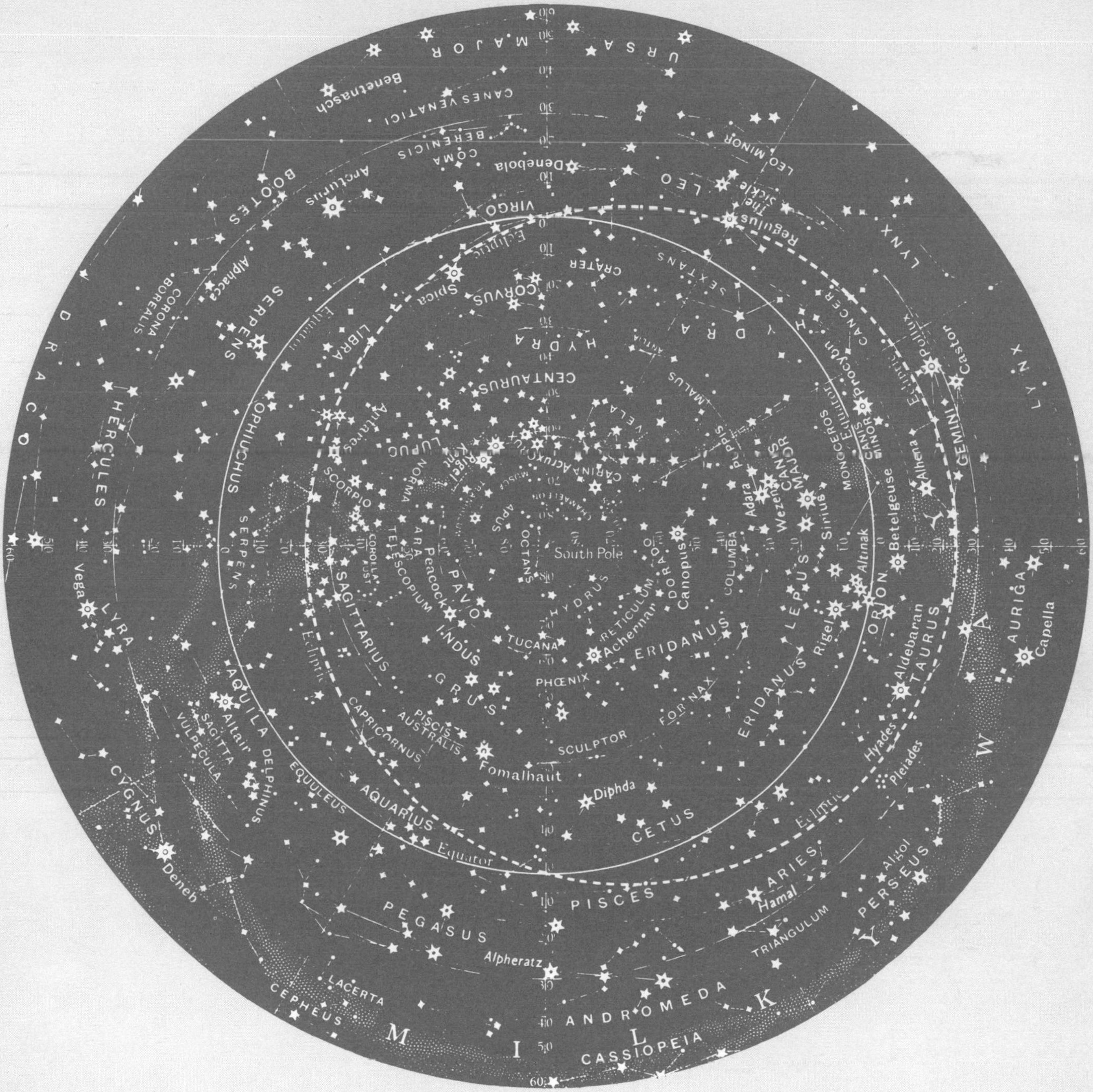

CONSTELLATIONS OF THE SOUTHERN HEMISPHERE

The star-glittering night sky whose teeming myriads populate space in every direction . . . they guide the mariner, the pilot, the way-farer . . . they are the friends of man, the delight of the world.

The New

WEBSTER
Encyclopedic
DICTIONARY
of The English Language

The New WEBSTER Encyclopedic DICTIONARY of The English Language

1980 Edition

VIRGINIA S. THATCHER
Editor in chief

ALEXANDER McQUEEN
Advisory Editor and Lexicographer

Editorial Staff
Margaret L. Smith • Clarice Geels
Anne Tomkin • Peter Morrison
Walter Eckart • David Phelps
George Malayil
Willard Grayson Smythe • Ava Friedmann

AVENEL BOOKS
New York

Library of Congress Catalog Card Number: 73-1877
ISBN: 0-517-457946
s r q p o n m

Preface

This dictionary is based on a wider experience with the usage of words than any one person can ever have in his own lifetime. A great body of information about words has been built up over many years, and lexicographers have made it their business to collect it and to organize it in dictionary form. We have endeavored to bring you authoritative data on every word you are likely to use in school, office, or home and in your daily contacts with people.

A great quantity of matter has been compiled in this work in very moderate compass, and the wide scope of this volume should meet the needs of the most exacting dictionary user. It is recognized that a dictionary suited to the popular demand for such a work should possess the three important qualities of accuracy, completeness, and convenience. This work carries an outstanding background of authority and scholarship and is a source to which you may turn with complete confidence for an understanding of the meaning, pronunciation, spelling, and proper use of the words with which you are unfamiliar.

In selecting the words for inclusion in this dictionary, the net has been cast fairly widely. The greatest importance is naturally attached to words in literary and colloquial use at the present day. At the same time, a large number of purely technical and scientific words and terms have been included since many of these necessarily play a considerable part in the lives of important sections of the community. Meanings and shades of meaning are carefully distinguished and explained, not with synonyms or confusing technical terms, but in clearly worded, simplified form, illustrated by quotations or brief phrases whenever necessary for lucidity.

The compilers of this dictionary have made it possible for the reader to find instantly the word or information he seeks, including at the same time such details as the spelling and pronunciation, as well as the origin of words so that he can appreciate how far reaching are the sources of our language. For easy reference, main entries are displayed in large, extra bold type the full width of the column, with definitions and other text matter slightly indented.

In order to carry out the principle of conciseness, the method of grouping related words in a single paragraph has been adopted. Particularly, primary words followed by a number of derivatives are thus grouped, and compounds are listed under the word that forms their first element.

We have included the name of WEBSTER, the great American lexicographer, in the title of this dictionary in recognition of his important contribution to the principles of lexicography.

The Publishers

ON THE ORIGIN OF WORDS

Alexander McQueen

On almost every page of this dictionary are clues to the origin and development of our language. Such clues may be traced from mankind's earliest days—through the ancient civilizations of Greece and Rome—and into the modern period, where, with the piling up of new discoveries in the arts and sciences, the invention of new words has become almost commonplace.

Every word we use has a history, and in almost every case it is a story of action—a story of something happening. This word-forming activity has been going on for thousands of years, ever since the first human beings uttered the first human sounds. We have inherited a rich legacy from the past.

SOUND AND SENSE

Many of our most stirring impressions come to us through elementary speech sounds. Conclusive proof of this statement can be found in the radio script that depends for dramatic effect not only on words but also on other sounds—of closing doors, tramping feet, rippling water, howling wind, ticking clocks, crashing collisions, and no end of other noises.

The use of sound effects is as old as man. Early men got along with a small stock of words, and they probably began with sound effects. For telling about violence, such as shattering or breaking, they made noises with smashing sounds, which in time became such dictionary words as *smash, dash, bash, mash, clash, crash.* It is easy to add to such a list of words ending in *-sh,* meaning something to do with violence.

To show how a sound might suggest a whole group of words, let us take an imaginary situation. Suppose that an ancient Teuton has gone to sleep. He sleeps with his mouth open, and as he breathes he makes a queer noise, a mixture of whistling and nasal humming. Someone observing the sleeping man imitates him like this: "Sss-norr!" In the evolution of language these sounds have been retained; today when we refer to this noise made by a sleeper, we call it a *snore.* Other nasal words have been built on the same pattern. A more abrupt sound, in waking hours, became a *snort.* A growl through the nose was called a *snarl.* A sudden breathing into the nose was called a *sniff.* A laugh like "eh-eh-eh" was called a *snicker.* The nose of an animal was called a *snout.* A scornful glance, with upturned nose, became a *sneer.* And a sort of nasal explosion became a *sneeze.* One could make a long list of words starting with *sn,* all related to the nose. It isn't by accident that sense and sound go together. The Choctaws have a very expressive word for *sneeze;* it has three syllables, *ha-bish-ko.* When the Choctaw says it quickly, with stress on the *bish,* it's a perfect sound effect for a sneeze.

In a dictionary are hundreds of these imitative words: the *tick-tick* of the clock, the *ding-dong* of the bell, the *boom* of the cannon. To describe an overabundance of talking, we use such words as *chatter* or *jabber.* Then there is *babble,* not very different from jabbering. It is possible that *babble* came from the simple sound *ba-ba* and from the prattle of a baby, whose first words are usually made with the lips. The sound *ba-ba* reminds us of a more complicated word—*barbarian.* In ancient times, when there was little travel from one land to another, men seldom had a chance to learn foreign languages. When they met a foreigner, they had to talk through an interpreter. And although most of the men of the Old World knew only one language, they despised people of other countries who also knew only their own native tongue. In fact, the Greeks used to say that the language of foreigners sounded like "bar-bar-bar." In time foreigners began to be nicknamed the "bar-bar" people. That particular nickname found its way into the regular language of the Greeks, then of the Romans, and we have it in a form that came through the Latin—*barbarian.* So even the ancient Greeks, with their keen sense of the niceties of language, sometimes made a dictionary word out of a simple sound. In doing so they were giving a sort of classic approval to the methods of our remotest ancestors, who enriched our speech with sounds that made sense.

WORDS FROM GREEK

The classic tongue of Greece – the language of Homer and Plato and Aristotle – is one of the most important sources of our everyday speech. You have already learned something of the Greek language. You started when you learned your ABC's; when you referred to the alphabet, you were just saying the names of the two Greek letters alpha and beta, that is, A and B. A little later, when you talked about arithmetic, you were very nearly saying *arithmos,* the Greek word for "numbers."

You can't go into the kitchen and wash dishes without handling something with a Greek name. The very word *dish* is Greek. At first it was *diskos,* meaning "quoit." Later the meaning was extended to include dishes.

One word from the ancient Greek shows how meanings change. The rich men in Greece had an easy life —no tiresome work to do—plenty of leisure time. To this spare time they gave the name of *scho-le*. In their *scho-lē* they were devoted to discussion, study, and instruction. Because they studied in their *scho-lē*, they were called scholars; and the place where they studied came to be called school. So schooltime was spare time, and the pleasure found in that spare time was the pleasure of study.

Among familiar personal names are many that come from the Greek, as George, Philip, and Eugene. The name George means "landman, or farmer." The *geo* in the name George is simply the Greek word for "earth." It is in *geography* and *geology* and *geometry;* they all have something to do with the earth.

The name Philip means one who loves horses; *philos,* "loving"; *hippos,* "horse." A hippodrome is a racecourse where horses run. A hippopotamus is a river horse; *potamos* is Greek for "river."

The name Eugene means "well-born": *eu-,* "good, well"; *genesis,* "birth." Most words starting with *eu* have a sense that is good, pleasant, or beautiful. *Euphony* has to do with pleasant sounds; *eulogy,* pleasant sayings or words. A speech praising someone is a eulogy.

Now for some girls' names: Margaret, she's a pearl; Dora, she's a gift; Catherine, she's pure; Irene, she's peaceful—that is, if you go by their Greek names. And the Greeks did have a name for almost everything. When you say that this great nation of ours is a democracy, you're talking Greek—*demos-kratein,* "people-governing." Democracy is government by the people. The same Greeks who gave us the name of our kind of government gave us the word *politics*. It comes from the Greek *polis,* "city." The Greeks gave us also the precious word *economy*. They called it *oikonomos,* from *oikos,* "house," and *nomos,* "management." That's the spirit of economy—the management of a house. And because economy has so much to do with the home, some of the world's best economists are women.

Speaking of women and housekeeping, marriage customs in ancient Greece emphasized business rather than romance. Sometimes the man never saw his wife until the wedding day. However, even if he didn't see her face, he always wanted to be sure about her dowry, that is, the money and other things of value that she would bring to him, as a sort of premium. Almost everything she owned became his. But under the old Greek law every bride was allowed to keep certain articles as her own, such as personal belongings and articles of adornment. These things would be carefully listed, and it was understood that the husband would have no control over them. What he got was the *phernē*, or dowry. The things the bride kept were the *parapherna: para,* "independent of"; *phernē,* "dowry." On the day of an ancient Greek wedding the bride came home, taking great care to keep her own special treasures separate from the ones that would belong to her husband. It might be a strange collection of unrelated things, but it was her very own —her *parapherna*. And that's how we came by our word *paraphernalia,* meaning "a miscellaneous collection of accessories or equipment."

People who guess at the derivation of words and then refer to the dictionary often find that their guess was wrong. Guessing is not safe. A comet and a comma look somewhat alike (each has a round part and a tail); so someone says, "They must be related." But they're not. *Comet* is from Greek *kometes,* "long-haired," because of the trail of light the comet leaves behind. *Comma,* Greek *komma,* means "a section or segment, something cut off"; a comma slightly cuts off part of a sentence. Now someone may say, "Is a comic long-haired?" No. He gets his name from Greek *kōsmos,* "a revel." Today many children give the word *comic* an entirely new meaning; they use it to mean any pictured story in strip form. They even talk about "Bible comics," an example of how the meaning of a word gets "pushed around."

Pharmacist is from Greek *pharmakon,* "poison." Many ancient medicinal drugs were more or less poisonous; hence the name of their dispenser.

Glamour is merely another form of *grammar*. Because *grammar* at one time meant "magic" or "fascination," *glamour* took on the meaning "witchery, allurement." This word also is Greek.

A dilemma is not an animal, in spite of its two horns. The word comes from Greek *di,* "double," and *lemma,* "proposition or assumption." When we have to choose between two propositions, each unfavorable to us, we are said to be "on the horns of a dilemma."

WORDS FROM LATIN

Latin is not a dead language, for it plays a lively part in our everyday speech. Sometimes we recognize it and applaud it. That word *applaud* is Latin; in Latin it's *applaudere* and usually means the clapping of hands. It is one of the thousands of Latin words that help give life to our language. So were I to say that Latin is totally dead, I would not be entirely candid. *Candid* is another Latin word; it means "fair, frank, or just." *Candid,* the Latin *candidus,* really meant "white, pure." In ancient Rome when a politician was running for office and went on a speechmaking tour, he wore white garments as a sign of good, clean politics. So our own officeseekers are called candidates. Next time you burn a candle, remember that its name is also from the Latin *candidus,* "white." Our republic gets its name from Latin *respublica: res,* "thing, interest"; *publica,* "public." Many of our political terms are derived from the Latin. Take the word *senate;* it's just another form of the Latin *senatus,* "council of old men." Senators are supposed to be old enough to be wise. Men who are *junior* (pure Latin for "younger") are seldom found in a senate. The senate calls for men who are *senior* ("older"). In fact, *senior* and *senate* are of the same origin.

Many of the Latin words in our language are quite

lively. Take the word *rivals*. We know what rivals are. If several men are competitors in business or are running a race, they are rivals. If several young men are courting the same girl, they are rivals in love. But why are they called rivals? The Latin word for stream is *rivus;* when two men lived near a stream and had to share that stream between them, they were called *rivales,* or rivals. The word originally meant "partners"; but when two persons have to share something, it is easy for partnership to lead to contention. So the Latin word for stream became our word for rivalry in sports, in business, in love, or in war.

Speaking of war, Roman soldiers usually got part of their wages in salt, because salt was considered essential to human life. The Latin word for salt was *sal;* the salt pay was called *salarium*. From that word came our word *salary*. Sometimes, if we consider that a man is lazy and isn't earning his salary, we say, "He isn't earning his salt." Note that word *consider,* which means "to study, to meditate, to reflect upon something." It's a simple word with a romantic origin. In Latin it was two words: *con,* "with"; *sider,* "a star." It comes from the days when men, for guidance in their decisions, turned for help to the stars. This use of *consider* is found in the English of Psalm 8: "When I consider Thy heavens . . . the moon and the stars, which thou hast ordained."

We take our words from old Roman politicians, stream dwellers, senators, soldiers—and farmers. When a Roman farmer was plowing and became careless, his plowshare would turn out of the furrow; and when his neighbors saw that his plowing had gone awry, they would say, "He has turned from the furrow." In Latin a furrow is *lira;* and "to turn out of the furrow" is *de-lira,* the source of our word *delirious*. When a man is temporarily out of his mind, he has turned aside from his proper mental furrow. When he comes to himself, and we might say that he's back on the right track, the old Romans said, "He's back in the right furrow."

The Rome of 20 centuries ago was built on seven hills. One was called the Palatium; on this Palatium, or Palatine Hill, the Emperor Augustus built a magnificent house. It was thought to be the last word in royal residences. But it wasn't, for a little later the Emperor Nero built another on the self-same hill. His house, called the Golden House, was still grander than the one built by Augustus. These royal houses gave their name to all royal houses to come. Because they were built on the Palatine Hill, they were called palatial; and it is from them that we get our word *palace*.

When you listen carefully, you are paying attention, or attending to what is being said. *Attention* is from *attentio,* the Latin word for a "stretching of the mind toward something." The same idea is in our word *tension,* which also means "stretching." And speaking of stretching, let us imagine a Roman strong man showing the remarkable development of his muscles. As he stretches out his arm and makes one of his muscles move between his elbow and his shoulder, somebody says, "It looks like a little mouse!" Now the Latin word for mouse is *mus,* and a little mouse is *musculus. Musculus* in time was changed to *muscule,* and now we call it *muscle*.

Consider the words *host* and *guest*. Both are derived from the Latin *hostis*. One offers hospitality, the other receives it—a friendly arrangement. But, oddly enough, *hostis* also meant "an enemy," which does not sound so friendly. The history of the words provides an explanation. In the days before hotels the person needing hospitality was a stranger, and all strangers were feared as possible enemies.

Another tricky word is *miniature*. Because a miniature is something small, one might suppose that it is related to *minus* and *minimum*. But it comes from the Latin *minium,* meaning "red lead," with which certain ancient pictures were painted. The word came to be connected with small pictures and then with small objects.

We have considered *candid* and *candidate,* both coming from Latin *candidus,* "white." What about candy? Did it, too, come from this source? No. Candy gets its name from the Arabic word *qand,* meaning "sugar."

Confute is a dignified word; it means "to disprove" or "to show that an argument is false." Its original significance, however, from the Latin was "to throw water on something." And *absurd,* another word from the Latin, joins *ab,* "from," to *surdus,* "deaf," suggesting an amusing misunderstanding by a deaf person.

WORDS THAT STAND OR STAY

One of the simplest words in our language is *stand*. It is very old and is related to many other words. It has been traced to an ancient Indo-European root, *sta,* which appears in many Greek and Latin words. *Sta* suggests stability, "strength to stand without being moved or overthrown." A stable is a place where horses stand. A stage is a platform whereon someone stands to act. An establishment is something that is fixed, reliable, standing. A standard is a flag or other sign around which loyal soldiers can stand; it is also a norm by which the standing of other things may be measured.

The *sta* root is seen unchanged in hundreds of words. A staple is an item of merchandise that is kept in stock, that is, a standing, always available, item. A staple is also a fastening device, to keep things, as it were, standing. A stall is a place where people stand to buy and sell goods. If the customer stands too long without buying, he may be charged with stalling. Things become stale from standing too long. A man's status indicates his standing in the community. When the man becomes old, he may need a staff to aid him in standing. Ecstasy might be described as a kind of "out-standing emotion."

To recite all of the *sta* words would be tiring. And even if we exhausted the list of *sta* words, we would encounter scores of related *ste* words. The homestead is where the home stands. One who is steady is one who is able to stand well. The printer's notation *stet* is pure Latin for "let it stand." In such words as *destiny,* the *sta* element appears as *sti;* destiny is a sort of predetermined stand in a person's future.

NONCLASSICAL WORD SOURCES

English, with its richness, power, and beauty, is indebted to many languages other than Greek and Latin. A few examples will illustrate this debt.

Long ago in a town in France a young man was in his workshop. As he worked, a group of his friends came by and called, "Come along, Pierre, don't work so hard. Come with us and have a good time; you can leave your shop." Now, the old French word for shop was *bauche* or *bawtch;* and the French word for luring a man away from his shop, or, as we might say, un-shopping him, was *dé-baucher*. Today if we entice a man away from his duty and attempt to corrupt him, we are said to be debauching him.

Among the ancient French a man and his wife sometimes had arguments. If the husband shouted at his wife, she might begin to look pathetic, with tear-filled eyes and pouting lips. Now her husband couldn't bear to see her lips sticking out like that, so he built a special little room into which she might retire to pout. Since the French word for pouting was *bouder,* the lady's pouting room came to be called the *boudoir,* a household word today.

In the days of Richard II of England men lost their heads for uttering a single word; it was the word *havoc*. *Havoc* was a dangerous word. In war the shout "Havoc" was a signal for soldiers to lay waste the countryside and to plunder and kill without mercy. That's what Shakespeare meant in his famous line in *Julius Caesar,* "Cry 'Havoc!' and let slip the dogs of war." When the cry "Havoc" was raised in a rebellion, it was a call to revolt against the government; for shouting "Havoc" in such a case, the shouter was condemned to lose his head.

The ancient Scottish Highlanders believed in battle cries. They called them army yells. In the Gaelic tongue, army is *sluagh;* yell is *ghairm*. Put them together, and it's *sluagh-ghairm,* or, as it is pronounced today, *slogan*. A good slogan is always short, something one can yell out easily while rushing full tilt at his opponent. Slogans are handy in advertising.

In Hungary, not far from the twin cities of Buda and Pest, is a town named Kocs. In Hungarian it's pronounced "kotch." In the little town of Kocs more than 500 years ago a man designed a special carriage for the king. It was a large four-wheeled carriage, with a roof. To make it ride easier on the rough roads, it was suspended on springs. In time such carriages became very popular. Because they were first made at the town of Kocs, they were called *coaches;* and that's what we call them today. Even when we use the word *coach* for a tutor or an athletic trainer, such as a football coach, we're carrying out the same idea. A human coach, like the oldtime carriage, helps the student get along faster.

Let's change the scene to East India, about a hundred years ago, and pay a visit to an Indian prince. He offers us a cool drink, of pleasant taste. We ask him what it is. He explains that it is made of arrack, tea, sugar, lemon, and water—five different elements. Now the Hindustani word for five is *panch,* pronounced almost like *punch*. So we call the drink punch.

In London, in the days of Queen Victoria, the people often wondered whether the national income was going to be enough to pay the national expenses. They called it "balancing the budget." The expression sounds perfectly natural to us, for we too have budgets to balance. But why is an annual statement of finances called a budget? It's from the old British custom of enclosing the annual estimates of revenue and expenditures in a leather purse or bag for presentation to the House of Commons. The name of the bag came from an old French word, *bougette,* or, as we pronounce it, "budget."

In delving into the history of the English language we find a group of unfortunates—people who have come down in the world: a villain, a hussy, a boor, a pagan, a savage, an imp, a knave, a silly, an idiot, and a hypocrite. All have seen better days. They are victims of change and, to some extent, of carelessness. Take, for example, the villain. He was a farm laborer working on a country estate. The estate was called a villa, and the man was called a villain. It was only after centuries, during which his master sometimes called to him impatiently, "Villain, come here!" that the name began to suggest a scoundrel.

So it is with the others. The hussy, at one time, was a respectable housewife. But *housewife* was pronounced *huzzif;* that word, shortened to *hussy,* was sometimes applied jokingly to a girl. Today we forget the good meaning and remember only the disrespectful one. A boor was merely a farmer; that's what *boor* meant, not very long ago. The pagan was simply a countryman, a peasant; *paganus* in Latin meant "a dweller in the country." The savage, as shown by his Franco-Latin name, was simply a *sauvage,* "a dweller in the woods."

We usually employ the word *imp* for the boy next door when we want to suggest that he's up to mischief. Yet the name comes from the days when *imp* was merely another word for "child." In one oldtime book a young English prince is called "that most angelic imp." *Knave* today means "a rascal, a rogue." At one time it was the word for "boy" or "youth."

The final trio—the silly, the idiot, and the hypocrite—were all perfectly normal. A silly today is one who is weak in intellect; in ancient times, *silly* meant "happy, fortunate, blessed." Our idiot received his name many centuries ago, when *idiot* meant "a private person." As to the hypocrite—he dates his name from the old days in classic Greece, when a hypocrite was not a deceitful person at all but merely a mimic, an actor.

AMERICA'S CONTRIBUTIONS

If a language belongs to the people who speak it, the English language surely belongs to America. Today about 60 percent of the world's English-speaking people are citizens of the United States; about 20 percent are found in the British Isles; the other 20 percent live elsewhere.

Since the establishment of the first English settlement in America in the 17th century, American influence on the language of the mother country has grown so great that today an Englishman cannot speak his own language without using words and expressions originating in the New World. Some years ago Dr. Mitford M. Mathews, of the University of Chicago, began to make a list of English words of American origin, and at last count he had reached a total of well over 50,000. These words were not merely terms of American Indian origin (such as *tomahawk, wampum, squaw)* or of Spanish origin (such as *bronco, lariat, stampede)* but a host of others that can fairly be classed as household words. Here are a few of them:

advertising agent
anesthesia
appendicitis
automobile
balance (remainder)
beeline
belittle
boss
boy friend
cablegram
cafeteria
casket (coffin)
chop suey
cute
elevator (lift)
faculty (of school)
filibuster
fraternity (college)
gerrymander
girl friend
governmental
hamburger
interview
iron lung
lengthy
lipstick
moron
movie
O.K.
overcoat
phonograph
refrigerator
Santa Claus
single tax
sorority
telephone
typewriter
undershirt

Multiplying this list by 1,100 will give some idea of the vast number of words in the English language that are of American origin. The British can accept the situation without embarrassment, for they know that English, the language of Shakespeare and Lincoln, was not created by the people of any single nation. English is a polyglot river, fed by the streams of every land and age, forever changing, ever flowing on. And we have done our share to keep it flowing.

OUR HOSPITABLE LANGUAGE

Our language is rich because it is hospitable. It receives, naturalizes, and uses words from many tongues. Thousands of words of Greek, Latin, French, and German origin will be found in the dictionary pages. In addition, there are many words from other languages.

From Arabic we get *coffee, cotton, magazine, mattress, sofa, syrup, tariff, zero.* Also from Arabic are such words as *alcohol, alcove, algebra,* and *alkali,* in all of which the *al-* means "the."

Among Chinese contributions are *tea, china, typhoon.*

From Dutch we borrow *boss, skate, snoop, skipper, yacht,* and many other seafaring terms.

From Hebrew: *amen, hallelujah, cherub,* and *satan.*

From Hindustani: *khaki* and probably *calico.*

From Hungarian: *coach, hussar, shako.*

From Italian: *alarm, bandit, bankrupt, carnival, ditto, gazette, influenza, piano, sonnet, stucco, studio, umbrella, volcano.*

From Japanese: *geisha, mikado.*

From Malay: *bamboo, bantam, caddy* (for tea), *gong, sago, gutta-percha, ketchup, batik.*

From Persian: *bazaar, check, shawl, turban, paradise.*

From Portuguese: *caste, marmalade, cobra.*

From Russian: *babushka, czar, knout, soviet.*

From the Scandinavian languages: *fiord, ski, skoal, viking.*

From Turkish: *ottoman, tulip, caviar.*

BEAUTIFUL WORDS

Every few years, presumably when there is a shortage of news, some enterprising reporter asks a number of prominent men and women to make lists of the ten "most beautiful" words in the language. As might be expected, the nominations include a great diversity of words; no two persons have the same eye or ear for words. Beauty in words is somewhat elusive, but ugliness is easy to recognize. No one would give a beauty prize to *scratch,* or *shredded,* or *eschew.*

Popular in many lists of beautiful words are *mother, love, truth,* and *justice,* yet all of these have been disallowed on the ground that they are not euphonious. They are beautiful in concept but not in sound. Love may be supremely beautiful in our thoughts, but as a word it is a mere monosyllable that closes on the uninspiring sound of *v.* The Romance languages are much more fortunate in their words for love: Latin and Spanish *amor,* French *amour,* and, notably, the flowing Italian *amore,* ah-mo'reh, which sounds and sings very well.

The word *lullaby* is a great vote getter, partly from its sound but probably also from its association with the slumber of innocent infants. *Slumber,* by the way, is a popular word.

High on many lists are *golden, murmuring,* and *melody;* also *glow, noble,* and *soul.* The *o* sound is always liked. *Twilight, home,* and *romance* are favored by many voters, and it will be noticed that two of these words contain the *o* sound, unstressed in *romance* but definite in *home.* (The word *home* also profits from its sentimental associations.)

Smoothness seems to be the deciding factor in judging verbal beauty. The "good round *O*" is smooth sounding; perhaps even more so is the *oo* sound as in *moon, coo,* and the Irish pet name *mavourneen.* The 18th-century Emanuel Swedenborg, whose studies in words are unique, pictured the language of heaven as containing many long-vowel sounds, with *oo* as the most important. The *oo* sound can be tested in a sort of one-sided conversation with a young baby by gently saying "oo" and then waiting for the infantile response. You may have to wait as long as 15 or 20 seconds, but the reaction is almost sure to come in the form of a pleased smile.

Famous among allegedly beautiful English words is *cellar-door.* This word was chosen many years ago by the Italian patriot Mazzini, when he began to learn

English. To him the sound of *cellar-door* was fascinating. As he formed his opinion in England, we may assume that he heard the word with its 19th-century British pronunciation of *selladaw*.

George Whitefield, 18th-century English preacher, who spent some years in America, gave a vogue to the long word *Mesopotamia*. It is said that by merely uttering that word he could reduce a great audience to tears. To this day some public speakers talk about "the true Mesopotamia ring," referring to an utterance with more ring to it than reason.

NEW WORDS

New words are always entering the language. The ways in which new words come into existence are many, and the rate at which they enter varies with the times. Four of the main sources of new words are borrowing, construction, compounding, and affixing. In the past, as we have seen, English borrowed a large number of words, called loan-words, from other languages.

In our own time, constructed words probably account for most of the additions to the vocabulary. Constructed words are formed from word elements of other languages, usually Greek or Latin. For instance, *bathyscaph* is from the Greek *bathys,* deep, and *skaphe,* boat. Most constructed words appear in technical vocabularies. Some, however, do gain wide currency: *antibiotic* and *transistor,* for example.

Another important source of new words is compounding, the joining of two existing words: *paperback* and *spacewalk,* for example.

Many new words are formed by affixing, the addition of living prefixes or suffixes (such as *pre-, non-,* and *-ize*) to a word. Affixed words often originate in conversation to satisfy the needs of a particular situation. Thus, even an unabridged dictionary does not contain all of the many affixed words in use.

A short description of some other sources of new words follows: Conversion is the transfer of a word from one part of speech to another. Conversion of a noun to a verb, for example, *to invoice* and *to contact,* is common. Blending is the combination of parts of different words: *brunch* from *br*eakfast and l*unch*. Acronyms are words formed from the initial letters of a phrase: *laser* and *radar*. Proper or trade names are sometimes adapted as common nouns: *diesel* and *nylon*. Shortening usually involves a single word, rather than a phrase: *phone* from *telephone*.

Many words are transitory and are not in currency long enough to be included in a dictionary. Other words (such as the Latin additions of the 16th century or new words of the Space Age) are relatively permanent members of the language and are altered or eliminated only in the long, slow, complex process of language change.

The following list is composed of three types of current words: (1) new words, such as *spacewalk,* (2) words with new meanings or applications, such as *abort* and *Augmented Roman,* and (3) existing words that are new to popular usage, such as *LSD-25*.

abort, a•bärt′, *v.t.* To cancel or cut short a space flight, usually because of the craft's failure to perform its purposes.

aerospace, âr′ō•spās′, *a.* Referring to the earth's atmosphere and space.

aquanaut, ak′wa•nat, *n.* One who explores underwater phenomena.

Augmented Roman, *n.* A phonetic alphabet system that utilizes 43 characters to represent the speech sounds of English, used in teaching reading.

bathyscaph, bath′i•skaf, *n.* A submarine-like craft used in exploring extreme depths of the oceans and in other oceanographic research.

biodegrade, bi′ō•di•grād″, *v.t.* To break down a substance by means of bacterial action.

bistatic radar, *n.* A radar system that utilizes three bodies: the earth, the object of study, and an artificial satellite, which carries receiving equipment (conventional, monostatic radar having the transmitter and receiver in one place).

booster rocket, *n.* A rocket engine that provides the necessary thrust, or pushing force, to launch a spacecraft and place it in orbit. (Also referred to as a *launch vehicle.)*

centrifuge, sen′tri•fūj, *n.* An apparatus in which equipment, human beings, or animals are rotated and subjected to conditions simulating the accelerations encountered in a spacecraft.

collision course, *n.* A course taken by a craft, especially a missile, that will cause it to intercept and collide with another craft.

comsat, käm′sat, *n.* A blending of *com*munications and *sat*ellite.

countdown, kount′doun, *n.* The period during which the sequence of actions necessary to launch a spacecraft is carried out.

deep space probe, *n.* A space vehicle designed to explore regions near the moon and beyond.

destruct, dē•strukt′, *v.t.* To deliberately destroy a spacecraft before it has completed its course, usually because of a malfunction that makes the craft a hazard.

docking, dok′ing, *n.* The operation of bringing together and joining two craft in space.

escape velocity, *n.* The speed that a body must attain in order to leave the gravitational pull of a celestial body.

exobiology, eks′ō•bi•o″lo•ji, *n.* The study of living organisms that exist on celestial bodies other than the earth.

garbage, gar′bij, *n.* Miscellaneous objects in orbit that have been ejected or have broken away from spacecraft.

hold, hōld, *n.* The temporary halt of a countdown to remove an impediment so that the countdown can be continued (compare with **abort** and **scrub**).

laser, lā′zer, *n.* [An acronyn for *l*ight *a*mplification by *s*timulated *e*mission of *r*adiation.] A device that generates a concentrated light beam that can be used to carry communications signals, to weld hard materials (such as the exotic metals used in the aerospace industry), to perform some kinds of surgery, etc.

LEM, lem, *n.* [An acronym for *l*unar *e*xcursion *m*od-ule.] A small spacecraft that is designed to carry two men and equipment and to be launched from another manned craft in order to make a landing on the moon.

LSD-25 (lysergic acid diethylamide), *n.* A drug that can cause hallucinations and other simulated symptoms of mental disorders, used primarily in psychological experimentation.

magnetosphere, mag•net″ō•sfēr′, *n.* The region of space around a celestial body that is dominated by that body's magnetic field.

microelectronics, mi′krō•ē•lek•tron″iks, *n.* A branch of electronics concerned with extreme miniaturization of components, especially circuits. [Amplifier circuits smaller than an aspirin tablet have been produced.]

module, mod′ūl, *n.* A self-contained unit of a spacecraft that serves as a functional part of the craft.

op art, *n.* A form of painting that evinces strong visual responses by utilizing various optical effects; optical art.

OSO, ō′sō, *n.* [An acronym for *o*rbiting *s*olar *o*bservatory.] A series of U.S. artificial satellites used in solar research.

plus count, *n.* The count, in seconds, that immediately follows the launching of a spacecraft, used to check the sequence of events after the countdown has ended.

pop art, *n.* A form of painting and sculpture that uses as subject matter such things as comic strip characters, advertisements, product packages, etc.

rendezvous, ran′dā•vö, *n.* The meeting of two or more spacecraft in space at a prescheduled time and place.

retrorocket, re″trō•rok′et, *n.* A rocket used to retard the forward motion of a spacecraft.

roll, rōl, *n.* The rotational movement of a craft about its longitudinal axis.

scrub, skrub, *v.t.* To cancel a rocket firing, either before or during the countdown.

shutdown, shut′doun, *n.* The automatic switching off of the booster rocket in order to prevent a liftoff, possibly because of a malfunction in one of the spacecraft's systems.

soft landing, *n.* A landing, on a celestial body other than the earth, that avoids a crash of the landing vehicle.

spacewalk, spās′wak, *n.* The activity of an astronaut that takes place outside the spacecraft; extra vehicular activity (EVA).

staging, stāg′ing, *n.* The method of using a booster and one or more rockets in a spacecraft, in which each state, as it burns out, is jettisoned.

sustainer engine, *n.* A rocket that maintains the velocity a spacecraft attains from its booster rocket.

tracking, trak′ing, *n.* The various means of observing the movements of spacecraft.

T-time, *n.* Any specific time either before or after the launching of a spacecraft, for instance, "T minus 40," meaning 40 minutes prior to launch.

voiceprint, vois′print, *n.* A spectograph, or visible representation, of the sound patterns of the human voice.

weightlessness, wāt′les•nes, *n.* The absence of apparent gravitational pull on an object.

yaw, ya, *n.* The lateral rotational movement of a craft about its vertical axis.

HOW TO USE THIS DICTIONARY

For most users of this dictionary the entries will explain themselves. None the less, a few words of introduction may be useful.

To find a word, we must know how it is spelled. When several spellings are in use, they appear under cross-entries. Thus the main entry for *czar* is indexed also under *tsar* and *tzar*. The order of information is as follows: (1) The word itself. (2) Its pronunciation, according to the sound-spelling system at the foot of each page and explained in the key to pronunciation. Stress is shown by this sign (′) *after* the stressed syllable. In some words an additional heavier stress is indicated by the same sign doubled (″). (3) The part of speech, shown by *n.* for noun, *v.* for verb, *a.* for adjective, and so forth, and explained in the list of abbreviations and signs used in this dictionary. (4) The derivation of the word, in brackets, with related words in other languages. (5) The meaning or meanings of the word, often followed by idioms or familiar phrases.

PRONUNCIATION

In speaking, choice of the right word is important, but that word must be given an acceptable pronunciation. Absolute uniformity of pronunciation is neither possible nor necessary. A dictionary noting local speech variations heard in all fifty States of the Union would be confusing. The pronunciations in the present work represent an American standard, acceptable wherever English is spoken.

Sometimes a sound-spelling may seem strange, as when *exhibit* is spelled ig•zib′it. Possibly at one time the word was pronounced eks•hib′it, but not now. Long ago the *eks,* because it was unstressed, was worn down to *igs,* and the *h,* because its utterance called for more breath, was dropped entirely. Today only a foreign student would carefully say eks-hib-it. *Exhibition,* on the other hand, is pronounced eg′zi•bish″on, because here the *eks,* somewhat stressed, was protected from vowel change.

Stress, in speech as in music, is a valuable aid to expression, but when it is placed on the wrong syllable, the effect is absurd, especially when it is put on an unaccented syllable. A person may be heard talking about CREE-ation, YEW-nited States, DEE-mocracy, REE-publicanism, and so forth. Such a practice, presumably used to emphasize the words, only distorts them. The case is similar with final unstressed syllables; for example, there is no *age* in damage, no *page* in rampage, no *sage* in message. The accepted pronunciations are, respectively, dam′ij, ramp′ij, mes′ij.

Stress is important even with monosyllables. In the sentence "He asked her boy to call James" (hē askt hėr boi tų kal jāmz), the word *to* is pronounced tu, because it is obscure and unstressed. Only when stressed is it given its full sound tö, rhyming with "moo."

Early in the 20th century an American publisher issued a book entitled *25,000 Words Frequently Mispronounced*. This is a most discouraging title, until we realize that the list included many geographic, theological, scientific, and foreign terms seldom used by the average citizen.

Pronunciation of English varies to some extent, which is not to be wondered at, for the language is spoken by about 300 million people. Some variation is noted even in the pronunciation of the well educated.

Here is a short list of words that are often mispronounced. Preferred pronunciations for them are found in the dictionary entries.

accessory	column	liqueur
accompanist	coupé	perfume *(n.)*
address	decade	presentation
adult	envoy	program
ally	exemplary	promulgate
anti-	exquisite	respite
arctic	genuine	semi-
athletic	gesture	statistics
bade	gist	suite
bulwark	lingerie	vagary

KEY TO PRONUNCIATION

In showing the pronunciation the simplest and most easily understood method has been adopted, that of rewriting the word with a set of letters that have invariably the same sound, no matter by what letter or letters the sounds may be expressed in the word whose pronunciation is shown. The key by this means is greatly simplified, the reader having only to bear in mind one mark for each sound. Sounds and letters, it must be remembered, are often very different things. In English there are a great many more sounds than letters to represent them, so that some of the letters stand for more than one sound. The letter *a,* for instance, has at least six or seven, namely, those given in the accompanying table and two more, as in the words *any* and *quality,* which may be better represented by *e* and *o* respectively. Our alphabet is therefore very far from being a perfect alphabet, which would have a distinct letter for each sound and would always represent the same sound by the same letter. The following is a list of characters and key-words used to show the pronunciation in the dictionary.

VOWELS

ā	as in *fa*te	i	as in p*i*n
ä	as in f*a*r	ō	as in n*o*te
â	as in f*a*re	o	as in n*o*t
a	as in f*a*t	ö	as in m*o*ve
a̤	as in f*a*ll	ū	as in t*u*be
ē	as in m*e*	u	as in t*u*b
e	as in m*e*t	u̇	as in b*u*ll
ė	as in h*e*r	oi	as in *oi*l
ī	as in p*i*ne	ou	as in p*ou*nd

CONSONANTS

ch	as in *ch*ain	ng	as in si*ng*
ch	as in Sc. lo*ch*, Ger. na*ch*t	TH	as in *th*en
		th	as in *th*in
g	as in *g*o	w	as in *w*ig
j	as in *j*ob	hw	as in *wh*ig
zh	as in a*z*ure		

This system, it is believed, will be sufficient for all practical purposes, and the intelligent reader will not care for greater nicety. Consonants not in the list are used simply with their ordinary sounds.

Accent.—Words consisting of more than one syllable receive an accent, as the first syllable of the word *labor,* the second of *delay,* and the third of *comprehension.* The accented syllable is the most prominent part of the word and is denoted by the mark (′), as in the words *la′bor, delay′*, and *comprehen′sion.*

Many polysyllabic words are pronounced with two accents, the primary and the secondary accent, as the word *excommunication,* in which the third as well as the fifth syllable is commonly accented. The accent on the fifth syllable is the primary accent, and when it requires to be indicated in the pronunciation it receives a double mark, thus (″), the secondary or inferior accent receiving only the single mark (′), as in *excommu′nica″tion.*

ABBREVIATIONS AND SIGNS USED IN THIS DICTIONARY

a. or *adj.* adjective
abbrev. abbreviation, abbreviated
acc. accusative
adv. adverb
agri. agriculture
alg. algebra
Amer. American
anat. anatomy
anc. ancient
anthropol. anthropology
antiq. antiquities
aor. aorist, aoristic
Ar. Arabic
arch. architecture
archaeol. archaeology
arith. arithmetic
Armor. Armoric
art. article
A.Sax. Anglo-Saxon
astrol. astrology
astron. astronomy
at. no. atomic number
at. wt. atomic weight
aug. augmentative
avi. aviation
bact. bacteriology
biol. biology
bot. botany
Bret. Breton (=Armoric)
Carl. Carlyle
carp. carpentry
caus. causative
Celt. Celtic
chem. chemistry
chron. chronology
Class. Classical (=Greek and Latin)
cog. cognate, cognate with
colloq. colloquial
com. commerce
comp. compare
compar. comparative
conch. conchology
conj. conjunction

contr. contraction, contracted
crystal. crystallography
D. Dutch
Dan. Danish
dat. dative
def. definite
dial. dialect, dialectal
dict. dictionary
dim. diminutive
distrib. distributive
dram. drama, dramatic
dyn. dynamics
E., Eng. English
eccles. ecclesiastical, in ecclesiastical affairs
econ. economics
educ. education
elect. electricity
engin. engineering
engr. engraving
entom. entomology
ethn. ethnology
etym. etymology
exclam. exclamation
fem. feminine
fig. figuratively
Fl. Flemish
fort. fortification
Fr. French
freq. frequentative
Fris. Frisian
fut. future
G. German
Gael. Gaelic
galv. galvanism
genit. genitive
geog. geography
geol. geology
geom. geometry
Goth. Gothic
Gr. Greek
gram. grammar
gun. gunnery
Heb. Hebrew
her. heraldry
Hind. Hindustani, or Hindi
hist. history
hort. horticulture
Hung. Hungarian
hydros. hydrostatics
Icel. Icelandic
ich. ichthyology
imper. imperative
imperf. imperfect
impers. impersonal
incept. inceptive
ind. indicative
Ind. Indian
indef. indefinite
Indo-Eur. Indo-European
inf. infinitive
intens. intensive
interj. interjection
Ir. Irish
It. Italian
L. Latin
L.G. Low German
lit. literal, literally
Lith. Lithuanian
L.L. Late Latin
mach. machinery
manuf. manufactures
masc. masculine
math. mathematics
mech. mechanics
med. medicine
Med. L. Medieval Latin
mensur. mensuration
metal. metallurgy
metaph. metaphysics
meteor. meteorology
M.H.G. Middle High German
Mil. Milton
milit. military, in military affairs
mineral. mineralogy
Mod. Fr. Modern French
Ms manuscript
Mss manuscripts
mus. music
myth. mythology
N. Norse, Norwegian
n. noun
nat. hist. natural history
nat. order natural order
nat. phil. natural philosophy
naut. nautical
navig. navigation
neg. negative
neut. neuter
N.H.G. New High German
N.L. New Latin
nom. nominative
Norm. Norman
North. E. Northern English
N.T. New Testament
numis. numismatics
obj. objective
obs. obsolete
obsoles. obsolescent
O.E. Old English (*i.e.*, English between A. Saxon and Modern English)
O.Fr. Old French
O.H.G. Old High German
O. Sax. Old Saxon
O.T. Old Testament
ornith. ornithology
p. or *part.* participle
paint. painting
paleon. paleontology
pass. passive
pathol. pathology
pejor. pejorative
Per. Persian
perf. perfect
pers. person
persp. perspective
Pg. Portuguese
phar. pharmacy
philol. philology
philos. philosophy
Phoen. Phoenician
photog. photography
phren. phrenology
phys. physics
phys. geog. physical geography
physiol. physiology
pl. plural
pneum. pneumatics
poet. poetical
Pol. Polish
poss. possessive
pp. past participle
ppr. present participle
Pr. Provençal
prep. preposition
pres. present
pret. preterite
print. printing
priv. privative
pron. pronunciation, pronounced
pron. pronoun
pros. prosody
prov. provincial
psych. psychology
rail. railways
refl. reflexively, with a reflexive pronoun
R. Cath. Ch. Roman Catholic Church
rhet. rhetoric
Rom. antiq. Roman antiquities
Rus. Russian
Sax. Saxon
Sc. Scottish
Scand. Scandinavian
Scrip. Scripture
sculp. sculpture
Shak. Shakespeare
sing. singular
Skr. Sanskrit
Slav. Slavonic, or Slavic
sociol. sociology
Sp. Spanish
sp. gr. specific gravity
subj. subjunctive
superl. superlative
surg. surgery
surv. surveying
Sw. Swedish
sym. symbol
syn. synonym
technol. technology
tel. telegraphy and telephony
teleg. telegraphy
Tenn. Tennyson
term. termination
Teut. Teutonic
Thack. Thackeray
theol. theology
trigon. trigonometry
Turk. Turkish
typog. typography
v.i. verb intransitive
v.t. verb transitive
W. Welsh
zool. zoology
† rare
‡ obsolete
= equivalent to
. . comparison of synonyms

Cross-references in this dictionary are printed in two kinds of type. When a word is printed in small capital letters, as NAIL, *the reader should look under that entry for more information. When a word is capitalized and italicized, it is a variant and directs the reader to the desired information.*

PREFIXES AND SUFFIXES

PREFIXES

A-. From A. Sax. *a-* intensive, as in *arise, awake.*
A-. From A. Sax. *of,* as in *adown, athirst, anew, akin.*
A-. From A. Sax. *of, o',* as in *o'clock (a-clock).*
A-. From A. Sax. *on,* as in *afoot, abed, aboard.*
A-. From L. *ab,* from, as in *avert.*
A-. From L. *ad,* to, as in *achieve, ascend.*
A-. From A. Sax. *and-, against,* as in *along.*
A-. From L. *ex,* out, modified by Angl. Fr. *a* from O. Fr. *e,* as in *amend, affray.*
A-. From Gr. *a-* privative or negative, sometimes through L. or Fr. as in *abysm, agnostic, amorphous*
Ab-, from, away, as in *abduct, abjure.* From L. *ab,* from, preposition and prefix; allied to E. *of, off,* Gr. *apo,* from or away. Before *c* and *t,* generally assumes the lengthened form *abs,* also appears as *a-* (*see* **A-**).
Abs-. *See* **Ab-**.
Ac-. A form of **Ad-**.
Ad-, to, toward, at or near, as in *adapt, admit.* From L. *ad,* to, preposition and prefix; allied to E. *at.* Takes by assimilation the forms *ac-, af-, ag-, al-, an-, ap-, ar-, as-, at-,* as in *accede, affirm, aggregate, allude, annex, applaud, arrogant, assume, attribute,* also appears as *a-* in *ascend.*
Af-, Ag-, Al-. Forms of **Ad-**.
Al- (Arabic *al,* the), as in *alchemy, alcohol, algebra, alkali.*
Ambi-, Amb-, about, around, as in *ambition, amputate.* From L. *ambi-, amb-,* on both sides, around; allied to Gr. *amphi,* about, L. *ambo,* both; A. Sax. *emb, ymb,* G. *um,* about.
Amphi-, about, around, on both or all sides, as in *amphibious, amphitheater.* From Gr. *amphi,* about, around, preposition and prefix. *See* **Ambi-**.
An-. (1)=**Ad-**. (2) Not, negation or privation, from Gr. *an-* or *a-,* the negative prefix, as in *anarchy.* Allied to E. *un-,* L. *in-,* not. (3)=A. Sax. *and-,* against, opposite, as in *answer.* Appears as *a-,* in *along.* Same as Goth. *and-,* Gr. *ant-, ent-,* Gr. *anti.*
Ana-, up, through, throughout, as in *analysis, anatomy, anabasis.* From Gr. *ana,* up, preposition and prefix; allied to E. *on.*
Ant-, against, as in *antagonist, antacid.* Same as **Anti-**.
Ante-, before, as in *antecedent, antedate.* From L. *ante,* before, preposition and prefix. *See* **Anti-**.
Anti-, against, in opposition, as in *antichrist, anticlimax.* From Gr. *anti,* against, preposition and prefix; allied to L. *ante,* before, and to the A. Sax. prefix *and-, an-,* seen in *answer. See* **An-**.
Ap-. A form of **Ad-**.
Apo-, Aph-, away, apart, off, as in *apostle, apostate, aphelion.* From Gr. *apo,* from, away, preposition and prefix; allied to L. *ab,* from, E. *off. See* **Ab-**.
Ar-. A form of **Ad-**.
Arch-, Archi-, chief, head, ruling, as in *archbishop, architect, archangel.* From Gr. *archi-,* chief, from *archē,* rule, beginning.
As-, At-. Forms of **Ad-**.
Auto-, self, of one's self, as in *autograph, automatic.* From Gr. *auto-,* from pronoun *autos,* self.
Be-. From A. Sax. *be-, bi-,* from *bi, big*=E. *by.* Has various meanings: by or near, or denoting locality, as in *beside, beneath, below;* with a causative or intensive force, as in *benumb, besprinkle, bemire;* with a privative force, in *behead;* upon or against, as in *befall.*
Bi-, twice, two ways, double, as in *bicycle, biennial, bisect.* From L. *bi-,* double, for older *dui-,* akin to *duo,* two (compare *bellum,* war, for *duellum),* and to E. *two.*
Bis-, twice, double, as in *biscuit.* Longer form of **Bi-**.
Cata-, Cath-, Cat-, down, downward, through, according to, as in *cataract, cataclysm, catarrh, catholic, catechism.* From Gr. *kata,* down, through; preposition and prefix.
Circum-, around, all round, as in *circumnavigate, circumspect, circumstance.* From L. *circum,* round, preposition and prefix; from *circus,* a circle. Seen also in *circuit.*
Cis-, on this side of, as in *cisalpine.* From L. *cis,* preposition and prefix.
Co-, Col-. Same as **Com-**.
Com-, with, together, altogether (intensively), as in *combine, compound, command.* From L. *com-,* prefix, used for preposition *cum,* with, allied to Gr. *syn, Skr. sam,* with. Appears also as *co-, col-, con-, cor-,* as in *co-exist, collect, connect, correspond.*
Con-. Same as **Com-**.
Contra-, against, as in *contradict, contravene.* From L. *contra,* against, preposition and prefix, from *con-,* or *cum-* and *-tra* (as in *intra,* within, *extra,* beyond), akin to *trans,* across, Skr. *tar,* to pass.
Cor-. Same as **Com-**.
Counter-, against; same as **Contra,** but directly from Fr. *contre,* against.
De-, down, from, away, as in *descend, denude, depart, describe.* From L. *de,* from, out of, preposition and prefix. In some cases, represents O. Fr. *des-,* from L. *dis-,* apart, as in *decry, defeat.*
Demi-, half, semi-. From Fr. *demi. See* dictionary.
Di-, double, as in *dimorphous.* From Gr. *di-,* double, akin to *dis-, bis-.*
Dia-, through, between, double, as in *diameter, diagnosis, dialogue.* From Gr. *dia,* through, between, preposition and prefix; akin to *di-, dis-.*
Dif-. A form of **Dis-**.
Dis-, apart, asunder, in two, as in *disarm, discharge, distract;* also used negatively, as in *disbelief, disapprove.* From L. *dis,* asunder, preposition and prefix; allied to Gr. *dis, di-,* double, and to L. *bis,* twice.
Dys-, bad, ill, difficult, as in *dysentery, dyspepsia.* From Gr. *dys-,* prefix.
E. Same as **Ex-**. In *enough, e-* represents A. Sax. prefix *ge-*; in *esquire, estate,* it is a mere euphonic element prefixed for ease in pronunciation.
Ec-, Ex-, out, as in *ecstasy, eclectic, exodus.* From Gr. *ek, ex,* out, preposition and prefix, akin to L. *ex.*
Ef-. A form of **Ex-**.
Em-, En-, in, as in *embrace, enclose, enlist;* or used with a causal force, as in *enable, enlarge.* From Fr. *em-, en-,* L. *im-, in-,* preposition and prefix. *See* **In-**.
En-, in, as in *encaustic, energy.* From Gr. *en,* in, preposition and prefix, akin to L. *in,* A. Sax. *in,* in.
Enter-, between, among, as in *enterprise.* From Fr. *entre,* L. *inter. See* **Inter-**.

Epi-, Eph-, Ep-, upon, over, as in *epitaph, epithet, epidermis, ephemeral*. From Gr. *epi*, upon; akin to Skr. *api*.

Es-, out, away, as in *escape, escheat*. From L. *ex*, *q.v.*

Eu-, well, as in *eulogy, euphony*. From. Gr. *eu-*, well, prefix, neuter of *eus*, good, for *esus*, from root *as*, to be (seen in E. *is*).

Ex-, out of, out, from, as in *exceed, exclude;* also used intensively, as in *exacerbate, exasperate*. From L. *ex*, out, akin to Gr. *ek, ex*, out. *See* **Ec-**. Appears also as *e-, ef-, es-*.

Extra-, beyond, without, as in *extraordinary, extrajudicial*. From L. *extra*, without, preposition and prefix, from *ex and -tra*. *See* **Contra-**.

For-. Used intensively or almost negatively, as in *forgive, forbid, forgo*. From A. Sax. *for-*, same as Icel. and Dan. *for-*, D. and G. *ver-*, Goth. *fra-;* allied to *far*, L. *per*.

Fore-, beforehand, in advance, as in *foretell, foreshow, foreground*. *See* FORE, in dictionary.

Hemi-, half, as in *hemisphere*. From Gr. prefix *hēmi-*, half, akin to L. *semi*.

Hetero-, other, different, as in *heterodox, heterogeneous*. From Gr. *heteros*, other.

Holo-, whole, entire, as in *holograph, holocaust*. From Gr. *holos*, whole.

Homo-, same, as in *homonym*. From Gr. *homos*, same; allied to E. *same*.

Hyper-, over, beyond, too; *hyperborean, hypercritical*. From Gr. *hyper*, above, over, preposition and prefix; allied to L. *super*, E. *over, up*.

Hypo-, under, beneath, as in *hypocaust, hypotenuse, hypothesis*. From Gr. *hypo*, under, preposition and prefix; allied to L. *sub*, under.

Il-. A form of **In-** (2 and 3).

Im-. A form of **In-**.

In-. (1) In, as in *inborn, insight*. From A. Sax. and E. preposition *in*, cog. with L. *in*, in (whence next **In-**). It may become *im-*, as in *imbed, imbody*. (2) In, into, as in *include, inclose*. From L. *in*, in, preposition and prefix; cog. with Gr. *en*, E. and Goth. *in*, Icel, *inn*, G. *ein*. Before *m, b, p*, it becomes *im-*, as in *immune, imbibe, implant;* before *l, il-;* before *r, ir-*. (3) Not–the negative prefix, as in *inactive, incapable*. From L. *in-*, not, prefix; Gr. *an-*, E. *un-*, not (see **Un-**). Like the preceding it appears also as *il-, im-, ir-*, as in *illegitimate, immaculate, irrational*.

Infra-, below, as in *infracostal, infraorbital, infrared*. From L. *infra*, below.

Inter-, between, among, as in *intercede, intermingle, interchange*. From L. *inter*, between, among, preposition and prefix; a comparative form akin to *intra-, intro-*, within, *interior*, inner, *internus*, internal. *See* UNDER in dictionary. It also takes the form **Intel-**, as in *intellect*.

Intra-, within, as in *intramural*. From L. *intra*, within. *See* **Inter-**.

Intro-, within, into, as in *introduce, introspection*. *See* **Inter-**.

Ir-. A form of **In-**.

Juxta-, near, nigh, as in *juxtaposition*. From L. preposition *juxta*, near.

Kata-. *See* **Cata-**.

Mal-, Male-, ill, badly, as in *maladministration, maladroit, malcontent, malefactor*. From Fr. *mal-*, L. *male*, badly, *malus*, evil.

Meta-, Met-, after, beyond, among, or denoting change, as in *metaphysics, metaphor, metamorphosis, metathesis, metonymy*. From Gr. *meta*, with, among, preposition and prefix; cog. with A. Sax. *mid*, G. *mit*, Goth. *mith*, with.

Mis-. (1) Wrong, wrongly, bad, badly, as in *misdeed, mistake, misshapen, mishap, misinformed*. From A. Sax., Icel., Dan., and D. *mis-*, Sw. *miss-*, Goth. *missa-*, wrongly; akin to verb *miss*. (2) Ill, unfortunate, as in *misadventure, misalliance, mischance*. From O. Fr. *mes-*, from L. *minus*, less. *See* dictionary.

Mono-, Mon-, single, sole, having only one, as in *monarch, monody, monogram, monomaniac*. From Gr. *monos*, sole, single.

Multi-, Mult-, many, as in *multangular, multiform, multivalve*. From L. *multus*, many, much.

N-, negative element, as in *never, none*. From A. Sax. *ne*, not; cog. with L. *ne*, not, Skr. *na*, E. *no*. *See* NO in dictionary.

Non-, not; often used as *in-*, negative, or as *un-*. From L. *non*, not, from *ne unum*, not one. *See* above.

Ob-, against, before, in the way of, as in *object, obstacle, obstruct*. From L. *ob*, against, preposition and prefix; allied to Gr. *epi*, upon, Skr. *api*, moreover. It appears also as *o-, oc-, of-, op-*, as in *omit, occur, offend, oppress*.

Oc-, Of-. Forms of **Ob-**.

Off-, from, as in *offshoot, offspring*. *See* OFF in dictionary.

On-, on, against, as in *onset, onslaught*. *See* ON in dictionary.

Op-. A form of **Ob-**.

Out-, out, beyond, as in *outbid, outburst*. *See* OUT in dictionary.

Over-, above, beyond, too much, as in *overhead, overhang, overburden, overcharge*. *See* OVER in dictionary.

Palin-, back again, as in *palindrome*. From Gr. *palin*, again.

Pan-, Panto-, all, as in *panacea, pantheism, pantograph*. From Gr. *pan, pantos*, all.

Para-, Par-, beside, beyond or aside from, as in *parallel, paradox, parable, parody*. From Gr. *para*, beside, preposition and prefix; allied to *peri*, around, L. *per*, through, E. *for-*. *See* **For-**.

Pel-. A form of **Per-**.

Pen-, almost, as in *peninsula, penultimate*. From L. *pene, paene*, almost.

Per-, through, throughout, thoroughly, as in *perforate, pervade, perfect, perdition;* sometimes has the effect of E. *for-* (in *forswear, forget*), as in *perfidy, perjury*. From L. *per*, through, preposition and prefix; allied to Gr. *para*, E. *for-;* in *pellucid* it appears as *pel*.

Peri-, around, about, as in *periphery, peripatetic, periphrasis*. From Gr. *peri*, about, preposition and prefix; allied to Gr. *para*, L. *per*.

Pol-. A form of **Por-**.

Poly-, many, as in *polygamy, polygon, polysyllable*. From Gr. *polys*, many; same root as E. *full*.

Por-, Pol-, forward, forth, as in *portend, pollute*. From L. prefix *por-, pol-*, akin to *pro*, before, Gr. *pro*, Skr. *pra*, E. *forth*.

Post-, after, behind, as in *postdate, postpone*. From L. *post*, after, preposition and prefix.

Pre-, Prae-, before, beforehand, in advance, as in *predict, prefer, prefigure, preeminent*. From L. *prae*, before, preposition and prefix; akin to *pro, per, primus*. It is the *pr* of *prison*, the *pro* of *provost*.

Preter-, beyond, above, as in *preternatural, preterit*. From L. *praeter*, beyond, a comparative form of *prae*. *See* **Prae**.

Pro-, before, forth, forward, as in *produce, project, pro-*

fess, promise, also instead of, as in *pronoun, proconsul.* From L. *pro,* before, for, preposition and prefix; akin to *prae* and to Gr. *pro,* before, Skr. *pra,* away, E. *for-, q.v.* In some words *pro-* is the Gr. *pro,* as in *prologue.*

Pros-, toward, in addition, as in *proselyte, prosody.* From Gr. *pros,* toward, preposition and prefix; akin to Skr. *prati,* toward, E. *forth.*

Proto-, **Prot-**, first, original, as in *protocol, protoplasm, protagonist.* From Gr. *prōtos,* first, akin to *pro,* before.

Re-, **Red-**, back, again, as in *recall, regain, return, retract;* also change of place, as in *remove.* From L. *re-, red-,* prefix, the latter form being used before vowels, as in *redeem, redolent, redundant.*

Retro-, backward, as in *retroact, retrograde.* From L. prefix *retro-,* backward, a comparative of **Re-** (compare *intro-* and *in-*).

Se-, aside, apart, as in *secede, seduce, seclude;* also without, as in *secure.* From L. *se-,* originally *sed-,* only used as a prefix.

Semi-, half, as in *semicircle.* From L. prefix *semi-,* half; akin to Skr. *sāmi,* half, Gr. *hēmi-. See* **Hemi-.**

Sine-, without, as in *sinecure.* From L. *sine,* without, preposition and prefix, from *si,* if, and *ne,* not.

Sub-, under, beneath, inferior, as in *subject, subordinate, submarine, submerge, submit;* also slightly, as in *subacid, subobtuse.* From L. *sub,* under, preposition and prefix; allied to Gr. *hypo,* under, Skr. *upa,* near, and to E. *up, over;* appears also as *su-, suc-, suf-, sug-, sum-, sup-, sur-,* as in *suspect, succeed, suffer, suggest, summon, suppress, surreptitious.*

Subter-, beneath, as in *subterfuge.* From L. *subter,* beneath, preposition and prefix; comparative of *sub, q.v.*

Suc-, Suf-, Sug-, Sum-, Sup-. Forms of **Sub-.**

Super-, above, over, more than, as in *superabound, superadd, supersede, superhuman.* From L. *super,* over, above, preposition and prefix; a comparative form akin to *sub* and to Gr. *hyper,* over, E. *over. See* SUPER in dictionary.

Supra-, above, as in *supracostal.* From L. *supra,* above, akin to *super.*

Sur-, over, above, as in *surface, surmount;* from Fr. *sur,* above, from L. *super, q.v.*

Sur-. A form of **Sub-.**

Syn-, Sym-, Syl-, with, together with, in company, as in *synagogue, synclinal, symmetry, sympathy, syllable, syllogism.* From Gr. *syn,* with, preposition and prefix; allied to L. *cum. See* **Com-.**

To-, this, on this, as in *today, tonight, together, toward.* From preposition *to.*

Trans-, Tra-, across, over, through, beyond, as in *transmit, transport, transfix, transgress, traverse, traduce.* From L. *trans,* across, preposition and prefix; same root as E. *through. See* THROUGH in dictionary.

Tri-, three, thrice, threefold, as in *triangle, tricolor, trident, trilobite, trilogy.* From L. and Gr. *tri-,* prefix, three, thrice; allied to E. *three.*

Ultra-, beyond, as in *ultramarine, ultramontane.* From L. *ultra,* beyond, preposition and prefix. *See* ULTRA in dictionary.

Un- (1) The negative prefix = not, as in *unavailing, unanswerable.* From A. Sax. *un-,* not; allied to L. *in-,* not. (2) Denoting reversal of an action; as in *undo, untie.* From A. Sax. *un-,* akin to G. *ent-,* Goth. *and-,* E. *an-* in *answer. See* UN- in dictionary.

Under-, below, beneath, as in *undercurrent, underlie, underhand, undersell. See* UNDER in dictionary.

Up-, up, as in *upheave. See* UP in dictionary.

Utter-, outer, further, as in *uttermost.* From A. Sax. *uter,* comparative of *ut,* out.

With-, against, back, as in *withstand, withdraw, withhold.* From A. Sax. *with,* against, same as preposition *with. See* dictionary.

SUFFIXES

-able, that may be, capable of being, as in *lovable, affable.* L. *-abilis.*

-ac, pertaining to, as in *cardiac, demoniac.* Gr. *-akos.*

-aceous, partaking of the properties of, as in *arenaceous, herbaceous.* L. *-aceus.*

-acious, characterized by, as in *tenacious, pugnacious.* Fr. *-acieux,* L. *-ax, -acis.*

-acity, character, quality, as in *veracity.* From L. *acitas.*

-ad, toward, as in *ventrad, dorsad.* From Lat. *-ad,* toward.

-ade, a more or less continuous action, usually by a group of persons, as in *cavalcade, cannonade, fusillade.* From L. suffix *-ata,* through F., Sp., etc.

-age, abstract or collective, also locality, as in *advantage, foliage, parsonage.* Fr. *-age,* L.L. *-aticum,* L. *-aticus,* adjective termination.

-ain, giving adjectives and nouns, as in *certain, captain.* Fr. *-ain,* L. *-anus.*

-air, -aire, as in *corsair, millionaire.* From L. *arius,* through F. *aire.*

-al, pertaining to, as in *annual, filial.* L. *-alis.*

-an, noun and adjective suffix, as in *pagan, Roman, human.* L. *-anus.*

-ana (iana), items of information about places, persons, or things, as in *Americana, Swedenborgiana, Californiana.* From L. *ana,* pertaining to.

-ance, -ancy, denoting state or action, as in *abundance, acceptance.* L. *-antia. See* **-nce.**

-ane, adjective suffix, as in *mundane, humane.* L. *-anus.*

-aneous, belonging to, as in *contemporaneous.* L.*-aneus.*

-ant, equivalent to E. suffix *-ing,* as in *abundant, accordant.* L. *-ans, -antis,* termination of present participle.

-ar, pertaining to, as in *angular, familiar, polar.* L. *-aris.*

-ard, denoting disposition or character, as in *coward, niggard, sluggard.* Partly from A. Sax. *-heard,* literally hard, partly from Fr. *-ard,* from G. *hart,* hard.

-ary, adjective and noun suffix, as in *auxiliary, contrary, library, secretary, antiquary, seminary.* L. *-arius,-arium.*

-asm. *See* **-ism.**

-aster, denoting contempt, as in *poetaster, criticaster.* O. Fr. *-astre,* L. *-aster,* having somewhat of, adjective termination.

-ate, seen in verbs, adjectives, and nouns, as *animate, agitate.* From L. *-atus,* termination of past participle.

-ble. *See* **-able, -ible.**

-ble, as in *treble. See* **-ple.**

-cle, -cule, diminutive suffix, as in *article, particle, animalcule.* L. *-culus, -cula, -culum.*

-cy, state of, as in *idiocy.* Fr. *-cie,* L. *-tia.*

-d. *See* **-ed.**

-dom, power or jurisdiction, state, as in *kingdom, earldom, wisdom, martyrdom.* A. Sax. *dóm,* judgment, authority; akin G. *-thum. See* DOOM in dictionary.

-ed, -d, suffix of past tense. A. Sax. *-de,* shortened for *-dide,* past tense of *dón,* E. to do.

-ed, -d, suffix of past participle and some adjectives and nouns, as in *loved, booted, horned.* Originally *-th,* and corresponding to L. *-tus,* of past participle; same as the *-d, -t, -th,* of *cold, dead, fight, height, death, health.*

-ee, denoting one who is acted on, a recipient, as in *legatee, referee, trustee.* Fr. *-é, -ée,* from L. *-atus* of past participle. *See* **-ate.**

-eer, -ier, denoting profession or employment, as in *brigadier, charioteer.* Fr. *-ier,* L. *-arius.*

-el, diminutive. *See* **-le.**

-en, -n, made of, as in *golden, waxen, leathern;* also pertaining to, as in *heathen.* A. Sax. *-en,* G. *-en,* Goth. *-ein;* akin to L. *-nus,* Gr. *-nos,* Skr. *-nas.*

-en, diminutive, as in *chicken, kitten.* A. Sax. *-en.*

-en, plural, as in *oxen, kine, shoon.* A. Sax *-an.*

-en, to make, verbal termination, as in *soften, whiten.* A. Sax and Goth. infinitive *-nan,* originally an intransitive form.

-ence, -ency. Similar to **-ance, ancy.**

-eous, pertaining to, containing, as in *aqueous.* L. *-eus.* [In *courteous, -eous* is from L. *-ensis;* in *righteous,* also of different origin.]

-er, one who does, as in *baker, singer, writer.* A. Sax. *ere,* G. *-er,* Goth. *-areis,* allied to L. *-arius.* Sometimes takes *y* before it, as in *bowyer, lawyer, sawyer,* in *liar* takes form of *-ar.*

-er, frequentative, as in *flicker, sputter.* A. Sax. *-erian,* G. *-ern.*

-er, comparative suffix. A. Sax. *-er, -or,* G. *-er,* L. *-or.*

-erel, diminutive, as in *cockerel, mongrel.* O. Fr. *-erel.*

-erly, to or from in direction, as in *northerly, easterly.* For *-ern-ly.*

-ern, expressing direction, as in *southern.* A. Sax. *-ern.*

-ery, business or place where it is carried on, also with collective force, as in *archery, brewery, cutlery, finery, soldiery.* From nouns in *-er* with Fr. *-ie,* L. *-ia.*

-es, -s, denoting plurals. A. Sax. *-as;* common to the Aryan languages.

-escent, becoming gradually, as in *convalescent, effervescent.* L. *-escens, -escentis,* present participle of inceptive verbs in *-esco.*

-ese, belonging to a country or city, as in *Siamese, Maltese.* Fr. *-ais, -ois,* It. *-ese,* from L. *-ensis.*

-esque, partaking of, as in *picturesque.* Fr. *-esque,* from L. *-iscus,* a form of *-icus.*

-ess, feminine suffix, as in *authoress, countess, giantess.* Fr. *-esse,* L. *-issa,* from Gr. *-issa.*

-est, suffix of superlatives. A. Sax. *-est, -ost,* G. *-est;* allied to Gr. *-istos,* Skr. *-ishthas.*

-et, -ette, diminutive suffix, as in *billet, coronet, palette.* Fr. *-et, -ette.*

-ey, adjective suffix. *See* **-y.**

-ferous, bearing, producing, as in *auriferous, quartziferous.* L. *-fer,* from *fero,* to bear.

-fold, denoting multiplication, as in *threefold, manifold.* From *fold,* noun or verb.

-ful, full of, as in *fanciful, mournful.* A. Sax. *-ful*=E. *full.*

-fy, to make, as in *beautify.* Fr. *-fier,* L. *ficare,* from *facio,* to make.

-geneous, -genous, as in *homogeneous.* From Gr. and L. root *-gen,* to produce.

-graph, -graphy. From Gr. *-graphos, -graphia,* from *grapho,* to write.

-head, -hood, state, condition, as in *Godhead, widowhood.* A. Sax. *had,* state, rank=G. *-heit.*

-iana. *See* **-ana.**

-ible, same meaning as **-able,** as in *accessible.*

-ic, pertaining to, as in *botanic, periodic, public.* L. *-icus,* Gr. *-ikos,* Skr. *-ikas.*

-ical, pertaining to, as in *logical.* From L. *-icus* and *-alis* combined.

-ics, properly plural, but used as a singular in names of branches of knowledge, as in *mathematics, ethics.* Gr. *ika,* literally things belonging to.

-id, adjective suffix, as in *arid, fluid, torpid.* L. *-idus.*

-id, -idae, suffix of family names of animals. Gr. *-ides,* denoting descent.

-ide, suffix of certain chemical compounds, as *chloride.* Gr. *-eidos,* form.

-ie, -y, diminutive suffix, as in *wifie, Johnnie.* From *-ick,* weaker form of *-ock.*

-ier. Same as **-eer.**

-ile, capable of being, as in *docile, fragile.* L. *-ilis.*

-ile, belonging to, as in *puerile, senile, Gentile.* L. *-ilis.*

-im, a Hebrew plural sign, as in *cherubim.*

-ine, feminine suffix, as in *heroine.* Fr. *-ine,* L. *-ina.*

-ine, suffix of adjectives and nouns, as in *divine, iodine.* L. *-inus, -ina.*

-ing, noun suffix, as in *whiting, shilling.* A. Sax. *-ing.*

-ing, termination of present participles. Corrupted from A. Sax. *-ende.*

-ing, termination of verbal nouns. A. Sax. *-ung.*

-ion. *See* **-sion, -tion.**

-ique, adjective suffix, as in *antique, unique.* Fr. *-ique,* L. *-iquus,* a form of *-icus.*

-ise. *See* **-ize.**

-ish, pertaining to, having somewhat of, as in *childish, foolish, dwarfish, whitish, English.* A. Sax. *-isc,* G. *-isch,* Goth. *-isk.*

-ish, verbal suffix, as in *nourish, perish.* From forms in *-iss-* of French verbs, from L. *-esc-* of inceptive verbs (as *abolesco—abolish*).

-ism, -asm, suffix of nouns, often implying state, system, doctrines, as in *barbarism, atheism, organism, skepticism, pleonasm.* L. *-ismus, -asmus,* from Gr. *-ismos, -asmos.*

-ist, -ast, one who; suffix often corresponding to *-ism, -asm,* as in *atheist, gymnast.*

-ite, one of, a follower of, as in *Israelite, Spinozite.* L. *-ita,* Gr. *-itēs.*

-ite, a geological suffix=*-lite.* Also a chemical suffix, from L. adjective suffix *-itus.*

-itis, suffix denoting inflammation; used in medical terms, as in *laryngitis.* Gr. *-itis.*

-ity, state, as in *ability.* L. *-itas.* *See* **-ty.**

-ix. *See* **-trix.**

-ize, -ise, to make, to act, as in *civilize, economize.* Fr. *-iser,* O. Fr. *-izer,* L.L. *izare,* from Gr. *-izein.*

-kin, diminutive suffix, as in *lambkin.* Not in A. Sax.; same as D. *-ek-en,* Gr. *-ch-en;* equivalent to *-ock-en,* and thus a double diminutive.

-le, -el, a suffix in nouns denoting instrument, as in *needle, saddle, steeple, navel, weasel.* A. Sax. *-el, -ol, -ul, -ela,* G. *-el,* Aryan *-al, -ar.* Also in some adjectives, as *idle.*

-le, diminutive and frequent suffix of verbs, as in *frizzle, nibble, sparkle.*

-lence, suffix in abstract nouns, corresponds to **-lent.**

-lent, full of, as in *violent, purulent.* L. *-lentus.*

-less, free from, without, as in *artless, fatherless.* A. Sax. *-leás,* G. *-los;* akin *lose, loss.*

-let, diminutive suffix, as in *leaflet, streamlet.* From *-le* or *-el,* and *-et.*

-ling, diminutive suffix, as in *darling, lordling, starveling.* From *-ing,* A. Sax. *-ing,* with prefixed *-le* or *-el.*

-ling, -long, adverbial suffix, as in *darkling, endlong.* A. Sax. *-linga, -lunga,* adverbial datives.

-lite, in mineralogical terms, stone, as in *aerolite.* Gr. *lithos,* a stone.

-logy, doctrine, science, as in *biology.* Gr. *-logia,* from *logos,* a word, speech.

-ly, like, an adjective and adverbial suffix, as in *lovely, truly.* A form of adjective *like;* A. Sax. *-lic,* adjective suffix, *-lice,* adverbial suffix.

-ment, act of, state of, as in *agreement, argument, experiment.* Fr. *-ment,* L. *mentum.*

-meter, a measure, as in *hydrometer.* Gr. *metron,* a measure.

-mony, state, as in *matrimony, parsimony.* L. *-monium, -monia.*

-most, suffix in superlatives, as *foremost.* Not the same as *most,* superlative of *much,* but a double superlative composed of superlative suffixes *-ma* and *-est. See* FOREMOST in dictionary.

-nce, -ncy, suffix of abstract nouns usually denoting state, as in *vigilance, brilliancy, abhorrence, excellency.* Fr. *-nce,* L. *-ntia,* from present participles in *-ans, -antis, ens, -entis,* with suffix *-ia.*

-ness, denoting state of being, as in *barrenness, fullness, redness.* A. Sax. *-nes,* same as G. *-nis,* Goth. *-nassus.*

-ock, diminutive suffix, as in *hillock, bullock.* A. Sax. *-uca.*

-oid, -oidal, resembling, as in *elephantoid, spheroidal.* Gr. *-oeidēs,* from *eidos,* form.

-on, noun suffix, as in *dragon, falcon.* Fr. *-on,* L. *-onem,* accusative suffix of nouns in *-o, -onis.*

-or, one who, as in *emperor, sailor.* Fr. *-eur,* from L. *-torem,* accusative of nouns in *-tor.*

-ory. *See* **-tory.**

-our, -or, suffix of abstract nouns, as in *colour* or *color, favor, honor.* Fr. *eur,* L. *-oreum,* accusative of nouns in *-or, -oris.*

-ous, -ose, full of, abounding with, as in *copious, famous, operose, verbose.* Fr. *-eux,* L. *-osus.*

-pathy, state of feeling, as in *antipathy.* Gr. *-pathia,* from *pathos,* suffering.

-phorous, bearing, carrying, as in *phyllophorous.* Gr. *-phoros,* from *pherō,* to bear.

-ple, same sense as *-fold,* as in *triple, quadruple.* L. *-plus,* akin to *-pleo,* to fill.

-red. *See* HATRED in dictionary.

-ric. *See* BISHOPRIC in dictionary.

-ry, collective noun suffix, an art, as in *nunnery, cookery, poetry.* Fr. *-rie,* L. *-ria.*

-'s, suffix of the possessive. A. Sax. *-es*=G. *-s, -es,* L. *-is.* [The old notion that it stands for *his* is quite erroneous, though this may be the origin of the apostrophe sign.]

-scope, -scopy, what assists sight, a seeing. Gr. *-skopes, -skopia,* from *skopeō,* to see.

-ship, state of, office of, as in *apprenticeship, censorship, rectorship.* A. Sax. *-scipe,* akin to *ship, shape.*

-sion, state or action abstractly, as in *explosion, tension.* L. *-sio, sionis,* akin *-tion.*

-some, full of, abounding in, as in *gladsome, frolicsome, troublesome.* A. Sax. *-sum,* Icel. and G. *-sam;* akin to *same.*

-some, noun suffix for two or more persons working or playing together, as in *twosome, foursome.*

-ster, one who, as in *gamester, maltster, songster.* A. Sax. *-estre,* originally a feminine suffix, as still in *spinster.*

-sy, state, as in *heresy, fantasy.* Gr. *-sis, -sia.*

-t, suffix of nouns, as in *height, flight.* Same as *-th.*

-teen, ten, as in *fifteen.* A. Sax. *-tyne.*

-ter, -ther, a comparative suffix, as in *after, other.* A. Sax. *-ter, -der, -ther. See* AFTER in dictionary.

-th, suffix of abstract nouns, as in *breadth, death, health.* A. Sax. *-th,* allied to L. *-tus,* as in *juventus,* youth.

-th, suffix of ordinals, as *sixth.* A. Sax. *-tha;* allied to *-tus,* in L. *sextus,* sixth.

-ther, an agent, as in *father, mother, brother.* A. Sax. *-der, -dor, thor;* allied to L. *-tor,* Skr. *-tar,* denoting an agent.

-tion, state or action abstractly, as in *conception, perception.* L. *-tio, -tionis;* akin *-sion.*

-tor, an agent, as in *actor. See* **-ther.**

-tory, adjective suffix, as in *amatory, confirmatory, explanatory.* L. *-torius,* corresponding to nouns in *-tor.* From the neuter *-torium* comes the termination when signifying place, as in *dormitory, lavatory.*

-trix, feminine suffix corresponding to *-tor,* as in *testatrix.* L. *-trix.*

-tude, suffix of abstract nouns, as in *fortitude, gratitude.* L. *-tudo, -tudinis.*

-ture, *See* **-ure.**

-ty, suffix of abstract nouns, as in *gravity, levity.* Fr. *-té,* L. *-tas, -tatis.*

-ty, ten times, as in *fifty.* A. Sax. *-tig;* akin to *ten, -teen.*

-ule, diminutive suffix, as in *globule.* L. *-ulus, -ula, -ulum.*

-ure, act, thing produced, as in *capture, gesture, creature, picture.* L. *-ura.*

-ward, -wards, suffix of direction, as in *homeward, homewards;* when with *-s* an adverbial genitive. A. Sax. *-weard, -weardes;* akin to *worth* (verb), L. *verto,* to turn.

-way, -ways, suffix of manner, as in *always, straightway.* From *way,* manner; *-ways* is an adverbial genitive.

-wise, suffix of manner, as in *lengthwise, likewise. See* WISE in dictionary.

-y, -ey, adjective suffix, as in *bloody, clayey, dirty, filthy, skyey, woody.* A. Sax. *-ig,* G. *-ig;* allied to L. *-icus,* Gr. *-ikos.* In *hasty, jolly,* represents Fr. *-if,* L. *-ivus.*

-y, noun suffix. Sometimes, as in *company, fallacy,* it represents Fr. *-ie,* L. *-ia,* or Gr. *-ia* (as in *apology);* sometimes L. *-ium,* as in *remedy, subsidy;* sometimes L. *-ius,* as in *notary;* sometimes L. *-atus,* as in *deputy.*

A

A, a, ā, the first letter in the English and other alphabets derived from the Latin and Greek alphabets. In *music,* it designates the sixth note of the model or diatonic scale of C, the note sounded by the open second string of the violin.

a, ā, the indefinite article, a contraction of *an,* used before nouns singular beginning with a consonant sound. AN.

aardvark, ärd′värk, *n.* [D.=earth pig.] The groundhog of South Africa, a burrowing, insectivorous, edentate animal.

aardwolf, ärd′wu̧lf, *n.* [D.=earth wolf.] The earth wolf of South Africa, an animal allied to the hyenas and civets.

Aaronic, Aaronical, â•ron′ik, â•ron′ik•al, *a.* Pertaining to Aaron, or to his priesthood.

abaca, ab′a•ka, *n.* Native name of the plant which yields Manila hemp.

aback, a•bak′, *adv.* [Prefix *a,* on, and *back.*] Backward: *naut.* catching the wind so as to urge a sailing vessel backward; *fig.* by surprise; unexpectedly: as, to take a person *aback.*

ab•a•cus ab′a•kus, *n.* [L.] A frame holding beaded rods for making calculations; *arch.* a slab or table forming the crowning of a column and its capital.

Abaddon, a•bad′on, *n.* [Heb. destruction.] Hell. Rev. ix. 11.

abaft, a•bäft′, *adv.* or *prep.* [Prefix *a,* and A. Sax. *be-aeftan, baeftan.* AFT.] On or toward the aft or hinder part of a ship.

abalone, ab•a•lō′ni, *n.* [Spanish, of unknown origin.] A name in California for a marine mollusk, a species of ear shell which furnishes mother-of-pearl.

abandon, a•ban′dun, *v.t.* [Fr. *abandonner,* from *a,* to, and O.Fr. *bandon,* control, liberty; to leave at liberty. BAN.] To detach or withdraw one's self from; desert; forsake; give up; resign; yield up; *refl.* to yield one's self up without attempt at restraint; as, to *abandon one's self* to grief.—*n.* Abandonment†; heartiness; frank, unrestrained demeanor (a French usage).—**abandoned,** a•ban′dund, *a.* Given up to vice; shamelessly and recklessly wicked; profligate; depraved; vicious.—**abandoner,** a•ban′dun•ėr, *n.* One who abandons.—**abandonment,** a•ban′dun•ment, *n.* The act of abandoning or state of being abandoned; relinquishment; desertion; giving up.

abase, a•bās′, *v.t.—abased, abasing.* [Fr. *abaisser—a,* to, and *baisser,* to lower, from L.L. *bassus,* low. BASE.] To lower or depress (of material objects)‡; to reduce lower, as in rank; humble; degrade.—**abasement,** a•bās′ment, *n.* The act of abasing; a state of depression, degradation, or humiliation.

abash, a•bash′, *v.t.* [O.Fr. *esbahir,* ppr. *esbahissant,* from *es=ex,* intens., *bair, baer,* to gape; Mod.Fr. *s'ebahir,* to be astonished; probably from *bah!* exclamation of astonishment.] To confuse or confound, as by consciousness of guilt, inferiority, etc; make ashamed; put to confusion. *Abash* is a stronger word than *confuse,* but not so strong as *confound.* —**abashment,** a•bash′ment, *n.* Act of, state of being, abashed.

abate, a•bāt′, *v.t.—abated, abating.* [Fr. *abattre,* to beat down, from L. *batere,* a form of *batuere,* to beat. BATTER.] To beat down‡; to lessen; diminish; remit; moderate (zeal, a demand, a tax); *law,* to annul; put an end to.—*v.i.* To decrease or become less in strength or violence.—**abatable,** a•bāt′a•bl, *a.* Capable of being abated.—**abatement,** a•bāt′ment, *n.* The act of, or state of being, abated; decrease; decline; mitigation; amount or sum deducted; deduction; decrease.—**abater,** a•bāt′ėr, *n.* One who or that abates.

abatis, ab′a•tis, *n.* [Fr. *abattis, abattis,* from *abattre,* to beat down. ABATE.] *Fort.* a collection of felled trees, from which the smaller branches have been cut off, and which are laid side by side, with the branched ends toward assailants, forming an obstruction to their progress.

abattoir, a•bat•wär′, *n.* [Fr., from *abattre,* to beat or knock down. ABATE.] A public slaughterhouse.

abaxial, ab•ak′si•al, *a.* [Prefix *ab,* from, *axis.*] Not in the axis.

abbacy, ab′ba•si, *n.* The dignity, rights, and privileges of an abbot.—**abbatial,** ab•bā′shi•al), *a.* Belonging to an abbey.

abbé, ab′bā, *n.* [Fr., an abbot.] In France, especially before the Revolution, one who devoted himself to divinity, or who had pursued a course of study in a theological seminary; many of them became tutors, professors, and men of letters.

abbess, ab′bes, *n.* [Fr. *abbesse,* L.L. *abbatissa.*] A female superior of an abbey, possessing, in general, the same dignity and authority as an abbot, except that she cannot exercise the spiritual functions appertaining to the priesthood.—**abbey,** ab′bi, *n.* [Fr. *abbaye,* from L.L. *abbatia,* an abbey. ABBOT.] A monastery or monastic establishment of the highest rank; a society of persons of either sex, secluded from the world, and devoted to religion and celibacy, governed by an *abbot* or *abbess.*—**abbot,** ab′but, *n.* [Formerly *abbat,* L.L. *abbas, abbatis,* from Syr. and Chal. *abba,* father.] The male head or superior of an abbey or monastery. Some abbots were *mitred* abbots, almost equal in rank with bishops. Laymen were sometimes abbots, enjoying the abbey revenues.—*Abbot of Misrule,* of unreason; burlesque figure in medieval mystery plays and revels.—**abbotship,** ab′but•ship, *n.* The state or office of an abbot.

abbreviate, ab•brē′vi•āt, *v.t.—abbreviated, abbreviating.* [L. *abbrevio, abbreviatum,* to shorten—*ab* for *ad,* and *brevis,* short. BRIEF, ABRIDGE (which is really the same word).] To make briefer; shorten; abridge; reduce to smaller compass.—**abbreviation,** ab•brē′vi•ā″shon, *n.* Act of abbreviating, shortening, or contracting; that which is abbreviated; a syllable, letter, or series of letters, standing for a word or words; as *Ph.D.* for *doctor of philosophy; D.A.R.* for *Daughters of the American Revolution.*—**abbreviator,** ab•brē′vi•ā•tėr, *n.* One who abbreviates.

abdicate, ab′di•kāt, *v.t.—abdicated,*

abdicating. [L. *abdico*, *abdicatum*—*ab*, from, and *dico*, *dicatum*, to declare publicly.] To give up, renounce, lay down, or withdraw from in a voluntary, public, or formal manner, as a throne, duties, etc.; vacate; resign.—*v.i.* To renounce or give up power voluntarily.—**abdication,** ab•di•kā'shon, *n.* The act of abdicating an office, especially the kingly office. —**abdicator,** ab'di•kāt•ėr, *n.* One who abdicates.

abdomen, ab•dō'men or ab'do•men, *n.* [L.] That part of the human body which lies between the thorax and the pelvis, containing the stomach, liver, spleen, pancreas, kidneys, bladder, and intestines; the posterior of the three parts of a perfect insect.—**abdominal,** ab•dom'in•al, *a.* Pertaining to the abdomen or belly. —*abdominal regions*, certain regions into which the abdomen in man is arbitrarily divided for convenience in anatomical or medical descriptions.—**abdominous,**† ab•dom'in•us, *a.* Abdominal; potbellied.

abduce, ab•dūs', *v.t.*—*abduced*, *abducing*. [L. *abduco*, to lead away—*ab*, and *duco*, to lead, to draw. DUKE.] To draw or conduct away.—**abducent,** ab•dūs'ent, *a.* Drawing away; pulling back.—*Abducent muscles*, muscles which pull back certain parts of the body from the mesial line.—**abduct,** ab•dukt', *v.t.* To draw or lead away; to take away surreptitiously, and by force.—**abduction,** ab•duk'shon, *n.* The act of abducting; *anat.* the action by which muscles withdraw a limb or other part from the axis of the body; *law*, the unlawful leading away of a person, as a young woman, by fraud, persuasion, or open violence.—**abductor,** ab•duk'tėr, *n.* One who or that which abducts; *anat.* a muscle which moves certain parts from the axis of the body.

abeam, a•bēm', *adv. Naut.* in the direction of the beams, that is, at right angles to the keel of a ship.

abecedarian, ā'bē•sē•dâ''ri•an, *n*, [From the letters *a*, *b*, *c*, *d*.] One who teaches the letters of the alphabet, or a learner of the letters.—**abecedary,**†, ā•bē•sē'dâ•ri, *a.* Pertaining to or formed by the letters of the alphabet.—*n.* A first principle or element; rudiment.

abed, a•bed', *adv.* In bed; gone to bed.

abele, a•bēl', *n.* [D. *abeel*, G. *albele*, L. *albus*, white.] The white poplar.

aberr, ab•er', *v.i.* [L. *aberro*, *aberratum*—*ab*, from, and *erro*, to wander, to err.] *Obs.* To wander; to err.—**aberrance,**† **aberrancy,**† ab•er'rans, ab-er'ran-si, *n.* A wandering; aberration.—**aberrant,** ab•er'rant, *a.* Characterized by aberration; wandering; straying from the right way; differing from a common type.—**aberration,** ab•er•rā'shon, *n.* [L. *aberratio*.] The act of wandering from the right way; deviation from truth or rectitude or from a type or standard; partial alienation of mind; mental wandering; the difference between the true and the observed position of a heavenly body.

abet, a•bet', *v.t.*—*abetted*, *abetting*. [O.Fr. *abetter*, *abeter*, to incite, to lure; *abet*, a bait—prefix *a*, and word = *bait*, to incite, set on. BAIT, BITE.] To encourage by aid, countenance, or approval: used chiefly in a bad sense; incite; support, encourage; back up.—**abetment,** a•bet'ment, *n.* The act of abetting; aid. —**abetter, abettor,** a•bet'ėr, *n.* One who abets or incites; a supporter or encourager, generally of something bad.

abeyance, a•bā'ans, *n.* [O.Fr. *abbaiaunce*, expectation, from *abbayer*, to listen with the mouth open, from *bayer*, *baer*, to gape, as in crying *bah!* ABASH.] A state of expectation, or waiting for an occupant or holder: said of lands, honors, or dignities; a state of temporary suspension.—**abeyant,** a•bā'ant, *a.* Being in abeyance.

abhor, ab•hąr', *v.t.*—*abhorred*, *abhorring*. [L. *abhorreo*, to shrink back—*ab*, from, and *horreo*, to feel horror. HORRIBLE.] To hate extremely or with loathing; loathe, detest, or abominate; shrink from with horror; fill with horror and loathing (*Shak.*)‡.—**abhorrence,** ab•hor'rens, *n.* Extreme hatred; detestation; great aversion.—**abhorrent,** ab•hor'rent, *a.* Struck with abhorrence; hating; detesting; utterly repugnant: in the last sense used formerly with *from*, now with *to*.—**abhorrently,** ab•hor'rent•li, *adv.* With abhorrence.—**abhorrer,** ab•hor'ėr, *n.* One who abhors; petitioner to Charles II in 1680 against the change of succession.

abide, a•bīd', *v.i.*—*abode* (pret. and pp.), *abiding*. [A. Sax. *abîdan*, *gebîdan*, to abide, from *bîdan*, to bide. See BIDE.] To take up one's abode; dwell; stay; not to depart.—*To abide by*, to remain beside; to adhere to: to maintain; to remain satisfied with. —*v.t.* To be prepared for; to await; be able to endure or sustain; remain firm under; to put up with; to tolerate.—**abider,** a•bīd'ėr, *n.* One who abides.—**abiding,** a•bīd'ing, *a.* Continuing; permanent; steadfast; as an *abiding* faith.—**abidingly,** a•bīd'•ing•li, *adv.* In such a manner as to continue; permanently.

Abigail, ab'i-gāl, *n.* [From the title of *handmaid* assumed to herself by *Abigail*, wife of Nabal. See 1 Sam. xxv. 3.] A general name for a waiting woman or lady's-maid. [Colloq.]

ability, a•bil'i•ti, *n.* [Fr. *habilité*, L. *habilitas*, ableness. ABLE.] The state or condition of being able; power, whether bodily or mental; *pl.* talents; powers of the mind; mental gifts or endowments.

abiogenesis, abiogeny, a•bī'ō•jen''e•sis, a•bī•oj'en•i, *n.* [Gr. *a*, not, *bios*, life, and *genesis*, generation.] The doctrine that living matter may be produced by nonliving matter. BIOGENESIS, HETEROGENESIS.—**abiogenist,** a•bī•oj'en•ist, *n.* A believer in the doctrine of abiogenesis.—**abiogenetic,** a•bī'ō•jen•et'ik, *a.* Of, pertaining to, or produced by abiogenesis.—**abiogenetically,** a•bī'ō•jenet''ik•al•li, *adv.* In an abiogenetic manner.

abject, ab'jekt, *a.* [L. *abjectus*, from *abjicio*, to throw away—*ab*, and *jacio*, to throw.] Sunk to a low condition; worthless, mean, despicable; low, groveling.—*n.* A person in a low or abject condition.—**abjection,** ab•jek'shon, *n.* A low state; meanness of spirit; abjectness.—**abjectly,** ab•jekt'li, *adv.* In an abject or contemptible manner; meanly; servilely.—**abjectness,** ab•jekt'nes, *n.* The state of being abject; meanness; servility.

abjure, ab•jūr', *v.t.*—*abjured*, *abjuring*. [L. *abjuro*, to deny upon oath—*ab*, and *juro*, to swear. JURY.] To renounce upon oath; to reject or withdraw from with solemnity; abandon (as allegiance, errors); to recant or retract.—**abjurer,** ab•jūr'ėr, *n.* One who abjures.—**abjuration,** ab•jū•rā'shon, *n.* The act of abjuring; a renunciation upon oath; a rejection or denial with solemnity; a total abandonment.—**abjuratory,** ab•jū'ra•to•ri, *a.* Pertaining to abjuration.

ablactate, ab-lak'tāt, *v.t.* [L. *ablacto*, to wean—*ab*, from, and *lac*, milk.] To wean from the breast.—**ablactation,** ab•lak•tā'shon, *n.* The weaning of a child from the breast; *hort.* same as *inarching*.

ablative, ab'la•tiv, *a.* [L. *ablativus*, from *ablatus*, carried away—*ab*, away, and *latus*, carried.] Taking or tending to take away†: applied to a case of nouns in Sanskrit, Latin, and some other languages, originally given to the case in Latin because separation from was considered to be one of the chief ideas expressed by it.—**ablation,**† ab•lā'shon, *n.* A carrying or taking away.

ablaut, ab'lout, *n.* [G., from *ab*, off, and *laut*, sound.] *Philol.* a substitution of one vowel for another in the body of a word, to indicate a corresponding modification of use or meaning; as, *bind*, *band*, *bound*, *bond;* especially the change of a vowel to indicate tense change in verbs, instead of the addition of a syllable (•*ed*); as, *sink*, *sank*, *sunk*.

ablaze, a•blāz', *adv.* or *a.* In a blaze; in a state of eager excitement or desire.

able, ā'bl, *a.* [O. Fr. *able*, *hable*, *habile*, skillful, fit, from L. *habilis*, suitable, fit, from *habeo*, to have; akin are *ability*, *habiliment*, *habit*, suffix•*able*.] Having the power, means, or qualification sufficient; competent; qualified; having strong or unusual powers of mind, or intellectual qualifications; gifted; vigorous; active.—**able,**‡ ā'bl, *v.t.* To make able; to enable; to warrant or answer for. [*Shak.*]—**able-bodied,** *a.* Having a sound, strong body; having strength sufficient for work; often applied to a seaman who is well skilled in seamanship, and classed in the ship's books as A.B.—**ably,** ā'bli, *adv.* In an able manner; with ability.

abloom, a•blöm', *a.* or *adv.* In a blooming state.

abluent, ab'lū•ent, *a.* [L. *abluens*, *abluentis*, ppr. of *abluo*, to wash off—*ab*, from, and *luo*, to wash.]

Washing clean; cleansing by water or liquids.—*n.* That which washes or carries off impurities; a detergent.—**ablution,** ab•lū′shon, *n.* The act of washing; cleansing or purification by water or other liquid; specifically, a washing of the body preparatory to religious rites.—**ablutionary,** ab•lū′shon•a•ri, *a.* Pertaining to ablution.

abnegate, ab′nē•gāt, *v.t.*—*abnegated, abnegating.* [L. *abnego, abnegatum*—*ab,* from, and *nego,* to deny. NEGATIVE, DENY.] To deny; to renounce.—**abnegation,** ab•nē•gā′shon, *n.* [L. *abnegatio.*] The act of abnegating; denial; renunciation.—**abnegator,** ab′nē•gā•tėr, *n.* One who abnegates, denies, or renounces.

abnormal, ab•nạr′mal, *a.* [L. *abnormis*—*ab,* from, and *norma,* a rule. NORMAL.] Not conformed or conforming to rule; deviating from a type or standard; irregular; contrary to system or law.—**abnormality,** ab•nor•mal′i•ti, *n.* The state or quality of being abnormal; deviation from a standard, rule, or type; irregularity; that which is abnormal.—**abnormity,**† ab•nor′mi•ti, *n.* Abnormality.

aboard, a-bōrd′, *adv.* On board; within a ship or boat.—*prep.* On board; into (to go *aboard* a ship).

abode, a•bōd′, pret. of *abide.*—**abode,** a•bōd′, *n.* [From *abide.*] Residence or place of residence; a place where a person abides, a dwelling; habitation.—*To make abode,* to dwell or reside.

abolish, a•bol′ish, *v.t.* [Fr. *abolir*; L. *abolere,* to annul, abolish—*ab,* from, and *oleo,* to grow. ADULT.] To do away with; to put an end to; to destroy; to efface or obliterate; to make void; to annul; to put out of existence.—**abolishable,** a•bol′ish•a•bl, *a.* Capable of being abolished.—**abolisher,** a•bol′ish•ėr, *n.* One who or that which abolishes.—**abolishment,**† a•bol′ish•ment, *n.* Abolition.—**abolition,** ab•ō•li′shon, *n.* The act of abolishing, or the state of being abolished.—**abolitionism,** ab•ō•li′shon-izm, *n.* The principles of an abolitionist.—**abolitionist,** ab•ō•li′shon•ist, *n.* A person who favors the abolition of anything; applied especially to those who favored the abolition of slavery in the United States.

abomasus, abomasum, ab•ō•mā′sus, ab•ō•mā′sum, *n.* [L. prefix *ab,* from, and *omasum.*] The fourth stomach of ruminating animals, lying next to the omasum or third stomach.

abominate, a•bom′in•āt, *v.t.*—*abominated, abominating.* [L. *abominor, abominatus, to deprecate, as of ill* omen—*ab,* from, and *omen,* an omen.] To hate extremely; to abhor; to detest.—**abominable,** abom′in•a•bl, *a.* Deserving or liable to be abominated; detestable; loathsome; odious in the utmost degree; execrable.—**abominableness,** a•bom′in•a•bl•nes, *n.* The quality or state of being abominable, detestable, or odious.—**abominably,** a•bom′in•a•bli, *adv.* In an abominable manner or degree.—**abomination,** a•bom′in•ā″shon, *n.* The act of abominating or state of being abominated; detestation; that which is abominated or abominable; hence, hateful or shameful vice.

aboriginal, ab•o•rij′in•al, *a.* [L. *ab,* from, and *origo,* origin.] Inhabiting a country from the earliest known times; as, *aboriginal* tribes.—*n.* An original inhabitant; one of an aboriginal race.—**aboriginally,** ab•o•rij′in•al•li, *adv.* In or of first origin; originally; from the very first.—**aborigines,** ab•o•rij′in•ēz, *n. pl.* [L.] The people found in a country at the time of the earliest known settlement.

abort, a•bạrt′, *v.i.* [L. *aborior, abortus,* to miscarry—*ab,* and *orior, ortus,* to arise. ORIENT.] To miscarry in giving birth; to appear in a rudimentary or undeveloped state.—**abortion,** a•bor′shon, *n.* The act of miscarrying, or producing young before the natural time, or before the fetus is perfectly formed; the product of untimely birth; a misshapen being; a monster; anything which fails before it is matured or perfect, as a design.—**abortive,** a•bort′iv, *a.* Brought forth in an immature state; rudimentary; imperfectly formed or developed; producing or intended to produce abortion; not brought to completion or to a successful issue; coming to nought.—**abortive,** a•bort′iv, *n.* A drug causing or thought to cause abortion.—**abortively,** a•bort′iv•li, *adv.* In an abortive manner; immaturely.—**abortiveness,** a•bort′iv•nes, *n.* The state of being abortive.

abound, a•bound′, *v.i.* [Fr. *abonder,* from L. *abundare,* to overflow—*ab,* and *unda,* a wave. UNDULATE, WATER.] To be in great plenty; be very prevalent; have or possess in great quantity; be copiously supplied: in the latter sense followed by *with* or *in.*

about, a•bout′, *prep.* [A.Sax. *âbûtan, onbûtan,* about, around—prefixes *â, on,* on, and *bûtan,* without. BUT.] Around; on the outside or surface of; in a circle surrounding; round (two yards *about* the stem); near to in place, time, size, number, quantity, etc.; near to in action; on the point of (to be *about* to speak): in this sense followed by the infinitive; concerned in; engaged in (what is he *about?*) concerning; relating to; respecting.—*adv.* Around the outside; in circuit; in a circle; near to in number, time, place, quality, or degree (*about* as high); here and there; around; in one place and another; in different directions.—*To bring about,* to cause to happen; to effect or accomplish.—*To come about,* to come to pass; to happen.—*To go about,* to prepare to do.—*Turn about, week about,* etc.; alternately, on each alternate week, and the like.

above, a•buv′, *prep.* [A.Sax. *âbûfan,* above: a triple compound of *â,* on, at, *be,* by, and *ûfan,* upward, akin to E. *over,* L. *super,* Gr. *hyper,* above.] In or to a higher place than; superior to in any respect; too high for (*above* mean actions); more in number, quantity, or degree than; in excess of (*above* a ton).—*Above all,* above or before everything else; before every other consideration.—*adv.* In or to a higher place; overhead; before, in rank or order, especially in a book or writing (what has been said *above*); besides, in the expression *over and above. Above* is often used elliptically as a noun, meaning (1) heaven; (2) the aforesaid; as, from the *above* you will learn. It is equal to an adjective in such phrases as, the *above* particulars, in which *cited* or *mentioned* is understood.—**aboveboard,** *adv.* [Said to mean lit. above the table, not with hands below the table, as one trying to cheat at cards.] In open sight; without tricks or disguise.—**aboveground,** *adv.* Alive; not buried.

abracadabra, ab′ra•ka•dab″ra, *n.* A word of eastern origin used in incantations. When written on paper so as to form a triangle, the first line contained the word in full, the one below it omitted the last letter, and so on each time until only one letter remained. Worn as an amulet, it was supposed to be an antidote against certain diseases.

abrade, a•brād′, *v.t.*—*abraded, abrading.* [L. *abrado,* to scrape off—*ab,* away, and *rado,* to scrape, whence *raze, razor,* etc.] To rub or wear down; to rub or grate off.—**abradant,** a•brād′ant, *n.* A material for grinding, usually in powder, such as emery, sand, glass, etc.—**abrasion,** ab•rā′zhon, *n.* The act of abrading, wearing, or rubbing off; an injury of the skin by removal of cuticle.—**abrasive,** ab•rā′ziv, *a.* and *n.* Serving to abrade; an abradant.

Abrahamic, ā•bra•ham′ik, *a.* pertaining to Abraham, the patriarch.

abranchiate, a•brang′ki•āt, *a.* [Gr. *a,* without, and *branchia,* gills.] Devoid of branchiae or gills.—*n.* A vertebrate animal (mammal, bird, reptile) that at no period of its existence possesses gills.

abrasion. See ABRADE.

abreaction, ab′rē•ak″shon, *n.* [L. *ab.* away, and *reaction.*] In psychoanalysis, getting rid of a past disagreeable experience by living it through again in speech or action in the course of treatment.

abreast, a•brest′, *adv.* Side by side, with the breasts in a line; hence, up to a level or standard (to keep *abreast* of science).

abridge, a•brij′, *v.t.*—*abridged, abridging.* [Fr. *abréger,* from L. *abbreviare,* to shorten. ABBREVIATE.] To make shorter; to curtail; to epitomize; to shorten by using fewer words; to condense; to lessen; to diminish; to deprive or cut off from: in the last sense followed by *of* (to *abridge* one *of* his *rights*).—**abridger,** a•brij′ėr, *n.* One who or that which abridges.—**abridgment,** a•brij′ment, *n.* The act of abridging or state of being; that which is abridged; an epitome; a summary, as of a book; an abstract. An *abridgment* is a larger work shortened; a *compendium* is a condensed view of a particular subject regarded as complete in itself; an *epitome* has more reference to the selection of essential facts than an *abridgment*; an *abstract* is a bare statement of facts contained in, or of the leading features of, a work.

abroach, a•brōch′, *a.* or *adv.* Tapped; in a position for letting out liquor: said of a cask; broached.

abroad, a•brạd′, *adv.* At large; without being confined to narrow limits; with expansion (to spread its branches *abroad*); beyond or out of the walls of a house or other inclosure; beyond the bounds of a country; in foreign countries.

abrogate, ab′rō•gāt, *v.t.—abrogated, abrogating.* [L. *abrogo,* to repeal—*ab,* from, and *rogo,* to ask, propose as a law.] To repeal; to make void; to do away with; to annul by an authoritative act.—**abrogable,** ab′rō•ga•bl, *a.* Capable of being abrogated. —**abrogation,** ab•rō•gā′shon, *n.* The act of abrogating; repeal by authority.—**abrogative,** ab′rō•gā•tiv, *a.* Capable of abrogating; tending to abrogate.

abrupt, ab•rupt′, *a.* [L. *abruptus,* from *abrumpo,* to break off—*ab,* off, from, and *rumpo, ruptum,* to break, whence *rupture,* etc.] Steep; craggy (of rocks, precipices, etc.); sudden; without notice to prepare the mind for the event (an *abrupt* entrance); disconnected; having sudden transitions (an *abrupt* style).—*Abrupt leaf, root, bot.,* one terminating suddenly as if the end were cut off.—**abruption,** ab•rup′shon, *n.* A sudden and violent breaking off.—**abruptly,** ab•rupt′li, *adv.* In an abrupt manner; suddenly; without any notice or warning; precipitously.—**abruptness,** ab•rupt′nes, *n.* The state or quality of being abrupt; precipitousness; suddenness; unceremonious haste or vehemence.

abscess, ab′ses, *n.* [L. *abscessus,* from *abscedere,* to separate, to gather into an abscess—*abs,* away, and *cedo, cessum,* to go, whence *cession, cede,* etc.] A collection of purulent matter in the tissue of a body organ or part, with pain and heat.

abscind, ab•sind′, *v.t.* L. *abscindo, abscissum,* to cut off—*ab,* from, and *scindo,* to cut.] To cut off.—**abscissa,** ab•sis′sa, *n.* Any part of the diameter or transverse axis of a conic section (as an ellipse), intercepted between the vertex and a line at right angles to the axis; the *x*-coordinate of a point.—**abscission,** ab•si′zhon, *n.* The act of cutting off; severance; removal.

abscond, ab•skond′, *v.i.* [L. *abscondo,* to hide—*abs,* from, and *condo,* to hide.] To withdraw or absent one's self in a private manner; run away in order to avoid a legal process; decamp.—**absconder,** ab•skond′•ėr, *n.* One who absconds.

absence, ab′sens, *n.* L. *absentia,* from *absens, absentis,* absent, pres. part. of *absum,* to be absent—*ab* or *abs,* away, and *sum, esse,* to be.] The state of being absent; opposite of *presence;* the state of being at a distance in place; the state of being wanting; nonexistence within a certain sphere (*absence* of evidence); inattention.—**absent,** ab′sent, *a.* Not present; away; somewhere else; wanting; having the mind withdrawn from what is passing; characterized by absence of mind (an *absent* man).—**absent,** ab•sent′, *v.t.* To keep away intentionally: used *refl.*; as, to *absent* one's self from a meeting.—**absentee,** ab•sen•tē′, *n.* One who is absent; one who absents himself: often applied to landlords who, deriving their income from one country, reside and spend it in another.—**absenteeism,** ab•sen•tē′-izm, *n.* The practice or habit of an absentee.—**absenter,** ab•sent′ėr, *n.* One who absents himself.—**absently,** ab′sent•li, *adv.* In an absent or inattentive manner.—**absent-minded,** ab′sent•mīn′ded, *a.* Preoccupied; forgetful of one's immediate surroundings.

absinthe, ab•saṅt′ or ab′sinth, *n.* [Fr., from L. *absinthium,* wormwood.] A popular French liqueur or cordial consisting of brandy flavored with wormwood. The sale and consumption of absinthe are prohibited because of its harmful effects on the nervous system.

absolute, ab′sō•lūt, *a.* [L. *absolutus.* ABSOLVE.] Freed from limitation or condition; unconditional (an *absolute* promise); unlimited by extraneous power or control (an *absolute* government or prince); complete in itself; finished; perfect (*absolute* beauty); free from mixture (*absolute* alcohol); positive; decided; peremptory (now rare); *metaph.* (*a*) not relative; considered without reference to other things; (*absolute* knowledge); (*b*) existing independent of any other cause; self-existing; unconditioned; *gram.* applied to the case which is not determined by any other word in the sentence.—**absolute temperature.** Temperature measured in degrees centigrade from absolute zero, which is -273.16° centigrade.—**absolutely,** ab′sō•lūt•li, *adv.* In an absolute manner; completely; without restriction, limitation, or qualification; unconditionally; positively.—**absoluteness,** ab′sō•lūt•nes, *n.* The state of being.—**absolutism,** ab′sō•lūt•izm, *n.* State of being absolute, or principles of absolute government.—**absolutist,** ab′sō•lūt•ist, *n.* An advocate for absolute government.—**absolutistic, absolutist,** ab′sō•lūt•ist″ik, ab′sō•lūt•ist, *a.* Pertaining to absolutism.

absolution, ab•sō•lū′shon, *n.* The act of absolving or state of being absolved; specifically, in the Roman Catholic and some other churches, a remission of sins pronounced by a priest in favor of a penitent.

absolve, ab•solv′, *v.t.—absolved, absolving.* [L. *absolvo, absolutum,* to set free—*ab,* from, and *solvo,* to loose. SOLVE.] To set free or release from some duty, obligation, or responsibility (to *absolve* a person *from* a promise); acquit; to forgive or grant remission of sins to (with *from*).—**absolvable,** ab•solv′-a•bl, *a.* Capable of being absolved.—**absolver,** ab•solv′ėr, *n.* One who absolves.

absorb, ab•sorb′, *v.t.* [L. *absorbeo—ab,* from, and *sorbeo,* to suck in.] To drink in; suck up; imbibe, as a sponge; take in by capillarity; swallow up; engross or engage wholly.—**absorbability,** ab•sorb′a•bil″i•ti, *n.* The state or quality of being absorbable.—**absorbable,** ab•sorb′a•bl, *a.* Capable of being absorbed or imbibed.—**absorbent,** ab•sorb′ent, *a.* Capable of absorbing fluids; performing the function of absorption.—**absorbent,** ab•sorb′-ent, *n.* Anything which absorbs; a vessel in an animal body which takes in nutritive matters into the system; a substance applied to a wound to stanch or arrest the flow of blood.—**absorption,** ab•sorp′shon, *n.* The act or process of absorbing; state of being absorbed or engrossed. —**absorptive,** ab•sorp′tiv, *a.* Having power to absorb or imbibe.—**absorptivity,** ab•sorp•tiv′i•ti, *n.* The power or capacity of absorption.

abstain, ab•stān′, *v.i.* [O.Fr. *abstener,* Mod.Fr. *abstenir,* from L. *abstineo,* to keep from—*abs,* from, and *teneo,* to hold, whence *contain, tenant, tenacious,* etc.] To forbear or refrain voluntarily; to withhold.—**abstainer,** ab•stān′ėr, *n.* One who abstains; specifically, one who abstains from the use of intoxicating liquors.—**abstention,** ab•sten′shon, *n.* The act of holding off or abstaining; abstinence.—**abstinence,** ab′sti•nens, *n.* The act or practice of voluntarily refraining from the use of anything within our reach, especially from some bodily indulgence; partaking sparingly of food or drink.—**abstinent,** ab′sti•nent, *a.* Practicing abstinence.—**abstinently,** ab′sti•nent•li, *adv.* In an abstinent manner.

abstemious, ab•stē′mi•us, *a.* [L. *abstemius—abs,* and root seen in *temetum,* strong drink, *temulentus,* drunken; Skr. *tim,* to be wet.] Sparing in diet; refraining from a free use of food and strong drinks; temperate; devoted to or spent in abstemiousness or abstinence (an *abstemious* life); very moderate and plain; very sparing (*abstemious* diet). —**abstemiously,** ab•stē′mi•us•li, *adv.* In an abstemious manner.—**abstemiousness,** ab•stē′mi•us•nes, *n.*

abstention. See ABSTAIN.

absterge, ab•stėrj′, *v.t.—absterged, absterging.* [L. *abstergeo,* to wipe off—*abs,* and *tergeo, tersum,* to wipe, whence *terse.*] To wipe, or make clean by wiping; to wash away; to deterge.—**abstergent,** ab•stėrj′ent, *a.* Having cleansing or purgative properties.—**abstergent,** ab•stėrj′ent, *n.* Whatever aids in scouring or cleansing; a detergent.—**abstersion,** ab•stėr′shon, *n.* The act of absterging or cleansing.

abstinence, abstinent, abstinently. See ABSTAIN.

abstract, ab•strakt′, *v.t.* [From L. *abstraho, abstractum,* to draw away—

abs, and *traho*, *tractum*, to draw, seen also in *trace*, *contract*, *detract*, *retract*, etc.] To draw or take away; to withdraw; to purloin; to take away mentally; consider separately; epitomize or reduce to a summary.—**abstract,** ab′strakt, *a.* Considered or thought of in itself; not concrete; considered and treated apart from any particular object (*abstract* mathematics; *abstract* logic). In *gram.* and *logic*, *abstract nouns* or *terms* are names of qualities, in opposition to *concrete*, which are names of things. —*n.* A summary or epitome containing the substance; a bare or brief statement of facts detailed elsewhere. *Syn.* under ABRIDGMENT. —**abstracted,** ab•strakt′ed, *a.* Absent in mind; inattentive.—**abstractedly,** ab•strakt′ed•li, *adv.* In an abstracted or absent manner.—**abstractedness,** ab•strakt′ed•nes, *n.*—**abstracter,** ab•strakt′ėr. *n.* One who abstracts or purloins.—**abstraction,** ab•strak′shon, *n.* The act of abstracting or separating; the act of withdrawing; the act of considering separately what is united in a complex object; something abstract; an idea or notion of an abstract character; absence of mind; the state of being entirely engrossed in thought.—In *art*, an artistic composition intended to suggest an idea or emotion without imitating recognizable objects.—**abstractive,** ab•strakt′iv, *a.* Having the power or quality of abstracting.—**abstractively,** ab•strakt′iv•li, *adv.* In an abstractive manner.

abstriction,† ab•strik′shon, *n.* [L. *ab*, from, and *stringo*, *strictum*, to bind.] The act of unbinding.

abstruse, ab•strūs′, *a.* [L. *abstrusus*, pp. of *abstrudo*, to thrust away.] Remote from ordinary minds or notions; difficult to be comprehended or understood; profound; recondite. —**abstrusely,** ab•strūs′li, *adv.* In an abstruse manner; profoundly; with terms or notions remote from such as are obvious.—**abstruseness,** ab•strūs′nes, *n.* The quality of being abstruse.

absurd, ab•sėrd′, *a.* [L. *absurdus*—*ab*, and *surdus*, deaf, insensible. SURD.] Inconsistent with reason or common sense; ridiculous; nonsensical; logically contradictory.—**absurdity,** ab•sėrd′i•ti, *n.* The state or quality of being absurd; that which is absurd; an absurd action, statement, etc.—**absurdly,** ab•sėrd′li, *adv.* In an absurd manner.—**absurdness,** ab•sėrd′nes, *n.* The quality of being absurd.

abundance, a•bun′dans, *n.* [L. *abundantia*, abundance, from *abundo*, to abound (which see).] A fullness or plenteousness great to overflowing; ample sufficiency; plenteousness; copiousness.—**abundant,** a•bun′dant, *a.* Plentiful; ample; fully sufficient; abounding; overflowing. —**abundantly,** a•bun′dant•li, *adv.* In a plentiful or sufficient degree; amply; plentifully.

abuse, a•būz′, *v.t.*—*abused*, *abusing*. [Fr. *abuser*; L. *abutor*, *abusus*—*ab*, and *utor*, to use. USE.] To misuse; to put to a wrong or bad use; to do wrong to; injure; dishonor; violate; deceive; impose on; take undue advantage of.—**abuse,** a•būs′, *n.* Improper treatment or employment; improper use or application; misuse; a corrupt practice or custom (the *abuses* of government); injury; scurrilous or contumelious language.—**abuser,** a•būz′ėr, *n.* One who abuses, in speech or behavior.—**abusive,** a•būs′iv, *a.* Practicing abuse; offering harsh words or ill-treatment; scurrilous; opprobrious; insulting.—**abusively,** a•būs′iv•li, *adv.* In an abusive manner.—**abusiveness,** a•bū′siv•nes, *n.* The quality of being abusive; rudeness of language.

abut, a•but′, *v.i.*—*abutted*, *abutting*. [Fr. *aboutir*, to meet at the end, to border on—*a*, at, and *bout*, extremity. BUTT.] To be contiguous; to join at a border or boundary; to form a point or line of contact: with *on*, *upon*, *against*.—**abutment,** a•but′ment, *n.* The condition of abutting; the part abutting; the solid part of a pier or wall against which an arch abuts or from which it springs.—**abuttal,** a•but′al, *n.* The abutting part of a piece of land.—**abutter,** a•but′ėr, *n.*—That which abuts.

abyss, a•bis′, *n.* [L. *abyssus*, Gr. *abyssos*, bottomless—*a*, not, and *byssos*, bottom.] A bottomless gulf; anything profound and unfathomable, literally or figuratively.—**abysmal,** a•biz′mal, *a.* Pertaining to an abyss; profound; immeasurable.—**abyssal,** a•bis′al, *a.* Relating to or like an abyss; pertaining to the deeper parts of the sea.

Abyssinian, ab•is•sin′i•an, *a.* Belonging to Abyssinia or its inhabitants.—*n.* A native or inhabitant of Abyssinia; a member of the Abyssinian Church.

Acacia, a•kā′shi•a, *n.* [L. *acacia*, Gr. *akakia*, from *ake*, a point.] A genus of ornamental plants, some species of which produce catechu, and some exude gum arabic. *Acacia-tree*, a name sometimes given to the locust-tree, *Robinia pseudoacacia*.

academy, a•kad′e•mi, *n.* [L. *academia*, Gr. *academeia*, the Academy, from the hero *Acadēmus*, to whom the ground originally belonged which formed the garden in which Plato taught.] A school holding a rank between a college and an elementary school; a seminary of learning of the higher class; an association for the promotion of literature, science, or art, established sometimes by government, and sometimes by the voluntary union of private individuals, the members of which are called *academicians*. The Academy of Plato was the philosophical school founded by that Greek philosopher.—**academe,** *n.* An academy. [Poet.]—**academic, academical,** ak•a•dem′ik, ak•a•dem′ik•al, *a.* Belonging to an academy, or to a college or university; as, *academic* studies.—**academic,** ak•a•dem′ik, *n.* A student in a college or university.—**academical,** ak•a•dem′i•kal, *n.* A member of an academy; *pl.* the costume proper to the officers and students of a school or college.—**academically,** ak′a•dem″ik•al•li, *adv.* In an academical manner.—**academician,** a•kad′e•mish″an, *n.* A member of an academy or society for promoting arts and sciences.—**academicism,** ak•a•dem′i•sizm, *n.* The system or mode of teaching at an academy; an academical mannerism.

Acadian, a•kā′di•an, *a.* Belonging to Acadia, a former name of Nova Scotia.—*n.* A native or inhabitant of Acadia.

Acalephae, a•ka•lē′fē, *n. pl.* [Gr. *akalēphē*, a nettle.] A name sometimes applied to the marine animals commonly known as sea nettles, jellyfish, etc.—**acaleph, acalephan,** ak′a•lef, ak•a•lē′fan, *n.* A member of the Acalephae.—**acalephoid,** a•ka•lē′foid, *a.* Like an acaleph or medusa; medusoid.

acantha, a•kan′tha, *n.* [Gr. *akantha*, a spine or thorn.] A prickle of a plant; a spine of an animal; one of the acute processes of the vertebrae of animals.—**acanthaceous,** ak•an•thā′shus, *a.* Armed with prickles, as a plant.—**acanthine,** a•kan′thīn, *a.* Pertaining to or resembling the plant acanthus; prickly.—**acanthocephalous,** a•kan•thō•sef′a•lus, *a.* [Gr. *akantha*, thorn, *kephalē*, head.] *Zool.* having spines or hooks on the head, as certain intestinal worms (the Acanthocephala), which are thus attached within the bodies of animals.—**acanthoid, acanthous,** a•kan′thoid, a•kan′thus, *a.* Spiny.—**acanthophorous,** ak•an•tho′for•us, *a.* Having or producing spines.

acanthus, a•kan′thus, *n.* [Gr. *akanthos*, from its prickly leaves.] Any of a genus of plants of the Mediterranean region having large spiny leaves; an architectural ornament used in capitals of the Corinthian and Composite orders, and resembling somewhat the foliage of this plant.

Acanthopterygii, a•kan′thop•te•rij″i•ī, *n. pl.* [Gr. *akantha*, a thorn, and *pterygion*, the fin of a fish, from *pteryx*, a wing.] One of the two primary divisions of the osseous fishes, characterized by having one or more of the first rays of the fins in the form of spines.—**acanthopterygian,** a•kan′thop•te•rij″i•an, *a.* Of or pertaining to the Acanthopterygii. —**acanthopterygian,** a•kan′thop•te•rij″i•an, *n.* An acanthopterygian fish.

acanthus, a•kan′thus, *n.* See ACANTHA.

Acarida, a•kar′i•da, *n. pl.* (Gr. *akarēs*, too short to be cut, small, tiny—*a*, not, and *keirō*, to cut.] A division of Arachnida, including the mites, ticks, and water mites. The mouth in all is formed for suction.—**acarid,** ak′a•rid, *n.* One of the Acarida.—**acaricide,** a•kär′i•sīd, *n.* A substance that destroys mites.

acaroid resin, ak′a•roid rez′in, *n.* A resin that exudes from the grass trees of Australia, used in varnishes.

acarpous, a•kär′pus, *a.* [Gr. *akarpos*,

unfruitful—*a*, not, and *karpos*, fruit.] *Bot.* not producing fruit; sterile; barren.

acatalectic, a′kat•a•lek″tik, *a.* [Gr. *akatalēktos.*] Having the complete number of syllables (an *acatalectic* verse).

acaulous, acaulescent, a•kạl′us, a•kạl•es′ent, *a.* [Gr. *a*, not, and *kaulos*, a stalk.] *Bot.* without a conspicuous stem; stemless; *acauline, acaulose*, are also used in same sense.

accede, ak•sēd′, *v.i.*—*acceded, acceding.* [Fr. *accéder*, to assent, from L. *accedo*—*ad*, to, and *cedo*, to move, to give place. CEDE.] To agree or assent, as to a proposition, or to terms proposed by another; to become a party by agreeing to terms; to join or be added; to succeed, as an heir; come to by inheritance: said especially of a sovereign.—**accession,** ak•se′shon, *n.* The act of acceding; the act of agreeing or assenting; increase by something added; that which is added; the act of succeeding to a throne, office, or dignity; the attack or commencement of a disease.

accelerate, ak•sel′ėr•āt, *v.t.*—*accelerated, accelerating.* [L. *accelero, acceleratum*, to hasten—*ad*, to, and *celer*, swift. CELERITY.] To make quicker; to cause to move or advance faster; hasten; add to the velocity of; bring about or help to bring about more speedily.—**acceleration,** ak′-sel•ėr•ā″shon, *n.* The act of accelerating or state of being accelerated; increase of velocity.—**acceleration of gravity.** *Phys.* the acceleration of a falling body due to gravity, which is a little more than 32 feet per second per second at sea level and which varies with latitude and altitude.—**accelerative,** ak•sel′ėr•ā•tiv, *a.* Tending to accelerate; adding to velocity.—**accelerator,** ak•sel′ėr•-āt•ėr, *n.* One who or that which accelerates; a hastener. In *chem.* a catalyst; *phys.* any device that increases the speed of charged particles.—**acceleratory,** ak•sel′ėr•-a•to•ri, *a.* Accelerating or tending to accelerate.

accent, ak′sent, *n.* [L. *accentus*, an accent—*ad*, to, and *cano, cantum*, to sing. CHANT.] A superior stress or force of voice upon certain syllables of words, which distinguishes them from the other syllables, and forms an element in correct pronunciation; a mark or character used in writing to direct the stress of the voice in pronunciation, or to mark a particular tone, length of vowel sound, or the like; a peculiar or characteristic modulation or modification of the voice, such as that found in a given district; *pl.* words or expressions; *music*, stress or emphasis on particular notes.—*v.t.* ak•sent′. To give an accent or accents to in speaking; mark with an accent or accents.—**accentual,** ak•sent′ū•al, *a.* Pertaining to accent. —**accentuate,** ak•sent′ū•āt, *v.t.*—*accentuated, accentuating.* To mark or pronounce with an accent or with accents; to emphasize or give prominence to.—**accentuation,** ak•sent′-ū•ā″shon, *n.* The act of accentuating or state of being accentuated.

accept, ak•sept′, *v.t.* [L. *acceptare*, freq. of *accipio, acceptum*, to accept—*ad*, to, and *capio*, to take. CAPABLE, HAVE.] To take or receive, as something offered; receive with approbation or favor; take as it comes; accede or assent to (a treaty, a proposal); to acknowledge, especially by signature, and thus to promise to pay (a bill of exchange).—**acceptable,** ak•sep′ta•bl, *a.* Capable, worthy, or sure of being accepted or received; pleasing to a receiver; gratifying; agreeable; welcome.—**acceptableness, acceptability,** ak•-sep′ta•bl•nes, ak•sep′ta•bil″i•ti, *n.* The quality of being acceptable.—**acceptably,** ak•sep′ta•bli, *adv.* In an acceptable manner; in a manner to please.—**acceptance,** ak•sep′tans, *n.* The act of accepting; a taking or receiving; favorable reception; an agreeing to terms; a written engagement to pay money, made by a person signing his name across or at the end of a bill of exchange; an accepted bill, or the amount contained in it.—**acceptation,** ak•-sep•tā′•shon, *n.* The act of accepting or receiving; kind or favorable reception; the meaning or sense in which a word or expression is understood, or generally received.—**accepter, acceptor,** ak•sept′ėr, ak•-sept′or, *n.* A person who accepts; specifically, the person who accepts a bill of exchange.

access, ak′ses, *n.* [L. *accessus*, from *accedo*, to come near, to approach. ACCEDE.] A coming to; near approach; admittance; admission; the means or way of approach; passage allowing communication; increase or accession; attack or return of a disease.—**accessibility,** ak′ses•si•bil″i•ti, *n.* The condition or quality of being accessible or of admitting approach. —**accessible,** ak•ses′si•bl, *a.* Capable of being approached or reached; easy of access; approachable; attainable. —**accession,** ak•se′shon, *n.* See ACCEDE.—**accessional,** ak•se′shon•-al, *a.* Additional.

accessory, accessary, ak•ses′o•ri, ak•ses′a•ri, *a.* [L. *accessorius*, from *accessus, accedo.* ACCEDE.] Contributing; aiding in producing some effect, or acting in subordination to the principal agent: contributing to a general effect; belonging to something else as principal; accompanying.—*n.* One who aids or gives countenance to a crime; that which belongs to something else, as its principal; that which contributes to the effect of something more important; an accompaniment.—**accessorial,** ak•ses•sō′ri•al, *a.* Pertaining to an accessory.—**accessorily,** ak′ses•so″ri•li, *adv.* In the manner of an accessory; not as principal but as a subordinate agent.—**accessoriness,** ak′ses•so•ri•nes, *n.* The state of being accessory, or of being or acting in a secondary character.

accident, ak′si•dent, *n.* [L. *accidens*, falling—*ad*, and *cado*, to fall, whence *case, cadence, casual, decadence*, etc.] Chance or what happens by chance; an event that happens when quite unlooked for; an unforeseen and undesigned injury to a person; casualty; mishap; a property or quality of a thing which is not essential to it nor is one of its invariable signs (as whiteness in paper).—**accidence,** ak′si•dens, *n.* [A corruption of *accidents* in the old sense of inflections of words.] That part of grammar which treats of the inflection of words, or the declension of nouns, adjectives, etc., and the conjugation of verbs; a small book containing the rudiments of grammar.—**accidental,** ak•si•dent′-al, *a.* Happening by chance or accident, or unexpectedly; casual; fortuitous; nonessential; not necessarily belonging; adventitious.—*n.* A casualty; a property not essential; *music*, a sharp, flat, or natural which does not occur in the clef, and which implies some change of key or modulation different from that in which the piece began.—**accidentally,** ak•si•dent′al•li, *adv.* In an accidental manner; by chance; fortuitously; not essentially.

accipiter, ak•sip′i•tėr, *n.* [L. *accipiter*, a bird of prey, from root *ak*, signifying sharpness and swiftness, and *pet*, to fly, like Gr. *ōkypteros*, swift-winged.] A genus of the order of birds Falconiformes.—**accipitres,** ak•sip′i•trēz, *n. pl.* An order of rapacious birds, now usually called Falconiformes.—**accipitral, accipitrine,** ak•sip′i•tral, ak•sip″i•trin, *a.* Of or pertaining to a hawk; having the character of a bird of prey; rapacious.

acclaim,† ak•klām′, *v.t.* [L. *acclamo* —*ac* for *ad*, and *clamo*, to cry out, whence *claim*, clamor, etc.] To applaud; to declare or salute by acclamation.—**acclaim,** ak•klām′, *n.* A shout of joy; acclamation.—**acclamation,** ak•kla•mā′shon, *n.* A shout or other demonstration of applause made by a multitude, indicating joy, hearty assent, approbation, or good wishes.—**acclamatory,** ak•klam′a•to•ri, *a.* Expressing joy or applause by acclamation.

acclimate, acclimatize, ak•klī′māt, ak•klī′mat•īz, *v.t.*—*acclimated, acclimating; acclimatized, acclimatizing.* [Fr. *acclimater*, to acclimate. CLIMATE.] To habituate to a foreign climate; to render proof against the prejudicial influences of a foreign climate; to adopt for permanent existence and propagation in a foreign climate.—**acclimation, acclimatization,** ak•kli•mā′shon, ak′klī•-mat•iz•ā″shon, *n.* The act or process of acclimating or acclimatizing, or state of being acclimatized.

acclivity, ak•kliv′i•ti, *n.* [L. *acclivitas*, an acclivity—*ac* for *ad*, to, and *clivus*, a slope, from root *cli* seen in *clino, inclino*, to incline, Gr. *klinō*, to bend, incline; akin E. to *lean.*] A slope or inclination of the earth, as the side of a hill, considered as *ascending*, in opposition to *declivity.*

—**acclivitous, acclivous,** ak•kliv′i•tus, ak•klīv′us, *a.* Rising, as a hill with a slope; sloping upwards.

accolade, ak•kō•lād′, *n.* Fr. *accolade,* the accolade, lit. an embracing of the neck—L. *ad,* to, and *collum,* the neck; Fr. *accoler,* to embrace, *donner l'accolade,* to dub a knight. COLLAR.] A ceremony used in conferring knighthood, anciently consisting in putting the hand on the knight's neck, now usually a blow over the neck or shoulder with the flat of a sword; a salutation or rite performed in recognition of special merit; an award.

accommodate, ak•kom′mō•dāt, *v.t.* —*accommodated, accommodating.* [L. *accommodo,* to apply or suit—*ac* for *ad,* to, and *commodo,* to profit or help, from *con,* with, and *modus,* measure, proportion, limit, or manner. MODE.] To make suitable, correspondent, or consistent; to fit; adapt; conform; adjust; reconcile (with *to* after the object); to supply or furnish with required conveniences (with *with* after the object, as a friend *with* money).—**accommodating,** ak•kom′mo•dat•ing, *a.* Obliging; yielding to the desires of others; disposed to comply and to oblige another.—**accommodation,** ak•kom′mō•dā″shon, *n.* The act of accommodating; adjustment; adaptation; adjustment of differences; anything which supplies a want, as in respect of ease, refreshment, and the like; a convenience; lodgings; a loan of money.—*Accommodation bill,* a bill of exchange not given like a genuine bill of exchange in payment of a debt, but merely intended to accommodate the drawer.—*Accommodation ladder,* a light ladder hung over the side of a ship to facilitate ascending from, or descending to, boats.—**accommodative,** ak•kom′mō•dāt•iv, *a.* Furnishing accommodation.

accompany, ak•kum′pa•ni, *v.t.*—*accompanied, accompanying.* [Fr. *accompagner,* to accompany—*ac* for *ad,* to, and *compagnon,* a companion. COMPANION.] To go with or attend as a companion or associate; to go together; to be associated or connected with; to play a subordinate musical part to, as to a singer or other performer of a musical composition.—**accompaniment,** ak•kum′pa•ni•ment, *n.* Something that attends as a circumstance, or which is added by way of ornament to the principal thing, or for the sake of symmetry; the subordinate part or parts performed by instruments accompanying a voice, or several voices, or a principal instrument.—**accompanist,** ak•kum′pan•ist, *n.* The performer in music who plays the accompaniment.

accomplice, ak•kom′plis, *n.* [Prefix *ac* for *ad,* to, and the older E. *complice,* Fr. *complice,* L. *complex, complicis,* confederate, participant—*con,* with, and *plico,* to fold, *plica,* a fold, a stem which appears also in E. *comply, ply, triple,* etc. PLY, etc.] An associate or confederate, especially in a crime; a partner or partaker in guilt.

accomplish, ak•kom′plish, *v.t.* [Fr. *accomplir,* to finish—prefix *ac* for *ad,* to, and L. *compleo,* to complete. COMPLETE.] To complete; to finish entirely; to execute; to carry out; to fulfill or bring to pass.—**accomplishable,** ak•kom′plish•a•bl, *a.* Capable of accomplishment.—**accomplished,** ak•kom′plisht, *a.* Perfected; finished; consummate; having the attainments and graces regarded as necessary for cultivated or fashionable society.—**accomplisher,** ak•kom′plish•ėr, *n.* One who accomplishes.—**accomplishment,** ak•kom′plish•ment, *n.* The act of accomplishing or carrying into effect; fulfillment; acquirement; attainment, especially such as belongs to cultivated or fashionable society.

accord, ak•kord′, *n.* [Fr. *accord,* agreement—prefix *ac* for *ad,* to, and L. *cor, cordis,* the heart, formed like L. *concors, discors,* E. *concord, discord.*] Agreement; harmony of minds; as, to do a thing with one *accord;* just correspondence of things; concord; harmony of sound; voluntary or spontaneous impulse or act; in this sense in such phrases as *of my, of his, of its, of their own accord.*—*v.t.* To make to agree or correspond†; to grant; to give; to concede; as, to *accord* to one due praise.—*v.i.* To be in correspondence or harmony.—**accordance,** ak•kord′ans, *n.* The state of being in accord; agreement with a person; conformity with a thing.—**accordant,** ak•kord′ant, *a.* Corresponding; consonant; agreeable; of the same mind.—**accordantly,** ak•kord′ant•li, *adv.* In accordance or agreement.—**according,** ak•kord′ing, *a.* Agreeing; agreeable; in accordance.—*According as,* agreeably, conformably, or proportionately as.—*According to,* agreeably to or in accordance with (zeal *according to* knowledge): followed by a personal object it refers to a statement of the person (*according to him* you are wrong).—**accordingly,** ak•kord′ing•li, *adv.* Agreeably; suitably; in a manner conformable; consequently.

accordion, ak•kord′i•on, *n.* [From *accord.*] A small keyed wind instrument, whose tones are generated by the play of wind upon metallic reeds.—**accordionist,** ak•kord′i•on•ist, *n.* A player on the accordion.

accost, ak•kost′, *v.t.* [Fr. *accoster,* L.L. *accostare*—*ac* for *ad,* to, and L. *costa* (Fr. *côte*), a rib, a side. COAST.] To speak first to; to address before oneself is addressed.

accoucheur, ak•kö•shėr′, *n.* [Fr., a man-midwife—*ac* for *ad,* and *coucher,* to lie or lay down. COUCH.] A surgeon who attends women in childbirth.—**accoucheuse,** ak•kö•shėz′, *n.* A midwife.—**accouchement,** ak•kösh′ment, *n.* Childbirth.

account, ak•kount′, *n.* [O.E. *accompt*—*ac* for *ad,* and O.Fr. *compte,* a calculation, from L. *computo,* to compute, reckon. The Mod.Fr. *conte, conter,* present the same change of *m* into *n* as our own word.] A reckoning, enumeration, or computation; a list of debits and credits, or charges; a statement of things bought or sold, of payments, services, etc.; an explanatory statement of particulars, facts, or events; narrative; relation; description; reason or consideration; ground (on all *accounts*); profit; advantage (to turn to *account*); regard; behalf; sake (trouble incurred on one's *account*); *stockbroking,* the operations on the stock exchange performed during the period before the ordinary settlement day.—*To make account of,* to hold in estimation or esteem; to value: with an adjective of quantity, as *much, little, no,* etc.—*Account current,* the statement of the successive mercantile transactions of one person with another, drawn out in the form of debtor and creditor, and in the order of their dates.—**account,** ak•kount′, *v.t.* To deem, judge, think, or hold in opinion,—*v.i.* To render an account or relation of particulars; to answer in a responsible character; to give reasons; to explain: followed by *to* before a person, *for* before a thing.—**accountability,** ak•kount′a•bil″i•ti, *n.* The state of being accountable or answerable.—**accountable,** ak•kount′a•bl, *a.* Liable to pay or make good in case of loss; responsible for a trust; liable to be called to account; answerable to a superior.—**accountableness,** ak•kount′a•bl•nes, *n.* The state of being accountable; accountability.—**accountably,** ak•kount′a•bli, *adv.* In an accountable manner.—**accountant,** ak•kount′ant, *n.* One who makes the keeping or examination of accounts his profession; an officer in a public office who has charge of the accounts.—**accountantship,** ak•kount′ant•ship, *n.* The office or employment of an accountant.—**accounting,** a•koun′ting, *n.* The theory and system of setting up, maintaining, and auditing the books of a firm; the art of analyzing the financial position and operating results of a business house from a study of its sales, purchases, etc.

accouter, accoutre, ak•kö′tėr, *v.t.*—*accoutred, accoutring.* [Fr. *accoutrer*—prefix *ac* for *ad,* to, and *couture,* a seam, from L. *consutura,* a stitching together, from *con,* together, and *suo, sutum,* to sew.] To equip or furnish with personal trappings; especially, to array in a military dress and arms; to equip for military service.—**accouterments,** ak•kö′tėr•ments, *n. pl.* Military dress and arms; fighting array.

accredit ak•kred′it, *v. t.* [Fr. *accréditer,* to accredit—L. *ad,* to, and *credo, creditum,* to trust.] To repose confidence in; to trust (a person); to give credit to; to believe (a story); to confer credit or authority on; to send with credentials, as an envoy.

accresce, ak•kres′, *v.i.* [L. *accresco, accretum,* to increase, to grow to—*ad,* to, and *cresco,* to grow, increase.] To accrue (which see).—**accrescence,** ak•kres′ens, *n.* Act of increasing;

gradual growth or increase; accretion.—**accrescent,** ak•kres′ent, *a.* Increasing; growing.—**accrete,**† ak•krēt′, *v.i.* To grow by accretion; to be added by growth.—**accretion,** ak•krē′shon, *n.* The act of accreting or accrescing; a growing to; an increase by natural growth; an increase by an accession of parts externally; *med.* the growing together of parts naturally separate, as the fingers or toes; the thing added by growth; an accession.—**accretive,** ak•krēt′iv, *a.* Of or pertaining to accretion.

accrue, ak•krö′, *v.i.*—*accrued, accruing.* [Fr. *accrue*, increase, from *accrû*, pp. of *accroitre*, to increase, from L. *accrescere*—*ac* for *ad*, to, and *cresco*, to grow, seen also in *crescent, decrease, increase.*] To be gained or obtained; to proceed, arise, or spring; as, a profit or a loss *accrues* from a commercial transaction.—**accrual,** a•krö′al, *n.* Act or process of accruing; accretion.—**accrument,**† ak•krö′ment, *n.* That which accrues; addition; increase.

accumbent, ak•kum′bent, *a.* [L. *accumbens*, ppr. of *accumbo*, from *ad*, to, and *cumbo*, to lie down.] Leaning or reclining; lying against anything.—**accumbency,** ak•kum′ben•si, *n.* State of being accumbent.

accumulate, ak•kū′mū•lāt, *v.t.*—*accumulated, accumulating.* [L. *accumulo, accumulatum*, to heap up—*ad*, to, and *cumulus*, a heap.] To heap or pile up; to amass; to collect or bring together.—*v.i.* To grow to be extensive in number or quantity; to increase greatly.—**accumulation,** ak•kū′mū•lā″shon, *n.* The act of accumulating; a collecting or being heaped up; that which has accumulated; a mass that has been collected.—**accumulative,** ak•kū′mū•lāt•iv, *a.* Causing accumulation; heaping up.—**accumulatively,** ak•kū′mū•lāt•iv•li, *adv.* In an accumulative manner; in heaps.—**accumulator,** ak•kū′mū•lāt•ėr, *n.* One who or that which accumulates; a contrivance, such as a spring, that by being coiled up serves as a store of force.

accurate, ak′kū•rāt, *a.* [L. *accuratus*, prepared with care—*ac* for *ad*, to, and *cura*, care. CURE.] In exact conformity to truth, or to a standard or rule, or to a model; free from error or defect; exact; precise; strictly correct; adhering to exactness or correctness.—**accuracy, accurateness,** ak′kū•ra•si, ak′kū•rāt•nes, n. The condition or quality of being accurate; extreme precision or exactness; exact conformity to truth, or to a rule or model; correctness.—**accurately,** ak′kū•rāt•li, *adv.* In an accurate manner.

accurse, ak•kėrs′, *v.t.* [Prefix *ac* for *ad*, or A. Sax. *â*, intens., and *curse.*] To call down curses on; to curse.—**accursed, accurst,** ak•kėrst′ or ak•kėrs′ėd, ak•kėrst′, *a.* Lying under a curse; blasted; ruined; execrable; cursed.

accuse, ak•kūz′, *v.t.*—*accused, accusing.* [L. *accuso*, to call to account, blame, indict—*ad*, to, and *causa*, cause, process. CAUSE.] To charge with a crime, offense, or fault; to blame (with *of* before the crime or offense). ∴ *Accuse* is both a legal and a general term, and commonly expresses something more formal than *charge.* The construction of the two verbs is also different: *accuse of, charge with.*—**accusation,** ak•kū•zā′shon, *n.* The act of accusing; that of which one is accused; a charge brought against one.—**accusative,** ak•kūz′at•iv, *a.* Accusatory. —**accusative,** ak•kūz′at•iv, *n.* The fourth case of nouns and other declinable words in Latin, Greek, etc., corresponding to the *objective* in English.—**accusatively,** ak•kūz′at•iv•li, *adv.* By way of accusation; in the position or relation of an accusative case.—**accusatory, accusatorial,** ak•kūz′a•to•ri, ak•kūz′a•tō″ri•al, *a.* Accusing; containing an accusation; as, an *accusatory* libel.—**accused,** ak•kūzd′, *pp.* used as a *noun.* A person or persons charged with a crime.—**accuser,** ak•kūz′ėr, *n.* One who accuses; one who formally brings a charge.

accustom, ak•kus′tum, *v.t.* [O.Fr. *accoustumer*, to accustom—*ac* for L. *ad*, to, and O.Fr. *coustume*, custom. CUSTOM.] To familiarize by use or habit; to habituate or inure.—**accustomed,** ak•kus′tumd, *a.* Often practiced; customary; habitual; wonted; familiar; as, in their *accustomed* manner.

ace, ās, *n.* [Fr. *as*, ace at dice or cards; L. *as*, a unit, a pound, a foot, etc., from Doric Gr. *as, ais*, Attic Gr. *heis*, one.] A unit; a single pip on a card or die, or the card or face of a die so marked; a trifle or insignificant quantity or distance (within an *ace* of it); the ace in certain card games counting as ten; an expert; a champion; one proficient in a particular field of endeavor. In *aviation*, the name given to a combat pilot officially credited with shooting down five or more enemy planes.—*a.* Excellent; first in quality.

Aceldama, a•kel′da•ma, *n.* [Heb.] Field of blood. Acts, i. 19.

acentric, a•sen′trik, *a.* [Prefix *a*, neg., and *centre.*] Not centric; away from a center.—*n.* An airplane so designed that the line of the propeller thrust does not pass through the center of gravity.

Acephala, a•sef′a•la, *n. pl.* [Gr. *akephalos*, headless—*a*, not, and *kephalē*, head.] Molluscous animals, like the oyster and scallop, that do not have a distinct head.—**acephalist,** a•sef′al•ist, *n.* One who acknowledges no head or superior.—**acephalous,** a•sef′al•us, *a.* Without a head; headless.

acerb, a•sėrb′, *a.* [L. *acerbus*, unripe, harsh, sour, from *acer*, sharp; same root as in *acid.*] Sour, bitter, and harsh to the taste; sour with astringency and roughness.—**acerbity,** a•sėrb′it•i, *n.* Sourness, with roughness or astringency of taste; poignancy or severity; painfulness; sharpness; harshness or severity of temper; sourness.

acerous, acerose, as′ėr•us, as′ėr•ōz, *a.* [L. *acerosus*, chaffy, from *acus, aceris*, chaff.] *Bot.* resembling chaff; narrow and slender, with a sharp point.

acervate,† a•sėrv′āt, *v.t.* [L. *acervo*, to heap up, from *acervus*, a heap.] To heap up.

acetabulum, as•ē•tab′ū•lum, *n.* pl. **acetabula,** as•ē•tab′ū•la. [L., vinegar cruet, a cup-shaped vessel, from *acetum*, vinegar. ACID.] The cavity which receives the head of the thigh bone; the socket in which the leg of an insect is inserted; the cuplike sucker with which the arms of the cuttlefish are provided; the cuplike or saucer-like fructification of many lichens; the receptacle of certain fungi.

acetic, a•set′ik, *a.* [L. *acetum*, vinegar.] Having the properties of vinegar; sour.—*Acetic acid*, an acid often prepared by the oxidation of alcohol (acetous fermentation), and along with water forming the chief ingredient of vinegar.—**acetate,** as′ē•tāt, *n.* A salt formed by the union of acetic acid with a base; a product made from cellulose acetate, for example, acetate rayon.—**acetification,** a•set′i•fi•kā″shon, *n.* The act of acetifying or making acetous or sour; the process of becoming acetous; the operation of making vinegar.—**acetifier,** a•set′i•fī•ėr, *n.* An apparatus used in making vinegar. —**acetify,** a•set′i•fī, *v.t.*—*acetified, acetifying.* To convert into acid or vinegar.—*v.i.* To become acid; to be converted into vinegar.—**acetimeter, acetometer,** as•et•im′et•ėr, as•et•om′et•ėr, *n.* An instrument for ascertaining the strength or purity of acids; an acidimeter.—**acetone,** as′ē•tōn, *n.* [*acetic* and *ketone.*] A chemical compound used as a solvent for fats, rubber, and plastic.

acetylcholine, as′e•til•ko″lēn, *n.* A chemical compound liberated from nerve endings, involved in transmission of nerve impulses.

acetylene, a•set′i•lēn, *n.* [From *acetic*, and Gr. *hylē*, matter.] A flammable gas made with calcium carbide and water; used as a fuel in welding.

acetylsalicylic acid, as′e•til•sal′e•sil″ik as′id, *n.* Aspirin.

ache, āk, *n.* [A.Sax, *ace, æce, ece*, ache, pain; *acan*, to ache; akin to Icel. *aka*, to drive, press hard; cog. L. *ago*, to drive.] Pain, or continued pain, in opposition to sudden twinges, or spasmodic pain; a continued gnawing pain as in toothache or earache; feeling of distress (heartache).—*v.i.*—*ached, aching.* To suffer from an ache or pain.

achene, a•kēn′, *n.* [Gr. *a*, priv., and *chainō*, to yawn, to gape.] *Bot.* a small dry carpel, containing a single seed, which does not open when ripe.

achieve, a•chēv′, *v.t.*—*achieved, achieving,* [Fr. *achever*, to finish—*a*, to, and O.Fr. *cheve*, Fr. *chef*, the head or end, from L. *caput*, the head. CHIEF.] To perform or execute; to finish or carry on to a final and prosperous close; to obtain or bring about, as by effort.—**achievable,** a•chēv′a•bl, *a.* Capable of being achieved or performed.—**achievement,** a•chēv′ment, *n.* The act of achieving or performing; accomplishment; an exploit; a great or heroic deed; an escutcheon or ensign armorial; a hatchment.—**achiever,** a•chēv′ėr, *n.* One who achieves or accomplishes.

achlamydate, a•klam′id•āt, *a.* [Gr. *a,* not, and *chlamys, chlamydos,* a cloak.] *Zool.* not possessing a mantle, as certain mollusks.—**achlamydeous,** a•kla•mid′ē•us, *a. Bot.* having neither calyx nor corolla, the flowers being without floral envelope.

achromatic, ak•rō•mat′ik, *a.* [Gr. *a,* not, and *chrōma, chrōmatos,* color.] Destitute of color; transmitting light without decomposing it into its primary colors; as, an *achromatic* lens or telescope.—**achromaticity, achromatism,** ak′rō•ma•tis″i•ti, ak•rō′ma•tizm, *n.* The state of being achromatic; want of color.—**achromatize,** a•krō′ma•tīz, *v.t.* To deprive of color; to render achromatic.

acicula, a•sik′ū•la, *n.* pl.—**aciculae,** a•sik′ū•lē. [L., dim. of *acus,* a needle. ACID.] A name given by naturalists to a spine or prickle of an animal or plant.—**acicular, aciculate, aciform,** a•sik′ū•lėr, a•sik′ū•lāt, as′i•form, *a.* Having the shape of a needle; having sharp points like needles; needle shaped.—**acicularly,** a•sik′ū•lėr•li, *adv.* In an acicular manner.

acid, as′id, *a.* [L. *acidus,* sour, from root *ac, ak,* a point, seen in *acus,* a needle; *acuo,* to sharpen; *acer,* sharp; *aceo,* to be sour; *acetum,* vinegar; giving such English words as *acrid, acumen, acute, ague, eager,* etc.] Sour, sharp, or biting to the taste; not sweet; not alkaline.—**acid,** as′id, *n.* A sour substance; specifically, in *chem.* a compound of which hydrogen is an essential constituent. Acids possess a sour taste, change blue vegetable colors to red, and combine with bases to form salts.—**acidic,** a•sid′ik, *a. Chem.* pertaining to acid; containing a large amount of an acid constituent.—**acidify,** a•sid′i•fī, *v.t.—acidified, acidifying.* To make acid; to convert into an acid.—**acidifiable,** a•sid′i•fī•a•bl, *a.* Capable of being acidified or converted into an acid.—**acidification,** a•sid′i•fi•kā″shon, *n.* The act or process of acidifying.—**acidimeter,** as•id•im′et•ėr, *n.* Same as *acetimeter.*—**acidity,** a•sid′i•ti, *n.* The quality of being acid or sour; sourness; tartness.—**acidulate,** a•sid′ū•lāt, *v.t.—acidulated, acidulating.* [Pr. *aciduler,* to make slightly sour; L. *acidulus,* slightly sour.] To make acid in a moderate degree.—**acidulent,** a•sid′ū•lent, *a.* Somewhat acid or sour; tart; peevish.—**acidulous,** a•sid′ū•lus, *a.* Slightly sour; subacid; as cream of tartar, oranges, etc.

aciform, as′i•fąrm, *a.* See ACICULA.

acinaceous, as•in•ā′shus, *a.* [L. *acinus,* a grapestone or kernel.] Full of kernels.—**acinarious,** as•in•ā′ri•us, *a. Bot.* covered with little spherical stalked vesicles resembling grapeseeds, as in some algae.—**aciniform,** a•sin′i•form, *a.* Having the form of grapes, or being in clusters like grapes.—**acinose, acinous,** as′in•ōs, as′in•us, *a.* Consisting of minute, granular concretions.

acinaciform, as•in•as′i•fąrm, *a.* [L. *acinaces,* Gr. *akinakēs,* a scimitar.] Formed like or resembling a scimitar; as, an *acinaciform* leaf.

ack•ack, ak•ak, *a.* [From pronunciation of AA, antiaircraft, by British radio operators.] Pertaining to antiaircraft.—*n.* An antiaircraft gun; antiaircraft artillery; antiaircraft fire.

acknowledge, ak•nol′ej, *v.t.—acknowledged, acknowledging.* [Prefix *a,* on, and *knowledge.*] To own or recognize by avowal or by some act; to assent to the truth or claims of; to admit to be; to own or confess; to avow receiving. ...We *acknowledge* what is in some way brought or set before our notice; when we *confess* we make known, and often of our own free will.—**acknowledger,** ak•nol′ej•ėr, *n.* One who acknowledges.

acknowledgment, ak•nol′ej•ment, *n.* The act of acknowledging; owning; recognition; avowal; confession; expression of thanks; something given or done in return for a favor; a receipt for money received.

acme, ak′mē, *n.* [Gr. *akmē,* a point. Root *ak.* ACID.] The top or highest point; the furthest point attained; maturity or perfection; the height or crisis of a disease.

acne, ak′nē, *n.* [Origin unknown.] An eruption of hard, inflamed tubercles or pimples on the face.

acolyte, ak′o•līt, *n.* [Fr. from L.L. *acolythus,* an acolyte; Gr. *akolouthos,* a follower.] An attendant; in the *R. Cath. Ch.* one of an inferior order of clergy, who attends during service on the superior orders; a lay attendant so employed.

aconite, ak′on•īt, *n.* L. *aconitum,* Gr. *akoniton,* a poisonous plant, like monkshood.] The plant wolfsbane or monkshood, *Aconitum napellus.*

acorn, ā′korn, *n.* [A. Sax. *æceren, æcern,* an acorn; Goth. *akram,* fruit; Icel. *akarn,* Dan. *agern,* O.H.G. *ackeran,* an acorn; the word originally meant simply fruit, fruit of the field, being allied to *acre.*] The fruit of the oak, a one-celled, one-seeded, oval nut, which grows in a permanent cup.

acotyledon, a•kot′il•ē″don, *n.* [Gr. *a,* not, and *kotylēdōn,* any cup-shaped cavity, from *kotylē,* a hollow.] *Bot.* a plant whose seeds, called spores, are not furnished with cotyledons or seed lobes.—**acotyledonous,** a•kot′il•ē″don•us, *a.* Having no seed lobes.

acoustic, acoustical, a•kös′tik, a•kös′tik•al, *a.* [Gr. *akoustikos,* from *akouō,* to hear.] Pertaining to the sense or organs of hearing, or to the science of acoustics.—**acoustic,** *n.* A remedy for deafness or imperfect hearing.—**acoustically,** a•kös′tik•al•li, *adv.* In relation to or in a manner adapted to acoustics.—**acoustics,** a•kös′•tiks, *n.* The science of sound, teaching the cause, nature, and phenomena of the vibrations of elastic bodies which affect the organ of hearing.

acquaint, ak•kwānt′, *v.t.* [O.Fr. *accointer;* L.L. *accognitare,* to make known, from L. *ad,* to, and *cognitus,* known, from *cognosco, cognitum,* to know; same root as in *know.*] To make to know; to make aware of; to apprise; to make familiar; inform: *with* is used before the subject of information, if a noun (*acquaint* a person *with* facts).—**acquaintance,** ak•kwānt′ans, *n.* A state of being acquainted, or of having more or less intimate knowledge; knowledge; familiarity (followed by *with*); a person known to one; the whole body of those with whom one is acquainted.—**acquaintanceship,** ak•kwānt′ans•ship, *n.* State of being acquainted.—**acquainted,** ak•kwānt′ed, *a.* Having acquaintance; knowing, but not a close or intimate friend.

acquiesce, ak•kwi•es′, *v.i.—acquiesced, acquiescing.* [Fr. *acquiescer,* L. *acquiesco,* to rest, to acquiesce—*ad,* to, and *quiesco,* to be quiet. QUIET.] To rest satisfied, or apparently satisfied, or to rest without opposition and discontent; to assent quietly; to agree.—**acquiescence,** ak•kwi•es′ens, *n.* The act of acquiescing or giving a quiet assent.—**acquiescent,** ak•kwi•es′ent, *a.* Disposed to acquiesce; disposed to submit; quietly assenting.—**acquiescently,** ak•kwi•es′ent•li, *adv.*

acquire, ak•kwīr′, *v.t.—acquired, acquiring.* [L. *acquiro,* to get—*ad,* to and *quaero,* to look or search for. QUEST.] To get or gain, the object being something which is more or less permanent (as fortune, title, habits, etc.) A mere temporary possession is not expressed by *acquire,* but by *obtain, procure,* etc.; as, to *obtain* (not *acquire*) a book on loan.—**acquirable,** ak•kwīr′a•bl, *a.* Capable of being acquired.—**acquirement,** ak•kwīr′ment, *n.* The act of acquiring, or of making acquisition; that which is acquired; attainment, especially personal attainment (as contrasted with a natural *gift* or *endowment*).—**acquirer,** ak•kwīr′ėr, *n.* A person who acquires.—**acquisition,** ak•kwi•zi′shon, *n.* The act of acquiring; the thing acquired or gained: generally applied to material gains.—**acquisitive,** ak•kwiz′it•iv, *a.* Disposed to make acquisitions; having a propensity to acquire property.—**acquisitively,** ak•kwiz′it•iv•li, *adv.* In an acquisitive manner; by way of acquisition.—**acquisitiveness,** ak•kwiz′i•tiv•nes, *n.* Quality of being acquisitive.

acquired character, *n.* A biological change that results from use or environment rather than from heredity.

acquit, ak•kwit′, *v.t.—acquitted, acquitting.* [Fr. *acquitter,* to discharge, to set at rest with respect to a claim—L. *ad,* to, and *quietus,* at rest, quiet. QUIET.] To release or discharge from an obligation, accusation, or the like; to pronounce not guilty (with *of* before the thing; *refl.* to behave; to bear or conduct one's self.—**acquittal,** ak•kwit'al, *n.* The act of acquitting; a judicial setting free from the charge of an offense.—**acquittance,** ak•kwit'ans, *n.* An acquitting or discharging from a debt or any other liability; the writing which is evidence of such a discharge.

acre, ā'kėr, *n.* [A.Sax, *acer, æcer,* a field=D. *akker,* Icel. *akr,* Dan. *ager,* G. *acker,* Goth. *akrs,* arable land, a field; L. *ager,* Gr. *agros,* Skr. *ajra,* a field. From root, *ag, ak,* as in L. *ago.* Icel. *aka,* to drive; the word probably meaning originally the place to or over which cattle were driven; a pasture. *Acorn* is from this root.] A definite quantity of land. The United States and British statute acre contains 160 square rods or perches, or 4,840 square yards.—**acreage,** ā'kėr•āj, *n.* The number of acres in a piece of land; acres taken collectively.

acrid, ak'rid, *a.* [From L. *acer, acris, acre,* sharp: with *id,* from the common L. adjective termination *-idus.* ACID.] Sharp or biting to the taste; pungent; bitter; virulent; bitter (as in temper or disposition).—**acrid,** ak'rid, *n.* An acrid or irritant poison.—**acridity, acridness,** a•krid'i•ti, ak'rid•nes, *n.* The quality of being acrid or pungent.

acrimony, ak'ri•mo•ni, *n.* [L. *acrimonia,* from *acris,* sharp.] Acridity; pungency; sharpness or severity of temper; bitterness of expression; acerbity; asperity.—**acrimonious,** ak•ri•mō'ni•us, *a.* Abounding in acrimony; severe; bitter; virulent; caustic; stinging.—**acrimoniously,** ak•ri•mō'ni•us•li, *adv.* In an acrimonious manner; sharply; bitterly; pungently.—**acrimoniousness,** ak•ri•mō'ni•us•nes, *n.* The quality of being acrimonious.

acrobat, ak'rō•bat, *n.* [Gr. *akrobatos-akros,* high, and *bainō,* to go.] A rope-dancer; also, one who practices vaulting, tumbling, throwing somersaults, etc.—**acrobatic,** ak'rō•bat•ik, *a.* Of or pertaining to an acrobat or his performance.

acrocarpous, ak•rō•kärp'us, *a.* [Gr. *akros,* highest, and *karpos,* fruit.] *Bot.* applied to mosses whose flower terminates the growth of a primary axis.

acrogen, ak'rō•jen, *n.* [Gr. *akros,* high, on the top, and root *gen,* to produce.] A plant (as a moss, fern, horsetail) increasing by extension of the stem or axis of growth at the top.—**acrogenous,** a•kroj'en•us, *a.* Increasing by growth at the summit, as the tree ferns; pertaining to the acrogens.

acromegaly, ak'ro•meg"a•le, *n.* [Gr. *akros,* an extremity; *megale,* large.] A rare disease, associated with overgrowth of bone, especially in the jaws, hands, and feet.

acronical, a•kron'ik•al, *a.* [Gr. *akros,* extreme, and *nyx,* night.] *Astron,* culminating at midnight: said of a star which rises as the sun sets, and sets as the sun rises.—**acronically,** a•kron'ik•al•li, *adv.* In an acronical manner.

acronym, ak'ru•nim, *n.* [From *acro-* and Gr. *onoma,* name.] A word formed from the initial syllables or letters of other words, as *radar* from "*ra*dio *d*etecting *a*nd *r*anging."

acrophobia, ak'ro•fo"bi•a, *n.* [Gr. *akron,* a height; *phobos,* fear.] A pathological dread of high places.

acropolis, a•krop'o•lis, *n.* [Gr. *akros,* high, and *polis,* a city.] The citadel or highest part of a Grecian city, usually situated on an eminence commanding the town.

acrospire, ak'rō•spīr, *n.* [Gr. *akros,* highest, and *speira,* a spire or spiral line.] The first leaf which rises above the ground when corn germinates; also the rudimentary stem or first leaf which appears in malted grain.

across, a•kros', *prep.* and *adv.* [Prefix *a,* and *cross.*] From side to side: opposed to *along*; athwart; quite over; intersecting; passing over at any angle; from one side to another; crosswise.

acrostic, a•kros'tik, *n.* [Gr. *akrostichion,* an acrostic—*akros,* extreme, and *stichos,* order or verse.] A composition in verse, in which the first, or the first and last, or certain other letters of the lines, taken in order, form a name, title, motto, etc., which is the subject of the poem.—*a.* Relating to or containing an acrostic. —**acrostically,** a•kros'tik•al•li, *adv.* In the manner of an acrostic.

acrotic, a•krot'ik, *a.* [L.L. *acroticus,* from Gr. *akros,* extreme.] *Med.* belonging to or affecting external surfaces.

acrotism, ak'rō•tizm, *n.* [Gr. *a,* not, and *krotos,* a beating.] An absence or weakness of the pulse.

acrylic, a'kril"ik, *adj.* Pertaining to the acid CH_2: CH.COOH obtained from acrolein.—**acrylic resin,** *n.* Thermoplastic resin from polymerization of acrylic or methacrylic acid esters, used for transparent airplane parts, lenses, dentures.

act, akt, *v.i.* [L. *ago, actum,* to exert power, to put in motion, to do; Gr. *agō,* to lead; allied to Icel. *aka,* to drive, and to E. *acre* (which see).] To exert power; to produce effects; to be in action or motion; to carry into effect a purpose or determination of the mind; to behave, demean, or conduct oneself; to perform, as an actor.—*v.t.* To transact; to do or perform; to represent as real; to perform on or as on the stage; to play; hence, to feign or counterfeit.—**act,** akt, *n.* That which is being done or which has been done; a deed; an exploit; the exertion of power; the effect of which power exerted is the cause; a state of reality or real existence, as opposed to a possibility; actuality; a part or division of a play, generally subdivided into smaller portions called *scenes*; a decree, edict, or law, especially one proceeding from a legislative body. ACTION.—*In the act,* in the actual performance or commission of some misdeed.—*In act to,* prepared or ready to, by being in a suitable posture.—**actable,** akt'a•bl, *a.* Capable of being acted or performed; practically possible.—**acting,** akt'ing, *a.* Performing duty, service, or functions; doing the real work of an office for a nominal or honorary holder of the post.—*n.* A playing on the stage.—**actor,** ak'tėr, *n.* One who acts or performs; one who represents a character or acts a part in a play.—**actress,** ak'tres, *n.* A female actor.

ACTH, ā'sē'tē'āch', *n.* Initials for *a*dreno*c*ortico*t*ropic *h*ormone, a pituitary hormone that stimulates the cortex of the adrenal glands.

actinia, ak•tin'i•a, *n.* pl. **actiniae,** [Gr. *aktis, aktinos,* a ray; from their tentacles being ray-like.] A sea anemone; a polyp having the mouth surrounded by tentacles in concentric circles, which when spread resemble the petals of a flower: often of brilliant colors.

actinic, ak•tin'ik, *a.* [Gr. *aktis, aktinos,* a ray.] Pertaining to rays; pertaining to the chemical rays of the sun.—**actinism,** ak'tin•izm, *n.* The radiation of heat or light; the property of the chemical part of the sun's rays, which, as seen in photography, produces chemical combinations and decompositions.—**actinium,** ak•tin'i•um, *n.* Radioactive element discovered in pitchblende. Symbol, Ac; at. no., 89; at. wt., 227. —**actinoid,** ak'tin•oid, *a.* Resembling a ray or rays; radiated.—**actinograph,** ak•tin'ō•graf, *n.* An instrument for measuring and registering the variations of actinic or chemical influence in the solar rays.—**actinology,** ak•ti•nol'ō•ji, *n.* The science which investigates the power of sunlight to cause chemical action.—**actinolitic,** ak•tin'ō•lit"ik, *a.* Like or pertaining to actinolite.—**actinometer,** ak•tin•om'et•ėr, *n.* An instrument for measuring the intensity of the sun's actinic rays.—**actinometric,** ak•tin'ō•met"rik, *a.* Of or belonging to the actinometer or its use.

action, ak'shon, *n.* [L. *actio.* ACT.] The state or manner of acting or being active, as opposed to *rest*; activity; an act or thing done; the performance of a function; a deed; an exploit; a battle or engagement; the mechanism or movement of a compound instrument, or the like; agency; operation; impulse; the connected series of events on which the interest of a drama or work of fiction depends; gesture or gesticulation; a suit or process at law. . . *Action* and *Act* have some meanings in common, but others are peculiar to each. Thus, the meanings battle, lawsuit, mechanism, belong only to the former; those of law, part of a play, to the latter. So we speak of a *course of action.* But we may speak of performing a noble *action* or a noble *act.*—**actionable,** ak'shon•a•bl, *a.* Furnishing ground for an action at law.—**actionably,** ak'shon•a•bli, *adv.* In an actionable manner.

active, ak'tiv, *a.* [Fr. *actif, active*; L. *activus.* ACT.] Having the power or property of acting; exerting or having the power to exert an influence (as opposed to *passive*); performing actions quickly; quick; nimble; brisk; agile; constantly engaged in action; busy; assiduous; accompanied or characterized by action, work, or by the performance of business (an *active* demand for goods); actually proceeding (*active* hostilities); *gram.* expressing action, especially action affecting an object; transitive.—**actively,** ak′tiv•li, *adv.* In an active manner.—**activity,** ak•tiv′i•ti, *n.* The state or quality of being active; the active faculty; active force; nimbleness; agility; briskness.—**activeness,** ak′tiv•nes, *n.* State of being active.

actor, actress. See ACT.

actual, ak′tū•al, *a.* Acting or existing really and objectively; real; effectively operative; effectual: opposed to *potential* or *nominal*; now existing; present.—*n.* Something actual or real.—**actualness,** ak′tū•al•nes, *n.* The quality of being actual.—**actuality,** ak•tū•al′i•ti, *n.* The state of being actual; that which is real or actual.—**actualization,** ak′tū•al iz•ā″shon, *n.* A making real or actual. —**actualize,** ak′tū•al•īz, *v.t.*—*actualized, actualizing.* To make actual.—**actually,** ak′tū•al•li, *adv.* In fact; really; with active manifestation.

actuary, ak′tū•a•ri, *n.* [L. *actuarius,* a clerk, a registrar, from *acta,* records, acts.] A registrar or clerk; an official in a joint-stock company, particularly an insurance company, whose duty it is to make the necessary computations, especially computations of some complexity.—**actuarial,** ak•tū•ā′ri•al, *a.* Of or pertaining to an actuary or to his business.

actuate, ak′tū•āt, *v.t.*—*actuated, actuating,* [From *act.*] To put into action; to move or incite to action.—**actuation,** ak•tū•ā′shon, *n.* The state of being put in action.—**actuator,** ak′tū•āt•ėr, *n.* One who actuates or puts in action.

aculeate, aculeated, a•kū′lē•āt, a•kū′lē•āt•ed, *a.* [L. *aculeus,* a spine, a prickle, dim. of *acus,* a needle. ACID.] *Bot.* having prickles or sharp points; *zool.* having a sting.

acumen, a•kū′men, *n.* [L. *acumen,* from *acuo,* to sharpen. ACID.] Quickness of perception; mental acuteness or penetration; keenness of insight; sagacity.—**acuminate,** a•kū′min•āt, *a.* [L. *acuminatus,* sharpened.] Pointed; acute.—**acuminate,** a•kū′min•āt, *v.t.* —*acuminated, acuminating.* To render sharp or keen.—*v.i.* † To taper to a point.—**acumination,** a•kū′min•ā″shon, *n.* Act of acuminating or sharpening; a pointed extremity; a sharp point or jag.

acupuncture, ak•ū•pungk′tūr, *n.* [L. *acus,* a needle, and *punctura,* a pricking. PUNCTURE.] A surgical operation resorted to in certain complaints, as in headaches, neuralgia, rheumatism, etc., and consisting in the insertion of a delicate needle or set of needles beneath the tissues.

acute, a•kūt′, *a.* [L. *acutus,* sharp-pointed, from *acuo,* to sharpen. From root, *ac, ak,* a point. ACID.] Sharp at the end; ending in a sharp point: opposed to *blunt* or *obtuse*; intellectually sharp; perceiving minute distinctions, or characterized by the use of such; characterized by keenness of insight: opposed to *dull* or *stupid*; having nice or quick sensibility; susceptible of slight impressions (*acute* hearing); keen; sharp; said of pain; high in pitch; shrill: said of sound; *med,* a term applied to a disease which is attended with more or less violent symptoms, and comes speedily to a crisis; *geom.* less than a right angle.—**acutely,** a•kūt′li, *adv.* In an acute manner; sharply; keenly; with nice discrimination.—**acuteness,** a•kūt′nes, *n.* The quality of being acute; sharpness; keenness; sagacity; acumen.

adage, ad′āj, *n.* [Fr. *adage,* L. *adagium,* a proverb.] A proverb; an old saying, which has obtained credit by long use.

adagio, a•dä′jō, *a.* and *adv.* [It.] *Music,* slow; slowly, leisurely, and with grace.—*n.* A slow movement.

Adam, ad′am, *n.* The name of the first man; hence, the frailty inherent in human nature.—*Adam's apple,* the prominence on the fore part of the throat.—*Adam's needle,* the popular name of the plants otherwise called *Yucca.*—**Adamic,** a•dam′ik, *a.* Pertaining to Adam.

adamant, ad′a•mant, *n.* [L. *adamas, adamantis,* Gr. *adamas,* the hardest iron or steel, anything inflexibly hard, the diamond, lit. the unconquerable—Gr. *a,* not, and *damaō,* to tame. TAME, DIAMOND.] Any substance of impenetrable hardness: chiefly a rhetorical or poetical word. (Formerly it sometimes meant the diamond, sometimes loadstone, from confusion with L. *adamantem* through the loving-attractive quality). — **adamantean, adamantine,** ad′a•mant•ē″an, ad•a•mant′īn, *a.* Made of adamant; having the qualities of adamant; impenetrable.

adapt, a•dapt′, *v.t.* [L. *adapto*—*ad,* to, and *apto,* to fit. APT.] To make suitable; to make to correspond; to fit or suit; to proportion; to remodel, work up, and render fit for representation on the stage, as a play from a foreign language or a novel. — **adaptability, adaptableness,** a•dapt′a•bil″i•ti, a•dapt′a•bl•nes, *n.* The quality of being capable of adaptation.—**adaptable,** a•dapt′a•bl, *a.* Capable of being adapted.—**adaptation,** ad•ap•tā′shon, *n.* The act of adapting or making suitable; the state of being suitable or fit; that which is adapted.—**adapter,** a•dapt′ėr, *n.* One who or that which adapts.—**adaptive,**† a•dapt′iv, *a.* Tending to adapt; suitable.

Adar, ā′där, *n.* A Hebrew month, answering to the latter part of February and the beginning of March, the twelfth of the sacred and sixth of the civil year.

add, ad, *v.t.* [L. *addo,* to add—*ad,* to, and *do,* to put, to place, to give.] To set or put together; to join or unite; to put into one sum; to annex; subjoin; say further.—*v.i.* To be or serve as an addition (with *to*); also, to perform the arithmetical operation of addition.—**addible,** ad′i•bl, *a.* Capable of being added.—**addition,** ad•di′shon, *n.* The act or process of adding; the uniting of two or more numbers in one sum; the rule or branch of arithmetic which treats of adding numbers; an increase; something added; a title coming after a personal name (*Shak.*).—**additional,** ad•di′shon•al, *a.* Added; supplementary.—**additionally,** ad•di′shon•al•li, *adv.* By way of addition.—**additive,** ad′it•iv, *a.* Additional; helping to increase.

addax, ad′aks, *n.* A species of large antelope inhabiting Africa, with long and beautifully twisted horns.

addendum, ad•den′dum, *n.* pl. **addenda,** ad•den′da. [L.] A thing to be added; an addition; an appendix to a work.

adder, ad′ėr, *n.* [O.E. *addre, addere,* by loss of initial *n* from A. Sax. *nædre, næddre,* O. and Prov. E. *nedder,* Icel. *nadr.* Goth. *nadrs,* G. *natter.*] A variety of venomous serpents, as the common viper, found in America and over Europe. —**adder's-tongue,** *n.* A species of fern.—Adderwort, *n.* Snakeweed, a kind of plant.

addible. See ADD.

addict, ad•dikt′, *v.t.* [L. *addico, addictum,* to devote—*ad,* to, and *dico,* to dedicate.] To apply habitually; to habituate: generally with a reflexive pronoun, and usually in a bad sense (followed by *to*); as, to *addict* one's self to intemperance. —*n.* (ad′dikt). One who is addicted. —**addicted,** ad•dikt′ed, *a.* Habitually practicing; given up; devoted; habituated (followed by *to*).—**addiction,** ad•dik′shon, *n.* The act of devoting or giving up one's self to a practice; the state of being devoted; devotion.

addition, additional, etc. See ADD.

addle, ad′l, *a.* [From A.Sax. *adela,* filth; Sw. *adel* (seen in *ko adel,* cow urine), urine; Sc. *addle,* putrid water, urine.] Having lost the power of development and become rotten, putrid: applied to eggs; hence, barren; producing nothing.—*v.t.*— *addled, addling.* To make rotten, as eggs.—**addleheaded, addlepated,** *a.* Stupid; muddled.

address, ad•dres′, *v.t.* [Fr. *adresser.* DRESS.] To direct or aim words; to pronounce; to apply to by words or writings; to accost; to speak to; to direct in writing; to write an address on; to court or make suit to.—*To address one's self to,* to speak to; to address.—*n.* The act of addressing one's self to a person; a speaking to; any speech or writing in which one person or set of persons makes a communication to another person or set of persons; manner of speaking to another; a person's bearing in conversation; courtship (in this sense generally in the plural); skill; dexterity; adroitness; direction of a letter.—**addressee,** ad•-

dres•ē′, *n.* One who is addressed.—**addresser,** ad•dres′ėr, *n.* One who addresses or petitions.

adduce, ad•dūs′, *v.t.—adduced, adducing.* [L. *adduco,* to lead or bring to—*ad,* to, and *duco,* to lead. DUKE.] To cite; to name or instance as authority or evidence; to bring to notice as bearing on a subject.—**adducent,** ad•dūs′ent, *a.* Bringing forward or together (an *adducent* muscle).—**adducer,** ad•dūs′ėr, *n.* One that adduces.—**adducible,** ad•dūs′i•bl, *a.* Capable of being adduced.—**adduction,** ad•duk′shon, *n.* The act of adducing; *anat.* the action by which a part of the body is drawn towards the bodily axis.—**adductive,** ad•dukt′iv, *a.*

adenalgy, ad•en•al′ji, *n.* [Gr. *aden,* a gland, and *algos,* pain.] Pain in a gland.—**adenoid,** ad′en•oid, *a.* Of a glandlike shape or character; glandular.—**adenitis,** ad•e•nī′tis, *n.* Inflammation of one or more of the lymphatic glands.—**adenoids,** ad′e•noidz, *n. pl.* Glandlike morbid growths in the throat behind the soft palate.—**adenoma,** ad•e•nō′ma, *n.* A tumor originating in a gland.

adenosine diphosphate, ad•en″o•sin dī•fos′fāt, *n.* A coenzyme important to the transfer of energy through the cell.

adenosine triphosphate, ad•en″o•sin trī•fos′fāt, *n.* A nucleotide that occurs in all cells. It represents the reserve energy of muscle and is important to many biochemical processes that produce or require energy.

adept, a•dept′, *n.* [L. *adeptus,* pp. of *adipiscor,* to obtain. Alchemists who were reputed to have *obtained* the philosopher's stone were termed *adepts;* hence *adept,* a proficient.] One fully skilled or well versed in any art; a proficient.—*a.* Well skilled.

adequate, ad′ē•kwāt, *a.* [L. *adaequatus,* made equal, pp. of *adaequo—ad,* to, and *aequus,* equal.] Equal; proportionate; exactly correspondent; fully sufficient.—**adequacy,** ad′ē•kwa•si, *n.* The state of being adequate; a sufficiency for a particular purpose.—**adequately,** ad′ē•kwāt•li, *adv.* In an adequate manner; sufficiently.—**adequateness,** ad′ē•kwāt•nes, *n.* The state of being adequate; sufficiency.

adhere, ad•hēr′, *v.i.—adhered, adhering.* [L. *adhaereo—ad,* to, and *haereo,* to stick, whence *hesitate.*] To stick together; to cleave; to become closely joined or united; to be fixed in attachment or devotion.—**adherence,** ad•hēr′ens, *n.* The quality or state of adhering; fidelity; steady attachment.—**adherent,** ad•hēr′ent, *a.* Sticking fast to something; clinging; attached.—**adherent,** ad•hēr′ent, *n.* One who adheres; one who follows a leader, party, or profession; a follower or partisan.—**adherently,** ad•hēr′ent•li, *adv.* In an adherent manner.—**adhesion,** ad•hē′zhon, *n.* L. *adhaesio,* from *adhaereo,* to adhere.] The act or state of adhering, or being united and attached; a sticking together of the surface of bodies; close connection or association; steady attachment of the mind or feelings; assent; concurrence (*adhesion* to a treaty).—**adhesive,** ad•hē′siv, *a.* Sticky; tenacious.—**adhesively,** ad•hē′siv•li, *adv.* In an adhesive manner.—**adhesiveness,** ad•hē′siv•nes, *n.* The state or quality of being adhesive; *phren.* an organ which is said to promote attachment to objects.

adhibit, ad•hib′it, *v.t.* [L. *adhibeo, adhibitum—ad,* to, and *habeo,* to hold.] To apply†; to attach (one's signature).—**adhibition,** ad•hi•bi′shon, *n.* The act of adhibiting.

adiabatic, a•di•a•bat′ik, *n.* [Gr. *a,* not, *diabainō,* pass through.] Of physical changes without gain or loss of heat; *adiabatic curve,* curve showing relation between the volume and the pressure of a fluid which changes its volume without gain or loss of heat.

adieu, a•dū′. [Fr. *à,* to, and *Dieu,* God, It. *addio,* Span. *a dios,* all forms of L. *ad,* to, and *Deus,* God.] *Lit.* to God: an ellipsis for I commend you to God; farewell; an expression of kind wishes at the parting of friends.—*n.* pl. **adieus,** or **adieux,** a•dūz′. A farewell or commendation to the care of God.

adipocere, ad′i•pō•sēr, *n.* [L. *adeps,* fat, and *cera,* wax.] A soft, unctuous, or waxy substance, into which the flesh of dead animals is converted when protected from atmospheric air, and under certain circumstances of temperature and humidity.

adipose, ad′i•pōs, *a.* [From L. *adeps, adipis,* fat.] Fatty; consisting of or resembling fat.—*n.* Fat; the fat on the kidneys.

adit, ad′it, *n.* [L. *aditus—ad,* to, and *eo, itum,* to go.] Approach; access; passage; a more or less horizontal passage into a mine.

adjacent, ad•jā′sent, *a.* [L. *adjacens, adjacentis,* pp. of *adjaceo,* to lie contiguous—*ad,* to, and *jaceo,* to lie.] Lying near or close; bordering upon; neighboring; adjoining.—**adjacency,** ad•jā′sen•si, *n.* The state of being adjacent.—**adjacently,** ad•jā′sent•li, *adv.* So as to be adjacent.

adjective, ad′jek•tiv, *n.* [L. *adjectivum, adjectivus,* added—*ad,* to, and *jacio,* to throw.] *Gram.* a word used with a noun to express a quality of the thing named, or something attributed to it, or to specify or describe a thing as distinct from something else, and so to limit and define it.—**adjectival,** ad•jek•tīv′al, *a.* Belonging to or like an adjective; having the import of an adjective.—**adjectivally, adjectively,** ad•jek•tī•v′al•li, ad′jek•tiv•li, *adv.* By way of, or as, an adjective.

adjoin, ad•join′, *v.t.* [Fr. *adjoindre;* L. *adjungo—ad,* to, and *jungo,* to join. JOIN.] To join or add; to unite; to annex or append.—*v.i.* To lie or be next or in contact; to be contiguous.—**adjoining,** ad•join′ing, *a.* Adjacent; contiguous; neighboring.

adjourn, ad•jėrn′, *v.t.* [Fr. *ajourner,* O.Fr. *ajorner, adjorner*—prefix *a, ad,* to, and O.Fr. *jorn* (now *jour*), a day, L. *diurnus,* diurnal, from *dies,* a day. DIURNAL.] To put off or defer to another day or until a later period; to suspend the meeting of, as of a public or private body, to a future day; to postpone to a future meeting of the same body.—*v.i.* To cease sitting and carrying on business for a time.—**adjournment,** ad•jėrn′ment, *n.* The act of adjourning; the period during which a public body adjourns its sittings.

adjudge, ad•juj′, *v.t.—adjudged, adjudging.* [Prefix *ad,* and *judge.* JUDGE.] To award judicially; to adjudicate upon; to settle.—

adjudicate, ad•jū′di•kāt, *v.t.—adjudicated, adjudicating.* [L. *adjudico,* to give sentence—*ad,* to, and *judico,* to judge. JUDGE.] To adjudge; to award judicially.—*v.i.* To sit in judgment; to give a judicial decision.—**adjudication,** ad•jū′di•kā″shon, *n.* The act of adjudicating; the act or process of trying and determining judicially; judgment or decision of a court.—**adjudicator,** ad•jū′di•kāt•ėr, *n.* One who adjudicates.

adjunct, ad′jungkt, *n.* [L. *adjunctus,* joined, from *adjungo—ad,* to, and *jungo, junctum,* to join. JOIN.] Something added to another, but not essentially a part of it.—*a.* United with in office or in action of any kind; conjoined with.—**adjunctive,** ad•jungk′tiv, *a.* Joining; having the quality of joining.—*n.* One who or that which is joined.

adjure, ad•jūr′, *v.t.—adjured, adjuring.* [L. *adjuro—ad,* to, and *juro,* to swear.] To charge, bind, or command, earnestly and solemnly.—**adjuration,** ad•jū•rā′shon, *n.* The act of adjuring; a solemn charging on oath; a solemn oath.—**adjuratory,** ad•jūr′a•to•ri, *a.* Containing an adjuration, or characterized by adjurations.—**adjurer,** ad•jūr′ėr, *n.* One who adjures.

adjust, ad•just′, *v.t.* [Fr. *ajuster,* Mod.Fr. *adjouter,* L.L. *adjuxtare,*] to bring together—*ad* and *juxta.* To fit; to make correspondent; to adapt; to accommodate; to put in order; to regulate or reduce to system; to settle or bring to a satisfactory state, so that parties are agreed in the result.—**adjustable,** ad•just′a•bl, *a.* Capable of being adjusted.—**adjuster,** ad•just′ėr, *n.* One who or that which adjusts.—**adjustment,** ad•just′ment, *n.* The act of adjusting.

adjutant, ad′jū•tant, *n.* [L. *adjutans,* ppr. of *adjuto,* to assist—*ad,* and *juvo, jutum,* to help.] *Milit.* an officer whose business is to assist a commanding officer by receiving and communicating orders.—**adjutancy,** ad′jū•tan•si, *n.* The office of an adjutant.—**adjutant bird, adjutant crane, adjutant stork,** *n.* A very large grallatorial bird allied to the storks, a native of the warmer parts of India. It feeds on carrion, and is most voracious.

adjutor, ad•jūt′ėr, *n.* obs. A helper; a coadjutor.—**adjutrix,†** ad•jū′triks, *n.* A female assistant.—**adjuvant,** ad′jū•vant or ad•jū′vant, *n.* An assistant; *med.* a substance added to a prescription to aid the operation of the principal ingredient or basis.

admeasure, ad•me′zhūr, *v.t.—admeasured, admeasuring.* [L. *ad,* to, and E. *measure.* MEASURE.] To ascertain the dimensions, size, or capacity of; to measure.—**admeasurement,** ad•me′zhūr•ment, *n.* The act of admeasuring; the measure of a thing, or dimensions ascertained.

adminicular, ad•min•ik′ū•lėr, *a.* [L. *adminiculum,* a prop, stay, or support.] Supplying help; helpful; lending aid or support.

administer, ad•min′is•tėr, *v.t.* [L. *administro—ad,* to, and *ministro,* to serve. MINISTER.] To manage or conduct as chief agent or directing and controlling official; to direct or superintend the execution of, as of laws; to afford, give, furnish, or supply; to give, as a dose of medicine; to dispense or distribute; to tender, as an oath; *law,* to manage, as the estate of a deceased person, collecting debts, paying legacies, etc. —*v.i.* To contribute assistance; to bring aid or supplies: with *to;* as, to *administer to* one's necessities; *law,* to perform the office of administrator.—**administrable,** ad•min′is•tra•bl, *a.* Capable of being administered.—**administration,** ad•min′is•trā″shon, *n.* The act of administering; direction; management; government of public affairs; the executive functions of government; the persons, collectively, who are intrusted with such functions; the executive; *law,* the management of the estate of a deceased person, consisting in collecting debts, paying debts and legacies, and distributing the property among the heirs.—**administrative,** ad•min′is•trāt•iv, *a.* Pertaining to administration.—**administrator,** ad•min′is•trāt•ėr, *n.* One who administers, or who directs, manages, distributes, or dispenses; one who has the charge of the goods and estate of a person dying without a will.—**administratorship,** ad•min′is•trāt•ėr•ship, *n.* The office of an administrator.—**administratrix,** ad•min′is•trāt•riks, *n.* A female administrator.

admirable, etc. See ADMIRE.

admiral, ad′mi•ral, *n.* [O.E. *amiral,* Fr. *amiral,* from Ar. *amir, emir,* a prince, chief, with the Ar. article suffixed.] Commander in chief of a fleet; highest rank of naval officer; high rank of naval officer. In U.S. Navy grades are fleet admiral, admiral, vice admiral, and rear admiral. Two species of butterflies, *Vanessa atalanta,* or red admiral, and *Limenitis camilla,* or white admiral.—**admiralship,** ad′mi•ral•ship, *n.* The office or power of an admiral.—**admiralty,** ad′mi•ral•ti, *n.* Jurisdiction of an admiral; department of state having charge of naval affairs.—**the admiralty,** official building of British commission for naval affairs in London.

admire, ad•mīr′, *v.t.—admired, admiring.* [Fr. *admirer,* L. *admiror—ad,* and *miror,* to wonder.] To wonder at‡; to regard with wonder mingled with approbation, esteem, reverence, or affection; to take pleasure in the beauty of; to look on or contemplate with pleasure.—*v.i.* To feel or express admiration.—**admirer,** ad•mīr′ėr, *n.* One who admires; one who esteems greatly; one who openly shows his admiration of a woman; a lover.—**admiringly,** ad•mīr′ing•li, *adv.* In an admiring manner; with admiration.—**admiration,** ad•mi•rā′shon, *n.* Wonder‡; wonder mingled with pleasing emotions, as approbation, esteem, love, or veneration; an emotion excited by something beautiful or excellent.—**admirable,** ad′mi•ra•bl, *a.* Worthy of admiration; most excellent.—**admirableness,** ad′mi•ra•bl•nes, *n.* —**admirably,** ad′mi•ra•bli, *adv.* In an admirable manner; excellently; exceedingly well.

admissible, etc. See ADMIT.

admit, ad•mit′, *v.t.—admitted, admitting.* [L. *admitto—ad,* to, and *mitto, missum,* to send, seen also in *commit, submit, mission,* etc.] To suffer to enter; to grant entrance to; to give right of entrance to; to grant in argument; to receive as true; to permit, grant, or allow, or to be capable of; to acknowledge; to own; to confess.—*v.i.* To give warrant or allowance; to grant opportunity; to permit: with *of* (the words do not *admit of* this interpretation).—**admittance,** ad•mit′ans, *n.* The act of admitting; permission to enter; entrance.—**admittedly,** ad•mit′ed•li, *adv.* By admission, acknowledgment, or concession.—**admissible,** ad•mis′i•bl, *a.* [Fr. *admissible,* L.L. *admissibilis,* from *admitto, admissum,* to admit.] Capable of being admitted, allowed, or conceded.—**admissibility,** ad•mis′i•bil″i•ti, *n.* The quality of being admissible.—**admissibly,** ad•mis′i•bli, *adv.* In an admissible manner; so as to be admitted.—**admission,** ad•mi′shon, *n.* [L. *admissio.*] The act of admitting; power or permission to enter; entrance; access; power to approach; the granting of an argument or position not fully proved; a point or statement admitted; acknowledgment; confession of a charge, error, or crime.—**admissive,** ad•mis′iv, *a.* Having the nature of an admission.

admix, ad•miks′, *v.t.* [Prefix *ad,* to, and *mix.*] To mingle with something else.—**admixture,** ad•miks′tūr, *n.* The act of mingling or mixing; that which is formed by mingling.

admonish, ad•mon′ish, *v.t.* [O.E. *amoneste,* O.Fr. *amonester,* to admonish—prefix *a, ad,* and L.L. *monestum,* for L. *monitum,* pp. of *moneo,* to warn. MONITION.] To warn or notify of a fault; to reprove with mildness; to counsel against wrong practices; to caution or advise; to instruct or direct; to remind; to recall or incite to duty.—**admonisher,** ad•mon′ish•ėr, *n.* One who admonishes.—**admonishment,**† ad•mon′ish•ment, *n.* Admonition.—**admonition,** ad•mō•ni′shon, *n.* The act of admonishing; counsel or advice; gentle reproof; instruction in duties; caution; direction.—**admonitor,** ad•mon′it•ėr, *n.* An admonisher; a monitor.—**admonitory,** ad•mon′i•to•ri, *a.* Containing admonition; tending or serving to admonish.

adnascent,† ad•nas′ent, *a.* [L. *ad,* to, *nascens,* growing.] Growing on something else.—**adnate,** ad′nāt, *a.* [L. *adnatus—ad,* to, and *natus,* grown.] Growing attached: chiefly a term in *bot.*

ado, a•dö′, *n.* [Prefix *a* for *at,* and *do,* that is, to do; *at* being here the sign of the infinitive, as in Icelandic.] Bustle; trouble; labor; difficulty.

adobe, a•dō′be, *n.* [Sp.] A sun-dried brick.

adolescence, ad•ō•les′ens, *n.* [L. *adolescentia—ad,* and *olesco,* to grow.] The state of growing: applied almost exclusively to the young of the human race; youth, or the period of life between childhood and the full development of the frame.—**adolescent,** ad•ō•les′ent, *a.* Growing up; advancing from childhood to manhood.

Adonic, Adonean, a•don′ik, ad•ō•nē′an, *a.* [From *Adonis,* a mythical personage among the Greeks, originally the Phoenician sun god.] Of or pertaining to Adonis.—*Adonic verse,* in Greek and Latin poetry, a verse consisting of a dactyl and a spondee or trochee.—**Adonis,** a•dōn′is, *n.* Beautiful person; a beau.

adopt, a•dopt′, *v.t.* [L. *adopto—ad,* and *opto,* to desire or choose. OPTION.] To take into one's family and treat as one's own child; to take to one's self by choice or approval, as principles, opinions, a course of conduct, etc.—**adoptable,** a•dopt′a•bl, *a.* Capable of, fit for, or worthy of being adopted.—**adopter,** a•dopt′ėr, *n.* One who adopts.—**adoption,** a•dop′shon, *n.* [L. *adoptio.*] The act of adopting, or the state of being adopted.—**adoptive,** a•dopt′iv, *a.* [L. *adoptivus.*] Constituted by adoption; adopting or adopted; assumed.

adore, a•dōr′, *v.t.—adored, adoring.* [L. *adoro,* to pray, to adore,—*ad,* to, and *oro,* to ask. ORACLE.] To worship with profound reverence; to pay divine honors to; to regard with the utmost esteem, love, and respect; to love in the highest degree, as a man a woman.—**adorability,** a•dōr′a•bil′i•ti, *n.* Quality of being adorable.—**adorable,** a•dōr′a•bl, *a.* Demanding adoration; worthy of being adored; exquisitely charming; lovable.—**adorableness,** a•dōr′a•bl•nes, *n.*—**adorably,** a•dōr′a•bli, *adv.* In a manner worthy of adoration.—**adoration,** ad•ō•rā′shon, *n.* The act of adoring; the act of paying honors, as to a divine being; worship addressed to a deity; the highest degree of love, as of a man for a woman.—**adorer,** a•dōr′ėr, *n.* One who adores; one who worships or honors as divine; a lover; an admirer.—**adoringly,** a•dōr′ing•li, *adv.* With adoration.

adorn, a•dorn′, *v.t.* [L. *adorno—ad,* to, and *orno,* to deck or beautify.]

To deck or decorate; to add to the attractiveness of by dress or ornaments; to set off to advantage; beautify; embellish.—**adornment,** a•dorn′ment, *n.* An ornament or decoration.

ADP. See ADENOSINE DIPHOSPHATE.

adrenal, ad•rē′nal, *a.* [L. *ad*, near, and *renes*, kidney.] On or near the kidney.—*n.* An adrenal gland.—**adrenal gland,** ad•rē′nal gland, *n.* A small endocrine gland attached to the kidney.

adrenalin, ad•ren′al•in, *n.* A name for epinephrine, a hormone secreted by the medulla of the adrenal gland; a drug used as a heart stimulant, muscle relaxant, etc.

adrift, a•drift′, *a.* or *adv.* [Prefix *a*, on, and *drift*, a driving or floating. DRIVE.] Floating at random; impelled or moving without direction; at the mercy of winds and currents; swayed by any chance impulse; at sea; at a loss.

adroit, a•droit′, *a.* [Fr. *adroit*, dexterous—*a*, to, and *droit*, right, as opposed to left (comp. *dexterous*, from L. *dexter*, right); from L. *directus*, straight, direct.] Dexterous; skillful; expert; active in the use of the hand, and, figuratively, in the exercise of the mental faculties; ready in invention or execution.—**adroitly,** a•droit′li, *adv.*—**adroitness,** a•droit′nes, *n.*

adsorb, ad•sorb′, *v.t.* To collect, as molecules of gases, dissolved substances, or liquids, in a thin layer on a surface.—**adsorption,** ad•sorp′shun, *n.* The adhesion of molecules to a surface, to be distinguished from *absorption*.

adularia, ad•ū•lā′ri•a, *n.* [From *Adula*, the summit of the St. Gothard, where fine specimens are got.] A very pure, limpid, translucent variety of the common feldspar, called also *Moonstone*.

adulation, ad•ū•lā′shon, *n.* [L. *adulatio*, *adulationis*, a fawning, *adulor*, *adulatus*, to flatter.] Servile flattery; praise in excess, or beyond what is merited; high compliment.—**adulate,** ad′ū•lāt, *v.t.* To show feigned devotion to; to flatter servilely.—**adulator,** ad′ū•lāt•ėr, *n.* A flatterer.—**adulatory,** ad′ū•lāt•o•ri, *a.* Flattering.

adult, a•dult′, *a.* [L. *adultus*, grown to maturity, from *ad*, to, *oleo*, to grow. ADOLESCENCE.] Having arrived at mature years, or to full size and strength; pertaining or relating to full strength; suitable for an adult.—**adult,** a•dult′, *n.* A person grown to full size and strength.

adulterate, a•dul′tėr•āt, *v.t.*—*adulterated*, *adulterating*. [L. *adultero*, from *adulter*, mixed, an adulterer—*ad*, to, and *alter*, other.] To debase or deteriorate by an admixture of foreign or baser materials.—**adulterant,** a•dul′tėr•ant, *n.* The person or thing that adulterates.—**adulteration,** a•dul′tėr•ā″shon, *n.* The act of adulterating, or the state of being adulterated or debased by foreign mixture.—**adulterator,** a•dul′tėr•ā•tėr, *n.* One who adulterates.

adultery, a•dul′tėr•i, *n.* [L. *adulterium*, from *adulter*, an adulterer. ADULTERATE.] Violation of the marriage bed; sexual commerce by a married person with one who is not his or her wife or husband.—**adulterer,** a•dul′tėr•ėr, *n.* A man guilty of adultery.—**adulteress,** a•dul′tėr•es, *n.* A woman guilty of adultery.—**adulterine,** a•dul′tėr•īn, Proceeding from adulterous commerce.—**adulterous,** a•dul′tėr•us, *a.* Guilty of adultery; pertaining to adultery; illicit.—**adulterously,** a•dul′tėr•us•li, *adv.* In an adulterous manner.

adumbrate, ad•um′brāt, *v.t.*—*adumbrated*, *adumbrating*. [L. *adumbro*, to shade—*ad*, and *umbra*, a shade.] To give a faint shadow of; to exhibit a faint resemblance of, like a shadow; to shadow forth.—**adumbration,** ad•um•brā′shon, *n.* The act of adumbrating or shadowing forth; a faint or imperfect representation of a thing.—**adumbrative,** ad•um′bra•tiv, *a.* Shadowing forth; faintly resembling.—**adumbratively,** ad•um′bra•tiv•li, *adv.* In an adumbrative manner.

aduncous, ad•ungk′us, *a.* [L. *aduncus*, hooked—*ad*, to, and *uncus*, a hook.] Hooked; bent or made in the form of a hook.—**aduncity,** ad•un′si•ti, *n.* Hookedness.

adust, a•dust′, *a.* [L. *adustus*, burned—*ad*, to, and *uro*, *ustum*, to burn.] Burned; scorched; parched up; looking as if burned or scorched.

advance, ad•vans′, *v.t.*—*advanced*, *advancing*. [Fr. *avancer*, from *avant*, forward (whence also E. *van*), L. *abante*, from before, in front—*ab*, from, *ante*, before.] To bring forward; to move further in front; to promote; to raise to a higher rank; to forward or further; to encourage the progress of; to enhance (price); to accelerate the growth of; to offer or propose; to bring to view or notice, as something one is prepared to abide by; to allege; to supply beforehand; to furnish on credit, or before goods are delivered, or work done.—*v.i.* To move or go forward; to proceed; to make progress; to grow better, greater, wiser, or older; to rise in rank, office, or consequence.—*n.* A moving forward or toward the front; a march forward; gradual progression; improvement; advancement; promotion; a proposal; a first step toward; addition to price; rise in price; a giving beforehand; that which is given beforehand, especially money.—*In advance*, in front, before; beforehand; before an equivalent is received.—**advancement,** ad•vans′ment, *n.* The act of advancing; the state of being advanced; the act of promoting; preferment; promotion; improvement; furtherance.

advantage, ad•van′tāj, *n.* [O.Fr. *advantage*, Fr. *avantage*, from *avant*, before. ADVANCE.] Any state, condition, circumstance, opportunity, or means specially favorable to success, prosperity, or any desired end (the *advantage* of a good constitution, of an excellent education); superiority; benefit; gain; profit.—*v.t.*—*advantaged*, *advantaging*. To bring advantage to; to be of service to; to benefit; to yield profit or gain to.—**advantageous,** ad•van•tā′jus, *a.* Being of advantage; profitable; useful; beneficial.—**advantageously,** ad•van•tā′jus•li, *adv.* In an advantageous manner.—**advantageousness,** ad•van•tā′jus•nes, *n.*

advene, ad•vēn′, *v.i.* [L. *advenio*, to come to—*ad*, to, and *venio*, to come. VENTURE.] To accede or be superadded; to become a part, though not essential.—**advent,** ad′vent, *n.* [L. *adventus*, an arrival.] A coming; approach; visitation; [*cap*] the coming of the Saviour; an ecclesiastical division of the year embracing the four weeks before Christmas.—**adventitious,** ad•ven•tish′us, *a.* [L. *adventitius*.] Added extrinsically; not essentially inherent; accidentally or casually acquired.—**adventitiously,** ad•ven•tish′us•li, *adv.*—**adventitiousness,** ad•ven•tish′us•nes, *n.*

adventure, ad•ven′tūr, *n.* [O.Fr. *adventure*, Fr. *aventure*, L.L. *adventura*, *aventura*, from L. *adventurus*, about to arrive, fut. part. of *advenio*, to arrive. ADVENE.] Hazard; risk; chance; a hazardous enterprise; a bold and dangerous undertaking of uncertain issue; a commercial speculation; a speculation in goods sent abroad; a remarkable occurrence in one's personal history; a noteworthy event or experience in one's life.—*v.t.*—*adventured*, *adventuring*. To risk or hazard; to venture on; to attempt.—**adventurer,** ad•ven′tūr•ėr, *n.* One who engages in an adventure or speculation; one who attempts or takes part in bold, novel, or extraordinary enterprises; one who lives by underhand means, or by a system of imposition.—**adventuress,** ad•ven′tūr•es, *n.* A female adventurer.—**adventurous,** ad•ven′tūr•us, *a.* Bold to encounter danger; daring; courageous; enterprising; full of hazard; attended with risk.—**adventurously,** ad•ven′tūr•us•li, *adv.* In an adventurous manner.—**adventurousness,** ad•ven′tūr•us•nes, *n.*

adverb, ad′vėrb, *n.* [L. *adverbium*—*ad*, to, and *verbum*, a word, a verb.] *Gram.* one of the indeclinable parts of speech, so called from being frequently joined to verbs for the purpose of limiting or extending their signification.—**adverbial,** ad•vėrb′i•al, *a.* Pertaining to or having the character or structure of an adverb.—**adverbially,** ad•vėrb′i•al•li, *adv.* In the manner or with the force or character of an adverb.

adversary, ad′vėr•se•ri, *n.* [L. *adversarius*. ADVERSE.] An enemy; a foe; an antagonist; an opponent... An *adversary* is one who is opposed to another, without necessarily having hostile feelings; an *antagonist* is one who strives personally against another for victory; an *enemy* is one who entertains feelings of personal hostility.

adversative, ad•vėrs′at•iv, *a.* Expressing difference, contrariety, or opposition (an *adversative* conjunction).—*n.* A word denoting contrariety or opposition.

adverse, ad′vėrs, *a.* [L. *adversus,* opposite—*ad,* to, and *versus,* turned, from *verto,* to turn.] Acting in a contrary direction; counteracting; opposing (*adverse* winds; hostile; inimical (a party, criticism); unfortunate; calamitous; unprosperous (fate or circumstances).—**adversely,** ad′vėrs•li, *adv.* In an adverse manner. —**adverseness,** ad′vėrs•nes, *n.* The state or quality of being adverse.—**adversity,** ad•vėrs′i•ti, *n.* An event, or series of events, which oppose success or desire; misfortune; calamity; affliction; distress; state of unhappiness.

advert, a•dvėrt′, *v.i.* [L. *advert—ad,* to, and *verto,* to turn.] To turn the mind or attention; to regard, observe, or notice; to refer or allude: followed by *to.* ∴ *Advert* is to turn directly, and it may be abruptly; *allude* is to touch slightly, and it may be in a very vague and uncertain manner; *refer, lit.* to carry back, is to bring a thing already well known into notice; to mention or speak of directly.—**advertence, advertency,** ad•vėrt′ens, ad•vėrt′en•si, *n.* Attention; notice; regard; heedfulness.—**advertent,** ad•vėrt′ent, *a.* Attentive; heedful.—**advertently,** ad•vėrt′ent•li, *adv.* In an advertent manner.

advertise, ad•vėr•tīz′, *v.t.—advertised, advertising.* [Fr. *avertir, avertissant,* to warn, inform, from L. *adverto,* to turn towards—*ad, verto,* to turn.] To inform or give notice; to make public intimation of, especially by printed notice.—*v.i.* To announce one's wishes or intentions by a public and usually a printed notice.—**advertisement,** ad•vėr′tiz•ment, *n.* Warning, advice, or admonition (*Shak.*); a written or printed notice intended to make something known to the public; especially a printed and paid notice in a newspaper or other public print.—**advertiser,** ad•vėr•tīz′ėr, *n.* One who advertises.

advice, ad•vīs′, *n.* [O.Fr. *advis,* opinion, counsel—L. *ad,* to, and *visum,* what is seen or judged proper. VISION.] An opinion recommended, or offered, as worthy to be followed; counsel; suggestion; information; notice; intelligence; a notification in respect of a business transaction.—*To take advice,* to consult with others; specifically, to take the opinion of a professional or skillful man, as a physician or lawyer.—**advisability,** ad•vīz′a•bil″i•ti, *n.* Advisableness; expediency.—**advisable,** ad•vīz′a•bl, *a.* Proper to be advised; expedient; proper to be done or practiced; open to advice.—**advisableness,** ad•vīz′a•bl•nes, *n.* The quality of being advisable or expedient.—**advisably,** ad•vīz′a•bli, *adv.* With advice.—**advise,** ad•vīz′, *v.t.—advised, advising.* [Fr. *aviser.* ADVICE.] To give counsel to; to counsel; to give information to; to inform; to acquaint. *v.i.* To consider; to reflect; to take counsel. —**advised,** ad•vīzd′, *a.* Cautious; prudent; done, formed, or taken with advice or deliberation (an *advised* act).—**advisedly,** ad•vīz′ed•li, *adv.* With deliberation or advice; heedfully; purposely; by design.—**advisedness,** ad•vīz′ed•nes, *n.* The state of being advised; prudent procedure. —**adviser,** ad•vīz′ėr, *n.* One who gives advice or admonition; a counsellor.—**advisory,** ad•vīz′o•ri, *a.* Having power to advise; containing advice.

advocate, ad′vō•kāt, *n.* [L. *advocatus,* one summoned to aid—*ad,* to, and *voco, vocatum,* to call. VOICE, VOCAL.] One who pleads the cause of another in a court of law; one who defends, vindicates, or espouses a cause by argument; a pleader in favor of something; an upholder; a defender. —*v.t. advocated, advocating.* To plead in favor of (a thing, not a person); to defend by argument before a tribunal; to support or vindicate.—**advocacy,** ad′vō•ka•si, *n.* The act of pleading for; intercession; defense.

advocation, ad•vō•kā′shon, *n.* The act of advocating; a pleading for.

advowson, ad•vou′sn, *n.* [O.Fr. *advoeson, advouson,* protection, patronage; L. *advocatio, advocationis,* a calling to one for help. ADVOCATE.] The right of presentation to a vacant benefice in the Established Church of England.

adynamia, ad″i•nā′mi•a, *n.* [Gr. *a,* not, and *dynamis,* power.] Weakness; want of strength occasioned by disease; a deficiency of vital power.—**adynamic,** a•di•nam′ik, *a.* Weak; destitute of strength.

adytum, ad′i•tum, *n.* pl. **adyta,** ad′i•ta. [L. *adytum,* Gr. *adyton,* lit. a place not to be entered—*a,* not, and *dyō,* to enter.] An innermost sanctuary or shrine; the chancel or altar-end of a church.

adz, adze, adz, *n.* [O.E. *addice,* A.Sax. *adese,* an adze.] An instrument of the ax kind used for chipping the surface of timber, the cutting edge being at right angles to the handle.—*v.t.* To chip or shape with an adz.

aedile. Same as *Edile.*

aegis, ē′jis, *n.* [Gr. *aigis.*] Among the ancient Greeks the shield of Zeus; in later times part of the armor of Pallas Athena, a kind of breastplate; hence, anything that protects or shields; protecting power or influence.

aeolian. Same as *Eolian.*

aeolotropic, ē′ol•ō•trop″ik, *a.* [Gr. *aiolos,* varied, *tropē,* a turn.] Applied to bodies unequally elastic in different directions: opposed to *isotropic.*

aeon, *n.* Same as *Eon.*

aerate, ā′ėr•āt, *v.t.—aerated, aerating.* [L. *aer,* air. AIR.] To combine with carbonic acid or other gas, or with air.—**aerial,** ā•ē′ri•al, *a.* [L. *aerius.*] Belonging or pertaining to the air or atmosphere; inhabiting or frequenting the air; produced by or in the air; reaching far into the air; high; lofty; possessed of a light and graceful beauty.—*n.* Radio or television antenna.—**aerially,** ā•ē′ri•al•li, *adv.*—**aerify,** ā′ėr•i•fī, *v.t.—aerified, aerifying.* To infuse air into; to fill with air, or to combine air with; to change into an aeriform state.

aerie, ė′rē or ā′ėr•i, *n.* [Fr. and Pr. *aire,* L.L. *aeria, aerea, area,* an aerie; origin doubtful.] The nest of a bird of prey, as of an eagle or hawk; a brood of eagles or hawks.

aerify. See AERATE.

aerobic, ā•ėr•ob′ik, *a.* [Gr. *aēr,* air, *bios,* life.] Requiring air or free oxygen in order to live and thrive, as certain bacteria.

aerodynamics, ā′ėr•ō•dī•nam″iks, *n.* [Gr. *aēr, dynamis,* power.] The science treating of the motion of the air and gases, and of their effects when in motion.

aerolite, ā′ėr•ō•līt, *n.* [Gr. *aēr,* air, and *lithos,* a stone.] A meteoric stone; a meteorite.—**aerolitic,** ā′ėr•ō•lit″ik, *a.* Relating to aerolites.

aerology, ā•ėr•ol′o•ji, *n.* [Gr. *aēr, aeros,* air, *logos,* description, *gnōsis,* knowledge.] That branch of physics which treats of the air, its constituent parts, properties, and phenomena.—**aerologic, aerological,** ā′ėr•ō•loj″ik, ā′ėr•ō•loj″ik•al, *a.* Pertaining to aerology.—**aerologist,** ā•ėr•ol′o•jist, *n.* One who is versed in aerology.

aeromechanics, ā′ėr•ō•me•kan″iks, *n.* [Gr. *aer,* and *mechanikos, mechane,* a machine.] Study of air and other gases in motion or equilibrium, or of solid bodies immersed in gases.

aerometer, ā•ėr•om′et•ėr, *n.* [Gr. *aēr,* air, and *metron,* measure.] An instrument for weighing air, or for ascertaining the density of air and gases.—**aerometric,** ā′ėr•ō•met″rik, *a.* Pertaining to aerometry.—**aerometry,** ā•ėr•om′et•ri, *n.* The science of measuring the weight or density of air and gases.

aeronaut, ā′ėr•ō•nạt, *n.* [Gr. *aēr,* air, and *nautes,* a sailor, from *naus,* a ship.] An aerial navigator; a balloonist.—**aeronautic, aeronautical,** ā′ėr•ō•nạt″ik, ā′ėr•ō•nạt″ik•al, *a.* Pertaining to aeronautics or aerial sailing.—**aeronautics,** ā′ėr•ō•nạt″iks, *n.* The doctrine, science, or art of floating in the air, as by means of a balloon.

aeropause, ā′ėr•ō•pạz, *n.* [Gr. *aer,* air, and *pausis,* stop.] The dividing line between outer space and areas in which man and aircraft can function.

aerophore, ā′ėr•o•for, *n.* [Gr. *aēr, pherō,* to bring.] A kind of ventilating apparatus; a portable receptacle by which air is supplied artificially under water or elsewhere.

aerophysics, ā′ėr•ō•fiz′iks, *n.* [*aer,* and physics.] A branch of physics that deals with the design, construction, and operation of high-speed, rocket-type aircraft.

aerophyte, ā′ėr•o•fīt, *n.* [Gr. *aēr,* air, and *phyton,* a plant.] A plant which lives exclusively in air; an air plant.

aerosol, ā″er•o•sōl′, *n. Phys. Chem.* A suspension of fine particles, solid or liquid, in a gas; a smoke or fog.—**aerosol bomb.** A device that sprays insecticide in a mist.

aerostat, ā′ėr•ō•stat, *n.* [Fr. *aérostat,* a balloon—Gr. *aēr,* air, and *statos,* standing, from *histemi,* to stand.] A machine or vessel sustaining weights in the air; a name given to air balloons.—**aerostatic, aerostatical,**

ā′ėr·ō stat″ik, ā′ėr·ō·stat″ik·al, *a.* Pertaining to aerostatics; pertaining to aerostation, or aerial navigation.—**aerostatics,** ā′ėr·ō·stat″iks, *n.* The science which treats of the weight, pressure, and equilibrium of air and other elastic fluids, and of the equilibrium of bodies sustained in them. —**aerostation,** ā′ėr·ō·stā″shon, *n.* Aerial navigation.

aery, ā′ėr·i, *a.* Airy; breezy; aerial. [Poetic.]

Aesculapian, ēs·kul·āp′i·an, *a. Med.* of or pertaining to Aesculapius, the ancient healing god.

aesthete, ēs′thēt, *n.* [From *aesthetic.*] One devoted to the principles or doctrines of aesthetics; a lover of the beautiful.—**aesthetic, aesthetical,** ēs·thet′ik, ēs·thet′ik·al, *a.* [Gr. *aisthētikos,* from *aisthanomai,* to perceive by the senses.] Pertaining to the science of taste or beauty; pertaining to the sense of the beautiful. —**aesthetically,** ēs·thet′ik·al·li, *adv.* According to the principles of aesthetics; with reference to the sense of the beautiful.—**aestheticism,** ēs·thet′i·sizm, *n.* The principles or doctrines of aesthetics; attachment to aesthetics.—**aesthetics,** ēs·thet′iks, *n.* The theory of the fine arts; the science or that branch of philosophy which deals with the beautiful; the doctrines of taste.

afar, a·fär′, *adv.* At a distance in place; to or from a distance: often with *from* preceding or *off* following, or both.

affable, af′fa·bl, *a.* [L. *affabilis,* affable—*af* for *ad,* to, *fari,* to speak.] Easy of conversation; admitting others to free conversation without reserve; courteous; complaisant; of easy manners; condescending.—**affability, affableness,** af·fa·bil′i·ti, af′fa·bl·nes, *n.* The quality of being affable.—**affably,** af′fa·bli, *adv.* In an affable manner; courteously.

affair, af·fār′, *n.* [Fr. *affaire—a,* to, and *faire,* to do, L. *facere,* to make, to do.] Business of any kind; that which is done, or is to be done; matter; concern; sometimes used by itself in the plural with the specific sense of public affairs or pecuniary affairs; special business; personal concern; a rencontre; a skirmish.—*Affair of honor,* a duel.

affect, af·fekt′, *v.t.* [L. *affecto,* to desire, to strive after, freq. of *afficio, affectum,* to affect the mind or body—*af* for *ad,* to, and *facio,* to do.] To act upon; to produce an effect or change upon; to influence; to move or touch by exciting the feelings; to aspire to; to endeavor after; to choose commonly; to habitually follow after; make a show of; to assume the appearance of; to pretend.—**affectation, affectedness,** af·fek·tā′shon, af·fekt′ed·nes, *n.* [L. *affectatio.*] An attempt to assume or exhibit what is not natural or real; false pretense, especially of what is praiseworthy or uncommon; artificial appearance or show.—**affected,** af·fekt′ed, *a.* Inclined or disposed (especially with *well, ill,* etc.); given to affectation; assuming or pretending to possess what is not natural or real; assumed artificially; not natural.—**affectedly,** af·fekt′ed·li, *adv.* In an affected or assumed manner; with affectation.—**affecter,** af·fekt′ėr, *n.* One who affects, pretends, or assumes.—**affecting,** af·fekt′ing, *a.* Having power to excite emotion; suited to affect; pathetic.—**affectingly,** af·fekt′ing·li, *adv.* In an affecting or impressive manner.

affection, af·fek′shon, *n.* [L. *affectio, affectionis,* the being affected or touched. AFFECT.] The state of having one's feelings affected in some way; bent or disposition of mind; sentiment or moral feeling (as esteem, envy, jealousy); appetite; inclination; a settled good-will, love, or zealous attachment; a property or attribute inseparable from its object (as figure from bodies); any particular morbid state of the body (a gouty *affection*). —**affectionate,** af·fek′shon·āt, *a.* Having great love or affection; warmly attached; fond; kind; loving; proceeding from affection; tender.—**affectionately,** af·fek′shon·āt·li, *adv.* In an affectionate manner; fondly; tenderly; kindly.—**affectionateness,** af·fek′shon·āt·nes, *n.* The quality of being affectionate; fondness; affection.

affenpinscher, af″en·pin′·shėr, *n.* Breed of small dog having stiff red, black, or gray coat, pointed ears, and shaggy hairs about nose, eyes, and chin; also called *monkey dog* from monkeyish expression.

afferent, af′fėr·ent, *a.* [L. *afferens, afferentis,* ppr. of *affero—af* for *ad,* to, and *fero,* to carry. Carrying to or inward (of vessels or nerves in animals).

affiance, af·fī′ans, *n.* [O.Fr., from *af* for *ad,* to, and *fiancer,* to betroth. L. *fidans, fidantis,* ppr. of *fido,* to pledge one's faith, *fides,* faith.] Marriage contract or promise; faith pledged; confidence; reliance.—*v.t.*—*affianced, affiancing.* To betroth; to bind by promise of marriage.

affidavit, af·fi·dā′vit, *n.* [3rd pers. sing. perf. ind. of L.L. *affido,* to pledge one's faith—L. *af* for *ad,* to, and *fides,* faith.] A written declaration upon oath; a statement of facts in writing signed by the party, and sworn to or confirmed by declaration before an authorized magistrate.

affiliate, af·fil′i·āt, *v.t.*—*affiliated, affiliating.* [L.L. *adfiliare,* to adopt as a son—L. *ad,* to, and *filius,* a son.] To adopt; to receive into a family as a son; to establish the paternity of, as of a bastard child; to connect in the way of descent; to receive into a society as a member.—**affiliation,** af·fil′i·ā″shon, *n.* The act of one who affiliates; the settlement of the paternity of a child on its true father.

affined,‡ af·fīnd′, *a.* [O.Fr. *affiner* to unite. AFFINITY.] Joined in affinity; akin; bound or impelled by any kind of affinity. [*Shak.*]

affinity, af·fin′i·ti, *n.* [L. *affinitas,* from *affinis,* adjacent, related—*af* for *ad,* to, and *finis,* boundary.] The relation contracted by marriage, in contradistinction from *consanguinity,* or relation by blood; relation, connection, or alliance in general (as of languages, sounds, etc.); similarity in kind or nature; *chem.* that force by which bodies of dissimilar nature unite in certain definite proportions to form a compound, different in its nature from any of its constituents.

affirm, af·fėrm′, *v.t.* [L. *affirmo—af* for *ad,* to, and *firmo,* to make firm.] To assert positively; to tell with confidence; to aver; declare; allege: opposed to *deny;* to confirm or ratify.—*v.i.* To make a solemn assertion or declaration; to make a legal affirmation.—**affirmable,** af·fėrm′abl, *a.* Capable of being affirmed, asserted, or declared.—**affirmably,** af·fėrm′a·bli, *adv.* In a way capable of affirmation.—**affirmance,†** af·fėrm′ans, *n.* Confirmation; ratification; affirmation. — **affirmant, affirmer,** af·fėrm′ant, af·fėrm′ėr, *a.* One who affirms or asserts; one who makes affirmation instead of an oath.—**affirmation,** af·fėr·mā′shon, *n.* The act of affirming or asserting as true; that which is asserted; averment; confirmation; ratification; a solemn declaration made in lieu of an oath by one who has scruples about taking the oath.—**affirmative,** af·fėrm′at·iv, *a.* Affirming or asserting, opposed to *negative.*—*n.* A word or phrase expressing assent or affirmation or answering a question affirmatively; the opposite of a negative.—*The affirmative,* that side of a debated question which maintains the truth of the affirmative proposition.—**affirmatively,** af·fėrm′at·iv·li, *adv.* In an affirmative manner; positively.

affix, af·fiks′, *v.t.* [L. *affigo, affixum—af* for *ad,* to, and *figo, fixum,* to fix.] To subjoin, annex, unite, or add at the close or end; to append; to attach.—**affix,** af′fiks, *n.* A syllable or letter added to the end of a word; a suffix; a post-fix.

afflation, af·flā′shon, *n.* [L. *afflo, afflatum—af* for *ad,* to, and *flo,* to blow.] A blowing or breathing on.—**afflatus,** af·flā′tus, *n.* [L.] A breath or blast of wind; inspiration; the inspiration of the poet.

afflict, af·flikt′, *v.t.* [L. *afflicto,* intens. of *affligo,* to dash down—*af* for *ad,* to, and *fligo,* to strike.] To give (to the body or mind) pain which is continued or of some permanence; to trouble, grieve, harass, or distress.—**afflicter,** af·flikt′ėr, *n.* One who afflicts.—**affliction,** af·flik′shon, *n.* The state of being afflicted; a state of acute pain or distress of body or mind; the cause of continued pain of body or mind… *Affliction* is stronger than *grief,* and *grief* than *sorrow. Affliction* is acute mental suffering caused by the loss of something cherished, as friends, health, or fortune.—**afflictive,** af·flikt′iv, *a.* Painful; distressing.—**afflictively,** af·flikt′iv·li, *adv.*

affluence, af′flu·ens, *n.* [L. *affluentia,* from *affluo,* to flow to—*ad,* to, and *fluo,* to flow. FLUENT.] A flowing to or concourse; an abundant supply; great plenty of worldly goods; wealth. — **affluent,** af′flu•ent, *a.* Flowing to; wealthy; abundant.—*n.* A tributary stream.—**affluently,** af′-flu•ent•li, *adv.*

afflux, af′fluks, *n.* [From L. *affluo, affluxum.* AFFLUENCE.] The act of flowing to; a flowing to, or that which flows to.

afford, af•fōrd′, *v.t.* [O.E. *aforth,* to afford, from prefix *a,* and *forth;* A.Sax. *forthian,* to further.] To give forth; to yield, supply, or produce (fruit, profit); to grant or confer (as consolation, gratification); to buy, sell, expend, etc., from having a sufficiency of means; to bear the expense of (with *can, could, may, might.* etc.).

afforest, af•for′est, *v.t.* [Prefix *af* for *ad,* to, and *forest.*] To convert into a forest; to turn into forest land.—**afforestation,** af•for′es•tā″shon, *n.* The act of converting into a forest.

affranchise, af•fran′chiz, *v.t.* [Prefix *af,* and *franchise.*] To make free; to liberate from servitude.

affray, af•frā′, *v.t.* [O. or Prov. Fr. *affraier, effroyer,* Fr. *effrayer,* to frighten; from L.L. *exfrediare*—L. *ex,* intens., and O.H.G. *fridu,* G. *friede,* peace. AFRAID.] To frighten; to terrify.—*n.* Fear‡; a noisy quarrel; a brawl; a tumult; disturbance.

affright, af•frīt′, *v.t.* [A. Sax. *afyrhtian, afyrhtan*—prefix *a,* intens., and *fyrhtan,* to frighten. FRIGHT.] To impress with sudden fear; to frighten.—*n.* Sudden or great fear, terror.

affront, af•frunt′, *v.t.* [Fr. *affronter,* to encounter face to face—*af* for *ad,* to, and L. *frons, frontis,* front, face.] To confront (*Shak.*)‡; to offend by an open manifestation of disrespect; to insult; to put out of countenance. —*n.* An open manifestation of disrespect or contumely; an outrage to the feelings; an insult; anything producing a feeling of shame or disgrace.—**affronter,** af•frunt′ėr, *n.* One who affronts.

affuse, af•fūz′, *v.t.*—*affused, affusing.* [L. *affundo, affusum*—*af* for *ad,* to, and *fundo, fusum,* to pour out.] To pour upon; to sprinkle, as with a liquid.—**affusion,** af•fū′zhon, *n.* The act of pouring or sprinkling liquid upon; *med.* the act of pouring water on the body as a curative means.

afield, a•fēld′, *adv.* To the field; in the field; astray.

afire, a•fīr′, *a.* or *adv.* On fire.

aflame, a•flām′, *a.* or *adv.* Flaming; glowing.

afloat, a•flōt′, *a.* or *adv.* Borne on the water; floating; passing from one person to another; in circulation (as a rumor).

afoot, a•fu̦t′, *a.* or *adv.* On foot; borne by the feet; walking; in a state of being planned for execution (as a plan or plot).

afore, a•fōr′, *adv.* [Prefix *a,* at, and *fore;* A.Sax. *onforan.*] Before in time or place: now mainly a nautical term; in the fore part of a vessel.—*prep.* Before in time, position, rank, etc.; in presence of: now a *naut.* term.; more toward the head of a ship than; nearer the stem than.—*Afore the mast,* applied to a common sailor.—**aforesaid,** a•fōr′sed, *a.* Mentioned before in the same writing or discourse.—**aforethought,** a•fōr′-tha̦t, *a.* Thought of beforehand; premeditated; prepense. — **aforetime,‡** a•fōr′tīm, *adv.* In time past; formerly. [N.T.]

afraid, a•frād′, *a.* or *pp.* [O.E. *affrayd, afrayde,* etc., pp. of *affray.* AFFRAY.] Impressed with fear or apprehension; fearful: not used attributively. [Colloquially, *I am afraid* is often nearly equivalent to I suspect, I am inclined to think, or the like.]

afreet, af•rēt′. *n. Mohammedan myth.* a powerful evil jinni or demon. Written also *Efreet, Afrite.*

afresh, a•fresh′, *adv.* Anew; again; after intermission.

African, af′rik•an, *a.* Pertaining to Africa.—*n.* A native of Africa.

Afrikaans, af′ra•käns″, *n.* [Variation of D. *Afrikansch.*] An official language of the Republic of South Africa, developed from Dutch.

Afrikaner, af′ra•kän″ėr, *n.* [D.] A native of the Republic of South Africa of European (especially Dutch) descent.

aft, aft, *a.* or *adv.* [A.Sax. *æft, eft,* after, behind; Goth. *afta;* from A.Sax. *af, æf,* Goth. *af,* E. *of, off.*] *Naut.* a word used to denote position at or near, or direction toward the stern of a ship.

after, aft′ėr, *a.* [A.Sax. *æfter,* a compar. from *af,* E. *of, off, -ter* being the compar. syllable, seen as *-ther* in *whether, hither,* as *-der* in *under.* OF.] Later in time; subsequent; succeeding; as, an *after* period of life: in this sense often combined with the following noun.—*prep.* Behind in place; later in time; in pursuit of; in search of; with or in desire for; in imitation of, or in imitation of the style of (*after* a model); according to; in proportion to (*after* our deserts); below in rank or excellence; next to; concerning (inquire *after*).—*After all,* at last; upon the whole; at the most; notwithstanding.—*adv.* Later in time; behind; in pursuit.—**afterbirth,** *n.* That which is expelled from the uterus after the birth of a child. —**afterburner,** *n.* A turbojet device that provides extra thrust by forcing fuel into hot exhaust gases; tail-pipe burner.—**aftereffect,** *n.* A delayed effect; *med.* a result appearing after the immediate effect; secondary effect.—**afterglow,** *n.* The glow in the west after sunset.—**afterimage,** *n.* The image of a bright object left for a time on the retina.—**afternoon,** *n.* The part of the day which follows noon, between noon and evening. —**afterthought,** *n.* Reflection after act to which it refers.—**aftertime,** *n.* Succeeding time: more commonly in the plural.

aftermost, aft′ėr•mōst, *a. superl.* [A.Sax. *æftemest,* a double superlative, *mest* being from *ma+st,* two superlative suffixes.] Hindmost: opposed to *foremost.*

afterward, afterwards, aft′ėr•wėrd, aft′ėr•wėrdz, *adv.* [A.Sax. *æfterweard. Afterwards* is an adverbial genitive. WARD.] In later or subsequent time.

again, a•gen′ or a•gān′, *adv.* [A.Sax. *ongeân,* again; *geân,* against. AGAINST.] A second time; once more; on another occasion; on the other hand; moreover; besides; further; in return; back; in answer.

against, a•genst′, *prep.* [O.E. *agayns, ongaenes,* A.Sax. *ongeân,* against. The *es* is an adverbial or genitive termination and the *t* has been added, like that in *amidst, betwixt.* A.Sax. *geân,* again or against, is the same as *gain* in *gainsay;* G. *gegen,* against.] Opposite in place (often preceded by *over*); in opposition to; adverse or hostile to (*against* law or public opinion); towards or upon; so as to meet (to strike *against* a rock); bearing or resting upon (to lean *against*); in preparation for (an event).

agamic, a•gam′ik, *a.* [Gr. *a,* not, and *gamos,* marriage.] Reproduced without the congress of individuals of the opposite sex.

agamogenesis, a•gam′ō•jen″e•sis, *n.* [Gr. *a,* not, *gamos,* marriage, and *genesis,* production.] The production of young without the congress of the sexes.—**agamogenetic,** a•gam′ō•jen•et″ik, *a.* Of or pertaining to agamogenesis.

agape, a•gāp′, *adv.* or *a.* Gaping as with wonder; having the mouth wide open.

agape, ag′a•pē, *n.* [Gr. *agapē,* love.] Among the primitive Christians a love feast or feast of charity, held before or after the communion, when contributions were made for the poor.

agar-agar, āgar•ā′gar, *n.* The native name of a dried seaweed much used in the East for soups and jellies.

agaric, a•gar′ik, *n.* [Gr. *agarikon.*] A name of various fungi. Many of the species are edible like the common mushroom, while others are deleterious and even poisonous.

agate, ag′āt, *n.* [Fr. *agate,* from L. *achates,* so called because found near a river of that name in Sicily.] A semipellucid mineral, consisting of bands or layers of various colors blended together, the base generally being chalcedony, and this mixed with jasper, amethyst, quartz, opal, etc.: used for rings, seals, cups, beads, etc.; an instrument used by gold-wire drawers, so called from the agate in the middle of it; a gilder's tool; a kind of type, called also *Ruby.*

agave, a•gā′vē, *n.* [Gr. *agauos,* noble. A genus of plants, comprehending the American aloe. They live for many years—ten to seventy—before flowering.

age, āj, *n.* [Fr. *âge,* O.Fr. *eage,* L.L. *aetaticum,* from L. *aetas, aetatis,* abbrev. of *aevitas,* from *aevum,* an age. EVER.] A period of time representing the whole or a part of the duration of any individual thing or being; the time during which an individual has lived; the latter part of life; the state of being old; oldness; old people collectively; the state of having arrived at legal maturity (the completion of the first twenty-one years of one's life); great length of time; a long or protracted period, sometimes definitely a century; a historical epoch; an epoch having a particular character; the people who live at a particular period.—*The age*, the times we live in.—*v.i.*—*aged* (ājd), *aging*. To grow old; to assume the appearance of old age.—*v.t.* To give the character of age or ripeness to (to *age* wine).—**aged,** āj′ed, *a.* Old; having lived long; having a certain age (*aged* forty years); in this sense often (ājd).—**agedly,** āj′ed•li, *adv.* Like an aged person.—**agedness,** āj′ed•nes, *n.* The state or condition of being aged; oldness.

agenda, a•jen′da, *n. pl.* [L., things to be done.] Memoranda; a memorandum-book; a church service; a ritual or liturgy.

agent, ā′jent, *n.* [L. *agens*, *agentis*, acting. ACT.] One who or that which acts; an actor; one that exerts power or has the power to act; an active power or cause; a body or substance that causes a certain action to begin; a person entrusted with the business of another.—**agency,** ā′jen•si, *n.* The state of being in action or of exerting power; operation; instrumentality; the office or business of an agent or factor.—**agential,** ā•jen′shal, *a.* Pertaining to an agent or agency.

agglomerate, ag•glom′ėr•āt, *v.t.*—*agglomerated*, *agglomerating*. [L. *agglomero*—*ad*, and *glomus*, *glomeris*, a ball of yarn.] To collect or gather into a mass.—*v.i.* To become collected into a ball or mass.—*n. Geol.* a collective name for masses consisting of angular fragments ejected from volcanoes.—**agglomeration,** ag•glom′ėr•ā″shon, *n.* The act of agglomerating; a collection; a heap.—**agglomerative,** ag•glom′ėr•āt•iv, *a.* Disposed to agglomerate.

agglutinate, ag•glū′tin•āt, *v.t.*—*agglutinated*, *agglutinating*. [L. *agglutino*—*ad*, and *glutino*, from *gluten*, glue. GLUE.] To unite or cause to adhere, as with glue or other viscous substance; to glue together.—*a.* United as by glue; joined.—*Agglutinate* or *Agglutinating languages*, in *philol.* those languages in which the suffixes for inflection retain a kind of independence, and are felt to be distinct from the root or main significant element of the word.—**agglutinant,** ag•glū′tin•ant, *a.* Uniting as glue; tending to cause adhesion.—*n.* Any viscous substance which agglutinates or unites other substances.—**agglutination,** ag•glū′-tin•ā″shon, *n.* The act of agglutinating or the state of; adhesion of parts; the marked feature of agglutinate languages.—**agglutinative,** ag•glū′-tin•āt•iv, *a.* Tending or having power to agglutinate.

aggrandize, ag′gran•dīz, *v.t.*—*aggrandized*, *aggrandizing*. [Fr. *agrandir*—L. prefix *a* for *ad*, to, and *grandis*, grand.] To make great or greater: especially to make greater in power, wealth, rank, or honor; to exalt; to elevate; extend; enlarge.—**aggrandizement,** ag′gran•dīz•-ment or ag•gran′diz•ment, *n.* The act of aggrandizing; the act of increasing one's own power, rank, or honor; advancement.—**aggrandizer,** ag′gran•dīz•ėr, *n.* One that aggrandizes.

aggravate, ag′gra•vāt, *v.t.*—*aggravated*, *aggravating*. [L. *aggravo*—*ad*, to, and *gravis*, heavy. whence *grave*, *grief*, etc.] To make worse, more severe, or less tolerable; to make more enormous, or less excusable; to intensify; to exaggerate; to provoke; irritate; tease.—**aggravating,** ag′gra•vāt•ing, *a.* Provoking; annoying.—**aggravatingly,** ag′gra•vāt•-ing•li, *adv.* In an aggravating manner.—**aggravation,** ag′gra•vā″-shon, *n.* The act of aggravating or making worse; addition to that which is evil or improper; provocation; irritation.

aggregate, ag′grē•gāt, *v.t.*—*aggregated*, *aggregating*. [L. *aggrego*, *aggregatum*—*ad*, and *grex*, *gregis*, a herd or band.] To bring together; to collect into a sum, mass, or body.—*a.* Formed by the conjunction or collection of particulars into a whole mass or sum; total.—*n.* A sum, mass, or assemblage of particulars; a whole or total.—*In the aggregate*, taken altogether; considered as a whole; collectively.—**aggregately,** ag′grē•gāt•li, *adv.* Collectively; taken in a sum or mass.—**aggregation,** ag•grē•gā′shon, *n.* The act of aggregating; the state of; an aggregate.—**aggregative,** ag′grē•-gāt•iv, *a.* Tending to aggregate; collective.

aggress, ag•gres′, *v.i.* [L. *aggredior*, *aggressus*—*ad*, and *gradior*, to go.] To make a first attack; to commit the first act of hostility or offence.—*v.t.*† To attack.—**aggression,** ag•-gre′shon, *n.* The first attack or act of hostility; the first act leading to a war or controversy.—**aggressive,** ag•gres′iv, *a.* Characterized by aggression; tending to aggress.—**aggressiveness,** ag•gres′iv•nes, *n.* The quality of being aggressive.—**aggressor,** ag•gres′ėr, *n.* The person who aggresses; an assaulter; an invader.

aggrieve, ag•grēv′, *v.t.*—*aggrieved*, *aggrieving*. [O.Fr. *agrever*, to weigh down, from *grever*, to oppress, from L. *gravis*, heavy, whence also *grief*, *grave*, etc.] To give pain or sorrow; to afflict; to grieve; to bear hard upon; to oppress or injure in one's rights.

aghast, a•gast′, *a.* or *p.* [A participial form from O.E. *agasten*, *agesten*, to terrify—prefix *a*, intens., and A.Sax. *gaestan*, to terrify; allied to Goth. *gaisjan*; *usgaisjan*, to terrify; comp. Prov. E. *gast*, to terrify, *gast*, fear, *gastful*.] Struck with amazement; stupefied with sudden fright or horror. Written also *agast*, which is etymologically the better spelling.

agile, aj′il, *a.* [Fr. *agile*; L. *agilis*, from *ago*. ACT.] Nimble; quick in movement; brisk; active.—**agilely,** aj′il•li, *adv.* In an agile or nimble manner.—**agility, agileness,** a•jil′i•ti, aj′il•nes, *n.* The state or quality of being agile; nimbleness; briskness; activity.

agio, a•ji•ō, *n.* [It.] The difference in value between one sort of money and another, especially between paper money and metallic coin.—**agiotage,** a•ji•ot•āj, *n.* The maneuvers by which speculators in stocks contrive to lower or enhance their price; stock jobbing.

agitate, aj′it•āt, *v.t. agitated*, *agitating*. [L. *agito*, *agitatum*, freq. from *ago*. ACT.] To move or force into violent irregular action; to shake or move briskly; to disturb; to perturb; to discuss; debate; arouse public attention to, as by speeches, pamphlets, etc.—*v.i.* To engage in agitation.—**agitable,** aj′it•a•bl, *a.* Capable of being agitated.—**agitated,** aj′it•āt•ed, *a.* Disturbed; perturbed; excited; expressing agitation (countenance, manner).—**agitation,** aj•it•-ā′shon, *n.* The act of agitating, or state of being agitated; perturbation of mind or feelings; commotion; disturbance.—**agitator,** aj′it•āt•ėr, *n.* One who or that which agitates, rouses, or stirs up.

aglet, ag′let, *n.* [Fr. *aiguillette*, a point, from *aiguille*, a needle; L. *acus*, a needle.] A metal tag at the end of a lace or point, formerly worn on dresses.

aglow, a•glō′, *a.* In a glow; glowing.

agnail, ag′nāl, *n.* [A.Sax. *angnægl*=*ange*, pain, and *nægl*, nail.] A sore hard as a nail; a corn; corrupted to *hangnail*, from false idea of sore on fingernail.

agnate, ag′nāt, *n.* [L. *agnatus*—*ad*, and *nascor*, *natus*, to be born.] Any male relation by the father's side.—*a.* Related or akin by the father's side.—**agnatic,** ag•nat′ik, *a.* Pertaining to descent by the male line, of ancestors.—**agnation,** ag•nā′shon, *n.* Relation by the father's side only or descent in the male line.

agnomen, ag•nō′men, *n.* [L.—*ag* for *ad*, to, and *nomen*, a name.] An additional name or epithet conferred on a person.

agnostic, ag•nos′tik, *n.* [Gr. *agnōstos*, unknowing, unknown, from *a*, not, and stem of *gignōskō*, to know. Same root as *know*.] One of those persons who disclaim any knowledge of God or of the origin of the universe or of anything but material phenomena, holding that with regard to such matters nothing can be known.—*a.* Pertaining to the agnostics or their doctrines.—**agnosticism,** ag•nos′ti•sizm, *n.* The doctrines or belief of agnostics.

agnus, ag′nus, *n.* [L., a lamb.] An image of a lamb as emblematical of the Saviour; an Agnus Dei.—*Agnus Dei.* [L., Lamb of God.] A medal, or more frequently a cake of wax, consecrated by the pope, stamped with the figure of a lamb supporting the banner of the cross; supposed to possess great virtues, such as preserving those who carry it in faith from accidents, etc.

ago, a•gō′, *a.* or *adv.* [Really a *pp.*, being shortened form of *agone*, formerly used in same sense; A. Sax. *âgân*, gone by—*â*, away, *gân*, to go.] Past; gone; as, a year ago.

agog, a•gog′, *adv.* [Prefix *a*, on, and W. *gog*, activity, *gogi*, to shake.] In eager excitement; highly excited by eagerness for an object.

agone,‡ a•gon′, *adv.* Ago, [O.T.]

agonic, a•gon′ik, *a.* [Gr. *a*, not, and *gōnia*, an angle.] Not forming an angle.—*Agonic lines*, two lines on the earth's surface, on which the magnetic needle points to the true north, or where the magnetic meridian coincides with the geographical.

agonist,† ag′ō•nist, *n.* [Gr. *agōnistēs*. AGONY.] One who contends for the prize in public games; a combatant; a champion.—**agonistics,** ag•ō•nist′iks, *n.* The art of contending in public games.

agony, ag′ō•ni, *n.* [Gr. *agōnia*, struggle, anguish, from *agōn*, a contest or struggle, from *agō*, to lead, to bring together.] A violent contest or striving‡; the struggle, frequently unconscious, that precedes natural death; the death throe or pang (often in plural); extreme bodily or mental pain; intense suffering; anguish; torment. ∴ *Agony* is extreme bodily pain; *anguish* is mental pain or the effect of extreme distress on the mind.—**agonize,** ag′ō•nīz, *v.i.*—*agonized, agonizing*. To writhe with agony or extreme pain.—*v.t.* To distress with extreme pain; to torture.

agoraphobia, ag″ō•ra•fō′bē•a, *n.* [L., from Gr. *agora*, a marketplace, Gr. *phŏbŏs*, fear.] Morbid fear of open spaces.

agouta, a•gö′ta, *n.* [W. Indian name.] An insectivorous animal peculiar to Haiti, of the tanrec family, and rather larger than a rat.

agouti, a•gö′ti, *n.* The native American name of several species of rodent mammals allied to the guinea pig.

agraffe, a•graf′, *n.* [Fr. *agrafe.*] A sort of hook or clasp, often jewelled.

agraphia, a•graf′i•a, *n.* [Gr. *a*, not, and *graphō*, to write.] A form of aphasia, in which the patient is unable to express ideas by written signs.

agrarian, a•grā′ri•an, *a.* [L. *agrarius*, from *ager*, a field. ACRE.] Relating to lands, especially public lands; growing wild in fields†.—*Agrarian laws*, in ancient Rome, laws for regulating the distribution of the public lands among the citizens.—*n.* One in favor of an equal division of landed property.—**agrarianism,** a•grā′ri•an•izm, *n.* The upholding of an equal division of lands and property; the principles of one who does so.

agree, a•grē′, *v.i.*—*agreed, agreeing*. [Fr. *agréer*—*a*, to, and *gré*, O.Fr. *gret*, good-will, favor, from L. *gratus*, pleasant, whence *gratitude*, *grateful*, etc.] To be of one mind; to harmonize in opinion; to live in concord or without contention; to come to an arrangement or understanding; to arrive at a settlement (*agree to* a proposal; *agree with* a person); to be consistent; to harmonize; not to contradict or be repugnant (stories *agree with* each other); to tally; to match; to correspond; to suit; to be accommodated or adapted (food *agrees with* a person); *gram.* to correspond in number, case, gender, or person.—**agreeability,** a•grē′a•bil″i•ti, *n.* Agreeableness.—**agreeable,** a•grē′a•bl, *a.* Suitable; conformable; correspondent; pleasing, either to the mind or senses (*agreeable* manners; *agreeable* to the taste); willing or ready to agree or consent; giving consent; with *to*.—**agreeableness,** a•grē′a•bl•nes, *n.* The state or quality of being agreeable; the quality of pleasing.—**agreeably,** a•grē′a•bli, *adv.* In an agreeable manner; suitably; consistently; conformably; in a manner to give pleasure; pleasingly.—**agreement,** a•grē′ment, *n.* The state of agreeing or being agreed; harmony; conformity; union of opinions or sentiments; bargain; compact; contract.

agrestic,† a•gres′tik, *a.* [L. *agrestis*, from *ager*, a field.] Rural; rustic.

agriculture, ag′ri•kul•tūr, *n.* [L. *agricultura*—*ager*, a field, and *cultura*, cultivation. ACRE and CULTURE.] The cultivation of the ground, more especially with the plough and in large areas or fields; it may include also the raising and feeding of cattle or other live stock; husbandry; tillage; farming.—**agricultural,** ag•ri•kul′tūr•al, *a.* Pertaining to, connected with, or engaged in agriculture.—**agriculturist, agriculturalist,** ag•ri•kul′tūr•ist, ag•ri•kul′tūr•al•ist, *n.* One engaged or skilled in agriculture; a husbandman.

agrimony, ag′ri•mon•i, *n.*]L. *argemonia*, from Gr. *argema*, a whitish ulceration on the eye (which this plant was supposed to cure), from *argos*, white.] A British plant formerly of much repute as a medicine. Its leaves and rootstock are astringent, and the latter yields a yellow dye.

agriology, ag•ri•ol′o•ji, *n.* [Gr. *agrios*, pertaining to a wild state, and *logos*, a discourse.] The comparative study of human customs, especially of the customs of man in a rude or uncivilized state.—**agriologist,** ag•ri•ol′o•jist, *n.* A student of agriology.

agronomy, a•gron′ō•mi, *n.* [Gr. *agronomos*, rural, from *agros*, a field.] Agriculture and other rural pursuits. —**agronomic, agronomical,** ag•rō•nom′ik, ag•rō•nom′ik•al, *a.* Relating to agronomy.—**agronomist,** a•gron′ō•mist, *n.* One who studies agronomy.

agrostography, a•gros•tog′ra•fi, *n.* [Gr. *agrōstis*, a grass.] A description of grasses.—**agrostology,** a•gros•tol′o•ji, *n.* That part of botany which relates to grasses.

aground, a•ground′, *adv.* or *a.* On the ground; run ashore; stranded.

ague, ā′gū, *n.* [Fr. *aigu*, acute; *fièvre aiguë* (L.L. *febris acuta*), acute fever; L. *acutus*, sharp.] The cold fit or rigor which precedes a fever or a paroxysm of fever in intermittents; a fever coming in periodical fits accompanied by shivering; a chill or state of shaking not resulting from disease.—**aguish,** ā′gū•ish, *a.* Having the qualities of an ague; productive of agues; chilly, shivering.—

ah, ä. [A natural cry expressive of sudden emotion; comp. G. *ach*, L. *ah*, Skr. *â*, *âh*, ah.] An exclamation expressive of pain, surprise, pity, compassion, complaint, contempt, dislike, joy, exultation, etc., according to the manner of utterance.

aha, ä•hä′, [A lengthened form of *ah*, or formed of *ah* and *ha*; comp. G. *aha*, Skr. *ahô*, *ahaha*.] An exclamation expressing triumph, contempt, surprise, etc.

ahead, a•hed′, *adv.* Headlong; head foremost‡; in or to the front; in advance; before; further on (to walk *ahead of* a person; *naut.* opposite to *astern*.

ahoy, a•hoi′, *exclam.* [Longer form of *hoy!*] A word used chiefly at sea in hailing.

ai, ä′ē, *n.* The three-toed sloth, so called from its cry.

aid, ād, *v.t.* [Fr. *aider*, O.Fr. *ajuder*, from L. *adjutare*, freq. of *adjuvo*, *adjutum*, to help—*ad*, to, and *juvo*, *jutum*, to help.] To help; to assist; to come to the support or relief of; to succor;—**aid,** ād, *n.* [Fr. *aide.*] Help; succor; support; assistance; the person or thing that aids or yields assistance; a helper; an auxiliary; an assistant; a subsidy or tax formerly granted by Parliament to the crown; a tax paid by a feudal tenant to his lord.—**aider,** ād′ėr, *n.*

aide, ād, *n.* [Fr.] A person acting as an assistant.

aide-de-camp, ād′de•koṅ, *n.* pl. **aides-de-camp,** ādz′de•koṅ. [Fr., lit. field assistant.] *Milit.* an officer whose duty is to receive and communicate the orders of a general officer, to act as his secretary, etc.

aigrette, ā•gret′, *n.* [EGRET.] A plume or ornament for the head composed of feathers or precious stones.

aiguille, ā′gwil, *n.* [Fr., a needle.] A name given to the needle-like points or tops of rocks and mountain masses, or to sharp-pointed masses of ice on glaciers, etc.

ail, āl, *v.t.* [O.E. *eylen*, A.Sax. *eglian*, to feel pain; to ail; *eglan*, to give pain; *egle*, trouble, grief; comp. Goth. *aglo*, affliction, Sw. *agg*, a prick.] To affect with pain or uneasiness, either of body or mind; to trouble; to be the matter with. —*v.i.* To be in pain or trouble. —**ailment,** āl′ment, *n.* Disease; indisposition; morbid affection of the body.

ailanthus, ā•lan′thus, *n.* [From *ailanto*, the Malacca name.] A handsome Asiatic tree, the tree-of-heaven, widely grown in cities.

aileron, ā′ler•on, *n.* [Fr. *aile*, wing.]

Any one of certain small movable planes fixed to the main planes of an airplane and used as balancing flaps, or to give stability, being actuated by suitable leverage.

aim, ām, *v.i.* [O. Fr. *esmer, aesmer*—L. *ad*, to, and *aestimare*, to estimate.] To direct a missile towards an object; to direct the mind or intention; to make an attempt; to endeavor (followed by *at* before the object).—*v.t.* To direct or point to a particular object with the intention of hitting it; to level at.—*n.* The pointing or directing of a missile; the point intended to be hit, or object intended to be affected; the mark; a purpose; intention; design; scheme.—**aimless,** ām′les, *a.* Without aim; purposeless.—**aimlessly,** ām′les•li, *adv.* Purposelessly.

air, âr, *n.* [Fr. *air*, L. *aēr*, from Gr. *aēr, air*.] A heterogeneous mixture of tasteless, odorless, colorless, and invisible gases surrounding the earth, which consists of 78.03% nitrogen, 20.99% oxygen, 0.94% argon, 0.03% carbon dioxide, 0.01% hydrogen, and traces of krypton, neon, helium, and xenon; that which we breathe and which is essential to all plant and animal life; a breeze; air in motion; a tune; a melody; the principal melody part in a harmonized piece of music; outward appearance, mien, bearing, manner of a person or thing as, an *air of importance;* semblance; an affected manner as, *to put on airs.*—*v.t.* To expose to, put out in, the air; to let air into, to ventilate, as *to air a room;* to state publicly, as *to air one's views, one's grievances*, etc. —**air base,** *n.* The base of operations for aircraft.—**air bladder,** *n.* A sac or vesicle filled with air located under the backbone of most fishes, and responsible for their buoyancy.—**air brake,** *n.* A mechanical brake worked by air pressure.—**airbrush,** *n.* A device attached to a compressed-air hose, for the spraying of paint.—**air castle,** *n.* A daydream; an unrealizable scheme.—**air cell,** *n.* A minute cavity containing air; one of the cells of the lungs.—**air chamber,** *n.* Any cavity filled with air.—**air compressor,** *n.* A device used for compressing air.—**air conditioning,** *n.* The process of controlling the quality, temperature, humidity, and circulation of air in a space enclosure. —**aircooled,** *a.* Cooled by air, as in an engine that is cooled by a current of air.—**aircraft,** *n.* Any kind of flying machine.—**aircraft carrier,** *n.* A ship designed to carry naval airplanes, with special decks for taking off and landing.—**airfield,** *n.* A level area where airplanes take off and land; an airport.—**airfoil,** *n.* Wing, rudder, or any aircraft surface designed to obtain reaction from a moving air stream.—**air force,** *n.* That branch of the armed forces which fights in the air.—**air gun,** *n.* A gun that uses compressed air to propel bullets.—**air hole,** *n.* A hole made to allow air to pass in or out; an *air pocket.*—**airily,** *adv.* In an airy manner; in a light, gay manner. —**airing,** *n.* An exposure to air as, *to give clothes an airing;* a short walk or drive out of doors.—**air lane,** *n.* A particular route through the air traversed by aircraft.—**airless,** *adj.* Lacking air; stuffy.—**airlift,** *n.* A supply line operated by aircraft.—*v.* To transport by air.—**airline,** *n.* A transportation system of airplanes making regularly scheduled flights and transporting passengers and freight between its points of flight. —**air lock,** *n.* Airtight area at the entrance of a pressure chamber.—**air mail,** *n.* Mail carried by airplanes. —**airman,** *n.* A flier; an aviator. —**airminded,** *a.* Interested in, and approving of, air travel or things aeronautic.—**airplane,** *n.* Any one of the different kinds of flying machines which are heavier than air and which are supported in the air by planes or wings, driven forward by a propeller or a jet.—**air pocket,** *n.* A disturbance of the atmosphere that causes aircraft to drop suddenly for a considerable distance; an air hole.—**airport,** *n.* An airfield; a field, with a hangar or hangars, for the landing, taking-off, and servicing of aircraft.—**air raid,** *n.* A hostile destructive incursion by enemy aircraft.—**air rifle,** *n.* A rifle that uses compressed air to propel bullets. —**air shaft,** *n.* A passage for admitting fresh air into a mine or tunnel; a passage in a building which affords ventilation and light.—**airship,** *n.* A machine for navigating the air, capable of being steered, supported by gas bags, and propelled by an engine or engines; a dirigible. —**airsickness,** *n.* Illness when flying at high altitudes.—**airtight,** *a.* Impermeable to air; hermetically sealed. —**airway,** *n.* A passage for air currents; a chartered route for aircraft.—**airy,** *a.* Consisting of or having the character of air; ethereal; exposed to air; gay and sprightly; lively.—**air-cushion vehicle,** *n.* A vehicle that hovers and travels near the ground or water on a cushion of air; GEM.

Airedale, ar′dāl, *n.* [From *Airedale*, Yorkshire, Eng.] A large terrier with coarse wiry hair.

aisle, īl, *n.* [O.Fr. *aisle.* Fr. *aile*, a wing, an aisle; L. *ala*, a wing; the *s* does not properly belong to the word.] A lateral division of a cathedral or other church, separated from the central part, called the nave, by pillars or piers.—**aisled,** īld, *a.* Furnished with aisles.

ait, āt, *n.* [A form of *eyot*, an islet.] A small island in a river or lake.

aitchbone, āch′bōn, *n.* [For *natchbone* (by loss of initial *n* as in *apron*), from Fr. *nache*, L.L. *naticae*, L. *nates*, the rump.] The rump-bone of an ox. Called also *Edgebone* (by false etymology).

ajar, a•jar′, *adv.* [O.E. *achar, onchar*, lit. on the turn—prefix *a*, on, *jar, char*, A. Sax. *cerre*, a turn, seen also in *chare, char*-woman.] On the turn; neither quite open nor shut; partly opened; said of a door.

akimbo, a•kim′bō, *a.* or *adv.* [Prefix *a*, on, and *kimbo*, from Icel. *kengboginn*, lit. crook-bowed, *kengr*, a crook.] With the elbow pointing outwards and the hand resting on the hip; said of the arm.

akin, a•kin′, *a.* or *adv.* [Prefix *a*, of, and *kin.*] Related by blood; allied by nature; partaking of the same properties.

alabaster, al′a•bas•tėr, *n.* [L. *alabaster*, Gr. *alabastros*, from Alabastron, a village in Egypt where it was got.] A soft, semi-transparent, marble-like mineral of which there are two well-known varieties—the gypseous and the calcareous. Small works of art are often made of it.—**alabastrine,** al•a•bas′trīn, *a.* Of or pertaining to.

alack, a•lak′, *interj.* [Probably a corruption of *alas;* but comp. *lauk!* euphemism for Lord.] An explanation expressive of sorrow.—**alackaday,** a•lak′a•dā, *interj.* [Comp. *Well-a-day!*] An exclamation uttered to express regret or sorrow.

alacrity, a•lak′ri•ti, *n.* [L. *alacritas*, from *alacer, alacris*, cheerful.] A cheerful readiness or promptitude to do some act; cheerful willingness; briskness.

alamode, a•la•mōd′, *adv.* [Fr. *à la mode*, after the fashion.] According to the fashion or prevailing mode: sometimes used as an adjective.

alar, ā′lėr, *a.* [L. *ala*, a wing.] Pertaining to wings; having the character of a wing.

alarm, a•lärm′, *n.* [Fr. *alarme*, alarm, from It. *all'arme*=L. *ad arma*, to arms.] A summons to arms; an outcry or other notice of approaching danger; a tumult; a disturbance; a sudden fear or painful suspense excited by an apprehension of danger; apprehension; terror; a mechanical contrivance for awakening persons from sleep or rousing their attention.—*v.t.* To call to arms for defense; to give notice of danger; to rouse to vigilance; to disturb with terror; to fill with anxiety by the prospect of evil.—**alarming,** a•lärm′-ing, *a.* Calculated to rouse alarm; causing apprehension.—**alarmingly,** a•lärm′ing•li, *adv.* In an alarming manner.—**alarmist,** a•lärm′ist, *n.* One that excites alarm; one who is prone to take alarm, and to circulate and exaggerate any sort of bad news.

alary, ā′la•ri, *a.* Alar.

alas, a•las′, *exclam.* [O.Fr. *alas*, from interj. *a, ah*, L. *lassus*, weary.] An exclamation expressive of sorrow, grief, pity, concern, or apprehension of evil.

alate, ā′lāt, *a.* [L. *alatus*, winged, *ala*, a wing.] Winged; having membranous expansions like wings.

alb, alb, *n.* [L. *alba*, white (*vestis*, garment, understood).] A clerical vestment worn by priests, a long robe of white linen bound with a girdle.

albacore, al′ba•kōr, *n.* [Sp. *albacora*, Fr. *albicore*, from Ar. *al*, the, *bakr*, a young cow or heifer.] A name given to several fishes of the tunny kind, especially to the Pacific tunny.

albata, al•bā′ta, *n.* [L. *albus*, white.]

An alloy consisting of a combination of nickel, zinc, tin, and copper, often with antimony and silver; German silver.

albatross, al′ba•tros, *n.* [Fr. *albatros*, a corruption of Sp. and Pg. *alcatraz*, a pelican, from Ar. *al-qādūs*, the bucket of a water wheel, the pelican being supposed to carry water to its young ones in the pouch below its bill.] An aquatic bird, the largest sea bird known, some measuring 17½ feet from tip to tip of the wings, met with at immense distances from land.

albeit, ạl•bē′it, *conj.* [*Al* in old sense of though, *be*, and *it*, and equivalent to *be it so*,] Be it so; admit all that; although; notwithstanding; even though.

albescent, al•bes′ent, *a.* [L. *albesco*, to grow white, an incept. from *albus*, white.] Becoming white or rather whitish; moderately white; of a pale, hoary aspect.

Albigenses, al•bi•jens′ez, *n. pl.* A party of religious reformers in the twelfth century, who were ruthlessly persecuted: so called from *Albi*, a town of Languedoc in France, where they resided.

albino, al•bī′nō, *n.* pl. **albinos,** al•bī′nōz. [Pg., from L. *albus*, white.] A person of abnormally pale, milky complexion, with light hair and pink eyes; an animal characterized by the same peculiarity in physical constitution.—**albinism,** al′bin•izm, *n.* The state or condition of an albino; leucopathy.

albite, al′bīt, *n.* [L. *albus*, white.] A name given to feldspar whose alkali is composed of soda instead of potash.

album, al′bum, *n.* [L., from *albus*, white.] A book originally blank, in which may be inserted autographs of celebrated persons or favorite pieces of poetry or prose, generally contributed by friends; a book for preserving photographs, drawings, portraits, etc.

albumen, al•bū′men, *n.* [L., from *albus*, white.] The white of an egg.—**albumenize,** al•bū′men•īz, *v.t.*—*albumenized, albumenizing.* To convert into albumen; to cover or impregnate with albumen.—**albumin,** al•bū′min, *n.* Any of a group of simple proteins widely found in plant and animal tissues, especially in the white of eggs.—**albuminoid,** al•bū′min•oid, *a.* Like albumin.—*n.* A substance resembling albumin; proteide.—**albuminose, albuminous,** al•bū′min•ōs, al•bū′min•us, *a.* Pertaining to or having the properties of albumin; applied to plants whose seeds have a store of albumin, as all kinds of grain, palms, etc.—**albuminuria,** al•bū′mi•nū″ri•a. [*Albumen* and Gr. *ouron*, urine.] *Pathol.* a condition in which the urine contains albumin, indicating a diseased state of the kidneys.

alburnum, al•bėr′num, *n.* [L. *alburnum*, sapwood, from *albus*, white.] The white and softer part of the wood of exogenous plants between the inner bark and the heartwood; the sapwood.

Alcaic, al•kā′ik, *a.* [L. *alcaicus.*] Pertaining to *Alcaeus*, a lyric poet of Mitylene.—*Alcaic verse*, a variety of verse used in Greek and Latin poetry, consisting of five feet, a spondee or iambus, an iambus, a long syllable, and two dactyls.

alcalde, alcaide, äl•käl′dā, äl•kä′i•dā, *n.* [Sp. and Pg. from Ar.] In Spain, Portugal, etc., a commander of a fortress; the chief civil magistrate of a town; also, a jailer.

alchemy, alchymy, al′ke•mi, al′ki•mi, *n.* [O.F. *alquimie*, L.L. *alchimia*, from Ar. *al-Kimia—al*, the, and *Khemia*, the name of Egypt; confusion with Gr. *kheō*, I pour, *khumeia*, gives alchymy. CHEMISTRY.] The art which had for its main objects the transmuting of the baser metals into gold or silver, the discovery of an elixir of life, a universal solvent, etc.—**alchemic, alchemical, alchemistic, alchemistical,** al•kem′ik, al•kem′ik•al, al•kem•ist′ik, al•kem•ist′ik•al, *a.* Relating to, produced by, or practicing alchemy. Also spelled with *y* for *e*.—**alchemically,** al•kem′ik•al•li, *adv.* In the manner of alchemy.—**alchemist,** al′kem•ist, *n.* One who practices alchemy.—**alchemise,**† al′kem•iz, *v.t.* To change by alchemy; to transmute, as metals.—**alchymy,** A mixed metal (Mil.).

alcohol, al′kō•hol, *n.* [Sp. Pg. *alcohol*—Ar. *al*, the, and *kohl*, a fine powder of antimony, hence anything very fine or purified, as rectified spirits.] Any of a class of chemical compounds derived from hydrocarbons by replacing one or more of the hydrogen atoms with an equal number of hydroxyl radicals; term for ethyl alcohol (ethanol), the alcohol of commerce and medicine.—**alcoholic,** al•kō•hol′ik, *a.* Pertaining to alcohol, or partaking of its qualities.—*n.* An alcoholic liquid.—**alcoholism,** al′kō•hol•izm, *n.* A disease condition due to over-indulgence of alcohol; dipsomania.—**alcoholize,** al′kō•hol•īz, *v.t.* To convert into alcohol; to rectify (spirit) till it is wholly purified.—**alcoholometer,** al′kō•hol•om″et•er, *n.* An instrument for determining the quantity of pure alcohol in any liquid.—**alcoholometry,** al′kō•hol•om″et•ri, *n.* The determination of the percentage of absolute alcohol in a liquid.

Alcoran. See ALKORAN.

alcove, al′kōv, *n.* [Fr. *alcove*, Sp. *alcoba*—Ar. *al*, the, and *kubbeh*, an alcove, a little chamber.] A wide and deep recess in a room, intended for the reception of a bed or seats, etc.; any natural recess.

aldehyde, al′dē•hīd, *n.* [*Al*, first syllable of *alcohol*, and *dehyd*, the first two of *dehydrogenatus*, deprived of hydrogen.] A transparent colorless liquid produced by the oxidation of pure alcohol; one of a class of organic compounds, derived from alcohol by the abstraction of two atoms of hydrogen, and converted into acids by the addition of one atom of oxygen.

alder, ol′dėr, *n.* [O.E. *aller* (the *d* being a more modern insertion), A. Sax. *aler, alr;* Icel. *ölr*, G. *eller;* allied to L. *alnus*, an alder.] The popular name of plants of the genus *Alnus. A. glutinosa* is the common alder, usually growing in moist land.

alderman, ol′dėr•man, *n.* pl. **aldermen,** ol′dėr•men. [A.Sax. *aldorman, ealdorman—ealdor*, an elder, from *eald*, old, and *man.*] Anciently, an Anglo-Saxon nobleman, often a governor of a shire; now a magistrate or officer of a town corporate, next in rank below the mayor.—**aldermanic,** ol•dėr•man′ik, *a.* Relating to or becoming an alderman.

Aldine, ol′dīn, *a.* Proceeding from the printing press of *Aldus* Manutius, of Venice, and his family, from 1490 to 1597.—**Aldine type**=Italic type invented by the printer for his 1501 edition of Virgil.

ale, āl, *n.* [A.Sax. *ealu*, Dan. Sw. and Icel. *öl*, ale.] A liquor made from an infusion of malt by fermentation; beer, or a kind of beer; a merry meeting in English country places, so called from the liquor drunk.—**alehouse,** *n.* A house where ale is retailed; a beer shop.—**alewife,** *n.* A woman who keeps an alehouse.

aleatory, al′ē•a•to•ri, *a.* [L. *alea*, a die, chance.] Pertaining to chance or contingency; depending on a contingency.

alee, a•lē′, *adv. Naut.* on the lee side; on the side opposite to that on which the wind strikes: opposite of *a-weather.*

alembic, a•lem′bik, *n.* [L.L. *alembicum;* Sp. *alambique*—Ar. *al*, the, *ambik*, an alembic, from Gr. *ambix*, a cup.] A chemical vessel formerly used in distillation, usually made of glass or copper.

alert, a•lėrt′, *a.* [Fr. *alerte*, alert, and (as noun) alarm or notice of danger, formerly *allerte*, and *a l'erte*, from It. *all'erta*, to the watchtower, the lookout—*erta*, fem. p.p. of L. *erigere*, erect.] Active in vigilance; watchful; vigilant; brisk; nimble.—*On* or *upon the alert*, upon the watch; on the lookout; guarding against surprise or danger.—**alertness,** a•lėrt′nes, *n.* The state or quality of being alert.

aleurone, a•lū′rōn, *n.* [Gr. *aleuron*, fine flour.] Albuminoid granules found in seeds.

alewife, āl′wīf, *n.* A fish of the shad genus, caught in the Severn; also a similar N. American fish much used as food.

Alexandrian, al•egz•an′dri•an, *a.* Pertaining to *Alexandria* in Egypt, more especially ancient Alexandria.—**alexandrine,** al•egz•an′drīn, *n.* A kind of verse consisting of twelve syllables in English poetry, or in French of twelve and thirteen in alternate couplets: so called from a poem written in French on the life of *Alexander the Great.*

alexipharmic, a•lek′si•farm″ik, *a.* [Gr. *alexō*, to ward off, *pharmakon*, a drug, remedy, poison.] Acting as a means of warding off disease or the effects of poison; acting as a remedy.—*n.* A remedy; an antidote.

alfalfa, alf•al′fa, *n.* [Sp.] A common name in the United States for the fodder plant lucerne.

alga, al′ga, *n.* pl. **algae,** al′jē, [L.] A seaweed; one of an order of cryptogamic plants found for the most part in the sea and fresh water, comprising seaweeds.—**algal,** al′gal, *n.* One of the Algae.—**algal,** al′gal, *a.* Of or pertaining to the Algae; having the nature of the Algae.—**algology,** al•gol′o•ji, *n.* The study or science of Algae.

algebra, al′je•bra, *n.* [Sp. *algebra,* from Ar. *al-jabr,* the putting together of broken things, reduction of fractions to whole numbers, from Ar. *jabara,* to bind together, to consolidate.] That branch of mathematical analysis in which signs are employed to denote arithmetical operations, and letters are used to represent numbers and quantities; a kind of universal arithmetic.—**algebraic, algebraical,** al•je•brā′ik, al•je•brā′ik•al, *a.* Pertaining to algebra; containing an operation of algebra.—**algebraically,** al•je•brā′-ik•al•li, *adv.* By algebraic process.—**algebraist,** al•je•brā′ist, *n.* One versed in the science of algebra.

algid, al′jid, *a.* [L. *algidus,* cold, *algeo,* to be cold.] Cold.—*Algid cholera,* Asiatic cholera.—**algidity, algidness,** al•jid′i•ti, al′jid•nes, *n.* The state of being algid; chilliness; coldness.—**algific,** al•jif′ik, *a.* [L. *algificus.*] Producing cold.—**algor,** al′gor, *n.* [L.] An unusual coldness in the human system.—**algose,** al′gōs, *a.* [L. *algosus.*] Cold in a high degree.

algology. See ALGA.

algorithm, algorism, al′gō•rithm, al′gō•rizm, *n.* [O.F. *augorisme,* L. *algorismus,* Ar. *al-khowarazmi,* the man of Khiva, name of a mathematician; confused with Gr. *arithmos,* number.] Arabic decimal notation; the art of computing or reckoning in reference to some particular subject, or in some particular way (the *algorithm* of the differential calculus).

Alhambresque, al•am′bresk, *a.* Of or pertaining to the *Alhambra* (lit. red house), a Moorish palace near Granada in Spain; built or decorated after the fanciful manner of the Alhambra, in which arabesques are a notable feature.

alias, ā′li•as, *adv.* [L.] Otherwise; used especially of persons who assume various names (John Smith *alias* Thomas Jones).—*n.* pl. **aliases,** ā′li•as•ez. An assumed name; another name.

alibi, al′i•bī, *n.* [L., elsewhere.] *Law,* a plea which avers that the accused was in another place at the time of the commission of the offense, and therefore cannot be guilty.

alien, āl′yen, *a.* [L. *alienus,* alien, from *alius,* another. The same root appears in E. *else.*] Not belonging to the same country, land, or government; foreign; different in nature; estranged; adverse: with *to* or *from.* —*n.* A foreigner; one born in or belonging to another country; one who is not a denizen, or entitled to the privileges of a citizen.—**alienability,** āl′yen•a•bil″i•ti, *n.* The state or quality of being alienable.—**alienable,** āl′yen•a•bl, *a.* Capable of being alienated, sold, or transferred to another.—**alienage,** āl′yen•āj, *n.* The state of being an alien.—**alienate,** āl′yen•āt, *v.t.*—*alienated, alienating.* [L. *alieno, alienatum,* to alienate.] To transfer or convey, as title, property, or other right, to another; to withdraw, as the affections; to make indifferent or averse, where love or friendship before existed; to estrange; to wean; with *from.*—**alienation,** āl•yen•ā′shon, *n.* [L. *alienatio.*] The act of alienating or the state of being alienated.—**alienator,** āl•yen•ā′tėr, *n.* One who alienates.—**alienee,** āl•yen•ē′, *n.* One to whom the title of property is transferred.—**alienism,** āl′yen•izm, *n.* The state of being an alien; the scientific study and treatment of mental alienation or insanity.—**alienist,** āl′yen•ist, *n.* One who studies or practices alienism.—**alienor,** āl′yen•or, *n.* One who transfers property.

aliferous, aligerous, a•lif′ėr•us, a•lij′ėr•us, *a.* [L. *ala,* wing, and *fero, gero,* to bear.] Having wings.—**aliform,** ā′li•form, *a.* [L. *ala,* wing, and *forma,* shape.] Having the shape of a wing or wings.

alight, a•līt′, *v.i.* [A.Sax. *âlihtan, gelihtan,* to alight or light. See LIGHT in this sense.] To get down or descend, as from horseback or from a carriage; to settle or lodge, as a bird on a tree; to light down.

alight, a•līt′, *a.* or *adv.* Lighted; kindled; made to burn by having a light applied.

align, a•līn′, *v.t.* [Fr. *aligner,* to align—*a,* to, and *ligne,* L. *linea,* a line.] To lay out or regulate by a line; to form in line, as troops.—**alignment,** a•līn′ment, *n.* The act of aligning; an adjusting to a line; the line of adjustment; the ground-plan of a railway or other road; a row of things.

alike, a•līk′, *a.* [Prefix *a,* and *like;* A.Sax. *gelic,* alike. LIKE.] Having resemblance or similitude; similar; without difference (always used as a predicate).—**alike,** a•līk′, *adv.* In the same manner, form, or degree; in common (all have erred *alike*).

aliment, al′i•ment, *n.* [L. *alimentum,* nourishment—*alo,* to nourish.] That which nourishes; food; nutriment.—**alimental,** al•i•ment′al, *a.* Of or pertaining to aliment.—**alimentally,** al•i•ment′al•li, *adv.* In an alimental manner.—**alimentary,** al•i•ment′a•ri, *a.* Pertaining to aliment or food.—**alimentary canal,** *n. Anat.* the canal from the mouth to the anus through which food passes; digestive tract.—**alimentation,** al′i•ment•ā″-shon, *n.* The act or power of affording nutriment; the state of being nourished.

alimony, al′i•mo•ni, *n.* [L. *alimonia.*] An allowance out of her husband's estate made for the support of a woman legally separated from him.

aliped, al′i•ped, *a.* [L. *ala,* wing, and *pes, pedis,* a foot.] Wing-footed; having the toes connected by a membrane, which serves as a wing, as the bats.—*n.* An animal whose toes are so connected.

aliquant, al′i•kwant, *a.* [L. *aliquantum,* somewhat.] *Arith.* applied to a number which does not measure another without a remainder.—**aliquot,** al′i•kwot, *a.* [L. *aliquot,* some, several.] *Arith.* applied to a part of a number or quantity which will measure it without a remainder.

alive, a•līv′, *a.* [Prefix *a* for *on,* and *life;* in old English it was written *on live, on lyve,* where *live, lyve* is a dat. form of *life.*] Having life; living; not dead; in a state of action; in force or operation (keep an agitation *alive*); full of alacrity; sprightly (*alive* with excitement); easily impressed; sensitive to; susceptible (*alive* to the beauties of nature); used always after its noun.

alizarin, al′i•za•rin, *n.* [Fr. *alizarine,* from *alizari,* an Eastern name of madder, from the (Ar.) root of *azure,* with the article prefixed.] A red coloring matter obtained from madder, but made for commercial purposes from coal-tar products, and now largely used instead of madder.

alkahest, al′ka•hest, *n.* [Etym. unknown.] The pretended universal solvent or menstruum of the alchemists.

alkali, al′ka•lī, *n.* pl. **alkalies,** or **alkalis,** al′ka•līz. [Sp. Fr. *alcali,* Ar. *al-qali,* the plant from which soda was first obtained.] A term applied to an important class of bases which combine with acids to form salts, turn vegetable yellows to red and vegetable blues to green, and unite with oil or fat to form soap. The proper alkalies are hydroxide of potassium (potash), hydroxide of sodium (soda), hydroxide of lithium (lithia), and hydroxide of ammonium (an aqueous solution of ammonia).—**alkalescent,** al•ka•les′ent, *a.* Tending to the properties of an alkali; slightly alkaline. — **alkalescence, alkalescency,** al•ka•les′ens, al•ka•les′en•si, *n.* A tendency to become alkaline.—**alkalifiable,** al′ka•li•fī•a•bl or al•kal′-i•fī•a•bl, *a.* Capable of being alkalified. —**alkalify,** al′ka•li•fī or al•kal′i•fī, *v.t.*—*alkalified, alkalifying*; **alkalize,** al′ka•līz, *v.t.*—*alkalized, alkalizing.* To form or to convert into an alkali; to make alkaline.—*v.i.* To become an alkali.—**alkalimeter,** al•ka•lim′-et•ėr, *n.* An instrument for ascertaining the strength of alkalies.—**alkalimetry,** al•ka•lim′et•ri, *n.* The finding of the amount of real alkali in an alkaline mixture or liquid.—**alkaline,** al′ka•līn, *a.* Having the properties of an alkali.—**alkaline earths,** oxides of barium, strontium, calcium, and sometimes magnesium. —**alkalinity,** al•ka•lin′i•ti, *n.* The state of being alkaline; the quality which constitutes an alkali.—**alkalization,** al′ka•liz•ā″shon, *n.* The act or process of rendering alkaline.—**alkaloid,** al′ka•loid, *n.* A term applied to a class of nitrogenized compounds found in living plants, and containing their active principles, such as *morphine*, *quinine*, *aconitine*, *caffeine*, etc.—*a.* Relating to or containing alkali.

alkanet, al′ka•net, *n.* [Sp. *alcaneta*, dim. of *alcana*, *alcanna*, from Ar. *al-hinna*, henna.] A plant, *Alkanna* (*Anchusa tinctoria*) whose root yields a red dye.

Alkoran, al•kō•ran′ or al′kō•ran, *n.* [Ar. *al*, the, *qurân*, book.] The book which contains the religious and moral code of the Mohammedans, and by which indeed all their transactions, civil, legal, military, etc., are regulated; the Koran.

all, al, *a.* [A.Sax. *eal* (sing.), *ealle* (pl.); Icel. *allr*, Goth. *alls*, G. *all*, all. Common to all the Teutonic tongues; also in Celtic.] Every one of; the whole number or quantity of. It goes before an article or adj. belonging to the same noun: *all the* men, *all good* men, *all my* labor, etc. With nouns of time it is equivalent to during the whole (*all* day, *all* night).—*adv.* Wholly; completely; entirely; altogether; quite (*all* alone, *all* unarmed).—*All but*, nearly; almost; not quite.—*All one*, the same thing in effect; quite the same.—*n.* The whole number; the entire thing; the aggregate; the total.—*At all*, in the least degree; to the least extent; under any circumstances.—*In all*, everything reckoned or taken into account; all included.—*All*, in composition, has often the force of an adverb; as in *almighty*, *all-powerful*, *all-perfect*, *all-important;* sometimes of a noun in the objective case; as, *all-seeing*.—**All Fools' Day.** The first day of April.—**all fours.** A game of cards, so called from the four chances of which it consists, for each of which a point is scored.—**On all fours,** on four legs, or on two legs and two arms or hands; hence, fig. even or evenly; as a parallel case.—**all hail,** *exclam.* and *n.* All health: a phrase of salutation.—**Allhallows,** *n.* All Saints' Day.—**Allhallowmas, Allhallowtide,** *n.* The time near All Saints or November 1.—**allheal,** *n.* A plant, cat's or common wild valerian, so called from its medicinal virtues.—**All Saints' Day.** A church festival held on November 1; Hallowmas.—**All Souls' Day.** A church festival held on November 2, when prayers are offered up for the dead.—**allspice,** *n.* A spice of a mildly pungent taste, the fruit of a West Indian tree, so called from being regarded as combining many different flavors; pimento.

Allah, al′la, *n.* The Arabic name of the Supreme Being.

allantois, al•lan′tois, *n.* [Gr. *allas*, *allantos*, a sausage, and *eidos*, form.] A sac developed from the posterior end of the abdominal cavity in vertebrate embryos.—**allantoic,** al•lan•tō′ik, al•lan•toid′al, *a.* Pertaining to or contained in the allantois.

allay, al•lā′, *v.t.* [A.Sax. *âlecgan*, to lay down, suppress, tranquilize, from prefix *â*, and *lecgan*, to lay. LAY.] To make quiet; to pacify or appease (a tumult); to abate, mitigate, or subdue; to relieve or alleviate (grief, thirst).—*v.i.* To subside; to grow calm.—**allayer,** al•lā′ėr, *n.* One who or that which allays.

allege, al•lej′, *v.t.*—*alleged*, *alleging*. [O.Fr. *esligier*, L.L. *exlitigare*, to clear at law (confused with L.L. *allegare*).] To assert; to pronounce with positiveness; to declare; to affirm; to assert; to produce as an argument, plea, or excuse; cite; quote; bring forward.—**allegation,** al•lē•gā′shon, *n.*—**alleged,** al•lej′id, *a.*—**allegedly,** al•lej′id•li, *adv.*

allegiance, al•lē′jans, *n.* [Prefix *a*, to, and O.Fr. *ligence*, allegiance, loyalty, from *lige*, loyal. LIEGE.] The tie or obligation of a subject to his sovereign or government; the duty of fidelity to a king, government, or state.

allegory, al′lē•go•ri, *n.* [Gr. *allegoria*—*allos*, other, and *agoreuō*, to speak, from *agora*, a forum, an oration.] A figurative discourse, in which the principal subject is described by another subject resembling it in its properties and circumstances; a narrative in which abstract ideas are personified; a continued metaphor.—**allegoric, allegorical,** al•lē•gor′ik, al•lē•gor′ik•al, *a.* Pertaining to allegory; in the manner of allegory.—**allegorically,** al•lē•gor′ik•al•li, *adv.* In an allegorical manner; by way of allegory.—**allegorist, allegorizer,** al′lē•go•rist, al′lē•go•rīz•ėr, *n.* One who allegorizes; a writer of allegory.—**allegorize,** al′lē•go•rīz, *v.t.*—*allegorized*, *allegorizing*. To turn into allegory; to narrate in allegory; to explain in an allegorical sense.—*v.i.* To use allegory.—**allegorization,** al′lē•gor•ī•zā″shon, *n.* The act of turning into allegory.

allegro, äl•lā′grō, *a.* and *n.* [It., merry, cheerful.] *Music*, a word denoting a brisk movement; a sprightly part or strain.—**allegretto,** äl•lē•gret′to. Time quicker than *andante*, but not so quick as *allegro*.

alleluia, al•lā•lū′ya, *n.* and *interj.* [Heb. *halelûyâh*, praise to Jah—*halal*, to praise, and *Yâh*, Jehovah.] Praise Jehovah; a word used to denote pious joy and exultation, chiefly in hymns and anthems. Written also *hallelujah*.

allergen, al′ėr•jin, *n.* [Gr. *allos*, other, *ergon*, work, and *gen*, to produce.] Any substance that induces allergy.

allergy, al′ėr•ji, *n.* [Gr. *allos* other and *ergon* work.] Excess sensitiveness to certain substances, as food, pollen, drugs, or heat or cold, which are harmless to most persons. Common allergies are hay fever, hives, and asthma.—**allergic,** al•ėr′jik, *a.*

alleviate, al•lē′vi•āt, *v.t.*—*alleviated*, *alleviating*. [L.L. *alleviare*, *alleviatus*, L. *allevare*, *allevatus*—*ad*, to, and *levo*, to ease, from *levis*, light. LEVITY.] To make light, in a figurative sense; to lessen, mitigate, or make easier to be endured (sorrow, pain, distress).—**alleviation,** al•lē′vi•ā″shon, *n.* The act of alleviating: that which lessens, mitigates, or makes more tolerable.—**alleviative,** al•lē′vi•āt•iv, *a.* Tending to alleviate; mitigative.—*n.* That which alleviates or mitigates.—**alleviator,** al•lē′vi•āt•ėr, *n.* One who or that which alleviates.

alley, al′li, *n.* [Fr. *allée*, from *aller*, to go, from O.Fr. *aner*, from L. *adnare*, lit. to swim to—*ad*, to, and *nare*, to swim.] A passage; especially, a narrow passage or way in a town.

alliaceous, al•li•ā′shus, *a.* [L. *allium*, garlic.] Pertaining to garlic and allied plants; having the properties of garlic.

alliance. See ALLY.

alligator, al′li•gā•tėr, *n.* [A corruption of Sp. *el lagarto*, lit. the lizard—*el.*, the, and *lagarto*, a lizard, from L. *lacertus*, whence E. *lizard*.] A large reptile of the crocodile family found in tropical America. The alligators differ from the true crocodiles in having a shorter and flatter head, in having cavities or pits in the upper jaw, into which the long canine teeth of the under jaw fit, and in having the feet much less webbed.

alliteration, al•lit•ėr•a′shon, *n.* [L. *al* for *ad*, to, and *litera*, a letter.] The repetition of the same letter at the beginning of two or more words immediately succeeding each other, or at short intervals (as in 'apt *alliteration's* artful aid').—**alliterative,** al•lit′ėr•āt•iv, *a.* Pertaining to or consisting in alliteration; characterized by alliteration.—**alliterativeness,** al•lit′ėr•āt•iv•nes, *n.* Quality of being alliterative.

allocate, al′lō•kāt, *v.t.*—*allocated*, *allocating*. [L. *ad*, to, and *loco*, *locatum*, to place, from *locus*, a place.] To assign or allot to a person or persons; to set apart for a particular purpose; to apportion or distribute (shares in a public company or the like).—**allocation,** al•lō•kā′shon, *n.* The act of allocating, alloting, or assigning; allotment; assignment; apportionment.

allocution, al•lō•kū′shon, *n.* [L. *allocutio*—*ad*, to, and *loquor*, to speak.] A speaking to; an address, especially a formal address.

allodium, al•lō′di•um, *n.* [L.L. *allodium*, of Ger. or Scand. origin *allod*, all, *od*, estate. UDAL. Comp. Icel. *odal*, Dan. and Sw. *odel*, a patrimonial estate.] Freehold estate; real estate held in absolute independence, without being subject to any rent, service, or acknowledgment to a superior.—**allodial,** al•lō′di•al, *a.* Pertaining to allodium or freehold; held independent of a lord paramount: opposed to *feudal*.

allomorphism, al•lō•mar′fizm, *n.* [Gr. *allos*, other, and *morphē*, form.] That property of certain substances of assuming a different form, the substance remaining otherwise unchanged.—**allomorphic,** al•lō•mar′fik, *a.* Pertaining to, or possessing the qualities of allomorphism.

allopathy, al•lop′a•thi, *n.* [Gr. *allos*, other, and *pathos*, morbid condition.] That method of treating disease by which it is endeavored to produce a condition of the system either different from, opposite to, or incompatible with the condition essential to the disease: it is opposed to *homeopathy*, and is the common method of treatment.—**allopathic,** al•lo•path′ik, *a.* Pertaining to allopathy.—**allopathically,** al•lo•path′-ik•al•li, *adv.* In a manner conformable to allopathy.—**allopathist,** al•-lop′a•thist, *n.* One who practices allopathy.

allophane, al′lō•fān, *n.* [Gr. *allos*, other, and *phainō*, to appear.] A mineral of a pale blue, or sometimes of a green or brown color.

allot, al•lot′, *v.t.—allotted, allotting.* O.Fr. *allotir, alloter*, to divide, part—*al* for *ad*, to, and *lotir*, to cast lots for, from *lot*, a share, which itself is a Teutonic word=A. Sax. *hlot.* LOT.] To distribute or parcel out in parts or portions; to assign; to set apart; to destine.—**allotment,** al•lot′ment, *n.* The act of allotting; that which is allotted; a share, part, or portion granted or distributed; a place or piece of ground appropriated.—*Allotment-system*, the system of allotting small portions of land to farm laborers or others, to be cultivated, after regular work, by themselves and families.—**allottee,** al•lot′tē, *n.* One to whom anything is allotted.

allotropy, allotropism, al•lot′ro•pi, al•lot′ro•pizm, *n.* [Gr. *allos*, another, and *tropos*, condition.] The capability exhibited by some substances of existing in more than one form, and with different characteristics (thus carbon forms both the diamond and charcoal).—**allotropic,** al•lō•-trop′ik, *a.* Of or pertaining to allotropy.

allow, al•lou′, *v.t.* [Fr. *allouer*, to grant, settle, L.L. *allocare—ad*, to, and *locare*, to place. (ALLOCATE.) O.Fr. *allouer*, to approve or praise, from L. *ad*, and *laudare*, to praise, from *laus, laudis*, praise, has also influenced the meaning.] To grant, give, or make over; to assign (to *allow* him $300 a year); to admit; to own or acknowledge (*allow* a claim); to abate or deduct; to set apart (*allow* so much for loss); to grant permission to; to permit.—*v.i.* To concede; to make abatement or concession.—**allowable,** al•lou′-a•bl, *a.* Proper to be or capable of being allowed or permitted; not forbidden; permissible.—**allowably,** al•lou′a•bli, *adv.* In an allowable manner; with propriety.—**allowance,** al•lou′ans, *n.* Permission; license; sanction; a quantity allowed or granted; relaxation of severity in censure; a deduction or abatement.—**allowance,** al•lou′ans, *v.t.* To put upon allowance.—**allowedly,**† al•-lou′ed•li, *adv.* Admittedly.

alloy, al•loi′, *n.* [Originally *allay*, O.F. *aley*, L. *alligare*, bind, with confusion of Fr. *aloi*, legal standard of coin, *a*, according, and *loi*, law.] A baser metal mixed with a finer; a mixture of different metals; any metallic compound; *fig.* evil mixed with good.—**alloy,** al•loi′, *v.t.* To reduce the purity of (a metal) by mixing with it a portion of less valuable metal; to reduce, abate, or impair by mixture.

allspice, al′spīs, *n.* See ALL.

allude, al•lūd′, *v.i.—alluded, alluding*, [L. *alludo*, to play upon, to allude—*ad*, and *ludo*, to play.] To refer to something not directly mentioned; to hint at by remote suggestions (followed by *to*). *Syn.* under ADVERT.—**allusion,** al•lū′zhon, *n.* The act of alluding; a reference to something not explicitly mentioned; an indirect or incidental suggestion; a hint.—**allusive,** al•lū′siv, *a.* Having allusion or reference to something not fully expressed; containing allusions.—**allusively,** al•lū′-siv•li, *adv.* In an allusive manner; by way of allusion.—**allusiveness,** al•-lū′siv•nes, *n.*

allure, al•lūr′, *v.t.—allured, alluring.* [Prefix *al* for *ad*, to, and *lure*, Fr. *leurrer*, to decoy. LURE.] To tempt by the offer of some good, real or apparent; to draw or try to draw by some proposed pleasure or advantage; to entice, decoy, tempt, attract.—**allurement,** al•lūr′ment, *n.* The act of alluring, or that which allures.—**allurer,** al•lūr′ėr, *n.* One who, or that which, allures.—**alluring,** al•lūr′ing, *a.* Inviting; having the quality of attracting or tempting.—**alluringly,** al•lūr′ing•li, *adv.* In an alluring manner; enticingly.

alluvium, al•lū′vi•um, *n.* [L. *alluvius*, alluvial—*ad*, to, and *luo*=Gr. *louō*, L. *lavo*, to wash; akin *deluge, lotion, dilute*, etc.] Soil deposited by means of the action of water, often washed down from mountains or high grounds.—**alluvial,** al•lū′vi•al, *a.* Pertaining to or having the character of alluvium; deposited by the action of waves or currents of water.

ally, al•lī′, *v.t.—allied, allying.* [Fr. *allier*, to join, to unite, *s'allier*, to confederate or become allied—*al* for *ad*, to, and *lier*, to tie or unite; L. *ligare*, to bind, whence *league, ligament*.] To unite by marriage, treaty, league, or confederacy; to connect by formal agreement; to bind together or connect (as by friendship or pursuits).—*v.i.* To be closely united.—*n.* A prince or state united by treaty or league: a confederate.—**alliance,** al•lī′ans, *n.* [O.Fr. *alliance*.] The state of being allied or connected; the relation or union between families, contracted by marriage; a union between nations, contracted by compact, treaty, or league; any union or connection of interests; a compact or treaty; the persons or parties allied.

almagest, al′ma•jest, *n.* [Ar. *al*, the, Gr. *megistē*, greatest.] The great astronomical and geographical compilation of Ptolemy; great books on astrology and kindred arts.

Alma Mater, al′ma mā′tėr. [L., benign mother, fostering mother.] An epithet applied by students to the university where they have been trained.

almanac, a̤l′ma•nak, *n.* [Fr. *almanach*. Sp. *almanaque*, Ar. *al-manakh*, probably from a root meaning to reckon; Heb. *manah*.] A table, book, or publication of some kind, generally annual, comprising a calendar of days, weeks, and months, with the times of the rising of the sun and moon, changes of the moon, eclipses, stated festivals of churches, etc., for a certain year or years.

almandine, al′man•dīn, *n.* [Fr. *almandine*, L.L. *alamandina, alavandina, alabandina*, a gem brought from *Alabanda*, a city in Asia Minor.] A name given to the violet or violet-red varieties of the spinel ruby, and also to precious or noble garnet.

alme, almeh, al′mē, *n.* The name given in some parts of the East, and especially in Egypt, to singing and dancing girls.

almighty, a̤l•mī′ti, *a.* [*All* and *mighty*.] Possessing all power; omnipotent; being of unlimited might.—*The Almighty*, the omnipotent God.—**almightily,**† a̤l•mī′ti•li, *adv.* In an almighty manner; with almighty power.—**almightiness,** a̤l•mī′ti•nes, *n.* The quality of being almighty; omnipotence.

almond, ä′mund, *n.* [O. Fr. *almandre*, Fr. *amande*, It. *amandola*, corrupted from L. *amygdala*, Gr. *amygdale*, an almond.] The seed or kernel of a tree allied to the peach; the tree itself. There are two varieties, *sweet* and *bitter*. The name is also given to the seeds of some other species of plants; also to a tonsil or gland of the throat.

almoner, al′mon•ėr, *n.* [O.Fr. *almosnier*, L.L. *eleemosynarius*, from Gr. *eleēmosynē*=E. *alms*.] A dispenser of alms or charity; more especially an officer who directs or carries out the distribution of charitable doles in connection with religious communities, hospitals, or almshouses, or on behalf of some superior.—**almonry,** al′mon•ri, *n.* The place where an almoner resides, or where alms are distributed.

almost, a̤l′mōst, *adv.* [*All* and *most*.] Nearly; well nigh; for the greatest part.

alms, ämz, *n.* [O.E. *almesse, almes*, A. Sax, *almes, aelmesse*, borrowed from L. *eleemosyna*, alms, from Gr. *eleēmosynē*, pity.] Anything given gratuitously to relieve the poor; a charitable dole; charity. [This word (like *riches*) is strictly a singular, but its form has caused it to be often regarded as grammatically plural.]—**almsgiver,** *n.* One who gives alms.—**almsgiving,** *n.* The act of giving alms.—**almsman,** *n.* A person supported by charity or by public provision.

aloe, al′ō, *n.* [Gr. *aloē*.] The common name of the plants of the genus *Aloe*, of the same order as the lily. They are natives of warm climates, and especially abundant in Africa. Several species yield *aloes*, the well-known bitter purgative medicine.—**aloetic,** al•ō•et′ik, *a.* Pertaining to or obtained from the aloe or aloes; partaking of the qualities or containing the properties of aloes.

aloft, a•loft′, *adv.* [Icel. *à lopt* (pron. loft). LOFT.] On high; in the air; high above the ground; *naut.* on the higher yards or rigging.

alone, a•lōn′, *a*, or *adv.* [*All* and *one*—the *all* and *one* being formerly printed as separate words; G. *allein*, Dan. *allene*, D. *alleen*, alone, are formed in the same way.] Apart from another or others; single; solitary (to remain *alone*, to walk *alone*); only; to the exclusion of other persons or things; solely (he *alone* remained, two men *alone* returned). Rarely used before a noun, as one *alone* verse.—*To let alone*, to leave untouched or not meddled with.

along, a•long′, *adv.* [A.Sax, *andlang*, *anlong*—prefix *and*, *an* (in *an*swer), and *lang*, *long*.] By the length; lengthwise; in a line with the length (stretched *along*); in a line or with a progressive motion; onward (to walk *along*); in company; together (followed by *with*).—*prep.* By the length of, as distinguished from *across*; in a longitudinal direction over or near.—**alongshore,** along′shōr, *adv.* By the shore or coast; lengthwise and near the shore.—**alongside,** a•long′sīd, *adv.* Along or by the side; beside each other (to lie *alongside* or *alongside of*).—*prep.* Beside; by the side of.

aloof, a•löf′, *adv.* (O.E. *a-lofe*—prefix *a*, on, and *loof* or *luff*, windward.] At a distance, but within view; apart; separated.

alopecia, al′o•pe″shi•a, *n.* [L. *alopecia*, Gr. *alòpekia*, from *alòpex*, a fox, because foxes are said to be subject to this disease.] Loss of hair; baldness.

aloud, a•loud′, *adv.* With a loud voice or great noise; loudly.

alow, a•lō′, *adv.* In a low place, or a lower part; opposed to *aloft*.

alp, alp, *n.* [From the *Alps*, well-known mountains in Central Europe.] A high mountain.—**alpenhorn,** al′pen•horn, *n.* [G. *Alpen*, the Alps, and *horn*, a horn.] A very long, powerful, nearly straight horn, but curving slightly and widening towards its extremity, used on the Alps to convey signals. Called also *Alphorn*.—**alpenstock,** al′pen•stok, *n.* [G. *Alpen*, the Alps, and *stock*, a stick.] A strong tall stick shod with iron, pointed at the end, used in climbing the Alps and other high mountains.—**Alpine,** al′pīn, *a.* Of, pertaining to, or connected with the Alps, or any lofty mountain; mountainous. [*not cap.*]

alpaca, al•pak′a, *n.* [Peruv. *alpaco.*] A ruminant mammal, of the camel tribe, a native of the Andes, valued for its long, soft, and silky wool, which is woven into fabrics of great beauty: a fabric manufactured from the wool of the alpaca.

alpha, al′fa, *n.* The first letter in the Greek alphabet, answering to A, sometimes used to denote what is first or a beginning.—*Alpha and Omega*. The first and last letters of the Greek alphabet; the beginning and the end.—**alphabet,** al′fa•bet, *n.* [Gr. *alpha* and *beta*, A and B.] The letters of a language arranged in the customary order; any series of elementary signs or symbols used for a similar purpose; hence, first elements; simplest rudiments.—**alphabetic, alphabetical,** al•fa•bet′ik, al•fa•bet′ik•al, *a.* Pertaining to an alphabet; furnished with an alphabet; expressed by an alphabet; in the order of an alphabet.—**alphabetically,** al•fa•bet′ik•al•li, *adv.* In an alphabetical manner; in the customary order of the letters.—**alphabetize,** al′fa•bet•īz, *v.t.* To arrange alphabetically.—**alpha particle,** *Phys.* a positively charged particle composed of two protons and two neutrons and therefore the equivalent of the nucleus of a helium atom.

already, a̤l•red′i, *adv.* [*All* and *ready*.] Before the present time; before some specified time.

Alsatian, al•sā′shon, *a.* Of or pertaining to Alsace in France.—*n.* A native of Alsatia.

also, a̤l′so, *adv.* and *conj.* [*All* and *so*; A.Sax. *eall-swâ*, *ealswâ*, *alswâ*, from *eall*, *eal*, all, quite, and *swâ*, so. *As* is this word contracted.] In like manner; likewise; in addition; too; further.

Altaic, Altaian, al•tā′ik, al•tā′yan, *a.* Pertaining to the Altai, a vast range of mountains in Eastern Asia.—*Altaic* or *Altaian family of languages*, a family of languages which includes Hungarian, Finnish, Turkish, etc. Also called *Scythian* and *Turanian*.

altar, a̤l′tėr, *n.* [L. *altare*, from a root seen in L. *altus*, high.] An elevated place on which sacrifices were offered or incense burned to a deity; a table in a church for the celebration of the eucharist.—**altarpiece,** *n.* A painting or piece of sculpture placed behind or above an altar in a church.

altazimuth, alt•az′i•muth, *n.* [From *altitude* and *azimuth*.] An astronomical instrument for determining the altitude and azimuth of heavenly bodies, consisting of a vertical circle and attached telescope, the two having both a vertical and a horizontal motion.

alter, a̤l′tėr, *v.t.* [L.L. *altero*, to change, from L. *alter*, another of two—root *al*, another (seen in *alius*, Gr. *allos*, another, E. *else*), and compar. suffix *-ter* = E. *-ther* in *other*, etc.] To make other or different; to make some change in; to vary in some degree, without an entire change;—*v.i.* To become, in some respects, different; to vary; to change.—**alterability,** a̤l′tėr•a•bil″i•ti, *n.* The quality of being susceptible of alteration.—**alterable,** a̤l′tėr•a•bl, *a.* Capable of being altered, varied, or made different.—**alterableness,** a̤l′tėr•a•bl•nes, *n.* The quality of being alterable.—**alterably,** a̤l′tėr•a•bli, *adv.* In an alterable manner; so as to be altered or varied.—**alteration,** a̤l•tėr•ā′shon, *n.* The act of altering; the state of being altered; also, the change made.—**alterative,** al′tėr•āt•iv, *a.* Causing alteration; having the power to alter; *med.* having the power to restore healthy functions of the body without sensible evacuations.—*n.* A medicine having this character.

altercate, al′tėr•kāt, *v.i.* [L. *altercor*, *altercatus*, to wrangle, from *alter*, another. ALTER.] To contend in words; to wrangle.—**altercation,** al•tėr•kā′shon, *n.* The act of altercating; warm contention in words; heated argument; a wrangle.

altern,† al′tėrn, *a.* [L. *alternus*, from *alter*, another. ALTER.] Acting by turns; alternate. [*Mil.*]—**alternate,** al•tėr′nāt, *a.* [L. *alternatus*, pp. of *alterno*, to do by turns.] Being by turns; following one another in time or place by turns; first one, then another successively; reciprocal; having one intervening between each pair; occupying every second place; consisting of parts or members proceeding in this way (an *alternate* series).—*Alternate generation*, that species of generation among animals by which the young do not resemble their parent, but their grandparent or some remote ancestor; heterogenesis.—**alternate,** al′tėr•nāt or a̤l•tėr′nāt, *v. t.*—*alternated*, *alternating*. To perform by turns or in succession; to cause to succeed or follow by turns.—*v.i.* To follow one another in time or place by turns.—**alternating current.** *Elect.* a current that reverses direction in cycles.—**alternately,** al•tėr′nāt•li, *adv.* In an alternate manner.—**alternation,** al•tėr•nā′shon, *n.* The act of alternating, or state of being alternate; the act of following and being followed in turn.—**alternative,** al•tėr′na•tiv, *a.* Offering a choice or possibility of one of two things.—*n.* A choice between two things, so that if one is taken the other must be left; a possibility of one of two things, so that if one thing is false the other must be true.—**alternatively,** al•tėr′na•tiv•li, *adv.* In an alternative manner.—**alternativeness,** al•tėr′na•tiv•nes, *n.*

although, a̤l•THō′, *conj.* [*All*, if, even, and *though*; comp. *albeit.*] Grant all this; be it so; suppose that; admit all that. *Although* differs very little from *though*, but is perhaps rather stronger.

altimeter, al•tim′et•ėr, *n.* [L. *altus*, high, and Gr. *metron*, measure.] An instrument for taking altitudes by geometrical principles, as a quadrant.—**altimetry,** al•tim′et•ri, *n.* The art of ascertaining altitudes.

altitude, al′ti•tūd, *n.* [L. *altitudo*, from *altus*, high (whence *exalt*, *haughty*).] Height; amount of space to a point above from one below; measure of elevation; *pl.* haughty airs (colloq.).

alto, al′tō or äl′tō, *n.* [It., from L. *altus*, high, being above the tenor.] *Mus.* contralto; the deepest voice among women and boys, and the highest among men, a special voice above the tenor; a singer in this voice.—*a.* Pertaining to this voice.—**altorilievo,** äl′tō•rē•lyā″vo, *n.* High relief; sculpture in which the figures stand out prominently from the background; sculpture in high relief.

altogether, a̤l·tu̇·geᴛʜ′ėr, *adv.* [*All,* quite, and *together.*] Wholly; entirely; completely; quite.

altruism, al′trö·izm, *n.* [It. *altrui,* others, from L. *alter,* another.] Devotion to others or to humanity: the opposite of *selfishness.*—**altruist,** al′trö·ist. *n.* One who practices altruism.—**altruistic,** al·trö·ist′ik, *a.* Pertaining to altruism.

alum, al′um, *n.* [L. *alumen.*] A general name for a class of double sulfates containing aluminum and such metals as potassium, ammonium, iron, etc. Common or potash alum is used medicinally as an astringent and a styptic; in dyeing, as a mordant; in tanning, for restoring the cohesion of skins.—*v.t.* To steep in or impregnate with a solution of alum.—**alumina,** al·ū′min·a, *n.* The oxide of aluminum, the most abundant of the earths, widely diffused in the shape of clay, loam, etc.—**aluminiferous,** al·ū′min·if″ėr·us, *a.* Containing alum or alumina.—**aluminum,** al·ū′min·um, *n.* Chemical sym. Al; sp. gr., 2.7; at. no., 13; at. wt., 26.98. The metallic base of alumina; a white metal with a bluish tinge, and a luster somewhat resembling, but far inferior to, that of silver.—*Aluminum bronze,* an alloy of aluminum and copper, possessed of great tenacity, for industrial purposes.—*Aluminum gold,* an alloy of 10 parts of aluminum to 90 of copper.—**aluminous,** al·ū′min·us, *a.* Pertaining to or containing alum or alumina.—**alumroot,** *n.* A name given to the astringent root of several plants.

alumnus, a·lum′nus, *n.* pl. **alumni,** a·lum′nī. [L., a disciple, from *alo,* to nourish.] Formerly a pupil; now a graduate of an educational institution.—**alumna,** a·lum′na, *n.* Feminine for alumnus.

alveary, al′vē·a·ri, *n.* [L. *alvearium,* a bee-hive.] A beehive, or something resembling a beehive; the hollow of the external ear.—**alveolar,** al′vē·o·lėr, *a.* Containing sockets, hollow cells, or pits; pertaining to sockets, specifically the sockets of the teeth.—**alveolate,** al′vē·o·lāt, *a.* Deeply pitted, so as to resemble a honeycomb.—**alveolus,** al·vē′o·lus, *n.* pl. **alveoli,** al·vē′o·lī. [L., a little hollow, dim. of *alveus.*] A cell, as in a honeycomb or in a fossil; the socket of a tooth.

alvine, al′vīn, *a.* [From L. *alvus,* the belly.] Belonging to the belly or intestines; relating to the intestinal excrements.

always, a̤l′wāz, *adv.* [*All* and *way, -ways* being an adverbial genitive.] Perpetually; uninterruptedly; continually (*always* the same); as often as occasion recurs (he is *always* late).

am, am. [For hypothetical *arm, asm*; comp. Goth. *im* for *ism,* Icel. *em* for *erm, esm,* Lith. *esmi,* L. *sum,* Skr. *asmi,* made up of root *as,* to breathe, exist, be, and *mi,* cognate with E. *me.* In the conjugation of this verb three different roots are employed; seen in *am, was, be.* BE, WAS.] The first person of the verb *to be,* in the indicative mood, present tense.

amadavat, am·a·da·vat′, *n.* [East Indian name.] A small granivorous bird of India, having a red conical beak and red and black plumage, often imported as a cage bird.

amadou, am′a·dö, *n.* [Fr. *amadou,* a word of Scandinavian origin.] A soft leathery substance used for tinder, prepared from a fungus growing on trees; German tinder.

amain, a·mān′, *adv.* [Prefix *a,* in, on, and *main,* force.] With force, strength, or violence; suddenly; at once.

amalgam, a·mal′gam, *n.* [Fr. *amalgame,* Gr. *malagma,* a soft mass.] A compound of mercury or quicksilver with another metal; any metallic alloy of which mercury forms an essential constituent part; a mixture or compound of different things.—**amalgamate,** a·mal′gam·āt, *v.t.*—*amalgamated, amalgamating.* To compound or mix (a metal) with quicksilver; commonly, to blend, unite, or combine generally into one mass or whole.—*v.i.* To combine to form an amalgam; to unite or coalesce generally; to become mixed or blended together.—**amalgamation,** a·mal′ga·mā″shon, *n.* The act or operation of amalgamating; the state of being amalgamated; union or junction into one body or whole; the process of separating gold and silver from their ores by combining them with mercury, which dissolves and separates the other metal, and is afterward driven off by heat.

amanuensis, a·man′ū·en″sis, *n.* pl. **amanuenses,** a·man′ū·en″sēz. [L. *a,* by, and *manus,* the hand.] A person whose employment is to write what another dictates, or to copy what has been written by another.

amaranth, am′a·ranth, *n.* [Gr. *amarantos,* unfading—*a,* not, and *marainō,* to wither.] A poetical name loosely used to signify a flower supposed never to fade; a color inclining to purple.—**amaranthine,** am·a·ranth′in, *a.* Belonging to, consisting of, or resembling amaranth; never fading; of a purplish color.

Amaryllis, am·a·ril′lis, *n.* [Greek female name.] A genus of bulbous-rooted plants with fine flowers. Some of them, called lilies, form the type of a natural family of plants, the Amaryllidaceae.

amass, a·mas′, *v.t.* [Fr. *amasser*—*a,* to, and *masse,* L. *massa,* a mass.] To collect into a heap; to gather a great quantity or number of; to accumulate.—**amassment,** a·mas′ment, *n.* The act of amassing.

amateur, am′a·tūr, am·a·tėr (ė long), *n.* [Fr., from L. *amator, amatoris,* a lover, from *amo,* to love.] One who cultivates any study or art from taste or attachment without pursuing it professionally or with a view to gain; one who has a taste for the arts.—**amateurish,** am·a·tūr′ish, *a.* Pertaining to or characteristic of an amateur; wanting the skill, finish, or other faculties of a professional.

amative, am′at·iv, *a.* [L. *amo, amatum,* to love.] Full of love; amorous; amatory.—**amativeness,** am′at·iv·nes, *n. Phren.* that propensity which impels to sexual passion.—**amatorial,**† am·a·tō′ri·al, *a.* Pertaining to love; amatory.—**amatory,** am′a·to·ri, *a.* Pertaining to or producing love; expressive of love (verses, sighs, etc.).

amaurosis, am·a̤·rō′sis, *n.* [Gr. *amaurōsis,* from *amauros,* obscure.] A partial or complete loss of sight from loss of power in the optic nerve or retina, without any visible defect in the eye except an immovable pupil.—**amaurotic,** a·ma̤·rot′ik, *a.* Pertaining to or affected with amaurosis.

amaze, a·māz′, *v.t.* [Prefix *a,* on or in, and *maze* (which see),] To confound with fear, sudden surprise, or wonder; to confuse utterly; to perplex; to astound; to astonish; to surprise.—*n.* Astonishment; confusion; amazement: used chiefly in poetry.—**amazedly,** a·māz′ed·li, *adv.* With amazement.—**amazedness,** a·māz′ed·nes, *n.* The state of being amazed; amazement.—**amazement,** a·māz′ment, *n.* The state of being amazed or astounded; astonishment; great surprise.—**amazing,** a·māz′ing, *a.* Very wonderful; exciting astonishment.—**amazingly,** a·māz′ing·li, *adv.* In an amazing manner or degree.

Amazon, am′a·zon, *n.* [Gr. *amazōn*: of unknown origin.] One of a fabled race of female warriors who are mentioned by the ancient Greek writers; hence, a warlike or masculine woman; a virago.—**Amazonian,** am·a·zō′ni·an, *a.* Pertaining to or resembling an Amazon; of masculine manners; also, belonging to the river Amazon in South America.

ambages,† am·bā′jēz, *n. pl.* [L.] Windings or turnings; hence, circumlocution; subterfuges; evasions.—**ambagious,**† am·bā′jus, *a.* Circumlocutory; roundabout.

ambassador, am·bas′sa·dor, *n.* [Fr. *ambassadeur,* from *ambassade,* an embassy, from L. *ambactus,* a vassal, a dependent, from a Teutonic word = Goth. *andbahts,* A.Sax. *ambiht, ambeht,* a servant, from prefix *and* (the *an* in *an*swer), and a root allied to Skr. *bhaj,* to serve or honor.] A minister of the highest rank employed by one prince or state at the court of another to transact state affairs. [The spelling *Embassador* is obsolete, though *Embassy,* not *Ambassy* is used.]—**ambassadorial,** am·bas′sa·dō″ri·al, *a.* Belonging to an ambassador.—**ambassadress,** am·bas′sa·dres, *n.* The wife of an ambassador; a female ambassador.

amber, am′bėr, *n.* [Fr. *ambre,* It. *ambra,* Sp. *ambar,* from Ar. *ambar,* ambergris, from its resemblance to this.] A mineralized pale-yellow, and sometimes reddish or brownish, resin of extinct pine trees, found most abundantly on the shores of the Baltic. *a.* Of or like amber.

ambergris, am′bėr·grēs, *n.* [Fr. *ambre gris* (*gris*, gray), gray amber.] A solid, opaque, ash-colored substance used in perfumery. It is a morbid secretion obtained from the sperm whale.

ambidexter,† am·bi·deks′tėr, *n.* [L. *ambo*, both, and *dexter*, the right hand.] A person who uses both hands with equal facility; one equally ready to act on either side. —**ambidexterity,**† **ambidextrousness,**† am′bi·deks·ter″i·ti, am·bi·deks′trus·nes, *n.* The quality of being ambidextrous; double-dealing. —**ambidextrous,** am·bi·deks′trus, *a.* Having the faculty of using both hands with equal ease; double-dealing.

ambient, am′bi·ent, *a.* [L. *ambiens*, *ambientis*—*amb*, around, and *iens*, ppr. of *ire*, to go]. Surrounding; encompassing on all sides: applied to fluids or diffusible substances (the *ambient* air).

ambiguous, am·big′ū·us, *a.* [L. *ambiguus*, from *ambigo*, to go about—*ambi*, about, and *ago*, to drive.] Doubtful or uncertain, especially in respect to signification; liable to be interpreted two ways; equivocal; indefinite.—**ambiguously,** am·big′ū·us·li, *adv.* In an ambiguous manner; with doubtful meaning.—**ambiguity, ambiguousness,** am·bi·gū′i·ti, am·big′ū·us·nes, *n.* The state or quality of being ambiguous; doubtfulness or uncertainty, particularly of signification.

ambition, am·bi′shon. *n.* [L. *ambitio*, *ambitionis*, the going about of candidates for office in Rome, hence flattery, ambition—*amb*, around, round about, and *eo*, *itum*, to go, from L. Gr. and Skr. root *i*, to go.] An eager and sometimes inordinate desire after honor, power, fame, or whatever confers distinction; desire to distinguish one's self among others.—*v.t.*† To seek after ambitiously.—**ambitious,** am·bi′shus, *a.* [L. *ambitiosus.*] Possessing ambition; eagerly or inordinately desirous of power, honor, fame, office, superiority, or distinction; strongly desirous (with *of* or *after*); springing from, indicating, or characterized by ambition; showy; pretentious (*ambitious* ornament).—**ambitiously,** am·bi′shus·li, *adv.* In an ambitious manner. —**ambitiousness,** am·bi′shus·nes, *n.* The quality of being ambitious.

ambivalence, am·biv′a·lans, *n.* [L. *ambo*, both, and *valere*, to be strong.] Coexistence of contradictory feelings about a particular person, object, or action.

amble, am′bl, *v.i.*—*ambled*, *ambling*, [O.Fr. *ambler*, to amble, from L. *ambulo*, to walk, from *amb*, about.] To move by lifting both legs on each side alternately: said of horses, etc.; hence, to move easily and gently.—*n.* The pace of a horse or like animal when ambling; easy motion; gentle pace.—**ambler,** am′blėr, *n.* One who ambles.

amblygon, am′bli·gon, *n.* [Gr. *amblys*, obtuse, and *gōnia*, an angle.] An obtuse-angled triangle.—**amblygonite,** am·blig′on·īt, *n.* A greenish-colored mineral, of different pale shades, marked with reddish and yellowish brown spots.

amblyopia, am·bli·ō′pi·a, *n.* [From Gr. *amblys*, dull, and *ōps*, *ōpos*, the eye.] Dullness or dimness of eyesight without any apparent defect in the organs—the first stage in amaurosis.

ambo, am′bo, *n.* [Gr. *ambōn*, a stage, a pulpit.] In early Christian churches a raised desk or pulpit.

Amboina wood, am·boi′na wụd, *n.* [*Amboyna*, one of the Molucca Islands.] A beautifully mottled and curled wood employed in cabinet work.

ambrosia, am·brō′zhi·a, *n.* [Gr. *ambrosia*, from *ambrotos*, immortal—*a*, not, and same root as L. *mors*, death, E. *murder*.] The fabled food of the ancient Greek gods, which conferred immortality on those who partook of it; hence, anything pleasing to the taste or smell, as a perfumed draught, unguent, or the like. —**ambrosial,** am·brō′zhi·al, *a.* Of or pertaining to ambrosia; anointed or fragrant with ambrosia; delicious; fragrant.—**ambrosially,** am·brō′zhi·al·li, *adv.* In an ambrosial manner; with an ambrosial odor.

ambry, am′bri, *n.* [From L. *armarium*, tool chest. Scottish *aumry*, through French.] An almonry‡; a niche or recess in the wall of ancient churches near the altar in which the sacred utensils were deposited; a cupboard†.

ambsace, āmz′ās, *n.* [O.F. *ambes ace.*] Ambsace; complete bad luck, the two aces being the lowest throw at dice.

ambulacrum, am·bū·lā′krum, *n.* pl. **ambulacra,** am·bū·lā′kra. [L. *ambulacrum*, an alley.] One of the perforated spaces or avenues through which are protruded the tube feet, by means of which locomotion is effected in the sea urchins, etc.—**ambulacral,** am·bū·lā′kral, *a.* Pertaining to ambulacra.

ambulance, am′bū·lans, *n.* [Fr. AMBULATE.] A vehicle fitted with suitable appliances for conveying the injured and sick. Also a mobile hospital unit which accompanies an army in its movements in the field.

ambulate,† am′bū·lāt, *v.i.*—*ambulated*, *ambulating*. [L. *ambulo*, *ambulatum*, to go about. AMBLE.] To move backward and forward; to walk.—**ambulant,** am′bū·lant, *a.* Walking; moving from place to place.—**ambulation,** am·bū·lā′shon, *n.* The act of ambulating or walking about.—**ambulatory,** am′bū·la·to·ri, *a.* Having the power or faculty of walking; adapted for walking; pertaining to a walk; accustomed to move from place to place; not stationary (an *ambulatory* court).—*n.* Any part of a building intended for walking in.

ambuscade, am·bus·kād′, *n.* [Fr. *embuscade*, from It. *imboscare*, to lie in bushes—*in*, in, and *bosco*, a wood, the same word as E. *bush*.] A lying in wait and concealed for the purpose of attacking an enemy by surprise; a place where one party lies concealed with a view to attack another by surprise; those lying so concealed; ambush.—*v.t.* and *i.*—*ambuscaded*, *ambuscading*. To lie in wait in order to attack from a concealed position.—**ambush,** am′bụsh, *n.* [O. Fr. *embusche*, verb *embuscher*, to lie in wait.] Same as *Ambuscade*.—*v.t.* To post or place in ambush.—*v.i.* To lie or be posted in ambush.—**ambushment,** am′bụshment, *n.*

ameba. See AMOEBA.

ameer, amir, a·mēr′, *n.* [Ar.] A nobleman; a chief; a ruler; an emir.

ameliorate, a·mēl′yor·āt, *v.t.*—*ameliorated*, *ameliorating*. [Fr. *améliorer*, from L. *ad*, to, and *melioro*, *melioratum*, to make better, from *melior*, better.] To make better; to improve; to meliorate.—*v.i.* To grow better; to meliorate.—**ameliorable,** a·mēl′yor·a·bl, *a.* Capable of being ameliorated.—**amelioration,** a·mēl′yor·ā″shon, *n.* The act of ameliorating; improvement; melioration.—**ameliorative,** a·mēl′yor·āt·iv, *a.* Producing, or having a tendency to produce, amelioration.—**ameliorator,** a·mēl′yor·āt·ėr, *n.* One who ameliorates.

Amen, ä·men′, ā·men′. [Heb. āmen, verily, certainly.] A term occurring generally at the end of a prayer, and meaning *So be it*. In the N. T. it is used as a noun to denote Christ as being one who is true and faithful, and as an adjective to signify made true, verified, fulfilled.

amenable, a·mē′na·bl, *a.* [Fr. *amener*, to bring or lead to—*a*, to, and *mener*, to lead. DEMEAN.] Liable to answer or be called to account; responsible; ready to yield or submit, as to advice; submissive.—**amenableness, amenability,** a·mē′na·bl·nes, a·mē′na·bil″i·ti, *n.* The state of being amenable.—**amenably,** a·mē′na·bli, *adv.* In an amenable manner.

amend, a·mend′, *v.t.* [Fr. *amender*, for *emender*, to correct, from L. *emendo*, to free from faults—*e*, out, out of, and *menda*, a fault. MEND.] To make better, or change for the better, by removing what is faulty; to correct; to improve; to reform.—*v.i.* To grow or become better by reformation or rectifying something wrong in manners or morals.∴ *Amend* differs from *impróve* in this, that to *amend* implies something previously wrong, while to *improve* does not necessarily do so.—**amendable,** a·mend′a·bl, *a.* Capable of being amended or corrected.—**amendatory,** a·mend′a·to·ri, *a.* Supplying amendment; corrective.—**amender,** a·mend′ėr, *n.* One who amends.—**amendment,** a·mend′ment, *n.* The act of amending, or changing for the better, in any way; the act of becoming better, or state of having become better; an alteration proposed to be made in the draft of a parliamentary bill, or in the terms of any motion under discussion before a meeting.—**amends,** a·mendz′, *n. pl.* Compensation for a loss or injury; recompense; satisfaction; equivalent.

amende, ä·mänd′, *n.* [Fr. *amende*, L.L. *amenda*, a penalty, reparation. AMEND.] A pecuniary punishment or fine; a recantation or reparation.—*Amende honorable*, a public or open recantation and reparation to an injured party.

amenity, a•men′i•ti, *n.* [Fr. *amenité*, L. *amaenitas, amaenus*, pleasant.] The quality of being pleasant or agreeable, in respect of situation, prospect, climate, etc., as also of temper, disposition, or manners.

amenorrhea, a•men•o•rē′a, *n.* [Gr. *a*, not, *mén*, month, *rheo*, to flow.] *Med.* a morbid or unnatural suppression of menstruation.

amentia, a•men′shi•a, *n.* [L., want of reason—*a*, from, and *mens, mentis*, mind.] Imbecility of mind; idiocy or dotage.

amentum, ament, a•men′tum, am′ent, *n.* pl. **amenta,** a•men′ta. *Bot.* a kind of inflorescence consisting of unisexual apetalous flowers in the axils of scales or bracts ranged along a stalk or axis; a catkin.—**amentaceous,** a•men•tā′shus, *a.* Consisting of, resembling, or furnished with an amentum or amenta.

amerce, a•mėrs′, *v.t.*—*amerced, amercing.* [Fr. *amercié*, fined at the mercy of the court—*a*, at, and *merci*, mercy.] To punish by a pecuniary penalty, the amount of which is left to the discretion of the court; hence, to punish by deprivation of any kind†.—**amerceable,** a•mėrs′a•bl, *a.* Liable to amercement.—**amercement,** a•mėrs′ment, *n.* The act of amercing; a pecuniary penalty inflicted on an offender at the discretion of the court.—**amercer,** a•mėrs′ėr, *n.* One who amerces.

American, a•mer′i•kan, *a.* Pertaining to America; often, in a restricted sense, pertaining to the United States.—*n.* A native of America; in a restricted sense, one of the inhabitants of the United States.—**Americanism,** a•mer′i•kan•izm, *n.* The feelings of nationality which distinguish American citizens; the exhibition of national prejudice by Americans; a word, phrase, or idiom peculiar to Americans.—**Americanize,** a•mer′i•kan•īz, *v.t.*—*Americanized, Americanizing.* To render American or like what prevails in or is characteristic of America (especially the United States); to naturalize in America.

americium, am′er•ish″i•um, *n.* Radio-active element produced by the bombardment of uranium with high-energy helium ions. Symbol, Am; at. no., 95.

amethyst, am′ē•thist, *n.* [Gr. *amethystos*—*a*, not, and *methyō*, to inebriate, from its supposed power of preventing or curing intoxication.] A violet-blue or purple variety of quartz which is wrought into various articles of jewelry.—*Oriental Amethyst*, a rare violet-colored gem, a variety of corundum, of extraordinary brilliancy and beauty.—**amethystine,** a•mē•thist′īn, *a.* Pertaining to, composed of, or resembling amethyst.

amiable, ā′mi•a•bl, *a.* [Partly from Fr. *aimable*, lovely, amiable, from L. *amabilis*, from *amo*, to love, partly from Fr. *amiable*, amicable, L. *amicabilis*.] Worthy of love; delightful or pleasing (said of things)‡; possessing agreeable moral qualities; having an excellent and attractive disposition; lovable.—**amiability, amiableness,** ā′mi•a•bil″i•ti, ā′mi•a•bl•nes, *n.* The quality of being amiable or lovable; sweetness of temper.—**amiably,** ā′mi•a•bli, *adv.* In an amiable manner.

amianthus, am•i•an′thus, *n.* [Gr. *amiantos*—*a*, not, and *miainō*, to pollute or vitiate; so called from its incombustibility.] Flexible asbestos, earth flax, or mountain flax; an incombustible mineral composed of delicate filaments, very flexible, and somewhat elastic, often long and resembling threads of silk.

amicable, am′ik•a•bl, *a.* [L. *amicabilis*, from *amicus*, a friend, from *amo*, to love.] Characterized by or exhibiting friendship, peaceableness, or harmony; friendly; peaceable; harmonious in social or mutual transactions. *Amicable* is a weaker word than *friendly*. *Friendly* is active and positive; *amicable* simply implies a degree of friendship such as makes us unwilling to disagree with those with whom we are on harmonious terms.—**amicability, amicableness,** am′ik•a•bil″i•ti, am′ik•a•bl•nes, *n.* Quality of being amicable.—**amicably,** am′ik•a•bli, *adv.* In an amicable or friendly manner; with harmony.

amice, am′is, *n.* [Confusion of O.F. *amit*, L. *amictus*, garment, with O.F. *amusse*, cap, mutch.] A flowing cloak formerly worn by priests and pilgrims; an oblong embroidered piece or strip of fine linen, falling down the shoulders like a cope, worn under the alb by priests in the service of the mass.

amid, amidst, a•mid′, a•midst′, *prep.* [Prefix *a*, on, in, and *mid, midst.* O.E. *amidde, amiddes* (the latter a genitive form); A.Sax. *on-middan*; the *t* has been tacked on as in *against*.] In the midst or middle of; surrounded or encompassed by; mingled with; among.—**amidships,** a•mid′ships, *adv.* In or towards the middle or the middle line of a ship.

amide, am′id, *n.* [From *am* of *ammonia*.] *Chem.* any chemical compound derived from ammonia by the substitution of acid or acyl groups for the atoms of hydrogen.

amine, am′in, *n.* [From *am* of *ammonia*.] Chemical compound formed from ammonia by replacing one or more hydrogen atoms of the ammonia molecule with a corresponding number of organic radicals.—**aminic,** a•mi′nik, *a.*

amino acid, a•mē′no as′id. *Chem.* an acid containing the amino group, NH_2. These acids are the basic constituents of proteins.

amiss, a•mis′, *a.* [Prefix *a*, on, and *miss*.] Wrong; faulty; out of time or order; improper.—*adv.* In a faulty manner.—*To be not amiss*, to be passable or suitable.

amity, am′i•ti, *n.* [Fr. *amitié*, from L.L. *amicitas*, friendship; L. *amicus*, a friend, from *amo*, to love.] Friendship; harmony; good understanding, especially between nations.

ammeter, am′ mē•ter, *n.* [*Ampere* and *meter*.] An instrument for measuring electric current.

ammonia, am•mō′ni•a, *n.* [Gr. *ammoniakon*, sal ammoniac, from being first obtained near the Temple of *Ammon* in Libya.] A gaseous compound whose molecules contain one atom of nitrogen and three of hydrogen. Very soluble in water and easily liquefied, it is widely used in industry, agriculture, and medicine, frequently in solution in water, under the names of *liquid ammonia* or *spirits of hartshorn*.—**ammoniac, ammoniacal,** am•mō′ni•ak, am•mō•ni′ak•al, *a.* Pertaining to ammonia, or possessing its properties.—**ammoniac,** am•mō′ni•ak, *n.* An exudation of an umbelliferous plant with a fetid smell, used as an antispasmodic and expectorant, and in plasters.—**ammonium,** am•mo′ni•um, *n.* The radical NH_4 formed by the reaction of ammonia with acids.

ammonite, am′mon•īt, *n.* [Resembling the horns with which Jupiter *Ammon* was furnished when represented by statues.] One of the fossil shells of an extensive genus of extinct cuttle-fishes, coiled in a plane spiral, and chambered within like that of the nautilus, to which the ammonites were allied.

ammunition, am•mū•ni′shon, *n.* [Fr. *amunition*, L. *munitio*, defence, from *munio*, to fortify.] Military stores, especially such articles as are used in the discharge of firearms and ordnance of all kinds, as powder, balls, shells, shot, etc.

amnesia, am•nē′zha, *n.* [Gr. *a.* not, and *mnēsis*, memory.] Loss of memory.

amnesty, am′nes•ti, *n.* [L. *amnestia*, from Gr. *amnestia*, oblivion—*a*, not, and root *mna*, to remember.] An act of oblivion; a general pardon of the offenses of subjects against the government, or the proclamation of such pardon.—*v.t.*—*amnestied, amnestying.* To grant an amnesty to; to pardon.

amnion, am′ni•on, *n.* [Gr.] The innermost membrane surrounding the fetus of mammals, birds, and reptiles; also a thin, semitransparent, gelatinous fluid, in which the embryo of a seed is suspended when it first appears.

amoeba, a•mē′ba, *n.* [Gr. *amoibē*, change.] The generic name of various microscopic Protozoa, one of which is common in our fresh-water ponds and ditches. It consists of a gelatinous mass, and from continually altering its shape it received this as well as its former name of *proteus-animalcule*.—**amoeboid,** a•mē′boid, *a.* Of or pertaining to or resembling the amoeba.

amok, a•mok′, *n.* Same as *Amuck*.

among, amongst, a•mung′, a•mungst′, *prep.* [O.E. *amonge, amonges, amongest*, A.Sax. *amang, onmang*, from *mengan*, to mingle; the *es* being an adverbial genitive termination, and the *t* tacked on, as in *amidst*. MINGLE.] Mixed or mingled with (implying a number); in or into the midst of; in or into the number of (one *among* a thousand); jointly or with a reference to some one or other (they killed him *among* them).

amontillado, a•mon'til•ä"dō, *n.* [Sp.] A dry kind of sherry of a light color.

amoral, ā•mor'al, *a.* [*a*, not, and *moral*.] Lacking, or indifferent to, moral responsibility; independent of moral distinctions.

amoretto, am•o•ret'tō (pl. **amoretti**); **amorino,** am•o•rē'nō (pl. **amorini**), *n.* [It. from *amor*, love.] Terms in art for loves or cupids.

amorous, am'or•us, *a.* [Fr. *amoureux*, L.L. *amorosus*, L. *amor*, love; akin *amity*, *amiable*, etc.] Inclined to love persons of the opposite sex; having a propensity to love, or to sexual enjoyment; loving; fond; pertaining or relating to love; produced by love; indicating love; enamored (in this sense with *of*).—**amorously,** am'or•us•li, *adv.* In an amorous manner; fondly, lovingly. — **amorousness,** am'or•us•nes, *n.*

amorphous, a•mor'fus, *a.* [Gr. *amorphos*—*a*, neg., and *morphē*, form.] Having no determinate form; of irregular shape; not having the regular forms exhibited by the crystals of minerals; being without crystallization; formless; characterless.—**amorphism,** a•mor'fizm, *n.*

amortize, a•mor'tīz, *v.t.*—*amortized, amortizing*. [L.L. *amortisare*, to sell in *mort*-main—L. *ad*, to, and *mors, mortis*, death.] To extinguish a debt by means of a sinking fund.—**amortization,** a•mor'tiz•ā"shon, *n.*

amount, a•mount', *v.i.* [O.Fr. *amonter* to advance, increase, *amont*, upwards—*a*, to, and *mont*, L. *mons, montis*, a hill.] To add up to a sum; to reach a certain total by an accumulation of particulars; to come in the aggregate or whole; to result in; to be equivalent: followed by *to*.—*n.* The sum total of two or more particular sums or quantities; the aggregate; the effect, substance, or result.

amour, a•mör', *n.* [Fr., from L. *amor*, love.] A love intrigue; an affair of gallantry.

amperage, am•pâr'ij, *n.* [From *Ampere*, a French physicist.] The strength of an electric current measured in amperes.

ampere, am•pār', *n.* *Elect.* the unit employed in measuring the strength of an electric current.

ampersand, am'pėr•sand, *n.* [*and, per se*, and *and*.] The character &, symbol for *and*.

amphetamine, am•fet'a•min, *n.* [*alphamethyl-phenethyl*, and *amine*.] A drug used as an inhalant in colds or hay fever, or internally as a mental stimulant.

amphibian, am•fib'i•an, *n.* [Gr. *amphibios*, living a double life—*amphi*, both, and *bios*, life.] Any of a class of vertebrates intermediate between fishes and reptiles; an animal or plant that is adapted to live both on land and in the water; sea plane; hydroplane.—*a.* Amphibious. —**amphibious,** am•fib'i•us, *a.* Capable of living both on land and in water; *mil.* executed by the combined action of sea, land, and air forces; trained for such action; having two lives, natures, characteristics, etc.—**amphibiously,** am•fib'i•us•li, *adv.*—**amphibiousness,** am•fib'i•us•nes, *n.*

amphibole, am'fi•bōl, *n.* [Gr. *amphibolos*, doubtful, equivocal.] A name given to hornblende, from its resemblance to augite, for which it may readily be mistaken.—**amphibolic,** am•fi•bol'ik, *a.* Pertaining to or resembling amphibole.—**amphibolite,** am•fib'o•līt, *n.* A rock with a base of amphibole or hornblende.

amphibology, am•fi•bol'o•ji, *n.* Gr. *amphibologia*—*amphi*, in two ways, *ballō*, to throw, and *logos*, discourse.] A phrase or discourse susceptible of two interpretations; and hence, a phrase of uncertain meaning.—**amphibological,** am•fib'o•loj"ik•al, *a.* Of or pertaining to amphibology; of doubtful meaning; ambiguous.

amphibrach, am'fi•brak, *n.* [Gr.—*amphi*, on both sides, and *brachys*, short.] *Pros.* a foot of three syllables, the middle one long, the first and last short.

amphictyonic, am•fikt'i•ōn•ik, *a.* Of or belonging to the Amphictyonic Council, or council of amphictyones or neighbors, meeting in spring at Thermopylae, in autumn at Delphi.

amphigory, am'fi•gōr•i, *n.* [Fr. *amphigouri*.] A meaningless rigmarole; a nonsensical parody.—**amphigoric,** am•fi•gor'ik, *a.* Of, relating to, or consisting of amphigory; absurd; nonsensical.

amphimacer, am•fim'a•sėr, *a.* [Gr. *amphimakros*, long on both sides.] *Pros.* a foot of three syllables, the middle one short and the others long.

amphioxus, am•fi•oks'us, *n.* [Gr. *amphi*, on both sides, and *oxus* or *oxys*, sharp, because sharp at both ends.] A kind of fish of a very rudimentary type, the lancelet.

amphipod, am'fi•pod, *n.* [Gr. *amphi*, on both sides, and *pous, podos*, a foot.] Any of a large group of crustaceans having both swimming and leaping appendages, as beach fleas, sand hoppers, and fresh-water shrimps.—*a.* Of or pertaining to amphipods.

amphiprostyle, am•fip'ro•stīl, *a.* [Gr. *amphi*, on both sides, *pro*, before, and *stylē*, a column.] Having a prostyle or portico on both ends or fronts, but with no columns on the sides.

amphisbaena, am•fis•bē'na, *n.* [Gr. *amphisbaina*—*amphis*, on both sides, and *bainō*, to go, from the belief that it moved with either end foremost.] The generic name of small serpent-like reptiles, formerly but erroneously deemed poisonous.

amphiscii, amphiscians, am•fish'i•ī, am•fish'i•anz, *n. pl.* [Gr. *amphi*, on both sides, and *skia*, shadow.] The inhabitants of the intertropical regions, whose shadows at noon in one part of the year are cast to the north and in the other to the south.

amphitheater, am•fi•thē'a•tėr, *n.* [Gr. *amphitheatron*—*amphi*, on both sides, and *theatron*, theater.] An ancient edifice of an oval form, having a central area encompassed with rows of seats, rising higher as they receded from the center, on which people used to sit to view some spectacle or performance; a similar modern edifice; anything, as a natural hollow among hills, resembling an amphitheater in form. —**amphitheatric, amphitheatrical,** am'fi•thē•at"rik, am'fi•thē•at"rik•al, *a.* Pertaining to or resembling an amphitheater; exhibited in an amphitheater.

Amphitryon, am•fit'ri•ōn, *n.* King of Thebes, used for host, the man who provides dinner, from Molière's play of that name.

amphora, am'fo•ra, *n.* pl. **amphorae,** am'fo•rē. [L. *amphora*, Gr. *amphoreus*—*amphi*, on both sides, and *phoreō*, to carry, from its two handles.] Among the Greeks and Romans, a vessel, usually tall and narrow, with two handles or ears and a narrow neck, used for holding wine, oil, honey, and the like.

ample, am'pl, *a.* [Fr. *ample*, L. *amplus* —prefix *am, amb*, round, about, and root of *pleo*, to fill; akin *double*.] Large in dimensions; of great size, extent, capacity, or bulk; wide; spacious; extended (*ample* room); fully sufficient for some purpose intended; abundant; copious; plentiful (an *ample* supply; *ample* justice). —**ampleness,** am'pl•nes, *n.* The state of being ample; largeness; sufficiency; abundance.—**amplification,** am'pli•fi•kā"shon, *n.* The act of amplifying; an enlargement; extension; diffusive description or discussion.—**amplificatory,** am'pli•fi•kā•to•ri, *a.* Serving or tending to amplify.—**amplifier,** am'pli•fī•ėr, *n.* One who amplifies or enlarges.—*Elect.* a device for increasing the amplitude of electric waves or impulses, commonly including one or more vacuum tubes.—**amplify,** am'pli•fī, *v.t.*—*amplified, amplifying*. [Fr. *amplifier*, to enlarge—L. *amplus*, ample, and *facio*, to make.] To make more ample, larger, more extended, more copious, and the like. *v.i.*—To grow or become ample or more ample; to be diffuse in argument or description.—**amplitude,** am'pli•tūd, *n.* [L. *amplitudo*.] State of being ample; largeness of dimensions; extent of surface or space; greatness; *astron.* an arc of the horizon intercepted between the east or west point and the center of the sun or star at its rising or setting.—**amplitude modulation.** *Elect.* a system of radio transmission in which the amplitude of the carrier wave is modulated (contrasted with frequency modulation).—**amply,** am'pli, *adv.* In an ample manner; largely; sufficiently; copiously.

amplectant, am•plek'tant, *a.* [L. *amplectens, amplectentis*, ppr. of *amplector*, to embrace.] *Bot.* embracing; clasping.—**amplexicaul,** am•plek'si•kal, *a.* [L. *amplexus*, embracing, and *caulis*, a stem.] *Bot.* nearly surrounding, clasping, or embracing the stem, as some leaves do at their base.

ampulla, am•pul′la, *n.* pl. **ampullae,** am•pul′lē. [L.] A more or less globular bottle, used by the Romans for holding oil; a vessel for holding the consecrated oil used in various church rites and at the coronation of kings; a small sac or baglike appendage of a plant; a hollow flask-shaped leaf.—**ampullaceous,** am•pul•lā′shus, *a.* Of or pertaining to or like an ampulla.

amputate, am′pū•tāt, *v.t.*—*amputated, amputating.* [L. *amputo, amputatum*—*amb,* about, and *puto,* to prune.] To cut off, especially a human limb or that of an animal.—**amputation,** am•pū•tā′shon, *n.* The act of amputating; the operation of cutting off a limb or other projecting part of the body.

amuck, a•muk′, *n.* [Malay or Javanese.] A furious, reckless onset; a term used in the Eastern Archipelago by Malays, who are occasionally seen to rush out in a frantic state with daggers in their hands, yelling 'Amuck, amuck,' and attacking all that come in their way.—*To run amuck,* to rush about frantically, attacking all that come in the way; to attack all and sundry.

amulet, am′ū•let, *n.* [L. *amuletum,* Fr. *amulette,* from Ar. *hamâlat,* anything worn, from *hamala,* to carry, to wear.] Something worn or carried about the person, intended to act as a charm or preservative against evils or mischief, such as diseases and witchcraft.

amuse, a•mūz′, *v.t.*—*amused, amusing.* [Fr. *amuser,* to amuse, to divert, to hold in play—*a,* to, and O.Fr. *muser,* to muse. MUSE, *v.*] To entertain the mind of agreeably; to occupy or detain the attention of in a pleasant manner or with agreeable objects; to divert; entertain; often *refl.;* to keep in expectation, as by flattery, plausible pretenses and the like; to keep in play. ∴ *Amuse* is to occupy lightly and pleasantly; *divert* generally implies something absolutely lively or sportive; *entertain,* to keep in a continuous state of interest, often by something instructive.—**amusable,** a•mūz′a•bl, *a.* Capable of being amused.—**amusement,** a•mūz′ment, *n.* The act of amusing, or state of being amused; a slight amount of mirth or tendency towards merriment; that which amuses; entertainment; sport; pastime.—**amuser,** a•mūz′ėr, *n.* One who amuses.—**amusing,** a•mūz′ing, *a.* Giving amusement; pleasing; diverting.—**amusingly,** a•mūz′ing•li, *adv.* In an amusing manner.

amygdalate, a•mig′da•lāt, *n.* [L. *amygdalus,* an almond.] An emulsion made of almonds; milk of almonds.—**amygdaline,** a•mig′da•līn, *a.* Pertaining to, resembling, or made of almonds.—**amygdaloid,** a•mig′da•loid, *n.* A term applied to igneous rock, especially trap, containing round or almond-shaped vesicles or cavities partly or wholly filled with crystalline nodules of various minerals.—**amygdaloidal,** a•mig′da•loid″al, *a.* Pertaining to amygdaloid; shaped like an almond.

amyl, am′il, *n.* [Gr. *amylon,* starch.] *Chem.* a hypothetical radical said to exist in many compounds, as amylic alcohol, etc.—*Nitrite of amyl,* an amber-colored fluid with a pleasant odor, having the property when inhaled of quickening the heart's action.—**amylaceous,** am•il•ā′shus, *a.* Pertaining to starch, or the farinaceous part of grain; resembling starch.—**amylene,** am′il•ēn, *n.* A hydrocarbon obtained from amylic alcohol, and possessing anesthetic properties.—**amylic,** am•il′ik, *a.* Pertaining to amyl.—**amyloid,** am′il•oid, *a.* Resembling or being of the nature of amyl.—*n.* A semigelatinous substance, analogous to starch, met with in some seeds.

amylase, am′i•lās, *n.* [Gr. *amylon,* starch.] A digestive enzyme that converts starch into sugar, as in saliva and germinating seeds.

an, a, an, ā, *indef. art.* [A.Sax. *án,* one, an, the former being the original, the latter a developed meaning; the same word as *one.* ONE.] A word used before nouns in the singular number to denote an individual as one among more belonging to the same class, and not marking singleness like *one,* nor pointing to something known and definitive like *the.* The form *a* is used before consonants (including the name sound of *u* as in *unit, European=yu*); *an* is used before words beginning with a vowel sound, or the sound of *h* when the accent falls on any syllable except the first, as, *an inn, an umpire, an heir, an historian* (but also *a historian*).

ana, ā′na, *n. pl.* [The neuter plural termination of Latin adjectives in *-anus,* often forming an affix to the names of eminent men to denote a collection of their memorable sayings —thus *Scaligeriana, Johnsoniana.*] The sayings of notable men; personal gossip or anecdotes.

Anabaptist, an•a•bap′tist, *n.* [Gr. *ana,* again, and *baptistēs,* a baptist.] One who holds the invalidity of infant baptism, and the necessity of re-baptism, generally by immersion, at an adult age.—**Anabaptism,** an•a•bap′tizm, *n.* The doctrine or practices of the Anabaptists.

anabasis, an•ab′a•sis, *n.* [Gr.—*ana,* up, and *basis,* a going, from *bainō,* to go.] A going up; an expedition from the coast inland; [*cap.*] the expedition of Cyrus the Younger against Persia in 401 B.C. described by Xenophon.

anabolism, an•ab′o•lizm, *n.* [*anabole,* build up, and *ism.*] Constructive metabolism.

anachronism, an•ak′ron•izm, *n.* [Gr. *ana,* implying inversion, error, and *chronos,* time.] An error in computing historical time; any error which implies the misplacing of persons or events in time; anything foreign to or out of keeping with a specified epoch (as where Shakespeare makes Hector quote Aristotle). —**anachronous, anachronistic,** an•ak′ron•us, an•ak′ron•ist″ik, *a.*

anaclastic, an•a•klas′tik, *a.* [Gr. *anaklasis,* a bending back—Gr. *ana,* back, and *klasis,* a breaking, from *klaō,* to break.] Pertaining to or produced by the refraction of light; bending back; flexible.

anacoluthon, an′a•kol•ū″thon, *n.* [Gr. *anakolouthos,* wanting sequence—neg. prefix *an,* and *akolouthos,* following.] *Gram.* want of sequence in a sentence, owing to the latter member of it belonging to a different grammatical construction from the preceding; as, 'He that curseth father or mother, let him die the death.'—Mat. xv. 4.—**anacoluthic,** an′a•kol•ū″thik, *a.*

anaconda, an•a•kon da, *n.* The popular name of two of the largest species of the serpent tribe, namely, a Ceylonese species and a South American species, both growing to the length of over 30 feet.

Anacreontic, a•nak′rē•on″tik, *a.* Pertaining to or after the manner of *Anacreon;* relating to the praise of love and wine; convivial; amatory.—**Anacreontic,** a•nak′rē•on″tik, *n.* A poem by Anacreon, or composed in the manner of Anacreon; a little poem in praise of love or wine.

anacrusis, an′a•krü•sis, *n.* [Gr. *anakrousis,* striking up.] The unstressed syllable at the beginning of a verse.

anadem, an′a•dem, *n.* [Gr. *anadēma,* a head-band or fillet—*ana,* up, and *deō,* to bind.] A band, fillet, garland, or wreath.

anadromous, a•nad′rom•us, *a.* [Gr. *ana,* up, and *dromos,* course.] Passing from the sea into fresh waters at stated seasons, as the salmon.

anaerobe, an•âr′ōb, *n.* [Gr. *an,* without, *aer,* air, and *bios,* life.] A micro-organism that lives without air or free oxygen.—**anaerobic,** an•âr•ōb′ik, *a.*

anaglyph, an′a•glif, *n.* [Gr. *anaglyphon,* embossed work—*ana,* up, and *glyphō,* to engrave.] An ornament in relief chased or embossed.—**anaglyphic,** an•a•glif′ik, *a.*

anagoge, anagogy, an′a•gō•jē, an′a•go•ji, *n.* [Gr. *anagōgē*—*ana,* upward, and *agōgē,* a leading, from *agō,* to lead.] An elevation of mind to things celestial; the spiritual meaning or application of words; a mysterious or allegorical interpretation, especially of Scripture.—**anagogic, anagogical,** an•a•goj′ik, an•a•goj′ik•al, *a.* Of or pertaining to anagoge; mysterious; elevated; spiritual.—**anagogically,** an•a•goj′ik•al•li, *adv.*

anagram, an′a•gram, *n.* [Gr. *ana,* up, again, and *gramma,* a letter.] A transposition of the letters of a word or sentence, to form a new word or sentence.—**anagrammatic, anagrammatical,** an′a•gram•mat′ik, an′a•gram•mat″ik•al, *a.* Pertaining to or forming an anagram.—**anagrammatize,** an•a•gram′mat•īz, *v.t.* To transpose, as the letters of a word, so as to form an anagram,—*v.i.* To make anagrams.

anal, ā′nal, *a.* [L, *anus,* the fundament.] Pertaining to or situated near the anus.

analcime, a•nal′sim, *n.* [Gr. *an,* priv., and *alkimos,* strong, from *alkē,* strength.] A mineral of frequent occurrence in traprocks, especially in the cavities of amygdaloids. By friction it acquires a *weak* electricity; hence its name.

analecta, analects, an•a•lek′ta, an′•a•lekts, *n. pl.* [Gr. neut. pl. of *analektos*, select—*ana*, up, and *legō*, to gather.] Extracts or small pieces selected from different authors.

analepsis, an•a•lep′sis, *n.* [Gr., from *ana*, up or again, and *lepsis*, a taking, from *lambanō*, to take.] *Med.* recovery of strength after disease.—**analeptic,** an•a•lep′tik, *a.* Invigorating; giving strength after disease; awakening, especially from drug stupor.—*n.* an analeptic remedy.

analgesia, an•al•jēz′i•a, *n.* [Gr. *analgesia*—*an*, not, and *algos*, pain.] *Pathol.* incapacity for feeling pain in some part of the body.

analogy, an•al′o•ji, *n.* [Gr. *analogia*—*ana*, according to, and *logos*, ratio, proportion.] An agreement or likeness between things in some circumstances or effects, when the things are otherwise entirely different; relationship; conformity; parallelism; likeness. ∴ *Analogy* is sometimes confounded with *similarity*, but the latter properly denotes general likeness or resemblance; the former implies general difference, with identity or sameness in one or more relations. Thus there is *analogy*, but no *similarity* between the wing of a bird and that of a bat. [We say analogy *between* things, one thing has an analogy *to* or *with* another.]—**analogical,** an•a•loj′ik•al, *a.* Having analogy; analogous; used by way of analogy; expressing or implying analogy.—**analogically,** an•a•loj′ik•al•li, *adv.* In an analogical manner.—**analogist,** an•al′o•jist, *n.* One who adheres to analogy.—**analogize,** an•al′o•jīz, *v.t.*—*analogized, analogizing.* To explain by analogy; to consider with regard to its analogy to something else.—**analogous,** an•al′og•us, *a.* Having analogy; bearing some resemblance in the midst of differences (followed by *to* or *with*).—**analogously,** an•al′og•us•li, *adv.* In an analogous manner.—**analogue,** an′a•log, *n.* Something having analogy with something else.—**analogue computer.** A calculating machine that uses directly measurable quantities (voltages, resistances, etc.) to solve problems by physical analogy. Also spelled *analog computer*.

analysis, an•al′i•sis, *n.* pl. **analyses,** an•al′i•sēz. [Gr.—prefix *ana*, implying distribution, and *lysis*, a loosing, resolving, from *lyō*, to loosen.] The resolution of a compound object whether of the senses or the intellect into its constituent elements or component parts; a consideration of anything in its separate parts and their relation to each other; opposed to *synthesis;* the process of subjecting to chemical tests to determine ingredients; a syllabus or table of the principal heads of a discourse or treatise.—**analyzable,** an•a•līz′a•bl, *a.* Capable of being analyzed.—**analyzation,** an′a•līz•ā″shon, *n.* The act of analyzing.—**analyze,** an′a•līz, *v.t.*—*analyzed, analyzing.* [Fr. *analyser.*] To resolve into its elements; to separate, as a compound subject, into its parts or propositions.—**analyzer,** an′a•līz•ėr, *n.* One who or that which analyzes.—**analyst,** an′a•list, *n.* One who analyzes or is versed in analysis; one who subjects articles to chemical tests to find out their ingredients.—**analytic, analytical,** an•a•lit′ik, an•a•lit′ik•al, *a.* Pertaining to analysis; resolving into first principles or elements.—**analytically,** an•a•lit′ik•al•li, *adv.* In an analytical manner; in the manner of analysis.—**analytics,** an•a•lit′iks, *n.* The science of analysis.

anandrous, an•an′drus, *a.* [Gr. *an*, not, and *anēr*, *andros*, a male or stamen.] *Bot.* applied to flowers that are destitute of a stamen (female flowers).

anapaest, anapest, an′a•pest, *n.* [L. *anapaestus*, from Gr. *anapaistos.*] A poetical foot consisting of three syllables, the first two short or unaccented, the last long or accented.—**anapaestic,** an•a•pes′tik, *a.* Pertaining to an anapest; consisting of anapests.

anaphrodisiac, an•af′ro•diz″i•ak, *n.* [Gr. neg. prefix *an*, and *aphrodisiakos*, venereal.] A substance capable of dulling sexual appetite.

anaplasty, an′a•plas•ti, *n.* [Gr. *ana*, again, and *plassō*, to fashion.] *Surg.* an operation to supply by the employment of adjacent healthy structure the loss of small portions of flesh.—**anaplastic,** an•a•plas′tik, *a.* Of or pertaining to anaplasty.

anarchy, an′ar•ki, *n.* [Gr. *anarchia*, lawlessness—*an*, not, and *archē*, rule.] Want of government; a state of society when there is no law or supreme power; political confusion.—**anarchic, anarchical,** an•ärk′ik, an•ärk′ik•al, *a.* Of or pertaining to anarchy or anarchism; in a state of anarchy or confusion; lawless.—**anarchism,** an′ärk•izm, *n.* The doctrine of the abolition of formal government, free action for the individual, land and other resources being common property.—**anarchist, anarch,** an′ärk•ist, an′ärk, *n.* One who excites disorder in a state; an advocate of anarchy or anarchism.

anastomose, a•nas′tō•mōz, *v.i.*—*anastomosed, anastomosing.* [Fr. *anastomoser*, Gr. *anastomoō*—*ana*, again, anew, and *stoma*, a mouth.] *Anat.* and *bot.* to inosculate or run into each other, to communicate with each other by minute branches or ramifications, as the arteries and veins.—**anastomosis,** a•nas•tō•mō′sis, *n.* The inosculation of vessels in vegetable or animal bodies.—**anastomotic,** a•nas′tō•mot″ik, *a.* Pertaining to anastomosis.

anastrophe, a•nas′tro•fe, *n.* [Gr.—*ana*, back, *strephō*, to turn.] An inversion of the natural order of words.

anathema, a•nath′ē•ma, *n.* [Gr. *anathema*, a thing devoted to evil, from *anatithēmi*, to dedicate—*ana*, up, and *tithēmi*, to place.] A curse or denunciation pronounced with religious solemnity by ecclesiastical authority, and accompanied by excommunication; execration generally; curse.—**anathematization,** a•nath′ē•mat′iz•a″shon, *n.* The act of anathematizing.—**anathematize,** a•nath′ē•mat•īz, *v.t.*—*anathematized, anathematizing.* To pronounce an anathema against.—*v.i.* To pronounce anathemas; to curse.

anatomy, a•nat′o•mi, *n.* [Gr. *anatomē*—*ana*, up, and *tomē*, a cutting.] The art of dissecting or artificially separating the different parts of an organized body, to discover their situation, structure, and economy; the science which treats of the internal structure of organized bodies, as elucidated by dissection; when used alone it refers to the human body, *vegetable anatomy* being the anatomy of plants, *zootomy* that of the lower animals; the act of taking to pieces something for the purpose of examining in detail (the *anatomy* of a discourse); a skeleton (colloq.); hence, a thin meager person.—**anatomic, anatomical,** an•a•tom′ik, an•a•tom′ik•al, *a.* Belonging to anatomy or dissection.—**anatomically,** an•a•tom′ik•al•li, *adv.* In an anatomical manner; by means of dissection.—**anatomist,** a•nat′o•mist, *n.* One who is skilled in dissection, or in the doctrine and principles of anatomy.—**anatomization,** a•nat′o•miz•ā″shon, *n.* The act of anatomizing.—**anatomize,** a•nat′o•mīz, *v.t.*—*anatomized, anatomizing.* To cut up or dissect for the purpose of displaying or examining the structure; *fig.* to lay open or expose minutely; to analyze (to *anatomize* an argument).

ancestor, an′ses•tėr, *n.* [O.Fr. *ancestre, ancessor*, Fr. *ancêtre*, an ancestor, from L. *antecessor*, a predecessor—*ante*, before, and *cedo*, *cessum*, to go. CEDE.] One from whom a person descends, either by the father or mother, at any distance of time; a progenitor; a forefather; one from whom an inheritance is derived.—**ancestress,**† an′ses•tres, *n.* A female ancestor.—**ancestry,** an′ses•tri, *n.* A series of ancestors; lineage; honorable descent; high birth.

anchor, ang′kėr, *n.* [A.Sax. *ancor*, borrowed from L. *ancora*, Gr. *angkyra*, an anchor. From a root meaning crooked, bent, seen in L. *angulus*, a corner, E. *ankle, angle*, a fish-hook.] An iron implement, consisting usually of a straight bar called the shank, at the upper end of which is a transverse piece called the stock, and of two curved arms at the lower end of the shank, each of which arms terminates in a triangular plate called a fluke, and used for holding a ship or other vessel at rest in comparatively shallow water; something serving a purpose analogous to that of a ship's anchor; *fig.* that which gives stability or security; that on which we place dependence for safety.—*At anchor*, floating attached to an anchor; anchored.—*v.t.* To hold at rest by lowering the anchor; to place at anchor; *fig.* to fix or fasten on; to fix in a stable condition.—*v.i.* To cast anchor; to come to anchor.—**anchorage,** ang′kėr•aj, *n.* Anchoring ground; a place where a ship can anchor; a duty imposed on ships for anchoring in a harbor.

anchoret, anchorite, ang′kō•ret, ang′kō•rīt, *n.* [L. *anachoreta;* Gr. *anachorētēs—ana,* back, and *chōreō,* to retire, from *chōros,* a place.] A hermit; a recluse; one who retires from society to avoid the temptations of the world and devote himself to religious duties.—**anchoress,** ang′-kō•res, *n.* A female anchoret.—**anchoretic,** ang•kō•ret′ik, *a.* Pertaining to a hermit, or his mode of life.

anchovy, an•chō′vi, *n.* [Pg. and Sp. *anchova,* an anchovy, from Basque *anchua, anchuva,* dry.] A small fish belonging to the herring family, caught in vast numbers in the Mediterranean, and pickled for exportation. An esteemed sauce is also made from them.

anchylose, ang′ki•lōs. A common but erroneous spelling of *Ankylose.*

ancient, ān′shent, *a.* [Fr. *ancien,* L.L. *antianus,* from L. prep. *ante,* before. The final *t* has no right to its place in this word.] That happened or existed in former times, usually at a great distance of time; associated with, or bearing marks of the times of long ago (*ancient* authors); of long standing; having lasted from a remote period; of great age; old (an *ancient* city); having lived long (an *ancient* man—poetical). ∴ *Old* refers to the duration of the thing itself; *ancient,* to the period with which it is associated. *Ancient* is opposed to *modern; old* to *young, new, fresh.* An *old* dress, custom, etc., is one which has lasted a long time, and which still exists; an *ancient* dress, custom, etc., is one which prevailed in former ages.—*n.* A person living at an early period of history (generally in plural, and opposed to *moderns*); a very old man; an elder or person of influence.—**anciently,** ān′shent•li, *adv.* In old times; in times long past.—**ancientness,** ān′shent•nes, *n.* The state or character of being ancient; antiquity.

ancillary, an′sil•la•ri, *a.* [L. *ancillaris,* from *ancilla,* a maid-servant.] Subservient; aiding; auxiliary; subordinate.

ancipital, an•sip′it•al, *a.* [L. *anceps, ancipitis,* two-headed, ambiguous—*an* for *amb,* on both sides, and *caput,* the head.] Doubtful or double; ambiguous; *bot.* two-edged.

ancon, ang′kon, *n.* pl. **ancones,** ang•-kō′nēz. [L. *ancon,* Gr. *angknō,* the elbow.] *Anat.* the upper end of the ulna or elbow; *arch.* a console, cantilever, corbel, or other stone projection.

and, and, *conj.* [A.Sax. *and,* D. *en, ende,* G. *und,* O.H.G. *anti,* all signifying and; Icel. *enda,* and yet, and if]. A particle joining words and sentences, and expressing the relations of connection or addition; sometimes used to introduce interrogative and other clauses.

andalusite, an•da•lū′sīt, *n.* A pellucid mineral of the garnet family, of a gray, green, bluish, flesh or rose-red color: so called from *Andalusia* in Spain, where it was first discovered.

andante, an•dan′tā, *a.* [It. *andante,* walking moderately, from *andare,* to go.] *Music,* moving with a moderate, even, graceful, onward progression.—*n.* A movement or piece composed in *andante* time.—**andantino,** an•-dan•tē′no, *a.* Applied to a movement quicker than *andante.*

Andean, an•dē′an, *a.* Pertaining to the Andes, the great mountain chain of South America.

andiron, and′ī•ėrn, *n.* [O.E. *andiren, aundirin, aundire,* O.F. *andier;* origin unknown.] A horizontal iron bar raised on short legs, with an upright standard at one end, used to support pieces of wood when burning on an open hearth, one being placed on each side; a firedog.

andraecium, an•drē′si•um, *n.* [Gr. *anēr, andros,* a man, a male, and *oikos,* a house.] *Bot.* the male system of a flower; the assemblage of the stamens.

androgynal, androgynous, an•-droj′in•al, an•droj′in•us, *a.* [Gr. *androgynos—anēr, andros,* a man, and *gynē,* woman.] Having two sexes; being male and female; hermaphroditical; having or partaking of the mental and physical characteristics of both sexes.

androsphinx, an′dro•sfingks, *n.* [Gr. *anēr, andros,* a man, and *sphingx,* a sphinx.] A sphinx with a human head.

androus, an′drus, *a.* [Gr. *anēr, andros,* a male.] *Bot.* producing stamens only; staminate; male.

anecdote, an′ek•dōt, *n.* [Gr. *anekdotos,* not published—*a,* neg., *ek,* out, and *dotos,* given, from *didōmi,* to give.] A short story, narrating a detached incident or fact of an interesting nature; a biographical incident; a single passage of private life.—**anecdotage.** The garrulity of dotage, or old age.—**anecdotic, anecdotal, anecdotical,** an•ek•dot′ik, an′ek•dōt•al, an•ek•dot′ik•al, *a.* Pertaining to anecdotes; consisting of or of the nature of anecdotes.—**anecdotist,** an′ek•dōt•ist, *n.* One who deals in anecdotes.

anele, an•ēl′ *v.t.* [O.E. *ele,* L. *oleum,* oil.] Anoint, with extreme unction. [*Shak.*]

anelectric, an•ē•lek′trik, *a.* [Gr. *an,* not, and E. *electric.*] Having no electric properties; nonelectric.

anemia, a•nē′mi•a, *n.* [Gr. *an,* not, and *haima,* blood.] *Med.* a deficiency of blood; a state of the system marked by a deficiency in certain constituents of the blood.—**anemic,** a•ne′mik, *a.* Pertaining to or affected with anemia.

anemograph, a•nem′o•graf, *n.* [Gr. *anemos,* the wind.] An instrument for measuring and recording the force and direction of the wind.—**anemology,** an•e•mol′o•ji, *n.* The doctrine of or a treatise on winds.—**anemometer,** an•e•mom′et•ėr, *n.* An instrument for measuring force and velocity of the wind.—**anemometry,** an•e•mom′et•ri, *n.* The process of determining the pressure or force of the wind by an anemometer.

anemone, a•nem′o•nē, *n.* [Gr. *anemōnē,* the wind-flower, from *anemos,* the wind, being easily stripped of its petals by the wind.] Any plant of the genus *Anemone,* especially *Anemone quinquefolia,* a spring flower with slender stem and delicate whitish blossoms. *Sea anemone.* ACTINIA.

anemophilous, an•e•mof′i•lus, *a.* [Gr. *anemos,* wind, *philos,* loving.] *Bot.* having the pollen conveyed and fertilization effected by the wind.

anemoscope, a•nem′o•skōp, *n.* [Gr. *anemos,* wind, and *skopeō,* to view.] A contrivance which shows the direction of the wind; a weathercock; a wind vane.

anent, a•nent′, *prep.* [A.Sax. *on efn, on emn,* on a level, near, lit. on even. The *t,* as in *ancient,* is superfluous.] About; respecting; regarding.

anergy, an′ėr•ji, *n.* [Gr. *an,* not, *ergon,* work.] *Pathol.* morbid loss of energy.

aneroid, an′ē•roid, *a.* [Gr. *a,* not, *nēros,* moisture, and *eidos,* form.] Dispensing with fluid, as with quicksilver.—*Aneroid barometer,* a barometer the action of which depends on the pressure of the atmosphere on a circular metallic box exhausted of air, hermetically sealed, and having a slightly elastic top, the vacuum serving the purpose of the column of mercury in the ordinary barometer.

anesthesia, an•es•thē′zha, *n.* [Gr. *anaisthēsia—an,* not, and *aisthanomai,* to feel.] Diminished or lost sense of feeling; an artificially produced state of insensibility, especially to the sense of pain.—**anesthetic,** an•es•thet′ik, *a.* Of or belonging to anesthesia; having the power of depriving of feeling or sensation.—*n.* A substance which has the power of depriving of feeling or sensation, as chloroform when its vapor is inhaled.—**anesthetize,** an•es′the•tīz, *v.t.*—*anesthetized, anesthetizing.* To bring under the influence of an anesthetic agent; to render insensible to the feeling of pain.

anew, a•nū′, *adv.* [Prefix *a,* of or on, and *new.*] Over again; in a new form; afresh.

anfractuous, an•frak′tū•us, *a.* [Fr. *anfractueux,* L. *anfractus,* winding—*frango, fractum,* to break.] Winding; full of windings and turnings; sinuous.—**anfractuose,** an•frak′tū•ōs, *a.* *Bot.* twisted or sinuous.—**anfractuosity,** an•frak′tū•os″i•ti, *n.* A state of being anfractuous; *anat.* a sinuous depression.

angel, ān′jel, *n.* [L. *angelus,* Gr. *anggelos,* a messenger.] A divine messenger; a spiritual being employed in the service of God; also applied to an evil being of similar powers; a gold coin, formerly current in England, varying in value from 6*s.* 8*d.* to 10*s.*, bearing the figure of the archangel Michael.—**angelic, angelical,** an•jel′lik, an•jel′ik•al, *a.* Resembling or belonging to, or partaking of the nature and dignity of angels.—*Angelic doctor,* Thomas Aquinas.—**angelica,** an•jel′ik•a, *n.*

[From possessing what were regarded as *angelic* powers or virtues.] Any plant of the genus *Angelica*, tall umbelliferous plants found in both hemispheres, especially *Angelica Archangelica*, cultivated in Europe for its aromatic odor and its medicinal roots, also for its roots, which are candied.—**angelically,** an•jel′ik•al•li, *adv.* In an angelic manner.—**angelology,** ān•jel•ol′o•ji, *n.* A discourse on angels, or the doctrine of angelic beings.—**Angelus,** an′jel•us, *n. R. Cath. Ch.* a solemn devotion in memory of the Incarnation; the bell tolled to indicate the time when the Angelus is to be recited.—**angelfish,** ān′jel•fish, *n.* A fish nearly allied to the sharks: so called from its pectoral fins, which are so large as to spread like wings.

anger, ang′gėr, *n.* [Originally grief, from Icel. *angr*, grief, sorrow, *angra*, to grieve, annoy; Dan. *anger*, sorrow; same root as in A.Sax. *ange*, vexed, narrow, G. *enge*, narrow; L. *ango*, to trouble, *angor*, vexation, Gr. *angchō*, to choke.] A violent, revengeful passion or emotion, excited by a real or supposed injury to one's self or others; passion; ire; choler; rage; wrath. ∴ *Anger* is more general and expresses a less strong feeling than *wrath* and *rage*, both of which imply a certain outward manifestation, and the latter violence and want of self-command.—*v.t.* To excite to anger; to rouse resentment in; to make angry; to exasperate.—**angrily,** [*Tenn.*] —**angrily,** ang′gri•li, *adv.* In an angry manner.—**angriness,** ang′gri•nes, *n.* The state of being angry.—**angry,** ang′gri, *a.* Feeling resentment; provoked; showing anger; caused by anger; raging; tumultuous.

Angevin, an′je•vin, *a.* Of or pertaining to *Anjou*, a former province of France.

angina, an•jī′na, *n.* [L. from *ango*, to choke. ANGER.] *Med.* an inflammatory affection of the throat or fauces.—*Angina pectoris*, a fatal disease characterized by paroxysms of intense pain and a feeling of constriction in the chest. (Also pron. an′ji•na.)

angiocarpous, an′ji•ō•kär″pus, *a.* [Gr. *angeion*, a capsule, and *karpos*, fruit.] *Bot.* having a fruit whose seed vessels are enclosed within a covering that does not form a part of themselves, as the acorn.

angiography, angiology, an•ji•og′ra•fi, an•ji•ol′o•ji, *n.* [Gr. *angeion*, a vessel.] *Med.* a description of the vessels of the body.

angioma, an•ji•ō′ma, *n.* [Gr. *angeion*, a vessel.] *Med.* a tumor produced by the enlargement of a blood vessel.

angiosperm, an′ji•ō•spėrm, *n.* [Gr. *angeion*, a vessel, and *sperma*, seed.] *Bot.* a plant which has its seeds enclosed in a seed vessel.—**angiospermous,** an′ji•ō•spėrm″us, *a. Bot.* having seeds enclosed in a seed vessel.

angle, ang′gl, *n.* [L. *angulus*, a corner. ANCHOR.] The point where two lines or planes meet that do not run in the same straight line; a corner; the degree of opening or divergence of two straight lines which meet one another.—**angled,** ang′gld, *a.* Having angles: used chiefly in compounds.—**angular,** ang′gū•lėr, *a.* Having an angle or angles; having corners; pointed; consisting of or forming an angle.—*Angular motion, angular velocity*, the motion or velocity of a body or a point moving circularly.—**angularity,** ang•gū•lar′i•ti, *n.* The quality of being angular.—**angularly,** ang′gū•lėr•li, *adv.* In an angular manner.—**angularness,** ang′gū•lėr•nes, *n.* The quality of being angular. —**angulate, angulated,** ang′gū•lāt, ang′gū•lāt•ed, *a.* Angled; cornered.—**angulation,** ang•gū•lā′shon, *n.* The state of being angulated; that which is angulated.—**angle iron,** *n.* A piece of rolled iron in the shape of the letter L, used for forming the joints of iron plates in girders, boilers, etc., to which it is riveted.

angle, ang′gl, *v.i.—angled, angling.* [A. Sax. *angel*, a fishhook; G. *angel*, Icel. *öngull*, a hook; from a root meaning crooked, seen also in ANCHOR.] To fish with an angle, or with line and hook.—**angler,** ang′glėr, *n.* One who fishes with an angle; a fish having long filamentous appendages in its head, which attract the smaller fishes and thus provide it with prey. —**angleworm,** ang′gl•wėrm, *n.* An earth worm used as bait.—**angling,** ang′gling, *n.* The act or art of fishing with a rod and line.

Angles, ang′glz, *n. pl.* [A.Sax. *Angle*, *Engle*, the Angles.] A Low German tribe who in the fifth century and subsequently crossed over to Britain along with bands of Saxons, Jutes, and others, and colonized a great part of what from them has received the name of England.—**Anglian,** ang′gli•an, *a.* Of or pertaining to the tribe of the Angles.—*n.* A member of the tribe of the Angles.

Anglican, ang′glik•an, *a.* [L.L. *anglicus*, English.] English; pertaining to the English Church.—*Anglican Church*, the Church of England and the Protestant Episcopal churches in Ireland, Scotland, and the colonies; sometimes including also the Episcopal churches of the United States.—*n.* A member of the Anglican Church. —**Anglicanism,** ang′glik•an•izm, *n.* The principles of or adherence to the Established Church of England.—**Anglicism,** ang′gli•sizm, *n.* The quality of being English; an English idiom.—**Anglicize, Anglify,** ang′gli•sīz, ang′gli•fī, *v.t.—anglicized, anglicizing.* To make English; to render conformable to the English idiom or to English analogies.

Anglo-, ang′glō, prefix. [L.L. *Anglus*, an Englishman.] A prefix signifying *English*, or connected with England. —**Anglo-American,** *n.* A descendant from English ancestors born in America or the United States: used also as an adj.—**Anglo-Catholic,** *n.* A member of the Church of England who lays stress on the claim that his church is historically a part of the Catholic Church: used also as an adj.—**Anglo-Catholicism,** *n.* The principles or doctrines of the Anglo-Catholics.—**Anglo-Indian,** *n.* One of the English race born or resident in the East Indies. Also as an adj.—**Anglo-Irish,** *n. pl.* English people born or resident in Ireland; descendants of parents English on the one side and Irish on the other. Also as an adj.—**Anglomania,** ang•glō•mā′ni•a, *n.* [Gr. *mania*, madness.] An excessive or undue attachment to, respect for, or imitation of Englishmen or English institutions and customs by a foreigner.—**Anglophobia,** ang•glō•fō′bi•a, *n.* [Gr. *phobos*, fear.] An excessive hatred or dread of English people, customs, or institutions.—**Anglo-Saxon,** *n.* [ANGLES, SAXON.] One of the nation formed by the union of the Angles, Saxons, and other early Teutonic settlers in Britain, or one of their descendants; one belonging to the English race; the language of the Anglo-Saxons, or the English language in its first stage.—*a.* Pertaining to the Anglo-Saxons or to the oldest form of English.

Angora, an•gō′ra, *n.* A light cloth, made from the wool or long silky hair of the Angora goat, a native of Asia Minor.—**Angora cat.** A large variety of the domestic cat originally from Angora, with beautiful long silky hair.

angostura, ang•gos•tū′ra, *a.* Belonging to or brought from the town of Angostura in Venezuela—an epithet of a kind of bark having febrifugal properties and of a kind of bitters made from it.

angrily, angriness, angry. See ANGER.

angstrom unit, angstrom, ang′strum. [After A. J. Angström (1814-1874), Sw. physicist.] One tenth of a millimicron or one hundred-millionth of a centimeter; a unit used to express the length of light waves.

anguish, ang′gwish, *n.* [O.E. *anguis*, *angoise*, Fr. *angoisse*, from L. *angustia*, a strait, perplexity, from *angustus*, narrow; root *ang* as in E. *anger*.] Extreme pain, either of body or mind; any keen affection of the emotions or feelings ('an *anguish* of delight.' *Thack.*)—**anguish,**† ang′gwish, *v.t.* To distress extremely.

angular, angularity, etc. See ANGLE.

angustifoliate, ang•gus′ti•fō′li•āt, *a.* [L. *angustus*, narrow, and *folium*, a leaf.] *Bot.* having narrow leaves.

anhydrous, an•hī′drus, *a.* [Gr. *anydros*, dry—neg. prefix *an*, and *hydōr*, water.] Destitute of water; specifically, *chem.* destitute of the water of crystallization.—**anhydride,** an•hī′drid, *n.* One of a class of oxygen compounds in which there is no water.—**anhydrite,** an•hī′drīt, *n.* Anhydrous sulfate of calcium, a mineral resembling a coarse-grained granite.

anil, an′il, *n.* [Sp. *anil*, Ar. *neel*, Skr. *nîlam*, indigo, *nîli*, the indigo-plant.] A shrub from whose leaves and stalks the West Indian indigo is made.—**aniline,** an′i•lin, *n.* A substance obtained from indigo and other organic substances, though the aniline of commerce is obtained from benzol, a product of coal tar. It furnishes a number of brilliant dyes.

anile, an′īl, *a.* [L. *anilis*, from *anus*, an old woman.] Old-womanish; aged; imbecile.—**anility,** a•nil′i•ti, *n.* The state of being anile.

animadvert, an″i•mad•vėrt′, *v.i.* [L. *anidmadverto—animus*, mind, and *adverto*, to turn to.] To perceive or take cognizance; usually, to make remark by way of criticism; to pass strictures or criticisms (followed by *on*, *upon*). —**animadversion,** an″i•mad•vėr′-shon, *n.* The act of one who animadverts; a remark by way of criticism or censure; stricture; censure.

animal, an′i•mal, *n.* [L. *animal*, a living being, from *anima*, air, breath, life, the soul, from a root *an*, to breathe or blow.] A living being characterized by sensation and voluntary motion; an inferior or irrational being, in contradistinction to man; also often popularly used to signify a quadruped.—*a.* Belonging or relating to animals (*animal* functions); pertaining to the merely sentient part of a living being, as distinguished from the intellectual or spiritual part (*animal* passions); of or pertaining to, or consisting of, the flesh of animals.—**animalism,** an′i•mal•izm, *n.* The state of a mere animal; the state of being actuated by sensual appetites only; sensuality. —**animality,** an•i•mal′i•ti, *n.* The state of being an animal; *physiol.* those vital phenomena which, superadded to vegetative powers, constitute animal existence.—**animalization,** an′i•mal•iz•ā″shon, *n.* The act of animalizing; conversion into animal matter by the process of assimilation.—**animalize,** an′i•mal•īz, *v.t.* —*animalized, animalizing.* To give animal life to; to convert into animal matter; to bring under the sway of animal appetites.

animalcule, an•i•mal′kūl, *n.* [L.L. *animalculum*, dim. of L. *animal*, an animal.] A minute animal, especially one that is microscopic or invisible to the naked eye.—**animalcular,** an•i•mal′kū•lėr, *a.* Pertaining to or resembling animalcules.—**animalculum,** an•i•mal′kū•lum, *n.* pl. **animalcula,** an•i•mal′kū•la. An animalcule.

animate, an′i•māt, *v.t.—animated, animating.* [L. *animatus*, animated, pp. of *animo*, to fill with breath. ANIMAL.] To give natural life to; to quicken; to make alive; to give life, spirit, or liveliness to; to heighten the powers or effect of; to stimulate or incite; to inspirit; rouse.—**animate,** an′i•māt, *a.* Alive; possessing animal life.—**animated,** an′i•māt•ed, *a.* Endowed with animal life; lively; vigorous; full of spirit (an *animated* discourse).—**animater, animator,** an′i•māt•ėr, *n.* One who animates.—**animating,** an′i•māt•ing, *a.* Giving life; infusing spirit; enlivening; rousing.—**animatingly,** an′i•māt•ing•li, *adv.* So as to animate. —**animation,** an•i•mā′shon, *n.* The act of animating or state of being animated; state of having life; liveliness; briskness; vivacity.

animé, an′i•mā, *n.* [Sp.] A resin exuding from a large American tree, called in the West Indies *locust tree.* It produces a fine varnish. The name is also given to Indian copal.

animism, an′i•mizm, *n.* [L. *anima*, the soul.] The old hypothesis of a force (*Anima mundi*, soul of the world) immaterial but inseparable from matter, and giving to matter its form and movements; the attribution of spirit or soul to inanimate things.—**animist,** an′i•mist, *n.* One who holds to or believes in animism. —**animistic,** an•i•mist′ik, *a.* Pertaining to, or founded on, animism.

animosity, an•i•mos′i•ti, *n.* [L. *animositas*, from *animosus*, full of courage, ardent, from *animus*, the mind, courage, pride.] Courage‡; rancorous feeling; bitter and active enmity.

animus, an′i•mus, *n.* [L., spirit, temper.] Intention; purpose; spirit; temper; especially, hostile spirit or angry temper.

anion, an′i•on, *n.* [Gr. *ana*, upward, and *iōn*, going.] *Elect.* the element of an electrolyte which is evolved at the positive pole or *anode*.

anise, an′is, *n.* [Fr., from L. *anisum.*] An annual umbelliferous plant (*Pimpinella Anisum*), the seeds of which have an aromatic smell and a pleasant warm taste, and are employed in the manufacture of liqueurs.—**aniseed,** an′i•sēd, *n.* The seed of the anise.— **anisette,** an•i•set, *n.* [Fr.] A liqueur flavored with anise.

anisotrope, anisotropic, an′i•sō-trōp, an•i•sō•trōp′ik, *a.* Same as *Aelotropic.*

ankle, ang′kl, *n.* [A.Sax. *ancleow*, O. Fris. *ankel*, Dan. and Sw. *ankel*, G. *enkel*; from a root *ang*, meaning crooked. ANCHOR.] The joint which connects the foot with the leg.— **anklet,** ang′klet, *n.* An ornament, support, or protection for the ankle.

ankylosis, ang•ki•lō′sis, *n.* [Gr., from *angkylos*, crooked.] Stiffness and immovability of a joint; morbid adhesion of the articular ends of contiguous bones.—**ankylose,** ang′-ki•lōs, *v.t.—ankylosed, ankylosing.* To affect with ankylosis.—*v.i.* To become ankylosed.—**ankylotic,** ang•-ki•lot′ik, *a.* Pertaining to ankylosis.

anna, an′na, *n.* In the East Indies, the sixteenth part of a rupee, or about 1 English penny.

annals, an′nalz, *n. pl.* [L. *annales* (*libri*, books, understood), *annalis*, pertaining to a year, from *annus*, a year.] A history or relation of events in chronological order, each event being recorded under the year in which it happened.—**annalist,** an′nal•ist, *n.* A writer of annals.— **annalistic,** an•nal•ist′ik, *a.* Pertaining or peculiar to an annalist.

annats, annates, an′nats, an′nāts, *n. pl.* [L.L. *annata*, from L. *annus*, a year.] The first year's income of a see or benefice.

annatto, an•nät′tō, *n.* A small tropical American tree, the seeds of which yield an orange-red dyestuff.

anneal, an•nēl′, *v.t.* [A.Sax. *anaelan*, *onaelan*, to set on fire, to anneal—*an* or *on*, on, and *ælan*, to kindle.] To heat, as glass or iron vessels, in an oven or furnace, and then cool slowly, for the purpose of rendering less brittle; to temper by a gradually diminishing heat; to heat in order to fix colors; to bake.

annelid, annelidan, an′ne•lid, an•-nel′i•dan, *n.* [L. *annellus*, a little ring, and Gr. *eidos*, form.] One of an extensive division or class of annulose animals, so called because their bodies are formed of a great number of small rings, as in the earthworm.

annex, an•neks′, *v.t.* [L. *annecto*, *annexum*, to bind to—*ad*, to, and *necto*, *nexum*, to bind.] To unite at the end; to subjoin; to unite, as a smaller thing to a greater; to connect, especially as a consequence (to *annex* a penalty).—*n.* Something annexed.—**annexation,** an•neks•ā′-shon, *n.* The act of annexing; what is annexed; addition; union.—**annexationist,** an•neks•ā′shon•ist, *n.* One favorable to annexation, as of a portion of another country to his own.

annihilate, an•nī′hil•āt, *v.t.—annihilated, annihilating.* [L. *annihilo—ad*, to, and *nihil*, nothing.] To reduce to nothing; to destroy the existence of; to cause to cease to be; to destroy the form or peculiar distinctive properties of.—**annihilable,** an•-nī′hil•a•bl, *a.* Capable of being annihilated.—**annihilation,** an•nī′-hi•lā•shon, *n.* The act of annihilating or the state of being annihilated.— **annihilator,** an•nī′hil•āt•ėr, *n.* One who, or that which annihilates.

anniversary, an•ni•vėrs′a•ri, *a.* [L. *anniversarius—annus*, a year, and *verto*, *versum*, to turn.] Returning with the year at a stated time; annual; yearly.—*n.* A stated day on which some event is annually celebrated; the annual celebration in honor of an event.

annotate, an′nō•tāt, *v.t.—annotated, annotating.* [L. *annoto*, *annotatum— ad*, to, and *noto*, to note.] To comment upon; to make remarks on by notes.—*v.i.* To act as an annotator; to make annotations or notes (with *on*).—**annotation,** an•nō•tā′ shon, *n.* The act of annotating or making notes on; an illustrative note on some passage of a book.—**annotator,** an′nō•tāt•ėr, *n.* A writer of annotations or notes; a commentator.

announce, an•nouns′, *v.t.—announced, announcing.* [Fr. *annoncer*, from L. *annuncio—ad*, and *nuncio*, to tell, from *nuncius*, a messenger.] To publish; to proclaim; to give notice or first notice of.—**announcement,** an•nouns′ment, *n.* The act of announcing or giving notice; proclamation; publication.—**announcer,** an•-nouns′ėr, *n.* One that announces; a proclaimer.

annoy, an•noi′, *v.t.* [O.Fr. *anoier*, from *anoi*, annoyance, vexation, from L. *in odio*, in hatred, common in such phrases as *est mihi in odio*, it is hateful to me. ODIUM.] To torment or disturb, especially by continued or repeated acts; to tease, vex, pester, or molest.—*n.* Molestation; annoyance (chiefly a poetical word).—**annoyance,** an•noi′ans, *n.* The act of annoying; the state of being annoyed; that which annoys; trouble.—**annoyer,** an•noi′ėr, *n.* One that annoys.—**annoying,** an•noi′ing, *a.* Vexatious; troublesome.

annual, an′nū•al, *a.* [L.L. *annualis,* from L. *annus,* a year.] Returning every year; coming yearly; lasting or continuing only one year or one yearly season; performed in a year; reckoned by the year.—*n.* A plant that grows from seed, flowers, and perishes in the course of the same season; a literary production published annually.—**annually,** an′nū•al•li, *adv.* Yearly; returning every year; year by year.

annuity, an•nū′i•ti, *n.* [Fr. *annuité,* from *annus,* a year.] A yearly payment of money which a person receives for life or for a term of years, the person being usually entitled to such payment in consideration of money advanced to those who pay.—**annuitant,** an•nū′it•ant, *n.* One receiving an annuity.

annul, an•nul′, *v.t.*—*annulled, annulling.*[Fr. *annuler,* from L. *ad nullum,* to nothing.] To reduce to nothing or annihilate (*Mil.*)‡; to make void; to nullify; to abrogate; cancel (laws, decrees, compacts, etc.).—**annulment,** an•nul′ment, *n.* The act of.

annular, † an′nū•lėr, *a.* [L. *annularis,* from *annulus, anulus,* dim. of *anus,* a ring, akin to *annus,* a year, ANNUAL.] Having the form of a ring; pertaining to a ring.—*Annular eclipse,* an eclipse of the sun in which a ring of light formed by the sun's disk is visible around the dark shadow of the moon.—**annularly,** an′nū•lėr•li, *adv.* In the manner of a ring.—**annulate, annulated,** an′nū•lāt, an′nū•lāt•ed, *a.* Furnished with rings, or circles like rings; having belts.—**annulation,** an•nū•lā′shon, *n.* A circular or ringlike formation.—**annulet,** an′nū•let, *n.* [A dim. from L. *annulus,* a ring.] A little ring or ringlike body.—**annulose,** an′nū•lōs, *a.* Furnished with rings; having a body composed of rings; a term applied to animals forming a subkingdom which embraces the worms, leeches, crabs, spiders, insects.

annunciate, an•nun′shi•āt, *v.t.*—*annunciated, annunciating.* [ANNOUNCE.] To bring tidings of; to announce. —**annunciation,** an•nun′shi•ā″shon, *n.* The act of announcing; announcement. [*cap.*] The tidings brought by the angel to Mary of the Incarnation of Christ; the church festival in memory of this announcement, falling on March 25.—**annunciator,** an•nun′shi•āt•ėr, *n.* One who announces.

anode, an′ōd, *n.* [Gr. *ana,* upwards, and *hodos,* a way.] The part of the surface of an electrolyte which the electric current enters: opposed to *cathode.*—**anodize,** an′ōd•īz, *v.t.* To coat a metal with a protective film by subjecting it to electrolytic action as the anode of a cell.

anodyne, an′ō•dīn, *n.* [Gr. neg. prefix *an,* and *odynē,* pain.] Any medicine which allays pain.—*a.* Assuaging pain.

anoint, a•noint′, *v.t.* [O.E. *anointen, enointen*; O.Fr. *enoindre,* part. *enoint,* from L. *inungere, inunctum,* from *in,* in, on, and *ungo, unctum,* to anoint. UNGUENT.] To pour oil upon; to smear or rub with oil or unctuous substances; to consecrate by unction, or the use of oil.—**anointer,** a•noint′ėr, *n.* One who anoints.—**anointment,** a•noint′ment, *n.* The act of anointing.

anomaly, a•nom′a•li, *n.* [Fr. *anomalie*; L. *anomalia,* Gr. *anōmalia,* inequality, neg. prefix *an,* and *homalos,* equal, similar, from *homos,* the same. SAME.] Deviation from the common rule; something abnormal; irregularity; *astron.* the angular distance of a planet from its perihelion, as seen from the sun; also the angle measuring apparent irregularities in the motion of a planet.—**anomalism,** a•nom′al•izm, *n.* An anomaly; a deviation from rule.—**anomalistic,** a•nom′a•list″ik, *a.* Pertaining to an anomaly.—*Anomalistic year,* the interval between two occasions when the earth is in perihelion, rather longer than the civil year.—**anomalous,** a•nom′a•lus, *a.* [L. *anomalus,* Gr. *anomalos.*] Forming an anomaly; deviating from a general rule, method, or analogy; irregular; abnormal.—**anomalously,** a•nom′a•lus•li, *adv.* —**anomalousness,** a•nom′a•lus•nes, *n.*

anon, a•non′, *adv.* [O.E. *anan, anoon,* A.Sax. *on ân, an ân*=on one, that is, without break.] Forthwith; immediately; quickly; at another time; thereafter; sometimes.—*Ever and anon,* every now and then.

anonymous, a•non′im•us, *a.* [Gr. *anōnymos*—neg. prefix *an,* and *onoma,* name. NAME.] Wanting a name; without any name acknowledged as that of author, contributor, and the like.—**anonymously,** a•non′im•us•li, *adv.* In an anonymous manner; without a name.—**anonyme,** an′on•īm, *n.* An assumed or false name.—**anonymity, anonymousness,** an•o•nim′i•ti, a•non′im•us•nes, *n.* The state of being anonymous.

anorthic, an•or′thik, *a.* [Gr. neg. prefix *an,* and *orthos,* straight, right.] Without right angles; *mineral.* having unequal oblique axes.—**anorthite,** an•or′thīt, *n.* A mineral of the feldspar family.

anosmia, an•os′mi•a, *n.* [Gr. neg. prefix *an,* and *osmē,* smell.] *Med.* a loss of the sense of smell.

another, an•uTH′ėr, *a.* [*An,* indefinite art., and *other.*] Not the same; different; one more, in addition to a former number; any other; any one else. Often used without a noun, as a substitute for the name of a person or thing, and much used in opposition to *one*; as, *one* went *one* way, *another another.* Also frequently used with *one* in a reciprocal sense; as, 'Love *one another*'; any other; some other.

anserine, an′sėr•īn, *a.* [L. *anserinus,* from *anser,* a goose.] Relating to or resembling a goose, or the skin of a goose: applied to the skin when roughened by cold or disease.—**anserous,**† an′sėr•us, *a.* Of or pertaining to a goose; foolish; silly.

answer, an′sėr, *v.t.* [A.Sax. *andswerian,* to answer—*and,* a prefix meaning against (=*a* in *along,* L. *ante,* before, Gr. *anti,* against), and *swerian,* to swear.] To speak or write in return to; to reply to; to refute; to say or do in reply; to act in compliance with, or in fulfilment or satisfaction of; to render account to or for; to be security for (*Shak.*); to be equivalent or adequate to; to serve; to suit.—*v.i.* To reply; to speak or write by way of return; to respond to some call; to be fit or suitable.—*To answer for,* to be accountable for; to guarantee.—*To answer to,* to be known by; to correspond to, in the way of resemblance, fitness, or correlation.—**answer,** an′sėr, *n.* A reply; that which is said, written, or done, in return to a call, question, argument, challenge, allegation, petition, prayer, or address; the result of an arithmetical or mathematical operation; a solution; something done in return for, or in consequence of, something else; *law,* a counterstatement of facts in a course of pleadings.—**answerable,** an′sėr•a•bl, *a.* Capable of being answered: obliged to give an account; amenable; responsible; correspondent.—**answerableness,** an′sėr•a•bl•nes, *n.* The quality of being answerable.—**answerably,** an′sėr•a•bli, *adv.* In due proportion, correspondence, or conformity; suitably.

ant, ant, *n.* [From A.Sax, *aemete,* an emmet (like *aunt,* from L. *amita*). EMMET.] An emmet; a pismire; a hymenopterous insect living in communities which consist of males, females, and neuters. The name is also given to the neuropterous insects more correctly called *Termites.*—**antbear,** *n.* A kind of large anteater.—**anteater,** *n.* A quadruped that eats ants, especially an edentate animal (genus *Myrmecophaga*) which feeds on ants and other insects, catching them by thrusting among them the long tongue covered with a viscid saliva.—**ant lion,** *n.* The larva of a neuropterous insect which prepares a kind of pitfall for the destruction of ants, etc.

antacid, ant•as′id, *n.* [*Anti,* against, and *acid.*] An alkali, or a remedy for acidity in the stomach.—*a.* Counteracting acidity.

antagonist, an•tag′ō•nist, *n.* [Gr. *antagōnistēs*—*anti,* against, and *agōnistēs,* a champion, a combatant, from *agōn,* a contest (whence *agony*).] One who contends with another; an opponent; a competitor; an adversary. ∴ *Syn.* under ADVERSARY.—*a.* Counteracting; opposing (said of muscles).—**antagonistic,** an•tag′ō•nist″ik, *a.* Contending against; acting in opposition; opposing.—**antagonistic,** *n.* A muscle whose action counteracts that of another.—**antagonistically,** an•tag′-ō•nis″tik•al•li, *adv.* In an antagonistical manner.—**antagonize,** an•tag′-ō•niz, *v.i.*—*antagonized, antagonizing* To contend against; to act in opposition.—**antagonism,** an•tag′ō•nizm, *n.* Character of being an antagonist or antagonistic; counteraction or contrariety of things or principles.

antalkali, ant•al′ka•li, *n.* [*Anti* against, and *alkali.*] A substance which neutralizes an alkali.—**antalkaline,** ant•al′ka•līn, *a.* Having the property of neutralizing alkalies.

antarctic, ant•ärk′tik, *a.* [L. *antarcticus*, Gr. *antarktikos*—*anti*, against, and *arktos*, the north. ARCTIC.] Opposite to the northern or arctic pole; relating to the southern pole or to the region near it, and applied to a circle parallel to the equator and distant from the pole 23° 28′.

ante, an′tē, *prefix.* [L. *ante*, before, in front.] Before.—*n.* Poker stake.

antebellum, an′ti•bel′lum, *a.* [*ante*, before, and *bellum*, war.] Before the war; before the American Civil War.

antecede, an•tē•sēd′, *v.t.*—*anteceded, anteceding.* [L. *ante*, before, and *cedo*, to go. CEDE.] To go before in time; to precede.—**antecedence,** an•tē•sē′dens, *n.* The act or state of going before in time; precedence. —**antecedent,** an•tē•sē′dent, *a.* Going before; prior; anterior; preceding.—*n.* One who or that which goes before in time or place; *gram.* the noun to which a relative or other pronoun refers; *pl.* the earlier events of a man's life; previous course, conduct, or avowed principles.

antechamber, anteroom, an′tē•-chām•bėr, an′tē•röm, *n.* A chamber or room before or leading to another apartment.

antedate, an′tē•dāt, *n.* [Prefix *ante*, before, and *date.*] Prior date; a date antecedent to another.—*v.t. antedated, antedating.* To date before the true time or beforehand; to give an earlier date than the real one to; to anticipate or give effect to before the due time.

antediluvian, an′tē•di•lū″vi•an, *a.* [L. *ante*, before, and *diluvium*, a flood.] Existing, happening, or relating to what happened before the deluge.—*n.* One who lived before the deluge.

antelope, an′tē•lōp, *n.* [Doubtfully derived from a Gr. *antholōns*, an antelope, supposed to be compounded of *anthos*, a flower, and *ōps*, an eye.] A name applied to many species of ruminant mammals resembling the deer in general appearance, but essentially different in nature from them, having hollow, unbranched horns that are not deciduous.

antemeridian, an′tē•me•rid″i•an, *a.* [L. *ante*, before, and *meridies*, noon.] Being before noon; pertaining to the forenoon.

antenna, an•ten′na, *n.* pl. **antennae,** an•ten′nē. [L. *antenna*, a sail-yard.] One of the hornlike filaments that project from the head in insects, crustacea, and myriapods, and are considered as organs of touch and hearing; a feeler.

antepast, an′tē•past, *n.* [L. *ante*, before, *pastus*, food.] A foretaste.

antependium, ant•ē•pen′di•um, *n.* [L. *ante*, before, and *pendo*, to hang.] The hanging with which the front of an altar is covered.

antepenult, an′tē•pē•nult, *n.* [L. *ante*, before, *pene*, almost, and *ultimus*, last.] The last syllable of a word except two.—**antepenultimate,** an′-tē•pē•nul″ti•māt, *a.* Pertaining to the last syllable but two.—*n.* The antepenult.

anterior, an•tē′ri•ėr, *a.* [L., a comparative from *ante*, before.] Before in time; prior; antecedent; before in place; in front.—**anteriority,** an•-tē′ri•or″i•ti, *n.* The state of being anterior in time or place.—**anteriorly,** an•tē′ri•ėr•li, *adv.* In an anterior manner; before.

anteroom, an′tē•röm, *n.* See ANTECHAMBER.

anteroposterior, an•tē″rō•pos•tē′-ri•ėr, *a.* [L. *anterior*, from *ante*, before, and *posterior*, from *post*, behind.] Lying in a direction from behind forward.

anthelion, ant•hē′li•on, *n.* pl. **anthelia,** ant•hē′li•a. [Gr. *anti*, opposite to, and *hēlios*, the sun.] A luminous ring, or rings, caused by the diffraction of light, seen in alpine and polar regions opposite the sun when rising or setting.

anthelmintic, an•thel•min′tic, *a.* [Gr. *anti*, against, and *helmius*, *helminthos*, a worm.] *Med.* destroying or expelling worms in the intestines. —*n.* A vermifuge; a remedy for worms in the intestines.

anthem, an′them, *n.* [O.E. *antempne*, *antemne*, *antefne*, etc., A.Sax. *antefen*, an anthem; from L.L. *antiphona*, from Gr. *antiphōnon*, an antiphon—*anti*, against, and *phōne*, sound, the voice.] A hymn sung in alternate parts; in modern usage, a sacred tune or piece of music set to words taken from the Psalms or other parts of the Scriptures.

anther, an′thėr. *n.* [Gr. *anthēros*, flowery, from *anthos*, a flower.] The essential part of the stamen of a plant containing the pollen or fertilizing dust.

anthesis, an•thē′sis, *n.* [Gr., from *antheō*, to bloom, from *anthos*, a flower.] The period when flowers expand; expansion into a flower.

anthocyanin, an•tho•sī′an•in, *n.* [Gr. *anthos* a flower, and *kyanos*, blue.] The blue coloring matter of plants.

anthodium, an•thō′di•um, *n.* [Gr. *anthōdēs*, from *anthos*, a flower.] *Bot.* the head of flowers of composite plants, as of a thistle or daisy.

anthology, an•thol′o•ji, *n.* [Gr. *anthologia*, from *anthologos*, flower-gathering—*anthos*, a flower, and *legō*, to gather.] A collection of passages from authors; a collection of selected poems.—**anthological,** an•tho•loj′ik•al, *a.* Pertaining to anthology.

anthophore, an′tho•fōr, *n.* [Gr. *anthos*, a flower, and *phereīn*, to bear.] *Bot.* a columnar process arising from the bottom of the calyx, and having at its apex the petals, stamens, and pistil.

anthracene, an′thra•sēn, *n.* [ANTHRACITE.] A hydrocarbon obtained from coal tar and furnishing alizarine.

anthracite, an′thra•sīt, *n.* [Gr. *anthrax*, *anthrakos*, coal.] Glance or blind coal, a nonbituminous coal of a shining luster, approaching to metallic, and which burns without smoke, with a weak or no flame, and with intense heat.—**anthracitic,** an•thra•sit′ik, *a.* Pertaining to anthracite.

anthrax, an′thraks, *n.* [Gr.] *Med.* a carbuncle; a malignant ulcer.

anthropogeny, an•thrō•poj′en•i, *n.* [Gr. *anthrōpos*, a man, and root *gen.* to beget.] the science of the origin and development of man.

anthropography, an•thrō•pog′ra•fi, *n.* [Gr. *anthrōpos*, a man, and *graphē*, a description.] A description of man or of the human race; ethnography.

anthropoid, an′thrō•poid, *a.* [Gr. *anthrōpos*, a man, and *eidos*, resemblance.] Resembling man: specifically applied to such apes as most closely approach the human race.

anthropology, an•thrō•pol′o•ji, *n.* [Gr. *anthrōpos*, a man, and *logos*, discourse.] The science of man and mankind, including the study of the physical and mental constitution of man, or his whole nature, as exhibited both in the present and the past.—**anthropologic, anthropological,** an•thrō′pō•loj″ik, an•-thrō′pō•loj″ik•al, *a.* Pertaining to anthropology.—**anthropologist,** an•-thrō•pol′o•jist, *n.* One who writes on or studies anthropology.

anthropometry, an•thrō•pom′et•ri, *n.* [Gr. *anthrōpos*, a man, and *metron*, measure.] The measurement of the human body.

anthropomorphism, an•thrō′pō•-morf″izm, *n.* [Gr. *anthrōpos*, a man, and *morphē*, form.] The representation or conception of the Deity under a human form, or with human attributes and affections.—**anthropomorphic,** an′thrō•pō•mor″fik, *a.* Relating to or characterized by anthropomorphism; resembling man. —**anthropomorphist,** an•thrō′pō•-morf″ist, *n.* One who believes that the Supreme Being has a human form and human attributes.— **anthropomorphitism,** an•thrō′pō•-morf″it•izm, *n.* The doctrines of anthropomorphites.—**anthropomorphous,** an•thrō′pō•morf″us, *a.* Having the figure of or resemblance to a man.

anthropophagi, an•thrō•pof′a•ji, *n. pl.* [Gr. *anthrōpos*, a man, and *phagō*, to eat.] Maneaters; cannibals; men that eat human flesh.— **anthropophagite,** an•thrō•pof′a•jīt *n.* A cannibal.—**anthropophagous,** an•-thrō•pof′a•gus, *a.* Feeding on human flesh.—**anthropophagy,** an•thrō•-pof′a•ji, *n.* Cannibalism.

antiaircraft, an′ti•âr″kraft, *adj.* Used for defense against enemy aircraft.

antiar, an′ti•är, *n.* [Javanese.] The milky juice which exudes from wounds made in the upas-tree, and which is one of the most acrid and virulent vegetable poisons.

antibiotic, an′ti•bi•ot″ik, *n.* A substance produced by living organisms (a bacterium or fungus) and having the power to kill or inhibit the growth of bacteria, as penicillin.

antibody, an′ti•bod″i, *n.* [*anti* and *body*.] A substance produced by body tissue as a reaction to the introduction of a foreign substance; an antigen.

antic, an′tik, *a.* [A form of *antique*, L. *antiquus*, ancient. The modern sense of this word is derived from the grotesque figures seen in the antique sculpture of the Middle Ages. ANTIQUE.] Odd; fanciful; grotesque; fantastic (tricks, postures).—*n.* An absurd or ridiculous gesture, an odd gesticulation; a piece of buffoonery; a caper.

antichlor, an′ti•klōr, *n.* [Gr. *anti*, against, and the *chlor-* of *chlorine*.] A substance employed to remove, or neutralize the effects of, the free chlorine left in goods bleached by means of chloride of lime, etc.

antichrist, an′ti•krīst, *n.* An opponent of Christ; a person or power antagonistic to Christ.—**antichristian,** an•ti•kris′tyan, *a.* Opposite to or opposing the Christian religion.

anticipate, an•tis′i•pāt, *v.t.*—*anticipated, anticipating.* [L. *anticipo* for *antecipo*, to *take* beforehand—*ante*, before, and *capio*, to take.] To be before in doing something; to prevent or preclude by prior action; to forestall; to realize beforehand; to foretaste or foresee; to look forward to; to expect.—*v.i.* To treat of something, as in a narrative, before the proper time.—**anticipant,** an•tis′i•pant, *a.* Anticipating; anticipative.—**anticipation,** an•tis′i•pā″shon, *n.* The act of anticipating; expectation; foretaste; realization beforehand; previous notion; preconceived opinion.—**anticipative,** an•tis′i•pāt•iv, *a.* Anticipating or tending to anticipate; containing anticipation.—**anticipatively,** an•tis′i•pāt•iv•li, *adv.* By anticipation.—**anticipator,** an•tis′i•pāt•ėr, *n.* One who anticipates.—**anticipatory,** an•tis′i•pā•to•ri, *a.* Anticipative.

anticlimax, an•ti•klī′maks, *n.* A passage in which the ideas first increase in force, and then terminate in something less important and striking: opposed to *climax*.

anticlinal, an•ti•klī′nal, *a.* [Gr. *anti*, opposite, and *klinō*, to incline.] Inclining in opposite directions.—*Anticlinal axis, geol.* a line from which strata dip on either side as from the ridge of a house: opposed to *synclinal*.—*n.* An anticlinal line or axis.

anticyclone, an″ti•sī′klōn, *n.* A meteorological phenomenon consisting of a region of high barometric pressure, the pressure being greatest in the center, with light winds flowing outward from the center and not inward as in the cyclone.

antidote, an′ti•dōt, *n.* [L. *antidotum*, from Gr. *antidoton*, an antidote—*anti*, against, and *dotos*, given, from *didōmi*, to give.] A medicine to counteract the effects of poison, or of anything noxious taken into the stomach; *fig.* anything that prevents or counteracts evil.—**antidotal,** an•ti•dōt′al, *a.* Having the qualities of an antidote; serving as an antidote.

antifebrile, an•ti•feb′ril or an•ti•fē′bril, *a.* Having the quality of abating fever; opposing or tending to cure fever.

antifederal, an•ti•fed′ėr•al, *a.* Opposed to or opposing federalism or a federal constitution.—**antifederalism,** an•ti•fed′ėr•al•izm, *n.* Opposition to federalism.—**antifederalist,** an•ti•fed′ėr•al•ist, *n.* One who is averse to federalism.

antifreeze, an′ti•frēz″, *n.* A substance added to water to lower its freezing temperature and used to keep the cooling systems of internal-combustion engines from freezing during the cold weather.

antifriction, an•ti•frik′shon, *a.* Obviating or lessening friction.

antigen, an′ti•jen, *n.* [Gr. *anti*, against, and *gen*, to form.] A substance that gives rise to an antibody when introduced into blood or tissue.

antihistamine, an′ti•his″ta•mēn, *n.* *Med.* any of a number of compounds that inactivate histamine in the body, used mainly for the treatment of allergy.

antilogy, an•til′o•ji, *n.* [Gr. *antilogia*—*anti*, against, and *legō*, to speak.] A contradiction between any words or passages in an author, or between members of the same body.

antimacassar, an′ti•ma•kas″ar, *n.* [Gr. *anti*, against, and E. *macassar*-oil.] A covering for charts, sofas, couches, etc., made of open cotton or worsted work, to preserve them from being soiled.

antimatter, an′ti•mat′ėr, *n.* [*anti* and *matter*.] Matter composed of particles with charges opposite to those of ordinary matter.

antimere, an′ti•mēr, *n.* [Gr. *anti*, opposite, *meros*, part.] *Biol.* one of two or more corresponding parts on opposite sides of animals.

antimissile, an′ti•mis″il, *adj.* Designed for use in the defense against enemy missiles, such as rockets.

antimonarchic, an′ti•mon•ärk″ik, *a.* Opposed to monarchy; opposing a kingly government.

antimony, an′ti•mo•ni, *n.* [L. of twelfth century *antimonium;* origin doubtful.] A metallic element, brittle, lustrous, and white in color, used chiefly in alloys and (in compounds) in medicine and pigments. Symbol, Sb (stibium); at. no., 51; at. wt., 121.75.—**antimonial,** an•ti•mō′ni•al, *a.* Pertaining to antimony, or partaking of its qualities.

antineutrino, an′ti•nu•trē″nō, *n. Phys.* a hypothetical subnuclear particle having the same relation to the neutrino as the positron has to the electron, having near zero mass, no electric charge, and a spin opposite in direction to that of the neutrino.

antineutron, an′ti•nū″tron, *n. Phys.* a hypothetical particle of mass equal to that of the neutron, without electric charge, and with a magnetic moment opposite to that of the neutron.

antinomy, an•tin′om•i, *n.* [Gr. *anti*, against, and *nomos*, a law.] The opposition of one law or rule to another law or rule; anything, as a law, statement, etc., opposite or contrary.— **antinomian,** an•ti•nō′mi•an, *a.* Opposed to law; pertaining to the Antinomians.—*n.* One of a sect who maintains that, under the gospel dispensation, the moral law is of no use or obligation.—**antinomianism,** an•ti•nō′mi•an•izm, *n.* The tenets of the Antinomians.

antioxidant, an′ti•ok″si•dant, *n.* A substance added to rubber that inhibits its deterioration; any substance inhibiting oxidation.

antipathy, an•tip′a•thi, *n.* [Gr. *antipatheia*—*anti*, against, and *pathos*, feeling. PATHOS.] Natural aversion; instinctive contrariety or opposition in feeling; an aversion felt at the presence of an object; repugnance; contrariety in nature: commonly with *to* before the object.—**antipathetic, antipathetical,** an′ti•pa•thet″ik, an′ti•pa•thet″ik•al, *a.* Having antipathy.

antipersonnel, an″ti•pėr″so•nel′, *adj.* *Milit.* used to destroy or obstruct individuals rather than matériel.

antiphlogistic, an′ti•flo•jis″tik, *a.* Opposed to the theory of phlogiston; counteracting inflammation, or an excited state of the system.—*n.* A medicine which checks inflammation.

antiphon, antiphony, an′ti•fon, an•tif′o•ni, *n.* [Gr. *anti*, in response to, and *phōnē*, voice. *Anthem* is the same word.] The answer of one choir or one portion of a congregation to another when an anthem or psalm is sung alternately; alternate singing; a short versicle sung before and after the psalms.—**antiphonal, antiphonary,** an•tif′o•nal, an•tif′o•na•ri, *n.* A book of antiphons or anthems.—**antiphonal, antiphonic,** an•tif′on•al, an•ti•fon′ik, *a.* Pertaining to antiphony or alternate singing.

antipodes, an•tip′o•dēz, *n. pl.* [Gr.—*anti*, opposite, and *pous, podos*, foot.] Those who live on the opposite side of the globe; the region directly on the opposite side of the globe; *fig.* anything diametrically opposite or opposed to another; a contrary.—**antipodal, antipodean,** an•tip′o•dal, an•tip′o•dē″an, *a.* Pertaining to antipodes.—**antipode,** an′ti•pōd, *n.* One who or that which is in opposition or opposite.

antipope, an′ti•pōp, *n.* One who usurps the papal power in opposition to the pope; a pretender to the papacy.

antiproton, an′ti•prō″ton, *n. Phys.* a hypothetical particle with mass equal to that of a proton but carrying a negative charge, postulated as existing in the nuclei of hypothetical inverted atoms.

antipyretic, an′ti•pi•ret″ik, *n.* [Gr. *anti*, against, and *pyretos*, fever.] *Med.* a remedy efficacious against fever.

antiquary, an′ti•kwa•ri, *n.* [L. *anti-*

quarius, from *antiquus*, old, ancient, from *ante*, before.] One devoted to the study of ancient times through their relics; one versed in antiquity: an archaeologist.—**antiquarian,** an-ti•kwā'ri•an, *a.* Pertaining to antiquaries or to antiquity.—*n.* An antiquary. —**antiquated,** an'ti•kwāt•ed, *a.* Grown old fashioned; obsolete; out of use; behind the times.—**antique,** an•tēk', *a.* [Fr., from L. *antiquus*, ancient. *Antic* is a form of this word.] Having existed in ancient times; belonging to or having come down from antiquity; ancient (an *antique* statue); having the characteristics of an earlier day; smacking of bygone days; of old fashion (an *antique* robe).—*n.* Anything very old; specifically, a term applied to the remains of ancient art, more especially to the works of Grecian and Roman antiquity.—**antiquity,** an•tik'wi•ti, *n.* [L. *antiquitas* from *antiquus*, ancient.] The quality of being ancient; ancientness; great age; ancient times; former ages; the people of ancient times; *pl.* the remains of ancient times; institutions, customs, etc., belonging to ancient nations.

antirrhinum, an•ti•rī'num, *n.* [Gr. *anti*, like, and *rhin*, a nose. The flowers of most of the species bear a resemblance to the snout of some animal.] Snapdragon, the generic name of various plants with showy flowers, much cultivated in gardens.

antiscorbutic, an"ti•skạr•bū'tik, *a.* *Med.* counteracting scurvy or a scorbutic tendency.—*n.* A remedy for or preventive of scurvy.

anti-Semitism, an•ti•sem'i•tizm, *n.* Hostility or discrimination against Jews.

antisepsis, an'ti•sep'sis, *n.* [Gr. *anti*, against, and *septos*, putrid, from *sepō*, to putrefy.] The inhibition or destruction of microorganisms; prevention of sepsis.—**antiseptic,** an•ti•sep'tik, *a.*—*n.* An agent that inhibits the growth of microorganisms.

antislavery, an'ti•slā•vėr•i, *a.* Against slavery.

antisocial, an'ti•sō'shal, *a.* Contrary to the laws and standards of society.

antispasmodic, an'ti•spaz•mod"ik, *a.* *Med.* opposing spasm; resisting convulsions.—*n.* A remedy for spasm.

antistrophe, an•tis'tro•fe, *n.* [Gr.—*anti*, opposite, and *strophē*, a turning.] A part of an ancient Greek choral ode alternating with the strophe.—**antistrophic,** an•ti•strof'ik, *a.* Relating to the antistrophe.

antisyphilitic, an•ti•sif'il•it"ik, *a.* Efficacious against syphilis, or the venereal poison.—*n.* A medicine of this kind.

antithesis, an•tith'e•sis, *n.* pl. **antitheses,** an•tith'e•sēz. [Gr. *antithesis* —*anti*, against, and *thesis*, a setting, from *tithēmi*, to place.] Opposition; contrast; *rhet.* a figure by which contraries are opposed to contraries; a contrast or opposition of words or sentiments; as, the prodigal *robs his heir*, the miser *robs himself*.—**antithetic, antithetical,** an•ti•thet'ik, an•ti•thet'ik•al, *a.* Pertaining to or characterized by antithesis.—**antithetically,** an•ti•thet'ik•al•li, *adv.* In an antithetical manner.

antitoxin, an•ti•tok'sin, *n.* [Gr. *anti*, against. TOXIC.] *Med.* a fluid introduced into the blood to counteract the poison of a disease.

antitrades, an'ti•trādz, *n.* A tropical wind blowing above a trade wind and in the opposite direction.

anti-Trinitarian, an•ti•trin'i•tā"ri•an, *n.* One who denies the doctrine of the Trinity, or the existence of three persons in the Godhead.—*a.* Opposing the doctrine of the Trinity.

antitrust, an'ti•trust, *a.* Against monopoly.

antitype, an'ti•tīp, *n.* That which is correlative to a type; that which is prefigured or represented by the type.—**antitypical,** an•ti•tip'ik•al, *a.*

antler, ant'lėr, *n.* [O.Fr. *antoillier, entoillier*; origin doubtful.] A branch of the horn of a deer, particularly of a stag; one of the horns of the cervine animals.—**antlered,** ant'lėrd, *a.*

antonym, ant'ō•nim, *n.* [Gr. *anti*, against, *onoma*, name.] A word of directly contrary signification to another: the opposite of a synonym.

antrorse, an•trors', *a.* [From L. *ante*, before, and *versus*, turned.] *Bot.* forward or upward in direction.

antrum, an'trum, *n.* [Gr. *antron*, cave.] Chamber or cavern; *anat.* cavity in a hollow organ; a sinus, esp. the maxillary antrum.

anus, ā'nus, *n.* [L.] *Anat.* the inferior opening of the alimentary canal; the fundament.

anvil, an'vil, *n.* [A.Sax. *anfilt*, O.H.G. *anafalz*—*an*, on, and A.Sax. *fealdan*, G. *falten, falzen*, to *fold*.] An iron block with a smooth, usually steel, face, and often a projecting horn, on which metals are hammered and shaped.—*v.t.*† To form or shape on an anvil.

anxiety, ang•zī'e•ti, *n.* [L. *anxietas*, from *anxius*, solicitous, from *ango*, to vex. ANGER.] Pain or uneasiness of mind respecting some event, future or uncertain; concern; solicitude; care; disquietude.—**anxious,** angk'shus, *a.* Full of anxiety or solicitude respecting something future or unknown; being in painful suspense (of persons); attended with or proceeding from solicitude or uneasiness (of things): followed often by *for*, *about*, *on account of*.—**anxiously,** angk'shus•li, *adv.* In an anxious manner; solicitously.—**anxiousness,** angk'shus•nes, *n.* Anxiety.

any, en'ni, *a.* [A.Sax. *ænig*, from *ân*, one, and term. *ig* (parallel to *naenig*, none); like G. *einig*, D. *eenig*, any.] One out of many indefinitely (*any* man); some; an indefinite number or quantity (*any* men, *any* money): often used as a pronoun, the noun being understood.—*adv.* In any degree; to any extent; at all (*any* better).—**anybody,** en'ni•bo•di, *n.* Any one person.—**anyhow,** en'ni•hou, *adv.* In any manner, at any rate; in any event; on any account.—**anyone,** en'ni•wun, *pron.* Any person at all; anybody.—**anything,** en'ni•thing, *pron.* Any object or fact whatever.—**anyway,** en'ni•wā, *adv.* Anyhow; at least.—**anywhere,** en'ni•whār, *adv.* In any place.—**anywise,** en'ni•wīz, *adv.* [*wise*=*guise*.] In any way.

Anzac, an'zak, *n.* The *A*ustralian—*N*ew *Z*ealand *A*rmy *C*orps, at Gallipoli during the war of 1915: from the initial letters.

aorist, ā'or•ist, *n.* [Gr. *aoristos*, indefinite—*a*, not, and *horos*, limit.] *Gram.* a tense in the Greek verb which expresses past time indefinitely (like E. *did* or *saw*).—**aoristic,** ā•or•ist'ik, *a.* Pertaining to or having the character of an aorist.

aorta, ā•or'ta, *n.* [Gr. *aortē*, from *aeirō*, to lift, to heave.] *Anat.* the great artery or trunk of the arterial system, proceeding from the left ventricle of the heart, and giving origin to all the arteries except the pulmonary.—**aortal, aortic,** ā•or'tal, ā•or'tik, *a.* Pertaining to the aorta.

apace, a•pās', *adv.* With a quick pace; fast; speedily; with haste.

apache, a•pash', *n.* [American Indian tribe.] A French street ruffian or desperado.

apart, a•pärt', *adv.* [Fr. *à part*, aside, separate—*à*, from L. *ad*, to, *part*=E. *part*, side.] Separately; in a state of separation; distinct or away from others; at some distance.—**apartment,** a•pärt'ment, *n.* [Fr. *appartement*.] A room in a building; a division in a house separated from others by partitions; *pl.* a suite, or set, of rooms; lodgings (a French usage).

apartheid, a•pärt'āt, *n.* [Afrik. lit, separateness.] The system of separation of the racial groups in the Republic of South Africa.

apathy, ap'a•thi, *n.* [L. *apathia*, Gr. *apatheia*—*a*, not, and *pathos*, suffering.] Want of feeling; privation of passion, emotion, or excitement; insensibility; indifference.—**apathetic, apathetical,** ap•a•thet'ik, ap•a•thet'ik•al, *a.* Affected with or proceeding from apathy; devoid of feeling; insensible.

apatite, ap'a•tīt, *n.* [From Gr. *apatē*, deceit, it having been mistaken for other minerals.] A mineral consisting chiefly of phosphate of lime, used as a fertilizer.

ape, āp, *n.* [A.Sax. *apa*, Icel. *api*, D. *aap*, Dan. *abe*, G. *affe*, O.H.G. *affo*, Ir. and Gael. *apa*: an initial guttural has been lost, seen in Gr. *kēpos*, Skr. *kapi*, an ape.] One of a family of quadrumanous animals found in both continents, having the teeth of the same number and form as in man, and possessing neither tails nor cheek pouches; *fig.* one who imitates servilely.—*v.t.* *aped, aping.* To imitate servilely; to mimic.—**apish,** āp'ish, *a.* Having the qualities of an ape; inclined to imitate superiors.—**apishly,** āp'ish•li, *adv.* In an apish manner.—**apishness,** āp'ish•nes, *n.*

apeak, a•pēk', *adv.* [Fr. *à-pic*, to the summit.] On the point; in a posture to pierce; *naut.* perpendicular, or inclining to the perpendicular: said of the anchor or yards.

aperient, a•pē'ri•ent, *a.* [L. *aperiens*, *aperientis*, part. of *aperio*, to open.]

Med. gently purgative; having the quality of opening; deobstruent; laxative.—*n.* A medicine which gently opens the bowels; a laxative.

apert, a•pėrt′, *a.* [L. *apertus*, open.] Open; evident.—**aperture,** ap′ėr•tūr, *n.* [L. *apertura*, from *aperio*, *apertum*, to open.] An opening; a mouth, entrance, gap, cleft, etc.; a passage; a perforation; the diameter of the exposed part of the object glass of a telescope or other optical instrument.

apetalous, a•pet′al•us, *a.* [Gr. *a*, neg., and *petalon*, a petal.] *Bot.* having no petals or corolla.—**apetalousness,** a•pet′al•us•nes, *n.*

apex, ā′peks, *n.* pl. **apices, apexes,** ā′pi•sēz, ā′peks•ez. [L. *apex*, pl. *apices*.] The tip, point, or summit of anything.

aphaeresis, apheresis, a•fe′re•sis, *n.* [Gr. *aphairesis*, a taking away—*apo*, from, and *haireō*, to take.] *Gram.* the taking of a letter or syllable from the beginning of a word; *med.* the removal of anything noxious; *surg.* amputation.

aphanite, af′an•īt, *n.* [Gr. *aphanēs*, indistinct—*a*, not, and *phainō*, to appear.] A name of fine-grained minerals whose structure cannot be detected by the naked eye.—**aphanitic,** af•an•it′ik, *a.* Pertaining to aphanite or of similar character.

aphasia, a•fā′zha, *n.* [Gr. *a*, not, *phasis*, speech.] Loss of the faculty of speech, or of connecting words and ideas, owing to morbid conditions of brain, while the speech organs and general intelligence remain unaffected.

aphelion, a•fē′li•on, *n.* pl. **aphelia,** a•fe′li•a. [Gr. *apo*, from, and *hēlios*, the sun.] That point of a planet's or comet's orbit which is most distant from the sun: opposed to *perihelion*.

aphesis, af′e•sis, *n.* [Gr. *aphesis*, a letting go.] Loss of a short unaccented syllable at the beginning of a word; as *squire* for *esquire*.—**aphetic,** a•fet′ik, *a.* Pertaining to.

aphid, ā′fid, *n.* pl. **aphides,** af′i•dēz. [A term of modern origin, perhaps from Gr. *aphyssō*, to draw or drink up liquids.] A plant louse. The aphides are small insects, some of them wingless; they are very numerous and destructive, almost every species of plant supporting a different variety.—**aphidian,** a•fid′i•an, *a.* Pertaining to the aphides.

aphonia, a•fō′ni•a, *n.* [Gr. *a*, not, and *phōnē*, voice.] A loss of voice; dumbness; speechlessness.—**aphonous,** af′ō•nus, *a.* Destitute of voice.

aphorism, af′or•izm, *n.* [Gr. *aphorismos*, from *aphorizō*, to mark out, to define—*apo*, from, and *horos*, a boundary.] A precept or principle expressed in a few words; a brief sentence containing some important truth; a maxim. ∴ *Aphorism* is the brief statement of a doctrine. *Axiom*, a statement claiming to be considered as a self-evident truth. *Maxim*, a formula referring rather to practical than to abstract truth; a rule of conduct. *Apophthegm*, a terse sententious saying.—**aphorist,** af′or•ist, *n.* A writer of aphorisms.—**aphoristic,** af•or•ist′ik, *a.* Pertaining to, resembling, or containing aphorisms; in the form of an aphorism.—**aphoristically,** af•or•ist′ik•al•li, *adv.* In the form or manner of aphorisms.—**aphorize,** af′or•īz, *v.i.* To make aphorisms.

aphrodisiac, af•ro•diz′i•ak, *a.* [Gr. *aphrodisios*, *aphrodisiakos*, from *Aphrodite*, goddess of love.] Exciting venereal desire.—**aphrodisiac,** *n.* Food or a medicine exciting sexual desire.

aphyllous, af′il•lus or a•fil′us, *a.* [Gr. *a*, neg., and *phyllon*, a leaf.] *Bot.* destitute of leaves.

apiary, ā′pi•a•ri, *n.* [L. *apiarium*, from *apis*, a bee.] The place where bees are kept; a stand or shed for bees.—**apiarian,** ā•pi•ā′ri•an, *a.* Relating to bees.—*n.* A bee keeper; an apiarist.—**apiarist,** ā′pi•a•rist, *n.* One who keeps bees.—**apiculture,** āp•i•kul′tūr, *n.* The art of managing bees in hives; beekeeping.

apical, ap′ik•al, *a.* [L. *apex*, an apex, a sharp point or peak.] Relating to the apex or top; belonging to the pointed end of a cone-shaped body.—**apices, apexes,** pl. of *apex*.—**apiculate,** a•pik′ū•lāt, *a. Bot.* tipped with a short and abrupt point.

apiece, a•pēs′, *adv.* To each; as the share of each; each by itself; by the individual.

apish, apishly. See APE.

aplacental, ap•la•sen′tal, *a.* [Prefix *a*, not, and *placental*.] Applied to those mammals in which the young are destitute of a placenta (as the kangaroo, duck mole, etc.).

aplanatic, ap•la•nat′ik, *a.* [Gr. *a*, not, and *planaō*, to wander.] *Optics*, corrective of the defect by which rays of light diverge and do not come to a focus (an *aplanatic* lens).

aplomb, a•plom′, *n.* [Fr., lit. the state of being perpendicular, or true to the *plumb*-line.] Self-possession springing from perfect self-confidence; assurance.

apocalypse, a•pok′a•lips, *n.* [Gr. *apokalypsis*, from *apokalyptō*, to disclose—prefix *apo*, and *kalyptō*, to cover.] Revelation; discovery; disclosure. The name of the last book of the New Testament.—**apocalyptic, apocalyptical,** a•pok′a•lip″tik, a•pok′a•lip″tik•al, *a.* Containing or pertaining to revelation; pertaining to the Revelation of St. John.—**apocalyptic,** a•pok′a•lip″tik, *n.* A writer on the Apocalypse.—**apocalyptically,** a•pok′a•lip″tik•al•li, *adv.* In an apocalyptic manner; by revelation.

apocarpous, ap•o•kär′pus, *a.* [Gr. *apo*, denoting separation, and *karpos*, fruit.] In *bot.* having the carpels, or at least their styles, disunited.

apocope, a•pok′o•pe, *n.* [Gr. *apokopē*, a cutting off—*apo*, and *kopē*, a cutting.] The cutting off or omission of the last letter or syllable of a word, as *th'* for *the*.—**apocopate,** a•pok′ō•pāt, *v.t.*—*apocopated*, *apocopating*. To cut off or drop the last letter or syllable of.

Apocrypha, a•pok′ri•fa, *n.* [Gr. *apokryphos*, hidden, spurious—*apo*, away, and *kryptō*, to conceal. CRYPT.] The collective name of certain books admitted by the R. Catholics into the Old Testament canon, but whose authenticity as inspired writings is not generally admitted.—**apocryphal,** a•pok′ri•fal, *a.* Pertaining to the Apocrypha; not canonical; of uncertain authority or credit; fictitious.—**apocryphally,** a•pok′ri•fal•li, *adv.* In an apocryphal manner; equivocally; doubtfully.—**apocryphalness,** a•pok′ri•fal•nes, *n.*

apodal, ap′o•dal, *a.* Having no feet: also said of fishes having no ventral fins, as the eel, swordfish, etc.

apodictic, apodictical, ap•o•dik′tik, ap•o•dik′tik•al, *a.* [Gr. *apodeiktikos*—*apo*, forth, and *deiknymi*, to show.] Demonstrative; evident beyond contradiction.—**apodictically,** ap•o•dik′-tik•al•li, *adv.* Demonstratively.

apodosis, a•pod′o•sis, *n.* [Gr. *apodosis*, a giving back—*apo*, from, and *didōmi*, to give.] *Gram.* the latter part of a conditional sentence (or one beginning with *if*, *though*, etc.), dependent on the *protasis* or condition.

apogee, ap′o•jē, *n.* [Gr. *apo*. from, and *gē*, the earth.] That point in the orbit of a planet or other heavenly body which is at the greatest distance from the earth; properly this particular point of the moon's orbit.—**apogean,** ap•o•jē′an, *a.* Pertaining to or connected with the apogee.

Apollyon, a•pol′yon, *n.* [Gr. *apollūmi*, to destroy.] The Devil.

apologue, ap′o•log, *n.* [Gr. *apologos*, an apologue, a fable—*apo*, from, and *logos*, discourse.] A moral fable; a relation of fictitious events intended to convey useful truths, such as the fables of Aesop.

apology, a•pol′o•ji, *n.* [Gr. *apologia*, a speech in defence—*apo*, away from, and *logos*, a discourse.] Something said or written in defense; justification; vindication; an acknowledgment, usually accompanied by an expression of regret, for some improper remark or act; a temporary substitute or makeshift (colloq.)—**apologetic, apological,** a•pol′o•jet″-ik, a•pol′o•jet″ik•al, *a.* Of or pertaining to or containing apology; defending by words or arguments.—**apologetically,** a•pol′o•jet″ik•al•li, *adv.* In an apologetic manner; by way of apology.—**apologetics,** a•pol′-o•jet″iks, *n.* That branch of theology by which Christians are enabled scientifically to justify and defend the peculiarities of their faith, and to answer its opponents.—**apologist, apologizer,** a•pol′o•jist, a•pol′o•jīz•er, *n.* One who makes an apology.—**apologize,** a•pol′o•jīz, *v.i.*—*apologized*, *apologizing*. To make an apology.

aponeurosis, ap′o•nū•rō″sis, *n.* pl. **aponeuroses,** ap′o•nū•rō″sēz. [Gr. *aponeurōsis*—*apo*, from, and *neuron*, a nerve, because formerly supposed to be an expansion of a nerve or nerves.] A white, shining, and very resisting membrane, composed of interlaced fibers, found surrounding the voluntary muscles, large arteries, and other parts of the body.—**aponeurotic,** ap′o•nū•rot″ik, *a.* Relating to the aponeuroses.

apophthegm, ap′o•them, *n.* [Gr. *apo,* from, and *phthēgma,* word.] A short, pithy, and instructive saying; a sententious precept or maxim. Written also *Apothegm. Syn.* under APHORISM.—**apophthegmatic, apophthegmatical,** ap′o•theg•mat″ik, ap′o•theg•mat″ik•al, *a.* Pertaining to or having the character of an apophthegm; sententious.—**apophthegmatize,** ap•o•theg′mat•īz, *v.i.* To utter apophthegms.

apophyllite, a•pof′i•līt, *n.* [Gr. *apo,* from, and *phyllon,* a leaf, from its tendency to exfoliate.] A mineral of a foliated structure, and readily separating into thin laminae, with a peculiar luster.

apophysis, a•pof′i•sis, *n.* pl. **apophyses,** a•pof′i•sēz. [Gr.—*apo,* from, and *physis,* growth.] *Anat.* a prominence; a prominent part of a bone.

apoplexy, ap′o•plek•si, *n.* [Gr. *apoplēxia,* apoplexy—*apo,* from, and *plēssō, plēxō,* to strike.] Abolition or sudden diminution of sensation and voluntary motion, resulting from congestion or rupture of the blood vessels of the brain.—**apoplectic, apoplectical,** ap•o•plek′tik, ap•o•plek′tik•al, *a.* Pertaining to or consisting in apoplexy; predisposed to apoplexy.—**apoplectic,** ap•o•plek′tik, *n.* A person affected with apoplexy.

aposiopesis, ap′ō•sī•ō•pē″sis, *n.* [Gr.—*apo,* from, and *siopaō,* to be silent.] *Rhet.* sudden stopping short and leaving a statement unfinished for the sake of effect.

apostasy, a•pos′ta•si, *n.* [Gr. *apostasia,* a standing away from, a defection—*apo,* from, and root *sta,* to stand.] An abandonment of what one has professed; a total desertion or departure from one's faith, principles, or party.—**apostate,** a•pos′tāt, *n.* One who has forsaken his faith, principles, or party.—*a.* False, traitorous.—**apostatize,** a•pos′ta•tīz, *v.i.*—*apostatized, apostatizing.* To turn apostate; to abandon principles, faith, or party.

a posteriori, a pos•tē′ri•ō″ri. [L. *posterior,* after.] A phrase applied to a mode of reasoning founded on observation of effects, consequences, or facts, whereby we reach the causes; inductive: opposed to *a priori.*

apostle, a•pos′l, *n.* [Gr. *apostolos, lit.* one sent forth, a messenger—*apo,* forth, and *stellō,* to send.] One of the twelve disciples of Christ, who were commissioned to preach the gospel; one regarded as having a similar mission.—**apostleship,** a•pos′l•ship, *n.* The office or dignity of an apostle.—**apostolate,** a•pos′tol•āt, *n.* The dignity or office of an apostle; a mission; the dignity or office of the pope, the holder of the apostolic see.—**apostolic, apostolical,** ap•os•tol′ik, ap•os•tol′ik•al, *a.* Pertaining or relating to or characteristic of an apostle, more especially of the twelve apostles; according to the doctrines of the apostles; proceeding from an apostle.—*Apostolic see,* the see of the bishop of Rome, as directly founded by the apostle Peter.—*Apostolic succession,* the uninterrupted succession of bishops, and, through them, of priests and deacons, in the church by regular ordination from the first apostles down to the present day.—**apostolicism, apostolicity,**† ap•os•tol′i•sizm, ap•os′tol•is″i•ti, *n.* The character of being apostolical.

apostrophe, a•pos′tro•fe, *n.* [Gr. *apo,* from, and *strophē,* a turning.] A sudden change in discourse; a sudden and direct address to a person or thing in the course of a speech; *gram.* the omission of a letter or letters from a word marked by a sign ('); the sign used to mark the omission, or merely as the sign of the possessive case in nouns.—**apostrophic,** ap•os•trof′ik, a. Pertaining to an apostrophe.—**apostrophize,** a•pos′trof•īz, *v.t.*—*apostrophized, apostrophizing.* To address by apostrophe; to make a direct address to in course of a speech; to mark with an apostrophe.—*v.i.* To make an apostrophe in speaking.

apothecary, a•poth′e•ka•ri, *n.* [L.L. *apothecarius,* a shopkeeper, from Gr. *apothēkē,* a repository—*apo,* away, and *thēkē,* a chest, from *tithēmi,* to place.] One who practices pharmacy; a skilled person who prepares drugs for medicinal uses, and keeps them for sale.

apothecium, ap•o•thē′si•um, *n.* pl. **apothecia,** ap•o•thē′si•a. [APOTHECARY.] *Bot.* the receptacle of lichens, the sporecase.

apothegm, apothegmatic, ap′o•them, ap′o•theg•mat″ik. Same as *Apophthegm, Apophthegmatic.*

apotheosis, ap″o•thē•ō′sis or -thē′o•sis, *n.* [Gr. *apo,* away, and *theos,* God.] Deification; the placing or ranking of a person among deities.—**apotheosize,** ap•o•thē′ō•sīz, *v.t.* To exalt to the dignity of a deity; to deify.

appall, appal, ap•pal′, *v.t.*—*appalled, appalling.* [O.Fr. *appalir,* to make pale, from prefix *ap* for *ad,* and *palle,* pale, from L. *pallidus,* pallid.] To impress with overpowering fear; to confound with terror; to dismay.—*n.* Terror; affright; dismay. [*Cowper.*]—**appalling,** ap•pal′ing, *a.* Calculated to cause dismay or horror.—**appallingly,** ap•pal′ing•li, *adv.* In a manner to appall.

appanage, ap′pan•āj, *n.* [Fr. *appanage, apanage,* from O.Fr. *apaner,* L.L. *apanare,* to furnish with bread—L. *ad,* to, and *panis,* bread.] An allowance to the younger branches of a sovereign house out of the revenues of the country, generally together with a grant of public domains; whatever belongs or falls to one from rank or station in life.

apparatus, ap•pa•rā′tus, *n. sing.* and *pl.;* pl. rarely **apparatuses,** ap•pa•rā′tus•ez. [L. from *apparo,* to prepare—*ad,* and *paro,* to make ready.] Things provided as means to some end; a collection or combination of articles or materials for the accomplishment of some purpose, operation, or experiment; *physiol* a collection of organs all ministering to the same function.

apparel, ap•par′el, *n.* (no pl.). [Fr. *appareil,* dress, *appareiller,* to match, to fit. to suit—*a,* to, and *pareil,* like, L.L. *pariculus,* from L. *par,* equal.] Clothing; vesture; garments; dress; external array; the furniture of a ship.—*v.t.*—*appareled, appareling.* To dress or clothe; to cover as with garments.

apparent, ap•pā′rent, *a.* [L. *apparens, apparentis,* ppr. of *appareo.* APPEAR.] Visible to the eye; within sight or view; appearing to the eye or to the judgment; seeming (often in distinction to *real*); obvious; plain; evident: in the latter sense now used only as a predicate.—*Heir apparent,* the heir who is certain to inherit if he survive the present holder.—*n.*† Heir apparent; one who has a claim. [*Shak.*]—**apparently,** ap•pā′rent•li, *adv.* Openly; evidently; seemingly; in appearance.—**apparentness,** ap•pā′rent•nes, *n.*

apparition, ap•pa•ri′shon, *n.* [APPEAR.] The act of appearing; appearance; the thing appearing; especially, a ghost; a specter, a visible spirit.—**apparitional,** ap•pa•ri′shon•al, *a.* Pertaining to an apparition.

apparitor, ap•par′it•or, *n.* [L., from *appareo,* to attend. APPEAR.] A messenger or officer who serves the process of a spiritual court; the beadle in a university.

appeal, ap•pēl′, *v.i.* [Fr. *appeler,* from L. *appellare,* to call, address, appeal to.] To call, as for aid, mercy, sympathy, and the like; to refer to another person or authority for the decision of a question controverted; to refer to a superior judge or court for a final settlement.—*v.t.* To summon or to challenge†; to remove (a cause) from an inferior to a superior judge or court; to charge with a crime; to accuse.—*n.* A call for sympathy, mercy, aid, and the like; a supplication; an entreaty; the removal of a cause or suit from an inferior to a superior tribunal, that the latter may, if needful, amend the decision of the former; a challenge; a reference to another for proof or decision; resort; recourse (*appeal* to arms).—**appealable,** ap•pēl′a•bl, *a.* Liable to be appealed; removable to a higher tribunal for decision.—**appealer,** ap•pēl′ėr, *n.* One who appeals; an appellant.—**appellant,** ap•pel′ant, *n.* One who appeals; one who removes a cause from a lower to a higher tribunal.—**appellate,** ap•pel′āt, *a.* Relating to appeals; having cognizance of appeals.—**appellee,** ap•pel•lē′, *n.* One against whom an appeal is brought.—**appellor,** ap•pel′or, *n.* One who appeals.

appear, ap•pēr′, *v.i.* [O.Fr. *apparoir,* L. *appareo*—*ad,* to, and *pareo,* to show one's self.] To come or be in sight; to be or become visible to the eye; to stand in presence of some one; to be obvious; to be clear or made clear by evidence; to seem; to look like.—**appearance,** ap•pēr′ans, *n.* The act of appearing or coming into sight; a coming into the presence of a person or persons; the thing seen; a phenomenon; an apparition; external show; semblance, in opposition to reality or substance; mien; build and carriage; figure.

appease, ap•pēz′, *v.t.—appeased, appeasing.* [Fr. *appaiser,* to pacify—*a,* from L. *ad,* to, and O.Fr. *pais* (Fr. *paix*), L. *pax, pacis,* peace.] To make quiet; to still; to assuage (hunger); to tranquilize; to calm or pacify (a person, anger).—**appeasable,** ap•pēz•a•bl, *a.* Capable of being appeased.—**appeasement,** ap•pēz′ment, *n.* Act of appeasing; appeased state. —**appeaser,** ap•pēz′ėr, *n.* One who appeases.

appellant, appellate, etc. See APPEAL.

appellation, ap•pel•ā′shon, *n.* [L. *appellatio,* from *appellare,* to address, accost, appeal to.] The word by which a thing or person is known; name; title.—**appellative,** ap•pel′a•tiv, *a.* Serving as an appellation; naming or marking out; denominative. *n.* An appellation.

append, ap•pend′, *v.t.* [L. *appendo*—*ad,* to, and *pendo,* to hang. PENDANT.] To hang on or attach; to add, as accessory or adjunct to a thing; to subjoin; to annex.—**appendage,** ap•pend′āj, *n.* Something appended or attached; what is attached to a greater thing.—**appendectomy,** ap•pen•dek′to•mi, *n.* [Gr. *appendix* and *ectomy,* excision.] Removal of the appendix by surgical operation.—**appendix,** ap•pen′diks, *n.* pl. **appendixes** and **appendices,** ap•pen′di•sez. [L. *appendix, appendicis,* from *appendo.*] Something appended or added; an addition appended to a book relating, but not essential, to the main work; *anat.* an appendage, process, or projecting part.—**appendicitis,** ap•pen′di•sī″tis, *n.* Inflammation of the vermiform appendix, a small hollow blind process attached to the cecum in man and some animals, an ailment sometimes fatal.

apperception, ap•pėr•sep′shon, *n.* [Prefix *ap* for *ad,* and *perception.*] Perception that reflects upon itself; consciousness; spontaneous thought.

appertain, ap•pėr•tān′, *v.i.* [Fr. *appartenir*—L. *ad,* and *pertineo,* to pertain.] To belong or pertain: with *to.*

appetence, appetency, ap′pē•tens, ap′pē•ten•si, *n.* [L. *appetentia,* from *appetens, appetentis,* ppr. of *appeto,* to desire—*ad,* and *peto,* to desire. PETITION.] Desire; inclination; propensity; strong natural craving or tendency; appetite.—**appetite,** ap′pe•tīt, *n.* [L. *appetitus,* desire.] The natural desire of pleasure or good; taste; inclination; a desire to supply a bodily want or craving; a desire for food or drink; eagerness or longing.—**appetizer,** ap′pē•tīz•ėr, *n.* That which appetizes or whets the appetite.—**appetizing,** ap′pē•tīz•ing, *a.* Whetting the appetite; appealing to the appetite.

applaud, ap•pla̤d′, *v.t.* [L. *applaudo, applausum*—*ad,* and *plaudo,* to make a noise by clapping the hands.] To show approbation of by clapping the hands, acclamation, or other significant sign; to praise highly; to extol.—*v.i.* To give praise; to express approbation.—**applause,** ap•pla̤z′, *n.* Praise loudly expressed; approbation expressed by clapping the hands or shouting; commendation; approval.—**applausive,** ap•pla̤z′iv, *a.* Applauding; containing applause.

apple, ap′l, *n.* [A. Sax, *aeppel, aepl,* a word common to the Teutonic, Celtic, Slavonic, and Lithuanian tongues; root unknown.] A fruit of a well-known fruit tree, or the tree itself; also a name popularly given to various exotic fruits or trees having little or nothing in common with the apple, as the pineapple, etc.—*Apple of the eye,* the pupil.—*Apple of Sodom,* a fruit described by old writers as externally of fair appearance, but turning to ashes when plucked.—*Adam's apple,* a prominence on the throat.

appliqué, ap•pli•kā′, *a.* [Fr. *appliqué,* applied.] Cut out from one material and fastened on another as an ornament.—*n.* Any such ornament.

apply, ap•plī′, *v.t.—applied, applying.* [O. Fr. *applier,* from L. *applicare,* to fasten to —*ad,* to, and *plico,* to fold. PLY.] To lay on (the hand to a table); to put or place on another thing; to use or employ for a particular purpose or in a particular case (a remedy, a sum of money); to put, refer, or use as suitable or relative to some person or thing (a proverb, etc.); to engage and employ with attention; to occupy (the mind, or *refl.*).—*v.i.* To suit; to agree; to have some connection, agreement, analogy, or reference; to make request; to solicit; to have recourse with a view to gain something; followed by *to.*—**appliance,** ap•plī′ans, *n.* The act of applying; the thing applied; means to an end; a device; an application; a remedy (*Shak.*)—**applicability,** ap′pli•ka•bil″i•ti, *n.* The quality of being applicable.—**applicable,** ap′pli•ka•bl, *a.* Capable of being applied; fit to be applied; having relevance.—**applicableness,** ap′pli•ka•bl•nes, *n.* The state or quality of being applicable.—**applicably,** ap′pli•ka•bli, *adv.* In an applicable manner.—**applicant,** ap′pli•kant, *n.* One who applies; a petitioner; a candidate.—**application,** ap•pli•kā′shon, *n.* The act of applying or putting to; the thing applied; the act of making request or soliciting; the employment of means; close study; attention; the testing of something theoretical by applying it in practice.—**applicative, applicatory,** ap′pli•kāt•iv, ap′pli•ka•to•ri, *a.* Having an application; that which may be applied.—**applier,** ap•plī′ėr, *n.* One that applies.

appoggiatura, ap•poj′a•tö″ra, *n.* [It.] *Mus.* a grace note: an added note of embellishment to an original passage.

appoint, ap•point′, *v.t.* [Fr. *appointer,* from L.L. *appunctare,* to bring to the point—L. *ad,* to, and *punctum,* a point. POINT.] To make firm, establish, or secure (O.T.)‡; to constitute, ordain, or decree; to allot, set apart, or designate; to nominate, as to an office; to settle; to fix, name, or determine by authority or upon agreement; to equip.—*v.i.* To ordain; to determine.—**appointer,** ap•point′ėr, *n.* One who appoints.—**appointment,** ap•point′ment, *n.* The act of appointing; designation to office; an office held; the act of fixing by mutual agreement; arrangement; decree; direction; command; equipment, furniture, etc. (*Shak.*); an allowance; a salary or pension.

apportion, ap•pōr′shon, *v.t.* [O.Fr. *apportioner*—L. *ad,* and *portio,* portion.] To divide and assign in just proportion; to distribute in proper shares; to allot.—**apportionment,** ap•pōr′shon•ment, *n.* The act of apportioning.

apposite, ap′pō•zit, *a.* [L. *appositus,* set or put to, from *appono, appositum*—*ad,* and *pono,* to put or place.] Suitable; fit; appropriate; very applicable; well adapted; followed by *to,* and said of answers, arguments, etc.—**appositely,** ap′pō•zit•li, *adv.* In an apposite manner; suitably; fitly.—**appositeness,** ap′pō•zit•nes, *n.* The state or quality of being apposite; fitness.—**apposition,** ap•pō•zi′shon, *n.* The act of adding to; addition; a setting to; *gram.* the relation in which a noun or a substantive phrase or clause stands to a noun or pronoun when it explains without being predicated of it, at the same time agreeing in case; as, Cicero, the orator, was there.—**appositional,** ap•pō•zi′shon•al, *a.* Pertaining to apposition.—**appositive,** ap•poz′it•iv, *a.* Placed in apposition.

appraise, ap•prāz′, *v.t.—appraised, appraising.* [O. Fr. *appreiser*; L. *appretiare,* to set a price on—*ad,* to, and *pretium,* a price. PRAISE, PRICE, PRECIOUS.] To set a price upon; to estimate the value of under the direction of a competent authority; to estimate generally.—**appraisement,** ap•prāz′ment, *n.* The act of appraising; the value fixed; the valuation.—**appraiser,** ap•prāz′ėr, *n.* One who appraises; a person licensed and sworn to estimate and fix the value of goods and estate.

appreciate, ap•prē′shi•āt, *v.t.— appreciated, appreciating.* [Fr. *apprécier,* to set a value, L. *appretio, appreciatum.* APPRAISE.] To set a just price, value, or estimate on; to estimate or value properly.—*v.i.* To rise in value; to become of more value.—**appreciable,** ap•prē′shi•a•bl, *a.* Capable of being appreciated or estimated; sufficiently great to be capable of estimation.—**appreciably,** ap•prē′shi•a•bli, *adv.* To a degree that may be appreciated or estimated; perceptibly.—**appreciation,** ap•prē′shi•ā″shon, *n.* The act of appreciating; the act of valuing or estimating; the act of setting a due price or value on.—**appreciative,** ap•prē′shi•ā•tiv, *a.* Capable of appreciating; manifesting, due appreciation.—**appreciatory,** ap·prē'shi·a·to·ri, *a.* Pertaining to appreciation.

apprehend, ap·prē·hend', *v.t.* [L. *apprehendo—ad,* and *prehendo,* to take or seize, *prae,* before, and *hendo* (not used), to seize.] To take or seize (a person); to arrest; to take or lay hold of by the mind; to become cognizant of; to understand; to entertain suspicion or fear of; to dread or be apprehensive of.—*v.t.* To form a conception; to conceive; to believe or be of opinion without positive certainty; to be apprehensive; to be in fear of a future evil.—**apprehensible,** ap·prē·hen'si·bl, *a.* Capable of being apprehended or conceived.—**apprehension,** ap·prē·hen'shon, *n.* The act of apprehending; a seizing or arresting by legal process; the operation of the mind in contemplating ideas, or merely taking them into the mind; opinion; belief; the power of perceiving and understanding; distrust or fear at the prospect of future evil, accompanied with uneasiness of mind.—**apprehensive,** ap·prē·hen'siv, *a.* Quick of apprehension (*Shak.*); inclined to believe, fear, or dread; anticipating, or in expectation of, evil (*apprehensive of* evil; *apprehensive for* our lives).—**apprehensively,** ap·prē·hen'siv·li, *adv.* In an apprehensive manner.—**apprehensiveness,** ap·prē·hen'siv·nes, *n.* The character of being apprehensive.

apprentice, ap·pren'tis, *n.* [L.L. *apprenticius,* from L. *apprehendo, apprendo,* to seize, to apprehend. APPREHEND.] One bound, often by legal document, to learn some art, trade, or profession; a learner in any subject; one not well versed in a subject.—*v.t. apprenticed, apprenticing.* To make an apprentice of; to put under the care of a master, for the purpose of learning a trade or profession.—**apprenticeship,** ap·pren'tis·ship, *n.* The state or condition of an apprentice; the term during which one is an apprentice.

apprize, ap·prīz', *v.t.—apprized, apprizing.* [O.E. *apprise,* notice, information, from Fr. *appris, apprise,* pp. of *apprendre,* to inform, to learn, L. *apprehendo.* APPREHEND.] To give notice, verbal or written; to inform; followed by *of* before that of which notice is given.

approach, ap·prōch', *v.i.* [Fr. *approcher,* from L.L. *appropiare,* to approach—L. *ad,* to, and *prope,* near. PROPINQUITY.] To come or go near in place or time; to draw near; to advance nearer; to approximate.—*v.t.* To bring near; to advance or put near; to come or draw near to, either literally or figuratively; to come near to, so as to be compared with,—*n.* The act of approaching or drawing near; a coming or advancing near; access; a passage or avenue by which buildings are approached.—**approachable,** ap·prōch'a·bl, *a.* Capable of being approached; accessible.

approbate, † ap'prō·bāt, *v.t.* [L. *approbo, approbatum,* to approve. APPROVE.] To express satisfaction with; to express approval of; to approve.—**approbation,** ap·prō·bā'shon, *n.* [L. *approbatio.*] The act of approving; that state or disposition of the mind in which we assent to the propriety of a thing with some degree of pleasure or satisfaction; approval.—**approbative,** ap'prō·bāt·iv, *a.* Approving; implying approbation.

appropriate, ap·prō'pri·āt, *v.t.—appropriated, appropriating.* [L. *approprio, appropriatum,* to make one's own—*ad,* to, *proprius,* one's own. PROPER, PROPRIETY.] To claim or take to one's self in exclusion of others; to claim or use as by an exclusive right; to set apart for or assign to a particular purpose.—*a.* Set apart for a particular use or person; hence, belonging peculiarly; peculiar; suitable; fit; proper.—**appropriable,** ap·prō'pri·a·bl, *a.* Capable of being appropriated, set apart, or assigned to a particular use.—**appropriately,** ap·prō'pri·āt·li, *adv.* In an appropriate manner.—**appropriateness,** ap·prō'pri·āt·nes, *n.* The quality of being appropriate.—**appropriation,** ap·prō'pri·ā"shon, *n.* The act of appropriating; application to a special use or purpose; the act of making one's own; anything appropriated or set apart.—**appropriative,** ap·prō'pri·āt·iv, *a.* Appropriating; making appropriation.—**appropriator,** ap·prō'pri·āt·ėr, *n.* One who appropriates.

approve, ap·pröv', *v.t.—approved, approving.* [Fr. *approuver, approver,* from L. *approbo,* to approve, to find good—*ad,* to and *probare,* to try, test, prove, from *probus,* good.] To admit the propriety or excellence of; to think or judge well or favorably of; to find to be satisfactory; to show to be real or true (to *approve* one's bravery); to prove by trial (*Shak,*)‡.—*v.i.* To be pleased; to feel or express approbation; to think or judge well or favorably: followed by *of.*—**approvable,** ap·pröv'a·bl, *a.* Capable of being approved.—**approval,** ap·pröv'al, *n.* The act of approving; approbation; commendation; sanction; ratification.—**approver,** ap·pröv'ėr, *n.* One who approves; one who confesses a crime and accuses another.—**approvingly,** ap·pröv'ing·li, *adv.* In an approving manner.

approximate, ap·prok'si·māt, *v.t.—approximated, approximating.* [L.L. *approximo, approximatum,* to bring or come near—L. *ad,* to, and *proximus,* nearest. PROXIMATE, APPROACH.] To carry or advance near; to cause to approach (especially said of amount, state, or degree).—*v.i.* To come near; to approach (especially as regards amount, state, or character).—*a.* Being near in state, place, or quantity; approaching; nearly equal or like.—**approximately,** ap·prok'si·māt·li, *adv.* In an approximate manner; by approximation.—**approximation,** ap·prok'si·mā"shon, *n.* The act of approximating; an approximate estimate or amount; approach.

appurtenance, ap·pėr'ten·ans, *n.* [Fr. *appartenance.* APPERTAIN.] That which appertains or belongs to something else; something belonging to another thing as principal; an adjunct; an appendage.—**appurtenant,** ap·pėr'ten·ant, *a.* Appertaining or belonging; pertaining; being an appurtenance.

apricot, ā'pri·kot, *n.* [O.E. *apricock, abricot,* Fr. *abricot,* Sp. *albarcoque,* from Ar. *alburqūq,* from *al,* the article, and L. Gr. *praikokkion,* from L. *praecox, praecoquus,* early ripe. PRECOCIOUS.] A roundish fruit of a delicious flavor, the produce of a tree of the plum kind.

April, ā·pril, *n.* [L. *aprilis,* the month in which the earth opens for the growth of plants, from *aperio,* to open.] The fourth month of the year.—*April fool,* one who is sportively imposed upon by others on April 1, as by being sent on some absurd errand.

a priori, ā prī·ō'ri. [L., from something prior or going before.] A phrase applied to a mode of reasoning by which we proceed from the cause to the effect, as opposed to *a posteriori* reasoning, by which we proceed from the effect to the cause; also a term applied to knowledge independent of all experience.

apron, ā'prun, *n.* [O.E. *napron,* Fr. *napperon,* from *nape, nappe,* a tablecloth, etc. (whence E. *napkin*), *nappe* being another form of *mappe,* E. *map. Apron,* like *adder, auger,* has lost the initial *n.*] A piece of cloth or leather worn on the forepart of the body to keep the clothes clean or defend them from injury; a covering for the front part of a body.—*v.t.* To put an apron on; to furnish with an apron.

apropos, ap"ro·pō', *a.* [Fr.—*à,* to, according to, and *propos,* purpose, L. *propositum,* a thing proposed.] Opportune; seasonable; to the purpose (an *apropos* remark).

apse, aps, *n.* [Gr. (*h*)*apsis,* (*h*)*apsīdos,* an arch, vault. joining, from (*h*)*aptō,* to join.] A portion of any building forming a termination or projection semicircular or polygonal in plan, and having a dome or vaulted roof; especially such a structure at the east end of a church.—**apsidal,** ap·sī'dal, *a.* Pertaining to or resembling an apse; pertaining to apsides.—**apsis,** ap'sis, *n.* pl. **apsides,** ap·sī'dēz. *Arch.* an apse; *astron.* one of the two points in the orbit of a heavenly body which mark its greatest and its least distance from the primary round which it revolves.

apt, apt, *a.* [L. *aptus,* fitted, fit.] Fit; suitable; apposite; pertinent; appropriate; having a tendency; liable; inclined; disposed; ready; prompt.—**aptitude,** ap'ti·tūd, *n.* The state or quality of being apt; disposition; tendency; fitness; suitableness; readiness in learning; docility.—**aptly,** apt'li, *adv.* In an apt or suitable manner; justly; pertinently; readily;

quickly; cleverly.—**aptness,** apt′nes, *n.* The state or quality of being apt; fitness; tendency; quickness of apprehension; readiness in learning; docility.

apteral, apterous, ap′ter•al, ap′ter••us, *a.* [Gr. *apteros,* without wings—*a,* not, and *pteron,* a wing.] Destitute of wings.

apteryx, ap′tėr•iks, *n.* [Gr. *a,* not, and *pteryx,* a wing.] A bird peculiar to but now nearly extinct in New Zealand, having no tail and very short rudimentary wings.

aqua, ak′wa, *n.* [L.] Water: a word forming an element in various terms; also used by itself as a commercial name of whisky.—*Aqua fortis* (= strong water), a name given to weak and impure nitric acid.—*Aqua regia* (= royal water), a mixture of nitric and hydrochloric acids, so called from its power of dissolving gold and other noble metals.—*Aqua vitae* (=water of life), ardent spirits, as whisky, brandy, etc.—**aquarium,** a•kwā′ri•um, *n.* A case, vessel, tank, or the like, in which aquatic plants and animals are kept; a place containing a collection of such vessels or tanks.—**Aquarius,** a•kwā′ri•us, *n.* [L.] The Water-bearer; a sign in the zodiac which the sun enters about 15 January.—**aquatic,** a•kwat′ik, *a.* Pertaining to water; living in or frequenting water.—*n.* A plant which grows in water; *pl.* sports or exercises practiced on or in water, as rowing or swimming.—**aqueous,** ak′wē•us, *a.* Partaking of the nature of water, or abounding with or formed by it; watery.

aquacade, ak′wa•kād, *n.* Water show with musical accompaniment including exhibitions of swimming, diving, and acrobatics.

aqualung, ak′wa•lung, *n.* A device to permit breathing under water, consisting of a watertight face mask and cylinders of compressed air.

aquamarine, ak′wa•ma•rēn, *n.* [L. *aqua,* water, and *marinus,* pertaining to the sea.] The finest beryl, so called from its bluish or sea-green tint.

aquanaut, ak′wa•nạt, *n*• [*Aqua,* water, and *nautēs,* sailor.] A deep-sea explorer who uses a capsule, resting on the ocean floor, as a base for his exploration.

aquaplane, ak′wa•plān″, *n.* A board on which a person stands as it is pulled over the water by a speedboat.—*v.i.* To ride an aquaplane.

aquarelle, ak•wa•rel′, [Fr., from L. *aqua,* water.] Watercolor painting.

aquatint, ak′wa•tint, *n.* [L. *aqua,* water, and It. *tinta,* dye, tint.] A method of etching on copper by which a beautiful effect is produced, resembling a fine drawing in watercolors or India ink.

aqueduct, ak′wē•dukt, *n.* [L. *aquaeductus—aqua,* water, and *ductus,* a pipe or canal, from *duco,* to lead.] A conduit or channel for conveying water from one place to another; a structure for conveying water for the supply of a town.

aqueous. See AQUA.

aquiline, ak′wil•in, *a.* [L. *aquilinus,* from *aquila,* an eagle.] Of or belonging to the eagle; resembling an eagle's beak; curving; hooked.

Arab, ar′ab, *n.* A native of Arabia; a neglected outcast boy or girl of the streets.—*a.* Of or pertaining to the Arabs or Arabia.—**arabesque,** ar′-ab•esk, *n.* [Fr., from the *Arabs,* who brought the style to high perfection.] A species of architectural ornamentation for enriching flat surfaces, either painted, inlaid, or wrought in low relief, often consisting of fanciful figures, human or animal, combined with floral forms.—**Arabian,** a•rā′bi•an, *a.* Pertaining to Arabia.—*n.* A native of Arabia; an Arab.—**Arabic,** ar′ab•ik, *a.* Belonging to Arabia or the language of its inhabitants.—*n.* The language of the Arabians.

arable, ar′a•bl, *a.* [Fr. *arable,* L. *arabilis,* from *aro,* to plow, from root seen also in A.Sax. *erian,* E. to *ear,* Icel. *erja,* Goth. *erjan,* Lith. *arti,* Rus. *orati,* to plow, to till; Ir. and W. *ar,* tillage; W. *aru,* to plow.] Fit for plowing or tillage.

Arachnida, a•rak′ni•da, *n. pl.* [Gr. *arachnē,* a spider.] A class of annulose, wingless animals, intermediate between the insects and the Crustacea, including spiders, mites, and scorpions.—**arachnidan,** a•rak′ni••dan, *n.* One of the Arachnida.—**arachnoid,** a•rak′noid, *a.* Resembling a spider's web; *anat.* applied to a semitransparent thin membrane which is spread over the brain and pia mater; *bot.* having hair that gives an appearance of being covered with cobweb.

Aramaic, ar•a•mā′ik, *n.* [From *Aram,* a son of Shem, the supposed ancestor of the Chaldeans and Syrians.] A language or group of languages anciently spoken in Syria, the earliest specimens being the Chaldee passages in the Old Testament and Apocrypha; Chaldaic; Chaldee.

Araucaria, ar•ạ•kā′ri•a, *n.* [From the *Araucanos,* a tribe of Indians in Chili.] The generic name of some fine coniferous trees found chiefly in South America, but now also commonly grown in Britain.—**Araucarian,** ar•ạ•kā′ri•an, *a.*

arbalist, arbalest, är′bal•ist, är′bal••est, *n.* [O.Fr. *arbaleste,* from L. *arcus,* a bow, and *ballista, balista,* an engine to throw stones.] A kind of powerful crossbow formerly used.—**arbalister,** är′bal•ist•ėr, *n.* A crossbowman.

arbiter, är′bit•ėr, *n.* [L., an arbiter, umpire, judge.] A person appointed or chosen by parties in controversy to decide their differences; one who judges and determines without control; one whose power of deciding and governing is not limited; an arbitrator.—**arbitrage,** är′bi•trāj, *n.* The calculation of the best mode by which advantage may be taken of differences in the value of money, stocks, etc., at different places in the same time; the dealing in bills of exchange, stocks, etc., for the purpose of making profit by such calculations.—**arbitrament,** är•bit′-ra•ment, *n.* Determination; decision; settlement; award (the *arbitrament* of the sword).—**arbitrary,** är′bi•tra•ri, *a.* [L. *arbitrarius.*] Given, adjudged, or done according to one's will or discretion; exercised according to one's will or discretion; capricious; despotic; imperious; tyrannical; uncontrolled.—**arbitrarily,** är′bi•tra•ri•li, *adv.* In an arbitrary manner; capriciously.—**arbitrariness,** är′bi•tra•ri•nes, *n.* The quality of being arbitrary.—**arbitrate,** är′bi••trāt, *v.i. arbitrated, arbitrating.* [L. *arbitror, arbitratus.*] To act as an arbiter or umpire; to hear and decide in a dispute.—*v.t.* To hear and decide on.—**arbitration,** är••bi•trā′shon, *n.* The act of arbitrating; the hearing and determination of a cause between parties in controversy, by a person or persons chosen by the parties.—**arbitrator,** är′bi•trāt•ėr, *n.* One who arbitrates; an arbiter.

arbor, är′bor, *n.* [L., a tree, a wooden bar, etc.] The principal spindle or axis of a machine, communicating motion to the other moving parts.—**arboreous, arboreal,** är•bō′rē•us, är•bō′rē•al, *a.* Pertaining to trees; living on or among trees; having the character of a tree.—**arborescence,** är•bor•es′ens, *n.* The state of being arborescent; an arborescent form or growth.—**arborescent,** är•bor•es′ent, *a.* [L. *arborescens,* pp. of *arboresco,* to grow to a tree.] Resembling a tree; *bot.* partaking of the nature and habits of a tree; dendritic.—**arboretum,** är•bo•rē′tum, *n.* [L.] A place in which a collection of different trees and shrubs is cultivated for scientific or educational purposes.—**arborization,** är′bor•i•zā″shon, *n.* A mineral or other body with a treelike form.

arbor, arbour, är′bėr, *n.* [O.E. *herber,* O.Fr. *herbier,* L. *herba,* herb; the spelling influenced by L. *arbor,* tree.] A seat in the open air sheltered by intertwining branches or climbing plants; a bower.—**arborous,** är′bor•us, *a.* Having the appearance or nature of an arbor. (*Mil.*)

arboriculture, är″bo•ri•kul′tūr, *n.* [L. *arbor,* a tree, and *cultura,* cultivation. CULTURE.] The cultivation of trees; the art of planting, dressing, and managing trees and shrubs.—**arboricultural,** är•bor′i••kul″tūr•al, *a.* Relating to arboriculture.—**arboriculturist,** är″bo•ri•kul′-tūr•ist, *n.* One who practices arboriculture.

arbor vitae, är′bor vī′tē, *n.* [L., the tree of life.] A common name of certain coniferous trees; a treelike arrangement which appears in the medullary substance of the brain when the cerebellum is cut vertically.

arbutus, är•bu′tus, *n.* [L., the strawberry-tree.] The generic name of an evergreen tree or shrub, with bright red or yellow berries, somewhat like the strawberry, having an unpleasant taste and narcotic properties.

arc, ärk, *n.* [L. *arcus*, a bow. ARCH.] *Geom.* a curve line forming or that might form part of the circumference of a circle; formerly also an arch.—**arcade,** är•kād′, *n.* [Fr., L.L. *arcata*, L. *arcus*, an arch.] A series of arches supported on pillars, often used as a roof support or as an ornamental dressing to a wall; a covered-in passage containing shops or stalls.

Arcadian, ar•kā′di•an, *a.* Pertaining to Arcadia, a mountainous district in southern Greece; hence, rustic; rural; pastoral.

arcanum, är•kā′num, *n.* pl. **arcana,** är•kā′na. [L.] A secret; a mystery: generally used in the plural (the *arcana* of nature).

arch, ärch, *n.* [Fr. *arche*, L.L. *archia*, from L. *arcus*, a bow, arch, arc.] A structure composed of separate wedge-shaped pieces, arranged on a curved line, so as to retain their position by mutual pressure; a covering, or structure, of a bow shape; a vault.—*Court of arches*, an ecclesiastical court of appeal pertaining to the archbishopric of Canterbury, anciently held in the church of St. Mary-le-bow, called also St. Mary-of-the-arches.—*v.t.* To cover or span with an arch.—**archway,** ärch′wā, *n.* A passage under an arch.

arch, ärch, *a.* [From next word, from being often used in such phrases as *arch* wag, *arch* rogue.] Cunning, sly, shrewd; waggish; mischievous for sport; roguish.—**archly,** ärch′li, *adv.* In an arch or roguish manner.—**archness,** ärch′nes, *n.*

arch, ärch, *a.* [From Gr. *archi*, in compound words, from stem of *archē*, power or rule.] Chief; of the first class or rank: principally used in composition as the first part of many words; as, *arch*bishop, *arch*priest, etc.—*n.*‡ A leader; a chief. (*Shak.*)

Archaean, är•kē′an, *a.* [Gr. *archaios*, ancient.] *Geol.* applied to the oldest rocks of the earth's crust, crystalline in character, and embracing granite, syenite, gneiss.

archaeology, är•kē•ol′o•ji, *n.* [Gr. *archaios*, ancient, and *logos*, discourse.] The science of antiquities, especially prehistoric antiquities, which investigates the history of peoples by the remains belonging to the earlier periods of their existence.—**archaeological, archaeologic,** är′ke•o•loj″ik•al, är′kē•o•loj″ik, *a.* Pertaining to ärchaeology.—**archaeologist,** är•kē•ol′o•jist, *n.* One skilled in archaeology.

archaeopteryx, är•kē•op′tėr•iks, *n.* [Gr. *archaios*, ancient, and *pteryx*, wing.] A fossil bird of the size of a rook, having two claws representing the thumb and forefinger projecting from the wing, and about twenty tail vertebrae prolonged as in mammals.

archaic, är•kā′ik, *a.* [Gr. *archaïkos*, old-fashioned, from *archaios*, ancient.] Old fashioned; obsolete; antiquated.—**archaism,** är′kā•izm, *n.* An ancient or obsolete word or idiom; antiquity of style or use; obsoleteness.

archangel, ärk•ān′jel, *n.* An angel of the highest order in the celestial hierarchy.—**archangelic,** ärk•an•jel′ik, *a.* Of or pertaining to archangels.

archbishop, ärch•bish′up, *n.* A bishop who has the supervision of other bishops (the sees of whom form his province), and also exercises episcopal authority in his own diocese.—**archbishopric,** ärch•bish′up•rik, *n.*

archdeacon, ärch•dē′kn, *n.* In England, an ecclesiastical dignitary, next in rank below a bishop, who has jurisdiction either over a part of or over the whole diocese.—**archdeaconate,** ärch•dē′kn•āt, *n.*

archdiocese, ärch•dī′ō•sēs, *n.* [*arch* and *diocese*.] Diocese of an archbishop.

archduke, ärch•dūk′, *n.* A prince belonging to the reigning family of the Austrian empire.—**archducal,** ärch•dūk′al, *a.* Pertaining to an archduke.—**archduchess,** ärch•duch′es, *n.* The wife of an archduke.—**archduchy,** ärch•duch′i, *n.* The territory or rank of an archduke or archduchess.

archenemy, ärch•en′ē•mi, *n.* A principal enemy; Satan.

archer, ärch′ėr, *n.* [Fr. *archer*, from *arc*, L. *arcus*, a bow. ARCH.] One who uses, or is skilled in the use of the bow and arrow; a bowman.—**archery,** ärch′ėr•i, *n.* The practice, art, or skill of shooting with a bow and arrow.

archetype, är′kē•tīp, *n.* [Gr. *archetypon*—*archē*, beginning, and *typos*, form.] A model or first form; the original pattern after which a thing is made, or to which it corresponds.—**archetypal,** är′kē•tīp•al, *a.* Of or pertaining to an archetype.

archidiaconal, är′ki•dī•ak″on•al, *a.* [Gr. *archi*, chief, *diakonos*, deacon.] Pertaining to an archdeacon.

archiepiscopacy, archiepiscopate, är′ki•ē•pis″kō•pa•si, är′ki•ē•pis″kō•pāt, *n.* The dignity, office, or province of an archbishop.—**archiepiscopal,** är′ki•ē•pis″kō•pal, *a.* Belonging to an archbishop.

archil, är′kil, *n.* A violet, mauve, or purple coloring matter obtained from lichens.

archimandrite, är•ki•man′drīt, *n.* [Gr. *archi*, chief, *mandra*, a monastery.] *Greek Ch.* an abbot, or abbot general, who has the superintendence of other abbots and convents.

Archimedean, är′ki•mē•dē″an, *a.* Pertaining to Archimedes, the Greek philosopher.—*Archimedean screw*, an instrument for raising water, formed by winding a flexible tube round a cylinder in the form of a screw, being placed in an inclined position, and the lower end immersed in water; by causing the screw to revolve, the water is raised to the upper end.

archipelago, är•ki•pel′a•gō, *n.* [Gr. *archi*, chief, and *pelagos*, the sea.] Originally the Aegean Sea, which is studded with a number of small islands; hence any water space interspersed with many islands; a group of many islands.—**archipelagic,** är′ki•pe•laj″ik, *a.* Relating to an archipelago.

architect, är′ki•tekt, *n.* [Fr. *architecte*, L. *architectus*, Gr. prefix *archi*, chief, and *tektōn*, a workman.] A person skilled in the art and science of building; one who makes it his occupation to form plans and designs of buildings, and superintend their erection; a former or maker. **architectonic,** är′ki•tek•ton″ik; *a.* Pertaining to or skilled in architecture.—**architectonics,** är′ki•tek•ton″iks, *n.* The science of architecture.—**architectural,** är•ki•tek′tūr•al, *a.* Pertaining to architecture or the art of building.—**architecture,** är′ki•tek•tūr, *n.* [L. *architectura*.] The art or science of building; that branch of the fine arts which has for its object the production of edifices pleasing to a cultivated and artistic taste; construction.

architrave, är′ki•trāv, *n.* [It. *architrave*—prefix *archi*, chief, and *trave*, from L. *trabs*, a beam.] *Arch.* the lower division of an entablature, or that part which rests immediately on the column.

archive, är′kīv, *n.* [L.L. *archivum*, a place for keeping public records, from Gr. *archeion*, a government building, from *archē*, rule, government.] A record or document preserved in evidence of something; almost always in plural and signifying documents or records relating to the affairs of a family, corporation, community, city, or kingdom.—**archival,** är′kīv•al, *a.* Pertaining to or contained in archives or records.—**archivist,** är′kīv•ist or är′ki•vist, *n.* The keeper of archives or records.

archon, är′kon, *n.* [Gr.] One of the chief magistrates of ancient Athens chosen to superintend civil and religious concerns.

arctic, ärk′tik, *a.* [L. *arcticus;* Gr. *arktikos*, from *arctos*, a bear, the northern constellation Ursa Major.] Northern; surrounding or lying near the north pole. The *arctic* circle is a circle parallel to the Equator, 23° 28′ from the north pole.

Arcturus, ärk•tū′rus, *n.* [Gr. *arktos*, a bear, and *oura*, tail.] A fixed star of the first magnitude near the tail of the Great Bear.

arcuate, ạrk′ū•āt, *a.* [L. *arcuatus*, from *arcus*, a bow.] Bent or curved in the form of a bow.

ardent, är′dent, *a.* [L. *ardens*, *ardentis*, pp. of *ardeo*, to burn, to be eager.] Burning; causing a sensation of burning; warm: applied to the passions and affections; vehement; passionate; eager; fervent; fervid; zealous.—*Ardent spirits*, alcoholic drinks, as brandy, whisky, rum, etc.—**ardently,** är′dent•li, *adv.* In an ardent manner; with warmth.—**ardency,** är′den•si, *n.* The quality of being ardent; warmth; ardor; eagerness.—**ardor,** är′dėr, *n.* [L. *ardor*.] Heat in a literal sense; warmth or heat, as of the passions and affections; eagerness.

arduous, är′dū•us, *a.* [L. *arduus;* allied to Ir. and Gael, *ard*, high.]

Steep, and therefore difficult of ascent; hard to climb; attended with great labor; difficult; hard (task or employment).—**arduously,** är'•dū•us•li, *adv.* In an arduous manner.—**arduousness,** är'dū•us•nes, *n.*

are, är. [O. Northumbrian *aron, arn,* we (you, they) are; the A.Sax. form proper is *sind* or *sindon.* The *r* is changed from *s,* the root being *as.* AM.] The present tense plural of the verb *to be, art* being the second pers. sing.

are, är or ãr, *n.* [L. *area.*] The unit of French superficial or square measure, containing 100 square meters or 119.6 square yards.

area, ā'rē•a, *n.* [L. *area,* a threshing floor, then any level open piece of land.] Any plain surface within boundaries, as the floor of a hall, etc.; a space sunk below the general surface of the ground before windows in the basement story of a building; a yard; the superficial contents of any space; a surface, as given in square inches, feet, yards, etc.—**areal,** ā'rē•al, *a.* Pertaining to an area.

areca, a•rē'ka, *n.* [The Malabar name.] A genus of palms, including the betel nut and cabbage trees.

arena, a•rē'na, *n.* [L. *arena,* lit. sand, a sandy place.] The inclosed space (usually covered with sand) in the central part of the Roman amphitheater; hence, the scene or theater of exertion or contest of any kind.—**arenaceous,** ar•ē•nā'shus, *a.* Abounding with sand; having the properties of sand; granular.

areola, a•rē'ō•la, *n.* pl. **areolae,** a•rē'-ō•lē. [L., dim. of *area* (which see).] A small area or space; a small interstice; the colored circle or halo surrounding the nipple or surrounding a pustule.—**areolar,** a•rē'ō•lėr, *a.* Pertaining to an areola.—**areolate,** a•rē'ō•lāt, *a.* Marked by areolae or small spots.—**areolation,** a•rē'ō•lā"-shon, *n.* Any small space or spot differing from the rest of a surface in color, texture, etc.

areometer, ar•ē•om'et•ėr, *n.* [Gr. *araios,* rare, thin, and *metron,* a measure.] An instrument for measuring the specific gravity of liquids; a hydrometer.

Areopagus, ar•ē•op'a•gus, *n.* [Gr., lit. hill of Ares or Mars.] A tribunal at ancient Athens, so called because held on a hill of this name.—**Areopagite,** ar•ē•op'a•jīt, *n.* A member of the Areopagus.—**Areopagitic,** ar•-ē•op'a•jit"ik, *a.* Pertaining to the Areopagus.

argal, argol, är'gal, är'gol, *n.* Unrefined or crude tartar; a hard crust formed on the sides of vessels in which wine has been kept.

argali, är'ga•lī, *n.* [Mongolian name.] A species of wild Asiatic sheep with very large horns, nearly as bulky as a moderately sized ox.

argent, är'jent, *n.* [Fr., from L. *argentum,* silver: cog. Gr. *argyros,* silver, *argos,* white; Ir. *arg,* white, *airgiod,* silver, money.] Silver†; whiteness, like that of silver; *her.* the white color in coats of arms, intended to represent silver, etc.—*a.* Resembling silver; bright like silver; silvery.—**argentic,** är•jent'ik, *a.* Pertaining to, like, or containing silver.—**argentiferous,** är•jen•tif'ėr•us, *a.* Producing or containing silver (*argentiferous* ore).—**argentine,** är'jen•tīn, *a.* Pertaining to, resembling, or sounding like silver; silvery.—*n.* White metal coated with silver; the Argentine Republic, S. America.—**argentite,** är'jen•tīt, *n.* Sulfide of silver, a valuable ore of this metal, a blackish, lead-gray mineral.

argil, är'jil, *n.* [L. *argilla,* white clay, allied to *argentum,* silver. ARGENT.] Clay or potter's earth; sometimes, pure clay or alumina.—**argillaceous,** är•jil•lā'shus, *a.* Partaking of the nature of argil or clay; clayey.—**argilliferous,** är•jil•lif'ėr•us, *a.* Producing or containing clay or argil.—**argillite,** är'jil•līt, *n.* Clay-slate.

Argive, är'jīv, *n.* A native or inhabitant of Argos, in ancient Greece; an ancient Greek. [Poetical.]

argon, är'gon, *n.* [Gr. *argos,* inert.] A colorless, odorless, gaseous element, chemically inactive. Symbol, A; at. no., 18; at. wt., 39.948.

Argonaut, är'gō•nạt, *n.* [Gr. *Argō,* and *nautēs,* a sailor.] One of the persons who, in the Greek legend, sailed with Jason, in the ship Argo, in quest of the golden fleece; a kind of cuttlefish, the paper nautilus or paper sailor of the Mediterranean, the female having a boatlike shell, in which its eggs are received. It was fabled to float with its arms extended to catch the breeze, and with other arms as oars.—**Argonautic,** är•gō•-nạ'tik, *a.*

argosy, är'go•si, *n.* [From *Ragusa.*] A large merchantman or other ship, especially if richly laden. [Poetical.]

argot, är'gō, *n.* [Fr.] Slang.

argue, är'gū, *v.i.*—*argued, arguing.* [L. *arguo,* to show, argue, to make clear.] To offer reasons to support or overthrow a proposition, opinion, or measure; to reason; to discuss; to debate; to dispute.—*v.t.* To debate or discuss (*argue* a cause in court); to prove, show, or evince; to cause to be inferred (his conduct *argued* suspicion).—**arguable,** är'gū•-a•bl, *a.* Capable of being argued.—**arguer,** är'gū•ėr, *n.* One who argues.—**argument,** ar'gū•ment, *n.* [L. *argumentum,* proof, theme, subject-matter.] The subject of a discourse or writing; an abstract or summary of a book or section of a book; a reason offered for or against something; a debate, controversy, or discussion; a process of reasoning.—*Argumentum ad hominem,* an argument which presses a man with consequences drawn from his own principles and concessions, or his own conduct.—**argumentation,** är'gū•men•tā"shon, *n.* The act of arguing, discussing, or debating; reasoning.—**argumentative,** är•gū•ment'a•tiv, *a.* Consisting of argument; addicted to argument, disputing, or debating.—**argumentatively,** är•gū•ment'a•tiv•li, *adv.*—**argumentativeness,** är•gū•ment'a•-tiv•nes, *n.*

Argus, är'gus, *n.* A being in Greek mythology having a hundred watchful eyes; hence, any watchful person; a species of pheasant having its plumage marked with eyelike spots.

Argyrol, ar'ji•rol, *n.* [Gr. *argyros,* silver.] Trade-mark for a silver-protein compound used as a mild local antiseptic.

aria, ä'ri•a, *n.* [It. *aria.*] A song; an operatic air for single voice.

Arian, ā'ri•an, *n.* One maintaining the doctrines of *Arius* (fourth century A.D.), who held Christ to be a created being inferior to God.—**Arian,** ā'ri•-an, *a.* Pertaining to Arius or to his doctrines.—**Arianism,** ā'ri•an•izm, *n.*

arid, ar'id, *a.* [L. *aridus.*] Dry; exhausted of moisture; parched with heat.—**aridity,** a•rid'i•ti, *n.* The state of being arid; dryness; want of interest.

Aries, ā'ri•ēz, *n.* [L. *aries,* a ram.] The Ram, a northern constellation, the first of the twelve signs in the zodiac, which the sun enters at the vernal equinox.

aright, a•rīt', *adv.* In a right way or form; properly; correctly; rightly.

aril, ar'il, *n.* [L. *areo,* to be dry, because it falls off when dry.] An extra covering of the seed of some plants (as the nutmeg) outside the true seed coats, falling off spontaneously.

arise, a•rīz', *v.i.*—*arose* (pret.), *arisen* (pp.), *arising.* [Prefix *a,* and *rise;* A.Sax. *arisan.* RISE.] To move to a higher place; to mount up; to ascend; to come into view; to get out of bed, or quit a sitting or lying posture; to spring; to originate; to start into action; to rise.

arista, a•ris'ta, *n.* [L.] *Bot.* an awn or beard.—**aristate,** a•ris'tāt, *a.* Awned.

aristocracy, ar•is•tok'ra•si, *n.* [Gr. *aristokratia—aristos,* best, and *kratos,* rule.] Government by the nobility or persons of rank in the state; the nobility or chief persons in a state.—**aristocrat,** a•ris'to•krat, *n.* A member of the aristocracy; one who favors an aristocracy; one who apes the aristocracy.—**aristocratic, aristocratical,** a•ris'to•krat'ik, a•ris'to•krat"-ik•al, *a.* Pertaining or belonging to the aristocracy or to the rule of aristocrats; resembling the aristocracy.—**aristocratically,** a•ris'to•-krat'ik•al•li, *adv.*

Aristotelian, a•ris'to•tē"li•an, *a.* Pertaining to *Aristotle* (born 384 B.C.), the celebrated Greek philosopher, and founder of the Peripatetic school.—*n.* A follower of Aristotle; a peripatetic.—**Aristotelianism,** a•ris'to•tē"-li•an•izm, *n.* The philosophy or doctrines of Aristotle.

arithmetic, a•rith'met•ik, *n.* [Gr. *arithmētikē,* from *arithmos,* number.] The science of numbers or the art of computation by figures or numerals.—**arithmetical,** ar•ith•met'-ik•al, *a.* Pertaining to arithmetic; according to the rules or methods used in arithmetic.—*Arithmetical progression,* series of numbers showing increase or decrease by a constant quantity, as 1, 2, 3, 4, etc.—9, 7, 5, 3; opposed to *geometrical progression,* *q.v.*—**arithmetically,** ar•ith•met′ik•al•li, *adv.* By the rules or methods of arithmetic.—**arithmetician,** a•rith′me•ti″shan, *n.* One skilled in arithmetic.

ark, ärk, *n.* [A.Sax. *arc*, from L. *arca*, a chest.] A small chest or coffer‡; *Scrip.* the repository of the covenant or tables of the law, over which was placed the golden covering or mercy seat; the large floating vessel in which Noah and his family were preserved during the deluge; hence, a place of safety or shelter.

arm, ärm, *n.* [A.Sax. *arm, earm*=Goth. *arms*, Icel. *armr*, G. Fris. D. Dan. and Sw. *arm;* cog. L. *armus*, the shoulder; Gr. *armos*, a fitting, from *arō*, to fit.] The limb of the human body which extends from the shoulder to the hand; an anterior limb; anything projecting from a main body, as a branch of a tree, a narrow inlet of waters from the sea; *fig.* power, might, strength.—**armful,** ärm′ful, *n.* As much as the arms can hold; that which is embraced by the arms.—**armchair,** *n.* A chair with arms to support the elbows.—**armhole,** *n.* The armpit†; a hole for the arm in a garment.—**armpit,** *n.* The cavity under the shoulder or upper arm.

arm, ärm, *n.* [Fr. *arme*, a weapon, from L. *arma*, arms.] A weapon; a branch of the military service; *pl.* war; the military profession; armor; armorial bearings.—*Small arms*, arms that can be carried by those who use them.—*A stand of arms*, a complete set of arms for one soldier.—*v.t.* To furnish or equip with arms or weapons; to cover or provide with whatever will add strength, force, or security; to fortify.—*v.i.* To provide one's self with arms; to take arms.—**armada, är•mä′da,** *n.* [Sp.] A fleet of armed ships; a squadron. [*cap.*] Usually applied to the Spanish fleet intended to act against England in the reign of Queen Elizabeth I, A.D. 1588.—**armadillo,** är•ma•dil′lō, *n.* [Sp. dim. of *armado*, one who is armed, so called from its bony shell.] A mammal peculiar to South America, covered with a hard bony shell, divided into belts, composed of small separate plates like a coat of mail.—**armament,** är′ma•ment, *n.* A body of forces equipped for war; a land force or a naval force.—**armature,** är′ma•tūr, *n.* Armor; hence, anything serving as a defense, as the prickles and spines of plants; a piece of iron connecting the two poles of a magnet.

Armageddon, är′ma•ged″on, *n.* [Possibly from Plain of Megiddo.] The scene of the final conflict of nations. *Rev.* xvi. 16.

Armenian, är•mē′ni•an, *a.* Pertaining to Armenia.—*n.* A native of Armenia; the language of the Armenians.

armilla, är•mil′la, *n.* [L., from *armus*, the shoulder.] An armlet; a bracelet; an iron ring, hoop, or brace, in which the gudgeons of a wheel move; a circular ligament of the wrist binding the tendons of the whole hand.—**armillary,** är′mil•la•ri, *a.* Resembling an armilla; consisting of rings or circles.—*Armillary sphere*, an arrangement of rings, all circles of one sphere, intended to show the relative positions of the principal circles of the heavens.

Arminian, är•min′i•an, *n.* A member of the Protestant sect who follows the teaching of *Arminius*, a Dutch theologian (died 1609), specially opposed to the Calvinistic doctrine of predestination.—*a.* Pertaining to Arminius or his principles.—**Arminianism,** är•min′i•an•izm, *n.* The peculiar doctrines or tenets of the Arminians.

armipotent, är•mip′ō•tent, *a.* [L. *armipotens, armipotentis*—*arma*, arms, and *potens*, powerful.] Powerful in arms; mighty in battle.

armistice, är′mis•tis, *n.* [L. *arma*, arms, *sisto*, to stand still.] A temporary suspension of hostilities by agreement of the parties; a truce.

armor, armour, är′mėr, *n.* [O.E. *armure*, O.Fr. *armeure*, from L. *armatura*, armor, from *armare*, to arm.] Defensive arms; any covering worn to protect the body in battle: also called *Harness*; the steel or iron covering intended as a protection for a ship of war.—**armorial,** är•mō′ri•al, *a.* Belonging to armor, or to the arms or escutcheon of a family.—**armorer,** är′mėr•ėr, *n.* A maker of armor or arms, or one who keeps them in repair; one who has the care of arms and armor.—**armory, armoury,** är′mėr•i, *n.* A place where arms and instruments of war are made or deposited for safekeeping; a collection of arms.

Armoric, Armorican, är•mor′ik, är•mor′ik•an, *a.* [Celt. *ar*, upon, and *mor*, the sea.] Pertaining to the northwestern part of France, formerly called *Armorica*, now Brittany.—*n.* The language of the Celtic inhabitants of Brittany, allied to the Welsh.

army, är′mi, *n.* [Fr. *armée*, an armed force or army, from *armer*, to arm. ARM, a weapon.] A collection or body of men armed for war, and organized in regiments, brigades, or similar divisions, under proper officers; a host; a vast multitude; a great number.—**army worm,** *n.* The larva of a moth, so called from its marching in compact and enormous bodies, devouring green things.

arnica, är′ni•ka, *n.* A composite plant, otherwise called mountain tobacco. The roots yield tannin, and a tincture of the plant is used as an application to wounds and bruises.

aroint, *v.t.* AROYNT.

aroma, a•rō′ma, *n.* [Gr. *arōma*, spice, sweet herb.] An agreeable odor; fragrance; perfume; *fig.* delicate intellectual quality; flavor.—**aromatic,** ar•ō•mat′ik, *a.* Giving out an aroma; fragrant; sweetscented; odoriferous. Also **aromatical,** ar•ō•mat′ik•al.—*Aromatic vinegar*, a perfume made by adding oil of lavender, cloves, etc., to acetic acid.—**aromatic,** ar•ō•mat′ik, *n.* A plant or drug which yields a fragrant smell, and often a warm, pungent taste.—**aromatize,** a•rō′mat•īz, *v.t.*—*aromatized, aromatizing.* To impregnate with aroma; to render fragrant; to perfume.

arose, a•rōz′, pret. of *arise.*

around, a•round′, *prep.* About; on all sides; encircling; encompassing.—*adv.* In a circle; on every side.

arouse, a•rouz′, *v.t.*—*aroused, arousing.* [Prefix *a*, with intens. force, and *rouse.*] To excite into action that which is at rest; to stir or put in motion or exertion; to rouse; to animate; to awaken.

arpeggio, är•ped′jē•ō, *n.* [It., from *arpa*, a harp.] The distinct sound of the notes of a chord, heard when the notes are struck in rapid succession.

arquebus, är′kwē•bus, *n.* [Fr. *arquebuse*, corrupted from D. *haakbus*, a gun fired from a rest, from *haak*, a hook, a forked rest, and *bus*, a gun=E. *hagbut, hackbut.*] An old-fashioned hand gun fired from a rest. Spelled also *Harquebus*, etc.—**arquebusier,** är′kwē•bus•ēr″, *n.* A soldier armed with an arquebus.

arrack, ar′ak, *n.* [Ar. *araq*, juice, spirits, from *araqa*, to sweat.] A spirituous liquor distilled in the East Indies from rice, the juice of the coconut, and other palms, etc.

arraign, a•rān′, *v.t.* [O.Fr. *arraigner, aresner*, etc., to arraign—L. *ad*, to, and *ratio, rationis*, account, a pleading in a suit. REASON.] To call or set at the bar of a court of justice; to call before the bar of reason or taste; to accuse or charge; to censure publicly; to impeach.—**arraignment,** a•rān′ment, *n.* The act of arraigning.

arrange, a•rānj′, *v.t.*—*arranged, arranging.* [Fr. *arranger*—*ar*=L. *ad*, and *ranger*, to range, from *rang*, a rank. RANGE, RANK.] To put in proper order; to dispose or set out; to give a certain collocation to; to adjust; to settle; to come to an agreement or understanding regarding.—*v.i.* To make or come to terms; to come to a settlement or agreement.—**arrangement,** a•rānj′ment, *n.* The act of arranging; disposition in suitable form; that which is arranged; preparatory measure; preparation; settlement; adjustment.—**arranger,** a•rānj′ėr, *n.* One that arranges or puts in order.

arrant, ar′ant, *a.* [A form of *errant*, wandering, hence vagrant, vagabond, thorough, in a bad sense.] Wandering‡; vagrant‡; shameless; notorious; thorough; out-and-out; downright.—**arrantly,** ar′ant•li, *adv.* In an arrant manner.

arras, ar′as, *n.* [From *Arras*, in France, where this article was manufactured.] Tapestry; hangings, consisting of woven stuffs ornamented with figures.

array, a•rā′, *n.* [O.Fr. *arrai*, order, arrangement, dress—prefix *ar-* (L. *ad*, to), and *rai*, order, from the Teutonic root seen in E. *ready.*] A collection or assemblage of men or things disposed in regular order, as an army in order of battle; raiment; dress; apparel.—*v.t.* To place or dispose in order, as troops for battle; to marshal; to deck or dress; to attire.

arrear, a•rēr′, *n.* [Fr. *arrière*, behind

—L. *ad*, to, and *retro*, behind.] The state of being behindhand; that which remains unpaid or undone when the due time is past: usually in the plural.

arrest, a·rest′, *v.t.* [O.Fr. *arrester*, Fr. *arrêter*—L. *ad*, to, and *restare*, to remain. REST.] To check or hinder the motion or action of; to stop; to seize or apprehend by virtue of a warrant from authority; to seize and fix (attention); to engage; to secure; to catch.—*n.* The act of arresting; apprehension; stoppage; stay; restraint.—**arrester, arrestor,** a·rest′·ėr, a·rest′or, *n.* One who arrests.—**arrestment,** a·rest′ment, *n.* The act of arresting; detention; arrest.

arride, a·rīd′, *v.t.* [L. *arrideo*—*ad*, and *rideo*, to smile.] To please or gratify. (*C. Lamb.*)

arris, ar′is, *n.* [O.Fr. *areste*, an arris.] The line in which two meeting surfaces of a body form an angle.

arrive, a·rīv′, *v.i.*—*arrived, arriving.* [Fr. *arriver*, from L.L. *adripare*, to come to shore—L. *ad*, to, and *ripa*, Fr. *rive*, the shore or bank.] To come to a certain place or point; to get to a destination; to reach a point or stage; to attain to a certain result or state: followed by *at*.—*v.t.*† To reach or arrive at. (*Mil.*)—**arrival,** a·rī′val, *n.* The act of arriving; a coming to or reaching; attainment; the person or thing which arrives.

arrogance, a′rō·gans, *n.* [L. *arrogantia, arrogo, arrogatum*—*ad*, to, and *rogo*, to ask or desire.] The character of being arrogant; the disposition to make exorbitant claims of rank, dignity, or estimation; the pride which exalts one's own importance; pride with contempt of others; presumption; haughtiness; disdain.—**arrogant,** a′rō·gant, *a.* Making exorbitant claims on account of one's rank, power, worth; presumptuous; haughty; overbearing; proud and assuming.—**arrogantly,** a′rō·gant·li, *adv.* In an arrogant manner.—**arrogate,** a′rō·gāt, *v.t.*—*arrogated, arrogating.* To claim or demand unduly or presumptuously; to lay claim to in an overbearing manner.—**arrogation,** a·rō·gā′shon, *n.* The act of arrogating; the claiming of superior consideration or privileges.

arrow, a′rō, *n.* [A.Sax. *arewe, aruwe, arwe*; allied to A.Sax. *earu*, swift, Icel. *ör*, pl. *örvar*, an arrow, *örr*, swift.] A missile weapon, straight, slender, pointed, and barbed, to be shot with a bow; anything resembling this.—**arrowy,** a′rō·i, *a.* Resembling an arrow in shape, in rapidity of flight, or the like.—**arrowroot,** *n.* A flour or starch obtained from the rootstocks of several West Indian reedlike plants, and much used as an article of food.

arsenal, är′se·nal, *n.* [Fr. *arsenal*, Sp. *arsenal*, from an Ar. word.] A repository or magazine of arms and military stores for land or naval service; a public establishment where arms or warlike equipments are manufactured or stored.

arsenic, är′sen·ik, *n.* [From Ar. *azzernikh*, the orpiment (q.v.).] An element, a grayish-white substance having a metallic luster and forming poisonous compounds. Symbol, As; at. no., 33; at. wt., 74.92.—**arsenic trioxide,** *n.* As_2O_3, a white or transparent, highly poisonous substance.—**arsenical,** är·sen′ik·al, *a.*

arsis, är′sis, *n.* [Gr. *arsis*, from *airō*, to elevate.] Elevation of the voice at a word or syllable, in distinction from *thesis*, or its depression; *pros.* a greater stress or force on a syllable.

arson, är′son, *n.* [O.Fr. *arson*, from L. *ardeo, arsum*, to burn.] The malicious burning of a house, shop, church, or other building, agricultural produce, ship, etc., which by the common law is felony.

art, ärt. Second pers. sing. ARE.

art, ärt, *n.* [L. *ars, artis*, art, from same root as Gr. *arō*, to join, to fit. ARM.] The use or employment of things to answer some special purpose; the employment of means to accomplish some end: opposed to *nature*; a system of rules to facilitate the performance of certain actions; skill in applying such rules (the *art* of building or of engraving; the fine *arts*): opposed to *science*; one of the fine arts or the fine arts collectively, that is those that appeal to the taste or sense of beauty, as painting, sculpture, music; the profession of a painter or sculptor; the special skill required by those who practice these arts; artistic faculty; skill; dexterity; knack; artfulness; cunning; duplicity.—*Art union*, an association for encouraging art.—**artful,** ärt′fu̇l, *a.* Cunning; sly; deceitful; crafty.—**artfully,** ärt′fu̇l·li, *adv.* In an artful manner; cunningly; craftily.—**artfulness,** ärt′fu̇l·nes, *n.* The quality of being artful.—**artless,** ärt′les, *a.* Devoid of art, skill, or cunning; natural; simple.—**artlessly,** ärt′les·li, *adv.* In an artless manner; naturally; simply.—**artlessness,** ärt′les·nes, *n.* Naturalness; simplicity; ingenuousness.

artery, är′tėr·i, *n.* [L. *artēria*, Gr. *arteria.*] One of a system of cylindrical vessels or tubes, which convey the blood from the heart to all parts of the body, to be brought back again by the veins.—**arterial,** är·tē′ri·al, *a.* Pertaining to or contained in an artery or the arteries.—**arterialization,** är·tē′ri·al·iz·ā″shon, *n.* The conversion of the venous into the arterial blood.—**arterialize,** är·tē′ri·al·īz, *v.t.*—*arterialized, arterializing.* To communicate, as to venous blood, the qualities of arterial blood, a result effected by the oxygen of the air taken into the lungs.

sclerosis, är·tėr′ri·o·skli·rō″sis, *n.* [Gr. *arteria*, artery, and *scleros*, hard.] A disease in which thickening of the walls of arteries impedes circulation of the blood.

artesian, är·tē′zi·an, *a.* [Fr. *artésien*, lit. pertaining to *Artois.*] Term descriptive of a kind of well formed by a perpendicular boring into the ground, often of great depth, through which water rises to the surface of the soil by natural gravitation, producing a constant flow or stream.

arthritis, är·thrī′tis, *n.* [Gr., from *arthron*, a joint.] Any inflammation of the joints; the gout.—**arthritic,** är·thrit′ik, *a.*

arthropod, är′thro·pod, *n.* [Gr. *arthron*, joint, and *podos, poús*, foot.] Any member of the Arthropoda, a phylum of invertebrates with segmented bodies and jointed limbs. Included are myriapods, arachnids, crustaceans, and insects.

artichoke, är′ti·chōk, *n.* [It. *articiocco*, probably of Ar. origin.] A composite plant somewhat resembling a thistle, cultivated in gardens for the thick and fleshy receptacle (or part supporting the flower), which is eaten. The *Jerusalem artichoke* is quite different, being a species of sunflower whose roots are used like potatoes. See GIRASOLE.

article, är′ti·kl, *n.* [L. *articulus*, a joint, division, part, or member, dim. of *artus*, a joint.] A single clause, item, point, or particular; a point of faith, doctrine, or duty; a prose contribution to a newspaper, magazine, or other periodical; a particular commodity or substance; a part of speech used before nouns to limit or define their application—in English *a* or *an* and *the*.—*v.t.*—*articled, articling.* To draw up under distinct heads or particulars; to bind, as an apprentice; to indenture.—**articular,** är·tik′ū·lėr, *a.* [L. *articularis.*] Belonging to the joints or to a joint.—**articulate,** är·tik′ū·lāt, *a.* [L. *articulatus*, jointed, distinct.] Jointed; formed with joints (an *articulate* animal); formed by the distinct and intelligent movement of the organs of speech; pronounced distinctly; expressed clearly; distinct (*articulate* speech or utterance).—*v.t. articulated, articulating.* To joint; to unite by means of a joint; to utter by intelligent and appropriate movement of the vocal organs; to enunciate, pronounce, or speak; to draw up or write in separate particulars or in articles (*Shak.*)‡.—*v.i.* To utter articulate sounds; to utter distinct syllables or words; to treat or stipulate (*Shak.*)‡.—**articulately,** är·tik′ū·lāt·li, *adv.* In an articulate manner; with distinct utterance.—**articulateness,** är·tik′ū·lāt·nes, *n.* The quality of being articulate.—**articulation,** är·tik′ū·lā″shon, *n.* The act or manner of articulating or being articulated; a joining or juncture, as of the bones; a joint; a part between two joints.—**articulator,** är·tik′ū·lāt·ėr, *n.* One who articulates.

artifact, är′ti·fakt, *n.* [L. *arte*, by art, and *factum*, made.] Any man-made object; *biol.* any unnatural change in structure or tissue.

artifice, är′ti·fis, *n.* [L. *artificium*—*ars, artis*, art, and *facio*, to make.] Artful, skillful, or ingenious contrivance; a crafty device; trick; shift; stratagem; deception; cunning; guile; fraud.—**artificial,** är·ti·fish′al, *a.* Made or contrived by art, or by human skill and labor; feigned; fictitious; assumed; affected; not genuine or natural.—**artificiality,** är·ti·fish′i·al″i·ti, *n.* The quality of being artificial.—**artificially,** är·ti·-fish′al·li, *adv.* In an artificial manner; by human skill and contrivance.—**artificialness,** är·ti·fish′al·nes, *n.* Artificiality.

artillery, är·til′lėr·i, *n.* (No pl.) [Fr. *artillerie*, from *artiller*, to work with art, to fortify, from L. *ars*, *artis*, art.] Formerly offensive weapons of war in general whether large or small (see 1 *Sa.* xx. 40); now, cannon; great guns; ordnance; ordnance and its equipment both in men and material; the men and officers that manage the guns; the science which treats of the use and management of great guns.—**artillerist,** är·til′lėr·-ist, *n.* A person skilled in gunnery.—**artilleryman,** *n.* A man engaged in the management of large guns.

artiodactyl, är′ti·ō·dak″til, *n.* [Gr. *artios*, even-numbered, and *daktylos*, a toe.] A hoofed mammal in which the number of toes is even (two or four), as the ox and other ruminants, the pig, etc.

artisan, är′ti·zan, *n.* [Fr. *artisan*, It. *artigiano*, L.L. *artitianus*, from L. *ars*, *artis*, art.] One skilled in any art or trade; a handicraftsman; a mechanic.

artist, ärt′ist, *n.* [Fr. *artiste*, It. *artista*, from L. *ars*, *artis*, art.] One skilled in an art or profession, especially, one who professes and practices one of the fine arts, as painting, sculpture, engraving, and architecture; specifically, and most frequently, a painter.—**artiste,** är·tēst′, *n.* [Fr.] One who is peculiarly skillful in almost any art, as a public singer, an opera dancer, and even a cook.—**artistic, artistical,** är·tist′ik, är·-tist′ik·al, *a.* Pertaining to art or artists; trained in art; conformable to or characterized by art.—**artistically,** är·tist′ik·al·li, *adv.* In an artistic manner.

artless, etc. See ART.

arum, ā′rum, *n.* [L. *arum*, Gr. *aron*.] The generic name of certain plants, one of which is the common arum, wake-robin, or lords-and-ladies.

arundinaceous, a·run′di·nā″shus, *a.* [L. *arundo*, a reed.] Pertaining to reeds; resembling a reed.

aruspex, a·rus′peks, *n.* [L. *aruspex* or *haruspex*.] One of a class of priests in ancient Rome whose business was to inspect the entrails of victims killed in sacrifice, and by them to foretell future events.—**aruspicy,** a·rus′pi·si, *n.* The art of an aruspex; augury; prognostication.

Aryan, är′i·an or ā′ri·an, *n.* [Skr. *ârya*, noble, eminent.] An Indo-European; a member of that division of the human race which includes the Hindus and Persians and most Europeans (except Turks, Hungarians, Finns, etc.).—*a.* Pertaining or belonging to the Aryans; Indo-European.

as, az, *adv.* and *conj.* [Contr. from A.Sax. *eallswa*, that is, *all so*, through the forms *alswa*, *also*, *alse*, *als*, *ase;* similarly G. *als*, *also*, as.] A word expressing equality, similarity of manner or character, likeness, proportion, accordance; in the same manner in which (ye shall be *as* gods; I live *as* I did); while; when (he whistled *as* he went); for example; for instance; thus; because; since (*as* the wind was fair we set sail); often equivalent to the relative *that* after *such* (give us *such* things *as* you please).

as, as, *n.* pl. **asses** as′ez, A Roman weight of 12 oz.; also, a Roman copper or bronze coin, latterly weighing ½ oz.

asafetida, asafoetida, as·a·fe′tid·a, *n.* [Per. *aza*, gum, and L. *fœtidus*, fetid.] A fetid inspissated sap from a large umbelliferous plant found in Central Asia, used in medicine as an antispasmodic, in flatulency, hysteric paroxysms, etc.

asbestos, asbestus, as·bes′tos, as·-bes′tus, *n.* [Gr. *asbestos*, inextinguishable—*a*, neg., and *sbennynai*, to extinguish.] A fibrous variety of several members of the hornblende family, having fine, elastic, flexible filaments, which are incombustible, and are made into fireproof cloth, paper, etc.—**asbestine,** as·bes′tin, *a.* Pertaining to asbestos, or partaking of its nature and qualities.

ascend, as·send′, *v.i.* [L. *ascendo*—*ad*, to, and *scando*, to climb. SCAN.] To move upward; to mouut; to go up from a lower to a higher place; to rise; to proceed from an inferior to a superior degree, from mean to noble objects, from particulars to generals, etc.; to pass from a grave tone to one more acute.—*v.t.* To go or move upward upon; to climb; to move upward along; to go toward the source of (a river).—**ascendable, ascendible,** as·send′a·bl, as·send′-i·bl, *a.* Capable of being ascended.—**ascendant,** as·send′ant, *n.* An ancestor, or one who precedes in genealogy or degrees of kindred; superiority or commanding influence; predominance.—**ascendant, ascendent,** as·send′ant, as·send′ent, *a.* Directed upward; rising; superior; predominant; surpassing.—**ascendancy,** as·send′en·si, *n.* Governing or controlling influence; power; sway; control.—**ascension,** as·sen′-shon, *n.* [L. *ascensio*.] The act of ascending; a rising; *the Ascension*, the visible elevation of the Saviour to heaven.—*Ascension Day*, the day on which the ascension of the Saviour is commemorated, falling on the Thursday but one before Whitsuntide.—*Right ascension* of the sun or of a star, the arc of the equator intercepted between the first point of Aries and that point of the equator which comes to the meridian at the same instant with the star.—**ascensional,** as·sen′-shon·al, *a.* Relating to ascension; ascending or rising up.—**ascent,** as·sent′, *n.* The act of rising; motion upward; rise; the way by which one ascends; acclivity; an upward slope; the act of proceeding from an inferior to a superior degree, from particulars to generals, etc.

ascertain, as·sėr·tān′, *v.t.* [O.Fr. *ascertainer*—*as* for *ad*, to, *certain*, from L. *certus*, sure. CERTAIN.] To make certain; to make sure or find out by trial or examination; to establish; to determine with certainty.—**ascertainable,** as·sėr·tān′-a·bl, *a.* Capable of being ascertained. —**ascertainment,** as·sėr·tān′ment, *n.* The act of ascertaining.

ascetic, as·set′ik, *a.* [Gr. *askētos*, exercised, disciplined, from *askeō*, to exercise.] Excessively strict or rigid in devotions or mortifications; severe; austere.—**ascetic,** as·set′ik, *n.* One who retires from the world and devotes himself to a strictly devout life; one who practices excessive rigor and self-denial; a hermit; a recluse.—**asceticism** as·-set′i·sizm, *n.* The condition or practice of ascetics.

ascidian, as·sid′i·an, *n.* [Gr. *askidion*, a little bottle.] One of certain marine molluscous animals of a low type; a tunicate animal.—**ascidium,** as·-sid′i·um, *n.* *Bot.* a pitcher-like appendage found in some plants.

ascites, as·sī′tēz, *n.* [Gr. *askos*, a bladder.] *Med.* dropsy of the abdomen, or of the peritoneal cavity.

ascorbic acid, a·skor′bik. The antiscorbutic vitamin, vitamin C, abundant in citrus fruits, tomatoes, and green vegetables and also occurring in animal products.

ascot, as′kot, *n.* [*Ascot* Heath, a racetrack in England.] A wide neck scarf that is looped under the chin.

ascribe, as·krīb′, *v.t.*—*ascribed*, *ascribing*. [L. *ascribo*—*ad*, to, and *scribo*, to write. SCRIBE.] To attribute, impute, or refer, as to a cause; to assign; to set down; to attribute, as a quality or appurtenance.—**ascribable,** as·krīb′a·bl, *a.* Capable of being ascribed or attributed.—**ascription,** as·krip′shon, *n.*

ascus, as′kus, *n.* pl. **asci,** as′kī. [Gh *askos*, a leather bottle.] *Bot.* one of the little membranous bags or cells in which the spores of lichens, some fungi, and some other cryptogams are produced.

asepsis, a·sep′sis, *n.* [Gr. *a*, without, and *sepsis*, putrefaction.] Absence of microorganisms; prevention of sepsis.—**aseptic,** a·sep′tik, *a.* Free or freed from septic material.

asexual, a·seks′ū·al, *a.* [Prefix *a*, neg., *sexual*.] Not sexual; having no distinctive organs of sex, or imperfect organs; performed without the union of males and females.—**asexually,** a·seks′ū·al·li, *adv.*

ash, ash, *n.* [A.Sax. *æsc* = Icel. *askr*, Sw. and Dan. *ask*, D. *esh*, G. *esche*.] A well-known tree cultivated extensively for its hard and tough timber; the timber of this tree.—**ash, ashen,** ash, ash′en, *a.*

ash, ash, *n.* [A.Sax. *æsce*, *asce*—a word common to the Teutonic tongues.] What remains of a body that is burnt; the dust or powdery substance to which a body is reduced by the action of fire: generally used in the plural; incombustible residue; the remains of a human body when burnt or otherwise decayed; *fig.* a corpse.—*Ash Wednesday*, the first day of Lent, so called from the ancient custom of sprinkling ashes on the heads of penitents on that day.—**ashy,** ash′i. *a.* Composed of or resembling ashes; lifeless and pale.

ashame, a•shām′, *v.t.—ashamed, ashaming.* [Prefix *a*, intens., for *of*, and *shame.*] To make ashamed; to shame.—**ashamed,** a•shāmd′, *p.* and *a.* Affected or touched by shame; feeling shame; exhibiting shame (an *ashamed* look): with *of* before the object.—**ashamedly,** a•shām′ed•li, *adv.* In a shamefaced manner.

ashlar, ashler, ash′lėr, *n.* [O.Fr. *aisselle, aissil*, a shingle, from L. *assula*, a small board, a chip or splinter.] Common freestones rough from the quarry; a facing made of squared stones on the front of buildings; hewn stone for such facing.

ashore, a•shōr′, *adv* On the shore, bank, or beach; on the land adjacent to water, to the shore.

Asian, ā′zhen, *a.* Pertaining to Asia, one of the continents of the globe.—**Asiatic,** ā•zhi•at′ik, *a.* Belonging to Asia or its inhabitants.—*n.* A native of Asia.

aside, a•sīd′, *adv.* On or to one side; to or at a short distance off; apart; away from some normal direction; out of one's thoughts, consideration, or regard; away; off (to lay cares *aside*); so as not to be heard, or supposed not to be heard, by someone present.—**aside,** a•sīd′, *n.* Something spoken and not heard, or supposed not to be heard, by someone present, as something uttered by an actor on the stage.

asinine. See ASS.

ask, ask, *v.t.* [A.Sax. *ascian, acsian, axian,* = Dan. *æske,* D. *eischen,* O.Fris. *askia,* O.G. *eiscôn.*] To request; to seek to obtain by words; to petition (with *of* before the person); to require, expect or claim; to demand; to interrogate or inquire of; to question; to inquire concerning; to seek to be informed about (to *ask* the way); to invite. [This verb may take two objects; as, to *ask* a person the time.]—*v.i.* To make a request or petition (with *for* before an object); to inquire or seek by request (often followed by *after*).—**asker,** ask′ėr, *n.* One who asks; a questioner, inquirer, petitioner.

askance, a•skans′, *adv.* [Etymology doubtful; perhaps It. *scansare,* to slip aside.] Sideways; obliquely; out of one corner of the eye.—**askant,** a•skant′, *adv.* A less common form of *Askance.*

askew, a•skū′, *adv.* In an oblique or skew position; obliquely; awry.

aslant, a•slant′, *a.* or *adv.* Slantwise; on one side; obliquely; not perpendicularly or at right angles.

asleep, a•slēp′, *a.* or *adv.* In or into a state of sleep; at rest.

aslope, a•slōp′, *a.* or *adv.* Sloping; deflected from the perpendicular.

asp, aspic, asp, as′pik, *n.* [L. and Gr. *aspis,* an asp.] A deadly species of viper found in Egypt; also, a species of viper found on the continent of Europe.

asparagus, as•par′a•gus, *n.* [Gr. *asparagos.*] A perennial herb of the lily family cultivated in gardens, the young shoots being used at table.

aspect, as′pekt, *n.* [L. *aspectus,* from *aspicio,* to look on—*ad,* to, and *specio,* to see or look.] Look; view; appearance to the eye or the mind (to present a subject in its true *aspect*); countenance; look or particular appearance of the face; mien; air (a severe *aspect*); view commanded; prospect; outlook (a house with a southern *aspect*); *astrol.* the situation of one planet with respect to another.

aspen, asp′en, *n.* [A.Sax. *æspen, æspe,* the aspen; D. *esp,* Icel, *ösp,* Sw. and Dan. *asp,* G. *espe,* the aspen-tree.] A species of poplar that has become proverbial for the trembling of its leaves, which move with the slightest impulse of the air.

aspergillum, as′pėr•jil″um, *n.* [Dim. from L. *aspergo,* to sprinkle—*ad,* to, and *spargo,* to sprinkle.] *R. Cath. Ch.* the brush used for sprinkling holy water on the people, said to have been originally made of hyssop.

asperity, as•per′i•ti, *n.* [L. *asperitas,* from *asper,* rough.] The quality or state of being rough; roughness or harshness to the touch, taste, hearing, or feelings; tartness; crabbedness; severity; acrimony.

asperse, as•pėrs′, *v.t.—aspersed, aspersing.* [L. *aspergo, aspersus—ad,* and *spargo,* to scatter or sprinkle.] To bespatter with foul reports or false and injurious charges; to slander or calumniate.—**aspersion,** as•pėr′zhun, *n.* A sprinkling, as of water (*Shak.*)†; the spread of calumnious reports or charges; calumny; censure.

asphalt, as′fạlt′, [Gr. *asphaltos,* from the Phoenician.] The most common variety of bitumen; mineral pitch; a black or brown substance which melts readily and has a strong pitchy odor; a mixture of asphalt or bitumen and sand or other substances, used for pavements, floors, the lining of tanks, etc.—*Asphalt rock* or *stone,* a dark-colored bituminous limestone.—**asphaltic,** as•fạlt′ik, *a.* Pertaining to or containing asphalt; bituminous.

asphodel, as′fō•del, *n.* [Gr. *asphodelos.*] The name given to various species of plants of the lily family: the asphodel of the older English poets is the daffodil.

asphyxia, as•fik′si•a, *n.* [Gr. *asphyxia—a,* not, and *sphyxis,* the pulse, from *sphyzō,* to throb.] Suspended animation or loss of consciousness, with temporary stoppage of the heart's action, caused by interrupted respiration, particularly from suffocation or drowning, or the inhalation of irrespirable gases.—**asphyxiate,** as•fik′ si•āt, *v.t.* To bring to a state of asphyxia; to cause asphyxia in.—**asphyxiation,** as•fik′-si•ā″shon, *n.* The act of causing asphyxia; a state of asphyxia.

aspic. See ASP.

aspic, as′pik, *n.* [Fr.; origin unknown.] A dish consisting of a clear, savory, meat jelly, and containing fowl, game, fish, etc.

aspire, as•pīr′, *v.i.—aspired, aspiring.* [L. *aspiro,* to breathe—*ad,* to, and *spiro,* to breathe, to endeavor after (in *expire, respire,* etc.). SPIRIT.] To desire with eagerness; to pant after a great or noble object; to aim at something elevated or above one; to be ambitious: followed by *to* or *after;* to ascend; to tower; to point upward; to soar.—**aspirant,** as•pīr′ant, *n.* One who aspires or seeks with eagerness; a candidate.—**aspirate,** as′pi•rāt, *v.t.—aspirated, aspirating.* To pronounce with a breathing or audible emission of breath; to pronounce with such a sound as our letter *h* has; to add an *h*-sound to (the word *horse* is aspirated, but not the word *hour*).—*n.* An aspirated sound like that of *h;* the letter *h* itself, or any mark of aspiration.—**aspiration,** as•pi•rā′shon, *n.* The act of aspirating; an aspirated sound; the act of aspiring or of ardently desiring; an ardent wish or desire chiefly after what is great and good.—**aspirator,** as′pi•rā•tėr, *n.* A device that uses suction to move air, liquids, or granular substances.

aspirin, as′pi•rēn, *n. Pharm.* a white crystalline derivative of salicylic acid, $C_9H_8O_4$, used to relieve pain and reduce fever.

asportation, as•pōr•tā′shon, *n.* [L. *asportatio—abs,* from, and *porto,* to carry.] A carrying away; specifically, the felonious removal of goods from the place where they were deposited.

asquint, a•skwint′, *adv.* In a squinting manner; not in the straight line of vision; obliquely.

ass, as, *n.* [A.Sax. *assa,* a male ass, *assen,* the female, also *esol, asal;* Goth. *asilus,* D. *ezel,* G. *esel,* Icel. *asni, asna,* Dan. *asen,* Lith. *asilas,* Gael. *asal,* W. *asyn,* L. *asinus;* ultimate origin unknown.] A well-known quadruped of the horse family, supposed to be a native of Asia, in parts of which vast troops roam in a wild state; from the slowness and want of spirit of the domestic ass, the type of obstinacy and stupidity; hence, a dull, stupid fellow; a dolt; a blockhead.—**asinine,** as′i•nīn, *a.* [L. *asininus,* from *asinus,* an ass.] Belonging to or having the qualities of an ass.

assafetida, *n.* Same as *Asafetida.*

assagai, as′sa•gā, *n.* [Pg. *azagaia,* Ar. *alzagāya—al,* the, and *zagaya,* a Berber word for a kind of weapon.] An instrument of warfare among the Kaffirs; a throwing spear; a species of javelin.

assail, as•sāl′, *v.t.* [Fr. *assaillir,* from L. *assilio,* to leap or rush upon—*ad,* to, and *salio,* to leap, to rise. ASSAULT.] To fall upon with violence; to set upon; assault; attack, with actual weapons or with arguments, censure, abuse, criticism, entreaties, or the like. *Assail* is not so strong as *assault,* which implies more violence, and is more frequently used in a figurative sense.—**assailable,** as•sāl′a•bl, *a.* Capable of being assailed.—**assailant,** as•sāl′-ant, *n.* One who assails, attacks, or assaults.—*a.* Assaulting; attacking.—**assailer,** as•sāl′ėr, *n.* One who assails.

assassin, as•sas′in, *n.* [Ar. *hashāshin, hashishin,* one who murders when infuriated by *hashish,* a maddening drink made from hemp.] One of a strange sect in Palestine in the time of the Crusades, the followers of the Old Man of the Mountains, distinguished for their secret murders; one who kills or attempts to kill by surprise or secret assault; a secret murderer; a cut-throat.—**assassinate,** as•sas′sin•āt, *v.t.*—*assassinated, assassinating.* To kill or attempt to kill by surprise or secret assault; to murder by sudden violence.—*n.*‡ [Fr. *assassinat.*] An assassin; assassination.—**assassination,** as•sas′sin•ā″shon, *n.* The act of assassinating; a killing or murdering by surprise or secret assault.—**assassinator,** as•sas′sin•āt•ėr, *n.* An assassin.

assault, as•sa̤lt′, *n.* [O.Fr. *assault* (Fr. *assaut*), from L.L. *assaltus,* from L. *ad,* to, and *saltus,* a leap, from *salio,* to leap. *Assail, insult, result,* etc., are akin.] An attack or violent onset; an onslaught; a violent attack with the intention of injuring a person; specifically, a sudden and vigorous attack on a fortified post; a storm.—*Assault at arms,* a name sometimes given to an exhibition of fencing or similar military exercises.—*v.t.* To fall upon by violence or with a hostile intention; to fall on with force; to assail. ASSAIL.—**assaulter,** as•sa̤lt′ėr, *n.* One who assaults.

assay, as•sā′, *n.* [O.Fr. *assai, essay,* a trial, examination, *essayer,* to test, from L. *exagium,* Gr. *exagion,* a weighing—*ex,* out, *agō,* to bring. *Essay* is the same word.] Examination; trial; the trial of the goodness, purity, weight, value, etc., of metals or metallic substances, especially gold and silver, their ores and alloys.—**assay,** as•sā′, *v.t.* To make an assay of; to examine by trial; to test the purity or metallic constituents of; to attempt, endeavor, essay (*Shak.*)‡.—**assayer,** as•sā′ėr, *n.* One who assays.

assegai, *n.* Same as *Assagai.*

assemble, as•sem′bl, *v.t.*—*assembled, assembling.* [Fr. *assembler,* from L.L. *assimulo,* to assemble—L. *ad,* to, and *simul,* together; akin, *similar, simulate, assimilate,* etc.; same root as E. *same.*] To collect into one place or body; to bring or call together; to convene; to congregate; to fit together (pieces of mechanism).—*v.i.* To meet or come together; to gather; to convene.—**assemblage,** as•sem′blāj, *n.* The act of assembling, or state of being assembled; a collection of individuals or of particular things; a gathering or company.—**assembler,** as•sem′blėr, *n.* —**assembly,** as•sem′bli, *n.* [Fr. *assemblée.*] A company or collection of human beings in the same place, usually for the same purpose; the name given to the legislative body or one of the divisions of it in various states.—*General Assembly,* the legislative body of the United Nations.—**assembly line,** as•sem′bli līn, *n.* Production line along which successive operations are performed until the final product is made.—**assemblyman,** as•sem′bli•man, *n.* Member of a law-making body, usually the lower house.

assent, as•sent′, *n.* [O.Fr. *assent*—L. *ad,* and *sentio,* to think (also in *consent, dissent, sense,* etc.)] The act of the mind in admitting or agreeing to the truth of a proposition; consent; concurrence; acquiescence; agreement to a proposal; accord; agreement; approval.—*Royal assent,* the approbation given by the British sovereign in parliament to a bill which has passed both houses, after which it becomes law.—*v.i.* To express an agreement of the mind to what is alleged or proposed; to concur; to acquiesce.—**assentation,** as•sen•tā′shon, *n.* [L. *assentatio,* flattery; from *assentor,* to assent from interested motives, to flatter.] Flattery; adulation.—**assentor,** as•sent′ėr, *n.* One who assents.

assert, as•sėrt′, *v.t.* [L. *assero, assertum*—*ad,* to, and *sero, sertum,* to join, connect, bind, from root of *series.*] To support the cause or claims of (rights, liberties); to vindicate a claim or title to; to affirm positively; to asseverate; to aver; *refl.* to come forward and assume one's rights, claims, etc.—**assertion,** as•sėr′shon, *n.* The act of affirming; the maintaining of a claim; a positive declaration or averment; an affirmation.—**assertive, assertory,** as•sėrt′iv, as•sėrt′o•ri, *a.* Positive; affirming confidently; peremptory; declaratory.—**assertively,** as•sėrt′iv•li, *adv.* In an assertive manner; affirmatively.—**assertor, asserter,** as•sėrt′ėr, *n.* One who asserts; one who affirms positively; one who maintains or vindicates.

assess, as•ses′, *v.t.* [O.Fr. *assesser,* L.L. *assessare,* from L. *assideo, assessum,* to sit beside, and hence to act as assessor—*ad,* to, and *sedeo,* to sit; akin, *assiduous, reside, sedentary,* etc.] To set, fix, or charge a certain sum upon (a person), by way of tax; to value, as property or the amount of yearly income, for the purpose of being taxed; to settle or determine the amount of (damages).—**assessable,** as•ses′a•bl, *a.* Capable of being assessed; liable to be assessed.—**assessably,** as•ses′a•bli, *adv.* By assessment.—**assessment,** as•ses′ment, *n.* The act of assessing; a valuation of property, profits, or income, for the purpose of taxation; a tax or specific sum charged on a person or property.—**assessor,** as•ses′ėr, *n.* One appointed to make assessments; an officer of justice who sits to assist a judge.—**assessorial,** as•ses•sō′ri•al, *a.* Pertaining to an assessor or assessors.

asset, as′set, *n.* [O.Fr. *aset, assetz,* Fr. *assez,* enough, from L. *ad.* to, and *satis,* enough.] An article of goods or property available for the payment of a person's obligations or debts: generally used in the plural; any portion of the entire effects belonging to a person.

asseverate, as•sev′ėr•āt, *v.t.*—*asseverated, asseverating.* [L. *assevero, asseveratum*—*ad,* to, and *severus,* serious, severe.] To affirm or aver positively, or with solemnity.—**asseveration,** as•sev′ėr•ā″shon, *n.* The act of asseverating; positive affirmation or assertion.

assiduous, as•sid′ū•us, *a.* [L. *assiduus,* from *assideo,* to sit close—*ad,* and *sedeo,* to sit. ASSESS.] Constant in application; attentive; devoted; unremitting; performed with constant diligence or attention.—**assiduously,** as•sid′ū•us•li, *adv.* In an assiduous manner.—**assiduousness, assiduity,** as•sid′ū•us•nes, as•si•dū′i•ti, *n.* The quality of being assiduous; constant or diligent application to any business or enterprise; diligence.

assign, as•sīn′, *v.t.* [Fr. *assigner,* L. *assigno,*—*ad,* and *signo,* to allot, mark out, from *signum,* a mark (whence *sign, consign,* etc.).] To mark out as a portion allotted; to apportion; to allot; to fix or specify; *law,* to transfer or make over to another.—*n.* A person to whom property or an interest is transferred; an assignee.—**assignable,** as•sīn′a•bl, *a.* Capable of being assigned. —**assignation,** as•sig•nā•shon, *n.* The act of assigning or allotting; the act of fixing or specifying; a making over by transfer of title; an appointment of time and place for meeting: used chiefly of love meetings.—**assignee,** as•sin•ē′, *n.* A person to whom an assignment is made; a person appointed or deputed to perform some act or business, or enjoy some right.—**assigner, assignor,** as•sīn′ėr, as•sīn′or, *n.* One who assigns or appoints.—**assignment,** as•sīn′ment, *n.* The act of assigning, fixing, or specifying; the writing by which an interest is transferred.—**assignat,** as′sig•nat or as•sin•yä′, *n.* [Fr., from L. *assignatus,* assigned.] A public note or bill in France during the first revolution.

assimilate, as•sim′il•āt, *v.t.*—*assimilated, assimilating.* [L. *assimilo*—*ad,* to, and *similis,* like. ASSEMBLE.] To make alike; to cause to resemble; to absorb and incorporate (food) into the system; to incorporate with organic tissues; to liken or compare†.—*v.i.* To become similar; to harmonize; to become incorporated with the body; to perform the act of converting food to the substance of the body.—**assimilability,** as•sim′il•a•bil″i•ti, *n.* The quality of being assimilable.—**assimilable,** as•sim′il•a•bl, *a.* Capable of being assimilated.—**assimilation,** as•sim′il•ā″shon, *n.* The act or process of assimilating or being assimilated; the process by which animals and plants convert and absorb nutriment so that it becomes part of the substances composing them.—**assimilative, assimilatory,** as•sim′il•āt•iv, as•sim′il•a•to•ri, *a.* Having the power of assimilating; tending to assimilate; producing assimilation.

assist, as•sist′, *v.t.* [Fr. *assister*, to stand by, help; L. *assisto—ad*, to, and *sisto*, to stand.] To help; to aid; to succor.—*v.i.* To lend aid; to be present; to take part in a ceremony or discussion.—**assistance,** as•sist′-ans, *n.* Help; aid; succor; a contribution in aid.—**assistant,** as•-sist′ant, *a.* Helping; lending aid or support; auxiliary.—*n.* One who aids or assists another; one engaged to work along with another; an auxiliary.

assize, as•sīz′, *n.* [Fr. *assises*, assizes, *assise*, a fixed rate, a tax, from L. *assideo*, to be an assessor. ASSESS.] A jury or similar assembly‡; the periodical sessions held at stated intervals by at least two judges in each of the counties of England and Wales (except Middlesex), for the purpose of trying criminal and certain other cases before a jury; generally in the plural; an ordinance; a decree; an assessment; particularly, an ordinance formerly fixing the weight, measure, and price of articles (hence the word *size*).—*v.t.—assized, assizing; assised, assising.* To fix the weight, measure, or price of; to fix the rate of; to assess‡.

associate, as•sō′shi•āt, *v.t.—associated, associating.* [L. *associo, associatum—ad*, to, and *socius*, a companion. SOCIAL.] To join in company (another with ourselves); to adopt as a partner, companion, and the like; to join or connect intimately (things together); to unite; to combine.—*v.i.* To unite in company; to join in a confederacy or association.—*a.* Joined in interest, object, office, etc.; combined together; joined with another or others.—*n.* A companion; a mate; a fellow; a partner; a confederate; an accomplice; an ally.—**associable,** as•-sō′shi•a•bl, *a.* Capable of being associated; companionable; social.—**associability, association,** as•sō′-shi-a•bil″i•ti, as•sō-shi•ā″shon, *n.* The act of associating or state of being associated; connection; union; a society, the members of which are united by mutual interests or for a common purpose; *philos.* the tendency which one idea, feeling, etc., has for one reason or another to recall another.—**associational,** as•sō′shi•ā″shon•al, *a.* Pertaining to association.—**associative,** as•sō′shi•-āt•iv, *a.* Capable of associating; tending to associate or unite; leading to association.

assonant, as′sō•nant, *a.* [L. *assonans*, ppr. of *assono—ad*, to, and *sono*, to sound.] Having a resemblance of sounds; *pros.* rhyming only so far as the vowels are concerned.—**assonance,** as′sō•nans, *n.* Resemblance of sounds; *pros.* a species of imperfect rhyme which consists in using the same vowel with different consonants.

assort, as•sort′, [Fr. *assortir*, to sort, to assort—*as* for L. *ad*, to, and *sors, sortis*, a lot. SORT.] To separate and distribute into sorts, classes, or kinds; to furnish with a suitable variety of goods (to *assort* a cargo); to adapt or suit.—*v.i.* To agree; to suit together; to associate; to keep company.—**assortment,** as•sort′-ment, *n.* The act of assorting; a collection of things assorted.

assuage, as•swāj′, *v.t.—assuaged, assuaging.* [O.Fr. *assouager, assouagier*, from L. *ad*, to, and *suavis*, sweet.] To allay, mitigate, ease, or lessen (pain or grief); to moderate; to appease or pacify (passion or tumult).—**assuagement,** as•swāj′ment, *n.* The act of assuaging; mitigation; abatement.

assume, as•sūm′, *v.t.—assumed, assuming,* [L. *assumo—ad*, to, and *sumo*, to take, also seen in *consume, presume, sumptuous*, etc.] To take upon one's self; to take on; to appear in (*assume* a figure or shape); to appropriate; to take for granted; suppose as a fact; to pretend to possess; to put on (*assume* a wise air).—*v.i.* To be arrogant; to claim more than is due; *law*, to undertake or promise.—**assuming,** as•sum′ing, *a.* Putting on airs of superiority; haughty; arrogant; overbearing.—**assumption,** as•sum′shon, *n.* [L. *assumptio.*] The act of assuming; a taking upon one's self; the act of taking for granted; supposition; the thing supposed; a postulate or proposition assumed; a church festival in honor of the miraculous ascent to heaven of the Virgin Mary's body after death, celebrated August 15.—**assumptive,** as•sum′-tiv, *a.* Capable of being assumed; assumed.

assure, a•shör′, *v.t.—assured, assuring,* [Fr. *assurer*, O.Fr. *asseürer*, L.L. *assecurare*—L. *ad*, to, and *securus*, secure.] To make (a person) sure or certain; to convince (to *assure* a person of a thing); to declare or affirm solemnly to; to confirm; to ensure; to secure (to *assure* success to a person); to insure; to embolden or make confident (N.T.); to affiance or betroth (*Shak.*).—**assurable,** a•-shör′a•bl, *a.* Capable of being assured; suitable for insurance.—**assurance,** a•shör′ans, *n.* The act of assuring; a pledge furnishing ground of full confidence; firm persuasion; certain expectation; undoubting steadiness; intrepidity; excess of boldness; impudence; laudable confidence; self-reliance; insurance.—**assured,** a•shörd′, *a.* Certain, convinced; not doubting or doubtful; bold to excess; confident; having life or goods insured (in this sense often a noun, sing. or pl.).—**assuredly,** a•shör′ed•li, *adv.* Certainly; indubitably.—**assuredness,** a•shör′ed•nes, *n.* The state of being assured; certainty; full confidence.—**assurer,** a•shör′ėr, *n.* One who assures; an insurer or underwriter.

assurgent, as•sėr′jent, *a.* [L. *assurgens, assurgentis*, ppr. of *assurgo—ad*, to, and *surgo*, to rise. SURGE.] Rising or directed upward.—**assurgency,**† as•sėr′jen•si, *n.* The act of rising upward.

Assyrian, as•sir′i•an, *a.* Pertaining or relating to Assyria or to its inhabitants.—*n.* A native or inhabitant of Assyria; the language of the Assyrians.—**Assyriologist,** as•sir′-i•ol″o•jist, *n.* One skilled in the antiquities, language (as exhibited in the cuneiform inscriptions), etc., of ancient Assyria.

astatic, a•stat′ik, *a.* [Gr. *a*, not, and root *sta*, to stand.] Being without polarity.—*Astatic needle*, a magnetic needle having its directive property destroyed by the proximity of another needle of the same intensity fixed parallel to it, but with the poles reversed.—**astatically,** a•stat′-ik•al•li, *adv.* In an astatic manner.

astatine, as′ta•tēn, *n.* [Gr. *astatos* unstable.] An unstable element belonging to the halogen family and produced by bombardment of bismuth with alpha particles. Symbol, At; at. no., 85.

aster, as′tėr, *n.* [Gr. *astēr*, a star.] A large genus of composite plants, the flowers of which somewhat resemble stars.—**asterisk,** as′tėr•isk, *n.* [Gr. *asteriskos*, a little star.] The figure of a star, thus *, used in printing and writing, as a reference to a note or to fill the space where something is omitted.—**asterism,** as′tėr•izm, *n.* [Gr. *asterismos.*] A small collection of stars; an asterisk, or several asterisks together†.

astern, a•stėrn′, *adv.* In or at or toward the stern of a ship; behind a ship; backward; with the stern foremost.

asteroid, as′tėr•oid, *n.* [Gr. *astēr*, a star, and *eidos*, form.] One of the small planets between the orbits of Mars and Jupiter, more accurately called *planetoids.*—**asteroid, asteroidal,** as′tėr•oid, as•tėr•oid′al, *a.* Resembling a star; pertaining to the asteroids, or to the starfishes.

asthenia, as•thē•nī′a, *n.* [Gr. *astheneia—a*, not, and *sthenos*, strength.] Debility; want of strength.—**asthenic,** as•then′ik, *a.* Characterized by asthenia or debility.

asthma, as′ma, *n.* [Gr. *asthma*, short-drawn breath.] A chronic disorder of respiration, characterized by difficulty of breathing, a cough, and expectoration.—**asthmatic, asthmatical,** ast•mat′ik, ast•mat′ik•al, *a.* Pertaining to asthma: affected by asthma.—*n.* A person troubled with asthma.—**asthmatically,** ast•mat′-ik•al•li, *adv.* In an asthmatical manner.

astigmatism, a•stig′mat•izm, *n.* [Gr. *a*, neg., and *stigma, stigmatos*, a mark.] A malformation of the lens of the eye, such that rays of light are not brought to converge in the same point.

astir, a•stėr′, *adv.* or *a.* On the stir; on the move; stirring; active; not used attributively.

astomatous, as•tom′a•tus, *a.* [Gr. *a*, without, and *stoma*, a mouth.] Without a mouth.

astonish, as•ton′ish, *v.t.* [Partly from O.Fr. *estonner*, L.L. *extonare*, lit. to make thunder-struck, from *ex*, intens., and *tono*, to thunder; partly from A.Sax. *âstunian—â*, intensive, and *stunian*, to stun.] To strike or impress with wonder, surprise, or admiration; to surprise; to amaze; to stun†; to confound‡.—**astonishing,** as·ton′ish·ing, *a.* Calculated to astonish; amazing; wonderful.—**astonishingly,** as·ton′ish·ing·li, *adv.* In an astonishing manner.—**astonishment,** as·ton′ish·ment, *n.* The state or feeling of being astonished; amazement; great surprise; a cause or matter of astonishment (O.T.).—**astound,** as·tound′, *v.t.* [For old *astoune*, A.Sax. *astunian*, with *d* added, as in *sound*, *expound*.] To astonish; to strike dumb with amazement.—**astounding,** as·tound′ing, *a,* Fitted or calculated to astound; causing terror; astonishing.

astraddle, a·strad′l, *adv.* Straddling; with one leg on either side; astride.

astragal, as′tra·gal, *n.* [Gr. *astragalos*, a huckle-bone, a moulding.] A small semi-circular molding separating the shaft of a column from the capital; one of the bars which hold the panes of a window; the huckle or ankle bone; the upper bone of the foot.

astrakhan, as′tra·kan, *n.* [From *Astrakhan* in the U.S.S.R.] A rough kind of cloth with a curled pile.

astral, as′tral, *a.* [L. *astralis*, from *astrum*, a star.] Belonging to the stars; starry.

astray, a·strā′, *adv.* Having strayed; out of the right way or proper place.

astrict,† as·trikt′, *v.t.* [L. *astrictum*. ASTRINGE.] To constrict; to contract; to limit.—**astriction,** as·trik′shon. *n.* The act of binding close, contracting, or restricting; limitation.—**astrictive,** as·trikt′iv, *a.* Binding; compressing.

astride, as·trīd′, *adv.* With one leg on each side; with the legs wide apart.

astringent, as·trin′jent, *a.* [L. *astringo*—*ad*, to, and *stringo*, to strain. STRAIN.] Contracting; especially contracting the organic tissues and canals of the body, and thereby checking or diminishing excessive discharges.—*n.* An astringent substance.

astrodynamics, as′trō·dī·nam″iks, *n.* [Gr. *astron*, star, and *dynamis*, power.] The science of adapting celestial mechanics to space flight.

astrolabe, as′trō·lāb, *n.* [Gr. *astēr*, a star, and root *lab*, seen in *lambanō*, to take.] An instrument formerly used for taking the altitude of the sun or stars at sea, now superseded by the quadrant and sextant.

astrology, as·trol′o·ji, *n.* [Gr. *astron*, a star, and *logos*, discourse, theory.] The pseudoscience which pretends to enable men to discover effects and influences of the heavenly bodies on human and other mundane affairs and to foretell the future.—**astrologer,** as·trol′o·jėr, *n.* One who practices astrology.—**astrological,** as·trō·loj′ik·al, *a.*—**astrologically,** as·trō·loj′ik·al·li, *adv.*

astronaut, as′tro·nąt, *n.* A person who travels through interplanetary space; a space-age enthusiast.—**astronautics,** as·tro·ną′tiks, *n.* The science of space flight.

astronomy, as·tron′o·mi, *n.* [Gr. *astron*, a star, and *nomos*, a law or rule.] The science which treats of the celestial bodies, their nature, magnitudes, motions, distances, periods of revolution, etc.—**astronomer,** as·tron′o·mėr, *n.* One who is versed in astronomy.—**astronomic, astronomical,** as·trō·nom′ik, as·trō·nom′ik·al, *a.*—**astronomically,** as·trō·nom′ik·al·li, *adv.*—**astronomical unit,** as·trō·nom′ik·al ū′nit, *n.* A basic measurement of astronomy. It is the mean distance between the earth and the sun.

astrophysics, as′tro·fiz″iks, *n.* Astronomical physics, the science that deals with the physical properties and phenomena of celestial bodies.

astucious, as·tū′shus, *a.* [Fr. *astucieux*, L. *astus*, craft.] Astute; crafty.

astute, as·tūt′, *a.* [L. *astutus*, from *astus*, craft, subtlety.] Of a shrewd and penetrating turn; cunning; sagacious; keen.—**astutely,** as·tūt′li, *adv.* In an astute manner; shrewdly; sharply; cunningly.—**astuteness,** as·tūt′nes, *n.* The quality of being astute; cunning; shrewdness.

astylar, a·stī′lėr, *a.* [Gr. *a*, not, and *stylos*, a column.] *Arch.* having no columns.

asunder, a·sun′dėr, *adv.* In sunder; apart; into parts; separately.

asylum, a·sī′lum, *n.* [L. *asylum*, Gr. *asylon*—*a*, not, and *sylaō*, to strip, plunder.] A sanctuary or place of refuge; any place of retreat and security; an institution for receiving and maintaining persons laboring under certain bodily defects or mental maladies; a refuge for the unfortunate.

asymmetry, a·sim′met·ri, *n.* [Gr. *a*, not, and *symmetria*, symmetry.] The want of symmetry or proportion between the parts of a thing.—**asymmetrical,** a·sim·met′rik·al, *a.* Not having symmetry; inharmonious; not reconcilable.

asymptote, as′im·tōt, *n.* [Gr. *asymptōtos*, not falling together—*a*, not, *syn*, with, and *piptō*, to fall.] *Math.* a line which approaches nearer and nearer to some curve, but though infinitely extended would never meet it.—**asymptotic, asymptotical,** as·im·tot′ik, as·im·tot′ik·al, *a.* Belonging to or having the character of an asymptote.—**asymptotically,** as·im·tot′ik·al·li, *adv.* In an asymptotic manner.

asyndeton, a·sin′de·ton, *n.* [Gr. *a*, not, *syn*, together, *deō*, to bind.] A figure of speech by which connectives are omitted; as, *veni, vidi, vici*; I came, I saw, I conquered.—**asyndetic,** as·in·det′ik, *a.* Pertaining to or characterized by the use of asyndeton.

at, at, *prep.* [A.Sax. *æt*, Goth. O.Sax. Icel. *at*, Dan. *ad*, O.H.G. *az;* allied to L. *ad*, to, Skr. *adhi*, upon.] Denoting coincidence or contiguity: *in time* (*at* first); *in space* (*at* home, *at* church); *in occupation* or *condition* (*at* work, *at* prayer); *in degree* or *condition* (*at* best, *at* the worst); *in effect*, as coincident with the cause (*at* the sight); *in relation*, as existing between two objects (*at* your command); *in value* (*at* a dollar a head); also, direction toward (fire *at* the target).—*At large*, at liberty; unconfined; also, generally; as a whole (the country *at large*).

Atabrine, at′a·brin, *n.* Trade-mark for quinacrine hydrochloride. It is used in the treatment of malaria.

ataractic, at·a·rak′tik, *n.* [Gr. *ataraktos*, without confusion.] A drug that decreases anxiety or tension.—*a.* tranquillizing.

atavism, at′a·vizm, *n.* [L. *atavus*, an ancestor.] The resemblance of offspring to a remote ancestor; the return or reversion among animals to the original type; *med.* the recurrence of any peculiarity or disease of an ancestor.

ataxia, a·tak′si·a, *n.* [Gr. *a*, not, and *taxis*, order.] Want of order; disturbance; *med.* irregularity in the functions of the body or in the crisis and paroxysms of disease.—**ataxic,** a·tak′sik, *a.*

atelier, at′el·yā, *n.* [Fr., a workshop.] A workshop; specifically, the workroom of sculptors and painters.

Athanasian, ath·a·nā′zhen, *a.* Pertaining to *Athanasius*, bishop of Alexandria, in the fourth century.—*Athanasian creed*, a creed of the Christian church, erroneously attributed to Athanasius, and also ascribed to Hilary, bishop of Arles (about A.D. 430). It defines the doctrines of the Trinity and the Incarnation in very precise and emphatic language, declaring damnation to be the lot of those who do not hold the right faith.

atheism, ā′thē·izm, *n.* [Gr. *atheos*, an atheist—*a*, not, and *theos*, God.] The disbelief in the existence of a God or Supreme Being.—**atheist,** ā′thē·ist, *n.* One who professes atheism or disbelief in God.—**atheistic, atheistical,** ā·thē·ist′ik, ā·thē·ist′ik·al, *a.*

atheling, ath′el·ing [A.Sax. *ætheling*, from *æthele*, noble = G. *edel*, noble.] In Anglo-Saxon times, a prince; one of the royal family; a nobleman.

athenaeum, atheneum, ath·e·nē′um, *n.* [L. from Gr. *Athēnē*, the goddess of wisdom.] An institution for the encouragement of literature and art, where a library, periodicals, etc., are kept for the use of the members.

athermanous, a·thėr′man·us, *a.* [Gr. *a*, not, and *thermainō*, to heat, from *thermē*, heat.] A term applied to those substances which have the power of absorbing radiant heat.—**athermancy,** a·thėr′man·si, *n.* The power or property of absorbing radiant heat.

athirst, a·thėrst′, *a.* or *adv.* Thirsty; wanting drink; having a keen appetite or desire (with *for*).

athlete, ath′lēt, *n.* [Gr. *athlētēs*, from *athlon*, a contest.] One trained to exercises of agility and strength.—**athletic,** ath·let′ik, *a.* Pertaining to athletes or such exercises as are practiced by athletes; strong; robust; vigorous.—**athletics,** ath·let′iks, *n. pl.* Athletic exercises.—**athletically,** ath·let′ik·al·li, *adv.* In an athletic manner.—**athleticism,** ath·let′i·sizm, *n.* The practice of athletics; the profession of an athlete.

athwart, a·thwąrt′, *prep.* Across; from side to side of; *naut,* across the line of a ship's course.—*adv.* In a manner to cross and perplex; crossly; wrong. (*Shak.*)

atilt, a·tilt′, *adv.* In the manner of a tilter; in the manner of a cask tilted up.

atlas, at′las, *n.* [Gr. *Atlas,* one of the Titans, who, according to the legend, bore the earth on his shoulders.] A collection of maps in a volume; a volume of plates or tables illustrative or explanatory of some subject; the first vertebra of the neck (so named because it supports the head).—**Atlantean,** at·lan·tē′an, *a.* Pertaining to Atlas; resembling Atlas.—**atlantes,** at·lan′tēz, *n. pl.* [Gr., pl. of *Atlas.*] Sculptured figures or half figures of men used in the place of columns or pilasters in buildings, supporting or seeming to support some mass above them.—**Atlantic,** at·lan′tik, *a.* Pertaining to or descended from Atlas (*Mil.*); pertaining to that division of the ocean which lies between Europe and Africa on the east and America on the west (named from *Mt. Atlas*).

atmosphere, at′mos·fēr, *n.* [Gr. *atmos,* vapor, and *sphaira,* a sphere.] The whole mass of aeriform fluid surrounding the earth and generally supposed to extend to the height of 40 or 50 miles above its surface; any similar gaseous envelope or medium; the amount of pressure of a column of the atmosphere on a square inch (=14.69 lbs.); *fig.* pervading influence (to live in an *atmosphere* of doubt).—**atmospheric, atmospherical,** at·mos·fer′ik, at·mos·fer′ik·al, *a.* Pertaining to, existing in, or consisting of the atmosphere; caused, produced, or operated on by the atmosphere.—*Atmospheric railway,* a railway, the motive power of which is derived from the pressure of the atmosphere, brought to act when air is exhausted from a tube of uniform bore, laid from one place to another.

atoll, a·tol′, *n.* [Name in the Maldive group.] A coral island, consisting of a strip or ring of coral surrounding a central lagoon or lake: such islands are very common in the Pacific Ocean.

atom, at′om, *n.* [L. *atomus,* Gr. *atomos,* an atom, lit. what is indivisible—*a,* not, and *temnō,* to cut.]—*Chem.* & *Phys.* the smallest particle of an element; it is composed of subatomic particles (protons, neutrons, electrons) whose number and arrangement characterize the element. A minute quantity.—**atomic,** a·tom′ik, *a.* Pertaining to atoms; consisting of atoms; extremely minute.—**atomic bomb.** A bomb whose explosive power is derived from the splitting (fission) of nuclei of atoms (plutonium, uranium) by bombardment with neutrons to release atomic energy.—**atomic energy.** Energy obtained from changes within the nucleus of an atom, by fission of a heavy nucleus or by fusion of light nuclei into heavier ones with loss of mass.—**atomic number.** *Chem* & *Phys.* a number giving the position of an element in the periodic table of elements; it is the number of positive charges on the nucleus of an atom of a given element.—**atomic philosophy,** a system of philosophy which taught that atoms, by virtue of their own properties, brought all things into being without the aid of a Creator.—**atomic theory,** the theory that all chemical combinations take place in a definite manner between the ultimate particles or atoms of bodies.—**atomic weight.** *Chem* & *Phys.* the weight of an atom of an element relative to the weight of a carbon atom, which is taken as 12.—**atomical,** a·tom′ik·al, *a.* Atomic.—**atomist,** at′om·ist, *n.* An adherent of the atomic philosophy or theory.—**atomism,** at′om·izm, *n.* The doctrine of atoms; atomic philosophy.—**atomistic,** at·om·ist′ik, *a.* Pertaining to atomism.—**atomize,** at′om·īz, *v.t.* —*atomized, atomizing.* To reduce to atoms.—**atomizer,** at′om·īz·ėr, *n.* One who or that which atomizes or reduces to atoms; an apparatus for reducing a liquid into spray for disinfecting, cooling, perfuming, etc. —**atomy,** at′om·i, *n.* An atom; a minute creature. (*Shak.*)

atone, a·tōn′, *v.i.*—*atoned, atoning.* [Compounded of *at* and *one,* often found together in such phrases as 'to be *at one,*' 'to set *at one.*'] To be at one‡; to agree or accord (*Shak.*)‡; to make reparation, amends, or satisfaction, as for an offense or a crime.—*v.t.* To expiate; to answer or make satisfaction for; to reconcile, as parties at variance.‡—**atonement,** a·tōn′ment, *n.* The act of atoning, reconciling, or making reparation; reconciliation after enmity or controversy; specifically, the reconciliation of God with man through Christ; satisfaction; expiation.—**atoner,** a·tōn′ėr, *n.* One who makes atonement.

atony, at′o·ni, *n.* [Gr. *atonia*—*a,* not, *tonos,* tone.] *Med.* a want of tone; defect of muscular power; weakness of every organ; debility.—**atonic,** a·ton′ik, *a. Med.* characterized by atony.

atop, a·top′, *adv.* On or at the top.

atrabilarian, atrabilarious, at′ra·bi·lā″ri·an, at′ra·bi·lā″ri·us, *a.* [L. *atra bilis,* black bile.] Affected with melancholy, which the ancients attributed to black bile; very bilious.—**atrabiliar, atrabilious,** at·ra·bil′i·ar, at·ra·bil′i·us, *a.* Melancholic or hypochondriacal; atrabilarian.

atrip, a·trip′, *a.* Of anchor loosed from bottom by means of a cable: of sails turned from horizontal to vertical position.

atrium, ā′tri·um, *n.* [L.] The entrance hall and usually the most splendid apartment of an ancient Roman house; *zool.* the chamber into which the intestine opens in ascidians.

atrocious, a·trō′shus, *a.* [L. *atrox, atrocis,* fierce, cruel.] Extremely heinous, criminal, or cruel; enormously or outrageously wicked; enormous; horrible.—**atrociously,** a·trō′shus·li, *adv.* In an atrocious manner.—**atrociousness,** a·trō′shus·nes, *n.* The quality of being atrocious.—**atrocity,** a·tros′i·ti, *n.* The state or quality of being atrocious; enormous wickedness or cruelty; a specific act of extreme heinousness or cruelty.

atrophy, at′ro·fi, *n.* [Gr. *atrophia*—*a,* not, and *trephō,* to nourish.] A wasting of the flesh with loss of strength; emaciation.

atropin, atropine, at′rō·pin, *n.* A very poisonous substance obtained from the deadly nightshade (*Atrōpa belladonna*).

attach, at·tach′, *v.t.* [Fr. *attacher,* same word as *attaquer,* to attack, from Arm. *tach,* Ir. *taca,* a peg, a nail=E. *tack,* a small nail.] To make to adhere; to tie, bind, or fasten; to connect or associate; to gain over, win, charm, or attract; to arrest or seize (a person or goods) by lawful authority, as in case of debt, etc.—*v.i.* To be attached or connected; to be joined or bound up with; to belong: with *to* (interest *attaches* to a subject).—**attachable,** at·tach′a·bl, *a.* Capable of being attached.—**attache,** a·ta·shā′, *n.* [Fr.] One attached to an embassy or legation to a foreign court.—**attachment,** at·tach′ment, *n.* The act of attaching; the state of being attached; close adherence or affection; any passion or liking which binds one person to another or to a place, etc.; love; regard; that which attaches one object to another; the object attached; an adjunct; *law,* a taking of a person or goods by legal means to secure a debt.

attack, at·tak′, *v.t.* [Fr. *attaquer.* ATTACH.] To assault; to fall upon with force or violence; to make a hostile onset on; to assail; to endeavor to injure by any act, speech, or writing; to come or fall upon; to seize, as a disease.—*v.i.* To make an attack or onset; to begin an assault.—*n.* A falling on, with force or violence, or with calumny, satire, etc.; an onset; an assault; a seizure by a disease.

attain, at·tān′, *v.t.* [O.Fr. *ataindre,* Fr. *atteindre,* L. *attingere*—*ad,* to, and *tango,* to touch. Akin *attaint, attainder, tact, tangent,* etc.] To reach by effort; to achieve or accomplish; to acquire; to gain: said of an end or object; to come to; to arrive at; to reach: said of a place.—*v.i.* To reach; to come or arrive; followed by *to.*—**attainable,** at·tān′a·bl, *a.* Capable of being attained, reached, achieved, or accomplished.—**attainability, attainableness,** at·tān′a·bil″i·ti, at·tān′a·bl·nes, *n.* The quality of being attainable.—**attainment,** at·tān′ment, *n.* The act of attaining; that which is attained, an acquisition; an acquirement.

attainder, at·tān′dėr, *n.* [O.Fr. *atteindre, attaindre,* to touch or reach, as with law; to attaint, from L. *attingo.* ATTAIN, *v.t.*] The act or legal process of subjecting a person to the consequences of judgment of death or outlawry pronounced in respect of treason or felony; forfeiture of civil privileges; a bringing under some disgrace or dishonor (*Shak*).—**attaint,** at·tānt′, *v.t.* [O.Fr. *attaint*, pp. of *attaindre, ataindre.*] To affect with attainder; to find guilty of a crime, as of felony or treason, involving forfeiture of civil privileges.

attaint,‡ at·tānt′, *n.* [Prefix *at*, from L. *ad*, to, and *taint*, from L. *tinctus*, pp. of *tingo*, to dye. TAINT.] A spot, taint, stain, disgrace. (*Shak.*)—*a.*‡ Tainted; corrupted; infected. (*Shak.*)

attar, at′tär, *n.* [Ar. *atr*, perfume.] A perfume from flowers.—*Attar* or *otto of roses*, an essential oil made from various species of roses, which forms a valuable perfume.

attemper, at·tem′pėr, *v.t.* [L. *attempero*—*ad*, and *tempero*, to temper, mix, or moderate. TEMPER.] To reduce, mollify, or moderate by mixture; to soften, modify, or regulate; to accommodate or make fit.

attempt, at·temt′, *v.t.* [O.Fr. *attempter*, from L. *attemptare*—*ad*, to and *tempto*, to try.] To make an effort to effect; to endeavor to perform; to undertake; to try; to attack; to make an effort upon (a person's life); to try to win or seduce.—*n.* An essay, trial, or endeavor; an effort to gain a point; an attack, onset, or assault.—**attemptable,** at·temt′a·bl, *a.* Capable of being attempted.

attend, at·tend′, *v.t.* [Fr. *attendre*, L. *attendo*, to turn one's mind to, to turn to—*ad*, to, and *tendo*, to stretch. TEND.] To accompany or be present with, as a companion or servant; to be present at or in for some purpose (church, a concert, etc.); to accompany or follow in immediate sequence, especially from a causal connection (a cold *attended* with fever); to wait for‡.—*v.i.* To pay regard or heed; to be present, in pursuance of duty; to act as an attendant; to be concomitant: by itself or followed by *on* or *upon.*—**attendance,** at·tend′ans, *n.* The act of attending or attending on; the act of waiting on or serving; service; ministry; the persons attending for any purpose; a train; a retinue.—**attendant,** at·tend′ant, *a.* Accompanying; being present or in attendance upon; connected with, or immediately following.—*n.* One who attends or accompanies another; one who belongs to a person's retinue; a follower; one who is present or regularly present; that which accompanies or is consequent on.—**attention,** at·ten′shon, *n.* [L. *attentio, attentionis*, from *attendo.*] The act of attending or heeding; the application of the ear to sounds, or of the mind to objects presented to its contemplation; heedfulness; observation; an act of civility or courtesy.—**attentive,** at·tent′iv, *a.* Paying or giving attention; heedful; intent; observant; regarding with care; mindful; habitually heedful or mindful; sedulous.—**attentively,** at·tent′iv·li, *adv.* In an attentive manner.—**attentiveness,** at·tent′iv·nes, *n.* The state of being attentive; attention.

attenuate, at·ten′ū·āt, *v.t.*—*attenuated, attenuating.* [L. *attenuo, attenuatum*—*ad*, and *tenuo*, to make thin; *tenuis*, thin; same root as in E. *thin, tender.*] To make thin, fine, or slender; to reduce the thickness of either liquids or solid bodies; to reduce the strength of; to render meager or jejune.—*v.i.* To become thin, slender, or fine; to diminish; to lessen.—**attenuation,** atten′ū·ā″shon, *n.* The act of attenuating or making thin, as fluids, or slender and fine, as solid bodies.—**attenuant,** at·ten′ū·ant, *a.* Attenuating; making thin, as fluids; diluting.—*n.* A medicine which increases the fluidity of the humors; a diluent.

attest, at·test′, *v.t.* [Fr. *attester*, L. *attestor*—*ad*, and *testor*, to witness. TESTAMENT, DETEST.] To bear witness to; to certify; to affirm to be true or genuine; to declare the truth of; to manifest (one's joy, etc.).—**attestation,** at·test·ā′shon, *n.* The act of attesting; a solemn declaration, verbal or written, in support of a fact; evidence; testimony.

Attic, at′tik, *a.* [L. *Atticus*, Gr. *Attikos.*] Pertaining to *Attica*, in Greece, or to its principal city, Athens; marked by the qualities characteristic of the Athenians; as, *Attic wit, Attic salt*, a delicate wit for which the Athenians were famous.—*n.* The dialect spoken in Attica or Athens; the chief literary and most elegant language of ancient Greece; [*not cap.*] *arch.* a low story erected over a principal; an apartment in the uppermost part of a house, with windows in the cornice or the roof; a garret.—**Atticism,** at′ti·sizm, *n.* A peculiarity or characteristic of the Attic dialect of Greek; elegance of diction.—**Atticize,** at′ti·sīz, *v.t.* and *i.* To conform to the Attic dialect.

attire, at·tīr′, *v.t.*—*attired, attiring.* [O.Fr. *attirer*, to array, from prefix *at*, L. *ad*, to, and same word as G. *zier*, ornament, A.Sax. *tir*, splendor, Dan. *ziir*, ornament.] To dress; to deck; to array; to adorn with elegant or splendid garments.—*n.* (no pl.). Dress; clothes; garb; apparel.

attitude, at′ti·tūd, *n.* [Fr., from It. *attitudine*, fitness, posture, L.L. *aptitudo*, fitness, L. *aptus*, fit. APT.] Posture or position of a person, or the manner in which the parts of his body are disposed; state, condition, or conjuncture, as likely to have a certain result; aspect (the *attitude* of affairs).—**attitudinize,** at·ti·tūd′in·īz, *v.i.*—*attitudinized, attitudinizing.* To assume affected attitudes, airs, or postures.

attorney, at·tėr′ni, *n.* [O.Fr. *attorné*, pp. of *attorner*, to transfer—*at*, L. *ad*, to, and *torner*, to turn. TURN.] One who is appointed or admitted in the place of another to transact any business for him.—*Letter* or *power of attorney*, a formal instrument by which one person authorizes another to do some act or acts for him.—*v.t.*‡—**district attorney,** the prosecuting officer of a Federal judicial district, or of a state, or any district thereof.—**attorney general,** *n.* Head of the Federal Department of Justice; also the chief officer of a Federal judicial district; also legal adviser to the state legislature.

attract, at·trakt′, *v.t.* [L. *attraho, attractum*—*ad*, to, and *traho*, to draw, whence *tract, treat, trace*, etc.] To draw to or toward, either in a physical or mental sense; to cause to draw near or close to by some influence; to invite or allure; to entice; to win.—*v.i.* To possess or exert the power of attraction; to be attractive or winning.—**attractable,** at·trakt′a·bl, *a.* Capable of being attracted; subject to attraction.—**attractor,** *n.* One who or that which attracts.—**attraction,** at·trak′shon, *n.* The act, power, or property of attracting; *physics*, the tendency, force, or forces through which all particles of matter, as well as all individual masses of matter are attracted or drawn towards each other; the inherent tendency in bodies to approach each other, to unite and to remain united; the power or act of alluring, drawing to, inviting, or engaging; allurement; enticement; that which attracts; a charm; an allurement.—**attractive,** at·trakt′iv, *a.* [Fr. *attractif.*] Having the quality of attracting; having the power of charming or alluring; inviting; engaging; enticing.—*n.* That which attracts; a charm or allurement.—**attractively,** at·trakt′iv·li, *adv.* In an attractive manner.—**attractiveness,** at·trakt′iv·nes, *n.* The quality of being attractive or engaging.

attrahent,† at′tra·hent, *a.* [L. *attrahens, attrahentis*, ppr. of *attraho.* ATTRACT.] Drawing to; attracting; dragging or pulling.

attribute, at·trib′ūt, *v.t.*—*attributed, attributing.* [L. *attribuo, attributum*—*ad*, and *tribuo*, to assign.] To ascribe; to impute; to consider as belonging or as due; to assign.—**attribute,** at′tri·būt, *n.* Any property, quality, or characteristic that can be ascribed to a person or thing; *fine arts*, a symbol of office or character added to any figure (thus the eagle is the *attribute* of Jupiter).—**attributable,** at·trib′ūt·a·bl, *a.* Capable of being, or liable to be attributed; ascribable; imputable.—**attribution,** at·tri·bū′shon, *n.* The act of attributing; that which is ascribed; attribute.—**attributive,** at·trib′ū·tiv, *a.* Pertaining to or expressing an attribute; *gram.* coming before the noun it qualifies. —*n. Gram.* a word expressive of an attribute; an adjective.—**attributively,** at·trib′ū·tiv·li, *adv. Gram.* in an attributive manner; used before the noun.

attrition, at·tri′shon, *n.* [L. *attritio*, from *attero, attritum*, to rub down—*ad*, to, and *tero, tritum*, to rub.] The act of wearing or rubbing down; the state of being worn down or smoothed by friction; abrasion.

attune, at·tūn′, *v.t.*—*attuned, attuning.* [Prefix *at* for *ad*, to, and tune.] To tune or put in tune; to adjust one sound to another; to make accordant; *fig.* to arrange fitly; to bring into harmony, concord, or agreement.

atypic, a·tip′ik, *a.* [Gr. *a*, not, and *typos*, a type.] Devoid of typical character; irregular.

auburn, a̧′bėrn, *a.* [L.L. *alburnus*, whitish, from L. *albus*, white.] Originally, whitish or flaxen colored; now reddish brown or rich chestnut; generally applied to hair.

auction, a̧k′shon, *n.* [L. *auctio*, from *augeo, auctum*, to increase (from the rising in successive bids); allied to Icel. *auka*, Goth. *aukan*, E. *ake*, to increase. AUGMENT, AUXILIARY.] A public sale of property to the highest bidder.—*v.t.* To sell by auction.—**auctioneer,** a̧k′shon·ēr′, *n.* One whose business it is to sell things by auction.—*v.t.*† To sell by auction.

audacious, a̧·dā′shus, *a.* [L. *audax, audacis*, from *audeo*, to dare.] Over bold or daring; bold in wickedness; insolent; imprudent; shameless; unabashed.—**audaciously,** a̧·dā′shus·li, *adv.* In an audacious manner.—**audaciousness, audacity,** a̧·dā′shus·nes, a̧·das′i·ti, *n.* The quality of being audacious; impudence; effrontery; insolence.

audible, a̧′di·bl, *a.* [L. *audibilis*, from *audio*, to hear; same root as in E. *ear.*] Capable of being heard; perceivable by the ear; loud enough to be heard.—**audibleness, audibility,** a̧′di·bl·nes, a̧·di·bil′i·ti, *n.* The quality of being audible.—**audibly,** a̧′di·bli, *adv.* In an audible manner.—**audience,** a̧′di·ens, *n.* [L. *audientia.*] The act of listening; a hearing; liberty or opportunity of being heard before a person or assembly; an assembly of hearers.

audiofrequency, a̧′di·ō·frē″kwen·si, *adj. Elec.* Pertaining to a frequency corresponding to audible frequencies of sound waves, that is, from 15 to 20,000 cycles per second.

audiometer, a̧·di·om′et·ėr, *n.* [L. *audio*, to hear, and Gr. *metron*, measure.] An instrument for testing the sense of hearing.

audio-visual aid, nontextual materials such as films, recordings, and charts used in teaching; so called because of their appeal to sight and hearing.

audiphone, a̧′di·fōn, *n.* [L. *audio*, to hear, and Gr. *phōnē*, voice.] An instrument for enabling the deaf to hear, essentially consisting of a fan-shaped vibratory plate of caoutchouc which is applied to the upper teeth, through which the sound vibrations are conveyed to the auditory nerve.

audit, a̧′dit, *n.* [L. *audit*, he hears, or *auditus*, a hearing, from *audio*, to hear. AUDIBLE.] An examination into accounts or dealings with money or property by proper officers, or persons appointed for that purpose, hence, a calling to account; an examination into one's actions; also, an audience or hearing†.—*v.t.* To make audit of; to examine, as an account or accounts.—**audition,** a̧·di′shon, *n.* [L. *auditio*, a hearing.] The act of hearing; a hearing or listening.—**auditor,** a̧′dit·ėr, [L.] A hearer; a listener; a person appointed and authorized to audit or examine an account or accounts.—**auditorium,** a̧·di·tō′ri·um, *n.* [L.] In an opera house, public hall, etc., the space allotted to the hearers.—**auditory,** a̧′di·to·ri, *a.* [L. *auditorius.*] Relating to hearing or to the sense or organs of hearing.—*n.* [L. *auditorium.*] An audience; an assembly of hearers; a place for hearing or for the accommodation of hearers; an auditorium.

Augean, a̧·jē′an, *a.* Of or pertaining to the mythical *Augeas*, King of Elis, in Greece.—*Augean stable*, the stable of this king, in which he kept 3000 oxen, and the cleaning out of which, after it had remained uncleaned for thirty years, was assigned as a task to Hercules, who accomplished it in a single day. Hence cleaning the Augean stables became a synonym for the removal of accumulated nuisances, abuses, etc.

auger, a̧′gėr, *n.* [For *nauger*, initial *n* having been lost (as in *adder, apron*), this word being from A. Sax. *nafe-gâr, nafugâr*, from *nafu, nafa*, the nave of a wheel; and *gâr*, a sharp-pointed thing, a dart or javelin. NAVE, GORE, to pierce.] An instrument for boring holes larger than those bored by a gimlet, chiefly used by carpenters, joiners, etc., and made in a great many forms; instruments on the same plan are used for boring into the soil.

aught, a̧t, *n.* [A.Sax. *áwiht*, from *á* for *án*, one, and *wiht*=E. *whit, wight*; lit. a whit, its negative being *naught*, not a whit.] Anything, indefinitely; any part or quantity.

augite, a̧′jīt, *n.* [Gr. *augē*, brightness.] The name given to a class of minerals, greenish black, pitch or velvet black, or leek green in color, and consisting of silicates of lime, magnesia, and iron, with alumina in the darker varieties.—**augitic,** a̧·jit′ik, *a.* Pertaining to, consisting of, resembling, or containing augite.

augment, a̧g·ment′, *v.t.* [Fr. *augmenter*, L. *augmento*, from *augmentum*, increase, from *augeo*, to increase. AUCTION.] To increase; to enlarge in size or extent; to swell; to make bigger.—*v.i.* To increase; to grow larger.—**augment,** a̧g′ment, *n.* Increase; enlargement by addition†; *gram.* an increase at the beginning of certain inflectional forms of a verb, as the *e* prefixed in certain tenses of the Greek verb, and the *ge* in the past participle of the German verb.—**augmentable,** a̧g·ment′a·bl, *a.* Capable of being augmented or increased.—**augmentation,** a̧g·men·tā′shon, *n.* The act of augmenting; the act of adding to or enlarging; the state or condition of being made larger; increase; enlargement; accession; the thing added by way of enlargement; addition.—**augmentative,** a̧g·ment′a·tiv, *a.* Having the quality or power of augmenting.—*n.* A word formed to express greatness: opposed to a *diminutive.*—**augmenter,** a̧g·ment′ėr, *n.* One who or that which augments.

augur, a̧′gėr, *n.* [L. *augur*, from *avis*, a bird, and L. *garrio*, to chatter.] Among the ancient Romans a functionary whose duty was to derive signs concerning future events from the flight or other actions of birds, from certain appearances in quadrupeds, from lightning and other unusual occurrences; hence, one who foretells future events by omens; a soothsayer; a prophet.—*v.i.* To guess; to conjecture, as from signs or omens; to be a sign; to bode (to *augur* well or ill for a project).—*v.t.* To guess or conjecture; to predict; to anticipate: said of persons; to betoken; to forebode: said of things.—**augury,** a̧′gū·ri or a̧′gėr·i, *n.* The art or practice of an augur; that which forebodes; that from which a prediction is drawn; a prognostication.

august, a̧·gust′, *a.* [L. *augustus*, from *augeo*, to increase, the same word as the name *Augustus.* AUGMENT, AUCTION.] Grand; magnificent, majestic; impressing awe; inspiring reverence.—**augustly,** a̧·gust′li, *adv.* In an august manner.—**augustness,** a̧·gust′nes, *n.* The quality of being august.

August, a̧′gust, *n.* [L. *Augustus*, from the Roman Emperor Augustus.] The eighth month of the year, containing thirty-one days.—**Augustan,** a̧·gust′an, *a.* Pertaining to the Emperor *Augustus*; as, the *Augustan* Age, which was the most brilliant period in Roman literature; hence, any brilliant period in the literary history of other countries.

Augustinian, a̧·gust·in′i·an, *n.* A member of one of the fraternities who follow rules framed by St. Augustine or deduced from his writings.

auk, a̧k, *n.* [Dan. *alke*, Icel. *alka, álka*, an auk.] The name of several swimming birds found in the colder parts of the Northern Hemisphere, having their legs placed so far back as to cause them to stand nearly upright, and with very short wings more useful for swimming and diving than for flight.

aulic, a̧′lik, *a.* [L. *aulicus*, from *aula*, Gr. *aulē*, a court.] Pertaining to a royal court.

aunt, änt, *n.* [O.Fr. *ante*, from L. *amita*, contracted in the same way as *emmet* is contracted into *ant.*] The sister of one's father or mother, a term correlative to nephew or niece.

aura, a̧′ra, *n.* [L. *aura*, a breath of air.] An air; an effluvium or odor; an exhalation.—**aural,** a̧′ral, *a.* Pertaining to an aura.

aural, a̧′ral, *a.* [L. *auris*, the ear.] Relating to the ear (*aural* surgery).—**auriform,** a̧′ri·form, *a.* Ear-shaped; having the form of the human ear.—**aurist,** a̧′rist, *n.* One skilled in disorders of the ear, or who professes to cure them; an otologist.

aureate, a̤′rē•āt, *a.* [L. *aureatus.*] Golden; gilded.

aureola, aureole, a̤•rē′ō•la, a̤′rē•ōl, *n.* [Fr. *auréole,* from L. *aureolus,* dim. of *aureus,* golden, from *aurum,* gold.] *Painting,* an illumination surrounding a holy person, as Christ, a saint, etc.; anything resembling an aureola; a halo.

aureomycin, a̤′re•o•mī″sin, *n.* Antibiotic isolated from *Streptomyces aureofaciens* and effective against certain diseases.

auricle, a̤′ri•kl, *n.* [L. *auricula,* dim. from *auris,* the ear.] The external ear, or that part which is prominent from the head; either of the two cavities in the mammalian heart, placed above the two ventricles, and resembling in shape the external ear.—**auricula,** a̤•rik′ū•la, *n.* A garden flower of the primrose family, found native in the Swiss Alps, and sometimes called bear's-ear from the shape of its leaves.—**auricular,** a̤•rik′ū•lėr, *a.* Pertaining to the ear or the sense of hearing, or to an auricle; confided to one's ear, especially privately confided to the ear of a priest (*auricular* confession).—**auriculate,** a̤•rik′ū•lāt, *a.* Shaped like the ear; having ears or some kind of expansions resembling ears; eared, as a leaf.

auriferous, a̤•rif′ėr•us, *a.* [L. *aurifer—aurum,* gold, and *fero,* to produce.] Yielding or producing gold; containing gold.

aurist. See AURAL.

aurochs, a̤′roks, *n.* [G.] A species of wild bull or buffalo, once abundant on the continent of Europe, but now reduced to a few herds inhabiting the forests of Lithuania.

aurora, a̤′rō′ra, *n.* [L., the goddess of morning, the dawn; same root as L. *uro,* to burn, *aurum,* gold.] The dawn, or morning twilight; the goddess of the morning, or dawn deified; the aurora borealis (in this sense with the plural *auroræ*).—*Aurora borealis,* the northern lights or streamers, a luminous meteoric phenomenon of varying brilliancy seen in the northern heavens, and in greatest magnificence in the arctic regions, believed to be electric in origin.—*Aurora australis,* the aurora of the Southern Hemisphere, quite a similar phenomenon to that of the north.—**auroral,** a̤•rō′ral, *a.* Belonging to or resembling the dawn; belonging to or resembling the polar lights; roseate; rosy.

auscultation, a̤s•kul•tā′shon, *n.* [L. *auscultatio,* a listening, from *ausculto,* to listen, from *auris,* the ear.] *Med.* a method of distinguishing the state of the internal parts of the body, particularly of the chest, by observing the sounds arising there either through the application of the ear or by the stethoscope.—**auscultator,** a̤s′kul•tāt•ėr, *n.* One who practices auscultation.—**auscultatory,** a̤s•kul′ta•to•ri, *a.* Pertaining to auscultation.

auspice, a̤′spis, *n.* [L. *auspicium,* from *auspex,* an augur—*avis,* a bird, and *specio,* to view.] An augury from birds; an omen or sign in general; protection; favorable influence.—**auspicate,**† a̤′spi•kāt, *v.t.* [L. *auspicor,* to take the auspices.] To initiate with pomp or ceremony; to inaugurate.—**auspicious,** a̤•spi′shus, *a.* Having omens of success, or favorable appearances; propitious; favorable; prosperous; happy.—**auspiciously,** a̤•spi′shus•li, *adv.* In an auspicious manner.—**auspiciousness,** a̤•spi′shus•nes, *n.*

austere, a̤•stēr′, *a.* [L. *austerus,* Gr. *austēros,* harsh.] Harsh; tart; sour; rough to the taste; *fig.* severe; harsh; rigid; rigorous; stern.—**austerely,** a̤•stēr′li, *adv.* In an austere manner; severely; rigidly; harshly.—**austereness, austerity,** a̤•stēr′nes, a̤•ste′ri•ti, *n.* The state or quality of being austere; severity; rigor; strictness; harshness.

austral, a̤s′tral, *a.* [L. *australis,* from *auster,* the south wind, or south.] Southern; lying or being in the south.—**Australian,** a̤s•trā′li•an, *a.* Pertaining to Australia.—*n.* A native or inhabitant of Australia.

autarchy, a̤′tär•ki, *n.* [Gr. *autos,* self, and *archos,* ruler.] Absolute rule; despotism.

autarky, a̤′tär•ki, *n.* [Gr. *atarkeia,* sufficiency.] Economic self-sufficiency; an economically independent area.

authentic, a̤•then′tik, *a.* [L. *authenticus,* from Gr. *authentikos,* original, genuine, from *authentēs,* one who does anything with his own hand.] Being what it purports to be; not false or fictitious; genuine; valid; authoritative; reliable.—**authentically,** a̤•then′tik•al•li, *adv.*—**authenticate,** a̤•then′ti•kāt, *v.t.*—*authenticated, authenticating.* To render authentic; to give authority to by proof, attestation, etc.; to prove authentic; to determine as genuine.—**authenticity,** a̤•then•tis′i•ti, *n.*

author, a̤′thor, *n.* [O.F. *autheur,* L. *auctor,* improperly written *autor, author,* from *augeo,* auctum, to increase, to produce. AUGMENT.] The beginner, former, or first mover of anything (*author* of our being): the originator or creator; efficient cause; the original composer of a literary work; the writer of a book or other literary production.—**authoress,** a̤′thor•es, *n.* A female author.—**authoritative,** a̤•thor′i•tā•tiv, *a.* Having authority; having the sanction or appearance of authority; positive; peremptory; dictatorial.—**authoritatively,** a̤•thor′i•tā•tiv•li, *adv.* In an authoritative manner; with a show of authority.—**authoritativeness,** a̤•thor′i•tā•tiv•nes, *n.* The quality of being authoritative.—**authority,** a̤•thor′i•ti, *n.* [O.Fr. *authorité.*] Power or right to command or act; dominion; control; the power derived from opinion, respect, or esteem; influence conferred by character, station, mental superiority, etc.; a person or persons exercising power or command: generally in the plural (the civil and military *authorities*); that to which or one to whom reference may be made in support of any fact, opinion, action, etc. (a person's *authority* for a statement); credit or credibility (a work of no *authority*).—**authorize,** a̤′thor•īz, *vt.*—*authorized, authorizing.* To give authority, warrant, or legal power to; to give a right to act; to empower; to make legal; to establish by authority or by usage or public opinion (an *authorized* idiom); to warrant; to sanction; to justify.—**authorization,** a̤′thor•iz•ā″shon, *n.* The act of authorizing.—**authorship,** a̤′thor•ship, *n.* The character or state of being an author; the source from which a work proceeds.

autobiography, a̤′tō•bī•og″ra•fi, *n.* [Gr. *autos,* self, and E. *biography.*] Biography or memoirs of a person written by himself.—**autobiographer,** a̤′tō•bī•og″ra•fėr, *n.* One who writes an autobiography.—**autobiographic, autobiographical,** a̤•tō•bī′o•graf″ik, a̤•tō•bī′o•graf″ik•al, *a.* Pertaining to, consisting of, or containing autobiography.—**autobiographically,** a̤•tō•bī′o•graf″ik•al•li, *adv.* In an autobiographical manner.

autochthon, a̤•tok′thon, *n.* pl. **autochthones,** a̤•tok′thon•ēz. [Gr. *autochthōn—autos,* self, and *chthōn,* the earth.] One of the primitive inhabitants of a country; an aboriginal inhabitant; that which is original to a particular country.—**autochthonous,** a̤•tok′thon•us, *a.* Aboriginal; primitive; indigenous.

autoclave, a̤′tō•klāv, *n.* [Gr. *auto,* self, and L. *clavism,* key.] Airtight vessel for sterilizing, cooking, etc., by high-pressure steam; pressure cooker.

autocracy, a̤•tok′ra•si, *n.* [Gr. *autokrateia—autos,* self, and *kratos,* power.] Supreme power invested in a single person; the government or power of an absolute monarch.—**autocrat,** a̤′tō•krat, *n.* [Gr. *autokratēs.*] An absolute sovereign; a monarch who governs without being subject to restriction: a title assumed by the emperors of Russia; hence, one who is invested with or assumes unlimited authority in any relation.—**autocratic, autocratical,** a̤″tō•krat′ik, a̤″tō•krat′ik•al, *a.* Pertaining to autocracy; absolute; holding unlimited powers of government.—**autocratically,** *adv.* In an autocratic manner.

auto-da-fé, a̤′tō•da•fā″, *n.* pl. **autos-da-fé,** a̤′tōz•da•fā″. [Sp., lit. act (in sense of decree, judgment, sentence) of faith—*auto* = L. *actum,* an act, *de,* of, and *fe* = L. *fides,* faith.] A public solemnity, formerly held by the courts of the Inquisition in Spain and Portugal and their dependencies at the execution of heretics condemned to the stake.

autogenous, a̤•toj′en•us, *a.* [Gr. *autos,* self, and root *gen,* to generate.] Self-produced; self-generated; produced independently.

autograph, a̤′tō•graf, *n.* [Gr. *autos,* self, and *graphē,* writing.] A person's own handwriting; an original manuscript or signature.—**autographic, autographical,** a̤•tō•graf′ik, a̤•tō•graf′ik•al, *a.* Pertaining or relating to an autograph, or one's own handwriting; relating to or used in the process of autography.—**autography,** ạ·tog′ra·fi. *n.* A person's own handwriting†; a process in lithography by which a writing or drawing is transferred from paper to stone.

automatic, ạ·tō·mat′ik, *a.* [Gr. *automatos*, self-acting—*autos*, self, and root *ma*, to strive.] Belonging to or proceeding by spontaneous movement; having the power of self-motion; self-acting: said especially of mechanism.—**automat,** ạ′tō·mat, *n.* A restaurant in which food is delivered through self-operating mechanical devices.—**automaton,** ạ·tom′a·ton, *n.* That which is self-moving; a self-acting machine; a mechanical contrivance which imitates the arbitrary or voluntary motions of living beings; a person who acts mechanically.—**automation,** ạ′to·mā″shun, *n.* The technique of making an industrial process or system operate automatically; the use of electronic devices for controlling processes or systems.

automobile, ạ·tō·mō·bil′, *n.* [Gr. *autos*, self. MOBILE.] A vehicle propelled by self-contained power and used for carrying passengers.—**automotive,** ạ·to·mō′tiv, *a.* Self-moving; related to automobiles.

autonomy, ạ·tono′·mi, *n.* [Gr. *autonomia*—*autos*, self, and *nomos*, law, rule.] The power or right of self-government.—**autonomic, autonomous,** ạ·tō·nom′ik, ạ·ton′o·mus, *a.* Relating to autonomy; independent in government.

autoplasty, ạ·tō·plas·ti, *n.* [Gr. *autos*, self, and *plassō*, to form.] *Surg.* same as *Anaplasty*.

autopsy, ạ′top·si, *n.* [Gr., from *autos*, self, and *opsis*, sight.] Personal observation; ocular view; *med.* post-mortem examination.

autotype, ạ′tō·tīp, *n.* [Gr. *autos*, self, *typos*, a stamp.] A photographic process resembling heliotype; a picture produced by the process.

autumn, ạ′tum, *n.* [L. *autumnus*, for *auctumnus*, the season of increase, from *augeo*, *auctum*, to increase. AUGMENT.] The third season of the year, or the season between summer and winter, popularly regarded as comprising Aug., Sept., and Oct., but astronomically beginning at the autumnal equinox, September 23, and ending at the winter solstice, December 21.—**autumnal,** ạ·tum′-nal, *a.* Belonging to autumn; produced or gathered in autumn; *fig.* belonging to the period past the middle stage of life.

auxiliary, ạg·zil′i·a·ri, *a.* [L. *auxiliaris*, from *auxilium*, aid, from *augeo*, to increase, whence also *auction*, *augment*, *autumn*, etc.] Conferring aid or support; helping; aiding; assisting; subsidiary.—**auxiliary,** ạg·zil′i·a·ri, *n.* A helper; an assistant; an associate in some undertaking; *pl.* foreign troops in the service of a nation at war; *gram.* a verb which helps to form the moods and tenses of other verbs; as, *have*, *may*, *shall*, and *will*.

auxin, ạk′sän, *n.* [Gr. *auxein*, to increase, and *in*, of, or belonging to.] *Biol.* any of several organic compounds, acting as plant hormones, which in minute quantities promote plant cell growth.

avail, a·vāl′, *v.t.* [O.Fr. *valeir*, to be worth, from L. *valeo*, to be strong, with prefix *a* for L. *ad.*] To be for the advantage of; to assist or profit; to benefit.—*To avail one's self of*, to take advantage of.—*v.i.* To be of use, benefit, or advantage; to answer a purpose; to have strength, force, or efficacy sufficient.—*n.* Advantage tending to promote success; benefit; service; utility; efficacy: used in such phrases as, of little *avail*; of much *avail*.—**available,** a·vāl′a·bl, *a.* Advantageous; having efficacy: capable of being used; attainable; accessible.—**availableness, availability,** a·vāl′a·bl·-nes, a·vāl′a·bil″i·ti, *n.* State of being available; power or efficacy; legal force; validity.—**availably,** a·vāl′-a·bli, *adv.* In an available manner.

avalanche, av′a·lansh, *n.* [Fr. *avalanche*, from *avaler*, to descend—*a*, to, *val*, a valley.] A vast body of snow or ice sliding down a mountain, or over a precipice.

avant-courier, a·vaṅ′kö′rēr, *n.* [Fr. *avant*, before, from L. *ab*, from *ante*, before.] A person despatched before another person or a company, to give notice of their approach.—**avant-guard,** a·väṅ·gärd′, *n.* [Fr. *avant-garde*.] The van or advanced body of an army; the vanguard.

avarice, av′a·ris, *n.* [L. *avaritia* from *avarus*, greedy, from *aveo*, to covet.] An inordinate desire of gaining and possessing wealth; covetousness; cupidity; greediness.—**avaricious,** av·-a·ri′shus, *a.* Characterized by avarice; greedy of gain; miserly; covetous.—**avariciously,** av·a·ri′shus·li, *adv.* In an avaricious manner; covetously; greedily.—**avariciousness,** av·a·ri′shus·nes, *n.* The quality of being avaricious.

avast, a·vast′, *exclam.* [From D. *houd vast*, hold fast, stop.] *Naut.* the order to stop, hold, cease, or stay in any operation: sometimes used colloquially, without reference to ships.

avatar, av·a·tär′, *n.* [Skr. *avatāra*—*ava*, down, and root *tri*, to go,] A descent from heaven; the incarnation of the Hindu deities, or their appearance in some manifest shape upon earth.

avaunt, a·vạnt′, *interj.* [Fr. *avant*, *en avant*, forward, march!—from L. *ab.* from *ante*, before. *Van* is the same word.] Begone; depart; an exclamation of contempt or abhorrence.

ave, ä′vā, *interj.* [L.] Hail! farewell! God bless you! [*cap.*] Sometimes used as a noun for an Ave Maria.—**Ave Maria,** ä′vā ma·rē′a, *n.* [L.= hail Mary!—the first words of Gabriel's salutation to the Virgin Mary.] Devotional words often repeated in the Roman Catholic Church, chaplets and rosaries being divided into a certain number of Ave Marias and paternosters.

avenaceous, av·e·nā′shus, *a.* [L. *avena*, oats.] Belonging to or partaking of the nature of oats.

avenge, a·venj′, *v.t.*—*avenged*, *avenging*. [O.Fr. *avengier*—prefix *a*, and L. *vindicare*, to avenge, vindicate.] To vindicate by inflicting pain or evil on the wrong doer; to deal punishment for injury done to, with a person as object; to take satisfaction for, by pain or punishment inflicted on the injuring party; to deal punishment on account of: with a thing as object.—**avenger,** a·venj′ėr, *n.* One who avenges; one who takes vengeance.

avens, av′enz, *n.* The popular name of several species of rosaceous plants growing wild: common avens is also called herb bennet.

aventurine, a·ven′tū·rin, *n.* [Fr. *aventure*, chance.] A variety of artificial gem consisting of glass, oxide of copper, and oxide of iron: a compound discovered accidentally (*par aventure*); also, a variety of quartz rock containing spangles of mica or quartz.

avenue, av′e·nū, *n.* [Fr., from *avenir*, to arrive, L. *advenio*. ADVENE ADVENT.] A passage; a way or opening for entrance; a wide straight roadway or street; an alley or walk planted on each side with trees; *fig.* means of access or attainment.

aver, a·vėr′, *v.t.*—*averred*, *averring*. [Fr. *averer*, from L. *ad*, to, and *verus*, true.] To affirm with confidence; to declare in a positive or peremptory manner; to assert.—**averment,** a·vėr′ment, *n.* The act of averring; affirmation; a positive assertion or declaration.

average, av′ėr·āj, *n.* [Fr. *avarie*, Sp. *averia*, damage sustained by goods at sea; from Ar. *avär*, defect, flaw, modified by the influence of L.L. *averagium*, the carriage of goods by *averia* or draft cattle, a contribution towards loss of things carried; from O.Fr. *aver*, a work horse, from L. *habere*, to have.] A contribution falling on the owners of a ship's freight and cargo, in proportion to their several interests, to make good a loss that has been sustained; a sum or quantity intermediate to a number of different sums or quantities; a mean or medial amount; a general estimate based on comparison of a number of diverse cases; a medium.—*a.* Exhibiting a mean proportion or mean quality; forming an average; medium; not extreme; ordinary; *com.* estimated in accordance with the rules of average.—*v.t.*—*averaged*, *averaging*. To find the average of; to reduce to a mean sum or quantity; to show or have as an average or mean (trees average 50 feet in height).

avert, a·vėrt′, *v.t.* [L. *averto*, *aversum*, to turn away—*a*, from, and *verto*, *versum*, to turn, whence *verse*, *convert*, *converse*, *diverse*, etc.] To turn or direct away from; to turn or to cause to turn off or away (the eyes, calamity, etc.).—**averse,** a·vėrs′, *a.* [L. *aversus*, turned from, pp. of *averto*.] Turned away from;

averted (*Mil.*); unwilling; having repugnance; now regularly followed by *to*, not by *from*.—**aversely**, a·vėrs′li, *adv.* In an averse manner; with repugnance; unwillingly.—**averseness**, a·vėrs′nes, *n.* The state of being averse.—**aversion**, a·vėr′zhen, *n.* Opposition or repugnance of mind; dislike; disinclination; reluctance; hatred: used absolutely or with *to*; the cause of dislike; the object of repugnance.

Avesta, a·ves′ta, *n.* The sacred writings attributed to Zoroaster; the Zend-Avesta.—**Avestan**, a·ves′tan, *n.* The language of the Avesta; Zend.

avian, ā′vi·an, *a.* [L. *avis*, a bird.] Pertaining to birds.—**aviary**, ā′vi·a·ri, *n.* [L. *aviarium*.] A building or enclosure for the breeding, rearing, and keeping of birds.—**aviation**, ā·vi·ā′shon, *n.* Aerial navigation by machines heavier than air.—**aviator**, ā′vi·ā·tėr, *n.* One who engages in aviation.—**aviculture**, ā′vi·kul″tūr, *n.* The breeding and rearing of birds.—**avifauna**, ā′vi·fạ·na, *n.* A collective name for the birds or avian fauna of a district.

avid, av′id, *a.* [L. *avidus*, from *aveo*, to desire; akin *avarice*.] Eager; greedy: with *of*.—**avidity**, a·vid′i·ti, *n.* [L. *aviditas*.] Greediness; strong appetite; eagerness; intenseness of desire.

avocado, av·ō·kä′dō, *n.* [Corrupted from Mexican name.] The fruit of a small tree of the laurel family, common in tropical America and the West Indies: also called *alligator pear*.

avocate,† av′ō·kāt, *v.t.* [L. *avoco*, *avocatum*—*a*, from, and *voco*, to call.] To call off or away; to remove from an inferior to a superior court.—**avocation**, av·ō·kā′shon, *n.* A chosen spare-time occupation, distinct from one's regular calling; the authoritative removal of a case from an inferior to a superior court; that which calls a man away from his proper business; a distraction; a hindrance.

avocet, av′ō·set, *n.* Same as *Avoset*.

avoid, a·void′, *v.t.* [Originally to empty; from prefix *a*, and *void*.] To make void (in legal phraseology); to shun; to keep away from; to eschew; to evade; to elude (expense, danger, bad company).—*v.i.* To become void or vacant; to retire‡; to withdraw‡.—**avoidable**, a·void′a·bl, *a.* That may be vacated or annulled; capable of being avoided, shunned, or escaped.—**avoidance**, a·void′ans, *n.* The act of annulling or making void; the act of avoiding or shunning.

avoirdupois, av·ėr′dū·poiz″, *n.* [O.Fr. *avoir du pois*, to have weight—L. *habeo*, to have, *pensum*, something weighed out. POISE.] A system of weight of which 1 lb. contains 16 oz., in distinction to troy weight, which has only 12—the system by which commodities in general are weighed.

avoset, av′ō·set, *n.* [Fr. *avocette*, It. *avocetta*.] A wading bird of the size of a lapwing, with very long legs, feathers variegated with black and white, and a long slender bill bent upward toward the tip.

avouch, a·vouch′, *v.t.* [Prefix *a* (=L. *ad*, to), and *vouch;* O.Fr. *avochier*, *avocher*.] To affirm openly; to avow; to maintain, vindicate, or justify (a statement); to establish; guarantee; substantiate.—*n.*‡ Evidence; testimony. (*Shak.*).

avow, a·vou′, *v.t.* [Fr. *avouer*—*a* (from L. *ad*, to), and *vouer*, to vow. VOW.] To declare openly, with a view to justify, maintain, or defend (sentiments, etc.); to acknowledge; to own.—**avowal**, a·vou′al, *n.* An open declaration; frank acknowledgment.—**avowed**, a·voud′, *a.* Declared; open (an *avowed* enemy).—**avowedly**, a·vou′ed·li, *adv.* In an avowed or open manner; with frank acknowledgment.—**avower**, a·vou′ėr, *n.* One who avows, owns, or asserts.

avulsion, a·vul′shon, *n.* [L. *avulsio*, from *avello*—*a*, from, away, and *vello*, *vulsum*, to pull.] A pulling or tearing asunder or off.

avuncular, a·vung′kū·lėr, *a.* [L. *avunculus*, an uncle.] Of or pertaining to an uncle.

await, a·wāt′, *v.t.* To wait for; to look for or expect; to be in store for; to be ready for (a reward *awaits* him).

awake, a·wāk′, *v.t.*—*awoke* or *awaked* (pret. & pp.), *awaking*. [Prefix *a*, intens., and *wake;* A.Sax. *áwacan*, pret. *áwóc*, also *áwacian*, to awake. WAKE.] To rouse from sleep or from a state resembling sleep; to put into action or new life.—*v.i.* To cease to sleep; to bestir or rouse one's self from a state resembling sleep.—*a.* [A.Sax. *áwacen*, pp. of *áwacan*.] Not sleeping; in a state of vigilance or action.—**awaken**, a·wāk′n, *v.i.* [A.Sax. *áwacnan*, *áwacnian*, to awake (intrans.).] To become awake; to awake.—*v.t.* To rouse from sleep; to awake.—**awakening**, a·wāk′n·ing, *n.* Act of awaking from sleep; a revival of religion.—*a.* Rousing; alarming.

award, a·wạrd′, *v.t.* [O.Fr. *awarder*, to have under *ward*, to inspect, to pronounce as to the sufficiency of. WARD.] To adjudge; to assign judicially or by sentence (as an arbitrator pronouncing upon the rights of parties).—*v.i.* To make an award.—*n.* Judgment; decision; the decision of arbitrators on points submitted to them.—**awarder**, a·wạrd′er, *n.* One that awards or makes an award.

aware, a·wâr′, *a.* [Prefix *a*, and *ware* (as in be*ware*); A.Sax. *gewær*, wary, cautious; G. *gewahr*, aware. WARE, WARY.] Apprised; cognizant; informed; conscious; followed by *of*. [Not used attributively.]

away, a·wā′, *adv.* [A.Sax. *onweg*—*on*. on and *weg*, way.] Absent; at a distance; apart; to a distance (to go *away*). It is often used elliptically (whither *away* so fast?). With many verbs it conveys a notion of using up or consuming (to squander *away*, to idle or loiter *away*); it has also merely an intensive force (eat *away*, laugh *away*).—*int.* Begone! depart! go away.

awe, ạ, *n.* [O.E. *aghe*, *eghe*, A.Sax. *ege*, fear, dread; Icel. *agi*, awe, terror; Goth. *agis*, fear; allied to Gael. *agh*, fear; Gr. *achos*, anguish—from root seen in *anguish*, *anger*, etc. ANGER.] Dread or great fear; fear mingled with admiration or reverence; reverential fear; feeling inspired by something sublime.—*v.t.*—*awed*, *awing*. To strike with awe; to influence by fear, reverence, or respect.—**aweless, awless**, ạ′les, *a.* Devoid of awe; wanting the power of inspiring reverence or awe.—**awful**, ạ′fụl, *a.* Striking or inspiring with awe; filling with dread, or dread mingled with profound reverence; proceeding from awe; extraordinary or highly remarkable (colloq.).—**awfully**, ạ′fụl·li, *adv.* In an awful manner; in a manner to fill with awe; terribly; excessively.—**awfulness**, ạ′fụl·nes, *n.* The quality of being awful, or of striking with awe, reverence, or terror.

aweary, a·wē′ri, *a.* Weary. [Poetical.]

aweather, a·weTH′ėr, *a.* or *adv.* On or to the weather side of a ship: opposed to *alee*.

awhile, a·hwīl′, *adv.* [O.E. *ane hwile*, a while.] For a space of time; for some time.

awkward, ạk′wėrd, *a.* [O.E. *awk*, *awke*, wrong, backward, reverse. and term. *-ward*. *Awk* corresponds to Icel. *öfigr*, *öfugr*, Sw. *afvig*, turned the wrong way, from *af*=E. *off*.] Wanting dexterity in the use of the hands or of instruments; bungling; clumsy; ungraceful in manners; uncouth.—**awkwardly**, ạk′wėrd·li, *adv.* In an awkward manner; clumsily.—**awkwardness**, ạk′wėrd·nes, *n.* The quality of being awkward.

awl, ạl, *n.* [A.Sax. *awul*, *ael*, *ál;* Icel. *alr*, G. *ahle*.] A pointed instrument for piercing small holes in leather, wood, etc.

awn, ạn, *n.* [Icel. *ōgn*, Dan. *avne*, Sw. *agne*, chaff, husk; akin to Gr. *achnē*, chaff.] The bristle or beard of corn or grass, or any similar bristlelike appendage.—**awned**, *a.* Having awns.

awning, ạn′ing, *n.* [L.G. *havenung*, a shelter, from *haven*, a haven.] A covering of canvas or other cloth spread over any place as a protection from the sun's rays.

awry, a·rī′, *a.* or *adv.* In a wry position; turned or twisted toward one side; asquint; crooked; perverse.

ax, axe, aks, *n.* [A.Sax. *ax*, *æx*, Icel. *ox*, Dan. *oxe*, D. *aakse*, G. *ax*, *axt;* allied to Gr. *axinē*, L. *ascia* for *acsia*—an axe. From root *ac*, *ak*, a point. ACID.] An instrument, consisting of a head, with an arching edge of steel in the plane of the sweep of the tool, attached to a handle, and used for hewing timber and chopping wood.

axial, axially, etc. See AXIS.

axil, axilla, aks′il, aks·il′la, *n.* [L. *axilla*, the arm-pit.] The armpit; a cavity under the upper part of the arm or shoulder, *bot.* the angle on the upper side between an axis and any organ growing from it.—**axillar, axillary**, aks′il·lėr, aks′il·la·ri, *a.* Pertaining to the armpit or to the axil of plants.

axiom, aks′i·om, *n.* [Gr. *axiōma*.]

A self-evident truth or proposition; a proposition whose truth is so evident at first sight that no process of reasoning or demonstration can make it plainer; an established principle in some art or science; a principle universally received.—*Syn.* under APHORISM.—**axiomatic, axiomatical,** aks′i•ō•mat″ik, aks′•iō•mat″-ik•al, *a.* Pertaining to, consisting of, or having the character of an axiom.—**axiomatically,** aks′i•ō•mat″ik•al•li, *adv.* In an axiomatic manner.

axis, aks′is, *n.* pl. **axes,** aks′ēz. [L.] The straight line, real or imaginary, passing through a body or magnitude, on which it revolves, or may be supposed to revolve; an agreement between two or more leading powers by which lesser powers may align themselves for or against the general principles set forth; specifically the Rome-Berlin axis; *bot.* the central line or column about which other parts are arranged; *anat.* the second vertebra of the neck.—**axial,** aks′i•al, *a.* Pertaining to an axis.—**axially,** aks′i•al•li, *adv.* According to or in line with the axis.

axle, axletree, aks′l, aks′l•trē, *n.* [A dim. from A.Sax. *eax, ex,* an axle; same root as L. *axis,* namely, *ag,* to drive. ACRE.] A piece of timber or bar of iron on which the wheels of a vehicle, etc., turn.

axolotl, aks′o•lotl, *n.* [Mexican name.] A remarkable member of the tailed amphibians found in Mexican lakes, possessing four limbs resembling those of a frog, and usually having throughout life both lungs and gills, but sometimes losing the latter.

ay, aye, ī, *adv.* [Of doubtful origin.] Yes; yea; a word expressing assent or affirmation; truly; certainly; indeed.—*n.* The word by which assent is expressed in Parliament; hence, an affirmative vote.—*The ayes have it,* the affirmative votes are in a majority.

ayah, ā′yä, *n.* In the East Indies, a native lady's maid.

aye-aye, ī•ī, *n.* [From its cry.] A nocturnal quadruped, about the size of a hare, found in Madagascar, allied to the lemurs, and in its habits resembling the sloth.

azalea, a•zā′lē•a, *n.* [Gr. *azaleos,* dry, from inhabiting dry localities.] The generic name of certain plants belonging to the heath family, remarkable for the beauty and fragrance of their flowers, and distinguished from the rhododendrons chiefly by the flowers having five stamens instead of ten.

azimuth, az′i•muth, *n.* [Ar. *as-sumuth,* pl. of *as-samt,* a way, a path. *Zenith* has the same origin.] *Astron.* an arc of the horizon intercepted between the meridian of a place and the vertical circle passing through the center of a celestial object and the zenith.—*Azimuth circle,* a circle passing through the zenith and cutting the horizon perpendicularly.—*Azimuth compass,* a kind of compass used for finding the azimuth of a heavenly object.—**azimuthal,** az′i•muth•al, *a.* Pertaining or relating to the azimuth.

azoic, a•zō′ik, *a.* [Gr. *a,* not, and *zōē,* life.] Destitute of any vestige of organic life: applied to rocks, especially some very old rocks, in which no fossils have as yet been found.

azote, az′ōt, *n.* [Gr. *a,* not, and *zōē,* life.] A name formerly given to nitrogen because it is unfit for respiration.

Aztec, az′tek, *n.* and *a.* One of or pertaining to the Aztecs, the ruling tribe in Mexico at the time of the Spanish invasion.

azure, a′zhūr, *a.* [Fr. *azur,* L.L. *azurrum, lazurum,* etc., from Arab. *lazwerd,* blue.] Resembling the clear blue color of the sky; sky blue.—*n.* The fine blue color of the sky; a name common to several sky-colored or blue pigments, as ultramarine or smalt; the sky or vault of heaven.—*v.t.* To color blue.—**azurite,** a′zhūr•īt, *n.* A blue mineral, an ore of copper, composed chiefly of hydrous carbonate: called also *Azure stone.*

azygous, az′i•gus, *a.* [Gr. *azygos—a,* not, and *zygon,* a yoke.] Not one of a pair; single: applied to certain muscles, etc.

B

B, b, bē, the second letter and the first consonant in the English and most other alphabets; *mus.* the seventh note of the model diatonic scale or scale of C.

baa, bä, *v.i.* [Imitation of the sound.] Bleating of a sheep.

Baal, bā′al, *n.* [Heb. *ba′al,* lord.] A deity worshiped among the Canaanites, Phoenicians, etc., and supposed to represent the sun.—**Baalism,** bā′al•izm, *n.* The worship of Baal; gross idolatry.—**Baalite,** bā′al•īt, *n.* A worshiper of Baal; a grovelling idolizer.

Babbitt metal, bab′it•met•al, *n.* [From the name of the inventor.] An alloy of copper, zinc, and tin, used for obviating friction in the bearing of cranks, axles, etc.

babble, bab′bl, *v.i.* [From *ba,* a sound uttered by an infant; D. and G. *babbeln,* Icel. *babbla,* Dan. *bable,* Fr. *babiller.*] To utter words imperfectly or indistinctly; to talk idly or irrationally; to make a continuous murmuring sound; to prate; to tell secrets.—*v.t.* To utter idly or irrationally.—*n.* Idle talk; senseless prattle; murmur as of a stream.—**babblement,**† bab′bl•ment, *n.* Idle talk; babble. (*Mil.*)—**babbler,** bab′blėr, *n.* One who babbles; a teller of secrets.

babe, baby, bāb, bā′bi, *n.* [From the Celtic; W. Ir. and Gael. *baban,* Gael. and Ir. *bab,* child, infant.] An infant; a young child of either sex.—**babyish,** bā′bi•ish, *a.* Like a babe; childish.—**babyhood,** bā′bi•hud, *n.* The state of being a baby; infancy.—**baby farm,** *n.* The establishment of a baby farmer.—**baby farmer,** *n.* One who receives infants, generally illegitimate, along with a sum of money for their bringing up, and whose object is to get rid of the children, by neglect or ill usage, as soon as possible.—**baby farming,** *n.* The system or practices of a baby farmer.

Babel, bā′bel, *n.* The city mentioned in Scripture where the confusion of tongues took place; any great city where confusion may be supposed to prevail; a confused mixture of sounds; confusion; disorder.

babiroussa, bab•i•rös′sa, *n.* A species of the swine family with long curved tusks in the upper jaw, inhabiting the islands of the East Indies and the Malayan Peninsula, and allied to the wild boars of Europe.

bablah, bab′la, *n.* The pod of several species of acacia sometimes used in dyeing, to produce a drab color.

baboo, babu, ba•bö′, *n.* A Hindu title of respect paid to gentlemen, equivalent to master, sir.—**babu.** *Babu-English.* The broken English of Bengal.

baboon, ba•bön′, *n.* [Fr. *babouin.*] A term applied to certain quadrumanous animals of the Old World having elongated muzzles like a dog, strong canine teeth, short tails, cheek pouches, small deep eyes with huge eyebrows, and naked callosities on the hips.

baby, etc. See BABE.

Babylon, bab′i•lōn, *n.* Type of any great or evil city; capital of Chaldean Empire.—**Babylonian, Babylonish,** bab•i•lō′ni•an, ba•bi•lo′nish, *a.* Pertaining to Babylon; like the confusion of tongues at Babel; mixed; confused.

bacca, bak′ka, *n.* [L.] *Bot.* a berry; a one-celled fruit, with several naked seeds immersed in a pulpy mass.—**baccate,** bak′kāt, *a. Bot.* having a pulpy texture like a berry; bearing berries; berried.—**bacciferous,** bak•sif′ėr•us, *a.* [L. *bacca,* and *fero,* to bear.] Bearing or producing berries.—**baccivorous,** bak•siv′ō•rus, *a* [L. *bacca,* and *voro,* to devour.] Eating or subsisting on berries.

baccalaureate, bak•ka•la′rē•āt, *n.* [L.L. *baccalaureatus,* from *baccalaureus,* a corrupted form, through *bacca lauri,* laurel berry, of L.L. *baccalarius,* Fr. *bachelier,* a *bachelor,* or one who has attained the lowest degree in a university. BACHELOR, LAUREATE.] The degree of Bachelor of Arts.—*a.* Pertaining to a Bachelor of Arts.

baccarat, bak′ka•rat or bak•ka•rä, *n.* [Fr.] A game of cards played by any number of players or rather betters.

bacchanal, bacchanalian, bak′a•nal, bak•a•nā′li•an, *a.* [L. *bacchanalis,* from *Bacchus,* the god of wine.] Revelling in or characterized by intemperate drinking; riotous; noisy.—*n.* A votary of Bacchus; one who indulges in drunken revels; a drunken feast.—**Bacchanalia,** bak•a•nā′li•a, *n. pl.* [L.] Feasts or festive rites in honor of Bacchus.—**bacchanalianism,** bak•a•nā′li•an•izm, *n.* The practice of bacchanalian rites; drunken revelry.—**bacchant,** ba•kant′, *n.* [L. *bacchans*, ppr. of *bacchor*, to celebrate the feast of Bacchus.] A priest of Bacchus; a bacchanal.—**bacchante,** ba•kan′tē, *n.* [It. *baccante*.] A priestess of Bacchus, or one who joined in the feasts of Bacchus, one in a state of Bacchic frenzy; a female bacchanal. — **Bacchic, Bacchical,** bak′ik, bak′ik•al, *a.* Relating to Bacchus; jovial; drunken; mad with intoxication.

bachelor, bach′el•ėr, *n.* [O.Fr. *bacheler*, *bachiler*, Fr. *bachelier*, from L.L. *baccalarius*, the owner of a small farm or a herd of cows, a vassal, from *bacca*, for L. *vacca*, a cow.] Formerly, a young man in the first or probationary stage of knighthood; hence, a man who has not been married; one who has taken the degree below that of Master or Doctor in Arts, Science, or other subjects at a university.—*Knight bachelor*, a man who has been knighted without being made a member of any of the orders of knighthood, as the Bath.—**bachelorhood, bachelorship,** bach′el•ėr•hụd, bach′el•ėr•ship, *n.* The state of being a bachelor.

bacillus, ba•sil′us, *n.* pl. **bacilli,** ba•sil′lī. [L., a little rod.] Any rod-shaped bacteria that produce spores in the presence of free oxygen; a bacterium.—**bacillary,** ba•sil′a•ri, *a.* Relating to bacilli.

back, bak, *n.* [A.Sax. *bæc*, Icel. Sw. and L.G. *bak*.] The posterior part of the trunk; the region of the spine; the hinder part of the body in man and the upper in other animals; that which is behind or furthest from the face or front; the rear (the *back* of a house); that which is behind or in the furthest distance; the part which comes behind in the ordinary movements of a thing, or when it is used (the *back* of the hand, a knife, saw, etc.); a reserve or secondary resource; a support or second; *pl.* among leather dealers the thickest and best-tanned hides.—*Behind one's back*, in secret, or when one is absent.—*adv.* [Short for *aback*, A.Sax. *on bæc*, back.] To or toward a former place, state, or condition; not advancing; in a state of restraint or hindrance (to keep *back*); toward times or things past (to look *back*); again; in return (to give *back*); away from contact; by reverse movement; in withdrawal or resilement from an undertaking or engagement (to draw *back*).—*To go or give back*, to retreat, to recede; to give way; to succumb. —*a.* Belonging to the back; lying in the rear; remote; in a backward direction: chiefly in compounds.—*v.t.* to furnish with a back or backing; to support; to second or strengthen by aid (often with *up*); to bet or wager in favor of; to get upon the back of; to mount; to write something on the back of; to endorse; to put backward; to cause to move backwards or recede.—*v.i.* To move or go back; to move with the back foremost.—**backed,** bakt, *a.* Having a back: used chiefly in composition. —**backer,** bak′ėr, *n.* One who backs or gets on the back; one who supports another; one who bets in favor of a particular party in a contest.—**backing,** bak′ing, *n.* Something put at or attached to the back of something else by way of support or finish.

back, bak, *n.* [Fr. *bac*, a back or ferry-boat, a brewer's or distiller's back; Armor. *bac*, a boat; D. *bak*, a bowl; Dan. *bakke*, a tray. The word may be originally Celtic. *Basin* is akin to this word.] A ferryboat, especially one adapted for carrying vehicles, and worked by a chain or rope fastened on each side of the ferry; *brewing* and *distilling*, a large tub or vessel into which the wort, etc., is drawn for the purpose of cooling, straining, mixing, etc.

backbite, bak′bīt, *v.t.*—*backbit* (pret.), *backbit* or *backbitten* (pp.), *backbiting*. To censure, slander, or speak evil of, in the absence of the person traduced. —**backbiter,** bak′bīt•ėr, *n.* One who backbites; a calumniator of the absent.

backboard, bak′bōrd, *n.* A board for the back; a board used to support the back and give erectness to the figure.

backbone, bak′bōn, *n.* The bone of the back; the spine; the vertebral column; *fig.* firmness; decision of character; resolution.—*To the backbone*, to the utmost extent; out and out; all through or over (a soldier *to the backbone*).

backdoor, bak′dōr, *n.* A door in the back part of a building.

backgammon, bak•gam′mon, *n.* [Dan. *bakke*, a tray, *gammen*, mirth.] A game played by two persons upon a table or board made for the purpose, with pieces or men, diceboxes, and dice.

background, bak′ground, *n.* The part of a picture represented as farthest from the spectator; *fig.* a situation little seen or noticed; a state of being out of view (to keep a fact in the *background*).

backhand, bak′hand, *n.* Writing sloping backwards or to the left.—**backhand, backhanded,** bak′hand, bak′hand•ed, *a.* With the hand turned backward (a *backhanded* blow); unfair; oblique; indirect; sloping back or to the left (of writing).—**backhandedness,** bak′hand•ed•nes, *n.*

backshish, backsheesh, bak′shēsh, *n.* Same as BAKSHISH.

backside, bak′sīd, *n.* The back part of anything; the side opposite to the front or behind that which is presented to the spectator.

backslide, bak′slīd, *v.i.* (conjugated as *slide*). To slide back; to fall off or turn away from religion or morality; to apostatize.—**backslider,** bak′slīd•ėr, *n.* One who backslides; one who falls away from religion or morality.

backstair, backstairs, bak′stãr, bak′stãrz, *n.* A stair or stairs in the back part of a house; private stairs.—*a.* Of or pertaining to backstairs; hence, indirect; underhand; secret and unfair (*backstairs* influence).

backstay, *n.* A long rope or stay, extending from the top of a mast backwards to the side of a ship to assist the shrouds in supporting the mast.

backward, backwards, bak′wėrd, bak′wėrdz, *adv.* [*Back* and *ward*, denoting direction.] With the back in advance; toward the back; in a direction opposite to forward; toward past times or events; from a better to a worse state; in a contrary or reverse manner, way, or direction.—**backward,** *a.* Being in the back or at the back; turned or directed back (a *backward* look); unwilling; reluctant; slow; dull; not quick of apprehension; late; behind in time. —**backwardly,** bak′wėrd•li, *adv.* Unwillingly; reluctantly; aversely; perversely†.—**backwardness,** bak′wėrd•nes, *n.* The state or quality of being backward.—**backwater,** *n.* Ebbtide. —*v.i.* To fall back in the boat course.

backwoods, bak′wụdz, *n. pl.* Woody or forest districts of a country situated back or away from the more thickly settled parts: more especially used in regard to the United States and Canada.—**backwoodsman,** bak′wụdz•man, *n.* An inhabitant of the backwoods.

bacon, bā′kn, *n.* [O.Fr. *bacon*, from O.D. *baken*, bacon, from *bak*, *bake*, a pig; G. *bache*, a wild sow.] Swine's flesh salted or pickled and dried, usually in smoke.

Baconian, bā•kō′ni•an, *a.* Pertaining to Francis *Bacon*, or his system of philosophy.

bacteria, bak•tē′ri•a, *n.* pl. [Gr. *bakterion*, a stick.] Simple microscopic organisms that reproduce themselves by fission. Some, such as pathogenic bacteria, cause disease; others, such as denitrifying bacteria, are useful.—**bactericide,** bak•tėr′i•sīd, *n.* Anything capable of destroying bacteria. —**bacteriology,** bak•tē′ri•ol″o•ji, *n.* The study of bacteria.—**bacteriologist,** bak•tē′ri•ol″o•jist, *n.*—**bacteriophage,** bak•tē′ri•o•fāj, *n.* Any of various viruses that destroy bacteria.

bactericide, bak•tėr′i•sīd, *n.* Anything capable of destroying bacteria.

bacteriostasis, bak•tėr′i•o•stā″sis, *n.* *Bact.* prevention of the development of bacteria without killing them.

Bactrian, bak′tri•an, *a.* Of or pertaining to Bactria, an ancient province of the Persian empire (the *Bactrian* camel).

bad, bad, *a*, compar. (from quite a different root) *worse*, superl. *worst*. [Perhaps of Celtic origin; comp. Corn. *bad*, Gael. *baodh*, *baoth*, vain, foolish, etc.] The opposite of good; wanting good qualities, physical or moral; not coming up to a certain type or standard or the average of individuals of the particular class; wicked, unprincipled, depraved, immoral, vicious; pernicious, debasing, corrupting (influence, habits); ill, infirm (health); unwholesome, noxious (air, climate, food); defective, insufficient (work, crop); infertile, sterile (soil); unfortunate or unhappy (result, marriage); incompetent (workman), etc. etc.—*n.* That which is bad.—*To go to the bad*, to fall into bad company, bad ways, or bad circumstances; to fall into vicious courses and ruin one's life.—**badly,** bad'li, *adv.* In a bad manner; not well; unskillfully.—**badness,** bad'nes, *n.* The state of being bad; want of good qualities, physical or moral.

badderlocks, bad'ėr•loks, *n.* A common name for a seaweed found on the shores of the north of Europe, the midrib of which is edible.

badge, baj, *n.* [L.L. *bagia*, a sign, probably from O.Sax. *bag*, A.Sax. *beag*, Icel. *baugr*, a bracelet, ring, garland.] A mark, sign, token, or cognizance worn to show the relation of the weaver to any person, occupation, or order.—*v.t.*† To mark or distinguish with a badge or as with a badge. (*Shak.*)

badger, baj'ėr, *n.* [For *bladger*, from O.Fr. *blaage*, store of corn (the animal being supposed to steal corn), from L.L. *bladum*, wheat (Fr. *blé*), lit. grain carried off the field; L. *ablatum*—*ab*, from, and *latum*, carried.] A plantigrade carnivorous mammal belonging to a family intermediate between the bears and the weasels, living in a burrow, nocturnal in habits, and feeding on vegetables, small quadrupeds, etc.—*v.t.* To attack (a person), as the badger is attacked when being drawn or baited; to assail (as with importunities, commands, etc.); to worry; to pester.

badinage, bad'i•nāj or bä•dē•näzh, *n.* [Fr., from *badin*, facetious.] Light or playful discourse.

badminton, bad'min•ton, *n.* [From a residence of the Dukes of Beaufort.] An outdoor game, the same as lawn tennis but played with shuttlecocks; a kind of claret cup or summer beverage.

baffle, baf'fl, *v.t.*—*baffled, baffling.* [Origin unknown.] To elude; to foil; to frustrate; to defeat; to thwart.—*n.* A plate or screen that deflects or regulates flow of a gas, liquid, or the distribution of soundwaves.—**baffler,** baf'flėr, *n.*

bag, bag, *n.* [Icel. *baggi*, *böggr*, a bag, a bundle; comp. O.Fr. *bague*, a bundle, Gael. *bag*, a bag.] A sack; a wallet; a pouch; what is contained in a bag (as the animals shot by a sportsman); a definite quantity of certain commodities.—*v.t.*—*bagged, bagging.* To put into a bag; to distend; to swell; to shoot or otherwise lay hold of (game).—*v.i.* To swell or hang like a bag.—**bagging,** bag'ing, *n.* The cloth or other materials for bags.—**baggy,** bag'i, *a.* Having the appearance of a bag; puffy.—**bagginess,** bag'i•nes, *n.* Character of being baggy.—**bagpipe,** bag'pīp, *n.* A musical wind instrument consisting of a leathern bag which receives the air from the mouth or from a bellows; and of pipes into which the air is pressed from the bag by the performer's elbow.—**bagpiper,** bag'pīp•ėr, *n.* One who plays on a bagpipe.—**bagwig,** *n.* A wig with a sort of purse attached to it.

bagasse, ba•gas', *n.* [Fr.] The sugar cane in its dry crushed state as delivered from the sugar mill.

bagatelle, bag•a•tel', *n.* [Fr., from It. *bagatella*, a dim. of *bagata*, a trifle, L.L. *baga*, a bundle, a bag.] A trifle; a thing of no importance; a game played on a board having at the end nine holes, into which balls are to be struck with a cue or mace.

baggage, bag'āj, *n.* [Fr. *bagage*, baggage, O.Fr. *bague*, a bundle. BAG.] The necessaries of an army, or other body of men on the move; luggage; things required for a journey.

baggage, bag'āj, *n.* [Fr. *bagasse*, It. *bagascia*, Sp. *bagazo*, a strumpet.] A low worthless woman; a strumpet; now usually a playful epithet applied familiarly to any young woman.

bagnio, bän'yo, *n.* [It. *bagno*, from L. *balneum*, a bath.] A bath; a brothel; a stew.

bah, bä, *interj.* An exclamation expressing contempt, disgust, or incredulity.

bail, bāl, *v.t.* [O.Fr. *bailler*, to bail, to guard, from L. *bajulus*, a bearer, later a tutor or governor. Hence *bailiff*.] To liberate from arrest and imprisonment, upon security that the person liberated shall appear and answer in court.—*n.* The person or persons who procure the release of a prisoner from custody by becoming surety for his appearance in court; the security given for the release; not used with a plural termination (we were his *bail*).—**bailable,** bāl'a•bl, *a.* Capable of being admitted to bail; admitting of bail (a *bailable* offense).—**bailer,** bāl'ėr, *n.* One who or that which bails.

bail, bāl, *n.* [O.Fr. *baille*, a palisade, from L. *baculum*, a rod or staff.] A little stick laid on the tops of the stumps in playing cricket.

bail, bāl, *v.t.* [Fr. *baille*, a bucket, Armor. *bal*, a tub.] To free (a boat) from water with a bucket or other utensil.

bailiff, bā'lif, *n.* [O.Fr. *baillij*, *bailli*, from *baillir*, *bailler*, to hold, to govern, L. *bajulare*, to bear, *bajulus*, a porter. BAIL, to liberate.] A civil officer or functionary, a sheriff's deputy, a court officer who executes writs, processes, distraints, and arrests; who also acts as a messenger or usher in court.—**bailiwick,** bā'li•wik, *n.* [-*wick* from A.Sax. *wic*, dwelling, station, L. *vicus*, a village.] The precincts in which a bailiff has jurisdiction.

bailment, bāl'ment, *n.* The act of bailing an arrested person.

Baily's beads, *n.* [From F. *Baily*, astronomer.] The belt of bright sunlight shining through mountains on the moon's surface that is seen just before and just after a total eclipse of the sun.

Bairam, bā'ram, *n.* The name of two Mohammedan festivals, one held at the close of the fast Ramadan, the other seventy days after.

bait, bāt, *v.t.* [From Icel. *beita*, to make to eat, to feed, to bait a hook—a causative of *bita*, E. *bite*.] To give a portion of food and drink to a beast when traveling; to furnish with a piece of flesh or other substance which acts as a lure to fish or other animals (to *bait* a hook); to provoke and harass by dogs (as a bull, badger, or bear); to annoy.—*v.i.* To take a portion of food and drink for refreshment on a journey.—*n.* A portion of food and drink, or a refreshment taken on a journey; any substance used as a lure to catch fish or other animals; an allurement; enticement.

bait, bāt, *v.i.* [Fr. *battre*, to beat. BATE.] To clap the wings; to hover above prey. (*Shak.*)

baize, bāz, *n.* [A modified plural; O.E. *bayes*, Fr. *baie*, coarse woolen cloth, originally of a bay color; from L. *badius*, bay-colored.] A coarse woolen stuff with a long nap, sometimes friezed on one side.

bake, bāk, *v.t.*—*baked, baking* (old pp. *baken*). [A.Sax. *bacan*=Icel. and Sw. *baka*, Dan. *bage*, D. *bakken*, G. *backen*.] To dry and harden by heat, in an oven, kiln, or furnace, or by the solar rays (as bread, bricks, pottery); to prepare in an oven.—*v.i.* To do the work of baking; to dry and harden in heat.—**baker,** bāk'ėr, *n.* One whose occupation is to bake bread, biscuit, etc.—**baker's dozen.** Thirteen, the extra as retailer's profit.—**bakery,** bāk'ėr•i, *n.* A place used for the business of baking bread, etc.

bakelite, bā'ke•līt, *n.* [From L. H. *Baekeland*, chemist.] Trade name of a substance of coal tar origin used in making plastic ware.

baking powder, *n.* A mixture of baking soda, starch or flour, and an acid substance, used as a leavening agent.—**baking soda,** *n.* Sodium bicarbonate.

bakshish, bak'shēsh, *n.* [Pers., from *bakkshidan*, to give.] A present or gratuity of money: used in Eastern countries.

balance, bal'ans, *n.* [Fr., from L. *bilanx*—*bis*, double, and *lanx*, a dish, the scale of a balance.] An instrument for ascertaining the weight of bodies, consisting in its common form of a beam or lever suspended exactly at the middle, and having a scale or basin hung to each extremity of exactly the same weight, so that the beam rests horizontally when nothing is in either scale or when they are loaded with equal weights; the excess by which one thing is greater than another; surplus; the difference of two sums; the sum due on an account; an equality of weight, power, advantage, and the like; the part of a clock or watch which regulates the beats; the balance wheel.—*v.t.*—*balanced, balancing.* To bring to an equipoise; to keep in equilibrium on a small support; to poise; to compare by estimating the relative importance or value of; to weigh; to serve as a counterpoise to; to settle (an account) by paying what remains due; to examine (a merchant's books) by summations and show how debits and credits stand.—*v.i.* To be in equipoise; to have equal weight or importance; to be employed in finding balances on accounts.—**balancer,** bal′ans•ėr, *n.* One who or that which balances; an organ of an insect useful in balancing the body.—**balance sheet,** A statement of the assets and liabilities of a trading concern.—**balance wheel,** *n.* That part of a watch or chronometer which, like a pendulum, regulates the beat or strike.

balas, bal′as, ba•las′, *n.* [From Ar. *balakhsh,* from *Badakhshan,* in Central Asia.] A variety of spinel ruby, of a pale rose-red color, sometimes inclining to orange.

balata, ba•lä′ta, *n.* A gum obtained from a S. American tree, used for similar purposes to india-rubber, and in the United States as a chewing-gum. BULLET TREE.

balcony, bal′kō•ni (nineteenth century), bal•kō′ni (previously), *n.* [It. *balcone,* from *balco,* a scaffold, from O.H.G. *balcho,* G. *balken*=E. *balk,* a beam.] A platform projecting from the front of a building, supported by columns, pillars, or consoles, and encompassed with a balustrade, railing, or parapet; a projecting gallery in the interior of a building, as of a theater.

bald, bạld, *a.* [O.E. *balled,* lit. marked with a white spot; of Celtic origin, comp. Armor. *bal,* a white mark on an animal's face; Ir. and Gael. *bal,* a spot.] Having white on the face (said of animals); destitute of hair, especially on the top and back of the head; destitute of the natural or usual covering of the head or top; destitute of appropriate ornament; unadorned (said of style or language); *bot.* destitute of beard or awn.—**baldly,** bạld′li, *adv.* Nakedly; meanly; inelegantly.—**baldness,** bạld′nes, *n.* The state or quality of being bald.—**bald eagle,** the white-headed eagle of America.—**bald-faced,** *a.* Having a white face or white on the face; said of animals.—**bald head,** *n.* A person bald on the head. [O.T.] **bald-headed,** *a.* (*to go*). Having a bald head. In a wild, reckless manner.

baldachin, baldaquin, bal′da•kin, bal′da•kin, *n.* [It. *baldacchino,* Sp. *baldaquino,* from *Baldacco,* Italian form of *Bagdad,* where the cloth was manufactured.] A canopy or covering; a canopy on four poles held over the pope; a canopy on four columns over an altar; a canopy over a throne.

balderdash, bạl′dėr•dash, *n.* [W. *baldordus,* prattling, *baldordd,* prattle.] Senseless prate; a jargon of words; noisy nonsense.

baldpate, *n.* Same as *Bald head.*

baldric, bạld′rik, *n.* [O.E. *baudric, baldric,* etc., O.Fr. *baudric,* from O.G. *balderich,* from *balz,* a belt. BELT.] A broad belt, stretching from the right or left shoulder diagonally across the body, either as an ornament or to suspend a sword, dagger, or horn.

bale, bāl, *n.* [O.Fr. *bale,* the same word as *ball,* meaning originally a round package.] A bundle or package of goods.—*v.t.*—*baled, baling.* To make up into a bale or bundle.

bale, bāl, *v.t.*—*baled, baling.* To free from water by laving; to bail.

bale, bāl, *n.* [A.Sax. *bealu,* O.Sax. *balu,* Icel. *böl,* calamity, sorrow.] Misery; calamity; that which causes ruin, destruction, or sorrow.—**baleful,** bāl′fụl, *a.* Full of bale, destruction, or mischief; destructive; pernicious; calamitous; deadly.—**balefully,** bāl′fụl•li, *adv.* In a baleful or calamitous manner.—**balefulness,** bāl′fụl•nes, *n.* The state or quality of being baleful.

baleen, ba•lēn′, *n.* [Fr. *baleine,* from L. *balæna,* a whale.] The whalebone of commerce.

balefire, bāl′fīr, *n.* [A.Sax. *bael,* fire, flame, a funeral pile; Icel. *bal,* flame, a funeral pile.] A signal fire; an alarm fire.

balk, bạk, *n.* [A.Sax. *balca,* a balk or ridge, a beam; Icel. *balkr,* Sw. *balk,* a balk, a partition; Dan. *bjelke,* G. *balken,* a beam.] A ridge of land left unplowed; an uncultivated strip of land serving as a boundary; a beam or piece of timber of considerable length and thickness; a barrier or check; a disappointment.—*v.t.* To bar the way of; to disappoint. to frustrate.—*v.i.* To turn aside or stop in one's course (as a horse).—**balker,** bạk′ėr, *n.* One who balks.—**balkingly,** bạk′ing•li, *adv.* In a manner to balk or frustrate.

ball, bạl, *n.* [Fr. *balle,* from O.H.G. *balla,* G. *ball,* Icel. *böllr,* ball. *Bale,* a package, is another form, and *balloon, ballot* are derivatives.] A round body; a small spherical body often covered with leather and used in many games; any part of a thing that is rounded or protuberant; *farriery,* a form of medicine, corresponding to the term *bolus* in pharmacy; *metal.* a mass of half-melted iron; a loop; the projectile of a firearm; a bullet (in this sense also used collectively).—*Ball-and-socket joint,* a joint (as in the human hip) formed by a ball or rounded end playing within a socket so as to admit of motion in all directions.—**ball,** bal, *v.t.* To make into a ball.—*v.i.* To form or gather into a ball.—**ball cock,** *n.* A kind of self-acting stop cock opened and shut by means of a hollow sphere or ball of metal floating on the surface of a liquid, and attached to the end of a lever connected with the cock.—**ballpoint pen.** A pen with a tiny steel ball as a writing point, inked by rotating against an inking magazine.

ball, bạl, *n.* [Fr. *bal,* L.L. *ballare,* to dance, to shake, from Gr. *ballizō,* to dance. Akin *ballad, ballet.*] A social assembly of persons of both sexes for the purpose of dancing.

ballad, bal′lad, *n.* [Fr. *ballade,* from L.L. (and It.) *ballare,* to dance. BALL, a dance, BALLET]. A short narrative poem, especially such as is adapted for singing; a poem partaking of the nature both of the epic and the lyric.—**ballad,**† bal′lad, *v.t.* To celebrate in a ballad. (*Shak.*)—**ballade,** ba•lad, *n.* [Fr. *ballade.*] Poem consisting in its normal form of three stanzas of eight lines each, with a closing stanza or envoy of four lines, the rhymes throughout being not more than three.

ballast, bal′ast, *n.* [D. *ballast,* ballast, literally worthless load (being worthless in itself), from *bal* (akin to E. *bale,* misery, bad, and *last,* a load. LAST.) In Danish it was modified to *baglast,* lit. a back-load—*bag,* back after, and *last,* load.] Heavy matter, as stone, sand, or iron, carried in the bottom of a ship or other vessel, to prevent it from being readily overset (the vessel being said to be in *ballast* when she sails without a cargo); sand carried in bags in the car of a balloon to steady it, and enable the aeronaut to lighten the balloon by throwing part of it out; material filling up the space between the rails on a railroad in order to make it firm and solid; *fig.* that which confers steadiness on a person.—*v.t.* To place ballast in or on (a ship, a railroad track); *fig.* to steady; to counterbalance.

ballerina, bal•e•rē′na, *n.* A female ballet dancer.

ballet, bal•lā′or bal′let, *n.* [Fr. *ballet,* It. *balletto.* BALL, a dance.] A dance, more or less elaborate, in which several persons take part; a theatrical representation, in which a story is told by gesture, accompanied with dancing, scenery, etc.

ballista, bal•lis′ta, *n.* pl. **ballistae,** bal•lis′tē, [L., from Gr. *ballō,* to throw.] A military engine used by the ancients for discharging heavy stones or other missiles especially against a besieged place.—**ballistic,** bal•lis′tik, *a.* —**ballistic missile,** a projectile that uses rocket power in its first stage but continues to its target unguided and without propulsion.—**ballistics,** bal•lis′tiks, *n.* The science that studies the motion of projectiles.

balloon, bal•lön′, *n.* [Fr. *ballon,* an aug. of *balle,* a ball. BALL.] A large hollow spherical body; a very large bag, usually made of light fabric or plastic material and filled with hydrogen gas or heated air, or any other gaseous fluid lighter than common air, the contained gas causing the balloon to rise and float in the atmosphere.—**balloonist,** bal•lön′ist, *n.*

ballot, bal′lot, *n.* [Fr. *ballotte,* a ball used in voting, dim. of *balle,* a ball. BALL.] A ball, ticket, paper, or the like, by which one votes, and which gives no indication of who the voter is; the system of voting by means of this kind.—*v.i.* To vote or decide by ballot: frequently with *for.*—**balloter,** bal′lot•ėr, *n.* One who ballots or votes by ballot.

balm, bäm, *n.* [O.Fr. *baulme,* Fr. *baume;* a contr. of *balsam.*] A name common to several species of odoriferous or aromatic trees or shrubs, and to the fragrant medicinal exudations from them; any fragrant or valuable ointment; anything which heals, soothes, or mitigates pain.—**balm,** bäm, *v.t.* To anoint as with balm or with anything fragrant or medicinal; to soothe; to mitigate; to assuage; to heal.—**balmily,** bäm′i·li, *adv.* In a balmy manner.—**balminess,** bäm′i·nes, *n.* The state or quality of being balmy.—**balmy,** bäm′i, *a.* Having the qualities of balm; aromatic; fragrant; healing; soothing; assuaging; refreshing.

balsam, bal′sam, *n.* [L. *balsamum,* Gr. *balsamon,* a fragrant gum.] An oily, aromatic, resinous substance, flowing spontaneously or by incision from certain plants and used in medicine and perfumery; balm. —**balsamic,** bal·sam′ik, *a.* Having the qualities of balsam, stimulating; unctuous; soft; mitigating; mild.—*n.* A warm, stimulating, demulcent medicine, of a smooth and oily consistence.—**balsamiferous,** bal·sam·if′ėr·us, *a.* Producing or yielding balm or balsam.

baluster, bal′us·tėr, *n.* [Fr. *balustre,* It. *balaustro,* a baluster, from L. *balaustium,* Gr. *balaustion,* the flower of the wild pomegranate, being so called from some resemblance of form.] A small column or pilaster, of various forms and dimensions, used for balustrades.—**balustrade,** bal·us·trād′, *n.* [Fr. *balustrade.*] A row of small columns or pilasters, joined by a rail, serving as an enclosure for altars, balconies, staircases, terraces, etc., or used merely as an ornament.

bamboo, bam·bö, *n.* [Malay.] A tropical plant of the family of the grasses, with large jointed stems, the thickest being much used in India, China, etc., for building purposes, and the slenderest for walking canes.—**bamboo curtain.** The condition of censorship, prohibition of free travel, and secrecy in Communist China.

bamboozle, bam·bö′zl, *v.t.* [Origin doubtful.] To impose or practice upon; to hoax; to humbug; to deceive.—**bamboozler,** bam·bö′zlėr, *n.* One who bamboozles.

ban, ban, *n.* [A.Sax. *ban, gebann,* interdict, proclamation, edict; D. *ban,* excommunication; Icel. and Sw. *bann,* proclamation; Dan. *band.* a ban, *bande,* to curse. Akin *bandit, banish, abandon,* etc.] An edict or proclamation in general; an edict of interdiction or proscription; interdiction; prohibition; curse; excommunication; anathema; *pl.* proclamation of marriage (BANNS).—*v.t.*—*banned, banning.* To curse; to execrate; to prohibit; to interdict.—*v.i.* To curse.

ban, ban, *n.* [Serv. *ban,* a lord.] A Croatian or Hungarian military chief or ruler.

banal, ban′al, *a.* [Fr.] Hackneyed; commonplace; vulgar; properly, a *bannal mill* was by feudal custom the mill common by *ban* or order to *all* the vassals.—**banality,** ban·al′i·ti, *n.* Banal character; what is banal.

banana, ba·nä′na, *n.* [Sp., from the native name.] A herbaceous plant closely allied to the plantain, and extensively cultivated in tropical countries for its soft luscious fruit, which is the staple food of millions of people.

band, band, *n.* [A.Sax. *bend,* a band, from *bindan,* to bind; D. Icel. Sw. and G. *band,* in sense of body of men, from Fr. *bande,* G. *bande,* from same root. BIND.] That which binds together; a bond or means of attachment in general; a fetter or similar fastening; a narrow strip or ribbon-shaped ligature, tie, or connection; a fillet; a border or strip on an article of dress; that which resembles a band, tie, or ligature; pl. the linen ornament about the neck of a clergyman, with the ends hanging down in front; a company of persons united together by some common bond, especially a body of armed men; a company of soldiers; an organized body of instrumental musicians; an orchestra.—*v.t.*—To bind with a band; to mark with a band; to unite in a troop, company, or confederacy.—*v.i.* To associate or unite for some common purpose.—**bandage,** ban′dij, *n.* A fillet, roller, or swathe used in dressing and binding up wounds, restraining hemorrhages, etc.; a band or ligature in general.—*v.t. bandaged, bandaging.* To put a bandage on.—**bandbox,** band′box, *n.* A box made of pasteboard, or thin flexible pieces of wood and paper, for holding bands, bonnets, or other light articles.—**bandmaster,** *n.* The conductor and trainer of a band of musicians.—**bandsaw,** *n.* A saw formed of a long flexible belt of steel revolving on pulleys.—**bandwagon,** *n.* A wagon in which a band of musicians rides.—*Get on the bandwagon,* side with the apparent victor in a contest or cause.

bandana, bandanna, ban·dan′a, *n.* [Hind. *bândhnû,* to tie.] An Indian silk handkerchief having a pattern formed by tying little bits so as to keep them from being dyed; hence, a silk or cotton handkerchief having a somewhat similar pattern, that is, a uniform ground, usually of bright red or blue, with white or yellow figures of simple form.

bandeau, ban′dō, *n.* pl. **bandeaux,** ban′dō. [Fr., dim. from *bande,* a band.] A fillet worn round the head; a head band.

banderole, ban′de·rōl, *n.* [Fr. *banderole,* Sp. *banderola,* a little banner, from *bandera,* a banner, from G. *band.* BAND.] A little flag or streamer affixed to a mast, a military weapon, or a trumpet; a pennon; a banderole. *Arch.* stone band with inscription.

bandicoot, ban′di·kut, *n.* [Corruption of the Telinga name *pandikoku,* lit. pig-rat.] A large species of rat, attaining the weight of 2 or 3 lbs., a native of India and Ceylon, where its flesh is a favorite article of food among the coolies.

bandit, ban′dit, *n.* pl. **bandits, banditti,** ban′dits, ban·dit′ti. [It. *bandito,* pp. of *bandire,* L.L. *bannire,* to banish. BAN, BANISH.] An outlaw; more commonly a robber; a highwayman.

bandog, ban′dog, *n.* [*Band* and *dog,* lit. bound-dog.] A large, fierce kind of dog, generally a mastiff, usually kept chained.

bandoleer, ban·dō·lēr′, *n.* [Sp. *bandolera,* Fr. *bandoulière,* from Sp. *banda,* a sash.] A large leather belt carrying a bag for balls and a number of charges of gunpowder, worn by musketeers; a shoulder belt carrying ball cartridges.

bandoline, ban′dō·lēn, *n.* A gummy perfumed substance used to impart a glossiness and stiffness to the hair.

bandore, ban′dōr, *n.* [Fr., from It. *pandora,* L. *pandura,* Gr. *pandoura,* a musical instrument ascribed to *Pan.*] A musical stringed instrument like a lute.

bandy, ban′di, *n.* [Fr. *bandé,* bent, from *bander,* to bend a bow, to bind, to swathe, from G. *band,* a band. BAND.] A club bent at the end for striking a ball at play; a game played with such clubs.—*v.t.*—*bandied, bandying.* To beat to and fro, as a ball in play; to toss from one to another; to exchange contentiously; to give and receive reciprocally (words, compliments).—*v.i.* To contend; to strive. (*Shak.*)—**bandy,** ban′di, *a.* Bent, especially having a bend or crook outwards: said of a person's legs.—**bandy-legged,** *a.* Having bandy or crooked legs.

bane, bān, *n.* [A.Sax. *bana,* destruction, death, bane; Icel. *bani,* Dan. and Sw. *bane,* O.H.G. *bana;* allied to Gr. *phonos,* murder.] Any fatal cause of mischief, injury, or destruction; ruin; destruction; deadly poison.—**baneful,** bān′ful, *a.* Destructive; pernicious; poisonous.—**banefully,** bān′ful·li, *adv.* In a baneful manner.—**banefulness,** bān′ful·nes, *n.* The quality of being baneful.

bang, bang, *v.t.* [Comp. Icel. *bang,* a knocking; G. *bängel,* a club, the clapper of a bell; D. *bangel,* a bell.] To beat, as with a club or cudgel; to thump; to cudgel; to beat or handle roughly or with violence (*Shak.*); to bring a loud noise from or by, as in slamming a door, and the like.—*v.i.* To resound with a loud noise; to produce a loud noise; to thump violently.—*n.* A loud, sudden, resonant sound; a blow as with a club; a heavy blow.

bang, *n.* See BHANG.

bangle, bang′gl, *n.* [Hind. *bangri.*] An ornamental ring worn upon the arms or ankles in India, Africa, and elsewhere.

banian, ban′yan, *n.* [Hind. *banyá,* a merchant.] An Indian trader or merchant; a Hindu trader strict in regard to food.

banish, ban′ish, *v.t.* [Fr. *bannir,* ppr. *bannissant,* to banish, from L.L. *bannire,* to proclaim, denounce, from O.H.G. *bannan,* to proclaim. BAN.] To condemn to exile; to send (a person) from a country as a punishment; to drive away; to exile; to cast from the mind (thoughts, care, business).—**banisher,** ban′ish•ėr, *n.* One who banishes.—**banishment,** ban′ish•ment, *n.* The act of banishing; the state of being banished; enforced absence; exile.

banister, ban′is•tėr, *n.* [Form of *baluster.*] A baluster; an upright in a stair rail.

banjo, ban′jō, *n.* [Negro corruption of *bandore.*] A musical instrument having six strings, a body like a tambourine, and a neck like a guitar.

bank, bangk, *n.* [A.Sax. *banc,* a bank, a hillock, also *benc,* a bench; Sw. and Dan. *bank, bänk,* Icel. *bakki* (for *banki*), D. and G. *bank,* a bank, a bench. In sense of establishment dealing in money the word is directly from the Fr. *banque,* a banking establishment; It. *banco,* a bench, counter, a bank, this being from the German. *Bench* is the same word.] A mound or heap of earth; any steep acclivity, as one rising from a river, the sea, or forming the side of a ravine or the like; a rising ground in the sea, partly above water or covered everywhere with shoal water; a shoal; the face of coal at which miners are working; a bench or seat for the rowers in a galley; one of the rows of oars; an establishment which trades in money; an establishment for the deposit, custody, remittance, and issue of money; the office in which the transactions of a banking company are conducted; the funds of a gaming establishment; a fund in certain games at cards.—*v.t.* To enclose, defend, or fortify with a bank; to embank; to lay up or deposit in a bank.—*v.i.* To deposit money in a bank.—*To bank* (*upon*), to stake or rest hopes upon an event (recent use).—**bankable,** bangk′a•bl, *a.* **banker,** bangk′-ėr, *n.* One who keeps a bank; one who traffics in money, receives and remits money, negotiates bills of exchange, etc.—**banking,** bangk′ing, *n.* The business or profession of a banker; the system followed by banks in carrying on their business; the tilting up of an airplane at a sharp angle sideways when flying swiftly round a curve, on the same principle as that on which a cycle track is ‘ banked ’ steeply at corners rounded at high speed.—**banknote,** *n.* A promissory note issued by a banking company payable on demand.

bankrupt, bangk′rupt, *n.* [*Bank,* a bench, and L. *ruptus,* broken, lit. one whose bench has been broken, the bench or table which a merchant or banker formerly used in the exchange having been broken on his bankruptcy.] A person declared by legal authority unable to pay his debts; popularly, one who has wholly or partially failed to pay his debts; one who has compounded with his creditors; an insolvent.—*a.* Insolvent; unable to meet one's obligations.— **bankruptcy,** bangk′-rupt•si, *n.* The state of being a bankrupt; inability to pay all debts; failure in trade.

banner, ban′ėr, *n.* [Fr. *bannière,* L.L. *banderia,* from *bandum,* banner, standard, from G. *band,* a band or strip of cloth, from *binden,* to bind.] A piece of cloth usually bearing some warlike or heraldic device or national emblem, attached to the upper part of a pole or staff; an ensign; a standard; a square flag.—**bannerol,** ban′ėr•ol, *n.* A little flag; a banderole.—**banneret,** ban′ėr•et, *n.* A knight of a rank between a baron and an ordinary knight, raised to this rank for bravery on the field.

bannock, ban′ok, *n.* [A.Sax. *bannue,* Gael. *bannach.*] An unleavened cake of oatmeal or other meal baked at an open fire, and generally on an iron plate. [Scotch.]

banns, banz, *n.pl.* [See BAN.] The proclamation in church previous to a marriage, made by calling over the names of the parties intending matrimony.

banquet, bang′kwet, *n.* [Fr. *banquet,* dim. of *banque,* a bench, a seat, and hence a feast. BANK.] A feast; a rich entertainment of meat and drink; *fig.* something specially delicious or enjoyable.—*v.t.* To treat with a feast or rich entertainment.—*v.i.* To feast; to regale one's self; to fare daintily.—**banqueter,** bang′-kwet•ėr, *n.* A feaster; one who provides feasts or rich entertainments.

banquette, ban•ket′, *n.* [Fr. from *banc,* a bench, a bank.] *Fort.* A little raised way or bank running along the inside of a parapet, on which musketeers or riflemen stand to fire upon the enemy in the moat or covered way; the footway of a bridge when raised above the carriage way.

banshee, ban′shē, *n.* [Ir. *bean-sith,* Gael. *ban-sith,* from Ir. and Gael. *bean, ban,* woman, and *sith,* fairy.] A kind of female fairy believed in Ireland and some parts of Scotland to attach herself to a particular house, and to appear before the death of one of the family.

Bantam, ban′tam, *n.* A small but spirited breed of domestic fowl with feathered shanks, first brought from the East Indies, and supposed to derive its name from *Bantam* in Java;—*a.* [*not cap.*] Pertaining to or resembling the bantam; of the breed of the bantam; hence, diminutive; puny.

banter, ban′tėr, *v.t.* [Origin unknown.] To address humorous raillery to; to attack with jokes or jests; to make fun of; to rally.—*n.* (no pl.) A joking or jesting; humorous raillery: pleasantry with which a person is attacked.—**banterer,** ban′-tėr•ėr, *n.* One who banters.

bantling, bant′ling, *n.* [Probably from *band,* a wrapping, and the dim. suffix- *ling,* meaning properly a child in swaddling clothes.] A young child; an infant: a term carrying with it a shade of contempt.

banyan, ban′yan, *n.* [From the connection of one such tree with certain *banians* or Indian merchants.] An Indian tree of the fig genus, remarkable for its horizontal branches sending down shoots which take root when they reach the ground and enlarge into trunks, which in their turn send out branches; the tree in this manner covering a prodigious extent of ground.

baobab, bā′ō•bab, *n.* [The name in Senegal.] A large African tree usually from 40 to 70 feet high, and often 30 feet in diameter, having an oblong pulpy fruit called monkey bread; the sour-gourd or calabash tree.

baptism, bap′tizm, *n.* [Gr. *baptisma,* from *baptizō,* to baptize, from *baptō,* to dip in water.] The application of water by sprinkling or immersion to a person, as a sacrament or religious ceremony.—**baptismal,** bap•tiz′mal, *a.* Pertaining to baptism.—**baptismally,** bap•tiz′mal-li, *adv.* In a baptismal manner.—**Baptist,** bap′tist, *n.* [Gr. *baptistēs.*] One who administers baptism: specifically applied to John, the forerunner of Christ; as a contraction of *Anabaptist,* one who objects to infant baptism.—**baptistery,** bap′-tis•tėr•i, *n.* A building or a portion of a building in which is administered the rite of baptism.—**baptize,** bap•tīz′, *v.t.*—*baptized, baptizing.* [Gr. *baptizō.*] To administer the sacrament of baptism to; to christen.—**baptizer,** bap•tīz′ėr, *n.* One who baptizes.

bar, bär, *n.* [Fr. *barre*; from the Celtic; W. and Armor. *bar,* the top branch of a tree, a rail, a bar. *Barrier, barrister, barricade, embarrass,* etc., are derivatives.] A piece of wood, metal, or other solid matter, long in proportion to its thickness; a pole; a connecting piece in various positions and structures, often for a hindrance or obstruction; anything which obstructs, hinders, or impedes; an obstruction; an obstacle; a barrier; a bank of sand, gravel, or earth forming an obstruction at the mouth of a river or harbor; the railing enclosing the place which counsel occupy in courts of justice; the place in court where prisoners are stationed for arraignment, trial, or sentence; all those who can plead in a court; lawyers in general; the profession of the law; the railing or partition which separates a space near the door from the body of either house of parliament; a tribunal in general; the enclosed place of a tavern, inn, or other establishment where liquors, etc., are served out; the counter over which such articles are served out; military mark of distinction, stripe added to medal; *music,* a line drawn perpendicularly across the staff dividing it into equal measures of time; the space and notes included between two such lines.—*v.t.*—*barred, barring.* To fasten with a bar or as with a bar; to hinder; to obstruct; to prevent; to prohibit; to restrain; to except; to exclude by exception; to provide with a bar or bars; to mark with bars; to cross with one or more stripes or lines.—**barmaid,** *n.* A maid or woman who serves at the bar of an inn or other place of refreshment.— **Bar-room,** *n.* The room in a public house, hotel, etc., containing the bar or counter where refreshments are served.

barb, bärb, *n.* [Fr. *barbe,* L. *barba,* beard.] The sharp point projecting backward from the penetrating extremity of an arrow, fishhook, or other instrument for piercing, intended to prevent its being extracted; a barbel; a beard.—*v.t.* To shave or dress the beard‡; to furnish with barbs, as an arrow.

barb, bärb, *n.* [Contr. from *Barbary.*] A horse of the Barbary breed, remarkable for speed, endurance, and docility.

barbarian, bär•bā′ri•an, *n.* [L. *barbarus,* from Gr. *barbaros,* one whose language is unintelligible, a foreigner.] A foreigner‡ (N.T.); a man in his rude savage state; an uncivilized person; a cruel, savage, brutal man; one destitute of pity or humanity.—*a.* Of or pertaining to savages; rude; uncivilized; cruel; inhuman.—**barbaric,** bär•bar′ik, *a.* Of or pertaining to, or characteristic of a barbarian; uncivilized; savage; wild; ornate without being in accordance with sound taste.—**barbarism,** bär′bar•izm, *n.* An uncivilized state; want of civilization; rudeness of manners; an act of barbarity, cruelty, or brutality; an outrage; an offense against purity of style or language; any form of speech contrary to correct idiom. —**barbarity,** bär•bar′i•ti, *n.* The state of being barbarous; barbarousness; savageness; ferociousness; inhumanity; a barbarous act.—**barbarization,** bär′bar•iz•ā″shon, *n.* The act or process of rendering barbarous or of becoming barbarous.—**barbarize,** bär′bar•īz, *v.i.* To become barbarous.—*v.t.* To make barbarous.—**barbarous,** bär′ba•rus, *a.* Unacquainted with arts and civilization; uncivilized; rude and ignorant; pertaining to or characteristic of barbarians; adapted to the taste of barbarians; barbaric; cruel; ferocious; inhuman.—**barbarously,** bär′ba•rus•li, *adv.* In a barbarous manner; without knowledge or arts; savagely; cruelly; ferociously; inhumanly.—**barbarousness,** bar′ba•rus•nes, *n.* The state or quality of being barbarous; barbarity.

barbecue,† bär′bē•kū, *n.* [Conjectured to be from Fr. *barbe-à-queue,* from beard to tail; more probably from Carib *barbacoa,* a kind of large gridiron.] a hog or other large animal dressed whole;—*v.t.*— *barbecued, barbecuing.* To dress and cook whole by splitting to the backbone and roasting on a gridiron; to cook meat on a revolving spit, often drenching it in a sauce.

barbel, bär′bel, *n.* [O.Fr. *barbel,* from L. *barbus,* a barbel (the fish), from *barba,* a beard. In sense of appendage it is rather for *barbule.*] A fresh-water fish having four beard-like appendages on its upper jaw; a vermiform process appended to the mouth of certain fishes, serving as an organ of touch.

barber, bär′bėr, *n.* [Fr. *barbier,* from *barbe,* L. *barba,* a beard.] One whose occupation is to shave the beard or to cut and dress hair.—*v.t.* To shave and dress the hair of. (*Shak.*)

barberry, bär′be•ri, *n.* [Fr. *berberis,* from Ar. *barbāris,* the barberry, but the spelling has been modified so as to give the word an English appearance.] A shrubby plant bearing small acid and astringent, red berries, common in hedges.

barbet, bär′bet, *a.* [Fr. *barbet,* from L. *barba,* a beard.] A variety of dog having long, curly hair; a poodle; one of a group of climbing birds, approaching the cuckoos, having a large conical beak, and at its base tufts of stiff bristles.

barbette, bär•bet′, *n.* [Fr. *barbette.*] A fixed armored shelter on a warship, inside which a gun revolves on a turntable.

barbican, bär′bi•kan, *n.* [Fr. *barbacane,* It. *barbacane,* from Ar. *bâbkhânah,* a gateway or gatehouse.] A kind of watchtower; an advanced work defending the entrance to a castle or fortified town, as before the gate or drawbridge.

barbiturate, bär•bit′ū•rāt, *n. Chem.* a derivative of barbituric acid; any **of a group of drugs used as sedatives.—barbital,** bär′bi•tal, ***n.* A drug containing barbituric acid, used as a hypnotic.—barbituric acid,** **bär•bi•tūr′ik as′id, *n.* A crystalline substance, $C_4H_4O_3N_2$, that is the basis for many sedative and hypnotic drugs.**

barbule, bär′būl, *n.* [L. *barbula,* dim. of *barba,* a beard.] A small barb; a little beard.

barcarole, bär′ka•rōl, *n.* [Fr., from It. *barcarolo,* a boatman, from *barca,* a boat or barge.] A simple song or melody sung by Venetian gondoliers; a piece of instrumental music composed in imitation of such a song.

bard, bärd, *n.* [Celtic.] A poet and singer among the ancient Celts; a poet generally.—**bardic,** bärd′ik, *a.* Pertaining to bards or to their poetry.

bare, bâr, *a.* [A.Sax. *bær,* Icel. *ber,* Sw. Dan. *bar,* D. *bāar,* G. *bar, baar,* probably from root meaning shining seen in Skr. *bhas,* to shine.] Naked; without covering; laid open to view; detected; no longer concealed; poor; destitute; indigent; ill-supplied; empty; unfurnished; unprovided: often followed by *of* (bare *of* money); threadbare; much worn.—*v.t.*— *bared, baring.* To strip off the covering from; to make naked.—**barely,** bâr′li; *adv.* In a bare manner; nakedly; poorly; without decoration; scarcely; hardly.—**bareness,** bâr′nes, *n.* The state of being bare; want of clothing or covering; nakedness; deficiency of appropriate covering, ornament, and the like; poverty; indigence.—**barefaced,** bâr′fāst, *a.* Having the face uncovered; unreserved; shameless; impudent.—**barefoot, barefooted,** bâr′fu̧t, bâr′fu̧t•ed, *a.* and *adv.* Without shoes or stockings.

barege, ba•räzh′, *n.* [From *Baréges,* a village of the Pyrenees.] A thin, gauzelike fabric for ladies' dresses, usually made of silk and worsted, but, in the inferior sorts, with cotton instead of silk.

bargain, bär′gin, *n.* [O.Fr. *bargaine,* L.L. *barcania,* a bargain, traffic; believed to be from L. L. *barca,* a bark.] A contract or agreement between two or more parties; a compact settling that something shall be done, sold, transferred, etc.; the thing purchased or stipulated for; what is obtained by an agreement; something bought or sold at a low price.—*v.i.* To make a bargain or agreement; to make an agreement about the transfer of property.—*v.t.* To sell; to transfer for a consideration: generally followed by *away.*—**bargainer,** bär′gin•ėr, *n.* One who bargains or stipulates.

barge, bärj, *n.* [O.Fr. *barge,* L.L. *bargia, barga, barca,* bark. BARQUE.] A vessel or boat elegantly fitted up and decorated, used on occasions of state and pomp; a flat-bottomed vessel for loading and unloading ships or conveying goods from one place to another.—**bargee,** bär•jē′, *n.* One of the crew of a barge or canal-boat. —**bargeman,** bärj′man, *n.* The man who manages a barge.

barilla, ba•ril′la, *n.* [Sp.] An impure soda or carbonate and sulfate of soda obtained in Spain and elsewhere by burning several species of plants; a kind of kelp; Spanish soda.

baritone, bar′i•tōn, *a.* [Gr. *barys,* heavy, and *tonos,* tone.] Ranging between tenor and bass; having a voice ranging between tenor and bass.—*n.* A male voice, the compass of which partakes of the bass and the tenor, but which does not descend so low as the one nor rise as high as the other; a person with a voice of this quality; a deep brass instrument.

barium, bâr′i•um, *n.* [Gr. *barys,* heavy.] Chemical element belonging to the alkaline-earth series, a whitish malleable metal occurring in combination. Symbol, Ba; at. no., 56; at. wt., 137. 34.

bark, bärk, *n.* [Dan. and Sw. *bark,* Icel. *börkr,* G. *borke,* bark.] The outer rind of a tree, shrub, etc.; the exterior covering of exogenous plants, composed of cellular and vascular tissue.—*v.i.* To strip bark off; to peel; to apply bark to; to treat with bark in tanning.—**barker,** bärk′ėr, *n.* One who barks; one who removes the bark from trees.

bark, bärk, *n.* Same as *Barque.*

bark, bärk, *v.i.* [A.Sax. *beorcan.*] To emit the cry of a dog, or a similar sound.—*n.* The cry of the domestic dog; a cry resembling that of the dog.—**barker,** bärk′ėr, *n.* An animal that barks; a person who clamors unreasonably.

barley, bär′li, *n.* [O.E. *barlic, berlic,* from A.Sax. *bere* (=Sc. *bear*), barley, and *leac,* a plant (also a *leek*); comp. *garlic.*] A kind of grain commonly grown and used especially for making malt; the plant yielding the grain.—

barleycorn, bär′li•korn, *n.* A grain of barley; a measure equal to the third part of an inch.—John Barleycorn, a surname of malted drink.

barm, bärm, *n.* [A.Sax. *beorma*=Sw. *bärma*, Dan. *bärme*, L.G. *barme*, G. *bärme*, barm; from root of *brew*.] Yeast.—**barmy,** bärm′i, *a.* Containing or consisting of barm; frothy, as beer.

Barmecidal, bar′me•sīd•al, *a.* Disappointing, fallacious.—**Barmecide feast.** Rich apparent feast given in the *Arabian Nights*, by prince to guest, with nothing but names for the dishes.

barn, bärn, *n.* [A.Sax. *berern*—*bere*, barley, and *ern*, a house.] A covered building for securing grain, hay, or other farm produce.—*v.t.* To store up in a barn.

barnacle, bär′na•kl, *n.* [Fr. *bernacle*, *barnacle*, L.L. *bernacula*, for *pernacula*, dim. of L. *perna*, a ham, a kind of shellfish. In sense of goose origin doubtful.] A stalked cirriped, often found on the bottoms of ships, on timber fixed below the surface of the sea, etc.; a species of goose found in the northern seas, but visiting more southern climates in winter.

barnacle, bär′na•kl, *n. pl.* [Origin unknown.] An instrument to put upon a horse's nose, to confine him for shoeing, bleeding, or dressing.

barograph, bar′ō•graf, *n.* [Gr. *baros*, weight, and *graphō*, to write.] A self-registering barometric instrument for recording the variations in the pressure of the atmosphere.

barometer, ba•rom′et•ėr, *n.* [Gr. *baros*, weight, and *metron*, measure.] An instrument for measuring the weight or pressure of the atmosphere, consisting ordinarily of a glass tube containing a column of mercury, its lower end dipping into a cup containing the same metal; the mercury in the tube, having a vacuum above it, rises and falls according to the varying pressure of the air on the mercury in the cup. In the aneroid barometer no fluid is used.—**barometric, barometrical,** bar•ō•met′rik, bar•ō•met′rik•al, *a.* Pertaining or relating to the barometer; made by a barometer.—**barometrically,** bar•ō•met′rik•al•li, *adv.* By means of a barometer.

baron, bar′on, *n.* [Fr. *baron*, from O.H.G. *bar*, a man, from *beran*=E. to *bear*, the original sense being probably that of one who could *bear*, as being strong and robust.] In Great Britain, a title or degree of nobility; one who holds the lowest rank in the peerage; a title of certain judges or officers; as, *barons of the exchequer*, the judges of the court of exchequer.—*Baron of beef*, two sirloins not cut asunder.—**baronage,** bar′on•āj, *n.* The whole body of barons or peers; the dignity or condition of a baron.—**baroness,** bar′on•es, *n.* A baron's wife or lady; a holder of the title in her own right.—**baronet,** bar′on•et, *n.* [Dim. of *baron*.] One who possesses a hereditary rank or degree of honor next below a baron, and therefore not a member of the peerage; one belonging to an order founded by James I in 1611.—**baronetage,** bar′on•et•āj, *n.* The baronets as a body; the dignity of a baronet.—**baronetcy,** bar′on•et•si, *n.* The title and dignity of a baronet.—**baronial,** bar•ō′ni•al, *a.* Pertaining to a baron or a barony.—**barony,** bar′on•i, *n.*

baroque, ba•rōk′, *a.* [Fr., from It. *barocco*.] Pertaining to a style of architecture, music, and literature that involves elaborate and sometimes grotesque forms; ornate.

baroscope, bar′o•skōp, *n.* [Gr. *baros*, weight, *skopeō*, to view.] An instrument for exhibiting changes of atmospheric pressure; a kind of weatherglass.

barouche, ba•rösh′, *n.* [From G. *barutsche*, from It. *baroccio*, *biroccio*, from L. *birotus*, two-wheeled—*bis*, double, and *rota*, a wheel.] A four-wheeled carriage with a falling top.

barque, bärk, *n.* [Fr. *barque*, L.L. *barca*, a barque, through a dim. form *barica*, from Gr. *baris*, a skiff. *Barge* is a form of this word.] A sailing vessel of any kind; *naut.* a three-masted vessel with only fore-and-aft sails on the mizzenmast, the other two masts being square rigged.—**barquentine,** bärk′an•tīn, *n.* [From *barque*, in imitation of *brigantine*.] A three-masted vessel square rigged in the foremast and fore-and-aft rigged in the main and mizzenmasts.

barrack, bar′ak, *n.* [Fr. *baraque*, It. *baracca*, from L.L. *bárra*, a bar, from the Celtic; comp. Ir. *barrachad*, a hut or booth.] A hut or house for soldiers, especially in garrison; permanent buildings in which both officers and men are lodged; a large building, or a collection of huts for a body of workpeople: generally in pl.—**barracoon,** bar•a•kön′, *n.* A Negro barrack; a slave depot or bazaar.

barracuda, ba•ra•kö′da, *n.* A large voracious game fish of tropical seas related to gray mullets.

barrage, ba•räzh′, *n.* [Fr. *barre*.] Damming up; the discharge of artillery so as to keep a zone under continuous fire.

barranca, bar•rang′ka, *n.* [Sp.] A deep gully or ravine.

barrator, bar′a•tor, *n.* [O.Fr. *barateur*, a cheater, *barate*, deceit. BARTER.] One who frequently excites suits at law; an encourager of litigation; the master or one of the crew of a ship who commits any fraud in the management of the ship or cargo, by which the owner, freighters, or insurers are injured.—**barratrous,** bar′a•trus, *a.* Characterized by or tainted with barratry.—**barratrously,** bar′a•trus•li, *adv.*—**barratry,** bar′a•tri, *n.* The act or practice of a barrator; the exciting and encouraging of lawsuits and quarrels; fraud in a shipmaster to the injury of the owners, freighters, or insurers, as by running away with the ship, sinking, or deserting her.

barrel, bar′el, *n.* [O.Fr. *bareil*, Fr. *baril*, from Celt; comp. W. *baril*, Gael. *barail*, a barrel; so called because made of *bars* or staves. BAR.] A somewhat cylindrical wooden vessel made of staves and bound with hoops; a cask; anything resembling a barrel in shape; a hollow cylinder or tube (as the *barrel* of a gun).—*v.t.*—*barreled*, *barreling*. To put in a barrel.—**barrel organ,** *n.* An organ in which a barrel or cylinder furnished with pegs or staples, when turned round, opens a series of valves to admit a current of air to a set of pipes, or acts on wires, so as to produce a tune.

barren, bar′en, *a.* [From O.Fr. *baraigne*, *brehaine*, *brehaigne*, sterile, possibly from Armor. *brec'han*, sterile.] Incapable of producing its kind; not prolific: applied to animals and vegetables; unproductive; unfruitful; sterile: applied to land; *fig.* not producing or leading to anything (*barren* speculation, *barren* of ideas); unsuggestive; uninstructive.—*n.* A barren or unproductive tract of land.—**barrenly,** bar′en•li, *adv.* Unfruitfully.—**barrenness,** bar′en•nes, *n.* The state or quality of being barren; sterility; want of fertility, instructiveness, interest, or the like (*barrenness* of invention).

barret, bar′et, *a.* [Fr. *barrette*.] Flat cap, or biretta.

barricade, bar•i•kād′, *n.* [From Sp. *barricada*, blocking with *barricas* or casks.] A temporary fortification made of trees, earth, stones, or anything that will obstruct the progress of an enemy or serve for defense or security against his shot; a fence around or along the side of a space to be kept clear; any barrier or obstruction.—*v.t.*—*barricaded*, *barricading*. To stop up by a barricade; to erect a barricade across; to obstruct.

barrier, bar′i•ėr, *n.* [Fr. *barrière*, a barrier, from *barre*, a bar. BAR.] A fence; a railing; any obstruction; what hinders approach, attack, or progress; what stands in the way; an obstacle; a limit or boundary of any kind; a line of separation.—*Barrier reef*, a coral reef rising from a great depth to the level of low tide, encircling an island like a barrier, or running parallel to a coast, with a navigable channel inside, as on the northeast coast of Australia.

barring, bär′ing, *part.* of verb to *bar*, used as *prep.* Excepting; leaving out of account. (Colloq.).

barrister, bar′is•tėr, *n.* [From *bar*.] A counselor or advocate admitted to plead at the bar of a court of law in protection and defense of clients: a term more especially used in England and Ireland, the corresponding term in Scotland being *advocate*, in the United States lawyer.

barrow, bar′ō, *n.* [A.Sax. *beorg*, *beorh*, *berg*, a hill or funeral mound; Dan. Sw. G. *berg*, a hill; allied to *burgh*.] A prehistoric or at least ancient sepulchral mound formed of earth or stones, found in Britain and elsewhere, and met with in various forms: often containing remains of the dead, implements, etc.

barter, bär′tėr, *v.i.* [O.Fr. *bareter*,

barater, to cheat, to barter, *barat*, *barate*, deceit, barter; origin doubtful.] To traffic or trade by exchanging one commodity for another (and not for money).—*v.t.* To give in exchange; to exchange, as one commodity for another.—*n.* The act of exchanging commodities; the thing given in exchange.—**barterer,** bär′tėr•ėr, *n.* One who barters or traffics by exchanging commodities.

bartizan, bär′ti•zan, *n.* [Comp. O.Fr. *bretesche*, a fortification of timber; G. *bret*, a board.] A small turret projecting from the top part of a tower or wall, with apertures for archers to shoot through.

baryta, ba•rī′ta, *n.* [Gr. *barys*, heavy, *barytēs*, weight.] Oxide of barium, called sometimes *heavy earth*, generally found in combination with sulfuric and carbonic acids, forming sulfate and carbonate of baryta, the former of which is called *heavy spar*. Baryta is a gray powder with a sharp caustic alkaline taste.—**barytes,** ba•rī′tēz, *n.* A name of baryta or its sulfate (heavy spar).—**barytic,** ba•rī′tik, *a.* Of or containing baryta.

barytone, bar′i•tōn, *a.* [Gr. *barys*, heavy, and *tonos*, tone.] *Greek gram.* having no accent marked on the last syllable, the grave being understood.

basal metabolism, *n.* The heat produced by an organism in the resting and fasting state. It represents the minimum amount of energy needed to maintain respiration, circulation, and other vital functions.

basalt, ba•sạlt′, *n.* [Gr. *basaltēs*, of unknown origin.] A well-known igneous dark-gray or black rock, remarkable as often assuming the form of regularly prismatic columns.

bascule, bas′kūl, *n.* [Fr.] An arrangement in bridges by which one portion balances another.—*Bascule bridge*, a kind of drawbridge in which the roadway may be raised at will and kept in an upright position by means of weights or otherwise.

base, bās, *a.* [Fr. *bas*, low, from L.L. *bassus*, low, short, allied to Ir, *bass*, W. *bas*, Armor. *baz*, shallow.] Of little or no value; coarse in comparison (the *base* metals); worthless; fraudulently debased in value; spurious (*base* coin); of or pertaining to humble or illegitimate birth; of low station; lowly; of mean spirit; morally low; showing or proceeding from a mean spirit; deep; grave: applied to sounds.—*n. pl.* An old name for a skirt or something similar worn by knights, etc. (*Mil.*)—**basely,** bās′li, *adv.* In a base manner or condition; meanly; humbly; vilely.—**baseness,** bās′nes, *n.* The state or quality of being base; meanness; lowness; vileness; worthlessness.—**baseborn,** *a.* Born in a base condition; of illegitimate birth.

base, bās, *n.* [Fr. *base*, L. *basis*, a base, a pedestal, from Gr. *basis*, a going, a foot, a base, from *bainō*, to go.] The bottom of anything, considered as its support, or the part of a thing on which it stands or rests; the opposite extremity to the apex; *arch.* the part between the bottom of a column and the pedestal or the floor; *chem.* one of those compound substances which unite with acids to form salts; *dyeing*, a mordant; *geom.* the line or surface forming that part of a figure on which it is supposed to stand; *mus.* the bass; *milit.* a tract of country protected by fortifications, or strong by natural advantages, from which the operations of an army proceed; the place from which racers or tilters start; a starting post; the game of baseball or prisoner's base, or an old game somewhat similar.—*v.t.*—*based, basing.* To lay the base or foundation of; to place on a basis; to found.—**basal, basilar basilary,** bās′al, bas′il•ėr, bas′il•a•ri, *a.* Of or pertaining to a base; situated at the base.—**baseless,** bās′les, *a.* Without a base; without grounds or foundation (a *baseless* rumor).—**basement,** bās′ment, *n. Arch.* the lowest story of a building, whether above or below the ground.—**basic,** bās′ik, *a.* Relating to a base; *chem.* performing the place of a base in a salt, or having the base in excess.—**basic slag,** *n.* The slag or refuse matter got in making basic steel, a valuable fertilizer from the phosphate of lime it contains.—**basicity,** bās′is′•iti, *n. Chem.* the state of being a base; the power of an acid to unite with one or more atoms of a base.

baseball, *n.* The national American game or sport played with bat and ball, four bases indicating the points of the diamond marking the course each player takes in making a run (scoring), played by two teams of nine players each, one team being at bat while the other is in the field alternately; a horsehide-covered ball used in the game of baseball.

bash, bash, *v.t.* [Scand., Dan. *bask*, a slap, *baske*, to slap; akin to *box*, to fight.] To beat violently; to knock out of shape. (Colloq.)

bashaw, ba•shạ′, *n.* [Per. *bâshâ*, *pâshâh.*] A pasha.

bashful, bash′ful, *a.* [For *abashful.*] Easily put to confusion; modest to excess; diffident; shy.—**bashfully,** bash′ful•li, *adv.*—**bashfulness,** bash′ful•nes, *n.*

bashi-bazouk, bash′ē•ba•zök″, *n.* [Turk.] A kind of irregular soldier in the Turkish army, a member of a corps collected hastily in a time of emergency.

Basic English, *n.* A simplified system of English consisting of 850 essential words.

basic, basicity. See BASE.

basidium, ba•sid′i•um, *n.* pl. **basidia,** ba•sid′i•a. [Gr. *basis*, a base, and *eidos*, likeness.] *Bot.* the cell to which the spores of some fungi are attached.

basil, baz′il, *n.* [Shortened from O.Fr. *basilic*, from Gr. *basilikos*, royal, *basileus*, a king.] A plant, a native of India, cultivated in Europe as an aromatic potherb, and used for flavoring dishes.

basilar. See BASE, *n.*

basilica, ba•sil′ik•a, *n.* [L., from Gr. *basilikē*, a colonnade; lit. a royal colonnade or porch, from *basileus*, a king.] Originally, the name applied by the Romans to their public halls: usually of rectangular form, with a middle and two side aisles and an apse at the end. The ground plan of these was followed in the early Christian churches, and the name is now applied to some of the churches in Rome by way of distinction, or to other churches built in imitation of the Roman basilicas.—**basilican,** ba•sil′ik•an, *a.* In the manner of or pertaining to a basilica.

basilisk, bas′il•isk, *n.* [Gr. *basiliskos*, lit. little king, from *basileus*, king.] A fabulous creature formerly believed in, and variously regarded as a kind of serpent, lizard, or dragon, and sometimes identified with the cockatrice; a name of several reptiles of the lizard tribe with a crest or hood; a large piece of ordnance formerly used.

basin, bā′sn, *n.* [Fr. *bassin*, O.Fr. *bacin*, a dim. of *bac*, a wide open vessel, same as E. *back*, a brewer's vat. BACK.] A vessel or dish of some size, usually circular, rather broad and not very deep, used to hold water for washing, and for various other purposes; any reservoir for water, natural or artificial; the whole tract of country drained by a river and its tributaries; *geol.* an aggregate of strata dipping toward a common axis or center; strata or deposits lying in a depression in older rocks.

basis, bās′is, *n.* pl. **bases,** bās′ēz. [L. and Gr. *basis*, the foundation. BASE.] A base; a foundation or part on which something rests; *fig.* grounds or foundation. BASE.

bask, bask, *v.i.* [Formerly to bathe, a word of Scandinavian origin = Icel. *batha sik*, to bathe one's self—*sik* being the reflexive pronoun. *Busk* is a similar form.] To lie in warmth; to be exposed to genial heat; *fig.* to be at ease and thriving under benign influences.—*v.t.* To warm by continued exposure to heat; to warm with genial heat.

basket, bas′ket, *n.* [Possibly of Celtic origin; comp. W. *basged* or *basgawd*, Ir. *bascaid*, a basket; W. *basg*, a netting or piece of wickerwork.] A vessel made of twigs, rushes, thin strips of wood, or other flexible materials interwoven; as much as a basket will hold.—*v.t.* To put in a basket.

basketball, bas′ketbạl, *n.* A game played by teams of five, using basket-like nets as goals.

Basque, bask, *n.* A language of unknown affinities spoken in parts of France and Spain on both sides of the Pyrenees at the angle of the Bay of Biscay, supposed to represent the tongue of the ancient Iberians, the primitive inhabitants of Spain; Biscayan or Euskarian.—*a.* Pertaining to the people or language of Biscay.

bas-relief, basso-rilievo, bas′ or bä′rē•lēf, bäs′sō•rē•lyā′vō, *n.* [Fr. *bas*, It. *basso*, low, and *relief*, It. *rilievo*, relief.] A sculpture in low relief; a mode of sculpturing figures on a flat surface, the figures being raised above the surface, but not so much as in high relief or *alto-rilievo*.

bass, bas, *n.* [A corruption of *barse*, A.Saxi *bœrs*, G. *bars*, D. *baars*, a perch.] The name of various British and American sea fishes allied to the perch, some of them of considerable size and used as food.

bass, bas, *n.* [Same as *bast*, the *t* being dropped or changed to *s*. BAST.] The American linden or lime tree; a mat made of bast; a hassock.—**basswood** *n.* The American lime tree or its timber.

bass, bās, *n.* [It. *basso*, deep, low. BASE, *a.*] *Mus.* the lowest part in the harmony of a musical composition, whether vocal or instrumental; the lowest male voice.—*a. Mus.* low; deep; grave.—**bass clef,** *n.* The character shaped like an inverted C put at the beginning of the bass staff. —**bass drum,** *n.* A large drum having two heads and producing a deep sound when struck.—**bass horn,** *n.* A tuba.

basset, bas′set or bas•set′, *n.* [Fr. *bassette;* It. *bassetta.*] An old game at cards, resembling modern faro.

basset, bas′set, *n.* A miner's term for the outcrop or surface edge of any inclined stratum.—*v.i. Mining*, to incline upward, so as to appear at the surface; to crop out.

basset, bas′set, *n.* [Fr. *basset*, diminutive of *bas*, low.] A dog with short crooked legs and a long body, used for hunting; also *basset hound*.

basset horn, bas′set•horn, *n.* [It. *bassetto*, somewhat low, and E. *horn*.] A musical instrument, a sort of clarinet of enlarged dimensions and extended compass.

bassinet, bas′i•net, *n.* [Probably a dim. from Fr. *berceau*, a cradle.] A wicker basket with a covering or hood over one end, in which young children are placed by way of cradle.

bassoon, bas•sön′, *n.* [Fr. *basson;* It. *bassone*, aug. of *basso*, low.] A musical wind instrument of the reed order, blown with a bent metal mouthpiece.

bast, bast, *n.* [A.Sax. *bœst*=Icel. Sw. D. Dan. and G. *bast*, bark, perhaps from root of *bind*.] The inner bark of exogenous trees, especially of the lime, consisting of several layers of fibers; rope or matting made of this.

bastard, bas′tėrd, *n.* [O.Fr. *bastard*, from *bast* (Fr. *bât*), a packsaddle, with the common termination *-ard* added to it, referring to the old locution *fils de bast*, son of a pack-saddle, the old saddles being often used by way of beds or to serve as pillows.] A natural child; a child begotten and born out of wedlock; an illegitimate or spurious child; what is spurious or inferior in quality; a kind of impure, soft, brown sugar; a kind of sweet, heady Spanish wine (*Shak.*).—*a.* Begotten and born out of lawful matrimony; illegitimate; spurious; not genuine; false; adulterate; impure; not of the first or usual order or character.—**bastardize,** bas′tėrd•īz, *v. t.*—*bastardized, bastardizing*. To make or prove to be a bastard.—**bastardly,** bas′tėrd•li, *a.* Bastard; spurious.—**bastardy,** bas′tėrd•i, *n.* The state of being a bastard, or begotten and born out of lawful wedlock.—**bastard wing,** *n.* A group of stiff feathers attached to the bone of a bird's wing that represents the thumb.

baste, bāst, *v.t.*—*basted, basting*. [Allied to Icel. *beysta*, to strike, to beat, Dan. *böste*, to beat. As term in cookery the origin may be different.] To beat with a stick; to cudgel; to give a beating to; to drip butter or fat upon meat in roasting it.

baste, bāst, *v.t.* [O.Fr. *bastir*, lit. to sew with *bast*, the fibers of bast having been used as thread. BAST.] To sew with long stitches, and usually to keep parts together temporarily; to sew slightly.—**basting,** bāst′ing, *n.* The long stitches by which pieces of garments are loosely attached to each other.

bastille, bastile, bas•tēl′ *n.* [Fr. *bastille*, a fortress, O.Fr. *bastir*, to build.] A tower or fortification.—*The Bastille*, an old castle in Paris used as a state prison, demolished by the enraged populace in 1789.

bastinado, bas•ti•nā′dō, *n.* [Sp. *bastonada*, from *baston*, a stick, a baton.] A sound beating with a stick or cudgel; a mode of punishment in oriental countries, especially Mohammedan, by beating the soles of the feet with a rod.—*v.t.* To beat with a stick or cudgel; to beat on the soles of the feet, as a judicial punishment.

bastion, bas′ti•on, *n.* [Fr. and Sp. *bastion*, from O.Fr. and Sp. *bastir*, Fr. *bâtir*, to build.] *Fort.* a huge mass of earth, faced with sods, brick, or stones, standing out with an angular form from the rampart at the angles of a fortification.—**bastioned,** bas′ti•ond, *a.* Provided with bastions.

bat, bat, *n.* [A Celtic word: Ir. and Armor. *bat*, a stick.] A heavy stick or club; a piece of wood used in driving the ball in baseball and similar games; a turn at batting; a piece of a brick; a brickbat.—*v.t.* and *i.*—*batted, batting*.—**batsman, batter,** bats′man, bat′ėr, *n.*

bat, bat, *n.* [Corruption of O.E. *back*, *bak;* Sc. *bak*, *bakie-bird*, a bat. Dan. *bakke* (in *aften-bakke*, a bat, lit. evening-bird), the word having lost an *l*, seen in Icel. *lethrblaka*, 'leather-flapper', a bat, from *blaka*, to flutter.] One of a group of mammals possessing a pair of leathery wings which extend between the fore and the posterior limbs, the former being specially modified for flying, the bones of the forefeet being extremely elongated.—**batty,** bat′i, *a.* Pertaining to or resembling a bat. (*Shak.*)—**batfowling,** *n.* A mode of catching birds at night by means of a light and nets; the birds being roused fly toward the light and are entangled in the nets.

batch, bach, *n.* [From the verb to *bake*.] The quantity of bread baked at one time; any quantity of a thing made at once; a number of individuals or articles similar to each other.

bate, bāt, *v.t.*—*bated, bating*. [Abbrev. of *abate*.] To abate, lessen, or reduce; to leave out; to take away; to weaken, dull, or blunt (*Shak.*)‡.—*v.i.*‡ To grow or become less; to lessen.—**bating,** bāt′ing, *ppr.* used as *prep.* Abating; taking away; deducting; excepting.

bateau, bä•tō′, *n.* [Fr.] A light broad and flat boat used in Canada; also the pontoon of a floating bridge.

bath, bäth, *n.* [A.Sax. *bœth*, a bath= Icel. *bath*, Dan. D. G. *bad;* from root of *bake; bask* is akin.] The immersion of the body or a part of it in water or other fluid or medium; an apparatus or contrivance for exposing the surface of the body to water or other diffusible body (as oil, medicated fluids, steam, etc.); a building in which people may bathe; an apparatus for regulating the heat in chemical processes, by interposing a quantity of sand, water, etc., between the fire and the vessel to be heated.—*Knights of the Bath*, a British order established in 1725 by George I, patterned after a legendary order connected with the coronation of Henry IV in 1399. Candidates were put into a bath the preceding evening, to denote a purification or absolution from evil deeds.—**bathe,** bāTH, *v.t.*—*bathed, bathing*. [A.Sax. *bathian*, from *bœth*. a bath=Icel. *batha*. Dan. *bade*. D. and G. *baden*. BATH.] To subject to a bath; to immerse in water, for pleasure, health, or cleanliness; to wash, moisten, or suffuse with any liquid; to immerse in or surround with anything analogous to water.—*v.i.* To take a bath; to be or lie in a bath; to be in water or in other liquid; to be immersed or surrounded as if with water.—**bather,** bāTH′ėr, *n.* One who bathes.—**bathroom,** *n.* A room for bathing in.

bath, bäth, *n.* [Heb.] A Hebrew liquid measure, the tenth part of a homer.

Bath brick, bäth′brik, *n.* [From the town of *Bath*, in Somersetshire.] A preparation of siliceous earth in the form of a brick, used for cleaning knives, etc.—**bath chair,** *n.* A small carriage capable of being pushed along by an attendant; used by invalids.

bathometer, ba•thom′e•tėr, *n.* [Gr. *bathos*, depth, and *metron*, a measure.] An apparatus for taking soundings, especially one in which a sounding line is dispensed with.

bathos, bā′thos, *n.* [Gr. *bathos*, from *bathys*, deep.] A ludicrous descent from the elevated to the mean in writing or speech.

bathyscaph, bath′i•skaf, *n.* [Gr.—*bathys*, deep, and *skaphe*, light boat.] A deep-sea craft that uses gasoline and lead pellets for ballast control.

bathysphere, bath′i•sfēr, *n.* A diving sphere for deep-sea observation and study developed by William Beebe.

bating. See BATE.

batiste, ba•tēst′, *n.* [Fr. *batiste*, from its inventor *Baptiste*.] A fine linen cloth made in Flanders and Picardy, a kind of cambric.

batman, bạ′man, *n.* [Fr. *bât*, a pack-saddle.] In the British army a person having charge of the cooking utensils of each company of a regiment of soldiers on foreign service, and of the horse (bat horse) that carries them.—**bat money,** bạ'mun•i, *n.* Money paid to a batman.

baton, ba•ton', *n.* [Fr. *bâton*, O.Fr. *baston;* akin *baste*, to beat.] A staff or club; a truncheon, the official badge of various officials of widely different rank; the stick with which a conductor of music beats time.

batrachian, ba•trā'ki•an, *a.* [Gr. *batracheios*, of a frog.] Relating to or pertaining to a frog.—*n.* A frog, toad, or other froglike animal.

battalion, bat•tal'yon, *n.* [Fr. *bataillon*, It. *battaglione*, aug. of *battaglia*, a battle or body of soldiers. BATTLE.] A body of infantry usually forming part of a regiment.

batten, bat'n, *v.t.* [Icel. *batna*, to grow better, from root *bat*, *bet* in *better*.] To fatten; to make fat; to make plump by plenteous feeding.—*v.i.* To grow or become fat; to feed greedily; to gorge.

batten, bat'n, *n.* [Fr. *bâton*, a stick.] A long piece of wood from 1 inch to 7 inches broad, and from ½ in. to 2½ in. thick; a plank; *naut.* one of the slips of wood used to keep a tarpaulin close over a hatchway; *weav.* a lathe.—*v.t.* To fasten with battens (to *batten* down the hatches).

batter, bat'ėr, *v.t.* [Fr. *battre*, It. *battere*, from L.L. *batere*, a form of L. *batuere*, to beat, whence also *battle*.] To beat with successive blows; to beat with violence, so as to bruise or dent; to assail by a battering-ram or ordnance; to wear or impair, as by beating, long service, or the like (usually in pp.).—*v.i.* To make attacks, as by a battering-ram or ordnance.—**batter,** bat'ėr, *n.* A mixture of several ingredients, as flour, eggs, etc., beaten together with some liquor into a paste, and used in cookery.—**battering-ram,** *n.* An engine formerly used to beat down the walls of besieged places, consisting of a large beam, with a head of iron somewhat resembling the head of a ram, whence its name.—**battery,** bat'ėr•i, *n.* [Fr. *batterie*.] The act of battering‡; a small body of cannon for field operations, with complement of wagons, artillerymen, etc.; a parapet thrown up to cover a gun or guns and the men employed in loading, etc.; a number of guns placed near each other and intended to act in concert; *elect.* an apparatus for originating an electric current; a series of connected Leyden jars that may be discharged together; *law*, the unlawful beating of a person.

battle, bat'l, *n.* [Fr. *bataille*, from L.L. *batalia*, *batualia*, a fight; from L. *batuere*, to beat, to fence. BATTER.] A fight or encounter between enemies or opposing armies; an engagement; more especially a general engagement between large bodies of troops; a combat, conflict, or struggle; a division of an army‡.—*To give battle*, to attack; *to join battle*, to meet in hostile encounter. ∴ *Battle* is the appropriate word for great engagements. *Fight* has reference to actual conflict; a man may take part in a *battle*, and have no share in the *fighting*. *Combat* is a word of greater dignity than *fight*, but agrees with it in denoting close encounter.—*v.i.* —*battled, battling*. To join in battle; to contend; to struggle; to strive or exert one's self.—**battle-ax,** *n.* An ax anciently used as a weapon of war.—**battlefield,** *n.* The field or scene of a battle.—**battlement,** bat'l•ment, *n.* [Perhaps from O.Fr. *bastille*, a fortress, *bastiller*, to fortify, to embattle modified by the influence of E. *battle*.] A notched or indented parapet, originally constructed for defenses, afterward for ornament, formed by a series of rising parts called cops or merlons, separated by openings called crenelles or embrasures, the latter intended to be fired through.

battledore, bat'l•dōr, *n.* [From Sp. *batidor*, a beater, from *batir*, to beat.] An instrument with a handle and a flat board or palm, used to strike a ball or shuttlecock; a racket.

battue, bat•tü', *n.* [Fr., from *battre*, to beat.] A kind of sport in which the game is driven by a body of beaters from under cover into a limited area where the animals may be easily shot.

bauble, bạ'bl, *n.* [O.Fr. *babole*, a toy or baby-thing; from same Celtic root as *babe*.] A short stick with a fool's head, anciently carried by the fools attached to great houses; a trifling piece of finery; something showy without real value; a gewgaw; a trifle.

baulk, bạk. Same as *Balk*.

bauxite, bạx'īt, *n.* [From Fr. *Baux*, near Arles, France.] A clay mineral from which aluminum is derived.

bawd, bạd, *n.* [O.Fr. *baud*, bold, wanton, from G. *bald*=E. *bold*.] A person who keeps a house of prostitution or acts as a go-between in illicit amours.—**bawdy,** bạ'di, *a.* Obscene; lewd; indecent; smutty; unchaste. Hence **bawdily, bawdiness.**

bawl, bạl, *v.i.* A word imitative of sound; akin, *bell*, *bellow;* L. *balo*, to bleat.] To cry out with a loud full sound; to make vehement or clamorous outcries; to shout.—*v.t.* To proclaim by outcry; to shout out. —*n.* A vehement cry or clamor.—**bawler,** bạl'ėr, *n.* One who bawls.

bay, bā, *n.* [Fr. *baie*, L.L. *baia*, a bay; of doubtful origin.] A rather wide recess in the shore of a sea or lake; the expanse of water between two capes or headlands; a gulf; any recess resembling a bay.—**bay rum,** bā-rum', *n.* A spirituous liquor containing the oil of the bayberry of Jamaica, a species of pimento, and used for the hair.—**baywood,** *n.* A variety of mahogany exported from Honduras, or the Bay of Honduras.

bay, bā, *n.* [Fr. *baie*, L. *bacca*, a berry.] The laurel tree, noble laurel, or sweet bay; a garland or crown bestowed as a prize for victory or excellence, consisting of branches of the laurel; hence, fame or renown, laurels: in this sense chiefly in plural.

bay, bā, *n.* [O.Fr. *abai*, *abbai*, a barking, *abbayer*, to bark; Mod. Fr. *aboi*, a barking, *aux abois*, at bay; comp. Fr. *bayer*, to gape, or stand gaping. ABASH.] The bark of a dog; especially, a deep-toned bark.—*At bay*, so hard pressed by enemies as to be compelled to turn round and face them from impossibility of escape.—*v.i.* To bark; to bark with a deep sound. —*v.t.* To bark at; to follow with barking (*Shak.*); to express by barking.

bay, bā, *n.* [Fr. *bai*, L. *badius*, brown or chestnut colored; akin *baize*.] Red or reddish, inclining to a chestnut color.—**Bayard,** bā'yard, *n.* A brave man, from the Chevalier Bayard; [*not cap.*] a horse, from *Bayard*, the horse given by Charlemagne to Renaud.

bayadere, bā•ya•dēr', *n.* [Pg. *bailadeira*, from *bailar*, to dance.] In the East Indies, a professional dancing girl.

bayberry, bā'be•ri, *n.* The fruit of the bay tree; also the wax myrtle and its fruit.

bayonet, bā'on•et, *n.* [O.Fr. *bayonnette*, Fr. *baïonnette*, usually derived from *Bayonne* in France, because bayonets are said to have been first made there.] A short triangular sword or dagger, made so that it may be fixed upon the muzzle of a rifle or musket.—*v.t.* To stab with a bayonet; to compel or drive by the bayonet.

bayou, bī'ö, *n.* [Fr. *boyau*, a gut, a long narrow passage.] A channel proceeding from a lake or a river.

bazaar, bazar, ba•zär', *n.* [Per. *bâzâr*.] In the East, a place where goods are exposed for sale, usually consisting of small shops or stalls in a narrow street or series of streets; a series of connected shops or stalls in a European town; a sale of miscellaneous articles in furtherance of some charitable or other purpose; a fancy fair.

bazooka, ba•zö'ka, *n.* [From *bazooka*, a musical instrument.] An antitank rocket weapon; a rocket launcher.

bdellium, del'li•um, *n.* [L. *bdellium*, Gr. *bdellion*, from Heb.] An aromatic gum resin brought chiefly from Africa and India, in pieces of different sizes and figures, used as a perfume and a medicine, externally of a dark reddish brown, internally clear, and not unlike glue.

be, bē, *v.i. substantive verb*, pres. *am*, *art*, *is*, *are;* pret. *was*, *wast* or *wert*, *were;* subj. pres. *be;* pret. *were;* imper. *be;* pp. *been;* ppr. *being*. [One of the three verbal roots required in the conjugation of the substantive verb, the others being *am* and *was*. A.Sax. *beó*, I am, *beón* to be; G. *bin*, I am; allied to L. *fui*, I was, Skr. *bhû*, to be. It is now chiefly used in the subjunctive, imperative, infinitive, and participles, being seldom used in the present tense. AM and WAS.] To have a real state or existence; to exist in the world of fact, whether physical or mental; to exist in or have a certain state or quality, to become; to remain. ∴ The most common use of the verb *to be* is to assert connection between a subject and a predicate, forming what is called the copula; as, he *is* good; John *was* at home; or to form the compound tenses of other verbs.—**being,** bē'ing, *n.* Existence, whether real or only in the mind; that which has life; a living existence; a creature.

beach, bēch, *n.* [Origin doubtful; comp. Icel. *bakki*, Sw. *backe*, Dan. *bakke*, a bank, the shore; or from old *bealch*, to belch, alluding to the washing up of pebbles, etc.] That part of the shore of a sea or lake which is washed by the tide and waves; the strand.—*Raised beaches*, in *geol.* a term applied to those long terraced level pieces of land, consisting of sand and gravel, and containing marine shells, now, it may be, a considerable distance above and away from the sea.—*v.t.* To run (a (vessel) on a beach.—**beachcomber,** bēch'kōm•ėr, *n.* A long rolling wave breaking on the beach; a seashore idler or vacationist.—**beachhead,** bēch'hed, *n.* A foothold on enemy **shore from which further attacks can be made.**

beacon, bē•kn, *n.* [A.Sax. *bécn*, *beácen*, a beacon; hence *beck*, *beckon*.] An object visible to some distance, and serving to denote the presence of danger, as a light or signal shown to signify the approach of an enemy, or to warn seamen of the presence of rocks, shoals, etc.; hence, anything used for a kindred purpose. A revolving light supported by a structure for the guidance of aviators.—*v.t.* To light up by a beacon; to illuminate; to signal.

bead, bēd, *n.* [A.Sax. *bed*, *bead*, a prayer, from *biddan*, to pray. From beads being used to count prayers (as in the rosary), the word which originally meant prayer came to mean what counted the prayers. BID.] A little perforated ball of gold, amber, glass, etc., strung with others on a thread, and often worn round the neck as an ornament, or used to form a rosary; any small globular body, as a drop of liquid and the like; *arch.* and *joinery*, a small round molding sometimes cut so as to resemble a series of beads or pearls; an astragal. —*v.t.* To mark or ornament with beads.—**beady,** bēd'i, *a.* Consisting of or containing beads; beadlike.—**bead roll,** *n.* A list of persons for the repose of whose souls a certain number of prayers is to be said; hence, any list or catalogue.—**beads man,** *n.* A man employed in praying, generally in praying for another; one privileged to claim certain alms or charities.—**beads woman,** *n.* The feminine equivalent of *beads man.*

beadle, bē'dl, *n.* [A.Sax. *bydel*, a herald, a beadle, from *beódan*, to bid. BID.] A messenger or crier of a court; a parish officer whose business is to punish petty offenders; a church officer with various subordinate duties.

beagle, bē'gl, *n.* [Comp. Ir. and Gael. *beag*, little.] A small smooth-haired, hanging-eared hound, formerly kept to hunt hares.

beak, bēk, *n.* [Fr. *bec*, from the Celtic—Armor. *bek*, *beg*, Ir. and Gael. *bec*, a beak.] The bill or neb of a bird; anything in some way resembling a bird's bill; the bill-like mouth of some fishes, reptiles, etc.; a pointed piece of wood fortified with brass, fastened to the prow of ancient galleys, and intended to pierce the vessels of an enemy; a similar, but infinitely more powerful appendage of iron or steel in modern warships; a magistrate. (Colloq.)—**beaked,** bēkt, *a.* Having a beak or something resembling a beak; beak shaped; rostrate.

beaker, bēk'ėr, *n.* [Icel. *bikarr*, D. *beker*, G. *becher*, from L.L. *bicarium*, a cup, from Gr. *bikos*, a wine-jar.] A large drinking cup or glass.

beam, bēm, *n.* [A.Sax. *beam*, a beam, a post, a tree, a ray of light; D. *boom*, G. *baum*, a tree.] A long straight and strong piece of wood or iron, especially when holding an important place in some structure, and serving for support or consolidation; a horizontal piece of timber in a structure; the part of a balance from the ends of which the scales are suspended; the pole of a carriage which runs between the horses; a cylindrical piece of wood, making part of a loom, on which the warp is wound before weaving; one of the strong timbers stretching across a ship from one side to the other to support the decks and retain the sides at their proper distance; the oscillating lever of a steam engine forming the communication between the piston rod and the crankshaft; a ray of light, or more strictly a collection of parallel rays emitted from the sun or other body; a constant unidirectional radio signal to guide airplane pilots.—*v.i.* To emit rays of light or beams; to give out radiance; to shine.—**beamy,** bēm'i, *a.* Like a beam; heavy or massive; emitting beams or rays of light: radiant.

bean, bēn, *n.* [A.Sax. *beán*=Icel. *baun*, Sw. *bōna*, Dan. *bonne*, D. *boon*, G. *bohne*.] A name given to several kinds of valuable leguminous seeds contained in a bivalve pod, and to the plants producing them, as the common bean, cultivated both in fields and gardens for man and beast, the French. bean, the kidney bean, etc.—**bean caper,** *n.* A small tree growing in warm climates, the flowerbuds of which are used as capers.

bear, bâr, *v.t.* pret. *bore* (formerly *bare*); pp. *borne*; ppr. *bearing*. [A. Sax. *beran*=Icel. *bera*, Dan. *bære*, to bear, to carry, to bring forth; D. *baren*, G. *(ge)bären*, to bring forth; cog. L. *ferre*, Gr. *pherein*, Skr. *bhri*, to bear, to support. Akin are *birth*, *burden*, *bairn*, *barrow*.] To support, hold up, or sustain, as a weight; to suffer, endure, undergo, or tolerate, as pain, loss, blame, etc.; to carry or convey; to have, possess, have on, or contain; to bring forth or produce, as the fruit of plants or the young of animals. [*Born* is the passive participle in the sense of brought forth by a female, as the child was *born*; but we say actively, she has *borne* a child. *Born* is also used attributively, *borne* not.]—*To bear down*, to overcome by force.—*To bear out*, to give support or countenance to (a person or thing); to uphold, corroborate, establish, justify.—*To bear up*, to support; to keep from sinking. —*To bear a hand*, to lend aid; to give assistance.—*To bear in mind*, to remember.—*v.i.* To suffer, as with pain, to be patient; to endure; to produce (fruit); to be fruitful; to lean, weigh, or rest burdensomely; to tend; to be directed or move in a certain way (to *bear* back, to *bear* out to sea, to *bear* down upon the enemy); to relate; to refer: with *upon;* to be situated as to some point of the compass, with respect to something else.—*To bear up*, to have fortitude; to be firm; not to sink.—*To bear with*, to tolerate; to be indulgent; to forbear to resent, oppose, or punish.—**bearable,** bâr'a•bl, *a.* Capable of being borne, endured, or tolerated.—**bearably,** bâr'a•bli, *adv.* In a bearable manner.—**bearer,** bâr'ėr, *n.* One who or that which bears, sustains, supports, carries, conveys, etc.—**bearing,** bâr'ing, *n.* The act of one who bears; manner in which a person comports himself; carriage, mien, or behavior; import, effect, or force (of words); that part of a shaft or axle which is in connection with its support; the direction or point of the compass in which an object is seen; relative position or direction; a figure on a heraldic shield.—**bearing rein,** *n.* The rein by which the head of a horse is held up in driving.

bear, bâr, *n.* [A.Sax. *bera*, a bear=D. *beer*, G. *bär*, Icel. *bera*.] A name common to various quadrupeds of the carnivorous order and of the plantigrade group, having shaggy hair and a very short tail, the most notable being the brown or black bear of Europe, the grizzly bear of the Rocky Mountains, the white or Polar bear, etc.; the name of two constellations in the northern hemisphere, called the Greater and Lesser Bear; *fig.* a rude or uncouth man; in stock-exchange slang, a person who does all he can to bring down the price of stock in order that he may buy cheap: opposed to a *bull*, who tries to raise the price that he may sell dear.—**bearish,** bâr'ish, *a.* Resembling a bear; rude; violent in conduct; surly.—**bearbaiting,** *n.* The sport of baiting bears with dogs.—**bear garden,** *n.* A place in which bears are kept for sport, as bear-baiting, etc.; *fig.* a place of disorder or tumult.—**bearberry,** bâr'ber•i, *n.* An evergreen shrub of the heath family, growing on barren moors in the colder parts of the northern hemisphere, the leaves being used as an astringent and tonic under the name *uva-ursi.*—**bear's-ear,** *n.* A species of primrose, so called from the shape of the leaf.—**bear's-foot,** *n.* A herbaceous plant of the hellebore genus, having a rank smell and purgative and emetic properties.

bear, bĕr, *n.* Same as *Bere.*

beard, bērd, *n.* [A.Sax. *beard,* a beard=D. *baard,* G. *bart;* L. *barba,* W. and Armor. *barf*—beard.] The hair that grows on the chin, lips, and adjacent parts of the face of male adults; anything resembling this; a hairy, bristly, or threadlike appendage of various kinds, such as the filaments by which some shellfish attach themselves to foreign bodies, etc.; the awn on the ears of grain; a barb, as of an arrow.—*v.t.* To take by the beard; to oppose to the face; to set at defiance.—**bearded,** bērd′ed, *a.* Having a beard in any of the senses of that word.—**beardless,** bērd′les, *a.* Without a beard; hence, of persons of the male sex, young; not having arrived at manhood.

beast, bēst, *n.* [O.Fr. *beste,* from L. *bestia,* a beast.] Any four-footed animal, as distinguished from birds, insects, fishes, and man; as opposed to *man,* any irrational animal; a brutal man; a disgusting person.—**beastliness,** bēst′li•nes, *n.* The state or quality of being beastly; brutality; filthiness.—**beastly,** bēst′li, *a.* Like a beast; brutish; brutal; filthy; contrary to the nature and dignity of man.

beat, bēt, *v.t.* pret. *beat;* pp. *beat, beaten;* ppr. *beating.* [A.Sax. *beatan* =Icel. *bauta, bjáta,* O.H.G. *pózan,* to beat; akin *butt, abut, beetle* (a mallet).] To strike repeatedly; to lay repeated blows upon; to knock, rap, or dash against often; to pound; to strike for the purpose of producing sound (a drum); to shape by hammer; to scour with bustle and outcry in order to raise game; to overcome, vanquish, or conquer in a battle, contest, competition, etc.; to surpass or excel; to be too difficult for; to be beyond the power or skill of; to baffle; to fatigue utterly; to prostrate; to flutter (the wings).—*To beat back,* to compel to retire or return.—*To beat down,* to dash down by beating or battering, as a wall; to lay flat; to cause to lower a price by importunity or argument; to lessen the price or value of; to depress or crush.—*To beat off,* to repel or drive back.—*To beat out,* to extend by hammering.—*To beat up,* to attack suddenly; to alarm or disturb, as an enemy's quarters.—*To beat time,* to regulate time in music by the motion of the hand or foot.—*To beat a retreat,* to give a signal to retreat by a drum; hence, generally, to retreat or retire.—*v.i.* To strike or knock repeatedly; to move with pulsation; to throb (as the pulse, heart, etc.); to dash or fall with force or violence (as a storm, flood, etc.); to summon or signal by beating a drum; *naut.* to make progress against the direction of the wind by sailing in a zigzag.—*To beat about,* to make search by various means or ways.—*To beat up for,* to go about in quest of (recruits); to search earnestly or carefully for.—*n.* A stroke; a blow; a pulsation; a throb; a footfall; a round or course which is frequently gone over, as by a policeman, etc.; *music,* the beating or pulsation resulting from the joint vibrations of two sounds of the same strength, and all but in unison.—**beaten,** bēt′n, *p.* and *a.* Made smooth by beating or treading; worn by use; conquered; vanquished; exhausted; baffled. [*Beat* is so far synonymous with *beaten,* but is less of an adjective, not being used attributively as the latter is; thus we do not say *beat* gold.]—**beater,** bēt′ėr, *n.* One who or that which beats; an instrument for pounding or comminuting substances; the striking part in various machines.

beatify, bē•at′i•fī, *v.t.*—*beatified, beatifying.* [Fr. *beatifier,* L. *beatificare*—*beatus,* blessed, and *facere,* to make.] To make happy; to bless with the completion of celestial enjoyment; *R. Cath. Ch.* to declare that a person is to be reverenced as blessed, though not canonized.—**beatific,** bē•a•tif′ik, *a.* Blessing of making happy; imparting bliss.—**beatification,** bē•at′i•fi•kā″shon, *n.* The act of beatifying; the state of being blessed; blessedness; *R. Cath. Ch.* an act of the pope by which he declares a person beatified; an inferior kind of canonization.—**beatitude,** bē•at′i•tūd, *n.* [L. *beatitudo.*] Blessedness; felicity; one of the declarations of blessedness to particular virtues, made by the Saviour in the Sermon on the Mount.

beatnik, bēt′nik, *n.* [Beat, and *nik,* Rus. suffix meaning person.] A person (often) characterized by unconventional behavior and dress and by an emotional disengagement from society.

beau, bō, *n.* pl. **beaux,** bōz. [Fr. *beau,* O.Fr. *bel,* from L. *bellus,* beautiful.] One whose great care is to deck his person according to the first fashion of the times; male sweetheart or lover.—**beau ideal,** bō i•dē′al or ē•dā′al, *n.* [Fr. *beau idéal,* beautiful ideal.] A conception of any object in its perfect typical form; a model of excellence in the mind or fancy.—**beau monde,** bō″ mond′, *n.* [Fr. *beau,* fine, and *monde,* world.] The fashionable world.

beauty, bū′ti, *n.* [O.Fr. *biaute,* Fr. *beauté,* beauty, from L.L. *bellitas, bellitatis,* beauty, from L. *bellus,* beautiful.] An assemblage of perfections through which an object is rendered pleasing to the eye; those qualities in the aggregate that give pleasure to the aesthetic sense; qualities that delight the eye, the ear, or the mind; loveliness; elegance; grace; a particular grace or ornament; that which is beautiful; a part which surpasses in beauty that with which it is united; a beautiful person, especially, a beautiful woman.—**beauty shop,** an establishment where a woman may receive a hairdress, manicure, and other beauty treatments.—**beauteous,** bū′tē•us, *a.* Possessing beauty; beautiful.—**beauteously,** bū′tē•us•li, *adv.*—**beautician,** bū•tish′an, one whose business is to improve the appearance of women's hair, nails, complexion, etc.—**beautification,** bū′ti•fi•kā″shon, *n.* The act of beautifying or rendering beautiful; decoration; adornment; embellishment.—**beautiful,** bū′ti•fụl, *a.* Having the qualities that constitute beauty; highly pleasing to the eye, the ear, or the mind (a *beautiful* scene, melody, poem, character, but not a *beautiful* taste or smell); beauteous; lovely; handsome; fair; charming; comely.—*The beautiful,* all that possess beauty; beauty in the abstract.—**beautifully,** bū′ti•fụl•li, *adv.* In a beautiful manner.—**beautifulness,** bū′ti•fụl•nes, *n.* The quality of being beautiful; beauty.—**beautify,** bū′ti•fī, *v.t.*—*beautified, beautifying.* To make or render beautiful; to adorn; to deck; to decorate.

beaver, bē′vėr, *n.* [A.Sax. *befer*=D. *bever,* Dan. *bæver,* Sw. *bäfver,* Icel. *bjórr,* G. *biber,* L. *fiber.*] A rodent quadruped valued for its fur, about 2 feet in length, haunting streams and lakes, now found in considerable numbers only in North America, and generally living in colonies, with large webbed hind feet and a flat tail covered with scales on its upper surface; beaver fur; a hat or cap made of beaver fur.

beaver, bē′vėr, *n.* [O.Fr. *baviere,* a child's bib, a beaver, *bave,* slaver.] The faceguard of a helmet, so constructed with joints or otherwise that the wearer could raise or lower it to eat and drink; a visor.

bebeeru, bē•bē′rö, *n.* [Native name.] A tree of British Guiana of the laurel family, the timber of which, known as *greenheart,* is used for building ships and submarine structures.

bebop, bē″bop′, *n.* Jazz style characterized by dissonance, complex rhythms, and experimental instrumentation.

becalm, bē•käm′, *v.t.* To render calm, still, or quiet (the sea, passions, etc.)†; to keep from motion for want of wind (as a ship); to delay (a person) by a calm.

became, bi•kām′, pret. of *become.*

because, bē•kạz′, *conj.* [*Be* for *by,* and *cause;* O.E. *bicause, bycause*=by or for the cause that.] By cause, or by the cause that; on this account that; for the cause or reason next explained; as, he fled *because* (as the reason given) he was afraid.

beccafico, bek•a•fē′kō, *n.* [It., lit. figpecker.] A bird resembling the nightingale; the greater pettichaps or garden warbler.

bechamel, besh′a•mel, *n.* [Named after its inventor.] A fine white broth or sauce thickened with cream.

bechance,† bē•chans′, *v.t.* To befall; to happen to. (*Shak.*)

beck, bek, *v.i.* [Shortened form of *beckon.*] To nod or make a significant gesture.—*v.t.* To call by a nod; to intimate a command or desire to by gesture.—*n.* A nod of the head or other significant gesture intended as a sign or signal.

becket, bek′et, *n.* A contrivance in ships for confining loose ropes, etc.

beckon, bek′n, *v.i.* [A.Sax. *beácnian, bécnian,* to beckon, from *beácn, bécn,* a beacon.] To make a sign to another by a motion of the hand or finger, etc., intended as a hint or intimation.—*v.t.* To make a significant sign to; to direct by making signs (*beckon* him to us).

become, bē·kum′, *v.i.*—*became* (pret.) *become* (pp.), *becoming.* [A.Sax. *becuman, bicuman,* to arrive, happen, turn out—prefix *be=by,* and *cuman,* to come, to happen.] To pass from one state to another; to change, grow, or develop into (the boy *becomes* a man).—*To become of* (usually with *what* preceding), to be the fate of; to be the end of; to be the final or subsequent condition.—*v.t.* To suit or to be suitable to (anger *becomes* him not); to befit; to accord with, in character or circumstances; to be worthy of, or proper to; to grace or suit as regards outward appearance (a garment *becomes* a person).—**becoming,** bē·kum′ing, *a.* Suitable; meet: proper; appropriate; befitting; seemly.—**becomingly,** bē·kum′ing·li, *adv.* After a becoming or proper manner.

bed, bed, *n.* [A.Sax. *bed*=D. *bed, bedde,* Dan. *bed,* Goth. *badi,* G. *bett.*] That on or in which one sleeps, or which is specially intended to give ease to the body at night; especially, a large flat bag filled with feathers or other soft materials: the word may include or even be used for the bedstead; a plat or piece of tilled ground in a garden; the bottom of a river or other stream, or of any body of water; a layer; a stratum; an extended mass of anything, whether upon the earth or within it; that on which anything lies, rests, or is supported.—*v.t.*—*bedded, bedding.* To place in, or as in, a bed; to plant, as flowers, in beds.—**bedding,** bed′-ing, *n.* A bed and its furniture; materials of a bed.—**bedrid, bedridden,** bed′rid, bed′rid·n, *a.* [A.Sax. *bed-rida,* lit. a bedrider.] Long confined to bed by age or infirmity.—**bedstead,** bed′sted, *n.* The framework of a bed.—**bedstraw,** bed′stra̤, *n.* Straw for packing into a bed; also, a herbaceous perennial plant bearing yellow or white flowers growing in waste places in Britain.—**bedchamber,** *n.* An apartment intended for sleeping in, or in which there is a bed; a bedroom.—**bedclothes,** *n. pl.* Blankets, coverlets, etc., for beds.—**bedfellow,** *n.* One who occupies the same bed with another.—**bed linen,** *n.* Sheets, pillow covers, etc., for beds.—**bedpan,** *n.* A pan for warming a bed; also a necessary utensil for bedridden persons.—**bedplate.** The soleplate or foundation plate of an engine, etc.—**bedpost,** *n.* One of the posts forming part of the framework and often supporting the canopy of a bed.—**bedroom,** *n.* A room intended for sleeping in; a sleeping room or bedchamber.—**bedsore,** *n.* A sore liable to occur on bedridden persons on the parts of the body subjected to most pressure.—**bedtick,** *n.* A tick or stout linen or cotton bag for containing the feathers or other packing material of a bed.—**bedtime,** *n.* The time to go to bed; the usual hour of retiring to rest.

bedaub, bē·da̤b′, *v.t.* To daub over; to soil with anything thick, slimy, and dirty.

bedeck, bē·dek′, *v.t.* To deck; to adorn; to grace.

bedell, bedel, bē′dl, *n.* [L.L. *bedellus* =E. *beadle.*] A beadle in a university or connected with a law court.

bedevil, bē·dev′il, *v.t.* To throw into utter disorder and confusion; spoil or corrupt, as by evil spirits.

bedizen, bē·diz′n, *v.t.* [DIZEN.] To deck or trick out; especially, to deck in a tawdry manner or with false taste.

bedlam, bed′lam, *n.* [Corrupted from *Bethlehem,* the name of a religious house in London, afterward converted into a hospital for lunatics.] A madhouse; a place appropriated for lunatics; hence, any scene of wild uproar and madness.—**bedlamite,** bed′lam·īt, *n.* A madman.

Bedouin, bed′ö·in, *n.* [Ar. *bedâwî,* dwellers in the desert.] A nomadic Arab living in tents in Arabia, Syria, Egypt, and elsewhere.

bedraggle, bē·drag′l, *v.t.*—*bedraggled, bedraggling.* To soil by draggling; to soil by drawing along on mud.

bee, bē, *n.* [A.Sax. *beó, bi*=Icel. *by,* Sw. Dan. *bi,* D. *bij, bije,* O. and Prov. G. *beie,* Ir. and Gael. *beach,* a bee.] An insect, of which there are numerous species, the honey or hive bee being the most familiar and typical species, having been kept in hives from the earliest periods for its wax and honey.—**bee bread,** *n.* A brown substance, the pollen of flowers, collected by bees as food for their young.—**bee eater,** *n.* A bird of several species that feeds on bees.—**beehive,** *n.* A case or box intended as a habitation for bees, and in which they may store honey for the use of their owners.—**beeline,** *n.* The direct line or nearest distance between two places.—**beeswax,** *n.* The wax secreted by bees, and of which their cells are constructed.—**beeswing,** *n.* A gauzy film in port wines indicative of age, and much esteemed by connoisseurs.

beech, bēch, *n.* [A.Sax. *béce,* from *bóc,* a beech, a book=Icel. *bók,* Dan. *bög,* D. *beuk,* G. *buche,* a beech; cog. L. *fugus,* a beech; Gr. *phēgos,* the esculent oak, from root seen in Gr. *phagein,* Skr. *bhag,* to eat, from its nuts being eaten. BOOK.] A large-sized tree with a smooth bark yielding a hard timber made into tools, etc., and nuts from which an oil is expressed.—**beechen,** bēch′en, *a.* Consisting of the wood of the beech; belonging to the beech.—**beechnut,** *n.* One of the nuts or fruits of the beech.

beef, bēf, *n.* [Fr. *bœuf,* from L. *bos, bovis,* an ox; cog. Ir. and Gael. *bo,* W. *buw,* Skr. *go,* a cow.] Originally an animal of the ox kind in the full-grown state (in this sense with the plural *beeves,* but the singular is no longer used); the flesh of an ox, bull, or cow when killed.—**beefeater,** bēf′-ēt·ėr, *n.* An eater of beef; a yeoman of the royal guard (of England), a body of men who attend the sovereign at state banquets and on other occasions; an African bird that picks the larvae of insects from the hides of oxen.—**beefsteak,** *n.* A steak or slice of beef for broiling.—**beef-witted,** *a.* With no more wit than an ox; dull; stupid. (*Shak.*)

Beelzebub, bē·el′zē·bub, *n.* [Heb. *baal,* lord, and *zebub,* a fly.] A god of the Philistines; in the N.T. the prince of devils.

beer, bēr, *n.* [A.Sax. *beór*=D. and G. *bier;* origin doubtful.] A fermented alcoholic liquor made from any farinaceous grain, but generally from malted barley flavored with hops, and yielding a spirit on being distilled; a fermented drink prepared with various substances, as ginger, molasses, etc.—**beery,** bē′ri, *a.* Pertaining to beer; soiled or stained with beer; affected by beer; intoxicated.

beestings, bēst′ingz, *n. pl.* [A.Sax. *býsting, byst, beóst,* D. *biest, biestemelk* G. *biestmilch.*] The first milk given, by a cow after calving.

beet, bēt, *n.* [A.Sax. *béte,* D. *biet,* G. *beeta,* from L. *beta,* beet.] A plant of various species cultivated for its thick fleshy roots, the red varieties of which are much used as a kitchen vegetable, while the white varieties yield a large portion of sugar, and are now extensively cultivated.

beetle, bē′tl, *n.* [A.Sax. *bytl, bitel,* a mallet from *bedtan,* to beat; L.G. *betel, bötel.*] A heavy wooden mallet used to drive wedges, consolidate earth, etc.—*v.t.* To use a beetle on; to beat with a heavy wooden mallet as a substitute for mangling.

beetle, bē′tl, *n.* [A.Sax. *bítel,* from *bítan,* to bite.] A general name of many insects having four wings, the anterior pair of which are of a horny nature and form a sheath or protection to the posterior pair; a coleopterous insect.

beetle, bē′tl, *v.i.* [From A.Sax. *bítel,* sharp, hence prominent, from *bítan,* to bite.] To be prominent (as a cliff, a battlement); to hang or extend out; to overhang; to jut.—**beetle-browed,** *a.* Having prominent brows.

befall, bē·fa̤l′, *v.t.*—*befell, befallen, befalling.* [A.Sax. *befeallan*—prefix *be,* and *feallan,* to fall.] To happen to; to occur to.—*v.i.* To happen; to come to pass.

befit, bē·fit′, *v.t.*—*befitted, befitting.* [Prefix *be,* and *fit.*] To be fitting for; to suit; to be suitable or proper to.

befog, bē·fog′, *v.t.*—*befogged, befogging.* To involve in fog; hence, to confuse.

befool, bē·föl′, *v.t.* To fool; to make a fool of; to delude or lead into error.

before, bē·fōr′, *prep.* [A.Sax. *beforan*—prefix *be,* and *foran,* fore.] In front of; preceding in space; in presence of; in sight of; under the cognizance or consideration of (a court, a meeting); preceding in time; earlier than; ere; in preference to; prior to; having precedence of in rank, dignity, etc.—*Before the mast,* in or into the condition of a common sailor, the portion of a ship behind the mainmast being reserved for the officers.—*adv.* Further onward in place; in front; in the forepart; in time preceding; previously; formerly; already.—**beforehand,** bē•fōr′hand, *a.* In good pecuniary circumstances; having enough to meet one's obligations and something over.—*adv.* In anticipation; in advance.—**beforetime,**‡ bē•fōr′tīm, *adv.* Formerly; of old time. (O.T.)

befoul, bē•foul′, *v.t.* To make foul; to soil.

befriend, bē•frend′, *v.t.* To act as a friend to; to aid, benefit, or assist.

beg, beg, *v.t.—begged, begging.* [Contr. it is believed from A.Sax. *bedegian* or *bedecian,* to beg; from stem of *bid,* A.Sax. *biddan,* to beg, to ask; comp. Goth. *bidagwa,* a beggar, from same root.] To ask or supplicate in charity; to ask for earnestly (alms); to ask earnestly (a person); to beseech; to implore; to entreat or supplicate with humility; to take for granted; to assume without proof. [The phrase *I beg to* is often used as a polite formula for introducing a question or communication; as, *I beg to* inquire, *I beg to* state. It may be regarded as elliptical for *I beg leave to.*]—*v.i.* To ask alms or charity; to live by asking alms.—**beggar,** beg′ėr, *n.* One that begs; a person who lives by asking alms; one who supplicates with humility; a petitioner.—*v.t.* To reduce to beggary; to impoverish; to exhaust the resources of (to *beggar* description); to exhaust.—**beggarliness,** beg′ėr•li•nes, *n.* The character of being beggarly; meanness; extreme poverty.—**beggarly,** beg′ėr•li, *a.* Like or belonging to a beggar; poor; mean; contemptible.—**beggary,** beg′ėr•i, *n.* The state of a beggar; a state of extreme indigence.

began, bē•gan′, pret. of *begin.*

beget, bē•get′, *v.t.—begot, begat* (pret. the latter now almost obsolete), *begot, begotten* (pp.), *begetting.* (A. Sax. *begitan, bigitan*—prefix *be,* and *gitan,* to get.] To procreate, as a father or sire; to produce, as an effect; to cause to exist; to generate.—**begetter,** bē•get′ėr, *n.* One who begets or procreates; a father.

begin, bē•gin′, *v.i.—began* (pret.), *begun* (pp.), *beginning.* [A.Sax. *beginnan,* to begin—prefix *be,* and *ginnan,* to begin.] To take rise; to originate; to commence; to do the first act; to enter upon something new; to take the first step.—**begin,** bē•gin′, *v.t.* To do the first act of; to enter on; to commence.—**beginner,** bē•gin′ėr, *n.* A person who begins or originates; the agent who is the cause; one who first enters upon any art, science, or business; a young practitioner; a novice; a tyro.—**beginning,** bē•gin′ing, *n.* The first cause; origin; the first state; commencement; entrance into being; that from which a greater thing proceeds or grows.

begird, bē•gėrd′, *v.t.—begirt* (pret. etc. pp.), *begirding.* [A.Sax. *begyrdan.*] To gird or bind with a band or girdle; to surround; to encompass.

begone, bē•gon′, *interj.* Go away; hence!—the imperative *be* and pp. *gone* combined.

begonia, bē•gō′ni•a, *n.* [From M. *Begon,* a French botanist.] The generic name of tropical plants much cultivated in hothouses for the beauty of their leaves and flowers.

begot, bē•got′ (pret. and pp.) **begotten,** bē•got′n. pp. of *beget.*

begrudge, bē•gruj′, *v.t.—begrudged, begrudging.* To grudge; to envy the possession of: with two objects (to *begrudge* a person something).

beguile, bē•gīl′, *v.t.—beguiled, beguiling.* To practice guile upon; to delude; to deceive; to cheat; to trick; to dupe; to impose on by artifice or craft; to dispel or render unfelt by diverting the mind (cares); to while away (time).—**beguilement,** bē•gīl′ment, *n.* The act or state of beguiling.—**beguiler,** bē•gīl′ėr, *n.* One who beguiles.

Beguine, bā•gēn′, *n.* [Fr. *béguine;* from founder's name. Lambert Begue, 1180.] One of an order of females in Holland, Belgium, and Germany, who, without taking the monastic vows, form societies for the purposes of devotion and charity.

begum, bē′gum, *n.* In the East Indies, a princess or lady of high rank.

begun, bē•gun′, pp. of *begin.*

behalf, bē•häf′, *n.* [Prefix *be,* and *half,* in old sense of side.] Interest; profit; support; defense; always in such phrases as in or on *behalf* of, in my, his, some person's *behalf.*

behave, bē•hāv′, *v.i.—behaved, behaving.* [Prefix *be,* and *have.*] To conduct one's self; to demean one's self: used *refl.*—*v.i.* To act; to conduct one's self.—**behavior,** bē•hāv′yėr, *n.* Manner of behaving; conduct; deportment; mode of acting (of a person, a machine, etc.).

behead, bē•hed′, *v.t.* To cut off the head of; to sever the head from the body of.

beheld, bē•held′, pret. and pp. of *behold.*

behemoth, bē′hē•moth, *n.* [Heb.] An animal described in Job xl. 15-24, and which some suppose to be an elephant, others a hippopotamus, crocodile, etc.

behest, bē•hest′, *n.* [Prefix *be,* and *hest;* A.Sax. *behaes.* HEST.] A command; precept; mandate. [Poetical.]

behind, bē•hīnd′, *prep.* [A.Sax. *behindan,* behind—prefix *be,* and *hindan,* behind. HIND.] On the side opposite the front or nearest part of, or opposite to that which fronts a person; at the back of; toward the back or back part of; remaining after; later in point of time than; farther back than; in an inferior position to.—*adv.* At the back; in the rear; out of sight; not exhibited; remaining; toward the back part; backward; remaining after one's departure.—**behindhand,** bē•hīnd′hand, *adv.* or *a.* In a state in which means are not adequate to the supply of wants in arrear; in a backward state; not sufficiently advanced; not equally advanced with another; tardy.

behold, bē•hōld′, *v.t.—beheld* (pret. and pp.), *beholding.* [A.Sax. *behealdan*—prefix *be,* and *healdan,* to hold.] To fix the eyes upon; to look at with attention; to observe with care; to contemplate, view, survey, regard, or see.—*v.i.* To look; to direct the eyes to an object; to fix the attention upon an object; to attend or fix the mind; in this sense chiefly in the imperative, and used interjectionally.—**beholden,** bē•hōld′n, *a.* Under obligation; bound in gratitude; obliged; indebted.—**beholder,** bē•hōld′ėr, *n.* One who beholds; a spectator.

behoof, bē•höf′, *n.* [A.Sax. *behóf*= D. *behoef,* G. *behuf*—prefix *be,* and word equivalent to Icel. *hóf,* measure, moderation.] That which is advantageous to a person; behalf; interest; advantage; profit; benefit: always in such phrases as in or for *behoof* of, for a person's *behoof.*—**behoove,** bē•höv′, *v.t.*—behooved, behooving. [A. Sax. *behófian,* from the noun.] To be fit or meet for, with respect to necessity, duty, or convenience; to be necessary for: used impersonally (*it behooves* us, or the like.)

belabor, bē•lā′bėr, *v.t.* [Prefix *be,* and *labor;* comp. G. *bearbeiten,* to labor, and to beat soundly—prefix *be,* and *arbeit,* work.] To beat soundly; to deal blows to; to thump.

belay, bē•lā′, *v.t.* [Prefix *be,* and *lay.*] *Naut.* to make fast by winding round something.—**belaying pin,** *n. Naut.* a pin for belaying ropes to.

belch, belsh, *v.t.* [O.E. *belken, belke,* A. Sax. *bealcian,* to belch.] To throw out or eject with violence, as from the stomach or from a deep hollow place; to cast forth (a volcano *belches* flames or ashes).—*v.i.* To eject wind from the stomach; to issue out, as with eructation.—*n.* The act of one who or that which belches; eructation.

beldam, beldame, bel′dam, bel′dām, *n.* [Fr. *belle,* fine, handsome, and *dame,* lady; it was at one time, applied respectfully to elderly females.] A grandmother (*Shak.*)‡; an old woman in general, especially an ugly old woman; a hag.

beleaguer, bē•lēg′ėr, *v.t.* [Prefix *be,* and *leaguer.*] To besiege; to surround with an army so as to preclude escape; to blockade.

belemnite, bel′em•nīt, *n.* [Gr. *belemnon,* a dart or arrow, from *belos,* a dart, from the root of *ballō,* to throw.] A straight, tapering, dart-shaped fossil; the internal bone or shell of animals allied to the cuttlefishes, common in the chalk formation; the animal to which such a bone belonged.

belfry, bel′fri, *n.* [O.Fr. *belfroi, beffroit,* etc., a watch-tower, from O.G. *bervrit, bercvrit,* a tower or castle for defense, from *bergen,* to protect, and *frid,* a strong place (Mod. G. *friede,* peace). False etymology connected the word with *bell,* hence its modern English meaning.] A bell tower, generally attached to a church or other building; that part of a building in which a bell is hung.

Belgian, bel′ji•an, *a.* Pertaining to Belgium.—*n.* A native of Belgium.

Belgravian, bel•grā′vi•an, *a.* Belonging to *Belgravia*, an aristocratic portion of London; aristocratic; fashionable.—*n.* An inhabitant of Belgravia; a member of the upper classes. (*Thack.*)

Belial, bē′li•al, *n.* [Heb. *belial—beli*, not, without, and *yaal*, use, profit.] Wickedness; a wicked and unprincipled person; an evil spirit; Satan.

belie, bē•lī′, *v.t.—belied, belying.* [Prefix *be*, and *lie*, to speak falsely; like G. *belugan*, to belie. LIE.] To tell lies concerning; to calumniate by false reports; to show to be false; to be in contradiction to (his terror *belies* his words); to fail to equal or come up to; to disappoint (*belie* one's hopes).

believe, bē•lēv′, *v.t.—believed, believing.* [O.E. *bileve, beleve*, from A.Sax. *gelyfan, geléfan*, to believe, the initial particle being changed; *-lieve* is akin to *lief* and *leave, n.*] To credit upon the ground of authority, testimony, argument, or any other circumstances than personal knowledge; to expect or hope with confidence.—*v.i.* To be more or less firmly persuaded of the truth of anything.—*To believe in*, to hold as an object of faith; to have belief of.—**belief,** bē•lēf′, *n.* An assent of the mind to the truth of a declaration, proposition, or alleged fact, on the ground of evidence, distinct from personal knowledge; *theol.* faith, or a firm persuasion of the truths of religion; the thing believed; the object of belief; the body of tenets held by the professors of any faith; a creed.—**believable,** bē•lēv′a•bl, *a.* Capable of being believed; credible.—**believer,** bē•lēv′ėr, *n.* One who believes; an adherent of a religious faith; a professor of Christianity.—**believingly,** bē•lēv′ing•li, *adv.* In a believing manner.

belittle, bē•lit′l, *v.t.* To make smaller; to lower; speak disparagingly of.

bell, bel, *n.* [A.Sax. *belle*; allied to *bellan*, to bellow, E. to *bell*, as a deer; akin *bellow*, and G. *bellen*, to bark.] A metallic vessel which gives forth a clear, musical, ringing sound on being struck, generally cup shaped; anything in form of a bell; *pl.* the phrase employed on shipboard to denote the divisions of daily time, from their being marked by strokes on a bell each half hour.—*To bear the bell*, to be the first or leader, in allusion to the bell wether of a flock.—*Passing bell*, a bell which used to be rung when a person was on the point of death.—*v.i.* To flower; to put out bell-shaped blossoms.—*v.t.* To put a bell on.—**bell bird,** *n.* A South American passerine bird, and also an Australian insessorial bird; so named from their bell-like notes.—**bell buoy,** *n.* A buoy on which is fixed a bell, which is rung by the heaving of the sea.—**bellflower,** *n.* A common name of plants of the genus *Campanula*, from the shape of the flower.—**bellman,** *n.* A public crier who uses a bell.—**bell metal,** *n.* An alloy of copper and tin, used for making bells.—**bellmouthed,** *a.* Gradually expanded at the mouth in the form of a bell.—**bell-punch,** *n.* A small punch fitted to the jaws of a pincers-shaped instrument, combined with a little bell which sounds when the punch makes a perforation, used as a check on streetcar conductors, etc.—**bellwether,** *n.* A wether or sheep which leads the flock, with a bell on his neck.

bell, bel, *v.i.* [A.Sax. *bellan*, Icel. *belja*, to bellow. BELLOW.] To roar; to bellow, as a bull or a deer in rutting time.

belladonna, bel•la•don′na, *n.* [It., beautiful lady.] A plant of the nightshade family, containing atropine; *med.* a drug prepared from the plant.

belle, bel, *n.* [Fr., from L. *bellus*, beautiful.] A young lady; a lady of superior beauty and much admired.

belles-lettres, bel•let•tr, *n. pl.* [Fr. BELLE and LETTER.] Polite or elegant literature, a term including rhetoric, poetry, history, criticism, with the languages in which the literature is written.

bellicose, bel′li•kōs, *a.* [L. *bellicosus*, from *bellum*, war.] Inclined to war; warlike; pugnacious; indicating warlike feelings.

belligerent, bel•lij′ėr•ent, *a.* [L. *bellum*, war, and *gerens, gerentis*, carrying on.] Waging war; carrying on war; pertaining to war or warfare.—*n.* A nation, power, or state carrying on war; one engaged in fighting.—**belligerence,**† bel•lij′ėr•ens, *n.* The act of carrying on war; warfare.

bellow, bel′lō, *v.i.* [A.Sax. *bylgean*, to bellow, allied to *bellan*, to bell, Icel. *belja*, to bellow. BELL.] To utter a hollow, loud sound, as a bull; to make a loud noise or outcry; to roar.—*n.* A loud outcry; roar.—**bellower,** bel′lō•ėr, *n.* One who bellows.

bellows, bel′lōz, *n. sing.* and *pl.* [Really a plural form of the word *belly*, A.Sax. *bælg, belg, bælig*, a bag, a belly, bellows. BELLY.] An instrument for producing a strong current of air, and principally used for blowing fire, either in private dwellings or in forges, furnaces, mines, etc., or for supplying the pipes of an organ with wind.

belly, bel′li, *n.* [A.Sax. *bælg, belg, bælig*, bag, belly=Icel. *belgr*, D. *balg*, Dan. *bælg*, G. *balg*, the belly; akin to *bulge*; comp. Gael. and Ir. *bolg, balg*, the belly, a bag, bellows. *Bellows* is a plural form of this word.] That part of the human body which extends from the breast to the thighs, containing the bowels; the abdomen; the corresponding part of a beast; the part of anything which resembles the human belly in protuberance or cavity.—*v.t. bellied, bellying.* To fill; to swell out.—*v.i.* To swell and become protuberant like the belly.—**bellyband,** *n.* A band that goes round the belly of a horse as part of its harness.

belong, bē•long′, *v.i.* [Prefix *be*, and O.E. *long*, to belong (to extend in length to), from the adjective *long*; comp. D. and G. *belangen*, to concern, from *lang*, long.] To be the property of; to appertain; to be the concern or affair; to be appendant or connected; to be suitable; to be due; to have a settled residence; to be domiciliated; to be a native of a place; to have original residence: in all senses followed by *to*.—**belonging,** bē•long′ing, *n.* That which belongs to one: used generally in plural; qualities, endowments, property, possessions, appendages.

beloved, bē•luv′ed, *a.* Loved; greatly loved; dear to the heart.

below, bē•lō′, *prep.* [Prefix *be*, and *low*.] Under in place; beneath; not so high as; inferior to in rank, excellence, or dignity.—*adv.* In a lower place, with respect to any object; beneath; on the earth, as opposed to the heavens; in hell, or the regions of the dead; in a court of inferior jurisdiction.

belt, belt, *n.* [A.Sax. *belt*=Dan. *bælte*, Icel. *belti*, a belt, a girdle, from L. *balteus*, a belt. Comp. Ir. and Gael. *balt*, a border, a welt.] A girdle; a band, usually of leather, in which a sword or other weapon is hung; anything resembling a belt; a strip; a stripe; a band; a band passing round two wheels, and communicating motion from one to the other.—*v.t.* To encircle; to surround.—**belted,** belt′ed, *a.* Wearing a belt; marked or distinguished with a belt.—**belting,** belt′ing, *n.* Belts taken generally; the material of which the belts used in machinery are made.

Beltane, bel′tān, *n.* [A Celtic word; Gael. *bealltainn*, Ir. *bealltaine*; the first of May; origin unknown.] The name of a sort of festival formerly observed among all the Celtic tribes of Europe. It was celebrated in Scotland on the first day of May (o.s.), and in Ireland on June 21 by kindling fires on the hills and eminences.

beluga, bē•lū′ga, *n.* [Rus. *bieluga*, from *bielyi*, white.] A kind of whale found in northern seas, the white whale or white fish, from 12 to 18 feet in length, killed for its oil and skin.

belvedere, bel′ve•dēr, *n.* [It., lit. a beautiful view—*bello, bel*, beautiful, and *vedere*, to see.] In Italy an open erection on the top of a house for the purpose of obtaining a view of the country; in France, a summerhouse on an eminence.

bema, bē′ma, *n.* [Gr.] A stage or platform for an orator; part of a church raised above the rest and reserved for the higher clergy.

bemire, bē•mīr′, *v.t.—bemired, bemiring.* To drag or stall in the mire; to soil, as by passing through mud.

bemoan, bē•mōn′, *v.t.* To moan or mourn for; to lament; to bewail; to express sorrow for.

bemock, bē•mok′, *v.t.* To treat with mockery; to mock.

bemused, bē•mūzd′, *a.* Originally, overcome with musing; sunk in reverie; hence, muddled; stupefied.

ben, ben, *n.* A tree of India, called also horse-radish tree, having seeds or nuts that yield an oil (*oil of ben*) which keeps without becoming rancid for many years.

bench, bensh, *n.* [A.Sax. *benc*, a bench = Dan. *bœnk*, a parallel form with *bank*. BANK.] A long seat; a strong table on which carpenters or other mechanics prepare their work; the seat on which judges sit in court; the seat of justice; the persons who sit as judges; the court. —*Bench of bishops*, or *episcopal bench*, a collective designation of the bishops who have seats in the House of Lords.—*King's* (or *Queen's*) *Bench*, a superior English court of civil and criminal jurisdiction, now incorporated in the High Court of Justice.—*v.t.* To furnish with benches; to seat on a bench or seat of honor (*Shak.*)‡.—*v.i.*‡ To sit on a seat of justice. (*Shak.*)

bend, bend, *v.t.—bended* or *bent* (pret. & pp.), *bending*. [A.Sax. *bendan*, to bend, lit. to bend and keep bent by the string, from *bend*, a band; comp. Fr. *bander un arc*, to bend a bow, from *bande*, a string.] To curve or make crooked; to deflect from a normal condition of straightness; to direct to a certain point (one's mind, course, steps); to subdue; to cause to yield.—*v.i.* To be or become curved or crooked; to incline; to lean or turn; to be directed; to bow or be submissive.—*n.* A curve; a crook; a turn; flexure; incurvation.

beneath, bē•nēth′, *prep.* [A.Sax. *beneoth*, *beneothan*—prefix *be*, and *neothan*, below. NETHER.] Under; lower in place than something which rests above; burdened or overburdened with; lower than in rank, dignity, or excellence; below the level of.—*adv.* In a lower place; below.

benedicite, ben•e•dis′i•tē, *n.* [L., lit. bless ye, the first word of the hymn.] A canticle or hymn in the Book of Common Prayer, as old as the time of St. Chrysostom.

benedick, benedict, ben′e•dik, ben′e•dikt, *n.* A sportive name for a married man, especially one who has been long a bachelor: from one of the characters (*Benedick*) in Shakespeare's *Much Ado about Nothing*.

Benedictine, ben•e•dik′tin, *a.* Pertaining to the monks of St. Benedict. —*n.* A Blackmonk; a member of the order of monks founded at Monte Cassino about the year 530 by St. Benedict, and wearing a loose black gown with large wide sleeves, and a cowl on the head; a liqueur made by the Benedictine monks at Fécamp, in Normandy, consisting of spirits containing juices of certain aromatic herbs. CHARTREUSE.

benediction, ben•e•dik′shon, *n.* [L. *benedictio*—*bene*, well, and *dictio*, speaking.] The act of invoking a blessing; blessing, prayer, or kind wishes uttered in favor of any person or thing; a solemn or affectionate invocation of happiness.—**benedictory,** ben•e•dik′to•ri, *a.* Giving a blessing; expressing a benediction, or wishes for good.

Benedictus, ben•e•dik′tus, *n.* [L., blessed—' Blessed be the Lord God of Israel ', etc.] The song of Zacharias in *Luke* i, used in the service of the Roman Catholic Church and introduced with English words into the morning prayer of the English Church.

benefaction, ben•e•fak′shon, *n.* [L. *benefactio*, from *benefacio*, to do good to one. BENEFICE.] The act of conferring a benefit; a benefit conferred, especially a charitable donation.—**benefactor,** ben•e•fak′tėr, *n.* One who confers a benefit.—**benefactress,** ben•e•fak′tres, *n.* A female who confers a benefit.

benefice, ben′e•fis, *n.* [Fr. *bénéfice*, a benefice, from L. *beneficium*, a kindness, in late L. an estate granted for life—*bene*, well, and *facio*, to do.] An ecclesiastical living; a church endowed with a revenue for the maintenance of divine service, or the revenue itself.—**beneficed,** ben′e•fist, *a.* Possessed of a benefice or church preferment.—**beneficence,** be•nef′i•sens, *n.* [L. *beneficentia.*] The practice of doing good; active goodness, kindness, or charity. ∴ *Beneficence*, lit. well-doing, is the outcome and visible expression of *benevolence*, or well-willing. *Benevolence* may exist without *beneficence*, but *beneficence* always presupposes *benevolence*.—**beneficent, beneficient,**‡ be•nef′i•sent, ben•e•fi′shent, *a.* Doing good; performing acts of kindness and charity.—**beneficently,** be•nef′i•sent•li, *adv.* In a beneficent manner.—**beneficial,** ben•e•fi′shal, *a.* Contributing to a valuable end; conferring benefit; advantageous; useful; profitable; helpful. —**beneficially,** ben•e•fi′shal•li, *adv.* In a beneficial manner; advantageously; profitably; helpfully.—**beneficialness,** ben•e•fi′shal•nes, *n.*—**beneficiary,** ben•e•fi′shi•a•ri, *a.* Connected with the receipt of benefits, profits, or advantages.—*n.* One who holds a benefice; one who is in the receipt of benefits, profits, or advantages; one who receives something as a free gift.

benefit, ben′e•fit, *n.* [O.E. *benfite*, *bienfete*, O.Fr. *bienfet*, from L. *benefactum*, a benefit. BENEFICE.] An act of kindness; a favor conferred; whatever is for the good or advantage of a person or thing; advantage; profit; a performance at a theater or other place of public entertainment, the proceeds of which go to one of the actors, or towards some charitable object.—*v.t.* To do good to; to be of service to; to advantage.—*v.i.* To gain advantage; to make improvement.

benevolence, bē•nev′ō•lens, *n.* [L. *benevolentia*—*bene*, well, and *volens*, *volentis*, ppr. of *volo*, to will or wish.] The disposition to do good; the love of mankind, accompanied with a desire to promote their happiness; good will; kindness; charitableness; an act of kindness; a contribution or tax illegally exacted by arbitrary kings of England. ∴ BENEFICENCE.—**benevolent,** bē•nev′ō•lent, *a.* Possessing love to mankind, and a desire to promote their prosperity and happiness; inclined to charitable actions.—**benevolently,** bē•nev′ō•lent•li, *adv.* In a benevolent manner.

bengali, ben•gal•ē′, *n.* The language or dialect spoken in Bengal.—**bengal light,** *n.* A species of fireworks used as signals by night or otherwise, producing a steady and vivid blue-colored fire.

benign, bē•nīn′, *a.* [L. *benignus* for *benigenus*, kind-hearted—*benus* for *bonus*, good, and *genus*, kind, race.] Of a kind disposition; gracious; kind (*benign* sovereign); proceeding from or expressive of gentleness, kindness, or benignity; salutary (*benign* influences); *med.* mild; not severe or violent.—**benignant,** bē•nig′nant, *a.* Kind; gracious; favorable: frequently, like *benign*, used of the kindness of superiors; but *benign* is more a poetical word.—**benignantly,** bē•nig′nant•li, *adv.* In a benignant manner.—**benignity,** bē•nig′ni•ti, *n.* The state or quality of being benign or benignant; kindness of nature; graciousness; beneficence.—**benignly,** bē•nīn′li, *adv.* In a benign manner; favorably; kindly; graciously.

benison, ben′i•zn, *n.* [O.Fr. *beneison*, from L. *benedictio*, a benediction. *Benediction* is thus the same word.] A blessing uttered by a person; a benediction.

Benjamin, ben′ja•min, *n.* [Proper name. O.T.] The youngest son of family.

benjamin, ben′ja•min, *n.* [Fr. *benjoin*, benzoin.] A common form of the name of the gum *benzoin*.

benne, ben′e, *n.* [Malay.] Sesame.

bent, bent, pret. & pp. of *bend*.—*n.* Originally, a condition of being bent (as a bow); flexure; hence, *fig.* turn; inclination; disposition; natural tendency; leaning or bias of the mind.

bent, bent grass, bent, bent′gras, *n.* [A.Sax. *beonet* = G. *binse*, a rush.] A wiry grass, such as grows on common or neglected ground.

Benthamism, ben′tham•izm, *n.* The doctrine according to Jeremy Bentham, by which man's actions are regulated purely by utilitarian considerations; profit-and-loss morality.

benumb, bē•num,′ *v.t.* [NUMB.] To make numb or torpid; to deprive of sensation; to stupefy; to render inactive; to drug, deaden, or paralyze.

benzene, ben′zēn, *n.* A clear, colorless, flammable liquid obtained from coal or petroleum and used as a solvent, an ingredient of motor fuel, and a chemical raw material.

benzine, ben′zēn, *n.* A volatile,

highly flammable liquid composed chiefly of hydrocarbons of the methane series obtained from the distillation of petroleum and used as a cleaning agent and an ingredient of paints and varnishes.

benzoin, ben•zō′in, or ben′zoin, *n.* [Of Ar. origin=Fr. *benjoin*, Pg. *beijoim.*] Gum benjamin; a concrete resinous juice or balsam flowing from incisions made in the stem of a tree of Sumatra, etc., chiefly used in cosmetics and perfumes, and in incense, having a fragrant and agreeable smell.—**benzoic,** ben•zō′ik, *a.* Pertaining to or obtained from benzoin.

bequeath, bē•kwēTH′, *v.t.* [A.Sax. *becwethan*—prefix *be*, and *cwethan*, to say. QUOTH.] To give or leave by will; to devise by testament; to hand down; to transmit.—**bequest,** bē•kwest′, *n.* The act of bequeathing or leaving by will; something left by will, a legacy.

berate, bē•rāt′, *v.t.*—*berated, berating.* To rate or chide vehemently; to scold.

Berber, bėr′bėr, *n.* A person belonging to, or the language spoken by, certain tribes of North Africa (Barbary).

berberine, bėr′bėr•in, *n.* A substance obtained from the root of the barberry tree, used in dyeing yellow.

bere, bēr, *n.* [A.Sax. *bere*, barley. BARLEY.] A species of barley having six rows in the ear.

bereave, bē•rēv′, *v.t.*—*bereaved* or *bereft* (pret. & pp.), *bereaving.* [Prefix *be*, and *reave*; A.Sax. *bereafian.* REAVE.] To deprive of something that is prized; to make destitute; to rob; to strip; with *of* before the thing taken away.—**bereavement,** bē•rēv′ment, *n.* The act of bereaving, or state of being bereaved, deprivation, particularly the loss of a friend by death.

berg, bėrg, *n.* [A.Sax. and G. *berg*, a hill.] A large mass or mountain, as of ice; an iceberg.

bergamot, bėr′ga•mot, *n.* [Fr. *bergamote*, It. *bergamotta*, from *Bergamo*, in Italy.] A variety of pear; the lime or its fruit, the rind of which yields a fragrant oil; an essence or perfume from the fruit of the lime; a coarse tapestry manufactured originally at *Bergamo*, in Italy.

beri-beri, ber′i•ber′i, *n.* [Singhalese, *beri*, weakness.] A dangerous disease endemic in parts of India and Ceylon, characterized by paralysis, difficult breathing, and other symptoms. It is due to a lack of vitamin B.

berkelium, bėr•kē′li•um, *n.* [From *Berkeley*, Calif., where it was discovered.] Radioactive element first produced by helium-ion bombardment of americium 241. Symbol, Bk; at. no., 97.

berlin, bėr′lin or bėr•lin′, *n.* A fourwheeled vehicle of the chariot kind, first made at Berlin; Berlin wool; a knitted glove.—*Berlin blue*, Prussian blue.—*Berlin wool*, a kind of fine dyed wool used for tapestry, knitting, etc.—*Berlin work*, fancy work in Berlin wools or worsted.

berm, berme, bėrm, *n.* [O.Fr. *barme*, from G. *brame*, *bräme*=E. *brim*, border.] *Fort.* a space of ground of 3, 4, or 5 feet in width, between the rampart and the moat or fosse; the bank or side of a canal which is opposite to the towpath.

berry, be′ri, *n.* [A.Sax. *berie*, a berry; Icel. *ber*, Sw. and D. *bär*, G. *beere*, Goth. *basi*; root seen in Skr. *bhas*, to eat.] A succulent or pulpy fruit, containing many seeds, and usually of no great size, such as the gooseberry, the strawberry, etc.; what resembles a berry, as one of the eggs of the lobster.—*v.i.* To bear or produce berries.—**berried,** be′rid, *a.* Furnished with berries.

berserk, bėr′sėrk, or bėr•sėrk′, *n.* [Icel. *berserkr*, lit. 'bearsark', or bear-shirt.] A berserker.—*a.* Extremely agitated; crazed; frenzied. —**berserker,** bėr′sėr•kėr, *n.* A wild warrior in Scandinavian folklore.

berth, bėrth, *n.* [From the root of *bear.*] A station in which a ship lies or can lie; a small room in a ship set apart for one or more persons; a box or place for sleeping in a ship or railroad car; a post or appointment; a situation.—*v.t.* To assign a berth or anchoring ground to; to allot a berth or berths to.

beryl, ber′il, *n.* [L. *beryllus*, Gr. *bēryllos*, of Eastern origin.] A colorless, yellowish, bluish, or less brilliant green variety of emerald, the prevailing hue being green.—**beryllium,** be•ril′li•um, *n.* A hard, light metallic element (also called glucinum) always occurring in combination. Symbol, Be (also Gl); at. no., 4; at. wt., 9.0122.

beseech, bē•sēch′, *v.t. besought* (pret. & pp.), *beseeching.* [O.E. *beseke*, *biseke*—prefix *be*, and *seek.*] To entreat; to supplicate; to implore; to beg eagerly for; to solicit.—**beseecher,** bē•sēch′ėr, *n.* One who beseeches.—**beseechingly,** bē•sēch′ing•li, *adv.* In a beseeching manner.

beseem, bē•sēm′, *v.t.* [Prefix *be*, and *seem*, in old sense of become, be seemly.] To become; to be fit for or worthy of.

beset, bē•set′, *v.t.*—*beset, besetting.* [A.Sax. *besettan.* to set near, to surround—prefix *be*, and *settan*, to set.] To distribute over; to intersperse through or among; to surround; to enclose; to hem in (*beset* with enemies, a city *beset* with troops; to press on all sides, so as to perplex (temptations that *beset* us); to press hard upon.—**besetment,** bē•set′ment, *n.* The condition of being beset; the sin or failing to which one is most liable; a besetting sin.—**besetting,** bē•set′ing, *a.* Habitually attending or assailing us (a *besetting* sin).

beshrew, bē•shrö′, *v.t.* [Prefix *be*, and *shrew.* SHREWD.] To wish a curse to; to execrate: generally used impersonally in phrases intended as mild imprecations or maledictions (*beshrew* me! *beshrew* the fellow!).

beside, bē•sīd′, *prep.* [Prefix *be*, by, and *side.*] At the side of a person or thing; near to; apart from; not connected with (*beside* the present subject).—*To be beside one's self*, to be out of one's wits or senses.—**beside, besides,** bē•sīdz′, *adv.* Moreover; over and above; not included in the number, or in what has been mentioned. [*Besides* is now the commoner form.]—**besides,** *prep.* Over and above; separate or distinct from; in addition to.

besiege, bē•sēj′, *v.t.*—*besieged, besieging.* To lay siege to; beset or surround with armed forces for the purpose of compelling to surrender; to beset; to harass (*besieged* with applications).—**besieger,** bē•sēj′ėr, *n.* One who besieges.

besmear, bē•smēr′, *v.t.* To smear all over; to bedaub; to overspread with some viscous, glutinous, or soft substance that adheres; to foul; to soil.

besom, bē′zum, *n.* [A.Sax. *besema*, *besma*, a besom=D. *bezem*, G. *besem*, *besen*: root unknown.] A broom; a brush of twigs or other materials for sweeping.—*v.t.*† To sweep, as with a besom. (*Cowper.*)

besot, bē•sot′, *v.t.*—*besotted, besotting.* To make sottish, as with drink; to infatuate; to stupefy; to make dull, stupid, or senseless.—**besotted,** bē•sot′ed, *a.* Made sottish by drink; indicating or proceeding from gross stupidity; stupid; infatuated.

bespatter, bē•spat′ėr, *v.t.* To soil by spattering; *fig.* to asperse with calumny or reproach.

bespeak, bē•spēk′, *v.t.*—*bespoke* (pret.), *bespoke, bespoken* (pp.), *bespeaking.* To speak for (something wanted) beforehand; to order or engage against a future time; to betoken; to indicate by outward appearance (an action that *bespoke* a kind heart).—*n.* Among actors, a benefit.

bespread, bē•spred′, *v.t.* To spread over; to cover or form a coating over.

besprent, bē•sprent′, pp. [A participle of the obsolete verb *besprenge*, to besprinkle.] Sprinkled or scattered. [Poetical.]

besprinkle, bē•spring′kl, *v.t.* To sprinkle over; to cover by scattering or being scattered over.

Bessemer steel, bes′e•mėr•stēl, *n.* [From Sir H. *Bessemer*, the inventor of the process.] Steel made directly from molten cast iron by driving through it currents of air so as to oxidize and carry off the carbon and impurities, the proper quantity of carbon for making steel being then introduced.

best, best, *a. superl.* [A.Sax. *betest*, *betst*, *best*, serving as the superl. of *gód*, *good*=D. and G. *best*, Dan. *beste*, Icel. *bestr*, Sw. *bästa.* The root is *bat*, *bet*, seen also in *better*, Goth. *batista*, best. BETTER.] Most good; having good qualities or attainments in the highest degree; possessing the highest advantages.—*Best man*, the right-hand man or supporter of the bridegroom at a wedding.—*adv.* In the highest degree.—*n.* Highest possible state of excellence (*Shak.*); all that one can do, or show in one's self: often used in this sense with the possessive pronouns *my, thy, his, their,* etc. —*At best,* considered or looked at in the most favorable light.—*To make the best of,* to use to the best advantage; to get all that one can out of; to put up with as well as one can.

bestead, bē-sted′, pp. of an obs. verb. [Prefix *be,* and *stead,* place.] Placed, disposed, or circumstanced as to convenience, benefit, and the like; situated: now always with *ill, well, sore,* etc.

bestial, bes′ti•al, *a.* [L. *bestialis,* from *bestia,* a beast.] Belonging to a beast or to the class of beasts; animal; having the qualities of a beast; brutal; brutish.—**bestiality,** bes•ti•al′i•ti, *n.* The quality of a beast; beastliness.—**bestialize,** bes′ti•al•īz, *v.t.*—*bestialized, bestializing.* To make like a beast; to bring or reduce to the condition of a beast.—**bestially,** bes′ti•al•li, *adv.* In a bestial manner.

bestir, bē•stėr′, *v.t.* To stir; to put into brisk or vigorous action; usually *refl.*

bestow, bē•stō′, *v.t.* To stow away; to lay up in store: to deposit; to lodge; to place (often *refl.*); to give; to confer; to impart: followed by *on* or *upon* before the recipient.—**bestowal,** bē•stō′al, *n.* The act of bestowing.

bestrew, bē•strū′ or bē•strō′, *v.t.* To scatter over; to besprinkle; to strew.

bestride, bē•strīd′, *v.t.*—*bestrid, bestrode* (pret.), *bestrid, bestridden* (pp.), *bestriding.* To stride over; to stand or sit on with the legs on either side; to step over; to cross by stepping (*Shak.*).

bet, bet, *v.t.* and *i.*—*bet* or *betted, betting.* [A contraction of *abet,* to encourage, back up.] To lay or stake in wagering; to stake or pledge something upon the event of a contest; to wager.—*n.* A wager; that which is laid, staked, or pledged on any uncertain question or event; the terms on which a bet is laid.—**better, bettor,** bet′ėr, bet′or, *n.* One who lays bets or wagers.

beta, bā′ta, *n.* The second letter of the Greek alphabet.—**beta particle,** *n. Phys.* one of the high-speed electrons ejected from the nucleus during radioactive disintegration.—**beta ray,** *n. Phys.* a stream of high-speed electrons from radioactive disintegration.

betake, bē•tāk′, *v.t.*—*betook* (pret.), *betaken* (pp.), *betaking.* [Prefix *be,* and *take.*] To repair; to resort; to have recourse: with the reflexive pronouns.

betatron, bē′ta•tron, *n. Phys.* a device for the high-speed acceleration of electrons to form a beam of beta rays.

betel, bē′tl, *n.* [An Oriental word.] A species of pepper, a creeping or climbing plant, cultivated throughout the East Indies for its leaf, which is chewed with the betel nut and lime.—**betel nut,** *n.* The kernel of the nut of the betel palm.—**betel palm,** *n.* An Asiatic palm tree.

bethink, bē•thingk′, *v.t.* [Prefix *be,* and *think.*] To call or recall to mind; to bring to consideration: always with a reflexive pronoun (to *bethink* one's self *of* a thing). —*v.i.*† To have in recollection; to consider.

betide, bē•tīd′, *v.t.* *betid, betided* (pret.), *betid* (pp.), *betiding.* [Prefix *be,* and *tide,* from A.Sax. *tidan,* to happen. TIDE.] To happen to; to befall; to come to.—*v.i.* To come to pass; to happen.

betimes, bē•tīmz′, *adv.* [Prefix *be* for *by* and *time,* with adverbial genitive termination.] Seasonably; in good season or time; early; at an early hour; soon; in a short time.

betoken, bē•tō′kn, *v.t.* To be or serve as a token of; to foreshow; to indicate as future by that which is seen.

betony, bet′o•ni, *n.* [L. *betonica.*] A plant formerly much employed in medicine, and sometimes used to dye wool of a fine dark yellow.

betook, bē•tu̧k′, pret. of *betake.*

betray, bē•trā′, *v.t.* [Prefix *be,* and O.Fr. *traïr,* Fr. *trahir,* to betray, from L. *tradere,* to give up or over. TRADITION.] To deliver into the hands of an enemy by treachery in violation of trust; to violate by fraud or unfaithfulness (to *betray* a cause or trust); to play false to; to reveal or disclose (secrets, designs) to let appear or be seen inadvertently (to *betray* ignorance).—**betrayal,** bē•trā′al, *n.* Act of betraying.—**betrayer,** bē•trā′ėr, *n.* One who betrays; a traitor.

betroth, bē•trōth′, *v.t.* [Prefix *be,* and *troth.* TROTH.] To contract to any one in order to a future marriage; to affiance; to pledge one's troth to (O.T.).—**betrothal, betrothment,** bē•trōth′al, bē•trōth′ment, *n.* The act of betrothing.

better, bet′ėr, *a.* serving as the compar. of *good.* [A.Sax. *betera, betra,* with corresponding forms in the other Teutonic languages. BEST.] Having good qualities in a greater degree than another; preferable, in regard to use, fitness, or the like; improved in health.—*To be better off,* to be in improved or in superior circumstances.—*adv.* In a more excellent or superior manner; more correctly or fully; in a higher or greater degree; with greater advantage; more, in extent or amount (*better* than a mile).—*v.t.* To make better; to improve; to ameliorate; to increase the good qualities of (soil, etc.); to advance the interest or worldly position of; to surpass; to exceed; to improve on (as a previous effort).—*v.i.* To grow better; to become better; to improve.—*n.* A superior; one who has a claim to precedence; generally in the plural, and with possessive pronouns.—*The better,* a state of improvement; generally in adverbial phrase *for the better* (to alter a thing *for the better*); advantage; superiority; victory (to have or get *the better* of).—**betterment,** bet′ėr•ment, *n.* A making better; improvement; value added to property from public improvements.

between, bē•twēn′, *prep.* [A.Sax. *betweónum, betweónan*—prefix *be,* and dat. pl. of *tweon,* twain, from *twá,* two; akin *twain, twin.*] In the space, place, or interval of any kind separating; in intermediate relation to; from one to another of (letters passing *between* them); in partnership among (shared *between* them); so as to affect both of; pertaining to one or other of two (the blame lies *between* you).—**betwixt,** bē•twikst′, *prep.* [A.Sax. *betweox, betweohs*—prefix *be,* and *tweoh,* from *twá,* two. The *t* is excrescent as in *amidst,* etc.] Between; passing between; from one to another.

bevel, bev′el, *n.* [O.Fr. *bevel;* origin unknown.] The obliquity or inclination of one surface of a solid body to another surface of the same body; an instrument for drawing or measuring angles.—*a.* Having the form of a bevel; slant; not upright, (*Shak.*).—*v.t.*—*beveled, beveling.* To cut to a bevel.—*v.i.* To slant or incline on to a bevel angle.—**bevel gear,** *n.*—A species of wheel-work in which the axis or shaft of the driving wheel forms an angle with the axis or shaft of the wheel driven.—**beveled,** bev′eld, *a.* Having a bevel; formed with a bevel angle.—**beveling,** bev′el•ing, *a.* Inclining from a right line; slanting towards a bevel angle.

beverage, bev′ėr•āj, *n.* [O.Fr. *beuvrage,* from *boivre, bevre,* L. *bibere,* to drink.] Drink; liquor for drinking.

bevy, bev′i, *n.* [Perhaps of similar origin with *beverage,* and originally a drinking company, or animals collected at a watering-place.] A flock of birds; a company of females.

bewail, bē•wāl′, *v.t.* and *i.* To wail or weep aloud for; to lament.

beware, bē•wār′, *v.t.* and *i.* [*Be,* imperative of verb to *be,* and *ware*= wary. WARE, WARY.] To be wary or cautious; to be suspicious of danger; to take care; now used only in imperative and infinitive, with *of* before the noun denoting what is to be avoided.

bewilder, bē•wil′dėr, *v.t.* [Prefix *be,* and old *wilder,* to lead astray. WILD.] To lead into perplexity or confusion; to perplex; to puzzle; to confuse.—**bewilderingly,** bē•wil′dėr•ing•li, *adv.* So as to bewilder.—**bewilderment,** bē•wil′dėr•ment, *n.* State of being bewildered.

bewitch, bē•wich′, *v.t.* To subject to the influence of witchcraft; to throw a charm or spell over; to please to such a degree as to take away the power of resistance.—**bewitcher,** bē•wich′ėr, *n.* One that bewitches or fascinates. — **bewitchery,** bē•wich′ėr•i, *n.* Witchery; fascination; charm.—**bewitching,** bē•wich′ing. *a.* Having power to bewitch or to control by the arts of pleasing. —**bewitchingly,** bē•wich′ing•li, *adv.* **bewitchment,** bē•wich′ment, *n.* Fascination; the power of charming.

bey, bā, *n.* [Turk. *beg*, pron. as *bey*.] A governor of a town or district in the Turkish dominions; also, a prince; a beg.

beyond, bē•yond′, *prep.* [A.Sax. *begeond, begeondam*—prefix *be*, and *geond*, yond, yonder.—YON.] On the further side of; out of reach of; further than the scope or extent of; above; in a degree exceeding or surpassing.

bezant, bez′ant, *n.* [From *Byzantium*.] A gold coin of Byzantium; a coin current in England from the tenth century till the time of Edward III.

bezel, bez′el, *n.* [A form of *basil*, Fr. *beseau*, a slope. BASIL.] The part of a finger ring which surrounds and holds fast the stone; the groove in which the glass of a watch is set.

bezique, be•zēk′, *n.* [Fr.] A simple game at cards, played by two, three, or four persons.

bezoar, bē′zōr, *n.* [O.Fr. *bezoar*, from Per. *pâdzahr—pâd*, dispelling, and *zâhr*, poison.] A name for certain concretions found in the intestines of some animals (especially ruminants), formerly (and still in some places) supposed to be an antidote to poison.

bhang, bang, *n.* An Indian variety of the common hemp.

biangular, bī•ang′gū•lėr, *a.* Having two angles or corners.

biannual, bī•an′nū•al, *a.* [Prefix *bi*, twice, and *annual*.] Occurring twice a year.

bias, bī′as, *n.* [Fr. *biais*, from L.L. *bifax, bifacis*, two-faced—L. *bi*, double, and *facies*, the face.] A weight on the side of a bowl which turns it from a straight line; that which causes the mind to incline towards a particular object or course; inclination; bent; prepossession.—*v.t.*—*biassed* or *biased, biassing* or *biasing*. To give a bias or particular direction to; to prejudice; to prepossess.—*adv.* In a slanting manner; obliquely.

biaxial, bī•aks′i•al, *a.* Having two axes, as in biaxial polarization.

bib, bib, *n.* A fish of the cod family, about a foot in length.

bib,‡ bib, *v.t.* and *i.*—*bibbed, bibbing*. [L. *bibo, bibere*, to drink.] To sip; to tipple; to drink frequently.—*n.* A small piece of linen or other cloth worn by children over the breast, so called because protective of the child's dress when drinking.—**bibber,** bib′ėr, *n.* A tippler; a man given to drinking.—**bibulous,** bib′ū•lus, *a.* [L. *bibulus*.] Having the quality of imbibing fluids; spongy; addicted to drinking intoxicants; pertaining to the drinking of intoxicants (*bibulous* propensities).

Bible, bī′bl, *n.* [Fr. *bible*, Gr. *biblia*, the books, pl. of *biblion*, dim. from *biblos*, papyrus, paper, a book.] Originally a book, but specifically restricted now to THE BOOK, by way of eminence; the sacred Scriptures, consisting of two parts, the Old Testament, originally written in Hebrew, the New Testament in Greek.—**Biblical,** bib′lik•al, *a.* Pertaining to the Bible or to the sacred writings.—**Biblically,** bib′-lik•al•li, *adv.* In a Biblical manner; according to the Bible.—**Biblicist,** bib′li•sist, *n.* One skilled in the knowledge and interpretation of the Bible.—**Biblist,** bī′blist, *n.* One conversant with the Bible; one who makes the Bible the sole rule of faith.

bibliography, bib•li•og′ra•fi, *n.* [Gr. *biblion*, a book, and *grapho*, to write.] A history or description of books or manuscripts, with notices of the different editions, the times when they were printed, etc.—**bibliographer,** bib•li•og′ra•fėr, *n.* One versed in bibliography; one who composes or compiles the history of books.—**bibliographic, bibliographical,** bib′li•o•graf″ik, bib′-li•ō•graf″ik•al, *a.* Pertaining to bibliography.

bibliolatry, bib•li•ol′a•tri, *n.* [Gr. *biblion*, a book, and *latreia*, worship.] Worship or homage paid to books; excessive reverence for any book, especially the Scriptures.

bibliology, bib•li•ol′o•ji, *n.* [Gr. *biblion*, a book, and *logos*, discourse.] Biblical literature, doctrine, or theology; a treatise on books; bibliography.

bibliomancy, bib′li•ō•man•si, *n.* [Gr. *biblion*, a book, and *manteia*, divination.] Divination performed by means of a book; divination by means of the Bible, consisting in selecting passages of Scripture at hazard and drawing from them indications concerning future things.

bibliomania, bib′li•ō•mā″ni•a, *n.* [Gr. *biblion*, a book, and *mania*, madness.] Book-madness; a rage for possessing rare and curious books.—**bibliomaniac,** bib′li•ō•mā″ni•ak, *n.* One affected with bibliomania.—**bibliomaniacal,** bib′li•ō•ma•nī″ak•al, *a.* Pertaining to bibliomania.

bibliopegy, bib•li•op′e•ji, *n.* [Gr. *biblion*, a book, and *pegnymi*, to make firm.] The art of bookbinding.

bibliophile, bib′li•ō•fīl, *n.* [Gr. *biblion*, book, and *phileō*, to love.] A lover of books.—**bibliophilism,** bib•li•of′il•izm, *n.* Love of bibliography or of books.—**bibliophilist,** bib•li•of′il•ist, *n.* A bibliophile.

bibliopole, bib′li•ō•pōl, *n.* [Gr. *biblion*, a book, and *pōleō*, to sell.] A bookseller.—**bibliopolist,** bib•li•op′-ol•ist, *n.* A bibliopole.

bibliotheca, bib′li•ō•thē″ka, *n.* [L., from Gr. *biblion*, a book, and *thēkē*, a repository.] A library.

bibulous. See BIB.

bicameral, bī•kam′ėr•al, *a.* [L. prefix *bi*, twice, and *camera*, a chamber]. Pertaining to or consisting of two legislative or other chambers.

bicarbonate, bī•kär′bon•āt, *n.* A carbonate containing two equivalents of carbonic acid to one of a base.

bice, bīs, *n.* [Fr. *bis*; etymology unknown.] A name given to two colors used in painting, one •blue, the other green, and both native carbonates of copper.

bicentenary, bī•sen′te•na•ri, *n.* [L. *bi*, twice, and E. *centenary*.] The period of two hundred years; the commemoration of an event that happened two hundred years before.—*a.* Relating to a bicentenary; occurring once in two hundred years.

biceps, bī′•seps, *n.* [L., from *bi*, double, and *caput*, the head.] A muscle having two heads or origins; the name of two muscles, one of the arm the other of the thigh.—**bicipital,** bī•sip′it•al, *a.* Having two heads; two-headed; pertaining to a biceps.

bicker, bik′ėr, *v.i.* [W. *bicra*, to fight, *bicre*, conflict.] To skirmish; to quarrel; to contend in words; to scold; to run rapidly; to move quickly with some noise, as a stream; to quiver; to be tremulous, like flame or water; to make a confused noise; to clatter.—*n.* A fight, especially a confused fight.

biconcave, bī•kon′kāv, *a.* Hollow or concave on both sides.

bicorn, bī′korn, *a.* [L. *bi*, double, and *cornu*, a horn.] Having two horns or antlers; crescent-shaped.

bicuspid, bī•kus′pid, *a.* [L. prefix *bi* two, and *cuspis*, a prong.] With two, cusps or points; two-fanged: often applied to teeth, as to the two first pairs of grinders in each jaw.

bicycle, bī′si•kl, *n.* [L. prefix *bi*, two, and Gr. *kyklos*, a circle or wheel.] A two-wheeled velocipede; a vehicle consisting of two wheels, one behind the other, connected by a light metal frame carrying a seat, the vehicle being propelled by the feet of the rider pressing on treadles which act directly or through gearing.—**bicyclist,** bī′sik•list, *n.* One who rides on a bicycle.

bid, bid, *v.t.*—*bid* or *bade* (pret.), *bid, bidden* (pp.), *bidding*. [Partly from A.Sax. *biddan*, to pray, ask, declare, command=Icel. *bidja*, G. *bitten*, Goth. *bidjan*, to ask, to pray; partly from A. Sax. *beódan*, to offer, to bid=Goth. *biudan*, G. *bieten*, to offer, command.] To ask, request, or invite (a person); to pray; to wish; to say to by way of greeting or benediction (to *bid* good-day, farewell); to command; to order or direct; to enjoin: followed by an objective and infinitive without *to* (*bid* him come); to offer; to propose, as a price at an auction.—*n.* An offer of a price, especially at an auction.—**bidder,** bid′ėr, *n.* One who bids or offers a price.

bide, bīd, *v.i.* [A. Sax. *bidan*=Icel. *bida*, D. *beiden*, Goth. *beidan*. Hence *abide*.] To be or remain in a place or state; to dwell; to inhabit.—*v.t.* To endure; to suffer; to bear; to wait for (chiefly in phrase *to bide one's time*).

bidentate, bī•den′tāt, *a.* [L. *bidens*—prefix *bi*, and *dens*, a tooth.] Having two teeth, or processes like teeth; two-toothed.

biennial, bī•en′ni•al, *a.* [L. *biennium*, a space of two years—prefix *bi*, twice, *annus*, a year.] Happening or taking place once in two years; *bot.* continuing for two years and then perishing; taking two years to produce its flowers and fruit.—*n.* A biennial plant.—**biennially,** bī•-

en′ni•al•li, *adv*. Once in two years; at the return of two years.

bier, bēr, *n*. [O.E. *beere*, *bere*, A. Sax. *baer*, a bier; from the root of *bear*, to carry.] A carriage or frame of wood for conveying a corpse to the grave.

biestings, bēst′ingz. See BEESTINGS.

bifacial, bī•fā′shi•al, *a*. [L. prefix *bi*, twice, *facies*, a face.] Having the opposite surfaces alike.

bifid, bī′fid, *a*. [L. *bifidus*—prefix *bi*, twice, *findo*, *fidi*, to split.] Cleft or divided into two parts; forked; *bot*. divided half-way down into two parts; opening with a cleft.

bifilar, bī•fī′lėr, *a*. [L. prefix *bi*, twice, and *filum*, a thread.] Two-threaded; fitted or furnished with two threads (a *bifilar* micrometer).

bifocal, bī•fō′kal, *a*. Having two focuses.—**bifocal lens,** a lens with two parts: one for near vision and one for distant vision.—*n*. pl. Eyeglasses with bifocal lenses.

bifoliate, bī•fō′li•āt, *a*. [L. *bi*, twice, two, and *folium*, a leaf.] In *bot*. having two leaves.

biform, biformed, bī′form, bī′formd, *a*. [L. *biformis*, double-formed —*bi*, twice, and *forma*, form.] Having two forms, bodies, or shapes; double-bodied.

bifurcate, bī•fėr′kāt, *a*. [L. *bi*, twice, and *furca*, a fork.] Forked; divided into two branches.—**bifurcation,** bī•fėr•kā′shon, *n*. A forking or division into two branches.

big, big, *a*. [Etymology doubtful; perhaps connected with Sc. or North. E. to *big*, Icel. *byggja*, Dan. *bygge*, to build.] Having size, whether large or small; more especially, great; large; bulky; great with young; pregnant; hence, *fig*. full of something important; teeming; distended; full, as with grief or passion; tumid; haughty in air or mien; pompous. —**bighorn,** *n*. The Rocky Mountain sheep.—**bigwig,** *n*. A person of great importance.

bigamy, big′a•mi, *n*. [Prefix *bi*, twice, and Gr. *gamos*, marriage.] The crime, fact, or state of having two wives or husbands at once.—**bigamist,** big′a•mist, *n*. One who has committed bigamy.—**bigamous,** big′a•mus, *a*. Of or pertaining to bigamy; guilty of bigamy.

biggin, big′in, *n*. [Fr. *beguin*, the cap of the *Beguines*.] A child's cap; a nightcap; a coif. (*Shak.*)

bight, bīt, *n*. [A.Sax. *byht*, from *bigan*, *bugan*, to *bow* or bend=L.G. Dan. Icel. *bugt*, a bending, a bay. BOW.] A bend in a coastline; a bay; the double of a rope when folded; a bend anywhere except at the ends; a loop.

bignonia, big•nō′ni•a, *n*. [After M. *Bignon*, librarian to Louis XIV.] The generic name of a number of plants, inhabitants of hot climates, usually climbing shrubs with beautiful trumpet-shaped flowers, hence their name of *trumpet flower*.

bigot, big′ot, *n*. [Fr. *bigot*, a bigot; It. *bigotto*, *bigozzo*. Etymology uncertain; Some suppose it a corruption of *Visigoth*, as intolerant Arians, persecuting in Spain, others refer it to the oath *bi Gott* (by God) common among the Norse settlers in Normandy.] A person obstinately and unreasonably wedded to a particular religious creed, opinion, or practice; a person blindly attached to any opinion, system, or party.—**bigoted,** big′ot•ed, *a*. Having the character of a bigot; belonging to a bigot; showing blind attachment to opinions.—**bigotedly,** big′ot•ed•li, *adv*. In a bigoted manner.—**bigotry,** big′ot•ri, *n*. The practice or tenets of a bigot; obstinate or blind attachment to a particular creed or to certain tenets; unreasoning zeal; intolerance.

bijou, bē′zhö, *n*. [Fr.] A jewel; something small and pretty.—**bijouterie,** bē•zhö′trē, *n*. Jewelry; trinkets.

bijugous, bijugate, bī′jū•gus, bī′jū•gāt, *a*. [L. *bijugus*—*bi*, two, *jugum*, a yoke.] Having two pairs of leaflets.

bike, bīk, *n*. A bicycle. [Colloq.]

bilabiate, bī•lā′bi•āt, *a*. [L. *bi*, twice, and *labium*, a lip.] *Bot*. applied to a corolla having two lips, the one placed over the other.

bilander, bī′lan•dėr, *n*. [D. *bijlander* —*bij*, by, near, and *land*, land.] A small merchant vessel with two masts, used chiefly in the Dutch canals; a kind of hoy.

bilateral, bī•lat′ėr•al, *a*. [L. *bi*, twice, and *latus*, *lateris*, a side.] Having two sides; of or pertaining to two sides; two sided.

bilberry, bil′be•ri, *n*. [Dan. *böllebœr*, bilberry—*bölle*, of doubtful meaning, and *bœr*, a berry.] Any of several species of blueberry of the genus *Vaccinium*; the European whortleberry (*Vaccinium myrtillus*).

bilbo,‡ bil′bō, *n*. [From *Bilbao* in Spain, famous for their manufacture.] A rapier; a sword.—**bilboes,** bil′bōz, *n. pl*. A contrivance for confining the feet of prisoners—a long bar or bolt of iron with shackles sliding on it and a lock at the end.

bile, bīl, *n*. [Fr. *bile*, L. *bilis*, bile, also anger, spleen.] A yellow bitter liquid, separated from the blood by the action of the liver, and discharged into the gallbladder, its most obvious use being to assist in the process of digestion; ill-nature; bitterness of feeling; spleen.—**biliary,** bil′i•a•ri, *n*. Pertaining to or containing bile.—**bilious,** bil′i•us, *a*. Consisting of, or affected by bile; having an excess of bile; having the health deranged from excess of bile in the system.—**biliousness,** bil′i•us•nes, *n*. The state or quality of being bilious, or of suffering from an excessive secretion of bile.

bilge, bilj, *n*. [A different orthography of *bulge*.] The protuberant part of a cask; the breadth of a ship's bottom, or that part of her floor which approaches to a horizontal direction.—*v.i. Naut*. to spring a leak in the bilge.—**bilge water,** *n*. A water which enters a ship and lies upon her bilge or bottom.

bilingual, bī•ling′gwal, *a*. [L. *bilinguis*—*bi*, double, and *lingua*, a tongue, a language.] Containing, or expressed in, two different languages (a *bilingual* dictionary).

bilk, bilk, *v.t*. [Probably a form of *balk*.] To deceive or defraud by nonfulfillment of engagement; to leave in the lurch; to decamp without paying (a person).

bill, bil, *n*. [A.Sax. *bile*, a beak.] The beak of a fowl.—*v.t*. To join bills or beaks, as doves; to caress fondly.

bill, bil, *n*. [A.Sax. *bil*, *bill*, a bill, a sword, etc.; D. and G. *bille*, a pick; Dan. *biil*, D. *bijl*, G. *beil*, a hatchet; root in Skr. *bhil*, to split.] A cutting instrument hook-shaped toward the point, or with a concave cutting edge, used in pruning, etc.; a billhook; an ancient military weapon, consisting of a broad hook-shaped blade, having a short pike at the back and another at the summit, attached to a long handle.—**billhook,** *n*. A small variety of hatchet with a hook at the end of the cutting edge.

bill, bil, *n*. [O.Fr. *bille*, a label or note, from L.L. *billa*, *bulla*, a seal, a letter, a roll, from L. *bulla*, a boss, a stud, whence *bull*, a papal edict.] A sheet or piece of paper containing a statement of certain particulars; a sheet containing a public notice or advertisement; a note of charges for goods supplied, work done, or the like, with the amount due on each item; a declaration of certain facts in legal proceedings; a written promise to pay or document binding one to pay a specified sum at a certain date; a bill of exchange (see below); a draft of a law presented to a legislature to be passed into an act: also applied to various measures that are really acts.—*Bill of divorce*, a writing given by a husband to his wife among the Jews by which their marriage was dissolved.—*Bill of entry*, a written account of goods entered at the custom house.—*Bill of exchange*, an order drawn by one person (the drawer) on another (the drawee) who is either in the same or in some distant country, requesting or directing him to pay money at a specified time to some person assigned (the payee), who may either be the drawer himself or some other person. The person on whom the bill is drawn becomes the ‘ acceptor ’ by writing his name on it as such.—*Bill of fare*, in a hotel, restaurant, etc., a list of refreshments ready to be supplied.—*Bill of health*, a certificate signed by consuls or other authorities as to the health of a ship's company at the time of her clearing any port, a *clean bill* being given when no disorder is supposed to exist, and a *foul bill* when it is known to exist.—*Bill of lading*, a memorandum of goods shipped on board of a vessel, signed by way of receipt by the master of the vessel.—*Bill of mortality*, an official return of the number of deaths occurring in a place within a certain time.—*Bill of sale*, a formal instrument for the transfer of personal property (as furniture, the stock in a shop), often given in security for a debt, empowering the receiver to sell the goods if the money is not repaid at the appointed time.—**billboard,** *n.* A board, fence, etc., on which advertisements are posted.

billet, bil′et, *n.* [A dim of *bill*=Fr. *billet.* BILL.] A small paper or note in writing; a short letter; a ticket directing soldiers at what house to lodge.—**billet,** bil′et, *v.t.* To quarter or place in lodgings, as soldiers in private houses.—*v.i.* To be quartered; to lodge: specifically applied to soldiers.

billet, bil′et, *n.* [Fr. *billot*, a log, from *bille*, the stock of a tree, from the Celtic.] A small stick or round piece of wood used for various purposes; *arch.* an imitation of a wooden billet placed in a hollow molding at intervals apart, usually equal to its own length.

billet-doux, bil•le•dö′, *n.* pl. **billets-doux,** bil•le•döz′. [Fr., lit. sweet billet or note.] A love note or short love letter.

billiards, bil′yėrdz, *n.* [Fr. *billard*, the game of billiards, a billiard cue, from *bille*, a piece of wood.] A game played on a long rectangular, cloth-covered table, without pockets, with three ivory balls. Scoring is made by the use of a cue to cause one ball to strike the other two. Pocket billiards are played on the same kind of table but having six pockets and fifteen numbered balls and one cue ball, the object being to drive the numbered balls into pockets with the cue ball.

billingsgate, bil′ingz•gāt, *n.* [From a fish-market of this name in London, celebrated for the use of foul language.] Profane or foul language; ribaldry.

billion, bil′yon, *n.* [Fr., contr. from L. *bis*, twice, and *million.*] A thousand millions, in the U.S. and France; a million millions in Great Britain and Germany.

billon, bil′on, *n.* [Fr.] An alloy of copper and silver, used in some countries for coins of low value.

billow, bil′ō, *n.* [Icel. *bylgja*, Dan. *bölge*, Sw. *bölja*, a swell, a billow, from root of *bulge*, *belly*, *bellows.*] A great wave or surge of the sea.—*v.i.* To swell; to rise and roll in large waves or surges.—**billowy,** bil′lō•i, *a.* Swelling into large waves; full of surges; belonging to billows; wavy.

billy goat, bil′i•gōt, *n.* A he-goat, after the man's name.

bilobate, bī•lō′bāt, *a.* [Prefix *bi*, and *lobate.*] Divided into two lobes (a *bilobate* leaf).

bilocular, bī•lok′ū•lėr, *a.* [L. *bi*, twice, and *loculus*, a cell, from *locus*, a place.] Divided into two cells or small compartments.

biltong, bil′tong, *n.* An African name for lean meat cut in strips and dried.

bimensal, bī•men′sal, *a.* [L. *bi*, two, twice, and *mensis*, a month.] Occurring once in two months.

bimetallic, bī•me•tal′ik, *a.* [Prefix *bi*, twice, and *metallic.*] Of or pertaining to two metals; pertaining to the use of a double metallic standard in currency.—**bimetallism,** bī•met′-al•izm, *n.* That system of currency which recognizes coins of two metals, as silver and gold, as legal tender to any amount.—**bimetallist,** met′-al•ist, *n.* One who favors bimetallism.

bimonthly, bī•munth′li, *a.* [Prefix *bi*, twice, and *monthly.*] Occurring every two months.

bin, bin, *n.* [A.Sax. *bin*, *binn*, a bin, a hutch; D. *ben*, G. *benne*, *binne*, a basket.] A box or enclosed place used as a repository of any commodity; one of the subdivisions of a cellar for wine bottles.

binary, bī′na•ri, *a.* [L. *binus*, double. two and two.] Consisting or composed of two or of two parts; double; twofold; dual.—*Binary compound*, *chem.* a compound of two elements or radicals.—*Binary system*, *math.* a system of numerical notation with a base of 2, used in digital computers. —*Binary star*, a double star, one of two stars associated together so as to form a system, the one revolving round the other, or both round their common center of gravity.

binaural broadcasting. Radio broadcasting via both FM and AM microphones so arranged that pickup on FM and AM receivers provides a stereophonic effect.

bind, bīnd, *v.t.*—*bound* (pret. & pp.), *binding*. [A. Sax. *bindan*, pret. *band*, pp. *bunden*=Icel. Sw. *binda*, Dan. *binde*, D. and G. *binden*, same root as Skr. *bandh*, to bind.] To tie or confine with a cord, or anything that is flexible; to fasten or encircle, as with a band or ligature; to put a ligature or bandage on; to put in bonds or fetters; to hold in, confine, or restrain; to engage by a promise, agreement, vow, law, duty, or any other moral or legal tie; to form a border on, or strengthen by a border; to sew together and cover (a book). —*v.i.* To exercise an obligatory influence; to be obligatory; to tie up; to tie sheaves up; to grow hard or stiff (of soil).—**binder,** bīnd′ėr, *n.* A person who binds; one whose occupation is to bind books; one who binds sheaves; anything that binds, as a fillet, cord, rope, or band; a bandage.—**bindery,** bīnd′ėr•i *n.* A place where books are bound.—**binding,** bīnd′ing, *a.* Serving to bind; having power to bind or oblige; obligatory; making fast; astringent.—*n.* The act of one who binds; anything which binds; the cover of a book, with the sewing and accompanying work; something that secures the edges of cloth.—**bindingly,** bīnd′-ing•li, *adv.* In a binding manner; so as to bind.—**bindingness,** bīnd′-ing•nes. *n.* The character of being binding or obligatory.—**bindweed,** *n.* The common name for twining or trailing plants of the convolvulus family, common in cornfields and waste places and overrunning hedges.

bine, bīn, *n.* [From the verb to *bind.*] The slender stem of a climbing plant: sometimes written *Bind.*

bing, bing, *n.* [Dan. *binge*, Icel. *bingr*, a heap.] A large heap, as of corn, coal, ore, etc.

binnacle, bin′a•kl, *n.* [Formerly, *bittacle*, from Fr. *habitacle*, a little house for pilot and steersman, from L. *habitaculum*, an abode, from *habito*, to dwell. HABITATION.] A box on the deck of a vessel, near the helm, containing the compass and lights by which it can be read at night.

binocular, bī•nok′ū•lėr, *a.* [L. *binus* double, and *oculus*, an eye.] Involving two eyes.—*n.* pl. Field glasses.

binomial, bī•nō′mi•al, *n.* [L. *bi*, two, twice, and *nomen*, a name.] *Alg.* an expression or quantity consisting of two terms connected by the sign *plus* (+) or *minus* (—).—*a.* Pertaining to binomials.—*Binomial theorem*, a celebrated theorem by Sir Isaac Newton, for raising a binomial to any power, or for extracting any root of it.

bioastronautics, bī•ō•as•trō•na̤′tiks, *n.* [Gr. *bios*, life, and E. *astronautics.*] The study of the effects of air flight and space travel on plant and animal life; space medicine.

biochemistry, bī•ō•kem′ist•ri, *n.* [Gr. *bios*, life, and *chemistry.*] The science that studies the chemical processes of plant and animal life.

biodynamics, bī′ō•dī•nam″iks, *n.* [Gr. *bios*, life, and E. *dynamics* (which see).] The doctrine of vital forces or energy.

biogenesis, bī•ō•jen′e•sis, *n.* [Gr. *bios*, life, and *genesis*, generation.] The origin of what has life (vegetable or animal) from living matter; the doctrine which holds that living organisms can spring only from living parents: as opposed to *abiogenesis;* the history of the life development of organized existences. —**biogenetic,** bī•ō•je•net′ik, *a.* Of or pertaining to biogenesis.

biography, bī•og′ra•fi, *n.* [Gr. *bios*, life, and *graphō*, to write.] The history of the life and character of a particular person; a life; a memoir. —**biographer,** bī•og′ra•fėr, *n.* One who writes a biography.—**biographic, biographical,** bī•ō•graf′ik, bī•-ō•graf′ik•al, *a.*—**biographically,** bī•-ō•graf′ik•al•li, *adv.*

biology, bī•ol′o•ji, *n.* [Gr. *bios*, life, and *logos*, a discourse.] The science of life, or which treats generally of the life of animals and plants, including their morphology, physiology, origin, development, and distribution.—**biologic, biological,** bī•ō•-loj′ik, bī•ō•loj′ik•al, *a.* Pertaining to biology.—**biological warfare.** Warfare using bacteria or viruses or their products against man, domestic animals, or food plants.—**biologist,** bī•ol′o•jist, *n.* One skilled in or who studies biology.

bioluminescence, bī•ō•lu•me•nes′-ens, *n.* [Gr. *bios*, life, and *luminescence.*] The emission of light from living organisms such as fireflies.

biopsy, bī′op•si, *n.* [Gr. *bios*, life, and *opsis*, appearance.] The examination of specimens of fluid, cells, or tissue taken from a living body.

biparous, bip′a•rus, *a.* [L. *bi*, twice, and *pario*, to bear.] Bringing forth two at a birth. *Bot.* bearing two axes.

bipartible, bipartile, bī·pär′ti·bl, bī·pär′til, *a.* [L. prefix *bi*, twice, and *partio*, to divide.] Capable of being divided into two parts.—**bipartite,** bī·pär′tīt, *a.* In two parts; having two correspondent parts; double; *bot.* divided into two parts nearly to the base, as leaves.—**bipartition,** bī·pär·ti′shon, *n.* The act of making bipartite.

bipartisan, bī·pär′ti·zan, *n.* [Prefix *bi* and *partisan.*] Composed or representative of two parties.

biped, bī′ped, *n.* [L. *bipes—bi*, twice, and *pes*, *pedis*, a foot.] An animal having two feet, as man.—**bipedal,** bī′ped·al, *a.* [L. *bipedalis.*] Having two feet.

bipinnate, bī·pin′nāt, *a.* [L. *bi*, double, and *pinnatus*, winged.] *Bot.* doubly pinnate; having pinnae which are pinnate.

biplane, bī′plān, *n.* [Prefix *bi*, and *plane.*] A flying machine with an upper and an under plane or carrying surface.

bipropellant, bī·prō·pel′ant, *n.* [Prefix *bi* and *propellant.*] Rocket fuel consisting of two unmixed chemicals that combine in a combustion chamber.

biquadratic, bī·kwod·rat′ik, *n.* [L. *bi*, double, twice, and *quadratus*, squared.] *Math.* the fourth power, arising from the multiplication of a square by itself; the square of the square.—*a.* Pertaining to this power.

birch, bėrch, *n.* [A. Sax. *byrc*, *beorc*= Icel. and Sw. *björk*, Dan. and Sc. *birk* (comp. Sc. *kirk*, E. *church*), D. *berk*, G. *birke*, Rus. *bereza*, Lith. *berzas*, Skr. *bhurja*—a birch.] A graceful tree having small leaves, slender, often drooping branches, and a smooth whitish bark; a kind of wine is made from its spring sap, its bark is much used in tanning, and its timber is employed in turnery; an instrument of punishment used by schoolmasters, generally made of the tough, slender twigs of the common birch.—

birchen, bėrch′en, *a.* Made of birch; consisting of birch.

bird, bėrd, *n.* [A. Sax. *brid*, a young bird, from the root of *brood*, *breed. Fowl* was originally the word for bird in general.] A feathered, warm-blooded animal, with two legs and two wings, producing young from eggs; one of the feathered class (Aves) of the vertebrate animals.—*v.i.* To catch birds.—**birdcall,** *n.* An instrument for imitating the cry of birds in order to attract or decoy them.—**bird cherry,** *n.* A species of cherry having the flowers in racemes and fruit only fit for birds.—**birdlime,** *n.* A viscous substance prepared from holly bark, etc., used for entangling birds, twigs being for this purpose smeared with it at places where birds resort.—*v.t.* To besmear with birdlime.—**bird of paradise,** *n.* One of a family of conirostral birds found in the islands of the Indian Archipelago, the male birds being celebrated for their gorgeous plumage.—**bird's-eye,** *n.* The popular name of a species of primrose or wild germander and several other plants; a kind of cut tobacco, the minute slices of the stems of which are marked somewhat like a bird's eye.—*Bird's-eye maple*, the wood of the sugar maple, which is marked by little knotty spots resembling birds' eyes, and is much used in cabinetmaking.—*Bird's-eye view*, a view or landscape shown as it might appear to a flying bird; hence, a rapid and comprehensive view of a subject.—**bird's-foot,** *n.* A common name for several plants, having legumes somewhat resembling the claws of a bird.—**bird's-nest,** *n.* A name of several plants, especially a British orchid having a root resembling a nest.

bireme, bī′rēm, *n.* [L. *biremis—bi*, two, and *remus*, an oar.] An ancient Greek or Roman vessel with two banks or tiers of oars.

biretta, beretta, bē·ret′ta, bā·ret′ta, *n.* [It. *berretta*, L.L. *birettum*, *birretum*, dim. of *birrus*, a hood.] A square cap worn by ecclesiastics; priests have it black, bishops purple, cardinals red: written also *Birretta.*

birr, bir, *n.* [Imitative of the sound.] A whirring noise.—*v.i.* To make a whirring noise.

birth, bėrth, *n.* [A. Sax. *beorth*, *byrth*, from *beran*, to bear; Goth. *gabaurths*, G. *geburt.*] The act or process of being born; the occasion of an individual's coming into life; the act of bearing or bringing forth; parturition; the condition in which a person is born; lineage; extraction; descent; that which is born or produced; origin; beginning.—**birthday,** *n.* The day on which any person is born, or the anniversary of the day; day or time of origin.—**birthmark,** *n.* Some congenital mark or blemish on a person's body.—**birthplace,** *n.* The place of one's birth; place of origin.—**birthright,** *n.* Any right or privilege to which a person is entitled by birth; right of primogeniture.—**birthroot,** *n.* A North American plant, the roots of which are esteemed as astringent, tonic, and antiseptic.

biscuit, bis′ket, *n.* [Fr. *bis*, twice, and *cuit* (L. *coctus*), cooked. COOK.] Bread baked in pieces from dough leavened with soda, yeast, or baking-powder; unraised bread, plain, sweet, or fancy, formed into flat cakes, and baked hard, commonly called *cracker* in the United States.

bisect, bī·sekt′, *v.t.* [L. *bi*, two, and *seco*, *sectum*, to cut.] To cut or divide into two parts, more especially into two equal parts, as a line, etc.—**bisection,** bī·sek′shon, *n.* The act of bisecting; the division of a line, angle, etc., into two equal parts.

bisexual, bī·seks′ū·al. *a.* Having the organs of both sexes in one individual; of two sexes; hermaphrodite; *bot.* having both stamen and pistil within the same envelope.

bishop, bish′up, *n.* [A. Sax. *biscop*, a bishop, from Gr. *episcopos*, an overseer—*epi*, over, and *skopeo*, to look. *Bishop* is the same word as Fr. *évêque* (a bishop), though they have not a letter in common.] A member of the highest order of the Christian ministry; a prelate having the spiritual direction and government of a diocese, the oversight of the clergy within it, and with whom rests the power of ordination, confirmation, and consecration; a piece in the game of chess having its upper section cleft in the form of a bishop's miter.—**bishopric,** bish′up·rik, *n.* [*Bishop*, and *ric*, jurisdiction= A. Sax. *rice*, D. *rijk*, G. *reich*, realm, dominion.] The office or dignity of a bishop; the district over which the jurisdiction of a bishop extends; a diocese.

bismuth, bis′muth or biz′muth, *n.* [G. *bismuth*, *wismuth.*] Chemical element. Symbol, Bi; at. no., 83; at. wt., 208.980.

bison, bī′son, n. [L. *bison*, Gr. *bisōn*, a name borrowed from the ancient Germans.] The name of two bovine quadrupeds, the European bison or aurochs, and the American bison, usually called the buffalo, having short, black, rounded horns, and on the shoulders a large hunch, consisting of a fleshy substance.

bisque, bisk, *n.* [Fr.] Unglazed white porcelain; a reddish-yellow color; a rich soup, usually of meat or fish.

bissextile, bis·seks′tīl, *n.* [L. *bisextilis* (*annus*), leap year, from *bi*, twice, and *sextus*, sixth, because the sixth day before the calends of March (=our 24th Feb.) was reckoned twice every fourth year, a day (the *bisextus*) being intercalated.] Leap year.—*a.* Pertaining to leap year.

bistort, bis′tort *n.* [L. *bistorta—bis*, twice, and *tortus*, twisted.] A plant, so called because of its twisted roots.

bistre, bister, bis′tėr, *n.* [Fr. *bistre.*] A brown pigment prepared from the soot of wood, especially of the beech.

bisulcate, bī·sul′kāt, *a.* [L. *bi*, double, and *sulcus*, a furrow.] Cloven-footed, or having two-hoofed digits, as oxen or swine.

bisulfate, bī·sul′fāt, *n.* In *chem.* a salt of sulfuric acid, in which one-half of the hydrogen of the acid is replaced by a metal.—**bisulfite,** bī·sul′fīt, *n.* A salt of sulfurous acid, in which one-half of the hydrogen of the acid is replaced by a metal.

bit, bit, *n.* [From the verbal stem *bite*. In sense of piece it is the A. Sax. *bita*, *bite*, Icel. *biti*, a bite, a morsel; in sense of part of a bridle it corresponds to A. Sax. *bitol*, D. *bit*, Icel. *bitill*, G. *gebiss.*] A small piece of anything; a piece, morsel, fragment, or part; any small coin; the metal part of a bridle which is inserted in the mouth of a horse, and its appendages, to which the reins are fastened; a boring tool for wood or metal, fixed in a stock, brace, lathe, or the like; the part of a key which enters the lock and acts on the bolts and tumblers; the cutting blade of a plane. ∴In certain phrases *a bit* often means somewhat, a little, a whit; as, he is *a bit* of a painter; not *a bit* better.—*A bit of* *one's mind*, one's candid opinions expressed in clear and unflattering terms.—*v.t.—bitted, bitting*. To put a horse's bit into the mouth of.

bit, bit, *n*. [A blend of *bi*nary and digi*t*.] *Communication theory*, the basic unit of the measurement of information.

bitch, bich, *n*. [A. Sax. *bicce*=Sc. *bick*, Icel. *bikkja*, Dan. *bikke*.] The female of canine animals, as of the dog, wolf, and fox; a term of reproach for a woman.

bite, bīt, *v.t. bit* (pret.), *bit, bitten* (pp.), *biting*. [A. Sax. *bítan*=Icel. *bíta*, D. *bijten*, Goth. *beitan*, G. *beiszen*; *allied* to L. *findo, fidi*, Skr. *bhid*, to split. *Bit, bitter, beetle* are from this stem.] To cut, break, or crush with the teeth; to penetrate or seize with the teeth; to cause a sharp or smarting pain to (pepper *bites* the mouth); to pinch or nip as with frost; to blast or blight; to grip or catch into or on, so as to act with effect (as an anchor, a file, etc.); to corrode or eat into, by aqua fortis or other acid.—*v.i.* To have a habit of biting persons; to seize a bait with the mouth; to grip or catch into another object, so as to act on it with effect (the anchor *bites*).—*n*. The seizure of anything by the teeth or with the mouth; a wound made by the mouth; a mouthful; a bit; a cheat, trick, fraud‡; catch or hold of one object on another.—**biter,** bīt′ėr, *n*. One who or that which bites; an animal given to biting; one who cheats or deceives‡ (in phrase now, ' the *biter* bit ').—**biting,** bīt′ing, *a*. Sharp; severe; cutting; pungent; sarcastic. —**bitingly,** bīt′ing•li, *adv*. In a biting manner; sarcastically; sneeringly.

bitt, bit, *n*. [Comp. Icel. *biti*, a crossbeam or girder.] *Naut*. a piece of wood or frame secured to the deck, on which to make fast the cables.

bitter, bit′ėr, *a*. [A.Sax. *biter*, from *bítan*, to bite, from causing the tongue to smart=D. G. Dan. and Sw. *bitter*, Icel. *bitr*.] Acrid, biting, pungent to taste; keen, cruel, poignant, severe, sharp, harsh, painful, distressing, piercing to the feelings or to the mind; reproachful, sarcastic, or cutting, as words.—**bitterish,** bit′ėr•ish, *a*. Somewhat bitter, especially to the taste.—**bitterly,** bit′ėr•li, *adv*. In a bitter manner; keenly, sharply, severely, intensely. —**bittern,** bit′ėrn, *n*. The residual brine in saltworks, used for making Epsom salts.—**bitterness,** bit′ėr•nes, *n*. The state or quality of being bitter in all its senses, whether to the taste, feelings, or mind.—**bitters,** bit′ėrz, *n. pl*. A liquor prepared with bitter herbs or roots, and used as a stomachic, etc.—**bittersweet,** *n*. The woody nightshade, a trailing plant with small scarlet berries and strongly narcotic leaves, so called because the root and branches when chewed produce first a bitter, then a sweet taste.

bittern, bit•ėrn, *n*. [O.E. *bitore, bittor, bittour*; Fr. *butor*, Sp. *bitor*; origin uncertain.] A name given to several grallatorial or wading birds of the heron family, celebrated for the singular booming or drumming noise they make.

bitumen, bi•tū′men, *n*. [L.] A mineral substance of a resinous nature and highly inflammable, appearing in a variety of forms which are known by different names, *naphtha* being the most fluid, *petroleum* and *mineral tar* less so, and *asphalt* being solid.—**bituminization,** bi•tū′min•iz•ā″shon, *n*. Transformation into a bituminous substance.—**bituminize,** bi•tū′min•īz, *v.t.—bituminized, bituminizing*. To form into or impregnate with bitumen; to convert (as wood) into a bituminous body.—**bituminous,** bi•tū′min•us, *a*. Having the qualities of bitumen; containing or yielding bitumen.

bivalve, bī′valv, *n*. [L. prefix *bi*, double, and *valva*, a valve.] An animal of the molluscous class, having two valves, or a shell consisting of two parts which open by an elastic hinge and are closed by muscles, as the oyster, cockle, mussel, etc.; *bot*. a pericarp in which the seedcase opens or splits into two parts.—**bivalve, bivalvular,** bī′valv, bī•val′vū•lėr, *a*. Having two valves: said especially of the shells of mollusks.

bivouac, biv′ö•ak, *n*. [Fr. *bivouac, bivac*, from G. *beiwache*; lit. by-or near-watch. WAKE, WATCH.] An encampment of soldiers in the open air without tents, each remaining dressed and with his weapons by him; a similar encampment of travelers, hunters, etc.—*v.i. bivouacked, bivouacking*. To encamp in bivouac; to pass the night in the open air without tents or covering.

biweekly, bī•wēk′li, *a*. Occurring or appearing every two weeks (a *biweekly* magazine).

bizarre, bi•zär′, *a*. [Fr., from Sp. *bizarro*, gallant, of Basque origin.] Old in appearance; fanciful; fantastical; formed of incongruous parts.

blab, blab, *v.t.—blabbed, blabbing*. [Allied to L.G. *blabben*, Dan. *blabbre*, G. *plappern*, to gabble; Gael. *blabaran*, a stutterer; *blubber*-lipped, *blob*, etc.] To utter or tell in a thoughtless or unnecessary manner what ought to be kept secret; to let out (secrets).—*v.i.* To talk indiscreetly; to tattle; to tell tales.—*n*. One who blabs; a telltale. (*Mil.*)—**blabber,** blab′ėr, *n*. A blab; a tattler; a telltale.

black, blak, *a*. [A.Sax. *blæc, blac*, black=Icel. *blakkr*, O.H.G. *plak*, black; comp. D. and L.G. *blaken*, to burn or scorch, Gr. *phlegō*, to burn, the original meaning perhaps referring to blackness caused by fire.] Of the darkest color; the opposite of white; very dark in hue (though not absolutely incapable of reflecting light; destitute of light, or nearly so; dismal, gloomy, sullen, forbidding, or the like; destitute of moral light or goodness; mournful; calamitous; evil; wicked; atrocious. —*Black art*, the art of performing wonderful feats by supernatural means, or aided by evil spirits; necromancy; magic.—*Black beer*, a kind of beer of a black color and syrupy consistence.—*Black cattle*, oxen, cows, etc., reared for slaughter, as distinguished from dairy cattle; used without reference to color.—*Black death*, an oriental plague which first visited Europe in the fourteenth century, characterized by inflammatory boils and black spots all over the skin.—*Black flag*, the flag formerly assumed by pirates.—*Black list*, a printed list circulated among commercial men, containing the names of persons who have become bankrupt or unable to meet their bills, etc.—*Black snake*, a name given to some snakes of a black color, such as a large non-venomous North American snake which feeds on birds and small quadrupeds.—*Black spruce*, a spruce tree belonging to North America, which furnishes the spruce deals of commerce.—*n*. The opposite of white; a black dye or pigment or a hue produced by such; a black part of something, as of the eye; a black dress of mourning; frequently in plural; a small flake of soot; a member of one of the dark-colored races; a Negro or other dark-skinned person. —*v.t.* To make black; to apply blacking to (shoes); to blacken; to soil.—**blacken,** blak′n, *v.t.* To make black; to polish with blacking; to sully; to stain; to defame; to vilify; to slander.—*v.i.* To become black or dark.—**blacking,** blak′ing, *n*. A composition for polishing boots, shoes, harness, etc., consisting usually of a mixture of lampblack, oil, vinegar. etc.—**blackish,** blak′ish, *a*. Somewhat black.—**blackly,** blak′li, *adv*. In a black manner; darkly; gloomily; threateningly; angrily; atrociously.—**blackness,** blak′nes, *n*. The state or quality of being black; black color; darkness; gloominess; somberness; sullen or severe aspect; atrocity.—**blackamoor,** blak′a•mör, *a*. [*Black*. and *Moor*. in the old sense of black man or Negro, formerly written also *blackmoor*.] A Negro; a black man or woman.—**blackball,** *v.t.* To reject, as a proposed member of a club; to exclude by vote.—**blackberry,** *n*. The berry of the bramble.—**blackbird,** blak′bėrd, *n*. An insessorial bird of the thrush family, the male bird being characterized by its black plumage and its rich mellow note; the merle. —**blackboard,** *n*. A board painted black, used in schools and lecture rooms for writing or drawing lines on for instruction.—**blackcap,** *n*. A dentirostral European bird of the warbler family, noted for the sweetness of its song, and so called from its black tufted crown; a species of raspberry having black fruit, native to North America.—**blackcock,** *n*. A bird of the grouse family, so called from the glossy black plumage of the male; the heath cock or black grouse.—**Black Friar,** *n*. A friar of the Dominican order, so called from the color of the dress; a Dominican.—**blackguard,** black′gärd or bla′gärd, *n.* [Formerly a name given to the scullions and lowest menials connected with a great household, who attended to the pots, coals, etc.] A man of coarse and offensive manners; a fellow of low character; a scamp; a scoundrel.—*v.t.* To revile in low or scurrilous language.—**blackguardism,** blak′gärd•izm, or bla′gärd•izm, *n.* The conduct or language of a blackguard.—**blackguardly,** blak′gärd•li or bla′gärd•li, *a.* Characteristic of a blackguard; rascally; villainous.—**black hole,** *n.* Formerly a dungeon or dark cell in a prison; now more specifically applied to a place of confinement for soldiers.—**blackjack,** *n.* A capacious can, now made of tin, but formerly of waxed leather; the flag or ensign of a pirate; a small leather-covered club or billy weighted at the head and having an elastic shaft; a card game.—**blacklead,** *n.* Amorphous graphite; plumbago. GRAPHITE.—**blackleg,** *n.* [Origin undecided.] One who systematically tries to win money by cheating in connection with races, or with cards, billiards, or other game; a rook; a swindler; also same as *Black-quarter*, a disease of cattle.—**black letter,** *n.* The old English or Gothic type used in early printed books, being an imitation of the written character in use before the art of printing, still in general use in German books.—**blackmail,** *n.* [*-mail* is from Icel. *mâl*, stipulation, agreement, *mæla*, to stipulate.] Money or an equivalent, anciently paid, in the north of England and in Scotland, to certain men allied with robbers, to be protected by them from pillage; hence, the act of demanding payment by means of intimidation; also extortion of money from a person by threats of public accusation or censure.—**black market,** *n.* Trade in violation of official prices or quantities.—**blackout,** *n.* The dimming of a city's lights as a precaution against air raids; temporary loss of consciousness.—**Black Rod,** *n.* In England, the usher belonging to the order of the Garter and one of the official messengers of the House of Lords, so called from the black rod which he carries.—**black sheep,** *n.* A member of a family or society distinguished from his fellows by low habits or loose conduct.—**blacksmith,** blak′smith, *n.* A smith who works in iron and makes iron utensils; an ironsmith: opposed to a *whitesmith* or tinsmith.—**blackthorn,** *n.* The sloe.—**black vomit,** *n.* A blackish substance vomited in yellow fever; the fever itself.—**black widow spider,** *n.* The name given to the female of an American spider that devours its mate. Its bite is poisonous.

bladder, blad′ėr, *n.* [A.Sax. *blædr*, *blæddre*, a bladder, pustule, blister = Icel. *blathra*, Sw. *blädra*, L.G. *bladere*, *bledder*, O.H.G. *plâtara*, a bladder, G. *blatter*, a pustule; the root is probably in E. to *blow*.] A thin membranous bag in animals, which serves as the receptacle of some secreted fluid, as the urine, the gall, etc.; any vesicle, blister, or pustule, especially if filled with air or a thin watery liquid; a hollow appendage in some plants.—*v.t.* To put up in a bladder, as lard; to puff up; to fill with wind†.—**bladdery,** blad′ėr•i, *a.* Resembling or containing bladders.

blade, blād, *n.* [A.Sax. *blæd*, a leaf = D. Dan. Sw. *blad*, Icel. *blath*, G. *blatt*, a leaf; from root of to *blow*, and allied to *bloom*, *blossom*.] The leaf of a plant, especially the leaf or the young stalk or spire of grass or corn plants; a thing resembling a blade in shape, etc., as the cutting part of an instrument; the broad part of an oar; a dashing or rollicking fellow; a swaggerer; a rakish fellow.—*v.t.* To furnish with a blade.—*v.i.* To come into blade; to produce blades.—**bladed,** blād′ed, *a.* Having a blade or blades.

blain, blān, *n.* [A.Sax. *blegen*—D. *blein*, Dan. *blegn*, *a* blain, a blister; probably from root of to *blow*, and allied to *bladder*.] A pustule; a botch; a blister.

blame, blām, *v.t.*—*blamed*, *blaming*. [Fr. *blâmer*, O. Fr. *blasmer*, from L.L. *blasphemare*, from Gr. *blasphemein*, to calumniate. *Blaspheme* is the same word.] To express disapprobation of (a person or thing); to find fault with; to censure; to reproach; to chide; to condemn; to upbraid. ∴In such phrases as 'he is *to blame*,' *to blame* has the passive meaning = to be blamed, like 'a house to let,' etc.—*n.* An expression of disapprobation for something deemed to be wrong; imputation of a fault; censure; reproach; reprehension; that which is deserving of censure (the *blame* is yours); fault; crime; sin.—**blamable,** blām′a•bl, *a.* Deserving of blame or censure; faulty; culpable; reprehensible; censurable.—**blamableness,** blām′a•bl•nes, *n.* The state or quality of being blamable.—**blamably,** blām′a•bli, *adv.* In a blamable manner; culpably.—**blameful,** blām′ful, *a.* Meriting blame; reprehensible; faulty; guilty; criminal.—**blameless,** blām′les, *a.* Not meriting blame or censure; without fault; undeserving of reproof; innocent; guiltless.—**blamelessly,** blām′les•li, *adv.* In a blameless manner.—**blamelessness,** blām′les•nes, *n.*—**blameworthy,** blām′wėr•THi, *a.* Deserving blame; censurable, culpable; reprehensible.—**blameworthiness,** blām′wėr•THi•-nes, *n.*

blanch, blansh, *v.t.* [Fr. *blanchir*, to whiten, from *blanc*, white. BLANK.] To whiten by depriving of color; to render white, pale, or colorless (fear *blanches* the cheek); *hort.* to whiten or prevent from turning green by excluding the light, a process applied to kitchen vegetables, such as celery, lettuce, sea kale, etc.; to whiten or make lustrous, as metals, by acids or other means.—*v.i.* To become white; to bleach.—**blancher,** blansh′ėr, *n.* One who blanches or whitens.

blanc-mange, blanc-manger, bla•-manzh′, blań•mań•zhā′, *n.* [Fr. *blanc*, white, and *manger*, food.] *Cookery*, a preparation of the consistency of a jelly, variously composed of dissolved isinglass, arrow root, cornstarch, etc., with milk and flavoring substances.

bland, bland, *a.* [L. *blandus*, mild.] Mild; soft; gentle (*bland* zephyrs); affable; suave (his manner is very *bland*); soothing; kindly.—**blandness,** bland′nes, *n.* State of being bland; mildness; gentleness.

blandish, blan′dish, *v.t.* & *i.* [O.Fr. *blandir*, *blandissant*, L. *blandior*, to flatter, from *blandus*, bland.] To render pleasing, alluring, or enticing; to caress, soothe, fawn, or flatter.—**blandisher,** blan′dish•ėr, *n.* One that blandishes; one that flatters with soft words.—**blandishment,** blan′dish•ment, *n.* Words or actions expressive of affection or kindness, and tending to win the heart; artful caresses; flattering attention; cajolery; endearment.

blank, blangk, *a.* [Fr. *blanc*, white, blank, from G. *blank*, white, lustrous, blank, from *blinken*, to *blink*, to glimmer; cog. D. Dan. and Sw. *blank*, white. BLINK.] White or pale†; void of written or printed characters, as paper; wanting something necessary to completeness; vacant; unoccupied; void; empty; pale from fear or terror; hence, confused; confounded; dispirited; dejected; unrhymed; applied to verse.—*n.* A piece of paper without writing or printed matter on it; a void space on paper or in any written or printed document; a document remaining incomplete till something essential is filled in; any void space; a void; a vacancy; a ticket in a lottery on which no prize is indicated; a lot by which nothing is gained; *archery*, the white mark in the center of a butt or target to which an arrow is directed; hence, the object to which anything is directed; aim; a piece of metal prepared to be formed into something useful by a further operation; a plate, or piece of gold or silver, cut and shaped, but not stamped into a coin.—*v.t.*‡ To make white or pale; confuse, confound, dispirit. (*Shak.*)—**blankly,** blangk′li, *adv.* In a blank manner; with paleness or confusion.—**blankness,** blangk′nes, *n.* State of being blank.

blanket, blang′ket, *n.* [O.Fr. *blanket*, dim. from *blanc*, white. BLANK.] A soft thick cloth made of wool loosely woven, and used as a covering in beds; any similar fabric used as covering, etc.—*v.t.* To toss in a blanket by way of punishment; to cover or clothe with a blanket (*Shak.*).

blare, blār, *v.i.*—*blared*, *blaring*. [Probably an imitative word; comp. D. *blaren*, L.G. *blarren*, *blaren*, G. *blarren*, *blärren*, to bellow, bleat, blare.] To give forth a loud sound like a trumpet; to give out a brazen sound; to bellow.— *v.t.* To sound loudly; to proclaim noisily.—*n.* Sound like that of a trumpet; noise; roar.

blarney, blär′ni, *n.* [From Castle *Blarney*, near Cork, in the wall of which is a stone said to endow any one who kisses it with skill in the use of flattery.] Excessively complimentary language; gross flattery; smooth, deceitful talk; gammon. (Colloq.)—*v.t.* To talk over by soft delusive speeches; to flatter; to humbug with talk (Colloq.).

blasé, blä•zā′. [Fr.] Lost to the power of enjoyment; used up; having the healthy energies exhausted.

blaspheme, blas•fēm′, *v.t.*—*blasphemed, blaspheming.* [L. *blasphemare*, Gr. *blasphēmein*, to calumniate—from *blapsis*, injury, and *phēmi*, to speak. *Blame* is a shortened form of this word.] To speak in terms of impious irreverence of; to revile or speak reproachfully of instead of reverentially: used of speaking against God or things sacred.—*v.i.* To utter blasphemy; to use blasphemous language.—**blasphemer,** blas•fēm′ėr, *n.* One who blasphemes; one who speaks of God in impious and irreverent terms.—**blasphemous,** blas′fē•mus, *a.* Containing or exhibiting blasphemy; impiously irreverent or reproachful toward God.—**blasphemously,** blas′fē•mus•li, *adv.* In a blasphemous manner.—**blasphemy,** blas′fē•mi, *n.* The language of one who blasphemes; words uttered impiously againt God; grossly irreverent or outrageous language.

blast, blast, *n.* [A.Sax. *blaest*, a puff of wind; from *blaesan*, to blow=Icel. *blástr*, Dan. *blœst*, a blowing; Icel. *blása*, Dan. *blœse*, G. *blasen*, to blow; same root as E. *blow, blase.*] A gust or puff of wind; a sudden gust ot wind; the sound made by blowing a wind-instrument, as a horn or trumpet; the sound produced by one's breath; a blight or sudden pernicious influence on animals or plants; a forcible stream of air from the mouth, bellows etc.; a violent explosion of gunpowder or other explosive in splitting rocks, etc.—*v.t.* To injure by a blast; to cause to fade, shrivel, or wither; to blight or cause to come to nothing; to ruin; to split by an explosion.—*v.i.* To wither or be blighted. (*Shak.*)—**blast furnace,** *n.* The smelting furnace used for obtaining iron from its ores with the aid of a powerful blast of air, usually a lofty furnace of masonry, in which the iron is smelted from its ore by being mixed with coal and the whole mass kept burning, the melted metal being run off at the bottom.—**blast-pipe,** *n.* The pipe of a locomotive steam engine which carries the waste steam up the chimney, and thus induces a stronger draught.

blastema, blas•tē′ma, *n.* [Gr. *blastēma*, a shoot, growth, from *blastano*, to bud.] *Bot.* the axis of growth of an embryo; that part of the embryo comprising the radicle and plumule, with the intervening portion.

blastocarpous, blas•tō•kär′pus, *a.* [Gr. *blastos*, a germ, and *karpos*, fruit.] Having the germ beginning to grow inside the pericarp of the fruit.—**blastoderm,** blas′tō•dėrm, *n.* [Gr. *derma*, a skin.] *Anat.* the germinal skin or membrane; the superficial layer of the embryo in its earliest condition.—**blastodermic,** blas•tō•dėr′mik, *a.* Relating to the blastoderm.—**blastogenesis,** blas•tō•jen′e•sis, *n. Biol.* reproduction by germination or budding.

blastula, blas′tū•la, *n.* [From Gr. *blastos*, a germ.] An embryo so far developed from a germ or ovum as to consist of a sack formed of a single layer of cells.

blatant, blā′tant, *a.* [From Prov. E. *blate*, to *bleat*, with suffix *-ant*, as in *errant*, etc.] Bellowing; bawling; noisy.

blaze, blāz, *n.* [A.Sax. *blœse*, a blaze, a torch, from root of *blow*; comp. Icel. *blys*, Dan. *blus*, a torch; akin to *blast.*] The stream of light and heat from any body when burning; a flame; brilliant sunlight; effulgence; brilliance; a bursting out; an active or violent display (a *blaze* of wrath). —*v.i.*—*blazed, blazing.* To flame; to send forth or show a bright and expanded light.—**blazer,** blāz′ėr, *n.* That which blazes; a bright-colored jacket or short coat suited for sports, etc.

blaze, blāz, *v.t.*—*blazed, blazing,* [A.Sax. *blaesan*, to blow=Icel. *blása*, Dan. *blœse*, G. *blasen*, to blow, to sound as a trumpet. BLAST, BLOW.] To make known to all; to noise or bruit abroad; to proclaim.

blaze, blāz, *n.* [D. *bles*, Icel. *blesi*, Dan. *blis*, a white spot or streak on the forehead.] A white spot on the forehead or face of a horse or other quadruped; a white spot on a tree by removing the bark with a hatchet.—*v.t.* To set a blaze on, by paring off part of the bark; to indicate or mark out, as a path, by paring off the bark of a number of trees in succession.

blazon, blā′zn, *n.* [O.E. *blasoun*, *blason*, Fr. *blason*, heraldry, *blasonner*, to blazon, from a G. word equivalent to E. *blaze*, to spread abroad or make known.] The drawing or representation on coats of arms; a heraldic figure; show; pompous display, by words or other means (*Shak.*).—*v.t.* To explain, in proper terms, the figures on ensigns armorial; to deck; to embellish; to adorn; to display; to publish; to celebrate.—**blazoner,** blā′zn•ėr, *n.* One that blazons; a herald; one prone to spread reports; a propagator of scandal.— **blazonment,** blā′zn•ment, *n.* The act of blazoning; emblazonment.—**blazonry,** blā′zn•ri, *n.* The art of describing or explaining coats of arms in proper heraldic terms and method; emblazonry.

bleach, blēch, *v.t.* [A.Sax. *blaecan*, from *blaec*, pale, white. BLEAK.] To make white or whiter by taking out color; to whiten; to blanch; to whiten by exposure to the action of the air and sunlight or of chemical preparations.—*v.i.* To grow white in any manner.—**bleacher,** blēch′ėr, *n.* One who bleaches; one whose occupation is to whiten cloth.—**bleachers,** blēch′ėrz, *n.* Seats, usually uncovered, for spectators at baseball and other outdoor sporting events.—**bleachery,** blēch′ėr•i, *n.* An establishment where bleaching textile fabrics or the like is carried on.—**bleaching powder,** *n.* Chloride of lime made by exposing slaked lime to the action of chlorine.

bleak, blēk, *a.* [A.Sax. *blaec*=Icel. *bleikr*, D. *bleek*, G. *bleich*, pale, pallid, white; allied to A.Sax. *blícan*, Icel. *blikja*, G. *blicken*, to shine, to gleam, E. to *blink. Bleach* is from this word.] Exposed to cold and winds (situation, tract of land); desolate; ungenial; cheerless; dreary; cold; chill (*bleak* winds).—**bleakish,** blēk′ish, *a.* Moderately bleak.—**bleakly,** blēk′li, *adv.* In a bleak manner; coldly.—**bleakness,** blēk′nes, *n.* State of being bleak; coldness; desolation.—**bleaky,**†blēk′i, *a.* Bleak; unsheltered; cold; chill.

bleak, blēk, *n.* [So called from the *bleak* or pale color of its scales.] A small river fish, 5 or 6 inches long, belonging to the carp family, occurring in many European rivers.

blear, blēr, *a.* [L.G. *blarr*, *blerr*, blear; Sw. *blira*, Dan. *blire*, *plire*, to twinkle, to wink; Dan. *pliiröiet*, blear-eyed.] Sore, with a watery rheum; said of the eyes.—*v.t.* To make sore so that the sight is indistinct; to affect with soreness of eyes; to make rheumy and dim; *fig.* to hoodwink or deceive.—**blear-eyed,** *a.* Having sore eyes; having the eyes dim with rheum; dim-sighted; wanting in perception or understanding.

bleat, blēt, *v.i.* [A.Sax. *blaetan*=D. *blaten*, *bleeten*, L.G. *blaten*, *bleten*, to bleat, probably an imitative word.] To utter the cry of a sheep or a similar cry.—**bleat,** *n.* The cry of a sheep.—**bleater,** blēt′ėr, *n.* One who bleats; a sheep.

bleed, blēd, *v.i.*—*bled* (pret. & pp.), *bleeding.* [A.Sax. *blédan*, from *blód*, blood=D. *blœden*, Icel. *blœtha*, Dan. *blóde*, to bleed.] To lose blood; to be drained of blood; to run with blood; to let sap or other moisture flow from itself; to trickle or flow, as from an incision; to have money extorted, or to part with it freely to some wheedling or unworthy party (colloq.).—*v.t.* To take blood from by opening a vein; to emit (a tree *bleeds* juice, sap, or gum); to extort or extract money from (colloq.).

blemish, blem′ish, *v.t.* [O.Fr. *blemir*, *blemissant*, to spot, to beat one blue, from Icel. *bláman*, the livid color of a wound, from *blár*, blue, livid. BLUE.] To injure or impair; to mar or make defective; to deface; to sully; to tarnish, as reputation or character; to defame.—*n.* A defect, flaw, or imperfection; something that mars beauty, completeness, perfection, or reputation; a blot or stain.

blench, blensh, *v.i.* [Probably a softened form of *blink*, in old sense to wink; hence, to turn aside, to flinch; *blanch* seems to have been partly confounded with it.] To shrink; to start back; to give way; to flinch; to turn aside, as from pain, fear, repugnance, etc.—*n.* A start back; a deviation; aberration.

blend, blend, *v.t.*—*blended* (pret.), *blended* or *blent* (pp.), *blending* [A.Sax. *blandan*, to mix=Icel. and Sw. *blanda*, Dan. *blande*, to mix; allied to *blind*, originally turbid. BLIND.] To mix or mingle together; to confound so that the separate things mixed cannot be distinguished.—*v.i.* To be mixed; to become united; to merge insensibly the one into the other (as colors).—*n.* A mixture, as of liquids, colors, etc.; a mixture of spirits from different distilleries.

blende, blend, *n.* [G. *blende*, blend. from *blenden*, to blind, to dazzle.] An ore of zinc, of which there are several varieties; a native sulfide of zinc. This word is also employed in such compound terms as manganese blende, zinc blende, ruby blende.

Blenheim, blen'em, *n.* One of a breed of dogs of the spaniel kind, preserved in perfection at Blenheim Palace in Oxfordshire, England.

blenny, blen'i, *n.* [L. *blennius*, from Gr. *blennos*, slime.] The name of several small fishes frequenting rocky coasts.

blepharitis, blef•a•rī'tis, *n.* [Gr. *blehparon*, eyelid.] Inflammation of the eyelids.

blesbok, bles'bok, *n.* [D. *bles*, a blaze or spot on the forehead, and *bok*, a buck.] An antelope of Cape Colony, with a white face.

bless, bles, *v.t.*—*blessed* or *blest*, *blessing*. [A.Sax. *bletsian*, *bledsian*, to bless, from *blód*, blood; originally perhaps to consecrate by sprinkling blood.] To invoke the divine favor on; to express a wish for the good fortune or happiness of; to bestow happiness, prosperity, or good things of any kind upon (*blest* with peace and plenty); to make and pronounce holy; to consecrate; to glorify for benefits received; to extol for excellencies (to *bless* the Lord; to esteem or account happy: with the reflexive pronoun.—*Bless me! bless my soul*! expressions of surprise.—**blessed,** bles'ed, *a.* [As pret. and pp. *blessed* is now commonly pronounced *blest*]. Enjoying happiness; favored with blessings; highly favored; happy; fortunate; enjoying spiritual blessings and the favor of God; fraught with or imparting blessings; sacred; hallowed; holy.—**blessedly,** bles'ed•li, *adv.* In a blessed or fortunate manner; joyfully.—**blessedness,** bles'ed•nes, *n.* The state of being blessed; happiness; felicity; heavenly joys; the favor of God.—*Single blessedness*, the unmarried state; celibacy.—**blessing,** bles'ing, *n.* The act of one who blesses; a prayer or solemn wish imploring happiness upon another; a benediction; the act of pronouncing a benediction or blessing; that which promotes temporal prosperity and welfare or secures immortal felicity; any good thing falling to one's lot; a mercy.

blew, blö, pret. of *blow*.

blight, blīt, *n.* [Possibly from prefix *be*, and *light*, the original meaning being perhaps to scorch or blast as by lightning.] Something that nips, blasts, or destroys plants; a diseased state of plants; smut, mildew, or other plant disease; *fig.* something that frustrates, blasts, destroys, brings to nought, etc.—*v.t.* To affect with blight; to cause to wither or decay; to blast; to frustrate.—*v.i.* To injure or blast as blight does.

blimp, blimp, *n.* A nonrigid airship of the smallest size.

blind, blīnd, *a.* [A.Sax. D. Icel. Sw. Dan. G. *blind*; originally meaning turbid or cloudy, and allied to *blend*, to mix.] Destitute of the sense of sight; not having sight; not having the faculty of discernment; destitute of intellectual, moral, or spiritual light; not easily discernible; dark; obscure (*blind* paths, *blind* mazes); indiscriminate; heedless (*blind* wrath); without openings for admitting light (*blind* window), or otherwise wanting something ordinarily essential; closed at one end; having no outlet (a *blind* alley).—*v.t.* To make physically, morally, or intellectually blind; to render incapable of clear vision (*blinded* by passion); to darken; to obscure to the eye or to the mind; to conceal (' to *blind* the truth '. *Tenn.*); to eclipse.—*n.* Something to hinder sight, to intercept a view, or keep out light; a screen of some sort to prevent too strong a light from shining in at a window, or to keep people from seeing in; something ostensible to conceal a covert design; a cover; a pretext.—**blinder,** blīnd'ėr, *n.* One who or that which blinds; a blinker on a horse's bridle.—**blindfold,** blīnd'fōld, *a.* Having the eyes covered, as with a bandage; having the mental eye darkened (*Shak.*).—*v.t.* To cover the eyes of; to hinder from seeing by binding something round the eyes.—**blinding,** blīnd'ing, *a.* Making blind: preventing from seeing clearly; depriving of sight or of understanding.—**blindingly,** blīnd'ing•li, *adv.* In a blinding manner; so as to blind.—**blindly,** blīnd'li, *adv.* In a blind manner; without sight or understanding; without examination; regardlessly; recklessly.—**blindman's buff,** *n.* A play in which one person is blindfolded and tries to catch some one of the company and tell who it is.—**blindness,** blīnd'nes, *n.* State of being blind; want of bodily sight; mental darkness; ignorance.—**blindworm,** *n.* [So called because, its eyes being very minute, it has popularly been supposed to be blind.] A small harmless wormlike reptile, called also slowworm, connecting the serpents and lizards.

blink, blingk, *v.i.* [Same word as D. *blinken*, Dan. *blinke*, Sw. *blinka*, G. *blinken*, to shine, glance, twinkle; allied to A. Sax. *blican*, to gleam, D. *blikken*, Dan. *blikke*, G. *blicken*, to glance, to glimpse. Akin *blank*, *blench*, *bleach*.] To wink; to twinkle; to see with the eyes half shut or with frequent winking; to get a glimpse; to peep (*Shak.*); to intermit light; to glimmer.—*v.t.* To shut one's eyes to; to avoid or purposely evade (to *blink* a question or topic).—*n.* A glance of the eye; a glimpse; a gleam; a glimmer; the gleam or glimmer reflected from ice in the Arctic regions.—**blinker,** bling'kėr, *n.* One who blinks; a leather flap placed on either side of a horse's head, to prevent him from seeing sideways or backward; a warning light.

bliss, blis, *n.* [A.Sax. *blis*, *bliss*, joy, alacrity, exultation, from *blithe*, blithe. BLITHE.] The highest degree of happiness; blessedness; felicity; often specifically heavenly felicity.—**blissful,** blis'fu̥l, *a.* Full of, abounding in, enjoying, or conferring bliss.—**blissfully,** blis'fu̥l•li, *adv.* In a blissful manner.—**blissfulness,** blis'fu̥l•nes, *n.* Exalted happiness; felicity; fullness of joy.

blister, blis'tėr, *n.* [Connected with *blast*, to blow or puff, from same root as to *blow*. com. G. *blase*, a blister, a bladder.] A thin vesicle on the skin, containing watery matter or serum; a pustule; an elevation made by the separation of an external film or skin, as on plants; something applied to the skin to raise a blister; a vesicatory.—*v.t.* To raise a blister or blisters on.—*v.i.* To rise in blisters or become blistered.—**blister beetle,** *n.* A beetle used to raise a blister on the skin; the Spanish fly.—**blister steel,** *n.* Iron bars which, when converted into steel, have their surface covered with blisters.—**blistery,** blis'tėr•i, *a.* Full of blisters.

blithe, blīTH, *a.* [A.Sax. *blithe*, blithe, joyful; O.Sax. *blithi*, clear, joyful; Goth. *bleiths*, merciful; Icel. *blithr*, Dan. *blid*, bland; D. *blijde*, blithe. Hence *bliss*.] Gay; merry; joyous; sprightly; mirthful; characterized by blitheness or joy.—**blithely,** blīTH'li, *adv.* In a blithe, gay, or joyful manner.—**blithesome,** blīTH'sum, *a.* Full of blitheness or gaiety; gay; merry; cheerful.

blitzkrieg, blits'krēg, *n.* [G. *Blitz*, lightning, and *Krieg*, war.] A technique of warfare developed by German strategists, consisting of swift strokes designed to pierce the enemy's lines, disrupt his communications and supply systems, and separate his forces so that they can be destroyed piecemeal.

blizzard, bliz'ard, *n.* [Akin to *blaze*, *blast*. Originally provincial English, but general in American literature since 1880.] A biting-cold snowstorm.

bloat, blōt, *v.t.* [Allied to Icel. *blautr*, soaked and soft; Sw. *blōt*, soaked, *blōta*, to soak, to cure fish by soaking.] To make turgid or swollen, as with air, water, etc.; to cause to swell, as in adenia; to inflate; to make vain; to cure by smoking, as herrings.—*v.i.* To become swollen; to dilate.

blob, blob, *n.* [Also in form *bleb*, and allied to *blab*, *blubber*.] A small globe of liquid; a dewdrop; a blister.

bloc, blok, *n.* [Fr. for block or lump.] A combination of groups or nations united to further their joint interests.

block, blok, *n.* [Same word as D. and Dan. *blok*, G. and Sw. *block*, a block, a log, a lump; Ir. *blog*, a fragment.] Any solid mass of matter, usually with one or more plane or approximately plane faces; a lump; a stock or stupid person; the mass of wood on which criminals lay their necks when they are beheaded; any obstruction or cause of obstruction; a stop; the state of being blocked or stopped up; a casing or shell containing one or more pulleys over which a rope or chain works; a connected mass of buildings; a portion of a city enclosed by streets; a mold or piece on which something is shaped, or placed to make it keep in shape; a piece of wood on which an engraving is cut.—*v.t.* To hinder egress or passage from or to; to stop up or barricade; to obstruct; to act in opposition or by interference, as in boxing, football, cricket; to mold, shape, or stretch on a block.—*To block out*, to begin to reduce to the required shape; to shape out.—**blockade,** blok·ād′, *n.* [Comp. such words as *barricade*, *stockade*, *palisade*, etc.] The shutting up of a place by surrounding it with hostile troops or ships with a view to compel a surrender, by hunger and want, without regular attacks.—*To raise a blockade*, to remove or break up a blockade.—*v.t. blockaded*, *blockading*. To subject to a blockade; to prevent ingress to or egress from by warlike means; to shut up or in by obstacles of any kind; to obstruct.

block and tackle, *n.* A set of pulleys and ropes for lifting or hauling.—**blockhead,** blok′hed, *n.* A stupid fellow.—**blockhouse,** *n. Milit.* a building of one or more stories, so named because constructed chiefly of logs or beams of timber, having loopholes for musketry.—**blockish,** blok′ish, *a.* Like a block; stupid; dull; deficient in understanding. (*Shak.*)—**block system,** *n.* The system of working the traffic on a railroad, according to which the line is divided into short sections, and no train is allowed to enter upon any one section till it is signalled wholly clear, so that between two successive trains there is an interval of time as well as one of space.—**block tin,** *n.* Tin cast into ingots or blocks.

blond, blonde, blond, *a.* [Fr. *blond*, *blonde*, a word of Teutonic origin; comp. D. and G. *blond*, fair, flaxen; A.Sax. *blonden*, grayish or grizzled; allied to *blend*.] Of a fair color or complexion.—*n.* A person (especially a woman) of very fair complexion, with light hair and light-blue eyes.

blood, blud, *n.* [O.E. *blod*, *blode*, etc., A.Sax. *blód*=Goth. *bloth*, Icel. *blóth*, Dan. Sw. *blod*, L.G. *blood*, D. *bloed*, G. *blut;* root probably seen in to *blow* (as a flower), *bloom*, from the brightness of its color.] The fluid which circulates through the arteries and veins of the human body and that of other animals, and which is essential to life and nutrition—in man and the higher animals of a more or less red color; relationship by descent from a common ancestor (allied by *blood*); consanguinity; lineage; kindred; family; birth; extraction; often high birth; good extraction; natural disposition; temper; spirit (to do a thing in hot *blood* or cold *blood*, that is in anger or deliberately); mettle; passion; anger (his *blood* was up).—*The blood*, royal family or royal lineage; thus it is common to speak of princes of *the blood*.—*Flesh and blood*, human nature; mortal man.—*v.t.* To let blood; to bleed; to stain with blood; to inure to blood; to give a taste of blood.—**bloodguiltiness,** *n.* The state of being blood-guilty; the guilt or crime of shedding blood.—**blood-guilty,** *a.* Guilty of murder.—**bloodhound,** *n.* A large variety of dog with long smooth and pendulous ears, remarkable for the acuteness of its smell, and employed to recover game or prey by scent.—**bloodily,** blud′i·li, *adv.* In a bloody manner; cruelly.—**bloodiness,** blud′i·nes, *n.* The state of being bloody; disposition to shed blood; murderousness.—**bloodless,** blud′les, *a.* Without blood; drained of blood; dead; without shedding of blood or slaughter (a *bloodless* victory); without spirit or activity.—**bloodlessly,** blud′les·li, *adv.* In a bloodless manner; without bloodshed.—**bloodletting,** blud′let·ing, *u.* The act of letting blood by opening a vein.—**blood money,** *n.* Money earned by the shedding of blood or by laying, or supporting, a charge implying peril to the life of an accused person.—**bloodshed,** blud′shed, *n.* The shedding or spilling of blood; slaughter; waste of life.—**blood-shedder,** blud′shed·ėr, *n.* One who sheds blood; a murderer.—**blood-shedding,** blud′shed·ing, *n.* The crime of shedding blood or taking human life.—**bloodshot,** blud′shot, *a.* Red and inflamed by a turgid state of the blood vessels: said of the eye.—**bloodstained,** *a.* Stained with blood; guilty of slaughter.—**bloodstone,** *n.* A stone worn as an amulet, to prevent bleeding at the nose; red hematite; a species of heliotrope dotted with spots of jasper.—**bloodsucker,** *n.* Any animal that sucks blood, as a leech, a fly, etc.; a hard niggardly man; an extortioner.—**bloodthirstiness,** blud′thėrs·ti·nes, *n.* Thirst for shedding blood.—**bloodthirsty,** blud thėrs·ti, *a.* Desirous to shed blood; murderous.—**blood vessel,** *n.* Any vessel in which blood circulates in an animal body; an artery or a vein.—**bloody,** blud′i, *a.* Of or pertaining to blood; consisting of, containing, or exhibiting blood; bloodstained; cruel; murderous; given to the shedding of blood; attended with much bloodshed.

bloom, blöm, *n.* [Same word as Icel. *blóm*, Sw. *blomma*, Dan. *blomme*, Goth. *bloma*, D. *bloem*, G. *blume*, a flower, from stem of *blow*, to blossom; akin *blossom*.] A blossom; the flower of a plant; the act or state of blossoming; fullness of life and vigor; a period of high success; a flourishing condition; the delicate rose hue on the cheek indicative of youth and health; a glow; a flush; a superficial coating or appearance upon certain things, as the delicate powdery coating upon certain fruits when newly gathered.—*v.i.* To produce or yield blossoms; to blossom; to flower; to show the beauty of youth; to glow.—*v.t.*‡ To put forth, as blossoms. (O.T.)—**blooming,** blöm′ing, *a.* Showing blooms; glowing as with youthful vigor.—**bloomingly,** blöm′ing·li, *adv.* In a blooming manner.—**bloomy,** blö′mi, *a.* Full of bloom or blossoms; flowery; having freshness or vigor as of youth; having a delicate powdery appearance, as fresh fruit.

bloom, blöm, *n.* [A.Sax, *blóma*, a mass or lump of metal.] A lump of puddled iron, which leaves the furnace in a rough state, to be subsequently rolled into the bars or other material into which it may be desired to convert the metal.—**bloomery,** blöm′ėr·i, *n.* The first forge through which iron passes after it is melted from the ore.

bloomers, blöm′ėrz, *n.* A woman's knee-length undergarment; originally loose trousers, gathered at the ankles; named for Amelia Bloomer, American, who advocated their use in 1849.

blossom, blos′om, *n.* [A.Sax. *blóstma*, a blossom, from same root as *bloom* (which see).] The flower of a plant, consisting of one or more colored leaflets, generally of more delicate texture than the leaves; the bloom; blooming state or period (the plant is in *bloom*).—*v.i.* To put forth blossoms or flowers; to bloom; to flourish.—**blossomy,**† blos′om·i, *a.* Full of or covered with blossoms.

blot, blot, *n.* [Same word as Icel. *blettr*, Dan. *plet*, a blot; Dan. dial. *blat*, a drop, a spot of something wet.] A spot or stain, as of ink on paper; a blur; an obliteration of something written or printed; a spot in reputation; a blemish.—*v.t.*—*blotted*, *blotting*. To spot, to stain, as with ink; to stain with infamy; to tarnish; to obliterate or efface: in this sense generally with *out;* to dry by means of blotting paper or the like.—**blotter,** blot′ėr, *n.* One who or that which blots.—**blotting paper,** *n.* A species of unsized paper, serving to imbibe the superfluous ink from newly written manuscript, etc.

blotch, bloch, *n.* [For *blatch*, *blach*, a softened form of *black* (comp. *bleak*, *bleach*), the meaning being influenced by *botch*, a pustule.] A pustule or eruption on the skin; an irregular spot.—*v.t.* To mark with blotches.—**blotchy,** bloch′i, *a.* Marked with blotches, spots, or blurs.

blouse, blouz or blous, *n.* [Fr.] A light loose upper garment, resembling a smock frock, made of linen or cotton, and worn by men as a protection from dust or in place of a coat; also, a garment of nearly the same form and of various materials worn by women and children.

blow, blō, *v.i.—blew, blown, blowing.* [A.Sax. *bláwan;* allied to G. *blähen,* to blow, Icel. *blása,* Goth. *blésan,* G. *blasen,* to blow, to blow a wind instrument; also to E. *blow,* to bloom, *bladder, blast,* etc., and L. *flo, flare,* to breathe or blow.] To make a current of air, as with the mouth, a bellows, etc.; to constitute or form a current of air; to be a wind: often used with an indefinite *it* for the subject (*it blew* strongly yesterday); to pant; to puff; to breathe hard or quick; to give out sound by being blown, as a horn or trumpet; to boast; to brag: in this sense colloq.—*To blow over,* to pass away after having spent its force (the storm *blew over*).—*To blow up,* to be broken and scattered by an explosion.—*To blow upon,* to bring into disfavor or discredit; to render stale, unsavory, or worthless; also to inform upon.—*v.t.* To throw or drive a current of air upon; to drive by a current of air; to sound by the breath (a wind instrument); to form by inflation (to *blow* a glass bottle); to swell by injecting air into; to put out of breath by fatigue; to scatter or shatter by explosives (to *blow* up, to *blow* to pieces).—*To blow out,* to extinguish by a current of air; to scatter (one's brains) by firearms.—*To blow up,* to fill with air; to swell; to inflate; to puff up; to blow into a blaze; to burst in pieces and scatter by explosion; to scold: in this sense colloq.—*n.* A gale of wind; a blast; the breathing or spouting of a whale. —**blower,** blō′ėr, *n.* One who or that which blows; a blowing engine. —**blowy,** blō′i, *a.* Windy; gusty.—**blowfly,** *n.* A name of various species of flies (dipterous insects) which deposit their eggs on flesh, and thus taint it.—**blowhole,** *n.* The nostril of a cetacean, situated on the highest part of the head; a hole in the ice to which whales and seals come to breathe.—**blowpipe,** *n.* An instrument by which a current of air or gas is driven through a flame so as to direct it upon a substance, an intense heat being created by the rapid supply of oxygen and the concentration of the flame; a pipe or tube through which poisoned arrows are blown by the breath, used by South American Indians and natives of Borneo.

blow, blō, *v.i.—blew, blown.* [A.Sax. *blówan,* to bloom or blossom; D. *bloeijen,* G. *blühen;* allied to the other verb *to blow,* and to L. *florere,* to bloom.] To flower; to blossom; to bloom, as plants.—*v.t.*‡ To make to blow or blossom.—*n.* A mass of blossoms; the state or condition of blossoming or flowering; the highest state of anything; bloom; an ovum or egg deposited by a fly; a flyblow.—

blown, blōn, *p.* and *a.* Fully expanded or opened, as a flower.

blow, blō, *n.* [Akin to O.D. *blauwen,* to strike; D. *blouwen,* to beat flax; G. *bleuen,* to cudgel; and perhaps also with *blue.* BLUE.] A stroke with the hand or fist, or a weapon; a knock; an act of hostility; a sudden calamity; a sudden or severe evil; mischief or damage received.—*At a blow,* by one single action; at one effort; suddenly.

blowze, blouz, *n.* [From the same root as *blush.*] *Obs.* A ruddy fat-faced woman; a blowzy woman.—**blowzed, blowzy,** blouzd, blou′zi, *a.* Ruddyfaced; fat and ruddy; high-colored.

blubber, blub′ėr, *n.* [A lengthened form of *blub, blob, bleb;* perhaps from same root as that of *blow, bladder.*] The fat of whales and other large sea animals, from which train oil is obtained; a gelatinous mass of various kinds; the sea-nettle; a jellyfish.—*v.i.* To weep, especially in such a manner as to swell the cheeks or disfigure the face.—*v.t.* To disfigure with weeping.

blucher, blöch′ėr, *n.* A strong leather half boot or high shoe, named after Field Marshal von *Blücher.*

bludgeon, bluj′on, *n.* [Origin unknown; perhaps allied to G. *blotzen,* to strike, D. *blutsen,* to bruise.] A short stick, with one end loaded or thicker and heavier than the other, and used as an offensive weapon.

blue, blū, *n.* [Same as Sc. *blae,* Icel. *blár,* livid; Dan. *blaa,* D. *blaauw,* G. *blau,* blue; connected with *blow,* a blow producing a blue color. Akin *blemish.*] One of the primary colors; the color of the clear sky or deep sea; azure; what is blue; a dye or pigment of this hue.—*a.* Of the color of blue; sky-colored; azure.—*v.t.—blued, bluing.* To make blue; to dye of a blue color.—**bluely,** blū′li, *adv.* With a blue hue or shade. —**blueness,** blū′nes, *n.* The quality of being blue; a blue hue or color.—**blues,** blūz, *n.* A type of song of melancholy character and slow tempo written in characteristic key.—**bluish,** blū′ish, *a.* Blue in a slight degree; somewhat blue.—**bluishness,** blū′ish•nes, *n.*—**blue baby,** An infant with a bluish color from congenital heart disease.—**Bluebeard,** *n.* Personage in medieval tale, synonymous with wife-murderer.—**bluebird,** *n.* A small bluish bird with a red breast very common in the United States.—**bluebook,** *n.* In the U. S. a directory of persons of social prominence. In colleges, a blue-covered booklet for writing examinations.—**bluebottle,** *n.* A composite plant found frequently in cornfields; a fly with a large blue belly.—**bluecap,** *n.* The blue titmouse.—**bluecoat,** *n.* A person wearing a blue coat as a special dress.—**bluefish,** *n.* A name of certain American fishes, one of them a food fish allied to the mackerel, common on the Atlantic coast of N. America. —**blue devils,** *n. pl.* A colloquial phrase for dejection, hypochondria, or lowness of spirits; also for delirium tremens. Often called simply *the blues.*—**bluegrass,** *n.* A name of several grasses, more especially a grass of Kentucky, highly valued for pasturage and hay.—**blue gum,** *n.* A species of Eucalyptus or gum-tree with valuable medicinal properties, and now planted in malarious localities with beneficial results. It yields the drug Eucalyptol.—**bluejacket,** *n.* A sailor, from the color of his jacket. —**blueprint,** *n.* A photographic printing method using sensitized paper for the reproduction of engineering drawings; the print itself.—**blue ribbon,** *n.* The broad, dark-blue ribbon, worn by members of the order of the Garter; a piece of blue ribbon, usually with suitable words or markings, awarded as evidence of the winning of a highest award; hence a prize, a distinction.—**bluestone, blue vitriol,** *n.* Sulfate of copper.

bluff, bluf, *a.* [Perhaps from or allied to O.D. *blaf,* applied to a broad full face, also to a forehead rising straight up.] Broad and full: specially applied to a full countenance, indicative of frankness and good humor; rough and hearty; somewhat boisterous and unconventional; having a steep front (a *bluff* bank).—*v.t.* To deceive or impose upon, by boisterous talk or action.—*n.* A high bank with a steep front; a bold headland; bold words or acts intended to daunt or test an opponent.

bluing, blū′ing, *n.* A blue liquid used in laundering to offset the yellow tinge of linen or cotton.

blunder, blun′dėr, *v.i.* [Allied to Icel. *blunda,* to doze, *blundr,* slumber, Dan. and Sw. *blund,* a nap, also to *blind, blend.*] To make a gross mistake, especially through mental confusion; to err stupidly; to move without direction or steady guidance; to flounder; to stumble, literally or figuratively.—*n.* A mistake through precipitance or mental confusion; a gross and stupid mistake.—**blunderer,** blun′dėr•ėr, *n.* One who is apt to blunder or to make gross mistakes.—**blunderingly,** blun′dėr•ing•li, *adv.* In a blundering manner.

blunderbuss, blun′dėr•bus, *n.* [A humorous corruption of D. *donderbus,* a blunderbuss—*donder,* thunder, and *bus,* a tube, gun, originally a box.] A short gun or firearm, with a large bore.

blunt, blunt, *a.* [Akin to Prov. G. *bludde,* a dull or blunt knife; Dan. *blunde,* Sw. and Icel. *blunda,* to doze, E. *blunder.*] Having a thick edge or point, as an instrument; dull; not sharp; dull in understanding; slow of discernment; abrupt in address; plain; unceremonious.—*v.t.* To dull the edge or point of, by making it thicker; to impair the force, keenness, or susceptibility of.—**bluntly,** blunt′li, *adv.* In a blunt manner; plainly; abruptly; without delicacy or the usual forms of civility.—**bluntness,** blunt′nes, *n.* The state or quality of being blunt.

blur, blėr, *n.* [Probably a form of *blear.*] Something that obscures or soils; a blot; a stain; confused appearance, as produced by indistinct vision.—*v.t.*—*blurred, blurring.* To obscure without quite effacing; to render indistinct; to confuse and bedim; to cause imperfection of vision in; to dim; to sully; to stain; to blemish (reputation).

blurt, blėrt, *v.t.* [Perhaps imitative of abrupt sound made by the lips.] To utter suddenly or inadvertently; to divulge unadvisedly: commonly with *out.*

blush, blush, *v.i.* [A.Sax. *blísian, blysian,* allied to Dan. *blusse,* to blaze, to blush, D. *blos,* a blush, *blozen,* to blush; akin *blaze, blow.*] To redden in the cheeks or over the face, as from a sense of guilt, shame, confusion, or modesty; to exhibit a red or rosy color; to bloom.—*n.* The act of blushing; the suffusion of the cheeks or the face generally with a red color through confusion, shame, diffidence, or the like; a red or reddish color; a rosy tint.—*At the first blush,* at the first review or consideration of a matter.—**blushful,** blush′fu̦l, *a.* Full of blushes.—**blushingly,** blush′ing•li, *adv.* In a blushing manner; with blushes.

bluster, blus′tėr, *v.i.* [A kind of intens. of *blow;* akin to *blast, blister.*] To roar and be tumultuous, as wind; to be boisterous; to be loud, noisy, or swaggering; to bully; to swagger.—*v.t.* To utter or effect in a blustering manner or with noise and violence; with *out,* or other prep.—*n.* A violent blast of wind; a gust; noisy talk; swaggering; boisterousness.—**blusterer,** blus′tėr•ėr, *n.* One who blusters; a swaggerer; a bully.—**blusteringly,** blus′tėr•ing•li, *adv.* In a blustering manner.—**blusterous, blustery,** blus′tėr•us, blus′tėr•i, *a.* Noisy; tumultuous; tempestuous.

boa, bō′a, *n.* [L., a water-serpent.] The generic and common name of certain serpents destitute of fangs and venom, having a prehensile tail, and including some of the largest species of serpents, the constrictor being 30 or 40 feet long; a long round article of dress for the neck, made of fur.

boar, bōr, *n.* [A.Sax. *bár*=D. *beer,* O.H.G. *pér,* M.H.G. *ber,* a boar; perhaps akin to *bear* (the animal).] The male of swine: when applied to the wild species the term is used without reference to sex.—**boarish,** bōr′ish, *a.* Pertaining to or resembling a boar; swinish; brutal.

board, bōrd, *n.* [A.Sax. *bord,* table, plank, deck or side of a ship=Icel. Dan. G. *bord,* Goth. *baurd,* D. *boord;* allied probably to verb *bear. Border, broider,* are akin.] A piece of timber sawed thin, and of considerable length and breadth compared with the thickness; a table; hence, what is served on a board or table; food; diet; specifically, daily food obtained for a stipulated sum at the table of another; a council table; a number of persons having the management, direction, or superintendence of some public or private office or trust; the deck or side of a ship or boat, or its interior part (on *board,* to fall over *board*); a table or frame for a game, as chess, checkers, etc.; a kind of thick stiff paper; a sheet of substance formed by layers of paper pasted together, usually in compounds (as, card*board,* mill-*board*); one of the two stiff covers on the sides of a book.—*The boards,* the stage of a theater.—*v.t.* To lay or spread with boards; to cover with boards; to place at board, or where food or food and lodging are to be had; to furnish with food, or food and lodging, for a compensation; to go on board a vessel; to enter a vessel by force in combat.—*v.t.* To live at board; to live as a boarder.—**boarder,** bōrd′ėr, *n.* One furnished with food or food and lodging at another's house at a stated charge; one who boards a ship in action.—**boarding-house,** *n.* A house where board or board and lodging is furnished.—**boarding school,** *n.* A school in which pupils are boarded and lodged as well as taught.

boast, bōst, *v.i.* [Probably of Celtic origin; comp. W. *bost,* a boast, *bostio,* to boast. Corn. *bostye,* to boast.] To speak in high praise of one's self or belongings; to use exulting, pompous, or pretentious language; to brag; to exult; to glory; to vaunt; to bluster.—*v.t.* To display in ostentatious language; to speak of with pride, vanity, or exultation; to magnify or exalt (strength, genius); to vaunt; often *refl.*—*n.* A statement expressive of ostentation, pride, or vanity; a vaunting or bragging; a brag; the cause of boasting; occasion of pride, vanity, or laudable exultation.—**boaster,** bōst′ėr, *n.* One who boasts, glories, or vaunts with exaggeration or ostentatiously; a bragger.—**boastful,** bōst′ful, *a.* Given to boasting.—**boastfully,** bōst′fu̦l•li, *adv.* In a boastful manner.—**boastfulness,** bōst′fu̦l•nes, *n.*—**boastingly,** bōst′ing•li, *adv.* Boastfully; with boasting.

boat, bōt, *n.* [A.Sax. *bát*=Icel. *bátr,* D. L.G. and G. *boot,* a boat. Similar forms occur also in Celtic, as Ir. W. *bad.* Cael. *bata.*] A small open vessel or watercraft, usually moved by oars or rowing; any sailing vessel, but usually described by another word denoting its use or mode of propulsion; as, a packet-*boat,* steam*boat,* etc.—*v.t.* To transport in a boat.—*v.i.* To go or sail in a boat.—**boatbill,** *n.* A bird of the heron family, inhabiting South America, and named from having a bill resembling a boat with the keel uppermost.—**boat hook,** *n.* An iron hook with a point on the back, fixed to a long pole, to pull or push a boat.—**boathouse,** *n.* A house or shed for protecting boats from the weather.—**boatman,** bōt′man, *n.* A man who manages a boat; a rower of a boat.—**boatswain,** bōt′swān or bō′sn, *n.* [A.Sax, *bátswan*—*bát,* boat, and *swan,* swain.] A ship's officer who has charge of the sails, rigging, anchors, cables, etc., and who pipes or summons the crew to their duty.

bob, bob, *n.* [Perhaps imitative or suggestive of abrupt, jerky motion; in some of its senses allied to Gael. *babag, baban,* a tassel.] A general name for any small round object playing loosely at the end of a cord, line, chain, etc., as a knot of worms on a string used in fishing for eels, the bail or weight at the end of a pendulum, plumbline, and the like; a short jerking action or motion; a shake or jog; a blow.—**bob,** bob, *n.* A shilling. [Colloq.] *Bell-ringing,* a peal of courses or sets of changes.—*v.t. bobbed, bobbing.* To move in a short, jerking manner; to perform with a jerky movement; to cut short, as hair or a horse's tail; to beat or strike; to deceive; to defraud of (*Shak.*)‡.—*v.i.* To play backward and forward; to play loosely against anything; to make a quick, jerky motion, as a rapid bow or obeisance; to angle or fish with a bob, or by giving the hook a jerking motion in the water.—**bobtail,** bob′tāl, *n.* A short tail or a tail cut short; the rabble; used in contempt, as in the phrase *ragtag and bobtail.*

bobbin, bob′in, *n.* [Fr. *bobine,* from L. *bombus,* a humming sound, or more probably connected with E. *bob.*] A small cylindrical piece of wood with a head or flange at one or both ends, on which thread or yarn is wound for use in sewing, weaving, etc.—**bobbinet,** bob′in•et, *n.* A machine-made cotton net, originally imitated from the lace made by means of a pillow and bobbins.

bobolink, bob′ō•lingk, *n.* American migratory bird known in southern U. S. as the reedbird or ricebird.

Boche, bosh, *n.* [Fr. of disputed origin. Perhaps short form of *Alboche,* slang for *Allemand,* a German.] A term of opprobrium for a German.

bode, bōd, *v.t.*—*boded, boding.* [A. Sax. *bodian,* to announce, to proclaim, from *bod,* an edict. a message; Icel, *botha,* to proclaim; to bode; A. Sax. *boda,* D. *bode,* G. *bote,* a messenger; allied to *bid.*] To portend; to foreshow; to presage; to indicate something future by signs; to be the omen of.—*v.i.* To be ominous.—**bodement,** bōd′ment, *n.* An omen; portent; prognostic.—**boding,** bōd′-ing, *a.* Portentous; ominous.—*n.* A portent; an omen.

bode, bōd, pret. of *bide.*

bodice, bod′is, *n.* [Formerly *bodies,* pl. of *body,* being originally in two pieces.] The body part of a woman's dress; a kind of waistcoat; stays; a corset.

bodkin, bod′kin, *n.* [From W. *bidogyn,* a dagger, dim. of *bidog,* Gael. *biodag,* a short sword.] Originally a dagger; now a pointed pin of steel, ivory, or the like, for piercing holes in cloth; a blunted needle for drawing a ribbon, cord, or string through a loop, or a pin for keeping up the hair; to sit *bodkin,* to sit squeezed between two persons.

body, bod′i, *n.* [A.Sax. *bodig,* a body—O.H.G. *potach,* later *botech, bodech,* body; comp. Gael. *bodhaig,* the body.] The frame or material organized substance of an animal, in distinction from the soul, spirit, or vital principle; the main central or principal part of anything, as distinguished from subordinate parts, such as the extremities, branches, wings, etc.; a person; a human being; now generally forming a compound with *some* or *no* preceding; a number of individuals spoken of collectively, united by some common tie or by some occupation; a corporation; any extended solid substance; matter; any substance or mass distinct from others; a united mass; a general collection; a code; a system; a certain consistency or density; substance; strength (as of liquors, paper, etc.).—*v.t.*—*bodied, bodying.* To produce in some form; to embody; to invest with a body.—**bodiless,** bod′i•les, *a.* Having no body or material form; incorporeal. —**bodily,** bod′i•li, *a.* Pertaining to or concerning the body; of or belonging to the body or to the physical constitution; not mental; corporeal. ∴ *Bodily*, relating to or connected with the body as a whole; opposed to *mental; corporal*, relating to the body as regards outward bearings; *corporeal*, relating to its nature; opposed to *spiritual*. Hence *bodily* form, *corporal* punishment, *corporeal* existence.—*adv.* Corporeally; united with a body or matter; entirely; completely (to remove a thing *bodily*). —**bodyguard,** *n.* The guard that protects or defends one's person; lifeguard.—**body snatcher,** *n.* One who robs burying-places of dead bodies.

Boeotian, bē•ō′shun, *a.* Of or relating to Boeotia, thick-witted, dull, in distinction from *Attic*, the inhabitants of Attica.

Boer, bör or bö′er, *n.* [D., a peasant, farmer.] The name applied to the Dutch colonists of South Africa engaged in agriculture or cattle-breeding.

bog, bog, *n.* [Gael. and Ir. *bog*, soft, moist, *bogan, bogach*, a quagmire.] A piece of wet, soft, and spongy ground, where the soil is composed mainly of decaying and decayed vegetable matter; a piece of mossy ground or where peat is found; a quagmire or morass.—*v.t.*—*bogged, bogging.* To whelm or plunge in mud or mire.—**boggy,** bog′i. *a.* Pertaining to or resembling a bog; full of bogs; marshy; swampy; miry.—**bogtrotter,** *n.* A derisive term for an inhabitant of a boggy country, applied especially to the Irish peasantry.

bogey, bogy, bō′gi, *n.* [W. *bwg, bwgan*, a hobgoblin, scarecrow, *bugbear*.] A hobgoblin; a wicked spirit. —*Old Bogey*, the devil.

boggle, bog′l, *v.i.*—*boggled, boggling.* [Probably connected with *bogey*, Prov. E. *bogle*, a goblin.] To doubt; to hesitate; to stop, as if afraid to proceed or as if impeded by unforeseen difficulties; to waver; to shrink; to play fast and loose; to shilly-shally.—**boggler,** bog′lėr, *n.* A doubter; a timorous man; a waverer; an inconstant person.

bogus, bō′gus, *a.* [A word of uncertain origin. It first appeared in America, having been originally applied, it is said, in 1827, to an apparatus for coining spurious money.] Counterfeit; spurious; sham; pretended. [Originally Amer.]

bohea, bō•hē′ *n.* [Said to be from a mountain in China called *Voo-y*.] An inferior kind of black tea: sometimes applied to black teas in general.

Bohemian, bō•hē′mi•an, *n.* [Fr. *Bohémien*, a gypsy, because the first of that wandering race that entered France were believed to be Hussites driven from Bohemia, their native country.] A person, especially an artist or literary man, who leads a free, often somewhat dissipated life, despising conventionalities generally. —**Bohemianism,** bō•hē′mi•an•izm, *n.* The life or habits of a Bohemian.

boil, boil, *v.i.* [O.Fr. *boiller*, Fr. *bouillir*, L. *bullare, bullire*, to boil, to bubble, from *bulla*, a bubble. *Bill* (a paper), *billet, bullet*, are of same origin.] To be in a state of ebullition; to bubble by the action of heat, as water or other fluids; to exhibit a swirling or swelling motion; to seethe, as waves; to be violently agitated or excited, as the blood; to be subjected to the action of boiling water in cooking, etc., as meat.—*v.t.* To put into a state of ebullition; to cause to be agitated or bubble by the application of heat; to collect, form, or separate by the application of heat, as sugar, salt; to subject to the action of heat in a boiling liquid, as meat in cooking; to prepare in a boiling liquid; to seethe.—**boiler,** boil′ėr, *n.* A person who boils; a vessel, generally a large vessel of iron, copper, etc., in which anything is boiled in great quantities; a strong metallic vessel, usually of wrought iron or steel plates riveted together, in which steam is generated for driving engines or other purposes.—*Boiling point*, the degree of heat at which a fluid is converted into vapor with ebullition, as water at 212° Fahr., mercury at 675°, etc.—*Boiling springs*, springs or fountains which give out water at the boiling point or at a high temperature, as the geysers of Iceland and in the Yellowstone region in the United States.

boil, boil, *n.* [O.E. *bile, byle*, A.Sax. *byl*, a blotch, a sore; D. *buil*, G. *beule*, a boil; Icel. *bóla*, a blain or blister; Dan. *byld*, a boil.] An inflamed and painful suppurating tumor.

boisterous, bois′tėr•us, *a.* [Probably from W. *bwystus*, brutal, ferocious, *bwyst*, wildness, ferocity; perhaps connected with *boast*.] Violent; stormy; turbulent; furious; tumultuous; noisy.—**boisterously,** bois′tėr•us•li, *adv.* In a boisterous manner.—**boisterousness,** bois′tėr•us•nes, *n.* The state or quality of being boisterous.

bold, bōld, *a.* [A.Sax. *beald, bald*, bold, courageous = Icel. *ballr*, D. *bout*, O.H.G. *bald*, bold.] Daring; courageous; brave; intrepid; fearless, as a man; requiring or exhibiting courage in execution; executed with courage and spirit, as a deed; rude; forward; impudent; overstepping usual bounds; presuming upon sympathy or forbearance; showing liberty or license; striking to the eye; markedly conspicuous; steep; abrupt; prominent.—**boldly,** bōld′li, *adv.* In a bold manner; courageously; intrepidly; forwardly; insolently; abruptly, etc.—**boldness,** bōld′nes, *n.* The quality of being bold, in all the senses of the word; courage; bravery; confidence; assurance; forwardness; steepness; abruptness.—**bold-faced,** *a.* Impudent.

bole, bōl, *n.* [From Icel. *bolr, bulr*, Dan. *bul*, trunk, stem of a tree; probably of same root as *bowl, bulge*, etc.] The body or stem of a tree.

bole, bōl, *n.* [Fr. *bol*, bole, a bolus, L. *bolus*, from Gr. *bolos*, a clod of earth.] A friable clayey shale or earth of various kinds used as a pigment, generally yellow, or yellowish-red, or brownish-black, from the presence of iron oxide. These earths were formerly employed as astringent, absorbent, and tonic medicines, and they are still in repute in the East; they are also used occasionally as veterinary medicines in Europe. Armenian bole is used as a coarse red pigment.

bolero, bō•ler′ō, *n.* [Sp., from *bola*, a ball.] A favorite dance in Spain.

boll, bōl, *n.* [G. *bolle*, a seed vessel of flax, D. *bol*, a round body; same root as *bole*, a stem.] The pod or capsule of a plant, as of flax.—**boll weevil,** *n.* A weevil, the larva of which feeds on cotton bolls.

bollard, bol′lärd, *n.* [Allied to *bole*, the stem of a tree.] A strong post fixed vertically into the ground on a wharf or quay; a kind of stanchion in a ship or boat.

bologna, bo•lō′nya, *n.* A large sausage made of bacon, veal, and pork suet, chopped fine, and enclosed in a skin.

Bolshevik, bōl•she′vik, *n.* The Russian name for the majority party, as opposed to the minority (*mensheviki*), that took over the government in 1917.—**bolshevism,** bōl′she•vizm, *n.*

bolster, bōl′stėr, *n.* [A.Sax. D. Dan. and Sw. *bolster*, Icel. *bólstr*, G. *polster*, a cushion, a bolster; root *bol, bul*, as in *bulge*, etc., and term. *-ster*, as in *holster*.] A long pillow or cushion used to support the head of persons lying on a bed; something resembling a bolster more or less in form or application, as a pad or quilt used to prevent pressure; a compress, a cushioned or padded part of a saddle; the part of a cutting tool which joins the end of the handle; a hollow tool for punching holes, etc.—*v.t.* To furnish or support with a bolster, pillow, or any soft pad; to pad; to stuff; *fig.* to support; to maintain: usually implying support of an unworthy cause or object and generally with *up* (to *bolster up* his pretentions with lies).—**bolsterer,** bōl′stėr•ėr, *n.* One who bolsters; a supporter; an upholder; a standby.

bolt, bōlt, *n.* [A.Sax. *bolt*, an arrow, a bolt; Dan. *bolt*, a bolt, an iron peg, a fetter, G. *bolz, bolzen*, an arrow, a bolt or large nail.] An arrow; a thunderbolt; a stream of lightning; a stout metallic pin used for holding objects together, frequently screw-threaded at one extremity to receive a nut; a movable bar for fastening a door, gate, window sash, or the like; especially that portion of a lock which is protruded from or retracted within the case by the action of the key; an iron to fasten the legs of a prisoner; a shackle.—*v.t.* To fasten or secure with a bolt or iron pin, as a door, a plank, fetters, etc.; to swallow hurriedly or without chewing, as food (colloq.); to start or spring game.—*v.i.* To shoot forth suddenly; to spring out with speed and suddenness; to start forth like a bolt; to run out of the regular path; to start and run off; to take flight; to make one's escape (colloq.).—*adv.* As straight as a bolt; suddenly; with sudden meeting or collision (to come *bolt* against a person).—**bolter,** bōlt′-ėr, *n.* One who fastens with a bolt; one who makes his escape or runs away; a horse given to starting off or running away.

bolt, bōlt, *v.t.* [O.Fr. *buleter, bulter* (Mod. Fr. *bluter*), with change of *r* into *l*, from an older form *bureter*, from *bure*, the thick woolen cloth of which bolting-sieves are made, from L. *burra*, coarse cloth.] To sift or pass through a sieve so as to separate the coarser from the finer particles, as bran from flour; *fig.* to sift or separate good from bad, or the like.—**bolter,** bōlt′ėr, *n.* One who bolts; a sieve or apparatus for bolting.—**bolthead,** *n.* A long straight-necked glass vessel for chemical distillations; a matrass or receiver.—**boltrope,** *n.* A rope to which the edges of sails are sewed to strengthen them.

bolus, bō′lus, *n.* [L. *bolus*, a bit, a morsel, a lump, Gr. *bōlos*, a clod, a lump.] A soft round mass of anything medicinal to be swallowed at once, larger and less solid than an ordinary pill.

bomb, bom, *n.* [Fr. *bombe*, a bomb, from L. *bombus*, Gr. *bombos*, a hollow deep sound. Probably imitative, like E. *bum, boom*, to make a deep hollow sound.] A projectile filled with explosive or flammable materials fired from a mortar or dropped from an airplane.—**bombproof,** *a.* Secure against the force of bombs; capable of resisting the shock or explosion of shells.—**bombshell,** *n.* A spherical shell; a bomb.—**bombsight,** bom′-sīt, *n.* A sighting device for controlling the dropping of aerial bombs on a specific target.—**bombard,** bom′bärd, *n.* [Fr. *bombarde*, a piece of ordnance.] A piece of short thick ordnance with a large mouth, formerly used; a barrel; a drinking vessel (*Shak.*).—*v.t.*, bom•bärd′. To attack with bombs; to fire shells at or into; to shell: sometimes used somewhat loosely for to assault with artillery of any kind.—**bombardier,** bom•bär•dēr′, *n.* In the British army, a noncommissioned artillery officer; a crew member on a bomber who aims and releases aerial bombs.—*Bombardier beetle*, the common name of many coleopterous insects, possessing a remarkable power of violently expelling from the anus a pungent, acrid fluid, accompanied by a smart report.—**bombardment,** bom•bärd′ment, *n.* The act of bombarding; the act of throwing shells and shot into a town, fortress, etc.—**bombardon,** bom•bär′don, *n.* [Fr., ultimately from L. *bombus*, a hollow sound.] A large-sized and grave-toned musical instrument of the trumpet kind, in sound not unlike the ophicleide.

bombasine, bombazine, bom•ba•-zēn′, *n.* [Fr. *bombasin, bombasine*, It. *bombicina*, bombasin, L. *bombycinus*, made of silk or cotton, from Gr. *bombyx, bombykos*, a silkworm, silk.] A slight twilled fabric, of which the warp is silk (or cotton) and the weft worsted.

bombast, bom′bast, *n.* [Originally padding made of cotton, of same origin as *bombasine*.] Cotton or other stuff of soft, loose texture used to stuff garments‡; hence, high-sounding words; inflated or turgid language; fustian; words too big and high-sounding for the occasion.—**bombastic,** bom•bas′tik, *a.* Characterized by bombast; high-sounding; turgid; inflated. —**bombastically,** bom•bas′tik•al•li, *adv.* In a bombastic or inflated manner or style.

bona fide, bō′na fi′dē. [L.] With good faith; without fraud or deception: frequently used as a sort of adjective.

bonanza, bo•nan′zä, *n.* [Sp. good weather, L. *bonus*.] Good luck, good output of farms, mines, stocks.

Bonapartist, bō′na•pärt•ist, *n.* One attached to the policy or the dynasty of the Bonapartes; one who favors the claims of the Bonaparte family to the throne of France.

bonbon, bon′bon, *n.* [Fr.] Some article of sugar confectionery; a sugarplum.

bond, bond, *n.* [A form of *band*. BAND, BIND.] Anything that binds, fastens, confines, or holds things together, as a cord, a chain, a rope; hence, *pl.* fetters, chains, and so imprisonment, captivity; a binding power or influence; a uniting tie (the *bond* of affection); an obligation imposing a moral duty, as by a vow or promise; an obligation or deed by which a person binds himself, his heirs, etc., to do or not to do a certain act, usually to pay a certain sum on or before a certain day; *masonry*, the connection of one stone or brick with another by lapping them over each other in building so that an inseparable mass may be formed, which could not be the case if every vertical joint were over that below it; the state of being bonded, as goods in bond, that is stored in a bonded warehouse until customs or excise duties have been paid on them.—*a.* [For *bound*.] In a state of servitude or slavery; captive.—*v.t.* To put in bond or into a bonded warehouse, as goods liable for customs or excise duties, the duties remaining unpaid till the goods are taken out.—*Bonded warehouse*, a licensed warehouse or store in which goods liable to government duties may be lodged after bond has been given on behalf of the owners of the goods, for the payment of such duty on their removal for home consumption.—**bondage,** bon′dij, *n.* Slavery or involuntary servitude; thraldom; captivity; imprisonment; restraint of a person's liberty by compulsion.—**bonder,** bon′dėr, *n.* One who bonds; one who deposits goods in a bonded warehouse; one of the stones which reach a considerable distance into or entirely through a wall for the purpose of binding it together.—**bondholder,** *n.* A person who holds a bond for money lent.—**bondmaid,** bond′mād, *n.* A female slave, or one bound to service without wages, in opposition to a hired servant.—**bondman, bondsman,** bond′man, bondz′man, *n.* [Dan. *bonde*, pl. *bōnder*, yeoman, peasant. Same as A.S. *bonda*, a house-holder, the *-band* of *husband*.] Serf, with mistaken meaning of one bound by bond. At the Norman Conquest the yeoman sank to a serf, and the meaning changed to suit. A man slave, or one bound to service without wages. —**bond servant,** *n.* A slave; a bondman or bondwoman.—**bondwoman,** *n.* A woman slave.

bone, bōn, *n.* [A.Sax. *bān*, a bone; cog. D. and Dan. *been*, Icel. and G. *bein*, a bone, the lower part of the leg.] One of the pieces of which the skeleton of an animal is composed; the substance of which the skeleton of vertebrate animals is composed; a firm hard substance of a dull white color, more or less hollow or cellular internally, and consisting of earthy matters (chiefly calcium phosphate and some calcium carbonate) about 67 per cent, and animal matter 33 per cent; *pl.* pieces of bone held between the fingers somewhat after the manner of castanets, and struck together in time to music of the Negro minstrel type.—*Bone of contention*, a subject of dispute and rivalry, probably from the manner in which dogs quarrel over a bone.—*To make no bones*, to make no scruple: a metaphor taken from a dog, which greedily swallows meat, bones included.—*v.t.*—*boned, boning*. To take out the bones from, as in cookery; to put whalebone into (stays).—**bony,** bō′-ni, *a.* Pertaining to, consisting of, or resembling bone; having prominent bones.—**bone black,** *n.* Animal charcoal; the black carbonaceous substance into which bones are converted by charring in close vessels.

bonfire, bon′fīr, *n.* [M. E. *banfyre*, bone-fire, a ceremonial burning of bones.] A fire made as an expression of public joy and exultation.

Boniface, bon'i•fās, *n.* [The name of the landlord in Farquhar's *Beaux' Stratagem.*] A sleek, jolly, good-natured landlord or innkeeper.

bonito, bo•nē'to, *n.* [Sp.] A fish of several species, one of which is the striped-bellied tunny common in tropical seas, one of the fishes which pursue the flying fish.

bon-mot, bon•mō', *n.* [Fr. *bon,* good, and *mot,* a word.] A witticism; a witty repartee.

bonnet, bon'et, *n.* [Fr. *bonnet,* Sp. and Pg. *bonete,* L.L. *bonetus, boneta,* originally a sort of stuff so called; perhaps of Oriental origin.] A covering for the head worn by men; a cap; a covering for the head worn by women, and distinguished from a hat by details which vary according to the fashion; anything that covers the head or top of an object, as the cowl or wind-cap of a chimney, etc.—*v.t.* To force the hat over the eyes of, with the view of mobbing or hustling.—*v.i.* To pull off the bonnet; to make obeisance. (*Shak.*)

bonny, bon'i, *a.* [Doubtfully derived from Fr. *bonne,* good.] Handsome; beautiful; fair or pleasant to look upon; pretty; fine.

bonspiel, bon'spēl, *n.* [Dan. *bondespil,* a rustic game, from *bonde,* a rustic (A.Sax. *bonda*), and *spil,* G. *spiel,* a game.] In Scotland, a match in the game of curling between parties belonging to different districts.

bon ton, bon ton', *n.* [Fr. 'good tone'.] The style of persons in high life; high mode or fashion; fashionable society.

bonus, bō'nus, *n.* [L. *bonus,* good.] A sum given or paid over and above what is required to be paid, as a premium given for a loan, or for a charter or other privilege granted to a company; an extra dividend or allowance to the shareholders of a joint stock company, holders of insurance policies, etc., out of accumulated profits; a sum paid to an employe over and above his stated pay in recognition of successful exertions.

bony, *a.* See BONE.

bonze, bonz, *n.* [Pg., a corruption of Japanese *busso,* a pious man.] The European name for a priest or monk of the religion of Fo or Buddha in China, Burma, Japan, etc.; there are both male and female bonzes living in monasteries.

booby, bö'bi, *n.* [Sp. *bobo,* a fool, the bird called the booby.] A dunce; a stupid fellow; a lubber; a bird allied to the gannet, apparently so stupid as to allow itself to be knocked on the head by a stick or caught by the hand.

boodle, bö'dl, *n.* [D. *boedel,* goods, lumber.] Goods fraudulently obtained; gain made by cheating in public office; lot, crowd, or pack.

boogie-woogie, bö'gi wö'gi, *n.* A blues style using melodic variations over a persistent bass rhythm.

book, bu̦k, *n.* [A.Sax. *boc,* a book, originally a beech tree; Icel. *bók,* a beech; D. *boek,* a book, a beech; G. *buch,* a book, *buche,* a beech; Slav. *bukva,* a book, *buk,* a beech. The words *book* and *beech* are closely akin, beechen tablets or pieces of beech bark having probably formed the early books.] A number of sheets of paper or other material folded, stitched, and bound together on edge, blank, written, or printed; a volume; a particular part (generally including several chapters or sections) of a literary composition; a division of a subject in the same volume; a register or record; a register containing commercial transactions or facts in proper form.—*v.t.* To enter, write, or register in a book; to secure the carriage or transmission of by purchasing a ticket for coach, rail, or steamer.—**bookish,** bu̦k'ish, *a.* Given to reading or study; more acquainted with books than with the world; pertaining to, contained in, or learned from books; theoretical.—**bookishness,** bu̦k'ish•nes, *n.* Addictedness to books; fondness for study.—**booklet,** bu̦k'let, *n.* A little book.—**bookbinder,** bu̦k'bīnd•ėr, *n.* One whose occupation is to bind books.—**bookbindery,** bu̦k'bīnd•ėr•i, *n.* A place where books are bound.—**bookbinding,** bu̦k'bīnd•ing, *n.* The act or practice of binding books; or of sewing the sheets and covering them with leather or other material.—**bookcase,** *n.* An upright case with shelves for holding books.—**bookkeeper,** *n.* One who keeps accounts; a person who has the charge of entering or recording business transactions or items of debit and credit in the regular set of books belonging to business houses.—**bookkeeping,** *n.* The art of recording mercantile transactions by keeping accounts in a book or set of books in such a manner as to give a permanent record of business transactions, so that at any time the true state of one's pecuniary affairs and mercantile dealings may be exhibited.—**bookmaker,** *n.* One who writes and publishes books; especially, a compiler; in betting phraseology, a person, generally a professional betting man, who wagers on the defeat of a specified horse or other competitor in a race; a layer as opposed to a backer.—**bookseller,** bu̦k'sel•ėr, *n.* One whose occupation is to sell books.—**bookstall,** *n.* A stall on which books are placed which are offered for sale.—**bookstand,** *n.* A stand or support to hold books for reading or reference.—**bookworm,** *n.* A worm or mite that eats holes in books; a person too much addicted to books or study.

boom, böm, *n.* [Akin to *beam,* from D. *boom,* a tree, a pole, a beam, Dan. *bom,* a rail or bar.] A long pole or spar run out from various parts of a vessel for extending the bottom of particular sails, as the jib-*boom,* main-*boom,* etc.; a strong beam, or an iron chain or cable, extended across a river or harbor to prevent ships from passing.

boom, böm, *v.i.* [An imitative word; comp. D. *bomme,* a drum; *bommen,* to drum; L. *bombus,* a humming sound. BOMB.] To make a sonorous, hollow, humming, or droning sound.—*n.* A deep hollow noise, as the roar of waves or the sound of distant guns: applied also to the cry of the bittern and the buzz of the beetle; a sudden briskness or rise in prices.

boomerang, böm'e•rang, *n.* A missile formed generally of a piece of hard wood, parabolic in shape, used by the Australian aborigines, and remarkable from the fact that when thrown returns near the thrower; a scheme or plan that recoils upon the user.—*v.i.* To reverse or recoil like a boomerang.

boon, bön, *n.* [Icel. *bón,* a request, a boon, Dan. and Sw. *bón*=A.Sax. *ben,* Icel. *bœn,* a prayer.] Originally a prayer, petition, or request; hence, that which is asked; a petition, favor; a grant; a benefaction; a benefit; a blessing; a great privilege.

boon, bön, *a.* [Norm. Fr. *boon,* Fr. *bon,* from L. *bonus,* good.] Gay; jovial; merry (a *boon* companion).

boor, bör, *n.* [A.Sax. *(ge)búr,* a countryman or farmer=D. *boer,* G. *bauer;* from A.Sax. *buan,* Icel. *búa,* to dwell, to inhabit, to cultivate; D. *bouwen,* G. *bauen,* to cultivate.] A countryman; a peasant; a rustic; a clown; hence, one who is rude in manners and illiterate.—**boorish,** bör'ish, *a.* Clownish; rustic; awkward in manners; illiterate.—**boorishly,** bör'ish•li, *adv.* In a clownish manner.—**boorishness,** bör'ish•nes, *n.* The state of being boorish.

boost, böst, *n.* A push that helps one over an obstacle; any help given; an increase in price, etc.—*v.t.* To give a boost to.—**booster,** böst'er, *n.* A person who enthusiastically promotes the welfare of another person or thing; a device that increases pressure or force.

boot, böt, *n.* [A.Sax. *bót,* reparation, amends; Icel. *bót,* remedy, amends; same root as in *better.*] Profit; gain; advantage; that which is given to supply the deficiency of value in one of the things exchanged.—*To boot* [A.Sax. *to-bóte*], in addition to; over and above; into the bargain.—*v.t.* To profit; to advantage; to avail; used impersonally (it *boots* us little; what *boots* it?).—**bootless,** böt'les, *a.* Without boot, profit, or advantage; unprofitable; unavailing; useless.—**bootlessly,** böt'les•li, *adv.* In a bootless or unprofitable manner.—**bootlessness,** böt'les•nes, *n.*

boot, böt, *n.* [Fr. *botte,* a butt, and also a boot, from resemblance in shape. BUTT.] An article of dress, generally of leather, covering the foot and extending to a greater or less distance up the leg; an instrument of torture fastened on to the leg, between which and the boot wedges were introduced and hammered in, often crushing both muscles and bones; the luggage box in a stagecoach, either on the front or the hind part; *pl.,* used as a singular noun, the servant in hotels who cleans the shoes of the guests, or part of whose work was originally to do so.—*v.t.* To put boots on.—**booted,** böt′ed, *a.* Equipped with boots having boots on.—**bootee,** böt•ē′, *n.* A half or short boot; also a child's knitted boot.—**bootjack,** *n.* An instrument for drawing off boots.—**bootrack,** *n.* A frame or stand to hold boots, especially with their tops downward.—**boot tree,** *n.* A shoe tree; an instrument for blocking or stretching boots or shoes.

Boötes, bo•ō′tēz, *n.* [Gr. *boōtēs,* a herdsman, from *bous,* an ox or cow.] A northern constellation, containing the star Arcturus.

booth, böth, *n.* [Icel. *búth,* Dan. and Sw. *bod,* G. *bude,* a booth; allied to Gael. *buth,* Slav. *bauda, buda,* Lith. *buda,* a booth, a hut.] A covered stall at a fair, market, exposition or polling place; a closed stall for privacy when telephoning.

booty, bö′ti, *n.* [Same as Icel. *byii,* Dan. *bytte,* exchange, barter, booty, from *byta,* to divide into portions, to deal out.] Spoil taken from an enemy in war; that which is seized by violence and robbery; plunder; pillage.

booze, böz, [M.E. *baus,* a drink.] *n.* Intoxicating liquor, generally of inferior quality.—*v.i.* To drink intoxicating liquor, especially excessively.—**boozer,** böz′er, *n.* One who boozes; a drunkard.

borage, bor′ij, *n.* [L.L. *borrago, borago,* from *borra,* hair, from its hairy leaves.] A plant allied to the forget-me-not, having very rough hairy leaves and pretty blue flowers, which were supposed to be cordial and were infused in drinks.

borax, bō′raks, *n.* [Sp. *borax,* Ar. *búrag,* saltpeter, from *barak,* to shine.] A natural salt, sodium tetraborate; also, obtained from boric acid in reaction to soda: used as a flux in soldering metals, and in making glass and artificial gems.—**boracic,** bō•ras′ik, *a.* Of, pertaining to, or produced from boron: same as *boric.*

border, bor′dėr, *n.* [Fr. *bordure, bord,* a border, *border,* to border, from the German. BOARD.] The outer part or edge of anything, as of a garment, piece of cloth, a country, etc.; margin; verge; brink; boundary; confine; frontier.—*v.i.* To have the edge or boundary adjoining; to be contiguous or adjacent; to approach; to come near: with *on* or *upon.*—*v.t.* To make a border to; to adorn with a border of ornaments; to form a border to; to touch at the edge or end; to be contiguous to; to limit.—**borderer,** bor′dėr•ėr, *n.* One who dwells on a border, or at the extreme part or confines of a country, region, or tract of land.—**borderland,** *n.* Land forming a border or frontier; an uncertain intermediate district.

bore, bōr, *v.t.*—*bored, boring.* [A.Sax. *borian;* Icel. *bora,* Sw. *borra,* Dan. *bore,* D. *boren,* G. *bohren,* to bore; of same root with L. *foro,* to bore.] To pierce or perforate and make a round hole in; to drill a hole in; to form by piercing or drilling (to *bore* a hole); to force a narrow and difficult passage through; to weary by tedious iteration or repetition; to tire by insufferable dullness; to tease; to annoy; to pester.—*v.i.* To pierce or enter by drilling, etc.; to push forward toward a certain point.—*n.* The hole made by boring; hence, the cavity or hollow of a gun, cannon, pistol, or other firearm; the caliber whether formed by boring or not; a person that tires or wearies, especially by trying the patience; a dull person who forces his company and conversation upon us; anything troublesome or annoying.—**boredom,** bōr′dum, *n.* The domain of bores; bores collectively; the state of being bored or of being a bore.—**borer,** bōr′ėr, *n.* One who or that which bores; a term sometimes applied to certain worms, insects, fishes, which penetrate foreign bodies.

bore, bōr, *n.* [Icel. *bára,* a wave or swell.] A sudden influx of the tide into the estuary of a river from the sea, the inflowing water rising and advancing like a wall and rushing with a tremendous noise against the current for a considerable distance.

bore, bōr, pret. of *bear* (which see).

boreal, bō′rē•al, *a.* [L. *borealis,* from *boreas,* the north wind.] Northern; pertaining to the north or the north wind.

boric, bōr′ik, *a.* [From *boron.*] Of, or pertaining to, the element boron.—*Boric acid,* boron in combination with oxygen and hydrogen.—**borate,** bō′rāt, *n.* A salt of boric acid.

born, born, pp. of *bear,* to bring forth.

borne, bōrn, pp. of *bear,* to carry, etc.

boron, bō′ron, *n.* [From *borax.*] Nonmetallic element present in combination, as in borax. Symbol, B; at. no., 5; at. wt., 10.811.

borough, bur′ō, *n.* [A.Sax. *burg, burh,* a fort, town, city; Icel. Sw. Dan. *borg,* Goth. *baurgo,* G. D. *burg;* root in A. Sax. *beorgan,* Goth. *bairgan,* G. *bergen,* to protect. From same root are *bury, borrow, burrow, barrow* (grave mound), etc.] A corporate town or township; a town with a properly organized municipal government.—**borough-English,** *n.* *Law,* a customary descent of estates to the youngest son instead of the eldest, or, if the owner leaves no son, descent to the youngest brother.

borrow, bor′rō, *v.t.* [A.Sax. *borgian,* properly to take on security, from *borg, borh,* security, from *beorgan,* to protect; G. and D. *borgen,* to borrow. BOROUGH.] To ask and obtain on loan, trust, or on credit, with the intention of returning or giving an equivalent for; to take or adopt from another or from a foreign source and use as one's own; to adopt; to appropriate; to imitate; to copy—**borrower,** bor′rō•ėr, *n.* One who borrows; one who takes what belongs to another and uses it as his own; a copier; an imitator; a plagiarist.

bort, bort, *n.* Diamonds too coarse for ornamental setting, or small fragments of pure diamonds, used, when reduced to a powder, for polishing and grinding.

boscage, bos′kij, *n.* [O.Fr. *boscage,* from the German. BUSH.] A mass of growing trees or shrubs; woods; groves or thickets; sylvan foliage.

bosh, bosh, *n.* [Turk., empty, vain, useless.] Nonsense; absurdity; trash.

bosk,† bosk, *n.* [An old form of *bush.*] A thicket; a small close natural wood, especially of bushes. (*Tenn.*)—**boskage,** *n.* BOSCAGE.—**bosky,** bos′ki, *a.* Bushy; covered with groves or thickets. (*Mil.*)

bosom, bu̦′zum, *n.* [A.Sax. *bósm,* D. *boezem,* G. *busen,* probably from root of *bow,* meaning literally a swelling or protruding part.] The breast of a human being; the folds of the dress about the breast; the seat of the tender affections, passions, inmost thoughts, wishes, secrets, etc.; embrace or compass (the *bosom* of the church); something likened to the human bosom (the *bosom* of the earth, of a lake, etc.).—*a.* Intimate; familiar; close; dear.—*v.t.* To enclose or harbor in the bosom; to embrace; to keep with care; to cherish intimately; to conceal; to embosom.

boss, bos, *n.* [Fr. *bosse,* a swelling, from O.H.G. *bózo,* a bunch or bundle, same root as G. *boszen,* to beat; E. *beat.*] A protuberant part; a round, swelling body; a projecting mass; a stud or knob; a protuberant ornament of silver, ivory, or other material, used on bridles, harness, etc.; *arch.* an ornament placed at the intersection of the ribs or groins in vaulted or flat roofs.—*v.t.* To ornament with bosses; to bestud; to emboss. (*Shak.*)—**bossy,** bos′i, *a.* Containing a boss; ornamented with bosses.

boss, bos, *n.* [D. *baas,* a master.] An employer; a master; a superintendent; a chief man.—*v.t.* and *i.* To control; to superintend.

bot, botfly. See BOTT.

botany, bot′a•ni, *n.* [As if from a form *botaneia,* from Gr. *botane,* herbage, a plant, from *boskō,* to feed.] The science which treats of the vegetable kingdom, dealing with the forms, structure, and tissues of plants, the laws or conditions which regulate their growth or development, the functions of their various organs, the classification of the various specific forms of plants, their distribution over the face of the globe, and their condition at various geological epochs.—*Botany Bay,* Sydney, N.S.W., from its botanical richness when discovered by Captain Cook, 1770; as a penal settlement, in 1787.—**botanic, botanical,** bo•tan′ik, bo•tan′ik•al, *a.* Pertaining to botany; relating to plants in general.—**botanically,** bo•tan′ik•al•li, *adv.* In a botanical manner; after the manner of a botanist;

according to a system of botany.—**botanist,** bot′an•ist, *n.* One skilled in botany; one versed in the knowledge of plants or vegetables, their structure, and generic and specific differences.—**botanize,** bot′an•īz, *v.i.* —*botanized, botanizing.* To study plants; to investigate the vegetable kingdom; to seek for plants with a view to study them.

botch, boch, *n.* [O.E. *bocche, botche,* a sore, a swelling, O.Fr. *boce,* a boss, a botch, a boil, a parallel form of *boss;* comp. O.D. *butse,* a boil, a swelling.] A swelling on the skin; a large ulcerous affection; a boil or blotch; a patch, or the part of a garment patched or mended in a clumsy manner; a part in any work bungled or ill-finished; bungled work generally.—*v.t.* To mark or cover with botches or boils†; to mend or patch in a clumsy manner; to perform or express in a bungling manner.—**botcher,** boch′ėr, *n.* One who botches; a clumsy workman at mending; a mender of old clothes; a bungler.—**botchery,**† boch′ėr•i, *n.* A botching, or that which is done by botching; clumsy workmanship. —**botchy,** boch′i, *a.* marked with botches; full of botches.

both, bōth, *a.* and *pron.* [A Scandinavian word=Icel. *báthir, baethi,* Sc. *baith,* Dan. *baade,* Goth. *bajoths,* G. *beide,* both. The first element is seen in A.Sax. *bátwa,* bothtwo, both, Goth. *bai,* both, L. *ambo,* G. *amphö,* Skr. *ubha,* both.] The one and the other; the two; the pair or the couple. In such a sentence as '*both* men were there', it is an adjective; in 'he invited James and John, and *both* went', it is a pronoun; in 'the men *both* went', 'he took them *both*', it is a pronoun in apposition to *men, them.* It is often used as a conjunction in connection with *and—both.* ∴ *and* being equivalent to as well the one as the other; not only this but also that; equally the former and the latter.

bother, boTHėr, *v.t.* [Probably a word of Irish origin; comp. Ir. *buaidhirt,* trouble, affliction; *buaidhrim,* I vex, disturb; Ir. and Gael. *buair,* to vex, trouble.] To perplex; to perturb; to tease; to annoy.—*v.i.* To trouble or worry one's self; to make many words or much ado.—*n.* A trouble, vexation, or plague.—**botheration,** boTH•ėr•ā′shon, *n.* The act of bothering, or state of being bothered; annoyance; trouble; vexation; perplexity.

bothy, both′i, *n.* [Gael. *bothag,* a cot, from same root as *booth.*] In Scotland a house for the accommodation of workpeople engaged in the same employment; a farm building in which the unmarried male or female servants or laborers are lodged.

botryoid, botryoidal, bot′ri•oid, bot•ri•oi′dal, *a.* [Gr. *botrys,* a bunch of grapes, and *eidos,* form.] Having the form of a bunch of grapes; like grapes, as a mineral presenting an aggregation of small globes.

bott, bot, bot, *n.* [Gael. *botus,* a bott, *boithag,* a maggot.] A name given to the larvae or maggots of several species of gadfly when found in the intestines of horses, under the hides of oxen, in the nostrils of sheep, etc.; generally in plural.—**botfly,** *n.* A fly that produces botts.

bottle, bot′l, *n.* [Fr. *bouteille,* from L.L. *buticula,* a dim. from *butica,* a kind of vessel, from Gr. *boutis,* a flask.] A hollow vessel of glass, leather, or other material, with a narrow mouth, for holding and carrying liquors; the contents of a bottle; as much as a bottle contains; hence, *fig. the bottle* is used as equivalent to strong drink in general; the practice of drinking (to be fond of *the bottle*).—*v.t.*—*bottled, bottling.* To put into bottles.—**bottler,** bot′lėr, *n.* One whose occupation it is to bottle wines, spirits, beer, or the like.—**bottlenose,** *n.* A whale measuring from 22 to 28 feet long, and having a beaked snout, occurring in high north latitudes; also, the caaing whale.

bottom, bot′om, *n.* [A.Sax. *botm,* bottom=D. *bodem,* Icel. *botn,* O.H.G. *podam,* Mod. G. *boden,* from same root as L. *fundus,* Gr. *pythmen,* base, bottom.] The lowest or deepest part of anything, as distinguished from the top; that on which anything rests or is founded; utmost depth either literally or figuratively; base; foundation; the ground under any body of water; the lower or hinder extremity of the trunk of an animal; the buttocks; the portion of a chair for sitting on; the seat; low land formed by alluvial deposits along a river; a dale; a valley; the part of a ship below the wales; hence, the ship itself; power of endurance; stamina; native strength.—*a.* At the bottom; lowest; undermost; having a low situation; alluvial.—*v.t.* To found or build upon; to base; to furnish with a bottom.—**bottomless,** bot′om•les, *a.* Without a bottom; hence, fathomless; whose bottom cannot be found by sounding.—**bottomry,** bot′om•ri, *n.* The act of borrowing money, and pledging the *bottom* of the ship, that is, the ship itself, as security for the repayment of the money.

bottom, bot′om, *n.* [W. *botwm,* a boss, a bud, a button.] A ball or skein of thread; a cocoon.—*v.t.* To wind round something, as in making a ball of thread.

botulism, bot′ū•lizm, *n.* [L. *botulus.*] Poisoning caused by a toxin from the bacillus *Clostridium botulinum,* occurring in improperly preserved food, usually home canned, and affecting the nervous system.

boudoir, bö′dwär, *n.* [Fr., from *bouder,* to pout, to sulk.] A small room to which a lady may retire to be alone, or in which she may receive her intimate friends.

bough, bou, *n.* [A. Sax. *bóg, bóh,* an arm, a shoulder, a bough; Icel. *bógr,* Dan. *boug, bov,* the shoulder, a vessel's bow; allied to Gr. *péchys,* the fore-arm, Skr. *bāhus,* the arm. *Bow* (of a ship) is the same word]. An arm or large branch of a tree.

bought, ba̤t, pret. & pp. of *buy* (which see).

bougie, bö′zhē, *n.* [Fr., a wax-candle, from Sp. *bugia,* from *Bugia,* in North Africa, whence wax candles were first brought.] A wax taper; *surg.* a slender flexible cylinder made of waxed linen or silk cord, or of caoutchouc, steel, German silver, etc., intended for introduction into the urethra, esophagus, or rectum, when those passages are obstructed, as by stricture.

bouillon, bö′yon, *n.* [Fr.] Broth; soup.

boulder, bōl′dėr, *n.* From Dan. *buldre,* E. dial. *bolder,* Sw. *bullra,* to make a loud noise, to thunder; Sw. dial *bullersten* (*sten*=stone), a large pebble; lit. a stone that makes a thundering noise.] A waterworn roundish stone of considerable size, and larger than a pebble; *geol.* applied to iceworn and smoothed blocks lying on the surface of the soil, or imbedded in the clays and gravels of the drift formation.

boule, boule-work, böl, böl′wėrk, *n.* Same as *Buhl.*

boulevard, böl′e•värd, *n.* [Fr., older forms *boulevert, bouleverse,* borrowed and altered from G. *bollwerk.* BULWARK.] Originally, a bulwark or rampart of a fortification or fortified town; hence a public walk or street occupying the site of demolished fortifications; now sometimes extended to any wide street or walk.

bounce, bouns, *v.i.*—*bounced, bouncing.* [O.E. *bounsen, bunsen,* to strike suddenly; L.G. *bunsen,* to knock; D. *bonzen,* to strike, bounce; *bons,* a bounce; imitative of the noise of a blow.] To make a sudden leap or spring; to jump or rush suddenly; to knock or thump; to boast or bluster; to brag.—*v.t.* To drive against anything suddenly and violently.—*n.* A heavy blow, thrust, or thump; a loud heavy sound; a sudden crack or noise; a boast; a piece of brag or bluster; boastful language; exaggeration; a bold or impudent lie.—*adv.* With a bounce or abrupt movement; abruptly (to come *bounce* into a room).—**bouncer,** bouns′ėr, *n.* One that bounces; a boaster; a bully; a bragging liar; a barefaced lie; something big or large of its kind.—**bouncing,** bouns′ing, *a.* Vigorous; strong; stout; exaggerated; excessive; big.

bound, bound, *n.* [O.Fr. *bodne, bonne,* a bound, limit (Fr. *borne*), from L.L. *bodina, bonna,* a boundary, from Armor. *boden,* a cluster of trees serving as a boundary.] That which limits or circumscribes; the external or limiting line of any object or of space (to pass beyond the *bounds*); hence, that which keeps in or restrains; limit (to set *bounds* to ambition).—*v.t.* To set bounds or limits to; to act as a bound or limit to; to limit; to terminate; to restrain or confine; to circumscribe.—**boundary,** boun′dė•ri, *n.* [From *bound,* with a Latin termination.] That which marks a bound or limit; a limit; a bound.—**bounder,** boun′dėr, *n.* One who or that which bounds; assertive, unduly forceful person. [Colloq.] **boundless,** bound′les, *a.* Without bounds or limits; unlimited; limitless; immeasurable; illimitable; infinite.—**boundlessly,** bound′les•li, *adv.* In a boundless manner; infinitely. —**boundlessness,** bound′les•nes, *n.* The state or quality of being boundless or without limits.

bound, bound, *v.i.* [Fr. *bondir,* to leap, O.Fr. to ring, to echo; from L.L. *bombitare,* to resound, from L. *bombus,* a humming. BOMB.] To leap; to jump; to spring; to move forward by leaps; to rebound.—*n.* A leap; a spring; a jump; a rebound.

bound, bound, pp. of *bind* (also pret.). Made fast by a band or by chains, fetters, etc.; hemmed in; kept back; tied; having a binding; obliged by moral ties; confined; restrained. Colloquially the word is often used as equivalent to certain, sure; as, he is *bound* to succeed; the town is *bound* to increase.

bound, bound, *a.* [Formerly *boun,* from Icel. *buinn,* pp. of *bua,* to till, prepare, get ready. The *d* is parasitic, as in *sound,* from L. *sonus.* Same root as *boor, bower.*] Prepared; ready, hence, going or intending to go (outward *bound*); destined: often with *to* or *for* (a ship *bound for* London).

bounden, boun′den, *a.* [An old participle of *bind*] Obliged or beholden†; appointed; indispensable; obligatory (our *bounden* duty).

bounty, boun′ti, *n.* [O.Fr. *bonteit,* Fr. *bonte,* goodness, favor, from L. *bonitas,* goodness, from *bonus,* good.] Liberality in bestowing gifts and favors; generosity; munificence; a favor bestowed from a benevolent disposition; that which is given bounteously; a free gift; a premium offered to induce men to enlist into the public service, or to encourage some branch of industry.—**bounteous,** boun′tē•us, *a.* Disposed to give freely; free in bestowing gifts; bountiful; liberal; generous; munificent.—**bounteously,** boun′tē•us•li, *adv.* In a bounteous manner; liberally.—**bounteousness,** boun′tē•us•nes, *n.* The quality of being bounteous.—**bountiful,** boun′ti•fụl, *a.* Liberal in bestowing gifts, favors, or bounties; munificent; generous.—**bountifully,** boun′ti•fụl•li, *adv.* In a bountiful manner; liberally.—**bountifulness,** boun′ti•fụl•nes, *n.*

bouquet, bö•kā′, *n.* [Fr., O.Fr. *bousquet, bosquet,* a little wood, dim. of *bosc,* a wood. BUSH.] A nosegay; a bunch of flowers; something resembling a bunch of flowers; an agreeable aromatic odor, such as that of the finer wines.

bourbon, bėr′bon, *n.* [Bourbon County, Kentucky.] A whiskey made from corn or rye.

bourdon, bör′don, *n.* [Fr.] The drone of the bagpipe; a bass stop in the organ or harmonium having a drone-like quality of tone.

bourgeois, börzh•wä′, *n.* [Fr., sing. & pl.] A member of the middle class; a kind of printing type.—*a.* Ordinary.

bourgeon, bėr′jon, *n.* [Fr. *bourgeon,* a bud.] A bud.—*v.i.* To sprout; to put forth buds.

bourn, börn, bōrn, *n.* [Fr. *borne,* a limit, corruption of *bonne,* a boundary. BOUND.] A bound; a limit.

bourn,‡ börn, *n.* [Prov. E. and Sc. *burn,* A.Sax. *burna,* a stream = D. *born,* Icel. *brunnr,* Sw. *brunn,* Goth. *brunna,* G. *brunnen,* a spring, a well.] A brook; a torrent; a rivulet; a burn. (*Shak.*)

bourse, börs, *n.* [Fr., a purse, an exchange, from L. *bursa,* a hide, leather.] An exchange; a place where merchants assemble for general business.

bout, bout, *n.* [Older form *bought;* same word as Dan. *bugt,* a bend, a bight; closely akin to E. *bight,* and verb to *bow.*] A twist or turn; a bend or flexure; a going and returning, as in plowing, reaping, etc.; as much as is performed at one time; a trial; a set-to; a contest; a debauch.

boutonnière, bö•tan•yēr′, *n.* [Fr. *boutonnière,* buttonhole.] A small flower worn in the buttonhole.

bovine, bō′vīn, *a.* [L.L. *bovinus,* from L. *bos, bovis,* an ox.] Pertaining to oxen and cows, or other quadrupeds of the same family.

bow, bou, *v.t.* [A.Sax. *búgan,* to bend (trans. and intrans.) = D. *buigen,* Dan. *boie,* Goth. *biugan,* G. *beugen;* cog. L. *fugio,* Gr. *pheugō,* to flee; Skr. *bhuj,* to bend. From same stem are *bow* (for arrows), *bight, bout.*] To make crooked or curved; to bend; to bend or incline, as the head or the body, in token of respect or civility; to bend or cause to yield; to subdue (to *bow* the will); to make a bow to (to *bow* a person out, etc.).—*v.i.* To bend in token of reverence, respect, or civility; to be bent or inflected; to curve.—*n.* An inclination of the head, or a bending of the body, in token of reverence, respect, or submission. —**bower,** bou′ėr, *n.* One who bows.

bow, bou, *n.* [Icel. *bógr,* Dan. *bov, boug,* a shoulder, the bow of a vessel; same words as *bough.*] *Naut.* the rounding part of a ship's side forward, on either side, terminating at the stem or prow.—**bower,** bou′ėr, *n.* One of two anchors at the bow of a vessel, which are both kept in constant working use: called also *Bower-anchor.*—**bowline,** bō′līn, *n.* A rope fastened near the middle of the perpendicular edge of the square sails, and used to keep the weather edge of the sails tight forward toward the bow.—**bowsprit,** bō′sprit, *n.* The large spar or boom projecting over the bow or stem of a vessel.

bow, bō, *n.* [A.Sax. *boga,* Icel. *bogi,* Dan. *bue,* D. *boog;* from root of verb to *bow.*] A missile weapon made of a strip of wood or other elastic material, which, being bent by means of a string fastened to its two ends, can discharge an arrow placed endwise on the string by the latter being drawn back and suddenly let go; anything bent or in form of a curve, as the rain*bow;* an implement strung with horsehair, by means of which the tone is produced from instruments of the violin kind; an instrument in use among smiths for turning a drill, with turners for turning wood, with hatters for breaking fur and wool, and consisting of a piece of wood more or less curved, and having a string extending from one extremity to the other; a kind of ornamental knot of ribbon or other material.—*v.t.* or *i. Mus.* to perform or play with the *bow.*—**bowman,** bō′man, *n.* One who shoots with or is skilled in the use of the bow; an archer.—**bowyer,** bō′yėr, *n.* An archer or bowman; a maker of bows. —**bowknot,** *n.* A slipknot made by a ribbon or other material.—**bowleg,** *n.* A crooked or bandy leg.—**bowlegged,** *a.* Having crooked or bandy legs.—**bowshot,** *n.* The distance a bow can propel an arrow.—**bowstring,** *n.* The string with which a bow is bent; a similar string used by the Turks for strangling offenders.—*v.t.* To strangle with a bowstring.—**bow window,** *n.* A window built so as to project from a wall, properly one that forms a segment of a circle.

bowdlerize, boud′lėr•īz, *v.t.* To abbreviate, or expunge texts of objectionable matter, on moral grounds. From Thomas Bowdler, who in 1818 issued an edition of Shakespeare in which “ those words and expressions are omitted which cannot with propriety be read aloud in a family. ”

bowel, bou′el, *n.* [O.Fr. *boel,* from L. *botellus,* a small sausage, an intestine.] One of the intestines of an animal; a gut, especially of man; *pl.* the supposed seat of pity or tenderness; hence kindness, compassion, or affection; the interior part of anything (the *bowels* of the earth).—*v.t.*—*boweled, boweling.* To take out the bowels of; to eviscerate.

bower, bou′ėr, *n.* [A.Sax. *búr,* a chamber, from *búan,* to dwell; Icel. *búr,* a chamber, from *búa,* to live; akin *boor, bound* (ready).] A woman's private apartment; any room in a house except the hall (in these senses now only poetical); a shelter made with boughs or twining plants; an arbor; a shady recess.—**bowerbird,** *n.* A name of certain Australian birds of the oriole family, about the size of a large starling, and remarkable for erecting bowers and adorning them with gay feathers, shells, and other bright-colored objects, these bowers being used as places of resort, but not as nests.

bower, bou′ėr, *n.* [G. *bauer,* peasant, knave.] One of two cards at Euchre. The right bower is the knave of trumps, the left is the knave of same color.

bowie knife, bō′i, *n.* [After its inventor, Colonel James *Bowie.*] A knife from 10 to 15 inches long and about 2 inches broad.

bowl, bōl, *n.* [O.E. *bolle,* A.Sax. *bolla,* a bowl; Icel. *bolli,* M.H.G. *bolle,* a bowl; allied to *ball.*] A concave vessel of a somewhat semiglobular shape; a large cup with roundish outlines; a goblet: often used as the emblem of festivity; the hollow part of anything, as of a spoon or of a tobacco pipe.

bowl, bōl, *n.* [O.E. *bowle*, Fr. *boule*, from L. *bulla*, a bubble (whence verb to *boil*).] A ball of wood or other material used for rolling on a level surface at play; a ball of wood loaded on one side used in a game played on a level plat of greensward; *pl.* the game played with such balls.—*v.i.* To play with bowls or at bowling; to roll a bowl, as in the game of bowls; to deliver the ball to be played by the batsman at cricket; to move rapidly and like a ball (*bowl* along).—*v.t.* To roll in the manner of a bowl; to pelt with or as with bowls.—**bowler,** bōl′ėr, *n.* One who plays at bowls; *cricket*, the player who delivers the ball in order to be played by the batsman.—**bowling alley,** *n.* A covered place for the game of bowls.—**bowling green,** *n.* A level piece of greensward kept smooth for bowling.—**bowlder,** bōl′dėr, *n.* Same as *boulder*.

box, boks, *n.* [A.Sax. *box*, a box, from L. *buxus*, *buxum*, the box tree, and something made of its wood.] A case or receptacle of any size and made of any material; the driver's seat on a carriage; a present, especially a Christmas present; a compartment for the accommodation of a small number of people, as in a theater; a narrow confined enclosed place; a place of shelter for one or two men engaged in certain duties, as sentries, signalmen, etc.; a small house for sportsmen during the shooting season or the like.—*v.t.* To enclose, as in a box; to confine.—*To box the compass*, to repeat or go over the points of the compass in order, or to answer any questions regarding the divisions of the compass; to perform a swift change in politics.—**Boxing day,** *n.* The day after Christmas day when Christmas boxes and presents are given [in England].

box, boks, *n.* [Corresponding by metathesis to Dan. *bask*, a slap, *baske*, to beat; akin *bash*.] A blow with the fist.—*v.t.* To strike with the fist or hand.—*v.i.* To fight with the fists; to practice fighting with the fists.—**boxer,** bok′sėr, *n.* One who fights with his fists; a pugilist; a breed of short-haired, medium-sized dog.—**boxing,** *n.* Fist fighting with padded gloves, practiced as a sport. —**boxing glove,** *n.* A large padded glove used for sparring.

box, boks, *n.* [L. *buxus*, Gr. *pyxos*, the box-tree. Box, a case.] The name given to several species of trees or shrubs, the most important being a small evergreen tree with small shining leaves, and yielding a hard close-grained wood, and the dwarf variety used as edgings of garden walks.—**boxwood,** *n.* The fine hard-grained timber of the box tree, much used by wood engravers and in the manufacture of musical and mathematical instruments, etc.

boy, boi, *n.* [Fris. *boi*, *boy*, a boy; allied to D. *boef*, G. *bube*, Sw. *bue*, a boy.] A male child from birth to the age of puberty; a lad; a man wanting in vigor, experience, judgment; a familiar term applied in addressing or speaking of grown persons, especially one's associates; in compounds sometimes applied to grown men without any idea of youth or contempt; as, a post*boy*, a pot*boy*. —**boyhood,** boi′hụd, *n.* The state of being a boy or of immature age.—**boyish,** boi′ish, *a.* Belonging to a boy; pertaining to boyhood; in a disparaging sense; childish; trifling; puerile.—**boyishly,** boi′ish•li, *adv.* In a boyish manner.—**boyishness,** boi′ish•nes, *n.* The quality of being boyish.

boyar, boi′är, *n.* A member of an order of the old Russian aristocracy next in rank to the ruling princes.

boycott, boi′kot, *v.t.* [From Capt. *Boycott*, an Irish land agent, the first prominent victim of the system in 1880.] To combine in refusing to work for, to buy from or sell to, or to have any dealings with, as a means to show disapproval or to coerce.—*n.* The process of boycotting.

brabble, brab′l, *n.* [D. *brabbelen*, to confound, to stammer.] A broil; a wrangle.—*v.i.*—*brabbled, brabbling*. To dispute or quarrel noisily.—**brabblement,** brab′l•ment, *n.* A clamorous contest; a brabble.

brace, brās, *n.* [O.Fr. *brace*, *brasse*, etc., from L. *brachia*, the arms, pl. of *brachium*, an arm; allied to Gael. *brac*, W. *braic*, the arm.] That which holds anything tight, tense, firm, or secure, or which supports, binds, or strengthens, as a piece of timber placed near and across the angles in the frame of a building; a thick strap which supports a carriage on wheels; the crank-shaped stock in which boring tools, etc., are held, serving as a lever for turning them, etc.; a mark { or } used in written or printed matter connecting two or more words or lines; a couple or pair (not of persons unless in contempt).—*v.t.*—*braced, bracing*. To bind or tie closely; to make tense; to strain up; to increase the tension, tone, or vigor of (the nerves, the system); to strengthen; to invigorate. —**bracer,** brās′ėr, *n.* One who or that which braces; an archery guard for the left forearm.—**bracing,** brās′ing, *a.* Giving vigor or tone to the bodily system.

bracelet, brās′let, *n.* [Fr. *bracelet*, a dim. of O.Fr. *bracel*, *brachel*, an armlet, from L. *brachile*, from *brachium*, the arm. BRACE.] An ornament encircling the wrist, now worn mostly by ladies.

brachial, brā′ki•al, *a.* [L. *brachium*, the arm.] Belonging to the arm; of the nature of an arm; resembling an arm.—**brachiate,** brā′ki•āt, *a. Bot.* having branches in pairs, nearly horizontal, and each pair at right angles with the next.

Brachiopoda, brā•ki•op′o•da, *n. pl.* [Gr. *brachiōn*, an arm, and *pous*, a foot.] A class of marine, bivalve, molluscoid animals, including the lamp shells, etc., so named from the development of a long spirally-coiled fringed respiratory appendage or arm on either side of the mouth.—**brachiopod,** brā′ki•o•pod, *n.* One of the Brachiopoda.

brachycephalic, brachycephalous, brak′i•se•fal′ik, brak•i•sef′al•us, *a.* [Gr. *brachys*, short, and *kephalē*, the head.] In *ethn.* terms applied to heads (or races possessing such heads) whose diameter from side to side is not much less than that from front to back, their ratio being as 8 to 10, as those of the Mongolian type.

Brachyura, brak•i•ū′ra, *n. pl.* [Gr. *brachys*, short, and *oura*, tail.] A section of ten-footed crustaceans (Decapoda), with the abdomen forming a very short, jointed tail, folded forward closely under the thorax, as in the common edible crab.—**brachyurous,** brak•i•ū•rus, *a.* Short-tailed: applied to certain Crustacea, as the crab, to distinguish them from the macrurous or long-tailed crustaceans, as the lobster.—**brachyuran,** brak•i•ū′ran, *n.* One of the Brachyura.

bracken, brak′en, *n.* [A Scandinavian word; same as Sw. *bräken*, Dan. *bregne*, fern; closely allied to *brake*.] Fern. BRAKE.

bracket, brak′et, *n.* [Ultimately perhaps from L. *brachium*, an arm.] A kind of short supporting piece projecting from a perpendicular surface, either plain or ornamentally carved, as an ornamental projection from the face of a wall to support a statue; a triangular wooden support for a shelf or the like; an ornamental piece supporting a hammer beam; one of two projecting pieces attached to a wall, beam, etc., for carrying or supporting a line of shafting; *printing*, one of two marks [ ] used to enclose a reference, note, or explanation, to indicate an interpolation, rectify a mistake, etc.; a gas pipe projecting from a wall, usually more or less ornamental.—*v.t.* To furnish with a bracket or with brackets; *printing*, to place within brackets; to connect by brackets.

brackish, brak′ish, *a.* [D. and L.G. *brak*, G. *brack*, brackish.] Possessing a salt or somewhat salt taste; salt in a moderate degree; applied to water.—**brackishness,** brak′ish•nes, *n.* The quality of being brackish.

bract, brakt, *n.* [L. *bractea*, a thin plate of metal.] *Bot.* a modified leaf differing from other leaves in shape or color, and generally situated on the peduncle near the flower.—**bracteate,** brak′tē•it, *a.* Furnished with bracts.—**bracteole, bractlet,** brak′tē•ōl, brakt′let, *n.* A little bract on a partial flower stalk or pedicel in a many-flowered inflorescence.

brad, brad, *n.* [Same word as Icel. *broddr*, a spike, a nail; Dan. *brodde*, a frost nail; A.Sax. *brord*, a prick, a spire of grass; comp. Gael. and Ir. *brod*, goad, sting.] A finishing nail with little or no head used where it is deemed proper to drive nails entirely into the wood.—**bradawl,** *n.*

An awl to make holes for brads or other nails.

brae, brā, *n.* [Icel. *brá,* eyelid, akin to G. *braue,* eyebrow.] A sloping bank, acclivity. [Scottish.]

brag, brag, *v.i.—bragged, bragging.* [From the Celtic; W. *bragiaw,* Ir. *braghaim,* to boast; Gael. *bragaire-achd,* boasting; Armor. *braga,* to make a display; from root of *break.*] To use boastful language; to speak vaingloriously; to boast; to vaunt; to swagger; to bluster.—*n.* A boast or boasting; a vaunt; the thing boasted of; a game at cards: so called because one player *brags* he has a better hand than the others, staking a sum of money on the issue.—**braggadocio,** brag·a·dō′shi·ō, *n.* [From *Braggadochio,* a boastful character in Spenser's 'Faery Queen', from the verb to *brag.*] A boasting fellow; a braggart; empty boasting; brag.—**braggart,** brag′ärt, *n.* [*Brag,* and suffix *-art, -ard.*] A boaster; a vain fellow.—*a.* Boastful; vainly ostentatious.

Brahman, brä′man, *n.* Among the Hindus a member of the sacred or sacerdotal caste, who claim to have proceeded from the mouth of Brahmā (the Creator, one of the deities of the Hindu triad or trinity), and who are noted for their many minute religious observances, their abstemiousness, and their severe penances.—**Brahmanic, Brahmanical,** brä·man′ik, brä·man′ik·al, *a.* Of or pertaining to the Brahmans or their doctrines and worship.—**Brahmanism,** brä′man·izm, *n.* The religion or system of doctrines of the Brahmans.—**Brahmanist,** brä′man·ist, *n.* An adherent of Brahmanism. These words are also spelled *Brahmin, Braminic,* etc.

braid, brād, *v.t.* [A.Sax. *bredan, bregdan,* to weave, to braid; Icel. *bregtha,* to braid, *bragth,* a sudden movement; O.H.G. *brettan,* to braid.] To weave or intertwine, as hair, by forming three or more strands into one; to plait.—*n.* A sort of narrow textile band formed by plaiting or weaving several strands of silk, cotton, woolen, etc., together; a plait or plaited tress of hair.—**braiding,** brād′ing, *n.* Braid, or trimming made of braid collectively.

brail, brāl, *n.* [O.Fr. *braiel, braieul,* etc., a trouser band, from *braies,* breeches, from L. *bracae,* breeches.] BREECHES.] *Naut.* a rope attached to a fore-and-aft sail, or a jib to assist in taking in the sail.—*v.t.* To haul in by means of the brails: followed by *up.*

braille, brāl, *n.* [Fr. *Braille,* inventor's name.] A system of reading with raised letters for the blind.

brain, brān, *n.* [A.Sax. *braegen, bregen,* D. and O.Fris. *brein.*] The soft whitish mass enclosed in the skull in man and other vertebrate animals, forming the center of the nervous system, and the seat of consciousness and volition, and in which the nerves and spinal marrow terminate; the cerebrum: sometimes used to include also the cerebellum; the understanding; the fancy; the imagination.—*v.t.* To dash out the brains of; to kill by beating out the brains.—**brainless,** brān′les, *a.* Without understanding or judgment; silly; stupid.—**brainy,** brān′i, *a.* Provided with brains; intellectual.—**brainpan,** *n.* The skull which encloses the brain. (*Shak.*)—**brainsick,** *a.* Disordered in the understanding; fantastic; crotchety; crazed.—**brainsickness,** *n.* Disorder of the understanding.—**brainstorming,** brān′storm·ing, *n.* A group technique for stimulating creative thinking.—**brain washing.** Systematic indoctrination by psychological manipulation to undermine or change political beliefs.

braise, brāz, *v.t.* [Fr. *braiser,* to braise, from Dan. *brase,* to fry; Sw. *brasa,* to flame. BRASS.] To bake, broil, or stew with herbs, spices, etc., in a closely covered pan.

brake, brāk, *n.* [A.Sax. *bracce,* fern, bracken; L.G. *brake,* brushwood; allied to D. *braak,* Dan. *brak,* G. *brach,* fallow.] A fern; bracken; a place overgrown with brakes or brushwood, shrubs, and brambles; a thicket, as of canes, etc.

brake, brāk, *n.* [From the verb to *break;* comp. L.G. *brake,* G. *breche,* an instrument for breaking flax; O.D. *brake,* a fetter for the neck, *braake,* an instrument for holding an animal by the nose.] An instrument or machine to break flax or hemp; a pump handle; a kneading trough; a sharp bit or snaffle; a frame for confining refractory horses while shoeing; a large heavy barrow for breaking clods; a kind of wagonette; a strong heavy vehicle with a seat only for the driver, used for breaking in young horses to harness; an appliance used to stop or retard the motion of a machine or vehicle by friction, and generally consisting of a simple or compound lever which can be pressed forcibly against the rim of a wheel on one of the axles of the machine or carriage.—**brakeman,** brāk′man, *n.* The man whose business is to stop a railroad train by applying the brake; *mining,* the man in charge of a winding engine.

bramble, bram′bl, *n.* [A.Sax. *bremel, brembel,* from stem *bram, brem* (seen also in *broom*), *el* being simply a termination and *b* inserted as in *number,* etc., comp. L.G. *brummel*-beere, Dan. *bram*bär, G. *brom*beere, Sw. *brom*-bär, a blackberry.] A prickly trailing shrub of the rose family growing in hedges and waste places, and bearing a black berry somewhat like a raspberry; the berry itself; the blackberry.—**brambly,** bram′bli, *adv.* Full of brambles.

bran, bran, *n.* [A Celtic word = W. Ir. Gael. *bran,* bran, chaff; Armor. *brenn,* bran, whence O.Fr. *bren.*] The outer coat of wheat, rye, or other farinaceous grain, separated from the flour by grinding.

branch, bransh, *n.* [From Fr. *branche,* a branch, from Armor. *branc,* an arm; connected with L.L. *branca,* a claw, W. *braich,* L. *brachium,* an arm.] A portion of a tree, shrub, or other plant springing from the stem, or from a part ultimately supported by the stem; a bough; a shoot; something resembling a branch; an offshoot or part extending from the main body of a thing; any member or part of a body or system; a department, section, or subdivision; a line of family descent, in distinction from some other line or lines from the same stock.—*v.i.* To spread in branches; to send out branches as a plant; to divide into separate parts or subdivisions; to diverge (a road *branches* off); to ramify.—*v.t.*† To divide, as into branches; to adorn, as with needlework, representing branches, flowers, or twigs.

branchiae, brang′ki·ē, *n. pl.* [L.] The respiratory organs of fishes, etc.; the gills.—**branchial,** brang′ki·al, *a.* Relating to the branchiae or gills; performed by means of branchiae.

Branchiopoda, brang·ki·op′o·da, *n. pl.* [Gr. *branchia,* gills, and *pous, podos,* a foot.] An order of crustaceous animals, so called because their branchiae, or gills, are situated on the feet, as in the water fleas, brine shrimps, etc.—**branchiopod,** brang′-ki·o·pod, *n.* An animal belonging to the order Branchiopoda.

brand, brand, *n.* [A.Sax. *brand,* a burning, a sword = Icel. *brandr,* firebrand, sword; Dan. D. and G. *brand,* a burning. The sword is so called from its gleaming. Akin to verb *burn.*] A piece of wood burning or partly burned; a sword; a mark made by burning with a hot iron or by other means, as on commodities to indicate the quality or manufacturer, on sheep to indicate the owner, or on criminals to indicate their crime or for identification; a trademark; hence, kind or quality; a mark of infamy; a stigma; a disease in vegetables by which their leaves and tender bark are partially destroyed as if they had been burned.—*v.t.* To burn or impress a mark upon with a hot iron, or to distinguish by a similar mark; to fix a mark or character of infamy upon; to stigmatize as infamous.—**brander,** brand′-ėr, *n.* One who brands.—**brand-new,** *a.* A more correct form of *bran-new* (which see).

brandish, bran′dish, *v.t.* [From Fr. *brandir, brandissant,* from Teut. *brand,* a sword. BRAND.] To move or wave, as a weapon; to raise and move in various directions; to shake or flourish.—**brandisher,** bran′dish·-ėr, *n.* One who brandishes.

brandling, brand′ling, *n.* The parr or young of the salmon, so named from having, as it were, branded markings; also, a small red worm used for bait in fresh-water fishing.

brandy, bran′di, *n.* [O.E. *brandywine,* D. *brandewijn,* lit. burnt wine—D. *branden,* to burn, to distil, and *wijn,* wine, like G. *branntwein*—*brennen,* to burn, and *wein,* wine. BRAND.] A spirituous liquor obtained by the distillation of wine, or of the refuse of the wine press; a name now also given to spirit distilled from other liquors or from some fruit juices.

brangle, brang′gl, *n.* [Perhaps for *braggle,* from *brag.*] A wrangle; a squabble; a noisy contest or dispute. —*v.i.* To wrangle; to dispute contentiously; to squabble.

branks, brangks, *n.* [From the Celtic: Gael. *brangas,* a kind of pillory; Ir. *brancas,* a halter.] An instrument of the nature of a bridle formerly used for correcting scolding women; a scolding bridle.

bran-new, bran′nū, *a.* [For *brand-new,* the original form, from *brand,* a burning, and *new.*] *Lit.* glowing like metal newly out of the fire or forge; hence, quite new.

brash, brash, *n.* [From Fr. *brèche,* a breach, broken stuff, breccia.] A confused heap of fragments, as masses of loose, broken, or angular fragments of rocks; small fragments of crushed ice, collected by winds or currents, near the shore; refuse boughs of trees.

brasier, brā′zi•ėr, *n.* [Fr. *brasier, braisier,* from *braise,* embers, live coals; same origin as *braze, brass.*] An open pan for burning wood or coal.

brasier, brā′zi•ėr, *n.* [From *brass* or from *braze.*] An artificer who works in brass.

brass, bras, *n.* [A.Sax. *braes,* brass = Icel. *bras,* solder; from verbal stem seen in Icel. *brasa,* to harden by fire; Sw. *brasa,* to blaze; Dan. *brase,* to fry (whence Fr. *braise,* live embers, *braser,* to braze, *braiser,* to braise).] A malleable and fusible alloy of copper and zinc, of a yellow color, usually containing about one-third of its weight of zinc; a utensil, ornament, or other article made of brass, as a monumental plate bearing effigies, coats of arms, etc., inlaid in a slab of stone, common in the pavements of medieval churches; *pl.* musical instruments of the trumpet kind; brazenness or impudence (colloq.); money (colloq.).—*v.t.* To cover or coat over with brass.—**brassy,** bras′i, *a.* Resembling or composed of brass; brazen.—*n.* A golf club shod with brass.—**brassiness,** bras′i•nes, *n.*

brassard, bras′ėrd, *n.* [Fr., from *bras,* arm.] A protecting piece, or a badge, for the arm. Also *Brassart.*

brassiere, bras•yâr′, bra•zēr′, *n.* (Fr., from *bras,* arm.) An undergarment worn by women to support the breasts. Also (colloq.) **bra,** brä.

brat, brat, *n.* [Ir. and Gael. *brat,* a rag, an apron.] A child: so called in contempt.

brattice, brat′is, *n.* [O.Fr. *bretesche,* a bartizan; probably from G. *bret,* a board, a plank.] A partition which divides a mining shaft into two chambers, serving as the upcast and downcast shafts for ventilation, or placed across a gallery to keep back noxious gases, or prevent the escape of water; a fence put round dangerous machinery.

bravado, bra•vä′dō, *n.* [Sp. *bravada,* Fr. *bravade.* BRAVE.] An arrogant menace, intended to intimidate; a boast; a brag.

brave, brāv, *a.* [Fr. *brave,* brave, gay, proud, braggard; Sp. and It. *bravo,* brave, courageous; perhaps from the Celtic; comp. Armor. *brao, brav,* gaily dressed, fine, handsome; also O.Sw. *braf,* good.] Courageous; bold; daring; intrepid; high-spirited; valiant; fearless; making a fine display in bearing, dress, or appearance generally; excellent‡; capital‡.—*n.* A brave, bold, or daring person; a man daring beyond discretion; a North American Indian warrior.—*v.t.*—*braved, braving.* To encounter with courage and fortitude, or without being moved; to defy; to dare.—**bravely,** brāv′li, *adv.* In a brave manner; courageously; gallantly; prosperously.—**braveness,** brāv′nes, *n.* The quality of being brave.—**bravery,** brāv′ėr•i, *n.* The quality of being brave; courage; undaunted spirit; intrepidity; gallantry; splendor‡; show‡; bravado‡.

bravo, brä′vō, *interj.* [It. BRAVE.] Well done! The word being an Italian adjective, the correct usage is to say *bravo* to a male singer or actor, *brava* to a female, and *bravi* to a company.

bravo, brä′vō, *n.* pl. **bravoes,** brä′vōz. [It. and Sp., lit. a daring man.] A daring villain; an assassin or murderer for hire.

bravura, brä•vö′ra, *a.* [It., bravery, spirit.] *Mus.* applied to a florid air, serving to display a performer's flexibility of voice and distinctness of articulation.

brawl, bral, *v.i.* [Perhaps from W. *brawl,* a boast, *broliaw,* to boast, *bragal,* to vociferate; or akin to D. *brallen,* to boast, Dan. *bralle,* to jabber, to prate, *brölle,* to roar.] To be clamorous or noisy; to quarrel noisily; to make the noise of rushing or running water; to flow with a noise (a brook *brawls* along).—*n.* A noisy quarrel; loud angry contention; an uproar, row, or squabble; a kind of dance‡.—**brawler,** bral′ėr, *n.* One who brawls; a noisy fellow; a wrangler.

brawn, bran, *n.* [O.Fr. *braon,* the muscular parts of the body, from O.H.G. *brato, braton,* meat for roasting, from *braten,* to roast.] Boar's flesh; the flesh of the boar or swine, collared so as to squeeze out much of the fat, boiled, and pickled; the flesh of a pig's head and ox feet cut in pieces and boiled, pickled, and pressed into a shape; a fleshy, protuberant, muscular part of the body, as on the thigh or the arm; muscular strength; muscle; the arm‡.—**brawniness,** bra′ni•nes, *n.* The quality of being brawny; strength, hardiness.—**brawny,** bra′ni, *a.* Having large strong muscles; muscular; fleshy; bulky; strong.

braxy, brak′si, *n.* [Perhaps from the verb to *break;* comp. G. *brechen,* vomiting, *brechen,* to break; or from Gael. *bragsaidh,* a disease of sheep.] The name given to several diseases of sheep; a sheep having the braxy; the mutton of such a sheep.—*a.* Affected or tainted with braxy.

bray, brā, *v.t.* [O.Fr. *brayer* (Fr. *broyer*), to pound, from G. *brechen,* to break.] To pound, beat, or grind small, especially in a mortar.

bray, brā, *v.i.* [Fr. *braire,* to bray; L.L. *bragire, bragare,* to bray, from Celtic root seen in *brag.*] To utter a harsh cry: said especially of the ass; to make a loud, harsh, disagreeable sound.—*v.t.* To utter with a loud harsh sound: sometimes with *out.*—*n.* The harsh sound or roar of an ass; a harsh or grating sound.—**brayer,** brā′ėr, *n.* One that brays like an ass.

braze, brāz, *v.t.*—*brazed, brazing.* [Fr. *braser,* to braze, from the Scandinavian. BRASS.] To solder with hard solder, such as an alloy of brass and zinc; to cover or ornament with brass; to harden; to harden to impudence (*Shak.*)‡.—**brazen,** brā′zn, *a.* Made of brass; also, from brass often serving as a type of strength or impenetrability, extremely strong; impenetrable; pertaining to brass; proceeding from *brass* (a *brazen* sound); impudent; having a front like brass.—*v.t.* To behave with insolence or effrontery: with an indefinite *it.*—*To brazen out,* to persevere in treating with effrontery: with an indefinite *it,* or a noun like *matter, affair, business.*—**brazenly,** brā′zn•li, *adv.* In a brazen manner; boldly; impudently.—**brazenness,** brā′zn•nes, *n.* Appearance like brass; brassiness; impudence. — **brazier,** brā′zi•ėr, *n.* Same as *Brasier.*—**brazenface,** *n.* An impudent person; one remarkable for effrontery.—**brazen-faced,** *a.* Impudent; bold to excess.

brazil, brazil-wood, bra•zil′, *n.* [Pg. *brasil,* from *braza,* a live coal, the name being given to the wood from its color, and the country being called after the wood.] A very heavy wood of a red color, growing in Brazil and other tropical countries, used for dyeing red.—**brazilin,** braz′il•in, *n.* The red coloring matter of Brazil-wood.—**Brazil nut,** *n.* The seeds of a very lofty tree growing throughout tropical America. The fruit is nearly round and about 6 inches in diameter, having an extremely hard shell, and containing from eighteen to twenty-four triangular wrinkled seeds, which, besides being eaten, yield an oil, used by watchmakers and others.

breach, brēch, *n.* [From A.Sax. *brece, brice,* a breach or breaking, from *brecan,* to break; partly also from Fr. *brèche,* a breach, from the same stem, but directly from the German.] The act of breaking in a figurative sense; the act of violating or neglecting some law, contract, obligation, or custom; the space between the several parts of a mass parted by violence; a rupture; a break; a gap (a *breach* in a wall); separation between persons through ill feeling; difference; quarrel; injury; wound (O.T.); the breaking of waves; the surf (*Shak.*).—*v.t.* To make a breach or opening in.

bread, bred, *n.* [A.Sax. *bread* = D. *brood,* Sw. and Dan. *brōd,* G. *brod, brot.* Root doubtful; perhaps *brew.*] A kind of food made by moistening and kneading the flour or meal of some species of grain, or that prepared from other plants, and baking it, the dough being often caused to ferment; food or sustenance in general.—**breadfruit,** *n.* The fruit of a tree which grows in the islands of the Pacific Ocean, producing a large round fruit used as a substitute for bread, and forming the principal food of a considerable population.—**breadstuff,** bred′stuf, *n.* Breadcorn: used frequently in the plural to signify all the different varieties of grain and flour from which bread is made collectively.—**breadwinner,** *n.* One who works for the support of himself or of himself and a family.

breadth, bredth, *n.* [O.E. *brede*, with *th* added, from A.Sax. *braedu*, breadth, from *brád*, broad; comp. *length*, *width*. BROAD.] The measure or extent of any plane surface from side to side; width; *fig.* largeness of mind; liberality; wide intellectual grasp; *fine arts*, an impression of largeness, freedom, and space produced by bold or simple touches and strokes of the pencil.—**breadthways,** bredth′wāz, *adv.* In the direction of the breadth.

break, brāk, *v.t.*—*broke* (pret. *brake* is still used in archaic style); *broken* or *broke* (pp.); *breaking*. [A.Sax. *brecan*, to break, weaken, vanquish, etc.=D. *breken*, Dan. *braekke*, G. *brechen*, Goth. *brikan*, to break, to crush, etc.; Icel. *braka*, to creak; same root as L. *frango*, Gr. (*f*)*rēgnymi*, to break.] To part or divide by force and violence (as a stick, a rope); *fig.* to sever or interrupt (connection, friendship); to cause to give way (to *break* an enemy's lines); to destroy, weaken, or impair (health, constitution); to subdue; to quell (to *break* one's spirit); to train to obedience; to make tractable (to *break* a horse); to dismiss or cashier; pay off (troops); to reduce in rank or condition (an officer); to give a superficial wound to so as to lacerate (the skin); to violate, as a contract, law, or promise; to stop; to interrupt (sleep); to cause to discontinue (to *break* a person *of* a habit); to check; to lessen the force of (a fall or a blow); to make a first and partial disclosure of; to impart or tell cautiously so as not to startle or shock (to *break* unwelcome news); to destroy the completeness of; to remove a part from (a sum of money, a set of things).—*To break off*, to sever by breaking; to put a sudden stop to (a marriage); to discontinue; to leave off (intimacy, a conversation).—*To break up*, to open forcibly (a door); to lay open (to *break up* ground); to dissolve or put an end to (a meeting); to separate; to disband.—*To break ground*, to begin to plow or dig; to commence excavation; *fig.* to begin to execute any plan.—*To break the heart*, to afflict grievously; to cause to die of grief.—*To break one's mind to*, to reveal one's thoughts to.—*To break the ice*, to overcome obstacles and make a beginning; to get over the feeling of restraint incident to a new acquaintanceship. —*v.i.* To become broken; to burst forth violently (a storm, a deluge); to open spontaneously or by force from within; to burst (a bubble, a tumor); to show the first light of morning; to dawn (the day, the morning *breaks*); to become bankrupt; to decline or fail in health and strength; to fail, change in tone, or falter, as the voice.—*To break away*, to disengage one's self abruptly; to rush off.—*To break down*, to come down by breaking; to fail and be unable to proceed in an undertaking.—*To break forth*, to burst out; to be suddenly manifested (rage, light, noise); to rush or issue out; to give vent to one's feelings.—*To break from*, to disengage one's self from; to leave abruptly or violently.—*To break in* or *into*, to enter by force; to start into suddenly (*break* into a gallop).—*To break loose*, to get free by force; to shake off restraint.—*To break off*, to part; to become separated; to desist suddenly.—*To break out*, to issue forth; to arise or spring up (fire, fever, sedition); to appear in eruptions.—*To break up*, to dissolve and separate (as a company).—*To break with*, to cease to be friends with; to quarrel; to broach a subject to (*Shak.*)†.—*n.* An opening made by force; a rupture; a breach; an interruption of continuity (five years without a *break*); a line in writing or printing, noting a suspension of the sense or a stop in the sentence; a contrivance to check the velocity of a wheeled carriage; a brake; a contrivance for interrupting or changing the direction of electric currents; a large high-set four-wheeled vehicle; a brake; in *cricket*, a sudden swerve of the ball after pitching, in direction of the batsman; in *billiards*, a continuous score of points.—*Break of day*, the dawn.—**breakable,** brāk′a·bl, *a.* Capable of being broken.—**breakage,** brāk′ij, *n.* The act of breaking; allowance for what is accidentally broken.—**breakdown,** *n.* An overthrow, as of a carriage; a downfall; a crash; a failure; a collapse; a lively, noisy dance.—**breaker,** brāk′ėr, *n.* The person who or that which breaks anything; a violator or transgressor; a wave broken into foam against the shore, a sand bank, or a rock near the surface; a small flat water cask (in this sense perhaps a corruption of Sp. *barrica*, a keg.—**breakfast,** brek′fast, *n.* The first meal in the day; the meal which enables one to break the fast lasting from the previous day; the food eaten at the first meal.—*v.t.* To furnish with breakfast.—*v.i.* To eat breakfast.—**breakneck,**† brāk′nek, *n.* A fall that breaks the neck; a dangerous business (*Shak.*).—*a* Endangering life; extremely hazardous.—**breakthrough,** brāk′thrö, *n. Milit.* penetration beyond an enemy's defense line; a major advance in solving a problem.—**breakup,** *n.* A disruption; a dissolution of connection; a disintegration; a disbandment.—**breakwater,** brāk′wa̤·tėr, *n.* Any structure or contrivance serving to break the force of waves.

bream, brēm, *n.* [Fr. *brème*, O.Fr. *bresme*, from O.H.G. *brahsema*, G. *bressem*, the bream.] The name of several fresh-water soft-finned fishes belonging to the carp family; the name is also given to some spiny-finned sea fishes resembling the perches.

bream, brēm, *v.t.* [D. *brem*, broom, furze, from the materials commonly used; the verb *broom* is also used in same sense.] *Naut.* to clear of shells, seaweed, ooze, etc., by fire—an operation applied to a ship's bottom.

breast, brest, *n.* [A.Sax. *breóst*=Icel. *brjóst*, Sw. *bröst*, Dan. *bryst*, D. *borst*, Goth. *brusts*, G. *brust*; allied to E. *burst*, and primarily signifying a protuberance, a swelling.] The soft protuberant body adhering to the thorax in females, in which the milk is secreted for the nourishment of infants; the fore part of the thorax, or the fore part of the body between the neck and the belly in man or animals; *fig.* the seat of the affections and emotions; the repository of consciousness, designs, and secrets; anything resembling or likened to the breast.—*To make a clean breast*, to make full confession. —*v.t.* To meet in front boldly or openly; to oppose with the breast; to bear the breast against (a current); to stem.—**breastbone,** *n.* The bone of the breast; the sternum.—**breastplate,** brest′plāt, *n.* A plate worn on the breast as a part of defensive armor; *Jewish antiq.* a part of the vestment of the high priest.—**breast stroke,** *n.* A swimming stroke in which both arms are simultaneously moved forward and then backward.—**breastwork,** *n. Fort*, a hastily constructed work thrown up breasthigh for defense; the parapet of a building.

breath, breth, *n.* [A.Sax. *braeth*, odor, scent, breath, allied to G. *bradem*, *brodem*, steam, vapor, breath, *brod*, vapor, a bubble; same root as E. *broth* and *brew*.] The air inhaled and expelled in the respiration of animals, the power of breathing, life; the state or power of breathing freely (to be out of *breath* from violent exercise), a pause; time to breathe, a single respiration; the time of a single respiration; a very slight breeze; air in gentle motion, an exhalation; an odor, a perfume.—*Out of breath*, breathless.—**breathable,** brēᴛʜ′a·bl, *a.* Capable of being breathed.—**breathe,** brēᴛʜ, *v.i.*—*breathed*, *breathing*. To respire; to inspire and expire air; to live; to make a single respiration; to take breath; to rest from action; to pass or blow gently, as air; to exhale, as odor; to emanate; *fig.* to be instinct with life; to be alive.—*v.t.* To inhale and exhale in respiration; to inspire or infuse (*breathe* life into), to exhale; to send out; to utter; to speak; to whisper (vows, etc.); to suffer to take or recover breath (a horse); to put out of breath; to exhaust.—**breathed,** bretht, *a.* Endowed with breath; *philol.* uttered with breath as distinguished from *voice;* surd or mute.—**breather,** brēTH'ėr, *n.* One who breathes; one who lives (*Shak.*); a sharp spell of exercise.—**breathing,** brēTH'ing, *n.* Respiration; the act of inhaling and exhaling air; a gentle breeze; *fig.* a gentle influence or operation; inspiration; soft or secret utterance (*Shak.*); time taken to recover breath; a stop; a delay; *gram.* an aspiration; an aspirate.—**breathless,** breth'les, *a.* Being out of breath; spent with labor or violent action; without breath; dead; incapable of breathing, as with wonder or admiration.—**breathlessness,** breth'les•nes *n.* The state of being breathless.

breccia, brech'i•a, *n.* [It., a breach, a breccia.] *Geol.* an aggregate composed of angular fragments of the same rock or of different rocks united by a matrix or cement.

bred, bred, pp. of *breed.*

breech, brēch, *n.* [A singular developed from a plural. BREECHES.] The lower part of the body behind; the hinder part of anything: the large thick end of a cannon or other firearm.—*v.t.* To put into breeches; to whip on the breech; to fit or furnish with a breech; to fasten by a breeching.—**breechblock,** *n.* A movable piece at the breech of a breech-loading gun which is withdrawn for the insertion of the charge, and closed before firing.—**breeches,** brēch'ez, *n. pl.* [A double plural, from A.Sax. *bréc,* breeches, pl. of *bróc,* as *feet* is the pl. of *foot*=Fris. *brôck,* pl. *brêk,* breeches; D. *broek,* breeches; Dan. *brog,* breeches, the breeching of a gun; Icel. *brók,* pl. *brœkr,* breeches; Ir. *brog,* Gael. *briogais,* Armor. *brœges*—breeches.] A garment worn by men, covering the hips and thighs; less properly used in the sense of trousers.—*To wear the breeches,* to usurp the authority of the husband: said of a wife.—**breeching,** brēch'ing, *n.* A whipping on the breech; a strong rope to prevent a cannon from recoiling too much when fired; that part of a horse's harness attached to the saddle and hooked on the shafts, which enables him to push back the vehicle to which he is harnessed; a bifurcated smoke pipe of a furnace.—**breechloader,** *n.* A cannon or smaller firearm loaded at the breech instead of the muzzle.—**breech-loading,** *a.* Receiving the charge at the breech instead of the muzzle: applied to firearms.

breed, brēd, *v.t.*—*bred, breeding.* [A.Sax. *brédan,* to nourish, cherish, keep warm; allied to D. *broeden,* G. *brüten,* to brood, hatch, and to E. *brew,* W. *brwd,* warm.] To procreate; to beget; to engender; to hatch; to cause; to occasion; to produce; to originate (to *breed* dissension); to produce; to yield or give birth to; to bring up; to nurse and foster; to train; to rear, as live stock.—*v.i.* To beget or bear a child or children; to be fruitful; to be produced; to take rise (dissensions *breed* among them); to engage in raising live stock.—*n.* A race or progeny from the same parents or stock; kind or sort in a general sense.—**breeder,** brēd'ėr, *n.* One who breeds, procreates, or produces young; one who or that which rears or brings up; one who or that which produces, causes, brings about; one who takes care to raise a particular breed or breeds, as of horses or cattle.—**breeding,** brēd'ing, *n.* The act of generating or producing; the raising of cattle or live stock of different kinds; upbringing; nurture; education; deportment or behavior in social life; manners, especially good manners.—*Cross breeding,* breeding from individuals of two different offsprings or varieties.—*In-and-in breeding,* breeding from animals of the same parentage.

breeze, brēz, *n.* [Fr. *brise,* Sp. *brisa,* a breeze.] A wind, generally a light or not very strong wind; a gentle gale.—**breezy,** brēz'i, *a.* Fanned with gentle winds or breezes; subject to frequent breezes; vivacious; hilarious.

breeze, brēz, *n.* [A.Sax. *briosa, breosa,* a gadfly; comp. A.Sax. *brimse,* a gadfly, a horsefly; D. *brems,* G. *bremse;* O.H.G. *bremen,* to hum.] A name given to flies of various species, the most noted of which is the great horsefly, which sucks the blood of horses.

breeze, brēz, *n.* [Fr. *bris, débris,* rubbish, fragments, from *briser,* to break.] House sweepings, as fluff, dust, ashes, etc.; small ashes and cinders used for burning bricks.

brent, brant, brent, brant, *n.* [D. and G. *brent-gans,* Icel. *brand-gás,* probably from its color being likened to that caused by burning. BRAND.] A species of goose much smaller than the common goose, which breeds in the far north, but migrates for the winter as low down as the middle of France.

brethren, breTH'ren, *n.* pl. of *brother.*

Breton, bret'on, *a.* Relating to Brittany, or Bretagne in France, or the language of its people.—*n.* The native language of Brittany; Armoric.

breve, brēv, *n.* [From L. *brevis,* short.] *Music,* a note or character of time, 𝅜, equivalent to two semibreves or four minims; *printing,* a mark (˘) used to indicate that the syllable over which it is placed is short.

brevet, bre•vet', *n.* [Fr., commission, license. BRIEF.] A commission to an officer which entitles him to a rank in the army above that which he holds in his regiment, without, however, conferring a right to receive corresponding advance in pay; a patent; a warrant; license.—*a.* Taking rank by brevet.—*v.t.* To confer brevet rank upon.

breviary, brē'vi•e•ri, *n.* [Fr. *breviaire,* L. *breviarium,* from *brevis,* short. BRIEF.] *R. Cath. Ch.* a book containing the daily offices which all who are in orders are bound to read. It consists of prayers or offices to be used at the canonical hours, and is an abridgment (whence the name) of the services of the early church.

brevier, bre•vēr', *n.* [G. *brevier,* Fr. *breviaire:* so called from being originally used in printing breviaries.] A kind of printing type in size between bourgeois and minion.

brevipennate, brev'i•pen•āt, *a.* [L. *brevis,* short, and *penna,* a feather, a wing.] Having short wings: said of such birds as the ostrich, emu, cassowary, dodo, etc.—*n.* A bird having short wings.

brevirostrate, brev•i•ros'trāt, *a.* [L. *brevis,* short, and *rostrum,* a beak.] Having a short beak or bill.

brevity, brev'i•ti, *n.* [L. *brevitas,* from *brevis,* short. BRIEF.] The state or character of being brief; shortness; conciseness; fewness of words.

brew, brö, *v.t.* [A.Sax. *breówan,* to brew; D. *brouwen,* Icel. *brugga,* Dan. *brygge,* G. *brauen,* to brew; akin *broth.*] To prepare, as beer, ale, or other similar liquor is prepared, from malt or other materials, by steeping, boiling, and fermentation; to mingle; to mix; to concoct (a bowl of punch, a philter); to contrive; to plot.—*v.i.* To perform the business of brewing or making beer; to be mixing, forming, or collecting (a storm *brews*).—*n.* The mixture formed by brewing; that which is brewed.—**brewage,** brö'ij, *n.* A mixed drink; drink brewed or prepared in any way.—**brewer,** brö'ėr, *n.* One who brews; one whose occupation is to brew malt liquors.—**brewery,** brö'ėr•i, *n.* The establishment and apparatus where brewing is carried on.—**brewing,** brö'ing, *n.* The act or process of making ale, or other fermented liquor; the quantity brewed at a time.

briar, briary, etc. See BRIER, BRIERY.

Briarean, bri•â'ri•an, *a.* Pertaining to or resembling *Briareus,* a giant with a hundred hands.

bribe, brīb, *n.* [Fr. *bribe,* Prov. Fr. *brife,* broken victuals, such as are given to beggars, something given away; from root seen in Armor. *breva,* to break; W. *briw,* a fragment.] A price, reward, gift, or favor bestowed or promised with a view to pervert the judgment or corrupt the conduct.—*v.t.*—*bribed, bribing.* To induce to a certain course of action, especially a wrong course, by the gift or offer of something valued; to gain over by a bribe.—*v.i.* To practice bribery; to give a bribe to a person.—**bribable,** brī'ba•bl, *a.* Capable of being bribed; liable to be bribed.—**briber,** brī'bėr, *n.* One who bribes or pays for corrupt practices.—**bribery,** brī'bėr•i, *n.* The act or practice of giving or taking a bribe or bribes; the giving or receiving of money by which one's conduct in some public capacity is influenced.

bric-a-brac, brik'a"brak, *n.* [Fr.

Origin doubtful.] Articles of vertu; a collection of objects having a certain interest or value from their rarity, antiquity, or the like.

brick, brik, *n.* [Fr. *brique*, a brick, also a piece, a fragment, from O.D. *brick*, a piece, a fragment, a brick or tile, from *breken*, to *break*.] A kind of artificial stone made principally of clay moistened and made fine by kneading, formed usually into a rectangular shape in a mold and hardened by being burned in a kiln; bricks collectively or as designating the material of which any structure is composed; a mass or object resembling a brick; a jolly good fellow (colloq. or slang.)—*a.* Made of brick; resembling brick.—*v.t.* To lay or pave with bricks, or to surround, close, or wall in with bricks.—**brickbat,** brik′bat, *n.* A piece or fragment of a brick.—**brickkiln,** *n.* A kiln or furnace in which bricks are baked or burned; or a pile of bricks, laid loose, with arches underneath to receive the fuel.—**bricklayer,** brik′lā·ėr, *n.* One whose occupation is to build with bricks.—**bricklaying,** brik′lā·ing, *n.* The art of building with bricks.—**brickwork,** brik′wėrk, *n.* The laying of bricks; masonry consisting of bricks; a place where bricks are made.

bride, brīd, *n.* [A.Sax. *brýd*, *brid*; cog. D. *bruid*, Icel. *brúthr*, Dan. *brud*, Goth. *bruths*, G. *braut*—a bride.] A woman newly married, or on the eve of being married.—**bridal,** brī′dal, *n.* [Formerly *bride-ale*, from *bride*, and *ale*, in the sense of a feast; comp. *church-ale*, etc.] A nuptial festival; a marriage; a wedding.—*a.* Belonging to a bride or to a wedding.—**bridegroom,** brīd′-gröm, *n.* [A.Sax. *brydguma*, from *bryd*, a brīde, and *guma*, a man—D. *bruidegom*, Icel. *brúthgumi*, Dan. *brudgom*, G. *bräutigam*. A.Sax. is cognate with L. *homo*, a man.] A man newly married, or just about to be married.—**bridesmaid,** brīdz′-mād, *n.* A woman or girl who attends on or accompanies a bride at her wedding.

bridewell, brīd′wel, *n.* A house of correction for the confinement of disorderly persons: so called from the palace of King John, 1210, built near *St. Bride's* or *Bridget's Well*, in London, which was turned into a penal workhouse by Edward VI in 1553.

bridge, brij, *n.* [O.E. *brig*, *brigge*, Sc. *brig*, A.Sax. *bricg*, *brycg*, Icel. *bryggja*, Dan. *brygge*, a pier, D. *brug*, G. *brücke*, a bridge; akin to Icel. *bru*, Dan. *bro*, a bridge.] Any structure of wood, stone, brick, or iron, raised over a river, pond, lake, road, valley, or the like, for the purpose of a convenient passage; in *furnaces*, a low wall or vertical partition for compelling the flame and heated vapor to ascend; the part of a stringed instrument over which the strings are stretched, and by which they are raised above the sounding board; the upper bony part of the nose; a platform above the deck of a ship for the commanding officer; a device for fastening false teeth to natural teeth; a card game.—**bridgehead,** brij′hed, *n.* A commanding position in hostile territory.—*v.t.*—*bridged*, *bridging*. To build a bridge on or over; to make a bridge or bridges for (a road); *fig.* to find a way of overcoming or getting over: generally with *over* (to *bridge over* a difficulty).

bridle, brī′dl, *n.* [A.Sax. *bridel*, a bridle=D. *bridel*, O.H.G. *bridel*. Probably from A.Sax. *bredan*, to braid.] The portion of gear or harness fitted to the head of a horse (or animal similarly used), and by which he is governed and restrained; a restraint; a curb; a check.—*v.t.*—*bridled*, *bridling*. To put a bridle on; to restrain, guide, or govern; to check, curb, or control.—*v.i.* To hold the head up and backward; to assume a lofty manner so as to assert one's dignity or express indignation at its being offended; to toss the head: generally with *up*.—**bridle path,** *n.* A path or road which can be traveled on horseback but not by wheeled carriages.

bridoon, bri·dön′, *n.* [Fr. *bridon*, from *bride*, a bridle.] A light snaffle or bit of a bridle in addition to the principal bit, and having a distinct rein.

brief, brēf, *a.* [O.Fr. *brief*, Fr. *bref*, from L. *brevis*, short, seen also in *brevity*, *breve*, *abbreviate*, *abridge*.] Short in duration; lasting a short time; short in expression; using few words; concise; succinct.—*In brief*, in few words; in short.—*n.* An epitome; a short or concise writing (*Shak.*); an abridged relation of the facts of a litigated case drawn up for the instruction of an advocate or barrister in conducting proceedings in a court of justice; a formal letter from the pope on some matter of discipline.—*v.t.* To furnish (a barrister) with a brief.—**briefless,** brēf′les, *a.* Receiving or having received no briefs (a *briefless* barrister).—**briefly,** brēf′li, *adv.* In a brief manner; concisely; in few words.—**briefness,** brēf′nes, *n.* The state or quality of being brief; shortness; conciseness; brevity.

brier, briar, brī′ėr, *n.* [A.Sax. *braer*, *brér*, a brier; probably borrowed from the Celtic; comp. Ir. *briar*, a thorn, a pin, a brier; Gael. *preas*, a bush, a brier.] A prickly plant or shrub in general; the sweetbrier and the wild brier, species of the rose; the wild rose.—**briery, briary,** brī′-ėr·i, *a.* Full of briers; rough; thorny.

brig, brig, *n.* [An abbrev. of *brigantine*.] A vessel with two masts, square rigged nearly like a ship's mainmast and foremast.

brigade, bri·gād′, *n.* [Fr. *brigade*, from It. *brigata*, a brigade, from *brigare*, to fight. BRIGAND.] A party or division of troops, consisting of several regiments, squadrons, or battalions; in the U.S. army formation, three regiments ordinarily constitute a *brigade*, and three *brigades* a division; an organized body of individuals, usually wearing a uniform, and acting under an authorized head (a fire *brigade*).—**brigadier,** brig·a·dēr′, **brigadier general,** *n.* The general officer next in rank below a major general.

brigand, brig′and, *n.* [Fr. *brigand*, from It. *brigante*, a pirate, a brigand, from *brigare*, to intrigue, to quarrel (whence also *brigade*), from *briga*, an intrigue, a quarrel.] A robber; a freebooter; a highwayman; especially, one of those robbers who live in gangs in secret retreats in mountains or forests.—**brigandage,** brig′an·dij, *n.* The life and practices of a brigand; highway robbery.

brigandine, brig′an·dēn, *n.* [Fr. *brigandine*, from *brigand*, in old sense of foot soldier. BRIGAND.] Body armor composed of iron rings or small thin iron plates sewed upon canvas, linen, or leather, and covered over with similar materials.

brigantine, brig′an·tēn, *n.* [Fr. *brigantin*, from It. *brigantino*, a pirate vessel, from *brigante*, a pirate. BRIGAND. *Brig* is an abbrev. of this word.] A kind of light sailing vessel formerly much used by corsairs; a two-masted vessel partly square rigged and resembling a brig.

bright, brīt, *a.* [A.Sax. *beorht*, *bryht*, clear, shining=Goth. *bairhts*, O.H.G. *berht*, bright; same root as L. *flagro* (anciently *fragro*), to flame, *flamma* (*flagma*), flame, Skr. *bhraj*, to shine.] Radiating or reflecting light; blazing with light; brilliant; shining; luminous; resplendent; sparkling; illustrious; glorious (name, period); quick in wit; witty; clever; not dull; lively; vivacious; animated; cheerful.—**brighten,** brīt′n. *v.t.* To make bright or brighter; to shed light on; to make to shine; to cheer; to make gay or cheerful; to heighten the splendor of; to add luster to; to make acute or witty; to sharpen the faculties of.—*v.i.* To grow bright or more bright; to clear up; to become less dark or gloomy.—**brightly,** brīt′li, *adv.* In a bright manner; splendidly; with luster.—**brightness,** brīt′nes, *n.* The state or quality of being bright; splendor; luster; acuteness of mental faculties; sharpness of wit.—**Bright's disease** (Dr. Bright). Granular kidney degeneration.

brill, bril, *n.* [Probably from Corn. *brithel*, a mackerel, pl. *brithelli*, *brilli*, from *brith*, streaked, variegated.] A kind of flatfish resembling the turbot, but inferior to it both in size and quality.

brilliant, bril′yant, *a.* [Fr. *brillant*, sparkling, from *briller*, to shine or sparkle, L.L. *beryllare*, to shine like a beryl, from L. *beryllus*, a beryl.] Sparkling or gleaming with luster; glittering; bright; distinguished by such qualities as command admiration; splendid; shining (a *brilliant* achievement, a *brilliant* writer).—*n.* A diamond of the finest cut, formed into faces and facets so as to reflect and refract the light in the most vivid manner possible; *printing*, a very small type, a size less than diamond.—**brilliance, brilliancy,** bril'yans, bril'yan•si, *n.* Great brightness; splendor; luster.—**brilliantly,** bril'yant•li, *adv.* In a brilliant manner; splendidly.—**brilliantness,** bril'-yant•nes, *n.*

brim, brim, *n.* [A.Sax. *brim*, the surf, the sea = Icel. *brim*, the surf; akin Dan. *braemme*, G. *bräme*, the edge, border; from root seen in L. *fremere*, to roar, Skr. *bhram*, to whirl, *bhrimi*, a whirlpool, *brim* being thus the part where the surf roars or rages.] The brink, edge, or margin of a river or sheet of water; the upper edge of anything hollow, as a cup; a projecting edge, border, or rim round anything hollow, as a hat.—*v.t.*—*brimmed, brimming*. To fill to the brim, upper edge, or top; to furnish with a brim, as a hat.—*v.i.* To be full to the brim; to be full to overflowing.—*To brim over*, to run over the brim; to be so full as to overflow.—**brimful,** brim'fu̦l, *a.* Full to the top; completely full; used predicatively.—**brimmer,** brim'ėr, *n.* A bowl or glass full to the top.

brimstone, brim'stōn, *n.* [O.E. *bremstone, brenston*, etc., Sc. *bruntstane, brunstane*; lit. *burn-stone*, or *burning-stone*, like Icel. *brennisteinn*, brimstone.] Sulfur.

brinded, brin'ded, *a.* [Equivalent to Prov. E. and Sc. *branded*, of a reddish-brown color with darker markings; lit. of a burnt color, the root being in *burn, brand*, etc.] Obs., of a gray or tawny color with bars or streaks of a darker hue; having a hide variegated by streaks or blotches lighter and darker in hue.—**brindled,** brin'dld, *a.* Same as *Brinded*, and now the more commonly used word.

brine, brīn, *n.* [A.Sax. *bryne*, brine, so called from its burning taste = A.Sax. *bryne*, a burning. BURN.] Water saturated or strongly impregnated with salt, like the water of the ocean; salt water; hence used for tears, and for the sea or ocean.—*v.t.*—*brined, brining*. To steep in brine.—**brinish,** brī'nish, *a.* Like brine; somewhat salt; saltish.—**briny,** brī'ni, *a.* Consisting of or resembling brine; of the nature of brine; salt.

bring, bring, *v.t.*—*brought, bringing*. [A.Sax. *bringan, brang, brungen*, later *brengan, brohte, broht* = D. *brengen*, Goth. *briggan* (pron. *bringan*), G. *bringen*; same root as *bear*, to carry.] To bear or convey from a distant to a nearer place, or to a person; to fetch; to carry; to make to come (honor, wisdom, strength, sleep); to procure; to conduct or attend in going; to accompany; to change in state or condition (*bring* to nought, etc.); to persuade (*bring* to reason, to terms).—*To bring about*, to effect; to accomplish.— *To bring down*, to cause to come down; to lower; to humiliate; to abase.—*To bring forth*, to produce, as young or fruit; to beget; to cause.—*To bring forward*, to produce to view or notice (*bring forward* arguments).—*To bring in*, to introduce; to supply; to furnish (income, rent).—*To bring off*, to bear or convey from a place; to procure to be acquitted; to clear from condemnation.—*To bring on*, to cause to begin (a battle, etc.); to originate (*bring on* a disease).—*To bring over*, to convey over; to convert by persuasion or other means; to cause to change sides or an opinion.—*To bring* (*a ship*) *to*, to check the course of (a ship) by making the sails counteract each other and keep her nearly stationary.—*To bring to light*, to reveal.—*To bring to mind*, to recall what has been forgotten or out of the thoughts.—*To bring to pass*, to effect.—*To bring under*, to subdue; to reduce to obedience.—*To bring up*, to nurse, feed, and tend; to rear; to educate; to introduce to notice (to *bring up* a subject); to cause to advance near (troops); to cause to stop (a horse); to pull up.—*To bring up the rear*, to move onward in the rear; to form the rear portion.—**bringer,** bring'ėr, *n.* One who brings or conveys.

brink, bringk, *n.* [A Scandinavian word; Dan. and Sw. *brink*, a hill, declivity; allied to W. *bryncyn*, a hillock, from *bryn*, a hill.] The edge, margin, or border of a steep place, as of a precipice or the bank of a river; verge; hence, close proximity to danger.

briquette, bri•ket', *n.* [Dim. of Fr. *brique*, a brick.] A lump of fuel, in the form of a brick, made from coal dust, with some binding material such as coal tar.

brisk, brisk, *a.* [From the Celtic: W. *brysg*, Ir. *brisg*, quick, lively.] Lively; active; nimble; gay; sprightly; vivacious; effervescing vigorously; sparkling (liquor); burning freely; rapid; quick (movement, pace).—*v.t.* To make brisk.—*v.i.* To become brisk, lively, or alert: often with *up*.—**briskly,** brisk'li, *adv.* In a brisk manner; actively; vigorously; with life and spirit.—**briskness,** brisk'nes, *n.* The state or quality of being brisk.

brisket, bris'ket, *n.* [O.Fr. *brischet* or *bruschet* (Fr. *bréchet*), from Armor. *brusk*, the breast.] The breast of an animal, or that part of the breast that lies next to the ribs; in a horse, the fore part of the neck at the shoulder down to the forelegs.

bristle, bris'l, *n.* [A diminutive from A. Sax. *byrst*, a bristle = D. *borstel*, a bristle; akin Icel. *burst*, Dan. *börste*, G. *borste*, a bristle.] One of the stiff, coarse, glossy hairs of the hog and the wild boar, especially one of the hairs growing on the back; a stiff roundish hair or similar appendage.—*v.t.*—*bristled, bristling*. To erect in bristles; to make bristly; to erect in defiance or anger, like a swine; to furnish with bristles or stiff hairs.—*v.i.* To rise up or stand on end like bristles; to appear as if covered with bristles; to show anger, resentment, or defiance: generally followed by *up*.—**bristly,** bris'li, *a.* Thick set with bristles, or with hairs like bristles; rough; resembling a bristle or bristles.

Bristol board, *n.* [From the city of *Bristol*, in England.] A fine kind of pasteboard, smooth, and sometimes glazed on the surface.

britannia metal, *n.* A metallic compound or alloy of tin, with a little copper and antimony, used chiefly for teapots, spoons, etc.

Britannic, bri•tan'ik, *a.* Pertaining to Britain.—**British,** brit'ish, *a.* Pertaining to Great Britain or its inhabitants: sometimes applied distinctively to the original Celtic inhabitants.—**Britisher,** brit'ish•ėr, *n.* A patriotic or typical British subject.—**Briton,** brit'on, *n.* A native of Britain or the British islands.

British Thermal Unit. The amount of heat needed to raise one pound of water one degree Fahrenheit. Abbrev. B.T.U.

brittle, brit'l, *a.* [O.E. *britel*, from A.Sax. *brytan, breótan*, to break = Icel. *brjóta*, Dan. *bryde*, to break.] Easily broken, or easily breaking short, without splinters or loose parts rent from the substance; fragile; not tough or tenacious.—**brittleness,** brit'l•nes, *n.* Aptness to break; fragility.

britzska, brits'ka, *n.* [A Polish word.] An open carriage with a calash top, and space for reclining when used for a journey.

broach, brōch, *n.* [Fr. *broche*, from L.L. *brocca*, a spit, a point; allied to Gael. *brog*, to goad, *brog*, an awl.] A spit‡; a spire, especially a spire springing directly from a tower; a general name for all tapered boring bits or drills.—*v.t.* To pierce with or as with a spit‡; to open for the first time for the purpose of taking out something; more especially to tap: to pierce, as a cask in order to draw the liquor; to begin conversation or discussion about; to open up (a topic or subject).—*To broach to* (*naut.*), to incline suddenly to windward, so as to lay the sails aback and expose the vessel to the danger of oversetting; to overset, by death.—**broacher,** brōch'ėr, *n.* One who broaches, opens, or utters.

broad, bra̦d, *n.* [A.Sax. *brád* = D. *breed*, Icel. *breithr*, Dan. and Sw. *bred*, Goth. *braids*, G. *breit*, broad; root unknown.] Having extent from side to side, as distinguished from *long*, or extended from end to end; having breadth; having a great extent from side to side, as opposed to *narrow;* wide; extensive; vast; *fig.* not limited or narrow; liberal; comprehensive; enlarged; widely diffused; open; full (*broad* daylight); plain or unmistakable; free; unrestrained (*broad* humor); somewhat gross, coarse, or unpolished; indelicate; indecent; bold; unreserved; characterized by vigor, boldness, or freedom of style, as in art, so that strong and striking effects or impressions are produced by simple unelaborate means.—*Broad Church,* a section of the Church of England contrasted with the High Church and the Low Church; a section of any church holding moderate or not very rigid views.—**broaden,** bra̤d'n, *v.t.* To make broad or broader; to increase the width of; to render more comprehensive, extensive, or open.—*v.i.* To become broad or broader.—**broadly,** bra̤d'li, *adv.* In a broad manner; widely; comprehensively; fully; openly; plainly. —**broad arrow** *n.* A stamp resembling the barbed head of an arrow put upon stores, etc., belonging to the British government.—**broadbrim,** *n.* A hat with a very broad brim, such as is worn by members of the Society of Friends; *cap.* hence, a member of said society; a Quaker. (Colloq.)—**broadcast,** bra̤d'kast, *n. Agri.* a casting or throwing seed from the hand for dispersion in sowing; act of disseminating; transmission by radio or television.—*v.t.* To scatter widely; to send out by radio or television.—*a.* Widely scattered; made public by radio or television.—**broadcaster,** *n.*—**broadcloth,** *n.* A kind of fine woolen cloth woven about twice the usual breadth, and dyed in the piece.—**broadside,** bra̤d'sīd, *n.* The side of a ship above the water from the bow to the quarter; a simultaneous discharge of all the guns on one side of a ship; a sheet of paper, one side of which is covered by printed matter, often of a popular character.—**broadsword,** bra̤d'sōrd, *n.* A sword with a broad blade and cutting edges.

Brobdingnagian, brob•ding•nag'i•an, *a.* Gigantic, like an inhabitant of the fabled region of Brobdingnag in Swift's *Gulliver's Travels.*

brocade, brō•kād', *n.* [Sp. *brocado,* from an old *brocar,* equivalent to Fr. *brocher,* to pick, emboss. BROACH.] Silk stuff variegated with gold and silver, or having raised flowers, foliage, and other ornaments; also applied to other stuffs wrought and enriched in like manner.—**brocaded,** brō•kād'ed, *a.* Woven or worked into a brocade; dressed in brocade.

brocatel, brok•a•tel', *n.* [Sp. *brocatel,* Fr. *brocatelle,* It. *brocatello,* from root of *brocade.*] Sienna marble, a species of brecciated marble composed of fragments of various colors; a kind of light thin woolen cloth of silky surface used for linings, etc.; linsey-woolsey. Spelled also *Brocatelle.*

broccoli, brok'o•li, *n.* [It. *broccoli,* pl. of *broccolo,* sprout, cabbage sprout, dim. of *brocco,* a skewer, a shoot. BROACH.] One of the many varieties of the common cabbage, closely resembling the cauliflower.

brochure, brō•shör', *n.* [Fr., from *brocher,* to stitch.] A pamphlet, especially a slight pamphlet, or one on a matter of transitory interest.

brock, brok, *n.* [A.Sax. *broc*=Dan. *brok,* Ir. and Gael. *broc,* W. *broch,* a badger, from the white-streaked face of the animal; comp. Gael. *brocach,* speckled; Dan. *broget,* Sw. *brokug,* parti-colored.] A badger.

brocket, brok'et, *n.* [Fr. *brocart,* because it has one *broche* or snag to its antler.] A red deer two years old; a pricket.

brogue, brōg, *n.* [Ir. and Gael. *brog,* a shoe of rough hide. From this shoe being used by the Irish the word came to designate their manner of speaking English.] A kind of shoe made of raw or half-tanned leather, of one entire piece; a stout, coarse shoe; a dialectical manner of pronunciation; especially the pronunciation peculiar to the Irish.

broil, broil, *n.* [Fr. *brouiller,* to jumble or mix up, to throw into bustle or confusion; origin doubtful.] A tumult; a noisy quarrel; contention; discord; a brawl.—**broiler,** broil'ėr, *n.* One who excites broils or quarrels, or who readily takes part in tumults or contentions.

broil, broil, *v.t.*[O.Fr. *bruiller;* origin doubtful.] To dress or cook over a fire, generally upon a gridiron; to subject to a strong heat.—*v.i.* To be subjected to the action of heat, like meat over the fire; to be greatly heated or to sweat with heat.—**broiler,** broil'ėr, *n.* One who or that which dresses by broiling; a gridiron.

broke, brōk. Pret. and obsolescent or poetical pp. of *break.*—**broken,** brō'kn, pp. of *break,* often used as an *a.* Parted by violence; separated into fragments, as by a blow; not integral or entire; fractional, as numbers; humble; contrite; violated; transgressed (a *broken* vow); interrupted by sobs or imperfect utterance.—**brokenly,** brō'kn•li, *adv.* In a broken interrupted manner.—**brokenness,** brō'kn•nes, *n.* The state of being broken.—**brokenhearted,** *a.* Having the spirits quite crushed by grief or despair.—**broken wind,** *n.* A disease in horses, characterized by a difficult expiration of the air from the lungs, and often accompanied with an enlargement of the lungs and heart. —**broken-winded,** *a.* Affected with broken wind.

broker, brō'kėr, *n.* [O.Fr. *brokeor, brokiere,* from a verb meaning to tap or *broach;* originally a retailer of liquor.] An agent who buys and sells goods or shares or transacts other business for others, being generally paid at a rate per cent on the value of the transaction, such as exchange brokers, ship brokers, stockbrokers, etc.; one who deals in second-hand household goods, clothes, and the like.—**brokerage,** brō'kėr•ij, *n.* The fee, reward, or commission given or charged for transacting business as a broker; the business or employment of a broker.

brom, brōm, *n.* [Gr. *bromos,* oats.] A name of several oatlike species of grass.

bromine, brō'mīn or brō'min, *n.* [Gr. *brômos,* a fetid odor.] An element occurring as a dark-red fuming liquid, the vapor being irritating and evil smelling. Symbol, Br; at. no., 35; at. wt., 79.904.—**bromal,** brō'mal, *n.* A colorless oily fluid of a penetrating odor, obtained by the action of bromine on alcohol.—**bromate,** brō'māt, *n.* A salt formed of bromic acid.—**bromic,** brō'mik, *a.* Pertaining to or obtained from bromine, as *bromic* acid, a compound of oxygen and bromine.—**bromide,** brō'mīd, *n.* A compound formed by the union of bromine with another element.

bronchia, brong'ki•a, *n. pl.* [Gr. and L.] The two tubes, with their ramifications, arising from the bifurcation of the windpipe in the lungs, and conveying air to the latter; the bronchi.—**bronchial,** brong'ki•al, *a.* Belonging to the bronchia.—*Bronchial tubes,* the ramifications of the bronchia, terminating in the bronchial cells, or air cells of the lungs.—**bronchic,** brong'kik, *a.* Same as *Bronchial.*—**bronchitis,** brong•kī'tis, *n.* [The term. *-itis* signifies inflammation.] An inflammation of the lining membrane of the bronchi or bronchia, often a troublesome ailment.—**bronchotomy,** brong•kot'o•mi, *n.* [Gr. *tome,* a cutting.] *Surg.* an incision into the windpipe or larynx between the rings, to afford a passage for the air into and out of the lungs when respiration in the usual way is prevented.—**bronchus,** brong'kus, *n.* pl. **bronchi,** brong'kī. [Gr. *bronchos,* the windpipe.] One of the two bronchia or bifurcations of the trachea.

brontosaurus, bron•to•sa̤'rus, *n.* [Gr. *bronte,* thunder, *sauros,* a lizard.] A fossil reptile with a remarkably small skull.

bronze, bronz, *n.* [Fr. *bronze,* from It. *bronzo,* bronze, L. *Aes Brundusianum,* the brass of Brundusium.] A compound or alloy of from 2 to 20 parts of copper to 1 of tin, to which other metallic substances are sometimes added, especially zinc, used for statues, bells, cannon, coins, etc.; any statue, bust, urn, medal, or other work of art, cast of bronze; a brown color resembling bronze; a pigment prepared for the purpose of imitating bronze.—*v.t.*—*bronzed, bronzing.* To give the appearance or color of bronze to, by covering with bronze leaf, copper dust, etc.; to make brown or tan, as the skin by exposure to the sun.—**bronzy,** bron'zi, *a.* Belonging to or resembling bronze.

brooch, brōch, *n.* [A form of *broach* (which see).] An ornamental pin or clasp used for fastening the dress or merely for display.

brood, bröd, *n.* [A.Sax. *brod,* a brood=D. *broed,* G. *brut,* a brood; from root of *breed.*] Offspring; progeny; the young birds hatched at once; that which is bred or produced.—*v.i.* To sit upon eggs or upon young, as a hen for the purpose of hatching, warming, or protecting them; hence, to remain steadfastly settled over something; to have the mind dwelling for a long time uninterruptedly on a subject; with *on* or *over.*—*v.t.* To sit over, cover, and cherish; to nourish; to foster.

brook, bru̦k, *n.* [A.Sax. *bróc,* a spring, a brook, from *brecan,* to burst forth; comp. D. *brock,* G. *bruch,* a marsh.

A brook is a breaking forth of water; comp. *spring*.] A small natural stream of water, or a current flowing from a spring or fountain less than a river.—**brooklet,** bruk'let, *n.* A small brook.

brook, bruk, *v.t.* [A.Sax. *brúcan*, to use, enjoy=D. *gebruiken*, Icel. *bruka*, Goth. *brukjan*, to use; allied to L. *frui*, to enjoy (whence *fruition*).] To bear; to endure; to support; usually in negative or interrogative sentences (they cannot *brook* restraint).

broom, bröm, *n.* [A.Sax. *bróm*=L.G. *brâm*, D. *brem*, broom; allied to *bramble*. BRAMBLE, BRIM.] A leguminous shrub growing abundantly on sandy pastures and heaths, distinguished by having large, yellow, papilionaceous flowers, leaves in threes, and single, and the branches angular; a besom or brush with a long handle for sweeping floors; so called from being originally made of the broom plant.—**broomcorn,** *n.* The common millet or Guinea corn, a cereal plant so called from its branched panicles being made into carpet brooms.—**broomrape,** *n.* A parasitic plant growing on the roots of broom, furze, etc.—**broomstick,** bröm'stik, *n.* The stick or handle of a broom.

broth, broth, *n.* [A.Sax. *broth*, from root of *brew*.] Liquor in which flesh is boiled and macerated, usually with certain vegetables to give it a better relish.

brothel, broth'el, *n.* [O.E. *brothel*, a wretch, from *brothen*, ruined, destroyed, from *breóthan*, to destroy.] A house appropriated to the purposes of prostitution; a bawdyhouse.

brother, bruTH'ėr, *n.* pl. **brothers,** bruTH'ėrz, or **brethren,** breTH'ren. [A.Sax. *bróthor*=D. *broeder*, Icel. *bróthir*, Dan. and Sw. *broder*, Goth. *brothar*, G. *bruder*, Ir. and Gael. *brathair*, W. *brawd*, Rus. *brat'*, Bohem. *brátr*, L. *frater*, Gr. *phrater*, Skr. *bhratr*, brother; the root meaning of the word is unknown.] Strictly a human male born of the same father and mother (also used of animals); a male born of the same father or mother (more strictly called a *half*-brother); a relation or kinsman; an associate; one of the same rank, profession, or occupation; or more generally, a fellow creature; specifically, a member of a religious order; one that resembles another in manners or disposition. [The plural *brethren* is now used only in the wider meanings of the word.]—**brotherhood,** bruTH'ėr·hud, *n.* The state of being a brother or brotherly; an association of men for any purpose; a class of individuals of the same kind, profession, or occupation; a fraternity.—**brotherly,** bruTH'ėr·li, *a.* Pertaining to brothers; such as is natural for brothers; becoming brothers (*brotherly* love).—**brotherliness,** bruTH'ėr·li·nes, *n.* State of being brotherly.—**brother-in-law,** *n.* The brother of one's husband or wife; also, a sister's husband.

brougham, brö'am or bröm, *n.* [After the first Lord *Brougham*.] A onehorse closed carriage, either two or four wheeled, and adapted to carry either two or four persons.

brought, brat, pret. & pp. of *bring*.

brow, brou, *n.* [A.Sax. *brú*, the eyebrow=D. *braauw*, Icel. *brun*, G. *braue*, the eyebrow; cog. with Gr. *ophrys*, Per. *abru*, Skr. *bhrû*, the eyebrow.] The prominent ridge over the eye, forming an arch above the orbit; the arch of hair over the eye; the eyebrow; the forehead; the edge of a steep place; the upper portion of a slope.—**browbeat,** brou'bēt, *v.t.* To abash or bear down with haughty, stern looks, or with arrogant speech and dogmatic assertions.

brown, broun, *a.* [A.Sax. *brun*=Icel. *brúnn*, Dan. *bruun*, Sw. *brun*, D. *bruin*, G. *braun*, brown; lit. of a *burnt* color, from root of *burn*, *bronze*, etc.] Of a dark or dusky color, inclining to redness.—*n.* A dark color inclining to red or yellow of various degrees of depth, and resulting from a mixture of red, black, and yellow.—*Brown bread*, wheaten bread made from unbolted flour, which thus includes the bran, and hence is of a brown color.—*Brown coal*, lignite. —*Brown study*, a fit of mental abstraction or meditation; a reverie.—*v.t.* To make brown or dusky; to give a brown color to.—*v.i.* To become brown.—**brownie,** *n.* Household servant of a fairy or goblin nature, in Scottish mythology. Milton's 'drudging-goblin', 'lubberfiend'.—**brownish,** broun'ish, *a.* Somewhat brown; inclined to brown.

browse, brouz, *v.t.*—*browsed*, *browsing*. [O.Fr. *brouster* (Fr. *brouter*), to browse, from *brost*, *broust*, a sprout, a shoot, from O.H.G. *broz*, G. *bross*, sprout.] To feed on: said of cattle, deer, etc.; to pasture on; to graze.—*v.i.* To feed on pasture or on the leaves, shoots, etc., of shrubs and trees: said of cattle, deer, etc.—*n.* The tender shoots or twigs of trees and shrubs, such as cattle may eat; green food fit for cattle, deer, etc.

brucine, brö'sin, *n.* [From name *Bruce*.] A vegetable alkaloid akin to strychnine, bitter and acid, but less powerful in its action.

bruin, brö'in, *n.* [The bear's name in the celebrated fable Reynard the Fox; from the D. *bruin*, brown.] A name given to the bear.

bruise, bröz, *v.t.*—*bruised*, *bruising*. [O.Fr. *bruiser*, *bruser*, *briser*, to break, to shiver, from O.G. *brestan*, to break, to burst.] To injure by a blow without laceration; to contuse; to crush by beating or pounding; to pound; to bray, as drugs or articles of food; to make a dent or dint in.—*v.i.* To fight with the fists; to box (colloq.).—*n.* A contusion; a hurt upon the flesh of animals, upon plants or other bodies, with a blunt or heavy object.—**bruiser,** bröz'ėr, *n.* The person or thing that bruises; an instrument or machine for bruising substances; a pugilist, boxer, or prize fighter (colloq.).

bruit, bröt, *v.t.* [Fr. *bruit*, noise, uproar, rumor, from *bruire*, to make a noise.]—*v.t.* To announce with noise; to report; to noise abroad.

brumal, brumous, brö'mal, brö'mus, *a.* [L. *brumalis*, from *bruma*, winter.] Belonging to the winter.

brunet, brö·net', *n.* [Fr., a dim. from *brun*, brown. BROWN.] A woman with a brown or dark complexion.

brunt, brunt, *n.* [From the root or stem of to *burn*; comp. Sc. *brunt*, burnt; Icel. *bruni*, a burning; Dan. *brynde* and *brunst*, ardor, ardency, burning heat. BURN.] The heat or utmost violence of an onset; the first or severest shock of a battle or struggle; the force of a blow; violence; shock of any kind.

brush, brush, *n.* [O.Fr. *broche*, *brosse*, brushwood; Mod.Fr. *brosse*, a brush; from O.H.G. *broz*, a sprout. BROWSE.] An instrument made of bristles or other similar material bound together, used for various purposes, as for dressing the hair, removing dust from clothes, laying on colors, whitewash, and the like; the small trees and shrubs of a wood, or a thicket of small trees; electricity issuing in a diverging manner from a point; the bushy tail of some animals, as the fox, squirrel, etc.; the act of using a brush, or of applying a brush to; a slight encounter; a skirmish.—*v.t.* To sweep or rub with a brush; to strike lightly by passing over the surface; to pass lightly over; to remove by brushing or by lightly passing over.—*To brush up*, to furbish; to polish; to improve; especially, to improve the appearance of.—*v.i.* To move nimbly in haste; to move so lightly as scarcely to be perceived; to move over lightly.—**brushy,** brush'i, *a.* Resembling a brush; rough; shaggy; having long hair.—**brushwood,** *n.* Small trees or shrubs forming a thicket or coppice; branches of trees cut off.

brusque, brusk, brusk, *a.* [Fr. *brusque*, from It. *brusco*, brusque, sharp, sour.] Abrupt in manner; blunt; rude.—**brusqueness,** brusk'nes, *n.* A rude, abrupt, or blunt manner.

Brussels carpet, *n.* A carpet having a heavy linen web enclosing worsted yarns of different colors, which are raised in loops to form the patterns. —**Brussels sprouts,** *n. pl.* A variety of cabbage, characterized by little clusters of leaves which form miniature heads of cabbage.

brute, bröt, *n.* [L. *brutus*, stupid, insensible, irrational.] A beast; any animal destitute of reason; a brutal person; a savage in disposition or manners; a low-bred, unfeeling human being.—*a.* Insensible, irrational, or unintelligent; not proceeding from or inspired by reason and intelligence (*brute* force, the *brute* earth).—**brutal,** brö'tal, *a.* Pertaining to a brute; like a brute; savage; cruel; inhuman; brutish.—**brutality,** brö·tal'i·ti, *n.* The quality of being brutal; inhumanity; savageness; gross cruelty; insensibility to pity or shame; a savage, shameless, or inhuman act.—**brutalize,** brö'tal·īz, *v.t.*—*brutalized*, *brutalizing*. To make brutal, coarse, gross, or inhuman; to degrade to the level of a brute.—**brutally,** brö'tal·li, *adv.* In a brutal manner; cruelly; inhumanly; in a coarse, gross, or unfeeling manner.—**brutify,** brö'ti•fī, *v.t.—brutified, brutifying.* To make a person a brute; to make senseless, stupid, or unfeeling.—**brutish,** brö'tish, *a.* Pertaining to or resembling a brute; uncultured; ignorant; stupid; unfeeling; savage; brutal; gross; carnal; bestial.—**brutishly,** brö'tish•li, *adv.* In a brutish manner.—**brutishness,** brö'tish•nes, *n.* The quality of being brutish.

bryology, brī•ol'o•ji, *n.* [Gr. *bryon,* moss, and *logos,* discourse.] The science of mosses, their structure, affinities, classification, etc.—**bryological,** brī•o•loj'ik•al, *a.* Pertaining to bryology, or to the mosses.

bryony, brī'o•ni, *n.* [L. *bryonia,* Gr. *bryōnia,* bryony, from *bryō,* to swell, to sprout, from the quick growth of the stems.] A climbing plant of various species; *white bryony,* found in the hedgerows of England, has small red berries and abounds in an acrid fetid juice, which acts as a cathartic and emetic; *black bryony* is a plant of the yam family, and has a tuberous rootstalk, also with cathartic and emetic properties.

Bryozoa, brī•o•zō'a, *n. pl.* [Gr. *bryon,* moss, and *zōon,* animal.] A group of minute molluscoid animals living together in mosslike masses; now commonly called *Polyzoa* (which see).—**bryozoan,** brī•o•zō'an, *n.* One of the Bryozoa.

bubble, bub'l, *n.* [Dan. *boble,* Sw. *bubbla,* D. *bobbel,* a bubble; akin to *blob.*] A small vesicle of water or other fluid inflated with air; a blob of air in a fluid; *fig.* something that wants firmness or solidity; a vain project; a false show; a delusive or fraudulent scheme of speculation; a fraud.—*v.i. bubbled, bubbling.* To rise in bubbles, as liquids when boiling or agitated; to run with a gurgling noise; to gurgle.—*v.t.* To cause to bubble; to cheat; to deceive; to trick.—**bubbly,** bub'li, *a.* Full of bubbles.

bubo, bū'bō, *n.* [Gr. *boubōn,* the groin, a swelling in the groin.] A tumor or abscess, with inflammation, which rises in certain glandular parts of the body, as in the groin or armpit.

buccal, buk'al, *a.* [L. *bucca,* the cheek.] Pertaining to the cheek.—*Buccal glands,* the small glands of the mouth which secrete a viscous fluid that mixes with the saliva.

buccaneer, buk•a•nēr', *n.* [Fr. *boucanier,* a pirate, originally a hunter who smoked the flesh of the animals killed, from *boucaner,* to smoke meat, from *boucan,* a place for smoking meat, a Carib word.] A pirate; a sea robber; more especially, one of the piratical adventurers, English and French, who combined to make depredations on the Spaniards in America in the 17th and 18th centuries.—*v.i.* To act the part of a pirate or sea robber.

bucentaur, bū•sen'tạr, *n.* [Gr. *bous,* an ox, and *kentauros,* a centaur.] A mythological monster, half man and half ox; the state barge of Venice, in which the doge and senate went to wed the Adriatic.

Bucephalus, bū•sef'a•lus, *n.* A war horse, the steed of Alexander the Great.

buck, buk, *n.* [Ir. and Gael. *buac,* cow dung used in bleaching, bleaching liquid, lye; from W. *bu, buw,* Gael. *bo,* a cow.] Lye or suds in which clothes are soaked in the operation of bleaching.—*v.t.* To soak or wash in lye, a process in bleaching; to break up and pulverize, as ores.

buck, buk, *n.* [A.Sax. *bucca,* a he-goat, a buck=D. *bok,* Icel. *bokkr,* a he-goat; Dan. *buk,* a buck, a he-goat, a ram; G. *bock,* a he-goat, a buck; W. *bwch,* a buck, Ir. *boc,* a he-goat.] The male of the fallow deer, of the goat, the rabbit and hare; often used specifically of the male of the fallow deer; a roebuck; a dashing fellow; a fop, swell, or dandy.—**buckish,** buk'ish, *a.* Pertaining to a buck or dashing fellow; foppish.—**buckeye,** *n.* A name for several species of American horse chestnut.—**buckhound,** *n.* A kind of hound, less than the staghound, for hunting bucks or fallow deer.—**buckskin,** buk'skin, *n.* A kind of soft, yellowish or grayish leather originally made of the skin of the deer, but now of that of the sheep; *pl.* breeches made of this leather.—**buckshot,** *n.* A large kind of shot used for killing deer or other large game.—**buckthorn,** *n.* A somewhat spiny shrub of various species; as the purging buckthorn, a native of Britain, having small shining black berries with powerful cathartic properties; another species yields the Persian or yellow berries of commerce.—**bucktooth,** *n.* A projecting tooth in a person's jaw; a prominent canine tooth.

bucket, buk'et, *n.* [A.Sax. *buc,* a bucket, a flagon, a pitcher, with dim. term. added. Probably allied to *back,* a vessel.] A vessel made of wood, leather, metal, or other material, for drawing or holding water or other liquids; one of the cavities on the circumference of a water wheel, into which the water is delivered to move the wheel; the scoop of a dredging machine or of a grain elevator.—**bucketful,** buk'et•fụl, *n.* As much as a bucket will hold.

buckle, buk'l, *n.* [Fr. *boucle,* buckle, from L.L. *buccula,* the central part of the buckler, the boss, dim. of L. *bucca,* a cheek.] An instrument, usually made of some kind of metal, and consisting of a rim with a chape and tongue, used for fastening harness, belts, or parts of dress together; a curl of hair; a state of being curled or crisped (as a wig).—*v.t. buckled, buckling.* To fasten with a buckle or buckles; *refl.* to set vigorously to work at anything; to join together, as in marriage (colloq.).—*v.i.* To bend or bow (*Shak.*)‡; to apply with vigor; to engage with zeal: followed by *to.*

buckler, buk'lėr, *n.* [O.Fr. *bocler,* Fr. *bouclier,* a protuberance, a boss on the shield. BUCKLE.] A kind of shield, a piece of defensive armor anciently used in war, and worn on the left arm.—*v.t.*† To be a buckler or shield to; to shield; to defend.

buckra, buk'ra, *n.* [W. African word meaning supernatural being or demon.] A Negro term for a white man.

buckram, buk'ram, *n.* [O.E. *bokeram,* from O.Fr. *boucaran, boqueran,* M.H.G. *buckeram, buckeran,* L.L. *boquerannus,* etc.; perhaps stuff made originally of goat's hair (G. *bock,* a goat) BUCK.] A coarse linen cloth, stiffened with glue, used in garments to keep them in the form intended, and for wrappers to some kinds of merchandise; imaginary or phantom foemen, *men in buckram* (Shak. 1 *Henry IV*).—*a.* Made of buckram or resembling buckram; hence, stiff, precise, formal.

buckshot, buk'shot, *n.* A coarse leaden pellet used as a projectile for killing large game.

buckwheat, buk'hwēt, *n.* [From Prov. E. *buck,* beech and *wheat,* D. *boekweit,* G. *buchweizen* (D. *boek,* G. *buche* a beech); from the resemblance of its triangular seeds to beech-nuts.] A plant with a branched and jointed herbaceous stem, somewhat arrow-shaped leaves, purplish-white flowers, and bearing small triangular seeds, which are ground into flour.

bucolic, bū•kol'ik, *a.* [L. *bucolicus,* from Gr. *boukolikos,* pertaining to cattle, pastoral, from *bous,* an ox.] Pastoral, relating to country affairs and to a herdsman's life and occupation.—*n.* A pastoral poem.

bud, bud, *n.* [Allied to D. *bot,* a bud; O.Fr. *boter,* to bud; Fr. *bouton,* a bud; E. *button.*] A small, generally more or less ovoid, protuberance on the stem or branches of a plant, being the form in which leaves or flowers exist before expanding; a prominence on or in certain animals of low organization, as polyps, which becomes developed into an independent being, which may or may not remain permanently attached to the parent organism.—*v.i.—budded, budding.* To put forth or produce buds; to sprout; to begin to grow from a stock like a bud, as a horn, *fig.* to be in an early stage of development.—*v.t.* To graft by inserting a bud under the bark of another tree.

Buddhism, böd'izm, *n.* [*Buddha,* from Skr. *buddh; pp.* from Skr. *budh,* to awake, the Enlightened, known otherwise as Sakyamuni, Gautama: the sacred name of the founder of the system, who appears to have lived in the 6th cent. B.C.] The religious system founded by Buddha, one of the most prominent doctrines of which is that *nirvâna,* or an absolute release from existence, is the chief good; it prevails in China, Japan, Kashmir, Tibet, Burma, Ceylon, etc., its adherents comprising about a third of the human race.—**Buddhist,** böd'ist, *n.* A worshiper of Buddha; one who adheres to the system of Buddhism.—**Buddhistic,** böd•ist'ik, *a.* Relating to Buddha or to Buddhism.

buddle, bud'l, *n.* [Comp. G. *butteln,* to shake.] *Mining,* a large square frame of boards used in washing metalliferous ore.—*v.t.* or *i.* To wash ore in a buddle.

budge, buj, *v.i.* [Fr. *bouger*, to stir, to move = Pr. *bolegar*, to be agitated, It. *bolicare*, to bubble, from L. *bullire*, to boil. BOIL.] To move off; to stir; to remove from a spot a little; to flinch; to take one's self off.

budge, buj, *n.* [O.Fr. *bouge*, L. *bulga*, a leather bag, from a Gallic word seen in Ir. and Gael. *balg*, *bolg*, a bag; akin *bellows*, *belly*.] Lambskin with the wool dressed outward, formerly used as an ornamental border for scholastic habits.—*a.*‡ Trimmed or adorned with budge; scholastic; pedantic; austere; stiff; formal. (*Mil.*)

budget, buj'et, *n.* [O.E. *boget*, *bouget*, from Fr. *bougette*, dim. of *bouge*, a leather bag. BUDGE, *n.*] A little sack, with its contents; hence, a stock or store; a financial statement of estimated income and expenditures of a country for a fiscal year; a plan of financing a government, based on such a statement; in general, the *weekly budget* of a family, estimating costs of living.

buff, buf, *n.* [Abbrev. of *buffalo*, O.F. *buffle*, Fr. *buffle*, a buffalo.] A sort of leather prepared from the skin of the buffalo, ox, etc., dressed with oil, like shammy; the color of buff; a light yellow.—*a.* Made of buff; of the color of buff.—**buffing wheel,** *n.* A wheel covered with cloth or leather, used in polishing metal.

buffalo, buf'fa•lō, *n.* [From Sp. *bufalo*, Fr. *buffle*, L. *bubalus*, *bufalus*, from Gr. *boubalos* from *bous*, an ox.] A ruminant mammal of the ox family somewhat larger than the common ox and with stouter limbs; in North America, it is called the *bison*, while in India it is named *water buffalo*, in Africa, the *cape buffalo*.—*v.t.* To bewilder; to bamboozle; to get one *buffaloed*. [*American Slang*.]—**buffalo grass,** *n.* A species of short grass growing on the prairies of North America.

buffer, buf'ėr, *n.* [O.E. *buff*, to strike; *buffet*, a blow.] Any apparatus for deadening the concussion between a moving body and the one on which it strikes; an apparatus with powerful springs attached to railroad carriages to prevent injury from violent contact.—**buffer state,** *n.* [Name invented by Archibald Forbes to express the position of Afghanistan in relation to India.] A state between two rival nations.

buffer, buf'ėr, *n.* [From O.E. *buffe*, to stammer, Fr. *bufer*, to puff out the cheeks; comp. Sc. *buff*, nonsense.] A foolish fellow; a fellow: a term expressive of extreme familiarity, and generally having a flavor of contempt.

buffet, bụ•fā', *n.* [Fr. *buffet*, a sideboard, a cupboard.] A cupboard, sideboard, or closet, to hold china, crystal, plate, and other like articles; the space set apart for refreshments in public places.

buffet, buf'et, *n.* [O.Fr. *buffet*, *bufet*, a slap, a blow, dim. from *buffe*, *bufe*, a blow.] A blow with the fist; a box; a cuff; a slap; hence, hard usage of any kind suggestive of blows (Fortune's *buffets*).—*v.t.* To strike with the hand or fist; to box; to beat; to beat in contention; to contend against (*buffet* the billows).—*v.i.* To deal blows or buffets; to make one's way by buffeting.

buffoon, buf•fön', *n.* [Fr. *bouffon*, from It. *buffone*, from *buffare*, to jest or sport, from *buffa*, a trick, a piece of sport.] A man who makes a practice of amusing others by low tricks, odd gestures and postures, jokes, etc.; a merry-andrew; a clown; a jester.—*v.t.* To make ridiculous.—*v.i.* To play the buffoon.—*a.* Characteristic of a buffoon.—**buffoonery,** buf•fön'ėr•i, *n.* The arts and practices of a buffoon; low jests; ridiculous pranks.—**buffoonish,** buf•fön'ish, *a.* Like a buffoon; consisting in low jests or gestures.

bug, bug, *n.* [W. *bwg*, a hobgoblin, a scarecrow; akin to E. *bogey*, Sc. *bogle*.] A hobgoblin, specter, or bugbear (*Shak.*)‡; a name applied to insects of various kinds, as the may-*bug*, the lady-*bug*.—**bugaboo,** bug'a•bö, *n.* An imagined object of fright; a bogeyman; a bugbear.—**bugbear,** bug'bâr, *n.* [Lit. a *bug* or hobgoblin in the shape of a *bear*.] Something real or imaginary that causes terror.—**buggy,** bug'i, *a.* Abounding with bugs.

buggy, bug'i, *n.* A name given to several species of light one-horse carriages or gigs.

bugle, bū'gl, *n.* [Lit. a buffalo-horn, from O.E. *bugle*, a buffalo, from L. *buculus*, a young bullock.] A hunting horn; a military musical brass wind instrument, now frequently furnished with keys so as to be capable of producing all the notes of the scale.—**bugler,** būg'lėr, *n.* One who plays a bugle; a soldier whose duty is to convey the commands of the officers by sounding a bugle.

bugle, bū'gl, *n.* [L.L. *bugulus*, a female ornament, from root seen in A.Sax. *bugan*, to bend, to *bow*, G. *bügel*, a bent piece of metal.] A shining elongated glass bead, usually black, used in decorating female apparel, etc.—*a.*‡ Black as a bugle or bead; jet black. (*Shak.*)

bugloss, bū'glos, *n.* [L. *buglossus*, Gr. *bouglōssos*—*bous*, an ox, and *glōssa*, tongue.] A bristly plant of several species, with narrow oblong leaves and deep purple flowers, a common weed, and so called from the shape and roughness of its leaves; oxtongue.

buhl, būl, *n.* [From *Boule*, an Italian woodcarver, who introduced this style of work into France in the reign of Louis XIV.] Unburnished gold, brass, or mother-of-pearl worked into complicated and ornamental patterns, used for inlaying; articles ornamented in this style.—**buhlwork,** būl'wėrk, *n.* Work in which wood, tortoise-shell, etc., is inlaid with buhl.

buhrstone, bör'stōn, *n.* Same as *Burrstone*.

build, bild, *v.i.*—*built*, *building*. The pret. & pp. *builded* are now confined to poetry. [Of obscure origin, but connected with A.Sax. *bold*, a house, a building; Icel. *ból*, Dan. *bol*, a house, a dwelling, from same root as Icel. *búa*, to dwell, G. *bauen*, to build or cultivate.] To frame, construct, and raise, as an edifice or fabric of almost any kind; to construct; to frame; to raise on a support or foundation; to rear; to erect; to settle or establish (fame, hopes, etc.).—*v.i.* To exercise the art or practice the business of building; to rest or depend (to *build* on another's foundation); to base; to rely.—*n.* Construction; make; form.—**builder,** bil'dėr, *n.* One who builds; one whose occupation is to build, as an architect, shipwright, mason, etc.—**building,** bild'ing, *n.* The act of one who builds; the thing built, as a house, a church, etc.; fabric; edifice.—**built,** bilt, *p.* and *a.* Formed; shaped (of the human body, etc.): frequently in composition; constructed of different pieces instead of one, as a mast, beam, etc.

bulb, bulb, *n.* [L. *bulbus*, a bulbous root.] The rounded part or head of an onion or similar plant; strictly, a modified leaf bud, consisting of imbricated scales or concentric coats or layers, formed on a plant usually beneath the surface of the ground, emitting roots from its base, and producing a stem from its center, as in the onion, lily, hyacinth, etc.; any protuberance or expansion resembling a bulb, especially an expansion at the end of a stalk or long and slender body, as in the tube of a thermometer.—*v.i.* To project or be protuberant: with *out*.—**bulbil,** bul'bil, *n. Bot.* a separable bulb formed on certain flowering plants; a small axillary bulb.—**bulbiferous,** bul•bif'ėr•us, *a.* Producing bulbs.—**bulbous,** bul'bus, *a.* Having or pertaining to bulbs or a bulb; growing from bulbs; resembling a bulb in shape; swelling out.

bulbul, bụl'bụl, *n.* The Persian name of the nightingale, or a species of nightingale; an Eastern name of other singing birds.

Bulgarian, bul•gâ'ri•an, *a.* Pertaining to Bulgaria.—*n.* A Bulgarian; the language of the Bulgarians, a Slavonic tongue.

bulge, bulj, *v.i.*—*bulged*, *bulging*. [From the Scandinavian; O.Sw. *bulgja*, to swell; Icel. *bólginn*, swollen; the same word as A.Sax. *belgan*, to swell, in sense of be angry; akin, *belly*, *bellows*, *bowl*, *billow*, *bulk*, etc. *Bilge* is another spelling.] To swell out; to be protuberant; to bilge, as a ship.

bulimia, bulimy, bū•lim'i•a, bū'li•mi, *n.* [Gr. *boulimia*—*bous*, an ox, in composition, huge, great, and *limos*, hunger.] Morbidly voracious, insatiable appetite.

bulk, bulk, *n.* [Same root as *bulge*; Icel. *bulki*, a heap, the freight of a vessel; Dan. *bulk*, a lump, a clod; O.Sw. *bolk*, a crowd, a mass.] Magnitude of material substance; whole dimensions; size; the gross; the majority; the main mass or body (the *bulk* of a nation); the whole contents of a ship's hold.—*In bulk*, loose or open, that is not packed in bags, boxes, etc.—*v.i.* To grow large; to swell; to appear large or important.—**bulky,** bul'ki, *a.* Of great bulk or dimensions; of great size; large.—**bulkiness,** bul'ki•nes, *n.* The state or quality of being bulky.—**bulkhead,** *n.* A partition in a ship made with boards, to form separate apartments.

bull, bu̦l, *n.* [A.Sax. *bull* (only found in dim. *bulluca*, a bullock); L.G. *bulle*, *bolle*, D. *bul*, Icel. *boli*, a bull. The root may be in A.Sax. *bellan*, to bellow.] The male of any bovine quadruped or animal of the ox or cow kind; an old male whale; *stock-exchange slang*, one who operates in order to effect a rise in the price of stock in order to sell out at a profit; the opposite of a *bear*;—*a.* Male, or of large size; characteristic of a bull, as coarse, loud, obstinate, or the like: used in composition; as, a *bull*trout, *bull*head, *bul*rush, etc.—**bullock,** bu̦l'ok, *n.* [A.Sax. *bulluca*, dim. of *bull.*] An ox or castrated bull; a full-grown steer.—**bulldog,** *n.* A very strong muscular variety of dog, with large head, broad muzzle, short hair, and of remarkable courage and ferocity: formerly much used in bullbaiting.—**bullfight,** *n.* A combat between armed men and bulls in a closed arena; a popular amusement in Spain, Portugal, and Latin America.—**bullfighter,** *n.* A man who engages in bullfights.—**bullfinch,** *n.* A species of finch, distinguished by the large size of the head, the stoutness of the bill, and by having the beak and crown of the head black; a European songbird.—**bullfrog,** *n.* A large species of frog living in marshy places, having a loud bass voice which resembles the bellowing of a bull.—**bullhead,** *n.* A name given to several species of fish with wide and flattened heads, as the *catfish*; **bullheaded,** *a.* Headstrong; obstinate; opinionated.—**bull's-eye,** *n.* *Arch.* any circular opening for the admission of light or air; a round piece of thick glass convex on one side let into the deck, port, or skylight of a vessel for the purpose of admitting light; a small lantern with a lens on one side to concentrate the light in a given direction; the center of a target of a different color from the rest of it, and usually round, also a shot that hits the bull's-eye.—**bull terrier,** *n.* Breed of dog with characteristics of terrier and bulldog.

bull, bu̦l, *n.* [L. *bulla*, a boss, an ornament worn on a child's neck, later a leaden seal.] Originally the seal appended to the edicts and briefs of the pope, hence, a letter, edict, or rescript of the pope, published or transmitted to the churches over which he is head, containing some decree, order, or decision.

bull, bu̦l, *n.* [Origin doubtful.] A gross inconsistency in language; a ludicrous blunder involving a contradiction in terms.

bullate, bu̦l'lāt, *a.* [L. *bullatus*, from *bulla*, a bubble.] In *bot.* having elevations like bubbles or blisters, as a leaf whose membranous part rises between the veins in elevations like blisters.

bullet, bu̦l'et, *n.* [Fr. *boulet*, a dim. from *boule*, a ball, from L. *bulla*, a bubble, a boss, a seal. Akin *bullion*, *bulletin*, to *boil*, a papal *bull.*] A small ball; a projectile generally of lead intended to be discharged from small arms, as rifles, muskets, pistols, etc.—**bulletproof,** *a.* Capable of resisting the force of a bullet.

bulletin, bu̦l'e•tin, *n.* [Fr. from It. *bulletino*, dim. of *bulla*, an edict of the pope.] An official report concerning some public event, such as military operations, etc., issued for the information of the public; any public announcement, especially of news recently received.

bullion, bu̦l'yon, *n.* [From L.L. *bullio*, *bulliona*, a mass of gold or silver, from L. *bulla*, a boss, a stud, a seal. BULLET.] Uncoined gold or silver in the mass; gold or silver not in the form of current coin; the precious metals in bars, ingots, or in any uncoined form; foreign or uncurrent coins; a kind of heavy twisted fringe frequently made of silk and covered with fine gold or silver wire.

bullock. See BULL.

bully, bu̦l'i, *n.* [From root of *bull*, *bellow*; originally the first element in compounds such as *bully-rook*, *bully-Jack*, and other old terms; comp. Sw. *bullerbas*, a noisy person, from *bullra*, to make a noise.] A blustering, quarrelsome, overbearing fellow, more distinguished for insolence than for courage; a swaggerer; one who domineers or browbeats; a brisk, dashing fellow: a familiar term of address (*Shak.*)‡.—*v.t.*—*bullied*, *bullying*. To act the bully toward; to overbear with bluster or menaces.—*v.i.* To be loudly arrogant and overbearing; to be noisy and quarrelsome; to bluster, swagger, hector, or domineer.

bully, bu̦l'i, [Fr. *bouilli.*] Tinned beef.

bulrush, bu̦l'rush, *n.* [From *bull*, implying largeness, and *rush.*] A name given to large rushlike plants, of various genera, growing in marshes.—**bulrushy,** bu̦l'rush•i, *a.* Abounding in bulrushes, resembling or pertaining to bulrushes.

bulwark, bu̦l'wėrk, *n.* [Lit. a *work* built of the *boles* or trunks of trees, from Dan. *bulwerk*, D. *bolwerk*, G. *bollwerk*, rampart; hence by corruption Fr. *boulevard.*] A mound of earth round a place, capable of resisting cannon shot, and formed with bastions, curtains, etc.; a rampart; a fortification; that which protects or secures against attack; means of protection and safety; the boarding round the sides of a ship, above the level of the decks, to prevent them being swept by the waves, etc.—*v.t.* To fortify with a bulwark or rampart; to protect; defend.

bum,† bum, *v.i.* [A different spelling of *boom*, D. *bommen*, to boom or sound hollow.] To make a hollow noise; to boom.—*n.* A droning or humming sound, as that made by the bee; a hum.

bum, bum, *n.* An inebriate; a mendicant; a loafer; one who prefers charity to work; a panhandler.—*v.i.* To travel without expense to oneself, by begging or stealing food and lodging.

bumblebee, bum'bl•bē, *n.* [From *bum*, to hum or boom.] A large bee; a humblebee: so named from its sound.

bumboat, bum'bōt, *n.* [D. *bumboot*, a wide fishing-boat, from *bun*, a tank in a boat in which fish are kept alive, and *boot*, a boat.] A boat for carrying provisions to a ship at a distance from shore.

bump, bump, *v.t.* [Perhaps imitative of sound; comp. L G. *bumsen*, to strike or fall on with a hollow noise; also W. *pwmp*, a round mass; *pwmpiaw*, to thump.] To make to come in violent contact; to give a shock to; to strike; to thump.—*v.i.* To come in collision; to strike against something.—*n.* A swelling or protuberance (especially on the body); *phren.* one of the natural protuberances on the surface of the skull regarded as indicative of distinct qualities, affections, propensities, etc. of the mind; a shock from a collision.

bumper, bum'pėr, *n.* [Corrupted from older *bumbard*, *bombard.*] A cup or glass filled to the brim; something well or completely filled; device for absorbing shock in a collision, especially a bar across the end of an automobile.

bumpkin, bump'kin, *n.* [For *bumkin*, a short boom, a bumpkin being a blockish fellow, a blockhead.] An awkward, clumsy rustic; a clown or country lout.

bumptious, bump'shus, *a.* [For *bumpish*, from *bump*, apt to strike against or come in contact with others.] Offensively self-assertive; disposed to quarrel; domineering. (Colloq.)—**bumptiousness,** bump'shus•nes, n. (Colloq.)

bun, bun, *n.* [O.Fr. *bugne*, a swelling; Fr. *bugnet*, a little puffed loaf.] A kind of cake; a kind of sweet bread.

bunch, bunsh, *n.* [From O.Sw. and Dan. *bunke*, Icel. *bunki*, a heap. BUNK.] A protuberance; a bunch; a knob or lump; a collection, cluster, or tuft of things of the same kind connected together in growth or tied together; any cluster or aggregate.—*v.i.* To swell out in a protuberance; to cluster, as into bunches.—*v.t.* To form or tie in a bunch.—**bunchy,** bunsh'i, *a.* Having a bunch or hunch; having knobs or protuberances; growing in a bunch; like a bunch.

bundle, bun'dl, *n.* [A dim. from *bind*; equivalent to D. *bondel*, G. *bundel*, bundle.] A number of things bound or rolled into a convenient form for conveyance or handling; a package.—*v.t.*—*bundled*, *bundling*. To tie or bind in a bundle or roll: often followed by *up*; to place or dispose of in a hurried unceremonious manner.—*To bundle off*, to send a person off in a hurry; to send off unceremoniously.—*To bundle out*, to expel summarily.—*v.i.* To depart in a hurry or unceremoniously; often with *off*.

bung, bung, *n.* [Allied to D. *bom*, O.D. *bonne*, a bung; Ir. *buinne*, a tap, a spigot; W. *bwng*, a bung hole.] A large cork or stopper for closing the hole in a cask through which it is filled.—*v.t.* To stop the orifice of with a bung; to close up.—**bunghole,** *n.* The hole or orifice in a cask through which it is filled, and which is closed by a bung.

bungalow, bung′ga•lō, *n.* [Per. *bangalah*, from *Bengal*; lit. a Bengalese house.] A house or residence, generally of a single floor, and surrounded by a veranda.

bungle, bung′gl, *v.i.—bungled, bungling.* [Akin to *bang*, G. dial. *bungen* O.Sw. *bunga*, to beat, to bang.] To perform in a clumsy awkward manner.—*v.t.* To make or mend clumsily; to botch; to manage awkwardly; to perform inefficiently.—*n.* A clumsy performance; a piece of awkward work; a botch.—**bungler,** bung′glėr, *n.* One who bungles; one who performs without skill.—**bungling,** bung′gling, *a.* Prone to bungle, clumsy; characterized by bungling.—**bunglingly,** bung′gling•li, *adv.* In a bungling manner; clumsily; awkwardly.

bunion, bun′yon, *n.* [From It. *bugnone*, a round knot or bunch, a boil. *Bun* is of the same origin.] An excrescence or knob on some of the joints of the feet, generally at the side of the ball of the great toe, which causes an inflammation of the small membranous sac called *bursa mucosa*.

bunk, bungk, *n.* [Sw. *bunke*, a wooden vessel, a coop, in O.Sw. also part of a vessel's deck.] A wooden box or case, serving as a seat during the day and a bed at night; one of a series of sleeping berths arranged above each other.—**bunker,** bung′kėr, *n.* A sort of fixed chest or box; a large bin or receptacle (a coal-*bunker*).

bunker, *n.* A sandy hollow in golf links.—**bunker,** *v.t.* To block, to check.

bunkum, buncombe, bung′kum, *n.* [From *Buncombe*, in N. Carolina, whose member of Congress had on one occasion admitted that he was talking simply ‘for Buncombe’, that is, to please his constituents.] Talking for talking's sake; bombastic speechmaking; mere words.

bunny, bun′i, *n.* [Ir. and Gael. *bun*, root, stump; lit. the short-tailed animal.] A sort of pet name for the rabbit.

Bunsen burner, bun′sen, *n.* [From inventor, Baron *Bunsen*.] A kind of lamp or gas burner producing an intensely hot flame.

bunt, bunt, *v.t.* To tap a baseball lightly with a loosely held bat.—

buntline, bunt′lin, *n. Naut.* one of the ropes fastened on the bottoms of square sails, to draw them up to their yards.

bunt, bunt, *n.* [Supposed to be a corruption of *burnt*.] A disease of wheat; smut; also, the fungus producing the disease.

bunting, bun′ting, *n.* [O.E. *bunting*, *bounting*, *buntel*, Sc. *buntlin*; origin unknown.] The popular name of a number of insessorial birds closely allied to finches and sparrows.

bunting, buntine, bun′ting, bun′tin, *n.* [Probably from G. *bunt*, D. *bont*, particolored, of different colors.] A thin woolen stuff, of which the colors, or flags and signals, of ships are made; a vessel's flags collectively.

buoy, boi, *n.* [D. *boei*, a buoy, a fetter, O.Fr. *boye*, from L. *boiae*, a kind of fetter or shackle; a buoy being fettered at a fixed point.] A floating object fixed at a certain place to show the position of objects beneath the water, as shoals, rocks, etc., or to mark out the course a ship is to follow, etc.; a floating object used to throw overboard for a person who has fallen into the water to lay hold of, and to keep him afloat till he can be taken out; more particularly called a *life buoy*.—*v.i.* To keep afloat in a fluid, as in water or air; generally with *up*; *fig.* to keep from sinking into despondency; to fix buoys in as a direction to mariners.—**buoyancy,** boi′an•si, *n.* The quality of being buoyant, that is of floating on the surface of water or in the atmosphere; *fig.* lightheartedness; cheerfulness; hopefulness; elasticity of spirit.—**buoyant,** boi′ant, *a.* Floating; light; having the quality of rising or floating in a fluid; *fig.* cheerful; hopeful; not easily depressed.—**buoyantly,** boi′ant•li, *adv.* In a buoyant manner.

bur, burr, bėr, *n.* [A.Sax. *burr*, a bur, a burdock; Dan. *borre*, Sw. *kardborre*, a burdock; the root is probably seen in Ir. *borr*, a knob, *borraim*, to swell.] A rough prickly covering of the seeds of certain plants, as of the chestnut and burdock; the plant burdock; *engr.* a slight ridge of metal left by the graver on the edges of a line, and which is removed by a scraper; the guttural pronunciation of the rough *r* common in some of the northern counties of England.

Burberry, bėr′be•ri, *n.* [Maker's name.] Waterproof overcoat of material specially treated by Burberry process.

burbot, bėr′bot, *n.* [Fr. *barbote*, from *barbe* L. *barba*, a beard.] A fish of the cod family, shaped like an eel but shorter, with a flat head and two small beards on the nose and another on the chin.

burden, burthen, bėr′dn, bėr′THn, *n.* [A.Sax. *byrthen*, from *beran*, to bear, like Icel. *byrthr*, *byrthi*, Dan. *byrde*, Goth. *baurthei*, G. *bürde*, a burden. BEAR.] That which is borne or carried; a load; that which is grievous, wearisome, or oppressive; the quantity or number of tons a vessel will carry.—*v.t.* To load; to lay a heavy load on; to encumber with weight; to oppress with anything grievous; to surcharge.—**burdensome,** bėr′dn•sum, *a.* Weighing like a heavy burden; grievous to be borne; causing uneasiness or fatigue; oppressive; heavy; wearisome.—**burdensomely,** bėr′dn•sum•li, *adv.* In a burdensome manner.—**burdensomeness,** bėr′dn•sum•nes, *n.* The quality of being burdensome; heaviness; oppressiveness.

burden, bėr′dn, *n.* [Fr. *bourdon*, a drone or bass, the humble-bee, from L.L. *burdo*, a drone.] The part in a song which is repeated at the end of each verse; the chorus or refrain; a subject on which one dwells.

burdock, bėr′dok, *n.* [*Bur* and *dock*.] The popular name of a large rough-leaved perennial plant belonging to the composite family, common on roadsides and waste places, and a troublesome weed in cultivated grounds.

bureau, bū′rō, pl. **bureaux, bureaus,** bū′rōz, *n.* [Fr. *bureau*, an office, a desk or writing table, originally a kind of russet stuff with which writing tables were covered, from L. *burrus*, red or reddish.] An office or place where business is transacted; a department for the transaction of public business; a chest of drawers for clothes, etc.—**bureaucracy,** bū•ro′kra•si, *n.* The system of centralizing the administration of a country, through regularly graded series of government officials; such officials collectively.—**bureaucrat,** bū′rō•krat, *n.* An advocate for or supporter of bureaucracy.—**bureaucratic,** bū•rō•krat′ik, *a.* Relating to bureaucracy.

burette, bū•ret′, *n.* [Fr. from *buire*, a flagon, L. *bibere*, to drink.] A tube used in chemistry for accurately measuring out quantities of fluids.

burgee, bėr′jē, *n.* A flag or pennant which ends in two points; a kind of small coal suited for burning in furnaces.

burgeon, bėr′jon, *n.* and *v.i.* Same as *Bourgeon*.

burgh, bėrg, bu′rė, *n.* [BOROUGH.] A corporate town or borough; the Scotch term corresponding to the English *borough*, applied to several different kinds of corporations.—**burgess,** bėr′jes, *n.* [O.Fr. *burgeis*, Fr. *bourgeois*, from *bourg*, L.L. *burgus*, a borough.] An inhabitant of a borough or walled town, especially one who possesses a tenement therein; a citizen or freeman of a borough; a parliamentary representative of a borough.—**burgher,** bėr′gėr, *n.* An inhabitant of a burgh or borough, who enjoys the privileges of the borough of which he is a freeman.

burglar, bėrg′lėr, *n.* [From Fr. *bourg*, a town, and O.Fr. *laire*, Pr. *lairo*, L. *latro*, a thief.] One guilty of housebreaking. — **burglarious,** bėrg•lâ′ri•us, *a.* Pertaining to burglary; constituting the crime of burglary.—**burglariously,** bėrg•lâ′ri•us•li, *adv.* With an intent to commit burglary; in the manner of a burglar. —**burglary,** bėrg′la•ri, *n.* The act or crime of housebreaking, with an intent to commit a felony.

burgomaster, bėr′go•mas•tėr, *n.* [D. *burgemeester* = E. *borough-master.*]The chief magistrate of a municipal town in Holland, Flanders, and Germany, nearly corresponding to *mayor* in England and the United States.

burgonet, bėr′go•net, *n.* [Fr. *bourguignotte,* properly a Burgundian helmet.] A kind of helmet with a small visor formerly worn.

burgoo, bėr′gö, *n.* A kind of oatmeal porridge, a dish used at sea; contemptuous Russian anarchist expression for middle-class or bourgeois politics.

burgrave, bėr′grāv, *n.* [L.L. *burggravius,* from G. *burggraf—burg,* a town, and *graf,* a count, an earl.] In some European countries an hereditary governor of a town or castle.

Burgundy, bėr′gun•di, *n.* A kind of wine, so called from Burgundy, in France.—*Burgundy pitch,* a pitch obtained from the Norway spruce, used in plasters.

burial, be′ri•al, *n.* See BURY.

burin, bū′rin, *n.* [Fr. *burin,* from root of *bore.*] A graver; an instrument for engraving made of tempered steel, of a prismatic form, and with the graving end ground off obliquely so as to produce a sharp point.

burke, bėrk, *v.t.* [From the name of an Irishman who first committed the crime, in 1829, in Edinburgh, with the view of selling the dead bodies for dissection.] To murder by suffocation; *fig.* to smother.

burl, bėrl, *n.* [Fr. *bourre,* a flock of wool as for stuffing, L.L. *burra,* a flock of wool.] A small knot or lump in thread, whether woven into cloth or not.—*v.t.* To pick knots, loose threads, etc., from, as in finishing cloth.—**burler,** bėr′lėr, *n.* One who burls cloth.

burlap, bėr′lap, *n.* [Origin uncertain.] A fabric made from jute and used to make bags and upholstery.

burlesque, bėr•lesk′, *a.* [Fr. *burlesque,* from It. *burlesco,* ridiculous, from *burlare,* to ridicule, *burla,* mockery.] Tending to excite laughter by ludicrous images, or by a contrast between the subject and the manner of treating it.—*n.* That kind of literary composition which exhibits a contrast between the subject and the manner of treating it so as to excite laughter or ridicule; travesty; caricature; a kind of dramatic extravaganza with more or less singing in it; a ludicrous or debasing caricature of any kind; a gross perversion.—*v.t.*—*burlesqued, burlesquing.* To make ridiculous by burlesque representation; to turn into a burlesque.—*v.i.*† To use burlesque. —**burlesquer,** bėr•lesk′ėr, *n.* One who burlesques or turns to ridicule.

burly, bėr′li, *a.* [Of same origin as *bur, burr,* Ir. and Gael. *borr,* a knob, with term. *-ly.*] Great in bodily size; bulky; lusty: the word, now used only of persons, includes the idea of some degree of coarseness.—**burliness,** bėr′li•nes, *n.* The state or quality of being burly.

Burmese, bur•mēz′, *a.* Of or pertaining to Burma.—*n.* An inhabitant or inhabitants of Burma; the language of the people of Burma.

burn, bėrn, *v.t.*—*burned* or *burnt, burning.* [A.Sax. *bernan, byrnan, beornan, brinnan,* to burn = Icel. *brenna,* Dan. *braende,* O.D. *bernen,* Goth. *brinnan,* G. *brennen,* to burn, *Brand, brown, brine, brim*stone, etc., are akin.] To consume with fire; to reduce to ashes; to injure by fire; to scorch, to act on with fire; to expose to the action of fire (limestone, bricks), to make into by means of fire (to *burn* charcoal), to affect with a burning sensation; to apply a cautery to; to cauterize.—*To burn daylight,* to use artificial light before it is dark; to waste time. (*Shak*).—*v.i.* To be on fire, to flame, to suffer from or be injured by an excess of heat; to shine; to sparkle; to glow; to gleam; to be inflamed with passion or desire; to be affected with a sensation of heat (the cheeks *burn*), in certain games, to be near a concealed object which is sought; hence, to be nearly right in guessing (colloq.).—*n.* A hurt or injury of the flesh caused by the action of fire.—**burner,** bėr′nėr, *n.* A person who burns or sets fire to anything, the part of a lamp from which the flame issues; the part that holds the wick, the jet-piece from which a gasflame issues.—**burning,** bėr′ning, *a.* Much heated; flaming; scorching; vehement; powerful; causing excitement, ardor, or enthusiasm (a *burning* question).—**burning glass,** *n.* A double-convex lens of glass, which, when exposed to the direct rays of the sun, collects them into a focus, where an intense heat is produced, so that combustible matter may be set on fire.

burn, bėrn, *n.* [A.Sax. *burna,* a stream, a well; Icel. *brunnr,* D. *born,* Goth. *brunna,* G. *brunnen,* akin to verb to *burn;* comp. *torrent,* from L. *torreo,* to burn.] A rivulet; a brook. [Prov. E. and Sc.]

burnish, bėr′nish, *v.t.* [O.Fr. *burnir, burnissant,* to polish, to embrown, from *brun,* O.H.G. *brun,* brown. BROWN.] To cause to glow or become resplendent; to polish and make shining by friction; to make smooth and lustrous.—*v.i.*† To grow bright or brilliant; to show conspicuously. —*n.*† Gloss; brightness; luster.—**burnisher,** bėr′nish•ėr, *n.* One who or that which burnishes or makes glossy.

burnoose, bėr•nös′, *n.* [Fr. *burnous, bournous,* from Sp. *al-bornoz,* a kind of Moorish cloak. An Ar. word.] A white woolen mantle, with hood, woven in one piece, worn by the Arabs.

burr, burstone, bėr, bėr′stōn, *n.* A name given to certain siliceous or siliceocalcareous stones, whose dressed surfaces present a burr or keen-cutting texture, whence they are much used for millstones.

burro, bur′ō, *n.* A small donkey, used as a pack animal.

burrow, bur′ō, *n.* [The same word with *burgh, borough,* from A.Sax. *beorgan,* to protect, shelter.] A hole in the ground excavated by rabbits, hares, and some other animals, as a refuge and habitation.—*v.i.* To make a hole or burrow to lodge in; to work a way into or under something; to lodge in a burrow or in any deep or concealed place; to hide.—**burrower,** bur′ō•ėr, *n.* One who burrows; an animal which excavates and inhabits burrows.

bursa, bėr′sa, *n.* [L.] *Anat.* a kind of sac.—*Bursa mucosa,* a sac situated at a joint and containing the synovial fluid.

bursar, bėr′sėr, *n.* [BURSE.] A treasurer or cash keeper of a college or of a monastery; a purser; a student to whom a bursary is paid.

burse, bėrs, *n.* [Fr. *bourse,* a purse, bursary, exchange, from L.L. *bursa,* a purse, a skin, leather. PURSE.] A purse to hold something valuable; one of the official insignia of the lord high chancellor of England.

bursitis, bėr•sī′tis, *n.* [From *bursa* and Gr. *-itis,* inflammation.] Inflammation of a bursa.

burst, bėrst, *v.i.*—*burst, bursting.* [A.Sax. *berstan* = Icel. *bersta,* Dan. *briste, bröste,* D. *bersten,* O.G. *bresten,* Mod. G. *bersten,* to burst; same root in Ir. *brisaim,* Gael. *bris, brisd,* to break.] To fly or break open from internal force and with sudden violence, to suffer a violent disruption; to explode; to become suddenly manifest; to rush; with prepositions, adverbs, and adverbial phrases (to *burst* out, to *burst* into life).—*v.t.* To break or rend by force or violence; to open suddenly (to *burst* one's bonds, to *burst* a cannon). —*n.* A sudden disruption; a violent rending; a sudden explosion or shooting forth; a rush; an outburst.

burthen. See BURDEN.

burton, bėr′ton, *n.* A small tackle formed by two blocks or pulleys, used in ships to set up or tighten the topmost shrouds and for various other purposes.

bury, ber′i, *v.t.*—*buried, burying.* [A.Sax. *byrgan, byrigan,* to bury; allied to *beorgan,* to protect, and thus to *burgh, borough, burrow, barrow,* etc.] To cover with earth or other matter; to deposit in a grave when dead; to inter; to entomb; to hide; to conceal; to withdraw or conceal in retirement: used *refl.*; to hide in oblivion (to *bury* injuries, etc.).—**burying,** ber′i•ing, *n.* Burial; sepulture. (N.T.)—**burial,** ber′i•al, *n.* The act of burying, especially the act of burying a deceased person; sepulture; interment; the act of depositing a dead body in the earth, in a tomb or vault, or in the water.—**burier,** ber′i•ėr, *n.* One who buries; that which buries or covers.

bus, bus, *n.* An abbreviation of *omnibus,* a public vehicle; a motor coach, a large public carriage.

busby, buz'bi, *n.* A military headdress consisting of a fur hat with a bag, of the same color as the facings of the regiment, hanging from the top over the right side.

bush, bụsh, *n.* [Scandinavian: Dan. *busk.* Sw. *buske*, a bush = D. *bosch*, a grove; G. *busch*, a bush. The word passed from the Teutonic into the Romance languages, and *ambush*, *ambuscade*, *bosky*, *bouquet*, etc., are akin.] A shrub with branches; a thick shrub; a branch of a tree, properly of ivy, fixed or hung out as a tavern sign (*Shak.*), a stretch of shrubby vegetation; a district covered with brushwood, or shrubs, trees, etc.—*To beat about the bush*, to use circumlocution; to dilly-dally.—*v.i.* To grow thick or bushy. —*v.t.* To set bushes about; to support with bushes; to use a bush harrow on.—**bushiness,** bụsh'i•nes, *n.* The quality of being bushy.—**bushy,** bụsh'i, *a.* Full of bushes; overgrown with shrubs; resembling a bush; thick and spreading, like a bush.—**bushbuck,** bụsh'buk, *n.* [D. *bosch-bok.*] The name given to several species of South African antelopes.—**bushman,** bụsh'man, *n.* A woodsman; a settler in the bush or forest districts of a new country, as Australia; [*cap.*] an aboriginal of Bushmanland, near the Cape of Good Hope; a Bosjesman.—**bushranger,** *n.* In Australia, one who takes to the 'bush', or woods, and lives by robbery.

bush, bụsh, *n.* [Parallel form of *box*, from D. *bus*, a box, a bush; G. *büchse*, a box, the bush of a wheel.] A lining of harder material let into an orifice (as for an axle) to guard against wearing by friction.—*v.t.* To furnish with a bush.

bushel, bụsh'el, *n.* [O.Fr. *bussel*, L.L. *bussellus*, a dim. form from *bussida*, for *buxida*, *pyxida*, from Gr. *pyxis*, a box.] A dry measure containing 8 gallons or 4 pecks. The standard bushel in the United States has a capacity of 2,150.42 cubic inches, and holds 77.627 lbs. avoirdupois of distilled water at the temperature of 39.2° Fahr.; a vessel of the capacity of a bushel.

business, biz'nes, *n.* [This word, though with the form of an ordinary abstract noun from *busy*, has lost the meaning of state of being busy, *busy-ness.*] A matter or affair that engages a person's time, care, and attention; that which one does for a livelihood; occupation; employment; mercantile concerns, or traffic in general; the proper duty; what belongs to one to do; task or object undertaken; concern; right of action or interposing; affair; point; matter. —*a.* Relating to or connected with business, traffic, trade, etc.

buskin, bus'kin, *n.* [For *broskin*, *bruskin*, a dim. from D. *broos*, a buskin, akin to *brogue.*] A kind of half-boot or high shoe covering the foot and leg to the middle of the calf; the high shoe worn by ancient tragic actors; the tragic drama as opposed to comedy.

bust, bust, *n.* [Fr. *buste*, It. and Sp. *busto*, L.L. *bustum*, from *busta*, a small box, L. *buxida.* BOX.] A sculptured figure of a person showing only the head, shoulders, and breast; the chest or thorax.

bustard, bus'tėrd, *n.* [O.Fr. *bistarde*, a corruption of L. *avis tarda*; lit. slow bird.] A bird belonging to the order of the runners, but approaching the waders. The great bustard is the largest European bird, the male often weighing 30 lbs.

bustle, bus'l, *v.i.*—*bustled*, *bustling*. [Same word as Icel. *bustla*, to bustle, to plash in water; *bustl*, bustle, a plash.] To display activity with a certain amount of noise or agitation; to be active and stirring.—*n.* Activity with noise and agitation; stir; hurry-scurry; tumult.

bustle, bus'l, *n.* [Perhaps for *buskle*, a dim. of *busk*, a support for a lady's stays.] A pad, cushion, or wire framework worn at one time, about 1880, beneath the skirt of a woman's dress, expanding and supporting it behind.

busy, biz'i, *a.* [O.E. *bisy*, A.Sax. *bysig*, *bisig* = D. *bezig*, L.G. *besig*, busy; further affinities doubtful.] Employed with constant attention; engaged about something that renders interruption inconvenient; occupied without cessation; constantly in motion; meddling with or prying into the affairs of others; officious; causing or spent in much employment (a *busy* day).—*v.t.*—*busied*, *busying*. To employ with constant attention; to keep engaged; to make or keep busy; often *refl.*—**busybody,** biz'i•bod•i, *n.* One who officiously concerns himself or herself with the affairs of others.—**busily,** biz'i•li, *adv.* In a busy manner; with constant occupation; importunately; officiously.

but, but. Originally a prep. and still often to be so regarded, though also an adv. and frequently a conj. [A.Sax. *butan*, without, out of, unless—*be*, by, and *utan*, out, without.] Except; besides; unless (all, none *but* one); save or excepting that; were it not (commonly followed by *that*); only; merely; simply (I do *but* jest); sometimes equivalent to, that...not (who knows *but* or *but that* he may); as an adversative conj. equivalent to, on the contrary; on the other hand; yet; still; however; nevertheless.

butadiene, bū•ta•dī'ēn, *n.* A flammable colorless gas obtained from oil and carbon dioxide, used chiefly in making synthetic rubber.

butane, bū'tān, *n.* [From L. *buytrum*, Gr. *boutyron*, butter.] A hydrocarbon gas obtained from petroleum.

butcher, bụch'ėr, *n.* [Fr. *boucher*, from *bouc*, a he-goat (from G. *bock*, a goat = E. *buck*), the males being killed for food, the females kept for milk.] One whose trade is to kill beasts for food; one who deals in meat; one who kills in a cruel or bloody manner.—*v.t.* To kill or slaughter for food or for market; to murder in a bloody or barbarous manner.—**butcherly,**‡ bụch'ėr•li, *a.* Cruel; savage; murderous. (*Shak.*)—**butchery,** bụch'ėr•i, *n.* The business of slaughtering cattle for the table or for market; murder committed with unusual barbarity; great slaughter.—**butcherbird,** *n.* A name given to the shrikes from their habit of suspending their prey, as a butcher does his meat, and then pulling it to pieces and devouring it at their leisure.—**butcher's-broom,** *n.* A stiff, erect, spiny-leaved shrub belonging to the lily family, often made into brooms for sweeping butchers' blocks.

butler, but'lėr, *n.* [O.E. *boteler*, from L.L. *botellarius*, a butler, from *botellus*, a bottle. BOTTLE.] A servant or officer in a house-hold whose principal business is to take charge of the liquors, silverware, etc.—**butlership,** but'lėr•ship, *n.* The office of a butler.

butt, but, *n.* [O.Fr. *bot*, *bout*, the end or extremity of a thing, Fr. *but*, an end, aim, goal, also *butte*, a butt used in shooting; from M.H.G. *bózen*, to strike, to beat, a word akin to E. *beat.*] The end or extremity of a thing, particularly the larger end of a thing, as of a piece of timber or of a felled tree; the thick end of a musket, fishing rod, whip handle, etc.; thickest and stoutest part of tanned ox hides; a mark to be shot at; the point where a mark is set or fixed to be shot at; the object of aim; the person at whom ridicule, jests, or contempt is directed; a goal; a bound (*Shak.*); *rifle-practice*, the hut, embankment, or other protection in which the marker sits.—**butt-end,** *n.* The largest, thickest, or blunt end of anything.—**butt shaft,**‡ *n.* An arrow. (*Shak.*)

butt, but, *v.t.* & *i.* [Fr. *bouter*, O.Fr. *boter*, to push, to butt. BUTT, an end.] To strike by thrusting the head against, as an ox or a ram; to have a habit of so striking.—*n.* [In the first sense directly from the verb; in second from Fr. *botte*, a pass or thrust in fencing.] A push or thrust given by the head of an animal; a thrust in fencing.

butt, but, *n.* [O.Fr. *boute*, Fr. *botte*, a boot, a butt, the two having a considerable resemblance. BOOT.] A large cask; a measure of 126 gallons of wine or 2 hogsheads.

butte, būt, *n.* [Fr.] A term applied to a detached hill or ridge of no great height rising abruptly.

butter, but'ėr, *n.* [A.Sax. *buter*, *butor*, from L. *butyrum*, from Gr. *boutyron*, butter, from *bous*, an ox, and *tyros*, cheese.] An oily or unctuous substance obtained from cream or milk by churning; *old chem.* a term applied to certain anhydrous, metallic chlorides of buttery consistency and fusibility.—*Vegetable butters*, a name given to certain vegetable oils, from their resemblance to butter.—*Rock butter*, a peculiar mineral composed of alum combined with iron, of the consistence and appearance of soft butter, appearing as a pasty exudation from aluminiferous rocks.—*v.t.* To smear with butter; to flatter grossly (vulgar).—**buttercup,** but'ėr•kup, *n.* A name given to several species of Ranunculus, a common field plant with bright yellow flowers.—**butterfly,** but′ėr•flī, *n.* [The reason for the name is doubtful; probably it was originally given to a common yellow species.] The common name of all the diurnal lepidopterous insects (the nocturnal ones being moths), in their last and fully developed state, having four wings often decked with the most beautiful colors, and a suctorial mouth; *fig.* a person whose attention is given up to a variety of trifles of any kind; a showily dressed, vain and giddy person.—**buttermilk,** *n.* The milk that remains after the butter is separated from it.—**butternut,** *n.* The fruit of a North American tree akin to the walnut, so called from the oil it contains; also the fruit of one or two lofty hardwood trees growing in Guiana.—**butterscotch,** but′ėr•skoch, *n.* The name given to a kind of toffee containing a considerable admixture of butter.—**butter tree,** *n.* A species of African tree, the seeds of which yield a substance like butter, called shea butter.—**butterwort,** but′ėr•wėrt, *n.* A European plant growing in bogs or soft grounds, the leaves of which are covered with soft, pellucid, glandular hairs, which secrete a glutinous liquor that catches small insects.—**buttery,** but′ėr•i, *a.* Having the qualities or appearance of butter.

buttery, but′ėr•i, *n.* [Originally *botelerie,* a place for bottles, but altered to *buttery* from butter being also kept in it.] An apartment in a household, in which wines, liquors, and provisions are kept; in some colleges, a room where refreshments are kept for sale to the students.

buttock, but′ok, *n.* [Dim. of *butt.*] The rump, or the protuberant part of an animal behind.

button, but′n, *n.* [Fr. *bouton,* a button, a bud, from *bouter,* to push. BUTT, to thrust, BUTT, an end.] A small round or roundish object of bone, ivory, metal, wood, mother-of-pearl, etc., used for fastening the parts of dress, by being passed into a hole, slit, or loop, or sometimes attached as mere ornament; something resembling a button; a round knob or protuberance; the small disk at the end of fencing foils, etc. The plural used as a singular is a colloquial or slang term for a page boy, from the buttons on his jacket.—*v.t.* To attach a button or buttons to; to fasten with a button or buttons; to enclose or make secure with buttons.—*v.i.* To be capable of being buttoned (his coat will not *button*).—**buttonbush,** *n.* A North American shrub of the cinchona family so called on account of its globular flower heads.—**buttonhole,** *n.* The hole or loop in which a button, or flower, is fastened.—*v.t.* To seize a man by the button or buttonhole and detain him in conversation against his will.—**buttonwood,** *n.* A common name in America for the western plane tree; also the same as *buttonbush.*

buttress, but′res, *n.* [O.E. *butrasse, boterase,* etc., from Fr. *bouter,* to thrust (BUTT), or a modification of *brattice, bretèche.*] A projecting support of masonry built on to the exterior of a wall, especially common in churches in the Gothic style; *fig.* any prop or support (a *buttress* of the constitution).—*v.t.* To support by a buttress; to prop.

butyraceous, bū•ti•rā′shus, *a.* [From L. *butyrum,* butter. BUTTER.] Having the qualities of butter; resembling butter.—**butyric,** bū•tir′ik, *a.* Pertaining to or derived from butter; a term applied to an acid obtained from butter, and also occurring in perspiration.

buxom, buk′sum, *a.* [A.Sax. *buhsom,* compliant, obedient, from *búgan,* to bend, to *bow,* and term. *-som, -some,* as in *blithesome,* etc.; D. *buigzaam,* G. *biegsam,* flexible, tractable, are exactly similar.] Yielding to pressure‡; flexible or elastic (*Mil.*)‡; obedient‡; healthy and cheerful; brisk; jolly; lively and vigorous; applied especially to women.—**buxomly,** buk′sum•li, *adv.* In a buxom manner; briskly; vigorously.—**buxomness,** buk′sum•nes, *n.*

buy, bī, *v.t.*—*bought* (pret. & pp.), *buying.* [O.E. *bygge, bugge,* A.Sax. *bicgan, bycgan,* to buy; Goth. *bugjan,* to buy. Hence *aby.*] To acquire by paying a price to the satisfaction of the seller; to purchase: opposed to *sell;* to get, acquire, or procure for any kind of equivalent (to *buy* favor with flattery); to bribe; to corrupt or pervert by paying a consideration.—*To buy in,* to buy for the owner at a public sale, especially when an insufficient price is offered.—*To buy off,* to release from military service by a payment; to get rid of the opposition of by paying; to purchase the non-intervention of.—*To buy out,* to purchase the share or shares of a person in a commercial concern, the purchaser thus taking the place of the seller.—*To buy over,* to detach by a bribe or consideration from one party and attach to the opposite party.—**buyer,** bī′ėr, *n.* One who buys; a purchaser.

buzz, buz, *v.i.* [Purely imitative of the sound. Comp. It. *buzzicare,* to buzz, whisper.] To make a low hissing sound, as that of bees; to whisper; to speak with a low hissing voice.—*v.t.* To whisper; to spread or report by whispers; to spread secretly.—*n.* A continuous humming sound, as of bees; a low whispering hum; a report circulated secretly and cautiously; a general confused conversation.—**buzzer,** buz′ėr, *n.* One who buzzes; a whisperer; one who is busy in telling tales secretly. (*Shak.*)

buzzard, buz′ėrd, *n.* [Fr. *buzard, busard,* from *buse,* a buzzard, and term. *-ard, buse* being from L.L. *busio,* for L. *buteo,* a buzzard.] A name for several large raptorial birds of the falcon family, with short weak toes; a blockhead; a dunce.

by, bī, *prep.* [A.Sax. *bi, big,* by; O.Sax. O.Fris. *bi,* D. *bij,* G. *bei,* Goth. *bi.* Often as a prefix in form *be.*] Near; close to; near along with motion past; through or with, denoting the author, producer, or agent, means, instrument, or cause; according to; by direction, authority; or example of (*by* his own account, ten *by* the clock, a rule to live *by*); at the rate of; in the ratio or proportion of (*by* the yard, *by* the dozen); to the amount or number of (larger *by* half, older *by* ten years); during the course of; within the compass or period of (*by* day); not later than (*by* this time, *by* two o'clock). In oaths or adjurations it comes before what is invoked or appealed to (*by* heaven).—*Two by two, day by day, piece by piece,* etc., each two, each day, each piece, taken separately or singly.—*Five feet by four,* measuring five feet one way and four the other.—*a.* Side; secondary: used only in composition, as *by*-path, *by*-play, *by*-street, etc.—*adv.* Near; in the same place with; at hand; aside (to stand *by,* to lay a thing *by*); so as to pass (to run *by*); so as to be past or over (the time went *by*).—*By and by,* in the near future; soon; presently.—**by, bye,** bī, *n.* A thing not directly aimed at; something not the immediate object of regard; as, by the *by,* or by the *bye,* that is, by the way, in passing; an odd or side run gained at cricket.—**by-blow,** *n.* A side or accidental blow (*Mil.*); an illegitimate child (vulgar).—**bygone,** bī′gon, *a.* Past; gone by.—*n.* What is gone by and past.—**byname,**‡ *n.* Nickname.—**bypast,** bī′past, *a.* Past; gone by. (*Shak.*)—**bypath, byroad, bystreet, byway,** *n.* A path, road, street, or way which is secondary to a main road, street, etc.; a lesser, private, or obscure way.—**byplay,** *n.* Action carried on aside, and commonly in dumb show, while the main action proceeds; action not intended to be observed by some of the persons present.—**by-product,** *n.* A secondary product; something obtained, as in a manufacturing process, in addition to the principal product or material.—**bystander,** *n.* One who stands by or near; an onlooker or spectator; one present but taking no part in what is going on.—**byword,** *n.* A common saying; a proverb.

bylaw, byelaw, bī′la̤, *n.* [From the Scand. *by,* a town, the termination in Whit-*by* and other names, and *law;* Dan. *by-lov,* a municipal law; Sw. *by-lag,* a by-law.] A law made by an incorporated body, as a railroad company, for the regulation of its own affairs, or the affairs entrusted to its care.

byre, bīr, *n.* [A Scandinavian word = E. *bower.*] A cow house. [Scotch.]

byssus, bis′us, *n.* pl. **byssi,** bis′ī. [L. *byssus,* Gr. *byssos,* fine linen or cotton.] *Zool.* a long, lustrous, and silky bunch of filaments by which certain bivalve mollusks, as the oyster, are attached to fixed objects; *bot.* the stipe of certain fungi.

Byzantine, biz•an′tin or biz′an•tīn, *a.* Pertaining to *Byzantium,* at one time the capital of the Eastern Roman Empire, afterward Constantinople, now, Istanbul, the largest city and seaport of the Turkish Republic.

C

C, c, sē, the third letter in the English alphabet and the second of the consonants, originally having the sound of *k,* now having also the sharp sound of *s* (before *e, i,* and *y*); *music,* the name of the first or key note of the modern normal scale, answering to the *do* of the Italians and the *ut* of the French.

Caaba, kä'a•ba, *n.* [Ar. from *ka'b,* a cube.] An oblong stone building forming the great temple at Mecca, containing at the northwest corner the famous black stone (an aerolite), presented in Arab tradition by the angel Gabriel to Abraham.

cab, kab, *n.* [Heb.] A Hebrew dry measure containing according to one estimate 2 pints, according to another 4.

cab, kab, *n.* [Abbrev. of *cabriolet.*] A closed four-wheel vehicle, usually for public hire; a taxicab. The covered part of a locomotive.

cabal, ka•bal', *n.* [Fr. *cabale,* the *cabala,* an intrigue, a cabal. CABALA.] Intrigue; secret artifices of a few persons united in some design; a number of persons united in some close design, usually to promote their private views in church or state by intrigue; a junto; specifically, a name given to a ministry of Charles II., consisting of Clifford, Ashley, Buckingham, Arlington, and Lauderdale, the initials of whose names happened to compose the word.—*v.i.*— *caballed, caballing.* To form a cabal; to intrigue; to unite in secret artifices to effect some design.

cabala, cabbala, kab'a•la, *n.* [Heb. *qabbâlâ,* reception, the cabala or mysterious doctrine received traditionally, from *qâbal,* to take or receive.] A mysterious kind of science or learning among Jewish rabbis, transmitted by oral tradition, serving for the interpretation of difficult passages of Scripture.—**cabalism,** kab'al•izm, *n.* The science of the cabalists.—**cabalist,** kab'al•ist, *n.* A Jewish doctor who professes the study of the cabala.—**cabalistic, cabalistical,** kab•al•ist'ik, kab•al•ist'ik•al, *a.* Pertaining to the cabala; containing an occult meaning.

cabaret, kab'a•rā, *n.* [Fr.] A restaurant where dancers and singers entertain.

cabbage, kab'ij, *n.* [O.E. *cabbish, cabage,* from Fr. *cabus,* O.Fr. *choux cabus,* a large-headed cabbage—*cabus, cabuce,* large-headed, from L. *caput,* a head.] A well-known vegetable of several varieties, the kinds most cultivated being the common cabbage, the savoy, the broccoli, and the cauliflower; the common cabbage forms its leaves into dense rounded heads, the inner leaves being blanched.—*v.i.* To form a head like that of a cabbage in growing.—**cabbage palm, cabbage tree,** *n.* A West Indian palm, having a simple unbranched slender stem growing to a great height, and so called from the young unexpanded leaves being eaten as a vegetable.

cabbage, kab'ij, *v.t.*—*cabbaged, cabbaging.* [Fr. *cabasser,* to put in a *cabas* or basket; hence, to hoard, steal. CABAS.] To purloin, especially to purloin pieces of cloth after cutting out a garment.—*n.* A cant name for anything filched, more particularly, cloth purloined by one who cuts out garments.

cabbala, cabbalism, etc., *n.* See CABALA, CABALISM, etc.

cabby, kab'i, *n.* Driver of cab. (Colloq.)

caber, kā'ber, *n.* [Gael. *cabar,* a pole, a stake, a rafter.] In Highland games, a long undressed stem of a tree, used for tossing as a feat of strength.

cabin, kab'in, *n.* [From W. *caban,* a cabin, dim. of *cab,* a kind of hut; Ir. and Gael. *caban,* a cabin.] A small room or enclosed place; a cottage; a hut or small house or habitation, especially one that is poorly constructed; an apartment in a ship for officers or passengers—*v.i.* To live in a cabin; to lodge. (*Shak.*)—*v.t.* To confine as in a cabin. (*Shak.*)—**cabin boy,** *n.* A boy whose duty is to wait on the officers and passengers on board a ship.

cabinet, kab'in•et, *n.* [Fr. *cabinet,* a closet, receptacle of curiosities, etc., a dim. form, ultimately from the Celtic. CABIN.] A small room, closet, or retired apartment; a private room in which consultations are held hence, the select or secret counsel of a prince or executive government; [*often cap.*] the collective body of ministers who direct the government of a nation or country: so called from the apartment in which the meetings were originally held; a piece of furniture consisting of a chest or box, with drawers and doors.—**cabinetmaker,** *n.* A man whose occupation is to make household furniture, such as cabinets, sideboards, tables, etc.

cable, kā'bl, *n.* [Fr. *câble,* a rope, from L.L. *capulum, caplum,* a rope, a halter, from L. *capio,* to take.] A large strong rope, usually of 3 or 4 strands of hemp, or a chain, such as is used to retain a vessel at anchor; a cablegram; *arch.* a molding with its surface out in imitation of the twisting of a rope; also, a cylindrical molding in the flute of a column and partly filling it.—*Cable's length,* a United States nautical measure, 720 feet or 120 fathoms.—*Sub-marine,* or *electric telegraph cable,* a cable by which telegraphic messages are conveyed through the ocean, usually composed of a single wire of pure copper, or of several wires, embedded in a compound of gutta-percha and resinous substances, so as to be compacted into one solid strand, encircled by layers of gutta-percha or india rubber, hemp or jute padding, and coils of iron wire.—*v.t.*—*cabled, cabling.* To fasten with a cable; to send a message by electric cable; *arch.* to fill (the flutes of columns) with cables or cylindrical pieces.—**cablegram,** kā'bl•gram, *n.* A message by cable.

cabob, ka•bob', *n.* [Per.] An oriental dish, consisting generally of a neck or loin of mutton cut in pieces and roasted, dressed with onions, eggs, spices, etc.

caboose, ka•bös', *n.* [From D. *kabuis,* a caboose or ship's galley; Dan., *kabys,* Sw. *kabysa, kabyssa,* a caboose. L.G. *kabuse, kabüse,* a little room or hut; probably from same root as *cabin.*] The cookroom or kitchen of a ship; last car of a freight train.

cabriole, kab'ri•ōl, *n.* [Fr. *cabriole,* a goat-leap; L.L. *capriolus,* a goat, from L. *caper,* a goat.] A leap or curvet of a horse; a capriole.—**cabriolet,** kab•rē•o•lā', *n.* [Fr. *cabriolet,* dim. from *cabriole,* a goat-leap.] A one-horse carriage; a cab.

cacao, ka•kā'ō, *n.* [Fr. Sp. Pg. *cacao,* from Mexican *cacauatl,* cacao.] The chocolate tree, a small tree 16 to 18 feet high, a native of the West Indies, and much cultivated in the tropics of both hemispheres on account of its seeds, from which cocoa (a corruption of the word *cacao*) and chocolate are prepared.

cachalot, kash'a•lot or kash•a•lō, *n.* [Fr. *cachalot,* from Catalan *quichal,* a tooth, lit. therefore toothed whale.] A very large cetaceous mammal, the blunt-headed sperm whale, having a head of enormous size, containing a large receptacle filled with spermaceti; sperm oil and ambergris are also obtained from this animal.

cache, kash, *n.* [Fr.] A hole in the ground in which travelers hide and preserve provisions which it is inconvenient to carry.

cachet, ka•shā', *n.* [Fr., from *cacher,* to conceal.] A seal.—*Lettre de cachet,* a private letter of state; a name given especially to letters bearing the private seal of the French kings, often employed as arbitrary warrants of imprisonment for an indefinite period.

cachexy, cachexia, ka•kek'si, ka•kek'si•a, *n.* [Gr. *kachexia,* from *kakos,* ill, and *hexis,* habit, from *echō,* to have.] A morbid state of the bodily system, the result of disease or of intemperate habits.—**cachectic, cachectical,** ka•kek'tik, ka•kek'tik•al, *a.* Having or pertaining to cachexy.

cachinnation, kak•in•nā'shon, *n.* [L. *cachinnatio,* from *cachinno,* to laugh; imitative of the sound.] Loud or immoderate laughter.

cachou, ka•shö', *n.* [Fr. Same as *cashew.*] A sweetmeat generally in the form of a pill, and made of the extract of licorice, cashew nut, gum, etc., used to remove an offensive breath.

cachucha, ka•chö'cha, *n.* [Sp.] A Spanish dance similar to the bolero, a piece of music for it.

cacique, ka•sēk', *n.* The native name of the princes or head chiefs of Haiti, Cuba, Peru, Mexico, and other regions of America, who were found reigning there when these countries were discovered.

cackle, kak'l, *v.i.*—*cackled, cackling.* [D. and L.G. *kakelen,* Sw. *kackla,* Dan. *kagle;* of imitative origin like *giggle, cachinnation,* etc.] To utter a noisy cry such as that often made by a goose or a hen; to laugh with a broken noise, like the cackling of a goose; to giggle; to prate; to prattle; to tattle.—*n.* The broken cry of a goose or hen; idle talk; silly prattle.—**cackler,** kak′lėr, *n.* A fowl that cackles; a telltale; a tattler.

cacodemon, cacodaemon, kak•o•dē′mon, *n.* [Gr. *kakos*, evil, and *daimōn*, a demon.] An evil spirit; a devil. (*Shak.*)

cacodyle, kak′o•dil, *n.* [Gr. *kakos*, bad, *odōdē*, smell, and *hylē*, matter.] A compound of hydrocarbon and arsenic; a clear liquid of an insupportably offensive smell and poisonous vapor.

cacoëthes, kak•ō•ē′thēz, *n.* [L. *cacoethes*, from Gr. *kakoēthes*, a bad habit, an itch for doing something—*kakos*, vicious, and *ēthos*, custom, habit.] A bad custom or habit.—*Cacoethes scribendi*, a diseased propensity for writing; an itch for authorship.

cacophony, ka•kof′o•ni, *n.* [Gr. *kakophōnia*—*kakos*, bad, and *phōnē*, sound, voice.] A disagreeable vocal sound; discord.—**cacophonous,** ka•kof′o•nus, *a.* Sounding harshly.

cactus, kak′tus, *n.* [L., from Gr, *kaktos*, a prickly plant.] A succulent. spiny, and usually leafless shrub of numerous species, natives of tropical America, the fruit of some being edible, and many being cultivated in conservatories for their showy flowers and curious stems.—**cactaceous,** kak•tā′shus, *a.* Relating to or resembling the cactus.

cad, kad, *n.* [An abbreviation of *cadet.*] A slang term applied originally to various classes of persons of a low grade, as hangers-on about inn yards, messengers or errand boys, etc.; now extended to any mean, vulgar fellow of whatever social rank.

cadastre, ka•das′tėr, *n.* [Fr. *cadastre*, a survey and valuation of property, from L.L. *capitastrum*, register for a poll tax, from L. *caput*, the head.] A detailed survey of a country, as the basis of an assessment for fiscal purposes, etc.

cadaver, ka•da′vėr, *n.* [L. *cadere*, to fall.] A dead body.—**cadaverous,** ka•dav′ėr•us, *a.* Of or like a cadaver; pale; sickly; especially, having the appearance or color of a dead human body; pale; wan; ghastly.—**cadaverously,** ka•dav′ėr•us•li, *adv.* In a cadaverous manner.—**cadaverousness,** ka•dav′ėr•us•nes, *n.*

caddice, caddis, kad′is, *n.* [From W. *cadach*, a rag, *cadas*, a kind of cloth, from the rough or ragged covering of the larva.] The larva of the caddice fly.—**caddice fly, caddis fly,** *n.* A neuropterous insect, called also the *May fly*, the larva or grub of which forms for itself a case of small roots, stalks, stones, shells, etc., and lives under water till ready to emerge from the pupa state.

caddie, caddy, kad′i, *n.* One who carries clubs for a golfer.—*v.i.* to serve as a caddie.—**caddy,** *n.* A small box for keeping tea.

cadence, kā′dens, *n.* [L.L. *cadentia*, a falling, from L. *cado*, to fall. *Chance* is the same word.] A decline; a state of falling or sinking; the general tone or modulation of the voice in reading or reciting; tone; sound; rhythm; measure; *mus.* a short succession of notes or chords at the close of a musical passage or phrase; also a shake or trill, run, or division, introduced as an ending or as a means of return to the first subject.—**cadent,**‡ kā′dent, *a.* Falling down; sinking. (*Shak.*)—**cadenza,** ka•den′za, *n.* [It.] *Mus.* an embellishment made at the end of a melody, either actually extempore or of an impromptu character; also, a running passage at the conclusion of a vocal piece.

cadet, ka•det′, *n.* [Fr. *cadet*, O.Fr. *capdet*, contr. from L.L. *capitettum*, dim. of L. *caput*, the head; lit. little head or chief.] A younger or youngest son; a junior male member of a noble family; a young man in training for the rank of an officer in the army or navy; cadets of the U. S. Naval Academy at Annapolis are officially called *midshipmen.*—**cadetship,** ka•det′ship, *n.* The state of being a cadet; the rank or office of a cadet.

cadge, kaj, *v.t.* and *i.* [Perhaps from noun *cadger.*] To carry about for sale; to hawk, go about begging.

cadger, kaj′ėr, *n.* [Perhaps from O.Fr. *cagier*, one who carried about falcons or other birds in a *cage* for sale.] An itinerant huckster or hawker.

cadi, käd′i or kā′di, *n.* [Turk.] A judge in civil affairs among the Turks; usually the judge of a town or village.

Cadmean, kad•mē′an, *a.* Relating to *Cadmus*, a legendary prince of ancient Greece, who is said to have introduced the sixteen simple letters of the Greek alphabet, thence called *Cadmean* letters.—*Cadmean victory*, a victory in which the victors suffer as much as the vanquished.

cadmium, kad′mi•um, *n.* [L. *cadmia*, Gr. *kadmia*, *kadmeia*, calamine.] A metallic element, malleable, ductile, and looking like tin. Symbol, Cd; at. no., 48; at. wt., 112.40.

cadre, kä′dr, *n.* [Fr. from L. *quadra*, a square.] The permanent skeleton or frame-work of a regiment, which may be filled up as need requires.

caduceus, ka•dū′sē•us, *n.* [L.] Mercury's rod represented as a winged rod entwisted by two serpents, in modern times used as a symbol of a physician.—**caducean,** ka•dū′sē•an, *a.* Belonging to the caduceus or wand of Mercury.

caducous, ka•dū′kus, *a.* [L. *caducus*, from *cado*, to fall.] Having a tendency to fall or decay; specifically applied to organs of animals and plants that early drop off, as branchiae, floral envelopes, etc.

caecum, sē′kum, *n.* pl. **caeca,** sē′ka. [L. *caecus*, blind.] The blind gut or intestine; a branch of an intestine with one end closed; mammals have generally only one caecum, birds usually two caeca, while in fishes they are often numerous.—**caecal,** sē′kal, *a.* Of or belonging to the caecum; having the form of a caecum; bag-shaped.

Caesar, sē′zėr, *n.* A title, originally a surname of the Julian family at Rome, which, after being dignified in the person of the dictator C. Julius Caesar, was adopted by successive Roman emperors, and latterly came to be applied to the heir presumptive to the throne; personification of the civil power, the State.—**Caesarean,** sē•zâ′rē•an, *a.* Of or pertaining to Caesar.—*Caesarean operation*, the operation by which the fetus is taken out of the uterus by an incision through the abdomen and uterus, when delivery of a living child is otherwise impossible; said to be so named because Julius Caesar was brought into the world in this way.—**Caesarism,** sē′zėr•izm, *n.* Despotic sway exercised by one who has been raised to power by popular will; imperialism.

caesium, sē′zi•um, *n.* [L. *caesius*, blue.] A rare metal originally discovered in mineral waters, and so named because its spectrum exhibits two characteristic blue lines. It is always found in connection with rubidium.

caesura, sē•zū′ra, *n.* [L. *caesura*, a cutting, from *caedere*, *caesum*, to cut.] A pause or division in a verse; a separation, by the ending of a word or by a pause in the sense, of syllables rhythmically connected.

cafe, ka•fā′, *n.* [F. *café*, coffee.] A coffee house; a restaurant.—**cafeteria,** ka′fe•tēr″i•ä, *n.* A self-service restaurant.

caffeic, ka•fē′ik, *a.* Of or pertaining to coffee.—**caffeine,** ka•fē′in, *n.* A slightly bitter alkaloid found in coffee, tea, etc., which, when taken in large doses, is poisonous.

caftan. See KAFTAN.

cage, kāj, *n.* [Fr. *cage*, from L. *cavea*, a hollow, from *cavus*, hollow (whence E. *cave*).] A box, or enclosure, a large part of which consists of latticework of wood, wicker, wire, or iron bars, for confining birds or beasts; a prison or place of confinement for petty malefactors‡; a skeleton framework of various kinds; the framework of a hoisting apparatus, as the framework in which miners ascend and descend the shaft, and by which hutches are raised and lowered.—*v.t.*—*caged*, *caging*. To confine in a cage; to shut up or confine.—**cageling,** kāj′ling, *n.* A bird kept in a cage; a cage bird.

caiman, *n.* See CAYMAN.

Cain, kān, *n.* [Biblical.] Murderer, fratricide.

Cainozoic, kā•no•zō′ik, *a.* [Gr. *kainos*, recent, and *zōē*, life.] *Geol.* a term applied to the latest of the three divisions into which strata have been arranged, with reference to the age of the fossils they include, embracing the tertiary and posttertiary systems.

caïque, ka•ēk′, *n.* [Fr. from Turk. *kaik.*] A light skiff used in the Bosporus, where it almost monopolizes the boat traffic.

cairn, kârn, *n.* [Gael. Ir. W. *carn*, a heap, a cairn.] A heap of stones, common in Scotland and Wales, and generally of a conical form, erected as a sepulchral monument, to commemorate some event, as a landmark, etc.

cairngorm, Cairngorm stone, kärn′-gorm, *n.* A yellow or brown variety of rock crystal, found in great perfection on *Cairngorm* and the neighboring mountains in Scotland, and much used for brooches, seals, and other ornaments.

caisson, kās′son, *n.* [Fr., *caisson,* from *caisse,* a chest, a case, from L. *capsa,* a chest.] A wooden chest filled with explosives to be fired when approached by an enemy; also, an ammunition wagon, or an ammunition chest; a vessel in the form of a boat used as a floodgate in docks; a watertight structure or case filled with air and placed under sunken vessels to raise them; a kind of floating dock; a watertight box or cylindrical casing used in founding and building structures in water too deep for the cofferdam, such as piers of bridges, quays, etc.

caitiff, kā′tif, *n.* [O.Fr. *caitif,* captive, unfortunate; from L. *captivus,* a captive, from *capere,* to take.] A mean villain; a despicable knave; one who is both wicked and mean.—*a.* Belonging to a caitiff; servile; base.

cajeput, kaj′i•pụt, *n.* [Malay *kâyû,* a tree, and *putih,* white.] A pungent, volatile oil, having stimulant and antispasmodic properties, obtained from the cajeput tree of the Moluccas.

cajole, ka•jōl′, *v.t.*—*cajoled, cajoling.* [Fr. *cajoler,* to cajole; O.Fr. *cageoler,* to sing or chatter like a bird in a cage, from *cage.*] To deceive or delude by flattery, specious promises, etc.; to wheedle; to coax.—**cajoler,** ka•jōl′ėr, *n.* One who cajoles; a wheedler.—**cajolery,** ka•jōl′ėr•i, *n.* The act of cajoling; coaxing language or tricks; a wheedling to delude.

cake, kāk, *n.* [Icel. and Sw. *kaka,* Dan. *kage,* D. *koeck,* G. *kuchen,* cake; probably from L. *coquere,* to cook. COOK.] A mass of fine light dough baked, and generally sweetened or flavored with various ingredients; something made or concreted in the form of a cake; a mass of matter in a solid form relatively thin and extended.—*To take the cake,* complete the victory, to surpass. (Colloq.)—*v.t.*—*caked, caking.* To form into a cake or mass.—*v.i.* To concrete or become formed into a hard mass, as dough in an oven, etc.

calabash, kal′a•bash, *n.* [Pg. *calabaca,* Sp. *calabaza,* from Ar. *qar,* a gourd, and *aibas,* dry.] A gourd shell dried; the fruit of the calabash tree; a vessel made of a dried gourd shell or of a similar shell, used for containing liquors or goods, as pitch, resin, and the like.—**calabash tree,** *n.* A name of several American trees bearing large gourdlike fruits, the hard shells of which are made into numerous domestic utensils, as basins, cups, spoons, bottles, etc.

calamander wood, kal•a•man′dėr, *n.* [Supposed to be a corruption of *Coromandel.*] A beautiful species of wood, a kind of ebony obtained from a Ceylonese tree resembling rosewood, and so hard that it is worked with great difficulty.

calamint, kal′a•mint, *n.* [Gr. *kalaminthe, kalaminthos.*] A name for labiate plants akin to mint.

calamity, ka•lam′i•ti, *n.* [L. *calamitas, calamitatis.*] Any great misfortune or cause of misery; a disaster accompanied with extentive evils; misfortune; mishap; affliction; adversity.—**calamitous,** ka•lam′i•tus, *a.* [Fr. *calamiteux,* L. *calamitosus.*] Producing or resulting from calamity; making wretched; distressful; disastrous; miserable; baleful.—**calamitously,** ka•lam′i•tus•li, *adv.* In a calamitous manner.—**calamitousness,** ka•lam′i•tus•nes, *n.*

calamus, kal′a•mus, *n.* [L. *calamus,* a reed, a reed pen; same root as in E. *haulm.*] A reed or reedlike plant; a perennial tufted Indian grass, called also sweet-scented lemon grass, yielding an aromatic oil used in perfumery; the root of the sweet rush; the generic name of the palms yielding rattans.

calash, ka•lash′, *n.* [Fr. *calèche,* from G. *kalesche,* a word of Slavonic origin: Bohem. *kolesa,* Pol. *kolaska.*] A light carriage with very low wheels and a folding top; the folding hood or top fitted to such a carriage; a kind of headdress worn by ladies, and consisting of a frame of cane or whalebone covered with silk.

calcaneum, kal•kā′nē•um, *n.* [L., the heel.] *Anat.* the largest bone of the tarsus; the bone that forms the heel.

calcar, kal′kär, *n.* [L. *calcar,* a spur, from *calx, calcis,* the heel.] *Bot.* a spur; a hollow projection from the base of a petal.—**calcarate,** kal′-ka•rāt, *a. Bot.* furnished with a spur, as the corolla of larkspur.

calcar, kal′kär, *n.* [L. *calcaria,* a limekiln, from *calx,* lime.] A kind of oven or reverberating furnace, used in glassworks for the calcination of sand and salt of potash, and converting them into frit.

calcareous, kal•kä′rē•us, *a.* [L. *calcarius,* from *calx,* lime.] Partaking of the nature of, having the qualities of, containing calcium carbonate.

calceoralia, kal•sē•o•lä′ri•a, *n.* [L. *calceolus,* a slipper, from the shape of the inflated corolla resembling a shoe or slipper.] The generic name of a number of ornamental herbaceous or shrubby plants, natives of South America, and now very common in gardens, most having yellow flowers, some puce colored, and some with the two colors intermixed, while others are white.

calcic, kal′sik, *a.* [L. *calx, calcis,* lime.] Of or pertaining to lime; containing calcium. — **calciferous,** kal•sif′ėr•us, *a.* [L. *calx,* and *fero,* to produce.] Producing or containing lime, especially when in considerable quantity (*calciferous* strata).—**calcification,** kal′si•fi•kā″shon, *n.* A changing into lime; the process of changing into a stony substance by the disposition of lime.—**calcify,** kal′si•fī, *v.i.*—*calcified, calcifying.* [L. *calx,* and *facio,* to make.] To become gradually changed into a stony condition by the deposition or secretion of lime.—*v.t.* To make stony by depositing lime.—**calcimine,** kal′si•mīn, *n.* [From L. *calx.*] A superior kind of white or colored wash for the walls of rooms, ceilings, etc.—**calcine,** kal•sīn′, *v t.*—*calcined, calcining.* [Fr. *calciner,* from L. *calx.*] To reduce to a powder or to a friable state by the action of heat, to free from volatile matter by the action of heat, as limestone from carbonic acid, iron ore from sulfur; to oxidize or reduce to a metallic calx.—*v.i.* To be converted into a powder or friable substance by the action of heat.—**calcination,** kal•si•na′shon, *n.* The act or operation of calcining.—**calcite,** kal′sīt, *n.* A term applied to various minerals, including limestone, all the white and most of the colored marbles, chalk, Iceland spar, etc.—**calcium,** kal′si•um, *n.* [From L. *calx.*] A silver-white metallic element occurring only in combination such as in limestone, milk, bones, etc. Symbol, Ca; at. no., 20; at. wt., 40.08.—*Calcium carbide,* a compound of calcium and carbon used in the preparation of acetylene.—*Calcium carbonate,* a mineral occurring in bones and teeth.—*Calcium chloride,* a compound of calcium and chloride used as a drying agent and in refrigeration.

calc-sinter, kalk′sin•tėr, *n.* [L. *calx,* lime, and G. *sinter,* a stalactite.] A stalactitic calcium carbonate, a variety of calcite, consisting of deposits from springs holding calcium carbonate in solution.—**calc-spar,** kalk′-spär, *n.* Calcareous spar, or crystallized calcium carbonate.—**calc-tuff,** kalk′tuf, *n.* An alluvial formation of calcium carbonate.

calculate, kal′kū•lāt, *v.t.*—*calculated, calculating.* [L. *calculo, calculatum,* from *calculus,* a counter or pebble used in calculations, from *calx,* a small stone, a counter.] To ascertain by computation; to compute; to reckon up; to estimate (value, cost); to make the necessary or usual computations regarding (an eclipse, etc.); to fit or prepare by the adaptation of means to an end; to make suitable: generally in pp. in this sense=suited or suitable; adapted (a scheme *calculated* to do much mischief).—*v.i.* To make a computation; to weigh all the circumstances; to deliberate.—**calculable,** kal′kū•la•bl, *a.* Capable of being calculated or ascertained by calculation.—**calculating,** kal′kū•lāt•-ing, *a.* Having the power or habit of making arithmetical calculations; given to forethought and calculation; deliberate and selfish; scheming (a *calculating* disposition).—**calculation,** kal•kū•lā′shon, *n.* The act of calculating; the art or practice of computing by numbers; reckoning; computation; a series of arithmetical processes set down in figures and bringing out a certain result; estimate formed by comparing the circumstances bearing on the matter in hand.—**calculative,** kal′kū•lā•tiv, *a.* Pertaining to calculation; tending to calculate.—**calculator,** kal′kū•lā•tėr, *n.* One who calculates.

calculus, kal′kū•lus, *n.* pl. **calculi,** kal′kū•lī. [L., a pebble used for calculating, from *calx*, a small stone, a counter.] A general term for hard concretions of various kinds formed in various parts of the body, the more important being those formed in the gall bladder, called *biliary calculi* or gallstones, and those formed by a deposition from the urine in the kidney or bladder, called *urinary calculi*; the stone; gravel; a method of mathematical computation using algebraic symbols.—**calculous,** kal′kū•lus, *a.* Stony; gritty; hard like stone; arising from calculi, or stones in the bladder.

caldron, cauldron, kạl′dron, *n.* [O.Fr. *caldron*=Sp. *calderon*, It. *calderone*, from L. *caldus*, *calidus*, hot.] A large kettle or boiler of copper or other metal.

calefacient, kal•i•fā′shi•ent, *a.* [L. *calefacio*, to make warm, from *caleo*, to be warm, and *facio*, to make.] Warming; heating.—*n.* That which warms or heats; *med.* a substance which excites a degree of warmth in the part to which it is applied, as mustard, pepper, etc.—**calefaction,** kal•i•fak′shon, *n.* The act or operation of warming or heating; the state of being heated.—**calefactive, calefactory,** kal•i•fak′tiv, kal•i•fak′te•ri, *a.* Adapted to make warm or hot; communicating heat.

calendar, kal′en•dėr, *n.* [L. *calendarium*, an account book, a calendar, from *calendae*, the first day of each month, the calends; root in *calo*, Gr. *kalein*, to call.] A register of the year, in which the months, weeks, and days are set down in order, with the feasts observed by the church, etc.; an orderly table or enumeration of persons or things, as a list of criminal causes which stand for trial; a list; a catalogue; a register.—*v.t.* To enter or write in a calendar; to register.—**calends,** kal′endz, *n. pl.* [L. *calendæ*.] Among the Romans the first day of each month.—*The Greek calends*, a time that never occurred or never will occur, a phrase which originated in the fact that the Greeks had nothing corresponding to the Roman calends.

calender, kal′en•dėr, *n.* [Fr. *calandre*, L.L. *celendra*, a calender, from L. *cylindrus*, Gr. *kylindros*, a cylinder.] A machine consisting of two or more cylinders revolving so nearly in contact with each other that cloth or paper passing through between them is smoothed and glazed by their pressure.—*v.t.* To press or finish in a calender.—**calenderer,** kal′en•dėr•ėr, *n.* A person who calenders cloth.

calender, kal′en•dėr, *n.* [From the founder of the order.] One of an order of dervishes in Turkey and Persia, of not very strict morals, nor held in very high esteem by the Mohammedans.

calenture, kal′en•tūr, *n.* [Fr. *calenture*, Sp. *calentura*, heat, a calenture, from *calentar*, to heat, from L. *caleo*, to be hot.] A kind of delirium caused within the tropics, especially on board ship, by exposure to excessive heat.

calescence, ka•les′ens, *n.* [From L. *calesco*, to grow warm, incept. of *caleo*, to be hot.] Growing warmth; growing heat.

calf, käf, *n.* pl. **calves,** kävz. [A.Sax. *cealf*=D. *kalf*, Icel. *kálfr*, Sw. *kalf*, Dan. *kalv*, G. *kalb*, a calf.] Properly the young of the cow or the bovine genus of quadrupeds, but applied also to the young of the marine mammalia, as the whale; an ignorant, stupid person; a dolt; a weak or cowardly man; leather made from the skin of a calf.—**calf love,** *n.* A youthful romantic passion or affection.—**calfskin,** *n.* The hide or skin of a calf; leather made of the skin.

calf, käf, *n.* [Icel. *kálfi*, the calf of the leg.] The thick fleshy part of the leg behind, below the knee.

caliber, calibre, kal′i•bėr, *n.* [Fr. *calibre*, possibly from Ar. *kâlib*, Pers. *kâlab*, a mould.] The diameter of a body, as of a column or a bullet; usually the diameter of the bore of a firearm; *fig.* compass or capacity of mind; the extent of one's intellectual endowments.—*Caliber-compasses*, *calibers*, or *callipers*, compasses made either with arched legs to measure the diameters of cylinders or globular bodies, or with straight legs and points turned outward to measure the interior diameter or bore of anything.—**calibrate,** kal′i•brāt, *v.t.* To ascertain the caliber of.—**calibration,** kal•i•brā′shon, *n.* The act or process of calibrating, especially of ascertaining the caliber of a thermometer tube, with the view of graduating it to a scale.

calico, kal′i•kō, *n.* [From *Calicut* in India, whence the cloth was first introduced.] A printed cotton cloth; originally, a white cotton cloth imported from India.

calif, caliph, kā′lif, *n.* [Fr. *calife*, from Ar. *khalîfa*, successor, from *khalafa*, to succeed.] A title given to the acknowledged successors of Mohammed, regarded among Mohammedans as being vested with supreme dignity and power in all matters relating to religion and civil policy. Written also *Kalif*, *Khalif*, etc. —**califate,** kal′i•fāt, *n.* The office or dignity of a calif; the government of a calif. Written also *Kalifate*, *Caliphate*.

californium, kal′i•for″ni•um, *n.* [From California, the university and state where first identified.] A radioactive element. Symbol, Cf; at. no., 98.

caliginous, ka•lij′i•nus, *a.* [L. *caliginosus*, from *caligo*, *caliginis*, darkness.] Dim; obscure; dark.

calipash, kal′i•pash, *n.* [A form of *calabash*, with sense of *carapace*, the upper shell of the tortoise.] That part of a turtle which belongs to the upper shield, consisting of a fatty, gelatinous substance of a dull, greenish color; spelled also *Callipash*.—**calipee,** kal′i•pē, *n.* That part of a turtle which belongs to the lower shield, of a light yellow color; spelled also *Callipee*.

caliph, caliphate, *n.* See CALIF, CALIFATE.

calisaya, kal•i•sä′a, *a.* A name for the yellow, or orange-yellow, febrifugal barks of several species of cinchona trees, consisting of the inner bark.

calisthenics, kal•is•then′iks, *n.* [Gr. *kalos*, beautiful, and *sthenos*, strength.] The art or practice of taking exercise for health, strength, or grace of movement.—**calisthenic,** kal•is•then′ik, *a.* Relating to calisthenics.

calk, caulk, kạk, *v.t.* [O.E. *cauke*, O.Fr. *cauquer*, to tread, from L. *calcare*, to tread, to tread on, from *calx*, *calcis*, a heel.] To drive oakum into the seams of (a ship or other vessel), to prevent leaking, the seams being then smeared with melted pitch.—**calker, caulker,** kạ′kėr, *n.* One who calks.

calk, kạk, *n.* [Perhaps from L. *calcar*, a spur, from L. *calx*, the heel.] The prominent part of either extremity of a horseshoe, bent downward and brought to a sort of point; the semicircular ring of iron nailed on to the heel of a strong shoe or boot.—**calk,** kạk, *v.t.* To furnish with a calker or calkin.

call, kạl, *v.t.* [A.Sax. *ceallian*=Icel. and Sw. *kalla*, Dan. *kalde*, to call; D. *kallen*, to talk, to prattle; same root as Gr. *gēryō*, to cry; Skr. *gar*, to call.] To name; to denominate: with the name or appellation as well as the person or thing named to pronounce the name of; to designate or characterize as; to affirm to be; to invite or command to come or assemble (a person, a cab, a meeting); to summon; to select or appoint, as for an office, duty, or employment; to invoke or appeal to; to arouse, as from sleep; to awaken; to proclaim or utter loudly.—*To call back*, to recall; to summon or bring back.—*To call forth*, to bring or summon to action (one's energies).—*To call in*, to collect (as debts or money); to draw from circulation (coin).—*To call names*, to use opprobrious epithets to.—*To call out*, to challenge to a duel; to summon into service or action (the military).—*To call over*, to go over by reading aloud name by name.—*To call to mind*, to recollect; to revive in memory.—*To call up*, to bring into view or recollection; to recall; to require payment of.—*v.i.* To utter a loud sound; or to draw a person's attention by name; often with *to*; to make a short stop or pay a short visit; often followed by *at*, *for*, or *on*.—*To call at*, to visit a place in passing; *to call for* (a person or thing) is to visit in order to obtain the company of the person to some other place, or to get the thing; also, to demand, require, claim (crime *calls for* punishment).—*To call on* or *upon*, to visit (a person); to demand from or appeal to; to invoke.—*To call out*, to utter in a loud voice; to bawl.—*n.* A summons or invitation made vocally or by an instrument; a demand; requisition; claim (the *calls* of justice or humanity; *calls* on one's time); divine vocation or summons; invitation or request to a clergyman by a congregation to become their minister; a short or passing visit paid to a person; the cry of a bird to its mate or young; a whistle or pipe used by a boatswain and his mate to summon sailors to their duty; a pipe to call birds by imitating their voice.—**callboy,** *n.* A boy whose duty it is to call actors on to the stage at the proper moment.—**caller,** kạl′ėr, *n.* One who calls.—**calling,** kạl′ing, *n.* A vocation; profession; trade; usual occupation or employment; a collective name for persons following any profession; state of being divinely called (N.T.).

calligraphy, kal•lig′ra•fi, *n.* [Gr. *kalligraphia*—*kalos*, beautiful, and *graphō*, to write.] The art of beautiful writing; fair or elegant writing or penmanship.—**calligrapher, calligraphist,** kal•lig′ra•fėr, kal•lig′ra•fist, *n.* One skilled in calligraphy.—**calligraphic,** kal•i•graf′ik, *a.* Relating to calligraphy.

calliope, ka•lī′o•pē, *n.* A set of musical whistles, played like an organ.

callipash, kal′i•pash. See CALIPASH.

callisthenic, callisthenics. See CALISTHENICS.

callous, kal′us, *a.* [L. *callosus*, from *callus*, *callum*, hard thick skin. CALLID.] Hardened or thickened from continuous pressure or friction: said of the skin; having a hardened skin; hence, hardened in mind or feelings; insensible; unfeeling.—**callosity,** kal•los′i•ti, *n.* [L. *callositas*.] The state or quality of being hardened or indurated; any thickened or hardened part on the surface of the human body or that of any other animal; any part of a plant unusually hard.—**callously,** kal′us•li, *adv.* In a callous, hardened, or unfeeling manner.—**callousness,** kal′us•nes, *n.* The state or character of being callous; insensibility; apathy; indifference.—**callus,** kal′us, *n.* A callosity; a new growth of osseous matter between the extremities of fractured bones; any part of a plant unusually hard; the new formation over the end of a cutting before it sends forth rootlets.

callow, kal′ō, *a.* [A.Sax. *calu*, bald=D. *kaal*, Sw. *kal*, G. *kahl*, bald; cog. L. *calvus*, bald.] Destitute of feathers, as a young bird; naked; unfledged; pertaining to the condition of a young bird.

calm, käm, *a.* [Fr. *calme*, calm, from L.L. *cauma*, the heat of the sun, hence the hot part of the day, the time for rest; from Gr. *kauma*, heat, from *kaiō*, to burn.] Still; quiet; undisturbed; not agitated; not stormy: said of the weather, the sea, etc.; undisturbed by passion; not agitated or excited in feeling; tranquil, as the mind, temper, etc.—*n.* Freedom from motion, agitation, or disturbance; stillness; tranquility; quiet; especially, a state or period at sea when there is neither wind nor waves.—*Region of calms* or *calm latitudes*, the tracts in the Atlantic and Pacific Oceans on the confines of the trade winds, where calms of long duration prevail.—*v.t.* To make calm; to still; to quiet; to appease, allay, or pacify (grief, anger, anxiety, etc.); to becalm (*Shak.*).—*v.i.* To become calm or serene.—**calmly,** käm′li, *adv.* In a calm manner; without agitation; quietly.—**calmness,** käm′nes, *n.* The state of being calm, quiet, or unruffled; quietness; stillness; tranquility.

calomel, kal′o•mel, *n.* [Gr. *kalos*, fair, good, and *melas*, black, perhaps because it was good for black bile.] A preparation of mercury, a compound of this metal and chlorine, usually in the form of a whitish powder, much used in medicine.

caloric, ka•lor′ik, *n.* [L. *calor*, heat.] In chemistry and physics, an obsolete term referring to the hypothetical fluid to which heat and combustion were attributed.—*Caloric engine*, an engine similar in principle to the steam engine, the motive power being the expansive force of heated air.—**calorie,** kal′o•rē, *n.* The quantity of heat, equivalent to 1/860 watthour, required to raise a gm. of water one degree C.; or the quantity required to raise a kg. of water the same amount (called a kilocalorie), used to express the heat-producing or energy value of food.—**calorific,** kal•o•rif′ik, *a.* Capable of producing heat; causing heat; heating.—*Calorific rays*, invisible rays emanating from the sun, manifested only by their effects on the thermometer.

calorimeter, kal•o•rim′e•tėr, *n.* [L. *calor*, heat, and Gr. *metron*, measure.] An apparatus for measuring absolute quantities of heat.—**calorimetric,** ka•lor′i•met″rik, *a.* Of or belonging to the use of the calorimeter.—**calorimetry,** kal•o•rim′et•ri, *n.* The art or process of using the calorimeter.

calotte, ka•lot′, *n.* [Fr. *calotte*, a skull-cap, dim. of *cale*. CAUL.] A skull-cap worn by ecclesiastics, etc.

caloyer, kal′o•yėr, *n.* [Fr. from Mod. Gr. *kalogeros*, from Gr. *kalos*, beautiful, and *gerōn*, Mod. Gr. *geros*, an old man.] One of a sect of monks of the Greek Church.

caltrop, kal′trop, *n.* [L.L. *calcitrapa*, from L. *calx*, *calcis*, a heel, and L.L. *trappa*, a snare.] *Milit.* an instrument with four iron points disposed in such a manner that any three of them being on the ground the other points upward, used as an obstacle to the advance of troops; *bot.* a term applied to several plants from the resemblance of their heads or fruits to the military instrument.

calumet, kal′ū•met, *n.* [Fr. *calumet*, from L. *calamus*, a reed.] The North American Indians' pipe of peace, the smoking of which was a pledge of amity and good faith.

calumniate, ka•lum′ni•āt, *v.t.*—*calumniated, calumniating*. [L. *calumnior, calumniatus*, to calumniate, from *calumnia*, calumny.] To speak evil of falsely; to cast aspersions on; to charge falsely and knowingly with some crime, offense, or something disreputable; to slander.—*v.i.* To propagate evil reports with a design to injure the reputation of another.—**calumniation,** ka•lum′ni•ā″shon, *n.* The act of calumniating; calumny.—**calumniator,** ka•lum′ni•ā″tėr, *n.* One who calumniates or slanders.—**calumniatory, calumnious,** ka•lum′ni•ā″to•ri, ka•lum′ni•us, *a.* Using calumny; containing or implying calumny; injurious to reputation; slanderous.—**calumniously,** kalum′ni•us•li, *adv.* In a calumnious manner; slanderously.—**calumny,** kal′um•ni, *n.* [L. *calumnia*.] False accusation of a crime or offense, knowingly or maliciously made or reported, to the injury of another; a defamatory or slanderous report; slander; defamation.

Calvary, kal′vâ•ri, *n.* [L. *calvaria*, a skull, from *calva*, a bare scalp.] Golgotha, the place where Christ was crucified, west of Jerusalem.

calve, käv, *v.i.*—*calved, calving*. [From *calf*=D. *kalven*, Dan. *kalve*, to calve.] To bring forth a calf or calves: used specifically of cows, whales, and seals.

Calvinism, kal′vin•izm, *n.* The theological tenets or doctrines of *Calvin*, the celebrated reformer, and his followers, among the distinguishing doctrines of whose system are, predestination, original sin, the irresponsible sovereignty of God, etc.—**Calvinist,** kal′vin•ist, *n.* A follower of Calvin; one who embraces the theological doctrines of Calvin.—**Calvinistic,** kal•vin•ist′ik, *a.* Pertaining to Calvin or to his opinions in theology.

calx, kalks, *n.* pl. **calxes, calces,** kalk′sēz, kal′sēz, [L. *calx*, limestone.] Lime or chalk; an old term for the substance of a metal or mineral which remains after being subjected to violent heat or calcination; an oxide; lime recently prepared by calcination; broken and refuse glass, which is restored to the pots in glassmaking.

calypso, ka•lip′sō, *n.* [Origin uncertain.] A type of improvised, often satirical folksong native to the West Indies.

calyptra, ka•lip′tra, *n.* [Gr. *kalyptra*, a veil or covering.] *Bot.* the hood of the theca or capsule of mosses.

calyx, kā′liks, *n.* pl. **calyces, calyxes,** kā′li•sēz, kā′lik•sez, [L. *calyx*, from Gr. *kalyx*, a calyx, a covering.] *Bot.* the exterior covering of a flower within the bracts and external to the corolla, which it encloses and supports, and consisting of several verticillate leaves called sepals, either united or distinct, usually of a green color and of a less delicate texture than the corolla.—**calycinal,**

calycine, ka•lis′i•nal, kal′i•sīn, *a.* *Bot.* pertaining to a calyx; situated on a calyx.—**calycle,** kal′i•kl, *n.* [L. *calyculus,* dim. of *calyx.*] *Bot.* an outer accessory calyx, or set of leaflets or bracts looking like a calyx; *zool.* same as *Calice.*

cam, kam, *n.* [O.E. *camb,* a comb, a crest; comp. Dan. *kam-hiul,* G. *kamm-rad,* a cogweel, from *kam, kamm,* a comb.] *Mach.* a projecting part of a wheel or other revolving piece so placed as to give an alternating motion, especially in a rectilinear direction, to another piece (often a rod) that comes in contact with it and is free to move only in a certain direction. The eccentric is a kind of cam.

camaraderie, kam′a•räd•ėr•ē, *n.* [Fr.] Mutual good fellowship as comrades.

camarilla, kam•a•ril′a, Sp. pron. ka•ma•rēl′ya, *n.* [Sp., a small room, a dim. from *camara,* L. *camera, camara,* a vault. CHAMBER.] A company of secret counselors or advisers; a cabal; a clique.

camber, kam′bėr, *n.* [Fr. *cambrer,* to arch, to vault, from L. *camera,* a vault.] A convexity upon an upper surface, as a ship's deck, a bridge, a beam, a lintel; the curve of a ship's plank.—*Camber window,* a window arched at the top.—*v.t.* To arch; to bend; to curve ship planks.

cambist, kam′bist, *n.* [Fr. *cambiste,* from L. *cambio,* to exchange. CHANGE.] One who has to do with exchange, or is skilled in the science of exchange; one who deals in notes and bills of exchange; a banker.

cambium, kam′bi•um, *n.* [L. *cambio,* to exchange, from the alterations occurring in it.] The layer of soft tissue between the bark and the wood of vascular plants that produces new secondary growth.

Cambrian, kam′bri•an, *a.* Relating or pertaining to Wales or *Cambria.*—*n.* A Welshman; a series of strata on the base of the Paleozoic system of rocks.

cambric, kām′brik, *n.* A species of fine white linen fabric, said to be named from *Cambray* in Flanders.

came, kām, pret. of *come.*

camel, kam′el, *n.* [L. *camelus,* from Gr. *kamelos,* from Heb. *gâmâl,* camel.] A large hoofed quadruped of the ruminant class, with one or two humps on its back, used in Asia and Africa for carrying burdens, and for riding on; a watertight structure placed beneath a vessel in the water, being first filled with water and sunk, after which the water is pumped out, when the camel gradually rises, lifting the vessel with it.

camellia, ka•mel′i•a, or ka•mēl′ya, *n.* [After George Joseph *Kamel,* a Moravian Jesuit.] A genus of beautiful trees or shrubs belonging to the tea family, with showy flowers somewhat resembling the rose, and elegant dark-green, shining, laurel-like leaves.

camelopard, ka•mel′o•pärd or kam′-el•o•pard, *n.* [L. *camelus,* a camel, and *párdalis,* a leopard.] The giraffe.

cameo, kam′ē•ō, *n.* [It. *cameo, cammeo,* from L.L. *cammæus,* a word of uncertain origin.] A stone or shell composed of several different colored layers having a subject in relief cut upon one or more of the upper layers, an under layer of a different color forming the ground.

camera, kam′ėr•a, *n.* [L., a vault, a chamber, from Gr. *kamara,* anything arched. CHAMBER.] An apparatus that takes photographs by means of a light-proof enclosure fitted with a lens that focuses the image of an object on light-sensitive film or plates; the part of a television transmitter in which images to be televised are converted into electric impulses.—*Camera lucida* [L., lit. clear chamber], an optical instrument for facilitating the delineation of distant objects, by producing a reflected picture of them upon paper by means of a glass prism suitably mounted, and also for copying or reducing drawings.—*Camera obscura* [L., dark chamber], an apparatus in which the images of external objects, received through a double-convex lens, are exhibited in their natural colors, on a white surface placed at the focus of the lens.

camisade, kam•i•säd′, *n.* [Fr. *camisade,* Sp. *camisado,* O.Fr. *camise,* a shirt. CHEMISE.] A shirt worn by soldiers over their armor in a night attack to enable them to recognize each other; an attack by soldiers wearing the camisade; an attack made in the dark.

camisole, kam′i•sōl, *n.* [Fr. dim. or O.Fr. *camise,* L.L. *camisa,* a chemise.] A short light garment worn by ladies when dressed in *negligee;* strait jacket for lunatics or criminals condemned to the guillotine.

camlet, kam′let, *n.* [Fr. *camelot,* from *camel.*] A stuff originally made of camel's hair, now made sometimes of wool, sometimes of silk, sometimes of hair, especially that of goats, with wool or silk.

camomile, kam′o•mīl, *n.* Any plant of the genus *Anthemis,* especially *Matricaria chamomilla.* Foliage and flowers are strong-scented and contain essential oils of medicinal value.

camouflage, kam′ö•fläzh, *n.* [Fr.] The art of disguising; especially the art of disguising material in warfare.—*v.* To alter the appearance so as to mislead or render difficult to recognize.

camp, kamp, *n.* [Fr. *camp,* a camp, formerly a field, from L. *campus,* a plain. *Campaign, champion, decamp, scamper,* are from same source.] The place where an army or other body of men is or has been encamped; the collection of tents or other erections for the accommodation of a number of men, particularly troops in a temporary station; an encampment.—*v.t.*† To put into or lodge in a camp, as an army; to encamp; to afford camping ground for (*Shak.*). *v.i.* To live in a camp, as an army; to encamp.—**camp follower,** *n.* One who follows or attaches himself or herself to a camp or army without serving.—**camp meeting,** *n.* In *Amer.* a religious meeting in the open air, where the frequenters encamp for some days for continuous devotion.—**campstool,** *n.* A stool with crossed legs, so made as to fold up when not used.

campaign, kam•pān′, *n.* [Fr. *campagne* country, open country, campaign, from L. *campania,* a level country, *campus,* a plain. CAMP.] An open field or open plain‡; the time, or the operations of an army during the time it keeps the field in one season.—*v.i.* To serve in a campaign; a political, commercial or other contest.—**campaigner,** kam-pān′er, *n.* One who has served in an army in several campaigns.

campanile, kam•pa•nē′la, or kam′-pa•nīl, *n.* pl. **campanili,** kam•pa•-nē′lē. [It. *campanile,* from It. and L.L. *campana,* a bell.] *Arch.* a clock or bell tower; a term applied especially to detached buildings in some parts of Italy, erected for the purpose of containing bells.

campanology, kam•pa•nol′o•ji, *n.* [L.L. *campana,* a bell, and Gr. *logos,* discourse.] The art or principles of bell ringing; a treatise on the art.—**campanologist,** kam•pa•nol′o•jist, *n.* One skilled in the art of bell ringing or campanology.

campanula, kam•pan′ū•la, *n.* [L.L., a dim. of *campana,* a bell, from form of the corolla.] The bellflowers, a large genus of herbaceous plants, with bell-shaped flowers usually of a blue or white color.—**campanulate,** kam•pan′ū•lāt, *a.*

camphene, kam′fēn, *n.* The commercial term for purified oil of turpentine, obtained by distilling the oil over quicklime to free it from resin, and used in lamps.

camphor, kam′fėr, *n.* [L.L. *camphora,* L.Gr. *kaphoura,* from Ar. *kâfûr,* camphor, said to be from a Malay word signifying chalk.] A whitish translucent substance belonging to the class of vegetable oils, with a bitterish aromatic taste and a strong characteristic smell, found in many plants and sometimes secreted naturally in masses, obtained also by distillation of the wood, and used in medicine as a diaphoretic, antispasmodic, etc.—**camphorate,** kam′fėr•āt, *v.t.* To impregnate with camphor.—**camphoric,** kam•for′ik, *a.* Pertaining to or obtained from camphor, or partaking of its qualities.

campion, kam′pi•on, *n.* [Probably from L. *campus,* a field.] The popular name of certain English plants belonging to the genera *Lychnis* and *Silene,* such as bladder campion, sea campion, rose campion, etc.

campus, kam′pus, *n.* [L. field.] The grounds and buildings of a school or college.

can, kan, *v.i.*—pret. *could.* [A.Sax. *can,* pres. ind. of *cunnan,* to know, to know how to do, to be able; *could*=O.E. *coude* (with *l* erroneously inserted), A.Sax. *cúthe,* pret. of *cunnan.* Akin D. *kunnen,* to be able;

Sw. *kunna*, Dan. *kunde*, Icel. *kunna*, to know, to be able; G. *können*, to be able. The root is the same as that of *ken* and *know*. KNOW.] (A verb now used only as an auxiliary and in the indicative mood.) To be able, physically, mentally, morally, legally, or the like; to possess the qualities, qualifications, or resources necessary for the attainment of any end or the accomplishment of any purpose, the specific end or purpose being indicated by the verb with which *can* is joined.—*Can but*, can do no more than; can only (we *can but* fail).—*Cannot but*, cannot help doing or being; cannot refrain from (*cannot but* remember, *cannot but* acknowledge).

can, kan, *n.* [A.Sax. *canne*=D. *kan*, Icel. *kanna*, G. *kanne*, a can.] A rather indefinite term applied to various vessels of no great size, now more especially to vessels made of sheet metal, for containing liquids, preserves, etc.—*v.t.*—*canned*, *canning*. To put into a can (to *can* preserved meat, fruit, etc.).

Canaanite, kā′nan•īt, *n.* An inhabitant of the land of *Canaan*; specifically, one of the inhabitants before the return of the Israelites from Egypt.—**Canaanitish,** kā•nan•īt′ish, *a.* Of or pertaining to Canaan or the Canaanites.

Canadian, ka•nā′di•an, *a.* Pertaining to Canada.—*n.* An inhabitant or native of Canada.—*Canadian balsam*, *Canada balsam*, a fluid resin mixed with a volatile oil, obtained from fir trees, and much valued for optical purposes on account of its perfect transparency and its refractive power.—*Canada rice*, a plant growing in deep water in the northern states of America and Canada, the seeds of which form much of the food of the American Indians, and of the great flocks of waterfowl.

canaille, ka•nāl′ or ka•nä′ya, *n.* [Fr., from It. *canaglia*, a pack of dogs, from L. *canis*, a dog.] The lowest orders of the people; the rabble; the vulgar.

canal, ka•nal′, *n.* [Fr. *canal*, from L. *canalis*, a channel, from the same root as Skr. *khan*, to dig.] An artificial watercourse, particularly one constructed for the passage of boats or ships; *arch.* a channel; a groove or a flute; *anat*, any cylindrical or tubular cavity in the body through which solids, liquids, or certain organs pass; a duct; *zool.* a groove observed in different parts of certain univalve shells.—**canaliculate, canaliculated,** kan•a•lik′ū•lāt, kan•a•lik′ū•lāt•ed, *a.* [L. *canaliculatus* from *canaliculus*, a little pipe, from *canalis*.] Channelled; furrowed; grooved.—**canalize,** ka•nal′īz, *v.t.* To make a canal through (to *canalize* an isthmus); to make like a canal, to *canalize* a river.—**canalization,** ka•nal′i•zā″shon, *n.* The act of canalizing.

canard, kä•när′ or ka•närd′, *n.* [Fr., a duck, from L.L. *canardus*, a kind of boat, from G. *kahn*, a boat or skiff.] An absurd story which one attempts to impose on his hearers or readers; a false rumor set afloat by way of news.

canary, ka•nâ′ri, *n.* Wine made in the Canary Islands; an old dance introduced from the Canary Islands into Europe; a singing bird, belonging to the finch family, a native of those islands, and which has long been very common as a cage bird in various countries.—**canary grass,** *n.* A kind of grass, a native of the Canary Isles, the seeds of which are much used under the name of *Canary seed*, as food for cage birds.

canasta, ka•nas′ta, *n.* [Sp. basket.] A card game, similar to rummy, played with two decks of 52 cards and four jokers.

cancan, kan′kan, *n.* A kind of French dance performed by men and women, who indulge in extravagant postures and lascivious gestures.

cancel, kan′sel, *v.t.*—*cancelled*, *cancelling*. [Fr. *canceller*, to cancel; whence also *chancel*, *chancellor*.] To draw lines across (something written) so as to deface; to blot out or obliterate; to annul or destroy (an obligation, a debt); to throw aside as no longer useful (sheets of a printed book, etc.).—*n.* Latticework‡; that which is cancelled or thrown aside.—**cancellation,** kan•sel•lā′shon, The act of cancelling.

cancer, kan′sėr, *n.* [L., a crab, a cancer.] *Pathol.* a general term for any malignant growth, most tending to metastasize; any destructive condition; *astron.* [*cap.*] one of the twelve signs of the zodiac.—**cancerous,** kan′sėr•us, *a.* Like a cancer; having the qualities of a cancer; virulent.—**cancroid,** kang′kroid, *a.* Like cancer: applied to morbid growths somewhat like cancer, but not really cancerous.—*n.* A skin disease approaching in its nature to cancer.

candelabrum, kan•de•lä′brum, *n.* pl. **candelabra,** kan•de•lä′bra, [L., from *candela*, a candle.] A tall candlestick; a stand by which lamps were supported; a branched highly ornamental candlestick; a chandelier.

candent, kan′dent, *a.* [L. *candens*, *candentis*, from *candeo*. to be white or hot. CANDID.] Heated to whiteness; glowing with white heat.—**candescence,** kan•des′ens, *n.* [L. *candesco*, incept. of *candeo*.] A state of glowing; incandescence.

candid, kan′did, *a.* [L. *candidus*, white, bright, frank, sincere, from *candeo*, to be white; akin *candle*, *incense*, *incendiary*, etc.] White‡; honest and frank; open and sincere; ingenuous; outspoken; fair; just; impartial.—*A candid friend*, a person disposed to tell unpleasant truths or to say ill-natured things under the guise of candor.—**candid camera,** a small camera of hand size with powerful lens and quick shutter that permits the photographing of unposed pictures.—**candidly,** kan′did•li, *adv.* Openly; frankly.—**candidness,** kan′did•nes, *n.* Candor.—**candor,** kan′dėr, *n.* The quality or trait of being candid; readiness to make known anything relating to one's self; openness of heart; frankness; sincerity.

candidate, kan′di•dāt, *n.* [L. *candidatus*, from *candidus*, white; those who sought offices in Rome wearing a white robe during their candidature.] A person who aspires or is put forward by others as an aspirant to an office or honor.—**candidature, candidacy,** kan′di•dā•chėr, kan′di•da•si, *n.* The state of being, or act of standing as, a candidate.

candle, kan′dl, *n.* [L. *candela*, a candle, from *candere*, to shine. CANDID.] A taper; a cylindrical body of tallow, wax, spermaceti, or other fatty material, formed on a wick, and used for a portable light.—*Not fit to hold the candle to one*, not fit to act as a mere attendant; to be very inferior.—*The game is not worth the candle*, a phrase of French origin, indicating that an object is not worth the pains requisite for its attainment.—**candleberry, candlenut,** *n.* The fruit of the candleberry tree, a name given to several species of myrtle, especially the wax myrtle, a shrub common in North America, the berries of which are covered with a greenish-white wax, of which candles are made.—**candlefish,** *n.* A small sea fish of the salmon family, frequenting the northwestern shores of America, so extremely oily that it is used for making oil, and as a natural candle. whence its name.—**candle power,** *n.* The illuminating power of a candle, taken as a unit in estimating the luminosity of any illuminating agent (as gas), the standard usually employed being a spermaceti candle burning at the rate 120 grains of sperm per hour.—**Candlemas,** kan′dl•mas, *n.* [So named from the blessing or consecration of candles on this day, in the R. Cath. Ch.] An ecclesiastical festival held on the second day of February in honor of the purification of the Virgin Mary; in *Scot.* a quarterly money term.—**candlestick,** kan′dl•stik, *n.* An instrument to hold a candle when burning, made in different forms and of different materials.—**candlewood,** *n.* The wood of a West Indian resinous tree.

candor. See CANDID.

candy, kan′di, *n.* [It. *candi*, candy, from Ar. *qandi*, made of sugar, from *qand*, sugar.] A solid preparation of sugar or molasses, either alone or in combination with other substances, to flavor, color, or give it the desired consistency.—*v.t.*—*candied*, *candying*. To conserve with sugar so as to form a thick mass; to boil in sugar; to form into congelations or crystals.—*v.i.* To become incrusted by candied sugar; to become crystallized or congealed.—**candied,** kan′did, *p.* and a. Preserved or incrusted with sugar; *fig.* honeyed, flattering; glozing.

candytuft, kan′di•tuft, *n.* [From *Candia*, the ancient Crete.] The popular name of a tufted flower brought from the island of Candia.

cane, kān, *n.* [Old spelling also *canne*, from L. *canna*, Gr. *kanna*, a reed.] A term applied to the stems of some palms, grasses, and other plants, such as the bamboo, rattan, and sugarcane; a cane used as a walking stick.—*v.t.*—*caned, caning.* To beat with a cane or walking stick. to furnish or complete with cane (as chairs).—**canebrake,** *n.* A thicket of canes.—**cane sugar,** *n.* Sugar obtained from the sugarcane, as distinguished from beet root sugar, grape sugar, maple sugar, etc.

canella, ka•nel′la, *n.* [Dim. of L. *canna*, a reed, from the cylindrical form of the bark when peeled off.] A kind of aromatic bark, also called white cinnamon, brought from the West Indies and used as a tonic.

canescent, ka•nes′ent, *a.* [L. *canescens, canescentis*, ppr. of *canesco*, to grow white, from *caneo*, to be white.] Growing white or hoary; tending or approaching to white; whitish.

canine, kā′nīn, *a.* [L. *caninus*, from *canis*, a dog.] Pertaining to dogs; having the properties or qualities of a dog.—*Canine teeth*, or *canines*, two sharp pointed teeth in both jaws of man and other mammalia, one on each side, between the incisors and grinders, most highly developed in the Carnivora.

canister, kan′is•tėr, *n.* [L. *canistrum*, Gr. *kanastron*, from *kanna*, a reed.] A small basket‡; a small box or case, usually of tin, for tea, coffee, etc.; a case containing shot which bursts on being discharged; case shot.

canker, kang′kėr, *n.* [From L. *cancer*, properly pronounced *canker*, a crab, a cancer.] A kind of cancerous, gangrenous, or ulcerous sore or disease, whether in animals or plants; an eating, corroding, or other noxious agency producing ulceration, gangrene, rot, decay, and the like; anything that insidiously or persistently destroys, corrupts, or irritates, as care, trouble, annoyance, grief, pain, etc.; a kind of wild, worthless rose; the dog rose (*Shak.*).—*v.t.* To infect with canker either literally or figuratively; to eat into, corrode or corrupt; to render ill-conditioned, crabbed, or ill-natured.—*v.i.* To grow corrupt; to be infected with some poisonous or pernicious influence; to be or become malignant.—**cankerous,** kang′kėr•us, *a.* Corroding, destroying, or irritating like a cancer; cancerous.—**cankerworm,** *n.* A worm or larva destructive to trees or plants.

cannel coal, kan′el•kōl, *n.* A glistening grayish-black hard bituminous coal, so called because it burns with a bright flame like a candle; it is chiefly used in making gas.

cannery, kan′ėr•i, *n.* An establishment for canning or preserving meat, fish, or fruit in tins hermetically sealed.

cannibal, kan′i•bal, *n.* [Sp. *canibal*, a cannibal, a corruption of *Caribal*, a Carib, the Caribs being reputed cannibals.] A human being that eats human flesh; a man-eater or anthropophagite; an animal that eats the flesh of its own or kindred species.—**cannibalism,** kan′i•bal•izm, *n.* The act or practice of eating human flesh by mankind; anthropophagy; murderous cruelty.

cannon, kan′un, *n.* pl. **Cannons** or **cannon.** [Fr. *canon*, a tube, barrel, cannon, from L. *canna*, Gr. *kanna*, a cane or reed. Akin *canister, canon, cane.*] A large military firearm for throwing balls and other missiles by the force of gunpowder; a big gun or piece of ordnance; *billiards*, the act of hitting your adversary's ball with your own, so that your ball flies off and strikes the red, or vice versa.—*v.i.* To make a cannon at billiards; to fly off or asunder from the force of collision.—**cannonade,** kan•un•ād′, *n.* The act of discharging cannon and throwing balls, for the purpose of destroying an army or battering a town, ship, or fort.—*v.t.* and *i.*—*cannonaded, cannonading.* To attack with ordnance or artillery; to batter with cannon.—**cannoneer,** kan•un•ēr′, *n.* A man who manages cannon.—**cannoneering,** kan•un•ēr′ing, *n.* The act or art of using cannons; practice with cannons.—**cannon bone,** *n.* (1) In horses, etc., the large metacarpal or metatarsal of the single digit. (2) In ruminants, the bone formed by fusion of third and fourth metacarpals or metatarsals.—**cannon shot,** *n.* A ball or shot for cannon; the range or distance a cannon will throw a ball.—**cannon ball,** *n.* A ball or solid projectile to be thrown from cannon.

cannot, kan′ot. *Can* and *not.* [These words are usually written as one word, being colloquially so pronounced.]

cannula, kan′ū•la, *n.* [L., dim. of *canna*, a reed.] A small tube used by surgeons for various purposes.—**cannular,** kan′ū•lėr, *a.* Having the form of a cannula or small tube.

canny, kan′i, *a.* [Akin to *can, ken.*] Cautious; prudent; wary; watchful; expert; not extortionate or severe; gentle; quiet in disposition; tractable; easy; comfortable.

canoe, ka•nö′, *n.* [Sp. *canoa*, from the native West Indian name.] A light narrow boat made by hollowing out and shaping the trunk of a tree, such as is used by savage tribes; any light boat narrow in the beam, and propelled by paddles.—**canoeist,** ka•nö′ist, *n.* One who uses a canoe.

canon, kan′on, *n.* [A.Sax. *canon*, from L. *canon*, Gr. *kanōn*, a straight rod, a rule or standard—from *kanē*, a form of *kanna, kannē*, a reed, a cane, whence also *cannon.*] A law or rule in general; a law or rule regarding ecclesiastical doctrine or discipline, especially one enacted by a council and duly confirmed; the books of the Holy Scriptures universally received as genuine by Christian churches; the rules of a religious order; a dignitary who possesses a prebend or revenue allotted for the performance of divine service in a cathedral or collegiate church; the catalogue of saints acknowledged in the Roman Catholic Church; *mus.* a kind of perpetual fugue, in which the different parts, beginning one after another, repeat incessantly the same air; *printing*, one of the largest kinds of type or letter, supposed to be so named because it was used in the printing of canons.—**canoness,** kan′on•es, *n.* A female canon; a woman who enjoys a prebend without having to make religious vows.—**canonical,** ka•non′ik•al, *a.* Pertaining or according to a canon or rule, especially according to ecclesiastical canons or rules; belonging to the canon of Scripture.—*Canonical books*, those books of the Bible which are admitted to be of divine origin.—*Canonical hours*, hours appointed in Roman Catholic Church by canon law for the celebration of marriage, 8 a.m. to 3 p.m. Also the times, from midnight onward, at which certain parts of the daily service are recited. They are matins, prime, tierce, sext, nones, vespers, and compline (*Ps.* cxix. 164: 'Seven times a day do I praise thee').—**canonically,** ka•non′ik•al•li, *adv.* In a canonical manner; in accordance with a canon or canons.—**canonicals,** ka•non′ik•alz, *n. pl.* The dress or habit prescribed by canon to be worn by the clergy when they officiate; certain articles or appurtenances of dress sometimes worn by university men, English barristers, etc.—**canonicity,** kan•o•nis′i•ti, *n.* The quality of being canonical; the state of belonging to the canon or genuine books of Scripture.—**canonist,** kan′on•ist, *n.* A professor of canon law; one skilled in the study and practice of ecclesiastical law.—**canonistic,** kan•o•nis′tik, *a.* Pertaining to the canonists.—**canonization,** kan′on•i•zā″shon, *a.* The act of canonizing a person; the act of ranking a deceased person in the catalogue of saints, called a canon.—**canonize,** kan′on•īz, *v.t.*—*canonized, canonizing.* To declare a man a saint, and rank him in the catalogue or canon of saints, this act being in the power of the popes.—**canonry, canonship,** kan′on•ri, kan′on•ship, *n.* The benefice filled by a canon.—**canon law,** *n.* A collection of ecclesiastical constitutions for the regulation of a church; specifically those of the Roman Catholic Church.

canopy, kan′o•pi, *n.* [Fr. *canapé*, O.Fr. *conopé*, L. *conopeum*, Gr. *kōnōpeion*, lit. a net to keep off gnats, from *kōnōpos*, a gnat.] A covering fixed at some distance above a throne or a bed; any somewhat similar covering; a covering held over a person's head in a procession or public ceremony; *arch.* a decoration, often richly sculptured, above a tomb, niche, pulpit, etc.—*v.t.*—*canopied, canopying.* To cover with a canopy, or as with a canopy.

canorous, ka•nō′rus, *a.* [L. *canorus,* from *cano,* to sing.] Musical; tuneful. —**canorousness,** ka•nō′rus•nes, *n.*

cant, kant, *v.i.* [From L. *canto,* freq. of *cano,* to sing.] To speak with a whining voice or in an affected, assumed, or supplicating tone (as a beggar); to make whining pretensions to goodness; to affect piety without sincerity; to sham holiness. —*n.* A whining manner of speech; the whining speech of beggars, as in asking alms; the language or jargon spoken by gypsies, thieves, professional beggars, etc.; a kind of slang; the words and phrases peculiar to or characteristic of a sect, party, or profession; a pretentious assumption of a religious character; a hypocritical addiction to the use of religious phrases, etc.; religious phrases hypocritically used.—*a.* Of the nature of cant or slang.—**canter,** kan′tėr, *n.* One who cants, whines, or uses an affected hypocritical style of speech.

cant, kant, *n.* [Same word as Dan. Sw. and D. *kant,* edge, border, margin, etc.; G. *kante,* a side, a border or brim; O.Fr. *cant,* corner, angle.] An external or salient angle; an inclination from a perpendicular or horizontal line; a toss, thrust, or push with a sudden jerk.—*v.t.* To turn about or over by a sudden push or thrust; to cause to assume an inclining position; to tilt; to toss; to cut off an angle from (a square block).

can't, kant. A colloquial contraction of *can not.*

Cantab, kan•tab′. An abbreviation of *Cantabrigian.* — **Cantabrigian,** kan•ta•brij′i•an, *n.* [L.L. *Cantabrigiensis,* pertaining to Cambridge.] A student or graduate of Cambridge University.

cantaloupe, kan′ta•löp, *n.* [Fr. *canteloup,* from *Cantalupo,* Italian estate where grown.] A delicately flavored muskmelon.

cantankerous, kan•tang′kėr•us, *a.* [Comp. O.E. *contek, contak,* debate, strife.] Ill-natured; ill-conditioned; cross; waspish; contentious; disputatious. [Colloq.]—**cantankerously,** kan•tang′kėr•us•li, *adv.* In a cantankerous manner.—**cantankerousness,** kan•tang′kėr•us•nes, *n.*

cantata, kan•tä′tä, *n.* [It., from *cantare,* L. *cantare,* freq. of *cano,* to sing.] *Mus.* a short composition in the form of an oratorio, but without *dramatis personæ.*

canteen, kan•tēn′, *n.* [Fr. *cantine,* from It. *cantina,* a wine-cellar, a vault, from *canto,* an angle, a corner. CANT, an angle.] A shop in barracks, camps, garrisons, etc., where provisions, liquids, etc., are sold to noncommissioned officers and privates; a vessel used by soldiers, when on the march or in the field, for carrying liquid for drink; a box, fitted up with compartments, in which officers on foreign service pack bottles, knives, forks, etc.

canter, kan′tėr, *v.i.* [An abbrev. of *Canterbury Gallop,* the gallop of pilgrims in olden times riding to Canterbury.] To move in a moderate gallop, raising the two forefeet nearly at the same time, with a leap or spring: said of horses.—*n.* A moderate gallop; a gallop by a winner at the end of an easy race.

Canterbury bell, *n.* A species of Campanula, so named because it is abundant around Canterbury.

cantharides, kan•thar′i•dēz, *n. pl.* [Gr. *kantharis, kantharidis,* a blistering fly.] Coleopterous insects of several species, the best known being the Spanish or blistering fly, which is, when bruised, extensively used as the active element in blistering plasters, having a very powerful effect.

canticle, kan′ti•kl, *n.* [L. *canticulum,* a little song, from *canto,* to sing. CANT.] A song, especially a little song; an unmetrical hymn taken from Scripture, arranged for chanting, and used in church service; [*cap.*] *pl.* The Song of Songs or Song of Solomon, one of the books of the Old Testament.

cantilever, kan′ti•lev•ėr, *n.* A beam or member projecting beyond a single support at one end; either of two beams projecting toward each other from piers to be joined to form the span of a cantilever bridge.

cantle, kan′tl, *n.* [O.Fr. *cantel,* cornerpiece, dim. of *cant.* CANT, an angle.] A corner; a fragment; a piece; a portion (*Shak.*); the protuberant part of a saddle behind; the hind-bow.—*v.t.*—*cantled, cantling.* To cut into pieces; to cut a piece out of.

canto, kan′tō, *n.* pl. **cantos,** kan′tōz, [It. *canto,* a song; L. *cantus.* CHANT, CANT.] A part or division of a poem of some length; *mus.* the highest voice part in concerted music.

canton, kan′ton, *n.* [Fr. *canton;* It. *cantone,* aug. of *canto,* a corner. CANT. CANTLE.] A distinct or separate portion or district of territory; one of the states of the Swiss republic; a distinct part or division, as of a painting or of a flag.—*v.t.* To divide into cantons or distinct portions; to separate off; to allot separate quarters to each regiment of.—**cantonal,** kan′ton•al, *a.* Pertaining to a canton or cantons.—**cantonment,** kan•ton′ment, *n.* A part or division of a town or village assigned to a particular regiment of troops; a permanent military station of a slighter character than barracks; military towns at some distance from any city, such as are formed in India.

cantor, kan′tor, *n.* [L. *cantor,* singer.] A leader of the singing in a cathedral or other church; a synagogue official in charge of music.

canvas, kan′vas, *n.* [Fr. *canevas,* Pr. *canabas,* It. *canavaccis,* L.L. *canabacius,* from L. *cannabis,* hemp.] A coarse cloth made of hemp or flax, used for tents, sails of ships, painting on, and other purposes; hence sails in general; a painting.—*Under canvas,* in a tent or tents; with sails spread.—**canvasback,** *n.* A sea duck of North America, with delicate flesh: so called from the color of its back.

canvass, kan′vas, *v.t.* [From *canvas,* canvas, and formerly also a sieve, a strainer, because sieves were made of canvas; like O.Fr. *canabasser,* to examine, search, sift.] To examine; to scrutinize; to sift or examine by way of discussion; to discuss; to debate; to visit or apply to in order to obtain orders for goods, votes, or support for a candidate for an office or appointment, etc.—*v.i.* To seek or go about to solicit votes or interest, or to obtain mercantile orders.—*n.* The act of canvassing; close inspection; scrutiny; discussion; debate; a seeking; solicitation of votes, orders for goods, etc.—**canvasser,** kan′vas•ėr, *n.* One who canvasses or solicits votes, mercantile orders, etc.

canyon, cañon, kan′yun, kä•nyon′ *n.* [Sp. *cañon,* a canon, a tube, a canyon.] A narrow chasm with steep sides, formed by erosion.

canzonet, kan•zo•net′, *n.* [It. *canzonetta.*] *Mus.* a little or short song, shorter and less elaborate than airs of oratorio or opera; a short concerted air; a madrigal‡.

caoutchouc, kö′chök, *n.* [A South American word.] An elastic gummy substance, which is the inspissated juice of several tropical plants, much used in the industrial arts for covering fabrics to render them waterproof, making elastic webbing, flexible tubes, etc.: india rubber, gum elastic.

cap, kap, *n.* [A.Sax. *caeppe,* a cap, cope, cape, hood, from L.L. *capa, cappa* (of unknown origin), a cape, whence Sp. *capa,* It. *cappa,* Fr. *chape,* a cloak, cape, cover. *Cape* and *cope* are forms of the same word.] A part of dress made to cover the head, generally of softer material than a hat, and without a brim; an act of respect made by uncovering the head; the summit, top, or crown; anything resembling a cap in appearance, position, or use, as the inner case which covers the movement of some kinds of watches, etc.; a percussion cap (which see).—*v.t.*—*capped, capping.* To put a cap on; to cover with a cap or as with a cap; to cover the top or end of; to place a cap on the head of, when conferring official distinction, admitting to professional honors, etc.; to complete; to consummate; to crown; to follow up with something more remarkable than what has previously been done. —*To cap verses, texts,* or *proverbs,* to quote verses, texts, or proverbs alternately in emulation or contest.—*To set one's cap at,* to use measures to gain the affections of someone with a view to matrimony.

capable, kā′pa•bl, *a.* [Fr. *capable,* capable, able, sufficient L.L. *capabilis,* from L. *capio,* to take, which appears also in *captious, captive, accept, except, conception, susceptible, recipient, occupy,* etc.] Able to receive; open to influences; impressible; susceptible; admitting; with *of* (*capable of* pain, *of* being broken); having sufficient power, skill, ability: with *of* (*capable of* judging); able; competent; fit; duly qualified (a *capable* instructor).—**capability, capableness,** kā•pa•bil′i•ti, kā′pa•bl•-nes, *n.* The state or quality of being capable.

capacious, ka•pā′shus, *a.* [L. *capax*, *capacis*, able to take in or contain, spacious, capable, from *capio*, to take. CAPABLE.] Capable of containing much, either in a physical or mental sense; large; wide; spacious; extensive; comprehensive.—**capaciously,** ka•pā′shus•li, *adv.* In a capacious manner or degree.—**capaciousness,** ka•pā′shus•nes, *n.* The state or quality of being capacious.— **capacitate,** ka•pas′i•tāt, *v.t.* —*capacitated, capacitating.* To make capable; to enable; to qualify.—**capacity,** ka•pas′i•ti, *n.* [L. *capacitas*, from *capax*, capacious.] The power of receiving or containing; specifically, the power of containing a certain quantity exactly; cubic contents; the extent or comprehensiveness of the mind; the power of receiving ideas or knowledge; the receptive faculty; active power; ability (a man with the *capacity* of judging); ability in a moral or legal sense; legal qualification (to attend a meeting in the *capacity* of an elector); character (to give advice in the *capacity* of a friend); used in *phys.* in various ways with the general notion of power of containing or receiving; in *electrostatics*, the capacity of a conductor is the quantity of electricity required to charge it to unit potential; in *heat*, the thermal capacity of a body of any mass is the quantity of heat required to raise its temperature one degree.

capacitor, ka•pas′i•tėr, *n. Elect.* a condenser.

cap-a-pie, kap•a•pē′, *adv.* [O.Fr., lit. head to foot.] From head to foot; all over.

caparison, ka•par′i•son, *n.* [O.Fr. *caparasson*, from Sp. *caparazon*, a cover for a saddle, aug. of *capa*, a cover. CAP, CAPE.] A cloth or covering, more or less ornamented, laid over the saddle or furniture of a horse, especially a sumpter horse, or horse of state; hence, clothing, especially gay clothing.—*v.t.* To cover with a caparison; to adorn with rich dress.

cape, kāp, *n.* [O.Fr. *cape*, L.L. *capa*, a kind of covering for the shoulders. CAP.] The part of a garment hanging from the neck behind and over the shoulders; a loose cloak or garment, hung from the shoulders, and worn as a protection against rain, cold weather, etc.

cape, kāp, *n.* [Fr. *cap*, It. *capo*, a cape, from L. *caput*, the head.] A piece of land jutting into the sea or a lake beyond the rest of the coast line; a headland; a promontory; [*usually cap.*] by pre-eminence, the Cape of Good Hope, Cape Colony.

capeline, kap′e•lin, *n.* [Fr. *capeline*, hood, dim. from L. *capa.*] A kind of hood worn by ladies going to evening entertainments; a surgical bandage for the head.

caper, kā′pėr, *n.* [O.Fr. *capriole*, It. *capriola*, a caper, from L. *caper*, *capra*, a goat. Akin *caprice*, *cab.*] A leap; a skip; a spring, as in dancing or mirth, or in the frolic of a goat or lamb; a sportive or capricious action; a prank.—*To cut capers*, to leap or dance in a frolicsome manner; to act sportively or capriciously.—*v.i.* To cut capers; to skip or jump; to prance; to spring.—**caperer,** kā′-pėr•ėr, *n.* One who capers.

caper, kā′pėr, *n.* [Fr. *capre*, O.Fr. *cappre*, L. *capparis*, Gr. *kapparis*, from Per. *kabar*, the caper.] The bud of a bush (the caperbush), pickled and used as a condiment; the plant itself, a low prickly shrub, growing in rocky or stony places in the countries bordering on the Mediterranean.—**caper tea,** *n.* A kind of black tea with a knotted curled leaf regarded as resembling the caper.

capercailzie, capercaillie, kā•pėr•-kāl′yi, kā•pėr•kāl′ē, *n.* [Gael. *capull-choile*—*capull*, a horse, and *coille*, a wood—so named from its great size.] The wood grouse or cock of the woods, the largest of the gallinaceous birds of Europe.

Capetian, ka•pē′shan, *a.* Pertaining to the dynasty of the *Capets*, founded about the close of the tenth century, when Hugh *Capet* ascended the French throne.

capias, kā′pi•as, *n.* [L., you may take.] *Law*, a writ of various kinds authorizing a person or his goods to be laid hold of.

capillary, kap′il•la•ri or ka•pil′la•ri, *a.* [L. *capillaris*, from *capillus*, hair, from root of *caput*, the head.] Resembling a hair; fine, minute, small in diameter though long; filiform; as, a *capillary* tube, that is, a tube with a very minute bore; a *capillary* vessel in animal bodies (see the *n.*); pertaining to capillary tubes, or to the capillary vessels or capillaries in organic structures.—*Capillary action*, the spontaneous elevation or depression of liquids in fine hairlike tubes, or in bodies of a porous structure, when these are dipped in the liquid; the term *capillary attraction* being applied when the liquid rises, as the sap in trees, water in a sponge, etc.; and *capillary repulsion* when it sinks, as mercury does in a fine glass tube. —*n.* A tube with a small bore; a minute blood vessel constituting the termination of an artery or vein; one of the minute vessels which intervene between the terminal arteries and veins.—**capillarity,** kap•il•lar′i•ti, *n.* The state or condition of being capillary; capillary action.

capital, kap′i•tal, *a.* [L. *capitalis*, capital, deadly, also pre-eminent, from *caput*, *capitis*, the head, seen also in *captain*, *chapter*, *chief*, *cadet*, etc.] First in importance; chief; principal; notable; affecting the head or life (*capital* punishment); incurring the forfeiture of life (a *capital* offense); punishable with death; excellent; very good; firstclass; splendid; a term applied to a type or letter of a certain form and a larger size than that generally used in the body of written or printed matter.—*n.* The uppermost part of a column, pillar, or pilaster, serving as the head or crowning, and placed immediately over the shaft and under the entablature; the chief city or town in a kingdom or state; a metropolis; a type or letter of a certain form, and of a larger size than that commonly used in the body of a piece of writing or printing; a capital letter; money or wealth in some shape employed in trade, in manufactures, or in any business; stock in trade, in money, goods, property, etc.; *fig.* stock of any kind, whether physical or moral; wealth; influence.—**capitalism,** kap′-i•tal•izm, *n.* An economic system characterized by private ownership of natural resources and means of production.—**capitalist,** kap′i•tal•ist, *n.* One who owns or controls wealth; an advocate of capitalism.—**capitalistic,** kap′i•tal•is″tik, *adj.* Pertaining to capitalism or capitalists; based on or favoring capitalism.—**capitalization,** kap′i•tal•i•zā″shon, *n.* The act of capitalizing or being capitalized; the total investment in a business.—**capitalize,** kap′i•tal•īz, *v.t.*—*capitalized, capitalizing.* To write in capital letters; to convert into capital; to supply capital for; to turn to one's advantage.—**capitally,** kap′i•tal•li, *adv.* In a capital manner; excellently; so as to involve life; in a pre-eminent degree; excellently; finely.—**capitate,** kap′i•tāt, *a.* [L. *capitatus.*] *Bot.* growing in a head; having a rounded head; applied to a flower, etc.—**capitation,** kap•i•tā′shon, *n.* [L. *capitatio.*] Numeration by the head; a numbering of persons.—*Capitation grant*, a grant given to a certain number of persons, a certain amount being allowed for each individual among the number.—*Capitation tax*, a poll tax.

Capitol, kap′i•tol, *n.* [L. *capitolium*, from *caput*, the head.] In ancient Rome, the name of a hill crowned by a temple dedicated to Jupiter; the temple itself, in which the senate assembled; the edifice occupied by the United States Congress in their deliberations at Washington; [*often not cap.*] also, in some states the state house or house in which the legislature holds its sessions; a government house.—**Capitoline,** kap′-i•tol•īn, *a.* Pertaining to the Capitol in Rome.

capitular, capitulary, ka•pit′ū•lėr, ka•pit′ū•le•ri, *n.* [L.L. *capitulare*, from L. *capitulum*, a chapter, a capital. CAPITAL.] An act passed in a chapter, as of knights or canons; the body of laws or statutes of a chapter or of an ecclesiastical council; the member of a chapter.—**capitular,** ka•pit′ū•lėr, *a.* Belonging to a chapter; capitulary; *bot.* growing in a capitulum or head, as composite plants. —**capitularly,** ka•pit′ū•lėr•li, *adv.* In the form of an ecclesiastical chapter.

—**capitulary,** ka•pit′ū•la•ri, *a.* Relating to the chapter of a cathedral.

capitulate, ka•pit′ū•lāt, *v.i.—capitulated, capitulating.* [L.L. *capitulo, capitulatum,* to arrange in heads or chapters, from L. *capitulum,* a chapter, dim. of *caput,* the head.] To draw up articles of agreement; to arrange terms of agreement; to treat (*Shak.*); more usually to surrender, as an army or garrison, to an enemy on certain stipulated conditions.

capitulation, ka•pit′ū•lā″shon, *n.* The act of capitulating or surrendering to an enemy upon stipulated terms or conditions; the treaty or instrument containing the conditions of surrender; an article of agreement; formal agreement†.

capitulum, ka•pit′ū•lum, *n. Bot.* a close head of sessile flowers.

capon, kā′pon, *n.* [L. *capo,* Gr. *kapōn*—a capon, from a root seen in Gr. *koptō,* to cut.] A castrated cock; a cock-chicken castrated for the purpose of improving the flesh for table. —**caponize,** kā′pon•iz, *v.t.—caponized, caponizing.* To make a capon of.

capote, ka•pōt′, *n.* [Fr. *capote,* from *cape,* a hood or cape, L.L. *capa.* CAP.] A kind of long cloak. (*Byron*).

capreolate, kap′rē•ō•lāt, *a.* [From L. *capreolus,* a wild goat, a tendril of a vine, from *caper,* a goat.] *Bot.* having tendrils, or filiform spiral claspers, by which plants fasten themselves to other bodies, as in vines, etc.

capriccio, ka•prē′chō, *n.* [It., a caprice.] A caprice; a whim (*Shak.*); a musical piece in which the composer is guided more by fancy than by strict rule.

caprice, ka•prēs′, *n.* [Fr. *caprice,* It. *capriccio,* whim, freak, originally a fantastical goat leap, from L. *caper, capra,* a goat; akin *caper, capriole.*] A sudden start of the mind; a sudden change of opinion or humor; a whim or freak; capriciousness; fickleness. —**capricious,** ka•prish′us, *a.* Characterized by caprice; apt to change opinions suddenly, or to start from one's purpose; unsteady; changeable; fickle; subject to change or irregularity.—**capriciously,** ka•prish′us•li, *adv.* In a capricious manner.—**capriciousness,** ka•prish′us•nes, *n.* The quality of being capricious.

Capricorn, kap′ri•korn, *n.* [L. *capricornus—caper,* a goat, and *cornu,* a horn.] One of the twelve signs of the zodiac; the tenth sign, marking the winter solstice.

caprification, kap′ri•fi•kā″shon, *n.* [L. *caprificatio,* from *caprificus,* the wild figtree—*caper,* a goat, and *ficus,* a fig, from goats feeding on it.] A process intended to accelerate the ripening of the fig by causing a species of gall insect to spread over the plant, the supposed beneficial effect being produced by the insects either distributing the pollen of the male flowers or by puncturing the fruit.

capriole, kap′ri•ōl, *n.* [O.Fr. *capriole,* now *cabriole,* lit. a goat-leap, from L. *capriolus,* a wild goat, from *caper,* a goat.] A caper or leap, as in dancing; an active bound; a spring; a leap, accompanied with a jerking out of the hind legs, which a horse makes without advancing.—*v.i.* To execute a capriole.

capsicum, kap′si•kum, *n.* [From L. *capsa,* a box, from the shape of the fruit.] The generic name of some South American and Asiatic plants, many species of which are cultivated for their pods, used in cookery under the name of chillies, and when dried and ground called Cayenne pepper, to which the name capsicum is also sometimes given.—**capsaïcin,** kap′-sā′e•sin, *n.* An alkaloid, the active principle of the capsules of Cayenne pepper.

capsize, kap•sīz′, *v.i.—capsized, capsizing.* [Origin doubtful; probably the first syllable means head or top, ultimately from L. *caput.*] To upset or overturn.—*v.i.* To be upset or overturned.

capstan, kap′stan, *n.* [Fr. *cabestan,* O.Fr. *cabestron,* from Latin *capistrum.* a halter.] An apparatus working on the principle of the wheel and axle, and consisting of a cylinder or barrel adjusted on an upright axis, the barrel being made to turn round by means of horizontal bars or levers, the ends of which are inserted in holes near the top of the barrel, so that a rope is thus wound round it and a weight, such as an anchor, raised or moved.

capsule, kap′sūl, *n.* [L. *capsula,* a little chest, dim. of *capsa,* a chest, from *capio,* to take.] Any membranous sac enclosing an organ of the body; a soluble case of gelatin for enclosing a dose of medicine; a sealed, detachable compartment of an airplane or spaceship; a dry fruit, containing seeds, and opening of itself by valves or pores when mature; *chem.* a small saucer used for roasting or melting ores, for evaporations, solutions, etc.; seal or cover for going over the cork or stopper of a bottle.—**capsular,** kap′sū•lėr, *a.* Hollow like a capsule; pertaining to a capsule.—**capsulate, capsulated,** kap′sū•lāt, kap′sū•lāt•ed, *a.* Enclosed in a capsule.

captain, kap′tn, *n.* [Fr. *capitaine,* O.Fr. *capitain,* from L.L. *capitanus,* from L. *caput,* the head.] One who is at the head of or has authority over others; a chief; a leader; a commander, especially in military affairs; more specifically, the military officer who commands a company, whether of infantry, cavalry, or artillery; an officer in the navy commanding a ship of war; the commander or master of a merchant vessel.—**captaincy,** kap′tn•si, *n.* The rank, post, or commission of a captain.—**captainship,** kap′tn•ship, *n.* The condition or post of a captain or chief commander; skill in military affairs.

caption, kap′shon, *n.* [L. *captio,* a taking, fraud, deceit, from *capio,* to seize.] The heading or title of a chapter, page, or article; the title or explanation under an illustration or picture.—*v.t.* To put a caption on.

—**captious,** kap′shus, *a.* [L. *captiosus,* from *captio,* a taking.] Apt to find fault or raise objections; apt to cavil; difficult to please; carping; cavilling; proceeding from a captious or cavilling disposition; fitted to ensnare or perplex (a *captious* question).—**captiously,** kap′shus•li, *adv.* In a captious manner.—**captiousness,** kap′shus•nes, *n.* The quality of being captious.

captive, kap′tiv, *n.* [From L. *captivus,* a captive, from *capio, captus,* to seize. *Caitiff* is the same word derived through the French.] One who is taken prisoner, especially a prisoner taken in war; one who is charmed or subdued by beauty or excellence; one whose affections are seized, or who is held by strong ties of love.—*a.* Made prisoner in war; kept in bondage or confinement; bound by the ties of love or admiration; captivated.—**captivate,** kap′ti•vāt, *v.t.—captivated, captivating.* [L. *captivo, captivatum.*] To capture or make prisoner‡; to overpower and gain with excellence or beauty; to charm; to engage the affections of; to fascinate, enslave, subdue, enchant. —**captivation,** kap•ti•vā′shon, *n.* The act of captivating; the act of gaining over or winning one's affections.—**captivity,** kap•tiv′i•ti, *n.* [L. *captivitas.*] The state of being a captive; subjection; a state of being under control; bondage; servitude.—**captor,** kap′tėr, *n.* [L. *captor.*] One who captures or takes by force, stratagem, etc.—**capture,** kap′chėr, *n.* [L. *captura.*] The act of one who captures; the act of making prize of something; seizure; arrest; the thing taken; a prize.—*v.t.—captured, capturing.* To take or seize by force, surprise, or stratagem, as an enemy or his property; to make a prize or prisoner of.

Capuchin, kap′ū•shin, *n.* [Fr. *capuchon, capucine,* from *capuce,* a hood or cowl, from *cape,* a cape.] A monk of the order of St. Francis, so called from the *capuchon,* a stuff cap or cowl, the distinguishing badge of the order; [*not cap.*] a garment for females, consisting of a cloak and hood in imitation of the dress of Capuchin monks.

capybara, kap•i•bä′ra, *n.* [The native Brazilian name.] A rodent quadruped, allied to the guinea pig, abounding in rivers of South America, feeding on vegetables and fish, over 3 feet in length, tailless, with a large head and blunted muzzle, and toes imperfectly webbed.

car, kär, *n.* [O.Fr. *car* (Mod.Fr. *char*), from L. *carrus,* a four-wheeled vehicle, from the Celtic Armor. *carr,* a chariot, W. *car,* Ir. and Gael, *carr,* a dray, wagon, etc. Akin *carry, charge, cargo,* etc.] A name applied to various kinds of wheeled vehicles, as railroad cars, freight cars, passenger cars, dining cars, sleeping cars, street cars, motor cars.

caracara, kä•ra•kä′ra, *n.* [From its hoarse cry.] American bird of prey of several species, akin to the eagles and vultures, and feeding on carrion.

caracole, kar′a•kōl, *n.* [Fr., from Sp. and Pg. *caracol*, a winding staircase, a caracole.] A half turn which a horseman makes, either to the right or left; *arch.* a spiral staircase.—*v.i.* —*caracoled, caracoling.* To move in a caracole; to wheel.

caracul, kar′a•kul, *n.* [From *karakul.*] A flat, glossy, curly fur made from the skin of newborn lambs; karakul sheep.

carafe, kar′af or ka•raf′, *n.* [Fr.] A glass water bottle or decanter.

carageen, caragheen, kar′a•gēn, *n.* See CARRAGEEN.

caramel, kar′a•mel, *n.* [Fr. *caramel*, caramel, from Sp. *caramelo*, a lozenge, of Ar. origin.] Anhydrous or burnt sugar, a product of the action of heat upon sugar; it dissolves readily in water, is of a brown color, and is used to color spirits and wines.

carapace, kar′a•pās, *n.* [Fr., from Sp. *carapacho*, a carapace or shell.] The shell which protects the body of chelonian reptiles; also the covering of the anterior upper surface of the crustaceans.

carat, kar′at, *n.* [Fr. *carat*, Ar. *qirrât*, a carat, from Gr. *keration*, lit. a little horn, also the seed of the carob-tree, used for a weight, a carat.] A weight, about 3 1/6 grains, used in weighing precious stones and pearls; a term used to express the proportionate fineness of gold, gold of twenty-four carats being pure gold, gold of sixteen (for instance) having eight parts of alloy.

caravan, kar′a•van, *n.* [Fr. *caravane*, from Sp. *caravana*, Ar. *qairawân*, Per. *kârwân*, a caravan.] A company of travelers who associate together in many parts of Asia and Africa that they may travel with greater security; a large close carriage for conveying traveling exhibitions or the like from place to place.—**caravansary, caravanserai,** kar•a•van′sa•ri, kar•a•van′se•rī, *n.* [Per. *kârwân*, a caravan, and *sarâi*, an inn.] In the East, a place appointed for receiving and lodging travelers.

caravel, carvel, kar′a•vel, kär′vel, *n.* [Sp. and It. *caravela*, a caravel, dim. of L. *carabus*, Gr. *karabos*, a light ship, a boat, also a crab.] A small galley-rigged ship formerly used by the Spanish and Portuguese; also a small fishing vessel.

caraway, kar′a•wā, *n.* [Sp. *al-carahweya*, from Ar. *karwiyâ, karawiyâ*, caraway; probably from Gr. *karon*, L. *careum*, caraway.] A biennial plant belonging to the carrot family, the seeds of which are used to flavor food.

carbide, kär′bīd, *n.* A compound of carbon with a metal; a carburet.

carbine, carabine, kär′bīn, kar′a•bīn, *n.* [Fr. *carabine*, a carabine; O.Fr. *carabin, calabrin*, a musketeer, from *calabre*, an engine of war, from L.L. *chadabula*, an engine for throwing stones, from Gr. *katabolē*, a throwing down—*kata*, down, and *ballo*, to throw.] A gun or firearm commonly used by cavalry, shorter in the barrel than the infantry musket or rifle.—**carbineer, carabineer,** kär•bin•ēr′, kar′a•bin•ēr″, *n.* One armed with a carbine or carabine.

carbohydrate, kär•bo•hī′drāt, *n.* [L. *carbo*, charcoal, Gr. *hydōr*, water.] A chemical compound made of carbon, hydrogen, and oxygen, the two latter being commonly in the same proportion as in water (H_2O).

carbolic acid, kär•bol′ik as′id, *n.* [L. *carbo*, coal, *oleum*, oil, and *acid.*] An acid obtained from the distillation of coal tar, an oily, colorless liquid, with a burning taste, employed as an antiseptic and disinfectant and in industry.

carbon, kär′bon, *n.* [L. *carbo, carbonis*, a coal.] An element forming a constituent of all organic compounds, of carbonates, such as coal, and occurring in pure form in diamond. Symbol, C; at. no., 6; at. wt., 12.011—*Carbon-12*, the most common form of carbon and the standard for the atomic weights of elements.—*Carbon-14*, a radioactive isotope of carbon used as a tracer in biochemical studies and in archaeological and geological dating. Also called *radiocarbon.*—*Carbon cycle*, the process by which living organisms utilize carbon; the process by which hydrogen is converted into helium.—**carbonaceous,** kär•bō•nā′shus, *a.*—**carbonate,** kär′bon•āt, *n.* A salt or ester of carbonic acid.—*v.t.* To change into a carbonate; to charge with carbon dioxide.—**carbon dioxide,** *n.* A heavy, colorless, noncombustible gas present in the atmosphere and formed from the decay and combustion of organic substances.—**carbonic,** kär•bon′ik, *a.* —*Carbonic acid*, a weak acid formed when carbon dioxide is dissolved in water.—**carboniferous,** kär•bon•if′ėr•us, *a.* Containing or yielding carbon or coal; [*cap.*] pertaining to a geological period or system.—**carbon monoxide,** *n.* A poisonous gas that is the result of incomplete combustion of carbon.

carbonado, kär•bo•nā′dō, *n.* [From L. *carbo*, a coal.] An old name for a piece of meat, fowl, or game, cut across, seasoned, and broiled; a chop.

Carbonari, kar•bon•ä′rē, *n.* Members of a Neapolitan secret revolutionary society who took their name from the charcoal burners of the Abruzzi, among whom many of them were obliged to take refuge, and with whom they identified themselves.

carborundum, kär•bo•run′dum, *n.* [*Carbon* and *corundum.*] Silicon carbide, a very hard substance used as a substitute for emery.

carboxyl, karb•oks′īl, *n.* [L. *carbo*, charcoal, Gr. *oxys*, acid.] The group CO . OH, typical of organic acids.

carboy, kär′boi, *n.* [Per. *karabâ*, a large vessel for containing wine.] A large, strong, glass bottle, protected by an outside covering.

carbuncle, kär′bung•kl, *n.* [L. *carbunculus*, a little coal, from *carbo*, a coal.] A beautiful gem of a deep red color, with a mixture of scarlet, found in the East Indies; an inflammatory tumor.

carburet, kär′bū•ret, *n.* Same as *Carbide.*—**carburetor,** kär′bū•ret•ėr, *n.* In an internal combustion engine the device for vaporizing gasoline or other fuel.—**carburize.** kär′bū•rīz, *v.t.* To combine with carbon or a compound of it.

carcajou, kär′ka•jö, *n.* [Fr. *carcajou*, from native name.] An American name for the wolverine or glutton, and erroneously for the badger and lynx.

carcanet, kär′ka•net, *n.* [Fr. *carcan*, a carcanet, from Armor. *kerchen*, the neck or bosom.] A necklace or collar of jewels.

carcass, carcase, kär′kas, *n.* [Fr. *carcasse*, the carcass, a framework, a kind of bomb, same word as *carquois*, a quiver, from L.L. *tarcasius*, a quiver, from Ar. and Per. *tarkash*, a quiver.] The body, usually the dead body, of an animal; a corpse; the decaying remains of a bulky thing; the frame or main parts of a thing unfinished; a kind of bomb or shell filled with combustible matter, and having apertures for the emission of flame, so as to set fire to buildings, etc.

carcinoma, kär•si•nō′ma, *n.* [Gr. *karkinōma*, from *karkinos*, a cancer.] A kind of cancer or cancerous growth.

card, kärd, *n.* [From Fr. *carte*, a card, from L. *charta*, paper, from Gr. *chartē, chartēs*, a layer of papyrus bark.] A rectangular piece of thick paper or pasteboard; such a piece with certain devices, marks, or figures, used for playing games; a piece having one's name, etc., written or printed on it, used in visiting; a larger piece written or printed, and conveying an invitation, or some intimation or statement; the dial or face of the mariner's compass.—**cardboard,** kärd′bōrd, *n.* A stiff kind of paper or pasteboard for making cards, etc.—**cardsharper,** *n.* One who cheats in playing cards; one who makes it a trade to fleece the unwary in games of cards.

card, kärd, *n.* [Fr. *carde*, from L.L. *cardus*, L. *carduus*, a thistle, from *carere*, to card—thistles having been used as cards.] An instrument for combing, opening, and breaking wool or flax, freeing it from the coarser parts and from extraneous matter.—*v.t.* or *i.* To comb or open wool, flax, hemp, etc., with a card.—**carder,** kär′dėr, *n.* One who cards; the machine employed in carding.

cardamom, kär′da•mum, *n.* [L. *cardamomum*, Gr. *kardamōmon.*] The aromatic capsule of various plants of the ginger family, employed in medicine as well as an ingredient in sauces and curries.

cardiac, cardiacal, kär′di•ak, kär•dī′ak•al, *a.* [L. *cardiacus*, Gr. *kardiakos*, from *kardia*, the heart.] Pertaining to the heart, exciting action in the heart through the medium of the stomach; having the quality of stimulating action in the system, invigorating the spirits, and giving strength and cheerfulness.—**cardiac,** *n.* A medicine which excites action in the stomach and animates the spirits; a cordial.—**cardiography,** kär•di•og′ra•fi, *n.* An anatomical description of the heart.—**cardialgia,** kär•di•al′ji•a, *n.* [Gr. *algos,* pain.] *Med.* heart burn.

cardigan, kär′di•gan, *n.* [After Earl of *Cardigan.*] A kind of knitted waistcoat worn over or instead of the waistcoat.

cardinal, kär′di•nal, *a.* [L. *cardinalis,* from *cardo,* a hinge.] Chief, principal, preeminent, or fundamental.—*Cardinal numbers,* the numbers *one, two, three,* etc., in distinction from *first, second, third,* etc., called ordinal numbers.—*Cardinal points,* north and south, east and west.—*Cardinal virtues,* justice, prudence, temperance, and fortitude.—*n.* An ecclesiastical prince in the Roman Catholic Church, next in rank to the pope, and having a distinguishing dress of a red color.—**cardinalate, cardinalship,** kär′di•nal•āt, kär′di•nal•ship, *n.* The office, rank, or dignity of a cardinal.—**cardinal bird,** *n.* A North American bird, with a fine red plumage, and a crest on the head.—**cardinal flower,** *n.* The name commonly given to a species of lobelia because of its large, very showy, and intensely red flowers.

cardiogram, kär′di•o•gram, *n.* [Gr. *kardia,* heart, and *gramma,* mark.] The tracing produced by a cardiograph.—**cardiograph,** kär′di•o•graf, *n.* [Gr. *kardia,* heart, and *graphō,* to write.] An instrument that registers the movement of the heart.—**cardiology,** kär•di•ol′o•ji, *n.* [Gr. *kardia,* heart, and *logos,* discourse.] The study of the heart and its diseases.—**cardiologist,** kär•di•ol′o•jist, *n.*—**cardiovascular,** kär•di•o•vas′ku•lar, *a.* Pertaining to the heart and blood vessels.

care, kâr, *n.* [A.Sax. *caru, cearu,* care, sorrow = O.Sax. *cara,* Icel. *kaeri,* complaint, Goth. *kara,* sorrow, O.H.G. *chara,* lamentation; from a root signifying to cry, seen also in E. *call.*] Some degree of pain in the mind from apprehension of evil; a painful load of thought; mental trouble; concern; anxiety; solicitude; attention or heed; a looking to; caution; regard; watchfulness; charge or oversight, implying concern for safety and prosperity; the object of care or watchful regard and attention. ∴*Care* denotes mental trouble regarding the present, the future, or even the past; *solicitude* and *concern* denote affections of the mind of a more active kind than *care,* and relate to the present and the future, while the latter may also be excited by something past.—*v.i.*—*cared, caring.* To be anxious or solicitous; to be concerned; to be inclined or disposed; to like.—**careful,** kâr′fụl, *a.* Full of care; anxious; solicitous; attentive to support and protect; giving good heed; watchful, cautious; showing or done with care or attention: generally with *of* before the object.—**carefully,** kâr′fụl•li, *adv.* In a careful manner.—**carefulness,** kâr′fụl•nes, *n.* The state or quality of being careful.—**careless,** kâr′les, *a.* Free from care or anxiety; heedless; negligent, unthinking, inattentive; regardless, unmindful, with *of* or *about* before an object, done or said without care; unconsidered.—**carelessly,** kâr′les•li, *adv.* In a careless manner or way.—**carelessness,** kâr′les•nes, *n.* The state or quality of being careless.—**careworn,** *a.* Worn, oppressed, or burdened with care; showing marks of care or anxiety.

careen, ka•rēn′, *n.* [Fr. *caréner,* from *carène,* the side and keel of a ship, L. *carina,* a keel.] To heave or bring (a ship) to lie on one side for caulking, repairing, cleansing, or the like.—*v.i.* To incline to one side, as a ship under a press of sail, or a motor car turning a corner on two wheels.

career, ka•rēr′, *n.* [Fr. *carrière,* O.Fr. *cariere,* road, race-course, course, career, from L. *carrus,* a car. CAR.] A race or running, course of proceeding; a specific course of action or occupation forming the object of one's life.—*v.i.* To move or run rapidly (as a horse, a ship, etc.).

caress, ka•res′, *n.* [Fr. *caresse,* from It. *carezza,* L.L. *caritia* from L. *carus,* dear.] An act of endearment, any act or expression of affection.—*v.t.* To treat with caresses; to fondle; to embrace with tender affection.—**caressingly,** ka•res′ing•li, *adv.* In a caressing manner.

caret, ka′ret, *n.* [L. *caret,* there is (something) wanting, from *carere* to want.] In *writing,* a mark made thus, ∧ which shows that something, omitted in the line, is interlined above or inserted in the margin, and should be read in that place.

cargo, kär′gō, *n.* [Sp., from *cargar,* to load, L.L. *carricare,* to load, from L. *carrus,* a car. CAR, CHARGE.] The lading or freight of a ship.

Carib, kar′ib, *n.* One of a native race inhabiting certain portions of Central America, and formerly also the Caribbean Islands.

caribou, kar′i•bö, *n.* [Probably of Indian origin.] A North American variety of the reindeer.

caricature, kar′i•ka•chụr″, *n.* [It. *caricatura,* an overloaded representation, from *caricare,* to load. CHARGE.] A representation, pictorial or descriptive, in which beauties are concealed and peculiarities or defects exaggerated so as to make the person or thing ridiculous, while a general likeness is retained.—*v.t.*—*caricatured, caricaturing.* To make or draw a caricature of; to represent in a ridiculous and exaggerated fashion.—**caricaturist,** kar′i•ka•chụr″ist, *n.* One who caricatures others.

caries, kâ′ri•ēz, *n.* [L.] Ulceration of bony substance; the gangrenous eating away of a bone; decay of teeth.—**carious,** kâ′ri•us, *a.* Affected with caries; ulcerated: said of a bone.

carillon, kar′il•lon, *n.* [Fr., from L.L. *quadrilio,* from L. *quattuor,* four, because *carillons* were played formerly on four bells.] A chime of bells, properly tuned, and rung by means of finger keys like those of the pianoforte; a simple air adapted to be performed on a set of bells.

carina, ka•rī′na, *n.* [L., the keel of a boat.] *Bot.* the two partially united lower petals of papilionaceous flowers; *zool.* a prominent median ridge or keel in the sternum or breastbone of all existing birds except the runners (ostrich, etc.).—**carinate, carinated,** kar′i•nāt, kar′i•nāt•ed, *a.* [L. *carinatus.*] Shaped like a keel; having a carina or keel; keeled; *bot.* having a longitudinal ridge like a keel; *zool.* applied to those birds whose sternum is keeled, or to their sternum.

cariole, kar′i•ōl, *n.* [Fr., from L. *carrus,* a car.] A small open carriage; a kind of calash; a covered cart.

carious. See CARIES.

carl, carle, kärl, *n.* [A Scandinavian word = Icel. Dan. Sw. *karl,* a man; A.Sax. *carl,* male, as in *carl-catt,* a he-cat.] A man; a robust, strong, or hardy man; an old man. [O.E. and Sc.] Hence **carline,** a woman.

carline, carling, kär′lin, kär′ling, *n.* [Fr. *carlingue* or *escarlingue.*] One of the fore-and-aft deck timbers in a ship.

Carlist, kär′list, *n.* A follower of Don *Carlos* of Spain, the heir to the crown but for the repeal of the Salic law; an adherent and supporter of the family of Don Carlos.—**Carlism,** kär′lizm, *n.* The principles of the Carlists.

Carlovingian, kär•lo•vin′ji•an, *a.* Pertaining to or descended from Charlemagne.

carmagnole, kär•ma•nyōl′, *n.* [Fr. *Carmagnole* in Piedmont.] A revolutionary dance and song in France during 1789-93 Revolution, from the street-dancing Savoyards; any bombastic harangue.

Carmelite, kär′mel•īt, *n.* A mendicant friar of the order of our Lady of Mount *Carmel;* a sort of pear; the White Friars founded at Mount Carmel; gray woolen stuff.

carminative, kär′mi•nā•tiv or kär•min′a•tiv, *n.* [L. *carmino, carminatum,* to card wool (hence to make fine or thin), from *carmen,* a card.] A medicine which tends to expel wind from the stomach and remedy flatulency.—*a.* Expelling wind from the stomach; antispasmodic.

carmine, kär′mīn, *n.* [Sp. *carmin,* from *carmesino,* carmine, crimson, from *carmes,* kermes (which see). *Crimson* has the same origin.] The pure coloring matter or principle of cochineal; a red or crimson pigment made from cochineal.

carnage, kär′nij, *n.* [Fr. *carnage,* slaughter, from L.L. *carnaticum,* from L. *caro, carnis,* flesh.] Slaughter; great destruction of men; butchery; massacre.

carnal, kär′nal, *a.* [L. *carnalis,* carnal, from *caro, carnis,* flesh.] Pertaining to the body, its passions and appetites; not spiritual; fleshly; sensual; lustful; impure.—**carnality,** kär•nal′i•ti, *n.* The state of being carnal; want of spirituality; fleshliness; fleshly lusts or desires, or the indulgence of those lusts; sensuality.—**carnally,** kär′nal•li, *adv.* In a carnal manner; according to the flesh; not spiritually.

carnallite, kär′nal•līt, *n.* [After a German called Von *Carnall*.] A pink-colored mineral obtained from the Stassfurt salt mines.

carnation, kär•nā′shon, *n.* [Fr. *carnation*, the naked part of a picture, flesh color; from L. *caro, carnis*, flesh.] Flesh color; the parts of a picture which exhibit the natural color of the flesh; the representation of flesh; a perennial plant found in many varieties, much prized for the beautiful colors of their sweet-scented double flowers.

carnauba, kär•nou′ba, *n.* The Brazilian name of a tall South American palm which has its leaves coated with small waxy scales, yielding a straw-colored wax by boiling. Also written *Carnahuba*.

carnelian, kär•nē′li•an, *n.* [More correctly *cornelian*, from Fr. *cornaline*, a carnelian, from L. *carnis*, flesh, from its fleshlike color.] A variety of chalcedony, of a deep red, flesh-red, or reddish-white color, tolerably hard, capable of a good polish.

carnival, kär′ni•val, *n.* [Fr. *carnaval*, It. *carnevale*, from L.L. *carnelevamen*, for *carnis levamen*, solace of the body, permitted in anticipation of any fast—L. *caro*, flesh, and *levare*, to solace, to lighten.] The feast or season of rejoicing before Lent; feasting or revelry in general; an amusement place.

carnivorous, kär•niv′o•rus, *a.* [L. *caro, carnis*, flesh, and *voro*, to devour.] Eating or feeding on flesh: an epithet applied to animals which naturally seek flesh for food, as the lion, tiger, wolf, dog, etc.; also applied to some plants that can assimilate animal substances.—**Carnivora,** kär•niv′o•ra, *n. pl.* [L.] A term applicable to any creatures that feed on flesh or animal substances, but generally denoting an order of mammals which prey upon other animals.—**carnivore,** kär′ni•vōr, *n.* A carnivorous animal; one of the Carnivora.

carob, kar′ob, *n.* [O.Fr. *carobe*, from Ar. *kharrûb*, bean-pods.] A tree growing in the countries skirting the Mediterranean, the pods of which, known as locust beans, contain a sweet nutritious pulp.

carol, kar′ol, *n.* [O.Fr. *carole*, a kind of dance, also a Christmas song or carol; from the Celtic: Armor. *koroll*, a dance; W. *carol*, a carol, a song.] A song, especially one expressive of joy; a religious song or ballad in celebration of Christmas.—*v.i.*—*caroled, caroling*. To sing; to warble; to sing in joy or festivity.—*v.t.*—To praise or celebrate in song.

Carolingian, kar•ō•lin′ji•an, *a.* Same as *Carlovingian*.

carotic, ka•rot′ik, *a.* [Gr. *karos*, torpor, stupor.] Relating to stupor or carus; also same as carotid.—**carotid,** ka•rot′id, *a.* [Gr. pl. *karōtides*, the carotids, said to be from *karos*, a deep sleep, because the ancients believed that sleep was caused by an increased flow of blood to the head through these arteries, or by the compression of these arteries.] Of or pertaining to the two great arteries, one on either side of the neck, which convey the blood from the aorta to the head and brain.—*n.* One of these arteries.

carouse, ka•rouz′, *v.i.*—*caroused, carousing*. [O.Fr. *carousser*, to quaff, to carouse, from *carous*, a carouse, a bumper, from G. *garaus!* quite out! that is, empty your glasses! an old German drinking exclamation.] To drink freely and with jollity; to quaff; to revel.—**carousal, carouse,** ka•rou′zal, ka•rouz′, *n.* A feast or festival; a noisy drinking bout or revelling.—**carouser,** ka•rouz′ėr, *n.* One who carouses; a drinker; a toper; a noisy reveler or bacchanalian.

carp, kärp, *v.i.* [Formerly to speak, tell, from Icel. *karpa*, to boast, its modern sense being due to L. *carpo*, to seize, catch, pick.] To censure, cavil, or find fault, particularly without reason or petulantly: used absolutely or followed by *at*.—**carper,** kärp′ėr, *n.* One who carps; a caviller.—**carping,** kärp′ing, *a.* Cavilling; captious; censorious.—**carpingly,** kärp′ing•li, *adv.* In a carping manner; captiously.

carp, kärp, *n.* [Same as D. *karper*, Dan. *karpe*, Sw. *karp*, a carp.] A fresh-water fish found in lakes, rivers, ponds, etc. The most noted species are the common carp and the gold fish. The carp has been introduced in America, where it has become so numerous as to be a pest.

carpal. See CARPUS.

carpel, kär′pel, *n.* [Mod. L. *carpellum*, dim. from Gr. *karpos*, fruit.] *Bot.* a single-celled ovary or seed vessel, or a single cell of an ovary or seed vessel together with what belongs to that cell.—**carpellary,** kär′pel•la•ri, *a.* Belonging to a carpel or carpels.

carpenter, kär′pen•tėr, *n.* [O.Fr. *carpentier* (Mod. Fr. *charpentier*); L.L. *carpentarius*, a carpenter, from L. *carpentum*, a chariot, a word of Celtic origin.] An artificer who works in timber; a framer and builder of houses and of ships.—**carpenter bee,** *n.* The common name of different species of bees, so called from their habit of excavating nests in decaying wood.—**carpentry,** kär′pen•tri, *n.* The art of cutting, framing, and joining timber; an assemblage of pieces of timber connected by framing or letting them into each other.

carpet, kär′pet, *n.* [O.Fr. *carpite*, a carpet, from It. and L.L. *carpita*, a woolly cloth, from *carpere*, to tease wool, L. *carpo*, to pluck, to pull in pieces, etc.] A thick fabric used for covering floors, stairs, etc.; a covering resembling a carpet (a *carpet* of moss).—*To be on the carpet*, is to be under consideration; to be the subject of deliberation.—*Carpet knight*, a knight who has not known the hardships of the field.—*v.t.* To cover with or as with a carpet; to spread with carpets.—**carpeting,** kär′pet•ing, *n.* Cloth for carpets; carpets in general.—**carpetbag,** *n.* A traveling bag made of the same material as carpets.—**carpetbagger,** *n.* A new comer to a place, having all his property in a carpet bag; a newcomer or political candidate, without possessing property in a community.

carpologist, kär•pol′o•jist, *n.* One who studies or treats of carpology.

carpology, kär•pol′o•ji, *n.* [Gr. *karpos*, fruit, *logos*, discourse.] The division of botany relating to the structure of seeds and seed vessels.

carpophore, kär′po•fōr, *n.* [L. *carpophorum*, from Gr. *karpos*, fruit, and *pherō*, to bear.] *Bot.* the prolongation of the floral axis which bears the pistil beyond the stamens.

carpus, kär′pus, *n.* [L., the wrist.] *Anat.* that part of the skeleton between the forearm and hand; the *wrist* in man and the corresponding bones in other animals.—**carpal,** kär′pal, *a.* Pertaining to the carpus.

carrageen, carragheen, kar′ra•gēn, *n.* [From *Carragheen*, near Waterford, Ireland, where it abounds.] A seaweed which, when dried, becomes whitish, and in this condition is known as Irish moss, being used for making soups, jellies, etc.

carriage, kar′ij, *n.* [O.Fr. *cariage*, from *carier*, to carry. CARRY.] The act of carrying, bearing, transporting, or conveying; the price or expense of carrying; the manner of carrying one's self; behavior; conduct; deportment; a wheeled vehicle for persons, especially a four-wheeled vehicle supported on springs and with a cover, belonging to a private person and not used for hire; in composition, a wheeled stand or support; as, a gun-*carriage*; *print.* the frame on rollers by which the bed carrying the types is run in and out from under the platen.

carrick bend, kar′ik, a kind of knot.—**carrick bitts,** supports for the windlass of a ship.

carrier. See CARRY.

carrion, kar′ri•on, *n.* [O.Fr. *caroigne*, from L.L. *caronia*, from L. *caro, carnis*, flesh.] The dead and putrefying body or flesh of animals; flesh so corrupted as to be unfit for food.—*a.* Pertaining to carrion; feeding on carrion.—**carrion crow,** *n.* The common crow, so called because it often feeds on carrion.

carronade, kar•on•ād′, *n.* [From *Carron* in Scotland, where it was first made.] A short piece of ordnance of confined range, formerly used in the navy.

carrot, kar′ot, *n.* [Fr. *carotte*; L.L. *carota*.] A plant having a long esculent root of a reddish color much used as a culinary vegetable and also for feeding cattle.—**carroty,** kar′ot•i, *a.* Like a carrot in color.

carry, kar′i, *v.t.*—*carried, carrying*. [O.E. *carie*, from O.Fr. *carier*, to convey in a car, from O.Fr. *car*, a cart or car. CAR.] To bear, convey, or transport by sustaining and moving with the thing carried; to drive, drag, or fetch (*carry* a person off prisoner); to transfer, as from one column, page, book, etc., to another; to convey or take with one generally (as a message, news, etc.); to urge, impel, lead, or draw, in a moral sense (anger *carried* him too far); to effect, accomplish, achieve, bring to a successful issue (a purpose, etc.); to gain; *milit.* to gain possession of by force; to capture (to *carry* a fortress); to extend or continue in any direction, in time, in space, or otherwise: commonly with such words as *up*, *back*, *forward*, etc. (to *carry* a history on to the present, to *carry* improvements far); to bear; to have in or on; to bear or bring as a result (words *carry* conviction); to import, contain, or comprise (the words *carry* a promise); to manage; to conduct (matters or affairs).—*To carry off*, to remove to a distance; to kill or cause to die (to be *carried off* by sickness or poison).—*To carry on*, to manage or prosecute; to continue to pursue (a business).—*To carry out*, *to carry through*, to sustain to the end; to continue to the end; to accomplish; to finish; to execute (a purpose, an undertaking).—*v.i.* To act as a bearer; to convey; to propel, as a gun.—*n.* Range or distance.—**carrier**, kar′i•ėr, *n.* One who or that which carries; a person or thing that transmits a disease; an underwriter or insurer; an aircraft carrier. —**carrier current** or **carrier wave**, *n.* An electric current, the modulations of which are used as radio or telegraphic signals.—**carrier pigeon**, *n.* A pigeon used to carry messages; a homing pigeon.

cart, kärt, *n.* [From W. *cart*, a cart or wagon, Ir. *cairt*. CAR.] A carriage usually without springs for the conveyance of heavy goods.—*v.t.* To carry or convey on a cart.—**cartage**, kär′tij, *n.* The act of carrying in a cart; the price for carting.—**carter**, kär′tėr, *n.* One who drives a cart. —**cart wheel**, *n.* The wheel of a cart; a large coin; a sideways handspring or somersault.

carte, kärt, *n.* [Fr., a card.] A card; a bill of fare at a tavern; a carte-de-visite photograph.—**carte blanche**, kärt blänsh′, *n.* [Fr., white paper.] A blank paper; a paper duly authenticated with signature, etc., and intrusted to a person to be filled up as he pleases; hence, unconditional terms; unlimited power to decide.

cartel, kär′tel, *n.* [Fr., from L. *chartula*, dim. of *charta*, paper, a paper.] A writing or agreement between states at war, for the exchange of prisoners or for some mutual advantage. In Europe, an organization controlling the commercial policy of a number of independent companies, the equivalent of the American pool or trust.

Cartesian, kär•tē′zi•an, *a.* Pertaining to the philosopher René *Descartes*, or to his philosophy.—*n.* One who adopts the philosophy of Descartes. —**Cartesianism**, kär•tē′zi•an•izm, *n.* The philosophy of Descartes.

Carthusian, kär•thu′zi•an, *n.* One of an order of monks, founded in 1086, under Benedictine rule, by St. Bruno, so called from *Chartreuse*, in France, the place of their institution; pupil of the Charterhouse School, founded on the site of the London monastery.

cartilage, kär′ti•lij, *n.* [Fr. *cartilage*, L. *cartilago*.] An elastic tissue occurring in vertebrate animals, and forming the tissue from which bone is formed by a process of calcification; gristle.—**cartilaginous**, kär•ti•laj′i•nus, *a.* Pertaining to or resembling a cartilage; gristly; consisting of cartilage; having cartilage only and not true bones (as many fishes).

cartography, kär•tog′ra•fi, *n.* [E. *chart*, L. *charta*, paper, and Gr. *graphē*, writing, description.] The making of maps or charts.—**cartographer**, kär•tog′ra•fėr, *n.*

carton, a box with cover made of various kinds of board, as pasteboard, fiberboard, for shipping light articles.

cartoon, kär•tön′, *n.* [Fr. *carton*, pasteboard, a cartoon, from It. *cartone* (same sense), aug. of *carta*, L. *charta*, paper.] A pictorial design drawn on strong paper as a study for a picture intended to be painted of same size, and more especially for a picture to be painted in fresco; a caricature, often satirical, commenting on political and public events; a comic strip; a short, animated motion picture.—*v.t.* To represent by, or draw, cartoons.

cartouch, cartouche, kär•tösh′, *n.* [Fr. *cartouche*, O.Fr. *cartoche*, from It. *cartoccio*, a cartridge, a roll of paper, from *carta*, L. *charta*, paper. *Cartridge* is a corruption of this.] A case of wood filled with shot to be fired from a cannon; a cartridge; a portable box for charges for firearms; on Egyptian monuments, papyri, etc., a group of hieroglyphics in a small oblong area; *arch.* a sculptured ornament in the form of a scroll unrolled.

cartridge, kär′trij, *n.* [Formerly also *cartrage*, a corruption of *cartouch*.] A case of pasteboard, parchment, copper, tin, etc., holding the exact charge of any firearm.—*Blank cartridge*, a cartridge without ball or shot.

cartulary, kär′chu̧•le•ri, *n.* Same as *Chartulary*.

caruncle, kar′ung•kl, *n.* [L. *caruncula*, dim. from *caro*, flesh.] A small fleshy excrescence; a fleshy excrescence on the head of a fowl, as a wattle or the like; *bot.* a protuberance surrounding the hilum of a seed.—**caruncular, carunculous**, ka•rung′kū•lėr, ka•rung′kū•lus, *a.* Pertaining to or in the form of a caruncle.—**carunculate, carunculated**, ka•rung′kū•lāt, ka•rung′kū•lāt•ed, *a.* Having a fleshy excrescence.

carve, kärv, *v.t.*—*carved, carving.* [A.Sax. *ceorfan*=D. *kerven*, Icel. *kyrfa*, to carve; Dan. *karve*, G. *kerven*, to notch or indent; same root as *grave*.] To cut (some solid material) in order to produce the representation of an object or some decorative design; to make or shape by cutting; to form by cutting or hewing; to cut into, hew, or slash; to cut into small pieces or slices, as meat at table.—*v.i.* To exercise the trade of a carver; to engrave or cut figures; to cut up meat at table.—**carver**, kär′vėr, *n.* One who carves, as one who cuts ivory, wood, or the like, in a decorative way; one who cuts meat for use at table; a large tableknife for carving.—**carving**, kär′ving, *n.* A branch of sculpture usually limited to works in wood, ivory, etc.; the device or figure carved.

carvel, kär′vel, *n.* Same as *Caravel*.—**carvel-built**, *a.* A term applied to a ship or boat the planks of which are all flush and not overlapping, as in clincherbuilt boats.

caryatid, kar′i•at•id, *n.* pl. **caryatids, caryatides**, kar′i•at•idz, kar•i•at′i•dēz. [L., from Gr. *Karyatis*, name of a priestess of Diana.] Arch. a figure of a woman dressed in long robes, serving to support entablatures.

caryophyllaceous, kar′i•o•fil•lā″shus, *a.* [Gr. *karyophyllon*, the clove-tree.] Pertaining or similar to the plants known as pinks, and their allies; applied to flowers having five petals with long claws in a tubular calyx.

caryopsis, kar•i•op′sis, *n.* [Gr. *karyon*, a nut, and *opsis*, an appearance.] *Bot.* a small, one-seeded, dry, indehiscent fruit, in which the seed adheres to the thin pericarp throughout, as in wheat and other grains.

cascade, kas•kād′, *n.* [Fr. *cascade*, It. *cascata*, from *cascare*, to fall, from L. *cado*, *casum*, to fall.] A fall or flowing of water over a precipice in a river or other stream; a waterfall.—*v.i.* To fall in a cascade.—*v.t.* To cause to fall like a cascade.

cascara sagrada, kas•kâ′ra säg•rä′da, *n.* [Sp. sacred bark.] A purgative medicine obtained from the bark of an American tree.

cascarilla, kas•ka•ril′la, *n.* [Sp. dim. of *cascara*, peel, bark.] The aromatic bitter bark of a small tree chiefly in Eleuthera, one of the Bahamas, employed as a substitute for cinchona.

case, kās, *n.* [O.Fr. *casse* (now *caisse*), from *capio*, to take, receive, contain. *Cash* is really the same word.] A covering, envelope, box, frame, or sheath; that which encloses or contains; the skin of an animal‡; a case with its contents; hence, a certain quantity; *print.* a partitioned tray for types, from which the compositor gathers them and arranges them in lines and pages to print from.—*v.t.*—*cased, casing.* To cover with a case; to surround with any material that shall enclose or defend; to coat or cover over; to put in a case or box; to skin (*Shak.*)‡.—**casing**, kās′ing, *n.* The act of putting a case on, or of putting into a case; a case or covering.—**caseharden**, *v.t.* To harden the outer part or surface of (iron tools, etc.) by converting it into steel.—**case history,** *n.* A record of facts of an individual's personal history for use in analyzing his case for treatment, compensation, etc.—**case knife,** *n.* A long knife kept in a case or sheath; a large table-knife.—**case law,** *n.* Law made by decided cases that serve as precedents; judge-made laws.—**case shot,** *n.* A collection of shot or small projectiles enclosed in cases to be discharged from cannon; an iron case holding a number of bullets.—**casework,** *n.* A detailed study of persons in need of social assistance that can be used for diagnosis and treatment. —**caseworker,** *n.*

case, kās, *n.* [Fr. *cas*, a case, L. *casus*, a falling, from *cado*, *casum*, to fall.] The particular state, condition, or circumstances that befall a person, or in which he is placed; an individual occurrence or specific instance as of disease; a question or group of facts involving a question for discussion or decision; a cause or suit in court; a cause; one of the forms in the declension of a noun, pronoun, or adjective.—*In case*, in the event or contingency; if it should so fall out or happen.

casein, kā'sē•in, *n.* A white amorphous phosphoprotein contained in the milk of all mammals. Acids precipitate it as in souring milk. It is used for paints and glues, the coating of paper and, after treatment with formaldehyde, as artificial ivory; it is likewise the raw material in the manufacture of synthetic wool.

casemate, kās'māt, *n.* [Fr. *casemate*, from It. *casamatta*, a casemate, from *casa*, a house, and *matto*, obscure, dark.] *Fort.* a bomb-proof vault for the protection of the garrison, and sometimes used as a barrack or hospital; a loopholed gallery excavated in a bastion, from which the garrison could fire on an enemy in possession of the ditch.

casement, kās'ment, *n.* [From *case*, in the sense of a frame, as of a door, etc.]. A window frame, or portion of one made to turn and open on hinges; a compartment between the mullions of a window.

cash, kash, *n.* [O.Fr. *casse*, Mod. Fr. *caisse*, It *cassa*, a chest, box, coffer, from L. *capsa*, a box or case. CASE.] A receptacle for money‡; a money-box‡; money, primarily, ready money; money in chest or on hand, in bank or at command; Chinese copper coin of very small value, often strung on cord.—*v.t.* To turn into money, or to exchange for money (to *cash* a bank-note).—**cashier,** kash•ēr', *n.* One who has charge of cash; one who keeps an account of the monetary transactions of a commercial or trading establishment.—**cashier's check,** in the United States a check drawn by a bank upon itself and signed by its cashier.—**cashbook,** *n.* A book in which is kept a register or account of money received and paid.—**cash register,** *n.* A device recording the amount of cash received. It contains an automatic adding machine and a money drawer.

cashew, ka•shö', *n.* [From native name.] The tree which produces cashew nuts, a native of tropical America.—**cashew nut,** *n.* The kidney-shaped fruit of an American tree, having a kernel abounding in a sweet milky juice; the inner layer of the shell contains a black acrid caustic oil.

cashier, kash•ēr', *v.t.* [Du. *casseere*, G. *kassiren*, from O.Fr. *casser*, to break, to cashier, from L. *cassare*, to annul, from *cassus*, void, empty.] To dismiss from an office, place of trust, or service for bad conduct; to discharge; to discard.

cashmere, kash'mēr, *n.* A fine costly shawl made of the downy wool of the Cashmere goat and the wild goat of Tibet, and so called from the country where first made.

casino, ka•sē'nō, *n.* [It., a small house, from L. *casa*, a cottage.] A building used for social meetings or public amusements, for dancing, gambling, etc.

cask, kask, *n.* [Sp. *casco*, helmet, winecask, skull, potsherd, peel or rind, from a L.L. *quassicare*, to break or burst, from L. *quassare*, to break, whence E. *quash.*] A closed vessel for containing liquors, formed by staves, heading, and hoops; a general term comprehending the pipe, hogshead, butt, barrel, etc.—*v.t.* To put into a cask.

casket, kas'ket, *n.* [In form a dim. of *cask*, but in meaning from Fr. *cassette*, a coffer or casket, dim. of *casse*, a box. CASH.] A small chest or box for jewels, etc.; a coffin. —*v.t.* To put in a casket.

casque, kask, *n.* [Fr., from Sp. *casco*, a helmet. CASK.] A helmet generally, but more precisely a headpiece wanting a visor, but furnished with cheek-pieces and earpieces, and frequently elaborately ornamented and embossed.

cassava, kas•sā'va or kas•sä'va, *n.* [Pg. *cassave*, Sp. *casabe*, *cazabe*, from Haytian name *kasabi.*] A slender erect shrub belonging to the spurge family extensively cultivated in tropical America and the West Indies on account of the nutritious starch obtained from the root, and formed into cakes (cassava-bread) and into tapioca.

casserole, kas'e•rōl, *n.* [Fr., of same origin as *kettle.*] A kind of stewpan or saucepan; a kind of stew; rice, potatoes, etc., formed into a cup to hold some other kind of food; a small dish with a handle, used for chemical operations.

cassia, kash'i•a, *n.* [L. *cassia*, Gr. *kasia*, *kassia*, from the Hebrew or Phoenician name.] A tropical leguminous plant of many species, consisting of trees, shrubs, or herbs, the leaflets of several of which constitute the drug called senna, while the pulp from the legumes of another species is used as a purgative.—**cassia bark,** *n.* The bark of a species of cinnamon, used as a substitute for the true cinnamon.

cassimere, kas'si•mēr, *n.* [Fr. *cassimir*, same word as *cashmere.*] A twilled woolen cloth woven in imitation of Cashmere shawls; kerseymere.

Cassiopeia, kas'si•o•pē"ya, *n.* A constellation in the northern hemisphere with five of its stars forming a kind of W.

Cassiterite, kas'si•tėr•īt, *n.* [Gr. *kassiteros*, tin.] The most common ore of tin; it is a peroxide, consisting of tin 79, and oxygen 21.

cassock, kas'ok, *n.* [Fr. *casaque*, from It. *casaca*, from *casa*, a house, L. *casa*, a cottage.] A sort of long coat or tight-fitting garment worn by clergymen.

cassowary, kas'so•wa•ri, *n.* [Malay *casuwaris.*] A large cursorial bird inhabiting the islands of the Indian Archipelago, nearly as large as the ostrich, which it resembles; but its legs are thicker and stronger in proportion, and it has three toes on the foot; its head is surmounted by a large horny crest.

cast, kast, *v.t.*—*cast, casting.* [Dan. *kaste*, Sw. and Icel. *kasta*, to throw: a Scandinavian word.] To throw, fling, or send; to hurl; to shed or throw off (leaves, the skin); to discard, dismiss, or reject; to shed or impart (*cast* light); to turn or direct (a look, the eyes); to throw down (as in wrestling); to decide against at law; to condemn; to bring forth abortively (young); to form by pouring liquid metal, etc., into a mold; to compute, reckon, or calculate; to distribute (the parts of a drama) among the actors; to assign a part to, the work of the casting director in the movies. —*To cast aside*, to dismiss or reject.—*To cast away*, to reject; to lavish or waste by profusion; to wreck (a ship). —*To cast down*, to throw down; *fig.* to deject or depress.—*To cast forth*, to throw out or reject; to emit or send out.—*To cast a vote*, to enter a checkmark in the ballot for the candidate of one's choice.—*To cast off*, to discard or reject; to drive away; *naut.* to loosen from or let go. —*To cast out*, to reject or turn out.—*To cast up*, to compute; to reckon; to calculate; to eject; to vomit; to twit or upbraid with.—*To cast one's self on* or *upon*, to resign or yield one's self to the disposal of.—*To cast in one's lot with*, to share the fate or fortune of.—*To cast* (something) *in the teeth*, to upbraid (with something); to charge; to twit.—*v.i.* To throw or fling; to throw the line in angling, especially one with a fly; to work arithmetical calculations; to turn or revolve in the mind; to calculate; to consider; to warp or twist.—*n.* The act of casting; a throw; the distance passed by a thing thrown; motion or turn of the eye; direction, look, or glance; a throw of dice; the form or shape into which something is cast; anything formed in a mold, as a figure in bronze, plaster, etc.; *fig.* shape; mold; impression generally; a tinge or slight coloring or slight degree of a color (a *cast* of green); manner; air; mien; style; the company of actors to whom the parts of a play are assigned.—*Cast in the eye*, squint.—**castaway,** kast'a•wā, *n.* One who or that which is cast away or shipwrecked; one ruined in fortune or character.—*a.* Thrown away; rejected; useless; abandoned.—**caster,** kas'tėr, *n.* One who or that which casts; specifically, one who makes castings; a founder; a small cruet or bottle for holding sauce, pepper, etc., for the table; spelled also *Castor;* a small wheel attached by a vertical pivot to the legs of a chair, sofa, table, etc., to facilitate their being moved without lifting: spelled also *Castor.*—**casting,** kas'ting, *n.* The act of one who casts; that which is cast; especially, something cast or formed in a mold; something formed of cast-metal.—*a.* Throwing; sending; computing; turning; deciding; determining.—*Casting-vote,* a vote given by a president or chairman which decides when the votes are equally divided.—**cast iron, cast steel,** *n.* Iron, and steel melted and cast into pigs, ingots, or molds, which renders the metal hard and non-malleable.—**castoff,** *a.* Laid aside as worn out or useless; rejected.

Castalian, kas•tā'li•an, *a.* Pertaining to Castalia; the spring on Mount Parnassus, sacred to the Muses.

castanet, kas•ta•net', *n.* [Sp. *castañeta,* from L. *castanea,* a chestnut, from resembling that fruit.] One of a pair of small concave pieces of ivory or hard wood, shaped like spoons, fastened to the thumb, and beat with the middle finger in certain Spanish dances.

caste, kast, *n.* [Fr. *caste,* Pg. *casta,* breed, race, caste.] One of the classes or distinct hereditary orders into which the Hindus are divided according to the religious law of Brahmanism; a class or order of the same kind prevailing in other countries; a rank or order of society; social position; in social insects, a set of similar individuals, e.g. the 'workers' in ants, bees, etc.

castellan, kas'tel•lan, *n.* [L.L. *castellanus,* from L. *castellum,* a castle. CASTLE.] A governor or constable of a castle.—**castellated,** kas'tel•lāt•ed, *a.* Furnished with turrets and battlements like a castle; built in the style of a castle.

castigate, kas'ti•gāt, *v.t.*—*castigated, castigating.* [L. *castigo, castigatum,* from *castus,* pure.] To chastise; to punish; to correct; to criticize for the purpose of correcting; to emend. —**castigation,** kas•ti•gā'shon, *n.* The act of castigating; punishment by whipping; correction; chastisement; discipline; critical scrutiny and emendation; correction of textual errors.—**castigator,** kas'ti•gā•tėr, *n.* One who castigates or corrects.

Castile soap, kas•tēl', *n.* A kind of fine hard, white or mottled soap, originally from Castile, made with olive oil and a solution of caustic soda.—**Castilian,** kas•til'i•an, *a.* Pertaining to Castile in Spain.—*n.* An inhabitant or native of Castile; the language of Castile, the classic or literary language of Spain.

castle, kas'l, *n.* [L. *castellum,* dim. of *castrum,* a fort.] A building, or series of connected buildings, fortified for *defense* against an enemy; a house with towers, often surrounded by a wall and moat, and having a donjon or keep in the center; a fortified residence; a fortress; the house or mansion of a person of rank or wealth: somewhat vaguely applied, but usually to a large and more or less imposing building; a piece made in the form of a castle, used in the game of chess; the rook. —*Castle in the air,* a visionary project; a scheme that has no solid foundation. —*v.t.* or *i. Chess,* to move the king two squares to the right or left and bring up the castle to the square the king has passed over.—**castled,** cas'ld, *a.* Furnished with a castle or castles.

castor, kas'tėr, *n.* [L. *castor;* Gr. *kastōr,* a beaver.] A substance of a strong penetrating smell, secreted by special glands of the beaver, and used in medicine and perfumery; a beaver hat.—**castor oil,** *n.* [Probably from some resemblance to the substance *castor.*] The oil, used in medicine as a purgative, obtained from the seeds, or beans, of the castor-oil plant.

castrametation, kas'tra•mi•tā''shon, *n.* [L. *castrametari,* to encamp—*castra,* camp, and *metior,* to measure.] The art or act of encamping; the marking or laying out of a camp.

castrate, kas'trāt, *v.t.*—*castrated, castrating.* [L. *castro, castratum,* to castrate.] To deprive of the testicles; to geld; to take the vigor or strength from; to emasculate; to remove something objectionable from, as obscene parts from a writing; to expurgate.—*n.* A man (as a eunuch) or male animal (as an ox) that has been castrated.—**castration,** kas•trā'shon, *n.* The act of castrating.

casual, kazh'ū•al, *a.* [L. *casualis,* from *casus,* a chance or accident, from *cado, casum,* to fall; akin *case, chance, accident,* etc.] Happening or coming to pass, without design in the person or persons affected, and without being foreseen or expected; accidental; fortuitous; coming by chance; not happening or coming regularly; occasional; incidental.—*n.* A person who receives relief and shelter for one night at the most in the workhouse of a parish or union to which he does not belong. —**casualist,** kazh'ū•al•ist, *n.* A believer in casualism.—**casually,** kazh'ū•al•li, *adv.* In a casual manner; accidentally; fortuitously.—**casualness,** kazh'ū•al•nes, *n.* The fact of being casual.—**casualty,** kazh'ū•al•ti, *n.* Chance, or what happens by chance; accident; contingency; an unfortunate chance or accident, especially one resulting in death or bodily injury; loss suffered by a body of men from death, wounds, etc.

casuist, kaz'ū•ist, *n.* [Fr. *casuiste,* from L. *casus,* a case.] One versed in or using casuistry; one who studies and resolves cases of conscience, or nice points regarding conduct.—**casuistic, casuistical,** kaz•ū•is'tik, kaz•ū•is'tik•al, *a.* Pertaining to casuists or casuistry; partaking of casuistry.—**casuistically,** kaz•ū•is'tik•al•li, *adv.* In a casuistic manner.—**casuistry,** kaz'ū•ist•ri, *n.* The science, doctrine, or department of ethics dealing with cases of conscience; frequently used in a bad sense for quibbling in matters of morality, or making too nice moral distinctions.

cat, kat, *n.* [A.Sax. *cat, catt*=D. and Dan. *kat,* Sw. *katt,* Icel. *kōttr,* G. *katze, kater,* O.Fr. *cat,* Mod. Fr. *chat,* Ir. *cat,* W. *cath,* Rus. and Pol. *kot,* Tur. *kedi,* Ar. *qitt*—a cat; origin unknown.] A name applied to certain species of carnivorous quadrupeds of the feline tribe; a strong tackle or combination of pulleys, to hook and draw an anchor perpendicularly up to the cat-head of a ship; a double tripod having six feet: so called because it always lands on its feet as a cat is proverbially said to do; an abbreviation of cat-o'-nine-tails (which see).—*To let the cat out of the bag,* to disclose a trick; to let out a secret.—**catamount, catamountain,** kat'a•mount, kat'a•moun•tān, *n.* The cat of the mountain; the wild cat; the North American puma or cougar.—**catbird,** *n.* A North American singing bird, a species of thrush which utters a cry of alarm like the mew of a cat.—**catcall,** kat'kạl, *n.* A sound like the cry of a cat, such as that made by a dissatisfied audience in a theater; a small squeaking instrument for producing such a sound.—**catgut,** kat'gut, *n.* The intestines of sheep (sometimes of the horse or the ass) dried and twisted into strings for the violin and for other purposes: so called from a notion that the material was the gut or intestines of the cat.—**catkin,** kat'kin, *n.* The blossom of the willow, birch, hazel, etc., which resembles a kitten or cat's tail.—**catnip,** kat'nip, *n.* A plant resembling mint, having a strong odor and taste, and which cats are said to be fond of.—**cathead,** *n.* A strong beam projecting over a ship's bows, and furnished with a block and tackle to lift an anchor.—**cat-o'-nine-tails,** *n.* An instrument consisting generally of nine pieces of knotted cord, used to flog offenders on the bare back.—**cat's-eye,** *n.* A hard and semi-transparent variety of quartz, having an opalescent radiation or play of colors like a cat's eye.—**cat's-paw,** *n.* The instrument used by a person to accomplish his designs; a tool; a dupe: so called from the story of the monkey which, instead of using his own paw, used that of the cat to draw nuts from the fire.—**cat walk,** *n.* A narrow footpath.

catabolism, ka•ta'bo•lizm, *n.* [Gr. *katabolē,* throwing down.] Destructive metabolism.

catachresis, kat•a•krē'sis, *n.* [Gr. *katachrēsis,* abuse—*kata,* against, and *chraomai*, to use.] The wresting of a word from its true signification; the employment of a word under a false form through misapprehension in regard to its origin (*crayfish* for example).—**catachrestic, catachrestical,** kat•a•kres′tik, kat•a•kres′tik•al, *a.* Belonging to catachresis; wrested from its natural sense, use, or form.—**catachrestically,** kat•a•kres′tik•al•li, *adv.* In a catachrestical manner.

cataclysm, kat′a•klizm, *n.* [Gr. *kataklysmos*, a deluge, from *kataklyzō*, to inundate—*kata*, down, and *klyzō*, to wash.] A deluge, flood, or inundation sweeping over a territory.—**cataclysmal, cataclysmic,** kat•a•kliz′mal, kat•a•kliz′mik, *a.* Of or belonging to a cataclysm.

catacomb, kat′a•kōm, *n.* [It. *catacomba*, L.L. *catacumba*, from Gr. *kata*, down, and *kumbe, kumbos*, a hollow or recess.] A cave or subterranean place for the burial of the dead, in which the bodies are deposited in recesses hollowed out of the sides of the cave, the most notable being those near Rome, supposed to be the cells and caves in which the primitive Christians concealed themselves, and in which were deposited the bodies of the martyrs.

catafalque, kat′a•falk, *n.* [Fr. *catafalque*, from It. *catafalco*, from *falco*, for O.H.G. *palcho* (G. *balke*), a beam, with *cata* (as in Sp. *catar*, to view) prefixed. *Scaffold* is the same word with French prefix es.] A temporary structure representing a tomb placed over the coffin of a distinguished person in churches or over the grave.

Catalan, kat′a•lan, *a.* Pertaining to Catalonia, a province of Spain.—*n.* A native of Catalonia; the language of Catalonia; an old Spanish literary dialect early cultivated.

catalectic, kat•a•lek′tik, *a.* [Gr. *katalēktikos*, from *katalēgo*, to leave off, to stop.] *Pros.* having the measure incomplete; ending abruptly, as a verse wanting a syllable of its proper length.

catalepsy, kat′a•lep•si, *n.* [Gr. *katalēpsis*, a seizing, from *katalambanō*, to seize.] A condition marked by loss of voluntary motion, muscular rigidity, and fixity of posture.—**cataleptic,** kat•a•lep′tik, *a.*

catalog, catalogue, kat′a•log, *n.* [Fr. *catalogue*, from Gr. *katalogos*, a counting up—*kata*, thoroughly, and *logos*, a reckoning.] A list or enumeration of the names of men or things disposed in a certain order, often in alphabetical order; a list; a register. —*v.t.*—*catalogued, cataloguing.* To make a catalogue of.—*Catalogue raisonné*, a catalogue of books, paintings, etc., classed according to their subjects.

catalysis, ka•tal′i•sis, *n.* [Gr. *kata*, down, an *lyō*, to loose.] A modification (usually increase) in the speed of a chemical reaction, induced by a catalyst.—**catalyst,** kat′a•list, *n.* An agent that induces catalysis but is not itself chemically changed.—**catalytic,** kat•a•lit′ik, *a.*

catamaran, kat′a•ma•ran″, *n.* [Said to be from a Tamil word signifying ‘tied logs’.] A kind of float or raft used as a substitute for a surfboat, particularly in the East and West Indies, and consisting usually of three pieces of wood lashed together, the middle piece being longer than the others, and having one end turned up in the form of a bow.

catamenia, kat•a•mē′ni•a, *n. pl.* [Gr. *katamēnios*—*kata*, down, and *mēn*, a month.] The menstrual discharge of females.—**catamenial,** kat•a•mē′ni•al, *a.*

cataplasm, kat′a•plazm, *n.* [Gr. *kataplasma*, from *kataplasso*, to anoint or to spread as a plaster.] *Med.* a soft and moist substance to be applied to some part of the body; a poultice.

catapult, kat′a•pult, *n.* [L. *catapulta*, from Gr. *katapeltēs*—*kata*, against, and *pallō*, to brandish, hurl.] A military engine anciently used for discharging missiles against a besieged place; originally an engine of the nature of a powerful bow.

cataract, kat′a•rakt, *n.* [L. *cataracta*, Gr. *katarraktēs*, from *kata*, down, and *rhēgnymi*, to break.] A great fall of water over a precipice; a waterfall; any furious rush or downpour of water; a disease of the eye consisting in an opacity of the crystalline lens or its capsule, by which the pupil seems closed by an opaque body, usually whitish, vision being thus impaired or destroyed.

catarrh, ka•tär′, *n.* [From Gr. *katarrheō*, to flow down.] A discharge or increased secretion of mucus from the membranes of the nose, fauces, and bronchia, characteristic of the ailment commonly called a *cold* in the head.—**catarrhal, catarrhous,** ka•tär′ral, ka•tär′rus, *a.* Pertaining to catarrh, produced by it, or attending it (a *catarrhal* fever).

catastrophe, ka•tas′tro•fe, *n.* [Gr. *katastrophe*, an overthrowing, a sudden turn, from *katastrephō*, to subvert—*kata*, down, and *strephō*, to turn.] The unfolding and winding up of the plot, clearing up of difficulties, and closing of a dramatic piece; the dénouement; a notable event terminating a series; a finishing stroke or windup; an unfortunate conclusion; a calamity or disaster; a supposed change in the crust of the earth from sudden physical violence, causing elevation or subsidence of the solid parts; a cataclysm.—**catastrophic,** kat•as•trof′ik, *a.* Pertaining to a catastrophe or catastrophes; pertaining to the theory of great changes on the globe being due to violent and sudden physical action.

catatonia, ka′ta•tō″ni•a, *n.* [Gr. *kata*, down, and *tonos*, tension.] A mental disorder characterized by muscular inactivity and apparent, although not actual, insensitiveness to the outside world.—**catatonic,** ka′ta•ton″ik, *a.* and *n.*

Catawba, ka•tą′ba, *n.* A variety of grape much cultivated in Ohio, discovered on the *Catawba* river; the wine made from the grape.

catch, kach, *v.t.* pret. & pp. *caught* (*catched* is obsolete or vulgar). [O.E. *cacche*, O.Fr. *cachier, chacier*, etc., to hunt (Mod. Fr. *chasser*), from L.L. *captiare*, from L. *captare*, from *capere*, to take (whence *capable, captious*, etc.). *Chase* is the same word.] To lay sudden hold on; to seize, especially with the hand; to grasp; to snatch; to perceive or apprehend; to seize, as in a snare or trap; to ensnare; to entangle; to get entangled with, or to come into contact or collision with (the branch *caught* his hat); to get; to receive (to *catch* the sunlight; especially, to take or receive as by sympathy, contagion, or infection; to take hold of; to communicate to; to fasten on (the flames *caught* the woodwork); to seize the affections of; to engage and attach; to charm; to captivate.—*To catch it*, to get a scolding, a beating, or other unpleasant treatment. (Colloq.)—*To catch hold of*, to take or lay hold of.—*To catch up*, to snatch; to take up suddenly; to lay hold suddenly of something said.—*v.i.* To take or receive something; to be entangled or impeded; to spread by or as by infection; to be eager to get, use, or adopt: with *at*.—*n.* The act of seizing; seizure; anything that seizes or takes hold, that checks motion or the like, as a hook, a ratchet, a pawl, a spring bolt for a door or lid, etc; a choking or stoppage of the breath; something caught or to be caught, especially anything valuable or desirable obtained or to be obtained; a gain or advantage; one desirable from wealth as a husband or wife (*colloq.*); *mus.* a kind of canon or round for three or four voices, the words written to which are so contrived that by the union of the voices a different meaning is given by the singers *catching* at each other's words.—**catcher,** kach′ėr, *n.* One who or that which catches. —**catching,** kach′ing, *a.* Communicating, or liable to be communicated, by contagion; infectious; captivating; charming; attracting.—**catchment,** kach′ment, *n.* A surface of ground of which the drainage is capable of being directed into a common reservoir.—**catchpenny,** *n.* Something of little value got up to hit the popular taste, and thereby catch the popular penny; anything got up merely to sell.—**catchpoll,** *n.* [Med. L. *cacepollus*, Fr. *chacepol.*] A *chaser* of *fowls.* (L. *pullus.*) A sheriff's officer, bailiff, constable, or other person whose duty is to arrest persons.—**catchword,** *n.* The word formerly often, now rarely, placed at the bottom of each page, on the right hand under the last line, and forming the first word on the following page; in a play the last word of one actor to be caught up by another as a reminder that he is to speak next; cue; a word caught up and repeated for effect.—**catchy,** *a.* Attractive, infectious, easily picked up, of tunes and songs.

catchup, kach′ip, *n.* Same as *Ketchup.*

cate, kāt, *n.* [O.E. *acates*, provisions purchased, from O.Fr. *acat*, buying. CATER.] Food, more particularly rich, luxuriant, or dainty food; a delicacy; a dainty: commonly used in the plural.

catechetic, catechetical, kat•e•ket′-ik, kat•e•ket′ik•al, *a.* [CATECHISE.] Relating to catechising, or one who catechises; consisting in asking questions and receiving answers, as in teaching pupils.

catechize, catechise, kat′e•kīz, *v.t.* —*catechized, catechised, catechizing, catechising,* [Gr. *katēchisō,* to catechize, from *katēcheō,* to utter sound, to teach by the voice—*kata,* down, and *ēchcō,* to sound, whence *echo.*] To instruct by asking questions, receiving answers, and offering explanations and corrections; to question; to interrogate; to examine or try by questions, especially such questions as would implicate the answerer.—**catechizer,** kat′e•kīz•ėr, *n.* One who catechizes.—**catechism,** kat′e•kizm, *n.* [Gr. *katēchismos,* instruction.] A book containing a summary of principles in any science or art, but especially in religion, reduced to the form of questions and answers. —**catechist,** kat′e•kist, *n.* One who instructs question and answer; a catechizer.—**catechistic, catechistical,** kat•e•kist′ik, kat•e•kist′ik•al, *a.* Pertaining to a catechist or catechism.

catechu, kat′e•shū, *n.* [Tamil *katti,* tree, and *shu,* juice.] A name common to several astringent extracts prepared from the wood, bark, and fruits of various plants, especially from some species of acacia, and used in dyeing, tanning, and medicine.

catechumen, kat•e•kū′men, *n.* [Gr. *katēchoumenos,* instructed. CATECHISE.] One who is under instruction in the first rudiments of Christianity; a neophyte.

category, kat′e•gor•i, *n.* [Gr. *katēgoria,* a class or category, from *katēgoreō,* to accuse, show, demonstrate —*kata,* down, etc., and *agoreō,* to speak in an assembly, from *agora,* a forum or market.] One of the highest classes to which objects of thought can be referred; one of the most general heads under which everything that can be asserted of any subject may be arranged; in a popular sense, any class or order in which certain things are embraced.—**categorical,** kat•e•gor′ik•al, *a.* Pertaining to a category; absolute; positive; express; not relative or hypothetical (statement, answer).—**categorically,** kat•-e•gor′ik•al•li, *adv.* In a categorical manner; absolutely; directly; expressly; positively.

catenary, catenarian, ka•tē′ne•ri or kat′ē•ne•ri, kat•e•nâ′ri•an, *a.* [L. *catenarius,* from *catena,* a chain.] Relating to a chain; like a chain.—*Catenary curve,* that variety of curve which is formed by a rope or chain, of uniform density and thickness, when allowed to hang freely with its ends attached to two fixed points.—**catenate,** ‡ kat′e•nāt, *v.t.* To connect in a series of links or ties; to concatenate.—**catenation,**‡ kat•e•nā′shon, *n.* Connection of links; union of parts, as in a chain; regular connection; concatenation.

cater, kā′tėr, *v.i.* [From obs. *cater,* a caterer, O.Fr. *acateur, acator,* from *acater,* L.L. *accaptare,* to buy, from L. *ad,* to, and L. *captare,* intens. of *capere,* to take.] To buy or provide something for use, enjoyment, or entertainment; to purvey food, provisions, amusement, etc.: followed by *for.*—**caterer,** kā′tėr•ėr, *n.* One who caters; a provider or purveyor of provisions; one who provides for any want or desire.—**cateress,** kā′-tėr•es, *n.* A woman who caters; a female provider. (*Mil.*)

cateran, kat′ėr•an, *n.* [Gael. and Ir. *ceatharnach,* a soldier.] A kern; a Highland or Irish irregular soldier; a Highland freebooter.

cater-cousin,† kā′tėr•kuz•n, *n.* [*Cater*=Fr. *quatre,* four.] A distant cousin; a remote relation. (*Shak.*)

caterpillar, kat′ėr•pil•lėr, *n.* [O.E. *catyrpel* (comp. *caterwaul*); from *cat,* and L. *pilosus,* hairy.] The hairy, wormlike larva or grub of the lepidopterous insects (butterflies and moths), but also sometimes applied to the larvae of other insects.

caterwaul, kat′ėr•wąl, *v.i.* [From *cat,* and *waul,* in imitation of the sound made by a cat; O.E. *caterwawe.*] To utter noisy and disagreeable cries: said of cats; to make a disagreeable howling or screeching.

catharsis, ka•thär′sis, *n.* [Gr. *katharsis,* a cleansing.] Purgation; purging of the effects of emotional stress; discharge of repressed emotions or ideas.—**cathartic,** ka•thär′tik, *a.*—*n.* *Med.* a laxative or purgative.

cathedra, ka•thed′ra, *n.* [L. *cathedra,* a teacher's or professor's chair, a bishop's chair, Gr. *kathedra,* a chair or seat—*kata,* down, and *hedra,* a seat.] The throne or seat of a bishop in the cathedral or episcopal church of his diocese.—**cathedral,** ka•thē′dral, *n.* The principal church in a diocese, that which is specially the church of the bishop: so called from possessing the episcopal chair called *cathedra.*—*a.* Pertaining to the bishop's or head church of a diocese (a *cathedral* church).

catheter, kath′e•tėr, *n.* [Gr. *kathetēr,* from *kathiēmi,* to thrust in—*kata,* down, and *hiēmi,* to send.] In *surg.* a tubular instrument, usually made of silver, to be introduced through the urethra into the bladder to draw off the urine when the natural discharge is arrested.—**catheterize,** kath′e•tėr•īz, *v.t.* To operate on with a catheter.

cathode, kath′ōd, *n.* [Gr. *kata,* down, and *hodos,* a way.] The negative pole of an electric current, or that by which the current leaves: opposed to *anode.*—**cathode ray,** a stream of electrons projected from cathode to anode in a vacuum tube; the source of X rays.

catholic, kath′o•lik, *a.* [Gr. *katholikos* —*kata,* down, throughout, and *holos,* the whole; L. *catholicus,* Fr. *catholique.*] Universal or general; embracing all true Christians (the *catholic* church or faith); not narrowminded, partial, or bigoted; free from prejudice; liberal (*catholic* tastes or sympathies); [*cap.*] pertaining to or affecting the Roman Catholics.—*n.* A member of the universal Christian church; often restricted to members of the Church of Rome.—**catholicism,** ka•thol′i•sizm, *n.* The state of being catholic or universal; catholicity; [*cap.*] adherence to the Roman Catholic Church; the Roman Catholic faith.—**catholicity,** kath•o•lis′i•ti, *n.* The state or quality of being catholic or universal; catholic character or position; universality; the quality of being catholic or liberal-minded.—**catholicize,** ka•thol′i•sīz, *v.i.* To become a Catholic.—**catholicon,**‡ ka•-thol′i•kon, *n.* [Gr. *katholikon iama,* universal remedy.] A remedy for all diseases; a panacea.

cation, kat′ī•on, *n.* [Gr. *kata,* down, and *ion,* going.] A positive ion; the ion that moves toward the cathode in electrolysis.

catkin, *n.* See CAT.

catoptric, ka•top′trik, *a.* [Gr. *katoptrikos,* from *katoptron,* a mirror—*kata,* against, and *optomai,* to see.] Pertaining to incident and reflected light; pertaining to catoptrics.—**catoptrics,** ka•top′triks, *n.* That branch of optics which explains the properties of incident and reflected light, and particularly that which is reflected from mirrors or polished bodies.

catsup, *n.* See KETCHUP.

cattle, kat′l, *n. pl.* [O.E. *catel,* goods, cattle, from O.Fr. *catel, chatel,* property in general, from L.L. *capitale, captale,* property, capital, from L. *capitalis,* chief, capital, from *caput,* the head. *Cattle*=*chattel, capital.*] A term applied collectively to domestic quadrupeds, such as serve for tillage or other labor, or for food to man, including camels, horses, asses, cows, sheep, goats, and perhaps swine, but now chiefly restricted to domestic beasts of the cow kind.

catty, kat′i, *n.* A Chinese weight of $1\frac{1}{3}$ lbs.

Caucasian, ką•kā′zi•an or ką•kā′zhi•-an, *a.* [From the Caucasus Mountains.] Pertaining to the Caucasus or its inhabitants; a designation of race; one of the races into which the human family has been divided.—*n.* An ethnological term applied to the highest type of the human family, including nearly all Europeans, the Circassians, Armenians, Persians, Indians, Jews, etc., being invented by Blumenbach, who regarded a skull he had got from Caucasus as representing the standard of perfection.

caucus, ką′kus, *n.* [Med. Gr. *kaukos,* a drinking cup, referring to convivial meetings of 18th-century U.S. political leaders in Boston and elsewhere.] A private meeting of citizens to agree upon candidates to be proposed for election to offices, or to concert measures for supporting a party.

caudal, ką′dal, *a.* [L. *cauda,* a tail.] Pertaining to a tail; of the nature of a tail; having the appearance of a tail. —**caudate, caudated,** ką′dāt, ką′dāt•-ed, *a.* Having a tail or tail-like attachment: a term applied in *bot.* to seeds which have a taillike appendage.

caudex, ka̤'deks, *n.* L. pl. **caudices,** ka̤'di•sēz, E. pl. **caudexes,** ka̤'deks•ez. [L.] In *bot.* the stem of a tree; specially the scaly trunk of palms and tree ferns.

caudle, ka̤'dl, *n.* [O.Fr. *caudel, chaudel,* a dim. form from L.L. *calidum, caldum,* a kind of hot drink, from L. *calidus,* warm.] A kind of warm drink made of spiced and sugared wine or ale, given to sick persons, women in childbed, or the like.—*v.t.* To make into caudle; to refresh or make warm, as with caudle (*Shak.*).—**caudle cup,** *n.* A vessel or cup for holding caudle.

caught, ka̤t, pret. & pp. of *catch.*

caul, ka̤l, *n.* [From O.Fr. *cale,* a kind of little cap; from the Celtic; comp. Ir. *calla,* Gael. *call,* a veil, a hood.] A kind of head covering worn by females; a net enclosing the hair; the hinder part of a cap; a membrane investing some part of the viscera (O.T.); a portion of the amnion or membrane enveloping the fetus, sometimes encompassing the head of a child when born, and superstitiously supposed to be a preservative against drowning.

cauldron, ka̤l'dron. Same as *Caldron.*

caulescent, ka̤•les'ent, *a.* [L. *caulis,* a stalk.] *Bot.* having a caulis or obvious stem rising above the ground.—**caulicle,** ka̤'li•kl, *n.* [L. *cauliculus.*] *Bot.* a little or rudimentary stem.—**cauline,** ka̤'līn, *a. Bot.* of or belonging to a stem (*cauline* leaves).—**caulis,** ka̤'lis, *n. Bot.* the stem of a plant rising above the ground.

cauliflower, kol'i•flou•ėr, *n.* [Lit. cabbage-flower, from its appearance, from L. *caulis,* colewort, cabbage, and E. *flower*; comp. Fr. *choufleur* (*chou,* cabbage, *fleur,* flower), cauliflower.] A garden variety of cabbage, the inflorescence of which is condensed while young into a depressed fleshy head, which is highly esteemed as a table vegetable.

caulk, ka̤k. Same as *calk.*

cause, ka̤z, *n.* [Fr. *cause,* L. *causa,* a cause.] That which produces an effect; that which brings about a change; that from which anything proceeds, and without which it would not exist; the reason or motive that urges, moves, or impels the mind to act or decide; a suit or action in court; any legal process which a party institutes to obtain his demand, or by which he seeks his right; any subject of question or debate; case; interest; matter; affair; that object or side of a question to which the efforts of a person or party are directed.—*v.t.*—*caused, causing.* To be the cause of; to effect by agency; to bring about; to be the occasion of; to produce.—**causable,** ka̤'za•bl, *a.* Capable of being caused, produced, or effected.—**causal,** ka̤'zal, *a.* [L. *causalis.*] Relating to a cause or causes; implying, containing, or expressing a cause or causes.—*n.* A verb signifying to make to do something; as *fell,* to make to fall.—**causality,** ka̤•zal'i•ti, *n.* The state of being causal; the fact of acting as a cause; the action or power of a cause, in producing its effect; the doctrine or principle that every change implies the operation of a cause.—**causally,** ka̤'zal•li, *adv.* In a causal manner; by tracing effects to causes; by acting as a cause.—**causation,** ka̤•zā'shon, *n.* The act of causing or producing; the doctrines as to the connection of causes and effects.—**causative,** ka̤'za•tiv, *a.* Effective as a cause or agent: often followed by *of*; *gram.* expressing a cause on reason; causal.—*n.* A word expressing a cause.—**causatively,** ka̤'za•tiv•li, *adv.* In a causative manner.—**causeless,** ka̤z'les, *a.* Having no cause or producing agent; self-originated; uncreated; without just ground, reason, or motive.—**causer,** ka̤z'ėr, *n.* One who or that which causes.

causerie, kōz•rē', *n.* [Fr.] Newspaper light talk; literary conversation; an informal lecture.

causeway, ka̤z'wā, *n.* [Original spelling *causey,* from O.Fr. *caucis* (Mod. Fr. *chaussée*), from L.L. *calciata* (*via,* understood), a road in making which lime or mortar is used, from L. *calx, calcis,* lime (whence *chalk, calcareous*).] A road or path raised above the natural level of the ground by stones, earth timber, etc., serving as a passage over wet or marshy ground or the like; a raised and paved roadway.—*v.t.* To provide with a causeway; to pave, as a road or street, with blocks of stone.—**causey,** ka̤'zi, *v.* and *n.* Causeway: a less common but more correct spelling.

caustic, ka̤s'tik, *a.* [Gr. *kaustikos,* from *kaiō, kausō,* to burn.] Capable of burning, corroding, or destroying the texture of animal substances; *fig.* severe; cutting; stinging; pungent; sarcastic.—*n. Med.* any substance which burns, corrodes, or disintegrates the textures of animal structures; an escharotic: sometimes popularly restricted to lunar caustic or nitrate of silver when cast into sticks for surgeons' use; *math.* the name given to the curve to which the rays of light reflected or refracted by another curve are tangents.—**caustically,** ka̤s'ti•kal•li, *adv.* In a caustic or severe manner.—**causticity,** ka̤s•tis'i•ti, *n.* The quality of being caustic or corrosive; *fig.* severity of language; pungency; sarcasm.

cauterize, ka̤'tėr•īz, *v.t.*—*cauterized, cauterizing.* [L.L. *cauterizo,* from Gr. *kautēriazō,* from *kautērion, kautēr,* a burning or branding iron, from *kaiō,* to burn.] To burn or sear with fire or a hot iron or with caustics, as morbid flesh.—**cauterization,** ka̤'tėr•īz•ā"shon, *n. Surg.* the act or the effect of cauterizing.—**cautery,** ka̤'tėr•i, *n.* [L. *cauterium,* Gr. *kautērion.*] A burning or searing, as of morbid flesh, by a hot iron or by caustic substances; the instrument or drug employed in cauterizing.

caution, ka̤'shon, *n.* [L. *cautio,* from *caveo, cautum,* to be on one's guard, beware.] Provident care; prudence in regard to danger; wariness; watchfulness, forethought, or vigilance; a measure taken for security; a security or guarantee‡; a warning or admonition.—*v.t.* To give notice of danger to; to warn; to exhort to take heed.—**cautionary,** ka̤'shon•ar•i, *a.* Containing caution, or warning to avoid danger; given as a pledge or in security.—**cautious,** ka̤'shus, *a.* Possessing or exhibiting caution; attentive to examine probable effects and consequences of actions with a view to avoid danger or misfortune: prudent; circumspect; wary; watchful; vigilant; careful.—**cautiously,** ka̤'shus•li, *adv.* In a cautious manner.—**cautiousness,** ka̤'shus•nes, *n.* The quality of being cautious; caution.

cavalcade, kav'al•kād, *n.* [Fr. *cavalcade,* It. *cavalcata,* from L. *caballus,* a horse. CAVALIER, CAVALRY.] A procession of persons on horseback, or consisting mostly of persons on horseback.

cavalier, kav•a•lēr', *n.* [Fr. *cavalier,* L.L. *caballarius,* from L. *caballus,* a horse, whence also *cavalry, chivalry, cavalcade,* etc. *Chevalier* is a parallel form.] A horseman, especially an armed horseman; a knight; [*cap.*] a partisan of Charles I, as opposed to a Roundhead or adherent to the Parliament; a gallant; *fort.* a work commonly situated within the bastion, and raised higher than the other works so as to command all the adjacent works and the surrounding country.—*a.* Gay; sprightly; easy; offhand; haughty; disdainful; supercilious (a *cavalier* answer).—**cavalierly,** kav•a•lēr'li, *adv.* In a cavalier manner; haughtily; arrogantly; disdainfully.—**cavalry,** kav'al•ri, *n.* [Fr. *cavalerie,* from It. *cavalleria,* from *cavallo,* L. *caballus,* a horse. *Chivalry* is a parallel form.] A body of troops, mounted on horseback or moving in motor vehicles.

cavatina, kav•a•tē'na, *n.* [It.] *Music,* a melody of short simple character, and without a second part and a return part.

cave, kāv, *n.* [Fr. *cave,* from L. *cavus,* hollow, whence also *cavity, cavern,* and *cage.*] A hollow place in the earth; a subterranean cavern; a den.—**cave,** *n.* A political party: desertion; seceders; applied by John Bright in 1866 to deserters, with reference to the Cave of Adullam, 1 *Sam.* xxii. 1-2—*v.t.* To make hollow.—*v.i.*† To dwell in a cave.—*To cave in,* to fall in and leave a hollow, as earth on the side of a well or pit or the roof of a subterranean passage.—**cave dweller, cave man,** *n.* One who dwells in caves, a name given to such of the earliest races of prehistoric man as dwelt in natural caves, subsisting on shellfish and wild animals.

caveat kā'vi•at, *n.* [L. *caveat,* let him beware, from *caveo,* to beware.] In *law,* a process in a court to stop proceedings; hence, an intimation of caution; hint; warning; admonition.—*v.i.* To enter a caveat.—**caveat emptor,** [L., let the buyer beware.] At the buyer's risk.

cavendish, kav'en•dish, *n.* Tobacco which has been softened and pressed into quadrangular cakes.

cavern, kav'ėrn, *n.* [L. *caverna,* from *cavus,* hollow. CAVE.] A deep hollow place in the earth; a cave.—**cavern-**

ous, kav′ėrn•us, *a.* [L. *cavernosus.* Hollow, or containing a cavern or caverns; filled with small cavities.

cavetto, ka•vet′tō, *n.* [It., from *cavo,* hollow, L. *cavus.*] *Arch.* a hollow member, or round concave molding, containing the quadrant of a circle.

caviar, kav′•i•är, *n.* [Fr. *caviar,* Turk *haviâr.*] A delicacy made from the salted roe of sturgeon and other large fish. —*Caviar to the general,* a delicacy beyond the reach of most; a reasoning beyond the popular grasp.

cavil, kav′il, *v.i.*—*cavilled, cavilling.* [O.Fr. *caviller,* from L. *cavillor,* to cavil, *cavilla,* a quibble, trick, shuffle.] To raise captious and frivolous objections; to find fault without good reason: frequently followed by *at.* —*n.* A captious or frivolous objection; captious or specious argument. —**caviller,** kav′il•ėr, *n.* One who cavils; one who is apt to raise captious objections; a captious disputant.—**cavilling,** kav′il•ling, *a.* Given to cavil or making captious objections.

cavity, kav′i•ti, *n.* [Fr. *cavité,* L. *cavitas,* from L. *cavus,* hollow. CAVE.] A hollow place; a hollow; a void or empty space in a body; an opening; a hollow part of the human body.

cavy, kā′vi, *n.* The name common to certain South American rodent animals, the most familiar species being the well-known guinea pig.

caw, kạ, *v.i.* [Imitative of the sound; comp. Sc. *kae,* D. *kaauw,* Dan. *kaa,* a jackdaw.] To cry like a crow, rook, or raven.—*n.* The cry of the rook or crow.

cay, kā, *n.* [Sp. *cayo,* a rock, a shoal, an islet.] An islet; a range or reef of rocks lying near the surface of the water: used especially in the West Indies and sometimes written *Key.*

cayenne, kī•en′ or kā•en′. *n.* [From *Cayenne* in South America.] A kind of pepper, a powder made from the dried and ground fruits, and more especially the seeds, of various species of *Capsicum.*

cayman, kā′man, *n.* [Native Guiana name.] A name applied popularly to the alligator of the West Indies and South America.

cayuse, kī•ūs′, *n.* A small horse; an Indian pony: a bronco.

cease, sēs, *v.i.*—*ceased, ceasing.* [Fr. *cesser,* L. *cesso, cessare,* to cease, a freq. from *cedere,* to yield, to *cede.* CEDE.] To stop moving, acting, or speaking; to leave off; to give over; to desist: followed by *from* before a noun; to come to an end; to terminate; to become extinct; to pass away (the storm *ceases*).—*v.t.* To put a stop to; to put an end to; to desist from.—**ceaseless,** sēs′les, *a.* Without a stop or pause; incessant; continual; without intermission; enduring for ever; endless.

cedar, sē′dėr, *n.* [L. *cedrus,* Gr. *kedros,* a kind of juniper.] A coniferous evergreen tree which grows to a great size, and is remarkable for its durability, forming fine woods on the mountains of Syria and Asia Minor, and often called distinctively the cedar of Lebanon. The deodar cedar is closely akin to it, and the name is also given to various other trees.—*a.* Made of cedar, belonging to cedar.—**cedarn,** sē′dėrn, *a.* Pertaining to the cedar; made of cedar. (*Tenn.*)

cede, sēd, *v.t.*—*ceded, ceding.* [L. *cedo, cessum,* to retire, yield, grant, give up, a word which appears also in *accede, concede, exceed, precede, recede, decease, abscess, antecedent, ancestor, predecessor, cease,* etc.] To yield; to surrender, to give up; to resign; to relinquish.—*v.i.* To yield; to submit; to pass over; to be transferred; to fall to; to lapse.

cedilla, si•dil′la, *n.* [Fr. *cédille,* It. *zediglia,* a dim. of *zeta,* the name of *z* in Greek; because formerly, in order to give *c* the sound of *s,* it was customary to write *cz*: thus *leczon,* for modern *leçon.*] A mark placed under the letter *c,* especially in French (thus ç), to show that it is to be sounded like *s.*

ceil, sēl, *v.t.* [O.E. *seile,* a canopy, from Fr. *ciel,* It. *cielo,* a canopy, heaven, from L. *cælum,* heaven, same root as Gr. *koilos,* hollow, and E. *hollow.*] To overlay or cover the inner roof of a room or building; to provide with a ceiling.—**ceiling,** sēl′ing, *n.* The inside lining of surface of an apartment above; the horizontal or curved surface of an apartment opposite the floor, usually finished with plastered work; maximum height to which an airplane can climb under certain conditions; the upper limit of wages, prices, etc.

celandine, sel′an-din, *n.* [O.Fr. *celidoine,* Fr. *chélidoine,* from L. *chelidonium,* Gr. *chelidonion,* swallowwort, from *chelidōn,* a swallow.] A name given to two plants belonging to the poppy family, which yield an acrid juice used in medicine.

Celanese, sel′an•ēz, *n.* A trademarked name for a type of rayon material.

celebrate, sel′e•brāt, *v.t.*—*celebrated, celebrating.* [L. *celebrare, celebratum,* to celebrate, from *celeber,* famous, frequented, populous.] To make known or mention often, especially with honor or praise; to extol; to distinguish by any kind of observance or ceremony (to *celebrate* a birthday). —**celebrant,** sel′e•brant, *n.* One who celebrates; one who performs a public religious rite.—**celebrated,** sel′e•brāt•ed, *a.* Having celebrity; distinguished; well known; famous.—**celebrator,** sel′e•brā•tėr, *n.* One who celebrates.—**celebration,** sel•e•brā′shon, *n.* The act of celebrating; the act of praising or extolling; honor or distinction bestowed; the act of observing with appropriate rites or ceremonies.—**celebrity,** se•leb′ri•ti, *n.* [L. *celebritas.*] The condition of being celebrated; fame; renown (the *celebrity* of the Duke of Wellington, of Homer, or of the Iliad); a person of distinction.

celerity, se•ler′i•ti, *n.* [L. *celeritas,* from *celer,* swift.] Rapidity of motion; swiftness; quickness; speed. ∴ As distinguished from *velocity, celerity* is now generally applied to the motions or actions of living beings, *velocity* to inanimate objects.

celery, sel′e•ri, *n.* [Fr. *céleri,* It. *seleri,* from Gr. *selinon,* parsley.] A plant indigenous to marshy places and long cultivated in gardens as a salad and culinary vegetable.

celestial, se•les′chel, *a.* [O.Fr. *celestial, celestiel,* L. *cælestis,* from *cælum,* heaven, whence also *ceiling.*] Heavenly; belonging or relating to heaven; dwelling in heaven; supremely excellent or delightful; belonging to the upper regions or visible heaven; pertaining to the heavens.—*Celestial Empire,* China, so called because the first emperors are fabled to have been deities.—*n.* An inhabitant of heaven; [*usually cap.*] a native of China, the so-called Celestial Empire.—**celestially,** se•les′chel•li, *adv.* In a celestial or heavenly manner.—**celestial navigation,** *n.* Navigation using celestial bodies for reference.

celibacy, sel′i•ba•si, *n.* [L. *cælibatus,* a single life, celibacy, from *cælebs,* unmarried.] The state of being celibate or unmarried; a single life.—**celibate,** sel′i•bāt, *n.* One who adheres to or practices celibacy.—*a.* Unmarried; single.

cell, sel, *n.* [L. *cella,* a cell, a small room, a hut, from same root as *celare,* whence *concelare,* to conceal. *Hole* and *hollow* are from same root.] A small apartment, as in a convent or a prison; a small or mean place of residence, such as a cave or hermitage; a small cavity or hollow place: variously applied (the *cells* of the brain, the *cells* of a honey comb, the *cells* of a galvanic battery); *eccles.* a lesser religious house, especially one subordinate to a greater; *arch.* the part of the interior of a temple where the image of a god stood; *biol.* a small, usually microscopic, mass of contractile protoplasm with a membranous envelope forming the most elementary constituent or the structural unit in the tissues of animals and plants.—**cellophane,** sel′lo•fān, *n.* Transparent moisture-proof cellulose sheets or film, used extensively as coverings and wrappings for cigarettes, cigars, foodstuffs, and other kinds of merchandise.—**cellular,** sel′lū•lėr, *a.* [L. *cellula,* a little cell.] Consisting of cells, or containing cells.—**Celluloid,** sel′lū•loid, *n.* An artificial substance, chiefly composed of cellulose or vegetable fibrin, used as a substitute for ivory, bone, coral, etc.—**cellulose,** sel′lū•lōs, *a.* Containing cells.—*n. Bot.* the substance of which the permanent cell membranes of plants are always composed, in many respects allied to starch.—*n. Chem.* a chief constituent of wood, cotton, paper, etc.

cellar, sel′lėr, *n.* [L. *cellarium.* CELL.] A room in a house or other building, either wholly or partly under ground, used for storage purposes.—**cellarage,** sel′lėr•ij, *n.* The space occupied by cellars; cellars collectively; charge for storage in a cellar.—**cellarer,** sel′lėr•ėr, *n.* An officer in a monastery who has the care of the cellar; a butler; one who keeps wine or spirit cellars; a spirit-dealer.—**cellaret,** sel•lėr•et′, *n.* [Dim. of *cellar.*] A case of cabinet work for holding bottles of liquors.

Celt, selt, *n.* [L. *Celtæ*, Gr. *Keltoi*, *Keltai*, connected with W. *celt*, a covert or shade; Gael. *ceiltach*, an inhabitant of the forest.] One of a distinct group of men inhabiting many parts of ancient Europe; the Celts now speaking a distinctive language are the Bretons, Welsh, Scotch Highlanders, and a portion of the Irish. [The word with its derivaties is frequently written with an initial *K*—*Kelt*, *Keltic*, etc.]—**Celtic,** sel′tik, *a.* Pertaining to the Celts, or to their language.—*n.* The language or group of dialects spoken by the Celts.—**Celticism,** sel′ti•sizm, *n.* The manners and customs of the Celts; a Celtic expression or mode of expression.

cement, si•ment′, *n.* [O.Fr. *cement*, L. *cæmentum*, chips of stone made into cement, contr. from *cædimentum*, from *cædo*, to cut.] Any glutinous or other substance capable of uniting bodies in close cohesion; a kind of mortar consisting of those hydraulic limes which contain silica and therefore set quickly; *fig.* bond of union; that which unites persons firmly together.—*v.t.* To unite by cement or other matter that produces cohesion of bodies; *fig.* to unite firmly or closely.—*v.i.* To unite or become solid; to unite and cohere.—**cementation,** si•men•tā′shon, *n.* The act of cementing; the conversion of iron into steel by heating the iron in a mass of ground charcoal, and thus causing it to absorb a certain quantity of the latter.—**cementer,** si•men′tėr, *n.* The person or thing that cements.

cemetery, sem′e•te•ri, *n.* [L. *cœmeterium*, a burying place, from Gr. *koimētērion*, a sleeping place, afterward a burying place, from *koimaō*, to sleep.] A place set apart for interment; a graveyard; a necropolis.

cenobite, sen′o•bīt, *n.* [L. *cœnobita*, from Gr. *koinobios*, living in common, from *koinos*, common, and *bios*, life.] One of a religious order living in a convent or in community; in opposition to an anchorite or hermit, who lives in solitude.—**cenobitic,** sen•o•bit′ik, sen•o•bit′ik•al, *a.* Living in community, as men belonging to a convent.—**cenobitism,** sen′o•bīt•izm, *n.* The state of being a cenobite; the principles or practice of a cenobite.

cenotaph, sen′o•taf, *n.* [Gr. *kenotaphion*—*kenos*, empty, and *taphos*, a tomb.] A sepulchral monument erected to one who is buried elsewhere.

cense,† sens, *v.t.*—*censed, censing*. [Fr. *encenser*. INCENSE.] To perfume with incense.—*v.i.* To scatter incense.—**censer,** sen′sėr, *n.* [A shortened form for *incenser;* Fr. *encensoir*.] A vase or pan in which incense is burned; a vessel for burning and wafting incense; a thurible.

censor, sen′sėr, *n.* [L. *censor*, from *censeo*, to value, enrol, tax.] An officer in ancient Rome whose business was to draw up a register of the citizens, to keep watch over their morals, and to superintend the finances of the state; one empowered to examine all manuscripts, pamphlets, newspapers, and books before they are published, and to see that they contain nothing obnoxious; a war official employed to open, destroy, or revise correspondence, or sources of information calculated to instruct the enemy; one who censures, blames, or reproves.—**censor,** *v.t.* To revise in this sense.—**censorial,** sen•sō′ri•al, *a.* Belonging to a censor or to the correction of public morals; censorious.—**censorious,** sen•sō′ri•us, *a.* Addicted to censure; apt to blame or condemn; ready to pass severe remarks on a person's conduct; implying or expressing censure.—**censoriously,** sen•sō′ri•us•li, *adv.* In a censorious manner.—**censoriousness,** sen•sō′ri•us•nes, *n.* The quality of being censorious; disposition to blame and condemn.—**censorship,** sen′sėr•ship, *n.* The office or dignity of a censor; the period of his office.

censure, sen′shör, *n.* [Fr. *censure;* L. *censura*, an opinion or judgment; from *censere*, to value, to estimate, whence *censor*, *census*.] Judgment or opinion‡; the act of blaming or finding fault and condemning as wrong; expression of blame or disapprobation; faultfinding; condemnation; animadversion.—*v.t.*—*censured, censuring*. To find fault with and condemn as wrong; to blame; to express disapprobation of.—*v.i.*† To pass an opinion, especially a severe opinion. (*Shak.*)—**censurable,** sen′shör•a•bl, *a.* Worthy of censure; blamable; culpable; reprehensible; blameworthy.—**censurably,** sen′shör•a•bli, *adv.* In a censurable manner; in a manner worthy of blame.—**censurer,** sen′shör•ėr, *n.* One who censures or expresses blame.

census, sen′sus, *n.* [L., from *censere*, to register, enroll, whence *censure*, *censor*.] In ancient Rome a registered statement of the particulars of a person's property for taxation purposes; an enumeration and register of the Roman citizens and their property; in modern times, an enumeration of the inhabitants of a state or part of it, taken by order of its legislature; any official enumeration of population.—**censual,** sen′shö•al, *a.* [L. *censualis*.] Relating to or containing a census.

cent, sent, *n.* [Contr. of L. *centum*, a hundred.] A hundred, commonly used with *per;* as, ten *per cent*, that is in the proportion of ten to the hundred; in various countries a coin equal to the hundredth part of the monetary unit; in the United States the hundredth part of the dollar.—**cental,** sen′tal, *n.* A weight of 100 lbs.—*a.* Pertaining to or consisting of a hundred; reckoned or proceeding by the hundred.—**centesimal,** sen•tes′i•mal, *a.* [L. *centesimus*, from *centum*.] Hundredth; by the hundred.—*n.* Hundredth part; the next step of progression after decimal.

centaur, sen′ta̤r, *n.* [L. *centaurus;* Gr. *kentauros*, lit. bull-pricker; the Centaurs probably represented some race that hunted wild cattle and lived almost constantly on horseback.] *Greek myth*, a member of a race of fabulous beings supposed to be half man and half horse; [*cap.*] the name given to a constellation in the southern hemisphere.—**centaury,** sen′ta̤•ri, *n.* [L. *centaurea*, Gr. *kentaurion*, after the *Centaur* Cheiron, because said to have cured a wound in his foot.] The popular name of various plants. Common centaury is an annual herb of the gentian family in high repute among the old herbalists for its medicinal properties.

centenary, sen′te•ne•ri, *n.* [L. *centenarius*, consisting of a hundred, relating to a hundred, from *centum*, a hundred.] What consists of or comprehends a hundred; the space of a hundred years; the commemoration of any event which occurred a hundred years before.—*a.* Relating to or consisting of a hundred; relating to a hundred years.—**centenarian,** sen•te•nâ′ri•an, *n.* A person a hundred years old or upward.—*a.* Of or pertaining to a centenary or centenarian.—**centennial,** sen•ten′ni•al, *a.* [L. *centum*, and *annus*, a year.] Consisting of or lasting a hundred years; aged a hundred years or upward; happening every hundred years.—*n.* The commemoration or celebration of any event which occurred a hundred years before.—**centennially,** sen•ten′ni•al•li, *adv.* Once in every hundred years.

center, sen′tėr, *n.* [Fr., from L. *centrum*, Gr. *kentron*, a prick or point, from *kenteō*, to prick.] That point of a line, plane figure, or solid body which is equally distant from the extremities; the middle point, portion, or place; the middle or central object; a point of concentration; the nucleus around which or into which things are collected (a *center* of attraction); the part of a target next the bull's-eye; the men of the moderate party in politics.—*Center of buoyancy*, in hydrostatics, the center of gravity of the liquid displaced by a floating body. It is the point through which the upward thrust of the liquid may be conceived to act.—*Center of gravity*, the point of a body about which all the parts of the body exactly balance each other, and which being supported, the whole body will remain at rest though acted on by gravity.—*Center of magnitude*, that point in a body which is equally distant from all the similar external parts of it. In the regular solids this point coincides with the center of gravity.—*Center of mass*, that point in a body through which the resultant of absolutely parallel forces exerted on its particles always acts, whatever the direction of the forces.—*Center of motion*, the point which remains at rest while all the other parts of a body move round it.—*Center of* *oscillation*, the point of a body suspended, at which, if all the matter were concentrated, the oscillations would be performed in the same time.—*Center of pressure*, the point in a submerged plane area through which the resultant of the fluid-pressures upon it acts.—*v.t.*—*centered, centering*. To place on a center; to fix on a central point; to collect to a point.—*v.i.* To be placed in a center or in the middle; to be collected to one point; to be concentrated or united in one.—**central,** sen′tral, *a.* [L. *centralis.*] Relating or pertaining to the center; placed in the center or middle; constituting or containing the center; originating or proceeding from the center.—**centralism,** sen′tral•izm, *n.* The quality of being central; the combination of several parts into one whole; centralization.—**centralist,** sen′tral•ist, *n.* One who promotes centralization.—**centrality,** sen•tral′-i•ti.—**centralization,** sen′tral•iz•ā″-shon, *n.* The act of centralizing or bringing to one center.—**centralize,** sen′tral•īz, *v.t.*—*centralized, centralizing*. To draw to a central point; to bring to a center; to render central; to concentrate in some particular part: often applied to the process of transferring local administration to the capital or seat of government of a country.—**centrally,** sen′tral•li, *adv.* In a central manner or position; with regard to the center.—**center bit,** *n.* A carpenter's tool for boring large circular holes, which turns on an axis or central point when in operation.—**centerboard,** *n.* A kind of movable keel in American yachts, capable of being raised and lowered in a well extending longitudinally amidships, to prevent leeway.—**centerpiece,** *n.* An ornament intended to be placed in the middle or center of something, as of a table.

centesimal, sen•tes′i•mal, *a.* [L. *centesimus*, hundredth.] Pertaining to division into a hundred parts.—**centesimally,** *adv.* By division into hundreds.

centigrade, sen′ti•grād, *a.* [From L. *centum*, a hundred, *gradus*, a degree.] Consisting of a hundred degrees; graduated into a hundred divisions or equal parts; pertaining to the scale which is divided into a hundred degrees.—*Centigrade thermometer*, a thermometer which divides the interval between the freezing and boiling points of water into 100 degrees, while in Fahrenheit's thermometer the same interval is divided into 180 degrees.

centime, sän•tēm′ or sän′tēm, *n.* [Fr.] French coin, the hundredth part of a franc.

centimeter, sen′ti•mē•tr, *n.* [Fr. *centimètre*, from L. *centum*, a hundred, and Gr. *metron*, measure.] A metric measure of length, the hundredth part of a meter; rather more than 0.39 of an inch.—**centimeter-gram-second,** *a.* Pertaining to a system of measurement in which the centimeter is the unit of length, the gram is the unit of mass, and the second (1/86,400 of the mean solar day) is the unit of time.

centipede, sen′ti•pēd, *n.* [L. *centipeda*—*centum*, a hundred, and *pes*, *pedis*, a foot.] A term applied to various long, flatbodied animals having many feet, popularly called insects, but belonging to the Myriapoda.

Centner, sent′nėr, *n.* [G., from L. *centenarius*, from *centum*, a hundred.] A name in several European countries for a weight nearly equivalent to a hundredweight.

cento, sen′tō, *n.* [L. *cento*, patchwork, a poem made up of selections from different poems.] A composition (whether literary or musical) made up of selections from the works of various authors or composers.

centrifugal sen•trif′ū•gal, *a.* [L. *centrum*, a center, and *fugio*, to flee.] Tending to recede from the center; acting by or depending on centrifugal force or action; *bot.* expanding first at the summit and later at the base, as an inflorescence.—*Centrifugal force*, that force by which all bodies moving round another body in a curve tend to fly off at any point of their motion in the direction of a tangent to the curve.—**centripetal,** sen•trip′e•tal, *a.* [L. *centrum*, a center, and *peto*, to seek.] Tending toward the center; progressing by changes from the exterior of an object to its center.—*Centripetal force* is that force which draws a body toward a center, and thereby acts as a counterpoise to the centrifugal force in circular motion.

centrosome, sen′tro•sōm, *n.* [L. *centrum*, centre, *soma*, a body.] In cells, a minute particle outside the nucleus which plays an active part in indirect division.

centuple, sen′tū•pl, *a.* [L. *centuplus*—*centum*, a hundred, and root of *plica*, a fold.] Multiplied or increased a hundredfold.—*v.t.*—*centupled, centupling*. To multiply a hundredfold.—**centuplicate,** sen•tū′•pli•kāt, *v.t.*—*centuplicated, centuplicating*. [L. *centum*, and *plicatus*, folded.] To make a hundredfold; to repeat a hundred times.

century, sen′tū•ri, *n.* [L. *centuria*, from *centum*, a hundred.] An aggregate of a hundred; anything consisting of a hundred in number; a period of a hundred years; often such a period reckoned from the birth of Christ.—**centurial,**†sen•tū′ri•al,*a.*[L. *centurialis.*] Relating to or occurring once in a century.—**centurion,** sen•-tū′ri•on, *n.* [L. *centurio*, from *centum*, a hundred.] In ancient Rome a military officer who commanded a century or company of infantry consisting of a hundred men.

Cephalata, sef•a•lā′ta, *n. pl.* [Gr. *kephalē*, the head.] A division of mollusks which have a distinct head, with eyes, as the gasteropods, cuttlefishes, etc.—**cephalate,** sef′al•āt, *n.* A mollusk of the division Cephalata.

cephalic, se•fal′ik, *a.* [Gr. *kephalikos*, from *kephalē*, the head.] Pertaining to the head.—*n.* A medicine for headache or other disorder in the head.—**cephalic index,** *n.* A number denoting the ratio of the transverse to the longitudinal (front to back) diameter of the skull, and according to which skulls and races of people are called brachycephalic or dolichocephalic.—**cephalitis,** sef•a•lī′tis, *n.* [The term. *-itis* signifies inflammation.] Inflammation of the brain.—**cephalous,** sef′a•lus, *a.* Having a head: applied specifically to the cephalates.

cephalopod, sef′a•lo•pod, *n.* [Gr. *kephalē*, a head, and *pous*, *podos*, a foot.] Any member of the class Cephalopoda.—**Cephalopoda,** sef•a•-lop′o•da, *n. pl.* A class of mollusks, the highest in organization, characterized by having the organs of prehension and locomotion, called tentacles or arms, attached to the head, and including the cuttlefishes, squids, ammonites, etc.

cephalothorax, sef′a•lo•thō″raks, *n.* [Gr. *kephalē*, the head, and *thōrax*, the thorax.] The anterior division of the body in crustaceans, spiders, scorpions, etc., which consists of the head and thorax blended together.

ceraceous, si•rā′shus, *a.* [L. *ceraceus*, waxy, from *cera*, wax.] *Bot.* waxy: a term applied to bodies which have the texture and color of new wax.

ceramic, se•ram′ik, *a.* [Gr. *keramikos*, from *keramos*, potter's clay, a piece of pottery.] Of or belonging to the fictile arts or pottery; pertaining to the manufacture of porcelain and earthenware.—**ceramics,** se•ram′iks, *n.* The art of the potter; pottery.

cerate, sē′rāt, *n.* [L. *ceratum*, from cera, wax.] A thick kind of ointment composed of wax, lard, or oil, with other ingredients, applied externally in various diseases.

ceratite, ser′a•tīt, *n.* [Gr. *keras*, *keratos*, a horn.] A genus of fossil cephalopods, allied to and resembling the ammonites.—**ceratodus,** se•rat′-o•dus, *n.* [Gr. *keras*, horn, *odous*, tooth.] A fish of Australia, one of the few that have lungs, said to be able to leave the water for some time.

Cerberus, sėr′ber•us, *n.* [L.] *Class. myth.* the three-headed watchdog of the infernal regions; hence, any watchful and dreaded guardian.—**Cerberean,** sėr•bē′rē•an, *a.* Relating to Cerberus.

cere, sēr, *n.* [L. *cera*, wax; from its appearance.] The term applied to the space destitute of feathers, and having a waxy appearance, generally observed at the base of the bill in birds.

cereal, si′rē•al, *a.* [From *Ceres*, the goddess of corn.] Pertaining to edible grain, as wheat, rye, barley, oats, corn, rice, millet.—*n.* A grain plant, such as wheat, oats, barley, etc.

cerebellum, ser•e•bel′lum, *n.* [L. dim. of *cerebrum*, the brain.] The little brain; that portion of the brain in vertebrate animals which is posterior to and underlies the great cerebral mass or cerebrum.—**cerebellar,** ser•e•bel′lėr, *a.* Relating to the cerebellum.—**cerebral, cerebric,** ser′e•bral, se•rē′brik, *a.* Pertaining to the cerebrum or brain.—*Cerebral letters*, in *philol.* certain consonants in the Sanskrit alphabet, formed by bringing the tip of the tongue backward and applying its under surface against the roof of the mouth. —**cerebrate,** sėr′e•brāt, *v.i.* To have the brain in action; to exhibit brain action.—**cerebration,** sėr•e•brā′shon, *n.* Exertion or action of the brain, conscious or unconscious—**cerebrospinal,** se•rē′brō•spī″nal, *a.* Pertaining to the brain and spinal cord together; consisting in the brain and spinal cord.—**cerebrospinal meningitis,** men′in•jīt″is, *n.* [Gr. *meninx*, *meningos*, a membrane, *-itis*, inflammation.] Spotted fever; a virulent bacterial disease, associated with inflammation of the membranes covering the brain and spinal cord. —**cerebrum,** ser′e•brum, *n.* [L.] The superior and chief portion of the brain, occupying the whole upper cavity of the skull.

cerecloth, cerement, sēr′kloth, sēr′ment, *n.* [L. *cera*, wax.] Cloth dipped in melted wax, with which dead bodies are enfolded when embalmed; hence, *pl.* graveclothes (poetical).

ceremony, ser′e•mo•ni, *n.* [Fr. *cérémonie*, from L. *cærimonia*, a rite or ceremony, veneration, sanctity; probably from same root as Skr. *kri*, *kar*, to do.] A religious or other rite or observance; a solemn or formal display or performance; a solemnity; a usage of politeness, or such usages collectively; formality; punctilio; punctiliousness.—*Master of ceremonies*, a person who regulates the forms to be observed by the company or attendants on a public occasion. —**ceremonial,** ser•e•mō′ni•al, *a.* [L. *cærimonialis*.] Relating to ceremonies or external forms or rites; ritual; pertaining to the forms and rites of the Jewish religion (the *ceremonial* law).—*n.* A system of rites; ceremonies or formalities to be observed on any occasion.—**ceremonialism,** ser•e•mō′ni•al•izm, *n.* Adherence to or fondness for ceremony.—**ceremonially,** ser•e•mō′ni•al•li, *adv.* In a ceremonial manner; according to rites and ceremonies.—**ceremonialness,** ser•e•mō′ni•al•nes, *n.*—**ceremonious,** ser•e•mō′ni•us, *a.* Full of ceremony; accompanied with rites; according to prescribed or customary formalities or punctilios; formally respectful or polite; observant of conventional forms; fond of using ceremony.—**ceremoniously,** ser•e•mō′ni•us•li, *adv.* In a ceremonious manner; formally; with due forms.—**ceremoniousness,** ser•e•mō′ni•us•nes, *n.* The quality of being ceremonious; the practice of much ceremony; formality.

Ceres, sē′rēz, *n.* A Roman goddess watching over the growth of grain and other plants; hence, grain; also a name of one of the asteroids or planetoids.

cerise, se•rēz′, *n.* [Fr., a cherry.] Cherry-color.—*a.* Of the color of cerise; cherry-colored.

cerium, sē′ri•um, *a.* [From the planet *Ceres*, discovered a year or two before.] A malleable, ductile, metallic element of the rare-earth series. Symbol, Ce; at. no., 58; at. wt., 140.12.—**cerite,** sē′rīt, *n.* A rare mineral, of a pale rose-red color, from which cerium was first obtained.

cermet, sėr″met′, *n.* A strong heat-resistant alloy, for example, nickel and titanium.

cernuous, sėr′nū•us, *a.* [L. *cernuus*.] *Bot.* drooping; pendulous.

ceroplastic, sē•ro•plas′tik, *a.* [Gr. *kēros*, wax, and *plastikē* (*techné*), the art of the modeler or carver.] Pertaining to the art of modeling in wax; modeled in wax.—*n.* The art of modeling or of forming models in wax.

certain, sėr′tin, *a.* [Fr. *certain*, as if from a L. adjective *certanus*, formed from *certus*, certain, by adding suffix *-anus*. *Certus* is connected with *cerno*, *certum*, to distinguish, dis*cern*.] Sure; undoubtedly true; established as a fact; undoubtedly existing or impending (death, danger); capable of being counted or depended on; unfailing; infallible; of things (a sign, a remedy); capable of being counted upon or able to count on; of persons (he is *certain* to be there, you are *certain* to find him); assured in mind; free from doubt; having no doubt or suspicion regarding: often with *of;* stated; fixed; determinate; definite (a *certain* rate); not specifically named; indefinite; one or some (a *certain* person, a *certain* pleasure in something).—*For certain*, certainly.—**certainly,** sėr′tin•li, *adv.* Without doubt or question; in truth and fact; without fail; assuredly; of a certainty.—**certainty,** sėr′tin•ti, *n.* The fact of being certain; exemption from failure to happen or produce the natural result; a fact or truth certainly established; that which cannot be questioned; full assurance of mind; exemption from doubt.—**certify,** sėr′ti•fī, *v.t.*—*certified*, *certifying*. [Fr. *certifier*, from L.L. *certifico*, to certify—L. *certus*, certain, and *facio*, to make.] To assure or make certain; to give certain information *to* (a person); to give certain information *of;* to make clear or definite; to testify to in writing; to make known or establish as a fact.—**certificate,** sėr•tif′i•kit, *n.* [Fr. *certificat*.] A written testimony to the truth of a certain fact or facts; a testimonial; a legally authenticated voucher or testimony of certain facts; sometimes a kind of license.—*v.t.* To give a certificate to, as to one who has passed an examination; to attest or certify by certificate.—**certification,** sėr′ti•fi•kā″shon, *n.* The act of certifying.—**certifier,** sėr′ti•fī•ėr, *n.* One who certifies.—**certiorari,** sėr′shi•o•râ″rī, *n.* [Lit. to be informed of, L.L. *certioro*, to inform, from L. *certus*, certain.] *Law*, a writ to call up the records of an inferior court or remove a cause there depending, that it may be tried in a superior court.—**certitude,** sėr′ti•tūd, *n.* [L.L. *certitudo*.] Certainty; assurance; freedom from doubt.

cerulean, sē•rö′lē•an, *a.* [L. *cæruleus*, azure, for *cæluleus*, sky-colored, from *cælum*, the sky.] Sky-colored; azure; blue.

cerumen, se•rö′men, *n.* [From L. *cera*, wax.] The wax or yellow matter secreted by certain glands lying in the external canal of the ear.—**ceruminous,** sē•rö′mi•nus, *a.* Relating to or containing cerumen.

ceruse, sē′rös, *n.* [Fr., from L. *cerussa*, white lead, from *cera*, wax.] White lead, composed of hydroxide and carbonate of lead, produced by exposing the metal in thin plates to the vapor of vinegar. It is much used in painting, and a cosmetic is prepared from it.—*v.t.* To wash with ceruse; to apply ceruse to as a cosmetic.—**cerussite,** se′rṵs•īt, *n.* A native carbonate of lead; a common lead ore.

cervical, sėr′vi•kal, *a.* [L. *cervix*, *cervicis*, the neck.] Belonging to the neck.

cervine, sėr′vīn, *a.* [L. *cervinus*, from *cervus*, a deer.] Pertaining to the deer family.

Cesarean, Cesarian, si•zâ′rē•an, si•zä′ri•an, *n.* See CAESAREAN.

cesium, sē′zi•um, *n.* The most electropositive of the elements. Symbol, Cs; at. no., 55; at. wt., 132.905.

cespitose, ses′pi•tōs, *a.* [L. *caespes*, *cespitis*, turf.] Pertaining to turf; turfy; *bot.* growing in tufts.

cess, ses, *v.t.* [Shortened and corrupted from *assess*.] To impose a tax; to assess.—*n.* A rate or tax. (Colloq.)

cessation, ses•sā′shon, *n.* [L. *cessatio*, from *cesso*, from *cedo*, *cessum*, to cease. CEDE.] A ceasing; a stop; a rest; the act of discontinuing motion or action of any kind, whether temporary or final.

cession, sesh′on, *n.* [L. *cessio*, from L. *cedo*, *cessum*. CEDE.] The act of ceding, yielding, or surrendering, as of territory, property, or rights; a giving up, resignation, or surrender.

cesspool, ses′pöl, *n.* [The better spelling seems to be *sess-pool*, the word being from A.Sax. *sessian*, to settle; or from prov. *soss*, *suss*, a mess. filth; Gael. *sos*.] A cavity or well in a drain or privy to receive the sediment or filth.

cestoid, ses′toid, *a.* [L. *cestus*, a girdle, from their shape.] A term used to characterize certain intestinal worms, such as tapeworms.

cestus, ses′tus, *n.* [L. *cestus*, *cæstus*, from *cædo*, *cæsum*, to strike.] Among the Greeks and Romans, a kind of boxing glove, loaded with lead or iron, which boxers fastened on their hands and arms by leather thongs.

cesura. See CAESURA.

Cetacea, si•tā′sha, *n. pl.* [L. *cetus*, Gr. *kēto*, any large sea monster, a whale.] An order of marine mammals comprising the whales and dolphins.—**cetacean,** si•tā′shan, *n.* An animal of the order Cetacea.—**cetaceous,** si•tā′shus, *a.* Pertaining to the whale; belonging to the Cetacea or whale kind.

C.G.S. The standard contraction for the centimeter=gram=second system of units now in universal use for scientific purposes: named from the fundamental units of length, mass, and time.

Chablis, shab'lē, *n.* A celebrated white French wine, having good body and an exquisite perfume, so called from the town of that name near which it is produced.

chabouk, chabuk, cha•bụk', *n.* [Hind. *chabuk*, a horsewhip.] A long whip; the whip used in the East for inflicting corporal punishment.

chacma, chak'ma, *n.* A baboon found in South Africa.

chafe, chāf, *v.t.*—*chafed, chafing.* [O.E. *chaufe*, Fr. *chauffer*, O.Fr. *chaufer*, to warm, from L. *calefacere*, to warm, from *caleo*, to grow warm, and *facere*, to make.] To excite heat in (some part of the body) by friction: to stimulate to warmth by rubbing; to excite the passions of; to inflame; to anger; to excite violent action in; to cause to rage (the wind *chafes* the ocean); to fret and wear by rubbing (the rope was *chafed*).—*v.i.* To be excited or heated; to rage; to fret; to dash, as in anger; to rage or boil (as the sea); to be fretted and worn by rubbing.—*n.* A state of being angry or annoyed; heat; fret.—**chafer,** chā'fėr, *n.* One who or that which chafes; a chafing-dish.—**chafing dish,** *n.* A dish or vessel to hold coals for heating anything set on it or for cooking.

chafer, chā'fėr, *n.* [A.Sax. *ceafor*, a chafer: D. *kever*, G. *käfer*, a beetle.] A beetle: especially applied to such as are destructive to plants, and generally in compounds; as, cock-*chafer*, rose-*chafer*, bark-*chafer*, etc.

chaff, chaf, *n.* [A.Sax. *ceaf*=D. *kaf*, G. *kaff*, chaff.] The glumes or husks of corn and grasses, but more commonly restricted to the husks when separated from the corn by thrashing, sifting, or winnowing; worthless matter, especially that which is light and apt to be driven by the wind; refuse.—**chaffy,** chaf'i, *a.* Like chaff; full of chaff; light; frivolous; worthless.

chaff, chaf, *v.t.* and *i.* [A corruption of *chafe*, to irritate or annoy.] To assail with sarcastic banter or raillery; to banter; to make game of. (Colloq.)—*n.* Banter, especially slangy banter; sarcastic raillery. (Colloq.)—**chaffer,** chaf'ėr, *n.* One who employs chaff or slangy banter. (Colloq.)

chaffer, chaf'ėr, *v.i.* [O.E. *chapfare, chaffare*, bargaining, merchandise, from *chap*, A.Sax. *ceáp*, a bargain, and *fare*, procedure, journey, A.Sax. *faru*, a journey. Akin *cheap, cheapen*. CHEAP.] To treat about a purchase; to bargain; to haggle; to talk much and idly.—**chafferer,** chaf'ėr•ėr. *n.* One who chaffers; a bargainer; a buyer.

chaffinch, chaf'finsh, *n.* [Perhaps from its note; comp. *chiff-chaff*, the name of a British bird, from its cry.] A European bird of the finch family.

chagrin, sha•grin', *n.* [Fr., said to be another form of *shagreen*, which from being used to polish wood, has come to be employed as a type of grinding or gnawing care.] Ill humor, as from disappointment, wounded vanity, etc., vexation; peevishness; mortification, fretfulness.—*v.t.* To excite ill humor in; to vex; to mortify.

chain, chān, *n.* [Fr. *chaîne*, O.Fr. *chaene, cadene*, from L. *catena*, a chain.] A series of links or rings connected or fitted into one another, generally of some kind of metal, and used for various purposes; *fig.* that which binds, restrains, confines, or fetters; a bond; a fetter; bondage; slavery: in this sense often in the plural (the *chains* of evil habit); a series of things linked together; a series, line, or range of things connected or following in succession (*chain* of causes, events, etc.); *weaving*, the warp threads of a web, so called because they form a long series of links or loops; *pl. naut.* strong links or plates of iron bolted to a ship's sides, and forming part of the attachments of the shrouds; *surv.* a measuring instrument, generally consisting of 100 links, and having a total length of 66 feet.—*v.t.* To fasten, bind, restrain, or fetter with a chain or chains; to put in chains; to restrain; to hold in control; to unite firmly; to link.—**chain gang,** *n.* A gang of convicts chained together.—**chain mail,** *n.* Flexible armor of linked metal rings.—**chain reaction,** *n.* Any series of events each of which is initiated by a preceding one; *phys.* a nuclear reaction that continues automatically and becomes self-sustaining once started.—**chain saw,** *n.* A power saw that has teeth on a continuous band or chain.—**chain shot,** *n.* Two cannon balls connected by a chain, formerly much used in naval warfare for carrying away rigging.—**chain-stitch,** *n.* Sewing consisting of threads or cords linked together in the form of a chain; also, a kind of machine sewing, which consists in looping the upper thread into itself on the under side of the fabric, or in using a second thread to engage the loop of the upper thread: in contradistinction to *lock stitch*.

chair, châr, *n.* [Fr. *chaire*, O.Fr. *chayere*, L. *cathedra*, Gr. *kathedra*, a seat. CATHEDRAL. *Chaise* is a corruption of *chaire*.] A movable seat, with a back, for one person; a seat of office or authority; hence, the office itself, especially the office of a professor, and sometimes the person occupying the chair; a chairman or president; a sedan chair; one of the iron blocks which support and secure the rails in a railroad.—*v.t.* To place or carry in a chair; to carry publicly in a chair in triumph.—**chairman,** châr'man, *n.* The presiding officer of an assembly, association, or company, committee or public meeting; one whose business is to carry a sedan chair.—**chairmanship,** châr'man•ship, *n.* The office of a chairman.

chaise, shāz, *n.* [Fr., a corruption of *chaire*, a chair.] A two-wheeled carriage drawn by one or more horses.—**chaise longue,** shāz•long, *n.* [Fr. long chair.] A long couchlike seat with a back at one end.

chalaza, ka•lā'za, *n.* [Gr. *chalaza*, a pimple.] *Bot.* that part of the ovule or seed where the integuments cohere with each other and with the nucleus; *zool.* one of the two membranous twisted cords which bind the yolk bag of an egg to the lining membrane at the two ends of the shell.

chalcedony, kal•sed'o•ni, *n.* [From *Chalcedon*, an ancient Greek town in Asia Minor.] A kind of quartz, resembling milk diluted with water, and more or less clouded or opaque, with veins, circles, and spots.

chalcography, kal•kog'ra•fi, *n.* [Gr. *chalkos*, copper, brass, and *graphō*, to engrave.] The art of engraving on copper or brass.—**chalcographer, chalcographist,** kal•kog'raf•ėr, kal•kog'raf•ist. *n.* An engraver on brass or copper.—**chalcographic,** kal•ko•graf'ik, *a.* Pertaining to chalcography.

Chaldaic, Chaldean, Chaldee, kal•dā'ik, kal•dē'an, kal'dē, *a.* Pertaining to Chaldea or Chaldæa, anciently a country on the Euphrates in Asia.—*n.* The language or dialect of the Chaldeans; Aramaic.

chalet, shal'ā, *n.* [Fr.; properly a Swiss word.] A cottage, cabin, or hut for sheltering the herdsmen and their cattle in the Swiss mountains; a small dwelling house built in a similar style.

chalice, chal'is, *n.* [Fr. *calice*, from L. *calix, calicis*, a cup or goblet.] A drinking cup or bowl, a cup used to administer the wine in the celebration of the Lord's supper.

chalk, chạk, *n.* [A.Sax. *cealc*, from L. *calx*, lime, limestone.] A well-known earthy limestone, an impure carbonate of lime of an opaque white color, soft, and admitting no polish.—*v.t.* To rub with chalk; to mark with chalk; to trace out; to describe: from the use of chalk in making lines.—*Black chalk.* See under BLACK.—*Brown chalk*, a name for umber.—*Red chalk*, a natural clay containing 15 to 20 per cent of protoxide and carbonate of iron.—*French chalk*, steatite or soapstone.—**chalky,** chạ'ki, *a.* Resembling chalk; consisting of or containing chalk.—**chalkstones,** *n.* Certain concretions in the joints of persons violently affected by the gout.

challenge, chal'lenj, *n.* [O.Fr. *chalenge, calenge, calonge*, etc., claim, accusation, dispute, from L. *calumnia*, a false accusation, a calumny. *Calumny* is thus the same word.] An invitation to a contest or trial of any kind; a calling or summons to fight in a single combat; the letter or message containing the summons to a contest; the calling in question or taking exception to something; the act of a sentry in demanding the countersign from any one who appears near his post; the claim of a party that certain jurors shall not sit in trial upon him or his cause, a right given both in civil and criminal trials when the impartiality of the jurors may be reasonably questioned.—*v.t.*—*challenged, challenging.* To address a challenge to; to call to a contest; to summon to fight, or to a duel; to demand the countersign or password from: said of a sentry; to claim as due, to demand as a right; *law,* to demand the removal of from among the jurymen; to object to (a person or thing); to take exception to; to call in question (a statement).—**challengeable,** chal′-len•ja•bl, *a.* Capable of being challenged or called to an account.—**challenger,** chal′len•jėr, *n.* One who challenges; one who defies another to a contest; an objector; one who calls in question.

chalybeate, ka•lib′ē•āt, *a.* [From Gr. *chalyps, chalybos,* steel.] Impregnated with iron: applied to medicines containing iron, and especially to springs and waters impregnated with iron, or holding iron in solution.—*n.* Any water or other liquid into which iron enters.

cham,‡ kam, *n.* The sovereign prince of Tartary: now written *Khan.*

chamade, sha•mäd′ or sha•mäd′, *n.* [Fr., from It. *chiamata,* a calling, *chiamare,* to call, from L. *clamare,* to call = E. *claim.*] The beat of a drum or sound of a trumpet inviting an enemy to a parley.

chamber, chām′bėr, *n.* [Fr. *chambre,* from L. *camera,* Gr. *kamara,* a vault or arched roof.] A room of a dwelling house; an apartment; a room where professional men, as lawyers, conduct their business; especially the room in which judges sit for the disposing of matters not sufficiently important to be heard in court; a hall or place where an assembly, association, or body of men meets; the assembly or body itself, as a *chamber* of commerce or of agriculture; a hollow or cavity in a thing, especially when of definite form and use; the part of a pump in which the bucket or plunger works; that part of a firearm where the powder lies.—*v.i.* To reside in or occupy as a chamber; to indulge in wantonness‡.— *v.t.* To shut up in, or as in, a chamber. (*Shak*).—**chambered,** chām′bėrd, *a.* Having or divided into a number of chambers or compartments.—**chamberer,** chām′bėr•ėr, *n.* One who intrigues or indulges in wantonness; a gallant. (*Shak.*).—**chamberlain,** chām′bėr•lin, *n.* [O.Fr. *chamberlain,* from O.H.G. *chamarling, chamarlinc—chamar,* chamber, and suffix *-ling.*] A person charged with the direction and management of a chamber or chambers; specifically, an officer charged with the direction and management of the private apartments of a monarch or nobleman; the treasurer of a city, corporation, or the like.—**chambermaid,** *n.* A woman who has the care of chambers, making the beds and cleaning the rooms.—**chamber pot,** *n.* A vessel for urine and other wastes, used in bedrooms.

chameleon, ka•mē′lē•on, *n.* [Gr. *chamaileōn—chamai,* on the ground, and *leōn,* lion; lit. ground-lion.] An insectivorous lizard, having a naked body, a prehensile tail, four feet suited for grasping branches, and the eye covered by a single circular eyelid with an aperture in the center. It has long been remarkable for its faculty of changing its color; and its powers of fasting and inflating itself gave rise to the notion that it lived on air.

chamfer, cham′fėr, *n.* [Fr. *chanfrein,* a chamfer.] A small gutter or furrow cut in wood or other hard material; a bevel or slope; the corner of anything originally right-angled cut aslope equally on the two sides which form it.—*v.t.* To cut a chamfer in or on; to flute; to channel; to cut or grind so as to form a bevel.

chamfron, cham′fron, *n.* [O.Fr. *chamfrein,* from *champ,* field, battlefield, and *frein,* L. *frenum,* a bridle.] The defensive armor for the fore part of the head of a war horse.

chamois, shäm•wä′ or sham′i, *n.* [Fr.] A species of goatlike antelope inhabiting high inaccessible mountains in Europe and Western Asia, about the size of a wellgrown goat, and extremely agile; a kind of soft leather made from various skins dressed with fish oil; so called because first prepared from the skin of the chamois: in this sense often written *Shammy.*

champ, champ, *v.t.* [From O.Fr. *champayer,* to graze, from *champ,* L. *campus,* a field, or a modification of obsolete *cham,* to chew.] To bite with repeated action of the teeth and with a snapping noise; to bite into small pieces; to chew; to munch; to craunch.

champagne, sham•pān′, *n.* A kind of light sparkling wine made chiefly in the department of Marne, in the former province of *Champagne,* in France.

champaign, sham•pān′, *n.* [O.Fr. *champaigne,* from *champ,* L. *campus,* a field. CAMPAIGN.] A flat open country.—*a.* Level; open; having the character of a plain.

champignon, sham•pin′yon, *n.* [Fr., a mushroom, from L.L. *campinio,* what grows in fields, from L. *campus,* a field.] A name for two edible mushrooms, one the common mushroom, the other a species growing in fairy rings.

champion, cham′pi•on, *n.* [Fr. *champion,* L.L. *campio, campionis,* a champion, from L. *campus,* a field, later a combat, duel.] One who comes forward in defense of any cause; especially one who engages in single combat in the cause of another; more generally, a hero; a brave warrior; one who has acknowledged superiority in certain matters decided by public contest or competition; one open to contend with all comers, or otherwise required to resign the title.—*v.t.* To challenge to a combat; to come forward and maintain or support (a cause or a person).—**championship,** cham′pi•on•ship, *n.* State of being a champion; support or maintenance of a cause.

chance, chans, *n.* [Fr. *chance,* chance, hazard, from L.L. *cadentia,* a falling (E. *cadence*), from L. *cadere,* to fall; in allusion to the falling of the dice.] A casual or fortuitous event; an accident; that which is regarded as determining the course of events in the absence of law, ordinary causation, or providence (to happen by *chance*); accident; what fortune may bring; fortune; possibility of an occurrence; opportunity (to lose a *chance*).—*v.i.* To happen; to fall out; to come or arrive without design or expectation.—*v.t.* To put under the influence of chance; to risk; to hazard.—*a.* Happening by chance; casual.—**chanceful,**† chans′fụl, *a.* Full of chances or accidents; hazardous.—**chance-medley,** *n.* Originally, a casual affray or riot, without deliberate or premeditated malice; now, the killing of another in self-defense upon a sudden and unpremeditated encounter.

chancel, chan′sel, *n.* [So named from being railed off from the rest of the church by lattice-work—L. *cancelli.* CANCEL.] That part of the choir of a church between the altar or communion table and the balustrade or railing that encloses it, or that part where the altar is placed.—**chancellor,** chan′sel•ėr, *n.* [L.L. *cancellarius,* from L. *cancelli,* a lattice-work railing, from the chancellor formerly standing *ad cancellos* (at the latticed railing), to receive petitions, etc.] A state official in various European states, invested with judicial powers, and particularly with the superintendence of charters, letters, and other official writings of the government, varying in degree of political importance and responsibility. In the ecclesiastical sense, the chancellor of a cathedral is an official who superintends arrangements for religious ceremonies and services. The head of some universities; as the *chancellor* of McGill University, or of the University of Kansas. The usual title of university heads in the United States is *president.* In U. S. law courts, a judge in a court of chancery or equity; especially the presiding judge as distinguished from the vice-chancellors. — **chancellorship,** chan′sel•ėr•ship, *n.* The office of a chancellor.

chancery, chan′se•ri, *n.* [Modified from older *chancelry,* from Fr. *chancellerie.* CHANCELLOR.] A court or department of public affairs at the head of which is a chancellor; in England, formerly the highest court of justice next to parliament, but since 1873 a division of the High Court of Justice, which is itself one of the two departments of the Supreme Court of Judicature.

chancre, shang′kėr, *n.* [Fr. = *canker.*] A sore or ulcer which arises from the direct application of the venereal virus.—**chancrous,** shangk′rus, *a.* Having the qualities of a chancre; ulcerous; affected with ulcers.

chandelier, shan•de•lēr′, *n.* [Fr. *chandelier*, a chandelier, from L. *candela*, a candle. CANDLE.] A stand with branches to hold a number of candles, to light up a room.

chandler, chand′lėr, *n.* [Fr. *chandelier*, a dealer in candles, from L. *candela*, a candle.] One who makes or sells candles; a dealer in general: the particular meaning of the term being determined by a prefix; as, tallow-*chandler;* ship-*chandler*, etc. —**chandlery,** chand′lėr•i, *n.* The commodities sold by a chandler; a chandler's warehouse; a storeroom for candles.

change, chānj, *v.t.—changed, changing.* [Fr. *changer*, to change, from L.L. *cambiare*, from L. *cambire*, to change, to barter.] To cause to turn or pass from one state to another; to vary in form or essence; to alter or make different; to substitute another thing or things for (to *change* the clothes); to shift; to give or procure another kind of money for (to *change* a bank note); to give away for a money equivalent of a different kind; to exchange (to *change* places with a person).—*v.i.* To suffer change; to be altered; to undergo variation; to be partially or wholly transformed; to begin a new revolution, or to pass from one phase to another, as the moon.—*n.* Any variation or alteration in form, state, quality, or essence; a passing from one state or form to another; a succession of one thing in the place of another (*change* of seasons); the passing from one phase of the moon to another; alteration in the order of a series; permutation; that which makes a variety or may be substituted for another (two *changes* of clothes); small money, which may be given for larger pieces; the balance of a sum of money returned when the price of goods is deducted; a place where merchants and others meet to transact business: in this sense an abbreviation for *Exchange*, and often written *Change*.—**changeable,** chān′ja•bl, *a.* Liable to change; subject to alteration; fickle; inconstant; mutable; variable. — **changeableness, changeability,** chān′ja•bl•nes, chān•ja•bil′i•ti, *n.* The quality of being changeable.—**changeably,** chān′ja•bli, *adv.* In a changeable manner.—**changeful,** chānj′fụl, *a.* Full of change; inconstant; mutable; fickle; uncertain; subject to alteration.—**changefully,** chānj′fụl•li, *adv.* In a changeful manner.—**changefulness,** chānj′fụl•nes, *n.*—**changeless,** chānj′les, *a.* Constant; not admitting alteration.—**changeling,** chānj′ling, *n.* A child, often a deformed or stupid child supposed to be substituted by fairies for another.—**changer,** chānj′ėr, *n.* One who changes or alters the form of anything; one that is employed in changing and discounting money; a moneychanger; one given to change; one who is inconstant or fickle.

channel, chan′el, *n.* [From O.Fr. *chanel*, *canel*, L. *canalis*, a water pipe; whence also *canal* and *kennel*, a gutter.] The bed of a stream of water; the hollow or course in which a stream flows; the deeper part of an estuary, bay, etc., where the current flows, or which is most convenient for the track of a ship; a strait or narrow sea between two islands, two continents, or a continent and an island; that by which something passes or is transmitted (as news, information); means of passing, conveying, or transmitting; a furrow or groove.—*v.t.—channeled, channeling.* To form a channel in; to cut channels in; to groove. (*Shak.*)

channel, chan′el, *n.* [A corruption of *chain-wale*.] One of the pieces of plank projecting edgewise from a ship's sides and over which the shrouds are extended to keep them clear of the gunwale.

chant, chänt, *v.t.* [Fr. *chanter*, from L. *cantare*, aug. of *cano*, *cantum*, to sing. Akin *cant*.] To utter with a melodious voice; to warble; to sing; to celebrate in song; to repeat the words of, in a kind of intoning voice or in a style between air and recitative.—*v.i.* To sing; to make melody with the voice; to intone, or perform a chant.—*n.* A song or singing; melody; specifically, a short musical composition consisting generally of a long reciting note, on which an indefinite number of words may be intoned, and a melodic phrase or cadence.—**chanter,** chän′tėr, *n.* One who chants; a singer or songster; in bagpipes, the tube with finger holes for playing the melody.—**chanticleer,** chan′ti•klēr, *n.* [From *chant* and *clear*.] A cock, so called from the clearness or loudness of his voice in crowing.—**chantress,**† chänt′res, *n.* A female singer. (*Mil.*)—**chantry,** chän′tri, *n.* [O.Fr. *chanterie*, from *chant*.] A church or chapel endowed for the maintenance of one or more priests daily to sing or say mass for the souls of the donors or such as they appoint.

chanterelle, shan•trel′ or shan•tėr•el′, *n.* [Fr., perhaps from O.Fr. *chanterelle*, a small bell, from its shape, from *chanter*, to sing.] An English edible mushroom, having a bright orange color, a fragrant fruity smell, and being found frequently in woods under trees.

chaos, kā′os, *n.* [Gr. *chaos*, from a root *cha*, to gape, to yawn, whence also *chasm*.] That confusion or confused mass out of which the universe was created; a confused mixture of parts or elements; a scene of extreme confusion; disorder.—**chaotic,** kā•ot′ik, *a.* Resembling chaos; confused. —**chaotically,** kā•ot′ik•al•li, *adv.* In a chaotic state.

chap, chap or chop, *v.t.—chapped, chapping.* [Same word as *chop*, to cut.] To cause to cleave, split, crack, or open longitudinally, as the surface of the earth or the skin and flesh of the hand.—*v.i.* To crack; to open in long slits; to have the skin become cracked and sore, as from frost. *n.* A crack in the surface of the hands or feet.

chap, chop, chop, *n.* [A form standing for *chaf* or *chof*, and equivalent to Sc. *chäft*, Icel. *kjaptr*, Dan. *kjaeft*, Sw. *kaft*, a jaw, without the *t*.] The upper or lower part of the mouth; the jaw; either of the two planes or flat parts of a vise or pair of tongs or pliers, for holding anything fast.—**chapfallen,** chop′fạ•ln, *a.* Having the lower chap or jaw depressed; hence, dejected or dispirited; silenced.

chap, chap, *n.* [An abbrev. of *chapman;* as regards its modern use compare *customer*, in senses of regular purchaser and fellow or chap.] A buyer‡; a chapman (*Steele*)‡; a man or a boy; a youth: used familiarly and laxly, much as the word *fellow* is.—**chapbook,** *n.* A kind of small book or tract formerly much sold among the people by chapmen, containing generally lives of heroes, giants, etc., fairy lore, ghost and witch stories, ballads, songs, and the like.

chape, chāp, *n.* [Fr. *chape*, a catch, hook, chape, also a *cope;* same origin as *cape*, *cap*.] The part by which an object is attached, as the back piece by which a buckle is fixed on the article or garment; the transverse guard of a sword for a protection to the hand; the metal tip at the end of a scabbard, or at the end of a belt or girdle.

chapel, chap′el, *n.* [Fr. *chapelle*, from L.L. *capella*, dim. of *capa*, a cape, hood, canopy, covering of the altar, a recess or chapel attached to the altar. CAP, CAPE, CHAPLET.] A subordinate place of worship usually attached to a large church or cathedral, connected with a palace or private residence, or subsidiary to a parish church; a place of worship used by dissenters from the Church of England; a meetinghouse; a union or society formed by the workmen in a printing office; printing office, from Caxton's establishment in Westminster Abbey.

chaperon, shap′ėr•ōn or shap•ron, *n.* [Fr. *chaperon*, from *chape*, a cope. CHAPEL.] A kind of ancient hood or cap; a lady, especially a married lady, who attends a young lady to public places as a guide or protector.—*v.t.* To attend on as chaperon, guide, or the like.—**chaperonage,** shap′ėr•ōn•ij, *n.* The protection or countenance of a chaperon.

chapiter,‡ chap′i•tėr, *n.* [From O.Fr. *chapitel*, from L.L. *capitellum*, L. *capitulum*, dim. of *caput*, a head; *chapter* is the same word.] The upper part or capital of a column or pillar. (*O.T.*)

chaplain, chap′lin, *n.* [Fr. *chapelain;* L.L. *capellanus*, from *capella*, a chapel. CHAPEL.] An ecclesiastic who performs divine service in a chapel; more generally, an ecclesiastic who officiates at court, in the household of a nobleman, or in an army, garrison, ship, institution, etc.—**chaplaincy, chaplainship,** chap′lin•si, chap′lin•ship, *n.* The office or post of a chaplain.

chaplet, chap′let, *n.* [Fr. *chapelet*, a dim. of O.Fr. *chapel*, Mod.Fr. *chapeau*, a hat, from *chape*, L.L.

capa, a hood, a cape; akin *chapel*, *chape*, etc.] A garland or wreath to be worn on the head; a string of beads used by Roman Catholics, by which they count their prayers; a small rosary; *arch*. a small round molding, carved into beads, pearls, olives, or the like.

chaps, chaps, *n*. [From Mexican Spanish *chaparreras*, from *chaparro*, evergreen oak.] Leather trousers, usually open at the back, worn by cowboys as protection against thorns.

chapter, chap′tėr, *n*. [Fr. *chapitre*, formerly *chapitle*, *capitel*, from L. *capitulum*, dim. of *caput*, the head, whence also *capital*, *cattle*, etc.] A division of a book or treatise; the council of a bishop, consisting of the canons or prebends and other clergymen attached to a collegiate or cathedral church, and presided over by a dean; the place in which the business of the chapter is conducted; a chapter house; the meeting of certain organized orders and societies; a branch of some society or brotherhood.—**chapter house,** *n*. The building in which a chapter meets for the transaction of business.

char, charr, chär, *n*. [It. and Gael. *cear*, red; from its having a red belly.] A name given to at least two species of the salmon family, inhabiting lakes in many parts of the north of Europe.

char, chare, chär, chār, *n*. [From A.Sax. *cerr*, *cyrr*, a turn, time, occasion; *cerran*, *cyrran*, to turn=D. *keeren*, G. *kehren*, to turn, move or change. Hence *char*coal.] A turn of work; a single job or piece of work; household work.—*v.i.* To work at others' houses by the day without being a hired servant; to do small jobs.—**charwoman,** chär• or chār•, *n*. A woman employed by the day on odd jobs about a house; one employed in the house of another to do occasional or miscellaneous work.

char, chär, *v.t.*—*charred*, *charring*. [O.E. *char*, to turn, from A.Sax. *cerran*, to turn, to *char* wood is to turn or change it; *charcoal* is wood turned into coal. CHAR, a turn.] To burn with slight admission of air; to reduce to charcoal; to burn (wood) slightly or partially, and on the surface.—**charcoal,** chär′kōl, *n*. Coal made by charring wood; or more generally, the carbonaceous residue of vegetable, animal, or combustible mineral matter when they undergo smothered combustion. Wood-charcoal is much employed in the manufacture of gunpowder, and, like coke or *mineral charcoal*, as a more or less smokeless fuel; while *animal charcoal* from oils, fats, and bones, is the basis of lampblack and printer's ink.

character, kar′ak•tėr, *n*. [L. *character*, an engraved mark, from Gr. *charakter*, from *charattō*, *charaxō*, to cut, engrave.] A distinctive mark made by cutting, stamping, or engraving, as on stone, metal, or other hard material; a mark or figure, written or printed, and used to form words and communicate ideas; a letter, figure, or sign; the peculiar form of letters, written or printed, used by a particular person or people (the Greek *character*); the peculiar qualities impressed by nature or habit on a person, which distinguish him from others; a distinctive quality assigned to a person by repute; reputation; sometimes restricted to good qualities or reputation; strongly marked distinctive qualities of any kind; an account or statement of qualities or peculiarities; especially, an oral or written account of a servant's or employee's character or qualifications; a person; a personage; especially applied to individuals represented in fiction or history, to persons of eminence, and to persons marked by some prominent trait.—*v.t.* To mark with or as with characters; to engrave; to inscribe.—**characteristic,** kar′ak•tėr•is″tik, *a*. [Gr. *charakteristikos*.] Pertaining to or serving to constitute the character; exhibiting the peculiar qualities of a person or thing; peculiar; distinctive.—*n*. That which serves to constitute a character; that which characterizes; that which distinguishes a person or thing from another.—**characteristical,** kar′ak•tėr•is″tik•al, *a*. Characteristic.—**characteristically,** kar′ak•tėr•is″tik•al•li, *adv*. In a characteristic manner.—**characterization,** kar′ak•tėr•iz•ā″shon, *n*. Act of characterizing.—**characterize,** kar′ak•tėr•īz, *v.t.* [Gr. *charaktērizō*.] To give a special stamp or character to; to constitute a peculiar characteristic or the peculiar characteristics of; to stamp or distinguish (*characterized* by benevolence); to give a character or an account of the personal qualities of a man; to describe by peculiar qualities.—**characterless,** kar′ak•tėr•les, *a*. Destitute of any peculiar character.

charade, sha•räd′ or sha•räd′, *n*. [Fr. Etymology unknown.] An enigma, the solution of which is a word of two or more syllables, each of which is separately significant, the word and its syllables being intended to be discovered from description, or in other cases from representation, when it is called an *acting charade*.

charcoal, *n*. See CHAR.

chard, chärd, *n*. [Fr. *charde*, from L. *carduus*, a thistle or artichoke.] The leaves of artichoke, covered with straw in order to blanch them, and to make them less bitter; the vegetable, Swiss chard.

chare, chār, *n*. and *v*. See CHAR.

charge, chärj, *v.t.*—*charged*, *charging*. [Fr. *charger*, from L.L. *carricare*, from L. *carrus*, a *car*, whence also *carry*, *cargo*, *caricature*.] To lay a load or burden on; to burden; to load; to fill; to occupy (to *charge* the memory); to impute or register as a debt; to put down to the debt of; to register as indebted or as forming a debt (to *charge* a person *for* a thing; to *charge* a thing *to* or *against* a person); to fix the price of: with *at* before the price or rate; to accuse; to impeach (to *charge* a person *with* a crime); to lay to one's charge; to impute; to ascribe the responsibility of (to *charge* guilt *on* a person); to entrust; to commission (a person *with*); to command; to enjoin; to instruct; to urge earnestly; to exhort; to adjure; to give directions to (a jury, etc.); to instruct authoritatively; to make an onset on; to attack by rushing against violently. ∴ Syn. under ACCUSE.—*v.i.* To make an onset; to rush to an attack; to place the price of a thing to one's debit.—*n*. That which is laid on or in; in a general sense, any load or burden; the quantity of anything which an apparatus, as a gun, an electric battery, etc., is intended to receive and fitted to hold, or what is actually in as a load; an attack, onset, or rush; an order, injunction, mandate, or command; hence, a duty enjoined on or entrusted to one; care, custody, or oversight; the person or thing committed to another's custody, care, or management; a trust; instructions given by a judge to a jury, or an exhortation given by a bishop to his clergy; what is alleged or brought forward by way of accusation; accusation; the sum payable as the price of anything bought; cost; expense; rent, tax, or whatever constitutes a burden or duty.—**chargeable,** chärj′a•bl, *a*. Capable of being charged; falling to be set, laid, or imposed, as a tax or duty; subject to a charge or tax, as goods; capable of being laid to one's charge; capable of being imputed to one; subject to accusation; liable to be accused; causing expense, and hence burdensome.—**charger,** chärj′ėr, *n*. One who or that which charges; a large dish (N.T.); a war horse.

chargé d'affaires, shär•zhā′ dä•fâr′, *n*. [Fr., lit. charged with affairs.] One who transacts diplomatic business at a foreign court during the absence of his superior the ambassador, or at a court where no functionary so high as an ambassador is appointed.

charily, chariness. See CHARY.

chariot, char′i•ot, *n*. [Fr. *chariot*, from *char*, a car. CAR.] A stately four-wheeled pleasure or state carriage with one seat; a two-wheeled car formerly used in war, in processions, and for racing, drawn by two or more horses.—*v.t.*† To convey in a chariot. (*Mil*.)—**charioteer,** char′i•o•tēr″, *n*. The person who drives or conducts a chariot.

charity, char′i•ti, *n*. [Fr. *charité*, O.Fr. *charitet*, *cariteit*, from L. *caritas*, *caritatis*, from *carus*, dear, whence also *caress*.] The good affection, love, or tenderness which men should feel toward their fellows, and which should induce them to do good to and think favorably of others; benevolence; liberality in thinking or judging; liberality in giving to the poor; whatever is bestowed gratuitously on the poor for their relief; alms; any act of kindness or benevolence; a charitable institution; a hospital.—**charitable,** char′it•a•bl, *a*. Pertaining to or characterized by charity; full of good will or tenderness; benevolent and kind; liberal in benefactions to the poor and in relieving them in distress; pertaining to almsgiving or relief to the poor; springing from charity or intended for charity; lenient in judging of others; not harsh; favorable.—**charitableness,** char′it•a•bl•nes, *n.* The quality of being charitable.—**charitably,** char′it•a•bli, *adv.* In a charitable manner.

charlatan, shär′la•tan, *n.* [Fr., from It. *ciarlatano,* a quack, from *ciarlare,* to prate, to chatter like birds.] One who prates much in his own favor and makes unwarrantable pretensions to skill; a quack; an empiric; a mountebank.—**charlatanic,** shär•la•tan′ik, *a.* Pertaining to or resembling a charlatan; quackish.—**charlatanism, charlatanry,** shär′la•tan•izm, shär′la•tan•ri, *n.* The behavior of a charlatan; undue pretensions to skill; quackery.

Charles's Wain, chärlz′iz•wān, *n.* [A corruption of *churl's* (that is farmer's or peasant's) *wain.*] The seven brightest stars in the constellation called Ursa Major or the Great Bear: known also as the *Plow.*

charlock, chär′lok, *n.* [A.Sax. *cerlic;* the termination is the same as in *garlic, hemlock,* and meant properly *leek.*] A weedy annual of the mustard family, with bright yellow flowers, occurring in cornfields.

charm, chärm, *n.* [Fr. *charme,* a charm, an enchantment, from L. *carmen,* a song, a verse, a charm.] A melody‡; a song‡ (*Mil.*); anything believed to possess some occult or supernatural power, such as an amulet or spell or some mystic observance; something which exerts an irresistible power to please and attract; fascination; allurement; attraction; a trinket, such as a locket, seal, etc., worn on a watch guard.—*v.t.* To subdue or control by incantation or magical or supernatural influence; to fortify or make invulnerable with charms; to subdue or soothe as if by magic; to allay or appease by what gives delight; to give exquisite pleasure to; to fascinate; to enchant.—*v.i.* To act as a charm or spell; to produce the effect of a charm.—**charmer,** chär′mėr, *n.* One who charms, fascinates, enchants, allures, or attracts.—**charming,** chär′ming, *a.* Pleasing in the highest degree; delighting; fascinating; enchanting; alluring.—**charmingly,** chär′ming•li, *adv.* In a charming manner.

charnel, chär′nel, *a.* [Fr. *charnel,* O.Fr. *carnel,* carnal, from L. *carnalis,* from *caro, carnis,* flesh.] Containing dead bodies.—**charnel house,** *n.* A place under or near churches where the bones of the dead are deposited.

charqui, chär′kē, *n.* [The Chilian name, of which the term *jerked* beef is a corruption.] Jerked beef; beef cut into strips of about an inch thick and dried by exposure to the sun.

charr, *n.* A kind of fish, the char.

chart, chärt, *n.* [L. *charta,* paper, a leaf of paper. *Card* is the same word.] A sheet of any kind on which information is exhibited in a methodical or tabulated form; specifically, a marine map, with the coasts, islands, rocks, soundings, etc., to regulate the courses of ships.—*v.t.* To delineate, as on a chart; to map out.—**chartaceous,** kär•tā′shus, *a. Bot.* papery; resembling paper: applied to the paper-like texture of leaves, bark, etc.—**charter,** chär′tėr, *n.* [O.Fr. *chartre,* from L. *chartarius,* from *charta,* paper.] A writing given as evidence of a grant, contract, etc.; any instrument executed with form and solemnity bestowing or granting powers, rights, and privileges; privilege; immunity; exemption.—*v.t.* To hire or let (a ship) by charter or contract; to establish by charter; to grant; to privilege.—**charterer,** chär′tėr•ėr, *n.* One who charters.—**charter party,** *n.* [Fr. *charte-partie,* a divided charter, from the practice of cutting the instrument in two, and giving one part to each of the contractors.] *Com.* an agreement respecting the hire of a vessel and the freight, signed by the proprietor or master of the ship, and by the merchant who hires or freights it.—**Chartism,** chär′tizm, *n.* The political principles or opinions of the Chartists.—**Chartist,** chär′tist, *n.* One of a body of political reformers in England that sprung up about the year 1838, and advocated as their leading principles universal suffrage, no property qualification for a seat in parliament, annual parliaments, equal representation, payment of members, and vote by ballot, all which privileges they demanded as constituting the people's charter.

chartreuse, shär•trėz′, *n.* A highly esteemed liqueur made with fine spirits and aromatic plants growing on the Alps, and so called from the monastery of the same name, where it used to be made.

chartulary, kär′chū•le•ri, *n.* [Fr. *cartulaire,* L.L. *cartularius,* from *chartula,* dim. of L. *charta,* paper.] A record or register, as of a monastery.

charwoman, chär′wu̧m•an, *n.* [From A. Sax. *cerr, cyrr,* a turn, time, occasion; *cerran, cyrran,* to turn = D. *keeren,* G. *kehren,* to turn, move or change. CHORE.] A woman employed by the day on odd jobs about a house.

chary, châ′ri, *a.* [A.Sax. *cearig,* full of care, sad, from *cearu, caru,* care. CARE.] Careful; cautious; frugal; sparing: with *of* before an object.—**charily,** châ′ri•li, *a.* In a chary manner; carefully; sparingly.—**chariness,** châ′ri•nes, *n.*

chase, chās, *v.t.*—*chased, chasing.* [Also written *chace,* from O.Fr. *chacier,* Mod.Fr. *chasser,* to chase, a parallel form with *catch,* being like it from L.L. *captiare.* CATCH.] To pursue for the purpose of taking, as game; to hunt; to follow after or search for with eagerness; to pursue for any purpose; to follow with hostility; to drive off.—*n.* Pursuit; hunting; ardent search for or following after; that which is pursued or hunted; specifically, a vessel pursued by another; an open piece of ground or place well stored with game, and belonging to a private proprietor.—**chaser,** chās′ėr, *n.* One who or that which chases; a pursuer or hunter; a ship that pursues another; a chase-gun.—**chase gun,** *n.* In warships, a gun used in chasing an enemy or in defending a ship when chased.

chase, chās, *n.* [Fr. *châsse,* from L. *capsa,* box, case. *Case,* for holding things, is a form of the same word.] An iron frame used by printers to confine types when set in columns or pages; the part of a gun between the trunnions and the muzzle; a wide groove.

chase, chās, *v.t.* [Shortened from *enchase.*] To enchase; to cut a thread on, so as to make a screw.—**chaser,** chās′ėr, *n.* One who chases or enchases; an enchaser; a steel tool used for cutting or finishing the threads of screws.

chasm, kazm, *n.* [Gr. *chasma,* from root *cha,* as in *chaos.*] A gaping or yawning opening, as in the earth; an abyss; a wide and deep cleft; a fissure; a void space.—**chasmy,** kaz′mi, *a.* Abounding with chasms.

chasseur, shas•sėr′, *n.* [Fr., a huntsman.] One of a body of soldiers, light and active, both mounted and on foot, trained for rapid movements; a person dressed in a sort of military style in attendance upon persons of rank.

chassis, shä′sē, *n.* [Fr.] The framework of an automobile, carrying the body and other parts.

chaste, chāst, *a.* [Fr. *chaste,* from L. *castus,* chaste.] Pure from all unlawful sexual commerce; free from libidinous desires; continent; virtuous; free from obscenity or impurity in thought and language; as applied to literary style, free from barbarous words and phrases, affected or extravagant expressions, or the like; in art, free from meretricious ornament or affectation, not gaudy. — **chastely,** chāst′li, *adv.* In a chaste manner.—**chasteness,** chāst′nes, *n.* The state or quality of being chaste.—**chastity,** chas′ti•ti, *n.* The state or property of being chaste, pure, or undefiled; sexual purity; continence.

chasten, chās′n, *v.t.* [O.Fr. *chastier,* from L. *castigare,* to castigate or chastise, from *castus,* pure, whence *chaste;* comp. *chastise.*] To inflict pain, trouble, or affliction on for the purpose of reclaiming from evil; to correct; to chastise; to punish; not now used of corporal punishment, which is expressed by *chastise;* to purify, as the taste; to refine.—**chastener,** chās′n•ėr, *n.* One who chastens.

chastise, chas•tīz′, *v.t.*—*chastised, chastising.* [Same word as *chasten,* but with a different verbal termination; O.E. *chastie, chasty,* from O.Fr. *chastier.* CHASTEN.] To inflict pain on by stripes or in any other manner, for the purpose of punishing and recalling to duty; to correct by punishment; to free from faults or excesses; to correct; to restrain.—

chastisement, chas′tiz•ment, *n.* The act of chastising; pain inflicted for punishment and correction, either by stripes or otherwise.—**chastiser,** chas•tīz′ėr, *n.* One who chastises; a punisher; a corrector.

chasuble, chas′ū•bl, *n.* [Fr. *chasuble,* from L.L. *casubula,* from L. *casula,* a little cottage, a hooded garment, dim. of *casa,* a cottage.] A rich vestment or garment worn uppermost by a priest at the celebration of the eucharist.

chat, chat, *v.i.*—*chatted, chatting.* [An abbreviated form of *chatter.*] To talk idly or in a familiar manner; to talk without form or ceremony.—*n.* Free, familiar talk; idle talk; prate.—**chatty,** chat′i, *a.* Inclined to chat; talkative.

chat, chat, *n.* [From the chattering sound of its voice.] A name of several small, lively birds of the warbler family, species of which are found in Europe and America.

château, shä•tō′, *n.* pl. **châteaux,** shä•tōz′, Fr. tō. [Fr. *château,* O.Fr. *chastel,* a castle, from L. *castellum.* CASTLE.] A castle; a mansion in the country; a country seat.—**chatelaine,** shat′ė•lān, *n.* [Fr. *châtelaine,* lit. a female castellan or castle-keeper.] A female castellan; a bunch of chains worn at a lady's waist, having attached such articles as a key, thimble case, penknife, corkscrew, etc.

chatoyant, sha•toi′ant, *a.* [Fr., pp. of *chatoyer,* to change luster like the eye of a cat, from *chat,* a cat.] Having a changeable, undulating luster or color, like that of a cat's eye in the dark.

chattel, chat′el, *n.* [O.E. *chatel,* also *catel,* really the same word as *cattle* (which see).] An item or article of goods, specifically applied in law to goods movable or immovable, except such as have the nature of freehold.

chatter, chat′ėr, *v.i.* [Probably an imitative word, allied to D. *kwetteren,* Dan. *kviddre,* Sw. *kvittra,* to chirp, to chatter.] To utter sounds rapidly and indistinctly, as a magpie or a monkey; to make a noise by repeated rapid collisions of the teeth; to talk idly, carelessly, or rapidly; to jabber. —*v.t.* To utter as one who chatters. —*n.* Sounds like those of a magpie or monkey; idle talk.—**chatterbox,** *n.* One that talks incessantly: applied chiefly to children. (Colloq.)—**chatterer,** chat′ėr•ėr, *n.* One who chatters; a prater; an idle talker; the popular name of sundry insessorial birds, one of which is the waxwing, or Bohemian chatterer.

chauffer, cha̧′fėr, *n.* [Fr. *chauffer,* to heat. CHAFE.] A small portable furnace, usually of sheet iron, with a grating near the bottom.—**chauffeur,** shō•fėr′, *n.* [Fr.] The driver of a motor vehicle.

chauvin, shō•van′, *n.* [From Nich. *Chauvin,* an enthusiastic military adherent of Napoleon I.] Originally, one of the veterans of the first French Empire who professed, after the fall of Napoleon, a sort of adoration for his person and his acts; hence, anyone possessed by an absurdly exaggerated patriotism or military enthusiasm.—**chauvinism,** shō′vin•izm, *n.* The sentiments of a chauvin; absurdly exaggerated patriotism or military enthusiasm.

chaw, cha̧, *v.t.* To chew: an old form now vulgar.

chay, chā, *n.* An Indian root yielding a red dye.

cheap, chēp, *a.* [Strictly a noun, being = A.Sax. *ceáp,* price, bargain; from the use of the phrase *good cheap,* as to buy a thing *good cheap,* that is a good bargain, the noun came to be used as an adjective. Cog. D. *koop,* a purchase, *koopen,* to buy; Icel. *kaup,* a bargain; *kaupa,* to buy; G. *kaufen,* to buy; Goth. *kaufon,* to traffic. *Cheapen, chop, chaffer, chapman,* are akin.] Bearing a low price in market; capable of being purchased at a low price, either as compared with the usual price of the commodity, or with the real value, or more vaguely with the price of other commodities; being of small value; common; not respected.—**cheapen,** chē′pn, *v.t.* To ask the price of; to chaffer or bargain for; to beat down the price of; to lessen the value of; to depreciate.—**cheapener,** chē′pn•ėr, *n.* One who cheapens or bargains.—**cheaply,** chē′pli, *adv.* At a small price; at a low rate.—**cheapness,** chēp′nes, *n.* The state or quality of being cheap.

cheat, chēt, *v.t.* [Abbrev. of *escheat,* to act like an escheater, who held an office giving great opportunities of fraud. ESCHEAT.] To deceive and defraud; to impose upon; to trick (to *cheat* a person *of* or *out of* something); to illude; to deceive; to mislead.—*v.i.* To act dishonestly; to practice fraud or trickery.— *n.* A fraud committed by deception; a trick, imposition, or imposture; a person who cheats; a fraudulent person; a swindler.—**cheater,** chēt′ėr, *n.* One who cheats; an escheater (*Shak.*)‡.—**cheatingly,** chēt′ing•li, *adv.* In a cheating manner.

check, chek, *n.* [From *chequer,* or *exchequer,* in old sense of banker's or moneychanger's office or counter; or from *check,* in sense of counterfoil.] An order for money drawn on a banker or bank, payable to the bearer.—**checkbook,** *n.* A book containing blank bankchecks.

check, chek, *n.* [Fr. *échec,* O.Fr. *eschec,* a check, a check at chess, lit. king, the call of king! in chess, from Per. *shâh,* king, the chief piece at chess. CHESS, CHEQUE, CHEQUER.] The act of suddenly stopping or restraining; a stop; hindrance; restraint; obstruction; a term or word of warning in chess when one party obliges the other either to move or guard his king; a reprimand; rebuke; censure; slight; a species of cloth, in which colored lines or stripes cross each other rectangularly, making a pattern resembling the squares of a chessboard; the pattern of such cloth; a mark put against names or items on going over a list; a duplicate, or counterpart, used for security or verification; a counterfoil; a ticket or token given for identification.—*v.t.* To stop or moderate the motion of; to restrain in action; to hinder; to curb; to rebuke; to chide or reprove; *chess,* to make a move which puts the adversary's king in check; to compare with a counterfoil or something similar, with a view to ascertain authenticity or accuracy.—*v.i.* To make a stop; to stop; to pause.—*a.* Made of check; chequered.—**checker,** chek′ėr, *n.* One who checks.—**checkmate,** chek′māt, *n.* [From Per. *shâh mât,* the king is dead (*shâh,* the king, *mât,* he is dead).] *Chess,* the position of a king when he is in check, and cannot release himself, which brings the game to a close; hence, defeat; overthrow.—*v.t.*—*checkmated, checkmating.* To put in check, as an opponent's king in chess. —**check point,** *n.* A place where traffic is stopped for inspection and clearance; a geographical location on land or water used by a flier to determine his position.—**check up,** *n.* An examination; a thorough medical examination.

checker, chek′ėr, *n.* [O.Fr. *eschequier,* Mod. Fr. *échiquier,* a chessboard, an exchequer, from O.Fr. *eschecs,* chess. CHECK, CHESS.] Pl. a game for two players; one of the divisions of a pattern that consists of squares; the pattern itself.—*v.t.* To mark with little squares, like a chessboard, by lines or stripes of different colors; to mark with different colors; *fig.* to variegate with different qualities; to impart variety to (events that *checker* one's career).—**checkered, chequered,** chek′ėrd, *a.* Marked with or exhibiting squares of different colors; varied with a play of different colors; *fig.* variegated with different qualities, scenes, or events; crossed with good and bad fortune (a *checkered* life or narrative).—**checkerboard,** *n.* A board on which checkers or draughts are played.—**checkerwork,** *n.* Work exhibiting checkers or squares of varied color or materials.

cheddar, ched′ėr, *n.* A rich fine-flavored cheese made at *Cheddar* in Somersetshire, England; any cheese of similar character.

cheek, chēk, *n.* [A.Sax. *ceáce,* cheek; cog. D. *kaak,* Sw. *kek,* the jaw, *kak,* the cheek; probably same root as *chaw, jaw, chaps.*] The side of the face below the eyes on each side; something regarded as resembling the human cheek in position or otherwise; one of two pieces, as of an instrument, apparatus, framework, etc., which form corresponding sides or which are double and alike, as the *cheeks* of a vise, of a lathe, of a door, etc.; cool confidence; brazen-faced impudence; impudent or insulting talk (in these senses rather vulgar).

cheep, chēp, *v.i.* & *t.* [Imitative.] To pule or peep, as a chicken; to chirp; to squeak.—*n.* A chirp; a squeak.

cheer, chēr, *n.* [O.E. *chere,* face, look, mien, from O.Fr. *chere, chiere,* face, countenance, from L.L. *cara*, the face, from Gr. *kara*, the head.] Expression of countenance, as noting a greater or less degree of good spirits (*Shak.*); state or temper of the mind; state of feeling or spirits; a state of gladness or joy; gaiety; animation; that which makes cheerful or promotes good spirits; provisions for a feast; viands; fare; a shout of joy, encouragement, applause, or acclamation.—*v.t.* To gladden; to make cheerful; to encourage; to salute with shouts of joy or cheers; to applaud.—*v.i.* To grow cheerful; to become gladsome or joyous: often with *up*; to utter a cheer or shout of acclamation or joy.—**cheerer,** chēr′ėr, *n.* One who or that which cheers.—**cheerful,** chēr′fu̜l, *a.* Of good cheer; having good spirits; gay; moderately joyful; associated with or expressive of agreeable feelings; lively; animated; promoting or causing cheerfulness; gladdening; animating; genial.—**cheerfully,** chēr′fu̜l•li, *adv.* In a cheerful manner; with alacrity or willingness; readily; with life, animation, or good spirits.—**cheerfulness,** chēr′fu̜l•nes, *n.* The state or quality of being cheerful.—**cheerily,** chē′ri•li, *adv.* In a cheery manner.—**cheeriness,** chēr′i•nes, *n.* Quality or state of being cheery.—**cheerless,** chēr′les, *a.* Without joy, gladness, or comfort; gloomy; destitute of anything to enliven or animate the spirits.—**cheerlessly,** chēr′les•li, *adv.* In a cheerless manner; dolefully.—**cheerlessness,** chēr′les•nes, *n.* State of being cheerless.—**cheerly,** chēr′li, *adv.* Cheerily; cheerfully; heartily; briskly. (*Shak.*)—**cheery,** chē′ri, *a.* Showing cheerfulness or good spirits; blithe; hearty; gay; sprightly; promoting cheerfulness.

cheese, chēz, *n.* [A.Sax. *cése*, *cyse*, cheese; derived like G. *käse*, D. *kaas*, from L. *caseus*, cheese.] An article of food consisting of the curd or casein of milk, coagulated by rennet or some acid, separated from the whey, and usually pressed into a solid mass in a mold.—**cheesy,** chē′zi, *a.* Having the qualities, taste, odor, or form of cheese; resembling or pertaining to cheese.—**cheesiness,** chē′zi•nes, *n.* The quality of being cheesy.—**cheesecake,** *n.* A cake filled with a jelly made of soft curds, sugar, and butter; a small cake made in various ways and with a variety of different ingredients.—**cheeseparing,** *a.* Meanly economical; parsimonious.

cheetah, chē′ta, *n.* [Native name, meaning spotted.] The hunting leopard, trained in India to hunt such game as deer, etc.

chef, shef, *n.* [Fr., lit. head, from L. *caput.*] Head or chief; specifically, the head cook of a great establishment, as a nobleman's household, a club, etc.—**chef-d'oeuvre,** shā•dė′•vr, *n.* pl. **chefs-d'oeuvre,** shā•dė′•vr. [Fr.] A masterpiece; a fine work in art, literature, etc.

chela, kē′la, *n.* pl. **chelae,** kē′lē. [Gr. *chēlē*, a claw.] One of the prehensile claws possessed by certain crustacea, as the crab, lobster, etc.—**chelate, cheliferous,** kē′lāt, ki•lif′ėr•us, *a.* Furnished with chelae.—**cheliform,** kē′li•form, *a.* Having the form of a chela or prehensile claw.

chelonian, ki•lō′ni•an, *a.* [Gr. *chelōnē*, a tortoise.] Pertaining to or designating animals of the tortoise kind.—*n.* A tortoise or turtle.

chemise, she•mēz′, *n.* [Fr. *chemise*, L.L. *camisia*, a shirt, from Ar. *qamis*, a shirt, an undergarment of linen.] A shift or smock worn by females; a wall that lines the face of an earthwork; a breast wall.—**chemisette,** shem•i•zet′, *n.* [Fr.] A short undergarment worn on the breast over the chemise.

chemist, kem′ist, *n.* [Shortened from *alchemist*, from *alchemy*, O.Fr. *alchemie*, from Ar. *al*, the, and *qīmiā*, chemistry, from L. Gr. *chēmeia*, chemistry, from Gr. *cheō*, to pour, to drop.] A person versed in chemistry; one whose business is to make chemical examinations or investigations.—**chemistry,** kem′ist•ri, *n.* The science that investigates the composition of the various kinds of matter, the changes of composition that occur, the energy phenomena that accompany these changes, and the relationships involved; chemical properties, reactions, etc.—*Organic chemistry*, the study of carbon compounds.—*Inorganic chemistry*, the study of elements and compounds other than those of carbon.—**chemical,** kem′i•kal, *a.* Pertaining to chemistry.—*n.* A substance obtained by or used in a chemical process.—**chemically,** kem′i•kal•li, *adv.*—**chemical engineering,** *n.* A branch of chemistry that deals with the industrial uses of chemistry.—**chemical warfare,** *n.* Warfare with incendiary mixtures, poisonous gases, etc.

chemosmosis, kem•os•mō′sis, *n.* [*Chem-* in *chemistry*, and *osmosis.*] Chemical action acting through an intervening membrane, as parchment, etc.

chemotherapy, kem′o•ther″a•pi, *n.* Treatment of disease with chemicals having a specific destructive effect on the micro-organisms causing the disease.

chenille, she•nēl′, *n.* [Fr., a caterpillar.] A tufted cord of silk or worsted, somewhat resembling a caterpillar, used for making rugs, bedspreads, etc.

cherish, cher′ish, *v.t.* [O.Fr. *cherir*, *cherissant* (Fr. *chérir*), to hold dear, from *cher*, L. *carus*, dear, whence also *caress.*] To treat with tenderness and affection; to take care of; to foster; to hold as dear; to indulge and encourage in the mind; to harbor; to cling to.—**cherisher,** cher′ish•ėr, *n.* One who cherishes; an encourager; a supporter.—**cherishingly,** cher′ish•ing•li, *adv.* In an affectionate or cherishing manner.

cheroot, she•röt′, *n.* [Tamil *shuruttu*, a roll.] A kind of cigar of a cylindrical or often somewhat tapering shape, with both ends cut square off.

cherry, cher′i, *n.* [O.E. *cheri*, *chiri*, from Fr. *cerise*, L. *cerasus*, from Gr. *kerasos*, a cherry.] The fruit of a tree belonging to the plum family, consisting of a pulpy drupe inclosing a one-seeded smooth stone; the tree itself; also the name of other fruits.—*a.* Like a red cherry in color; red; ruddy; blooming.

chersonese, kėr′so•nēz, *n.* [Gr. *chersonēsos*—*chersos*, land, and *nēsos*, an isle.] A peninsula.

chert, chėrt, *n.* [Probably Celtic; comp. Ir. *ceart*, a pebble.] A variety of quartz, more or less translucent, less hard than common quartz, with a fracture usually conchoidal and dull, sometimes splintery.—**cherty,** chėr′ti, *a.* Like chert; full of chert; flinty.

cherub, cher′ub, *n.* pl. **cherubs;** Hebrew pl. **cherubim,** cher′ub•im. [Heb. *kerub.*] One of an order of angels; a beautiful child. [In the latter sense the plural is always *cherubs.*]—**cherubic,** che•röb′ik, *a.* Pertaining to or resembling cherubs; angelic.

chervil, chėr′vil, *n.* [A.Sax. *cerfille*, from L. *chœrophyllum*, from Gr. *chairephyllon*—*chairō*, to rejoice, and *phyllon*, leaf, from their agreeable odor.] A hairy herb of the carrot family, with longish grooved fruits, common in fields and waste places.—*Garden chervil*, an annual plant cultivated as an aromatic potherb.

chess, ches, *n.* [O.Fr. *eschecs*, Fr. *échecs*, chess, really a plural, meaning lit. kings, from Per. *shâh*, a king, the principal figure in the game, whence also *check.*] An ingenious game played by two persons or parties with different pieces on a checkered board, divided into sixty-four squares.—**chessboard,** *n.* The board used in the game of chess.—**chessman,** *n.* A piece used in playing the game of chess.

chest, chest, *n.* [A.Sax. *cyste*, from L. *cista*, Gr. *kistē*, a chest, a box.] A box of considerable size; *com.* a case in which certain kinds of goods, as tea, indigo, etc., are packed for transit; hence, the quantity such a chest contains; the trunk of the body from the neck to the belly; the thorax.—*Chest of drawers*, a piece of furniture with sliding boxes or drawers for holding various articles of dress, linen, etc.—*v.t.* To deposit in a chest; to hoard.

chestnut, ches′nut, *n.* [For *chestennut*, O.E. *chestrine*, *chesteyne*, from O.Fr. *chastaigne*, from L. *castanea*, the chestnut tree, from Gr. *kastanon*, from *Castana* in Pontus, where this tree abounded.] The seed or nut of a forest tree allied to the beech, inclosed in a prickly pericarp, containing two or more edible seeds; the tree itself or its timber; the color of the husk of a chestnut; a reddish-brown color; an old joke (colloq.).—*a.* Of the color of a chestnut; reddish-brown.

cheval-de-frise, she•val′de•frēz, *n.* pl. **chevaux-de-frise,** she•vō′de•frēz. [Fr. *cheval*, a horse, pl. *chevaux*, and *Frise*, Friesland, where first employed.] A horizontal piece of timber or iron with long spikes transversely through it, set on the ground to bar a passage, form an obstacle to the advance of cavalry, etc.

cheval glass, *n.* A swing looking glass mounted on a frame, and large enough to reflect the whole figure.

chevalier, shev•a•lēr′, *n.* [Fr., from *cheval*, a horse. CAVALRY, CAVALIER.] A horseman; a cavalier; a member of certain orders of knighthood.—*Chevalier d'industrie*, one who gains a living by dishonest means; a sharper; a swindler; a thief.

Cheviot, che′vi•ot, *n.* and *a.* A name for a variety of sheep, noted for their large carcass and valuable wool, so called from the Cheviot Hills between Scotland and England.

chevron, shev′run, *n.* [Fr., a rafter, from *chèvre*, L. *capra*, a goat, because rafters are reared on end like butting goats.] *Her.* a figure on a shield representing two rafters of a house meeting at the top; *arch.* a variety of fret ornament; a zigzag; *milit.* the distinguishing marks on the sleeves of noncommissioned officers' coats.

chew, chö, *v.t.* [From A.Sax. *ceówan*, to chew=D. *kaauwen*, to chew. *Jaw*, *jowl*, *chaps*, *chops* are from the same root.] To bite and grind with the teeth; to masticate.—*To chew the cud*, to ruminate, and *fig.* to ruminate or meditate on something.—*v.i.* To perform the act of chewing; to champ.—*n.* That which is chewed; a quid of tobacco.

chewing gum, *n.* Vegetable gum, usually chicle, sweetened and flavored, for chewing.

chi, kī, *n.* The twenty-second letter of the Greek alphabet, written as *ch* in English.

chiaroscuro, chiaro-oscuro, ki•ä′-rō•skö″rō, ki•ä′rō•os•kö″rō, *n.* [It., lit. clear-obscure, from L. *clarus*, clear, and *obscurus*, obscure; Fr. *clair-obscur*.] That department of painting which relates to light and shade; the art of judiciously distributing the lights and shadow in a picture.

chiasma, kī•az′ma, *n.* [Gr. *chiasma*, from the Greek letter χ.] *Anat.* the central body of nervous matter, where the optic nerves cross each other proceeding from the brain to the eyes; a cross arrangement [X] of clauses e.g. *I cannot sing, to laugh I would be ashamed.*

chibouque, chibouk, shi•bök′, *n.* [Turk.] A Turkish tobacco pipe.

chic, shēk, *n.* [Fr., from G. *schick*, due order, tact.] Easy elegance; smartness; adroitness; knowingness.—*a.* Smart.

chicane, chicanery shi•kān′, shi•-kān′ėr•i, *n.* [Fr. *chicane*, *chicanerie*, originally a kind of game and the maneuvers in playing it, from Per. *chaugan*, the game of golf played on horseback, polo.] The art of protracting a contest or discussion by the use of evasive stratagems or trickery; sophistry; artifice.—*v.t.* and *i.* To use chicane.

chickadee, chik′a•dē, *n.* [Amer. imitative of its call.] A small North American bird with black, white, and gray feathers.

chicken, chik′en, *n.* [A.Sax. *cicen*, *cycen*, a chicken; cog. L.G. *kiken*, *küken*, Prov. G. *küchen*.] A young fowl; particularly a young domestic fowl; a person of tender years: generally used of females, as in the phrase, she is no *chicken*.—**chick,** chik, *n.* A chicken.—**chickenhearted,** *a.* Having no more courage than a chicken; timid; cowardly.—**chicken pox,** *n.* A mild contagious eruptive disease generally appearing in children.—**chickweed,** *n.* A common weed with small white blossoms much used for feeding cage birds.

chickling, chickling vetch, chik′-ling, *n.* [From Fr. *chiche*, It. *cece*, from L. *cicer*, the chick-pea.] A vetch or pea extensively cultivated in the south of Europe for its seed.—**chick-pea,** *n.* A plant cultivated for its seeds, which form an important article in French cookery.

chicle, chi′kl, *n.* [Mex.] Elastic gum of the sapodilla tree, usual base of chewing gum.

chicory, chik′o•ri, *n.* [Fr. *chicorée*, L. *cichorium*, from Gr. *kichōrion*, chicory.] The popular name of a composite plant common in Europe and America, with a fleshy tapering root which is extensively employed as a substitute for coffee, or to mix with coffee.

chide, chīd, *v.t.*—*chid* (pret.), *chid* or *chidden*, *chiding*. [A.Sax. *cidan*, to chide; connections unknown.] To scold; to reprove; to rebuke; to find fault with or take exception to (a thing); to strike by way of punishment or admonition (*Tenn.*).—*v.i.* To scold; to find fault; to contend in words of anger.—**chider,** chīd′ėr, *n.* One who chides, reproves, or rebukes.—**chidingly,** chīd′-ing•li, *adv.* In a scolding or reproving manner.

chief, chēf, *a.* [O.Fr. *chef*, *chief* (Fr. *chef*), the head, top, chief; from L. *caput*, the head, whence also *capital*, *cattle*, *captain*, etc.] Highest in office, authority, or rank; principal or most eminent, in any quality or action; most important; at the head; leading; main.—*n.* The person highest in authority, the head or head man; a military commander; the person who heads an army; the principal person of a clan, tribe, family, etc.—**chiefly,** chēf′li, *adv.* Principally; above all; in the first place; for the most part; mostly.—**chief justice,** *n.* The presiding officer of a court.—**chief of state,** *n.* The formal or symbolic head of a country as distinguished from the head of government.

chieftain, chēf′tan, *n.* [O.Fr. *chevetaine*, *chieftaine*, etc.; from L.L. *capitanus*, from *caput*, the head; really the same word as *captain*.] A leader or commander; a chief; the head of a clan or family.—**chieftaincy, chieftainship,** chēf′tan•si, chēf′tan•ship, *n.* The rank and dignity or office of a chieftain.

chiffonnier, shif•o•nēr′, *n.* [Fr., a chiffonnier, a rag-picker, from *chiffon*, a rag.] A kind of small sideboard; a wooden stand with shelves.

chignon, shē•nyon′, *n.* [Fr., the nape of the neck, a chignon.] The term applied to ladies' back hair when raised and folded up, usually round a pad of artificial hair.

chigoe, chig′ō, *n.* [Of West Indian or South American origin.] An insect closely resembling the common flea, but of more minute size, found in the West Indies and South America, which burrows beneath the skin of the foot, and becoming distended with eggs produces a troublesome ulcer.

chihuahua, chi•wä′•wä, *n.* [Mexican Sp. from *Chihuahua*, Mexico.] A very small dog of ancient Mexican breed.

chilblain, chil′blān, *n.* [*Chill*, cold, and *blain*.] A blain or inflamed sore on the hands or feet produced by cold.—*v.t.* To afflict with chilblains; to produce chilblains in.

child, chīld, *n.* pl. **children,** chil′dren. [A.Sax. *cild*, a child, pl. *cildru*, afterward *cildre*, *childre*, to which *n* or *en* another plural termination was added. The root is the same as that of *kin*, *kind*, etc., G. *kind*, a child.] A son or a daughter of any age; a male or female descendant in the first degree; a very young person of either sex; one of crude or immature knowledge, experience, judgment, or attainments; *pl.* descendants; offspring.—*Child's play*, a trivial matter of any kind; anything easily accomplished or surmounted.—*With child*, pregnant.—**childhood,** chīld′hụd, *n.* The state of a child; the time in which persons are still classed as children.—**childing,**† chīld′ing, *a.* Bearing children; productive; fruitful.—**childish,** chīld′ish, *a.* Of or belonging to a child or to childhood; like a child, or what is proper to childhood; with the disparaging senses of trifling, puerile, ignorant, silly, weak.—**childishly,** chīld′ish•li, *adv.* In a childish manner.—**childishness,** chīld′ish•nes, *n.* The state or quality of being childish.—**childless,** chīld′les, *a.* Destitute of children or offspring.—**childlessness,** chīld′les•nes, *n.* State of being without children.—**childlike,** chīld′-līk, *a.* Resembling a child or that which belongs to children; meek; submissive; dutiful; never used in a disparaging sense.—**childly,**† chīld′-li, *a.* Like a child; acquired or learned when a child. (*Tenn.*).—**childbearing,** *n.* The act of producing or bringing forth children; parturition.—**childbed,** *n.* The state of a woman who is lying-in or in labor.—**childbirth,** *n.* The act of bringing forth a child; travail; labor.—**Childermas,** chil′dėr•mas, *n.* [*Childer*, pl. of *child*, and *mass*.] An anniversary of the Church of England, held on the 28th of December: Innocents Day.

chiliad, kil′i•ad, *n.* [Gr. *chilias*, from *chilioi*, a thousand.] A thousand; a collection or sum containing a thousand individuals or particulars; the period of a thousand years.—**chiliarch,** kil′i•ärk, *n.* [Gr. *archos*, a chief.] The military commander or chief of a thousand men.—**chiliasm,** kil′i•azm, *n.* A millennium.—**chiliast,** kil′i•ast, *n.* A millenarian.—**chiliastic,** kil•i•as′tik, *a.* Relating to the millennium; millenarian.

chill, chil, *n.* [A.Sax. *cele, cyle,* a cold, chill, from *cól,* cool; akin D. *kill,* chill, *killen,* to chill; Sw. *kyla,* to chill; same root as in L. *gelidus,* gelid. COOL.] A shivering with cold; a cold fit; sensation of cold in an animal body; chilliness; coldness or absence of heat in a substance; *fig.* the feeling of being damped or discouraged; a depressing influence. *a.* Cold; tending to cause shivering (*chill* winds); experiencing cold; shivering with cold; *fig.* depressing; discouraging; distant; formal; not warm (a *chill* reception).—*v.t.* To affect with chill; to make chilly; *fig.* to check in enthusiasm or warmth; to discourage; to dispirit; to depress; *metal.* to reduce suddenly the temperature of (a piece of castiron), with the view of hardening (a *chilled* shot).—**chiller,** chil′ėr, *n.* One who or that which chills.—**chillingly,** chil′ing•li, *adv.* In a chilling manner; coldly.—**chilly,** chil′i, *a.* [*Chill,* and term. *-y.*] Experiencing or causing the sensation of chillness; disagreeably cold; chilling.—*adv.*, chil′li, [*Chill,* and term. *-ly.*] In a chill or chilly manner.—**chilliness,** chil′i•nes, *n.* The state or quality of being chilly.

chime, chīm, *n.* [O.E. *chimbe, chymbe,* a cymbal, a shortening of *chymbale,* A.Sax. *cimbal,* from L. *cymbalum,* a cymbal.] The harmonious sound of bells or musical instruments; a set of bells (properly five or more) tuned to a musical scale, and struck by hammers, not by the tongues.—*v.i.* To sound in consonance, rhythm, or harmony; to give out harmonious sounds; hence, to accord; to agree; to suit; to harmonize; to express agreement; often with *in with* (to *chime in with* one's sentiments or humor).—*v.t.* To cause to sound harmoniously, as a set of bells.—**chimer,** chīm′ėr, *n.* One who chimes.

chime, chimb, chīm, *n.* [D. *kim,* Sw. *kim, kimb,* the edge of a cask, G. *kimme,* edge, brim.] The edge or brim of a cask or tub, formed by the ends of the staves projecting beyond the head.

chimera, chimaera, ki•mē′ra, *n.* [L. *chimæra,* from Gr. *chimaira,* a chimaera.] *Class. myth.* a fire-breathing monster, the fore parts of whose body were those of a lion, the middle of a goat, and the hinder of a dragon; *ornamental art.* a fantastic assemblage of animal forms so combined as to produce one complete but unnatural design; hence, a vain or idle fancy; a mere phantasm of the imagination; also the name of a cartilaginous fish of extraordinary appearance inhabiting the northern seas, and sometimes called king of the herrings.—**chimeric, chimerical,** ki•mer′ik, ki•mer′ik•al, *a.* Merely imaginary; fanciful; fantastic; wildly or vainly conceived.—**chimerically,** ki•mer′ik•al•li, *adv.* In a chimerical manner.

chimere, shi•mēr′, *n.* [Fr. *simarre,* It. *zimarra.*] The upper robe, to which the lawn sleeves of a bishop are attached.

chimney, chim′ni, *n.* [Fr. *cheminée,* L.L. *caminata,* a chimney, from L. *caminus,* a furnace, a flue, from Gr. *kaminos,* an oven.] An erection, generally of stone or brick, containing a passage by which the smoke of a fire or furnace escapes to the open air; a chimney stack; a flue; the funnel of a steam engine; a tall glass to surround the flame of a lamp to protect it and promote combustion.—**chimney pot,** *n.* A pipe of earthenware or sheet metal placed on the top of chimneys to prevent smoking.—**chimney piece,** *n.* The assemblage of architectural dressings around the open recess constituting the fire place in a room.—**chimneysweep,** *n.* One whose occupation is to clean chinneys of the soot that adheres to their sides.

chimpanzee, chim•pan′zē or chim•pan•zē′, *n.* [The native Guinea name.] A large West African ape belonging to the anthropoid or manlike monkeys, and most nearly related to the gorilla.

chin, chin, *n.* [A.Sax. *cin*=D. *kin,* G. *kinn,* the chin; Icel. *kinn,* Dan. *kind,* Goth. *kinnus,* the cheek; Cog. Armor. *gen,* the cheek; W. *gen.* the chin; L. *gena,* the cheek; Gr. *genys,* the jaw, the chin; Skr. *hanu,* the jaw.] The lower extremity of the face below the mouth.—*v.t.* To lift oneself up by the arms until the chin is level with the support.—*v.i.* To talk. (Slang).

china, chinaware, chī′na, chī′na•wâr, *n.* A species of earthenware made in *China,* or in imitation of that made there, and so called from the country; porcelain.—**China aster,** *n.* The common name of a hardy and free-flowering composite plant.—**China rose,** *n.* The name given to a number of varieties of garden rose, natives of China.

chinch, chinch, *n.* [Sp. *chinche,* a bug, from L. *cimex.*] The common bedbug; also the popular name of certain fetid American insects resembling the bedbug, very destructive to wheat, corn, etc.

chinchilla, chin•chil′la, *n.* [Spanish name.] A genus of rodent animals peculiar to the South American continent, one species of which produces a fine pearly-gray fur; the fur of the chinchilla.

chincough, chin′kof, *n.* [For *chinkcough, chink* being for *kink,* as in Sc. *kinkhost* (*host,* a cough), D. *kinkhoest.*] Whooping-cough.

chine, chīn, *n.* [Fr. *échine,* O.Fr. *eschine,* the spine.] The backbone or spine of an animal; a piece of the backbone of an animal, with the adjoining parts, cut for cooking.—*v.t.* To cut through the backbone, or into chine pieces.

Chinese, chī•nēz′, *a.* Pertaining to China.—*Chinese fire,* a composition used in fireworks.—*Chinese lantern,* a lantern made of colored paper used in illuminations.—*Chinese white,* the white oxide of zinc.—*n. sing.* and *pl.* A native or natives of China; the language of China.

chink, chingk, *n.* [Akin to O.E. *chine,* A.Sax. *cinu,* a chink, a fissure, *cinan,* to gape.] A narrow aperture; a cleft, rent, or fissure of greater length than breadth; a cranny, gap, or crack.—*v.t.* To cause to open or part and form a fissure; to make chinks in; to fill up chinks in.—*v.i.* To crack; to open.

chink, chingk, *v.i.* [Imitative; comp. *jingle.*] To make a small sharp metallic sound.—*v.t.* To cause to sound as by shaking coins or small pieces of metal.—*n.* A short, sharp, clear, metallic sound; a term for money (vulgar); the reed bunting.

chinquapin, ching′ka•pin, *n.* [Of Amer.-Indian origin.] The dwarf chestnut of the U.S. yielding edible nuts; also an American tree allied to the oak.

chintz, chints, *n.* [Hind. *chint,* Per. *chinz,* spotted, stained.] Cotton cloth or calico printed with flowers or other devices, generally glazed.

chip, chip, *v.t.*—*chipped, chipping.* [Closely connected with *chop* and *chap*; O.D. *kippen,* to knock to pieces; O.Sw. *kippa,* to chop; G. *kippen,* to clip or cut money.] To cut into small pieces; to diminish by cutting away a little at a time or in small pieces.—*v.i.* To break or fly off in small pieces.—*n.* A piece of wood, stone, or other substance separated from a body by a blow of an instrument; a flat counter used in games.

chipmunk, chip′mungk, *n.* The popular name of the ground squirrel.

chipper, chip′ėr, *a.* [Probably from North. E. *kipper,* lively.] Cheerful; sprightly.

Chippendale, chip′en•dāl, *a.* [Inventor's name.] A style of drawing-room furniture.

chirographer, kī•rog′ra•fėr, *n.* [Gr. *cheir,* the hand, *graphō,* to write.] One who exercises or professes the art of writing; one who tells fortunes by examining the hand.—**chirographic, chirographical,** kī•ro•graf′ik, kī•ro•graf′ik•al, *a.* Pertaining to chirography.—**chirography,** kī•rog′ra•fi, *n.* The art of writing; handwriting; the art of telling fortunes by examining the hand.

chiromancy, kī′ro•man•si, *n.* [Gr. *cheir,* the hand, and *manteia,* divination.] Divination by the hand; the art or practice of foretelling one's fortune by inspecting the lines and lineaments of his hand; palmistry.—**chiromancer,** kī′ro•man•sėr, *n.* One who practices chiromancy.

chiropodist, kī•rop′od•ist, *n.* [Gr. *cheir,* the hand, and *pous, podos,* the foot.] One who treats diseases of the feet.

chiropractic, kī•ro•prak′tik, *n.* [Gr. *cheir,* hand, and *praktikos,* practice.] Manipulation of the spine to cure disease.—**chiropractor,** kī′ro•prak•tėr, *n.* One who practices chiropractic by method of manipulation.

chiropter, kī•rop'tėr, *n.* [Gr. *cheir,* a hand, and *pteron,* a wing.] A bat. BAT.

chirp, cherp, *v.i.* [Akin to G. *zirpen, tschirpen, schirpen,* to chirp, *chirrup* being a lengthened form; the same root is in D. *kirren,* to coo, L. *garrio,* to chatter.] To make a short sharp shrill sound, as is done by small birds or certain insects; to cheep.—*n.* A short, shrill note, as of certain birds or insects.

chirrup, chir'up, *v.i.* [A lengthened form of *chirp.*] To chirp.—*n.* A chirp.

chisel, chiz'el, *n.* [O.Fr. *cisel* (Fr. *ciseau*). L.L. *cisellus,* from L. *cædo, cæsum,* to cut.] An instrument of iron or steel, used in carpentry, joinery, cabinet work, masonry, sculpture, etc., for paring, hewing, or gouging.—*v.t.*—*chiseled, chiseling.* To cut, pare, gouge, or engrave with a chisel (a statue *chiseled* out of marble); *fig.* to cut close, as in a bargain; to cheat (slang).—**chiseled,** chiz'eld, *a.* Worked with a chisel or as with a chisel; clear-cut; statuesque.

chit, chit, *n.* [A.Sax. *cith,* a shoot or twig.] A shoot or sprout; the first shoot of a seed or plant; a child or babe; a young and insignificant person.

chitchat, chit'chat, *n.* [A reduplication of *chat.*] Prattle; familiar or trifling talk.

chitin, kī'tin, *n.* [Gr. *chitōn,* a tunic.] The organic substance which forms the wing covers and integuments of insects and the carapaces of crustacea, having a somewhat horny character.—**chitinous,** kī'tin•us, *a.* Consisting of, or having the nature of chitin.

chiton, kī'ton, *n.* [Gr. *chitōn,* a tunic, a cuirass, a coat of mail.] The name of certain mollusks, the shell of which is formed of successive portions, often in contact and overlapping each other, but never truly articulated.

chitterling, chit'ėr•ling, *n. Cookery,* part of the small intestines, as of swine, fried for food: generally used in the plural.

chivalry, shiv'al•ri, *n.* [Fr. *chevalerie,* from *chevalier,* a knight or horseman, from *cheval,* a horse. CAVALRY.] Knighthood; the system to which knighthood with all its laws and usages belonged; the qualifications of a knight, as courtesy, valor, and dexterity in arms; knights or warriors collectively; any body of illustrious warriors, especially cavalry.—**chivalric, chivalrous,** shiv'al•rik, shiv'al•rus, *a.* Pertaining to chivalry or knight errantry; warlike; bold; gallant.—**chivalrously,** shiv'al•rus•li, *adv.* In a chivalrous manner or spirit.—**chivalrousness,** shiv'al•rus•nes, *n.* The quality of being chivalrous.

chive, chīv, *n.* [Fr. *cive,* L. *cepa,* an onion.] A small perennial plant of the same genus as the leek and onion, cultivated in kitchen gardens as a potherb.

chlamys, kla'mas, klā'mas, *n.* [L. *chlamys,* from Gr.] A short, oblong mantle usually clasped at the shoulder, worn by young men in ancient Greece.

chloral, klō'ral, *n.* [From *chlor,* the first part of *chlorine,* and *al,* the first syllable of *alcohol.*] An oily liquid with a pungent odor and slightly astringent taste, produced from chlorine and alcohol; also the name popularly applied to chloral hydrate, a white crystalline substance used in medicine for producing sleep.

chlorine, klō'rēn, *n.* [Gr. *chlōros,* greenish-yellow, from its color.] A gaseous element, yellowish green in color with a suffocating odor, used as a bleach and in industrial processes. Symbol, Cl; at. no., 17; at. wt., 35.453.—**chlorate,** klō'rāt, *n.* A salt of chloric acid.—**chloric,** klō'rik, *a.* Pertaining to or containing chlorine.—*Chloric acid,* a colorless unstable solution that has strong oxidizing properties.—**chloride,** klō'rīd, *n.* A compound of chlorine with another element.—*Chloride of lime,* chlorine and lime, used as a bleaching agent.—**chlorinate,** klō're•nāt, *v.t.* To treat or combine with chlorine.—**chlorination,** klō•re•nā'shon, *n.*—**chlorite,** klō'rīt, *n.* A green mineral silicate of aluminum.—**chlorous,** klō'rus, *a.*

chloroform, klo'ro•form, *n.* [*Chlor-,* from *chloride* or *chlorine,* and *-form,* from *formic* acid, from chemical connection.] A volatile colorless liquid, of an agreeable, fragrant, sweetish apple taste and smell, prepared by distilling together a mixture of alcohol, water, and chloride of lime, and much used as an anesthetic, for which purpose its vapor is inhaled.—*v.t.* To put under the influence of chloroform; to treat with chloroform.

chlorophyll, klō'ro•fil, *n.* [Gr. *chlōros,* green, and *phyllon,* a leaf.] The green coloring matter of plants, which is developed by the influence of light; hence arises the etiolation or blanching of plants by privation of light.

chlorosis, klo•rō'sis, *n.* [Gr. *chlōros,* greenish-yellow.] The greensickness, a peculiar form of anemia or bloodlessness which affects young females, and is characterized by a pale greenish hue of the skin.

chlorous. See CHLORINE.

chock-full, chok'fu̧l, *a.* As full as possible; crammed.

chocolate, chok'o•lit, *n.* [Sp. *chocolate;* Mex. *chocolatl—choco,* cocoa, and *latl,* water.] A paste or cake composed of the kernels of the cacao nut ground and combined with sugar and vanilla, cinnamon, cloves, or other flavoring substance; the beverage made by dissolving chocolate in boiling water or milk.—*a.* Having the color of chocolate; of a dark, glossy brown.

choice, chois, *n.* [O.Fr. *chois,* a choice, from *choisir,* to choose; from the German. CHOOSE.] The act or power of choosing; a selecting or separating from two or more things that which is preferred; selection; election; option; preference; the thing chosen; the best part of anything.—*a.* Carefully selected; worthy of being preferred; select; precious.—**choicely,** chois'li, *adv.* In a choice manner or degree.—**choiceness,** chois'nes, *n.* The quality of being choice or select; excellence; value.

choir, kwīr, *n.* [O.Fr. *chœur,* L. *chorus,* Gr. *choros,* a dance in a ring, a band; same word as *chorus, quire.*] A band of dancers‡; a collection of singers, especially in a church; that part of a church appropriated for the singers in cruciform churches; that part eastward of the nave, and separated from it usually by a screen of open work; a chancel.—*v.t.* and *i.* To sing in company.

choke, chōk, *v.t.*—*choked, choking.* [Akin to *cough,* and to Icel. *koka,* to gulp, *kyka,* to swallow; perhaps imitative of the convulsive sound made when the throat is impeded.] To deprive of the power of breathing by stopping the passage of the breath through the windpipe; to compress the windpipe of; to strangle; to stop by filling (any passage); to obstruct; to block up; to hinder by obstruction or impediments (as plants from growing); to enrich the fuel mixture of an engine by decreasing the air supply.—*v.i.* To have the windpipe stopped; to have something stick in the throat.—*n.* The act of choking; the valve that chokes a gasoline engine.—**choker,** chōk'ėr, *n.* One who or that which chokes; a short necklace.

choler, kol'ėr, *n.* [O.Fr. *cholere* (Fr. *colère*), choler, anger, L. *cholera,* a bilious ailment, from Gr. *cholera,* from *cholē,* bile, anger.] The bile, the excess of which was formerly supposed to produce anger, etc.; hence, anger, wrath, irascibility.—**choleric,** kol'ėr•ik, *a.* Abounding with choler or bile; easily irritated; irascible; inclined to anger; proceeding from anger.

cholera, kol'ėr•a, *n.* [L. bile, a bilious complaint. CHOLER.] A serious gastrointestinal infection marked by diarrhea, vomiting, and dehydration.

cholesterol, ko•les'ter•ōl, *n.* [Gr. *cholē,* bile, and *stereos,* solid.] A white crystalline solid found in all animal fats, gallstones, egg yolk, milk, etc.

chondrite, kon'drīt, *n.* [L. *chondrus,* a species of seaweed.] A fossil marine plant of the chalk and other formations resembling Irish moss.

chondrotomy, kon•drot'o•mi, *n.* [Gr. *chondros,* cartilage, and *tome,* a cutting.] A dissection of cartilages.

choose, chöz, *v.t.*—*chose* (pret.), *chosen, choosing.* [A.Sax. *ceósan*=D. *kiezen,* Icel. *kjosa,* G. *kiesen,* to choose, Goth. *kiusan,* to choose, to prove; from root seen in L. *gustare,* Gr. *geuomai,* to taste.] To take by preference; to make choice or selection of; to pick out; to select; to prefer; to wish; to be inclined or have an inclination for (colloq.).—*v.i.* To make a choice.—**chooser,** chöz'ėr, *n.* One that chooses; one that has the power or right of choosing.

chop, chop, *v.t.*—*chopped, chopping.* [Same word as *chap,* to split, with a slightly different form and meaning=D. and G. *kappen*, to chop, to mince, to cut; Dan. *kappe*, to cut, to lop.] To cut into pieces; to mince; to sever or separate by striking with a sharp instrument: usually with *off*.—*v.i.* To chap or crack, as the skin.—*n.* A piece chopped off; a slice, particularly of meat.—**chopper,** chop′ėr, *n.* One who or that which chops; a tool for chopping or mincing meat; a cleaver.—**chophouse,** *n.* A house where meat chops are dressed ready for eating; an eating house.

chop, chop, *v.t.*—*chopped, chopping.* [Same origin as *cheap.*] To buy, or rather to barter; to truck or exchange.—*To chop logic*, to dispute or argue in a sophistical manner or with an affectation of logical terms or methods.—*v.i.* To bargain‡; to bandy words or dispute‡; to turn, vary, change, or shift suddenly: said of the wind.—*n.* A turn of fortune; change; vicissitude, especially in the phrase *chops and changes*.

chop, chop, *n.* The chap; the jaw; *pl.* the mouth or entrance to a channel. CHAP.—**chopfallen,** *a.* Dejected; chapfallen.

chop, chop, *n.* [Hind. *chhap*, stamp, print.] An eastern customhouse or other stamp on goods; hence, quality or brand (silk or tea of the first *chop*).

chopine, cho•pēn′, *n.* [From Sp. *chapin*, a clog or chopine.] A sort of very lofty clog or patten formerly worn.

choppy, chop′i, *a.* [From *chop*, change.] Showing short broken waves.

chopstick, chop′stik, *n.* One of two small sticks of wood, ivory, etc., used by the Chinese and Japanese for conveying food to the mouth.

choragus, kō•rā′gus, *n.* [Gr. *choragos* —*choros*, a chorus, and *agō*, to lead.] The leader or superintendent of a chorus or of a theatrical representation in ancient Greece; the person who had to provide at his own expense the choruses for dramatic representations and religious festivals.—**choragic,** kō•rā′jik, *a.* Pertaining to or connected with a choragus.

choral, etc. See CHORUS.

chord, kord, *n.* [L. *chorda*, from Gr. *chordē*, an intestine, of which strings were made. *Cord* is the same word.] The string of a musical instrument; *mus.* the simultaneous combination of different sounds, consonant or dissonant; *geom.* a straight line drawn or supposed to extend from one end of an arc of a circle to the other.—*v.t.* To furnish with chords or musical strings.

chore, chōr, *n.* [An alteration of E. *chare*, an odd job.] A task; a duty; a small odd job.

chorea, kō′rē•a or ko•rē′a, *n.* [Gr. *choreia*, a dance.] *Med.* St. Vitus's dance; convulsive motions of the limbs.

choreography, kōr•ē•og′ra•fi, *n.* [Gr. *choreia*, dance, and *graphy*, *graphein*, to write.] The art of designing and arranging dances for a ballet.—**choreographer,** kōr•ē•og′ra•fėr, *n.*

choriamb, kō•ri•amb′, *n.* [Gr. *choreios*, a trochee, and *iambos*, iambus.] *Pros.* a foot consisting of four syllables, the first two forming a trochee and the second two an iambus.

chorion, kō′ri•on, *n.* [Gr.] *Anat.* the external vascular membrane which invests the fetus in the womb; *bot.* the external membrane of the seeds of plants.—**choroid,** kor′oid, *a.* and *n.* A term applied to a membrane resembling the chorion, especially to one of the membranes of the eye of a very dark color.

chorister, etc. See CHORUS.

chorography, kō•rog′ra•fi, *n.* [Gr. *chōros*, a place or region, and *graphō*, to describe.] The art or practice of making maps of or of describing particular regions, countries, or districts. — **chorographer,** kō•rog′ra•fėr, *n.* One skilled in chorography. —**chorographic, chorographical,** kō•ro•graf′ik, kō•ro•graf′ik•al, *a.* Pertaining to chorography; descriptive of particular regions or countries.

choroid. See CHORION.

chorus, kō′rus, *n.* [L. *chorus*, from Gr. *choros*, a dance in a ring, a chorus.] Originally a band of dancers accompanied by their own singing or that of others; the performers in a Greek play who were supposed to behold what passed in the acts, and sing their sentiments between the acts; the song between the acts; now, usually, verses of a song in which the company joins the singer, or the singing of the company with the singer; a union or chiming of voices in general (a *chorus* of laughter or ridicule); *mus.* a composition in parts sung by many voices; the whole body of vocalists other than soloists, whether in an oratorio, opera, or concert.—*v.t.* To sing or join in the chorus of; to exclaim or call out in concert.—**choral,** kō′ral, *a.* Belonging, relating, or pertaining to a chorus, choir, or concert.—**choral, chorale,** ko•ral′, ko•räl′, *n.* A psalm or hymn tune, often sung in unison by the congregation, the organ supplying the harmony.—**choric,** kō′rik, *a.* Pertaining to a chorus; choral. (*Tenn.*)—**chorister,** kor′ist•ėr, *n.* A singer in a choir or chorus; a singer generally.

chose, chōz, pret. of *choose.*—**chosen,** chō′zn, pp. of *choose.* As an adjective, choice; select.

chough, chuf, *n.* [A.Sax. *ceó*, a chough or jackdaw; D. *haauw*, Dan. *kaa.*] A bird of the crow family, genus *Pyrrhocorax*, of a black color with red beak, legs, and toes.

chowchow, chou′chou, *n.* A Chinese term for any mixture, but in trade circles confined generally to mixed pickles.

chrestomathy, kres•tom′a•thi, *n.* [Gr. *chrēstos*, useful, and *mathein*, to learn.] A book of extracts from a foreign language, with notes, intended to be used in acquiring the language.

chrism, krizm, *n.* [Gr. *chrisma*, an unguent, from *chriō*, to anoint, whence also *Christ.*] Holy or consecrated oil or unguent used in the administration of baptism, confirmation, ordination, and extreme unction, more especially in the Latin and Greek churches; the baptismal cloth laid upon the head of a child newly baptized; the baptismal vesture; the chrisom.—**chrismal,** kriz′mal, *a.* Pertaining to chrism.—*n.* The vessel holding the consecrated oil or chrism; the white cloth laid over the head of one newly baptized, after the unction with chrism.—**chrisom,** kris′um, *n.* [A form of *chrism.*] A cloth anointed with chrism laid on a child's face at baptism; the white consecrated vesture put about a child when christened.—*Chrisom child*, a newly baptized infant; a child that dies within a month after christening.

Christ, krīst, *n.* [L. *Christus*, Gr. *Christos*, lit. anointed, from *chriō*, to anoint.] THE ANOINTED: an appellation given to the Saviour of the World, and synonymous with the Hebrew MESSIAH.—**christen,** kris′n, *v.t.* [A.Sax. *cristnian*, to christen, from *Cristen*, a Christian, from *Crist*, Christ.] To initiate into the visible church of Christ by the application of water; to name and baptize; to baptize; to name or denominate generally.—**Christendom,** kris′n•dum, *n.* [A.Sax. *cristendom*—*Cristen*, Christian, and term. *-dom.*] The territories, countries, or regions chiefly inhabited by Christians or those who profess to believe in the Christian religion; the whole body of Christians. — **Christian,** kris′chen, *n.* [L. *christianus*, from *Christus*, Christ.] One who believes, professes to believe, or who is assumed to believe, in the religion of Christ; a believer in Christ who is characterized by real piety.—*a.* Pertaining to Christ or to Christianity.—*Christian name*, the name given or announced at baptism, as distinguished from the family name.—*Christian era* or *period*, the period from the birth of Christ to the present time.—**Christianity,** kris•chi•an′i•ti, *n.* The religion of Christians, or the system of doctrines and precepts taught by Christ; conformity to the laws and precepts of the Christian religion. —**Christianization,** kris′chen•iz•ā″shon, *n.* The act or process of converting to Christianity.—**Christianize,** kris′chen•iz, *v.t.*—*christianized, christianizing.* To make Christian; to convert to Christianity.—**Christless,** krīst′les, *a.* Having no interest in Christ; without the spirit of Christ.—**Christmas,** kris′mas, *n.* [*Christ*, and *mass*, A.Sax. *mæssa*, a holy day or feast.] The festival of the Christian church observed annually on the 25th day of December, in memory of the birth of Christ; Christmas day or Christmastide.—**Christmas day,** *n.* The 25th day of December, when Christmas is celebrated.—**Christmas eve,** *n.* The evening of the day before Christmas.—**Christmastide,** *n.* The season of Christmas.—**Christmas tree,** *n.* A small evergreen tree set up by a family, etc., at Christmas, from which are hung ornaments and lights, with gifts placed underneath. —**Christ's thorn,** *n.* A deciduous shrub with large hooked spines, a native of Palestine and the south of Europe: so named from a belief that it supplied the crown of thorns for Christ.

chromatic, krō•mat′ik, *a.* [Gr. *chromatikos,* from *chrōma,* color.] Relating to color, or to colored inks or pigments; *mus.* including notes not belonging to the diatonic scale.—*Chromatic scale,* a scale made up of thirteen successive semitones, that is, the eight diatonic tones and the five intermediate tones.—**chromatically,** krō•mat′ik•al•li, *adv.* In a chromatic manner.—**chromatics,** krō•mat′iks, *n.* The science of colors; that part of optics which treats of the properties of the colors of light and of natural bodies.—**chromatography,** krō•ma•tog′ra•fi, *n. Chem.* separation of closely related compounds by a method in which the compounds in solution are separately adsorbed in colored layers of an adsorbent.—**chromatology,** krō•ma•tol′o•ji, *n.* The doctrine of or a treatise on colors.—**chromatophore,** krō•mat′ō•fōr, *n.* [Gr. *chrōma,* and *pherein,* to bear.] One of the pigment cells in animals, well seen in the chameleons and cuttlefishes.

chromatin, krō′ma•tin, *n.* [Gr. *chrōma, -atos,* color.] In cells, that part of the nucleus which can be deeply stained.

chrome, chromium, krōm, krō′mi•um, *n.* [Gr. *chrōma,* color.] **A hard, grayish-white, metallic element, used as a plating and in chrome steel. Symbol, Cr; at. no., 24; at. wt., 51.996.**—**chromic,** krōm′ik, *a.* Pertaining to chrome or obtained from it.—**chromite,** krō′mīt, *n.* A mineral containing chromium.

chromogen, krō′mo•jen, *n.* [Gr. *chrōma,* color, and root *gen,* to produce.] A chemical compound containing color-forming groups; a substance that becomes a coloring matter.

chromolithography, krō′mo•li•thog″ra•fi, *n.* A method of producing colored lithographic pictures by using stones having different portions of the picture drawn upon them with inks of different colors, and so arranged as to blend into a complete picture.—**chromolithograph,** *n.* A picture obtained by means of chromolithography.—**chromolithographer,** *n.* One who practices chromolithography.—**chromolithographic,** *a.* Pertaining to chromolithography.

chromosome, krō′mo•sōm, *n.* [Gr. *chrōma,* color, and *sōma,* body.] Any of the small, elongated bodies in the cell nucleus that control the activity of the cell and play an important role in inheritance.

chromosphere, krō′mo•sfēr, *n.* [Gr. *chrōma,* color, and *sphaira,* a sphere.] The red layer of the sun's atmosphere, just beyond the solar disk, that is composed chiefly of hydrogen; a similar layer around any star.—**chromospheric,** krō•mo•sfer′ik, *a.*

chronic, kron′ik, *a.* [Gr. *chronikos,* from *chronos,* time, duration.] Pertaining to time; having reference to time; continuing a long time, as a disease.—**chronicle,** kron′i•kl, *n.* [Fr. *chronique,* a chronicle.] An account of facts or events disposed in the order of time; a history, more especially one of a simple unpretentious character; *pl.* the title of two books of the Old Testament consisting mainly of the annals of the kingdom of Judah.—*v.t. chronicled, chronicling.* To record in history or chronicle; to record; to register.—**chronicler,** kron′i•klėr, *n.* One who chronicles; a writer of a chronicle.

chronogram, kron′o•gram, *n.* [Gr. *chronos,* time, and *gramma,* a letter or writing.] A word or words in which a date is expressed by the numeral letters occurring therein.—**chronogrammatic,** kron′o•gram•mat″ik, *a.* Belonging to a chronogram; containing a chronogram.

chronograph, kron′o•graf, *n.* [Gr. *chronos,* time, and *graphō,* to write.] A chronogram; a device of various kinds for measuring and registering very minute portions of time with extreme precision, generally consisting of a revolving hand, disk, or cylinder, moved by clockwork, the time of the event being indicated by a point or pen marking the disk or cylinder, such marking being controlled either by the observer himself or by electricity.

chronology, kro•nol′o•ji, *n.* [Gr. *chronologia—chronos,* time, and *logos,* discourse or doctrine.] The science of ascertaining the true periods or years when past events or transactions took place, and arranging them in their proper order according to their dates.—**chronologic, chronological,** kron•o•loj′ik, kron•o•loj′ik•al, *a.* Relating to chronology; containing an account of events in the order of time; according to the order of time.—**chronologically,** kron•o•loj′ik•al•li, *adv.* In a chronological manner.—**chronologist, chronologer,** kro•nol′o•jist, kro•nol′o•jėr, *n.* One versed in chronology; a person who investigates the dates of past events and transactions.

chronometer, kro•nom′et•ėr, *n.* [Gr. *chronos,* time, and *metron,* measure.] Any instrument that measures time, as a clock, watch, or dial; specifically, a timekeeper of great perfection of workmanship, made much on the principle of a watch, but rather larger, used (in conjunction with observations of the heavenly bodies) in determining the longitude at sea.—**chronometric, chronometrical,** kron•o•met′rik, kron•o•met′rik•al, *a.* Pertaining to a chronometer; measured by a chronometer.—**chronometry,** kro•nom′et•ri, *n.* The art of measuring time; the measuring of time by periods or divisions.

chronoscope, kron′o•skōp, *n.* [Gr. *chronos,* time, and *skopeō,* to observe.] An instrument for measuring the duration of extremely short-lived phenomena; more especially, the name given to instruments of various forms for measuring the velocity of projectiles.

chrysalis, chrysalid, kris′a•lis, kris′a•lid, *n.* [Gr. *chrysallis,* a grub, from *chrysos,* gold, from its golden color.] The form which butterflies, moths, and most other insects assume when they change from the state of larva or caterpillar and before they arrive at their winged or perfect state. Called also *Aurelia* and *Pupa.*

chrysanthemum, kri•san′the•mum, *n.* [Gr. *chrysos,* gold, and *anthemon,* a flower.] The generic and common name of numerous species of composite plants, some of which are common weeds, such as the ox-eye daisy, while the florists' chrysanthemum, in its numerous varieties, is equally well known.—**chryselephantine,** kris′el•e•fan″tin, *a.* [Gr. *elephas, elephantos,* ivory.] Composed or partly composed of gold and ivory: a term specially applied to statues overlaid with gold and ivory, as made among the ancient Greeks.—**chrysoberyl,** kris′o•ber•il, *n.* [Gr. *beryllion,* beryl.] A gem of a yellowish-green color, next to the sapphire in hardness, and employed in jewelry, being found in Ceylon, Peru, Siberia, Brazil, etc.—**chrysolite,** kris′ō•līt, *n.* [Gr. *lithos,* stone.] A greenish, sometimes transparent, gem, composed of silica, magnesium, and iron, not of great value.—**chrysoprase,** kris′o•prāz, *n.* [Gr. *prason,* a leek.] A translucent mineral of an apple-green color, a variety of chalcedony much esteemed as a gem.

chthonian, thōn′i•an, *a.* [Gr. *chthonios,* from *chthōn,* the earth.] Pertaining to the earth; belonging to the underworld or divinities of subterraneous regions, preceding the Olympian system.

chub, chub, *n.* [So called probably from its *chubbiness* or plumpness.] A river fish of the carp family, having the body oblong, nearly round; the head and back green, the sides silvery, and the belly white.

chubby, chub′i, *a.* [Akin to E. *chump*; Sw. dial. *kubbug,* plump, *kubb,* a lump, a block.] Having a round plump face or plump body; round and fat; plump.—**chubbiness,** chub′i•nes, *n.* The state of being chubby.

chuck, chuk, *n.* [Imitative; comp. *cluck.*] The voice or call of a hen and some other birds, or a sound resembling that.—*v.i.* To make the noise which a hen and some other birds make when they call their chickens.

chuck, chuk, *v.t.* [A modification of *shock.* Fr. *choquer,* and formerly written *chock.*] To strike, tap, or give a gentle blow; to throw, with quick motion, a short distance; to pitch.—*n.* A slight blow or tap under the chin; a toss; a short throw.

chuck, chuk, *n.* [Variant of *chock.*] A cut of beef between the neck and the shoulder; a device for holding a tool in a machine.—**chuck wagon,** *n.* A wagon that carries food and cooking equipment.

chuckle, chuk′l, *v.i.—chuckled, chuckling.* [A freq. and dim. from *chuck,* to cry like a hen; or connected with *choke.*] To laugh in a suppressed or broken manner; to feel inward triumph or exultation.

chuff,† chuf, *n.* [Perhaps from W. *cyff*, a stock or stump.] A coarse, heavy, dull, or surly fellow; a niggard; an old miser.

chum, chum, *n.* [Perhaps an abbrev. of *chamber-fellow*; or, a rather more probable suggestion, of *chimney-fellow*.] One who lodges or resides in the same room or rooms; hence, a close companion; a bosom friend; an intimate.—*v.i.* To occupy the same room or rooms with another; to be the chum of some one.

chump, chump, *n.* [Same as Icel. *kumbr*, a log, akin to *kubba*, to chop, and therefore allied to E. *chop*, *chub*, *chubby*.] A short, thick, heavy piece of wood; a blockhead.

chunk, chungk, *n.* Lump of bread, cheese, wood; a short, heavy-set person.

church, chėrch, *n.* [O.E. *chirche*, *cherche*, etc., A.Sax. *circe*, *cirice*, *cyrice* (the c's all hard), from Gr. *kyriakon*, a church, the Lord's house, from *Kyrios*, the Lord=Sc. *kirk*, D. *kerk*, Dan. *kirke*, G. *kirche*.] A house consecrated to the worship of God among Christians; in England often restricted to a place of public worship belonging to the Established Church (as opposed to *chapel* and *meeting-house*); the collective body of Christians; a particular body of Christians united under one form of ecclesiastical government, in one creed, and using the same ritual and ceremonies; ecclesiastical power or authority.—*v.t.* To perform with or for anyone the office of returning thanks in the church, as a mother after childbirth.—**churchgoer,** *n.* One who habitually attends church.—**churchgoing,** *a.* Usually attending church; summoning to church, as a bell.—**churchman,** chėrch′man, *n.* An ecclesiastic or clergyman; in England, a member of the Established Church.—**churchmanship,** chėrch′man•ship, *n.* State of being a churchman.—**churchwarden,** *n.* A functionary appointed by the minister, or elected by the parishioners, to superintend a church and its concerns, to represent the interests of the parish, etc.

churl, chėrl, *n.* [A.Sax. *ceorl*, a countryman of the lowest rank; Icel. Dan. Sw. *karl*, a man, a male; G. *kerl*, a fellow.] A rustic; a peasant; a countryman or laborer; a rude, surly, sullen, selfish, or rough-tempered man.—**churlish,** chėr′lish, *a.* Like or pertaining to a churl; rude; surly; sullen; unfeeling; uncivil; selfish; narrowminded; avaricious.—**churlishly,** chėr′lish•li, *adv.* In a churlish manner.—**churlishness,** chėr′lish•nes, *n.* The quality of being churlish.

churn, chėrn, *n.* [A.Sax. *cyrn*, Sc. *kirn*, Icel. *kirna*, Dan. *kierne*, a churn; probably from same root as *corn*, *kernel*, butter being as it were the kernel or best portion of the milk.] A vessel in which cream or milk is agitated for separating the oily parts from the caseous and serous parts, to make butter.—*v.t.* To stir or agitate (milk or cream) in order to make into butter; to make (butter) by the agitation of milk or cream; to shake or agitate with violence or continued motion.

chute, shöt, *n.* [Fr., a fall.] A river-fall or rapid over which timber is floated; an inclined trough or tube through which articles are passed from a higher to a lower level.

chutney, chutnee, chut′ni, chut′nē, *n.* An East Indian condiment compounded of ripe fruit, spices, sour herbs, cayenne, lemon juice, pounded and boiled together and bottled for use.

chyle, kīl, *n.* [Gr. *chylos*, juice, chyle, from *cheo*, to flow, whence also *chyme*.] A white or milky fluid separated from aliments while in the intestines, taken up by the lacteal vessels and finally entering the blood.—**chylous,** kī′lus, *a.* Consisting of, pertaining to, or resembling chyle.

chyme, kīm, *n.* [Gr. *chymos*, juice. CHYLE.] The pulpy mass of partially digested food before the chyle is extracted from it.—**chymous,** kīm′-us, *a.* Pertaining to chyme.

cicada, si•kā′da, *n. pl.* **cicadae** or **cicadas,** si•kā′dē, si•kā′daz. [L.] The popular and generic name of certain insects, the males of which have on each side of the body an organ with which they can make a considerable noise.—**cicala,** si•kä′la; It. pron. chi•kä′la, *n.* [It., from L. *cicada*.] A cicada.

cicatrice, sik′a•tris, *n.* [Fr. *cicatrice*, L. *cicatrix*.] A scar; a little seam or elevation of flesh remaining after a wound or ulcer is healed. Also **cicatrix,** si•kā′triks, pl. **cicatrices,** sik•a•trī′sēz.—**cicatricle,** sik′a•tri•kl, *n.* [L. *cicatricula*, dim. of *cicatrix*.] The germinating point in the embryo of a seed; the point in the yolk of an egg at which development is first seen.—**cicatrize,** sik′•a•trīz, *v.t.*—*cicatrized*, *cicatrizing*. To induce the formation of a cicatrice on; to heal up (a wound).—*v.i.* To become healed leaving a cicatrice; to skin over.—**cicatrization,** sik′a•tri•zā″shon, *n.* The process of healing or forming a cicatrice.

cicely, sis′e•li, *n.* [L. *seseli*, Gr. *seseli*.] Popular name applied to several umbelliferous plants, *sweet cicely*, or sweet chevril, being an aromatic plant with fine, fernlike foliage.

cicerone, sis•e•rō′ne; It. pron. chē•-chā•rō′nā, *n.* [It., from *Cicero*, the Roman orator.] A name given by the Italians to the guides who show travelers the antiquities of the country; hence, in a general sense, one who explains the curiosities of a place; a guide.—**Ciceronian,** sis•e•rō′ni•an, *a.* Resembling the style of Cicero; eloquent.

cichoraceous, sik•o•rā′shus, *a.* [L. *cichorium*, chicory.] Having the qualities of or belonging to plants of the succory or chicory family.

cider, sī′dėr, *n.* [Fr. *cidre*, from L. *sicera*, Gr. *sikera*, strong drink, from Heb. *shakar*, to intoxicate.] The pressed juice of apples used as a beverage or for making a vinegar.

cigar, si-gär′, *n.* [Fr. *cigare*, Sp. *cigarro*, originally the name of a kind of tobacco in Cuba.] A small roll of tobacco leaf, with a pointed end for putting into the mouth, used for smoking.—**cigarette,** sig•a•ret′, *n.* [Fr. dim. of *cigare*.] A little cut tobacco rolled up in tissue paper, used for smoking.

cilia, sil′i•a, *n. pl.* [L. *cilium*, an eyelash.] The hairs which grow from the margin of the eyelids; eyelashes; hairs or bristles situated on the margin of a vegetable body; small, generally microscopic, hairlike vibratile processes which project from animal membranes, and have usually important functions.—**ciliary,** sil′i•-a•ri, *a.* Belonging to the eyelids or eyelashes; pertaining to or performed by vibratile cilia (*ciliary* motion).—**ciliate, ciliated,** sil′i•āt, sil′i•āt•ed, *a.* Furnished with cilia; bearing cilia.

Cimmerian, sim•mē′ri•an, *a.* Pertaining to the *Cimmerii* or *Cimmerians*, a mythical people described as dwelling where the sun never shines, and perpetual darkness reigns; hence, very dark (*Mil.*).

cinch, sinch, *n.* [Sp. *cincha*, same as *cincture*.] A saddle girth, in United States; firm hold, a sure thing.

cinchona, sin•kō′na, *n.* [From the Countess of *Chinchon*, vice-queen of Peru, who was cured of fever by it in 1638, and assisted in spreading the remedy.] The name of a number of South American trees and shrubs, some of which yield the bark whence quinine is obtained; the bark of such trees, called also *Peruvian bark*.—**cinchonic,** sin•kon′ik, *a.* Of or belonging to cinchona; derived from cinchona; having the properties of cinchona.—**cinchonine,** sin′ko•nin, *n.* An alkaloid obtained from the bark of several species of cinchona, along with quinine, and one of the medicinal active principles of this bark, being valuable as a febrifuge.—**cinchonism,** sin′kon•izm, *n.* A disturbed condition of the system, the result of overdoses of cinchona or quinine.

cincture, singk′chėr, *n.* [L. *cinctura*, from *cingo*, *cinctum*, to gird, seen also in *precinct*, *succinct*.] A belt, girdle, or something similar; that which rings, encircles, or encloses; enclosure; *arch.* a ring round a column.

cinder, sin′dėr, *n.* [A.Sax. *sinder*, dross, cinder=Icel. *sindr*, Sw. *sinder*, Dan. *sinder*, *sinner*, a cinder; D. *sintel*, G. *sinter*.] A solid piece of matter remaining after having been subjected to combustion; especially, a piece of coal more or less completely burnt, but not reduced to ashes.—**Cinderella,** *n.* A dance ending at twelve at night, from the French fairy tale of that name; a household drudge.—**cindery,** sin′dėr•i, *a.* Resembling cinders; containing cinders, or composed of them.

cinematograph, sin•e•mat′o•graf, *n.* [Gr. *kinēma*, motion, and *-graph*.] *Brit.* A motion picture camera taking a large series of instantaneous pictures, at least sixteen images per second, to obtain consecutive, continuous, uninterrupted movement.

cinereous, si•nē′rē•us, *a.* [L. *cineraceus, cinereus,* from *cinis, cineris,* ashes.] Like ashes: having the color of the ashes of wood.—**cinerary,** sin′e•ra•ri, *a.* [L. *cinerarius.*] Pertaining to ashes; a term applied to the urns in which the ashes of bodies which had been burned were deposited.—**cineritious,** sin•e•ri′shus, *a.* [L. *cineritius.*] Having the color or consistence of ashes; ash-gray; *anat.* a term applied to the exterior or cortical part of the brain.

cinnabar, sin′na•bär, *n.* [L. *cinnabaris,* Gr. *kinnabari,* a word of Eastern origin; Per. *quinbâr.*] Red sulfide of mercury, which, when sublimed and used as a pigment, is called *vermilion*; a red resinous juice obtained from an East Indian tree formerly used as an astringent: called also *Dragon's-blood.*

cinnamon, sin′na•mon, *n.* [L. *cinnamomum*; from Gr. *kinnamōmon,* through Phœn. from Heb. *kinnamon.*] The inner bark of a tree of the laurel family, a native of Ceylon and other parts of tropical Asia, dried and having a fragrant smell, moderately pungent taste, with some degree of sweetness and astringency, being one of the best cordial, carminative, and restorative spices.—*White cinnamon.* CANELLA.—**cinnamic,** sin-nam′ik, *a.* Pertaining to or obtained from cinnamon.—**cinnamon stone,** *n.* A variety of garnet of a cinnamon color.

cinque, singk, *n.* [Fr., L. *quinque,* five.] A five: a word used in certain games.—**cinquefoil,** *n.* [L. *folium, a* leaf.] An ornament in the pointed style of architecture somewhat resembling five leaves about a common center, the apertures of circular windows being often in this form; the name of various plants having quinate leaves, as the five-bladed clover, etc.

cipher, sī′fėr, *n.* [O.Fr. *cifre,* Mod.Fr. *chiffre,* It. *cifra,* Ar. *sifr,* cipher, from Ar. *sifr,* empty.] The numerical character or figure 0 or nothing; any numerical character; some person or thing of no consequence, importance, or value; a monogram or literal device formed of the intertwined initials of a name; a kind of secret writing.—*v.i.* To use figures; to practice arithmetic. —*v.t.* To write in occult or secret characters.

Circean, sėr•sē′an, *a.* Pertaining to *Circe,* in Greek mythology a celebrated sorceress, who transformed the companions of Ulysses into swine by a magical beverage; hence, fascinating but brutifying or poisonous; magical.

circinate, sėr′si•nāt, *a.* [From L. *circinus,* a compass, a circle, from *circus,* a circle.] *Bot.* rolled up on itself like a shepherd's crook or bishop's crosier, as the fronds of ferns in a young state.

circle, sėr′kl, *n.* [L. *circulus,* dim. of *circus,* a circle.] A plane figure, comprehended by a single curve line, called its circumference, every part of which is equally distant from a point within it called the center; the line bounding or forming such a figure, or something in a similar form; a ring; a round body; compass; circuit; a series (as of actions) ending where it begins; an ending where one began; a number of particulars regarded as having a central point; a number of persons associated by some tie; a coterie; a set.—*v.t.*—*circled, circling.* To encircle; to encompass; to surround; to enclose; to move round; to revolve round.—*v.i.* To move circularly; to circulate; to revolve.—*Great circle,* a circle on a sphere having as its center the center of the sphere: opposed to a *small* or *lesser circle.* The equator is a great circle; any parallel of latitude a small circle.—*Great circle sailing,* the manner of conducting a vessel between one place and another so that her track may always be along or nearly along the arc of a great circle. —*Polar circles,* the Arctic and the Antarctic circles 23½° from the respective poles.—**circlet,** sėr′klet, *n.* A little circle; a ring-shaped ornament for the head; a chaplet; a headband.

circuit, sėr′kit or sėr′kūt, *n.* [Fr. *circuit,* L. *circuitus—circum,* round, and *eo, itum,* to go.] The act of moving or passing round; a circular journey; a revolution; the distance round any space whether circular or otherwise; a boundary line encompassing an object; circumference; the journey of judges or other persons through certain appointed places for the purpose of holding courts or performing other stated duties; the district or portion of country in which a particular judge or judges hold courts and administer justice; the arrangement by which a current of electricity is kept up between the two poles of a galvanic battery; the path of a voltaic current.—**circuitous,** sėr•kū′it•us, *a.* Having a roundabout or devious course; not direct; roundabout.—**circuitously,** sėr•kū′it•us•li, *adv.* In a circuitous manner.—**circuitousness, circuity,** sėr•kū′it•us•nes, sėr•kū′i•ti, *n.* The character or condition of being circuitous.

circular, sėr′kū•lėr, *a.* [L. *circularis.* CIRCLE.] In the form of a circle; round; circumscribed by a circle; passing over or forming a circle, circuit, or round; addressed to a number of persons having a common interest (a *circular* letter).—*Circular note,* a note or letter of credit furnished by bankers to persons about to travel abroad, and which is payable at any one of a number of places.—*Circular numbers,* those whose powers terminate in the roots themselves, as 5 and 6, whose squares are 25 and 36. —*n.* A letter, notice, or intimation, generally printed or multiplied by some other rapid process, of which a copy is sent to several persons on some common business.—**circularity,** sėr•kū•lar′i•ti, *n.* The state or quality of being circular; a circular form.—**circulate,** sėr′kū•lāt, *v.i.*—*circulated, circulating.* [L. *circulo, circulatum.*] To move in a circle; to move round and return to the same point: to flow in the veins or channels of an organism; to pass from one person or place to another; to be diffused.—*v.t.* To cause to pass from place to place or from person to person; to put about; to spread. —*Circulating* or *recurring decimals,* interminate decimals in which two or more figures are continually repeated.—*Circulating library,* a library the books of which circulate among the subscribers.—**circulation,** sėr•kū•lā′shon, *n.* The act of circulating or moving in a course which brings or tends to bring the moving body to the point where its motion began; the act of flowing through the veins or channels of an organism; recurrence in a certain order or series; the act of passing from place to place or from person to person (as of money, news, etc.); the extent to which anything is circulated (a newspaper with a large *circulation*); currency; circulating coin, or notes, bills, etc., current and representing coin.—**circulative,** sėr′kū•lā•tiv, *a.* Circulating; causing circulation.—**circulator,** sėr′kū•lā•tėr, *n.* One who or that which circulates: specifically applied to a circulating decimal fraction.—**circulatory,**‡ sėr′kū•la•to•ri, *a.* Passing round a certain circuit; circular.

circumambient, sėr•kum•am′bi•ent, *a.* [L. *circum,* around, and *ambio,* to go about.] Surrounding; encompassing; enclosing or being on all sides, as the air about the earth.—**circumambiency,** sėr•kum•am′bi•en•si, *n.* The state or quality of being circumambient.

circumambulate, sėr•kum•am′bū•lāt, *v.i.* [L. *circum,* around, and *ambulo,* to walk.] To walk round about. —**circumambulation,** sėr•kum•am′-bū•la″shon, *n.* The act of circumambulating.

circumcise, sėr′kum•sīz, *v.t.*—*circumcised, circumcising.* [L. *circumcido, circumcisum—circum,* about, and *caedo,* to cut.] To cut off the prepuce or foreskin of, a ceremony or rite among the Jews, Mohammedans, and others.—**circumciser,** sėr′kum•sīz•ėr, *n.* One who performs circumcision.—**circumcision,** sėr•kum•si′zhon, *n.* The act of circumcising.

circumference, sėr•kum′fėr•ens, *n.* [L. *circumferentia—circum,* round, and *fero,* to carry.] The line that bounds a circle or any regular curvilinear figure; periphery; measure round a circular or spherical body.—**circumferential,** sėr•kum′fėr•en″shal, *a.* Pertaining to the circumference.

circumflect, sėr′kum•flekt, *v.t.* [L. *circum,* round, and *flecto, flexum,* to bend.] To bend round; to circumflex.—**circumflex,** sėr′kum•fleks, *n.* A wave of the voice, embracing both a rise and a fall on the same syllable; an accent placed only on long vowels, and indicating different things in different languages. In Greek it is marked by the signs ~ and ^, in French and some other languages by the sign ^.—*a.* Term for the above accent; *anat.* applied to several curved parts in the body.—*v.t.* To mark or pronounce with the circumflex; to curve or bend around.

circumfluence, sėr•kum′flu•ens, *n.* [L. *circumfluens—circum,* round, and *fluo,* to flow.] A flowing round on all sides; an enclosure of waters.—**circumfluent, circumfluous,** sėr•-kum′flu•ent, sėr•kum′flu•us, *a.* Flowing round; surrounding as a fluid.

circumfuse, sėr•kum•fūz′, *v.t.—circumfused, circumfusing.* [L. *circumfundo, circumfusus—circum,* round, and *fundo, fusus,* to pour.] To pour round; to spread round (*Mil.*).—**circumfusion,** sėr•kum•fū′zhon, *n.* The act of circumfusing.

circumgyrate, sėr•kum•jī′rāt, *v.t.* and *i.* [L. *circum,* round, and *gyro,* to turn, from *gyrus,* a circle.] To roll or turn round.—**circumgyration,** sėr•kum′jī•rā″shon, *n.* The act of circumgyrating; a circular motion.

circumjacent, sėr•kum•jā′sent, *a.* [L. *circumjacens—circum,* round, and *jaceo,* to lie.] Lying round; bordering on every side.

circumlocution, sėr′kum•lō•kū″shon, *n.* [L. *circum,* round, and *locutio,* a speaking, *loquor,* to speak.] A roundabout way of speaking; the use of more words than necessary to express an idea; a periphrasis.—**circumlocutory,** sėr•kum•lok′ū•to•ri, *a.* Exhibiting circumlocution; periphrastic.

circumnavigate, sėr•kum•nav′i•gāt, *v.t.—circumnavigated, circumnavigating.* [L. *circumnavigo—circum,* round, and *navigo,* to sail, from *navis,* a ship.] To sail round; to pass round by water (the globe, an island, etc.)—**circumnavigable,** sėr•kum•nav′i•-ga•bl, *a.* Capable of being circumnavigated or sailed round.—**circumnavigation,** sėr•kum•nav′i•gā″shon, *n.* The act of sailing round.—**circumnavigator,** sėr•kum•nav′i•gā•tėr, *n.* One who circumnavigates: generally applied to one who has sailed round the globe.

circumpolar, sėr•kum•pō′lėr, *a.* Surrounding either pole of the earth or heavens.

circumscissile, sėr•kum•sis′sil, *n.* [L. *circum,* round, and *scindo, scissum,* to cut.] *Bot.* opening or divided by a transverse circular line: a term applied to a mode of dehiscence in some fruits, as in the henbane, monkeypot, etc.

circumscribe, sėr′kum•skrīb, *v.t.—circumscribed, circumscribing.* [L. *circumscribo—circum,* round, and *scribo,* to write.] To inscribe or draw a line round; to mark out certain bounds or limits for; to enclose within certain limits; to limit, bound, confine, restrain (authority, etc.)—**circumscriber,** sėr•kum•skrīb′ėr, *n.* One who or that which circumscribes.—**circumscription,** sėr•kum•skrip′-shon, *n.* The act of circumscribing or state of being circumscribed; limitation; restriction; also a periphery or circumference. — **circumscriptive,** sėr•kum•skrip′tiv, *a.* Circumscribing or tending to circumscribe; limiting; restricting. (*Mil.*)

circumspect, sėr′kum•spekt, *a.* [L. *circumspectus—circum,* round, and *specio,* to look.] Examining carefully all the circumstances that may affect a determination; watchful on all sides; wary; vigilant; prudent; cautious.—**circumspection,** sėr•kum•spek′shon, *n.* The quality of being circumspect; observation of the true position of circumstances; watchfulness; vigilance; wariness; caution.—**circumspective,**† sėr•kum•spek′tiv, *a.* Circumspect; cautious.—**circumspectly,** sėr′kum•spekt•li, *adv.* In a circumspect manner; cautiously; watchfully.—**circumspectness,** sėr′kum•spekt•nes, *n.* Circumspection.

circumstance, sėr′kum•stans, *n.* [L. *circumstantia,* from *circumstans,* standing about—*circum,* round, and *sto,* to stand.] Something attending, appendant, or relative to a fact or case; something incidental; some fact giving rise to a certain presumption, or tending to afford some evidence; detail; incident; event; *pl.* situation; surroundings; state of things; especially, condition in regard to worldly estate.—*v.t. circumstanced, circumstancing.* To place in a particular situation or in certain surroundings: usually in pp.—**circumstantial,** sėr•-kum•stan′shal, *a.* Consisting in or pertaining to circumstances; attending; incidental; relating to, but not essential; exhibiting all the circumstances (account or recital); minute; particular; obtained or inferred from the circumstances of the case; not direct or positive (*circumstantial* evidence),—*n.* Something incidental and of subordinate importance: opposed to *essential.*—**circumstantiality,** sėr•-kum•stan′shi•al″i•ti, *n.* The quality of being circumstantial; minuteness; fullness of detail;—**circumstantially,** sėr•kum•stan′shal•li, *adv.* In a circumstantial manner; minutely; in full detail; indirectly; not positively.—**circumstantiate,** sėr•kum•stan′-shi•āt, *v.t.* To confirm by circumstances; to describe circumstantially or in full detail.

circumvallate,† sėr•kum•val′lāt, *v.t.* [L. *circum,* round, and *vallum,* a rampart.] To surround with a rampart.—**circumvallation,** sėr•kum′val•lā″-shon, *n.* The act of surrounding with a rampart; a line of field fortifications consisting of a rampart or parapet with a trench, surrounding a besieged place or a camp.

circumvent, sėr•kum•vent′, *v.t.* [L. *circumvenio, circumventum—circum,* about, and *venio,* to come.] To gain advantage over by artfulness, stratagem, or deception; to defeat or get the better of by cunning; to outwit; to overreach.—**circumvention,** sėr•-kum•ven′shon, *n.* The act of circumventing; outwitting or overreaching; stratagem. — **circumventive,** sėr•-kum•vent′iv, *a.* Tending or designed to circumvent.—**circumventor,** sėr•-kum•vent′ėr, *n.* One who circumvents.

circumvolve, sėr•kum•volv′, *v.t.—circumvolved, circumvolving.* [L. *circum,* round, and *volvo, volutum,* to roll.] To turn or cause to roll round; to cause to revolve.—**circumvolution,** sėr•kum′vo•lū″shon, *n.* A rolling or being rolled round; one of the windings of a thing wound or twisted; a convolution; a roundabout procedure.

circus, sėr′kus, *n.* pl. **circuses,** sėr′-kus•ez. [L.] Among the ancient Romans a kind of theater or amphitheater adapted for horse races, the exhibition of athletic exercises, contests with wild beasts, etc.; in modern times, a place of amusement where feats of horsemanship and acrobatic displays form the principal entertainment.

cirque, sėrk, *n.* [Fr., a circle, a circus.] A kind of circular valley among mountains; an amphitheater.

cirrhosis, sir•rō′sis, *n.* [Gr. *kirrhos,* orange-tawny, from the appearance of the diseased liver.] A disease consisting of diminution and deformity of the liver, often seen in drunkards.—**cirrhotic,** sir•rot′ik, *a.* Affected with or having the character of cirrhosis.

cirribranch, sir′ri•brangk, *a.* [L. *cirrus,* a tendril, and *branchiæ,* gills.] Having tendril-like gills: a term applied to certain mollusks.—**cirriped,** sir′ri•ped, *n.* [L. *cirrus,* and *pes, pedis,* the foot.] A member of an order of lower crustaceous animals, so called from the cirri or filaments with which their transformed feet are fringed.—**cirrose, cirrous,** sir′-rōs, sir′rus, *a. Bot.* having a cirrus or tendril; resembling tendrils or coiling like them. Written also *Cirrhose, cirrhous.*—**cirrus,** sir′rus, *n.* pl. **cirri,** sir′rī. A tendril; a long threadlike organ by which a plant climbs; a soft curled filamentary appendage to parts serving as the feet of certain lower animals, as barnacles, and the jaws of certain fishes; one of the forms which clouds assume; a light fleecy cloud at a high elevation, *cirro-cumulus* and *cirro-stratus* being intermediate forms partaking partly of this character, partly of that of the cumulus and stratus.

cisalpine, sis•al′pīn, *a.* [L. *cis,* on this side, and *Alpes,* Alps.] On this side of the Alps, with regard to Rome; that is, on the south of the Alps.—**cismontane,** sis•mon′tān, *a.* Existing on this side of the mountains; specifically, on this side of the Alps: opposed to *Ultramontane.*—**cispadane,** sis′pa•dān, *a.* [L. *Padus,* the river Po.] On this side of the Po, with regard to Rome; that is, on the south side.

cist, sist, *n.* [L. *cista,* Gr. *kistē,* a chest. *Chest* is another form of this word.] A place of interment of an early or prehistoric period, consisting of a stone chest formed of two parallel rows of stones fixed on their ends, and covered by similar flat stones.

Cistercian, sis•tėr′shi•an, *n.* A member of a religious order, which takes its name from its original convent, *Cistercium* or Citeaux, near Dijon, where the society was founded in 1098.

cistern, sis′tėrn, *n.* [L. *cisterna,* from *cista,* a chest.] An artificial reservoir or receptacle for holding water, beer, or other liquor.

citadel, sit′a•del, *n.* [Fr. *citadelle.* Same origin as *city.*] A fortress or castle in or near a city, intended to keep the inhabitants in subjection, or, in case of a siege, to form a final point of defense.

cite, sīt, *v.t.—cited, citing.* [Fr. *citer,* from L. *cito, citare,* freq. of *cieo,* to call, to summon; seen also in *excite, incite, recite.*] To call upon officially or authoritatively to appear; to summon before a person or tribunal; to quote, adduce, or bring forward; to refer to in support, proof, or confirmation (to *cite* an authority).—**citable,** sīt′a•bl. *a.* Capable of being cited or quoted.—**citation,** sī•tā′shon, *n.* A summons; an official call or notice given to a person to appear, as in a court; the act of citing a passage from a book or person; the passage or words quoted; quotation.

cithara, sith′a•ra, *n.* [L., from Gr. *kithara,* whence *gittern, guitar.*] An ancient stringed instrument resembling the more modern cittern or guitar.—**cithern, cittern,** sith′ėrn, sit′tėrn, *n.* An old instrument of the guitar kind, strung with wire instead of gut.

citizen, etc. See CITY.

citron, sit′ron, *n.* [Fr. *citron,* from L. *citreum,* from *citrus,* the lemon or citron.] The fruit of the citron tree, a large lemonlike fruit; the tree itself.—**citric acid,** sit′rik as′id, *n.* An organic acid obtained from citrus fruits or by fermentation of sugars.—*Citric acid cycle,* a series of chemical reactions occurring in the living organism, by which food is oxidized to create energy.—**citrus,** sit′rus, *n.* Any of a genus of trees or shrubs that bear citrons, lemons, grapefruit, etc.—*a.* Pertaining to such trees or shrubs.

cittern, sit′tėrn, *n.* See CITHARA.

city, sit′i, *n.* [Fr. *cité,* from L. *civitas, civitatis,* a city, state, from *civis,* a citizen, whence also *civil.*] In a general sense, a large and important town; in Great Britain, a town corporate that is or has been the seat of a bishop and of a cathedral church; in the United States an incorporated town governed by a mayor and aldermen; the inhabitants of a city collectively.—*a.* Pertaining to a city.—**citied,** sit′ēd, *a.* Belonging to a city; having the qualities of a city; covered with cities.—**citizen,** sit′i•zen, *n.* [O.E. *citezein,* from O.Fr. *citeain, citeien,* etc. (Mod. Fr. *citoyen*), from *cité,* a city. The *z* is a corruption of the old symbol used for *y.*] The native of a city, or an inhabitant who enjoys the freedom and privileges of the city in which he resides; a member of a state with full political privileges.—*a.* Having the qualities of a citizen; townbred.—**citizenship,** sit′i•zen•ship, *n.* The state or principles of a citizen.

civet, siv′et, *n.* [Fr. *civette,* It. *zibetto,* from Ar. *zabad,* the substance civet.] A strong smelling substance taken from the anal glands of the civet cats, and yielding a perfume; the animal that yields this substance.—*v.t.* To scent with civet.—**civet cat,** *n.* The name of several carnivorous mammals natives of North Africa and Asia, having a gland near the anus containing the odoriferous substance civet.

civic, siv′ik, *a.* [L. *civicus,* from *civis,* a citizen; whence also *city.*] Pertaining to a city or citizen: relating to civil affairs or honors.—*Civic crown, Rom. antiq.* a crown of oak leaves given to a soldier who saved the life of a citizen in battle.—**civics,** siv′iks, *n.* The science of the rights and duties of citizens.—**civil,** siv′il, *a.* [L. *civilis,* from *civis.*] Relating to the community, or to the policy and government of the citizens and subjects of a state (*civil* rights, government, etc.); political; municipal or private, as opposed to criminal; not ecclesiastical or military; exhibiting some refinement of manners; civilized; courteous; obliging; well bred; affable; polite.—*Civil engineering,* that branch of engineering which relates to the forming of roads, bridges, railroads, canals, aqueducts, harbors, etc.—*Civil law,* law of a state, city, or country.—*Civil liberty,* the absence of arbitrary governmental restraint on individual freedom.—*Civil marriage,* marriage performed by a government official rather than a clergyman.—*Civil rights,* the legal and political rights enjoyed by the inhabitants of a country; especially the rights guaranteed by the United States Constitution and bills passed by Congress.—*Civil service,* that branch of the public service in which the nonmilitary employees of a government are engaged, or those persons collectively.—*Civil war,* a war between the people of the same state.—**civilly,** siv′il•li, *adv.* In a civil manner; as regards civil rights or privileges; in a well-bred manner.—**civilian,** si•vil′yen, *n.* One skilled in the Roman or civil law; one whose pursuits are those of civil life, not military or clerical.—**civility,** si•vil′i•ti, *n.* [L. *civilitas,* from *civilis.*] The state of being civilized‡; good breeding; politeness, or an act of politeness; courtesy; kind attention.—**civilizable,** siv′il•īz•a•bl, *a.* Capable of being civilized.—**civilization,** siv′il•iz•ā″shon, *n.* The act of civilizing, or state of being civilized; the state of being refined in manners from the rudeness of savage life, and improved in arts and learning.—**civilize,** siv′il•īz, *v.t.—civilized, civilizing.* [Fr. *civiliser,* formerly also *civilizer.*] To reclaim from a savage state; to introduce order and civic organization among; to refine and enlighten; to elevate in social life.

clack, klak, *v.i.* [An imitative word; comp. Fr. *claque,* a clap or clack; D. *klakken,* to clap; E. *clap, crack.*] To make a sudden sharp noise, as by striking or cracking; to rattle; to utter sounds or words rapidly and continually, or with sharpness and abruptness.—*v.t.* To cause to make a sharp, short sound; to clap; to speak without thought; to rattle out.—*n.* A sharp, abrupt sound, continually repeated; a kind of small windmill for frightening birds; continual talk; prattle.—**clacker,** klak′ėr, *n.* One who or that which clacks.—**clack valve,** *n.* A valve in pumps with a single flap, hinged at one edge.

clad, klad, *pp.* Clothe.

claim, klām, *v.t.* [O.Fr. *claimer,* from L. *clamo, clamare,* to shout, whence also *clamor, acclaim, acclamation, exclaim, reclaim,* etc.] To ask or seek to obtain by virtue of authority, right, or supposed right; to assert a right to; to demand as due.—*v.i.* To be entitled to a thing; to have a right; to derive a right; to assert claims; to put forward claims.—*n.* A demand of a right or supposed right; a calling on another for something due or supposed to be due; a right to claim or demand; a title to anything; the thing claimed or demanded; specifically, in America, Australia, etc., a piece of land allotted to one.—**claimable,** klām′a•bl, *a.* Capable of being claimed or demanded as due.—**claimant, claimer,** klām′ant, klām′ėr, *n.* A person who claims; one who demands anything as his right.

clairvoyance, klâr•voi′ans, *n.* [Fr. *clair,* clear, and *voyant,* seeing, ppr. of *voir* (L. *videre*), to see.] A power attributed to persons in the mesmeric state, by which the person (called a clairvoyant or clairvoyante) discerns objects concealed from sight, tells what is happening at a distance, etc. —**clairvoyant,** klâr•voi′ant, *a.* Of or pertaining to clairvoyance.—**clairvoyant,** klâr•voi′ant, *n.* A man or woman in a certain stage of mesmerism, in which state the subject is said to see things not present to the senses.

clam,† klam, *v.t.—clammed, clamming.* [A.Sax. *clam,* mud, clay, that which is clammy; Dan. *klam,* clammy, *klamme,* to clog.] To clog with glutinous or viscous matter.—*v.i.*† To be glutinous or moist; to stick like clammy matter or moisture.—**clammy,** klam′mi, *a.* Viscous; adhesive; soft and sticky; glutinous; tenacious.—**clamminess,** klam′mi•nes, *n.* The state of being clammy or viscous; viscosity; stickiness.

clam, klam, *n.* [Shortened from *clamp,* the former name, given from the firmness with which some of these animals adhere to rocks. CLAMP.] The popular name of certain bivalvular shellfish, of several genera and many species.

clamant, klam′ant, *a.* [CLAIM.] Clamorous; beseeching; pressing; urgent; crying.

clamber, klam′bėr, *v.i.* [O.E. *clamer, clammer,* akin to *clam,* to adhere, *clamp,* and *climb.*] To climb with difficulty or with hands and feet; to rise up steeply (*Tenn.*)†.—*v.t.*† To ascend by climbing; to climb with difficulty. (*Shak.*)—*n.* The act of clambering or climbing with difficulty.

clamor, klam′ėr, *n.* [L. *clamor,* an outcry, from *clamo,* to cry out, whence E. *claim.*] A great outcry; vociferation made by a loud human voice continued or repeated, or by a number of voices; loud complaint; urgent demand; loud and continued noise.—*v.t.* To utter in a loud voice;

to shout.—*v.i.* To make a clamor; to utter loud sounds or outcries; to vociferate; to make importunate complaints or demands.—**clamorer,** klam′ėr•ėr, *n.* One who clamors.—**clamorous,** klam′ėr•us, *a.* Making a clamor or outcry; noisy; vociferous; loud.—**clamorously,** klam′ėr•us•li, *adv.* In a clamorous manner; with loud noise or words.—**clamorousness,** klam′ėr•us•nes, *n.* State of being clamorous.

clamp, klamp, *n.* [Most closely connected with L.G. and D. *klamp,* Dan. *klampe,* G. *klampe,* a clamp; from root seen in E. *climb, clamber, clem* (to pinch with hunger), *clam.*] Something rigid that fastens or binds; a piece of wood or metal fastening two pieces together, or strengthening any framework; an instrument of wood or metal used by joiners, etc., for holding pieces of timber closely together until the glue hardens.—*v.t.* To fasten with clamps; to fix a clamp on.

clamp, klamp, *n.* [Imitative; comp. *clank, clink.*] A heavy footstep or tread; a tramp; a heap of turnips, potatoes, etc., covered over with straw earth for winter keeping; pile of bricks for burning.—*v.i.* To tread heavily. (*Thack.*)

clan, klan, *n.* [Gael. and Ir. *clann,* family, tribe.] A race; a family; a tribe; the common descendants of the same progenitor, under the patriarchal control of a chief; a clique, sect, society, or body of persons closely united by some common interest or pursuit.—**clannish,** klan′ish, *a.* Imbued with the feelings, sentiments, and prejudices peculiar to clans; blindly devoted to those of one's own clan, set, or locality, and illiberal toward others.—**clannishly,** klan′ish•li, *adv.* In a clannish manner.—**clannishness,** klan′ish•nes, *n.* The state or quality of being clannish.—**clansman,** klanz′-man, *n.* A member of a clan.

clandestine, klan•des′tin, *a.* [L. *clandestinus,* from *clam,* in secret.] Secret; private; hidden; withdrawn from public view; generally implying craft, deception, or evil design.—**clandestinely,** klan•des′tin•li, *adv.* In a clandestine manner; secretly; privately; in secret.—**clandestineness,**† klan•des′tin•nes, *n.* The state or quality of being clandestine.

clang, klang, *n.* [Imitative of sound, and akin to *clank, clink, clack*; G. *klingen,* to sound; Dan. Sw. G. *klang,* D. *klank,* a sound; L. *clangor,* Gr. *klangē.*] A loud sound produced from solid bodies, especially that produced by the collision of metallic bodies; a clank; clangor.—*v.i.* To give out a clang; to clank; to resound —*v.t.* To cause to sound with a clang. —**clangorous,** klang′gėr•us, *a.* Making a clangor; having a hard or ringing sound.—**clangor,** klang′gėr, *n.* [Directly from L. *clangor.*] A sharp, hard, ringing sound as of a trumpet.

clank, klangk, *n.* [CLANG.] The loud sound made by collision of metallic or other similarly sounding bodies (as chains, iron armor, etc.): generally expressing a less resounding sound than *clang,* and a deeper and stronger sound than *clink.*—*v.t.* To cause to sound with a clank.—*v.i.* To sound with or give out a clank.

clap, klap, *v.t.*—*clapped* or *clapt* (pret. & pp.), *clapping.* [Same as Icel. and Sw. *klappa,* Dan. *klappe,* D. and L.G.*klappen,* to clap, to pat, etc.; perhaps imitative of sound.] To strike with a quick motion; to slap; to thrust; to drive together; to shut hastily; followed by *to* (to *clap to* the door); to place or put by a hasty or sudden motion (to *clap* the hand to the mouth, to *clap* spurs to a horse).—*To clap hands,* to strike the palms of the hands together, as a mark of applause or delight.—*To clap the wings,* to flap them, or to strike them together so as to make a noise.—*To clap hold of,* to seize roughly and suddenly.—*v.i.* To come together suddenly with noise; to clack; to strike the hands together in applause.—*n.* A collision of bodies with noise; a bang; a slap; a sudden act or motion (in phrase *at a clap,* that is at a blow, all at once); a burst or peal of thunder; a striking of hands to express approbation.—**clapper,** klap′ėr, *n.* A person who claps or applauds by clapping; that which claps or strikes, as the tongue of a bell; a kind of small noisy windmill to scare birds.—**claptrap,** *n.* An artifice or device to elicit applause or gain popularity; high-flown sentiments or other rhetorical device by which a person panders to an audience; bunkum.—*a.* Designing or designed merely to catch applause.

claque, klak, *n.* [Fr., from *claquer,* to clap the hands, to applaud.] A name applied collectively to a set of men who in theaters (as in those of Paris) are regularly hired to applaud the piece or the actors.

clarabella, klarä•bel′a, *n.* An 8-foot organ stop with open wooden pipes, giving a soft sweet tone.

clarence, klar′ens, *n.* [After the Duke of *Clarence,* William IV.] A closed fourwheeled carriage, with inside seats for four.

clarendon type, klar′en•don, *n.* In printing, a style of type.

claret, klar′et, *n.* [Fr. *clairet,* from *clair,* clear; It. *claretto.*] The name given to the red wines of the Bordeaux district.—*a.* Having the color of claret wine.

clarify, klar′i•fī, *v.t.*—*clarified, clarifying.* [Fr. *clarifier,* from L. *clarificare*—*clarus,* clear, *facio,* to make.] To make clear, to purify from feculent matter; to defecate; to fine (liquor).—*v.i.* To grow or become clear or free from feculent matter; to become pure, as liquors.—**clarifier,** klar′i•fī•ėr, *n.* One who or that which clarifies or purifies; a vessel in which liquor is clarified.—**clarification,** klar′i•fi•kā″shon, *n.* The act of clarifying; particularly the clearing or fining of liquid substances from all feculent matter.

clarinet, clarionet, klar′i•net, klar′i•on•et, *n.* [Fr. *clarinette*—L. *clarus,* clear.] A wind instrument of music, made of wood, having finger holes and keys, and a fixed mouthpiece, containing a reed, forming the upper joint of the instrument.—**clarion,** klar′i•on, *n.* [L.L. *clario, clarionis,* a clarion, Fr. *clairon,* from L. *clarus,* clear, from its clear sound.] A kind of trumpet whose tube is narrower and tone more acute and shrill than that of the common trumpet.

clash, klash, *v.i.* [An imitative word; comp. D. *kletsen,* G. *klatschen,* Dan. *klatsche,* to clap.] To make a loud, harsh noise, as from violent or sudden collision; to dash against an object with a loud noise; to come into violent collision; *fig.* to act with opposite power or in a contrary direction; to meet in opposition (their opinions and their interests *clash* together).—*v.t.* To strike against with sound; to strike noisily together. —*n.* The noise made by the meeting of bodies with violence; a striking together with noise; collision or noisy collision of bodies; *fig.* opposition; contradiction, as between differing or contending interests.

clasp, klasp, *n.* [By metathesis for O.E. *clapse,* to clasp, *claps,* a clasp: allied to O.E. *clip,* to embrace, in the same way as *grasp,* to *grip,* and *gripe.*] A catch to hold something together; a hook for fastening, or for holding together the covers of a book, or the different parts of a garment, of a belt, etc.; a clinging, grasping, or embracing; a close embrace; bar on medal ribbon for additional service in a campaign.—*v.t.* To shut or fasten together with a clasp; to catch and hold by twining or embracing; to surround and cling to; to embrace closely; to catch with the arms or hands; to grasp.—*v.i.*† To cling. (*Shak.*)—**clasp knife,** *n.* A knife the blade of which folds into the handle.

class, klas, *n.* [L. *classis,* a class.] An order or rank of persons; a number of persons in society supposed to have some resemblance or equality in rank, education, property, talents, and the like; a number of pupils in a school, or students in a college, of the same standing or pursuing the same studies; *nat. hist.* a large group of plants or animals formed by the union or association of several orders.—*v.t.* To arrange in a class or classes; to rank together; to refer to a class or group; to classify.—*v.i.* To be arranged or classed.—**classible,** klas′i•bl, *a.* Capable of being classed.—**classic,** klas′ik, *n.* [L. *classicus,* pertaining to the first or highest of the classes or political divisions into which the Roman people were anciently divided, hence the use of the word in reference to writers.] An author of the first rank; a writer whose style is pure, correct, and refined: primarily, a Greek or Roman author of this character; a literary production of the first class or rank; *the classics,* specifically, the literature of ancient Greece and Rome.—*a.* Same as

Classical.—**classical,** klas′ik•al, *a.* Pertaining to writers of the first rank; being of the first order; more specifically relating to Greek and Roman authors of the first rank or estimation; pertaining to ancient Greece or Rome; relating to localities associated with great ancient or modern authors, or to scenes of great historical events; pure, chaste, correct, or refined (taste, style, etc.). —*Classic orders, arch.* the Doric, Ionic, and Corinthian orders.—**classicalism,** klas′ik•al•izm, *n.* A classic idiom or style; classicism; *art,* close adherence to the rules of Greek or Roman art.—**classicalist,** klas′ik•al•ist, *n.* A devoted admirer of classicalism; one who scrupulously adheres to the canons of Greek or Roman art.—**classicality,** klas•i•kal′i•ti, *n.* The quality of being classical.—**classically,** klas′ik•al•li, *adv.* In a classical manner; according to the manner of classical authors. —**classicism,** klas•i•sizm, *n.* A classic idiom or style.—**classicist,** klas′i•sist, *n.* One versed in the classics.—**classify,** klas′i•fī, *v.t.*—*classified, classifying.* [L. *classis,* a class, and *facio,* to make.] To arrange in a class or classes; to arrange in sets.—**classifiable,** klas′i•fī•a•bl, *a.* Capable of being classified.—**classification,** klas′i•fi•kā″shon, *n.* The act of classifying or forming into a class or classes, so as to bring together those beings or things which most resemble each other, and to separate those that differ; distribution into sets, sorts, or ranks.—**classificatory,** klas′-i•fi•kā•to•ri, *a.* Belonging to classification; concerned with distribution into sets, sorts, or ranks.—**classified,** klas′i•fīd, *a.* Confidential, restricted; secret.—**classified ad,** *n.* A want ad. —**classifier,** klas′i•fī•ėr, *n.*—**classmate,** *n.* One of the same class at school or college.

clatter, klat′ėr, *v.i.* [From the sound. A.Sax. *clatrung,* a clattering, a rattle; D. *klater,* a rattle; *klateren,* to rattle.] To make rattling sounds; to make repeated sharp sounds, as when sonorous bodies strike or are struck rapidly together; to rattle.—*v.t.* To strike so as to produce a rattling noise from.—*n.* A rapid succession of abrupt, sharp sounds; rattling sounds; tumultuous and confused noise.—**clatterer,** klat′ėr•ėr, *n.* One who clatters; a babbler.

clause, kla̦z, *n.* [Fr. *clause,* from L.L. *clausa,* for L. *clausula,* a conclusion, a clause, from *claudo, clausum,* to close, whence *close, exclude,* etc.]. A member of a compound sentence containing both a subject and its predicate; a distinct part of a contract, will, agreement, charter, commission, or the like; a distinct stipulation, condition, proviso, etc.

claustral, kla̦s′tral, *a.* [L.L. *claustralis,* from L. *claustrum,* an inclosure, a cloister, from *claudo,* to shut.] Relating to a cloister; cloister-like; secluded.

claustrophobia, kla̦s″tro•fō′bē•a, *n.* [L. *claustrum,* an enclosure, Gr. *phōbōs,* fear.] Morbid fear of narrow spaces or closed rooms.

clavate, claviform, klā′vāt, klav′i•form, *a.* [L. *clava,* a club.] *Bot.* and *zool.* club-shaped; having the form of a club; growing gradually thicker toward the top, as certain parts of a plant.

clave, klāv, pret. of *cleave.*

clavichord, klav′i•kord, *n.* [L. *clavis,* a key, and *chorda,* a string.] An old stringed instrument, a precursor of the spinet and harpsichord.

clavicle, klav′i•kl, *n.* [L. *clavicula,* a little key or fastener, from *clavis,* a key.] The collarbone.—**clavicular,** kla•vik′ū•lėr, *a.* Pertaining to the collarbone or clavicle.

clavicorn, klav′i•korn, *n.* [L. *clava,* a club, and *cornu,* a horn.] A member of a family of beetles, so named from the antennae being thickened at the apex so as to terminate in a club-shaped enlargement.

clavier, klav′i•ėr, *n.* [Fr. *clavier,* from L. *clavis,* a key.] The key board of a pianoforte or other instrument whose keys are arranged similarly; the instrument itself.

claw, kla̦, *n.* [A.Sax. *cláwu, clá,* a claw = D. *klaauw,* Icel. *kló,* Dan. and Sw. *klo,* G. *klaue,* a claw; allied to *cleave,* to adhere.] The sharp hooked nail of a quadruped, bird, or other animal; the whole foot of an animal with hooked nails; a hooked extremity belonging to any animal member or appendage; anything shaped like the claw of an animal, as the crooked forked end of a hammer used for drawing nails; *bot.* the narrow base of a petal.—*v.t.* To tear, scratch, pull, or seize with claws or nails; to scratch.—**claw hammer,** *n.* A hammer furnished with two claws, for convenience of drawing nails out of wood; evening-dress coat, or coat with tails.

clay, klā, *n.* [A.Sax. *claeg* = Dan. *klaeg,* L.G. *klei,* D. *klai, klei,* G. *klei,* clay; same root as in *cleave, clog, glue.*] The name common to various earths, compounds of silica and alumina; earth which is stiff, viscid, and ductile when moistened, and many kinds of which are used in the arts, as pipe *clay,* porcelain *clay,* etc.; earth in general, especially as the material of the human body. —*a.* Formed or consisting of clay.—*v.t.* To cover or mingle with clay; to purify and whiten (sugar) with clay. —**clayey,** klā′i, *a.* Consisting of clay; abounding with clay; partaking of clay; like clay; bedaubed or besmeared with clay.

claymore, klā′mōr, *n.* [Gael. *claidheammor*—*claidheam,* a sword, and *mor,* great.] Formerly the large two-handed sword of the Scottish Highlanders; now a basket-hilted, double-edged broadsword.

clean, klēn, *a.* [A.Sax. *claene,* clean, pure, bright; cog. with W. *glain, glan,* Ir. and Gael. *glan,* clean, pure, radiant.] Clear of dirt or filth; having all impurities or foreign matter removed; pure, without fault, imperfection, or defect (timber, a copy); well-proportioned; shapely (*clean* limbs); not bungling; dexterous; adroit (a *clean* leap); complete or thorough; free from moral impurity, guilt, or blame; among the Jews, not defiled or polluted; not forbidden by the ceremonial law for use in sacrifice and for food.—*adv.* Quite; perfectly; wholly; entirely; fully.—*v.t.* To make clean; to remove all foreign matter from; to purify; to cleanse.—*To clean out,* to exhaust the pecuniary resources of. (Colloq.)—**cleaner,** klēn′ėr, *n.* One who or that which cleans.—**cleanly,** klen′li, *a.* Free from dirt, filth, or any foul matter; neat; carefully avoiding filth.—**cleanlily,**† klen′li•li, *adv.* In a cleanly manner.—**cleanliness,** klen′li•nes, *n.* The state or quality of being cleanly.—**cleanly,** klēn′li, *adv.* In a clean manner; neatly; without filth; adroitly; dexterously.—**cleanness,** klēn′nes, *n.* The state or quality of being clean. —**cleanhanded** *a.* Having clean hands; *fig.* free from moral taint or suspicion.—**clean-limbed,** *a.* Having well-proportioned limbs.

cleanse, klenz, *v.t.*—*cleansed, cleansing.* [A.Sax. *claensian,* from *claene,* clean.] To make clean; to free from filth, or whatever is unseemly, noxious, or offensive; to purify.—**cleanser,** klen′zėr, *n.* One who or that which cleanses.

clear, klēr, *a.* [O.Fr. *cleir* (Fr. *clair*), from L. *clarus,* clear; akin *claret, clarify, clarinet.*] Free from darkness or opacity; brilliant; light; luminous; unclouded; not obscured; free from what would dim transparency or bright color (*clear* water); free from anything that confuses or obscures; acute, sagacious, or discriminating (intellect, head); perspicuous; lucid (statement); evident; manifest; indisputable; undeniable; free from accusation, imputation, distress, imprisonment, or the like; followed by *of* or *from*; free from impediment or obstruction; unobstructed (a *clear* view); sounding distinctly; distinctly audible; in full; net (*clear* profit or gain),—*Clear days* (preceded by a numeral), days reckoned exclusively of those on which any proceeding is commenced or completed.—*adv.* Clearly; quite; entirely; clean; indicating entire separation.—*v.t.* To make or render clear; to free from whatever diminishes brightness, transparency, or purity of color; to free from obscurity, perplexity, or ambiguity: often followed by *up*; to free from any impediment or encumbrance, or from anything noxious or injurious; to remove; with *off, away,* etc.; to free from the imputation of guilt; to acquit; to make by way of gain or profit beyond all expenses and charges; to leap over or pass without touching or failure; *naut.* to pay the customs on or connected with; to obtain permission to sail for (a cargo, a ship).—*v.i.* To become free from clouds or fog; to become fair or serene; to pass away or disappear from the sky; often followed by *up, off,* or *away*; to exchange checks and bills and settle balances, as is done in clearing-houses; *naut.* to leave a port: often followed by *out* or *outward*.—**clearance,** klē′rans, *n.* The act of clearing.—**clearer,** klē′rėr, *n.* One who or that which clears.—**clearing,** klēr′ing, *n.* The act of one who clears; among *bankers,* the act of exchanging drafts on each other's houses and settling the differences; among *railroads,* the act of distributing among the different companies the proceeds of the through traffic passing over several railroads; a place or tract of land cleared of wood or cultivation.—**clearing-house,** *n.* An institution through which the claims of banks against one another are settled. These claims are represented in the form of bank checks in the case of bank clearing-houses. At the Stock Exchange and the Board of Trade similar clearing-houses exist for the facilitation of trading in stocks and in grain.—**clearly,** klēr′li, *adv.* In a clear manner; brightly; luminously; plainly; evidently.—**clearness,** klēr′nes, *n.* The state or quality of being clear.—**clearheaded,** *a.* Having a clear head or understanding; having acute discernment or keen intelligence.—**clearsighted,** *a.* Seeing with clearness; having acuteness of mental discernment; discerning; perspicacious.—**clear-sightedness,** *n.*—**clearstarch,** *v.t.* To stiffen and dress with clear or colorless starch.

cleat, klēt, *n.* [Allied to G. *klate, klatte,* a claw.] A piece of wood or iron used in a ship to fasten ropes upon; a piece of iron worn on a shoe; a piece of wood nailed on transversely to a piece of joinery for the purpose of securing it in its proper position, or for strengthening.—*v.t.* To strengthen with a cleat or cleats.

cleave, klēv, *v.i.*—pret. *clave* or *cleaved*; pp. *cleaved*; ppr. *cleaving.* [A.Sax. *clifian, cleofian,* pret. *clifode,* pp. *clifod* (*cleaved* is therefore historically the correct pret. and pp.); cog. D. and L.G. *kleven,* Dan. *klaebe,* G. *kleben,* to adhere, to cleave. *Climb* is akin.] To stick; to adhere; to be attached physically, or by affection or other tie.

cleave, klēv, *v.t.*—pret. *clove,* or *clave* (the latter antiquated), also *cleft*; pp. *cloven, cleft* or *cleaved*; ppr. *cleaving.* [A.Sax. *cleófan,* pret. *cleáf,* pp. *clofen,* (the historically correct conjugation is therefore *cleave, clave* or *clove, cloven*), to cleave or split; cog. D. *kloven,* Icel. *kljúfa,* Dan. *klóve,* G. *klieben.*] To part or divide by force; to split or rive; to sever forcibly; to hew; to cut.—*v.i.* To divide; to split; to open.—**cleavable,** klē′va•bl, *a.* Capable of being cleaved or divided.—**cleavage,** klē′vij, *n.* The act of cleaving or splitting; the manner in which rocks or mineral substances regularly cleave or split according to their natural joints, or regular structure; in animals, early divisions of fertilized egg cell.—**cleaver,** klē′vėr, *n.* One who or that which cleaves; a butcher's instrument for cutting carcasses into joints or pieces.

cleek, klēk, *n.* An iron club with a narrow face and a long shaft used as a golf club.

clef, klef, *n.* [Fr. *clef,* L. *clavis,* a key.] A character in music, placed at the beginning of a staff, to determine the degree of elevation to be given to the notes belonging to it as a whole.

cleft, kleft, pret. & pp. of *cleave,* to divide.—*n.* A space or opening made by splitting; a crack; a crevice.—**cleft palate,** *n.* A malformation in which more or less of the palate is wanting, so as to leave a longitudinal gap in the upper jaw, often an accompaniment of harelip.

cleistogamic, cleistogamous, klīs•to•gam′ik, klīs•tog′a•mus, *a.* [Gr. *kleiō,* to close or shut up, and *gamos,* marriage.] *Bot.* having minute, bud-like, self-fertilizing flowers as well as other flowers conspicuously colored.

clematis, klem′a•tis, *n.* [Gr. *klēmatis.*] The generic name of woody climbing plants of the crowfoot family having white or purple blossoms.

clemency, klem′en•si, *n.* [L. *clementia,* from *clemens, clementis,* merciful.] Mildness of temper as shown by a superior to an inferior; disposition to spare or forgive; mercy; leniency; softness or mildness of the elements.—**clement,** klem′ent, *a.* Mild in temper and disposition; gentle; lenient; merciful; kind; tender, compassionate.—**clemently,** klem′ent•li, *adv.* With mildness of temperature; mercifully.

clench, klench, *v.t.* [Shortened form =Sc. *clink,* Dan. *klinke,* Sw. *klinka,* to clinch, to rivet; akin *clink.*] To secure or fasten, as a nail, by beating down the point when it is driven through anything; to rivet; to establish, settle, or confirm (a denial, argument, etc.); to bring together and set firmly; to double up tightly (the teeth or the hands); to grasp firmly.—*n.* A catch; a grip; a persistent clutch; a clinch.

clepe,‡ klēp, *v.t.*—pp. *yclept.* [A.Sax. *clipian, cleopian.*] To call or name. (*Shak.*)

clepsydra, klep′si•dra, *n.* [Gr. *klepsydra*—*kleptō,* to steal, to hide, and *hydōr,* water.] A name common to devices of various kinds for measuring time by the discharge of water; a water clock.

cleptomania, klep•to•mā′ni•a, *n.* See KLEPTOMANIA.

clergy, klėr′ji, *n.* [O.Fr. *clergie,* from L. *clericus,* Gr. *klērikos,* clerical, from *klēros,* a lot, an allotment, the clergy. Akin *clerical, clerk.*] The body of men set apart and consecrated, by due ordination, to the service of God in the Christian church; the body of ecclesiastics, in distinction from the laity; *law,* benefit of clergy.—*Benefit of clergy, law,* the exemption of clergymen from criminal process before a secular judge; in cases of felony, an immunity latterly extended to any person who could read, though laymen could only claim it once; abolished in 1827.—**clergyman,** klėr′ji•man, *n.* A man in holy orders; the minister of a Christian church.

clerical, kler′ik•al, *a.* [L. *clericus,* Gr. *klērikos.* CLERGY, CLERK.] Relating or pertaining to the clergy; relating to a writer or copyist.—*Clerical error,* an error in the text of a document made by carelessness or inadvertence on the part of the writer or transcriber.—**cleric,** kler′-ik, *n.* A clergyman or scholar.—**clericalism,** kler′ik•al•izm, *n.* Clerical power or influence; undue influence of the clergy; sacerdotalism.—**clerisy,†** kler′i•si, *n.* A body of clerks or learned men; the literati; the clergy, as opposed to the laity.

clerk, klėrk, *n.* [A.Sax. *clerc,* a priest; O.Fr. *clerc*; from L. *clericus.* Gr. *klērikos.* CLERGY.] A clergyman or ecclesiastic; a man in holy orders, especially in the Church of England; formerly also any man of education; the layman who leads in reading the responses in the service of the Anglican Church; one who is employed in keeping records or accounts; an officer attached to courts, municipal and other corporations, associations, etc., whose duty generally is to keep records of proceedings, and transact business under direction of the court, body, etc., by whom he is employed; in America, an assistant in a shop; a shopman.—*St. Nicholas' clerk,* a thief. (*Shak.*)—**clerkly,** klėrk′li, *a.* Pertaining to a clerk or to penmanship; scholarly.—*adv.*† In a scholarly manner. (*Shak.*)—**clerkship,** klėrk′ship, *n.* The office or business of a clerk or writer.

clever, klev′ėr, *a.* [Connected with O.E. *cliver,* a claw, and with *cleave,* to adhere.] Performing or acting with skill or address; possessing ability of any kind, especially such as involves quickness of intellect or mechanical dexterity; indicative of or exhibiting cleverness; dexterous; adroit; able.—**cleverish,** klev′ėr•ish, *a.* Tolerably clever.—**cleverly,** klev′-ėr•li. *adv.* In a clever manner; dexterously; skillfully; ably.—**cleverness,** klev′ėr•nes, *n.* The quality of being clever; dexterity; adroitness; skill; ingenuity; smartness.

clew, *n.* or *v.t.* See CLUE.

cliché, klē•shā′, *n.* [Fr., from *clicher,* to stereotype, from older *cliquer,* to fasten, make firm, from root of *clinch, clench* (omitting the nasal).] Hackneyed jest or stereotyped phrase. A stereotype plate, especially one derived from an engraving.

click, klik, *v.i.* [An imitative word expressing a slighter sound than *clack*; comp. *clack, cluck, clink, clank*; D. *klikken,* Fr. *cliquer,* to click.] To make a small sharp sound, or a succession of small sharp sounds, as by a gentle striking; to tick.—*v.t.* To move with a clicking sound.—*n.* A small sharp sound; the cluck of the natives of South Africa; the piece that enters the teeth of a ratchet wheel; a detent or ratchet; the latch of a door.

client, klī′ent, *n.* [L. *cliens, clientis,* a client, from O.L. *cluo,* to hear.] An ancient Roman citizen who put himself under the protection of a man of distinction and influence (his *patron*); one whose interests are represented by any professional man; especially one who applies to a lawyer, or commits his cause to his management.—**clientage,** kli′en•tij, *n.* The state or condition of being a client; a body of clients.—**cliental,** klī′en•tal, *a.* Pertaining to a client or clients.—**clientele, clientelage,** klī′en•tel, kli•en′tēl•ij, *n.* [L. *clientela.*] A body of clients or dependents; one's clients collectively.

cliff, klif, *n.* [A.Sax. *clif*, a rock. a cliff=D. *klif*, Icel. *klif*, a cliff; comp. also Dan. *klippe*, Sw. *klippa*, G. *klippe*, a crag.] A precipice; the steep and rugged face of a rocky mass; a steep rock; a headland.

climacteric, klī•mak′tėr•ik, *n.* [Gr. *klimakter*, the step of a ladder, from *klimax*, a ladder or scale. CLIMAX.] A critical period in human life, or a period in which some great change is supposed to take place in the human constitution; the *grand* or *great climacteric* being the 63d year. —*a.* Pertaining to a climacteric.

climate, klī′mit, *n.* [L. *clima*, Gr. *klima*, *klimatos*, a slope, a zone of the earth, a clime, from *klinō*, to bend, referring to the inclination of the earth from the equator to the pole.] The condition of a tract or region in relation to the various phenomena of the atmosphere, as temperature, wind, moisture, miasmata, etc., especially as they affect the life of animals or man.—**climatic,** klī•mat′ik, *a.* Pertaining to a climate or climates; limited by a climate.—**climatology,** klī•ma•tol′o•ji, *n.* The science of climates; an investigation of the causes on which the climate of a place depends.—**climatological,** klī′mat•o•loj″ik•al, *a.* Pertaining to climatology.—**clime,** klīm, *n.* A tract or region of the earth. (Poetical.)

climax, klī′maks, *n.* [L., from Gr. *klimax*, a ladder, from *klinō*, to slope. CLIMATE, CLIMACTERIC.] A figure of speech or rhetorical device in which the language rises step by step in dignity, importance, and force; the highest point of anything; the culmination; acme.

climb, klīm, *v.i.*—(*clomb* for pret. & pp. *climbed* is now only poetical). [A.Sax. *climban*, G. and D. *klimmen*; from same root as *cleave*, to adhere, *clip*, to embrace.] To mount or ascend anything steep with labor and difficulty; especially, to ascend by means of the hands and feet; of things, to rise with a slow motion, to ascend, as certain plants, by means of tendrils, etc.— *v.t.* To climb up.—**climbable,** klīm′a•bl, *a.* Capable of being climbed.—**climber,** klīm′ėr, *n.* One who climbs; a plant that rises by attaching itself to some support; one of an order of birds, including the parrots, woodpeckers, etc., so called from their climbing habits.

clime. See CLIMATE.

clinanthium, klī•nan′thi•um, *n.* [Gr. *klinē*, a bed, *anthos*, a flower.] *Bot.* a term for the receptacle of a composite plant.

clinch, klinsh, *v.t.* [A variant of CLENCH.] To secure a driven nail, bolt, etc. by flattening the protruding point; to fasten in this way; to settle a matter conclusively.—*v.i.* *Boxing*, to grasp firmly.—*n.* The act of clinching; a grasp; a grapple.—**clincher,** klinsh′ėr, *n.*

cling, kling, *v.i.*—*clung*, *clinging*. [A.Sax. *clingan*, to adhere, to dry up or wither; Dan. *klynge*, to grow in clusters; *klynge*, a heap, a cluster.] To adhere closely; to stick; to hold fast, especially by winding round or embracing.

clinic, klin′ik, *n.* [Gr. *klinikos*, from *klinē*, a bed, from *klinō*, to recline.] A medical institution in which a group of physicians jointly examine and treat patients; also, the examination and treatment of patients in the presence of medical students.—**clinical,** klin′i•kal, *adj.* Pertaining to a clinic or sickroom; pertaining to direct observation of a patient; analytical.—**clinically,** klin′ik•al•li, *adv.*

clink, klingk, *v.i.* [An imitative word, akin to *click* and *clank*; comp. D. *klinken*, to tinkle; Dan. *klinge*, to jingle; Icel. *klingja*, G. *klingen*, to ring, to chink.] To ring or jingle; to give out a small sharp sound or a succession of such sounds, as by striking small metallic bodies together; to rhyme.—*v.t.* To cause to produce a small sharp ringing sound. —*n.* A sharp sound made by the collision of sonorous bodies.—**clinker,** klingk′ėr, *a.* A partially vitrified brick; a kind of hard brick used for paving; a mass of incombustible slag which forms in grates and furnaces. —**clinkstone,** *n.* [From its sonorousness.] A feldspathic rock of the trachytic group with a slaty structure, sometimes used as roofing slates.

clinker-built, klingk′ėr, *a.* *Naut.* built with the planks of the side so disposed that the lower edge of each overlies the upper edge of the next below it, like slates on a roof.

clinometer, klī•nom′et•ėr, *n.* [Gr. *klinō*, to lean, and *metron*, measure.] An instrument for measuring the dip of rock strata.—**clinometric, clinometrical,** klī•no•met′rik, klī•no•met′rik•al, *a.* Of or pertaining to a clinometer; ascertained or determined by a clinometer; pertaining to crystals which have oblique angles between the axes.

Clio, klī′ō, *n.* The muse who was supposed to preside over history; the name of an asteroid; a genus of pteropodous mollusks.

clip, klip, *v.t.*—*clipped*, *clipt*; *clipping*. [Icel. *klippa*, to clip, to cut the hair; Dan. *klippe*, Sw. *klippa*, to clip or shear.] To cut off or sever with shears or scissors; to trim or make shorter (the hair) with scissors; to diminish (coin) by paring the edge; to curtail; to cut short (words); to pronounce shortly and indistinctly. —*n.* The quantity of wool shorn at a single shearing of sheep; a season's shearing; a clasp or spring holder for letters or papers.—**clipper,** klip′ėr, *n.* A full-rigged ship of a type developed in America about 1840, characterized by a sharp bow, graceful lines, tall masts and a large sail area.

clique, klēk, *n.* [Fr. *clique*, probably a mere variant of *claque*, with a somewhat different sense. CLAQUE.] A party; a set; a coterie: used generally in a bad sense.—**cliquish,** klēk′ish, *a.* Relating to a clique or party; disposed to form cliques; having a petty party spirit.—**cliquishness,** klēk′ish•nes, *n.* The state or quality of being cliquish.

cloaca, klō•ā′ka, *n.* [L., a common sewer.] An underground conduit for drainage; a common sewer; the excrementory cavity in birds, reptiles, many fishes, and lower mammalia, formed by the extremity of the intestinal canal and the outlet of the urinary organs.—**cloacal,** klō•ā′kal, *a.* Pertaining to a cloaca.

cloak, klōk, *n.* [O. and Prov.Fr. *cloque*, L.L. *cloca*, *clocca*, a bell, a kind of horseman's cape of a bell-shape; same word as *clock*.] A loose outer garment worn over other clothes; *fig.* that which conceals; a disguise or pretext; an excuse.—*v.t.* To cover with a cloak; to hide; to conceal.

clock, klok, *n.* [Originally a bell. A.Sax. *clucga*, Icel. *klukka*, Dan. *klokke*, Sw. *klocka*, D. *klok*, G. *glocke*, a bell or clock; Ir. and Gael. *clog*, a bell or clock. *Cloak* is the same word.] A machine for measuring time, indicating the hours, minutes, and often seconds by means of hands moving over a dial plate, and generally marking the hours by the strokes of a hammer on a bell, the motion being kept up by weights or springs, and regulated by a pendulum or a balance wheel. ∴ *O'clock*, in such phrases as, 'it is one *o'clock*', is contracted from *of the clock*.—**clockwork,** *n.* The machinery of a clock; a complex mechanism of wheels producing regularity of movement.

clock, klok, *n.* [Possibly originally applied to a bell-shaped ornament or flower.] A figure or figured work embroidered on the side of a stocking.

clod, klod, *n.* [A slightly modified form of *clot*; comp. Dan. *klode*, a globe or ball, *klods*, a block or lump.] A lump or mass in general‡; a lump of earth, or earth and turf; a lump of clay; a dull, gross, stupid fellow; a dolt.—**cloddish,** klod′ish, *a.* Clownish; boorish; doltish; uncouth; ungainly.—**cloddy,** klod′i, *a.* Consisting of clods; abounding with clods; earthy; gross in sentiments or thoughts.—**clodhopper,** klod′hop•ėr, *n.* A clown; a dolt; a boor.—**clodpoll,** klod′pōl, *n.* [*Poll*=head.] A stupid fellow; a dolt; a blockhead.

clog, klog, *n.* [Comp. Sc. *clag*, a clog, an impediment, *clag*, to clog, as with something viscous or sticky, from A.Sax. *clæg*, clay. CLAY.] An encumbrance that hinders motion, or renders it difficult, as a piece of wood fastened to an animal's leg; hindrance; encumbrance; impediment; a sort of shoe with a wooden sole; a wooden shoe; a sabot; a patten.

—*v.t.*—*clogged, clogging.* To impede the movements of by a weight, or by something that sticks or adheres; to encumber, restrain, or hamper; to choke up (a tube, etc.); to obstruct so as to hinder passage through; to throw obstacles in the way of; to hinder; to burden; to trammel.—*v.i.* To become loaded or encumbered with extraneous matter.—**cloggy,** klog'i, *a.* Clogging or having power to clog; adhesive; viscous.—**clog dance,** *n.* A dance in which the feet, shod with clogs, are made to perform a noisy accompaniment to the music.

cloister, klois'tėr, *n.* [O.Fr. *cloistre,* Fr. *cloître*; from L. *claustrum,* a bolt, enclosed place, from *claudo, clausum,* to shut. CLOSE.] An arched way or covered walk running round the walls of certain portions of monastic and collegiate buildings; a place of religious retirement; a monastery; a convent; any arcade or colonnade round an open court; a piazza.—*v.t.* To confine in a cloister or convent; to shut up in retirement from the world; to furnish with a cloister or cloisters.—**cloistral,** klois'tral, *a.* Of or pertaining to a cloister.—**cloistress,**† klois'tres, *n.* A nun; a woman who has vowed religious retirement. (*Shak.*)

cloke, klōk, *n.* and *v.* Same as *cloak.*

clonic, klon'ik, *a.* [From Gr. *klonos,* a shaking.] *Pathol.* convulsive, with alternate relaxation.—*Clonic spasm,* a spasm in which the muscles or muscular fibers rapidly contract and relax alternately, as in epilepsy: used in contradistinction to *tonic spasm.*

close, klōz, *v.t.*—*closed, closing.* [Fr. *clos,* pp. of *clore,* to shut up; from L. *claudo, clausum,* to shut; seen also in *conclude, exclude, include, seclude, cloister,* etc.] To bring together the parts of; to shut (a door, window, book, eyes, hands); make fast; to end, finish, conclude, complete; to fill or stop up; to consolidate: often followed by up; to encompass or enclose; to shut in.—*v.i.* To come together; to unite; to coalesce; to end, terminate, or come to a period; to engage in close encounter; to grapple; to accede or consent to (to *close with* terms); to come to an agreement (to *close with* a person). —*n.* Conclusion; termination; end; pause; cessation; a grapple, as in wrestling.—**closer,** klō'zėr, *n.* One who or that which closes.—**closure,** klō'zhėr, *n.* The act of closing; an end or conclusion; the act of bringing a parliamentary debate to an end, by special vote or otherwise.—**cloture,** klō'chėr, *n.* The act of bringing a parliamentary debate to an end.

close, klōs, *a.* [Fr. *clos,* L. *clausus,* shut. CLOSE, *v.t.*] Shut fast; made fast so as to leave no opening; strictly confined; strictly watched (a *close* prisoner); retired; secluded; hidden; private; secret; having the habit or disposition to keep secrets; secretive; reticent; confined within narrow limits; narrow; without motion or ventilation; difficult to breathe; oppressive: of the air or weather; in direct contact or nearly so; adjoining; with little or no intervening distance in place or time; with little difference, as between antagonists or rival parties; almost evenly balanced (*close* contest); having the parts near each other; compact; dense; firmly attached; intimate; trusty; confidential (*close* friends); firmly fixed on a given object (*close* attention); keen and steady; not deviating from a model or original (a *close* translation); niggardly; stingy; penurious.—*n.* [Fr. *clos,* an inclosed place.] An enclosed place; any place surrounded by a fence; specifically, the precinct of a cathedral or abbey; a narrow passage or entry leading off a street.—*adv.* Tightly, so as to leave no opening; in strict confinement; in contact, or very near in space or time.—**closely,** klōs'li, *adv.* In a close manner.—**closeness,** klōs'nes, *n.*—**closed circuit,** *a.* Pertaining to television broadcasting that is limited to a specified group of interconnected receivers.—**closed shop,** *n.* A business in which an employer hires only members of labor unions.—**close-fisted,** klōs'fis"ted, *a.* Stingy.—**close up,** *n.* A picture taken at close range; an intimate view.

closet, kloz'et, *n.* [O.Fr. *closet,* dim. of *clos,* an enclosure. CLOSE, *n.*] A small room or apartment for retirement; any room for privacy; a small side room or recess for storing utensils, furniture, provisions, etc.—*v.t.* To put in or admit into a closet, as for concealment or for private consultation: usually in pp. *closeted.*

closure, *n.* See CLOSE, *v.t.*

clot, klot, *n.* [Older form of *clod,* and formerly used in same sense; A.Sax. *clot,* a mass; D. *kloot,* a ball or globe; Sw. *klot,* a sphere; *klots,* a block; G. *kloss,* a clod, a lump, *klotz,* a block; akin *cloud.*] A coagulated mass of soft or fluid matter, as of blood, cream, etc.—*v.i.*—*clotted, clotting.* To coagulate, as soft or fluid matter, into a thick, inspissated mass. —*v.t.* To cause to coagulate; to make or form into clots.—**clotty,** klot'i, *a.* Full of clots; resembling a clot; coagulated.

cloth, kloth, *n.* [A.Sax. *cláth*=D. *cleed,* Icel. *klæthi,* Dan. and Sw. *klæde,* G. *kleid,* cloth.] A fabric of wool or hair, or of cotton, flax, hemp, etc., or of mineral filaments, formed by weaving; frequently, a fabric of wool in contradistinction to that made of other material; a piece of linen for covering a table at meals; a tablecloth; a professional dress, specifically that of a clergyman; hence, with the definite article or other defining word, the office of a clergyman; the members of the clerical profession.—**clothe,** klōTH, *v.t.*—*clothed* or *clad; clothing.* To put garments on; to dress; to furnish or supply with clothes or raiment; *fig.* to cover or spread over with anything; to invest; to put on or over.—**clothes,** klōTHz, *n. pl.* [A plural of *cloth,* though it cannot now be said to have a singular.] Garments for the human body; dress; vestments; vesture; the covering of a bed; bedclothes.—**clothes-horse,** *n.* A frame to hang clothes on.—**clothier,** klōTH'i•ėr, *n.* A seller of cloth or of clothes.—**clothing,** klōTH'ing, *n.* Garments in general; clothes.

cloud, kloud, *n.* [Originally a mass or rounded mass in general; A.Sax. *clúd,* a rock, a hillock, the root being that seen in *clod*; so in O.D. *klot,* a clod, and *klote,* a cloud.] A collection of visible vapor or watery particles suspended in the atmosphere at some altitude, the principal forms being designated as the *cirrus,* the *cumulus,* and the *stratus* (see these words); something resembling a cloud, as a body of smoke or flying dust; a dark area of color in a lighter material; that which obscures, darkens, sullies, threatens, or the like; a multitude; a collection; a mass.—*v.t.* To overspread with a cloud or clouds: hence, to obscure; to darken; to render gloomy or sullen; to darken in spots; to variegate with colors. —*v i.* To grow cloudy; to become obscured with clouds.—**cloudberry,** kloud'be•ri, *n.* A plant of the bramble family, with large and white flowers and orange-red berries of an agreeable taste.—**cloudy,** kloud'i, *a.* Overcast with clouds; obscured with clouds, as the sky; consisting of a cloud or clouds; obscure; dark; not easily understood; having the appearance of gloom; indicating gloom, anxiety, sullenness, or ill-nature; not open or cheerful; marked with spots or areas of dark or various hues.—**cloudily,** kloud'i•li, *adv.* In a cloudy manner; with clouds; darkly; obscurely.—**cloudiness,** kloud'i•nes, *n.* The state of being cloudy.—**cloudless,** kloud'les, *a.* Being without a cloud; unclouded; clear; bright.—**cloudlet,** kloud'let, *n.* A small cloud.—**cloudburst,** *n.* A tremendous downpour of rain over a limited area.

clout, klout, *n.* [A.Sax. *clút,* a clout, a patch; Dan. *klud,* Sw. *klut,* a clout; also W. *clwt,* Ir. and Gael. *clud,* a clout.] A patch or rag; a piece of cloth or the like used to mend something; any piece of cloth, especially a worthless piece; *archery,* the mark fixed in the center of a target; a hard blow, struck usually with the fist; in baseball, a long hard-hit ball; a dull or stupid person.

clout, clout nail, klout, klout' nāl, *n.* [Fr. *clouet,* a dim. of *clou,* a nail.] A short, large-headed nail worn in the soles of shoes; also, a nail for securing small patches of iron, as on axle trees, etc.—*v.t.* To stud or fasten with nails.

clove, klōv, pret. of *cleave.*

clove, klōv, *n.* [Sp. *clavo,* a clove, a nail, from L. *clavus,* a nail, from its resemblance to a nail in shape.] The dried flower bud of an evergreen tree of the myrtle tribe, a native of the Molucca Islands, such buds forming a very pungent aromatic spice; the tree yielding cloves.

clove, klōv, *n.* [A.Sax. *clufe,* a bulb.] One of the small bulbs formed in the axils of the scales of a mother bulb, as in garlic; a denomination of weight of cheese, etc., being about 8 lbs.

cloven, klōv′n, pp. of *cleave.* Divided; parted.—**cloven footed,** *a.* Having the hoof divided into two parts, as the ox; bisulcate.

clover, klō′vėr, *n.* [A.Sax. *clœfre*=D. *klaver,* L.G. *klever,* Dan. *klover,* Sw. *klofver,* perhaps from root of *cleave,* from its trifid leaves.] A herbaceous leguminous plant of numerous species bearing three-lobed leaves and roundish heads or oblong spikes of small flowers, several species being widely cultivated for fodder.—*To be* or *to live in clover,* to be in most enjoyable circumstances; to live luxuriously or in abundance.

clown, kloun, *n.* [Icel. *klunni,* a clumsy, boorish fellow; Fris. *klonne,* a bumpkin; allied to Sw. *klunn,* a block.] An awkward country fellow; a peasant; a rustic; a man of coarse manners; a person without refinement; a boor; a lout; a churl; a jester, merryman, or buffoon, as in a theater, circus, or other place of entertainment.—*v.i.* To act as a clown; to play the clown.—**clownish,** kloun′ish, *a.* Of or pertaining to clowns or rustics; rude; coarse; awkward; ungainly; abounding in clowns.—**clownishly,** kloun′ish•li, *adv.* In a clownish manner. — **clownishness,** kloun′ish•nes, *n.* Boorishness; rusticity.

cloy, kloi, *v.t.* [O.Fr. *cloyer,* to stop up, equivalent to *clouer, cloer,* originally to fasten with a nail, O.Fr. *clo,* Fr. *clou,* from L. *clavus,* a nail.] To gratify to excess so as to cause loathing; to surfeit, satiate, or glut.

club, klub, *n.* [A Scandinavian word; Icel. *klubba, klumba,* Sw. *klubba,* Dan. *klub,* a club.] A stick or piece of wood. with one end thicker and heavier than the other, suitable for being wielded with the hand; a thick heavy stick used as a weapon; a cudgel; a staff with a crooked and heavy head for driving the ball in the game of golf, etc.; a card of the suit that is marked with trefoils; *pl.* the suit so marked; a select number of persons in the habit of meeting for the promotion of some common object, as social intercourse, literature, science, politics; a club house.—*v.i. clubbed, clubbing.* To form a club or combination for a common purpose; to combine to raise a sum of money; often with *for* before the object; to combine generally.—*v.t.* To beat with a club; to convert into a club; to use as a club by brandishing with the small end; to add together, each contributing a certain sum.—**clubbable,** klub′a•bl, *a.* Having the qualities that make a man fit to be a member of a club; social.—**clubfoot,** *n.* A short, distorted foot, generally of congenital origin.—**clubfooted,** *a.* Having a clubfoot or clubfeet.—**club moss,** *n.* A mosslike plant; a lycopod.

cluck, kluk, *v.i.* [A.Sax. *cloccian*=D. *klokken,* Dan. *klukke,* an imitative word like *clack, click,* etc.] To utter the call or cry of a brooding hen. —*n.* A sound uttered by a hen; a similar sound, or click, characteristic of the languages of South Africa, especially the Kaffir and Hottentot.

clue, clew, klū, *n.* [A.Sax. *cliwe, cliwen,* a ball of thread=D. *kiuwen,* a clue; akin to L. *globus, glomus,* a mass.] A ball of thread; the thread that forms a ball; *fig.* anything that guides or directs one in an intricate case (there being sundry stories of persons being guided in intricate mazes or labyrinths by a clue of thread); *naut.* the lower corner of a square sail.

clump, klump, *n.* [Same as D. *klomp,* Dan. Sw. and G. *klump,* a lump, a clod; from same root as *clumsy, club,* etc.] A shapeless mass; a lump; a cluster of trees or shrubs.—**clumpy,** klump′i, *a.* Consisting of clumps; shapeless.

clumsy, klum′zi, *a.* [From old *clumsen, clomsen,* to benumb or stupefy; allied to Sw. *klummsen,* benumbed, Icel. *klumsa,* lockjaw, D. *kleumen,* to be benumbed; the root being same as in *clump,* etc.] Awkward; ungainly; without readiness, dexterity, or grace; ill-made; badly constructed; awkwardly done; unskillfully performed.—**clumsily,** klum′zi•li, *adv.* In a clumsy manner.—**clumsiness,** klum′zi•nes, *n.* The quality of being clumsy.

clung, klung, pret. & pp. of *cling.*

cluster, klus′tėr, *n.* [A. Sax. *cluster*; same root as Sw. and Dan. *klase,* Icel. *klasi,* a cluster.] A number of things, as fruits, growing naturally together; a bunch; a number of individuals of any kind collected or gathered into a body; an assemblage; a group; a swarm; a crowd.—*v.i.* To grow or be assembled in clusters or groups.—*v.t.* To collect into a cluster or group; to produce in a cluster or clusters.—*Clustered column, arch.* a column or pier which appears to consist of several columns or shafts clustered together.

clutch, kluch, *v.t.* [O.E. *clucche, cloche,* from *cloche,* a claw, a softened form of older *cloke,* a claw, Sc. *cluik, cluke,* a claw; allied to *claw.*] To seize, clasp, or grip with the hand; to close tightly; to clench.—*n.* A gripping or pinching with the fingers; seizure; grasp; a paw, talon, or grasping merciless hand; hence such phrases as, to fall into a person's *clutches*; *mach.* a contrivance for connecting shafts with each other or with wheels, so that they may be disengaged at pleasure.

clutch, klutch, *n.* [A form of *cluck,* cry of a brooding hen.] The eggs laid and hatched by a bird at one time.

clutter, klut′tėr, *n.* [A modification of *clatter.*] Confused noise; bustle; confusion; litter.—*v.t.* To put in a clutter; to crowd together in disorder. —*v.i.* To make a bustle or disturbance.

clypeate, clypeiform, klip′ē•āt, klip′ē•i•form, *a.* [L. *clypeus,* a shield.] Shaped like a round buckler; shield-shaped; scutate.

clyster, klis′tėr, *n.* [Gr. *klystēr,* from *klyzō,* to wash or cleanse.] A liquid substance injected into the lower intestines to purge or cleanse them, or to relieve from costiveness; an injection.

coach, kōch, *n.* [Fr. *coche,* from Hung. *kocsi* (pron. ko-chi), from *Kocs,* in Hungary.] A vehicle drawn by horses and intended to carry passengers; more particularly a four-wheeled, closed vehicle of considerable size; a two-door automobile; a railroad passenger car; a private tutor, often one employed to prepare pupils for examination; an instructor in athletics, expecially an adviser and trainer for contests.—*v.t.* To carry in a coach; to prepare for an examination by private instruction; to train for an athletic contest; to direct the actions of a player (*Baseball*).—**coach dog,** *n.* A dog of Dalmatian breed, generally white spotted with black, kept to accompany carriages. —**coachman,** kōch′man, *n.* The person who drives a coach.—**coachmanship,** kōch′man•ship, *n.* Skill in coaching.

coact, kō•akt′, *v.i.* [Prefix *co,* and *act.*] To act together.—**coactive,** kō•ak′tiv, *a.* Acting in concurrence; also forcing or compelling; compulsory (in this sense from L. *cogo, coactum,* to compel).

coadjutor, kō•ad•jū′tėr, *n.* [L. *coadjutor*—prefix *co, ad,* to, and *juvo, jutum,* to help.] One who aids another; an assistant; a fellow helper; an associate; a fellow worker; a colleague; the assistant of a bishop or other prelate.—**coadjutress, coadjutrix,** kō•ad•jū′tres, kō•ad•jū′triks, *n.* A female assistant or fellow helper.

coadunate, kō•ad′ū•nit, *a.* [L. *coadunatus*—prefix *co, ad,* to, *unus,* one.] United or joined together: especially used in *bot.* and applied to leaves united at the base.

coagulate, kō•ag′ū•lāt, *v.t.*—*coagulated, coagulating.* [L. *coagulo, coagulatum,* from *coagulum,* rennet—*con,* together, and *ago,* to bring, drive, etc.] To change from a fluid into a curd-like or inspissated solid mass; to curdle, congeal, or clot.—*v.i.* To curdle or congeal.—**coagulability,** kō•ag′ū•la•bil″i•ti, *n.* The capacity of being coagulated.—**coagulable,** kō•ag′ū•la•bl, *a.* Capable of becoming coagulated.—**coagulant,** kō•ag′ū•lant, *n.* That which produces coagulation. —**coagulation,** ko•ag′ū•lā″shon, *n.* The act of coagulating or clotting; the state of being coagulated; the substance formed by coagulation.—**coagulative,** kō•ag′ū•lā•tiv, *a.* Causing coagulation.—**coagulator,** kō•ag′ū•lā•tėr, *n.* That which causes coagulation.—**coagulum,** kō•ag′ū•lum, *n.* A coagulated mass, as curd, etc; *med.* a blood clot.

coal, kōl, *n.* [A.Sax. *col*=D. *kool,* Dan. *kul.* Icel. and Sw. *kol.* G. *kohle.*] A piece of wood or other combustible substance burning or charred; charcoal; a cinder; now, usually, a solid black substance found in the earth, largely employed as fuel, and formed from vast masses of vegetable matter deposited through the luxurious growth of plants in former epochs of the earth's history.—*v.t.* To supply with coal, as a steam vessel or locomotive engine.—*v.i.* To take in coals. —*To haul,* (*take,* etc.) *over the coals,* to call to a strict or severe account; to reprimand.—*To carry coals to Newcastle,* to take things where there are already plenty; to perform unnecessary labor.—**coalfish,** *n.* A species of cod, growing to the length of 2 feet or more, found on the northern coasts of Europe, and so named from the color of its back.—**coal gas,** *n.* A variety of carbureted hydrogen which produces the ordinary gaslight. GAS.—**coal heaver,** *n.* One who is employed in carrying coal, and especially in discharging it from coal-ships.—**coal measures,** *n. pl. Geol.* the upper division of the carboniferous system, consisting of alternate layers of sandstone with thinly laminated beds of clay, between which the coal seams occur.—**coal mine,** *n.* A mine or pit in which coal is dug. —**coal tar,** *n.* A thick, black, viscid, opaque liquid which condenses in the pipes when gas is distilled from coal.

coalesce, kō•a•les′, *v.t.*—*coalesced, coalescing.* [L. *coalesco*—prefix *co,* and *alesco,* to grow up, from *alo,* to nourish.] To unite by growth into one body; to grow together physically; to combine or be collected into one body or mass; to join or unite into one body, party, society, or the like.—**coalescence,** kō•a•les′ens, *n.* The act of coalescing or uniting; the state of being united or combined.—**coalescent,** kō•a•les′ent, *a.* Growing together; uniting.—**coalition,** kō•a•li′shon, *n.* Union in a body or mass; voluntary union of individual persons, parties, or states for a common object or cause.—**coalitionist,** kō•a•li′shon•ist, *n.* One who favors or joins a coalition.

coaming, kōm′ing, *n.* [For *combing,* from *comb.*] *Naut.* a raised border or edge round the hatches to keep out water.

coarse, kōrs, *a.* [The same word as *course,* a thing *of course,* or *in course,* being what is natural, ordinary, common.] Of ordinary or inferior quality; wanting in fineness of texture or structure, or in elegance of form; rude; rough; unrefined; gross; indelicate (*coarse* language).—**coarsely,** kōrs′li, *adv.* In a coarse manner; rudely; uncivilly; without art or polish; grossly.—**coarsen,**† kōr′sn, *v.t.* To render coarse or wanting in refinement; to make vulgar.—**coarseness,** kōrs′nes, *n.* The state or quality of being coarse.

coast, kōst, *n.* [O.Fr. *coste,* Fr. *côte,* rib, hill, shore, coast, from L. *costa,* a rib, side.] The exterior line, limit, or border of a country (O.T.); the edge or margin of the land next to the sea; the seashore.—*The coast is clear,* a phrase equivalent to danger is over; the enemies have gone.—*v.i.* To sail near a coast; to sail by or near the shore, or in sight of land; to slide down without using power. —**coaster,** kōs′tėr, *n.* One that coasts; a ship that trades between coastal ports; a sled; a tray or mat to hold a glass or bottle.—**coaster brake,** *n.* A brake on the rear wheel of a bicycle, etc.—**coastwards,** kōst′wėrdz, *adv.* Toward the coast.—**coastways, coastwise,** kōst′wāz, kōst′wīz, *adv.* By way of or along the coast.—**Coast Guard,** *n.* That branch of the U. S. naval service detailed to ice patrol, lifesaving, and enforcement of customs, navigation and immigration laws.

coat, kōt, *n.* [O.Fr. *cote,* Fr. *cotte,* a coat, from L.L. *cota,* a coat, from O.G. *cotte,* a coarse mantle, G. *kutte,* a cowl: allied to *cot.*] An upper garment, in modern times generally applied to the outer garment worn by men on the upper part of the body; an external covering; a layer of one substance covering another; a coating.—*Coat of arms,* a representation of the armorial insignia which used to be depicted on a coat worn by knights over their armor; an escutcheon or shield of arms.—*Coat of mail,* armor worn on the upper part of the body, and consisting of a network of iron or steel rings, or of small plates, usually of tempered iron, laid over each other like the scales of a fish, and fastened to a strong linen or leather jacket.—*v.t.* To cover with a coat; to spread over with a coating or layer of any substance.—**coat card,** *n.* A card bearing a coated figure, as the king, queen, or knave: now corrupted into *Court-card.*—**coating,** kōt′ing, *n.* Any substance spread over for cover or protection; a thin external layer, as of paint or varnish; cloth for coats.

coax, kōks, *v.t.* [From O.E. *cokes,* a fool; to *coax* one being thus to make a *cokes,* or fool, of him.] To soothe, appease, or persuade by flattery and fondling; to wheedle; to cajole.—**coaxer,** kōk′sėr, *n.* One who coaxes; a wheedler.—**coaxingly,** kōk′sing•li, *adv.* In a coaxing manner.

coaxial, kō•ak′si•al, *a.* Having a common axis.

cob, kob, *n.* [Probably, in some of the meanings, from W. *cob,* a top, a tuft.] A roundish lump of anything; the receptacle on which the grains of corn grow in rows; a short-legged stout horse or pony; clay mixed with straw.—**cob coal,** *n.* A large round piece of coal.

cobalt, kō′balt, *n.* [G. *kobalt, kobolt,* the same word as *kobold,* a goblin, the demon of the mines.] A silver-white metallic element occurring with iron and nickel. Symbol, Co; at. no., 27; at. wt., 58.9332; a blue pigment.—*Cobalt*-60, a radioactive isotope of cobalt used in medicine.

cobble, kob′l. *n.* [From *cob,* a lump.] A roundish stone: a stone rounded by the attrition of water; a boulder; a cobstone.

cobble, kob′l, *v.t.*—*cobbled, cobbling.* [O.Fr. *cobler,* to join or knit together, from L. *copulare,* to couple.] To make or mend coarsely (shoes); to botch; to make or do clumsily or unhandily.—*v.i.* To work as a cobbler; to do work badly.—**cobbler,** kob′lėr, *n.* One who cobbles; a mender of boots and shoes; a clumsy workman; a cooling beverage, composed of wine, sugar, lemon, and finely pounded ice.

coble, kob′l, *n.* [W. *ceubal,* a coble.] A flattish-bottomed boat, clinker-built, with a square stern.

cobra, cobra de capello, kōb′ra, kōb′ra de ka•pel′lō, *n.* [Pg., snake of the hood.] The hooded or spectacle snake, a reptile of the most venomous nature, found in different countries of Asia and Africa, especially in India.

cobweb, kob′web, *n.* [O.E., also *copweb,* A.Sax. *coppe,* a spider, seen in *attor-coppe,* a spider.] The network spun by a spider to catch its prey; something to entangle the weak or unwary; something flimsy and worthless; old musty rubbish. —**cobwebby,** kob′web•i, *a.* Covered with cobwebs; *bot.* covered with a thick interwoven pubescence.

coca, kō′ka, *n.* [Native name.] The dried leaf of a South American plant which is chewed by the inhabitants of countries on the Pacific side of South America, giving great power of enduring fatigue; the plant itself.

cocaine, kō•kān′ *n.* The active principle of coca, which has invigorating properties, and is also used as a local anesthetic in minor surgical operations.

coccus, kok′us, *n.* [Gr. *kokkos,* a berry.] In bacteria, a spheroidal type.

coccyx, kok′siks, *n.* [Gr. *kokkyx.*] An assemblage of small bones attached to the lower extremity of the backbone; the rump.—**coccygeal,** kok•sij′ē•al, *a.* Of or belonging to the coccyx.

Cochin China, kōch′in chī′na, *n.* and *a.* A term applied to a large variety of the domestic fowl, which was imported from Cochin China.

cochineal, koch′i•nēl, *n.* [Fr. *cochenille,* from Sp. *cochinilla,* a wood louse, cochineal, dim. of *cochina,* a sow.] A dyestuff consisting of the dried bodies of a species of insect, a native of the warmer climates of America, found on the cochineal fig tree.—**cochineal fig,** *n.* A treelike cactaceous plant, a native of America, cultivated for the sake of the cochineal insect.

cochlea, kok′lē•a, *n.* [L., a snail or snail's shell.] A bony structure in the internal ear, so called from resembling a snail shell.—**cochleate, cochleated,** kok′lē•āt, kok′lē•āt•ed, *a.* Having a form like the spiral of a snail shell; spiral. Also *Cochleous,* kok′lē•us.

cock, kok, *n.* [A.Sax. *coc, cocc;* comp. O.Fr. *coc,* Fr. *coq,* a cock; probably like *cuckoo,* a word of onomatopoetic origin.] The male of birds, particularly of the gallinaceous, domestic or barn-door fowls: often used adjectively and occasionally to signify the male of certain animals other than birds (a *cock* lobster); a kind of faucet or turn valve, for permitting or arresting the flow of fluids through a pipe; a prominent portion of the lock of a firearm, the hammer; the act of cocking or setting up, or the effect or form produced by such an act (a *cock* of the head, nose, etc.).—*Cock of the wood*, the capercailzie.—*v.t.* [Probably from the strutting of the animal.] To set erect (the ears); to turn up with an air of pertness; to set or draw back the cock in order to fire (to *cock* a gun).—*v.i.* To hold up the head; to look big, pert, or menacing.—**cockerel,** kok′ėr•el, *n.* A young cock.—**cock and bull,** *a.* [From some old tale about a cock and a bull; comp. Fr. *coq-à-l'âne* (cock-and-ass), a cock-and-bull story.] A term applied to idle or silly fictions, stories having no foundation; canards. (Colloq.)—**cockcrow, cockcrowing,** *n.* The time at which cocks crow; early morning.—**cockeye,** *n.* A squinting eye.—**cockeyed,** *a.* Having a squinting eye.—**cockfight, cockfighting,** *n.* A fight between gamecocks; the practice of fighting gamecocks.—**cockhorse,** *n.* A child's rocking horse: now commonly used in the adverbial phrase, *a-cock-horse*, on horseback; in an elevated position; on the high horse.—**cockloft,** *n.* [Lit. a loft for cocks to roost in.] A small loft in the top of a house; a small garret immediately under the roof.—**cockpit,** *n.* A pit or area where gamecocks fight; a space in the fuselage of an airplane for seating pilots or passengers.—**cockscomb,** koks′kōm, *n.* A cock's crest; an annual plant with feathery red or gold flowers.

cock, kok, *n.* [Dan. *kok*, a heap, a pile; Icel. *kökkr*, a lump.] A small conical pile of hay, so shaped for shedding rain.—*v.t.* To put into cocks or piles.

cock, kok, *n.* [O.Fr. *coque*, a kind of boat; Sp. *coca*, It. *cocca*, from L. *concha*, a kind of shell, a vessel.] A small boat. (*Shak.*)

cock, kok, *n.* [It. *cocca*, Fr. *coche*, a notch.] The notch of an arrow or crossbow.

cockade, ko•kād′, *n.* [Fr. *cocarde*, O.Fr. *coquarde*, from *coq*, a cock, from its resemblance to the comb of the cock.] A ribbon or knot of ribbon worn in the hat; a rosette of leather worn on the hat by gentlemen's servants.—*White Cockade*, white rosette, the emblem of the French and English Jacobites.—**cockaded,** ko•kā′ded, *a.* Wearing a cockade.

cockatoo, kok•a•tö′, *n.* [Malay *kakatûa*, from its cry.] A name common to numerous beautiful birds of the parrot kind, chiefly inhabiting Australia and the Indian islands, having crests composed of a tuft of elegant feathers, which they can raise or depress at pleasure.

cockatrice, kok′a•tris, *n.* [O.Fr. *cocatrice*, L.L. *cocatrix*, a crocodile, a cockatrice, a corrupted form of L. *crocodilus*, crocodile. In time the first syllable was thought = *cock.*] A fabulous monster said to be hatched by a serpent from a cock's egg, and represented as possessing characters belonging to both animals; a basilisk.

cockchafer, kok′chā•fėr, *n.* [*Cock* is probably for *clock*, Prov. E. and Sc. for a beetle.] A lamellicorn beetle, the larvae or caterpillars of which feed on the roots of corn, etc., and the insects in their winged state do much injury to trees.

cocker, kok′ėr, *v.t.* [M.Dan. *kokre*, Norweg. *kokla*, to pet, pamper, fondle.] To fondle; to indulge; to treat with tenderness; to pamper.

cocker, kok′ėr, *n.* A dog of the spaniel kind, used for raising woodcocks (whence probably the name) and snipes from their haunts.

cockle, kok′l, *n.* [A.Sax. *coccel*, tares; comp. Gael. *cogal*, Fr. *coquiole*, cockle.] A plant that grows among corn, the corn cockle.

cockle, kok′l, *n.* [Dim. from Fr. *coque*, a cockle, a shell, from L. *concha*, Gr. *kongchē*, a mussel or cockle.] A heart-shaped mollusk with wrinkled shells, common on the sandy shores of Europe and much used as food; a kind of stove, a stove in which the fuel chamber is surrounded by an open space.—*v.t.* and *i.*—*cockled, cockling.* [Perhaps from *cockle*, the shell, marked with wrinkles.] To wrinkle or ridge; to give or assume a wrinkled or ridged surface (as a piece of paper).

cockney, kok′ni, *n.* [Usually connected with the old term *Cockaigne*, land of abundance, perhaps from L. *coquo*, to cook.] A native or resident of London: used slightingly or by way of contempt.—*a.* Related to or like cockneys.—**cockneydom,** kok′-ni•dum, *n.* The region or home of cockneys, a contemptuous or humorous name for London and its suburbs.—**cockneyfy,** kok′ni•fī, *v.t.* To make like a cockney.—**cockneyish,** kok′ni•ish, *a.* Relating to or like cockneys.—**cockneyism,** kok′-ni•izm, *n.* The condition, qualities, manner, or dialect of the cockneys; a peculiarity of the dialect of the Londoners.

cockroach, kok′rōch, *n.* [Sp. *cucaracha*, a wood louse, a cockroach.] An orthopterous insect, the so-called black beetle, very troublesome in houses, where they often multiply to a great extent, infesting kitchens and pantries.

cocksure, kok′shör, *a.* [Said to be derived from the *cock* of a musket, as being much more reliable than the match of the old matchlock.] Perfectly secure (*Shak.*)‡; confidently certain. (Colloq.)

cockswain, kok′swān or kok′sn, *n.* [*Cock*, a boat, and *swain.*] The person who steers a boat; a person on board a ship who has the care of a boat. Also *coxswain.*

coco, kō′kō, *n.* [Pg. *coco*, from *coco*, a bugbear, a distorted mask, from the monkey-like face at the base of the nut.] The coconut palm.—**coconut,** kō′kō•nut, *n.* The large, egg-shaped fruit of the coconut palm.—**coconut palm,** *n.* A tall, slender tropical tree.

cocoa, kō′kō, *n.* [Corruption of *cacao.*] Roasted and pulverized cacao seeds; a drink made from this powder.

cocoon, ko•kön′, *n.* [Fr. *cocon*, from *coque*, a shell, from L. *concha*, a shell-fish.] The silky tissue or envelope which the larvae of many insects spin as a covering for themselves while they are in the chrysalis state.

cod, codfish, kod, kod′fish, *n.* [D. *kodde*, a club, from its large club-shaped head.] A species of fish of great commercial importance, inhabiting northern seas; used as food either fresh, salted, or dried, and yielding cod-liver oil.—**codling,** kod′-ling, *n.* A young cod.—**cod-liver oil,** *n.* An important medical oil obtained from the liver of the common cod.

cod, kod, *n.* [A.Sax. *cod*, *codd*, a small bag; Icel. *koddi*, a pillow; Sw. *kudde*, a cushion.] Any husk, envelope, or case containing the seeds of a plant; a pod.—*v.t.* To enclose in a cod.—**codling,** kod′ling, *n.* A term applied to several cultivated varieties of kitchen apple.—**codling moth,** *n.* A small moth, the larva of which feeds on the apple.

coda, kō′da, *n.* [It., from L. *cauda*, a tail.] *Music*, an adjunct to the close of a composition, for the purpose of enforcing the final character of the movement.

coddle, kod′l, *v.t.*—*coddled, coddling.* [O.Fr. *cadeler*, to cocker, pamper, make much of, *cadel*, an animal cast or born out of time, from L. *cado*, to fall.] To make effeminate by pampering; to make much of; to treat tenderly like an invalid; to pamper; to cocker.—*n.* An over-indulged, pampered being.

code, kōd, *n.* [Fr., from L. *codex*, the trunk of a tree, a tablet, a book.] A systematic collection or digest, of laws; any system or body of rules or laws relating to one subject; a system of signals or the like agreed upon; *teleg.* a set of words representing others for purposes of secrecy.—**codify,** kod′i•fī, *v.t.* To reduce to a code or digest, as laws.—**codification,** kod′i•fi•kā″shin, *n.* The act or process of codifying.—**codifier,** kod′i•fī•ėr, *n.* One who codifies.—**codex,** kō′deks, *n.* pl. **codices,** kō′di•sēz. A manuscript volume, as of a Greek or Latin classic, or of the Scriptures.

codger, koj′ėr, *n.* [Probably a form of *cadger* (which see).] A mean miserly man; a curious old fellow; an odd fish; a character; a familiar term of address. (Slang.)

codical, kod′i•kal, *a.* Relating to a codex or to a code.—**codicil,** kod′i•sil, *n.* [L. *codicillus*, dim. of *codex.*] A writing by way of supplement to a will, containing anything which the testator wishes to add, or any revocation or explanation of what the will contains.—**codicillary,** kod•-i•sil′la•ri, *a.* Of the nature of a codicil.

coed, kō′ed, n. [Short for *coeducational student.*] A female student in a coeducational institution.—**coeducation,** kō′ed•ū•kā″shon, *n.* Joint education of both sexes in the same institution.—**coeducational,** kō′ed•-ū•kā″shon•al, *a.*

coefficient, kō•ef•fish′ent, *a.* Cooperating, acting in union to the same end.—*n.* That which unites in action with something else to produce the same effect; *alg.* a number or known quantity put before letters or quantities, known or unknown, into which it is supposed to be multiplied.—*Coefficient of expansion*, in heat, for a given material a small fraction denoting the portion of its size by which it increases when heated through one degree of temperature.—*Coefficient of friction*, the constant ratio of the retarding force of friction between two surfaces to the mutual pressure between them. —*Coefficient of performance* (marine engineering), coefficient involving the efficiency of the engine and the efficiency of the screw, required in obtaining the speed of a ship in terms of engine power.—*Coefficient of restitution*, the radio of the relative velocity of two bodies after impact to their relative velocity before impact.

coelenterate, sē•len′tėr•āt, *n.* [Gr. *koilos*, hollow, *enteron*, an intestine.] Any of a group of aquatic invertebrates having a hollow saclike body but no head or segmentation, including corals, sea anemones, jellyfishes, etc.—**Coelenterata,** sē•len′-tėr•ā″ta, *n. pl.* The coelenterate animals; the phylum consisting of the Hydrozoa, the Scyphozoa, and the Anthozoa.—**coelenteron,** sē•len′tėr•-on, *n.* The digestive body cavity of coelenterates.

coeliac, celiac, sē′li•ak, *a.* [Gr. *koiliakos*, from *koilia*, the belly, *koilos*, hollow.] Pertaining to the cavity of the abdomen.

coelodont, sē′lo•dont, *a.* [Gr. *koilos*, hollow, *odous*, *odontos*, a tooth.] Having hollow teeth: said of certain lizard-like reptiles.—**coelom,** sē′-lom, *n.* [Gr. *koilōma*, a cavity.] In animals, a secondary body cavity; the body cavity of metazoans.

coenesthesis, sē•nes•thē′sis, *n.* [Gr. *koinos*, common, and *aisthēsis*, perception.] The general sensibility of the system, as distinguished from the special sensations (sight, smell, etc.).

coenobite, sē′no•bīt. Same as *Cenobite*.

coequal, kō•ē′kwal, *a.* Equal with another person or thing; of the same rank, dignity, or power.—*n.* One who is equal to another.—**coequality,** kō•ē•kwol′i•ti, *n.* The state of being coequal.—**coequally,** kō•ē′kwal•li, *adv.* With joint equality.

coerce, kō•ėrs′, *v.t.* [L. *coerceo*—prefix *co*, and *arcere*, to shut up, confine.] To restrain by force, particularly by moral force, as by law or authority; to repress; to compel to compliance; to constrain.—**coercible,** kō•ėr′si•bl, *a.* Capable of being coerced.—**coercion,** kō•ėr′-shon, *n.* The act of coercing; restraint; compulsion; constraint.—**coercive,** kō•ėr′siv, *a.* Capable of coercing; restrictive; able to force into compliance.—*n.* That which coerces; that which constrains or restrains.—**coercively,** kō•ėr′siv•li, *adv.* By constraint or coercion.

coessential, kō•es•sen′shal, *a.* Having the same essence.—**coessentiality,** kō•es•sen′shi•al″i•ti, *n.* The fact of having the same essence.

coetaneous,† kō•ē•tā′nē•us, *a.* [L. *coætaneus*—prefix *co*, and *ætas*, age.] Of the same age with another; beginning to exist at the same time; coeval.—**coetaneously,** kō•ē•tā′nē•-us•li, *adv.* Of or from the same age or beginning.

coeternal, kō•ē•tėr′nal, *a.* Equally eternal with another.—**coeternally,** kō•ē•tėr′nal•li, *adv.* With coeternity or equal eternity.—**coeternity,** kō•-ē•tėr′ni•ti, *n.* Existence from eternity equal with another eternal being; equal eternity.

coeval, kō•ē′val, *a.* [L. *coævus*—*con*, and *ævum*, age.] Of the same age; having lived for an equal period; existing at the same time, or of equal antiquity in general (*coeval with* a person).—*n.* One who is coeval; one who lives at the same time.

coexecutor, kō•ek•sek′ū•tėr, *n.* A joint executor.—**coexecutrix,** ko•ek•-sek′ū•triks, *n.* A joint executrix.

coexist, kō•eg•zist′, *v.i.* To exist at the same time with another (to *coexist with*).—**coexistence,** kō•eg•-zis′tens, *n.* Existence at the same time with another; contemporary existence.—**coexistent,** kō•eg•zis′-tent, *a.* Existing at the same time with another.

coextend, kō•eks•tend′, *v.t.* and *i.* To extend through the same space or duration with another; to extend equally.—**coextension,** kō•eks•ten′-shon, *n.* The fact or state of being equally extended with something else.—**coextensive,** kō•eks•ten′siv, *a.* Equally extensive; having equal scope or extent.—**coextensively,** kō•-eks•ten′siv•li, *adv.* So as to exhibit coextension.

coffee, kof′i, *n.* [Fr. *café*, from Turk. *qahveh*, coffee.] The berries or the ground seeds of a tree, a native of Arabia and tropical Africa, but now extensively cultivated throughout tropical countries, each berry containing two seeds, commonly called coffee beans; a drink made from the roasted and ground seeds of the coffee tree, by infusion or decoction. —**coffee bean,** *n.* A coffee seed.—**coffeehouse** *n.* A house of entertainment where guests are supplied with coffee and other refreshments. —**coffeepot,** *n.* A covered pot in which the decoction or infusion of coffee is made, or in which it is brought upon the table for drinking. —**coffeeroom** *n.* A public room in an inn or hotel where guests are supplied with refreshments.— *n.* **coffee tree,** *n.* The tree which produces coffee.

coffer, kof′ėr, *n.* [Fr. *coffre*, O.Fr. *cofre*, *cofin*, a coffer, from L. *cophinus*, Gr. *kophinos*, a basket. *Coffin* is the same word.] A chest, trunk, or casket for holding jewels, money, or other valuables; a sunk panel or compartment in a ceiling of an ornamental character; a kind of caisson or floating dock.—*v.t.* To deposit or lay up in a coffer.—**cofferdam,** *n.* A wooden enclosure formed in a river, etc., by driving two or more rows of piles close together, with clay packed in between the rows to exclude the water, and so obtain a firm and dry foundation for bridges, piers, etc.

coffin, kof′in, *n.* [O.Fr. *cofin*, a chest, L. *cophinus*, a basket. COFFER.] The chest or box in which a dead human body is buried or deposited in a vault; a casing of paste for a pie (*Shak.*)‡; the hollow part of a horse's hoof.—*v.i.* To put or enclose in a coffin.—**coffin bone,** *n.* A small spongy bone enclosed in the hoof of a horse.

cog, kog, *v.t.*—*cogged*, *cogging*. [W. *coegio*, *coegiaw*, to trick, from *coeg*, empty, vain.] To flatter; to wheedle; to draw from by flattery; to foist or palm: now hardly used except in regard to dice, *to cog a die* being to load it so as to direct its fall, for the purpose of cheating.—*v.i.* To cheat; to wheedle; to lie.—*n.* A trick or deception.

cog, kog, *n.* [Sw. *kugg*, *kugge*, a cog.] The tooth of a wheel, by which it drives another wheel or body, or any similar mechanical contrivance. —**cogwheel,** *n.* A wheel with cogs or teeth.—*v.t.*—*cogged*, *cogging*. To furnish with cogs.

cogent, kō′jent, *a.* [L. *cogens*, *cogentis*, forcing, compelling, from *cogo*—*con*, together, and *ago*, to lead or drive.] Compelling in a physical sense†; resistless†; convincing; having the power to compel conviction; powerful; not easily resisted; forcible; irresistible: of arguments, proofs reasoning, etc.—**cogently,** kō′jent•li, *adv.* In a cogent manner; powerfully; forcibly.—**cogency,** kō′jens•si, *n.* The quality of being cogent; power of moving the will or reason; power of compelling conviction; force; conclusiveness.

cogitate, koj′i•tāt, *v.i.*—*cogitated*, *cogitating*. [L. *cogito*, *cogitatum*—*co* for *con*, together, and *agito*, to shake, to agitate. AGITATE.] To think; to meditate; to ponder.—**cogitation,** koj•i•tā′shon, *n.* The act of cogitating or thinking; thought; meditation; contemplation.—**cogitative,** koj′i•-tā•tiv, *a.* Thinking; having the power of cogitating; meditative; given to thought.—**cogitatively,** koj′i•tā•tiv•-li, *adv.* In a cogitative or thinking manner.—**cogitable,** koj′i•ta•bl, *a.* Capable of being thought; capable of being conceived.—*n.* Anything capable of being the subject of thought.

cognac, kō•nyak′, *n.* [Fr.] A kind of French brandy, so called from the town of the same name, where large quantities are made.

cognate, kog′nāt, *a.* [L. *cognatus*—prefix *co* for *con*, with, and *gnatus*, old form of *natus*, born.] Allied by blood; kindred by birth; *law*, connected by the mother's side; related in origin generally; proceeding from the same stock or root; of the same family (words, roots, languages);

allied in nature; having affinity of any kind (*cognate* sounds).—*n.* One connected with another by ties of kindred; *law,* a relation connected by the mother's side; anything related to another by origin or nature.—**cognation,** kog•nā′shon, *n.* [L. *cognatio.*] Relationship by descent from the same original; affinity; resemblance in nature or character.

cognition, kog•ni′shon, *n.* [L. *cognitio*; *cognosco, cognitus*—*co* for *con,* and *nosco,* anciently *gnosco,* to know.] Knowledge from personal view or experience; perception; a thing known.—**cognitive,** kog′ni•tiv, *a.* Knowing or apprehending by the understanding.—**cognizable,** kog′•niz•a•bl or kon′, *a.* Capable of falling under notice or observation; capable of being known, perceived, or apprehended; capable of falling under judicial notice.—**cognizably,** kog′niz•a•bli or kon′, *adv.* In a cognizable manner.—**cognizance,** kog′ni•zans or kon′, *n.* [O.Fr. *cognoissance, connoissance.*] Knowledge or notice; perception; observation; *law,* judicial or authoritative notice or knowledge, also right to try and determine causes; a crest; a badge; a badge worn by a retainer, soldier, etc., to indicate the person or party to which he belongs.—**cognizant,** kog′ni•zant or kon′, *a.* Acquainted with; having obtained knowledge of; competent to take legal or judicial notice.—**cognize,** kog•nīz′, *v.t.*—*cognized*; *cognizing.* To recognize as an object of thought; to perceive; to become conscious of; to know.

cognomen, kog•nō′men, *n.* [L. *cognomen*—prefix *co* for *con,* and *nomen,* formerly *gnomen,* a name.] Strictly the last of the three names by which a Roman of good family was known, indicating the family to which he belonged; hence a surname or distinguishing name in general.

cognoscible, kog•nos′i•bl, *a.* [From L. *cognosco.* COGNITION.] Capable of being known; subject to judicial investigation.—**cognoscibility,** kog•-nos′i•bil″i•ti, *n.* The quality of being cognoscible.

cohabit, kō•hab′it, *v.i.* [L. *cokabito,* from *eo,* with, and *habito,* to dwell.] To dwell or live together as husband and wife; often applied to persons not legally married, and suggesting sexual intercourse.—**cohabitation,** kō•hab′l•tā″shon, *n.* The state of living together as man and wife.

coheir, kō•âr′, *n.* A joint heir; one who succeeds to a share of an inheritance divided among two or more.—**coheiress,** kō′âr•es, *n.* A joint heiress.

cohere, kō•hēr′, *v.i.*—*cohered, cohering.* [L. *cohæro*—*co* for *con,* and *hæro,* to stick together.] To stick or cleave together; to be united; to keep in close contact as parts of the same mass, or as two substances that attract each other; to hang well together; to agree or be consistent (as parts of a discourse or an argument).—**coherence, coherency,** kō•hē′rens, kō•hē′ren•si, *n.* The state of cohering; a cleaving together of bodies by means of attraction; suitable connection or dependence; due agreement as of ideas; consistency.—**coherent,** kō•hē′rent, *a.* Cohering or sticking together; united; having a due agreement of parts; hanging well together; consecutive; observing due agreement; consistent (a *coherent* argument or discourse, a *coherent* speaker).—**coherently,** kō•-hē′rent•li, *adv.* In a coherent manner.—**coherer,** kō•hēr′ėr, *n.* In wireless telegraphy, the essential part of the receiving instrument.—**cohesion,** kō•hē′zhon, *n.* [Fr. *cohésion.*] The act or state of cohering, uniting, or sticking together; logical connection; *physics,* the state in which, or the force by which, the particles of bodies of the same nature are kept in contact so as to form a continuous mass.—**cohesion,** kō•hē′-zhun, *n.* [L. *cohæro, cohesum,* I stick to.] In flowers, the union of like parts, e.g. petals.—**cohesive,** kō•hē′-siv, *a.* Causing cohesion.—**cohesively,** kō•hē′siv•li, *adv.* In a cohesive manner; with cohesion.—**cohesiveness,** kō•hē′siv•nes, *n.* The quality of being cohesive; the tendency to unite by cohesion.

cohort, kō′hort, *n.* [L. *cohors, cohortis.*] In Roman armies, the tenth part of a legion, a body of about 500 or 600 men; a band or body of warriors in general.

coif, koif, *n.* [Fr. *coiffe,* L.L. *cofia, cufia,* from M.H.G. *kuffe, kupfe,* a kind of cap.] A close-fitting cap or headdress worn usually by nuns, a hood without a cape; a cap of mail.—*v.t.* To cover with a coif.—**coiffure,** kwä•für, *n.* A style of arranging the hair.

coign,‡ koin, *n.* A corner; a coin or quoin. (*Shak.*)

coil, koil, *v.t.* [O.Fr. *coillir, cueillir,* from L. *colligere,* to collect. COLLECT.] To gather (a rope, chain, etc.) into a series of rings above one another; to twist or wind spirally.—*v.i.* To form rings or spirals; to wind.—*n.* A ring or series of rings or spirals into which a rope or other pliant body is wound.

coin, koin, *n.* [Fr. *coin,* a wedge, the die with which money is stamped, a coin, a corner, from L. *cuneus,* a wedge.] A piece of metal, as gold, silver, copper, or some alloy, converted into money by impressing some stamp on it; such pieces collectively; metallic currency; money; also, a quoin.—*v.t.* To stamp and convert into money; to mint; to make, fabricate, or invent.—**coinage,** koi′nij, *n.* The stamping of money; coin; money coined; the act of inventing, forming, or producing; invention; fabrication; what is fabricated or produced.—**coiner,** koi′-nėr, *n.* One who coins; a maker of money; often a maker of base or counterfeit coin; an inventor or maker, as of words.

coincide, kō•in•sīd′, *v.i.*—*coincided, coinciding.* [L.L. *coincido,* from L. prefix *co,* with, and *incido,* to fall in—*in,* and *cado,* to fall.] To occupy the same place in space, or the same position in a scale or series; to happen at the same point of time; to be exactly contemporaneous; to correspond exactly; to concur; to agree (to *coincide with* a person *in* an opinion).—**coincidence,**† kō•in′-si•dens, *n.* The fact of coinciding; exact correspondence in position; a happening or agreeing in time; contemporaneousness; agreement in circumstance, character, etc.; exact correspondence generally, or a case of exact correspondence.—**coincident, coincidental,** kō•in′si•dent, kō•in•si•den′tal, *a.* Coinciding; happening at the same time; concurrent; exactly corresponding.—**coincidently,** kō•in′si•dent•li, *adv.* In a coincident manner; with coincidence.

coinheritance, kō•in•her′it•ans, *n.* Joint inheritance.—**coinheritor,** kō•-in•her′it•ėr, *n.* A joint heir; a coheir.

coir, koir, *n.* A species of yarn manufactured from the husk of cocoanuts, and formed into cordage, sailcloth, matting, etc.

coition, kō•i′shon, *n.* [L. *coitio*—*con,* and *eo, itum,* to go.] A coming together; copulation.

coke, kōk, *n.* [Perhaps from *cook* or *cake*; comp. *caking* coal.] Coal deprived of its bitumen, sulfur, or other extraneous or volatile matter by fire.—*v.t.*—*coked, coking.* To convert into coke; to deprive of volatile matter, as coal.

col, kol, *n.* [Fr., neck.] An elevated mountain pass between two higher summits; the most elevated part of a mountain pass.

colander, kul′an•dėr or kol′an•dėr, *n.* [From L. *colans, colantis,* ppr. of *colo,* to strain, from *colum,* a colander.] A vessel with a bottom perforated with little holes for straining liquids; a strainer.

colatitude, kō•lat′i•tūd, *n.* [Abbrev. of *complement* and *latitude.*] The complement of the latitude, or what it wants of 90°.

colchicum, kol′chi•kum, *n.* [L., a plant with a poisonous root, from *Colchis,* the native country of Medea, the famous sorceress.] A genus of liliaceous plants, the most familiar species being the meadow saffron, a plant with a solid bulblike rootstock and purple, crocus-like flowers, found in various parts of Europe.—**colchicine,** kol′chi•sin, *n.* An alkaloid obtained from colchicum bulbs, and used for the alleviation or cure of gout and rheumatism.

colcothar, kol′ko•thär, *n.* [Probably of Ar. origin.] The brownish-red peroxide of iron, used for polishing glass and other substances.

cold, kōld, *a.* [A.Sax. *cald, ceald, a,* and *n.*=Dan. *kold,* Icel. *kaldr,* Sw. *kall,* D. *koud,* Goth. *kaldo,* G. *kalt;* from root of *cool, chill,* which also appears in L. *gelidus,* gelid.] Not warm or hot; gelid; frigid; chilling; cooling; having the sensation of coolness; wanting warmth or animal heat; chill; wanting passion, zeal, or ardor; insensible; not animated or easily excited into action; not affectionate, cordial, or friendly;

unaffecting; not animated or animating; not able to excite feeling or interest; spiritless.—*In cold blood*, without excitement, emotion, or passion.—*To give, show*, or *turn the cold shoulder*, to treat a person with studied coldness, neglect, or contempt.—*n.* The relative absence or want of heat; the cause of the sensation of coolness; the sensation produced in animal bodies by the escape of heat; an indisposition occasioned by cold; a catarrh.—**coldly,** kōld′li, *adv.* In a cold manner; without warmth; without concern; without apparent passion, emotion, or feeling; with indifference or negligence; dispassionately; calmly.—**coldness,** kōld′nes, *n.* The state or quality of being cold; frigidity; indifference.—**cold-blooded,** *a.* Having cold blood; without sensibility or feeling; *zool.* a term applied to those animals the temperature of whose blood is a very little higher than that of their habitat.—**cold chisel,** *n.* A chisel for cutting metal in its cold state.—**cold cream,** *n.* A kind of cooling unguent for the skin, variously prepared.

cole, kōl, *n.* [From L. *colis, caulis*, a cabbage-stalk, a cabbage.] The general name of all sorts of cabbage.—**coleslaw,** kōl′slạ. A salad made of sliced cabbage leaves.

colemanite, kōl′man•īt, *n.* A mineral.

Coleoptera, kol•ē•op′tėr•a, *n. pl.* [Gr. *koleos*, a sheath, and *pteron*, a wing.] An order of insects commonly known by the name of *beetles*, and characterized by having four wings, of which the two anterior, called elytra, are not suited for flight, but form a covering and protection to the two posterior, and are of a hard and horny or parchment-like nature.—**coleopteran,** kol•ē•op′tėr•an, *n.* A member of the order Coleoptera.—**coleopterous,** kol•ē•op′tėr•us, *a.* Pertaining or belonging to the Coleoptera.

coleorhiza, kol′ē•o•rī″za, *n.* [Gr. *koleos*, a sheath, and *rhiza*, a root.] *Bot.* the sheath which covers the young radicle of monocotyledonous plants.

colic, kol′ik, *n.* [L. *colicus*, Gr. *kōlikos*, from *kōlon*, the colon.] A painful spasmodic affection of the intestines.—**colicky,** kol′ik•i, *a.*

colin, kol′in, *n.* [Fr.] The Virginian quail or American partridge.

collaborate, kol•lab′o•rāt, *v.i.* [L. *collaboratus*, from *com*, together, and *labore*, to labor.] To work together, especially on scientific or literary efforts; to cooperate with the enemy.

collaborator, kol•lab′o•rā•tėr, *n.* [Fr. *collaborateur*—L. *col* for *con*. together, and *laboro*, to labor.] An assistant; an associate in labor, especially in literary or scientific pursuits.—**collaboration,** kol•lab′o•rā″shon, *n.*

collapse, kol•laps′, *v.i.*—*collapsed, collapsing.* [L. *collabor, collapsus*—*col* for *con*, and *labor, lapsus*, to slide or fall (whence *lapse*).] To fall in or together, as the two sides of a vessel; to close by falling together; hence, to come to nothing; to break down.—*n.* A falling in or together, as of the sides of a hollow vessel; a more or less sudden failure of the vital powers; a sudden and complete failure of any kind; a breakdown.—**collapsible,** kol•lap′si•bl, *a.* Capable of collapsing or being made to collapse.

collar, kol′ėr, *n.* [L. *collare*, Fr. *collier*, a collar, from L. *collum*, the neck.] Something worn round the neck, whether for use or ornament or both, or it may be for restraint; the necklace or chain worn by knights, and having the badge of the order appended to it; part of the harness of an animal used for draft; an article of dress or part of a garment going round the neck; something resembling a collar; anything in the form of a ring, especially at or near the end of something else.—*To slip the collar*, to escape or get free; to disentangle one's self.—*v.t.* To seize by the collar; to put a collar on; to roll up and bind with cord (a piece of meat) for keeping for a time.

collarbone, *n.* The clavicle; one of the two bones of the thorax in man and many quadrupeds joined at one end to the shoulder bone and at the other to the breastbone.

collate, kol•lāt′, *v.t.*—*collated, collating.* [L. *confero, collatum*, to bring together, compare, bestow—*col* for *con*, and *fero, latum*, to carry.] To bring together and compare; to examine critically, noting points of agreement and disagreement (manuscripts and books); to confer or bestow (a benefice) on (to *collate* a person *to* a church); to gather and place in order, as the sheets of a book for binding.—**collation,** kol•lā′shon, *n.* The act of collating; a comparison, especially the comparison of manuscripts or editions of books; the presentation of a clergyman to a benefice by a bishop who has the benefice in his own gift, or by neglect of the patron has acquired the patron's rights; the reading of passages in Scripture and in the Fathers, in Benedictine monasteries, followed by a discussion and light repast.—**collator,** kol•lā′tėr, *n.* One who collates.

collateral, kol•lat′ėr•al, *a.* [L.L. *collateralis*—*col* for *con*, and L. *lateralis*, from *latus*, a side.] At the side; belonging to the side or what is at the side; acting indirectly; acting through side channels; accompanying but subordinate; auxiliary; subsidiary; descending from the same ancestor, but not in a direct line, as distinguished from *lineal*.—*n.* Pertaining to an obligation or security attached to another to secure its performance; hence, guaranteed by security as in a loan.

colleague, kol′lēg, *n.* [L. *collega*, a colleague—*col* for *con*, and stem of *lego, legatum*, to send on a mission.] A partner or associate in the same office, employment, or commission, civil or ecclesiastical.—**colleagueship,** kol′lēg•ship, *n.* The state of being a colleague in office or special work.

collect, kol•lekt′, *v.t.* [L. *colligo, collectum*—*col* for *con*, and *lego*, to gather, which appears also in *neglect, select, analect*, etc., also *coil, cull.*] To gather into one body or place; to assemble or bring together; to gather; to infer or conclude (in this sense now rare).—*To collect one's self*, to recover from surprise or a disconcerted state.—*v.i.* To run together; to accumulate.—*n.* (kol′lekt). A short comprehensive prayer; a form of prayer adapted to a particular day or occasion.—**collectanea,** kol•lek•tā′nē•a, *n. pl.* [L., things collected.] A selection of passages from various authors, usually made for the purpose of instruction; a miscellany.—**collected,** kol•lek′ted, *p.* and *a.* Gathered together; not disconcerted; cool; firm; prepared; self-possessed.—**collectedly,** kol•lek′ted•li, *adv.* In one view; together; in a cool, firm, or self-possessed manner.—**collectedness,** kol•lek′ted•nes, *n.* The state of being collected.—**collectible,** kol•lek′ti•bl, *a.* Capable of being collected.—**collection,** kol•lek′shon, *n.* The act or practice of collecting or of gathering; that which is collected or gathered together (as pictures or objects of interest); that which is collected for a charitable, religious, or other purpose; the jurisdiction of a collector; a collectorship; the act of deducing from premises, or that which is deduced (*Mil.*)‡—**collective,** kol•lek′tiv, *a.* [L. *collectivus*, Fr. *collectif.*] Formed by collecting; gathered into a mass, sum, or body; aggregate, *gram.* expressing a number or multitude united, though in the singular number (a *collective noun*).—*Collective note*, in *diplomacy* an official communication signed by the representatives of several governments.—*n. Gram.* a noun with a singular form comprehending in its meaning several individuals, such as *people, infantry, crowd*.—**collectively,** kol•lek′tiv•li, *adv.* In a collective manner; in a mass or body; in the aggregate; unitedly.—**collectivism,** kol•lek′tiv•izm, *n.* The socialistic doctrine that the land and means of production should belong to the people collectively. Also **collectivist.**—**collector,** kol•lek′tėr, *n.* One who collects; especially, one who collects objects of interest; an officer appointed to collect and receive customs, duties, taxes, etc., within a certain district.—**collectorship,** kol•lek′tėr•ship, *n.* The office or jurisdiction of a collector.

college, kol′ej, *n.* [L. *collegium*, a society, guild, or fraternity, from *collega*, a colleague. COLLEAGUE.] A society of men invested with certain powers and rights, performing certain duties, or engaged in some common pursuit, a guild, a corporation, especially a society or institution for purposes of instruction and scientific research in the higher branches of knowledge; the edifice belonging to a college.—**collegial,**† kol•lē′ji•al, *a.* Pertaining to a college; collegiate.—**collegian,** kol•lē′ji•an, *n.* A member of a college, particularly of a literary institution so called; a student.—**collegiate,** kol•lē′ji•āt, *a.* Pertaining to a college (*collegiate* studies); constituted after the manner of a college.—*Collegiate church,* a church that has no cathedral, but does have a college of canons, or a dean, as Westminster Abbey; in the U. S., a church in an association of churches.

collenchyma, kol•len′ki•ma, *n.* [Gr. *kolla,* glue, and *enchyma,* an infusion.] *Bot.* the cellular matter in which pollen is generated.

collet, kol′et, *n.* [Fr. *collet,* a collar or necklace, from *col.* L. *collum,* the neck.] A band or collar; among jewelers, the horizontal face or plane at the bottom of brilliants, and the part of a ring containing the bezel in which the stone is set; *bot.* the neck or part of a plant from which spring the ascending and descending axes.

collide, kol•līd′, *v.i.*—*collided, colliding.* [L. *collido*—*col* for *con,* and *lædo,* to strike.] To strike or dash against each other; to meet in shock; to meet in opposition or antagonism. —**collision,** kol•li′zhon, *n.* [L. *collisio.*] The act of striking or dashing together; the meeting and mutual striking of two or more moving bodies, or of a moving body with a stationary one; opposition; antagonism; interference.

collie, kol′•i, *n.* [Origin doubtful.] A variety of dog especially common in Scotland, and much esteemed as a sheep dog.

collier, kol′yėr, *n.* [From *coal*; comp. *lawyer, sawyer.*] A digger of coal; one who works in a coal mine; a vessel employed in the coal trade.—**colliery,** kol′yėr•ri, *n.* The place where coal is dug; a coal mine or pit.

colligate, kol′li•gāt, *v.t.*—*colligated, colligating.* [L. *colligo*—*col* for *con,* and *ligo,* to bind.] To bind or fasten together; to connect by observing a certain relationship or similarity (to *colligate* phenomena).—**colligation,** kol•li•gā′shon, *n.* The act of colligating; that process by which many isolated facts are brought together under one general conception or observation.

collimation, kol•li•mā′shon, *n.* [From a fancied L. verb *collimare,* really a false reading for *collineare*—*col,* together, and *linea,* a line.] The act of leveling or of directing the sight to a fixed object.—*Line of collimation,* in an astronomical instrument, the straight line which passes through the center of the object glass, and intersects at right angles the fine wires which are fixed in the focus.—*Error of collimation,* the deviation of the actual line of sight in a telescope from the focus and center of the object glass, or from the proper position.—**collimate,** kol′li•māt, *v.t.* To adjust the line of collimation in. —**collimator,** kol•lim′ā•tėr, *n.* A small telescope used for adjusting the line of collimation.

collinear, kol•lin′ē•er, *a.* [L. *col* for *con,* and *linea,* a line.] Pertaining to or situated in a corresponding line.

collision. See COLLIDE.

collocate, kol′lo•kāt, *v.t.*—*collocated, collocating.* [L. *colloco*—*col* for *con,* together, and *loco,* to place, *locus,* a place.] To set or place; to set; to station.—**collocation,** kol•lo•kā′shon, *n.* [L. *collocatio.*] The act of collocating, placing, disposing, or arranging along with something else; the manner in which a thing is placed with regard to something else; disposition; arrangement.

collodion, kol•lō′di•on, *n.* [Gr. *kolla,* glue, and *eidos* resemblance.] A substance prepared by dissolving guncotton in ether, or in a mixture of ether and alcohol, used as a substitute for adhesive plaster in the case of slight wounds, and as the basis of a photographic process.—**colloid,** kol′loid, *a* Like glue or jelly; *chem.* applied to uncrystallizable liquids; *geol.* applied to partly amorphous minerals.—*n.* The name given to a transparent, viscid, yellowish, structureless or slightly granular matter, resembling liquid gelatine. CRYSTALLOID.—**colloidal,** kol•loi′dal, *a.* Of or pertaining to the nature of colloids.

collogue, ko•lōg′, *v.i.* To plot together. (Colloq.)

collop, kol′op, *n.* [Perhaps lit. a piece of meat made tender by beating; Sw. *kollops,* G. *klopps,* meat that has been beaten; D. *kloppen,* G. *klopfen,* to beat; E. to *clap.*] A slice or lump of flesh.

colloquy, kol′lo•kwi, *n.* [L. *colloquium*—*col,* together, and *loquor,* to speak.] The mutual discourse of two or more; a conference; a dialogue; a conversation.—**colloquial,** kol•lō′kwi•al, *a.* Pertaining to conversation; peculiar to the language of common conversation.—**colloquialism,** kol•lō′kwi•al•izm, *n.* A word or phrase peculiar to the language of common conversation.—**colloquially,** kol•lō′kwi•al•li, *adv.* In a colloquial or conversational manner; in colloquial language.

collotype, ko′lo•tīp, *n.* [Gr. *kolla,* glue.] Thin gelatinous plate etched by actinic rays and then printed from.

collude, kol•lūd′, *v.i.*—*colluded, colluding.* [L. *colludo*—*col,* together, and *ludo,* to play, as in *allude, delude.*] To play into the hands of each other; to conspire in a fraud; to act in concert; to connive.—**colluder,** kol•lūd′ėr, *n.* One who colludes.—**collusion,** kol•lū′zhon, *n.* Secret agreement for a fraudulent purpose.—**collusive,** kol•lū′siv, *a.* Fraudulently concerted between two or more.—**collusively,** kol•lū′siv•li, *adv.* In a collusive manner; by collusion.—**collusiveness,** kol•lū′siv•nes, *n.* The quality of being collusive.

collyrium, kol•lir′i•um, *n.* [L.] Eye salve; eyewash.

colocynth, kol′o•sinth, *n.* [Gr. *kolokynthis,* a gourd or pumpkin.] A kind of cucumber, the fruit of the wild gourd, indigenous in the warmer parts of Asia, but now widely cultivated on account of its medicinal properties, being a purgative.

Cologne earth, ko•lōn′, *n.* A kind of ochre of a deep-brown color, used in watercolor painting.—**Cologne water,** *n.* Eau de Cologne.

colon, kō′lon, *n.* [Gr. *kōlon,* the colon, a member or limb, a clause.] The largest portion of the human intestine, forming the middle section of the large intestine, and terminating in the rectum; a punctuation mark formed thus [:], used to mark a pause greater than that of a semicolon, but less than that of a period.

colonel, kėr′nel, *n.* [Formerly also *coronel,* which is an old French form and has given the modern pronunciation; Fr. *colonel,* O.Fr. *colonnel,* from It. *colonello,* a colonel, a little column, dim. of *colonna,* L. *columna,* a column; the name was originally given to the leading company in a regiment.] The chief commander of a regiment of troops, in any branch of service.—**colonelcy, colonelship,** kėr′nel•si, kėr′nel•ship, *n.* The office, rank, or commission of a colonel.

colonnade, kol•on•nād′, *n.* [It *colonnata,* from *colonna,* a column. COLUMN.] *Arch.* any series or range of columns placed at certain intervals from each other, such intervals varying according to the rules of art and the order employed.

colony, kol′o•ni, *n.* [L. *colonia,* from *colo, cultum,* to till (hence *cultivate, culture*).] A body of people transplanted from their mother country to a remote province or country, and remaining subject to the jurisdiction of the parent state; a body of settlers or their descendants; the country planted or colonized; a number of animals or plants living or growing together.—**colonial,** ko•lō′ni•al, *a.* Pertaining to a colony.—*n.* A person belonging to a colony.—**colonist,** kol′on•ist, *n.* An inhabitant of or settler in a colony; a member of a colonizing expedition. — **colonize,** kol′on•īz, *v.t.*—*colonized, colonizing.* To plant or establish a colony in; to send a colony to; to migrate and settle in.—*v.i.* To move and settle in a distant country.—**colonization,** kol′on•iz•ā″shon, *n.* The act of colonizing or state of being colonized.—**colonizationist,** kol′on•iz•ā″shon•ist, *n.* An advocate for colonization.—**colonizer,** kol′on•īz•ėr, *n.* One who colonizes; one who establishes colonies.

colophon, kol′o•fon, *n.* [Gr. *kolophōn,* a summit, top, finishing.] A device, or printer's name, place of publication, and date, formerly put at the conclusion of a book; from the acme or finish of horsemanship displayed by the Ionians of Colophon.

colophony, kol′o•fo•ni, *n.* [Gr. *kolophōnia,* from *Colophōn,* a city of Ionia, whence the Greeks obtained it.] Black resin or turpentine boiled in water and dried.

coloquintida, kol•o•kwin′ti•da, *n.* The colocynth or bitter apple.

color, kul′ėr, *n.* [L. *color,* color.]

That in respect of which bodies have a different appearance to the eye independently of their form; any tint or hue distinguished from white; that which is used for coloring; a pigment; paint; the blood-red hue of the face; redness; complexion; false show; pretense; guise; *pl.* a flag, ensign, or standard borne in an army or fleet; a color used as a badge. —*Complementary colors*, colors which together make white; thus, any of the three primary colors is complementary to the other two.—*Primary colors*, red, green, and violet (or blue); or in a looser sense the colors into which white light is divided by a glass prism.—viz. red, orange, yellow, green, blue, indigo, and violet.—*v.t.* To impart color to; to dye; to tinge; to paint; to stain; *fig.* to clothe with an appearance different from the real; to give a specious appearance to; to make plausible.—*v.i.* To blush.—**colorable,** kul′ėr•a•bl, *a.* Specious; plausible; giving an appearance of right or justice (pretense, grounds); intended to deceive (a *colorable* imitation of a trademark). ∴ *Colorable*, having such an appearance as would not lead to the suspicion of anything underhand; *specious*, having a fair outside show, and likely to mislead thereby; *plausible*, apparently reasonable or satisfactory, though not convincing; *ostensible*, put forward as having a certain character but not really having it.—**colorableness,** kul′ėr•a•bl•nes, *n.* Speciousness.—**colorably,** kul′ėr•a•bli, *adv.* In a colorable manner.—**colored,** kul′ėrd, *p.* and *a.* Having a color; dyed, painted, or stained; having some other color than white or black; having a specious appearance; a term applied to the darker varieties of mankind; *bot.* applied to a leaf, calyx, seed, etc., to express any color except green. —**coloring,** kul′ėr•ing, *n.* The act or art of applying colors; color applied; tints or hues collectively, as in a picture; a specious appearance; show.—**colorist,** kul′ėr•ist, *n.* One who colors; a painter whose works are remarkable for beauty of color. —**colorless,** kul′ėr•les, *a.* Destitute of color.—**colorblind,** *a.* Incapable of accurately distinguishing colors; having an imperfect perception of colors.—**colorblindness,** *n.* Total or partial incapability of distinguishing colors, arising from some defect in the eye, though otherwise vision may be perfect.

colorate, kul′ėr•āt, *a.* [L. *coloratus.*] [*obs.*] Colored; dyed or tinged with some color.—**coloration,** kul•ėr•ā′shon, *n.* Coloring; the state of being colored; the tints of an object.—**colorific,** kul•ėr•if′ik, *a.* Having the quality of tingeing; able to give color or tint to other bodies.—**colorimeter,** kul•o•rim′et•ėr, *n.* An instrument for measuring the depth of color in a liquid by comparison with a standard liquid of the same tint.

colossus, ko•los′sus, *n.* pl. **colossi,** ko•los′sī, or rarely **colossuses,** ko•los′sus•ez. [Gr. *kolossos*, a colossal statue.] A statue of a gigantic size or of size much greater than the natural, such as the statue of Apollo which anciently stood at the entrance to the port of Rhodes.—**colossal,** ko•los′sal, *a.* Like a colossus; much exceeding the size of nature; very large; huge; gigantic.

colostrum, ko•los′trum, *n.* [L.] The first milk secreted in the breasts after childbirth.

colporteur, kol′por•tėr, ė long, *n.* [Fr.—*col*, from L. *collum*, the neck, and *porteur*, a carrier, from L. *porto*, to carry.] A hawker of wares; a hawker of books and pamphlets, particularly a hawker of religious books and pamphlets.—**colportage,** kol′por•tij, *n.* The system of distributing religious books, tracts, etc., by colporteurs.

colt, kōlt, *n.* [A.Sax. *colt*, a young ass, a young camel; comp. Sw. *kult*, a young boar, a stout boy.] A young horse, or a young animal of the horse genus; commonly and distinctively applied to the male, *filly* being the female; a young camel or a young ass (O.T.)‡.—**coltish,** kōl′tish, *a.* Like a colt; wanton; frisky; gay. —**coltsfoot,** *n.* The popular name of a composite plant whose leaves were once much employed in medicine; *Tussilago*.

colubrine, kol′ū•brīn, *a.* [L. *colubrinus*, from *coluber*, a serpent.] Relating to serpents; cunning; crafty.

columbarium, kol•um•bâ′ri•um, *n.* [L. *columba*, pigeon.] An ancient sepulchre with recesses for urns containing the ashes of the dead.

Columbian, ko•lum′bi•an, *a.* [From *Columbia*, a name sometimes given to the United States, after Christopher *Columbus*.] Pertaining to the United States or to America.

columbine, kol′um•bīn, *a.* [L. *columbinus*, from, *columba*, a pigeon.] Like or pertaining to a pigeon or dove; of a dove color; resembling the neck of a dove in color.—*n.* [L. *columbina.*] A plant of the buttercup family, so called from the curved petals being in shape somewhat like pigeons, the sepals forming the wings; [*cap.*] the name of the mistress of Harlequin in pantomimes.

columbium, ko•lum′bi•um, *n.* [From *Columbia*, America.] A rare metal; niobium.—**columbite,** ko•lum′bīt, *n.* The ore of columbium.

columella, kol•ū•mel′a, *n.* [L. dim. of *columna*, column.] A name for various plants having column-like parts.

column, kol′um, *n.* [L. *columna*, a column, from root which appears in *collis*, a hill, *culmen*, a summit.] A solid body of considerably greater length than thickness, standing upright, and generally serving as a support to something resting on its top; a pillar; anything resembling a column in shape (a *column* of water, air, or mercury); *bot.* the united stamens and styles of plants when they form a solid central body, as in orchids; *milit.* a formation of troops, narrow in front, and deep from front to rear; *naut.* a body of ships following each other; *printing* and *writing*, a division of a page; a perpendicular set of lines separated from another set by a line or blank space.—**columella,** kol•ū•mel′la, *n.* [L. *columella*, dim. of *columen* or *columna*, a column.] *Bot.* the central column in the capsule of mosses, from which the spores separate; the axis round which the parts of a fruit are arranged; *conch.* the upright pillar in the center of most of the univalve shells.—**columnar,** ko•lum′nėr, *a.* Formed in columns; like the shaft of a column.—**columned,** kol′umd, *a.* Furnished with columns; supported on or adorned by columns.—**columniation,** ko•lum′ni•ā″shon, *n.* *Arch.* the employment of columns in a design.

colure, kol′ūr, *n.* [Gr. *kolouros*, docktailed (with *grammē*, a line, understood)—*kolos*, stunted, and *oura*, a tail, because a part is always beneath the horizon.] Either of the two great circles supposed to intersect each other at right angles in the poles of the world, one of them passing through the solstitial and the other through the equinoctial points of the ecliptic, the points where they intercept the ecliptic being called cardinal points.

colza, kol′za, *n.* [Fr. *colza*, O.Fr. *colzat*, from D. *koolzaad*, lit. cabbage seed—*kool*, cabbage, and *zaad*, seed.] A variety of cabbage whose seeds afford an oil much employed for burning in lamps, and for many other purposes.

coma, kō′ma, *n.* [Gr. *kōma*, lethargy.] A state of more or less complete insensibility and loss of power of thought or motion; lethargy.—**comatose,** kō′ma•tōs, *a.* Pertaining to coma; drowsy; lethargic.

coma, kō′ma, *n.* [L., the hair.] *Bot.* the empty leaf or bract terminating the flowering stem of a plant, in a tuft or bush; also, the silky hairs at the end of some seeds; *astron.* the nebulous hairlike envelope surrounding the nucleus of a comet.—**comate,** kō′māt, *a.* [L. *comatus.*] Hairy; furnished with a coma.

comb, kōm, *n.* [A.Sax. *camb*, a comb, a crest=D. *kam*, Icel. *kambr*, a comb, a crest; Dan. *kam*, a comb, a cam; G. *kamm*, a comb.] An instrument with teeth for separating, cleansing, and adjusting hair, wool, or flax; also, an instrument used by women for keeping the hair in its place when dressed; the crest, caruncle, or red fleshy tuft growing on a cock's head; the top or crest of a wave; honeycomb.—*v.t.* To dress with a comb.—*v.i.* To roll over, as the top of a wave, or to break with a white foam.—**comber,** kōm′ėr, *n.* One who combs; one whose occupation is to comb wool, etc.

combat, kom′bat or kum′bat, *v.i.* [Fr. *combattre*—*com*, and *battre*, to beat. BATTER.] To fight; to struggle or contend.—*v.t.* To fight with; to oppose by force; to contend against; to resist: now chiefly *fig.* (he *com-*

bated their scruples.)—*n.* A fight; a struggle to resist, overthrow, or conquer; contest; engagement; battle.—*Single combat*, a fight between two individuals; a duel. ∴ Syn. under BATTLE.—**combatable,** kom•bat′a•bl, *a.* Capable of being combated, disputed, or opposed.—**combatant,** kom′ba•tant, *a.* Contending; disposed to combat or contend.—*n.* A person who combats; any person engaged in active war; a person who contends with another in argument or controversy.—**combative,** kom•bat′iv, *a.* Disposed to combat; showing such a disposition; pugnacious.—**combatively,** kom•bat′iv•li, *adv.* In a combative manner; pugnaciously.—**combativeness,** kom•bat′iv•nes, *n.* State of being combative; disposition to contend or fight.

combine, kom•bīn′, *v.t.*—*combined, combining.* [Fr. *combiner*, from the L.L. *combino*—*com*, and L. *binus*, two and two, or double.] To unite or join; to link closely together.—*v.i.* To unite, agree, or coalesce; to league together; to unite by affinity or chemical attraction.—kom′bīn, *n.* Group of persons or associations leagued together in a joint undertaking; a harvesting machine which cuts and threshes grain while traveling across a field.—**combinable,** kom•bī′na•bl, *a.*—**combination,** kom•bi•nā′shon, *n.* The act of combining; the act of joining, coming together, or uniting; union of particulars; concurrence; meeting; union or association of persons or things for effecting some object by joint operation; commixture; union of bodies or qualities in a mass or compound; chemical union; *math.* the union of a number of individuals in different groups, each containing a certain number of the individuals.—**combinative,** kom•bī′na•tiv, *a.* Tending to combine; uniting.—**combiner,** kom•bī′nėr, *n.* One who or that which combines.

combustible, kom•bus′ti•bl, *a.* [Fr. *combustible*, from L. *comburo*, *combustum*, to consume—*comb*, for *cum* or *con*, and *uro*, to burn; same root as Gr. *auein*, to kindle; Skr. *ush*, to burn.] Capable of taking fire and burning; flammable; *fig.* fiery or irascible; hot tempered.—*n.* A substance that will take fire and burn.—**combustibility, combustibleness,** kom•bus′ti•bil″i•ti, kom•bus′ti•bl•nes, *n.* The state or quality of being combustible.—**combustion,** kom•bus′chen, *n.* The operation of fire on flammable substances; burning; or, in chemical language, the union of a flammable substance with oxygen or some other supporter of combustion, attended with heat, and in most instances with light.—*Spontaneous combustion*, the ignition of a body by the internal development of heat without the application of an external flame.

come, kum, *v.i.*—*came* (pret.), *come* (pp.); *coming.* [A.Sax. *cuman* or *cwiman*=D. *komen*, Icel. *koma*, Dan. *komme*, Sw. *komma*, G. *kommen*, Goth. *kwiman*: also from same root, L. *venio*, to come; Gr. *bainō*, to go.] To move hitherward; to advance nearer in any manner and from any distance; to approach the person speaking or writing, or the person addressed; opposed to *go*; to arrive; to take place; to reach a certain stage or point of progress; to arrive at: followed by an infinitive (I now *come* to consider the next subject); to get into a certain state or condition; especially followed by *to be*; to happen or fall out; to befall (*come* what will); to advance or move into view; to appear (color *comes* into the face); to accrue or result; to be formed (knowledge *comes*): frequently with *of* (this *comes* of not taking heed). *Come*, in the imperative, is used to excite attention, or to invite to motion or joint action; or it expresses earnestness, or haste, impatience, remonstrance, etc.—*To come and go*, to alternate; to appear and disappear.—*To come about*, to happen; to fall out (how did these things *come about*?).—*To come at*, to reach; to arrive within reach of; to gain.—*To come away*, to leave; to germinate; to sprout.—*To come by*, to pass near; to obtain, gain, acquire.—*To come down*, to descend; to be humbled or abased.—*To come home*, to come to one's dwelling; to touch nearly; to touch the feelings, interest, or reason.—*To come in*, to enter, as into an enclosure or a port; to become fashionable; to be brought into use.—*To come in for*, to get a share of; to get; to obtain.—*To come into*, to acquire by inheritance or bequest.—*To come near* or *nigh*, to approach in place; to approach in quality; to arrive at nearly the same degree.—*To come off*, to escape; to get free; to emerge (to *come off* with honor); to happen; to take place.—*To come on*, to advance; to progress; to thrive.—*To come out*, to remove from within; to become public; to be introduced to general society: said of a young lady; to appear after being obscured by clouds (the sun has *come out*); to result from calculation.—*To come out of*, to issue forth; to get clear of (he has *come out of* that affair very well).—*To come out with*, to give publicity to; to let out or disclose.—*To come over*, to pass above or across, or from one side to another.—*To come round*, to recover; to revive; to regain one's former state of health.—*To come short*, to fail; not to reach; to be inadequate.—*To come to*, to fall or be allotted to; to amount to.—*To come to one's self*, to get back one's consciousness; to recover.—*To come to pass*, to happen.—*To come true*, to be verified.—*To come up*, to ascend; to rise; to spring; to shoot or rise above the earth.—*To come up to*, to attain to; to equal; to amount to.—*To come up with*, to overtake in following or pursuit.—*Come your ways*, come along; come hither.—*To come*, future; in future (time *to come*).—**comer,** kum′ėr, *n.* One that comes; one who has arrived and is present.—*All comers*, any one that may come; everybody, without exclusion.—**coming,** kum′ing, *p.* and *a.* Drawing nearer or nigh; approaching; moving toward; advancing; future; next in the future.

comedy, kom′e•di, *n.* [L. *comœdia*, Gr. *kōmōdia*, a comedy, from *kōmos*, a revel or feast, and *ōdē*, a song.] A dramatic composition of a light and amusing class, its characters being represented as in the circumstances or meeting with the incidents of ordinary life.—**comedian,** ko•mē′di•an, *n.* An actor or player in comedy; a player in general; a writer of comedy.

comely, kum′li, *a.* [A.Sax. *cymlic*, comely, from *cyme*, suitable, from *cuman*, to *come*.] Handsome; graceful; symmetrical; well proportioned; decent; suitable; proper; becoming.—**comeliness,** kum′li•nes, *n.* The quality of being comely.

comestible, ko•mes′ti•bl, *n.* [Fr. *comestible*, from L. *comedo*, *comesum* or *comestum*, to eat up—*com*, and *edo*, to eat.] An eatable; an article of solid food.

comet, kom′et, *n.* [L. *cometa*, from Gr. *komētēs*, long-haired, a comet, from *komē*, hair; from the appearance of its tail.] The name given to certain celestial bodies consisting of a star-like nucleus, surrounded by a luminous envelope, called the *coma*, and usually accompanied with a tail or train of light, appearing at irregular intervals, moving through the heavens in paths which seem to correspond with parabolic curves, or in a few instances in elliptical orbits of great eccentricity.—**cometic, cometary,** ko•met′ik, kom′et•a•ri, *a.* Pertaining to a comet.

comfit, kum′fit, *n.* [Fr. *confit*, pp. of *confire*, to preserve, to make into a sweetmeat, from L. *conficere*—*con*, together, and *facio*, to make.] A dry sweetmeat; any kind of fruit or root preserved with sugar and dried; a bonbon; a lollipop.

comfort, kum′fėrt, *v.t.* [O.E. *confort*, from O.Fr. *conforter*, to comfort, from L.L. *confortare*, to strengthen—*con*, intens., and L. *fortis*, brave.] To raise from depression; to soothe when in grief or trouble; to bring solace or consolation to; to console; to cheer; to hearten; to solace; to enliven.—*n.* Relief from affliction, sorrow, or trouble of any kind; solace; consolation; a state of quiet or moderate enjoyment, resulting from the possession of what satisfies bodily wants and freedom from all care or anxiety; a feeling or state of well-being, satisfaction, or content; that which furnishes moderate enjoyment or content.—**comfortable,** kum′fėrt•a•bl, *a.* Being in comfort or in a state of ease or moderate enjoyment; giving comfort; affording help, ease, or consolation.—**comfortableness,** kum′fėrt•a•bl•nes, *n.* The state of being comfortable.—**comfortably,** kum′fėrt•a•bli, *adv.* In a comfortable manner; in a manner to give comfort or consolation.—**comforter,** kum'fėrt•ėr, *n.* One who comforts; a knit woolen fabric for tying round the neck in cold weather. —**comfortless,** kum'fėrt•les, *a.* Without comfort; without affording or without being attended by any comfort.

comfrey, kum'fri, *n.* [Fr. *conferve,* L. *conferva,* from *conferveo,* to heal, to grow together, from prefix *con,* and *ferveo,* to boil, from the plant's supposed healing power.] A name given to several species of rough herbaceous European and Asiatic plants of the borage family.

comic, kom'ik, *a.* [L. *comicus,* Gr. *kōmikos.* COMEDY.] Relating or belonging to comedy, as distinct from tragedy; also comical.—*n.* A comic actor or singer.—**comical,** kom'ik•al, *a.* Exciting mirth; ludicrous; laughable; diverting; sportive; droll.—**comicality,** kom•i•kal'i•ti, *n.* The quality of being comical; ludicrousness; that which is comical or ludicrous.—**comically,** kom'ik•al•li, *adv.* In a comical manner; in a manner to raise mirth; laughably; ludicrously. —**comicalness,** kom'ik•al•nes, *n.* The quality of being comical; comicality.

comitia, ko•mish'i•a, *n. pl.* [L.] Legislative assemblies or meetings among the ancient Romans.—**comitial,** ko•mish'i•al, *a.* Pertaining to the comitia.

comity, kom'i•ti, *n.* [L. *comitas,* from *comis,* mild, affable.] Mildness and suavity of manners; courtesy; civility; good breeding.—*Comity of nations* (*comitas gentium*), that kind of courtesy by which the laws and institutions of one state or country are recognized and to some extent given effect to by the government of another within its territory.

comma, kom'ma, *n.* [Gr. *komma,* a segment, from *koptō,* to cut off.] A punctuation mark [,] denoting the shortest pause in reading, and separating a sentence into divisions or members, according to the construction; *mus.* an enharmonic interval, being the difference between a major and a minor tone.

command, kom•mand' or kom•mänd', *v.t.* [Fr. *commander,* L. *commendo,* to entrust, later to enjoin, to command—*com* for *con,* and *mando,* to commit to, to command.] To order with authority; to lay injunction upon; to direct; to charge; to have or to exercise supreme authority, especially military authority, over; to have control over; to dominate through position, often specifically military position; to have within the range of the eye; to overlook; to exact or compel by moral influence; to challenge (to *command* respect); to have at one's disposal and service (to *command* assistance). —*v.i.* To act as or have the authority of a commander; to exercise influence or power.—*n.* The power of governing with chief authority; supreme power; control; exercise of authority; a commandment; mandate; order; power or control, as from holding an advantageous military position; the power of overlooking from elevated position; a force under the command of a particular officer.—**commandant,** kom•man•dant', *n.* [Fr.] A commander.—**commander,** kom•man'dėr, *n.* One who commands; a chief; one who has supreme authority; a leader; the chief officer of an army or of any division of it; a naval officer next in rank above lieutenant and under the captain; one on whom is bestowed a commandery.—*Commander-in-chief,* a supreme military commander; the highest staff appointment in the British army.—**commandeer,** kom•mand•ēr', *v.t.* [African-Dutch.] To impress or force men or stores for military purposes.—**commandership,** kom•mand'dėr•ship, *n.* The office of a commander.—**commandery,** kom•man'dėr•i, *n.* [Fr. *commanderie.*] Among several orders of knights, and in certain religious orders, a district under the control of a member of the order called a commander or preceptor; the office of such a member; the official building of a commandery.—**commanding,** kom•man'ding, *a.* Governing; bearing rule; exercising supreme authority; controlling by influence, authority, or dignity (*commanding* eloquence); dominating; overlooking a wide region without obstruction (a *commanding* eminence).—**commandingly,** kom•man'ding•li, *adv.* In a commanding manner.—**commandment,** kom•mand'ment, *n.* A command; a mandate; an order or injunction given by authority; charge; precept; a precept of the decalogue; authority; power of commanding.—**commando,** kom•man'dō, *n.* [D. *commando,* lit. a command.] A body of armed men raised for military service among the Boers or other whites of South Africa; a military expedition undertaken by such a body of men.

commeasure,† kom•mezh'ūr, *v.t.* To coincide with; to be coextensive with.—**commeasurable,**† kom•mezh'ūr•a•bl, *a.* Commensurate; equal.

commemorate, kom•mem'or•āt. *v.t.* —*commemorated, commemorating.* [L. *commemoro*—*com,* and *memoro,* to mention. MEMORY.] To preserve the memory of by a solemn act; to celebrate with honor and solemnity. —**commemoration,** kom•mem'o•rā"shon, *n.* The act of commemorating or calling to remembrance by some solemnity; the act of honoring the memory of some person or event by solemn celebration.—**commemorative,** kom•mem'or•āt•iv, *a.* Tending to commemorate or preserve the remembrance of something.—**commemorator,** kom•mem'or•āt•ėr, *n.* One who commemorates.

commence, kom•mens', *v.i.*—*commenced, commencing.* [Fr. *commencer,* from a (hypothetical) L.L. *cominitiare*—L. prefix *com,* and *initiare,* to begin. INITIATE.] To begin; to take rise or origin; to have first existence; to begin to be, as in a new state or character.—*v.t.* To begin; to enter upon; to perform the first act of.—**commencement,** kom•mens'ment, *n.* The act or fact of commencing; beginning; rise; origin; first existence; the day when, or the ceremonies at which, degrees are conferred.

commend, kom•mend', *v.t.* [L. *commendo,* to commit, to commend—*com,* and *mando,* to commit to; the same word as *command* with a different signification.] To commit, deliver, entrust, or give in charge (N.T.); to represent as worthy of confidence, notice, regard, or kindness; to recommend; with reflexive pronoun sometimes to call for notice or attention (this subject *commends itself* to our attention); to mention with approbation; to mention by way of keeping in memory; to send greetings or compliments from (*Shak.*).—*v.i.* To approve; to praise. **commendable,** kom•men'da•bl, *a.* Capable or worthy of being commended or praised; praiseworthy; laudable. — **commendably,** kom•men'da•bli, *adv.* In a commendable or praiseworthy manner.—**commendam,** kom•men'dam, *n.* [L.L.] An ecclesiastical benefice or living commended to the care of a qualified person to hold till a proper pastor is provided. When a beneficed parson was made a bishop, and was empowered to retain his benefice, he was said to hold it *in commendam.*—**commendation,** kom•men•dā'shon, *n.* [L. *commendatio.*] The act of commending; praise; favorable representation in words; declaration of esteem; respects; greeting; message of love.—**commendatory,** kom•men'da•to•ri, *a.* Serving to commend; presenting to favorable notice or reception; containing praise; holding a benefice *in commendam.*

commensal, kom•men'sal, *n.* [L. *com,* with, and *mensa,* table.] One that eats at the same table‡; one of two animals or plants that are always found together; an animal which lives on or in another without being parasitic.—*a.* Having the character of a commensal.—**commensalism,** kom•men'sal•izm, *n.* The state of being commensal.

commensurable, kom•men'shu̥•ra•bl, *a.* [L. prefix *com,* and *mensura,* measure. MEASURE.] Having a common measure; reducible to a common measure.—**commensurability,** kom•men'shu̥•ra•bil"i•ti, *n.* The state of being commensurable, or of having a common measure.—**commensurably,** kom•men'shu̥•ra•bli, *adv.* In a commensurable manner.—**commensurate,** kom•men'shu̥•rāt, *a.* Reducible to a common measure; of equal size; having the same boundaries; corresponding in amount, degree, or magnitude; adequate.—**commensurately,** kom•men'shu̥•rāt•li, *adv.* In a commensurate manner; so as to be commensurate; correspondingly; adequately.—**commensuration,** kom•men'shu̥•rā"shon, *n.* Proportion; a state of being commensurate.

comment, kom•ment', *v.i.* [L. *com-*

mentor, from *commentus*, pp. of *comminiscor*, to reflect on—*com*, with, together with, and stem *min*, seen in *memini*, to remember, and in E. *mind*.] To make remarks or observations, either on a book or writing, or on actions, events, or opinions; to write notes on the works of an author, with a view to illustrate his meaning, or to explain particular passages; to make annotations.—*n*. (kom′ment). A remark or observation; a note intended to illustrate a difficult passage in an author; annotation; exposition; talk; discourse.—**commentary,** kom′men•ta•ri, *n*. A series or collection of comments or annotations; a historical narrative; a memoir of particular transactions (the *Commentaries* of Caesar).—**commentator,** kom′men•tā•tėr, *n*. One who writes a commentary; one who writes annotations; an annotator.

commerce, kom′mėrs, *n*. [Fr. *commerce*, L. *commercium*—*com*, together with, and *merx*, *mercis*, merchandise.] An interchange of goods, merchandise, or property of any kind between countries or communities; mercantile pursuits; trade; traffic; mutual dealings in common life; intercourse.—*v.i*. To carry on trade‡; to hold intercourse; to commune.—**commercial,** kom•mėr′shal, *a*. Pertaining to commerce or trade; dealing with or depending on commerce; carrying on commerce.—*Commercial announcement*, an announcement made over the radio concerning the product of the advertiser who sponsors the program.—**commercialism,** kom•mėr′shal•izm, *n*. The doctrines, tenets, or practices of commerce or of commercial men.

commination, kom•mi•nā′shon, *n*. [L. *comminatio*—*com*, and *minatio*, a threatening, from *minari*, to threaten. MENACE.] A threat or threatening; a denunciation of punishment or vengeance; an office in the liturgy of the Church of England, appointed to be read on Ash Wednesday or on the first day of Lent.—**comminatory,** kom•min′a•to•ri, *a*. Threatening; denouncing punishment.

commingle, kom•ming′gl, *v.t*. or *i*. —*commingled*, *commingling*. [Prefix *com*, and *mingle*.] To mix together; to mingle in one mass or intimately; to blend.

comminute, kom′mi•nūt, *v.t*.—*comminuted*, *comminuting*. [L. *comminuo*, *comminutum*, to make small—*com*, with, and *minuo*, to lessen; root *min*, as in *minor*, less.] To make small or fine; to reduce to minute particles or to a fine powder; to pulverize; to triturate; to levigate.—*a*. Divided into very small parts or particles.—**comminution,** kom•mi•nū′shon, *n*. The act of comminuting or reducing to a fine powder or to small particles; pulverization.

commiserate, kom•miz′ėr•āt, *v.t*.—*commiserated*, *commiserating*. [L. *commiseror*—*com*, and *miseror*, to pity. MISERABLE.] To feel sorrow, pain, or regret for, through sympathy; to compassionate; to pity.—**commiseration,** kom•miz′ėr•ā″shon, *n*. The act of commiserating: a sympathetic suffering of pain or sorrow for the afflictions or distresses of another; pity; compassion.—**commiserative,** kom•miz′ėr•ā•tiv, *a*. Compassionate. —**commiseratively,** kom•miz′ėr•ā•tiv•li, *adv*.

commissar, kom′mis•sär, *n*. [Fr. *commissaire*, L.L. *commissarius*, one to whom something is entrusted.] A Communist party official in charge of teaching party doctrine; formerly, the head of a government department in Soviet Russia.

commissary, kom′mis•â•ri, *n*. [Fr. *commissaire*, L.L. *commissarius*, one to whom any trust or duty is delegated; L. *committo*, *commissum*, to commit.] In a general sense, a commissioner; one to whom is committed some charge, duty, or office by a superior; a representative; a store that supplies provisions, as in a camp; *Scots law*, the judge in a commissary-court; *milit*. a name given to officers or officials of various kinds, especially to officers of the commissariat department.—**commissarial,** kom•mis•sâ′ri•al, *a*. Pertaining to a commissary.—**commissariat,** kom•mis•sâ′ri•at, *n*. The department of an army whose duties consist in supplying transport, provisions, forage, camp equipage, etc., to the troops; also, the body of officers in that department; the office or employment of a commissary; the district or country over which the authority or jurisdiction of a commissary extends.

commission, kom•mish′on, *n*. [L. *commissio*, *commissionis*. COMMIT.] The act of committing; the act of doing something wrong; the act of perpetrating (the *commission* of a crime); the act of entrusting, as a charge or duty; the thing committed, entrusted, or delivered; a duty, office, charge, or piece of work entrusted to any one; the warrant by which any trust is held, or any authority exercised (as that of an officer in an army); mandate; authority given; a number of persons joined in an office or trust; commissioners; the state of acting in the purchase and sale of goods for another; position or business of an agent; agency; the allowance made to an agent for transacting business.—*Commission of the Justice of the Peace*, a warrant of authority issued by the state for the granting of certain powers to, and the appointment of, Justices of the Peace.—*To put a ship into commission*, to equip and man a vessel, and place it in service after it has been in dry dock for repairs.—*v.t*. To give a commission to; to give special powers and instructions for the accomplishment of an act; to empower or authorize by special commission; to send with a mandate or authority.—**commission merchant,** *n*. One who buys or sells goods for another on commission.—**commissionnaire,** kom•mēs•yōn•âr′, *n*. [Fr.] At European hotels and terminals, a kind of messenger or light porter. —**commissioner,** kom•mish′on•ėr, *n*. One who commissions; a person who has a commission or warrant from proper authority to perform some office or execute some business; an officer having charge of some department of the public service, which is put into commission; a steward or agent who manages affairs on a large estate.

commissure, kom•e•shųr′, *n*. [Fr. *commissure*, from L. *commissura*, a joining together, joint, seam—*com*, together, and *mitto*, *missum*, to send.] A joint or seam; the place where two parts of a body meet and unite; a juncture; a suture: used chiefly in *anat*.—**commissural,** kom•mis•shų′ral, *a*. Belonging to a commissure.

commit, kom•mit′ *v.t*.—*committed*, *committing*. [L. *committo*, to make over in trust, to set to work, do wrong—*com*, together, and *mitto*, to send, whence also *admit*, *permit*, *dismiss*, *mission*, *missile*, etc.] To give in trust; to put into charge or keeping; to entrust; to surrender, give up, consign: with *to*; *refl*. to bind to a certain line of conduct, or to expose or endanger by a preliminary step or decision which cannot be recalled; to compromise; to order or send into confinement; to imprison (the magistrate *commits* a guilty person); to refer or entrust to a committee or select number of persons for their consideration and report; to do (generally something wrong); to perpetrate.—*To commit to memory*, to learn by heart.—**committable,** kom•mit′a•bl, *a*. Capable of being committed. —**commitment, committal,** kom•mit′ment, kom•mit′al, *n*. The act of committing; commission (but we do not say the *committal* or *commitment* of crimes, but the *commission*).—**committee,** kom•mit′tē, *n*. A body of persons elected or appointed to attend to any matter or business referred to them, often a section of a larger body.—*Committee of the whole house*, an arrangement by which matters are discussed in a particular manner in congress, the chair being occupied by the chairman of committee, and members being allowed to speak more than once on a question.—**committeeman,** *n*. A member of a committee, as of the national, state, county, and city district.

commix, kom•miks′, *v.t*. or *i*. [L. *commisceo*, *commixtus*—*com*, together, and *misceo*, to mix. MIX.] To mix or mingle; to blend.—**commixture,** kom•miks′chėr, *n*. The act of mixing; the state of being mingled; the mass formed by mingling; a compound.

commode, kom•mōd′, *n*. [Fr., from L. *commodus*, convenient. COMMODIOUS.] A kind of headdress formerly worn by ladies; a chest of drawers, often with shelves and other conveniences added; a night stool.

commodious, kom•mō′di•us, *a*. [L.L. *commodiosus*, from L. *commodus*, useful.—*com*, together, and *modus*, measure, mode.] Roomy and convenient; spacious and suitable; serviceable. —**commodiously,** kom•mō′di•us•li, *adv*. So as to be commodious.—**commodiousness,** kom•mō′di•us•nes, *n*.

The state or quality of being commodious.—**commodity,** kom•mod′i•ti, *n.* [Fr. *commodité*, convenience, commodity; L. *commoditas*, fitness, convenience.] Suitableness or convenience‡; what is useful; specifically, an article of merchandise; anything movable that is bought and sold, as goods, wares, produce of land and manufactures.

commodore, kom′mo•dōr, *n.* [From Sp. *commendador*, a commander, or from Pg. *capitao mor*, superior captain.] An officer who commands a detachment of ships in the absence of an admiral; a title given by courtesy to the senior captain when three or more ships of war are cruising in company, to the senior captain of a line of merchant vessels, and to the president of a yachting club; the leading ship in a fleet of merchantmen.

common, kom′on, *a.* [Fr. *commun*, L. *communis*—*com*, together, and *munis*, ready to be of service, obliging.] Belonging or pertaining equally to more than one, or to many indefinitely; belonging to all; general; universal; public; of frequent or usual occurrence; not extraordinary; frequent; usual; ordinary; habitual; not distinguished by rank or character; not of superior excellence; of low or mean rank or character; *gram.* applied to such nouns as are both masculine and feminine, and to those that are the names of all the objects possessing the attributes denoted by the noun (river, etc.).—*Common council*, the council of a city or corporate town, empowered to make bylaws for the government of the citizens.—*Common law*, the unwritten law, the law that receives its binding force from immemorial usage and universal reception, in distinction from the written or statute law.—*Common measure*, a number or quantity that divides two or more numbers or quantities without leaving a remainder.—*Common Pleas*, formerly one of the three superior courts of common law in England, now a division of the High Court of Justice.—*Common Prayer*, the liturgy or public form of prayer prescribed by the Church of England to be used in all churches and chapels.—*Common seal*, a seal used by a corporation as the symbol of their incorporation.—*Common sense*, sound practical judgment; the natural sagacity or understanding of mankind in general.—*Common time*, musical time or rhythm with two, four, or eight beats to a bar.—*In common*, equally with another or with others.—*n.* A tract of ground, the use of which is not appropriated to an individual, but belongs to the public or to a number; in all other senses *pl.*: the common people; the untitled; the vulgar, the lower house of the British Parliament, consisting of the representatives of cities, boroughs, and counties; food provided at a common table, as at colleges; food or fare in general.—*Short commons*, stinted allowance.—*Extra commons*, increased allowance.—**commonage,** kom′on•ij, *n.* The right of pasturing on a common; the joint right of using anything in common with others.—**commonalty,** kom′on•al•ti, *n.* The common people; all below the rank of nobility.—**commoner,** kom′on•ėr, *n.* A person under the degree of nobility; a student of the second rank in the University of Oxford, not dependent on the foundation for support.—**commonly,** kom′on•li, *adv.* In a common manner; usually; generally; ordinarily; frequently; for the most part.—**commonness,** kom′on•nes, *n.* The state or fact of being common.—**commonplace,** kom′on•plās, *a.* Not new or extraordinary; common; trite.—*n.* A memorandum of something that is likely to be frequently referred to; a well-known or customary remark; a trite saying; a platitude.—**commonweal,** kom′on•wēl, *n.* A commonwealth; the body politic; a state.—**commonwealth,** kom′on•welth, *n.* [Here *wealth* means strictly well-being.] The body politic; the public; a republican state; the form of government which existed in England from the death of Charles I in 1649 to the abdication of Richard Cromwell in 1659.

commotion, kom•mō′shon, *n.* [L. *commotio*, from *commoveo*, *commotum*—*com*, with, and *moveo*, to move. MOVE.] Agitation; tumult of people; disturbance; perturbation; disorder of mind; excitement.—**commove,**† kom•möv′, *v.t.*—*commoved*, *commoving*. [L. *commoveo*.] To put in motion; to disturb; to agitate; to unsettle.

commune, kom•mūn′, *v.i.*—*communed*, *communing*. [Fr. *communier*; L. *communico*, to communicate, from *communis*, common. COMMON.] To converse; to talk together familiarly; to impart sentiments mutually; to interchange ideas or feelings.—*n.* (kom′mūn). Familiar interchange of ideas or sentiments; communion; intercourse; friendly conversation (to hold *commune*, to be in *commune*).

commune, kom′mūn, *n.* [Fr., from *commun*, common.] A small territorial district in France and in some other countries, under the government of a mayor; the inhabitants of a commune; the members of a communal council.—*The commune of Paris*, a revolutionary committee which took the place of the municipality of Paris in the French revolution of 1789; also, a committee or body of communalists who in 1871 for a brief period ruled over Paris after the evacuation of the German troops.—**communal,** kom′mū•nal, *a.* Pertaining to a commune or to communalism.—**communalism,** kom′mū-nal•izm, *n.* The theory of governments by communes or other local self-governing bodies.—**communalist,** kom′mū•na•list, *n.* One who adheres to communalism.—**communalistic,** kom′mū•na•lis″tik, *a.* Pertaining to communalism.—**communism,** kom′mūn•izm, *n.* [Fr. *communisme*.] The system or theory which upholds the absorption of all proprietary rights in a common interest; the doctrine of a community of property.—**communist,** kom′mūn•ist, *n.* One who holds the doctrines of communism.—**communistic,** kom•mū•nis′tik, *a.* Relating to communists or communism, according to the principles of communism.—**communistically,** kom•mū•nis′tik•al•li, *adv.* In accordance with communism; in a communistic way or form.

communicate, kom•mū′ni•kāt, *v.t.*—*communicated*, *communicating*. [L. *communico*, from *communis*, common.] To impart to another or others; to bestow or confer for joint possession, generally or always something intangible, as intelligence, news, opinions, or disease; with *to* before the receiver.—*v.i.* To share; to participate: followed by *in*; to have a communication or passage from one to another (one room *communicates with* another); to have or hold intercourse or interchange of thoughts; to partake of the Lord's supper or communion.—**communicability,** kom•mū′ni•ka•bil″i•ti, *n.* The quality of being communicable; capability of being imparted.—**communicable,** kom•mū′ni•ka•bl, *a.* Capable of being communicated or imparted from one to another; capable of being recounted; communicative; ready to impart information, news, etc.—**communicableness,** kom•mū′ni•ka•bl•nes, *n.*—**communicant,** kom•mū′ni•kant, *n.* One who communicates or partakes of the sacrament at the celebration of the Lord's supper.—**communication,** kom•mū′ni•kā″shon, *n.* The act of communicating; means of communicating; connecting passage; means of passing from place to place; that which is communicated or imparted; information or intelligence imparted by word or writing; a document or message imparting information.—**communicative,** kom•mū′ni•kā•tiv, *a.* Inclined to communicate; ready to impart to others; free in communicating; not reserved; open.—**communicatively,** kom•mū′ni•kā•tiv•li, *adv.* In a communicative manner; by communication.—**communicativeness,** kom•mū′ni•kā•tiv•nes, *n.* The state or quality of being communicative; readiness to impart to others; freedom from reserve.—**communicator,** kom•mū′ni•kā•tėr, *n.* One who or that which communicates.

communion, kom•mūn′yon, *n.* [L. *communio*, *communionis*, participation.] Participation of something in common; fellowship; concord; bond or association; intercourse between two or more persons; interchange of thoughts or acts; union in religious worship, or in doctrine and discipline; union with a church; a body of Christians who have one common faith and discipline; [*cap.*] the act of partaking in the sacrament of the eucharist; the celebration of the Lord's supper.—*Communion elements*, the bread and wine used in the sacrament of the Lord's supper.

communiqué, kom•mū•ni•kā′, *n.* [Fr.] An official communication, a statement given to the press.

communism, etc. See COMMUNE.

community, kom•mū′ni•ti, *n.* [L. *communitas.* COMMON.] Common possession or enjoyment (a *community* of goods); a society of people having common rights and privileges; a society of individuals of any kind; the body of people in a state; the public, or people in general: used in this sense always with the definite article; common character (individuals distinguished by *community* of descent).

commute, kom•mūt′, *v.t.*—*commuted, commuting.* [L. *commuto*—prefix *com,* and *muto,* to change. MUTABLE, MUTATION.] To exchange; to put one thing in the place of another; to give or receive one thing for another; to exchange, as one penalty or punishment for one of less severity; to pay in money instead of in kind or in duty; to travel back and forth daily between places, as to and from a city. —**commuter,** one who travels to and from a city daily.—**commutability,** kom•mūt′a•bil″i•ti, *n.* The quality of being commutable; interchangeableness.—**commutation,** kom•mū•tā′shon, *n.* [L. *commutatio.*] The act of commuting; the act of substituting one thing for another; the change of a penalty or punishment from a greater to a less.—*Commutation ticket.* A railroad ticket at a reduced rate for a number of trips, between stations.—**commutative,** kom•mūt′a•tiv, *a.* Relating to exchange; interchangeable; mutual.—**commutator,** kom′mū•tā•tėr, *n.* [L. *commutatio,* a change.] *Elect.* A device for converting an alternating current into a direct one; the rotating terminal of the armature of an electric motor or generator.

comose, kō•mōs′, *a.* [L. *coma,* hair.] Hairy; comate.

compact, kom•pakt′, *a.* [L. *compactus,* pp. of *compingo, compactum,* to join or unite together—*com,* together and *pango,* to fix.] Closely and firmly united, as the parts or particles of solid bodies; having the parts or particles close; solid; dense; not diffuse; not verbose; concise; composed; made up: with *of* (*Shak.*).—*v.t.* To thrust, drive, or press closely together; to join firmly; to consolidate; to make close; to unite or connect firmly, as in a system.—**compactly,** kom•pakt′li, *adv.* In a compact or condensed manner; closely; concisely; briefly; tersely; neat. —**compactness,** kom•pakt′nes, *n.* State of being compact.

compact, kom′pakt, *n.* [L. *compactum,* a compact, from *compaciscor, compactus,* to make an agreement—*com,* together, and *paciscor,* to fix, settle, covenant.] An agreement; a contract, covenant, bargain, or settlement between parties.

companion, kom•pan′yon, *n.* [O.Fr. *compainon, companion*; Fr. *compagnon*—L. *com,* together, and *panis,* bread; lit. a sharer of one's bread; a mess fellow.] One with whom a person frequently associates and converses; a mate; a comrade; one who accompanies another; a person holding the lowest rank in an order of knighthood (as of the Bath).—*a.* Accompanying; united with.—*v.t.* To be a companion to; to accompany; to put on the same level (*Shak.*)‡.—**companionable,** kom•pan′yon•a•bl, *a.* Fit for good fellowship; qualified to be agreeable in company; sociable.—**companionableness,** kom•pan′yon•a•bl•nes, *n.* The quality of being companionable; sociableness.—**companionably,** kom•pan′yon•a•bli, *adv.* In a companionable manner.—**companionless,** kom•pan′yon•les, *a.* Having no companion.—**companionship,** kom•pan′yon•ship, *n.* The state or fact of being a companion; fellowship; association.—**company,** kum′pa•ni, *n.* [Fr. *compagnie*; O.Fr. also *companie.*] The state of being along with; companionship; fellowship; society; any assemblage of persons; a collection of men or other animals, in a very indefinite sense; guests at a person's house; a number of persons united for performing or carrying on anything jointly, as some commercial enterprise, the term being applicable to private partnerships or to incorporated bodies; a firm (but this word usually implies fewer partners than *company*); the members of a firm whose names do not appear in the style or title of the firm: usually contracted when written (Messrs. Smith & *Co.*); a subdivision of an infantry regiment or battalion commanded by a captain; the crew of a ship, including the officers.—*To bear* or *keep* (a person) *company,* to accompany; to attend; to go with; to associate with.—*To be good company,* to be an entertaining companion.—*v.t.* and *i.*† To associate or associate with; to frequent the company of.

companion, kom•pan′yon, *n.* [Comp. O.Sp. *compaña,* an outhouse.] *Naut.* the framing and sash lights upon a quarter deck, through which light passes to the cabins below; a raised cover to the cabin stair of a merchant vessel.—*Companion ladder,* the steps or ladder between the main deck and the quarter deck.—*Companion way,* the staircase at the entrance to the cabin of a vessel.

compare, kom•pâr′ *v.t.*—*compared, comparing.* [L. *compaño,* to put together, unite, match, compare—*com,* together, and *par,* equal, whence *peer, pair, parity.* PAIR.] To set or bring together in fact or in contemplation, and examine the relations they bear to each other, especially with a view to ascertain agreement or disagreement, resemblances or differences (to *compare* one thing *with* another); to liken; to represent as similar for the purpose of illustration (to *compare* one thing *to* another); *gram.* to inflect by the degrees of comparison. —*v.i.* To hold or stand comparison; to contrast favorably.—*n.* Comparison; scope or room for comparison (rich beyond *compare*).—**comparable,** kom′pa•ra•bl, *a.* [L. *comparabilis.*] Capable of being compared; worthy of comparison; being of equal regard.—**comparableness,** kom′pa•ra•bl•nes, *n.* State of being comparable.—**comparably,** kom′pa•ra•bli, *adv.* By comparison; so as to be compared.—**comparative,** kom•par′a•tiv, *a.* [L. *comparativus.*] Estimated by comparison; not positive or absolute; proceeding by comparison; founded on comparison, especially founded on the comparison of different things belonging to the same science or study (*comparative* anatomy, etc.); having the power of comparing different things (the *comparative* faculty; *gram.* expressing a greater degree; expressing more than the positive but less than the superlative: applied to forms of adjectives and adverbs.—*n. Gram.* the comparative degree.—**comparatively,** kom•par′a•tiv•li, *adv.* By comparison; according to estimate made by comparison; not positively, absolutely, or in itself.—**comparison,** kom•par′i•son, *n.* [Fr. *comparaison,* L. *comparatio.*] The act of comparing; the act of examining in order to discover how one thing stands with regard to another; the state of being compared; relation between things such as admits of their being compared; something with which another thing is compared; a similitude, or illustration by similitude; a parallel; *gram.* the inflection of an adjective or adverb to express degrees of the original quality.

compartment, kom•pärt′ment, *n.* [Fr. *compartiment,* L.L. *compartimentum,* from L. *compartior,* to divide, share, from *pars, partis,* a part.] A division or separate part of a general design, as of a building, railroad car, picture, plan, or the like.

compass, kum′pas, *n.* [Fr. *compas,* from L.L. *compassus,* a circuit—L. *com,* and *passus,* a step. PACE.] A passing round; a circular course; a circuit (to fetch a *compass,* that is, to make a circuit or round); limit or boundary; extent; range: applied to time, space, sound, etc.; moderate estimate; moderation; due limits (to keep within *compass*); an instrument consisting essentially of a magnet suspended so as to have as complete freedom of motion as possible, and used to indicate the magnetic meridian or the position of objects with respect to that meridian; a mathematical instrument for describing circles, measuring figures, distances between two points, etc.: often with the plural designation *compasses,* or a *pair of compasses.*—*v.t.* To stretch round; to encompass; to enclose, encircle, environ, surround; to go or walk about or round; to obtain; to attain to; to accomplish (to *compass* one's purposes); *law,* to plot; to contrive (a person's death).—**compassable,** kum′pas•a•bl, *a.* Capable of being compassed.—**compass plant,** *n.* A composite plant, common on the prairies of North America: so called from being disposed to present the edges of its leaves north and south.

compassion, kom•pa′shon, *n.* [Fr. *compassion,* L. *compassio.* PASSION.] A suffering with another; sympathy; pity; commiseration; an act of mercy (O.T.)‡.—**compassionate,** kom•pa′-

shon•it, *a.* Characterized by compassion; full of pity; tender-hearted. —*v.t.*— *compassionated, compassionating.* To pity; to commiserate; to have compassion for.—**compassionately,** kom•pa′shon•it•li, *adv.* In a compassionate manner; with compassion; mercifully.—**compassionateness,** kom•pa′shon•it•nes, *n.* The quality of being compassionate.

compatible, kom•pat′i•bl, *a.* [Fr. *compatible,* L.L. *compatibilis*—L. *com,* together, and *patior,* to suffer.] Capable of coexisting or being found together in the same subject; capable of existing together in harmony; suitable; agreeable; not incongruous (things *compatible* with one another). —**compatibility, compatibleness,** kom•pat′i•bil″i•ti, kom•pat′i•bl•nes, *n.* The quality of being compatible; consistency; suitableness. **compatibly,** kom•pat′i•bli, *adv.* In a compatible manner; fitly; suitably; consistently.

compatriot, kom•pā′tri•ot, *n.* [Fr. *compatriote.*] One of the same country.—*a.*† Of the same country; patriotic.

compeer, kom•pēr′, *n.* [L. *com,* and *par,* equal. PEER.] An equal; a companion; an associate; a mate.—*v.t.*‡ To equal; to match. (*Shak.*)

compel, kom•pel′, *v.t.*—*compelled, compelling.* [L. *compello, compulsum,* to drive together—*com,* and *pello,* to drive; hence *compulsion, compulsory,* etc.] To drive or urge with force or irresistibly; to constrain; to oblige; to necessitate; to subject; to cause to submit; to take by force or violence (*Shak.*).—**compellable,** kom•pel′a•bl, *a.* Capable of being compelled or constrained.—**compeller,** kom•pel′ėr, *n.* One who compels or constrains.—**compellingly,**— kom•pel′ing•li, *adv.* In a compelling or constraining manner; compulsively; in a way to force attention or obedience.

compellation, kom•pel•lā′shon, *n.* [L. *compellatio,* the act of accosting, from *compello, compellare,* to address.] Style or manner of address; word of salutation.

compendium, kom•pen′di•um, *n.* [L. *compendium,* a shortening, abbreviating—*com,* with, and *pendo,* to weigh.] A brief compilation or composition containing the principal heads or general principles of a larger work or system; an abridgment; a summary; an epitome. ∴ Syn. under ABRIDGMENT.—**compendious,** kom•-pen′di•us, *a.* [L. *compendiosus.*] Containing the substance or general principles of a subject or work in a narrow compass; succinct; concise. —**compendiously,** kom•pen′di•us•li, *adv.* In a compendious manner; summarily; concisely; in epitome.— **compendiousness,** kom•pen′di•us•-nes, *n.* The state of being compendious.

compensate, kom•pen′sāt or kom′-pen•sāt, *v.t.*—*compensated, compensating.* [L. *compenso, compensatum*— *com,* together, and *penso,* freq. of *pendo, pensum,* to weigh; lit. to weigh together, hence to balance, give an equivalent for.] To give equal value to; to recompense; to give an equivalent to (to *compensate* a laborer for his work); to make up for; to counterbalance; to make amends for (losses, defects, etc.).—*v.i.* To supply or serve as an equivalent: followed by *for*; to make amends.—**compensation,** kom•pen•sā′shon, *n.* The act of compensating; that which is given or serves as an equivalent for services, debt, want, loss, or suffering; amends; indemnity; recompense; that which supplies the place of something else or makes good a deficiency.—*Compensation Act for Workmen,* any of a number of state laws providing for the compensation of a workman by his employer in case of accident.—**compensative,** kom•pen′sa•tiv, *a.* Making amends or compensation.—*n.*† That which compensates; compensation.—**compensator,** kom′pen•sā•tėr, *n.* One who or that which compensates.— **compensatory,** kom•pen′sa•to•ri, *a.* Serving for compensation; making amends.

compete, kom•pēt′, *v.i.*—*competed, competing.* [L. *competo,* to strive after—*com,* together, and *peto,* to seek.] To seek or strive for the same thing as another, to carry on a contest or rivalry for a common object; to vie (to *compete with* a person *for* a thing). —**competition,** kom•pe•ti′shon, *n.* [L.L. *competitio.*] The act of competing; mutual contest or striving for the same object; rivalry; a trial of skill proposed as a test of superiority or comparative fitness. ∴ In a *competition* the persons strive to attain a common end, and may have the most friendly feelings toward each other; in *rivalry* there is rather the desire of one to supplant or get before another, and usually a certain hostility.—**competitive,** kom•pet′i•-tiv, *a.* Relating to competition; carried out by competition.—**competitor,** kom•pet′i•tėr, *n.* [L. *competitor* (*i* long).] One who competes; one who endeavors to obtain what another seeks; one who claims what another claims; a rival.—**competitory,**† kom•-pet′i•to•ri, *a.* Acting in competition; rival.

competent, kom′pe•tent, *a.* [Fr. *compétent,* from *competer,* to be sufficient; L. *competo,* to be meet or suitable— *com,* together, and *peto,* to seek.] Answering all requirements; suitable; fit; sufficient or fit for the purpose; adequate; having legal capacity or power; rightfully or lawfully belonging.—**competently,** kom′pe•tent•li, *adv.* In a competent manner; sufficiently; adequately; suitably.—**competence, competency,** kom′pe•tens, kom′pe•ten•si, *n.* State of being competent; fitness; suitableness; adequateness; ability; sufficiency; such a quantity as is sufficient; especially, property or means of subsistence sufficient to furnish the necessaries and conveniences of life, without superfluity.

compile, kom•pīl′ *v.t.*—*compiled, compiling.* [L. *compilo,* to plunder, pillage—*com,* together, and *pilo,* to pillage.] To draw up, write out, or compose by collecting materials from various sources; to collect or put together by utilizing the writings of others,—**compilation,** kom•pi•lā′-shon, *n.* The act of compiling or collecting from written or printed documents or books; that which is compiled; a book or treatise drawn up by compiling.—**compiler,** kom•-pīl′ėr, *n.* One who compiles.

complacent, kom•plā′sent, *a.* [L. *complacens, complacentis,* pleasing, ppr. of *complaceo,* to please—*com,* and *placeo,* to please (whence *pleasure*).] Accompanied with a sense of quiet enjoyment; displaying complacency; gratified; satisfied.—**complacence, complacency,** kom•plā′-sens, kom•plā′sen•si, *n.* A feeling of quiet pleasure; satisfaction; gratification; complaisance or civility‡. —**complacently,** kom•plā′sent•li, *adv.* In a complacent manner.

complain, kom•plān′, *v.i.* [Fr. *complaindre,* from L.L. *complangere*— L. *com,* together, and *plango,* to beat the breast in sorrow. PLAINT.] To utter expressions of grief, pain, uneasiness, censure, resentment, or the like; to lament; to murmur; to bewail; to make a formal accusation against a person; to make a charge: now regularly followed by *of* before the cause of grief or censure.— **complainant,** kom•plā′nant, *n.* One who complains or makes a complaint; a complainer; *law,* one who prosecutes by complaint, or commences a legal process against an offender; a plaintiff; a prosecutor.—**complainer,** kom•plā′nėr, *n.* One who complains; one who finds fault; a murmurer.— **complainingly,** kom•plā•ning•li, *adv.* In a complaining manner; murmuringly.—**complaint,** kom•plānt′, *n.* [Fr. *complainte.*] Expression of grief, regret, pain, censure, or resentment; lamentation; murmuring; a finding fault; the cause or subject of complaint or murmuring; a malady; an ailment; a disease: usually applied to disorders not violent; a charge; a representation of injuries suffered; accusation.

complaisance, kom′plā•zans, *n.* [Fr. *complaisance,* from *complaisant,* ppr. of *complaire,* to please = L. *complacere.* COMPLACENT.] A pleasing deportment; affability; civility; courtesy; desire of pleasing; disposition to oblige.— **complaisant,** kom′plā•-zant, *a.* Pleasing in manners; courteous; obliging; desirous to please; proceeding from an obliging disposition.

complected, kom•plek′ted, *a.* [L. prefix *com,* and *plecto,* to weave.] Woven together; interwoven.

complement, kom′ple•ment, *n.* [L. *complementum,* that which fills up or completes, from *compleo,* to complete. COMPLETE, *Compliment* is the same word.] Full quantity or number; full amount; what is wanted to complete or fill up some quantity or thing; difference; *math.* what is wanted in an arc or angle to make it up to 90°; outward show (*Shak.*)‡; courtesy or compliment (*Shak.*)‡.

—**complemental,** kom•ple•men′tal, *a.* Forming a complement; completing; complementary.—**complementary,** kom•ple•men′ta•ri, *a.* Completing; supplying a deficiency; complemental.—*Complementary colors.* COLOR.

complete, kom•plēt′, *a.* [L. *completus,* pp. of *completo, completum,* to fill up—*com,* intens., and *pleo,* to fill; same root as E. *fill.*] Having no deficiency; wanting no part or element; perfect; thorough; consummate; in every respect; finished; ended; concluded. ∴ 'Nothing is *whole* that has anything taken from it; nothing is *entire* that is divided; nothing is *complete* that has not all its parts and those parts fully developed. *Complete* refers to the perfection of parts; *entire* to their unity; *whole* to their junction; *total* to their aggregate' (*Angus*).—*v.t.—completed, completing.* To make complete; to finish; to end; to perfect; to fulfill, to accomplish; to realize.—**completely,** kom•plēt′li, *adv.* In a complete manner; fully; perfectly; entirely; wholly; totally; utterly; thoroughly; quite.—**completeness,** kom•plēt′nes, *n.* The state of being complete.—**completion,** kom•plē′shon, *n.* Act of completing, finishing, or perfecting; state of being complete or completed; perfect state; fulfillment; accomplishment.—**completive,** kom•plē′tiv, *a.* Completing or tending to complete; making complete.

complex, kom′pleks, *a.* [L. *complexus,* pp. of *complector, complexus,* to fold or twine together—*com,* together, and stem *plec, plic,* to fold; seen also in *ply, apply, complicate, display,* etc.] Composed of various parts or things; including sundry particulars connected; composite; not simple (being, idea); involved; intricate; complicated; perplexed (process).—*n.* Assemblage of things related as parts of a system; *Psychoanalysis* (which see), a series of emotionally accentuated ideas in a repressed state.—**complexity, complexness,** kom•plek′si•ti, kom′pleks•nes, *n.* The state of being complex; anything complex; intricacy; involvement; entanglement.—**complexly,** kom′pleks•li, *adv.* In a complex manner; not simply.

complexion, kom•plek′shon, *n.* [L. *complexio, complexionis,* a combination, in L.L. physical constitution, from *complector, complexus.* COMPLEX.] The temperament, habitude, or natural disposition of the body or mind; physical character or nature‡; the color or hue of the skin, particularly of the face; the general appearance of anything; aspect (*Shak.*).—**complexioned,** kom•plek′shond, *a.* Having a complexion of this or that kind; having a certain hue, especially of the skin; used in composition.

compliance, etc. See COMPLY.

complicate, kom′ pli•kāt, *v.t.— complicated, complicating.* [L. *complico—com,* and *plico,* to fold, weave, or knit. COMPLEX, PLY.] To intertwine; to interweave; to render complex or intricate; to involve.—*a.* Composed of various parts intimately united; complex; involved; intricate; *bot.* folded together, as the valves of the glume or chaff in some grasses.—**complicated,** kom′pli•kāt•ed, *p.* and *a.* Complicate; involved; intricate.—**complicacy,** kom′pli•ka•si, *n.* A state of being complex or intricate.—**complication,** kom•pli•kā′shon, *n.* The act of complicating or state of being complicated; entanglement; complexity; something complicated; an aggregate of things involved, mixed up, or mutually united; what complicates or causes complication.

complice,‡ kom′plis, *n.* [Fr. *complice,* ACCOMPLICE.] An accomplice. (*Shak.*)—**complicity,** kom•plis′i•ti, *n.* The state of being an accomplice; partnership in crime.

compliment, kom′pli•ment, *n.* [Fr. *compliment,* It. *complimento,* from *complire,* to fill up, to satisfy, L. *compleo, complere,* to complete: same word as *complement,* which formerly was used in this sense.] An act or expression of civility, respect, or regard; delicate flattery; expression of commendation or admiration; praise.—*v.t.* To pay a compliment to; to flatter or gratify by expressions of approbation, esteem, or respect, or by acts implying the like.—**complimentary,** kom•pli•men′ta•ri, *a.* Full of or using compliments; intended to express or convey a compliment or compliments; expressive of civility, regard or praise.—**complimentarily,** kom•pli•men′ta•ri•li, *adv.* In a complimentary manner.

compline, kom′plīn, *n.* [From Fr. *complie,* from L. *completae* (*horae*), 'complete hours': so called because this service completes the religious exercises of the day.] The last of the seven canonical hours in the Roman Catholic breviary; the last prayer at night, to be recited after sunset.

complot, kom′plot, *n.* [Fr. *complot,* a plot, from L. *complicitum.* COMPLICATE.] A plotting together; a plot; a conspiracy. (*Shak.*)—*v.t.* To plan together; to contrive; to plot.—*v.i.—complotted, complotting.* To plot together; to conspire; to form a plot.—**complotter,** kom•plot′ėr, *n.* One joined in a plot; a conspirator.

comply, kom•plī′, *v.i.—complied, complying.* [From L. *complere,* to fill up, satisfy (whence *complete, compliment*), like *supply* from *supplere—com,* with, and *plere,* to fill. The meaning has been affected by *ply* and *pliant.*] To adopt a certain course of action at the desire of another; to yield; to acquiesce; to consent; to agree; used alone or followed by *with.*—**compliable,**‡ kom•plī′a•bl, *a.* Compliant. (*Mil.*)—**compliance,** kom•plī′ans, *n.* The act of complying; a yielding as to a request, wish, desire, etc; a disposition to yield to others; complaisance.—**compliancy,** kom•plī′an•si, *n.* A disposition to yield, or a habit of yielding to others.—**compliant,** kom•plī′ant, *a.* Given to comply; yielding to request or desire; ready to accommodate; obliging.—**compliantly,** kom•plī′ant•li, *adv.* In a compliant or yielding manner.

component, kom•pō′nent, *a.* [L. *componens—com,* together, and *pono,* to place.] Composing; constituting; entering into as a part.—*n.* A constituent part.—**component,** kom•pō′nent, *n.* [L. *compono,* I construct.] The effective part of a force, velocity, etc., in a given direction; one of any number of constituent forces, velocities, etc., of which the given force, velocity, etc., is the resultant.

comport, kom•pōrt′, *v.i.* [Fr. *comporter,* to admit of, allow, endure, from L. *comportare,* to bear or carry together—*com,* and *porto,* to carry.] To be suitable; agree; accord; fit; suit: with *with* (pride *comports* ill *with* poverty).—*v.t.* To behave; to conduct; used *refl.*—**comportment,** kom•pōrt′ment, *n.* Behavior; demeanor; deportment.

compose, kom•pōz′, *v.t.—composed, composing.* [From Fr. *composer,* to *compose,* from prefix *com,* and *poser,* to place, L. *pausare* (see POSE), but early identified with L. *compono, compositum,* to compound, from *com,* and *pono,* to place; so also *dispose, expose.*] To form by uniting two or more things; to form, frame, or fashion; to form by being combined or united; to constitute; to make; to write, as an author; to become the author of (a book, a piece of music); to calm; to quiet; to appease; to settle; to adjust (differences, etc.); to place in proper form; to dispose; *fine arts,* to arrange the leading features of; *printing,* to set in proper order for printing, as types in a composing stick.—*v.i.* To practice literary, musical, or artistic composition.—**composed,** kom•pōzd′, *a.* Free from disturbance or agitation; calm; sedate; quiet; tranquil.—**composedly,** kom•pō′zed•li, *adv.* In a composed manner; calmly; without agitation; sedately.—**composure, composedness,** kom•pō′zhėr, kom•pō′zed•nes, *n.* The state of being composed; a settled state of mind; sedateness; calmness; tranquillity.

composer, kom•pō′zėr, *n.* One who or that which composes; one who writes an original work; most commonly, one who composes musical pieces.—**composite,** kom′po•zit, *a.* [L. *compositus,* from *compono, compositum,* to compound.] Made up of distinct parts, elements, or substances; compounded; *arch.* a term applied to one of the orders because the capital belonging to it is *composed* out of those of the other orders, exhibiting leaves, volutes, etc.; *bot.* applied to plants forming a vast order, and having flowers forming dense heads composed of many florets, as in the daisy, dandelion, etc.—*Composite number*—A product of two or more integers each greater than 1.—*Composite ship,* a ship having a wooden skin on an iron framework.—*n.* Anything made up of parts or of different elements; a compound; a composition.—

composition, kom•po•zi′shon, *n.* [L. *compositio*, Fr. *composition*, in meaning akin partly to *compose*, partly to the verb *compound.*] The act of composing or compounding, or the state of being composed or compounded; the act of producing some literary or musical piece; what is composed, as a literary, musical, or artistic production; the act of writing for practice in English or a foreign language; the act of making a mutual agreement for the discharge of a debt, or the agreement itself; the amount or rate paid in compounding with creditors; *gram.* the act of forming compound words, the arrangement of parts in a whole; mode of arrangement; a material compounded of two or more ingredients; a compound; *printing*, the act of setting types or characters in the composing stick, to form lines, and of arranging the lines in a galley to make a column or page, and from this to make a form.—**compositor,** kom•poz′i•tėr, *n. Printing*, one who sets types and makes up the pages and forms.—**composing stick,** *n.* A printer's instrument in which types are arranged into words and lines.

compost, kom′pōst, *n.* [O.Fr. *composte*, It. *composta*, a mixture, from L. *compositum*, from *compono.* COMPOUND.] A mixture or composition of various manuring substances for fertilizing land; a composition for plastering the exterior of houses.—*v.t.* To manure with compost; to plaster.

composure. See COMPOSE.

compotation, kom•pō•tā′shon, *n.* [L. *compotatio—com*, with, and *potatio*, from *poto*, to drink.] The act of drinking or tippling together.—**compotator,** kom•pō•tā′tėr, *n.* One who drinks with another.

compote, kom′pōt, *n.* [Fr.] Fruit, generally stone fruit, stewed or preserved in syrup.

compound, kom′pound, *a.* [Originally a participle of O.E. *compoune*, *compone*, to compound. See the verb.] Composed of two or more elements, parts, or ingredients; not simple; *bot.* made up of smaller parts of like kind with or similar to the whole.—*Compound animals*, animals, such as coral polyps, in which individuals, distinct as regards many of the functions of life, are yet connected by some part of their frame so as to form a united whole.—*Compound fracture*, *surg.* a fracture in which a bone is broken and there is also laceration of the tissues.—*Compound interest*, that interest which arises from the principal with the interest added.— *Compound quantities*, *alg.* such quantities as are joined by the signs + and —, plus and minus; *arith.* quantities which consist of more than one denomination (as of dollars and cents); hence the operations of adding, subtracting, multiplying, and dividing such quantities are termed *compound addition*, *subtraction*, *multiplication*, and *division.*—*Compound word*, a word composed of two or more words.—*n.* Something produced by compounding two or more ingredients, parts, or elements, as a substance or a word.—*v.t.* (kom•pound′). [O.E. *compone*, *compoune*, with *d* added (as in *expound*, *propound*, *sound*, vulgar *drownd*, etc.), from L. *compono—com*, together, and *pono*, *positum*, to set or put, whence *position.* COMPOSE.] To mix up or mingle together; to form by mingling two or more ingredients or elements into one; to combine: to settle amicably; to adjust by agreement (a controversy); to fail to prosecute (an offense) for a consideration; to discharge (a debt) by paying a part.—*v.i.* To agree upon concession; to come to terms of agreement; to arrange or make a settlement by compromise; especially, to settle with creditors by agreement, and discharge a debt by paying a part of its amount; or to make an agreement to pay a debt by means or in a manner different from that stipulated or required by law (to *compound with* a person, and *for* a debt).—**compoundable,** kom•poun′da•bl, *a.* Capable of being compounded.—**compounder,** kom•poun′dėr, *n.* One who compounds.

compound, kom′pound, *n.* [From Malay *kampong*, a yard or court.] In the Orient, an enclosure containing European establishments; any large enclosed area; the enclosure in which isolated houses stand.

comprehend, kom•prē•hend′ *v.t.* [L. *comprehendo—com*, together, *præ*, before, and an obs, *hendere*, to catch.] To take in or include within a certain scope; to include by implication or signification; to embrace; to comprise; to take into the mind; to grasp by the understanding; to possess or have in idea; to understand.—**comprehensible,** kom•prē•hen′si•bl, *a.* [L. *comprehensibilis.*] Capable of being comprehended; capable of being understood; conceivable by the mind; intelligible; also **comprehendible,** kom•prē•hen′di•bl. — **comprehensibility,** kom•prē•hen′si•bil″i•ti, *n.* The quality of being comprehensible; the capability of being understood.—**comprehensibly,** kom•prē•hen′si•bli•, *adv.* In a comprehensible manner; conceivably.—**comprehension,** kom•prē•hen′shon, *n.* [L. *comprehensio.*] The act of comprehending, including, or embracing; a comprising; inclusion; capacity of the mind to understand; power of the understanding to receive and contain ideas; capacity of knowing.—**comprehensive,** kom•prē•hen′siv, *a.* Having the quality of comprehending or embracing a great number or a wide extent; of extensive application; wide in scope; comprehending much in a comparatively small compass; having the power to comprehend or understand.—**comprehensively,** kom•prē•hen′siv•li, *adv.* In a comprehensive manner; with great extent of scope; so as to contain much in small compass.—**comprehensiveness,** kom•prē•hen′siv•nes, *n.* The quality of being comprehensive.

compress, kom•pres′, *v.t.* [L. *comprimo*, *compressum—com*, together, and *premo*, *pressum*, to press.] To press together; to force, urge, or drive into a smaller compass; to condense.—*n.* (kom′pres). *In surg.* a soft mass formed of tow, lint, or soft linen cloth, so contrived as by the aid of a bandage to make due pressure on any part.—**compressed,** kom•prest′, *p.* and *a.* Pressed into narrow compass; condensed; *bot.* and *zool.* flattened laterally or lengthwise.—**compressibility,** kom•pres′i•bil″i•ti, *n.* The quality of being compressible, or yielding to pressure.—**compressible,** kom•pres′i•bl, *a.* Capable of being compressed or forced into a narrower compass, yielding to pressure; condensable.—**compression,** kom•presh′on, *n.* The act of compressing; the act of forcing into closer union or density; the state of being compressed; condensation.—**compressive,** kom•pres′iv, *a.* Having power to compress; tending to compress.—**compressor,** kom•pres′ėr, *n.* [L.] One who or that which compresses.

comprise, kom•priz′, *v.i.—comprised*, *comprising.* [Fr. *compris*, part. of *comprendre*, L. *comprehendo*, to comprehend. COMPREHEND.] To comprehend; to contain; to include (the United States *comprises* various states).—**comprisal,**† kom•pri′zal, *n.* The act of comprising; inclusion.

compromise, kom′pro•mīz, *n.* [Fr. *compromis*, a compromise, originally a mutual promise to refer to arbitration, from *compromettre*, L. *compromitto—com*, and *promitto*, *promissum*, to promise. PROMISE.] A settlement of differences by mutual concessions; a combination of two rival systems, principles, etc., in which a part of each is sacrificed to make the combination possible; what results from, or is founded on, such an agreement; a mutual concession.—*v.t.—compromised*, *compromising.* To adjust or combine by a compromise; to settle by mutual concessions; to put to risk or hazard, or expose to serious consequences, by some act or declaration which cannot be recalled; to put in jeopardy; to endanger the interests of: often *refl.* (he *compromised himself* by his rash statements).—*v.i.* To make a compromise.

Comptometer, komp•tom′e•tėr, *n.* A name applied to a kind of calculating machine; hence, a machine bearing this trademark.

comptroller, kon•trōl′er, *n.* A controller; an officer who examines expenditures.—**comptrollership,** kon•trōl′ėr•ship, *n.* The office of comptroller.

compulsion, kom•pul′shon, *n.* [L. *compulsio*, *compulsionis*, constraint, compulsion, from *compello*, *compulsum*, to compel. COMPEL.] The act of compelling or driving by force, physical or moral; an obsessive impulse.—**compulsive,** kom•pul′siv, Exercising compulsion; compulsory.—**compulsively,** kom•pul′siv•li, *adv.*

By or under compulsion; by force.—**compulsorily,** kom•pul′so•ri•li, *adv.* In a compulsory manner; by force or constraint.—**compulsory,** kom•pul′so•ri, *a.* Exercising compulsion; compelling; constraining; enforced; due to compulsion; obligatory (a *compulsory* contribution).

compunction, kom•pungk′shon, *n.* [L. *compunctio, compungo—com,* and *pungo,* to prick or sting. PUNGENT.] The stinging or pricking of the conscience; contrition; remorse.

compurgation, kom•pėr•gā′shon, *n.* [L. *compurgo—com,* and *purgo,* to purge or purify.] An ancient mode of trial in England, where the accused was permitted to call a certain number of persons who joined their oaths to his in testimony to his innocence.

compute, kom•pūt′, *v.t.—computed, computing.* [L. *computo,* to calculate—*com,* together, and *puto,* to reckon, esteem, whence also *dispute, impute.* To *count* is really the same as this word.] To determine by calculation; to count; to reckon; to calculate; to estimate.—*v.i.* To reckon.—**computability,** kom•pū′ta•bil″i•ti, *n.* The quality of being computable.—**computable,** kom•pū′ta•bl, *a.* Capable of being computed, numbered, or reckoned.—**computation,** kom•pū•tā′shon, *n.* [L. *computatio.*] The act or process of computing, reckoning, or estimating; calculation; the result of a computation.—**computer,** kom•pū′tėr, *n.* One who computes; a reckoner; a calculator.

comrade, kom′rad, *n.* [O.E. *camarade, camerade,* from Sp. *camarada,* Fr. *camarade,* one who occupies the same chamber, from L. *camera,* a chamber.] An associate in occupation or friendship; a close companion; a mate.—**comradeship,** kom′rad•ship, *n.* The state or feeling of being a comrade; companionship; fellowship.

comsat, käm′sat, *n.* [From *com*munications and *sat*ellite.] A satellite linked to a global communications network.

Comtism, kom′tizm, *n.* The philosophical system founded by Auguste *Comte*; positivism.—**Comtist,** kom′tist, *n.* A disciple of Comte; a positivist. Used also adjectively.

con, kon, *adv.* and *n.* [Abbrev. from L. *contra,* against.] Against, in the phrase *pro and con,* for and against, as a noun, a statement, argument, point, or consideration supporting the negative side of a question (to (discuss the *pros* and *cons*).

con, kon, *v.t.—conned, conning.* [A form of *can.*] To peruse carefully and attentively; to study over; to learn; to direct the steering of (a ship).—**conning tower,** a turret on a ship from which the vessel's movements are directed.

con, kon, *v.t.* [From *confidence.*] (Slang) To swindle.—*a.* Confidence.

conation, ko•nā′shon, *n.* [L. *conor, conatus,* to attempt.] *Metaph.* the faculty of voluntary agency, embracing desire and volition.—**conative,** kon′a•tiv, *a.* Relating to the faculty of conation.

concatenate, kon•kat′e•nāt, *v.t.—concatenated, concatenating.* [L. *concateno, concatenatum,* to link together—*con,* together, and *catena,* a chain. CHAIN.] To link together; to unite in a successive series or chain, as things depending on each other.—**concatenation,** kon•kat′e•nā″shon, *n.* The state of being concatenated or linked together; a series of links united.

concave, kon′kāv, *a.* [L. *concavus—con,* and *cavus,* hollow. CAVE.] Hollow and curved or rounded, as the inner surface of a spherical body; presenting a hollow or incurvation towards some direction expressed or understood; incurved.—*n.* A hollow; an arch or vault; a cavity.—*v.t.*†*—concaved, concaving.* To make hollow.—**concavely,** kon′kāv•li, *adv.* So as to be concave; in a concave manner.—**concaveness,** kon′kāv•nes, *n.* The state of being concave.—**concavity,** kon•kav′i•ti, *n.* Hollowness; a concave surface, or the space contained in it.—**concavo-concave,** kon•kā′vō•kon•kāv, *a.* Concave or hollow on both surfaces, as a lens.—**concavo-convex,** kon•kā′vō•kon•veks, *a.* Concave on one side and convex on the other.

conceal, kon•sēl′, *v.t.* [From L. *concelo,* to conceal—*con,* together, and *celo,* to hide.] To hide; to withdraw from observation; to cover or keep from sight; to keep close or secret; to forbear to disclose; to withhold from utterance or declaration.—**concealable,** kon•sēl′a•bl, *a.* Capable of being concealed, hid, or kept close.—**concealment,** kon•sēl′ment, *n.* The act of concealing, hiding, or keeping secret; the state of being hid or concealed; privacy; shelter from observation; cover from sight.

concede, kon•sēd′, *v.t.—conceded, conceding.* [L. *concedo, concessum,* to yield, grant—*con,* together, and *cedo,* to yield. CEDE.] To admit as true, just, or proper; to grant; to let pass undisputed; to grant as a privilege; to yield up; to allow; to surrender.—*v.i.* To make concession; to grant a request or petition; to yield.—**conceder,** kon•sē′dėr, *n.* One who concedes.—**concession,** kon•sesh′on, *n.* [L. *concessio.*] The act of conceding, admitting, or granting; a yielding to demand or claim; the thing yielded; a grant; a grant empowering some scheme or work to be done.—**concessionary, concessionnaire,** kon•sesh′on•a•ri, kon•sesh′on•âr″, *n.* [Fr. *concessionnaire.*] A person to whom a concession for carrying out some scheme has been made; a member of a company to whom special powers have been granted by a government for carrying out some work.—**concessive,** kon•ses′iv, *a.* Implying or containing concession.

conceit, kon•sēt′, *n.* [O.E. *conceipt,* O.Fr. *concept,* from L. *conceptus,* a conception, from *concipio,* to conceive—*con,* and *capio,* to take; comp. *deceit, receipt.*] Opinion, estimation, view, or belief (wise in one's own *conceit*); an ill-grounded opinion; a baseless fancy; a crotchety notion; an ill-grounded opinion of one's own importance; self-conceit; vanity; a witty, happy, or ingenious thought or expression; a quaint or humorous fancy; now commonly a thought or expression intended to be striking or poetical, but rather farfetched, insipid, or pedantic.—*Out of conceit with,* not now having a favorable opinion of; no longer pleased with.—*v.t.* To imagine wrongly; to err in believing: used *refl.*—**conceited,** kon•sē′ted, *a.* Entertaining a flattering opinion of one's self; self-conceited; vain; egotistical.—**conceitedly,** kon•sē′ted•li, *adv.* In a conceited manner; with vanity or egotism.—**conceitedness,** kon•sē′ted•nes, *n.* The state of being conceited.

conceive, kon•sēv′, *v.t.—conceived, conceiving.* [O.Fr. *concever, conceveir,* Fr. *concevoir,* from L. *concipere,* to conceive. CONCEIT.] To become pregnant with; to develop in the womb in an embryonic state; to form in the mind; to devise (an idea, a purpose); to realize in the mind; to form a conception of; to place distinctly before the thoughts; to comprehend; often used as a specific term in philosophy; to think; to imagine; to suppose possible.—*v.i.* To have a fetus formed in the womb; to become pregnant; to have or form a conception or idea; to think (to *conceive of* a thing).—**conceivable,** kon•sē′va•bl, *a.* Capable of being conceived, thought, imagined, or understood.—**conceivability, conceivableness,** kon•sē′va•bil″i•ti, kon•sē′va•bl•nes, *n.* The quality of being conceivable.—**conceivably,** kon•sē′va•bli, *adv.* In a conceivable or intelligible manner.—**conceiver,** kon•sē′vėr, *n.* One that conceives.

concentrate, kon•sen′trāt, or kon′, *v.t.—concentrated, concentrating.* [Fr. *concentrer*—L. *con,* together, and *centrum,* a center.] To bring to a common center or point of union; to cause to come together to one spot or point; to bring to bear on one point; to direct toward one object; in chemical manipulations, to intensify by removing nonessential matter; to reduce to a state of great strength and purity.—*v.i.* To approach or meet in a common point or center.—**concentration,** kon•sen•trā′shon, *n.* The act of concentrating; the act of collecting into a central point or of directing to one object; the state of being concentrated; the act of increasing the strength of fluids by volatilizing part of their water.—*Concentration camp.* Barracks with stockade, patrolled by the military, used for the detention and punishment of people politically, economically, or morally adverse to the policies of the government, esp., in Europe.—**concenter,** kon•sen′tėr, *v.i.—concentered, concentering.* To converge to or meet in a common center; to combine or be united in one object.—*v.t.* To draw or direct to a common center; to concentrate—**concentric, concentrical,** kon•sen′trik, kon•sen′tri•kal, *a.* [L. *concen-*

tricus.] Having a common center (circles, etc.).—**concentrically,** kon•sen′tri•kal•li, *adv.* In a concentric manner.—**concentricity,** kon•sen•tris′i•ti, *n.* State of being concentric.

concept, kon′sept, *n.* [L. *conceptum,* what is conceived, from *concipio.* CONCEIVE.] *Philos.* the subject of a conception; the object conceived by the mind; a notion.—**conceptacle,** kon•sep′ta•kl, *n.* [L. *conceptaculum.*] That in which anything is contained; a receptacle; *bot.* a hollow sac containing bodies connected with reproduction or fructification†.—**conception,** kon•sep′shon, *n.* [L. *conceptio.*] The act of conceiving; the first formation of the embryo of an animal; the act or power of conceiving in the mind; that which is conceived in the mind; product of the imaginative or inventive faculty; *philos.* that mental act or combination of acts by which an absent object of perception is brought before the mind by the imagination; the mental operation by which such notions or conceptions are formed; a general notion; that which constitutes the meaning of a general term; thought, notion, or idea in the loose sense (you have no *conception* how clever he is).—*Immaculate conception.* IMMACULATE.—**conceptional,** kon•sep′shon•al, *a.* Pertaining to or having the nature of a conception or notion.—**conceptive,** kon•sep′tiv, *a.* Capable of conceiving either physically or mentally.—**conceptual,** kon•sep′chū•al, *a.* Pertaining to conception, mental or physical.—**conceptualism,** kon•sep′chū•al•izm, *n.* The doctrine of the conceptualists, in some sense intermediate between realism and nominalism.—**conceptualist,** kon•sep′chū•al•ist, *n.* One who holds the doctrine that the mind has the power of assigning an independent existence to general conceptions.—**conceptualistic,** kon•sep′chū•a•lis″tik, *a.* Pertaining to conceptualism or conceptualists.

concern, kon•sėrn′, *v.t.* [Fr. *concerner,* to concern, from L. *concerno,* to mix, as in a sieve—*con,* together, and *cerno,* to sift, akin to Gr. *krinō,* to separate. Akin *decree, discreet, secret,* etc.] To relate, pertain, or belong to; to affect the interest of; to be of importance to (that does not *concern* me); *refl.* to take or have an interest in, occupy or busy one's self; to disturb, make uneasy, or cause concern to: in this sense generally in pp.—*n.* That which relates or belongs to one; business; affair; matter of importance; that which affects one's welfare or happiness; solicitude; anxiety; agitation or uneasiness of mind; disturbed state of feeling; an establishment, such as a manufacturing or commercial establishment. ∴ *Syn.* under CARE.—**concerned,** kon•sėrnd′, *p.* and *a.* Having concern; interested; engaged; anxious.—**concerning,** kon•sėr′ning, *prep.* In regard to; regarding; with relation to; about.—**concernment,** kon•sėrn′ment, *n.* A thing in which one is concerned or interested; concern; affair; business; interest; importance; participation; concern; solicitude.

concert, kon•sėrt′, *v.t.* [Fr. *concerter,* from It. *concertare,* to concert, misspelled from L. *consero, consertus,* to join together—*con,* and *sero,* to join, from root of *series.*] To contrive and settle by mutual communication of opinions or propositions; to plan; to devise.—*n.* (kon′sėrt). [From above verb, but in musical meanings L. *concentus,* a singing together, seems to have had an influence.] Agreement of two or more in a design or plan; accordance in a scheme; cooperation; concord; the music of a company of players or singers, or of both united; a public or private musical entertainment, at which a number of vocalists or instrumentalists, or both, perform singly or combined.—**concerted,** kon•sėr′ted, *p.* and *a.* Mutually contrived or planned.—*Concerted piece,* in *music,* a composition in parts for several voices or instruments.—**concertina,** kon•sėr•tē′na, *n.* A musical instrument held between the hands in playing, and composed of a bellows, with two faces or ends, in which are the keys or stops by pressing which with the fingers air is admitted to the free metallic reeds producing the sounds.—**concerto,** kon•chăr′tō, *n.* [It.] A musical composition, usually in a symphonic form, written for one principal instrument, with accompaniments for a full orchestra.

concession, etc. See CONCEDE.

conch, kongk, *n.* [L. *concha,* Gr. *kongchē,* Skr. *çankha,* a shell.] A marine shell, especially a large spiral shell of a trumpet shape, which may be blown like a trumpet; the external portion of the ear, more especially the hollow part of it.—**conchiferous,** kong•kif′ėr•us, *a.* Belonging to the chonchifers.—**conchoidal,** kong•koi′dal, *a. Mineral,* having convex elevations and concave depressions like shells.—**conchological,** kong•ko•loj′ik•al, *a.* Pertaining to conchology.—**conchologist,** kong•kol′o•jist, *n.* One versed in conchology.—**conchology,** kong•kol′o•ji, *n.* That department of zoology which treats of the nature, formation, and classification of the shells with which the bodies of many Mollusca are protected, or of the animals themselves.

concierge, kon•syârzh′, *n.* [Fr.] A doorkeeper to a hotel, house, prison, etc.; a janitor, male or female; a porter.

conciliar, kon•sil′i•ėr, *a.* [From L. *concilium,* a council.] Pertaining or relating to a council.

conciliate, kon•sil′i•āt, *v.t.*—*conciliated, conciliating.* [L. *concilio, conciliatum,* to unite in thought or feeling, from *concilium,* plan, council. COUNCIL.] To bring to entertain a friendly feeling; to make friendly from being antagonistic; to pacify; to soothe; to win, gain, or engage (to *conciliate* one's affection or regard); to show to be compatible (statements, etc.).—**conciliation,** kon•sil′i•ā″shon, *n.* The act of conciliating; the act of making friendly; the act of winning or gaining favor or esteem.—**conciliative,** kon•sil′i•ā•tiv, *a.* Tending to conciliate; conciliatory.—**conciliator,** kon•sil′i•ā•tėr, *n.* One who conciliates or reconciles.—**conciliatory,** kon•sil′i•a•to•ri, *a.* Tending to conciliate or bring to a friendly state of feeling; pacific.

concise, kon•sīs′, *a.* [L. *concisus,* cut off, brief, from *concido*—*con,* and *caedo,* to cut.] Comprehending much in few words; brief and comprehensive; employing as few words as possible;succinct. ∴ *Concise* refers mainly to style or manner in speaking or writing; *succinct* refers rather to the result produced by conciseness; thus we speak of a *concise* style or phrase; a *succinct* narrative or account.—**concisely,** kon•sīs′li, *adv.* In a concise manner; briefly; in few words.—**conciseness,** kon•sīs′nes, *n.* The quality of being concise.

concision,‡ kon•si′zhon, *n.* Conciseness; a sect or faction; those in the apostles' time who laid too much stress on circumcision (N.T.).

conclave, kon′klāv, *n.* [L. *conclave,* a private room, a closet—*con,* together, and *clavis,* a key.] The assembly or meeting of the cardinals shut up for the election of a pope; hence, the body of cardinals; a private meeting; a close assembly.—**conclavist,** kon′klā•vist, *n.* An attendant whom a cardinal is allowed to take with him into the conclave for the choice of a pope.

conclude, kon•klūd′, *v.t.*—*concluded, concluding.* [L. *concludo*—*con,* and *claudo,* to shut; whence also *clause, close.*] To shut up or enclose‡; to include or comprehend (N.T.)‡; to infer or arrive at by reasoning; to deduce, as from premises; to judge; to end, finish, bring to a conclusion; to settle or arrange finally (to *conclude* an agreement, a peace).—*v.i.* To infer; to form a final judgment; to come to a decision; to resolve; to determine; generally followed by an infinitive or a clause; to end; to make a finish.—**concluder,** kon•klū′dėr, *n.* One who concludes.—**conclusion,** kon•klū′zhon, *n.* [L. *conclusio.*] The end, close, or termination; the last part: often in the phrase *in conclusion*=finally, lastly, determination; final decision; inference; *logic,* the inference of a syllogism as drawn from the premises; an experiment (obsolete except in the phrase *to try conclusions*).—**conclusive,** kon•klū′siv, *a.* Putting an end to debate or argument; leading to a conclusion or determination; decisive; bringing out or leading to a regular logical conclusion.—**conclusively,** kon•klū′siv•li, *adv.* In a conclusive manner.—**conclusiveness,** kon•klū′siv•nes, *n.* The quality of being conclusive or decisive.

concoct, kon•kokt′, *v.t.* [L. *concoquo, concoctum*—*con,* and *coquo,* to cook. COOK.] To digest by the stomach‡; to ripen or mature‡; to form and prepare in the mind; to devise; to plan; to plot (a scheme); to mix by combining different ingredients. —**concoction,** kon•kok′shon, *n.* [L. *concoctio.*] Digestion‡; the act of mixing ingredients, as for a dish in cookery.—**concoctive,** ‡ kon•kok′tiv, *a.* Maturing; ripening.

concomitant, kon•kom′i•tant, *a.* [From L. *com,* together, and *comitor,* to accompany, from *comes,* a companion.] Accompanying; conjoined with; concurrent; attending: of things, circumstances, etc.—*n.* A thing, that accompanies another; an accompaniment; an accessory. —**concomitance, concomitancy,** kon•kom′i•tans, kon•kom′i•tan•si, *n.* The state of being concomitant; a being together or in connection with another thing.—**concomitantly,** kon•kom′i•tant•li, *adv.* So as to be concomitant; concurrently; unitedly.

concord, kon′kord or kong′kord, *n.* [Fr. *concorde,* L. *con,* and *cor, cordis,* the heart. ACCORD.] Agreement or union in opinions, sentiments, views, or interests; harmony; agreement between things; suitableness; *music,* the pleasing combination of two or more sounds; the relation between two or more sounds which are agreeable to the ear; *gram.* agreement of words in construction.—**concordance,** kon•kor′dans, *n.* The state of being concordant; agreement; harmony; a book in which the principal words used in any work, as the Scriptures, Shakespeare, etc., are arranged alphabetically, and the book, chapter, verse, act, scene, line, or other subdivision in which each occurs are noted.—**concordant,** kon•kor′dant, *a.* [L. *concordans,* ppr. of *concordare,* to agree.] Agreeing; agreeable; correspondent; harmonious.—**concordantly,** kon•kor′dant•li, *adv.* In a concordant manner.—**concordat,** kon•kor′dat, *n.* [Fr.] An agreement; compact; convention; especially, a formal agreement between the see of Rome and any secular government.

concourse, kon′kōrs or kong′kōrs, *n.* [Fr. *concours,* from L. *concursus,* from *concurro,* to run together—*con,* and *curro,* to run.] A moving, flowing, or running together; confluence; a meeting or coming together of people; the people assembled; a throng; a crowd; an assemblage of things; agglomeration.

concrete, kon′krēt or kong′krēt, *a.* [L. *concretus,* from *concresco,* to grow together—*con,* and *cresco,* to grow; seen also in *decrease, increase, crescent,* etc.] Formed by union of separate particles in a mass; united in a solid form; *logic,* a term applied to an object as it exists in nature, invested with all its attributes, or to the notion or name of such an object. ABSTRACT.—*n.* A mass formed by concretion of separate particles of matter in one body; a compound; *logic,* a concrete term; a compact mass of gravel, coarse pebbles, or stone chippings cemented together by hydraulic or other mortar, employed extensively in building.—*v.i.* and *t.*—*concreted, concreting.* To coagulate; to congeal; to thicken.—**concretely,** kon•krēt′li, *adv.* In a concrete manner; not abstractly.—**concretion,** kon•krē′shon, *n.* The act of concreting or growing together so as to form one mass; the mass or solid matter formed by growing together; a clot; a lump; *geol.* a lump or nodule formed by molecular aggregation as distinct from crystallization.—*Morbid concretions,* hard substances which occasionally make their appearance in different parts of the body.—**concretionary,** kon•kre′sho•na•ri, *a.* Pertaining to concretion; formed by concretion; consisting of concretions.

concubine, kong′kū•bīn, *n.* [L. *concubina,* from *concumbo,* to lie together—*con,* and *cumbo* or *cubo,* to lie down.] A paramour, male or female‡; a woman who cohabits with a man without being legally married to him; a kept mistress; a wife of inferior condition, such as were allowed in ancient Greece and Rome; a lawful wife, but not united to the man by the usual ceremonies.—**concubinage,** kon′kū•bi•nij, *n.* The act or practice of having a concubine or concubines; the state of being a concubine; a living as man and wife without being married.—**concubinary,** kon•kū′bi•na•ri, *a.* Relating to concubinage; living in concubinage.

concupiscence, kon•kū′pi•sens, *n.* [L. *concupiscentia,* from *concupisco,* to lust after—*con,* and *cupio,* to desire.] Lustful feeling; lust; sinful desire.—**concupiscent,** kon•kū′pi•sent, *a.* Desirous of unlawful pleasure; libidinous; lustful.—**concupiscible,**† kon•kū′pis•i•bl, *a.* Concupiscent; lustful.

concur, kon•kėr′, *v.i.*—*concurred, concurring.* [L. *concurro,* to run together—*con,* and *curro,* to run; seen also in *course, current, incur, recur,* etc.] To run or meet together‡; to agree, join, or unite, as in one action or opinion (to *concur with* a person *in* an opinion (to assent: with *to* (*Mil.*)†; to unite or be conjoined; to meet together; to be combined; to unite in contributing to a common object (causes that *concur* to an effect); to coincide or have points of agreement (*Shak.*).—**concurrence, concurrency,** kon•kur′ens, kon•kur′en•si, *n.* The act of concurring; conjunction; combination of agents, circumstances, or events; agreement in opinion; union or consent as to a design to be carried out; approbation; consent with joint aid or contribution of power or influence.—**concurrent,** kon•kur′ent, *a.* Concurring or acting in conjunction; agreeing in the same act; contributing to the same event or effect; operating with; conjoined; associate; concomitant; joint and equal; existing together and operating on the same objects (the *concurrent* jurisdiction of law courts).—*n.* One who concurs; one agreeing to or pursuing the same course of action; that which concurs; joint or contributory cause.—**concurrently,** kon•kur′ent•li, *adv.* So as to be concurrent; in union or combination; unitedly.

concuss, kon•kus′, *v.t.* [L. *concutio, concussum,* to shake, and as a law term to extort—*con,* together, and *quatio, quassum* (in composition *cutio, cussum*), to shake. QUASH.] To shake or agitate†; to force by threats to do something, especially to give up something of value; to intimidate into a desired course of action; to coerce.—**concussive,** kon•kus′iv, *a.* Having the power or quality of shaking; agitating.—**concussion,** kon•kush′on, *n.* [L. *concussio, concussionis,* a shock, extortion.] The act of shaking, particularly by the stroke or impulse of another body; the shock occasioned by two bodies coming suddenly into collision; a shock; *surg.* applied to injuries sustained by the brain and other organs from falls, blows, etc.; the act of extorting by threats or force; extortion.

condemn, kon•dem′, *v.t.* [L. *condemno*—*con,* intens., and *damno,* to condemn, whence *damn.*] To pronounce to be utterly wrong; to utter a sentence of disapprobation against; to pronounce to be guilty; to sentence to punishment; to utter sentence against judicially: opposed to *acquit* or *absolve*; to judge or pronounce to be unfit for use or service, or to be forfeited.—*Condemned cell* or *ward,* in *prisons,* the cell in which a prisoner sentenced to death is detained till his execution.—**condemnable,** kon•dem′na•bl, *a.* Worthy of being condemned.—**condemnation,** kon•dem•nā′shon, *n.* [L. *condemnatio.*] The act of condemning; the state of being condemned; the cause or reason of a sentence of condemnation (N.T.).—**condemnatory,** kon•dem′na•to•ri *a.* Condemning; bearing condemnation or censure.—**condemner,** kon•dem′ėr, *n.* One who condemns.

condense, kon•dens′, *v.t.*—*condensed, condensing.* [L. *condenso*—*con,* and *denso,* to make dense. DENSE.] To make more dense or compact; to reduce the volume or compass of; to bring into closer union of parts; to consolidate; to compress (to *condense* a substance, an argument, etc.); to reduce (a gas or vapor) to the condition of a liquid or solid.—*v.i.* To become close or more compact, as the particles of a body; to change from the vaporous to the liquid state.—**condensed,** kon•denst′, *a.* Made dense or close in texture or composition; compressed; compact (a *condensed* style of composition).—**condenser,** kon•den′sėr, *n.* One who or that which condenses; a pneumatic instrument or syringe in which air may be compressed; a vessel in which aqueous or spirituous vapors are reduced to a liquid form by coldness; a lens to gather and concentrate rays collected by a mirror and direct them upon an object; an instrument employed to collect and render sensible very small quantities of electricity.—**condensability,** kon•den′sa•bil″i•ti, *n.*

Quality of being condensable.—**condensable, condensible,** kon•den′-sa•bl, kon•den′si•bl, *a.* Capable of being condensed; capable of being compressed into a smaller compass, or made more compact.—**condensate,**† kon•den′sāt, *v.t.* and *i.*—*condensated, condensating.* To condense. —**condensation,** kon•den•sā′shon, *n.* [L. *condensatio.*] The act of condensing or making more dense or compact; the act of bringing into smaller compass; consolidation; the act of reducing a gas or vapor to a liquid or solid form.

condescend, kon•dē•send′, *v.i.* [Fr. *condescendre*—L. *con,* with, and *descendo.* DESCEND.] To descend voluntarily for a time to the level of an inferior; to stoop; to lower one's self intentionally: often followed by the infinitive or a noun preceded by *to.*—**condescending,** kon•dē•sen′-ding, *a.* Marked or characterized by condescension; stooping to the level of one's inferiors.—**condescendingly,** kon•dē•sen′ding•li, *adv.* In a condescending manner.—**condescension,** kon•dē•sen′shon, *n.* The act of condescending; the act of voluntary stooping to an equality with inferiors; affability on the part of a superior.

condign, kon•dīn′, *a.* [L. *condignus,* well worthy—*con,* and *dignus,* worthy. DIGNITY.] Well deserved; merited; suitable: now always applied to punishment or something equivalent. —**condignly,** kon•dīn′li, *adv.* In a condign manner.

condiment, kon′di•ment, *n.* [L. *condimentum,* from *condio,* to season, pickle.] Something used to give relish to food, and to gratify the taste; sauce; seasoning.

condisciple, kon•di•sī′pl, *n.* A comrade disciple or student associate; a fellow learner; a schoolmate.

condition, kon•di′shon, *n.* [L. *condicio, condicionis* (also *conditio*) situation, compact, etc.—*con,* and *dico,* to declare. DICTION.] A particular mode of being; situation; predicament; case; state; state with respect to the orders or grades of society or to property; rank in society; that which is requisite to be done, happen, exist, or be present in order to something else being done, taking effect, or happening; a clause in a contract embodying some stipulation, provision, or essential point. —*v.t.* To form the condition or essential accompaniment of; to regulate or determine; to stipulate; to arrange.—**conditional,** kon•di′shon•-al, *a.* Imposing conditions; containing or depending on a condition or conditions; made with limitations; not absolute; made or granted on certain terms; *gram.* and *logic,* expressing or involving a condition. —**conditionality,** kon•di′sho•nal″i•-ti, *n.* The quality of being conditional or limited; limitation by certain terms.—**conditionally,** kon•di′-shon•al•li, *adv.* In a conditional manner; with certain limitations; on particular conditions, terms, or stipulations.—**conditioned,** kon•di′-shond, *a.* Having a certain state or qualities, usually preceded by some qualifying term, as *well conditioned, ill conditioned*; *metaph.* placed or cognized under conditions or relations.

condole, kon•dōl′, *v.i.*—*condoled, condoling.* [L.L. *condoleo*—*con,* with, and L. *doleo,* to grieve, whence *doleful, dolor.*] To express pain or grief at the distress or misfortunes of another; to express sympathy to one in grief or misfortune: followed by *with.*—*v.t.*‡ To lament or grieve over.—**condolence,** kon•-dō′lens, *n.* The act of condoling; expression of sympathy with another's grief.—**condoler,** kon•dō′lėr, *n.* One who condoles.

condominium, kon•do•min′i•um, *n.* [L. *con,* and *dominium,* rule.] Joint rule or control.

condone, kon•dōn′, *v.t.*—*condoned, condoning.* [L. *condonare,* to pardon—*con,* and *donare,* to present, from *donum,* a gift. DONATION.] To pardon; to forgive; to overlook an offense (never with a personal object); *law,* to forgive, or to act so as to imply forgiveness of a violation of the marriage vow.—**condonation,** kon•-dō•nā′shon, *n.* [L. *condonatio.*] The act of condoning or pardoning a wrong act; *law,* an act or course of conduct by which a husband or a wife is held to have pardoned a matrimonial offense committed by the other, the party condoning being thus barred from a remedy for that offense.

condor, kon′dor, *n.* [Sp., from Peruv. *cuntur.*] A south American bird, one of the largest of the vulture tribe, found most commonly in the Andes at heights from 10,000 to 15,000 feet above the level of the sea.

conduce, kon•dūs′, *v.i.*—*conduced, conducing.* [L. *conduco,* to conduce—*con,* and *duco,* to lead; *conduct* is from the same verb.] To combine with other things in bringing about or tending to bring about a result; to lead or tend; to contribute: followed by the infinitive or a noun preceded by *to.*—**conducible,**‡ kon•-dū′si•bl, *a.* [L. *conducibilis.*] Conducive.—**conducibleness,**‡ kon•dū′-si•bl•nes, *n.* Conduciveness.—**conducive,** kon•dū′siv, *a.* Having the quality of conducing, promoting, or furthering; tending to advance or bring about; followed by *to.*—**conduciveness,** kon•dū′siv•nes, *n.* The quality of being conducive.

conduct, kon′dukt, *n.* [L.L. *conductus,* L. *conductus,* pp. of *conduco.* CONDUCE. DUKE.] The act of guiding or commanding; mode of carrying on or conducting; mode of handing or wielding; administration; management; personal behavior; deportment: applied indifferently to a good or bad course of action; the act of convoying or guarding; guidance or bringing along under protection.—*v.t.* (kon-dukt′). To accompany and show the way; to guide; to lead; to escort; to lead, as a commander; to direct; to command; to manage (affairs, etc.); *refl.* to behave; *physics,* to carry, transmit, or propagate, as heat, electricity, etc.; to lead or direct as musical conductor.—*v.i.* To carry, transmit, or propagate heat, electricity, sound, etc.; to act as musical conductor.—**conductibility,** kon•-duk′ti•bil″i•ti, *n.* Capacity of being conducted; conductivity.—**conductible,** kon•duk′ti•bl, *a.* Capable of being conducted or conveyed.—**conduction,** kon•duk′shon, *n. Physics,* the mode of transference of heat through the substance of solids and of electricity through any suitable body called a *conductor.*—**conductive,** kon•duk′tiv, *a. Physics,* having the power or quality of conducting.—**conductivity,** kon•duk•tiv′i•ti, *n. Physics,* the power of conducting heat, electricity, etc.; the quality of being conductive; the quantity of heat that flows in unit time through unit area of a plate of any substance of unit thickness, with one degree of difference of temperature between its faces.—**conductor,** kon•duk′tėr, *n.* One who conducts; a leader; a guide; a commander; one who leads an army; a director or manager; the director of a chorus or orchestra; the person who attends to the passengers in a bus or a streetcar, or the like, as contradistinguished from the driver; *physics,* a body that receives and transmits or communicates heat, electricity, or force in any of its forms; hence, specifically, a lightning rod.—**conductory,** kon•duk′-to•ri, *a.* Having the property of conducting.

conduit, kon′dit, or kon′du̧it, *n.* [Fr. *conduit,* pp. of *conduire,* L. *conducere, conductum,* to conduct.] A pipe, tube or other channel for the conveyance of fluids; a tube or pipe for protecting electric wires or cables.

conduplicate, kon•dū′pli•kāt, *a.* Doubled or folded over or together; *bot.* applied to leaves in the bud when they are folded down the middle, so that the halves of the lamina are applied together by their faces.

condyle, kon′dīl, *n.* [L. *condylus,* Gr. *kondylos,* a knuckle, a joint.] *Anat,* a protuberance on the end of a bone serving to form an articulation with another bone.—**condyloid,** kon′-di•loid, *a. Anat.* resembling or shaped like a condyle.

cone, kōn, *n.* [L. *conus,* Gr. *kōnos,* a cone, from root seen in E. *hone,* Skr. *co,* to sharpen.] A solid figure rising from a circular base and regularly tapering to a point; anything shaped like, or approaching the shape of, a cone; one of the fruits of fir trees, pines, etc.; a strobilus; the name of certain molluscous shells; the hill surrounding the crater of a volcano, formed by the gradual accumulation of ejected material; a form of storm signal.—**conic,** kon′ik, *a.* [L. *conicus,* Gr. *kōnikos.*] Having the form of a cone; conical; pertaining to a cone.—*Conic sections,* the figures formed by the outlines of the cut surfaces when a cone is cut by a plane, more especially the parabola, ellipse, and hyperbola, the first of which is seen when the section is made parallel to the slope of the cone.—*n.* A conic section.—**conical,** kon′-ik•al, *a.* Having the form of a cone; cone shaped.—**conically,** kon′ik•al•li, *adv.* In the form of a cone.—**conics,** kon′iks, *n.* That part of geometry which treats of the cone and the several curve lines arising from the sections of it.—**conifer,** kō′ni•fėr, *n.* [L. *conus,* and *fero,* to bear.] *Bot.* a plant producing cones, or hard, dry, scaly seed vessels of a conical figure, as the pine, fir, etc.—**coniferous,** kō•nif′ėr•us, *a.* Bearing cones; belonging or relating to the conifers.—**conoid,** kō′noid, *n. Geom.* a solid formed by the revolution of a conic section about its axis; *anat,* the pineal gland.—**conoid, conoidal,** kō′-noid, kō•noi′dal, *a.* Approaching to a conical form; nearly conical.

coney, *n.* See CONY.

confabulate, kon•fab′ū•lāt, *v.i.* [L. *confabulor—con,* and *fabulor,* to talk. FABLE.] To talk familiarly together; to chat; to prattle. This word is sometimes shortened colloquially to **confab,** kon•fab′.—**confabulation,** kon•fab′ū•lā″shon, *n.* [L. *confabulatio.*] A talking together; familiar talk; easy, unrestrained conversation. Often shortened to **confab,** kon′fab.

confect,‡ kon•fekt′, *v.t.* [L. *conficio, confectum,* to prepare—*con,* and *facio,* to make. COMFIT.] To compose, mix, put together; to make into sweetmeats.—*n.*‡ (kon′fekt). A confection; a sweetmeat.—**confection,** kon•fek′shon, *n.* Anything prepared or preserved with sugar, as fruit; a sweetmeat; a composition or mixture‡.—**confectionary,**‡ kon•-fek′sho•ne•ri, *n.* A confectioner (O.T.).—*a.* Relating to confections.—**confectioner,** kon•fek′shon•ėr, *n.* One whose occupation is to make or sell sweetmeats or confections.—**confectionery,** kon•fek′sho•ne•ri, *n.* Sweetmeats; things prepared or sold by a confectioner; confections.

confederacy, kon•fed′ėr•a•si, *n.* [L. L. *confœderatio—con,* and L. *fœdus,* a league. FEDERAL.] A contract between two or more persons, bodies of men or states, combined in support of each other, in some act or enterprise; a league; compact; alliance; the persons, states, or nations united by a league.—**confederate,** kon•fed′ėr•āt, *a.* [L.L. *confœderatus.*] United in a league; allied by treaty; engaged in a confederacy; pertaining to a confederacy.—*Confederate States of America,* the alliance formed by eleven southern states after secession from the United States in 1860 and 1861.—**confederation,** kon•fed′ėr•ā″shon, *n.* A confederacy; a league; alliance; [*cap.*] the Government of the American Colonies from 1781-1789, previous to the adoption of the Constitution of the United States.—**confederative,** kon•fed′ėr•ā•tiv, *a.* Of or belonging to a confederation.

confer, kon•fėr′, *v.t.—conferred, conferring.* [L. *confero,* to bring together, compare, bestow, consult, etc.—*con,* together, and *fero,* to bring.] To give or bestow: with *on* or *upon* before the recipient. ∴ *Confer* differs from *bestow,* inasmuch as it always implies a certain amount of condescension or superiority on the part of the giver.—*v.i.* To consult together on some special subject; to compare opinions; formerly often simply to discourse or talk, but *confer* now implies conversation on some serious or important subject.—**conferee,** kon•fėr•ē′, *n.* One on whom something is conferred.—**conference,** kon′fėr•ens, *n.* [Fr. *conférence.*] The act of conferring or consulting together; a meeting for consultation, discussion, or instruction; a meeting of the representatives of different foreign countries in regard to some matter of importance to all; talk or conversation (*Shak.*)‡.—**conferrable,** kon•fėr′a•bl, *a.* Capable of being conferred or bestowed.—**conferrer,** kon•fėr′ėr, *n.* One who confers.

conferva, kon•fėr′va, *n.* pl. **confervae,** kon•fėr′vē. [L.] A name for various aquatic plants belonging to the algae, and chiefly composed of simple or branching filaments.—**confervoid,** kon•fėr′void, *a.* Resembling a conferva; partaking of the character of the confervae.

confess, kon•fes′, *v.t.* [Fr. *confesser,* from L. *confiteor, confessum—con,* and *fateor,* to own or acknowledge.] To own, acknowledge, or avow, as a crime, a fault, a charge, a debt, or something that is against one's interest or reputation; to own to; to disclose; *eccles.* to disclose or recapitulate (sins) to a priest in private with a view to absolution: in this sense sometimes *refl.*; to hear or receive the confession of: said of the priest; to acknowledge as having a certain character or certain claims; to declare belief in; to grant, concede, admit; not to dispute, to attest, reveal, let be known (poet.). ∴ Syn. under ACKNOWLEDGE.—*v.i.* To make confession or avowal; to disclose faults; to make known one's sins to a priest.—**confessedly,** kon•fes′ed•li, *adv.* By general confession or admission; admittedly.—**confesser,** kon•fes′ėr, *n.* One who confesses.—**confession,** kon•fesh′on, *n.* The act of confessing; the act of making an avowal; profession (N.T.); a disclosing of sins or faults to a priest; the disburdening of the conscience privately to a confessor.—*Confession of Faith,* a formulary which comprises the articles of faith that a person, a church, etc., accepts as true.—**confessional,** kon•fesh′on•al, *n.* [Fr. *confessional,* L.L. *confessionale.*] A compartment or cell in which a priest sits to hear confession, having a small opening or hole at each side through which the penitent, kneeling without, makes confession.—*a.* Of or pertaining to a confession.—**confessionary,** kon•fesh′o•ne•ri, *a.* Pertaining to auricular confession.—**confessor,** kon•fes′ėr, *n.* One who confesses; one who acknowledges a crime or fault; a priest who hears confession and assumes power to grant absolution; one who made a profession of his faith in the Christian religion, and adhered to it in the face of persecution.

confide, kon•fīd′, *v.i.—confided, confiding.* [L. *confido—con,* and *fido,* to trust. FAITH.] To rely with full assurance of mind; to rest the mind firmly without anxiety; to trust; to believe: followed by *in.*—*v.t.—confided, confiding.* To entrust; to commit with full reliance on the party to whom the thing is committed (to *confide* a thing *to* a person).—**confidant,** kon′fi•dant, *n. masc.*—**confidante,** kon•fi•dant′, *n. fem.* [O.Fr.] A person entrusted with the confidence of another; one to whom secrets are confided; a confidential friend.—**confidence,** kon′fi•dens, *n.* [L. *confidentia.*] Assurance of mind; firm belief; trust; reliance; reliance on one's own abilities, resources, or circumstances; self-reliance; assurance; boldness; courage; that in which trust is placed; ground of trust; a secret; a private or confidential communication (to exchange *confidences* together).—**confident,** kon′fi•dent, *a.* Full of confidence; having full belief; fully assured; relying on one's self; full of assurance; bold, sometimes overbold.—**confidential,** kon•fi•den′shal, *a.* Enjoying the confidence of another; entrusted with secrets or with private affairs; intended to be treated as private, or kept in confidence; spoken or written in confidence; secret.—**confidentially,** kon•fi•den′-shal•li, *adv.* In a confidential manner.—**confidently,** kon′fi•dent•li, *adv.* In a confident manner; with firm trust; with strong assurance; positively; dogmatically.—**confider,** kon•fī′dėr, *n.* One who confides; one who trusts in or entrusts to another.—**confiding,** kon•fī′ding, *p.* and *a.* Trusting; reposing confidence; trustful; credulous.—**confidingly,** kon•-fī′ding•li, *adv.* In a confiding manner; trustfully.

configure,† kon•fig′ūr, *v.t.—configured, configuring.* [L. *configuro—con,* and *figuro,* to form; *figura,* figure.] To form; to dispose in a certain form, figure, or shape.—**configuration,** kon•fig′ū•rā″shon, *n.* [L. *configuratio.*] External form, figure, or shape of a thing as resulting from the disposition and shape of its parts; external aspect or appearance; shape or form.

confine, kon′fīn, *n.* [L. *confinis,* bordering, adjoining, *confine,* a border—*con,* and *finis,* end, border, limit. FINE.] Border; boundary; frontier; the part of any territory which is at or near the end or extremity: generally in the plural and in regard to contiguous regions—*v.t.* (kon-fīn′)—*confined, confining.* [Fr. *confiner.*] To restrain within limits; to circumscribe; hence, to imprison; to immure; to shut up; to limit or restrain voluntarily in some act or practice (to *confine one's self to* a subject).—*To be confined*, to be in childbed.—**confinable,** kon•fī′na•bl, *a.* Capable of being confined or limited.—**confined,** kon•fīnd′, *p.* and *a.* Restrained within limits; limited; circumscribed; narrow (a *confined* scope or range).—**confinement,** kon•fīn′ment, *n.* The state of being confined; restraint within limits; any restraint of liberty by force or other obstacle or necessity; imprisonment; the lying-in of a woman.—**confiner,** kon•fī′nėr, *n.* One who or that which confines.

confirm, kon•fėrm′, *v.t.* [L. *confirmo—con*, and *firmo*, to make firm, from *firmus*, firm.] To make firm or more firm; to add strength to; to strengthen; to settle or establish; to make certain; to put past doubt; to assure; to verify; to sanction; to ratify (an agreement, promise); to strengthen in resolution, purpose, or opinion; to administer the rite of confirmation to.—**confirmable,** kon•fėr′ma•bl, *a.* Capable of being confirmed.—**confirmation,** kon•fėr•mā′shon, *n.* The act of confirming; the act of establishing; establishment; corroboration; the act of rendering valid or ratifying; the ceremony of laying on hands by a bishop in the admission of baptized persons to the full enjoyment of Christian privileges, a rite of the Roman, Greek, and English churches; that which confirms; additional evidence; proof; convincing testimony.—**confirmative,** kon•fėr′ma•tiv, *a.* Tending to confirm or establish; confirmatory.—**confirmatory,** kon•fėr′ma•to•ri, *a.* Serving to confirm; giving additional strength, force, or stability, or additional assurance or evidence.—**confirmed,** kon•fėrmd′, *p.* and *a.* Fixed; settled; settled in certain habits, state of health, etc. (a *confirmed* drunkard or invalid); having received the rite of confirmation.—**confirmedly,** con•fėr′med•li, *adv.* In a confirmed manner.

confiscate, kon′fis•kāt or kon•fis′kāt, *v.t.—confiscated, confiscating*. [L. *confisco, confiscatum—con*, together, and *fiscus*, the state treasury.] To adjudge to be forfeited to the public treasury; to appropriate to public use by way of penalty; to appropriate under legal authority as forfeited.—*a.* Confiscated. (*Shak.*)—**confiscable,**† kon•fis′ka•bl, *a.* Capable of being confiscated; liable to forfeiture.—**confiscation,** kon•fis•kā′shon, *n.* The act of confiscating or appropriating as forfeited.—**confiscator,** kon′fis•kā•tėr or kon•fis′, *n.* One who confiscates.—**confiscatory,** kon•fis′ka•to•ri, *a.* Confiscating; relating to confiscation.

conflagration, kon•fla•grā′shon, *n.* [L. *conflagratio—con*, with, and *flagro*, to burn, whence *flagrant*.] A great fire, or the burning of any great mass of combustibles.

conflict, kon′flikt, *n.* [L. *conflictus*, a conflict, from *confligo—con*, together, and *fligo*, to strike, to dash.] A fighting or struggle for mastery; a combat; a striving to oppose or overcome; active opposition; contention; strife.—kon•flikt′, *v.i.* To meet in opposition or hostility; to contend; to strive or struggle; to be in opposition; to be contrary; to be incompatible or at variance.—**conflicting,** kon•flik′ting, a. Being in opposition; contrary; contradictory; incompatible.—**confliction,**† kon•flik′shon, *n.* Act of conflicting or clashing.

confluence, kon′flū•ens, *n.* [L. *confluentia*, from *confluo—con*, and *fluo*, to flow.] A flowing together; the meeting or junction of two or more streams of water; also, the place of meeting; the running together of people; a crowd; a concourse.—**confluent,** kon′flū•ent, *a.* [L. *confluens*.] Flowing together; meeting in their course, as two streams; meeting; running together; *bot.* united at some part.—*Confluent smallpox*, smallpox in which the pustules run together or unite.—*n.* A tributary stream.—**conflux,** kon′fluks, *n.* A flowing together; a crowd; a multitude collected.

conform, kon•form′, *v.t.* [L. *conformo—con*, and *forma*, form.] To make of the same form or character; to make like (to *conform* anything *to* a model); to bring into harmony or correspondence; to adapt; to submit: often *refl.*—*v.i.* To act in conformity or compliance; *eccles.* to comply with the usages of the Established Church. —*a.* [L. *conformis—con*, and *forma*, form.] Conformable.—**conformability,** kon•for′ma•bil″i•ti, *n.* The state or quality of being conformable.—**conformable,** kon•for′ma•bl, *a.* Corresponding in form, character, manners, opinions, etc.; in harmony or conformity; agreeable; suitable; consistent; adapted; compliant; submissive; disposed to obey; *geol.* lying in parallel or nearly parallel planes, and having the same dip and changes of dip: said of strata or groups of strata.—**conformableness,** kon•for′ma•bl•nes, *n.* State of being conformable.—**conformably,** kon•for′ma•bli, *adv.* In a conformable manner; in conformity; suitably; agreeably.—**conformation,** kon•for•mā′shon, *n.* The manner in which a body is formed; the particular disposition of the parts which compose it; configuration; form; structure.—**conformer,** kon•for′mėr, *n.* One who conforms; one who complies with established forms or doctrines.—**conformist,** kon•for′mist, *n.* One who conforms or complies; one who complies with the worship of the Church of England, as distinguished from a Dissenter or Non-conformist. —**conformity,** kon•form′i•ti, *n.* Correspondence in form or manner; agreement; congruity; likeness; harmony; correspondence with decrees or dictates; submission; accordance; compliance with the usages or principles of the English Church.

confound, kon•found′, *v.t.* [Fr. *confondre*, from L. *confundo—con*, together, and *fundo*, *fusum*, to pour out, whence *fuse, confuse, refuse*, etc.] To mingle confusedly together; to mix in a mass or crowd so that individuals cannot be distinguished; to throw into disorder; to confuse; to mistake one for another; to make a mistake between; to throw into consternation; to perplex with terror, surprise, or astonishment; to astound; to abash; to overthrow, ruin, baffle, or bring to nought. ∴ Syn. under ABASH.—**confounded,** kon•foun′ded, *a.* Excessive; odious; detestable. (Colloq.)—**confoundedly,** kon•foun′ded•li, *adv.* Enormously; greatly; shamefully; odiously; detestably. (Colloq.)—**confounder,** kon•foun′dėr, *n.* One who or that which confounds.

confraternity, kon•fra•tėr′ni•ti, *n.* A fraternity or brotherhood.

confront, kon•frunt′, *v.t.* [Fr. *confronter*—L. *con*, together, and *frons, frontis*, the countenance or front.] To stand facing; to face; to stand in front of; to meet in hostility; to oppose; to set face to face; to bring into the presence of: followed by *with*.—**confrontation,**† **confrontment,**† kon•frun•tā′shon, kon•frunt′ment, *n.* The act of confronting.—**confronter,** kon•frun′tėr, *n.* One who confronts.

Confucian, Confucianist, kon•fū′shi•an, kon•fū′shi•an•ist, *n.* A follower of Confucius, the famous Chinese philosopher.—**Confucianism,** kon•fū′shian•izm, *n.* The doctrines or system of morality taught by Confucius, which has been long adopted in China, and inculcates the practice of virtue but not the worship of any god.

confuse, kon•fūz′, *v.t.—confused, confusing*. [L. *confusus*, from *confundo*. CONFOUND.] To mix up without order or clearness; to throw together indiscriminately; to derange, disorder, jumble; to confound; to perplex or derange the mind or ideas of; to embarrass; to disconcert. ∴ Syn. under ABASH.—**confusedly,** kon•fū′zed•li, *adv.* In a confused manner; in a mixed mass; without order; indiscriminately; with agitation of mind.—**confusedness,** kon•fū′zed•nes, *n.* A state of being confused.—**confusion,** kon•fū′zhon, *n.* [L. *confusio*.] A state in which things are confused; an indiscriminate or disorderly mingling; disorder; tumultuous condition; perturbation of mind; embarrassment; distraction; abashment; disconcertment; overthrow; defeat; ruin.

confute, kon•fūt′, *v.t.—confuted, confuting*. [L. *confuto*, to cool down by cold water, to confute—*con*, together, and *futis*, a pitcher, from root of *fundo*, to pour.] To prove (an argument, statement, etc.) to be false, defective, or invalid; to disprove; to overthrow; to prove (a person) to be wrong; to convict of error by argument or proof.—**confutation,** kon•fū•tā′shon, *n.* The act of confuting, disproving, or proving to be false or invalid.—**confutative,** kon•fū′ta•tiv, *a.* Adapted or designed to confute.—**confuter,** kon•fū′tėr, *n.* One who confutes.

congeal, kon•jēl′, *v.t.* [L. *congelare*—

con, together, and *gelare*, to freeze, from *gelu*, cold, whence also *gelid*, *jelly*.] To change from a fluid to a solid state by cold or a loss of heat; to freeze; to coagulate; to check the flow of; to make (the blood) run cold. —*v.i.* To pass from a fluid to a solid state by cold; to coagulate.—**congealable,** kon•jēl′a•bl, *a.* Capable of being congealed.—**congealment,** kon•jēl′ment, *n.* Congelation.—**congelation,** kon•je•lā′shon, *n.* [L. *congelatio*.] The act or process of congealing; the state of being congealed; what is congealed or solidified; a concretion.

congener, kon′jē•nėr, *n.* [L.—*con*, together, and *genus*, *generis*, a kind or race.] A thing of the same kind or nearly allied; a plant or animal belonging to the same genus.—**congeneric,** kon•je•ner′ik, *a.* Being of the same kind or nature; belonging to the same genus.—**congenerous,** kon•jen′ėr•us, *a.* Congeneric; *anat.* applied to muscles which concur in the same action.

congenial, kon•jē′ni•al, *a.* [L. *con*, and *genialis*, E. *genial*.] Partaking of the same nature or natural characteristics; kindred; sympathetic; suited for each other.—**congeniality,** kon•jē′ni•al″i•ti, *n.* The state of being congenial; natural affinity; suitableness.—**congenially,** kon•jē′ni•al•li, *adv.* In a congenial manner.

congenital, kon•jen′i•tal, *a.* [L. *congenitus*—*con*, and *genitus*, born, root *gen*, to produce.] Belonging or pertaining to an individual from hirth (a *congenital* deformity).

conger, conger eel, kong′gėr, *n.* [L. *conger*, a conger eel.] The sea eel, a large voracious species of eel, sometimes growing to the length of 10 feet, and weighing 100 lbs.

congeries, kon•jē′ri•ēz, *n. sing.* and *pl.* [L., from *congero*, to amass—*con*, and *gero*, to bear.] A collection of several particles or bodies in one mass or aggregate; an aggregate; a combination.

congest, kon•jest′, *v.t.* [L. *congero*, *congestum*—*con*, and *gero*, to bear.] To heap together‡; *med.* to cause an unnatural accumulation of blood in.—**congested,** kon•jes′ted, *a. Med.* containing an unnatural accumulation of blood; affected with congestion.—**congestion,** kon•jest′yon, *n.* [L. *congestio*.] *Med.* an excessive accumulation of blood in an organ, the functions of which are thereby disordered.—**congestive,** kon•jes′tiv, *a.* Pertaining to congestion; indicating an unnatural accumulation of blood in some part of the body.

conglobate, kon′glō•bāt, *a.* [L. *conglobatus*—*con*, and *globus*, a ball. GLOBE.] Formed or gathered into a ball or small spherical body; combined into one mass.—*v.t.*†—*conglobated*, *conglobating*. To collect or form into a ball; to combine into one mass.—*v.i.* To assume a round or globular form.—**conglobation,** kon•glō•bā′shon, *n.* The act of forming or gathering into a ball; a round body.—**conglobe,**† kon•glōb′, *v.t.* and *i.*—*conglobed*, *conglobing*. To conglobate.

conglomerate, kon•glom′ėr•āt, *a.* [L. *conglomero*, *conglomeratum*—*con*, and *glomus*, *glomeris*, a ball, a clew.] Gathered into a ball or round body; crowded together; clustered.—*v.t.*—*conglomerated*, *conglomerating*. To gather into a ball or round body; to collect into a round mass.—*n.* A kind of rock made up of rounded fragments of various rocks cemented together by a matrix of siliceous, calcareous, or other cement; gravel solidified by cement into a rock; pudding stone.—**conglomeration,** kon•glom′ėr•ā″shon, *n.* The act of conglomerating; collection; accumulation; what is conglomerated; a mixed mass; a mixture.

conglutinate, kon•glū′ti•nāt, *v.t.*—*conglutinated*, *conglutinating*. [L. *conglutino*—*con*, and *glutino*, from *gluten*, glue. GLUE.] To glue together; to unite by some glutinous or tenacious substance; to reunite; to cement.—*v.i.* To coalesce; to unite by the intervention of some glutinous substance.—*a.* Glued together; *bot.* united by some adhesive substance, but not organically united.—**conglutination,** kon•glū′ti•nā″shon, *n.* The act of gluing together; a joining by means of some tenacious substance; union; coalescence.

congou, kong′gö, *n.* [Chinese *kung-fu*, labor.] The second lowest quality of black tea, being the third picking from a plant during the season.

congratulate, kon•grat′ū•lāt, *v.t.*—*congratulated*, *congratulating*.—[L. *congratulor*—*con*, and *gratulor*, from *gratus*, grateful, pleasing. GRACE.] To address with expressions of sympathetic pleasure on some piece of good fortune happening to the party addressed; to compliment upon an event deemed happy; to wish joy to; to felicitate; also *refl.* to have a lively sense of one's own good fortune; to consider one's self lucky.—**congratulant,** kon•grat′ū•lant, *a.* Congratulating; expressing pleasure in another's good fortune.—**congratulation,** kon•grat′ū•lā″shon, *n.* The act of congratulating; words used in congratulating; expression to a person of pleasure in his good fortune; felicitation.—**congratulator,** kon•grat′ū•lā•tėr, *n.* One who congratulates.—**congratulatory,** kon•grat′ū•la•to•ri, *a.* Containing or expressing congratulation.

congregate, kong′grē•gāt, *v.t.*—*congregated*, *congregating*. [L. *congrego*—*con*, and *grex*, *gregis*, a herd. GREGARIOUS.] To collect into an assemblage; to assemble; to bring into one place or into a crowd or united body.—*v.i.* To come together; to assemble; to meet in a crowd.—*a.* Collected; compact; close.—**congregation,** kong•grē•gā′shon, *n.* The act of congregating; the act of bringing together or assembling; a collection or assemblage of persons or things; an assembly, especially an assembly of persons met for the worship of God; or a number of people organized as a body for the purpose of holding religious services in common.—**congregational,** kong•grē•gā′shon•al, *a.* Pertaining to a congregation; [*cap.*] pertaining to the Independents or Congregationists, or to Congregationalism.—**congregationalism,** kong•gre•gā′shon•al•izm, *n.* A system of administering church affairs by which each congregation has the right of regulating the details of its worship, discipline, and government.—**Congregationalist,** kong•gre•gā′shon•al•ist, *n.* One who belongs to a Congregational church or society; an Independent.

congress, kong′gres, *n.* [L. *congressus*, a meeting, from *congredior*, *congressum*, to come together—*con*, and *gradior*, to go; *gradus*, a step, whence *grade*, *degree*, etc.] A meeting together of individuals; an assembly of envoys, commissioners, deputies, etc.; a meeting of sovereign princes or of the representatives of several courts, for the purpose of arranging international affairs; [*cap.*] the legislative assembly of the United States of America, consisting of the Senate and House of Representatives.—*v.i.*† To come together; to assemble; to meet.—**congressional,** kon•gresh′on•al, *a.* Pertaining to a congress or to the Congress of the United States. —**congressman,** *n.* A member of the United States Congress.

congrue, kon•grö′, *v.i.* [L. *congruo*, to suit, to be congruous.] [*obs.*] To be consistent; to agree. (*Shak.*)—**congruence, congruency,** kong′grụ•ens, kong′grụ•en•si, *n.* [L. *congruentia*.] Suitableness of one thing to another; agreement; consistency.—**congruent,** kong′grụ•ent, *a.* Suitable; agreeing; corresponding.—**congruently,** kong′grụ•ent•li, *adv.* In a congruent manner.—**congruity, congruousness,** kong•grū′i•ti, kong′grū•us•nes, *n.* The state or quality of being congruous; agreement between things; suitableness; pertinence; consistency; propriety.—**congruous,** kong′grụ•us, *a.* [L. *congruus*.] Accordant; harmonious; well adapted; appropriate; meet; fit.—**congruously,** kong′grụ•us•li, *adv.* In a congruous manner; suitably; pertinently; agreeably; consistently.

conic, conifer, etc. See CONE.

conidium, -ia, kon•id′i•um, *n.* [Gr. dim. of *kōnis*, dust.] In fungi, a minute asexual spore.

coniine, kōn•i′ēn, *n.* [From *conium*, the hemlock.] An alkaloid poison contained in hemlock.

conjecture, kon•jek′chėr, *n.* [Fr. *conjecture*, L. *conjectura*, a conjecture, lit. a throwing or putting of things together, from *conjicio*, to throw together—*con*, and *jacio*, to throw.] A guess or inference based on the supposed possibility or probability of a fact, or on slight evidence; an opinion formed on insufficient or presumptive evidence; surmise.—*v.t.*—*conjectured*, *conjecturing*. To judge by guess or conjecture; to guess.—*v.i.* To form conjectures.—**conjecturer,** kon•jek′chėr•ėr, *n.* One who conjectures; a guesser.—**conjecturable,** kon•jek′chėr•a•bl, *a.* Capable of being guessed or conjectured. —**conjectural,** kon•jek′chėr•al, *a.* Depending on conjecture; implying guess or conjecture.—**conjecturally,** kon•jek′chėr•al•li, *adv.* In a conjectural manner; by conjecture; by guess.

conjoin, kon•join′, *v.t.* [*Con* and *join*; Fr. *conjoindre.*] To join together or in one; to unite; to associate or connect.—*v.i.* To unite; to join; to league.—**conjoint,** kon•joint′, *a.* United; connected; associated.—**conjointly,** kon•joint′li, *adv.* In a conjoint manner; jointly; unitedly; in union; together.

conjugal, kon′jū•gal, *a.* [L. *conjugalis* —*con,* together, and *jugum,* a yoke, from *jug,* root of *jungo,* to join, seen also in E. *yoke.* YOKE.] Belonging to marriage or married persons; matrimonial; connubial.—**conjugally,** kon′jū•gal•li, *adv.* Matrimonially; connubially.

conjugate, kon′jū•gāt, *v.t.*—*conjugated, conjugating.* [L. *conjugo, conjugatus,* to couple—*con,* and *jugo,* to yoke. CONJUGAL.] *Gram.* to inflect (a verb) through its several voices, moods, tenses, numbers, and persons, or so many of them.—*a.* United in pairs; joined together; coupled; *bot.* applied to a pinnate leaf which has only one pair of leaflets; *chem.* containing two or more radicals acting the part of a single one; *gram.* applied to words from the same root, and having the same radical signification, but modified by the affix added, or to words which have the same form but are different parts of speech; *math.* applied to two points, lines, etc., when they are considered together, with regard to any property, in such a manner that they may be interchanged without altering the way of enunciating the property. —*Conjugate foci,* in a mirror or lens, are two points such that rays proceeding from either are reflected or refracted to the other.—*n.* What is conjugate; a conjugate word.—**conjugation,** kon•jū•gā′shon, *n.* [L. *conjugatio.*] The inflection of a verb in its different forms; a class of verbs conjugated in the same way; *biol.* the union of two sex cells (gametes) of similar appearance.—**conjugational,** kon•jū•gā′shon•al, *a.* Of or belonging to conjugation.

conjunct, kon•jungkt′, *a.* [L. *conjunctus,* from *conjungo.* CONJOIN.] Conjoined; united; concurrent.—**conjunction,** kon•jungk′shon, *n.* [L. *conjunctio.*] Union; connection; association; *astron.* that position of a planet in which it is in a line with the earth or another planet and the sun; *gram.* an indeclinable particle, serving to unite words, sentences, or clauses of a sentence, and indicating their relation to one another.—**conjunctional,** kon•jungk′shon•al, *a.* Belonging or relating to a conjunction.—**conjunctionally,** kon•jungk′shon•al•li, *adv.* In a conjunctional manner.—**conjunctiva,** kon•jungk•tī′va, *n. Anat.* the mucous membrane which lines the inner surface of the eyelids, and is continued over the fore part of the globe of the eye.—**conjunctive,** kon•jungk′tiv, *a.* [L. *conjunctivus.*] Uniting; serving to unite.—*Conjunctive mood, gram.* the mood which follows a conjunction or expresses some condition or contingency; the subjunctive.—**conjunctively,** kon•jungk′tiv•li, *adv.* In a conjunctive manner.—**conjunctivitis,** kon•junk•tiv•īt′is, *n.* [From *conjunctiva,* and Gr. *-itis,* inflammation.] Inflammation of the conjunctiva.—**conjunctly,** kon•jungkt′li, *adv.* In a conjunct manner; in union; jointly; together.—**conjuncture,** kon•jungk′chėr, *n.* Combination of circumstances or affairs; especially, a critical time, proceeding from a union of circumstances; a crisis of affairs.

conjure, *v.t.*—*conjured, conjuring.* [L. *conjuro,* to swear together, to conspire —*con,* with, and *juro,* to swear, whence also *jury, perjure.*] With pron. kon•jūr′, to call on or summon by a sacred name or in a solemn manner; to implore with solemnity; to adjure: with pron. kun′jėr, to affect or effect by magic or enchantment; to bring about by affecting the arts of a conjurer.—*To conjure* (kun′jėr) *up,* to call up or bring into existence by conjuring or as if by conjuring.—*v.i.* (kun′jėr). To practice the arts of a conjurer; to use magic arts.—**conjuration,** kon•jū•rā′shon, *n.* The act of conjuring or imploring with solemnity; the act of binding by an oath; adjuration; an incantation; a spell.—**conjurer, conjuror,** kun′jėr•ėr, *n.* An enchanter; one who practices legerdemain; a juggler.

connascency, kon•nas′en•si, *n.* [L. *con,* and *nascor, natus,* to be born.] The common birth of two or more at the same time; the act of growing together or at the same time.—**connate,** kon′nāt, *a.* [L. *con,* and *natus,* born.] Belonging to from birth; implanted at birth: applied chiefly in *philos.* to ideas or principles; *bot.* united in origin; growing from one base, or united at their bases (a leaf, an anther); *med.* congenital.

connature, kon•nā′chėr, *n.* Likeness in nature; identity or similarity of character.—**connatural,** kon•nach′ė•rel, *a.* Connected by nature; united in nature; belonging to by nature.—**connaturally,** kon•nach′ė•rel•li, *adv.* In a connatural manner; by the act of nature; originally.

connect, kon•nekt′ *v.t.* [L. *connecto, connexum*—*con,* and *necto,* to bind.] To fasten together; to join or unite; to conjoin; to combine; to associate. —*v.i.* To join, unite, or cohere.—**connectedly,** kon•nek′ted•li, *adv.* By connection; in a connected manner; conjointly.—**connection, connexion,** kon•nek′shon, *n.* [L. *connexio.*] The act of connecting or state of being connected; also that which connects; union by something physical or by relation of any kind; relationship by blood or marriage, but more specifically by marriage; a person connected with another by this relationship; circle of persons with whom any one is brought into contact.—*In this connection,* in connection with what is now under consideration.—**connective,** kon•nek′tiv, *a.* Having the power of connecting; tending to connect; connecting.—*n.* That which connects; *gram.* a word that connects other words and sentences; a conjunction.—**connectively,** kon•nek′tiv•li, *adv.* In a connective manner; jointly.—**connector,** kon•nek′tėr, *n.* One who or that which connects.

conning tower, *n.* An armored structure on a warship from which the officer in charge issues his orders during the time the ship is in action.

connive, kon•nīv′, *v.i.*—*connived, conniving.* [L. *conniveo,* to wink, to connive at—*con,* together, and *niveo,* to wink.] To wink or close and open the eyelids rapidly‡; *fig.* to close the eyes upon a fault or other act; to pretend ignorance or blindness; to forbear to see; to wink at or overlook a fault or other act and suffer it to pass unnoticed: followed by *at.*—**connivance,** kon•nī′vans, *n.* The act of conniving; voluntary blindness to an act.—**conniver,** kon•nī′vėr, *n.* One who connives.

connoisseur, kon′is•sėr, *n.* [O.Fr. *connoisseur,* Mod.Fr. *connaisseur,* from the verb *connoitre, connaître,* from L. *cognoscere,* to know. COGNIZANCE.] A critical judge; one competent to pass a critical judgment upon anything.

connote, connotate, kon•nōt′, kon′ō•tāt, *v.t.*—*connoted, connoting; connotated, connotating.* [L. *con,* and *noto, notatum,* to mark. NOTE.] To include in the meaning; to comprise among the attributes expressed; to imply. ∴ *Connote* and *denote* are contrasted in logic. Thus the word ‘ horse ’ *connotes* the qualities that distinguish a horse from other animals, and *denotes* the class of animals which are characterized by having these qualities. ‘ Thames ’, however, *connotes* nothing, being simply the name of the particular river which it *denotes.*—*v.i.* To have a meaning or signification in connection with another word.—**connotation,** kon•o•tā′shon, *n.* That which constitutes the meaning of a word; the attributes expressed by a word.—**connotative,** kon•no′ta•tiv, *a.* Connoting; significant.

connubial, kon•nū′bi•al, *a.* [L. *connubialis,* from *connubium,* marriage—*con,* and *nubo,* to marry.] Pertaining to marriage; nuptial; belonging to the state of husband and wife.—**connubiality,** kon•nū′bi•al″i•ti, *n.* The state of being connubial; anything pertaining to the state of husband and wife.—**connubially,** kon•nū′bi•al•li, *adv.* In a connubial manner; as man and wife.

conoid, conoidal, etc. See CONE.

conquer, kong′kėr, *v.t.* [O.Fr. *conquerre, conquerrer,* Mod.Fr. *conquérir,* from L. *conquiro,* to seek for, procure —*con,* and *quæro,* to seek (whence *quest* and *query*).] To overcome and bring to subjection in war; to reduce by physical force till resistance is no longer made; to vanquish; to gain by force; to overcome or surmount (obstacles, difficulties); to gain or obtain by effort. ∴ *Conquer* is wider and more general than *vanquish*, denoting usually a succession of struggles or conflicts; while *vanquish* refers more commonly to a single conflict, and has regularly a personal object. *Subdue* implies a continued process and a complete and thorough subjection.—*v.i.* To overcome; to gain the victory.—**conquerable,** kong′kėr•a•bl, *a.* Capable of being conquered, overcome, or subdued.—**conqueror,** kong′kėr•ėr, *n.* One who conquers or gains a victory.—*The Conqueror*, an epithet applied to William I of England, as expressing his conquest of the country.—**conquest,** kong′kwest, *n.* [O.Fr. *conquest*, Fr. *conquête*.] The act of conquering; the act of overcoming or vanquishing opposition by force, physical or moral; subjugation; that which is conquered; a possession gained by force.—*The Conquest*, by preeminence the conquest of England by William of Normandy.—**conquistador,** kong•kwis′ta•dōr, *n.* [Sp.] A term applied to the early Spanish leaders who conquered Spanish America.

consanguinity, kon•sang•gwin′i•ti, *n.* [L. *consanguinitas*—prefix *con*, and *sanguis, sanguinis*, blood.] The relation of persons by blood, the relation or connection of persons descended from the same stock or common ancestor, in distinction from *affinity* or relation by marriage.—**consanguineous,** kon•sang•gwin′i•us, *a.* [L. *consanguineus*.] Of the same blood; related by birth; descended from the same parent or ancestor.

conscience, kon′shens, *n.* [L. *conscientia*, from *conscio*, to know, to be privy to—*con*, with, and *scio*, to know. SCIENCE.] Private or inward thoughts or real sentiments (*Shak.*); the faculty, power, or principle within us, which decides on the rightness or wrongness of our own actions and affections; the sense of right and wrong; the moral sense; morality; what a good conscience would approve.—*A bad conscience*, a reproving conscience.—*A good conscience*, an approving conscience.—*In all conscience*, to be reasonable, to keep within the bounds of moderation: a form of asseveration.—*Conscience clause*, a clause or article in an act or law which specially relieves persons having conscientious scruples in taking judicial oaths, or having their children present at school during the time of religious instruction or service.—**conscientious,** kon′shi•en′shus, *a.* Influenced by conscience; governed by a strict regard to the dictates of conscience, or by the known or supposed rules of right and wrong.—**conscientiously,** kon•shi•en′shus•li, *adv.* In a conscientious manner; according to the direction of conscience.—**conscientiousness,** kon•shi•en′shus•nes, *n.* The state or quality of being conscientious.

conscious, kon′shus, *a.* [L. *conscius*—*con*, and *scio*, to know. CONSCIENCE.] Knowing what affects or what goes on in one's own mind; having direct knowledge of a thing; having such a knowledge as is conveyed by immediate sensation or perception; aware; sensible (*conscious of* something); having become the subject of consciousness; known to one's self (*conscious* guilt).—**consciously,** kon′shus•li, *adv.* In a conscious manner; with knowledge of one's own mental operations or actions.—**consciousness,** kon′shus•nes, *n.* The faculty of knowing what affects or what goes on in one's own mind; immediate knowledge, such as is given in sensation and perception; internal persuasion.

conscript, kon′skript, *a.* [L. *conscriptus*, from *conscribo*, to enroll—*con*, with, and *scribo*, to write.] Enrolled.—*Conscript fathers*, a title of the senators of Rome.—*n.* One who is compulsorily enrolled for military or naval service.—kon•skript′, *v.t.* to draft; to enroll by compulsion for military service.—**conscription,** kon•skrip′shon, *n.* [L. *conscriptio*.] A compulsory enrollment of individuals of a certain age, held liable to be drafted for military or naval service.

consecrate, kon′se•krāt, *v.t.*—*consecrated, consecrating*. [L. *consecro*—*con*, with, and *sacro*, to consecrate, from *sacer*, sacred. SACRED.] To make or declare to be sacred with certain ceremonies or rites; to appropriate to sacred uses; to enroll among deities or saints; to canonize; to give episcopal rank to; to dedicate with solemnity; to render venerable; to make respected; to hallow.—**consecrate,** kon′se•krāt, *a.* Sacred; consecrated; devoted; dedicated. [Obs. or poet.]—**consecration,** kon•se•krā′shon, *n.* The act or ceremony of consecrating or separating from a common to a sacred use; dedication of a person or thing to the service and worship of God, by certain rites or solemnities; dedication; the ceremony of elevating a priest to the dignity of a bishop; the giving of the bread and wine of the eucharist their sacred character in the mass or communion service.—**consecrator,** kon′se•krā•tėr, *n.* One who consecrates.

consecution, kon•se•kū′shon, *n.* [L. *consecutio*—*con*, and *sequor*, to follow (whence *sequence*); same root as *second*.] A following; a train or series; the state of being consecutive.—**consecutive,** kon•sek′ū•tiv, *a.* Uninterrupted in course or succession; succeeding one another in a regular order; successive; following; succeeding.—**consecutively,** kon•sek′ū•tiv•li, *adv.* In a consecutive manner; in regular succession; successively.—**consecutiveness,** kon•sek′ū•tiv•nes, *n.* State of being consecutive.

consent, kon•sent′, *v.i.* [L. *consentio*, to agree—*con*, with, and *sentio, sensum*, to feel, perceive, think; akin *sense, sentiment*, etc.] To agree; to accord; to yield, as to persuasion or entreaty; to comply; to acquiesce or accede.—*n.* Voluntary accordance with what is done or proposed by another; a yielding of the mind or will to that which is proposed; acquiescence; concurrence; compliance; accord of minds; agreement in opinion or sentiment; *law*, intelligent concurrence in the terms of a contract or agreement, of such a nature as to bind the party consenting.—**consensual,** kon•sen′shū•al, *a.* *Law*, formed or existing by mere consent; *physiol.* excited or caused by sensation or sympathy and not by conscious volition.—**consensus,** kon•sen′sus, *n.* [L.] Unanimity; agreement; concord.—**consentaneous,** kon•sen•tā′ni•us, *a.* [L. *consentaneus*.] Accordant; agreeing; consistent; suitable.—**consentaneously,** kon•sen•tā′ni•us•li, *adv.* Agreeably; consistently; suitably.—**consentaneousness,** kon•sen•tā′ni•us•nes, *n.* Agreement; accordance; consistency.—**consenter,** kon•sen′tėr, *n.* One who consents.—**consentient,** kon•sen′shi•ent, *a.* Agreeing; accordant; unanimous.

consequence, kon′se•kwens, *n.* [L. *consequentia*, from *consequor*. CONSECUTION.] That which follows from any act, cause, principles, or series of actions; an event or effect produced by some preceding act or cause; inference; deduction; conclusion from premises; importance (a matter *of consequence*, a man *of* great *consequence*).—*In consequence of*, as the effect of; by reason of; through.—**consequent,** kon′se•kwent, *a.* [L. *consequens*.] Following as the natural effect: with *to* or *on*.—*n.* That which follows; *logic*, that member of a hypothetical proposition which contains the conclusion.—**consequential,** kon•se•kwen′shal, *a.* Following as the effect; produced by the connection of effects with causes; affecting airs of great self-importance, or characterized by such affectation; pompous.—*n.* An inference; a deduction; a conclusion.—**consequentially,** kon•se•kwen′shal•li, *adv.* In a consequential manner; with just deduction of consequences; with assumed importance; pompously.—**consequentialness,** kon•se•kwen′shal•nes, *n.* The quality of being consequential.—**consequently,** kon′se•kwent•li, *adv.* By consequence; by necessary connection of effects with their causes; in consequence of something.

conservatoire, kon•sâr•va•twär, *n.* [Fr., from It. *conservatorio*.] A name given to an establishment for promoting the study of any special branch, especially music.

conserve, kon•sėrv′, *v.t.*—*conserved, conserving*. [L. *conservo*—*con*, and *servo*, to preserve.] To keep in a safe or unimpaired state; to uphold and keep from decay, waste, or injury; to guard or defend from violation (institutions, customs, buildings, etc.); to preserve with sugar, etc., as fruits.—*n.* (kon′sėrv). That which is conserved; a sweetmeat made of the inspissated juice of fruit boiled with sugar.—**conserver,** kon•sėr′vėr, *n.* One who conserves or preserves.—

conservable, kon•sėr′va•bl, *a.* That may be conserved.—**conservation,** kon•sėr•vā′shon, *n.* [L. *conservatio.*] The act of conserving, preserving, guarding, or protecting; preservation from loss, decay, injury, or violation. —*Conservation of energy*, the principle that energy or force is indestructible, the sum of all the energy in the universe being constant.—**conservational,** kon•sėr•vā′shon•al, *a.* Tending to preserve; preservative. —**conservatism,** kon•sėr′va•tizm, *n.* The political principles and opinions maintained by Conservatives; tendency to preserve what is established; opposition to change.—**conservative,** kon•sėr′va•tiv, *a.* Tending to conserve; traditional; cautious; inclining to keep up old institutions, customs, and the like; having a tendency to uphold and preserve entire the institutions of a country, both civil and ecclesiastical; opposed to radical changes or innovations; [*cap.*] pertaining to the Conservatives or their principles.—*n.* One who aims to preserve from ruin, innovation, injury, or radical change; [*cap.*] one of the political party the professed object of which is to support and preserve all that is good in the existing institutions of a country, and to oppose undesirable changes.—**conservator,** kon′sėr•vā•tėr or kon•sėr′ve•tėr, *n.* One who conserves; one who preserves from injury or violation; one appointed to conserve or watch over anything.—**conservatory,** kon•sėr′ve•to•ri, *a.* Having the quality of preserving from loss, decay, or injury.—*n.* A large greenhouse for preserving exotics and other tender plants.—Same as CONSERVATOIRE.

consider, kon•sid′ėr, *v.t.* [L. *considero*, to view attentively, to consider: originally (like *contemplor*) an augurial term—*con*, together, and *sidus, sideris*, a constellation.] To fix the mind on, with a view to a careful examination; to think on with care; to ponder; to study; to meditate on; to observe and examine; to regard with pity or sympathy, and hence relieve (the poor); to have regard or respect to; to respect; to take into view or account, or have regard to, in examination, or in forming an estimate; to judge to be; to reckon (to *consider* a man wise).—*v.i.* To think seriously, maturely, or carefully; to reflect.—**considerable,** kon•sid′ėr•a•bl, *a.* Worthy of consideration on account of its amount; more than a little; moderately large; somewhat important or valuable.—**considerably,** kon•sid′ėr•a•bli, *adv.* In a degree deserving notice; in a degree not trifling or unimportant.—**considerate,** kon•sid′ėr•it, *a.* [L. *consideratus.*] Given to consideration or to sober reflection; circumspect; discreet; prudent; characterized by consideration or regard for another's circumstances and feelings; thoughtful or mindful of others.—**considerately,** kon•sid′ėr•it•li, *adv.* In a considerate manner.—**considerateness,** kon•sid′ėr•it•nes, *n.* The state or quality of being considerate.—**consideration,** kon•sid′ėr•ā″shon, *n.* [L. *consideratio.*] The act of considering; mental view; regard; notice; mature thought; serious deliberation; thoughtful, sympathetic, appreciative, or due regard or respect; contemplation; meditation; some degree of importance or claim to notice or regard; motive of action; ground of conduct; ground of concluding; reason; recompense or remuneration (colloq.).—*In consideration of*, in respect or regard of; in return for.—**considering,** kon•sid′ėr•ing, *prep.* Having regard to; taking into account; making allowance for.

consign, kon•sīn′, *v.t.* [L. *consigno*, to seal or sign—*con*, and *signum*, a sign, seal, or mark. SIGN.] To give or hand over; to transfer or deliver over into the possession of another or into a different state (to *consign* a body to the grave); to deliver or transfer in charge or trust; to entrust (as goods to a factor for sale); to commit for permanent preservation (to *consign* to writing).—**consignation,**† kon•sig•nā′shon, *n.* The act of consigning.—**consignee,** kon•sī•nē′, *n.* The person to whom goods or other things are consigned for sale or superintendence; a factor.—**consigner, consignor,** kon•sī′nėr, kon•sī′nor, *n.* The person who consigns. —**consignment,** kon•sīn′ment, *n.* The act of consigning; the act of sending off goods to an agent for sale; goods sent or delivered to a factor for sale.

consist, kon•sist′, *v.i.* [L. *consisto*—*con*, and *sisto*, to stand.] To hold together or remain fixed‡; to be, exist, subsist‡; to stand or be; to be comprised or contained: followed by *in*; to be composed; to be made up: followed by *of*; to be compatible, consistent, or harmonious; to accord: followed by *with*.—**consistence, consistency,** kon•sis′tens, kon•sis′ten•si, *n.* An indefinite degree of density or viscosity; agreement or harmony of all parts of a complex thing among themselves, or of the same thing with itself at different times; congruity, agreement, or harmony.—**consistent,** kon•sis′tent, *a.* [L. *consistens.*] Having a certain substance or firmness; standing in agreement; compatible; congruous; not contradictory or opposed; not out of harmony with other acts or professions of the same person.—**consistently,** kon•sis′tent•li, *adv.* In a consistent manner; in agreement; suitably or agreeably to one's other acts or professions.

consistory, kon•sis′tor•i, *n.* [L. *consistorium*, a place of assembly, a council. CONSIST.] A spiritual or ecclesiastical court; the court of a bishop for the trial of ecclesiastical causes arising within the diocese; an assembly of prelates; the college of cardinals at Rome; a solemn assembly or council; in some Reformed churches, an assembly or council of ministers and elders.—**consistorial,** kon•sis•tō′ri•al, *a.* Pertaining or relating to a consistory.

console, kon•sōl′, *v.t.*—*consoled, consoling.* [L. *consolor*, to console—*con*, and *solor*, to comfort; akin *solace.*] To cheer the mind in distress or depression; to comfort; to soothe; to solace.—**consolable,** kon•sōl′a•bl, *a.* Capable of receiving consolation. —**consolation,** kon•sōl•ā′shon, *n.* [L. *consolatio.*] The act of consoling; alleviation of misery or distress of mind; a comparative degree of happiness in distress or misfortune, springing from any circumstance that abates the evil or supports and strengthens the mind, as hope, joy, courage, and the like; comfort of the mind; that which comforts or refreshes the spirits; the cause of comfort.—**consolatory,** kon•sōl′a•tor•i, *a.* Tending to console or give comfort; refreshing to the mind; assuaging grief.—**consoler,** kon•sōl′ėr, *n.* One that consoles.—**consoling,** kon•sōl′ing, *a.* Adapted to console or comfort.

console, kon′sōl, *n.* [Fr., from *consoler*, in sense of to support.] A variety of bracket, either useful or ornamental; an ornamental bracket projecting from a wall, employed to support a cornice, bust, vase, or the like; the desklike part of an organ containing keyboards, pedals, etc.

consolidate, kon•sol′id•āt, *v.t.*—*consolidated, consolidating.* [L. *consolido, consolidatum*—*con*, and *solidus*, solid.] To make solid or compact; to harden or make dense and firm; to bring together into one close mass or body; to make firm or establish (power).—*v.i.* To grow firm and hard; to unite and become solid.—*a.* Formed into a solid mass. (*Tenn.*).—**consolidation,** kon•sol′id•ā″shon, *n.* The act of consolidating; a making or process of becoming solid; the act of forming into a firm compact mass, body, or system.—**consols,** kon′solz, *n. pl.* [Contr. for *consolidated annuities.*] A term used to denote a considerable portion of the public debt of Britain, more correctly known as the three per cent consolidated annuities.

consonance, consonancy, kon′sō•nans, kon′sō•nan•si, *n.* [L. *consonantia*, from *consono*, to sound together—*con*, and *sono*, to sound. SOUND.] Accord or agreement of sounds; *mus.* an accord of sounds which produces an agreeable sensation in the ear, as the third, fifth, and octave; hence, agreement; accord; congruity; consistency; suitableness. —**consonant,** kon′so•nant, *a.* Like in sound; agreeing generally; according; congruous; consistent: followed by *to* or *with*.—*n.* A letter that receives its proper sound only in connection with a vowel; one of the closings or junctions of the organs of speech, which precede or follow the openings of the organs with which the vowels are uttered.—**consonantal,** kon•so•nant′al, *a.* Relating to or partaking of the nature of a consonant.—**consonantly,** kon′so•nant•li, *adv.* In a consonant manner; consistently; in agreement.

consort, kon′sort, *n.* [L. *consors*—*con*, and *sors*, a lot. SORT.] A partner;

an intimate associate; particularly, a wife or husband; *naut.* any vessel keeping company with another.—*Queen consort*, the wife of a king, as distinguished from a *queen regnant*, who rules alone, and a *queen dowager*, the widow of a king.—*v.i.* (kon•sort′). To associate; to unite in company; to keep company: followed by *with.*—*v.t.*‡ To marry; to unite in company; to accompany.

conspectus, kon•spek′tus, *n.* [L.] A comprehensive view of a subject; an abstract or sketch.

conspicuous, kon•spik′ū•us, *a.* [L. *conspicuus*, from *conspicio*, to look or see—*con*, and *specio*, to see. SPECIES.] Obvious or prominent to the eye; easy to be seen; manifest; clearly or extensively known, perceived, or understood; eminent; distinguished (*conspicuous* abilities).—**conspicuously,** kon•spik′ū•us•li, *adv.* In a conspicuous manner; in a manner to be clearly seen; prominently; eminently; remarkably.—**conspicuousness,** kon•spik′ū•us•nes, *n.* The state of being conspicuous.

conspire, kon•spīr′, *v.i.*—*conspired, conspiring*. [L. *conspiro*, to plot—*con*, and *spiro*, to breathe; lit. to breathe together.] To agree by oath, covenant, or otherwise to commit a crime; to plot; to form a secret plot; to hatch treason; to agree, concur, or conduce to one end (circumstances *conspired* to defeat the plan).—*v.t.* To plot; to plan; to devise; to contrive; to concur to produce.—**conspiracy,** kon•spir′a•si, *n.* [L. *conspiratio*, from *conspiro*.] A secret combination of men for an evil purpose; an agreement or combination to commit some crime in concert; a plot; concerted treason.—**conspirator, conspirer,** kon•spir′at•ėr, kon•spī′rėr, *n.* One who conspires; one who engages in a plot to commit a crime, particularly treason.

constable, kun′sta•bl, *n.* [O.Fr. *conestable*, from L. *comes stabuli*, count of the stable.] An officer of high rank in several of the medieval monarchies; the keeper or governor of a castle belonging to the king or to a great baron; now usually a peace officer; a police officer.—**constableship,** kun′sta•bl•ship, *n.* The office of a constable.—**constabulary,** kon•stab′ū•le•ri, *a.* Pertaining to constables; consisting of constables.—*n.* The body of constables of a district, city, or country.

constant, kon′stant, *a.* [L. *constans*, pp. of *consto*—*con*, and *sto*, to stand.] Not undergoing change; continuing the same; permanent; immutable; fixed or firm in mind, purpose, or principle; not easily swayed; firm or unchanging in affection or duty; faithful; true; loyal.—*n.* That which is not subject to change; *math.* a quantity which remains the same throughout a problem.—**constantly,** kon′stant•li, *adv.* Firmly; steadily; invariably; continually; perseveringly.—**constancy,** kon′stan•si, *n.* [L. *constantia.*] Fixedness; a standing firm; immutability; steady, unshaken determination; fixedness or firmness of mind under sufferings; steadiness in attachments; perseverance in enterprise.

constellation, kon•stel•lā′shon, *n.* [L. *constellatio*—*con*, together, and *stella*, a star.] A group of the fixed stars to which a definite name has been given; an assemblage of splendors or excellences (a *constellation* of poetic genius).

consternation, kon•stėr•nā′shon, *n.* [L. *consternatio*, from *consterno*—*con*, and *sterno*, to throw or strike down.] Astonishment; amazement or horror that confounds the faculties, and incapacitates a person for consultation and execution; excessive terror, wonder, or surprise.

constipate, kon′sti•pāt, *v.i.*—*constipated, constipating*. [L. *constipo*, *constipatum*, to crowd together—*con*, together, and *stipo*, to crowd, to cram.] To stop up by filling a passage‡; to make costive.—**constipation,** kon•sti•pā′shon, *n.* A state of the bowels in which the evacuations do not take place as frequently as usual, or are very hard and expelled with difficulty; costiveness.

constituent, kon•stit′ū•ent, *a.* [L. *constituens*, ppr. of *constituo*—*con*, and *statuo*, to set. STATUE, STATUTE.] Forming or existing as an essential component or ingredient; composing, or making up as an essential part; component, elementary (the *constituent* parts of water); having the power of constituting or appointing.—*n.* One who or that which establishes or determines; that which constitutes or composes, as a part, or an essential part; an essential ingredient; one who elects or assists in electing another as his representative in a deliberative or administrative assembly; one who empowers another to transact business for him.—**constituency,** kon•stit′ū•en•si, *n.* A body of constituents who appoint or elect persons to any office or employment, especially to state or national offices.

constitute, kon′sti•tūt, *v.t.*—*constituted, constituting*. [L. *constituo*, *constitutum*—*con*, and *statuo*, to set. STATUE, STATUTE.] To settle, fix, or enact; to establish; to form or compose: to make up; to make a thing what it is; to appoint, depute, or elect to an office or employment; to make and empower.—**constitution,** kon•sti•tū′shon, *n.* The act of constituting, enacting, establishing, or appointing; the peculiar structure and connection of parts which makes or characterizes a system or body; natural condition of the human body as regards general health or strength; the established form of government in a state; a system of fundamental rules, principles, and ordinances for the government of a state or nation.—*Constitution of the U. S.*, the document, ratified in 1789, creating the federal system of government, with twenty-two amendments, embodying the fundamental law.—**constitutional,** kon•sti•tū′shon•al, *a.* Pertaining to a constitution; connected with the constitution, or natural condition of body or mind; consistent with the constitution of a state; authorized by the constitution or fundamental rules of a government.—*n.* A walk taken for health and exercise.—**constitutionalism,** kon•sti•tū′shon•al•izm, *n.* The theory or principle of constitutional rule or authority; constitutional principles; adherence to a constitution.—**constitutionalist,** kon•sti•tū′shon•al•ist, *n.* An adherent to the constitution of government; an upholder of the constitution of his country.—**constitutionality,** kon•sti•tū′shon•al″i•ti, *n.* The state of being constitutional.—**constitutionally,** kon•sti•tū′shon•al•li, *adv.* In a constitutional manner; in consistency with a national constitution; in accordance with the constitution of mind or body; naturally.—**constitutive,** kon′sti•tūt•iv, *a.* Forming, composing, enacting, or establishing; constituting; instituting. *Constitutively*, kon′sti•tūt•iv•li, *adv.* In a constitutive manner.

constrain, kon•strān′, *v.t.* [O.Fr. *constraindre*, Fr. *contraindre*, from L. *constringo*, to bind together—*con*, and *stringo*, to strain. STRAIN.] To compel or force; to urge with a power sufficient to produce the effect; to drive; to necessitate; to confine by force; to restrain, check, repress, confine, bind.—**constrainable,** kon•strā′na•bl, *a.* Capable of being constrained; liable to constraint or to restraint.—**constrainedly,** kon•strā′ned•li, *adv.* In a constrained manner; with constraint; by compulsion.—**constrainer,** kon•strā′nėr, *n.* One who constrains.—**constraint,** kon•strānt′, *n.* A constraining, compelling, or restraining; force; compulsion; restraint; confinement; feeling of reserve or being kept in check.

constrict, kon•strikt′, *v.t.* [L. *constringo, constrictum.* CONSTRAIN.] To draw together; to cramp; to contract or cause to shrink: said of canals, etc., of the body.—**constriction,** kon•strik′shon, *n.* The state of being constricted or drawn together as by some spasm, as distinguished from compression or the pressure of extraneous bodies.—**constrictive,** kon•strik′tiv, *a.* Tending to contract or compress.—**constrictor,** kon•strik′tėr, *n.* That which draws together or contracts; a muscle which draws together or closes an orifice of the body; one of the larger class of serpents which envelop and crush their prey in their folds.—**constringe,** kon•strinj′, *v.t.*—*constringed, constringing*. To strain into a narrow compass; to constrict.—**constringent,** kon•strin′jent, *a.* Having the quality of constringing.

construct, kon•strukt′, *v.t.* [L. *construo*, *constructum*—*con*, and *struo*, to pile up. STRUCTURE.] To put together the parts of in their proper place and order; to build up; to erect; to form; to form by the mind.—**constructer, constructor,** kon•struk′ter, *n.* One who constructs or frames.—**construction,** kon•struk′shon, *n.* [L. *constructio.*] The act of building, devising, or forming; fabrication; the form of building; the manner of putting together the parts; structure; conformation; the arrangement and connection of words in a sentence; syntactical arrangement; attributed sense or meaning to language; explanation; interpretation; the manner of describing a figure or problem in geometry for the purpose of any demonstration.—**constructional,** kon•struk′shon•al, *a.* Pertaining to construction; deduced from construction or interpretation. —**constructive,** kon•struk′tiv, *a.* Pertaining to construction or building; having ability to construct; created or deduced by construction or mode of interpretation.—**constructively,** kon•struk′tiv•li, *adv.* In a constructive manner, by way of construction or interpretation; by fair inference.—**constructiveness,** kon•struk′tiv•nes, *n.* State of being constructive; *phren.* a faculty supposed to produce constructive power.

construe, kon′strö, *v.t.—construed, construing.* [L. *construo.* CONSTRUCT.] To arrange words so that their grammatical bearing and meaning are apprehended; to analyze grammatically; as applied to a foreign language, to translate; to interpret or draw a certain meaning from; to explain (to *construe* actions wrongly).

consubstantial, consubstantiate, kon•sub•stan′shal, kon•sub•stan′shi•āt, *a.* [L. *consubstantialis—con* and *substantia.* SUBSTANCE.] Having the same substance or essence; coessential.—**consubstantiality,** kon•sub•stan′shi•al″i•ti, *n.* The quality of being consubstantial; the existence of more than one in the same substance; participation of the same nature.—**consubstantially,** kon•sub•stan′shi•al•li, *adv.* In a consubstantial manner.—**consubstantiate,**† kon•sub•stan′shi•āt, *v.t.* and *i.—consubstantiated, consubstantiating.* To unite in one common substance or nature, or regard as so united.—**consubstantiation,** kon•sub•stan′shi•ā″shon, *n.* The union of the body of the blessed Saviour with the sacramental elements; impanation.

consuetude,† kon′swi•tūd, *n.* [L. *consuetudo,* custom. CUSTOM.] Custom; usage.—**consuetudinary,** kon•swi•tūd′in•e•ri, *a.* Customary.—*Consuetudinary law,* in contradistinction to written or statutory law, is that law which is derived by immemorial custom from antiquity.

consul, kon′sul, *n.* [L. *consul—con,* together, and root seen also in *consulo, consultum,* to consult.] The title of the two chief magistrates of the ancient Roman republic, invested with legal authority for one year; the title given to the three supreme magistrates of the French republic after the dissolution of the Directory in 1799; a person commissioned by a sovereign or state to reside in a foreign country as an agent or representative, to protect the interests (especially the commercial interests) of his own country.—**consular,** kon′sul•ėr, *a.* Pertaining to a consul.—**consulate,** kon′sul•it, *n.* [L. *consulatus.*] The office or jurisdiction of a consul; the official dwelling or residence of a consul; consular government.—**consulship,** kon′sul•ship, *n.* The office of a consul, or the term of his office.

consult, kon•sult′, *v.i.* [L. *consulto,* intens. from *consulo,* to consult.] To seek the opinion or advice of another; to take counsel together; to deliberate in common.—*v.t.* To ask advice of; to seek the opinion of as a guide to one's own judgment; to have recourse to for information or instruction; to regard or have reference or respect to, in judging or acting (to *consult* one's safety, one's means.) —**consultation,** kon•sul•tā′shon, *n.* The act of consulting; deliberation of two or more persons with a view to some decision; a meeting of experts, as physicians or counsel, to consult about a specific case.—**consultatory,** kon•sult′a•tō•ri, *a.* Having the privilege of consulting or deliberating; deliberative: often opposed to *executive.*—**consultant,** kon•sul′tent, *n.* One who consults.—**consulting,** kon•sult′ing, *a.* In the practice of giving advice; making the giving of advice one's business (a *consulting* attorney); used for consultations (*consulting* room).—**consultive,**† kon•sult′iv, *a.* Consultatory; advisory.

consume, kon•sūm′, *v.t.—consumed, consuming.* [L. *consumo,* to take wholly or completely—*con,* intens., and *sumo,* to take, seen also in *assume, resume,* etc.] To destroy by separating the component parts and annihilating the form of the substance, as by fire or by eating; to destroy by dissipating or by use; to expend; to waste; to spend; to pass (time); to waste slowly; to bring to ruin.—*v.i.* To waste away slowly; to be exhausted.—**consumable,** kon•sūm′a•bl, *a.* That may be consumed, destroyed, dissipated, or wasted.—**consumer,** kon•sūm′ėr, *n.* One who or that which consumes; *pol. econ.* one who uses commodities as distinguished from the producer of them.—**consumption,** kon•sum′shon, *n.* [L. *consumptio.*] The act of consuming, or state of being consumed; a progressive wasting of the body, especially from pulmonary tuberculosis; a decline; *pol. econ.* the use or expenditure of the products of industry, or of all things having an exchangeable value.—**consumptive,** kon•sum′tiv, *a.* Consuming, wasting, or exhausting; having the quality of consuming or dissipating; affected with or having a tendency to the disease consumption.—**consumptively,** kon•sum′tiv•li, *adv.* In a consumptive manner.—**consumptiveness,** kon•sum′tiv•nes, *n.* A state of being consumptive or a tendency to consumption.

consumedly, kon•sūm′ed•li, *adv.* [*Consumed* formerly had sense of deuced, confounded.] Greatly; hugely; deucedly.

consummate, kon′sum•āt, *v.t.—consummated, consummating.* [L. *consummo, consummatus—con,* and *summa,* sum. SUM.] To finish by completing what was intended; to perfect; to bring or carry to the utmost point or degree; to make complete.—*a.* (kon•sum′at). Complete; perfect; carried to the utmost extent or degree; thorough.—**consummately,** kon•sum′at•li, *adv.* Completely; perfectly.—**consummation,** kon•sum•ā′shon, *n.* [L. *consummatio.*] Completion; end; termination; perfection of a work, process, or scheme. —**consummative,** kon•sum′at•iv, *a.* Pertaining to consummation; consummating; final.

contact, kon′takt, *n.* [L. *contactus,* from *contingo, contactum,* to touch—*con,* and *tango* (root *tag*), to touch, whence also E. *tact, tangent,* etc.] A state or condition of touching; touch; proximity or association; connection; a junction of two electrical conductors through which current flows; a carrier of contagion. —*v.t.* To bring into contact; to get in touch with.—*v.i.* To be in contact.

contagion, kon•tā′jon, *n.* [L. *contagio —con,* and root *tag.* CONTACT.] The communication of a disease by contact; infection; that which propagates mischief (the *contagion* of vice); pestilential influence.—**contagium,** kon•tā′ji•um, *n.* That which carries the infectious element in diseases from one person to another. —**contagious,** kon•tā′jus, *a.* Containing or generating contagion; communicated by contagion or contact; catching; containing contagion; containing mischief that may be propagated; spreading from one to another, or exciting like affections in others (*contagious* fear).—**contagiously,** kon•tā′jus•li, *adv.* By contagion.—**contagiousness,** kon•tā′jus•nes, *n.*

contain, kon•tān′, *v.t.* [L. *contineo—con,* and *teneo,* to hold, seen also in *attain, retain, tenant, tempt,* etc.] To hold within fixed limits; to comprehend; to comprise; to include; to hold or be capable of holding; to comprise, as a writing; to have for contents; to keep in check an enemy's forces; to keep occupied, to hinder progress.—*To contain one's self,* to restrain one's feelings or prevent them showing themselves.—**containable,** kon•tā′na•bl, *a.* Capable of being contained or comprised.—**container,** kon•tā′nėr, *n.* One who, or that which, contains.

contaminate, kon•tam′in•āt, *v.t.—contaminated, contaminating.* [L. *contamino, contaminatum,* from *contamen,* contact, contamination contr. for *contagmen,* from root of *tango,* to touch. CONTAGION, CONTACT.] To defile; to pollute: usually in a figurative sense; to sully; to tarnish; to taint.—**contamination,** kon•tam′in•ā″shon, *n.* The act of contaminating, what contaminates; pollution; defilement; taint.

contemn, kon•tem′, *v.t.* [L. *contemno, contemptum,* to despise (whence also *contempt*)—*con,* intens., and *temno,* to despise.] To despise; to consider and treat as mean and despicable;

to scorn; to reject with disdain.—**contemner,** kon•tem′ėr, *n.* One who contemns; a despiser; a scorner.

contemplate, kon′tem•plāt, *v.t.*—*contemplated, contemplating.* [L. *contemplor, contemplatus,* to mark out a *templum,* to view attentively, contemplate—*con,* and *templum,* the space marked out by the augur as that within which the omens should be observed. TEMPLE.] To view or consider with continued attention; to study; to meditate on; to consider or have in view in reference to a future act or event; to intend.—*v.i.* To think studiously; to study; to muse; to mediate.—**contemplation,** kon•tem•plā′shon, *n.* [L. *contemplatio.*] The act of contemplating; meditation; continued attention of the mind to a particular subject; a looking forward to the doing or happening of something; expectation.—**contemplative,** kon•tem′plat•iv, *a.* Given to contemplation, or continued application of the mind to a subject; thoughtful; meditative; having the power of thought or meditation (the *contemplative* faculty).—**contemplatively,** kon•tem′plat•iv•li, *adv.* With contemplation; thoughtfully. —**contemplativeness,** kon•tem′plat•iv•nes, *n.* State of being contemplative.—**contemplator,** kon″tem•plā′ter, *n.* One who contemplates.

contemporary, kon•tem′po•re•ri, *a.* [L. *con,* and *tempus, temporis,* time.] Living, existing, or occurring at the same time: of persons and things.—*n.* One who lives at the same time with another. —**contemporaneous,** kon•tem′po•rā″nē•us, *a.* [L. *contemporaneus.*] Contemporary: most commonly of things.—**contemporaneously,** kon•tem′po•rā″ni•us•li, *adv.* At the same time with some other event.—**contemporaneousness,** kon•tem′po•rā″ni•us•nes, *n.* Contemporaneity.

contempt, kon•temt′, *n.* [L. *contemptus,* from *contemno.* CONTEMN.] The feeling that causes us to consider and treat something as mean, vile, and worthless; disdain; scorn for what is mean; the state of being despised; *law,* disobedience to the rules or orders of a court, or a disturbance of its proceedings.—**contemptibility,** kon•tem′ti•bil″i•ti, *n.* Quality of being contemptible.—**contemptible,** kon•tem′ti•bl, *a.* [L. *contemptibilis.*] Worthy of contempt; deserving scorn or disdain; despicable; mean; vile; despised or neglected from insignificance (a *contemptible* plant). ∴ *Contemptible,* deserving of being scorned or looked down upon from meanness or worthlessness; *despicable,* implies a stronger feeling, scorn, and loathing, often on moral grounds; *paltry* or *pitiful,* too insignificant to waken any active feeling.—**contemptibleness,** kon•tem′ti•bl•nes, *n.* The state of being contemptible.—**contemptibly,** kon•tem′ti•bli, *adv.* In a contemptible manner; meanly; in a manner deserving of contempt.—**contemptuous,** kon•tem′tū•us, *a.* Manifesting or expressing contempt or disdain; scornful; apt to despise; haughty; insolent.—**contemptuously,** kon•tem′tū•us•li, *adv.* In a contemptuous manner; with scorn or disdain; despitefully. —**contemptuousness,** kon•tem′tū•us•nes, *n.* Disposition to contempt; scornfulness; haughtiness.

contend, kon•tend′, *v.i.* [L. *contendo,* to strive, contend—*con,* intens., and *tendo,* stretch; whence E. *tend, tent, attend, pretend*; root also in *tender.*] To strive; to struggle in opposition; absolutely, or with *against* or *with* preceding an object; to use earnest efforts to obtain, or to defend and preserve: with *for* before the object. —**contender,** kon•tend′ėr, *n.* One who contends; a combatant or rival. —**contention,** kon•ten′shon, *n.* [L. *contentio.*] The act of contending; contest, struggle, or strife; strife in words; debate; angry contest; quarrel; controversy; competition; emulation; a point that a person maintains, or the argument in support of it.—**contentious,** kon•ten′shus, *a.* [Fr. *contentieux.*] Apt to contend; given to angry debate; quarrelsome; perverse; relating to or characterized by contention or strife; involving contention.—**contentiously,** kon•ten′shus•li, *adv.* In a contentious manner.—**contentiousness,** kon•ten′shus•nes, *n.* The state or quality of being contentious; a disposition to contend; peevishness; quarrelsomeness.

content, kon•tent′, *a.* [L. *contentus,* from *contineo,* to contain—*con,* and *teneo,* to hold. CONTAIN.] Having a mind at peace; satisfied, so as not to repine, object, or oppose; not disturbed; contented; easy.—*v.t.* To make content; to quiet, so as to stop complaint or opposition; to appease; to make easy in any situation; to please or gratify.—*n.* The state of being contented; contentment.—*n.* (kon•tent′ or kon′tent.) That which is contained; the thing or things held, included, or comprehended within a limit or line; *geom.* the area or quantity of matter or space included in certain lines. [Usually in the pl.]—*Table of contents,* a summary or index of all the matters treated in a book.—**contented,** kon•tent′ed, *a.* Satisfied with what one has or with one's circumstances; easy in mind; not complaining, opposing, or demanding more.—**contentedly,** kon•tent′ed•li, *adv.* In a contented manner; quietly; without concern.—**contentedness,** kon•tent′ed•nes, *n.* State of being contented.—**contentment,** kon•tent′ment, *n.* [Fr. *contentement.*] The state or feeling of being contented; content; a resting or satisfaction of mind without disquiet or craving for something else; acquiescence in one's own circumstances. ∴ *Contentment* is passive, *satisfaction* is active. The former implies the absence of fretting or craving, the latter an active feeling of pleasure.

contention, etc. See CONTEND.

conterminous, kon•tėr′min•us, *a.* [L. *conterminus*—*con,* and *terminus,* a border.] Terminating at a common point; having common boundaries or limits; touching at the boundary.

contest, kon•test′, *v.t.* [Fr. *contester,* from L. *contestari,* to call to witness, to call witnesses—*con,* together, and *testis,* a witness. DETEST.] To make a subject of contention or dispute; to enter into a struggle for; to struggle to defend; to controvert: to oppose; to call in question; to dispute (statements).—*v.i.*† To strive; to contend; followed by *with.*—*n.* (kon′test). A struggle for victory, superiority, or in defense; struggle in arms; dispute; debate; controversy; strife in argument.—**contestable,** kon•tes′ta•bl, *a.* Capable of being disputed or debated; disputable; controvertible.—**contestant,**† kon•tes′tant, *n.* One who contests.

context, kon′tekst, *n.* [L. *contextus,* connection, from *contexo*—*con,* and *texo,* to weave.] The parts of a book or other writing which immediately precede or follow a sentence quoted. —**contexture,** kon•teks′chėr, *n.* The manner of interweaving several parts into one body; the disposition and union of the constituent parts of a thing with respect to each other; constitution.

contiguous, kon•tig′ū•us, *a.* [L. *contiguus*—*con,* and *tango,* to touch. CONTACT.] Situated so as to touch; meeting or joining at the surface or border; close together; neighboring; bordering or adjoining.—**contiguity,** kon•ti•gū′i•ti, *n.* The state of being contiguous; closeness of situation or place; a linking together, as of a series of objects.—**contiguously,** kon•tig′ū•us•li, *adv.* In a contiguous manner; without intervening space.—**contiguousness,** kon•tig′ū•us•nes, *n.* The state or quality of being contiguous; contiguity.

continence, continency, kon′ti•nens, kon′ti•nen•si, *n.* [L. *continentia,* from *contineo,* to hold or withhold. CONTAIN.] The restraint which a person imposes upon his desires and passions; the restraint of the passion for sexual enjoyment; forbearance of lewd pleasures; chastity.—**continent,** kon′ti•nent, *a.* [L. *continens.*] Refraining from sexual commerce; chaste; also moderate or temperate in general.—**continently,** kon′ti•nent•li, *adv.* In a continent manner; chastely.

continent, kon′ti•nent, *n.* [L. *continens,* a continent or mainland, lit. land holding together.] An arbitrary term applied to a connected tract of land of great extent; one of the great divisions of the land on the globe.—**Continental,** kon•ti•nent′al, *a.* Pertaining or relating to the continent of Europe; pertaining to the confederated colonies at the time of the American Revolution; a soldier in the Continental Army; [*not cap.*] the least bit;—*not worth a Continental*—from the low value of Continental currency at the time.

contingency, kon•tin′jen•si, *n.* [L. *contingens,* ppr. of *contingo*—to fall or happen to—*con,* and *tango,* to touch. CONTACT.] The quality of being contingent; the possibility of happening or coming to pass; fortuitousness; something that may happen; a possible occurrence; a fortuitous event, or one which may occur. Also **contingence,** kon•tin′jens.—**contingent,** kon•tin′jent, *a.* Possibly occurring; liable to occur; not determinable by any certain rule; accidental; casual; dependent upon what is undetermined or unknown; dependent upon the happening of something else.—**contingent,** kon•tin′jent, *n.* A contingency‡; a quota or suitable proportion, as of troops furnished for some joint enterprise.—**contingently,** kon•tin′jent•li, *adv.* In a contingent manner.

continue, kon•tin′ū, *v.i.—continued, continuing.* [L. *continuo,* to carry on, to keep on, continue, from *continuus,* unbroken, continuous—*con,* together, and *teneo,* to hold. CONTAIN.] To remain in a state or place; to abide for any time indefinitely; to last; to endure; to be permanent; to persevere; to be steadfast or constant in any course.—*v.t.* To protract or lengthen out; not to cease from or to terminate; to extend; to make longer; to persevere in; not to ease to do or use; to suffer or cause to remain as before.—**continuable,** kon•tin′ū•a•bl, *a.* Capable of being continued—**continual,** kon•tin′ū•al, *a.* [Fr. *continuel;* L. *continuus.*] Proceeding without interruption or cessation; not intermitting; unceasing; of frequent recurrence; often repeated; incessant. ∴ Syn. under CONTINUOUS.—**continually,** kon•tin′ū•al•li, *adv.* Without pause or cessation; unceasingly; very often; in repeated succession; from time to time. Syn. under CONTINUOUSLY.—**continuance,** kon•tin′ū•ans, *n.* The state or continuing or remaining in a particular state or course; permanence, as of habits, condition, or abode; a state of lasting: constancy; perseverance; duration; the act of continuing; continuation. ∴ Syn. under CONTINUATION.—**continuation,** kon•tin′ū•a″shon, *n.* [L. *continuatio.*] The act of continuing or prolonging; extension or carrying on to a further point; the portion continued or extended; a prolongation or extension. ∴ *Continuation* is the act of continuing (also the part prolonged), *continuance* the state of continuing.—**continuative,** kon•tin′ū•āt•iv, *a.* Tending to continue, extend, prolong, or persist.—*n.* What is continuative. —**continuator, continuer,** kon•tin′ū•āt•ėr, kon•tin′ū•ėr, *n.* One who or that which continues; one who carries forward anything that had been begun by another.—**continued,** kon•tin′ūd, *p.* and *a.* Protracted or extended; proceeding without cessation; unceasing.—*Continued fraction,* one whose denominator is an integer with a fraction, which latter fraction has for its denominator an integer with a fraction, and so on.—**continuity,** kon•ti•nū′i•ti, *n.* [L. *continuitas.*] Connection uninterrupted; cohesion; close union of parts; unbroken texture.—**continuous,** kon•tin′ū•us, *a.* [L. *continuus.*] Joined without intervening space or time; proceeding from something else without interruption or without apparent interruption; uninterrupted; unbroken. ∴ *Continuous* means unbroken, uninterrupted; *continual* does not imply unceasing continuity, but the habitual or repeated renewals of an act, state, etc. *Perpetual* is *continuous* with the idea of lastingness.—**continuously,** kon•tin′ū•us•li, *adv.* In a continuous manner; in continuation; without interruption. ∴ *Continuously,* like its adjective, denotes unbroken continuity, *continually* close succession.—**continuousness,** kon•tin′ū•us•nes, *n.* State or quality of being continuous.

contort, kon•tort′, *v.t.* [L. *contorqueo, contortum,* to twist—*con,* intens., and *torqueo, tortum,* to twist, whence also *torture, torment, extort,* etc.] To twist together; to bend or curve in irregular forms; to writhe.—**contortion,** kon•tor′shon, *n.* [L. *contortio.*] The act of contorting, or state of being contorted; a twist or twisting; a writhing, especially spasmodic writhing; a wry motion or position; *med.* a twisting or wresting of a limb or member of the body out of its natural situation.—**contortionist,** kon•tor′shon•ist, *n.* An acrobat who practices contortions of the body.

contour, kon′tör, *n.* [Fr. *contour*—*con,* and *tour,* a turn, revolution, turner's lathe, from L. *tornus,* Gr. *tornos,* a lathe; hence also Fr. *tourner,* E. *turn.*] The outline of a figure or body; the line that defines or bounds a solid body; the periphery considered as distinct from the object.—*v.t.* To delineate or draw by the contour.

contraband, kon′tra•band, *a.* [Fr. *contrebande*—It. *contra,* against, and *bando,* a proclamation, a ban. BAN.] Prohibited or excluded by proclamation, law, or treaty.—*Contraband goods* are such as are prohibited to be imported or exported, either by the laws of a particular kingdom or state, or by the law of nations, or by special treaties.—*n.* Illegal or prohibited traffic; articles prohibited to be imported or exported.—**contrabandist,** kon′tra•band•ist, *n.* One who deals in contraband goods. —**contrabass,** kon′tra•bās, *n.* [It.] The largest of the violin species of instruments, of which it forms the lowest bass; usually called the double bass.

contract, kon•trakt′, *v.t.* [Fr. *contracter,* L. *contraho, contractum—con,* and *traho,* to draw, whence also *tract, treat. trace, train,* etc.] To draw together or closer; to draw into a less compass, either in length or breadth; to abridge, narrow, lessen; to wrinkle; to betroth or affiance; to bring on, incur, acquire (vicious habits, debts); to shorten by omission of a letter or syllable.—*v.i.* To be drawn together; to become shorter or narrower; to shrink; to bargain; to make a mutual agreement as between two or more persons.—*n.* (kon′trakt). An agreement or mutual promise upon lawful consideration or cause which binds the parties to a performance; a bargain; a compact; the act by which a man and woman are betrothed each to the other; the writing which contains the agreement of parties.—**contractibility, contractibleness,** kon•trakt′i•bil″i•ti, kon•trakt′i•bl•nes, *n.* Quality of being contractible.—**contractible,** kon•trakt′i•bl, *a.* Capable of contraction. —**contractile,** kon•trakt′il, *a.* Tending to contract; having the power of shortening or of drawing into smaller dimensions.—**contractility,** kon•trakt•il′i•ti, *n.* The inherent quality or force by which bodies shrink or contract; *physiol.* that vital property which gives to certain parts the power of contracting.—**contraction,** kon•trak′shon, *n.* [L. *contractio.*] The act of contracting, drawing together, or shrinking; the act of shortening, narrowing, or lessening dimensions by causing the parts to approach nearer to each other; the state of being contracted; an abbreviation employed with the view of saving labor in writing, as *recd.* for *received;* the shortening of a word by the omission of one or more letters or syllables.—**contractive,** kon•trakt′iv, *a.* Tending to contract.—**contractor,** kon•trakt′ėr, *n.* One who contracts; one of the parties to a bargain; one who covenants to do anything for another; one who contracts to perform any work or service, or to furnish supplies, at a certain price or rate.

contradict, kon•tra•dikt′, *v.t.* [L. *contradico, contradictum—contra,* and *dico,* to speak, whence *diction,* etc.] To assert not to be so, or to assert to be the contrary to what has been asserted; to meet (a person, an assertion) with a statement quite different or opposite; to deny; to be directly contrary to.—**contradictable,** kon•tra•dik′ta•bl, *a.* Capable of being contradicted; deniable; disputable.—**contradicter,** kon•tra•dik′tėr, *n.* One who contradicts or denies.—**contradiction,** kon•tra•dik′shon, *n.* [L. *contradictio.*] The act of contradicting; an assertion of the contrary to what has been said or affirmed; denial; contrary declaration; direct opposition or repugnancy; inconsistency with itself; incongruity or contrariety of things, words, thoughts, or propositions; the person who, or thing that, contradicts or is inconsistent with him, her, or its self.—**contradictious,** kon•tra•dik′shus, *a.* Contradictory; given to contradict.—**contradictive,**† kon•tra•dik′tiv, *a.* Contradictory; inconsistent.—**contradictorily,** kon•tra•dik′tor•i•li, *adv.* In a contradictory way; in a manner inconsistent with itself.—**contradictoriness,** kon•tra•dik′tor•i•nes, *n.* The state or character of being contradictory; contrariety in assertion or effect.—**contradictory,** kon•tra•-dik′tor•i, *a.* Contradicting; given to contradict; affirming the contrary; implying a denial of what has been asserted; inconsistent with one another; directly opposite.—*n.* A proposition which denies or opposes another in all its terms.

contradistinction, kon′tra•dis•-tingk″shon, *n.* Distinction by opposite qualities or characteristics; a setting or bringing (terms, notions) into contrast or opposition.—**contradistinctive,** kon′tra•dis•tingkt″iv, *a.* Having the quality of, or characterized by, contradistinction; opposite in qualities.—*n.* A mark of contradistinction.—**contradistinguish,** kon′tra•dis•ting″gwish, *v.t.* To distinguish or set distinctly forward, not merely by different but by opposite qualities; used of ideas, terms, etc.

contraindicate, kon•tra•in′di•kāt, *v.t.* or *i.*—*contraindicated, contraindicating.* To indicate, suggest, or point to something contrary or opposite.—**contraindication,** kon•tra•in′di•kā″-shon, *n.* What contraindicates.

contralto, kon•tral′tō, *n.* [It.] *Mus.* the lowest voice of a woman or boy, called also the *Alto*; generally a female voice below the mezzo soprano and soprano; also the countertenor; the person who sings with this voice.—*a.* Pertaining to, or possessed of the quality of, contralto.

contraposition, kon′tra•po•zi″shon, *n.* A placing over against; opposite position.

contrapuntal, kon•tra•punt′al, *a.* Pertaining to counterpoint.—**contrapuntist,** kon•tra•punt′ist, *n.* One skilled in counterpoint.

contrary, kon′tra•ri, *a.* [L. *contrarius*, from *contra*, against; Fr. *contraire*.] Opposite; adverse; moving against or in an opposite direction (*contrary* winds); contradictory; not merely different, but inconsistent or repugnant; perverse or froward (*colloq.*). [This adjective, in many phrases, is to be treated grammatically as an adverb, or as an adjective referring to a sentence or affirmation; as, this happened *contrary* to my expectations.]—*n.* A thing that is contrary or of opposite qualities; a proposition contrary to another, or fact contrary to what is alleged.—*On the contrary*, on the other hand; quite oppositely.—*To the contrary*, to an opposite purpose or fact.—**contrariety,** kon•-tra•rī′e•ti, *n.* [L. *contrarietas*.] The state or quality of being contrary; opposition in fact, essence, quality, or principle; repugnance; inconsistency; quality or position destructive of its opposite.—**contrarily,** kon′tra•-ri•li, *adv.* In a contrary manner; in opposition; on the other hand; in opposite ways.—**contrariness,** kon•-trâr′i•nes, *n.* Contrariety; opposition.—**contrariwise,** kon′tra•ri•wīz, *adv.* On the contrary; oppositely; on the other hand (N.T.).

contrast, kon•trast′, *v.t.* [Fr. *contraster*, from L. *contra*, opposite, and *stare*, to stand.] To set in opposition so as to show the difference between, and to exhibit the excellence of the one and the defects of the other; to compare so as to point out dissimilarity.—*v.i.* To stand in contrast or opposition to something else; followed by *with*.—*n.* (kon′trast). The viewing or comparing of things together in order to render any difference between them more vividly marked; comparison by contrariety of qualities; opposition or dissimilitude of things or qualities.

contravallation, kon′tra•val•lā″shon, *n.* [Fr. *contrevallation*—L. *contra*, against, and *vallum*, a rampart.] *Fort.* a chain of redoubts and breastworks raised by the besiegers about a fortress to prevent sorties of the garrison.

contravene, kon•tra•vēn′, *v.t.*—*contravened, contravening.* [L. *contravenio*—*contra*, against, and *venio*, to come, as in *convene*, etc.] To come or be in conflict with; to obstruct in operation; to act so as to violate; to transgress.—**contravener,** kon•-tra•vē′nėr, *n.* One who contravenes.—**contravention,** kon•tra•ven′shon, *n.* The act of contravening, violating, or transgressing; violation; opposition.

contre-temps, kon•tre•täṅ′, *n.* [Fr.] An unexpected and untoward accident; an embarrassing conjuncture; a hitch.

contribute, kon•trib′ūt, *v.t.*—*contributed, contributing.* [L. *contribuo*—*con*, and *tribuo*, to grant, assign, or impart. TRIBE, TRIBUTE.] To give or grant in common with others; to give to a common stock or for a common purpose; to pay as a share.—*v.i.* To give a part; to lend a portion of power, aid, or influence; to have a share in any act or effect; with *to*.—**contributable,** kon•trib′-ūt•a•bl. *a.* Capable of being contributed.—**contribution,** kon•tri•bū′-shon, *n.* The act of contributing; the payment of a share along with others; that which is given to a common stock or purpose, either by an individual or by many; the sum or thing contributed.—**contributive,** kon•trib′ūt•iv, *a.* Tending to contribute; contributing.—**contributor,** kon•trib′ūt•ėr, *n.* One who contributes, one who gives or pays money to a common fund; one who gives aid to a common purpose.—**contributory,** kon•trib′ū•to•ri, *a.* Contributing to the same stock or purpose; bringing assistance to some joint design, or increase to some common stock.—*n.* A contributor.

contrite, kon′trīt, *a.* [L. *contritus*, from *contero*, to break or bruise—*con*, and *tero*, to bruise. TRITE.] Brokenhearted for sin; deeply affected with grief and sorrow for sin; humble; penitent,—*n.* A contrite person; a penitent.—**contritely,** kon′-trīt•li, *adv.* In a contrite manner; with penitence.—**contriteness, contrition,** kon′trīt•nes, kon•trish′on, *n.* [L. *contritio*.] Grief of heart for sin; sincere penitence.

contrive, kon•trīv′, *v.t.*—*contrived, contriving.* [O.Fr. *controver*, Fr. *controuver*, to invent, to fabricate—*con*, and *trouver*, to find.] To invent; to devise; to plan.—*v.i.* To form schemes or designs; to plan; to scheme.—**contrivable,** kon•trī′va•-bl, *a.* Capable of being contrived, planned, invented, or devised.—**contrivance,** kon•trī′vans, *n.* The act of contriving, inventing, devising, or planning; the thing contrived; an artifice; scheme; invention.—**contriver,** kon•trī′vėr, *n.* One who contrives, plans, or devises.

control, kon•trōl′, *n.* [Fr. *contrôle*, lit. counter-roll, from *contre*, against, and *rôle*, a roll, list. ROLL.] Restraining power or influence; check; restraint; power; authority; government; command.—*v.t.*—*controlled, controlling.* To exercise control over; to hold in restraint or check; to subject to authority; to regulate; to govern; to subjugate.—**controllable,** kon•trōl′a•bl, *a.* Capable of being controlled, checked, or restrained; subject to command.—**controller,** kon•trōl′ėr, *n.* One who controls; one that has the power or authority to govern or control; one who governs or regulates; an officer appointed to keep a counter register of accounts, or to oversee, control, or verify the accounts of other officers; a comptroller.—**controllership,** kon•trōl′ėr•ship, *n.* The office of a controller; comptrollership.—**controlment,** kon•trōl′ment, *n.* The power or act of controlling; control; restraint.

controvert, kon′tro•vėrt, *v.t.* [L. *contra*, against, and *verto*, *versum*, to turn.] To dispute; to oppose by reasoning; to contend against in words or writings; to deny and attempt to disprove or confute.—**controversial,** kon•tro•vėr′shal, *a.* Relating to controversy.—**controversialist,** kon•tro•vėr′shal•ist, *n.* One who carries on a controversy; a disputant.—**controversially,** kon•-tro•vėr′shal•li, *adv.* In a controversial manner.—**controversy,** kon′-tro•vėr•si, *n.* [L. *controversia*.] Debate; agitation of contrary opinions; a disputation or discussion between parties, particularly in writing; a litigation.—**controverter,** kon′tro•-vėr•tėr, *n.* One who controverts; a controversial writer.—**controvertible,** kon•tro•vėr′ti•bl, *a.* Capable of being controverted or disputed; disputable; not too evident to exclude difference of opinion.

contumacious, kon•tū•mā′shus, *a.* [L. *contumax*, *contumacis*—*con*, and *tumeo*, to swell, seen also in *tumid*, *tumult*, *contumely*.] Resisting legitimate authority; disobedient; froward or perverse; *law*, wilfully disobedient to the orders of a court.—**contumaciously,** kon•tū•mā′shus•li, *adv.* In a contumacious manner; obstinately; stubbornly; in disobedience of orders.—**contumaciousness,** kon•tū•mā′shus•nes, *n.* State of being contumacious; obstinacy; perverseness; contumacy.—**contumacy,** kon′tū•ma•si, *n.* [L. *contumacia*.] Contumacious conduct; character or state of being contumacious; willful and persistent resistance to legitimate authority; unyielding obstinacy; stubborn perverseness; *law*, wilful disregard of the orders of a court.

contumely, kon′tū•me•li, *n.* [L. *contumelia*, from *contumeo—con*, and *tumeo*. CONTUMACIOUS.] Haughtiness and contempt in language or behavior; contemptuous or insulting language; haughty insolence.—**contumelious,** kon•tū•mē′li•us, *a.* [L. *contumeliosus.*] Indicating or expressive of contumely; contemptuous; insolent; rude and sarcastic; disposed to utter reproach or insult; insolent; proudly rude.—**contumeliously,** kon•tū•mē′li•us•li, *adv.* In a contumelious manner; rudely; insolently.—**contumeliousness,** kon•tū•mē′li•us•nes, *n.* State of being contumelious.

contuse, kon•tūz′, *v.t.—contused, contusing.* [L. *contundo, contusum—con*, and *tundo*, to beat, same root as Skr. *tud*, to beat.] To wound or injure by bruising; to injure without breaking the flesh.—**contusion,** kon•tū′zhon, *n.* [L. *contusio.*] A severe bruise on the body; a hurt or injury as to the flesh or some part of the body without breaking of the skin, as by a blunt instrument or by a fall.

conundrum, ko•nun′drum, *n.* [Origin uncertain.] A sort of riddle, in which some odd resemblance is proposed for discovery between things quite unlike, the answer involving a pun.

convalescence, kon•va•les′ens, *n.* [L. *convalesco*, to grow stronger—*con*, and *valesco*, to get strength, *valeo*, to be strong. VALID, AVAIL.] The gradual recovery of health and strength after disease; the state of a person renewing his vigor after sickness or weakness.—**convalesce,** kon•va•les′, *v.i.—convalesced, convalescing.* To grow better after sickness; to recover health.—**convalescent,** kon•va•les′ent, *a.* Recovering health and strength after sickness or debility.—*n.* One who is recovering his health after sickness.

convection, kon•vek′shon, *n.* [L. *convectio*, from *conveho*, to convey.] The act of carrying or conveying; a process of transmission, as of heat or electricity by means of particles of matter affected by them.—**convective,** kon•vek′tiv, *a.* Resulting from or caused by convection.—**convectively,** kon•vek′tiv•li, *adv.* In a convective manner; by means of convection.

convene, kon•vēn′, *v.i.—convened, convening.* [L. *convenio—con*, and *venio*, *ventum*, to come: seen also in *intervene*, *advent*, *event*, *revenue*, etc.] To come together, to meet, to meet in the same place; to assemble: rarely said of things.—*v.t.* To cause to assemble; to call together; to convoke; to summon judicially to meet or appear.—**convener,** kon•vē′nėr, *n.* One who convenes or meets with others; one who convenes or calls a meeting.

convenience, conveniency, kon•vē′ni•ens, kon•vē′ni•en•si, *n.* [L. *convenientia*, from *convenio*, to convene; lit. a coming together.] The state or quality of being convenient; freedom from discomfort or trouble; ease; comfort; that which gives ease or comfort; that which is suited to wants; opportune conjunction of affairs; opportunity.—**convenient,** kon•vē′ni•ent, *a.* Suitable or proper; giving certain facilities or accommodation; commodious; opportune; at hand or readily available (*colloq.*).—**conveniently,** kon•vē′ni•ent•li, *adv.* in a convenient manner or situation: suitably; with adaptation to the end or effect; with ease; without trouble or difficulty.

convent, kon′vent, *n.* [O.Fr. *convent*, from L. *conventus*, a meeting—*con*, together, and *venio*, *ventum*, to come. CONVENE.] A community of persons devoted to religion; a body of monks or nuns; a house for persons devoted to religion and celibacy; an abbey, monastery, or nunnery.—**conventual,** kon•ven′tū•al, *a.* Of or belonging to a convent; monastic.—**conventual,** kon•ven′tū•al, *n.* One who lives in a convent; a monk or nun.

conventicle, kon•ven′ti•kl, *n.* [L. *conventiculum*, dim. of *conventus*, a meeting. CONVENT.] An assembly or gathering, especially a secret assembly; a meeting of dissenters from the established church for religious worship; a secret meeting for religious worship held by the Scottish Covenanters.—**conventicler,** kon•ven′ti•klėr, *n.* One who supports or frequents conventicles.

convention, kon•ven′shon, *n.* [L. *conventio*. CONVENE.] The act of coming together; a meeting; an assembly; an assembly of delegates or representatives for consultation on important concerns, civil, political, or ecclesiastical; a special agreement or contract between two countries or parties; an agreement previous to a definitive treaty; conventionality†. — **conventional,** kon•ven′shon•al, *a.* [L. *conventionalis.*] Formed by agreement; tacitly understood; arising out of custom or tacit agreement; sanctioned by or depending on general concurrence and not on any principle; resting on mere usage.—**conventionalism,** kon•ven′shon•al•izm, *n.* That which is conventional; something received or established by convention or agreement; a conventional phrase; form, or ceremony; anything depending on conventional rules and precepts.—**conventionalist,** kon•ven′shon•al•ist, *n.* One who adheres to a convention or agreement.—**conventionality,** kon•ven′shon•al″i•ti, *n.* The character of being conventional; what is conventional; a conventional mode of living, acting or speaking, as opposed to what is natural.—**conventionalize,** kon•ven′tion•al•īz, *v.t.—conventionalized, conventionalizing.* To render conventional; to bring under the influence of conventional rules; to render observant of the conventional rules of society.—**conventionally,** kon•ven′shon•al•li, *adv.* in a conventional manner.

conventual. See CONVENT.

converge, kon•vėrj′, *v.i.—converged, converging.* [L. *con*, together, and *vergo*, to incline. VERGE.] To tend to one point; to incline and approach nearer together in position; to approach in character.—**convergence, convergency,** kon•vėr′jens, kon•vėr′jen•si, *n.* The quality of converging; tendency to one point.—**convergent,** kon•vėr′jent, *a.* Converging; tending to one point; approaching each other.

converse, kon•vėrs′, *v.i.—conversed, conversing.* [Fr. *converser*; L. *conversor*, to associate with—*con*, and *versor*, to be engaged in anything, from *verto*, *versum*, to turn; seen also in *convert*, *reverse*, *verse*, *version*, etc. VERSE.] To associate, hold intercourse or communion; to talk familiarly; to have free intercourse in mutual communication of thoughts and opinions; to chat; to discourse.—*n.* [kon′vėrs). Acquaintance by frequent or customary intercourse; intercourse; communion; familiarity; free interchange of thoughts or opinions.—**conversable,** kon•vėr′sa•bl, *a.* [Fr. *conversable.*] Disposed to conversation; ready or inclined to mutual communication of thoughts; sociable; free in discourse. —**conversableness,** kon•vėr′sa•bl•nes, *n.* The quality of being conversable; disposition or readiness to converse; sociability.—**conversance,** † **conversancy,** † kon′vėr•sans, kon′vėr•san•si, *n.* The state of being conversant.—**conversant,** kon•vėr′sant, *a.* Keeping company; having frequent intercourse; intimately associating; followed by *with* or *among*; but the common meaning now is, acquainted by familiar use or study; having an intimate or thorough knowledge (of things); followed generally by *with*).—**conversantly,** kon•vėr′•sant•li, *adv.* In a conversant or familiar manner.—**conversation,** kon•vėr•sā′shon, *n.* [Fr. *conversation*, L. *conversatio*, intercourse.] Manners, behavior, or deportment, especially as respects morals; familiar discourse; general interchange of sentiments; chat; unrestrained talk, opposed to a formal conference (now the usual meaning); also sexual intercourse.—**conversational,** kon•vėr•sā′shon•al, *a.* Pertaining to conversation.—**conversationalist, conversationist,** kon•ver•sā′shon•al•ist, kon•vėr•sā′shon•ist, *n.* One who excels in conversation.

converse, kon′vers, *a.* [L. *conversus*, turned round, *converto*, *conversum*, to turn round—*con*, and *verto*, *versum*, to turn. CONVERSE, *v.i.*] Turned so as to be transposed or inverted, put the opposite, reverse, or contrary way (*converse* statement, proposition, way).—*n.* Something forming a counterpart; what is contrary or opposite; a statement or proposition produced by inversion or interchange of terms; thus the *converse* of ‘religion is true wisdom’, is ‘true wisdom is religion '.—**conversely,** kon•vėrs′•li, *adv.* In a converse manner; with inversion of order; put the converse way.—**conversion,** kon•ver′zhon, *n.* [L. *conversio.*] The act of turning or changing from one state to another; the state of being so turned or changed; transmutation; the act of changing or state of being changed in opinions or conduct; a change of heart or dispositions, succeeded by a reformation of life; a change from heathenism or from irreligion to Christianity.—**convert,** kon•vert′, *v.t.* [L. *converto.*] To change or turn into another substance or form; to change from one state to another; to change or turn from one religion to another, or from one party or sect to another; to change from heathenism to Christianity; to turn from a bad life to a good, religious, and holy one; to turn from one use or destination to another; to interchange conversely.—*v.i.* To turn or be changed; to undergo a change.—*n.* (kon′vėrt). A person who turns from one opinion or practice to another: a person who renounces one creed, religious system, or party, and embraces another; one who is turned from sin to holiness. ∴ A *convert* is one who changes opinions, and thus goes over to another side, party, or religion; a *proselyte* is one who changes his religion; but proselytism does not, like conversion, necessarily imply conviction.—**converter,** kon•vėr′tėr, *n.* One who converts; one who makes converts; that which converts, especially an iron retort used in the Bessemer process of steelmaking.—**convertibility, convertibleness,** kon•vėr′ti•bil″i•ti, kon•vėr′ti•bl•nes, *n.* The condition or quality of being convertible; the capability of being converted.—**convertible,** kon•vėr′ti•bl, *a.* Capable of being converted; susceptible of change, transmutable; transformable; capable of being used the one for the other, as terms of similar signification; interchangeable. —**convertibly,** kon•vėr′ti•bli, *adv.* In a convertible manner; with interchange of terms.

convex, kon′veks, *a.* [L. *convexus,* carried round, rounded—*con,* together, and *veho, vexum,* to carry; whence also *vehicle.*] Rising or swelling into a spherical or rounded form on the exterior surface: opposed to *concave.*—*n.* A convex part. —**convexly,** kon•veks′li, *adv.* In a convex form.—**convexity,** kon•vek′si•ti, *n.* State of being convex; the exterior surface of a convex body; roundness.—**convexo-concave,** *a.* Convex on one side and concave on the other: said of a lens.—**convexo-convex,** *a.* Convex on both sides: said of a lens.

convey, kon•vā′, *v.t.* [O.Fr. *conveier, convoyer,* L.L. *conviare,* to convey, to convoy—L. *con,* with, and *via,* a way; whence also *voyage, devious, deviate, obvious,* etc.] To carry, bear, or transport; to transmit, hand over, or transfer from one person to another (rights, landed estate); to transmit or carry by any medium (air *conveys* sound, words *convey* meaning).—**conveyable,** kon•vā′a•bl, *a.* Capable of being conveyed or transferred.—**conveyance,** kon•vā′ans, *n.* The act of conveying; the act of bearing, carrying, or transporting; transmission; transference; the transmitting or transferring of property from one person to another; the document by which property is transferred; the means by which anything is conveyed, especially a vehicle or carriage of some kind.—**conveyancing,** kon•vā′ans•ing, *n.* The act or practice of drawing deeds, leases, or other writings for transferring the title to property from one person to another.—**conveyer,** kon•vā′ėr, *n.* One who or that which conveys.

convict, kon•vikt′, *v.t.* [L. *convinco, convictum*—*con,* and *vinco,* to vanquish. CONVINCE.] To determine the truth of a charge against; to prove or find guilty of a crime charged; to determine or decide to be guilty: with *of* before the crime.—*n.* (kon′vikt). A person convicted or found guilty of a crime; a person undergoing penal servitude.—**conviction,** kon•vik′shon, *n.* The act of convicting or the state of being convicted; the act of a legal tribunal adjudging, finding, or determining a person to be guilty of an offense charged against him; strong belief on the ground of satisfactory evidence; settled persuasion. ∴ *Conviction* is assent founded on satisfactory proofs which appeal to the reason; *persuasion* is assent founded on what appeals to the feelings and imagination.—**convictive,**† kon•vik′tiv, *a.* Having the power to convince or convict.

convince, kon•vins′, *v.t.*—*convinced, convincing.* [L. *convinco, convictum*—*con,* and *vinco,* to vanquish, whence *victor, vanquish, evince.*] To persuade or satisfy by evidence; to bring to full belief or acquiescence by satisfactory proofs or arguments; to compel to yield assent; to convict or prove guilty (N.T.)‡; to overpower (*Shak.*)‡.—**convincible,** kon•vin′si•bl, *a.* Capable of conviction.—**convincingly,** kon•vin′sing•li, *adv.* In a convincing manner; in a manner to leave no room to doubt, or to compel assent.—**convincingness,** kon•vin′sing•nes, *n.* The power of convincing.

convivial, kon•viv′i•al, *a.* [L. *conviva,* a guest—*con,* and *vivo, victum,* to live, whence *victuals, vital, vivid,* etc.] Relating to a feast or entertainment; festal; social; jovial.—**conviviality,** kon•viv′i•al″i•ti, *n.* The good humor or mirth indulged at an entertainment; a convivial spirit or disposition.—**convivially,** kon•viv′i•al•li, *adv.* In a spirit of conviviality; in a convivial manner; festively.

convoke, kon•vōk′, *v.t.*—*convoked, convoking.* [L. *convoco,* to convoke—*con,* and *voco,* to call. VOICE, VOCAL.] To call together; to summon to meet; to assemble by summons.—**convocation,** kon•vo•kā′shon, *n.* The act of convoking or assembling by summons; an assembly; a convention; a congress; a council; in England, an assembly of the clergy, by their representatives, to consult on ecclesiastical affairs—a sort of ecclesiastical parliament.—**convocational,** kon•vo•kā′shon•al, *a.* Relating to a convocation.

convolve, kon•volv′, *v.t.*—*convolved, convolving.* [L. *convolvo*—*con,* and *volvo,* to roll, whence *involve, revolve, volume, vault.* WALLOW.] To roll or wind together; to roll one part on another; to coil up.—**convolute,** kon′vo•lūt, *a.* Rolled together, or one part on another; presenting convolutions.—**convolution,** kon•vo•lū′shon, *n.* [L. *convolutio, convolutionis.*] The act of rolling or winding together, or one thing on another; a winding motion; the state of being rolled round upon itself or rolled or wound together; a turn or winding; a twisted or tortuous part of something.

convolvulus, kon•vol′vū•lus, *n.* [L., from *convolvo,* to entwine, in reference to their twining habit.] Bindweed, a genus of plants consisting of slender twining herbs, with milky juice, and somewhat bell-shaped flowers, many of them beautiful.—**convolvulaceous,** kon•vol′vū•lā″shus, *a.* Relating to the convolvulus or allied plants.

convoy, kon•voi′, *v.t.* [Fr. *convoyer. Convoy*=*convey.* CONVEY.] To accompany on the way for protection, either by sea or land; to escort, as a guard against enemies.—*n.* (kon′voi). A protecting force accompanying ships or property on their way from place to place either by sea or land; that which is conducted by such a force.

convulse, kon•vuls′, *v.t.* [L. *convello, convulsum*—*con,* and *vello,* to pull or pluck.] To draw together or contract spasmodically, as the muscular parts of an animal body; to affect by irregular spasms; to affect by violent irregular action; to agitate violently.—**convulsion,**kon•vul′shon, *n.* [L. *convulsio.*] A violent and involuntary contraction of the muscular parts of an animal body, with alternate relaxations; violent and irregular motion; a violent and far-reaching disturbance in nature or among peoples; turmoil; a violent commotion.—**convulsional,**† **convulsionary,**† kon•vul′shon•al, kon•vul′shon•e•ri, *a.* Pertaining to convulsion; of the nature of convulsion.—**convulsive,** kon•vul′siv, *a.* Producing or tending to produce convulsion; attended with, or characterized by, convulsion or spasms.—**convulsively,** kon•vul′siv•li, *adv.* In a convulsive manner; with convulsion.

cony, coney, kō′ni, *n.* [O.E. *coning, cunning,* perhaps from O.Fr. *conil, conin,* from L. *cuniculus,* a rabbit; comp. W. *cwning,* Gael. *coinean,* Ir. *coinin,* Manx *connee*—rabbit.] A rabbit; a rabbit-like animal found in Syria and Palestine; the hydrax, or daman, a small Old World mammal.

coo, kö, *v.i.* [Imitative of the noise of doves; comp. D. *korren*, Icel. *kurra*, Fr. *roucouler*, to coo like a dove.] To cry or make the characteristic sound uttered by pigeons or doves; to act in a loving manner.

cooey, cooee, kö′i, *n.* [Imitative.] The cry or call of the Australian aborigines.—*v.t.* To cry or call like the aborigines of Australia.

cook, kuk, *v.t.* [A.Sax. *cóc*, a cock, borrowed, like Dan. *koge*, G. *kochen*, D. *kooken*, to boil, to cook, from L. *coquo*, to cook, *coquus*, a cook.] To prepare for the table by boiling, roasting, baking, broiling, etc.; to dress, as meat or vegetables, for eating; to dress up or give a color to for some special purpose, especially, to tamper with accounts so as to give them a more favorable aspect than they ought to have; to garble; to falsify.—*n.* One whose occupation is to cook or prepare victuals for the table.—**cookery,** kuk′ėr•i, *n.* The art or the practice of dressing and preparing victuals for the table.

cool, köl, *a.* [A.Sax. *col*=G. *kuhl*, cool; Icel. *kul*, D. *koel*, a cold blast; same root as in *chill*, *cold*, L. *gelu*, frost, *gelidus*.] Moderately cold; being of a temperature between hot and cold; not ardent or zealous; not excited by passion of any kind; not angry; not fond; indifferent; apathetic; chilling; frigid; deliberate; calm; quietly impudent and selfish: of persons and acts (*colloq.*).—*n.* A moderate state of cold; moderate temperature of the air between hot and cold (the *cool* of the day).—*v.t.* To make cool; to reduce the temperature of; to moderate or allay, as passion of any kind; to calm; to abate, as desire, zeal, or ardor; to render indifferent.—*v.i.* To become less hot; to lose heat; to lose the heat of excitement, passion, or emotion; to become less ardent, zealous, or affectionate.—**cooler,** köl′ėr, *n.* That which cools; a vessel in which liquids or other things are cooled.—**coolish,** köl′ish, *a.* Somewhat cool.—**coolly,** köl′li, *adv.* Without heat or sharp cold; in a cool or indifferent manner; without passion or ardor; without haste; calmly; deliberately.—**coolness,** köl′nes, *n.* The state or quality of being cool; a moderate degree of cold; a moderate degree or a want of passion; want of ardor or zeal; indifference; want of affection.

coolie, kö′li, *n.* An East Indian porter or carrier; an emigrant laborer from India, China, and other eastern countries.

coom, köm, *n.* [Perhaps from Fr. *écume*, foam, dross.] Soot; dirty refuse matter; the matter that works out of the naves or boxes of carriage wheels; coal dust.

coomb, comb, köm, kōm, *n.* [A.Sax. *cumb*, a liquid measure, a valley= Dan. and G. *kumme*, a bowl, a basin; D. *kom*, a trough, a chest.] An English dry measure of 4 bushels or half a quarter; a valley between hills (see COMB).

coon, kön, *n.* An abbreviation of *Raccoon*. A raccoon (colloq.).

coop, köp, *n.* [From L. *cupa*, a cask or vessel; akin *cup*.] A box of boards grated or barred on one side for keeping fowls in confinement; an enclosed place for small animals; a pen.—*v.t.* To put in a coop; to confine in a coop; to shut up or confine in a narrow compass: followed by *up*, *in*, or *within*.—**cooper,** kö′pėr, *n.* One whose occupation is to make barrels, tubs, etc.—*v.t.* and *i.* To do the work of a cooper.—**cooperage,** kö′pėr•ij, *n.* A place where coopers' work is done; the work or business of a cooper.—**coopery,** kö′pėr•i, *n.* The trade of a cooper; a cooper's workshop.

co-operate, kō•op′ėr•āt, *v.i.*—*co-operated*, *co-operating*. To act or operate jointly with another or others to the same end; to work or labor to promote a common object; to unite in producing the same effect.—**co-operation,** kō•op′ėr•ā″shon, *n.* The act of working or operating together to one end; joint operation, concurrent effort or labor.—**co-operative,** kō•op′ėr•ā•tiv, *a.* Operating jointly to the same end; established for the purpose of providing the members with goods at wholesale prices or at prime cost and cost of management (*co-operative* societies or stores).—**co-operator,** kō•op′ėr•ā•tėr, *n.* One who co-operates.

co-opt, kō•opt′, *v.t.* [L. *co-opto*.] To elect by co-optation into some body of which the electors are members.

co-ordinate, kō•or′din•āt, *a.* [L. *co* for *con*, and *ordinatus*, from *ordo*, order. ORDER.] Being of equal order, or of the same rank or degree; not subordinate.—*v.t.*—*co-ordinated*, *co-ordinating*. To make co-ordinate; to arrange in due and relative order; to harmonize.—*n.* What is co-ordinate; *geom.* any straight line which, with another or others, serves to determine the position of certain points under consideration.—**co-ordinately,** kō•or′di•nāt•li, *adv.* In the same order or rank; without subordination.—**co-ordinateness,** kō•-or′di•nāt•nes, *n.* The state of being co-ordinate.—**co-ordination,** kō•or′-di•nā″shon, *n.* The act of making co-ordinate or state of being co-ordinated.—**co-ordinative,** kō•or′di•-nā•tiv, *a.* Expressing or indicating co-ordination.

coot, köt, *n.* [Same as D. *koet*, a coot; comp. W. *cwta*, short-tailed.] A wading bird of the rail family, with a bald forehead, a black body, short tail, and lobated toes, and about 15 inches in length.

copaiba, kō•pā′ba, *n.* [Sp. and Pg.] A liquid resinous juice or balsam, flowing from incisions made in the stem of certain South American trees, used in medicine, especially in affections of the mucous membranes.

copal, kō′pal, *n.* [Mex. *copalli*, a generic name of resins.] A hard, shining, transparent, citron-colored, and odoriferous resinous substance, the product of several different tropical trees: when dissolved and diluted with spirit of turpentine it forms a beautiful transparent varnish.

coparcener, kō•pär′sen•ėr, *n.* [Prefix *co*, and *parcener*, ultimately from L. *pars*, a part.] A coheir; one who has an equal portion of the inheritance of his or her ancestor with others.—**coparcenary,** kō•pär′sen•e•ri, *n.* Partnership in inheritance; joint heirship.

copartner, kō•pärt′nėr, *n.* A partner with others; one who is jointly concerned with one or more persons in carrying on trade or other business; a sharer; a partaker.—**copartnership,** kō•pärt′nėr•ship, *n.* The state of being a copartner; joint concern in business; the persons who have a joint concern.

cope, kōp, *n.* [A form of *cap* and *cape*, a hood.] An ecclesiastical vestment resembling a cloak, worn in processions, at vespers, at consecration, and other sacred functions; something spread or extended over the head; hence, the arch or concave of the sky, the roof or covering of a house, the arch over a door; a coping.—*v.t.*—*coped*, *coping*. To cover as with a cope.—**copestone,** *n.* A head or top stone, as on a wall or roof.—**coping,** kō′ping, *n.* The covering course of a wall, parapet, buttresses, etc.

cope, kōp, *v.i.*—*coped*, *coping*. [O.Fr. *coper*, to strike (Fr. *couper*, to cut), from *colp*, *cop* (Fr. *coup*), a blow. COPPICE.] To strive or contend on equal terms or with equal strength; to match; to oppose with success; to encounter: followed by *with*.

copeck, kō′pek, *n.* A Russian coin, the hundredth part of a silver rouble.

Copernican, kō•pėr′ni•kan, *a.* Pertaining to Copernicus, who taught the solar system now received, called the *Copernican* system.

coping. See COPE, *n.*

copious, kō′pi•us, *a.* [L. *copiosus*, from *copia*, plenty—*co*, and *ops*, *opis*, property.] Abundant; plentiful; in great quantities; furnishing abundant matter: rich in supplies.—**copiously,** kō′pi•us•li, *adv.* In a copious manner; abundantly; plentifully; in large quantities; fully; amply; diffusely.—**copiousness,** kō′pi•-us•nes, *n.* The state or quality of being copious.

copper, kop′ėr, *n.* [L.L. *cuprum*, from L. *cyprium* (*aes*), Cyprian brass, from *Cyprus*, whence the Romans got their best copper.] A malleable, ductile metallic element, red in color and a good conductor; symbol, Cu; at. no., 29; at. wt., 63.546; vessel made of copper, particularly a large boiler; a coin made of copper or partly of copper; *pl.* the cast-iron apparatus used on board ship for cooking, and erected in the cook-house or galley.—*a.* Consisting of or resembling copper.—*v.t.* To cover or sheathe with sheets of copper; as, to *copper* a ship.—**copperhead,** *n.* [From its color.] A poisonous American serpent.—**copperplate,** *n.* A plate of polished copper on which some figure or design has been engraved, and from which an impression can be printed; a print or impression from such a plate.—**coppersmith,** *n.* One whose occupation is to manufacture copper utensils.—**coppery,** kop'ėr•i, *a.* Mixed with or containing copper; like copper in taste, smell, or color.

copperas, kop'ėr•as, *n.* [From L. *cuprirosa*, rose of copper, It. *copparosa*, Sp. Pg. *caparrosa*, Fr. *couperose.*] Sulfate of iron or green vitriol, a salt of a peculiar astringent taste and of various colors, but usually green.

coppice, copse, kop'is, kops, *n.* [O.Fr. *copeiz*, *coupiez*, wood newly cut, from *couper*, *coper*, to cut, from L.L. *colpus*, L. *colaphus*, Gr. *kolaphos*, a blow.] A wood of small growth, or consisting of underwood or brushwood; a wood cut at certain times for fuel or other purposes.

copra, kop'ra, *n.* The dried kernel of the coconut, from which the oil has yet to be expressed.

coprolite, kop'ro•līt, *n.* [Gr. *kopros*, dung, and *lithos*, a stone.] The petrified dung of extinct animals, such as lizards or sauroid fishes, found chiefly in the lias and coal measures.

coprophagous, kop•rof'a•gus, *a.* [Gr. *kopros*, dung, and *phâgo*, to eat.] Feeding upon dung or filth: a term particularly applied to certain insects.

copse, kops, *n.* See COPPICE.

Copt, kopt, *n.* A descendant of the ancient Egyptian race, and usually professing Christianity.—**Coptic,** kop'tik, *a.* Pertaining to the Copts.—*n.* The language of the Copts, an ancient Hamitic tongue, used in Egypt till superseded as a living language by Arabic.

copula, kop'ū•la, *n.* [L. *copula*, a band, a link, whence E. *couple.*] *Logic*, the word which unites the subject and predicate of a proposition; as in 'man is mortal', where *is* is the copula.—**copulate,** kop'ū•lāt, *v.i.* —*copulated, copulating.* To unite in sexual embrace.—**copulation,** kop•ū•lā'shon, *n.* [L. *copulatio.*] The act of copulating; coition.—**copulative,** kop'ū•lā•tiv, *a.* Uniting or coupling. —*Copulative conjunction, gram.* a conjunction (such as *and*) which connects two or more subjects or predicates in an affirmative or negative proposition.—*n.* A copulative conjunction.—**copulatively,** kop'ū•lā•tiv•li, *adv.* In a copulative manner.

copy, kop'i, *n.* [Fr. *copie*, from L. *copia*, plenty.] A writing like another writing; a transcript from an original; a book printed according to the original; one of many books containing the same literary matter; what is produced by imitating; a thing made in close imitation of another; that which is to be imitated; a pattern; a model; an archetype; writing engraved or penned by a master to be imitated by a pupil; written or printed matter given to a printer to be put in type.—*v.t.*—*copied, copying.* To make a copy from; to write, print, engrave, construct, draw, paint, etc., according to an original; to transcribe; to imitate; to follow as in language, style, manners, or course of life; take as one's model.—*v.i.* To make or produce a copy.—**copybook,** *n.* A book in which copies are written or printed for learners to imitate.—**copyhold,** kop'i•hōld, *n. English law*, a tenure for which the tenant has nothing to show except the copy of the rolls made on the tenant's being admitted to the possession of the subject; land held in copyhold.—**copyholder,** kop'i•hōl•dėr, *n.* One who is possessed of land in copyhold; a device for holding copy; a proofreader's assistant.—**copyright,** kop'i•rīt, *n.* The exclusive privilege which the law allows an author (or his assignee) of printing, reprinting, publishing, and selling his own original work; an author's exclusive right of property in his work for a certain time.—*a.* Relating to, or protected by the law of copyright.—*v.t.* To secure by copyright, as a book.

coquet, kō•ket', *v.t.*—*coquetted, coquetting.* [Fr. *coqueter*, lit. to demean one's self as a cock amongst hens, to swagger, to strut, from *coq*, a cock.] To entertain with compliments and amorous tattle.—*v.i.* To act the lover from vanity; to endeavor to gain admirers.—**coquetry,** kōk'et•ri, *n.* [Fr. *coquetterie.*] The arts of a coquette; attempts to attract admiration, notice, or love, from vanity; affectation of amorous advances.—**coquette,** kō•ket', *n.* [Fr. *coquette.*] A vain, airy, trifling girl, who endeavors to attract admiration and advances in love, from a desire to gratify vanity; a flirt.—**coquettish,** kō•ket'ish, *a.* Of or pertaining to coquetry; characterized by coquetry; practicing coquetry.—**coquettishly,** kō•ket'ish•li, *adv.* In a coquettish manner.

coquilla nut, ko•kēl'ya, *n.* The seed of one of the coconut palms, a native of Brazil, extensively used in turnery.

coracoid, kor'a•koid, *a.* [Gr. *korax*, *korakos*, a crow, and *eidos*, resemblance.] Shaped like a crow's beak.—*Coracoid process*, in *anat.* a small sharp process of the scapula in mammals; *coracoid bone*, a bone connecting the shoulder joint and sternum in birds.

coral, kor'al, *n.* [Fr. *corail* or *coral*, L. *corallium* or *corallum*, Gr. *korallion.*] A general term for the hard calcareous substance secreted by marine coelenterate polyps for their common support and habitation, exhibiting a great variety of forms and colors; a toy or plaything for an infant, made of coral; the unimpregnated eggs in the lobster, so called from being of a bright red color.—*a.* Made of coral; resembling coral.—**coralliferous, coralligerous,** kor•a•lif'ėr•us, kor•a•lij'ėr•us, *a.* Containing or consisting of coral; producing coral.—**coralline,** kor'al•īn, *a.* Consisting of coral; like coral; containing coral.—*n.* One of the coral polyps or other zoophytes; a seaweed with calcareous fronds; an orange-red color.—**coralloid, coralloidal,** kor'al•oid, kor'al•oi•dal, *a.* Having the form of coral; branching like coral.

corban, kor'ban, *n.* [Heb. *corbân*, an offering, sacrifice.] *Jewish antiq.* a solemn consecration of anything to God, as of one's self, one's services, or possessions; an alms basket; a treasury of the church.

corbeil, kor'bēl, *n.* [Fr. *corbeille*, from L. *corbicula*, dim. of *corbis*, a basket.] *Fort.* a basket, to be filled with earth and set upon a parapet to shelter men; *arch.* a carved basket with sculptured flowers and fruits.—**corbel,** kor'bel, *n.* [L.L. *corbella*, a dim. from L. *corbis*, a basket.] *Arch.* a piece of stone, wood, or iron projecting from the vertical face of a wall to support some superincumbent object.—*v.t. corbelled, corbelling. Arch.* to support on a corbel or corbels; to provide with corbels.

cord, kord, *n.* [Fr. *corde*, from L. *chorda*, Gr. *chordē*, a string or gut, the string of a lyre.] A string or small rope composed of several strands twisted together; a quantity of wood, originally measured with a cord or line, containing 128 cubic feet, or a pile 8 feet long, 4 feet high, and 4 feet broad; *fig.* what, binds, restrains, draws, or otherwise in moral effects resembles a cord: corded cloth; corduroy.—*v.t.* To bind with a cord or rope; to pile up for measurement and sale by the cord.—**cordage,** kor'dij, *n.* Ropes or cords collectively; the ropes in the rigging of a ship.—**corded,** kor'ded, *p.* and *a.* Fastened with cords; made of cords (*Shak.*); striped or furrowed, as by cords (*corded* cloth).

cordate, kor'dāt, *a.* [L. *cor*, *cordis*, the heart.] Having the form of a heart; heart-shaped.—**cordately,** kor'dāt•li, *adv.* In a cordate form.—**cordiform,** kor'di•form, *a.* Heart-shaped.

Cordelier, kor'de•lēr, *n.* [Fr., from *corde*, a girdle or cord worn by the order.] A Franciscan friar under the strictest rules and wearing a girdle of knotted cord.

cordial, kor'di•al, *a.* [Fr. *cordial*, from L. *cor*, *cordis*, the heart; same root as E. *heart.*] Proceeding from the heart; hearty; sincere; not hypocritical; warm; affectionate; reviving the spirits; refreshing; invigorating (a *cordial* liquor).—*n.* Anything that strengthens, comforts, gladdens, or exhilarates; an exhilarating liquor; an aromatized and sweetened spirit employed as a beverage.—**cordiality, cordialness,** kor•di•al'i•ti, kor'di•al•nes, *n.* The state of being cordial; sincere affection and kindness; genial sincerity; hearty warmth of heart; heartiness.—**cordially,** kor'di•al•li, *adv.* In a cordial manner; heartily; sincerely; without hypocrisy; with real affection.

cordiform. See CORDATE.

cordillera, kor•dēl•yā'ra, *n.* [Sp., from L. *chorda*, a string. CORD.] A ridge or chain of mountains; specifically, the mountain range of the Andes in South America.

cordite, kor'dīt, *n.* [From being made in *cord*-like forms.] A smokeless gunpowder, for use in ordnance.

cordon, kor'don, *n.* [Fr. and Sp.

cordon. CORD.] A line or series of military posts enclosing or guarding any particular place; a line of posts on the borders of a district infected with disease, to cut off communication; a ribbon worn across the breast by knights of the first class of an order.

cordovan, cordwain, kor′dō•van, kord′wān, *n.* [O.Fr. *cordouan,* Sp. *cordoban,* from *Cordova* or *Cordoba,* in Spain, where it is largely manufactured.] Spanish leather; goat skin tanned and dressed.—**cordwainer,** kord′wān•ėr, *n.* A shoemaker.

corduroy, kor•dū•roi′, *n.* [Fr. *corde du roy,* the king's cord.] A thick cotton stuff corded or ribbed on the surface.

core, kōr, *n.* [O.Fr. *cor, coer,* from L. *cor,* the heart, whence *cordial.*] The heart or inner part of a thing; particularly the central part of fruit containing the kernels or seeds; a center or central part, as the iron bar of an electromagnet round which is wound a coil of insulated wire, the conducting wires of a submarine telegraph cable, the interior part of a column, the internal mold which forms a hollow in the casting of metals; *fig.* the heart or deepest and most essential part of anything (the *core* of a question).—*v.t.* To remove the core of.

co-respondent, kō•ri•spon′dent, *n.* *Law,* a joint respondent, or one opposed, along with another or others, to the plaintiff; a person charged with adultery, and made a party to a suit for dissolution of marriage.

coriacoues, kō•ri•ā′shus, *a.* [L. *coriaceus,* from *corium,* leather.] Consisting of leather or resembling leather; tough and leathery.

coriander, kōr•i•an′dėr, *n.* [L. *coriandrum,* from Gr. *koriannon,* coriander, from *koris,* a bug, from the smell of its leaves.] An annual plant of the carrot family, the seeds of which have a strong smell, and are stomachic and carminative, being used in sweetmeats, in certain liqueurs, and also in cookery.

Corinthian, ko•rin′thi•an, *a.* Pertaining to *Corinth,* a celebrated city of Greece.—*Corinthian order,* an architectural order distinguished by fluted columns and capitals adorned with acanthus leaves.—*n.* An inhabitant of Corinth; a gay, fast, or spirited fellow.—**Corinthian,** kor•in′thi•an, *n.* A gentleman who does the work on his own or a friend's yacht, opposed to a paid hand; a gentleman jockey who rides his own horse; *pl.* two epistles written by St. Paul to the church of Corinth.

corium, kō′ri•um, *n.* [L., leather.] Leather body armor worn by the Roman soldiers; the innermost layer of the skin in mammals; the true skin.

cork, kork, *n.* [G. Dan. and Sw. *kork,* Sp. *corcho,* from L. *cortex, corticis,* bark.] The outer bark of a kind of oak (the cork oak or cork tree) growing in Spain and elsewhere, stripped off and made into such articles as stoppers for bottles and casks; a stopper for a bottle or cask cut out of cork.—*v.t.* To stop or fit with cork; to confine or make fast with a cork.—**corkscrew,** kork′skrö, *n.* A screw to draw corks from bottles.—*v.t.* To direct or work along in a spiral; to wriggle forward.—**corky,** kor′ki, *a.* Consisting of cork; resembling cork.

corm, korm, *n.* [Gr. *kormos,* a stem.] *Bot.* a bulblike part of a plant, consisting of the dilated base of the stem, as in the crocus; a solid bulb.

cormorant, kor′mo•rant, *n.* [Fr. *cormoran,* from L. *corvus marinus,* sea raven.] A web-footed sea bird of the pelican family, of several species, catching fish by swimming and diving, and extremely voracious; *fig.* a greedy fellow; a glutton.

corn, korn, *n.* [A.Sax. *corn,* a word found throughout the Teutonic languages, of same root as L. *granum,* a seed. Akin *kernel, grain.*] A grain grown extensively in many parts of the United States, particularly the central west (corn belt) and southwest, and also throughout the world in most temperate zones. It is used as food for human consumption, but its principal use is for stock food. In Great Britain, corn means any of a variety of grains such as wheat, barley, etc.—*v.t.* To preserve and season with salt in grains; to sprinkle with salt (to *corn* beef.)—**corn cockle,** *n.* The common name of a plant with purple flowers, a frequent weed among grain crops.—**corn crake,** *n.* The crake or land rail, which frequents cornfields and is noted for its strange harsh cry.—**corn laws,** *n. pl.* In England, legislative enactments and restrictions relating to the exportation and importation of grain.—**corny,** kor′ni, *a.* Of the nature of, or furnished with, grains of corn; producing corn; containing corn; produced from corn; tasting of corn or malt.

corn, korn, *n.* [L. *cornu,* a horn.] A hard excrescence or induration of the skin on the toes or some other part of the feet, occasioned by the pressure of the shoes.

cornea, kor′ni•a, *n.* [L. *corneus,* horny, *cornu,* a horn.] The horny transparent membrane in the fore part of the eye through which the rays of light pass.

cornel, kor′nel, *n.* [L. *cornus,* from *cornu,* a horn, from the hardness of the wood.] A species of dogwood found in Europe and Northern Asia, which produces a small, red, acid, cherry-like fruit, used in preserves and confectionery. Sometimes called *Cornelian tree.*

cornelian, kor•nē′li•an, *n.* Same as *Carnelian.*

corneous, kor′ni•us, *a.* [L. *corneus,* from *cornu,* a horn.] Horny; like horn; consisting of a horny substance, or a substance resembling horn; hard.

corner, kor′nėr, *n.* [Fr. *cornière,* from L. *cornu,* a horn, projection.] The point where two converging lines or surfaces meet, or the space between; an angle; a secret or retired place; a nook or out-of-the-way place; any part (every *corner* of the forest); a combination to raise the price of goods in the market.—*v.t.* In trading, to secure a monopoly or sufficient quantity of any stock or commodity, so that prospective buyers will be forced to pay the seller's price.—**cornerstone,** *n.* The stone which forms the corner of the foundation of an edifice; hence, that which is of the greatest importance; that on which any system is founded.

cornet, kor′net, *n.* [Fr., dim. of *corne,* L. *cornu,* a horn.] A kind of brass wind instrument; a cornet-à-pistons; a troop of horse: said to be so called because each company had a cornet player; formerly the title of the officer who carried the ensign or colors in a troop of horse in the British army. — **cornet-à-pistons,** kor′net•a•pis″tonz, *n.* [Fr., cornet with pistons.] A brass or silver wind instrument, capable of producing the notes of the chromatic scale from the valves and pistons with which it is furnished.—**cornetcy,** kor′net•si, *n.* The commission or rank of a cornet.

cornice, kor′nis, *n.* [O.Fr. *cornice,* It. *cornice,* from Gr. *korōnis,* a summit, from *korōne,* a crown. CROWN.] *Arch.* any molded projection which crowns or finishes the part to which it is affixed; specifically, the highest part of an entablature resting on the frieze.

Cornish, korn′ish, *a.* Pertaining to Cornwall, in England.—*Cornish engine,* a single-acting steam engine used for pumping water.—*n.* The ancient language of Cornwall, a dialect of the Celtic.

cornucopia, kor•nū•kō′pi•a, *n.* [L. *cornucopiae,* the horn of plenty.] A wreathed horn, filled to overflowing with richest fruit, flowers, and grain, used in sculpture, etc., as a symbol of plenty, peace, and concord.

corolla, ko•rol′la, *n.* [L. *corolla,* dim. of *corona,* a crown.] *Bot.* the part of a flower inside the calyx, surrounding the parts of fructification, and composed of one or more petals, generally to be distinguished from the calyx by the fineness of its texture and the gayness of its colors.—**corollate, corollated,** kor′ol•āt, kor′ol•āt•ed, *a.* *Bot.* like a corolla; having corollas.

corollary, kor′ol•le•ri, *n.* [Fr. *corollaire,* from L. *corolla,* a little crown, from as it were crowning what it refers to.] That which follows over and above what is directly demonstrated in a mathematical proposition; any consequence necessarily concurrent with or following from the main one; an inference; a conclusion; a surplus (*Shak.*)‡.

corona, ko•rō′na, *n.* [L., a crown. CROWN.] A technical term for various things supposed to have some resemblance to a crown; *astron.* a halo or luminous circle around one of the heavenly bodies; a luminous appearance observed during total eclipses of the sun, which lies outside the chromosphere; *arch.* the lower member or drip of a classical cornice having a broad vertical face, usually of considerable projection; *bot.* the circumference or margin of a radiated composite flower; also an appendage of the corolla or petals of a flower proceeding from the base of the limb.—**coronal,** ko•rō′nal, *a.* Pertaining to a corona†; belonging to the crown or top of the head: in this sense pron. kor′o•nal.—*n.* (kor′o•nal). A crown; wreath; garland.—**coronary,** kor′o•ne•ri, *a.* Relating to a crown; of or like a crown; pertaining to either or both of the two arteries of the heart. —*n.* A coronary artery; coronary thrombosis.—**coronary thrombosis,** *n.* Clotting of blood in one of the arteries of the heart.—**coronation,** kor•o•nā′shon, *n.* The act or solemnity of crowning a sovereign or investing him; the pomp attending on a coronation.—**coroner,** kor′-o•nėr, *n.* [L.L. *coronator,* originally a crown officer of extensive powers, from L. *corona,* a crown.] An officer appointed to hold inquests on the bodies of such as either die, or are supposed to die, a violent death.—**coronet,** kor′o•net, *n.* An inferior crown worn by princes and noblemen, bearing crosses, fleurs-de-lis, strawberry leaves, pearls; the lower part of the pastern of a horse.—*v.t.* To adorn with a coronet or something similar.—**coroneted,** kor′o•net•ed, *a.* Wearing or entitled to wear a coronet.

coronach, kor′o•nach, *n.* [Gael. and Ir.] A dirge; a lamentation for the dead among the Highlanders and Irish.

corporal, kor′po•ral, *n.* [Corrupted from Fr. *caporal,* It. *caporale,* from *capo,* L. *caput,* the head.] The noncommissioned officer of a company of infantry next below a sergeant; in *ships-of-war,* a petty officer who attends to police matters.

corporal, kor′po•ral, *a.* [L. *corporalis,* from *corpus,* body.] Belonging or relating to the body; bodily; also material or not spiritual†. ∴ Syn. under BODILY.—**corporality,** kor•-po•ral′i•ti, *n.* The state of being corporal; corporation; confraternity. —**corporally,** kor′po•ral•li, *adv.* Bodily; in or with the body (*corporally* present).—**corporate,** kor′po•rit, *a.* [L. *corporatus.*] United in a body, as a number of individuals who are empowered to transact business as an individual; formed into a body; united; collectively one (*Shak.*); belonging to a corporation.—**corporately,** kor′po•rit•li, *adv.* In a corporate capacity.—**corporation,** kor•po•rā′shon, *n.* A body corporate, formed and authorized by law to act as a single person; a society having the capacity of transacting business as an individual; the body or bodily frame of a man (*colloq.*).—**corporeal,** kor•pō′ri•al, *a.* Of or pertaining to a body; having a body; consisting of a material body; material; opposed to *spiritual* or *immaterial.* ∴ Syn. under BODILY.—**corporeality,** kor•pō′ri•al″i•ti, *n.* The state of being corporeal.—**corporeally,** kor•pō′ri•al•li, *adv.* In body; in a bodily form or manner.—**corporeity,** kor•pō•re′i•ti, *n.* The state of having a body or of being embodied; materiality†.

corposant, kor′pō•zant, *n.* [It. *corpo santo,* holy body.] A name given to a ball of electric light often observed on dark tempestuous nights about the rigging; St. Elmo's light.

corps, kōr, *n.* pl. **corps,** kōrz. [Fr., from L. *corpus,* body.] A body of troops; any division of an army.—*Corps d'armée,* a large division of an army.—**corpse,** korps, *n.* The dead body of a human being.—**corpse-candle,** *n.* A local name for the will-o′-the-wisp.—**corpse gate,** *n.* A covered gateway at the entrance to churchyards, a lich gate.

corpulence, corpulency, kor′pū•-lens, kor′pū•len•si, *n.* [L. *corpulentia,* from *corpulentus,* corpulent, *corpus,* a body.] Fleshiness or stoutness of body; excessive fatness.—**corpulent,** kor′pū•lent, *a.* Having a great bulk of body; stout; fat; obese.

corpus, kor′pus, *n.* A collected whole; a material substance; *anat.* a name for certain small bodies of various kinds.

Corpus Christi, kor′pus kris′ti, *n.* [L., body of Christ.] *R. Cath. Ch.* the host or eucharist; an annual festival in its honor.

corpuscle, kor′pus•l, *n.* [L. *corpusculum,* dim. of *corpus,* body.] A minute particle, molecule, or atom; a minute animal cell generally enclosing granular matter, and sometimes a spheroidal body called a nucleus.—**corpuscular,** kor•pus′kū•ler, *a.* Relating to corpuscles or small particles, supposed to be the constituent materials of all large bodies.—*Corpuscular theory,* a theory which supposes light to consist of minute particles emitted by luminous bodies, and traveling through space with immense rapidity till they reach the eye.

corral, kor•ral′, *n.* [Sp., from *corro,* a circle; Pg. *curral,* a cattle-pen.] A pen or enclosure for horses or cattle, and also an enclosure formed of wagons employed by emigrants as a means of defense [Amer.]; a strong stockade or enclosure for capturing wild elephants in Ceylon.—*v.t.*—*corralled, corralling.* To form into a corral; to form a corral or enclosure by means of.

correct, ko•rekt′, *a.* [L. *correctus,* from *corrigo*—*con,* and *rego,* to set right. REGENT, RIGHT.] Set right or made straight; in accordance with a certain standard; conformable to truth, rectitude, or propriety; not faulty; free from error.—*v.t.* To make correct or right; to bring into accordance with a certain standard; to remove error or defect from; to amend or emend; to punish for faults or deviations from moral rectitude; to chastise; to discipline; to counteract or obviate, as by adding some new ingredient.—**correction,** ko•rek′-shon, *n.* [L. *correctio.*] The act of correcting; the removal of faults or errors; something written to point out an error, or substituted in the place of what is wrong; punishment; discipline; chastisement; critical notice; animadversion; the counteraction of what is inconvenient or hurtful in its effects.—*House of correction,* a house where disorderly persons are confined; a bridewell.—**correctional,** ko•rek′shon•al, *a* Tending to correction.—**corrective,** ko•-rek′tiv, *a.* Having the power to correct; having the quality of removing or obviating what is wrong or injurious.—*n.* That which has the power of correcting; that which has the quality of altering or obviating what is wrong or injurious.—**correctly,** ko•rekt′li, *adv.* In a correct manner; according to a standard; in conformity with a copy or original; exactly; accurately; without fault or error.—**correctness,** ko•rekt′nes, *n.* The state of being correct; conformity to a standard or rule; exactness; accuracy.—**corrector,** ko•rek′tėr, *n.* One who corrects; one who amends faults; one who punishes for correction; that which corrects.

correlate, kor′e•lāt, *n.* [L. *cor* for *con,* and *relatus.* RELATE.] One who or that which stands in a reciprocal relation to something else, as father and son.—*v.i.*—*correlated, correlating.* To have a reciprocal relation; to be reciprocally related, as father and son.—*v.t.* To place in reciprocal relation; to determine the relations between, as between several objects or phenomena which bear a resemblance to one another.—**correlation,** kor•e•lā′shon, *n.* Reciprocal relation; corresponding similarity or parallelism of relation or law.—**correlative,** ko•rel′a•tiv, *a.* Having a reciprocal relation, so that the existence of one in a certain state depends on the existence of another; reciprocal.—*n.* That which is correlative; that of which the existence implies the existence of something else; one of two terms either of which calls up the notion of the other, as *husband* and *wife*; *gram.* the antecedent to a pronoun.—**correlatively,** ko•rel′a•tiv•li, *adv.* In a correlative relation.

correspond, kor•e•spond′, *v.i.* [*Cor* for *con,* and *respond.*] To be adapted or suitable; to have a due relation; to be adequate or proportionate; to accord; to agree; to answer; to fit: used absolutely or followed by *with* or *to*; to communicate or hold intercourse with a person by letters sent and received.—**correspondence,** kor•e•spon′dens, *n.* The state of corresponding or being correspondent; mutual adaptation of one thing or part to another; intercourse between persons by means of letters sent and received; the letters collectively which pass between correspondents; friendly intercourse; reciprocal exchange of offices or civilities.—**correspondency,** kor•e•-spon′den•si, *n.* Correspondence, in sense of relation, congruity, adaptation, friendly intercourse.—**correspondent,** kor•e•spon′dent, *a.* Corresponding; suitable; duly related; congruous; agreeable; answerable; adapted.—*n.* One who corresponds; one with whom an intercourse is carried on by letters or messages; a person who sends regular communications to a newspaper from a distance.—**correspondently,** kor•e•spon′dent•li, *adv.* In a corresponding manner.—**corresponding,** kor•e•spon′ding, *a.* Answering; agreeing; suiting; correspondent.—**correspondingly,** kor•e•spon′ding•li, *adv.* In a corresponding manner.—**corresponsive,** kor•e•spon′siv, *a.* Answerable; adapted. (*Shak.*)

corridor, kor′i•dor, *n.* [It. *corridore,* from *correre,* L. *currere,* to run, CURRENT.] *Arch.* a passage in a building leading to several chambers at a distance from each other; a strip of land through foreign territory.

corrie, kor′i, *n.* [Gael.] A steep hollow in a hill.

corrigendum, kor•i•jen′dum, *n.* pl. **corrigenda,** kor•i•jen′da, [L.] A thing or word to be corrected or altered.

corrigible, kor′i•ji•bl, *a.* [Fr., from L. *corrigo,* to correct. CORRECT.] Capable of being corrected, amended or reformed; deserving punishment or correction; punishable.

corroborate, ko•rob′o•rāt, *v.t.*—*corroborated, corroborating.* [L. *corroboro, corroboratum—con,* and *roboro,* to strengthen, from *robur,* strength.] To strengthen or give additional strength to; to confirm; to make more certain; to add assurance to (to *corroborate* testimony, news).—**corroborant,** ko•rob′o•rant, *a.* Strengthening the body; having the power or quality of giving strength.—*n.* A medicine that strengthens the body when weak; a tonic.—**corroboration,** ko•rob′o•rā″shon, *n.* The act of corroborating; confirmation; that which corroborates.—**corroborative,** ko•rob′o•rā•tiv, *a.* Having the power of corroborating or confirming.—*n.* A medicine that strengthens; corroborant.—**corroboratory,** ko•rob′o•ra•to•ri, *a.* Corroborative.

corrode, ko•rōd′, *v.t.*—*corroded, corroding.* [L. *corrodo—cor* for *con,* and *rodo,* to gnaw, whence also *rodent, erode.*] To eat away by degrees; to wear away or diminish by gradually separating small particles (nitric acid *corrodes* copper); *fig.* to gnaw or prey upon; to consume by slow degrees; to envenom or embitter; to poison, blight, canker.—**corrodible,** ko•rō′di•bl, *a.* That may be corroded.—**corrosion,** ko•rō′zhon, *n.* The action of corroding, eating, or wearing away by slow degrees, as by the action of acids on metals; *fig.* the act of cankering, fretting, vexing, envenoming, or blighting.—**corrosive,** ko•rō′siv, *a.* Having the power of corroding or eating into a substance; having the quality of fretting, envenoming, blighting.—*Corrosive sublimate,* a compound of chlorine and mercury, forming a white crystalline solid, an acrid poison of great virulence, and a powerful antiseptic.—*n.* That which has the quality of eating or wearing gradually; anything which irritates, preys upon one, or frets.—**corrosively,** ko•rō′siv•li, *adv.* In a corrosive manner.—**corrosiveness,** ko•rō′siv•nes, *n.* The quality of being corrosive.

corrugate, ko′rū•gāt, *v.t.*—*corrugated, corrugating.* [L. *corrugo, corrugatum—cor* for *con,* and *rugo,* to wrinkle.] To wrinkle; to draw or contract into folds.—*a.* Wrinkled; showing wrinkles or furrows.—**corrugated,** ko′rū•gā•ted, *p.* and *a.* Wrinkled; furrowed or ridged.—*Corrugated iron,* common sheet iron or 'galvanized' iron, bent into a series of regular grooves and ridges by being passed between powerful rollers. Iron thus treated will resist a much greater strain than flat iron, each groove representing a half tube; it is used for roofing, etc.—**corrugation,** ko•ru•gā′shon, *n.* A wrinkling; contraction into wrinkles.

corrupt, ko•rupt′, *v.t.* [L. *corrumpo, corruptum—con,* and *rumpo, ruptum,* to break; whence also *rupture, abrupt, disrupt,* etc.] To change from a sound to a putrid or putrescent state; to cause to rot; *fig.* to deprave; to pervert; to impair; to debase; to defile, taint, pollute, or infect; to bribe; to debase or render impure by alterations or innovations (language); to falsify (a text).—*v.i.* To become putrid; to putrefy; to rot; to become vitiated; to lose purity.—*a.* Changed from a sound to a putrid state; changed from the state of being correct, pure, or true to a worse state; vitiated; perverted; debased; impure; ready to be influenced by a bribe; infected with errors or mistakes (a *corrupt* text).—**corrupter,** ko•rup′tėr, *n.* One who or that which corrupts.—**corruptibility,** ko•rup′ti•bil″i•ti, *n.* The possibility of being corrupted.—**corruptible,** ko•rup′ti•bl, *a.* Capable of being made corrupt, putrid, or rotten; subject to decay and destruction, debasement, depravation, etc.—**corruptibleness,** ko•rup′ti•bl•nes, *n.*—**corruptibly,** ko•rup′ti•bli, *adv.* In such a manner as to be corrupted or vitiated.—**corruption,** ko•rup′shon, *n.* [L. *corruptio.*] The act of corrupting, or state of being corrupt, putrid, or rotten; putrid matter; pus; depravity; wickedness; loss of purity or integrity; debasement; impurity; depravation; pollution; defilement; vitiating influence, more specifically, bribery; *law,* an immediate consequence of attainder by which a person was formerly disabled from holding, inheriting, or transmitting lands.—**corruptive,** ko•rup′tiv, *a.* Having the power of corrupting, tainting, or vitiating.—**corruptly,** ko•rupt′li, *adv.* In a corrupt manner; with corruption; impurely; by bribery.—**corruptness,** ko•rupt′nes, *n.* Corrupt quality or state; putrid state.

corsage, kor•säzh′, *n.* [Fr.] A small bouquet for a woman; the waist of a woman's dress.

corsair, kor′sâr, *n.* [Fr. *corsaire,* It. *corsare,* from *corsa,* a course, a cruise, from L. *cursus,* a course. COURSE.] A pirate; a sea robber; a rover; a piratical vessel.

corselet, kors′let, *n.* [Fr., a dim. of O.Fr. *cors,* L. *corpus,* the body.] A small cuirass, or armor to cover and protect the body; a type of lightly boned corset for women; that part of a winged insect to which the wings and legs are attached; the thorax.

corset, kor′set, *n.* [Dim. of O.Fr. *cors.*] A tight, boned undergarment, reaching from the bust to below the hips, worn by women, occasionally by men, to support and mold the body.

cortege, kor•tezh′, *n.* [Fr., from It. *corteggio,* from *corte,* court.] A train of attendants to a great personage on a ceremonial occasion.

Cortes, kor′tez, *n. pl.* [Sp., pl. of *corte,* court.] The present legislative assembly of Portugal and formerly, the single legislative chamber of Republican Spain.

cortex, kor′teks, *n.* [L. *cortex, corticis,* bark; whence *cork.*] Bark, as of a tree; hence, an outer covering; *anat.* a membrane forming a covering or envelope for any part of the body. *Of brain,* external layer of cerebral hemispheres and cerebellum: that of cerebral hemispheres divided into *motor areas,* controlling muscles, and *sensory areas,* concerned with sensations.—**cortical,** kor′ti•kal, *a.* Belonging to, consisting of, or resembling bark or rind; external; belonging to the external covering.—**corticate, corticated,** kor′ti•kāt, kor′ti•kā•ted, *a.* [L. *corticatus.*] Resembling the bark or rind of a tree.—**corticose, corticous,** kor′ti•kōz, kor′ti•kus, *a.* Barky; full of bark.

cortisone, kor′ti•sōn, *n.* A compound extracted from the cortex of the adrenal gland of animals or produced synthetically and used in treatment of disease, as arthritis.

corundum, ko•run′dum, *n.* [Hind. *kurand.*] A mineral, next in hardness to the diamond, and consisting of nearly pure anhydrous alumina; the amethyst, ruby, sapphire, topaz, and emery are considered as varieties.

coruscate, kor′us•kāt, *v.i.*—*coruscated, coruscating.* [L. *corusco, coruscatum,* to flash.] To flash; to lighten; to gleam; to glitter.—**coruscation,** kor•us•kā′shon, *n.* [L. *coruscatio.*] A sudden burst of light in the clouds or atmosphere; a flash; glitter; a blaze.

corvette, kor•vet′, *n.* [Fr. *corvette,* from L. *corbita,* a ship of burden, from *corbis,* a basket.] A flush-decked vessel, ship-rigged, but without a quarter-deck, and having only one tier of guns.

corvine, kor′vīn, *a.* [L. *corvus,* a crow.] Pertaining to the crow, or the crow family of birds.

Corybant, kor′i•bant, *n.pl.* **Corybants,** or **Corybantes,** kor•i•ban′tēz. [L. *corybas, corybantis,* Gr. *korybas.*] A priest of Cybele who celebrated the mysteries with mad dances to the sound of drum and cymbal.—**Corybantic,** kor•i•ban'tik, *a.* Madly agitated like the Corybantes.

corymb, ko'rimb, *n.* [L. *corymbus*, Gr. *korymbos*, a cluster of fruit or flowers.] *Bot.* an inflorescence in which the flowers or blossoms are so arranged as to form a mass of flowers with a convex or level top, as in the hawthorn, candytuft, etc.—**corymbose,** ko•rim'bōz, *a. Bot.* relating to or like a corymb.—**corymbous,** ko•rim'bus, *a.* Corymbose.

coryphaeus, kor•i•fē'us, *n.* [L. *coryphæus*, Gr. *koryphaios*, from *koryphē*, the head.] The chief of a chorus; the chief of a company.—**coryphee,** ko•ri•fā', *n.* [Fr.] A ballet dancer.

coryza, ko•rī'za, *n.* [Gr.] *Med.* a cold in the head.

cosecant, kō•sē'kant, *n.* [From *complement* and *secant.*] *Geom.* in a right-angle triangle, the cosecant of the base angle that is not 90° is the number obtained after dividing the hypotenuse by the perpendicular. Multiplied by the sine it equals one.

cosey, cosy, kō'zi. Same as *cozy.*

cosher, kosh'ėr, *v.i.* [Ir. *coisir*, a feast.] To levy exactions in the shape of feasts and lodgings, as formerly Irish landlords with their trains did on their tenants.—*v.t.* To treat with dainties or delicacies; to fondle; to pet.

cosignatory, kō•sig'na•to•ri, *n.* One who signs a treaty or other agreement along with another or others. Also used as an adj.

cosine, kō'sīn, *n.* [*Complement* and *sine.*] *Geom.* in a right-angle triangle, the cosine of the base angle that is not 90° is the number obtained after dividing the base by the hypotenuse. Multiplied by the secant it equals one.

cosmetic, koz•met'ik, *a.* [Gr. *kosmētikos*, from *kosmos*, order, beauty.] Beautifying; improving beauty, particularly the beauty of the complexion.—*n.* Any preparation that renders the skin soft, pure, and white, or helps to beautify and improve the complexion.

cosmic, cosmical, koz'mik, koz'mi•kal, *a.* [Gr. *kosmikos*, from *kosmos*, the universe.] Relating to the universe and to the laws by which its order is maintained; hence, harmonious as the universe; orderly.—**cosmically,** koz'mi•kal•li, *adv.* In a cosmic manner; with the sun at rising or setting; said of a star.—**cosmic ray,** *n.* An electromagnetic ray of extremely high frequency and energy content that originates in outer space and bombards the earth, penetrating barriers impervious to all other radiation. Molecules of the earth's atmosphere are ionized upon impact with cosmic rays.

cosmogony, koz•mog'o•ni, *n.* [Gr. *kosmogonia—kosmos*, world, and root *gen*, to bring forth.] The origin or creation of the world or universe; the doctrine of the origin or formation of the universe.

cosmography, koz•mog'ra•fi, *n.* [Gr. *kosmographia—kosmos*, the world, and *graphō*, to describe.] A description of the world or universe; the science which treats of the construction of the universe.—**cosmographer,** koz•mog'ra•fėr, *n.* One who describes the world or universe; one versed in cosmography.—**cosmographic, cosmographical,** koz•mo•graf'ik, koz•mo•graf'ik•al, *a.* Relating to cosmography.

cosmology, koz•mol'o•ji, *n.* [Gr. *kosmologia—kosmos*, the universe, and *logos*, discourse.] The science of the universe; a theory relating to the structure and laws of the universe; cosmogony.—**cosmological,** koz•mo•loj'ik•al, *a.* Pertaining to cosmology.—**cosmologist,** koz•mol'o•jist, *n.* One versed in cosmology.

cosmonaut, koz'mo•nạt, *n.* Traveler in interplanetary space.—**cosmonette,** *n. fem.*

cosmopolitan, cosmopolite, koz•mo•pol'i•tan, koz•mop'o•lit, *n.* [Gr. *kosmos*, world, and *politēs*, a citizen.] A person who is nowhere a stranger, or who is at home in every place; a citizen of the world.—*a.* Free from local, provincial, or national prejudices or attachments; at home all over the world; common to all the world.—**cosmopolitanism, cosmopolitism,** koz•mo•pol'i•tan•izm, kos•mop'o•lit•izm, *n.* The state of being a cosmopolitan; disregard of local or national prejudices, attachments, or peculiarities.

cosmos, koz'mos, *n.* [Gr. *kosmos*, order, ornament, and hence the universe as an orderly and beautiful system.] The universe as an embodiment of order and harmony; the system of order and harmony combined in the universe.

Cossack, kos'ak, *n.* [Rus. *kosak*, Turk. *kazâk*, a robber.] One of a warlike people, very expert on horseback, inhabiting the steppes in the south of the Soviet Union.

cosset,‡ kos'et, *n.* [Comp. old *coss*, Icel. *koss*, a *kiss.*] A pet; a pet lamb.

cost, kost, *n.* [O.Fr. *cost*, from *coster*, *couster* (Mod.Fr. *coûter*), to cost, from L. *constare*, to cost—*con*, and *stare*, to stand. STATE.] The price, value, or equivalent of a thing purchased; amount in value expended or to be expended; charge; expense; *law.* the sum to be paid by the party losing in favor of the party prevailing, etc.; outlay, expense, or loss of any kind, as of time, labor, trouble, or the like; detriment: pain; suffering (he learned that to his *cost*).—*v.t.*—pret. and pp. *cost.* To require to be given or expended in order to purchase; to be bought for; to require to be undergone, borne, or suffered; often with two objects (to *cost* a person money or labor).—**costly,** kost'li, *a.* Of a high price; costing much; expensive; dear.—**costliness,** kost'li•nes, *n.* The state or quality of being costly, high in price, or expensive.

costal, kos'tal, *a.* [L. *costa*, a rib.] Pertaining to the side of the body or the ribs.—**costate,** kos'tāt, *a.* Ribbed; marked with elevated lines.

costard, kos'tėrd, *n.* [Lit. a *ribbed* apple, O.Fr. *coste*, L. *costa*, a rib.] An apple; hence, humorously for the head. (*Shak.*)

costive, kos'tiv, *a.* [Contr. from It. *costipativo*, from L. *constipo*, to cram, to stuff. CONSTIPATE.] Suffering from a morbid retention of fecal matter in the bowels, in a hard and dry state; having the bowels bound; constipated. — **costively,** kos'tiv•li, *adv.* With costiveness.—**costiveness,** kos'tiv•nes, *n.* The state of being costive; constipation.

costmary, kost'ma•ri, *n.* [L. *costus*, Gr. *kostos*, an aromatic plant, and *Mary* (the Virgin).] A perennial composite plant, a native of the south of Europe, cultivated for the agreeable fragrance of the leaves.

costrel, kos'trel, *n.* [L. *costa*, O.Fr. *coste*, rib, side.] A small vessel, generally with ears for suspending at side, used by laborers in harvest time; a vessel for holding wine.

costume, kos'tūm, *n.* [Fr. *costume*, custom. CUSTOM.] An established mode of dress; the style of dress peculiar to a people or nation, to a particular period, or a particular class of people; a dress of a particular style.—**costumier, costumer,** kos•tū'mi•ėr, kos'tūm•ėr, *n.* One who prepares costumes, as for theaters, fancy balls, etc.; one who deals in costumes.

cosy, kō'zi, *a.* Same as *cozy.*

cot, kot, *n.* [A.Sax. *cot*, *cott*, a cot, chamber; Icel. and D. *kot*, a cot, G. *kot*, *kote*, a hut; *cote* is the same word. From this comes *cottage.*] A small house; a hut or cottage; a small bed or crib for a child to sleep in; *naut.* a sort of bed frame suspended from the beams.

cotangent, kō•tan'jent, *n.* [*Complement* and *tangent.*] In a right-angle triangle, the cotangent of the base angle that is not 90° is the number obtained after dividing the base by the perpendicular. Multiplied by the tangent it equals one.

cote, kōt, *n.* [COT.] A shelter or habitation for animals, as a dove-*cote*; a sheepfold; a cottage or hut.

cotemporaneous, cotemporary, kō•tem'po•rā''ni•us, kō•tem'po•re•ri. See CONTEMPORANEOUS, CONTEMPORARY.

cotenant, kō•ten'ant, *n.* A tenant in common.

coterie, kō'te•rē, *n.* [Fr., from L.L. *coteria*, an association of villagers, *cota*, a cottage. COT.] A set or circle of friends who are in the habit of meeting for social or literary intercourse or other purposes; a clique.

coterminous, kō•tėr'mi•nus, *a.* See CONTERMINOUS.

cothurnus, cothurn, kō•thėr'nus, kō'thėrn, *n.* [L. *cothurnus.*] A buskin; a kind of high laced shoe, such as was anciently worn by tragic actors; hence, *fig.* tragedy.

cotidal, kō•tī'dal, *a.* Marking an equality of tides.

cotillion, cotillon, ko•til'yon, *n.* [Fr. *cotillon.*] A kind of brisk dance; a tune which regulates the dance.

Cotswold, kots'wōld, *n.* A large sheep of a breed belonging to the Cotswold Hills in Gloucestershire.

cottage, kot′ij, *n*, [From *cot*.] A cot or small dwelling house; a small country residence or detached suburban house, adapted to a moderate scale of living.—**cottager,** kot′ij•ėr, *n*. One who lives in a hut or cottage.—**cotter, cottier,** kot′ėr, kot′i•ėr, *n*. A cottager; one who inhabits a cot or cottage, dependent upon a farm, having sometimes a piece of land. Written also *cottar*.

cotton, kot′n, *n*. [Fr. *coton*, from Ar. *qoton*.] A soft downy substance resembling fine wool, growing in the pods or seed vessels of certain plants, being the material of a large proportion of cloth for apparel and furniture; cloth made of cotton.—*a*. Pertaining to cotton; made of cotton.—*v.i.* To fraternize; to agree or get on (with). (*Colloq*.)—**cottony,** kot′n•i, *a*. Downy or soft like cotton; pertaining to or resembling cotton. —**cotton gin,** *n*. A machine to separate the seeds from raw cotton. **cotton grass,** *n*. A name of plants of the sedge family with white cottony spikes.—**cottonwood,** *n*. A tree of the poplar genus, a native of North America.—**cotton wool,** *n*. A name sometimes given to raw cotton.

cotyledon, kot•i•lē′don, *n*. [Gr. *kotylēdōn*, from *kotylē*, a hollow.] *Bot*. the seed leaf; the first leaf or leaves of the embryo plant, forming, together with the radicle and plumule, the embryo, which exists in every seed capable of germination; *anat*. a tuft of vessels adhering to the chorion of some animals.—**cotyledonal,** kot•i•lē′do•nal, *a*. Belonging to a cotyledon; resembling a cotyledon.—**cotyledonary,** kot•i•lē′do•ne•ri, *a*. *Anat*. having the tuft called cotyledon (*cotyledonary* placenta).—**cotyledonous,** kot•i•lē′do•nus, *a*. Pertaining to cotyledons; having cotyledons.

couch, kouch, *v.i.* [Fr. *coucher*, O.Fr. *colcher*, Pr. *colcar*, It. *colcare*, from *collocare*, to lay, to place—*col* for *con*, and *locare*, to place.] To lie down, as on a bed or place of repose; to recline; to lie or crouch with body close to the ground, as a beast; to stoop; to bend the body or back (O.T.); to lie or be outspread (O.T.). —*v.t.* To lie down; to spread on a bed or floor (to *couch* malt); to express in obscure terms that imply what is to be understood: with *under*; to fix a spear in the rest in the posture of attack; *surg*. to cure of cataract in the eye by depressing the crystalline lens.—*n*. A bed; a seat for repose or on which one may lie down undressed; any place for repose, as the lair of a wild beast, etc.; a heap of steeped barley spread out on a floor to allow germination to take place, and so convert the grain into malt.—**couchant,** kouch′ant, *a*. Lying down; squatting. (*Tenn*.).

couch grass, kouch′gras, *n*. [A corruption of *quitch* or *quick grass*.] A species of grass which infests arable land, spreading over a field with great rapidity, being propagated both by seed and by its creeping rootstock.

cougar, kö′gär, *n*. [Native name modified.] A quadruped of the cat kind, 7 or 8 feet in length, one of the most destructive of all the animals of America, particularly in the warmer parts. Called also *puma* and *red tiger*.

cough, kof, *n*. [Imitative of the sound; like D. *kuch*, a cough; G. *keichen*, *keuchen*, to pant, cough.] A deep inspiration of air followed by a spasmodic and sonorous expiration, excited by the sensation of the presence of some irritating cause in the air passages.—*v.i.* To give a cough; to expel the air from the lungs suddenly with noise.—*v.t.* To expel from the lungs by a violent effort with noise; to expectorate; with *up* (to *cough up* phlegm).—*To cough down*, to put down an unpopular or too lengthy speaker by simulated coughs.—**cougher,** kof′ėr, *n*. One that coughs.

could, kụd, *v*., pret. of *can*. [O.E. *coude*, A.Sax. *cúthe*, pret. of *cunnan*, to be able. See CAN. *L* has been improperly introduced through the influence of *would* and *should*.] Was able, capable, or susceptible.

coulee, kö′li, *n*. [Fr., from *couler*, to flow.] *Geol*. a stream of lava, whether flowing or consolidated.

coulisse, kö•lēs′, *n*. [Fr.] One of the side scenes of the stage in a theater or the space included between the side scenes.

coulomb, kö•lom′, *n*. [From *Coulomb*, the French physicist.] In *current elect*., the practical unit of quantity, that transferred by a current of one ampere in one sec., equal to 1/10 of the absolute electromagnetic unit of quantity.

coulter, kōl′tėr, *n*. [L. *culter*, a knife, a coulter.] An iron blade or knife inserted into the beam of a plow for the purpose of cutting the ground and facilitating the separation of the furrow slice by the plow-share.

coumarine, kö′ma•rēn, *n*. [From *coumaron*, a tree of Guiana.] A vegetable principle obtained from the tonka bean, used in medicine and to give flavor to the Swiss cheese called schabzieger.

council, koun′sil, *n*. [Fr. *concile*, from L. *concilium*—*con*, together, and root *cal*, to summon; akin *conciliate*, *reconcile*. This word is often improperly confounded with *cousel*.] An assembly of men summoned or convened for consultation, deliberation, and advice (a common *council*, an ecumenical *council*, the privy-*council*); act of deliberation; consultation, as of a council.—*Council of war*, an assembly of officers of high rank called to consult with the commander-in-chief of an army or admiral of a fleet on matters of supreme importance.—**councilor,** koun′sil•ėr, *n*. The member of a council; specifically, a member of a common council or of the privy-council.—**councilman,** *n*. A member of a city common council.

counsel, koun′sel, *n*. [Fr. *conseil*, from L. *consilium*, advice, from *consulo*, to consult, deliberate. Akin *consult*.] Opinion or advice, given upon request or otherwise, for directing the judgment or conduct of another; consultation; interchange of opinions; deliberation; the secrets entrusted in consultation; secret opinions or purposes (to keep one's *counsel*); intent or purpose; one who gives counsel in matters of law.—*v.t.*—*counseled*, *counseling*. To give advice or deliberate opinion to, for the government of conduct; to advise, exhort, warn, admonish, or instruct; to recommend or give an opinion in favor of.—**counselor,** koun′sel•ėr, *n*. Any person who gives counsel or advice; an adviser; one whose profession is to give advice in law, and manage causes for clients; a barrister. —**counselorship,** koun′sel•ėr•ship, the office of a counselor.

count, kount, *v.t.* [Fr. *conter*, *compter*, from L. *computare*, to compute. COMPUTE.] To tell or name one by one, or by small numbers, in order to ascertain the whole number of units in a collection; to reckon; to number; to compute; to esteem, account, think, judge or consider. *To count out*, to bring (a meeting) to a close by numbering the members and finding a quorum not present, as in the House of Commons, where this is done by the speaker.—*v.i.* To be added or reckoned in with others; to reckon; to rely; in this sense with *on* or *upon* (to *count on* assistance).—*n*. The act of numbering; reckoning; number; *law*, a particular charge in an indictment, or narration in pleading, setting forth the cause of complaint.—**countable,** koun′ta•bl, *a*. Capable of being counted or numbered.—**count down,** the count by seconds prior to the firing of a missile, with the precise moment of firing designated as zero.—**counter,** koun′tėr, *n*. One who counts, numbers, or reckons; that which is used to keep an account or reckoning, as in games, such as a small plate of metal, ivory, wood, etc.; a counterfeit or imitation of a coin; a registering apparatus or telltale; a table or board on which money is counted; a table in a store over which sales are made, and on which goods are exposed for sale.—**countless,** kount′les, *a*. Not capable of being counted; innumerable.—**countinghouse,** *n*. A house or room appropriated by mercantile men to the business of keeping their books, accounts, etc.

count, kount, *n*. [Fr. *comte*, from L. *comes*, *comitis*, a companion, a companion of the emperor or a king—*com* for *con*, with, and stem of *eo*, *itum*, to go, seen also in *ambition*, *exit*, *transit*, *perish*, etc.] A title of foreign nobility, equivalent to the English *earl*, and whose domain is a *county*.—**countess,** koun′tes, *n*. The wife of an earl or count, or a lady possessed of the same dignity in her own right.

countenance, koun′te•nans, *n*. [Fr. *contenance*, demeanor, way of acting or holding one's self, from *contenir*, to contain. CONTAIN.] The whole form of the face; the features considered as a whole; the visage; the face; appearance or expression of the face; favor expressed toward a person; good will; support.—*In countenance,* in favor or estimation; free from shame or dismay.—*Out of countenance,* confounded; abashed; not bold or assured.—*v.t. countenanced, countenancing.* To favor; to encourage; to aid; to support; to abet.

counter, koun′tėr, *adv.* [Fr. *contre,* from L. *contra—con,* and *tra,* denoting direction, as in *intra, extra, ultra.*] In an opposite direction; in opposition; contrariwise.—*n.* The opposite; a stiffener around the heel of a shoe.—*v.t.* To act in opposition to.—*v.i.* To make an opposing move. —*a.* Adverse; opposite; opposing.

counteract, koun•tėr•akt′, *v.t.* To act in opposition to; to hinder, defeat, or frustrate by contrary agency; to oppose.—**counteraction,** koun′tėr•ak•shon, *n.* Action in opposition; hindrance; resistance.—**counteractive,** koun′tėr•ak•tiv, *a.* Tending to counteract.—*n.* One who or that which counteracts.

counterattraction, koun′tėr•at•trak″shon, *n.* Opposite attraction.

counterbalance, koun•tėr•bal′ans, *v.t.—counterbalanced, counterbalancing.* To weigh against with equal force; to counteract.—*n.* Weight, power, etc. balancing or counteracting another; counterpoise.

counterchange, koun′tėr•chānj, *n.* Exchange; reciprocation. (*Shak.*)—*v.t.* To give and receive; to cause to make alternate changes; to alternate. (*Tenn.*)

countercharge, koun′tėr•chärj, *n.* An opposite charge.

counterclockwise, koun′tėr•klok″wīz, *adv.* and *a.* In a direction opposite to that in which the hands of a clock rotate.

countercurrent, koun′tėr•kur•ent, *n.* A current in an opposite direction.

counterespionage, koun″tėr•es′pi•o•nij, *n.* The measures taken by a nation to detect and defeat enemy espionage.

counterfeit, koun′tėr•fit, *a.* [Fr. *contrefait,* made to correspond—*contre,* against, and *faire,* to make.] Made in imitation of something else, with a view to pass the false copy for genuine or original; forged; not genuine; base; assuming the appearance of something; false; spurious; hypocritical.—*n.* One who pretends to be what he is not; an impostor; a cheat; that which is made in imitation of something with a view to defraud by passing the false for the true.—*v.t.* To copy or imitate with a view to pass off as original or genuine; to make a likeness or resemblance of with a view to defraud; to forge; to imitate or copy generally; to sham or pretend. —*v.i.* To feign; to dissemble; to carry on a fiction or deception.—**counterfeiter,** koun′tėr•fit•ėr, *n.* One who counterfeits; a forger; one who assumes a false appearance, or who makes false pretenses.

counterfoil, koun′tėr•foil, *n.* [*Counter,* and *foil,* from L. *folium,* a leaf.] A portion of a document, such as a bank check or draft, which is retained by the person giving the other part, and on which is noted the main particulars contained in the principal document.

counterirritant, koun′tėr•ir•i•tant, *n. Med.* an irritant substance employed to relieve another irritation or inflammation, as mustard, croton oil, Spanish flies.

countermand, koun•tėr•mand′, *v.t.* [Fr. *contremander—contre,* and *mander,* L. *mando,* to command.] To revoke, as a former command; to order or direct in opposition to an order before given, thereby annulling it.—*n.* A contrary order; revocation of a former order or command by a subsequent order.

countermarch, koun•tėr•märch′, *v.i.* To march back.—*n.* A marching back; a returning; a change of measures.

countermine, koun′tėr•mīn, *n. Milit.* a mine sunk in search of the enemy's mine or till it meets it, to defeat its effect; *fig.* a stratagem or project to frustrate any contrivance; an opposing scheme or plot.—*v.t.* To mine so as to discover or destroy an enemy's mine; *fig.* to frustrate by secret and opposite measures.—*v.i.* To make a countermine; to counterplot.

counterpane, koun′tėr•pān, *n.* [From older *counterpoint,* O.Fr. *contrepoinct,* corruptly derived from L.L. *culcita puncta,* lit. stitched quilt. QUILT, POINT.] A bedcover; a coverlet for a bed; a quilt.

counterpart, koun′tėr•pärt, *n.* A part that answers to or resembles another, as the several parts or copies of an indenture corresponding to the original; a thing or person exactly resembling another; a copy; a duplicate; the thing that supplements another thing or completes it; a complement.

counterplot, koun′tėr•plot, *v.t.* To oppose or frustrate by another plot or stratagem.—*n.* A plot or artifice set afoot in order to oppose another.

counterpoint, koun′tėr•point, *n.* The art of writing music in several distinct parts or themes proceeding simultaneously, as distinguished from harmony, which depends more for its effects on the composition and progression of whole chords than on the melody of each separate part; so called because the points which formerly represented musical notes were written under or against each other on the lines; often used, but improperly, as equivalent to *harmony.*

counterpoise, koun′tėr•poiz, *v.t.* To weigh against with equal weight; to equal in weight; to counterbalance; to act against with equal power or effect; to balance.—*n.* A weight equal to and acting in opposition to another weight; equal power or force acting in opposition; state of being in equilibrium by being balanced by another weight or force.

counterrevolution, koun′tėr•rev•o•lū•shon, *n.* A revolution opposed to a former one, and restoring a former state of things.

counterscarp, koun′tėr•skärp, *n. Fort.* the slope of the ditch nearest the enemy and opposite the scarp; the face of the ditch sloping down from the covered way.

countersign, koun′tėr•sīn, *v.t.* To sign (a document) formally or officially in proof of its genuineness; to attest or witness by signature.—*n.* A private signal, word, or phrase given to a guard with orders to let no man pass unless he first give that sign; a watchword; also, the signature of a subordinate to a writing signed by his superior, to attest its authenticity.—**countersignature,** koun′tėr•sig″ne•chėr, *n.* The name of a secretary or other subordinate officer countersigned to a writing.

countersink, koun′tėr•singk, *v.t.* To form a cavity in timber or other materials so as to receive the head of a bolt, screw, etc., and make it flush with the surface; to sink below or even with a surface, as the head of a screw, bolt, etc., by making a depression for it in the material.—*n.* A drill or brace bit for countersinking; the cavity made by countersinking.

countertenor, koun′tėr•ten•ėr, *n. Mus.* the highest male adult voice, having about the same compass as the alto, with which term this is sometimes confounded; a singer with this voice.

countervail, koun′tėr•vāl, *v.t.* [Fr. *contrevaloir.* AVAIL.] To act with equivalent force or effect against anything; to balance; to compensate; to equal.—*n.* Equal weight, strength, or value; compensation; requital.

counterview, koun′tėr•vū, *n.* An opposite or opposing view; a posture in which two persons front each other; opposition; contrast.

counterweigh, koun′tėr•wā, *v.t.* To weigh against; to counterbalance.—**counterweight,** koun′tėr•wāt, *n.* A weight in the opposite scale; a counterpoise.

counterwork, koun′tėr•wėrk, *v.t.* To work in opposition to; to counteract; to hinder any effect by contrary operations.—*n.* A work in opposition or in answer to another.

country, kun′tri, *n.* [Fr. *contrée,* from L.L. *contrata,* country, from L. *contra,* against, opposite; *country* being thus literally the land opposite or before us. Akin *counter,* adv., *encounter.*] A tract of land; a region; the land occupied by a particular race of people; a state; a person's native or adopted land.—*The country,* the rural parts of a region, as opposed to cities or towns; the inhabitants of a region; the people; the public; the parliamentary electors of a state, or the constituencies of a state, collectively.—*a.* Pertaining to the country or to a district at a distance from a city; rural; rustic.—**countrified,** kun′tri•fīd, *a.* Having the airs or manner of a rustic.—**countryman,**

kun′tri•man, *n.* One born in the same country with another; one who dwells in the country as opposed to the town; a rustic; an inhabitant or native of a region.—**countrywoman,** kun′tri•wu̧•man, *n.* A woman belonging to the country, as opposed to the town; a woman born in the same country; a female inhabitant or native of a region.—**country-dance,** *n.* [*Country* and *dance*; not from Fr. *contre-danse,* which is a kind of quadrille.] A dance in which the partners are arranged opposite to each other in lines.

county, koun′ti, *n.* [L.L. *comitatus,* from *comes, comitis,* a count. COUNT.] Originally, the district or territory of a count or earl; now, an administrative unit in various countries; in the United States, the political unit below a State; a shire (which see); a count; an earl or lord‡.—*a.* Pertaining to a county. —*County town,* the chief town of a county; that town where the various courts of a county are held.

coup, kö, *n.* A French term for stroke or blow, and used in various connections, to convey the idea of promptness, force, or violence.—*Coup d'état* (kö•dā•tä), a sudden decisive blow in politics; a stroke of policy; specifically, a daring or forcible alteration of the constitution of a country without the consent or concurrence of the people.—*Coup de grâce* (köd•gräs), the finishing stroke.—*Coup de main* (köd•mań), a sudden attack or enterprise.—*Coup d'œil* (kö•dė′i), glance of the eye; a comprehensive or rapid view.—*Coup de soleil* (köd•so•lā′i), sunstroke.

coupé, coupe, kö•pā, köp, *n.* [From Fr. *carosse coupé,* cut-off coach.] An enclosed carriage seating two inside and a driver outside; an enclosed two-door automobile, generally seating two but sometimes four persons.

couple, kup′l, *n.* [Fr. *couple,* from L. *copula,* a band, bond, connection.] Two of the same class or kind, connected or considered together; a brace; a pair; a male and female connected by marriage, betrothed, or otherwise allied; *mech.* two equal and parallel forces acting in opposite directions; *elect.* one of the pairs of plates of two metals which compose a battery, called a *galvanic* or *voltaic couple*; *carp.* one of a pair of opposite rafters in a roof, united at the top where they meet.—*v.t.*—*coupled, coupling.* To link, chain, or otherwise connect; to fasten together; to unite, as husband and wife; to marry.—*v.i.* To copulate.—**coupler,** kup′lėr, *n.* One who or that which couples; specifically, the mechanism by which any two of the ranks of keys, or keys and pedals, of an organ are connected together.—**couplet,** kup′let, *n.* Two verses or lines of poetry, especially two that rhyme together; a pair of rhymes.—**coupling,** kup′ling, *n.* The act of one who couples; that which couples or connects; a coupler; a contrivance for connecting one portion of a system of shafting with another; the chains or rods connecting the carriages, etc., of a train.

coupon, kö′pon, *n.* [Fr., from *couper,* to cut.] An interest certificate printed at the bottom of transferable bonds, and so called because it is cut off or detached and given up when a payment is made; hence, generally one of a series of tickets which binds the issuer to make certain payments, perform some service, or give value for certain amounts at different periods, in consideration of money received.

courage, kur′ij, *n.* [Fr. *courage,* from L. *cor,* the heart, whence also *cordial,* etc.] That quality of mind which enables men to encounter danger and difficulties with firmness, or without fear; bravery; intrepidity; valor; boldness; resolution; disposition or frame of mind (*Shak.*)‡.—**courageous,** ku•rā′jus, *a.* Possessing or characterized by courage; brave; bold; daring; intrepid.—**courageously,** ku•rā′jus•li, *adv.* In a courageous manner.—**courageousness,** ku•rā′jus•nes, *n.*

courier, kö′ri•ėr, *n.* [Fr. *courrier,* from *courir,* L. *curro,* to run.] A messenger sent express with letters or dispatches; an attendant on a party traveling abroad whose especial duty is to make all arrangements at hotels and on the journey.

course, kōrs, *n.* [Fr. *cours, course,* a course, a race, direction; way, etc.; from L. *cursus,* L.L. also *cursa,* from *curro, cursum,* to run (whence *current, incur, recur,* etc.).] A running, race, flight, career, a moving or motion forward in any direction; a continuous progression or advance; the direction of motion; the line in which a body moves; the ground or path marked out for a race; continuous or gradual advance; progress; order or succession; stated or orderly method of proceeding; customary or established sequence; series of successive and methodical proceedings; systematized order in arts or sciences for illustration or instruction (*course* of studies, etc.); way of life or conduct; line of behavior (to follow evil *courses*); the part of a meal served at one time; *arch.* a continued range of stones or bricks of the same height throughout the face or faces of a building; *naut.* one of the sails that hang from a ship's lowest yards; *pl.* the menstrual flux; catamenia.—*v.t. coursed, coursing.* To hunt; to pursue; to chase; to hunt (hares) with greyhounds; to drive with speed; to run through or over.—*v.i.* To move with speed; to run or move about.—*Of course,* by consequence; in regular or natural order; naturally; without special direction or provision.—**courser,** kōr′sėr, *n.* One who courses; a swift horse; a war horse: used chiefly in poetry; a swift-footed cream-colored bird of the plover tribe; any bird of the cursorial order, or runners.

court, kōrt, *n.* [O.Fr. *cort, court* (Fr. *cour*), from L. *cors, cortis,* contracted from *cohors, cohortis,* a yard, a *court*—*co* for *con,* and *hor,* a root seen in *hortus,* a garden, also in *garden, garth.*] An enclosed uncovered area, whether behind or in front of a house, or surrounded by buildings; a courtyard; an alley, lane, close, or narrow street; the place of residence of a king or sovereign prince; all the surroundings of a sovereign in his regal state; the collective body of persons who compose the retinue or council of a sovereign; a hall, chamber, or place where justice is administered; the persons or judges assembled for hearing and deciding causes, as distinguished from the counsel or jury; any judicial body, civil, military, or ecclesiastical; the sitting of a judicial assembly; attention directed to a person in power to gain favor; civility; flattery; address to gain favor (to pay *court* to a person).—*v.t.* To endeavor to gain the favor of or win over by attention and address; to flatter; to seek the affections or love of; to woo; to solicit for marriage; to attempt to gain by address; to solicit; to seek (to *court* applause); to hold out inducements to; to invite. —*v.i.* To pay one's addresses; to woo. —**courteous,** kėr′ti•us, *a.* Having courtly, refined, or elegant manners; characterized by courtesy; affable; condescending, polite.—**courteously,** kėr′ti•us•li, *adv.* In a courteous manner.—**courteousness,** kėrt′i•us•nes, *n.*—**courtesan, courtezan,** kōr′ti•zan, *n.* A prostitute.—**courtesy,** kėr′ti•si, *n.* Politeness of manners, combined with kindness; polished manners or urbanity shown in behavior toward others; an act of civility or respect; a curtsy (in this sense pronounced kėrt′si); favor or indulgence, as contradistinguished from right.—*Courtesy of England,* the husband's tenure of certain kinds of property after his wife's death.—*Courtesy title,* a title assumed or popularly accorded and to which the individual has no valid claim, as the title marquis to the eldest son of a duke, viscount to the eldest son of an earl, etc.—**courtier,** kōr′ti•ėr, *n.* One who attends or frequents the court of a sovereign; one who courts or flatters another with a view to obtain favor, etc.—**courtly,** kōrt′li, *a.* Relating or pertaining to a prince's court; refined and dignified; elegant; polite; courteous.—**courtliness,** kōrt′li•nes, *n.* The state or quality of being courtly.—**courtship,** kōrt′ship, *n.* The act of courting or soliciting favor; wooing.—**courtcard,** *a.* A corruption of *coat-card* (which see).—**court hand,** *n.* The old manner of writing used in records and judicial proceedings.—**courthouse,** *n.* A house in which established courts are held.—**court-martial,** *n.* pl.—**courts-martial.** A court consisting of military or naval officers, for the trial of military or naval offenses.—**court plaster,** *n.* A fine kind of sticking plaster.—**courtyard,** *n.* A court or enclosure round a house or adjacent to it.

cousin, kuz′n, *n.* [Fr. *cousin,* from L.L. *cosinus,* for L. *consobrinus,* a cousin—*con*, and *sobrinus*, akin to *soror*, a sister.] The son or daughter of an uncle or aunt; in a wider and now less usual sense, one collaterally related more remotely than a brother or sister; a kinsman or kinswoman; a blood-relation; a title given by a monarch to a nobleman.—**cousinhood,** kuz′n•hụd, *n.* The state of being cousins; the individuals connected with a family regarded collectively.—**cousinly,** kuz′n•li, *a.* Like or becoming a cousin.—**cousinship,** kuz′n•ship, *n.* The state of being cousins; cousinhood.—**cousin-german,** *n.* A first or full cousin.

couvade, kö•väd, *n.* [Fr. *couver*, to hatch; L. *cubare*, to lie. COVEY.] A custom among primitive races (Basques, Corsicans, etc.) of men, by which, at the birth of a child, the father takes to bed and is attended by mother. Perhaps to prove paternity, by a survival from earlier days of promiscuity of intercourse.

cove, kōv, *n.* [A.Sax. *cófa*, a chamber, a cave; allied to Icel. *kofi*, Sw. *kofwa*, a hut.] A small inlet, creek, or bay; a sheltered recess in the seashore; *arch.* any kind of concave molding; the concavity of a vault.—*v.t. coved, coving.* To arch over.

covenant, kuv′e•nant, *n.* [O.Fr. *covenant*, for *convenant*, from L. *convenire*, to agree—*con*, and *venio*, to come. CONVENE.] A mutual consent or agreement of two or more persons to do or to forbear some act or thing; a contract; a compact; a bargain, arrangement, or stipulation; a writing containing the terms of agreement or contract between parties.—*v.i.* To enter into a formal agreement; to contract; to bind one's self by contract.—*v.t.* To grant or promise by covenant. [O.T.]—**covenantee,** kuv′e•nan•tē″, *n.* The person to whom a covenant is made.—**covenanter,** kuv′e•nan•tėr, *n.* One who makes a covenant; [*cap.*] a term specially applied to those who joined in the Solemn League and Covenant in Scotland, and in particular those who resisted the government of Charles II, and fought and suffered for adherence to their own form of worship.—**covenantor,** kuv′e•nan•tėr, *n. Law*, the person who makes a covenant and subjects himself to the penalty of its breach.

cover, kuv′ėr, *v.t.* [O.Fr. *covrir*, Fr. *couvrir*, from L. *cooperire*—*con*, intens., and *operire*, to cover.] To overspread the surface of with another substance; to lay or set over; to overspread so as to conceal; to envelop; to wrap up; to clothe; to shelter; to protect; to defend; to cloak; to screen; to invest with; to brood over; to be sufficient for; to include; to comprehend; to be equal to; to be coextensive with.—*n.* Anything which is laid, set, or spread over another thing; anything which veils or conceals; a screen; disguise; superficial appearance; shelter; defense; protection; concealment and protection; shrubbery, woods, underbrush, etc., which shelter and conceal game; the articles laid at table for the use of one person.—plate, spoon, knife and fork, etc.—**coverer,** kuv′ėr•ėr, *n.* One who or that which covers.—**covering,** kuv′ėr•ing, *n.* That which covers; anything spread or laid over another, whether for security, protection, shelter, or concealment; clothing; dress; wrapper; envelope.—**coverlet,** kuv′ėr•let, *n.* [O.Fr. *covre-lit*, *couvre-lit*, a bed-cover—*covrir*, to cover, and *lit*, L. *lectus*, a bed.] The upper covering of a bed.—**coverlid,** kuv′ėr•lid, *n.* A coverlet. (*Tenn.*)

covert, kuv′ėrt, *a.* [O.Fr. *covert*, part. of *covrir*, to cover.] Kept secret or concealed; not open (*covert* fraud or enmity); *law*, under cover, authority, or protection.—*n.* A place which covers and shelters; a shelter; a defense; a thicket; a shady place or a hiding place; *pl.* feathers covering the bases of the quills of the wing or tail of birds.—**covertly,** kuv′ėrt•li, *adv.* Secretly; in private; insidiously.—**coverture,** kuv′ėr•chėr, *n.* Covering; shelter; defense; *law*, the state of a married woman, who is considered as under the cover or power of her husband.

covet, kuv′et, *v.t.* [From O.Fr. *coveiter* (Fr. *convoiter*), from L. *cupidus*, desirous, *cupio*, to desire.] To desire or wish for with eagerness; to desire earnestly to obtain or possess; to desire inordinately; to desire with a greedy or envious longing; to long for; to hanker after.—*v.i.* To have or indulge inordinate desire.—**covetable,** kuv′e•ta•bl, *a.* That may be coveted.—**coveter,** kuv′e•tėr, *n.* One who covets.—**covetous,** kuv′e•tus, *a.* Very desirous; eager to obtain; inordinately desirous; excessively eager to obtain and possess; avaricious.—**covetously,** kuv′e•tus•li, *adv.* With a strong or inordinate desire; eagerly; avariciously.—**covetousness,** kuv′e•tus•nes, *n.* The state or quality of being covetous; avarice; cupidity; greediness; craving.

covey, kuv′i, *n.* [O.Fr. *covee*, Fr. *couvée*, a brood, from *couver*, *cover*, to sit on or brood, L. *cubare*, to lie; seen also in *incubate*.] A brood or hatch of birds; an old fowl with her brood of young; a small flock: usually confined to partridges.

cow, kou, *n.* pl. **cows,** kouz, old pl. **kine,** kīn. [A.Sax. *cú*, pl. *cý*; G. *kuh*, D. and Dan. *koe*, Icel. *kú*; the same root appears in Skr. *go*, nom. *gaus*, a cow, an ox., *Kine* is a double plural, the *en* form as in *oxen* being added to the older form.] The general term applied to the females of the bovine genus or ox, the most valuable to man of all the ruminating animals, on account of her milk, flesh, hide, etc.—**cowbane,** *n.* A kind of hemlock, water hemlock, highly poisonous, being sometimes fatal to cattle who eat its leaves.—**cowberry,** *n.* Red whortleberry.—**cowboy,** *n.* Boy who has charge of cows; a man who looks after cattle on a large stock farm and does this work on horseback.—**cow bunting,** *n.* An American bird belonging to the starling tribe, remarkable for dropping its eggs into the nests of other birds to be hatched.—**cowcatcher,** *n.* A strong frame in front of locomotives for removing obstructions, such as strayed cattle, from the rails.—**cowhide,** *n.* The hide or skin of a cow, made or to be made into leather; a strong whip made of such leather.—*v.t.* To thrash or whip with a lash of cowhide.—**cowpea,** *n.* A kind of clover having bright red flowers.—**cowpox,** *n.* A disease which appears on the teats of the cow in the form of vesicles or blisters, the fluid or virus contained in which is capable of communicating the disease to the human subject, and of conferring, in the great majority of instances, security against smallpox.—**cowslip,** kou′slip, *n.* [A.Sax. *cu-slyppe*, *cu-sloppe*, the latter part of the name apparently meaning dung.] A perennial herb of the primrose family, growing in moist places in Britain.—*Cowslip wine*, a beverage made by fermenting cowslips with sugar, and used as a domestic soporific.

cow, kou, *v.t.* [Dan. *kue*, Icel. *kúga*, to depress, subdue, keep under.] To sink the spirits or courage of; to daunt, dishearten, intimidate, overawe.

coward, kou′ėrd, *n.* [Fr. *couard*, It. *codardo*, from L. *cauda*, a tail, the name being originally applied to the timid hare from its short tail.] A person who wants courage to meet danger; a poltroon; a craven; a dastard; a faint-hearted, timid, or pusillanimous man.—*a.* Destitute of courage; timid; of, proceeding from, or expressive of fear or timidity.—**cowardice,** kou′ėr•dis, *n.* [Fr. *couardise.*] Want of courage to face danger; timidity; pusillanimity; fear of exposing one's person to danger.—**cowardly,** kou′ėrd•li, *a.* Wanting courage to face danger; timid; timorous; pusillanimous; fainthearted; mean; base; proceeding from fear of danger; befitting a coward.—*adv.* In the manner of a coward.—**cowardliness,** kou′ėrd•li•nes, *n.* Cowardice.

cower, kou′ėr, *v.i.* [Same word as Sc. *curr*, to squat; Icel. *kúra*, Dan. *kure*, Sw. *kura*, to doze, to rest; G. *kauern*, to cower.] To squat; to stoop or sink downward, as from terror, discomfort, etc.

cowhage, cowitch, kou′ij, kou′ich, *n.* [Hind. *kawanch*, cowhage.] The short, brittle hairs of the pods of a leguminous plant, which easily penetrate the skin, and produce an intolerable itching; they are administered in honey or molasses as a vermifuge.

cowl, koul, *n.* [A.Sax. *cufle*, Icel. *kufl*, *kofl*, a cowl; comp. also O.Fr. *coule*, from L. *cucullus*, a cowl.] A hood, especially a monk's hood; a chimney covering designed to increase draft; the part of an automobile body on which the windshield and dashboard are mounted. —**cowled,** kould, *a.* Wearing a cowl; hooded in shape of a cowl (*cowled* leaf).

cowl, koul, *n.* [O.Fr. *cuvel*, dim. of *cuve*, a tub, from L. *cupa*. CUP.] A vessel to be carried on a pole betwixt two persons, for the conveyance of water.—**cowlstaff,** *n.* Same as *Colstaff.*

co-work, kō•wėrk′, *v.i.* To work jointly; to co-operate.—**co-worker,** kō•wėr′kėr, *n.* One that works with another; a co-operator.

cowry, kou′ri, *n.* [Hind. *kauri.*] A small univalve shell used for coin on the coast of Guinea, and in many parts of Southern Asia.

coxa, kok′sa, *n.* [L.] *Anat.* the hip, haunch, or hip joint; *entom.* the joint of an insect's limb which is next the body.

coxcomb, koks′kōm, *n.* [*Cock's comb.*] The comb resembling that of a cock which licensed fools wore formerly in their caps; hence used often for the cap itself; the top of the head, or the head itself; a vain showy fellow; a superficial pretender to knowledge or accomplishments; a fop; a dandy.—**coxcombical,** koks•kom′i•kal, *a.* Like or indicating a coxcomb; conceited; foppish.—**coxcombry,** koks′kōm•ri, *n.* The manners of a coxcomb; foppishness.

coxswain, *n.* Same as *Cockswain.*

coy, koi, *a.* [O.Fr. *coi, coy, coit,* from L. *quietus,* quiet. QUIET.] Shrinking from familiarity; shy; modest; reserved; distant; backward; bashful. —**coyly,** koi′li, *adv.* In a coy manner; with disinclination to familiarity.—**coyness,** koi′nes, *n.* The quality of being coy; bashfulness; shyness; reserve; modesty.

coyote, koi•ōt′, koi•ō′ti, *n.* [Sp. *coyote,* Mex. *coyotl.*] The American prairie wolf.

coypu, koi′pö, *n.* The native name of a South American rodent, beaver-like, semiaquatic mammal, valued for its fur.

cozen, kuz′n, *v.t.* [A form of *cousin;* Fr. *cousiner,* to sponge upon people (under pretext of relationship), from *cousin,* a cousin.] To cheat; to defraud; to deceive; to beguile.—*v.i.* To cheat; to act deceitfully.—**cozenage,** kuz′n•ij, *n.* Trickery; fraud; deceit.—**cozener,** kuz′n•ėr, *n.* One who cozens.

cozy, cosy, kō′zi, *a.* [Akin to Norse *koselig,* cosy, *kose sig,* to enjoy one's ease.] Well sheltered; snug; comfortable; social.—*n.* A kind of padded covering or cap put over a teapot to keep in the heat after the tea has been infused.—**cozily,** kō′zi•li, *adv.*

crab, krab, *n.* [A.Sax. *crabba*=D. *krab,* Icel. *krabbi,* Sw. *krabba,* G. *krabbe,* a crab; all perhaps from L. *carabus,* Gr. *karabos,* a kind of crab.] A popular name for all the ten-footed, short-tailed crustaceans, having the tail folded under the body, the two forefeet not used for locomotion, but furnished with strong claws or pincers, and several species being highly esteemed as food; Cancer, a sign in the zodiac; a name given to various machines, as a kind of portable windlass or machine for raising weights, etc.

crab, krab, *n.* [Sw. *krabbāple,* a crab apple, perhaps from *crab,* the animal, in allusion to its pinching or astringent juice.] A small, wild, very sour apple; the tree producing the fruit; a sour-tempered, peevish, morose person‡.—**crab apple,** *n.* A wild apple.—**crabbed,** krab′ed, *a.* Rough or harsh as regards temper or disposition; sour; peevish; morose; difficult; perplexing; uninviting (a *crabbed* author).—**crabbedly,** krab′ed•li, *adv.* In a crabbed manner; peevishly; morosely.—**crabbedness,** krab′ed•nes, *n.* The state or quality of being crabbed.—**crabstick,** *n.* A walking stick made of the wood of the crab tree.—**crab tree,** *n.* The tree that bears crabs; the wild apple tree.

crack, krak, *v.t.* [An imitative word; A.Sax. *cracian,* to crack; G. *krachen,* to crack; D. *krak,* a crack; Gael. *knac,* a crack, as of a whip, etc.] To rend, break, or burst; to break partially; to break without an entire severance of the parts; to throw out or utter with smartness (to *crack* a joke); to snap; to cause to make a sharp sudden noise (a whip).—*v.i.* To break with a sharp sound; to burst; to open in chinks; to be fractured without quite separating into different parts; to give out a loud or sharp sudden sound; to boast or brag: with *of* (*Shak.*)‡.—*n.* A chink or fissure; a partial separation of the parts of a substance, with or without an opening; a burst of sound; a sharp or loud sound uttered suddenly; a violent report; injury or impairment to the intellect or to the character; flaw; blemish; an instant; a trice.—*a.* Having qualities to be proud of; first-rate; excellent (a *crack* regiment, a *crack* horse).—**cracked,** krakt, *p.* and *a.* Burst or split; rent; broken; impaired; crazy, as regards the mind.—**cracker,** krak′ėr, *n.* One who or that which cracks; a noisy, boasting fellow (*Shak.*); a small kind of firework filled with powder, which explodes with a sharp crack or with a series of sharp cracks; a small hard biscuit.—**crackle,** krak′l, *v.i.*—*crackled, crackling.* [Dim. of *crack.*] To make slight cracks; to make small abrupt noises, rapidly or frequently repeated; to decrepitate. —**crackling,** krak′l•ing, *n.* A noise made up of small cracks or reports frequently repeated; the browned skin of roast pig; a kind of cake used for dog's food, made from the refuse of tallow melting.—**cracknel,** krak′nel, *n.* A hard brittle cake or biscuit. —**crackbrained,** *a.* Having a disordered intellect; insane; lunatic; mad.

cradle, krā′dl, *n.* [A.Sax. *cradel, cradal;* comp. G. *krätze,* a basket.] A small bed, crib, or cot in which an infant is rocked; hence, the place where any person or thing is nurtured in the earlier stage of existence; something resembling a cradle in construction or use, as a case in which a broken limb is placed after being set; a rocking machine in which gold is washed from the earth, etc., containing it; a vessel or basket attached to a line or lines between a wrecked ship and the shore for bringing off the crew or passengers, etc.—*v.t.*—*cradled, cradling.* To lay in a cradle; to rock in a cradle; to compose or quiet by rocking; to nurse in infancy.—*v.i.* To lie or lodge as in a cradle. (*Shak.*)

craft, kraft, *n.* [A.Sax. *craeft,* craft, cunning, force, a craft=G. Sw. Icel. and Dan. *kraft,* D. *kracht,* power, faculty; from root of which *cramp* is a nasalized form, akin to Skr. *grabh.* to grasp.] Cunning art, or skill, in a bad sense; artifice; guile; dexterity in a particular manual occupation; hence, the occupation or employment itself; manual art; trade; the members of a trade collectively; *naut.* a vessel: often used in a collective sense for vessels of any kind.—**craftsman,** krafts′man, *n.* An artificer; a mechanic; one skilled in a manual occupation.—**craftsmanship,** krafts′man•ship, *n.* The skilled work of a craftsman.—**crafty,** kraf′ti, *a.* Characterized by, having, or using craft; cunning; wily; sly; deceitful; subtle; dexterous; skillful.—**craftily,** kraf′ti•li, *adv.* In a crafty manner; cunningly; slyly; deceitfully; skillfully; dexterously.—**craftiness,** kraf′ti-nes, *n.* The state or quality of being crafty.

crag, krag, *n.* [Gael. *creag,* Ir. *craig,* W. *careg,* a rock, stone.] A steep, rugged rock; a rough broken rock, or point of a rock; a cliff; *geol.* shelly deposits in Norfolk and Suffolk, usually of gravel and sand, of the older pliocene period.—**cragged,** krag′ed, *a.* Full of crags or broken rocks; craggy.—**craggy,** krag′i, *a.* Full of crags; abounding with broken rocks; rugged with projecting points of rocks.—**cragginess,** krag′i•nes, *n.* The state of being craggy.—**cragsman,** kragz, *n.* One who is dexterous in climbing or descending rocks; one who takes seafowls or their eggs from crags.

crake, krāk, *n.* [Imitative of the bird's cry, like *croak, creak;* comp. L. *crex,* Gr. *krex,* a landrail; Icel. *kraka,* to croak, etc.] A grallatorial bird of various species belonging to the family of the rails, the best known species being the corncrake or land rail.

cram, kram, *v.t.*—*crammed, cramming.* [A.Sax. *crammian,* to cram; Dan. *kramme,* to crush; Sw. *krama,* to press; akin *cramp.*] To press or drive, particularly in filling or thrusting one thing into another; to stuff; to crowd; to fill to superfluity; to fill with food beyond satiety; to stuff; *fig.* to endeavor to qualify for an examination, in a comparatively short time, by storing the memory with only such knowledge as is likely to serve the occasion; to coach.—*v.i.* To eat greedily or beyond satiety; to stuff; to prepare for an examination by rapidly storing the memory with crude facts.—*n.* Information got up hurriedly for an examination or other special purpose.—**crammer,** kram′ėr, *n.* One who crams or stuffs; one who crams in study.

crambo, kram′bō, *n.* [Origin doubtful.] A game in which one person gives a word, to which another finds a rhyme; a word rhyming with another.

cramp, kramp, *n.* [Same as D. *kramp,*

Dan. *krampe*, Sw. *kramp*, *krampa*, G. *krampf*, *krampe*, cramp, a cramp-iron; from root seen in *cram*, *crimp*, *crumple*.] The contraction of a limb or some muscle of the body, attended with pain; spasm; a feeling of restraint; a piece of iron bent at the end, serving to hold together pieces of timber, stones, etc.; a cramp iron; a portable kind of iron screw press for closely compressing the joints of a timber framework.—*v.t.* To pain or affect with spasms or cramps; to confine, restrain, or hinder from action or expansion; to fasten, confine, or hold with a cramp or cramp iron.—*a.* Difficult; knotty.—**crampon,** kram′pon, *n.* [Fr. *crampon*.] *Bot.* an adventitious root which serves as a fulcrum or support in climbing, as in the ivy.—**crampoon,** kram′pön, *n.* An iron fastened to the shoes of a storming party, to assist them in climbing a rampart; an apparatus used in raising timber or stones for building, consisting of two hooked pieces of iron hinged together.

cranberry, kran′be•ri, *n.* [That is *craneberry*, perhaps because the berries are eaten by cranes.] The globose, dark red berry, about the size of a currant, produced by several species of small shrubs growing in peat bogs or swampy land in Europe and North America; the shrub producing this berry. Called also *Mossberry* and *Moorberry*.

crane, krān, *n.* [A.Sax. *cran*; cog. D. *kraan*, G. *krahn*, *kranich*, Icel. *trani*, Dan. *trane* (with *tr* for *kr*), W. *garan*, Gr. *geranos*, L. *grus*, the bird, also the lifting apparatus; from a root *gar*, seen in L. *garrio*, Gr. *geryō*, to call.] A large migratory grallatorial bird of several species, having long slender legs, a long neck, and powerful wings; a machine for raising great weights, and depositing them at some distance from their original place, the most common form consisting of a vertical shaft, with projecting arm or jib, at the outer end of which is a fixed pulley, carrying the rope or chain to receive the weight, which is raised by coiling the rope or chain round a cylinder; a movable iron arm or beam attached to the back or side of a fireplace for supporting a pot or kettle; a siphon or crooked pipe for drawing liquors out of a cask.—*v.i.—craned*, *craning*. To stretch out one's neck like a crane; hence, *hunting*, to look before one leaps; to pull up at a dangerous jump.—**crane fly,** *n.* A dipterous insect having very long legs, and lanceolate spreading wings; the daddy longlegs is a well-known species.—**crane's-bill,** *n.* The popular name given to the species of Geranium, from the long slender beak of their fruit.

cranium, krā′ni•um, *pl.* **crania,** krā′ni•a, *n.* [L.L. *cranium*, from Gr. *kranion*, a skull.] The bones which enclose the brain; the skull.—**cranial,** krā′ni•al, *a.* Relating to the cranium.—**craniofacial,** krā′ni•o•fā•shal, *a.* Pertaining to the cranium and face.—**craniology,** krā•ni•ol′o•ji, *n.* The knowledge of the cranium or skull; the art of determining the intellectual and moral peculiarities of individuals by the shape of their skulls; phrenology.—**craniological,** krā′ni•o•loj″ik•al, *a.* Pertaining to craniology.—**craniologist,** krā•ni•ol′o•jist, *n.* One who treats of or is versed in craniology.—**craniometer,** krā•ni•om′et•ėr, *n.* An instrument for measuring skulls.—**craniometrical,** krā′ni•o•met″ri•kal, *a.* Pertaining to craniometry.—**craniometry,** krā•ni•om′et•ri, *n.* The art of measuring skulls.

crank, krangk, *n.* [Allied to *cringe*, *crinkle*; D. *krinkel*, something bending, a curve, *krinkelen*, to bend.] An iron axis with the end bent like an elbow, serving as a handle for communicating circular motion (as in a grindstone), for changing circular motion into motion backward and forward or the reverse (steam engine), or for merely changing the direction of motion (as in bell hanging); any twisting or turning in speech; a whim; any perversity of action or manner; a crotchety or perverse person.—*v.t.* To bend into the shape of a crank; to furnish with a crank; to start by turning a crank.—*v.i.* To turn a crank.

crank, krangk, *a.* [A.Sax. *cranc*, weak, sick; D. and G. *krank*, Icel. *krankr*, sick, ill.] Liable to be overset, as a ship when she has not sufficient ballast to carry full sail; in a shaky or crazy condition; loose; disjointed.—**cranky,** krang′ki, *a.* Liable to overset; full of crotchets or whims; not to be depended on; unsteady; crazy.

cranny, kran′i, *n.* [Fr. *cran*, a notch, from L. *crena*, a notch; comp. G. *krinne*, a rent.] A small narrow opening, fissure, crevice, or chink, as in a wall or other substance.—*v.i.* To become intersected with or penetrated by crannies or clefts; to enter by crannies (*Shak.*).—**crannied,** kran′id, *p.* or *a.* Having chinks, fissures, or crannies.

crape, krāp, *n.* [Fr. *crêpe*, O.Fr. *crespe*, from L. *crispus*, curled. CRISP.] A thin transparent cloth with a crinkled surface; crepe; a band of black crepe worn in mourning.

crapulence, krap′ū•lens, *n.* [L. *crapulo*, intoxication.] Drunkenness; the sickness occasioned by intemperance.—**crapulent, crapulous,** krap′ū•lent, krap′ū•lus, *a.* Drunk; sick by intemperance; connected or associated with drunkenness.

crash, krash, *v.t.* [Imitative. Comp. *crack*, *clash*, *crush*, etc.] To break to pieces violently; to dash with tumult and violence.—*v.i.* To make the loud multifarious sound of a thing or things falling and breaking; or to make any similar noise.—*n.* The loud sound of a thing or things falling and breaking; a sound made by dashing; the collapse of a commercial undertaking; bankruptcy; failure.

crash, krash, *n.* [L. *crassus*, thick.] A coarse kind of linen cloth, mostly used for towels.

crasis, krā′sis, *n.* [Gr. *krasis*, a mixing.] *Med.* the mixture of the constituents of a fluid, as the blood; hence, temperament; constitution; *gram.* a figure by which two different letters are contracted into one long letter or into a diphthong: called also *Synaeresis*.

crass, kras, *a.* [L. *crassus*.] Gross; thick; coarse; not thin, nor fine: applied to fluids and solids; *fig.* gross; dense; stupid; obtuse.—**crassitude,** kras′i•tūd, *n.* Grossness; coarseness; thickness. — **crassness,** kras′nes, *n.* Grossness.

crate, krāt, *n.* [L. *crates*, wickerwork.] A kind of basket or hamper of wickerwork, used for the transportation of china, glass, etc.; also for fruit; framework made of wooden slats.—*v.t.* To pack in a crate.

crater, krā′tėr, *n.* [L. *crater*, from Gr. *kratēr*, a great cup, a mixing vessel, from *kerannymi*, to mix.] The orifice or mouth of a volcano; a hole made by a bomb or a meteorite.

craunch, kra̤nsh, *v.t.* [Imitative, same as *crunch*, *scranch*.] To crush with the teeth; to crunch.

cravat, kra•vat′, *n.* [Fr. *Cravate*, a Croat, and hence a cravat, because this piece of dress was adopted in the seventeenth century from the Croats who entered the French service.] A neckcloth; an article of muslin, silk, woolen, or other material worn by men about the neck.

crave, krāv, *v.t.—craved*, *craving*. [A.Sax. *crafian*, to ask—Icel. *krefja*, Sw. *krāfva*, Dan. *kraeve*, to crave, to ask.] To ask for with earnestness or importunity; to ask (a thing) with submission or humility; to beg, entreat, implore, solicit; to call for, as a gratification; to long for; to require or demand, as a passion or appetite.—*v.i.* To beg, ask, beseech, or implore; to long or hanker eagerly: with *for*.—**craver,** krā′vėr, *n.* One who craves.—**craving,** krā′ving, *n.* Vehement or inordinate desire; a longing.—*a.* Ardently or inordinately desirous or longing.

craven, krā′vn, *n.* [O.Fr. *cravanter*, to overthrow, from a L.L. *crepantare*, from L. *crepare*, to break; akin *crevice*, *crepitate*.] Formerly one vanquished in trial by battle, and yielding to the conqueror; hence, a recreant; a coward; a weak-hearted, spiritless fellow.—*a.* Cowardly; base.

craw, kra̤, *n.* [Of same origin as Dan. *kro*, D. *kraag*, G. *kragen*, the throat, craw.] The crop or first stomach of fowls; the stomach, in a general sense.

crawfish, *n.* The crayfish; also the spiny lobster, a marine crustacean.

crawl, kra̤l, *v.i.* [Of same origin as Sw. *krāla*, also *krafla*, Icel. *krafla*, Dan. *kravle*, G. *krabbeln*, to crawl.] To move slowly by thrusting or drawing the body along the ground; to move on hands and knees; to move slowly or cautiously; to swarm with crawling things; to feel overrun by crawling things; to behave abjectly.—*n.* The act of crawling; a method of swimming consisting of double overarm strokes combined with fluttering leg movements; a creeping motion.—**crawler,** kra̤′lėr, *n.* One who or that which crawls;

a creeper; a reptile; a mean, cringing fellow.—**crawlingly,** krą'ling•li, *adv.* In a crawling manner.

crayfish, crawfish, krā'fish, krą'fish, *n.* [A curious corruption of comparatively modern origin; formerly *crevise, creveys,* from O.Fr. *crevice,* O.H.G. *krebiz,* G. *krebs* — crab. CRAB.] The river lobster, a ten-footed crustacean found in streams, and resembling the lobster, but smaller, used as food; also the spiny lobster.

crayon, krā'on, *n.* [Fr. *crayon,* from *craie,* L. *creta,* chalk, whence *cretaceous.*] A pencil or cylinder of colored pipe clay, chalk, or charcoal, used in drawing upon paper; a composition pencil made of soap, resin, wax, and lampblack, used for drawing upon lithographic stones —*v.t.* To sketch with a crayon; hence, to sketch roughly.

craze, krāz, *v.t.*—*crazed, crazing.* [Same as Sw. *krasa,* to crush, break; Dan. *krase,* to crackle; from sound of crushing. Akin *crush, crash,* etc.] To break in pieces, grind or crush‡; to put out of order; to impair the natural force or energy of; to derange the intellect of; to render insane. —*v.i.* To become crazy or insane; to become shattered; to break down.—*n.* Craziness; an inordinate desire or longing; a passion; a wild fancy or notion.—**crazy,** krā'zi, *a.* Decrepit; feeble; shattered; unsound: of the body or any structure; disordered, deranged, weakened, or shattered in mind.—**crazily,** krā'zi•li, *adv.* In a crazy manner.—**craziness,** krā'zi•nes, *n.* The state of being crazy; imbecility or weakness of intellect; derangement.

creak, krēk, *v.i.* [Imitative of a more acute and prolonged sound than *crack*; comp. Fr. *criquer,* to creak; W. *crecian,* to scream.] To make a sharp harsh grating sound of some continuance, as by the friction of hard substances.—*v.t.* To cause to make a harsh protracted noise.—*n.* A sharp, harsh, grating sound.

cream, krēm, *n.* [Fr. *crème,* from L.L. *cremum* (or *crema*), cream—a word suggested by L. *cremor,* thick juice or broth; It. Sp. and Pg. *crema,* cream.] Any part of a liquor that separates from the rest, rises, and collects on the surface; more particularly, the richer and butyraceous part of milk, which rises and forms a scum on the surface, as it is specifically lighter than the other part of the liquor; the best part of a thing; the choice part; a sweetmeat prepared from cream (as, ice *cream*).—*Cream of tartar,* the scum of a boiling solution of tartar; a salt obtained from the tartar of argol that forms on the inside of wine casks, frequently employed in medicine.—*v.t.* To skim; to take the cream off by skimming; to take off the best part of.—*v.i.* To gather cream; to gather a covering on the surface; to flower or mantle. (*Shak.*)—**creamy,** krē'mi, *a.* Full of cream; having the nature of or resembling cream.—**creaminess,** krē'mi•nes, *n.* The state of being creamy.—**cream cheese,** *n.* A cheese made with milk to which a certain quantity of cream is added.—**creamer,** krē'mėr, *n.* A pitcher for holding cream; a machine that separates cream from milk.—**creamery,** krē'mėr•i, *n.* An establishment to which farmers send their milk to be made into butter and cheese.

crease, krēs, *n.* [Prob. related to O.Fr. *creast,* a line, ridge, or furrow.] A line or mark made by folding or doubling anything; hence, a similar mark, however produced; specifically, the name given to certain lines marking boundaries near the wickets in the game of cricket.—*v.t. creased, creasing.* To make a crease or mark in, as by folding or doubling.—**creasy,** krē'si, *a.* Full of creases; characterized by creases. (*Tenn.*)

crease, krēs, *n.* [Malay.] A Malay dagger.

creaser, krēs'ėr, *n.* A tool, or a sewing machine attachment for making creases on leather or cloth, as guides to see by; in *bookbinding,* a tool for making the band impression distinct on the back or for making blind lines or creases on covers.

create, krē•āt', *v.t.*—*created, creating.* [L. *creo, creatum,* to create; same root as Skr. *kri,* to make.] To originate or cause; to bring into being; to cause to exist; to make or form, by investing with a new character; to constitute; to appoint (to *create* a peer); to be the occasion of; to bring about; to cause; to produce (*create* a disturbance).—**creation,** kri•ā'shon, *n.* The act of creating, producing, or causing to exist; especially, the act of bringing this world into existence; the act of investing with a new character; appointment; formation; the things created; that which is produced or caused to exist; the world; the universe.—**creational,** kri•ā'shon•al, *a.* Pertaining to creation.—**creative,** kri•ā'tiv, *a.* Having the power to create, or exerting the act of creating. —**creator,** kri•ā'tėr, *n.* [L.] One who, or that which, creates, produces, causes, or constitutes; [*cap.*] distinctively, the almighty Maker of all things.—**creatorship,** kri•ā'tėr•ship, *n.* The state or condition of a creator. —**creature,** krē'chėr, *n.* [O.Fr. *creature,* L.L. *creatura.*] Anything created‡; a thing‡; a created being: any living being; a human being, in contempt or endearment; a person who owes his rise and fortune to another; one who is entirely subject to the will or influence of another; a mere tool.—*a.* Of or belonging to the body (*creature* comforts).

creatic, krē•at'ik, *a.* [Gr. *kreas, kreatōs,* flesh.] Relating to flesh or animal food.—**creatin,** krē'a•tin, *n.* Substances obtained from animal flesh by chemical processes.

creche, krāsh, *n.* [Fr. *crèche,* manger.] An institution or establishment where, for a small payment, children are fed and taken care of during the day, in cases where the mothers daily go from home to work; an asylumn for foundlings; a representation of the manger and the Holy Family.

credence, krē'dens, *n.* [L.L. *credentia,* belief, from L. *credens, credentis,* pp. of *credo,* to believe. CREED.] Reliance on evidence derived from other sources than personal knowledge, as from the testimony of others; belief or credit (to give a story *credence*); the small table by the side of the altar or communion table, on which the bread and wine are placed before they are consecrated: called also *Credence-table.*—**credendum,** kri•den'dum, *n.* pl. **credenda,** kri•den'da. [L.] A thing to be believed; an article of faith.—**credent,**† krē'dent, *a.* Believing; giving credit; easy of belief; having credit; not to be questioned. (*Shak.*)—**credential,** kri•den'shal, *n.* That which gives a title or claim to confidence†; *pl.* testimonials or documents given to a person as the warrant on which belief, credit, or authority is claimed for him among strangers, such as the documents given to an ambassador when sent to a foreign court.

credible, kred'i•bl, *a.* [L. *credibilis.*] Capable of being believed; such as one may believe; worthy of credit, reliance, or confidence as to truth and correctness: applied to persons and things.—**credibility, credibleness,** kred•i•bil'i•ti, kred'i•bl•nes, *n.* The state or quality of being credible.—**credibly,** kred'i•bli, *adv.* In a credible manner; so as to command belief (to be *credibly* informed).

credit, kred'it, *n.* [Fr. *crédit*; L. *creditum.* CREED.] Reliance on testimony; belief; faith; trust; good opinion founded on a belief of a man's veracity, integrity, abilities, and virtue; reputation derived from the confidence of others; esteem; honor; what brings some honor or estimation; reputation for commercial stability or solvency; the selling of goods or lending of money in confidence of future payment; trust; *bookkeeping,* the side of an account in which payment or other item lessening the claim against a debtor is entered: opposed to *debit*; the time given for payment for goods sold on trust.—*v.t.* To believe; to confide in the truth of; to sell, or lend in confidence of future payment; to trust; to enter upon the credit side of an account; to give credit for.—*Letter of credit,* an order given by bankers or others at one place to enable a specified person to receive money from their agents at another place.—**creditable,** kred'i•ta•bl, *a.* Accompanied with reputation or esteem; the cause of credit or honor; honorable; estimable.—**creditability,** kred'i•ta•bil''i•ti, *n.* The quality of being creditable.—**creditably,** kred'i•ta•bli, *adv.* Reputably; with credit; without disgrace.—**creditor,** kred'i•tėr, *n.* [L.] One who gives goods or money on credit; one to whom money is due; one having a just claim for money; correlative to *debtor.*

credulous, kred'ū•lus, *a.* [L. *credulus,* from *credo,* to believe.] Apt to believe without sufficient evidence; unsuspecting; easily deceived.—**credulously,** kred'ū•lus•li, *adv.* With credulity.—**credulousness, credulity,** kred′ū•lus•nes, kre•dū′li•ti, *n.* The state or quality of being credulous; disposition or readiness to believe without sufficient evidence.

creed, krēd, *n.* [A.Sax. *creda,* from L. *credo,* I believe, the first word of the Apostles' Creed, whence also *credence, credit, credible,* also *grant, recreant.*] A brief and authoritative summary of the articles of Christian faith; hence, a statement or profession of fundamental points of belief; a system of principles of any kind which are believed or professed.

creek, krēk, *n.* [O.E. *creke, cryke,* a creek, a bay; D. *kreek,* Icel. *kriki,* a crack, a corner; akin to *crook.*] A small inlet, bay, or cove; a recess in the shore of the sea or of a river; a stream of water smaller than a river but larger than a brook; a narrow winding passage.

creel, krēl, *n,* [Gael. *craidhleag*; same root as *cradle.*] An osier basket or pannier; specifically, a large deep fish basket for carrying on the back.

creep, krēp, *v.i.* pret. et pp. *crept.* [A.Sax. *creópan*—D. *kruipen,* Icel. *krjúpa,* Sw. *krypa,* Dan. *krybe,* to creep or crawl; akin *cripple, cramp.*] To move with the belly on the ground or any surface, as a reptile, or as many insects with feet and very short legs; to crawl; to move along a surface in growth (as a vine); to move slowly, feebly, or timorously; to move slowly and insensibly, as time; to move secretly or insidiously; to move or behave with extreme servility or humility; to cringe; to fawn; to have a sensation such as might be caused by worms or insects creeping on the skin.—**creeper,** krē′pėr, *n.* One who or that which creeps; a creeping plant, which moves along the surface of the earth, or attaches itself to some other body, as ivy; an instrument of iron with hooks or claws for dragging the bottom of a well, river, or harbor; a popular name of birds which resemble the woodpeckers in their habits of creeping on the stems of trees in quest of insect prey.—*n.* The act of creeping, or moving slowly and insensibly.

creese, krēs, *n.* A crease or Malay dagger.

cremate, kri•māt′, *v.t.*—*cremated, cremating.* [L. *cremo, crematum,* to burn.] To burn; to dispose of (a human body) by burning instead of interring.—**cremation,** kri•mā′shon, *n.* The act or custom of cremating; the burning of a dead body instead of burial.—**crematory,** krē′ma•to•ri, *a.* Connected with or employed in cremation.—*n.* A place for cremation.

Cremona, kri•mō′na, *n.* A general name given to the unrivalled violins made at *Cremona* in North Italy in the seventeenth and eighteenth centuries.

crenate, crenated, krē′nāt, kri′nā•ted, *a.* [L. *crenatus,* notched, *crena,* a notch.] Notched; intented; scalloped; *bot.* applied to a leaf having its margin cut into even and rounded notches or scallops.—**crenature,** kren′a•chėr, *n.* A tooth of a crenate leaf, or any other part that is crenate.

crenel, crenelle, kren′el, kre•nel′, *n.* [O.Fr. *crenel,* from L. *crena,* a notch.] An embrasure in an embattled parapet or breastwork to fire through; an indentation; a notch.—**crenelate,** kren′e•lāt, *v.t.* To furnish with crenels or similar openings; to embattle.—**crenelation,** krē•nel•lā′shon, *n.* The act of crenelating: a crenel or indentation.—**crenulate, crenulated,** kre′nū•lāt, kre′nū•lā•ted, *a.* Having the edge cut into very small scallops.

Creole, krē′ōl, *n.* [Fr. *créole,* Sp. *criollo*; said to be of Negro origin.] A white descendant of early French settlers in Louisiana; a Latin American descended from French or Spanish conquerors; [*often not cap.*] a person of mixed Spanish, French, and Negro ancestry.—*a.* Of or relating to Creoles.

creosote, krē′ō•sōt, *n.* A heavy, oily colorless liquid of strong odor obtained from wood tar, used as a powerful antiseptic.

crepe, krāp, *n.* [Fr. *crêpe.*] Thin crinkled fabric, often of silk, but also of other textiles; crape.—*Crepe paper,* paper resembling crepe.

crepitate, krep′i•tāt, *v.i.*—*crepitated, crepitating.* [L. *crepito, crepitatum,* freq. from *crepo,* to crackle (whence *crevice*).] To make a crackling noise; to rattle.—**crepitation,** krep′i•tā″shon, *n.*

crepuscular, kri•pus′kū•lėr, *a.* [L. *crepusculum,* twilight.] Pertaining to twilight; glimmering; flying or appearing in the twilight or evening, or before sunrise, as certain insects.

crescendo, kre•shen′dō. [It.] *Mus.* a term signifying that the notes of the passage are to be gradually swelled: usually written *Cres.,* and marked thus <.

crescent, kres′ent, *a.* [L. *crescens, crescentis,* from *cresco,* to grow, seen also in *increase, decrease, accrue, concrete,* etc.] Increasing; growing; waxing. (*Mil.*)—*n.* The increasing or new moon, which, when receding from the sun, shows a curving rim of light terminating in points or horns; anything shaped like a new moon, as a range of buildings whose fronts form a concave curve; the figure or likeness of the new moon, as that borne in the Turkish flag or national standard; the standard itself, and figuratively, the Turkish power.

cress, kres, *n.* [A.Sax. *caerse, cresse*—D. *kers,* G. *kresse,* Sw. *karse.*] The name of various plants, mostly cruciferous, in general use as a salad, such as water cress, common in streams, and having a pungent taste; garden cress, a dwarf cultivated species; Indian cress, a showy garden annual whose fruits are made into pickles.

cresset, kres′et, *n.* [O.Fr. *crusset, crasset*; akin to E. *cruse,* G. *kruse,* a jar.] A term most commonly applied to a lamp or firepan suspended on pivots and carried on a pole, or to a beacon light in a kind of iron basket; also a large lamp formerly hung in churches, etc.

crest, krest, *n.* [O.Fr. *creste,* L. *crista,* a crest.] A tuft or other excrescence upon the top of an animal's head, as the comb of a cock, etc.; anything resembling, suggestive of, or occupying the same relative position as a crest, as the plume or tuft of feathers, or the like, affixed to the top of the helmet; *her.* a figure placed upon a wreath, coronet, or cap of maintenance above both helmet and shield; the foamy, feather-like top of a wave; the highest part or summit of a hill, ridge, slope, or the like; the rising part of a horse's neck; *fig.* pride, high spirit, courage, daring (*Shak.*).—*v.t.* To furnish with a crest; to serve as a crest for; to adorn as with a plume or crest.—**crested,** kres′ted, *a.* Furnished with a crest or crests.—**crestless,** krest′les, *a.* Without a crest; without a family crest, and hence of low birth (*Shak.*).—**crestfallen,** *a.* Dejected; sunk; bowed; dispirited; spiritless.

cretaceous, kri•tā′shus, *a.* [L. *cretaceus,* from *creta,* chalk.] Composed of or having the qualities of chalk; like chalk; abounding with chalk; chalky.—*Cretaceous group,* in *geol.* the upper strata of the secondary series, immediately below the tertiary series, and superincumbent on the oölite system, containing immense chalk beds.

cretin, krē′tin, *n.* [Swiss dial. *crétin,* a Christian, a man, from L. *christianus.*] One afflicted with cretinism.—**cretinism,** krē′tin•izm, *n.* A congenital condition due to thyroid deficiency and characterized by physical and mental stunting.

cretonne, kri•ton′, *n.* [Fr.] A cotton cloth with various textures of surface printed with pictorial and other patterns, and used for curtains, covering furniture, etc.

crevasse, kre•vas′, *n.* [Fr. *crevasse.* CREVICE.] A fissure or rent: generally applied to a fissure across a glacier, and in the United States to a breach in the embankment of a river.

crevice, krev′is, *n.* [Fr. *crevasse,* from *crever,* L. *crepare,* to burst, to crack; akin *craven, crepitate, decrepit.*] A crack; a cleft; a fissure; a cranny; a rent.—*v.t.* To crack; to flaw.

crew, krū, *n.* [From O. Icel. *krú,* a swarm; or for old *accrue,* number added, company. ACCRUE.] A company of people; an assemblage; a crowd; a band; a gang; a herd; a horde; a company; the company of seamen who man a ship, vessel, or boat; the company belonging to a vessel.

crew, krū, pret. of *crow.*

crewel, krū′el, *n.* [From D. *krul,* a curl.] A kind of fine worsted or thread of silk or wool, used in embroidery and fancy work.

crib, krib, *n.* [A.Sax. *crib, cribb,* D. *kribbe,* Dan. *krybbe,* Icel. and Sw. *krubba,* G. *krippe,* a crib.] A small habitation or cottage; a hovel; the manger or rack of a stable or house for cattle; a feeding place for cattle; a small frame or bed for a child to sleep in; a theft, or the thing stolen (*colloq.*); a literal translation of a classic author for the use of students (*colloq.*); in the game of cribbage, a set of cards made up of two thrown from the hand of each player.—*v.t. cribbed, cribbing.* To shut or confine in a narrow habitation; to cage (*Shak.*), to pilfer or purloin (*colloq.*).—**cribbage,** krib′ij, *n.* A game at cards played with the whole pack by two, three, or four persons: so called because the dealer receives a *crib*, or additional hand partly drawn from the hands of his opponent or opponents.—*Cribbage board*, a board used for marking in the game of cribbage.

crick, krik, *n.* [Akin to *crook.*] A spasmodic affection of some part of the body, as of the neck or back, making motion of the part difficult.

cricket, krik′et, *n.* [O.Fr. *criquet*, from its sharp creaking sound; comp. D. *kriek*, a cricket, *krieken*, to chirp. Akin *creak*, *crack.*] An orthopterous insect of several species, nearly allied to the grasshoppers, noted for the chirping or creaking sound produced by the friction of the bases of its wing cases against each other.

cricket, krik′et, *n.* [Fr. *criquet*, a kind of game.] A favorite open-air game played in England, Australia, and other British possessions, generally by two sides of eleven each, with bats, ball, and wickets.—*v.i.* To engage in the game of cricket.

cricoid, krī′koid, *a.* [Gr. *krikos*, a ring, and *eidos*, appearance.] Ringlike: applied to a round ringlike cartilage of the larynx.

crier, krī′ėr, *n.* See CRY.

crime, krīm, *n.* [Fr. *crime*, L. *crimen*, an accusation, a crime; allied to *cerno*, to sift, *cribrum*, a sieve; Gr. *krinō*, to separate, judge, condemn.] A violation of a law whether human or divine; specifically, a gross violation of law, as distinguished from a misdemeanor, trespass, or other slight offense; any great wickedness or iniquity; a foul wrong; offense.—**criminal,** krim′i•nal, *a.* Guilty of a crime; culpable; wicked; iniquitous; atrocious; abandoned; villainous; felonious; nefarious; partaking of the nature of a crime; involving a crime; that violates public law, divine or human; relating to crime: opposed to *civil.*—*Criminal conversation*, in *law*, adultery; illicit intercourse with a married woman.—*n.* A person guilty of crime; a person indicted or charged with a public offense and found guilty; a culprit; a malefactor.—**criminality,** krim•i•nal′i•ti, *n.* The quality or state of being criminal; that which constitutes a crime; guiltiness.—**criminally,** krim′i•nal•li, *adv.* In a criminal or wicked manner.—**criminate,** krim′i•nāt, *v.t.*—*criminated, criminating.* [L. *criminor*, *criminatus.*] To accuse or charge with a crime; to involve in a crime or the consequences of a crime.—**crimination,** krim•i•nā′shon, *n.* The act of criminating; accusation; charge.—**criminative, criminatory,** krim′i•nā•tiv, krim′i•na•to•ri, *a.* Relating to accusation; accusing.—**criminology,** krim′i•nol″o•ji, *n.* The science of crime.

crimp, krimp, *v.t.* [A lighter form of *cramp*; D. *krimpen*, Dan. *krympe*, G. *krimpen*, to shrink; akin *crumple.*] To curl or crisp, as the hair; to flute or make regular ridges on, as on a frill; to crimple; to pinch and hold; to seize; hence, to decoy for service in the army or navy (see noun); *cookery*, to gash the flesh of a live fish with a knife, to give it greater hardness and make it more crisp.—*n.* One who decoys another into the naval or military service; one who decoys sailors by treating, advancing money, boarding and lodging, giving goods on credit, etc., and when he has them in his power, induces them to engage with a shipmaster whom it is the crimp's interest to serve.

crimson, krim′zn, *n.* [O.Fr. *cramoisin*, from L.L. *carmesinus*, from Ar. *kermez*, *qirmiz*, the kermes insect, which yields the dye; akin *carmine.*] A deep red color; a rich red slightly tinged with blue; a red color in general.—*a.* Of a deep red color.—*v.t.* To dye with crimson; to make red.—*v.i.* To become of a crimson color; to be tinged with red; to blush.

cringe, krinj, *v.i. cringed, cringing.* [A.Sax. *cringan*, *crincan*, to cringe, succumb, from root of *crank*, *crinkle*, etc.] To bend or crouch with servility; to fawn; to stoop or truckle.—*n.* A mean or fawning obeisance.—*v.t.*‡ To contract; to draw together; to distort.—**cringer,** krin′jėr, *n.* One who cringes or bows and flatters with servility.

cringle, kring′gl, *n.* [D. *kring*, *krinkel*, a curl, bend, ring; Icel. *kringla*, an orb, from *kringr*, a circle; A.Sax. *kring*, a ring. Akin *ring*, *cringe.*] A withe for fastening a gate; *naut.* an iron ring, or a short rope worked into the boltrope of a sail so as to form a ring or eye, etc.

crinite, krī′nīt, *a.* [L. *crinitus*, from *crinis*, hair.] Having the appearance of a tuft of hair†; *bot.* having tufts of long weak hairs on the surface.

crinkle, kring′kl, *v.i.*—*crinkled, crinkling.* [D. *krinkelen*, to turn or wind; akin *crank.*] To turn or wind; to bend; to wrinkle; to run in and out in little or short bends or turns; to curl.—*v.t.* To form with short turns or wrinkles; to make with many flexures.—*n.* A wrinkle; a winding or turn; sinuosity.

crinoid, krī′noid, *n.* [Gr. *krinon*, a lily, *eidos*, likeness.] A lily star or sea lily; one of an order of echinoderms having starshaped bodies, supported by a long, slender, calcareous jointed stem; most of the species are fossil.—**crinoid,** krī′noid, *a.* Containing or consisting of the fossil remains of crinoids.

crinoline, krin′o•lin, *n.* [Fr., from *crin*, L. *crinis*, hair, and *lin*, L. *linum*, flax.] A stiff fabric of horsehair, etc.; a skirt or petticoat stiffened by horsehair, hoops, etc.

criosphinx, krī′ō•sfingks, *n.* [Gr. *krios*, a ram, and *sphinx*, sphinx.] A sphinx having the head of a ram.

cripple, krip′l, *n.* [A.Sax. *crypel*—G. *krüppel*, Icel. *kryppil*, a cripple, D. *kreupel*, lame; from stem of *creep.*] One who halts or limps; one who has lost or never enjoyed the use of his limbs; a lame person.—*a.* Lame.—*v.t.*—*crippled, crippling.* To disable by injuring the limbs, particularly the legs or feet; to lame; to deprive of the power of exertion; to disable (a *crippled* fleet).

crisis, krī′sis, *n.* pl. **crises,** krī′sēz. [L. *crisis*, Gr. *krisis*, from the root of *krinō*, to separate, to determine. CRIME.] The change of a disease which indicates recovery or death; the decisive state of things, or the point of time when an affair has reached its height, and must soon terminate or suffer a material change; turning point; conjuncture.

crisp, krisp, *a.* [A.Sax. *crisp*, *crips*, from L. *crispus*, curled, crisp.] Curling in small stiff or firm curls; indented or winding†; easily broken or crumbled; brittle; friable; possessing a certain degree of firmness and freshness; fresh; brisk, effervescing or foaming; sparkling.—*v.t.* To curl; to contract or form into ringlets; to wrinkle or curl into little undulations; to ripple.—*v.i.* To form little curls or undulations; to curl. (*Tenn.*)—**crisper,** kris′pėr, *n.* One who or that which crisps or curls; an instrument for friezing or crisping cloth.—**crisply,** krisp′li, *adv.* In a crisp manner.—**crispness,** krisp′nes, *n.* State of being crisp.—**crispy,** kris′pi, *a.* Curled; formed into ringlets; brittle; dried so as to break short.

cristate, cristated, kris′tāt, kris′tā•ted, *a.* [L. *cristatus*, from *crista*, a crest.] *Bot.* having an appendage like a crest or tuft, as some anthers and flowers; crested; tufted.

criterion, krī•tē′ri•on, *n.* pl. **criteria,** krī•tē′ri•a. [Gr. *kriterion*, from root of *krinō*, to judge. CRIME.] A standard of judging; any established law, rule, principle, or fact by which a correct judgment may be formed.

critic, krit′ik, *n.* [L. *criticus*, Gr. *kritikos*, from *kritēs*, a judge, from *krinō*, to judge. CRIME.] A person skilled in judging of the merit of literary works; a judge of merit or excellence in the fine arts generally; a writer whose chief function it is to pass judgment on matters of literature and art; a reviewer; one who judges with severity; one who censures or finds fault.—**critical,** krit′i•kal, *a.* Relating to criticism; belonging to the art of a critic; passing judgment upon literary and artistic matters; inclined to make nice distinctions; nicely judicious; exact; fastidious; inclined to find fault or to judge with severity: *med.* pertaining to the crisis or turning point of a disease; pertaining to any crisis; decisive; important, as regards consequences (a *critical* time or juncture); momentous; attended with danger or risk; dangerous; hazardous (a *critical* undertaking.—*Critical angle. Optics*, the angle of incidence of a ray passing from one medium into a less refracting medium, when it emerges along the bounding surface.—*Critical temperature*, that temperature of a gas above which no pressure, however great, can liquefy it.—**critically,** kri'tik•al•li, *adv.* In a critical manner; with nice discernment or scrutiny; at the crisis: at the exact time; in a critical situation, place, or condition.—**criticalness,** krit'i•kal•nes, *n.* The state of being critical.—**criticaster,** krit'i•kas•tėr. *n.* A small or inferior critic.—**criticize,** krit'i•sīz, *v.i.—criticized, criticizing.* To judge critically, estimating beauties and defects; to pick out faults; to utter censure.—*v.i.* To examine or judge critically; to notice beauties and blemishes or faults in; to pass judgment on with respect to merit or blame; to animadvert upon.—**criticizable,** krit'i•sī•za•bl, *a.* Capable of being criticized.—**criticism,** krit'i•sizm, *n.* The art of judging with propriety of the beauties and faults of a literary performance or of any production in the fine arts; the art of judging on the merit of any performance; a critical judgment; a detailed critical examination; a critique.—**critique,** kri•tēk', *n.* [Fr.] A written estimate of the merits of a performance, especially of a literary or artistic performance; a criticism.

croak, krōk, *v.i.* [Purely imitative, like M.H.G. *krochzen*, G. *krächzen*, Fr. *croasser*, L. *crocire*, *crocitare*, Gr. *krōzein*, to croak.] To make a low, hoarse noise in the throat, as a frog, a raven, or crow; to produce any low harsh sound; to speak with a low, hollow voice; to forebode evil; to complain; to grumble.—*v.t.* To utter in a low hollow voice; to murmur out; to announce or herald by croaking.—*n.* The low, harsh sound uttered by a frog or a raven, or a like sound.—**croaker,** krō'kėr, *n.* One that croaks, murmurs, or grumbles; one who complains unreasonably; one who takes a desponding view of everything; an alarmist.—**croaky,** krō'ki, *a.* Having or uttering a low harsh sound; hoarse; grumbling.

crochet, krō•shā', *n.* [Fr., dim. of *croc*, a hook.] A species of knitting performed by means of a small hook, the material being worsted, cotton, or silk.—*v.t.* To knit in this style.

crocidolite, krō•sid'o•līt, *n.* [Gr. *krokis*, nap of cloth, *lithos*, stone.] A sort of fibrous quartz, made into trinkets, etc.

crock, krok, *n.* [A.Sax. *crocca*—D. *kruik*, Icel. *krukka*, Dan. *krukke*, G. *krug*, an earthen vessel, pitcher.] An earthen vessel; a pot or pitcher; the soot or smut from pots, kettles, etc.—**crockery,** krok'ėr•i, *n.* Earthenware; vessels formed of clay, glazed and baked.

crocket, krok'et, *n.* [Akin to *crochet* or to *crook*.] An architectural ornament, usually in imitation of curved and bent foliage, etc., placed on the angles of the inclined sides of pinnacles, canopies, gables, etc.; one of the terminal snags on a stag's horn.

crocodile, krok'o•dīl, *n.* [L. *crocodilus*, Gr. *krokodeilos*.] A large aquatic reptile of the lizard kind, sometimes reaching the length of 30 feet, and having a long and powerful tail flattened at the sides, the body covered with square bony plates, the jaws long, and the gape of enormous width; the best known species haunt the Nile.—*a.* Of or pertaining to or like a crocodile.—*Crocodile tears*, false or affected tears: in allusion to the old fiction that crocodiles shed tears over their victims.—**crocodilian,** krok•o•dil'i•an, *a.* Relating to the crocodile.—**crocodilian,** *n.* A reptile of the order (*Crocodilia*) which includes the true crocodile, the alligator, the gavial, etc.

crocus, krō'kus, *n.* [L. *crocus*, Gr. *krokos*, saffron, also the *crocus*.] A beautiful genus of plants of the iris family; deep yellow; saffron.

Cro-Magnon, krō•mag'non, *a.* [*Cro-Magnon*, a cave near Les Eyzies, France.] Pertaining to a group of tall, erect, prehistoric people who lived in southwestern Europe and used bone and stone implements.—*n.* One of this group.

cromlech, krom'lek, *n.* [W. *cromlech*—*crom*, bent, concave, and *llech*, a flat stone.] An ancient structure (probably a sepulchral monument) consisting of two or more large unhewn stones fixed upright in the ground supporting a large flat stone in a horizontal position.

crone, krōn, *n.* [Formerly *crony*, from D. *karonje*, a hussy, a slut, lit. a *carrion*. CARRION.] A contemptuous term for an old woman.—**crony,** krō'ni, *n.* A crone‡; an intimate companion; an associate.

crony, krō'ni, *n.* [Origin uncertain.] An intimate companion; an associate.

crook, kruk, *n.* [Same as Icel. *krókr*, Sw. *krok*, Dan. *krog*, a hook or crook; D. *kruk*, a crutch; comp. W. *crwg*, Gael. *crocan*, a crook, a hook. Akin *crutch*, *crouch*.] Any bend, turn, or curve; curvature; flexure; any bent or curved instrument; especially, a shepherd's staff, curving at the end, or the staff of a bishop or abbot, fashioned in the form of a shepherd's staff, as a symbol of his sway over and care for his flock; a pastoral staff; a small curved tube applied to a trumpet, horn, etc., to change its key; an artifice; a trick; a swindler, sharper.—*v.t.* To bend; to turn from a straight line; to make a curve or hook.—*v.i.* To bend or be bent; to be turned from a straight line.—**crooked,** kru'ked, *a.* Deviating from a straight line; bent, curved, or winding; wry or deformed; deviating from the path of rectitude; perverse, deceitful, devious, or froward.—**crookedly,** kru'ked•li, *adv.* In a crooked, curved, or perverse manner.—**crookedness,** kru'ked•nes, *n.* The state or quality of being crooked.

croon, krön, *v.t.* and *i.* [Imitative of sound; D. *kreunen*, to groan, to lament.] To sing in a low humming tone; to hum; to utter a low, continued, plaintive sound.

crop, krop, *n.* [A.Sax. *crop*, top, bunch, craw of a bird; D. *krop*, G. *kropf*, a bird's crop; Icel. *kroppr*, a hump, bunch.] The first stomach of a fowl; the craw; that which is cropped, cut, or gathered from a single field; the quantity of a particular kind of grain, fruit, etc., obtained from a single field or in a single season; the corn or fruits of the earth collected; harvest; corn and other cultivated plants while growing; the act of cutting or clipping off, as hair.—*Hunting crop*, a riding whip with loop at end, with no lash.—*Neck and crop*, bodily; altogether; bag and baggage.—*v.t.—cropped, cropping.* To cut off the ends of; to eat off or browse; to pull off; to pluck; to mow: to reap; to cause to bear a crop; to raise crops on.—*v.i.* To yield harvest‡. (*Shak.*)—*To crop out*, to appear on the surface; to appear incidentally and undesignedly; to come to light.—**cropper,** krop'ėr, *n.* A breed of pigeons with a large crop; one who raises crops, generally receiving his wages in the form of shares of the crops. Known also as a *sharecropper*.

croquet, krō•kā', *n.* [Fr. *croquer*, to crack.] An open-air game played by two or more persons with mallets, balls, pegs or posts, and a series of iron hoops or arches, the object of each party being to drive their balls through the hoops and against the posts in a certain order before their opponents.

crore, krōr, *n.* In the East Indies, ten millions (a *crore* of rupees).

crosier, *n.* See CROZIER.

cross, kros, *n.* [Prov. *cros*, Fr. *croix*, from L. *crux*, *crucis*, a cross used as a gibbet, from same root as that of W. *crog*, a cross, *crwg*, a hook; Ir. *crohaim*, to hang; Gael. *crocan*, a hook.] An instrument on which malefactors were anciently put to death, consisting of two pieces of timber placed across each other, either in form of +, T, or ×, variously modified, such as [*cap.*] that on which Christ suffered; hence, the symbol of the Christian religion; and hence, *fig.* the religion itself; an ornament in the form of a cross; a monument with a cross upon it to excite devotion, such as were anciently set in market places; any figure, mark, or sign in the form of a cross, or formed by two lines crossing each other, such as the mark made instead of a signature by those who cannot write; anything that thwarts, obstructs, or perplexes; hindrance, vexation, misfortune, or opposition; a mixing of breeds; a hybrid.—*a.* Transverse; passing from side to side; falling athwart; adverse; thwarting; untoward; snappish; perverse; intractable; peevish; fretful; ill-humored; contrary; contradictory; perplexing; made or produced by the opposite party, as a *cross* question or examination.—*v.t.* To draw or run a line or lay a body across another; to erase by marking crosses on or over; to cancel; to make the sign of the cross upon; to pass from side to side of; to pass or move over; to thwart, obstruct, hinder, embarrass; to contradict; to counteract; to clash with; to be inconsistent with; to cause to interbreed; to mix the breed of.—*v.i.* To lie or be athwart; to move or pass across.—*To cross one's path*, to thwart or oppose one's interest, purpose, designs, etc.; to stand in one's way.—*Crossed check*, in Britain, a check crossed with two lines, between which may be written the name of a banking firm or the words 'and Co.', such marks being made as an additional security that the sum shall be paid to the proper party.—**crossing,** kros′ing, *n.* The act of one who crosses; an intersection; a place specially set apart or adapted for passing across, as on a street or line of rails.—**crosslet,** kros′let, *n.* A little cross.—**crossly,** kros′li, *adv.* In a cross manner; athwart; transversely; *fig.* adversely; in opposition; unfortunately; peevishly; fretfully. **crossness,** kros′nes, *n.* The state or quality of being cross; peevishness; ill-humor; fretfulness; perverseness.—**crosswise,** kros′wīz, *adv.* In the form of a cross; across.—**crossbill,** *n.* A bird of several species belonging to the finch family, the mandibles of whose bill curve opposite ways and cross each other at the points.—**crossbones,** *n. pl.* A symbol of death, consisting of two human thigh or arm bones placed crosswise, generally in conjunction with a skull.—**crossbow,** *n.* An ancient missile weapon formed by placing a bow athwart a stock.—**crossbred,** *a.* A term applied to an animal produced from a male and female of different breeds.—**crossbreed,** *n.* A breed produced from parents of different breeds.—**crossbreeding,** *n.* The system of breeding animals, such as horses, cattle, dogs, and sheep, from individuals of two different strains or varieties.—**crosscut,** *v.t.* To cut across.—*Crosscut saw*, a saw adapted for cutting timber across the grain.—**cross-examine,** *v.t.* To examine a witness of one party by the opposite party in the suit or his counsel.—**cross-examination,** *n.* The examination or interrogation of a witness called by one party by the opposite party or his counsel.—**cross-eye,** *n.* That sort of squint by which both eyes turn toward the nose.—**cross-fertilization,** *n. Bot.* the fertilization of the ovules of one plant by the pollen of another; the fecundation of a pistilliferous plant by a staminiferous one, which is effected by the agency of insects, the action of the wind, water, etc.—**cross fire,** *n. Milit.* a term used to denote that the lines of fire from two or more parts of a work cross one another.—**cross-grained,** *a.* Having the grain or fibers transverse or irregular, as timber; *fig.* perverse; intractable; crabbed.—**crosshatching,** *n.* Engraved lines which cross each other regularly to increase or modify the depth of shadow.—**crosshead,** *n.* A beam or rod stretching across the end of the piston of a steam engine and moving between parallel guides.—**cross-pollination,** *n.* Same as *Cross-fertilization.*—**cross-purpose,** *n.* A contrary purpose; a misunderstanding; an inconsistency; *pl.* a sort of conversational game consisting in the mixing up of questions and answers.—*To be at cross-purposes*, to misunderstand each other, and so to act counter without intending it.—**cross-question,** *v.t.* To cross-examine.—**cross reference,** *n.* A reference from one part of a book to another where additional information on the subject is to be had.—**crossroad,** *n.* A road that crosses another, or the place where one road intersects another; a byroad.—**cross section,** *n.* Strictly, the cutting of any body at right angles to its length, but often used to denote the area of the surface thus exposed.—**crosstree,** *n. pl. Naut.* horizontal pieces of timber at the upper ends of the lower and top masts, to sustain the frame of the tops and extend the shrouds.

crotch, kroch, *n.* [Same as CRUTCH.] A fork or forking; the parting of two branches.

crotchet, kroch′et, *n.* [Fr. *crochet*, dim. from *croc*, a hook. CROCHET, CROOK.] A peculiar turn of the mind; a whim or fancy; a perverse conceit; *print.* a bracket; *music*, a black-faced note with a stem.—**crotchety,** kroch′e•ti, *a.* Full of crotchets; whimsical; fanciful; odd.—**crotchetiness,** kroch′e•ti•nes, *n.* The state of being crotchety.

croton, krō′ton, *n.* [Gr. *krotōn*, a tick, from the appearance of the seeds.] A genus of East Indian shrubs from the seeds of which is extracted an oil of active and dangerous purgative properties, and which, when applied externally, acts as an irritant and suppurative.

crouch, krouch, *v.i.* [A softened form of *crook*, with modification of meaning.] To bend down; to stoop low; to lie close to the ground, as an animal; to bend servilely; to stoop meanly; to fawn; to cringe.—*v.t.* To bend or cause to bend lowly.

croup, kröp, *n.* [Fr. *croupe*, the rump, croup. Same origin as *crop.*] The rump or buttocks of certain animals, especially of a horse; hence, the place behind the saddle.

croup, kröp, *n.* [Sc. *croup*, *roup*, hoarseness; allied to Goth. *hropjan*, to croak, to call; A.Sax. *hreópan*, to call.] A dangerous disease mostly attacking children, and consisting of inflammatory affection of the windpipe, accompanied with a short barking cough and difficult respiration, generally brought on by exposure to cold.

croupier, krö′pi•ėr, *n.* [Fr. *croupier*, from *croupe*, the rump or hinder part.] One who superintends and collects and pays the money at a gaming table; one who at a public dinner party sits at the lower end of the table as assistant chairman.

crow, krō, *n.* [A.Sax. *cráwe*, a crow, *cráwan*, to crow or croak, from the cry; like G. *krähe*, a crow, *krähen*, to crow; Goth. *kruk*, a croaking; L. *crocio*, Gr. *krazō*, to croak. Comp. *crake*, *croak.*] The general name of such conirostral birds as the raven, rook, jackdaw, carrion crow, hooded crow, etc.; usually of a black color, and having the voice harsh and croaking; the cry of the cock; a crowbar (which see).—*As the crow flies*, in a direction straight forward, resembling the flight of the crow.—*To have a crow to pluck with one*, to have something demanding explanation from one; to have some fault to find with one; to have a disagreeable matter to settle.—*v.i. crowed* or *crew*; pp. *crowed.* [A.Sax. *cráwan.*] To cry or make a noise as a cock in joy, gaiety, or defiance; to boast in triumph; to vaunt; to vapor; to swagger; to utter a sound expressive of pleasure, as a child.—**crowbar,** krō′bär, *n.* A bar of iron with a bent and sometimes forked end, used as a lever for forcing open doors or raising weights.—**crowfoot,** *n. Naut.* a complication of small cords spreading out from a long block, used to suspend the awnings, etc.; a popular name for the species of buttercups, from the leaf being supposed to have the shape of the foot of a crow.—**crow's-feet,** *n. pl.* The wrinkles brought on by age under and around the outer corners of the eyes.—**crow's-foot,** *n.* A caltrop (which see).—**crow's-nest,** *n.* A barrel or box fitted up on the main-topmast cross-trees of a vessel for the shelter of the lookout man.

crowd, kroud, *n.* [A.Sax. *crúdan*, to press; O.D. *cruden*, to press, to push; L.G. *krüden*, to oppress.] A number of persons or things collected or closely pressed together; a number of persons congregated without order; a throng; the lower orders of people; the populace; the vulgar; the mob.—*v.t.* To press into a crowd; to drive together; to fill by pressing numbers together without order; to fill to excess; to throng about; to press upon; to encumber or annoy by multitudes or excess of numbers.—*v.i.* To press in numbers; to swarm; to press or urge forward.

crown, kroun, *n.* [O.Fr. *corone*, Fr. *couronne*, L. *corona*—crown; Gr. *korōnē*, anything curved, a crown; akin W. *crwn*, Ir. *cruin*, round.] An ornament for the head, in the form of a wreath or garland, worn as a symbol of honor, victory, joy, etc.; a rich head covering of gold, gems, etc., worn by monarchs on state occasions as a badge of sovereignty; hence, regal power; royalty; kingly government or executive authority; the wearer of a crown; the sovereign, as head of the state; honorary distinction; reward; honor; completion; accomplishment; highest or most perfect state; acme; the top part of anything, as of the head, or of a covering for the head, of a mountain or other elevated object; the portion of a tooth which appears above the gum; the end of the shank of an anchor, or the point from which the arms proceed; a coin anciently stamped with a crown (the English crown being a silver piece); paper of a particular size (15 by 20 inches), so called from formerly having the watermark of a crown.—*v.t.* To cover, decorate, or invest with, or as if with, a crown; hence, to invest with regal dignity and power; to honor; to reward; to dignify; to form the topmost or finishing part of; to terminate or finish; to complete; to consummate; to perfect.—*a.* Relating to, pertaining to, or connected with, the crown or government.—*Crown* or *demesne lands*, the lands, estate, or other real property belonging to the crown or sovereign.—**crown glass,** *n.* The finest sort of common window glass.—**crown prince,** *n.* The prince royal who is apparently successor to the crown.—**crown saw,** *n.* A species of circular saw formed by cutting the teeth round the edge of a cylinder, as the surgeon's trepan.

crownwork, *n. Fort.* an outwork running into the field, consisting of two demibastions at the extremes, and an entire bastion in the middle, with curtains.

crozier, crosier, krō'zhi•ėr, *n.* [O.E. *croisier, croysier*, from Fr. *crois*, a cross. CROSS.] A staff about 5 feet long, surmounted by an ornamental cross or crucifix, borne by or before an archbishop on solemn occasions; also (and more properly) a bishop's pastoral staff terminating in a crook.

crucial, krö'shi•al, *a.* [Fr. *crucial*, from L. *crux, crucis*, a cross. CROSS.] Relating to or like a cross; having the shape of a cross; transverse; intersecting; trying or searching, as if bringing to the cross; decisive (a *crucial* experiment).—**cruciate,**† krö'shi•āt, *v.t.* [L. *crucio, cruciatum*, to torture.] To torture; to torment; to afflict with extreme pain or distress.—*a.* Tormented†; *bot.* having four parts arranged like the arms of a cross; cruciform.—**crucifer,** krö'si•fėr, *n.* [L. *crux*, and *fero*, to bear.] A plant belonging to a very extensive order, all the members of which have flowers with six stamens, two of which are short, and four sepals and petals, the spreading limbs of which form a Maltese cross, whence the name.—**cruciform,** krö'si•form, *a.* Cross-shaped; disposed in the form of a cross.

crucible, krö'si•bl, *n.* [L.L. *crucibulum*, from the root seen in G. *kruse*, E. *cruse*, D. *kroes*, pitcher; akin *cresset.*] A chemical vessel or melting pot, made of earth, black lead, platina, etc., and so tempered and baked as to endure extreme heat without fusing; *fig.* a severe or searching test.

crucify, krö'si•fī, *v.t.*—*crucified, crucifying.* [Fr. *crucifier*, L. *crux*, cross, and *figo*, to fix. CROSS, FIX.] To nail to a cross; to put to death by nailing the hands and feet to a cross or gibbet, sometimes anciently by fastening a criminal to a cross with cords; to subdue or mortify; also, to torture.—**crucifix,** krö'si•fiks, *n.* [L. *crucifixus*, crucified.] A cross with the figure of Christ crucified upon it.—**crucifixion,** krö•si•fik'shon, *n.* The act of nailing or fastening a person to a cross, for the purpose of putting him to death; death upon a cross; [*cap.*] the death of Christ.

crude, kröd, *a.* [L. *crudus*, raw, unripe; akin *crudelis*, cruel; from same root as E. *raw.* RAW.] Raw; not cooked; in its natural state; not digested in the stomach; not altered, refined, or prepared by any artificial process (*crude* salt or alum); unripe; not having reached the mature or perfect state; not brought to perfection; unfinished; immature; not matured; not well formed, arranged, or prepared in the intellect (notions, plan, theory).—**crudely,** kröd'li, *adv.* In a crude manner; without due preparation; without form or arrangement; without maturity or digestion.—**crudeness,** kröd•nes, *n.* The state or quality of being crude; rawness; unripeness; a state of being unformed or undigested; immatureness.—**crudity,** krö'di•ti,*n.* [L. *cruditas.*] Crudeness; that which is crude.

cruel, krö'el, *a.* [Fr. *cruel*, from L. *crudelis*, cruel. CRUDE.] Disposed to give pain to others in body or mind; destitute of pity, compassion, or kindness; hard-hearted: applied to persons; exhibiting or proceeding from cruelty; causing pain, grief, or distress; inhuman; tormenting, vexing, or afflicting (disposition, mood, manner, act, words, etc.).—**cruelly,** krö'el•li, *adv.* In a cruel manner; with cruelty; inhumanly; barbarously; painfully; with severe pain or torture; extremely (*colloq.*).—**cruelty,** krö'el•ti, *n.* [O.Fr. *crueltė*, L. *crudelitas.*] The state or character of being cruel; savage or barbarous disposition; any act which inflicts unnecessary pain; a wrong; an act of great injustice or oppression.

cruet, krö'et, *n.* [Contr. from Fr. *cruchette*, dim. of *cruche*, a pitcher. Akin *crock, cruse.*] A vial or small glass bottle for holding vinegar, oil, etc.

cruise, kröz, *v.i.*—*cruised, cruising.* [D. *kruisen*, to cross, to cruise, from *kruis*, a cross. CROSS.] To sail hither and thither, or to rove on the ocean in search of an enemy's ships for capture, for protecting commerce, for pleasure, or any other purpose.—*n.* A voyage made in various courses; a sailing to and fro, as in search of an enemy's ships, or for pleasure.—**cruiser,** krö'zėr, *n.* A person or a ship that cruises; an armed ship that sails to and fro for capturing an enemy's ships, for protecting commerce, or for plunder.

cruller, krul'ėr, *n.* [O.E. *crull*, curled; D. *krullen*, to curl.] A cake shaped in the form of a curl or twist, composed of a rich batter, and fried crisp in deep fat.

crumb, krum, *n.* [A.Sax. *cruma*=D. *kruim*, Dan. *krumme*, G. *krume*, a crumb, from root of *crimp.*] A small fragment or piece; usually, a small piece of bread or other food, broken or cut off; the soft part of bread: opposed to *crust.*—*v.t.* To break into small pieces with the fingers; to cover (meat, etc.) with bread crumbs.—**crumble,** krum'bl, *v.t.*—*crumbled, crumbling.* [A dim. form from *crumb*; like D. *kruimelen*, G. *krümeln*, to crumble.] To break into crumbs or small pieces.—*v.i.* To fall into small pieces, as something friable; to molder; to become frittered away.—**crumbly,** krum'bli, *a.* Apt to crumble; brittle; friable.

crumpet, krum'pet, *n.* [Allied to *crimp*, brittle.] A sort of muffin or tea cake, very light and spongy.

crumple, krum'pl, *v.t.*—*crumpled, crumpling.* [Closely allied to *crimp* and *cramp.*] To draw or press into wrinkles or folds; to rumple.—*v.i.* To contract; to shrink; to shrivel.

crunch, krunsh, *v.t.* [See CRAUNCH.] To crush with the teeth; to chew with violence and noise.—*v.i.* To press with force and noise through a brittle obstacle.

crupper, krup'ėr, *n.* [Fr. *croupière*, from *croupe*, the buttocks. CROUP.] The buttocks of a horse; a strap of leather buckled to a saddle and passing under a horse's tail, to prevent the saddle from sliding forward on to the horse's neck.

crural, krö'ral, *a.* [L. *cruralis*, from *crus, cruris*, the leg.] Belonging to the leg.—*Crural arch*, the ligament of the thigh.

crusade, krö•sād', *n.* [Fr. *croisade*, from L. *crux*, a cross.] [*often cap.*] A military expedition under the banner of the cross, undertaken by Christians in the eleventh, twelfth, and thirteenth centuries, for the recovery of the Holy Land from the power of infidels or Mohammedans; any enterprise undertaken through enthusiasm.—*v.i.*—*crusaded, crusading.* To engage in a crusade; to support or oppose any cause with zeal.—**crusader,** krö•sā'dėr, *n.* A person engaged in a crusade.

crusado, krö•sā'dō, *n.* A Portuguese coin, so called from having the cross stamped on it. (*Shak.*)

cruse, kröz, *n.* [Icel. *krús*, Dan. *krúus*, D. *kroes*, pot, mug; akin *cresset, crucible.*] A small cup; a bottle or cruet (O.T.).

crush, krush, *v.t.* [O.Fr. *cruisir, croissir*, to crack or crash, from the Teutonic; comp. Dan. *kryste*, Sw. *krysta*, Icel. *kreista*, to squeeze; Goth. *kriustan*, to gnash.] To press and bruise between two hard bodies; to squeeze so as to force out of the natural shape; to press with violence; to force together into a mass; to beat or force down, by an incumbent weight, with breaking or bruising; to bruise and break into fine particles by beating or grinding; to comminute; to subdue or conquer beyond resistance.—*v.i.* To press, bruise, or squeeze.—*n.* A violent pressing or squeezing; the act or effect of anything that crushes; violent pressure caused by a crowd; a crowding or being crowded together.—**crusher,** krush′ėr, *n.* One who or that which crushes; a machine for crushing rocks, oilseeds or other materials; a worker who tends such a machine; a conclusive or overwhelming retort.

crust, krust, *n.* [O.Fr. *crouste*, L. *crusta*.] A hard or comparatively hard external coat or covering; a hard coating on a surface; the hard outside portion of a loaf; an incrustation; a deposit from wine, as it ripens, collected on the interior of bottles, etc.—*Crust of the earth*, the exterior portion of our globe which is so far accessible to our inspection and observation.—*v.t.* To cover with a crust; to spread over with hard matter; to incrust.—*v.i.* To gather or form into a crust.—**Crustacea,** krus•tā′shi•a, *n. pl.* [From their crusty covering or shell.] An important division of animals, comprising crabs, lobsters, crayfish, shrimp, etc., having an external calcareous skeleton or shell in many pieces, and capable of being molted or cast; a number of jointed limbs; head and thorax united into a single mass; abdomen often forming a kind of tail.—**crustacean,** krus•tā′shi•an, *n.* and *a.* One of, or pertaining to the crustaceans.—**crustaceous,** krus•tā′shus, *a.* Having a crustlike shell; belonging to the Crustacea; crustacean.—**crustily,** krus′ti•li, *adv.* In a crusty manner; peevishly; harshly; morosely.—**crustiness,** krus′ti•nes, *n.* The quality of being crusty; hardness; snappishness; surliness.—**crusty,** krus′ti, *a.* Like crust; of the nature of a crust; pertaining to a hard covering; hard; peevish; snappish; surly.

crutch, kruch, *n.* [A.Sax. *crycc*, *cricc*, a staff, a crutch; D. *kruk*, G. *krücke*, Dan. *krykke*, Sw. *krycka*, a crutch; same root as in *crook*.] A staff with a curving crosspiece at the head, to be placed under the arm or shoulder to support the lame in walking; any fixture or adjustment of similar form; used in various technical meanings.—*v.t.* To support on crutches; to prop or sustain with miserable helps.

crux, kruks, *n.* [L. *crux*, a cross.] Anything that puzzles greatly; a basic or essential point.

cry, krī, *v.i.*—*cried, crying.* [Fr. *crier*, from L. *quiritare*, to invoke the aid of the *Quirites*, or citizens.] To utter a loud voice; to speak, call, or exclaim with vehemence; to utter a loud voice by way of earnest request or prayer; to utter the voice of sorrow; to lament; to weep or shed tears; to utter a loud voice in giving public notice; to utter a loud inarticulate sound, as a dog or other animal.—*To cry out*, to exclaim; to vociferate; to clamor; to utter a loud voice; to utter lamentations.—*To cry out against*, to complain loudly against; to blame or censure.—*I cry you mercy*,‡ I beg pardon.—*v.t.* To utter loudly; to sound abroad; to proclaim; to name loudly and publicly, so as to give notice regarding; to advertise by crying.—*To cry down*, to decry; to dispraise; to condemn.—*To cry up*, to praise; to applaud; to extol.—*n.* Any loud sound articulate or inarticulate uttered by the mouth of an animal; a loud or vehement sound uttered in weeping or lamentation; a fit of weeping; clamor; outcry; an object for which a party professes great earnestness; a political catchword or the like.—**crier,** krī′ėr, *n.* One who cries; especially, an officer whose duty it is to proclaim the orders or commands of a court, to keep silence, etc.—**crying,** krī′ing, *a.* Calling for vengeance and punishment; clamant; notorious; common; great (*crying* sins).

cryogenics, krī•o•jen′iks, *n.* [Gr. *kryos*, cold, and *gen*, to bring forth.] The physical science dealing with the phenomena of extreme cold.

cryolite, krī′o•līt, *n.* [Gr. *kryos*, cold, and *lithos*, stone—ice-stone.] A fluoride of sodium and aluminum.

crypt, kript, *n.* [L. *crypta*, Gr *cryptē*, from *kryptō*, to hide.] A subterranean cell or cave, especially one constructed for interment.—**cryptic, cryptical,** krip′tik, krip′ti•kal, *a.* Hidden; secret; occult.

cryptogam, krip′tō•gam, *n.* [Gr. *kryptos*, concealed, and *gamos*, marriage.] One of those plants forming a large division of the vegetable kingdom which do not bear true flowers consisting of stamens and pistils, and which are divided into cellular and vascular cryptogams, the former including algæ, fungi, lichens, mosses, etc., the latter the ferns, horsetails, lycopods, etc.—**cryptogamic, cryptogamous,** krip•to•gam′ik, krip•tog′a•mus, *a.*

cryptogram, krip′tō•gram, *n.* [Gr. *kryptos*, concealed, and *gramma*, a letter.] A message or writing in secret code or cipher.—**cryptogrammic,** krip•to•gram′ik, *a.*

cryptograph, krip′to•graf, *n.* [Gr. *kryptos*, concealed, and *graphō*, to write.] Something written in secret characters or cipher.—**cryptographer,** krip•tog′ra•fėr, *n.* One who writes in secret characters.—**cryptographic, cryptographical,** krip•to•graf′ik, krip•to•graf′i•kal, *a.* Written in secret characters or in cipher; pertaining to cryptography.—**cryptography,** krip•tog′ra•fi, *n.* The act or art of writing in secret characters; also, secret characters or cipher.

crystal, kris′tal, *n.* [L. *crystallus*, Gr. *krystallos*, from *kryos*, frost.] Quartz that is clear and transparent or nearly so; glass of superior quality; the transparent cover of a watch dial; *chem.* and *mineral.* a solid substance bounded by plane surfaces that show a symmetrical arrangement; anything made of, or similar to, such a substance; a natural or synthetic crystalline material used for rectification or frequency control. *Rock crystal*, a general name for all the transparent crystals of quartz, particularly of limpid or colorless quartz.—*a.* Consisting of crystal, or like crystal; clear; transparent; pellucid.—**crystalline,** kris′tal•in, *a.* Consisting of crystal; relating or pertaining to crystals or crystallography; resembling crystal; pure; clear; transparent; pellucid.—*Crystalline lens*, a lens-shaped pellucid body situated in the anterior part of the eye, and serving to produce that refraction of the rays of light which is necessary to cause them to meet in the retina, and form a perfect image there.—**crystallizable,** kris′ta•līz•a•bl, *a.* Capable of being crystallized.—**crystallization,** kris′tal•i•zā″shon, *n.* The act of crystallizing or forming crystals; the act or process of becoming crystallized, so that crystals are produced with a determinate and regular form, according to the nature of the substance; a body formed by the process of crystallizing.—*Water of crystallization*, the water which unites chemically with many salts during the process of crystallizing.—**crystallize,** kris′ta•līz, *v.t.*—*crystallized, crystallizing.* To cause to form crystals.—*v.i.* To be converted into a crystal; to become solidified, as the separate particles of a substance into a determinate and regular shape.—**crystallographer,** kris•ta•log′ra•fėr, *n.* One who treats of crystallography, crystals, or the manner of their formation.—**crystallographic, crystallographical,** kris′tal•o•graf″ik, kris′tal•o•graf″i•kal, *a.* Pertaining to crystallography.—**crystallographically,** kris′tal•o•graf″i•kal•li, *adv.* In the manner of crystallography.—**crystallography,** kris•ta•log′ra•fi, *n.* The doctrine or science of crystallization, teaching the principles of the process, and the forms and structure of crystals.—**crystalloid,** kris′tal•oid, *a.* Resembling a crystal.—*n.* The name given to a class of bodies which have the power, when in solution, of passing through membranes, as parchment-paper, easily: opposed to *colloids*, which have not this power; in *seeds*, etc., a minute crystal-shaped mass of albuminoid matter.

ctenoid, ten′oid, *a.* [Gr. *kteis*, *ktenos*, a comb, and *eidos*, form.] Comb-shaped; pectinated; having the posterior edge with teeth: said of the scales of certain fishes, those of the perch and flounder being of this kind; having scales of this kind.—*n.* A fish having ctenoid scales; one of an order of fishes, mostly fossil, having scales jagged or pectinated like the teeth of a comb.

cub, kub, *n.* [Etymology unknown.] The young of certain quadrupeds, as of the lion, bear, or fox; a whelp; a young boy or girl: in contempt; a junior member of the Boy Scouts. —*v.t.*—*cubbed, cubbing.* To bring forth a cub or cubs.

cubane, kū•bān, *n.* A molecule of boxlike structure.

cube, kūb, *n.* [Fr. *cube*, from L. *cubus*, Gr. *kybos*, a cube, a cubical die.] A solid body that is exactly square; a regular solid body with six equal sides, all squares, and containing equal angles; the product of a number multiplied into itself, and that product multiplied into the same number (4×4=16, and 16×4=64, the cube of 4).—*Cube root*, the number or quantity which, multiplied into itself, and then into the product, produces the cube (thus 4 is the cube root of 64).—*v.t.*—*cubed, cubing*. To raise to the cube or third power by multiplying into itself twice.—**cubature,** kū′ba•chėr, *n.* The finding of the solid or cubic contents of a body.—**cubic, cubical,** kū′bik, kū′bi•kal, *a.* [L. *cubicus*.] Having the form or properties of a cube; pertaining to the measure of solids (a *cubic* foot, *cubic* contents).—**cubically,** kū′bi•kal•li, *adv.* In a cubical method.—**cubicalness,** kūb′i•kal•nes, *n.* The state or quality of being cubical.—**cubiform,** *a.* Having the form of a cube.—**cuboid, cuboidal,** kū′boid, kū•boi′dal, *a.* Having the form of a cube or differing little from it.

cubeb, kū′beb, *n.* [Ar. *kabâbah*.] The small spicy berry of a kind of pepper, a native of Java and other East India Isles.

cubicular, kū•bik′ū•lėr, *a.* [L. *cubiculum*, a sleeping room.] Belonging to a bedchamber.—**cubicule,**‡ kū′bi•kūl, *n.* A bedchamber; a chamber.

cubit, kū′bit, *n.* [L. *cubitus, cubitum*, the elbow, an ell or cubit, from root of L. *cubo*, to lie or recline.] *Anat.* the forearm; the ulna, a bone of the arm from the elbow to the wrist; a lineal measure, being the length of a man's arm from the elbow to the extremity of the middle finger: usually taken at 18 inches.

cucking stool, kụk′ing•stöl, *n.* [Icel. *kúka*, to ease one's self, *kúkr*, dung.] A chair in which an offender was placed, usually before her or his own door, to be hooted at or pelted by the mob; or it might be used for ducking its occupant.

cuckold, kuk′old, *n.* [Lit. one who is *cuckooed*, from O.Fr. *coucoul*, L. *cuculus*, a cuckoo; from the cuckoo's habit of depositing her eggs in the nests of other birds.] A man whose wife is false to his bed; the husband of an adulteress.—*v.t.* To make a cuckold of.—**cuckoldly,** kuk′old•li, *a.* Having the qualities of a cuckold. (*Shak.*)—**cuckoldry,** kuk′old•ri, *n.* The debauching of other men's wives; the state of being made a cuckold.

cuckoo, kụ′kö, *n.* [Fr. *coucou*, from L. *cuculus*, like G. *kukuk*, D. *koekoek*, Gr. *kokkux*, Skr. *kokila*, names derived from its cry.] A migratory bird remarkable for its striking call note and its habit of depositing its eggs in the nests of other birds; also the name of many allied birds in various parts of the world.—**cuckoo spit, cuckoo spittle,** *n.* A froth found on plants in summer, being a secretion formed by the larva of a small insect.

cucullate, cucullated, kū•kul′āt, kū•kul′ā•ted, *a.* [L. *cucullatus*, from *cucullus*, a hood or cowl.] Hooded; cowled; covered as with a hood; having the shape or resemblance of a hood.

cucumber, kū′kum•bėr, *n.* [Fr. *concombre*, from L. *cucumis, cucumeris*, a cucumber.] An annual plant of the gourd family, extensively cultivated and prized as an esculent; in an unripe state used in pickles under the name of gherkins.—**cucumber tree,** *n.* A beautiful American tree, a species of *Magnolia*, abounding in the Alleghanies.—**cucumiform,** kū•kū′mi•form, *a.* Shaped like a cucumber.

cucurbit, kū•kėr′bit, *n.* [Fr. *cucurbite*, L. *cucurbita*, a gourd.] A chemical vessel originally in the shape of a gourd, but sometimes shallow, with a wide mouth, used in distillation.—**cucurbitaceous,** kū•kėr′bi•tā″shus, *a.* Resembling a gourd.

cud, kud, *n.* [A.Sax. *cud*, the cud, what is chewed, from *ceówan*, to chew.] The food which going into the first stomach of ruminating animals is afterward brought up and chewed at leisure; a portion of tobacco held in the mouth and chewed; a quid.—*To chew the cud* (*fig.*), to ponder; to reflect; to ruminate.

cuddle, kud′l, *v.i.*—*cuddled, cuddling*. [Origin doubtful; perhaps same as *coddle*.] To lie close or snug; to squat; to join in an embrace; to fondle.—*v.t.* To hug; to fondle; to press close, so as to keep warm.—*n.* A hug; an embrace.

cuddy, kud′i, *n.* [Probably a word of East Indian origin.] *Naut.* a room or cabin abaft and under the poop deck; also a sort of cabin or cook room in lighters, barges, etc.

cudgel, kuj′el, *n.* [A.Sax. *cycgel*, perh. from *cog*, a short piece of wood.] A short thick stick; a club.—*To take up the cudgels*, to stand boldly forth in defense.—*v.t.*—*cudgelled, cudgelling*. To beat with a cudgel or thick stick; to beat in general.—*To cudgel one's brains*, to reflect deeply and laboriously.

cue, kū, *n.* [Fr. *queue*, L. *cauda*, the tail; or partly from Q, the first letter of L. *quando*, when, which was marked on the actors' copies of the plays, to show when they were to enter and speak.] The end of a thing, as the long curl of a wig, or a long roll of hair; a queue; the last words of a speech which a player, who is to answer, catches and regards as an intimation to begin; a hint on which to act; the part which any man is to play in his turn; turn or temper of mind; the straight tapering rod used in playing billiards.

cuff, kuf, *n.* [Akin to Sw. *kuffa*, Hamburg dialect *kuffen*, to cuff.] A blow with the fist; a stroke; a box.—*v.t.* To strike with the fist, as a man; to buffet.—*v.i.* To fight; to scuffle.

cuff, kuf, *n.* [Perhaps from Fr. *coiffe*, It. *cuffia*, a coif, hence a covering for the hand.] The fold at the end of a sleeve; anything occupying the place of such a fold, as a loose band worn over the wristband of a shirt.

Cufic, kū′fik, *a.* [From *Cufa*, near Bagdad.] Applied to the characters of the Arabic alphabet used in the time of Mohammed, and in which the Koran was written; Kufic.

cuirass, kwi•ras′, *n.* [Fr. *cuirasse*, from *cuir*, L. *corium*, leather. The cuirass was originally made of leather.] A breastplate; a piece of defensive armor made of iron plate, well hammered, and covering the body from the neck to the girdle.—**cuirassier,** kwi•ras•sēr′, *n.* A soldier armed with a cuirass or breastplate.

cuisine, kwē•zēn′, *n.* [Fr., from L. *coquina*, art of cooking, a kitchen, from *coquo*, to cook. COOK.] A kitchen; the cooking department; manner or style of cooking; cookery.

cul-de-sac, kul′de•sak, *n.* [Fr., lit. the bottom of a bag.] A place that has no thoroughfare; a blind alley; any natural cavity, bag, or tubular vessel, open only at one end.

culinary, kū′li•ne•ri, *a.* [L. *culinarius*, from *culina*, a kitchen.] Relating to the kitchen, or to the art of cooking; used in kitchens.

cull, kul, *v.t.* [Fr. *cueillir*, from L. *colligere*, to collect—*col*, and *legere*, to gather. COLLECT, COIL.] To pick out; to separate one or more things from others; to select from many; to pick up; to collect.

cullender, kul′en•dėr, *n.* A colander.

cullet, kul′et, *n.* Broken glass for melting up with fresh materials.

cullis, kul′is, *n.* [Fr. *coulisse*, a groove, from *couler*, to run.] *Arch.* a gutter in a roof.

culm, kulm, *n.* [L. *culmus*, a stalk.] *Bot.* the jointed stem of grasses, which is herbaceous in most, but woody and treelike in the bamboo.—**culmiferous,** kul•mif′ėr•us, *a.* Bearing culms.

culm, kulm, *n.* [Perhaps another spelling of *coom*; or akin to *coal*.] Anthracite shale, an impure shaly kind of coal.—**culmiferous,** kul•mif′ėr•us, *a.* Abounding in culm.

culmen, kul′men, *n.* [L.] Top; summit; highest ridge.—**culminant,** kul′mi•nant, *a.* Being vertical, or at the highest point of altitude; hence, predominating.—**culminate,** kul′mi•nāt, *v.i.*—*culminated, culminating*. To come or be in the meridian; to be in the highest point of altitude, as a planet; to reach the highest point, as of rank, power, size, numbers, or quality.—**culminating,** kul′mi•nāt•ing, *p.* or *a.* Being at the meridian; being at its highest point, as of rank, power, size, etc.—**culmination,** kul•mi•nā′shon, *n.* The transit of a heavenly body over the meridian, or highest point of altitude for the day; *fig.* the condition of any person or thing arrived at the most brilliant or important point of his or its progress.

culpable, kul′pa•bl, *a.* [L. *culpabilis*, from *culpa*, a fault.] Deserving censure; blamable; blameworthy; immoral: said of persons or their conduct.—**culpability, culpableness,** kul•pa•bil′i•ti, kul′pa•bl•nes, *n.* State of being culpable; blamableness; guilt.—**culpably,** kul′pa•bli, *adv.* In a culpable manner; blamably; in a faulty manner; criminally; immorally.

culprit, kul′prit, *n.* [Probably for *culpat*, from old law Latin *culpatus*, one accused, from L. *culpo*, to blame, accuse.] A person arraigned in court for a crime; a criminal; a malefactor.

cult, cult, *n.* [Fr. *culte*, L. *cultus*, worship, from *colo*, *cultum*, to till, worship.] Homage; worship; a system of religious belief and worship; the rites and ceremonies employed in worship.

cultch, kulch, *n.* The spawn of the oyster.

cultivate, kul′ti•vāt, *v.t.—cultivated, cultivating.* [L.L. *cultivare, cultivatum*, from L. *cultus*, pp. of *colo*, *cultum*, to till.] To till; to prepare for crops; to manure, blow, dress, sow, and reap; to raise or produce by tillage; to improve by labor or study; to refine and improve; to labor to promote and increase; to cherish; to foster (to *cultivate* a taste for poetry); to devote study, labor, or care to; to study (to *cultivate* literature); to study to conciliate or gain over; to labor to make better; to civilize.—**cultivable, cultivatable,** kul′ti•va•bl, kul′ti•vā•ta•bl, *a.* Capable of being tilled or cultivated.—**cultivation,** kul•ti•vā′shon, *n.* The act or practice of cultivating; husbandry; study, care, and practice directed to improvement or progress; the state of being cultivated or refined; culture; refinement.—**cultivator,** kul′ti•vā•tėr, *n.* One who cultivates; especially, a farmer or agriculturist; an agricultural implement used for the purpose of loosening the earth about the roots of growing crops.

culture, kul′chėr, *n.* [L. *cultura*, from *colo*, *cultum*, to till.] Tillage; cultivation; intellectual development; improvement by mental or physical training; education; refinement; the way of life of a people; growth of bacteria, fungi, etc. in a prepared medium.—*v.t.* To grow in a prepared medium.—**cultural,** kul′chėr•al, *a.*—**cultured,** kul′chėrd, *a.* Enlightened; cultivated; produced under artificial conditions.

culver, kul′vėr, *n.* [A.Sax. *culfre.*] A pigeon; a dove.

culverin, kul′vėr•in, *n.* [Fr. *couleuvrine*, from L. *coluber*, a serpent.] A long, slender piece of ordnance or artillery, serving to carry a ball to a great distance.

culvert, kul′vėrt, *n.* [O.Fr. *culvert*; Fr. *couvert*, a covered walk, from *couvrir*, to cover. COVER.] An arched drain of brickwork or masonry carried under a road, railroad, canal, etc., for the passage of water.

cumber, kum′bėr, *v.t.* [O.Fr. *combrer*, from L.L. *combrus*, *cumbrus*, a mass, from L. *cumulus*, a heap (whence also *cumulate*), by insertion of *b* (comp. *number*) and change of *l* to *r*.] To overload, to overburden; to check, stop, or retard, as by a load or weight; to make motion difficult; to obstruct; to perplex or embarrass; to distract or trouble; to cause trouble or obstruction in, as by anything useless.—**cumber,** kum′bėr, *n.* Hindrance; burdensomeness; embarrassment. —**cumbersome,** kum′bėr•sum, *a.* Troublesome; burdensome; embarrassing; vexatious; unwieldy; unmanageable; not easily borne or managed.—**cumbersomely,** kum′bėr•sum•li,*adv.*—**cumbersomeness,** kum′bėr•sum•nes, *n.*—**cumbrance,** kum′brans, *n.* That which cumbers or encumbers; an encumbrance.—**cumbrous,** kum′brus, *a.* Serving to cumber or encumber; burdensome; troublesome; rendering action difficult or toilsome; unwieldy.—**cumbrously,** kum′brus•li, *adv.* In a cumbrous manner.—**cumbrousness,** kum′brus•nes, *n.*

cumin, cummin, kum′in, *n.* [L. *cuminum*, Gr. *kyminon*, Heb. *kamon*, cumin.] An annual umbelliferous plant found wild in Egypt and Syria, and cultivated for the sake of its agreeable aromatic seeds, which possess well-marked stimulating and carminative properties.

cummerbund, kum′ėr•bund, *n.* [Hind. *kamar*, the waist, and *bandhna*, to tie.] A girdle or waistband.

cumshaw, kum′sha̤, *n.* [Chinese *komtsie.*] In the East, a present or bonus.

cumulate, kū′mū•lāt, *v.t.—cumulated, cumulating.* [L. *cumulo, cumulatum*, to heap up, from *cumulus*, a heap, seen also in *accumulate*; akin *cumber.*] To form a heap of; to heap together; to accumulate.—**cumulation,** kū•mū•lā′shon, *n.* The act of heaping together; a heap.—**cumulative,** kū′mū•lāt•iv, *a.* Forming a mass; aggregated; increasing in force, weight, or effect by successive additions (arguments, evidence).—*Cumulative system*, in elections, that system by which each voter has the same number of votes as there are persons to be elected, and can give them all to one candidate or distribute them as he pleases.—**cumulostratus,** kū′mū•lō•strā″tus, *n.* A species of cloud in which the cumulus at the top, mixed with cirri, overhangs a flattish stratum or base.—**cumulus,** kū′mū•lus, *n.* A species of cloud which assumes the form of dense convex or conical heaps, resting on a flattish base.

cuneal, kū′ni•al, *a.* [L. *cuneus*, a wedge, whence also *coin.*] Having the form of a wedge.—**cuneate, cuneated,** kū′ni•āt, kū′ni•āt•ed, *a.* Wedge-shaped; cuneiform.—**cuneiform, cuniform,** kū•nē′i•form, kū′-ni•form, *a.* Having the shape or form of a wedge; wedge-shaped; the epithet applied to the arrow-headed inscriptions found on old Babylonian and Persian monuments, from the characters resembling a wedge.

cunning, kun′ing, *a.* [O.E. *cunnand*, from A.Sax. *cunnan*, Icel. *kunna*, Goth. *kunnan*, to know; akin *can*, *ken*, *know.*] Having skill or dexterity; skillful; wrought with skill; ingenious; shrewd; sly; crafty; astute; designing; subtle.—*n.* Knowledge‡; skill‡; artifice; artfulness; craft; deceitfulness or deceit; fraudulent skill or dexterity.—**cunningly,** kun′ing•li, *adv.* In a cunning manner; artfully; craftily; with subtlety; with fraudulent contrivance; skillfully; artistically.—**cunningness,** kun′ing•nes, *n.* Cunning.

cup, kup, *n.* [A.Sax. *cuppe*, from L. *cupa*, a tub, a cask, in later times a cup.] A vessel of small capacity, used commonly to drink from; a chalice; the contents of a cup; the liquor contained in a cup, or that it may contain; anything formed like a cup (the *cup* of an acorn, of a flower).—*In his cups*, intoxicated; tipsy.—*v.t.—cupped, cupping.* To perform the operation of cupping upon.—**cupbearer,** *n.* An attendant at a feast who conveys wine or other liquors to the guests.—**cupboard,** kub′bėrd, *n.* Originally, a board or shelf for cups to stand on; now, a case or enclosure in a room with shelves to receive cups, plates, dishes, and the like.—**cupful,** kup′ful, *n.* As much as a cup holds.—**cupping,** kup′ing, *n. Surg.* a species of bloodletting performed by a scarificator and a glass called a cupping glass from which the air has been exhausted.

cupel, kū′pel, *n.* [L. *cupella*, dim. of *cupa*, a tub.] A small, shallow, porous, cuplike vessel: generally made of the residue of burned bones rammed into a mold, and used in refining metals.—**cupellation,** kū•pel•lā′shon, *n.* The refining of gold or silver by a cupel.

Cupid, kū′pid, *n.* [L. *Cupido*, from *cupido*, desire, from *cupio*, to desire.] The god of love, and *fig.* love.

cupidity, kū•pid′i•ti, *n.* [L. *cupiditas*, from *cupidus*, desirous, from *cupio*, to desire; akin *covet.*] An eager desire to possess something; inordinate or unlawful desire, especially of wealth or power; avarice; covetousness.

cupola, kū′po•la, *n.* [It. *cupola*, dim. of L. *cupa*, a cup. CUP.] *Arch.* a spherical vault on the top of an edifice; a dome, or the round top of a dome; the round top of any structure, as of a furnace; the furnace itself.

cupreous, kū′pri•us, *a.* [L. *cupreus*, from *cuprum*, copper.] Coppery; consisting of copper; resembling copper or partaking of its qualities.—**cupric, cuprous,** kū′prik, kū′prus, *a.* Of or belonging to copper.—**cupriferous,** kū•prif′ėr•us, *a.* Producing or affording copper.—**cuprite,** kū′prīt, *n.* The red oxide of copper; red copper ore.

cupule, kū′pūl, *n.* [From L. *cupa*. CUP.] *Bot.* a form of involucrum, occurring in the oak, the beech, and the hazel, and consisting of bracts cohering by their bases, and forming a kind of cup.—**cupuliferous,** kū•pū•lif′ėr•us, *a.* In *bot.* bearing cupules.

cur, kėr, *n.* [Sw. *kurre*, D. *korre*, a dog, from root of Icel. *kurra*, to grumble or mutter.] A degenerate dog; a worthless or contemptible man; a hound.—**currish,** kėr′ish, *a.* Like a cur; having the qualities of a cur; snappish; snarling; churlish; quarrelsome; malignant.—**currishly,** kėr′ish•li, *adv.* In a currish manner.

curable, kūr′a•bl, *a.* See CURE.

curaçao, kö•ra•sou′, *n.* A liquor or

cordial flavored with orange peel, cinnamon, and mace: so named from the island of *Curaçao* where it was first made.

curacy. See CURATE.

curari, curara, ku′rä•ri, ku′rä•rä, *n.* A brown-black resinous substance obtained from a small tree of the nux-vomica family; and forming a deadly poison; used by the South American Indians for poisoning arrows, especially for hunting, the animals killed by it being quite wholesome; a muscle relaxant.

curassow, kū•ras′sō, *n.* The name given to several species of gallinaceous birds found in the warmer parts of America, about the size of turkeys, and easily domesticated and raised.

curate, kū′rit, *n.* [L.L. *curatus*, one intrusted with the cure of souls, from L. *cura*, care.] One who has the cure of souls; a clergyman in Episcopal churches who is employed to perform divine service in the place of the incumbent, parson, or vicar.—**curacy,** kū′ra•si, *n.* The office or employment of a curate.—**curator,** kū•rā′tėr, *n.* [L., from *cura*, *curatum*, to take care of.] One who has the care and superintendence of anything, as a public library, museum, fine art collection, or the like; *Scots law*, a guardian.—**curatorship,** kū•rā′tėr•ship, *n.* The office of a curator.—**curé,** kü•rā, *n.* [Fr.] A curate; a parson.

curative, kū′ra•tiv, *a.* See CURE.

curb, kėrb, *v.t.* [Fr. *courber*, to bend or crook, from L. *curvare*, to curve, from *curvus*, curved.] To bend to one's will; to check, restrain, hold back; to keep in subjection; to restrain (a horse) with a curb; to guide and manage by the reins; to strengthen by a curbstone.—*n.* What checks, restrains, or holds back; restraint; check; hindrance; a chain or strap attached to a bridle, and passing under the horse's lower jaw, against which it is made to press tightly when the rein is pulled; the edge stone of a sidewalk or pavement; a curbstone.—**curb roof,** *n.* A roof formed with an upper and under set of rafters on each side, the under set being less inclined to the horizon than the upper; a mansard roof.—**curbstone,** *n.* A stone placed against earth or stonework to hold the work together; the outer edge of a foot pavement.

curd, kėrd, *n.* [Probably connected with W. *crwd*, a round lump, and perhaps with *crowd*.] The coagulated or thickened part of milk; the coagulated part of any liquid.—*v.t.* to cause to coagulate; to turn to curd; to curdle; to congeal.—*v.i.* To become curdled or coagulated; to become curd.—**curdle,** kėr′dl, *v.i.*—*curdled*, *curdling*. To coagulate or concrete; to thicken or change into curd; to run slow with terror; to freeze; to congeal.—*v.t.* To change into curd; to coagulate; to congeal or make run slow.

cure, kūr, *n.* [O.Fr. *cure*, L. *cura*, care.] Care‡; a spiritual charge; care of the spiritual welfare of people; the employment or office of a curate; curacy; remedial treatment of disease; method of medical treatment; remedy for disease; restorative; that which heals; a healing; restoration to health from disease and to soundness from a wound.—*v.t.*—*cured*, *curing*. To restore to health or to a sound state; to heal; to remove or put an end to by remedial means; to heal, as a disease; to remedy; to prepare for preservation, as by drying, salting, etc.—*v.i.* To effect a cure.—**curability,** kūr•a•bil′i•ti, *n.* The quality of being curable.—**curable,** kū′ra•bl, *a.* Capable of being healed or cured; admitting a remedy.—**curableness,** kūr′a•bl•nes, *n.* Possibility of being cured.—**curative,** kū′ra•tiv, *a.* Relating to the cure of diseases; tending to cure.—**cureless,** kūr′les, *a.* Incurable; not admitting of a remedy.—**curer,** kū′rėr, *n.* One who or that which cures or heals; a physician; one who preserves provisions, as beef, fish, and the like, from speedy putrefaction by means of salt, or in any other manner.

curé, *n.* See CURATE.

curfew, kėr′fū, *n.* [Fr. *couvre-feu*, coverfire, from L. *cooperire*, to cover, and *focus*, hearth, fireplace.] A bell formerly rung in the evening as a signal to the inhabitants to rake up their fires and retire to rest; a signal to withdraw from the streets; the time of such a signal.

curious, kū′ri•us, *a.* [L. *curiosus*, from *cura*, care, attention. CURE.] Eager to know things interesting; inquisitive; addicted to research or inquiry; wrought with care and art or with nice finish; singular; exciting surprise; awakening curiosity; odd or strange.—**curiosity,** kū•ri•os′i•ti, *n.* [L. *curiositas*.] The state or feeling of being curious; a strong desire to see something novel or to discover something unknown; a desire to see what is new or unusual, or to gratify the mind with new discoveries; inquisitiveness; a curious or singular object.—**curio,** kū′ri•ō, *n.* A curiosity; a small interesting article or object.—**curiously,** kū′ri•us•li, *adv.* In a curious manner; inquisitively; attentively; in a singular manner; unusually.—**curiousness,** kū′ri•us•nes, *n.*

curium, kū′ri•um, *n.* [From Pierre and Marie Curie.] A metallic element produced artificially by helium-ion bombardment of plutonium. Symbol, Cm; at. no., 96.

curl, kėrl, *v.t.* [Akin to D. *krullen*, Dan. *krölle*, to curl.] To bend or twist circularly; to bend or form into ringlets; to crisp (the hair); to writhe; to twist; to coil; to curve; to raise in breaking waves or undulations.—*v.i.* To bend or twist in curls or ringlets; to move in or form curves or spirals; to rise in waves; to writhe; to twist: to play at the game called curling.—*n.* A ringlet of hair or anything of a like form; something curled or bent round; a waving; sinuosity; flexure.—**curled,** kėrld, *a.* Having the hair curled; curly.—**curler,** kėrl′ėr, *n.* One who or that which curls; one who engages in the amusement of curling.—**curliness,** kėrl′i•nes, *n.* State of being curly.—**curling,** kėrl′ing, *n.* A winter amusement on the ice (especially in Scotland), in which contending parties slide large smooth stones of a circular form from one mark to another, called the tee.—**curling irons, curling tongs,** *n.* An instrument for curling the hair.—**curling stone,** *n.* A stone shaped somewhat like a cheese with a handle in the upper side, used in the game of curling.—**curly,** kėr′li, *a.* Having or forming curls; tending to curl.

curlew, kėr′lū, *n.* [O.Fr. *corlieu*; imitative of the cry of the bird; Fr. *courlis*.] A bird allied to the snipe and woodcock, with a long, slender, curved bill, longish legs, and a short tail.

curmudgeon, kėr•muj′on, *n.* [Word of uncertain origin.] An avaricious churlish fellow; a miser; a niggard; a churl.—**curmudgeonly,** kėr•muj′on•li, *a.* Avaricious; covetous; niggardly; churlish.

currant, kur′ant, *n.* [From *Corinth*, whence it was probably first brought.] A small kind of dried grape, brought in large quantities from Greece; the name of several species of shrubs belonging to the gooseberry family, and of their fruits, as the red currant, the white currant, and the black currant.

current, kur′ent, *a.* [L. *currens*, *currentis*, ppr. of *curro*, to run, seen also in *concur*, *incur*, *occur*, *course*, *cursive*, etc.] Running†; passing from person to person, or from hand to hand (report, coin); circulating; common, general, or fashionable; generally received, adopted, or approved (opinions, beliefs, theories); popular; established by common estimation (the *current* value of coin); fitted for general acceptance or circulation (*Shak.*); now passing, or at present in its course (the *current* month; often in abbreviated expressions, such as, 20th *curt.*).—*Current coin*, coin in general circulation.—*n.* A flowing or passing; a stream; a body of water or air moving in a certain direction; course; progressive motion or movement; connected series; successive course (the *current* of events); general or main course (the *current* of opinion).—*Electric current*, the passage of electricity from one pole of an apparatus to the other.—**currency,** kur′en•si, *n.* The state of being current; a passing from person to person; a passing from mouth to mouth among the public; a continual passing from hand to hand, as coin or bills of credit; circulation; that which is in circulation, or is given and taken as having value, or as representing property; circulating medium (the *currency* of a country).—*Metallic currency*, the gold, silver, and copper in circulation in any country.—*Paper currency*, bank notes, or other documents serving as a substitute for money or a

representative of it.—**currently,** kur′ent•li, *adv.* Commonly; generally; popularly; with general acceptance.—**currentness,** kur′ent•nes, *n.* The state of being current; currency.
curricle, kur′i•kl, *n.* [L. *curriculum*, from *curro*, to run.] A chaise or carriage with two wheels, drawn by two horses abreast.
curriculum, ku•rik′ū•lum, *n.* [L.] A specified fixed course of study in a university, academy, school, or the like.
currish, kėr′ish, *a.* See CUR.
curry, kur′i, *v.t.*—*curried, currying.* [Fr. *courroyer, corroyer*, originally to prepare, put right, or make ready in general, from the prefix *con*, and the Germanic stem to which belong E. *ready*, *ray* in *array*.] To dress leather after it is tanned by scraping, cleansing, beating, and coloring; to rub and clean (a horse) with a comb; to beat, drub, or thrash (*colloq.*).—*To curry favor*, to seek favor by officiousness, kindness, flattery, caresses, and the like; the phrase being corrupted from 'to *curry favel*', from *favel*, an old name for a chestnut horse.—**currier,** kur′i•ėr, *n.* A man who curries leather or a horse.—**curriery,** kur′i•ėr•i, *n.* The trade of a currier or the place where the trade is carried on.—**currycomb,** *n.* An iron instrument or comb with very short teeth, for combing and cleaning horses.—*v.t.* To rub down or comb with a currycomb.
curry, currie, kur′i, *n.* [Per. *khur*, flavor, relish.] A kind of sauce much used in India, containing cayenne pepper, garlic, turmeric, coriander seed, ginger, and other strong spices; a dish of fish, fowl, etc., cooked with curry.—*v.t.*—*curried, currying.* To flavor with curry.—**curry powder,** *n.* A condiment used for making curry.
curse, kėrs, *v.t.*—*cursed, cursing.* [A. Sax. *cursian*, from *curs*, a curse—a word of doubtful connections.] To utter a wish of evil against one; to imprecate evil upon; to call for mischief or injury to fall upon; to execrate; to bring evil to or upon; to blast; to blight; to vex, harass, or torment with great calamities.—*v.i.* To utter imprecations; to use blasphemous or profane language; to swear.—*n.* A malediction; the expression of a wish of evil to another; an imprecation; evil solemnly or in passion invoked upon one; that which brings evil or severe affliction; torment; great vexation; condemnation or sentence of divine vengeance on sinners.—**cursed,** kėr′sed, *a.* Blasted by a curse; deserving a curse; execrable; hateful; detestable; abominable; wicked; vexatious; troublesome.—**cursedly,** kėr′sed•li, *adv.* In a cursed manner; miserably; in a manner to be cursed or detested.—**cursedness,** kėr′sed•nes, *n.* The state of being cursed.—**curst,** kėrst, *a.* Cursed; having a violent temper; snarling; peevish; forward.
cursive, kėr′siv, *a.* [L.L. *cursivus*, L. *cursus*, a running. COURSE, CURRENT.] Running; flowing: said of handwriting.—**cursively,** kėr′siv•li, *adv.* In a cursive manner.—**cursorial,** kėr•sō′ri•al, *a.* Adapted for running.—**cursorily,** kėr′so•ri•li, *adv.* In a cursory or hasty manner; slightly; hastily; without attention.—**cursoriness,** kėr′so•ri•nes, *n.* The state of being cursory.—**cursory,** kėr′so•ri, *a.* [L. *cursorius.*] Rapid or hurried, as if running; hasty; slight; superficial; careless; not exercising close attention (a *cursory* view, a *cursory* observer).
curst, *a.* See CURSE.
curt, kėrt, *a.* [L. *curtus*, short, docked.] Short; concise; brief and abrupt; short and sharp.—**curtly,** kėrt′li, *adv.* In a curt manner; briefly.—**curtness,** kėrt′nes, *n.* Shortness; conciseness; abruptness, as of manner.
curtail, kėr•tāl′, *v.t.* [O.Fr. *courtault*, Mod.Fr. *courteau*, from *court*, L. *curtus*, short.] To cut off the end or a part of; to make shorter; to dock; hence, to shorten in any manner; to abridge; to diminish.—**curtailer,** kėr•tā′lėr, *n.* One who curtails.—**curtailment,** kėr•tāl′ment, *n.* The act of curtailing.
curtain, kėr′tin, *n.* [Fr. *curtine*, L.L. *cortina*, a little court, a curtain, from L. *cors. cortis*, an enclosure, a court. COURT.] A hanging cloth or screen before a window, around a bed, or elsewhere, that may be moved at pleasure so as to admit or exclude the light, conceal or show anything; the movable screen in a theater or like place serving to conceal the stage from the spectators; what resembles a curtain; *fort.* that part of a rampart which is between the flanks of two bastions, or between two gates.—*v.t.* To enclose or furnish with curtains.—**curtain lecture,** *n.* A lecture or reproof given behind the curtains or in bed by a wife to her husband.—**curtain raiser,** *n.* In the theater, a short piece, usually of one scene with few characters, used to open a performance.
curtsy, curtesy, kėrt′si, kėr′te•si, *n.* [A modification of *courtesy.*] An obeisance or gesture of respect by a woman, consisting in bending the knees and slightly dropping the body.—*v.i.*—*curtsied, curtsying.* To drop or make a curtsy.
curule, kū′röl, *a.* [L. *curulis.*] *Rom. antiq.* applied to a chair of state, something like a campstool, which belonged to certain of the magistrates of the republic in virtue of their office; hence, privileged to sit in such a chair.
curve, kėrv, *a.* [L. *curvus*, crooked. CURB.] Bending circularly, or so as in no part to be straight; having a bent form; crooked.—*n.* A bending in a circular form; a bend or flexure such that no part forms a straight line; *geom.* a line which may be cut by a straight line in more points than one; a line which changes its direction at every point.—*v.t.*—*curved, curving.* To bend into the form of a curve; to crook.—*v.i.* To have a curved or bent form; to bend round.—**curvature,** kėr′va•chėr, *n.* A bending in a regular form; the manner or degree in which a thing is curved.
curvet, kėr′vet or kėr•vet′, *n.* [It. *corvetta*, from L. *curvare*, to bend or curve.] The leap of a horse when he raises both forelegs at once, and as they are falling also his hind legs; a gambol; a leap.—*v.i.*—*curvetted, curvetting.* To make a curvet; to bound or leap; to prance; to frisk or gambol.—*v.t.* To cause to make a curvet.
curvicostate, kėr•vi•kos′tāt, *a.* [L. *curvus*, crooked, and *costa*, a rib.] Marked with small bent ribs.—**curvilinear, curvilineal,** kėr•vi•lin′i•ėr, kėr•vi•lin′•ial, *a.* [L. *linea*, a line.] Having the shape of a curved line; consisting of curved lines; bounded by curved lines.
cushat, kush′at, *n.* [A.Sax. *cusceote.*] The ring dove or wood pigeon.
cushion, kush′on, *n.* [Fr. *coussin*, It. *cuscino*; from a hypothetical *culcitinum*, dim. of L. *culcita*, a cushion, a quilt.] A pillow for a seat; a soft pad to be placed on a chair or attached to some kind of seat; any stuffed or padded appliance; the padded side or edge of a billiard table.—*v.t.* To furnish or fit with cushion or cushions.
cusk, kusk, *n.* A large edible marine fish, allied to the cod; the burbot.
cusp, kusp, *n.* [L. *cuspis*, a point, a spear.] A sharp projecting point; the point or horn of the crescent moon or other similar point; a prominence on a molar tooth; a projecting point formed by the meeting of curves, as in heads of Gothic windows and panels, etc.—**cusped,** kuspt, *a.* Furnished with a cusp or cusps; cusp-shaped.—**cuspidate, cuspidated,** ku′spi•dāt, kus′pi•dā•ted, *a.* Cusp-shaped or having cusps; terminating in a cusp or spine (as leaves).
cuspidor, kus′pi•dor, *n.* [Pg. from *cuspir*, to spit.] A spittoon.
custard, kus′tėrd, *n.* [Probably a corruption of old *crustade*, a kind of stew served up in a raised *crust.*] A composition of milk and eggs, sweetened, and baked or boiled, forming an agreeable kind of food.—**custard apple,** *n.* [From the yellowish pulp.] The large, dark-brown, roundish fruit of a West Indian tree, now cultivated in all tropical countries.
custody, kus′to•di, *n.* [L. *custodia*, from *custos, custodis*, a watchman, a keeper.] A keeping; a guarding; guardianship; care, watch, inspection, for keeping, preservation, or security; restraint of liberty; confinement; imprisonment.—**custodial,** kus•tō′di•al, *a.* Relating to custody or guardianship.—**custodian,** kus•tō′di•an, *n.* One who has the care or custody of anything, as of a library, some public building, etc.—**custodianship,** kus•tō′di•an•ship, *n.* The office or duty of a custodian.
custom, kus′tum, *n.* [O.Fr. *custume*, from L. *consuetudo, consuetudonis*, custom—*con*, with, and *sueo, suetum*,

to be wont or accustomed. *Costume* is the same word.] Frequent or common use or practice; established manner; habitual practice; a practice or usage; an established and general mode of action, which obtains in a community; practice of frequenting a shop, manufactory, etc., and purchasing or giving orders; tribute, toll, or tax; *pl.* the duties imposed by law on merchandise imported or exported. *Custom* is the frequent repetition of the same act, *habit* being a custom continued so long as to develop a tendency or inclination to perform the customary act.—**customable,** kus'tum•a•bl, *a.* Subject to the payment of the duties called customs.—**customarily,** kus'tum•e•ri•li, *adv.* Habitually; commonly.—**customariness,** kus'tum•e•ri•nes, *n.* State of being customary; frequency; commonness.—**customary,** kus'-tum•e•ri, *a.* According to custom or to established or common usage; wonted; usual; habitual; in common practice.—*n.* A book containing an account of the customs and municipal rights of a city, province, etc.—**customer,** kus'tum•ėr, *n.* A purchaser; a buyer; a dealer; one that a person has to deal with, or one that comes across a person; a queer fellow.—**customhouse,** *n.* An office where the customs on merchandise are paid or secured to be paid; the whole establishment by means of which the customs revenue is collected and its regulation enforced.

cut, kut, *v.t.*—*cut* (pret. & pp.), *cutting.* [Of Celtic origin; comp. W. *cwt,* a short piece, *cwtogi,* to curtail; Ir. *cut,* a short tail; *cutach,* bob-tailed.] To separate or divide the parts of by an edged instrument, or as an edged instrument does; to make an incision in; to sever; to sever and cause to fall for the purpose of removing; to fell, as wood; to mow or reap, as corn; to sever and remove, as the nails or hair; to fashion by, or as by, cutting or carving; to hew out; to carve; to wound the sensibilities of; to affect deeply; to intersect; to cross (one line *cuts* another); to have no longer anything to do with; to quit (*colloq.*); to shun the acquaintance of (*colloq.*).—*To cut down,* to cause to fall by severing; to reduce as by cutting; to retrench; to curtail (expenditure).—*To cut off,* to sever from the other parts; to bring to an untimely end; to separate; to interrupt; to stop (communication); to intercept; to hinder from return or union.—*To cut out,* to remove by cutting or carving; to shape or form by, or as by, cutting; to fashion; to take the preference or precedence of; *naut.* to seize and carry off, as a vessel from a harbor or from under the guns of the enemy.—*To cut short,* to hinder from proceeding by sudden interruption; to shorten; to abridge.—*To cut up,* to cut in pieces; to criticize severely; to censure; to wound the feelings deeply; to affect greatly.—*To cut and run,* to cut the cable and set sail immediately; to be off; to be gone.—*To cut off with a penny*; to bequeath one's natural heir a penny; a practice adopted by a person dissatisfied with his heir, as a proof that the disinheritance was not the result of neglect—*To cut capers,* to leap or dance in a frolicsome manner.—*To cut a dash* or *figure,* to make a display.—*To cut a joke,* to joke; to crack a jest.—*To cut a knot,* to take short measures with anything; in allusion to the well-known story of Alexander the Great and the Gordian knot.—*To cut a pack of cards,* to divide it into portions before beginning to deal or for other purposes.—*To cut one's stick,* to move off; to be off at once. (*Slang.*)—*To cut the teeth,* to have the teeth pierce the gums.—*v.i.* To do the work of an edge tool; to serve in dividing or gashing; to admit of incision or severance; to use a knife or edge tool; to divide a pack of cards, to determine the deal or for any other purpose; to move off rapidly (*colloq.*).—*To cut across,* to pass over or through in the most direct way (*colloq.*).—*To cut in,* to join in suddenly and unceremoniously (*colloq.*).—*p.* and *a.* Gashed; carved; intersected; pierced; deeply affected.—*Cut and dry,* or *cut and dried,* prepared for use: a metaphor from hewn timber.—*Cut glass,* glass having the surface shaped or ornamented by grinding and polishing.—*Cut nail,* a nail manufactured by being cut from a rolled plate of iron by machinery.—*n.* The opening made by an edged instrument; a gash; a notch; a wound; a stroke or blow as with an edged instrument; a smart stroke or blow, as with a whip; anything that wounds one's feelings deeply, as a sarcasm, criticism, or act of discourtesy; a part cut off from the rest; a near passage, by which an angle is cut off; the block on which a picture is carved, and by which it is impressed; the impression from such a block; the act of dividing a pack of cards; manner in which a thing is cut; form; shape; fashion; the act of passing a person without recognizing him, or of avoiding him so as not to be recognized by him.—*To draw cuts,* to draw lots, as of paper, etc., cut of unequal lengths.—**cutter,** kut'ėr, *n.* One who or that which cuts; one who cuts out cloth for garments according to measurements; *naut.* a small boat used by ships of war; a vessel rigged nearly like a sloop, with one mast and a straight running bowsprit.—**cutting,** kut'ing, *a.* Penetrating or dividing by the edge; serving to penetrate or divide; sharp; piercing the heart; wounding the feelings; sarcastic; satirical; severe.—*n.* The act or operation of one who cuts; a piece cut off; a portion of a plant from which a new individual is propagated; an excavation made through a hill or rising ground in constructing a road, railroad, canal, etc.—**cuttingly,** kut'ing•li, *adv.* In a cutting manner.—**cutpurse** *n.* One who cuts purses for the sake of stealing them or their contents; one who steals from the person; a thief; a robber.—**cutaway,** *n.* A coat, the skirts of which are rounded or cut away; used also adjectively.—**cutoff,** *n.* That which cuts off or shortens; that which is cut off; *steam engines,* a contrivance for economizing steam.—**cutthroat,** *n.* A murderer; an assassin; a ruffian.—*a.* Murderous; cruel; barbarous.—**cutwater,** *n.* The fore part of a ship's prow which cuts the water; the lower portion of the pier of a bridge formed with an angle or edge directed up stream.

cutaneous. See CUTICLE.

cutchery, kuch'ėr•i, *n.* In the East Indies, a court of justice or public office.

cute, kūt, *a.* [An abbrev. of *acute.*] Acute; clever; sharp.—**cuteness,** kūt'nes, *n.* The quality or character of being cute; attractive by reason of daintiness, usually with the idea of smallness, as a child.

cuticle, kū'ti•kl, *n.* [L. *cuticula,* dim. of *cutis,* skin.] *Anat.* the outermost thin transparent skin which covers the surface of the body; the epidermis or scarfskin; *bot.* the thin external covering of the bark of a plant; the outer pellicle of the epidermis.—**cutaneous,** kū•tā'ni•us, *a.* Belonging to the skin; existing on or affecting the skin.—**cutin,** kū'tin, *n.* A peculiar modification of cellulose, contained in the epidermis of leaves, petals, and fruits.—**cutis,** kū'tis, *n.* [L.] *Anat.* the dense resisting skin which forms the general envelope of body below the cuticle; the dermis or true skin.

cutlass, kut'las, *n.* [Fr. *coutelas,* from O.Fr. *coutel* (Fr. *couteau*), a knife; from L. *cultellus,* dim. of *culter,* a knife.] A broad curving sword used by cavalry, seamen, etc.

cutler, kut'lėr, *n.* [Fr. *coutelier,* from L. *culter,* a knife. CUTLASS.] One whose occupation is to make or deal in knives and other cutting instruments; one who sharpens or repairs cutlery; a knife grinder.—**cutlery,** kut'lėr•i, *n.* The business of a cutler; edged or cutting instruments.

cutlet, kut'let, *n.* [Fr. *côtelette,* lit. a little side or rib, from *côte,* side. COAST.] A piece of meat, especially veal or mutton, cut for cooking; generally cut from the short ribs or shank.

cuttle, cuttlefish, kut'l, *n.* [A.Sax. *cudele,* a cuttlefish; G. *kuttel-fisch.*] A two-gilled cephalopodous mollusk, having a body enclosed in a sac, eight arms or feet covered with suckers, used in locomotion and for seizing prey, a calcareous internal shell, and a bag or sac from which the animal has the power of ejecting a black inklike fluid (sepia) so as to darken the water and conceal it from pursuit.—**cuttlebone,** *n.* The internal calcareous plate of the cuttlefish, used for polishing wood, as also for pounce and tooth-powder.

cyanic, sī•an'ik, *a.* [Gr. *kyanos,* blue.] Of or pertaining to the color blue; *chem.* containing cyanogen.—**cyanide,** sī'an•id, *n.* A combination of cyanogen with a metallic base.—*Cyanide of potassium,* a poisonous substance used in photography and electrotyping.—**cyanogen,** sī•an'o•-jen, *n.* A gas of a strong and peculiar odor composed of carbon and nitrogen.—**cyanosis,** sī•a•nō'sis, *n.* A condition in which the skin has a blue tint.

cybernetics, sī•bėr•net'iks, *n.* [Gr. *kybernetes,* helmsman, from *kybernan,* to steer. GOVERN.] The science that compares the communication and control systems in animals and machines.—**cybernetic,** sī•bėr•net'ik, *a.*—**cyberneticist,** sī•bėr•net'i•sist, *n.*

cycad, sī'kad, *n.* [Gr. *kykas,* a kind of plant.] One of a natural order of gymnospermous plants, resembling palms in their general appearance, inhabiting India, Australia, Cape of Good Hope, and tropical America.—**cycadaceous,** sī•ka•dā'shus, *a.* Belonging to the cycads.—**cycadiform,** sī•kad'i•form, *a.* Resembling in form the cycads.

cyclamen, sik'la•men, *n.* [From Gr. *kyklos,* a circle, referring to the roundshaped rootstock.] A genus of low-growing herbaceous plants, with fleshy rootstocks and very handsome flowers.

cycle, sī'kl, *n.* [Gr. *kyklos,* a circle or cycle.] A circle or orbit in the heavens; a circle or round of years, or a period of time, in which a certain succession of events or phenomena is completed; a long period of years; an age; the aggregate of legendary or traditional matter accumulated round some mythical or heroic event or character (as the siege of Troy or King Arthur); a bicycle or similar conveyance.—*v.i.* —*cycled, cycling.* To use a cycle; *bot.* a complete turn of leaves, etc., arranged spirally.—*Cycle of the moon,* or golden number, a period of nineteen years, after the lapse of which the new and full moons return on the same days of the month.—*Cycle of the sun* is a period of twenty-eight years, which having elapsed, the dominical or Sunday letters return to their former place according to the Julian calendar.—*v.i.*—*cycled, cycling.* To recur in cycles.—**cyclic,** sī'klik, *a.* Pertaining to or moving in a cycle or circle; connected with a cycle in the sense it has in literature.—*Cyclic poets,* Greek poets who wrote on matters and personages connected with the Trojan war.—**cyclical,** sī'kli•kal, *a.* Pertaining to a cycle; cyclic.—**cyclist,** sīk'list, *n.* One who uses a cycle.—**cycloid,** sī'kloid, *n.* A curve generated by a point in the circumference of a circle when the circle is rolled along a straight line and kept always in the same plane, that is, such a line as a nail in the circumference of a carriage wheel describes in the air while the wheel runs.—*a.* Having a circular form; belonging to the Cycloidians.—**cycloidal,** sī'kloi•dal, *a.* Of or pertaining to a cycloid.

cyclone, sī'klōn, *n.* [From Gr. *kyklos,* a circle.] A circular or rotary storm of immense force, revolving at an enormous rate round a calm center, and at the same time advancing at a rate varying from 20 to 40 miles an hour. In the northern hemisphere they rotate from right to left, and in the southern from left to right.—**cyclonic,** sī•klon•ik, *a.* Relating to a cyclone.

cyclopedia, cyclopaedia, sī•klo•-pē'di•a, *n.* [Gr. *kyklos,* circle, and and *paideia,* discipline.] A work containing definitions or accounts of the principal subjects in one or all branches of science, art, or learning; an encyclopedia.—**cyclopedic, cyclopaedic, cyclopedical, cyclopaedical,** sī•klo•pē'dik, sī•klo•-pē'di•kal, *a.* Belonging to a cyclopedia.

Cyclops, sī'klops, *n. sing,* and *pl.* [Gr. *kyklōps,* a Cyclops, pl. *kyklōpes* —*kyklos,* a circle, and *ōps,* an eye.] *Class. myth.* a race of giants who had but one circular eye in the middle of the forehead.

cyclostome, sī'klo•stōm, *n.* [Gr. *kyklos,* a circle, and *stoma,* a mouth.] One of a family of cartilaginous fishes which have circular mouths, as the lamprey.—**cyclostomous,** sī•-klos'to•mus, *a.* Having a circular mouth or aperture.

cyclotron, sī'klo•tron, *n. Phys.* an apparatus using electromagnetic and electrostatic means to cause electrified particles to move in circles at high speeds.

cygnet, sig'net, *n.* [Dim. of Fr. *cygne,* from L. *cygnus,* a swan.] A young swan.

cylinder, sil'in•dėr, *n.* [Gr. *kylindros,* from *kylindō,* to roll.] A body shaped like a roller; an elongated, round, solid body, of uniform diameter throughout its length, and terminating in two flat circular surfaces which are equal and parallel; that chamber of a steam engine in which the force of steam is exerted on the piston; in certain printing machines, a roller by which the impression is made, and on which stereotype plates may be secured.—**cylindric, cylindrical,** si•lin'drik, si•lin'dri•kal, *a.* Having the form of a cylinder, or partaking of its properties.—**cylindrically,** si•lin'dri•kal•li, *adv.* In the manner or shape of a cylinder.—**cylindroid,** sil'in•droid, *n.* A solid body resembling a cylinder, but having the bases elliptical.

cyma, sī'ma, *n.* [Gr. *kyma,* a wave, a sprout, from *kyō,* to swell.] *Arch.* a molding of a cornice, the profile of which is a double curve, concave joined to convex; an ogee molding; *bot.* a cyme.

cymar, si•mär', *n.* [Fr. *simmare.*] Woman's light garment.

cymbal, sim'bal, *n.* [L. *cymbalum,* Gr. *kymbalon,* a cymbal, from *kymbos,* hollow.] A musical instrument, circular and hollow like a dish, made of brass or bronze, two of which are struck together, producing a sharp ringing sound.—**cymbalist,** sim'ba•list, *n.* One who plays the cymbals.

cyme, sīm, *n.* [Gr. *kyma,* a wave, a sprout. CYMA.] *Bot.* an inflorescence of the definite or determinate class, in which the flowers are in racemes, corymbs, or umbels, the successive central flowers expanding first.—**cymose,** sī'mōs, *a.* Containing a cyme; in the form of a cyme.

cymophane, sī'mō•fān, *n.* [Gr. *kyma,* a wave, and *phainō,* to show.] A siliceous gem of a yellowish-green color, the same as chrysoberyl.

Cymric, kim'rik, *a.* Of or pertaining to the Cymry (kim'ri), the name given to themselves by the Welsh; Welsh; pertaining to the ancient race to which the Welsh belong.—*n.* The language of the Cymry or ancient Britons; Welsh.

cynic, sin'ik, *n.* [L. *cynicus,* Gr. *kynikos,* from Gr. *kyōn, kynos,* a dog.] [*cap.*] One of an ancient sect of Greek philosophers who valued themselves on their contempt of riches, of arts, sciences, and amusements; a man of a currish temper; a surly or snarling man; a sneering faultfinder; a misanthrope.—**cynical,** sin'i•kal, *a.* surly; sneering; captious.—**cynically,** sin'i•kal•li, *adv.* In a cynical, sneering, captious, or morose manner.—**cynicalness,** sin'-i•kal•nes, *n.* The state or character of being cynical.—**cynicism,** sin'i•-sizm, *n.* The practice of a cynic; a morose contempt of the pleasures and arts of life.

cynosure, sī'no•shör, *n.* [Gr. *kynosoura,* lit. dog's tail, the Little Bear—*kyōn, kynos,* a dog, and *oura,* tail.] [*cap.*] An old name of the constellation Ursa Minor or the Little Bear, which contains the polestar, and thus has long been noted by mariners and others; hence, anything that strongly attracts attention; a center of attraction.

cyperaceous, sī•pėr•ā'shus, *a.* [Gr. *kyperos,* an aromatic plant.] Belonging to the sedge family of plants; having the characters of the sedges.

cypher, sī'fėr, *n.* Same as *cipher.*

cypress, sī'pres, *n.* [O.Fr. *cypres,* Gr. *kyparissos.*] The popular name of a genus of coniferous trees, some species of which have attained much favor in shrubberies and gardens as ornamental evergreen trees, while the wood of others is highly valued for its durability; the emblem of mourning for the dead, cypress branches having been anciently used at funerals.

Cyprian, sip'ri•an, *a.* Belonging to the island of *Cyprus;* a term applied to a lewd woman, from the worship of Venus in Cyprus and women of this island having anciently a bad character.—*n.* A native of Cyprus; a lewd woman; a courtesan; a strumpet.—**Cypriot,** sip'ri•ot, *n.* A native of Cyprus.

cypsela, sip'se•la, *n.* [Gr. *kypselē,* any hollow vessel.] *Bot.* the one-celled, one-seeded, indehiscent, inferior fruit of composite plants.

Cyrillic, si•ril′ik, *a.* [From St. *Cyril*, its reputed inventor.] The term applied to an alphabet adopted by all the Slavonic peoples belonging to the Eastern Church.

cyst, sist, *n.* [Gr. *kystis*, a bladder.] A close sac or bag of vegetable or animal nature; a bladder-like body; a hollow organ with thin walls (as the urinary bladder); a bladder-like bag or vesicle which includes morbid matter in animal bodies.—**cystic,** sis′tik, *a.* Pertaining to, or contained in, a cyst; having cysts; formed in, or shaped like, a cyst.—**cysticercus,** sis•te•ser′kus. [Gr. *kystis*, a bladder, *kerkos*, a tail.] In tapeworms, a simple cyst with only one head.—**cystitis,** sis•tī′tis, *n.* Inflammation of the bladder.—**cystocele,** sis′to•sēl, *n.* [Gr. *kelē*, a tumor.] A hernia or rupture formed by the protrusion of the urinary bladder.—**cystoscope,** sis′to•skōp. [Gr. *kystis*, a bladder, *skōpeō*, I look at.] An instrument for inspecting the interior of the bladder.—**cystotomy,** sis•tot′o•mi, *n.* The act or practice of opening encysted tumors; the operation of cutting into the bladder for the extraction of a calculus.

Cytherean, sith•e•rē′an, *a.* [From *Cythera*, now Cerigo, where Venus was specially worshiped.] Pertaining to Venus.

cytogenesis, sī•tō•jen′e•sis, *n.* [Gr. *kytos*, a cell, and *genesis*, origin.] *Biol.* the development of cells in animal and vegetable structures.—**cytogenetic,** sī′tō•je•net″ik, *a. Biol.* relating or pertaining to cell formation.—**cytology,** sī•tol′o•ji, *n.* The biological doctrine of cells; the study of cells.—**cytolysis,** sīt•ol′is•is. [Gr. *kytōs*, a cell, *lysis*, a loosing.] The dissolving of poisoned cells.—**cytoplasm,** sīt′o•plasm. [Gr. *kytōs*, a cell, *plasma*, anything formed.] Of a cell, the part of the protoplasm outside the nucleus.

czar, zär or tsär, *n.* [Perhaps a corruption of L. *Cæsar*.] A title of the Emperor of Russia.—**czarevna,** zä•rev′na, *n.* The wife of the czarevitch.—**czarina,** zä•rē′na, *n.* A title of the Empress of Russia.—**czarevitch,** zä′re•vich, *n.* The title of the eldest son of the Czar of Russia.

Czech, che*ch*, *n.* A Bohemian; one of the Slavonic inhabitants of Bohemia; the language of the Czechs or Bohemians.

D

D, d, dē, in the English alphabet, is the fourth letter and the third consonant, representing a dental sound; as a numeral equivalent to 500; *mus.* the second note of the natural scale, answering to the French and Italian *re.*

dab, dab, *v.t.*—*dabbed, dabbing.* [Allied to O.D. *dabben*, to dabble, probably also to *dub.*] To strike quickly but lightly with the hand or with some soft or moist substance.—*n.* A gentle blow with the hand or some soft substance; a quick but light blow; an expert (*colloq.*); a small lump or mass of anything soft or moist; a name common to many species of the flatfish, but especially to a kind of flounder which is found along the European and American coasts of the Atlantic Ocean.—**dabber,** dab′ėr, *n.* One who dabs.

dabble, dab′l, *v.t.*—*dabbled, dabbling.* [A dim. and freq. from *dab.*] To wet; to moisten; to spatter; to sprinkle.—*v.i.* To play in water, as with the hands; to splash in mud or water; to do or engage in anything in a slight or superficial manner; to occupy one's self with slightly; to dip into; to meddle.—**dabbler,** dab′lėr, *n.* One who dabbles in water or mud; one who partakes casually without going thoroughly into an activity; a superficial, casual participant, as one who *dabbles* in politics.

dabchick, dab′chik, *n.* [*Dab*, equivalent to *dip*, and *chick*, from its habit of dipping or diving below the water.] The little grebe, a small swimming bird of the diver family.

dace, dās, *n.* [O.Fr. *dars*, a dace, a dart; comp. also Fr. *vandoise*, the dace.] A small river fish resembling the roach, chiefly inhabiting the deep and clear waters of quiet streams.

dachshund, daks′hu̦nt, *n.* [G. *dachs*, badger, *hund*, dog.] Badger dog; a long-bodied, short-legged dog, with pendulous ears and short hair, black with yellow extremities.

dacoit, dacoity. See DAKOIT, DAKOITY.

dactyl, dak′til, *n.* [Gr. *daktylos*, a finger, a dactyl, which, like a finger, consists of one long and two short members.] A poetical foot consisting of three syllables, the first long and the others short, or the first accented, the others not, as in hăppily.—**dactylic,** dak•til′ik, *a.* Pertaining to or consisting chiefly or wholly of dactyls.—*n.* A dactylic verse.—**dactylology,** dak•ti•lol′o•ji, *n.* The art of communicating ideas or thoughts by the fingers; the language of the deaf and dumb.

dad, daddy, dad, dad′i, *n.* [Comp. W. *tad*, Skr. *tata*, Hind. *dada*, Gypsy *dad, dada*, L. *tata*, Gr. *tata*, Lapp *dadda*—father.] A childish or pet name for father.—**daddy longlegs,** *n.* A kind of spider, called also *harvest-man.*

dado, dā′dō, *n.* [It., a die, a dado, same word as *die, n.*] That part of a pedestal which is between the base and the cornice; the finishing of the lower part of the walls in rooms, made somewhat to represent a continuous pedestal, and frequently formed by a lining of wood, by painting, or by a special wall paper.

daedal, dē′dal, *a.* [L. *Dædalus*, Gr. *Daidalos*, an ingenious artist.] Formed with art; showing artistic skill; ingenious; mazy; intricate.

daemon, dē′mon. Same as *Demon.*

daff,†‡ daf. *v.t.* [A form of *doff.*] To toss aside, to put off. (*Shak.*)

daffodil, daf′o•dil, *n.* [O.E. *affodille*, O.Fr. *asphodile*, Gr. *asphodelos.* ASPHODEL.] Common name of a plant of the amaryllis family with bright yellow bell-shaped flowers; a variety of narcissus; grows in woods and meadows; called also *Daffadowndilly, Daffadilly, Daffodilly.*

dag, dag, *n.* [Probably from same root as *dagger.*] A loose end, as of a lock of wool.

dagger, dag′ėr, *n.* [W. *dagr*, Ir. *daigear*, Armor. *dager, dag.* a dagger or poniard; Gael. *daga*, a dagger, a pistol; Fr. *dague*, a dagger.] A weapon resembling a short sword, with usually a two-edged, sometimes a three-edged, sharp-pointed blade, used for stabbing at close quarters; *printing*, a mark of reference in the form of a dagger, thus†.—*At daggers drawn*, on hostile terms; at war.—*To look* or *speak daggers*, to look or speak fiercely, savagely.—*v.t.* To stab with a dagger.

daggle, dag′l, *v.t.*—*daggled, daggling.* [A freq. form of the obsolete verb *dag*, to bedew, from Icel. *dögg*, Sw. *dagg*, dew.] To make limp by passing through water; to trail in mud or wet grass; to befoul; to draggle.—*v.i.* To run through mud and water.

Dago, dā′gō, *n.* [Sp. *Diego*, James.] A name applied to Spanish, Portuguese, or Italian immigrants, often scornfully.

Dagon, dā′gon, *n.* [Heb. *dag*, a fish.] The national god of the Philistines, represented with the upper part of a man and the tail of a fish.

daguerreotype, da•gâr′ō•tīp, *n.* [From *Daguerre* of Paris, the inventor.] A photographic process by which the picture is fixed on a chemically coated metallic plate solely by the action of the sun's actinic or chemical rays; a picture produced by the process.

dahabeah, dä•ha•bē′ä, *n.* [Egyptian name.] A kind of boat in use on the Nile for the conveyance of travelers, and having one or two masts with a long yard supporting a triangular sail.

dahlia, däl′ya, *n.* [From *Dahl*, a Swedish botanist.] A genus of American composite plants, consisting of tuberous-rooted herbs, putting forth solitary terminal flowers, well known from the varieties of one species being florists' plants.

daily, dā′li, *a. adv.* and *n.* See DAY.

daimio, dī′mi•ō, *n.* [Japanese.] The title of a class of feudal lords in Japan, the greater number of whom, previous to 1871, exercised the authority of petty princes in their domains.

dainty, dān′ti, *a.* [From O.Fr. *daintie, dainté*, pleasantness, an agreeable thing, same word as *dignity*, or from W. *dantaidd, dantaeth*, a dainty, what is toothsome, from *dant*, a tooth.] Pleasing to the palate; of exquisite taste; delicious, as food; of acute sensibility; nice in selecting what is tender and good;

delicate; squeamish; luxurious, as the palate or taste; scrupulous; affectedly fine; nice; ceremonious; elegant; pretty and slight; tender; effeminately beautiful.—*n.* Something delicate to the taste; that which is delicious; a delicacy.—**daintily,** dān'ti•li, *adv.* In a dainty manner.—**daintiness,** dān'ti•nes, *n.* The state or quality of being dainty.

dairy, dâ'ri, *n.* [From O.E. *dey*, a dairymaid = Sw. *deja*, a dairymaid. Icel. *deigja*, a maid servant, a dairymaid.] The place where milk is processed and prepared for sale; a shop where milk, butter, etc., are sold; also used as an adj.—**dairying,** dâ'ri•ing, *n.* The business of conducting a dairy.—**dairymaid,** dâ'ri•mād, *n.* A female whose business is to milk cows and work in the dairy.—**dairyman,** dâ'ri•man, *n.*

dais, dā'is, *n.* [O.Fr. *dais*, *deis*, a dining table, from L. *discus*, a dish, a quoit. *Disk*, *desk*, are the same word.] The high table at the upper end of an ancient dining hall at which the chief persons sat; the raised floor on which the table stood; the chief seat at the high table; often with a canopy; a canopy.

daisy, dā'zi, *n.* [A.Sax. *daeges-eáge*, day's eye, because it opens and closes its flower with the daylight.] The popular name of a composite plant, one of the most common wild flowers, being found in all pastures and meadows, and several varieties being cultivated in gardens; also the name of several other plants having a somewhat similiar blossom. North Carolina's state flower.—**daisied,** dā'zid, *a.* Full of daisies; adorned with daisies.

dak, däk, *n.* See DAWK.

dakoit, da•koit', *n.* An East Indian name for robbers who plunder in bands, but seldom take life.—**dakoity,** da•koi'ti, *n.* The system of robbing in bands.

dale, dāl, *n.* [A.Sax. *dael* = Icel. Sw. Goth. etc. *dal*, G. *thal*, a valley. *Dell* is akin; the root may be in *deal*.] A low place between hills; a vale or valley.—**dalesman,** dālz'man, *n.* One living in a dale or valley.

dally, dal'i, *v.i.*—*dallied*, *dallying*. [Probably allied to G. *dalen*, *dallen*, *tallen*, to speak or act childishly, to trifle, to toy; or perhaps E. *doll*.] To waste time in effeminate or voluptuous pleasures; to amuse one's self with idle play; to trifle; to linger; to delay; to toy and wanton; to interchange caresses; to fondle; to sport; to play; to frolic.—**dalliance,** dal'yans, *n.* The act of dallying, caressing, fondling, trifling, deferring, or delaying.—**dallier,** dal'i•ėr, *n.* One who dallies.

Dalmatian, dal•mā'shi•an, *a.* Of or pertaining to *Dalmatia*.—*Dalmatian dog*, a variety of dog of elegant shape, of a white color, thickly marked with black rounded spots; usually kept as a coach dog.—**dalmatic,** dal•mat'ik, *n.* The vestment used by the deacon at mass, and worn also by bishops under the chasuble, so called as coming originally from Dalmatia, long, loose, and wide-sleeved.

Daltonism, dal'ton•izm, *n.* [From *Dalton*, the chemist, who suffered from this defect, and was the first to call attention to it.] Color blindness.

dam, dam, *n.* [A form of *dame*.] A female parent: used now only of quadrupeds, unless in contempt.

dam, dam, *n.* [Indian.] Name of a small Indian coin of slight value—*not worth a dam*. RAP.

dam, dam, *n.* [Same word as Sw. and G. *damm*, Dan. and D. *dam* (as in Amster*dam*, Rotter*dam*, etc.); Lith. *tama*, a dam.] A bank, mound of earth, wall, or other structure, built across a current of water, to raise its level for the purpose of driving millwheels, or for other purposes.—*v.t.*—*dammed*, *damming*. To obstruct by a dam; to confine by constructing a dam.

damage, dam'ij, *n.* O.Fr. *damage*; Fr. *dommage*, from L.L. *damnaticum*, from L. *damnum*, loss, injury. DAMN.] Any hurt, injury, or harm to person, property, character, or reputation; the value in money of what is injured, harmed, or lost; the estimated money equivalent for detriment or injury sustained: in this sense commonly in pl.—*v.t.*—*damaged*, *damaging*. To injure; to impair; to lessen the soundness, goodness, or value of.—*v.i.* To become injured or impaired in soundness or value.—**damageable,** dam'ij•a•bl, *a.* Capable of being injured or impaired; susceptible of damage.

daman, dā'man, *n.* A rabbit-like animal, the hyrax, or cony of Scripture.

damascene, dam'as•sēn, *n.* [L. *damascenus*, from *Damascus*.] A kind of plum; a damson.—*v.t.* To damask; to damaskeen.

damask, dam'ask, *a.* Of or belonging to *Damascus*; of the color of the rose so called; pink or rosy.—*Damask steel*, a fine steel chiefly from Damascus, used for sword blades.—*n.* The name given to textile fabrics of various materials, more especially silk and linen, ornamented with raised figures of flowers, etc.; a pink color, like that of the damask rose.—*v.t.* To form or imprint the figures of flowers upon, as upon cloth; to variegate; to diversify; to adorn with figures, as steelwork.—**damaskeen,** dam'as•kēn, *v.t.* [Fr. *damasquiner*.] To ornament (particularly iron and steel) with designs produced by inlaying or incrusting with another metal, as gold, silver, etc., by etching, and the like; to damask.—**damask rose,** *n.* A pink species of rose.

dame, dām, *n.* [Fr. *dame*, from L. *domina*, a mistress, fem. of *dominus*, a lord, whence *dominate*, *dominion*, *damsel*, etc.; same root as E. *tame*.] A woman in authority; a title equivalent to *Lady*, *Madam*, *Miss*, used as a form of address; a woman in general; particularly, a woman of mature years; an honor similar to knighthood bestowed on women.

dammar, dam'är, *n.* A gum or resin used as a colorless varnish, and produced by various species of coniferous trees (dammar or dammara-pine) belonging to the South Asiatic islands and New Zealand, kauri gum being a variety.

damn, dam, *v.t.* [L. *damno*, to condemn, from *damnum*, damage, a fine, penalty, from root *da*, as in *dare*, to give.] To consign or send to punishment in a future state; to send to hell; to condemn, censure, reprobate severely; to condemn or destroy the success of by common consent, as by hissing in a theater or by criticisms in the press.—*n.* A profane oath; a curse or execration.—**damnable,** dam'na•bl, *a.* Liable to be damned or condemned; deserving damnation; odious, detestable, or pernicious.—**damnableness,** dam'na•bl•nes, *n.* The state or quality of being damnable.—**damnably,** dam'na•bli, *adv.* In a damnable manner; odiously; detestably; infernally.—**damnation,** dam•nā'shon, *n.* Sentence to punishment in a future state, or the state in which such punishment is undergone; eternal punishment; penalty inflicted for sin; condemnation.—**damnatory,** dam'na•to•ri, *a.* Containing a sentence of condemnation; condemning to damnation; condemnatory.—**damned,** damd, *p.* and *a.* Suffering punishment in hell; lost; hateful; detestable; abominable.—**damning,** dam'ning, dam'ing, *a.* Exposing to damnation; calling for damnation (a *damning* sin).

damp, damp, *a.* [Same word as D. and Dan. *damp*, G. *dampf*, steam, vapor, fog, smoke.] Being in a state between dry and wet; moderately wet; moist; humid; depressed or dejected.—*n.* Moist air; humidity; moisture; fog; dejection; depression of spirits; chill; a noxious exhalation issuing from the earth, and deleterious or fatal to animal life, such as exists in old disused wells, in mines and coal pits.—*v.t.* To make damp; to moisten; to chill, deaden; depress, or deject; to check or restrain; to discourage; to dispirit; to abate.—**dampen,** dam'pen, *v.t.* To make damp or moist.—*v.i.* To grow or become damp.—**damper,** dam'pėr, *n.* One who or that which damps; an iron plate sliding across a flue of a furnace, etc., to check or regulate the draft of air; a piece of mechanism in a pianoforte which, after the finger has left the key, checks a long-continued vibration of the strings; a cake made of flour and water without fermentation (a colonial word).—**dampish,** dam'pish, *a.* Moderately damp or moist.—**dampishness,** dam'pish•nes, *n.* The state of being dampish.—**dampness,** damp'nes, *n.* The state or condition of being damp; moistness; humidity.

damsel, dam'zel, *n.* [Fr. *demoiselle*, O.Fr. *damoisele*, *damisele*, from L.L. *dominicella*, dim. of L. *domina*, *domna*, a mistress. DAME.] A young unmarried woman; a maiden; a virgin.

damson, dam'zn, *n.* [Contr. from

damascene (which see).] A small black, dark-bluish, purple, or yellow plum.

Dan, dan, *n.* [O.Fr. *dan, dans,* a master, from L. *dominus.* DAME.] An old title of honor equivalent to *master, sir, don* ('*Dan* Chaucer').

dance, dans, *v.i.—danced, dancing.* [Fr. *danser,* from O.H.G. *danson,* to draw.] To leap or move with measured steps, regulated by music; to leap and frisk about; to move nimbly, as up and down, backward and forward.—*v.t.* To make to dance; to dandle.—*To dance attendance,* to be assiduous in attentions and officious civilities.—*n.* A leaping or stepping with motions of the body adjusted to the measure of a tune; the regular movements of one who dances; a tune by which dancing is regulated.—**dancer,** dan′sėr, *n.* One who dances.

dandelion, dan′di•lī•un, *n.* [Fr. *dent de lion,* lion's tooth.] A well-known composite plant, having a naked stalk, with one large bright yellow flower, and a tapering milky perennial root of aperient and tonic properties.

dandle, dan′dl, *v.t.—dandled, dandling.* [Allied to G. *tand,* prattle, frivolity, *tändeln,* to trifle, to dandle.] To shake or jolt on the knee, as an infant; to fondle, amuse, or treat as a child; to pet.—**dandler,** dand′lėr, *n.* One who dandles.

dandruff, dan′druf, *n.* [Etym. unknown.] A scurf which forms on the head and comes off in small scales or particles.

dandy, dan′di, *n.* [Fr. *dandin,* a ninny, akin to E. *dandle.*] A man who pays excessive attention to dress; one who dresses with special finery; a fop; a coxcomb.—*a.* Finely or foppishly dressed; foppish; trim; gay.—**dandify,** dan′di•fī, *v.t.* To make, form, or dress out as a dandy or fop.—**dandyish,** dan′di•ish, *a.* Like a dandy.—**dandyism,** dan′di•izm, *n.* The manners and dress of a dandy; foppishness.

Dane, dān, *n.* A native or inhabitant of Denmark.—**Danegelt, Danegeld,** dān′gelt, dān′geld, *n.* [*Gelt, geld*= A.Sax. *geld, gild,* a payment.] An annual tax laid on the English nation in early times for maintaining forces to oppose the Danes, or to furnish tribute to procure peace.—**Danish,** dā′nish, *a.* Belonging to the Danes or Denmark.—*n.* The language of the Danes.

danger, dān′jėr, *n.* [Formerly control, power, Fr. *danger,* O.Fr. *dangier, dongier,* a feudal term for right to woods and waters, from L.L. *dominiarium,* from L. *dominus,* a lord; akin *dominion, dame, damsel,* etc.] Exposure to destruction, ruin, injury, loss, pain, or other evil; peril; risk; hazard; jeopardy.—**dangerous,** dān′jėr•us, *a.* Attended with danger; perilous; hazardous; unsafe; full of risk; creating danger, causing risk of evil.—**dangerously,** dān′jėr•us•li, *adv.* In a dangerous manner or condition.—**dangerousness,** dān′jėr•us•nes, *n.* The state or quality of being dangerous.

dangle, dang′gl, *v.i.—dangled, dangling.* [Allied to Dan. *dingle,* Sw. and Icel. *dingla,* to swing.] To hang loose, flowing, shaking, or waving; to hang and swing; to be a humble officious follower, or to hang about a person (with *about* or *after*).—*v.t.* To cause to dangle; to swing.—**dangler,** dang′glėr, *n.* One who dangles; a man who hangs about women.

dank, dangk, *a.* [Nasalized form allied to *daggle* and Sw. *dagg,* dew.] Damp; moist; humid.—*n.*‡ Moisture; humidity; the watery element. (*Mil.*)

danseuse, dän•sėz′, *n.* [Fr.] A female stage dancer.

dap, dap, *v.i.* [Onomatopoeic.] To drop or let fall the bait gently into the water; an angling word.

dapper, dap′ėr, *a.* [Same word as D. *dapper,* Sw. and Dan. *tapper,* G. *tapfer,* brave.] Small and active; nimble; brisk; lively; neat.

dapple, dap′l, *a.* [Icel. *depill,* a spot; perhaps akin to *dip, deep.*] Marked with spots spotted; variegated with spots of different colors or shades of color.—*v.t. dappled, dappling.* To spot; to variegate with spots.

dare, dâr, *v.i.*—pret. *dared* or *durst*; pp. *dared*; ppr. *daring.* [A.Sax. *ic dear,* I dare, *he dear,* he dare, *we durran,* we dare; *ic dorste,* I durst; Goth. *daursan,* O.H.G. *turran*; cog. Gr. *tharsein,* Skr. *dharsh,* to be courageous.] To have courage for any purpose; to make up the mind to undertake something hazardous or dangerous; to be bold enough; to venture.—*v.t.—dared, daring.* To challenge, to provoke, to defy.—**daredevil,** *n.* A desperado; one who fears nothing and will attempt anything.—**daring,** dâ′ring, *a.* Bold; audacious; courageous; intrepid; adventurous.—*n.* Courage; boldness; fearlessness; audacity.—**daringly,** dâ′ring•li, *adv.* In a daring manner.—**daringness,** dâ′ring•nes, *n.* Boldness.

dare, dār, *v.t.* [A.Sax. *darian*; perhaps akin to Flemish *verdaren,* to amaze.] To stupefy by sudden terror; to daze.

dare, dār, *n.* See DACE.

dark, därk, *a.* [A.Sax. *deorc*; not found in the other Teutonic languages; comp. Gael. and Ir. *dorch,* dark, black.] Destitute of light; not radiating or reflecting light; wholly or partially black; having the quality opposite to white; gloomy; disheartening; not cheerful; concealed; secret; mysterious; not easily understood; not enlightened with knowledge; rude; ignorant (the *dark* ages); morally black; atrocious; wicked; sinister; keeping designs concealed; not fair; said of the complexion.—*n.* [Usually with *the.*] Darkness; the absence of light; a dark hue; a dark part; secrecy; obscurity; a state of ignorance.—**darken,** där′kn, *v.t.* To make dark or black; to deprive of light; to obscure, cloud, make dim; to deprive of vision; to render gloomy; to render ignorant or stupid; to render less clear or intelligible; to sully; to taint.—*v.i.* To grow dark or darker.—**dark horse,** *n.* A contestant about whom little is known or who unexpectedly wins.—**darkish,** därk′ish, *a.* Somewhat dark.—**darkling,** därk′ling, *adv.* In the dark.—*a.* Dark;lowering; gloomy. (*Thack.*)—**darkly,** därk′li, *adv.* In a dark manner; with imperfect light, clearness, or knowledge; obscurely; dimly; blindly; uncertainly.—**darkness,** därk′nes, *n.* The state or quality of being dark; the want of physical light; gloom; obscurity; deepness of shade or color; physical, intellectual, or moral blindness. —**darkroom,** *n.* A room with no light, or with a dim, colored light, used in treating and handling photographic or other light-sensitive materials.—**darksome,** därk′sum, *a. Poet.* gloomy; dark.

darling, där′ling, *a.* [A.Sax. *deórling —deóre,* dear, and dim. term. *-ling.* DEAR.] Dearly beloved; dear; favorite.—*n.* One much beloved; a favorite.

darn, därn, *v.t.* [W. and Armor. *darn,* Ir. *darne,* a piece, a patch.] To mend a rent or hole in, by imitating the texture of the cloth or stuff with yarn or thread and a needle; to sew or repair by crossing and recrossing the stitches.—*n.* A place mended by darning.

darnel, där′nel, *n.* [O.Fr. *darnelle*; same root as D. *door,* G. *thor,* a fool, Lith. *durnas,* foolish, mad; from its narcotic properties.] A troublesome weed in cornfields, with ryelike ears, which, when ground among corn, are said to be narcotic and stupefying.

dart, därt, *n.* [O.Fr. *dart,* Mod.Fr. *dard*; of Germanic origin = Sw. *dart,* A.Sax. *daroth,* O.H.G. *tart.*] A pointed missile weapon to be thrown by the hand; a short lance; anything which pierces and wounds; a sudden or rapid rush, leap, bound, spring, or flight.—*v.t.* To throw (a dart, etc.) with a sudden thrust; to throw swiftly; to shoot.—*v.i.* To fly, as a dart; to fly rapidly; to spring and run with velocity; to start suddenly and run.—**darter,** där′tėr, *n.* One that darts; a web-footed tropical bird of the pelican tribe, so called from darting after fish in the water.

Darwinian, där•win′i•an, *a.* Of or pertaining to Charles *Darwin,* the celebrated naturalist.—*n.* A believer in Darwinism.—**Darwinism,** där′win•izm, *n.* The doctrine as to the origin and modifications of the species of animals and plants taught by Darwin, the principal points being that there is a tendency to variation in organic beings, so that descendants may differ very widely from progenitors; that animals and plants tend naturally to multiply rapidly, so that if unchecked they would soon overstock the whole globe; that there is thus a continual struggle for existence among all organized beings; that the strongest and best fitted for particular surroundings naturally survive, and the others die out; that from a few forms (perhaps even one) sprang all existing species, genera, orders, etc., of animals and plants.

dash, dash, *v.t.* [A Scandinavian

word=Dan. *daske*, to slap, *dask*, a slap, Sw. *daska*, to beat.] To cause to strike or come against suddenly and with violence; to strike or throw violently or suddenly; to sprinkle or mix slightly; to disturb or frustrate (to *dash* courage); to confound, confuse, abash.—*To dash off*, to form or sketch out in haste carelessly; to execute hastily or with careless rapidity.—*v.i.* To rush with violence; to strike or be cast violently.—*n.* A violent striking together of two bodies; collision; something thrown into another substance; infusion; admixture; a sudden check; abashment; a rapid movement; a sudden onset; the capacity for unhesitating, prompt action; vigor in attack; a flourish or ostentatious parade; a mark or line [–] in writing or printing noting a break or pause.—**dasher,** dash′ėr, *n.* One who or that which dashes; the float of a paddle wheel, the plunger of a churn, and the like; also a dashboard.—**dashing,** dash′-ing, *a.* Impetuous spirited; showy; brilliant.—**dashboard,** *n* A board or leathern apron on the fore part of a vehicle to intercept mud, etc.; a partition below the windshield of an automobile (instrument board).

dastard, das′tėrd, *n.* [Icel. *daestr*, exhausted; akin to *daze*, the suffix being *-ard*.] A coward; a poltroon; one who meanly shrinks from danger. —*a.* Cowardly; meanly; shrinking from danger.—**dastardliness,** das′-tėrd•li•nes, *n.* Cowardliness.—**dastardly,** das′tėrd•li, *a.* Cowardly.

dasyure, dā′si•ūr, *n.* [Gr. *dasys*, hairy, and *oura*, a tail.] A carnivorous marsupial found in Australia.

data. See DATUM.

date, dāt, *n.* [Fr., from L. *datum*, given, used in a Roman letter as 'given' (at such a place and such a time).] That addition to a writing which specifies the year, month, and day when it was given or executed; the time when any event happened, when anything was transacted, or when anything is to be done; the period of time at or during which one has lived or anything has existed; an appointment made for a specified time; a social engagement with one of the opposite sex.—*Out of date*, obsolete; behind the times.—*Up to date*, modern; in the latest style.—*v.t.*—*dated, dating*. To write down the date on; to append the date to; to note or fix the time of; to make an appointment with a person of the opposite sex for a social engagement.—*v.i.* To reckon time; to begin at a certain date (to *date* from the 10th century) to have a certain date.—**dateless,** dāt′les, *a.* Having no date; undated; so old as to be beyond date; having no fixed limit; eternal.—**date line,** dāt•līn, *n.* A line in a newspaper, letter, etc., giving the date and place of origin; an imaginary line running north and south through the Pacific, approximately along the 180th meridian, where each calendar day begins.

date, dāt, *n.* [O.Fr. *date*, Fr. *datte*, from L. *dactylus*, Gr. *daktylos*, a finger, a date.] The fruit of the date palm, consisting of a soft fleshy drupe enclosing a hard seed and having a delicious flavor, used as food in North Africa and Western Asia, and imported into other countries.—**date palm,** *n.* A palm having a stem rising to the height of 50 or 60 feet, crowned with large feathery leaves, the female plant bearing 180 to 200 dates.

dative, dā′tiv, *a.* [L. *dativus*, from *do*, to give.] *Gram.* a term applied to the case of nouns which usually follows verbs that express giving, or the doing of something to or for.—*n.* The dative case.

datum, dā′tum, *n.* pl. **data,** dā′ta. [L.] Something given or admitted; some fact, proposition, quantity, or condition granted or known, from which other facts, propositions, etc., are to be deduced.—*Datum line*, *engin.* the base line of a section from which all the heights and depths are measured in the plans of a railroad, and so forth.

daub, dąb, *v.t.* [O.Fr. *dauber*, to plaster, from L. *dealbare*, to whitewash—*de*, intens., and *albus*, white.] To smear with soft adhesive matter, as with mud or slime; to plaster; to soil; to defile; to besmear; to paint coarsely; to lay or put on without taste; to load with affected finery.—*n.* A smear or smearing; a coarse painting.—**dauber,** dą′bėr, *n.* One who daubs; a builder of walls with clay or mud mixed with straw; a coarse painter; a low and gross flatterer.—**dauby,** dą′bi, *a.* Viscous; slimy; adhesive.

daughter, dą′tėr, *n.* [A.Sax. *dóhtor*= D. *dochter*, Dan. *dotter*, Icel. *dóttir*, G. *tochter*, Gr. *thygatēr*, Per. *doktarah*, Skr. *duhitri*, Lith. *dukté*, —daughter.] A female child of any age; a female descendant, a title of affection given to a woman by a person whose age, position, or office entitles the speaker to respect or esteem; the female offspring of an animal or plant.—**daughter-in-law,** *n.* A son's wife.—**daughterly,** dą′-tėr•li, *a.* Becoming a daughter; dutiful.

dauk, dąk, *n.* Same as *Dawk*.

daunt, dąnt, *v.t.* [O.Fr. *danter*, Fr. *dompter*, to tame, from L. *domitare*, a freq. of *domo*, to tame, from root of *dominus*, a lord. TAME.] To repress or subdue the courage of; to intimidate; to dishearten; to check by fear.—**dauntless,** dąnt′les, *a.* Bold; fearless; intrepid; not timid; not discouraged.—**dauntlessly,** dąnt′-les•li, *adv.* In a bold fearless manner. —**dauntlessness,** dąnt′les•nes, *n.* Fearlessness; intrepidity.

dauphin, dą′fin, *n.* [Fr. *dauphin*, the title originally of the lords of *Dauphiny*, and afterwards attached to the French crown along with this province, from L. *delphinus*, a dolphin, the crest of the lords of Dauphiny.] The eldest son of the King of France prior to the revolution of 1830.—**dauphiness,** dą′fin•es, *n.* The wife of the dauphin.

davit, da′vit, *n.* [Origin unknown.] *Naut.* either of the two projecting pieces of wood or iron on the side or stern of a vessel, used for suspending or lowering and hoisting the boats by means of pulleys.

Davy lamp, dā′vi lamp, *n.* A lamp whose flame is surrounded by wire, invented by Sir Humphry *Davy* to protect the miners from explosions of firedamp.

daw, dą, *n.* [From cry.] A jackdaw.

dawdle, dą′dl, *v.i.* [Akin to *daddle*, and probably to *dowdy*, a slattern.] To waste time; to trifle; to saunter.—*v.t.* To waste by trifling.—**dawdler,** dą′dlėr, *n.* One who dawdles; a trifler.

dawk, dąk, *n.* [Hind.] In the East Indies, the post; a relay of men, as for carrying letters, despatches, etc., or travelers in palanquins.

dawn, dąn, *v.i.* [A.Sax. *dagain*, to dawn or become day, from *daeg*, day.] To begin to grow light in the morning; to grow light; to begin to show intellectual light or knowledge; to begin to become visible or appear (the truth *dawns* upon me).—*n.* The break of day; the first appearance of light in the morning; first opening or expansion; beginning; rise; first appearance (the *dawn* of civilization, etc.).

day, dā, *n.* [A.Sax. *daeg*=D. Dan. and Sw. *dag*, Icel. *dagr*, Goth. *dags*, G. *tag*; not connected with L. *dies*, a day.] That space of time during which there continues to be light, in contradistinction to night; the time between the rising and setting of the sun; the period of one revolution of the earth on its axis, or twenty-four hours; light; sunshine (in the open *day*); any period of time distinguished from other time (the authors of that *day*); age; era; epoch; in the plural often=lifetime, earthly existence; the contest of a day or day of combat (to gain the *day*); an appointed or fixed time; time of commemorating an event; anniversary.—*Days of grace*, a certain number of days (usually three) allowed for the payment of a bill (not payable on demand) beyond the date marked on the face of it specifying when it becomes due.—*Astronomical, natural*, or *solar day*, the interval between the sun's leaving the meridian and its return to it.—*Mean solar day*, the mean of all the solar days in the year.—*Sidereal day*, the time of one apparent revolution of the fixed stars.—*Civil day*, the day beginning and ending at midnight.—*Jewish day*, the interval between sunset and sunset.—*Day's journey*, an indefinite measure of distance frequently mentioned in Scripture; the average distance one can travel in a day, say from 12 miles or more on foot, to 20 or over on horseback.—**daily,** dā′li, *a.* Happening, being, or appearing every day; done day by day; bestowed or enjoyed every day.—*adv.* Every day; day by day.—*n.* A newspaper published daily.—**day bed,** *n.* A bed used for rest during the day; a couch; a sofa. (*Shak.*)—**daybook,** *n.* A book in which are recorded the debts and credits or accounts of the day.—**daybreak,** dā'brāk, *n.* The dawn or first appearance of light in the morning.—**daydream,** dā'drēm, *n.* A visionary fancy indulged in when awake.—**daydreamer,** dā'drē•mėr, *n.*—**day laborer,** *n.* One who works by the day.—**daylight,** dā'līt, *n.* The light of the day; the light of the sun.—*Daylight saving time,* a method of reckoning time that provides more daylight for daytime activities by setting clocks ahead one or more hours in the spring and returning them to standard time in the fall.—**day lily,** *n.* A liliaceous plant, the flowers of which rarely last more than a day.—**day nursery,** *n.* A nursery for the care and training of small children during the day; a nursery school.—**daytime,** dā'tīm, *n.* The time of daylight.

daze, dāz, *v.t.* [The same word as Icel. *dasa,* to tire out; O.D. *daesen,* to be foolish; akin *doze, dizzy.*] To stun or stupefy, as with a blow, liquor, or excess of light; to blind by too strong a light.—*n.* The condition of being dazed.

dazzle, daz'l, *v.t.*—*dazzled, dazzling.* [Freq. of *daze.*] To overpower or blind with light; to dim by excess of light; *fig.* to overpower or confound by splendor or brilliancy, or with show or display of any kind.—*v.i.* To be overpoweringly bright or brilliant; to be overpowered or dimmed by light (as the eyes).—*n.* A dazzling light; glitter.—**dazzlingly,** daz'ling•li, *adv.*

DDT, *n.* [From dichloro-diphenyl-trichloro-ethane.] A symbol for a powerful water-soluble insecticide, $C_{14}H_9Cl_5$.

deacon, dē'kon, *n.* [L. *diaconus,* Gr. *diakonos,* a minister or servant.] In the Roman and Anglican churches, a member of the lowest of the three orders of priesthood (bishops, priests, and deacons); in Presbyterian churches, a functionary who attends to the secular interests of the church; among Congregationalists, Baptists and others, one who looks after the spiritual as well as temporal concerns of the congregation under the minister; in Scotland, the president of an incorporated trade.—**deaconess,** dē'kon•es, *n.* A female deacon in the primitive church.—**deaconry, deaconship,** dē'kon•ri, dē'kon•ship, *n.* The office of a deacon.

dead, ded, *a.* [A.Sax. *deád*=D. *dood,* Dan. *dod,* Icel. *dauthr,* Goth. *dauths.* DEATH, DIE.] Deprived, devoid, or destitute of life; having lost the vital principle; lifeless; inanimate; hence, wanting animation, activity, spirit, vigor; numb; callous; void of perception; resembling death; deep and sound (a *dead* sleep); perfectly still or motionless (a *dead* calm); monotonous; unvarying or unbroken by apertures or projections (a *dead* level, or wall); unemployed; useless (*dead* capital or stock); unreverberating, dull, heavy (a *dead* sound); tasteless, vapid, spiritless, flat, as liquors; producing death; sure or unerring as death (a *dead* shot); in a state of spiritual death; under the power of sin; cut off from the rights of a citizen; not communicating motion or power (*dead* steam); no longer spoken, or in common use by a people (a *dead* language); having no gloss, warmth, or brightness (a *dead* color).—*The dead* (*sing.*), the time when there is a remarkable stillness or gloom; the culminating point, as the midst of winter or of night; (*pl.*), those who are dead; the deceased; the departed.—*adv.* To a degree approaching death; to the last degree; thoroughly; completely (*dead* tired, *dead* drunk).—**deaden,** ded'n, *v.t.* To take away or lessen the vigor, force, feeling, etc., of; to make dull, flat, etc.; to soundproof.—*v.i.* To lose vigor, force, etc.—**deadly,** ded'li, *a.* Causing death; fatal; implacable; deathlike; intense.—**deadness,** ded'nes, *n.*—**dead-beat,** *a.* Tired out.—**deadbeat,** *n.* One who avoids paying his bills; a loafer.—**dead center, dead point,** *n.* A position in a link motion such as that when the crank and connecting rod of an engine are in a straight line.—**dead-end,** *a.* Closed at one end; leading nowhere.—**dead end,** *n.* An end, as of a street or pipe, that has no opening—**deadeye,** *n.* A round block without a pulley pierced with three holes and used to extend the shrouds and stays, etc.—**deadhead,** ded'hed, *n.* A person who receives free tickets for theaters, or passes for conveyances.—*v.t.* To treat as a deadhead.—**dead heat,** *n.* The result, in a contest of speed, when two or more competitors finish at the same time so that no one is the winner.—**dead letter,** *n.* A letter which cannot be delivered from defect of address, and which is sent to the general post office to be opened and returned to the writer; anything, as a condition, treaty, etc., which has lost its force or authority, by lapse of time or any other cause, and has ceased to be acted on.—**deadlight,** *n. Naut.* a strong wooden shutter for protecting the windows of cabins, etc. —**deadline,** *n.* A line or limit that must not be crossed; the latest possible time for doing something.—**deadlock,** *n.* A complete standstill.—*v.t.* To bring to a deadlock.—*v.i.* To come to a deadlock.—**dead reckoning,** *n.* The calculation of the position of a ship or airplane by log, compass, etc., when celestial observation is impossible; guesswork.—**dead weight,** *n.* The unrelieved weight of inert matter.—**dead wood,** *n.* Dead branches or trees; anything that is useless or unsatisfactory.

deaf, def, *a.* [A.Sax. *deáf*=D. *doof,* Dan. *dov,* Icel. *daufr,* G. *taub*—deaf; akin Sc. *daft,* stupid, Icel. *dofi,* torpor.] Wanting the sense of hearing, either wholly or in part; disinclined to hear; inattentive; unheeding; unconcerned.—**deafen,** def'n, *v.t.* To make deaf; to deprive of the power of hearing; to stun; to prevent the passage of sound.—**deafly,** def'li, *adv.* Without sense of sounds; obscurely heard.—**deafness,** def'nes, *n.* The state of being deaf, or of being unable to hear sounds; want of hearing; unwillingness to hear; inattention.—**deaf-mute,** *n.* A person who is both deaf and dumb.

deal, dēl, *n.* [A.Sax. *dael,* a portion, a share=D. *deel,* a portion, a board or plank; Dan. *deel,* Sw. *del,* Goth. *dails,* G. *theil,* a part, a share. *Dole, dale* are akin.] A portion or part; an indefinite quantity, degree, or extent, generally implying that the amount is considerable (often qualified by *great* which hardly adds to the sense); the division or distribution of playing cards; a board or plank of fir, of some length and at least 7 inches wide; fir or pine timber.—*v.t.*—*dealt* (delt), *dealing.* [A.Sax. *daelan,* to divide.] To divide in portions; to give out; to part; to distribute; to scatter; to hurl (blows, destruction).—*v.i.* To distribute; to traffic; to trade; to negotiate; to transact; to have intercourse; to conduct one's self in relation to others; to act; to behave.—**dealer,** dēl'ėr, *n.* One who deals; one who has to do or has concern with others; a trader, merchant, or trafficker; one who distributes cards to the players.—**dealing,** dē'ling, *n.* Conduct; behavior; practice (double *dealing,* fair *dealing*); traffic; business; intercourse or business of friendship; concern:commonly in pl.—**dealfish,** *n.* [From *deal,* board.] A name for a fish with an extremely compressed body found in the northern seas.

dean, dēn, *n.* [O.Fr. *dean, deien,* Mod.Fr. *doyen,* from L. *decanus,* one set over ten persons, from *decem,* ten.] An ecclesiastical dignitary ranking next to the bishop; an administrative officer of a college or university, under the president, supervising students in regard to their choice of courses, heading the faculty of a division or college, or adviser to men or women; a senior member of a diplomatic corps; an acknowledged leader in a profession.—**deanery,** dē'nėr•i, *n.* The office or jurisdiction of a dean; the official residence of a dean.—**deanship,** dēn'ship, *n.* The office or title of a dean.

dear, dēr, *a.* [A.Sax. *deóre, dýre,* dear, beloved, high-priced; O.D. *dier,* Mod.D. *duur,* Icel. *dyrr,* Dan. and Sw. *dyr,* G. *theuer,* dear, beloved, high-priced, etc.] Bearing a high price in comparison with the usual price or the real value; high-priced: opposite to *cheap;* characterized by high prices resulting from scarcity (a *dear* year); greatly valued; beloved; precious; heartfelt‡; passionate or intense‡.—*n.* A darling; a term of affection or endearment.—*adv.* Dearly; tenderly; at a dear rate.—**dearly,** dēr'li, *adv.* At a high price; with great fondness; fondly; tenderly.—**dearness,** dēr'nes, *n.* The state or quality of being dear; high value in price, or estimation; preciousness; tender love.—**dearth,** dėrth, *n.* [Comp. *warm-th, heal-th, slo(w)-th,* etc.] Scarcity, which makes food dear; want, or time of want; famine; lack or absence.

death, deth, *n.* [A.Sax. *deáth*=Goth. *dauthus*, L.G. and D. *dood*, Sw. and Dan. *dōd*, G. *tod*—death. DEAD, DIE.] That state of a being, animal or vegetable, in which there is a total and permanent cessation of all the vital functions; the state of being dead; the state or manner of dying; cause, agent, or instrument of death; total loss or extinction (the *death* of one's faculties); capital punishment.—*Civil death*, deprivation of the rights of citizenship, as when a man is banished or becomes a monk.—**deathless,** deth′les, *a.* Not subject to death, destruction, or extinction; undying; immortal.—**deathly,** deth′li, *a.* and *adv.* Resembling death; cadaverously; wanly.—**deathbed,** *n.* The bed on which a person dies or is confined in his last sickness.—**deathblow,** *n.* A blow causing death; a mortal blow; any thing which extinguishes hope or blights one's prospects.—**death rate,** *n.* The proportion of deaths among the inhabitants of a town, country, etc.—**death rattle,** *n.* A peculiar rattling in the throat of a dying person.—**death's-head,** *n.* The skull of a human skeleton, or a figure representing one.—*Death's-head moth*, the largest lepidopterous insect having markings upon the back of the thorax very closely resembling a skull or death's-head.—**death warrant,** *n.* An order from the proper authority for the execution of a criminal.—**deathwatch,** *n.* A vigil kept over the dead or the dying; a small insect that makes a clicking noise.

debacle, di•bak′l, *n.* [Fr., from *débâcler*, to break up—*de*, not, and *bâcler*, to bar, from L. *baculus*, a bar.] A sudden breaking up of ice in a river; *geol.* a sudden outbreak of water; the complete collapse of an enterprise.

debar, di•bär′, *v.t.*—*debarred, debarring*. To bar or cut off from entrance; to preclude; to hinder from approach, entry, or enjoyment; to shut out or exclude.—**debarment,** di•bär′ment, *n.* The act of debarring.

debark, di•bärk′, *v.t.* and *i.* [Fr. *débarquer*—*de*, and *barque*, a boat or bark.] To land from a ship or boat; to disembark.—**debarkation,** di•bärk•ā′shon, *n.* The act of disembarking.

debase, di•bās′, *v.t.*—*debased, debasing*. To impart a certain baseness to; to reduce or lower in quality, dignity, character, etc.; to degrade; to vitiate; to adulterate; to abase.—**debasement,** di•bās′ment, *n.* The act of debasing, or state of being debased.—**debaser,** di•bā′sėr, *n.* One who or that which debases.

debate, di•bāt, *n.* [O.Fr. *debatre*, to debate—prefix *de*, and *batre*, to beat. BATTER, ABATE.] An argument or reasoning between persons of different opinions; dispute; controversy; quarrel; strife; contention. *v.t.*—*debated, debating*. To discuss by arguments for and against; to dispute; to argue; to contest.—*v.i.* To discuss disputed points; to examine different arguments in the mind (to *debate* with one's self whether).—*Debating society*, a society for the purpose of debate and improvement in extemporaneous speaking.—**debatable,** dē•bā′ta•bl, *a.* Capable of being debated; disputable; subject to controversy and contention.—**debater,** di•bā′tėr, *n.* One who debates; a disputant.

debauch, di•bạch′, *v.t.* [O.Fr. *desbaucher*, Fr. *débaucher*—*de*, *des*, and *bauche*, a workshop, a task; the original meaning would therefore be to draw one away from his work or duty.] To corrupt or vitiate (as principles, etc.); to corrupt with lewdness; to bring to be guilty of unchastity; to seduce; to lead astray from duty or allegiance.—*n.* Excess or a fit of excess in eating or drinking; intemperance; drunkenness.—**debauchedly,** di•bạch′ed•li, *adv.* In a profligate manner.—**debauchee,** deb′o•shē, *n.* A man given to debauchery.—**debauchery,** di•bạ′chėr•i, *n.* Excessive indulgence in sensual pleasures of any kind, as gluttony, intemperance, unlawful indulgence of lust.—**debauchment,** di•bạch′ment, *n.* The act of debauching.

debenture, di•ben′chėr, *n.* [L. *debentur*, there are owing (certain things), a word used in old acknowledgments of debt. Akin *debt*, *debit*.] A deed or document charging certain property with the repayment of money lent by a person therein named, and with interest on the sum lent at a given rate; a certificate or drawback of customs duties on the exportation of certain goods.

debilitate, di•bil′i•tāt, *v.t.*—*debilitated, debilitating*. [L. *debilito*, *debilitatum*, to weaken, from *debilis*, weak.] To weaken; to impair the strength of; to enfeeble; to make faint or languid.—**debilitation,** di•bil′i•tā″shon, *n.* The act of weakening; relaxation.—**debility,** di•bil′i•ti, *n.* [L. *debilitas*.] A state of general bodily weakness; feebleness; languor of body; faintness.

debit, deb′it, *n.* [L. *debitum*, something owed, from *debeo*, to owe—*de*, from, and *habeo*, to have.] That which is entered in an account as a debt; a recorded item of debt; that part of an account in which is entered any article of goods furnished, or money paid to or on account of a person.—*v.t.* To charge with as a debt (to *debit* a person *for* or *with* goods); to enter on the debtor side of a book.

debonair, deb•o•när′, *a.* [Fr. *débonnaire*—*de*, from, *bon*, good, and *aire* (L. *area*), place, extraction.] Characterized by courtesy, affability, or gentleness; elegant; well-bred; winning; accomplished.—**debonairly,** deb•o•när′li, *adv.* In a debonair manner.—**debonairness,** deb•o•när′nes, *n.* The character of being debonair.

debouch, di•bösh′, *v.i.* [Fr. *déboucher*—*de*, from, and *bouche*, mouth, L. *bucca*, the cheek.] To issue or march out of a narrow place, or from defiles, as troops.

debris, dā•brē′, *n.* [Fr., from *dé*, L. *dis*, asunder, apart, and *briser*, to break.] Fragments; rubbish; ruins; *geol.* any accumulation of broken and detached matter, as that which arises from the waste of rocks, and which is piled up at their base or swept away by water.

debt, det, *n.* [O.Fr. *debte* (now *dette*), L. *debita*, things due. DEBIT.] That which is due from one person to another; that which one person is bound to pay to or perform for another; what is incumbent on one to do or suffer; a due; an obligation; the state of owing something to another (to be in *debt*); a duty neglected or violated; a trespass; a sin (N.T.).—**debtor,** det′ėr, *n.* [L. *debitor*.] A person who owes another either money, goods, or services: the correlative of *creditor*; one who has received from another an advantage of any kind; one indebted or in debt.

debunk, di•bunk′, *v.t.* To show the error in false or high-flown statements. [*Colloq.*]

debut, dā•bü′, *n.* [Fr.—*de*, from, and *but*, mark, butt. Perhaps has its meaning from the bowl being brought from the butt on one commencing to play at bowls.] Entrance upon anything; first appearance before the public, as that of an actor or actress on the stage.—**debutant,** *fem.* **debutante,** dā•bü•tän′, dā•bü•tänt′, *n.* [Fr.] One who makes a debut or first appearance before the public.

decade, dek′ād, *n.* [L. *decas*, *decadis*, Gr. *dekas*, from *deka*, ten.] The sum or number of ten; an aggregate or group consisting of ten; specifically, an aggregate of ten years.

decadence, decadency, dek′a•dens, dek′a•den•si, *n.* [Fr. *décadence*, L.L. *decadentia*, from L. *de*, down, and *cado*, to fall.] Decay; a falling into a lower state.—**decadent,** dek′a•dent, *a.* In decadence; decaying; deteriorating.—*n.* An artist or writer of a morally weak fiber and style.

decagon, dek′a•gon, *n.* [Gr. *deka*, ten, and *gōnia*, a corner.] *Geom.* a plane figure having ten sides and ten angles.—**decagonal,** de•kag′o•nal, *a.* Of or belonging to a decagon.

decagram, decagramme, dek′a•gram, *n.* [Fr. *décagramme*, Gr. *deka*, ten, and Fr. *gramme*.] A French weight of 10 grams, equal to 5.644 drams avoirdupois.

decahedron, dek•a•hē′dron, *n.* [Gr. *deka*, ten, and *hedra*, a seat, a base.] *Geom.* a figure or body having ten sides.—**decahedral,** dek•a•hē′dral, *a.* Having ten sides.

decalcify, dē•kal′si•fī, *v.t.* [L. *de*, not, and *calx*, *calcis*, lime, chalk.] To deprive of lime, as bones of their hardening matter, so as to reduce them to gelatin.—**decalcification,** dē•kal′si•fi•kā″shon, *n.* The removal of calcareous matter, as from bones.

decalcomania, dē•kal′kō•mā″nia, *n.* [Fr. *decalcomanie*.] A process in printing which permits the transfer of the ink, forming a design or picture, from the paper on which it is printed to some object.

decaliter, decalitre, dek′a•lē•tėr, *n.* A metric measure of volume equal to ten liters.

Decalogue, dek′a•log, *n.* [Gr. *deka*, ten, and *logos*, a word.] The ten commandments.

decameter, decametre, dek′a•mē•tėr, *n.* A metric measure of length equal to ten meters.

decamp, di•kamp′, *v.i.* [Fr. *décamper* —*de*, from, and *camp*, a camp.] To remove or depart from a camp or camping ground; to march off; to depart; to take one's self off, especially in a secret or clandestine manner.—**decampment,** di•kamp′ment, *n.*

decant, dē•kant′, *v.t.* [Fr. *décanter*, to decant—*de*, and *canter*, from O.Fr. *cant*, a rim, an edge; lit. to pour out by canting or tilting. CANT.] To pour off gently, as liquor from its sediment, or from one vessel into another.—**decantation,** dē•kan•tā′shon, *n.* The act of decanting.—**decanter,** dē•kan′tėr, *n.* One who decants; a vessel used to decant liquors, or for receiving decanted liquors; a glass vessel or bottle used for holding wine or other liquors for filling drinking glasses.

decapitate, di•kap′i•tāt, *v.t.*—*decapitated, decapitating.* [L.L. *decapito, decapitatum*, to behead—L. *de*, and *caput*, head.] To behead; to cut off the head of.—**decapitation,** di•kap′i•tā″shon, *n.* The act of beheading.

decapod, dek′a•pod, *n.* [Gr. *deka*, ten, and *pous, podos*, a foot.] One of an order of crustaceans (crabs, lobsters) having ten feet; one of that division of the cuttlefishes which have ten prehensile arms.—*a.* Having ten feet; belonging to the decapods.

decarbonate, dē•kär′bo•nāt, *v.t.* To deprive of carbonic acid.—**decarbonization, decarburization,** dē•kär′bo•ni•zä″shon, dē•kär′bū•ri•zā″shon, *n.* The process of depriving of carbon.—**decarbonize, decarburize,** dē•kär′bo•nīz, dē•kär′bū•rīz, *v.t.* —*decarbonized, decarbonizing.* To deprive of carbon.

decasyllabic, dek′a•sil•lab″ik, *a.* [Gr. *deka*, ten, and *syllabē*, a syllable.] Having ten syllables.

decathlon, di•kath′lon, *n.* [Prefix *deca*, ten, and Gr. *athlon*, contest.] An athletic contest having ten events.

decay, di•kā′, *v.i.* [O.Fr. *decaer* from L. *de*, down, and *cadere*, to fall; seen also in *cadence, chance, casual, incident*, etc.] To pass gradually from a sound, prosperous, or perfect state, to a less perfect state, or toward weakness, or dissolution; to become decomposed or corrupted; to rot; to be gradually impaired; to waste or molder away.—*v.t.* To impair.—*n.* The state or process of decaying.

decease, di•sēs′, *n.* [Fr. *décès*, from L. *decessus*, departure—*de*, and *cedo, cessum*, to go. CEDE.] Departure from this life; death.—*v.i.* To depart from this life; to die.—**deceased,** di•sēst′, *p.* Departed from life; dead; frequently used as a noun.

deceit, di•sēt′, *n.* [O.Fr. *deceit*, L. *deceptus*, from *decipio, deceptum*, to deceive, lit. to take down—*de*, down, and *capio*, to take. CAPABLE.] The quality or act of deceiving; guilefulness; the act of misleading a person; any artifice, stratagem, or practice, which misleads another, or causes him to believe what is false; act of fraud; cheat; fallacy. ∴ Syn. under FRAUD.—**deceitful,** di•sēt′fu̧l, *a.* Given to deceive; full of deceit; tending to mislead, deceive, or ensnare; trickish; fraudulent; cheating.—**deceitfully,** di•sēt′fu̧l•li, *adv.* In a deceitful manner.—**deceitfulness,** di•sēt′fu̧l•nes, *n.* Disposition or tendency to mislead or deceive; the quality of being deceitful.—**deceive,** di•sēv′, *v.t.* and *i.*—*deceived, deceiving.* [Fr. *décevoir*, O.Fr. *decever*.] To mislead, especially intentionally; to cause to believe what is false, or disbelieve what is true; to cause to mistake; to impose on; to delude; to frustrate or disappoint (the hopes, etc.).—**deceiver,** di•sē′vėr, *n.*

decelerate, de•sel′ėr•āt, *v.t.* [Prefix *de*, not, and *accelerate*.] To decrease the velocity of.—*v.i.* To slow down. —**deceleration,** dē•sel•ėr•ā″shon, *n.* —**decelerator,** de•sel′ėr•ātėr, *n.*

December, di•sem′bėr, *n.* [L. from *decem*, ten, this being the tenth month among the early Romans, who began the year in March.] The twelfth and last month in the year, in which the sun is at his greatest distance south of the equator.

decemvir, di•sem′vėr, *n.* pl. **decemvirs, decemviri,** di•sem′vėrz, di•sem•vi•rī. [L. *decem*, ten, and *vir*, a man.] One of ten magistrates, who had absolute authority in ancient Rome, from B.C. 449 to 447.—**decemviral,** di•sem′vėr•al, *a.* Pertaining to the decemvirs.—**decemvirate,** di•sem′vėr•āt, *n.* The office of the decemvirs; the decemvirs collectively.

decency. See DECENT.

decennary, di•sen′na•ri, *n.* [L. *decennium*, a period of ten years—*decem*, ten, and *annus*, a year.] A period of ten years.—**decennial,** di•sen′ni•al, *a.* Continuing for ten years; consisting of ten years; happening every ten years.

decent, dē′sent, *a.* [L. *decens, decentis*, ppr. of *decet*, it becomes; akin *decorate, decorum*.] Becoming; having a character or show that gains general approval; suitable, as to words, behavior, dress, and ceremony; seemly; decorous; free from immodesty; not obscene; modest; moderate, tolerable, passable, respectable (*colloq.*).—**decency,** dē′sen•si, *n.* [L. *decentia*.] The state or quality of being decent; propriety in actions or discourse; decorum; modesty; freedom from ribaldry or obscenity; a decent or becoming ceremony or rite.—**decently,** dē′sent•li, *adv.* In a decent or becoming manner; tolerably, passably, or fairly (*colloq.*).—**decentness,** dē′sent•nes, *n.* The state of being decent; decency.

decentralize, dē•sen′tral•īz, *v.t.* To distribute what has been centralized; to remove from direct connection or dependence on a central authority. —**decentralization,** dē•sen′tra•lī•zā″shon, *n.* The act of decentralizing; *politics*, the act of distributing among a number of places throughout a country the administration of its internal affairs.

deception, di•sep′shon, *n.* [L. *deceptio, deceptionis*, a deceiving. DECEIVE.] The act of deceiving or misleading; habit of deceiving; the state of being deceived or misled; that which deceives; artifice; cheat. ∴ Syn. under FRAUD.—**deceptive,** di•sep′tiv, *a.* Tending to deceive; having power to mislead or impress false opinious; misleading.—**deceptively,** di•sep′tiv•li, *adv.* In a manner to deceive.—**deceptiveness,** di•sep′tiv•nes, *n.* The state of being deceptive; tendency or aptness to deceive.

decibel, des′i•bel, *n.* [Prefix *deci*, ten, and *bel*, from A.G. *Bell*.] A unit for measuring the relative intensity of sound.

decide, di•sīd′, *v.t.*—*decided, deciding.* [L. *decido*—*de*, and *cædo*, to cut, seen also in *concise, precise, excision*.] To determine, as a question, controversy, or struggle, finally or authoritatively; to settle by giving the victory to one side or the other; to determine the issue or result of; to conclude; to end.—*v.t.* To determine; to form a definite opinion; to come to a conclusion; to pronounce a judgment.—**decidable,** di•sī′da•bl, *a.* Capable of being decided. —**decided,** di•sī′ded, *a.* Well marked; clear; unequivocal; that puts an end to doubt; free from ambiguity or uncertainty; unmistakable; resolute; determined; free from hesitation or wavering.—**decidedly,** dē•sī′ded•li, *adv.* In a decided or determined manner; in a manner to preclude doubt.

deciduous, di•sid′ū•us, *a.* [L. *deciduus, decido*—*de*, and *cado*, to fall; akin *decay*.] Not perennial or permanent; *bot.* applied to trees whose leaves fall in autumn and to leaves or other parts of the plant that fall; *zool.* applied to parts which fall off at a certain stage of an animal's existence, as hair, horns, teeth.—**decidua,** di•sid′ū•a, *n.* [For *decidua membrana*, the membrane that falls off.] A membrane arising from alteration of the upper layer of the mucous membrane of the uterus, after the reception into the latter of the impregnated ovum, the name being given to it because it is discharged at parturition.—**deciduousness,** di•sid′ū•us•nes, *n.* The quality of being deciduous.

decigram, decigramme, des′i•gram, *n.* A French weight of one-tenth of a gram.—**deciliter, decilitre,** des′i•lē•tėr, *n.* A French measure of capacity equal to one-tenth of a liter.

decillion, di•sil′yon, *n.* In English notation, the number denoted by a unit with 60 zeros annexed, while in the French and American notation, 33 zeros are annexed.—**decillionth,** de•sil′yonth, *a.* Being one of a decillion equal parts.—*n.* One such part.

decimal, des′i•mal, *a.* [L. *decimus,* tenth, from *decem,* ten.] Of or pertaining to tens; numbered or proceeding by tens; having a tenfold increase or decrease.—*Decimal fraction,* a fraction whose denominator is 10, or some number produced by the continued multiplication of 10 as a factor, such as 100, 1000, etc., but written with the denominator omitted, its value being indicated by a point placed to the left of as many figures of the numerator as there are ciphers in the denominator; thus 7/10, 3/1000, are written .7, .003.—*Decimal system,* a system of weights, measures, and moneys based on multiples of ten; the metric system; *in libraries,* a classification for books, dividing all knowledge into ten classes, indicating the specific subject of each book by a number ranging from .001 to 999.—*n.* A decimal fraction.

decimate, des′i•māt, *v.t.*—*decimated, decimating.* [L. *decimo, decimatum,* to select by lot every tenth man for punishment, from *decem,* ten.] To select by lot and punish with death every tenth man of, as was done by the Romans in punishing bodies of troops, etc.; hence, to destroy a great but indefinite number of.—**decimation,** des•i•mā′shon, *n.* A selection of every tenth by lot, as for punishment, etc.; the destruction of a great but indefinite proportion of people.—**decimator,** des′i•mā•tėr, *n.* One who or that which decimates.

decimeter, decimetre, des′i•mē•tėr, *n.* A French measure of length equal to the tenth part of a meter, or 3.9371 inches.

decipher, di•sī′fėr, *v.t.* To explain what is written in ciphers, by finding what each character or mark represents; to read what is written in obscure or badly formed characters; to discover or explain the meaning of, as of something difficult to be understood.—**decipherable,** di•sī′fėr•a•bl, *a.* That may be deciphered or interpreted.—**decipherment,** di•sī′fėr•ment, *n.* The act of deciphering.

decision, di•si′zhon, *n.* [L. *decisio, decisionis.* DECIDE.] The act of deciding; determination, as of a question or doubt; final judgment or opinion in a case which has been under deliberation or discussion; determination, as of a contest or event; arbitrament; the quality of being decided in character; unwavering firmness.—**decisive,** di•sī′siv, *a.* Having the power or quality of determining; final; conclusive; putting an end to controversy; marked by decision or prompt determination.—**decisively,** di•sī′siv•li, *adv.* In a decisive manner.—**decisiveness,** di•sī′siv•nes, *n.* The quality of being decisive; conclusiveness; decision of character.

deck, dek, *v.t.* [Same word as D. *dekken,* Dan. *dække,* G. *decken,* to cover, with the nouns, D. *dek,* Dan. *dæk,* a cover, a ship's deck, G. *decke,* a cover, *deck,* a deck; closely akin to E. *thatch* (Sc. *thack*), the root being that of L. *tego,* to cover. THATCH.] To clothe; to dress the person; but usually, to clothe with more than ordinary elegance; to array; to adorn; to embellish; to furnish with a deck, as a vessel or other structure.

deck, dek, *n.* [From D. *dek,* a covering; akin to D. *dekken,* G. *decken,* to cover. THATCH.] A platform that serves as a ship's flooring; any surface similar to a ship's deck; a pack of cards.—**decker,** dek′ėr, *n.* One or more decks (a double-*decker,* a three-*decker*).—**deck hand,** *n.* One whose duties are confined to the deck of a vessel, he being unfit for the work of a seaman properly so called.

deck, dek, *n.* [Origin unknown.] A pack of cards.

deckle, dek′l, *n.* [G. *deckel,* dim. of *decke,* cover.] A frame or rubber band upon a paper-making machine to limit the size of sheet.—**deckle edge,** *a.* Rough uncut edge.

declaim, di•klām′ *v.i.* [L. *declamo,* to practice speaking in public—*de,* and *clamo,* to cry out. CLAIM, CLAMOR.] To speak a set oration in public; to make a formal speech or oration; to harangue; to inveigh; to speak or write for rhetorical display.—*v.t.* To utter with rhetorical force; to deliver with inflation of tone.—**declaimer,** di•klā′mėr, *n.* One who declaims; one who habitually speaks for rhetorical display; one who speaks clamorously; an inveigher.—**declamation,** dek•la•mā′shon, *n.* [L. *declamatio.*] The act or art of declaiming or making a rhetorical harangue in public; the delivery of a speech or exercise in oratory, as by the students of a college, etc.; a display of showy rhetorical oratory; pretentious rhetorical language, with more sound than sense.—**declamatory,** di•klam′a•to•ri, *a.* [L. *declamatorius.*] Relating to the practice of declaiming; pertaining to declamation; merely rhetorical, without solid sense or argument.

declare, di•klâr′, *v.t.*—*declared, declaring.* [L. *declaro,* to declare—*de,* intens., and *claro,* to make clear, from *clarus,* clear. CLEAR.] To make known by words; to tell explicitly; to manifest or communicate plainly in any way; to exhibit; to publish; to proclaim; to assert; to affirm; to make a full statement of, as of goods on which duty falls to be paid to the customhouse.—*To declare one's self,* to throw off reserve and avow one's opinion; to show openly what one thinks, or which side he espouses.—*v.i.* To make a declaration; to make known explicitly some determination; to proclaim one's self; to pronounce adhesion in favor of a party, etc.: with *for* or *against.*—*To declare off,* to refuse to cooperate in any undertaking; to break off from one's party engagements, etc.—**declarant,**† dē•klâ′rant, *n.* One who declares.—**declaration,** dek•la•rā′shon, *n.* [L. *declaratio.*] The act of declaring, making known, or announcing; affirmation; explicit assertion; open expression; avowal; that which is declared; the document or instrument by which an announcement is authoritatively made; *law,* that part of the process or pleadings in which the plaintiff sets forth at large his cause of complaint; a simple affirmation substituted in lieu of an oath, solemn affirmation, or affidavit.—**declarative,** di•klâr′a•tiv, *a.* Making declaration, proclamation, or publication; declaratory.—**declaratory,** di•klâr′a•to•ri, *a.* Making declaration; distinctly expressive of opinions or intentions.

declension. See DECLINE.

decline, di•klīn′, *v.i.*—*declined, declining.* [L. *declino,* to bend down or aside—*de,* down, and a hypothetical *clino*=Gr. *klinō,* to bend. Root seen in L. *clivus,* sloping, and also in E. to *lean.*] To lean downward; to bend over; to hang down, as from weakness, despondency, submission, or the like; to sink to a lower level; to stoop, as to an unworthy object; to lean or deviate from rectitude (O.T.); to approach or draw toward the close (day *declines*); to avoid or shun; to refuse; not to comply; to tend to a less perfect state; to sink in character or value; to become diminished or impaired (as health, reputation); to fall; to decay.—*v.t.* To bend downward; to cause to bend; to depress; to shun or avoid; to refuse; not to accept or comply with; *gram.* to inflect, through cases and numbers; to change the termination of a word, for forming the oblique cases.—*n.* A falling off; a tendency to a worse state; diminution or decay; deterioration; a popular name for almost all chronic diseases in which the strength and plumpness of the body gradually decrease until the patient dies; consumption.—**decliner,** di•klī′nėr, *n.* One who declines.—**declinometer,** dek•li•nom′et•ėr, *n.* An instrument for measuring the declination of the magnetic needle, and for observing its variations.—**declension,** di•klen′shon, *n.* [L. *declinatio, declinationis,* in the grammatical sense it refers to the leaning away or differing of the other cases from the nominative; so *case* is lit. a falling.] The act of declining; declination; slope; a falling or declining toward a worse state; refusal; nonacceptance; *gram.* the inflection of nouns, adjectives, and pronouns by change of termination to form the oblique cases; the act of declining a word; a class of nouns declined on the same type.—**declinable,** di•klī′na•bl, *a.* Capable of being declined; having case inflections.—**declination,** dek•li•nā′shon, *n.* The act or state of declining; a bending down; inclination; a falling into a worse state; a falling away; deterioration; a deviation from a straight line; oblique motion;

deviation from rectitude in behavior or morals; the act of refusing; refusal; *astron.* the distance of a heavenly body from the celestial equator, measured on a great circle passing through the pole and also through the body; *physics*, the variation of the magnetic needle from the true meridian of a place—declination of the compass or magnetic declination.—**declinatory,** di•klī′na•to•ri, *a.* Of or pertaining to declination; characterized by declining; intimating declinature or refusal. —**declinature,** di•klī′na•chūr, *n.* The act of declining or refusing; a refusal.

declivity, di•kliv′i•ti, *n.* [L. *declivitas*, a declivity, from *declivis*, sloping—*de*, and *clivus*, sloping; same root as in *decline*.] Slope or inclination downward; a slope or descent of the ground: opposed to *acclivity*, or ascent.—**declivitous,** di•kliv′i•tus, *a.* Sloping downward.

decoct, di•kokt′, *v.t.* [L. *decoquo, decoctum*, to boil down—*de*, and *coquo*, to cook, to boil. COOK.] To prepare by boiling; to extract the strength or flavor of by boiling; to heat up or excite (*Shak.*)†.—**decoction,** di•kok′shon, *n.* The act of decocting; an extract obtained by boiling a substance in water, for extracting its virtues; the water in which a substance has been thus boiled.

decode, dē•kōd′, *v.t.* To decipher a telegram by code. CODE.

decollate, di•kol′lāt, *v.t.—decollated, decollating.* [L. *decollo, decollatum*, to behead—*de*, from, and *collum*, the neck.] To behead.—**decollation,** dē•kol•lā′shon, *n.* The act of beheading.

decolleté, dā•kol•tā′, *a.* [Fr.] Low-necked style of dress.

decoloration, dē•kul′ėr•ā″shon, *n.* [L. *decoloratio, decolorationis*, discoloring—*de*, from, and *color*, color.] The removal of color; abstraction or loss of color.—**decolorant,** dē•kul′ėr•ant, *n.* A substance which removes color, or bleaches.—**decolorization,** dē•kul′ėr•i•zā″shon, *n.* The process of depriving of color.—**decolorize, decolor,** dē•kul′ėr•īz, dē•kul′ėr, *v.t.* To deprive of color; to bleach.

decompose, dē•kom•pōz′, *v.t.—decomposed, decomposing.* [Fr. *decomposer—de*, from, and *composer*, to compose. COMPOSE.] To separate the constituent parts or elementary particles of; to resolve into original elements.—*v.i.* To become resolved into constituent elements; to decay, rot, or putrefy.—**decomposable,** dē•kom•pō′za•bl, *a.* Capable of being decomposed or resolved into constituent elements.—**decomposition,** dē•kom′pō•zi″shon, *n.* The act of decomposing; analysis; resolution; the state of being decomposed; disintegration; decay; putrescence.

decompound, dē•kom•pound′, *a.* [Prefix *de*, intens., and *compound*.] Composed of things or words already compounded; compounded a second time; *bot.* divided into a number of compound divisions, as a leaf or panicle.—*n.* A decomposite.

décor, dā•kor′, *n.* [Fr. *décor*, from *décorer*, to decorate.] Decoration in general; stage scenery.

decorate, dek′o•rāt, *v.t.—decorated, decorating.* [L. *decoro, decoratum*, from *decus, decor*, comeliness, grace; akin *decent*.] To deck with something becoming or ornamental; to adorn; to beautify; to embellish; to make attractive the interiors of dwellings; to award a decoration of honor to.—*Decorated style, arch.* a style of Gothic architecture distinguished by the flowing or wavy lines of its tracery, and generally by profuse florid ornamentation.—**decoration,** dek•o•rā′shon, *n.* The act of adorning; ornamentation; that which decorates or adorns; ornament; any badge, as a medal, cross of honor, etc., bestowed for distinguished services.—**decorative,** dek′o•rā•tiv, *a.* Adorning; suited to embellish.—**decorativeness,** dek′o•rā•tiv•nes, *n.* Quality of being decorative.—**decorator,** dek′o•rā•tėr, *n.* One who decorates or embellishes.

decorous, dek′o•rus, *a.* [L. *decorus*, becoming.] Suitable to a character or to the time, place, and occasion; becoming; seemly; proper; befitting (speech, behavior, dress, etc.).—**decorously,** dek′o•rus•li, *adv.* In a becoming manner.—**decorousness,** dek′o•rus•nes, *n.* Decency or propriety of behavior.—**decorum,** di•ko′rum, *n.* [L., what is becoming.] Propriety of speech or behavior; seemliness; decency; opposed to rudeness, licentiousness, or levity.

decorticate, di•kor′ti•kāt, *v.t.—decorticated, decorticating.* [L. *decortico, decorticatum—de*, not, and *cortex*, bark.] To strip off the bark of; to peel; to husk.—**decortication,** di•kor′ti•kā″shon, *n.* The act of stripping off bark or husk.

decoy, dē•koi′, *n.* [D. *eende-kooi*, a duck-cage.] A place into which wild fowls are enticed in order to be caught, being a structure of network covering in a piece of water; a fowl, or the likeness of one, employed to entice other fowl into a net or within range of shot; a thing or person intended to lead into a snare; a stratagem employed to mislead or lead into danger; a lure.—*v.t.* To lead or lure by artifice into a snare, with a view to catch; to entrap by any means which deceive; to allure, attract, or entice.

decrease, di•krēs′, *v.i.—decreased, decreasing.* [L. *decresco—de*, down, and *cresco*, to grow, seen also in *increase, crescent, accrue*.] To be diminished gradually in extent, bulk, quantity, or amount, or in strength, influence, or excellence; to become less.—*v.t.* To lessen; to make smaller in dimensions, amount, quality, or excellence, etc.; to diminish gradually or by small deductions.—*n.* A becoming less; gradual diminution; wane (as applied to the moon); decay.—**decreasingly,** di•krēs′ing•li, *adv.* By decreasing or diminishing. —**decrement,** dek′ri•ment, *n.* [L. *decrementum*.] Decrease; waste; the quantity lost by gradual diminution or waste; *math.* the small part by which a variable quantity becomes less and less: opposed to *increment*.—**decrescent,** di•kres′ent, *a.* [L. *decrescens, decrescentis*.] Decreasing; becoming less by gradual diminution.

decree, di•krē′, *n.* [L. *decretum*, from *decerno*, to judge—*de*, and *cerno*, to judge; also seen in *concern, discern, secret*, etc.] Judicial decision or determination of a litigated cause; the judgment or award of an umpire in a case submitted to him; an edict, law, or order by a superior authority as a rule to govern inferiors.—*Decree nisi* (decree unless), *law*, the order made by an English court of divorce, after satisfactory proof is given in support of a petition for dissolution of marriage; it remains conditional for at least six months, after which, *unless* sufficient cause is shown, it is made absolute, and the dissolution takes effect.—*v.t.—decreed, decreeing.* To determine judicially; to resolve by sentence; to determine or resolve legislatively; to fix or appoint; to determine or decide on.—*v.i.* To determine immutably; to make an edict; to appoint by edict.—**decretal,** di•krē′tal, *a.* Appertaining to a decree; containing a decree.—*n.* An authoritative order of decree; a letter of the pope determining some point or question in ecclesiastical law; *pl.* the second part of the canon law, so called because it contains the decrees of sundry popes.—**decretist,** di•krē′tist, *n.* One who studies or professes a knowledge of the decretals.—**decretive,** di•krē′tiv, *a.* Having the force of a decree; pertaining to a decree.—**decretory,** dek′ri•to•ri, *a.* Judicial; definitive; established by a decree.

decrepit, di•krep′it, *a.* [L. *decrepitus*, broken down, worn out—*de*, from and *crepare*, to make a noise, hence originally noiseless; akin *crevice, discrepant*.] Broken down or weakened with age; wasted or worn by the infirmities of old age; being in the last stage of decay.—**decrepitude,** di•krep′i•tūd, *n.* The state of being decrepit; the broken, crazy state of the body, produced by decay and the infirmities of age.

decrepitate, di•krep′i•tāt, *v.t.—decrepitated, decrepitating.* [L. *decrepo*, to break or burst, to crackle—*de* and *crepo*. DECREPIT.] To roast or calcine in a strong heat, with a continual bursting or crackling of the substance. —*v.i.* To crackle when roasting.—**decrepitation,** di•krep′i•tā″shon, *n.* The act of flying asunder with a crackling noise on being heated, or the crackling noise, attended with the flying asunder of their parts, made by several salts and minerals when heated.

decrescendo, dā•kre•shen′dō, *n.* [It.] *Mus.* a term which denotes the gradual weakening of the sound.

decry, di•krī′, *v.t.—decried, decrying.* [Fr. *décrier*, O.Fr. *descrier—des* (=L. *dis*). and *crier*, to cry.] To cry down;

to censure as faulty, mean, or worthless; to clamor against; to discredit by finding fault.—**decrial,** di•krī′al, *n.* The act of decrying or crying down.—**decrier,** di•krī′ėr, *n.* One who decries.

decuman, dek′ū•man, *a.* [L. *decumanus,* from *decimus,* tenth, from *decem,* ten.] Tenth; hence, from the ancient notion that every tenth wave was the largest in a series; large; immense. Sometimes used substantively for the tenth or largest wave.

decumbent, di•kum′bent, *a.* [L. *decumbens,* from *decumbo,* to lie down—*de,* and *cumbo,* for *cubo,* to lie.] Lying down; reclining; prostrate; recumbent; *bot.* declined or bending down, as a stem which rests on the earth and then rises again.—**decumbence, decumbency,** di•kum′bens, di•kum′ben•si, *n.* The state of being decumbent or of lying down; the posture of lying down.

decuple, dek′ū•pl, *a.* [L.L. *decuplus,* from L. *decem,* ten.] Tenfold; containing ten times as many.—*n.* A number ten times repeated.—*v.t.*—*decupled, decupling.* To increase to a tenfold proportion.

decurion, di•kū′ri•on, *n.* [L. *decurio,* from *decem,* ten.] An officer in the Roman army who commanded a *decuria,* that is, a body of ten soldiers.

decurrent, di•kėr′ent, *a.* [L. *decurrens, decurrentis*—*de,* and *curro,* to run.] *Bot.* applied to a sessile leaf having its base extended downward along the stem.—**decurrently,** di•kėr′ent•li, *adv.* In a decurrent manner.

decussate, di•kus′āt, *v.t.*—*decussated, decussating.* [L. *decusso,* to divide crosswise in the form of a ×, from *decussis,* the number 10, which the Romans represented by X.] To intersect so as to make acute angles, thus ×; to intersect; to cross, as lines, rays of light, leaves, or nerves in the body.—**decussate,** di•kus′it, *a.* Crossed; intersected; *bot.* arranged in pairs alternately crossing each other at regular angles.—**decussately,** di•kus′it•li, *adv.* In a decussate manner.—**decussation,** di•kus•ā′shon, *n.* The act of crossing at right or at acute angles; the crossing of two lines, rays, nerves, etc., which meet in a point and then proceed and diverge.

dedicate, ded′i•kāt, *v.t.*—*dedicated, dedicating.* [L. *dedico*—*de,* and *dico, dicare,* to devote, dedicate; akin *abdicate, diction, predict,* etc.] To set apart and consecrate to a divine Being, or to a sacred purpose; to appropriate to any person or purpose; to give wholly or earnestly up to (often *refl.*); to inscribe or address to a patron, friend, or public character (to *dedicate* a book).—*a.* Consecrated, devoted; appropriated. —**dedication,** ded•i•kā′shon, *n.* The act of dedicating; consecration or devotion to a sacred use; solemn appropriation; an address prefixed to a book, and inscribed to a friend of the author, some public character, or other person, as a mark of esteem.—*Dedication day, dedication feast,* an annual festival commemorating the consecration of a church.—**dedicator,** ded′i•kā•tėr, *n.* One who dedicates.—**dedicatory,** ded′i•ka•to•ri, *a.* Serving to dedicate; serving as a dedication.

deduce, di•dūs′, *v.t.*—*deduced, deducing.* [L. *deduco*—*de,* and *duco,* to lead. DUKE.] To draw; to draw, bring out, or infer in reasoning; to attain or arrive at (a truth, opinion, or proposition), from premises; to infer from what precedes.—**deducible,** di•dū′si•bl, *a.* Capable of being deduced; inferable.—**deduct,** di•dukt′, *v.t.* To take away, separate, or remove, in numbering, estimating, or calculating; to subtract.—**deduction,** di•duk′shon, *n.* [L. *deductio, deductionis.*] The act of deducting or taking away; that which is deducted; sum or amount taken from another; abatement; the act or method of deducing from premises; that which is drawn from premises; inference; consequence drawn; conclusion.—**deductive,** di•duk′tiv, *a.* Deducible; pertaining to deduction; that is or may be deduced from premises.—*Deductive reasoning,* the process of deriving consequences from admitted or established premises, as distinguished from *inductive* reasoning, by which we arrive at general laws or axioms by an accumulation of facts.—**deductively,** di•duk′tiv•li, *adv.* By regular deduction; by deductive reasoning.

deed, dēd, *n.* [A.Sax. *daed,* a deed, from *dón,* to do=Icel. *dád,* D. and Dan. *daad,* Goth. *deds,* G. *that,* a deed. DO.] That which is done or performed; an act; a fact; anything that is done; an exploit; achievement; *law,* a writing containing some contract or agreement, and the evidence of its execution; particularly, an instrument conveying real estate to a purchaser or donee.—*In deed,* in fact, in reality; often united to form the single word *indeed.*

deem, dēm, *v.t.* [A.Sax. *déman,* to deem, to judge, from *dóm,* doom, judgment (same word as term. *-dom*); Icel. *dœma,* Dan. *dōmme,* Goth. (*ga*)*domjan,* to judge; from root of *do.*] To think, judge, believe, or consider to be so or so.—*v.i.* To think or suppose.

deep, dēp, *a.* [A.Sax. *deóp*=D. *diep,* Dan. *dyb,* G. *tief,* deep; from root of *dip. dive.*] Extending or being far below the surface; descending far downward; profound: opposed to *shallow* (*deep* water, a *deep* pit); low in situation; being or descending far below the adjacent land (a *deep* valley); entering far (a *deep* wound); absorbed; engrossed; wholly occupied; not superficial or obvious; hidden; abstruse; hard to penetrate or understand; profoundly learned; having the power to enter far into a subject; penetrating; artful; concealing artifice; insidious; designing; grave in sound; great in degree; intense; profound (silence, grief, poverty); measured back from the front.—*n.* Anything remarkable for depth; the sea; the abyss of waters; any abyss.—*adv.* Deeply; to a great depth; profoundly.—**deepen,** dē′pn, *v.t.* To make deep or deeper; to sink lower; to increase; to intensify; to make more grave (sound).—*v.i.* To become more deep, in all its senses.

deeply, dēp′li, *adv.* At or to a great depth; far below the surface; profoundly; thoroughly; to a great degree; intensely; gravely; with low or deep tone; with art or intricacy (a *deeply* laid plot).—**deepness,** dēp′nes, *n.*—**deep-freeze,** *v.t.*—*deep-froze, deep-frozen.* To put or store in a deep freeze.—**deep freeze,** *n.* A refrigerator that preserves food at freezing temperatures.—**deep-sea,** *a.* Of or in the deeper parts of the sea.

deer, dēr, *n. sing.* and *pl.* [A.Sax. *deór,* any wild animal, a deer=Goth. *dius,* D. *dier,* Dan. *dyr,* Icel. *dyr,* Sw. *diur,* G. *thier,* any animal or beast, especially a wild beast.] A name of many ruminant quadrupeds, distinguished by having solid branching horns which they shed every year, and eight cutting teeth in the lower jaw, and none in the upper; such as the red deer, fallow deer, roebuck, reindeer, moose, or elk, etc.—**deerhound,** *n.* A hound for hunting deer; a staghound.—**deerskin,** *n.* The skin of a deer; the leather made from it.—**deerstalker,** *n.* One who practices deerstalking.—**deerstalking,** *n.* The hunting of deer (especially the red deer) on foot by hiding and stealing within shot of them unawares.

deface, di•fās′, *v.t.*—*defaced, defacing.* To destroy or mar the face or surface of; to injure the beauty of; to disfigure; to erase or obliterate.—**defacement,** di•fās′ment, *n.* The act of defacing; injury to the surface or exterior; what mars or disfigures. —**defacer,** di•fā′sėr, *n.* One who defaces.

de facto, dē•fak′tō, *a.* and *adv.* [L.] In fact; actually existing.

defalcate, di•fal′kāt, *v.i.*—*defalcated, defalcating.* [L.L. *defalco, defalcatum,* to cut off with a sickle, hence to deduct—L. *de,* down, and *falx, falcis,* a sickle.] To take away or deduct, as money.—**defalcation,** di•fal•kā′shon, *n.* Deduction; abatement; a fraudulent deficiency in money matters.—**defalcator,** def′al•kā•tėr, *n.*

defame, di•fām′, *v.t.*—*defamed, defaming.* [L.L. *defamare*—*de,* not, and L. *fama,* fame.] To slander; to speak evil of; to calumniate; to libel; to bring into disrepute.—**defamation,** def•a•mā′shon, *n.* The uttering of slanderous words with a view to injure another's reputation; slander; calumny.—**defamatory,** di•fam′a•to•ri, *n.* Containing defamation; calumnious; slanderous.—**defamer,** di•fā′mer, *n.* One who defames; a slanderer; a calumniator.

default, di•fa̤lt′, *n.* [Fr. *défaut,* for *défault,* from *défaillir,* to fail—*de,* and *faillir,* to fail. FAIL, FAULT.] A failing or failure; an omission of that which ought to be done; *law,* a failure of appearance in court at a day assigned.

—*In default of*, in the absence or want of; hence, in place of; in lieu of.—*v.i.* To fail in fulfilling or satisfying an engagement, claim, contract, or agreement.—*v.t. Law*, to give judgment against on account of failing to appear and answer.—**defaulter**, di•fal′tėr, *n.* One who makes default; a delinquent; one who fails to meet his claims or to fulfill his engagements.

defeasance, di•fē′zans, *n.* [Fr. *défaisant*, from *défaire*, to undo—L. *dis*, and *facio*, to do.] A rendering null and void; *law*, a condition which being performed renders a deed null or void; the writing containing a defeasance.—**defeasible**, di•fē′zi•bl, *a.* Capable of being abrogated or annulled.—**defeasibleness**, di•fē′zi•bl•nes, *n.*

defeat, di•fēt′, *n.* [Fr. *défaite*, from *défaire*, to undo, O.Fr. *desfaire*—L. *dis*, and *facere*, to do.] An overthrow; loss of battle; check, rout, or destruction of an army by the victory of an enemy; a frustration by rendering null and void, or by prevention of success.—*v.t.* To overcome or vanquish; to overthrow; to frustrate; to prevent the success of; to disappoint; to render null and void.—**defeatism**, de•fē′tizm, *n.* An attitude of admitting defeat, as of one's own country, or of life itself, on the ground that failure is inevitable.

defecate, def′e•kāt, *v.t.*—*defecated, defecating.* [L. *defæco*—*de*, and *fæx*, dregs.] To clear from dregs or impurities; to clarify or purify; to void excrement.—*v.i.* To become clear or pure by depositing impurities; to clarify.—*a.* Purged from lees; defecated.—**defecation**, def•e•kā′shon, *n.* The act of defecating or separating from lees or dregs; purification.—**defecator**, def′e•kā•tėr, *n.* One who or that which defecates.

defect, di•fekt′, *n.* [L. *defectus*, pp. of *deficio, defectum*, to fail—*de*, from, and *facio*, to make, to do.] Want or absence of something necessary or useful toward perfection; a fault; an imperfection; that which is wanting to make a perfect whole; blemish; deformity.—*v.i.* To desert a cause or party in order to support another. —**defector**, di•fek′tėr, *n.*—**defection**, di•fek′shon, *n.* The act of abandoning a person or cause to which one is bound by allegiance or duty, or to which one has attached himself; a falling away; apostasy; backsliding. —**defective**, di•fek′tiv, *a.* [L. *defectivus*, imperfect.] Having some defect; wanting either in substance, quantity, or quality, or in anything necessary; imperfect; faulty; *gram.* wanting some of the usual forms of declension or conjugation (a *defective* noun or verb).—**defectively**, di•fek′tiv•li, *adv.* In a defective manner; imperfectly.—**defectiveness**, di•fek′tiv•nes, *n.* The state of being defective; faultiness.

defense, di•fens′, *n.* [Fr. *défense*, from L.L. *defensa*, defense, from L. *defendo, defensum*, to defend—*de*, and *fendo*, to strike, a verb used also in *offendo*, to offend.] The act of defending, upholding, or maintaining; anything that opposes attack, violence, danger, or injury; fortification; guard; resistance against attack; protection; that which defends; means or methods of defense; the science or art of defending oneself, as in boxing, fencing, etc.; speech, action, etc. in favor of something; a defendant's answer to an accusation; a defendant and his legal advisors.—**defenseless**, di•fens′les, *a.*—**defenselessness**, di•fens′les•nes, *n.*—**defense mechanism**, *n.* An involuntary or subconscious process by which an individual copes with painful situations that are unacceptable at the conscious level.—**defensibility**, di•fen′si•bil″i•ti, *n.*—the state of being defensible. defensibleness.—**defensible**, di•fen′si•bl, *a.* Capable of being defended, vindicated, maintained, or justified. —**defensive**, di•fen′siv, *a.* [Fr. *défensif.*] Serving to defend; proper for or suited to defense; carried on in resisting attack or aggression; in distinction from *offensive.*—*n.* That which defends.—*To be on the defensive*, or *to stand on the defensive*, to be or stand in a state or posture of defense or resistance, in opposition to aggression or attack.—**defensively**, di•fen′siv•li, *adv.* In a defensive manner.— **defend**, di•fend′, *v.t.* To protect or support against any assault or attack; to ward off an attack upon; to protect by opposition or resistance; to vindicate, uphold, or maintain uninjured by force or by argument (rights and privileges); *law*, to come forward as defendant in (to *defend* an action).—*v.i.* To make opposition; to make defense.—**defendant**, di•fen′dant, *a.* Defensive (*Shak.*)‡; making defense.—*n.* One who defends; *law*, the party that opposes a complaint, demand, or charge. —**defender**, di•fen′dėr, *n.* One who defends; a vindicator, either by arms or by arguments; a champion or an advocate.—*Defender of the Faith*, a title peculiar to the sovereigns of England, first conferred by Pope Leo X on Henry VIII in 1521, as a reward for writing against Luther.

defer, di•fėr′, *v.t.*—*deferred, deferring* [O.Fr. *differre*, L. *differo*, to delay—*dis*, from, and *fero*, to carry.] To delay; to put off; to postpone to a future time.—*v.i.* To delay; to procrastinate.—**deferment**, di•fėr′ment, *n.* The act of deferring; postponement or delay.—**deferrer**, di•fėr′ėr. *n.* One who defers or delays.

defer, di•fėr′, *v.i.* [L. *defero*, to carry down or away, hand over, refer—*de*, down, and *fero*, to carry.] To yield to another's opinion; to submit or give way courteously or from respect (to *defer to* a friend's judgment).—**deference**, def′ėr•ens, *n.* A yielding in opinion; submission of judgment to the opinion or judgment of another; respect; courteous consideration; obedience.—**deferential**, def•ėr•en′shal, *a.* Expressing deference; accustomed to defer.—**deferentially**, def•ėr•en′shal•li, *adv.* In a deferential manner; with deference.—**deferrer**, di•fėr′ėr, *n.* One who defers in regard to opinion.

defiance, defiant, etc. See DEFY.

deficient, di•fish′ent, *a.* [L. *deficiens, deficientis*, ppr. of *deficio*, to fail—*de*, and *facio*, to do.] Wanting; defective; imperfect; not sufficient or adequate; not having a full or adequate supply: with *in* (*deficient in* strength).—**deficiency**, di•fish′en•si, *n.* The state of being deficient; a failing or falling short; want, either total or partial; defect; absence; something less than is necessary.—**deficiently**, di•fish′ent•li, *adv.* In a defective manner.—**deficit**, def′i•sit, *n.* [L., there is wanting.] A falling short of a requisite sum or amount; a deficiency (a *deficit* in revenue).

defier, di•fī′ėr, *n.* See DEFY.

defilade, def′i•lād, *v.t.*—*defilated, defilading.* [Fr. *défilade.* DEFILE, *v.i.*] *Fort.* to surround by defensive works so as to protect the interior when in danger of being commanded by an enemy's guns.

defile, di•fīl′, *v.t.*—*defiled, defiling.* [L. prefix *de*, and A.Sax. *fȳlan* (O.E. and Sc. *file*, to defile), from *ful*, foul. FOUL.] To make unclean; to render foul or dirty; to soil or sully; to tarnish, as reputation, etc.; to make ceremonially unclean; to pollute; to corrupt the chastity of; to debauch; to violate.—**defilement**, di•fīl′ment, *n.* The act of defiling, or state of being defiled.—**defiler**, di•fī′lėr, *n.* One who or that which defiles.

defile, di•fīl′, *v.i.*—*defiled, defiling.* [Fr. *défiler*—*de*, and *file*, a row or line, from L. *filum*, a thread.] To march off in a line, or file by file; to file off.—*v.t. Fort.* to defilade.—*n.* A narrow passage or way, in which troops may march only in a file, or with a narrow front; a long narrow pass; as between hills, etc.

define, di•fīn′, *v.t.*—*defined, defining.* [L. *definio*—*de*, and *finio*, to limit, from *finis*, end, whence also *final, finish, finite*, etc.] To determine or set down the limits of; to determine with precision; to mark the limit of; to circumscribe, mark, or show the outlines of clearly; to determine the extent of the meaning of; to give or describe the signification of; to enunciate or explain the distinctive properties of.—*v.i.* To give a definition.—**definable**, di•fī′na•bl, *a.* Capable of being defined; capable of having the limits ascertained, fixed, and determined; capable of having its signification expressed with certainty or precision.—**definer**, di•fī′nėr, *n.* One who defines.—**definite**, def′i•nit, *a.* [L. *definitus.*] Having fixed or marked limits; bounded with precision; determinate; having well-marked limits in signification; certain; precise; *gram*, defining; limiting; applied to particular things; *bot.* same as *centrifugal.*—The *definite article*, the article *the.*—**definitely**, def′i•nit•li, *adv.* In a definite manner. —**definiteness**, def′i•nit•nes, *n.* State or character of being definite.—**definition**, def•i•ni′shon, *n.* [L. *definitio, definitionis.*] The act of defining; a brief and precise description of a thing by its properties; an explanation of the signification of a word or term; the quality or power in a telescope or other optical instrument of showing distinctly the outlines or features of any object.—**definitive,** di•fin′i•tiv, *a.* [L. *definitivus,* definitive.] Limiting; determinate; positive; express; conclusive; final.—*n. Gram,* a word used to define or limit the extent of the signification of an appellative or common noun, as *this, the,* etc.—**definitively** di•fin′i•tiv•li, *adv.* In a definite manner; positively; expressly; finally; conclusively; unconditionally.

deflagrate, def′le•grāt, *v.t.*—*deflagrated, deflagrating.* [L. *deflagro, deflagratum*—*de,* intens., and *flagro,* to burn, whence *flagrant.*] To set fire to; to cause to burn rapidly; to consume.—*v.i.* To burn rapidly, or with violent combustion.—**deflagration,** def•le•grā′shon, *n.* The act or process of deflagrating; a rapid combustion of a mixture, attended with much evolution of flame and vapor; the process of oxidizing substances by means of niter; the rapid combustion of metals by the electric spark.

deflate, di•flāt′, *v.t.* To reduce from an inflated state by releasing of the distending gas or air.—**deflation,** di•flā′shon, *n.* A deflating; a reduction in the volume of currency outstanding; a reduction in the volume of purchasing power.

deflect, di•flekt′, *v.i.* [L. *deflecto*—*de,* from, and *flecto,* to turn or bend. FLEXIBLE.] To turn away or aside; to deviate from a true course or right line; to swerve.—*v.t.* To cause to turn aside; to turn or bend from a straight line.—**deflection,** di•flek′shon, *n.* [L. *deflecto,* I bend down.] The strain produced by a transverse stress, such as the bending of a horizontal beam under a load; also used to denote amount of deflection.—**deflection,** di•flek′shon, *n.* Deviation; a turning from a true line or the regular course.—**deflective,** di•flek′tiv, *a.* Causing deflection or deviation.—**deflector,** di•flek′tėr, *n.* A diaphragm in a lamp, stove, etc., by means of which air and gas are mingled, and made to burn completely.

deflower, di•flou′ėr, *v.t.* [Fr. *déflorer*; L.L. *defloro*—L. *de,* from, and *flos, floris,* a flower.] To deprive of her viriginity; to violate, ravish, seduce.—**defloration,** di•flo•rā′shon, *n.* The act of deflowering or taking away a woman's virginity; rape.

defluxion, di•fluk′shon, *n.* [L. *defluxio, defluxionis,* from *defluo, defluxum,* to flow down—*de,* and *fluo,* to flow.] *Med.* a discharge, as from the nose or head in catarrh.

defoliate, di•fō′li•āt, *a.* [L. *de,* priv., and *folium,* a leaf.] Deprived of leaves.—**defoliation,** di•fō′li•ā″shon, *n.* The fall of the leaf or shedding of leaves.

deforce, di•fōrs′, *v.t.*—*deforced, deforcing. Law,* to keep out of lawful possession of an estate; *Scots law,* to resist (an officer of the law) in the execution of official duty.—**deforcement,** di•fōrs′ment, *n.* The act of deforcing.

deforest, dē•for′est, *v.t.* To clear of forests or trees.—**deforestation,** dē•for′es•ta″shon, *n.*

deform, di•form′, *v.t.* [L. *deformo*—*de,* and *forma,* form.] To mar or injure the form of; to disfigure; to render ugly or unpleasing; to disfigure the moral beauty of (vices *deform* the character).—**deformation,** di•for•mā′shon, *n.* A disfiguring or defacing.—**deformed,** di•formd′, *p.* and *a.* Disfigured; distorted; misshapen; ugly.—**deformedly,** di•for′med•li, *adv.* In a deformed manner.—**deformedness,** di•for′med•nes, *n.* The state or character of being deformed.—**deformity,** di•for′mi•ti, *n.* [L. *deformitas.*] The state of being deformed; some deformed or misshapen part of the body; distortion; irregularity of shape or features; ugliness; anything that destroys beauty, grace, or propriety.

defraud, di•frạd′, *v.t.* [L. *defraudo de,* intens., and *fraudo,* to cheat, *fraus,* fraud.] To deprive of right, either by obtaining something by deception or artifice, or by taking something wrongfully without the knowledge or consent of the owner; to cheat; to keep out of just rights; with *of* before the thing.—**defraudation,** dē•frạ•dā′shon, *n.* The act of defrauding.—**defrauder,** di•frạ′dėr, *n.* One who defrauds; one who takes from another his right by deception, or withholds what is his due; a cheat.

defray, di•frā′, *v.t.* [Fr. *defrayer*—*de,* and *frais,* expense, from L.L. *fractus* or *fractum,* expense, compensation, from L. *frango, fractum,* to break, whence *fraction, fragile,* etc.] To pay for; to disburse the amount of; to discharge or bear; with *cost, charge, expense* as the object.—**defrayal, defrayment,** di•frā′al, dē•frā′ment, *n.* The act of defraying.—**defrayer,** di•frā′ėr, *n.* One who defrays or pays expenses.

defrost, dē•frost′, *v.t.* To remove frost or ice from; to thaw.—**defroster,** dē•fros′tėr, *n.*

deft, deft, *a.* [A.Sax. *daeft,* fit, convenient from (*ge*)*dafam,* to become, to befit; Goth. *gadaban,* to befit.] Dexterous; clever; apt.—**deftly,** deft′li, *adv.*—**deftness,** deft′nes, *n.*

defunct, di•fungkt′, *a.* [L. *defunctus,* having finished, discharged, or performed, from *defungor,* to perform—*de,* intens., and *fungor,* to perform.] Having finished the course of life; dead; deceased; used with reference to *defunct* periodicals, commercial organizations, or other enterprises.

defy, di•fī′, *v.t.*—*defied, defying.* [Fr. *défier,* O.Fr. *desfier,* lit. to renounce faith or allegiance.—L. *dis,* apart, and *fides,* faith. FAITH.] To provoke to combat or strife, by appealing to the courage of another; to invite one to contest; to challenge; to dare; to brave; to set at nought; to despise or be regardless of.—*n.* A challenge.—**defiance,** di•fī′ans, *n.* [O.Fr.] The act of defying, daring, or challenging; a challenge to fight; invitation to combat; a challenge to meet in any contest, or to make good any assertion; contempt of opposition or danger; daring that implies contempt for an adversary, or of any opposing power.—*To bid defiance to,* or *to set at defiance,* to defy; to brave.—**defiant,** di•fī′ant, *a.* Characterized by defiance, boldness, or insolence.—**defiantly,** di•fī′ant•li, *adv.* In a defiant manner; with defiance; daringly; insolently.—**defier,** di•fī′ėr, *n.* One who defies; one who dares to combat or encounter; one who sets at nought.

degenerate, di•jen′ėr•āt, *v.i.*—*degenerated, degenerating.* [L. *degenero, degeneratum,* to become unlike one's race, from *degener,* ignoble, base—*de,* from, and *genus, generis,* race.] To fall off from the qualities proper to the race or kind, to become of a lower type, physically or morally; to pass from a good to a worse state.—*a.* (di•jen′ėr•et). Having degenerated; having declined in qualities from one's ancestors, or one's former self; having lower moral standards.—*n.* (di•jen′ėr•et). One who has degenerated; a pervert.—**degeneracy,** di•jen′ėr•a•si, *n.* The state of degenerating or of being degenerate; deterioration; lowness; meanness.—**degenerately,** di•jen′ėr•āt•li, *adv.* In a degenerate or base manner; unworthily.—**degenerateness,** di•jen′ėr•āt•nes, *n.* A degenerate state.—**degeneration,** di•jen′ėr•ā″shon, *n.* The state or process of becoming degenerate; degeneracy; gradual deterioration from a state physiologically superior.—**degenerative,** di•jen′ėr•ā•tiv, *a.* Tending to cause degeneration.

deglutition, dē•glū•ti′shon, *n.* [L. *deglutio, deglutitum,* to swallow—*de,* and *glutio.* GLUTTON.] The act or power of swallowing; the process by which animals swallow.

degrade, di•grād′, *v.t.*—*degraded, degrading.* [Fr. *dégrader*—L. *de,* down, and *gradus,* a step, a degree. GRADE.] To reduce from a higher to a lower rank or degree; to strip of honors; to reduce in estimation; to lower or sink in morals or character; to debase.—*v.i.* To degenerate; to become lower in character.—**degradation,** deg•ra•dā′shon, *n.* The act of degrading; a depriving of rank, dignity, or office; the state of being reduced from an elevated or more honorable station to one that is meaner or humbler; a mean or abject state to which one has sunk; debasement; degeneracy; *geol.* the lessening or wearing down of higher lands, rocks, strata, etc., by the action of water, or other causes.—**degraded,** di•grā′ded, *a.* Sunk to an abject or vile state; exhibiting degradation; debased; low.—**degrading,** di•grā′ding, *a.* Dishonoring; disgracing the character; causing degradation.

degree, di•grē′, *n.* [Fr. *degré,* from L. *de,* down, and *gradus,* a step. DEGRADE.] A step or single movement, upward or downward, toward any end; one of a series of progressive advances; measure, amount, or proportion (he is a *degree* worse); measure of advancement; relative position attained, rank; station (men of low *degree*); a certain distance or remove in the line of family descent, determining the proximity of blood (a relation in the third or fourth *degree*); the 360th part of the circumference of any circle, a *degree of latitude* being the 360th part of any meridian on the earth's surface, a *degree of longitude* the same part of any given parallel of latitude; an interval of musical sound, marked by a line on the scale; a division, space, or interval marked on a mathematical or other instrument, as a thermometer or barometer; in universities, a title of distinction (*bachelor, master, doctor*) conferred as a testimony of proficiency in arts and sciences, or merely as an honor.—*By degrees*, step by step; gradually; by moderate advances.—*To a degree*, to an extreme; exceedingly.

dehisce, dē•his′, *v.i.* [L. *dehisco*, to gape—*de*, intens., and *hisco*, to gape.] *Bot.* to open, as the capsules or seed vessels of plants.—**dehiscence,** dē•his′ens, *n. Bot.* the splitting of an organ in accordance with its structure, as the opening of the parts of a capsule or the cells of anthers, etc.—**dehiscent,** dē•his′ent, *a. Bot.* opening; dehiscing.

dehort, di•hort′, *v.t.* [L. *dehortor*—*de*, and *hortor*, to advise.] To dissuade; to exhort against.—**dehortation,** dē•hor•tā′shon, *n.* Dissuasion.—**dehortative,** di•hor′ta•tiv, *a.* Dissuasive; dehortatory.—**dehortatory,** dē•hor′ta•to•ri, *a.* Dissuading; belonging to dissuasion.—*n.* A dissuasive argument or reason.

dehumanize, dē•hū′man•īz, *v.t.* To deprive of the character of humanity.

dehumidify, dē•hū•mid′i•fī, *v.t.*—*dehumidified, dehumidifying.* To remove moisture from.

dehydrate, dē•hī′drāt, *v.t.*—*dehydrated, dehydrating.* To remove water or water elements from.—*v.i.* To lose water or moisture.—**dehydration,** dē•hī•drā′shon, *n.* The process of dehydrating; excessive loss of body fluids.

deicide,† dē′i•sīd, *n.* [Fr. *déicide*—L. *deus*, God, and *cædo*, to slay.] The act of putting to death Jesus Christ, the Saviour; one concerned in putting Christ to death.

deify, dē′i•fī, *v.t.*—*deified, deifying.* [L. *deus*, a god, and *facio*, to make.] To make a god of; to exalt to the rank of a deity; to enroll among deities; to treat as an object of supreme regard; to praise or revere as a deity; to make godlike.—**deification,** dē′if•i•kā″shon, *n.*

deign, dān, *v.i.* [Fr. *daigner*, from L. *dignor*, to think worthy, from *dignus*, worthy, whence *dignity*, etc.] To vouchsafe; to condescend: generally followed by an infinitive.—*v.t.* To grant or allow.

deism, dē′izm, *n.* [Fr. *déisme*, from L. *Deus*, God. DEITY.] The doctrine or creed of a deist.—**deist,** dē′ist, *n.* [Fr. *déiste.*] One who believes in the existence of a God or supreme being but denies revealed religion, basing his belief on the light of nature and reason. ∴ The term *deist* generally implies a certain antagonism to Christianity; while the similar term *theist* is applied to Christians, Jews, Mohammedans, and all believers in one god, being opposed to *atheist* or *pantheist.*—**deistic, deistical,** dē•is′tik, dē•is′ti•kal, *a.* Pertaining to deism or to deists; embracing or containing deism.—**deistically,** dē•is′ti•kal•li, *adv.* In a deistical manner.

deity, dē′i•ti, *n.* [L.L. *deitas*, the Godhead, divine nature, from L. *Deus*, God, akin to Gr. *Zeus* (genit. *Dios*), the supreme divinity; L. *Diespiter, Jupiter*, and *dies*, a day; Skr. *deva*, a god; W. *Duw*, God, *dyw*, day; Gael. and Ir. *dia*, God; *Tiw*, the A.Sax. god whose name appears in *Tuesday*; all from a root implying brightness.] Godhead; divinity; the Supreme Being, or infinite self-existing Spirit; God; a fabulous god or goddess; a divinity.

deject, di•jekt′, *v.t.* [L. *dejicio, dejectum*—*de*, down, and *jacio*, to throw; seen also in *abject, eject, jet, jut*, etc.] To cast down; to depress the spirits of; to dispirit; discourage, dishearten.—**dejected,** di•jek′ted, *p.* and *a.* Downcast; depressed; sad; sorrowful.—**dejectedly,** di•jek′ted•li, *adv.* In a dejected manner; sadly; heavily.—**dejectedness,** di•jek′ted•nes, *n.* Dejection.—**dejection,** di•jek′shon, *n.* The state of being downcast; depression of mind; melancholy; lowness of spirits occasioned by grief or misfortune.—**dejecta,** di•jek′ta, *n. pl.* Droppings; castings; excrement.

delaine, de•lān′, *n.* [Fr. *de*, of, and *laine*, L. *lana*, wool.] A muslin made originally of wool, afterwards more commonly of a mixed fabric, generally cotton and wool, and used chiefly as a printing cloth.

delation, di•lā′shon, *n.* [L. *delatio*, from *de*, down, and *latus*, part. of *fero*, to bear.] *Law*, accusation; act of charging with a crime; information against.

delay, di•lā′, *v.t.* [Fr. *délai*, It. *dilata*, delay, from L. *dilatus*, put off—*dis*, apart, and *latus*, pp. of *fero*, to carry.] To prolong the time of doing or proceeding with; to put off; to defer; to retard; to stop, detain, or hinder for a time; to restrain the motion of.—*v.i.* To linger; to move slowly; to stop for a time.—*n.* A lingering; a putting off or deferring; procrastination; protraction; hindrance.—**delayer,** di•lā′ėr, *n.* One who delays.

delectable, di•lek′ta•bl, *a.* [L. *delectabilis*, from *delectare*, to delight. DELIGHT.] Delightful; highly pleasing; affording great joy or pleasure.—**delectableness,** di•lek′ta•bl•nes, *n.* Delightfulness.—**delectably,** di•lek′ta•bli, *adv.* In a delectable manner; delightfully.—**delectation,** dē•lek•tā′shon, *n.* A giving delight; delight.

delegate, del′e•gāt, *v.t.*—*delegated, delegating.* [L. *delego, delegatum*—*de*, and *lego*, to send as an ambassador. LEGATE.] To depute; to send on an embassy; to send with power to act as a representative; to entrust, commit, or deliver to another's care and management (power, an affair).—*n.* A person appointed and sent by another or by others, with powers to transact business as his or their representative; a deputy; a commissioner; a representative.—**delegation,** del•e•gā′shon, *n.* The act of delegating; appointment to act as deputy; a person or body of persons deputed to act for another or for others.

delete, di•lēt′, *v.t.* [L. *deleo, deletum*, to blot out, to destroy.] To blot out; to erase; to strike or mark out, as with a pen, pencil, etc.—**deletion,** di•lē′shon, *n.* [L. *deletio.*] The act of deleting; an erasure; a passage deleted.

deleterious, del•e•ter′ē•us, *a.* [L.L. *deleterius*, from Gr. *dēlētērios*, noxious, from *dēlēomai*, to injure.] Having the quality of destroying life; noxious; poisonous; injurious; pernicious.

delf, delft, delf, delft, *n.* Earthenware, covered with enamel or white glazing in imitation of chinaware or porcelain, made at *Delft*, in Holland; glazed earthenware dishes.

deliberate, di•lib′ėr•āt, *v.i.*—*deliberated, deliberating.* [L. *delibero, deliberatum*—*de*, and *libro*, to weigh, from *libra*, a balance; akin *level.*] To weigh consequences or results in the mind previous to action; to pause and consider; to ponder, reflect, cogitate, or debate with one's self.—**deliberate,** dē•lib′ėr•it, *a.* Weighing facts and arguments with a view to a choice or decision; carefully considering probable consequences; slow in determining; formed with deliberation; well advised or considered; not sudden or rash; not hasty.—**deliberately,** di•lib′ėr•it•li, *adv.* In a deliberate manner; with careful consideration; not hastily or rashly.—**deliberateness,** di•lib′ėr•it•nes, *n.* The state or quality of being deliberate.—**deliberation,** di•lib′ėr•ā″shon, *n.* [L. *deliberatio.*] The act of deliberating; careful consideration; mature reflection; mutual discussion and examination of the reasons for and against a measure; the act or habit of doing anything coolly or without hurry or excitement.—**deliberative,** di•lib′ėr•ā•tiv, *a.* Pertaining to deliberation; proceeding or acting by deliberation or discussion; having or conveying a right or power to deliberate or discuss.—**deliberatively,** di•lib′ėr•ā•tiv•li. *adv.* By deliberation.

delicate, del′i•kit, *a.* [Fr. *délicat*, L. *delicatus*, from *deliciæ*, delight, *delicio*, to allure—*de*, and *lacio*, to draw gently; akin *delight, delectable.*] Pleasing to a cultivated taste; refinedly agreeable; dainty; of a fine texture; fine; soft; smooth; tender; sensitive; easily injured; not capable of standing rough handling; nice; accurate; light or softly tinted; slender; minute; peculiarly sensitive to beauty, harmony, or their opposites; refined in manner; polite; nice.—**delicately,**

del′i•kit•li, *adv.* In a delicate manner; with nice regard to propriety and the feelings of others; tenderly; daintily; luxuriously.—**delicateness,** del′i•kit•nes, *n.* The state of being delicate.—**delicacy,** del′i•ka•si, *n.* The quality of being delicate or highly pleasing to the taste or some other sense; fineness; smoothness; softness; tenderness; slenderness; that which is pleasing to the senses; a luxury; refined taste or judgment; nicety.—**delicious,** di•lish′us, *a.* [Fr. *délicieux,* from L. *deliciæ,* delight.] Highly pleasing to the taste; most sweet or grateful to the senses; affording exquisite pleasure; charming; delightful; entrancing.—**deliciously,** di•lish′us•li, *adv.* In a delicious manner; exquisitely; delightfully.—**deliciousness,** di•lish′us•nes, *n.* The quality of being delicious.

delicatessen, del′i•ka•te″sen, *n.* [G. pl. of *delikatesse,* delicacy.] A shop that sells prepared foods such as cooked meat, smoked fish, salads, etc.

delight, di•līt′, *v.t.* [O.E. *delite,* from O.Fr. *deliter, deleiter,* from L. *delecto,* to delight, from *delicio,* to allure. DELICATE.] To affect with great pleasure; to please highly; to give or afford high satisfaction or joy.—*v.i.* To have or take great pleasure; to be greatly pleased or rejoiced (to *delight in* a thing).—*n.* A high degree of pleasure or satisfaction of mind; joy; rapture; that which gives great pleasure; the cause of joy; charm.—**delighted,** di•lī′ted, *a.* Experiencing delight; overjoyed.—**delightedly,** di•lī′ted•li, *adv.* In a delighted manner; with delight.—**delightful,** di•līt′fu̦l, *a.* Giving delight; highly pleasing; charming; exquisite; delicious.—**delightfully,** di•līt′fu̦l•li, *adv.* In a delightful manner; charmingly; exquisitely.—**delightfulness,** di•līt′fu̦l•nes, *n.*

delimit, di•lim′it, *v.t.* To mark or settle distinctly the limits of.—**delimitation,** di•lim′i•tā″shon, *n.* The act of delimiting; the fixing or settling of limits or boundaries.

delineate, di•lin′ē•āt, *v.t.*—*delineated, delineating.* [L. *delineo, delineatum*—*de,* down, and *linea,* a line. LINE.] To draw the lines which exhibit the form of; to make a draught of; to sketch or design; to represent in a picture; to draw a likeness of; to portray to the mind or understanding; to depict, sketch, or describe.—**delineation,** di•lin′ē•ā″shon, *n.* The act or process of delineating; representation or portrayal, whether pictorially or in words; sketch; description.—**delineator,** di•lin′ē•ā•tėr, *n.* One who delineates.

delinquency, di•ling′kwen•si, *n.* [L. *delinquentia,* a fault, from *delinquo,* to abandon, fail, omit duty—*de,* out, and *linquo,* to leave.] Failure or omission of duty; a fault; a misdeed; an offense.—**delinquent,** di•ling′kwent, *a.* Failing in duty; offending by neglect of duty.—**delinquent,** di•ling′kwent, *n.* One who fails to perform his duty; one guilty of a delinquency; an offender; a culprit; a malefactor.—**delinquently,** di•ling′kwent•li, *adv.* So as to fail in duty.

deliquesce, del•i•kwes′, *v.i.*—*deliquesced, deliquescing.* [L. *deliquesco*—*de,* and *liquesco,* to melt, from *liqueo,* to become liquid. LIQUID.] To melt gradually and become liquid by attracting and absorbing moisture from the air, as certain salts, acids, and alkalies.—**deliquescence,** del•i•kwes′ens, *n.* The process of deliquescing; a gradual melting or becoming liquid by absorption of moisture from the atmosphere.—**deliquescent,** del•i•kwes′ent, *a.* Liquefying in the air; deliquescing.

delirium, di•lir′i•um, *n.* [L., from *deliro,* to draw the furrow awry in plowing, to deviate from the straight line, hence to be crazy, to rave—*de,* from, and *lira,* a furrow.] A temporary disordered state of the mental faculties occurring during illness, either of a febrile or of an exhausting nature; violent excitement; wild enthusiasm; mad rapture.—*Delirium tremens* (trē′menz), an affection of the brain which arises from the inordinate and protracted use of ardent spirits.—**delirious,** di•lir′i•us, *a.* Affected with delirium; lightheaded; disordered in intellect; crazy; raving; frenzied; characterized by, or proceeding from, delirium.—**deliriously,** di•lir′i•us•li, *adv.* In a delirious manner.—**deliriousness,** di•lir′i•us•nes, *n.* The state of being delirious; delirium.

deliver, di•liv′ėr, *v.t.* [Fr. *délivrer,* from L.L. *delibero,* to set free—L. *de,* from, *libero,* to free, from *liber,* free, whence also *liberal, liberate.*] To release, as from restraint; to set at liberty; to free; to rescue or save; to transfer, hand over, or commit (a letter, a person to enemies); to surrender, yield, give up, resign: often followed by *up;* to disburden of a child; to utter, pronounce, speak (a sermon, address, etc.); to direct, send forth, or discharge (a blow, a broadside).—**deliverable,** di•liv′ėr•a•bl, *a.* Capable of being delivered.—**deliverance,** di•liv′ėr•ans, *n.* The act of delivering; in modern usage most commonly release or rescue, as from captivity, oppression, danger, etc., *delivery* being used in other senses.—**deliverer,** di•liv′ėr•ėr, *n.* One who delivers; one who releases or rescues; a preserver; a savior.—**delivery,** di•liv′ėr•i, *n.* The act of delivering; release; rescue, as from slavery, restraint, oppression, or danger; the act of handing over or transferring; surrender; a giving up; a giving or passing from one to another; specifically, the distribution of letters, etc., from a post office to a district or districts; utterance; pronunciation, or manner of speaking; childbirth.

dell, del, *n.* [DALE.] A small narrow valley between hills or rising grounds; a ravine.

Delphian, Delphic, del′fi•an, del′fik, *a.* Relating to *Delphi,* a town in Greece, and to the celebrated oracle of that place; hence, oracular; inspired.

delphinine, delf′in•īn, *n.* [Gr. *delphinion,* larkspur.] A poisonous alkaloid used medicinally.

delphinium, del•fin′i•um, *n.* [Gr. *delphinion,* larkspur.] Larkspur.

delta, del′ta, *n.* The name of the Greek letter Δ, answering to the English D; the island formed by the alluvial deposits between the mouths of the Nile, from its resemblance in shape to this letter; any similar alluvial tract at the mouth of a river.—**deltaic,** del•tā′ik, *a.* Relating to or like a delta.—**deltoid,** del′toid, *a.* Resembling the Greek Δ; triangular.

delude, di•lūd′, *v.t.*—*deluded, deluding.* [L. *deludo*—*de,* and *ludo,* to play, *ludus,* sport, whence also *ludicrous, elude, illusion,* etc.] To cause to entertain foolish or erroneous notions; to impose on; to befool; to lead from truth or into error; to mislead; to beguile; to cheat: often *refl,* (to *delude one's self* with vain hopes).—**deluder,** di•lū′dėr, *n.* One who deludes; a deceiver; an impostor; one who holds out false pretenses.—**delusion,** di•lū′zhon, *n.* The act of deluding; a misleading of the mind; false impression or belief; illusion; error or mistake proceeding from false views; the state of being deluded or misled.—**delusive,** di•lū′siv, *a.* Apt to delude; tending to mislead the mind; deceptive; beguiling.—**delusively,** di•lū′siv•li, *adv.* In a delusive manner.—**delusiveness,** di•lū′siv•nes, *n.* The quality of being delusive.—**delusory,** di•lū′so•ri, *a.* Apt to deceive; deceptive.

deluge, del′ūj, *n.* [Fr. *déluge,* from L. *diluvium,* a flood, a deluge—*di* for *dis,* asunder, away, and *luo*=*lavo,* to wash; akin *lave, ablution,* etc.] An inundation; a flood; [*cap.*] but specifically, the great flood or overflowing of the earth by water in the days of Noah; anything resembling an inundation; anything that overwhelms, as a great calamity.—*v.t.*—*deluged, deluging.* To overflow, as with water; to inundate; to drown; to overwhelm.

de luxe, de•luks′, *a.* [Fr.] Elegant; of superior quality.

delve, delv, *v.t.*—*delved, delving.* [A.Sax. *delfan*=D. *delven,* to dig; probably connected with *dell,* a dale, Fris. *dollen,* to dig.] To turn up with a spade; to dig.—*v.i.* To dig; to labor with the spade.—**delver,** del′vėr, *n.* One who delves.

demagnetization, dē•mag′net•i•zā″shon, *n.* The act or process of depriving of magnetic or of mesmeric influence.—**demagnetize,** dē•mag′ne•tīz, *v.t.*

demagogue, dem′a•gog, *n.* [Gr. *dēmagōgos*—*demos,* the people, and *agōgos,* a leader, from *agō,* to lead.] A leader of the people; a person who sways the people by his oratory; generally, an unprincipled factious orator; one who acquires influence with the populace by pandering to their prejudices or playing on their ignorance.—**demagogic, demagogical,** dem•a•goj′ik, dem•a•goj′i•kal, *a.* Relating to or like a demagogue; factious.—**demagogism** dem′a•gog-izm, *n.* The practices and principles of a demagogue.

demand, di•mand′ *v.t.* [Fr. *demander*, from L. *demando*, in its late sense of to demand, the opposite of *mando*, to commit to, lit. to put into one's hand, from *manus*, the hand, and *do*, to give; akin *mandate, command.*] To claim or seek as due by right (to *demand* a thing *of* a person); to ask or claim generally (a price, a reward); to ask (a thing) by authority; to question authoritatively (O.T.); to require as necessary or useful; to necessitate (a task *demands* industry).—*v.i.* To make a demand; to inquire; to ask.—*n.* An asking for or claim made by virtue of a right or supposed right to the thing sought; an asking or request with authority; the asking or requiring of a price for goods offered for sale; question; interrogation; the calling for in order to purchase (there is no *demand* for the goods).—*In demand*, in request; much sought after or courted (goods are *in demand*, his company is *in* great *demand*).—*On demand*, on being claimed; on presentation (a bill payable *on demand*).—**demander,** di•man′dėr, *n.* One who demands.

demarcation, dē•mär•kā′shon, *n.* [Fr. *démarcation—de*, down, and *marquer*, to mark. MARK.] The act or process of marking off, or of defining the limits or boundaries of anything; separation; distinction. Also written *Demarkation.*—**demarcate,**† di•mär′kāt, *v.t.* To mark the limits or boundaries of.

dematerialize, dē•ma•tē′ri•al•īz, *v.t.* To divest of material qualities or characteristics.

deme, dēm, *n.* [Gr. *demos.*] A subdivision of ancient Attica and of modern Greece; a township.

demean, di•mēn′, *v.t.* [Fr. *démener*, formerly to behave—*de*, intens., and *mener*, to lead, to manage, from L. *minare*, to drive with threats, from *mina*, a threat, whence also *menace, minatory.*] To behave; to carry; to conduct; used *refl.* From confusion with the adj. *mean* the word is also sometimes used in sense of to lower or degrade (one's self).—**demeanor,** di•mē′nėr, *n.* Behavior, especially as regards air or carriage of the person, countenance, etc.; carriage; deportment; conduct.

demented, di•men′ted, *a.* [L. *demens, dementis*, out of one's mind—*de*, out of, and *mens*, the mind.] Infatuated; mad; insane; crazy.—**dementia,** di•men′shi•a, *n.* [L.] A form of insanity; in psychiatry, any condition of impaired mentality.—**dementia praecox,** prē′koks. Schizophrenia.

demerit, dē•me′rit, *n.* [Fr. *démérite—de*, and *mérite*, merit. MERIT.] Desert, or what one merits (*Shak.*)‡; the opposite or absence of *merit*; that which is blamable or punishable in moral conduct; vice or crime.

demesne, de•mān′, *n.* [O.Fr. *demaine, domaine*, from L. *dominus*, a lord; akin *dame, damsel, dominate*, etc.] *Law*, possession of land as one's own; an estate in land; the land adjacent to a manorhouse or mansion kept in the proprietor's own hands, as distinguished from lands held by his tenants.

demi-, dem′i [Fr. *demi*, from L. *dimidius*, half—*di* for dis, and *medius*, the middle.] A prefix signifying half. The hyphen is not always inserted in all these words.—**demibastion,** dem′i•bas•ti•on, *n. Fort.* a bastion that has only one face and one flank.—**demigod,** dem′i•god, *n.* Half a god; an inferior deity; one partaking partly of the divine; partly of the human nature.—**demimonde,** dem′i•mond, *n.* [Fr. *monde*, the world, society.] Women of questionable reputation; courtesans; the society which these women frequent.—**demirep,** dem′i•rep, *n.* [A contr. for *demi-reputation.*] A woman of doubtful reputation, an adventuress.—**demisemiquaver,** dem′i•sem•i•kwā•vėr, n. *Mus.* the half of a semiquaver, or one-fourth of a quaver.—**demitasse,** dem′i•täs, *n.* [Fr.] A small cup of, or for, black coffee.—**demivolt,** dem′i•vōlt, n. A kind of leap or curvet of a horse.

demijohn, dem′i•jon, *n.* [Fr. *damejeanne*, from Ar. *damagan*, from *Damaghan*, a town in Khorassan once famous for its glassworks.] A glass vessel or bottle with a large body and small neck, enclosed in wickerwork.

demise, di•mīz′, *n.* [Lit. a laying off or aside, from Fr. *démettre—de*, L. *dis*, aside, and *mettre*, to put, L. *mitto*, to send.] The death of a person, especially of a person of distinction; decease: used with possessives; *law*, a conveyance or transfer of an estate by lease or will.—*v.t.—demised, demising. Law*, to transfer or convey, as an estate; to bequeath; to grant by will.—**demisable,** di•mīz′a•bl, *a.* Capable of being demised.

demit, di•mit′, *v.t.—demitted, demitting.* [L. *demitto—de*, down, and *mitto*, to send.] To lay down formally, as an office; to resign; to relinquish; to transfer.—**demission,** di•mi′shon, *n.* The act of demitting; a laying down of office; resignation; transference.

demiurge, demiurgus, dem′i•ėrj, dem′i•ėr″gus, *n.* [Gr. *dēmiourgos*, from *dēmos*, the people, and *ergon*, a work.] A maker or framer; the maker of the world; the Creator; specifically, the name given by the Gnostics to the creator or former of the world of sense.—**demiurgic, demiurgical,** dem•i•ėr′jik, dem•i•ėr′ji•kal, *a.* Pertaining to a demiurge or to creative power.

demobilize, dē•mō′bi•līz, *v.t.—demobilized, demobilizing.* [L. *de*, not, and E. *mobilize.*] To disarm and dismiss (troops) home; to disband.—**demobilization,** dē•mō′bi•li•zā″shon, *n.* The act of demobilizing.

democracy, di•mok′ra•si, *n.* [Gr. *dēmokratia—dēmos*, people, and *kratos*, strength, power.] That form of government in which the supreme power rests with the people, ruling themselves either directly, as in the New England town meetings, or indirectly, through representatives—aptly expressed by Abraham Lincoln's phrase, "*of the people, by the people, for the people.*" The modern concept of democracy assumes the political equality of all individuals, the right to private freedom, and to petition authority for redress of grievances; a country so governed.—**democrat,** dem′o•krat, *n.* One who adheres to principles of democracy; [*cap.*] a member of the Democratic party in the U.S.—**democratically,** dem•o•krat′i•kal•li, *adv.* In a democratical manner.—**democratize,**† di•mok′ra•tīz, *v.t.* To render democratic.

Demogorgon, dē•mo•gor′gon, *n.* [Gr. *daimōn*, a demon, and *gorgos*, terrible.] A mysterious divinity in classical or ancient mythology, viewed as an object of terror rather than of worship. (*Mil.*)

demography, di•mog′ra•fi, *n.* [Gr. *dēmos*, people, *graphō*, to write.] The description of peoples or communities in regard to their social relations and institutions, especially as compared with other communities; study of the size, density, composition, etc. of human populations.—**demographer,** di•mog′ra•fėr, *n.*—**demographic,** di•mo•graf′ik, *a.*

demoiselle, dė•mwä•zel′, *n.* [Fr. DAMSEL.] A young lady; a damsel; a bird, the Numidian crane, so called from its gracefulness and symmetry of form.

demolish, di•mol′ish, *v.t.* [Fr. *démolir, démolissant*, from L. *demolior—de*, not, and *molior*, to build, from *moles*, mass, whence *molecule.*] To throw or pull down; to raze; to destroy, as a structure or artificial construction; to ruin.—**demolisher,** di•mol′ish•ėr, *n.* One who demolishes.—**demolition,** dem•o•lish′on, *n.* The act of demolishing; destruction; ruin.

demon, dē′mon, *n.* [L. *daemon*, from Gr. *daimōn*, a spirit, evil or good.] A spirit or immaterial being, holding a middle place between men and the celestial deities of the pagans; an evil or malignant spirit; a devil; a very wicked or cruel person.—**demoniac, demoniacal,** di•mō′ni•ak, di•mō•nī′a•kal, *a.* Pertaining to demons or evil spirits; influenced by demons; produced by demons or evil spirits; extremely wicked or cruel.—**demoniac,** di•mō′ni•ak, *n.* A human being possessed by a demon.—**demoniacally,** di•mō•nī′a•kal•li, *adv.* In a demoniacal manner.—**demonian,**† di•mō′ni•an, *a.* Having the characteristics of a demon. (*Mil.*)—**demonism,** dē′mon•izm, *n.* The belief in demons.—**demonist,** dē′mon•ist, *n.* A worshiper of or believer in demons.—**demonize,** dē′mon•īz, *v.t.* To render demoniacal or diabolical; to control by a demon.—**demonology,** dē•

mon•ol′o•ji, *n.* A treatise on evil spirits and their agency, or beliefs regarding them.

demonetize, dē•mon′e•tīz, *v.t.* To deprive of standard value, as money; to withdraw from circulation.—**demonetization,** dē•mon′e•tī•zā″-shon, *n.* The act of demonetizing.

demonstrate, dem′on•strāt, *v.t.*—*demonstrated, demonstrating.* [L. *demonstro—de,* intens., and *monstro,* to show, from *monstrum,* a portent, a monster.] To point out with perfect clearness; to show clearly; to make evident; to exhibit; to exhibit the merits and operation of; to show or prove to be certain; to prove beyond the possibility, of doubt.—**demonstrable,** di•mon′-stra•bl, *a.* Capable of being demonstrated, proved, or exhibited.—**demonstrability,** di•mon′stra•bil″i•ti, *n.* The state or quality of being demonstrable.—**demonstrably,** di•mon′stra•bli, *adv.* In a manner so as to preclude doubt.—**demonstration,** dem•on•strā′shon, *n.* The act of demonstrating; an exhibition; the exhibition of parts dissected for the study of anatomy; *milit.* an operation, such as the massing of men at a certain point, performed for the purpose of deceiving the enemy respecting the measures which it is intended to employ against him.—**demonstrative,** di•mon′stra•-tiv, *a.* Serving to demonstrate; showing or proving by certain evidence; invincibly conclusive; characterized by or given to the strong exhibition of any feeling; outwardly expressive of feelings or emotions.—*Demonstrative pronoun,* one that clearly indicates the object to which it refers, as *this* man, *that* book.—**demonstratively,** di•mon′stra•tiv•li, *adv.* In a demonstrative manner; by demonstration; with proof which cannot be questioned; with energetic outward exhibition of feeling.—**demonstrativeness,** di•mon′stra•-tiv•nes, *n.* Quality of being demonstrative.—**demonstrator,** dem′-on•strā•tėr, *n.* One who demonstrates or exhibits the merits or operation of something to the public, as a device or food product; an article or product used for purposes of demonstration, such as an automobile or radio.

demoralize, di•mor′a•līz, *v.t.*—*demoralized, demoralizing.* [Prefix *de,* not, and *moral.*] To corrupt or undermine the morals of; to destroy or lessen the effect of moral principles on; to render corrupt in morals; *milit.* to deprive (troops) of courage and self-reliance, to render them distrustful and hopeless.—**demoralization,** di•mor′a•-li•zā″shon, *n.* The act of demoralizing; the state of being demoralized.

demote, di•mōt′, *v.t.* [Prefix *de,* and *mote,* from *promote.*] To reduce to a lower rank or class.—**demotion,** di•-mō′shon, *n.*

demulcent, di•mul′sent, *a.* [L. *demulcens, demulcentis,* ppr. of *demulceo,* to stroke down—*de,* down, and *mulceo,* to stroke, to soften.] Softening; mollifying; lenient.—*n.* Any medicine which lessens the effects of irritation, as gums and other mucilaginous substances.

demur, di•mėr′, *v.i.*—*demurred, demurring.* [Fr. *demeurer,* to delay, to stay, from L. *demorari—de,* and *mora,* delay.] To pause in uncertainty, to hesitate; to have or to state scruples or difficulties; to object hesitatingly; to take exceptions; *law—n.* Stop; pause; hesitation as to the propriety of proceeding; suspense of proceeding or decision; exception taken; objection stated.—**demurrage,** di•mėr′ij, *n.* The time during which any common carrier, such as a vessel, railroad car, or express truck, is detained beyond that originally stipulated for loading or unloading; the payment made for such detainment; the charge made for the storage of freight or luggage beyond the collection period.—**demurrer,** di•mėr′ėr, *n.* One who demurs; *law,* a pleading which claims that the contentions submitted by the opposing party are insufficient in law to warrant his justification in bringing action.

demure, di•mūr′, *a.* [From Fr. *de moeurs,* of manners, having manners, from L. *mores,* manners, whence *moral,* etc.] Affectedly modest or coy; making a show of gravity or decorousness; grave or reserved consciously and intentionally.—**demurely,** di•mūr′li, *adv.* In a demure manner; with a show of solemn gravity.—**demureness,** di•mūr′nes, *n.* The state or quality of being demure; gravity of countenance, real or affected.

den, den, *n.* [A.Sax. *denn.* a cave or lurking-place; akin *denu,* E. *dene,* a valley.] A cave or hollow place in the earth; a cave, pit, or subterranean recess, used for concealment, shelter, protection, or security; any squalid place of resort or residence; a dell, wooded hollow, or ravine; a quiet, private retreat, as a room for reading.

denarius, di•nâ′ri•us, *n.* [L., from *decem,* ten.] An ancient Roman silver coin originally worth 10 asses or 10 lbs. of copper.

denationalize, dē•na′shon•al•īz, *v.t.* To divest of national character or rights.—**denationalization,** dē•na′-shon•al•i•zā″shon, *n.* The act of denationalizing.

denaturalize, dē•nat′ū•ra•līz, *v.t.* Tó render unnatural; to alienate from nature; to deprive of naturalization or acquired citizenship in a foreign country.—**denature,** dē•nā′chėr, *v.t.* To change the nature of; to render unfit for human consumption, without impairing usefulness for other purposes, as alcohol.

dendriform, den′dri•form, *a.* [Gr. *dendron,* a tree.] Having the form or appearance of a tree.—**dendrite,** den′drīt, *n.* A stone or mineral, on or in which are figures resembling shrubs, trees, or mosses, the appearance being due to arborescent crystallization, resembling the frost work on our windows.—**dendritic, dentritical,** den•drit′ik, den•drit′i•-kal, *a.* Resembling a tree; treelike; marked by figures resembling shrubs, moss, etc.—**dendroid, dendroidal,** den′droid, den•droi′dal, *a.* Resembling a small tree or shrub.—**dendrology,** den•drol′o•ji, *n.* The natural history of trees.—**dendrologist,** den•-drol′o•jist, *n.* One versed in dendrology.

dengue, deng′gā, *n.* [Sp.] A febrile epidemic disease of the East and West Indies, with symptoms resembling those of scarlet fever and rheumatism combined.

denial, denier. See DENY.

denigrate, den′i•grāt, *v.t.* To blacken, to soil, or to defile; to defame.

denim, den′em, *n.* [Fr. *serge de Nîmes,* serge of Nîmes, France.] A heavy, twilled cotton fabric used for upholstery, overalls, sports clothes, etc.

denitrate, dē•nī′trāt, *v.t.* To set nitric acid free from.—**denitration,** dē•nī•trā′shon, *n.* A disengaging of nitric acid.—**denitrify,** dē•nī′tri•fī, *v.t.* To deprive of niter.

denitrification, dē•nī′tri•fi•kā″shon, [L. *de,* from, *facio,* I make (nitrogen).] Liberation of nitrogen from organic matter by the action of bacteria. Cp. NITRIFICATION.

denizen, den′i•zn, *n.* [O.Fr. *deinzein,* one living within a city, from *deins, dens,* Fr. *dans,* in, within, a contr. of L. *de inius,* from within, and thus opposed to *foreign.*] An alien who is admitted to the privileges of citizenship; one granted membership in a society or fellowship; hence, a stranger admitted to residence and certain rights in a foreign country; a citizen; a dweller; an inhabitant.—*v.t.* To make a denizen.

denominate, di•nom′i•nāt, *v.t.*—*denominated, denominating.* [L. *denomino—de,* intens., and *nomino,* to nominate.] To give a name or epithet to; to name, call, style, or designate.—**denomination,** di•-nom′i•nā″shon, *n.* The act of naming; a name or appellation; a class, society, or collection of individuals called by the same name; a religious sect.—**denominational,** di•nom′i•-nā″shon•al, *a.* Pertaining to or characterizing a denomination; pertaining to particular religious denominations or bodies.—**denominationalism,** di•nom′i•nā″shon•al•izm, *n.* A denominational or class spirit; adherence or devotion to a denomination; the principle or system of religious sects having each their own schools.—**denominationally,** di•-nom′i•nā″shon•al•li, *adv.* By denomination or sect.—**denominative,** di•nom′i•nā•tiv, *a.* Giving or conferring a name or distinct appellation.—*n.* That which has the character of a denomination; *gram.* a verb formed from a noun or an adjective.—**denominatively,** di•nom′i•nā•-tiv•li, *adv.* By denomination.—**denominator,** di•nom′i•nā•tėr, *n.* One who or that which denominates; the number placed below the line in vulgar fractions, showing into how many parts the integer is divided.

denote, di•nōt′, *v.t.—denoted, denoting.* [L. *denoto,* to mark, to point out, to denote—*de,* intens, and *noto,* to mark, from *nota,* a mark.] To signify by a visible sign; to indicate, mark, or stand for; to be the name of or express; to be the sign or symptom of; to show; to indicate. ∴ Syn. under CONNOTE.—**denotable,** di•nō′ta•bl, *a.* That may be denoted or marked.—**denotation,** dē•nō•tā′shon, *n.* [L. *denotatio.*] The act of denoting or marking off; what any word or sign denotes.—**denotative,** di•nō′ta•tiv, *a.* Having power to denote.

denouement, dā•nö•moṅ′, *n.* [Fr., from *dénouer,* to untie—*de,* not, and *nouer,* to tie, from L. *nodus,* a knot.] The winding up or catastrophe of a plot, as of a novel, drama, etc.; the solution of any mystery; the issue, as of any course of conduct; the event.

denounce, di•nouns′, *v.t.—denounced, denouncing.* [Fr. *denoncer,* L. *denuntiare—de,* and *nuntiare,* to declare, *nuntius,* a messenger; seen also in *announce, pronounce, renounce.*] To declare solemnly; to proclaim in a threatening manner; to announce or declare, as a threat; to threaten; to inform against; to accuse.—**denouncement,**† di•nouns′ment, *n.* The act of denouncing; denunciation.—**denouncer,** di•noun′sėr, *n.* One who denounces.—**denunciate,**† di•nun′shi•āt, *v.t.* To denounce.—**denunciation,** di•nun′shi•ā″shon, *n.* The act of denouncing; proclamation of a threat; public menace.—**denunciative, denunciatory,** di•nun′shi•ā•tiv, di•nun′shi•a•to•ri, *a.* Relating to, containing, or implying denunciation; ready or prone to denounce.—**denunciator,** di•nun′shi•ā•tėr, *n.* One who denounces, or solemnly and publicly threatens.

dense, dens, *a.* [Fr. *dense,* L. *densus,* thick, whence, *condense.*] Having its constituent parts closely united; close; compact; thick; crass; gross; crowded.—**densely,** dens′li, *adv.* In a dense manner; compactly.—**denseness,** dens′nes, *n.* Density.—**density,** den′si•ti, *n.* [L. *densitas.*] The quality of being dense, close, or compact; closeness of constituent parts; compactness; either the mass of unit volume of a substance (*absolute density*) or the ratio of the mass of a given volume of the substance to that of an equal volume of some standard substance (*relative density*). The standard for solids and liquids is water (see SPECIFIC GRAVITY); for gases, either air or (usually in *chem.*) hydrogen.

dent, dent, *n.* [A form of *dint.*] A mark made by a blow; especially, a hollow or depression made on the surface of a solid body.—*v.t.* To make a dent on or in.

dental, den′tal, *a.* [L. *dentalis,* dental, from *dens, dentis,* a tooth, a word akin to E. *tooth.*] Of or pertaining to the teeth; having the characteristic sound given by the teeth and tip of the tongue (*d* and *t* are *dental* letters).—*n.* A dental letter, as *d, t,* and *th.*—*Dental formula,* a formula for showing briefly the number and kinds of teeth of an animal; thus the *dental formula* of cats is: I. $\frac{3-3}{3-3}$, C. $\frac{1-1}{1-1}$, P.M. $\frac{3-3}{2-2}$. M. $\frac{1-1}{1-1} = 30$; which signifies that they have on each side of each jaw three incisors and one canine tooth, three premolars in the upper and two in the lower jaw on each side, and behind these one true molar.—**dentate,** den′tāt, *a.* [L. *dentatus,* toothed.] Toothed; having sharp teeth, with concave edges, as a leaf.—**denticle,** den′ti•kl, *n.* [L. *denticulus.*] A small tooth or projecting point.—**denticulate, denticulated,** den•tik′ū•lāt, den•tik′ū•lā•ted, *a.* Having small teeth, as a leaf, calyx, or seed.—**denticulation,** den•tik′ū•lā″shon, *n.* The state of being denticulate.—**dentiform,** den′ti•form, *a.* Having the form of a tooth.—**dentifrice,** den′ti•fris, *n.* [L. *dens,* and *frico,* to rub.] A powder, paste, or liquid, to be used in cleaning the teeth.—**dentil,** den′til, *n. Arch.* the name of the little cubes or square blocks often cut for ornament on Greek cornices.—**dentin,** den′tēn, *n.* The hard tissue lying below the enamel and constituting the body of the tooth.—**dentist,** den′tist, *n.* One who makes it his business to clean and extract teeth, repair them when diseased, and replace them when necessary by artificial ones.—**dentistry,** den′tist•ri, *n.* The art or profession of a dentist.—**dentition,** den•tish′on, *n.* [L. *dentitio.*] The breeding or cutting of teeth in infancy; the time of growing teeth; the system of teeth peculiar to an animal.—**denture,** den′chėr, *n.* A dentist's term for one or more artificial teeth.

denude, di•nūd′, *v.t.—denuded, denuding.* [L. *denudo—de,* and *nudus,* naked.] To divest of all covering; to make bare or naked; to strip; to uncover or lay bare.

denunciate, denunciation, denunciator, etc. See DENOUNCE.

deny, di•nī′, *v.t.—denied, denying.* [Fr. *dénier,* from L. *denego—de,* intens., and *nego,* to say no, from *nec,* nor. NEGATION.] To declare not to be true; to affirm to be not so; to contradict; to gainsay; to refuse to grant; not to afford; to withhold (Providence *denies* us many things); to refuse or neglect to acknowledge; not to confess; to disavow; to disown; to reject.—*To deny one's self,* to decline the gratification of appetites or desires.—*To deny one's self something,* to abstain from it although desiring it.—*v.i.* To answer in the negative; to refuse; not to comply.—**denial,** di•nī′al, *n.* The act of denying; contradiction; a contradictory statement; refusal; rejection; disownment.—**deniable,** di•nī′a•bl, *a.* Capable of being denied.—**denier,** di•nī′ėr, *n.* One who denies.

deodand, dē′ō•dand, *n.* [L. *Deo dandus,* to be given to God.] *Law,* formerly a personal chattel which had been the immediate occasion of the death of a rational creature (as a horse that killed a man), and for that reason forfeited to the king to be applied to pious uses.

deodar, dē′ō•där, *n.* [Skr. *devadāru,* that is, divine tree.] A kind of Indian cedar, closely akin to the cedar of Lebanon, yielding valuable timber, and introduced into Europe and elsewhere as an ornamental tree.

deodorize, dē•ō′dėr•īz, *v.t.—deodorized, deodorizing.* To deprive of odor or smell, especially of fetid odor resulting from impurities.—**deodorizer, deodorant,** dē•ō′dėr•i•zėr, dē•ō′dėr•ant, *n.* That which deodorizes; a substance which has the power of destroying fetid effluvia, as chlorine, chloride of lime, etc.—**deodorization,** dē•ō′dėr•i•zā″shon, *n.* The act or process of deodorizing.

deontology, dē•on•tol′o•gi, *n.* [Gr. *deon, deontos,* that which is binding or right, duty, and *logos,* discourse.] The science of duty; that doctrine of ethics which is founded on the principle of judging of actions by their tendency to promote happiness.—**deontological,** dē•on′to•loj″i•kal, *a.* Relating to deontology.—**deontologist,** dē•on•tol′o•jist, *n.* One versed in deontology.

deoxidize, dē•ok′si•dīz, *v.t.* [Prefix *de,* not, and *oxide,* or the first part of *oxygen.*] To deprive of oxygen, or reduce from the state of an oxide; also called *deoxygenate* (dē•ok′si•je•nāt).—**deoxidize,** dē•ok′si•dīz, *v.t.*—*deoxidized, deoxidizing.* To deoxidate.

depart, di•pärt′, *v.i.* [Fr. *départir—de,* and *partir,* to separate. PART.] To go or move away; to go elsewhere; to leave or desist, as from a practice; to forsake, abandon, deviate, not to adhere to or follow (commonly with *from* in these senses); to leave this world; to die; to decease.—*v.t.* To leave; to retire from; with ellipsis of *from.*—**departed,** di•pär′ted, *p.* and *a.* Gone; vanished; dead; with the definite article used as a noun for a dead person.—**department,** di•pärt′ment *n.* A separate branch of business; a distinct province, in which a class of duties are allotted to a particular person; a distinct branch, as of science, etc.; a division of territory, as in France; a district into which a country is formed for governmental or other purposes.—*Department store,* a store that sells a wide variety of goods arranged in different departments.—**departmental,** di•pärt•men′tal, *a.* —**departure,** di•pär′chėr, *n.* The act of leaving a place; death; decease; a forsaking; abandonment; deviation, as from a standard, rule, or plan.

depasture, dē•pas′chėr, *v.t.* To put out in order to graze or feed; to pasture; to graze; to eat up by cattle.—*v.i.* To feed or pasture; to graze.

depend, di•pend′, *v.i.* [L. *dependeo,* to hang down—*de,* down, and *pendeo,* to hang, seen also in *pendant,* *pendulum, pendulous, impend,* etc.] To be sustained by being fastened or attached to something above; to hang down; followed by *from;* to be related to anything in regard to existence, operation, or effects; to be contingent or conditioned: followed by *on* or *upon* (we *depend on* air for respiration); to rest with confidence; to trust, rely, or confide; to believe fully; with *on* or *upon.*—**dependable,** di•pen′da•bl, *a.* Capable of being depended on; trustworthy.—**dependability,** di•pen′da•bil″i•ti, *n.* Reliableness.—**dependent, dependant,** di•pen′dent, dē•pen′dant, *n.* One who is sustained by another, or who relies on another for support or favor; a retainer; a follower; a servant.—*a.* Hanging down; relying on something else for support; subject to the power of or at the disposal of another; not able to exist or sustain itself alone; relying for support or favor (*dependent on* another's bounty); in grammar, subordinate, as a *dependent* clause.—**dependence,** di•pen′dens, *n.* A state of being dependent; connection and support; mutual connection; interrelation; a state of relying on another for support or existence; a state of being subject to the operation of any other cause; reliance; confidence; trust; a resting on.—**dependency,** di•pen′den•si, *n.* The state of being dependent; dependence; now generally a territory remote from the kingdom or state to which it belongs, but subject to its dominion (Malta is a *dependency* of Britain).—**dependably,** di•pen′da•bli, *adv.* In a dependent manner.

depict, di•pikt′, *v.t.* [L. *depingo, depictum*—*de,* and *pingo,* to paint. PAINT, PICTURE.] To form a likeness of in colors; to paint; to portray; to represent in words; to describe; to delineate.—**depicture,** di•pik′tūr, *v.t.* To depict; to picture; to imagine.

depilate, dep′i•lāt, *v.t.*—*depilated, depilating.* [L. *depilo, depilatum*—*de,* not, and *pilus,* hair.] To strip of hair.—**depilation,** dep•i•lā′shon, *n.* The removal of hair.—**depilatory,** di•pil′a•to•ri, *a.* Having the quality or power to remove hair from the skin.—*n.* An application which is used to remove hair without injuring the texture of the skin; a cosmetic employed to remove superfluous hairs from the human skin.

deplete, di•plēt′, *v.t.*—*depleted, depleting.* [L. *depleo, depletum,* to empty out—*de,* not, and *pleo,* to fill, as in *complete,* etc.] To empty, reduce, or exhaust by draining away.—**depletion,** di•plē′shon, *n.* The act of depleting; *med.* the act of diminishing the quantity of blood in the vessels by bloodletting.—**depletive,** di•plē′tiv, *a.* Tending to deplete; producing depletion.—*n.* That which depletes; any medical agent of depletion.—**depletory,** di•plē′to•ri, *a.* Calculated to deplete or exhaust.

deplore, di•plōr′, *v.t.*—*deplored, deploring.* [L. *deploro*—*de,* intens., and *ploro,* to wail, to let tears flow (same root as *flow, flood*); seen also in *explore, implore.*] To feel or express deep and poignant grief for; to lament; to mourn; to grieve for, to bewail; to bemoan.—**deplorable,** di•plō′ra•bl, *a.* Lamentable; sad; calamitous; grievous, miserable; wretched; contemptible or pitiable.—**deplorably,** di•plō′ra•bli, *adv.* In a manner to be deplored; lamentably.

deploy, di•ploi′, *v.t.* [Fr. *déployer*—*de,* not, and *ployer* (as in *employ*), equivalent to *plier,* to fold, from L. *plicare,* to fold. PLY.] *Milit.* to extend in a line of small depth, as a battalion which has been previously formed in one or more columns; to display; to open out.—*v.i.* To form a more extended front or line; to open out.—**deployment,** di•ploi′ment, *n.* The act of deploying.

deplume, di•plūm′, *v.t.*—*deplumed, depluming.* [L.L. *deplumo*—L. *de,* not, and *pluma,* a feather.] To strip of feathers; to deprive of plumage.

depolarize, dē•pō′lėr•īz, *v.t.* To deprive of polarity.—**depolarization,** dē•pō′lėr•i•zā″shon, *n.* The act of depriving of polarity; the restoring of a ray of polarized light to its former state.

depone, di•pōn′, *v.i.* [L. *depono*—*de,* down, and *pono, positum,* to place. POSITION.] To give testimony; to depose: chiefly a Scots law term.—**deponent,** di•pō′nent, *a.* Laying down.—*Deponent verb,* in *Latin gram.* a verb which has a passive termination, with an active signification.—*n.* One who depones; a deponent verb.

depopulate, dē•pop′ū•lāt, *v.t.*—*depopulated, depopulating.* [L. *de,* from, and *populus,* people.] To deprive of inhabitants, whether by death or by expulsion; to dispeople; to greatly diminish the inhabitants of.—**depopulation,** dē•pop′ū•lā″shon, *n.* The act of depopulating.—**depopulator,** dē•pop′ū•lā•tėr, *n.* One who or that which depopulates.

deport, di•pōrt′, *v.t.* [Fr. *déporter,* to banish; O.Fr. *se deporter,* to amuse one's self; L. *deporto,* to banish—*de,* down, away, and *porto,* to carry.] To carry, demean, or behave: used *refl.;* also, to transport; to carry away; to eject undesirable aliens from a country, under compulsory edict. (*Mil.*)—**deportation,** dē•pōr•tā′shon, *n.* A removal from one country to another, or to a distant place; exile; banishment.—**deportment,** di•pōrt′ment, *n.* Manner of acting in relation to the duties of life; behavior; demeanor; carriage; conduct.

depose, di•pōz′, *v.t.*—*deposed, deposing.* [Fr. *déposer*—*de,* from, and *poser,* to place. COMPOSE.] To remove from a throne or other high station; to dethrone; to divest of office; to give testimony on oath, especially in a court of law.—**deposable,** di•pō′za•bl, *a.* That may be deposed.—**deposal,** di•pō′zal, *n.* The act of deposing or divesting of office.—**deposition,** dep′o•zish″un, *n.* The act of deposing or giving testimony under oath; the attested written testimony of a witness; declaration; the act of dethroning a king, or removing a person from an office or station. See also under DEPOSIT.

deposit, di•poz′it, *v.t.* [L. *depositum,* something deposited, a deposit, from *depono, depositum.* DEPONE, POSITION.] To lay down; to place; to put; to lay in a place for preservation; to lodge in the hands of a person for safekeeping or other purpose; to entrust; to commit as a pledge.—*n.* That which is laid down; any matter laid or thrown down, or lodged; matter that settles down and so is separated from a fluid, as (*geol.*) an accumulation of mud, gravel, stones, etc., lodged by the agency of water; anything entrusted to the care of another; a pledge; a thing given as security or for preservation; a sum of money lodged in a bank.—**depositary,** di•poz′i•te•ri, *n.* A person with whom anything is left or lodged in trust; a guardian.—**deposition,** dē•po•zish′on, *n.* [L. *depositio.*] The act of depositing, laying, or setting down; placing; that which is deposited, lodged, or thrown down. See also under DEPOSE.—**depositor,** di•poz′i•tėr, *n.* One who makes a deposit.—**depository,** di•poz′i•to•ri, *n.* A place where anything is lodged for safekeeping; a person to whom a thing is entrusted for safekeeping.

depot, dē′pō or dep′ō, *n.* [Fr. *dépôt,* O.Fr. *depost,* from L. *depono, depositum,* to deposit.] A place of deposit; a depository; a building for receiving goods for storage or sale; *milit.* the headquarters of a regiment; also a station where recruits for different regiments are received and drilled; a railroad station.

deprave, di•prāv′, *v.t.*—*depraved, depraving.* [L. *depravo,* to make crooked, to deprave—*de,* intens., and *pravus,* crooked, perverse, wicked.] To make bad or worse; to impair the good qualities of; to vitiate; to corrupt.—**depravation,** dep•ra•vā′shon, *n.* [L. *depravatio.*] The act of depraving or corrupting; the state of being depraved; corruption; deterioration.—**depraved,** di•prāvd′, *p.* and *a.* Vitiated; tainted; corrupted (*depraved* taste); destitute of good principles; vicious; immoral; profligate; abandoned.—**depraver,** di•prā′vėr, *n.* One who depraves.—**depravity,** di•prav′i•ti, *n.* The state of being depraved; a vitiated state; especially, a state of corrupted morals; destitution of good principles; sinfulness; wickedness; vice; profligacy.

deprecate, dep′re•kāt, *v.t.*—*deprecated, deprecating.* [L. *deprecor, deprecatus,* to pray against, to ward off by prayer—*de,* off, and *precor,* to pray.] To pray deliverance from, or that something may be averted; to plead or argue earnestly against; to urge reasons against; to express strong disapproval of (as of anger, a scheme, etc.).—**deprecatingly,** dep′re•kā•ting•li, *adv.* In a deprecating manner.—**deprecation,** dep•re•kā′shon, *n.* The act of deprecating; a praying against; entreaty; disapproval; condemnation.—**deprecatory, deprecative,** dep′re•ka•to•ri, dep′re•kā•tiv, *a.* Serving to deprecate; having the character of deprecation.

depreciate, di•prē′shi•āt, *v.t.—depreciated, depreciating.* [L. *depretio,* to lower the price of—*de,* down, and *pretium,* price. PRICE.] To bring down the price or value of; to cause to be less valuable; to represent as of little value or merit, or of less value than is commonly supposed; to lower in estimation, undervalue, decry, disparage, or underrate.—*v.i.* To fall in value; to become of less worth.—**depreciation,** di•prē′shi•ā″shon, *n.* The act of depreciating; reduction in value or worth; a lowering or undervaluing in estimation; the state of being undervalued. —**depreciative, depreciatory,** di•prē′shi•ā•tiv, di•prē′shi•a•to•ri, *a.* Tending to depreciate.—**depreciator,** di•prē′shi•ā•tėr, *n.* One who depreciates.

depredate, dep′ri•dāt, *v.t.—depredated, depredating.* [L. *depraedor,* to pillage—*de,* intens., and *praedor,* to plunder, from *praeda,* prey. PREY.] To plunder; to pillage; to waste; to spoil.—**depredation,** dep•ri•dā′shon, *n.* The act of depredating; a robbing; a pillaging by men or animals; a laying waste.—**depredator,** dep′ri•dā•tėr, *n.* One who depredates; a spoiler; a waster.—**depredatory,** dep′ri•dā•to•ri, *a.* Consisting in pillaging.

depress, di•pres′, *v.t.* [L. *deprimo, depressum,* to depress—*de,* and *premo, pressum,* to press. PRESS.] To press down; to let fall to a lower state or position; to lower; to render dull or languid; to deject or make sad; to humble, abase, bring into adversity; to lower in value.—**depressed,** di•prest′, *p.* and *a.* Dejected; dispirited; discouraged; sad; humbled; languid; dull; *nat. hist.* flattened in shape; flattened as regards the under and upper surfaces.—**depressingly,** di•pres′ing•li, *adv.* In a depressing manner.—**depression,** di•presh′on, *n.* The act of pressing down or depressing; a sinking or falling in of a surface; a hollow; the state or feeling of being depressed in spirits; a sinking of the spirits; dejection; a low state of strength; a prolonged period of financial and commercial stagnation characterized by unemployment, restricted credit, low prices, and general social distress.—*Angle of depression. Astron.* The angle by which a straight line drawn from the eye to any object dips below the horizon.—**depressive,** di•pres′iv, *a.* Able or tending to depress or cast down.—**depressor,** di•pres′ėr, *n.* One who or that which depresses; *anat.* a muscle which depresses or draws down the part to which it is attached.

deprive, di•prīv′, *v.t.—deprived, depriving.* [L. *de,* intens., and *privo,* to take away. PRIVATE.] To take from; to dispossess; to despoil; to bereave of something possessed or enjoyed: followed by *of* (to *deprive* a person *of* a thing); to divest of an ecclesiastical preferment, dignity, or office.—**deprivation,** dep•ri•vā′shon, *n.* The act of depriving; a taking away; a state of being deprived; loss; want; bereavement; the act of divesting a clergyman of his spiritual promotion or dignity; the taking away of a preferment; deposition.

depth, depth, *n.* [From *deep;* comp. *width, breadth, length,* etc.] The distance or measure of a thing from the highest part, top, or surface to the lowest part or bottom, or to the extreme part downward or inward; the measure from the anterior to the posterior part; deepness: in a vertical direction opposed to *height;* a deep place; an abyss; a gulf; the inner, darker, or more concealed part of a thing; the middle, darkest, or stillest part (the *depth* of winter or of a wood); abstruseness; obscurity; immensity; infinity; intensity (the *depth* of despair or of love).—**depth charge,** *n.* A bomb designed to go off under water.

depurate, dep′ū•rāt, *v.t.—depurated, depurating.* [L.L. *depuro, depuratum,* to purify—L. *de,* intens., and *puro, puratum,* to purify, from *purus,* pure.] To free from impurities, heterogeneous matter, or feculence; to purify; to clarify.—**depuration,** dep′ū•rā′shon, *n.* The act of depurating; the cleansing of a wound.—**depurator,** dep′ū•rā•tėr, *n.* One who or that which depurates.

depute, di•pūt′, *v.t.—deputed, deputing.* [Fr. *députer,* from L. *deputo,* to destine, allot—*de,* and *puto,* to prune, set in order, reckon, as in *compute, dispute,* etc.] To appoint as a substitute or agent to act for another; to appoint and send with a special commission or authority to act for the sender.—*n.* (dep′ūt). A deputy; as, a sheriff-*depute.* (Scotch.)—**deputation,** dep•ū•tā′shon, *n.* The act of deputing or sending as a deputy; a special commission or authority to act as the substitute of another; the person or persons deputed to transact business for another.—**deputy,** dep′ū•ti, *n.* [Fr. *député.*] A person appointed or elected to act for another; a representative, delegate, agent, or substitute.

deracinate,† dē•ras′i•nāt, *v.t.* [Fr. *déraciner—de,* from, and *racine,* a root, from L. *radix,* a root.] To pluck up by the roots; to extirpate. (*Shak.*)

derange, di•rānj′, *v.t.—deranged, deranging.* [Fr. *déranger—de,* not, and *ranger,* to set in order, to range. RANGE.] To put out of order; to throw into confusion; to disorder; to confuse; to disturb; to unsettle; to embarrass; to discompose.—**derangement,** di•rānj′ment, *n.* The act of deranging or state of being deranged; a putting out of order; embarrassment; confusion; disorder; delirium; insanity; mental disorder.

derelict, der′e•likt, *a.* [L. *derelictus,* left behind, abandoned—*de,* intens., *re,* behind, and *linquo,* to leave.] Left; abandoned, especially abandoned at sea.—*n.* An article abandoned by the owner, especially a vessel abandoned at sea.—**dereliction,** der•e•lik′shon, *n.* The act of leaving with an intention not to reclaim; desertion; relinquishment; abandonment (a *dereliction* of duty).

deride, di•rīd′, *v.t.—derided, deriding.* [L. *derideo—de,* intens., and *rideo,* to laugh.] To laugh at in contempt; to turn to ridicule or make sport of; to treat with scorn by laughter; to mock; to ridicule.—**derider,** dē•rī′dėr, *n.* One who derides; a mocker; a scoffer.—**deridingly,** di•rī′ding•li, *adv.* By way of derision or mockery.—**derision,** di•rizh′on, *n.* [L. *derisio.*] The act of deriding, or the state of being derided; contempt manifested by laughter; mockery; ridicule; scorn.—**derisive,** di•rī′siv, *a.* Expressing or characterized by derision; mocking; ridiculing.—**derisively,** di•rī′siv•li, *adv.* With mockery or contempt.—**derisiveness,** di•rī′siv•nes, *n.* The state of being derisive.

derive, di•rīv′, *v.t.—derived, deriving.* [L. *derivo,* to divert a stream from its channel, to derive—*de,* from, and *rivus,* a stream, whence also *rivulet, rival.*] To divert or turn aside from a natural course‡; to draw from, as in a regular course or channel; to receive from a source or as from a source or origin (to *derive* power, knowledge, facts); to deduce or draw from a root or primitive word; to trace the etymology of.—*Derived units.* Units based upon and determined by the FUNDAMENTAL UNITS (which see).—*v.i.*† To come or proceed. (*Tenn.*)—**derivable,** di•rī′va•bl, *a.* Capable of being derived.—**derivation,** der•i•vā′shon, *n.* The act of deriving, drawing, or receiving from a source; the drawing or tracing of a word from its root or origin; etymology.—**derivational,** der•i•vā′shon•al, *a.* Relating to derivation.—**derivative,** di•riv′a•tiv, *a.* Taken or having proceeded from another or something preceding; derived; secondary.—*n.* That which is derived; that which is deduced or comes by derivation from another; a word which takes its origin in another word, or is formed from it.—**derivatively,** di•riv′a•tiv•li, *adv.* In a derivative manner; by derivation.—**deriver,** di•rī′vėr, *n.* One who derives.

derma, dermis, dėr′ma, dėr′mis, *n.* [Gr. *derma,* skin.] The true skin, or under layer of the skin, as distinguished from the cuticle, epidermis, or scarf skin.—**dermal,** dėr′mal, *a.* Pertaining to skin; consisting of skin.—**dermatitis,** dėr•ma•tī′is. [Gr. *derma,* skin, *-itis,* inflammation.] Inflammation of the skin.—**dermatogen,** dėr•mat′o•jen. [Gr. *derma, dermatos,* skin, *gen,* to produce.] A cellular layer at the tip of a root or stem from which the epidermis is produced.—**dermatologist,** dėr•ma•tol′o•jist, *n.* One versed in dermatology.—**dermatology,** dėr•ma•tol′o•ji, *n.* The branch of science which treats of the skin and its diseases.—**dermatophyte,** dėr′ma•to•fīt, *n.* [Gr. *phyton,* a plant.] A parasitic plant, infesting the cuticle and epidermis of men and animals, and giving rise to various forms of skin disease, as ringworm.—**dermic,** dėr′mik, *a.* Relating to the skin.

derogate, der′o•gāt, *v.t.—derogated, derogating.* [L. *derogo, derogatum,* to repeal part of a law, to restrict, to modify—*de,* not, and *rogo,* to ask, to propose.] To repeal, annul, or revoke partially, as a law: distinguished from *abrogate*; to lessen the worth of; to disparage‡.—*v.i.* To detract; to have the effect of lowering or diminishing, as in reputation; to lessen by taking away a part: with *from* (something *derogates* from a person's dignity).—**derogation,** der•o•gā′shon, *n.* The act of derogating; a taking away from, or limiting in extent or operation; a lessening of value or estimation; detraction; disparagement.—**derogatory,** di•rog′a•to•ri, *a.* Having the effect of derogating or detracting from; lessening the extent, effect, or value: with *to.*—**derogatoriness,** di•rog′a•to•ri•nes, *n.* The quality of being derogatory.—**derogatorily,** di•rog′a•to•ri•li, *adv.*

derrick, der′ik, *n.* [The name of a London hangman of the 17th century, applied first to the gallows, and hence to a contrivance resembling it.] An apparatus for hoisting heavy weights, usually consisting of a boom supported by a central post; a framework over an oil well, gas well, etc., that holds drilling and hoisting tackle.

derringer, der′in•jėr, *n.* [After the inventor, an American gunsmith.] A small pistol of large caliber.

dervish, dėr′vish, *n.* [Turkish *dervish,* Per. *darwesh,* poor, indigent, a dervish.] A Mohammedan friar or monk, who professes extreme poverty, and leads an austere life, partly in monasteries, partly itinerant.

descant, des′kant, *n.* [O.Fr. *deschant,* from L.L. *discantus*—L. *dis,* and *cantus,* singing, a song.] A discourse, discussion, or disputation; *mus.* an addition of a part or parts to a subject or melody; a song or tune with various modulations.—*v.i.* (des•kant′). To discourse, comment, or animadvert freely; to add a part or variation to a melody.

descend, di•send′, *v.i.* [Fr. *descendre* L. *descendere*—*de,* down, *scando,* to climb. SCAN.] To move from a higher to a lower place; to move, come, or go downward; to sink; to run or flow down; to invade or fall upon hostilely; to proceed from a source or origin; to be derived; to pass from one heir to another; to pass, as from general to particular considerations; to lower or degrade one's self; to stoop.—*v.t.* To walk, move, or pass downward upon or along; to pass from the top to the bottom of.—**descendable,** di•sen′da•bl, *a.* Capable of descending by inheritance; descendible.—**descendant,** di•sen′dant, *n.* An individual proceeding from an ancestor in any degree, offspring.—**descendent,** di•sen′dent, *a.* Descending.—**descendible,** di•sen′di•bl, *a.* Capable of being descended or passed down; capable of descending from an ancestor to an heir.—**descent,** di•sent′, *n.* [Fr. *descente.*] The act of descending or passing from a higher to a lower place; inclination downward; slope; declivity; decline, as in station, virtue, quality, or the like; an incursion, invasion, or sudden attack on a country; transmission by succession or inheritance; a proceeding from a progenitor; extraction; lineage; pedigree; a generation; a single degree in the scale of genealogy; issue†; descendants†.

describe, di•skrīb′, *v.t.—described, describing.* [L. *describo,* to write down, to delineate—*de,* down, and *scribo,* to write, as in *ascribe, inscribe,* etc.; akin *scribe, scripture.*] To delineate or mark the form or figure of; to trace out; to form or trace by motion; to show or represent orally or by writing; to depict or portray in words.—*v.i.* To use the power of describing.—**describable,** di•skrī′ba•bl, *a.* Capable of being described.—**describer,** di•skrī′bėr, *n.* One who describes.—**description,** di•skrip′shon, *n.* [L. *descriptio, descriptionis.*] The act of describing; delineation; an account of the properties or appearance of a thing, so that another may form a just conception of it; the combination of qualities which constitute a class, species, or individual; hence, class, species, variety, kind (a person of this *description.*)—**descriptive,** di•skrip′tiv, *a.* Containing description; having the quality of representing.—**descriptively,** di•skrip′tiv•li, *adv.* In a descriptive manner.—**descriptiveness,** di•skrip′tiv•nes, *n.* State of being descriptive.

descry, di•skrī′, *v.t.—descried, descrying.* [O.Fr. *descrier,* to decry, to make an outcry on discovering something. DECRY.] To espy; to discover by the sight; to see or behold from a distance; to examine by the sight (O.T.).

desecrate, des′i•krāt, *v.t.—desecrated, desecrating.* [From L. *de,* from, away, and *sacer,* sacred, being thus the opposite of *consecrate.*] To divert from a sacred purpose or sacred character; to render unhallowed; to profane.—**desecration,** des•i•krā′shon, *n.* The act of desecrating; profanation.

desegregate, dē•seg′re•gāt, *v.t.* To abolish racial segregation.—**desegregation,** dē•seg′re•gā″shon, *n.*

desensitize, dē•sen′si•tiz, *v.t.* To make less sensitive; *photog.* to make less sensitive to light.

desert, dez′ėrt, *a.* [L. *desertus,* pp. of *desero, desertum,* to forsake—*de,* not, and *sero, sertum,* to unite, to join together, from root seen in *series.*] Lying waste; uncultivated and uninhabited; in the natural state and unimproved by man; pertaining to a wilderness (the *desert* air).—*n.* An uninhabited tract of land; a wilderness; a solitude; often a vast sandy, stony, or rocky expanse, almost destitute of moisture and vegetation. *v.t.* (di•zėrt′). To forsake; to leave utterly; to abandon; to quit, leave, or depart from in defiance of duty. *v.i.* To quit a service or post without permission; to run away.—**deserter,** di•zėr′tėr, *n.* One who deserts; particularly, a soldier or seaman who quits the service without permission.—**desertion,** di•zėr′shon, *n.* The act of deserting; the state of being deserted or forsaken.

desert, di•zėrt′, *n.* [O.Fr. *deserte,* merit, from *deservir,* to deserve. DESERVE.] The quality of deserving either reward or punishment; merit or demerit; what is deserved on account of good or evil done; reward or punishment merited; due return.

deserve, di•zėrv′ *v.t.—deserved, deserving.* [O.Fr. *deservir, desservir,* from L. *deservio,* to serve diligently—*de,* intens., and *servio,* to serve.] To merit; to be worthy of, whether of good or evil; to merit by labor, services, or qualities; to be worthy of or call for on account of evil acts or qualities (actions that *deserve* censure).—*v.i.* To merit; to be worthy of or deserving (to *deserve* well of a person).—**deservedly,** di•zėr′ved-li, *adv.* According to desert, whether of good or evil; justly.—**deserver,** di•zėr′vėr, *n.* One who deserves or merits: used generally in a good sense.—**deserving,** di•zėr′ving, *a.* Worthy of reward or praise: meritorious.—**deservingly,** di•zėr′ving•li, *adv.* Meritoriously; with just desert.

deshabille, dez•a•bēl′, *n.* [Fr.—*des*= prefix *dis,* and *habiller,* to dress; akin *habiliment.*] The state of being in undress, or of not being properly or fully dressed.

desiccate, des′i•kāt, *v.t.—desiccated, desiccating.* [L. *desicco,* to dry up—*de,* intens., and *sicco,* to dry, from *siccus,* dry.] To exhaust of moisture; to exhale or remove moisture from; to dry.—*v.i.* To become dry.—**desiccant, desiccative,** des′ik•ant, de•sik′a•tiv, *a.* Drying.—*n.* A medicine or application that dries a sore.—**desiccation,** des•ik•kā′shon, *n.* The act of making dry; the state of being dried.

desiderate, di•sid′ėr•āt, *v.t.* [L. *desidero, desideratum,* to long for, to feel the want of, whence also *desire.*] To feel the want of; to miss; to want; to desire.—**desiderative,** di•sid′ėr•ā•tiv, *a.* Having or implying desire; expressing or denoting desire.—*n.* A verb formed from another verb and expressing a desire of doing the action implied in the primitive verb.—**desideratum,** di•sid′ėr•ā″tum, *n.* pl. **desiderata,** di•sid′ėr•ā″ta. [L.] That which is not possessed, but which is desirable; something much wanted.

design, di•zīn′, *v.t.* [L. *designo,*

to mark out, point out, contrive —*de*, and *signo*, to seal or stamp, from *signum*, a sign. SIGN.] To plan and delineate by drawing the outline or figure of; to sketch, as for a pattern or model; to project or plan; to contrive for a purpose; to form in idea (a scheme); to set apart in intention; to intend; to purpose.—*v.i.* To intend; to purpose. —*n.* A plan or representation of a thing by an outline; first idea represented by lines, as in painting or architecture; a sketch; a drawing; a tracing; a scheme or plan in the mind; purpose; intention; aim; the adaptation of means to a preconceived end; contrivance.—**designate,** dez′ig•nāt, *v.t.*—*designated, designating.* To mark out or indicate by visible lines, marks, description, etc.; to name and settle the identity of; to denominate; to select or distinguish for a particular purpose; to appoint, name, or assign.—**designation,** dez•-ig•nā′shon, *n.* The act of designating; a distinguishing from others; indication; appointment; assignment; distinctive appellation.—**designative,** dez′ig•nā•tiv, *a.* Serving to designate or indicate.—**designator,** dez′ig•nā•-tėr, *n.* One who designates or points out.—**designedly,** di•zī′ned•li, *adv.* By design; purposely; intentionally. —**designer,** di•zī′nėr, *n.* One who designs.—**designing,** di•zī′ning, *pp.* and *a.* Artful; insidious.

desire, di•zīr′, *v.t.*—*desired, desiring.* [Fr. *désirer*, from L. *desidero, desideratum*, to desire (*desiderate* being thus the same word)—prefix *de*, and *sidero*, as in *considero.* CONSIDER.] To wish for the possession or enjoyment of; to long for; to hanker after; to covet; to express a wish to obtain; to ask; to request; to petition.—*v.i.* To be in a state of desire or anxiety.—*n.* [Fr. *désir*, from the verb.] An emotion or excitement of the mind, directed to the attainment or possession of an object from which pleasure is expected; a wish, craving, or longing to obtain or enjoy; the object of desire; that which is desired.—**desirability, desirableness,** di•zī′ra•bil″i•ti, di•-zī′ra•bl•nes, *n.* The state or quality of being desirable.—**desirable,** di•-zī′ra•bl, *a.* Worthy of desire; calculated or fitted to excite a wish to possess.—**desirably,** di•zī′ra•bli, *adv.* In a desirable manner.—**desirous,** di•zī′rus, *a.* Filled with a desire; wishing to obtain; wishful; covetous: often with *of.*

desist, di•zist′, *v.i.* [L. *desisto*, to desist—*de*, away from, and *sisto*, to stand, as in *assist, consist, persist*, etc. STAND.] To cease to act or proceed; to forbear; to leave off; to discontinue; to cease.—**desistance, desistance,**† di•zis′tans, di•zis′tens, *n.* A ceasing to act or proceed; a stopping.

desk, desk, *n.* [A.Sax. *disc*, a table, a dish; L.L. *discus*, a desk, from L. *discus*, Gr. *diskos*, a disc, a quoit; *dais, dish, disk* are the same word.] A kind of table or piece of furniture for the use of writers and readers; a frame or case to be placed on a table for the same purpose.

desolate, des′o•lit, *v.t.*—*desolated, desolating.* [L. *desolo, desolatum*, to leave alone, to forsake—*de*, intens., and *solo*, to lay waste, from *solus*, alone. SOLE, *a.*] To deprive of inhabitants; to make desert; to lay waste; to ruin; to ravage.—*a.* [L. *desolatus*, pp. of *desolo, desolatum.*] Destitute or deprived of inhabitants; desert; uninhabited; laid waste; in a ruinous condition; without a companion; solitary; forsaken; forlorn; lonely.—**desolately,** des′o•lit•li, *adv.* In a desolate manner.—**desolateness,** des′o•lit•nes, *n.* A state of being desolate.—**desolater, desolator,** des′-o•lā•tėr, *n.* One who or that which desolates.—**desolation,** des•o•lā′shon, *n.* The act of desolating; devastation; havoc; ravage; a place depopulated, ravaged, or laid waste; the state of being desolate; gloominess; sadness; melancholy; destitution; ruin.

despair, di•spâr′, *v.i.* [O.Fr. *desperer* (now *desespérer*), from L. *despero*—*de*, not, and *spero*, to hope, allied to Skr. root *sprih*, to desire. *Prosper* is from same root.] To give up all hope or expectation: followed by *of*; to be sunk in utter want of hope. —*n.* The state of being without hope, combined with a dread of coming evil; hopelessness; desperation; that which causes despair; *theol.* loss of hope in the mercy of God.—**despairing,** di•spâr′ing, *a.* Indulging in despair; prone to despair; indicating despair.—**despairingly,** di•-spâr′ing•li, *adv.* In a despairing manner.

desperado, des′pėr•ā″dō, des′pėr•-ā″dō, *n.* A desperate fellow; one fearless or regardless of safety; a reckless ruffian.

desperate, des′pėr•it, *a.* [L. *desperatus*, pp. of *despero*, to despair. DESPAIR.] Without hope‡; regardless of safety; fearless of danger; reduced to extremity and reckless of consequences; frantic; proceeding from despair; reckless; beyond hope; irretrievable; past cure; hopeless (*desperate* disease, situation, undertaking).—**desperately,** des′pėr•it•li, *adv.* In a desperate manner; recklessly; violently; furiously; madly.—**desperateness,** des′pėr•it•nes, *n.* The state or quality of being desperate.—**desperation,** des•pėr•ā′shon, *n.* The state of being desperate; a giving up of hope; disregard of safety or danger; fury; rage; violence.

despicable, des′pi•ka•bl, *a.* [L.L. *despicabilis*, from L. *despicor, despicatus*, to despise, from *despicio.* DESPISE.] Deserving of being despised; contemptible; base; mean; vile; worthless. ∴ Syn. under CONTEMPTIBLE.—**despicableness,** des′-pi•ka•bl•nes, *n.* The quality or state of being despicable.—**despicably,** des′pi•ka•bli, *adv.* In a despicable manner; basely; vilely.

despise, di•spīz′, *v.t.*—*despised, despising.* [O.Fr. *despiz*, pp. of *despire*, to despise, from L. *despicere*, to despise—*de*, down, and *specio*, to look. SPECIES. Akin *despicable, despite.*] To look down upon; to have the lowest opinion of; to contemn; to disdain; to scorn.

despite, di•spīt′, *n.* [O.Fr. *despit*, Mod. Fr. *dépit*, from L. *despectus*, a looking down upon, a despising, from *despicio*, to despise. DESPISE. Hence the shorter form *spite.*] Extreme malice; malignity; contemptuous hate; aversion; spite; defiance with contempt, or contempt of opposition; contemptuous defiance; an act of malice or contempt.—*v.t.*† To vex; to offend; to spite; to tease.—*prep.* In spite of; notwithstanding.—**despiteful,** di•spīt′fu̧l, *a.* Full of despite or spite; malicious; malignant. —**despitefully,** di•spīt′fu̧l•li, *adv.* With despite; maliciously; contemptuously.—**despitefulness,** di•spīt′-fu̧l•nes, *n.*

despoil, di•spoil′, *v.t.* [O.Fr. *despoiller*, L. *despolio*, to rob, plunder—*de*, intens., and *spolio*, to spoil. SPOIL.] To take from by force; to rob; to strip; to divest; to deprive (to *despoil* a person *of* a thing).—**despoiler,** di•-spoi′lėr, *n.* One who despoils; a plunderer.—**despoliation,** di•spō′li•-ā″shon, *n.* The act of despoiling; a stripping.

despond, di•spond′, *v.i.* [L. *despondeo*, to promise in marriage, to promise away, to give up, to despond —*de*, away, and *spondeo, sponsum*, to promise solemnly, whence *sponsor, spouse, respond.*] To be quite cast down; to feel depressed or dejected in mind; to lose hope, heart, or resolution.—**despondency,** di•spon′-den•si, *n.* The state or quality of being despondent.—**despondent,** di•-spon′dent, *a.* Losing courage at the loss of hope; sinking into dejection.—**despondently, despondingly,** di•-spon′dent•li, di•spon′ding•li, *adv.* In a despondent manner.

despot, des′pot, *n.* [Gr. *despotēs, potēs* being from same root as Gr. *posis*, Lith. and Skr. *patis*, lord, husband; L. *potior*, to be master of, *potis*, able, *potestas*, power; Slav. *hospodar, gospodar*, lord, master.] A sovereign or monarch ruling absolutely or without control; a tyrant; one who enforces his will regardless of the interests or feelings of others.—**despotic, despotical,** des•pot′ik, des•pot′i•kal, *a.* Absolute in power; unrestrained by constitution, laws, or men; arbitrary; tyrannical.—**despotically,** des•pot′-i•kal•li, *adv.* In a despotic manner.—**despotism,** des′pot•izm, *n.* Absolute power; unlimited or uncontrolled authority; an arbitrary government; the rule of a despot; absolutism; autocracy; tyranny.

desquamate,† des′kwa•māt, *v.i.* [L. *desquamo, desquamatum*—*de*, off, and *squama*, a scale.] To scale off; to peel off.—**desquamation,** des•kwa•mā′-shon, *n.* A scaling off.

dessert, di•zėrt′, *n.* [Fr. *dessert*, from *desservir*, to clear the table—*des* (=L. *dis*), and *servir*, to serve.] A service of fruits or sweetmeats at the close of a dinner or entertainment.—**dessertspoon,** *n.* A spoon intermediate in size between a tablespoon and teaspoon, used for dessert.

destine, des′tin, *v.t.—destined, destining.* [L. *destino,* to place down, to make firm or secure—*de,* and a root *stan,* a stronger form of *sta,* root of *stare,* to stand, E. *stand, stay,* being of the same root.] To set, ordain, or appoint to a use, purpose, state or place; to fix unalterably, as by a divine decree; to doom; to devote; to appoint inevitably.—**destination,** des•ti•nā′shon, *n.* [L. *destinatio.*] The act of destining; the purpose for which anything is intended or appointed; predetermined object or use; the place to which a thing is appointed; the predetermined end of a journey or voyage.—**destinist,** des′ti•nist, *n.* A believer in destiny.—**destiny,** des′ti•ni, *n.* A person's destined fate or lot; ultimate fate; doom; fortune; invincible necessity; fate; order of things fixed or established by divine decree, or by connection of causes and effects.—*pl.* [*cap*] the Fates.

destitute, des′ti•tūt, *a.* [L. *destitutus,* pp. of *destituo, destitutum,* to set down, to forsake—*de,* down, and *statuo,* to set. STATE, STATUE, etc.] Not having or possessing; wanting: with *of;* not possessing the necessaries of life; in abject poverty; entirely without the means of subsistence.—**destitution,** des•ti•tū′shon, *n.* The state of being destitute; a state of utter want; poverty; indigence; deprivation†.

destroy, di•stroi′, *v.t.* [O.Fr. *destruire* (now *détruire*), from L. *destruo,* to destroy—*de,* not, and *struo,* to pile, to build. STRUCTURE.] To pull down; to knock to pieces; to demolish; to ruin; to annihilate; to put an end to; to cause to cease; to kill or slay; to ravage; to spoil.—**destroyer,** di•stroi′ėr, *n.* One who or that which destroys; a swift class of vessel intended for the destruction of torpedo craft, and itself armed with guns and torpedoes.—**destructible,** di•struk′ti•bl, *a.* Liable to destruction; capable of being destroyed.—**destructibility,** di•struk′ti•bil″i•ti, *n.* The state of being destructible.—**destruction,** di•struk′shon, *n.* [L. *destructio.*] The act of destroying; demolition; a pulling down; subversion; overthrow; ruin, by whatever means, extermination; death; murder; slaughter; the state of being destroyed; cause of destruction; a destroyer (O.T.).—**destructive,** di•struk′tiv, *a.* Causing destruction; having the quality of destroying; having a tendency to destroy; delighting in destruction; ruinous; mischievous; fatal; deadly: with *of* or *to.*—*Destructive distillation,* the distillation of organic products at high temperatures, by which the elements are separated or evolved in new forms, as in making gas from coal.—**destructively,** di•struk′tiv•li, *adv.* In a destructive manner.—**destructiveness,** di•struk′tiv•nes, *n.* The quality of being destructive; a propensity to destroy.—**destructor,** di•struk′tėr, *n.* A destroyer; a furnace for burning refuse.

desuetude, des′wi•tūd, *n.* [L. *desuetudo—de,* not, and *suesco,* to accustom one's self. CUSTOM.] A state of being no longer practiced or customary; disuse; discontinuance of practice, custom, or fashion.

desulfurate, desulfurize, dē•sul′fė•rāt, dē•sul′fė•rīz, *v.t.* To deprive of sulfur.—**desulfuration, desulfurization,** dē•sul′fė•rā″shon, dē•sul′fė•ri•zā″shon, *n.* The act of depriving of sulfur.

desultory, des′ul•to•ri, *a.* [L. *desultorius,* pertaining to a *desultor,* or rider in the circus, from *desilio, desultum,* to leap down—*de,* down, and *salio,* to leap.] Leaping or hopping about‡; passing from one thing or subject to another without order or natural connection; rambling; unconnected; immethodical; inconstant; unsettled; hasty.—**desultorily,** des′ul•to•ri•li, *adv.* In a desultory manner; without method; loosely.—**desultoriness,** des′ul•to•ri•nes, *n.* The character of being desultory.

detach, di•tach′, *v.t.* [Fr. *detacher—de,* not, and the root from which the English noun *tack* is derived TACK, ATTACH.] To separate or disunite; to disengage; to part from; to sever; to separate for a special purpose or service, especially some military purpose.—**detached,** di•tacht′, *a.* Separated; disunited; standing apart or separately; drawn and sent on a separate service.—**detachment,** di•tach′ment, *n.* The act of detaching; a body of troops or number of vessels selected or taken from the main army or fleet and employed on some special service or expedition.

detail, di•tāl′, *v.t.* [Fr. *détailler,* to cut in pieces—*de,* and *tailler,* L.L. *taleare, taliare,* to cut, from L. *talea,* a cutting. RETAIL, TAILOR.] To relate, report, or narrate in particulars; to recite the particulars of; to particularize; to relate minutely and distinctly; *milit.* to appoint to a particular service.—*n.* (dē′tāl). A fact, circumstance, or portion going along with others; an item; a particular; a minute account; a narrative or report of particulars; *milit.* an individual or small body; small detachment on special service.—*In detail,* circumstantially; item by item; individually; part by part.—**detailed,** di•tāld′, *p.* and *a.* Related in particulars; minutely recited; exact; minute; particular.

detain, di•tān′, *v.t.* [Fr. *détenir,* L. *detineo,* to detain—*de,* off, and *teneo,* to hold, as in *contain, retain,* etc., seen also in *tenant, tenacious.* TENANT.] To keep back or from; to withhold; to retain or keep what belongs to another; to keep or restrain from proceeding; to hinder; to stay or stop; to hold in custody.—**detainer,** di•tā′nėr, *n.* One who detains; *law,* a holding or keeping possession of what belongs to another.—**detainment,** di•tān′ment, *n.* The act of detaining; detention.—**detent,** di′tent′, *n.* [L. *detentus,* a keeping back.] A pin, stud, or lever forming a check in a clock, watch, tumblerlock, or other machine; a click or pawl.—**detention,** di•ten′shon, *n.* The act of detaining; a wrongful keeping of what belongs to another; state of being detained; confinement; restraint; delay from necessity or from accident.

detect, di•tekt′, *v.t.* [L. *detego, detectum,* to uncover, expose—*de,* not, and *tego,* to cover. DECK.] To discover; to find out; to bring to light (an error, crime, criminal).—**detectable, detectible,** di•tek′ta•bl, di•tek′ti•bl, *a.* Capable of being or liable to be detected.—**detection,** di•tek′shon, *n.* The act of detecting; the finding out of what is concealed, hidden, or formerly unknown; discovery.—**detective,** di•tek′tiv, *a.* Fitted for or skilled in detecting; employed in detecting crime.—*n.* A species of police officer, having no specific beat nor uniform, whose special duty it is to detect offenses and to apprehend criminals; also a private person who engages to investigate cases, often of a delicate nature, for hire.—**detector,** di•tek′tėr, *n.* One who, or that which, detects or brings to light; a revealer; a discoverer.

detent, detention. See DETAIN.

deter, di•tėr′, *v.t.—deterred, deterring.* [L. *deterreo,* to frighten from, to prevent—*de,* from, and *terreo,* to frighten. TERROR.] To discourage and prevent from acting or proceeding, the preventing agency being something anticipated as difficult, dangerous, or unpleasant.—**deterrent,** di•tėr′ent, *n.* and *a.* The act or cause of deterring; that which deters.

deterge, di•tėrj′, *v.t.—deterged, deterging.* [L. *detergeo—de,* from, and *tergeo, tersum,* to wipe. TERSE.] To cleanse (a sore); to clear away foul or offending matter from.—**detergence, detergency,** di•tėr′jens, di•tėr′jen•si, *n.* The state or quality of being detergent; cleansing or purging power.—**detergent,** di•tėr′jent, *a.* Cleansing; purging.—*n.* Anything that has a strong cleansing power.—**detersive,** di•tėr′siv, *a.* Having power to cleanse; cleansing.—*n.* That which has the power of cleansing; a detergent.

deteriorate, di•tē′ri•o•rāt, *v.i.—deteriorated, deteriorating.* [L. *deterioro, deterioratum,* from *deterior,* worse, from *de,* as *exterior* from *ex, interior* from *in.*] To grow worse or inferior in quality; to be impaired in quality; to degenerate.—*v.t.* To make worse; to reduce in quality.—**deterioration,** di•tē′ri•o•rā″shon, *n.* The process or state of growing worse.

determine, di•tėr′min, *v.t.—determined, determining.* [L. *determino,* to bound, to limit—*de,* intens., and *terminus,* a boundary, whence *terminate, term.*] To fix the bounds of; to set bounds or limits to; to mark off, settle, fix, establish; to end or settle conclusively, as by the decision of a doubtful or controverted point; to settle ultimately; to come to a fixed resolution and intention in respect of; to give a bent or direction to; to influence the choice of; to cause to come to a conclusion or resolution.—*v.i.* To resolve; to conclude; to decide; to settle on some line of conduct; to cease; to terminate.—**determinable,** di•tėr′-mi•na•bl, *a.* Capable of being determined, ascertained, decided, brought to a conclusion.—**determinant,** di•tėr′mi•nant, *a.* Serving to determine; determinative.—*n.* That which determines or causes determination; *math.* the sum of a series of products of several numbers, these products being formed according to certain specified laws; a group of BIOPHORES (which see).—**determinate,** di•tėr′mi•nit, *a.* [L. *determinatus.*] Limited; fixed; definite; established; settled; positive; decisive; conclusive; fixed in purpose; resolute.—*Determinate inflorescence,* in *bot.* same as *centrifugal inflorescence.*—*v.t.*‡ To bring to an end; to terminate (*Shak.*).—**determinately,** di•tėr′mi•nit•li, *adv.* In a determinate manner; precisely; with exact specification; resolutely.—**determinateness,** di•tėr•mi•nit•nes, *n.* The state of being determinate.—**determination,** di•tėr′mi•nā″shon, *n.* The act of determining or deciding; decision in the mind; firm resolution; settled purpose; the mental habit of settling upon some line of action with a fixed purpose to adhere to it; adherence to aims or purposes; resoluteness; *chem.* the ascertainment of the exact proportion of any substance in a compound body; *med.* afflux; tendency of blood to flow to any part more copiously than is normal.—**determinative,** di•tėr′mi•nā•tiv, *a.* Having power to determine or direct to a certain end; directing; conclusive; limiting; bounding; having the power of ascertaining precisely; employed in determining.—**determined,** di•tėr′-mind, *a.* Having a firm or fixed purpose; manifesting firmness or resolution; resolute.—**determinedly,** di•tėr′mind•li, *adv.* In a determined manner.—**determiner,** di•tėr′mi•nėr, *n.* One who decides or determines.—**determinism,** di•tėr′mi•nizm, *n.* A system of philosophy which denies liberty of action to man, holding that the will is not free, but is invincibly determined by motives.

deterrent. See DETER.

detersive, etc. See DETERGE.

detest, di•test′, *v.t.* [L. *detestor,* to invoke a deity in cursing, to detest—*de,* intens., and *testor,* to call to witness, from *testis,* a witness; so *attest, contest,* also *testify, testament.*] To abhor; to abominate; to hate extremely.—**detestable,** di•tes′ta•bl, *a.* Extremely hateful; abominable; very odious; deserving abhorrence.—**detestableness, detestability,** di•tes′ta•bl•nes, di•tes′ta•bil″i•ti, *n.* The state or quality of being detestable; extreme hatefulness.—**detestably,** di•tes′ta•bli, *adv.* In a detestable manner.—**detestation,** dē•tes•tā′-shon, *n.* Extreme hatred; abhorrence; loathing.—**detester,** di•tes′-tėr, *n.* One who detests.

dethrone, dē•thrōn′, *v.t.*—*dethroned, dethroning.* [Prefix *de,* from, and *throne.*] To remove or drive from a throne; to depose; to divest of royal authority and dignity; to divest of rule or power, or of supreme power.—**dethronement,** dē•thrōn′ment, *n.* Removal from a throne; deposition.—**dethroner,** dē•thrō′nėr, *n.* One who dethrones.

detonate, det′ō•nāt, *v.t.* and *i.*—*detonated, detonating.* [L. *detono, detonatum,* to thunder—*de,* and *tono,* to thunder.] To explode or cause to explode; to burn with a sudden report.—**detonation,** det•o•nā′shon, *n.* An explosion or sudden report made by the inflammation of certain combustible bodies.—**detonator,** det′o•nā•tėr, *n.* That which detonates; the device by which fulminate of mercury is made to explode the charge in a torpedo or submarine mine.

detour, de•tör′, *n.* [Fr. *détour*—prefix *de,* and *tour*=E. *turn.*] A roundabout or circuitous way; a going round instead of by a direct road or route.

detract, di•trakt′, *v.t.* [L. *detracto*—*de,* from, and *tracto,* to draw, from *traho, tractum,* to draw, whence *tract, trace,* etc.] To take away from a whole; to withdraw; to disparage†.—*v.i.* To take away a part; especially, to take away reputation; to derogate: followed by *from* (this *detracts from* his merit).—**detractor,** di•trak′tėr, *n.* One who detracts; a detractor.—**detraction,** di•trak′-shon, *n.* [L. *detractio.*] The act of detracting; an attempt, by calumny, or injurious or carping statements, to take something from the reputation of another; envious or malicious depreciation of a person, or denial of his merits.—**detractive,** di•trak′tiv, *a.* Having the quality or power to take away; having the character of detraction.—**detractor,** di•trak′tėr, *n.* One who uses detraction; one who tries to take somewhat from the reputation of another injuriously; a muscle that draws the part to which it is attached away from some other part.—**detractory,** di•trak′to•ri, *a.* Containing detraction; depreciatory.

detrain, dē•trān′, *v.t.* To remove from a railroad train; to cause to leave a train: said especially of bodies of men (to *detrain* troops).—*v.i.* To quit a railroad train.

detriment, det′ri•ment, *n.* [L. *detrimentum,* from *detero, detritum,* to rub off or down, to wear—*de,* down, and *tero,* to rub, whence *trite.*] A certain degree of loss, damage, or injury; injurious or prejudicial effect; harm; diminution.—**detrimental,** det•ri•men′tal, *a.*

detritus, di•trī′tus, *n.* [L. *detritus,* worn down. DETRIMENT.] *Geol.* a mass of substances worn off or detached from solid bodies by attrition; disintegrated materials of rocks.

detrude, di•tröd′, *v.t.*—*detruded, detruding.* [L. *detrudo*—*de,* down, and *trudo,* to thrust.] To thrust down; to push down.—**detrusion,** di•trö′zhon, *n.* The act of thrusting or driving down.

detruncate, di•trung′kāt, *v.t.*—*detruncated, detruncating.* [L. *detrunco*—*de,* and *trunco,* to maim, *truncus,* cut short. TRUNK.] To cut off; to lop; to shorten by cutting.—**detruncation,** di•trung•kā′shon, *n.* The act of detruncating.

deuce, dūs, *n.* [Fr. *deux,* two.] A playing card or a die with two spots; the two at dice, being the lowest throw.

deuce, dūs, *n.* [Perhaps from L. *deus,* God, used as an interjection; but comp. L.G. *duus,* G. *daus,* used similarly; Armor. *dus, teuz,* a goblin.] The devil; perdition: used only in exclamatory or interjectional phrases.

deuterium, dū•tēr′i•um, *n.* [N.L., from Gr. *deuteros,* second.] A nonradioactive isotope of hydrogen that has twice the mass of ordinary hydrogen.

deuterogamy, dū•tėr•og′a•mi, *n.* [Gr. *deuteros,* second, and *gamos,* marriage.] A second marriage after the death of the first husband or wife.—**deuterogamist,** dū•tėr•og′a•mist, *n.* One who marries a second time.

deuteron, dū′ter•on, *n.* *Phys.* the nucleus of the deuterium atom; a particle with one positive charge.

Deuteronomy, dū•tėr•on′o•mi, *n.* [Gr. *deuteros,* second, and *nomos,* law.] Lit. the second law or second statement of the law, the fifth book of the Pentateuch.

deutoplasm, dū′to•plazm, *n.* *Biol.* that portion of the yolk of ova which furnishes nourishment for the embryo (the *protoplasm*).

devaluate, dē•val′ū•āt, *v.t.* [Prefix *de,* and *value.*] To reduce the value of; to fix a lower legal value on currency.—**devaluation,** dē•val′ū•ā″shon, *n.*—**devalue,** dē•val′ū, *v.t.* To devaluate.

devastate, dev′as•tāt, *v.t.*—*devastated, devastating.* [L. *devasto, devastatum,* to lay waste—*de,* intens., and *vasto,* to lay waste. WASTE.] To lay waste; to ravage; to desolate.—**devastation,** dev•as•tā′shon, *n.* [L. *devastatio.*] The act of devastating; the state of being devastated; ravage; havoc; desolation.—**devastator,** dev•as•tā′tėr, *n.*

develop, di•vel′up, *v.t.* [Fr. *développer* O.Fr. *desveloper*—prefix *des,* L. *dis,* apart.] To unfold gradually, to lay open part by part; to disclose or show all the ramifications of; *biol.* to make to pass through the process of natural evolution; in photography, to bring out the latent image on a sensitized surface by the action of chemical agents.—*v.i.* To be unfolded; to become manifest in all its parts; to advance from one stage to another by a process of natural or inherent evolution; to grow or expand by a natural process; to be evolved; to proceed or come forth naturally from some vivifying source.—**developable,** di•vel′up•a•bl, *a.* Capable of developing or of being developed.—**developer,** di•vel′up•ėr, *n.* One who or that which develops or unfolds.—**development,**

di•vel′up•ment, *n.* The act or process of developing; unfolding; the unraveling of a plot; a gradual growth or advancement through progressive changes; the organic changes which take place in animal and vegetable bodies, from their embryo state until they arrive at maturity; *photog.* the process following exposure, by which the image on the plate is rendered visible.—*Development theory, biol.* the theory that plants and animals are capable of advancing, in successive generations and through an infinite variety of stages, from a lower to a higher state of existence, and that the more highly organized forms at present existing are the descendants of lower forms.

deviate, dē′vi•āt, *v.i.—deviated, deviating.* [L. *devio, deviatum—de,* from, and *via,* way; seen also in *convey, obvious, voyage,* etc.] To turn aside or wander from the common or right way, course, or line; to diverge; to err; to swerve; to vary from uniform state.—*v.t.* To cause to deviate.—**deviation,** dē•vi•ā′shon, *n.* A turning aside from the right way, course, or line; variation from a common or established rule or standard.—*Deviation of the compass,* the deviation of a ship's compass from the true magnetic meridian, caused by the near presence of iron.

device, di•vīs′, *n.* [O.Fr. *devise,* a device; Fr. *deviser,* to imagine, devise; from L. *divido, divisum,* to divide. DIVIDE.] That which is formed by design or invented; a scheme, contrivance, stratagem, project; invention or faculty of devising (*Shak.*); something fancifully conceived, as an ornamental design; an emblem or figure representative of a family, person, action, or quality, with or without a motto.

devil, dev′il, *n.* [A.Sax. *deófol,* from L. *diabolus,* Gr. *diabolos,* the accuser, from *diaballō,* to accuse.] An evil spirit or being; the evil one, represented in Scripture as the traducer, father of lies, tempter, etc.; a very wicked person; a ferocious marsupial animal of Tasmania; a printer's errand boy; a machine through which cotton or wool is first passed to prepare it for the carding machines; a teasing machine; a machine for cutting up rags and old cloth into flock and for other purposes; *cookery,* a dish, as a bone with some meat on it, grilled and seasoned with pepper.—*The devil,* is used as an expletive and also in various colloquial expressions, being equivalent to ruin or destruction, something very annoying or harassing, the deuce.—*Devil's advocate, R. Cath. Ch.* a person appointed to raise doubts against the claims of a candidate for canonization.—*v.t.—devilled, devilling.* To pepper or season excessively and broil; to tease or cut up by an instrument called a devil.—**devilish,** dev′il•ish, *a.* Partaking of the qualities of the devil; pertaining to the devil; diabolical; very evil and mischievous.—**devilishly,** dev′il•ish•li, *adv.* In a devilish manner.—**devilishness,** dev′il•ish•nes, *n.* The quality of being devilish.—**devilment,** dev′il•ment, *n.* Trickery; roguishness; devilry; prank. (*Colloq.*)—**devilry,** dev′il•ri, *n.* Devilment; extreme wickedness; wicked mischief.

devious, dē′vi•us, *a.* [L. *devius—de,* and *via,* way. DEVIATE.] Out of the common way or track; following circuitous or winding paths; rambling; erring; going astray.—**deviously,** dē′vi•us•li, *adv.* In a devious manner.—**deviousness,** dē′vi•us•nes, *n.* The character or state of being devious.

devise, di•vīz′, *v.t.—devised, devising.* [Fr. *deviser,* to devise or invent, to dispose of. See DEVICE.] To invent, contrive, or form in the mind; to strike out by thought; to plan; to scheme; to excogitate; *law,* to give or bequeath by will.—*v.t.* To consider; to contrive; to lay a plan; to form a scheme.—*n.* The act of bequeathing by will; a will or testament; a share of estate bequeathed. —**devisable,** di•vī′za•bl, *a.* Capable of being devised.—**devisee,** di•vī•zē′, *n.* The person to whom a devise is made.—**deviser,** di•vī′zėr, *n.* One who devises; a contriver; an inventor.—**devisor,** di•vī′zėr, *n.* One who gives by will.

devitalize, dē•vī′tal•īz, *v.t.* To deprive of vitality; to take away life from.

devitrify, dē•vit′ri•fī, *v.t.—devitrified, devitrifying.* To deprive of the character or appearance of glass.—**devitrification,** dē•vit′ri•fi•kā″shon, *n.* The act of devitrifying.

devoid, di•void′, *a.* [Prefix *de,* out, from, and *void.*] Destitute; not possessing: with *of* before the thing absent.

devoir, dev•wär′, *n.* [Fr., from L. *debere,* to owe, whence *debt.*] Service or duty; an act of civility or respect; respectful notice due to another.

devolution, dev•ō•lū′shon, *n.* [L.L. *devolutio.*] The act of rolling down; the act of devolving, transferring, or handing over; a passing to or falling upon a successor.

devolve, di•volv′, *v.t.—devolved, devolving.* [L. *devolvo, devolutum—de,* and *volvo,* to roll, seen also in *revolve, convolve, volume, voluble,* etc.] To roll down; to move from one person to another; to deliver over, or from one possessor to a successor.—*v.i.* To roll down; hence, to pass from one to another; to fall by succession from one possessor to his successor.

Devonian, de•vō′ni•an, *a.* Of or pertaining to *Devonshire* in England; *geol.* a term applied to a great portion of the paleozoic strata of North and South Devon, lying between the Silurian and carboniferous rocks, and sometimes used as synonymous with 'old red sandstone'.

devote, di•vōt′, *v.t.—devoted, devoting.* [L. *devoveo, devotum,* to vow anything to a deity, to devote—*de,* intens., and *voveo,* to vow. VOW, VOTE.] To appropriate by vow; to set apart or dedicate by a solemn act; to consecrate; to give up wholly; to direct the attention wholly or chiefly (to *devote* one's self or one's time to science); to give up; to doom; to consign over (to *devote* one to destruction).—**devoted,** di•vō′ted, *a.* Strongly attached to a person or cause; ardent; zealous.—**devotedness,** di•vō′ted•nes, *n.* The state of being devoted.—**devotee,** dev•ō•tē′, *n.* One who is wholly devoted; a votary; particularly, one who is superstitiously given to religious duties and ceremonies.—**devotement,** di•vōt′ment, *n.* The act of devoting.—**devoter,** di•vō′tėr, *n.* One that devotes.—**devotion,** di•vō′shun, *n.* The state of being devoted or set apart for a particular purpose; a yielding of the heart and affections to God, with reverence, faith, and piety, in religious duties, particularly in prayer and meditation; devoutness; performance of religious duties: now generally used in the plural; ardent attachment to a person or a cause; attachment manifested by constant attention; earnestness; ardor; eagerness.—**devotional,** di•vō′shon•al, *a.* Pertaining to devotion; used in devotion; suited to devotion.—**devotionally,** di•vō′shon•al•li, *adv.* In a devotional manner; toward devotion.

devour, di•vour′, *v.t.* [Fr. *dévorer,* L. *devorare—de,* intens., and *voro* to eat greedily, whence *voracious.*] To eat up; to eat with greediness; to eat ravenously; to destroy or consume; to waste.—*v.i.*† To act as a devourer; to consume (O.T.).—**devourer,** di•vou′rėr, *n.* One who devours.—**devouringly,** di•vou′ring•li, *adv.* In a devouring manner.

devout, di•vout′, *a.* [Fr. *dévot,* devout; L. *devotus.* DEVOTE.] Yielding a solemn and reverential devotion to God in religious exercises; pious; devoted to religion; religious; expressing devotion or piety; solemn; earnest.—**devoutly,** di•vout′li, *adv.* In a devout manner; piously; religiously; earnestly.—**devoutness,** di•vout′nes, *n.* The quality or state of being devout.

dew, dū, *n.* [A.Sax. *deáw,* D. *dauw,* Dan. *dug,* G. *thau*—dew.] The aqueous vapor or moisture which is deposited in small drops, especially during the night, from the atmosphere, on the surfaces of bodies when they have become colder than the surrounding atmosphere. —*v.t.* To wet with dew; to bedew. —**dewberry,** *n.* A species of bramble, the fruit of which is black, with a bluish bloom, and an agreeable acid taste.—**dewclaw,** *n.* The uppermost claw in a dog's foot, smaller than the rest, and not touching the ground.—**dewdrop,** dū•drop, *n.* A drop or spangle of dew.—**dewlap,** dū′lap, *n.* The fold of skin that hangs from the throat of oxen or cows, or a similar appendage in other animals.—**dewlapped,** dū′lapt, *a.* Furnished with a dewlap, or similar appendage. (*Shak*).—**dew point,** *n.*

The temperature when dew begins to be deposited, varying with the humidity of the atmosphere.—**dewy,** dū′i, *a.* Of or pertaining to dew; partaking of the nature or appearance of dew; like dew; moist with, or as with, dew; accompanied with dew; abounding in dew; falling gently, or refreshing, like dew (*dewy* sleep).

dexter, deks′tėr, *a.* [L. *dexter,* right, on the right side, akin to Gr. *dexios,* Skr. *daksha,* on the right hand.] Pertaining to or situated on the right hand; right as opposed to left. —**dexterity,** deks•ter′i•ti, *n.* [L. *dexteritas.*] Ability to use the right hand more readily than the left†; righthandedness†; expertness; skill; that readiness in performing an action which proceeds from experience or practice, united with activity or quick motion; readiness of mind or mental faculties, as in contrivance, or inventing means to accomplish a purpose; promptness in devising expedients.—**dexterous,** deks′tėr•us, *a.* Characterized by dexterity; skillful and active with the hands; adroit; prompt in contrivance and management; expert; quick at inventing expedients; skillful; done with dexterity. Sometimes written **dextrous,** deks′trus.—**dexterously,** deks′tėr•us•li, *adv.* With dexterity; adroitly.—**dexterousness,** deks′tėr•us•nes, *n.* Dexterity.—**dextral,** deks′tral, *a.* Right as opposed to left.—**dextrin,** deks′trin, *n.* A carbohydrate formed when starch is decomposed by heat, acids, or enzymes.—**dextrorse,** deks•trors′, *a.* [L. *dextrorsum,* towards the right side—*dexter,* right, and *vorsum,* for *versum,* turned.] Turned towards the right; rising from left to right, as a spiral line, helix, or climbing plant.—**dextrose,** deks′trōs, *n.* A name for grape sugar, from its solution rotating the plane of polarization of a ray of light to the right.

dextran, deks′tran, *n.* A polymer of glucose, produced by enzyme action of *Leuconostoc* bacteria in sucrose; used as a blood-plasma substitute.

dey, dā, *n.* [Turk, *dâi,* an uncle.] The title of the old governors or sovereigns of Algiers, Tunis, and Tripoli, under the Sultan of Turkey.

dhole, dōl, *n.* The Singalese name for the wild dog of India.

dhow, dou, *n.* An Arab vessel, generally with one mast, from 150 to 250 tons burden, employed in mercantile trading, and also in carrying slaves.

diabetes, dī•a•bē′tez, *n.* [Gr. *diabanō,* —*dia,* and *bano,* to pass through.] An abnormal metabolic condition marked by an excessive discharge of urine.—*Diabetes insipidus,* a disorder of the pituitary gland, marked by excessive thirst.—*Diabetes mellitus,* a disorder of metabolism marked by excessive amounts of sugar in the blood.—**diabetic,** dī•a•bē′tik, *a.* Pertaining to diabetes.

diablerie, diablery, di•ab′lėr•i, *n.* [Fr. *diablerie,* from *diable,* devil.] Devilry; mischief; wickedness; sorcery; witchcraft.

diabolic, diabolical, dī•a•bol′ik, dī•a•bol′i•kal, *a.* [L. *diabolus,* the devil. DEVIL.] Devilish; pertaining to the devil; infernal; impious; atrocious.—**diabolically,** dī•a•bol′i•kal•li, *adv.* In a diabolical manner.—**diabolicalness,** dī•a•bol′i•kal•nes, *n.* The state or quality of being diabolical.

diacaustic, dī•a•kąs′tik, *a.* [Gr. prefix *dia,* through, and E. *caustic.*] *Math.* belonging to a species of caustic curves formed by refraction.—*n.* *Math.* a diacaustic curve; *med.* cautery by a burning glass.

diachylon, diachylum, dī•ak′i•lon, dī•ak′i•lum, *n.* [Gr. *dia,* through, and *chylos,* juice.] *Med.* a plaster originally composed of the juices of herbs, now made of olive oil and finely pounded litharge.

diaconal, dī•ak′o•nal, *a.* [L. *diaconus,* Gr. *diakonos,* a deacon.] Pertaining to a deacon.—**diaconate,** dī•ak′o•nāt, *n.* The office or dignity of a deacon; a body of deacons.

diacritical, diacritic, dī•a•krit′i•kal, dī•a•krit′ik, *a.* [Gr. *diakritikos*—*dia,* and *krinō,* to separate.] Separating or distinguishing; distinctive.—*Diacritical mark,* a mark used in some languages to distinguish letters which are similar in form.

diactinic, dī•ak•tin′ik, *a.* [Gr. *dia,* through, and *aktis, aktinos,* a ray.] Capable of transmitting the actinic or chemical rays of the sun.

diadelph, dī′a•delf, *n.* [Gr. *di,* twice, and *adelphos,* a brother.] *Bot.* a plant the stamens of which are united into two bodies or bundles by their filaments.—**diadelphous,** dī•a•del′fus, *a.* *Bot.* having the stamens united in two bundles.

diadem, dī′a•dem, *n.* [Gr. *diadēma*—*dia,* and *deō,* to bind.] A head band or fillet formerly worn as a badge of royalty; anything worn on the head as a mark or badge of royalty; a crown; a coronet.—*v.t.*† To adorn with or as with a diadem; to crown.

diaeresis, dī•e′re•sis, *n.* [Gr. *diairesis,* from *diaireō,* to divide.] Separation of one syllable into two; a mark which signifies such a division, as in naïve, aërial.

diagnosis, dī•ag•nō′sis, *n.* [Gr. *diagnōsis*—*dia,* through, and *gignōskō,* to know.] Scientific discrimination of any kind; *med.* the discrimination of diseases by their distinctive marks or symptoms.—**diagnose,** dī•ag•nōs′, *v.t.*—*diagnosed, diagnosing.* To discriminate or ascertain from symptoms the true nature of.—**diagnostic,** dī•ag•nos′tik, *a.* Distinguishing; characteristic; indicating the nature of a disease.—*n.* A sign or symptom by which a disease is known.—*pl.* The department of medicine which treats of the diagnosis of diseases; symptomatology.

diagonal, dī•ag′o•nal, *a.* [Gr. *diagōnios,* from angle to angle—*dia,* and *gōnia,* an angle or corner.] Extending from one angle to the opposite of a quadrilateral figure, and dividing it into two triangles; lying in this direction.—*n.* A straight line drawn between the opposite angles of a quadrilateral figure.—**diagonally,** dī•ag′o•nal•li, *adv.*

diagram, dī′a•gram, *n.* [Gr. *diagramma*—*dia,* and *graphō,* to write.] A figure or drawing for the purpose of demonstrating the properties of any geometrical figure, as a triangle, circle, etc.; any illustrative figure that explains something.—*v.t.*—*diagramed, diagrammed, diagraming, diagramming.* To represent by, or make, a diagram. —**diagrammatic,** dī′a•gram•mat″ik, *a.* Pertaining to or partaking of the nature of a diagram.—**diagrammatically,** dī′a•gram•mat″i•kal•li, *adv.*

dial, dī′al, *n.* [L.L. *dialis,* daily, from L. *dies,* a day, whence also *diary, diurnal, journal,* etc.] An instrument for showing the hour of the day from the shadow thrown by means of a *stile* or *gnomon* upon a surface; the face of a watch, clock, or other timekeeper; any somewhat similar plate or face on which a pointer or index moves, as in a gas meter or telegraphic instrument.— *v.t. dialed, dialing.* To use or measure with, or as with, a dial.—**dialing,** dī′al•ing, *n.* The art of constructing dials; the science which explains the principles of measuring time by the sundial.

dialect, dī′a•lekt, *n.* [Fr. *dialecte,* from Gr. *dialektos*—*dia,* and *legō,* to speak.] The form or idiom of a language peculiar to a province or to a limited region or people, as distinguished from the literary language of the whole people; language; speech or manner of speaking.—**dialectal,** dī•a•lek′tal, *a.* Pertaining to a dialect.—**dialectic, dialectical,** dī′a•lek′tik, dī•a•lek′ti•kal, *a.* Pertaining to a dialect or dialects; pertaining to dialectics.—**dialectically,** dī•a•lek′ti•kal•li, *adv.* In a dialectic manner.—**dialectician,** dī•a•lek•tish″an, *n.* One skilled in dialectics; a logician; a reasoner.—**dialectics,** dī•a•lek′tiks, *n.* [Gr. *dialektike* (*techne*), the art of discussing.] The art of reasoning or disputing; that branch of logic which teaches the rules and modes of reasoning, or of distinguishing truth from error; the art of using forms of reasoning so as to make fallacies pass for truth; wordfence. Also **dialectic,** in same sense.

diallage, dī′a•lij, *n.* [Gr. *diallage,* an interchange, difference.] A silicomagnesian mineral of a lamellar or foliated structure, akin to augite and exhibiting sometimes a beautiful green color, at other times brownish or yellowish; it includes bronzite and hypersthene.

dialogue, dī′a•log, *n.* [Fr. *dialogue,* from Gr. *dialogos,* dialogue, from *dialegomai,* to dispute—*dia,* and *legō,* to speak.] A conversation between two or more persons; a formal conversation in theatrical performances; a composition in which two or more persons are represented as conversing on some topic.—**dialogistic,** dī•al′o•jis″tik, *a.* Pertaining to, or partaking of the nature of, a dialogue; having the form of a dialogue.—**dialogist,** dī-al′o•jist, *n.* A speaker in a dialogue; a writer of dialogues.

dialysis, dī-al′i•sis, *n.* [Gr. *dialysis,* a separation—*dia,* and *lyō,* to dissolve.] *Chem.* the act or process of separating the crystalloid elements of a body from the colloid by diffusion through a parchment-paper septum; *med.* debility; also, a solution of continuity; in *writing* or *printing,* same as *Diaeresis.*—**dialyze,** dī′a•līz, *v.t.* To separate by a dialyzer.—**dialyzer,** dī′a•li•zėr, *n.* The parchment paper, or septum, stretched over a ring used in the operation of dialysis.—**dialytic,** dī•a•lit′ik, *a.* Pertaining to dialysis.

diamagnetic, dī′a•mag•net″ik, *a.* [Prefix *dia,* and *magnetic.*] Applied to a class of substances which, when under the influence of magnetism, and freely suspended, take a position at right angles to the magnetic meridian, that is, point east and west.—**diamagnetism,** dī•a•mag′ne•tizm, *n.* The characteristic phenomena of diamagnetic bodies.

diameter, dī•am′e•tėr, *n.* [Gr. *diametros*—*dia,* and *metron,* measure.] A straight line passing through the center of a circle or other curvilinear figure, terminated by the circumference, and dividing the figure into two equal parts; a straight line through the center of any body; the measure transversely through a cylindrical body; thickness.—**diametric, diametrical, diametral,** di•a•met′rik, di•a•met′ri•kal, di•a•met′ral, *a.* Of or pertaining to a diameter; directly opposed.—**diametrically,** di•a•met′ri•kal•li, *adv.* In a diametrical direction or position.

diamond, dī′a•mond, *n.* [Fr. *diamant,* corrupted from *adamant* (which see).] A most valuable gem of extreme hardness, usually clear and transparent, but sometimes yellow, blue, green, black, etc., consisting of pure carbon; a small diamond fixed to a handle and used for cutting glass; a very small variety of printing type; a four-sided figure with the sides equal or nearly so, and having two obtuse and two acute angles, called also a lozenge or rhomb; one of a set of playing cards marked with one or more such figures in red.—*Black diamond,* a term applied colloquially to coal.—*a.* Resembling a diamond; consisting of diamonds; set with a diamond or diamonds.—**diamond type,** A kind of printing type.

diander, dī•an′dėr, *n.* [Gr. *di,* twice, and *anēr, andros,* a male.] *Bot.* a plant having two stamens.—**diandrous,** dī•an′drus, *a. Bot.* having two stamens.

dianoetic, dī′a•nō•et″ik, *a.* [Gr. *dianoētikos,* from *dia,* and *noeō,* to revolve in the mind.] Capable of thought; thinking; intellectual.

diapason, dī•a•pā′zon, *n.* [Gr. *diapasōn,* lit. through all (notes).] *Mus.* an old Greek term for the octave; proportion in the constituent parts of an octave; harmony; the entire compass of a voice or an instrument; a rule or scale by which the pipes of organs, the holes of flutes, etc., are correctly adjusted; a name of certain stops in the organ, given because they extend through the scales of the instrument.

diaper, dī′a•pėr, *n.* [Fr. *diapré,* pp. of *diaprer,* to variegate with colors; from L.L. *diasprus,* a kind of precious cloth, from It. *diaspro,* jasper. JASPER.] A fabric, either linen or cotton, or a mixture of the two, upon the surface of which a figured pattern is produced; an infant's breechcloth.—*v.i.* To furnish with a diaper pattern; to put a diaper on.

diaphane, dī′a•fān, *n.* [Gr. *dia,* through, and *phainō,* to show.] A woven silk stuff with transparent and colorless figures.—**diaphanous,** dī•af′a•nus, *a.* Having power to transmit rays of light, as glass; pellucid; transparent; clear.—**diaphanously,** dī•af′a•nus•li, *adv.* In a diaphanous manner.

diaphoresis, dī′a•fo•rē″sis, *n.* [Gr. *diaphorēsis,* perspiration—*dia,* and *phoreō,* to carry.] *Med.* a greater degree of perspiration than is natural.—**diaphoretic,** dī′a•fo•ret″ik, *a.* Having the power to increase perspiration.—**diaphoretic,** *n.* A medicine which promotes perspiration; a sudorific.

diaphragm, dī′a•fram, *n.* [Gr. *diaphragma,* a partition—*dia,* and *phrassō,* I fence in, I enclose.] The midriff, a muscle separating the chest or thorax from the abdomen, a partition or dividing substance, as a circular ring used in telescopes, etc., to cut off marginal portions of a beam of light; a calcareous plate which divides the cavity of certain molluscous shells.—**diaphragmatic,** dī′a•frag•mat″ik, *a.* Appertaining to or having the character of a diaphragm.

diarchy, dī′är•ki, *n.* [Gr. *di,* double, and *archē,* rule.] A form of government in which the supreme power is invested in two persons.

diarrhea, dī•a•rē′a, *n.* [Gr. *diarrhoia*—*dia,* through, and *rheō,* to flow.] An ailment consisting in a morbidly frequent evacuation of the intestines.—**diarrhetic,** dī•a•rē′tik, *a.* Producing diarrhea.

diarthrosis, dī•är•thrō′sis, *n.* [Gr., from *dia,* through, asunder, and *arthron,* a joint.] *Anat.* a joint in which the bones revolve freely in every direction, as in the shoulder joint.

diary, dī′a•ri, *n.* [L. *diarium,* a daily allowance of food, a journal, from *dies,* a day, whence also *dial, diurnal, journal.*] A book in which daily events or transactions are noted; a journal; a blank book dated for the record of daily memoranda.—**diarist,** dī′a•rist, *n.* One who keeps a diary.

diastase, dī′as•tās, *n.* [Gr. *diastasis,* separation—*dia,* asunder, and root *sta,* to stand.] A substance existing in barley and oats after germination: so called because in solution it possesses the property of causing starch to break up at 150° Fahr., transforming it first into dextrin and then into sugar.

diastole, dī•as′to•lē, *n.* [Gr. *diastolē,* a drawing asunder—*dia,* and *stellō,* to set.] *Physiol.* the dilatation of the heart with blood: opposed to *systole,* or contraction; *gram.* the lengthening of a syllable that is naturally short.—**diastolic,** dī•a•stol′ik, *a.* Pertaining to or produced by the diastole.

diatessaron, dī•a•tes′ar•on, *n.* [Gr. *dia tessaron,* by four.] A harmony of the four gospels.

diathermic, dī•a•thėr′mik, *a.* [Gr. *dia,* and *therme,* heat.] Pertaining to diathermy.—**diathermy,** dī″a•thėr′mi, *n.* The application of electric current to produce heat in tissues below the skin for therapeutic purposes.

diathesis, dī•ath′e•sis, *n.* [Gr.] *Med.* particular disposition or habit of body, good or bad; predisposition to certain diseases rather than to others.—**diathetic,** dī•a•thet′ik, *a.* Pertaining to diathesis; constitutional.

diatom, dī′a•tom, *n.* [Gr. *dia,* through, and *tomē,* a cutting, from forming often loosely connected chains.] One of a natural order of microscopic vegetable organisms with siliceous coverings, found in fresh and salt water, and in moist places.—**diatomaceous,** dī′a•to•mā″shus, *a.* Pertaining to diatoms; containing or made up of the siliceous parts of diatoms.

diatomic, dī•a•tom′ik, *a.* [Gr. *di,* twice, and *atomos,* an atom.] *Chem.* consisting of two atoms.—**diatomite,** dī•at′o•mīt, *n.* A name for certain earthy deposits, consisting of the minute siliceous parts of diatoms, forming when dry a fine powder, and used in making dynamite, glaze for pottery, polishing, etc.

diatonic, dī•a•ton′ik, *a.* [Gr. *dia,* by or through, and *tonos,* sound.] *Mus.* applied to the major or minor scales, or to chords, intervals, and melodic progressions belonging to one scale.—**diatonically,** dī•a•ton′i•kal•li, *adv.* In a diatonic manner.

diatribe, dī′a•trīb, *n.* [Gr. *diatribē,* a discussion, amusement, passing of time—*dia,* through, and *tribō,* to rub.] A continued disputation; a lengthy invective; a harangue in which a person inveighs against something.

dibasic, dī•bā′sik, *a.* [Gr. *di,* two and *basis,* base.] Containing two hydrogen atoms that can be replaced by basic atoms or radicals.

dibble, dib′l, *n.* [From *dib,* a form of *dip.*] A pointed instrument used in gardening and agriculture to make holes for planting seeds, bulbs, etc. Also called *Dibber* (dib′ėr).—*v.t.*—*dibbled, dibbling.* To plant with a dibble; to dig with a dibble.

dibranchiate, dī•brang′ki•āt, *a.* [Gr. *di,* double, and *branchia,* gills.] Having two gills.—*n.* A member of an order of cephalopods in which the branchiae are two in number, one situated on each side of the body.

dicast, dī′kast, *n.* [Gr. *dikastēs,* from

dikē justice.] *Greek antiq.* an officer answering nearly to the modern juryman.

dice, dīs, *n.* pl. of *die,* for gaming. DIE.—*v.i.*—*diced, dicing.* To play with dice.—**dicer,** dī′sėr, *n.* A player at dice.

dichogamy, dī•kog′a•mi, *n.* [Gr. *dicha,* in two parts, and *gamos,* marriage.] *Bot.* a provision in hermaphrodite flowers to prevent self-fertilization, as where the stamens and pistils within the same flower are not matured at the same time.—**dichogamous,** dī•kog′a•mus, *a. Bot.* exhibiting or characterized by dichogamy.

dichotomous, dī•kot′o•mus, *a.* [Gr. *dicha,* doubly, by pairs, and *temnō,* to cut.] *Bot.* regularly dividing by pairs from top to bottom.—**dichotomy,** dī•kot′o•mi, *n.*—A cutting in two‡; division‡; division or distribution of ideas by pairs; *bot.* a mode of branching by constant forking, as when the stem of a plant divides into two branches, each branch into two others, and so on.

dichroism, dī′krō•izm, *n.* [Gr. *di,* twice, and *chroa,* color.] *Optics,* a property possessed by several crystallized bodies of appearing under two distinct colors according to the direction in which light is transmitted through them.—**dichroic,** dī•krō′ik, *a.* Characterized by dichroism.—**dichroite,** dī′krō•īt, *n.* A mineral generally of a blue color, but exhibiting different colors in different positions.—**dichromatic,** dī•krō•mat′ik, *a.* [Gr. *di,* and *chrōma,* color.] Having or producing two colors.—**dichroscope,** dī′krō•skōp, *n.* [Gr. *di, chroa,* and *skopeō,* to see.] An instrument in which a prism of Iceland spar is used for testing the dichroism of crystals.—**dichroscopic,** dī•krō•skop′ik, *a.* Pertaining to the dichroscope.

dickens, dik′enz, *interj.* [Probably a fanciful euphemism for *devil;* comp. L.G. *duker, duks,* the deuce.] Devil; deuce: used interjectionally. (*Shak.*)

dicker, dik′ėr, *n.* [L.G. and Sw. *deker,* G. *decher,* ten hides, from L.L. *dacra, decara,* L. *decem,* ten.] The number or quantity of ten, particularly ten hides or skins.

dickey, dicky, dik′i, *n.* [Origin doubtful.] An article of dress like the front of a dress shirt, and worn instead.

diclinous, dī′kli•nus, *a.* [Gr. *di,* double, and *klinē,* a bed.] *Bot.* having the stamens in one flower and the pistil in another.

dicotyledon, dī′kot•i•lē″don, *n.* [Gr. *di,* and *kotylēdōn.*] A plant whose seeds contain a pair of cotyledons or seed leaves, which are always opposite to each other.—**dicotyledonous,** dī′-kot•i•lē″do•nus, *a.* Having two cotyledons.

dictate, dik′tāt, *v.t.*—*dictated, dictating.* [L. *dicto, dictatum,* a freq. of *dico, dictum,* to say. DICTION.] To deliver or enounce with authority, as an order, command, or direction; to instruct to be said or written; to utter, so that another may write out; to direct by impulse on the mind (an action *dictated* by fear); to instigate.—*n.* An order delivered; a command; a rule, maxim, or precept, delivered with authority; rule or direction suggested to the mind (the *dictates* of reason).—**dictation,** dik•tā′shon, *n.* The act of dictating; the act or practice of speaking or reading that another may write down what is spoken.—**dictator,** dik′tā•tėr, *n.* [L., a supreme magistrate appointed on special occasions with unlimited power.] One invested with absolute authority; a supreme leader or guide to direct the conduct or opinion of others.—**dictatorial,** dik•ta•tō′ri•al, *a.* Pertaining to a dictator; imperious; overbearing.—**dictatorially,** dik•ta•tō′ri•al•li, *adv.* In an imperious manner.—**dictatorship,** dik′tā•tėr•ship, *n.* The office of a dictator; authority; imperiousness.—**dictatress,** dik•tā′-tres, *n.* A female dictator.

diction, dik′shon, *n.* [L. *dictio,* from *dico, dictum,* to speak, appearing in a great many English words, as *dictate, addict, contradict, edict, condition, preach,* etc.] A person's choice or selection of words in speaking or writing, general mode of expressing one's self; style. ∴ *Diction* refers chiefly to the words used; *phraseology* refers more to the manner of framing the phrases, clauses, and sentences; *style* includes both, referring to the thoughts as well as the words, and especially comprehends the niceties and beauties of a composition.—**dictionary,** dik′shon•e•ri, *n.* (L.L. *dictionarium.*) A book containing the words of a language arranged in alphabetical order, with explanations or definitions of their meanings; a lexicon; a word book; any work which communicates information on an entire subject or branch of a subject, under entries or heads arranged alphabetically.—*a.* Pertaining to, contained in, or given by a dictionary or dictionaries.—**dictum,** dik′-tum, *n.* pl.—**dicta,** dik′ta. [L.] A positive assertion; an authoritative saying or decision.

did, did, pret. of *do.*

didactic, didactical, di•dak′tik, di•-dak′ti•kal, *a.* [Gr. *didaktikos,* from *didaskō,* to teach.] Adapted to teach; containing doctrines, precepts, principles, or rules; intended to instruct.—**didactically,** di•dak′ti•kal•li, *adv.* In a didactic manner; in a form to teach.—**didactics,** di•dak′tiks, *n.* The art or science of teaching.

didapper, did′a•pėr, *n.* [For *divedapper* (*Shak.*), from *dive,* and *dap=dip.* DABCHICK.] The dabchick or little grebe.

diddle, did′l, *v.t.* [A.Sax. *dyderian,* to deceive or delude, originally perhaps by rapid movements or sleight of hand.] To cheat or trick, especially in money matters (slang); to dandle (provincial).

didymium, dī•dim′i•um, *n.* [Gr. *didymos,* double, twin.] A rare metal discovered in 1841 in the oxide of cerium, and so named from being, as it were, the twin brother of lanthanum, which was previously found in the same body.—**didymous,** did′i•-mus, *a. Bot.* twin; growing double.

die, dī, *v.i.*—*died, dying.* [Not an A.Sax. word; closely allied to the O.Fris. *deja, deya,* Icel. *deya, deyja,* Dan. *dōe,* to die; A.Sax. *deád,* dead, a kind of participial form, *deáth,* death.] To cease to live; to expire; to decease; to perish; to become dead; to lose life: said of both animals and plants; to come to an end; to cease to have influence or effect (his fame will not *die*); to sink; to faint (his heart *died* within him); to languish with pleasure, tenderness, affection, or the like; to become gradually less distinct or perceptible to the sight or hearing.

die, dī, *n.* [Fr. *dé,* O.Fr. *de,* from L. *datum,* something given, hence what is thrown or laid on the table.] A small cube marked on its faces with numbers from one to six, used in gaming by being thrown from a box; a square body: in the above senses the plural is *dice; arch.* the cubical part of a pedestal between its base and cornice; a stamp used in coining money, in foundries, etc.: in the last two senses the plural is regular, *dies.*—*The die is cast,* everything is now put to hazard; all will depend upon fortune.—**diesinker,** *n.* An engraver of dies for stamping or embossing.—**diesinking,** *n.* The process of engraving dies.

dielectric, dī•e•lek′trik, *n.* [Gr. *dia,* through, and E. *electric.*] *Elect.* any medium through or across which electric induction takes place between two conductors.

dieresis, dī•e′re•sis, *n.* Same as *Diaeresis.*

diesel, dē′zel, *n.* [From Rudolf *Diesel,* the inventor.] A type of internal-combustion engine, in which high pressure of air or fuel causes the ignition; also *diesel engine.*

diet, dī′et, *n.* [O.Fr. *diète,* L.L. *dieta,* Gr. *diaita,* a way of living, diet.] A person's regular food or victuals: manner of living as regards food and drink; course of food prescribed and limited in kind and quantity; allowance of provision.—*v.t.* To furnish diet or meals for; to prescribe a particular diet for.—*v.i.* To eat according to rules prescribed; to eat; to feed.—**dietary,** dī′e•te•ri, *a.* Pertaining to diet or the rules of diet.—*n.* A system or course of diet; allowance of food.—**dieter,** dī′et•ėr, *n.* One who diets; one who prescribes rules for eating. (*Shak.*)—**dietetic, dietetical,** dī•e•tet′ik, dī•e•tet′i•kal, *a.* Pertaining to diet, or to the rules for regulating diet.—**dietetically,** dī•-e•tet′i•kal•li, *adv.* In a dietetical manner.—**dietetics,** dī•e•tet′iks, *n.* That department of medicine which relates to the regulation of diet.—**dietitian, dietician,** dī•e•ti′shon, *n.* One versed in dietetics; one who arranges diets.

diet, dī′et, *n.* [Fr. *diète,* from L.L. *dieta,* the space of a day, from L. *dies,* a day, whence also *dial, diary.*] A meeting, as of dignitaries or delegates, held from day to day for legislative, ecclesiastical, or other purposes; session; specifically [*often* *cap.*] the legislative or administrative assemblies, as the Japanese, etc.

differ, dif′ėr, *v.i.* [L. *differo*—prefix *dif, dis,* and *fero,* to bear, to carry, seen also in *confer, offer, refer, suffer, infer,* etc.; root also in *fertile.*] To be unlike, dissimilar, distinct, or various, in nature, condition, form, or qualities (men and things *differ* greatly; they *differ* from each other); to disagree; not to accord; to be of another opinion (we *differ with* or *from* a person); to contend; to be at variance; to dispute; to quarrel.—**difference,** dif′ėr•ens, *n.* The state or condition in virtue of which things differ from each other; a point or feature of disagreement; the being different; want of sameness; variation; dissimilarity; distinction; a dispute, contention, quarrel, controversy; the point in dispute; the remainder of a sum or quantity after a lesser sum or quantity is subtracted; the quantity by which one quantity differs from another.—*v.t.* —*differenced, differencing.* To cause a difference or distinction in; to distinguish; to discriminate.—**different,** dif′ėr•ent, *a.* Distinct; separate; not the same; various; of various natures, forms, or qualities; unlike; dissimilar.—**differential,** dif•ėr•en′shal, *a.* Making a difference; discriminating; distinguishing; *math.* an epithet applied to an infinitely small quantity by which two variable quantities differ; pertaining to mathematical processes in which such quantities are employed.—*Differential calculus,* an important branch of the higher mathematics which deals largely with the infinitely small differences of variable and mutually dependent quantities.—*Differential duties, pol. econ.* duties which are not levied equally upon the produce or manufactures of different countries, as when a heavier duty is laid on certain commodities from one country than on the same commodities from another country.—*n.* A coupling used to connect shafts, as in the driving axle of an automobile, so that a union is effected when moving straight, but allowing independent motion on a curve; *math.* an infinitesimal difference between two states of a variable quantity.—**differentiate,** dif•ėr•en′shi•āt, *v.t.* To produce, or lead to, a difference in or between; to mark or distinguish by a difference; to set aside for a definite or specific purpose; *math.* to obtain the differential of.—*v.i.* To acquire a distinct and separate character.—**differentiation,** dif•ėr•en′shi•ā″shon, *n.* The act of differentiating; the production or discrimination of differences or variations; the assignment of a specific agency to the discharge of a specific function; *biol.* the formation of different parts, organs, species, etc., by the production or acquisition of a diversity of new structures, through a process of evolution or development; *math.* the operation of finding the differential of any function.

difficulty, dif′i•kul•ti, *n.* [Fr. *difficulté;* L. *difficultas,* from *difficilis,* difficult—*dis,* priv., and *facilis,* easy to be made or done.] Hardness to be done or accomplished; the state of anything which renders its performance laborious or perplexing: opposed to *easiness* or *facility;* that which is hard to be performed or surmounted; perplexity; embarrassment of affairs; trouble; objection; cavil; obstacle to belief; an embroilment; a falling out; a controversy; a quarrel.—**difficult,** dif′i•kult, *a.* Hard to make, do, or perform; not easy; attended with labor and pains; arduous; hard to understand.—**difficultly,** dif′i•kult•li, *adv.* Hardly; with difficulty.

diffidence, dif′i•dens, *n.* [L. *diffidentia, diffidens,* ppr. of *diffido,* to distrust—*dis,* not, and *fido,* to trust. FAITH.] Distrust; want of confidence; especially distrust of one's self; a doubt respecting some personal qualification; modest reserve.—**diffident,** dif′i•dent, *a.* Characterized by diffidence; distrustful of one's self; not confident; backward; bashful.—**diffidently,** dif′i•dent•li, *adv.* In a diffident manner.

diffract, dif•frakt′, *v.t.* [L. *diffringo, diffractum*—prefix *dif, dis,* and *frango,* to break.] To break; to bend from a straight line; to deflect.—**diffraction,** dif•frak′shon, *n. Optics,* the peculiar modifications which light undergoes when it passes by the edge of an opaque body; deflection.—**diffractive,** dif•frak′tiv, *a.* Causing diffraction.

diffuse, dif•fūz′, *v.t.*—*diffused, diffusing.* [L. *diffundo, diffusum*—prefix *dif, dis,* and *fundo, fusum,* to pour, whence *fusion.*] To pour out and spread, as a fluid; to cause to flow and spread; to send out or extend in all directions (light, information, happiness).—*a.* (dif•fūs′). Widely spread; using too many words to express meaning; wanting conciseness and due condensation; verbose; prolix; *bot.* spreading widely, horizontally, and irregularly.—**diffusely,** dif•fūs′li, *adv.* In a diffuse manner; widely; extensively; with too many words.—**diffuseness,** dif•fūs′nes, *n.* The quality of being diffuse; want of conciseness or due concentration in expressing one's meaning.—**diffuser,** dif•fū′zėr, *n.* One who or that which diffuses.—**diffusibility,** dif•fū′zi•bil″i•ti, *n.* The quality of being diffusible. —**diffusible,** dif•fū′zi•bl, *a.* Capable of being diffused or spread in all directions.—**diffusion,** dif•fū′zhon, *n.* The act of diffusing or process of being diffused; a spreading abroad or scattering; dispersion; dissemination; extension; propagation; the tendency of two different gases to mix when separated by a porous partition.—**diffusive,** dif•fū′siv, *a.* Having the quality of diffusing or becoming diffused; extending in all directions; widely reaching (*diffusive* charity); diffuse as regards expression.—**diffusively,** dif•fū′siv•li, *adv.* In a diffusive manner; widely; extensively.—**diffusiveness,** dif•fū′siv•nes, *n.* The character of being diffusive.

dig, dig, *v.t.*—*digged* or *dug, digging.* [Probably connected with *dike* or *dyke, ditch;* A.Sax. *dic,* a dike or a ditch, *dician,* Dan. *dige,* to make a ditch.] To open and break, or turn up, with a spade or other sharp instrument; to excavate; to form in the ground by digging and removing the loose soil; to raise from the earth by digging (to *dig* coals, fossils, etc.).—*v.i.* To work with a spade or other similar instrument.—**digger,** dig′ėr, *n.* One who or that which digs; specifically, one who digs for gold.—**digging,** dig′ing, *n.* The act of one who digs; *pl.* a word applied to the different localities in California, Australia, New Zealand, etc., where gold is obtained by excavations in the earth.

digamma, dī′gam•ma, *n.* [Gr., lit. double gamma (gamma = E. *g* hard), because in form it resembled two gammas, the one set above the other, somewhat like our F.] A letter which once belonged to the alphabet of the Greeks, and appears to have had the force of *v* or *f.*

digastric, dī•gas′trik, *a.* [Gr. *di,* double, and *gastēr,* belly.] Having a double belly.—*Digastric muscle,* a double muscle that pulls the lower jaw downward and backward.

digest, di•jest′, *v.t.* [L. *digero, digestum,* to distribute, dispose, digest food—*di* for *dis,* asunder, and *gero, gestum,* to bear; also in *congest, suggest, gesture,* etc.] To arrange in suitable divisions or under proper heads or titles; to dispose in due method for being conveniently studied or consulted; to arrange methodically in the mind; to think out; to separate or dissolve in the stomach, preparing the nutritious elements for entering the system; *chem.* to soften and prepare by a heated liquid; *fig.* to bear with patience or with an effort; to brook; to put up with.—*v.i.* To undergo digestion, as food.—*n.* (dī′jest). A collection of Roman laws, digested or arranged under proper titles by order of the Emperor Justinian; any orderly or systematic summary, as of laws.—**digester,** di•jes′tėr, *n.* One who digests or disposes in order; that which assists the digestion of food; a vessel in which bones or other substances may be subjected to heat in water or other liquid.—**digestibility,** di•jes′ti•bil″i•ti, *n.* The quality of being digestible. —**digestible,** di•jes′ti•bl, *a.* Capable of being digested.—**digestion,** di•jes′chon, *n.* [L. *digestio.*] The act of methodizing or disposing in order; the process which food undergoes in the stomach, by which it is prepared for nourishing the body; *chem.* the operation of exposing bodies to heat in a liquid to prepare them for some action on each other; or the slow action of a solvent on any substance.—**digestive,** di•jes′tiv, *a.* Having the power to promote digestion in the stomach.—*n.* Any preparation or medicine which increases the tone of the stomach and aids digestion; a stomachic.

digger, digging, *n.* See DIG.

dight, dīt, *v.t.—dight.* [A.Sax. *dihtan*, from L. *dictare*, to dictate. DICTATE.] To put in order; to dress; to array. (Now only poet.)

digit, dij′it, *n.* [L. *digitus*, a finger; akin Gr. *daktylos*, a finger; root *dik*, to point out, as in Gr. *deiknymi*, to show, L. *dico*, to say.] A finger: sometimes used scientifically to signify toe, when speaking of animals; the measure of a finger's breadth or ¾ inch; *astron.* the twelfth part of the diameter of the sun or moon; *arith.* any integer under 10: so called from counting on the fingers.—**digital,** dij′i•tal, *a.* [L. *digitalis.*] Pertaining to the fingers or to digits.—*n.* One of the keys of instruments of the organ or piano class.—**digital computer.** A calculating machine with numbers expressed as digits.—**digitalin,** dij′i•ta•lin, *n.* A strong poison obtained from digitalis.—**digitalis,** dij•i•tā′lis, *n.* Any of a genus of Eurasian herbs of the figwort family; the dried and powdered leaf of the common foxglove, containing several important glucocides and serving as a powerful heart stimulant and a diuretic.—**digitately,** dij′i•tāt•li, *adv.* In a digitate manner. —**digitation,** dij•i•tā′shon, *n.* A division into finger-like processes.—**digitiform,** dij′i•ti•form, *a.* Formed like fingers.—**digitigrade,** dij′i•ti•grād, *n.* [L. *digitus*, and *gradior*, to go.] An animal that walks on its toes, as the lion, wolf, etc.—*a.* Walking on the toes.

dignify, dig′ni•fī, *v.t.—dignified, dignifying.* [Fr. *dignifier*—L. *dignus*, worthy, and *facere*, to make.] To invest with honor or dignity; to exalt in rank; to elevate to a high office; to honor; to make illustrious.—**dignified,** dig′ni•fīd, *p.* and *a.* Invested with dignity; honored; marked with dignity or loftiness; noble; stately in deportment.—**dignitary,** dig′ni•te•ri, *n.* One who holds an exalted rank or office.—**dignity,** dig′ni•ti, *n.* [L. *dignitas.*] Nobleness or elevation of mind; loftiness; honorable place or rank; degree of elevation; elevation of aspect; grandeur of mien; height or importance; an elevated office; one who holds high rank; a dignitary.

digraph, dī′graf, *n.* [Gr. *di*, twice, and *graphō*, to write.] A union of two vowels or of two consonants, representing a single sound of the voice (as *ea* in head).

digress, di•gres′, *v.i.* [L. *digredior, digressus*, to step apart—prefix *dis*, apart, and *gradior*, to step. GRADE.] To depart or wander from the main subject or tenor of a discourse, argument, or narration.—**digression,** di•gresh′on, *n.* [L. *digressio.*] The act of digressing; a departure from the main subject; the part or passage of a discourse, etc., which deviates from the main subject; transgression (*Shak.*)‡.—**digressional, digressive,** di•gresh′on•al, di•gres′iv, *a.* Pertaining to or consisting in digression.—**digressively,** di•gres′iv•li, *adv.* By way of digression.

dihedral, dī•hē′dral, *a.* [Gr. *di*, twice, and *hedra*, a seat or face.] Having two plane faces, as a crystal.

dike, dyke, dīk, *n.* [A.Sax. *dic*, D, *dijk*, Dan. *dige*, a bank of earth, a ditch, the ditch being excavated and the bank formed by the same operation. *Ditch* is a softened form of this.] A ditch or channel for water; a barrier of earth, stones, or other materials, intended to prevent low lands from being inundated by the sea or a river; a low wall forming a fence; *geol.* a vein of igneous rock which has intruded in a melted state into rents or fissures of other rocks.—*v.t.—diked, diking.* To surround with a dike; to secure by a bank; to drain by one or more dikes or ditches.

dilacerate, dī•las′ėr•āt, *v.t.* [L. *dilacero*—prefix *di* for *dis*, asunder, and *lacero*, to tear.] To tear; to rend asunder.—**dilaceration,** dī•las′ėr•ā″shon, *n.* The act of dilacerating.

dilapidate, di•lap′i•dāt, *v.i.—dilapidated, dilapidating.* [L. *dilapido, dilapidatum*—prefix *di* for *dis*, asunder, and *lapis, lapidis*, a stone.]—*v.t.* To suffer to go to ruin (buildings) by misuse or neglect; to waste; to squander.—*v.i.* To fall to ruin.—**dilapidated,** di•lap′i•dā•ted, *p.* and *a.* In a ruinous condition; suffered to go to ruin.—**dilapidation,** di•lap′i•dā″shon, *n.* The act of dilapidating; *eccles.* the ruinous neglect or actual wasting, by an incumbent, of any building or other property in his possession.

dilate, dī•lāt′, *v.t.—dilated, dilating.* [L. *dilato*, to make wider—*di* for *dis*, asunder, and *latus* broad.] To expand or swell out, especially by filling; to distend; to enlarge in all directions: opposed to *contract*; to tell copiously or diffusely (*Shak.*)‡.—*v.i.* To expand, swell, or extend in all directions; to speak largely and copiously; to dwell in narration; to descant: with *on* or *upon.*—**dilatability,** dī•lā′ta•bil″i•ti, *n.* The quality of being dilatable.—**dilatable,** dī•lā′ta•bl, *a.* Capable of being dilated; possessing elasticity; elastic.—**dilatation, dilation,** dī•lā•tā′shon, dī•lā′shon, *n.* The act of expanding, dilating, or state of being expanded or distended.—**dilater, dilator,** dī•lā′tėr, *n.* One who or that which dilates.—**dilative,** dī•lā′tiv, a. Tending to dilate.

dilatory, dil′a•to•ri, *a.* [Fr. *dilatoire*, L.L. *dilatorius*, from L. *differo, dilatum.* DELAY.] Marked with or given to procrastination or delay; making delay or resulting in delay; slow; tardy; not proceeding with diligence: of persons or things.—**dilatorily,** dil′a•to•ri•li, *adv.* In a dilatory manner; tardily.—**dilatoriness,** dil′a•to•ri•nes, *n.* The quality of being dilatory; delay in proceeding; tardiness.

dilemma, di•lem′ma, *n.* [Gr. *dilēmma*—prefix *di* for *dis*, double, and *lēmma*, an assumption, from *lambanō*, to take.] *Logic*, an argument in which the adversary is caught between two difficulties, by having two alternatives presented to him, each of which is equally conclusive against him; hence, a state of things in which evils or obstacles present themselves on every side, and it is difficult to determine what course to pursue.

dilettante, dil•e•tänt′, *n.* pl. **dilettanti,** dil•e•tan′tē. [It., from L. *delectare*, to delight. DELIGHT.] An admirer or lover of the fine arts; an amateur or trifler in art; one who pursues an art desultorily and for amusement. —**dilettantism,** dil•e•tan′tizm, *n.* The quality characteristic of a dilettante.

diligence, dil′i•jens, *n.* [L. *diligentia*, carefulness, diligence, from *diligo*, to love earnestly—*di* for *dis*, intens., and *lego*, to choose.] Steady application in business of any kind; constant effort to accomplish what is undertaken; due attention; industry; assiduity; care; heed; heedfulness; *Scots law*, a kind of warrant, and also a process by which persons or effects are attached.—**diligent,** dil′i•jent, *a.* [L. *diligens, diligentis.*] Steady in application to business; constant in effort to accomplish what is undertaken; assiduous; attentive; industrious; not idle or negligent: of persons or things.—**diligently,** dil′i•jent•li, *adv.* In a diligent manner.

diligence, dē•lē•zhäns, *n.* [Fr.] A kind of four-wheeled stagecoach.

dill, dil, *n.* [A.Sax. *dil*, Sw. *dill*, G. *dill*, dill; possibly from its soothing qualities in *dilling* or *dulling* pain. Comp. prov. E. *dill*, Icel. *dilla*, to lull a child.] A plant of the parsley family, seeds of which are moderately pungent and aromatic, and are used as a seasoning.

dillydally, dil′i•dal•i, *v.i.* [A reduplication of *dally.*] To loiter; to delay; to trifle.

dilute, di•lūt′, *v.t.—diluted, diluting.* [L. *diluo, dilutus*—prefix *di* for *dis*, and *luo*, to wash, as in *ablution.* DELUGE.] To render liquid or more liquid, especially by mixing with water; to weaken (spirit, acid, etc.) by an admixture of water.—*a.* Diluted; reduced in strength by intermixture.—**diluteness,** di•lūt′nes, *n.* The state or quality of being diluted. —**dilution,** di•lū′shon, *n.* The act of diluting.—**diluent,** dil′ū•ent, *a.* [L. *diluens, diluentis.*] Having the effect of diluting.—*n.* That which dilutes; *med.* a substance which increases the proportion of fluid in the blood.

diluvial, diluvian, di•lū′vi•al, di•lū′vi•an, *a.* [L. *diluvium*, a deluge, from *diluo.* DILUTE.] Pertaining to a flood or deluge, more especially to the deluge in Noah's days.—*Diluvial formation*, *geol.* a name of superficial deposits of gravel, clay, sand, etc., conveyed to their present sites by any unusual or extraordinary rush of water.

dim, dim, *a.* [A.Sax. *dim*, dark, obscure = O.Fris. *dim*, Icel. *dimmr*, dim; comp. Lith. *tamsa*, Skr. *tamas*, darkness.] Not seeing clearly; having the vision indistinct; not clearly seen; obscure; faint; vague; somewhat dark; not luminous; dull of apprehension; having the luster obscured; tarnished.—*v.t.—dimmed, dimming.* To render dim or less clear or distinct; to becloud; to obscure;

to tarnish or sully.—**dimly,** dim′li, *adv.* In a dim manner.—**dimness,** dim′nes, *n.* The state of being dim.

dime, dīm, *n.* [Fr. *dîme,* a tenth, a tithe, O.Fr. *disme,* from L. *decimus,* tenth, from *decem,* ten.] A silver coin of the United States, value ten cents; the tenth of a dollar.

dimension, di•men′shon, *n.* [L. *dimensio,* from *dimetior,* to measure—*di* for *dis,* and *metior, mensus,* to mete. METE, MEASURE.] Extension in a single direction, as length, breadth, and thickness or depth, a solid body having thus three dimensions ; *pl.* measure, size, extent, capacity; *fig.* consequence; importance; *alg.* same as *degree.*

dimerous, dim′ėr•us, *a.* [Gr. *di,* twice, and *meros,* part.] Having its parts in pairs; composed of two unrelated pieces or parts; *entom.* having the tarsi two-jointed.

dimeter, dim′e•tėr, *a.* [Gr. *dimetros*—*di,* twice, and *metron,* a measure.] Having two poetical measures.—*n.* A verse of two measures.

dimidiate, di•mid′i•āt, *a.* [L. *dimidiatus,* from *dimidium,* half—*dis,* asunder, and *medius,* the middle.] Divided into two equal parts; halved; *bot.* applied to an organ when half of it is so much smaller than the other as to appear to be missing; *zool.* having the organs of one side of different functions from the corresponding organs on the other.

diminish, di•min′ish, *v.t.* [O.Fr. *demenuiser,* from L. *diminuo,* to lessen—*di* for *dis,* asunder, and *minuere,* to lessen, from root *min,* in *minor,* less.] To lessen; to make less or smaller by any means: opposed to *increase* and *augment*; to impair, degrade, or abase (O.T.).—*v.i.* To lessen; to become or appear less or smaller; decrease.—**diminishable,** di•min′ish•a•bl, *a.* Capable of being diminished.—**diminuendo,** di•min′ū•en″dō. [It.] *Mus.* an instruction to the performer to lessen the volume of sound from loud to soft: opposite of *crescendo.*—**diminution,** dim•i•nū′shon, *n.* [L. *diminutio.*] The act of diminishing; a making smaller; the state of becoming or appearing less; discredit; loss of dignity; degradation.—**diminutive,** di•min′ū•tiv, *a.* [Fr. *diminutif.*] Considerably smaller than the normal size; small; little.—*n.* Anything of very small size (*Shak.*)‡; *gram.* a word formed from another word to express a little thing of the kind (as *manikin,* a little man).—**diminutively,** di•min′ū•tiv•li, *adv.* In a diminutive manner.—**diminutiveness,** di•min′ū•tiv•nes, *n.* State of being diminutive; smallness; littleness.

dimissory, di•mis′o•ri, *a.* [L.L. *dimissorius.* DISMISS.] Sending away; dismissing to another jurisdiction; granting leave to depart.

dimity, dim′i•ti, *n.* [It. *dimito,* L.L. *dimitum,* from Gr. *dimitos,* dimity—*di,* double, and *mitos,* a thread.] A stout cotton fabric ornamented in the loom by raised stripes or fancy figures, rarely dyed, but usually employed white for beds, etc.

dimly, dimness. See DIM.

dimorphism, dī•mor′fizm, *n.* [Gr. *di,* double, and *morphē,* form.] The property shown by some mineral bodies of crystallizing in two distinct forms not derivable from each other; the condition when analogous organs of plants of the same species appear under two very dissimilar forms; difference of form between animals of the same species.—**dimorphous, dimorphic,** dī•mor′fus, dī•mor′fik, *a.* Characterized by dimorphism.

dimple, dim′pl, *n.* [Probably a diminutive form connected with *dip* or *deep*; comp. G. *dümpel, tümpel,* a pool.] A small natural depression in the cheek or other part of the face, as the chin; a slight depression or indentation on any surface.—*v.i.*—*dimpled, dimpling.* To form dimples; to sink into depressions or little inequalities.—*v.i.* To mark with dimples.—**dimply,** dim′pli, *a.*

din, din, *n.* [A.Sax. *dyn, dyne,* noise, thunder; Icel. *dynr,* din, *dynia,* to resound; from same root as Skr. *dhvan,* to sound.] Noise; a clattering, or rumbling sound, long continued.—*v.t.* and *i.*—*dinned, dinning.* To strike with continued or confused sound; to stun with noise.

dine, dīn, *v.i.*—*dined, dining.* [Fr. *dîner,* O.Fr. *disner,* L.L. *disnare*—L. *de,* intens. (as in *devour*), and *cœnare,* to dine, from *cœna,* dinner.] To eat the chief meal of the day; to take dinner.—*To dine out,* to take dinner elsewhere than at one's own residence.—*v.t.* To give a dinner to; to supply with dinner; to afford convenience for dining.—**diner,** dī′nėr, *n.* One who dines; a dining car; a restaurant shaped like a railroad car.—**dinette,** dī•net′, *n.* A small dining room.—**dining car,** *n.* A railroad car in which meals are served.—**dining room,** *n.* A room used for dinner and other meals.—**dinner,** din′ėr, *n.* The chief meal of the day; a formal meal in honor of a person or an event.

ding, ding, *v.t.* and *i.*—*dung* or *dinged.* [Icel. *dengja,* Dan. *daenge,* Sw. *danga,* to knock, to beat.] To sound as a bell.—**dingdong,** ding′dong, *n.* The sound of bells, or any similar sound.

dinghy, dingey, ding′gi, *n.* [Hindi] An East Indian boat varying in size in different localities; a small boat used by a ship; a sailboat or yacht used in racing; a rubber life raft.

dingle, ding′gl, *n.* [Apparently a form of O.E. *dimble,* a dell or dingle, and *dimple.*] A narrow dale or valley between hills; a small secluded and embowered valley.

dingo, ding′gō, *n.* The wild Australian dog, of a wolflike appearance.

dingy, din′ji, *a.* [Probably connected with *dung.*] Of a dirty white or dusky color; soiled; sullied; dusky.—**dinginess,** din′ji•nes, *n.*

dinkey, dinky, dingk′i, *n.* [Amer.] A small locomotive used for hauling logs, shunting freight cars, etc.

dinky, dingk′i, *a.* [Sc. *dink,* neat.] Small; insignificant.

dinoceras, dī•nos′e•ras, *n.* [Gr. *deinos,* terrible, *keras,* horn.] A fossil animal as large as an elephant, with three horns.

dinosaur, dinosaurian, dī′nō•sạr, dī•nō•sạ′ri•an, *n.* [Gr. *deinos,* and *sauros,* a lizard.] One of a group of huge, terrestrial, fossil reptiles peculiar to the upper secondary formations, some of them carnivorous.—**dinothere,** dī′nō•thēr, *n.* [Gr. *deinos,* and *thērion,* wild beast.] A gigantic extinct mammal allied to the elephant, occurring in the strata of the tertiary formation, with two tusks curving downward. These words are also spelled *Dei-.*

dint, dint, *n.* [A.Sax. *dynt,* a blow, O.E. and Sc. *dunt,* Icel. *dyntr,* a stroke; perhaps akin to *din* and *ding. Dent* is the same word.] A blow or stroke‡; the mark made by a blow; a cavity or impression made by a blow or by pressure on a substance; a dent.—*By dint of,* by the force or power of; by means of.—*v.t.* To make a dint in; to dent.

diocese, dī′ō•sēs, *n.* [Gr. *dioikēsis,* administration, a province or jurisdiction—*dia,* and *oikēsis,* residence, from *oikeō,* to dwell, *oikos,* a house.] The circuit or extent of a bishop's jurisdiction; an ecclesiastical division of a state, subject to the authority of a bishop.—**diocesan,** dī•os′-es•an or dī•ō•sē′san, *a.* Pertaining to a diocese.—*n.* A bishop as related to his own diocese; one in possession of a diocese, and having the ecclesiastical jurisdiction over it.

dioecious, dī•ē′shus, *a. Bot.* having stamens on one plant and pistils on another; *zool.* having the germ cell or ovum produced by one individual (female), and the sperm cell, or spermatozoid, by another (male).

diopside, dī•op′sīd, *n.* [Gr. *dia,* through, and *opsis,* a view, from being sometimes transparent.] A variety of augite, of a vitreous luster and greenish or yellowish color.

dioptase, dī•op′tās, *n.* [Gr. *dia,* through, and *optazō,* from *optomai,* to see.] Emerald copper ore, a translucent mineral of a beautiful green, occurring crystallized in six-sided prisms.

diopter, di•op′ter, *n.* [Gr. *diopter,* a spy.] In lenses, the unit of refractive power, being that of a lens with a focal length of one meter.—**dioptric, dioptrical,** dī•op′trik, dī•-op′tri•kal, *a.* [Gr. *dioptrikos,* from *dia,* through, and the root *op,* to see.] Pertaining to dioptrics, or to the passing of light through instruments or substances.—*Dioptric system,* the mode of illuminating lighthouses in which the illumination is produced by a central lamp, sending its rays through a combination of lenses surrounding it.—**dioptrics,** dī•op′-triks, *n.* That part of optics which treats of the refractions of light passing through different mediums, as through air, water, or glass, and especially through lenses.

diorama, di•o•ra′ma, *n.* [Gr. *dia,* through, and *horama,* a view.] A painted scene in three dimensions, viewed through an aperture; a spectacular picture or scene of any size, with or without translucent features.

diorite, dī′o•rīt, *n.* [Gr. *dia*, through, and *horos*, boundary, the stone being formed of distinct portions.] A tough crystalline trap rock of a whitish color, speckled with black or greenish black.

dioxide, dī•ok′sīd, *n.* [Prefix *di*, double, and *oxide*.] An oxide consisting of one atom of a metal and two atoms of oxygen.

dip, dip, *v.t.—dipped* or *dipt, dipping.* [A.Sax. *dippan, dyppan*, to dip; Fris. *dippe*, D. *doopen*, G. *taufen*, to dip, to baptize, akin *deep, dive.*] To plunge or immerse in water or other liquid; to put into a fluid and withdraw; to lift with a ladle or other vessel; often with *out*; to baptize by immersion.—*v.i.* To plunge into a liquid and quickly emerge; to engage in a desultory way; to concern oneself to some little extent (to *dip* into a subject); to read passages here and there (to *dip* into a volume); to sink, as below the horizon; *geol.* to incline or slope.—*n.* An immersion in any liquid; a plunge; a bath; a candle made by dipping the wick in tallow; inclination or slope.—*Dip of the needle*, the angle which the magnetic needle makes with the plane of the horizon.—*The dip of strata*, in *geol.* the inclination or angle at which strata slope or dip.—**dipper,** dip′ėr, *n.* One who or that which dips, especially, a kind of ladle or scoop; [cap.] either of two groups of seven stars in the Northern Hemisphere resembling a dipper.

diphtheria, dif•thē′ri•a, *n.* [Gr. *diphthera*, a membrane.] An epidemic inflammatory disease of the air passages, and especially of the throat, characterized by the formation of a false membrane.—**diphtheritic,** dif•the•rit′ik, *a.* Connected with, relating to, or formed by diphtheria.

diphthong, dif′thong or dip′thong, *n.* [Gr. *diphthongos—di*, twice, and *phthongos*, sound.] A union of two vowels pronounced in one syllable (as in *bound, oil*).—**diphthongization,** dif′thong•gi•zā″shon or dip-, *n.* The formation of a diphthong; the conversion of a simple vowel into a diphthong.—**diphthongize,** dif′-thong•gīz or dip-, *v.t.* To form into a diphthong.

diphyllous, dī•fil′us, *a.* [Gr. *di*, twice, and *phyllon*, a leaf.] *Bot.* having two leaves, as a calyx, etc.

diplococcus, dip′lo•kok″us, *n.* [Gr. *diploos*, double, *kokkos*, a berry.] Of bacteria, a form consisting of a pair of cocci. See COCCUS.

diploma, di•plō′ma, *n.* [Gr. *diplōma*, a paper folded double, a license, from *diploō*, to fold, *diploos*, double.] A letter or writing, usually under seal and signed by competent authority, conferring some power, privilege, or honor, as that given to graduates of colleges on their receiving the usual degrees, to physicians who are licensed to practice their profession, and the like.—*v.t.* To furnish with a diploma; to fortify by a diploma.—**diplomacy,** di•plō′ma•si, *n.* The science or art of conducting negotiations, arranging treaties, etc., between nations; the forms of international negotiations; dexterity or skill in managing negotiations of any kind; artful management or maneuvering with the view of securing advantages.—**diplomat,** dip′lo•mat, *n.* A diplomatist.—**diplomatic,** dip•-lo•mat′ik, *a.* Pertaining to diplomacy or to the management of any negotiations; skillful in gaining one's ends by tact and cleverness; conferred by diploma; relating to diplomatics.—**diplomatically,** dip•lo•-mat′i•kal•li, *adv.* In a diplomatic manner; artfully.—**diplomatics,** dip•-lo•mat′iks, *n.* The science of deciphering old writings, to ascertain their authenticity, date, etc.; paleography.—**diplomatist,** di•plō′ma•tist, *n.* A person skilled in diplomacy; a diplomat.

diplopia, di•plō′pi•a, *n.* [Gr. *diploos*, double, and *ōps*, the eye.] A disease of the eye, in which the patient sees an object double or even triple.

dipper, dipping. See DIP.

dipsomania, dip•so•mā′ni•a, *n.* [Gr. *dipsa*, thirst, and *mania*, madness.] That morbid condition to which habitual drunkards of a nervous and sanguine temperament are liable to reduce themselves, and in which they manifest an uncontrollable craving for stimulants.—**dipsomaniac,** dip•so•mā′ni•ak, *n.* A victim of dipsomania.—**dipsomaniacal,** dip•-so•mā′ni•a•kal, *a.* Pertaining to dipsomania.

dipteral, dip′tėr•al, *a.* [Gr. *di*, double, and *pteron*, a wing.] *Entom.* having two wings only; dipterous; *arch.* a term applied to a temple having a double row of columns on each of its flanks.—*n. Arch.* a dipteral temple.—**dipteron,** dip′tėr•an, *n.* A dipterous insect.—**dipterous,** dip′tėr•us, *a. Entom.* having two wings. *bot.* a term applied to seeds which have their margins prolonged in the form of wings.

diptych, dip′tik, *n.* [Gr. *diptychos—di*, double, and *ptyssō*, to fold.] Anciently, a kind of register or list as of magistrates or bishops consisting usually of two leaves folded, a design, as a painting or carved work, on two folding compartments or tablets.

dire, dīr, *a.* [L. *dirus*, terrible.] Dreadful; dismal; horrible; terrible; evil in a great degree.—**direful,** dīr′fu̦l, *a.* Same as *Dire*.—**direfully,** dīr′fu̦l•li, *adv.* In a direful manner.—**direly,** dīr′li, *adv.* In a dire manner.—**direness,** dīr′nes, *n.* The state or quality of being dire. (*Shak.*)

direct, di•rekt′, *a.* [L. *dirigo, directum*, to set in a straight line, to direct—*di* for *dis.* intens., and *rego, rectum*, to make straight. RIGHT, REGENT.] Straight, right; opposite to *crooked, circuitous, winding, oblique*; *astron.* appearing to move from west to east; opposed to *retrograde*; in the line of father and son; opposed to *collateral*; straightforward; open; ingenuous; plain; not ambiguous,—*v.t.* To point or aim in a straight line toward something; to make to act or work, towards a certain end or object; to show the right road or course; to prescribe a course to; to order or instruct; to prescribe to; to inscribe (a letter) with the address.—*v.i.* To act as a guide; to point out a course.—*n. Mus.* the sign ᵥᵥ placed at the end of a stave to direct the performer to the first note of the next stave.—**direct current,** *Elect.* A current flowing in one direction in a circuit; abbreviated D.C.—**direction,** di•rek′shon, *n.* The act of directing; the course or line in which anything is directed; a being directed toward a particular end; the line in which a body moves, or to which its position is referred; course; the act of governing; administration; management; guidance; superintendence; instruction in what manner. to proceed; order; behest; the address on a letter, parcel, etc ; a body or board of directors; directorate —**directive,** di•rek′tiv, *a* Having the power of directing.—**directly,** di•rekt′li, *adv.* In a direct manner; in a straight line or course; straightway; immediately; instantly; soon; without delay; openly; expressly; without circumlocution or ambiguity.—**directness,** di•rekt′nes, *n.*—**direct object,** *n. Gram.* the person or thing that receives the action expressed by the verb.—**director,** di•rek′tėr, *n.* One who or that which directs; one who superintends; specifically, one of a body appointed to direct, control, or superintend the affairs of a company.—**directorate,** di•rek′-tėr•it, *n.* The office of a director; a body of directors.—**directorship,** di•-rek′tėr•ship, *n.* The condition or office of a director.—**directory,** di•-rek′te•ri, *n.* A rule to direct; a book containing directions for public worship or religious services; a book containing an alphabetical list of the inhabitants of a city, town, etc., with their places of business and abode; board of directors; directorate; [*cap.*] during the French Revolution, a body established by the Convention in 1795, and composed of five members.—**directress,** di•rek′tres, *n.* A female who directs or manages.—**directrix,** di•rek′triks, *n.* A directress; *geom.* a straight line of importance in the doctrine of conic sections.

direful. See DIRE.

dirge, dėrj, *n.* [A contraction of L. *dirige* ('direct', imperative of *dirigere*, to direct), the first word in a psalm or hymn formerly sung at funerals.] A song or tune intended to express, grief, sorrow, and mourning.

dirigible, di′ri•ji•bl, *a.* That may be directed, turned, or guided in any direction.—*n.* A balloon or airship driven by motors whose course can be directed by means of steering or directing apparatus.

dirk, dėrk, *n.* [Origin doubtful.] A kind of dagger or poniard; a dagger worn as essential to complete the Highland costume.—*v.t.* To poniard; to stab.

dirt, dėrt, *n.* [Icel. *drit,* dirt, excrement, *drita,* Sc. *drite,* A.Sax. *(ge) dritan,* to go to stool.] Any foul or filthy substance, as excrement, mud, mire, dust; whatever, adhering to anything, renders it foul or unclean; a gold-miner's name for the material, as earth, gravel, etc., put into his cradle to be washed.—*v.t.* To soil; to dirty.—**dirtily,** dėr′ti•li, *adv.* In a dirty manner; nastily; filthily; meanly; sordidly.—**dirtiness,** dėr′ti•nes, *n.* The condition of being dirty; filthiness; foulness; nastiness.—**dirty,** dėr′ti, *a.* Foul; nasty; filthy; not clean; impure; turbid; mean; base; despicable; sleety, rainy, or sloppy (weather).—*v.t.—dirtied, dirtying.* To defile; to make dirty or filthy; to soil.

disable, dis•ā′bl, *v.t.—disabled, disabling.* [Prefix *dis,* priv., and *able.*] To render unable; to deprive of competent strength or power, physical or mental; to injure so as to be no longer fit for duty or service; to deprive of adequate means, instruments, or resources; to impair; to deprive of legal qualifications; to incapacitate; to render incapable.—**disability,** dis•a•bil′i•ti, *n.* The state or quality of being disabled or unable; weakness; impotence; incapacity; inability; want of legal qualifications.—**disablement,**† dis•ā′bl•ment, *n.* The act of disabling; disability.

disabuse, dis•a•būz′, *v.t.—disabused, disabusing.* [Fr. *désabuser,* to disabuse.] To free from mistaken or erroneous notions or beliefs; to undeceive; to set right.

disaccustom, dis•ak•kus′tum, *v.t.* To destroy the force of habit in by disuse; to render unaccustomed.

disadvantage, dis•ad•van′tij, *n.* Absence or deprivation of advantage; that which prevents success or renders it difficult; any unfavorable circumstance or state, prejudice to interest, fame, credit, profit, or other good; loss; injury; harm; damage.—**disadvantageous,** dis•ad′van•tā″jus, *a.* Attended with disadvantage; unfavorable to success or prosperity; prejudicial.—**disadvantageously,** dis•ad′van•tā″jus•li, *adv.* In a disadvantageous manner.—**disadvantageousness,** dis•ad′van•tā″jus•nes, *n.*

disaffect, dis•af•fekt′, *v.t.* To alienate the affection of; to make less friendly or faithful, as to a person, party, or cause; to make discontented or unfriendly.—**disaffected,** dis•af•fek′ted, *p.* and *a.* Having the affections alienated; indisposed to favor or support; unfriendly; hostile to the governing power.—**disaffection,** dis•af•fek′shon, *n.* Alienation of affection, attachment, or good will; disloyalty.

disaffirm, dis•af•fėrm′, *v.t.* To deny; to contradict; to annul, as a judicial decision, by a contrary judgment of a superior tribunal.

disafforest, dis•af•for′est, *v.t.* To reduce from the privileges of a forest to the state of common ground; to strip of forest laws and their oppressive privileges.

disagree, dis•a•grē′, *v.t.—disagreed, disagreeing.* To be not accordant or coincident; to be not exactly similar; to differ; to be of an opposite or different opinion; to be unsuitable to the stomach; to be in opposition; not to accord or harmonize; to become unfriendly; to quarrel.—**disagreeable,** dis•a•grē′a•bl, *a.* The reverse of agreeable; unpleasing; offensive to the mind or to the senses; repugnant; obnoxious.—**disagreeableness,** dis•a•grē′a•bl•nes, *n.* The state or quality of being disagreeable.—**disagreeably,** dis•a•grē′a•bli, *adv.* In a disagreeable manner; unpleasantly.—**disagreement,** dis•a•grē′ment, *n.* Want of agreement; difference, as of form or character; difference of opinion or sentiments; a falling out; a quarrel; discord.

disallow, dis•al•lou′, *v.t.* To refuse permission or sanction for; not to grant; not to authorize; to disapprove of; to reject, as being illegal, unnecessary, unauthorized, and the like.—**disallowance,** dis•al•lou′ans, *n.* Disapprobation; refusal; prohibition; rejection.

disannul, dis•an•nul′, *v.t.* To make void; to annul; to deprive of force or authority; to cancel. (*Shak.*)—**disannulment,** dis•an•nul′ment, *n.* Annulment.

disappear, dis•ap•pēr′, *v.i.* To cease to appear or to be perceived; to vanish from the sight; to go away or out of sight; to cease, or seem to cease, to be or exist.—**disappearance,** dis•ap•pē′rans, *n.* Act of disappearing; removal from sight.

disappoint, dis•ap•point′, *v.t.* [Fr. *désappointer,* originally to remove from an appointment or office.] To defeat of expectation, wish, hope, desire, or intention; to frustrate; to balk; to hinder from the possession or enjoyment of that which was hoped or expected (*disappointed* of the expected legacy).—**disappointed,** dis•ap•poin′ted, *p.* and *a.* Having suffered disappointment; balked; unprepared (*Shak.*)‡.—**disappointment,** dis•ap•point′ment, *n.* The act of disappointing or feeling of being disappointed; defeat or failure of expectation, hope, wish, desire, or intention.

disapprobation, dis•ap′ro•bā″shon, *n.* The reverse of approbation; disapproval; censure, expressed or unexpressed.—**disapprove,** dis•a•pröv′, *v.t.—disapproved, disapproving.* To censure; to regard as wrong or objectionable.—*v.i.* To express or feel disapproval: with *of* before the object.—**disapproval,** dis•a•prö′val, *n.* Disapprobation; dislike.—**disapprovingly,** dis•a•prö′ving•li, *adv.* In a disapproving manner.

disarm, dis•ärm′, *v.t.* To take the arms or weapons from, usually by force or authority; to reduce to a peace footing, as an army or navy; to deprive of means of attack or defense, or of annoyance, or power to terrify; to render harmless.—*v.i.* To lay down arms; to disband armed forces.—**disarmament,** dis•är′ma•ment, *n.* Act of disarming.

disarrange, dis•a•rānj′, *v.t.* To put out of order; to unsettle or disturb the order or due arrangement of.—**disarrangement,** dis•a•rānj′ment, *n.* The act of disarranging; disorder.

disarray, dis•a•rā′, *v.t.* To undress; to divest of clothes; to throw into disorder.—*n.* Disorder; confusion; disordered dress.

disaster, diz•as′tėr, *n.* [Fr. *désastre*—*dis,* and L. *astrum,* a star; a word of astrological origin. Compare the adj. *disastrous* with *ill-starred.*] Any unfortunate event, especially a great and sudden misfortune; mishap; calamity; adversity; reverse.—**disastrous,** diz•as′trus, *a.* Occasioning or accompanied by disaster; calamitous.—**disastrously,** diz•as′trus•li, *adv.* In a disastrous manner.

disavow, dis•a•vou′, *v.t.* To deny to be true, as a fact or charge respecting one's self; to disown; to repudiate; to reject.—**disavowal,** dis•a•vou′al, *n.* Denial; repudiation.

disband, dis•band′, *v.t.* To dismiss from military service, to break up, as a band or body of men; to disperse.—*v.i.* To break up and retire from military service.—**disbandment,** dis•band′ment, *n.* The act of disbanding.

disbar, dis•bär′, *v.t.—disbarred, disbarring.* To expel from being a member of the bar; to remove from the list of lawyers.

disbelief, dis•bi•lēf′, *n.* Refusal of credit or faith; denial of belief; unbelief; infidelity; scepticism.—**disbelieve,** dis•bi•lēv′, *v.t.—disbelieved, disbelieving.* To refuse belief to; to hold not to be true or not to exist; to refuse to credit.—*v.i.* To deny the truth of any position; to refuse to believe.—**disbeliever,** dis•bi•lē′vėr, *n.* One who disbelieves or refuses belief; an unbeliever.

disburden, dis•bėr′den, *v.t.* To remove a burden from; to lay off or aside as oppressive; to get rid of.

disburse, dis•bėrs′, *v.t.—disbursed, disbursing.* [O.Fr. *desbourser*—prefix *dis,* and L.L. *bursa,* a purse. PURSE.] To pay out, as money; to spend or lay out; to expend.—**disbursement,** dis•bėrs′ment, *n.* The act of disbursing; a sum paid out.—**disburser,** dis•bėr′sėr, *n.* One who disburses.

disc. See DISK.

discard, dis•kärd′, *v.t.* and *i.* To throw out of the hand such cards as are not played in the course of the game; to dismiss from service or employment, or from society; to cast off.

discern, diz•zėrn′, *v.t.* [L. *discerno*—*dis,* and *cerno,* to separate or distinguish, akin to Gr. *krinō,* to judge (whence *critic*); Skr. *kri,* to separate. CRIME.] To perceive or note as being different; to discriminate by the eye or the intellect; to distinguish or mark as being distinct; to discover by the eye; to see.—*v.i.* To see or understand differences; to make distinction; to have clearness of mental vision.—**discerner,** diz•zėr′nėr, *n.* One who discerns; a clearsighted observer; one who knows and judges; one who has the power of distinguishing.—**discernible,** diz•zėr′ni•bl, *a.* Capable of being discerned; discoverable by the eye or the understanding; distinguishable.—**discernibleness,** diz•zėr′ni•bl•nes, *n.*—**discernibly,** diz•zėr′ni•bli, *adv.* So as to be discerned.—**discerning,** diz•zėr′ning, *p.* and *a.* Having power to discern; capable of discriminating, knowing, and judging; sharp-sighted; acute.—**discerningly,** diz•zėr′ning•li, *adv.* In a discerning manner.—**discernment,** diz•zėrn′ment, *n.* The act of discerning; the power or faculty of discerning by the mind; acuteness of judgment; power of perceiving differences of things or ideas, and their relations; penetration.

discharge, dis•chärj′, *v.t.*—*discharged, discharging.* To unload (a ship); to take out (a cargo); to free from any load or burden; to free of the missile with which anything is charged or loaded; to fire off; to let fly; to shoot; to emit or send out; to give vent to, *lit.* or *fig.*; to deliver the amount or value of to the person to whom it is owing; to pay (a debt); to free from an obligation, duty, or labor; to relieve (to *discharge* a person from a task); to clear from an accusation or crime; to acquit; to absolve; to set free; to perform or execute (a duty or office); to divest of an office or employment; to dismiss from service (a servant, a soldier, a jury); to release; to liberate from confinement. —*v.i.* To get rid of or let out a charge or contents.—*n.* The act of discharging, unloading or freeing from a charge; a flowing or issuing out, or a throwing out; emission; that which is thrown out; matter emitted; dismissal from office or service; release from obligation, debt, or penalty; absolution from a crime or accusation; ransom; price paid for deliverance; performance; execution, as of an office, trust, or duty; liberation; release from confinement; payment of a debt; a written acknowledgment of payment; a substance used in calico printing to remove color, and so form a pattern.—**discharger,** dis•chär′jėr, *n.* One who or that which discharges.

disciple, dis•sī′pl, *n.* [L. *discipulus,* from *disco,* to learn.] One who receives instruction from another; a learner; a scholar; a pupil; a follower; an adherent.—**discipleship,** dis•sī′pl•ship, *n.* The state of being a disciple.

discipline, dis′si•plin, *n.* [L. *disciplina,* from *discipulus,* a disciple, from *disco,* to learn.] Training, education; instruction and the government of conduct or practice; the training to act in accordance with rules; drill; method of regulating principles and practice; punishment inflicted by way of correction and training; instruction by means of misfortune, suffering, and the like; correction; chastisement.—*v.t.*—*disciplined, disciplining.* To subject to discipline; to apply discipline to; train; to teach rules and practice, and accustom to order and subordination; to drill; to correct, chastise, punish.—**discipliner,** dis′si•plin•ėr, *n.* One who disciplines.—**disciplinable,** dis′si•plin•a•bl, *a.* Capable of instruction and improvement in learning; capable of being made matter of discipline; subject or liable to discipline.—**disciplinarian,** dis′si•pli•nâ″ri•an, *n.* One who disciplines; one who instructs in military and naval tactics and maneuvers; one who enforces rigid discipline; a martinet.—*a.* Pertaining to discipline.—**disciplinary,** dis′si•pli•na•ri, *a.* Pertaining to discipline; intended for discipline; promoting discipline.

disclaim, dis•klām′, *v.t.* To deny or relinquish all claim to; to reject as not belonging to one's self; to renounce; to deny responsibility for or approval of; to disavow; to disown.—**disclaimer,** dis•klā′mėr, *n.* A person who disclaims; an act of disclaiming; abnegation of pretensions or claims; *law,* a renunciation, abandonment, or giving up of a claim.

disclose, dis•klōz′, *v.t.*—*disclosed, disclosing.* To uncover and lay open to the view; to cause to appear; to allow to be seen; to bring to light; to make known, reveal, tell, utter.—**discloser,** dis•klō′zėr, *n.* One who discloses.—**disclosure,** dis•klō′zhėr, *n.* The act of disclosing; exhibition; the act of making known or revealing; utterance of what was secret; a telling; that which is disclosed or made known.

discoid. See DISK.

discolor, dis•kul′ėr, *v.t.* To alter the hue or color of; to change to a different color or shade; to stain; to tinge.—**discoloration,** dis•kul′ėr•ā″shon, *n.* The act of discoloring; alteration of color; a discolored spot or marking.

discomfit, dis•kum′fit, *v.t.* [O.Fr. *disconfire, disconfit*—L. *dis,* not, and *conficere,* to achieve. COMFIT.] To rout, defeat, or scatter in flight; to cause to flee; to vanquish; to disconcert, foil, or frustrate the plans of.—*n.* A defeat; an overthrow. (*Mil.*)—**discomfiture,** dis•kum′fi•chėr, *n.* Rout; defeat; overthrow; frustration; disappointment.

discomfort, dis•kum′fėrt, *n.* Absence or opposite of comfort or pleasure; uneasiness; disturbance of peace; pain, annoyance, or inquietude.—*v.t.* To disturb the peace or happiness of; to make uneasy; to pain.—**discomfortable,**† dis•kum′fėr•ta•bl, *a.* Wanting in comfort; uncomfortable.

discommend,† dis•kom•mend′, *v.t.* To blame; to censure; to expose to censure or bad feeling.

discommode, dis•kom•mōd′, *v.t.*—*discommoded, discommoding.* To put to inconvenience; to incommode.

discommon, dis•kom′on, *v.t.* To make to cease to be common land; to deprive of the right of a common.

discompose, dis•kom•pōz′, *v.t.*—*discomposed, discomposing.* To disorder, disturb, or disarrange; to disturb the peace and quietness of; to agitate, ruffle, fret, or vex.—**discomposure,** dis•kom•pō′zhėr, *n.* The state of being discomposed; a certain agitation or perturbation of mind.

disconcert, dis•kon•sėrt′, *v.t.* To throw into disorder or confusion; to undo, as a concerted scheme or plan; to defeat; to frustrate; to discompose or disturb the self-possession of; to confuse.—**disconcertion,** dis•kon•sėr′shon, *n.* The act of disconcerting; the state of being disconcerted.

disconformable, dis•kon•for′ma•bl, *a.* Not conformable.—**disconformity,** dis•kon•for′mi•ti, *n.* Want of agreement or conformity; inconsistency.

disconnect, dis•kon•nekt′, *v.t.* To separate or sever the connection between; to disunite; to detach.—**disconnection,** dis•kon•nek′shon, *n.* The act of disconnecting; separation; want of union.

disconsolate, dis•kon′so•lit, *a.* [L. *dis,* not, and *consolatus,* pp. of *consolor,* to console, to be consoled. CONSOLE.] Destitute of consolation; hopeless; sad; dejected; melancholy; cheerless; saddening; gloomy.—**disconsolately,** dis•kon′so•lit•li, *adv.* In a disconsolate manner; without comfort.—**disconsolateness,** dis•kon′so•lit•nes, *n.*

discontent, dis•kon•tent′, *n.* Want of content; uneasiness or inquietude of mind; dissatisfaction; one who is discontented; a malcontent (*Shak.*). —*a.*‡ Uneasy; dissatisfied.—*v.t.* To make dissatisfied.—**discontented,** dis•kon•ten′ted, *a.* Not contented; dissatisfied; not pleased with one's circumstances; given to grumble.—**discontentedly,** dis•kon•ten′ted•li, *adv.* In a discontented manner or mood.—**discontentedness,** dis•kon•ten′ted•nes, *n.* The state of being discontented; dissatisfaction.—**discontentment,** dis•kon•tent′ment, *n.* The state of being discontented; discontent.

discontinue, dis•kon•tin′ū, *v.t.*—*discontinued, discontinuing.* [Prefix *dis,* neg., and *continue.*] To continue no longer; to leave off or break off; to give up, cease from, or abandon; to stop; to put an end to.—*v.i.* To cease; to stop.—**discontinuance,** dis•kon•tin′ū•ans, *n.* Want of continuance; breaking off; cessation; intermission; interruption.—**discontinuation,** dis•kon•tin′ū•ā″shon, *n.* Discontinuance.—**discontinuity,** dis•kon′ti•nū″i•ti, *n.* Want of continuity or uninterrupted connection; disunion of parts; want of cohesion.—**discontinuous,** dis•kon•tin′ū•us, *a.* Broken off; interrupted.

discord, dis′kord, *n.* [Fr. *discorde,* L. *discordia,* disagreement, from *discors,* discordant—*dis,* and *cor, cordis,* the heart, as in *concord, accord, cordial.*]

Want of concord or agreement; opposition of opinions; difference of qualities; disagreement; variance; contention; strife; *mus.* a union of sounds disagreeable or grating to the ear; dissonance; each of the *two* sounds forming a dissonance.—*v.i.* (dis-kord′). To disagree; to be out of harmony or concord; to clash.—**discordance, discordancy,** dis•kor′-dans, dis•kor′dan•si, *n.* Disagreement; opposition; inconsistency.—**discordant,** dis•kor′dant, *a.* Disagreeing; incongruous; being at variance; dissonant; not in unison; not harmonious; not accordant; harsh; jarring.—**discordantly,** dis•-kor′dant•li, *adv.* In a discordant manner.

discount, dis′kount, *n.* [Prefix *dis,* neg., and *count*; O.Fr. *descompte.*] A certain sum deducted from the credit price of goods sold on account of prompt payment, or any deduction from the customary price, or from a sum due or to be due at a future time; a charge made to cover the interest of money advanced on a bill or other document not presently due; the act of discounting.—*At a discount,* below par; hence, in low esteem; in disfavor.—*v.t.* (diskount′). To lend or advance the amount of (a bill or similar document), deducting the interest or other rate per cent from the principal; to leave out of account or disregard; to estimate or take into account beforehand; to enjoy or suffer by anticipation.—**discountable,** dis•koun′ta•bl, *a.* Capable of being discounted.—**discounter,** dis′koun•tėr, *n.* One who discounts bills, etc.

discountenance, dis•koun′te•nans, *v.t.* To put out of countenance; to put to shame; to abash; to set one's countenance against; to discourage, check, or restrain by frowns, censure, arguments, cold treatment, etc.—*n.* Cold treatment; disapprobation.

discourage, dis•kur′ij, *v.t.*—*discouraged, discouraging.* To check the courage of; to dishearten; to deprive of self-confidence; to attempt to repress or prevent by pointing out difficulties, etc.; to dissuade.—**discouragement,** dis•kur′ij•ment, *n.* The act of discouraging; the act of deterring or dissuading from an undertaking; that which discourages or damps ardor or hope; the state of being discouraged.—**discourager,** dis•kur′i•jėr, *n.* One who or that which discourages.—**discouraging,** dis•kur′i•jing, *a.* Tending to discourage or dishearten; disheartening. —**discouragingly,** dis•kur′i•jing•li, *adv.* In a discouraging manner.

discourse, dis′kōrs, *n.* [Fr. *discours,* from L. *discursus,* a running about, a conversation, from *discurro,* to ramble—*dis,* and *curro,* to run. CURRENT.] A running over a subject in speech; hence, a talking together or discussing; conversation; talk; speech; a treatise; a dissertation; a homily, sermon, or other production. —*v.i. (dis-kors′),—discoursing.* To communicate thoughts orally or in writing, especially in a formal manner; to hold forth; to expatiate; to converse.—*v.t.* To talk over or discuss‡; to utter or give forth.—**discourser,** dis•kōr′sėr, *n.* One who discourses.

discourteous, dis•kėr′tē•us, *a.* Wanting in courtesy; uncivil; rude.—**discourteously,** dis•kėr′tē•us•li, *adv.* In a discourteous manner.—**discourteousness,** dis•kėr′tē•us•nes, *n.*—**discourtesy,** dis•kėr′te•si, *n.* Want of courtesy; incivility; rudeness of manner; act of disrespect.

discover, dis•kuv′ėr, *v.t.* [Prefix *dis,* not, and *cover*; O.Fr. *descouvrir.*] To lay open to view; to disclose or reveal; to espy; to have the first sight of; to find out; to obtain the first knowledge of; to come to the knowledge of; to detect. ∴ We *discover* what before existed, though to us unknown; we *invent* what did not before exist.—**discoverable,** dis•kuv′-ėr•a•bl, *a.* Capable of being discovered, brought to light, exposed, found out, or made known.—**discoverer,** dis•kuv′ėr•ėr, *n.* One who discovers; one who first sees or espies; one who finds out or first comes to the knowledge of something.—**discovery,** dis•-kuv′ėr•i, *n.* The act of discovering; a disclosing or bringing to light; a revealing or making known; a finding out or bringing for the first time to sight or knowledge; what is discovered or found out.

discredit, dis•kred′it, *n.* Want of credit or good reputation; some degree of disgrace or reproach; disesteem; disrepute; want of belief, trust, or confidence; disbelief.—*v.t.* To give no credit to; not to credit or believe; to deprive of credit or good reputation; to bring into some degree of disgrace or disrepute; to deprive of credibility.—**discreditable,** dis•kred′i•ta•bl, *n.* Injurious to reputation; disgraceful; disreputable.—**discreditably,** dis•kred′i•ta•bli, *adv.* In a discreditable manner.

discreet, dis•krēt′, *a.* [Fr. *discret,* from L. *discretus,* pp. of *discerno,* to discern. DISCERN.] Wise in avoiding errors or evil, and in selecting the best course or means; prudent in conduct; circumspect; cautious; heedful; guarded.—**discreetly,** dis•-krēt′li, *adv.* In a discreet manner; prudently.—**discreetness,** dis•krēt′-nes, *n.* The quality of being discreet. —**discretion,** dis•kresh′on, *n.* [Fr. *discrétion,* L. *discretio.*] The quality or attribute of being discreet; discernment to judge critically of what is correct and proper, united with caution; prudence; sound judgment; circumspection; wariness; caution; liberty or power of acting without other control than one's own judgment (to leave an affair to one's *discretion,* to surrender at *discretion,* that is without stipulating for terms). —**discretionary,** dis•kresh′on•e•ri, *a.* Left to a person's own discretion or judgment; to be directed according to one's own discretion (*discretionary* powers).

discrepance, discrepancy, dis•krep′-ans, dis•krep′an•si, *n.* [L. *discrepantia,* from *discrepo,* to give a different sound, to vary—*dis,* and *crepo,* to creak. CREPITATE.] A difference or inconsistency between facts, stories, theories, etc.; disagreement; divergence.—**discrepant,** dis•krep′ant, *a.* Differing or diverging; not agreeing or according; disagreeing; dissimilar.

discrete, dis•krēt′, *a.* [L. *discretus,* separated, set apart. DISCREET.] Separate; distinct; disjunct; disjunctive.—*A discrete quantity,* quantity not continued in its parts, as any number, since a number consists of units.

discretion. See DISCREET.

discriminate, dis•krim′i•nāt, *v.t.*—*discriminated, discriminating.* [L. *discrimino, discriminatum,* to distinguish, from *discrimen,* difference—*dis,* asunder, and the root seen in *crimen,* accusation, *cerno,* to sift or separate. CRIME, DISCERN, DISCREET.] To distinguish from other things by observing differences; to perceive by a distinction; to discern; to separate; to select; to distinguish by some note or mark.—*v.i.* To make a difference or distinction; to observe or note a difference; to distinguish.—**discriminately,** dis•krim′i•nit•li, *adv.* With minute distinction; particularly.—**discriminating,** dis•krim′-i•nā•ting, *p.* and *a.* Serving to discriminate; distinguishing; distinctive; able to make nice distinctions.—**discrimination,** dis•krim′i•nā″shon, *n.* The act of discriminating; the faculty of distinguishing or discriminating; penetration; discernment; the state of being discriminated or set apart.—**discriminative,** dis•krim′-i•nā•tiv, *a.* Discriminating or tending to discriminate; forming the mark of distinction or difference; characteristic. — **discriminatively,** dis•-krim′i•nā•tiv•li, *adv.* By discrimination.—**discriminatory,** dis•krim′i•-na•to•ri, *a.* Discriminative.

discrown, dis•kroun′, *v.t.* To deprive of a crown.

discursive, dis•kėr′siv, *a.* [Fr. *discursif,* from L. *discursus.* DISCOURSE.] Passing rapidly from one subject to another; desultory; rambling; digressional; argumentative; reasoning; rational.—**discursively,** dis•kėr′-siv•li, *adv.* In a discursive manner.—**discursiveness,** dis•kėr′siv•nes, *n.*

discus, dis′kus, *n.* See DISK.

discuss, dis•kus′, *v.t.* [L. *discutio, discussum,* to scatter, dissipate—*dis,* asunder, and *quatio,* to shake, as in *concussion.* QUASH.] To drive away, dissolve, or resolve (a tumor, etc.: a medical use); to agitate by argument; to examine by disputation; to reason on; to debate; to argue; to make an end of, by eating or drinking; to consume (*colloq.*).—**discussion,** dis•ku′shon, *n.* The act of discussing; debate; disquisition; the agitation of a point or subject with a view to elicit truth.

disdain, dis•dān′, *v.t.* [O.Fr. *desdaigner,* Fr. *dédaigner,* from L. *dis,* not, and *dignor,* to deem worthy, from *dignus,* worthy. DEIGN.] To deem or regard as worthless; to consider to be unworthy of notice, care, regard, esteem, or unworthy of one's character; to scorn; to contemn.—*n.* A feeling of contempt, mingled with indignation; the looking upon anything as beneath one; haughtiness; contempt; scorn.—**disdainful,** dis•dān′fu̦l, *a.* Full of or expressing disdain; contemptuous; scornful; haughty.—**disdainfully,** dis•dān′fu̦l•li, *adv.* In a disdainful manner.—**disdainfulness,** dis•dān′-fu̦l•nes, *n.* The quality of being disdainful; haughty scorn.

disease, di•zēz′, *n.* Want or absence of ease‡; uneasiness, distress, or discomfort‡; any morbid state of the body, or of any particular organ or part of the body; ailment; distemper; malady; disorder; any morbid or depraved condition, moral, mental, social, political, etc.—**diseased,** di•-zēzd′, *a.* Affected with disease; having the vital functions deranged; disordered; deranged; distempered; sick.

disembark, dis•em•bärk′, *v.t.* To remove from on board a ship to the land; to put on shore; to land.—*v.i.* To leave a ship and go on shore; to land.—**disembarkation, disembarkment,** dis•em′bär•kā″shon, dis•em•-bärk′ment, *n.* The act of disembarking.

disembarrass, dis•em•bar′as, *v.t.* To free from embarrassment or perplexity; to clear; to extricate.—**disembarrassment,** dis•em•bar′as•-ment, *n.* The act of disembarrassing.

disembody, dis•em•bod′i, *v.t.* To divest of the body (a *disembodied* spirit=a ghost); to set free from the flesh; to disband (*military*).—**disembodiment,** dis•em•bod′i•ment, *n.* The act of disembodying; the condition of being disembodied.

disembogue, dis•em•bōg′, *v.t.* and *i.*—*disembogued, disemboguing.* To pour out or discharge at the mouth, as a stream; to discharge water into the ocean or a lake.—**disemboguement,** dis•em•bōg′ment, *n.* Discharge of waters by a stream.

disembowel, dis•em•bou′el, *v.t.*—*disemboweled, disemboweling.* To deprive of the bowels or of parts analogous to the bowels; to eviscerate; to gut.

disenchant, dis•en•chant′, *v.t.* To free from enchantment; to deliver from the power of charms or spells; to free from fascination or pleasing delusion.—**disenchanter,** dis•en•-chan′tėr, *n.* One who or that which disenchants.—**disenchantment,** dis•-en•chant′ment, *n.* Act of disenchanting.

disencumber, dis•en•kum′bėr, *v.t.* To free from encumbrance, clogs, and impediments.

disendow, dis•en•dou′, *v.t.* To deprive of an endowment or endowments, as a church or other institution.—**disendowment,** dis•en•dou′-ment, *n.* The act of disendowing.

disenfranchise, dis•en•fran′chīz, *v.t.* To disfranchise.

disengage, dis•en•gāj′, *v.t.*—*disengaged, disengaging.* To separate or set free from union or attachment; to detach; to disunite; to free; to disentangle; to extricate; to clear, as from difficulties or perplexities; to free, as from anything that occupies the attention; to set free by dissolving an engagement.—**disengagement,** dis•en•gāj′ment, *n.* The act or process of disengaging; the state of being disengaged; freedom from engrossing occupation; leisure.

disentail, dis•en•tāl′, *v.t.* To free from being entailed; to break the entail of.

disentangle, dis•en•tang′gl, *v.t.* To free from entanglements; to unravel; to extricate from perplexity or complications; to disengage.—**disentanglement,** dis•en•tang′gl•ment, *n.* Act of disentangling.

disenthrone, dis•en•thrōn′, *v.t.* To dethrone; to depose from sovereign authority. (*Mil.*)

disentomb, dis•en•töm′, *v.t.* To take out of a tomb; to disinter.

disestablish, dis•es•tab′lish, *v.t.* To cause to cease to be established; to withdraw (a church) from its connection with the state.—**disestablishment,** dis•es•tab′lish•ment, *n.* The act of disestablishing; the act of withdrawing a church from its connection with the state.

disesteem, dis•es•tēm′, *n.* Want of esteem; slight dislike; disregard.—*v.t.* To dislike in a moderate degree; to regard as unworthy of esteem.

disfavor, dis•fā′vėr, *n.* A feeling of some dislike or slight displeasure; unfavorable regard; disesteem; a state of being unacceptable, or not favored, patronized, or befriended; a disobliging act.—*v.t.* To withdraw or withhold favor, friendship, or support from.

disfigure, dis•fig′ūr, *v.t.*—*disfigured, disfiguring.* To mar the external figure of; to impair the shape or form of; to injure the beauty, symmetry, or excellence of; to deface; to deform.—**disfiguration,** dis•fig′-ū•rā″shon, *n.* The act of disfiguring; disfigurement.—**disfigurement,** dis•-fig′ūr•ment, *n.* The act of disfiguring or state of being disfigured; that which disfigures.—**disfigurer,** dis•-fig′ū•rėr, *n.* One who disfigures.

disforest, dis•for′est, *v.t.* Same as *Disafforest.*

disfranchise, dis•fran′chīz, *v.t.*—*disfranchised, disfranchising.* To deprive of the rights and privileges of a free citizen; to deprive of any franchise, more especially of the right of voting in elections, etc.—**disfranchisement,** dis•fran′chiz•ment, *n.* The act of disfranchising, or state of being disfranchised.

disgorge, dis•gorj′, *v.t.*—*disgorged, disgorging.* [O.Fr. *desgorger*, to vomit —*dis*, and *gorge.* GORGE.] To eject or discharge from, or as from, the stomach, throat, or mouth; to vomit; to belch; to discharge violently (a volcano *disgorges* lava); to yield up, as what has been taken wrongfully; to give up; to surrender.—*v.i.* To give up plunder or ill-gotten gains.

disgrace, dis•grās′, *n.* A state of being out of favor; disfavor; state of ignominy; dishonor; shame; infamy; cause of shame.—*v.t.*—*disgraced, disgracing.* To bring into disgrace; to put out of favor; to dismiss with dishonor; to treat ignominiously; to bring shame or reproach on; to humiliate or humble; to dishonor.—**disgraceful,** dis•grās′fu̦l, *a.* Entailing disgrace; shameful; infamous; dishonorable.—**disgracefully,** dis•grās′-fu̦l•li, *adv.* In a disgraceful manner. —**disgracefulness,** dis•grās′fu̦l•nes, *n.* The state or quality of being disgraceful.—**disgracer,** dis•grā′sėr, *n.* One who disgraces.

disguise, dis•gīz′, *v.t.*—*disguised, disguising.* [O.Fr. *desguiser*, Fr. *déguiser* —prefix *dis*, and *guise*, way, fancy, manner. GUISE.] To conceal the ordinary guise and appearance of by an unusual habit or mask; to hide by a counterfeit appearance; to cloak by a false show, false language, or an artificial manner (anger, intentions, etc.); to change in manners or behavior by the use of spirituous liquor; to intoxicate.—*n.* A counterfeit dress; a dress intended to conceal the identity of the person who wears it; a counterfeit show; artificial or assumed language or appearance intended to deceive.—**disguisedly,** dis•gī′zed•li, *adv.* With disguise.—**disguiser,** dis•gī′zėr, *n.* One who disguises.

disgust, dis•gust′, *n.* [O.Fr. *desgoust*, Fr. *dégoût*, from L. *dis*, not, and *gustus*, taste.] Aversion to the taste of food or drink; distate; disrelish; nausea; aversion in the mind excited by something offensive in the manners, conduct, language, or opinions of others; loathing; repugnance; strong dislike.—*v.t.* To cause to feel disgust; to excite aversion in the stomach of; to offend the taste of; to stir up loathing or repugnance in. —**disgustful,** dis•gust′fu̦l, *a.* Exciting the feeling of disgust.—**disgusting,** dis•gus′ting, *a.* Producing or causing disgust; nauseous; loathsome; nasty. —**disgustingly,** dis•gus′ting•li, *adv.* In a disgusting manner.

dish, dish, *n.* [A.Sax. *disc*, a dish; like D. *disch*, G. *tisch*, a table, from L. *discus*, Gr. *diskos*, a quoit or disk. DESK, DISK.] A broad open vessel made of various materials, used for serving up meat and various kinds of food at the table; the meat or provisions served in a dish; hence, any particular kind of food; the concavity of certain wheels, as those of vehicles.—*v.t.* To put in a dish after being cooked; to make (a wheel) concave in the center; to damage, ruin, completely overthrow (*slang*).—**dishcloth, dishclout,** *n.* A cloth used for washing and wiping dishes.—**dishwater,** *n.* Water in which dishes are washed.

dishabille, dis′a•bēl, *n.* Same as *Deshabille.*

dishearten, dis•här′tn, *v.t.* To discourage; to deprive of courage; to depress the spirits of; to deject; to dispirit.

dishevel, di•shev′el, *v.t.*—*disheveled, disheveling.* [O.Fr. *descheveler*, Fr. *décheveler*, to put the hair out of order—*des* for *dis*, not, and O.Fr. *chevel*, Fr. *cheveu*, hair, from L. *capillus*, the hair of the head.] To spread the locks or tresses of loosely and negligently; to suffer (the hair) to hang negligently and uncombed.

dishonest, dis•on′est, *a.* Void of honesty, probity, or integrity; not honest, fraudulent; inclined or apt to deceive, cheat, pilfer, embezzle, or defraud; proceeding from or marked by fraud; knavish; unchaste‡.—**dishonestly,** dis•on′est•li, *adv.* In a dishonest manner; fraudulently; knavishly.—**dishonesty,** dis•on′es•ti, *n.* The opposite of honesty; want of probity or integrity; a disposition to cheat, pilfer, embezzle, or defraud; violation of trust; fraud; treachery; deviation from probity or integrity; unchastity or incontinence‡.

dishonor, dis•on′ėr, *n.* The opposite of honor; want of honor; disgrace; shame; anything that disgraces.—*v.t.* To disgrace; to bring shame on; to stain the character of; to lessen in reputation; to treat with indignity; to violate the chastity of; to debauch; to refuse or decline to accept or pay (a bill of exchange).—**dishonorable,** dis•on′ėr•a•bl, *a.* Shameful; disgraceful; base; bringing shame; staining the character and lessening reputation; unhonored (*Shak.*).—**dishonorableness,** dis•on′ėr•a•bl•nes, *n.* Quality of being dishonorable.—**dishonorably,** dis•on′ėr•a•bli, *adv.* In a dishonorable manner.

disillusion, dis•il•lū′zhon, *v.t.* To disenchant; to free from illusion. —*n.* Disenchantment.—**disillusionment,** dis•il•lū′zhon•ment, *n.*

disincline, dis•in•klīn′, *v.t.* To excite slight aversion in; to make unwilling; to cause to hang back; to alienate.

disinfect, dis•in•fekt′, *v.t.* To cleanse from infection; to purify from contagious matter.—**disinfectant,** dis•in•fek′tant, *n.* A substance that disinfects, or is used for destroying the power or means of propagating diseases which spread by infection or contagion.—**disinfection,** dis•in•fek′shon, *n.* Purification from infecting matter.

disingenuous, dis•in•jen′ū•us, *a.* Not ingenuous; not open, frank, and candid; meanly artful; insincere; sly; uncandid.—**disingenuously,** dis•in•jen′ū•us•li, *adv.* In a disingenuous manner.—**disingenuousness,** dis•in•jen′ū•us•nes, *n.* The state or quality of being disingenuous.

disinherit, dis•in•her′it, *v.t.* To cut off from hereditary right; to deprive of the right to an inheritance.—**disinheritance,** dis•in•her′i•tans, *n.* Act of disinheriting.

disintegrate, dis•in′te•grāt, *v.t.* [L. *dis*, not, and *integer*, entire, whole.] To separate the component particles of; to reduce to powder or to fragments.—**disintegration,** dis•in′te•grā″shon, *n.* The act of separating the component particles of a substance; the gradual wearing down of rocks by atmospheric influence.

disinter, dis•in•tėr′, *v.t.*—*disinterred, disinterring.* To take out of a grave or out of the earth; to take out, as from a grave; to bring from obscurity into view.—**disinterment,** dis•in•tėr′ment, *n.* The act of disinterring; exhumation.

disinterested, dis•in′tėr•es•ted, *a.* Free from self-interest; having no personal interest or private advantage in a question or affair; not influenced or dictated by private advantage; unselfish; uninterested.—**disinterestedly,** dis•in′tėr•es•ted•li, *adv.* In a disinterested manner.—**disinterestedness,** dis•in′tėr•es•ted•nes, *n.* The state or quality of being disinterested.

disjoin, dis•join′, *v.t.* To part asunder; to disunite; to separate; to detach; to sunder.—*v.i.* To be separated; to part.—**disjoint,** dis•joint′, *v.t.* To separate, as parts united by joints; to put out of joint; to dislocate; to break the natural order and relations of; to put out of order; to derange; to render incoherent.—*v.i.* To fall in pieces.—**disjointed,** dis•join′ted, *a.* Unconnected; incoherent; out of joint; out of order; ill-joined together.—**disjointedness,** dis•join′ted•nes, *n.* State of being disjointed.—**disjointly,** dis•joint′li, *adv.* In a disjointed manner or state.

disjunct, dis•jungkt′, *a.* [L. *disjunctus*, pp. of *disjungo*—*dis*, and *jungo*, to join.] Disjoined; separated.—**disjunction,** dis•jungk′shon, *n.* The act of disjoining, disunion; separation.—**disjunctive,** dis•jungk′tiv, *a.* Tending to disjoin or separate; *gram.* marking separation or opposition, a term applied to a word or particle which unites words or sentences in construction, but disjoins the sense (as *neither, nor*); *logic*, applied to a proposition in which the parts are opposed to each other by means of disjunctives.—*n. Gram.* a word that disjoins (as *or, nor, neither*); *logic*, a disjunctive proposition.—**disjunctively,** dis•jungk′tiv•li, *adv.* In a disjunctive manner.

disk, disc, disk, *n.* [L. *discus*, a quoit. DESK, DISH.] A kind of ancient quoit; any flat circular plate or surface, as of a piece of metal, the face of the sun, moon, or a planet as it appears to our sight, etc.; *bot.* the whole surface of a leaf; also, the central part of a radiate compound flower, the part surrounded by what is called the ray.—**discoid,** dis′koid, *a.* Shaped like a disk; resembling a disk.

dislike, dis•līk′, *n.* A feeling the opposite of liking; disinclination; aversion; distaste; antipathy; repugnance.—*v.t.*—*disliked, disliking.* To feel dislike toward; to regard with some aversion; to have a feeling against; to disrelish.—**dislikable,**† dis•lī′ka•bl, *a.* Worthy of, or liable to dislike; distasteful; disagreeable.

dislocate, dis′lo•kāt, *v.t.*—*dislocated, dislocating.* To displace; to shift from the original site; particularly, to put out of joint; to move (a bone) from its socket, cavity, or place of articulation.—**dislocation,** dis•lo•kā′shon, *n.* The act of dislocating; particularly, the act of removing or forcing a bone from its socket; luxation; *geol.* the displacement of parts of rocks, or portions of strata, from the situations which they originally occupied.

dislodge, dis•loj′, *v.t.*—*dislodged, dislodging.* To drive from the fixed position or place occupied; to drive (enemies) from any place of hiding or defense, or from a position seized. —*v.i.* To go from a place of rest.—**dislodgment,** dis•loj′ment, *n.* The act of dislodging.

disloyal, dis•loi′al, *a.* Not loyal or true to allegiance; false to a sovereign or country; faithless; false; perfidious; treacherous; not true to the marriage bed; false in love.—**disloyally,** dis•loi′al•li, *adv.* In a disloyal manner.—**disloyalty,** dis•loi′al•ti, *n.* The character of being disloyal; want of fidelity to a sovereign; violation of allegiance; want of fidelity in love.

dismal, diz′mal, *a.* [Etym. doubtful. According to one derivation, from L. *dies malus*, an evil day; according to another, from O.Fr. *dismal*, L. *decimalis, decem*, ten, referring to the day of paying tithes.] Dark, gloomy, or cheerless to look at; depressing; sorrowful; dire; horrid; melancholy; calamitous; unfortunate; frightful; horrible.—**dismally,** diz′mal•li, *adv.* In a dismal manner.—**dismalness,** diz′mal•nes, *n.* The state of being dismal; gloominess; horror.

dismantle, dis•man′tl, *v.t.*—*dismantled, dismantling.* [O.Fr. *desmanteler, desmanteller*, lit. to deprive of cloak or mantle.] To deprive of dress; to strip; to divest; more generally, to deprive or strip (a thing) of furniture, equipments, fortifications, and the like.

dismast, dis•mast′, *v.t.* To deprive of a mast or masts; to break and carry away the masts from.

dismay, dis•mā′, *v.t.* [Same word as Sp. and Pg. *desmayar*, to fall into a swoon, but no doubt directly from the French; from prefix *dis*, and O.H.G. *magan*, to be able (=E. *may*).] To deprive entirely of strength or firmness of mind; to discourage, with some feeling of dread or consternation; to confound; to daunt; to strike aghast.—*v.i.* To be daunted; to stand aghast. (*Shak.*)—*n.* A complete giving way of boldness or spirit; loss of courage together with consternation; a yielding to fear.

dismember, dis•mem′bėr, *v.t.* To divide limb from limb; to separate the members of; to mutilate; to sever and distribute the parts of; to divide into separate portions (a kingdom, etc.).—**dismemberment,** dis•mem′bėr•ment, *n.* The act of dismembering.

dismiss, dis•mis′, *v.t.* [From L. *dimitto, dimissum*, to dismiss—*di, dis*, and *mitto*, as in *admit, commit*, etc.] To send away; to permit to depart, implying authority in a person to retain or keep; to discard; to remove from office, service, or employment; *law*, to reject as unworthy of notice, or of being granted.—**dismissal,** dis•mis′al, *n.* The act of dismissing; dismission; discharge; liberation; manumission. — **dismission,** dis•mish′on, *n.* The act of dismissing or sending away; leave to depart; removal from office or employment; discharge; *law*, rejection of something as unworthy of notice or of being granted.

dismount, dis•mount′, *v.i.* To alight from a horse or other animal; to come or go down.—*v.t.* To throw or remove from a horse; to unhorse; to throw or remove (cannon or other artillery) from their carriages.

disobedience, dis•o•bē′di•ens, *n.* Neglect or refusal to obey; violation of a command or prohibition; the omission of that which is commanded to be done, or the doing of that which is forbidden.—**disobedient,** dis•o•bē′di•ent, *a.* Neglecting or refusing to obey; guilty of disobedience; not observant of duty or rules prescribed by authority.—**disobediently,** dis•o•bē′di•ent•li, *adv.* In a disobedient manner.—**disobey,** dis•o•bā′, *v.t.* To neglect or refuse to obey; to omit or refuse obedience to; to transgress or violate an order or injunction.—*v.i.* To refuse obedience; to disregard orders.

disoblige, dis•o•blīj′, *v.t.* To offend by acting counter to the will or desires of; to offend by failing to oblige or do a friendly service to; to be unaccommodating to.—**disobliging,** dis•o•blī′jing, *a.* Not obliging; not disposed to gratify the wishes of another; unaccommodating.

disorder, dis•or′dėr, *n.* Want of order or regular disposition; irregularity; immethodical distribution; confusion; tumult; disturbance of the peace of society; disturbance or interruption of the functions of the animal economy or of the mind; distemper; sickness; derangement.—*v.t.* To break the order of; to derange; to throw into confusion; to disturb or interrupt the natural functions of; to produce sickness or indisposition in; to disturb as regards the reason or judgment; to craze.—**disordered,** dis•or′dėrd, *p.* and *a.* Disorderly; irregular; deranged; crazed.—**disorderliness,** dis•or′dėr•li•nes, *n.* State of being disorderly.—**disorderly,** dis•or′dėr•li, *a.* Being without proper order; marked by disorder; confused; immethodical; irregular; tumultuous; unruly; violating law and good order.

disorganize, dis•or′ga•nīz, *v.t.* To disturb or destroy organic structure or connected system in; to throw out of regular system; to throw into confusion or disorder (a government, society, etc.).—**disorganization,** dis•or′ga•ni•zā″shon, *n.*

disorient, dis•ō′ri•ent, *v.t.* To cause to lose bearings; to confuse.—**disorientate,** dis•ō′ri•en•tāt, *v.t.* To disorient.—**disorientation,** dis•ō′ri•en•ta″shon, *n.*

disown, dis•ōn′, *v.t.* To refuse to acknowledge as belonging to one's self; to refuse to own; to deny; to repudiate.

disparage, dis•par′ij, *v.t.*—*disparaged, disparaging.* [O.Fr. *desparager*, to offer to a woman, or impose on her as husband, a man unfit or unworthy; to impose unworthy conditions—prefix *des* for *dis*, and *parage*, equality, from L. par, equal, whence also *peer, pair*.] To dishonor by a comparison with something of less value or excellence; to treat with detraction or in a depreciatory manner; to undervalue; to decry; to vilify; to lower in estimation.—**disparagement,** dis•par′ij•ment, *n.* The act of disparaging; the act of undervaluing or depreciating; detraction; what lowers in value or esteem; disgrace; dishonor.—**disparager,** dis•par′i•jėr, *n.* One who disparages.—**disparagingly,** dis•par′i•jing•li, *adv.* In a manner to disparage.

disparate, dis′pa•rit, *a.* [L. *disparatus*, pp. of *disparo*, to part, separate —*dis*, asunder, and *paro*, to prepare.] Unequal; unlike; dissimilar.—*n.* One of two or more things so unequal or unlike that they cannot be compared with each other.

disparity, dis•par′i•ti, *n.* [Fr. *disparité*, from L. *dispar*, unequal—*dis*, and *par*, equal. DISPARAGE.] Inequality; difference in degree, in age, rank, condition, or excellence; dissimilitude; unlikeness.

dispart, dis•pärt′, *v.t.* To divide into parts; to separate, sever, burst, rend. —*v.i.* To separate; to open; to cleave.—*n.* (dis′pärt). The difference between the semi-diameter of the base ring at the breech of a gun, and that of the ring at the swell of the muzzle.

dispassionate, dis•pash′on•it, *a.* Free from passion; calm; composed; unmoved by feelings; not dictated by passion; not proceeding from temper or bias; impartial.—**dispassionately,** dis•pash′on•it•li, *adv.* Without passion; calmly; coolly.

dispatch, despatch, dis•pach′, des•pach′, *v.t.* [O.Fr. *despecher*, Fr. *dépêcher*, to despatch, to expedite, from L.L. *dispedico*—L. *dis*, apart, and *pedica*, a snare, or from a L.L. *dispactare*, from L. *dis*, and *pango*, *pactum*, to fasten, as in *compact*, *a*.] To send or send away; particularly applied to the sending of messengers, agents, and letters on special business, and often implying haste; to hasten; to expedite; to speed; to send out of the world; to put to death; to slay; to kill; to perform or execute speedily; to finish.—*n.* The act of dispatching; the getting rid of or doing away with something; dismissal; riddance; speedy performance; speed; haste; expedition; a letter sent or to be sent with expedition by a special messenger; a letter on some affair of state or of public concern; a letter, message, or document, sent by some public officer on public business.—**dispatcher,** dis•pach′ėr, *n.* One who dispatches.

dispel, dis•pel′, *v.t.*—*dispelled, dispelling.* [L. *dispello*—*dis*, asunder, and *pello*, to drive, as in *compel*, *repel*, etc.] To scatter by force; to disperse; to dissipate; to drive away (clouds, doubts, fears, etc.).—*v.i.* To be dispersed; to disappear.

dispense, dis•pens′, *v.t.*—*dispensed, dispensing.* [L. *dispenso*, to weigh out or pay, to manage, to act as steward—*dis*, distrib., and *penso*, freq. of *pendo*, to weigh, whence *pension, poise, expend, spend*.] To deal or divide out in parts or portions; to distribute; to administer; to apply, as laws to particular cases; to grant dispensation to; to relieve, excuse, or set free from an obligation.—*v.i.* To bargain for, grant, or receive a dispensation; to compound.—*To dispense with*, to permit the neglect or omission of, as a ceremony, an oath, and the like; to give up or do without, as services, attendance, articles of dress, etc.—**dispenser,** dis•pen′sėr, *n.* One who or that which dispenses or distributes; one who administers.—**dispensable,** dis•pen′sa•bl, *a.* Capable of being dispensed or administered; capable of being spared or dispensed with.—**dispensableness,** dis•pen′sa•bl•nes, *n.* The capability of being dispensed with.—**dispensary,** dis•pen′se•ri, *n.* A shop in which medicines are compounded and sold; a house in which medicines are dispensed to the poor, and medical advice given gratis.—**dispensation,** dis•pen•sā′shon, *n.* The act of dispensing or dealing out; the distribution of good and evil in the divine government; system established by God settling the relations of man towards him as regards religion and morality (the Mosaic *dispensation*); the granting of a license, or the license itself, to do what is forbidden by laws or canons, or to omit something which is commanded.—**dispensator,** dis•pen•sā′tėr, *n.* [L.] A dispenser.—**dispensatory,** dis•pen′sa•to•ri, *a.* Having power to grant dispensations.—*n.* A book containing the method of preparing the various kinds of medicines used in pharmacy; a pharmacopoeia.

dispeople, dis•pē′pl, *v.t.* To depopulate; to empty of inhabitants.

disperse, dis•pėrs′ *v.t.*—*dispersed, dispersing.* [Fr. *disperser*, L. *dispersus*, from *dispergo*—*di* for *dis*, distrib., and *spargo*, to scatter, whence also *sparse*.] To scatter; to cause to separate and go far apart; to dissipate; to cause to vanish. ∴ *Dissipate* is said of things that vanish or are not afterwards collected: *disperse* and *scatter* are applied to things which do not necessarily vanish, and which may again be brought together.—*v.i.* To scatter; to separate or move apart; to break up; to vanish, as fog or vapors.—**dispersedly,** dis•pėr′sed•li, *adv.* In a dispersed manner; separately.—**disperser,** dis•pėr′sėr, *n.* One who disperses.—**dispersion, dispersal** dis•pėr′shon, dis•pėr′sal, *n.* The act of dispersing or scattering; the state of being scattered or separated into remote parts; *optics*, the separation of the different colored rays of a beam of light by means of a prism, prisms of different materials causing greater or less dispersion.—**dispersive,** dis•pėr′siv, *a.* Tending to scatter or dissipate.

dispirit, dis•pir′it, *v.t.* To depress the spirits of; to deprive of courage; to discourage; to dishearten; to deject; to cast down.—**dispirited,** dis•pir′i•ted, *p.* and *a.* Discouraged;

depressed in spirits; spiritless; tame.—**dispiritedly,** dis•pir′i•ted•li, *adv.* Dejectedly.—**dispiritedness,** dis•pir′i•ted•nes, *n.* Want of courage; depression of spirits.

displace, dis•plās′, *v.t.—displaced, displacing.* To put out of the usual or proper place; to remove from its place; to remove from any state, condition, office, or dignity.—**displacement,** dis•plās′ment, *n.* The act of displacing; removal; the quantity of water displaced by a body floating at rest, as a ship.

display, dis•plā′, *v.t.* [O.Fr. *desployer,* Fr. *déployer—des,* equal to L. *dis,* not, and *ployer,* same as *plier,* from L. *plicare,* to fold, as in *deploy, employ.*] To spread before the view; to set in view ostentatiously; to show; to exhibit to the eyes or to the mind; to make manifest.—*v.i.* To make a show or display.—*n.* An unfolding; an exhibition of anything to the view; ostentatious show; exhibition; parade.

displease, dis•plēz′, *v.t.—displeased, displeasing.* To offend somewhat; to dissatisfy; to annoy; to make angry, usually in a slight degree; to excite aversion in; to be disagreeable to (the taste, the sense).—**displeasure,** dis•plezh′ūr, *n.* The feeling of one who is displeased; dissatisfaction; anger; vexation; annoyance; that which displeases; offense.

disport, dis•pōrt′, *n.* [O.Fr. *desport,* Fr. *déport,* properly diversion resorted to in order to divert the thoughts—prefix *dis,* and L. *porto,* to carry (whence *export,* etc.). *Sport* is an abbrev. of *disport.*] Play; sport; pastime.—*v.i.* To play; to sport.

dispose, dis•pōz′, *v.t.—disposed, disposing.* [Fr. *disposer,* to dispose, arrange—prefix *dis,* and *poser,* to place (E. *pose*). COMPOSE.] To arrange, place out, or distribute; to set in a particular order; to apply to a particular end or purpose; to set the mind of in a particular frame; to incline.—*v.i.* To regulate, determine, or settle; to bargain or make terms (*Shak.*).—*To dispose of,* to part with; to alienate; to sell; to put into another's hand or power; to bestow; to do with, make use of, use, or employ (one's self, one's time, etc.); to put away or get rid of.—**disposable,** dis•pō′za•bl, *a.* Subject to disposal; free to be used or employed as occasion may require.—**disposal,** dis•pō′zal, *n.* The act of disposing; a setting or arranging; power of ordering, arranging, or distributing; government; management; power or right of bestowing; the act of selling or parting with; alienation.—**disposer,** dis•pō′zėr, *n.* One who or that which disposes.—**disposition,** dis•po•zish′on, *n.* [L. *dispositio,* arrangement.] The act of disposing or state of being disposed; manner in which things or the parts of a complex body are placed or arranged; order; method; distribution; arrangement; natural fitness or tendency; temper or natural constitution of the mind; inclination; propensity; *Scots law,* disposal or settlement of property or effects.—**disposure,**† dis•pō′zhur, *n.* Disposal; management; distribution; allotment.

dispossess, dis•poz•zes′, *v.t.* To put out of possession; to deprive of the occupancy or ownership; to dislodge; with *of* before the thing taken away.—**dispossession,** dis•poz•zesh′on, *n.* The act of dispossessing.—**dispossessor,** dis•poz•zes′ėr, *n.* One who dispossesses.

dispraise, dis•prāz′, *n.* The opposite of praise, blame; censure.—*v.t. dispraised, dispraising.* To blame; to censure.—**dispraiser,** dis•prā′zėr, *n.* One who dispraises.

disproof, dis•pröf′, *n.* See DISPROVE.

disproportion, dis•pro•pōr′shon, *n.* Want of proportion of one thing to another, or between the parts of a thing; want of symmetry; want of proper quantity; according to rules prescribed; want of suitableness or adequacy; disparity; inequality.—*v.t.* To violate due proportion or symmetry in.—**disproportional, disproportionate,** dis•pro•pōr′shon•al, dis•pro•pōr′shon•it, *a.* Not having due proportion to something else; not having proportion or symmetry of parts; unequal; inadequate.—**disproportionateness,** dis•pro•pōr′shon•it•nes, *n.* Want of proportion or symmetry; unsuitableness in form, bulk, or value to something else.—**disproportionately,** dis•pro•pōr′shon•it•li, *adv.* With want of proportion or symmetry; unsuitably with respect to form, quantity, or value; inadequately; unequally.

disprove, dis•pröv′, *v.t.—disproved, disproving.* To prove to be false or erroneous; to confute; to refute.—**disprovable,** dis•prö′va•bl, *a.* Capable of being disproved or refuted.—**disproof,** dis•pröf′, *n.* Confutation; refutation; a proving to be false or erroneous.

dispute, dis•pūt′, *v.i.—disputed, disputing.* [L. *disputo,* to compute, to weigh, examine, investigate, discuss—*dis,* asunder, apart, and *puto,* to clean, prune, clear up, reckon. COMPUTE.] To contend in argument; to reason or argue in opposition; to debate; to altercate; to wrangle; to contend in opposition to a competitor.—*v.t.* To attempt to disprove by arguments or statements; to attempt to overthrow by reasoning; to controvert (an assertion, a claim, etc.); to call in question; to strive to maintain; to contest (to *dispute* every inch of ground).—*n.* Strife or contest in words or by arguments; a difference of opinion vigorously maintained; controversy in words; a wordy war; contention; strife; contest.—**disputer,** dis•pū′tėr, *n.* One who disputes or who is given to disputes.—**disputable,** dis•pū′ta•bl, *a.* Capable of being disputed; liable to be called in question, controverted, or contested; controvertible; disputatious (*Shak.*).—**disputant,** dis′pū•tant, *n.* One who disputes; one who argues in opposition to another; a reasoner in opposition—*a.* Disputing; engaged in controversy.—**disputation,** dis•pū•tā′shon, *n.* [L. *disputatio.*] The act of disputing; controversy; verbal contest respecting the truth of some fact, opinion, proposition, or argument.—**disputatious, disputative,** dis•pū•tā′shus, dis•pū′ta•tiv, *a.* Inclined to dispute; fond of arguing; characterized by disputes.—**disputatiously,** dis•pū•tā′shus•li, *adv.* In a disputatious manner.—**disputatiousness,** dis•pū•tā′shus•nes, *n.*

disqualify, dis•kwol′i•fī, *v.t.—disqualified, disqualifying.* To make unfit; to deprive of natural power, or the qualities or properties necessary for any purpose (weakness *disqualifies* a person *for* labor); to deprive of legal capacity, power, or right; to incapacitate.—**disqualification,** dis•kwol′i•fi•kā″shon, *n.* The act of disqualifying; the state of being disqualified; disability; legal disability or incapacity; that which disqualifies or incapacitates.

disquiet, dis•kwī′et, *n.* Want of quiet; uneasiness; anxiety.—*v.t.* To deprive of peace, rest, or tranquility; to make uneasy or restless; to disturb, harass, fret, or vex.—*a.* Unquiet; restless. (*Shak.*).—**disquieting,** dis•kwī′e•ting, *a.* Tending to disquiet; disturbing the mind.—**disquietly,** dis•kwī′et•li, *adv.* Unquietly; in a disquieting manner.—**disquietude,** dis•kwī′e•tūd, *n.* Want of peace or tranquility; uneasiness; disquiet.

disquisition, dis•kwi•zish′on, *n.* [L. *disquisitio,* from *disquiro, disquisitum,* to investigate—*dis,* distrib., and *quaero, quaesitum,* to ask, whence *query, question, inquire,* etc.] A formal or systematic inquiry into any subject, by discussion of the facts and circumstances bearing on it; an argumentative inquiry; a formal discussion or treatise on any matter; dissertation; essay.

disregard, dis•ri•gärd′, *n.* Want of regard, notice, or attention; neglect; slight.—*v.t.* To omit to take notice of; to neglect to observe; to pay no heed to; to treat as unworthy of regard or notice.—**disregardful,** dis•ri•gärd′fụl, *a.* Neglectful; heedless.

disrelish, dis•rel′ish, *n.* Distaste; dislike of the palate; some degree of disgust; dislike of the mind; aversion; antipathy.—*v.t.* To dislike the taste of; to feel some disgust at.

disrepair, dis•ri•pâr′, *n.* A state of being not in repair or good condition; state of requiring to be repaired.

disreputable, dis•rep′ū•ta•bl, *a.* Not reputable; disgracing reputation; dishonorable; discreditable; low; mean.—**disreputability,** dis•rep′ū•ta•bil″i•ti, *n.* The state of being disreputable.—**disreputably,** dis•rep′ū•ta•bli, *adv.* In a disreputable manner.—**disrepute,** dis•ri•pūt′, *n.* Loss or want of reputation; disesteem; discredit; dishonor.

disrespect, dis•ri•spekt′, *n.* Want of respect or reverence; incivility, irreverence, or rudeness; a slight or neglect.—*v.t.* To have no respect or esteem for; to show disrespect to.—**disrespectability,** dis•ri•spek′-

ta•bil″i•ti, *n.* The state or quality of being disrespectable.—**disrespectable,** dis•ri•spek′ta•bl, *a.* Not respectable; unworthy of respect.—**disrespectful,** dis•re•spekt′fu̇l, *a.* Wanting in respect; manifesting disrespect; irreverent; uncivil.—**disrespectfully,** dis•ri•spekt′fu̇l•li, *adv.* In a disrespectful manner.—**disrespectfulness,** dis•ri•spekt′fu̇l•nes, *n.*

disrobe, dis•rōb′, *v.t.—disrobed, disrobing.* To divest of a robe; to divest of garments; to undress; to strip of covering; to uncover.

disroot, dis•röt′, *v.t.* To tear up the roots of, or by the roots; to uproot.

disrupt,† dis•rupt′, *v.t.* [L. *disruptus*, pp. of *disrumpo* (*dirumpo*), to break or burst asunder—*dis*, asunder, and *rumpo*, to burst, whence *rupture*, etc.] To tear or rive away; to rend; to sever; to break asunder.—**disruption,** dis•rup′shon, *n.* [L. *disruptio.*] The act of rending asunder; the act of bursting and separating; breach; rent; breakup; the rupture which took place in the Established Church of Scotland in 1843, resulting in the foundation of the Free Church.—**disruptive,** dis•rup′tiv, *a.* Causing, or tending to cause, disruption; produced by or following on disruption.

dissatisfaction, dis•sat′is•fak″shon, *n.* The feeling caused by want of satisfaction; discontent; uneasiness proceeding from the want of gratification, or from disappointed wishes and expectations.—**dissatisfactory,** dis•sat′is•fak″to•ri, *a.* Causing dissatisfaction; giving discontent; mortifying; displeasing.—**dissatisfy,** dis•sat′is•fī, *v.t.—dissatisfied, dissatisfying.* To fail to satisfy; to render discontented; to displease; to excite displeasure in by frustrating wishes or expectations.

dissect, dis•sekt′, *v.t.* [L. *disseco, dissectum*—*dis*, asunder, and *seco, sectum*, to cut, whence *section, segment, intersect*, etc.] To divide (an animal body) with a cutting instrument, by separating the joints; to cut up (an animal or vegetable) for the purpose of examining the structure and character of the several parts, or to observe morbid affections; to anatomize; *fig.* to analyze for the purpose of criticism; to describe with minute accuracy.—**dissection,** dis•sek′shon, *n.* The act or art of dissecting or anatomizing.—**dissector,** dis•sek′tėr, *n.* One who dissects; an anatomist.

disseize, dis•sēz′, *v.t.—disseized, disseizing.* [Prefix *dis*, neg., and *seize*; Fr. *dessaisir*, to dispossess.] *Law*, to dispossess wrongfully; to deprive of actual seizin or possession: with *of* before the thing.—**disseizee,** dis•sē•zē′, *n.* One who is disseized.—**disseizin,** dis•sē′zin, *n.* The act of disseizing.—**disseizor,** dis•sē•zėr′, *n.* One who dispossesses another.

dissemble, dis•sem′bl, *v.t.—dissembled, dissembling.* [O.Fr. *dissembler* (Fr. *dissimuler*), from L. *dissimulo*—*dis*, and *simulo*, to make like, to simulate, from *similis*, like.—ASSEMBLE, SIMILAR. *Dissimulate* is the same word.] To hide under an assumed manner; to conceal or disguise by a false outward show; to hide by false pretenses (to *dissemble* love, hate, opinions, etc.).—*v.i.* To try to appear other than reality; to put on an assumed manner or outward show; to conceal the real fact, motives, intention, or sentiments under some pretense.—**dissembler,** dis•sem′blėr, *n.* One who dissembles; one who conceals his real thoughts or feelings.

disseminate, dis•sem′i•nāt, *v.t.—disseminated, disseminating.* [L. *dissemino, disseminatum*, to scatter seed—*dis*, and *semen*, seed.] To spread by diffusion or dispersion; to diffuse; to spread abroad among people; to cause to reach as many persons as possible (religious doctrines, knowledge, etc.).—**dissemination,** dis•sem′i•nā″shon, *n.* The act of disseminating.—**disseminative,** dis•sem′i•nā•tiv, *a.* Tending to disseminate or become disseminated.—**disseminator,** dis•sem′i•nā•tėr, *n.* One who disseminates.

dissent, dis•sent′, *v.i.* [L. *dissentio*, to think otherwise, to dissent—*dis*, asunder, and *sentio*, to perceive, as in *consent, resent*, etc. SENSE.] To disagree in opinion; to differ; to think in a different or contrary manner; with *from*; *eccles.* to differ from an established church in regard to doctrines, rites, or government.—*n.* Difference of opinion; disagreement; declaration of disagreement in opinion; *eccles.* separation from an established church.—**dissension,** dis•sen′shon, *n.* [L. *dissensio.*] Disagreement in opinion, usually a disagreement producing warm debates or angry words; strife; discord; quarrel; breach of friendship and union.—**dissentious,** dis•sen′shus, *a.* Disposed to dissension or discord.—**dissentaneous,** dis•sen•tā′nē•us, *a.* Disagreeing; inconsistent.—**dissenter,** dis•sen′tėr, *n.* One who dissents; one who differs in opinion, or one who declares his disagreement; *eccles.* one who separates from the service and worship of any established church.—**dissentient,** dis•sen′shi•ent, *a.* Disagreeing; declaring dissent; voting differently.—*n.* One who disagrees and declares his dissent.—**dissenting,** dis•sen′ting, *p.* and *a.* Disagreeing in opinion; having the character of dissent; belonging to or connected with a body of dissenters.

dissepiment, dis•sep′i•ment, *n.* [L. *dissepimentum*—*dis*, asunder, and *sepio*, to enclose, from *sepes*, a hedge.] A kind of small partition in certain hollow parts of animals and plants; one of the partitions in the ovary of some plants formed by the sides of cohering carpels.

dissertation, dis•sėr•tā′shon, *n.* [L. *dissertatio*, from *disserto*, a freq. of *dissero*, to argue, discuss—*dis*, asunder, and *sero*, to join, from root of *series.*] A formal discourse, intended to illustrate or elucidate a subject; a written essay, treatise, or disquisition.—**dissertator,** dis′sėr•tā•tėr, *n.* One who writes dissertations.

disserve, dis•sėrv′, *v.t.* To do the reverse of a service to; to do an injury or ill turn to.—**disservice,** *n.* An ill turn or injury; something done to one's injury.

dissever, dis•sev′ėr, *v.t.* To part in two; to divide asunder; to separate; to disunite;—**disseverance, disseverment,** dis•sev′ėr•ans, dis•sev′ėr•ment, *n.* The act of dissevering; separation.

dissident, dis′si•dent, *a.* [L. *dissidens, dissidentis*, ppr. of *dissideo*, to disagree—*dis*, asunder, and *sedeo*, to sit; seen also in *supersede, sedentary, session*, etc.] Dissenting; specifically, dissenting from an established church.—*n.* One who dissents from others; a dissenter; one who separates from an established religion.—**dissidence,** dis′si•dens, *n.* Disagreement; dissent; nonconformity.

dissilient, dis•sil′i•ent, *a.* [L. *dissilio*, to leap asunder—*dis*, and *salio*, to leap, whence *salient.*] Starting asunder; bursting and opening with an elastic force, as the dry pod or capsule of a plant.

dissimilar, dis•sim′i•ler, *a.* Not similar; unlike, either in nature, properties, or external form.—**dissimilarity,** dis•sim′i•lar″i•ti, *n.* Want of similarity; unlikeness; want of resemblance.—**dissimilation,** dis•sim•i•lā•shon, *n.* The act or process of rendering dissimilar or different; *philol.* the change of a sound to another and a different sound when otherwise two similar sounds would come together or very close to each other.—**dissimilitude,** dis•si•mil′i•tūd, *n.* [L. *dissimilitudo.*] Unlikeness; want of resemblance.

dissimulation, dis•sim′ū•lā″shon, *n.* [L. *dissimulatio*, from *dissimulo, dissimulatum*, to feign that a thing is not what it is—*dis*, and *simulo*, to make like, from *similis*, like. DISSEMBLE.] The act or practice of dissembling, usually from a mean or unworthy motive; a hiding under a false appearance; false pretension; hypocrisy.—**dissimulate,** dis•sim′ū•lāt, *v.i.* To dissemble; to make pretense; to feign.—**dissimulator,** dis•sim′ū•lā″tėr, *n.* One who dissimulates or dissembles.

dissipate, dis′si•pāt, *v.t.—dissipated, dissipating.* [L. *dissipo, dissipatum*—*dis*, asunder, and the rare *sipo, supo*, to throw, allied probably to E. verb to *sweep.*] To scatter, to disperse, to drive away (mist, care, energy, etc.); to scatter in wasteful extravagance; to waste. ∴ Syn. under DISPERSE.—*v.i.* To scatter, disperse, separate into parts and disappear; to vanish; to be wasteful or dissolute in the pursuit of pleasure.—**dissipated,** dis′si•pā•ted, *a.* Given to extravagance in the expenditure of property; devoted to pleasure and vice; dissolute.—**dissipation,** dis•si•pā′shon, *n.* The act of dissipating; the insensible loss of the minute particles of a body, which fly off, so that the body is diminished or may altogether disappear; indulgence in dissolute and irregular courses; a reckless and vicious pursuit of pleasure; dissolute conduct.—*Dissipation of energy*, the running down of energy from higher to lower or less available forms, a process constantly going on in nature, and tending to the ultimate production of an earth uninhabitable by man as at present constituted.

dissociate, dis•sō′shi•āt, *v.t.—dissociated, dissociating.* [L. *dissocio, dissociatum—dis,* and *socio,* to unite, from *socius,* a companion. SOCIAL.] To separate or take apart; to disunite; to part.—**dissociable,**† dis•sō′shi•a•bl, *a.* Not well associated, united, or assorted; not sociable; incongruous; not reconcilable.—**dissocial,** dis•sō′shal, *a.* Disinclined to or unsuitable for society; not social. —**dissociation,** dis•sō′shi•ā″shon, *n.* The act of dissociating; a state of separation; disunion; *chem.* the decomposition of a compound substance into its primary elements.—**dissociative,** dis•sō′shi•ā•tiv, *a.* Tending to dissociate; *chem.* resolving or reducing a compound to its primary elements.

dissoluble, dis•sol′ū•bl, *a.* [L. *dissolubilis.* DISSOLVE.] Capable of being dissolved or melted; having its parts separable, as by heat or moisture; susceptible of decomposition or decay.—**dissolubility,** dis•sol′ū•bil″i•ti, *n.* The state or quality of being dissoluble.

dissolute, dis′so•lūt, *a.* [L. *dissolutus,* pp. of *dissolvo.* DISSOLVE.] Loose in behavior and morals; given to vice or profligacy; debauched; devoted to or occupied in dissipation.—**dissolutely,** dis′so•lūt•li, *adv.* In a dissolute manner; profligately; in dissipation or debauchery.—**dissoluteness,** dis′so•lūt•nes, *n.* The state or character of being dissolute; looseness of manners and morals, vicious indulgence in pleasure, as in intemperance and debauchery; dissipation.—**dissolution,** dis•so•lū′shon, *n.* [L. *dissolutio,* a breaking up, a loosening, from *dissolvo.*] The act of dissolving, liquefying, or changing from a solid to a fluid state by heat; liquefaction; the reduction of a body into its smallest parts, or into very minute parts; the separation of the parts of a body by natural decomposition; decomposition; death; the separation of the soul and body; the separation of the parts which compose a connected system or body; the breaking up of an assembly, or the putting an end to its existence.

dissolve, diz•zolv′, *v.t.—dissolved, dissolving.* [L. *dissolvo,* to break up, to separate—*dis,* asunder, and *solvo, solutum,* to loose, to free, whence also *solve, soluble, solution, absolve,* etc.] To melt; to liquefy; to convert from a solid or fixed state to a fluid state, by means of heat or moisture; to disunite, break up, separate, or loosen; to destroy any connected system or body (parliament, a government); to break or make no longer binding (an alliance, etc.); to solve, explain, or resolve (doubts); to destroy the power of or render ineffectual (a spell or enchantment); to destroy or consume (O.T.).—*v.i.* To melt; to be converted from a solid to a fluid state; to fall asunder; to crumble; to waste away; to be decomposed; to be dismissed; to separate; to break up; *motion pictures,* to fade out one shot while fading in the next, causing the two shots to overlap during the process.—*n. Motion pictures,* a scene made using the process of dissolving —**dissolvable,** diz•zol′va•bl, *a.* Capable of being melted; capable of being converted into a fluid.—**dissolvent,** diz•zol′vent, *a.* Having power to melt or dissolve.—*n.* Anything that dissolves; a substance that has the power of converting a solid substance into a fluid, or of separating its parts so that they mix with a liquid.—**dissolver,** diz•zol′vėr, *n.* One who or that which dissolves.

dissonance, dis′so•nans, *n.* [Fr. *dissonance,* L. *dissonantia,* discordance —*dis,* asunder, and *sono,* to sound. SOUND.] Discord; a mixture or union of harsh, inharmonious sounds; incongruity; inconsistency.—**dissonant,** dis′so•nant, *a.* Discordant; harsh; jarring; unharmonious; unpleasant to the ear; disagreeing; incongruous.

dissuade, dis•swād′, *v.t.—dissuaded, dissuading.* [L. *dissuadeo,* to advise against—*dis,* not, and *suadeo,* to advise.] To advise or exhort against; to attempt to draw or divert from a measure by reasons or offering motives; to divert by persuasion; to turn from a purpose by argument; to render averse; the opposite of *persuade.*—**dissuader,** dis•swā′dėr, *n.* One who dissuades.—**dissuasion,** dis•swā′zhon, *n.* Advice or exhortation in opposition to something; dehortation; the opposite of *persuasion*—**dissuasive,** dis•swā′siv, *a.* Tending to dissuade.—*n.* Reason, argument, or counsel, employed to deter one from a measure or purpose; that which tends to dissuade.—**dissuasively,** dis•swā′siv•li, *adv.* In a dissuasive manner.

dissyllable, dis′sil•la•bl, *n.* [Gr. *dis,* twice, and *syllabe,* a syllable.] A word consisting of two syllables only.—**dissyllabic,** dis•sil•lab′ik, *a.* Consisting of two syllables only.

distaff, dis′taf, *n.* [A.Sax. *dist.f,* that is, *dis-* or *dise-staff—dis-* = O.E. *dise,* to put the flax on the distaff, allied to L.G. *diesse,* the flax on the distaff, G. *dusse,* tow, oakum.] The staff to which a bunch of flax or tow is tied, and from which the thread is drawn to be spun by the spindle; woman's work; woman or women.

distain, dis•tān′, *v.t.* [O.Fr. *desteindre,* Fr. *déteindre,* to cause to lose color—*des* for L. *dis,* not, and *teindre,* from L. *tingere,* to stain.] To stain; to discolor; to sully, defile, tarnish.

distal, dis′tal, *a.* [From *distant*: formed on the type of *central.*] Applied to the end of a bone, limb, or organ in plants and animals farthest removed from the point of attachment or insertion; situated away from or at the extremity most distant from the center.

distance, dis′tans, *n.* [Fr. *distance,* L. *distantia,* from *disto,* to stand apart—*dis,* apart, and *sto,* to stand. STATE, STATUE, etc.] An interval or space between two objects; the length of the shortest line which intervenes between things that are separate; remoteness of place; space of time, past or future; ideal space or separation, as between things that differ from each other; the remoteness or ceremonious avoidance of familiarity which respect requires; the remoteness or reserve which one assumes from being offended, from dislike, etc.; *mus.* the interval between two notes; *horse-racing,* a length of 240 yards from the winning post, marked by a post.—*v.t.—distanced, distancing.* To place at a distance or remote; to leave at a great distance; behind; to outdo or excel greatly.—**distant,** dis′tant, *a.* [L. *distans,* standing apart, ppr. of *disto.*] Separate or apart, the intervening space being of any indefinite extent; remote in place; in time, past or future; in a line of succession or descent; in natural connection or consanguinity; in kind or nature, etc.; as if remote or far off; hence, slight; faint (a *distant* resemblance); characterized by haughtiness, coldness, indifference, or disrespect; reserved; shy.—**distantly,** dis′tant•li, *adv.* Remotely; at a distance; with reserve.

distaste, dis•tāst′, *n.* Aversion of the taste; dislike of food or drink; disrelish; disinclination; a want of liking (a *distaste* for rural sports).—**distasteful,** dis•tāst′fụl, *a.* Causing distaste; unpleasant to the taste or liking; disagreeable; slightly repulsive.—**distastefully,** dis•tāst′fụl•li, *adv.* In a distasteful manner.—**distastefulness,** dis•tāst′fụl•nes, *n.* The state or character of being distasteful.

distemper, dis•tem′pėr, *n.* Any morbid state of an animal body or of any part of it; derangement of the animal economy; a disorder; malady; a disease of young dogs, commonly considered as a catarrhal disorder.—*v.t.* To derange the bodily functions of; to deprive of temper or moderation; to ruffle; to disturb; to make ill-humored.

distemper, dis•tem′pėr, *n.* [It. *distemperare,* to dissolve or mix with liquid.] *Painting,* a preparation of opaque color, ground with size and water; tempera; a kind of painting in which the pigments are mixed with size, and chiefly used for scene painting and interior decoration.

distend, dis•tend′, *v.t.* [L. *distendo—dis,* asunder, and *tendo,* to tend, as in *extend, contend.* TENT.] To stretch or swell out by force acting from within; to dilate; to expand; to swell; to puff out (a bladder, the lungs).—*v.i.* To become inflated or distended; to swell. **distensibility,** dis•ten′si•bil″i•ti, *n.* The quality or capacity of being distensible.—**distensible,** dis•ten′si•bl, *a.* Capable of being distended or dilated.—**distention, distension,** dis•ten′shon, *n.* [L. *distentio.*] The act of distending; the state of being distended; extent or space occupied by the thing distended.

distich, dis′tik, *n.* [Gr. *distichon—di,* twice, and *stichŏs,* a row, a line, a verse.] A couplet; a couple of verses or poetic lines making complete sense.—**distichous,** dis′ti•kus, *a.* Having two rows, or disposed in two rows, as the grains in an ear of barley.

distill, distil, dis•til′, *v.i.—distilled, distilling.* [Fr. *distiller,* from L. *destillo,* to trickle down—*de,* down, and *stillo,* to drop, from *stilla,* a drop.] To drop; to fall in drops or in a small stream; to trickle; to use a still; to practice distillation.—*v.t.* To yield or give forth in drops or a small stream; to let fall in drops; to drop; to obtain or extract by distillation; to subject to the process of distillation.—**distillable,** dis•til′a•bl, *a.* Capable of being distilled; fit for distillation.—**distillate,** dis′til•āt, *n.* A fluid distilled, and found in the receiver of a distilling apparatus.—**distillation,** dis•ti•lā′shon, *n.* The act of distilling or falling in drops; the volatilization and subsequent condensation of a liquid by means of an alembic, or still and refrigeratory, or of a retort and receiver; the operation of extracting spirit from a substance by evaporation and condensation.—**distiller,** dis•til′ėr, *n.* One who distills; one whose occupation is to extract spirit by distillation.—**distillery,** dis•til′ėr•i, *n.* The act or art of distilling; the building and works where distillation is carried on.

distinct, dis•tingkt′, *a.* [L. *distinctus,* pp. of *distinguo.* DISTINGUISH.] Separated or distinguished by some mark, note, or character; marked out; not the same in number or kind; different; having well-marked characteristics; standing clearly or boldly out; well defined; obvious; plain; unmistakable.—**distinction,** dis•tingk′shon, *n.* [L. *distinctio.*] The act of separating or distinguishing; that which distinguishes or marks as different; a note or mark of difference; distinguishing quality; eminence or superiority; elevation or honorable estimation; that which confers or marks eminence or superiority; a title or honor of some kind.—**distinctive,** dis•tingk′tiv, *a.* Marking or indicating distinction or difference.—**distinctively,** dis•tingk′tiv•li, *adv.* In a distinctive manner.—**distinctiveness,** dis•tingk′tiv•nes, *n.* The state or quality of being distinctive; distinctive character.—**distinctly,** dis•tingkt′li, *adv.* In a distinct manner; clearly; obviously; plainly; precisely. —**distinctness,** dis•tingkt′nes, *n.* The quality or state of being distinct; clearness; precision.

distinguish, dis•ting′gwish, *v.t.* [L. *distinguo,* to mark off, to distinguish —*di* for *dis,* asunder, and *stinguo,* to mark. STIGMA.] To mark or set apart as different or separate from others; to perceive or recognize the individuality of; to note as differing from something else by some mark or quality; to know or ascertain difference by the senses or the intellect; to classify or divide by any mark or quality which constitutes difference; to separate by definitions; to separate from others by some mark of honor or preference; to make eminent or known; to signalize.—*v.i.* To make a distinction; to find or show the difference.—**distinguishable,** dis•ting′gwish•a•bl, *a.* Capable of being distinguished or recognized; capable of being defined or classified; worthy of note or special regard.—**distinguishableness,** dis•ting′gwish•a•bl•nes, *n.* State of being distinguishable.—**distinguishably,** dis•ting′gwish•a•bli, *adv.* So as to be distinguished.—**distinguished,** dis•ting′gwisht, *p.* and *a.* Separated from others by superior or extraordinary qualities; eminent; extraordinary; transcendent; noted; famous; celebrated.—**distinguishing,** dis•ting′gwish•ing, *a.* Constituting difference or distinction from everything else; peculiar; characteristic.

distort, dis•tort′, *v.t.* [L. *distorqueo, distortum—dis,* asunder, and *torqueo,* to twist, as in *contort* (which see).] To twist out of natural or regular shape; to force or put out of the true bent or direction; to bias (the judgment); to wrest from the true meaning; to pervert.—**distorted,** dis•tor′ted, *p.* and *a.* Twisted out of natural or regular shape; shaped abnormally or awry.—**distortion,** dis•tor′shon, *n.* The act of distorting; a twisting or writhing motion; an unnatural direction of parts from whatever cause, as a curved spine, a wry mouth, squinting, etc.; a perversion of the true meaning of words.

distract, dis•trakt′, *v.t.* [L. *distraho, distractum,* to pull asunder, to perplex—*dis,* asunder, and *traho,* to draw; whence *tractable, trace,* etc.] To draw apart or pull separate‡; to turn or draw from any object or point; to divert toward various other objects (the attention); to perplex, confound, or harass (the mind); to disorder the reason of; to render insane or frantic.—**distracted,** dis•trak′ted, *p.* and *a.* Disordered in intellect; deranged; perplexed; crazy; frantic.—**distractedly,** dis•trak′ted•li, *adv.* In a distracted manner; insanely; wildly.—**distraction,** dis•trak′shon, *n.* The act of distracting; the state of being distracted; confusion from multiplicity of objects crowding on the mind and calling the attention different ways; perplexity; embarrassment; madness; frenzy; insanity; extreme folly; extreme perturbation or agony of mind, as from pain or grief; anything giving the mind a new and less onerous occupation; a diversion,—**distractive,** dis•trak′tiv, *a.* Causing perplexity.

distrain, dis•trān′, *v.t.* [O.Fr. *destraindre,* from L. *distringere,* to draw apart, bind, molest, later to exact a pledge—*dis,* asunder, and *stringere,* to strain (as in *constrain, restrain*). STRAIN. Akin *distress, district.*] To seize or take possession of (*Shak.*)‡; specifically, *law,* to seize, as goods and chattels, for debt. —**distrainable,** dis•trā′na•bl, *a.* Capable of being or liable to be distrained.—**distrainer, distrainor,** dis•trā′nėr, *n.* He who seizes goods for debt or service.—**distraint,** dis•trānt′, *n.* A distress or distraining.

distrait, dis•trā′, *a.* [Fr.] Abstracted; absent minded; inattentive.

distraught, dis•tra̤t′, *a.* [Old pp. of *distract.*] Distracted; perplexed.

distress, dis•tres′, *n.* [O.Fr. *destresse, destrece,* oppression, from *destrecer,* to oppress, from a hypothetical L.L. *destrictiare,* from L. *districtus,* pp. of *distringo,* to draw apart, hinder, molest. DISTRAIN.] Extreme pain; anguish of body or mind; that which causes suffering; affliction; calamity; adversity; misery; a state of danger; *law,* the act of distraining, the seizure of any personal chattel as a pledge for the payment of rent or debt, or the satisfaction of a claim.—*v.t.* To afflict with pain or anguish; to harass; to grieve; to perplex; to make miserable.—**distressful,** dis•tres′fu̥l, *a.* Inflicting or bringing distress; calamitous; proceeding from pain or anguish; indicating distress.—**distressfully,** dis•tres′fu̥l•li, *adv.* In a distressful manner.—**distressing,** dis•tres′ing, *a.* Very afflicting; affecting with severe pain.—**distressingly,** dis•tres′ing•li, *adv.* In a distressing manner; with great pain.

distribute, dis•trib′ūt, *v.t.—distributed, distributing.* [L. *distribuo, distributum,* to divide, distribute—*dis,* and *tribuo,* to give. TRIBUTE.] To divide among two or more; to deal out; to give or bestow in parts or portions; to dispense; to administer; to divide, as into classes, orders, genera; *printing,* to separate types and place them in their proper boxes or compartments in the cases.—**distributable,** dis•tri′bū•ta•bl, *a.* Capable of being distributed.—**distributer,** dis•trib′ū•tėr, *n.* One who or that which distributes or deals out; a dispenser.—**distribution,** dis•tri•bū′shon, *n.* [L. *distributio.*] The act of distributing or dealing out; the act of dispensing or administering; the act of separating into distinct parts or classes; *printing,* the separating of the types and arranging of them in their proper places in the case; the manner of being distributed or spread over the earth (the *distribution* of animals or plants).—**distributive,** dis•trib′ū•tiv, *a.* Serving to distribute; expressing separation or division; specifically, *gram.* an epithet applied to certain words (as *each, every*) which denote the persons or things that make a number taken separately and singly.—*n. Gram.* a distributive word, as *each* and *every.* —**distributively,** dis•trib′ū•tiv•li, *adv.* In a distributive manner.

district, dis′trikt, *n.* [L.L. *districtum,*

a district subject to one jurisdiction, from L. *districtus*, pp. of *distringo*. DISTRAIN.] A part of a country, city, etc., distinctly defined or marked out; a portion of country without very definite limits; a tract; a region, locality, quarter.—**district attorney,** *n.* The prosecuting attorney of a judicial district.

distrust, dis•trust′, *v.t.* To doubt or suspect the truth, fidelity, firmness, sincerity, reality, sufficiency, or goodness of; to have no faith, reliance, or confidence in; to be suspicious of. —*n.* Doubt or suspicion; want of confidence, faith, or reliance.—**distrustful,** dis•trust′fu̦l, *a.* Apt to distrust; wanting confidence; suspicious; mistrustful; apprehensive; not confident; diffident; modest.—**distrustfully,** dis•trust′fu̦l•li, *adv.* In a distrustful manner.—**distrustfulness,** dis•trust′fu̦l•nes, *n.* The state or quality of being distrustful.

disturb, dis•tėrb′, *v.t.* [L. *disturbo,* to throw into disorder—*dis,* asunder, and *turbo,* to confuse, from *turba,* a crowd, tumult, whence also *turbid, turbulent.*] To excite from a state of rest or tranquillity; to stir; to move; to discompose; to agitate; to throw into confusion or disorder; to excite uneasiness in the mind of; to disquiet; to render uneasy; to ruffle; to move from any regular course, operation, or purpose; to make irregular; to interfere with; to interrupt.—**disturbance,** dis•tėr′-bans, *n.* The act of disturbing; interruption of peace or quiet; interruption of a settled state of things; violent change; derangement; perturbation; agitation; disorder of thoughts; confusion; agitation in the body politic; a disorder; a tumult.—**disturber,** dis•tėr′bėr, *n.* One who disturbs; one who causes tumults or disorders.

disunion, dis•ūn′yon, *n.* A state of not being united; separation; disjunction; a breach of concord and its effect; contention; dissension.—**disunite,** dis•ū•nīt′, *v.t.* To separate; to disjoin; to part; to set at variance; to raise dissension between.—*v.i.* To fall asunder; to become separate.

disuse, dis•ūs′, *n.* Cessation of use, practice, or exercise.—*v.t.* (dis•ūz′). To cease to use; to neglect or omit to practice; to disaccustom.

disyoke, dis•yōk′, *v.t.* To unyoke; to free from any trammel. (*Tenn.*)

ditch, dich, *n.* [A softened form of *dike* (comp. *church* and *kirk,* etc.), both being formerly applied to the embankment as well as to the ditch. DIKE, DIG.] A trench in the earth made by digging, particularly a trench for draining wet land, or for making a fence to guard enclosures, or for preventing an enemy from approaching a town or fortress; any long artificial channel dug to contain water.—*v.i.* To dig or make a ditch or ditches.—*v.t.* To dig a ditch or ditches in; to drain by a ditch; to surround with a ditch.—**ditcher,** dich′ėr, *n.* One who digs ditches.

ditheism, dī′thē•izm, *n.* [Gr. *di,* double, and *theos,* a god.] The doctrine of the existence of two gods, especially that on which the old Persian religion was founded, or the opposition of the two (good and evil) principles; dualism; Manicheism.—**ditheist,** dī′thē•ist, *n.* One who believes in ditheism.—**ditheistic,** dī•-thē•is′tik, *a.* Pertaining to ditheism.

dither, diTH′ėr, *n.* [Origin uncertain] Trembling; quivering; a state of great agitation; confusion —*v.i.* To act hesitantly, irresolutely, or in a disturbed manner.

dithyramb, dith′i•ramb, *n.* [Gr. *dithyrambos.*] A hymn among the ancient Greeks, originally in honor of Bacchus, afterward of other gods, composed in an elevated or wildly enthusiastic style; hence, any poem of an impetuous and irregular character.—**dithyrambic,** *a.* Pertaining to or resembling a dithyramb; wild; enthusiastic.

dittany, dit′a•ni, *n.* [L. *dictamnus,* from growing abundantly on Mount *Dicte* in Crete.] A perennial plant found in the Mediterranean region, with large white or rose-colored flowers in terminal racemes, and having numerous glands containing a fragrant and very volatile oil.

ditto, dit′tō. [It. *ditto,* from L. *dictum,* something said. DICTION.] A word used chiefly in lists, accounts, etc., to save writing, equivalent to same as above, or aforesaid: often contracted into *Do.*, a symbol, (″).

ditty, dit′i, *n.* [O.Fr. *ditté,* story, poem, etc., from L. *dictatum,* pp. of *dictare,* to dictate. DICTION.] A song; a sonnet; a little poem to be sung.

diuretic, dī•ū•ret′ik, *a.* [Gr. *diourētikos,* from *dia,* through, and *ouron,* urine.] *Med.* having the power to excite the secretion of urine; tending to produce discharges of urine.—*n.* A medicine that excites the secretion of urine or increases its discharge.—**diuresis,** dī•ū•rē′sis, *n.* An excessive flow of urine.

diurnal, dī•ėr′nal, *a.* [L. *diurnalis,* from *diurnus,* daily, from *dies,* a day, whence also *dial, diary,* etc. *Journal* is the same word.] Relating to a day; pertaining to the daytime; happening daily.—**diurnally,** dī•ėr′nal•li, *adv.*

diva, dē′va, *n.* [It. from L. *diva,* goddess.] A great woman singer; a prima donna.

divan, di•van′, *n.* [Per. *divan,* a collection of writings, customhouse, council, raised seat.] Among the Turks and other orientals, a court of justice; a council; council chamber; a state or reception room; a kind of coffeehouse; a cushioned seat standing against the wall of a room; a collection of poems by one author.

divaricate, dī•var′i•kāt, *v.i.* [L. *divarico, divaricatum,* to spread asunder —*di* for *dis,* asunder, and *varico,* to straddle.] To fork; to part into two branches; *bot.* to diverge at an obtuse angle.—*v.t.* To divide into two branches; to cause to branch apart.—**divarication,** dī•var′i•kā″shon, *n.* A separation into two branches; a forking.

dive, dīv, *v.i.*—*dived, diving.* [A.Sax. *dýfan,* to dive = Icel. *dýfa,* to dip, to dive; akin *deep, dip.*] To descend or plunge into water head first; to go under water for the purpose of executing some work; to go deep into any subject; to plunge into any business or condition; to sink; to penetrate.—*n.* The act of diving; a plunge.—**diver,** dī′vėr, *n.* One who dives; one of a family of marine swimming birds, with short wings and tail, legs far back and toes completely webbed, preying upon fish, which they pursue under water. —**diving,** dī′ving, *n.* The act or practice of descending into water; especially, the art of descending below the surface of the water, and remaining there for some time, in order to remove objects from the bottom, etc.—**diving bell,** *n.* An apparatus, originally bell shaped, in which persons descend into the water and remain for a length of time, fresh air being pumped into the bell by assistants above.

diverge, di•vėrj′, *v.i.*—*diverged, diverging.* [L. *di* for *dis,* asunder, and *vergo,* to incline. VERGE.] To tend or proceed from a common point in different directions; to deviate from a given course or line: opposed to *converge*; to differ or vary.—**divergence, divergency,** di•vėr′jens, di•-vėr′jen•si, *n.* The act of diverging; a receding from each other; a going farther apart.—**divergent,** di•vėr′-jent, *a.* Diverging; separating or receding from each other, as lines which proceed from the same point.

divers, dī′vėrz, *a.* [Fr. *divers,* from L. *diversus,* diverse, turned away, from *di* for *dis,* asunder, and *verto, versum,* to turn. VERSE.] Different; various; several; sundry; more than one, but not a great number.—**diverse,** di•vers′ or dī′vėrs, *a.* [L. *diversus.*] Different; differing; unlike; not the same.—**diversely,** dī•-vėrs′li, *adv.* In a diverse manner; in different directions.—**diversification,** di•vėr′si•fi•kā″shon, *n.* The act of diversifying; the state of being diversified.—**diversified,** di•vėr′si•fīd, *p.* and *a.* Distinguished by various forms, or by a variety of objects.—**diversiform,** di•vėr′si•form, *a.* Of a different form; of various forms.—**diversify,** di•vėr′si•fī, *v.t.*—*diversified, diversifying.* [Fr. *diversifier*—L. *diversus,* and *facio,* to make.] To make diverse or various in form or qualities; to give variety or diversity to; to variegate.—**diversion,** di•vėr′-zhon, *n.* The act of diverting or turning aside from any course; that which diverts or turns the mind or thoughts away; what turns or draws the mind from care, business, or study, and thus relaxes and amuses; sport; play; pastime; a feint or other movement made to mislead an enemy as to the real point of attack.—**diversity,** di•vėr′si•ti, *n.* [L. *diversitas.*] The state of being diverse; difference; dissimilitude; unlikeness; multiplicity with difference; variety; distinctness or separateness of being, as opposed to *identity.*—**divert,** di•-vėrt′, *v.t.* [L. *diverto, diversum,* to turn aside.] To turn off from any course, direction, or intended application; to turn aside (to *divert* a stream, traffic, etc.); to turn from business or study; to turn from care or serious thoughts: hence, to please; to amuse; to entertain. ∴ Syn. under AMUSE.—**diverter,** di•vėr′tėr, *n.* One who or that which diverts.—**diverting,** di•vėr′ting, *a.* Causing diversion; amusing; entertaining.—**divertingly,** di•vėr′ting•li, *adv.* In a diverting manner.

Dives, dī′vēz, *n.* [L. *dives*, rich.] Name in Biblical parable; type of the rich man.

divest, di•vest′, *v.t.* [O.Fr. *devestir*, from L. *devestio*, to undress—*de*, not, and *vestio*, to clothe, from *vestis*, a garment, whence also *vest, vesture*.] To strip; to strip of dress or of anything that surrounds or attends; to deprive: with *of* before the thing removed.

divide, di•vīd′, *v.t.*—*divided, dividing*. [L. *divido*, to divide—*di* for *dis*, asunder, and *vid*, a root signifying to cut or separate, akin to Skr. *vyadh*, to penetrate.] To part or separate into pieces; to cut or otherwise separate into two or more parts; to cause to be separate; to keep apart, as by a partition or by an imaginary line or limit; to make partition of among a number; to disunite in opinion or interest; to set at variance.—*v.i.* To become separated; to part; to open; to cleave; to vote by the division of a legislative house, as in the British Parliament, into two parts, that is, the "ayes" dividing from the "noes."—*n.* The watershed of a district or region.—**dividable,** di•vī′da•bl, *a.* Capable of being divided.—**divided,** di•vī′ded, *p.* and *a.* Parted, separated, or disunited; showing divisions; at variance in feeling.—**dividend,** div′i•dend, *n.* [L., lit. a thing to be divided.] A sum or a number to be divided; the profit or gain made by a corporation and which falls to be divided among the stockholders according to the stock of each; the sum that falls to the share of each; the share of the fund realized from the effects of a bankrupt, and apportioned according to the amount of the debt of each creditor; a share of surplus allocated by an insurance company to policy holders.—**divider,** di•vī′dėr, *n.* One who or that which divides; *pl.* an instrument for dividing lines, etc.; compasses.

divi-divi, div′i•div′i, *n.* The native and commercial name of a tropical American tree and its remarkably curled pods which yield tannic acid and gallic acid.

divine, di•vīn′, *a.* [L. *divinus*, divine, religious, divinely inspired, godlike, from *divus*, divine, a deity or divinity. DEITY.] Pertaining to God, or to a heathen deity or false god; partaking of the nature of God; godlike; heavenly; sacred; holy; excellent in the highest degree; apparently above what is human; relating to divinity or theology.—*Divine right*, the claim set up by sovereigns to the unqualified obedience of their subjects on the assumption that they themselves were appointed by God to rule, and responsible to him only for their acts.—*n.* A minister of the gospel; a priest; a clergyman; a theologian.—*v.t.*—*divined, divining*. [L. *divino.*] To foretell; to predict; to prognosticate; to conjecture; to guess.—*v.i.* To use or practice divination; to utter presages or prognostications; to bode; to guess.—**divination,** div•i•nā′shon, *n.* [L. *divinatio.*] The act of divining; a foretelling future events, or discovering things secret or obscure, by the aid of superior beings, or by certain rites, experiments, observations, etc.—**divinatory,** di•vin′a•to•ri, *a.* Professing or pertaining to divination.—**divinely,** di•vīn′li, *adv.* In a divine manner; in a manner resembling deity; by the agency or influence of God; in a supreme degree; excellently.—**divineness,** di•vīn′nes, *n.* The state or quality of being divine, likeness to God; sacredness; superexcellence.—**diviner,** di•vī′nėr, *n.* One who professes divination; a soothsayer; one who guesses or conjectures.—**divining rod,** *n.* A rod, usually of hazel, which, if carried slowly along in suspension by an adept, dips and points downwards, it is affirmed, when brought over the spot where water or treasure is to be found.—**divinity,** di•vin′i•ti, *n.* [L. *divinitas.*] The state of being divine; divineness; deity; godhead; divine element; divine nature; a celestial being; one of the deities belonging to a polytheistic religion; supernatural power or virtue; awe-inspiring character or influence; sacredness; the science of divine things; theology. [*Cap.*] God; Deity.

divisible, di•viz′i•bl, *a.* [L. *divisibilis*, from *divido*. DIVIDE.] Capable of division; that may be separated or disunited; separable.—**divisibility, divisibleness,** di•viz′i•bil″i•ti, di•viz′i•bl•nes, *n.* The quality of being divisible; that general property of bodies by which their parts or component particles are capable of separation.—**divisibly,** di•viz′i•bli, *adv.* In a divisible manner.—**division,** di•vizh′on, *n.* [L. *divisio.*] The act of dividing or separating into parts; the state of being divided; separation; a dividing line; a partition; the part separated from the rest, as by a partition, line, etc., real or imaginary; a distinct segment or section; a part or distinct portion; a certain section or portion of an organized whole, as an army, a fleet; disunion; discord; dissension; variance; difference; the separation of members in a legislative house in order to ascertain the vote; *arith.* one of the four fundamental rules, the object of which is to find how often one number is contained in another. —*Milit.* an administrative and tactical organization, smaller than a corps but larger than a brigade or regiment. —**divisional,** di•vizh′on•al, *a.* Pertaining to division; noting or making division; belonging to a division or district.—**divisive,** di•vī′ziv, *a.* Forming division; tending to divide; creating division or discord.—**divisor,** di•vī′zėr, *n. Arith.* the number by which the dividend is divided.

divorce, di•vōrs′, *n.* [Fr. *divorce*, from L. *divortium*, a separation, a divorce, from *divorto*, same as *diverto*, to turn away. DIVERT.] A legal dissolution of the bond of marriage; a legal separation between husband and wife, after which either is free to marry again; the sentence or writing by which marriage is dissolved; disunion of things closely united; separation.—*v.t.*—*divorced, divorcing*. To dissolve the marriage contract between; to separate from the condition of husband and wife; to separate or disunite from close connection; to force asunder; to put away.—**divorcee,** di•vōr•sē′, *n.* A person divorced.—**divorcement,** di•vōrs′ment, *n.* Divorce, (O.T.)—**divorcer,** di•vōr′sėr, *n.* One who or that which divorces.

divulge, di•vulj′, *v.t.*—*divulged, divulging*. [L. *divulgo*, to spread among the people— *di* for *dis*, distrib., and *vulgus*, the common people, whence also *vulgar*.] To tell or make known what was before private or secret; to reveal; to disclose; to let be known.—**divulgement,**† di•vulj′ment, *n.* The act of divulging.—**divulger,** di•vul′jėr, *n.* One who divulges.

divulsion, di•vul′shon, *n.* [L. *divulsio*, a tearing asunder, from *divello, divulsum*, to pluck or pull asunder—*di* for *dis*, asunder, and *vello*, to pull.] The act of pulling or plucking away; a rending asunder; violent separation; laceration.—**divulsive,** di•vul′siv, *a.* Tending or having power to pull asunder or rend.

dizzy, diz′i, *a.* [A.Sax. *dysig*, foolish; akin to L.G. *dusig, dōsig*, O.D. *duyzigh*, Mod.D. *duizelig*, dizzy, Dan. *dosig*, drowsy. Allied are *daze, dazzle, dose*.] Having a sensation of whirling in the head with instability or proneness to fall; giddy; vertiginous; causing giddiness (a *dizzy* height); arising from, or caused by, giddiness; thoughtless; heedless; inconstant.—*v.t.*—*dizzied, dizzying*. To make dizzy or giddy; to confuse.—**dizzily,** diz′i•li, *adv.* In a dizzy manner.—**dizziness,** diz′i•nes, *n.* The state of being dizzy; giddiness; vertigo.

DNA, deoxyribonucleic acid, a nucleic acid constituting the genetic material of the chromosome. The molecule is a ladderlike helical chain in which purine bases determine the formation of RNA by a specific sequence.

do, dö, *v.t.* or *auxiliary*; pret, *did*; pp. *done*; ppr. *doing*. When transitive the present tense singular is, I *do*, thou *doest* or *dost* (dö′est, dust), he *does* or *doth* (duz, duth); when auxiliary, the second person is, thou *dost*. [A.Sax. *dón*, to do, *dó*, I do = D. *doen*, G. *thun*, to do, L. *do* in *abdo*, I put away, *condo*, I put together, Skr. *dhâ*, to place. From same stem are *deed, deem, doom*.] To perform; to execute; to carry into effect; to bring about, produce, effect; to give, confer, or pay (to *do* honor, reverence, etc.); to transact; to finish or complete; to hoax, cheat, swindle (*colloq.*); to inspect the sights or objects of interest in (*colloq.*); to prepare; to cook.—*To do away*, to remove; to put away; to annul; to put an end to.—*To do into*, to translate or render (in another language).—*To do over*, to perform again; to repeat; put a coating, as of paint, upon.—*To do up*, to put up, as a parcel; to tie up; to pack.—*To do with*, to dispose of; to employ; to occupy; to deal with; to get on with (as in what shall I *do with* it? I can *do* nothing *with* him, etc.).—*v.i.* [In this usage *do* is partly the intransitive form of the preceding verb, partly from A.Sax. *dugan*, to avail, be worth, same word as Icel. *duga*, Dan. *due*, D. *deugen*, Goth. *dugan*, G. *taugen*, to be worth, but the senses are so intermingled that it would be difficult to separate them.] To act or behave in any manner, well or ill; to conduct one's self; to fare; to be in a state with regard to sickness or health (how do you *do*?); to succeed; to accomplish a purpose; to serve an end; to suffice (will this plan *do*?); to find means; to contrive; to shift (how shall we *do* for money?).—*To do for*, to suit; to be adapted for; to answer in place of; to be sufficient for; to satisfy; to ruin; to put an end to (*vulg.*); attend on or do household duties for (*colloq.*).—*To do without*, to shift without; to put up without; to dispense with.—*To have done*, to have made an end; to have finished. —*To have done with*, to have finished; to cease to have part or interest in or connection with.—*Do* is often used for a verb to save the repetition of it; as, I shall probably come, but if I *do* not, you must not wait; that is, if I *come* not.—As an auxiliary it is used most commonly in forming negative and interrogative sentences; as, *do* you intend to go? *does* he wish me to come? *Do* is also used to express emphasis; as, I *do* love her. In the imperative, it expresses an urgent request or command; as, *do* come; help me, *do*; make haste, *do*. In the past tense it is sometimes used to convey the idea that what was once true is not true now. 'My lord, you once *did* love me.' (*Shak.*)—The past participle *done*, besides being used for all the ordinary meanings of the verb, has some colloquial or familiar uses; as *done!* an exclamation expressing agreement to a proposal, that is, it is agreed or I accept; *done up*, ruined in any manner, completely exhausted, very tired or fatigued.—**doable,** dö'a•bl, *a.* Capable of being done or executed.—**doer,** dö'ėr, *n.* One who does, executes, performs, or acts; one who performs what is required: as opposed to a mere talker or theorizer.—**doings,** dö'ingz, *n. pl.* Things done; transactions; feats; actions, good or bad; behavior; conduct.

do, dō, *n. Mus.* the name given to the first of the syllables used in solmization; the first or key note of the scale.

docile, dō'sīl or dos'il, *a.* [L. *docilis*, from *doceo*, to teach, whence also *doctor*, *document*.] Teachable; easily instructed; ready to learn; tractable; easily managed.—**docility,** dō•sil'i•ti, *n.* The state or quality of being docile.

dock, dok, *n.* [A.Sax. *docce*, G. *docke*.] The common name of various species of perennial herbs, most of them troublesome weeds with stout rootstalks, erect stems, and broad leaves.

dock, dok, *n.* [Icel. *dockr*, a short tail; G. *docke*, a thick short piece; Fris. *dok*, a small bundle, bunch; comp. also W. *toc*, anything short, *tociaw*, to curtail.] The tail of a beast cut short; the stump of a tail; the solid part of the tail.—*v.t.* To cut off, as the end of a thing; to curtail; to cut short; to clip; to shorten.

dock, dok, *n.* [D. *dok*, G. *docke*, Sw. *docka*, a dock, Flem, *docke*, a kind of cage; perhaps from L. *doga*, a kind of vessel; from Gr. *dochē*, receptacle, from *dechomai*, to receive.] The place where a criminal stands in court; a place artificially formed on the side of a harbor or the bank of a river for the reception of ships, the entrance of which is generally closed by gates; a landing pier for boats, a wharf; an elevated platform for loading freight cars.—*Dry* or *graving dock*, a dock so constructed that the water may be excluded at pleasure, allowing the bottom of a vessel to be inspected and repaired.—*Wet dock*, a dock in which there is always water.—*Floating docks* are composed of large pontoons carrying along each side pumps on suitable stiff frames. When the pontoons are filled with water, they sink to the desired depth, *e.g.*, beneath a vessel, that is raised with them when the water is pumped out of the pontoons.—**dockage,** dok'ij, *n.* Charges for the use of docks.—**docker,** *n.* A worker at the wharves or a longshoreman.—**dockyard,** dok'-yärd, *n.* A yard or repository near a harbor for containing all kinds of naval stores and timber.

docket, dok'et, *n.* [A dim. of *dock*, anything curtailed or cut short.] A summary of a larger writing; a small piece of paper or parchment containing the heads of a writing; an alphabetical list of cases in a court of law; a ticket attached to goods, containing the name of the owner, the place to which they are to be sent, or specifying their measurement, etc.—*v.t.* To make an abstract of, and enter, or write it down; to mark the contents of papers on the back; to add a docket to.

doctor, dok'tėr, *n.* [L., from *doceo*, *doctum*, to teach. DOCILE.] A teacher‡; an instructor‡; a learned man; a person who has received the degree of this name from a university, being thus a *doctor* of divinity, laws, medicine, etc., and supposed capable of teaching the particular subject; a person duly licensed to practice medicine; a physician; one who cures diseases.—*v.t.* and *i.* To treat medically; to repair or patch up; to adulterate (in all senses colloq.).—**doctoral,** dok'tėr•al, *a.*—**doctorate,** dok'tėr•it, *n.* The university degree of doctor.—**doctorship,** dok'tėr•ship, *n.* The degree of a doctor; doctorate.

doctrine, dok'trin, *n.* [L. *doctrina*, instruction, learning, from *doceo*, to teach, whence *doctor*, *docile*, etc.] In a general sense, whatever is taught; hence, a principle, view, or set of opinions maintained by any person or set of persons: whatever is laid down as true by an instructor or master; often instruction and confirmation in the truths of the gospel; one or more of the truths of the gospel.—**doctrinaire,** dok'tri•nâr", *n.* [Fr., from L. *doctrina*; the name was originally given to certain French politicians after the restoration of 1815.] One who theorizes or advocates important changes in political or social matters without a sufficient regard to practical considerations; a political theorist.—**doctrinal,** dok'-tri•nal, *a.* Pertaining to doctrine; containing a doctrine; pertaining to the act or means of teaching.—**doctrinally,** dok'tri•nal•li, *adv.* In the form of doctrine or instruction; by way of teaching or positive direction.—**doctrinarianism,** dok•tri•nâ'-ri•an•izm, *n.* The principles or doctrines of doctrinaires.

document, dok'ū•ment, *n.* [L. *documentum*, a lesson, a proof, from *doceo*, to teach. DOCTRINE.] Any official or authoritative paper containing instructions or proof, for information, establishment of facts, and the like. —*v.t.* To provide or support with documents.—**documental,** dok'ū•-men"tal, *a.*—**documentary,** dok'ū•-men"tė•ri, *a.* Certified in writing.—*n.* A documentary film.—**documentation,** dok'ū•men•tā"shon, *n.* The act of authenticating with documents.

dodder, dod'ėr, *n.* [Dan. *dodder*, Sw. *dodra*, G. *dotter*, of unknown derivation.] The name of certain slender, twining, leafless pink or white parasitic plants, the common English species of which are found on nettles, vetches, furze, flax, etc.—**doddered,** dod'ėrd, *a.* Overgrown with dodder. —**doddered oak,** *a.* With the top branches blasted or withered.

dodecagon, dō•dek'a•gon, *n.* [Gr. *dōdeka*, twelve, and *gōnia*, an angle.] A regular figure or polygon, consisting of twelve equal sides and angles. —**dodecahedral,** dō•dek'a•hē"dral, *a.* Pertaining to a dodecahedron: consisting of twelve equal sides.—**dodecahedron,** dō•dek'a•hē"dron, *n.* [Gr. *hedra*, a base or side.] A regular solid contained under twelve equal and regular pentagons, or having twelve equal bases.

dodge, doj, *v.i.*—*dodged*, *dodging*. [Perhaps connected with *duck*, to stoop or bend down the head, G. *ducken*, to bow, to stoop.] To start suddenly aside; to follow the footsteps of a person, but so as to escape his notice (obs.); to play tricks; to play fast and loose; to quibble.—*v.t.* To evade by a sudden shift of place; to escape by starting aside; to pursue by rapid movements in varying directions; to baffle by shifts and pretexts; to overreach by tricky knavery.—*n.* A trick; an artifice;

an evasion.—**dodger,** doj′ėr, *n.* One who dodges or evades; one who practices artful shifts or dodges.

dodo, dō′dō, *n.* [Pg. *doudo,* silly.] An extinct bird of Mauritius, having a massive, clumsy body, covered with down, short and extremely strong legs, and wings and tail so short as to be useless for flight.

doe, dō, *n.* [A.Sax. *dá,* Dan. *daa.*] The female of the fallow deer, the goat, the sheep, the hare, and the rabbit: corresponding to the masculine *buck.* —**doeskin,** *n.* The skin of a doe; a compact twilled woolen cloth.

doff, dof, *v.t.* [Contr. for *do off,* like *don* for *do on.*] To put, take, or lay off, as dress; to lay aside.—*v.i.* To lay off some article of dress; to take off the hat.

dog, dog, *n.* [A.Sax. *dogga* (very rare), a dog; same as D. *dog,* Dan. *dogge,* Sw. *dogg,* a large kind of dog. *Hound* (A.Sax. *hund*) was originally and long the common English word for dog.] A well-known domesticated carnivorous quadruped, closely allied to the wolf and the fox, noted for its sagacity, acute senses, and great attachment to man; a term of reproach or contempt given to a man; a mean, worthless fellow; a gay young man; a buck; a name applied to several tools, articles, etc., generally iron; as, an andiron, or kind of trestle to lay wood upon in a fireplace, an iron bar, with one or more sharp fangs or claws at one end, for fastening into a piece of wood or other heavy article, for the purpose of dragging or raising it, and the like. ∴ *Dog* is often used in composition for male; as, *dog*-fox, *dog*-otter, etc.; as also to denote meanness, degeneracy, or worthlessness; as, *dog*-Latin, *dog*-rose.—*To give* or *throw to the dogs,* to throw away as useless.—*To go to the dogs,* to go to ruin in life.—*v.t.—dogged, dogging.* To follow insidiously or indefatigably; to follow close; to hunt; to worry with importunity.—**dogged,** dog′ed, *a.* Having the bad qualities of a dog; sullen; sour; morose; surly; severe; obstinate.—**doggedly,** dog′ed•li, *adv.* In a dogged manner. —**doggedness,** dog′ed•nes, *n.* The quality of being dogged.—**doggish,** dog′ish, *a.* Snappish; surly; brutal.—**doggishness,** dog′ish•nes, *n.*—**dogbane,** *n.* A North American bitter plant used instead of ipecacuanha.—**dogberry,** *n.* The berry of the dogwood.—**dogcart,** *n.* A carriage with a box for holding sportsmen's dogs; a sort of double-seated gig, the occupants before and behind sitting back to back.—**dog days,** *n. pl.* The days when Sirius or the Dog Star (whence the term) rises and sets with the sun, extending from about July 3 to about August 11.—**dog-eared,** *a.* Having the corners of the leaves turned down from careless handling (a *dog-eared* book.)—**dogfight,** *n.* A fight, as of dogs; tenacious combat between fighter airplanes.—**dogfish,** *n.* A name given to several species of fishes closely allied to the sharks, but of no great size.—**dog Latin,** *n.* Barbarous Latin; a jargon having a superficial resemblance to Latin.—**dog paddle,** *n.* A form of swimming in which the arms, remaining in the water, alternately reach forward while the legs kick.—**dog tag,** *n.* A metal identification disk worn around the neck.—**Dog Star,** *n.* Sirius, a star of the first magnitude, whose rising and setting with the sun gives name to the dog days. —**dog's-tooth violet,** *n.* A bulbous garden plant with spotted leaves and purple flowers.—**dog-tired,** *a.* Quite tired.—**dogtooth,** *n.* A sharp-pointed human tooth situated between the foreteeth and grinders; a canine tooth; an eyetooth.—**dog-trot,** *n.* A gentle trot like that of a dog.—**dogvane,** *n. Naut.* a small vane placed on the weather gunwale of a vessel to show the direction of the wind.—**dogwatch,** *n. Naut.* the name of the two watches of two hours each instead of four (between 4 and 8 p.m.) arranged so as to alter the watches kept from day to day by each portion of the crew, otherwise the same men would form the watch during the same hours for the whole voyage.—**dog-weary,** *a.* Quite tired; much fatigued.—**dogwood,** dog′wụd, *n.* A name of several trees or shrubs.

doge, dōj, *n.* [It.] The chief magistrate of the former republics of Venice (697-1797) and Genoa (1339-1797).

dogger, dog′ėr, *n.* [D. *dogger-boot—dogger,* a codfish, and *boot,* a boat.] A Dutch fishing vessel having two masts, employed in the North Sea especially in the cod and herring fisheries.

doggerel, dog′ėr•el, *a.* [Possibly from *dog.*] An epithet originally applied to a kind of loose irregular measure in burlesque poetry, but now more generally to mean verses defective in rhythm and sense.—*n.* Doggerel or mean verses.

dogma, dog′ma, *n.* [Gr. *dogma,* that which seems true, an opinion, from *dokeō,* to seem.] A settled opinion or belief; a tenet; an opinion or doctrine received on authority, as opposed to one obtained from experience or demonstration.—**dogmatic, dogmatical,** dog•mat′ik, dog•mat′i•kal, *a.* Pertaining to a dogma or dogmas; having the character of a dogma; disposed to assert opinions with overbearing or arrogance; dictatorial; arrogant; authoritative; positive.—**dogmatically,** dog•mat′i•kal•li, *adv.* In a dogmatic manner.—**dogmatics,** dog•mat′iks, *n.* Doctrinal theology; the essential doctrines of Christianity.—**dogmatism,** dog′ma•tizm, *n.* The quality of being dogmatic: arrogant assertion.—**dogmatist,** dog′ma•tist, *n.* One who is dogmatic; an upholder of dogmas; an arrogant advancer of principles or opinions.—**dogmatize,** dog′ma•tīz, *v.i.* To teach opinions with bold and undue confidence; to assert principles arrogantly or authoritatively.—**dogmatizer,** dog′ma•tī•zėr, *n.* One who dogmatizes.

doily, doi′li, *n.* [Said to be named from the first maker.] A small ornamental mat used at table to put glasses on during dessert.

doit, doit, *n.* [D. *duit,* from Fr. *d'huit,* of eight, as the eighth part of a stiver.] A small Dutch copper coin, being the eighth part of a stiver, in value half a farthing; the ancient Scottish penny piece, of which twelve were equal to a penny sterling; any small piece of money; a trifle.

doldrums, dōl′drumz, *n. pl. Naut.* the parts of the ocean near the equator that abound in calms, squalls, and light baffling winds; low spirits; the dumps (*colloq.*).

dole, dōl, *n.* [DEAL.] That which is dealt out or distributed; a part, share, or portion; lot; fortune; that which is given in charity; gratuity; especially money distributed by the government during a financial depression.—*v.t.* To deal out; to distribute.

dole, dōl, *n.* [O.Fr. *dole,* Fr. *deuil,* mourning, from L. *doleo,* to grieve.] Grief; sorrow.—**doleful,** dōl′fụl, *a.* Full of dole or grief; sorrowful; expressing grief; mournful; melancholy; sad; dismal; gloomy.—**dolefully,** dōl′fụl•li, *adv.* In a doleful manner.—**dolefulness,** dōl′fụl•nes, *n.* The state or quality of being doleful.—**dolesome,**† dōl′sum, *a.* Doleful.

dolerite, dol′ėr•īt, *n.* [Gr. *doleros,* deceptive.] A variety of traprock composed of augite and labradorite; so named from the difficulty of discriminating its component parts.

dolichocephalic, dolichocephalous, dol′i•kō•se•fal″ik, dol′i•kō•sef″a•lus, *a.* [Gr. *dolichos,* long, and *kephalē,* the head.] A term used in ethnology to denote skulls in which the diameter from side to side bears a less proportion to the diameter from front to back than 8 to 10, as seen in the West African negro tribes.—**dolichocephalism,** dol′i•kō•sef″a•lizm, *n.* The condition of being dolichocephalic.

doll, dol, *n.* [Of doubtful origin; perhaps for *Doll,* contr. of *Dorothy.*] A puppet or small image in the human form for the amusement of children; a girl or woman more remarkable for good looks than intelligence.

dollar, dol′ėr, *n.* [D. Dan. and Sw. *daler,* from G. *thaler,* from *thal,* a dale, because first coined in Joachim's-*Thal,* in Bohemia, in 1519.] A silver coin of the United States, of the value of 100 cents.—*Dollar-diplomacy,* a diplomacy used to promote the financial or commercial interests of a country abroad.

dolly, dol′i, *n.* A child's name for a doll; a small, low platform on rollers, used for transporting heavy objects.

dolman, dol′man, *n.* [Fr. *dolman, doliman,* from Turk. *dōlāmān.*] A long outer robe, open in front, and having narrow sleeves buttoned at the wrist, worn by Turks; a kind of garment somewhat of the nature of a wide jacket, worn by ladies.

dolmen, dol′men, *n.* [Armor. *dolmen*; Gael. *tolmen—dol, tol,* a table, and *men,* a stone.] A rude ancient structure (probably of sepulchral origin) consisting of one large unhewn stone resting on two or more others placed erect; also applied to structures where several blocks are raised upon pillars so as to form a sort of gallery; a cromlech.

dolomite, dol′o•mīt, *n.* [After the French geologist *Dolomieu.*] A granular, crystalline, or schistose stone or rock, being a compound of carbonate of magnesia and carbonate of lime.

dolor, dolour, dō′lėr, *n.* [Fr. *douleur,* from L. *dolor, doloris,* grief, pain, from *doleo,* to grieve. Akin *dole, doleful.*] Grief; sorrow; lamentation. [Now only poetical.]—**dolorous,** dol′ėr•us, *a.* Sorrowful; doleful; exciting sorrow or grief; painful; expressing pain or grief.—**dolorously,** dol′ėr•us•li, *adv.* In a dolorous manner.—**dolorousness,** dol′ėr•us•nes, *n.* The state or quality of being dolorous.

dolphin, dol′fin, *n.* [O.Fr. *daulphin,* Mod. Fr. *dauphin,* a dolphin, the dauphin, from L. *delphinus,* a dolphin.] A name of several species of cetaceous mammals having numerous conical teeth in both jaws, as the dolphin proper, a peculiarly agile animal, the grampus, etc.; a fish about 5 feet long, celebrated for its swiftness and the brilliant and beautiful colors which it assumes in the act of dying; a spar or buoy made fast to an anchor, and usually supplied with a ring to enable vessels to ride by it; a mooring post placed at the entrance of a dock or along a quay or wharf.

dolt, dōlt, *n.* [Probably connected with E. *dull,* A.Sax. *dol,* dull, stupid; *dwelan,* to err, to be stupid.] A heavy, stupid fellow; a blockhead; a thickskull.—**doltish,** dōl′tish, *a.* Dull in intellect; stupid.—**doltishly,** dōl′tish•li, *adv.* In a doltish manner.—**doltishness,** dōl′tish•nes, *n.*

dom, dom, *n.* [L. *dominus,* lord.] Roman Catholic title of dignitaries of the Carthusian and Benedictine monks.

domain, dō•mān′, *n.* [Fr. *domaine,* from L.L. *domanium,* a form of L. *dominium,* ownership, property, from *dominus,* a lord.] The territory over which dominion is exercised; the territory ruled over; a dominion; an estate in land; the land about a mansion house and in the immediate occupancy of the owner; a demesne.

dome, dōm, *n.* [Fr. *dôme,* from Eccles, L. *dema,* a house, from Gr. *dōma,* a house, from *demō,* to build.] A roof rising up in the form of an inverted cup; a large cupola; the hemispherical roof of a building; anything shaped like a dome, as the steam chamber of a locomotive, rising above it with a rounded top, etc.—**domical,** dō′mi•kal, *a.* Shaped like a dome or cupola.

domestic, do•mes′tik, *a.* [L. *domesticus,* from *domus,* a house; from root seen in Gr. *demō,* to build, and in E. *timber*; akin *domicile.*] Belonging to the house or home; pertaining to one's place of residence and to the family; devoted to home duties or pleasures; living in or about the habitations of man; kept for the use of man; tame; not wild; pertaining to one's own country; intestine; not foreign.—*Domestic economy,* the economical management of all household affairs; the art of managing domestic affairs in the best and thriftiest manner.—*n.* One who lives in the family of another, and is paid for some service; a household servant.—**domestically,** do•mes′ti•kal•li, *adv.* In a domestic manner.—**domesticate,** do•mes′ti•kāt, *v.t.*—*domesticated, domesticating.* To make domestic; to accustom to remain much at home; to accustom (animals) to live near the habitations of man; to tame; to reduce from a wild to a cultivated condition (plants).—**domestication,** do•mes′ti•kā″shon, *n.* The act of domesticating; the state of being domesticated.—**domesticity,** do•mes•tis′i•ti, *n.* State of being domestic.

domicile, dom′i•sīl, *n.* [L. *domicilium,* a mansion, from *domus,* a house, and root of *cella,* a cell. DOMESTIC.] A place of residence; a dwelling house; the place where one lives in opposition to the place where one only remains for a time.—*v.t.*—*domiciled, domiciling.* To establish in a fixed residence.—**domiciliary,** dom•i•sil′i•a•ri, *a.* Pertaining to a domicile.—*Domiciliary visit,* a visit to a private dwelling, particularly for the purpose of searching it under authority.—**domiciliate,** dom•i•sil′i•āt, *v.t.*—*domiciliated, domiciliating.* To domicile.

dominant, dom′i•nant, *a.* [L. *dominans,* ppr. of *dominor,* to rule, from *dominus,* lord, master. DAME.] Ruling; prevailing; governing; predominant.—*Dominant chord, mus.* that which is formed by grouping three tones, rising gradually by intervals of a third from the dominant or fifth tone of the scale.—*n. Mus.* the fifth tone of the diatonic scale; thus G is the dominant of the scale of C, and D the dominant of the scale of G.—**dominance, dominancy,** dom′i•nans, dom′i•nan•si, *n.* Ascendency; rule; authority.—**dominate,** dom′i•nāt, *v.t.*—*dominated, dominating.* To have power or sway over; to govern; to prevail or predominate over.—*v.i.* To predominate.—**domination,** dom•i•nā′shon, *n.* The exercise of power in ruling; dominion; government; arbitrary authority; tyranny.—**dominations,** *n.* The fourth rank or order in the angelic hierarchy.—**dominative,** dom′i•nā•tiv, *a.* Presiding; governing; imperious; insolent.—**dominator,** dom′i•nā•tėr, *n.* One that dominates; a ruler or ruling power; the presiding or predominant power.—**domineer,** dom•i•nēr′, *v.i.* To rule with insolence or arbitrary sway; to bluster; to hector.—*v.t.* To govern harshly or overbearingly; to order or command insolently.—**domineering,** dom•i•nē′ring, *p.* and *a.* Given to domineer; overbearing.—**dominical,** do•min′i•kal, *a.* [L.L. *dominicalis,* connected with Sunday, from L. *dominicus* (*dies dominica,* Sunday), pertaining to a lord or master, from *dominus,* lord. DOMINANT.] Noting or marking the Lord's day or Sunday; relating to our Lord.—*Dominical letter,* one of the seven letters, A, B, C, D, E, F, G, used in almanacs, etc., to mark the Sundays throughout the year.

Dominican, do•min′i•kan, *a.* Of or pertaining to St. Dominic or the order founded by him.—*n.* A member of a religious order instituted in 1216 at Toulouse, by Dominic de Guzman (afterward St. *Dominic*) with the special purpose of combating the doctrines of the Albigenses: called also *Blackfriar,* from the color of the dress.

dominie, dom′i•ni, *n.* [From L. *domine,* vocative case of *dominus,* a lord or master.] A schoolmaster; a pedagogue. [Scotch.]

dominion, do•min′yon, *n.* [L. *dominium.* See DOMAIN.] Sovereign or supreme authority; the power of governing and controlling; government; sway; rule; ascendency; predominance; territory under a government; country or district governed, or within the limits of the authority of a prince or state; *pl.* an order of angels (N.T.).

domino, dom′i•nō, *n.* pl. **dominoes,** dom′i•nōz. [Fr., a covering for the head worn by priests, from *dominus,* lord.] A masquerade dress, consisting of an ample cloak or mantle, with a cap and wide sleeves; frequently, though incorrectly, applied to a half mask worn by ladies as a partial disguise for the features; a person wearing a domino; *pl.* a game played with twenty-eight flat, oblong pieces of ivory or bone, dotted, after the manner of dice, with a certain number of points.

don, don. [From L. *dominus,* a lord. The feminine is *donna* or *doña.*] A title in Spain, formerly given to noblemen and gentlemen only, but now used much more widely; a fellow or one holding high office in an English college (*colloq.*).

don, don, *v.t.*—*donned, donning.* [To *do on*: opposed to *doff.*] To put on; to invest one's self with.

donation, dō•nā′shon, *n.* [L. *donatio,* an offering, from *dono,* to give; *donum,* a gift, from *do,* to give.] The act of giving or bestowing; that which is gratuitously given; a grant; a gift.—**donative,** don′a•tiv, *n.* A gift; a largess; a gratuity; a present; a dole; *law,* a benefice given to a person by the founder or patron, without presentation, institution, or induction by the ordinary.—*a.* Vested or vesting by donation.—**donee,** dō•nē′, *n.* The recipient of a gift or grant.—**donor,** dō′nėr, *n.* One who gives, grants, or bestows; a giver.

done, dun, pp. of *do.*

donjon, don′jon, *n.* [Fr., from L.L. *domnio, domnionis,* for L. *dominio,* dominion.] The principal tower of a castle, which was usually situated in the innermost court, and into which the garrison could retreat in case of necessity, the lower part of it being commonly used as a prison: also called the *Keep*.

donkey, dong'ki, *n.* [Perh. a little *dun* animal, from *dun* and diminutive term. *-key*.] An ass; a stupid or obstinate and wrong-headed fellow. **—donkey engine,** *n.* A small steam engine used where no great power is required, and often to perform some subsidiary operation, as on board ships.

donna, don'na, *n.* [It., from L. *domina*, a lady or mistress.] A lady; as, *prima donna*, the first female singer in an opera, oratorio, etc.

donor. See DONATION.

dooly, doolie, dö'li, *n.* [Hind.] Light litter used in India.

doom, döm, *n.* [A.Sax. *dom*=O.Sax., O. Fris. *dom*, Goth. *doms*, Icel. *dómr*, the same word as the suffix *-dom* in king*dom*, etc., and derived probably from verb *to do*. Akin *deem*.] A judgment or judicial sentence; passing of sentence; the final judgment; the state to which one is doomed or destined; fate; fortune, generally evil; adverse issue; ruin; destruction.—*Crack of doom*, dissolution of nature.—*v.t.* To condemn to any punishment; to consign by a decree or sentence; to pronounce sentence or judgment on; to ordain as a penalty; to decree; to destine.—**doomsday,** dömz'dā, *n.* The day of doom or final judgment; a day of sentence or condemnation (*Shak.*).—*Doomsday Book*, a book compiled by order of William the Conqueror containing a survey of all the lands in England, giving the areas of estates, the amount of land under tillage, pasture, woods, etc., the number of villeins, etc.

door, dōr, *n.* [A.Sax. *dór*, *dúru*= O.Sax. *dur*, *dor*, Icel. *dyr*, Goth. *daur*, G. *thür*, L. *fores*, Gr. *thura*, Ir. *dorus*, Skr. *dvâra*, door.] An opening or passage into a house or apartment by which persons enter; the frame of boards or other material that shuts such an opening, and usually turns on hinges; means of approach or access.—*To lie* or *be at one's door* (*fig.*), to be imputable or chargeable to one.—*Next door to* (*fig.*), near to; bordering on (*colloq.*). —*Out of door* or *doors*, out of the house; in the open air; abroad.—*In doors*, within the house; at home.—**doorkeeper,** *n.* A porter; one who guards the entrance of a house or apartment.—**doornail,** *n.* The nail on which, in ancient doors, the knocker struck.—**doorplate,** *n.* A plate upon a door bearing the name of the resident.—**doorstep,** *n.* The stone at the threshold.—**doorway,** dōr'wā, *n.* The passage of a door; the entrance-way into a room or house.

dope, dōp, *v.t.* To drug; to dose.—*n.* A narcotic; a dull or stupid person. (*Slang.*)

Doric, Dorian, dor'ik, dō'ri•an, *a.* Pertaining to the Dorians, a people of ancient Greece.—*Doric order*, *arch.* the oldest and simplest of the three orders of Grecian architecture, characterized by the columns having no base, and the flutings few, large, and not deep, the capital of simple character.—*Dorian* or *Doric mode*, *mus.* a composition in which the second note of the normal scale acquires something of the dignity or force of a tonic, and upon it the melody closes.—**Doric,** *n.* The language of the Dorians, a Greek dialect characterized by broadness and hardness; hence, any dialect with similar characteristics, especially to the Scottish.

dorking, dor'king, *n.* A species of domestic fowl, distinguished by having five claws on each foot, so named because bred largely at *Dorking* in Surrey.

dormant, dor'mant, *a.* [Fr., from *dormir*, L. *dormio*, to sleep.] Sleeping; sunk in the winter sleep or torpid state of certain animals; at rest; not in action (*dormant* energies); neglected; not claimed, asserted, or insisted on (a *dormant* title or privileges); in *heraldry*, of beast with head on paws.—*Dormant partner*, a partner who takes no active part in a commercial concern.—**dormancy,** dor'man•si, *n.* State of being, dormant.—**dormer, dormer window,** dor'mėr, *n.* [Lit. the window of a sleeping apartment.] A window standing vertically on a sloping roof of a dwelling house, and so named because such windows are found chiefly in attic bedrooms.—**dormitory,** dor'mi•to•ri, *n.* [L. *dormitorium*.] A place, building, or room to sleep in.—**dormouse,** dor - mous, *n.* pl. **dormice,** dor'mīs. [Prov. E. *dorm*, to sleep, and *mouse*, lit. the sleeping-mouse.] A small rodent animal which passes the winter in a lethargic or torpid state, only occasionally waking and applying to its stock of provisions hoarded up for that season.

dorsal, dor'sal, *a.* [From L. *dorsum*, the back.] Of or pertaining to the back.—**dorsispinal,** *a.* Of or pertaining to the back and the spine.

dory, dō'ri, *n.* [Also called *John-Dory*, probably from Fr. *jaune dorée*, golden yellow, from its color.] A European fish of a beautiful yellow color, with a curious protrusible mouth, valued as food.

dory, dō'ri, *n.* A canoe or small boat.

dose, dōs, *n.* [Fr., from Gr. *dosis*, a giving, from *didōmi*, to give]. The quantity of medicine given or prescribed to be taken at one time; anything given to be swallowed; as much as a man can take; a quantity in general.—*v.t.*—*dosed*, *dosing*. To form into suitable doses; to give a dose or doses to; to physic. —**dosage,** dō'sij, *n. Med.* act of dosing; administering of medicine by doses.

dosimeter, do•sim'e•tėr, *n.* An apparatus for measuring minute amounts of liquid.

dossal, dos'al, *n.* [L.L. *dorsale*, from L. *dorsum*, back.] An ornamental cloth hung at the back of an altar or a seat.

dossier, dos'ē•ā, *n.* [Fr. word, from *dos*, back.] A collection of documents containing information about a person or incident.

dot, dot, *n.* [A.Sax. *dott*, a spot or speck (whence Sc. *dottle*, a small lump): comp. L.G. *dutte*, a plug, a stopper; D. *dot*, a small bundle.] A small point or spot made with a pen or other pointed instrument; a speck, used in marking a writing or other thing; a spot.—*v.t.*—*dotted*, *dotting*. To mark with dots; to mark or diversify with small detached objects (as clumps of trees).—*v.i.* To make dots or spots.

dotal, dō'tal, *a.* [Fr., from L. *dotalis*, from *dos*, dower. DOWER.] Pertaining to dower or a woman's marriage portion; constituting dower, or comprised in it.

dote, dōt, *v.i.*—*doted*, *doting*. [The same word as O.D. *doten*, to dote; akin to D. *dut*, a nap, *dutten*, to take a nap; Icel. *dotta*, to nod with sleep.] To have the intellect impaired by age, so that the mind wanders or wavers; to be in a state of senile silliness; to be excessively in love; to love to excess or extravagance (to *dote on* a person).—**doter,** dō'tėr, *n.* One who dotes.—**dotage,** dō'tij, *n.* Feebleness or imbecility of understanding or mind, particularly in old age; childishness of old age; senility; weak and foolish affection.—**dotard,** dō'tėrd, *n.* A man whose intellect is impaired by age; one in his second childhood. —**dotingly,** dō'ting•li, *adv.* In a doting manner; foolishly; in a manner characterized by excessive fondness.—**dotterel, dottrel,** dot'ėr•el, dot'rel, *n.* [From the bird's supposed stupidity.] A species of plover, breeding in the highest latitudes of Asia and Europe, and migrating to the shores of the Mediterranean; a booby; a dupe; a gull.

double, dub'l, *a.* [Fr. *double*, from L. *duplus*, double—*duo*, two, and term. *-plus*, from root of *pleo*, to fill. FILL.] Forming a pair; consisting of two in a set together; coupled; composed of two corresponding parts; twofold; twice as much; multiplied by two (a *double* portion); acting two parts, one openly, the other in secret; deceitful; *bot.* having two or more rows of petals produced by cultivation from stamens and carpels.—*v.t.*—*doubled*, *doubling*. To make double or twofold; to fold one part upon another part of; to increase by adding an equal sum, value, or quantity; to contain twice as much as; to pass round or by; to march or sail round, so as to proceed along both sides of (to *double* a cape).—*v.i.* To increase or grow to twice as much; to turn back or wind in running.—*n.* Twice as much; a turn in running to escape pursuers; a trick; a shift; an artifice to deceive; something precisely equal or like; a counterpart; a duplicate; a copy; a person's apparition or likeness; a wraith; a fold or plait; *milit.* the quickest step in marching next to the run.—

double bass, *n.* The largest musical instrument of the viol kind.—**double-breasted,** *a.* Applied to a waistcoat or coat, either side of which may be made to lap over the other and button.—**double cross,** *n.* An act of deception or cheating.—**double-dealer,** *n.* One who deceitfully acts two different parts.—**double entry,** *n.* Mode of bookkeeping in which two entries are made of every transaction, one on the Dr. side of one account, and the other on the Cr. side of another account, in order that the one may check the other.—**double-faced,** *a.* Deceitful; hypocritical; showing two faces.—**doubleheader,** *n.* Two games played consecutively on the same day.—**double-jointed,** *a.* Having joints that allow unusual freedom of motion.—**double-time,** *n. Milit.* the quickest step next to the run; a pace of 180 36-inch steps per minute; payment of twice one's normal wage.—**double star,** *n. Astron.* two stars so near each other that they are distinguishable only by the help of a telescope.—**doublet,** dub'let, *n.* [Dim. of *double.*] A close-fitting garment covering the body from the neck to a little below the waist; one of a pair; one of two (or more) words really the same but different in form (as *ant* and *emmet*).—**double-talk,** *n.* Purposely meaningless language that is made to appear sensible by mixing normal words with nonsense syllables; deliberately ambiguous language.

doubloon, dub•lön', *n.* [Fr. *doublon,* Sp. *doblon.*] A coin of Spain and the Spanish American States.

doubt, dout, *v.i.* [O.Fr. *doubter,* from L. *dubitare,* to doubt, from same stem as *dubius,* doubtful, from *duo,* two. Akin *dubious, dual,* etc.] To waver or fluctuate in opinion; to be in uncertainty respecting the truth or fact; to be undetermined.—*v.t.* To question or hold questionable; to withhold assent from; to hesitate to believe; to suspect; to be inclined to think (governing clauses: I *doubt* you are wrong) (*Scot.*); to distrust; to be diffident of (to *doubt* a person's ability),—*n.* A fluctuation of mind respecting the truth or correctness of a statement or opinion, or the propriety of an action; uncertainty of mind; want of belief; unsettled state of opinion; suspicion; apprehension.—**doubtable,** dou'ta•bl, *a.* Liable to be doubted.—**doubter,** dou'tėr, *n.* One who doubts.—**doubtful,** dout'fụl, *a.* Entertaining doubt; not settled in opinion; undetermined; wavering; dubious; ambiguous; not clear in its meaning; not obvious, clear, or certain; questionable; not without suspicion; not confident; not without fear; not certain or defined.—**doubtfully,** dout'fụl•li, *adv.* In a doubtful manner.—**doubtfulness,** dout'fụl•nes, *n.* The state or quality of being doubtful; uncertainty; suspense; ambiguity.—**doubtless,** dout'les, *adv.* Without doubt or question; unquestionably.—**doubtlessly,** *adv.* Unquestionably.

douche, dösh, *n.* [Fr.] A kind of bath consisting in a jet or current of water or vapor directed upon some part of the body.

dough, dō, *n.* [A.Sax. *dág, dáh*=D. *deeg,* Icel. and Dan. *deig,* Goth. *daigs,* G. *teig,* dough; akin Goth. *deigan,* to mold, to form.] Paste of bread; a mass composed of flour or meal moistened and kneaded but not baked.—**doughboy,** *n.* During World War I the nickname for an infantryman in the U.S. army.—**doughnut,** *n.* A small roundish cake, usually with a hole in the center.

doughty, dou'ti, *a.* [A.Sax. *dohtig, dyhtig,* from *dugan* (Sc. *dow*), to be able; Dan. *dygtig,* G. *tuchtig,* able, fit. Do, *v.i.*] Brave; valiant; noble; illustrious; now seldom used except in irony or burlesque.—**doughtily,** dou'ti•li, *adv.* With doughtiness.—**doughtiness,** dou'ti•nes, *n.* The character of being doughty; valor; bravery.

dour, dour, dụr, *a.* [L. *durus,* hard.] Sullen; gloomy; stern.—**dourly,** dour'li, dụr'li, *adv.*

douse, dous, *v.t.*—*doused, dousing.* [Origin doubtful; comp. Sw. *dunsa,* to plump; D. *doesen,* to strike.] To thrust or plunge into water; to immerse; to dip; *naut.* to strike or lower in haste; to slacken suddenly; to put out or extinguish (slang).—*v.i.* To fall or be plunged suddenly into water.

dove, duv, *n.* [A.Sax. *dúfa, dúfe,* from *dúfan,* to dive, to dip, probably from its habit of ducking the head, or from its manner of flight; D. *duif,* Dan. *due,* Sc. *doo,* G. *taube.*] A pigeon, some varieties being distinguished by an additional term prefixed, as *ring-dove, turtle-dove,* etc.; a word of endearment.—**dovecot, dovecote,** *n.* A small building or box in which domestic pigeons breed; a house for doves.—**dovetail,** *n. Carp.* a method of fastening the ends of boards together at right angles by letting one piece, cut into projections somewhat like a dove's tail spread, into corresponding cavities in another.—*v.t. Carp.* to unite by the above method; *fig.* to fit or adjust exactly and firmly.

dowager, dou'a•jėr, *n.* [From a form *dowage,* from Fr. *douer,* to endow. DOWER.] A name given to the widow of a person of title, as a prince or nobleman, to distinguish her from the wife of her husband's heir bearing the same title; thus when a duke dies leaving a widow, and his successor in the title has a wife, the widow becomes the duchess-*dowager.*

dowdy, dou'di, *n.* [Akin to O.E. *dowde, dowd,* dull, sluggish; E. *dawdle,* L.G. *dödeln,* to be slow; Prov. E. *daw,* a sluggard.] An awkward, ill-dressed woman; a woman with no elegance or grace.—*a.* Awkward; illdressed; vulgar looking; applied to females.—**dowdyish,** dou'di•ish, *a* Like a dowdy.

dowel, dou'el, *n.* [Fr. *douille,* a groove or socket; L.L. *ductile,* a gutter, from L. *duco,* to lead.] A wooden or iron pin or tenon used in joining together two pieces of any substance edgewise (as the pieces of a barrel end); a piece of wood driven into a wall to receive nails of skirtings, etc.—*v.t.*—*dowelled, dowelling.* To fasten by means of dowels, as two boards together by pins inserted in the edges.—**dowel pin,** *n.* A pin inserted in the edges of boards to fasten them together.

dower, dou'ėr, *n.* [Fr. *douaire,* from L.L. *dotarium,* from L. *doto, dotatum,* to endow, from *dos, dotis,* a dower, whence also *dotal, dowager.*] That with which one is endowed; the property which a woman brings to her husband in marriage; *law,* the right which a wife has in the third part of the real estate of which her husband died possessed —*v t.* To furnish with dower or a portion; to endow.—**dowry,** dou'ri, *n.* The money, goods, or estate which a woman brings to her husband in marriage; dower.

down, doun, *n.* [A.Sax. *dún,* a hill; L.G. *dünen,* Fris. *dunen,* D. *duin,* a dune; O.H.G. *dûn, dûna,* promontory, Sw. dial. *dun,* a hill; also W., Ir., and Gael. *dun,* a hill, hillock.] A hill or rising ground; a low, rounded, grassy hill; a tract of naked, hilly land, used chiefly for pasturing sheep; a term commonly used in the south of England; also a dune or sand hill near the sea.

down, doun, *prep.* [A.Sax. *adúne,* adown, for *of-dúne,* off or down the hill. DOWN, a hill.] Along in descent; from a higher to a lower part of; toward the mouth of and in the direction of the current.—*adv.* In a descending direction; from a higher to a lower position, degree, or place in a series; from the metropolis of a country to the provinces, or from the main terminus of a railway to the subordinate stations; on the ground, or at the bottom; in a low condition; in humility, dejection, calamity, etc.; below the horizon (the sun is *down*); into disrepute or disgrace (to write *down* folly, vice, an author); from a larger to a less bulk (to boil *down*); from former to more recent times; extended or prostrate on the ground or on any flat surface; paid or handed over in ready money (a thousand dollars *down*). It is often used elliptically or interjectionally for go down, kneel down, etc. (*down!* dog, *down!*); also with *with,* in energetic commands; as, *down with* the sail, that is, take it down.—*Up and down,* here and there; everywhere.—*Down in the mouth,* dispirited; dejected. (*Colloq.*)—*To be down at heel,* to have the back part of the upper, or heel, turned down, or to have on shoes with the heel turned down; to be slipshod or slovenly.—*n.* A downward fluctuation (ups and *downs*).—**downcast,** doun'kast, *a.* Cast downward; directed to the ground (*downcast* eyes); in low spirits; dejected.—*n.*

Mining, the ventilating shaft down which the air passes in circulating through a mine.—**downfall,** doun′fal, *n.* A falling down; a sudden descent or fall from a position of power, honor, wealth, fame, or the like; loss of rank, reputation, or fortune; loss of office; ruin; destruction.—**downfallen,** doun′fal′n, *a.* Fallen; ruined.—**downhearted,** doun′här•ted, *a.* Dejected in spirits. —**downhill,** doun′hil, *n.* A declivity; slope.—*a.* Sloping downwards; descending; sloping.—*adv.* Down a hill or slope.—**downpour,** doun′pōr, *n.* A pouring down; especially a heavy or continuous shower.—**downright,** doun′rīt, *adv.* Right down; perpendicularly; in plain terms; completely; thoroughly.—*a.* Directed straight or right down; coming down perpendicularly; directly to the point; plain; open; mere; sheer (*downright* nonsense); straightforward; unceremonious; blunt (a *downright* man).—**downrightly,** doun′rīt•li, *adv.* Plainly. —**downstairs,** *a.* Pertaining or relating to the lower floor of a house.—**down town,** *n.* The main part or business section of a town.—**downtown,** *a.* Pertaining to, or located in, the business section of a town.—*adv.* To or in the business section of a town.—**downtrodden, downtrod,** *a.* Trodden down; trampled upon; tyrannized over.—**downward, downwards,** doun′wėrd, doun′wėrdz, *adv.* From a higher place to a lower; in a descending course; in a course or direction from a spring or source; in a course of descent from an ancestor.—**downward,** *a.* Moving or extending from a higher to a lower place (a *downward* course); descending from a head, origin, or source; tending to a lower condition or state.

down, doun, *n.* [Same word as Icel. *dún*, Dan. *duun*, G. *daune*, down.] The fine soft covering of birds under the feathers, particularly on the breasts of waterfowl, as the duck and swan; the soft hair of the human face when beginning to appear; the pubescence of plants, a fine hairy substance; any fine feathery or hairy substance of vegetable growth.—*v.t.* To cover, stuff, or line with down.—**downiness,** dou′ni•nes, *n.* The quality of being downy; knowingness or cuteness (slang).—**downy,** dou′ni, *a.* Covered with down or nap; covered with pubescence or soft hairs, as a plant; made of down; soft, calm, soothing (sleep); knowing, cunning, or artful (slang).

dowry, *n.* See DOWER.

doxology, dok•sol′o•ji, *n.* [Gr. *doxologia*, a praising—*doxa*, praise, glory, and *legō*, to speak.] A short hymn or form of words ascribing glory to God, and used in worship.—**doxological,** dok•so•loj′i•kal, *a.* Pertaining to doxology.

doxy, dok′si, *n.* [Comp. G. *docke*, Sw. *docka*, a doll, a plaything.] An old low term for a sweetheart or mistress.

doyley, doi′li, *n.* Same as *Doily*.

doze, dōz, *v.i.*—*dozed, dozing*. [Akin to Dan. *döse*, to doze; *dōs*, drowsiness; G. *dōseln, doseln*, to doze; Prov. G. *dosen*, to slumber; allied to *dizzy* and to *daze*.] To slumber; to sleep lightly; to live in a state of drowsiness; to be dull or half asleep.—*v.t.* To pass or spend in drowsiness; to make dull; to stupefy. —*n.* A light sleep; a slumber.—**dozy,** dō′zi, *a.* Drowsy; heavy; inclined to sleep; sleepy.

dozen, duz′n, *n.* [Fr. *douzaine*, from *douze*, twelve, from L. *duodecim*—*duo*, two, and *decem*, ten.] A collection of twelve things of a like kind, or regarded as forming an aggregate for the time being; an indefinite or round number comprising more or less than twelve units, as the case may be.

drab, drab, *n.* [A Celtic word; Ir. *drabhog*, a slut, dregs, from *drab*, a spot, a stain; Gael. *drabach*, dirty, slovenly; *drabag*, a drab; akin to *draff*.] A strumpet; a prostitute; a low, sluttish woman; a slattern. *v.i.* To associate with strumpets.—**drabble,** drab′l, *v.t.*—*drabbled, drabbling*. To draggle; to make dirty; to wet and befoul.

drab, drab, *n.* [Fr. *drap*, L.L. *drappus*, cloth, from a Teut. root seen in E. *trappings*, horse furniture.] A thick woolen cloth of a dun or dull-brown color; a dull brownish-yellow color.—*a.* Being of a dull brown or pale brown color; like the cloth so called.

drachma, drak′ma, *n.* [L. from Gr. *drachmē*, a drachm, from *drassomai*, to grasp with the hand. *Dram* is the same word.] An ancient Greek silver coin; the monetary unit of modern Greece; an ancient Greek unit of weight; a small modern weight, especially a *dram*.

Draconic, Draconian, drā•kon′ik, drā•kō′ni•an, *a.* Relating to *Draco*, the Athenian lawgiver; hence (applied to laws), extremely severe; sanguinary.

draff, draf, *n.* [Icel. *draf*, D. *draf*, also *drab*, Dan. *drav*, dregs, hog's-wash; allied to *drab*, a slut.] Refuse: dregs; hogwash; the refuse of malt which has been brewed or distilled from, given to swine and cows.—**draffy,** draf′i, *a.* Like, or consisting of draff; waste; worthless.

draft or, mainly *Brit.*, **draught,** draft, *n.* [From *draw, drag*.] The action of pulling or hauling; that which is hauled; an outline, drawing, sketch, map, or plan; a written order from one person to another, directing payment; a check; a demand or drain on anything; a selection of persons or things for a special purpose; the persons selected; a current of air; a device for regulating the flow of air; the drawing in of a net to catch fish; the quantity of fish caught; the depth of water required to float a ship, especially when loaded; the depth a ship sinks in water; the drawing of liquid from a keg, etc., when ordered; the act of drinking; the amount taken in one drink; in the U.S., *draught* is sometimes the spelling for the fishing term, the drinking term, and air current.—*v.t.* To make a draft of; to make a rough sketch of; to outline; to select for a special purpose, as for military service.—**draftee,** draf′tē, *n.* One who is conscripted for military service.—**draftsman,** drafts′-man, *n.* One who makes drawings or diagrams, as of buildings or machinery.

drag, drag, *v.t.*—*dragged, dragging*. [A.Sax. *dragan*, to drag, to draw; Icel. *draga*, to drag, to carry; Goth. *dragan*, to draw, to carry; D. *dragen*, G. *tragen*, to carry, to bear. *Draw* is another form of the same word, *draggle* is a dim., and *drawl, dray, dredge*, are akin.] To pull; to haul; to draw along the ground by main force; to draw along slowly or heavily, as anything burdensome or troublesome; hence, to pass in pain or with difficulty; to search (a river, pond, etc.) with a net, hooked instrument, etc., for drowned persons, etc.—*To drag the anchor*, to draw or trail it along the bottom when it will not hold: said of a ship. —*v.i.* To be drawn along or trail on the ground, as a dress or as an anchor that does not hold; to move or proceed slowly, heavily, or laboriously; to move on lingeringly or with effort.—*n.* The act of dragging; any device used in dragging; that which is dragged; a sled for carrying heavy loads; a horse-drawn vehicle like a stage coach; an instrument for breaking up ground; anything that retards, hinders or obstructs; *aerodynamics*, the total force of the air acting parallel and opposite to an aircraft's direction of flight; a draw on a cigarette, etc.; a puff; an automobile race.—**dragnet,** *n.* A net drawn along the bottom of the water or along the ground to catch something; any system for catching or drawing in, as a police dragnet.

draggle, drag′l, *v.t.*—*draggled, draggling*. [Dim. from *drag*, or, as some think, a form of *drabble*.] To wet and dirty by drawing on damp ground or mud, or on wet grass; to drabble. —*v.i.* To be drawn on the ground; to become wet or dirty by being drawn on the mud or wet grass.

dragoman, drag′o•man, *n.* pl. **dragomans.** [Sp. *dragoman*, from Ar. *tarjuman*, an interpreter, from *tarjama*, to interpret; Chal. *targem*, to interpret.] An interpreter in Eastern countries.

dragon, drag′on, *n.* [Fr. *dragon*, from L. *draco*, Gr. *drakōn*, from root *drak* or *derk*, as in *derkomai*, to see; Skr. *darç*, to see; so called from its fiery eyes.] A fabulous animal, conceived as a sort of winged crocodile, with fiery eyes, crested head, and enormous claws, spouting fire, and often regarded as an embodiment of watchfulness; a kind of small lizard, having an expansion of the skin on each side, which forms a kind of wing, serving to sustain the animal when it leaps from branch to branch; a fiery, shooting meteor, or imaginary serpent (*Shak.*); a fierce, violent person, male or female; more generally now, a spiteful, watchful woman; a short carbine, carried by the original dragoons, having the representation of a dragon's head at the muzzle; a variety of carrier pigeons.—**dragonet,** drag'o•net, *n.* A little dragon; a small fish of the goby family.—**dragonfly,** *n.* The popular name of a family of insects, having large strongly reticulated wings, a large head with enormous eyes, a long body, and strong horny mandibles.—**dragon's blood,** *n.* The popular name of the inspissated juice of various plants, used for coloring spirit and turpentine varnishes, for tooth tinctures and powders, for staining marble, etc.—**dragon tree,** *n.* An evergreen tree of the Canary Islands, one of the plants that produce dragon's blood.

dragoon, dra•gön', *n.* [From *dragon*, the carbine carried by the original dragoons raised by Marshal Brissac in 1660, on the muzzle of which, from the old fable that the dragon spouts fire, the head of the monster was worked.] Originally a soldier serving both on foot and horseback; now a cavalry soldier, there being in the British army *heavy* and *light dragoons*, now nearly alike in weight of men, horses, and appointments.—*v.t.* To harass with or abandon to the rage of soldiers; to harass; to persecute; to compel to submit by violent measures.—**dragonnade,** drag•o•nād', *n.* A persecution of French Protestants in the reign of Louis XIV, from dragoons generally leading the persecuting force; a military attack upon civilians.

drain, drān, *v.t.* [Probably from A. Sax. *drehnigean*, to strain, and allied to *drag*.] To cause to pass through some porous substance; to filter; to exhaust any body of a liquid; to exhaust (land) of excessive moisture by causing it to flow off in channels; to exhaust; to deprive by drawing off gradually (to *drain* a country *of* men).—*v.i.* To flow off gradually; to be emptied or deprived of liquor by flowing or dropping.—*n.* The act of draining or drawing off, or of emptying by drawing off; gradual or continuous outflow or withdrawal; a channel through which water or other liquid flows off; a trench or ditch to convey water from wet land; a watercourse; a sewer; *pl.* the grain from the mash tub.—**drainage,** drā'nij, *n.* A draining; a gradual flowing off of any liquid; the system of drains and other works by which any town, surface, and the like, is freed from water; the mode in which the waters of a country pass off by its streams and rivers; the water carried away from a district by natural or other channels.—**drainer,** drā'nėr, *n.* One who or that which drains; one who constructs channels for draining land; *cookery*, a perforated plate for letting fluids escape.

drake, drāk, *n.* [Contr. from a form *enedrice, endrake* (Icel. *andrika*, O. H.G. *antrecho, antricho*), a hypothetical masculine of A.Sax. *ened*, a duck, the termination *ric*, being the same as that in *bishopric*, and akin to Goth. *reiks*, ruling, G. *reich*, empire. *Ened* is cog. with L. *anas, anatis*, a duck.] The male of the duck kind; a species of fly used as bait in angling.

dram, dram, *n.* [Contr. from *drachma*.] *Apothecaries' weight*, a weight of the eighth part of an ounce, or 60 grains; *avoirdupois weight*, the sixteenth part of an ounce; as much spirituous liquor as is drunk at once.—**dramshop,** *n.* A shop where spirits are sold in small quantities.

drama, drä'ma, *n.* [Gr. *drama*, from *draō*, to do, to act.] A poem or composition representing a picture of human life, and accommodated to action, generally designed to be spoken in character and represented on the stage; a series of real events invested with dramatic unity and interest; dramatic composition or literature; dramatic representation and all that is connected with it.—**dramatic, dramatical,** dra•mat'ik, dra•mat'i•kal, *a.* Of or pertaining to the drama or plays represented on the stage; appropriate to or in the form of a drama; theatrical; characterized by the force and fidelity appropriate to the drama (a *dramatic* description); striking.—**dramatics,** dra•mat'iks, *n.* sing. The art of producing or acting plays; pl. amateur theatrical productions.—**dramatically,** dra•mat'i•kal•li, *adv.*—**dramatis personae,** dram'a•tis per•sō'nē, *n.* pl. [L.] The characters in a play.—**dramatist,** dram'a•tist, *n.* A writer of plays.—**dramatize,** dram'a•tīz, *v.t.*—*dramatized, dramatizing*. To compose in the form of the drama; to adapt to the form of a play.—**dramaturgy,** dram'a•tėr•ji, *n.* [Gr. *dramatourgia*, dramatic composition —*drama*, and *ergon*, work.] The science which treats of the rules of composing dramas and representing them on the stage.—**dramaturgic,** dram•a•tėr'jik, *a.* Pertaining to dramaturgy; theatrical; hence, unreal.—**dramaturgist,** dram•a•tėr'jist, *n.* One skilled in dramaturgy.

drank, pret. of *drink*.

drape, drāp, *v.t.*—*draped, draping*. [Fr. *draper*, to drape, from *drap*, cloth. DRAB.] To cover or invest with clothing or cloth; to dispose drapery about for use or ornament.—**draperied,** drā'pėr•id, *a.* Furnished with drapery.—**drapery,** drā'pėr•i, *n.* [Fr. *draperie*.] Cloth or textile fabrics; the clothes or hangings with which any object is draped or hung.

drastic, dras'tik, *a.* [Gr. *drastikos*, from *draō*, to do, to act.] Acting with strength or violence; powerful; efficacious.—*n.* A strong purgative.

draught, draft, *n.* [From *draw, drag*.] The act of drawing; the capacity of being drawn (a cart or plough of easy *draught*); the drawing of liquor into the mouth and throat; the act of drinking; the quantity of liquor drunk at once.

Dravidian, dra•vid'i•an, *a.* Of or pertaining to *Dravida*, the name of an old province of India; applied to a distinct family of tongues spoken in South India, Ceylon, etc.

draw, dra̤, *v.t.*—*drew* (drö), *drawn* (dra̤n), *drawing*. [A softened form of *drag* (which see).] To pull along after one; to haul; to cause to advance by force applied in front of the thing moved or at the fore end; to pull out; to unsheathe; to bring out from some receptacle (to *draw* water); to let run out; to extract (blood, wine); to attract; to cause to move or tend toward; to allure; to lead by persuasion or moral influence; to lead, as a motive; to induce to move; to inhale; to take into the lungs; to pull more closely together, or apart (to *draw* a curtain); to lengthen; to extend in length; to form by extension (to *draw* wire); to form (a line) between two points; to represent by lines drawn on a plain surface; to form a picture or image; to describe in words or to represent in fancy; to derive, deduce, have, or receive from some source; to receive from customers or patrons; to receive or take (to *draw* money from a bank); to extort; to force out (groans, tears); to write in due form; to form in writing; to take out of a box or wheel, as tickets in a lottery; to receive or gain by such drawing; to require (so many feet of water) for floating; to bend (to *draw* the bow); to eviscerate; to finish, as a game, battle, etc., so as neither party can claim the victory.—*To draw a badger, fox*, etc., to drag or force it from its cover.—*To draw in*, to contract; to pull back; to collect or bring together; to entice, or inveigle.—*To draw off*, to draw away; to withdraw; to abstract (the mind); to draw or take from; to cause to flow from.—*To draw on*, to allure; to entice; to occasion; to cause.—*To draw over*, to persuade or induce to revolt from an opposing party, and to join one's own party.—*To draw out*, to lengthen; to extend; to compose or form in writing; to cause to issue forth; to elicit, by questioning or address; to cause to be declared; to call forth.—*To draw together*, to collect or be collected.—*To draw up*, to raise; to lift; to form in order of battle; to array; to compose in due form, as a writing; to form in writing.—*v.i.* To pull; to exert strength in drawing; to act or have influence, as a weight; to shrink; to contract; to advance; to approach; to resort or betake one's self to; to unsheathe a sword; to use or practice the art of delineating figures; to form a picture; to make a draft or written demand for payment of a sum of money upon a person.—*To draw back*, to retire; to move back; to withdraw.—*To draw near* or *nigh*, to approach; to come near.—*To draw off*, to retire; to retreat.—*To draw on*, to advance; to approach.—*To draw up*, to form themselves in regular order (as troops); to assume a certain order or arrangement; to stop a horse by pulling the reins.—*n.* The act of drawing; the lot or chance drawn; a drawn game.—**drawback,** dra̤'bak, *n.* What detracts from profit or pleasure; a discouragement or hindrance; a disadvantage; a certain amount of duties or customs dues paid back or remitted, as duty on spirits when they are sent abroad.—**drawbridge,** drą′brij, *n.* A bridge which may be drawn up or let down or opened or shut horizontally, to admit or hinder communication, as before the gate of a town or castle, or over a navigable river.—**drawee,** drą•ē′, *n.* The person on whom an order or bill of exchange is drawn.—**drawer,** drą′ėr, *n.* One who draws or pulls; one who takes water from a well; one who draws liquor from a cask; a waiter (*Shak.*); one who draws a bill of exchange or an order for the payment of money; a sliding box in a table, desk, etc., which is drawn out at pleasure; one of a set of such boxes in a case or bureau; *pl.* an under garment worn on the legs and lower part of the body by both sexes. CHEST.—**drawing,** drą′-ing, *n.* The act of one who draws; the representation or delineation of an object on a plain surface, by means of lines and shades, as with a pencil, crayon, pen. etc.; the amount of money taken for sales in a shop or other trading establishment.—**drawing room,** *n.* [For *with-drawing room*, a room to which the company withdraws from the dining room.] A room in a house appropriated for the reception of company; a room in which distinguished personages hold levees, or private persons receive parties; the formal reception of evening company at a royal court.—**drawn,** drąn, *p.* and *a.* Pulled, hauled, allured; unsheathed; extended; delineated, etc.; not decided, from both parties having equal advantage and neither a victory (a *drawn* battle).—**drawplate,** *n.* A stout plate of steel, pierced with a graduated series of conical holes, for drawing wire through in order to reduce and elongate it.

drawl, drąl, *v.t.* [A dim. form from *draw* or *drag.* DRAG.] To utter or pronounce in a slow lengthened tone; to while away in an indolent manner. —*v.i.* To speak with slow utterance. —*n.* A lengthened utterance of the voice.—**drawlingly,** drą′ling•li, *adv.* In a drawling manner.

dray, drā, *n.* [A.Sax. *dræge*, from *dragan.* DRAG, DRAW.] A low cart or carriage on heavy wheels, such as those used by brewers.—**drayage,** drā′ij, *n.* The use of a dray; charge for the use of a dray.—**drayman,** *n.* A man who attends a dray.

dread, dred, *n.* [A.Sax. *draedan, on-draedan*, to fear.] Great fear or apprehension of evil or danger; terror; awe; fear united with respect; the cause of fear; the person or the thing dreaded (O.T.).—*a.* Exciting great fear or apprehension; terrible; frightful; awful; venerable in the highest degree.—*v.t.* To fear in a great degree.—*v.i.* To be in great fear.—**dreadful,** dred′fụl, *a.* Impressing dread or great fear; terrible; formidable; awful; venerable.—*n.* A printed work chiefly devoted to the narration of stories of criminal life, frightful accidents, etc. (*Colloq.*)—**dreadfully,** dred′fụl•li, *adv.* In a manner to be dreaded.—**dreadfulness,** dred′fụl•nes, *n.* The quality of being dreadful.—**dreadnought,** dred′nąt, *n.* A person that fears nothing; a thick cloth with a long pile, used for warm clothing or to keep off rain; a garment made of such cloth; general term for battleship of the highest class.

dream, drēm, *n.* [A.Sax. *dreám*, joy, melody; O.Fris. *drâm*, D. *droom*, G. *traum*, O.Sax. *drôm*, dream.] The thought or series of thoughts of a person in sleep; *Scrip.* impressions on the minds of sleeping persons made by divine agency; a matter which has only an imaginary reality; a visionary scheme or conceit; a vain fancy; an unfounded suspicion.—*v.i.*—*dreamed* or *dreamt* (dremt), *dreaming.* To have ideas or images in the mind in the state of sleep; with *of* before a noun; to think; to imagine; to think idly.—*v.t.* To see in a dream.—*To dream away*, to pass in reverie or inaction; to spend idly. —**dreamer,** drē′mėr, *n.* One who dreams; a visionary; one who forms or entertains vain schemes.—**dreamful,** drēm′fụl, *a.* Full of dreams. (*Tenn.*)—**dreaminess,** drē′mi•nes, *n.* State of being dreamy.—**dreamland,** drēm′land, *n.* The land of dreams; the region of fancy or imagination; the region of reverie.—**dreamless,** drēm′les, *a.* Free from dreams.—**dreamy,** drē′mi, *a.* Full of dreams; associated with dreams; giving rise to dreams; dreamlike.

dreary, drē′ri, *a.* [A.Sax. *dreórig*, bloody, sad, sorrowful, *dreór*, blood, from *dreósan* (Goth. *driusan*), to fall, with common conversion of *s* into *r*; akin to G. *traurig*, sad, *trauern*, to mourn.] Dismal; gloomy; waste and desolate; distressing; oppressively monotonous.—**drear,** drēr, *a.* Dismal; gloomy with solitude.—**drearily,** drē′ri•li, *adv.* Gloomily; dismally.—**dreariness,** drē′ri•nes, *n.* The state of being dreary.—**drearisome,**† drē′-ri•sum, *a.* Very dreary.

dredge, drej, *n.* [From the stem of *drag*, the *g* being softened as in *bridge*, from older *brig.*] A dragnet for taking oysters, etc.; an apparatus for bringing up shells, plants, and other objects from the bottom of the sea for scientific investigation; a machine for clearing the beds of canals, rivers, harbors, etc.—*v.t.*—*dredged, dredging.* To take, catch, or gather with a dredge; to remove sand, silt, etc., from by the use of a dredge.—**dredger,** drej′ėr, *n.* One who or that which dredges.—**dredging machine,** *n.* A machine used to take up mud or gravel from the bottoms of rivers, docks, etc.

dredge, drej, *n.* [Fr. *dragée*, mixed provender for horses and cattle; It. *treggéa*, from Gr. *tragēmata*, dried fruits.] A mixture of oats and barley sown together.—*v.t.* To sprinkle flour on roast meat.—**dredger,** drej′-ėr, *n.* A utensil for scattering flour on meats when roasting.

dregs, dregz, *n. pl.* [Icel. *dregg*, Sw. *drägg*, dregs, lees; probably connected with *drag, drain*—the dregs being what remains after the liquor is drained off.] The sediment of liquors; lees; grounds; feculence; any foreign matter of liquors that subsides to the bottom of a vessel; dross; sweepings; refuse; hence, the most vile and worthless among men. *Dreg*, in the singular, is found in Spenser and Shakespeare.

drench, drensh, *v.t.* [A.Sax. *drencan, drencean*, to give to drink, to drench, from *drincan*, to drink. DRINK.] To wet thoroughly; to soak; to saturate; to purge violently (an animal) with medicine.—*n.* [A.Sax. *drenc*, a draught.] A draught; a dose of medicine for a beast, as a horse.—**drencher,** dren′shėr, *n.* One who drenches.

dress, dres, *v.t.*—*dressed* or *drest, dressing.* [Fr. *dresser*, to make right, prepare, from a L.L. verb *directiare, drictiare*, to make straight, from L. *directus*, straight. DIRECT.] To make straight or in a straight line (troops); to put to rights; to put in good order; to till or cultivate; to treat (a wound or sore) with remedies or curative appliances; to prepare, in a general sense; to make suitable or fit for something (leather, a lamp, etc.); to put clothes on; to invest with garments; to adorn; to deck.—*To dress up* or *out*, to clothe elaborately, pompously, or elegantly.—*v.i. Milit.* to arrange one's self in proper position in a line; to clothe one's self; to put on garments.—*n.* Clothes, garments, or apparel; collectively, a suit of clothes: a costume; a lady's gown.—**dress circle,** *n.* A portion of a theater, concert room; first gallery in a theater, etc. —**dress parade,** *n.* A ceremonial parade of soldiers or sailors in dress uniforms.—**dress rehearsal,** *n.* The final rehearsal of a play, etc., before the first performance.—**dresser,** dres′ėr, *n.* One who dresses; one employed in preparing, trimming, or adjusting anything; a hospital assistant, whose office is to dress wounds, ulcers, etc.—[Fr. *dressoir.*] A table or bench on which meat and other things are dressed or prepared for use; a kind of low cupboard for dishes and cooking utensils.—**dressing,** dres′ing, *n.* The act of one who dresses; what is used to dress; an application to a wound or sore; manure spread over land; gum, starch, paste, and the like, used in stiffening or preparing silk, linen, and other fabrics; *cookery*, the stuffing of fowls, pigs, etc., or the unctuous ingredients to complete a salad; *arch.* moldings round doors, windows, and other openings on an elevation.—**dressing gown,** *n.* A light gown or wide and flowing coat worn by a person while dressing, in the study, etc.—**dressing table,** *n.* A table provided with conveniences for the toilet; a toilet table.—**dressmaker,** dres′māk•ėr, *n.* A maker of ladies' dresses.—**dressy,** dres′i, *a.* Very attentive to dress; wearing rich or especially showy dresses.

drew, drö, *v.* pret. of *draw.*
dribble, drib'l, *v.t.—dribbled, dribbling.* [A dim. from *drip,* and properly *dripple.*] To give out or let fall in drops.—*v.i.* To fall in drops or small particles, or in a quick succession of drops.—**dribblet, driblet,** drib'let, *n.* One of a number of small pieces or parts; a small sum doled out as one of a series.
drier, drī'ėr, *n.* See DRY.
drift, drift, *n.* [From *drive;* A.Sax. *drīfan*=Icel. *drift,* a snow drift; Dan. *drift,* impulse, drove; D. *drift,* drove, course. DRIVE, and comp. *rive, rift; shrive, shrift; thrive, thrift.*] A drove or flock‡; a heap of matter driven together by the wind or water (a snow *drift*); a driving or impulse; overbearing power or influence; course of anything; tendency; aim (the *drift* of one's remarks); intention; design; purpose; a name in South Africa for a ford; *milit.* the deflection of a shell to the right of its proper course, due to the resistance of the air and the right-hand spin or rotation imparted by the rifling; the deviation of an aircraft due to the wind; *mining,* a passage cut between shaft and shaft; *naut.* the distance which a vessel drives through wind or current when lying-to or hove-to during a gale; *geol.* earth and rocks which have been conveyed by icebergs and glaciers and deposited over a country while submerged.—*Drift of a current,* the rate at which it flows.—*v.i.* To accumulate in heaps by the force of wind; to be driven into heaps; to float or be driven along by a current of water or air; to be carried at random by the force of the wind or tide; *mining,* to make a drift; to search for metals or ores.—*v.t.* To drive into heaps.—*a.* Drifted by wind or currents (*drift* sand, *drift* ice).—**drifter,** drif'tėr, *n.* A boat that uses drift nets.—**driftwood,** *n.* Wood drifted or floated by water.—**drifty,** drif'ti, *a.* Forming or characterized by drifts, especially of snow.
drill, dril, *v.t.* [From D. *drillen,* to bore, to drill soldiers; G. *drillen,* to bore; from same root as *through, thrill, -tril* in *nostril.* (In the agricultural sense, however, perhaps of different origin.)] To pierce or perforate by turning a sharp-pointed instrument of a particular form; to bore and make a hole by turning an instrument; *agri.* to sow in rows, drills, or channels; to teach and train soldiers or others to their duty by frequent exercises; hence, to teach by repeated exercise or repetition of acts.—*v.i.* To go through the exercises prescribed to recruits, etc.—*n.* A pointed instrument used for boring holes, particularly in metals and other hard substances; the act of training soldiers, etc., to their duty, or the exercises by which they are trained; *agri.* a row of seeds deposited in the earth, or the trench or channel in which the seed is deposited; also a machine for sowing seeds in rows.—**drillmaster,** *n.* One who trains others; one who drills soldiers in marching.—**drill press,** *n.* A machine armed with one or more drills for boring holes in metal.
drill, drilling, dril, dril'ing, *n.* [G. *drillich,* from *drei,* three, a fabric in which the threads are divided in a threefold way.] A kind of coarse linen or cotton cloth.
drily. See DRY.
drink, dringk, *v.i.—drank* or *drunk* (pret.), *drunk* or *drunken* (pp.). [A. Sax. *drincan*=D. *drinken,* Icel. *drekka,* G. *trinken,* Goth. *drigkan,* to drink. Hence *drench* and *drown.*] To swallow liquor, for quenching thirst or other purpose; especially, to take intoxicating liquor; to be intemperate in the use of intoxicating liquors; to be an habitual drunkard.—*To drink to,* to salute in drinking; to drink in honor of; to wish well to, in taking the cup.—*v.t.* To swallow (liquids); to imbibe; to suck in; to absorb; to take in through the senses (to *drink* delight); to inhale.—*To drink down,* to take away thought or consideration of (care, etc.) by drinking.—*To drink off,* to drink the whole at a draught.—*To drink in,* to absorb; to take or receive into.—*To drink up,* to drink the whole.—*To drink the health,* or *to the health of,* to drink while expressing good wishes for; to signify good will to by drinking; to pledge.—*n.* Liquor to be swallowed; a draught of liquor; intoxicating liquors.—*In drink,* drunk; tipsy.—**drinkable,** dring'ka•bl, *a.* Fit or suitable for drink; potable.—*n.* A liquor that may be drunk.—**drinker,** dring'kėr, *n.* One who drinks, particularly one who practices drinking spirituous liquors to excess; a drunkard.
drip, drip, *v.i.—dripped, dripping.* [A.Sax. *drypan,* to drip, to drop=Dan. *dryppe,* Icel. *drjúpa,* D. *druipen,* G. *triefen.* Akin *drop.*] To fall in drops; to have any liquid falling from it in drops.—*v.t.* To let fall in drops.—*n.* A falling or letting fall in drops; a dripping; that which falls in drops; dripping, or melted fat from meat while roasting; the edge of a roof; the eaves; *arch.* a large flat member of the cornice projecting so as to throw off water; a dripstone.—**dripping,** drip'ing, *n.* The fat which falls from meat in roasting.—**dripstone,** *n. Arch.* a projecting molding or cornice over doorways, windows, etc., to throw off the rain.
drive, drīv, *v.t.—drove* (formerly *drave*); *driven, driving.* [A.Sax. *drīfan*=Goth. *dreiban,* D. *drijven,* Dan. *drive,* G. *treiben,* to drive, to urge or carry on. *Drift* and *drove* are derivatives.] To impel or urge forward, or away from, by force; to force or move by physical means; to propel; to compel or urge by other means than absolute physical force, or by means that compel the will; to constrain; to press or carry to a great length (an argument); to chase or hunt; to keep horses or other animals moving onward while directing their course; to guide or regulate the course of an automobile or other vehicle; to guide or regulate a machine; to convey in a vehicle; to carry on, prosecute, engage in (a trade, a bargain); *mining,* to dig horizontally; to cut a horizontal gallery or tunnel.—*v.i.* To be forced along or impelled (a ship *drives* before the wind); to rush and press with violence (a storm *drives* against the house); to go in an automobile; to travel in a vehicle drawn by horses or other animals; to aim or tend; to aim a blow; to make a stroke.—*n.* A journey or airing in a vehicle; a course on which vehicles are driven; a road prepared for driving; a strong or sweeping blow or impulsion.—**drive-in,** *a.* A theater, restaurant, bank, etc., that caters to customers who remain in their automobiles.—**driver,** drī'vėr, *n.* One who or that which drives; the person who drives a vehicle, one who conducts a team; *naut.* a large fore-and-aft quadrilateral sail, called also the *Spanker,* on the mizzen mast; *mach.* the main wheel by which motion is communicated to a train of wheels; a driving wheel.—**driver ant,** *n.* A singular species of ant in West Africa, so named from its *driving* before it almost every animal that comes in its way.
drivel, driv'el, *v.i.—driveled, driveling.* [A modification of *dribble,* from root of *drib.*] To slaver; to let spittle drop or flow from the mouth, like a child, idiot, or dotard; to be weak or foolish; to dote.—*n.* Slaver; saliva flowing from the mouth; silly unmeaning talk; senseless twaddle.—**driveler,** driv'el•ėr, *n.* One who drivels; an idiot; a fool.
drizzle, driz'l, *v.i.—drizzled, drizzling.* [A dim. from A.Sax. *dreósan,* Goth. *driusan,* to fall; like Prov. G. *drieseln,* to drizzle. DREARY.] To rain in small drops; to fall from the clouds in very fine particles.—*v.t.* To shed in small drops or particles.—*n.* A small or fine rain; mizzle.—**drizzly,** driz'li, *a.* Shedding small rain, or small particles of snow.
droit, droit, *n.* [Fr., from L. *directus.*] Right; law; justice; a fiscal charge or duty.—*Droits of admiralty,* perquisites attached to the office of admiral of England, or lord high-admiral.
droll, drōl, *a.* [Same word as Fr. *drôle,* D. *drol,* G. *droll,* a thick, short person, a droll; Gael. *droll,* a slow, awkward person; perhaps from Icel. and Sw. *troll,* a kind of imp or hobgoblin.] Odd; merry; facetious; comical; ludicrous; queer; laughable; ridiculous.—*n.* One whose occupation or practice is to raise mirth by odd tricks; a jester; a buffoon; something exhibited to raise mirth or sport.—*v.i.* To jest; to play the buffoon.—**drollery,** drō'lėr•i, *n.* The quality of being droll; something done to raise mirth; sportive tricks; buffoonery; fun; comicalness; humor.
dromedary, drom'e•da•ri, *n.* [L. *dromedarius,* a dromedary, formed from Gr. *dromas, dromados,* running, from stem of *dramein,* to run.] A species of camel, called also the

Arabian camel, with one hump or protuberance on the back, in distinction from the Bactrian camel, which has two humps.

dromond, ‡drom′ond, *n.* [Gr. *dramein*, to run.] Fast-sailing ship of war.

drone, drōn, *n.* [A.Sax. *drán*, the dronebee; L.G. and Dan. *drone*, Sw. *dron*, *drōnje*, G. *drohne*, from the sound it makes; comp. *humble-bee*, G. *hummel*, and the verb *hum*.] The male of the honeybee; an idler; a sluggard; one who earns nothing by industry; a humming or low sound, or the instrument of humming; one of the largest tubes of the bagpipe, which emit a continued deep tone.—*v.i.*—*droned*, *droning*. [Dan. *dröne*, Sw. *dröna*, to drone; akin Goth. *drunjus*, a sound.] To give forth a low, heavy, dull sound; to hum; to snore; to make use of a dull monotonous tone; to live in idleness.—*v.t.* To read or speak in a dull, monotonous, droning manner.

drool, dröl, *v.i.* [Contraction of *drivel*.] To slaver; to drivel.

droop, dröp, *v.i.* [A form of *drip*, *drop*.] To sink or hang down; to bend downward, as from weakness or exhaustion; to languish from grief or other cause; to fail or sink; to decline; to be dispirited; to come towards a close (*Tenn.*).—*v.t.* To let sink or hang down.—*n.* The act of drooping or of falling or hanging down; a drooping position or state.—**drooper,** drö′pėr, *n.* One who or that which droops.—**droopingly,** drö′ping•li, *adv.* In a drooping manner.

drop, drop, *n.* [A.Sax. *dropa*, O.Sax. *dropo*, Icel. *dropi*, D. *drop*, G. *tropfe*, a drop; akin *dribble*, *drip*, *droop*.] A small portion of any fluid in a spherical form, falling or pendant, as if about to fall; a small portion of water falling in rain; what resembles or hangs in the form of a drop, as a hanging diamond ornament, a glass pendant of a chandelier, etc.; a very small quantity of liquid; a small quantity of anything (a *drop* of pity: *Shak.*); that part of a gallows which sustains the criminal before he is executed, and which is suddenly dropped; also the distance which he has to fall; the curtain which conceals the stage of a theater from the audience; *pl.* a liquid medicine, the dose of which is regulated by a certain number of drops.—*v.t.*—*dropped*, *dropping*. [A. Sax. *dropian*, from the noun=D. *droppen*, G. *tropfen*.] To pour or let fall in drops; to let fall, lower, or let down (to *drop* the anchor); to let go, dismiss, lay aside, break off from; to quit, leave, omit; to utter (words) slightly, briefly, or casually; to send in an off-hand informal manner (*drop* me a few lines).—*v.i.* To fall in small portions, globules, or drops, as a liquid; to let drops fall; to drip; to discharge itself in drops; to fall; to descend suddenly or abruptly; to sink lower; to cease; to die suddenly; to fall, as in battle; to come to an end; to be allowed to cease; to be neglected and come to nothing; to come unexpectedly: with *in* or *into*.—*To drop astern* (*naut.*), to slacken speed so as to let another vessel get ahead.—*To drop down*, to sail, row, or move down a river.—*Dropping fire* (*milit.*), a continuous irregular discharge of small arms.—**droplet,** drop′let, *n.* A little drop.—**dropper,** drop′ėr, *n.* One who or that which drops.—**dropping,** drop′-ing, *n.* The act of one who drops; a falling in drops; that which drops; pl. the dung of animals.—**drop kick,** *n.* A kick given to a football by dropping the ball and kicking it as it rises.—**dropout,** *n.* One who fails to complete a course, etc.

dropsy, drop′si, *n.* [Formerly *hydropsy*, from Gr. *hydrōps*, dropsy, from *hydōr*, water.] *Med.* an unnatural collection of water in any cavity of the body, or in the cellular tissue.—**dropsical,** drop′si•kal, *a.* Diseased with dropsy; inclined to dropsy; resembling or partaking of the nature of dropsy.—**dropsied,** drop′sid, *a.* Affected with dropsy; exhibiting an unhealthy inflation.

dropwort, drop′wėrt, *n.* A kind of spiraea or meadowsweet with fine-cut leaves.

drosky, dros′ki, *n.* [Rus. *drozhki*.] A kind of light four-wheeled carriage used in Russia and Prussia.

dross, dros, *n.* [A.Sax. *dros*, *drosn*, from *dreósan*, to fall; D. *droes*, Icel. *tros*, rubbish; Sc. *drush*, dregs; Dan. *drysse*, to fall. DREARY.] The refuse or impurities of metals; rust; waste matter; refuse; any worthless matter separated from the better part.—**drossy,** dros′i, *a.* Like dross; pertaining to dross; full of or abounding with refuse matter; worthless; foul; impure.

drought, drout, *n.* [Contr. from A.Sax. *drugath*, *drugoth*, from *drige*, *dryge*, dry; like D. *droogte*, from *droog*, dry. DRY.] Dry weather; want of rain; such a continuance of dry weather as affects the crops; aridness; thirst; want of drink; scarcity; lack.—**droughty,** drou′ti, *a.* Characterized by drought or the absence of rain or moisture; arid; thirsty.

drove, drōv, pret. of *drive*.

drove, drōv, *n.* [A.Sax. *dráf*, from *drifan*, to drive.] A number of animals, as oxen, sheep, or swine, driven in a body; a collection of animals moving forward; a crowd of people in motion; a flock.—**drover,** drō′vėr, *n.* One who drives cattle or sheep to market, or from one locality to another.

drown, droun, *v.t.* [From A.Sax. *druncnian*, to sink in water, to be drunk, from *druncen*, pp. of *drincan*, to drink; Dan. *drukne*, to drown. DRINK, DRENCH.] To deprive of life by immersion in water or other fluid; to overflow, overwhelm, or inundate; to put an end to, as if by drowning or overwhelming; to overpower (to *drown* care; to *drown* one's voice).—*v.i.* To be suffocated in water or other fluid; to perish in water.

drowse, drouz, *v.i.*—*drowsed*, *drowsing*. [A.Sax. *drúsan*, *drúsian*, to be slow, to languish; allied to *dreósan* to fall, to droop; D. *droosen*, to doze, to slumber. DREARY.] To sleep imperfectly or unsoundly; to slumber; to be heavy with sleepiness; to be heavy or dull.—*v.t.* To make heavy with sleep; to make dull or stupid.—*n.* A slight sleep; a doze; slumber.—**drowsily,** drou′zi•li, *adv.* In a drowsy manner.—**drowsiness,** drou′zi•nes, *n.* State of being drowsy.—**drowsy,** drou′zi, *a.* Inclined to sleep; sleepy; heavy with sleepiness; lethargic; sluggish; stupid; disposing to sleep; lulling.

drub, drub, *v.t.*—*drubbed*, *drubbing*. [Prov. E. *drab*; akin to Icel. and Sw. *drabba*, to beat; G. *treffen* to hit.] To beat with a stick; to thrash; to cudgel.—*n.* A blow with a stick or cudgel; a thump; a knock.—**drubber,** drub′ėr, *n.* One who drubs or beats.—**drubbing,** drub′ing, *n.* A cudgeling; a sound beating.

drudge, druj, *v.i.*—*drudged*, *drudging*. [Softened form of O.E. *drugge*, *drug*, to work laboriously; origin doubtful.] To work hard; to labor in mean offices; to labor with toil and fatigue.—*n.* One who labors hard in servile employments; a slave.—**drudgery,** druj′ėr•i, *n.* Ignoble toil; hard work in servile occupations.

drug, drug, *n.* [Fr. *drogue*; Pr. Sp. Pg. It. *droga*; all from D. *droog*, the same word as A.Sax. *dryge*, dry—because the ancient medicines were chiefly dried herbs.] Any substance, vegetable, animal, or mineral, used in the composition or preparation of medicines; any commodity that lies on hand or is not saleable; an article of slow sale or in no demand in the market.—*v.i.*—*drugged*, *drugging*. To prescribe or administer drugs or medicines.—*v.t.* To mix with drugs; to introduce some narcotic into with the design of rendering the person who drinks the mixture insensible; to dose to excess with drugs or medicines; to administer narcotics to; to render insensible with a narcotic drug.—**druggist,** drug′ist, *n.* One who deals in drugs; a pharmacist.—**drugstore,** *n.* A store where drugs, medicines, meals, etc., are sold.

drugget, drug′et, *n.* [Fr. *droguet*, dim. of *drogue*, drug, trash. DRUG.] A cloth or thin stuff of wool, or of wool and thread, used for covering carpets, and also as an article of clothing.

druid, drū′id, *n.* [Ir. and Gael. *druidh*, W. *derwydd*.] [*often cap.*] A priest or minister of religion who superintended the affairs of religion and morality, and performed the office of judges among the ancient Celtic nations in Gaul, Britain, and Germany.—**druidess,** drū′i•des, *n.* A female druid.—**druidic, druidical,** drū•id′ik, drū•id′i•kal, *a.* Pertaining to the druids.—*Druidical stones*, the name popularly given to large upright stones, found in various localities and sometimes forming circles, from an uncertain assumption that they were druidical places of worship.—**druidism,** drū′i•dizm, *n.* The doctrines, rites, and ceremonies of the druids.

drum, drum, *n.* [Probably, like *drone,* a word of imitative origin; Dan. *tromme,* G. *trommel,* a drum, Dan. *drum,* a booming sound; Goth. *drunjus,* a sound.] An instrument of music commonly in the form of a hollow cylinder, covered at the ends with vellum, the ends being beaten with sticks to produce the sound; a mechanical contrivance resembling a drum in shape, and used in connection with machinery of various kinds, etc.; the tympanum or barrel of the ear; a quantity packed in the form of a drum; a round box containing figs; a tea before dinner; a kettledrum; a name formerly given to a fashionable and crowded evening party; a storm drum.—*v.i.*—*drummed, drumming.* To beat a drum; to beat with rapid movements of the fingers; to beat with a rapid succession of strokes; to throb; to resound dully.—*v.t.* To perform on a drum; to expel with beat of drum (he was *drummed out* of the regiment); to summon by beat of drum; to din.—*To drum up,* to assemble or call together by beat of drum.—**drumhead,** *n.* The head or top of a drum; a variety of cabbage having a large, rounded, or flattened head.—*Drumhead court-martial,* a court-martial called suddenly on the field.—*Drumhead service,* religious service on the field, at the front.—**drum major,** *n.* The chief or first drummer of a regiment; the leader of a band in marching.—**drumlin,** drum'lin. [Celtic name.] An elongated mound of glacial material sorted by water action.—**drummer,** drum'ėr, *n.* One who drums; one whose office is to beat the drum; commercial traveler.—**drumstick,** *n.* The stick with which a drum is beaten; what resembles a drumstick, as the upper joint of the leg of a turkey.

drunk, drungk, *a.* [From *drunken.* DRINK.] Intoxicated; inebriated; overcome, stupefied, or frenzied by alcoholic liquor.—**drunkard,** drung'kėrd, *n.* One given to an excessive use of strong liquor; a person who habitually or frequently is drunk.—**drunken,** drung'ken, *a.* [Part. of *drink,* but now used chiefly as an adjective.] Intoxicated; drunk; given to drunkenness; proceeding from intoxication; done in a state of drunkenness (a *drunken* quarrel).—**drunkenly,†** drung'ken•li, *adv.* In a drunken manner. (*Shak.*)—**drunkenness,** drung'ken•nes, *n.* The state of being drunk; the habit of indulging in intoxication; intoxication; inebriety.

drupe, dröp, *n.* [Fr. *drupe,* L. *drupa,* Gr. *dryppa,* an overripe olive.] *Bot.* a stone fruit, such as the cherry or plum; a fruit in which the outer part is fleshy while the inner hardens like a nut, forming a stone with a kernel.

dry, drī, *a.* [A.Sax. *dryge, drige, drie* (D. *droog,* G. *trocken*), dry, whence *dryan, drigan,* to dry. *Drought* and *drug* are derivatives.] Destitute of moisture; free from water or wetness; free from juice, sap, or aqueous matter; not moist; arid; not giving milk; thirsty; craving drink; barren; jejune; plain; unembellished; destitute of interest; quietly sarcastic; caustic; discouraging; expressive of a degree of displeasure; cold and not friendly (a *dry* reception).—*Dry goods,* cloths, stuffs, silks, laces, ribbons, etc., in distinction from groceries.—*Dry steam,* superheated steam.—*Dry stone walls,* walls built of stone without mortar.—*Dry wines,* those in which no sweetness is perceptible.—*v.t.*—*dried, drying.* To make dry; to free from water or from moisture of any kind; to desiccate; to expose in order to evaporate moisture; to deprive of natural juice, sap, or greenness.—*To dry up,* to deprive wholly of water; to scorch or parch with thirst.—*v.i.* To grow dry; to lose moisture; to become free from moisture or juice; to evaporate wholly: sometimes with *up.*—**drier,** drī'ėr, *n.* One who or that which dries or makes dry; a desiccative; specifically a preparation to increase the hardening and drying properties of paint.—**dry cell,** *n.* An electric cell the contents of which are in the form of a paste.—**dry-clean,** *v.t.* To clean textiles with solvents other than water.—**dry dock,** *n.* A dock from which water may be shut or pumped out, used in constructing or repairing ships.—**Dry Ice,** *n.* A trademark for solidified carbon dioxide used as a substitute for ice.—**drying,** drī'ing, *a.* Adapted to exhaust moisture; having the quality of rapidly becoming dry and hard.—**dryly, drily,** drī'li, *adv.* Without moisture; coldly; frigidly; without affection; severely; sarcastically; barrenly; without embellishment; without anything to enliven, enrich, or entertain.—**dryness,** drī'nes, *n.* The state or quality of being dry.—**dry measure,** *n.* Measure for dry commodities by quarts, etc.; in this system two pints make one quart, eight quarts make one peck, four pecks make one bushel.—**dry nurse,** *n.* A nurse who attends and feeds a child by hand.—*v.t.* To act as dry nurse to; to feed, attend, and bring up without the breast.—**dry point,** *n.* A sharp etching needle, used to cut fine lines in copper without the plate being covered with etching ground or the lines bit in by acid.—**dry rot,** drī'rot, *n.* A well-known disease affecting timber, occasioned by various species of fungi, the mycelium of which penetrates the timber, destroying it.—**dry run,** *n.* A trial; a practice session.—**dry-shod,** *a.* and *adv.* Without wetting the feet.

dryad, drī'ad, *n.* [Gr. *dryas, dryados,* from *drys,* an oak, a tree.] *Myth.* a deity or nymph of the woods; a nymph supposed to preside over woods.

dual, dū'al, *a.* [L. *dualis,* from *duo,* two; akin *duel, double, doubt, dubious,* etc.] Expressing the number two; existing as two; consisting of two; twofold; a term applied to a special form of a noun or verb used in some languages when two persons or things are spoken of.—*n. Gram.* that number which is used when two persons or things are spoken of.—**dualism,** dū'a•lizm, *n.* A twofold division; *philos.* any system holding that all phenomena in the universe can be explained in terms of two fundamental and exclusive principles, such as mind and matter, being and nonbeing, etc.; *theol.* the doctrine that there are two distinct eternal principles, one good and the other evil; the belief that man embodies two irreducible elements such as body and soul; doctrine of those who maintain the existence of spirit and matter as distinct substances, in opposition to idealism, which maintains we have no knowledge or assurance of the existence of anything but our own ideas or sensations.—**dualist,** dū'a•list, *n.* One who holds the doctrine of dualism in any of its forms.—**dualistic,** dū•a•lis'tik, *a.* Pertaining to dualism; characterized by duality.—**duality,** dū•al'i•ti, *n.* The state of being two or of being divided into two.

dub, dub, *v.t.*—*dubbed, dubbing.* [A. Sax. *dubban,* to strike, to dub knight; Icel. *dubba,* to dub.] To strike with a sword and make a knight; to nickname; to make smooth by hammering; to make a blunder.—*n.* Something done poorly; a clumsy person.

dub, dub, *v.t.* [Shortening of *double.*] To insert music, dialogue, etc., into the sound track of a film.

dub, dub, *n.* [Probably of same root as *dip* and *deep.*] A puddle; a small pool of foul stagnant water.

dubious, dū'bi•us, *a.* [L. *dubius,* moving alternately in two opposite directions, from root of *duo,* two. DOUBT.] Doubtful; wavering or fluctuating in opinion; uncertain; not ascertained or known exactly; not clear or plain; occasioning or involving doubt; of uncertain event or issue.—**dubiously,** dū'bi•us•li, *adv.* In a dubious manner.—**dubiousness,** dū'bi•us•nes, *n.* The state of being dubious.—**dubiety,** dū•bī'e•ti, *n.* [L. *dubietas.*] Doubtfulness; a feeling of doubt.—**dubiosity,** dū•bi•os'i•ti, *n.* Dubiousness; doubtfulness.—**dubitable,†** dū'bi•ta•bl, *a.* [L. *dubito,* to waver in opinion.] Liable to be doubted; doubtful; uncertain.—**dubitation,†** dū•bi•tā'shon, *n.* [L. *dubitatio.*] The act of doubting or hesitating; doubt.

ducal, dū'kal, *a.* [L. *ducalis,* pertaining to a leader, from *dux, ducis,* a leader. DUKE.] Pertaining to a duke.—**ducally,** dū'kal•li, *adv.* After the manner of a duke; in relation with a duke or a ducal family.—**ducat,** duk'at, *n.* [Fr. *ducat,* It. *ducato,* from L.L. *ducatus,* a duchy (the particular duchy originating the name being uncertain), from L. *dux.* DUKE.] A gold coin.—**duchess,** duch'es, *n.* [Fr. *duchesse,* from *duc,* duke.] The consort or widow of a duke; a lady who has the sovereignty of a duchy.—**duchy,** duch'i, *n.* [Fr. *duché.*] The territory controlled or governed by a duke or duchess; a dukedom.

duck, duk, *n.* [Same word as D. *doek*, Sw. *duk*, G. *tuch*, cloth.] A species of coarse cloth or canvas, used for sails, sacking of beds, etc.

duck, duk, *n.* [Same word as Dan. *dukke*, G. *docke*, a baby or puppet; or the name of the bird used as a term of endearment.] A word of endearment or fondness.

duck, duk, *v.t.* [Akin to D. *duiken*, to bend the head, duck, dive, Dan. *dukke*, to dive, G. *tauchen*, to dip, to dive.] To dip or plunge in water and suddenly withdraw; to bow, stoop, or nod in order to escape a blow or the like.—*v.i.* To plunge into water and immediately withdraw; to dip; to plunge the head in water or other liquid; to drop the head suddenly; to bow; to cringe.—*n.* [From the verb to *duck*.] A name of various waterfowls akin to, but distinguished from swans and geese by having broader bills, a more waddling gait from their legs being placed further back, there being also a marked difference in the plumage of the sexes; a term of endearment (*colloq.*); an inclination of the head, resembling the motion of a duck in water.—*To make ducks and drakes*, to throw a flat stone, piece of slate, etc., along the surface of water so as to cause it to strike and rebound repeatedly; hence, *to make ducks and drakes of one's money*, to squander it in a foolish manner.—**duckbill,** *n.* A remarkable Australian animal with jaws which resemble the bill of a duck. ORNITHORHYNCHUS.—**ducker,** duk'ėr, *n.* One who ducks; a plunger; a diver; a cringer; a fawner.—**ducking stool,** *n.* A stool or chair in which common scolds were formerly tied and plunged into water.—**duckling,** duk'ling, *n.* A young duck.—**duckweed,** *n.* The popular name of several species of plants growing in ditches and shallow water, and floating on the surface, serving for food for ducks and geese.

duct, dukt *n.* [L. *ductus* a leading, conducting, from *duco*, *ductum*, to lead. DUKE.] Any tube or canal by which a fluid is conveyed, used especially of canals in the bodies of animals or in plants.—**ductile,** duk'til, *a.* [L. *ductilis.*] Easy to be led or influenced (persons); tractable; yielding to persuasion or instruction; capable of being drawn out into wire or threads (used of metals).—**ductility,** duk•til'i•ti, *n.* The property of solid bodies, particularly metals, which renders them capable of being extended by drawing, while their thickness or diameter is diminished, without any actual separation of their parts; a yielding disposition of mind; ready compliance.—**ductless glands.** Structures of various use, superficially resembling glands, but devoid of ducts for carrying off a liquid secretion, e.g. thymus, thyroid, and spleen.

dude, dūd, *n.* A dandy; a fop. *Western slang*, an Easterner or city-bred person.

dude ranch, *n.* A ranch operated for, or accommodating tourists, where they may board and get a taste of ranching.

dudgeon, duj'on, *n.* [Origin unknown.] Anger; resentment; malice; ill will; discord.

due, dū, *a.* [O.Fr. *deu*, Fr. *dû*, pp. of *devoir*, from L. *debere*, to owe. DEBT.] Falling to be paid or done to another; owed by one to another, and by contract, justice, or propriety required to be paid; liable or meriting to be given or devoted; owing to (the attention *due* to one's studies); proper; fit; appropriate; suitable; becoming; seasonable; required by the circumstances (to behave with *due* gravity); exact; correct; owing origin or existence; to be attributed or assigned as causing (an effect *due* to the sun's attraction); that ought to have arrived or to be present; bound or stipulated to arrive (the mails are *due*).—*adv.* Directly; exactly (to sail *due* east).—*n.* What is owed or ought to be paid or done to another; that which justice, office, rank, or station, social relations or established rules of decorum, require to be given, paid, or done; a toll, tribute, fee, or other legal exaction.—**duly,** dū'li, *adv.* In a due, fit, or proper manner; fitly; suitably; properly; at the proper time.

duel, dū'el, *n.* [Fr. *duel*, It. *duello*, from L. *duellum*, old form of *bellum*, war, from *duo*, two] A premeditated combat between two persons with deadly weapons for the purpose of deciding some private difference or quarrel; a single combat; a fight between two fortresses, two encamped armies, and the like, carried on without the tactics of a pitched battle or an assault —*v.i.*—*dueled*, *dueling*. To engage in a duel.—**dueling,** dū'el•ing, *n.* The practice of engaging in duels.—**duelist,** dū'el•ist, *n.* One who engages in a duel or in duels.—**duello,** dū•el'lō, *n.* A duel; the art or practice of *dueling*, or the code of laws which regulate it (*Shak.*).

duenna, dū•en'na, *n.* [Sp. *duenna*, *dueña*, a form of *doña*, fem. of *don*, from L. *domina*, a mistress.] An elderly female appointed to take charge of the younger female members of Spanish and Portuguese families; an elderly woman who is kept to guard a younger.

duet, dū•et', *n.* [It. *duetto*, from *duo*, two.] A musical composition for two voices or two instruments.

duffel, duffle, duf'el, duf'l, *n.* [From *Duffel*, a Belgian manufacturing town.] A kind of coarse woolen cloth having a thick nap; supplies as for camping.

duffer, duf'ėr, *n.* A peddler; a hawker of cheap, flashy articles; a hawker of sham jewelry; a person who is a sham; a useless character; a stupid person; a fogey (*colloq.*).

dug, dug, *n.* [Akin to Sw. *dägga*, Dan. *dægge*, to suckle; from root seen in Skr. *duh*, to milk.] The pap or nipple of a woman or (now generally) of an animal.

dug, dug, pret. & pp. of *dig*.

dugong, dū'gong, *n.* [Malayan.] A herbivorous mammal of the Indian Seas, allied to the manatee or sea cow.

dugout, dug'out, *n.* [Amer.] A boat made by hollowing out a large log; an underground shelter for troops in trenches; a shelter at the side of a baseball field containing the players' bench.

duke, dūk, *n.* [Fr. *duc*, from L. *dux*, *ducis*, a leader, from *duco*, to lead (seen also in *duct*, *ducat*, *conduct*, *produce*, *educate*, etc.); cog. A.Sax. *toga* a leader, E. *tug* and *tow.*] A chief, prince, or leader‡; in Great Britain, one of the highest order of nobility; a title of honor or nobility next below that of a prince; in some countries on the Continent, a sovereign prince, the ruler of a state.—**dukedom,** dūk'dum, *n.* The seigniory or possessions of a duke; the territory of a duke; the title or quality of a duke.

dulcet, dul'set, *a.* [O.Fr. *dolcet*, L. *dulcis*, sweet.] Sweet to the taste; luscious; exquisite; sweet to the ear; melodious; harmonious; agreeable to the mind.—**dulcification,** dul'si•fi•kā"shon, *n.* The act of dulcifying.—**dulcify,** dul'si•fī, *v.t.*—*dulcified*, *dulcifying*. [Fr. *dulcifier*, from L. *dulcis*, sweet, and *facio*, to make.] To sweeten; to free from acidity, saltness, or acrimony; to render more agreeable to the taste.

dulcimer, dul'si•mėr, *n.* [Sp. *dulcemele*, It. *dolcimello*, from L. *dulcis*, sweet.] A musical instrument consisting in its modern form of a shallow quadrilateral box without a top, across which runs a series of wires, tuned by pegs at the sides, and played on by being struck by two cork-headed hammers.

dulia, dū'li•a, *n.* [Gr. *douleia*, service, from *doulos*, a slave.] An inferior kind of worship or adoration, as that paid to saints and angels in the Roman Catholic Church.

dull, dul, *a.* [A.Sax. *dol*, *dwol*, erring, dull, from *dwelan*, to be torpid or dull; akin Goth. *dvals*, foolish; Icel. *dul*, foolishness; D. *dol*, L.G. *dull*, G. *toll*, mad.] Stupid; doltish; slow of understanding; heavy; sluggish; without life or spirit; slow of motion; wanting sensibility or keenness in some of the senses (sight, hearing); not quick; sad; melancholy; depressing; dismal; gross; inanimate; insensible; not pleasing; not exhilarating; cheerless; not bright or clear; tarnished; dim; obscure; blunt; obtuse; having a thick edge; cloudy; overcast.—*v.t.* To make dull; to stupefy; to blunt; to render less acute; to make less eager; to make sad or melancholy; to make insensible or slow to perceive; to render dim; to sully; to tarnish or cloud.—*v.i.* To become dull.—**dullard,** dul'ėrd, *n.* A stupid person; a dolt; a blockhead; a dunce.—**dullish,** dul'ish, *a.* Somewhat dull; somewhat stupid; tiresome.—**dully,** dul'i, *a.* Somewhat dull. (*Tenn.*)—*adv.* (dul'li). Stupidly; slowly; sluggishly; without life or spirit.—**dullness,**

dulness, dul′nes, *n.* The state or character of being dull.

dulse, duls, *n.* [Gael. *duilliasg*, Ir. *duileasg*, dulse.] A kind of edible seaweed having a reddish-brown, or purple, frond, several inches long, found at low water.

Duma, dö′ma, *n.* The Russian parliament created in 1905, and overthrown by the Bolshevist revolution in 1917.

dumb, dum, *a.* [A.Sax. *dumb* = Goth. *dumbs*, Dan *dum*, G. *dumm*, dumb, stupid; allied to *dim*, and perhaps Goth. *daubs*, deaf.] Mute; silent; not speaking; destitute of the power of speech; unable to utter articulate sounds; not accompanied with speech; effected by signs (*dumb* show).—*To strike dumb*, to confound; to astonish; to render silent by astonishment.—*v.t.* To silence; to overpower with sound (*Shak.*).—**dumbly,** dum′li, *adv.* Mutely; silently; without words or speech.—**dumbness,** dum′nes, *n.* State of being dumb.—**dumbbells,** *n. pl.* Weights, usually consisting of two iron balls with a short piece for grasping between them, swung in the hands for developing the chest, the muscles of the arms, etc.—**dumb show,** *n.* A sort of dramatic representation performed pantomimically; gesture without words; pantomime.—**dumb-waiter,** *n.* A framework with shelves, made to move from floor to floor in a house for conveying food, etc.; a side table or other portable piece of furniture in a dining room, on which dessert, etc., is placed until required.—**dumfound, dumbfound,** dum•found′, *v.t.* To strike dumb; to confuse. (*Colloq.*)—**dumfounder,** dum•foun′dėr, *v.t.* To confuse; to stupefy; to strike dumb; to confound. (*Colloq.*)—**dummy,** dum′i, *n.* One who is dumb; the fourth or exposed hand during the play of bridge or whist; also when there are only three playing; a sham object doing service for a real one, as sham packages, etc.; a lay figure on which merchants display clothing.—*a.* Silent; mute; sham; fictitious.

dumdum, dum′dum, *n.* [Indian name of station with arsenal.] A soft-nosed bullet which expands and lacerates on striking.

dump, dump, *v.t.* [Akin to *bump*, *thump*.] To put or throw down with a bang; to deposit carelessly; to sell more cheaply abroad than in the home market.—*n.* A pile of refuse or other waste material; a place for dumping; *milit.* a temporary storehouse.

dump, dump, *n.* [Allied to *damp*; Dan. *dump*, dull; G. *dampf*, steam, vapor; comp. *dumps*, melancholy, with *vapors*, in the sense of nervousness or depression.] A dull gloomy state of the mind; sadness; melancholy; low spirits; heaviness of heart: generally in the plural, and now used only when a ludicrous effect is intended; a melancholy tune (*Shak.*)‡.—**dumpish,** dum′pish, *a.* Sad; melancholy; depressed in spirits.—**dumpishly,** dum′pish•li, *adv.* In a moping manner.—**dumpishness,** dum′pish•nes, *n.* State of being dumpish.

dumpling, dump′ling, *n.* [Connected with Prov.E. *dump*, a clumsy leaden counter, a lump; also perhaps prov. *dump*, to knock.] A kind of pudding or mass of boiled paste, with or without fruit in it.—**dumpy,** dum′pi, *a.* Short and thick.—**dumpy level,** *n.* A spirit level having a short telescope with a large aperture, and a compass, used in surveying.

dun, dun, *a.* [A.Sax. *dunn*, perhaps from W. *dwn*, Gael. *donn*, dun.] Of a grayish-brown or dull-brown color; of a smoky color.—**dunnish,** dun′ish, *a.* Inclined to a dun color; somewhat dun.

dun, dun, *v.t.*—*dunned*, *dunning*. [A form of *din*.] To clamor for payment of a debt from; to demand a debt in a pressing manner from; to call on for payment repeatedly; to urge importunately.—*n.* One who duns.

dunce, duns, *n.* [From *Duns Scotus*, the leader of the Schoolmen of the fourteenth century, opposed to the revival of classical learning; hence this name was given to his followers in contempt by their opponents.] An ignoramus; a pupil too stupid to learn; a dullard; a thick-skull.

dunderhead, dunderpate, dun′dėr•hed, dun′dėr•pāt, *n.* [Comp. Dan. *dummerhoved*, a dunderhead, lit. stupid-head, from *dum*, stupid.] A dunce; a dull-head.—**dunderheaded,** dun′dėr•hed•ed, *a.* Stupid; thick-skulled.

dune, dūn, *n.* [A.Sax. *dún*. DOWN.] A low hill of sand accumulated on the sea-coast.

dung, dung, *n.* [A.Sax. *dung*, G. *dung*. Sw. *dynga*; connected with verb to *ding*.] The excrement of animals.—*v.t.* To manure with dung.—*v.i.* To void excrement.—**dunghill,** dung′-hil, *n.* A heap of dung; the place where dung is kept collected; a mean or vile abode or situation.—*a.* Sprung from the dunghill; mean; low; vile.

dungaree, dun•ga•rē′, *n.* [Anglo-Indian, low, common, vulgar.] A coarse unbleached Indian calico, generally blue, worn by sailors.

dungeon, dun′jon, *n.* [Fr. *dongeon*, *donjon*. DONJON.] The innermost and strongest tower of a castle; the donjon; a close prison; a deep, dark place of confinement.—*v.t.* To confine in a dungeon.

duniewassal, dū•ni•was′sal, *n.* [Gael. *duin' uasal*, from *duine*, a man, and *uasal*, gentle.] A gentleman of secondary rank among the Scottish Highlanders; a cadet of a family of rank.

dunk, dungk, *v.t.* and *i.* [Amer. from L.G. *dunken*, to dip.] To dip something into a liquid while eating.

Dunker, dung′kėr, *n.* A member of a sect of Baptists originating in Philadelphia.

dunlin, dun′lin, *n.* [From *dune* with dim. termination *-ling*; or from *dun*, adj.] A species of sandpiper, about eight inches in length, often occurring in vast flocks along sandy shores.

dunnage, dun′ij, *n.* [For *downage*, from *down*.] Faggots, boughs, or loose wood laid on the bottom of a ship to raise heavy goods above the bottom to prevent injury from water; also loose articles of lading wedged between parts of the cargo to hold them steady.

duo, dū′ō, *n.* [It. from L. *duo*, two.] *Mus.* a duet; a pair.

duodecimal, dū•ō•des′i•mal, *a.* [L. *duodecim*, twelve.] Proceeding in computation by twelves, *n. pl.* An arithmetical method of ascertaining the number of square feet and square inches in a rectangular area or surface, whose sides are given in feet and inches.—**duodecimo,** dū•o•des′-i•mō, *a.* Having or consisting of twelve leaves to a sheet.—*n.* A book in which a sheet is folded into twelve leaves; the size of a book consisting of sheets so folded: usually indicated thus, 12*mo*.

duodenum, dū•o•dē′num, *n.* [From L. *duodeni*, twelve each, so called because its length is about twelve fingers' breadth.] The first portion of the small intestines; the twelve-inch intestine.—**duodenal,** dū•o•dē′-nal, *a.* Connected with or relating to the duodenum.—**duodenary,** dū•-o•den′e•ri, *a.* [L. *duodenarius*.] Relating to the number twelve; twelvefold; increasing by twelves.—*Duodenary arithmetic*, that system in which the local value of the figures increases twelvefold from right to left, instead of tenfold.

duologue, dū′o•log, *n.* [L. *duo*, two, *-logue*, from *dialogue*.] A dialogue between two.

dupe, dūp, *n.* [Fr. *dupe*, a name sometimes given to the hoopoe, and hence, from the bird being regarded as stupid, applied to a stupid person. Comp. *pigeon*.] A person who is deceived, or one easily led astray by his credulity.—*v.t.*—*duped*, *duping*. [Fr. *duper*.] To make a dupe of; to trick; to mislead by imposing on one's credulity.—**dupable,** dū′pa•bl, *a.* Liable to be or capable of being duped.—**duper,** dū′pėr, *n.* One who dupes; a cheat; a swindler.—**dupery,** dū′pėr•i, *n.* The art of duping.

duple, dū′pl, *a.* [L. *duplus*, double. DOUBLE.] Double.—*Duple ratio*, that of 2 to 1, 8 to 4, etc.—*Sub-duple ratio* is the reverse, or as 1 to 2, 4 to 8, etc.—*v.t.*† To double.—**duplex,** dū′pleks, *a.* [L.] Double; twofold; an apartment of rooms on two floors; a house with two apartments.

duplicate, dū′pli•kit, *a.* [L. *duplicatus*, from *duplico*, to double, from *duplex*, double, twofold—*duo*, two, and *plico*, to fold. DUAL, PLY.] Double; twofold.—*Duplicate proportion* or *ratio*, the proportion or ratio of squares.—*n.* Another corresponding to the first; a second thing of the same kind; another example or specimen of the same kind.—*v.t.* dū′pli•-kāt.—*duplicated*, *duplicating*. To make an exact copy of; to repeat exactly.—**duplication,** dū•pli•kā′-shon, *n.* The act or process of duplicating; the state of being duplicated; a duplicate copy.—**dupli-**

cative, dū'pli•ka•tiv, *a.*—**duplicator,** dū'pli•kā•tėr, *n.* One who duplicates; a machine for producing copies.

duplicity, dū•plis'i•ti, *n.* [F. *duplicité*, from LL. *duplicitas.*] The state of being double; doubleness; especially, doubleness of heart or speech; the act or practice of exhibiting a different or contrary conduct, or uttering different or contrary sentiments at different times in relation to the same thing; double-dealing; dissimulation; deceit.

durable, dū'ra•bl, *a.* [L. *durabilis*, from *duro*, to last, *durus*, hard.] Having the quality of lasting or continuing long in being without perishing or wearing out; not perishable or changeable.—**durability, durableness,** dū•ra•bil'i•ti, dū'ra•bl•nes, *n.* The quality of being durable.—**durably,** dū'ra•bli, *adv.* In a durable manner.

Duralumin, dūr•al'ū•min, *n.* A composite material consisting mainly of aluminum as strong as mild steel under proper heat treatment.

dura mater, dū'ra mā•tėr. [L.; lit. hard mother: called *mother* as protecting the brain.] The outer membrane of the brain: so named from its hardness compared with the membrane which lies under it, called *pia mater* (pious mother), and which also surrounds the brain.

duramen, dū•rā'men, *n.* [L. *duramen*, hardness, *durus*, hard.] The central wood or heartwood in the trunk of an exogenous tree.

durance, dū'rans, *n.* [In the common sense apparently shortened from *endurance*, from the hardships of imprisonment; comp. *duress.*] Imprisonment; restraint of the person; custody; duration†.—**duration,** dū•rā'shon, *n.* Continuance in time; length or extension of existence, indefinitely; power of continuance.

durbar, dėr'bär, *n.* [Hind. and Per. *darbâr*—Per. *dâr*, door. and *bâr*, court, assembly.] An audience room in the palaces of the native princes of India; state levee or audience held by the governor-general of India, or by a native prince; an official reception.

duress, dū'res, *n.* [O.Fr. *duresse*, hardship, constraint, from L. *duritia*, harshness, hardness, from *durus*, hard.] Imprisonment; restraint of liberty; *law*, also restraint or constraint by threats of personal injury.

durian, dū'ri•an, *n.* [The Malay name.] A tree of the Malayan Archipelago; also its fruit, which is extremely luscious and enticing to eat, but has an abominably offensive odor.

during, dū'ring. [From the L. phrase *vita durante*, while life lasts.] Continuing; lasting; in the time of; throughout the course of.

durmast, dėr'mast, *n.* A highly valued species of oak, closely allied to the common oak.

durra, dur'a, *n.* [Ar.] A species of grain much cultivated in Africa, Asia, and the south of Europe; Indian millet; Guinea corn.

durst, dėrst, pret. of *dare.*

dusk, dusk, *a.* [Probably akin to Sw. *dusk*, dull weather; Icel. *doska*, to dawdle; L.G. *dusken*, to slumber.] Tending to darkness, or moderately dark; tending to a dark or black color; moderately black; swarthy.—*n.* An approach to darkness; incipient or imperfect obscurity; a middle degree between light and darkness; twilight; darkness of color.—*v.t.*† To make dusky, or somewhat dark.—*v.i.*† To begin to lose light or whiteness; to grow dark; to cause a dusky appearance.—**dusken,** dus'kn, *v.i.* To grow dusk; to become dark.—*v.t.* To make dusk, or somewhat dark.—**duskily,** dus'ki•li, *adv.* In a dusky manner.—**duskiness,** dus'ki•nes, *n.* The state of being dusky.—**duskish,** dus'kish, *a.* Moderately dusky.—**dusky,** dus'ki, *a.* Partially dark or obscure; not luminous; tending to blackness in color; dark-colored; not bright; gloomy.

dust, dust, *n.* [A.Sax. *dust*, dust; same word as Icel. and L.D. *dust*, D. *duist*, dust; akin to G. *dunst*, vapor.] Fine dry particles of earth or other matter, so attenuated that they may be raised and wafted by the wind; hence, *fig.* commotion and confusion accompanying a struggle; earth or earthy matter as symbolic of mortality; the body when it has moldered in the grave; the grave; a low condition; money (*colloq.*).—*To throw dust in one's eyes*, to mislead; to blind as to the true character of something.—*v.t.* To free from dust; to brush, wipe, or sweep away dust; to beat; to sprinkle with dust.—**dust bowl,** *n.* An area subject to violent and frequent dust storms.—**duster,** dus'tėr, *n.* One who or that which dusts; an overgarment that protects clothing from dust.—**dust jacket,** *n.* A paper cover for a book.—**dust storm,** *n.* A violent wind carrying masses of dust from or across a dry region.—**dusty,** dus'ti, *a.* Filled or sprinkled with dust; reduced to dust; like dust; of the color of dust.

Dutch, dutsh, *n.* [G. *deutsch*, German, Germanic, pertaining to the Germanic or Teutonic race; O.H.G. *diutisc*, from *diot*, A.Sax. *theod*, Goth. *thiuda*, people. The word has latterly been narrowed from its original meaning. The term *Low Dutch* means Dutch or Low German (*Plattdeutsch*), as opposed to *High Dutch* (*Hochdeutsch*), or German proper.] *Pl.* originally, the Germanic race; the German peoples generally; now only applied to the people of the Netherlands; *sing.* the language of the Netherlands.—*a.* Of or referring to the Netherlands or its inhabitants; pertaining to or characteristic of the Dutch.—*Dutch auction*, an auction at which the auctioneer starts with a high price, and comes down till he meets with a bidder; a mock auction.—*Dutch courage*, false or artificial courage; boldness inspired by intoxicating spirits.—*Dutch clover*, white clover, a valuable pasture plant.—*Dutch concert*, a concert in which a company join, each singing his own song at the same time as his neighbor, or in which each member sings a verse of a song, some well-known chorus being used as the burden after each verse.—*Dutch gold*, *Dutch metal*, an alloy of eleven parts of copper and two of zinc.—*Dutch leaf*, false gold leaf.—*Dutch mineral*, copper beaten out into very thin leaves.—*Dutch myrtle*, sweet gale; a fragrant shrub found in bogs and moors.—*Dutch oven*, a tin hanging screen for cooking before a kitchen range or ordinary fire grate; a metal utensil that opens in front, used for roasting before an open fire or on top of a stove; a heavy iron pot with a close-fitting cover; a brick oven in which the walls are preheated for cooking.—*Dutch treat*, a meal or treat at which each person pays for himself.—**Dutchman,** dutsh'man, *n.* A Netherlander.

duty, dū'ti, *n.* [From *due.*] That which a person is bound by any natural, moral, or legal obligation to do or perform; what has to be done as being due towards another; obligation to do something; obedience; submission; act of reverence or respect; any service, business, or office; particularly, military or similar service; a tax, toll, or impost; any sum of money required by government to be paid on the importation, exportation, or consumption of goods.—**duteous,** dū'tė•us, *a.* Performing that which is due, or that which law, justice, or propriety requires; dutiful; obedient; enjoined by duty (*Shak.*)†.—**duteously,** dū'tē•us•li *adv.* In a duteous manner.—**duteousness,** dū'tē•us•nes, *n.* Quality of being duteous.—**dutiable,** dū'ti•a•bl, *a.* Subject to the imposition of duty or customs.—**dutiful,** dū'ti•fųl, *a.* Performing the duties or obligations required by law, justice, or propriety; obedient; submissive to superiors; expressive of respect or a sense of duty; respectful; reverential; required by duty.—**dutifully,** dū'ti•fųl•li, *adv.* In a dutiful manner.—**dutifulness,** dū'ti•fųl•nes, *n.* The state or character of being dutiful.

duvetyn, duvetine, dū'vė•tēn, *n.* A soft fabric with a fine velvety nap, made of wool mixed with silk or cotton, or both.

dwarf, dwąrf, *n.* [A.Sax. *dwerg*, *dweorg*, D. *dwerg*, Sw. *dwerg*, *dwerf*, L.G. *dwarf*, a dwarf.] A general name for an animal or plant which is much below the ordinary size of the species or kind; a very diminutive man or woman.—*v.t.* To hinder from growing to the natural size; to prevent the due development of; to stunt; to cause to look small or insignificant by comparison.—*v.i.* To become less; to become dwarfish or stunted.—**dwarfish,** dwąr'fish, *a.* Like a dwarf; below the common stature or size; very small; low; petty; despicable,—**dwarfishly,** dwąr'fish•li, *adv.* In a dwarfish manner.—**dwarfishness,** dwąr'fish•-

nes, *n.* The state or quality of being dwarfish.

dwell, dwel, *v.i.—dwelled,* usually contracted into *dwelt, dwelling.* [From A.Sax. *dwellan,* to deceive, prevent, hinder; Icel. *dvelja,* to hinder, to delay; Dan. *dvaele,* to loiter, delay, dwell; akin *dull.*] To abide as a permanent resident; to live in a place; to have a habitation for some time or permanently; to be in any state or condition; to continue.—*To dwell on,* or *upon,* to keep the attention fixed on; to hang upon with fondness; to occupy a long time with; to be tedious over.—**dweller,** dwel′ėr, *n.* One who dwells; an inhabitant.—**dwelling,** dwel′ing, *n.* Habitation; place of residence; abode; continuance; residence.

dwindle, dwin′dl, *v.i.—dwindled, dwindling.* [Freq. from O.R. and Sc. *dwine*; A.Sax. *dwinan,* to pine, waste away=D. *dwijnen,* Icel. *dvína,* Dan. *tvine,* to pine.] To diminish gradually; to become small and insignificant; to shrink; to waste or consume away; to degenerate.—*v.t.* To cause to dwindle.—*n.* The process of dwindling; decline.

dyad, dī′ad, *n.* [Gr. *dyas, dyados,* from *dyo,* two.] Two units treated as one; a pair; a couple; *chem.* an elementary substance, each atom of which, in combining with other bodies, is equivalent to two atoms of hydrogen.—**dyadic,** dī•ad′ik, *a.* Pertaining or relating to the number two, or to a dyad; consisting of two parts or elements.

dyarchy, dī′är•ki, *n.* [Gr. *duo,* two, *archē,* rule.] The rule of two persons together.

dye, dī, *v.t.—dyed, dyeing.* [A.Sax. *deâgan,* from *deâg,* dye, color.] To give a new and permanent color to: applied particularly to cloth or the materials of cloth, as wool, cotton, silk, and linen; also to hair, skins, etc.; to stain; to color; to tinge.—*n.* A coloring liquid; color; stain; tinge.—**dyer,** dī′ėr, *n.* One whose occupation is to dye cloth and the like.—**dyer's-weed,** *n.* Any of several dye-yielding plants, as the woodwaxen.—**dyestuff,** *n.* Materials used in dyeing.—**dyewood,** *n.* A general name for any wood from which dye is extracted.

dying, dī′ing, *a.* Mortal; destined to death; given, uttered, or manifested just before death (*dying* words); pertaining to or associated with death (*dying* hour); drawing to a close; fading away.—*n.* The act of expiring; death.

dyke, *n.* and *v.* Same as *Dike.*

dynam, dī′nam, *n.* [Gr. *dynamis,* power.] A term proposed to express a unit of work equal to a weight of 1 lb. raised through 1 foot in a second; a foot-pound.—**dynameter,** di•nam′e•tėr, *n.* An instrument for determining the magnifying power of telescopes.—**dynamic, dynamical,** di•nam′ik, di•nam′i•kal, *a.* Pertaining to strength, power, or force; relating to dynamics; relating to the effects of the forces or moving agencies in nature.—*Dynamical electricity,* current electricity.—**dynamically,** di•nam′i•kal•li, *adv.* In a dynamical manner.—**dynamics,** di•nam′iks, *n.* That area of mechanics that deals with forces and their effects on bodies in motion or at rest; patterns of change or growth in objects.—**dynamism,** dī′na•mizm, *n.* The doctrine that all substance involves force.—**dynamite,** dī′na•mīt, *n.* An explosive substance consisting of a siliceous earth, and sometimes of charcoal, sawdust, etc., impregnated with nitroglycerin, and having a disruptive force estimated at about eight times that of gunpowder.—*v.t.* To shatter with dynamite.—**dynamiter,** dīn′a•mīt•ėr, *n.* One who uses dynamite for destroying public buildings or other criminal purposes.—**dynamo,** dī′na•mō, *n.* A generator; a machine that transforms mechanical input into electrical output; a forceful, energetic person.—**dynamometer,** dī′na•mom″e•tėr, *n.* An instrument for measuring force or power, especially that of men, animals, machines, the strength of materials, etc.—**dynamotor,** dī′na•mōt•ėr, *n.* A machine combining the generator and the electric motor.—**dynamometric, dynamometrical,** dī′na•mo•met″rik, dī′na•mo•met″ri•kal, *a.*—**dynamoelectric,** di•nam′ō•ē•lek″trik, *a.* With *machine,* an electric generator or motor.

dynasty, dīn′as•ti, *n.* [Gr. *dynasteia,* sovereignty, from *dynastēs,* a lord or chief, from *dynamai,* to be strong, *dynamis,* power.] A race or succession of rulers of the same line or family, who govern a particular country; the period during which they rule.—**dynastic,** dī•nas′tik, *a.* Relating to a dynasty or line of kings.

dyne, dīn, *n.* [Gr. *dynamis,* power.] *Physics,* a unit of force, being that force which, acting on a gram for one second, generates a velocity of a centimeter per second.

dyscrasia, dis•krā′si•a, *n.* [Gr. *dyskrasia—dys,* evil, and *krasis,* habit.] *Med.* a bad habit of body.

dysentery, dis′en•te•ri, *n.* [Gr. *dysenteria—dys,* bad, and *entera,* intestines.] An amoebic or bacillary inflammation of the mucous membrane of the large intestine, accompanied generally with much fever and great prostration, frequent stools, the discharges being mixed with blood and mucus.—**dysenteric,** dis•en•ter′ik, *a.*

dyslogistic, dis•lo•jis′tik, *a.* [Formed on the model of *eulogistic, dys* signifying ill, and the word having therefore the opposite signification of *eulogistic.*] Conveying censure, disapproval, or opprobrium; censorious; opprobrious.—**dyslogistically,** dis•lo•jis′ti•kal•li, *adv.* In a dyslogistic manner; so as to convey censure or disapproval.

dyspepsia, dyspepsy, dis•pep′si•a, dis•pep′si, *n.* [Gr. *dyspepsia—dys,* bad, and *peptō,* to concoct, to digest.] Indigestion, or difficulty of digestion; a state of the stomach in which its functions are disturbed, without the presence of other diseases, or when, if they are present, they are but of minor importance.—**dyspeptic, dyspeptical,** dis•pep′tik, dis•pep′ti•kal, *a.* Afflicted with dyspepsia; pertaining to or consisting in dyspepsy.—**dyspeptic,** *n.* A person afflicted with dyspepsy.

dysphagia, dis•fā′ji•a, *n.* [Gr. *dys,* ill, and *phagō,* to eat.] *Med.* difficulty of swallowing.

dysphonia, dis•fō′ni•a, *n.* [Gr. *dys,* bad, and *phōnē,* voice.] *Med.* a difficulty of speaking occasioned by an ill disposition of the organs of speech.

dyspnea, disp•nē′a, *n.* [Gr. *dyspnoia—dys,* ill, and *pneō,* to breathe.] *Med.* difficulty of breathing.—**dyspneic,** disp•nē′ik, *a.* Affected with or resulting from dyspnea.

dysprosium, dis•pro′shi•um, *n.* A metallic element, highly magnetic, of the rare-earth series. Symbol, Dy; at. no., 66; at. wt., 162.50.

dysuria, dis•ū′ri•a, *n.* [Gr. *dysouria—dys,* ill, and *ouron,* urine.] *Med.* difficulty in discharging the urine, attended with pain and a sensation of heat.

E

E, e, ē, the second vowel and the fifth letter of the English alphabet, occurring more frequently than any other letter of the alphabet; *mus.* the third note or degree of the natural or diatonic scale.

each, ēch, *distrib. a.* and *pron.* [O.E. *eche*; *ech, ych, uch, elch, elc, ilk*; A.Sax. *aelc,* from *á=aye,* ever, and *lic,* like; similar to D. and L.G. *elk,* G. *jeglich.* Comp. *such* and *which.*] Every one of any number separately considered or treated; every one of two or more considered individually. With *other* it is used reciprocally; as, it is our duty to assist *each other* (that is, each to assist the other).

eager, ē′gėr, *a.* [O.E. *egre,* O.Fr. *eigre,* Mod.Fr. *aigre,* eager, sharp, biting, from L. *acer, acris,* sharp, from root which appears in *acute acid, acrid,* etc.] Sharp, sour, acid (*Shak.*)‡; excited by ardent desire in the pursuit of any object; ardent to pursue, perform, or obtain; ardently wishing or longing; vehement; fervid; earnest; impetuous; keen.—**eagerly,** ē′gėr•li, *adv.* In an eager manner.—**eagerness,** ē′gėr•nes, *n.* The state or character of being eager; keenness; ardor; zeal.

eagle, ē′gl, *n.* [Fr. *aigle,* from L. *aquila,* an eagle, fem. of the rare adj. *aquilus,* dark-colored, swarthy.] A common name of many large birds of prey, characterized by a hooked beak and curved, sharp, and strong claws (talons), and by its great powers of flight and vision, often regarded as a symbol of royalty; the typical eagles constitute a genus (*Aquila*) in which the legs are feathered to the toes; a military standard having the figure of an eagle, such as that of ancient Rome and modern France; a gold coin of the United States, of the value of ten dollars, from the eagle on the reverse; a reading desk in churches in the form of an eagle with expanded wings; in golf, a score of two under par on any hole but a par-three hole.—**eaglet,** ē′glet, *n.* A small or young eagle.—**eaglestone,** *n.* A variety of argillaceous iron ore occurring in spherical, oval, or reniform masses varying from the size of a walnut to that of a man's head; so called from an ancient notion that they were often found in the nests of eagles.

eagre, ē′gėr, *n.* [A.Sax. *eágor*, *égor*, Icel. *ægir*, the sea.] A tidal wave moving up a river or estuary at spring tide; a bore.

ear, ēr, *n.* [A.Sax. *eáre*=D. *oor*, Icel. *eyra*, Dan. *ōre*, G. *ohr*, L. *auris*, G. *ous*.] The organ of hearing, which in man and higher animals is composed of the external ear, a cartilaginous funnel for collecting the sound waves and directing them inward; the middle ear, tympanum or drum; and the internal ear or labyrinth; the sense of hearing; the power of distinguishing sounds; the power of nice perception of the differences of musical sounds; a favorable hearing; attention; heed; a part of any inanimate object resembling an ear; a projecting part from the side of anything; a handle of a tub, pitcher, etc.—*All ear*, all attention.—*To set by the ears*, to make strife between; to cause to quarrel.—*Up to the ears*, *over head and ears*, deeply absorbed or engrossed; overwhelmed.—**eared,** ērd, *a.* Having ears: usually in compounds, as *long-eared*.—**earache,** *n.* Pain in the ear.—**eardrop,** *n.* An ornamental pendant for the ear.—**eardrum,** *n.* The tympanum (which see).—**earmark,** *n.* A mark on the ear for distinguishing sheep, pigs, cattle, etc.; hence any mark for distinction or identification.—*v.t.* To distinguish by putting an earmark on; to set apart funds for an overdue purpose or estimate.—**—ear phone,** *n.* A device worn over or in the ear that converts electrical energy into sound waves.—**earring,** *n.* An ornament that is worn in or on the lobe of the ear.—**ear shell,** *n.* One of a genus of gastropodous mollusks.—**earshot,** *n.* The distance the ear can perceive sound; hearing distance. —**earwax,** *n.* The waxy or viscous substance secreted by the ear; cerumen.—**earwig,** ēr′wig, *n.* [A.Sax. *wicga*, a beetle.] One of a family of insects having a long narrow body and a pair of nippers at the extremity of the abdomen: so called from a popular delusion that they have a propensity to creep into the ear.

ear, ēr, *n.* [A.Sax. *ear*, D. *aar*, G. *āhre*, an ear.] A spike or head of corn or grain; that part of cereal plants which contains the flowers and seeds.—*v.i.* To shoot, as an ear; to form ears, as corn.

earl, ėrl, *n.* [A.Sax. *eorl*, Icel. Dan., and Sw. *jarl*, an earl.] In Britain a nobleman, the third in rank, being next below a marquis, and next above a viscount.—**earldom,** ėrl′dum, *n.* The jurisdiction or dignity of an earl.—**earl marshal,** *n.* An officer of state in Great Britain, who, as the head of the College of Arms, determines all rival claims to arms, and grants armorial bearings, through the medium of the king-of-arms.

early, ėr′li, *a.* [A.Sax. *aerlice* (adv.), from *aer*, soon *lic*, like. ERE.] In advance of something else as regards time; sooner than ordinary; produced or happening before the usual time (*early* fruit, *early* maturity); forward; being at the beginning; first (in *early* manhood, *early* times).—*Early English architecture*, the style of architecture into which the Norman passed, the distinctive features of which are pointed arches, long, narrow, lancet-shaped windows without mullions, and a peculiar projecting ornament in the hollows of the moldings, called the dog-tooth ornament: called also the *First Pointed* or *Lancet Style*.—*Early Victorian*, of art, literature, or the state prevailing at the time, with a slight tinge of depreciation.—*adv.* Soon, or sooner than usual or than others; in good season; betimes.—**earliness,** ėr′li•nes, *n.* The state of being early.

earn, ėrn, *v.t.* [A.Sax. *earnian*, to earn, to reap the fruit of one's labors; O.D. *erne* G. *ernte* harvest.] To merit or deserve by labor or by any performance; to gain by labor, service, or performance; to deserve and receive as compensation.—**earnings,** ėr′ningz, *n. pl.* That which is earned; what is gained or deserved by labor, services, or performance; wages; reward; recompense.

earnest, ėr′nest, *a.* [A.Sax. *eornest*, earnestness, *eorneste* (adj.), earnest, serious; cog. D. and G. *ernst*, earnest, D. *ernsten*, to endeavor.] Ardent in the pursuit of an object; eager to obtain; having a longing desire; warmly engaged or incited; warm; zealous; intent; serious; grave.—*n.* Seriousness; a reality; a real event, as opposed to jesting or feigned appearance.—**earnestly,** ėr′nest•li, *adv.* In an earnest manner.—**earnestness,** ėr′nest•nes, *n.* The state or quality of being earnest.

earnest, ėr′nest, *n.* [From W. *ernes*, earnest or pledge, from *ern*, a pledge.] Something given by way of token or pledge, to bind a bargain and prove a sale; a part paid or delivered beforehand, as a pledge and security for the whole, or as a token of more to come; *fig.* anything which gives assurance, promise, or indication of what is to follow; first fruits; token.—**earnest money,** *n.* Money paid as earnest to bind a bargain or ratify and prove a sale.

earth, ėrth, *n.* [A.Sax. *eorthe*; Goth. *airtha*, Icel. *jōrth*, Sw. and Dan. *jord*, G. *erde*, allied to A.Sax. *eard*, soil, home, dwelling, and perhaps to Gr. *era*, Skr. *ira*—earth, and to L. *aro*, to plough.] The particles which compose the mass of the globe, but more particularly the particles which form the mold on the surface of the globe; the globe which we inhabit; the planet third in order from the sun; the world, as opposed to other scenes of existence; the inhabitants of the globe; dry land, as opposed to the sea; the ground; the hole in which a fox or other burrowing animal hides itself; *chem.* the name given to certain tasteless, inodorous, dry, and uninflammable substances, the most important of which are lime, baryta, strontia, magnesia, alumina, zirconia, glucina, yttria, and thoria.—*v.t.* To hide in the earth; to cover with earth or mold.—*v.i.* To retire under ground; to burrow.—*Earth currents*, in *elect.* strong irregular currents, which disturb telegraphic lines of considerable length, flowing from one part of the line to another, affecting the instruments and frequently interrupting telegraphic communication.—**earthen,** ėrth′n, *a.* Made of earth; composed of clay or other like substance.—**earthly,** ėrth′li, *a.* Pertaining to the earth or this world; worldly; temporal; gross; vile; carnal; mean; composed of earth; among the things of this earth; possible; conceivable.—**earthliness,** ėrth′li•nes, *n.* The state or quality of being earthly.—**earthling,** ėrth′ling, *n.* An inhabitant of the earth; a mortal; a frail creature; one much attached to worldly affairs; a worldling.—**earthy,** ėr′thi, *a.* Of or pertaining to earth; composed of earth; partaking of the nature of earth; like earth or having some of its properties.—**earthborn,** *a.* Born of the earth; springing originally from the earth; relating to or occasioned by earthly objects; of low birth; meanly born.—**earth-bound,** *a.* Fastened by the pressure of the earth; firmly fixed in the earth.—**earthenware,** ėrth′n•wâr, *n.* Every sort of household utensil made of clay hardened in the fire; crockery; pottery.—**earthnut,** *n.* An umbelliferous plant common in woods and fields, producing a brown sweetish farinaceous tuber or nut about the size of a chestnut, formed 4 to 6 inches below the surface, and of which swine are fond; also a name given to the groundnut.—**earthquake,** ėrth′kwāk, *n.* A shaking, trembling, or concussion of the earth, sometimes a slight tremor, at other times a violent shaking or convulsion, in which vast chasms open, swallowing up sometimes whole cities; at other times a rocking or heaving of the earth: probably due to internal igneous forces.—**earthshine,** *n.* The illumination of the dark portion of the moon, due to the sunlight reflected from the earth.—**earthwork,** *n.* A term applied to all operations where earth has to be removed or collected together, as in cuttings, embankments, etc.; a fortification constructed of earth.—**earthworm,** *n.* An annelid worm, living in wet soil, that is characterized by a long cylindrical body tapering at each end, minute bristles used in movement, and the digesting of decayed organic material obtained from the soil; a mean sordid wretch.

ease, ēz, *n.* [Fr. *aise*, ease; O.Fr. *eise*, *ayse*, *aize*, ease; Pr. *aise*, It. *agio*, O.It. *asio*, ease; all words of very doubtful origin.] Freedom from labor or exertion, or from physical pain, disturbance, excitement, or annoyance; freedom from concern, anxiety, solicitude or anything that frets or ruffles the mind; tranquility; repose; freedom from difficulty or great labor; facility; freedom from constraint, formality, stiffness, harshness, forced expressions, or unnatural arrangement; unaffectedness.—*Chapel of ease*, a chapel taking off the burdens of a large parish, and having right to most part of ecclesiastical duties.—*v.t.*—*eased*, *easing*. To free from pain, suffering, anxiety, care, or any disquiet or annoyance; to relieve; to give rest to; to mitigate; to alleviate; to assuage; to allay; to abate or remove in part (to *ease* pain, grief, a burden, etc.); to render less difficult; to facilitate; to release from pressure or restraint by moving gently; to shift a little.—**easeful,** ēz′fụl, *a.* Giving ease. [Poet.]—**easement,** ēz′ment, *n.* Convenience; accommodation; that which gives ease or relief; *law*, a privilege without profit which one proprietor has in the estate of another proprietor, distinct from the ownership of the soil, as a way, watercourse, etc.; Scots law, *servitude* (q.v.).—**easy,** ē′zi, *a.* Being at rest; having ease; free from pain, disturbance, suffering, annoyance, care, trouble, concern, anxiety, or the like; quiet; tranquil; giving no pain or disturbance; requiring no great labor or exertion; not difficult; not steep, rough, or uneven; gentle; not unwilling; ready; not constrained, stiff, or formal; not rigid or strict; smooth; flowing; not straitened or restricted as regards money or means; affluent; comfortable.—**easily,** ē′zi•li, *adv.* In an easy manner.—**easiness,** ē′zi•nes, *n.* The state or quality of being easy.

easel, ē′zel, *n.* [G. *esel*, an ass, a wooden horse, or stand.] The wooden frame on which painters place pictures while at work upon them.

east, ēst, *n.* [A.Sax. *eást*=D. *oost*, G. *ost*, Icel. *aust*; connected with L. *aurora* (anc. *ausosa*), Lith. *auszra*, the red of morning, Skr. *ushas*, the dawn, from a root *us*, to burn, as in L. *urere*, to burn.] One of the four cardinal points, being the point in the heavens where the sun is seen to rise at the equinox, or the corresponding point on the earth; that point of the horizon lying on the right hand when one's face is turned toward the north pole; [*cap.*] the regions or countries which lie east of Europe; the oriental countries.—*a.* Toward or in the direction of the rising sun; opposite from west.—*v.i.* To move in the direction of the east; to veer from the north or south toward the east.—*adv.* In an easterly direction; eastward.—**easterling,** ēs′tėr•ling, *n.* An old name for a native of some country lying eastward of Britain, especially a trader from the shores of the Baltic.—**easterly,** ēs′tėr•li, *a.* Coming from the east; moving or directed eastward; situated or looking toward the east.—*adv.* On the east; in the direction of east.—**eastern,** ēs′tėrn, *a.* [A.Sax. *eastern*.] [cap.] Being or dwelling in the east; oriental; [not cap.] situated toward the east; on the east part; going toward the east, or in the direction of east.—*Eastern Church*, the Greek Church, established in Russia, into which it was introduced from Constantinople.—*Eastern Hemisphere*, the half of the earth east of the Atlantic Ocean, comprising the land masses of Africa, Asia, Australia, and Europe.—**eastward, eastwards,** ēst′wėrd, ēst′wėrdz, *adv.* Toward the east; in the direction of east from some point or place.—**eastward,** *a.* Facing, pointing, or having its direction toward the east.

Easter, ēs′tėr, *n.* [A.Sax. *eástre*, Easter, from A.Sax. *Eástre*, *Eóstre*, O.H.G. *Ostarâ*, a goddess of light or spring, in honor of whom a festival was celebrated in April, whence this month was called *eastermônâth*; connected with *east*.] A movable festival of the Christian church observed in March or April in commemoration of the Saviour's resurrection. Easter is the first Sunday after the first full moon that falls on or next after the vernal equinox (March 21 in the Gregorian calendar); if the full moon happens on Sunday, Easter is celebrated one week later.

easy. See EASE.

eat, ēt, *v.i.* pret. *eat* or *ate* (et, āt); pp. *eat* or *eaten* (et, ē′tn). [A.Sax. *etan*=D. *eten*, Icel. *eta*, Dan. *æde*, Goth. *itan*, G. *essen*; from root seen also in L. *edo*, Gr. *edō*, Skr. *ad*, to eat.] To masticate and swallow; to partake of as food: said especially of solids; to corrode; to wear away; to gnaw into gradually.—*To eat one's heart*, to brood over one's sorrows or disappointments.—*To eat one's words*, to retract one's assertions.—*v.i.* To take food; to feed; to take a meal; to have a particular taste or character when eaten; to make way by corrosion; to gnaw; to enter by gradually wearing or separating the parts of a substance.—**eatable,** ē′ta•bl, *a.* Capable of being eaten; esculent.—*n.* Anything that may be eaten; that which is used as food; an edible or comestible.—**eater,** ē′tėr, *n.* One who eats; that which eats or corrodes.

Eau de Cologne, ō•dė•ko•lōn′, *n.* [Fr., from L. *aqua*, water.] A perfumed spirit, originally invented at *Cologne*, and consisting of spirits of wine flavored by a few drops of different essential oils blended so as to yield a fine fragrant scent.

eaves, ēvz, *n. pl.* [A.Sax. *efese*, *yfese* (sing.), the eave, the edge, whence *efesian*, to shave, to trim; same word as Goth. *ubizva*, O.H.G. *obisa*, a portico, a hall; from root of *over*.] That part of the roof of a building which projects beyond the wall and casts off the water that falls on the roof.—**eavesdrop,** *v.i.*—*eavesdropped*, *eaves-dropping*. To stand under the eaves, or near the windows of a house to listen and learn what is said within doors; to watch for an opportunity of hearing the private conversation of others.—*n.* The water which falls in drops from the eaves of a house.—**eavesdropper,** *n.* One who stands near the window or door of a house to catch what is said within doors; one who tries to hear private conversation.

ebb, eb, *n.* [A.Sax. *ebbe*, *ebba*; D. *eb*, *ebbe*, G. and Dan. *ebbe*, Sw. *ebb*; allied to E. *even*, G. *aben*, to fall off, to sink. EVENING.] The reflux of the tide; the return of tidewater toward the sea: opposed to *flood* or *flow*; a flowing backward or away; decline; decay (the *ebb* of prosperity or of life).—*v.i.* To flow back; to return, as the water of a tide toward the ocean: opposed to *flow*; to recede; to decrease; to decay; to decline.—**ebb tide,** *n.* The reflux of tidewater; the retiring tide.

ebony, eb′o•ni, *n.* [L. *ebenus*, Gr. *ebenos*.] A black colored wood of great hardness, heavier than water, and capable of taking on a fine polish, being much used in inlaid work and turnery; the most valuable variety is the heartwood of a large tree growing in Ceylon.—**ebon,** eb′on, *a.* Consisting of ebony; black like ebony; dark.—**ebonite,** eb′o•nīt, *n.* Same as *Vulcanite*.—**ebonize,** eb′-o•nīz, *v.t.* To make black or tawny; to tinge with the color of ebony.

ebracteate, ē•brak′tē•āt, *a.* [L. *e*, not, and *bractea*, a thin plate.] *Bot.* without bracts.

ebullition, eb•ụ•lish′on, *n.* [L. *ebullitio*; from *ebullio*—*e*, *ex*, out, up, and *bullio*, to boil, from *bulla*, a bubble. BOIL.] The operation or phenomenon of boiling; the bubbling up of a liquor by heat; the agitation produced in a fluid by the escape of a portion of it converted into an aeriform state by heat; effervescence; an outward display of feeling, as of anger; a sudden burst; a pouring forth; an overflowing.—**ebullience, ebulliency,** e•bụl′yens, e•bụl′yen•si, *n.* A boiling over; a bursting forth; overflow.—**ebullient,** e•bul′yent, *a.* Boiling over; hence, over-enthusiastic; over-demonstrative.

écarté, ā•kär•tā′, *n.* [Fr., discarded.] A game of cards for two persons with thirty-two cards, the small cards from two to six being excluded: so called because the players may discard or exchange their cards for others.

eccentric, ek•sen′trik, *a.* [L. *eccentricus*—*ex*, from, and *centrum*, center.] Deviating or departing from the center; not having the same center; not concentric though situated one within the other; having the axis out of the center; deviating from usual practice; given to act in a way peculiar to one's self and different from other people; anomalous; singular; odd.—*n.* An eccentric person; a term applied to several mechanical contrivances for converting circular into reciprocating rectilinear motion, consisting of variously shaped disks, attached to a revolving shaft.—**eccentrically,** ek•sen′tri•kal•li, *adv.* With eccentricity; in an eccentric manner.—**eccentricity,** ek•sen•tris′i•ti, *n.* The state of having a center different from that of another related circle; the ratio, to the semi-major-axis, of the distance of the center of a planet's orbit (an ellipse) from the center of the sun (a focus); eccentric conduct; departure or deviation from what is regular or usual; oddity; whimsicalness.

ecclesiastic, ecclesiastical, ek•klē′-zi•as″tik, ek•klē′zi•as″ti•kal, *a.* [Gr. *ekklēsiastikos,* from *ekklēsia,* an assembly, the church, from *ekkaleō,* to call forth or convoke—*ek,* and *kaleō,* to call.] Pertaining or relating to the church; not civil or secular.—**ecclesiastic,** *n.* A person in orders or consecrated to the services of the church and the ministry of religion.—**ecclesiastically,** ek•klē′zi•as″ti•kal•li, *adv.* In an ecclesiastical manner.—**Ecclesiastes,** ek•klē′zi•as″tēz, *n.* A canonical book of the Old Testament, placed between the book of Proverbs and the Song of Solomon; translation of *Koheleth,* the Preacher.—**ecclesiasticism,** ek•klē′-zi•as″ti•sizm, *n.* Strong adherence to the principles of the Church, or to ecclesiastical observances, privileges, etc.—**Ecclesiasticus,** *n.* Book in the Apocrypha, but allowed for use in the Church.—**ecclesiology,** ek•klē′zi•ol″o•ji, *n.* [Gr. *ekklēsia,* the church, and *logos,* discourse.] The science of antiquities as applied to churches and other ecclesiastical foundations; the science and theory of church building and decoration.

ecdysis, ek′di•sis, *n.* [Gr., from *ekdyō,* to strip off—*ek,* out of, and *dyō,* to enter.] The act of shedding or casting an outer coat or integument, as in the case of serpents, certain insects, etc.

echelon, esh′e•lon, *n.* [Fr., from *échelle,* a ladder, from L. *scala,* a ladder.] *Milit.* the position of an army in the form of steps, or in parallel lines, each line being a little to the left or right of the preceding one.

echidna, e•kid′na, *n.* [Gr., an adder, a fabulous monster.] A burrowing mammal of Australia belonging to the Monotremata and resembling the hedgehog, except that the muzzle is protracted and slender, with a small aperture at the extremity for the protrusion of a long flexible tongue, by means of which it catches its insect prey; the porcupine anteater.—**echidnine,** e•kid′nin, *n.* Serpent poison; the secretion from the poison glands of the viper and other serpents.

echinate, echinated, ek′i•nāt, ek′i•-nā•ted, *a.* [L. *echinus,* Gr. *echinos,* a hedgehog, a sea-urchin.] Set with prickles; prickly, like a hedgehog; having sharp points.

echinoderm, e•kī′no•derm, *n.* [Gr. *echinos,* sea urchin, and *dermos,* skin.] Any marine animal of the phylum Echinodermata, having radial appendages, symmetrical body structure, and a spiny calcareous exoskeleton, such as the sea urchin, starfish, etc.—**echinus,** e•kī′nus, *n.* The generic name for the sea urchin; *arch.* a rounded molding at the top of a Doric column.—**echinoid,** e•kī′-noid, *a.*

echo, ek′ō, *n.* pl. **echoes,** ek′ōz. [L. *echo,* from Gr. *ēchō,* an echo, a nymph, who, for love of Narcissus, pined away till nothing remained of her but her voice; a sound.] A sound reflected or reverberated from a distant surface; sound returned; repercussion of sound; repetition with assent; close imitation either in words or sentiments; a person who slavishly follows another in uttering sentiments.—*v.i.* To give forth an echo; to resound; to reflect sound; to be sounded back; to produce a sound that reverberates; to give out a loud sound.—*v.t.* To reverberate or send back the sound of; to repeat with assent.—**echolocation,** ek″ō•lō•kā′shon, *n.* A process by which the location or distance of an object is determined by the reflecting of sound waves off the object.

eclair, ā•klâr′, *n.* [Fr. *esclair,* lightning, and *esclairier,* to lighten.] An oblong pastry usually iced with chocolate and filled with custard.

éclat, ā•klä, *n.* [Fr., a splinter, noise, brightness, magnificence, from *éclater,* to split, to shiver, to glitter; from O.H.G. *skleizan,* G. *schleissen, schlitzen,* to split; E. *slit, slice, slate.*] A burst, as of applause; acclamation; approbation; brilliancy of success; splendor of effect; luster; renown; glory.

eclectic, ek•lek′tik, *a.* [Gr. *eklektikos* —*ek,* and *legō,* to choose.] Proceeding by the method of selection; choosing what seems best from others; not original nor following any one model or leader, but choosing at will from the doctrines, works, etc., of others; specifically applied to certain philosophers of antiquity who selected from the opinions and principles of various schools what they thought solid and good.—*n.* One who follows an eclectic method in philosophy, science, religion, and the like.—**eclectically,** ek•lek′ti•kal•li, *adv.* In an eclectic manner.—**eclecticism,** ek•lek′ti•sizm, *n.* The doctrine or practice of an eclectic.

eclipse, i•klips′, *n.* [L. *eclipsis,* from Gr. *ekleipsis,* defect, from *ekleipō,* to fail—*ek,* out and *leipō,* to leave.] An interception or obscuration of the light of the sun, moon, or other luminous body, by the intervention of some other body either between it and the eye or between the luminous body and that illuminated by it; an eclipse of the moon, for instance, being caused by the earth coming between it and the sun; *fig.* a darkening or obscuring of splendor, brightness, or glory.—*v.t.*—*eclipsed, eclipsing.* To cause the eclipse or obscuration of; to cloud; to darken, obscure, throw into the shade; to cloud the glory of.—*v.i.* To suffer an eclipse.—**ecliptic,** i•klip′tik, *n.* [L. *linea ecliptica,* the ecliptic line, or line in which eclipses take place.] A great circle of the celestial sphere supposed to be drawn through the middle of the zodiac, making an angle with the equinoctial of about 23° 27′; the path which the sun, owing to the annual revolution of the earth, appears to describe among the fixed stars; a great circle on the terrestrial globe, answering to and falling within the plane of the celestial ecliptic.—*a.* Pertaining to or described by the ecliptic; pertaining to an eclipse.

eclogue, ek′log, *n.* [L. *ecloga,* Gr. *eklogē,* selection, from *eklegō,* to select. ECLECTIC.] A poetical composition in which shepherds are introduced conversing with each other; a bucolic.

ecology, ek•ol′o•jē, *n.* [Gr. *oikos,* a dwelling, *logos,* a discourse.] The branch of biology that deals with the relation between organisms and their natural environment.

economy, i•kon′o•mi, *n.* [L. *œconomia,* Gr. *oikonomia—oikos,* house, and *nomos,* law, rule.] The management, regulation, and government of a household; especially, the management of the pecuniary concerns of a household; hence, a frugal and judicious use of money; that management which expends money to advantage and incurs no waste; a prudent management of all the means by which property is saved or accumulated; a judicious application of time, of labor, and of the instruments of labor; the disposition or arrangement of any work or the system of rules and regulations which control it; the operations of nature in the generation, nutrition, and preservation of animals and plants; the regular, harmonious system in accordance with which the functions of living animals and plants are performed; the regulation and disposition of the internal affairs of a state or nation, or of any department of government.—**economic, economical,** ek•o•nom′ik, ek•o•nom′i•kal, *a.* Managing domestic or public pecuniary concerns with frugality; frugal; thrifty; relating to the science of economics, or the pecuniary and other productive resources of a country; relating to the means of living.—**economically,** ē•ko•nom′i•kal•li, *adv.*—**economics,** ē•ko•nom′iks, *n.* A social science that investigates the conditions and laws affecting the production, distribution, and consumption of the national wealth; formerly political economy.—**economist,** i•kon′o•mist, *n.*—One who manages domestic or other concerns with frugality; one who practices economy; one versed in economics or the science of political economy.—**economize,** i•kon'o•mīz, *v.i.*—*economized, economizing.* To manage pecuniary concerns with frugality; to make a prudent use of money, or of the means of having or acquiring property.—*v.t.* To use with prudence; to expend with frugality.

ecstasy, ek'sta•si, *n.* [Gr. *ekstasis,* a standing out, a displacement, distraction, astonishment—*ek,* out, and *histēmi,* to stand (from root of *stand*).] A state in which the mind is carried away as it were from the body; a state in which the functions of the senses are suspended by the contemplation of some extraordinary or supernatural object; a kind of trance; excessive joy; rapture; a degree of delight that arrests the whole mind; extreme delight; madness or distraction (*Shak.*)‡.—**ecstatic, ecstatical,** ek•stat'ik, ek•stat'i•kal, *a.* Pertaining to or resulting from ecstasy; suspending the senses; entrancing; rapturous; transporting; delightful beyond measure.—**ecstatically,** ek•stat'i•kal•li, *adv.* In an ecstatic manner.

ectoblast, ek'to•blast, *n.* [Gr. *ektos,* outside, and *blastos,* bud, germ.] *Physiol.* the membrane composing the walls of a cell, as distinguished from *mesoblast,* the nucleus, and *entoblast,* the nucleolus.

ectoderm, ek'to•dėrm, *n.* [Gr. *ecto,* outermost, and *dermos,* skin.] *Zool.* the outermost of the three primary germ layers of an embryo.—**ectodermal,** ek•to•dėrm'al, *a.* Belonging to the ectoderm.—**ectoparasite,** ek•to•par'a•sīt, *n.* A parasitic animal infesting the outside of animals; as opposed to *endoparasite,* which lives in the body.—**ectosarc,** ek'to•särk, *n.* [Gr. *sarx, sarkos,* flesh.] *Zool.* the outer transparent sarcode-layer of certain Protozoa, such as the amoeba.

ectoplasm, ek'to•plazm, *n.* [Gr. *ektos,* outside, and *plasma.* PLASM.] *Biol.* the exterior portion of a cell; matter forming a cell wall.

ectype, ek'tīp, *n.* [Gr. *ektypos,* worked in high relief—*ek,* out, and *typos,* type.] A reproduction of, or very close resemblance to, an original; opposed to *prototype;* a copy in relief or embossed.—**ectypal,** ek•tī'pal, *a.* Taken from the original; imitated.

ecumenic, ecumenical, ek•ū•men'ik, ek•ū•men'i•kal, *a.* [L. *œcumenicus,* Gr. *oikoumenē,* the habitable earth, from *oikos,* a habitation.] General; universal; specifically, an epithet applied to an ecclesiastical council regarded as representing the whole Christian Church, or the whole Catholic Church.

eczema, ek'zē•ma, *n.* [Gr., from *ekzeō,* to boil out—*ek,* out, and *zeō,* to boil.] An eruptive disease of the skin, characterized by minute vesicles which burst and discharge a thin acrid fluid, often giving rise to excoriation; one form is popularly known as grocers' itch.—**eczematous,** ek•zem'a•tus, *a.* Pertaining to or produced by eczema.

edacious, i•dā'shus, *a.* [L. *edax,* from *edo,* to eat.] Eating; given to eating; greedy; voracious.—**edacity,** i•das'i•ti, *n.* [L. *edacitas.*] Greediness; voracity; ravenousness; rapacity.

Edam cheese, ē'dam•chēz, *n.* [From the village of *Edam,* near Amsterdam.] A pressed, fine-flavored, yellow, Dutch cheese made in balls, weighing three to four pounds, and colored dark red on the outside.

Edda, ed'a, *n.* [Icel., great-grandmother; a name given to indicate that it is the mother of all Scandinavian poetry.] The name of two Scandinavian books, dating from the eleventh to the thirteenth century: first, the *Elder* or *Poetic Edda,* a collection of pagan poems or chants of a mythic, prophetic, mostly all of a religious character; second, the *Younger* or *Prose Edda,* a kind of prose synopsis of Scandinavian mythology.

eddy, ed'i, *n.* [From Icel. *itha,* an eddy, from prefix *ith,* Goth. *id,* A.Sax. *ed,* again, back.] A current of air or water turning round in a direction contrary to the main stream; a whirlpool; a current of water or air moving circularly.—*v.i.*—*eddied, eddying.* To move circularly, or as an eddy.—*v.t.* To cause to move in an eddy; to collect as into an eddy.

edelweiss, ā'dl•vīs, *n.* [G. *edel,* noble, *weiss,* white.] A composite plant inhabiting the Alps, and having a specially woolly foliage and involucre.

edema, i•dē'ma, *n.* [Gr. *oidēma,* a swelling, from *oideō,* to swell.] *Med.* a puffiness or swelling of parts arising from water collecting.—**edematous, edematose,** i•dē'ma•tus, i•dē'mā•tōs, *a.* Relating to edema.

Eden, ē'den, *n.* [Heb, and Chal, *eden,* delight, pleasure, a place of pleasure.] The garden in which Adam and Eve were placed by God; hence, a delightful region or residence.

edentate, ē•den'tāt, *a.* [L. *edentatus*—*e, ex,* out of, and *dens, dentis,* a tooth.] Destitute or deprived of teeth; pertaining to the Edentata.—*n.* An animal belonging to the order Edentata.

edge, ej, *n.* [A.Sax. *ecg,* edge, whence *ecgian, eggian,* to sharpen, to egg= D. *egge,* Icel. and Sw. *egg,* G. *ecke,* edge, corner; from an Indo-European root *ak,* seen in L. *acies,* an edge, *acus,* a needle, *acuo,* to sharpen; akin *acid, acute, eager.*] The thin cutting side of an instrument; the abrupt border or margin of anything; the brink; the border or part adjacent to a line of division; the part nearest some limit; sharpness of mind or appetite; keenness; intenseness of desire; sharpness; acrimony.—*To set the teeth on edge,* to cause a tingling or grating sensation in the teeth.—*v.t.*—*edged, edging.* To sharpen; to furnish with an edge, fringe, or border; to exasperate; to embitter; to incite; to provoke; to instigate; to move sideways; to move by little and little.—*v.i.* To move sideways or gradually; to advance or retire gradually.—**edgewise,** ej'wīz, *adv.* With the edge turned forward or toward a particular point; in the direction of the edge; sideways; with the side foremost.—**edging,** ej'ing, *n.* That which is added on the border or which forms the edge, as lace, fringe, trimming, added to a garment for ornament; a row of small plants set along the border of a flower bed.—**edgebone,** *n.* AITCH-BONE.—**edge tool,** *n.* An instrument having a sharp or cutting edge; *fig.* something dangerous to deal or sport with.—**edgy,** ej'ē, *a.* Having an edge; nervous or anxious; eager; impatient; snappish.—**edgily,** ej'i•li, *adv.*—**edginess,** ej'ē•nes, *n.* Nervousness; irritability.

edible, ed'i•bl, *a.* [L.L. *edibilis,* from L. *edo,* to eat.] Fit to be eaten as food; eatable; esculent.—*n.* Anything that may be eaten for food; an article of food; a comestible.—**edibility, edibleness,** ed•i•bil'i•ti, ed'i•bl•nes, *n.* The quality of being edible.

edict, ē'dikt, *n.* [L. *edictum,* from *edico,* utter or proclaim—*e,* out, and *dico,* to speak. DICTION.] An order issued by a prince to his subjects, as a rule or law requiring obedience; a proclamation of command or prohibition; a decree.—**edictal,** ē•dik'tal, *a.* Pertaining to an edict.

edify, ed'i•fī, *v.t.*—*edified, edifying.* [Fr. *édifier,* from L. *ædificare,* to build, erect, construct—*ædes,* a house and *facio,* to make.] To build or construct‡; to instruct and improve in knowledge generally, and particularly in moral and religious knowledge, or in faith and holiness.—*v.i.* To cause or tend to cause a moral or intellectual improvement.—**edifier,** ed'i•fī•ėr, *n.* One who edifies.—**edifying,** ed'i•fī•ing, *a.* Adapted to edify; having the effect of instructing and improving.—**edification,** ed'i•fi•kā"shon, *n.* The act of edifying; improvement and progress of the mind in knowledge, in morals or in faith and holiness.—**edifice,** ed'i•fis *n.* [L. *ædificium,* a building. EDIFY.] A building; a structure; a fabric: chiefly applied to houses and other large structures.—**edificial,** ed•i•fish'al, *a.* Pertaining to an edifice or structure; structural.

edile, ē'dil, *n.* [L. *ædilis,* from *ædes,* a building.] A magistrate of ancient Rome who had the superintendence of buildings of all kinds, especially public edifices, and also the care of the highways, public places, weights and measures, etc.

edit, ed'it, *v.t.* [L. *edo, editum,* to give forth, to publish—*e* forth, and *do, datum,* to give, whence *date, dative.*] To superintend the publication of; to prepare, as a book or paper, for the public eye, by writing, correcting, or selecting the matter; to conduct or manage as regards literary contents or matter; to publish.—**edition,**

i•dish′on, *n.* A literary work as bearing a special stamp or form when first published or subsequently; a work as characterized by editorial labors; the whole number of copies of a work published at once.—**editor,** ed′i•tėr, *n.* One who edits; a person who superintends, revises, corrects, and prepares a book, newspaper, or magazine for publication.—**editorial,** ed•i•tō′ri•al, *a.* Pertaining to, proceeding from, or written by an editor.—*n.* An article, as in a newspaper, written by the editor; a leading article.—**editorially,** ed•i•tō′ri•al•li, *adv.* In the manner or character of an editor.—**editorship,** ed′i•tėr•ship, *n.* The business of an editor; the care and superintendence of a publication.

educate, ed′ū•kāt, *v.t.—educated, educating.* [L. *educo, educatum,* from *educo, eductum,* to lead forth, to bring up a child—*e,* out, and *duco,* to lead. DUKE.] To inform and enlighten the understanding of; to cultivate and train the mental powers of; to qualify for the business and duties of life; to teach; to instruct; to train; to rear.—**education,** ed•ū•kā′shon, *n.* The act of educating, teaching, or training; the act or art of developing and cultivating the various physical, intellectual, aesthetic, and moral faculties; instruction and discipline; tuition; nurture; learning; erudition.—**educational,** ed•ū•kā′shon•al, *a.* Pertaining to education; derived from education.—**educationalist, educationist,** ed•ū•kā′shon•al•ist, ed•ū•kā′shon•ist, *n.* One who is versed in or who advocates or promotes education.—**educative,** ed′ū•kā•tiv, *a.* Tending or having the power to educate.—**educator,** ed′ū•kā•tėr, *n.* One who or that which educates.

educe, i•dūs′, *v.t.—educed, educing.* [L. *educo, eductum—e,* out, and *duco,* to lead. EDUCATE.] To bring or draw out: to cause to appear; to extract.—**educible,** i•dū′si•bl, *a.* Capable of being educed.—**educt,** i′dukt, *n.* Extracted matter; a substance brought to light by separation, analysis, or decomposition; anything educed or drawn from another; an inference.—**eduction,** i•duk′shon, *n.* The act of educing, drawing out, or bringing into view.

edulcorate, i•dul′ko•rāt, *v.t.—edulcorated, edulcorating.* [L. *e,* out, and *dulcoro, dulcoratum,* to sweeten, from *dulcor,* sweetness, *dulcis,* sweet.] To remove acidity from; to sweeten†; *chem.* to free from acids, salts, or impurities by washing.—**edulcoration,** i•dul′ko•rā″shon, *n.* The act of sweetening by admixture of some saccharine substance†; *chem.* the act of freeing from acid or saline substances, or from any soluble impurities, by repeated affusions of water.—**edulcorative,** i•dul′ko•rā•tiv, *a.* Having the quality of sweetening or removing acidity.

eel, ēl, *n.* [A.Sax. *ael*=Dan. D. and G. *aal,* Icel. *all*; not connected with Gr. *echis,* Skr. *ahi,* a serpent; L. *anguilla,* an eel, *anguis,* a snake.] A fish characterized by its slimy serpent-like elongated body, by the absence of ventral fins, and the continuity of the dorsal and anal fins round the extremity of the tail; some species are marine, some fresh-water; all are remarkable for their voracity and tenacity of life, many are considered excellent food.—**eelpout,** *n.* [A.Sax. *aele-puta.*] The name of two different species of fish—the viviparous blenny and the burbot.

e'en, ēn, *adv.* A contraction for *Even.*

e'er, âr, *adv.* A contraction for *Ever.*

eerie, ē′ri, *a.* [A.Sax. *earh,* timid.] Calculated to inspire fear; dreary; lonely; weird; superstitiously affected by fear, especially when lonely.—**eeriness,** ē′ri•nes, *n.* The state or quality of being eerie.

efface, ef•fās′, *v.t.—effaced, effacing.* [Fr. *effacer*—L. *e,* out, and *facies,* a face. Comp. *deface.*] To destroy, as a figure, on the surface of anything, so as to render it invisible or not distinguishable; to blot out; to erase, strike, or scratch out; to remove from the mind; to wear away.—**effaceable,** ef•fā′sa•bl, *a.* Capable of being effaced.—**effacement,** ef•fās′ment, *n.* Act of effacing; state of being effaced.

effect, ef•fekt′, *n.* [L. *effectus,* from *efficio—ex,* and *facio,* to make. FACT.] That which is produced by an operating agent or cause; the result or consequence of the action of a cause or agent; consequence; result: power to produce consequences or results; force, validity, or importance; purport, import, tenor, or general intent; reality and not mere appearance; fact: preceded by *in*; the impression produced on the mind, as by natural scenery, a picture, musical composition, or other work of art, by the object as a whole, before its details are examined; *pl.* goods; movables; personal estate.—*v.t.* To produce, as a cause or agent; to bring about or cause to be; to bring to pass; to achieve; to accomplish.—**effecter,** ef•fek′tėr, *n.* One who effects, produces, causes, or brings about.—**effectible,**† ef•fek′ti•bl, *a.* Capable of being effected.—**effective,** ef•fek′tiv, *a.* Having the power to cause or produce effect; efficacious; operative; active; efficient; having the power of active operation; fit for duty.—**effectively,** ef•fek′tiv•li, *adv.* In an effective manner.—**effectiveness,** ef•fek′tiv•nes, *n.* The quality of being effective.—**effectual,** ef•fek′chū•al, *a.* Producing an effect, or the effect desired or intended; having adequate power or force to produce the effect.—**effectually,** ef•fek′chū•al•li, *adv.* In an effectual manner.—**effectuate,** ef•fek′chū•āt, *v.t.—effectuated, effectuating.* [Fr. *effectuer.*] To bring to pass; to achieve; to accomplish; to fulfill.—**effectuation,** ef•fek′chū•ā″shon, *n.* Act of effectuating.

effeminate, ef•fem′i•nit, *a.* [L. *effeminatus,* from *effeminor,* to grow or make womanish, from *ex,* out, and *femina,* a woman.] Having the qualities of a woman instead of those of a man; soft or delicate to an unmanly degree; weak and unmanly; womanish; voluptuous.—*v.t.—effeminated, effeminating.* To make womanish or effeminate.—*v.i.* To grow womanish or weak.—**effeminacy,** ef•fem′i•na•si, *n.* The state or character of being effeminate.

effendi, ef•fen′di, *n.* [Turk.] A title of respect frequently attached to the official title of certain Turkish officers, especially learned men and ecclesiastics.

efferent, ef′fėr•ent, *a.* [L. *ef* for *ex,* out of, and *fero,* to carry.] *Physiol.* conveying outward or discharging.

effervesce, ef•fėr•ves′, *v.i.—effervesced, effervescing.* [L. *effervesco—ef, ex,* out of, and *fervesco,* to begin boiling, from *ferveo,* to be hot. FERVENT.] To bubble and hiss or froth and sparkle, as fermenting liquors or any fluid when some part escapes in a gaseous form; to work, as new wine; *fig.* to exhibit signs of excitement; to exhibit feelings which cannot be suppressed.—**effervescence,** ef•fėr•ves′ens, *n.* That commotion, bubbling, frothing, or sparkling of a fluid which takes place when some part of the mass flies off in a gaseous form, producing innumerable small bubbles; strong excitement or manifestation of feeling; flow of animal spirits.—**effervescent,** ef•fėr•ves′ent, *a.* Effervescing.

effete, ef•fēt′, *a.* [L. *effetus,* exhausted, worn out by bearing—*ex,* and *fetus,* fruitful, pregnant.] Having the energies worn out or exhausted; having the vigor lost or dissipated; barren.

efficacious, ef•fi•kā′shus, *a.* [L. *efficax,* efficacious, from *efficio.* EFFECT.] Effectual; productive of effects; producing the effect intended; having power adequate to the purpose intended.—**efficaciously,** ef•fi•kā′shus•li, *adv.* In an efficacious manner.—**efficaciousness,** ef•fi•kā′shus•nes, *n.* The quality of being efficacious.—**efficacy,** ef′fi•ka•si, *n.* [L. *efficacia,* efficacy.] Power to produce effects; production of the effect intended; effectiveness; efficiency; virtue; energy.—**efficiency,** ef•fish′en•si, *n.* [L. *efficientia.*] The state or character of being efficient; effectual agency; power of producing the effect intended; active competent power; competence for one's duties; in any mechanical contrivance, the ratio of the useful work obtained to the energy expended.—**efficient,** ef•fish′ent *a.* Causing effects; causing anything to be what it is; efficacious; effectual; competent; able; operative.—*n.* One who is competent to perform the duties of a service.—**efficiently,** ef•fish′ent•li, *adv.* In an efficient manner.

effigy, ef′fi•ji, *n.* [L. *effigies,* from *effingo,* to fashion—*ef* for *ex,* and *fingo,* to form or devise. FEIGN.] The image, likeness, or representation of a person or thing; a likeness in sculpture, painting, or otherwise; an image; frequently applied to the figures on sepulchral monuments.—**effigial,**† ef•fij′i•al, *a.* Exhibiting or pertaining to an effigy.

effloresce, ef•flo•res′, *v.i.*—*effloresced, efflorescing.* [L. *effloresco*—*ef* for *ex,* and *floresco,* from *floreo,* to blossom, from *flos,* a flower. FLOWER.] To burst into bloom, as a flower; to break out into florid or excessive ornamentation; *chem.* to change over the surface or throughout to a whitish, mealy, or crystalline powder, from a gradual decomposition, on simple exposure to the air; to become covered with a whitish crust or light crystallization, from a slow chemical change.—**efflorescence,** ef•flo•res′-ens, *n.* The act or process of efflorescing; *bot.* the time of flowering; the production of blossoms; *med.* a redness of the skin; eruption; *chem.* the formation of a whitish substance on the surface of certain bodies, as salts; the powder or crust thus formed.—**efflorescent,** ef•flo•res′ent, *a.* Showing efflorescence; incrusted or covered with efflorescence; liable to effloresce.

effluence, ef′flū•ens, *n.* [Fr. *effluence,* from L. *effluo,* to flow out—*e, ex,* and *fluo,* to flow.] The act of flowing out; that which flows out or issues; an emanation.—**effluent,** ef′flū•ent, *a.* Flowing out; emanating; emitted.—*n. Geog.* a stream that flows out of another stream or out of a lake.

effluvium, ef•flū′vi•um, *n.* pl. effluvia, ef•flū′vi•a. [L., from *effluo,* to flow out, FLOW.] Something flowing out in a subtle or invisible form; exhalation; emanation; especially applied to noxious or disagreeable exhalations.—**effluvial,** ef•flū′vi•al, *a.* Pertaining to or containing effluvia.

efflux, ef′fluks, *n.* [L. *effluo, effluxum,* to flow out. EFFLUENCE.] The act or state of flowing out or issuing in a stream; outflow; that which flows out; emanation.

effort, ef′fėrt, *n.* [Fr. *effort*—L. *ef* for *ex,* out, and *fortis,* strong.] An exertion of strength or power, whether physical or mental; strenuous exertion to accomplish an object; a straining to do something; endeavor.—**effortless,** ef′fėrt•les, *a.* Making no effort.

effrontery, ef•frun′tėr•i, *n.* [Fr. *effronterie,* from L. *effrons, effrontis,* barefaced, shameless—*ef* for *ex,* and *frons,* the forehead. FRONT.] Audacious impudence or boldness; assurance entirely unabashed; shamelessness; brazenness.

effulge, ef•fulj′, *v.i.*—*effulged, effulging.* [L. *effulgeo*—*ef* for *ex,* out, and *fulgeo,* to shine.] To send forth a flood of light; to shine with splendor.—**effulgence,** ef•ful′jens, *n.* A flood of light; a shining forth of light or glory; great luster or brightness; splendor.—**effulgent,** ef•ful′jent, *a.* Shining; bright; splendid; diffusing a flood of light.—**effulgently,** ef•ful′-jent•li, *adv.* In a bright or splendid manner.

effuse, ef•fūz′, *v.t.*—*effused, effusing.* [L. *effundo, effusum,* to pour out—*ef* for *ex,* out, and *fundo, fusum,* to pour. FUSE.] To pour out, as a fluid; to spill; to shed.—*v.i.* To emanate; to come forth.—*a.* (ef′fūs). *Bot.* applied to a kind of panicle with a very loose one-sided arrangement; *conch.* applied to shells where the aperture is not whole behind, but the lips are separated by a gap or groove.—**effusion,** ef•fū′zhon, *n.* The act of pouring out; that which is poured out; *pathol.* the escape of any fluid out of the vessel containing it into another part; cordiality of manner; overflowing or demonstrative kindness.—**effusive,** ef•fū′siv, *a.* Pouring out; pouring forth largely; showing overflowing kindness or cordiality of manner.—**effusively,** ef•fū′siv•li, *adv.* In an effusive manner.—**effusiveness,** ef•fū′siv•nes, *n.*

eft, eft, *n.* [O.E. *evete, ewte,* A.Sax. *efete. Newt* is from *ewte,* the *n* of the art. *an* having adhered to the noun.] A newt.

egad, ē•gad′, *exclam.* [Probably a euphemistic corruption of 'by God'.] An exclamation expressing exultation or surprise.

egest, ē•jest′, *v.t.* [L. *egero, egestum,* to carry or bear out.—*e,* out, and *gero,* to carry.] To cast or throw out; to void excrement.—**egestion,** ē•jest′-yon, *n.* The act of voiding excrement.

egg, eg, *n.* [A.Sax. *æg*=Icel. *egg,* Dan. *æg,* Sw. *ägg,* G. and D. *ei;* allied in origin to L. *ovum,* Gr. *ōon,* Ir. *ugh,* Gael. *ubh,* an egg.] A roundish body covered with a shell or membrane, formed in a special organ of many female animals besides birds, and in which the development of the young animal takes place; an ovum. [Animals whose young do not leave the egg till after it is laid are called *oviparous;* those in which the eggs are retained within the parent body until they are hatched are called *ovoviviparous.*]—*Egg and anchor, egg and dart, egg and tongue, arch.* same as *Echinus.*—**egger,** eg′ėr, *n.* Any of various moths (family Lasiocampidae) whose larvae feed on leaves.—**egghead,** *n.* An intellectual; highbrow.—**eggnog,** *n.* A drink of eggs beaten with sugar, milk, and sometimes whiskey.—**eggplant,** *n.* A plant of the potato family (*Solanum melongena*) with egg-shaped fruits, which are boiled, stewed in sauces, etc., and served as a vegetable.

egg, eg *v.t.* [A.Sax. *ecgian, eggian,* to incite, to sharpen; Icel. *eggja,* to egg. EDGE.] To incite or urge on; to stimulate; to instigate; to provoke.

egis, ē′jis, *n.* Same as *Aegis.*

eglantine, eg′lan•tīn, *n.* [Fr. *églantine,* O.Fr. *aiglent,* from a form *aculentus,* prickly, from L. *aculeus,* a spine, a prickle, *acus,* a needle. ACID.] An old and poetical name for the sweetbrier or wild rose.

ego, ē′gō, *n.* [L. *ego,* I.] The self; the self as distinguished from any other self; one's will; self-esteem; *philos.* the complete man comprising body and soul; *psych.* that part of man that experiences and reacts to the outside world.—**egocentric,** ē′gō-sen″trik, *a.* Concern with the individual rather than society; selfish.—**egoism,** ē′gō•izm, *n.* Evaluating experience only by one's personal interest; the doctine that all action is motivated by self-interest.—**egoist,** e′go•ist, *n.* A selfish or self-centered person; egotist; one holding the doctrine of egoism.—**egoistic, egoistical,** ē•gō•is′tik, ē•gō•is′ti•kal, *a.* Pertaining to egoism; addicted to or manifesting egoism; egotistic.—**egoistically,** ē•gō•is′ti•kal•li, *adv.* In an egoistic manner.—**egotism,** ē′go•tizm, *n.* The practice of too frequently using the word *I;* hence, a speaking or writing much of one's self; a passionate and exaggerated love of self, leading one to refer all things to one's self, and to judge of everything by its relation to one's interests or importance. ∴ *Egotism* and *self-conceit* are based on what we think of ourselves, the former being the more deep-seated and powerful; *vanity,* on what we believe others think of us.—**egotist,** ē′go•tist, *n.* One who repeats the word *I* very often in conversation or writing; one who speaks much of himself or magnifies his own achievements.—**egotistic, egotistical,** ē•go•tis′tik, ē•go•tis′ti•kal, *a.* Addicted to egotism; manifesting egotism.—**egotistically,** ē•go•tis′ti•kal•li, *adv.* In an egotistical or self-conceited manner.

egregious, i•grē′ji•us, *a.* [L. *egregius,* lit. out of the common flock or herd—*e* or *ex,* out, and *grex, gregis,* a flock (whence *gregarious*).] Extraordinary; remarkable; enormous: now mostly used in a bad or ironical sense (an *egregious* fool, blunder, impudence).—**egregiously,** i•grē′ji•us•li, *adv.* In an egregious manner.—**egregiousness,** i•grē′ji•us•nes, *n.*

egress, ē′gres, *n.* [L. *egressus,* from *egredior*—*e,* and *gradior,* to step. GRADE.] The act of going or issuing out; the power of departing from any enclosed or confined place; *astron.* the passing of an inferior planet from the disk of the sun in a transit.—*v.i.* (ē•gres′) To go out; to depart; to leave.—**egression,**† ē•gresh′on, *n.* [L. *egressio.*] Egress.—**egressor,** ē•gres′-ėr, *n.* One who goes out.

egret, ē′gret, *n.* [Fr. *aigrette,* a dim. from an old form *aigre,* from O.H.G. *heigro,* a heron, Sw. *häger,* Icel. *hegri,* a heron. *Heron* has the same origin.] A name of those species of herons which have the feathers on the lower part of the back lengthened and the barbs loose, so that this part of the plumage is very soft and flowing; the small white heron; a plume of heron's feathers, or of feathers, diamonds, etc.; an aigret.

Egyptian, i•jip′shan, *a.* [From *Egypt,* Gr. *Aigyptos;* akin *Gypsy.*] Pertaining to Egypt.—*Egyptian vulture,* a vulture, about the size of a raven, which frequents the streets of eastern towns, where it is protected on account of its services as a scavenger. Called also *Pharaoh's chicken.*—*n.* A native of Egypt; an old designation for a gypsy, so called because believed to have come from Egypt.—**Egyptologist,** ē•jip•tol′o•jist, *n.* One well acquainted with the antiquities of

Egypt, especially the hieroglyphic inscriptions and documents.—**Egyptological,** i•jip′to•loj″i•kal, *a.* Pertaining to Egyptology; devoted to the study of Egyptology.—**Egyptology,** ē•jip•tol′o•ji, *n.* The science of Egyptian antiquities; that branch of knowledge which treats of the ancient language, history, etc., of Egypt.

eider, eider duck, ī′dėr, *n.* [G. *eider*, Sw. *eider*, Icel. *ædr.* Dan. *eder.*] A species of large duck, with down that is much valued for its warmth, lightness, and elasticity.

eidolon, ī•dō′lon, *n.* [IDOL.] An unreal or spectral form; a phantom.

eight, āt, *a.* [A.Sax. *eahta*=G. and D. *acht*, Icel. *átta*, Dan. *aatte*, L. *octo*, Gr. *oktō*, Ir. and Gael. *achd*, Skr. *ashtan, ashtau.*] One of the cardinal numeral adjectives; one more than seven and less than nine.—*n.* The number composed of seven and one; the symbol representing this number. —**eighteen,** ā′tēn, *a.* and *n.* Eight and ten; the sum of ten and eight; the symbol representing this sum.—**eighteenmo,** ā•tēn′mō, *n.* [From *eighteen* and *-mo*, in L. *decimo*, tenth.] The size of a book in which a sheet is folded into eighteen leaves: written often 18*mo*.—**eighteenth,** ā′tēnth, *a.* and *n.* Next in order after the seventeenth; one of eighteen equal parts of a thing.—**eightfold,** āt′fōld, *a.* Eight times the number or quantity. —**eighth,** āth, *a.* and *n.* Next in order after the seventh; one of eight equal parts of anything; an octave.—**eighth note,** *n.* A musical note having one eighth the time value of a whole note; a quaver.—**eightieth,** ā′ti•eth, *a.* and *n.* Next in order to the seventy-ninth; one of eighty equal parts of anything.—**eighty,** ā′ti, *a.* and *n.* Eight times ten; fourscore.

einsteinium, īn•stī′ni•um, *n.* [From Albert Einstein.] A synthetic, radioactive, metallic element. Symbol, Es; at. no., 99.

Einstein theory, *n.* The theory of *Relativity* developed by Albert Einstein.

eisteddfod, ās•teTH′vōd, *n.* [W.] A meeting of bards and minstrels in Wales; a periodical Welsh festival for the recitation of poems.

either, ē′THėr or ī′THėr; the former is more in accordance with analogy, *a.* or *pron.* [A.Sax. *aegther*; contracted from *aeghwæther*, compounded of *a*=*aye*, the augment *ge*, and *hwæther.* EACH, WHETHER.] One or the other; one of two things; each of two; the one and the other; both. —*conj.* A disjunctive conjunction always used as correlative to and preceding *or* (*either* the one *or* the other).

ejaculate, i•jak′ū•lāt, *v.t.*—*ejaculated, ejaculating.* [L. *ejaculor, ejaculatus*—*e*, out, and *jaculum*, a dart, from *jacio*, to throw, seen also in *reject, project*, etc.] To throw out, as an exclamation; to utter suddenly and briefly.—*v.i.*† To utter ejaculations.—**ejaculation,** i•jak′ū•lā″shon, *n.* The uttering of a short, sudden exclamation; the exclamation uttered; a prayer consisting of a few words.—**ejaculatory,** i•jak′ū•la•to•ri, *a.* Of the nature of an ejaculation.

eject, i•jekt′, *v.t.* [L. *ejicio, ejectum*—*e*, and *jacio*, to throw, as in *dejected, project*, etc.] To throw out; to cast forth; to thrust out; to drive away; to expel; to dismiss from office; to turn out.—**ejection,** i•jek′shon, *n.* [L. *ejectio.*] The act of ejecting; dismissal; dispossession; expulsion; rejection.—**ejectment,** i•jekt′ment, *n.* A casting out; a dispossession; *law*, the removal of a person from the wrongful possession of land or tenements.—**ejector,** i•jek′tėr, *n.* One who ejects.

eke, ēk, *v.t.*—*eked, eking.* [A.Sax. *écan*, to increase, to eke, Icel. *auka*, Goth. *aukan*, L. *augeo* (whence *augment*), Gr. *auxanō*, to increase.] To add to so as to make up for any deficiencies; to make a supply last by economy. ∴ Used with *out*, and refers to the supply, not to the result of the addition.

elaborate, i•lab′o•rāt, *v.t.*—*elaborated, elaborating.* [L. *elaboro, elaboratum*—*e*, out, and *laboro*, to labor, from *labor*, labor.] To produce with labor; to work out or complete with great care; to work out fully or perfectly.—*a.* Wrought with labor; finished with great care; executed with exactness; highly finished.—**elaborately,** i•lab′o•rit•li, *adv.* In an elaborate manner.—**elaborateness,** i•lab′o•rit•nes, *n.* The quality of being elaborate.—**elaboration,** i•lab′-o•rā″shon, *n.* The act of elaborating; careful or laborious finish bestowed; *physiol.* the process performed by the living organs in animals and plants by which something is produced (the *elaboration* of sap).—**elaborative,** i•lab′o•rā•tiv, *a.* Serving or tending to elaborate.—**elaborator,** i•lab′o-•ra•tėr, *n.* One who or that which elaborates.

eland, ē′land, *n.* [D. *eland*, an elk.] An African species of antelope, the largest of all antelopes; a name sometimes given to the moose.

elapse, i•laps′, *v.i.*—*elapsed, elapsing.* [L. *elabor, elapsus*, to slip away—*e*, out, and *labor, lapsus*, to glide. LAPSE.] To slip or glide away; to pass away silently: said of time.

elastic, i•las′tik, *a.* [Fr. *élastique*, L.L. *elasticus*, from Gr. *elastos*, beaten out, extensible, from *elaunō*, to drive, to beat out.] Having the power of returning to the form from which it is bent or extended; having the property of recovering its former figure or volume after being altered by pressure; rebounding; flying back; *fig.* possessing the power or quality of recovering from depression or exhaustion.—*Elastic limit*, for any material, is the maximum stress per unit area that can be applied without causing an appreciable permanent set.—**elastically,** i•las′ti•kal•li, *adv.* In an elastic manner; by elastic power.—**elasticity,** i•las•tis′i•ti, *n.*—**elastomer,** i•las′ta•mėr, *n.* Any elastic substance having the physical qualities of natural rubber.

elate, i•lāt′, *a.* [L. *elatus*, pp. of *effero*—*e*, out, and *latus*, borne or carried.] Raised or lifted up†; having the spirits lifted up; flushed, as with success; exultant; haughty.—*v.t.*—*elated, elating.* To raise; to exalt; to elevate with success; to cause to exult; to make proud.—**elatedly,** i•lā′ted•li, *adv.* With elation.—**elation,** i•lā′shon, *n.* Elevation of mind proceeding from self-approbation; haughtiness; pride of prosperity.

elater, el′a•tėr, *n.* [Gr. *elatēr*, a driver.] An elastic spiral filament generated in tubes in certain liverworts and scale mosses, and supposed to assist in the dispersion of spores; a name of various small leaping beetles.

elaterium, el•a•tē′ri•um, *n.* [Gr. *elatērion*, from *elatērios*, driving, purgative, from *elatēr*, a driver, from *elaunō*, to drive.] A substance obtained from the fruit of the squirting cucumber, serving as a drastic purge.

elbow, el′bō, *n.* [A.Sax. *elboga, elnboga*—*el, eln*, forearm, an ell (akin to L. *ulna*, Gr. *ōlenē*, the forearm), and *boga*, a bow; D. *elleboog*, G. *ellbogen, ellenbogen*, Icel. *alnbogi.* ELL, BOW.] The outer angle made by the bend of the arm; the joint which unites the upper arm with the forearm; a flexure, angle, or part of a structure somewhat resembling an elbow, or which supports the arm or elbow, as the raised arm of a chair or sofa.—*Out at elbows*, having holes in the elbows of one's clothes; shabbily dressed.—*v.t.* To push or jostle with the elbow; to make or gain (a path through a crowd) by pushing with the elbows.—*v.i.* To jut into an elbow or angle; to push one's way. —**elbow grease,** *n.* Vigorous physical exertion.—**elbowroom,** *n.* Room to extend the elbows on each side, hence, ample room for motion or action.

elder, el′dėr, *a.* [A.Sax. *yldra, eldra*, the compar. degree of *eald* old. OLD.] Having lived a longer time; of greater age; born, produced, or formed before something else; opposed to *younger*; prior in origin; senior; pertaining to earlier times; earlier.—*n.* [A.Sax. *ealdor*, an ancestor, a chief, a prince.] One who is older than another or others; an ancestor; a person advanced in life, and who, on account of his age, experience, and wisdom, is selected for office; a lay official in Presbyterian churches, who acts along with the minister in the administration of discipline and government, having an equal vote with the latter in all church courts.—**elderly,** el′dėr•li *a.* Somewhat old; advanced beyond middle age; bordering on old age.—**eldership,** el′dėr•ship, *n.* The office of an elder; elders collectively; order of elders.—**eldest,** el′dest, *a.* [A.Sax. *yldest*, superl. of *eald, ald*, old.] Oldest; most advanced in age; that was born before others.

elder, el′dėr, *n.* [A.Sax. *ellern, ellen*; the *d* has been inserted in later times; D. *elloorn*, the elder; perhaps akin to *alder.*] Any tree or shrub of the honeysuckle family of rapid growth with white flowers and purple berries, and containing an unusual quantity of pith.—**elderberry,** *n.* The fruit of the elder.

El Dorado, el do•rä'dō or el do•rā'dō, *n.* [Sp. the golden—*el*, the, and *dorado*, gilt.] A country formerly reputed to exist in South America, and possessing immense stores of gold; hence; any region rich in gold or treasure of any kind.

Eleatic, el•i•at'ik *a.* Of or pertaining to *Elea*, an ancient Greek town in southern Italy, or to a sect of philosophers that originated there.—*n.* An adherent of the Eleatic philosophy.

elecampane, el'i•kam•pān", *n.* [Fr. *énulecampane*, from L. *inula*, elecampane, and (probably) *campus*, a field.] A perennial plant with yellow-rayed flowers which grows in moist meadows and pastures, formerly regarded as expectorant; a coarse candy, professedly made from the root of the plant, but really composed of little else than colored sugar.

elect, i•lekt', *v.t.* [L. *eligo*, *electum*—*e*, out, and *lego*, *lectum*, to pick, choose, as in *collect*, *select*, etc.; *legend*, *lecture*, etc., being also akin.] To pick out or select; especially, to select or take for an office or employment; to choose from among others; to appoint to an office by vote or designation; to choose; to determine in favor of (often with an infinitive; he *elected* to go).—*a.* Chosen or elected; especially, chosen, but not inaugurated, consecrated, or invested with office (bishop-*elect*); *theol.* chosen, selected, or designated to eternal life; predestinated in the divine counsels.—*n. sing.* or *pl.* One or several chosen or set apart; *theol.* those especially favored by God.—**election,** i•lek'shon, *n.* [L. *electio.*] The act of electing; the act of selecting one or more from others; the act of choosing a person to fill an office or employment, by any manifestation of preference, as by vote, uplifted hands, *viva voce*, or ballot; power of choosing or selecting; choice; voluntary preference; liberty to choose or act (it is at his *election* to accept or refuse); *theol.* predetermination of God, by which persons are distinguished as objects of mercy, become subjects of grace, are sanctified and prepared for heaven.—**electioneer,** i•lek'shon•ēr", *v.i.* To work or exert one's self in any way to obtain the election of a candidate.—**electioneerer,** i•lek'shon•ē"rėr *n.* One who electioneers.—**elective,** i•lek'tiv, *a.* Chosen by election; dependent on choice; bestowed or passing by election; pertaining to or consisting in choice or right of choosing; exerting the power of choice.—**electively,** i•lek'tiv•lē, *adv.* By choice; with preference of one to another.—**elector,** i•lek'tėr, *n.* One who elects or has the right of electing; a person who has the right of voting for any functionary; specifically, one of the persons elected, by vote of the people, to the *electoral college*, whose function is to elect the President and Vice-President of the United States.—**electoral,** i•lek'tėr•al, *a.* Pertaining to election or electors; consisting of electors.—**electorate,** i•lek'tėr•āt, *n.* A body of electors; the dignity or territory of an elector.

electric, electrical, i•lek'trik, i•lek'tri•kal, *a.* [Fr. *électrique*, from L. *electrum*, Gr. *ēlektron*, amber, from the fact that the earliest electric phenomenon observed was the attraction of amber for light substances when rubbed.] Containing electricity, or capable of exhibiting it when excited by friction; pertaining to electricity; derived from or produced by electricity; conveying electricity; communicating a shock by electricity; *fig.* full of fire, spirit, or passion, and capable of communicating it to others.—*Electric battery*, a number of primary or secondary voltaic cells, connected with each other in one circuit.—*Electric charge*, a quantity of electricity existing on the surface of a body.—*Electric clock*, a clock in which the moving power, or the controlling power, is the action of a current of electricity.—*Electric condenser*, a system of two conducting surfaces, usually plane, facing each other across a narrow layer of air or other dielectric. A small difference of potential produces large charges on conductors so placed.—*Electric current*, a current or stream of electricity traversing a closed circuit formed of conducting substances, or passing by means of conductors from one body to another.—*Electric eel*, a fish which is capable of giving electric shocks.—*Electric eye*, a photoelectric cell.—*Electric lamp*, a lamp of any type depending on electricity, as the incandescent lamp, or the arc lamp.—*Electric light*, a light obtained by the conversion of electric energy into light energy. The usual method is to heat some material to incandescence by passing an electric current through it.—*Electric machine*, a machine for generating static electricity, by friction or by induction; the name is also given to the electric GENERATOR.—*Electric motor.* ELECTROMOTOR.—*Electric railway*, a railway on which electricity is the motor.—*Electric spark*, one of the forms in which accumulated electricity discharges itself.—*Electric telegraph.* TELEGRAPH.—**electrically,** i•lek'tri•kal•lē, *adv.* In the manner of electricity or by means of it.—**electrician,** i•lek•trish'an, *n.* One versed in the science of electricity; one who designs, sets up, repairs, or attends to electrical instruments and machinery.—**electricity,** i•lek•tris'i•tē, *n.* A phenomenon occurring in nature and based upon the imbalance of positive and negative charges.—*Static electricity*, electricity from the accumulation or deficiency of electrons (as manifest in lightning and the attraction of bodies electrified by friction).—*Current electricity*, electricity from the orderly movement of electrons through a circuit.—*Atmospheric electricity*, the electricity which is produced in the atmosphere, and which becomes visible in the form of lightning.—**electrification,** i•lek'tri•fi•kā"shon, *n.* The act of electrifying, or state of being electrified.—**electrify,** i•lek'tri•fī, *v.t.*—*electrified*, *electrifying*. To supply a community or region with electric power; to equip for the use of electric power; to charge with electricity; to affect by electricity; to give an electric shock to; *fig.* to give a sudden shock (as of surprise) to; to surprise with some sudden and brilliant effect; to thrill.—**electrocardiograph,** i•lek'trō•kärd"ē•o•graf, *n.* An instrument used to detect electrically the abnormal and irregular heartbeat.—**electrochemistry,** *n.* That branch of science which treats of, or is based upon, the relations between chemical and electrical phenomena.—**electrocute,** i•lek'tro•kūt, *v.t.* To execute by the agency of an electric current or shock.—**electrocution,** i•lek'trō•kū"shon, *n.*—**electrode,** i•lek'trōd, *n.* [-*ode* is from Gr. *hodos*, a way.] One of the conductors or terminals, either the cathode or anode, by which an electric current enters or leaves an electrolytic cell, vacuum tube, etc.—**electrodynamics,** i•lek'trō•dī•nam"iks, *n.* A science of mechanical actions exerted on one another by electric currents.—**electrodynamometer,** i•lek'trō•dī•na•mom"e•tėr, *n.* An instrument for measuring electric currents.—**electroencephalograph,** i•lek'trō•en•sef"a•lō•graf, *n.* An instrument used in electrically detecting and recording brain waves.—**electrokinetics,** i•lek'trō•ki•net"iks, *n.* That science which treats of electricity in motion.—**electrokinetic,** *a.* Of or pertaining to electrokinetics or electricity in motion.—**electrolyze,** i•lek'tro•līz, *v.t.* To decompose by direct action of the electric current.—**electrolyzation,** i•lek'tro•li•zā"shon, *n.* The act of electrolyzing.—**electrolysis,** i•lek•trol'i•sis, *n.* The resolution of compound bodies into their elements, or, in some cases, into groups of elements, under the action of a current of electricity.—**electrolyte,** i•lek'tro•līt, *n.* A compound which is decomposable, or is subjected to decomposition, by an electric current.—**electrolytic, electrolytical,** i•lek'tro•lit"ik, i•lek'tro•lit"i•kal, *a.* Pertaining to electrolysis.—**electromagnet,** *n.* A bar of soft iron rendered temporarily magnetic by a current of electricity having been caused to pass through a wire coiled round it.—**electromagnetic,** *a.* Having to do with the relations between electricity and magnetism.—*Electromagnetic units*, units employed in electrical measurement based upon the force exerted between two magnetic poles. The basis of the ordinary practical units.—**electrometallurgy,** *n* The art of depositing metals, as gold, silver, copper, etc., from solutions of their salts by electrolysis and of using the heating effects of the electric current—**electrometer,** i•lek•trom'e•ter, *n.* An instrument for measuring potential, or differences of electric potential between two conductors.—**electromotion,** *n.* The motion of electricity; mechanical motion produced by electricity.—**electromotive,** *a.* Causing or tending to cause an electric current.—*Electromotive force,* that which determines the flow of electricity along a conductor; proportional to difference of potential, and analogous to difference of level causing a flow in water, measured in volts.—**electromotor,** i•lek′tro•mō•tėr, *n.* A machine for transforming the energy of the electric current into mechanical energy.—**electron,** i•lek′tron, *n.* The elementary, subatomic, negatively charged particle orbiting about the atom's nucleus.—**electronegative,** i•lek′trō•neg″a•tiv, *a.* Repelled by bodies negatively electrified, and attracted by those positively electrified.—**electronics,** i•lek′tron″iks, *n.* The science of phenomena related to the emission, behavior, and effects of electrons, as in vacuum tubes, and their application, as in radio and television.—**electrophoresis,** i•lek′trō•fo•rē″sis, *n.* The movement of particles suspended in a fluid under the influence of currents.—**electrophorus,** i•lek′trof′o•rus, *n.* An instrument for collecting electricity, and showing the phenomena of induction.—**electroplate,** *v.t.* To plate or give a coating of silver or other metal by means of electric currents.—*n.* Articles coated with silver or other metal by the process of electroplating.—**electroplater,** *n.* One who practices electroplating.—**electropositive,** *a.* Attracted by bodies negatively electrified or by the negative pole of the galvanic arrangement.—**electroscope,** i•lek′tro•skōp, *n.* An instrument for observing or detecting the existence of free electricity, and, in general, for determining its kind.—**electroscopic,** i•lek′tro•skop″ik, *a.* Of or belonging to the electroscope.—**electrostatics,** *n.* The science which treats of the phenomena occasioned by electricity at rest, and of the production and discharge of stationary charges of electricity.—*Electrostatic units,* units employed in electrical measurement, based upon Coulomb's law of attraction and repulsion between quantities of statical electricity. All electrical quantities may be expressed in either electrostatic or electromagnetic units but the dimensions in the two systems differ, the velocity of light entering into the difference.—**electrotherapy,** i•lek′trō•ther″a•pi, *n.* The treatment of disease by the use of certain electrical techniques that change the structure or function of the affected body tissue.—**electrotype,** i•lek′trō•tīp, *n.* The act of producing copies of types, woodcuts, medals, etc., by means of the electric deposition of copper upon a mold taken from the original; a copy thus produced.—*v.t.*—*electrotyped, electrotyping.* To stereotype or take copies of by electrotype.—**electrotypic,** i•lek′tro•tī″pik, *a.* Pertaining to, or effected by means of, electrotype.—**electrotypist,** i•lek′tro•tī•pist, *n.* One who practices electrotypy.—**electrotypy,** i•lek′tro•tī•pi, *n.*

electuary, i•lek′tū•a•ri, *n.* [L.L. *electuarium,* a word of doubtful origin.] A medicine composed of powders or other ingredients, incorporated with some conserve, honey, or syrup.

eleemosynary, el•e•mos′i•ne•ri, *a.* [L.L. *eleemosynarius,* from Gr. *eleēmosynē,* alms, from *eleeō,* to pity, *eleos,* compassion. ALMS.] Given in charity or alms, appropriated to charity; founded by charity (an *eleemosynary* institution); relating to charitable donations; supported by charity.—*n.* One who lives by receiving alms or charity.

elegance, el′e•gans *n.* [Fr. *élégance,* from L. *elegantia,* from *elegans,* for *eligens,* from *eligo*—*e, ex,* out, and *lego,* to pick, to choose. ELECT.] The quality of being elegant; beauty resulting from perfect propriety, or from the absence of anything calculated to produce a disagreeable sensation; refinement; an elegant characteristic of feature.—**elegancy,** el′e•gan•si, *n.* Elegance.—**elegant,** el′e•gant, *a.* [Fr. *élégant,* L. *elegans.*] Having beauty or a pleasing effect resulting from grace, refinement, or polish; pleasing to good taste; graceful; refined (a lady with an *elegant* figure); having the words or style polished and appropriate (an *elegant* speech); giving expression to thought with propriety and grace; pleasing to the eye by grace of form or delicacy of color; free from coarseness, blemish, or other defect; showing fine harmony or symmetry.—**elegantly,** el′e•gant•li, *adv.* In an elegant manner.

elegy, el′e•ji, *n.* [L. *elegia,* from Gr. *elegeia,* from *elegos,* a lament.] A mournful or plaintive poem, or a funeral song; a poem or a song expressive of sorrow and lamentation; a dirge; *class. poetry,* any poem written in elegiac verse.—**elegiac,** i•lē′ji•ak, *a.* Belonging to elegy; plaintive; expressing sorrow or lamentation; used in elegies: said especially of a style of verse commonly used by the Greek and Latin poets, and composed of couplets consisting of alternate hexameter and pentameter lines.—**elegist,** el′e•jist, *n.* A writer of elegies.—**elegize,** el′e•jīz, *v.t.* and *i.* To write or compose elegies; to celebrate or lament in an elegy; to bewail.

element, el′e•ment, *n.* [L. *elementum,* an element, a first principle; same root as *aliment.*] One of the simplest constituent principles, or parts, of which anything consists, or upon which its constitution is based; a fundamental or ultimate part or principle, by the combination or aggregation of which anything is composed; an ingredient; *chem.* any of over 100 substances that alone or in combination constitute all matter; *pl.* the first or simplest rules or principles of an art or science; rudiments; one of the four constituents of the material world according to an old and still popular classification—fire, air, earth, water (hence such expressions as 'war of the *elements*' for a storm); the state or sphere natural to anything or suited to its existence (hence, *out of one's element,* out of one's natural sphere or position); a datum or value necessary to be taken into consideration in making a calculation or coming to a conclusion; *pl.* the bread and wine used in the Eucharist.—*v.t.* To constitute; to be an element in; to make a first principle.—**elemental,** el•e•men′tal, *a.* Pertaining to or produced by elements or primary ingredients; pertaining to the four so-called elements of the material world or some of them (hence '*elemental* war,' applied to a tempest); arising from or pertaining to first principles; elementary†.—**elementally,** el•e•men′tal•li, *adv.* In an elemental manner; according to elements.—**elementariness,** el•e•men′te•ri•nes, *n.* The state of being elementary.—**elementary,** el•e•men′te•ri, *a.* Having the character of an element or primary substance; primary; simple; uncompounded; uncombined; initial; rudimentary; containing, teaching, or discussing first principles, rules, or rudiments.—*Elementary particle,* any subatomic particle that is thought to be irreducible into further components (such as the proton, electron, positron, etc.).

elemi, el′e•mi, *n.* The resinous exudation from various trees, used in plasters and ointments and the manufacture of varnish.

eleoptene, el•ē•op′tēn, *n.* [Gr. *elaion,* olive oil, and *ptēnos,* winged.] The liquid portion of volatile oils, as distinguished from the solid portion called *stearoptene.*

elephant, el′e•fant, *n.* [L. *elephas, elephantis,* from Gr. *elephas, elephantos,* an elephant; probably from Heb. *aleph,* an ox.] The name of two species of huge quadrupeds, one inhabiting India, the other Africa, and both remarkable for having their nose prolonged into a long proboscis or trunk with the nostrils at its extremity, and for their large tusks.—**elephantiasis,** el″e•fan•tī′a•sis, *n.* [Gr., from *elephas,* elephant.] *Med.* the massive swelling of the limbs caused by the obstruction of the lymphatic vessels by filarial worms.—**elephantine,** el•e•fan′tin, *a.* Pertaining to the elephant; resembling an elephant.

Eleusinian, el•ū•sin′i•an, *a.* Relating to *Eleusis* in Greece; as, *Eleusinian mysteries* or *festivals,* the mysteries and festivals of Dēmētēr (Ceres), celebrated there.

elevate, el′e•vāt, *v.t.*—*elevated, elevating.* [L. *elevo, elevatum,* to lift up—*e,* out, up, and *levo,* to raise, from *levis,* light in weight, whence *levity, lever, levy,* etc.] To raise; in a literal sense, to raise from a low or deep place to a higher; to raise to a higher state or station; to improve, refine, or dignify; to raise from a low or common state, as by training or education; to exalt; to excite, cheer, animate; to augment or swell; to make louder.—**elevated,** el'e•vā•ted, *a.* Raised; exalted; dignified; raised above the natural pitch; somewhat loud.—**elevation,** el•e•vā'shon, *n.* [L. *elevatio.*] The act of elevating; the act of raising or conveying from a lower place or degree to a higher; the state of being raised or elevated; exaltation; that which is raised or elevated; an elevated place; a rising ground; height; degree of height; height above the surface of the earth; altitude; *astron.* altitude; *gun.* the angle which the axis of the bore of a firearm makes with the plane of the horizon; *arch.* a geometrical representation of a building in vertical section, as opposed to *ground-plan.*—**elevator,** el'e•vā•tėr, *n.* One who or that which elevates, raises, lifts, or exalts; a mechanical contrivance for raising passengers or goods from a lower place to a higher; an airfoil on the tail plane of an airplane for producing up-and-down motion.

eleven, i•lev'n, *a.* [A.Sax. *endleofan, endlufon*=Icel. *ellifu,* Dan. *elleve,* D. *elf,* Goth. *ainlif;* compounded of two elements meaning "one" and "left", or one left after ten.] Ten and one added.—*n.* The sum of ten and one; a symbol representing eleven units; *football* and *cricket,* the players selected to play as a team in a football game or cricket match.—**eleventh,** i•lev'nth, *a.* and *n.* Next in order after the tenth; one of eleven equal parts into which anything is divided.

elf, elf, *n.* pl. **elves,** elvz. [A.Sax. *ælf, elf*=L.G. *elf,* Dan. *alf,* Icel. *álfr,* O.H.G. *alp,* an elf. Original meaning a nightmare.] A kind of inferior spiritual being formerly believed in; a fairy; a goblin; a mischievous person; a pet name for a child.—**elfin,** el'fin, *a.* Relating or pertaining to elves.—*n.* A little elf; a little urchin.—**elfish,** el'fish, *a.* Of or pertaining to elves; resembling an elf; suggestive of elves.—**elflock,** *n.* A knot of hair twisted as if by elves.

elicit, i•lis'it, *v.t.* [L. *elicio, elicitum*—*e,* out, and *lacere,* to allure; akin *delicate, delight.*] To bring or draw out by reasoning, discussion, examination, or the like; to deduce or educe (as truth, facts, etc.).

elide, i•līd', *v.t.* [L. *elido*—*e,* out, and *lædo,* to strike.] *Gram.* to cut off or suppress, as a syllable.—**elision,** i•lizh'on, *n. Gram.* the act of eliding; the cutting off or suppression of a vowel or syllable.

eligible, el'i•ji•bl, *a.* [Fr. *éligible,* from L. *eligo*—*e,* out, and *lego,* to choose. ELECT.] Fit to be chosen for some purpose or duty; worthy of choice; desirable; legally qualified to be chosen.—**eligibility,** el'i•ji•bil"i•ti, *n.* The state or condition of being eligible; capability of being chosen.—**eligibly,** el'i•ji•bli, *adv.* In a manner to be worthy of choice; suitably.

eliminate, i•lim'i•nāt, *v.t.*—*eliminated, eliminating.* [L. *elimino, eliminatum*—*e,* out, and *limen,* threshold.] To discharge or throw off (as a secretion of the human body); to take out or separate as not being an element of value or necessary; to set aside as unimportant or not to be considered; to leave out of consideration; *alg.* to cause to disappear from an equation; to deduce or elicit† (incorrect in this sense).—**elimination,** i•lim'i•nā"shon, *n.* The act of eliminating.

elision. See ELIDE.

elite, ā•lēt, *n.* pl. [Fr., lit. elected or select.] Those who are choice or select; the best; a type style.

elixir, i•lik'sėr, *n.* [Fr. *elixir,* from Sp. *elixir,* from Ar. *el-iksir,* the philosopher's stone, from Gr. *xēros,* dry.] A liquor sought for by the alchemists for transmuting metals into gold or prolonging life; quintessence; a cordial; *med.* a tincture composed of various substances held in solution by alcohol in some form.

Elizabethan, i•liz'a•beth"an, *a.* Pertaining to Queen Elizabeth I of England or her period.—*Elizabethan architecture,* the architectural style of the times of Elizabeth and James I, when the debased Gothic and Italian were combined, characterized by large windows, tall and highly decorated chimneys, and much ornament.

elk, elk, *n.* [Icel. *elgr,* O.H.G. *elaho,* Sw. *elg;* akin to L. *alces,* an elk.] In Europe and Asia, the largest member of the deer family, similar to the moose; in America, the wapiti, a member of the deer family, next in size to the moose.

ell, el, *n.* [A.Sax. *eln;* D. *ell, elle,* G. *elle,* O.H.G. *elna,* Sw. *aln,* Icel. *alin,* Goth. *aleina;* akin to L. *ulna,* Gr. *ōlenē,* the forearm, and hence, a measure of length. Comp. *cubit.*] A measure of different lengths in different countries, used chiefly for measuring cloth; the English ell being 45 inches, the Flemish ell 27, the Scotch 37.2, and the French 54.

ellipse, el•lips', *n.* [Gr. *elleipsis,* an omission or defect, from *elleipō,* to leave out—*ek,* out, and *leipō,* to leave.] *Geom.* an oval figure produced when any cone is cut by a plane which passes through it, not parallel to nor cutting the base; a closed curve in which the distances of any point from two points called the *foci* have always the same sum.—**ellipsis,** el•lip'sis, *n. Gram.* the omission of one or more words which the hearer or reader may supply; *printing,* the marks,—or *** or . . . , denoting the omission or suppression of letters or words; *geom.* an ellipse‡.—**ellipsoid,** el•lip'soid, *n. Geom.* a solid figure, all plane sections of which are ellipses or circles.—**ellipsoidal,** el•lip•soi'dal, *a.* Pertaining to an ellipsoid; having the form of an ellipsoid.—**elliptic, elliptical,** el•lip'tik, el•lip'ti•kal, *a.* Pertaining to an ellipse; having the form of an ellipse; pertaining to ellipsis; having a word or words left out.—**elliptically,** el•lip'ti•kal•li, *adv.* According to the form of an ellipse; with a word or words left out.—**ellipticity,** el•lip•tis'i•ti *n.* The quality of being elliptical or having the form of an ellipse.

elm, elm, *n.* [A.Sax. *elm,* D. *olm,* Icel. *álmr,* Dan. *ælm, alm;* akin to L. *ulmus,* Bohem. *gilm* (pron. *yilm*), elm.] A valuable timber and shade tree, species of which are found in America and Europe.

elocution, el•o•kū'shon, *n.* [L. *elocutio,* from *eloquor, elocutus,* to speak out—*e,* out, and *loquor,* to speak, seen in *colloquy, eloquent, loquacious,* etc.] The art by which, in delivering a discourse before an audience, the speaker is enabled to render it effective and impressive; mode of utterance of delivery of an address, accompanied by gestures.—**elocutionary,** el•o•kū'shon•e•ri, *a.* Pertaining to elocution.—**elocutionist,** el•o•kū'shon•ist, *n.* One who is versed in elocution; a teacher of elocution.

Elohim, el•ō•hēm', *n.* One of the Hebrew names of God of frequent occurrence in the Bible, used both of the true God and of false gods, while *Jehovah* is used only of the true God.—**Elohistic,** ē•lō•his'tik, *a.* A term applied to certain passages in Scripture, especially in the Pentateuch, in which the Almighty is always spoken of as *Elohim.*

elongate, i•long'gāt, *v.t.*—*elongated, elongating.* [L.L. *elongo, elongatum*—L. *e,* out, and *longus,* long.] To lengthen; to extend.—*v.i.* To recede apparently from the sun: said of a planet in its orbit.—**elongation,** i•long•gā'shon, *n.* The act of elongating or lengthening; the state of being stretched out or lengthened; *astron.* the angular distance of a planet from the sun, as it appears to the eye of a spectator on the earth.

elope, i•lōp', *v.i.*—*eloped, eloping.* [From D. *loopen,* the same word as G. *laufen,* Goth. *hlaupan,* to run, to leap, E. *leap,* with prefix *e,* out, away.] To run away; to run away with a lover or paramour in defiance of duty or social restraints: said especially of a woman.—**elopement,** i•lōp'ment, *n.* The act of eloping; the running away of a woman, married or unmarried, with a lover.

eloquence, el'o•kwens, *n.* [Fr. *éloquence,* from L. *eloquentia.* ELOCUTION.] The art of expressing thoughts in such language and in such a way as to produce conviction or persuasion; oratory; that which is expressed with eloquence.—**eloquent,** el'o•kwent, *a.* Having the power of expressing strong emotions vividly and appropriately; adapted to express strong emotion with fluency and power; characterized by eloquence.—**eloquently,** el′o•-kwent•li, *adv.* In an eloquent manner.

else, els, *a.* or *adv.* [A.Sax. *elles*, else, otherwise; akin to O.H.G. *eli, ali*, Goth. *alis*; L. *alius* (see ALIEN), Gr. *allos*, another.] Other; besides; in addition; as in who *else*? nothing or nobody *else*, nowhere *else*.—*conj.* Otherwise; in the other case; if the fact were different; as, he was ill, *else* he would have come.—**elsewhere,** els′hwâr, *adv.* In another place; somewhere else.

elucidate, i•lū′si•dāt, *v.t.*—*elucidated, elucidating.* [L.L. *elucido, elucidatum* —L. *e*, out, and *lucidus*, bright. LUCID.] To make clear or manifest; to explain; to remove obscurity from and render intelligible; to illustrate.—**elucidation,** i•lū′si•dā″-shon, *n.* The act of elucidating; explanation; exposition; illustration.—**elucidative,** i•lū′si•dā•tiv, *a.* Making or tending to elucidate; explanatory.—**elucidator,** i•lū′si•-dā•tėr, *n.* One who elucidates or explains.

elude, i•lūd′, *vt.*.—*eluded, eluding.* [L. *eludo*—*e*, and *ludo*, to play, as in *allude, collude, delude*, etc.] To evade; to avoid by artifice, stratagem, wiles, deceit, or dexterity; to remain unseen, undiscovered, or unexplained by (to *elude* scrutiny).—**elusion,** i•lū′zhon, *n.* An escape by artifice or deception; an evasion.—**elusive,** i•lū′siv, *a.* Practicing elusion; using arts to escape.—**elusively,** i•lū′siv•li, *adv.* With or by elusion.—**elusory,** i•lū′so•ri, *a.* Tending to elude; tending to deceive; evasive; fallacious.

Elul, el•öl′, *n.* [Heb.] The twelfth month of the Jewish civil year, corresponding nearly to our August.

elutriate, i•lū′tri•āt, *v.t.*—*elutriated, elutriating.* [L. *elutrio, elutriatum*, from *eluo, elutum*, to wash off—*e*, off, and *luo*, to wash.] To purify (ores) by washing and straining off or decanting the liquid from the substance washed, the lighter matters being then separated from the heavier.—**elutriation,** i•lū′tri•ā″shon, *n.* The operation of elutriating.

elves, elvz, pl. of *elf*.—**elvish,** el′vish, *a.* Pertaining to elves or fairies; mischievous, as if done by elves; elfish.

Elysium, i•liz′i•um, *n.* [L., from Gr. *ēlysion* (*pedion*), the Elysian fields.] *Myth.* a place assigned to happy souls after death; the seat of future happiness; hence, any place exquisitely delightful.—**Elysian,** i•lizh′an, *a.* Pertaining to Elysium; exceedingly delightful.

elytron, elytrum, el′i•tron, el′i•-trum, *n.* pl. **elytra,** el′i•tra. [Gr., a cover, sheath, from *elyō*, to roll round.] The wing sheath or coriaceous membrane which forms the superior wing in certain insects, as beetles, serving to cover and protect the true wing.—**elytroid,** el′i•troid, *a.* Like an elytron.

Elzevir, el′ze•vėr, *a.* Of or belonging to the *Elzevir* family: applied to editions of the classics, etc., published by the Elzevir family at Amsterdam and Leyden, from about 1595 to 1680, and highly prized for their accuracy and elegance; a term applied to a variety of printing type consisting of tall thin letters.

em, em, *n. Print.* the unit of measurement, being a type whose breadth is equal to its depth.

emaciate, i•mā′shi•āt, *v.i.*—*emaciated, emaciating.* [L. *emacio, emaciatum* —*e*, intens., and *macies*, leanness.] To lose flesh gradually; to become lean from loss of appetite or other cause.—*v.t.* To cause to lose flesh gradually; to reduce to leanness.—*a.* Thin; wasted.—**emaciation,** i•-mā′shi•ā″shon, *n.* The act of making or becoming lean or thin in flesh; the state of being reduced to leanness.

emanate, em′a•nāt, *v.i.*—*emanated, emanating.* [L. *emano, emanatum*—*e*, out, and *mano*, to flow.] To flow forth or issue from a source: said of what is intangible, as light, heat, odor, power, etc.; to proceed from something as the source, fountain, or origin; to take origin; to arise; to spring.—**emanation,** em•a•nā′shon, *n.* The act of emanating; that which emanates, issues, flows, or proceeds from any source, substance, or body; efflux; effluvium; any person, power, or thing emanating or proceeding from the Divine Essence.—**emanative,**† em′a•nā•tiv, *a.* Tending to emanate.

emancipate, i•man′si•pāt, *v.t.*—*emancipated, emancipating.* [L. *emancipo, emancipatum*—*e*, out, *manus*, the hand, and *capio*, to take.] To set free from servitude or slavery by the voluntary act of the proprietor; to restore from bondage to freedom; to free from bondage, restriction, or restraint of any kind; to liberate from subjection, controlling power, or influence.—**emancipation,** i•man′-si•pā″shon, *n.* The act of emancipating, deliverance from bondage or controlling influence, liberation.—**emancipator,** i•man′si•pā•tėr, *n.* One who emancipates.

emarginate, emarginated, i•mär′-ji•nāt, i•mär′ji•nā•ted, *a.* [L. *emarginatus*—*e*, not, and *margo, marginis*, border, margin.] Having the margin or extremity taken away, having a blunt or obtuse notch in the margin; notched at the blunt apex; applied most commonly in *bot.* to a leaf, petal, etc.

emasculate, i•mas′kū•lāt, *v.t.*—*emasculated, emasculating.* [L. *e*, not, and *masculus*, dim. of *mas*, a male. MASCULINE.] To deprive of the properties of a male; to castrate; to geld; to deprive of masculine vigor; to render effeminate, to expurgate by removing coarse passages from (a book).—**emasculation,** i•mas′kū•lā″shon, *n.* The act of emasculating; the state of being emasculated.—**emasculatory,** i•-mas′kū•la•to•ri, *a.* Serving to emasculate.

embalm, em•bäm′, *v.t.* [Prefix *em*, and *balm.* balsam.] To preserve (a dead body) from decay by removing the intestines and filling their place with odoriferous and desiccative spices and drugs; to preserve from loss or decay; to cherish tenderly the memory of.—**embalmer,** em•bä′mėr, *n.* One who embalms.

embank, em•bangk′, *v.t.* [Prefix *em*, and *bank.*] To enclose with a bank, to defend by banks, mounds, or dikes; to bank up.—**embankment,** em•bangk′ment, *n.* The act of surrounding or defending with a bank; a mound or bank raised to protect land from being overflowed by a river or the sea, or to enable a road or railway to be carried over a valley.

embarcation, *n.* See EMBARKATION.

embargo, em•bar′gō, *n.* [Sp. *embargo*, an embargo, embarrassment, lit. what serves as a bar—prefix *em* for *in*, and L.L. *barra*, a bar; akin *embarrass.*] A restraint or prohibition imposed by the public authorities of a country on merchant vessels, or other ships, to prevent their entering or leaving its ports, sometimes amounting to an entire interdiction of commercial intercourse; a restraint or hindrance imposed on anything.—*v.t.* To put an embargo on; to subject to an embargo.

embark, em•bärk′, *v.t.* [Fr. *embarquer*—*en*, in, and *barque*, a bark. BARQUE.] To put or cause to enter on board a ship or boat; to engage, invest, or make to enter on in any affair.—*v.i.* To go on board of a ship, boat, or vessel; to engage or take a share in any affair; to enlist.—**embarkation,** em•bär•kā′shon, *n.* The act of embarking; that which is embarked or put on board.

embarrass, em•bar′as, *v.t.* [Fr. *embarrasser*, to embarrass, *embarras*, embarrassment—prefix *em*, and L.L. *barra*, a bar; akin *embargo.* BAR.] To derange, confuse, or entangle (affairs, business, etc.), so as to make a course of action difficult; to involve in pecuniary difficulties; to perplex, disconcert, or abash.—**embarrassing,** em•bar′as•ing, *a.* Perplexing; adapted to perplex or embarrass.—**embarrassingly,** em•-bar′as•ing•li, *adv.* In an embarrassing manner.—**embarrassment,** em•-bar′as•ment, *n.* The state of being embarrassed; entanglement; perplexity arising from inability to pay one's debts; confusion of mind; abashment.

embassador, em•bas′sa•dor, *n.* An ambassador. [This spelling is not now used, though *embassy* and not *ambassy* is the correct form.]—**embassy,** em′bas•si, *n.* [O.E. and Fr. *embassade.*] The mission of an ambassador; the charge or employment of an ambassador or envoy; the message of an ambassador; a message, especially a solemn or important message; the persons entrusted with ambassadorial functions; a legation; the business or official residence of an ambassador.

embattle, em•bat′l, *v.t.*—*embattled, embattling.* [Prefix *em*, and *battle.*] To arrange in order of battle; to array for battle; to furnish with battlements.—*v.i.* To be ranged in order of battle.

embay, em•bā′, *v.t.* [Prefix *em*, and *bay.*] To enclose in a bay or inlet; to landlock.—**embayment,** em•bā′-ment, *n.* A portion of the sea closed in and sheltered by capes or promontories.

embed, em•bed′, *v.t.*—*embedded, embedding.* [Prefix *em*, and *bed.*] To lay in or as in a bed; to lay in surrounding matter.

embellish, em•bel′lish, *v.t.* [Fr. *embellir*—prefix *em*, and *belle*, L. *bellus*, pretty, beautiful.] To make beautiful; to adorn; to beautify; to decorate; to deck.—**embellishment,** em•bel′lish•ment, *n.* The act of embellishing or adorning, or state of being embellished; that which embellishes or adorns; that which renders anything pleasing to the eye or agreeable to the taste; adornment; ornament; decoration.

ember, em′bėr, *n.* [A.Sax. *æmyrian*, cinders; Dan. *emmer*, Icel. *eimyrja*, embers.] A small live coal, glowing piece of wood, etc.; used chiefly in the plural to signify live cinders or ashes; the smoldering remains of a fire.

Ember days, *n. pl.* [A.Sax. *ymbrine, ymbren embren* the circle or course of the year, from *ymb* or *emb*, round, and *rinnan*, to run.] Days returning at certain seasons, being the Wednesday, Friday, and Saturday after the first Sunday in Lent, after Whitsunday, after Holyrood-day (September 14) and after St. Lucia's day (December 13), appointed in the Church of England and the Roman Catholic Church for fasting and abstinence: called also *Embering-days*†.—**Ember week,** *n.* A week in which ember days occur.

embezzle, em•bez′l, *v.t.*—*embezzled, embezzling.* [O.Fr. *embeasiler*, to filch, *besler*, to deceive; origin doubtful.] To appropriate fraudulently to one's own use what is entrusted to one's care; to apply to one's private use by a breach of trust, as a clerk or servant who misappropriates his employer's money or valuables.—**embezzlement,** em•-bez′l•ment, *n.* The act by which a clerk, servant, or person acting as such, fraudulently appropriates to his own use the money or goods entrusted to his care.—**embezzler,** em•bez′lėr, *n.* One who embezzles.

embitter, em•bit′ėr, *v.t.* [Prefix *em*, and *bitter.*] To make bitter or more bitter; to make unhappy or grievous; to render distressing; to make more severe, poignant, or painful; to render more violent or malignant; to exasperate.—**embitterment,** em•-bit′ėr•ment, *n.* The act of embittering.

emblaze,‡ em•blāz′, *v.t.*—*emblazed, emblazing.* [Prefix *em*, and *blaze.*] To kindle; to set in a blaze; to make to glitter or shine; to display or set forth conspicuously or ostentatiously; to blazon.

emblazon, em•blā′zon, *v.t.* [Prefix *em*, and *blazon.*] To adorn with figures of heraldry or ensigns armorial; to depict or represent, as an armorial ensign on a shield; to set off with ornaments; to celebrate in laudatory terms; to sing the praises of.—**emblazoner,** em•blā′zon•ėr, *n.* One that emblazons.—**emblazonment,** em•blā′zon•ment, *n.* The act of emblazoning; that which is emblazoned.—**emblazonry,** em•-blā′zon•ri, *n.* The act or art of emblazoning; blazonry; heraldic decoration, as pictures or figures on shields, standards, etc.

emblem, em′blem, *n.* [Fr. *emblême*; Gr. *emblēma*, from *emballō*—*em*, in, and *ballō*, to cast.] A kind of inlaid work or mosaic‡; a picture, figure, or other work of art representing one thing to the eye and another to the understanding; any object or its figure whose predominant quality symbolizes something else, as another quality or state; a symbolic figure; a type; a symbol; a device, as a balance used to symbolize justice.—**emblematic, emblematical,** em•ble•mat′ik, em•-ble•mat′i•kal, *a.* Pertaining to or comprising an emblem; serving as an emblem or symbolic figure; symbolic.—**emblematically,** em•-ble•mat′i•kal•li *adv.* In an emblematic manner.—**emblematize,** em•-blem′a•tīz *v.t.*—*emblematized, emblematizing*; *emblemized, emblemizing.* To represent by an emblem; to serve as the emblem of.

emblement, em′ble•ment *n.* [From O.Fr. *embleer*, to sow with corn—prefix *em*, and *blé, bled*, L.L. *bladum*, corn.] *Law*, the produce or fruits of land sown or planted; growing crops annually produced; used chiefly in the plural.

embody, em•bod′i, *v.t.*—*embodied, embodying.* [Prefix *em*, and *body.*] To lodge in a material body; to invest with a body; to incarnate; to clothe with a material form; to render obvious to the senses or mental perception (to *embody* thought in words); to form or collect into a body or united mass; to collect into a whole.—*v.i.* To unite into a body, mass, or collection; to coalesce.—**embodiment,** em•bod′-i•ment, *n.* Act of embodying or investing with a body; the state of being embodied; bodily or material representation; the act of collecting or forming into a body or united whole.

embolden, em•bōl′dn, *v.t.* [Prefix *em*, and *bold.*] To give boldness or courage to; to encourage.

embolism, em′bol•izm, *n.* [Gr. *embolismos*, from *emballō*, to throw in, to insert.] The insertion of days, months, or years in an account of time, to produce regularity, intercalation; *surg.* the obstruction of a vessel by a clot of fibrin, a frequent cause of paralysis, and of gangrene of the part beyond the obstacle.—**embolismic,** em•bo•liz′mik, *a.* Pertaining to embolism or to intercalation; intercalated; inserted.

embolus, em′bo•lus, *n.* [Gr. *embolos*, wedge or plug.] *Med.* an abnormal particle circulating in the bloodstream, as an air bubble, blood clot, etc.

embosom, em•bu̇′zum, *v.t.* [Prefix *em*, and *bosom.*] To take into or hold in the bosom; to admit to the heart or affection; to cherish; to enclose in the midst; to surround.

emboss, em•bos′, *v.t.* [Prefix *em*, and *boss.*] To form bosses on; to fashion relief or raised work on; to represent in worked figures.—**embosser,** em•bos′ėr, *n.* One who embosses.—**embossment,** em•bos′-ment, *n.* The act of embossing; work in relief.

embouchure, om•bö•shür′, *n.* [Fr., from prefix *em*, and *bouche*, mouth.] A mouth of a river; the mouth hole of a wind instrument of music; the shaping of the lips to the mouth-piece.

embowel, em•bou′el, *v.t.*—*emboweled, emboweling.* [Prefix *em*, and *bowel.*] To take out the bowels or entrails of; to eviscerate; to take out the internal parts of; to sink or enclose in; to embed; to bury.

embower, em•bou′ėr, *v.i.* [Prefix *em*, and *bower.*] To lodge or rest in a bower.—*v.t.* To cover with a bower; to shelter with, or as with, trees; to form a bower for.

embrace, em•brās′, *v.t.*—*embraced, embracing.* [Fr. *embrasser*, to embrace —*em*, in, and *bras*, the arm. BRACE.] To take, clasp, or enclose in the arms; to press to the bosom in token of affection; to enclose, encompass, or contain; to encircle; to seize eagerly, in a figurative sense; to accept with cordiality (doctrines, religion); to comprehend, include, or take in; to comprise; to submit to (*Shak*)‡.—*v.i.* To join in an embrace.—*n.* Enclosure or clasp with the arms; pressure to the bosom with the arms; sexual intercourse; conjugal endearment.—**embracement,** em•brās′ment, *n.* A clasp in the arms; a hug; embrace; sexual commerce (*Shak.*)‡—**embraceor,** em•brā′sėr, *n. Law*, one who practices embracery.—**embracer,** em•brā′sėr, *n.* One who embraces.—**embracery,** em•brā′sėr•i, *n. Law*, an attempt to influence a jury corruptly to one side, by promises, persuasions, entreaties, money, entertainments, or the like.

embrasure, em•brā′zhūr, *n.* [Fr., prefix *em*, and *braser*, to slope the edge of a stone.] *Fort.* an opening in a wall or parapet through which cannon are pointed and fired; the indent or crenelle of an embattlement; *arch.* the enlargement of the aperture of a door or window on the inside of the wall to give more room or admit more light.

embrocate, em′brō•kāt, *v.t.*—*embrocated, embrocating.* [L.L. *embroco, embrocatum*, from Gr. *embrochē*, a fomentation, from *embrechō*, to foment—prefix *em* for *en*, in, and *brechō*, to wet.] *Med.* to moisten and rub, as a diseased part, with a liquid substance, as with spirit, oil, etc.—**embrocation,** em•brō•kā'shon, *n.* The act of moistening and rubbing a diseased part with a cloth or sponge, dipped in some liquid substance, as spirit, oil, etc.; the liquid or lotion with which an affected part is rubbed or washed.

embroider, em•broi'dėr, *v.t.* [Prefix *em,* and *broider.* BROIDER.] To adorn with figures of needlework, often raised above the surface.—**embroiderer,** em•broi'dėr•ėr, *n.* One who embroiders.—**embroidery,** em•broi'dėr•i, *n.* Work in gold, silver, silk, or other fancy thread; elaboration with fictitious detail; anything pleasing but unimportant.

embroil, em•broil', *v.t.* [Prefix *em,* and *broil,* a noisy quarrel.] To mix up or entangle in a quarrel or disturbance; to intermix confusedly; to involve in contention or trouble.—**embroilment,** em•broil'ment, *n.* The act of embroiling; a state of contention, perplexity, or confusion.

embrown, em•broun', *v.t.* [Prefix *em,* and *brown.*] To make brown; to imbrown.

embrue, em•brö'. See IMBRUE.

embryo, em'bri•ō, *n.* [Gr. *embryon*—*em,* in, and *bryō,* to be full of anything.] The first rudiments of an animal in the womb, before the several members are distinctly formed, after which it is called a *fetus;* the rudimentary plant contained in the seed, produced by the action of the pollen on the ovule; the beginning or first state of anything, while yet in a rude and undeveloped condition; rudimentary state.—*Embryo buds,* spheroidal solid bodies formed in the bark of trees, and capable of developing into branches under favorable circumstances.—**embryogeny,** em•bri•oj'e•ni, *n.* [Gr. *embryon,* and root *gen,* to produce.] The formation and development of embryos; that department of science that treats of such formation and development.—**embryogenic,** em'bri•o•jen"ik, *a.* Pertaining to embryogeny.—**embryology,** em•bri•ol'o•ji, *n.* [Gr. *embryon,* and *logos,* discourse.] The doctrine of the development of embryos, whether in plants or animals.—**embryologic, embriological,** em'bri•o•loj"ik, em'bri•o•loj"i•kal, *a.* Of or belonging to embryology.—**embryon,**‡ em'bri•on, *n.* An embryo. (*Mil.*).—**embryonal, embryonic,** em'bri•on•al, em•bri•on'ik, *a.* Of or pertaining to an embryo, or the embryo stage.

emcee, em•sē', *v.t.*—*emceed, emceeing.* [From the abbrev. *M.C.,* master of ceremonies.] To act as master of ceremonies of.—*n.* The master of ceremonies.

emend, e•mend', *v.t.* [L. *emendo,* to correct—*e,* not, and *menda,* a spot or blemish. *Amend* and *mend* are virtually the same as this.] To remove faults or blemishes from; to amend; especially to amend by criticism of the text; to improve the reading of (an *emended* text of Vergil).—**emendation,** ē•men•dā'shon, *n.* The act of emending; removal of errors or corruptions from the text of a book or writing; a textual alteration or correction.—**emendator,** ē'men•dā•tėr, *n.* One who emends.—**emendatory,** ē•men'da•to•ri, *a.* Contributing to emendation or correction.

emerald, em'e•rald, *n.* [Fr. *emeraude,* Sp. *esmeralda,* It. *smeraldo;* from L. *smaragdus,* Gr. *smaragdos,* an emerald.] A precious stone whose colors are a pure lively green, varying to a pale, yellowish, bluish, or grass green, akin to the beryl, found especially in South America; a variety of printing type intermediate between minion and nonpareil.—*a.* Of a bright green, like emerald; printed with the size of type known as emerald.—*Emerald green,* a durable pigment of a vivid light-green color, prepared from the arsenate of copper.—*Emerald Isle.* Ireland. From the green verdure of the grass, or from its being set like an emerald in the sea. First so named in song by Drennan, 1754-1820.

emerge, i•mėrj', *v.i.*—*emerged, emerging.* [L. *emergo, emersum*—*e.* out, and *mergo,* to *plunge,* as in *immerge, submerge.* MERGE.] To rise out of a fluid or other covering or surrounding substance; to issue or proceed from something; to reappear after being eclipsed; to leave the sphere of the obscuring object; to rise out of a state of depression or obscurity; to come to notice.—**emergence,** i•mėr'jens, *n.* The act of emerging.—**emergency,** i•mėr'jen•si, *n.* The act of emerging; sudden occasion; unexpected casualty; unforeseen occurrence; any event or combination of circumstances calling for immediate action; pressing necessity.—**emergent,** i•mėr'jent, *a.* Emerging; rising into view or notice; coming suddenly; unexpected; calling for immediate action; urgent; pressing.—**emersion,** i•mėr'shon, *n.* The act of emerging or rising out of a fluid or other substance; the act of coming forth to view; the reappearance of a heavenly body after an eclipse or occultation.

emeritus, i•mer'i•tus, *a.* [L. *emeritus,* having served out his time.—*e* out, and *mereor, meritus,* to merit, earn, serve.] Discharged from the performance of public duty with honor, on account of infirmity, age, or long service; as, a professor *emeritus.* Sometimes used as a noun.

emersion. See EMERGE.

emery, em'e•ri, *n.* [Fr. *émeri,* O.Fr. *esmeril,* from It. *smeriglio,* from Gr. *smyris, smiris, smēris,* from *smaō,* to rub.] A mineral substance, an amorphous variety of corundum and sapphire, varying in color from deep gray to bluish or blackish gray, sometimes brownish, used for grinding and polishing metals, hard stones, and glass.

emetic, i•met'ik, *a.* [Gr. *emetikos,* from *emeō,* to vomit.] *Med.* inducing to vomit; exciting the stomach to discharge its contents by the mouth.—*n.* A medicine that provokes vomiting.—**emetin,** em'e•tin, *n.* The active principle of ipecacuanha.

emigrate, em'i•grāt, *v.i.*—*emigrated, emigrating.* [L. *emigro, emigratum,* to migrate, to emigrate—*e,* out, and *migro,* to migrate.] To quit one country, state, or region and settle in another; to remove from one country or state to another for the purpose of residence.—**emigrant,** em'i•grant, *a.* Emigrating; pertaining to emigration or emigrants.—**emigrant,** em'i•grant, *n.* One who emigrates.—**emigration,** em•i•grā'shon, *n.* The act of emigrating; departure of inhabitants from one country or state to another for the purpose of residence; a body of emigrants.

eminence, em'i•nens, *n.* [Fr. *éminence,* from L. *eminentia,* from *eminens, eminentis,* from *emineo*—*e,* out, and *mineo,* to project, to jut.] A rising ground; a hill of moderate elevation; a part rising or projecting beyond the rest or above the surface; a projection; a prominence; an elevated situation among men; station above men in general; rank; distinction; celebrity; conspicuousness; [*cap.*] a title of honor given to cardinals and others.—**eminency,**† em'i•nen•si, *n.* Same as *Eminence.*—**eminent,** em'i•nent, *a.* Standing out above other things‡; prominent‡; lofty‡; exalted in rank; high in office or public estimation; conspicuous; remarkable; distinguished.—**eminently,** em'i•nent•li, *adv.* In an eminent manner or position.

emir, em•ēr', *n.* [Ar. *amir,* a commander; from *amara,* Heb. *ámar,* to command.] The title given by Mohammedans to all independent chiefs, to the heads of certain departments, and to all the real or supposed descendants of Mohammed, through his daughter Fatimah.

emissary, em'is•se•ri, *n.* [L. *emissarius,* from *emitto, emissum,* to send out—*e,* out, and *mitto,* to send. EMIT.] A person sent on a mission; particularly, a secret agent, or one who carries on private negotiations or business; a spy; an outlet or channel by which water is drawn from a lake.—**emit,** i•mit', *v.t.*—*emitted, emitting.* [L. *emitto*—*e,* out, and *mitto, missum,* to send, whence *mission, missile, missive, message,* etc.] To throw or give out (light, heat, steam, etc.); to send forth; to vent; to cause or allow to issue or emanate.—**emission,** i•mish'on, *n.* [L. *emissio.*] The act of emitting or of sending or throwing out; that which is emitted, issued, sent, or thrown out.

emmenagogue, em•me'na•gog, *n.* [Gr. *emmena,* the menses—*em,* in, *mēn, mēnos,* month, and *agō,* to lead.] A medicine taken to promote the menstrual discharge.

emollient, i•mol'li•ent, *a.* [L. *emolliens, emollientis,* ppr. of *emollio.*] Softening; making supple; relaxing the solids.—*n.* A medicine which softens and relaxes living tissues that are inflamed or too tense.

emolument, i•mol′ū•ment, *n.* [L. *emolumentum*, a working out, from *e*, and *molior*, to exert one's self, from *moles*, a heavy mass.] The profit arising from office or employment; compensation for services; remuneration; salary; income; profit; advantage or gain in general.

emotion, i•mō′shon, *n.* [L. *emotio*, from *emoveo*, *emotum*—*e*, out, up, and *moveo*, to move.] A moving of the mind or soul; a state of excited feeling of any kind, as pleasure, pain, grief, joy, astonishment; one of the three fundamental properties of the human mind, the other two being *volition* and *intellect*.—**emotional,** i•mō′shon•al, *a.* Pertaining to or characterized by emotion; attended by or producing emotion; liable to emotion.—**emotionalism,** i•mō′shon•al•izm, *n.* The character of being emotional; tendency to emotional excitement.—**emotive,**† i•mō′tiv, *a.* Emotional; indicating or exciting emotion.—**emotively,**† i•mō′tiv•li, *adv.* In an emotive manner.—**emotiveness,**† i•mō′tiv•nes, *n.* The state or quality of being emotive.

empanel, empanelment, em•pan′el, em•pan′el•ment. See IMPANEL.

empathy, em′pa•thē, *n.* [Gr. *empatheia*, from *em*, in, and *pathos*, suffering, passion.] The imaginative projection of one's consciousness into the feelings of another person or object; sympathetic understanding.

emperor, em′pėr•ėr, *n.* [Fr. *empereur*, from L. *imperator*, from *impero*, *imperatum*, to command—prefix *im*, and *paro*, to prepare, to order.] The sovereign or supreme monarch of an empire; a title of dignity superior to that of king.—**empress,** em′pres, *n.* The consort or spouse of an emperor; a woman who rules an empire.—**empery,** em′pe•ri, *n.* Empire; power.

emphasis, em′fa•sis, *n.* [Gr. *emphasis*, a setting forth, from *emphainō*, to indicate—*em*, in, and *phainō*, to show (whence *phenomenon*).] A particular stress of utterance or force of voice given to the words or parts of a discourse whose signification the speaker intends to impress specially upon his audience; a peculiar impressiveness of expression or weight of thought; impressiveness; vividness.—**emphasize,** em′fa•sīz, *v.t.*—*emphasized*, *emphasizing*. To utter or pronounce with emphasis; to lay particular stress upon; to render emphatic.—**emphatic,** em•fat′ik, *a.* Having emphasis.—**emphatically,** em•fat′i•kal•li, *adv.*

emphysema, em•fi•sē′ma, *n.* [Gr. *emphysēma*, from *emphysaō*, to inflate.] *Med.* the presence of air in the intra-alveolar tissue of the lung due to the rupturing and distention of the alveoli.

empire, em′pīr, *n.* [Fr. *empire*, from L. *imperium*. EMPEROR.] Supreme power in governing; supreme dominion; sovereignty; imperial power; the territory or countries under the dominion of an emperor or other powerful sovereign; usually a territory of greater extent than a kingdom; supreme control; rule; sway.

empiric, em•pir′ik, *n.* [L. *empiricus*, from Gr. *empeirikos*, experienced—*en*, in, and *peira*, a trial.] One who relies only on experience and observation, as opposed to theory based on scientific conclusions; specifically, a physician who enters on practice without a regular professional education; an ignorant pretender to medical skill; a quack; a charlatan.—**empiric, empirical,** em•pir′i•kal, *a.* Pertaining to experiments or experience; depending altogether upon the observation of phenomena; depending upon experience or observation alone, without due regard to science and theory.—**empirically,** em•pir′i•kal•li, *adv.* In an empirical manner.—**empiricism,** em•pir′i•sizm, *n.* The quality or method of being empirical; the practice of an empiric; quackery.

emplacement, em•plās′ment, *n.* A position specially assigned to a gun or group of guns. A solid platform with accessories prepared for the support of a gun or guns.

employ, em•ploi′, *v.t.* [Fr. *employer*, from L. *implicare*, to infold, involve, engage—*in*, and *plicare*, to fold, seen also in *deploy*, *display*. PLY.] To occupy the time, attention, and labor of; to keep busy or at work; to make use of; to use as an instrument or means to, or as materials in forming anything; to engage in one's service; to use as an agent or substitute in transacting business; to apply or devote to an object; to occupy.—*n.* That in which one is employed; a state of being engaged by a master; occupation; employment.—**employable,** em•ploi′a•bl, *a.* Capable of being employed.—**employee,** em•ploi′ē, *n.* [The English form of the French *employé*, one who is employed, especially, a clerk.] One who works for an employer or master; a clerk, workman, or other person working for salary or wages.—**employer,** em•ploi′ėr, *n.* One who employs; one who uses; one who engages or keeps servants in employment.—**employment,** em•ploi′ment, *n.* The act of employing or using; the state of being employed; occupation; business; that which engages the head or hands; vocation; trade; profession; work.

empoison, em•poi′zn, *v.t* [Prefix *em*, and *poison*.] To poison; to taint with poison or venom; to embitter; to destroy all pleasure in.

emporium, em•pō′ri•um, *n.* [L., from Gr. *emporion*, an emporium or mart, from *emporos*, a merchant—*en*, in, and *poros*, a way, of same root as A.Sax. *faran*, to go, E. *fare*.] A town or city which is a center of commerce, or to which sellers and buyers resort from different countries; a commercial center; a department store.

empower, em•pou′ėr, *v.t.* [Prefix *em*, and *power*.] To give legal or moral power or authority to; to authorize, as by law, commission, letter of attorney, verbal license, etc.; to warrant; to license.

empress. *n.* See EMPEROR.

emprise, emprize, em•prīz′, *n.* [O. Fr. *emprise*—prefix *em*, and *prise*, a taking, from *prendre*, to take.] An undertaking; an enterprise; adventure. (*Poet.*)

empty, em′ti, *a.* [A.Sax. *aemti*, *aemtig*, *émtig*, vacant, free, idle; *aemtian*, to be at leisure, to be vacant; from *aemta*, *émta*, quiet, leisure.] Containing nothing, or nothing but air; void of contents or appropriate contents; destitute of solid matter; not filled; void; devoid; destitute of force or effect, or of sense or sincerity; wanting substance or solidity; wanting reality; unsatisfactory; not able to fill the mind or the desires; destitute of sense; knowledge, or judgment; vain; ignorant; unfruitful, or producing nothing (O.T.); without effect (O.T.)‡.—*n.* An empty packing case or the like.—*v.t. emptied*, *emptying*. To remove the contents from; to discharge; to render void.—*v.i.* To pour out or discharge contents; to become empty.—**emptier,** em′ti•ėr, *n.* One who or that which empties.—**emptiness,** em′ti•nes, *n.* A state of being empty.

empyema, em•pi•ē′ma, *n.* [Gr. *empyēma*, from *em*, in and *pyon*, pus.] *Med.* a collection of pus, blood, or other fluid matter, in some cavity of the body, especially in the cavity of the chest.

empyreal, em•pir′ē•al, or em•pi•rē′al, *a.* [L.L. *empyrœus*, from Gr. *empyros*, prepared by fire, fiery, scorched—*en*, and *pyr*, fire.] Formed of pure fire or light; refined beyond aerial substance; pertaining to the highest and purest region of heaven. —**empyrean,** em•pī•rē′an, *a.* Empyreal.—*n.* The highest heaven, where the pure element of fire was supposed by the ancients to exist.

emu, emeu, ē′mū, *n.* A large cursorial bird, closely allied to the ostrich and the cassowary, but differing from the former in having three toes, found in Australia.

emulate, em′ū•lāt, *v.t.*—*emulated*, *emulating*. [L. *œmulor*, *œmulatus*, to make one's self a rival, from *œmulus*, a rival.] To strive to equal or excel in qualities or actions; to vie with; to come forward as a rival of.—**emulation,** em•ū•lā′shon, *n.* The act of emulating; rivalry; desire of superiority, attended with effort to attain it; ambition to equal or excel; envy, jealousy, or malicious rivalry (*Shak.*).—**emulative,** em′ū•lā•tiv, *a.* Inclined to emulation; striving to emulate.—**emulatively,** em′ū•lā•tiv•li, *adv.* In an emulative manner.—**emulator,** em′ū•lā•tėr, *n.* One who emulates; a rival; a competitor.—**emulous,** em′ū•lus, *a.* Desirous or eager to imitate, equal, or excel another; desirous of like excellence with another (*emulous* of another's prowess); rivaling; engaged in competition; factious; contentious (*Shak.*) —**emulously,** em′ū•lus•li, *adv.* In an emulous manner.—**emulousness,** em′ū•lus•nes, *n.*

emulsion, ē•mul′shon, *n.* [From L. *emulgeo*, *emulsum*, to milk out—*e*, out, and *mulgeo*, to milk.] Any milky substance; *chem.* a mixture of two immiscible liquids, such as oil and water; a coating on photographic plates, paper, etc.—**emulsifier,** e•mul′si•fī•ėr, *n.* That which promotes the formation and stabilization of an emulsion.—**emulsify,** i•mul′si•fī, *v.t.* —*emulsified, emulsifying.* To make or form an emulsion.—**emulsive,** i•mul′siv, *a.* Softening; milklike; yielding oil by expression (*emulsive* seeds); producing a milklike substance.

emunctory, i•mungk′to•ri, *n.* [L. *emungo, emunctum,* to wipe.] *Anat.* any part of the body which serves to carry off excrementitious or waste matter; an excretory duct.

enable, en•ā′bl, *v.t.*—*enabled, enabling.* [Prefix *en,* and *able.*] To make able; to supply with power, physical, moral, or legal; to furnish with sufficient power, ability, or authority; to render fit or competent; to authorize.

enact, en•akt′, *v.t.* [Prefix *en,* and *act.*] To pass into an act or established law; to give sanction to (a bill or legislative proposal); to decree; to act or perform (*Shak.*)‡; to act the part of on the stage (*Shak.*)‡.—**enactive,** en•ak′tiv, *a.* Having power to enact, or establish as a law.—**enactment,** en•akt′ment, *n.* The passing of a bill or legislative proposal into a law; a law enacted; a decree; an act.

enamel, en•am′el, *n.* [Prefix *en,* and old *amel, ammel, amile,* enamel, from O.Fr. *esmail,* Mod.Fr. *émail,* enamel, from G. *schmelzen,* to smelt. SMELT.] A colored substance of the nature of glass, differing from it by a greater degree of fusibility or opacity, used as an ornamental coating for various articles; a smooth, glossy surface of various colors, resembling enamel; the smooth hard substance which covers the crown of a tooth, overlying the dentine.—*v.t.*—*enameled, enameling.* To lay enamel on; to paint in enamel; to form a glossy surface like enamel upon; to variegate or adorn with different colors.—*v.i.* To practice the use of enamel or the art of enameling.—**enameler, enamelist,** en•am′el•ėr, en•am′el•ist, *n.* One who enamels; one whose occupation is to lay on enamels.

enamor, en•am′ėr, *v.t.* [O.Fr. *enamourer*—*en,* and *amour,* L. *amor,* love.] To inflame with love; to charm; to captivate: commonly in the past participle, and with *of* or *with* before the person or thing that captivates.

enarthrosis, en•är•thrō′sis, *n.* [Gr. *enarthrōsis*—*en,* in, and *arthron,* a joint.] *Anat.* a ball-and-socket joint; an articulation which consists in the insertion of the round end of a bone in the cuplike cavity of another.

encaenia, en•sē′ni•a, *n.* [Gr. *enkainia.*] Dedication, festival of commemoration.

encage, en•kāj′, *v.i.*—*encaged, encaging.* [Prefix *en,* and *cage.*] To shut up or confine in a cage; to coop up.

encamp, en•kamp′, *v.i.* [Prefix *en,* and *camp.*] To take up position in a camp; to make a camp.—*v.t.* To form into or place in a camp (*Shak.*)†—**encampment,** en•kamp′ment, *n.* The act of encamping; the place where a body of men is encamped, together with the tents or other conveniences set in order for their accommodation; a camp.

encapsulate, in•kap′su•lāt, *v.t.* [L. *en,* and *capsula,* box.] To encase in a capsule.—*v.i.* To go into a capsule. —**encapsulation,** in•kap′su•lā″shon, *n.*

encaustic, en•ka̤s′tik, *a.* [Gr. *enkaustikos*—*en,* and *kaustikos,* caustic, from *kaiō,* to burn.] Pertaining to the art of enameling and to painting in colors that are fixed by burning.—*Encaustic painting,* a kind of painting in which, by heating or burning, the colors are rendered permanent in all their original splendor.—*Encaustic tiles,* decorated tiles of baked pottery, used in ornamental pavements, to cover parts of walls, etc.

encephalon, en•sef′a•lon, *n.* [Gr. *enkephalos,* within the head—*en,* in, and *kephalē,* the head.] The contents of the skull, consisting of the cerebrum, cerebellum, medulla oblongata, and membranes; the brain.—**encephalic,** en•se•fal′ik, *a.* Situated in the head; belonging to the head or brain.—**encephalalgia,** en′se•fa•lal″ji•a, *n.* [Gr. *en, kephalē,* and *algos,* pain.] *Med.* headache, cephalalgy.—**encephalitis,** en•sef′a•lī″tis, *n.* Inflammation of the brain.

enchain, en•chān′, *v.t.* [Prefix *en,* and *chain.*] To fasten with a chain; to bind or hold in chains; to hold in bondage; to hold fast, restrain, confine; to link together; to connect†. —**enchainment,** en•chān′ment, *n.* The act of enchaining or state of being enchained; concatenation.

enchant, en•chänt′, *v.t.* [Fr. *enchanter* —*en,* and *chanter,* to sing; L. *incanto* —*in,* and *canto,* freq. of *cano,* to sing. CHANT, CANT.] To practice sorcery or witchcraft on; to subdue by charms or spells; to hold as by a spell; to fascinate; to delight in a high degree; to charm, captivate, or enrapture.—**enchanter,** en•chän′tėr, *n.* One who enchants; a sorcerer or magician; one who practices enchantment or pretends to perform surprising things by the agency of demons; one who charms or delights.—**enchanting,** en•chän′ting, *a.* Charming; delighting; ravishing.—**enchantingly,** en•chän′ting•li, *adv.* In an enchanting manner.—**enchantment,** en•chänt′ment, *n.* The act of enchanting; the use of magic arts, spells, or charms; incantation; that which enchants; an influence or power which fascinates or delights; overpowering influence of delight.—**enchantress,** en•chänt′res, *n.* A female enchanter.

enchase, en•chās′, *v.t.*—*enchased, enchasing.* [Fr. *enchâsser*—*en,* and *châsse,* a frame, from L. *capsa,* a chest, a case, from *capio,* to take or receive.] To incase or enclose in a border or rim; to surround with an ornamental setting, as a gem with gold; to adorn by embossed work; to beautify by some design or figure in low relief.

enchorial, enchoric, en•kō′ri•al, en•kor′ik, *a.* [Gr. *enchōrios,* in or of the country—*en,* in, and *chōra,* a country.] Belonging to or used in a country; native; indigenous; demotic (which see).

encircle, en•sėr′kl, *v.t.*—*encircled, encircling.*] To form a circle about; to enclose or surround; to encompass; to environ; to embrace.

enclasp, en•klasp′, *v.t.* To clasp; to embrace.

enclave, en′klāv, *n.* [Fr.—*en,* in, and L. *clavis,* a key.] A place or country which is entirely surrounded by the territories of another power.

enclitic, en•klit′ik, *a.* [Gr. *enklitikos,* inclined, from *enklinō,* to incline—*en,* in, and *klinō,* to lean.] *Gram.* subjoined, and as it were leaning: said of a word or particle which always follows another word, and is so closely connected with the preceding word as to seem to be a part of it.—**enclitic,** *n. Gram.* an enclitic word.

enclose, en•klōz′, *v.t.*—*enclosed, enclosing.* [Prefix *en,* en, and *close.*] To surround, shut in, or confine on all sides; to shut up; to environ or encompass; to separate from common grounds by a fence (to *enclose* lands); to cover with a case, wrapper, or envelope.—**encloser,** en•klō′zėr, *n.* One who encloses.—**enclosure,** en•klō′zhėr, *n.* The act of enclosing; what is enclosed; a space enclosed or fenced; something enclosed along with a letter or the like.

encomium, en•kō′mi•um, *n.* [Gr. *enkōmion,* a laudatory ode, an encomium—*en,* in, and *kōmos,* a revel, a procession in honor.] A eulogy or commendation; a statement in praise of something or somebody; a panegyric.—**encomiast,** en•kō′mi•ast, *n.* [Gr. *enkōmiastēs.*] One who praises another; a panegyrist.—**encomiastic, encomiastical,** en•kō′mi•as″tik, en•kō′mi•as″ti•kal, *a.* Bestowing praise; laudatory.

encompass, en•kum′pas, *v.t.* To form a circle about; to encircle; to environ, enclose, or surround; to shut in; to go or sail round.—**encompassment,** en•kum′pas•ment, *n.* The act of encompassing or state of being encompassed.

encore, än′kōr, *adv.* [Fr., from L. (*in*) *hanc horam,* (to) this hour.] Again; once more: used by the auditors and spectators in calling for a repetition of a particular performance, song, or the like,—*v.t.*—*encored, encoring.* To call for a repetition of; to call upon to repeat.

encounter, en•koun′tėr, *n.* [Fr. *encontre*—*en,* and *contre,* L. *contra,* against.] A meeting, particularly a sudden or accidental meeting of two or more persons; a meeting in contest; a fight; a conflict; a skirmish; a battle; an intellectual or moral conflict or contest; controversy; debate —*v.t.* To meet face to face; to meet suddenly or unexpectedly; to meet in opposition or in a hostile manner; to engage with in battle; to come upon or light upon; to meet with; to meet and oppose; to resist.—

v.i. To meet face to face; to meet unexpectedly; to meet in hostile fashion; to come together in combat; to conflict.

encourage, in•kur′ij, *v.t.—encouraged, encouraging.* [Fr. *encourager—en,* and *courage.*] To give courage to; to inspire with courage; to embolden; to animate or inspirit; to help forward; to support or countenance. —**encouragement,** in•kur′ij•ment, *n.* The act of encouraging; that which encourages; incitement; incentive.—**encouraging,** in•kur′i•jing, *p.* and *a.* Exciting courage; furnishing ground to hope for success.—**encouragingly,** in•kur′i•jing•li, *adv.* In an encouraging manner.

encrinite, en′kri•nīt, *n.* [Gr. *en,* in, and *krinon,* a lily.] A crinoid, lily star, or stone lily; a common name for those fossil Echinodermata that have long many-jointed stalks supporting the somewhat flower-like animal.

encroach, en•krōch′, *v.i.* [Prefix *en,* and Fr. *crocher,* to hook on, from *croc,* a hook; E. *crook* (which see).] To trespass or intrude on the rights and possessions of another; to take possession of what belongs to another by gradual advances into his limits or jurisdiction (to *encroach on* one's privileges); to make inroads (the sea sometimes *encroaches on* the land); to assail gradually and stealthily.—**encroacher,** en•krō′chėr, *n.* One who encroaches. — **encroachment,** en•krōch′ment, *n.* The act of encroaching; undue or unlawful trespass on the privileges, jurisdiction, etc., of another; that which is taken by encroaching.

encumber, en•kum′bėr, *v.t.* [Prefix *en,* and *cumber*; Fr. *encombrer.*] To impede the motion of with a load, burden, or anything inconvenient; to clog; to load; to embarrass; to load, as an estate, with debts.—**encumbrance,** en•kum′brans, *n.* Anything that impedes action or renders it difficult and laborious; clog, load, burden, impediment; liability resting on an estate; a legal claim on an estate, for the discharge of which the estate is liable, as a mortgage, etc.

encyclical, en•sī′kli•kal, *a.* [Gr. *enkyklios—en,* in, and *kyklos,* a circle.] Sent to many persons or places; intended for many, or for a whole order of men.—*n.* A letter on some important occasion sent by the pope to the bishops.

encyclopedia, en•sī′klo•pē″di•a, *n.* [Gr. *enkyklopaideia—en,* in, *kyklos,* a circle, and *paideia,* instruction.] A work in which various branches of knowledge are discussed separately, and usually in alphabetical order; a kind of dictionary of things, not words; a cyclopedia; [*cap.*] specially of the great French encyclopedia projected by Diderot, D'Alembert, and others.—**encyclopedic, encyclopedical, encyclopedian,** en•sī′klo•pē″dik, en•sī′klo•pē″di•kal, en•sī′klo•pē″di•an, *a.* Pertaining to an encyclopedia; such as is embraced in an encyclopedia; universal as regards knowledge and information.—**encyclopedism,** en•sī′klo•pē•dizm, *n.* The making of encyclopedias; the possession of a wide range of information; extensive learning.—**encyclopedist,** en•sī′klo•pē•dist, *n.* The compiler of an encyclopedia, or one who assists in such compilation; a person whose knowledge is of a very wide range.

encyst, en•sist′, *v.t.* [Gr. *en,* in, and *kystis,* a bladder, a pouch.] To enclose in a cyst, sac, or vesicle.—**encystment,** en•sist′ment, *n.* A process undergone by certain Protozoa and Infusoria previous to fission, in which they become coated with a secretion of gelatinous matter, ultimately enclosing the body in a hard cyst.

end, end, *n.* [A.Sax. *ende*=Icel. *endi,* Dan. and G. *ende,* Goth. *andeis,* the end; Skr. *anta,* end, death.] The extreme point of a line, or of anything that has more length than breadth; the termination, conclusion, or last part of anything, as of a portion of time, of an action, of a state of things, of a quantity of materials; the close of life; death; consequence; issue; result; the ultimate point or thing at which one aims or directs his views; purpose intended; scope; aim; drift.—*On end,* resting on one end; upright; also, continuously; uninterruptedly.—*To make both ends meet,* to keep one's expenditure within one's income, or at least to keep them equal.—*v.t.* To put an end to or be the end of; to finish; to close, conclude, terminate; to destroy; to put to death.—*v.i.* To come to an end; to terminate; to close; to conclude; to cease.—**ender,** en′dėr, *n.* One who or that which ends or finishes.—**ending,** en′ding, *n.* The act of putting or coming to an end; conclusion; termination; the last part; the final syllable or letter of a word.—**endless,** end′les, *a.* Without end; having no end or conclusion: applied to length and duration; perpetually recurring; interminable; incessant; continual; without object, purpose, or use; fruitless; forming a closed loop and working continuously round two wheels or pulleys in the same plane (an *endless* rope, chain, saw).—*Endless screw,* a screw on a revolving shaft, the thread of which gears into a wheel with skew teeth.—**endlessly,** end′les•li, *adv.* In an endless manner.—**endlessness,** end′les•nes, *n.* The state or quality of being endless.—**endlong,** end′long, *a.* or *adv.* With the end forward; lengthwise. — **endways, endwise,** end′wāz, end′wīz, *adv.* On the end; erectly; in an upright position; with the end forward.

endamage, en•dam′ij, *v.t.—endamaged, endamaging.* To bring loss or damage to; to damage; to harm; to injure.

endanger, en•dān′jėr, *v.t.* To put in hazard; to bring into danger or peril; to expose to loss or injury.

endear, en•dēr′, *v.t.* To make dear; to make more beloved; to bind by ties of affection and love.—**endearment,** en•dēr′ment, *n.* The act of endearing; the state of being beloved; tender affection; a caress (in this sense chiefly plural).

endeavor, en•dev′ėr, *n.* [Fr. *en,* in, and *devoir,* duty, from the use of these words in such expressions as *se mettre en devoir,* to try to do, to set about; *devoir* (whence *due, duty*) is from L. *debere,* to owe, to be under obligation (whence *debt*).] An exertion of physical strength or the intellectual powers toward the attainment of an object; an effort; an essay; an attempt.—*v.i.* To labor or exert one's self for the accomplishment of an object; to strive; to try; to attempt; to essay.—*v.t.* To try to effect; to strive after: often governing an infinitive.—**endeavorer,** en•dev′ėr•ėr, *n.* One who endeavors.

endemic, endemical, en•dem′ik, en•dem′i•kal, *a.* [Fr. *endémique,* from Gr. *endēmios—en,* in, among, and *dēmos,* people.] Peculiar to a people, locality, or region: a term applied to diseases to which the inhabitants of a particular country are peculiarly subject.—*n.* A disease of an endemic nature. — **endemically,** en•dem′i•kal•li, *adv.* In an endemic manner.

endermic, en•dėr′mik, *a.* [Gr. *en,* and *derma,* skin.] *Med.* applied or effected by rubbing into the skin, especially after the cuticle has been removed, as by a blister.

endive, en′dīv, *n.* [Fr. *endive,* from L. *intybum*; probably from Ar. *hindeb.*] A composite herb used in salads; also called *escarole.*

endocardium, en•do•kär′di•um, *n.* [Gr. *endon,* within, and *kardia,* the heart.] *Anat.* a colorless transparent membrane which lines the interior of the heart.—**endocardiac,** en•do•kär′di•ak, *a.* Relating to the endocardium, or to the interior of the heart. —**endocarditis,** en′do•kär•dī″tis, *n.* An inflammatory disease of the internal parts of the heart, ending in the deposit of fibrin upon the valves.

endocarp, en′do•kärp, *n.* [Gr. *endon,* within, *karpos,* fruit.] *Bot.* the inner layer of the pericarp of fruits, when its texture differs from the outer layer, as the stone of a plum or the flesh of an orange.

endocrine, en′dō•krin, *a.* [L. *endon,* within, and *krinein,* separate.] Secreting internally; applied to those glands that secrete hormonal and metabolic substances into the blood or lymph.—*n.* An endocrine gland.

endoderm, en′dō•dėrm, *n.* [Gr. *endon,* within, and *derma,* skin.] The innermost germ layer of an embryo from which is derived the epithelium of the digestive and respiratory tracts.—**endodermal,** en•dō•dėrm′al, *a.*

endogamy, en•dog′a•mi, *n.* [Gr. *endon,* within, *gamos,* marriage.] A custom among some savage peoples of marrying only within their own tribe; opposite of *exogamy* (q.v.).—**endogamous,** en•dog′a•mus, *a.* Pertaining to, practicing, or characterized by endogamy.

endogenous, en•doj′e•nus, *a.* [Gr. *endon,* within, and *gen,* to produce.] Developing, originating from within. —**endogenously,** en•doj′e•nus•li, *adv.*

—**endogenously,** en•doj′e•nus•li, *adv.* In an endogenous manner; internally.

endolymph, en′do•limf, *n.* [Gr. *endon,* within, E. *lymph.*] *Anat.* a limpid fluid in the labyrinth of the ear.

endomorph, en′do•morf, *n.* [Gr. *endon,* within, *morphē,* form.] *Mineral.* a mineral enclosed in a crystal of another mineral.

endoparasite, en•do•par′a•sīt, *n.* [Gr. *endon,* within, and E. *parasite.*] A parasite living on the internal organs of animals, as opposed to an *ectoparasite.*

endoplasm, en′do•plazm, *n.* [Gr. *endon,* within, and *plasma.* PLASMA.] *Biol.* internal matter of a cell; internal protoplasm.

endorse, en•dors′, *v.t.*—*endorsed, endorsing.* [Prefix *en,* and L. *dorsum,* a back.] To write something on the back of, as one's name as payee on the back of (a check) in order to obtain the cash or credit represented on the face of the document; hence, to assign by writing one's name on the back; to assign or transfer by endorsement; to sanction, ratify, or approve; to acknowledge the receipt of (a sum specified) by one's signature.—**endorsable,** en•dors′a•bl, *a.* Capable of being endorsed.—**endorsement,** en•dors′ment, *n.* The act of endorsing; a note of the contents of any paper on its back; the signature of the holder of a note or bill of exchange written on its back; ratification, sanction, or approval; *insurance,* a provision added to an insurance contract whereby the scope of its coverage is restricted or enlarged.

endosarc, en′do•särk, *n.* [Gr. *endon,* within, *sarx,* flesh.] Endoplasm.

endoskeleton, en•do•skel′e•ton, *n.* [Gr. *endon,* within, and *skeleton.*] The internal bony structure of man and other animals, in contradistinction to *exoskeleton,* the outer hard covering of such animals as the crab, etc.

endosmosis, en•dos•mō′sis, *n.* [Gr. *endon,* within, *ōsmos,* impulsion, from *ōtheō,* to push.] The transmission of fluids or gases through porous septa or partitions, from the exterior to the interior.—**endosmotic,** en•dos•mot′ik, *a.* Of or pertaining to endosmosis; of the nature of or acting by endosmosis.

endosperm, en′do•spėrm, *n.* [Gr. *endon,* within, *sperma,* seed.] *Bot.* the albuminous tissue which surrounds the embryo in many seeds, and which contains the supply of food for the germinating embryo: called also *Albumen.*

endosteum, en•dos′ti•um, *n.* [Gr. *endon,* within, *osteon,* bone.] *Anat.* the lining membrane of the narrow cavity of a bone.

endothecium, en′di•thē″si•um, *n.* [Gr. *endon,* within, *thēkē,* a cell.] *Bot.* the fibrous cellular tissue lining an anther.

endothelium, en′do•the″li•um, *n.* [Gr. *endon,* without, *thēlē,* a nipple.] A delicate cellular membrane lining blood vessels and cavities.

endothermic, en•do•ther′mik, *n.* [Gr. *endon,* within, *thermos,* heat.] Of a chemical reaction, involving absorption of heat; or of the compound so formed.

endow, en•dou′, *v.t.* [Prefix *en,* and Fr. *douer,* to endow, from L. *dos, dotis,* a dowry, from root seen in L. *do,* Gr. *didōmi,* to give.] To furnish with a portion of goods or estate, called *dower;* to settle a dower on; to furnish with a permanent fund or provision for support; to enrich or furnish with any gift, quality, or faculty.—**endowment,** en•dou′ment, *n.* The act of endowing; property, fund, or revenue permanently appropriated to any object; that which is given or bestowed on the person or mind; gift of nature; natural capacity.

endue, en•dū′, *v.t.*—*endued, enduing.* [L. *induo,* to put on. INDUE.] To invest; to clothe; to indue (as with virtue or other qualities).

endure, en•dūr′, *v.i.*—*endured, enduring.* [Fr. *endurer,* from *en,* and *durer,* L. *durare,* to last.] To continue in the same state without perishing; to last; to remain; to abide; to suffer without resistance or without yielding; to hold out; to bear; to suffer.—*v.t.* To bear, sustain, or support without breaking or yielding; to bear with patience; to bear without opposition or sinking under the pressure; to undergo, suffer, experience.—**endurable,** en•dū′ra•bl, *a.* Capable of being endured.—**endurance,** en•dū′rans, *n.* A state of lasting or duration; permanence; lastingness; continuance; a bearing or suffering; a continuing under pain or distress without sinking or yielding; sufferance; patience; fortitude.—**enduring,** en•dū′ring, *a.* Lasting long; permanent. — **enduringly,** en•dū′ring•li, *adv.* Lastingly; for a time.—**enduringness,** en•dū′ring•nes, *n.*

enema, en′ė•ma or en•ē′ma, *n.* [Gr. *enema,* from *eniēmi,* to send in—*en,* in, and *hiēmi,* to send.] A liquid or gaseous substance injected into the rectum.

enemy, en′e•mi, *n.* [Fr. *ennemi,* from L. *inimicus*—*in,* neg., and *amicus,* a friend.] One hostile to another; one who hates another; a foe; an adversary; an antagonist; a hostile force, army, fleet, or the like.

energy, en′ėr•ji, *n.* [Gr. *energeia*—*en,* and *ergon,* work.] Internal or inherent power; the power of operating, whether exerted or not; power exerted; vigorous operation; force; vigor; effectual operation; efficacy; strength or force producing the effect; strength of expression; force of utterance; life; spirit; emphasis; *phys.* power to do work; it may be mechanical, electrical, thermal, chemical, etc.—*Conservation of energy.* CONSERVATION.—**energetic, energetical,** en•ėr•jet′ik, en•ėr•jet′i•kal, *a.* [Gr. *energētikos.*] Acting with or exhibiting energy; operating with force, vigor, and effect; forcible; powerful; efficacious; working; active; operative; vigorous.—**energetically,** en•ėr•jet′i•kal•li, *adv.* In an energetic manner; with energy and effect.—**energize,** en′ėr•jīz, *v.i.*—*energized, energizing.* To act with energy or force; to act in producing an effect.—*v.t.* To give strength or force to; to give active vigor to.

enervate, en′ėr•vāt, *v.t.*—*enervated, enervating.* [L. *enervo, enervatum.*—*e,* out, away, and *nervus,* a nerve.] To deprive of nerve, force, or strength; to weaken; to render feeble; to debilitate.—*a.* Without strength or force; weakened; debilitated.—**enervation,** en′ėr•vā′shon, *n.* The act of enervating; the state of being enervated; effeminacy.

enfeeble, en•fē′bl, *v.t.*—*enfeebled, enfeebling.* To make feeble; to deprive of strength; to weaken; to debilitate or enervate.—**enfeeblement,** en•fē′bl•ment, *n.* The act of enfeebling or state of being enfeebled.

enfeoff, en•fef′, *v.t.* [Prefix *en,* and L.L. *feoffo,* to confer a fief or feud. FIEF.] *Law,* to give a fief or feud to; to invest with the fee of an estate; to give any corporeal hereditament to in fee.—**enfeoffment,** en•fef′ment, *n. Law,* the act of enfeoffing; the instrument or deed by which one is enfeoffed.

Enfield, en′fēld, *n.* [From *Enfield,* Government factory, as *Carronades* at Carron foundry.] A rifle.

enfilade, en•fi•lād′, *v.t.*—*enfiladed, enfilading.* [Fr. *en,* and *file,* a row, a rank, from *fil,* a thread, L. *filum.*] *Milit.* to rake or sweep with shot through the whole length of, as, through a work or line of troops: to fire in the flank of a line.—*n.* A firing in such a manner; the line of fire.

enforce, en•fōrs′, *v.t.*—*enforced, enforcing.* [Prefix *en,* and *force;* Fr. *enforcir.*] To give strength to; to add force, emphasis, or impressiveness to; to inculcate, urge, or press earnestly; to make or gain by force or compulsion; to force; to compel, constrain, or force; to put in execution; to cause to take effect (to *enforce* the laws).—**enforceable,** en•fōr′sa•bl, *a.* Capable of being enforced.—**enforcement,** en•fōrs′ment, *n.* The act of enforcing; compulsion; that which gives force, energy, or effect; sanction; that which urges or constrains; constraining power; a putting in execution (the *enforcement* of law).—**enforcer,** en•fōr′sėr, *n.* One who enforces.

enfranchise, en•fran′chīz, *v.t.*—*enfranchised, enfranchising.* To set free; to liberate from slavery; to free or release, as from custody, bad habits, or any restraining power; to confer the franchise on; to endow with the right of voting.—**enfranchisement,** en•fran′chiz•ment, *n.* The act of enfranchising or the state of being enfranchised.

engage, en•gāj′, *v.t.*—*engaged, engaging.* [Fr. *engager*—*en,* and *gager,* from *gage,* a pledge. GAGE.] To bind or bring under an obligation, as by oath, pledge, contract, or promise: generally with reflexive pron.; to pawn, stake, or pledge; to enlist; to bring into a party; to bespeak, as for service or the like; to win and attach (to *engage* one's affections); to attract and fix (attention); to occupy (to *engage* a person in conversation); to employ the attention or efforts of (to make to embark or take concern in); to enter into contest with; to bring to conflict (to *engage* an enemy).—*v.i.* To promise or pledge one's word; to become bound; to embark in any business; to take a concern in; to undertake; to attack in conflict; to begin mutually a hostile encounter.—**engaged,** en•gājd′, *pp.* or *a.* Pledged; affianced; enlisted; attracted; occupied; earnestly employed.—*Engaged column, arch.* a column attached to a wall so that part of it is concealed.—**engagement,** en•gāj′ment, *n.* The act of engaging; obligation by agreement or contract; the act of betrothing or state of being betrothed; occupation; employment of the attention; affair of business; an appointment; a combat between bodies of troops or fleets; a fight; a conflict.—**engaging,** en•gā′jing, *a.* Winning; attractive; tending to draw the attention or the affections; pleasing.—**engagingly,** en•gā′jing•li, *adv.* In an engaging manner.

engender, en•jen′dėr, *v.t.* [Fr. *engendrer*, from L. *ingenero—in*, and *genero*, to beget, from *genus, generis*, birth, descent. GENUS.] To beget between the different sexes; more generally, to produce; to cause to exist; to cause, excite, stir up.—*v.i.* To be caused or produced; to meet in sexual embrace.

engine, en′jin, *n.* [Fr. *engin*, a machine, a tool, ingenuity, from L. *ingenium*, disposition, ability, invention—*in*, and root *gen*, to produce, as in *genius*. INGENIOUS.] Any instrument in any degree complicated; a tool, instrument, or appliance by which any effect is produced, as a musket, a cannon, the rack, a battering ram, etc.; a person regarded as a tool or instrument†; any mechanical instrument of complicated parts, which concur in producing an intended effect; a machine; especially, a machine for applying steam to drive machinery, to propel vessels, railway trains, etc.; a steam engine.—*v.t.* To furnish (a steam vessel) with an engine or engines.—**engineer,** en•ji•nēr′, *n.* [Formed on type of *charioteer*, *musketeer*, etc.] Originally one who managed military engines or artillery; now one who manages an engine or has to do with the construction of engines and machinery; or a person skilled in the principles and practice of engineering, either civil or military.—*v.t.* To direct or superintend the making of in the capacity of engineer; to perform the office of an engineer in respect of (to *engineer* a canal).—**engineering,** en•ji•nē′ring, *n.* The art of constructing and using engines or machines; the art of executing such works as are the objects of civil and military architecture, in which machinery is in general extensively employed.—*Military engineering*, that branch which relates to the construction and maintenance of fortifications, and the surveying of a country for the various operations of war.—*Civil engineering* relates to the forming of roads, bridges, and railroads, the formation of canals, aqueducts, harbors, drainage of a country, etc.—*Mechanical engineering* refers strictly to machinery.—*Electrical engineering* refers to electrical plant.—**enginery,**† en′jin•ri, *n.* Engines in general; artillery or instruments of war (*Mil.*); mechanism; machinery.

English, ing′glish, *a.* [A.Sax. *Englisc*, from the *Engle* or *Angles*, a North German tribe who settled in Britain.] Belonging to England or to its inhabitants.—*n.* One of the Low German group of languages, spoken by the people of England and the descendants of natives of that country, as the Americans, Canadian and Australian colonists, etc.; as a collective noun, the people of England; *print.* a size of type between great primer and pica.—*v.t.* To translate into the English language; to represent or render in English.—**Englishman,** ing′glish•man, *n.* A native or naturalized inhabitant of England.—**Englishry,** ing′glish•ri, *n.* A population of English descent; especially the persons of English descent in Ireland.

engorge, en•gorj′, *v.t.*—*engorged, engorging*. [Fr. *engorger*—prefix *en*, and *gorge*, the throat.] To swallow; to gorge; to swallow with greediness or in large quantities.—*v.i.* To devour; to feed with eagerness or voracity.—**engorgement,** en•gorj′ment, *n.* The act of swallowing greedily; *med.* congestion.

engraft, en•graft′, *v.t.* To ingraft.

engrail, en•grāl′, *v.t.* [Fr. *engrêler*, to engrail, from *grêle, gresle*, hail.] To variegate; to spot, as with hail; to indent in curved lines.

engram, en′gram, *n.* [Gr. *gramma*, a picture.] *Biol.* the impression left on protoplasm by any physiological happening.

engrave, en•grāv′, *v.t.*—*engraved*, pp. *engraved* or *engraven, engraving*. [Prefix *en*, and *grave*, to carve.] To cut figures, letters, or devices on, as on stone, metal, etc.; to delineate, copy, picture, or represent by incisions, as on stone, metal, wood, etc.; to imprint; to impress deeply; to infix.—**engraver,** en•grā′vėr, *n.* One who engraves; a cutter of letters, figures, or devices on stone, metal, or wood.—**engraving,** en•grā′ving, *n.* In its widest sense, the art of cutting designs, writing, etc., on any hard substance; specifically, the art of forming designs on the surface of metal plates or of blocks of wood for the purpose of taking off impressions or prints of these designs; that which is engraved; an engraved plate; an impression taken from an engraved plate; a print.

engross, en•grōs′, *v.t.* [Fr. *en*, and *grossir*, to enlarge, from *gros*, big. GROSS.] To increase in bulk or quantity (*Shak.*)‡; to seize, occupy, or take up the whole of (cares or duties *engross* one's time or attention); to purchase, with the purpose of making a profit by enhancing the price; to take or assume in undue quantity, proportion, or degree; to write a fair correct copy of in large or distinct legible characters (to *engross* a legal document).—*v.i.* To be employed in engrossing, or making fair copies of writings.—**engrosser,** en•grō′sėr, *n.* One who or that which engrosses; one who takes or assumes in undue quantity, proportion, or degree; one who copies a writing in large fair characters.

engulf, en•gulf′, *v.t.* To swallow up in or as in a gulf or whirlpool; to overwhelm by swallowing.—**engulfment,** en•gulf′ment, *n.* The act of engulfing.

enhance, en•hans′, *v.t.*—*enhanced, enhancing*. [Pr. *enanser*, to advance, enhance, from *enant, enans*, forward, from L. *in*, in, to, *ante*, before.] To heighten; to make greater; to increase (price, pleasure, difficulty, beauty, evil, or other nonphysical object).—*v.i.* To increase or grow larger.—**enhancement,** en•hans′ment, *n.* The act of enhancing or state of being enhanced; rise; augmentation; aggravation.

enharmonic, enharmonical, en•här•mon′ik, en•här•mon′i•kal, *a.* [Fr. *enharmonique*, Gr. *enarmonikos*, in harmony—*en*, in, and *harmonia*, harmony.] *Mus.* of or pertaining to that one of the three ancient Greek scales which consisted of quarter tones; pertaining to a scale of perfect intonation which recognizes intervals less than semitones.—**enharmonically,** en•här•mon′i•kal•li, *adv.* In the enharmonic style or system; with perfect intonation.

enigma, i•nig′ma, *n.* [L. *ænigma*, from Gr. *ainigma*, from *ainissomai*, to speak darkly, from *ainos*, a tale, a story.] A dark saying, in which something is concealed under obscure language; an obscure question; a riddle; something containing a hidden meaning which is proposed to be guessed; anything inexplicable to an observer, such as the means by which anything is effected, the motive for a course of conduct, the cause of any phenomenon, etc.; a person whose conduct or disposition is inexplicable.—**enigmatic, enigmatical,** i•nig•mat′ik, i•nig•mat′i•kal, *a.* Relating to or containing an enigma; obscure; darkly expressed; ambiguous.—**enigmatically,** i•nig•mat′i•kal•li, *adv.* In an enigmatic manner.

enjambment, en•jamb′ment, *n.* [Fr. *enjambement—en*, in, *jambe*, leg.] The prolongation of the words or sense beyond the second line of a couplet.

enjoin, en•join′, *v.t.* [Fr. *enjoindre*, from L. *injungo—in*, and *jungo*, to join.] To prescribe or impose with some authority; to lay, as an order or command; to put by way of injunction; to order, direct, or urge (to *enjoin* submission or obedience *upon* a person; duties *enjoined* by law); to admonish or instruct with authority; to command.—**enjoiner,** en•joi′nėr, *n.* One who enjoins.

enjoy, en•joi′, *v.t.* [O.Fr. *enjoier,* to receive with joy—prefix *en,* and *joie*=E. *joy.*] To feel or perceive with pleasure; to take pleasure or satisfaction in the possession or experience of; to have, possess, and use with satisfaction; to have, hold, or occupy, as a good or profitable thing, or as something desirable.—*To enjoy one's self,* to experience delight from the pleasures in which one partakes; to be happy.—**enjoyable,** en•joi′a•bl, *a.* Capable of being enjoyed; capable of yielding enjoyment.—**enjoyment,** en•joi′-ment, *n.* The condition of enjoying; the possession or occupancy of anything with satisfaction or pleasure; that which gives pleasure or satisfaction in the possession; cause of joy or gratification; delight.

enkindle, en•kin′dl′, *v.t.*—*enkindled, enkindling.* [Prefix *en,* and *kindle.*] To kindle; to set on fire; to inflame; to excite; to rouse into action.—*v.i.* To take fire.

enlace, en•lās′, *v.t.*—*enlaced, enlacing.* To fasten with or as with a lace; to lace; to encircle.—**enlacement,** en•lās′ment, *n.* Act of enlacing; state of being enlaced; an encircling.

enlarge, en•lärj′, *v.t.*—*enlarged, enlarging.* To make larger or greater in quantity or dimensions; to extend; to expand; to augment; to increase; to make more comprehensive (to *enlarge* the mind); to magnify to the eye; to set at liberty; to release from confinement or pressure.—*v.i.* To grow large or larger; to extend; to dilate; to expand; to expatiate in speaking or writing; to speak or write at length or in full detail.—**enlargement,** en•lärj′ment, *n.* The act of enlarging or state of being enlarged; augmentation; dilatation; expansion; something added on; an addition; expansion or extension, as applied to the mind or the intellectual powers; release from confinement; deliverance; a detailed discourse or argument.—**enlarger,** en•lär′jėr, *n.* One who or that which enlarges.

enlighten, en•lī′tn, *v.t.* [Prefix *en,* and *lighten,* to make light.] To shed light on; to give intellectual light to; to enable to see or comprehend.—**enlightenment,** en•lī′tn•ment, *n.* Act of enlightening; [cap.] a movement of the eighteenth century marked by the free use of reason and the rise of humanism.

enlist, en•list′, *v.t.* [Prefix *en,* and *list.*] *Lit.* to enroll or enter on a list; to hire for the public service, especially military service, by entering the name in a register; to employ in advancing some interest; to engage the services of (to *enlist* a person in the cause of truth).—*v.i.* To engage in public service, especially military service, voluntarily; to enter heartily into a cause, as being devoted to its interests.—**enlistment,** en•list′ment, *n.* The act of enlisting; the raising of soldiers by enlisting.

enliven, en•lī′vn, *v.t.* [Prefix *en,* and adj. *live.*] To give life, action, or motion to; to make vigorous or active; to stimulate; to give spirit or vivacity to; to animate; to make sprightly, gay, or cheerful.—**enlivener,** en•lī′vn•ėr, *n.*

en masse, en•mas′, *adv.* [Fr.] As a whole; altogether; in a body.

enmesh, in•mesh′, *v.t.* [Prefix *en,* and *mesh.*] To catch in; to entangle.

enmity, en′mi•ti, *n.* [Fr. *inimitié,* O.Fr. *enemistie,* corresponding to a L. form *inimicitas,* from *inimicus,* unfriendly—*in,* not, and *amicus,* a friend.] The quality or state of being an enemy; hostile or unfriendly disposition; hostility; ill will.

ennead, en′e•ad, *n.* [Gr. *ennea,* nine, *ad,* as in *monad, triad, myriad.*] A collection of nine books, discourses, or accounts.

ennoble, en•nō′bl, *v.t.*—*ennobled, ennobling.* [Prefix *en,* and *noble*; Fr. *ennoblier.*] To make noble; to raise to nobility; to dignify; to exalt; to elevate in degree, qualities, or excellence.—**ennoblement,** en•nō′-bl•ment, *n.* The act of ennobling; the state of being ennobled; exaltation; elevation.

ennui, än′wē, *n.* [Fr., O.Fr. *anui,* annoy, like O.Venet. *inodio,* from L. *in odio,* in hate, in disgust. ODIUM, ANNOY.] Languor of mind arising from lack of occupation; want of interest in present scenes and surrounding objects; listlessness; weariness; tedium.

enormous, i•nor′mus, *a.* [L. *enormis*—*e,* out of, and *norma,* a rule. NORMAL.] Great beyond or exceeding the common measure; excessively large; excessively wicked; flagitious; atrocious. ∴ *Enormous, lit.* out of rule, hence great, far beyond common: used especially of magnitude; *immense,* that cannot be measured: used especially of quantity, extent, and number; *excessive,* beyond bounds, beyond what is fit and right: said especially of degree.—**enormously,** i•nor′mus•li, *adv.* Excessively; beyond measure.—**enormousness,** i•nor′mus•nes, *n.* The state of being enormous.—**enormity,** i•nor′mi•ti, *n.* [L. *enormitas.*] The state or quality of being enormous, immoderate, or excessive; excessive degree; atrociousness; a very grave offense against order, right, or decency; an atrocious crime; an atrocity.

enough, i•nuf′, *a.* [O.E. *inoh, enow,* A.Sax. *genóh, genóg*=D. *genoeg,* Icel. *gnógr,* O.Fris. *enoch,* Goth. *ganohs,* G. *genug,* enough, from a verb meaning to suffice.] Satisfying desire or giving content; meeting reasonable expectations; answering the purpose; adequate to want or demand. [*Enough* usually follows the noun with which it is connected.]—*n.* A sufficiency; a quantity of a thing which satisfies desire or is adequate to the wants; what is equal to the powers or abilities.—*Enough!* an exclamation denoting sufficiency.—*adv.* Sufficiently; in a quantity or degree that satisfies or is equal to the desires or wants; fully; quite; denoting a slight augmentation of the positive degree (he was ready *enough* to embrace the offer); in a tolerable or passable degree (the performance is well *enough*).—**enow,** ē•nou′. An old form of *Enough.*

enounce, i•nouns′, *v.t.*—*enounced, enouncing.* [Fr. *énoncer,* L. *enuncio*—*e,* out, and *nuncio,* to declare, as in *announce, denounce, renounce.*] To declare; to enunciate; to state, as a proposition or argument.

enquire, in•kwīr′, *v.t.* and *i.* **enquirer,** in•kwī′rėr, *n.* **enquiry,** in•kwī′ri, *n.* Same as *Inquire, Inquirer, Inquiry.*

enrage, in•rāj′, *v.t.*—*enraged, enraging.* To excite rage in; to exasperate; to provoke to fury or madness; to make furious.

enrapture, in•rap′chėr *v.t.*—*enraptured, enrapturing.* To transport with rapture; to delight beyond measure.

enravish, in•rav′ish, *v.t.* To transport with delight; to enrapture.

enrich, in•rich′, *v.t.* To make rich, wealthy, or opulent; to supply with abundant property; to fertilize; to supply with an abundance of anything desirable; to fill or store; to supply with anything splendid or ornamental; to adorn.—**enrichment,** in•rich′ment, *n.* The act of enriching; something that enriches or adorns.

enrobe, en•rōb′, *v.t.*—*enrobed, enrobing.* To clothe with attire; to attire; to invest.

enroll, in•rōl′, *v.t.*—*enrolled, enrolling.* [O.Fr. *enroller*—*en,* and *rolle,* roll.] To write in a roll or register; to insert or enter the name of; to insert in records.—**enroller,** in•rōl′ėr, *n.* One who enrolls or registers.—**enrollment,** en•rōl′ment, *n.*

en route, en•röt′, *adv.* [Fr.] On the way; along the way.

ensanguine, en•sang′gwin, *v.t.*—*ensanguined, ensanguining.* [Prefix *en,* and L. *sanguis, sanguinis,* blood.] To stain or cover with blood; to smear with gore.

ensconce, en•skons′, *v.t.*—*ensconced, ensconcing.* To cover or shelter, as with a sconce or fort; to protect; to hide securely; to take shelter behind something; to hide; with the reflexive pronoun.

ensemble, on•som′bl, *n.* [Fr., from L. *insimul,* at the same time—*in,* and *simul,* together.] All the parts of anything taken together so that each part is considered only in relation to the whole; the general effect of a whole work of art, as a picture, piece of music, drama, etc.

enshrine, in•shrīn′, *v.t.*—*enshrined, enshrining.* To enclose in or as in a shrine or chest; to preserve with care and affection; to cherish.

enshroud, en•shroud′, *v.i.* To cover with or as with a shroud; to envelop with anything which conceals from observation.

ensiform, en′si•form, *a.* [L. *ensiformis,*—*ensis,* sword, and *forma,* form.] Having the shape of a sword;

sword-shaped: said of leaves of plants, also of a cartilage at the lower part of the human sternum or breastbone.

ensign, en′sīn, *n.* [Fr. *enseigne,* a sign, an ensign, from L. *insigne,* a sign, a badge—*in,* and *signum,* a mark, a sign. SIGN, SIGNAL.] A sign or token‡; a badge or mark of distinction, rank, or office; a symbol; a flag or standard; the flag or banner distinguishing a company of soldiers, an army, or vessel; the colors; *Military* (usually pronounced en′sin). The lowest commissioned officer in the United States Navy, ranking below a lieutenant, junior grade; formerly a commissioned officer of lowest rank in a British regiment of infantry, the equivalent rank now being that of second lieutenant.—**ensigncy, ensignship,** en′sin•si, en′sin•ship, *n.* The rank, office, or commission of an ensign.

ensilage, en′sil•ij, *n.* [Fr. *ensilage,* from Sp. *ensilar,* to store grain in an underground receptacle, from *en,* in, and *silo,* from L. *sirus,* a pit.] A mode of storing green fodder, vegetables, etc., by burying in pits or silos dug or built, the substance stored being pressed down with heavy weights, and undergoing a slight fermentation; the substance thus treated.—**ensile,** en•sīl′, *v.t.* To store by this process.

enslave, en•slāv′, *v.t.*—*enslaved, enslaving,* To make a slave of; to reduce to slavery or bondage; to subject to the dominant influence of; to master or overpower (*enslaved* by his passions).—**enslavement,** en•slāv′ment, *n.* The act of enslaving or state of being enslaved.—**enslaver,** en•slā′vėr, *n.* One who or that which enslaves.

ensnare, en•snâr′, *v.t.*—*ensnared, ensnaring.* To take in a snare; to entrap; to insnare.

ensue, en•sū′, *v.i.*—*ensued, ensuing.* [Prefix *en,* and *sue*; O.Fr. *ensuir,* from L. *insequor,* to follow upon.] To follow as a consequence; to follow in a train of events or course of time; to succeed; to come after. ∴ Syn. under FOLLOW.

ensure, in•shör′, *v.t.*—*ensured, ensuring.* To make sure or secure; to make certain to turn out, arise, or follow (to *ensure* peace, to *ensure* a good crop).

entablature, en•tab′la•chėr, *n.* [O.Fr. *entablature*—*en,* and *table*; L. *tabula,* a board, plank.] The superstructure which lies horizontally upon the columns in *class. arch.,* and consists of three principal divisions, the architrave, the frieze, and the cornice.

entail, in•tāl′, *n.* [Fr. *entaille,* a cutting, incision, from *entailler,* to cut in—*en,* and *tailler,* to cut, as in *detail, retail, tailor.*] *Law,* an estate or fee entailed or limited in descent to a particular heir or heirs, male or female; rule of descent settled for an estate.—*v.t. Law,* to settle the descent of (lands and tenements) by gift to a man and to certain heirs specified so that neither the donee nor any subsequent possessor can alienate or bequeath it; to transmit in an unalterable course; to devolve as a consequence or of necessity (crimes *entail* punishment).—**entailment,** in•tāl′ment, *n.* The act of entailing or state of being entailed.

entangle, in•tang′gl, *v.t.*—*entangled, entangling.* [TANGLE.] To interweave in such a manner as not to be easily separated; to make confused or disordered; to involve in anything complicated, and from which it is difficult to extricate one's self; to involve in difficulties or embarrassments; to puzzle; to perplex; to involve in contradictions; to hamper.—**entanglement,** in•tang′gl•ment, *n.* The act of entangling or state of being entangled.—**entangler,** in•tang′glėr, *n.* One who entangles.

entelechy, en•tel′e•ki, *n.* [Gr. *entelechia.*] The absoluteness, or actuality, of a thing, as opposed to simple capability or potentiality. A philosophic coinage by Aristotle, who styles the soul the *entelechy* of the body, that by which it actually is, though it had the capacity of existing before; actual, as opposed to virtual, or potential, power. In Rabelais, the kingdom of Queen Quintessence, the city of speculative science.

entellus, en•tel′lus, *n.* [Fr. *entelle,* from Gr. *entellō,* to command.] An East Indian species of monkey, the sacred monkey of the Hindus.

entente, äṅ•täṅt′, *n.* [Fr. *entente.*] An understanding, a good feeling between two or more nations; *entente cordiale, triple entente.*

enter, en′tėr, *v.t.* [Fr. *entrer,* from L. *intrare,* to enter, from *intro,* into the inside—*in,* in, and root seen in *trans,* across (a common prefix), and in Skr. *tri,* to pass.] To come or go into in any manner whatever; to pierce; to penetrate; to begin or commence upon, as a new period or stage in the progress of life, a new state of things, etc.; to engage or become involved in; to join; to become a member of (an army, a profession, a college); to initiate into a business, service, society, method, etc.; to set down in a book or other record; to enroll; to inscribe; to report (a ship) at the customhouse on arrival in port, by delivering a manifest; *law,* to go in or upon and take possession of (lands); to place in regular form before a court.—*v.i.* To come in; to go or pass in; sometimes with *in*; to embark or enlist in an affair; to become a member.—*To enter into,* to get into the inside or interior of; to penetrate; to engage in (to *enter into* business); to deal with or treat by way of discussion, argument, and the like; to be an ingredient in; to form a constituent part in.—*To enter on* or *upon,* to begin; to commence; to treat or deal with; to discuss or talk of; to examine.

enteric, en•ter′ik, *a.* [Gr. *enterikos,* from *enteron,* intestine.] Belonging to the intestines.—*Enteric fever,* same as *Typhoid Fever.*—**enteritis,** en•te•rī′tis, *n. Med.* inflammation of the intestines.—**enterology,** en•te•rol′o•ji, *n.* A treatise or discourse on the viscera or internal parts of the body.—**enterotomy,** en•te•rot′o•mi, *n.* [Gr. *enteron,* and *tomē,* a cutting.] Dissection of the bowels or intestines; incision of the bowels for the removal of strangulation, etc.

enterprise, en′tėr•prīz, *n.* [Fr., from *entreprendre,* pp. *entrepris, entreprise.*—*entre,* between, and *prendre,* to take, to lay hold of, from L. *prehendo, prendo,* as in *apprehend, comprehend.*] That which is undertaken or attempted to be performed; a project attempted; particularly, a bold, arduous, or hazardous undertaking; an active and enterprising spirit; readiness to engage in undertakings of difficulty, risk, or danger.—*v.t.*†—*enterprised, enterprising.* To undertake.—**enterpriser,** en′tėr•prī′zėr, *n.* An adventurer; one who engages in an enterprise.—**enterprising,** en′tėr•prī•zing, *a.* Having a disposition for or tendency to engage in enterprises; ready to start and carry on untried schemes.—**enterprisingly,** en′tėr•prī•zing•li, *adv.* In an enterprising manner.

entertain, en•tėr•tān′, *v.t.* [Fr. *entretenir,* to maintain—*entre*=L. *inter,* between, and *tenir*=L. *tenere,* to hold.] To receive into the house and treat with hospitality; to receive as a host his guests; to engage the attention of agreeably; to amuse with anything that causes the time to pass pleasantly; to take into consideration; to hold or maintain in the mind with favor; to harbor; to cherish (to *entertain* charitable sentiments). ∴ Syn. under AMUSE.—*v.i.* To give entertainments; to receive company.—**entertainer,** en•tėr•tā′nėr, *n.* One who entertains.—**entertaining,** en•tėr•tā′ning, *a.* Affording entertainment; pleasing; amusing; diverting.—**entertainingly,** en•tėr•tā′ning•li, *adv.* In an amusing manner.—**entertainingness,** en•tėr•tā′ning•nes, *n.* The quality of being entertaining.—**entertainment,** en•tėr•tān′ment, *n.* The act of entertaining; the receiving and accommodating of guests; food, lodging, or other things required by a guest; a hospitable repast; the pleasure which the mind receives from anything interesting, and which holds or arrests the attention; that which entertains; that which serves for amusement, as a dramatic or other performance; reception; admission.

enthrall, en•thrạl′, *v.t.* To reduce to the condition of a thrall; to enslave; to charm or to captivate; to hold spellbound.—**enthrallment,** en•thrạl′ment, *n.* The act of enthralling, or state of being enthralled.

enthrone, en•thrōn′, *v.t.*—*enthroned, enthroning.* To place on a throne; to invest with sovereign authority; to exalt to an elevated place or seat; to induct or install (a bishop) into the powers and privileges of a vacant see.—**enthronement,** en•thrōn′ment, *n.* Act of enthroning, or state of being enthroned.—**enthronization,** en•thrō′ni•zā″shon, *n.* The act of enthroning; the placing of a bishop on his throne in his cathedral.

enthusiasm, en•thū′zi•azm, *n.* [Gr. *enthousiasmos,* from *enthousiazō,* to infuse a divine spirit, from *enthous, entheos,* inspired, divine—*en,* and *theos,* god (whence *theist*).] An ecstasy of mind, as if from inspiration or possession by a spiritual influence; complete possession of the mind by any subject; ardent zeal in pursuit of an object; predominance of the emotional over the intellectual powers; elevation of fancy; exaltation of ideas.—**enthusiast,** en•thū′zi•ast, *n.* [Gr. *enthousiastēs.*] One full of enthusiasm; one whose mind is completely possessed by any subject; one who is swayed to a great or undue extent by his feelings in any pursuit; a person of ardent zeal; one of elevated fancy; a highly imaginative person.—**enthusiastic, enthusiastical,** en•thū′-zi•as″tik, en•thū′zi•as″ti•kal, *a.* Filled with or characterized by enthusiasm; prone to enthusiasm; ardent; devoted.—**enthusiastically,** en•thū′-zi•as″ti•kal•li, *adv.* With enthusiasm.

enthymeme, en′thi•mēm, *n.* [Gr. *enthymēma*—*en,* and *thymos,* mind.] *Rhet.* an argument consisting of only two premises or propositions, a third proposition required to complete the syllogism being suppressed or kept in mind; as, 'we are dependent, therefore we should be humble'—the proposition omitted being 'all dependent creatures should be humble'.

entice, en•tīs′, *v.t.*—*enticed, enticing.* [O.Fr. *enticer, entiser*=Mod. Fr. *attiser,* from *tison,* L. *titio,* a firebrand.] To draw on by exciting hope or desire; to allure, attract, invite; to lead astray; to induce to evil.—**enticement,** en•tīs′ment, *n.* The act or means of enticing; allurement; attraction; seduction.—**enticer,** en•tī′sėr, *n.* One who or that which entices.—**enticing,** en•-tī•sing, *p.* and *a.* Alluring; attracting; attractive.—**enticingly,** en•tī′sing•li, *adv.* In an enticing manner.

entire, en•tīr′, *a.* [Fr. *entier,* from L. *integer,* whole (whence *integer, integrity,* etc.).] Whole; unbroken; complete in its parts; perfect; not mutilated; not participated with others; mere; sheer. ∴ Syn. under COMPLETE.—*Entire horse,* an uncastrated horse; a stallion.—*n.* That kind of malt liquor known also as porter or stout: so called because it combined the qualities of various sorts of beer, and did not necessitate mixing.—**entirely,** en•tīr′li, *adv.* Wholly; completely; fully; altogether.—**entireness,** en•tīr′nes, *n.* Completeness; unbroken form or state.—**entirety,** en•tīr′ti, *n.* The state of being entire or whole; wholeness; completeness; the whole.

entitle, en•tī′tl, *v.t.*—*entitled, entitling.* [O.Fr. *entituler,* Fr. *intituler*—L. *in,* and *titulus,* a title.] To give a name or title to; to affix a name or appellation to; to designate; to denominate; to call; to name; to furnish with a title, right, or claim (a railway ticket *entitles* a person to travel).

entity, en′ti•ti, *n.* [L.L. *entitas,* from *ens, entis,* a thing. ENS.] Being; character of existence; essence; a being or species of being; an existing thing.

entomb, en•töm′, *v.t.* To deposit in a tomb; to bury; to inter.—**entombment,** en•töm′ment, *n.* The act of entombing; burial; sepulture.

entomology, en•to•mol′o•ji, *n.* [Gr. *entomon,* an insect, from *entomos,* cut in—*en,* in, and *temnō,* to cut; from the thorax being almost divided from the abdomen.] That branch of zoology which treats of the structure, habits, and classification of insects.—**entomologic, entomological,** en′to•mo•loj″ik, en′to•mo•-loj″i•kal, *a.* Pertaining to entomology.—**entomologically,** en′to•mo•loj″i•-kal•li, *adv.* In an entomological manner.—**entomologist,** en•to•mol′-o•jist, *n.* One versed in entomology.—**entomophagous,** en•to•mof′a•gus, *a.* Feeding on insects; insectivorous.

entophyte, en′to•fīt, *n.* [Gr. *entos,* within, and *phyton,* a plant.] A plant growing in the interior of animal or vegetable structures; a plant growing on or in living animals.—**entophytic,** en•to•fit′ik, *a.* Pertaining to entophytes.

entourage, än•tụ•räzh′, *n.* [Fr. *entour,* around—*en,* in, and *tour,* circuit.] The attendants to a person; one's associates; the surrounding environment.

entr'acte, äṅ•träkt′, *n.* [Fr.] The interval between the acts of a drama; a short musical entertainment performed during such interval.

entrails, en′trālz, *n. pl.* [Fr. *entrailles*; from L.L. *intralia,* from L. *inter,* within.] The internal parts of animal bodies; the bowels; the viscera; the guts.

entrain, en•trān′, *v.t.* To put on board a railroad train; opposed to *detrain.*—*v.i.* To take places in a railroad train.

entrance, en′trans, *n.* [From *enter.*] The act of entering into a place; the power or liberty of entering; admission; the doorway or passage by which a place may be entered; initiation; beginning; the act of taking possession, as of property or an office.—**entrant,** en′trant, *n.* One who enters; one who begins a new course of life; one becoming a member for the first time of any association or body.

entrance, en•trans′, *v.t.* or *i.*—*entranced, entrancing.* To throw into a trance; to put into an ecstasy; to ravish with delight or wonder; to enrapture.—**entrancement,** en•-trans′ment, *n.* The act of entrancing or state of being entranced.

entrap, en•trap′, *v.t.*—*entrapped, entrapping.* To catch as in a trap: to ensnare; to catch by artifices; to entangle.

entreat, en•trēt′, *v.t.* [Prefix *en,* and *treat*; O.Fr. *entraiter,* to treat of.] To ask earnestly (a person or a thing); to beseech; to supplicate; to solicit pressingly; to importune; to treat, handle, or deal with‡.—**entreatingly,** en•trē′ting•li, *adv.* In an entreating manner.—**entreaty,** en•trē′ti, *n.* Urgent prayer; earnest petition; pressing solicitation; supplication.

entree, äṅ′trā, *n.* [Fr.] Entry; freedom of access; a dish served between courses at dinner, or a dish served as the main course.—**entremets,** äṅ′-tr•mā, *n.* [Fr. *entre,* between, and *mets,* a dish.] A side dish or minor dish at table, as an omelet, a jelly, etc.

entrench, en•trensh′, *v.t.* [Prefix *en,* and *trench.*] To dig or cut a trench or trenches round, as in fortification; to fortify with a ditch and parapet; to lodge within or as within an entrenchment; to place in a strong position.—*v.i.* To invade; to encroach: with *on* or *upon.*—**entrenchment,** en•trensh′ment, *n.* The act of entrenching; *fort.* a work consisting of a trench or ditch and a parapet (the latter formed of the earth dug out of the ditch), constructed for a defense against an enemy; an inroad or encroachment on the rights of others.

entrepôt, äṅ′tre•pō, *n.* [Fr., from L. *inter,* between, *positum,* placed.] A warehouse for the depositing of goods; an emporium or center for the distribution of merchandise.

entrepreneur, än′trā•pre•nūr″, *n.* [Fr. *entreprendre,* to undertake.] The person who organizes, manages, and assumes the risks of a business; a successful businessman.

entresol, en′tėr•sol or äṅ•tr•sol, *n.* [Fr.] *Arch.* a low story between two others of greater height.

entropy, en′trop•i, *n.* [Gr. *en,* in, *tropē*—transformation.] A measure of the unavailability of thermal energy for conversion into mechanical work.

entrust, en•trust′, *v.t.* [Fr. *en,* in, and E. *trust.*] To deliver in trust; to trust or confide to the care of; to commit with confidence (to *entrust* a thing *to* a person, or a person *with* a thing); consign; commit; confide.

entry, en′tri, *n.* [Fr. *entrée.* ENTER.] The act of entering; entrance; ingress; the act of recording in a book; any single item entered or set down; the passage into a house or other building or into a room; a beginning; a first attempt; the giving an account of a ship's cargo or exhibition of her papers, and obtaining permission to land goods; *law,* the act of taking possession of lands or tenements.

entwine, en•twīn′, *v.t.* and *i.*—*entwined, entwining.* [Prefix *en,* and *twine.*] To twist or become twisted round.

enumerate, i•nū′me•rāt, *v.t.*—*enumerated, enumerating.* [L. *enumero, enumeratum*—*e,* out, and *numerus,* number.] To count or tell, number by number; to number; to count; to mention one by one; to recount.—**enumeration,** i•nū′me•rā″shon, *n.* The act of enumerating; an account of a number of things each by each.

—**enumerative,**† i•nū′me•rā•tiv, *a.* Counting; reckoning up.—**enumerator,** i•nū′me•rā•tėr, *n.* One who enumerates.

enunciate, i•nun′shi•āt, *v.t.*—*enunciated, enunciating.* [L. *enuncio, enunciatum*—*e,* out, and *nuncio,* to tell. NUNCIO.] To utter, as words or syllables; to pronounce; to declare; to proclaim; to announce; to state.—*v.i.* To utter words or syllables.—**enunciable,** i•nun′shi•a•bl, *a.* Capable of being enunciated or expressed.—**enunciation,** i•nun′shi•ā″shon, *n.* The act of enunciating; declaration; expression; utterance; announcement; statement.—**enunciative,** i•nun′shi•ā•tiv, *a.* Pertaining to enunciation; declarative.—**enunciatively,** i•nun′shi•ā•tiv•li, *adv.* Declaratively.—**enunciator,** i•nun′shi•ā•tėr, *n.* One who enunciates.—**enunciatory,** i•nun′shi•a•to•ri, *a.* Pertaining to enunciation or utterance.

enure, in•ūr′, *v.i.* [Same as *Inure.*] To take or have effect; to be available or of benefit.

enuresis, en•ū•rē′sis, *n.* [Gr. *en,* in, and *ouron,* urine.] *Pathol.* incontinence or involuntary discharge of urine.

envelop, en•vel′up, *v.t.* [Fr. *envelopper,* It. *invillupare,* to envelop—prefix *en,* in, and verb equivalent to E. *wrap,* an old form of which is *wlap;* so also *develop.*] To cover, as by wrapping or folding; to enwrap or wrap up; to surround entirely; to cover on all sides; to form a covering about; to lie around and conceal; to outflank or turn the enemy's line, so that it is partially surrounded.—**envelope,** en′ve•lōp, *n.* What is wrapped around or envelops something; a wrapper; an enclosing cover; an integument; *bot.* one of the parts of fructification surrounding the stamens and pistils; the outer covering of a balloon or airship distended by means of enclosed gas, usually a fabric into the construction of which a rubber enters.—**envelopment,** en•vel′up•ment, *n.* The act of enveloping; that which envelops.

envenom, en•ven′om, *v.t.* To taint or impregnate with venom; to poison; to imbue with bitterness or malice; to enrage; to exasperate.

enviable, envious, etc. See ENVY.

environ, en•vī′ron, *v.t.* [Fr. *environner*—*en,* and O.Fr. *vironner,* to veer, to environ, from *virer,* to veer. VEER.] To surround, encompass, or encircle; to hem in; to involve; to envelop.—**environment,** en•vī′ron•ment, *n.* Act of surrounding; state of being environed; that which environs; surroundings.—**environs,** en•vī′ronz, *n. pl.* The parts or places which surround another place, or lie in its neighborhood, on different sides.

envisage, en•viz′ij, *v.t.* [Fr. *envisager*—*en,* in, and *visage,* face.] To look in the face of; to face.

envoy, en′voi, *n.* [Fr. *envoyer,* to send *en,* and *voie,* L. *via,* a way, as in *convoy, voyage,* etc. WAY.] One dispatched upon an errand or mission; a messenger; a person deputed to negotiate a treaty, or transact other business, with a foreign ruler or government; a diplomatic agent sent on a special occasion; short poem or stanzas addressed by the author to the reader, sending him 'on his way' with the book.

envy, en′vi, *n.* [Fr. *envie,* from L. *invidia,* envy, from *invidus,* envious—*in,* against, and root *vid,* to look. VISION.] Pain, uneasiness, mortification, or discontent excited by the sight of another's superiority or success; a feeling that makes a person begrudge another his good fortune; malice; object of envy.—*v.t.*—*envied, envying.* [Fr. *envier.*] To feel envy toward or on account of; to repine at; to regard with malice and longing; to desire earnestly.—*v.i.* To be affected with envy; to have envious feelings.—**enviable,** en′vi•a•bl, *a.* Exciting or capable of exciting envy.—**enviably,** en′vi•a•bli, *adv.* In an enviable manner.—**envious,** en′vi•us, *a.* [Fr. *envieux.*] Feeling or harboring envy; tinctured with envy; excited or directed by envy.—**enviously,** en′vi•us•li, *adv.* In an envious manner.—**enviousness,** en′vi•us•nes, *n.*

enwrap, en•rap′, *v.t.* To envelop; to inwrap.

enzootic, en•zō•ot′ik, *a.* [Gr. *en,* among, and *zōon,* an animal.] Limited to the animals of a district: said of diseases,—*n.* A disease affecting the animals of a district.

enzyme, en′zīm, *n.* [Gr. *en,* in, *zymē,* leaven.] *Physiol.* a very large class of protein substances that are produced by living cells and that are essential to life by acting as catalysts in the metabolism of the cell.

Eocene, ē′o•sēn, *a.* and *n.* [Gr. *eōs,* the dawn, and *kainos,* recent.] *Geol.* a term applied to strata at the base of the tertiary formations, having a small proportion of living species among the fossils.

Eolian, Eolic, ē•ō′li•an, ē•ol′ik, *a.* A name of one of the ancient Greek races.—*Eolian mode, mus.,* the fifth of the authentic Gregorian modes; it consists of the natural notes A B C D E F G.—*n.* The Eolian dialect; one of the Eolian race.

Eolian, ē•ō′li•an, *a.* Pertaining to *Aeolus,* the god of the winds.—*Eolian lyre* or *harp,* a simple instrument that sounds by the air sweeping across its strings.

eolith, ē′o•lith, *n.* [Gr. *ēōs,* dawn, *lithos,* stone.] The oldest known type of prehistoric stone implements.

eolithic, ē•o•lith′ik, *a.* [Gr. *eos,* dawn, and *lithos,* stone.] *Archeol.* pertaining to the period 500,000 years ago during the use of the first stone tools.

eon, aeon, ē′on, *n.* [Gr. *aiōn,* age, duration, eternity.] A long indefinite space of time; an age; an era.

eosin, ē′o•sin, *n.* [Gr. *ēōs,* dawn.] A dye obtained from coal-tar products, giving a rose-red color.

Eozoic, ē•o•zō′ik, *a.* [Gr. *ēōs,* dawn, and *zoē,* life.] Of or pertaining to the oldest fossiliferous rocks, from their being supposed to contain the first or earliest traces of life in the stratified systems.

epact, ē′pakt, *n.* [Gr. *epaktos,* brought in or on—*epi,* on, and *agō,* to lead.] *Chron.* the excess of the solar month above the lunar synodical month, and of the solar year above the lunar year of twelve synodical months.

eparch, ep′ärk, *n.* [Gr. *eparchos*—*epi,* and *archē,* dominion.] In Greece, the governor of a province or eparchy.—**eparchy,** ep′är•ki, *n.* [Gr. *eparchia.*] The territory under the jurisdiction of an eparch.

epaule, e•pal′, *n.* [Fr. *épaule,* the shoulder, O.Fr. *espaule,* from L. *spatula, spathula,* a broad, flat thing; dim. of *spatha,* a broad blade; allied to *spade.*] *Fort.* the shoulder of a bastion, or the angle made by the face and flank.—**epaulet,** ep′e•let, *n.* [Fr. *épaulette.*] A shoulder piece; an ornamental badge worn on the shoulder, especially by military and naval officers.

epencephalon, ep•en•sef′a•lon, *n.* [Gr. *epi,* near, and *enkephalon,* the brain.] *Anat.* the hindmost of the four divisions or segments of the brain.—**epencephalic,** ep′en•se•fal″ik, *a. Anat.* of or belonging to the epencephalon.

epenthesis, e•pen′the•sis, *n.* [Gr. *epi,* on, *en,* in, and *tithēmi,* to put.] *Gram.* the insertion of a letter or syllable in the middle of a word.—**epenthetic,** ep•en•thet′ik, *a. Gram.* inserted in the middle of a word.

epergne, e•pėrn′, *n.* [Apparently from Fr. *épargne,* thrift, economy.] An ornamental stand with a large dish and branches for the center of a table.

epexegesis, e•pek′se•jē″sis, *n.* [Gr. *epi,* and *exegesis.* EXEGESIS.] A full explanation or interpretation of something immediately preceding; exegesis.—**epexegetical,** e•pek′se•jet″i•kal, *a.* Explanatory; exegetical.

epha, ephah, ē′fä, *n.* [Heb.] A Hebrew measure of capacity, containing, according to one estimate, 8.6696 gallons; according to another, 4.4286.

ephemeral, e•fem′e•ral, *a.* [Gr. *ephemeros,* lasting but a day, short-lived—*epi,* and *hēmera,* a day.] Beginning and ending in a day; continuing or existing one day only; short-lived; fleeting.—**ephemera,** e•fem′e•ra, *n.* A small fly that lives but for a day or for a very short time; the day fly.—**ephemeris,** e•fem′e•ris, *n.* pl. **ephemerides,** e•fe•mer′i•dēz. [Gr., a diary.] A journal or account of daily transactions; a diary; *astron.* a publication exhibiting the places of the heavenly bodies throughout the year, and giving other information regarding them; an astronomical almanac; a collective name for reviews, magazines, and all kinds of periodical literature.—**ephemeron,** e•fem′e•ron, *n.*

Ephesian, e•fē′zhi•an, *a.* Pertaining to Ephesus in Asia Minor.

Ephesians, e•fē′zhanz, *n.* pl. construed as sing. [L. *Ephesius.*] In the New Testament, the Epistle of St. Paul, the Apostle to the Ephesians.

ephod, ef′od, *n.* [Heb., from *aphad,* to put on.] A species of vestment worn by the Jewish high priest over the second tunic, and consisting of two main pieces, one covering the back, the other the breast and upper part of the body.

ephor, ef′or, *n.* [Gr. *ephoros.*] A name of certain magistrates among the ancient Spartans.

epiblast, ep′i•blast, *n.* [Gr. *epi,* upon, and *blastos,* a bud.] *Bot.* a second cotyledon, consisting of a small transverse plate, found on some grasses; *anat.* the upper of the two layers of cells (the under being the *hypoblast*) forming the blastoderm.

epic, ep′ik, *a.* [L. *epicus,* from Gr. *epikos,* from *epos,* a word, a song.] Composed in a lofty narrative style of poetry; pertaining to such a style; narrative; heroic.—*n.* A narrative poem of elevated character, describing often the exploits of heroes.

epicalyx, ep•i•kā′liks, *n.* [Gr. *epi,* upon, and *calyx.*] *Bot.* the outer calyx in plants with two calyces, formed either of sepals or bracts.

epicarp, ep′i•kärp, *n.* [Gr. *epi,* upon, and *karpos,* fruit.] *Bot.* the outer skin of fruits, the fleshy substance or edible portion being termed the *mesocarp,* and the inner portion the *endocarp.*

epicene, ep′i•sēn, *a.* [Gr. *epikainos,* common to a number—*epi,* and *koinos,* common.] *Gram.* a term applied to nouns which have but one form of gender, either the masculine or feminine, to indicate animals of both sexes.

epicentrum, ep•i•sent′rum, *n.* [Gr. *epicentros.*] The point at which an earthquake breaks out.

epicotyl, ep′i•kot″il, *n.* [Gr. *epi,* above, *cotyl*(edon).] In seedlings, that part of the stem immediately above the seed leaves (cotyledons).

epicure, ep′i•kūr, *n.* [After *Epicurus,* a Greek philosopher who taught that pleasure and pain are the chief good and chief evil.] One devoted to sensual enjoyments; especially one who indulges in the luxuries of the table.—**Epicurean,** ep′i•kū•rē″an, *a.* Pertaining to Epicurus or his teaching; luxurious; given to luxury.—*n.* A follower of Epicurus; a man devoted to sensual pleasures or luxuries; an epicure.—**Epicureanism,** ep′i•kū•rē″an•izm, *n.* The principles or philosophical doctrines of Epicurus; attachment to luxurious habits.—**epicurism,** ep′i•kū•rizm, *n.* The practices of an epicure.

epicycle, ep′i•sī•kl, *n.* [Gr. *epi,* and *kyklos,* a circle.] In old astronomy, a little circle, whose center moves round in the circumference of a greater circle.—**epicyclic,** ep•i•sī′klik, *a.* Pertaining to an epicycle.—**epicycloid,** ep•i•sī′kloid, *n. Geom.* a curve generated by the movement of a curve upon the convex or concave side of another fixed curve.—**epicycloidal,** ep′i•sī•kloi″dal, *a.* Pertaining to the epicycloid, or having its properties.—*Epicycloidal wheel,* a fixed wheel or ring toothed on its inner side, and having in gear with it another toothed wheel of half the diameter, fitted so as to revolve about the center of the larger.

epidemic, epidemical, ep•i•dem′ik, ep•i•dem′i•kal, *a.* [Gr. *epi,* upon, and *demos,* people.] Common to or affecting a whole people, or a great number in a community: said of diseases; prevalent; general; generally prevailing.—**epidemic,** *n.* A disease which, arising from a widespread cause, attacks many people at the same period and in the same country.—**epidemically,** ep•i•dem′i•kal•li, *adv.* In an epidemic manner.—**epidemiological,** ep•i•dē′mi•o•loj″i•kal, *a.* Pertaining to epidemiology.—**epidemiologist,** ep•i•dē′mi•ol″o•jist, *n.* One skilled in epidemiology.—**epidemiology,** ep•i•dē′mi•ol″o•ji, *n.* The doctrine of or method of investigating epidemic diseases.

epidermis, ep•i•dėr′mis, *n.* [Gr. *epidermis—epi,* and *derma,* skin.] *Anat.* the outermost layer of the skin; the cuticle or scarfskin of the body; a thin membrane covering the true skin of animals; *bot.* the cellular integument, or the exterior cellular coating of the leaf or stem of a plant.—**epidermal,** ep•i•dėr′mal, *a.* Relating to the epidermis; epidermic.—**epidermoid,** ep•i•dėr′moid, *a.* Resembling or pertaining to the epiderm.—**epidermic, epidermical,** ep•i•dėr′mik, ep•i•dėr′mi•kal, *a.* Pertaining to or like the epidermis.

epidote, ep′i•dōt, *n.* [Fr., from Gr. *epi,* over and above, and *didōmi,* to give, from the enlargement of the base of the primary in some of the secondary forms.] A mineral of a green or gray color, vitreous luster, and partial transparency, a member of the garnet family.

epigastric, ep•i•gas′trik, *a.* [Gr. *epi,* and *gastēr,* belly.] Pertaining to the upper and anterior part of the abdomen.—**epigastrium,** ep•i•gas′tri•um, *n.* The upper part of the abdomen.

epigene, ep′i•jēn, *a.* [Gr. *epi,* upon, and root *gen,* to produce.] *Geol.* formed or originating on the surface of the earth: opposed to *hypogene.*

epigenesis, ep•i•jen′e•sis, *n.* [Gr. *epi,* and *genesis,* generation.] The biological theory that organic bodies and parts are produced by superadded vital activity and not merely developed from pre-existing bodies.—**epigenetic,** ep′i•je•net″ik, *a.* Pertaining to or produced by epigenesis.—**epigenous,** ep•ij′e•nus, *a. Bot.* growing upon the surface of a part.

epigeous, ep•i•jē′us, *a.* [Gr. *epi,* upon, and *ge, gaia,* the earth.] *Bot.* growing on or close to the earth.

epiglottis, ep•i•glot′is, *n.* [Gr. *epiglōttis—epi,* upon, and *glōttis.*] *Anat.* a cartilaginous plate behind the tongue, which covers the glottis like a lid during the act of swallowing.

epigram, ep′i•gram, *n.* [Gr. *epigramma,* an inscription—*epi,* upon, and *gramma,* a writing, from *graphō,* to write.] A short poem usually keenly satirical, the last line of which generally contains the sting or pointed allusion; also an interesting thought represented happily in a few words, whether verse or prose; a pointed or antithetical saying.—**epigrammatic, epigrammatical,** ep′i•gram•mat″ik, ep′i•gram•mat″i•kal, *a.* Relating to, characterized by, or producing epigrams; like an epigram; antithetical; pointed.—**epigrammatically,** ep′i•gram•mat″i•kal•li, *adv.* In an epigrammatic manner or style; tersely and pointedly.—**epigrammatist,** ep•i•gram′ma•tist, *n.* One who composes epigrams or deals in them.—**epigrammatize,** ep•i•gram′ma•tīz, *v.t.* To represent or express by epigrams.

epigraph, ep′i•graf, *n.* [Gr. *epigraphē—epi,* and *graphō,* to write.] An inscription on a building, tomb, monument, statue, etc., denoting its use or appropriation; a quotation or motto at the commencement of a work, or at its separate divisions.—**epigraphic,** ep•i•graf′ik, *a.* Of or pertaining to an epigraph.—**epigraphy,** e•pig′ra•fi, *n.* That branch of knowledge which deals with the deciphering and explaining of inscriptions.—**epigraphist,** e•pig′ra•fist, *n.* One versed in epigraphics.

epigynous, e•pij′i•nus, *a.* [Gr. *epi,* upon, and *gyné,* female.] *Bot.* growing or appearing to grow upon the top of the ovary.

epilepsy, ep′i•lep•si, *n.* [Gr. *epilēpsia,* —*epi,* upon, and *lambanō, lēpsomai,* to take or seize.] A chronic nervous disease characterized by brief convulsive seizures and loss of consciousness.—**epileptic,** ep•i•lep′tik, *a.* Pertaining to, or affected with, epilepsy.—**epileptic,** *n.* One affected with epilepsy; a medicine for the cure of epilepsy.—**epileptoid,** ep•i•lep′toid, *a.* Of or pertaining to epilepsy; resembling epilepsy.

epilogue, ep′i•log, *n.* [L. *epilogus,* from Gr. *epilogos,* conclusion—*epi,* and *legō,* to speak.] A speech or short poem addressed to the spectators by one of the actors, after the conclusion of a drama.

epinasty, ep′i•nas•ti, *n.* [Gr. *epi,* on, *nastos,* pressed.] *Bot.* a bending downward of an organ owing to the more rapid growth of its upper than its under surface.

Epiphany, i•pif′a•nē, *n.* [Gr. *epiphaneia,* appearance, from *epiphainō,* to appear—*epi,* upon, and *phainō,* to show.] An appearance or a becoming manifest; specifically, a Christian festival celebrated on the sixth day of January in commemoration of the manifestation of the Saviour's birth to the wise men of the East.

epiphysis, i•pif′i•sis, *n.* [Gr. *epiphysis —epi,* upon, and *phyō,* to grow.] *Anat.* any portion of a bone separated from the body of the bone by a cartilage which becomes converted into bone by age.—**epiphyseal, epiphysial,** ep•i•fiz′ē•al, ep•i•fiz′i•al, *a.* Pertaining to or having the nature of an epiphysis.

epiphyte, ep′i•fīt, *n.* [Gr. *epi,* upon, and *phyton,* a plant.] A plant growing upon another plant, but not deriving its nourishment from it; an air plant.—**epiphytic, epiphytical,** ep•i•fit′ik, ep•i•fit′i•kal, *a.* Pertaining to or having the nature of an epiphyte.

episcopacy, i•pis′kō•pa•si, *n.* [L. *episcopatus,* from Gr. *episkopos,* a bishop. BISHOP.] That form of ecclesiastical government in which bishops are established, as distinct from and superior to priests or presbyters; the collective body of bishops.—**episcopal,** i•pis′ko•pl, *a.* Belonging to or vested in bishops or prelates; characteristic of or pertaining to a bishop or bishops.—**episcopalian,** i•pis′ko•pā″li•an, *a.* Pertaining to bishops or government by bishops; episcopal.—*n.* [*cap.*] One who belongs to an episcopal church or favors episcopacy.—**episcopalianism,** i•pis′ko•pā″li•an•izm, *n.* The system of episcopal religion, or government of the church by bishops.—**episcopally,** i•pis′ko•pal•li, *adv.* In an episcopal manner.—**episcopate,** i•pis′ko•pāt, *n.* A bishopric; the office and dignity of a bishop; the collective body of bishops.

episode, ep′i•sōd, *n.* [Gr. *epeisodion,* from *epi,* and *eisodos,* an entrance—*eis,* to, in, and *hodos,* a way.] A separate incident, story, or action, introduced for the purpose of giving a greater variety to the events related in a poem, romance, tale, etc.; an incident or action more or less connected with a complete series of events; that which follows on the entrance of the chorus into the orchestra.—*Greek play,* the part of the play or dialogue between two choral odes, incident.—**episodic, episodical,** ep•i•sod′ik, ep•i•sod′i•kal, *a.* Pertaining to an episode; contained in an episode or digression.—**episodically,** ep•i•sod′i•kal•li, *adv.* In an episodic manner.

epispastic, ep•i•spas′tik, *a.* [Gr. *epispaō,* to draw.] *Med.* drawing; blistering.—*n.* A vesicatory; a blister.

epistaxis, ep•i•stak′sis, *n.* [Gr. *epi,* upon, and *staxis,* a dropping.] Bleeding from the nose.

epistemology, i•pis′te•mol″o•jē, *n.* [Gr. *epistēmē,* knowledge, *logos,* discourse.] The theory of the method or ground of knowledge. ONTOLOGY.

episterna, ep•i•stėr′na, *n. pl.* [Gr. *epi,* upon, and *sternon,* the breastbone.] The lateral pieces of the lower surface of the segment of a crustacean.—**episternal,** ep•i•stėr′nal, *a.* *Anat.* a term applied to two bones forming part of the sternum, and situated upon its superior and lateral part.

epistle, i•pis′l, *n.* [L. *epistola,* Gr. *epistolē,* from *epistellō,* to send to—*epi,* on, and *stellō,* to send.] A writing, directed or sent, communicating intelligence to a distant person; a letter: applied particularly in dignified discourse or in speaking of the letters of the apostles or of the ancients.—**epistler,** i•pis′lėr, *n.* A writer of epistles; one who reads the epistle in a church service.—**epistolary,** i•pis′to•la•ri, *a.* Pertaining to epistles or letters; suitable to letters; contained in or consisting of letters.

epitaph, ep′i•taf, *n.* [Gr. *epi,* upon, and *taphos* or *taphē,* a tomb.] An inscription on a tomb or monument in honor or memory of the dead; or a composition such as might be so used.—**epitaphic,** ep•i•taf′ik, *a.* Pertaining to an epitaph; of the nature of or serving as an epitaph.

epithalamium, ep′i•tha•lā″mi•um, *n.* [Gr. *epithalamion—epi,* upon, and *thalamos,* a bed-chamber.] A nuptial song or poem, in praise of a bride and bridegroom; a poem in honor of a newly married pair.

epithelioma, ep′i•thē•li•ō″ma, *n.* Cancer of the skin.

epithelium, ep•i•thē′li•um, *n.* [Gr. *epi,* upon, and *thēlē,* the nipple.] *Anat.* any thin cellular tissue that lines a cavity or covers a free surface and performs the functions of protection, secretion, and assimilation.—**epithelial,** ep•i•thē′li•al, *a.*

epithet, ep′i•thet, *n.* [Gr. *epitheton,* a name added, from *epi,* upon, and *tithēmi,* to place.] An adjective expressing some real quality of the thing to which it is applied, or some quality ascribed to it; any word or name implying a quality attached to a person or thing.—**epithetic, epithetical,** ep•i•thet′ik, ep•i•thet′i•kal, *a.* Pertaining to an epithet or epithets: containing or consisting of epithets; abounding with epithets.

epitome, i•pit′o•mi, *n.* [Gr. *epitome,* from *epi,* upon, and *tomē,* a cutting, from *temnō,* to cut, seen also in *anatomy, entomology,* etc.] A brief summary or abstract of any book or writing; a compendium; abridgement; a summary; *fig.* anything which represents another or others in a condensed form. ∴ Syn. under ABRIDGE. —**epitomize,** i•pit′o•mīz, *v.t.—epitomized, epitomizing.* To make an epitome of; to abstract, in a summary, the principal matters of.

epizoon, ep•i•zō′on, *n.* pl. **epizoa,** ep•i•zō′a. [Gr. *epi,* upon, and *zōon,* animal.] A term applied to those parasitic animals which live on or in the skin of other animals.—**epizootic,** ep′i•zō•ot″ik, *a.* Applied to any disease that is prevalent among many animals of the same kind at the same time.—*n.* An epizootic disease.

epoch, ep′ok, *n.* [L. *epocha,* from Gr. *epochē,* retention, delay, from *epechō,* to hold back—*epi,* upon, and *echō,* to hold.] A fixed point of time from which succeeding years are numbered; a point from which computation of years begins; any fixed time or period; a memorable term of years; era; age; date.—**epochal,** ep′ok•al, *a.* Belonging to an epoch; of the nature of an epoch.

epode, ep′ōd, *n.* [Gr. *epōdē—epi,* upon, and *ōdē,* a song, an ode.] The third or last part of the ode, the ancient ode being divided into strophe, antistrophe, and epode; a species of lyric poem in which a longer verse is followed by a shorter one.

eponym, ep′o•nim, *n.* [Gr. *epi,* upon, and *onoma,* a name.] A name of a place or people derived from that of a person; a name of a personage called into existence to account for the name of a country or people, as *Italus, Romulus,* for *Italy, Rome.*—**eponymic, eponymous,** ep•o•nim′ik, e•pon′i•mus, *a.* Of or relating to or connected with an eponym.—*Eponymous archon.* The chief magistrate of Athens among the archons, giving his name to the year as a date or point of time.

epopee, epopoeia, ep•o•pē′, ep•o•pē′ya, *n.* [Fr. *épopée,* Gr. *epopoiïa—epos,* a word, an epic poem, and *poieō,* to make.] An epic poem; the subject of an epic poem.—**epos,** ep′os, *n.* [Gr.] An epic poem or its subject; an epopee; epic poetry.

epoxy, ep′äksē, *a.* [*epi,* and *oxy,* short for oxygen.] Containing oxygen attached to two different atoms, usually carbon, already united in a different manner.—**epoxy resin,** *n.* Any of various resins made by the polymerization of epoxy compounds and used as adhesives and coatings.

epsilon, ep′sä•län, *n.* [Gr. *e psilon,* simple e.] The fifth letter of the Greek alphabet, whose symbol is E.

Epsom salt, ep′som solt, *n.* The sulfate of magnesia, a cathartic producing watery discharges.

equable, ek′wa•bl, *a.* [L. *æquabilis,* from *æquo,* to make equal, from *æquus,* equal.] Characterized by uniformity, invariableness, or evenness; uniform in action or intensity; not varying; steady; even.—**equability, equableness,** ek•wa•bil′i•ti, ek′wa•bl•nes, *n.* State or quality of being equable.—**equably,** ek′wa•bli, *adv.* In an equable manner.

equal, ē′kwal, *a.* [L. *æqualis,* from *æquus,* equal (seen also in *equity, adequate, iniquity,* etc.); same root as Skr. *eka,* one, the same.] The same in size, value, qualities, or degree; neither inferior nor superior, greater nor less, better nor worse; uniform; not variable; being in just relation or proportion; of the same interest or importance; not unduly favorable to any party; just; equitable; fair; having competent power, ability, or means; adequate.—*n.* One not inferior or superior to another; a person having the same or a similar age, rank, station, office, talents, strength, etc.; a compeer.—*v.t.—equaled, equaling.* To make equal; to make of the same quantity or quality; to cause to be commensurate with or unsurpassed by; to equalize; to be equal to; to be adequate to; to be commensurate with; to rise to the same state, rank, estimation, or excellence with; to become equal to.—**equality,** i•kwol′i•ti, *n.* [L. *æqualitas.*] The state of being equal; likeness in size, number, quantity, value, qualities, or degree; the condition in which things or persons cannot be said to be inferior or superior, greater or less, one than another; parity; sameness in state or continued course.—**equalize,** ē′kwa•līz, *v.t.—equalized, equalizing.* To make equal; to cause to be equal in amount or degree; to adjust so that there shall be equality between.—

equalization, ē′kwal•i•zā″shon, *n.* The act of equalizing, or state of being equalized.—**equalizer,** ē′kwa•lī•zėr, *n.* One who or that which equalizes.—**equally,** ē′kwal•li, *adv.* In an equal manner or degree; in the same degree with another; alike; in equal shares or proportions; impartially.

equanimity, ek•wa•nim′i•ti, *n.* [L. *æquanimitas—æquus*, equal, and *animus*, mind.] Evenness of mind; that calm temper or firmness of mind which is not easily elated or depressed.

equate, i•kwāt′, *v.t.—equated, equating.* [L. *æquo, æquatum*, to make equal, from *æquus*, equal.] To make equal; to reduce to an average; to make such correction or allowance in as will reduce to a common standard of comparison, or will bring to a true result.—**equation,** i•kwā′shon, *n.* The act of equating; *alg.* a statement or expression asserting the equality of two quantities, equality being denoted by the sign = (equal to) between them; *astron.* a quantity which from some imperfect method has to be taken into account in order to give a true result.—*Equation of time*, the difference between mean and apparent time, or the difference between the time given by a dial and that given by a clock.—*Personal equation*, in astronomical observations the quantity of time by which a person is in the habit of noting a phenomenon wrongly.—**equator,** i•kwā′tėr, *n.* [L.L. *æquator*, from L. *æquo, æquatum*, to make equal.] That great circle of our globe which divides it into two hemispheres (the northern and southern), and every point of which is 90° from the poles, which are also its poles, its axis being also the axis of the earth; also, the equinoctial or celestial equator.—**equatorial,** ē•kwa•tō′ri•al, *a.* Pertaining to the equator.—*n.* An astronomical instrument, contrived for the purpose of directing a telescope upon any celestial object of which the right ascension and declination are known, and of keeping the object in view for any length of time, notwithstanding the diurnal motion.

equerry, ek′we•ri, *n.* [Fr. *écurie*, a stable, so that the word means really stable (man); from L.L. *scuria*, a stable; from O.H.G. *skiura*, the Mod.G. *scheuer*, a barn or shed.] An officer of nobles or princes who has the care and management of their horses: in England, equerries are certain officers of the royal household in the department of the master of the horse.

equestrian, i•kwes′tri•an, *a.* [L. *equestris*, from *eques*, horseman, from *equus*, horse; akin Gr. *hippos*, Skr. *açva*, horse; Gr. *ōkys*, swift.] Pertaining to horses or horsemanship; consisting in or accompanied with performances on horseback; representing a person on horseback (an *equestrian* statue); pertaining to the class or rank of knights in ancient Rome.—*n.* A rider on horseback; one who earns his living by performing feats of agility and skill on horseback in a circus.—**equestrienne,** i•kwes′tri•en, *n.* [Spurious French form.] A female rider or performer on horseback.

equiangular, ē•kwi•ang′gū•lėr, *a.* *Geom.* consisting of or having the angles all equal.

equidistance, ē•kwi•dis′tans, *n.* Equal distance.—**equidistant,** ē•kwi•dis′tant, *a.* Being at an equal distance from some point or place.—**equidistantly,** ē•kwi•dis′tant•li, *adv.* At an equal distance.

equilateral, ē•kwi•lat′ėr•al, *a.* [L. *æquus*, equal, and *latus, lateris*, a side.] Having all the sides equal.

equilibrate, ē•kwi•lī′brāt, *v.t.—equilibrated, equilibrating.* [L. *æquus*, equal, and *libro*, to poise, from *libra*, a balance.] To balance equally; to keep in equipoise.—**equilibration,** ē′kwi•lī•brā″shon, *n.* Equipoise; the state of being equally balanced.—**equilibrist,** ē•kwil′i•brist, *n.* One that balances equally; one who keeps his balance in unnatural positions and hazardous movements, as a rope dancer.—**equilibrium,** ē•kwi•lib′ri•um, *n.* [L. *æquilibrium.*] Equality of weight or force; a state of rest produced by two or more weights or forces counterbalancing each other, as the state of the two ends of a balance when both are charged with equal weights, and they maintain an even or level position; a state of just poise; the state where an organism is normally oriented to its environment.

equine, ē′kwīn, *a.* [L. *equinus*, from *equus*, a horse. EQUESTRIAN.] Pertaining to or resembling a horse.

equinox, ē′kwi•noks, *n.* [L. *æquinoctium*, from *æquus*, equal, and *nox*, night.] The time when the sun reaches one of the two equinoctial points, or points in which the ecliptic and celestial equator intersect each other, the *vernal equinox* being about March 21, the *autumnal equinox* about September 23, the day and the night being then of equal length all over the world.—**equinoctial,** ē•kwi•nok′shal, *a.* Pertaining to the equinoxes; occurring or manifested about that time (*equinoctial* gales); pertaining to the regions or climate under the equinoctial line or about the equator.—*Equinoctial points*, the two points of the heavens at which the equator and ecliptic intersect each other.—*n.* The celestial equator, so called because, when the sun is on it, the days and nights are of equal length in all parts of the world.

equip, i•kwip′, *v.t.—equipped, equipping.* [Fr. *équiper*, O.Fr. *esquiper*, to equip, to fit out a ship, from the Teut. stem *skip*, to provide, arrange, etc., as in Icel. *skipa*, to arrange; akin E. *ship, shape.*] To dress; to accouter; to prepare for some particular duty or service; specifically, to furnish with arms and munitions of war; to provide with everything necessary for an expedition or voyage; to fit out for sea, as a ship.—**equipage,** ek′wi•pij, *n.* [Fr. *équipage.*] Materials with which a person or thing is equipped; accouterments; equipment; the furniture and supplies of an armed ship, or the necessary preparations for a voyage; a train of dependents accompanying or following a person; a carriage with the horse or horses, harness, etc.; retinue.—**equipment,** i•kwip′ment, *n.* The act of equipping or fitting out; anything that is used in equipping; necessaries for an expedition, a voyage, etc.; equipage.

equipoise, ek′wi•poiz, *n.* [L. *æquus*, equal, and E. *poise.*] Equality of weight or force; due balance; equilibrium; a state in which the two ends or sides of a thing are balanced.

equipollence, equipollency, ē•kwi•pol′lens, ē•kwi•pol′len•si, *n.* [Fr. *équipollence*—L. *æquus*, equal, and *polleo*, to be able.] Equality of power or force; *logic*, an equivalence between two or more propositions.—**equipollent,** ē•kwi•pol′lent, *a.* Having equal power, force, or signification; equivalent.

equiponderate, ē•kwi•pon′dėr•āt, *v.i.—equiponderated, equiponderating.* [L. *æquus*, equal, and *pondero*, to weigh, from *pondus, ponderis*, weight.] To be equal in weight; to weigh as much as another thing.—*v.t.* To weigh equally in an opposite scale; to counterbalance. — **equiponderance, equiponderancy,** ē•kwi•pon′dėr•ans, ē•kwi•pon′dėr•an•si, *n.* Equality of weight; equipoise.—**equiponderant,** ē•kwi•pon′dėr•ant, *a.*

equisetum, ek•wi•sē′tum, *n.* [L. *equus*, a horse, and *seta*, a bristle.] Any plant belonging to the genus *Equisetum*, popularly known as horsetails, having hollow jointed stems, leaves in the form of whorls of teeth terminating the joints, and growing in marshy places.

equitable, ek′wi•ta•bl, *a.* [Fr. *équitable*, from L. *æquitas*, equity, from *æquus*, equal.] Possessing or exhibiting equity; equal in regard to the rights of persons; giving each his due; just; fair; impartial; pertaining to a court of equity.—**equitableness,** ek′wi•ta•bl•nes, *n.* The quality of being equitable.—**equitably,** ek′wi•ta•bli, *adv.* In an equitable manner; justly; impartially.—**equity,** ek′wi•ti, *n.* [Fr. *équité*, L. *æquitas.*] The giving or disposition to give to each man his due; justice; impartiality; fairness; uprightness; *law*, a doing justice between parties where there is no guidance or remedy in strict law; more strictly, a system of supplemental law founded upon defined rules, recorded precedents, and established principles, the judges, however, liberally expounding and developing these to meet new exigencies.

equitant, ek′wi•tant, *a.* [L. *equitans*, ppr. of *equito*, to ride, from *eques, equitis*, a horseman, from *equus*, a horse.] *Bot.* a term applied to unexpanded leaves in a leaf bud, that overlap each other entirely without any involution, as in the iris.—**equitation,** ek•wi•tā′shon, *n.* The act or art of riding on horseback; horsemanship.

equivalent, i•kwiv′a•lent, *a.* [Fr. *équivalent*—L. *æquus*, equal, and *valens, valentis*, ppr. of *valeo*, to be worth (seen also in *avail, prevail*, etc.).] Equal in value, force, power, effect, excellence, import, or meaning; interchangeable.—*n.* Something that is equivalent; that which is equal in value, weight, dignity, or force with something else; something given as a fair exchange; compensation; *chem.* the quantity by weight in which an element combines with or replaces a unit of hydrogen; *geol.* a stratum or series of strata in one district formed contemporaneously with a stratum or series of a different character in a different region, and holding a similar place.—**equivalently,** i•kwiv′a•lent•li, *adv.* In an equivalent manner.—**equivalence,** i•kwiv′a•lens, *n.* The condition of being equivalent; equality of value, signification, or force.—**equivalency,** i•kwiv′a•len•si, *n.* Same as *Equivalence*; *chem.* the quality in chemical elements of combining with or displacing one another in certain definite proportions.

equivocal, i•kwiv′ō•kal, *a.* [L. *æquus*, equal, and *vox, vocis*, voice.] Being of doubtful signification; capable of being or liable to be understood in different senses; ambiguous; uncertain; dubious; unsatisfactory; deserving to be suspected; capable of being ascribed to different motives; doubtful; questionable.—**equivocally,** i•kwiv′o•kal•li, *adv.* In an equivocal manner.—**equivocate,** i•kwiv′o•kāt, *v.i.*—*equivocated, equivocating.* To use ambiguous expressions with a view to mislead; to prevaricate; to quibble.—**equivocation,** e•kwiv′o•kā″shon, *n.* The act of equivocating; the use of words or expressions that are susceptible of a double signification, with a view to mislead; prevarication; quibbling.—**equivocator,** e•kwiv′o•kā•tėr, *n.* One who equivocates; a prevaricator; a quibbler.—**equivoque, equivoke,** ek′wi•vōk, ē′kwi•vōk, *n.* [Fr. *équivoque.*] An ambiguous term or expression; a quirk; pun or punning.

era, ē′ra, *n.* [L.L. *æra*, a date, an item of an account, from L. *æra*, counters, pl. of *æs*, brass.] A fixed point of time, from which any number of years is begun to be counted; a succession of years proceeding from a fixed point, or comprehended between two fixed points; an age or period.

eradicate, i•rad′i•kāt, *v.t.*—*eradicated, eradicating.* [L. *eradico, eradicatum*—*e*, out, and *radix, radicis*, a root (whence *radical*).] To pull up by the roots; to destroy at the roots; to root out; to destroy thoroughly; to extirpate.—**eradicable,** i•rad′i•ka•bl, *a.* That may be eradicated.—**eradication,** i•rad′i•kā″shon, *n.* The act of eradicating.—**eradicative,** i•rad′i•kā•tiv, *a.* Serving to eradicate, uproot, extirpate, or destroy.

erase, i•rās′, *v.t.*—*erased, erasing.* [L. *erado, erasum*—*e*, out, and *rado, rasum*, to scrape, to scratch. RAZE.] To rub or scrape out, as letters or characters written, engraved, or painted; to efface; to obliterate; to expunge; to remove or destroy, as by rubbing or blotting out.—**erasable,** i•rā′sa•bl, *a.* That may or can be erased.—**eraser,** i•rā′sėr, *n.* One who or that which erases; a sharp instrument, prepared caoutchouc and the like, used to erase writing, etc.—**erasure,** i•rā′zhėr, *n.* The act of erasing or scratching out; obliteration; the place where a word or letter has been erased.

Erastian, i•ras′ti•an, *n.* One whose opinions are the same or akin to those of Thomas *Erastus*, a German divine of the sixteenth century, who maintained the complete subordination of the ecclesiastical to the secular power.—*a.* Pertaining to the doctrines of Erastus or his followers.—**Erastianism,** i•ras′ti•an•izm, *n.* The doctrines or principles of Erastus or his followers; in a loose and inaccurate sense, the doctrine that an established church should be under the complete control of the state.

erbium, ėr′bi•um, *n.* [From *Ytterby*, in Sweden.] A metallic element of the rare-earth series. Symbol, Er; at. no., 68; at. wt., 167.26.

ere, âr, *adv.* or *conj.* [A.Sax. *aer*=D. *eer*, Icel. *ár*, Goth. *air*, before, sooner, earlier. It is the positive form, of which *erst* is the superlative.] Before; sooner than.—*prep.* Before, in respect of time.—**erelong,** âr•long′, *adv.* Before the lapse of a long time; before long; soon.—**erenow,** âr•nou′, *adv.* Before this time.—**erewhile,** âr′hwīl″, *adv.* Some time ago; a little time before.

Erebus, er′e•bus, *n.* [L. *erebus*, Gr. *erebos.*] According to the belief of the Greeks and Romans a dark and gloomy region under the earth, through which the shades passed into Hades.

erect, i•rekt′, *a.* [L. *erectus*, pp. of *erigo*, to erect—*e*, out, and *rego*, to straighten. REGENT.] In a perpendicular posture; upright; directed upward; raised; uplifted; firm; bold; unshaken.—*v.t.* To raise and set in an upright or perpendicular position, or nearly so; to set upright; to raise up; to construct; to set up; to build; to establish; to found; to form; to elevate; to exalt; to lift up; to encourage.—**erecter,** i•rek′tėr, *n.* One who or that which erects.—**erectile,** i•rek′til, *a.* Susceptible of erection.—**erectility,** i•rek•til′i•ti, *n.* The quality of being erectile.—**erection,** i•rek′shon, *n.* The act of erecting; a raising and setting perpendicular; a setting upright; the act of constructing or building; establishment; settlement; formation; anything erected; a building of any kind.—**erectly,** i•rekt′li, *adv.* In an erect posture.—**erectness,** i•rekt′nes, *n.* The state of being erect.—**erector,** i•rek′tėr, *n.* One who or that which erects.

eremite, er′e•mīt, *n.* [L. *eremita*; Late Gr. *erēmitēs*, from Gr. *erēmos*, alone, desert.] One who lives in a wilderness or in retirement; a hermit.—**eremitic, eremitical,** er•ē•mit′ik, er•e•mit′i•kal, *a.* Relating to, having the character of, or like an eremite or hermit.

erethism, er′e•thizm, *n.* [Gr. *erethismos*, irritation, from *erethizō*, to stir.] *Med.* a morbid energy or excitement in any organ or tissue.

erg, ėrg, *n.* [Gr. *ergon*, work.] *Physics.* a unit of work, being the work done by a force which, acting for one second upon a mass of one gram (15.4 grains), produces a velocity of a centimeter (.3937 inch) per second.

ergot, ėr′got, *n.* [Fr. *ergot, argot*, a spur, ergot.] A diseased state of rye and other grasses, caused by the attack of a minute fungus on the seeds or grains; the diseased grain itself.—**ergotism,** ėr′go•tizm, *n.* An epidemic occurring in moist districts from the use of ergoted rye in food.

ericaceous, er•i•kā′shus, *a.* [L. *erica*, heath.] Of or belonging to the nat. order of heaths.

Erin, â′rin, *n.* [Uncertain origin.] Ireland.

eringo, e•ring′gō, *n.* Same as *Eryngo.*

Erinys, i•rin′is, *n.* pl. **Erinyes,** i•rin′ni•ēz, *Greek myth.* one of the Furies; a goddess of discord.

eristic, eristical, ē•ris′tik, ē•ris′ti•kal, *a.* [Gr. *eristikos*, contentious, from *eris*, strife.] Pertaining to disputation or controversy; controversial; captious.

erlking, *n.* King of the elves, haunting the Black Forest, in poem by Goethe.

ermine, ėr′min, *n.* [O.Fr. *ermine*, Mod. Fr. *hermine*, from the Teut.; comp. Dan. Sw. and G. *hermelin*, O.G. *harm, harmo*, an ermine.] A quadruped of the weasel tribe found over temperate Europe, but common only in the north, much sought after in the winter on account of its fur, which is white at that season: known also as the *stoat*; the fur of the ermine, long considered as an emblem of purity; *fig.* the office or dignity of a judge, from his state robe being ornamented or bordered with ermine.—**ermined,** ėr′mind, *a.* Clothed or adorned with ermine.

erne, ėrn, *n.* [A.Sax. *earn*=Dan. and Sw. *ærn*, an eagle, allied to G. *aar*, an eagle, and to Skr. *ara*, swift, from *ri*, to go.] A name sometimes given to the white-tailed sea eagle, the bald eagle, and other allied species.

erode, i•rōd′, *v.t.*—*eroded, eroding.* [L. *erodo*—*e*, and *rodo*, to gnaw, whence *rodent.*] To eat into or away; to corrode.—**erose,** i•rōs′, *a.* [L. *erosus.*] *Bot.* having small irregular sinuses in the margin, as if gnawed.—**erosion,** i•rō′zhon, *n.* [L. *erosio.*] The act or operation of eating or wearing away; *geol.* the wearing away of soil or rock by the influence of water and ice (especially in the form of glaciers).—**erosive,** i•rō′siv, *a.* Having the property of eating, corroding or wearing away.

erotic, i•rot′ik, *a.* [Gr. *erōtikos,* from *erōs, erōtos,* love.] Pertaining to or prompted by love; treating of love.—*n.* An amorous composition or poem.

err, ėr, *v.i.* [L. *erro, erratum,* to wander, to err; allied to G. *irren,* to wander, to go astray.] To wander from the right way; to go astray; to deviate from the path of duty; to fail morally; to transgress; to mistake in judgment or opinion; to blunder; to misapprehend.—**errant,** er′rant, *a.* [L. *errans, errantis,* ppr. of *erro,* to err.] Wandering; roving; rambling: applied particularly to the knights of yore who wandered about to seek adventures. —**errantry,** er′rant•ri, *n.* A wandering; a roving or rambling about; the condition or way of life of a knight-errant.—**erratic,** er•rat′ik, *a.* [L. *erraticus.*] Wandering; devious; having no certain course; irregular or peculiar in movements or actions; eccentric; peculiar; queer.—*Erratic blocks,* or *Erratics,* in *geol.* boulders or fragments of rocks which appear to have been transported from their original sites by ice in the pleistocene period, and carried often to great distances.—**erratically,** er•rat′i•kal•li, *adv.* In an erratic manner. —**erratum,** er•rä′tum, *n.* pl. **errata,** er•rä′ta, [L. *erratum,* a blunder.] An error or mistake in writing or printing.—**erroneous,** er•rō′ni•us, *a.* [L. *erroneus.*] Characterized by or containing error or errors; wrong; mistaken; false; inaccurate.—**erroneously,** er•rō′ni•us•li, *adv.* In an erroneous manner.—**erroneousness,** er•rō′ni•us•nes, *n.* The state of being erroneous.—**error,** er′rėr, *n.* [L. *error.*] An unintentional wandering or deviation from truth or what is right; a going wrong; a mistake; a misapprehension; a mistake made in writing, printing, calculation, or other performance; an inaccuracy; an oversight; a transgression of law or duty; a fault; a sin.

errand, er′rand, *n.* [A.Sax. *aerend, aerynd.* Dan. *ærrende,* Icel. *eyrendi, erendi,* O.G; *âranti, ârunti,* an errand, a message; Goth. *airus,* a message, a messenger.] A special business entrusted to a messenger; something to be told or done by one expressly sent.

Erse, ėrs, *n.* [A variation of *Irish.*] The Celtic language spoken in the Highlands of Scotland, of Irish origin; Gaelic.

erubescence, er•ū•bes′ens, *n.* [L. *erubesco,* to become red—*e,* and *ruber,* red (whence *rubric*).] A becoming red; redness of the skin or surface of anything; a blushing.—**erubescent,** er•ū•bes′ent, *a.* Red or reddish; blushing.

eructate, i•ruk′tāt, *v.t.* [L. *eructo, eructatum—e,* out, and *ructo,* to belch.] To eject, as wind from the stomach; to belch.—**eructation,** i•ruk•tā′shon, *n.* [L. *eructatio.*] The act of belching wind from the stomach; a belch; a violent bursting forth or ejection of matter from the earth.

erudite, er′ū•dīt, *a.* [L. *eruditus,* from *erudio,* to polish, to instruct—*e,* out, and *rudis,* rough, rude.] Fully instructed; learned; deeply read; characterized by erudition.—**eruditely,** er′ū•dīt•li, *adv.* In an erudite manner.—**eruditeness,** er′ū•dīt•nes, *n.* The quality of being erudite.—**erudition,** er•ū•dish′on, *n.* Knowledge gained by study or from books and instruction; learning in literature, as distinct from the sciences; scholarship.

erupt, i•rupt′, *v.t.* [L. *erumpo, eruptum,* to break out—*e,* out, and *rumpo, ruptum,* to burst or break, as in *corrupt, disrupt,* etc.] To force out by internal action.—*v.i.* To become violent; to emit.—**eruption,** i•rup′shon, *n.* The act of breaking or bursting forth from enclosure or confinement; a violent emission of lava, etc.; the breaking out of a cutaneous disease; the rash, pustules, etc., accompanying the disease.—**eruptive,** i•rup′tiv, *a.*

erysipelas, er•i•sip′e•las, *n.* [Gr.—*erythros,* red, and *pella,* skin.] A contagious disease of the skin tissue, caused by a streptococcus and marked by inflammation of the infected area and high fever.

erythema, er•i•thē′ma, *n.* [Gr., from *erythros,* red.] A superficial redness of some portion of the skin without blisters and uninfectious.—**erythematic, erythematous,** er′i•thē•mat″ik, er•i•them′a•tus, *a.* Of the nature of erythema.

erythrite, e•rith′rīt, *n.* [Gr. *erythros,* red.] A mineral, a hydrous arsenate of cobalt; also a rose-red feldspar.

erythrocyte, i•rith′rä•sīt, *n.* [Gr. *erythro,* red, and *cyte,* hollow, vessel.] The red blood cell.

escalade, es•ka•lād′, *n.* [Fr., from L. *scala,* a ladder. SCALE.] A furious attack made by troops on a fortified place, in which ladders are used to pass a ditch or mount a rampart.—*v.t.—escaladed, escalading.* To climb up or over.—**escalate,** es′ka•lāt, *v.t.* To ascend slowly; to increase gradually the scope of a war, as calculated strategy, from the level of an incident to the level of nuclear warfare.—**escalation,** es′ka•lā″shon, *n.*—**escalator,** es″ka•lāt′ėr, *n.* A continuously ascending or descending stairway on an endless belt.

escalop, es•kal′op, *n.* [O.Fr. *escalope,* SCALLOP.] A kind of bivalve; a scallop.

escape, es•kāp′, *v.t.—escaped, escaping.* [O.Fr. *escaper,* Fr. *échapper,* Sp. Pg. Pr. *escaper,* to escape; from *ex,* out, and L.L. *cappa, capa,* a mantle (comp. *cape, cap*), lit. to slip out of one's mantle.] To flee from and avoid; to get out of the way of; to shun; to be unnoticed by.—*v.i.* To flee, shun, and be secure from danger; to be free, or get free, from any injury; to hasten or get away; to free one's self from custody or restraint; to regain one's liberty.—*n.* Flight to shun danger or injury; the act of fleeing from danger or imprisonment; the condition of being passed by without receiving injury, when danger threatens.—**escapable,** es•kā′pa•bl, *a.*—**escapade,** es•ka•pād′, *n.* A freakish or mad prank; a wild adventure.—**escapement,** es•kāp′ment, *n.* The general contrivance in a timepiece by which the rotatory motion of the wheels gives rise to or maintains the vibratory motion of the pendulum or balance wheel.—**escapism,** es•kāp′izm, *n.* Continually diverting the mind to fantasy, as an escape from reality.—**escape mechanism,** *n.* A mode of thinking devised to avoid unpleasant situations.—**escape velocity,** *n.* The minimum speed a vehicle requires to escape the gravitational field of the earth or other planet.

escarp, es•kärp′, *v.t.* [Fr. *escarper,* to cut steep, as rocks or slopes. SCARP.] *Fort.* to slope; to form a slope to.—*n.* Same as *Scarp.*—**escarpment,** es•kärp′ment, *n. Fort.* ground cut away nearly vertically about a position in order to make it inaccessible to an enemy; also, the precipitous side of any hill or rock; a steep ridge of land; a cliff.

eschar, es•kär′, *n.* [Gr. *eschara,* a fireplace, a scab.] The crust or scab occasioned on the skin by burns or caustic applications. —**escharotic,** es•ka•rot′ik, *a.* Caustic; having the power of searing or destroying the flesh.—*n.* An application which sears or destroys flesh.

eschatology, es•ka•tol′o•ji, *n.* [Gr. *eschatos,* last, and *logos,* discourse.] The doctrine of the last or final things, as death, judgment, etc.

escheat, es•chēt′, *n.* [O.Fr. *eschet,* from *escheir, escheoir,* Mod. Fr. *échoir,* from L. *excadere—ex,* and *cadere,* to fall (whence *cadence, decay,* etc.). *Cheat* is shortened from this.] The resulting back or reverting of any land or tenements to the state or sovereign through failure of heirs, and formerly also by forfeiture or attainder; the property which falls to the state in this way.—*v.i.* To become an escheat.—*v.t.* To cause to be an escheat; to forfeit.—**escheatable,** es•chē′ta•bl, *a.*

eschew, es•chö′, *v.t.* [O.Fr. *eschever,* Fr. *esquiver,* to avoid, to shun, from O.G. *skiuhan,* G. *scheuen,* to avoid; akin to E. *shy.*] To flee from; to shun; to seek to avoid; to avoid.

escort, es′kort, *n.* [Fr. *escorte,* from It. *scorta,* a guard or guide, from *scorgere,* to guide, from L. *ex,* and *corrigere,* to correct.] Persons attending one as a mark of respect, honor, or attention; protection or safeguard on a journey or excursion. —*v.t.* es•kort′. To accompany as a guard or protector.

escrow, es′krō, *n.* [Fr. *escroue,* scroll.] *Law.* a written agreement, such as a bond, deed, etc., that is deposited with a person, and to be delivered by him to the grantee only upon the fulfillment of a condition.

escritoire, es•kri•twär′, *n.* [O.Fr. *escriptoire,* from L. *scriptorium,* connected with writing, *scribo, scriptum,* to write. SCRIBE.] A desk or chest of drawers with an apartment for writing materials; a writing desk.

esculent, es′kū•lent, *a.* [L. *esculentus,*

from *esca*, food, from *edo*, to eat.] Capable of or fit for being used by man for food; edible.—*n.* Something that is eatable; an edible.

escutcheon, es•kuch′on, *n.* [O.Fr. *escusson*, from L. *scutum*, a shield. ESQUIRE.] The shield on which a coat of arms is represented; the shield of a family; a plate for protecting the keyhole of a door, or to which the handle is attached; a scutcheon.

esker, eskar, es′kėr, *n.* [Ir. *eiscir*.] In *geol.* a term for a long linear ridge of sand and gravel, common in regions where ice sheets have prevailed, and belonging to glacial phenomena.

Eskimo, es′ki•mō, *n.* pl. **eskimos,** es′ki•mōz. One of a race of men, generally short in stature, with broad oval faces and small oblique eyes, inhabiting the northern parts of North America and Greenland.

esophagus, ē•sof′a•gus, *n.* [Gr. *oisophagos*—*oisō*, I will bear, and *phagō*, to eat.] The gullet; the canal through which food and drink pass to the stomach.

esoteric, es•o•ter′ik, *a.* [Gr. *esōterikos*, from *esō*, within.] Taught only to a select number, and not intelligible to a general body of disciples; designed for, and understood only by, the initiated; private; opposed to *exoteric* or public.

espalier, es•pal′yėr, *n.* [Fr., from It. *spalliera*. a support for the shoulders, from *spalla*, a shoulder, L. *spathula*, *spatula*, a broad blade, dim. of *spatha*. EPAULET.] A broad piece of trellis work on which the branches of fruit trees or bushes are trained; a row of trees so trained.—*v.t.* To form an espalier of, or to train as an espalier.

esparto, es•pär′tō, *n.* [Sp., from L. *spartum*, Gr. *sparton*, *spartos*.] A name of two or three species of grass found in southern Spain and North Africa, and extensively exported to be used in the manufacture of paper, matting, baskets, etc.

especial, es•pesh′al, *a.* [O.Fr. *especial*, Fr. *spécial*, L. *specialis*, of particular sort or kind, special, from *species*, kind. SPECIES.] Of a distinct sort or kind; special; particular; marked; peculiar.—**especially,** es•pesh′al•li, *adv.* In an especial manner; particularly; specially; peculiarly.

Esperanto, es•per•ant′ō. A language formed for the purpose of enabling the inhabitants of all countries to converse with each other.

espial, espionage. See ESPY.

esplanade, es•pla•nād′, *n.* [Fr., from the old verb *esplaner*, to make level, from L. *explanare*—*ex*, and *planus*, plain, level.] *Fort.* a wide open space between the glacis of a citadel and the first houses of the town; any open level space near a town, especially a kind of terrace along the seaside, for public walks or drives.

espouse, es•pouz′, *v.t.*—*espoused*, *espousing*. [O.Fr. *espouser* (Fr. *épouser*), from L. *sponsare*, to betroth, to espouse, freq. of *spondeo*, *sponsum*, to pledge one's self, whence *despond*, *respond*.] To give or take in marriage; to promise, engage, or bestow in marriage by contract or pledge; to betroth; to marry; to wed; to become a partisan in; to embrace or to adopt (a cause, a quarrel).—**espousal,** es•pou′zal, *n.* [O.Fr. *espousailles*, L. *sponsalia*, espousals, pl. n. of *sponsalis*, relating to betrothal.] The act of espousing or betrothing: frequently used in the plural; the adopting or taking up of a cause.—**espouser,** es•pou′zėr, *n.* One who espouses.

espy, es•pī′, *v.t.*—*espied*, *espying*. [O.Fr. *espier*, It. *spiare*; same word as *spy*.] To see at a distance; to have the first sight of; to descry; to discover, as something concealed, or as if unexpectedly or unintentionally; to inspect; to spy.—**espial,** es•pī′al, *n.* The act of espying; observation; discovery.—**espionage,** es′pi•o•nij, *n.* The practice or employment of spies; the practice of watching the conduct and words of others as a spy.

esquire, es•kwīr′ or es′, *n.* [O.Fr. *escuyer*, Fr. *écuyer*, lit. a shield bearer, from L. *scutarius*, a soldier armed with a *scutum*, or shield, from root *sku*, to cover or protect.] Originally, a shield bearer or armor bearer; an attendant on a knight; hence, a title of dignity next in degree below a knight; a title properly given in Great Britain to the younger sons of noblemen, to justices of the peace, sheriffs, landed proprietors, etc. [*cap.*] A complimentary adjunct (usually abbreviated to *Esq.*) to a name in addressing letters, etc., to almost any person of respectable standing.

essay, es•sā′, *v.t.* [Fr. *essayer*. ASSAY.] To exert one's power or faculties on; to make an effort to perform; to try; to attempt; to endeavor to do; to make experiment of.—*n.* (es′sā). An effort made for the performance of anything; a trial, attempt; or endeavor; a test or experiment; a literary composition intended to prove some particular point or illustrate a particular subject, not having the importance of a regular treatise; a short disquisition on a subject of taste, philosophy, or common life.—**essayer,** *n.* One who essays (pronounced es•sā′ėr); one who writes essays; an essayist (pronounced es′sā•ėr).†—**essayist,** es′sā•ist, *n.* A writer of an essay or of essays.

essence, es′sens, *n.* [Fr., from L. *essentia*, from *esse*, to be; akin *entity*.] That which constitutes the particular nature of a thing, and which distinguishes it from all others; that which makes a thing what it is; existence; a being having existence; constituent substance; the predominant elements or principles of any plant or drug extracted, refined, or rectified from grosser matter; an extract; perfume; odor; scent; the most important or fundamental doctrines, facts, ideas, or conclusions (the *essence* of a lecture, a statement). —*v.t.* To perfume; to scent.—**essential,** es•sen′shal, *a.* Being of or pertaining to the essence; necessary to the constitution or existence of a thing; constituting a thing what it is; important in the highest degree; indispensable; volatile; diffusible (*essential* oils).—*n.* What is essential; fundamental or constituent principle; distinguishing characteristic.—**essentiality, essentialness,** es•sen′shi•al″i•ti, es•sen′shal•nes, *n.* The quality of being essential.—**essentially,** es•sen′shal•li, *adv.* In an essential manner; fundamentaly.

Essene, es•sēn′, *n. pl.* [Gr. *Essēnoi*, L. *Esseni*.] Among the Jews, a member of a sect remarkable for their strictness and abstinence.

establish, es•tab′lish, *v.t.* [O.Fr. *establir* (Fr. *établir*), from L. *stabilio*, to make firm, to establish, from *sta*, root of *sto*, to stand. STAND.] To make steadfast, firm, or stable; to settle on a firm or permanent basis; to set or fix unalterably; to institute and ratify; to enact or decree authoritatively and for permanence; to ordain; to strengthen; to prove; to confirm; to originate and secure the permanent existence of; to found permanently; to set up in connection with the state and endow (a church); to set up in business.—**establisher,** es•tab′lish•ėr, *n.* One who establishes. —**establishment,** es•tab′lish•ment, *n.* The act of establishing; the state of being established; settlement; fixed state; confirmation; a permanent civil or military force or organization, such as a fixed garrison or a local government; that form of doctrine and church government established by the legislature in any country; the place where a person is settled either for residence or for transacting business; a person's residence and everything connected with it, such as furniture, servants, carriages, etc.; an institution, whether public or private; the quota or number of men in an army, regiment, etc.

estafette, es•ta•fet′, *n.* [Fr. *estafette*, from It. *staffetta*, a courier, from *staffa*, a stirrup, from O.H.G. *stapho* =E. *step*.] A military courier; an express of any kind.

estate, es•tāt′, *n.* [O.Fr. *estat*, Fr. *état*, from L. *status*, a standing, state, from *sto*, *statum*, to stand. STAND.] Condition or circumstances of any person or thing; state; rank; quality; possessions; property; a piece of landed property; a definite portion of land in the ownership of some one; an order or class of men constituting a state; one of the classes of the nation invested with political rights, the *three estates of the realm*, in Britain, being the lords spiritual, the lords temporal, and the commons.—*The fourth estate*, the newspaper press; journalists.—*The Estates*, the old French and Scottish Parliament of nobles, clergy, burghers.—*The Third Estate*—*tiers état*, the commonalty.—*v.t.* To settle an estate upon (*Tenn.*)†; to bestow (*Shak.*)‡.

esteem, es•tēm′, *v.t.* [Fr. *estimer*, L. *æstimare*, *estimatum*, from same root as Skr. *esha*, a wish, G. *heischen*, to desire. Akin *aim*.] To set a value on, whether high or low; to estimate;

to value; to set a high value on; to regard with reverence, respect, or friendship; to prize.—*n.* Opinion or judgment of merit or demerit; estimation; high value or estimation; great regard; favorable opinion, founded on supposed worth.—**esteemable,** es•tē′ma•bl, *a.* Worthy of esteem; estimable.—**estimable,** es′ti•ma•bl, *a.* Capable of being estimated or valued; worthy of esteem or respect; deserving our good opinion or regard.—**estimableness,** es′ti•ma•bl•nes, *n.* The quality of being estimable.—**estimably,** es′ti•ma•bli, *adv.* In an estimable manner. —**estimate,** es′ti•māt, *v.t.*—*estimated estimating.* [L. *æstimare, æstimatum.*] To form a judgment or opinion regarding; especially applied to value, size, weight, degree, extent, quantity, etc.; to rate by judgment, opinion, or a rough calculation; to fix the worth of; to compute; to calculate; to reckon.—*n.* A valuing or rating in the mind; an approximate judgment or opinion as to value, degree, extent, quantity, etc.—**estimation,** es•ti•mā′shon, *n.* [L. *æstimatio.*] The act of estimating; calculation; computation; an estimate; esteem; regard; favorable opinion; honor.—**estimative,** es′ti•mā•tiv, *a.* Having the power of estimating.—**estimator,** es′ti•mā•tėr, *n.* One who estimates or values.

ester, es′tėr, *n.* [G. *essigäther,* ethyl acetate—from *essig,* vinegar, and *äther,* ether.] A compound formed by the reaction of alchohol plus an acid with the elimination of water.

esthesia, es•thē′zha, *n.* [Gr. *aisthēsis,* perception, sensibility.] Perception; feeling; sensibility.—**esthesiology,** es•thē′zi•ol″o•ji, *n.* The doctrine or branch of knowledge concerned with the sensations.

esthesiometer, es•thē′zi•om″et•ėr, *n.* [Gr. *aisthēsis,* perception, and *metron,* a measure.] An instrument for testing the tactile sensibility of the human body in health and disease.

esthete, esthetic, etc. Same as *Aesthete.*

estival,† es′ti•val, *a.* [L. *æstivus,* from *æstas,* summer.] Pertaining to summer.—**estivate,**† es′ti•vât, *v.i.* [L. *æstivo, æstivatum.*] To pass the summer.—**estivation, aestivation,** es•ti•vā′shon, *n. Bot.* the manner in which the parts of a flower bud are arranged with respect to each other before opening; the disposition of the petals within the flower bud—*vernation* being the disposition of leaves.

estop, es•top′, *v.t.*—*estopped, estopping.* [O.Fr. *estoper,* Fr. *étouper,* to stop with tow, from L. *stupa, stuppa,* tow.] *Law,* to impede or bar by one's own act.—**estoppel,** es•top′el, *n. Law,* a stop; a plea in bar, grounded on a man's own act.

estovers, es•tō′vėrz, *n. pl.* [O.Fr. *estoveir, estovoir,* to be needful.] *Law,* the right of taking the necessary amount of wood from an estate for fuel, fences, repairs, and other reasonable purposes.

estrange, es•trānj′, *v.t.*—*estranged, estranging.* [O.Fr. *estranger,* from L.L. *extraneus,* foreign, strange. STRANGE.] To keep apart or out of friendly relations; to make to cease from being familiar; to alienate; to turn from kindness to indifference or malevolence; to apply to a purpose foreign from its original or customary one.—**estrangement,** es•trānj′ment, *n.* The act of estranging or state of being estranged.

estray, es•trā′, *n.* A stray, or animal that has strayed from the custody of its owner.

estreat, es•trēt′, *n.* [O.Fr. *estraite,* from L. *extraho, extractum,* to draw out.] *Law,* a true copy of an original writing, under which fines are to be levied.—*v.t. Law,* to levy (fines) under an estreat.

estrogen, es′trä•jen, *n.* [L. *estrus,* frenzy, and *gen,* producer.] Any compound acting as a female hormone, causing sexual receptivity and the development of secondary sex characteristics.

estuary, es′tū•a•ri, *n.* [L. *æstuarium,* from *æstuo,* to boil or foam, *æstus,* heat, tide.] The wide mouth of a river where the tide meets the currents, or flows and ebbs; a firth.

eta, āt′ä, *n.* [Gr. *eta;* akin to Heb. *heth.*] The seventh letter of the Greek alphabet, whose symbol is H.

et cetera, et•set′ėr•a. [L. *et,* and *cætera,* other things.] And others of the like kind: written also *Etcaetera, Etcetera,* and commonly contracted *etc., &c.*

etch, ech, *v.t.* and *i.* [From D. *etsen,* G. *ätzen,* to corrode by acids, to etch; lit. to bite into; O.H.G. *ezan,* to eat. EAT.] To produce figures or designs upon a plate of steel, copper, glass, or the like, by means of lines drawn through a thin coating or ground covering the plate and corroded or *bitten in* by some strong acid, which can only affect the plate where the coating has been removed by the etching instrument.—**etcher,** ech′ėr, *n.* One who etches.—**etching,** ech′ing, *n.* The art or operation of an etcher; a design or picture produced by an etcher.

eternal, i•tėr′nal, *a.* [Fr. *éternel;* L. *æternus, æviternus,* from *ævum,* an age, and adj. suffix *-ternus.* AGE.] Having no beginning or end of existence; everlasting; endless; continued without intermission; ceaseless; perpetual.—*The Eternal,* an appellation of God.—**eternally,** i•tėr′nal•li, *adv.* In an eternal manner; without beginning or end of duration; perpetually; unceasingly; continually.—**eternity,** i•tėr′ni•ti, *n.* The condition or quality of being eternal; duration or continuance without beginning or end; endless past time or endless future time; the state or condition which begins at death.—**eternize,** i•tėr′nīz, *v.t.*—*eternized, eternizing.* [Fr. *éterniser.*] To make eternal or endless; to perpetuate; to make for ever famous; to immortalize.

etesian, i•tē′zhan, *a.* [L. *etesius,* from Gr. *etēsios,* annual, from *etos,* a year.] [*often cap.*] Recurring every year; blowing at stated times of the year: applied to the periodical winds in the Mediterranean.

ethane, eth′ān, *n.* A hydrocarbon (C_2H_6) allied to marsh gas (CH_4).

ether, ē′thėr, *n.* [L. *æther,* from Gr. *aithēr,* from *aithō,* to light up, to kindle, to burn or blaze; cog. L. *æstas,* summer heat, *Ætna,* Skr. *indh,* to set on fire, *iddhas,* bright.] The supposed subtle atmosphere in space beyond the earth's atmosphere; a hypothetical medium of extreme tenuity and elasticity supposed to be diffused throughout all space (as well as among the molecules of which solid bodies are composed), and to be the medium of the transmission of light and heat; a very light, volatile, and flammable fluid, obtained from alcohol, an excellent solvent of fats and resins, and used as a stimulant, antispasmodic, and anesthetic.—**ethereal,** i•thē′ri•al, *a.* Formed of ether or the fine atmosphere pervading all space; containing or filled with ether; belonging to the sky regions; heavenly; celestial.—**ethereality,** i•the′ri•al″i•ti, *n.* The state or quality of being ethereal.—**etherealize,** i•the′ri•al•īz, *v.t.*—*etherealized, etherealizing.* To convert into ether; to purify and refine; to render spirit-like or ethereal.—**etherealization,** i•thē′ri•al•i•zā″shon, *n.* An ethereal or subtle spirit-like state or condition.—**ethereally,** i•thē′ri•al•li, *adv.* In an ethereal, celestial, or heavenly manner.—**etherification,** i•thē′ri•fi•kā″shon, *n.* The process of ether formation.—**etherization,** ē′thėr•i•zā″shon, *n.* The act of administering ether to a patient; the state of the system when under the influence of ether.—**etherize,** ē′thėr•īz, *v.t.*—*etherized, etherizing.* To convert into ether; to subject to the influence of ether.

ethic, ethical, eth′ik, eth′i•kal, *a.* [L. *ethicus,* from Gr. *ēthikos,* from *ēthos,* custom, habit.] Relating to morals; treating of morality; containing precepts of morality; moral. —**ethically,** eth′i•kal•li, *adv.* In an ethical manner.—**ethics,** eth′iks, *n.* The science which treats of the nature and grounds of moral obligation; moral philosophy, which teaches men their duty and the reasons of it; the science of duty.

Ethiop, Ethiopian, ē′thi•op, ē•thi•ō′pi•an, *n.* [Gr. *Aithiops*—*aithō,* to burn, and *ōps,* countenance.] A native of Ethiopia; a Negro or black man.—**Ethiopian,** *a.* Relating to Ethiopia or to its inhabitants.—**Ethiopic,** ē•thi•op′ik, *n.* The language of Ethiopia; the literary and ecclesiastical language of Abyssinia, one of the Semitic tongues.—*a.* Relating to Ethiopia.

ethmoid, ethmoidal, eth′moid, eth•moi′dal, *a.* [Gr. *ēthmos,* a sieve, and *eidos,* form.] Resembling a sieve.—*Ethmoid bone,* a light spongy bone situated between the orbital processes at the root of the nose, its pores forming passages for the olfactory nerves.

ethnic, ethnical, eth′nik, eth′ni•kal,

a. [L. *ethnicus*, from Gr. *ethnikos*, from *ethnos*, nation, pl. *ta ethnē*, the nations, heathens, gentiles.] Not Christian or Jewish; heathen; relating to a people, or race, with common physical and cultural traits.—**ethnically,** eth′ni•kal•li, *adv.*—**ethnocentric,** eth•nō•sen′trik, *a.* Having race as a main interest; believing that one's own race is superior.—**ethnographer,** eth•nog′ra•fėr, *n.* One who cultivates ethnography.—**ethnographic, ethnographical,** eth•no•graf′ik, eth•no•graf′i•kal, *a.*—**ethnographically,** eth•no•graf′i•kal•li, *adv.*—**ethnography,** eth•nog′ra•fi, *n.* That branch of science which has for its subject the description of the different races of men, or the manners, customs, religion, etc., peculiar to different nations.—**ethnologic, ethnological,** eth•no•loj′ik, eth•no•loj′i•kal, *a.* Relating to ethnology.—**ethnologist,** eth•nol′o•jist, *n.* One skilled in ethnology; a student of ethnology.—**ethnology,** eth•nol′o•ji, *n.* That branch of science which investigates the mental and physical differences of mankind and the organic laws on which they depend.

ethology, eth•ol′o•ji, *n.* [Gr. *ethos* or *ēthos*, manners, morals, and *logos*, discourse.] The science of ethics; the science of character.—**ethological,** eth•o•loj′i•kal, *a.*

ethos, ē′thäs, *n.* [Gr. *ethos*, character.] One's character and disposition; the fundamental spiritual characteristics of a culture.

ethyl, eth′il, *n.* [*Ether*, and Gr. *hylē*, matter.] A univalent hydrocarbon radical.—**ethylene,** eth′i•lēn, *n.* A colorless, highly flammable gas found in coal gas and used as an anesthetic and fuel.

etiolate, ē′ti•o•lāt, *v.i.*—*etiolated, etiolating.* [Fr. *étioler*, to blanch, from *éteule*, stubble, from L. *stipula*, a straw.] To grow white from absence of the normal amount of green coloring matter in the leaves or stalks; to be whitened by excluding the light of the sun, as plants.—*v.t.* To blanch or whiten by excluding the light or by disease.—**etiolation,** ē′ti•o•lā″shon, *n.* The act of etiolating or state of being etiolated or blanched.

etiology, ē•ti•ol′o•ji, *n.* [Gr. *aitia*, cause, and *logos*, discourse.] An account of the causes of anything, particularly of diseases.—**etiological,** ē′ti•o•loj″i•kal, *a.* Pertaining to etiology.

etiquette, et′i•ket, *n.* [Fr.; O.Fr. *estiquette*, a thing attached, a label, from G. *stecken*, to stick, to put. *Ticket* is same word.] Conventional forms of ceremony or decorum; the forms which are observed toward particular persons, or in particular places; social observances required by good breeding.

etna, et′na, *n.* [From *Etna*, the Sicilian volcano.] A table cooking utensil, heated by an alcohol lamp.

Etruscan, i•trus′kan, *a.* Relating to Etruria, an ancient country in Central Italy.—*n.* A native of ancient Etruria.

étude, ā•tūd′, *n.* [Fr.] A musical or artistic composition designed to serve as a study.

etui, etwee, et•wē′, *n.* [Fr. *étui.*] A pocket case for small articles, such as needles, pins, etc.; a ladies' reticule.

etymology, et•i•mol′o•ji, *n.* [Gr. *etymos*, true or real, *to etymon*, the true or literal signification of a word, its root, and *logos*, discourse.] That part of philology which explains the origin and derivation of words; derivation; that part of grammar which comprehends the various inflections and modifications of words.—**etymologic, etymological,** et′i•mo•loj″ik, et′i•mo•loj″i•kal, *a.* Pertaining to or treating of etymology or the derivation of words.—**etymologically,** et′i•mo•loj″i•kal•li, *adv.* In an etymological manner.—**etymologist,** et•i•mol′o•jist, *n.* One versed in etymology; one who searches into the origin of words.—**etymologize,** et•i•mol′o•jīz, *v.i.* To search into the origin of words.—*v.t.* To trace the etymology of; to give the etymology of.—**etymon,** et′i•mon, *n.* The root of a word.

eucaine, ū•kān′, *n.* A complex synthetic substance used as a local anesthetic.

eucalyptol, ū′ka•lip″tol, *n.* [From *eucalyptus*, and *oleum*, oil.] The oil of the blue gum tree (*Eucalyptus globulus*), used as a remedy for asthma and other ailments.—**eucalyptus,** ū•ka•lip′tus, *n.* [Gr. *eu*, well, and *kalypto*, to cover—referring to the cover of the flower bud.] The eucalyptus, a genus of very large trees of the myrtle order, natives of Australia, called gum trees, from the gum that exudes from them, also stringy bark, ironbark, etc.

eucharis, ū′ka•ris, *n.* [Gr. *eucharis*, pleasing.] South American plant of the bulbous kind, with white flowers of bell shape.

Eucharist, ū′ka•rist, *n.* [Gr. *eucharistia*, thanksgiving, the Lord's Supper, *eucharistos*, grateful—*eu*, well, good, and *charis*, grace, favor.] The sacrament of the Lord's Supper; the Communion; the consecrated elements, and especially the bread; thanksgiving.—**Eucharistic, Eucharistical,** ū•ka•ris′tik, ū•ka•ris′ti•kal, *a.* Pertaining to the Eucharist.

euchre, ū′kėr, *n.* [Origin unknown.] A game of cards, played by two, three, or four players with the thirty-two highest cards of the pack.

euclase, ū′klās, *n.* [Gr. *eu*, and *klaō*, to break.] A mineral of the beryl family, of a pale-green color and very brittle.

eudemonism, ū•dē′mon•izm, *n.* [Gr. *eudaimōn*, happy.] The system of philosophy which makes human happiness the highest object, declaring that the production of happiness is the foundation of virtue.—**eudemonist,** ū•dē′mon•ist, *n.* A believer in eudemonism.

eudiometer, ū•di•om′e•tėr, *n.* [Gr. *eudios*, serene, and *metron*, measure.] An instrument usually in the form of a glass siphon with a graduated limb, originally designed for ascertaining the purity of the air, but now employed generally in the analysis of gases by the electric spark.—**eudiometric, eudiometrical,** ū′di•o•met″rik, ū′di•o•met″ri•kal, *a.* Pertaining to a eudiometer or to eudiometry.—**eudiometry,** ū•di•om′et•ri, *n.* The art or practice of using the eudiometer.

eugenics, ū•jen′iks, *n.* [Gr. *eu*, well, *genos*, race.] The science that deals with the improvement of the hereditary traits of a race.—**eugenic,** ū•jen′ik, *a.*—**eugenically,** ū•jen′i•kal•li, *adv.*—**eugenicist,** ū•jen′i•sist, *n.* A believer in eugenics.

euhemerism, ū•hem′ėr•izm, *n.* [After the Greek *Euēmeros*, who explained myths in this way.] That system of interpreting myths by which the gods are regarded as representing distinguished men who formerly lived, and so the myths are considered as founded on real histories.—**euhemerist,** ū•hem′ėr•ist, *n.* A believer in the doctrine of euhemerism.—**euhemeristic,** ū•hem′ėr•is″tik, *a.* Of or belonging to euhemerism.—**euhemerize,** ū•hem′ėr•īz, *v.t.* To treat or explain in the manner of Euemeros. Also written *Euemerism*, etc.

eulogy, ū′lo•ji, *n.* [Gr. *eulogia*—*eu*, well, and *logos*, speech, from *legō*, to speak.] Praise; encomium; panegyric; a speech or writing in commendation of a person on account of his valuable qualities or services.—**eulogically,** ū•loj′i•kal•li, *adv.* In a eulogic manner.—**eulogist,** ū•lo•jist, *n.* One who praises and commends another; one who pronounces a eulogy.—**eulogistic, eulogistical,** ū•lo•jis′tik, ū•lo•jis′ti•kal, *a.* Containing or pertaining to eulogy or praise; laudatory.—**eulogistically,** ū•lo•jis′ti•kal•li, *adv.* With commendation or eulogy.—**eulogium,** ū•lō′ji•um, *n.* A formal eulogy.—**eulogize,** ū′lo•jīz, *v.t.*—*eulogized, eulogizing.* To speak or write in commendation of another; to extol in speech or writing; to praise.

Eumenides, ū•men′i•dēz, *n. pl. Lit.* the gracious goddesses, a Greek name of the Furies, because it was considered unlawful and dangerous to name them under their true designation *Erinnyes.*

eunuch, ū′nuk, *n.* [Gr. *eunouchos*—*cunē*, a bed, and *echō*, to keep, to have charge of.] A castrated male of the human species; hence, from the employment to which eunuchs were commonly put, a chamberlain.

eupepsia, ū•pep′si•a, *n.* [Gr. *eupepsia*—*eu*, and *pepsis*, digestion, from *peptō*, to digest.] Good digestion; the opposite of dyspepsia.—**eupeptic,** ū•pep′tik, *a.* Having good digestion; easy of digestion.

euphemism, ū′fem•izm, *n.* [Gr. *euphēmismos*—*eu*, well, and *phēmi*, to speak.] A figure of speech in which a delicate word or expression is substituted for one which is offensive to good manners or to delicate ears.—**euphemistic, euphemistical,** ū•fem•is′tik, ū•fem•is′ti•kal, *a.* Pertaining to or containing euphemism.

—**euphemize,** ū′fem•īz, *v.t.* To express by a euphemism.

euphony, ū′fo•ni, *n.* [Gr. *euphōnia—eu*, well, and *phōne*, voice.] An agreeable sound; an easy, smooth enunciation of sounds; a pronunciation of letters, syllables, and words which is pleasing to the ear.—**euphonic, euphonical,** ū•fon′ik, ū•fon′i•kal, *a.* Of or pertaining to, or characterized by, euphony; agreeable in sound; pleasing to the ear.—**euphonious,** ū•fō′ni•us, *a.* Agreeable in sound; euphonic.—**euphoniously,** ū•fō′ni•us•li, *adv.* In a euphonious manner.—**euphonium,** ū•fō′ni•um, *n.* A brass bass instrument with three or four valves, used in military bands, and frequently in the orchestra as a substitute for the trombone. —**euphonize,** ū′fo•nīz, *v.t.* To make agreeable in sound.

euphorbia, ū•for′bi•a, *n.* [Gr. *euphorbia*, from the name of an ancient Greek physician.] A genus of exogenous plants, some of which are found in Britain, and are popularly called *spurges*, while the most remarkable are tropical shrubs or trees, often large, fleshy, and leafless, having the habit of a cactaceous plant.

euphoria, ū•fōr′i•a, *n.* [Gr. *eu*, well, *phoreō*, I possess.] Feeling of well-being.

euphrasy, ū′fra•si, *a.* [Gr. *euphrasia*, delight.] The herb popularly called eyebright, formerly a specific for diseases of the eye.

euphuism, ū′fū•izm, *n.* [From the name of the hero of two works by John Lyly, written in a strange and affected style, which became fashionable at the court of Elizabeth.—*Euphues* is the Gr. *euphyēs*, well-shaped—*eu*, well, and *phyē*, growth, stature.] Affectation of excessive elegance and refinement of language; high-flown artificial diction.—**euphuist,** ū′fū•ist, *n.* One addicted to euphuism: applied particularly to certain writers, at the head of which stood John Lyly.—**euphuistic,** ū•fū•is′tik, *a.* Belonging to the euphuists or to euphuism.

eupnea, ūp•nē′a, *n.* [Gr. *eu*, well, *pneō*, I breathe.] Easy, natural breathing.

Eurasian, ū•rā′zhi•an, *n.* [A contraction of *European* and *Asian.*] A person of mixed European and Asiatic descent.

eureka, ū•rē′ka. [Gr. (*h*)*eurēka*, I have found, perf. ind. act. of (*h*)*euriskō*, to find.] The exclamation of Archimedes, when, after long study, he discovered a method of detecting the amount of alloy in King Hiero's crown: hence, a discovery; especially, one made after long research; an expression of triumph at a discovery or supposed discovery.

eurhythmy, ū•rith′mi, *n.* Artistic harmony; proportion; harmonious movement. *Med.* regularity of the pulse.

European, ū•ro•pē′an, *a.* [L. *Europa*, Gr. *Eurōpē*, Europe.] Pertaining to Europe; native to Europe.—*n.* A native of Europe.—**Europeanize,** ū•ro•pē′an•īz, *v.t.* To cause to become European; to assimilate to Europeans in manners, character, and usages.

europium, u•rō′pi•um, *n.* [From *Europe.*] A metallic element of the rare-earth series. Symbol, Eu; at. no., 63; at. wt., 151.96.

Eustachian, ū•stā′ki•an, *a.* Named after *Eustachius* or *Eustachi*, an Italian physician, who died 1574.—*Eustachian tube*, the tube which forms a communication between the internal ear and the back part of the mouth.—*Eustachian valve*, a valve which separates the right auricle of the heart from the inferior vena cava.

euthanasia, ū•tha•nā′zha, *n.* [Gr.—*eu*, well, and *thanatos*, death.] An easy death; a putting to death by painless means; a means of putting to a painless death.

evacuate, i•vak′ū•āt, *v.t.—evacuated, evacuating.* [L. *evacuo, evacuatum—e*, out, and *vacuus*, empty, from *vaco*, to be empty. VACANT.] To make empty; to make empty by removing one's self from (an army *evacuates* a town or a country); to void or discharge from the bowels.—**evacuant,** i•vak′ū•ant, *a.* Producing evacuation; purgative.—*n.* A medicine which promotes the natural secretions and excretions.—**evacuation,** i•vak′ū•ā″shon, *n.* The act of evacuating; that which is evacuated or discharged, especially from the bowels. —**evacuator,** i•vak′ū•ā•tėr, *n.* One who or that which evacuates.

evade, i•vād′, *v.t.—evaded, evading.* [L. *evado—e*, and *vado*, to go, as in *invade, pervade*; akin to E. *wade.* WADE.] To avoid, escape from, or elude in any way, as by dexterity, artifice, sophistry, address, or ingenuity: to slip away from; to elude; to escape the grasp or comprehension of; to baffle or foil.—*v.i.* To escape; to slip away; to practice artifice or sophistry for the purpose of eluding.—**evadible,** i•vā′di•bl, *a.* Capable of being evaded.—**evasion,** i•vā′zhon, *n.* [L. *evasio.*] The act of evading, eluding, avoiding, or escaping; shift; subterfuge; equivocation; prevarication; shuffling.—**evasive,** i•vā′siv, *a.* Using evasion or artifice to avoid; shuffling; equivocating; containing or characterized by evasion.—**evasively,** i•vā′siv•li, *adv.* In an evasive manner.—**evasiveness,** i•vā′siv•nes, *n.*

evaluate, i•val′ū•āt, *v.t.* [Back formation of evaluation; L. *valere*, be worth.] To appraise carefully; to judge as to worth or amount.—**evaluation,** i•val′ū•ā″shon, *n.* Exhaustive appraisement.

evanesce, ev•a•nes′, *v.i.—evanesced, evanescing.* [L. *evanesco—e*, and *vanesco*, to vanish, from *vanus*, vain, empty. VAIN.] To vanish, to disappear; to be dissipated, as vapor.—**evanescence,** ev•a•nes′ens, *n.* The state or character of being evanescent.—**evanescent,** ev•a•nes′ent, *a.* Vanishing; subject to vanishing, fleeting; passing away; liable to disappear or come to an end.—**evanescently,** ev•a•nes′ent•li, *adv.*

evangel, i•van′jel, *n.* [L. *evangelium*, the gospel; Gr. *euangelion*, good tidings, the gospel—*eu*, well, good, and *angellō*, to announce.] The gospel; one of the gospels or four New Testament books under the names of Matthew, Mark, Luke, and John.—**evangelical, evangelic,** i•van•jel′i•kal, i•van•jel′ik, *a.*[L.L. *evangelicus.*] According to the gospel, or religious truth taught in the New Testament; sound in the doctrines of the gospel; adhering closely to the letter of the gospel; fervent and devout; *eccles.* a term applied to a section in the Protestant churches who give special prominence to the doctrines of the corruption of man's nature by the fall, of his regeneration and redemption through the Saviour and of free and unmerited grace; applied in Germany to Protestants as distinguished from Roman Catholics, and more especially to the national Protestant church formed in Prussia in 1817 by a union of the Lutheran and Calvinistic churches.—**evangelicalism,** i•van•jel′i•kal•izm, *n.* Adherence to evangelical doctrines.—**evangelically,** i•van•jel′i•kal•i, *adv.* In an evangelical manner.—**evangelist,** i•van′jel•ist, *n.* [*cap.*] One of the four writers of the gospels. A layman engaged in preaching or missionary work.—**evangelistic,** i•van′jel•is″tik, *a.* Evangelical, tending or designed to evangelize.—**evangelization,** i•van′jel•i•zā″shon, *n.* The act of evangelizing.—**evangelize,** i•van′jel•īz, *v.t.—evangelized, evangelizing.* To instruct in the gospel; to preach the gospel to and convert.—*v.i.* To preach the gospel.

evanish,† i•van′ish, *v.i.* To vanish; to disappear.

evaporate, ē•vap′ėr•āt, *v.i.—evaporated, evaporating.* [L. *evaporo, evaporatum—e*, out, and *vapor*, vapor. VAPOR.] To pass off in vapor; to escape and be dissipated, either in visible vapor or in particles too minute to be visible; *fig.* to escape or pass off without effect; to be dissipated; to be wasted.—*v.t.* To convert or resolve into vapor; to cause to evaporate; to vaporize.—**evaporable,** ē•vap′ėr•a•bl, *a.* Capable of being converted into vapor or of being dissipated by evaporation.—**evaporation,** ē•vap′ėr•ā″shon, *n.* The act or process of evaporating; the conversion of a liquid by heat into vapor or steam, which becomes dissipated in the atmosphere in the manner of an elastic fluid; vaporization; the matter evaporated; vapor. —**evaporative,** i•vap′ėr•ā•tiv, *a.* Causing evaporation; pertaining to evaporation.—**evaporometer,** i•vap′ėr•om″et•ėr, *n.* An instrument for ascertaining the quantity of a fluid evaporated in a given time; an atmometer.

evasion, evasive. See EVADE.

eve, ēv, *n.* [Short for *even, evening.*] The close of the day; the evening; the day or the latter part of the day before a church festival; the period just preceding some event (on the *eve* of a revolution).

even, ē'vn, *a.* [A.Sax. *efen,* even, level, equal=D. *even,* Dan. *jevn, jævn,* Icel. *jafn,* Goth. *ibns,* G. *eben,* even, level.] Level; smooth; flat; devoid of irregularities; straight or direct; uniform; equal; not easily ruffled; on a level or on the same level; in the same or in an equally favorable position; on a level in advantage; having accounts balanced; square; adjusted; fair; equitable; capable of being divided by 2 without a remainder: opposed to *odd.*—*v.t.* To make even; to level; to lay smooth; to place in an equal state; to balance.—*adv.* Expressing a level or equality; hence, just; exactly in consonance; according (*even* as he wished); expressing equality or sameness of time (I knew it *even* then); expressing, emphatically, identity of person (*even* he did it); expressing a strong assertion; not only this or so, but more, or but also.—**evenly,** ē'vn•li, *adv.* In an even manner; smoothly; equally; uniformly; impartially.—**evenness,** ē'vn•nes, *n.* The state or quality of being even.—**evenhanded,** *a.* Impartial; equitable; just.

even, ē'vn, *n.* [A.Sax. *aefen, éfen.* EVENING.] Evening. (*Poet.*)—**evenfall,** ē'vn•fal, *n.* The fall of evening; early evening; twilight.—**evensong,** ē'vn•song, *n.* A form of worship for the evening; vespers.

evening, ēv'ning, *n.* [A.Sax. *aefnung,* verbal noun (like *morning*), from *aefen, éfen,* evening; cog. G. *abend,* Sw. *afton,* Icel. *aftan,* Dan. *aften,* evening. The root meaning seems to be retiring, the word being akin to A.Sax. *af, of,* off; G. *ab,* of, from L. *ab,* Skr. *apa,* from.] The close of the day, and the beginning of darkness or night; the time from sunset until darkness; the latter part of the afternoon and the earlier part of the night; the decline or latter part of life: often used as an adjective.—**evening star,** *n.* Any planet visible in the western sky after sunset.

event, i•vent', *n.* [L. *eventus,* from *evenio, eventum,* to come out—*e,* out, and *venio,* to come, seen also in *advent, convene, prevent, venture,* etc.] That which happens or falls out; any incident good or bad; an occurrence; the consequence of anything; that in which an action, operation, or series of operations terminates; the issue, conclusion, end.—**eventful,** i•vent'ful, *a.* Full of events or incidents; characterized by great changes either in public or private affairs.—**eventual,** i•ven'tū•al, *a.* Coming or happening as a consequence or final result; consequential; final; ultimate.—**eventuality,** i•ven'tū•al"i•ti, *n.* That which eventuates or happens; a contingent result.—**eventually,** i•ven'tū•al•li, *adv.* In the event; in the final result or issue.—**eventuate,** i•ven'tū•āt, *v.i.* —*eventuated, eventuating.* To issue as an event or consequence; to fall out; to happen; to come to pass.

ever, ev'ėr, *adv.* [A.Sax. *aefre,* always; allied to Goth. *aivs,* time, *aiv,* ever; Icel. *æfi,* an age, the space of life; L. *ævum,* Gr. *aiōn,* Skr. *âyus,* an age. Akin *aye, every.*] At any time past or future; at all times; always; eternally; constantly; incessantly; continually; in any degree.—*For ever,* eternally; to perpetuity; sometimes with a repetition for the sake of emphasis (*for ever and ever*).—*Ever and anon,* now and then; again and again; time after time.—*Ever,* in *composition,* signifies always or continually, without intermission, or to eternity; as, *ever*-active; *ever*-living.—**evergreen,** ev'ėr•grēn, *a.* Always green; having verdant leaves throughout the year; *fig.* always fresh, vigorous, or in a good condition.—*n.* A plant that retains its verdure through all the seasons.—**everlasting,** ev•ėr•las'ting, *a.* Lasting or enduring for ever; existing or continuing without beginning or end; eternal; perpetual; endless; continual.—*n.* Eternity; a plant whose flowers retain their form, color, and brightness for many months after being gathered.—*The Everlasting,* the Eternal Being; God. —**everlastingly,** ev•ėr•las'ting•li, *adv.* Eternally; perpetually; continually. —**everlastingness,** ev•ėr•las'ting•nes, *n.*—**evermore,** ev'ėr•mōr, *adv.* Always; eternally; for ever; at all times; continually.

evert, i•vėrt', *v.t.* [L. *everto, eversum* —*e,* and *verto,* to turn, as in *convert, invert, revert, verse,* etc.] To overturn; to overthrow; to turn outward, or inside out.—**eversion,** i•vėr'shon, *n.* The act of everting; an overthrowing; destruction.—*Eversion of the eyelids,* a disease in which the eyelids are turned outward so as to expose the red internal tunic.

every, ev'ri, *a.* [O.E. *everich, everilk,* from A.Sax. *aefre,* ever, and *ælc,* each. EVER, EACH.] Each individual of the whole number; each of a number singly or one by one.—**everybody,** ev'ri•bod•i, *n.* Every person.—**everyday,** ev'ri•dā, *a.* Used, occurring, or that may be seen or met with every day; common; usual; ordinary.—**everywhere,** ev'ri•hwâr, *adv.* In every place; in all places.

evict, i•vikt', *v.t.* [L. *evinco, evictum,* to vanquish utterly—*e,* intens., and *vinco,* to overcome, as in *convince, convict, evince.* VICTOR.] To dispossess by a judicial process or course of legal proceedings; to expel from lands or tenements by law.—**eviction,** i•vik'shon, *n.* The act of evicting; the expulsion of a tenant from lands or tenements by law.

evidence, ev'i•dens, *n.* [Fr. *évidence,* from L. *evidentia*—*e,* and *video, visum,* to see. VISION.] That which demonstrates or makes clear that a fact is so; that which makes evident or enables the mind to see truth; proof arising from our own perceptions by the senses, or from the testimony of others, or from inductions of reason; testimony; *law,* that which is legally submitted to a competent tribunal as a means of ascertaining the truth of any alleged matter of fact under investigation.—*State's evidence,* evidence given by an accomplice, when the ordinary evidence is defective, on the understanding that he himself shall go free for his share of the crime.—*v.t.*—*evidenced, evidencing.* To render evident; to prove; to make clear to the mind.—**evident,** ev'i•dent, *a.* [L. *evidens.*] Open to be seen; clear to the mental or physical eye; manifest; obvious; plain.—**evidential,** ev•i•den'shal, *a.* Affording evidence; clearly proving. —**evidently,** ev'i•dent•li, *adv.* In an evident manner; clearly; manifestly.

evil, ē'vl, *a.* [A.Sax. *efel, yfel;* D. *euvel,* O.Fris. *evel,* G. *ubel,* Goth. *ubils.*] Having bad qualities of a natural kind; having qualities which tend to injury, or to produce mischief; injurious; pernicious; mischievous; having bad qualities of a moral kind; wicked; corrupt; perverse; wrong; vile; vicious; unfortunate; unpropitious; calamitous.—*The Evil One,* the devil.—*n.* Anything that causes injury, pain, or suffering; misfortune; calamity; mischief; injury; depravity; corruption of heart, or disposition to commit wickedness; malignity; the negation or contrary of good.—*adv.* Not well; ill.—**evildoer,** ē'vl•dö•ėr, *n.* One who does evil; one who commits sin, crime, or any moral wrong.—**evil eye,** *n.* A kind of influence superstitiously ascribed in former times to certain persons, their glance being supposed to injure.—**evil-minded,** *a.* Having evil dispositions or intentions; disposed to mischief or sin.—**evilness,** ē'vl•nes, *n.* Badness; viciousness; malignity of sin.

evince, i•vins', *v.t.*—*evinced, evincing.* [L. *evinco,* to vanquish, to prove or show. EVICT.] To show; to prove; to manifest; to make evident; to display as something belonging to one's own nature or character (to *evince* fear).—**evincible,** i•vin'si•bl, *a.* Capable of being evinced.

eviscerate, i•vis'ėr•āt, *v.t.*—*eviscerated, eviscerating.* [L. *eviscero*—*e,* and *viscera,* the bowels.] To take out the entrails of; to disembowel.—**evisceration,** i•vis'ėr•ā"shon, *n.* The act of eviscerating.

evoke, i•vōk', *v.t.*—*evoked, evoking.* [L. *evoco*—*e,* out, and *voco,* to call.] To call or summon forth.—**evocation,** ev•o•kā'shon, *n.* The act of evoking; a calling forth.

evolution, ev•o•lū'shon, *n.* [L. *evolutio,* from *evolvo, evolutum,* to unroll, to unfold. EVOLVE.] The act of unfolding, unrolling, or expanding; a gradual development or working out; the extraction of arithmetical or algebraic roots—the reverse of involution; a regulated or systematic series of movements which a body of troops, a fleet, or a ship makes when changing a previous formation or position; that theory which sees in the history of all things, organic and inorganic, a development from simplicity to complexity, a gradual advance from a simple or rudimentary condition to one that is more complex and of a higher character.—**evolutional, evolutionary,** ev•o•lū'shon•al, ev•o•lū'shon•e•ri, *a.* Of or pertaining to evolution; produced by or due to evolution.—**evolutionist,** ev•o•lū'shon•ist, *n.* One skilled in evolutions, specifically in military evolutions; a believer in the doctrine of evolution.

evolve, i•volv', *v.t.*—*evolved, evolving.* [L. *evolvo*—*e*, and *volvo*, to roll, which is cog. with E. to *wallow*, and is seen also in *convolve, devolve, revolve, voluble, volume,* etc.] To unfold; to open and expand; to disentangle; to unravel; to develop; to cause to pass from a simple to a complex state.—*v.i.* To open or disclose itself.—**evolvement,†** i•volv'ment, *n.* Act of evolving.

ewe, ū, *n.* [A.Sax. *eowu*; allied to Fris. *ei*, O.H.G. *avi, ou*, Icel. *â*, L. *ovis*, Gr. *oïs*, Skr. *avi*, a sheep.] A female sheep.

ewer, ū'ėr, *n.* [From O.Fr. *ewe*, Mod. Fr. *eau*, water, from L. *aqua*, water (whence *aquatic*, etc.).] A large pitcher or jug with a wide spout, used to bring water for washing the hands; a sort of pitcher that accompanies a wash basin for holding the water.

exacerbate, ek•sas'ėr•bāt, *v.t.*—*exacerbated, exacerbating.* [L. *exacerbo, exacerbatum*—*ex*, intens., and *acerbus*, harsh, sharp, sour.] To irritate, exasperate, or inflame; to increase the malignant qualities of; to increase the violence of (a disease).—**exacerbation,** ek•sas'ėr•bā″shon, *n.* The act of exacerbating; increase of malignity; a periodical increase of violence in a disease.

exact, eg•zakt', *a.* [L. *exactus*, pp. of *exigo*, to drive out, to measure—*ex*, out, and *ago*, to drive, to do, as in *agent, act, agitate,* etc.] Closely correct or regular; accurate; conformed to rule; precise; not different in the least; methodical; careful; observing strict method, rule, or order; punctual; strict.—*v.t.* [Fr. *exacter*, L.L. *exactare.*] To force or compel to be paid or yielded; to extort by means of authority or compulsion; to enforce a yielding of; to enjoin with pressing urgency.—**exacter,** eg•zak'tėr, *n.* One who exacts.—**exacting,** eg•zak'ting, *p.* and *a.* Demanding or disposed to demand without pity or justice; extorting; making unreasonable claims.—**exaction,** eg•zak'shon, *n.* The act of exacting; extortion; a wresting of contributions unjustly; that which is exacted; fees, rewards, or contributions levied with severity or injustice.—**exactitude,** eg•zak'ti•tūd, *n.* Exactness; accuracy; nicety.—**exactly,** eg•zakt'li, *adv.* In an exact manner.—**exactness,** eg•zakt'nes, *n.* The state or quality of being exact; accuracy; correctness; preciseness; regularity.—**exactor,** eg•zak'tėr, *n.* One who exacts.

exaggerate, eg•zaj'ėr•āt, *v.t.*—*exaggerated, exaggerating.* [L. *exaggero, exaggeratum*—*ex*, intens., and *aggero*, to heap, from *agger*, a heap—*ad*, to, and *gero*, to carry.] To represent as greater than truth or justice will warrant; to heighten unduly; to magnify.—**exaggeration,** eg•zaj'ėr•ā″shon, *n.* The act of exaggerating; a representation of things beyond the truth or reality.—**exaggerative,** eg•zaj'ėr•ā•tiv, *a.* Having the tendency to exaggerate.—**exaggeratory,** eg•zaj'ėr•a•to•ri, *a.* Containing exaggeration.

exalt, eg•za̤lt', *v.t.* [Fr. *exalter*, from L. *exaltare*—*ex*, and *altus*, high (whence *altitude, haughty*).] To raise high; to lift up; to elevate in power, wealth, rank, or dignity, character, and the like; to elevate with joy, pride, or confidence; to elate; to praise highly; to magnify; to extol; to elevate the tone of; to elevate in diction or sentiment.—**exaltation,** eg•za̤l•tā'shon, *n.* The act of exalting or state of being exalted; elevated state; state of greatness or dignity; a state of great elation; mental elevation.—**exaltedness,** eg•za̤l'ted•nes, *n.* The state of being exalted.—**exalter,** eg•za̤l'tėr, *n.* One who exalts.

examine, eg•zam'in, *v.t.*—*examined, examining.* [L. *examino, examinatum*, from *examen, examinis*, the tongue of a balance, for *exagmen*, from *ex*, out, and *ago*, to bring, to do (whence *agent*, etc.).] To inspect or observe carefully; to look into the state of; to view and consider in all its aspects; to question, as a witness or an accused person; to put judicial inquiries to; to inquire into the qualifications, capabilities, knowledge, or progress of, by interrogatories; to try or test.—**examinant,** eg•zam'i•nant, *n.* An examiner.—**examinee,** eg•zam'i•nē″, *n.* One who undergoes an examination.—**examiner,** eg•zam'i•nėr, *n.* One who examines; one who inspects; a person appointed to conduct an examination, as in a university.—**examinable,** eg•zam'i•na•bl, *a.* Capable of being examined.—**examen,†** eg•zam'en, *n.* An examination.—**examination,** eg•zam'i•nā″shon, *n.* The act of examining or state of being examined; a careful search or inquiry; careful and accurate inspection; a legal inquiry into facts by testimony; an attempt to ascertain truth by inquiries and interrogatories; a process for testing qualifications, knowledge, progress, of students, candidates, etc.; investigation; scrutiny; trial.

example, eg•zam'pl, *n.* [L. *exemplum*, from *eximo*, to take out or away—*ex*, out, and *emo, emptum*, to take, to purchase (as in *exempt*). *Sample* is the same word.] A sample or specimen; a pattern, in morals or manners, worthy of imitation; a copy or model; one who or that which is proposed or is proper to be imitated; a former instance, to be followed or avoided; one held out as a caution or warning to others; a particular case illustrating a general rule, position, or truth.

exanthema, ek•san•thē'ma, *n.* pl. **exanthemata,** ek•san•them'a•ta. [Gr. *exanthēma*, from *exantheō*, to blossom—*ex*, and *anthos*, a flower.] *Med.* an eruption or breaking out, as in measles, smallpox, etc.: frequently limited to such eruptions as are accompanied with fever.—**exanthematous, exanthematic,** ek•san•them'a•tus, ek•san'the•mat″ik, *a.* Of or pertaining to exanthema; eruptive.

exarch, ek'särk, *n.* [Gr. *exarchos*—*ex*, and *archos*, a chief.] A viceroy or governor of an Italian or African province under the Byzantine Empire.—**exarchate,** ek'sär•kāt, *n.* The office, dignity, or administration of an exarch.

exasperate, eg•zas'pėr•āt, *v.t.*—*exasperated, exasperating.* [L. *exaspero, exasperatum*, to irritate—*ex*, and *asper*, rough, harsh.] To irritate in a high degree; to provoke to rage; to enrage; to anger; to excite or inflame.—**exasperation,** eg•zas'pėr•ā″shon, *n.* The act of exasperating or state of being exasperated.

ex cathedra, eks•ka•thē'dra, *a.* [L. *ex*, from, and *cathedra*, Gr. *kathedra*, a chair (whence *cathedral*).] *Lit.* from the chair, as of authority or instruction; hence, applied to any decision, order, etc., given in an authoritative and dogmatic manner.

excavate, eks'ka•vāt, *v.t.*—*excavated, excavating.* [L. *excavo, excavatum*—*ex*, out, and *cavus*, hollow. CAVE.] To cut, scoop, dig, or wear out the inner part of anything and make it hollow; to hollow; to form by scooping or hollowing out.—**excavation,** eks•ka•vā'shon, *n.* The act of excavating; a hollow or a cavity formed by removing substance.—**excavator,** eks'ka•vā•tėr, *n.* One who or that which excavates; a machine for excavating.

exceed, ek•sēd', *v.t.* [L. *excedo*—*ex*, out, and *cedo*, to go. CEDE.] To pass or go beyond; to proceed beyond the given or supposed limit, measure, or quantity of; to outgo; to surpass; to excel.—*v.i.* To go too far; to pass the proper bounds or limits.—**exceeding,** ek•sē'ding, *a.* Great in extent, quantity, degree, or duration; very large.—*adv.* In a very great degree; unusually. (O.T.)—**exceedingly,** ek•sē'ding•li, *adv.* In an exceeding manner or degree; very greatly; very much.

excel, ek•sel', *v.t.*—*excelled, excelling.* [L. *excello*—*ex*, and root seen in Gr. *kellō*, to impel, L. *celsus*, raised high.] To surpass in good qualities or laudable deeds; to outdo in comparison; to surpass; to transcend; to exceed.—*v.i.* To be eminent or distinguished; to surpass others; to take a high rank.—**excellence,** ek'sel•lens, *n.* The state of excelling in anything; the state of possessing good qualities in an eminent or unusual degree; superiority; eminence; any valuable quality; anything highly laudable, meritorious, or esteemed; [*usually cap.*] a title of honor given to persons of high rank; excellency;—**excel-**

lency, ek′sel•len•si, *n.* Valuable quality; excellence; [*usually cap.*] a title of honor given to governors, ambassadors, ministers, and the like: with *your, his,* etc.—**excellent,** ek′-sel•lent, *a.* Being of great virtue or worth; eminent or distinguished for what is amiable, valuable, or laudable; virtuous; good; worthy; excelling or surpassing in any quality, power, or attainment; being of great value or use; remarkable for good properties.—**excellently,** ek′sel•lent•-li, *adv.* In an excellent manner; in an eminent degree.

excelsior, ik•sel′sē•ėr, *n.* [L. lofty; the compar. of *excelsus.*] Fine curled wood shavings used in packaging for protection.

except, ek•sept′, *v.t.* [Fr. *excepter,* L. *excipio, exceptum—ex,* out, and *capio,* to take, seen also in *captious, capacious, capable, accept, conceive,* etc.] To take or leave out of any number specified; to exclude.—*v.i.* To object; to take exception: usually followed by *to.*—*prep.* Being excepted or left out; with exception of; excepting.—*conj.* excepting; unless. —**excepting,** ek•sep′ting, *ppr.* used as a *prep.* and *conj.* With exception of; excluding; unless; except.—**exception,** ek•sep′shon, *n.* The act of excepting or excluding from a number designated, or from a description; exclusion; that which is excepted or excluded; the person or thing specified as distinct or not included; an objection; that which is or may be offered in opposition to a rule, proposition, statement, or allegation; offense; slight anger or resentment (to *take exception at* a severe remark; to *take exception to* what was said).—**exceptionable,** ek•-sep′shon•a•bl, *a.* Liable to exception or objection; objectionable.—**exceptional,** ek•sep′shon•al, *a.* Out of the ordinary course; relating to or forming an exception.—**exceptionally,** ek•sep′shon•al•li, *adv.* In an exceptional manner; unprecedentedly; extraordinarily; especially.—**exceptive,** ek•sep′tiv, *a.* Including an exception.

excerpt, ek•sėrpt′, *v.t.* [L. *excerpo, excerptum—ex,* out, and *carpo,* to pick.] To pick out or extract from a book or other literary composition; to cull; to select; to cite.—*n.* ek′sėrpt. An extract from a publication or from a writing of any kind.

excess, ek•ses′, *n.* [L. *excessus,* from *excedo,* to exceed. EXCEED.] That which exceeds any measure or limit; that which is beyond measure, proportion, or due quantity; superfluity; superabundance; any transgression of due limits; extravagance; wastefulness; riotous living; want of restraint in gratifying the desires; intemperance; overindulgence; the amount by which one number or quantity exceeds another.—**excessive,** ek•ses′iv, *a.* Beyond any given degree, measure, or limit, or beyond the common measure or proportion; immoderate; extravagant; extreme. —*Enormous, Excessive.* ∴ Syn. under ENORMOUS.—**excessively,** ek•ses′iv•li, *adv.* In an excessive manner or degree; exceedingly; vehemently; violently.

exchange, eks•chānj′, *v.t.—exchanged, exchanging.* [O.Fr. *exchanger—ex,* and *changer,* to change. CHANGE.] To give or take in return for another thing; to barter; to lay aside, quit, or resign (a thing, state, or condition), and take something else; to give and receive reciprocally; to give and take; to interchange.—*v.i.* To make an exchange; to pass or to be taken as an equivalent.—*n.* The act of giving one thing or commodity for another; barter; traffic by interchange of commodities; the act of giving up or resigning one thing or state for another; the act of giving and receiving reciprocally; the thing given or the thing received in return; the place where the merchants, brokers, and bankers of a city meet to transact business; the difference of value in the respective currencies of different countries.—**exchangeable,** eks•-chān′ja•bl, *a.* Capable of being exchanged; estimated by what may be procured in exchange.—**exchangeability,** eks•chān′ja•bil″i•ti, *n.* The quality or state of being exchangeable.

exchequer, eks•chek′ėr, *n.* [O.Fr. *eschequier,* Fr. *échiquier,* a chessboard: the term was applied to a court of finance from its having at first held its meetings round a table covered with *checked* cloth, because accounts were taken by means of counters on the checks. CHECK, CHEQUER, CHESS.] A state treasury; hence, pecuniary property in general; a person's finances or pecuniary resources; [*often cap.*] an ancient English tribunal and court, founded chiefly for the collection and care of the royal revenues, now a division of the High Court of Justice.—*Exchequer bills,* bills for money, or bills of credit issued from the exchequer, and pledging the government to repay the sum with a certain rate of interest; a species of paper currency emitted under the authority of the government, and in Britain forming a principal part of the public unfunded debt.—*v.t.*† To institute a process against in the court of exchequer.

excipient, ek•sip′i•ent, *n.* [L. *excipiens, excipientis,* ppr. of *excipio,* to take out. EXCEPT.] *Med.* an inert or slightly active substance employed as the medium or vehicle for the administration of the active medicine, as bread crust, sugar, jelly, etc.

excise, ek•sīz′, *n.* [From O.D. *aksijs,* G. *accise,* excise, corruption of O.Fr. *assise,* an assize, a tax. ASSIZE.] A tax or duty imposed on certain commodities of home production and consumption, as beer, spirits, etc.; or levied on persons for licenses to pursue certain callings, deal in certain commodities, as well as use certain things (armorial bearings, carriages, plate, etc.), or the like; that branch of the civil service which is connected with the collecting of such duties.—*v.t.—excised, excising.* To levy an excise on.—**excisable,** ek•sī′za•bl, *a.* Liable or subject to excise.—**exciseman,** ek•sīz′man, *n.* An inferior officer of the excise.

excise, ek•sīz′, *v.t.—excised, excising.* [From L. *excido, excisum—ex,* out, and *cædo,* to cut, as in *concise, circumcise.*] To cut out or off; to remove by cutting, as in surgery; to delete or expunge.—**excision,** ek•-sizh′on, *n.* The act of cutting out; removal by cutting; amputation; deletion.

excite, ek•sīt′, *v.t.—excited, exciting.* [Fr. *exciter,* from L. *excito—ex,* and *cito* (as in *cite, incite, recite*), intens. of *cieo* or *cio,* to excite, call; akin to Gr. *kiō,* to go, *kineō,* to move.] To call into action; to animate; to rouse, provoke, or to stir up; to cause to act, as that which is dormant, sluggish, or inactive; to give new or increased action to; to stimulate; to call forth or increase the vital activity of; to raise, create, or set afoot.—**excitable,** ek•sī′ta•bl, *a.* Susceptible of excitement; capable of being excited; easily excited or stirred up; prone to or characterized by excitement.—**excitability, excitableness,** ek•sī′ta•bil″i•ti, ek•sī′ta•-bl•nes, *n.* The state or quality of being excitable.—**excitant,** ek′si•-tant, *n.* That which produces or may produce increased action in a living organism; an agent or influence which arouses the vital activity of the body or of any of the tissues or organs; a stimulant.—**excitation,** ek•si•tā′shon, *n.* The act of exciting; excitement.—**excitative, excitatory,** ek•sī′ta•tiv, ek•sī′ta•to•ri, *a.* Having power to excite; tending or serving to excite.—**excitement,** ek•sīt′ment, *n.* The act of exciting; stimulation; the state of being excited; agitation; sensation; commotion; a state of aroused or increased vital activity in the body or any of its tissues or organs; a vitiated and abnormal state of the actions and sensations, or both, produced by stimulants, irritants, or the like; that which excites or rouses; that which moves, stirs, or induces action.—**exciter,** ek•sī′tėr, *n.* One who or that which excites.—**exciting,** ek•sī′ting, *p.* and *a.* Calling or rousing into action; producing excitement; deeply interesting; thrilling.—**excitingly,** ek•sī′ting•li, *adv.* So as to excite.

exclaim, eks•klām′, *v.i.* [L. *exclamo—ex,* and *clamo,* to call. CLAIM.] To utter with vehemence; to cry out; to shout; to declare with loud vociferation.—**exclaimer,** eks•klā′mėr, *n.* One who exclaims.—**exclamation,** eks•kla•mā′shon, *n.* The act of exclaiming or making an outcry; noisy talk; vehement vociferation; clamor; an emphatical or passionate utterance; the mark or sign [!] in printing by which emphatical utterance or interjectional force is marked; *gram.* a word expressing outcry; an interjection.—**exclamatory,** eks•klam′a•-to•ri, *a.* Pertaining to or characterized by exclamation; expressing exclamation.

exclude, eks•klūd′, *v.t.—excluded, ex-*

cluding. [L. *excludo*, to shut out—*ex*, out, and *claudo*, to shut, whence *clause*, *close*, etc.] To hinder from entering or from admission; to shut out; to hinder from participation or enjoyment; to debar; to except; not to comprehend or include in a privilege, grant, argument, description, etc.; to thrust out; to eject. —**exclusion,** eks•klū′zhon, *n*. The act of excluding, shutting out, debarring, expelling, excepting, or rejecting; the state of being excluded.—**exclusionism,** eks•klū′zhon•izm, *n*. Exclusive principles or practice.—**exclusionist,** eks•klū′zhon•ist, *n*. One who is in favor of exclusion.—**exclusive,** eks•klū′siv, *a*. Having the power or effect of excluding; possessed and enjoyed to the exclusion of others (an *exclusive* privilege); not taking into account something or certain individuals; not including or comprehending certain things (an *exclusive* estimate): often with *of* (500 men *exclusive of* officers); excluding from or chary in admitting to society or fellowship; fastidious as to the social rank of associates; illiberal; narrow.—*n*. One very fastidious as to the social position or breeding of his associates.—**exclusively,** eks•klū′siv•li, *adv*. Without admission of others; with the exclusion of all others; without comprehension in a number; not inclusively.—**exclusiveness,** eks•klū′siv•nes, *n*. State or quality of being exclusive.

excogitate, eks•koj′i•tāt, *v.t.*—*excogitated*, *excogitating*. [L. *excogito*—*ex*, out, and *cogito*, to think.] To strike out by thinking; to think out; to devise; to contrive.—**excogitation,** eks•koj′i•tā″shon, *n*. The act of excogitating.

excommunicate, eks•kom•mū′ni•kāt, *v.t.*—*excommunicated*, *excommunicating*. [L. *ex*, out, and *communico*, *communicatum*, to communicate, from *communis*, common.] To expel or eject from the communion of the church and deprive of spiritual advantages; hence, to expel from any association and deprive of the privileges of membership.—*n*. One who is excommunicated; one cut off from any privilege. — **excommunicable,** eks•kom•mū′ni•ka•bl, *a*. Liable or deserving to be excommunicated; punishable by excommunication.—**excommunication,** eks•kom•mū′ni•kā″shon, *n*. The act of excommunicating, or state of being excommunicated; expulsion from the communion of a church, and deprivation of its rights, privileges, and advantages.—**excommunicator,** eks•kom•mū′ni•kā•tėr, *n*. One who excommunicates.—**excommunicatory,** eks•kom•mū′ni•ka•tō•ri, *a*. Relating to or causing excommunication.

excoriate, eks•kō′ri•āt, *v.t.*—*excoriated*, *excoriating*. [L.L. *excorio*—L. *ex*, and *corium*, skin, hide.] To break or wear off the cuticle of; to abrade a part of the skin so as to reach the flesh; to gall.—**excoriation,** eks•kō′ri•ā″shon, *n*. The act of excoriating; a galling; abrasion.

excrement, eks′kre•ment, *n*. [L. *excrementum*, from *excerno*, *excretum*, to sift out—*ex*, out, and *cerno*, to separate. DISCERN.] Matter discharged from the animal body after digestion; alvine discharge.—**excremental, excrementitious,** eks•kre•men′tal, eks′kre•men•tish″us, *a*. Pertaining to or consisting of excrement; consisting of matter excreted from the animal body.

excrescence, excrescency, eks•kres′ens, eks•kres′en•si, *n*. [Fr. *excrescence*, from L. *excrescens*, pp. of *excresco*, to grow out—*ex*, out, and *cresco*, to grow (in *crescent*, *concrete*, *increase*, etc.).] Anything which grows out of something else and is useless or disfiguring (as a wart or tumor); a useless or troublesome outgrowth. —**excrescent,** eks•kres′ent, *a*.

excreta, eks•krē′tä, *n*. pl. [From L. *excrētus*, separated.] Matter excreted from the body, as sweat, feces, etc.

excrete, eks•krēt′, *v.t.*—*excreted*, *excreting*. [L. *excerno*, *excretum*. EXCREMENT.] To separate and throw off from the body by vital action; to discharge.—**excretion,** eks•krē′shon, *n*. A separation of some fluid from the blood by means of the glands; a discharge of animal fluids from the body; that which is discharged.—**excretory,** eks′krē•to•ri, *a*. Having the quality of excreting or throwing off excrementitious matter.—*n*. *Anat*. a duct or vessel destined to receive secreted fluids and to excrete them.

excruciate, eks•krö′shi•āt, *v.t.*—*excruciated*, *excruciating*. [L. *excrucio*, *excruciatum*—*ex*, and *crucio*, to torment, from *crux*, a cross. CROSS.] To cause extreme pain or torture to; to torment; to inflict most severe pain on.—**excruciating,** eks•krö′shi•ā•ting, *p*. and *a*. Extremely painful; distressing; torturing; tormenting.—**excruciatingly,** eks•krö′shi•ā•ting•li, *adv*. In an excruciating manner.—**excruciation,** eks•krö′shi•ā″shon, *n*. The act of excruciating; torture; extreme pain; vexation.

exculpate, eks′kul•pāt, *v.t.*—*exculpated*, *exculpating*. [L.L. *exculpo*, *exculpatum*—L. *ex*, and *culpo*, *culpatum*, to blame, from *culpa*, a fault.] To clear from a charge or imputation of fault or guilt; to vindicate from a charge of fault or crime; to relieve of or free from blame; to regard as innocent; to exonerate; to absolve; to excuse.—**exculpation,** eks•kul•pā′shon, *n*. The act of exculpating; what exculpates; an excuse.—**exculpatory,** eks•kul′pa•to•ri, *a*. Able to exculpate; containing excusatory evidence.

excurrent, eks•kur′ent, *a*. [L. *excurrens*, *excurrentis*, ppr. of *excurro*—*ex*, out, and *curro*, to run.] *Bot*. projecting or running beyond the edge or point, as when the midrib of a leaf projects beyond the apex.

excursion, eks•kėr′zhon, *n*. [L. *excursio*, from *excurro*—*ex*, out, and *curro*, to run.] Act of running out or forth; a deviation from a fixed or usual course; a wandering from a subject or main design; digression; a journey for pleasure or health, with the view of return; a trip.—*Excursion train*, a railroad train specially put on for carrying passengers on a pleasure trip for a certain distance and at a low fare.—**excursionist,** eks•kėr′zhon•ist, *n*. One who makes an excursion; specifically, one who travels by an excursion train; one who professionally provides the public with facilities for making excursions. —**excursive,** eks•kėr′siv, *a*. Given to making excursions; rambling; wandering.—**excursively,** eks•kėr′siv•li, *adv*. In an excursive manner.—**excursiveness,** eks•kėr′siv•nes, *n*. The condition or character of being excursive.—**excursus,** eks•kėr′sus, *n*. [L.] A dissertation appended to a book, discussing some important point or topic more fully than could be done in the body of the work.

excuse, eks•kūz′, *v.t.*—*excused*, *excusing*. [L. *excuso*—*ex*, out, and *causa*, a cause, a suit.] To free from accusation or the imputation of fault or blame; to relieve from blame; to exculpate; to absolve; to justify; to pardon (a fault), to forgive, or to admit to be little censurable, and to overlook; to free from an obligation or duty; to release by favor.—*n*. (eks•kūs′). A plea offered in extenuation of a fault or irregular deportment; apology; that which extenuates or justifies a fault.—**excusable,** eks•kū′za•bl, *a*. Capable of being excused; pardonable; admitting of excuse.—**excusably,** eks•kū′za•bli, *adv*. In an excusable manner; pardonably. —**excusatory,** eks•kū′za•to•ri, *a*. Making excuse; containing excuse or apology; apologetical.

execrate, ek′si•krāt, *v.t.*—*execrated*, *execrating*. [Fr. *exécrer*, from L. *execror*—*ex*, and *sacer*, consecrated or dedicated to a deity, accursed. SACRED.] To denounce evil against, or to imprecate evil on; to curse, hence, to detest utterly; to abhor; to abominate.—**execrable,** ek′si•kra•bl, *a*. Deserving to be execrated or cursed; very hateful; detestable; abominable.—**execrably,** ek′si•kra•bli, *adv*. In a manner deserving of execration; detestably.—**execration,** ek•si•krā′shon, *n*. The act of execrating; a curse pronounced; imprecation of evil; utter detestation; the object execrated.—**execrative, execratory,** ek′si•krā•tiv, ek′si•kra•to•ri, *a*. Denouncing evil; cursing; vilifying.

execute, ek′si•kūt, *v.t.*—*executed*, *executing*. [Fr. *exécuter*, from L. *exsequor*, *exsecutus*, to follow to the end—*ex*, and *sequor*, to follow, as in *sequence*, *prosecute*, *persecute*, *pursue*, *ensue*, etc.] To follow out; to perform; to do; to carry into complete effect; to complete; to accomplish; to finish; to give effect to; to put in force (a law or measure); to inflict; to inflict capital punishment on; to put to death; to perform what is required to give validity to (a writing), as by signing and sealing; to perform (a piece of music) on an instrument or with the voice.—**executable,** ek•si•kū′ta•bl, *a*. Capable of being executed.—**executant,**

eg•zek′ū•tant, *n.* One who executes or performs; a performer.—**executer,** ek′si•kū•tėr, *n.* One who performs or carries into effect.—**execution,** ek•si•kū′shon, *n.* The act of executing; performance; the mode of producing or performing an artistic work, and the dexterity with which it is accomplished; the carrying out of the sentence of the law by putting a criminal to death; a case of the infliction of capital punishment; the carrying out of the sentence of a court by arresting the goods or body of a debtor.—*To do execution,* to cause great damage; to have a destructive effect (as a storm or a cannon ball).—**executioner,** ek•si•kū′shon•ėr, *n.* One who inflicts a capital punishment in pursuance of a legal warrant.—**executive,** eg•zek′ū•tiv, *a.* Having the quality of executing or performing; designed or fitted for execution, administering, or carrying into effect, laws; governing.—*n.* The person (or body of persons) who superintends the execution of the laws; the person or persons who administer the government.—**executor,** ek′sė•kū•tėr, *n.* One who executes or performs; a performer or doer; *law,* the person appointed by a testator to execute his will or to see it carried into effect; in this sense pronounced eg•zek′ū•tėr.—**executorial,** eg•zek′ū•tō″ri•al, *a.* Pertaining to an executor.—**executory,** eg•zek′ū•to•ri, *a.* Performing official duties; carrying laws into effect; executive.—**executrix,** eg•zek′ū•triks, *n.* A female executor; a woman appointed by a testator to execute his will.

exegesis, ek•se•jē′sis, *n.* [Gr. *exēgēsis,* from *exēgeomai,* to explain—*ex,* and *hēgeomai,* to lead, to guide.] The exposition or interpretation of any literary production, but more particularly the exposition or interpretation of Scripture; also the principles of the art of sacred interpretation; exegetics; hermeneutics.—**exegetic, exegetical,** ek•se•jet′ik, ek•se•jet′i•kal, *a.* Explanatory; tending to illustrate or unfold; expository.—**exegetically,** ek•se•jet′i•kal•li, *adv.* By way of exegesis or explanation.—**exegetics,** ek•se•jet′iks, *n.* The science which lays down the principles of the art of scriptural interpretation; exegesis; hermeneutics. — **exegete,** ek′se•jēt, *n.* One skilled in exegesis; an expounder or interpreter.

exemplar, eg•zem′plėr, *n.* [L. EXAMPLE.] A model, original, or pattern to be copied or imitated; a person who serves as a pattern.—**exemplary,** eg′zem•ple•ri, *a.* Serving for a pattern or model for imitation; worthy of imitation; such as may serve for a warning to others; such as may deter.—**exemplarily,** eg′zem•ple•ri•li, *adv.* In an exemplary manner.—**exemplariness,** eg′zem•ple•ri•nes, *n.* The state or quality of being exemplary.

exemplify, eg•zem′pli•fī, *v.t.*—*exemplified, exemplifying.* [L.L. *exemplifico,* to exemplify—L. *exemplum,* an example, and *facio,* to make.] To show or illustrate by example; to serve as an example or instance of; to make an attested copy or transcript of.—**exemplification,** eg•zem′pli•fi•kā″shon, *n.* The act of exemplifying; a showing or illustrating by example; that which exemplifies.

exempt, ig•zemt′, *v.t.* [Fr. *exempter;* L. *eximo, exemptum,* to take out, to remove—*ex,* out, and *emo,* to buy, to take.] To free or permit to be free from any charge, burden, restraint, duty, etc., to which others are subject; to privilege; to grant immunity (no man is *exempted* from suffering).—*a.* Free from any service, charge, burden, tax, duty, requisition, or evil of any kind to which others are subject; not subject; not liable; not included; freed; free.—*n.* One who is exempted; one not subject.—**exemption,** ig•zem′shon, *n.* The act of exempting; the state of being exempt; immunity; privilege.

exequatur, ek•se•kwā′tėr, *n.* [L., let him perform or execute.] A written recognition of a person in the character of consul or commercial agent; an official permission to perform some act.

exercise, ek′sėr•sīz, *n.* [Fr. *exercice,* from L. *exercitium,* exercise, from *exerceo, exercitum,* to exercise—*ex,* out, and *arceo,* to inclose, to hinder.] A putting in action the powers or faculties of (the eyes, the limbs, the mind); use; employment; practice or performance; a carrying out in action, or performing the duties of anything (the *exercise* of an art, trade, occupation); exertion of the body as conducive to health; bodily exertion as a part of regimen; systematic exertion of the body for amusement or in order to acquire some art, dexterity, or grace; any such art or dexterity acquired by bodily training; training to acquire skill in the management of arms and in military evolutions; drill; moral training; discipline; a lesson or example for the practice of learners; a school task; puritan week-day service and sermon.—*v.t.*—*exercised, exercising.* To set in exercise or operation; to employ; to set or keep in a state of activity; to exert (the body, the mind) to put in practice; to carry out in action (to *exercise* authority); to train, discipline, or improve by practice; to task; to keep employed or busy; to cause to think earnestly and laboriously; to give anxiety to; to make uneasy; to task or try with something grievous; to pain or afflict.—*v.i.* To exercise one's self; to take exercise.—**exerciser,** ek′sėr•sī•zėr, *n.* One who or that which exercises.—**exercisable,** ek′sėr•sī•za•bl, *a.* Capable of being exercised, enjoyed, or enforced.

exergue, ig•zėrg′, *n.* [Gr. *ex,* out, and *ergon,* work.] The small space beneath the base line of a subject engraved on a coin or medal, left for the date, engraver's name, or something of minor importance.

exert, ig•zėrt′, *v.t.* [L. *exerto, exserto,* to stretch out, to thrust forth, freq. from *exsero, exsertum,* to thrust out or forth—*ex,* out, and *sero,* to join. SERIES.] To put forth (strength, force, ability); to put in action; to bring into active operation (the mind, the bodily powers); *refl.* to use efforts; to strive; to put forth one's powers.—**exertion,** eg•zėr′shon, *n.* The act of exerting; a putting forth of power; an effort; a striving or struggling; endeavor; trial.

exeunt. See EXIT.

exfoliate, eks•fō′li•āt, *v.i.*—*exfoliated, exfoliating.* [L. *exfolio, exfoliatum,* to strip of leaves—*ex,* and *folium,* a leaf.] To separate and come off in scales; to split into scales.—*v.t.* To free from scales or splinters.—**exfoliation,** eks•fō′li•ā″shon, *n.* The process of exfoliating or separation in scales; desquamation; separation into scales or laminae, as in a mineral.—**exfoliative,** eks•fō′li•ā•tiv, *a.* Having the power of causing exfoliation.

exhale, egz•hāl′, *v.t.*—*exhaled, exhaling.* [L. *exhalo*—*ex,* out, and *halo,* to breathe.] To breathe or send out (something of a vaporous or gaseous character); to emit, as vapor; also, to cause to be emitted in vapor or minute particles.—*v.i.* To rise or pass off, as vapor; to vanish.—**exhalant,** egz•hā′lant, *a.* Having the quality of exhaling or evaporating.—**exhalation,** egz•ha•lā′shon, *n.* [L. *exhalatio.*] The act or process of exhaling; evaporation; that which is exhaled; that which is emitted or which rises in the form of vapor; emanation; effluvium.

exhaust, eg•ząst′, *v.t.* [L. *exhaurio, exhaustum*—*ex,* out, up, and *haurio,* to draw, to draw water.] To draw out or drain off the whole of; to consume or use up; to empty by drawing out the contents; to use or expend the whole of by exertion; to wear out; to tire; to treat thoroughly; to leave nothing unsaid regarding.—*n.* Gaseous or other material exhausted, as from an internal combustion engine; also the muffler through which such material is passed.—**exhaustible,** eg•ząs′ti•bl, *a.* Capable of being exhausted, drained off, consumed, or brought to an end.—**exhaustibility,** eg•ząs′ti•bil″i•ti, *n.* Capability of being exhausted; the state of being exhaustible.—**exhaustion,** eg•ząst′shon, *n.* The act of exhausting; the state of being exhausted or emptied; the state of being deprived of strength or spirits; a state of complete fatigue and bodily weakness.—**exhaustive,** eg•ząs′tiv, *a.* Causing exhaustion; tending to exhaust; treating of a subject in such a way as to leave no part of it unexamined; thorough.—**exhaustless,** eg•ząst′les, *a.* Not to be exhausted; inexhaustible.

exhibit, eg•zib′it, *v.t.* [L. *exhibeo, exhibitum*—*ex,* out, and *habeo, habitum,* to hold, as in *prohibit,* etc. HABIT.] To hold out or present to view; to present for inspection; to show; to manifest publicly (to *exhibit* a noble example); *med.* to administer by way of medicine or remedy.—*v.i.* To show one's self in some particular capacity or character; to exhibit one's manufactures or productions at a public exhibition.—*n.* Anything exhibited, as at a public exhibition; a document or other thing shown to a witness when giving evidence, and referred to by him in his evidence.—**exhibitor, exhibiter,** ig•zib'i•tėr, *n.* One who exhibits; one who presents a petition.—**exhibition,** eg'zi•bish"on, *n.* [L. *exhibitio.*] The act of exhibiting; a showing or presenting to view; that which is exhibited; especially a public display, as of works of art, natural products, manufactures, feats of skill, and the like; formerly an allowance, pension, or salary; hence, a benefaction settled for the maintenance of scholars in English universities.—**exhibitionism,** eg'zi•bish"on•izm, *n.* The perversion of attaining gratification by indecent exposure; attempting to attract attention to oneself by boasting.

exhilarate, ig•zil'a•rāt, *v.t.—exhilarated, exhilarating.* [L. *exhilaro—ex,* and *hilaro,* to make merry, from *hilaris,* merry, jovial.] To make cheerful or merry; to inspire with hilarity; to make glad or joyous; to inspirit; to gladden; to cheer.—**exhilarant,** ig•zil'a•rant, *a.* Exhilarating.—*n.* That which exhilarates.—**exhilarating,** ig•zil'a•rā•ting, *a.* Such as to exhilarate or make cheerful.—**exhilaration,** ig•zil'a•rā"shon, *n.* The act of exhilarating; cheerfulness; enlivenment; gladness; gaiety.

exhort, ig•zort', *v.t.* [L. *exhortor—ex,* and *hortor,* to encourage, to advise.] To incite by words or advice; to animate or urge by arguments to laudable conduct or course of action; to advise, warn, or caution; to admonish.—*v.i.* To use words or arguments to incite to good deeds.—**exhortation,** ig•zor•tā'shon, *n.* The act or practice of exhorting; language intended to incite and encourage; a persuasive discourse; a homily; an admonition.—**exhortative, exhortatory,** ig•zor'ta•tiv, ig•zor'ta•to•ri, *a.* Containing exhortation; tending to exhort; serving for exhortation.—**exhorter,** ig•zor'tėr, *n.* One who exhorts or encourages.

exhume, eks•hūm', *v.t.—exhumed, exhuming.* [Fr. *exhumer,* to dig out of the ground—L. *ex,* out, and *humus,* earth, ground (akin *humble*).] To dig up after having been buried; to disinter.—**exhumation,** eks•hū•mā'shon, *n.* The act of exhuming.

exigence, exigency, ek'si•jens, ek'si•jen•si, *n.* [Fr. *exigence,* from L. *exigo,* to drive out or forth, to demand, to exact. EXACT.] The state of being urgent or pressing; urgent demand; urgency; a pressing necessity; emergency.—**exigent,** ek'si•jent, *a.* Pressing; requiring immediate aid or action.—**exigible,** ek'si•ji•bl, *a.* That may be exacted; demandable; requirable.

exiguous, ek•sig'ū•us, *a.* [L. *exiguus,* scanty.] Small; slender; minute; diminutive.—**exiguity,** ek•si•gū'i•ti, *n.* [L. *exiguitas.*] Smallness; slenderness.

exile, eg'zīl, *n.* [Fr. *exil,* banishment, *exilé,* an exiled person, from L. *exsilium,* banishment, *exsul,* a banished person—*ex,* out, and root of *salio,* to leap (whence *salient, sally*); Skr. *sar,* to go.] The state of being expelled from one's native country or place of residence by authority, and forbidden to return, either for a limited time or for perpetuity; banishment; a removal to a foreign country for residence; a separation from one's country and friends by distress or necessity; the person banished or expelled from his country, or who leaves his country and resides in another.—*v.t.—exiled, exiling.* To banish; to cause to be an exile.

exist, ig•zist', *v.i.* [Fr. *exister,* from L. *existo—ex,* and *sisto,* to stand, as in *assist, consist,* etc. STATE, STAND.] To have actual existence or being, whether in the form of matter or of spirit; to be; to live; to continue to have life or animation; to continue to be.—**existence,** ig•zis'tens, *n.* The state of being or existing; continuance of being; that which exists; an entity.—**existent,** ig•zis'tent, *a.* Having existence; being.—**existential,** eg•zis•ten'shal, *a.* Of or pertaining to, or consisting in existence.—**existentialism,** eg•zis•ten'shal•izm, *n. Philos.* a twentieth-century movement that stresses the indescribable nature of the world and the volition of man.—**existentialist,** eg•zis•ten'shal•ist, *n.*

exit, ek'sit, *n.* [L., he goes out, from *exeo,* to go out—*ex,* out, and *eo,* to go.] The departure of a player from the stage; a direction in a play to mark the time of an actor's quitting the stage; any departure; the act of quitting the stage of action; death; a way of departure; passage out of a place; a ramp by which an auto leaves a highway.—**exeunt,** ek'si•ụnt. They go out: a common direction in plays, referring to more of the actors than one.

exocarp, ek'sō•kärp, *n.* [Gr. *exō,* outside, *karpos,* fruit.] *Bot.* the outer layer of a pericarp.

exodus, ek'so•dus, *n.* [Gr. *exodos—ex,* and *hodos,* way.] Departure from a place; especially, the emigration of large bodies of people from one country to another; [*cap.*] the second book of the Old Testament, which gives a history of the departure of the Israelites from Egypt.

ex officio, eks•e•fish'ē•ō, *adv.* [L. from office.] By virtue of office or official position.—**ex-officio,** eks•e•fish'ē•ō, *a.*

exogamy, ek•sog'a•mi, *n.* [Gr. *exō,* without, and *gamos,* marriage.] Marriage outside of a specific group; reproduction by unrelated organisms; custom among certain savage tribes which prohibits a man from marrying a woman of his own tribe, and so leads the men to capture their wives from among other tribes.—**exogamous,** ek•sog'a•mus, *a.* Of or belonging to exogamy; characterized by exogamy.

exonerate, ig•zon'ėr•āt, *v.t.—exonerated, exonerating.* [L. *exonero, exoneratum—ex,* not, and *onus, oneris,* a load (whence also *onerous*).] To relieve of a charge or of blame; to clear of something that lies upon the character as an imputation; to discharge of responsibility, obligation, duty, or liability.—**exoneration,** ig•zon'ėr•ā"shon, *n.* The act of exonerating.—**exonerative,** ig•zon'ėr•ā•tiv, *a.* Freeing from a burden, or obligation.

exorable, ek'so•ra•bl, *a.* [L. *exorabilis,* from *ex,* and *oro,* to pray.] That may be moved or persuaded by entreaty.

exorbitance, exorbitancy, ig•zor'bi•tans, ig•zor'bi•tan•si, *n.* [L.L. *exorbitantia,* from *exorbito,* to go out of the track—L. *ex,* out, and *orbita,* a rut made by a wheel, from *orbis,* a circle. ORB.] A going beyond rule or ordinary limits; excess; extravagance (*exorbitance* of demands, of prices).—**exorbitant,** ig•zor'bi•tant, *a.* Going beyond the established limits of right or propriety; excessive; extravagant; enormous.—**exorbitantly,** ig•zor'bi•tant•li, *adv.* In an exorbitant manner.

exorcise, ek'sor•sīz, *v.t.—exorcised, exorcising.* [Fr. *exorciser,* from Gr. *exorkizō—ex,* intens., and *horkizō,* to bind by oath, from *horkos,* an oath.] To expel or cast out by conjurations, prayers, and ceremonies; to purify from unclean spirits by adjurations and ceremonies; to deliver from the influence or presence of malignant spirits or demons.—**exorciser, exorcist,** ek'sor•sī•zėr, ek'sor•sist, *n.* One who exorcises.—**exorcism,** ek'sor•sizm, *n.* The act of exorcising; a prayer or charm used to expel evil spirits.

exordium, ig•zor'di•um, *n.* [L., from *exordior,* to begin a web, to lay the warp—*ex,* and *ordior,* to begin a web, to begin.] The beginning of anything; specifically, the introductory part of a discourse, which prepares the audience for the main subject.—**exordial,** ig•zor'di•al, *a.* Pertaining to an exordium; introductory; initial.

exoskeleton, ek'sō•skel•e•ton, *n.* [Gr. *exō,* without, and *skeleton.*] The external skeleton; all those structures which are produced by the hardening of the integument, as the shells of the Crustacea, the scales and plates of fishes and reptiles; dermoskeleton.

exosmose, exosmosis, ek'sos•mōs, ek•sos•mō'sis, *n.* [Gr. *exō,* outside, and *ōsmos,* impulsion, from *ōtheō,* to thrust, to push.] The passage of gases or liquids through membranes or porous media, from within outward, the reverse process being called *endosmose.*—**exosmotic,** ek•sos•mot'ik, *a.* Pertaining or relating to exosmose.

exosphere, ek'sō•sfēr, *n.* [Gr. *exo,* outside, and *sphaira,* globe.] The outermost region of the atmosphere.

exostosis, ek•sos•tō'sis, *n.* [Gr. *ex,* and *osteon,* a bone.] *Path.* Any protuberance or enlargement of a bone which is not natural; *bot.* a disease of trees, in which knots or large tumors are formed.

exoteric, ek•so•ter′ik, *a.* [Gr. *exōterikos*, external, from *exōteros*, exterior —*exō*, without.] Suitable to be imparted to the public; hence, capable of being readily or fully comprehended; public; opposed to *esoteric* or secret.

exothermic, eks•o•ther′mik, *a.* [Gr. *exō*, outside, *thermos*, heat.] Of chemical compounds or reactions, formed with or involving evolution of heat. See ENDOTHERMIC.

exotic, eg•zot′ik, *a.* [Gr. *exōtikos*, from *exō*, outward.] Introduced from a foreign country; not native; foreign; extraneous.—**exotic,** *n.* Anything of foreign origin, as a plant, tree, word, practice, introduced from a foreign country.

expand, iks•pand′, *v.t.* [L. *expando*—*ex*, and *pando*, to spread out, to extend, to open (seen also in *pace*, *pass*, etc.).] To spread out so as to give greater extent to; to open out; to cause the particles or parts of to spread or stand apart, thus increasing the bulk; to dilate; to enlarge in bulk; to distend; to widen or extend. —*v.i.* To become opened, spread apart, dilated, distended, or enlarged. —**expanse,** iks•pans′, *n.* [L. *expansum*.] A widely expanded surface or space; a wide extent of space.—**expansible,** iks•pan′si•bl, *a.* Capable of being expanded, extended, dilated, or diffused.—**expansile,** iks•pan′sil, *a.* Capable of expanding or of being dilated.—**expansion,** iks•pan′shon, *n.* The act of expanding or spreading out; the state of being expanded; the increase of bulk which a body undergoes by the recession of its particles from one another so that it occupies a greater space, its weight remaining still the same; enlargement; dilatation; distention; an expanse or extended surface; extension.—**expansive,** eks•pan′siv, *a.* Having the power of expanding or dilating; having the capacity of being expanded; embracing a large number of objects; wide extending.—**expansively,** eks•pan′siv•li, *adv.* In an expansive manner.—**expansiveness,** eks•pan′siv•nes, *n.*

ex parte, eks•pär′te, *a.* [L.] Proceeding only from one part or side of a matter in question; one-sided; partial; *law*, made or done by or on behalf of one party in a suit.

expatiate, iks•pā′shi•āt, *v.i.*—*expatiated*, *expatiating*. [L. *exspatior*, *exspatiatus*—*ex*, and *spatior*, to walk about, from *spatium*, space. SPACE.] To move at large; to rove without prescribed limits; to enlarge in discourse or writing; to be copious in argument or discussion.—**expatiation,** eks•pā′shi•ā″shon, *n.* Act of expatiating.

expatriate, eks•pā′tri•āt, *v.t.*—*expatriated*, *expatriating*. [L. *ex*, out, and *patria*, one's fatherland, from *patrius*, fatherly, from *pater*, a father.] To banish from one's native country; to exile: often *refl.*—**expatriation,** eks•pā′tri•ā″shon, *n.* The act of banishing or state of being banished; banishment; exile.

expect, iks•pekt′, *v.t.* [L. *exspecto*, *exspectatum*—*ex*, and *specto*, to behold, from *specio*, to look. SPECIES.] To wait for‡; to await‡; to look forward to in the future; to look for to happen; to entertain at least a slight belief in the happening of; to anticipate; to reckon or count upon.—**expectance, expectancy,** iks•pek′tans, iks•pek′tan•si, *n.* The act or state of expecting; expectation; something on which expectations or hopes are founded; the object of expectation or hope.—**expectant,** iks•pek′tant, *a.* Expecting; looking for.—*n.* One who waits in expectation; one held in dependence by his belief or hope of receiving some good.—**expectation,** eks•pek•tā′shon, *n.* The act of expecting or looking forward to an event as about to happen; the state of being expected or awaited; prospect of future possessions, wealth, or other good fortune; wealth in prospect: in this sense usually in the plural; the value of anything depending on the happening of some uncertain event; prospect of reaching a certain age.—**expectative,** iks•pek′ta•tiv, *a.* Giving rise to expectation; anticipatory.

expectorate, iks•pek′to•rāt, *v.t.*—*expectorated*, *expectorating*. [L. *expectoro*, *expectoratum*—*ex*, and *pectus*, *pectoris*, the breast (whence *pectoral*).] To eject from the trachea or lungs; to discharge, as phlegm or other matter, by coughing, hawking, and spitting; to spit out.—*v.i.* To eject matter by coughing and spitting; to spit.—**expectorant,** iks•pek′to•rant, *a.* Having the quality of promoting discharges from the mucous membrane of the lungs or trachea.—*n.* A medicine which promotes such discharges. — **expectoration,** iks•pek′to•rā″shon, *n.* The act of expectorating; the matter expectorated.

expediency, expedience, iks•pē′di•en•si, iks•pē′di•ens, *n.* [L. *expediens*, pp. of *expedio*, to set free. EXPEDITE.] Propriety under the particular circumstances of a case; advisability, all things being duly considered or taken into account; the seeking of immediate or selfish gain or advantage at the expense of genuine principle; time-servingness.—**expedient,** iks•pē′di•ent, *a.* Tending to promote the object proposed; proper under the circumstances; conducive or tending to selfish ends.—*n.* That which serves to promote or advance; any means which may be employed to accomplish an end; means devised or employed in an exigency; shift; contrivance; resort; plan; device.

expedite, eks′pi•dīt, *v.t.*—*expedited*, *expediting*. [L. *expedio*, *expeditum*, to free one caught by the feet in a snare—*ex*, out, and *pes*, *pedis*, the foot, seen also in *pedal*, *pedestal*, *pedestrian*, *despatch*, etc.] To free from impediments; to accelerate or facilitate the motion or progress of; to render quicker or easier in progress.—*a.* Clear of impediments; easy; expeditious.—**expedition,** eks•pi•dish′on, *n.* Promptness in action from being free from encumbrance; speed; quickness; dispatch; the march of an army or the voyage of a fleet to a distant place for hostile purposes; any important journey or voyage made by an organized body of men for some valuable end; such a body of men, together with their equipments, etc.—**expeditionary,** eks•pi•dish′on•e•ri, *a.* Pertaining to or composing an expedition.—**expeditious,** eks•pi•dish′us, *a.* Performed with expedition or celerity; quick; hasty; speedy; nimble; active; swift; acting with celerity.—**expeditiously,** eks•pi•dish′us•li, *adv.* In an expeditious manner.—**expeditiousness,** eks•pi•dish′us•nes, *n.* The quality of being expeditious.

expel, iks•pel′, *v.t.*—*expelled*, *expelling*. [L. *expello*—*ex*, out, and *pello*, to drive, as in *impel*, *repel*, *compel*, etc.] To drive or force out from any enclosed place, or from that within which anything is contained or situated; to cast or thrust out; to banish; to exclude; to drive out, as from any society or institution.—**expellable,** iks•pel′a•bl, *a.* That may be expelled or driven out.

expend, iks•pend′, *v.t.* [L. *expendo*—*ex*, out, and *pendo*, to weigh out, to pay. The same word takes another form in *spend*.] To lay out in paying, purchasing, etc.; to disburse; to spend; to deliver or distribute, either in payment or in donations; to use, employ, consume (time, labor, material).—**expenditure,** iks•pen′di•chėr, *n.* The act of expending or laying out; disbursement; that which is expended; expense.—**expense,** iks•pens′, *n.* [L. *expensum*, from *expensus*, pp. of *expendo*.] A laying out or expending; that which is expended, laid out, or consumed; especially, money expended; cost; charge; cost, with the idea of loss, damage, or discredit (he did this at the *expense* of his character).—**expensive,** iks•pen′siv, *a.* Requiring much expense; costly; dear; extravagant; lavish.—**expensively,** iks•pen′siv•li, *adv.* In an expensive manner.—**expensiveness,** iks•pen′siv•nes, *n.* The quality of being expensive.

experience, iks•pē′ri•ens, *n.* [Fr. *expérience*, L. *experientia*, from *experior*, to try, to prove—*ex*, and a root *per*, to try, to pass through, same as in E. *ferry*, etc.] Personal trial, proof, or test; frequent trial; continued and varied observation; the knowledge gained by trial, or repeated trials, or observation; practical wisdom taught by the changes and trials of life.—*v.t.*—*experienced*, *experiencing*. To make practical acquaintance with; to try, or prove, by use, by suffering, or by enjoyment; to have happen to or befall.—**experienced,** iks•pē′ri•enst, *p.* and *a.* Taught by experience; skillful or wise by means of trials, use, or observation.—**experiential,** iks•pē′ri•en″shal, *a.* Relating to experience; derived from or based on experience, trial, or observation; empirical.

experiment, iks•per′i•ment, *n.* [L. *experimentum*, from *experior*. EXPERIENCE.] An act or operation designed to discover some unknown truth, principle, or effect, or to establish it when discovered; a trial. —*v.i.* To make trial; to make an experiment.—**experimental,** iks•per′i•men″tal, *a.* Pertaining to, derived from, founded on, or known by experiment; given to or skilled in experiment.—**experimentally,** iks•per′i•men″tal•li, *adv.* In an experimental manner; by experiment.—**experimentation,** iks•per′i•men•tā″shon, *n.* The act or practice of making experiments.—**experimenter,** iks•per′i•men•tėr, *n.* One who makes experiments.

expert, eks•pėrt′, *a.* [L. *experius,* having made trial, experienced, from *experior,* to try. EXPERIENCE.] Experienced; taught by use or practice; skillful; dexterous; adroit; having a facility of operation or performance from practice.—*n.* (eks′pėrt). A skillful or practiced person; a scientific or professional witness who gives evidence on matters connected with his profession.—**expertize,** ėks′pėr•tīz, *v.i.* To give an expert opinion.—**expertly,** eks•pėrt′li, *adv.*—**expertness,** eks•pėrt′nes, *n.*

expiate, eks′pi•āt, *v.t.*—*expiated, expiating.* [L. *expio, expiatum,* to make satisfaction—*ex,* out, and *pio,* to appease, to propitiate, from *pius,* pious.] To atone for; to make satisfaction or reparation for.—**expiable,** eks′pi•a•bl, *a.* Capable of being expiated.—**expiator,** eks′pi•ā•tėr, *n.* One who expiates.—**expiatory,** eks′pi•a•to•ri, *a.* Having the power to make atonement or expiation.

expire, iks•pīr′, *v.t.*—*expired, expiring.* [L. *exspiro*—*ex,* out, and *spiro,* to breathe. SPIRIT.] To breathe out; to expel from the mouth or nostrils in the process of respiration: opposed to *inspire;* to emit in minute particles; to exhale.—*v.i.* To emit breath; to emit one's last breath; to die; to come to an end; to close or conclude, as a given period; to terminate; to end.—**expiration,** eks•pi•rā′shon, *n.* [L. *exspiratio.*] The act of breathing out, or forcing the air from the lungs; emission of breath; exhalation; close, end, conclusion, or termination; expiry.—**expiratory,** iks•pī′ra•to•ri, *a.* Pertaining to the emission or expiration of breath.—**expiry,** ik•spī′ri, *n.* Expiration; termination.

explain, iks•plān′, *v.t.* [L. *explano*—*ex,* and *plano,* to make plain, from *planus,* level, plain. PLAIN.] To make plain, manifest, or intelligible; to clear of obscurity; to make clear or evident; to expound; to give or show the meaning or reason of.—*v.i.* To give explanations.—**explainable,** iks•plā′na•bl, *a.* Capable of being explained.—**explanation,** iks•pla•nā′shon, *n.* [L. *explanatio.*] The act of explaining; a making clear or understood; exposition; interpretation; the clearing up of matters between parties who have been at variance.—**explanatory,** iks•plan′a•to•ri, *a.* Serving to explain; containing explanation.

expletive, eks′pli•tiv, *a.* [Fr. *explétif,* from L. *expleo, expletum,* to fill full—*ex,* intens., and *pleo,* to fill (as in *complete,* etc.).] Added to fill a vacancy; superfluous: said of words. —*n.* A word or syllable inserted to fill a vacancy; an oath or a needless interjection.—**expletory,** eks′ple•to•ri, *a.* Expletive.

explicate, eks′pli•kāt, *v.t.*—*explicated, explicating.* [L. *explico, explicatum,* to unfold—*ex,* not, and *plico,* to fold, as in *complicate, implicate, apply,* etc. PLY.] To unfold the meaning or sense of; to explain; to interpret.—**explicable,** eks′pli•ka•bl, *a.* Capable of being explicated or explained.—**explication,** eks•pli•kā′shon, *n.* The act of explicating or explaining; explanation.—**explicative, explicatory,** eks′pli•kā•tiv, eks′pli•ka•to•ri, *a.* Serving to unfold or explain.

explicit, iks•plis′it, *a.* [L. *explicitus,* disentangled, from *explico, explicitum,* to unfold, to disentangle. EXPLICATE.] Not implied only, but distinctly stated; plain in language; open to the understanding; clear; not obscure or ambiguous; open; unreserved; outspoken.—**explicitly,** iks•plis′it•li, *adv.* In an explicit manner;expressly;plainly.—**explicitness,** iks•plis′it•nes, *n.* The quality of being explicit.

explode, iks•plōd′, *v.i.*—*exploded, exploding.* [L. *explodo,* to hoot off the stage, to cast out, reject—*ex,* and *plaudo,* to clap, as in *applaud, plaudit,* etc.] To burst with a loud report; to burst and expand with force and noise; to detonate; to burst into activity or into a passion.—*v.t.* To cause to explode or burst with a loud report; to drive from notice or practice and bring into disrepute; to cause to be no longer practiced, held, or believed in (generally in pp.; an *exploded* custom or theory).—**explodent,** iks•plō′dent, *n. Philol.* same as *explosive.*—**exploder,** iks•plō′dėr, *n.* One who or that which explodes.—**explosion,** iks•plō′zhon, *n.* [L. *explosio.*] The act of exploding; a bursting or sudden expansion of any elastic fluid with force and a loud report; a sudden and loud discharge caused by the application of fire, as of gunpowder or a flammable gas; *fig.* a violent outburst of feeling, as of rage, generally accompanied by excited language or by violent actions.—**explosive,** iks•plō′ziv, *a.* Causing explosion; readily exploding; *philol.* mute, forming a complete vocal stop: said of certain consonants.—*n.* Anything liable or with a tendency to explode, as gunpowder, dynamite, etc.; *philol.* a mute or noncontinuous consonant, as *k, t, b.*—**explosively,** iks•plō′ziv•li, *adv.* In an explosive manner.

exploit, eks′ploit, eks•ploit′, *n.* [Fr. *exploit,* O.Fr. *exploict,* from L. *explico, explicatum, explicitum,* to unfold, finish. EXPLICATE.] A deed or act of note; a heroic act; a deed of renown; a notable feat; a great or noble achievement.—*v.t.* eks•ploit′. [Fr. *exploiter.*] To utilize; to make use of basely for one's own advantage.—**exploitation,** eks•ploi•tā′shon, *n.* [Fr.] Utilization; the successful application of industry on any object, as in the cultivation of land, the working of mines, etc.; now, esp., selfish or unfair utilization.

explore, iks•plōr′, *v.t.*—*explored, exploring.* [L. *exploro,* to cry aloud, to explore—*ex,* out, and *ploro,* to bewail, as in *deplore.*] To travel or range over with the view of making discovery, especially geographical discovery; to search by any means; to scrutinize; to inquire into with care; to examine closely with a view to discover truth.—**exploration,** iks•plo•rā′shon, *n.* The act of exploring; close search; strict or careful examination.—**explorative, exploratory,** iks•plō′ra•tiv, iks•plō′ra•to•ri, *a.* Serving or tending to explore; searching; examining.—**explorer,** iks•plō′rėr, *n.* One who explores.

explosion. See EXPLODE.

exponent, iks•pō′nent, *n.* [L. *exponens, exponentis,* ppr. of *expono,* to expose or set forth—*ex,* out, and *pono,* to place.] One who expounds or explains anything; one who stands forth to explain the principles or doctrines of a party; *alg.* a small number placed above a quantity at the right hand to denote to what power the quantity must be understood to be raised: thus a^2 denotes *a* raised to the second power.—**exponential,** eks•pō•nen′shal, *a.* Of or pertaining to an exponent or exponents.

export, eks•pōrt′, *v.t.* (*often* eks′pōrt, *esp. in contrast with import*). [Fr. *exporter,* from L. *exporto*—*ex,* out, and *porto,* to bear, to carry, as in *import, report, support, sport.*] To send for sale or consumption in foreign countries; to send or furnish for conveyance to distant places, either by water or land.—*n.* (eks′pōrt). The act of exporting; exportation; the gross quantity of goods exported; that which is exported; a commodity that is exported.—**exportable,** eks•pōr′ta•bl, *a.* Capable of being exported.—**exportation,** eks•pōr•tā′shon, *n.* The act of exporting; the act of conveying or sending abroad commodities in the course of commerce.—**exporter,** eks•pōr′tėr, *n.* (*in contrast,* eks′pōr•tėr). One who exports.

expose, iks•pōz′, *v.t.* [Fr. *exposer*—prefix *ex,* and *poser,* to set, to place. POSE; also COMPOSE, DEPOSE, etc.] To set out or leave in a place unprotected and uncared for; to abandon; to make bare; to uncover; to disclose; to put forward or place in a position to be seen; to exhibit; to set out to view; to lay open to examination; to subject or place in the way of something to be avoided (this *exposed* him to danger); to put in danger; to hold up to censure by disclosing the faults of; to show the folly or ignorance of.—**exposé,** eks•po•zā′, *n.* [Fr.] Exposure; the exposure of something which it was desirable to keep concealed.—**exposed,** iks•pōzd′, *p.* and *a.* Put in danger; unprotected; liable; subject;

open to the wind or the cold; unsheltered.—**exposer,** iks•pō′zėr, *n.* One who exposes.—**exposition,** eks•po•zish′on, *n.* [Fr. *exposition,* L. *expositio.*] A laying open; a setting out to public view; explanation; interpretation; a laying open the sense or meaning; an exhibition or show.—**expositor,** iks•poz′i•tėr, *n.* One who expounds or explains; an interpreter.—**expository,** iks•poz′i•to•ri, *a.* Serving to explain; tending to illustrate.—**exposure,** iks•pō′zhėr, *n.* The act of exposing; abandonment; the state of being exposed; openness to view; openness or liability to danger, inconvenience, etc.; position in regard to the free access of light, air, etc.

ex post facto, eks•pōst•fak′tō, *a.* [L.] *Law,* done after another thing; after the deed is done; retrospective.

expostulate, iks•pos′che•lāt, *v.i.*—*expostulated, expostulating.* [L. *expostulo, expostulatum,* to demand vehemently, to find fault—*ex,* and *postulo,* to demand, from *posco,* to ask urgently, to beg. POSTULATE.] To reason earnestly with a person on some impropriety of his conduct; to remonstrate.—*v.t.*‡ To reason about; to discuss. (*Shak.*)—**expostulation,** iks•pos′che•lā″shon, *n.* The act of expostulating; the act of pressing on a person reasons or arguments against the impropriety of his conduct; an address containing expostulation.—**expostulator,** iks•pos′che•lā•tėr, *n.* One who expostulates.—**expostulatory,** iks•pos′che•la•to•ri, *a.* Consisting of or containing expostulation.

exposure. See EXPOSE.

expound, iks•pound′, *v.t.* [O.Fr. *expondre,* from L. *exponere,* to set forth, to explain—*ex,* out, and *pono,* to place. *Compound* is similarly formed.] To explain; to lay open the meaning of; to clear of obscurity; to interpret.—**expounder,** iks•poun′dėr, *n.* One who expounds.

express, iks•pres′, *v.t.* [O.Fr. *expresser.* L. *exprimo, expressum*—*ex,* out, and *premo,* to press. PRESS.] To press or squeeze out; to force out by pressure; to give utterance to or declare by words; to represent in words; to intimate; to indicate; to make known; to tell; to represent; to exhibit; to denote; to send or convey by special fast system; *refl.* to speak what one has got to speak.—*a.* Given in direct terms: not implied or left to inference; clearly expressed; not ambiguous; plain; explicit; intended or sent for a particular purpose or on a particular errand; traveling with special speed (an *express* train).—*n.* A messenger sent with haste on a particular errand or occasion; any regular provision made for the speedy transmission of parcels, money, goods; any vehicle or other conveyance sent on a special mission; a railroad train which travels at a specially high rate of speed; that sent by express.—**expression,** iks•presh′on, *n.* The act of expressing or forcing out by pressure, as juices and oils from plants; the act of uttering, declaring, or representing; utterance; declaration; power of expressing one's thoughts, feelings, ideas, etc.; something uttered; a phrase or mode of speech; the peculiar manner of utterance suited to the subject and sentiment; cast of countenance, as indicative of character; play of features, as expressive of feeling or any emotion; the natural and lively representation of any state or condition, as in a picture by the pose of the figure, the conformation of the features, etc.; the power or quality in a picture or other work of art of suggesting an idea; *mus.* sound suited to any particular subject; *alg.* any algebraic quantity, simple or compound, as $3a$, $\sqrt{4a+b}$, etc.—**expressionism,** iks•presh′on•izm, *n. Art,* the depiction of subjective qualities by an artist.—**expressive,** iks•pres′iv, *a.* Serving to express, utter, or represent (words *expressive of* gratitude); full of expression; emphatic.—**expressively,** iks•pres′iv•li, *adv.*—**expressiveness,** iks•pres′iv•nes, *n.* **expressly,** iks•pres′li, *adv.* In an express manner; of set purpose; in direct terms; plainly.—**expressway,** iks•pres′wā, *n.* A high-speed, nonstop highway.

expropriate, eks•prō′pri•āt, *v.t.* [L. *ex,* out of, from, and *proprius,* one's own. PROPER, PROPRIETY.] To disengage from appropriation; to give up a claim to the exclusive property of.—**expropriation,** eks•prō′pri•ā″shon, *n.* The act of expropriating; the act of dispossessing the owner of a property wholly or to a great extent of his proprietary rights.

expulsion, iks•pul′shon, *n.*[L. *expulsio,* a driving out, from *expello,* to expel.] The act of driving out or expelling; a driving away by violence; the state of being expelled, driven out, or away.—**expulsive,** iks•pul′siv, *a.* Having the power of expelling.

expunge, iks•punj′, *v.t.*—*expunged, expunging.* [L. *expungo,* to prick out, to cross or blot out—*ex,* out, and *pungo,* to prick. POINT.] To blot out, as with a pen; to rub out; to efface; to erase; to obliterate; to wipe out or destroy; to annihilate.

expurgate, eks′pėr•gāt, *v.t.*—*expurgated, expurgating.* [L. *expurgo, expurgatum*—*ex,* and *purgo,* to purge. PURGE, PURE.] To purify from anything noxious, offensive, or erroneous; to purge; to cleanse; to strike obscene, coarse, or offensive passages out of (a book).—**expurgation,** eks•pėr•gā′shon, *n.* The act of expurgating, purging, or cleansing; purification.—**expurgator,** eks•pėr′gā•tėr, *n.* One who expurgates.—**expurgatory,** iks•pėr′ga•to•ri, *a.* Cleansing; purifying; serving to expurgate.

exquisite, eks′kwi•zit, *a.* [L. *exquisitus,* carefully sought out, exquisite, from *exquiro, exquisitum*—*ex,* out, and *quæro,* to seek, whence *question, quest, query,* etc.] Of great excellence or fineness; choice; select; consummate; perfect; of keen or delicate perception; keen; nice; refined; delicate; pleasurable or painful in the highest degree; extreme.—*n.* One excessively nice in his dress; a dandy; a swell; a fop; a coxcomb.—**exquisitely,** eks′kwi•zit•li, *adv.* In an exquisite manner.—**exquisiteness,** eks′kwi•zit•nes, *n.*

exscind, ek•sind′, *v.t.* [L. *excsindo,* to cut out.] To cut out or off.

exsect, ek•sekt′, *v.t.* [L. *exseco,* to cut out.] To cut out or away.

exsert, exserted, ek•sėrt′, ek•ser′ted, *a.* [L. *exsertus,* from *exsero,* to stretch out or forth. EXERT.] Standing out; projected beyond some other part.—**exsertile,** ek•sėr′til, *a.* Capable of being protruded.

exsiccate, ek′sik•āt, *v.t.*—*exsiccated, exsiccating.* [L. *exsicco, exsiccatum,* to dry up—*ex,* intens., and *sicco,* to dry.] To exhaust of moisture; to dry up completely.—**exsiccation,** ek•sik•kā′shon, *n.* The act or operation of exsiccating or drying; dryness.—**exsiccator,** ek•sik′kā•tėr, *n.* An apparatus or contrivance for drying moist substances.

exstipulate, eks•tip′ū•lāt, *a. Bot.* having no stipules.

extant, eks′tant, *a.* [L. *extans, exstans, extantis, exstantis,* ppr. of *exsto,* to stand out—*ex,* out, and *sto,* to stand. STATE.] Still existing; in being; now subsisting; not destroyed or lost.

extemporaneous, extemporary, iks•tem′po•rā″ni•us, iks•tem′po•ra•ri, *a.* [L. *extemporaneus*—*ex,* not, and *tempus, temporis,* time.] Performed, uttered, or made at the time without previous thought or study; unpremeditated; off-hand.—**extemporaneously, extemporarily,** iks•tem′po•rā″ni•us•li, iks•tem′po•ra•ri•li, *adv.* In an extemporaneous manner.—**extemporaneousness,** iks•tem′po•rā″ni•us•nes, *n.* The quality of being extemporaneous.—**extempore,** iks•tem′po•ri, *adv.* [L. phrase *ex tempore,* same meaning.] Without previous thought, study, or meditation; without preparation.—*a.* Extemporary; extemporaneous.—**extemporization,** iks•tem′po•ri•zā″shon, *n.* The act of extemporizing.—**extemporize,** iks•tem′po•rīz, *v.i.*—*extemporized, extemporizing.* To speak without previous thought, study, or preparation; to discourse without notes or written composition.—*v.t.* To make without forethought; to provide for the occasion; to prepare in great haste with the means within one's reach (to *extemporize* a speech or a dinner).—**extemporizer,** iks•tem′po•rī•zėr, *n.* One who extemporizes.

extend, iks•tend′, *v.t.* [L. *extendo,* to stretch out—*ex,* out, and *tendo,* to stretch (as in *contend, pretend, tend*); same root as L. *tenuis,* thin, *tenax,* tenacious, E. *thin.*] To stretch in any direction; to carry forward or continue in length, as a line; to spread in breadth; to expand or dilate in size; to hold out or reach forth; to expand; to enlarge; to widen; to diffuse; to continue; to prolong; to communicate, bestow, or impart.—*v.i.* To stretch; to reach; to be continued in length, or breadth; to become larger or more comprehensive; to value land; to seize land for debt.—**extendedly,** eks•ten′ded•li, *adv.* In an extended manner.—**extendible,** iks•ten′di•bl, *a.* Capable of being extended.—**extensibility,** iks•ten′si•bil″i•ti, *n.* The quality of being extensible.—**extensible, extensile,** iks•ten′si•bl, iks•ten′sīl, *a.* Capable of being extended.—**extension,** iks•ten′shon, *n.* The act of extending; the state of being extended; enlargement; expansion; prolongation; that property of any body by which it occupies a portion of space, being one of the properties of matter; *logic,* the extent of the application of a general term, that is, the objects collectively which are included under it; compass.—**extensive,** iks•ten′siv, *a.* Having great or considerable extent; wide; large; embracing a wide area or a great number of objects; diffusive.—**extensively,** iks•ten′siv•li, *adv.* In an extensive manner.—**extensiveness,** iks•ten′siv•nes, *n.* The state or quality of being extensive.—**extensor,** iks•ten′sėr, *n. Anat.* a muscle which serves to extend or straighten any part of the body, as an arm or a finger: opposed to *flexor.*—**extent,** iks•tent′, *n.* [L.L. *extentus,* a stretching out; L. *extentus,* extended.] Space or degree to which a thing is extended; extension; length; compass; bulk; size; valuation of land; seizure of land for debt.

extensometer, eks•ten•som′e•tėr, *n.* [L. *extensio,* stretching, Gr. *metron,* a measure.] An instrument of precision for measuring small lengths.

extenuate, iks•ten′ū•āt, *v.t.*—*extenuated, extenuating.* [L. *extenuo, extenuatum,* to make thin or small, to lessen—*ex,* and *tenuis,* thin, fine (whence *tenuity*); same root as E. *thin.*] To lessen or diminish; to weaken the import or force of; to palliate; to mitigate.—**extenuation,** iks•ten′ū•ā″shon, *n.* The act of extenuating; palliation; mitigation, as opposed to *aggravation.*—**extenuator,** iks•ten′ū•ā•tėr, *n.* One who extenuates.—**extenuatory,** iks•ten′ū•a•to•ri, *a.* Tending to extenuate.

exterior, iks•tē′ri•ėr, *a.* [L., compar. of *exter* or *exterus,* on the outside, outward, from *ex,* out of; akin *external, extreme, estrange, strange.*] External; outer; outward; bounding or limiting outwardly; situated beyond the limits of; on the outside; not arising or coming from within.—*n.* The outer surface; the outside; the external features.—**exteriorly,** iks•tē′ri•ėr•li, *adv.* In an exterior manner; outwardly; externally.

exterminate, iks•tėr′mi•nāt, *v.t.*—*exterminated, exterminating.* [L. *extermino, exterminatum,* to remove—*ex,* and *termino,* to terminate, from *terminus,* a limit. TERM.] To destroy utterly; to extirpate; to root out; to eradicate.—**extermination,** iks•tėr′mi•nā″shon, *n.* The act of exterminating; destruction; eradication; extirpation.—**exterminator,** iks•tėr′mi•nā•tėr, *n.* One who or that which exterminates.—**exterminatory,** iks•tėr′mi•na•to•ri, *a.* Tending to exterminate; marked by extermination.

external, iks•tėr′nal, *a.* [L. *externus,* from *exter,* on the outside. EXTERIOR.] On the outside: opposite to *internal;* on the exterior; superficial; not being or arising within; outside of ourselves; relating to or connected with foreign nations; foreign.—*External-combustion engine,* an engine that derives its energy from the combustion of fuel outside the cylinder.—*n.* Something exterior; an outward rite or ceremony.—**externality,** iks•tėr•nal′i•ti, *n.* The state of being external; separation from the perceiving mind; exteriority.—**externalize,** iks•tėr′nal•īz, *v.t.* To embody in an outward form; to give shape and form to.—**externally,** iks•tėr′nal•li, *adv.* Outwardly; on the outside; apparently; exteriorly.

exterritorial, eks•ter′i•tō″ri•al, *a.* [Prefix *ex,* and *territorial.*] Beyond the jurisdiction of the laws of the country in which one resides.—**exterritoriality,** eks•ter′i•tō′ri•al″i•ti, *n.* Immunity from a country's laws, such as that enjoyed by an ambassador.

extinct, iks•tingkt′, *a.* [L. *extinctus,* pp. of *extinguo, exstinguo.* EXTINGUISH.] Extinguished; quenched; having ceased; being at an end; no longer in existence; having died out (a family or race is *extinct*).—**extinction,** iks•tingk′shon, *n.* The act of putting out or quenching flame or fire; the state of being extinguished; a putting an end to, or a coming to an end.

extinguish, iks•ting′gwish, *v.t.* [L. *extinguo, exstinguo—ex,* and *stinguo,* to scratch out, as in *distinguish.*] To put out; to quench; to stifle; to put an end to; to suppress; to destroy; to crush; to eclipse.—**extinguishable,** iks•ting′gwish•a•bl, *a.* Capable of being quenched, destroyed, or suppressed.—**extinguisher,** iks•ting′gwish•ėr, *n.* One who or that which extinguishes; a hollow conical utensil to put on a candle or lamp to extinguish it.—**extinguishment,**† iks•ting′gwish•ment, *n.* The act of extinguishing; extinction.

extirpate, eks′tėr•pāt, *v.t.*—*extirpated, extirpating.* [L. *extirpo, exstirpo, exstirpatum—ex,* out, and *stirps,* the trunk of a tree.] To pull or pluck up by the roots; to root out; to eradicate; to destroy totally; to exterminate.—**extirpation,** eks•tėr•pā′shon, *n.* The act of rooting out; eradication; total destruction.—**extirpator,** eks•tėr′pā•tėr, *n.* One who or that which extirpates.

extol, iks•tōl′, *v.t.*—*extolled, extolling.* [L. *extollo,* to raise up—*ex,* out, up, and *tollo,* to raise; from same root as in *tolero,* to endure, to tolerate.] To speak in laudatory terms of; to praise; to laud; to applaud; to eulogize; to magnify; to celebrate; to glorify.—**extoller,** iks•tōl′ėr, *n.* One who extols; a praiser or magnifier.

extort, iks•tort′, *v.t.* [L. *extorqueo, extortum—ex,* and *torqueo,* to twist, seen in *contort, distort, retort, torture,* etc.] To obtain from a person by force or compulsion; to wrest or wring by physical force, by menace, torture, or authority (to *extort* contributions, a confession, a promise, etc.).—**extorter,** iks•tor′tėr, *n.* One who extorts.—**extortion,** iks•tor′shon, *n.* The act of extorting; the act or practice of extorting or wringing money from people by any undue exercise of power; illegal compulsion to pay money; rapacity; that which is extorted.—**extortionary,** iks•tor′shon•e•ri, *a.* Practicing extortion; containing extortion.—**extortionate,** iks•tor′shon•at, *a.* Characterized by extortion; oppressive in exacting money.—**extortioner, extortionist,** iks•tor′shon•ėr, iks•tor′shon•ist, *n.*

extra, eks′tra, *a.* and *adv.* [Contr. from *extraordinary,* or directly from L. *extra,* beyond.] Beyond what is due, appointed, or expected; supplementary; additional.—*n.* Something in addition to what is due, expected, or usual; a special edition of a newspaper; one who plays small parts in a movie or stage show.

extract, iks•trakt′, *v.t.* [L. *extractus,* from *extraho—ex,* and *traho,* to draw; seen also in *contract, detract, retract, trace, tract,* etc.] To draw out; to take out; to pull out or remove from a fixed position; to draw out by distillation or other chemical process; to select as a specimen or sample; to take (a passage or passages) from a book or writing; to ascertain the root of a number.—*n.* (eks′trakt). That which is extracted or drawn from something; a passage taken from a book or writing; an excerpt; a quotation; anything drawn from a substance by heat, distillation, or a chemical process, as an essence, a tincture, and the like.—**extractable, extractible,** iks•trak′ta•bl, iks•trak′ti•bl, *a.* Capable of being extracted.—**extraction,** iks•trak′shon, *n.* [L. *extractio.*] The act of extracting or drawing out; descent; lineage; derivation of persons from a stock or family; the stock or family from which one has descended; operation of finding the root of a given number or quantity.—**extractive,** iks•trak′tiv, *a.* Capable of being extracted; extracting.—*n.* That which is extracted or extractable.—**extractor,** iks•trak′tėr, *n.*

extracurricular, eks′tra•kėr•ik″ū•lėr, *a.* [Prefix *extra,* and *curriculum.*] Being outside one's routine activities; not being in the regular school curriculum, such as athletics, clubs, etc.

extradition, eks•tra•dish′on, *n.* [L. *ex,* and *traditio,* a giving up, surrender, from *trado, traditum,* to give up.] Delivery of a criminal or fugitive from one state or nation, usually under a treaty or statute, to another having jurisdiction to try the charge.—**extradite,** eks′tra•dīt, *v.t.* To deliver or give up for extradition.

extragalactic, eks′tra•gal•âk″tik, *a.* [Prefix *extra,* and *galaxy.*] Lying outside or beyond a galaxy, especially the Milky Way.

extrajudicial, eks′tra•jū•dish″al, *a.* Out of the proper court, or the ordinary course of legal procedure.—

extrajudicially, eks′tra•jū•dish″al•li, *adv.* In an extrajudicial manner; out of court.

extramundane, eks•tra•mun′dān, *a.* Beyond the limit of the material world or mundane affairs.

extramural, eks•tra•mū′ral, *a.* [L. *extra,* beyond, and *murus,* a wall.] Without or beyond the walls, as of a fortified city or a university.

extraneous, eks•trā′ni•us, *a.* [L. *extraneus,* from *extra,* without, beyond; akin *strange.*] Foreign; not belonging to a thing; existing without; not intrinsic.—**extraneously,** eks•trā′ni•us•li, *adv.* In an extraneous manner.

extraofficial, eks′tra•of•fish″al, *a.* Not within the limits of official duty.

extraordinary, eks•tra•or′di•ne•ri, *a.* [L. *extraordinarius—extra,* and *ordo, ordinis,* order.] Beyond or out of the ordinary or common order or method; remarkable; uncommon; rare; wonderful; special; particular; sent for a special purpose or on a particular occasion (an ambassador *extraordinary*).—**extraordinarily,** eks•tra•or′di•ne•ri•li, *adv.*

extraphysical, eks•tra•fiz′i•kal, *a.* Not subject to physical laws or methods.

extrapolate, eks•trap′o•lāt, *v.t.* [L. *expolire,* to polish or refine—*extra,* beyond, and *polio,* polish. INTERPOLATE.] To project into an unknown field for the sake of knowledge by drawing parallelisms with a field that is known, under the assumption that they correspond.—**extrapolation,** eks•trap′o•lā″shon, *n.*

extraprofessional, eks′tra•pro•fesh″on•al, *a.* Not within the ordinary limits of professional duty or business.

extrasensory, eks′tra•sen″so•ri, *a.* [Prefix *extra,* and *sensory.*] Being beyond the ordinary sense perceptions; clairvoyant.

extraterritorial, eks′tra•ter′i•to″ri•al, *a.* [Prefix *extra,* and *territorial.*] Beyond the territorial limits of jurisdiction.—**extraterritoriality,** eks′tra•ter′i•to′ri•al″i•ti, *n.* Immunity from a country's laws.

extravagance, extravagancy, iks•trav′a•gans, iks•trav′a•gan•si, *n.* [Fr. *extravagance*—L. *extra,* beyond, and *vagans,* ppr. of *vago, vagor,* to wander. VAGABOND.] Want of restraint; wildness; irregularity; unreasonableness; prodigality; lavish spending or waste; excess; profusion; bombast.—**extravagant,** iks•trav′a•gant, *a.* Exceeding due bounds; unreasonable; excessive; not within ordinary limits of truth or probability or other usual bounds; unrestrained; profuse in expenses.—**extravagantly,** iks•trav′a•gant•li, *adv.*—**extravaganza,** iks•trav′a•gan″za, *n.* A literary or musical composition noted for its wildness and incoherence; a burlesque.

extravasate, iks•trav′a•sāt, *v.t.—extravasated, extravasating.* [L. *extra,* beyond, and *vas,* a vessel.] To force or let out of the proper vessels, as out of the blood vessels.—**extravasation,** iks•trav′a•sā″shon, *n.* The act of extravasating; the state of being forced or let out of the vessels or ducts of the body that contain it; effusion.—**extravascular,** eks•tra•vas′kūlėr, *a.* Being out of the proper vessels.

extreme, iks•trēm′, *a.* [Fr. *extrême,* from L. *extremus,* superl. of *exter* or *exterus,* on the outside, external. EXTERIOR.] Outermost; furthest; at the utmost point, edge, or border; worst or best that can exist or be supposed; carrying principles to the uttermost; ultra.—*n.* The utmost point of a thing; extremity; utmost limit or degree that can be supposed or tolerated; height or extravagant pitch; *math.* the first or the last term of a proportion.—**extremely,** iks•trēm′li, *adv.*—**extremism,** iks•trēm′izm, *n.* The quality or state of being extreme.—**extremist,** iks•trēm′ist, *n.* A supporter of extreme doctrines or practice.—**extremity,** iks•trem′i•ti, *n.* [L. *extremitas.*] The utmost point or side; the verge; the highest degree; the most aggravated or intense form; extreme or utmost distress, straits, or difficulties; a limb or organ of locomotion.

extricate, eks′tri•kāt, *v.t.—extricated, extricating.* [L. *extrico, extricatum—ex,* and *tricæ,* trifles, perplexity. See INTRICATE.] To free, as from difficulties or perplexities; to disembarrass; to disengage; to disentangle; to clear; to relieve.—**extricable,** eks′tri•ka•bl, *a.* Capable of being extricated.—**extrication,** eks•tri•kā′shon, *n.* The act of extricating, disentangling, or setting free.

extrinsic, extrinsical, eks•trin′sik, eks•trin′si•kal, *a.* [L. *extrinsecus,* from without—*exter,* outward (as in *exterior*), and *secus,* by, along with.] External; outward; coming from without; not intrinsic; not contained in or belonging to a body.—**extrinsically,** eks•trin′si•kal•li, *adv.* In an extrinsic manner; from without.

extrorsal, extrorse, eks•tror′sal, eks•trors′, *a.* [Fr. *extrorse,* from L. *extra,* on the outside, and *verto, versum,* to turn.] *Bot.* turned or directed outward, or turned away from the axis: opposed to *introrse.*—**extroversion,** eks•trō•vėr′shon, *n. Path.* a malformation consisting in an organ being turned inside out, as the bladder.

extrovert, ek′strō•vėrt, *n.* [L. *extro,* extra, and *vertere,* to turn.] One whose attentions are turned toward that which is outside the self.—**extroversion,** ek′strō•vėr″zhun, *n.*

extrude, eks•tröd′, *v.t.—extruded, extruding.* [L. *extrudo—ex,* and *trudo,* to thrust, as in *intrude.*] To thrust out; to urge, force, or press out; to expel; to drive away; to displace.—**extrusion,** eks•trö′zhon, *n.* The act of extruding; expulsion.

exuberance, exuberancy, igz•ū′bėr•ans, igz•ū′bėr•an•si, *n.* [Fr. *exubérance,* from L. *exuberantia—ex,* intens., and *ubero,* to be fruitful, from *uber,* rich, fruitful.] The state of being exuberant; superfluous abundance; an overflowing quantity; richness; excess; redundance; copiousness.—**exuberant,** igz•ū′bėr•ant, *a.* [L. *exuberans, exuberantis,* ppr. of *exubero.*] Characterized by abundance, richness, or luxuriance; plenteous; rich; overflowing; overabundant; superfluous.—**exuberantly,** igz•ū′bėr•ant•li, *adv.* In an exuberant manner.

exude, eks•ūd′, *v.t.—exuded, exuding.* [L. *exsudo,* to discharge by sweating—*ex,* and *sudo,* to sweat, from same root as E. *sweat.*] To discharge through the pores, as moisture or other liquid matter; to give out, like sweat or juice; to let ooze out.—*v.i.* To flow from a body through the pores; to ooze out like sweat.—**exudate,** eks′ū•dāt, *n.* [L. *exudare,* to sweat.] Material passing through the wall of a blood vessel into surrounding parts.—**exudation,** eks•ū′dā′shon, *n.* The act of exuding; that which is exuded.

exult, ig•zult′, *v.i.* [L. *exulto, exsulto,* to leap or jump about—*ex,* and *salio, saltum,* to leap, seen also in *insult, result, salient,* etc.] To rejoice in triumph; to rejoice exceedingly; to be glad above measure; to triumph.—**exultant,** ig•zul′tant, *a.* Rejoicing triumphantly.—**exultation,** eg•zul•tā′shon, *n.* The act of exulting; great gladness; rapturous delight; triumph.—**exultingly,** eg•zul′ting•li, *adv.* In an exulting manner.

exurb, ek′sėrb, *n.* [L. *ex,* outside, and *urb,* city.] A residential region located beyond the city and suburbs and usually inhabited by wealthy people.—**exurbanite,** ek•sėrb′an•īt, *n.*

exuviae, ig•zū′vi•ē, *n. pl.* [L., from *exuo,* to put off, to strip.] Cast skins, shells, or coverings of animals; any parts of animals which are shed or cast off, as the skins of serpents, etc.—**exuvial,** ig•zū′vi•al, *a.* Relating to or containing exuviae.—**exuviation,** ig•zū′vi•ā″shon, *n.* The rejection or casting off of exuviae.

eyas, ī′as, *n.* [Fr. *niais,* lit. a nestling falcon, from L.L. *nidax, nidacis,* still in the nest, L. *nidus,* a nest; with loss of *n* as in *adder.*] A young hawk just taken from the nest, not able to prey for itself. (*Shak.*)—*Eyas-musket,* a young sparrow hawk.

eye, ī, *n.* [O.E. *ye, eighe,* A.Sax. *eáge,* Dan. *öie,* D. *oog,* Icel. *auga,* G. *auge,* Goth. *augo*; cog. L. *oculus,* Skr. *akshi*—eye; from a root meaning sharp. ACID.] The nearly spherical hollow organ of sight filled with a vitreous fluid and located in a bony orbit in the anterior skull, consisting in man and the higher animals of the cornea, iris, pupil, lens, and retina that aid in transmitting, through the optic nerve, images to the brain; the faculty of seeing with the eye; delicate and accurate perception; anything resembling or suggesting an eye; the hole or aperture in a needle; the center of something; thus, the *eye* of a dome is the circular aperture at its apex.—*The wind's eye,* the direction right opposite to that of the wind.—*v.t.—eyed, eying or eyeing.* To fix the eye on; to look on; to observe narrowly, or with fixed attention.—**eyed,** īd, *a.* Furnished with eyes; having eyes of this or that character.—**eyeless,** ī′les, *a.* Without eyes.—**eyeball,** ī′bal, *n.* The ball, globe, or apple of the eye.—**eyebright,** ī′brīt, *n.* A pretty little annual European herb common in meadows, heaths, etc., which formerly enjoyed a great reputation in diseases of the eyes.—**eyebrow,** ī′brou, *n.* The brow or hairy arch above the eye.—**eyeglass,** *n.* A glass to assist the sight; the lens of a telescope, microscope, etc., to which the eye is applied.—**eyelash,** ī′lash, *n.* One of the hairs that edge the eyelid.—**eyelet,** ī′let, *n.* A small hole or perforation to receive a lace or small rope or cord, or for other purposes.—**eyelid,** ī′lid, *n.* That portion of movable skin that serves as a cover for the eyeball.—**eye opener,** *n.* Startling news; a drink of liquor, particularly the first of the day (*Slang*). **eyepiece,** *n.* In an optical instrument the lens or combination of lenses to which the eye is applied.—**eyeservant,** *n.* A servant who attends to his duty only when watched.—**eyeservice,** *n.* Service performed only under inspection or the eye of an employer.—**eyesight,** ī′sīt, *n.* The sight of the eye; view; observation; the sense of seeing.—**eyesore,** ī′sōr, *n.* Something offensive to the eye or sight.—**eyetooth,** ī′töth, *n.* A tooth under the eye; a fang; a canine tooth.—**eyewash,** *n.* A lotion to cleanse or treat the eye.—**eyewitness,** *n.* One who sees a thing done; one who has ocular view of anything.

eyre, âr, *n.* [O.Fr. *erre*, *eirre*, a journey, from L. *iter*, *itineris*, a journey.] A journey or circuit of a court; a court of itinerant justices.—*Justices in eyre*, itinerant justices who formerly traveled to hold courts in the different English counties.

eyrie, eyry, â′ri, *n.* Same as *Aerie*.

F

F, f, ef, the sixth letter of the English alphabet, a consonant, formed by the passage of breath between the lower lip and the upper front teeth; *mus.* the fourth note of the diatonic scale.

fa, fä, *n. Mus.* the Italian name of the fourth note of the diatonic scale.

fabaceous, fa•bā′shus, *a.* [L. *faba*, a bean.] Having the nature of the bean; like the bean.

Fabian, fā′bi•an, *a.* Like the generalship of *Fabius* Maximus, who harassed the troops of Hannibal but took care to avoid a battle (*Fabian* strategy).

fable, fā′bl, *n.* [Fr. *fable*, L. *fabula*, from *fari*, to speak; akin *fate*.] A fictitious narration intended to enforce some useful truth or precept; a fabricated story; a fiction; the plot or connected series of events in an epic or dramatic poem; subject of talk (*Tenn.*).—*v.i.*—*fabled*, *fabling*, To tell fables or falsehoods. —*v.t.* To invent or fabricate; to speak of as true or real.—**fabled,** fā′bld, *p.* and *a.* Celebrated in fables; fabulously imagined.—**fabler,** fā′blėr, *n.* One who fables; a writer of fables.—**fabliau,** fab′li•ō, *n.* pl. **fabliaux,** fab′li•ō. [Fr.] A kind of metrical tale common in French literature of the twelfth and thirteenth centuries.—**fabulist,** fab′ū•list, *n.* The inventor or writer of fables.—**fabulous,** fab′ū•lus, *a.* Having the nature of a fable; fictitious; invented; not real; mythical; hardly to be received as truth; incredible.—**fabulously,** fab′ū•lus•li, *adv.* In a fabulous manner.—**fabulousness,** fab′ū•lus•nes, *n.* The quality of being fabulous.

fabric, fab′rik, *n.* [Fr. *fabrique*, L. *fabrica*, from *faber*, a worker; same root as *facio*, to make. *Forge* is really the same word.] A structure; a building, edifice, or construction; the frame of a building; cloth manufactured; the structure of anything; the manner in which the parts are put together; texture.—**fabricant,** fab′ri•kant, *n.* [Fr.] A manufacturer.—**fabricate,** fab′ri•kāt, *v.t.*—*fabricated*, *fabricating*. [L. *fabrico*, *fabricatum*.] To frame, build, make, or construct; to form into a whole by connecting the parts; to form by art and labor; to invent and form; to forge; to devise falsely.—**fabrication,** fab•ri•kā′shon, *n.* The act of fabricating; construction; making; the act of devising falsely; forgery; that which is fabricated; a falsehood. —**fabricator,** fab′ri•kā•tėr, *n.* One who fabricates.

façade, fa•säd′ or fa•sād′, *n.* [Fr., from It, *faciata*, a façade, from *faccia*, L. *facies*, the face.] The face or front view or elevation of an edifice; exterior front or face.

face, fās, *n.* [Fr., from L. *facies*, face, figure, form, from *facio*, to make.] The front part of an animal's head, particularly of the human head, made up of the forehead, eyes, nose, mouth, cheeks, etc.; the visage; aspect or air of the face; cast of features; look; countenance; expression of the face; the surface of a thing, or the side which presents itself to the view of the spectator; the front; the forepart; a plane surface of a solid; one of the sides bounding a solid, appearance; aspect; effrontery; boldness; assurance; the dial of a clock, watch, compass card, or other indicator; the sole of a plane; operating edge or surface in certain implements.—*To make a face*, to distort the countenance; to make a grimace.—*To fly in the face of*, to act in direct opposition to or disregard of; to defy.—*Face to face*, both parties being present and confronting each other.—*v.t.*—*faced*, *facing*. To turn the face or front full toward; to meet in front; to stand up against in hostile encounter; to confront; to stand with the face or front toward; to finish or protect with a thin external covering over the front of; to smooth or dress the face of (a stone, etc.).—*To face down*, to oppose boldly or impudently.—*To face out*, to persist in, especially to persist in an assertion which is not true; to brave (an accusation) with effrontery.—*To face tea*, to adulterate it by mixing it with coloring matter and other substances.—*v.i.* To turn the face (to *face* to the right or left).—**faced,** fāst, *a.* Having a face; marked with a face (as a court card).—**facial,** fā′shel, *a.* Of or pertaining to the face.—*Facial angle*, an angle formed by lines drawn from nose to ear, and from nose to forehead; an angle formed by lines drawn to show to what extent the jaws are protruding and the forehead receding.—**facing,** fās′ing, *n.* A covering in front for ornament, protection, defense, or other purposes; a mode of adulterating tea by mixing with coloring matter and other substances; the movement of soldiers in turning round to the left, right, etc.; *pl.* the distinctive trimmings on a regimental coat or jacket.—*Put through his facings*, to be cross questioned; to be examined.

facet, fas′et, *n.* [Fr. *facette*, dim. of *face*.] A small flat portion of a surface; one of the small smooth surfaces on a gem or crystal,—*v.t.* To cut a facet or facets on.—**faceted,** fas′et•ed, *a.* Having facets; formed into facets.

facetiae, fa•sē′shi•ē, *n. pl.* [L., from *facetus*, merry, elegant, from root of *facio*, to make.] Witty or humorous sayings; jests; witticisms.—**facetious,** fa•sē′shus, *a.* Merry; jocular; witty; full of pleasantry; playful; exciting laughter.—**facetiously,** fa•sē′shus•li, *adv.* In a facetious manner.—**facetiousness,** fa•sē′shus•nes, *n.* The quality of being facetious; pleasantry.

facial. See FACE.

facile, fas′il, *a.* [L. *facilis*, easy to be done or made, from *facio*, to make.] Easy to be done or performed; not difficult; easy to be dealt with; easy of access or converse; not haughty or distant; easily persuaded to good or bad; yielding; ductile to a fault; ready; dexterous (an artist's *facile* pencil).—**facileness,**† fas′il•nes, *n.* The state of being facile.—**facilitate,** fa•sil′i•tāt, *v.t.*—*facilitated*, *facilitating*. [Fr. *faciliter*, from L. *facilitas*, easiness.] To make easy or less difficult; to lessen the labor of.—**facilitation,** fa•sil′i•tā″shon, *n.* The act of facilitating.—**facility,** fa•sil′i•ti, *n.* [Fr. *facilité*, L. *facilitas*.] Easiness to be performed; freedom from difficulty; ease; ease in performance; readiness proceeding from skill or use; dexterity; pliancy or ductility in character; easiness to be persuaded, usually implying a disposition to yield to solicitations to evil; the means by which the accomplishment of anything is rendered more easy: in this sense usually in the *pl.*

facsimile, fak•sim′i•li, *n.* [L. *facio*, to make, and *similis*, like.] An exact copy or likeness; an imitation of an original in all its proportions, traits, and peculiarities.

fact, fakt, *n.* [L. *factum*, a thing done,

a deed, a fact, from *facio*, to do or make, a stem which appears in many words, as *affect*, *affair*, *counterfeit*, *defeat*, *difficult*, *faculty*, *profits*, etc.] Anything done or that comes to pass; something known to exist; a statement based upon objective reality.—**factual,** fak′chū•al, *a.*

faction, fak′shon, *n.* [L. *factio*, from *facio*, *factum*, to do. FACT.] A party combined or acting in union, in opposition to another party or a government; a party unscrupulously promoting their private ends at the expense of the public good; discord; dissension.—**factious,** fak′shus, *a.* Given to faction; prone to clamor against public measures or men; pertaining to faction; proceeding from faction.—**factiously,** fak′shus•li, *adv.* In a factious, turbulent, or disorderly manner.—**factiousness,** fak′shus•nes, *n.* The state or character of being factious; disposition to clamor and raise opposition; clamorousness for a party.

factitious, fak•tish′us, *a.* [L. *factitius*, made by art, from *facio*, to make. FACT.] Made by art, in distinction from what is produced by nature; artificial; conventional.—**factitiously,** fak•tish′us•li, *adv.* In a factitious manner.—**factitiousness,** fak•tish′us•nes, *n.*

factitive, fak′ti•tiv, *a.* [From L. *facio*, *factum*, to make. FACT.] Causative; tending to make or cause; *gram.* expressing the result of an action that produces a new condition in the object (in 'he struck him dead', *struck* is factitive).

factor, fak′tėr, *n.* [L., a maker, doer, from *facio*, *factum*, to do. FACT.] An agent employed by merchants residing in other places to buy and sell or transact other business on their account; in Scotland, a person appointed by a landholder or house proprietor to manage an estate, collect rents, etc.; *arith.* the multiplier or multiplicand, from the multiplication of which proceeds the product; *alg.* any expression considered as part of a product; hence, generally, one of several elements or influences which tend to the production of a result.—*Factor of safety*, the ratio of the breaking load to the working load in any structure.—**factorage,** fak′tėr•ij, *n.* The allowance to a factor for his services; commission.—**factorial,** fak•tō′ri•al, *a.* Of or pertaining to a factor or factors.—**factory,** fak′te•ri, *n.* A name given to establishments of merchants and factors resident in foreign countries; (contr. from *manufactory*) a building or collection of buildings appropriated to the manufacture of goods; a manufactory.

factotum, fak•tō′tum, *n.* [L. *facio*, to do, and *totum*, the whole.] A confidential agent that manages all kinds of matters for his employer.

faculae, fak′ū•lē, *n. pl.* [L. *facula*, a little torch, dim. of *fax*, a torch.] *Astron.* spots sometimes seen on the sun's disk, which appear brighter than the rest of its surface.

facultative, fak′ul•tā″tiv, *a.* [L. *facultas*, capability.] Of bacteria and parasites, able to adapt themselves to certain conditions of life.

faculty, fak′ul•ti, *n.* [Fr. *faculté*, L. *facultas*, from *facio*, to do, to make. FACT.] Any mental or bodily power; capacity for any action or function; skill derived from practice, or practice aided by nature; special power or endowment; a right or power granted to a person by favor or indulgence, to do what by law he may not do; the body of individuals constituting one of the learned professions, and more specifically the medical profession; the teachers and professors of the several departments of a university, or one of the departments themselves, a *Faculty* of Arts, Law, Medicine; the teaching staff of any institution of learning.

fad, fad, *n.* A passing whim, hobby, style or fancy, pursued for a time with undue zeal.—**faddist,** fad′ist, *n.* One who is enthusiastic over a fad.—**faddish,** fad′ish, *a.* Pertaining or given to fads, faddy.

fade, fād, *v.i.*—*faded*, *fading*. [O.E. *vade*, to fade; comp. Fr. *fade*, insipid, from L. *vapidus*, vapid.] To wither; to lose strength, health, or vigor gradually; to decay; to lose freshness, color, or brightness; to tend from a stronger or brighter color to a more faint shade of the same color, or to lose color entirely; to grow dim or indistinct to view.—*v.t.* To cause to wither; to deprive of freshness or vigor.—**fadeless,** fād′les, *a.* Unfading.

fadge, faj, *v.i.* [A.Sax. *fægian*, to fit, akin to *faeger*, fair; comp. G. *fügen*, D. *voegen*, Sw. *foga*, to fit.] To suit; to fit; to be found suitable or successful.

faecal, fē′kal, *a.* See FECES.

fag, fag, *v.i.*—*fagged*, *fagging*. [Probably from verb to *flag*, by omission of *l*.] To become weary; to fail in strength; to be faint with weariness; to labor hard or assiduously; to work till wearied; to act as a fag.—*v.t.* To use or treat as a fag or drudge; to exhaust.—*n.* A laborious drudge; in certain English schools, a boy who performs menial services for another boy who is in the highest or next highest form or class; a cigarette.—**fag end,** *n.* [The end which *flags* or hangs loose.] The end of a web of cloth; the latter or meaner part of anything.

fagaceous, fa•gā′shus, *a.* Pertaining to the beech family of shrubs and trees.

fagot, faggot, fag′ot, *n.* [Fr. *fagot*, It. *fagotto*, a faggot, from L. *fax*, *facis*, a faggot, a torch.] A bundle of sticks or small branches used for fuel, or for filling ditches, and other purposes in fortification; a fascine; a bundle of pieces of iron or steel in bars; a person formerly hired to take the place of another at the muster of a military company or to hide deficiency in its number; a term of contempt for a dry, shriveled old woman.—*v.t.* To bind in a fagot or bundle; to collect promiscuously.

Fahrenheit, fa′ren•hīt, *a.* [After *Fahrenheit*, who first employed quicksilver in thermometers about 1720.] The name distinguishing that kind of thermometer in which the space between the freezing and the boiling points of water is divided into 180 degrees; the freezing point being marked 32°, and the boiling 212°.

faïence, fā•äns′ or fä•yäns′, *n.* [Fr.] A sort of fine pottery or earthenware glazed with a fine varnish, and painted in various designs, named from *Faenza* in Italy.

fail, fāl, *v.i.* [Fr. *faillir*, to fail, from L. *fallere*, to deceive, whence also *false*, *fallible*, *fault*, *falter*.] To become deficient; to be insufficient; to cease to be abundant for supply; to come short; not to have the due measure or degree; to decay, decline, sink, or be diminished; to become weaker; to become extinct; to be entirely wanting; to be no longer produced, furnished, or supplied; not to produce the effect; to miscarry; to be unsuccessful; to be guilty of omission or neglect; to become insolvent or bankrupt.—*v.t.* To cease or to neglect or omit to afford aid or strength to; to be wanting to; to disappoint; to desert; not to be at hand when required.—*n.* Miscarriage; failure; deficiency; want.—*Without fail*, without omission to perform something; without doubt; certainly.—**failing,** fāl′ing, *n.* Imperfection; a weakness in character or disposition; foible; fault.—*Failing whom. Failing* used either as preposition or *abl. absol.* 'who failing'.—**failingly,** fāl′ing•li, *adv.* By failing.—**failure,** fāl′yėr, *n.* A failing; deficiency; cessation of supply or total defect; omission; nonperformance; decay, or defect from decay; the act of failing or state of having failed to attain an object; want of success; a becoming insolvent or bankrupt.

faille, fāl or fī′y′, *n.* [Fr.] A heavy silk fabric of superior quality.

fain, fān, *a.* [A.Sax. *fægen*, joyful, *fægnian*, to rejoice; Goth. *faginon*, Icel. *fagna*, to be glad. *Fawn* (verb) is of same origin, and *fair* (adj.) is akin.] Glad or pleased under some kind of necessity; inclined; content to accept of or do something for want of better.—*adv.* Gladly; with joy or pleasure: with *would*.

fainéant, fā′ni•ent, *n.* [Fr. *faire*, do, *néant*, nothing.] An idler, a do-nothing, a puppet or phantom king in the Merovingian dynasty of the Franks.

faint, fānt, *v.i.* [O.Fr. *faint*, sluggish, negligent, pp. of *feindre*, L. *fingere*, to feign, whence also *feign*, *fiction*, etc.] To become feeble; to decline or fail in strength and vigor; to become temporarily unconscious, powerless, and motionless; to swoon; to sink into dejection; to lose courage or spirit; to become gradually weak or indistinct; to decay; to fade, disappear, or vanish.—*a.*

Weak; languid; feeble; exhausted; inclined to swoon; hardly perceptible by, or feebly striking, the senses; indistinct; wanting in brightness or vividness, loudness, sharpness, or force; not well defined; feeble; slight; imperfect; not carried on with vigor or energy; dejected; depressed; dispirited.—*n.* A fainting fit; a swoon; *pl.* the impure spirit which comes over first and last in the distillation of whisky.—**faint-hearted,** *a.* Cowardly; timorous; having lost courage; yielding to fear.—**faintheartedly,** *adv.* In a faint-hearted manner.—**faintheartedness,** *n.* Want of courage.—**faintish,** fānʹtish, *a.* Slightly faint.—**faintishness,** fānʹtish•nes, *n.* A slight degree of faintness.—**faintly,** fāntʹli, *adv.* In a faint, weak, feeble, or languid manner; without vigor or activity; without vividness or distinctness.—**faintness,** fāntʹnes, *n.* The state of being faint.

fair, fâr, *a.* [A.Sax. *fæger*, fair, pleasant, beautiful; Icel. *fagr*, Dan. *feir*, Sw. *fager*, Goth. *fagrs*, bright. FAIN.] Pleasing to the eye; beautiful; handsome; white or light colored in respect of skin or complexion; not dark or swarthy; not stormy or wet; not cloudy or overcast; clear (*fair* weather); free from obstruction, obstacle, or anything to impede (on the *fair* way to success); open, frank, or honest; not resorting to anything tricky or underhand; just; equitable; free from unfair or unfavorable circumstances or influences; civil, pleasing, or courteous (*fair* words); free from deletions, blots, and the like; perfectly or easily legible (a *fair* copy); free from stain or blemish; unspotted; untarnished (one's *fair* name); passably or moderately good; better than indifferent. —*Fair way*, the track or course that is clear of obstacles and is therefore taken by vessels in navigating a narrow bay, river, or harbor.—*adv.* Openly; frankly; civilly; complaisantly (especially in 'to speak a person *fair*'); on good terms (to keep *fair* with the world).—*To bid fair*, to promise well; to be in a fair way; to be likely.—*n.* Elliptically, a fair woman; a handsome female. (*Poet.*)—*The fair*, the female sex; specifically, the loveliest of that sex.—*v.t.* To make fair or beautiful.—**fairish,** fârʹish, *a.* Reasonably fair.—**fairly,** fârʹli, *adv.* In a fair manner; beautifully; handsomely; honestly; justly; equitably; tolerably.—**fairness,** fârʹnes, *n.* The quality or character of being fair; lightness of complexion, beauty; honesty; justice.—**fair-spoken,** *a.* Using fair speech; bland; civil, courteous, plausible.

fair, fâr, *n.* [Fr. *foire*, a fair, market; It. *feria*; L. *feriæ*, holidays, festivals.] A stated market in a particular town or city; a stated meeting of buyers and sellers for trade.—**fairing,** fârʹing, *n.* A present given at a fair.

fairy, fâʹri, *n.* [O.Fr. *faerie*, Fr. *féerie*, the power of a fairy, enchantment; from O.Fr. *fae*, Fr. *fée*, It. *fata*, a fairy, lit. a fate, from L. *fatum*, fate. FATE.] An imaginary being or spirit having a human form, though of a stature much below human and with sundry superhuman attributes; an elf or fay; any personage with superhuman power‡; fairyland‡.—*a.* Pertaining to or in some manner connected with fairies; coming from fairies; resembling a fairy.—*Fairy ring*, a ring (from a fungus) formed by the grass in certain places growing noticeably greener than that around, popularly supposed to be caused by fairies in their dances.—**fairyland,** *n.* The imaginary land or abode of fairies.—**fairy tale,** *n.* A tale relating to fairies.

faith, fāth, *n.* [O.E. *feid*, *feith*, O.Fr. *feid*, from L. *fides*, faith; akin *fidelity*, *confide*, *defy*, *infidel*, etc.] The assent of the mind to the truth of what is declared by another; firm and earnest belief on probable evidence of any kind; belief; belief in what is given forth as a revelation of man's relation to God and the infinite; a settled conviction in regard to religion; a system of religious belief; that which is believed on any subject, whether in science, politics, or religion; a doctrine or system of doctrines believed; faithfulness; fidelity; word or honor pledged; promise given.—*In good faith*, in real honesty; with perfect sincerity.—**faithful,** fāthʹfu̦l, *a.* Firm in faith; firmly adhering to religious or other duty; of true fidelity; loyal; true and constant to a person to whom one is bound; true to one's word; in conformity to the letter and spirit; conformable to truth; conformable to a prototype; true or exact; worthy of belief.—*The faithful*, those who adhere to the true faith, as contrasted with the adherents of another faith.—**faithfully,** fāthʹfu̦l•li, *adv.* In a faithful manner; sincerely; with strong assurance; earnestly; conformably to truth or fact; conformably to an example or prototype.—**faithfulness,** fāthʹfu̦l•nes, *n.* The quality or character of being faithful; fidelity; truth; loyalty; constancy.—**faithless,** fāthʹles, *a.* Without faith; not adhering to allegiance, vows, or duty; disloyal; not observant of promises.—**faithlessly,** fāthʹles•li, *adv.* In a faithless manner.—**faithlessness,** fāthʹles•nes, *n.* State of being faithless.

fake, fāk, *n.* [A.Sax. *faec*, a space or interval.] One of the circles or windings of a rope as it lies in a coil.

fake, fāk. *v. t.* [E. dial., to patch, alter.] To impart a false character to; to deceive. *n.* A counterfeit or imitation offered as genuine; a fraud.

fakir, fä•kẽrʹ, *n.* [Ar., lit. a poor man.] An oriental ascetic or begging monk.

falcate, falʹkāt, *a.* [L. *falcatus*, from *falx*, *falcis*, a sickle.] Hooked; in shape like a sickle or scythe.—**falciform,** falʹsi•form, *a.* In the shape of a sickle or reaping hook.

falchion, fa̦lʹshon, *n.* [L. *falx*, *falcis*, a sickle.] A broad short sword with a slightly curved point.

falcon, fa̦lʹkn, *n.* [O.Fr. *falcon*, Fr. *faucon*, L.L. *falco*, probably from L. *falx*, a reaping hook, from the curved claws and beak.] The common name of various raptorial birds inferior in size to the eagles and vultures, and remarkable for their elegant form and powers of flight; especially, one trained to hunt wild fowl or other game; a hawk. [The term falcon is by sportsmen restricted to the female, the male, which is smaller and less courageous, being called *tersel* or *tiercel*.] A small cannon. MUSKET.—**falconer,** fa̦ʹkn•ẽr, *n.* A person who breeds and trains falcons or hawks for sport; one who follows the sport of fowling with hawks.—**falcon-gentle,** *n.* The female of the goshawk. —**falconry,** fa̦ʹkn•ri, *n.* The art of training falcons to attack wild birds or game; the sport of pursuing wild fowls or game by means of falcons or hawks.

faldstool, fa̦ldʹstöl, *n.* [*Fald* or *fold*, and *stool*.] A folding stool similar to a campstool; a kind of stool at which the kings of England kneel at their coronation; a small desk at which in churches litany is said.

fall, fa̦l, *v.i.*—*fell* (pret.), *fallen* (pp.). [A.Sax. *feallen*=D. *vallen*, Dan. *falde*, Icel. *falla*, G. *fallen*, to fall. *Fell* is the causal of this.] To sink from a higher to a lower position; to descend by the power of gravity; to drop down; to sink; to ebb; to drop from an erect posture; to empty, disembogue, or discharge itself; said of a stream; to depart from the faith or from rectitude; to sink into sin; to die, particularly by violence; to come to an end suddenly; to perish, be overthrown, or ruined; to sink into weakness; to become faint or feeble (our hopes *fall*); to sink into disrepute or disgrace; to decline in power, wealth, or glory; to pass into a new state, especially with suddenness or through inadvertence or ignorance (to *fall* asleep, to *fall* into error); to decrease; to be diminished in weight, size, value, or intensity (the price *falls*, the wind *falls*); to assume an expression of dejection, discontent, sorrow, shame, etc.; applied to the countenance; to happen; to befall; to take place; to pass or be transferred by lot, inheritance, or otherwise (something *falls* to one's share); to belong or appertain; to have to be reckoned to; to be dropped or uttered carelessly; to sink in tone or loudness.—*To fall among*, to come among or into the society of, accidentally or unexpectedly.—*To fall away*, to lose flesh; to become lean or emaciated; to renounce or desert allegiance, faith, or duty; to revolt or rebel; to apostatize; to decline gradually; to languish or become faint.—*To fall back*, to recede; to give way; to go from better to worse; to retrograde; to fail of performing a promise or purpose; not to fulfill.—*To fall* *back upon,* to have recourse to, generally to some support or expedient formerly tried.—*To fall down,* to prostrate one's self in worship or supplication; to sink; to come to the ground.—*To fall foul of,* to attack; to make an assault upon.—*To fall from,* to recede from; to depart; not to adhere to.—*To fall in,* to take one's place in an organized body of men, as soldiers; to terminate or lapse (an annuity *falls in* when the annuitant dies).—*To fall in with,* to meet casually; to happen to meet; to concur, agree, or comply with.—*To fall off,* to be broken or detached from something; to apostatize; to fall away; to get into disuse; to decline from former excellence; to become less valuable or interesting; to become less; to decrease; *naut.* to deviate from the course to which the head of the ship was before directed.—*To fall on* or *upon,* to begin suddenly and eagerly; to begin an attack on; to assault; to assail; to come upon, usually with some degree of suddenness and unexpectedness; to drop on; to light on; to come upon.—*To fall out,* to quarrel; to begin to contend; to happen; to befall; to chance; to turn out; to prove.—*To fall short,* to be deficient.—*To fall to,* to begin hastily and eagerly; to apply one's self to.—*To fall under,* to come under or within the limits of; to be subjected to; to become the subject of.—*n.* The act of one who or that which falls; a dropping or descending; descent; a tumble; death; destruction; overthrow; downfall; degradation; declension of greatness, power, or dominion; ruin; diminution; decrease of price or value; a sinking of tone; cadence; descent of water; a cascade or cataract; extent of descent; the distance through which anything falls or may fall; amount of slope; declivity; the season when leaves fall from trees; autumn; that which falls; a shower; a kind of ladies' veil; lapse or declension from innocence or goodness; [*cap.*] specifically the lapse into sin of our first parents Adam and Eve; *naut.* the part of a tackle to which the power is applied in hoisting.—*To try a fall,* to try a bout at wrestling.—**fallen,** fal'en, *pp.* or *a.* Dropped; degraded; sunk in vice; lost to virtue; ruined; overthrown.—**fallout,** *n.* Particles of radioactive matter from nuclear explosions carried by air currents and dropped at a distance; the descent of such particles.—**falling sickness,** *n.* Epilepsy, a disease in which the patient suddenly loses his senses and falls.—**falling star,** *n.* A meteor appearing as a luminous point darting through the sky, and followed by a long train of light.

fallacious, fal•lā'shus, *a.* [Fr. *fallacieux,* from L. *fallax, fallacis,* deceitful, from *fallo,* to deceive. FAIL.] Pertaining to or embodying something deceptive or misleading; producing error or mistake; tending to mislead. ∴ *Fallacious* reasoning consists of arguments that deceive or mislead one, though not necessarily purposely. *Sophistical* reasoning is intendedly false reasoning, consisting of arguments so subtle as not to be easily detected and controverted, advanced purposely to mislead.—**fallaciously,** fal•lā'shus•li, *adv.* In a fallacious manner; sophistically; with purpose or in a manner to deceive.—**fallaciousness,** fal•lā'shus•nes, *n.* State of being fallacious.—**fallacy,** fal'la•si, *n.* [L. *fallacia,* deceit.] A misleading or mistaken argument; an argument or proposition apparently sound but really containing some undetected error, and therefore misleading; any unsound but specious mode of arguing.

fallible, fal'i•bl, *a.* [L.L. *fallibilis,* from L. *fallo,* to deceive. FALLACIOUS, FAIL.] Liable to fail or mistake; liable to deceive or to be deceived; liable to error or going astray.—**fallibility,** fal•i•bil'i•ti, *n.* The state of being fallible; liableness to deceive or to be deceived.—**fallibly,** fal'i•bli, *adv.* In a fallible manner.

Fallopian tube, fâ•lō'pē•en tūb, *n.* [From Gabriel *Fallopius,* a 16th—century Italian anatomist.] Either of the pair of tubes, arising from the uterus and each connected to an ovary, which conduct the egg into the uterus.

fallow, fal'ō, *a.* [O.E. *fealo, fealu,* pale yellow or dun; akin to G. *fahl,* pale, and Gr. *polios,* gray.] Of a pale yellow-brown; dun.—**fallow deer,** *n.* A small, pale yellow, European deer.

fallow, fal'ō, *a.* [O.E. *fealg, feahl,* plowed land.] Left to rest without a crop after plowing; untilled; uncultivated; neglected; unoccupied; unused.—*n.* Land that has lain a year or more untilled or unsown; land plowed without being sowed; the plowing of land, without sowing it, for a season.—*v.t.* To leave fallow or plowed but not sown in crop.

false, fols, *a.* [L. *falsus,* false, from *fallo, falsum,* to deceive. FAIL.] Not true; not conformable to fact; expressing what is contrary to that which exists, is done, said, or thought; intended to mislead; counterfeit; forged; not real or genuine; hypocritical; feigned; not agreeable to rule or propriety (*false* construction in language); not honest or just; fraudulent; not faithful or loyal; treacherous; perfidious; deceitful; unfaithful; inconstant; not well founded or based (*false* hopes); constructed for show or a subsidiary purpose (a *false* bottom, a *false* keel).—**falsehearted,** *a.* Treacherous; deceitful; perfidious.—**falsehood,** fols'höd, *n.* Contrariety or want of conformity to fact or truth; falseness; want of truth or veracity; untruthfulness; what is false or untrue; a lie; an untrue assertion; want of honesty; deceitfulness; perfidy; imposture.—**falsely,** fols'li, *adv.* In a manner contrary to truth and fact; not truly; untruly.—**falseness,** fols'nes, *n.* The state or quality of being false; untruthfulness; want of veracity; duplicity; deceit; unfaithfulness; perfidy.—**falsify,** fol'si•fī, *v.t.*—*falsified, falsifying.* [Fr. *falsifier,* from L. *falsus,* and *facio,* to make.] To represent falsely; to vitiate with false and misleading elements; to garble; to make not genuine; to disprove; to prove to be false; to cause to turn out false (to *falsify* a prediction); to violate or break by falsehood.—*v.i.* To violate the truth.—**falsification,** fol'si•fi•kā"shon, *n.* The act of falsifying; a counterfeiting; the giving to a thing an appearance of something which it is not.—**falsifier,** fol'si•fī•ėr, *n.* One who falsifies; one who counterfeits or gives to a thing a deceptive appearance.—**falsity,** fol'si•ti, *n.* The quality of being false; that which is false; a falsehood; a false assertion.

falsetto, fol•set'tō, *n.* [It., from L. *falsus,* false.] The tones above the natural compass of the voice.

falter, fol'tėr, *v.i.* [A freq. connected with *fault,* from a supposed Fr. verb corresponding to Sp. *faltar,* It. *faltare,* to fail, from L. *fallere,* to deceive. FAULT, FAIL.] To hesitate in the utterance of words; to speak with a broken or trembling utterance; to stammer; not to be firm and steady; to tremble.—*n.* The act of faltering; hesitation; trembling; quavering.—**faltering,** fol'tėr•ing, *a.* Trembling; hesitating.—**falteringly,** fol'tėr•ing•li, *adv.* With hesitation; with a trembling, broken voice.

fame, fām, *n.* [Fr. *fame,* from L. *fama,* fame, renown, from *fari,* to speak; whence also *fate.* FATE.] Public report or rumor; report or opinion widely diffused; renown; notoriety; celebrity.—**famed,** fāmd, *p.* and *a.* Much talked of; renowned; celebrated.—**famous,** fā'mus, *a.* [L. *famosus,* Fr. *fameux.*] Celebrated in fame or public report; renowned; much talked of; distinguished in story. —**famously,** fā'mus•li, *adv.* In a famous manner.—**famousness,**† fā'mus•nes, *n.* The state of being famous; renown; celebrity.

familiar, fa•mil'yėr, *a.* [L. *familiaris,* from *familia,* a household, the servants of a family, from *famulus,* a servant. FAMILY.] Well acquainted; closely intimate; well versed (in a subject of study); exhibiting the manner of an intimate friend; affable; accessible; characterized by ease or absence of stiffness of pedantry; easy; well known; well understood; of everyday occurrence or use. —*Familiar spirit,* a spirit or demon supposed to be constantly at the command of some person.—*n.* An intimate; a close companion; a familiar spirit; an officer of the Inquisition employed in apprehending and imprisoning persons accused.—**familiarity,** fa•mil'i•ar"i•ti, *n.* The state of being familiar; unconstrained intercourse; intimate acquaintance or knowledge; intimacy; *pl.* actions characterized by too much license; liberties.—**familiarization,** fa•mil'yėr•i•zā"shon, *n.* Act or process of making or becoming familiar.—**familiarize,** fa•mil'yėr•īz, *v.t.*—*fa-*

miliarized, *familiarizing*. To make familiar or intimate; to habituate; to accustom; to make intimately acquainted; to render conversant or fully acquainted by practice or customary use, or by intercourse.—**familiarly**, fa•mil′yėr•li, *adv*. In a familiar manner.

family, fam′i•li, *n*. [L. *familia*, a household, the slaves or servants of a house; from *famulus*, a servant, a slave, from Oscan *famel*, a servant, from *faama*, Skr. *dhâman*, a house.] The body of persons who live in one house and under one head; the parents and children alone; the children as distinguished from the parents; those who descend from one common progenitor; a tribe or race; kindred; lineage; line of ancestors; honorable descent; noble or respectable stock (a man of *family*); in scientific classifications, a group of individuals more comprehensive than a genus, and less so than an order.—**familial**, fä•mil′yäl, *a*. Of or pertaining to the family; hereditary.—*Family Compact*, the compact formed in 1733 between the divisions of the Bourbon family, Philip V of Spain and Louis XV of France, against British supremacy.—**family man**, *n*. One who has a family or household; a married man.

famine, fam′in, *n*. [Fr. *famine*, from L. *fames*, hunger.] Scarcity of food; dearth; a general want of provisions; destitution.—**famish**, fam′ish, *v.t.* [O.Fr. *famis*, starving, from L. *fames*.] To kill or destroy with hunger; to starve; to cause to suffer from hunger or thirst; to distress with hunger; to force or compel by famine.—*v.i.* To die of hunger; to suffer extreme hunger or thirst; to suffer by the deprivation of any necessary.

famous. See FAME.

fan, fan, *n*. [A.Sax. *fann*, *fan*, from L. *vannus*, a fan for winnowing; akin to L. *ventus*, wind, and E. *wind*, *winnow*.] The name of various instruments for exciting a current of air by the agitation of a broad surface, vanes or disks; a machine for winnowing grain; an instrument used by ladies to agitate the air and cool the face; anything resembling this; what fans or excites.—*v.t.*—*fanned*, *fanning*. To move or agitate as with a fan; to cool and refresh by moving the air with a fan; to winnow; to separate chaff from, and drive it away by a current of air; *fig*. to produce effects on analogous to those of a fan in exciting flame, to excite or stir up to activity; to stimulate.—**fanlight**, *n*. A fan-shaped window situated over a door in a circular-headed opening.—**fanner**, fan′ėr, *n*. One who fans; a rotatory contrivance with vanes for ventilating the interior of a chamber; an arrangement of vanes for blowing fires; *pl*. a fan or machine for winnowing grain.—**fantail**, *n*. A variety of the domestic pigeon; a form of gasburner.—**fanwindow**, *n*. A window having a semicircular outline and a sash formed of radial bars.

fanatic, fanatical, fa•nat′ik, fa•nat′i•kal, *a*. [L. *fanaticus*, inspired, enthusiastic, from *fanum*, a place dedicated to some deity, a temple.] Reckless and extravagant in opinions.—*n*. A person affected by excessive enthusiasm and devotion.—**fan**, fan, *n*. [From *fanatic*.] An admirer or devotee of someone or something.—**fanatically**, fa•nat′i•kal•li, *adv*.—**fanaticism**, fa•nat′i•sizm, *n*. The state or character of a fanatic; wild and extravagant notions of religion; religious frenzy; fervid zeal.—**fanaticize**, fa•nat′i•sīz, *v.t.* To make fanatic.

fancy, fan′si, *n*. [Contr. for *fantasy*, *phantasy*, from L. and Gr. *phantasia*, a fancy, from Gr. *phantazō*, to make visible, from *phainō*, to show; akin *phantom*, *phenomenon*.] A phase of the intellectual faculty of a lighter and less impressive cast than the imagination, or the active play of this lighter faculty; a new and pleasing thought or conception due to this faculty; the happy and poetical embodiment of such conception in words; a poetical illustration or ornament, as a simile, metaphor, and the like; an opinion or notion; an impression or supposition; a whim or conceit; inclination; liking; fondness; preference.—*The fancy*, a name for sporting characters, especially prize fighters.—*a*. Fine; elegant; ornamental (*fancy* goods); beyond intrinsic value; extravagant (a *fancy* price).—*v.i.*—*fancied*, *fancying*. To imagine; to figure to one's self; to believe or suppose without proof.—*v.t.* To form a conception of; to portray in the mind; to imagine; to like; to be pleased with.—**fancier**, fan′si•ėr, *n*. One who fancies; one who is influenced by his fancies.—**fanciful**, fan′si•fụl, *a*. Guided by fancy rather than by reason and experience; subject to the influence of fancy; whimsical: applied to persons; dictated or produced by fancy; appealing to or pleasing the fancy; full of wild images; curiously shaped: applied to things.—**fancifully**, fan′si•fụl•li, *adv*. In a fanciful manner.—**fancifulness**, fan′si•fụl•nes, *n*. The quality of being fanciful.—**fanciless**, fan′si•les, *a*. Destitute of fancy.—**fancy ball**, *n*. A ball in which persons appear in fancy dresses, imitations of antique costumes, etc.—**fancy-free**, *a*. Free from the power of love.—**fancywork**, *n*. Ornamental knitting, embroidery, etc., performed by ladies.

fandango, fan•dang′gō, *n*. A lively Spanish dance borrowed from the Moors, danced by two persons, male and female, the music being in triple time.

fanfare, fan′fâr, *n*. [Fr.] A flourish of trumpets; a short tune of a cheerful cast, played with hunting horns; an ostentatious parade or boast; bravado.—**fanfaron**, fan′fa•ron, *n*. [Fr.] A bully; a hector; a swaggerer; an empty boaster.—**fanfaronade**, fan•far′o•nād″, *n*. [Fr.] A swaggering; ostentation; bluster.

fang, fang, *n*. [A.Sax. *fang*, a taking, grasp, from *fôn* (for *fahan*), to seize (pret. *feng*, pp. *fangen*)=G. *fangen*, Goth. *fahan*, D. *vangen*, to take.] The tusk of a boar or other animal by which the prey is seized and held; a long pointed tooth; the hollow poison tooth of a serpent; a claw or talon; the catch of a pump.—*Off the fang*, out of sorts, listless.—*v.t.* To start a pump by pouring water on it.—**fanged**, fangd, *p*. and *a*. Furnished with fangs, tusks, or something resembling these.

fangled, fang′gld, *a*. [From old *fangle*, a gewgaw, something to catch the eye from old *fangen*, to catch.] Gaudy; showy; fond of finery. (Used by Shakespeare, but now only in the compound *new-fangled*.)

fanon, fan′on, *n*. [Fr. *fanon*, from Goth. *fana*, cloth, a banner.] *Eccles*. a kind of napkin or handkerchief used by the priest at mass; also an ornament attached to a priest's left arm.

fan palm, *n*. A name for the taliput and one or two other palms.

fantasia, fan•tä′zē•a, *n*. [It., lit. a fantasy or fancy, from L. and Gr. *phantasia*, a fancy, whence also E. *fancy*. FANCY.] A species of musical composition having no particular theme, but ranging amidst various airs and movements.—**fantasm**, fan′tazm, *n*. Same as *Phantasm*.—**fantast**, fan′tast, *n*. One whose mind is full of fantastic notions.—**fantastic, fantastical**, fan•tas′tik, fan•tas′ti•kal, *a*. [Fr. *fantastique*, from Gr. *phantastikos*, from *phantasia*, vision, fancy.] Fanciful; existing only in imagination; imaginary; chimerical; whimsical; capricious; indulging the vagaries of imagination; having oddness of figure or appearance; whimsically shaped; grotesque.—*n*. A whimsical person; a fop.—**fantasticality**, fan•tas′ti•kal″i•ti, *n*. Fantasticalness.—**fantastically**, fan•tas′ti•kal•li, *adv*. In a fantastic manner; capriciously; whimsically.—**fantasticalness**, fan•tas′ti•kal•nes, *n*. State of being fantastical.—**fantasy**, fan′ta•si, *n*. A mental image, especially of the unrestricted imagination; a daydream; a visionary idea; a caprice.

fantoccini, fan•to•chē′ni, *n. pl.* [It.] Puppets worked by concealed wires or strings; a puppet show; marionettes.

fantom, fan′tom, *n*. Same as *Phantom*.

far, fär, *a*. [A.Sax. *feor*; D. *ver*, Icel. *fjarri*, Goth. *fairra*, G. *fern*, far—allied to *fore*, *ferry*, *fare*; the root being same as that of L. *per*, through; G. *pera*, beyond; Skr. *para*, other.] Distant; separated by a wide space; hence, remote as regards wishes, feelings, affections; more distant of the two: applied to the right side of a horse.—*adv*. To a great extent or distance of space; to a remote period; in great part (the day *far* spent); in a great proportion; by many degrees; very much (*far* better or higher); to whatever point, degree, or distance (as *far* as).—*By far*, in a great degree; very much.—*From* *far*, from a great distance; from a remote place.—*Far other*, very different.—**far-fetched,** *p.* and *a.* Brought from a remote place; not easily or naturally introduced; elaborately strained (a *far-fetched* explanation).—**far-off,** *a.* Faraway; distant; remote in space or time.—**farsighted,** *a.* Seeing to a great distance; calculating carefully the distant results of present conduct or action; not capable of perceiving objects near at hand distinctly.—**farsightedness,** *n.* The state or quality of being farsighted.—**farther,** fär′THėr, *a. compar.* [Not the original compar. of *far*, which was *far-er* (*ferrer*), but assimilated to *further*.] More remote; more distant than something else; tending to a greater distance; additional.—*adv.* At or to a greater distance; more remotely; beyond; by way of progression in a subject; moreover.—**farthermost,** fär′THėr•mōst, *a. superl.* Being at the farthest distance; most remote.—**farthest,** fär′THest, *a. superl.* At the greatest distance either in time or place.—*adv.* At or to the greatest distance.

farad, far′ad, *n.* [In honor of *Faraday*.] The unit of electrical capacity in the practical system of units, being the capacity of a condenser which one coulomb of electricity raises to a potential of one volt.—**faradic,** fa•rad′ik, *a.* Applied to induction electricity.—**faradization, faradism,** far′a•di•zā″shon, far′ad•-izm, *n.* The medical application of the magneto-electric currents which *Faraday* discovered in 1837.

farce, färs, *v.t.*—*farced, farcing*. [Fr. *farcir*, L. *farcio*, to stuff.] To stuff with forcemeat; to fill with mingled ingredients.—*n.* [Fr. *farce*, It. *farsa*, from L. *farcio*, to stuff, from being stuffed or crammed with humor.] A dramatic composition of a broadly comic character; a comedy full of extravagant drollery; ridiculous parade; empty pageantry; mere show.—**farcical,** fär′si•kal, *a.* Belonging to a farce; of the character of a farce; droll; ludicrous; ridiculous.—**farcically,** fär′si•kal•li, *adv.* In a farcical manner.

farcy, fär′si, *n.* A disease of horses intimately connected with glanders, the two diseases generally running into each other.—**farcy bud,** *n.* A tumor which appears early in the disease farcy.

fare, fâr, *v.i.*—*fared, faring*. [A.Sax. *faran*, to go = Icel. Sw. *fara*, Dan. *fare*, D. *varen*, G. *fahren*, to go, same root as L. *per*, through, *porta*, gate, Gr. *poros*, passage, *peirō*, to pierce; E. *far, ferry*, etc.] To go; to pass; to move forward; to travel; to be in any state, good or bad; to be in a certain condition as regards bodily or social comforts; to be entertained with food; to happen; to turn out or result; to be; with *it* impersonally.—*n.* The sum paid or due for conveying a person by land, air, or water; food; provisions of the table; condition; treatment by circumstances; fortune; the person or persons conveyed in a vehicle.—**farewell,** fâr′wel, [From *fare*, in the imper., and *well*.] May you fare or prosper well; a wish of happiness to those who leave or those who are left: it sometimes has the pronoun inserted between its two elements, as *fare you well*. Sometimes it is an expression of mere separation (like 'good-bye' or 'adieu').—*n.* Good-bye; adieu; leave; departure; final look, reference, or attention.—*a.* Leave-taking; valedictory.

farina, fa•rē′na, *n.* [L. *farina*, flour, from *far*, a sort of grain.] Meal or flour; a soft, tasteless, and commonly white powder, obtained by trituration of the seeds of cereal and leguminous plants, and of some roots, as the potato.—**farinaceous,** far•i•nā′shus, *a.* Consisting or made of meal or flour; containing or yielding farina or flour; mealy.—**farinose,** far′i•nos, *a.* Yielding farina.

farm, färm, *n.* [A.Sax. *feorm, fyrm*, food, provisions, a feast, entertainment; hence, a piece of land that has to supply a certain quantity of provisions; from L.L. *firma* (from L. *firmus*, firm, established), farm rent, sum settled or fixed.] A tract of land cultivated by either the owner of the land or a tenant, and usually divided into fields.—*v.t.* To let to a tenant on condition of paying rent; to hold and cultivate either as tenant or as owner; to lease or let, as taxes or other duties, at a certain sum or a certain rate per cent.—*v.i.* To be employed in agriculture; to cultivate the soil.—**farmer,** fär′mėr, *n.* One who farms; one who cultivates a farm; an agriculturist; a husbandman; one who takes taxes, customs, excise, or other duties, to collect for a certain gross sum or a rate per cent.—**farmhouse,** färm′hous, *n.* A house attached to a farm for the residence of a farmer.—**farming,** fär′ming, *a.* Pertaining to agriculture.—*n.* The business of a farmer; husbandry.—**farmstead,** färm′sted, *n.* The system of buildings connected with a farm; a homestead.—**farmyard,** färm′yärd, *n.* The yard or enclosure surrounded by or connected with the farm buildings.

faro, fâ′rō, *n.* [Said to be from *Pharaoh* having formerly been depicted on one of the cards.] A game at cards in which a person plays against the bank.

farrago, fa•rā′gō, *n.* [L. from *far*, meal.] A mass composed of various materials confusedly mixed; a medley.—**farraginous,** fa•raj′i•nus, *a.* Formed of various materials mixed.

farrier, far′i•ėr, *n.* [O.Fr. *ferrier*, from *ferrer*, to shoe a horse, from L. *ferrum*, iron.] A shoer of horses; one who combines the art of horseshoeing with the profession of veterinary surgery.—*v.i.* To practice as a farrier.—**farriery,** far′i•ėr•i, *n.* The art of shoeing horses; the art of curing the diseases of horses, oxen, sheep, pigs, etc.; veterinary surgery.

farrow, far′ō, *n.* [A.Sax. *fearh*, a little pig; akin to O.H.G. *farah*, G. *ferkel*, D. *varken*, a pig; L. *porcus*, a pig, being also allied.] A litter of pigs.—*v.t.* and *i.* To bring forth pigs.

farther. See FAR.

farthing, fär′THing, *n.* [A.Sax. *ferthing, feorthing*, the fourth part of a thing, from *feorth*, fourth, from *feówer*, four.] The fourth of a penny, a small copper coin of Britain, the fourth of a penny in value.

farthingale, fär′THing•gal, *n.* [O.Fr. *vertugalle, vertugade*, from Sp. *verdugo*, a rod or shoot of a tree, hence a hoop.] A hoop petticoat formerly worn by ladies, or the circles of hoops used to extend the petticoat.

fasces, fas′sēz, *n. pl.* [L.] A bundle of rods, with an ax bound in along with them, anciently borne before the superior Roman magistrates as a badge of their power over life and limb; the symbol of the Fascist party in Italy.

fascia, fash′i•a, *n.* pl. **fasciae,** fash′i•ē. [L.] A band, sash, or fillet, or something resembling this in shape; a surgical bandage; *arch.* a long band of stone or brick forming a slight projection.—**fasciate,** fash′i•āt, *a.* Banded or bound together; fasciated.—**fasciated,** fash′i•ā•ted, *a.* Bound with a fillet, sash, or bandage; *bot.* applied to the peculiar flattened stems or branches which occur occasionally in trees.—**fasciation,** fash•i•ā′shon, *n.* The state of being fasciated; the act or manner of binding up diseased parts; bandage.

fascicle, fas′si•kl, *n.* [L. *fasciculus*, from *fascis*, a bundle.] A little bundle or collection; *bot.* a form of cyme in which the flowers are clustered together in a more or less compact bundle.—**fasciculate, fasciculated, fascicled, fascicular,** fas•sik′ū•lāt, fas•sik′ū•lā•ted, fas′si•kld, fas•sik′ū•lėr, *a. Bot.* growing in bundles or bunches from the same point: said of leaves, stems, roots, etc.—**fasciculately,** fas•sik′ū•lāt•li, *adv.* In a fasciculate manner.—**fascicule,** fas′si•kūl, *n.* A fascicle.—**fasciculus,** fas•sik′ū•lus, *n.* A fascicle; one of the separate divisions or numbers in which a book is published.

fascinate, fas′si•nāt, *v.t.*—*fascinated, fascinating*. [Fr. *fasciner*, L. *fascino, fascinatum*, to fascinate, bewitch.] To bewitch; to enchant; to operate on by some powerful or irresistible influence; to charm; to captivate; to allure irresistibly or powerfully.—*v.i.* To exercise a bewitching or captivating power.—**fascinating,** fas′si•nā•ting, *p.* and *a.* Bewitching; enchanting; charming; captivating.—**fascination,** fas•si•nā′shon, *n.* The act of fascinating, bewitching, or enchanting; enchantment; a charm.

fascism, fash′izm, *n.* A totalitarian form of government in Italy administered by the Fascisti (a political organization) which advocated the building of a highly nationalistic state, recognizing private ownership except when the state determined otherwise.—**Fascist,** fash′ist, *a.* Of or pertaining to fascism.—*n.* A member of the Fascisti.

fashion, fash′on, *n.* [O.Fr. *fachon*,

facion, from L. *factio*, a making, from *facio*, to make. FACT.] The make or form of anything; external form; shape; pattern; make according to the custom of the time; the prevailing mode of dress or ornament; manner, sort, way, or mode; custom; prevailing practice; genteel life or good breeding; genteel society.—*v.t.* To form; to give shape or figure to; to mold.—**fashionable,** fash′on•a•bl, *a.* Conforming to the fashion or established mode; taking the public taste and being in vogue; established by custom; current; prevailing; dressing or behaving according to the prevailing fashion; genteel; well-bred.—*n.* A person of fashion.—**fashionableness,** fash′on•a•bl•nes, *n.* The state of being fashionable.—**fashionably,** fash′on•a•bli, *adv.* In a manner according to fashion; according to the prevailing mode.—**fashioner,** fash′on•ėr, *n.* One who fashions.

fast, fast, *a.* [A.Sax. *fæst*, *fest*, fast, firm=D. *vast*, Icel. *fastr*. Dan. *fast*, G. *fest*, firm, solid. Hence *fast*, quick, and verb to *fast*.] Firmly fixed; close; tight; closely adhering; made close; strong against attack; firm in adherence; not easily alienated (a *fast* friend); steadfast; faithful; lasting; durable (a *fast* color).—*adv.* Firmly; immovably.—*To play fast and loose*, to act in an inconstant manner; to say one thing and do another.—**fasten,** fas′n, *v.t.* [A.Sax. *fæstnian*, to secure.] To fix firmly; to make fast or close; to secure, as by lock, bolt, or the like; to join in close union; to unite closely; to attach; to affix.—*v.i.* To fix one's self or itself, to become attached.—**fastener,** fas′n•ėr, *n.* One who or that which fastens.—**fastening,** fas′n•ing, *n.* Anything that fastens, binds, attaches, etc.—**fastness,** fast′nes, *n.* [A.Sax. *fæstnes*, firmness, a fortification.] The state of being fast, firm, or secure; strength; security; a stronghold; a fortified place; a castle; a fortress.

fast, fast, *a.* [The same word as *fast*, fixed firm or steadfast (one who runs fast runs steadfastly)=Icel. *fast*, rapidly, quickly, from *fastr*, firm.] Swift; moving rapidly; quick in motion; rapid; dissipated; devoted to pleasure; indulging in sensual vices: said of a man; imitating the manners or habits of a man: said of a female.—*adv.* In a fast or quick manner; swiftly; rapidly; with quick steps or progression; prodigally and wastefully; with dissipation.—**fastness,** fast′nes, *n.* The state or quality of being fast.

fast, fast, *v.i.* [A.Sax. *fæstan*, to fast; probably from *fæst*, firm, steadfast, the meaning being to be steadfast in abstaining=D. *vasten*, Dan. *faste*, Icel. and Sw. *fasta*, G. *fasten*, Goth. *fastan*, to fast.] To abstain from food beyond the usual time; to go hungry; to abstain from food, or particular kinds of food, voluntarily, especially for religious reasons.—*n.* Abstinence from food; a withholding from the usual quantity of nourishment; voluntary abstinence from food as a religious mortification or humiliation; the time of fasting.

fastidious, fas•tid′i•us, *a.* [L. *fastidiosus*, from *fastidium*, loathing, fastidiousness, from *fastus*, haughtiness.] Hard or difficult to please; squeamish; delicate to a fault; overnice; difficult to suit.—**fastidiously,** fas•tid′i•us•li, *adv.* In a fastidious manner.—**fastidiousness,** fas•tid′i•us•nes, *n.*

fastigiate, fastigiated, fas•tij′i•āt, fas•tij′i•ā•ted, *a.* [L. *fastigiatus*, pointed, from *fastigium*, a top or peak.] Peaked or pointed at top; *bot.* tapering to a narrow point like a pyramid, as a plant when the branches become gradually shorter from the base to the apex.

fat, fat, *a.* [A.Sax. *fæt*=D. *vet*, Dan. *fed*, Icel. *feitr*, G. *fett*, fat. Hence, to *fatten*, *fatling*.] Fleshy; plump; obese; corpulent; the contrary to *lean*; oily; greasy; unctuous; coarse; heavy; dull; stupid (especially in such compounds as *fat*-brained, *fat*-witted); producing a large income; rich; fertile; nourishing.—*n.* A solid oily substance of whitish or yellow color, a compound of carbon, hydrogen, and oxygen, found in certain parts of animal bodies, lard and tallow being varieties of it; the best or richest part of a thing.—*v.t.*—*fatted*, *fatting*. To make fat; to fatten.—*v.i.* To grow fat.—**fatling,** fat′ling, *n.* Any young animal fattened for slaughter, as a lamb, kid, or the like.—**fatly,** fat′li, *adv.* In a fat manner; grossly; greasily.—**fatness,** fat′nes, *n.* The state or quality of being fat; corpulence; plumpness; unctuousness; oiliness; richness; fertility.—**fatten,** fat′n, *v.t.* To make fat; to feed for slaughter; to enrich; to make fertile.—*v.i.* To grow fat; to become plump or fleshy.—**fattener,** fat′n•ėr, *n.* One who or that which fattens; that which gives fatness, richness, or fertility.—**fatty,** fat′i, *a.* Having the nature or qualities of fat; greasy.—**fatty acid,** *n.* Any of numerous saturated or unsaturated, aliphatic, monocarboxylic, organic acids, such as palmetic acid and stearic acid, that naturally occur as esters in fat.

fatal, fā′tal, *a.* [L. *fatalis*, from *fatum*, fate. FATE.] Mortal; destructive; calamitous; disastrous.—**fatalism,** fā′tal•izm, *n.* The doctrine that all events take place by inevitable necessity, and man is powerless to change them; the belief in, or the attitude of mind determined by, such a doctrine.—**fatalist,** fā′tal•ist, *n.*—**fatalistic,** fā•ta•lis′tik, *a.* Pertaining to fatalism; implying fatalism.—**fatality,** fa•tal′i•ti, *n.* The state of being fatal; a fixed unalterable course of things; a fatal occurrence; a calamitous accident.—**fatally,** fā′tal•li, *adv.*

fata morgana, fä′ta mor•gä′na, *n.* [It., because supposed to be the work of a *fata* or fairy called *Morgana*.] A striking optical illusion principally remarked in the Strait of Messina, between the coasts of Sicily and Calabria—a variety of mirage.

fate, fāt, *n.* [L. *fatum* (lit. that which has been spoken), destiny as pronounced by the gods, fate, from *fari*, to speak (whence also *fama*, fame, and *fanum*, a fane), from a root which appears also in Gr. *phanai*, to speak, and *phaos*, light; akin *fable*, *fairy*, *fay*, *affable*, etc.] A fixed decree or sentence, by which the order of things is prescribed; inevitable necessity settling how events are to befall; unavoidable concatenation and succession of events; destiny; predetermined lot; human destiny; the final fortune of anything; final event; death; destruction; [*cap.*] *pl.* (*myth.*) the Destinies or Parcae; [*cap.*] the three goddesses supposed to preside over the birth and life of men, called Clotho, Lachesis, and Atropos.—**fated,** fā′ted, *a.* Assigned or gifted with a certain fate; doomed; destined; regulated by fate.—**fateful,** fāt′fu̦l, *a.* Bringing or deciding fate or destiny; fatal.

father, fä′THėr, *n.* [A.Sax. *fæder*=D. *vader*, Icel. *fathir*, Dan. and Sw. *fader*, Goth. *fadar*, G. *vater*, L. *pater*, Gr. *patēr*, Per. *padar*, Skr. *pitri*—father; perhaps from a root *pa.* to feed.] He who begets a child; a male parent; a male ancestor more remote than a parent, especially the first ancestor; the founder of a race, family, or line; a respectful mode of address to an old man; one who exercises paternal care over another; a guardian, protector, or preserver; the first to practice any art; a distinguished example; a teacher; originator; cause; [*usually cap.*] the appellation of the first person in the Trinity; the title given to dignitaries of the church, confessors, and priests; the eldest member of a profession, or other body.—*Father of the House*, in England the member in the Commons who has sat the longest period of time—*Fathers of the Church*, the name given to the early teachers and expounders of Christianity, whose writings have thrown light upon the history, doctrines, and observances of the Christian church in the early ages.—*v.t* To beget as a father; to assume as one's own work; to profess or acknowledge one's self to be the author of; to ascribe or charge to one as his offspring or production (to *father* a book *on* a person).—**fatherhood,** fä′THėr•hu̦d, *n.* The state of being a father; the character or authority of a father.—**father-in-law,** *n.* The father of one's husband or wife.—**fatherland,** fä′THėr•land, *n.* [A literal translation of the G. *Vaterland*.] One's native country; the country of one's fathers or ancestors.—**fatherless,** fä′THėr•les, *a.* Destitute of a living father; without a known author.—**fatherliness,** fä′THėr•li•nes, *n.* The state or quality of being fatherly; parental kindness, care, and tenderness.—**fatherly,** fä′THėr•li, *a.* Like a father in affection and care; paternal; protecting; pertaining to a father.—*adv.* In the manner of a father.

fathom, faTH'um, *n.* [A.Sax. *fæthm*, the bosom, the space of both arms extended; Icel. *fathmr*, D. *vadem*, Sw. *famn*, G. *faden*, from a root meaning to stretch.] A measure of length containing 6 feet, being originally the space to which a man may extend his arms.—*v.t.* To try the depth of, to find the bottom or extent of; to sound; *fig.* to penetrate or comprehend.—**fathomable,** faTH'um•a•bl, *a.* Capable of being fathomed or comprehended.—**fathomless,** faTH'um•les, *a.* That of which no bottom can be found; bottomless; not to be penetrated or comprehended.

fatigue, fa•tēg', *v.t.*—*fatigued, fatiguing.* [Fr. *fatiguer*, from L. *fatigo*, to weary.] To weary with labor or any bodily or mental exertion; to harass with toil; to exhaust the strength by severe or long-continued exertion; to tire or wear out.—*n.* Weariness from bodily labor or mental exertion; lassitude or exhaustion of strength; the cause of weariness; labor undergone; toil; the labors of military men distinct from the use of arms.—**fatigue duty,** *n.* The work of soldiers distinct from the use of arms.

fatling, fatten, etc. See FAT.

fatuity, fa•tū'i•ti, *n.* [L. *fatuitas*, from *fatuus*, silly.] Weakness or imbecility of mind; feebleness of intellect; foolishness.—**fatuous,** fat'ū•us, *a.* [L. *fatuus.*] Feeble in mind; weak; idiotically silly; foolish.

fauces, fa̤'sēz, *n. pl.* [L., the throat, the gullet.] *Anat.* the gullet or windpipe; the posterior part of the mouth, terminated by the pharynx and larynx.—**faucal,** fa̤'kal, *a.* Pertaining to the fauces.

faucet, fa̤'set, *n.* [Fr. *fausset*, from L. *falsus*, false.] A spout fitted with a valve, for drawing liquids through a pipe; a spigot.

faugh, fa̤. Exclamation of contempt or abhorrence.

fault, folt, *n.* [O.Fr. *faulte*, Fr. *faute*, It. and Sp. *falta*, fault, defect, from a Romance verb (not recorded in French), from a L. freq. *fallitare*, from *fallo*, to deceive. FAIL.] A slight offense; a neglect of duty or propriety; something worthy of some blame or censure; a defect; a blemish; a flaw; among *sportsmen*, the act of losing the scent; a lost scent; *geol.* and *mining*, a break or dislocation of strata; an interruption in the continuity of strata such that the strata on either side appear elevated or depressed.—*At fault*, puzzled; in some difficulty or perplexity; also, to blame; deserving censure.—*To find fault*, to express blame; to take exception.—*To find fault with*, to take exception to; to censure.—**faultily,** fol'ti•li, *adv.* In a faulty manner.—**faultiness,** fol'ti•nes, *n.* The state of being faulty, defective, or erroneous.—**faultless,** folt'les, *a.* Without fault; not defective or imperfect; free from blemish, vice, or offense; perfect.—**faultlessly,** folt'les•li, *adv.* In a faultless manner.—**faultlessness,** folt'les•nes, *n.* Freedom from faults or defects.—**faulty,** fol'ti, *a.* Containing faults, blemishes, or defects; defective; imperfect; guilty of a fault or of faults; blamable.—**faultfinder,** *n.* One who censures or objects.

faun, fa̤n, *n.* [L. *Faunus*, a deity of the woods and fields.] *Rom. myth.* one of a kind of demigods or rural deities, differing little from satyrs.

fauna, fa̤'na, *n.* [N.L. *Fauna*, sister of Faunus.] The animals peculiar to a region, epoch, or geological stratum; the animals adapted to a specific environment.

faveolate, fa•vē'o•lāt, *a.* [L. *favus*, a honeycomb.]. Formed like a honeycomb; alveolate; cellular.

favonian, fa•vō'ni•an, *a.* [L. *favonius*, the west wind.] Pertaining to the west wind.

favor, fā'vėr, *n.* [Fr. *faveur*, from L. *favor, favoris*, from *faveo*, to favor, to befriend.] Kind regard; friendly disposition; a state of being looked on with good will or kindness; a kind act or office; kindness done or granted; an act of grace or good will; leave; good will; pardon; a token of love; a knot of ribbons worn at a marriage or on other festive occasions; something worn as a token of affection; convenience afforded for success (under *favor* of darkness); partiality; bias; aspect, look, or appearance (*Shak.*)‡.—*v.t.* To regard with favor or kindness; to support; to aid or have the disposition to aid; to be propitious to; to befriend; to show favor or partiality to; to afford advantages for success to; to render easier; to facilitate.—**favorable,** fā'vėr•a•bl, *a.* Kind; propitious; friendly; affectionate; manifesting partiality; conducive; contributing; tending to promote; advantageous; affording facilities.—**favorableness,** fā'vėr•a•bl•nes, *n.* The condition or quality of being favorable.—**favorably,** fā'vėr•a•bli, *adv.* In a favorable manner.—**favored,** fā'vėrd, *a.* Regarded or treated with favor; having special advantages or facilities; featured, now only in the compounds *well-favored, ill-favored.*—**favorer,** fā'vėr'ėr, *n.* One who favors.—**favorite,** fā'vėr•it, *n.* A person or thing regarded with peculiar favor, preference, and affection; one greatly beloved; often one unduly favored; one treated with undue partiality.—*The favorite,* the horse favored by betting on a horse race.—*a.* Regarded with particular affection or preference.—**favoritism,** fā'vėr•it•izm, *n.* The disposition to patronize favorites, or to promote the interest of a person or persons to the neglect of others having equal claims.

favus, fā'vus, *n.* [L., a honeycomb.] A kind of ringworm, a disease attacking the scalp, and characterized by yellowish dry incrustations somewhat resembling a honeycomb.

fawn, fa̤n, *n.* [Fr. *faon*, from a form *fetonus*, from L. *fetus*, progeny.] A young deer; a buck or doe of the first year.—*v.i.* To bring forth a fawn.—*a.* Resembling a fawn in color; light brown.

fawn, fa̤n, *v.i.* [A.Sax. *fægnian*, Icel. *fagna*, to rejoice, flatter. FAIN.] To show a servile attachment; to court favor by low cringing, and the like; to flatter meanly; to cringe and bow to gain favor; to cringe and frisk about a person (as a dog).—*n.* A servile cringe or bow; mean flattery.—**fawner,** fa̤'nėr, *n.* One who fawns.—**fawningly,** fa̤'ning•li, *adv.* In a fawning, servile way; with mean flattery.

fay, fā, *n.* [Fr. *fée*, L.L. *fata*, a fairy. FAIRY.] A fairy; an elf.

fay, fā, *v.t.* [A.Sax. *fægian*, to fit.] To fit two pieces of timber together so that they lie close and fair.

fayalite, fā'yal•īt, *n.* [*Fayal*, one of the Azores, where it is found.] A black, greenish, or brownish mineral, consisting mainly of silicate of iron.

fealty, fē'al•ti, *n.* [O.Fr. *fealté, feauté*, fealty, from L. *fidelitas*, faithfulness, fidelity; it is thus the same word as *fidelity.*] Fidelity to a superior; faithful adherence of a tenant or vassal to the superior of whom he holds his lands; faithfulness of any person to another; faith.

fear, fēr, *n.* [A.Sax. *faer*, fear, peril; Icel. *far*, harm, mischief; O.H.G. *fára*, danger, fright; Mod.G. *gefahr*, danger; from root of E. *fare*, to travel; seen also in L. *periculum*, danger (E. *peril*).] A painful emotion excited by an expectation of evil or the apprehension of impending danger; anxiety; solicitude; holy awe and reverence for God and his laws; respect; due regard, as for persons of authority or worth.—*v.t.* To feel fear or a painful apprehension of; to be afraid of; to suspect; to doubt; to reverence; to have a reverential awe of; to venerate; to affright or to terrify (*Shak.*)‡.—*v.i.* To be in fear; to be in apprehension of evil; to be afraid.—**fearer,** fē'rėr, *n.* One who fears.—**fearful,** fēr'fṳl, *a.* Affected by fear; apprehensive with solicitude; afraid; timorous; wanting courage; impressing fear; terrible; dreadful; awful.—**fearfully,** fēr'fṳl•li, *adv.* In a fearful manner.—**fearfulness,** fēr'fṳl•nes, *n.* The quality of being fearful.—**fearless,** fēr'les, *a.* Free from fear; bold; courageous; intrepid; undaunted.—**fearlessly,** fēr'les•li, *adv.* In a fearless manner.—**fearlessness,** fēr'les•nes, *n.* The state or quality of being fearless.—**fearsome,** fēr'sum, *a.* Alarming, terrible.

feasible, fē'zi•bl, *a.* [Fr. *faisible*, from *faire, faisant*, to do or make, L. *facere*, to do, to make. FACT.] Capable of being done, performed, executed, or effected; practicable.—**feasibility, feasibleness,** fē•zi•bil'i•ti, fē'zi•bl•nes, *n.* The quality of being feasible.—**feasibly,** fē'zi•bli, *adv.* In a feasible manner.

feast, fēst, *n.* [O.Fr. *feste* (Fr. *fête*), from L. *festum*, a holiday, a feast, from *festus*, solemn, festive.] A sumptuous repast or entertainment of which a number of guests partake; a banquet; a delicious meal; something particularly gratifying to the palate or the mind; a festival in commemoration of some great event, or in honor of some distinguished personage; a periodical or stated celebration of some event.—*v.i.* To take a meal of rich or sumptuous viands; to dine or sup on rich provisions; to be highly gratified or delighted.—*v.t.* To entertain with sumptuous food; to treat at the table magnificently; to pamper; to gratify luxuriously.—**feaster,** fēs′tėr, *n.* One who feasts.

feat, fēt, *n.* [Fr. *fait*, from L. *factum*, a deed, from *facio*, *factum*, to do. FACT.] An act; a deed; an exploit; in particular, any extraordinary act of strength, skill, or cunning.—*a.* [Fr. *fait*, made.] Neat; skillful; ingenious; deft. (*Shak.*)—**featly,** fēt′li, *adv.* Neatly; dexterously.

feather, feTH′ėr, *n.* [A.Sax. *fether*= D. *veder*, Sw. *fjäder*, Icel. *fjöthr*, G. *feder*; same root as L. *penna* (=*peina*), a feather: Skr. *pattra*, a wing, from root *pat*, to fly.] One of the growths which form the distinguishing covering of birds; a plume, consisting usually of a stem hollow at the lower part (called the quill), and having on each side of the upper part (called the shaft) the barbs, which with the shaft constitute the vane; something resembling a feather; a projection on the edge of a board which fits into a channel on the edge of another board.—*A feather in the cap*, an honor or mark of distinction.—*To be in high feather*, to appear in high spirits; to be elated.—*To show the white feather* to give indications of cowardice (a white feather in the tail of a fighting cock showed that it was not of the true game breed).—*v.t.* To dress in feathers; to fit with feathers; to cover with feathers.—*To feather one's nest*, to collect wealth, particularly from emoluments derived from agencies for others.—*To feather an oar*, to turn the blade horizontally, with the upper edge pointing aft as it leaves the water, to lessen the resistance of the air upon it.—**feathered,** feTH′ėrd, *a.* Clothed or covered with feathers; fitted or furnished with feathers; furnished with wings; winged.—**featheredge,** *n. Carp.* the thinner edge of a board or plank.—**feather-edged,** *a.* Having one edge thinner than the other and overlapping.—**featherless,** feTH′ėr•les, *a.* Destitute of feathers; unfledged.—**feathery,** feTH′ėr•i, *a.* Clothed or covered with feathers; resembling feathers in appearance, softness, or lightness.—**feather grass,** *n.* A wiry grass whose flowers are produced in loose panicles, which, when dried and colored, form ornaments for rooms.—**feather star,** *n.* A beautiful crinoid, consisting of a central body or disk, from which spring slender radiating arms, furnished on both sides with processes that give a feather-like appearance.—**featherweight,** *n.* A weight as light as a feather; the lightest weight that is placed on a race horse; a weight classification in boxing, wrestling, etc.

feature, fē′chėr, *n.* [O.Fr. *faiture*. *faicture* from L. *factura*, a making, from *facio*, *factum*, to make. FACT.] The make, form, or cast of any part of the face; any single lineament; the make or form of any part of the surface of a thing, as of a country or landscape; the prominent part of something.—*v.t.* To depict; to delineate the characteristics of; to be a distinctive mark of; to give prominence to.—**featureless,** fē′chėr•les, *a.*

febricula, fe•brik′ū•la, *n.* [L., dim. of *febris*, fever.] A slight fever.—**febrifacient,** feb′ri•fā′shi•ent, *a.* [L. *febris*, and *facio*, to make.] Causing fever.—**febriferous,** fe•brif′ėr•us, *a.* [L. *febris*, and *fero*, to bring.] Producing fever.—**febrifuge,** feb′ri•fūj, *n.* [L. *febris*, and *fugo*, to drive away.] Any medicine that mitigates or removes fever.—*a.* Having the quality of mitigating or subduing fever.—**febrile,** fē′bril, *a.* [L. *febrilis*.] Pertaining to fever; indicating fever, or derived from it.

February, feb′rụ•a•ri, *n.* [L. *februarius*, from *februa*, purification, because a great feast of purification was held on the 15th.] The second month in the year, consisting in common years of twenty-eight days, in leap-year of twenty-nine.

feces, fē′sēz, *n. pl.* [L. faeces.] Excrement; also, settlings; dregs; sediment.—**fecal,** fē′kal, *a.* Pertaining to feces.

feckless, fek′les, *a.* [Sc. for *effectless*.] Weak; impotent.

fecula, fek′ū•la, *n.* [L. *fæcula*, lees of wine, dim. of *fæx*, *fæcis*, dregs.] Powdery matter obtained from plants by crushing, washing with water, and subsidence; starch or farina.—**feculence,** fek′ū•lens, *n.* [L. *fæculentia*.] The quality or state of being feculent; sediment; dregs.—**feculent,** fek′ū•lent, *a.* [L. *fæculentus*.] Abounding with sediment, dregs, or impure and extraneous matter; dreggy; muddy; turbid; foul.

fecund, fē′kund, *a.* [L. *fecundus*, fruitful, from root *fe* (as in *fetus*), meaning to produce or bring forth.] Fruitful in children; prolific.—**fecundate,** fē′kun•dāt, *v.t.*—*fecundated*, *fecundating*. To make fruitful or prolific; to impregnate.—**fecundation,** fē•kun•dā′shon, *n.* The act of fecundating.—**fecundity,** fē•kun′di•ti, *n.* [L. *fæcunditas*.] The state or quality of being fecund or of bringing forth young abundantly; fertility; richness of invention.

fed, fed, pret. & pp. of *feed*.

federal, fed′ėr•al, *a.* [Fr. *fédéral*, from L. *foedus*, *foederis*, a league, seen also in *confederate*.] Pertaining to a league or contract, particularly between states, as the *federal* government of the United States is located in Washington, D.C.; united in a federation; founded on alliance between several states which unite for national or general purposes, each state retaining control of its home affairs, civil and criminal law, etc. of or relating to the central government of a federation; *hist.* applied to an early American political party advocating strong federal government.—*n.* [cap.] A supporter of the United States government during the Civil War; a soldier of the northern army during the Civil War.—**federalism,** fed′ėr•al•izm, *n.* The principles of federal government; the upholding and strengthening of the central government in a federal republic.—**federalist,** fed′ėr•al•ist, *n.* One who upholds federalism; a member or supporter of the Federal party.—**federalize,** fed′ėr•al•īz, *v.t.* or *v.i.*—*federalized*, *federalizing*. To unite in a federal compact.—**federate,** fed′ėr•āt, *a.* Leagued; united by compact, as states or nations.—**federation,** fed′ėr•ā″shon, *n.* The act of uniting in a league; a federal government; a league.

fedora, fa•dō′ra, *n.* [From *Fédora*, drama by V. Sardou.] A soft felt hat with the crown creased lengthwise.

fee, fē, *n.* [A.Sax. *feoh*, *feó*, cattle, property, money=D. *vee*, Icel. *fé*, G. *vieh*, cattle; Goth. *faihu*, goods, money—allied to L. *pecus*, cattle (whence *pecuniary*). *Fief* is really the same word.] A reward or compensation for services; recompense: applied particularly to the reward of professional services; a fief or piece of land held of a superior on certain conditions; a feud; *law*, a freehold estate liable to alienation at the pleasure of the proprietor, who is absolute owner of the soil; hence, absolute property, possession, or ownership; an inherited or heritable estate.—*v.t.*—*feed*, *feeing*. To give a fee to; to reward; to hire; to bribe.—**fee simple,** *n.* An estate in lands or tenements liable to alienation at the will of the owner: also called a *fee*.—**fee tail,** *n.* An estate limited to a man and the heirs of his body, or to himself and particular heirs of his body.

feeble, fē′bl, *a.* [Fr. *faible*, O.Fr. *fleble*, *floible*, *foible*, It. *flevole*, from L. *flebilis*, lamentable, from *fleo*, to weep.] Destitute of physical strength; infirm; debilitated; weak; wanting force, vigor, vividness, or energy.—**feebleness,** fē′bl•nes, *n.* The quality or condition of being feeble.—**feebly,** fē′bli, *adv.* In a feeble manner.—**feeble-minded,** *a.* Weak in mind; wanting firmness or constancy; irresolute.—**feeble-mindedness,** *n.*

feed, fēd, *v.t.*—pret. & pp. *fed*. [A.Sax. *fédan*, to feed, from *fóda*, food. FOOD.] To give food to; to supply with nourishment; *fig.* to entertain, indulge, delight (to *feed* one's self with hopes); to furnish with anything of which there is constant consumption, waste, use, or application for some purpose (to *feed* a lake, a fire); to supply.—*v.i.* To take food; to eat; to subsist by eating; to pasture; to graze; to satisfy a longing or craving.—*n.* That which is eaten; food; fodder; an allowance of provender given to a horse, cow, etc.; the material supplied at once to a machine or other contrivance to make it act.—**feeder,** fē′dėr, *n.* One who feeds; one who eats; that which supplies something.—**feedback,** fēd″bak′, *n. Elect.* a system in which part of the output of electric oscillation is returned and added to the input.—**feeding,** fē′-ding, *n.* Food; that which furnishes food, especially for animals.

feel, fēl, *v.t.*—*felt, feeling.* [A.Sax. *félan,* D. *voelen,* G. *fühlen,* to feel; root and connections doubtful.] To perceive by the touch; to have sensation excited by contact with the body or limbs; to have a sense of; to be affected by; to be sensitive of (pain, pleasure, disgrace); to experience; to suffer; to examine by touching.—*v.i.* To have perception by the touch, or by the contact of any substance with the body; to have the sensibility or the passions moved or excited; to produce an impression on the nerves of sensation (iron *feels* cold); to perceive one's self to be (to *feel* sick or well); to know certainly or without misgiving.—*n.* The act of feeling; sensation or impression on being touched.—**feeler,** fē′lėr, *n.* One who feels; an organ of touch in insects and others of the lower animals, as antennae, palpi, etc.; any device for the purpose of ascertaining the designs, opinions, or sentiments of others.—**feeling,** fē′ling, *a.* Expressive of great sensibility; affecting; tending to excite the passions; possessing great sensibility; easily affected or moved.—*n.* The sense of touch; the sense by which we perceive external objects which come in contact with the body, and obtain ideas of their tangible qualities; the sensation conveyed by the sense of touch; physical sensation not due to sight, hearing, taste, or smell (a *feeling* of warmth, pain, or drowsiness); mental sensation or emotion; mental state or disposition; mental perception; consciousness; conviction; tenderness of heart; nice sensibility; the quality of exciting or expressing emotion; *pl.* the emotional part of our nature; sensitiveness; susceptibility.—**feelingly,** fē′-ling•li, *adv.* In a feeling manner; tenderly; acutely; keenly.

feet, fēt, *n.* pl. of *foot.*

feign, fān, *v.t.* [Fr. *feindre,* from L. *fingere,* to shape, invent, feign, from root seen also in *figment, figure, fiction, faint,* etc.] To invent or imagine; to make a show of; to pretend; to assume a false appearance of; to counterfeit.—*v.i.* To represent falsely; to pretend.—**feigned,** fānd, *p.* and *a.* Devised; assumed; simulated; counterfeit.—**feint,** fānt, *n.* [Fr. *feinte,* from *feindre.*] A pretense; a mock attack; an appearance of aiming or thrusting at one part when another is intended to be struck.—*v.i.* To make a feint or mock attack.

feldspar, feld′spär, *n.* [G. *feldspath*—*feld,* field, and *spath,* spar.] A mineral, widely distributed, and usually of a foliated structure, consisting of silica and alumina, with potash, soda, or lime; it is a principal constituent in granite, gneiss, porphyry, etc. Called also *felspar, feldspath.*—**feldspathic, feldspathose,** feld•spath′ik, feld′spath•ōs, *a.* Pertaining to feldspar or containing it: written also *felspathic, felspathose.*

felicitate, fe•lis′i•tāt, *v.t.*—*felicitated, felicitating.* [Fr. *féliciter;* L.L. *felicito,* from L. *felix, felicis,* happy.] To congratulate; to express joy or pleasure to another at his good fortune; *refl.* to congratulate one's self.—**felicitation,** fe-lis′i•tā″shun, *n.* The act of felicitating; expression of joy at another's good fortune.—**felicitous,** fe•lis′i•tus, *a.* Happy; extremely appropriate, suitable, or well expressed; managed with extreme skill and success.—**felicitously,** fe•lis′i•tus•li, *adv.* In a felicitous manner.—**felicitousness,** fe•lis′i•tus•nes, *n.* The state of being felicitous.—**felicity,** fe•lis′i•ti, *n.* [L. *felicitas,* from *felix,* happy.] The state of being happy or in extreme enjoyment; happiness; bliss; blissfulness; blessing; source of happiness; skillfulness; a skillful or happy turn; appropriateness.

feline, fē′līn, *a.* [L. *felinus,* from *felis,* a cat.] Pertaining to cats or to their species; like a cat; belonging to the family Felidae.

fell, fel, pret. of *fall.*

fell, fel, *a.* [A.Sax. *fell,* D. *fel,* O.Fr. *fel, felle,* sharp, fierce, cruel, a word perhaps of Celtic origin.] Cruel; barbarous; inhuman; fierce; savage; rancorous; bloody.—**fellness,** fel′nes, *n.* The state or quality of being fell; cruelty; ruthlessness.

fell, fel, *n.* [A.Sax. *fell*=Icel. *fell,* G. *fell,* D. *vel,* Goth. *fill,* skin. Cog. L. *pellis,* skin.] A skin or hide of an animal; a seam or hem sewed down level with the cloth.—*v.t.* To lay a seam or hem and sew it down level with the cloth.—**fellmonger,** fel′-mung•gėr, *n.* One who deals in fells or hides.

fell, fel, *v.t.* [A.Sax. *fellan,* from *feallan,* to fall; causative form of *fall.* Comp. *sit, set; lie, lay; rise, raise;* etc.] To cause to fall; to bring to the ground, either by cutting or by striking; to hew down; to knock down.—**feller,** fel′ėr, *n.* One who fells or knocks or hews down.

fellah, fel′la, *n.* [Ar., a peasant; pl. *fellahin.*] An Egyptian peasant or agricultural laborer.

felloe, fel′ō. See FELLY.

fellow, fel′ō, *n.* [Icel. *félagi,* a partner, a sharer in goods, from *félag,* a community of goods (lit. a *fee-laying*), from *fé,* money, *fee,* and *lag,* partnership, a laying.] A companion; an associate; one of the same kind; an equal in rank, endowments, character, qualifications, etc.; a peer; a compeer; one of a pair, or of two things used together and suited to each other; an appellation of contempt for a man without good breeding or worth; an ignoble man; also, familiar for person, individual; in some universities and colleges, a member of the corporation or governing body; also a graduate appointed to a fellowship; a member of any incorporated society (as of the American College of Surgeons). [Used in composition to denote community in nature, station, or employment; mutual association on equal or friendly terms: as, *fellow*-citizen, *fellow*-laborer; bed-*fellow,* school-*fellow.*]—**fellowship,** fel′ō•-ship, *n.* The condition of being a fellow or associate; mutual association on equal and friendly terms; companionship; partnership; joint interest; an association of persons having the same tastes, occupations, or interests; a brotherhood; a foundation for the maintenance, under certain requirements, of a scholar called a fellow.—**fellow feeling,** *n.* Sympathy; a like feeling.

felly, fel′i, *n.* [A.Sax. *felg, felge*=Dan. *fælge,* D. *velg,* G. *felge,* a felly.] One of the curved pieces of wood which, joined together, form the circumference or circular rim of a wheel; the circular rim of a wheel. Written also *felloe.*

felon, fel′on, *n.* [Fr. *félon,* a traitor, from L.L. *felo,* a felon; origin doubtful.] A person who has committed felony; a person guilty of heinous crimes; a criminal; a malefactor; a whitlow.—*a.* Malignant; fierce; traitorous; disloyal.—**felonious,** fe•-lō′ni•us, *a.* Villainous; traitorous; perfidious; *law,* done with the deliberate purpose to commit a crime.—**feloniously,** fe•lō′ni•us•li, *adv.* In a felonious manner.—**feloniousness,** fe•lō′ni•us•nes, *n.* The quality of being felonious.—**felony,** fel′o•ni, *n.* A serious crime, such as murder, burglary, etc., punishable by death or more than a year's imprisonment.

felsite, fel′sīt, *n.* [From the *fels* of feldspar (q.v.).] An eruptive rock, made up of quartz and orthoclase feldspar, and very hard.—**felsitic,** fel•sit′ik, *a.* Pertaining to or containing felsite.

felspar. See FELDSPAR.

felt, felt, pret. & pp. of *feel.*

felt, felt, *n.* [A.Sax. *felt*=D. *vilt,* G. *filz,* felt; allied to Gr. *pilos,* wool wrought into felt, and to L. *pileus,* a felt hat or cap. Akin *filter.*] A cloth or stuff made of wool, or wool and hair or fur, matted or wrought into a compact substance by rolling, beating, and pressure; a hat made of wool felted.—*v.t.* To make into felt; to cover with felt.—**felting,** fel′ting, *n.* The process by which felt is made; the materials of which felt is made, or the felt itself.

felucca, fe•luk′a, *n.* [It. *felucca, feluca,* from Ar. *felûkah,* from *fulk,* a ship.] A long, narrow vessel, once common in the Mediterranean, with two large lateen sails, and capable of being propelled by oars.

female, fē′māl, *n.* [Fr. *femelle,* L. *femella,* a young girl, from *femina,* a woman.] An animal of that sex which conceives and brings forth young; that plant which produces fruit; the flower that bears the pistil and receives the pollen of the male flowers.—*a.* Belonging to the sex which produces young; feminine; delicate; weak; *bot.* pistil-bearing; producing pistillate flowers.—*Female rhymes,* double rhymes, such as *motion, notion,* the second syllable being unstressed.—*Female screw,* a concave screw, corresponding to the convex or male screw which works in it.—**feminine,** fem′in•in, *a.* [L. *femininus*, feminine, from *femina*, a woman.] Pertaining to a woman or to women, or to the female sex; having the qualities belonging to a woman; womanly; effeminate; womanish; *gram.* denoting the gender of words which signify females, or the terminations of such words.—**femininely,** fem′in•in•li, *adv.* In a feminine manner.—**feminineness, femininity,** fem′in•in•nes, fem•in•in′i•ti, *n.* The quality of being feminine.

femoral, fem′o•ral, *a.* [L. *femoralis*, from *femur*, the thigh.] Belonging to the thigh.—**femur,** fē′mėr, *n.* [L.] The first bone of the leg or pelvic extremity; the thighbone.

fen, fen, *n.* [A.Sax. *fen*, *fenn*, marsh, mud, dirt; D. *veen*, G. *fenne*, Icel. *fen*, fen, peatbog, Goth. *fani*, mud, clay.] Low land covered wholly or partially with water, but producing sedge, coarse grasses, or other plants; boggy land; a marsh.—**fenny,** fen′i, *a.* Having the character of a fen; marshy; boggy; inhabiting or growing in fens.

fence, fens, *n.* [Abbrev. from *defence.*] A wall, hedge, bank, railing, or paling forming a boundary to or enclosing some area; that which defends; defense; the art of fencing; skill in fencing or swordsmanship; hence, skill in argument and repartee; receiver of, or place for receiving, stolen goods.—*v.t.*—*fenced, fencing.* To enclose with a fence; to secure by an enclosure; to guard; to hedge in; to ward off or parry by argument or reasoning.—*v.i.* To use a sword or foil for the purpose of learning the art of attack and defense; to practice fencing; to fight and defend by giving and avoiding blows or thrusts; to parry arguments; to equivocate; to prevaricate.—**fenced,** fenst, *p.* and *a.* Enclosed with a fence; guarded; fortified.—**fenceless,** fens′les, *a.* Without a fence; unenclosed; open.—**fencer,** fen′sėr, *n.* One who fences; one who teaches or practices the art of fencing with sword or foil.—**fencible,** fen′si•bl, *n.* A soldier for defense of the country against invasion, and not liable to serve abroad.—**fencing,** fen′sing, *n.* The art of using skillfully a sword or foil in attack or defense; material used in making fences; that which fences; a protection put round a dangerous piece of machinery.

fend, fend, *v.t.* [Contr. from *defend*, from *de*, and obs. L. *fendo*, to thrust, to strike; seen also in *offendo*, to offend.] To keep off; to ward off; to shut out: usually followed by *off* (to *fend off* blows).—**fender,** fen′dėr, *n.* One who or that which fends or wards off; a low metal screen in front of a fireplace to stop falling coals; the stamped, metal part covering the wheels of an automobile; a piece of timber, foam plastic, etc., hung from the side of a boat for protection in docking.

fenestra, fe•nes′tra, *n.* [L.] A window; an aperture; a foramen.—**fenestral,** fe•nes′tral, *a.* [L. *fenestralis*, from *fenestra*, a window.] Pertaining to a window.—**fenestrate,** fe•nes′trāt, *a.* Having windows or openings; *bot.* applied to leaves in which the cellular tissue does not completely fill up the interstices between the veins, thus leaving openings.—**fenestration,** fen•es•trā′shon, *n.* The series or arrangement of windows in a building.

Fenian, fē′ni•an, *n.* [A name assumed from Ir. *Fionna*, a race of superhuman heroes in Irish legendary history.] A person belonging to a secret society having for its principal object the erection of Ireland into an independent republic.—*a.* Of or belonging to the Fenians.—**Fenianism,** fē′ni•an•izm, *n.* The principles or politics of the Fenians.

fennec, fen′ek, *n.* [Moorish name.] A North African animal allied to the fox.

fennel, fen′el, *n.* [A.Sax. *finol*, *finugl*, like G. *fenchel*, borrowed from the L. *fœniculum*, fennel, dim. from *fœnum*, hay.] A fragrant, umbelliferous, perennial, cultivated plant, having seeds which are carminative, and frequently employed in medicine, and leaves that are used in sauces.

fenugreek, fen′ū•grēk, *n.* [L. *fœnum græcum*, Greek hay.] A leguminous annual plant resembling clover, and whose bitter and mucilaginous seeds are used in veterinary practice.

feod, feodal, feodary, fūd, fū′dal, fū′da•ri. Same as *Feud*, etc.

feoff, fef, *n.* [A form of *fief.*] A fief or fee.—**feoffee,** fef′fē, *n.* A person who is invested with land in fee.—**feoffer, feoffor,** fef′ėr, *n.* One who enfeoffs or grants a fee.—**feoffment,** fef′ment, *n.* The legal gift or transference to a person of a fee or freehold estate; the instrument or deed by which such property is conveyed.

feracious,† fe•rā′shus, *a.* [L. *ferax*, *feracis*, from *fero*, to bear.] Fruitful; producing abundantly.

feral, fē′ral, *a.* [L. *fera*, a wild beast.] Relating to, or having the nature of, a wild beast; uncultivated; undomesticated; barbarous; wild.

fer-de-lance, fâr•de•läns′, *n.* [Fr., iron of a lance, lance-head.] The lance-headed viper, a very venomous serpent of tropical America.

feretory, fer′e•to•ri, *n.* [From L. *feretrum*, a bier or litter, from *fero*, to bear.] A shrine or repository for the relics of saints, variously adorned, and usually in the shape of a chest, with a roof-like top.

ferial, fē′ri•al, *a.* [L. *ferialis*, from *feriæ*, holidays.] Pertaining to holidays or days in which business is not transacted.

ferine, fē′rīn, *a.* [L. *ferinus*, from *fera*, a wild beast.] Relating to or resembling a wild beast; wild; untamed; savage.

Feringee, Feringhee, fe•ring′gē, *n.* [Probably a corruption of *Frank.*] The name given to Europeans by the Hindus.

ferment, fėr′ment, *n.* [L. *fermentum*, for *fervimentum*, from *fervo* or *ferveo*, to boil, to foam. FERVENT.] Any substance, as a yeast, whose presence in another body produces the peculiar effervescence and decomposition called fermentation; commotion; heat; tumult; agitation (as of a crowd, of the feelings, etc.).—*v.t.* (fėr•ment′). To cause fermentation in; to set in brisk motion or agitation; to warm; to excite.—*v.i.* To undergo fermentation; to work; to be in agitation or excited, as by violent emotions.—**fermentable,** fėr•men′ta•bl, *a.* Capable of fermentation.—**fermentation,** fėr•men•tā′shon, *n.* The act or process of fermenting; the decomposition or conversion of an organic substance into new compounds in presence of a ferment, generally indicated by a sensible internal motion, the development of heat, and the liberation of bubbles of gas; in common language, the process by which grape juice is converted into wine, and the wort of malt into beer; *fig.* the state of being in high activity or commotion; agitation; excitement.—**fermentative,** fėr•men′ta•tiv, *a.* Causing fermentation; consisting in or produced by fermentation.

fermium, fėr′mi•um, *n.* [After Enrico *Fermi*, American physicist.] A radioactive element. Symbol, Fm; at. no., 100.

fern, fėrn, *n.* [A.Sax. *fearn*=G. *farn*, *farren*, D. *varen*—fern; allied to Skr. *parna*, a wing or feather.] The name of many pteridophytes, consisting of herbaceous, shrubby, or arborescent plants, producing leaves called fronds, which are simple or more or less divided, and bear on their under surface or edge the capsules containing the minute spores.—**fernery,** fėr′nėr•i, *n.* A place where ferns are artificially grown —**fern seed,** *n.* The seed, or more correctly the spores, of fern, supposed to render the bearer invisible.—*To walk by fern seed*, to steal.—**ferny,** fėr′ni, *a.* Abounding or overgrown with fern.

ferocious, fe•rō′shus, *a.* [Fr. *féroce*; L. *ferox*, *ferocis*, fierce, allied to *ferus*, wild. FIERCE.] Fierce; savage; barbarous; ravenous; rapacious; indicating, or expressive of, ferocity.—**ferociously,** fe•rō′shus•li, *adv.* Fiercely; with savage cruelty.—**ferociousness,** fe•rō′shus•nes, *n.* State or quality of being ferocious; ferocity.—**ferocity,** fe•ros′i•ti, *n.* [Fr. *férocité*, L. *ferocitas.*] State of being ferocious; savage wildness or fierceness; fury; cruelty.

ferret, fer′et, *n.* [Fr. *furet*, It. *furetto*, a ferret, from L. *fur*, a thief.] A domesticated variety of the polecat, usually of a pale yellow color, with red eyes—used to drive rabbits out of their holes and to kill rats.—*v.t.* To hunt with ferrets; to drive out of a lurking place; (with *out*) to search out by perseverance and cunning.—**ferreter,** fer′e•tėr, *n.* One who ferrets.

ferret, fer'et, *n.* [Older *foret*, from It. *fioretti*, floss silk, from L. *flos*, *floris*, flower.] A kind of narrow tape, made of woolen thread, sometimes of cotton or silk.

Ferris wheel, fêr'is•hwēl, *n.* [G.W.G. *Ferris*, Amer. engineer and inventor.] A large, vertical, power-driven wheel used in amusement parks, having seats that remain in an upright position as it turns.

ferrite, fer'rīt, *n.* [L. *ferrum*, iron.] Layers of pure iron seen in sections of steel.

ferro-, [From L. *ferrum*, iron.] A prefix in various words naming substances that contain iron or form compounds with this metal.—**ferroconcrete,** fer•rō•kon'krēt, *n.* Reinforced concrete.—**ferromanganese,** fer'rō•mang"ga•nēz, *n.* An alloy of iron and manganese. See FERROUS.

ferrous, fer'us, *a.* [L. *ferrum*, iron.] Pertaining to, obtained from, or containing iron.—**ferric,** fer'ik, *a. Chem.* pertaining to or extracted from iron (*ferric* acid and *ferric* oxide).—**ferriferous,** fe•rif'ėr•us, *a.* [L. *ferrum*, and *fero*, to produce.] Producing or yielding iron.—**ferrocyanic,** fer'ō•sī•an"ik, *a.* Pertaining to or derived from iron and cyanogen.—**ferrotype,** fer'ō•tīp, *n. Photog.* a term applied to some photographic processes in which the salts of iron are the principal agents; a photograph taken on japanned sheet iron by a collodion process.—**ferruginous, ferrugineous,** † fe•rūj'i•nus, fe•rū•jin'i•us, *a.* [L. *ferrugineus*, rusty, from *ferrugo*, *ferruginis*, iron rust, from *ferrum*, iron.] Partaking of iron; irony; of the color of the rust or oxide of iron.

ferrule, fer'ūl, *n.* [Formerly *verril*, from Fr. *virole*, ferrule, from *virer*, to veer. VEER.] A ring of metal put round the end of a walking stick or other thing to strengthen it or prevent its splitting; a small cap or bushing placed in a joint to make it tight (as between pipes).

ferry, fer'i, *v.t.*—*ferried, ferrying.* [A.Sax. *ferian*, *farian*, to carry, to convey, causative of *faran*, to go. FARE.] To carry or transport over a river, strait, etc., in a boat or other conveyance.—*v.i.* To pass over a ferry.—*n.* The place or passage where boats pass over a narrow piece of water to convey passengers; the boat itself.—**ferryboat,** *n.* A boat that plies at a ferry.—**ferryman,** *n.* One who keeps a ferry.—**ferriage,** fer'i•ij, *n.* The price or fare to be paid at a ferry.

fertile, fėr'tīl or fėr'til, *a.* [Fr. *fertile*, from L. *fertilis*, from *fero*, to bear, to produce; same root as E. *bear* (BEAR); seen also in *confer*, *differ*, *refer*, etc.] Fruitful; producing fruit or crops in abundance; the opposite of barren; prolific or productive of anything, as of ideas, poetry, etc.; inventive; able to produce abundantly; *bot.* capable of producing fruit; fruit-bearing.—**fertilely,** fėr'til•li, *adv.* In a fertile manner; fruitfully.—**fertileness,** fėr'til•nes, *n.* Fertility.—**fertility,** fėr•til'i•ti, *n.* [L. *fertilitas*.] The state of being fertile or fruitful; fruitfulness; fecundity; productiveness; richness; fertile invention.—**fertilization,** fėr'til•i•zā"shon, *n.* The act or process of rendering fertile; the act of impregnation, insemination, pollination, etc., whereby the union of two germ cells initiates the formation of a new individual; the application of fertilizer.—**fertilize,** fėr'ti•līz, *v.t.*—*fertilized, fertilizing.* To make fertile or productive.—**fertilizer,** fėr'ti•lī•zėr, *n.* One who fertilizes; a chemical or organic compound used to enrich the soil.

ferula, fer'ū•la, *n.* [L.] A ferula, a genus of plants, members of which yield asafetida, galbanum, etc.

ferule, fer'ūl, *n.* [L. *ferula*, a twig, a cane, a switch, from *ferio*, to strike.] A flat piece of wood used to punish children by striking them on the palm of the hand; a cane or rod for the same purpose.—*v.t.*—*feruled, feruling.* To punish with a ferule.

fervent, fėr'vent, *a.* [L. *fervens*, *ferventis*, ppr. of *ferveo*, to boil, to ferment; akin *ferment*.] Hot; glowing; intensely warm; hot in temper; vehement; ardent; earnest; excited; animated; glowing with religious feeling; zealous.—**fervently,** fėr'vent•li, *adv.* In a fervent manner or degree; earnestly; ardently; vehemently.—**fervency,** fėr'ven•si, *n.* The state of being fervent; heat of mind; ardor; animated zeal; warmth of devotion.—**fervid,** fėr'vid, *a.* [L. *fervidus*, from *ferveo*.] Very hot; burning; glowing; fervent; very warm in zeal; vehement; ardent.—**fervidly,** fėr'vid•li, *adv.* Very hotly; with glowing warmth.—**fervidness,** fėr'vid•nes, *n.* Glowing heat; ardor.—**fervor,** fėr'vėr, *n.* [L. *fervor*, heat.] Heat or warmth; intensity of feeling; ardor; burning zeal; extreme earnestness in religion, particularly in prayer.

Fescennine, fes'en•īn, *a.* [From *Fescennia*, town in Etruria.] Sportive, ribald, licentious.

fescue, fes'kū, *n.* [O.E. *festue*, from O.Fr. *festu* (Fr. *fetu*), a straw; L. *festuca*, a shoot or twig.] A straw, wire, pin, or the like, used to point out letters to children; a kind of grass, some species being excellent meadow and pasture grasses.

fesse, fes, *n.* [O.Fr. *fesse*, Fr. *fasce*, L. *fascia*, a band.] *Her.* a band or girdle comprising the center third part of the escutcheon, which it crosses horizontally.

festal, fes'tal, *a.* [From L. *festum*, a feast. FEAST.] Pertaining to a feast; festive.—**festally,** fes'tal•li, *adv.* Joyfully; mirthfully.—**festival,** fes'ti•val, *a.* [L. *festivus*.] Pertaining to or befitting a feast; joyous; mirthful.—*n.* A time of feasting; an anniversary day of joy, civil or religious; a festive celebration.—**festive,** fes'tiv, *a.* [L. *festivus*.] Pertaining to or becoming a feast; joyous; gay; mirthful.—**festively,** fes'tiv•li, *adv.* In a festive manner.—**festivity,** fes•tiv'i•ti, *n.* [L. *festivitas*.] The condition of being festive; social joy or exhilaration at an entertainment; something forming part of a festal celebration.

fester, fes'tėr, *v.i.* [O.Fr. *festrir*, to fester.] To suppurate; to discharge or become full of pus or purulent matter; to rankle (passions, a sense of wrong, etc.).—*n.* Act of festering or rankling.

festinate,‡ fes'ti•nat, *a.* [L. *festino*, *festinatum*, to hasten] Hasty; hurried. (*Shak.*)

festoon, fes•tön', *n.* [Fr. *feston*, lit. a festal garland; It. *festone*, from L. *festum*, a feast.] A string, chain, or garland of flowers, foliage, etc., suspended so as to form one or more depending curves; *arch.* a sculptured ornament in imitation of this.—*v.t.* To adorn with festoons; to connect by festoons.

fetal, *a.* **fetation,** *n.* See FETUS.

fetch, fech, *v.t.* [A.Sax. *feccan*, *gefeccan*, to fetch, to draw, to take, to seek; akin to O.Fris, *faka*, to prepare.] To go and bring; to bring; to bear toward the person speaking; to recall or bring back; to make or perform, with certain objects (to *fetch* a blow or stroke, to *fetch* a sigh); to bring or obtain as its price. —*To fetch out*, to bring or draw out.—*To fetch to*, to restore; to revive, as from a swoon; to bring up; to stop suddenly in any course; to overtake.—*v.i.* To bring things; to move or turn.—*To fetch and carry*, to perform menial services; to become a servile drudge.—*n.* A stratagem by which a thing is indirectly brought to pass; a trick; an artifice; the apparition of a living person; a wraith.—**fetcher,** fech'ėr, *n.* One who fetches.

fête, fāt, *n.* [Fr., from L. *festum*, a feast.] A feast; a holiday; a festival day.—*v.t.*—*fêted, fêting.* To entertain with a feast; to honor with a festive entertainment.

feticide, foeticide, fē'ti•sīd, *n.* See FETUS.

fetid, fe'tid, *a.* [L. *fœtidus*, from *fœteo*, to stink.] Having an offensive smell; having a strong or rancid scent.—**fetidness,** fe'tid•nes, *n.* The quality of smelling offensively.—**fetor,** fē'tėr, *n.* [L. *fœtor*.] Any strong offensive smell; stench.

fetish, fē'tish, *n.* [Fr. *fétiche*, Pg. *feitiço*, sorcery, witchcraft, from L. *factitius*, artificial, from *facio*, to make. FACT.] Any object, animate or inanimate, natural or artificial, regarded by some uncivilized races with a feeling of awe, as having mysterious powers residing in it or as being the representative or habitation of a deity; hence, any object of exclusive devotion.—**fetishism,** fē'tish•izm, *n.* The worship of fetishes; emotional attachment to inanimate objects.—**fetishistic,** fē•tish•is'tik, *a.*

fetlock, fet'lok, *n.* [From *foot* or *feet* and *lock*.] A tuft of hair growing behind the pastern joint of horses; the joint on which the hair grows; an instrument fixed on the leg of a horse when put to pasture for the purpose of preventing him from running off.

fetor. See FETID.

fetter, fet′ėr, *n.* [A.Sax. *feter, fetor,* a fetter; O.G. *fezzera,* G. *fessel,* Icel. *fjöturr.* Probably connected with *foot.*] A chain for the feet; a chain by which a person or animal is confined by the foot; anything that confines or restrains from motion; a restraint.—*v.t.* To put fetters on; to bind; to confine; to restrain.

fettle, fet′l, *v.t.* [M. E. *fettlen,* to gird, fit, set in order.] To trim, put in order. *n.* Condition, state.

fetus, fē′tus, *n.* [L., from a root *fe,* implying fruitfulness, productiveness, as in *fecund.*] The young of viviparous animals in the womb, and of oviparous animals in the egg, after it is perfectly formed; before which time it is called *Embryo.*—**fetal,** fē′tal, *a.* Pertaining to a fetus. —**fetation,** fē•tā′shon, *n.* The formation of a fetus.—**feticide,** fē′ti•sīd, *n.* [L. *fetus,* and *cædo,* to kill.] The destruction of the fetus in the womb; the act by which criminal abortion is produced.

feud, fūd, *n.* [L.L. *feudum,* a fief; from O.Fr. or O.G., like *fief, feu, fee.*] A fief.—**feudal,** fū′dal, *a.* [L.L. *feudalis,* from *feudum.*] Pertaining to feuds or fiefs; founded upon or pertaining to the system of holding lands by military services.—*Feudal system,* a system according to which grants of land were made by the sovereign to the nobles, and by them to an inferior class, on the condition that the possessor should take an oath of fealty, and do military service.—**feudalism,** fū′dal•izm, *n.* An agricultural political organization developed in Europe during the early medieval period, with vestiges remaining up to 1917 characterized by complete subservience of vassal to lord, and under which all lands owned by the lords were held in fief to the vassals who worked the land. —**feudalization,** fū′dal•i•zā″shon, *n.* The act of feudalizing.—**feudalize,** fū′dal•īz, *v.t.*—*feudalized, feudalizing.* To reduce to a feudal tenure; to conform to feudalism.—**feudally,** fū′dal•li, *adv.* In a feudal manner; by feudal tenure.—**feudary,** fū′da•ri, *a.* Held by or pertaining to feudal tenure.—*n.* A tenant who holds his lands by feudal service; a feudatory. —**feudatory,** fū′da•to•ri, *a.* Holding from another by feudal tenure.—*n.* A tenant or vassal holding his lands on condition of military service; the tenant of a feud or fief.

feud, fūd, *n.* [O.E. *feide,* from A.Sax. *faehth,* hostility, from *fáh,* hostile (whence *foe*); D. *veede,* G. *fehde,* Dan. *fejde,* a feud; the spelling being modified through confusion with L.L. *feudum,* a feud or fief. Akin *fiend.*] A contention or quarrel; hostility; often, hostility or declared warfare between families or parties in a state.

fever, fē′vėr, *n.* [A.Sax. *fefer,* from L. *febris,* a fever; or from O.Fr. *fevre,* Mod. Fr. *fièvre,* of same origin.] An increase in body temperature above the normal; any disease accompanied by an increase in temperature, diminished strength, and often with excessive thirst; agitation or excitement by anything that strongly affects the passions.—*v.t.* To put in a fever.—*v.i.* To be seized with fever.—**feverish,** fē′vėr•ish, *a.* Having fever; affected with fever, especially with a slight degree of fever; indicating or pertaining to fever.—**feverishly,** fē′vėr•ish•li, *adv.* In a feverish manner.—**feverishness,** fē′vėr•ish•nes, *n.* The state of being feverish; anxious, heated excitement.—**feverous,** fē′vėr•us, *a.* Affected with fever or ague; feverish.—**feverously,**† fē′vėr•us•li, *adv.* In a feverous manner.—**feverfew,** fē′vėr•fū, *n.* [A.Sax. *feferfuge,* from L. *febrifugia,* from *febris,* fever, and *fugo,* to drive away.] A European composite plant with much-divided leaves, and white flowers; once supposed to be a valuable febrifuge, hence the name.

few, fū, *a.* [A.Sax. *feáwa, feáwe,* Dan. *faa,* Goth. *favs,* pl. *favai,* little, few; of cognate origin with L. *paucus,* few, *paulus,* Gr. *pauros,* little.] Not many; small in number: used frequently, by ellipsis of a noun, for not many persons or things. *A few* is often used and generally means more than *few* alone.—**fewness,** fū′nes, *n.* The state of being few; paucity.

fey, fā; *a.* [A.Sax. *fæge,* Icel. *feigr,* near to death.] On the verge of a sudden or violent death; fated soon to die, and often showing this in some peculiar way.

fez, fez, *n.* [From *Fez,* the principal town in Morocco, where such caps are largely manufactured.] A red cap of fine cloth, fitting closely to the head, with a tassel of blue silk or wool at the crown, once worn in Turkey, on the shores of the Levant, in Egypt, and North Africa generally.

fiacre, fi•ä′kr, *n.* [Fr., from the Hotel St. *Fiacre,* where the inventor of these carriages established in 1640 an office for the hire of them.] A small four-wheeled carriage; a hackney, coach or similar vehicle plying for hire.—*v.* To convey pilgrims and others to the shrine of the Irish saint Fiachra.

fiancé, fiancée, fē•än•sā′, *n. masc.* and *fem.* [Fr.] An affianced or betrothed person.

fiasco, fi•as′kō, *n.* [It. *fiasco,* a flask or bottle, a cry in Italy when a singer fails to please, perhaps in allusion to the bursting of a bottle.] A failure in a musical performance; an ignominious and notorious failure generally; a conspicuous or chagrining frustration; a breakdown.

fiat, fī′at, *n.* [L. let it be done, 3rd pers. sing. subj. of *fio,* to be done.] A command to do something; a decisive or effective command.—**fiat money,** *n.* Paper currency issued by a government as money, which does not represent coin or bullion, but is made legal tender by law.—*Fiat in Bankruptcy,* an order in chancery allowing the institution of proceedings in bankruptcy.

fib, fib, *n.* [Probably an abbreviation and corruption from *fable.*] A lie or falsehood: a word used as a softer expression than lie.—*v.i. fibbed, fibbing.* To lie; to speak falsely.—**fibber, fibster,** fib′ėr, fib′stėr, *n.* One who tells lies or fibs.

fiber, fibre, fī′bėr, *n.* [Fr. *fibre,* L. *fibra,* allied to *filum,* a thread.] A thread or filament; one of the fine slender threadlike or hairlike bodies of which the tissues of animals and plants are partly constituted; the small slender root of a plant.—**fiber glass,** *n.* Fibrous glass that is used in woven or molded products.—**fibriform,** fī′bri•form, *a.* Like a fiber or fibers.—**fibril,** fī′bril, *n.* [Fr. *fibrille.*] A small fiber; the branch of a fiber; a very slender thread.—**fibrilla,** fī•bril′la, *n.* pl. **fibrillae,** fī•bril′lē. [Dim. of L. *fibra.*] One of the elements or components of fiber; *bot.* one of the hairs produced from the epidermis which covers the young roots of plants.—**fibrillation,** fī•bri•lā′shon, *n.* The state of being reduced to fibrils or fibrillae.—**fibrillose,** fī•bril′ōs, *a. Bot.* covered with or composed of little strings or fibers.—**fibrin,** fī′brin, *n.* A tough white fibrous protein formed from fibrinogen as the blood coagulates.—**fibrinogen,** fī•brin′ō•jen, *n.* A globulant that is present in blood plasma and formed in the kidneys.—**fibrinous,** fī′brin•us, *a.* Having fibrin present.—**fibroid,** fī′broid, *a.* [From L. *fibra,* fiber.] Of a fibrous character.—**fibrosis,** fī•brō′sis, *n. Pathol.* a morbid growth or development of fibrous matter.—**fibroma,** fī•brō′ma, *n. Pathol.* a tumor or growth of fibrous matter.—**fibrous,** fī′brus, *a.* Containing or consisting of fibers.—**fibrovascular,** fī•brō•vas′kū•lėr, *a. Bot.* consisting of wood fibers and vessels.

fibula, fib′ū•la, *n.* pl. **fibulae,** fib′ū•lē. [L. a clasp, a brace, a pin.] An ancient clasp or buckle; *anat.* the outer and lesser bone of the lower leg; *surgery,* a needle for sewing up wounds.—**fibular,** fib′ū•lėr, *a.* Of or pertaining to the fibula.

fichu, fi•shö′, *n.* [Fr.] A light piece of dress worn by ladies covering the neck, throat, and shoulders.

fickle, fik′l, *a.* [A.Sax. *ficol,* inconstant; akin to G. *ficken,* to move quickly to and fro.] Wavering; inconstant; unstable; of a changeable mind; irresolute; not firm in opinion or purpose; capricious; liable to change or vicissitude.—**fickleness,** fik′l•nes, *n.* The state or quality of being fickle; inconstancy; unsteadiness in opinion or purpose; changeableness.

fico, fē′kō, *n.* [It. from *ficus,* fig.] A fig. used in expressions of contempt or scorn, originally with obscene gesture. (*Shak.*)

fictile, fik′tīl, *a.* [L. *fictilis,* from *fingo, fictum,* to form. FEIGN.] Molded into form by art; manufactured by the potter; suitable for the potter; made of molded earth or clay.

fiction, fik′shon, *n.* [L. *fictio*, a shaping, a fashioning, from *fingo, fictum*, to fashion. FEIGN.] The act of inventing or imagining; that which is feigned, invented, or imagined; a feigned or invented story; a tale or story composed for amusement or entertainment; fictitious literature; prose narrative in the form of romances, novels, tales, and the like.—**fictional,** fik′shon•al, *a.* Pertaining to or characterized by fiction. —**fictionist,** fik′shon•ist, *n.* A writer of fiction.—**fictitious,** fik•tish′us, *a.* [L. *fictitius.*] Feigned; imaginary; not real; counterfeit; false; not genuine; invented to give literary pleasure; dealing with imaginary characters and events.—**fictitiously,** fik•tish′us-li, *adv.* In a fictitious manner; falsely.—**fictitiousness,** fik•tish′us•-nes, *n.*—**fictive,** fik′tiv, *a.* Feigned; imaginary; hypothetical.

fid, fid, *n.* A bar or short piece of wood or metal, helping to support a topmast; a wooden pin for various purposes on board ship.

fiddle, fid′l, *n.* [A.Sax. *fithele*; L.G. *fidel*, Dan. *fiddel*, Icel. *fithla*, D. *vedel*; perhaps borrowed from L.L. *vidula*, a viol. VIOL.] A stringed instrument of music; a violin.—*v.i.*—*fiddled, fiddling.* To play on a fiddle or violin; to trifle.—**fiddle-faddle,** *a.* Trifling; making a bustle about nothing. (*Colloq.*)—*v.i.* To trifle.—**fiddler,** fid′lėr, *n.* One who plays on a fiddle.—**fiddlestick,** *n.* A fiddle bow: used often as an interjection equivalent to nonsense! pshaw! etc. —**fiddlewood,** *n.* A tropical American timber tree which yields a hard wood valuable for carpenter work.—**fiddling,** fid′ling, *a.* Trifling; trivial; fussily busy with nothing.

fidelity, fi•del′i•ti, *n.* [L. *fidelitas*, from *fidelis*, faithful, from *fides*, trust, faith, *fido*, to trust. FAITH.] Faithfulness; careful and exact observance of duty or performance of obligations; firm adherence to a person or to a party; loyalty; honesty; veracity; adherence to truth.

fidget, fij′et, *v.i.* [Dim. of provincial *fidge, fike, fyke*, to be restless; akin to Icel. *fika*, to hasten; G. *ficken*, O.Sw. *fika*, to move quickly to and fro.] To move uneasily one way and the other; to move irregularly or in fits and starts.—*n.* Irregular motion; restlessness.—**fidgetiness,** fij′et•i•nes, *n.* The state or quality of being fidgety.—**fidgety,** fij′et•i, *a.* Given to fidget; restless; uneasy.

fiducial, fi•dū′shal, *a.* [L.L. *fiducialis*, from L. *fiducia*, trust, trustiness, from *fido*, to trust. FAITH.] Confident in trust or belief; undoubting; fiduciary.—**fiducially,** fi•dū′shal•li, *adv.* With confidence.

fiduciary, fi•dū′shi•er•i, *a.* [L. *fiduciarius*, held in trust.] Confident in belief; trustful; undoubting; having the nature of a trust; held in trust. —*n.* One who holds a thing in trust; a trustee.

fie, fī, *interj.* [Interjectional expression corresponding to Sc. *feigh*, Fr. *fi*, G. *pfui, fi*, Dan. *fy*, etc.] An exclamation denoting contempt, dislike, or impatience.

fief, fēf, *n.* [Fr. *fief*, from O.H.G. *fihu*, property, lit. cattle. FEE, FEUD.] An estate held of a superior on condition of military or other service; an estate held on feudal tenure.

field, fēld, *n.* [A.Sax. *feld*, a field=D. *veld*, Dan. *felt*, G. *feld*; allied to *fold*, an enclosure, *fell*, a hill; Dan. *falle*, greensward; Sc. *fale, feal*, a turf.] A piece of land suitable for tillage or pasture; a distinct or separate division of a farm; cleared land; cultivated ground; the open country; the ground where a battle is fought or military operations carried on; hence, a battle or action (the *field* is lost); area of activity, especially in sports; *phys.* an area where a given effect exists (magnetic *field*); subject of study; profession; scope; compass; extent; sphere (a wide *field* for conjecture); space on which figures are drawn; the general surface of a heraldic shield or escutcheon; *cricket*, the fielders collectively; *sporting*, those taking part in a hunt; all the horses, dogs, or the like, taking part in a race.—*Field of vision* or *view*, in a telescope or microscope, the space or range within which objects are visible to an eye looking through the instrument.—*To keep the field*, to continue active military operations in the field.—*To take the field*, to begin military operations.—*v.i.* To be one of the field whose duty is to watch and catch or recover the ball in baseball.—**fielder,** fēl′dėr, *n.* A player who fields at baseball.—**field artillery,** *n.* Light ordnance fitted for active operations in the field.—**field day,** *n.* A day when troops are drawn out for instruction in field exercises and evolutions; any day of unusual display.—**field glass,** *n.* A kind of binocular, telescope or opera glass for looking at objects at a considerable distance from the spectator.—**field gun,** *n.* A small cannon for use in the field, acting with infantry or cavalry. A common *field gun* is the 18-pounder quick-firing gun.—**field marshal,** *n.* The highest rank conferred on general officers in practically all armies.—**field mouse,** *n.* One of several species of rodent animals that live in the field, burrowing in banks, etc. —**fieldwork,** *n.* All the out-of-doors operations of a surveyor, engineer, geologist, etc.—**field work,** *n.* A temporary fortification thrown up.

fiend, fēnd, *n.* [A.Sax. *feónd, fynd*, a fiend, an enemy, from *feón*, to hate; like D. *vijand*, Icel. *fjandi*, Goth. *fijands*, G. *feind*, originally a present participle. Akin *foe.*] An infernal being; a demon; the devil; a person with devilish qualities; a wicked, cruel, or malicious person; one who is addicted to something.—**fiendish,** fēn′dish, *a.* Having the qualities of a fiend; infernal; excessively cruel; diabolic; devilish.—**fiendishly,** fēn′dish•li, *adv.* In a fiendish manner. —**fiendishness,** fēn′dish•nes, *n.* The quality of being fiendish.

fierce, fērs, *a.* [O.Fr. *fers, fiers*, from L. *ferus*, wild, rude, cruel, whence *fera*, a wild beast; akin *feral* and *ferocious.*] Vehement; violent; furious; savage; ferocious; easily enraged; indicating ferocity or a ferocious disposition; very eager; vehement in anger or cruelty.—**fiercely,** fērs′li, *adv.* In a fierce manner; furiously; with rage; with a fierce expression or aspect.—**fierceness,** fērs′nes, *n.* The quality of being fierce, furious, or angry; violence; fury; ferocity; savageness.

fiery, fī′ėr•i, *a.* See FIRE.

fife, fīf, *n.* [Fr. *fifre*, a fife, from G. *pfeife*, (=E. *pipe*), a word of onomatopoetic origin. PIPE.] A small musical instrument of the flute kind, having but one key, and a compass of two octaves.—*v.i.* To play on a fife.—**fifer,** fī′fėr, *n.* One who plays on a fife; an inhabitant of the county of Fife.

fifteen, fif′tēn, *a.* [A.Sax. *fiftyne*, lit. five-ten.] Five and ten.—*n.* The number which consists of five and ten; a symbol representing this number, as 15 or XV.—*The Fifteen*, the old Scottish law court with its fifteen Lords of Session.—*The fifteen*, the '15, the Jacobite rebellion of 1715.—**fifteenth,** fif′tēnth, *a.* The fifth in order after the tenth; being one of fifteen equal parts into which a whole is divided.—*a.* A fifteenth part.—**fifth,** fifth, *a.* The ordinal of five; next after the fourth; being one of five equal parts of a whole.—*n.* One of five equal parts into which anything is divided; *mus.* an interval consisting of three tones and a semitone.—*Fifth-monarchy men*, believers in the last of the great monarchies of *Daniel*, ii. 44, expecting the advent of Christ, and denying all human organizations.—**fifth column,** *n.* The practice of sabotage and espionage by citizens of one country for the benefit of a foreign power; traitorous political activity.—**fifty,** fif′ti, *a.* [A.Sax. *fiftig.*] Five times ten.—*n.* The number which consists of five times ten; a symbol representing this number. —**fiftieth,** fif′ti•eth, *a.* and *n.*

fig, fig, *n.* [Fr. *figue*, like D. *vijg*, G. *feige*, from L. *ficus*, fig.] A fruit consisting of a hollow receptacle containing a great multitude of minute flowers, the ripe carpels of which, erroneously called the seed, are embedded in the pulp; the tree that bears this fruit; used also as a term of scorn or contempt (I do not care a *fig* for him; in this usage perhaps from O.Sp. *figo*, a motion denoting contempt.)

fig, fig, *n.* [A contr. for *figure.*] Dress; employed chiefly in the colloquial phrase *in full fig*, in full or official dress.

fight, fīt, *v.i.* pret. & pp. *fought.* [A.Sax. *feohtan*=G. *fechten*, D. *vechten*, Dan. *fegte*, Icel. *fikta*, to fight.] To contend for victory in battle or in single combat; to contend in arms or otherwise; to carry on active opposition; to strive or struggle to resist: with *with* or *against* before an object.—*To fight shy of*, to avoid from a feeling of dislike, fear, mistrust, etc.—*v.t.* To carry on or wage (a battle); to win or gain by struggle (to *fight* one's way); to contend with; to war against; to manage or maneuver in a fight (to *fight* one's ship).—*To fight it out,* to struggle till a decisive result is attained.—*n.* A contest; a battle; an engagement; a struggle for victory. Syn. under BATTLE.—**fighter,** fī′tėr, *n.* One that fights; a combatant.

figment, fig′ment, *n.* [L. *figmentum,* from *fingo,* to feign. FEIGN.] An invention; a fiction; something feigned or imagined.

figure, fig′ūr, *n.* [Fr. *figure,* from L. *figura,* figure, shape, from *fig,* root of *fingo,* to fashion, to shape; whence also *feign, fiction,* etc. FEIGN.] The form of anything as expressed by the outline or contour; shape; fashion; form; any form made by drawing, painting, carving, embroidering, etc.; especially the human body so represented; appearance or impression made by the conduct of a person (to cut a poor *figure*); *logic,* the form of a syllogism with respect to the relative position of the middle term; *arith.* a character denoting or standing for a number; hence, value, as expressed in numbers; price; *theol.* type or representative; *rhet.* a mode of speaking or writing in which words are deflected from their ordinary use or signification; a trope; a peculiar expression used for impressiveness as a metaphor, antithesis, etc.—*To cut a figure,* to make one's self celebrated or notorious; to appear to advantage or disadvantage.—*v.t.*—*figured, figuring.* To make a figure or likeness of; to represent by drawing, sculpture, carving, embroidery, etc.; to cover or adorn with figures or ornamental designs; to mark with figures; to represent by a typical or figurative resemblance; to typify; to imagine; to image in the mind.—*v.i.* To make a figure; to be a prominent figure or personage.—**figurant,** fig′ū•rant, *n. masc.*; **figurante,** fig′ū•rant, *n. fem.* [Fr.] One who dances at the opera in groups or figures; a character on the stage who figures in its scenes, but has nothing to say. —**figurate,** fig′ū•rāt, *a.* [L. *figuro, figuratum,* to form, to fashion.] Of a certain determinate form or shape. —*Figurate numbers,* such numbers as do or may represent some geometrical figure, being thus called triangular, square, pentagonal, etc., numbers.—**figuration,** fig•ū•rā′shon, *n.* The act of giving figure or determinate form.—**figurative,** fig′ū•rā•tiv, *a.* [Fr. *figuratif.*] Representing by means of a figure or type; typical; symbolical: used in a metaphorical sense; having the character of a figure or trope; metaphoric; not literal.—**figuratively,** fig′ū•re•tiv•li, *adv.* In a figurative manner; by a figure; in a sense different from that which words originally imply in a metaphorical sense.—**figurativeness,** fig′ū•re•tiv•nes, *n.* State of being figurative.—**figured,** fig′ūrd, *a.* Adorned with figures.—**figurehead,** *n.* The ornamental figure on a ship immediately under the bowsprit.—**figurine,** fig•ū•rēn′, *n.* [Fr. dim. of *figure.*] A small ornamental figure or piece of statuary; a statuette.

filament, fil′a•ment, *n.* [L.L. *filamentum,* a slender thread, from L. *filum* a thread.] A fine single thread or fiber from flesh, roots, minerals, etc.; a thread-like metallic conductor made incandescent by the flow of electricity, as in an electric bulb or electron tube.—**filamentary,** fil•a•men′te•ri, *a.* Having the character of or formed by a filament.—**filamentous,** fil•a•men′tus, *a.* Like a thread; consisting of fine filaments; *bot.* bearing filaments.—**filar,** fī′lėr, *a.* Pertaining to a thread: applied to a microscope, or other optical instrument, into whose construction one or more threads or fine wires are introduced.—**filature,** fil′a•chėr, *n.* A forming into threads; the reeling off silk from cocoons; a filatory.—**filiform,** fil′i•form, *a.* Having the form of a thread or filament.—**filose,** fī′lōs, *a. Zool.* and *bot.* applied to a part when it ends in a threadlike process.

filbert, fil′bėrt, *n.* [From St. *Philibert,* whose feast day is in the nutting season.] Either of two European hazels; the hazelnut.

filch, filch, *v.t.* [For *filk,* from O.E. *fele,* Icel. *fela,* to steal, like *talk* and *tell, stalk* (verb) and *steal.*] To steal, especially something of little value; to pilfer; to take in a thievish manner. —**filcher,** filch′ėr, *n.* One who filches.

file, fīl, *n.* [Fr. *file,* from L. *filum,* a thread, string.] A collection of papers arranged for ready reference; a container in which records are kept in order; a row of soldiers arranged one behind another, from front to rear; hence, *rank and file* (*milit.*), the lines of soldiers from side to side, and from front to back; an old *file,* a sharper.—*v.t.*—*filed, filing.* To arrange or place in a file; to bring before a court by presenting the proper papers (to *file* a bill in chancery).—*v.i.* To march in a file or line; to register as a candidate in an election.

file, fīl, *n.* [A.Sax. *feol*=D. *vijl,* Dan. *viil,* G. *feile,* O.H.G. *vihila,* a file.] A steel instrument, having minute teeth upon the surface for cutting, abrading, and smoothing metal, ivory, wood, etc.—*v.t.*—*filed, filing.* To rub smooth, or cut with a file, or as with a file; to polish.—**filing,** fī′ling, *n.* A particle rubbed off by a file.

filet, fi•lā′, fē•lā′, *a.* Indicating a lace or net of square mesh.

filial, fil′i•al, *a.* [Fr. *filial,* from L.L. *filialis,* from L. *filius,* a son, *filia,* a daughter.] Pertaining to a son or daughter; becoming a child in relation to his parents; bearing the relation of a child.—**filially,** fil′i•al•li, *adv.* In a filial manner.—**filiate,** fil′i•āt, *v.t.* To adopt as a son or daughter.—**filiation,** fil•i•ā′shon, *n.* The relation of a child to a father; adoption; the fixing of the paternity of a child.

filibuster, fil′i•bus•tėr, *n.* [Sp. *filibustero,* freebooter.] Any lawless adventurer who invades, with the view of occupying, a foreign country; an extreme stalling measure used to prevent action on, or to delay, legislation.—*v.i.* To engage in filibuster; to endeavor to defeat or to delay legislation by obstructionist tactics, as long speeches or motions.

filigree, fil′i•grē, *n.* [Formerly *filigrane,* from Fr. *filigrane,* It. *filigrana,* from L. *filum,* a thread, and *granum,* a grain: originally it is said to have had beads in it.] Ornamental open work executed in fine gold or silver wire, formed into flowers and arabesques.

fill, fil, *v.t.* [A.Sax. *fyllan,* to fill, from the adjective *ful,* full=Icel. and Sw. *fylla,* Goth. *fulljan,* G. *füllen,* D. *vullen,* to fill.] To make full; to cause to be occupied so that no space is left vacant; to put in so as to occupy a space; to occupy the whole space or capacity of; to repair cavities in teeth; to satisfy; to content; to glut; to press and dilate (a ship's sails); to supply with an occupant or holder; to possess and perform the duties of; to officiate in; to hold or occupy.—*To fill in,* to pour or put in for the purpose of filling something; to write in (items in a list).—*To fill out,* to distend or enlarge from within.—*To fill up,* to make quite full; to occupy or take up; to occupy the whole extent of; to engage or employ (time).—*v.i.* To grow or become full; to make something full.—*To fill out,* to become enlarged or distended.—*To fill up,* to grow or become full.—*n.* As much as fills or satisfies; material that fills a cavity or hole.—**filler,** fil′ėr, *n.* One who or that which fills; a utensil for conveying a liquid into a bottle, cask, etc.—**filling,** fil′ing, *a.* Calculated to fill, satisfy, or satiate.—*n.* Materials used for occupying some vacant space, stopping up a hole, or the like.

fillet, fil′et, *n.* [Fr. *filet,* a thread, a band, the chine of an animal, etc., dim. of *fil,* thread, from L. *filum,* a thread. FILE.] A little band to tie about the head; a band or narrow strip; *cookery,* fi•lā′, a boneless piece of lean meat, sometimes rolled and tied; fillet of beef, a slice of tenderloin; fillet of veal, a slice from the fleshy part of the calf's thigh.—*Arch.* A small molding having the appearance of a narrow band, generally used to separate ornaments and moldings; also the ridge between the flutes of a column.—*v.t.* To bind or adorn with a fillet; to cut into fillets.

fillip, fil′ip, *v.t.* [Same as *flip.*] To strike with the fore or middle finger by jerking it away from the ball of the thumb; to strike with a smart stroke.—*n.* A jerk of the finger forced suddenly from the thumb; a smart blow or stroke; something which sharply rouses or stimulates.

fillister, fil′is•tėr, *n.* A kind of plane used for grooving timber.

filly, fil′i, *n.* [A dim. form of *foal*= Icel. *fylja,* a filly, from *foli,* a foal. FOAL.] A young mare; a young girl.

film, film, *n.* [A.Sax. *filmen,* a skin; allied to *fell,* a skin.] A thin skin or membrane; a pellicle; a lamina; a thin layer for receiving a photographic negative; a motion picture. —*v.t.* To cover with a film; to take a motion picture of.—*v.i.* To become covered as with a film; to be suitable for photographing. —**filminess,** fil′mi•ness, *n.*—**filmstrip,** film′strip, *n.* A strip of film, showing diagrams, charts, or photographs, for still projection.—**filmy,** fil′mi, *a.*

filose, *a.* See FILAMENT.

filter, fil′tėr, *n.* [Fr. *filtre,* from L.L. *filtrum, feltrum,* felt or fulled wool, used originally as a strainer. FELT.] A strainer; any substance or apparatus through which liquids or gases are passed to separate suspended matter; a device that selects certain wave frequencies to pass through it.—*v.t.* To remove by passing through a filter.—*v.i.* To pass through a filter.—**filtrate,** fil′trāt, *v.t.*—*filtrated, filtrating.* [L.L. *filtro, filtratum.*] To filter.—*n.* The liquid which has been passed through a filter.—**filtration,** fil•trā′shon, *n.* The act or process of filtering.

filth, filth, *n.* [A.Sax. *fylth,* from *fúl,* foul. FOUL.] Anything that soils or defiles; dirt; foul matter; nastiness; corruption; pollution.—**filthily,** filth′-i•li, *adv.* In a filthy manner; foully.—**filthiness,** filth′i•nes, *n.* The state of being filthy; filth; foul matter; impurity.—**filthy,** filth′i, *a.* Dirty; foul; unclean; nasty; morally impure; licentious.

fimbriate, fim′bri•āt, *a.* [L. *fimbriæ,* threads, a fringe.] Fringed; having a sort of fringe or border; having the edge surrounded by fibers, hairs, or bristles.—*v.t.* To hem; to fringe.—**fimbriated,** fim′bri•ā•ted, *a.* Fimbriate.

fin, fin, *n.* [A.Sax. *fin, finn,* L.G. and Dan. *finne,* D. *vin,* Sw. *fena;* allied to L. *pinna, penna,* a feather.] One of the projecting winglike organs which enable fishes to balance themselves in an upright position, and assist in regulating their movements in the water.—**finless,** fin′les, *a.* Destitute of fins.—**finned,** find, *a.* Having a fin or fins or anything resembling a fin.—**finback,** fin′bak, *n.* A name given to several whales from their possessing a dorsal hump or fin.—**finny,** fin′i, *a.* Furnished with fins; relating to or abounding with fins.

final, fī′nal, *a.* [L. *finalis,* from *finis,* end; seen also in *fine,* adj. and noun, *confine, define, affinity, finance, finish,* etc.] Pertaining to the end or conclusion; last; ultimate; conclusive; decisive; respecting a purpose or ultimate end in view.—*n.* A final contest, test, etc.—**finale,** fē•nä′lā, *n.* *Mus.* the last part of a sonata, symphony, or opera; the closing part of any performance.—**finalist,** fī′nal•-ist, *n.* One who is in a final contest. —**finality,** fī•nal′i•ti, *n.* The state of being final; *philos.* the doctrine that nothing exists or was made except for a determinate end.—**finally,** fī′-nal•li, *adv.* At the end or conclusion; ultimately; lastly; completely; beyond recovery.

finance, fi•nans′, *n.* [Fr., from L.L. *financia,* a money payment, from *finare,* to pay a fine, from L. *finis,* end. FINE, *n.*] The system or science of public revenue and expenditure; pl. funds in the public treasury, or accruing to it; public resources of money.—*v.t.* and *i.* To raise or provide money for a charity or business; to provide on credit.—**financial,** fi•nan′-shal, *a.* Pertaining to finance or public revenue; having to do with money matters.—**financially,** fi•nan′-shal•li, *adv.* In relation to finances or public funds.—**financier,** fin•an•sēr′, *n.* One who is skilled in financial matters or in the principles or system of public revenue.

finch, finsh, *n.* [A.Sax. *finc*=G. Dan. and Sw. *fink, finke,* Gr. *spiza.*] A large family (Fringillidae) of small song-birds, including the bunting, sparrow, and goldfinch, having a small conical beak adapted to cracking seeds.

find, fīnd, *v.t.*—pret. and pp. *found.* [A.Sax. *findan,* to find=D. *vinden* G. *finden,* Dan. *finde,* Icel. *finna* (for *finda*), Goth. *finthan,* to find. From same root as in L. *peto,* to aim at, to seek.] To discover; to gain first sight or knowledge of (something lost); to recover; to get; to meet; to come or light upon; to gain, acquire, or procure (leisure, happiness); to supply, provide, or furnish (to *find* money for a purpose); to catch; to detect; *law,* to determine and declare by verdict.—*To find one's self,* to fare in regard to ease or pain, health or sickness; to provide one's necessaries at one's own expense.—*To find one in* (something), to supply, furnish, or provide one with (something).—*To find out,* to detect; to discover, as something before unknown, a mystery, secret, trick, etc.; to solve.—*To find fault with,* to censure.—*v.i. Law,* to give judgment on the merits or facts of a case.—*n.* A discovery of anything valuable; the thing found.—**finder,** fīn′dėr, *n.* One who or that which finds; *astron.* a smaller telescope attached to a larger, for the purpose of finding an object more readily.—**finding,** fīn′ding, *n.* Discovery; that which is found; *law,* the return of a jury to a bill; a verdict.

fine, fīn, *a.* [Fr. *fin,* fine, delicate, etc.; G. *fein,* D. *fijn,* Dan. *fiin,* Sw. *fin,* Icel. *finn,* from L. *finitus,* finished, perfect, pp. of *finio,* to finish, from *finis,* an end. FINAL.] Slender; minute; very small; of very small diameter; not coarse; in very small grains or particles; thin; keen; sharp; made of fine threads or material; delicate; pure; of excellent quality; refined; elegant; perceiving or discerning minute beauties or deformities (*fine* taste); handsome; beautiful; accomplished (a *fine* gentleman); elegant; showy; splendid; free from clouds or rain; sunshiny (*fine* weather); finically or affectedly elegant; aiming too much at show or effect.—*Fine arts,* the arts which depend chiefly on the labors of the mind or imagination, generally restricted to the imitative arts which appeal to us through the eye, such as painting and sculpture.—*v.t.*—*fined, fining.* To refine; to purify; to free from foreign matter.—**fine-draw,** fīn′dra, *v.t.* To sew up with so much nicety that the rent is not perceived.—**finely,** fīn′li, *adv.* In a fine or finished manner; admirably; beautifully; delicately.—**fineness,** fīn′nes, *n.* The state or quality of being fine.—**finery,** fī′nėr•i, *n.* Fineness; ornament; showy or excessive decoration; the forge in ironworks at which the iron is hammered into what is called a bloom or square bar.—**finespun,** fīn′spun, *a.* Drawn to a fine thread; minute, hence, overrefined; overelaborated; subtile.

fine, fīn, *n.* [From L. *finis,* an end, and in later times and in a feudal sense, a final settlement of a claim by composition or agreement. FINANCE, FINAL.] A payment of money imposed upon a person as a punishment for an offense.—*In fine,* in conclusion; to conclude; to sum up all.—*v.t.*—*fined, fining.* To set a fine on by judgment of a court; to punish by fine.

finesse, fi•nes′, *n.* [Fr., lit. fineness.] Artifice; stratagem; subtlety of contrivance to gain a point; in bridge, the attempt to win a trick by playing a low card while having a high card in reserve.—*v.i.* To use finesse.

finger, fing′gėr, *n.* [A.Sax. *finger*=D. *vinger,* G. Sw. and Dan. *finger,* Goth. *figgrs;* same root as in *fang.*] One of the five extreme members of the hand; any of them but the thumb; a digit; something resembling or serving the purpose of a finger; an index.—*To have a finger in,* to be concerned in.—*To have at one's finger ends,* to be quite familiar with; to be able to make available readily. —*v.t.* To touch with the fingers; to handle; to toy or meddle with; to touch or take thievishly; to apply the fingers to in order to produce musical effects.—*v.i.* To use the fingers in playing on an instrument. —**finger board,** *n.* The board at the neck of a violin, guitar, or the like, where the fingers act on the strings; also the whole range of keys of a piano, organ, etc; a. keyboard.—**fingerer,** fing′gėr•ėr, *n.* One who fingers or handles; a pilferer.—**fingering,** fing′gėr•ing, *n.* The act of touching lightly or handling; *mus.* the management of the fingers in playing on an instrument of music; the marking of the notes of a piece of music to guide the fingers in playing; a thick loose worsted used for knitting stockings.—**finger post,** *n.* A post set up to guide travelers, generally where roads cross or divide. —**fingerprint,** *n.* An impression made by fingers, often serving to identify the person.

finial, fin′i•al, *n.* [From L. *finio,* to

finish. FINAL.] The ornamental termination of a pinnacle, canopy, gable, or the like.

finical, fin′i•kal, *a.* [From *fine.*] Affecting great nicety or elegance; overnice; unduly particular about trifles.—**finicality,** fin•i•kal′i•ti, *n.* State of being finical; something finical.—**finically,** fin′i•kal•li, *adv.* In a finical manner.—**finicalness,** fin′i•kal•nes, *n.* Quality of being finical.—**finicking, finicky,** fin′i•king, fin′i•ki, *a.* [Equivalent to *finical.*] Precise in trifles; idly busy.

finis, fī′nis, *n.* [L.] An end; conclusion: often placed at the end of a book.

finish, fin′ish, *v.t.* [Fr. *finir*, ppr. *finissant*, from L. *finio*, *finitum*, to finish, from *finis*, end. FINAL.] To bring to an end; to make an end of; to arrive at the end of; to bestow the last required labor upon; to perfect; to polish to a high degree; to elaborate carefully.—*v.i.* To come to an end; to terminate; to expire.—*n.* The last touch to a work; polish; careful elaboration; a name for denatured alcohol.—**finished,** fin′isht, *p.* and *a.* Polished to the highest degree of excellence; complete; perfect.—**finisher,** fin′ish•ėr, *n.* One who finishes; something that gives the finishing touch to or settles anything (*colloq.*).

finite, fī′nīt, *a.* [L. *finitus*, from *finio*, to finish, from *finis*, limit. FINAL.] Having a limit; limited; bounded: opposed to *infinite*; *gram.* a term applied to those moods of a verb which are limited by number and person, as the indicative, subjunctive, and imperative.—**finitely,** fī′nīt•li, *adv.* In a finite manner; limitedly; to a certain degree only.—**finiteness,** fī′nīt•nes, *n.* State of being finite.—**finitude,** fin′i•tūd, *n.* State of being finite; limitation.

Finn, fin, *n.* [O.E. *Finnas.*] A native of Finland; person of the same race.—**Finnish,** fin′ish, *a.* Relating to the Finns or Finland.—*n.* A language spoken by the Finns.

finnan haddie, fin′an had′i, *n.* [From river *Findhorn.*] A split and cured haddock.

fiord, fjord, fyord, *n.* [Dan *fiord*; Icel. *fjörthr.* FIRTH.] An inlet from the sea, usually long, narrow, and very irregularly shaped, such as are common on the coast of Norway.

fir, fėr, *n.* [A.Sax. *furh*=Icel. Sw. *fura*, Dan. *fyr*, *fyrre*, G. *föhre. Fir* represents an ancient word, which appears in L. as *quercus*, an oak, and probably meant originally tree in general.] A general name for several species of coniferous trees, sometimes used as coextensive with the term pine (*Pinus*), but often restricted to trees of the genus *Abies*, which differ from the true pines in their leaves growing singly on the stem, and the scales of the cones being smooth, round, and thin.—**firry,** fėr′i, *a.* Of or pertaining to firs; consisting of fir; abounding in firs.

fire, fīr, *n.* [A.Sax. *fyr*=Icel. *fyri*, Dan. and Sw. *fyr*, G. *feuer*, fire; cog. Gr. *pyr*, fire; allied to Skr. *pu*, to purify, as fire is the great purifying element.] The evolution of heat and light during combustion; fuel in combustion; the burning of a house or town; a conflagration; the discharge of a number of firearms; a spark from hot iron accidentally lodged in the eye; light; luster; splendor; ardor of passion, whether of love, hate, anger, etc; consuming violence of temper; liveliness of imagination; vigor of fancy; animation; vivacity; force of sentiment or expression.—*On fire*, ignited; burning; hence, *fig.* eager; ardent.—*St. Anthony's fire*, erysipelas.—*v.t.*—*fired*, *firing*. To set on fire; to kindle; to inflame or irritate; to animate; to give life or spirit to; to cause to explode; to discharge (a gun, a shot).—*v.i.* To take fire; to be irritated or inflamed with passion; to discharge artillery or firearms.—*To fire away*, to begin; to go on. (*Colloq.*)—*Fireout*, to discharge or expel from office.—*To fire up*, to become irritated or angry; to fly into a passion. (*Colloq.*)—**fiery,** fī′ėr•i, *a.* Consisting of fire; burning; flaming; blazing; highly flammable; hot; ardent; vehement; impetuous; passionate; irritable; fierce; like fire; bright; glaring.—*Fiery cross*, a light wooden cross, the extremities of which were set fire to and then extinguished in blood; used in ancient times in Scotland as a signal to assemble under arms.—**fierily,** fī′ėr•i•li, *adv.* In a fiery manner.—**fieriness,** fī′ėr•i•nes, *n.* The state or quality of being fiery.—**firing,** fī′ring, *n.* The act of discharging firearms; a setting on fire; material for burning; fuel.—**firearm,** fīr′ärm, *n.* A weapon whose charge is expelled by the combustion of powder, as cannon, pistols, muskets, etc.—**fireball,** fīr′bal, *n.* A ball filled with combustibles to be thrown among enemies; a meteor having the appearance of a globular mass of light.—**firebox,** *n.* The box (generally made of copper) in which the fire in a locomotive is placed.—**firebrand,** fīr′brand, *n.* A piece of wood kindled; an incendiary; one who inflames factions, or causes contention and mischief.—**firebrick,** *n.* A brick of clay that will sustain intense heat without fusion.—**firebug,** *n.* An arsonist.—**fire clay,** *n.* A kind of clay capable of sustaining intense heat, and used in making firebricks, gas retorts, crucibles, etc.—**firecracker,** *n.* A firework consisting of a paper cylinder enclosing powder, through which a fuse is passed, and exploding with a sharp report when ignited.—**firedamp,** *n.* Light carburetted hydrogen gas, sometimes very abundantly evolved in coal mines, and productive of the most dreadful results when brought into contact with a naked flame, being highly explosive.—**firedog,** *n.* An andiron.—**fire-eater,** *n.* A juggler who pretends to eat fire; a fighting character or duelist; a fireman (*Colloq.*).—**fire engine,** *n.* An engine, acting on the force-pump principle, for throwing jets of water to extinguish fire and save buildings.—**fire escape,** *n.* An apparatus for escaping from the upper part of a building when on fire, a common form consisting of an arrangement of long ladders capable of being drawn out after the manner of a telescope.—**firefly,** fīr′flī, *n.* A name for any winged insect which possesses much luminosity.—**fireguard,** *n.* A framework of iron wire, to be placed in front of a fireplace to protect against fire.—**fire irons,** *n. pl.* Poker, tongs, and shovel.—**firelock,** fīr′lok, *n.* A musket or other gun with a lock furnished with a flint and steel.—**fireman,** fīr′man, *n.* A man whose business is to extinguish fires in towns; a member of a fire brigade; a man employed in tending fires, as of a steam engine.—**fireplace,** fīr′plās, *n.* The lower part of a chimney which opens into an apartment and in which fuel is burned; a hearth.—**fireplug,** *n.* A plug for drawing water from the pipes in the street to extinguish fire.—**fireproof,** fīr′pröf, *a.* Proof against fire; incombustible; rendered incombustible by some process.—**fire ship,** *n.* A vessel filled with combustibles to be set on fire for burning an enemy's ships.—**fireside,** fīr′sīd, *n.* The side of the fireplace; the hearth; home: often used adjectively.—**firestone,** fīr′stōn, *n.* Any kind of stone which resists the action of fire.—**fireweed,** *n.* A plant which appears abundantly on land over which a fire has passed.—**firewood,** fīr′wud, *n.* Wood for fuel.—**firework,** fīr′wėrk, *n.* A preparation of gunpowder, sulfur, and other flammable materials to be let off for the purpose of making a show.

firkin, fėr′kin, *n.* [From *four*, with dim. suffix *-kin*, being the fourth of a barrel.] An old measure of capacity equal to 7½ gallons; a small wooden vessel or cask.

firm, fėrm, *a.* [L. *firmus*, firm, seen also in *affirm*, *confirm*, *firmament*, *farm.*] Closely compressed; compact; hard; solid; fixed; steady; constant; stable; unshaken in purpose or will; resolute in mind; not easily moved; not giving way.—*n.* [Originally a signature by which a writing was *firmed* or rendered valid.] A partnership or association of two or more persons for carrying on a business; a commercial house; the name or title under which a company transacts business.—*v.t.* To make firm or solid; to solidify.—*v.i.* To become firm or solid.—**firmly,** fėrm′li, *adv.* In a firm manner.—**firmness,** fėrm′nes, *n.* The state or quality of being firm; compactness; solidity; stability; steadfastness; resolution.—**firmament,** fėr′ma•ment, *n.* [L. *firmamentum*, from *firmo*, *firmatum*, to make firm.] The region of the air; the sky or heavens.

firman, fėr′man or fėr•män′, *n.* [Per. *fermân*, *farmân*, a decree.] A decree, order, or grant of an Oriental sovereign, as of Turkey, etc., issued for various special purposes; a license or grant of privileges.

first, fėrst, *a.* [A superlative, of which *fore* may be regarded as the positive. A. Sax. *fyrst,* first, most to the fore. FORE.] The ordinal of *one;* preceding all others in a series; advanced before or further than any other in progression; foremost in place; preceding all others in time, rank, dignity, or excellence.—*n.* The beginning; number one in a series; the lowest forward gear.—*adv.* Before all others in place, time, etc.—*At first, at the first,* at the beginning or origin. *First and last,* within the whole time or period; altogether.— *First or last,* at one time or another.—**firstling,** fėrst′ling, *n.* The first produce or offspring of a beast.—**firstly,** fėrst′li, *adv.* In the first place; first.—**first-born,** *a.* First brought forth; eldest.—**first-class,** *a.* First-rate; of the highest excellence or quality. (*Colloq.*).—**firsthand,** *a.* Obtained direct from the first source; obtained direct from the producer, maker, etc.—*At firsthand,* directly; without the intervention of an agent. —**first-rate,** *a.* Of the first class or rate; of the highest excellence.—*n.* A war ship of the first or most powerful class.—**first water,** *n.* The first or highest quality; purest luster: applied principally to diamonds and pearls.

firth, fėrth, *n.* [From Icel. *fjörthr,* Dan. *fiord,* N. *fjord,* a firth; same root as *fare, ferry.*] A name given to several estuaries or bays into which rivers discharge themselves in Scotland; a channel or arm of the sea (the Pentland *Firth*): written also *Frith.*

fiscal, fis′kal, *a.* [From L. *fiscus,* the state treasury.] Pertaining to the public treasury or revenue; financial. —*Fiscal year,* the twelve months for which a complete financial accounting is made.

fish, fish, *n.* pl. **fishes,** fish′ez, instead of which the sing. is often used collectively. [A.Sax. *fisc*=Icel. *fiskr,* Dan. and Sw. *fisk,* D. *visch,* G. *fisch,* Goth. *fisks;* cog. L. *piscis,* W. *pysg,* Gael. and Ir. *iasg,* fish.] A vertebrate animal that lives in water, breathes by gills, and has cold blood, with limbs in the form of fins; popularly applied also to whales and various other marine animals; a contemptuous or familiar term for a person (in such phrases as, a queer or strange *fish;* a loose *fish*); the flesh of fish used as food; *naut.* a purchase used to raise the flukes of an anchor up to the gunwale.—*Neither flesh nor fish,* neither one thing nor another; having no decided character or qualities; nondescript.—*v.i.* To employ one's self in catching fish; to endeavor to take fish by a rod and line or other means; to seek to obtain by artifice, or indirectly (to *fish* for compliments).—*v.t.* To catch or attempt to catch fish; to draw out or up, especially when in water; to search by dragging, raking, or sweeping; to strengthen or unite by a piece that extends on both sides of a joint or a crack.—**fish cake,** *n.* A small ball of shredded fish, as codfish, mixed with potato, seasoned, and fried.—**fisher,** fish′ėr, *n.* One who fishes; one employed in catching fish. —**fisherman,** fish′ėr•man, *n.* One whose occupation is to catch fish.—**fishery,** fish′ėr•i, *n.* The business of catching fish; a place where fish are regularly caught, or other products of the sea or rivers are taken from the water.—**fishhook,** *n.* A hook for catching fish.—**fishing,** fish′ing, *n.* The art or practice of catching fish.—*a.* Used or employed in fishery or by fishermen.—**fish joint,** *n.* A railway contrivance for connecting two rails meeting end to end.—**fishtail,** fish′tāl, *a.* Shaped like a fish's tail.—*Fishtail burner,* a gas burner whose jet takes the form of a fish's tail.—**fishy,** fish′i, *a.* Pertaining to fishes; consisting of fish; inhabited by fish; having the qualities of fish; as a slang term, worn out, as if by dissipation; seedy; applied to persons; equivocal; unsafe; unsound; applied to a project or speculation; dull; without luster (*fishy* eyes).

fissile, fis′sil, *a.* [L. *fissilis,* from *findo, fissum,* to split or cleave, whence also *fissure,* the root being same as in E. *bite.*] Capable of being split in the direction of the grain (like wood), or in certain planes; readily splitting in flakes or plates.—**fissility,** fis•sil′i•ti, *n.* The quality of being fissile.—**fission,** fish′on, *n.* [L. *fissio.*] The act of cleaving, splitting, or breaking up into parts; *biol.* a species of reproduction or multiplication by means of a process of self-division seen in animals of a low type, the body becoming divided into two parts, each of which then becomes a separate and independent individual.—*Nuclear fission, phys.* the splitting of an atomic nucleus, either spontaneously or by bombardment with neutrons, etc., to release energy.

fissirostral, fis•si•ros′tral, *a.* [L. *findo, fissum,* to divide, and *rostrum,* a beak.] Characterized by a deeply-cleft bill, as swallows, goat suckers, etc., in which the gape is extended beneath the eyes.

fissure, fish′ėr, *n.* [Fr., from L. *fissura,* from *findo,* to split. FISSILE.] A cleft; a crack; a narrow chasm made by the parting of any substance; a longitudinal opening; a separation or disagreement in thought.—*v.t.* and *i.*—*fissured, fissuring.* To cleave or make a fissure in; to crack or fracture.

fist, fist, *n.* [A.Sax. *fyst*=G. *faust,* D. *vuist,* Rus. *pjast;* same root as L. *pugnus,* Gr. *pygmē,* the fist.] The hand clenched; the hand with the fingers doubled into the palm.—*v.t.* To strike or grip with the fist. —**fistic,** fis′tik, *a.* Pertaining to boxing; pugilistic.—**fisticuffs,** fis′ti•kufs, *n. pl.* Blows or a combat with the fists.—**fisty,** fis′ti, *a.* Pertaining to the fist or fists, or to pugilism.

fistula, fis′chụ•la, *n.* [L., a pipe.] A musical pipe; *surg.* a channel excavated between an internal part (as the rectum) and the skin surface, showing no tendency to heal, and generally arising from abscesses.—**fistular,** fis′chụ•lėr, *a.* Hollow, like a pipe or reed.—**fistulous,** fis′chụ•lus, *a.* Formed like a fistula; fistular.

fit, fit, *n.* [Of doubtful origin; comp. A.Sax. *fit, fitt,* a fight, a struggle, Icel. *fet,* a pace, a step.] A sudden effort, activity, or motion followed by an interval of relaxation; a temporary but violent mental affection or attack; a paroxysm; a temporary attack of a disease or pain; particularly a sudden and violent attack, accompanied with convulsions and loss of consciousness, as in hysteria, apoplexy, etc.—**fitful,** fit′fụl, *n.* Full of fits; varied by paroxysms; spasmodic; varied by events.—**fitfully,** fit′fụl•li, *adv.* In a fitful manner; by fits; at intervals.—**fitfulness,** fit′fụl•nes, *n.* The state of being fitful; impulsiveness; waywardness.

fit, fit, *a.* [Allied to Icel. *fitja,* to knit together, Goth. *fetjan,* to arrange, to adorn, E. *fettle;* or equivalent to *feat* (adj.), O.Fr. *feit,* L. *factum,* made.] Conformable to a standard of right, duty, taste, or propriety; of suitable kind; meet; becoming; appropriate; adapted to an end, object, or design; suitable; qualified; competent; prepared; ready.—*v.t.*—*fitted, fitting.* To make fit or suitable; to bring into some required form; to adapt; to suit; to furnish or accommodate with anything; to prepare; to put in order for; to qualify; to be properly fitted for or adjusted to; to suit; to become.—*To fit out,* to furnish; to equip; to supply with necessaries or means.—*To fit up,* to furnish (a house, etc.) with things suitable; to make proper for the reception or use of any person.—*v.i.* To be proper or becoming; to be adjusted to the shape intended; to suit or be suitable; to be adapted.—*n.* Nice adjustment; adaptation.—**fitly,** fit′li, *adv.* In a fit manner; suitably; properly.—**fitness,** fit′nes, *n.* The state or quality of being fit; suitableness; adaptation; preparation; qualification. The state of being fitted.—**fitter,** fit′ėr, *n.* One who fits; one who puts the parts of machinery together.—**fitting,** fit′ing, *a.* Fit or appropriate; suitable; proper.—*n.* Something fitted on or attached as subsidiary to another thing.—**fittingly,** fit′ing•li, *adv.* In a fitting manner; suitably.

fitch, fich, *n.* [O.D. *vitsche,* O.Fr. *fissau,* a polecat; akin *foist.*] The polecat; also its fur.—**fitchet, fitchew,** fich′et, fich′ū, *n.* The polecat.

five, fīv, *a.* [A.Sax. *fif*=Goth. *fimf,* Icel. *fimm,* Sw. and Dan. *fem,* D. *vijf,* G. *fünf,* Lith. *penki,* W. *pump,* Gael. *coig,* L. *quinque,* Gr. *pempe, pente,* Skr. *panchan*—five.] Four and one added; the half of ten.—*n.* The number which consists of four and one; the number of the fingers and thumb of one hand; a symbol representing this number.—**fivefold,** fīv′fōld, *a.* Consisting of five in one; five times repeated; in fives.—**fives,** fīvz, *n.* A kind of play with a ball, originally called hand tennis: so named probably because the ball is struck with the hand or *five* fingers.

fix, fiks, *v.t.* [Fr. *fixer*, from L. *figo, fixum*, to fasten, seen also in *affix, prefix, suffix.*] To make stable, firm, or fast; to set or place permanently; to establish firmly or immovably; to fasten; to attach firmly; to direct steadily, as the eye, the mind, the attention, etc.; to make solid; to congeal; to deprive of volatility; to stop or keep from moving.—*v.i.* To become firm or stable.—*n.* A predicament; dilemma; the position of an object (as a ship) determined by radio signals, bearing, etc.—**fixate,** fiks'āt, *v.t.*—*fixated, fixating.* To make fixed; to focus intently upon. —*v.i.* To concentrate one's attention. —**fixation,** fiks•ā'shon, *n.* The act or state of being fixed; an obsessive preoccupation upon an object.—**fixative,** fiks'a•tiv, *n.* A substance that fixes or sets.—*Fixed stars*, such stars as always retain the same apparent position and distance with respect to each other, and are thus distinguished from planets.—**fixedly,** fik'sed•li, *adv.* In a fixed manner.—**fixedness,** fik'sed•nes, *n.* A state of being fixed.—**fixity,** fik'si•ti, *n.* State of being fixed; fixed character; fixedness; stability.—**fixture,** fiks'chėr, *n.* Anything placed in a firm or fixed position; that which is fixed to a building; any appendage or part of the furniture of a house which is fixed to it, as by nails, screws, etc.

fizz, fiz, *v.i.* [Imitative.] To make a hissing sound; effervesce.—*n.* A hissing sound.—**fizzle,** fiz'l, *n.* Fizz; a failure.—*v.i.* To fail after starting well.

flabby, flab'i, *a.* [Akin to *flap*, and to G. *flabbe*, Sw. *flabb*, Dan. *flab*, hanging lips.] Soft and yielding to the touch; easily moved or shaken; hanging loose by its own weight; flaccid: said especially of flesh.—**flabbily,** flab'i•li, *adv.* In a flabby manner.—**flabbiness,** flab'i•nes, *n.* State of being flabby.

flabellum, fla•bel'lum, *n.* [L.] A fan; specifically, an ecclesiastical fan anciently used to drive away flies from the chalice during the Eucharist.—**flabellate, flabelliform,** fla•bel'lāt, fla•bel'li•form, *a.* Fan shaped.

flaccid, flak'sid, *a.* [L. *flaccidus*, from *flaccus*, flabby; comp. W. *llac*, slack, loose; Ir. *fluich*, flabby.] Soft and weak; limber; lax; drooping; hanging down by its own weight.—**flaccidly,** flak'sid•li, *adv.* In a flaccid manner.—**flaccidity,** flak•sid'i•ti, *n.* The state of being flaccid.

flag, flag, *n.* [Not found in A.Sax.; same as D. *vlag*, Sw. *flagg, flagga*, Dan. *flag*, G. *flagge*, banner; connected with *flag*, to hang loose.] A cloth, usually bearing emblems or figures and employed as a symbol or signal; any material used like a flag; an indication on a musical note of less than a ¼ beat; a deer's tail.—*Black flag*, a flag of a black color displayed on a piratical vessel as a sign that no mercy will be shown to the vanquished, or on a prison to indicate that an execution has taken place.—*White flag*, a flag of truce.—*Yellow flag*, flag as sign of infection or disease on board a vessel.—*Flag of truce*, a white flag displayed as an invitation to the enemy to confer, and in the meantime as a notification that the fighting shall cease.—*v.t.* To signal with a flag; to signal to stop (to *flag* a train).—**Flag Day,** *n.* June 14, a day in commemoration of the United States flag.—**flag officer,** *n.* The title for an admiral of any grade. —**flagship,** *n.* The ship that bears the flag officer and displays his flag.—**flagpole,** *n.* A pole used to display the flag.

flag, flag, *v.i.*—*flagged, flagging.* [Formerly written *flack*, and connected with Icel. *flaka*, to hang loosely, G. *flacken*, to become languid, O.D. *flaggeren*, to be loose; akin also *flicker*.] To hang loose without stiffness; to be loose and yielding; to grow spiritless or dejected; to droop; to grow languid; to grow stale or vapid; to lose interest or relish.—**flaggingly,** flag'ing•li, *adv.* In a drooping or listless manner.

flag, flag, *n.* [From Icel. *flaga*, a flag, Sw. *flaga*, a flake or scale; allied to L.G. *flage*, a flat marshy place, and Gr. *plax*, a tablet.] A flat stone used for paving.—*v.t.*—*flagged, flagging.* To lay with flags or flat stones.—**flagstone,** *n.* Any fissile sandstone that splits up into flags; a large flat paving stone; a flag.

flag, flag, *n.* [Probably named from its broad leaves resembling flags or standards.] A popular name for many endogenous plants with sword-shaped leaves, mostly growing in moist situations; particularly appropriated to a species of iris.

flagellate, flaj'el•lāt, *v.t.* [L. *flagello, flagellatum*, to beat or whip, from *flagellum*, a whip or scourge, akin to *flail.*] To whip; to scourge.—*a.* Having flagella.—**flagellant,** flaj'el•lant, *n.*—One who whips himself, specifically, one of a fanatical sect founded in Italy A.D. 1260, who maintained that flagellation was of equal virtue with baptism and other sacraments.—**flagellation,** flaj•el•lā'shon, *n.* A flogging; the discipline of the scourge.—**flagelliform,** fla•jel'li•form, *a.* [L. *flagelliformis*.] Long, narrow, and flexible, like the thong of a whip.—**flagellum,** fla•jel'lum, *n.* pl. **flagella,** fla•jel'la. *Bot.* a runner or creeping branch sent out from the bottom of a stem, as in the strawberry; *zool.* the lashlike appendage exhibited by many infusoria.

flageolet, flaj•el•et', *n.* [Fr. *flageolet*, dim. of O.Fr. *flajol*, from L.L. *flauta, flautus*, flute. FLUTE.] A small wind instrument of music, played by a mouthpiece inserted in the bulb-shaped head of the pipe, which is holed and keyed like the flute.

flagitious, fla•jish'us, *a.* [L. *flagitiosus*, from *flagitium*, a shameful act, from *flagito*, to demand or urge hotly or violently, from root *flag*, whence *flagro*, to burn (as in *flagrant*).] Deeply criminal; grossly wicked; vicious; abandoned; profligate; heinous; flagrant.—**flagitiously,** fla•jish'us•li, *adv.* In a flagitious manner. —**flagitiousness,** fla•jish'us•nes, *n.* The condition or quality of being flagitious.

flagon, flag'on, *n.* [Fr. *flacon, flascon*, L.L. *flasca*, a flask. FLASK.] A vessel with a narrow mouth, used for holding and conveying liquors.

flagrant, flā'grant, *a.* [L. *flagrans, flagrantis*, ppr. of *flagro*, to burn (seen in *conflagration*), the root being same as in *flamma*, flame, *flagitium*, a flagitious act.] Flaming into notice; glaring; notorious; enormous.—**flagrantly,** flā'grant•li, *adv.* In a flagrant manner.—**flagrancy,** flā'gran•si, *n.* The quality of being flagrant; heinousness; enormity.

flail, flāl, *n.* [O.Fr. *flael, flaiel, flaial*, from L. *flagellum*, a whip or scourge, whence also *flagellate.*] An instrument for thrashing or beating grain from the ear, consisting of the hand staff, which is held in the hand; the swiple, which strikes the grain; and a thong which connects the two.—*v.t.* and *i.* To beat as if with a flail.

flair, flâr, *n.* [O.Fr. odor, from L. *fragrare.*] Talent for discernment; taste and aptitude combined.

flak, also **flack,** flak, *n.* [From G. abbrev. of *flieger-abwehr-kanone.*] Anti-aircraft fire.

flake, flāk, *n.* [Allied to Icel. *flakna*, to flake off, *flyka*, a flake; E. *flag*, a stone for paving, and *flaw*; Sw. *flaga*, a flake.] A loose filmy or scale-like mass of anything; a scale; a small fleecy or feathery particle; a flock.—*v.t.* and *i.*—*flaked, flaking.* To break or separate in layers; to peel or scale off.—**flaky,** flā'ki, *a.*—**flakiness,** fla'ki•nes, *n.* The state of being flaky.

flambeau, flam'bō, *n.* pl. **flambeaux,** flam'bōz. [Fr., from *flambe*, a blaze, for *flamble*, from L. *flammula*, dim. of *flamma*, a flame.] A flaming torch; a light made of thick wicks covered with wax or other flammable material.—**flamboyant,** flam•boi'ant, *a.* [Fr., flaming.] Characterized by waving curves resembling flames, as in windows of French Gothic style of architecture; showy; ostentatious.—**flamboyance,** flam•boi'ance, *n.* Ostentation.

flame, flām, *n.* [Fr. *flamme*, from L. *flamma*, a flame, for *flagma*, from the root *flag*, whence *flagro*, to burn, to blaze, as in *flagrant, conflagration*; root also in Gr. *phlegō*, to burn.] A blaze; burning vapor or gas rising from matter in a state of visible combustion; fire in general; heat of passion; violent contention; passionate excitement or strife; a state of ardor; warmth of affection; the passion of love; one beloved.— —*v.t.* and *i.*—*flamed, flaming.* To blaze; to make a flame or blaze; to send out a flame or blaze; to shine like burning gas or any other luminous body; to break out in violence of passion.—**flaming,** flā'ming, *a.* Of a bright red or yellow color; burning; ardent; violent;

vehement.—**flamingly,** flā'ming•li, *adv.* In a flaming manner.

flamen, flā'men, *n.* [L.] The name in ancient Rome for any priest devoted to the service of one particular deity.

flamingo, fla•ming'gō, *n.* [Sp. and Pg. *flamenco,* from L. *flamma,* flame, from its red color.] A web-footed tropical bird, with long neck and long slender legs, standing from 5 to 6 feet high, and having scarlet plumage.

flange, flanj, *n.* [A form of *flank.*] A projecting edge or rim on any object, as the rims by which cast-iron pipes are connected together, or those round the wheels of railroad carriages to keep them on the rails.—*v.t.*—*flanged, flanging.* To furnish with a flange; to make a flange on.

flank, flangk, *n.* [Fr. *flanc,* Sp. and Pg. *flanco,* It. *fianco,* the flank; of Germanic origin ultimately, same as O.H.G. *hlanca,* side, loin, flank; akin G. *gelenk,* joint.] The fleshy or muscular part of the side of an animal, between the ribs and the hip; the side of anything, particularly the extreme right or left of an army, brigade, regiment, etc., the outer ships of a fleet, or the place occupied by such forces; any part of a fortified work defending another work by a fire along its face.—*v.t.* and *i.* To stand at the flank or side of; to place troops so as to command or attack the flank of; to pass round or turn the flank of.—**flanker,** flangk'ėr, *n.* One who or that which flanks; one employed on the flank of an army.

flannel, flan'el, *n.* [O.E. and Sc. *flannen,* from W. *gwlanen.* from *gwlan,* wool.] A soft nappy woolen cloth of loose texture.—**flannelette,** flan•el•et', *n.* A cotton cloth with a soft nap.

flap, flap, *n.* [Probably onomatopoetic, being imitative of a blow with a pliant flat surface; *flabby* is a kindred form.] Anything broad and flexible that hangs loose or is attached by one end or side and easily moved; a lappet, a lobe, a skirt or tail of a coat; the motion of anything broad and loose, or a stroke with it.—*v.t.*—*flapped, flapping.* To beat with or as with a flap; to move, as something broad or flaplike.—*v.i.* To move as wings, or as something broad or loose; to wave loosely or flutter.—**flapdragon,** *n.* A play in which the players snatch raisins out of burning brandy; snapdragon.—**flapjack,** *n.* A sort of broad, flat pancake; a fried cake.—**flapper,** flap'ėr, *n.* One who or that which flaps; young women who manifested a freedom of conduct and dress during 10 years after World War I.—**flappy,** flap'ē, *a.* Likely to flap; slack.

flare, flâr, *v.i.*—*flared, flaring.* [Comp. Dan. *flagre,* G. *flackern* (freq. of *flacken*), to flicker, to flare; perhaps akin to *flash.*] To waver or flutter in burning; to burn with an unsteady light; hence, to flutter with gaudy show; to shine out with sudden and unsteady light or splendor; to give out a dazzling light.—*To flare up,* to become suddenly angry or excited.—*n.* A bright unsteady light; a bright patch in the middle of a photographic print, caused by lens reflection; dazzling light used to signal.

flash, flash, *n.* [Comp. Icel. *flasa,* to rush, *flas,* a rush; also E. *flare.*] A sudden burst of light; a flood of light instantaneously appearing and disappearing; a gleam; a sudden burst of something regarded as resembling light, as wit, merriment, passion, etc.; a short and brilliant burst; momentary brightness or show; the time occupied by a flash of light; an instant.—*v.i.* To break or burst forth with a flash or flame; to give out a flash or gleam; to break forth into some new and dazzling condition; to burst out violently; to come, appear, or pass suddenly; to dart (a thought *flashes* through the mind).—*v.t.* To emit or send forth in a sudden flash or flashes; to convey or send instantaneously or startlingly.—*a.* Vulgarly showy or gaudy; forged; counterfeit (*flash* notes).—**flashy,** flash'i, *a.* Showy or gaudy; tawdry; fiery.—**flashily,** flash'i•li, *adv.*—**flashiness,** flash'i•nes, *n.*—**flash bulb,** *n.* Flash lamp that burns metal foil or wire to give momentary daylight brilliance in taking photographs.—**flash point,** flash point, *n.* Temperature at which vapor from oil or gaseous objects ignites.

flask, flask, *n.* [A.Sax. *flasc, flasca, flaxa,* Dan. *flaske,* Sw. *flasca;* ultimate origin doubtful; comp. O.Fr. *flasche, flascon;* Sp. *flasco,* It. *fiasco,* L.L. *flasco, flasca,* a flask; L. *vasculum,* dim. of *vas,* a vessel; also W. *fflasg,* a vessel of wickerwork, a basket.] A kind of bottle; a narrow-necked globular glass bottle; a metal or other pocket drambottle; a vessel for containing gunpowder, carried by sportsmen.—**flasket,** flas'ket, *n.* A vessel in which viands are served up; a long shallow basket.

flat, flat, *a.* [Not in A.Sax. = Icel. *flatr,* Sw. *flat,* Dan. *flad,* G. *flach,* flat; akin Gr. *platys,* Skr. *prithus,* broad.] Having an even and horizontal, or nearly horizontal surface, without elevations or depressions, hills or valleys; level without inclination; level with the ground; prostrate; fallen; laid low; tasteless; stale; vapid; insipid; depressed; without interest, point, or spirit; frigid; dull; peremptory; absolute; positive; downright (a *flat* denial); *mus.* below the natural or the true pitch; not sharp or shrill; not acute; *gram.* applied to consonants, in the enunciation of which voice (in contradistinction to breath) is heard; opposed to *sharp;* as, *b, d, g, z, v.*—*n.* A flat surface; a surface without relief or prominences; a level; a plain; a low tract of land; a shoal; a shallow; a sandbank under water; the flat part or side of anything (the *flat* of the hand, of a sword); *mus.* a mark (♭) placed on a line or in a space of the staff, which indicates that all notes on the same degree (or their octaves) are lowered a semitone; a story or floor of a building; a foolish fellow; a flat section of theatrical scenery; a tire that has been punctured; a flat-bottomed boat.—*v.t.* and *v.i.*—*flatted, flatting.* To flatten.—**flatboat,** *n.* A flat-bottomed boat used to transport bulky materials on shallow waters.—**flatfish,** *n.* One of a group of fish, having a flattened body, that swim with the flattened side up and have both eyes on one side.—**flatiron,** *n.* An iron.—**flatly,** flat'li, *adv.* In a flat manner; horizontally; evenly; positively; plainly.—**flatness,** flat'nes, *n.*—**flatten,** flat'n, *v.t.* To make flat or level; to lay flat; *mus.* to lower in pitch; to render less acute or sharp.—*v.i.* To grow or become flat.—**flattop,** *n.* An aircraft carrier.—**flatwise,** flat'wīz, *a.* and *adv.* With the flat side downward or next to another thing.

flatter, flat'ėr, *v.t.* [Fr. *flatter,* Pr. *flatar,* to pat, stroke, caress, flatter; perhaps from Icel. *flatr,* E. *flat;* comp. also Icel. *flathra,* to fawn or flatter, *flathr,* flattery.] To gratify by praise or obsequiousness; to please by applause, favorable notice, respectful attention, or anything that confirms one's good opinion of one's self; to encourage by favorable notice or by favorable representations or indications (to *flatter* hopes); to inspire with false hopes.—**flatterer,** flat'ėr•ėr, *n.* One who flatters; one who praises another with a view to please him, to gain his favor, or to accomplish some purpose.—**flatteringly,** flat'ėr•ing•li, *adv.* In a flattering manner.—**flattery,** flat'ėr•i, *n.* [Fr. *flatterie.*] The act of one who flatters; false, insincere, or venal praise; adulation; cajolery.

flatulent, flat'ū•lent, *a.* [L.L. *flatulentus,* from L. *flatus,* a blowing, from *flo, flatum,* to blow (as in *inflate*).] Affected with gases generated in the alimentary canal; generating or apt to generate wind in the stomach; windy.—**flatulence, flatulency,** flat'ū•lens, flat'ū•len•si, *n.* [L.L. *flatulentia.*] The state of being flatulent, or affected with an accumulation of gases in the alimentary canal.—**flatulently,** flat'ū•lent•li, *adv.* In a flatulent manner.

flaunt, flạnt, *v.i.* [Connected with prov. G. *flander,* a rag or tatter, *flandern,* to flutter, G. *flattern,* to flirt, to flutter.] To make an ostentatious display; to move or act ostentatiously; to be glaring or gaudy.—*v.t.* To display ostentatiously; to display impudently or offensively.—*n.* The act of flaunting; bold or impudent parade.—**flaunter,** flạn'tėr, *n.* One who flaunts.—**flauntingly,** flạn'ting•li, *adv.* In a flaunting way.—**flaunty, flaunting,** flạn'ti, flạn'ting, *a.* Ostentatious; vulgarly or offensively showy; gaudy.

flautist, flạ'tist, *n.* [It. *flauto,* a flute.] A player on the flute; a flutist.

flavescent, fla•ves'ent, *a.* [L. *flavesco,* to become yellow, from *flavus,* yellow.] *Bot.* yellowish or turning yellow.—**flavin,** flav'in, *n.* A yellow dye of vegetable origin.

flavor, flā'vėr, *n.* [O. F. *flauor, flaveur, flaur, flair,* an odor; all used also in reference to taste.] The quality of any substance which affects the taste; that quality which gratifies the palate; relish; zest; the quality of a substance which affects the smell; odor; fragrance.—*v.t.* To communicate flavor or some quality of taste or smell to.—**flavoring,** flā'vėr•ing, *n.* Any substance used for imparting flavor; seasoning.—**flavorless,** flā'vėr•les, *a.* Without flavor; tasteless.—**flavorous,** flā'vėr•us, *a.* Having a rich or pleasant flavor.

flaw, flạ, *n.* [A.Sax. *flóh,* that which has flown off, a fragment; Goth. *flaga,* a fragment; Sw. *flaga,* a flaw, *flaga sig,* to scale off, akin to *flake* and *flag*; comp. also W. *fflaw,* a splinter, *ffla,* a parting from.] A crack; a defect of continuity or cohesion; a gap or fissure; any blemish or imperfection; a defect; a fault; a sudden burst of wind; a sudden gust or blast of short duration.—*v.t.* To make or produce a flaw in.—**flawless,** flạ'les, *a.* Without flaw or defect.—**flawy,** flạ'i, *a.* Full of flaws; defective; faulty; subject to sudden gusts.

flax, flaks, *n.* [A.Sax. *fleax*=D. *vlas,* Fris. *flax,* G. *flachs,* flax; allied to Bohem. *vlas,* Rus. *volos,* Lith. *plaukas,* hair, from a root meaning to comb. weave, or twist, seen in L. *plecto,* Gr. *plekō,* to weave or plait.] A wiry, erect-stemmed annual plant, the fiber of which is used for making linen thread and cloth, lace, etc.; the fibrous part of the plant when broken and cleaned by scutching and hackling.—**flaxen,** flak'sn, *a.* Made of flax; resembling flax; of the color of flax; fair.

flay, flā, *v.t.* [A.Sax. *fleán,* to flay; O.D. *vlaegen, vlaen,* to flay; akin *flake, flaw.*] To skin; to strip off the skin of.—**flayer,** flā'ėr, *n.* One who flays.

flea, flē, *n.* [A.Sax. *fleá,* from *fleôn, fleôgan,* to fly; D. *vloo,* Icel. *fló,* Sc. *flech,* G. *floh,* a flea.] A hardbodied, wingless insect, with remarkable powers of leaping, that feeds on warm-blooded animals.—*A flea in the ear,* an annoying, unexpected hint or reply.—*v.t.* To clean from fleas.—**fleabane,** flē'bān, *n.* A name popularly given to several composite plants from their supposed power of destroying or driving away fleas.—**fleabite,** flē'bīt, *n.* The bite of a flea; a trifling wound or pain; a slight inconvenience; a thing of no moment.

fleam, flēm, *n.* [D. *vlijm,* Fr. *flamme,* O.H.G. *fliedimā,* from L.L. *flevotomum, flebotomum,* from Gr. *phlebs, phlebos,* a vein, and *tomos,* a cutting. PHLEBOTOMY.] A sharp instrument used by farriers for opening veins for letting blood; a lancet.

flèche, flāsh, *n.* [Fr.] A slight fieldwork, with two faces forming an angle pointing forward. A spire at the intersection of the nave and transepts of a church.

fleck, flek, *n.* [Icel. *flekkr,* D. *vlek,* G. *fleck,* a spot; allied to *flick.*] A spot; a streak; a dapple; a stain.—*v.t.* To spot; to streak or stripe; to variegate; to dapple.

flection, flek'shon, *n.* [L. *flectio.*] The act of bending or state of being bent; inflection.

fled, fled, pret. & pp. of *flee.*

fledge, flej, *v.t.*—*fledged, fledging.* [Icel. *fleygr,* able to fly, from *fljúga,* to fly; comp. G. *flück, flügge,* feathered, from *fliegen,* to fly.] To furnish with feathers; to supply with the feathers necessary for flight: chiefly in pp.—**fledgling,** flej'ling, *n.* A young bird just fledged.

flee, flē, *v.i.* pret. and pp. *fled*; ppr., *fleeing.* [A.Sax. *fleón,* to flee, *ic fleó,* I flee; akin to *fleógan,* to fly, Icel. *flyja,* Dan. *flye,* Sw. *fly,* G. *fliehen,* to flee. FLY.] To hasten or run away, as from danger or evil; to resort to shelter; sometimes apparently transitive, *from* being omitted before the object.

fleece, flēs, *n.* [A.Sax. *fleós, flýs,* a fleece, wool=D. *vlies,* G. *fliess*; root meaning doubtful.] The coat of wool that covers a sheep or that is shorn from a sheep at one time; any covering resembling wool.—*Golden Fleece,* the object of the Argonauts under Jason.—*Order of Golden Fleece,* the Flemish and Spanish order, commemorating the wool trade of Flanders, a sheep suspended by ribbon from the neck.—*v.t.*—*fleeced, fleecing.* To deprive of the fleece; to strip of money or property; to rob or cheat heartlessly.—**fleecer,** flē'sėr, *n.* One who fleeces or strips of money.—**fleecy,** flē'si, *a.* Covered with wool; woolly; resembling wool or a fleece.

fleer, flēr, *v.i.* [Comp. Dan. dial. *flire,* to laugh, to sneer, N. *flira,* to titter.] To make a wry face in contempt; to grin, sneer, mock, or gibe.—*v.t.* To mock; to flout at.—*n.* The act of one who fleers.

fleet, flēt, *n.* [A.Sax. *fleōt, fliēt,* a ship, from *fleōtan,* to float; akin D. *vloot,* G. *flotte,* fleet. FLOAT.] A body or squadron of ships; a number of ships, trucks, etc., operating in company; old London prison, from the ditch or stream of the Fleet, giving its name to Fleet Street, crossing it at right angles, and entering the city by the *fleet-gate, flood-gate.*—**Fleet Street,** *n.* Newspaper headquarters in London.

fleet, flēt, *a.* [Icel. *fljótr,* A.Sax. *fleótig.* quick; allied to *flit,* and *float.* FLIT, FLOAT.] Swift of pace; moving or able to move with rapidity; nimble; light and quick in motion.—*v.i.* To fly swiftly; to hasten; to flit, as a light substance.—*v.t.* To skim over the surface; to pass over rapidly.—**fleeting,** flē'ting, *p.* and *a.* Passing rapidly; transient; not durable (the *fleeting* moments). ∴ Syn. under TRANSIENT.—**fleetly,** flēt'li, *adv.* In a fleet manner; rapidly; swiftly.—**fleetness,** flēt'nes, *n.* The quality of being fleet; swiftness; rapidity; velocity; celerity; speed.

Fleming, flem'ing, *n.* A native of Flanders.—**Flemish,** flem'ish, *a.* Pertaining to Flanders.—*n.* The language of the Flemings, closely akin to Dutch; *pl.* the people of Flanders.

flense, flens, *v.t.*—*flensed, flensing.* [Dan. *flense*; D. *vlensen.*] To cut up and obtain the blubber of a whale.

flesh, flesh, *n.* [A.Sax. *flaesc*=D. *vleesch,* G. *fleisch,* flesh; Icel. and Dan. *flesk,* bacon or pork; further connections are doubtful.] The substance which forms a large part of an animal, consisting of the softer solids, as distinguished from the bones, the skin, and the fluids; animal food, in distinction from vegetable; beasts and birds used as food, in distinction from fish; the body, as distinguished from the soul; the bodily frame; the human race; mankind; human nature; bodily appetite; kindred; family; the soft pulpy substance of fruit; also that part of a root, fruit, etc., which is fit to be eaten.—*v.t.* To initiate to the taste of flesh (as dogs used in hunting); to accustom to flesh; to imbrue a sword in blood for the first time.—**fleshed,** flesht, *p.* and *a.* Fat; fleshy; having flesh of a particular kind.—**flesher,** flesh'ėr, *n.* A knife used for scraping flesh from hides.—**flesh fly,** *n.* Same as *Blowfly.*—**fleshiness,** flesh'i•nes, *n.* State of being fleshy; plumpness; corpulence.—**fleshing,** flesh'ing, *n.* [Generally in plural.] A kind of drawers worn by actors, dancers, etc., resembling the natural skin.—**fleshliness,** flesh'li•nes, *n.* State of being fleshly; carnal passions and appetites.—**fleshly,** flesh'li, *a.* Pertaining to the flesh; corporeal; carnal; lascivious; human—**fleshpot,** flesh'pot, *n.* High living; a luxurious abundance.—**fleshy,** flesh'i, *a.* Full of flesh; pulpy, as fruit; plump; fat; corpulent; corporeal; human.

fleur-de-lis, flėr•de•lē, *n.* [Fr., flower of the lily.] A heraldic figure representing either a lily or the head of a lance or some such weapon; the distinctive bearing of the kingdom of France; *bot.* the iris.

flew, flū, pret. of *fly.*

flex, fleks, *v.t.* [From L. *flecto, flexum,* to bend; seen also in *deflect, inflect, reflect,* etc.] To bend.—**flexed,** flekst, *p.* and *a.* Bent; having a bent shape.—**flexible,** flek'si•bl, *a.* [L. *flexibilis,* from *flecto, flexum.*] Capable of being flexed or bent; pliant; yielding to pressure; not stiff; capable of yielding to entreaties, arguments, or other moral force; manageable; tractable; easy and compliant; capable of being molded into different forms or styles; plastic; capable of being adapted or accommodated.—**flexibility,** flek•si•bil'i•ti, *n.* The quality of being flexible; pliancy; easiness to be persuaded; readiness to comply; facility.—**flexibly,** flek'si•bli, *adv.* In a flexible manner.—**flexile,** flek'sīl, *a.* [L. *flexilis.*] Pliant; pliable; flexible.—**flexion,** flek'shon, *n.* [L. *flexio.*] The act of bending; the bending of a joint which brings the connected parts closer together;

a bending; a part bent; *gram.* an inflection.—**flexor,** flek′sėr, *n. Anat.* a muscle whose office is to produce flexion.—**flexuous,** flek′sū•us, *a.* [L. *flexuosus.*] Winding or bending; having turns or windings; *bot.* changing its direction in a curve, from joint to joint, from bud to bud, or from flower to flower; in this sense written also *flexuose.*—**flexure,** flek′shėr, *n.* [L. *flexura.*] A bending; the form in which a thing is bent; part bent; a bend.

flick, flik, *n.* [Akin to *flip, flap.*] A sharp sudden stroke, as with a whip; a flip.—*v.t.* and *i.* To strike or move with a flick; to flip.

flicker, flik′ėr, *v.t.* and *i.* [A.Sax. *flicerian,* to flutter or move the wings; G. *flackern,* to flare, to blaze, to flutter; D. *flikkeren,* to twinkle; Icel. *flaka,* to flap.] To flutter or flap the wings; to fluctuate or waver, as a flame in a current of air.—*n.* A wavering or fluctuating gleam, as of a candle; a flutter; North American woodpecker marked with red at the back of the neck and having speckled underparts.

flight, flīt, *n.* [A.Sax. *fligt,* from *fleógan,* to fly. FLY.] The act of fleeing; hasty or precipitate departure; the act or power of flying; volitation; the manner or mode of flying; a flock of birds flying in company; the birds produced in the same season; a discharge; a mounting or soaring; an extravagant excursion or sally, as of the imagination; scheduled airplane trip; basic unit of military air forces; series of steps or stairs from one platform or landing to another.—**flightily,** flī′ti•li, *adv.* In a flighty, wild, capricious, or imaginative manner.—**flightiness,** flī′ti•nes, *n.* The state of being flighty; extreme volatility.—**flighty,** flī′ti, *a.* Fleeting‡; indulging in flights or sallies of imagination, humor, caprice, etc.; volatile; giddy; fickle.

flimsy, flim′zi, *a.* [Origin doubtful.] Without strength or solid substance; of loose and unsubstantial structure; without reason or plausibility.—*n.* A thin sort of paper.—**flimsily,** flim′zi•li, *adv.* In a flimsy manner.—**flimsiness,** flim′zi•nes, *n.* State or quality of being flimsy.

flinch, flinsh, *v.i.* [Perhaps corrupted from *blench,* or from O.E. *flecche,* Fr. *fléchir,* L. *flectere,* to bend.] To draw back from pain or danger; to show signs of yielding or of suffering; to shrink; to wince.—**flincher,** flinsh′ėr, *n.* One who flinches or fails.—**flinchingly,** flinsh′ing•li, *adv.* In a flinching manner.

flinder, *n.* Fragment; splinter.

fling, fling, *v.t.—flung, flinging.* [Akin to O.Sw. *flenga,* to strike or beat; Dan. *flenge,* to slash.] To cast, send, or throw; to hurl; to send or shed forth; to emit; to scatter; to throw to the ground; to prostrate.—*v.i.* To flounce; to throw out the legs violently; to start away with a sudden motion, as in token of displeasure; to rush away angrily.—*n.* A throw; a gibe; a sarcasm; a severe or contemptuous remark; enjoyment of pleasure to the full extent of one's opportunities (to take one's *fling*: *colloq.*); a Scotch dance, the Highland *fling.*

flint, flint, *n.* [A.Sax. and Dan. *flint,* Sw. *flinta;* same root as Gr. *plinthos,* a brick.] A species of quartz, of a yellowish or bluish-gray or grayish-black color, very hard and used to form an ingredient in fine pottery; a piece of flint used to strike fire with steel or in a flintlock.—**flinty,** flin′ti, *a.* Consisting or composed of flint; containing flints; like flint; very hard; cruel; unmerciful.—**flintiness,** flin′ti•nes, *n.*—**flintlock,** *n.* A musket gunlock with flint fixed in the hammer to strike against steel and produce sparks which ignite the charge.

flip, flip, *n.* [A form of *flap.*] A smart blow, as with a whip; a flick; a drink.—*v.t.* To flick; to put into motion quickly so as to cause to turn over in the air, as to *flip* a coin.—*v.i.* To make a small, abrupt movement.

flippant, flip′ant, *a.* [Formed from *flip, flap;* comp. Icel. *fleipr,* tattle, *fleipinn,* pert, petulant.] Speaking fluently and confidently, without knowledge or consideration; heedlessly pert; showing undue levity.—**flippancy, flippantness,** flip′an•si, flip′ant•nes, *n.* The state or quality of being flippant.—**flippantly,** flip′ant•li, *adv.* In a flippant manner; volubly.

flipper, flip′ėr, *n.* [Equivalent to *flapper,* from *flap.*] The paddle of a sea turtle; the broad fin of a fish; the arm of a seal; broad, flat, finlike rubber shoe used in skin diving.

flirt, flėrt, *v.t.* [A.Sax. *fleard,* trifle, folly; *fleardian,* to trifle; comp. G. *flirren,* trifles, *flirren,* to make a confused noise.] To throw with a jerk or sudden effort or exertion; to fling suddenly; to move with short, quick movements; to make coquettish motions with (a fan).—*v.i.* To run and dart about; to act with levity or giddiness; to play the coquette.—*n.* A sudden jerk; a quick throw or cast; one who flirts; a woman who plays at courtship; a coquette.—**flirtation,** flėr•tā′shon, *n.* A flirting; a playing at courtship; coquetry.—**flirtatious,**† flėr•tā′shus, *a.* Given to flirtation.

flit, flit, *v.i.—flitted, flitting.* [Dan. *flytte,* Sw. *flytta,* to remove; akin to *flee, fleet, flutter,* etc.] To fly away with a rapid motion; to dart along, as a bird; to move with celerity through the air; to move rapidly about; to flutter; to migrate.—*n.* The act of one who flits.

flitch, flich, *n.* [A.Sax. *flicce,* a flitch of bacon; Icel. *flikki,* a flitch.] The side of a hog salted and cured; *carp.* a plank fastened side by side with others to form a compound beam.

float, flōt, *v.i.* [A.Sax. *flotian,* to float, *fleótan,* to fleet; *fleet, flow, flood* are closely allied. FLOW.] To rest or glide on the surface of a fluid; to swim or be buoyed up; to move as if supported by a fluid; to move gently and easily through the air.—*v.t.* To cause to float; to cause to rest or be conveyed on the surface of a fluid; to flood; to inundate; to overflow.—*To float a scheme,* to bring it prominently before public notice; to raise funds for carrying it on.—*n.* That which floats on the surface of a fluid; a collection of timber fastened together and floated down a stream; a raft; a buoy; the cork or quill on an angling line, to support it and indicate the bite of a fish; a plasterer's tool for producing a plane surface; the float board of a water wheel or paddle wheel.—**floatage, flotage,** flō′tij, *n.* Anything that floats on the water.—**floatation,** flō•tā′shon, *n.* The science of floating bodies.—**floater,** flō′tėr, *n.* One that floats.—**floating,** flō′ting, *p.* and *a.* Resting on and buoyed up by a fluid; circulating; not fixed or invested; opposed to *sunk* (*floating* capital; *floating* debt); disconnected; unattached (*floating* ribs in fishes); fluctuating; unsettled (a *floating* population).—*Floating dock.* Under DOCK.

floccose, flok•ōs′, *a.* [L. *floccosus.*] *Bot.* composed of or bearing tufts of woolly, or long and soft, hairs.—**flocculence,** flok′ū•lens, *n.* The state of being flocculent; adhesion in small flakes.—**flocculent,** flok′ū•lent, *a.* Coalescing and adhering in locks or flakes.

flock, flok, *n.* [From O.Fr. *floc,* L. *floccus,* a lock of wool; comp. G. *flocke,* O.G. *floccho,* D. *vlok,* Sw. *flocka,* Dan. *flokke.*] A lock of wool or hair; the refuse of cotton and wool, or shreds of woolen goods, used for stuffing mattresses, etc.—**flocky,** flok′i, *a.* Abounding with flocks; floccose.

flock, flok, *n.* [A.Sax. *floc, flocc,* a flock, a company of men = Dan. *flok,* Sw. *flock,* Icel. *flokkr,* flock; perhaps same as *folk.*] A company or collection of living creatures, especially applied to birds and sheep; a Christian congregation in relation to their pastor, who takes charge of them in spiritual things.—*v.i.* To gather in flocks or crowds.

floe, flō, *n.* [Dan. *flage,* Sw. *flaga,* a floe; akin to *flake.*] A large mass of ice floating in the ocean.

flog, flog, *v.t.—flogged, flogging.* [Allied to Prov. E. *flack,* to beat; *flacket,* to flap about; perhaps also to *flap* or *flag.*] To beat or whip; to chastise with repeated blows.—*To flog a dead horse,* to try to revive interest in a stale subject.—**flogger,** flog′ėr, *n.* One who flogs.

flood, flud, *n.* [A.Sax. *flód,* a flood = Fris. Dan. and Sw. *flod,* Icel. *flód,* D. *vloed;* from the root of *flow.*] A great flow of water; a body of water rising and overflowing the land; a river (*poet.*); the flowing in of the tide: opposed to *ebb;* a flow or stream of anything fluid; a great quantity; an overflowing; abundance; superabundance.—*The Flood,* the deluge in the days of Noah.—*v.t.* and *i.* To overflow; to inundate;

to cause to be covered with water.—**floodgate,** *n.* A gate to be opened for letting water flow, or to be shut to prevent it.—**floodlight,** *n.* Lighting unit that casts a bright, broad beam.

floor, flōr, *n.* [A.Sax. *flór*, a floor = D. *vloer*, a floor; G. *flur*, a field, a floor; W. *llawr*, the ground, a floor.] That part of a building or room on which we walk; a platform; a story in a building; a suite of rooms on a level.—*v.t.* To furnish with a floor; to strike or knock down level with the floor (*colloq.*).—**floorer,** flō′rėr, *n.* One who or that which floors; a blow which floors a person (*colloq.*).—**flooring,** flō′ring, *n.* A floor; materials for floors.

flop, flop, *v.t.* [A form of *flap.*] To clap; to flap; to let fall or sink down suddenly.—*v.i.* To strike about with something broad and flat; to fail; to plump down suddenly.—*n.* A sudden sinking to the ground.—**floppy,** flop′i, *a.* Having a tendency to flop.

Flora, flō′ra, *n.* [L., from *flos, floris*, a flower (whence also *flower, flour, flourish*, etc.).] The Roman goddess of flowers; (*not. cap.*) a list of plants of a certain district or region; a collective term for the plants indigenous to any district, region, or period.—**floral,** flō′ral, *a.* Containing or belonging to the flower; pertaining to flowers in general; made of flowers.—**florally,** flō′ral•li, *adv.* In a floral manner.—**floriated,** flō′ri•ā•ted, *a.* Decorated with floral ornament; having florid ornaments.—**florescence,** flō•res′ens, *n.* [L. *florescens*, pp. of *floresco.*] *Bot.* a bursting into flower; the season when plants expand their flowers; inflorescence.—**florescent,** flō•res′-ent, *a.* Bursting into flower; flowering.—**floret,** flō′ret, *n.* A single small flower in a compact inflorescence.—**floriculture,** flō′ri•kul•chėr, *n.* [L. *flos, floris*, and *cultura.*] The culture or cultivation of flowers or flowering plants.—**floricultural,** flō•ri•kul′-chėr•al, *a.* Relating to floriculture.—**floriculturist,** flō•ri•kul′chėr•ist, *n.* One interested in floriculture.—**florid,** flor′id, *a.* [L. *floridus*, from *flos, floris.*] Flowery; bright in color; flushed with red; of a lively red color; embellished with profuse ornamentation, especially with flowers of rhetoric, or high-flown or elaborately elegant language.—**floridity, floridness,** flo•rid′i•ti, flor′id•nes, *n.* The quality or condition of being florid.—**floridly,** flor′id•li, *adv.* In a showy imposing way.—**floriferous,** flō•rif′ėr•us, *a.* Producing flowers.—**florist,** flor′ist, *n.* [Fr. *fleuriste*, a florist.] A cultivator of flowers; one who deals in flowers; one who writes a flora.

Florence, flor′ens, *n.* A kind of wine from *Florence* in Italy; a gold coin of the reign of Edward III, of Britain, value 6 shillings.—*Florence flask*, a globular bottle of thin transparent glass with a long neck.—**Florentine,** flor′en•tīn, *a.* Of or pertaining to Florence.—*n.* A native of Florence; a kind of silk cloth.

florin, flor′in, *n.* [Fr. *florin*, from It. *florino*, first applied to a Florentine coin, because stamped with a lily; It. *fiore*, a flower, from L. *flos, floris*, a flower.] A name given to different coins of gold or silver, of different values, and to moneys of account, in different countries; a British coin, value 2 shillings.

floss, flos, *n.* [It. *floscio, flosso*, soft, flaccid, from L. *fluxus*, flowing, loose.] A downy or silky substance in the husks of certain plants; untwisted filaments of the finest silk, etc.—**floss silk,** *n.* Floss; silk fibers broken off in unwinding the cocoons, and used for coarser fabrics.

flotation. See FLOATATION, under FLOAT.

flotilla, flō•til′la, *n.* [Sp. dim. of *flota*, a fleet.] A little fleet; a fleet of small vessels.

flotsam, flot′sam, *n.* [From *float.*] Such a portion of the wreck of a ship and the cargo as continues floating on the surface of the water. JETSAM.

flounce, flouns, *v.i.*—*flounced, flouncing.* [Akin N. and O.Sw. *flunsa*, to plunge about in water.] To throw one's self about with jerks, as if in displeasure or agitation.—*n.* A sudden jerking motion of the body.

flounce, flouns, *n.* [Originally *frounce*, from Fr. *froncis*, a plait, from *froncer, fronser*, to wrinkle, from L. *frons, frontis*, the front or forehead. FRONT.] A strip of cloth sewed horizontally round a frock or gown, with the lower border loose and spreading.—*v.t.* To deck with a flounce or flounces.

flounder, floun′dėr, *n.* [Gr. *flunder*, Sw. *flundra*, Dan. *flynder*, flounder.] One of the most common of the flat fishes, found in the sea and near the mouths of rivers.

flounder, floun′dėr, *v.i.* [Akin to D. *flodderen*, to flap like a loose garment.] To fling arms and body in clumsy struggle to move, stand or swim; to struggle, as a fish on land.

flour, flour, *n.* [Fr. *fleur*, a flower, *fleur de farine*, flour, lit. 'flour of meal', the finest part of the meal; comp. *flowers of sulfur*. *Flower* is merely another form.] The finely ground meal of wheat or of any other grain; the finer part of meal separated by bolting; the fine and soft powder of any substance.—*v.t.* To convert into flour; to sprinkle with flour.—**floury,** flou′ri, *a.* Consisting of or resembling flour; covered with flour.

flourish, flur′ish, *v.i.* [Fr. *fleurir, fleurissant*, L. *florere*, to flower, to bloom, from *flos, floris*, a flower. FLORA.] To grow luxuriantly; to increase and enlarge; to thrive; to be prosperous; to increase in wealth, comfort, happiness, or honor; to prosper; to live at a certain period (said of authors, painters, etc.); to use florid language; to make ornamental strokes in writing; to move or be moved in fantastic irregular figures; to play a bold prelude or fanfare.—*v.t.* To adorn with flowers or beautiful figures; to ornament with anything showy; to give a fair appearance to (*Shak.*); to make bold or irregular movements with; to hold in the hand and swing about; to brandish.—*n.* An ostentatious embellishment; parade of words and figures; show; a fanciful stroke of the pen or graver; a brandishing; the waving of a weapon or something held in the hand; the decorative notes which a singer or instrumental performer adds to a passage.—*Flourish of trumpets*, a trumpet call, fanfare, or prelude performed on the approach of any person of distinction; hence, any ostentatious preliminary sayings or doings.—**flourisher,** flur′ish•ėr, *n.* One who flourishes.—**flourishing,** flur′ish•ing, *p.* and *a.* Prosperous; thriving.—**flourishingly,** flur′ish•ing•li, *adv.* In a flourishing manner.

flout, flout, *v.t.* [D. *fluiten, fluyten*, to play on the flute, to whistle, to jeer, from *fluit*, a flute. FLUTE.] To mock or insult; to treat with contempt or disrespect; to jeer at; to jibe.—*v.i.* To behave with contempt: often with *at.*—*n.* A mock; an insult.—**flouter,** flou′tėr, *n.* One who flouts.

flow, flō, *v.i.* [A.Sax. *flówan*, to flow = D. *vloeijen*, to flow; Icel. *flóa*, to flood; O.H.G. *flawan*, to wash; from a root seen in L. *pluvius*, rain, Gr. *pleō*, to swim; Skr. *plu*, to flow. Akin are *flood, float, fleet*, etc.] To move along in the manner of liquids; to run like water; to melt; to proceed or issue as from a source; to abound; to have or be in abundance; to glide along smoothly, without harshness or roughness; to be smooth or pleasant to the ear; to be easily or smoothly uttered; to hang loose and waving; to rise, as the tide: opposed to *ebb.*—*v.t.* To cover with water; to overflow.—*n.* A stream of water or other fluid; a current; an outflow; the rise of the tide; abundance; copiousness; undisturbed and even movement.—**flowage,** flō′ij, *n.* Act of flowing; state of being flowed.—**flowingly,** flō′ing•li, *adv.* In a flowing manner.—**flowingness,** flō′ing•nes, *n.*

flower, flou′ėr, *n.* [O.Fr. *flour*, Mod. Fr. *fleur*, from L. *flos, floris*, a flower, whence also *floral, florid, florin*, etc. *Flour* is really the same word though it has taken a different signification and spelling.] The delicate and gaily-colored leaves or petals on a plant; a circle of leaves or leaflets of some other color than green; a bloom or blossom; more strictly, in *bot.* the organs of reproduction in a phenogamous plant, consisting of, when complete, stamens and pistils together with two sets of leaves which surround and protect them, the calyx and corolla; the early part of life or of manhood; the prime; youthful vigor; youth; the best or finest part; a figure of speech; an ornament of style; *pl.* a powdery or mealy substance (as *flowers* of sulfur); the menstrual discharge.—*v.i.* To blossom; to bloom; to flourish.—*v.t.* To embellish with figures of flowers; to adorn with imitated flowers.—**flowerage,** flou′ėr•ij, *n.* Flowers in general.—**floweret,** flou′ėr•et, *n.* A small flower; a floret.—**flower head,** *n. Bot.* a capitulum or head of sessile flowers, as in the daisy.—**floweriness,** flou′-ėr•i•nes, *n.* The state of being flowery; floridness of speech.—**flowering,** flou′ėr•ing, *p.* and *a.* Having or producing flowers.—**flowerless,** flou′-ėr•les, *a.* Having no flowers.—**flowerpot,** *n.* A pot in which flowering plants or other plants are grown.—**flowery,** flou′ėr•i, *a.* Full of flowers; abounding with blossoms; richly embellished with figurative language; florid.

flu, flö, *n.* [Short for *influenza.*] Contagious respiratory ailment.

fluctuate, fluk′tū•āt, *v.i.—fluctuated, fluctuating.* [L. *fluctuo, fluctuatum,* from *fluctus,* a wave, from *fluo,* to flow, whence *fluent,* etc. FLUENT.] To move as a wave; to wave; to float backward and forward; to be in an unsettled state.—*v.t.* To put into a state of fluctuating or wavelike motion.—**fluctuant,** fluk′-chū•ant, *a.* [L. *fluctuans, fluctuantis.*] Moving like a wave; wavering; unsteady. —**fluctuation,** fluk•chū•ā′-shon, *n.* [L. *fluctuatio.*] A motion like that of waves; a moving in this and that direction; a rising and falling; a wavering; unsteadiness.

flue, flö, *n.* [Comp. O.Fr. *flue,* a flowing, from *fluer,* L. *fluere,* to flow.] A passage for smoke in a chimney; a pipe or tube for conveying heat, as in certain kinds of steam boilers, etc.

flue, flö, *n.* [FLUFF.] Downy matter; fluff.

fluent, flö′ent, *a.* [L. *fluens, fluentis,* ppr. of *fluo, fluxum,* to flow, as in *affluence, confluence, influence, flux,* etc.; akin Gr. *phlyō,* to bubble over.] Flowing; ready in the use of words; having words at command and uttering them with facility and smoothness; voluble; smooth.—*n. Math.* the variable or flowing quantity in fluxions which is continually increasing or decreasing.—**fluently,** flö′ent•li, *adv.* In a fluent manner.—**fluency,** flö′en•si, *n.* The quality of being fluent; readiness of utterance; volubility.

fluff, fluf, *n.* [Also *flue;* akin to *flock,* L.G. *flog, flok,* flue.] Light down or nap such as rises from beds, cotton, etc.; flue.—**fluffy,** fluf′i, *a.* Containing or resembling fluff; giving off fluff; fluey.

flugelman. Same as fugleman.

fluid, flö′id, *n.* [L. *fluidus,* from *fluo,* to flow. FLUENT.] Capable of flowing or moving like water; liquid or gaseous.—*n.* A fluid body or substance; a body whose particles on the slightest pressure move and change their relative position without separation.—**fluid dram,** flö′id dram, *n.* A unit equal to $^1/_8$ fluid ounce.—**fluid ounce,** flö′id ounce, *n.* A unit of liquid capacity equal to $^1/_{16}$ pint.—**fluidity,** flö•id′i•ti, *n.*

fluke, flök, *n.* [Akin to G. *flunk,* a wing, the fluke of an anchor; comp. also Sw. *flik,* Dan. *flig,* a flap or lappet; Dan. *anker-flig,* anchor fluke.] The part of an anchor which catches in the ground; one of the two triangular divisions constituting the tail of a whale; *billiards,* an accidental successful stroke; hence, any unexpected or accidental advantage.—**fluky,** flö′ki, *a.*

fluke, flök, *n.* [A.Sax. *flóc,* a flatfish.] A flounder; a leaflike parasitic worm which infests the livers of sheep, cattle, etc.

flume, flöm, *n.* [Connected with *flow.*] The passage or channel for the water that drives a mill wheel; an artificial channel for gold washing.

flummery, flum′ėr•i, *n.* [W. *llymry,* flummery, oatmeal steeped until sour, from *llymyr,* harsh, *llym,* sharp.] A sort of jelly made of flour or meal; flour from oats steeped in water until sour and then boiled; flattery; empty compliment; nonsense.

flunk, flungk, *v.t.* and *i.* [Colloq. U.S.] To fail, as in an examination or course of study.

flunky, flung′ki, *n.* [L.G. *flunkern,* to flaunt; D. *flonkeren, flinkeren,* to glitter; or from *flank,* one that keeps at his master's flank.] A male servant in livery; a toady.

fluorite, flö′or•īt, *n.* Fluorspar.

fluorspar, flö′or•spär, *n.* [L. *fluor,* a flowing (from *fluo,* to flow), and *spar.*] Calcium fluoride, a crystalline mineral sometimes colorless and transparent, but more frequently exhibiting tints of yellow, green, blue, and red, manufactured into various ornamental articles.

fluorescence, flö•o•res′ens, *n.* [From L. *fluor,* L. *flux,* fr. *fluere,* to flow.] Property of emitting electromagnetic radiation in the form of light as the result of (and only during) the absorption of light from another source.—**fluorescent,** flö•o•res′ent, *a.* —**fluorescent lamp,** flö•o•res′cent lamp, *n.* An electron tube, coated on the inside with phosphor and containing mercury vapors, that converts ultraviolet discharge into visible light.—**fluoroscope,** flö′ro•-skōp, *n.* A machine for examining the body internally by studying shadows cast on a fluorescent screen by structures through which X-rays are sent.

fluorine, flö′o•rin, *n.* [L. *fluor.*] A nonmetallic, gaseous element, yellow and corrosive. Symbol, F; at. no., 9; at. wt., 18.9984.—**fluoride,** flö′o•rīd, *n.* Fluorine combined with another element; salt of hydrofluoric acid.—**fluoridate,** flö′or•i•dāt, *v.t.* To add a fluoride to, as to drinking water.—**fluoridation,** flö•o•ri•dā′shon, *n.*

flurry, flur′i, *n.* [Of doubtful origin and connections; comp. Sw. *flurig,* disordered, *flur,* disordered hair.] A sudden blast or gust of wind; a short snowfall; agitation; commotion; bustle.—*v.t.* To put in agitation; to excite or alarm.

flush, flush, *v.i.* [Perhaps akin to *flash;* or from O.Fr. *flux,* a flowing, a flush at cards, from L. *fluxus.* FLUX.] To flow and spread suddenly, as the blood to the face; to become suffused; to become suddenly red; to blush.—*v.t.* To cause to blush or redden suddenly; to elate; to excite; to animate with joy; to wash out by drenching with copious supplies of water; *sporting,* to cause to start up or fly off; to spring.—*n.* A sudden flow of blood to the face; the redness so produced; any warm coloring or glow; sudden thrill or shock of feeling; bloom; vigor; a rush or flow of water; a run of cards of the same suit.

flush, flush, *a.* [Origin doubtful.] Fresh; full of vigor; well supplied with money (*slang*); having the surface even or level with the adjacent surface.

fluster, flus′tėr, *v.t.* [Icel. *flauster,* fluster, *flaustra,* to be in a fluster; Norweg. *flosa,* passion.] To make hot with drinking; to heat; to agitate; to confuse.—*n.* Heat; glow; agitation; confusion of mind.

flute, flöt, *n.* [Fr. *flûte,* O.Fr. *flaüte,* from *flaüter,* from a L.L. *flatuare* (giving *flautare* by metathesis), from L. *flatus,* a blowing, from L. *flo, flatum,* to blow (as in *inflate*); akin *flageolet.*] A musical wind instrument consisting of a tube with six holes for the fingers, and from one to fourteen keys which open other holes; a perpendicular furrow or channel cut along the shaft of a column or pilaster; any similar groove or channel in any material.—*v.i.—fluted, fluting.* To play on a flute.—*v.t.* To play or sing in notes resembling those of a flute; to form flutes or channels in.—**fluted,** flö′ted, *p.* and *a.* Channeled; furrowed; *mus.* clear and mellow; flutelike.—**fluter,** flö′tėr, *n.* A flutist; one who makes grooves or flutes.—**fluting,** flö′ting, *n.* The act of forming a groove or flute; fluted work.—**flutist,** flö′tist, *n.* A performer on the flute.

flutter, flut′ėr, *v.i.* [A.Sax. *floterian,* to fluctuate, from *flot,* the sea; allied to *float,* and to L.G. *fluttern,* G. *flattern,* to flutter.] To move or flap the wings rapidly, without flying, or with short flights; to move about with bustle; to move with quick vibrations or undulations; to be in agitation.—*v.t.* To agitate; to disorder; to throw into confusion. —*n.* Quick and irregular motion; vibration; agitation of the mind; confusion; disorder.—**flutterer,** flut′-ėr•ėr, *n.* One who flutters.—**flutteringly,** flut′ėr•ing•li, *adv.* In a fluttering manner.

fluvial, flö′vi•al, *a.* [L. *fluvialis, fluviaticus, fluviatilis,* from *fluvius,* a river, from *fluo,* to flow.] Belonging to rivers; produced by river action; growing or living in fresh-water rivers.—**fluviomarine,** flö′vi•ō•ma•-rēn″, *a. Geol.* formed or deposited in estuaries or on the bottom of the sea at the embouchure of a river.

flux, fluks, *n.* [Fr., from L. *fluxus,* from *fluo,* to flow. FLUENT.] The act of flowing; a flow; the flow of the tide, in opposition to the ebb; *med.* an extraordinary evacuation from the bowels or other part; that which flows or is discharged; *metal.* any substance or mixture used to promote the fusion of metals or minerals; a liquid state from the operation of heat.—*v.t.* To melt or to fuse; make fluid.—*v.i.* To flow.—**fluxion,** *n.* A flux or flowing; a flow or determination of blood or other fluid toward any organ with greater force than natural; *math.* a differential, *fluxions* being an old method of mathematical analysis superseded by the differential calculus.—**fluxional, fluxionary,** fluk′shon•al, fluk′shon•e•ri, *a.* Pertaining to fluxions; variable.

fly, flī, *v.i.*—pret. *flew*, pp. *flown*, ppr. *flying*. [A.Sax. *fleógan*, G. *fliegen*, Icel. *fljuga*, Dan. *flyue*, to fly; akin *flee*, *flight*, *fledge*, etc.] To move through air by the aid of wings; to move through the air by the force of wind or other impulse; to rise in air, as light substances; to run or pass with swiftness; to depart swiftly; to run away; to flee; to escape; to ride in or operate an airplane; to pass quickly from mouth to mouth; to burst in pieces; to flutter, vibrate, or play, as a flag in the wind.—*To fly at*, to rush on; to fall on suddenly.—*To fly in the face of*, to set at defiance; to act in direct opposition to.—*To fly open*, to open suddenly or with violence.—*To let fly*, to discharge; to throw or drive with violence.—*v.t.* To flee from; to shun; to avoid; to cause to fly or float in the air; to transport by airplane.—*n.* A winged insect whose distinguishing characteristics are that the wings are transparent and have no cases or covers; a fishhook dressed so as to resemble a fly; *baseball*, ball hit by batter and caught by defensive fielder before it hits ground, automatically putting the batter out; an arrangement of vanes upon a revolving axis or other contrivance to regulate the motion of machinery; a flier; one of the arms that revolve round the bobbin in a spinning frame, and twist the yarn as it is wound on the bobbin; a light carriage formed for rapid motion; a hackney coach; a cab; a gallery in a theater running along the side of the stage at a high level, where the ropes for drawing up parts of the scenes, etc., are worked.—**flier, flyer,** flī′ėr, *n.* One that flies or flees; a runaway; a fugitive; a part of a machine which by moving rapidly equalizes and regulates the motion of the whole; a contrivance for taking off or delivering the sheets from a printing machine.—**flyblow,** flī′blō, *n.* The egg of a fly.—*v.t.* To deposit a fly's egg in; to taint with eggs which produce maggots.—**flyboat,** *n.* A large flat-bottomed Dutch vessel with a high stem; a long narrow passage boat, swifter than the cargo boats, formerly much used on canals.—**flycatcher,** *n.* One who or that which catches flies; especially, a name of various insessorial birds which feed on flies and other winged insects; the phoebe, bee-bird, or kingbird.—**fly-fishing,** *n.* The art or practice of angling for fish with flies, natural or artificial.—**flyleaf,** *n.* A blank leaf at the beginning or end of a book, pamphlet, etc.—**flypaper,** *n.* A kind of porous paper impregnated with poison for destroying flies.—**flytrap,** *n.* A trap to catch or kill flies; an American sensitive plant, the leaves of which close upon and capture insects.—**flywheel,** *n.* A wheel with a heavy rim placed on the revolving shaft of any machinery put in motion by an irregular or intermitting force, for the purpose of rendering the motion equable and regular by means of its momentum—**flying boat,** *n.* A seaplane supported on water by its hull.—**flying buttress,** *n.* A buttress springing from a solid mass of masonry, and abutting against and serving to support another part of the structure.—**flying fish,** *n.* One of those fishes which have the power of sustaining themselves for a time in the air by means of their large pectoral fins.—**flying fox,** *n.* A bat found in the islands of the Eastern Archipelago, so named from the resemblance of its head to that of a fox.—**Flying Dutchman,** *n.* A spectral or phantom ship seen off the Cape of Good Hope, believed to import foul weather or danger.—**flying jib,** *n. Naut.* a sail extended outside of the jib, upon a boom called the flying-jib boom.—**flying lemur,** *n.* An insectivorous mammal having the limbs connected by wide lateral folds of skin, which serve to bear it up when taking great leaps from tree to tree.—**flying phalanger,** *n.* A nocturnal marsupial.—**flying saucer,** *n.* Any of the unidentified flying objects, usually said to be saucer shaped, reported as seen in the sky.—**flying squirrel,** *n.* One of those squirrels that have a fold of skin extending between the fore and hind legs, so as to bear them up for a moment in the air, and enable them to make very great leaps; also a name of the flying phalanger.

foal, fōl, *n.* [A.Sax. *fola*, a foal; Icel. *foli*, Dan. *fole*, D. *veulen*, G. *fohlen*, *füllen*; Cog. Gr. *pōlos*, a foal; L. *pullus*, a young animal. *Filly* is a dim. from *foal*.] The young of the equine genus of quadrupeds, and of either sex; a colt; a filly.—*v.t.* To bring forth her young: said of a mare or a she-ass.—*v.i.* To bring forth a foal.

foam, fōm, *n.* [A.Sax. *fám*=G. *feim*, and dial. *faum*, foam; allied to L. *spuma*, foam, from *spuo*, to spit.] Froth; spume; the aggregation of bubbles which is formed on the surface of liquids by fermentation or violent agitation.—*v.i.* To gather foam; to froth; to be in a violent rage.—*v.t.* To cause to foam.—**foam rubber,** *n.* Fine-textured, spongy rubber used for mattresses, cushions, etc.—**foamy,** fō′mi, *a.* Covered with foam; frothy.

fob, fob, *n.* [Allied to Prov. G. *fuppe*, a pocket.] Small ornament or weight worn at the end of a watch chain.

fob, fob, *v.t.*—*fobbed*, *fobbing*. [Comp. G. *foppen*, to mock, to banter.] To cheat; to trick; to impose on. (*Shak*).

focus, fō′kus, *n.* pl. **focuses,** fō′kus-ez, or **foci,** fō′sī. [L. *focus*, a fire, the hearth, whence also *fuel*, *fusil*.] A point of concentration; a central point; a center of special activity; *optics*, a point in which any number of rays of light meet after being reflected or refracted; *geom.* a name of two important points on the principal axis of the ellipse (which see).—*v.t.* and *i.* To bring to a focus; to adjust to a focus; to focalize.—**focal,** fō′kal, *a.*—**focalize,** fō′kal•īz, *v.t.* To bring to a focus; to focus.

fodder, fod′ėr, *n.* [A.Sax. *fódder*, *fóder*, from *fóda*, food=Icel. *fóthr*, L.G. *foder*, D. *voeder*, G. *futter*, fodder. FOOD.] Food for cattle, horses, and sheep consisting of entire plants, such as corn.—*v.t.* To feed with fodder.

foe, fō, *n.* [A.Sax. *fá*, *fáh*, an enemy, from same stem as *fiend*. FIEND, FEUD.] An enemy; one who entertains personal enmity; an enemy in war; a hostile or opposing army; an adversary; one who opposes anything (a *foe* to virtue).—**foeman,** fō′man, *n.* An enemy in war; a personal antagonist.

fog, fog, *n.* [Comp. Dan. *snee-fog*, a snow storm *fyge*, to drive with the wind, Dan. dial. *fuge*, to rain fine and blow, Icel. *fok*, snow storm.] A dense watery vapor exhaled from the earth or from rivers and lakes, or generated in the atmosphere near the earth; a state of mental confusion or uncertainty.—*v.t.* To envelop with or as with fog.—*v.i.* To obscure by enclosing in fog; confuse; perplex; befog.—**foggily,** fog′i•li, *adv.* In a foggy manner.—**fogginess,** fog′i•nes, *n.*—**foggy,** fog′i, *a.* Filled or abounding with fog; damp with humid vapors; misty; dull; stupid; beclouded.—**foghorn,** *n.* A horn to sound as a warning signal in foggy weather; a sounding instrument for warning vessels of their proximity to the coast during a fog.

fog, fog, *n.* [W. *ffwg*, dry grass.] Aftermath; a second growth of grass; long grass that remains on land through the winter.

fogey, fogy, fō′gi, *n.* [Lit. one who is in a *fog*; or from *fog*, after grass.] One who is behind the times; a dull fellow, usually with *old*.—**fogeyism, fogyism,** fō′gi•izm, *n.* The habits or practices of a fogey.

foible, foi′bl, *n.* [O.Fr. weak. FEEBLE.] The weak part of a sword; opposed to *forte*; a particular moral weakness; a weak point; a fault of not a very serious character.

foil, foil, *v.t.* [Fr. *fouler*, to press, to crush, to oppress, from stem of L. *fullo*, a fuller.] To frustrate; to defeat; to render vain or nugatory, as an effort or attempt; to baffle; to balk.—*n.* Defeat; frustration; a blunt sword, or one that has a button at the end, used in fencing.

foil, foil, *n.* [Fr. *feuille*, L. *folium*, a leaf (whence *foliage*).] A leaf or thin plate of metal; a thin leaf of metal placed under precious stones to improve their appearance; anything of a different character which serves to set off something else to advantage; that which, by comparison or contrast, sets off or shows more conspicuously the superiority of something else; *arch.* one of the small arcs or hollow curves in the tracery of a Gothic window, panel, etc.—**foiled,** foild, *a. Arch.* having foils (a *foiled* arch).

foist, foist, *v.t.* [D. *vuist*, fist; originally, it would appear, to insert by clever movements of the *fist*; compare to *palm off*.] To insert surreptitiously, or without warrant; to pass off as genuine, true, or worthy. —*n.* A trick; an imposition.

Fokker, fok′ėr, *n.* A type of airplane named after the designer.

fold, fōld, *n.* [A.Sax. *fald*, *feald*, a plait, a fold, *fealdan*, to fold; cog. Fris. *fald*, G. *falte*, Goth. *falths*, a doubling, a plait; Icel. *falda*, Dan. *folde*, Goth. *falthan*, to fold; same as *fold* in *twofold*, *fivefold*.] The doubling or double of any flexible substance, as cloth; a plait; one part turned or bent and laid on another; a clasp; an embrace (*Shak.*). [Often used following a numeral in compounds, and then signifying ‘ times ’, as in two*fold*, four*fold*, ten*fold*.]—*v.t.* To lap or lay double or in plaits; to lay one part over another part of; to lay one over the other, as the hands or arms; to enfold; to embrace. —*v.i.* To become folded or doubled. **—folder,** fōl′dėr, *n.* An outer cover for loose papers; a brochure.

fold, fōld, *n.* [A.Sax. *fald*=Dan. *fold*, Sw. *falla*, a fold, a pen.] A pen or enclosure for sheep or like animals; a flock of sheep; hence, *Scrip.* the church, the flock of Christ.—*v.t.* To confine in a fold.

foliaceous, fō•li•ā′shus, *a.* [L. *foliaceus*, from *folium*, a leaf, akin to Gr. *phyllon*, a leaf.] Leafy; of the nature or form of a leaf; consisting of leaves or thin laminae.—**foliage,** fō′li•ij, *n.* Leaves collectively; the leaves of a plant; leafy growths represented by sculpture, etc.; the numbering of leaves in a book.—**foliate,** fō′li•āt, *v.t.* To beat into a leaf, thin plate, or lamina; to cover with tinfoil, etc.; furnish with leaves.—*v.i.* To form leaves.—**foliation,** fō′li•ā″shon, *n.* The leafing of plants; vernation; the act of beating metal into a thin plate or foil; the operation of spreading foil over a surface; the property in certain rocks of dividing into laminae or plates; the numbering of leaves in a book; *arch.* the foils, cusps, etc., in the tracery of Gothic windows.

folio, fō′li•ō, *n.* [Ablative case of L. *folium*, a leaf, short for *in folio*.] A book formed of sheets of paper folded once; a case for loose papers; *bookkeeping*, a page, or rather both the right and left hand pages, of an account book, expressed by the same figure; *printing*, the number appended to each page; *law*, a written page of a certain number of words.

folk, fōk, *n.* [A.Sax. *folc*, folk, a people or nation=L.G. Fris. Dan. and Sw. *folk*; Icel. *folk*; D. and G. *volk*; probably connected with E. *flock*; Lith. *pulkas*, multitude, crowd; but further connections doubtful.] People in general; a separate class of people; though plural in signification it is frequently used with the plural form especially with a qualifying adjective (rich *folks*); group of people forming a nation.—**folk song,** *n.* A song that originates among the common people of a country.—**folk tale,** *n.* A legend begun by the common people of any land, handed down by word of mouth.—**folklore,** *n.* Rural superstitions, tales, traditions, or legends.—**folkway,** *n.* Any way of acting or thinking that is characteristic of a people or social group.—**folksy,** fōk′sy, *a.* Sociable; friendly.

follicle, fol′li•kl, *n.* [L. *folliculus*, dim. of *follis*, a bag or bellows.] A little bag or vesicle in animals and plants; a dry seed vessel or pod opening on one side only; a vessel distended with air; a gland; a minute secreting cavity.—**follicular,** fol•lik′ū•lėr, *a.* Pertaining to, or consisting of follicles.—**folliculated,** fol•lik′ū•lā•ted, *a.* Having follicles; follicular.

follow, fol′ō, *v.t.* [A.Sax. *folgian*, *fyligean*=G. *folgen*, Dan. *folge*, Icel. *fylgja*, to follow. By some regarded as connected with *folk*, *full*, etc.] To go or come after or behind; to move behind in the same direction; to pursue; to chase; to pursue as an object of desire; to go with (a leader); to be led or guided by; to accept as authority; to take as an example; to copy; to come after in order of time, rank, or office; to result from, as an effect from a cause or an inference from premises; to keep the attention fixed upon while in progress (a speech, piece of music, etc.); to understand the meaning, connection, or force of; to walk in (a road or course); to practice (a trade or calling).—*To follow suit*, in *card playing*, to play a card of the same suit as that first played; hence, to follow the line of conduct adopted by a predecessor. —*v.i.* To go or come after another; to be posterior in time; to result, as an effect or an inference. . . *Follow* and *succeed* are applied to persons or things; *ensue*, in modern literature, to things only. *Succeed* implies a coming into the place previously occupied by another; *ensue*, generally that which follows is an effect or result.—**follower,** fol′ō•ėr, *n.* One who follows; an adherent; a disciple; an imitator; a dependent.—**following,** fol′ō•ing, *n.* A body of followers or retainers.—*p.* Being next after; succeeding; related, described, or explained next after.

folly, fol′i, *n.* [Fr. *folie*, folly, from *fol*, a fool. FOOL.] Weakness of intellect; imbecility of mind; a weak or foolish act; foolish, weak, or light-minded conduct; criminal weakness.

foment, fō•ment′, *v.t.* [Fr. *fomenter*, L. *fomento*, from *fomentum*, for *fovimentum*, a warm application, from *foveo*, to warm, to cherish.] To rouse; to instigate; to bathe with warm medicated liquids or warm water; to encourage; to abet, used especially in a bad sense (to *foment* quarrels).—**fomentation,** fō•men•tā′shon, *n.* The act of fomenting; encouragement; what is used to foment; a warm lotion.—**fomenter,** fō•men′tėr, *n.* One who foments.

fond, fond, *a.* [O.E. *fonne*, to be foolish, fond, stupid; *fon*, a fool; akin to Icel. *fána*, to play the fool; Sw. *fane*, fatuous. The word is properly a past participle, whence the final *d.*] Foolish; indiscreet; imprudent; foolishly tender and loving; doting; relishing highly; loving ardently; delighted with: followed by *of*; foolishly or extravagantly prized (*Shak.*).—**fondle,** fon′dl, *v.t.* —*fondled*, *fondling*. To treat with tenderness; to caress.—**fondly,** fond′li, *adv.* In a fond manner; with indiscreet or excessive affection; affectionately; tenderly.—**fondness,** fond′nes, *n.* The state of being fond; great affection or liking.

font, font, *n.* [From L. *fons*, *fontis*, a fountain. FOUNT.] The vessel used in churches as the receptacle of the baptismal water.—**fontal,**† fon′tal, *a.* Pertaining to a fount, source, or origin.

font, font, *n.* [Fr. *fonte*, from *fondre*, to melt or found, from L. *fundo*, to pour out, whence also *found*, *foundry*.] A complete assortment of printing types of one size.

fontanel, fon′ta•nel, *n.* [Fr. *fontanelle*, lit. a little fountain, from L. *fons*, a fountain.] *Anat.* a vacancy in the infant cranium between the frontal and parietal bones, and also between the parietal and occipital.

food, föd, *n.* [A.Sax. *fóda*, food, whence *fédan*, to feed; Dan. *fóde*, Sw. *foda*, food; from root meaning to feed, seen in L. *pasco*, to feed, *pastor*, a shepherd.] Whatever supplies nourishment to organic bodies; nutriment; aliment; victuals; provisions; whatever feeds, sustains, or nourishes.

fool, föl, *n.* [Fr. *fol*, *fou*, foolish, a fool, from L.L. *follus*, from L. *folles*, bellows, cheeks puffed out, the *follus* or fool being originally one who made grimaces.] One who is destitute of reason or the common powers of understanding; an idiot; a natural; a person who acts absurdly, irrationally, or unwisely; one who does not exercise his reason; a professional jester or buffoon.—*To make a fool of*, to cause to appear ridiculous.—*v.i.* To act like a fool.—*v.t.* To make a fool of; to befool; to deceive; to impose on; to cheat.—*To fool away*, to waste or spend foolishly. —**foolery,** föl′ėr•i, *n.* Folly; the practice of folly; an act of folly; object of folly.—**foolhardiness,** föl′här•di•nes, *n.* Quality of being foolhardy; mad rashness.—**foolhardily,** föl′här•di•li, *adv.* With foolhardiness. —**foolhardy,** föl′här•di, *a.* [O.Fr. *fol-hardi.*] Daring without judgment; madly rash and adventurous; foolishly bold. ∴ Syn. under RASH.—**foolish,** föl′ish, *a.* Characterized by or exhibiting folly; weak in intellect; unwise; silly; vain; trifling; ridiculous.—**foolishly,** föl′ish•li, *adv.* In a foolish manner.—**foolishness,** fōl′-ish•nes, *n.* The quality or condition of being foolish; folly.—**foolscap,** fōlz′-kap, *n.* Paper of the smallest regular size but one, its watermark in early times being the outline of a fool's head and cap.—**fool's errand,** *n.* An absurd or fruitless search or enterprise.—**fool's-parsley,** *n.* A British plant resembling parsley, commonly believed to be poisonous, but if so only in certain localities.

foot, fu̥t, *n.* pl. **feet,** fēt. [A.Sax. *fót*, pl. *fét*=Icel. *fótr*, Sw. *fot*, Goth. *fotus*, G. *fuss*; the same word also as L. *pes*, *pedis*, Gr. *pous*, *podos*, Skr. *pâda*, a foot, from a root *pad*, to go.] The terminal part of the leg upon which the body rests while standing; the muscular organ of locomotion in mollusks; step; tread; footfall; the part of a stocking, boot, etc., which receives the foot; the lower end of anything that supports a body; the part opposite to the head or top; the bottom; soldiers who march and fight on foot; infantry, as distinguished from cavalry; a measure consisting of 12 inches, taken from the length of a man's foot; *pros.* a certain number of syllables forming a distinct part of a verse.—*Square foot*, a square whose side is one foot or any equivalent area; 144 square inches.—*Cubic foot*, a cube whose side is one foot, and which therefore contains 1728 cubic inches or any equivalent solid.—*By foot*, *on foot*, by walking.—*To set on foot*, to originate; to begin; to put in motion. —*To put one's best foot foremost*, to adopt all the means at command.—*Foot-and-mouth disease*, a highly contagious infection of cattle.—*v.i.* To dance; to walk: commonly followed by *it*.—*v.t.* To sum up; to pay (a bill); to tread; to add or make a foot to (to *foot* a stocking or boot). —**footage,** fu̥t′aj, *n.* Length measurement expressed in feet.—**football,** fu̥t′ba̤l, *n.* An inflated oval ball made of a rubber bladder encased in pigskin; a field game in which each of two 11-member teams seeks to kick or carry the ball through or to the opposite goal line.—**footbridge,** fu̥t′brij, *n.* A narrow bridge for foot passengers.—**footfall,** fu̥t′fa̤l, *n.* A footstep; tread of the foot.—**footgear,** fu̥t′gēr, *n.* The covering of the feet; shoes or boots.—**foothill,** fu̥t′hil, *n.* Any of the minor hills at the base of a mountain.—**foothold,** fu̥t′hōld, *n.* That on which one may tread or rest securely; firm standing.—*Milit.* a position that provides a base for further advancement.—**footing,** fu̥t′ing, *n.* Ground for the foot; established place; permanent settlement; foothold; basis; foundation; state (on a *footing* of equality).—**footlights,** *n. pl.* A row of lights in a theater on the front of the stage, and serving to light it up.—**footman,** fu̥t′man, *n.* An infantry soldier; a male servant whose duties are to attend the door, the carriage, the table, etc.; a man in waiting.—**footmark,** fu̥t′märk, *n.* A track; mark of a foot.—**footnote,** *n.* A note of reference at the bottom of a page —**footpace,** *n.* A slow step, as in walking.—**footpad,** fu̥t′pad, *n.* A highwayman that robs on foot.—**footpath,** fu̥t′path, *n.* A narrow path for foot-passengers only.—**foot-pound,** *n.* In mechanics, a unit of work or energy; the work done in raising one pound of weight through a height of one foot against the force of gravity.—**footprint,** fu̥t′-print, *n.* The mark of a foot.—**foot soldier,** *n.* A soldier that serves on foot.—**footsore,** *a.* Having the feet rendered sore or tender, as by much walking.—**footstalk,** fu̥t′sta̤k, *n. Bot.* a petiole; the stalk supporting a leaf; *zool.* a process resembling the footstalk in botany; a peduncle.—**footstep,** fu̥t′step, *n.* The mark or impression of the foot; footprint; tread; footfall; sound of the step.—**footstool,** fu̥t′stöl, *n.* A stool for the feet when sitting.—**footway,** fu̥t′wā, *n.* A path for passengers on foot.—**footworn,** *p.* and *a.* Worn by the feet; footsore.

fop, fop, *n.* [D. *foppen*, to banter, to make a fool of, *fopper*, a wag.] A vain man of weak understanding and much ostentation; a gay, trifling man; a coxcomb; a dandy.—**foppery,** fop′ėr•i, *n.* The characteristics of a fop; showy folly; idle affectation; dandyism.—**foppish,** fop′ish, *a.* Pertaining to a fop; vain of dress; dressing in the extreme of fashion; affected in manners.—**foppishly,** fop′ish•li, *adv.* In a foppish manner. —**foppishness,** fop′ish•nes, *n.*

for, for, *prep.* [A.Sax. *for*, for, because of, instead of; D. *voor*, G. *für*, Goth. *faur*, for—allied to E. *fore*, *far*, *fare*; L. *pro*, for or in place of; Skr. *pra*, before: before, in advance, is the root-meaning. The prefix *for-* in *forbid*, etc., is different from this.] In the place of; instead of: indicating substitution or equivalence; corresponding to; accompanying (groan *for* groan); in the character of; as being (he took it *for* truth); toward; with the intention of going to; with a tendency to (an inclination *for* drink); conducive to; tending toward, in expectation of; with a view to obtain; in order to arrive at, get, or procure (to wait *for* money, he writes *for* money); suitable or proper to; against; with a tendency to resist and destroy (a remedy *for* the headache); because of; on account of; by reason of (*for* want of time) [in this usage *but* comes very often before the *for*]; on the part of; in relation to (easy *for* you, but difficult *for* me); in proportion to (tall *for* his age); through a certain space; during a certain time; according to; as far as; so far as concerns; notwithstanding (it may be so *for* anything I know); in favor of; on the part or side of (to vote *for* a person); desirous to have; willing to receive [in this sense often in interjections: O *for* revenge!]; to take up the part or character of (nature intended him *for* a usurer); having so much laid to one's account; to the amount of (he failed *for* ten thousand). ∴ *For* was at one time common before the infinitives of verbs to denote purpose; but this usage is now vulgar.—*For all the world*, of everything else in the world; in every respect; exactly (an animal *for all the world* like a mouse).—*For ever.* EVER.—*conj.* For the cause or reason that; because: a word by which a reason is introduced of something before advanced, being really a preposition governing a clause.—*For as much as*, or *forasmuch as*, in consideration that; seeing that; since.

forage, for′ij, *n.* [Fr. *fourrage*, O.Fr. *forrage*, from *forre*, forage; from the old German or Scandinavian word equivalent to E. *fodder*.] Food of any kind for horses and cattle; the act of searching for provisions.—*v.i.*—*foraged*, *foraging*. To collect forage; to roam in search of food or provender.—*v.t.* To collect forage from; to supply with forage.—**forager,** for′i•jėr, *n.* One that forages.

foramen, fō•rā′men, *n.* pl. **foramina,** fō•ram′i•na. [L., from *foro*, to bore.] A small natural opening or perforation in parts of animals or plants; an opening by which nerves or blood vessels obtain a passage through bones.—**foraminifer,** fō•ra•min′i•fėr, *n.* [L. *foramen*, *foraminis*, a hole, and *fero*, to bear.] An individual of the Foraminifera.—**Foraminifera,** fō•ram′i•nif″ėr•a, *n. pl.* An order of minute animals belonging to the protozoa, furnished with a shell, simple or complex, usually perforated by pores (whence the name).—**foraminiferal, foraminiferous,** fō•ram′i•nif″ėr•al, fō•ram′i•nif″ėr•us, *a.* Belonging to the Foraminifera.

forasmuch, for•az•much′, *conj.* See FOR.

foray, for′ā, *v.t.* [A form of *forage*.] To ravage; to pillage.—*n.* The act of foraging; a predatory excursion; booty.—**forayer,** for′ā•ėr, *n.* One who takes part in a foray; a marauder.

forbade, for•bad′, pret. of *forbid*.

forbear, for•bâr′, *v.i.*—*forbore* (pret.), *forborne* (pp.). [Prefix *for*, intens., and *bear*; A.Sax. *forberan*, *forbæran*.] To cease; to refrain from proceeding; to pause; to delay; to be patient; to restrain one's self from action or violence.—*v.t.* To avoid voluntarily; to abstain from; to omit; to avoid doing; to treat with indulgence‡.—**forbearance,** for•bâr′ans, *n.* The act of forbearing; restraint of passions; longsuffering; indulgence toward those who injure us; lenity.—**forbearer,** for•bâr′ėr, *n.* One who forbears.—**forbearing,** for•bâr′-ing, *p.* and *a.* Having forbearance; long-suffering.

forbid, for•bid′, *v.t.*—pret. *forbade*; pp. *forbid*, *forbidden*; *forbidding*. [Prefix *for*, implying negation, and *bid*.] To prohibit; to interdict; to command to forbear or not to do; to refuse access; to command not to enter or approach; to oppose; to hinder; to obstruct (a river *forbids* approach).—**forbiddance,**† for•bid′-

ans, *n.* Prohibition; command or edict against a thing.—**forbidden,** for•bid′n, *p.* and *a.* Prohibited; interdicted.—**forbidder,** for•bid′ėr, *n.* One who forbids.—**forbidding,** for•bid′ing, *a.* Repelling approach; repulsive; raising abhorrence, aversion, or dislike.—**forbiddingly,** for•bid′ing•li, *adv.* In a forbidding manner; repulsively.—**forbiddingness,** for•bid′ing•nes, *n.*

force, fōrs, *n.* [Fr., from L.L. *forcia, fortia,* from L. *fortis,* strong; seen also in *fort, fortitude, fortress, comfort, effort,* etc.] Active power; vigor; might; strength; energy; that which is the source of all the active phenomena occurring in the material world; that which produces or tends to produce change; one of the modes or forms in which energy is exhibited in nature, as heat or electricity; momentum; the quantity of energy or power exerted by a moving body; violence; power exerted against will or consent; moral power to convince the mind; influence; validity; power to bind or hold (the *force* of an agreement); a military or naval armament; a body of troops; an army or navy; a body of men prepared for action in other ways (a police *force*).—*v.t.*—*forced, forcing.* To compel; to constrain to do or to forbear, by the exertion of a power not resistible; to impel; to press, drive, draw, or push by main strength; to compel by strength of evidence (to *force* conviction on the mind); to ravish; to violate (a female); to twist, wrest, or overstrain; to assume, or compel one's self to give utterance or expression to (to *force* a smile); to ripen or bring to maturity by heat artificially applied. In contract bridge, to demand a bid from one's partner, as by bidding one more of a suit than is required by the preceding bid, or by making an opening bid of two.—**forced,** fōrst, *p.* and *a.* Unnaturally assumed; constrained; affected; overstrained; unnatural.—**forceful,** fōrs′fu̥l, *a.* Possessing force; powerful; driven with force; acting with power; impetuous (*Shak.*).—**forcefully,** fōrs′fu̥l•li, *adv.* Violently or impetuously.—**force pump,** *n.* A pump which delivers the water by means of pressure or force directly applied, so as to eject it forcibly to a great elevation; in contradistinction to a pump that raises water by the pressure of the air simply.—**forcer,** fōr′sėr, *n.* One who or that which forces.—**forcible,** fōr′si•bl, *a.* Having force; exercising force; powerful; strong; marked by force or violence; violent.—**forcibleness,** fōr′si•bl•nes, *n.* The condition or quality of being forcible.

force, fōrs, *v.t.* [Same as *farce*; or perhaps from *force,* in old sense of to season, *forcemeat* being thus highly seasoned meat.] *Obs.* To stuff; to farce.—**forcemeat,** fōrs′mēt, *n. Cookery,* meat chopped fine and seasoned, either served up alone or used as stuffing, *farced* meat, by corruption.

forceps, for′seps, *n.* [L., from *for* in *formus,* warm, and *capio,* to take.] A two-bladed instrument on the principle of pincers or tongs for holding anything difficult to be held by the hand: used by surgeons, dentists, jewelers, etc.

ford, fōrd, *n.* [A.Sax. *ford,* connected with *faran,* to go, to fare; comp. G. *furt,* a ford, *fahren,* to go; allied to Gr. *poros,* a passage; E. *ferry.*] A place in a river or other water where it may be passed by man or beast on foot or by wading.—*v.t.* To pass or cross (a stream) by wading; to wade through.—**fordable,** fōr′da•bl, *a.* Capable of being forded.

fordo, for•dö′, *v.t.*—*fordid* (pret.), *fordone* (pp.). [Prefix *for-*, intens., and *do.*] To exhaust, overpower, or overcome, as by toil.

fore, fōr, *a.* [A.Sax. *fore, foran,* before; D. *voor,* Dan. *for,* G. *vor,* before; Goth. *faura,* for; L. *præ,* before, *pro,* for, *por* (as in *porrigere,* to extend), Gr. *paros,* Skr. *pra, puras*—before. Akin *far, for, fare. First* and *foremost* are its superlatives.] Advanced, or, locally, in advance of something: opposed to *hind* or *hinder*; coming first in time: opposed to *after*; anterior; prior; antecedent; in front or toward the face; situated towards the stem of a ship.—*Fore and aft* (*naut.*), in a direction from stem to stern; *fore-and-aft* sail, a sail, such as a jib or spanker, that has a position more or less in this direction.—*n.* Toward the front as compared with another location; *golf,* warning cry to persons who may be in the path of a ball.

forearm, fōr•ärm′, *v.t.* To arm or prepare for attack or resistance before the time of need.

forearm, fōr′ärm, *n.* That part of the arm which is between the elbow and the wrist.

forebear, fōr′bâr, *n.* [Prefix *fore,* and *beer,* be,-er.] Ancestor; forefather.

forebode, fōr•bōd′, *v.t.*—*foreboded, foreboding.* To feel a secret sense of a misfortune about to happen.—**foreboder,** fōr•bō′der, *n.*—**foreboding,** fōr•bō′ding, *n.* Presentiment of approaching evil.

forecast, fōr•kast′, *v.t.*—pret. & pp. *forecast.* To cast or scheme beforehand; to plan before execution; to calculate beforehand; to estimate in the future.—*v.i.* To form a scheme previously; to contrive beforehand.—*n.* (fōr′kast). Prediction (a weather *forecast*).—**forecaster,** fōr′kas′tėr, *n.* One who forecasts.

forecastle, fōr′kas•l; sailors' pronunciation, fōk′sl, *n.* A short raised deck in the forepart of a ship; the forepart of a vessel where the sailors live.

foreclose, fōr•klōz′, *v.t.*—*foreclosed, foreclosing.* [*Fore* for Fr. prefix *for* (as in *forfeit*), from L. *foris,* away, out of doors.] To preclude; to stop; to prevent.—*To foreclose* a *mortgage,* to compel the mortgager to pay the money due on it, or forfeit his right to the estate.—**foreclosure,** fōr•klō′zhėr, *n.* The act of foreclosing.

foredate, fōr•dāt′, *v.t.* To date before the true time; to antedate.

foredeck, fōr′dek, *n.* The forepart of a deck of a ship.

foredo, fōr•dö′, *v.t.*—*foredid* (pret.), *foredone* (pp.). To do beforehand.

foredoom, fōr•döm′, *v.t.* To doom beforehand; to predestinate.

forefather, fōr′fä•THėr, *n.* An ancestor.

forefend, fōr•fend′, *v.t.* To fend off; to avert; to prevent the approach of; to forbid or prohibit.

forefinger, fōr′fing•gėr, *n.* The finger next to the thumb; the index.

forefoot, fōr′fu̥t, *n.* One of the anterior feet of a quadruped or multiped.

forefront, fōr′frunt, *n.* The foremost part or place.

foregather, fōr•gaTH′ėr, *v.i.* Same as *Forgather.*

forego, fōr•gō′, *v.t.* To forgo (which see).

forego, fōr•gō′, *v.t.*—*forewent* (pret.), *foregone* (pp.). To go before; to precede.—**foregoer,** fōr•gō′ėr, *n.* One who goes before another; an ancestor; a progenitor.—**foregoing,** fōr•gō′ing or fōr′gō•ing, *p.* and *a.* Preceding; going before, in time or place; antecedent.—**foregone,** fōr•gon′ or fōr′gon, *p.* and *a.* Past; preceding; predetermined; made up beforehand.

foreground, fōr′ground, *n.* The part of a picture which is represented so as to appear nearest the eye of the observer.

forehand, fōr′hand, *n.* The part of a horse which is before the rider; *tennis,* etc., a stroke made with palm forward (by a righthanded player on his right).—*a.* Anticipative; referring to a forehand stroke.

forehead, fōr′hed or for′ed, *n.* The part of the face which extends from the usual line of hair on the top of the head to the eyes; the brow.

foreign, for′in, *a.* [Fr. *forain,* from L.L. *foraneus,* from L. *foras,* out of doors (also in *forest*)—same root as E. *door.* As in *sovereign* the *g* has been improperly inserted.] Belonging or relating to another nation or country; not of the country in which one resides; alien; extraneous; not our own; remote; not belonging; not connected; irrelevant; not to the purpose: with *to* or *from.*—**foreigner,** for′in•ėr, *n.* A person born in or belonging to a foreign country; an alien.—**foreignism,** for′in•izm, *n.* Foreignness; a foreign idiom or custom.—**foreignness,** for′in•nes, *n.* The quality of being foreign.

forejudge, fōr•juj′, *v.t.* To judge beforehand or before hearing the facts and proof; to prejudge.—**forejudgment,** fōr•juj′ment, *n.* Judgment previously formed.

foreknow, fōr•nō′, *v.t.*—*foreknew* (pret.), *foreknown* (pp.). To have previous knowledge of; to know beforehand.—**foreknowable,** fōr•nō′a•bl, *a.* Capable of being foreknown.—**foreknowledge,** fōr•nol′ij, *n.* Knowledge of a thing before it takes place; prescience.

foreland, fōr′land, *n.* A promontory or cape; a headland.

foreleg, fōr′leg, *n.* One of the front or anterior legs, as of an animal, a chair, etc.

forelock, fōr′lok, *n.* The lock or hair that grows from the forepart of the head.—*To take time by the forelock,* to make prompt use of anything; to let no opportunity escape.

foreman, fōr′man, *n.* The first or chief man; the chief man of a jury who acts as their speaker; a chief workman who superintends others.

foremast, fōr′mast, *n.* The mast of a ship or other vessel which is placed before the other or the others.

foremost, fōr′mōst or fōr′most, *a.* [Should have been *formest* (to correspond with *former*), being the A.Sax. *formest,* a double superlative, from *forma,* first, foremost (itself a superlative), and the *-est* of superlatives: the spelling has been modified by confusion with *most;* so also *hindmost, inmost, outmost.*] First in place, station, honor, or dignity; most advanced; first in time.

forename, fōr′nām, *n.* A name that precedes the family name or surname.—**forenamed,** fōr′nāmd, *a.* Named or mentioned before.

forenoon, fōr′nön, *n.* The part of the day that comes before noon; the part from morning to mid-day.

forensic, forensical, fō•ren′sik, fō•ren′si•kal, *a.* [From L. *forensis,* from *forum,* a court, a forum; akin *forest.*] Belonging to courts of justice or to public discussion and debate; used in courts or legal proceedings, or in public discussions.—*Forensic medicine,* medical jurisprudence.

foreordain, fōr′or•dān, *v.t.* To ordain or appoint beforehand; to preordain; to predestinate.—**foreordination,** fōr•or′di•nā″shon, *n.* Predetermination; predestination.

forepart, fōr′pärt, *n.* The most advanced part, or the first in time or place; the anterior part; the beginning.

forepeak, fōr′pēk, *n. Naut.* the part of a vessel in the angle of the bow.

forerun, fōr•run′, *v.t.—foreran* (pret.), *forerun* (pp.), *forerunning* (ppr.). To run before; to come before, as an earnest of something to follow.—**forerunner,** fōr•run′ėr, *n.* A messenger sent before to give notice of the approach of others; a harbinger; a sign foreshowing something to follow.

foresaid, fōr′sed, *a.* Spoken of or mentioned before.

foresail, fōr′sāl, *n. Naut.* the principal sail set on the foremast.

foresee, fōr•sē′, *v.t.—foresaw* (pret.), *foreseen* (pp.). To see beforehand; to see or know before it happens; to have prescience of; to foreknow.—*v.i.* To exercise foresight.—**foreseer,** fōr•sē′ėr, *n.* One who foresees.

foreshadow, fōr•shad′ō, *v.t.* To shadow or typify beforehand.

foreshore, fōr′shōr, *n.* The sloping part of a shore between high and low watermark.

foreshorten, fōr•shor′tn, *v.t. Persp.* to represent or depict (as an arm, a branch, directed towards the spectator) with the due impression of length, prominence, and relative position.

foreshow, fōr•shō′, *v.t.—foreshowed,* (pret.), *foreshown* (pp.). To show, represent, or exhibit beforehand; to prognosticate; to foretell.

foreside, fōr′sīd, *n.* The front side.

foresight, fōr′sīt, *n.* The act or power of foreseeing; prescience; foreknowledge; provident care for the future; prudence in guarding against evil; wise forethought; the sight on the muzzle of a gun.—**foresighted,** fōr′-si•ted, *a.* Having foresight; prescient; provident.

foreskin, fōr′skin, *n.* The fold of skin that covers the anterior extremity of the male member of generation; the prepuce.

forest, for′est, *n.* [O.Fr. *forest,* Mod. Fr. *forêt,* from L.L. *foresta,* a forest, from L. *foris, foras,* out of doors, abroad; akin *foreign, forensic.*] An extensive wood, or a large tract of land covered with trees; a tract of mingled woodland and open uncultivated ground; *Eng. law.* a district wholly or chiefly devoted to hunting, and usually a royal domain.—*a.* Of or pertaining to a forest; sylvan; rustic.—*v.t.* To convert into a forest.—**forestation,** for′es•tā″shon, *n.* The act or process of planting a forest.—**forester,** for′es•tėr, *n.* A person who possesses a knowledge of forestry, particularly one appointed to inspect and care for forests or trees; various moths; the giant kangaroo.—**forestry,** for′est•ri, *n.* The art of forming or of cultivating forests, or of managing growing timber.

forestall, fōr•stąl′, *v.t.* [A.Sax. *foresteall,* an intercepting, a placing before from *fore,* before, and *steall,* a place, a stall.] To take too early action regarding; to realize beforehand; to anticipate; to take possession of in advance of something or somebody else; to hinder by preoccupation or prevention.—*To forestall the market,* to buy up merchandise on its way to market with the intention of selling it again at a higher price; formerly an offense at law.—**forestaller,** fōr•stąl′ėr, *n.* One who forestalls.

foretaste, fōr′tāst, *n.* A taste beforehand; anticipation; enjoyment in advance.—*v.t.* (fōr•tāst′). To taste before possession; to have a foretaste of.

foretell, fōr•tel′, *v.t.—foretold* (pret. & pp.). To tell before happening; to predict; to prophesy; to foretoken or foreshow; to prognosticate.—*v.i.* To utter prediction or prophecy.—**foreteller,** fōr•tel′ėr, *n.* One who foretells.

forethought, fōr′thąt, *n.* A thinking beforehand; provident care; foresight.

foretoken, fōr•tō′kn, *v.t.* To betoken beforehand; to foreshow; to presignify; to prognosticate.

fore-tooth, fōr′töth, *n.* pl. **fore-teeth,** fōr′tēth. One of the teeth in the forepart of the mouth; an incisor.

foretop, fōr′top, *n.* Hair on the forepart of the head; *naut.* the platform erected at the head of the foremast.—**fore-topmast,** *n.* The mast above the foremast, and below the foretop-gallant mast.

forewarn, fōr•wąrn′, *v.t.* To warn beforehand; to give previous notice to.

forewoman, fōr′wu̦•man, *n.* A woman who superintends others in a workshop or other establishment.

foreword, fōr′wėrd, *n.* A preface, an introduction to a book or reprint.

forfeit, for′fit, *v.t.* [Fr. *forfait,* a crime, misdeed, from *forfaire,* to transgress, L.L. *forisfacere,* to offend L. *foris,* out of doors, beyond (seen also in *foreclose, forest*), and *facere,* to do.] To lose the right to by some fault, crime, or neglect; to become by misdeed liable to be deprived of (an estate, one's life).—*n.* The act of forfeiting; that which is forfeited; a fine; a penalty; a sportive fine or penalty, whence the game of *forfeits.*—*p.* and *a.* Forfeited or subject to be forfeited; liable to deprivation or penal seizure.—**forfeitable,** for′-fit•a•bl, *a.* Liable to be forfeited; subject to forfeiture.—**forfeiter,** for′-fit•ėr, *n.* One who forfeits.—**forfeiture,** for′fi•chėr, *n.* The act of forfeiting; the losing of some right, privilege, estate, honor, etc., by an offense, crime, breach of condition, or other act; that which is forfeited.

forfend, for•fend′. Same as *Forefend.*

forgather, for•gaTH′ėr, *v.i.* [*For.,* intens., and *gather;* comp. O.Fris. *forgathera,* to assemble.] To meet; to convene; to come or meet together accidentally.

forgave, for•gāv′, pret. of *forgive.*

forge, fōrj, *n.* [Fr. *forge,* It. *forgia,* from L. *fabrica,* a workshop, from *faber,* a workman, a smith. So that *forge*=*fabric.*] A furnace in which iron or other metal is heated to be hammered into form; a workshop for this purpose; a smithy.—*v.t.*—*forged, forging.* To work into shape in a forge; to form or shape out in any way; to invent; to produce, as that which is counterfeit or not genuine; to counterfeit, as a signature or document.—*v.i.* To commit forgery.—**forger,** fōr′jėr, *n.* One who forges; especially, a person guilty of forgery.—**forgery,** fōr′jėr•i, *n.* The act of forging, fabricating, or producing falsely; the crime of counterfeiting a person's signature on a document; that which is forged, fabricated, or counterfeited.

forge, fōrj, *v.i.—forged, forging.* [Perhaps from Icel. *farga,* to press.] *Naut.* to move on slowly and laboriously; to work one's way; usually with *ahead, off, past,* etc.

forget, for•get′, *v.t.—forgot* (pret.), *forgot, forgotten* (pp.), *forgetting* (ppr.). [A.Sax. *forgitan—for,* not, or neg., and *gitan,* to get. GET.] To lose the remembrance of; to let go from the memory; to cease to have in mind; not to remember or think of; to slight; to neglect; *refl.* to be guilty of something unbecoming; to commit an oversight.—**forgettable,** for•get′a•bl, *a.* Capable of being forgotten.—**forgetful,** for•get′fụl, *a.* Apt to forget; easily losing remembrance; careless; neglectful; inattentive.—**forgetfully,** for•get′fụl•li, *adv.* In a forgetful manner.—**forgetfulness,** for•get′fụl•nes, *n.* The quality of being forgetful; a ceasing to remember; oblivion; neglect; negligence; inattention. — **forgetter,** for•get′ėr, *n.* One who forgets.—**forget-me-not,** *n.* A well-known plant, having bright blue flowers with a yellow eye, and considered to be the emblem of friendship and fidelity in many lands.

forgive, for•giv′, *v.t.*—*forgave* (pret.), *forgiven* (pp.), *forgiving* (ppr.) [A. Sax. *forgifan*—*for*, intens., and *gifan*, to give.] To give up resentment or claim to requital on account of; to remit, as an offense, debt, fine, or penalty; to pardon; to cease to feel resentment against; to free from a claim or the consequences of an injurious act or crime. Syn. under PARDON.—**forgivable,** for•giv′a•bl, *a.* Capable of being forgiven; pardonable.—**forgiveness,** for•giv′nes, *n.* The act of forgiving; disposition or willingness to forgive.—**forgiver,** for•giv′ėr, *n.* One who forgives.—**forgiving,** for•giv′ing, *p.* and *a.* Disposed to forgive; inclined to overlook offenses; mild; merciful; compassionate.—**forgivingness,** for•giv′ing•nes, *n.*

forgo, for•gō′, *v.t.*—*forwent* (pret.), *forgone* (pp.). [Also spelled less correctly *forego*; from prefix *for*, intens., or with sense of away, and *go*; A.Sax. *forgán*, to forgo, pass over. neglect.] To forbear to enjoy or possess; to voluntarily avoid enjoying or possessing; to give up, renounce, resign. —**forgoer,** for•gō′ėr, *n.* One who forgoes.

fork, fork, *n.* [A.Sax. *forc*, *furc*, from L. *furca*, a fork, which is also the parent of G. *furke*, D. *vork*, Fr. *fourche*.] An instrument, consisting of a handle with a shank, terminating in two or more parallel prongs, used for holding or lifting something; anything similar in shape; one of the parts into which anything is bifurcated; a prong.—*Forks of a road* or *river*, the point where a road parts into two, the point where two rivers meet and unite in one stream. —*v.i.* To divide into forks or branches.—*v.t.* To raise or pitch with a fork; to dig and break with a fork.—**forked,** forkt, *a.* Having prongs or divisions like a fork; opening into two or more prongs, points, or shoots; furcated.

forlorn, for•lorn′, *a.* [A.Sax. *forloren*, pp. of *forleósan*, to lose; prefix *for*, intens., *leósan*, to lose; comp. D. and G. *verloren*, forlorn, lost. LOSE.] Deserted; forsaken; abandoned; lost; helpless; wretched; solitary; bereft; destitute.—*Forlorn hope.* [D. *verloren hoop*—*hoop*, a troop.] A detachment of men appointed to lead in an assault, or perform other service attended with uncommon peril.—**forlornly,** for•lorn′li, *adv.* In a forlorn manner.—**forlornness,** for•lorn′nes, *n.*

form, form, *n.* [Fr. *forme*, form, shape, manner, bench, bed of a hare, from L. *forma*, form, whence *conform, inform, reform*, etc.] The shape or external appearance of a body, as distinguished from its material; the figure, as defined by lines and angles; appearance to the eye; configuration; a shape; a phantom; manner of arranging particulars; disposition of particular things (a *form* of words); general system or arrangement (a particular *form* of government); something on or after which things are fashioned; a model, draught, pattern; proper shape or trim; high condition or fitness for any undertaking; external appearance without the essential qualities; stated method; established practice; ceremony; a long seat; a bench; the bed of a hare; *printing*, the pages of type or stereotype plates arranged for printing a sheet, and fastened in an iron frame or chase.—*v.t.* To give form or shape to; to shape; to mold; to arrange; to combine in any particular manner; to model by instruction and discipline; to mold; to train; to devise; to contrive; to frame; to create; to be an element or constituent of; to combine to make up; to answer as; to take the shape of.—*v.i.* To take a form.—**formal,** for′mal, *a.* Given to outward forms, observances, or ceremonies; strictly ceremonious; done or made in due form or according to regular method; acting according to rule or established mode; having the form or appearance without the substance or essence; conventional; formative.—**formalism,** for′mal•izm, *n.* The quality of being formal or addicted to mere forms; outside and ceremonial religion.—**formalist,** for′mal•ist, *n.* One given to formalism.—**formality,** for-mal′i•ti, *n.* The condition or quality of being formal; form without substance; established order; rule of proceeding; mode; method; customary ceremony; ceremonial; conventionality.—**formalize,** for′mal•īz, *v.t.*—*formalized, formalizing.* To reduce to a form; to give a certain form to; to render formal.—**formally,** for′mal•li, *adv.* In a formal manner; ceremoniously; stiffly; precisely.—**format,** for′mat, *n.* [Fr.] Size of a book as regards length and breadth.—**formation,** for•mā′shon, *n.* The act of forming, making, creating, composing, shaping, etc.; production; the manner in which a thing is formed; *geol.* any series of rocks referred to a common origin or period; *milit.* an arrangement of troops, as in a square, column, etc.—**formative,** for′ma•tiv, *a.* Giving form; having the power of giving form; plastic; *gram.* serving to form; inflexional.—*n. Gram.* that which gives form to a word and is no part of the root.—**former,** for′mėr, *n.* One who forms.—**formless,** form′les, *a.* Wanting form or shape; shapeless.—**formlessness,** form′les•nes, *n.*

formaldehyde, form•al′de•hīd, *n.* [FORMIC and ALDEHYDE.] A colorless gas, with a strong odor, used chiefly in solution, as a preservative and disinfectant.

former, for′mėr, *a. compar.* [A compar. from A.Sax. *forma*, first. FOREMOST.] Before or preceding another in time: opposed to *latter*; ancient; long past (*former* ages); preceding; earlier, as between two things mentioned together; first mentioned.—**formerly,** for′mėr•li, *adv.* In time past, either in time immediately preceding or at an indefinite distance; of old; heretofore. ∴ *Formerly* means before the present time; *previously*, before some particular event.

formic, for′mik, *a.* [L. *formica*, an act.] Pertaining to or produced by ants.—*Formic acid*, a pungent acid with a peculiar odor, and acting as a corrosive on the skin, originally obtained from ants.—**formicary,** for′mi•ka•ri, *n.* A colony of ants; an anthill.—**formicate,** for′mi•kāt, *a.* Pertaining to an ant.

formidable, for′mi•da•bl, *a.* [L. *formidabilis*, from *formido*, fear.] Exciting fear or apprehension; adapted to excite fear or deter from approach, encounter, or undertaking.—**formidableness,** for′mi•da•bl•nes, *n.* The quality of being formidable.—**formidably,** for′mi•da•bli, *adv.* In a formidable manner.

formula, for′mū•la, *n.* pl. **formulae,** for′mū•lē, or **formulas,** [L. *formula*, dim. of *forma*, a form.] A prescribed form; a prescribed form of words in which something is stated; *med.* a prescription; *eccles.* a written confession of faith; a formal enunciation of doctrines; *math.* a rule or principle expressed in algebraic symbols; *chem.* an expression by means of symbols and letters of the constituents of a compound.—**formularization,** for′mū•lėr•i•zā″shon, *n.* The act of formularizing.—**formularize,** for′mū•lėr•īz, *v.t.*—*formularized, formularizing.* To reduce to a formula; to formulate.—**formulary,** for′mū•le•ri, *n.* A book containing stated and prescribed forms; a book of precedents.—*a.* Prescribed; ritual. —**formulate,** for′mū•lāt, *v.t.*—*formulated, formulating.* To reduce to or express in a formula; to put into a precise and comprehensive statement; to state precisely.—**formulation,** for•mū•lā′shon, *n.* The act of formulating.—**formulization,** for′mū•li•zā″shon, *n.* The act of formulizing.—**formulize,** for′mū•līz, *v.t.* To reduce to a formula or formulas; to formulate.

fornicate, for′ni•kāt, *v.i.* [L. *fornicor*, *fornicatus*, from *fornix*, a vault, a brothel, brothels in Rome being generally in vaults or cellars.] To have unlawful sexual intercourse.—**fornication,** for•ni•kā′shon, *n.* [L. *fornicatio.*] The incontinence or lewdness of unmarried persons, male or female.—**fornicator,** for′ni•kā•tėr, *n.* One guilty of fornication.

forsake, for•sāk′, *v.t.*—*forsook* (pret.), *forsaken* (pp.), *forsaking* (ppr.). [A. Sax. *forsacan*, to oppose, to renounce;

prefix *for*, intens., and *sacan*, to contend; Dan. *forsage*, D. *vérsaken*, to deny. SAKE.] To quit or leave entirely, often to leave that to which we are bound by duty or natural affection; to desert; to abandon; to depart or withdraw from; to renounce; to reject.
forsooth, for•söth′, *adv.* [*For* and *sooth*, that is, for or in truth. A.Sax. *forsoth.*] In truth; in fact; certainly.
forswear, for•swâr′, *v.t.—forswore* (pret.), *forsworn* (pp.). [Prefix *for* with negative sense.] To reject or renounce upon oath; to renounce earnestly or with protestations; *refl.* to swear falsely; to perjure one's self.—*v.i.* To swear falsely.—**forswearer,** for•swa′rėr, *n.*
forsythia, for•sith′•i•a, *n.* [After W. *Forsyth*, Brit. botanist.] Shrub of the oleaceous genus *Forsythia*, having bell-shaped yellow flowers that appear before the leaves in spring.
fort, fōrt, *n.* [Fr. *fort*, *lit.* strong place from *fort*, L. *fortis*, strong. FORCE.] A fortified place, usually small, occupied only by troops.—**forte,** fōr′tā, *a. Mus.* direction to sing or play with force of tone.—*adv.* Loudly, powerfully.—*n. Mus.* a passage played or sung powerfully.—**forte,** fōrt, *n.* [Fr. *fort*, strong part, also a person's forte (the final *e* being an English insertion).] The strong portion of a sword blade or rapier; peculiar talent or faculty a person has; a strong point; chief excellence.—**fortress,** fort′res, *n.* [Fr. *forteresse*, O.Fr. *fortelesse*: same word as *fortalice.*] A fortified place, especially one of considerable extent and complication; a stronghold; a place of security.
forth, fōrth, *adv.* [A.Sax. *forth*, from *fore*, before; G. *fort*, on, further; D. *voord*, forward. FORE.] Onward in time, place, or order (from that time *forth*); in advance from a given point; forward; out; abroad; from a state of concealment; from an interior; out into view.—**forthcoming,** fōrth′kum•ing, *a.* Ready to appear; making appearance.—**forthright,** fōrth′rīt, *adv.* Straightforward; straightway.—*a.* Straightforward; direct; immediate.—*n.* A straight way; opposed to meanders. (*Shak.*)—**forthwith,** fōrth′with, *adv.* [*Forth* and *with*, forth along with that.] Immediately; without delay; directly.
fortify, for′ti•fī, *v.t.—fortified, fortifying.* [Fr. *fortifier*, from L.L. *fortifico*—L. *fortis*, strong, and *facio*, to make.] To add strength to; to strengthen (an argument, resolution); to furnish with strength or means of resisting (to *fortify* one against cold); to surround, with a wall, ditch, palisades, or other works, with a view to defend against the attacks of an enemy; to increase the alcoholic strength of (wine) by means of adventitious spirit.—**fortification,** for′ti•fi•kā″shon, *n.* The act of fortifying; the art or science of strengthening military positions in such a way that they may be readily defended; the works constructed for the purpose of strengthening a position; a fortified place; a fort.—**fortifier,** for′ti•fī•ėr, *n.* One who fortifies.
fortissimo, for•tis′sē•mō, *adv. Mus.* a direction to sing with the utmost strength or loudness.
fortitude, for′ti•tūd, *n.* [L. *fortitudo*, from *fortis*, strong. FORCE.] That strength or firmness of mind or soul which enables a person to encounter danger or to bear pain with coolness and courage; passive courage; resolute endurance.
fortnight, fort′nīt, *n.* [Contr. from *fourteen nights*, time being formerly often reckoned by nights. SE′N-NIGHT.] The space of fourteen days; two weeks.—**fortnightly,** fort′nīt•li, *adv.* Once a fortnight; every fortnight.—*a.* Occurring or appearing once a fortnight.
fortress. See FORT.
fortuitous, for•tū′i•tus, *a.* [L. *fortuitus*, from *fors*, *fortis*, chance. FORTUNE.] Accidental; happening by chance; occurring without any known cause.—**fortuitously,** for•tū′i•tus•li, *adv.* In a fortuitous manner; accidentally; by chance.—**fortuitousness,** for•tū′i•tus•nes, *n.*—**fortuity,** for-tū′i•ti, *n.* Accident; chance; casualty.
fortune, for′chen, *n.* [L. *fortuna*, a lengthened form from stem of *fors*, *fortis*, chance, hap, luck, from *fero*, to bring (as in *fertile*).] Chance; accident; luck; fate; also, the personified or deified power regarded as determining the lots of life; the good or ill that befalls or may befall man; success, good or bad; what the future may bring; good success; prosperity; good luck; estate; possessions; especially, large estate; great wealth.—*v.i.* To befall; to fall out; to happen; to come casually to pass.—**fortunate,** for′che•nit, *a.* [L. *fortunatus.*] Coming by good fortune or favorable chance; bringing some unexpected good; having good fortune; lucky; successful. ∴ *Fortunate* refers to that which is deemed beyond our own control; *successful* denotes that effective effort has been made to gain the object; *prosperous* leaves both these notions out of account, simply conveying the fact of there being a flourishing state of matters.—**fortunately,** for′ché•nit•li, *adv.* In a fortunate manner; luckily; happily.—**fortunateness,** for′che•nit•nes, *n.*—**fortune hunter,** *n.* A man who seeks to marry a woman with a large fortune, with a view to enrich himself.—**fortuneless,** for′chen•les, *a.* Luckless; also, destitute of a fortune or wealth.—**fortuneteller,** *n.* One who pretends to tell people their fortune in life.—**fortunetelling,** *n.* The act or practice of telling fortunes.
forty, for′ti, *a.* [A.Sax. *feówertig*—*feówer*, four, and *tig*, ten. FOUR.] Four times ten; thirty-nine and one added.—*n.* The number which consists of four times ten; or a symbol expressing it.—*The roaring forties*, the stormy area of the Atlantic between 39° and 50° N. lat.—*The forty-five*, the Jacobite rebellion of 1745, following on the '15 of 1715.—*The forty thieves*, the tale of Ali Baba in the *Arabian Nights.*—*Forty winks*, short nap.—**fortieth,** for′ti•eth, *a.* Following the thirty-ninth; being one of forty equal parts into which anything is divided.—*n.* One of forty equal parts into which a whole is divided.
forum, fō′rum, *n.* [L., connected with *foris*, out of doors; hence *forensic.*] A public place in Rome where causes were judicially tried and orations delivered to the people; a tribunal; a court.
forward, for′wėrd, *adv.* [A.Sax. *foreweard*—*fore*, before, and *weard*, used to signify direction. Comp. G. *vorwärts.*] Toward a part or place before or in front; onward; progressively; opposed to *backward.*—*a.* Being at the front; anterior; fore; ready; prompt; ardent; eager; over bold; self-assertive; pert; saucy; advanced beyond the usual degree; advanced for the season.—*n.* One in advance; a front player in a game, such as basketball.—*v.t.* To advance or help onward; to further, promote, accelerate, hasten; to send toward the place of destination; to transmit; *bookbinding*, to prepare for the finisher.—**forwarder,** for′wėr•dėr, *n.* One who forwards.—**forwardly,** for′wėrd•li, *adv.* In a forward manner; eagerly; pertly; saucily.—**forwardness,** for′wėrd•nes, *n.* The quality of being forward; promptitude; pertness.—**forwards,** *adv.* Forward; toward the front.
fosse, foss, fos, *n.* [Fr. *fosse*, L. *fossa*, a ditch, a trench, from *fodio*, *fossum*, to dig, whence also *fossil.*] *Fort.* a ditch or moat, commonly full of water, outside the walls or rampart of a fortified place or post to be defended; *anat.* a kind of cavity in a bone with a large aperture.
fossil, fos′sil, *a.* [Fr. *fossile*, L. *fossilis*, from *fodio*, *fossum*, to dig. FOSSE.] Dug out of the earth; petrified and preserved in rocks.—*n.* Originally any substance dug out of the earth; now specifically applied to the petrified remains of plants and animals which occur in the strata that compose the surface of our globe; an antiquated person, a petrified fogey.—**fossiliferous,** fos•si•lif′ėr•us, *a.* Producing or containing fossils.—**fossilization,** fos′sil•i•zā″shon, *n.* The act or process of fossilizing; the state of being fossilized.—**fossilize,** fos′sil•īz, *v.t.—fossilized, fossilizing.* To convert into a fossil; *fig.* to render permanently antiquated; to cause to be out of harmony with present time and circumstances.—*v.i.* To become a fossil; to become antiquated, rigid, and fixed.
fossorial fos•sō′ri•al, *a.* [L. *fossor*, a digger, from *fodio*, *fossum*, to dig.] Pertaining to animals which dig dwellings and seek their food in the earth; adapted for digging.
foster, fos′tėr, *v.t.* [A.Sax. *fóstrian*, to nourish, from *fóster*, nourishment, from *fóda*, food. FOOD, FODDER.] To nourish or nurture; to bring up;

to cherish; to promote the growth of; to encourage; to sustain and promote.—**foster brother,** *n.* One who is a brother only by being nursed at the same breast.—**foster child,** *n.* A child nurtured by one who is not its mother or father.—**foster daughter,** *n.* One who is a daughter only by nursing.—**fosterer,** fos'tėr•ėr, *n.* One that fosters.—**foster father,** *n.* One who takes the place of a father in bringing up and educating a child.—**fosterling,** fos'-tėr•ling, *n.* A foster child.—**foster mother,** *n.* A woman who takes the place of a mother in bringing up a child.—**foster parent,** *n.* A foster father or foster mother.—**foster sister,** *n.* A female, not a sister, nursed by the same person.—**foster son,** *n.* One brought up like a son, though not the person's son by birth.

foul, foul, *a.* [A.Sax. *fúl*, foul=Icel. *fúll*, Dan. *fuul*, D. *vuil*, G. *faul*, Goth. *fuls*, putrid, corrupt; same root as L. *puteo*, Skr. *pûy*, to be putrid.] Covered with or containing extraneous matter, which is injurious, noxious, or offensive; filthy; dirty; not clean; turbid; muddy; scurrilous; obscene or profane; abusive; stormy, rainy, or tempestuous (*foul* weather); detestable; vile; shameful; odious; unfair; not lawful; *sports*, denoting, or pertaining to, an act committed contrary to the rules of the game; *naut.* entangled or in collision; opposed to *clear*.—*Foul ball, baseball*, a batted ball that falls or rolls outside the field of play bounded by two straight lines (*foul lines*) that extend from home plate past first base and third base to the boundary of the field.—*To run* or *fall foul of*, to rush upon; to attack; to run against; to stumble over or upon.—*v.t.* To make filthy; to defile; to dirty; to soil.—*v.i.* To become foul or dirty; to commit a foul; to hit a ball foul; *naut.* to come into collision; to become entangled or clogged.—*n.* The act of fouling; a colliding, or otherwise impeding due motion or progress.—**foully,** foul'li, *adv.* In a foul manner.—**foulness,** foul'nes, *n.* The quality or state of being foul or filthy.—**foulmouthed,** *a.* Using foul or vile language; uttering abuse, or profane or obscene words.

found, found, pret. & pp. of *find*.

found, found, *v.t.* [Fr. *fonder*, from L. *fundo*, to found, from *fundus*, the bottom of anything; hence also *fund, founder*.] To lay the basis of; to base; to establish on a basis literal or figurative; to take the first steps in erecting or building up; to originate.—*v.i.* To rest or rely: followed by *on* or *upon* (I *found upon* my own observation).—**foundation,** foun•dā'shon, *n.* The act of founding, establishing, or beginning to build; the masonry or the solid ground on which the walls of a building rest; the basis or groundwork of anything; that on which anything stands and is supported; fund invested for a benevolent purpose; endowment; an endowed institution or charity.—**founder,** foun'dėr, *n.* One who founds; one who fixes, originates, or establishes.

found, found, *v.t.* [Fr. *fondre*, to melt, to cast, from L. *fundo, fusum*, to pour out (hence *fusc*, etc.).] To form by melting a metal and pouring it into a mold; to cast.—**founder,** foun'dėr, *n.* One who founds; one who casts metals in various forms.—**foundry,** foun'dri, *n.* [Fr. *fonderie*.] The art of casting metals; the buildings and works occupied for casting metals.

founder, foun'dėr, *v.i.* [O.Fr. *fondrer, afondrer*, to founder—*fond*, ground, bottom, from L. *fundus*, bottom. FOUND, to establish.] To fill or be filled and sink; to go down: said of a ship; to fail; to miscarry; to go lame: said of a horse.—*n. Farriery*, a lameness occasioned by inflammation within the hoof of a horse; an inflammatory fever or acute rheumatism.

foundling, found'ling, *n.* [Dim. formed from *found*, as *bantling* from *band, darling* from *dear*.] A child found without a parent or any one to take care of it.

fount, fount, *n.* [L. *fons, fontis*. FONT.] A spring of water; a fountain.—*Fount of types*. FONT, in this sense.—**fountain,** foun'ten, *n.* [Fr. *fontaine*, L.L. *fontana*, from L. *fons, fontis*.] A spring or natural source of water; the head or source of a river; an artificial spout, jet, or shower of water; a basin or other structure kept constantly supplied with water for use or for ornament; the origin or source of anything.—**fountainhead,** *n.* Primary source; origin.—**fountain pen,** *n.* A writing pen with a reservoir for furnishing a continuous supply of ink.

four, fōr, *a.* [A.Sax. *feówer*=Fris. *fiower*, Icel. *fjórir*, Dan. *fire*, G. and D. *vier*, Goth. *fidwor*, L. *quatuor*, Gr. *tettares*, Russ. *cetvero*, W. *pedwar*, Ir. *ceathair*, Skr. *chatvâr*.] Twice two; three and one.—*n.* The number consisting of twice two; the symbol representing this number.—**four-cycle,** *a.* A four-stroke cycle, as for an internal-combustion engine.—**fourflusher,** *n.* One who bluffs, boasts or deceives.—**fourfold,** fōr'fōld, *a.* Four times folded; quadruple.—**four-in-hand,** *n.* A vehicle drawn by four horses and guided by one driver holding all the reins; a necktie tied with a slipknot at the collar and hanging down the shirt front.—**fourpence, fourpenny,** fōr'pens, fōr'pen•i, *n.* A British silver coin of an earlier era; the sum of four British pennies.—**four-poster,** *n.* A large bed having four posts or pillars for the curtains.—**fourscore,** fōr'skōr, *a.* Four times twenty; eighty; often elliptically for fourscore years.—*n.* Twenty taken four times; eighty units.—**foursome,** fōr'sum, *n.* Game of golf between two pairs; dance or reel of two pairs.

fourteen, fōr'tēn, *n.* [A.Sax. *feówertýne*.] The number consisting of ten and four, or the symbol representing it.—*a.* Four and ten; twice seven.—**fourteenth,** fōr'tēnth, *a.* The ordinal of fourteen; the fourth after the tenth.—*n.* One of fourteen equal parts in which a whole is divided.—**fourth,** fōrth, *a.* [A.Sax. *feórtha*.] The ordinal of four; the next after the third.—*n.* One of four equal parts into which a whole is divided; *mus.* an interval composed of two tones and a semitone.—*The Fourth of July*, in the U.S., the holiday celebrating the Declaration of Independence.—**fourth dimension,** *n.* The dimension that converts a three dimensional aggregate (length, breadth and thickness) into a space-time relationship; a thing outside the range of customary meaning.—**fourthly,** fōrth'li, *adv.*

fourchette, för•shet', *n.* [Fr. dim. of *fourche*, fork. FORK.] A small fork-shaped piece or implement; the furculum, or wishbone, of a bird.

Fourierism, fö'ri•ėr•izm, *n.* A socialistic system or form of communism propounded by Charles *Fourier*, a Frenchman.—**Fourierist, Fourierite,** fö'ri•ėr•ist, fö'ri•ėr•īt, *n.* An adherent of this system.

foveate, foveolate, fō'vē•āt, fō'vē•ō•lāt, *a.* [L. *fovea*, a pit.] *Bot.* marked by little depressions or pits; pitted.

fowl, foul, *n.* [A.Sax. *fugel, fugol*, a fowl, a bird=D. and G. *vogel*, Icel. and Dan. *fugl*, Goth. *fugls*, a bird; can hardly be connected with *fly*.] A bird: often unchanged in the plural (the *fowl* of the air); now very commonly a cock or hen; a barnyard or domestic fowl.—*v.i.* To catch or kill wild fowls.—**fowler,** fou'lėr, *n.* A sportsman who pursues wild fowls.—**fowling piece,** *n.* A light gun for shooting fowls or birds of any kind.

fox, foks, *n.* [A.Sax. *fox*; G. *fuchs*, L.G. *voss, vos*, Prov. E. *faws*, Goth. *fauho*, fox. *Fixen* (E. *vixen*) was the A.Sax. for she-fox.] A carnivorous animal closely allied to the dog, remarkable for his cunning; a sly cunning fellow.—*v.t.* and *i.* To trick.—**foxglove,** foks'gluv, *n.* A common plant, conspicuous by its tall spike of large showy flowers in long one-sided racemes; digitalis.—**foxhound,** *n.* A hound for chasing foxes.—**foxtail grass,** *n.* Any of certain grasses with tail-like spikelets.—**fox terrier,** *n.* A small, smooth-haired or wire-haired dog, first bred to dig out foxes.—**fox trot,** *n.* A form of ballroom dance in four-four time.—**foxy,** foks'i, *a.* Wily, as of one who is cunning or sly as a fox.—**foxily,** foks'•i•li, *adv.* In a foxy manner.—**foxiness,** foks'•i•nes, *n.* Slyness.

foyer, fwä'yā, *n.* [Fr., L.L. *focarium*, a hearth, L. *focus*.] A lobby or anteroom in a public building, as a theater.

fracas, frā'kes, *n.* [Fr., from *fracasser*, to crash; It. *fracassare*, to break.] An uproar; a noisy quarrel; a disturbance.

fraction, frak'shon, *n.* [Fr. *fraction*, from L. *fractio*, a breaking, from *frango, fractum*, to break; akin *frail*, *fragile, fragment, fracture, infringe,* etc.] A fragment; a portion; a very small part; *arith.* and *alg.* one or more of the equal parts into which a unit or whole number is divided or supposed to be divided (as $^2/_5$, $^1/_4$, .56, .004, decimal fractions); *chem.* one of several separable portions of a mixture or chemical compound.—*v.t.* To divide into fractions.—**fractional,** frak′shon•al, *a.*—*Fractional distillation,* the distillation of a mixture of liquids that have different boiling points, so that the most volatile comes over first, the others as more heat is applied, as in refining shale oil or petroleum.—**fractionary,** frak′shon•a•ri, *a.* Fractional; pertaining to a fraction or small portion of a thing.—**fractionize, fractionate,** frak•shon•īz′, frak•shon′āt, *v.t.* To separate into fractions.

fractious, frak′shus, *a.* [From Prov. E. *fratch,* to quarrel or chide.] Apt to quarrel; cross; snappish; peevish; fretful.—**fractiously,** frak′shus•li, *adv.* In a fractious manner; snappishly.—**fractiousness,** frak′shus•nes, *n.* A fractious temper.

fracture, frak′tūr, *n.* [L. *fractura,* from *frango, fractum,* to break. FRACTION.] A breakage; a breach in a body, especially caused by violence; a crack; a rupture; *surg.* the breaking of a bone; *mineral.* the characteristic manner in which a mineral breaks, and by which its texture is displayed.—*v.t.*—*fractured, fracturing.* To cause fracture in; to break; to crack.—*v.i.* To undergo fracture or breaking.

fragile, fraj′il, *a.* [L. *fragilis,* from *frango,* to break. FRACTION. *Frail* is the same word.] Brittle; easily broken; easily destroyed; frail.—**fragilely,** fraj′il•li, *adv.* In a fragile manner.—**fragileness, fragility,** fraj′il•nes, fra•jil′i•ti, *n.* The condition or quality of being fragile; brittleness; delicacy of substance.

fragment, frag′ment, *n.* [L. *fragmentum,* from *frango,* to break. FRACTION.] A part broken off; a piece separated from anything by breaking; anything left uncompleted; a part separated from the rest.—**fragmental,** frag•men′tal, *a.* Consisting of fragments; fragmentary.—**fragmentarily,** frag′men•te•ri•li, *adv.* In a fragmentary manner; by piecemeal.—**fragmentariness,** frag′men•ta•ri•nes, *n.*—**fragmentary,** frag′men•te•ri, *a.* Composed of fragments or broken pieces.—**fragmentation,** frag•men•tā′shun, *n.* Separation into fragments; *biol.* mitosis or cell division, beginning with the nucleus.

fragrant, frā′grent, *a.* [L. *fragrans, fragrantis,* ppr. of *fragro,* to emit a scent.] Sweet of smell; affecting the olfactory nerves agreeably; having an agreeable perfume; odoriferous.—**fragrantly,** frā′grent•li, *adv.* With sweet scent.—**fragrance, fragrancy,** frā′grens, frā′gren•si, *n.* The quality of being fragrant; sweetness of smell; pleasing scent; perfume.

frail, frāl, *a.* [Fr. *frele,* O.Fr. *fraile,* L. *fragilis,* fragile. FRAGILE.] Easily broken; fragile; liable to fail and decay; easily destroyed; perishable; not firm or durable; not strong against temptation to evil; liable to fall from virtue.—**frailly,** frāl′li, *adv.* In a frail manner; weakly.—**frailness,** frāl′nes, *n.* The condition or quality of being frail.—**frailty,** frāl′ti, *n.* The condition or quality of being frail; weakness of resolution; infirmity; liableness to be deceived or seduced; a fault proceeding from weakness; a foible.

frail, frāl, *n.* [O.Fr. *frael, frayel.*] A basket made of rushes, in which dried fruit is occasionally imported.

fraise, frāz, *n.* [Fr., same word as *frieze* (on a building).] *Fort.* a defense consisting of pointed stakes driven into the ramparts in a horizontal or inclined position.

framboesia, fram•bē′si•a, *n.* [Fr. *framboise,* a raspberry.] The yaws, a contagious disease prevalent in the Antilles and some parts of Africa, characterized by raspberry-like excrescences: whence the name.

frame, frām, *v.t.*—*framed, framing.* [A.Sax. *fremman,* to form, make, effect, from *fram, from,* strong, forward=*from,* prep.; O.Sax. *fremmian,* O.Fris. *frema,* Icel. *fremja,* to accomplish.] To construct by fitting and uniting together the several parts; to make, compose, contrive, devise, invent, fabricate; to fit, as for a specific end; to adjust, shape, conform; to surround or provide with a frame, as a picture.—*n.* Anything composed of parts fitted and united; fabric; structure; specifically, bodily structure; make or build of a person; the main timbers of a structure fitted and joined together for the purpose of supporting and strengthening the whole; framework; some kind of case or structure for admitting, enclosing, or supporting things; particular state, as of the mind; temper or disposition.—**frame house,** *n.* A house constructed with a wooden skeleton.—**framework,** frām′wėrk, *n.* A structure or fabric for supporting anything; a frame; fabric; structure.—**framing,** frā′ming, *n.* A framework or frame; a system of frames.

franc, frangk, *n.* [Fr., from the device *Francorum rex,* king of the French, on the coin when first struck by King John in 1360.] The French monetary unit, a silver coin worth 100 French centimes.

franchise, fran′chīz, *n.* [Fr., from *franc,* free. FRANK.] A particular privilege or right granted by a government, as the right to vote, to operate a railroad, or to form, and exercise the powers of, a corporate body.

Franciscan, fran•sis′kan, *n.* A mendicant of the order founded by St. Francis of Assisi about 1210, and also called *Minorites, Gray Friars,* from the former color of their habit, or *Black Friars,* from the color of the habit worn by the Conventuals.

francium, fran′si•um, *n.* An element of the alkali-metal series. Symbol, Fr; at. no., 87.

francolin, frang′ko•lin, *n.* [Dim. of Pg. *frango,* a hen.] A bird closely allied to the partridges, found throughout the warmer parts of Europe, as well as in Asia.

franc-tireur, frän′tē•rėr″, *n.* [Fr., lit. a free-shooter.] One of a body of irregular sharpshooters organized in France in the war of 1870, and employed in guerrilla warfare.

frangible, fran′ji•bl, *a.* [From L. *frango,* to break. FRACTION.] Capable of being broken; brittle.—**frangibility, frangibleness,** fran•ji•bil′i•ti, fran′ji•bl•nes, *n.* The state or quality of being frangible.

frangipani, fran•ji•pan′ni, *n.* A perfume prepared from, or imitating the odor of, the flower of a West Indian tree.

frank, frangk, *a.* [Fr. *franc,* free, originally free like the *Franks,* the word being from the name of this old Germanic tribe or nation.] Free in uttering real sentiments; not reserved.—*n.* The privilege granted by the federal government to its bureaus, legislators, and accredited representatives of foreign governments, of sending, postage free, mail concerned with official business.—*v.t.* To send by means of a frank; to transmit free of expense.—**frankly,** frangk′li, *adv.* In a frank manner; openly; candidly.—**frankness,** frangk′nes, *n.* The state or quality of being frank.—**frankpledge,** *n.* [A pledge given by free men.] An institution in early England by which the members of a tithing, composed of ten households, were made responsible for each other, so that if one committed an offense the others were bound to make reparation.

Frank, frangk, *n.* One of the Germanic race that entered the Roman Provinces and Gaul in A.D. 253, eventually establishing the Frankish Empire on the Rhine.—**Frankish,** frang′kish, *a.*

frankfurter, frangk′fėr•tėr, *n.* [From Frankfurt, German town.] Seasoned beef and pork sausage, linked and in casings.

frankincense, frangk′in•sens, *n.* [That is, pure, unadulterated incense.] A gum resin obtained from a tree inhabiting Africa and Asia, which, when burned, exudes a strong odor.

franklin, frangk′lin, *n.* [O.Fr. *frankeleyn, francheleyn,* from L.L. *franchilanus,* from *francus,* free. FRANK, *a.*] A freeholder; a yeoman; one whose estate was free of any feudal superior.

frantic, fran′tik, *a.* [Fr. *frénétique,* from L. *phreneticus,* from Gr. *phrenitis,* mental disorder, frenzy, from *phrēn,* the mind. FRENZY.] Mad; raving; furious; outrageous; distracted (a *frantic* person); characterized by violence, fury, and disorder (a *frantic* outburst).—**frantically, franticly,** fran′ti•kal•li, fran′tik•li, *adv.* In a frantic or furious manner.—**franticness,** fran′tik•nes, *n.*

frap, frap, *v.t.*—*frapped, frapping.*

[Fr. *frapper*, to strike, to frap, of Scandinavian origin.] *Naut.* to make fast or tight, as by passing ropes round a sail or a weakened vessel, or by binding tackle with yarn.

fraternal, fra•tėr′nal, *a.* [Fr. *fraternel*; L. *fraternus*, from *frater*, brother; a word cog. with E. *brother*.] Brotherly; pertaining to brothers; becoming or proceeding from brothers.—**fraternally,** fra•tėr′nal•li, *adv.* In a fraternal manner.—**fraternity,** fra•tėr′ni•ti, *n.* [Fr. *fraternité*; L. *fraternitas*.] The state or relationship of a brother; a body of men associated for their common interest, business, or pleasure; a brotherhood; a society; a class or profession of men.—**fraternization,** frat′ėr•ni•zā″shon, *n.* The act of fraternizing.—**fraternize,** frat′ėr•nīz, *v.i.* To associate or hold fellowship; to hold sympathetic intercourse; to have congenial sympathies and intercourse.—**fraternizer,** frat′ėr•nī•zėr, *n.* One who fraternizes.—

fratricide, frat′ri•sīd, *n.* [L. *fratricidium*, the crime, *fratricida*, the criminal—*frater*, and *caedo*, to kill.] The crime of murdering a brother; one who murders or kills a brother.—**fratricidal,** frat•ri•sī′dal, *a.* Pertaining to or involving fratricide.

fraud, frąd, *n.* [L. *fraus*, *fraudis*, Fr. *fraude*; hence *defraud*.] An act or course of deception deliberately practiced with the view of gaining an unlawful or unfair advantage; deceit; deception; imposition. ∴ *Deceit* is used of the mental process which underlies any proceeding intended to deceive; *deception* signifies the procedure by which deceit is carried out, and also that which deceives, misleads, or imposes on; while *fraud* is an act, or a series of acts of *deceit*, by which we attempt to benefit ourselves at the expense of another.—**fraudulence, fraudulency,** frą′dū•lens, frą′dū•len•si, *n.* [L. *fraudulentia*.] The quality of being fraudulent.—**fraudulent,** frą′dū•lent, *a.* [L. *fraudulentus*.] Using fraud in making bargains, contracts, etc.; given to using fraud; founded on fraud; proceeding from fraud.—**fraudulently,** frą′dū•lent•li, *adv.* In a fraudulent manner.

fraught, frąt, *a.* [A participial form from old verb *fraught*, to load, a form of *freight*. FREIGHT.] Freighted‡; *fig.* filled, stored, charged, abounding, pregnant (a scheme *fraught* with mischief).—**fraughtage,** † frą′tij, *n.* Loading; cargo. (*Shak.*)

fray, frā, *n.* [Abbrev. of *affray*.] An affray; a broil, quarrel, or violent riot.—*v.t.* To fright; to terrify.

fray, frā, *v.t.* [Fr. *frayer*, from L. *fricare*, to rub (whence also *friction*).] To rub; to rub away the surface of; to fret, as cloth by wearing or the skin by friction.—*n.* A frayed or rubbed place.

freak, frēk, *n.* [A.Sax. *frec*, greedy, bold = Icel. *frekr*, greedy, exorbitant; Dan. *fraek*, bold, G. *frech*, saucy.] A sudden causeless change or turn of the mind; a whim or fancy; a capricious prank; an odd, whimsical person.—**freakish,** frēk′ish, *a.* Addicted to freaks; whimsical; capricious; fanciful; grotesque.—**freakishly,** frēk′ish•li, *adv.* In a freakish manner.—**freakishness,** frēk′ish•nes, *n.* Capriciousness; whimsicalness.

freckle, frek′l, *n.* [O.E. *freckens*, *frekens*, freckles (akin to *freak*, to variegate); Icel. *freknur*, Dan. *fregner*, freckles; comp. G. *fleck*, a spot.] A spot of a yellowish color in the skin, particularly on the face, neck, and hands; any small spot or discoloration.—*v.t.* and *i.* To mark or become marked with freckles.—**freckled,** frek′ld, *pp.* and *a.* Marked with freckles.—**freckly,** frek′li, *a.* Covered with freckles.

free, frē, *a.* [A.Sax. *fri*, *freó* = Icel. *fri*, Dan. and Sw. *fri*, D. *vrij*, G. *frei*, Goth. *freis*, free; allied to *friend*, Goth. *frijon*, to love; Skr. *pri*, to love; perhaps also to L. *privus*, one's own, *privatus*, private.] Not being under necessity or restraint, physical or moral; exempt from subjection to the will of others; being at liberty; not in confinement; not under an arbitrary or despotic government; instituted by a free people; capable of being used, enjoyed, or taken advantage of without charge; unrestricted; open; not obstructed; going beyond due limits in speaking or acting; open; candid; frank; without care; unconcerned; liberal; not parsimonious; profuse; gratuitous; given with readiness or good will; clear; exempt; having got rid; not encumbered, affected, or oppressed; with *from*, and sometimes *of*; invested with or enjoying certain immunities; having certain privileges: with *of* (a man *free of* the city of London); *bot.* applied to parts which are not united together; *chem.* not chemically combined with any other body.—*Free agency*, the state of acting freely or without necessity or constraint of the will.—*Free Church of Scotland*, that ecclesiastical body which seceded from the Established Church at the Disruption in 1843.—*Free labor*, labor performed by free persons in contradistinction to that of slaves.—*Free love*, the right to consort with those we have conceived a passion for, regardless of the shackles of matrimony.—*To make free with*, to intermeddle with; to use liberties with; to help one's self to.—*Free and easy*, unconstrained; regardless of conventionalities.—*v.t.* —*freed*, *freeing*. To remove from a thing any encumbrance or obstruction; to disentangle; to disengage; to rid; to strip; to clear; to set at liberty; to rescue or release from slavery, captivity, or confinement; to manumit; to loose; to exempt, as from some oppressive condition or duty.—**freeboard,** *n. Naut.* the part of a ship's side between the gunwale and the line of flotation.—**freebooter,** frē′bö•tėr, *n.* [D. *vrijbuiter*, G. *freibeuter*. BOOTY.] One who wanders about for booty or plunder; a robber; a pillager; a plunderer.—**freeborn,** frē′born, *a.* Born free; not in vassalage; inheriting liberty.—**freedman,** frēd′man, *n.* A man who has been a slave and is manumitted.—**freedom,** frē′dum, *n.* The state of being free; exemption from slavery, servitude, confinement, or constraint; liberty; independence; frankness; openness; outspokenness; unrestrictedness.—*Freedom of the seas*, doctrine that merchant ships may traverse all waters, save those territorial, in both peace and war.—**free enterprise,** *n.* Economic system under which private businesses operate competitively to meet consumer demands and government limits its action to protecting rights of individuals.—**free fall,** *n.* Unconstrained fall of a body through air, as in a parachute jump.—**free-for-all,** *n.* An open competition; a promiscuous fight. (Colloq.)—**freehand,** frē′hand, *a.* Applied to drawing in which the hand is not assisted by any guiding or measuring instruments.—**freehanded,** *a.* Openhanded; liberal.—**freehearted,** *a.* Open; unreserved; liberal; charitable; generous.—**freehold,** frē′hōld, *n. Law*, an estate in real property, held either in fee simple or fee tail, or for life; the tenure by which such an estate is held.—**free lance,** *n.* One of the mercenary soldiers of the Middle Ages, who fought for any employer able to pay; one unattached to any political party; a writer (or artist or actor) not regularly employed by any one concern (*slang*).—**free liver,** frē′liv•ėr, *n.* One who eats and drinks abundantly; one who gives free indulgence to his appetites.—**freely,** frē′li, *adv.* In a free manner.—**freeman,** frē′man, *n.* A man who is free; one not a slave or vassal; one who enjoys or is entitled to a franchise or peculiar privilege.—**freemartin,** frē′mär•tin, *n.* A cow calf twinborn with a bull calf: generally barren.—**Freemason,** frē′mā•sn, *n.* A person belonging to a society or organization the members of which call themselves *free* and accepted *Masons*. — **Freemasonry,** frē′mā•sn•ri, *n.* The mysteries in which Freemasons are initiated.—**freeness,** frē′nes, *n.* The state or quality of being free.—**free port,** *n.* A port where ships may be unloaded and goods deposited without payment of customs.—**free-spoken,** frē′spō•kn, *a.* Outspoken.—**freestone,** frē′stōn, *n.* Any species of stone composed of sand or grit and easily cut or wrought; a kind of peach.—**freethinker,** frē′thingk•ėr, *n.* One whose opinions on religion are based on doubt and skepticism; a deist; an unbeliever; a sceptic.—**freethinking,** frē′thingk•ing, *n.*—*a.* Holding the principles of a freethinker.—**freethought,** frē′thąt, *a.* The beliefs or ways of thinking of freethinkers.—**free trade,** *n.* Trade or commerce free from restrictions, and in particular from customs duties levied on foreign commodities. —**free trader,** *n.* An advocate of free trade.—**free will,** *n.* The power of directing our own actions without constraint by necessity or fate; voluntariness; spontaneousness.—*a.* Voluntary; spontaneous.

freeze, frēz, *v.i.*—*froze* (pret.), *frozen* or *froze* (pp.), *freezing* (ppr.). [A.Sax. *frysan, freósan*=D. *vriezen,* Icel. *frjósa,* Dan. *fryse,* G. *frieren*; same root as L. *pruina,* hoarfrost. Akin *frore, frost.*] To be congealed by cold; to be changed from a liquid to a solid state by the abstraction of heat; to be hardened into ice; to be of that degree of cold at which water congeals: used impersonally (it *freezes* hard); to become chilled in body with cold.—*v.t.* To congeal or cause to freeze; to harden into ice; to chill; to give the sensation of cold and shivering.—*n.* The act of freezing; frost. (*Colloq.*).—**freezer,** frē´zėr, *n.* One who or that which freezes.—**freezing point,** *n.* That degree of a thermometer at which a liquid begins to freeze; the temperature at which ordinarily water freezes. By the centigrade thermometer the freezing-point of water is 0° or zero; by Fahrenheit's thermometer 32° above zero.—**frozen,** frō´zn, *p.* and *a.* Congealed by cold; frosty; subject to severe frost; void of sympathy; wanting in feeling or interest; unsympathetic.

freight, frāt, *n.* [Formerly *fraht*=D. *vragt,* Dan. *fragt,* Sw. *frakt,* G. *fracht,* a freight or cargo. FRAUGHT.] A burden or load; goods laden for transportation by land, water, or air; the price charged or paid for the transportation of goods; transportation by common carrier, as opposed to express; a freight train.—*v.t.* To transport by freight; *fig. to pay the freight,* to bear the burden.—**freightage,** frā´tij, *n.* The act or process of freighting; money paid for freight; freight or lading (*Mil.*).—**freighter,** frā´tėr, *n.* One who freights; a ship mainly transporting freight.

French, frensh, *a.* [O.Fr. *franchois, françois,* Mod.Fr. *français,* from *France,* which received its name from the *Franks.*] Pertaining to France or its inhabitants.—*n.* The language spoken by the people of France; collectively the French people.—**French chalk,** *n.* A variety of talc resembling chalk, of a pearly white or grayish color.—**French horn,** *n.* A musical instrument of brass having several curves, and gradually widening from the mouthpiece to the other end.—**Frenchify,** frensh´i•fī, *v.t.* To make French; to imbue with French tastes or manners.—**Frenchman,** frensh´man, *n.* A man of the French nation; a native or naturalized inhabitant of France.

frenetic, frenetical, fre•net´ik, fre•net´i•kal, *a.* [Same word as *frantic.* FRENZY.] Frenzied; frantic.—**frenetically,** fre•net´i•kal•li, *adv.* In a frenetic or frenzied manner.

frenzy, fren´zi, *n.* [O.Fr. *frenaisie,* Mod.Fr. *phrénésie*; from Gr. *phrenēsis, phrenitis,* mental derangement, from *phren,* the mind. FRANTIC.] Distraction; delirium; madness; any violent agitation of the mind approaching to distraction or temporary derangement of the mental faculties.—*v.t.*—*frenzied, frenzying.* To drive to madness; to render frenzied.—**frenzied,** fren´zid, *p.* and *a.* Affected with frenzy or madness; maddened; frantic.

frequent, frē´kwent, *a.* [Fr. *fréquent,* from L. *frequens, frequentis,* common, usual, full, crowded; same root as *farcio,* to cram (whence *farce*).] Often seen or done; often happening at short intervals; often repeated or occurring; doing a thing often; inclined to indulge in any practice.—*v.t.* (fri•kwent´). [L. *frequento*; Fr. *fréquenter.*] To visit often; to resort to often or habitually.—**frequence,**† frē´kwens, *n.* [L. *frequentia.*] A crowd; a throng; a concourse; an assembly.—**frequency,** frē´kwen•si, *n.* The state of being frequent; a frequent return or occurrence; the condition of being often repeated at short intervals.—**frequency modulation,** *Elect.* static-free broadcasting system in which the frequency of the transmitted waves is modulated in accordance with a signal.—**frequentation,** frē•kwen•tā´shon, *n.* The act or custom of frequenting.—**frequentative,** fri•kwen´ta•tiv, *a. Gram.* serving to express the frequent repetition of an action: applied to certain verbs.—*n.* A verb which denotes the frequent occurrence or repetition of an action.—**frequenter,** fri•kwen´tėr, *n.* One who frequents.—**frequently,** frē´kwent•li, *adv.* Often; many times, at short intervals; repeatedly; commonly.

fresco, fres´kō, *n.* pl. **frescoes** and **frescos,** fres´kōz. [It., fresh, from being executed on fresh plaster. FRESH.] A method of painting on walls with mineral and earthy pigments on fresh plaster, or on a wall laid with mortar not yet dry.—*v.t.* To paint in fresco, as walls.

fresh, fresh, *a.* [A.Sax. *fersc,* whence *fresh* by a common metathesis=D. *versch,* Icel. *ferskr, friskr,* Dan. *fersk, frisk,* G. *frisch*; hence It. Sp. and Pg. *fresco,* Fr. *frais, fraîche,* fresh. *Frisk* is a form of the same word.] Full of health and strength; vigorous; strong; brisk; lively; bright; not faded; undecayed; unimpaired by time; in good condition; not stale; not exhausted with labor or exertion; renewed in strength; reinvigorated; refreshing; health-giving: applied to pure cool water, and also to a rather strong wind; vivid; clearly remembered; new; recently grown, made, or obtained; not salt or salted.—*n.* A freshet; a spring of fresh water; a flood; an overflowing; an inundation.—**freshen,** fresh´n, *v.t.* To make fresh; to give a fresh appearance or character to; to make to feel fresh; to refresh; to revive.—*v.i.* To grow fresh; to grow strong (the wind *freshens*).—**freshet,** fresh´et, *n.* A small stream of fresh water; a flood or overflowing of a river, by means of heavy rains or melted snow.—**freshly,** fresh´li, *adv.* In a fresh manner.—**freshman,** fresh´man, *n.* A novice; a student of the first year in a university.—**freshness,** fresh´nes, *n.* The condition or quality of being fresh.—**fresh-water,** *a.* Pertaining to, produced by, or living in water that is fresh or not salt.

fret, fret, *v.t.*—*fretted, fretting.* [A. Sax. *fretan,* to eat, to gnaw, devour; D. *vreten,* G. *fressen,* O.H.G. *frezzan,* Goth. *fraïtan,* to eat, all from prefix =E. *for,* intens., and verb to *eat.*] To gnaw; to eat into; to rub or wear away; to fray; to chafe; to gall; to wear away so as to diminish; to impair; to agitate; to disturb (to *fret* the surface of the sea); *fig.* to chafe the mind of; to irritate; to tease; to make angry.—*v.i.* To become frayed or chafed; to be chafed or irritated; to become vexed or angry; to utter peevish expressions; to boil or work as angry feelings; to rankle.—*n.* A state of chafing or irritation; vexation; anger.—**fretful,** fret´fu̦l, *a.* Disposed to fret; ill-humored; peevish; in a state of vexation.—**fretfully,** fret´fu̦l•li, *adv.* In a fretful manner; peevishly.—**fretfulness,** fret´fu̦l•nes, *n.* Peevishness; ill-humor.

fret, fret, *n.* [O.Fr. *freter,* to interlace, *frettes,* a grating; from L. *ferrum,* iron. Comp. also A.Sax. *fraetwe,* ornaments.] A kind of ornament formed of bands or fillets variously combined, but most frequently arranged in rectangular forms; a piece of perforated ornamental work; one of the small crossbars or ridges on the fingerboards of some stringed instruments, to regulate the pitch of the notes.—*v.t.* To ornament or furnish with frets; to variegate; to diversify.—**fretty,** fret´i, *a.* Adorned with fretwork.—**fretwork,** fret´wėrk, *n.* Ornamental work consisting of a series or combination of frets; designs cut through a thin plate of wood.—**fret saw,** *n.* A small saw for cutting fretwork.

friable, frī´a•bl, *a.* [L. *friabilis,* from *frio, friatum,* to crumble down.] Easily crumbled or pulverized; easily reduced to powder.—**friability, friableness,** frī•a•bil´i•ti, frī´a•bl•nes, *n.* The quality of being friable.

friar, frī´ėr, *n.* [Formerly *frere,* Fr. *frère,* O.Fr. *freire,* a brother, from L. *frater, fratris,* a brother. BROTHER.] A person belonging to one of the Roman Catholic mendicant religious orders or brotherhoods—Dominicans, Franciscans, Carmelites, Augustines, etc.; a monk.—**friar's lantern,** *n.* Will o' the wisp; marsh light.—**friary,** frī´ėr•i, *n.* A convent of friars; a monastery.

fribble, frib´l, *a.* [Perhaps corrupted from Fr. *frivole,* frivolous.] Frivolous; trifling; silly.—*n.* A frivolous, trifling, contemptible fellow.—*v.i.*—*fribbled, fribbling.* To act the fribble; to trifle.—**fribbler,** frib´lėr, *n.* A trifler; a coxcomb.—**fribbling,** frib´ling, *a.* Frivolous; trifling.

fricandeau, frik•an•dō´, *n.* [Fr., etymology doubtful.] A fricassee or other preparation of veal.

fricassee, frik•as•sē´, *n.* [Fr. *fricassée,* from *fricasser,* to cook in this way: etymology doubtful.] A dish of food made by cutting chickens, veal, or other meat into pieces and stewing it in a gravy.—*v.t.*—*fricasseed, fricasseeing.* To dress in fricassee.

friction, frik′shon, *n.* [L. *frictio, frictionis,* from *frico, frictum,* to rub, to rub down.] The act of rubbing the surface of one body against that of another; attrition; *mech.* the effect of rubbing or the resistance which a moving body meets with from the surface on which it moves.—*Angle of friction,* the maximum angle at which one body will remain on another without sliding.—**fricative,** frik′a•tiv, *a.* A term applied to certain letters produced by the friction of the breath issuing through a narrow opening of the organs, as *f, v, s, z,* etc.—**frictional,** frik′shon•al, *a.* Relating to friction; moved by friction; produced by friction.—**friction clutch,** *n.* A species of loose coupling much used for connecting pieces in machines which require to be frequently engaged and disengaged. —**friction tape,** *elect.* a flat tape, both insulating and adhesive, used in repairs, etc.

Friday, frī′dā, *n.* [A.Sax. *Frige-dæg,* G. *Freytag,* the day sacred to *Frigga,* or *Freya,* the Teutonic goddess.] The sixth day of the week.—*Good Friday,* the Friday immediately preceding Easter, kept sacred as the day of Christ's crucifixion.

friend, frend, *n.* [A.Sax. *freónd,* virtually a pres. part. of *freón,* to love; like Goth. *frijonds,* from *frijon,* to love; D. *vriend,* Icel. *fraendi,* G. *freund,* a friend. *Fiend* is similarly formed. FREE.] One who is attached to another by affection; one who has esteem and regard for another and loves his society; one not hostile; one of the same nation, party, or kin; one who looks with favor upon a cause, institution, or the like; also a term of salutation or familiar address.—*Society of Friends,* the name assumed by the society of dissenters commonly called Quakers.—*To be friends with,* to feel as a friend toward; to be friendly toward: may be used when a single person is the friend of another.—*v.t.* To befriend; to support or aid.—**friendless,** frend′les, *a.* Destitute of friends.—**friendlessness,** frend′les•nes, *n.* The state of being friendless. — **friendlily,** frend′li•li, *adv.* In a friendly manner. —**friendliness,** frend′li•nes, *n.* The condition or quality of being friendly; a disposition to favor or befriend; good will; exercise of benevolence or kindness.—**friendly,** frend′li, *a.* Having the temper and disposition of a friend; disposed to promote the good of another; kind; amicable; befitting friends; not hostile; favorable; propitious.—*Friendly fire,* a fire kept within a container which has been provided for it, as a fire in a heater; opposed to *hostile fire,* a fire elsewhere than within a container provided for it. (*Fire Insurance.*) ∴ Syn. under AMICABLE.—*adv.*† In the manner of friends; amicably. (*Shak.*)—**friendship,** frend′ship, *n.* The feeling that subsists between friends or binds them to one another; attachment to a person; mutual attachment; kind regard; intimacy between friends; kindness.

Friese, frēz, [*obs.*] *n.* The language of Friesland; Frisian.—**friesic,** frē′zik, *a.* Frisian.

frieze, frēz, *n.* [Fr. *frise*=It. *fregio,* Sp. *friso,* probably from Ar. *ifriz,* a ledge or a wall.] *Arch.* that part of the entablature of a column which is between the architrave and cornice; a band enriched with figures or other ornaments.

frieze, frēz, *n.* [Fr. *frise,* probably from *Friesland,* once the principal seat of its manufacture.] A coarse woolen cloth having a shaggy nap on one side.—*Chevaux de Frieze,* 'horses of Friesland', pointed stakes planted to keep off cavalry.—*v.t.*—*friezed, friezing.* To form a shaggy nap on; to frizzle; to curl.

frigate, frig′it, *n.* [Fr. *frégate,* It. *fregata*; Sp. and Pg. *fragata*; origin doubtful.] Formerly a light vessel propelled by sails and oars; later, a war vessel, rigged with sails; a U.S. warship of 5,000 to 7,000 tons, in between a destroyer and cruiser in size.—**frigate bird,** *n.* A tropical sea bird allied to the cormorants, remarkable for its powers of flight.

fright, frīt, *n.* [A.Sax. *fyrhtu, fyrhto,* fear; Dan. *frygt,* G. *furcht,* D. *vrucht,* fear. *Fear* is probably akin in origin.] Sudden and violent fear; a sudden fit of fear or dread; terror; a person of a shocking, disagreeable, or ridiculous appearance in person or dress. —*v.t.* To frighten; to affright; to scare.—**frighten,** frī′tn, *v.t.* To strike with fright; to terrify; to scare; to alarm suddenly.—**frightful,** frīt′fụl, *a.* Causing fright; terrible; dreadful; awful; horrid; terrific.—**frightfully,** frīt′fụl•li, *adv.* In a frightful manner; dreadfully; horribly; terribly; shockingly.—**frightfulness,** frīt′fụl•nes, *n.* The quality of being frightful.

frigid, frij′id, *a.* [L. *frigidus,* from *frigeo,* to be cold, akin to *rigeo* to be numb or stiff; Gr. *rigos,* cold. *Frill* is of same origin.] Cold; wanting heat or warmth; of a very low temperature; cold in feeling or manner; wanting warmth of affection; wanting zeal, fire, energy, spirit, or animation; stiff; haughty; forbidding; lifeless.—*Frigid zones,* in *geog.* the two zones comprehended between the poles and the polar circles, which are about 23° 28′ from the poles.—**frigidity,** fri•jid′i•ti, *n.* The state or quality of being frigid; coldness; want of warmth; coldness of feeling or manner; want of animation, ardor, or vivacity.—**frigidly,** frij′id•li, *adv.* In a frigid manner.—**frigidness,** frij′id•nes, *n.* The state of being frigid.—**frigorific, frigorifical,** frig•o•rif′ik, frig•o•rif′i•kal, *a.* [L. *frigorificus*—*frigus, frigoris,* cold, and *facio,* to make.] Causing cold.

frill, fril, *n.* [Flemish *frul,* frill, *frullen,* to have frills.] Something purely decorative; a crimped or ornamental edging of fine linen on the bosom of a shirt; a somewhat similar trimming on something else; a ruffle; a fold of feathers or hair around the neck of a bird or beast. —*v.t.* To decorate with a frill.—**frilling,** fril′ing, *n.* Frills; ruffles.

fringe, frinj, *n.* [Fr. *frange,* fringe, It. *frangia,* from L. *fimbria,* fringe; akin to *fibra,* a fiber.] An ornament to the borders of garments, furniture, etc., consisting of threads attached at one end, the other hanging loose; something resembling a fringe; an edging; margin; extremity; *optics,* one of the colored bands of light in the phenomena of diffraction.—*v.t.* To adorn or border with or as with a fringe.—**fringed,** frinjd, *pp.* and *a.* Bordered or ornamented with a fringe or fringes.—**fringe tree,** *n.* A small American tree having snow-white flowers, which hang down like a fringe.

frippery, frip′ėr•i, *n.* [Fr. *friperie,* old clothes, from *friper,* to rumple, to spoil; from O.Fr. *frepe,* rag, tatter.] Old or castoff clothes; waste matter; useless things; trifles; traffic in old clothes; an old-clothes shop. (*Shak.*)—*a.* Trifling; contemptible.

Frisian, frizh′an, *a.* Belonging to Friesland.—*n.* A native of Friesland; the language of Friesland.

frisk, frisk, *v.i.* [O.Fr. *frisque,* brisk, lively, from the Germanic adjective corresponding to E. *fresh.* FRESH.] To leap, skip, dance, or gambol, as in gaiety or frolic; to frolic.—*v.t.* To search someone by running the hand over the clothing, also, to steal from in this manner.—*n.* A frisking; a gambol or romp.—**frisker,** fris′kėr, *n.* One who frisks.—**friskily,** fris′ki•li, *adv.* In a frisky manner.—**friskiness,** fris′ki•nes, *n.* The state or quality of being frisky.—**frisky,** fris′ki, *a.* Fond of frisking or capering; lively; frolicsome.

frit, frit, *n.* [Fr. *fritte,* from *frit,* fried. pp. of *frire,* from L. *frigo, frictum,* to roast. FRY.] The matter of which glass is made after it has been calcined or baked in a furnace.

frith, frith, *n.* Same as *Firth.*

fritillary, frit′il•la•ri, *n.* [L. *fritillus,* a dice box: from checkered markings.] The popular name of a genus of herbaceous bulbous plants.

fritter, frit′ėr, *n.* [Fr. *friture,* lit. a frying, fr. L. *frigere,* to fry.] A small amount of deep-fried batter, sometimes containing corn or fruit.

fritter, frit′ėr, *n.* [O.Fr. *freture, fraiture,* a breaking.] A fragment; a shred.—*v.t.* To break into fritters, meaning to scatter or fritter away; to waste piecemeal; to dwindle (away) little by little; to spend frivolously or in trifles.

frivolous, friv′o•lus, *a.* [L. *frivolus,* frivolous, silly, trifling; same root as *frico,* to rub (whence *friction*).] Of little weight, worth, or importance; not worth notice; trifling; trivial; given to trifling; characterized by unbecoming levity; silly; weak.—**frivolity,**† fri•vol′i•ti, *n.* The condition or quality of being frivolous or trifling; insignificance; also, the act or habit of trifling; unbecoming levity of mind or disposition.—**frivolously,** friv′o•lus•li, *adv.* In a frivolous manner. — **frivolousness,** friv'o•lus•nes, *n.* The quality of being frivolous.

friz, frizz, friz, *v.t.—frizzed, frizzing.* [Fr. *friser,* O.Fr. *frizer,* to curl, *frise,* frieze cloth. FRIEZE.] To curl; to crisp; to form into small curls or into little burs, as the nap of cloth.—*n.* That which is frizzed or curled.—**frizzle,** friz'l, *v.t.—frizzled, frizzling.* [Dim. from *frizz.*] To curl or crisp, as hair; to frizz.—*n.* A curl; a lock of hair crisped.—**frizzly, frizzy,** friz'li, friz'i, *a.* Curly.

fro, frō, *adv.* [A.Sax. or Icel. *frá,* from; short form of *from.*] From; away; back or backward; as in the phrase *to and fro.*

frock, frok, *n.* [Fr. *froc,* a monk's habit; L.L. *frocus, flocus.*] Primarily, a woman's dress; a gown or habit worn by monks or friars; a sailor's woolen jersey.—**frock coat,** *n.* A coat with full skirts having the same length before and behind; a surcoat.

frog, frog, *n.* [A.Sax. *frocga, froga, frosc, frox;* D. *vorsch,* G. *frosch,* Dan. *frö,* Icel. *froskr.*]. The name of various amphibians, having four legs with four toes on the forefeet and five on the hind, more or less webbed, a naked body, no ribs, and no tail, and with great powers of leaping; a condition of the throat that causes hoarseness; a tender section in the middle of the sole of a horse's foot.—**frogfish,** *n.* A fish with a wide and flattened head, larger than the body, a gaping mouth with many teeth, and spacious gill covers.—**froghopper,** *n.* A small leaping insect, the larvae of which are found on plants enclosed in a frothy liquid known as cuckoo spit.—**frog spit, frog spittle,** *n.* The frothy liquid of the larvae of the froghopper. —**frogman,** *n.* One who works underwater, usually for military reconnaissance.

frog, frog, *n.* A fastening for a frock or coat in the form of a tassel or large button passed through a loop on the breast; the loop of the scabbard of a bayonet or sword.—*v.t.—frogged, frogging.* To ornament or fasten with a frog.

frolic, frol'ik, *a.* [From D. *vrolijk,* from *vro*=O.Fris. *fro,* Dan. *fro,* glad, and *lijk*=E. *like;* so G. *fröhlich,* from *froh,* joyful, and *lich,* like.] Gay; merry; full of mirth; dancing, playing, or frisking about.—*n.* A wild or merry prank; a flight of levity or gaiety and mirth; a scene of gaiety and mirth; a merrymaking.—*v.i.—frolicked* (frol'ikt), *frolicking.* To play merry pranks; to play tricks of levity, mirth, and gaiety.—**frolicsome,** frol'ik•sum, *a.* Full of gaiety and mirth; given to frolics; sportive. — **frolicsomely,** frol'ik•sum•li, *adv.* In a frolicsome manner. —**frolicsomeness,** frol'ik•sum•nes, *n.*

from, from, *prep.* [A.Sax. *from, fram,* O.Sax. O.H.G. and Goth. *fram,* from; Icel. *fram,* forward, *frá,* from; Dan. *frem, fra,* from; cog. with L. *peren* in *perendie,* the day after tomorrow, Gr. *peran,* Skr. *param,* beyond. Allied to *far, forth,* etc.] Out of the neighborhood of; leaving behind; by reason of; out of; by aid of; denoting source, beginning, distance, absence, privation, or departure, sometimes literally and sometimes figuratively; the antithesis and correlative of *from* is *to.*

frond, frond, *n.* [L. *frons, frondis,* a leaf.] *Bot.* a term used to designate the leaf of the sporophyte generation of the fern.

Fronde, fronđ, *n.* [Fr.] The party in opposition to Mazarin, the French prime minister, 1648-53, with civil war as result.

front, frunt, *n.* [Fr. *front,* L. *frons, frontis,* the forehead (allied to E. *brow*); seen also in *affront, confront,* etc.] The forehead, or part of the face above the eyes; the whole face; boldness of disposition; impudence; the part or side of anything which seems to look out or to be directed forward; the face or forepart; the foremost rank; position directly before the face of a person or the foremost part of anything; a set of false hair or curls for a lady; the van of war; the area of warfare in campaign; shirt front, real or false.—*To come to the front,* to take a high rank in one's profession, in society, etc.—*a.* Relating to the front or face; having a position in the front.—*v.t.* To oppose face to face; to stand in front of or over against; to face; to appear in the presence of; to confront; to supply with a front; to adorn in front.—*v.i.* To have the face or front in some direction.—**frontage,** frun'tij, *n.* The front part of any structure or object; extent of front.—**frontal,** frun'tal, *n.* Something worn on the forehead; a frontlet; an ornamental band for the hair; *arch.* a little pediment over a door or window.—*a.* Belonging to the forehead.—*Frontal attack,* attack on the front, opposed to flank or rear.—**frontal bone,** *a.* The bone forming the upper front part of the cranium.–**frontier,** frun'tēr, *n.* [Fr. *frontière,* a frontier, a border.] That part of a country which fronts or faces another country; the confines or extreme part of a country bordering on another country; an unsettled area or new idea that offers a challenge (as *The New Frontier.*)—**frontiersman,** frun•tērz'man, *n.* A man living on the frontier.—**frontispiece,** frun'tis•pēs, *n.* An ornamental figure or engraving on the first page of a book or at the beginning. —**frontlet,** frunt'let, *n.* A fillet or band worn on the forehead.

frost, frost, *n.* [A.Sax. *frost, forst,* from *freósan,* to freeze; Icel. Dan. Sw. and G. *frost,* D. *vorst.* FREEZE.] That state or temperature of the air which occasions freezing or the congelation of water; freezing weather; frozen dew; rime; hoarfrost; coldness or severity of manner or feeling. —*v.t.* To injure by frost; to cover or ornament with anything resembling hoarfrost, as with white sugar; to furnish with frost nails.—*Frosted glass,* glass roughened on the surface, so as to destroy its transparency.—**frostbite,** *n.* A state of insensibility or deadness with arrested circulation in any part of the body, such as the nose and ears, occasioned by exposure to severe frost.—*v.t.—frostbit* (pret.), *frostbitten, frostbit* (pp.); *frostbiting* (ppr.). To affect with frostbite. —**frostily,** fros'ti•li, *adv.* In a frosty manner; with frost or excessive cold; without warmth of affection; coldly.—**frostiness,** fros'ti•nes, *n.* The state or quality of being frosty. —**frosting,** fros'ting, *n.* A coating resembling frost; the composition resembling hoarfrost used to cover cake, etc.—**frostwork,** frost'wėrk, *n.* The beautiful covering of hoarfrost deposited on shrubs or other natural objects.—**frosty,** fros'ti, *a.* Attended with frost; of a freezing temperature; affected by frost; without warmth of affection or courage; resembling hoarfrost; grayhaired.

froth, froth, *n.* [A.Scandinavian word =Icel. *frotha, frauth,* Dan. *fraade,* froth, foam.] The bubbles caused in liquors by fermentation or agitation; spume; foam; empty talk; mere words without sense; light, unsubstantial matter.—*v.t.* To cause to foam or produce froth; to vent, or give expression to what is light, unsubstantial, or worthless.—*v.i.* To foam; to throw up or out froth.—**frothily,** froth'i•li, *adv.* In a frothy manner.—**frothiness,** froth'i•nes, *n.* The state or quality of being frothy. —**frothy,** froth'i, *a.* Full of or accompanied with froth; consisting of froth or light bubbles; foamy; light, empty, or unsubstantial; given to empty display.

frounce, frouns, *v.t.—frounced, frouncing.* [Fr. *froncer,* D. *fronssen,* to wrinkle, from a hypothetical L.L. *frontiare,* to wrinkle the brows, from L. *frons,* the forehead (whence *front*). *Flounce* (of a dress) is the same work.] To form into plaits or wrinkles; to adorn with fringes, plaits, etc.—*n.* A wrinkle, plait, or curl; a flounce.

frow, frō, *n.* A wedge-shaped tool with a handle used for splitting wood.

froward, frō'wėrd, *a.* [From *fro*= from, and *-ward,* denoting direction, being thus the reverse of *to-ward,* and nearly equivalent to *way-ward* (*awayward*); A. Sax. *fromweard,* turned away, about to depart.] Not willing to comply with what is right or reasonable; perverse; ungovernable; refractory; disobedient; peevish.—**frowardly,** frō'wėrd•li, *adv.* In a froward manner.—**frowardness,** frō'wėrd•nes, *n.* The quality of being froward.

frown, froun, *v.i.* [Fr. *frogner,* in *se refrogner,* to knit the brow, to frown; of doubtful origin.] To express displeasure, severity, or sternness by contracting the brow; to put on a stern look; to scowl; to show displeasure or disapprobation; to be ominous of evil; to lower (the clouds *frown*).—*n.* A contraction or wrinkling of the brow, or a severe or stern look expressive of displeasure; a scowl; frown.—**frowningly,** frou'ning•li, *adv.* In a frowning manner.

frowzy, frowsy, frou′zi, *a.* [Comp. Prov. E. *froust,* a musty smell, also Prov. E. *frow,* a slattern, from D. *vrow,* G. *frau,* a woman.] Fetid; musty; rank; dingy; ill-colored; in a state of disorder; slovenly; slatternly.

froze, frozen, frōz, frō′zn. See FREEZE.

fructescence, fruk•tes′ens, *n.* [From L. *fructus,* fruit. FRUIT.] *Bot.* the time when the fruit of a plant arrives at maturity and its seeds are dispersed; the fruiting season.—**fructiferous,** fruk•tif′ėr•us, *a.* Bearing or producing fruit.—**fructification,** fruk′ti•fi•kā″shon, *n.* The act of forming or producing fruit; the act of fructifying or rendering productive of fruit; fecundation; the organs concerned in the production of the fruit of a plant.—**fructify,** fruk′ti•fī, *v.t.* [Fr. *fructifier.*] To make fruitful; to render productive; to fertilize.—*v.i.* To bear or produce fruit.—**fructose,** fruk′tōs, *n.* A variety of sugar from fruit.

frugal, frö′gal, *a.* [L. *frugalis,* from *frugi,* lit. fit for food, hence, worthy, temperate, dative case of *frux, frugis,* fruit; akin to *fruit.*] Economical in regard to expenditure; thrifty; sparing; not profuse, prodigal, or lavish; saving.—**frugality,** frö•gal′i•ti, *n.* The quality of being frugal; a prudent and sparing use of anything. —**frugally,** frö′gal•li, *adv.* In a frugal manner.—**frugalness,** frö′gal•nes, *n.* Frugality.

frugiferous, frö•jif′ėr•us, *a.* [L. *frugifer—frux, frugis,* fruit, and *fero,* to bear.] Producing fruit or crops; fruitful; fructiferous.—**frugivorous,** frö•jiv′ėr•us, *a.* [L. *frux, frugis,* and *voro,* to eat.] Feeding on fruits, seeds, or corn, as birds and other animals.

fruit, fröt, *n.* [Fr. *fruit,* from L. *fructus,* fruit, from *fruor, fructus,* to enjoy, from a root seen in E. verb to *brook,* originally to enjoy; akin *frugal, fruition.*] Whatever vegetable products the earth yields for the use of man and the lower animals (in this sense generally in the plural); in a more limited sense, the reproductive product of a tree or other plant; especially, the edible succulent products of certain plants, generally covering and including their seeds; such products collectively; *bot.* the seed of a plant, or the mature ovary, composed essentially of two parts, the pericarp and the seed; the produce of animals; offspring; young; something that results; effect, result, or consequence.—*v.i.* To produce or yield fruit.—**fruitage,** frö′tij, *n.* Fruit collectively; product or produce.—**fruitcake,** fröt′cake, *n.* A round or oblong loaf cake containing several varieties of spice and fruit; usually quite rich.—**fruitful,** fröt′fu̩l, *a.* Producing fruit in abundance; very productive; prolific; bearing children; not barren; producing or presenting in abundance; productive (*fruitful* in expedients).—**fruitfully,** fröt′fu̩•li, *adv.* In a fruitful manner; plenteously; abundantly.—**fruitfulness,** fröt′fu̩l•nes, *n.* The state or quality of being fruitful; productiveness; fertility; fecundity. —**fruitless,** fröt′les, *a.* Not bearing fruit; destitute of fruit or offspring; productive of no advantage or good effect; vain.—**fruitlessly,** fröt′les•li, *adv.* In a fruitless manner.—**fruitlessness,** fröt′les•nes, *n.* The state or quality of being fruitless or unprofitable.—**fruity,** frö′ti, *a.* Resembling fruit; having the taste or flavor of fruit.

fruition, frö•ish′on, *n.* [From L. *fruor, fructus* or *fruitus,* to use or enjoy. FRUIT.] Use or possession of anything, especially when accompanied with pleasure; the pleasure derived from use of possession; enjoyment.

frumentaceous, frö•men•tā′shus, *a.* [L. *frumentaceus,* from *frumentum,* corn; same root as *fructus,* fruit. FRUIT.] Having the character of or resembling wheat or other cereal.—**frumenty,** frö′men•ti, *n.* [L. *frumentum,* wheat.] A dish made of hulled wheat boiled in milk and seasoned; furmenty.

frump, frump, *n.* [Connected with *frampold,* or with Prov. E. *frumple,* D. *frommelen,* to wrinkle or crumple.] A cross tempered, old-fashioned female.—**frumpish,** frump′ish, *a.* Cross-tempered; cross-grained; scornful; old fashioned as to dress.—**frumpy,** frump′i, *a.* Cross tempered; frumpish.

frustrate, frus′trāt, *v.t.—frustrated, frustrating.* [L. *frustror, frustratus,* from *frustra,* in vain, same root as *fraus,* fraud.] To make to be in vain or of no avail; to bring to nothing; to prevent from taking effect; to defeat; to balk.—**frustration,** frus•trā′shon, *n.* The act of frustrating.—**frustrative,** frus′tra•tiv, *a.* Tending to frustrate or defeat.

frustum, frus′tum, *n.* [L., a piece, same root as *frustra,* in vain, *fraus,* fraud, etc.] *Geom.* the part of a solid (as a cone or a pyramid) left by cutting off the top portion by a plane; a truncated solid.

frutescent, frö•tes′ent, *a.* [From L. *frutex, fruticis,* a shrub.] *Bot.* having the appearance or habit of a shrub; shrubby.—**fruticose,** frö′ti•kōs, *a.* [L. *fruticosus.*] Pertaining to shrubs; shrubby.

fry, frī, *v.t.—fried, frying.* [Fr. *frire,* to fry, from L. *frigo,* to fry, roast, or parch; Skr. *bhrij,* to parch.] To cook in a pan over a fire along with fat or butter.—*v.i.* To be cooked as above; to simmer; to be agitated or vexed.—*n.* A dish of anything fried; state of vexation or mental agitation.—**fryer, frier,** frī′ėr, *n.* One who or that which fries; a young chicken, suitable for frying.

fry, frī, *n.* [Icel. *frae, frjo,* spawn; Goth. *fraiv,* seed.] Young of fishes at a very early stage; a swarm of little fishes; a swarm of small animals, or of young people; small or insignificant objects collectively.

fuchsia, fū′shi•a, *n.* [From the discoverer Leonard *Fuchs,* a German botanist.] A genus of beautiful flowering shrubs, natives of South America, Mexico, and New Zealand, having a funnel-shaped, colored, deciduous, four-parted calyx; a beautiful aniline color; magenta.

fuddle, fud′l, *v.t.—fuddled, fuddling.* [From a form *fuzzle,* akin to L.G. *fusslig,* G. *fusselig,* drunk.] To make foolish or stupid by drink; to make tipsy or intoxicated; to confuse or muddle.

fudge, fuj, *v.t.* and *i.—fudged, fudging.* [Origin unknown.] To make up or invent (a false story); to fabricate; to foist; to interpolate.—*n.* A made-up story; a creamy candy made of sugar, milk, and butter, often flavored with chocolate.

fuel, fū′el, *n.* [Norm. Fr. *fuayl, fouoyle, foualle,* from L.L. *focale,* from L. *focus,* a hearth, a fireplace. FOCUS.] Any matter used to produce heat or power; anything that feeds excitement.—*v.t.* and *i.—fueled, fueling.* To supply or get fuel.—**fuel cell,** fū′el sel, *n.* A device that produces electrical energy by direct conversion of chemical energy, combining hydrogen and oxygen to produce water and electricity.

fugacious, fū•gā′shus, *a.* [L. *fugax, fugacis,* from *fugio,* to flee.] Flying or disposed to fly; volatile; fleeting. —*Fugacious corolla, bot.* one that is soon shed.—**fugaciousness,** fū•gā′shus•nes, *n.* The quality of being fugacious.—**fugacity,** fū•gas′i•ti, *n.* The quality of being fugacious; fugaciousness; volatility; instability; transitoriness.—**fugitive,** fū′ji•tiv, *a.* [Fr. *fugitif,* L. *fugitivus,* from L. *fugio,* to flee.] Apt to flee away or be dissipated; volatile; staying or lasting but a short time; fleeting; not fixed or durable (*fugitive* dyes); fleeing or running from danger or pursuit, duty or service; as a literary term, applied to compositions which are short, unimportant, and published at intervals.—*n.* One who flees; a deserter; one who flees from danger or duty; one who flees for refuge.—**fugitively,** fū′ji•tiv•li, *adv.* In a fugitive manner.

fugleman, flugelman, fū′gl•man, flö′gl•man, *n.* † [G. *flügelmann,* a man at the head of a file or a wing, from *flügel,* a wing.] A soldier especially expert and well drilled, who takes his place in front of soldiers, as an example or model to the others in their exercises; a file leader; hence, any one who sets an example for others to follow.

fugue, fūg, *n.* [Fr., from L. *fuga,* a flight.] *Mus.* a composition in parts that do not all begin at once, but as it were, follow or pursue each other successively.

führer, fuehrer, fū′rėr, *n.* [G.] A leader or guide in Germany; the chancellor of the Third Reich.

fulcrum, ful′krum, *n.* pl. **fulcra, fulcrums,** [L., the post or foot of a couch, from *fulcio,* to support.] A prop or support; *mech.* the point about which a lever turns in lifting a body.

fulfill, fulfil, fu̩l•fil′, *v.t.—fulfilled,*

fulfilling. [A compound of *full* and *fill*; A.Sax. *fulfyllan*.] To accomplish or carry into effect, as a prophecy, promise, intention, design, desire, prayer, bargain, etc.; to perform; to complete by performance; to complete (a term of years)‡.—**fulfiller,** fu̥l•fil′ėr, *n.* One that fulfills or accomplishes.—**fulfillment, fulfilment,** fu̥l•fil′ment, *n.* Execution; performance.

fulgent, ful′jent, *a.* [L. *fulgens, fulgentis*, from *fulgeo*, to shine.] Shining; dazzling; exquisitely bright.—**fulgently,** ful′jent•li, *adv.* In a fulgent manner; dazzlingly; glitteringly.

fulguration, ful•gū•rā′shon, *n.* [L. *fulguratio*, from *fulgur*, lightning.] The flashing of lightning; *assaying*, the sudden brightening of the melted globules of gold and silver in the cupel.—**fulgurite,** ful′gū•rīt, *n.* Any rocky substance that has been fused or vitrified by lightning.—**fulgurous,** ful′gū•rus, *a.* Flashing like lightning.

fuliginous, fū•lij′i•nus, *a.* [L. *fuliginosus*, from *fuligo*, soot.] Pertaining to soot; sooty; smoky; resembling smoke; dusky.—**fuliginously,** fū•lij′i•nus•li, *adv.* In a smoky manner; duskily.

full, fu̥l, *a.* [A.Sax. *ful*=Icel. *fullr*, Sw. *full*, Dan. *fuld*, Goth. *fulls*, G. *voll*; same root as L. *plenus*, full, *pleo*, to fill (as in *complete*). *Fill* is a derivative.] Having within its limits all that it can contain; replete; completely or largely supplied or furnished; abounding; supplied; occupied; not vacant; plump; filled out; inclined to be stout or corpulent; saturated; sated; abundant in quantity; plenteous; not defective or partial; entire; adequate; mature; perfect (*full* supply, accomplishment, age; a *full* stop); loud, clear, and distinct (voice); giving ample details or arguments; copious (a *full* account; the speech was *full*).—*Full brothers* or *sisters*, children of the same father and the same mother.—*Full cousin*, the son or daughter of an aunt or uncle.—*Full cry*, a term in *hunting* signifying that all the hounds have caught the scent and give tongue in chorus; hence, hot pursuit; hard chase.—*Full dress*, a dress which etiquette requires to be worn on occasions of ceremony and the like.—*Full moon*, the moon with its whole disk illuminated; also, the time when the moon is in this position.—*n.* The state of being full; complete measure; utmost extent; highest state or degree (fed to the *full*; the *full* of the moon).— *Written in full*, written without contractions; written in words, not in figures.—*adv.* Quite; fully; equally; completely; altogether; exactly (*full* in the center); directly; straight (he looked him *full* in the face); to satiety (to sup *full* of horrors). ∴ *Full* is often used, especially in poetry, to heighten or strengthen the signification of adjectives and adverbs (*full* sad), and is prefixed to other words, chiefly participles, to express utmost extent or degree (*full*-blown, *full*-grown).—**fullback,** fu̥l′bak, *n.* In football, a back; originally the one standing farthest behind the line of scrimmage.—**full-blooded,** *a.* Having a full supply of blood; of pure blood or extraction; thoroughbred.—**full-blown** *a.* Fully expanded, as a blossom; mature (*full-blown* beauty).—**full house,** in poker, a hand containing three of a kind and a pair.—**fullness,** fu̥l′nes, *n.* The state or quality of being full or filled.—*In the fullness of time*, at the proper or destined time.—**fully,** fu̥l′li, *adv.* In a full manner; to the full extent; so as to be full; without lack or defect; completely; entirely.

full, fu̥l, *v.t.* [Partly from A.Sax. *fullian*, to whiten, *fullere*, a fuller, a bleacher, from L. *fullo*, a fuller; partly from Fr. *fouler*, to tread, to full or felt, from L.L. *fullare*, to full, also from L. *fullo*.] To thicken and condense the fibers of (woolen cloth) by wetting and beating; to scour, cleanse, and thicken in a mill.—*v.i.* To become fulled.—**fuller,** fu̥l′ėr, *n.* One who fulls; one whose occupation is to full cloth; one who bleaches or whitens (N.T.)‡.—**fuller's earth,** *n.* A variety of clay or marl, useful in scouring and cleansing cloth.

fulmar, fu̥l′mar, *n.* [Icel. *fúlmár*, lit. foul mew, from its feeding on putrid substances.] A marine swimming bird which inhabits the northern seas in prodigious numbers, and is valued for its feathers, down, and the oil it yields.

fulminate, ful′mi•nāt, *v.i.*—*fulminated, fulminating*. [L. *fulmino, fulminatum*, from *fulmen*, lightning, contr. for *fulgimen*, from *fulgeo*, to flash, whence *fulgent*.] To thunder; to explode with a loud noise; to detonate; to issue threats, denunciations, censures, and the like.—*v.t.* To cause to explode; to utter or hurl out (denunciation).—*n.* A kind of explosive compound.—**fulminant,** ful′mi•nant, *a.* [L. *fulminans, fulminantis*.] Thundering; making a loud noise.—**fulminating,** ful′mi•nā•ting, *p.* and *a.* Thundering; exploding; detonating.—*Fulminating powder*, a mixture of niter, sulfur, and potash.—**fulmination,** ful•mi•nā′shon, *n.* The act of fulminating; that which is fulminated or thundered forth, as a menace or censure.—**fulminatory,** ful′mi•na•to•ri, *a.* Sending forth thunders or fulminations.—**fulmine,** ful′min, *v.t.*—*fulmined, fulmining*. To fulminate or give utterance to in an authoritative or vehement manner.—*v.i.* To thunder; to fulminate or send forth denunciations, etc.—**fulminic,** ful•min′ik, *a.* Capable of detonation: applied to an acid.

fulsome, fu̥l′sum, *a.* [Partly from *full*, and term. *-some*, partly from old *ful*, foul.] Cloying‡; surfeiting‡; offensive from excess of praise; gross (flattery, compliments); nauseous; disgusting.—**fulsomely,** fu̥l′sum•li, *adv.* In a fulsome manner.—**fulsomeness,** fu̥l′sum•nes, *n.*

fulvous, ful′vus, *a.* [L. *fulvus*, yellow.] Yellow; tawny; of a tawny yellow color.

fumarole, fū′ma•rōl, *n.* [It. *fumarola*, from L. *fumus*, smoke.] A hole from which smoke or gases issue (in a volcanic locality).

fumble, fum′bl, *v.t.* [From D. *fommelen*, L.G. *fummelen*, to fumble, Sw. *fumla*, to handle feebly.] To feel or grope about; to grope about in perplexity; to seek or search for something awkwardly; to employ the hands or fingers in an awkward fashion; in football, baseball, and other games, to drop the ball or fail to handle it properly.—*n.* **A bungling try.—fumbler,** fum′blėr, *n.*

fume, fūm, *n.* [L. *fumus*, smoke, vapor, fume; akin to Skr. *dhûma*, smoke, the root being that of E. *dust*.] Smoky or vaporous exhalation, especially if possessing narcotic or other remarkable properties; volatile matter arising from anything; exhalation, generally in the plural; mental agitation clouding or affecting the understanding; an idle conceit or vain imagination (*Shak.*).—*v.i.*—*fumed, fuming*. To yield fumes or exhalations; to pass off in vapors; with *away*; to be in a rage; to be hot with anger.—*v.t.* To fumigate; to perfume; to offer incense to.—**fumette,** fū•met′, *n.* [Fr. *fumet*, from L. *fumus*.] The scent of meat, as venison or game when kept too long; the scent from meats cooking.—**fumigate,** fū′mi•gāt, *v.t.*—*fumigated, fumigating*. [L. *fumigo, fumigatum*.] To apply smoke to; to expose to fumes or vapors (as of sulfur) in cleansing infected apartments, clothing, etc.—**fumigation** fū•mi•gā′shon, *n.* The act of fumigating.

fumitory, fū′mi•to•ri, *n.* [O.E. *fumetere*, Fr. *fumeterre*, from L. *fumus*, smoke, and *terra*, the earth, because said to make the eyes water like smoke.] A common garden and field plant with much-divided leaves and purplish flowers, formerly much used in medicine.

fun, fun, *n.* [Perhaps connected with *fond*, O.E. *fon*, foolish, *fon, fonne*, to be foolish; or Ir. *fonn*, delight.] Sport; mirthful drollery; frolicsome amusement.—*To make fun of*, to turn into ridicule.—*Not to see the fun*, to be unwilling to regard something in the light of a joke.—**funnily,** fun′i•li, *adv.* In a funny, droll, or comical manner.—**funny,** fun′i, *a.* Making fun; droll; comical.—*n.* **Comic strip.—funny bone,** *n.* **Crazy bone; the elbow joint, where the ulnar nerve rests.**

funambulate, fū•nam′bū•lāt, *v.t.* [L. *funambulus*, a rope-walker, *funis*, rope, and *ambulo, ambulatum*, to walk on a rope.—**funambulist,** fū•nam′bū•list, *n.* A rope walker or rope dancer.

function, fungk′shon, *n.* [Fr. *fonction*, L. *functio*, from *fungor, functus*, to perform, to execute; same root as Skr. *bhuj*, to enjoy; akin *defunct*.] Office, duty, or business belonging to a person in virtue of a particular station or character; what a person or body of persons has specially to perform in some capacity (the *functions* of a bishop, of a parent); the specific office or action which any organ or system of organs performs in the animal or vegetable economy, as the body, the mind, or a faculty of the mind (the *function* of memory, of nutrition); a formal or ceremonious meeting; *math.* a quantity so connected with another that no change can be made in the latter without producing a corresponding change in the former.—**functional,** fungk'shon•al, *a.* Pertaining to a function or functions: thus a *functional* disease is one in which some one or other of the animal functions is deranged, and is often opposed to an *organic* disease, in which an organ is directly affected.—**functionally,** fungk'shon•al•li, *adv.*—**functionary,** fungk'shon•a•ri, *n.* One who holds an office or trust.—**functionalism,** fungk'shon•al•izm, *n.* Any doctrine that stresses function, use and adaptation.

fund, fund, *n.* [Fr. *fond,* land, fund, a merchant's stock, from L. *fundus,* foundation, a piece of land, estate, whence also *found, founder, profound.*] A stock or capital; a sum of money appropriated as the foundation of some commercial or other operation; money which an individual may possess or can employ for carrying on trade; in England, money lent to government and constituting part of the national debt (used in plural); money set apart for any object more or less permanent; a store laid up from which one may draw at pleasure; stock; supply (a *fund* of amusement, of anecdote).—*Sinking fund,* a fund or stock set apart, generally at certain intervals, for the reduction of a debt of a government or corporation.—*Consolidated fund.* Under CONSOLIDATE.—*v.t.* To provide and appropriate a fund or permanent revenue for the payment of the interest of; to put into the form of bonds or stocks bearing regular interest; to place in a fund.—*Funded debt,* a debt existing in the form of bonds bearing regular interest; a debt forming part of the permanent debt of a country at a fixed rate of interest.

fundament, fun'da•ment, *n.* [L. *fundamentum,* a groundwork or foundation, from *fundo, fundatum,* to found. FUND, FOUND.] The part of the body on which one sits; the anus.—**fundamental,** fun•da•men'tal, *a.* Pertaining to a groundwork, root, or basis; at the root or foundation of something; essential; elementary (a *fundamental* truth or principle).—*n.* A leading or primary principle, rule, law, or article; something essential.—**fundamentally,** fun•da•men'tal•li, *adv.* In a fundamental manner.

funeral, fū'nėr•al, *n.* [Fr. *funérailles,* from L. *funis, funeris,* a burial.] The ceremony of burying a dead human body; interment; burial; obsequies. —*a.* Pertaining to burial; used at the interment of the dead.—**funereal,** fū•nē'ri•al, *a.* [L. *funereus.*] Suiting a funeral; pertaining to or calling up thoughts of death or the grave; dismal; mournful; gloomy.—**funereally,** fū•nē•ri'al•li, *adv.*

fungus, fung'gus, *n.* pl. **fungi,** fun'jī. [L. *fungus,* mushroom.] Any of the parasitic plants that lack chlorophyll, or plants that live on dead tissue, such as the mushrooms, molds, mildew, smut, rust, dry rot, etc.—**fungal,** fung'gal, *n.* A plant of the class of fungi and lichens.—*a.* Relating to fungi.—**fungivorous,** fun•jiv'ėr•us, *a.* [L. *fungus,* and *voro,* to devour.] Feeding on mushrooms or fungi.—**fungoid,** fung'goid, *a.* Having the appearance or character of a fungus.—**fungosity,** fung•gos'i•ti, *n.* The quality of being fungous; fungous excrescence.—**fungous,** fung'gus, *a.* Like a fungus; having the character of one of the fungi; hence, growing or springing up suddenly, but not substantial or durable.—**fungus,** fung'gus, *n.* A member of the fungi; *med.* a spongy morbid excrescence; a diseased state dependent on the growth of vegetable parasites.

funicle, fū'ni•kl, *n.* [L. *funiculus,* dim. of *funis,* a cord.] A small cord; a small ligament; *bot.* the little stalk by which a seed is attached to the placenta.

funicular, fū•nik'ū•lėr, *a.* [L. *funiculus,* dim. of *funis,* a cord.] Pertaining to a small cord; dependent upon the tension of a cord.—**funicular railway,** fū•nik'ū•lėr rāl'wā, *n.* A cable railway.

funk, fungk, *n.* Fear; cowardice.—*v.i.* To be in terror. (*Colloq.*)

funnel, fun'el, *n.* [Prov. Fr. *enfounil,* a funnel, from L. *infundibulum,* a funnel—*in,* into, and *fundo, fusum,* to pour, whence *fuse,* to melt. FUSE.] A utensil for conveying fluids into vessels with small openings, being a kind of hollow cone with a pipe issuing from its apex; the shaft or hollow channel of a chimney; a cylindrical iron chimney in steamships for the furnaces, rising above the deck.—**funneled, funnelled,** fun'eld, *a.* Having a funnel or funnels; funnel-shaped.

funny, fun'i, *a.* See FUN.

fur, fėr, *n.* [Fr. *fourrure,* fur, O.Fr. *forre, fuere,* a case or cover, from an old German word corresponding to modern G. *futter,* covering, case, lining, *fur* being so called from the skins of animals being used for lining or trimming clothes.] The short, fine, soft hair of certain animals growing thick on the skin, and distinguished from the hair, which is longer and coarser; the skin of certain wild animals with the fur; peltry; a coating regarded as resembling fur, as morbid matter collected on the tongue.—*a.* Made of fur.—*v.t.*—*furred, furring.* To line, face, or cover with fur.—**furrier,** fėr'i•ėr, *n.* A dealer in or dresser of furs.—**furriery,** fėr'i•ėr•i, *n.* Furs in general; the trade of a furrier.—**furry,** fėr'i, *a.* Covered with fur; dressed in fur; consisting of fur or skins; resembling fur; coated with a deposit of morbid matter.

furbelow, fėr'bė•lō, *n.* [Fr. *falbala, farbala,* It. Sp. Pg. *falbala,* Sp. also *farfala,* flounce; origin unknown.] A kind of flounce; the plaited border of a petticoat or gown.

furbish, fėr'bish, *v.t.* [Fr. *fourbir,* from O.H.G. *furban,* to clean, to furbish, G. *fürben,* to sweep.] To rub or scour to brightness; to polish up; to burnish; *fig.* to clear from taint or stain; to brighten.—**furbisher,** fėr'bish•ėr, *n.* One who or that which furbishes.

furcate, fėr'kāt, *a.* [L. *furca,* a fork.] Forked; branching like the prongs of a fork.—**furcation,** fėr•kā'shon, *n.* A forking or branching.—**furcula,** fėr'kū•la, *n.* [L., dim. of *furca.*] The forked bone formed by the union of the collarbones in many birds; the wishbone.

furfur, fėr'fėr, *n.* [L.] Dandruff; scurf; scales like bran.—**furfuraceous,** fėr•fėr•ā'shus, *a.* [L. *furfuraceus.*] Branny; scurfy; like bran.

furious. See FURY.

furl, fėrl, *v.t.* [Fr. *ferler,* from *ferm, ferme,* firm, fast, and *lier,* to bind.] To roll up tightly, as a flag, or gather in firmly, as a sail.—*v.i.* To fold, as in being furled.—*n.* A furling.

furlong, fėr'long, *n.* [A.Sax. *furlang*—*furh,* a furrow, and *lang,* long.] A measure of length, being the eighth part of a mile; forty rods.

furlough, fėr'lō, *n.* [Dan. *forlov,* D. *verlof,* G. *verlaub,* leave, furlough, lit. leave off or away—*fur* being equivalent to *for-* in *forbear,* and *lough,* akin to *leave, lief.*] Leave or license given to a soldier to be absent from service for a certain time.—*v.t.* To furnish with a furlough.

furmenty, furmety, fėr'men•ti, fėr'me•ti, *n.* Same as *Frumenty.*

furnace, fėr'nes, *n.* [Fr. *fournaise,* from L. *fornax,* an oven.] An enclosed structure in which is kept up a strong fire for melting ores or metals, heating the boiler of a steam engine, and other such purposes; *fig.* an occasion of severe torture or trial.

furnish, fėr'nish, *v.t.* [Fr. *fournir,* to furnish; It. *fornire, frunire,* Pr. *formir, furmir,* to finish, perfect, to furnish; from O.H.G. *frumjan,* to perfect, of kindred origin with E. *frame.*] To supply with anything necessary or useful; to equip; to offer for use; to afford; to fit up; to supply with furniture.—**furnisher,** fėr'nish•ėr, *n.*—**furnishing,** fėr'nish•ing, *n.* Something that serves to equip or fit up; an appendage.—**furniture,** fėr'ni•chėr, *n.* That with which anything is furnished; equipment, specifically, the seats, tables, utensils, etc.; *print.* wood or metal bits smaller than type, placed between type to fill blank spaces or used with wedges to hold type in a metal frame (chase).

furor, fū'ror, *n.* See FURY.

furrier. See FUR.

furrow, fur'ō, *n.* [A.Sax. *furh*= O.H.G. *furich,* G. *furche,* furrow;

cog. with L. *porca*, a ridge between furrows.] A trench in the earth made by a plow; a narrow trench or channel; a groove; a wrinkle in the face.—*v.t.* To make furrows in; to plow; to mark with or as with wrinkles.

furry, fėr′i, *a.* See FUR.

further, fėr′THėr, *adv.* [A.Sax. *furthor, furthur*, further, more, besides, compar. of *forth*, or of *fore*, before.] More in advance; still onward; moreover; besides; farther: this word can hardly be said to differ in meaning from *farther.*—*a.* More distant; farther.—*v.t.* To help forward; to promote; to forward or assist.—**furtherance,** fėr′THėr•ans, *n.* The act of furthering; promotion; advancement.—**furtherer,** fėr′THėr-ėr, *n.* One who furthers; a promoter. —**furthermore,** fėr′THėr•mōr, *adv.* Moreover; besides; in addition to what has been said.—**furthest,** fėr′-THest, *a.* Most distant; farthest.

furtive, fėr′tiv, *a.* [L. *furtivus*, from *furtum*, theft, from *fur*, a thief.] Sly; accomplished by stealth; stealthy; thief-like.—**furtively,** fėr′tiv•li, *adv.* In a furtive manner; stealthily.

fury, fū′ri, *n.* [Fr. *furie*, L. *furia*, fury, one of the three goddesses of vengeance, from *furo*, to rage.] Rage; a storm of anger; madness; turbulence; a violent rushing; impetuous motion; inspired or supernatural excitement of the mind; a virago; an enraged woman; *class. myth.* one of the avenging deities, the daughters of Earth or of Night, three in number, and called respectively Tisiphone, Alecto, and Megaera.—**furious,** fū′ri•us, *a.* [L. *furiosus.*] Exhibiting fury; raging; violent; transported with passion; mad; frenzied; rushing with impetuosity; violent; boisterous.—**furiously,** fū′ri•us•li, *adv.* In a furious manner.—**furiousness,** fū′ri•us•nes, *n.*—**furor,** fū′ror, *n.* [L.] Fury; rage; mania.—**furore,** fö•rō′rā, *n.* [It.] Rage; fury; great excitement; intense commotion; enthusiasm.

furze, fėrz, *n.* [A.Sax. *fyrs.*] Whin or gorse; a spiny, almost leafless shrub, with yellow papilionaceous blossoms, growing abundantly in gravelly waste grounds in Western Europe.

fuscous, fus′kus, *a.* [L. *fuscus*, dark-colored.] Brown; of a dark color.

fuse, fūz, *v.t.*—*fused, fusing.* [L. *fundo, fusum*, to pour out, to melt, to cast; hence *found* (to cast), also *confound, confuse, diffuse, refuse*, etc.; akin also *futile.*] To melt or liquefy by heat; to render fluid; to dissolve; to blend or unite as if melted together.—*v.i.* To melt by heat; to become intermingled and blended.—**fusibility,** fū•zi•bil′i•ti, *n.* The quality of being fusible.—**fusible,** fū′zi•bl, *a.* Capable of being fused or melted.—*Fusible metal*, an alloy, usually of lead, tin, and bismuth, compounded in such definite proportions as to melt at a given temperature.—**fusil, fusile,** fū′zil, *a.* [Fr. *fusile*, L. *fusilis.*] Capable of being melted; fusible.—**fusion,** fū′-zhon, *n.* [Fr. *fusion*, L. *fusio.*] The act or operation of fusing; the state of being melted or dissolved by heat; the act or process of uniting or blending as if melted together; complete union; the combination of atomic nuclei of lighter elements to form a heavier nucleus, resulting in the release of enormous energy.

fuse, fuze, fūz, *n.* [From L. *fusus*, spindle.] A tube filled with combustible matter, used in blasting, or in discharging a shell, etc.; in an electric circuit, a piece of metal which melts when the load is too great, thus breaking the circuit and preventing possible damage; an electrical device used to set off torpedoes, etc.

fusee, fū•zē′, *n.* [Fr. *fusée*, a spindleful, from L.L. *fusata* (same sense), L. *fusus*, a spindle.] The cone or conical piece in a watch or clock round which is wound the chain or cord.—**fusiform** fū′zi•form, *a.* Shaped like a spindle.

fuselage, fū′zel•ij, *n.* [L. *fusus*, spindle.] The long, narrow, somewhat spindle-shaped body of an airplane.

fusel oil, fū′zel, *n.* [G. *fusel*, coarse spirits.] Amyl alcohol, a by-product of alcoholic fermentation, used as a solvent in making varnishes; a commercial pentyl alcohol.

fusil, fū′zil, *n.* [Fr. *fusil*, originally the part of the lock that struck fire, L.L. *focile*, from L. *focus*, a fire (whence also, *fuel*).] A light musket or firelock formerly used.—**fusilier, fusileer,** fū•zil•lēr′, *n.* Properly, a soldier armed with a fusil; an infantry soldier who bore firearms, as distinguished from a pikeman and archer.—**fusillade,** fū′zi•lād, *n.* [Fr. from *fusil.*] A simultaneous discharge of musketry.—*v.t.*—*fusilladed, fusillading.* To shoot down by a fusillade.

fuss, fus, *n.* [From A.Sax. *fús*, quick, ready; Icel. *fúss*, eager.] A tumult; a bustle; unnecessary bustle in doing anything; much ado about nothing. —*v.t.* and *i.* To make much ado about trifles; to make a fuss; to worry.—**fussily,** fus′i•li, *adv.* In a fussy manner.—**fussiness,** fus′i•nes, *n.* The state of being fussy; needless bustle. —**fussy,** fus′i, *a.* Moving and acting with fuss; bustling; making more ado than is necessary.

fust, [*obs.*] fust, *n.* [O.Fr. *fusté*, tasting or smelling of the cask, *fust*, a cask, from L. *fustis*, a stick.] A strong musty smell.—*v.i.* To become moldy or musty; to smell ill.—**fustiness,** fus′ti•nes, *n.* State or quality of being fusty.—**fusty,** fus′ti, *a.* Moldy; musty; ill-smelling; rank; rancid.

fustian, fus′tyan, *a.* [O.Fr. *fustaine*, Fr. *futaine*, It. *fustagno*, from *Fostat*, the name of a suburb of Cairo, whence this fabric was first brought.] A coarse cotton stuff, or stuff of cotton and linen, with a pile like velvet, but shorter, such as corduroy, moleskin, etc.; an inflated style of writing; bombast.—*a.* Made of fustian; ridiculously tumid; bombastic. —**fustianist,** fus′tyan•ist, *n.* One who writes bombast.

fustic, fus′tik, *n.* [Fr. and Sp. *fustoc*, from Sp. *fuste*, wood, timber, from L. *fustis*, a stick, a staff.] The wood of a tree growing in the West Indies, extensively used as an ingredient in the dyeing of yellow.

fustigate,† fus′ti•gāt, *v.t.* [L. *fustigo*, from *fustis*, a stick.] To beat with a cudgel.

futile, fū′t′l *a.* [Fr. *futile*, from L. *futilis*, leaky, vain, worthless, from *fundo, fusum*, to pour. FUSE.] Serving no useful end; of no effect; answering no valuable purpose; worthless; trivial.—**futilely,** fū′til•li, *adv.* In a futile manner.—**futility,** fū•til′i•ti, *n.* The quality of being futile, or producing no valuable effect; triflingness; unimportance.—**futilitarian,** fū•til′i•tâ″ri•an, *a.* [Formed on the type of *utilitarian.*] Devoted to the belief that all human aims and hopes are futile; pessimistic.

futtock, fut′ok, *n.* [Corrupted from *foothook.*] *Naut.* one of those timbers raised over the keel which form the breadth of the ship.

future, fū′chėr, *a.* [Fr. *futur*, from L. *futurus*, future part. of *sum, fui*, to be. BE.] That is to be or come hereafter; that will exist at any time after the present.—*Future tense*, that tense of a verb which expresses that something is yet to take place.—*n.* Time to come; time subsequent to the present; all that is to happen after the present time; the future tense.—**futurist,** fū′chėr•ist, *n.* Member of the art, music and literature movement of about 1910 that rejected tradition and sought to express the energy and movement of mechanical processes.—**futurity,** fū•tū′ri•ti, *n.* Future state of time; future event.—*Futurity race*, a race for which horses are entered a long time in advance, often even before they are born.

fuze, fūz, *n.* See FUSE.

fuzz, fuz, *v.i.* [Comp. Prov.E. *fozy*, spongy, soft and woolly; D. *voos*, spongy.] To fly off in minute particles.—*n.* Fine, light particles; loose, light particles of fluff.—**fuzzy,** fuz′i, *a.* Covered with fuzz; indistinct, as fuzzy shapes or sounds.

fylfot, fil′fot, *n.* A rectangular cross with arms of equal lengths and each bent at right angles at the end.

G

G, g, jē, the seventh letter in the English alphabet, with two sounds, a hard (guttural), as in *good*; a soft (=j) as in *gem*, the former being the original sound; *mus.* the fifth note and dominant of the normal scale of C, called also *sol.*

G. [Initial letter of *gravity.*] The symbol always used to denote the acceleration with which any body falls freely to the earth in vacuo. It varies from place to place on the earth's surface, its value being about 32 feet per second per second.

gab, gab, *v.i.* [Icel. *gabb*, mockery, *gabba*, to mock; akin D. *gabberen*, to joke, to chatter; Fr. *gaber*, to deceive; E. *gabble*, *gape*.] To talk much; to prate; to talk idly. (*Colloq.*)—*n.* (Dan. *gab*, Sw. *gap*, the mouth.) The mouth; idle talk; chatter. (*Colloq.*)

gabardine, gab′ėr•dēn″, gab″ėr•dēn′, *n.* A wool or cotton cloth, like serge in appearance, but twilled on one side only.

gabble, gab′l, *v.i. gabbled, gabbling.* [Freq. from *gab*; akin to *gobble*.] To talk noisily and rapidly, or without meaning; to prate; to utter rapid inarticulate sounds.—*n.* Loud or rapid talk without meaning; inarticulate sounds rapidly uttered, as of fowls.—**gabbler,** gab′lėr, *n.* One who gabbles.

gabelle, ga•bel′, *n.* [Fr. *gabelle*, O.It. *cabella*.] A tax or excise duty formerly imposed on salt in France.

gaberdine, gab′ėr•dēn″, gab″ėr•dēn, *n.* A coarse frock or loose upper garment, worn in medieval times.

gabion, gā′bi•on, *n.* [Fr. *gabion*, It. *gabbione*, a large cage, from *gabbia*, a cage, from L.L. *gabia* (= L. *cavea*), a cage. CAGE.] *Fort.* a large basket of wickerwork, of a cylindrical form, but without a bottom, filled with earth, and serving to shelter men from an enemy's fire.—**gabionade,** gā′bi•on•ād, *n.* A work consisting of gabions.

gable, gā′bl, *n.* [O.Fr. *gable*, L.L. *gabulum*, from the Teut.; comp. Dan. *gavl*, D. *gevel*, Icel. *gafl*, G. *giebel*, Goth. *gibla*, a gable.] *Arch.* the triangular end of a house from the level of the eaves to the top; also the end wall of a house.—**gable window,** *n.* A window in the end or gable of a building.

gaby, gā′bi, *n.* [Akin to *gape*, *gab*.] A silly, foolish person; a dunce. (*Colloq.*)

gad, gad, *n.* [Icel. *gaddr*, Sw. *gadd*, Goth. *gazds*, a goad, a spike, a sting; akin to *goad*; comp. also Ir. *gada*, a bar or ingot of metal.] A spike, style, or other sharp thing; a wedge or ingot of steel or iron; a pointed wedgelike tool used by miners.—**gadfly,** gad′flī, *n.* [From *gad*, for *goad*, and *fly*.] A two-winged insect which stings cattle, and deposits its eggs in their skin; called also *Botfly* and *Breeze*; any fly that bites and annoys cattle; a person who purposely annoys or provokes others.

gad, gad, *v.i.*—*gadded, gadding.* [Probably from the restless running about of animals stung by the *gadfly*.] To rove or ramble idly or without any fixed purpose; to act or move without restraint; to wander, as in thought or speech.—**gadabout,** gad′-a•bout, *n.* One who walks about idly; one who goes from one social entertainment to another.

gadget, gaj′ėt, *n.* A small object or device, usually of a mechanical nature; a part of a machine.

gadolinite, gad′ō•lin•īt, *n.* [From *Gadolin*, a Prussian chemist.] A blackish mineral, a silicate of yttrium and cerium.

gadolinium, gad′o•lin″i•um, *n.* [From *J. Gadolin*, Finnish chemist.] A metallic element of the rare-earth series. Symbol, Gd,; at. no., 64; at. wt., 157.25.

gadwall, gad′wal, *n.* [Origin doubtful.] A duck belonging to Europe, Asia, and North America, not so large as the common wild duck.

Gaelic, gāl′ik, *a.* [Gael. *Gaidhealach*, Gaelic, from *Gaidheal*, a Gael.] Of or pertaining to the Gaels, a Celtic race inhabiting the Highlands of Scotland.—*n.* The language of the Celts, that is, the Scottish, Irish, and Manx Celts.—**Gael,** gāl, *n.* A Scottish Highlander.

gaff, gaf, *n.* [Fr. *gaffe*, Sp. and Pg. *gafa*, a hook; of Celtic origin.] A harpoon; a gaff hook; *naut.* a spar with a forked end used to extend the upper edge of some fore-and-aft sails; an ordeal or something difficult to endure (slang).—*v.t.* To strike or secure (a salmon) by means of a gaff hook.

gaffer, gaf′ėr, *n.* [Contr. from *grandfather* or *good father*.] An old rustic; a word originally of respect, now rather of familiarity or contempt; (*Brit.*) the foreman of a squad of workmen; an overseer.

gag, gag, *v.t.*—*gagged, gagging.* [Perhaps from W. *cegiaw*, to choke, from *ceg*, a choking. Or it may be onomatopoetic; comp. *gaggle*.] To stop the mouth of by thrusting something into it so as to hinder speaking but permit breathing; hence, to silence by authority or violence.—*n.* Something thrust into the mouth to hinder speaking; interpolations, additions by actors to their verbal parts; a joke or trick.

gage, gāj, *n.* [Fr. *gage*, from L.L. *gadium*, *vadium*, from Goth. *wadi*, pledge, G. *wette*, a bet; or from L. *vas*, *vadis*, a surety, a pledge. Akin *wage*.] Something laid down or given as a security for the performance of some act by the person giving the gage; a pledge; something thrown down as a token of challenge to combat.—*v.t.*—*gaged, gaging.*‡ To give or deposit as a pledge or security for some act; to pledge or pawn; to bind by pledge.

gage, gāj, *n.* and *v.t.* Same as GAUGE.

gage, gāj, *n.* [The name of the person who first introduced them.] A name of several varieties of plum.

gaggle, gag′l, *v.t.*—*gaggled, gaggling.* —[Imitative.] To cackle like a goose. —*n.* A flock of geese.

gaiety, gaily. See GAY.

gain, gān, *v.t.* [Fr. *gagner*, anciently, to earn profit from pasturage, hence, to gain; from O.H.G. *weidanjan*, to pasture; partly also from Icel. and Sw. *gagn*, gain, profit.] To obtain by industry or the employment of capital; to get as profit or advantage; to acquire: opposed to *lose*; to win or obtain by superiority or success (to *gain* a battle, a prize); to obtain in general; to procure (fame, favor); to win to one's side; to conciliate; to reach, attain to, arrive at (to *gain* a mountain top).—*To gain over*, to draw to another party or interest; to win over.—*To gain ground*, to advance in any undertaking; to make progress.—*To gain time*, to obtain a longer time for a particular purpose.—*v.i.* To reap advantage or profit; to acquire gain.—*To gain on* or *upon*, to encroach on (the sea *gains on* the land); to advance nearer to, as in a race; to gain ground on.—*n.* Something obtained as an advantage; anything opposed to loss; profit; benefit derived.—**gainer,** gā′-nėr, *n.* One that gains or obtains profit or advantage.—**gainful,** gān′-fụl, *a.* Producing profit or advantage; profitable; advantageous; lucrative. —**gainfully,** gān′fụl•li, *adv.* In a gainful manner.—**gainfulness,** gān′-fụl•nes, *n.* The state or quality of being gainful.—**gainless,** gān′les, *a.* Not producing gain; unprofitable.—**gainlessness,** gān′les•nes, *n.*

gainly, gān′li, *a.* Handsome: now only in the compound *ungainly* (which see).

gainsay, gān′sā, *v.t.*—*gainsaid, gainsaying.* [A.Sax. *gegn*, against (as in *again*), and E. *say*.] To contradict; to deny or declare not to be true; to controvert; to dispute.—*n.* Opposition in words; contradiction.—**gainsayer,** gān′sā•ėr, *n.* One who gainsays.

'gainst, genst. Contr. for *Against*.

gait, gāt, *n.* [Akin Icel. *gata*, a way.] Walk; manner of walking or stepping; carriage.—**gaited,** gāt′ed, *a.* Having a particular gait: used in compounds (slow-*gaited*, heavy-*gaited*).

gaiter, gā′tėr, *n.* [Fr. *guêtre*, a gaiter—origin unknown.] A covering of cloth for the leg, fitting over the shoe; a spatterdash.—*v.t.* To dress with gaiters.

gala, gäl′a or gā′la, *n.* [Fr., show, pomp; It. *gala*, finery; of Teut. origin; akin *gallant*. GALLANT.] An occasion of public festivity.

galactic, ga•lak′tik, *a.* [Gr. *galaktikos*, milky, from *gala*, *galaktos*, milk.] Of or belonging to milk; obtained from milk; lactic; *astron.* pertaining to the Galaxy or Milky Way.—**galactagogue,** ga•lak′ta•gog, *n.* [Gr. *gala*, and *agō*, to induce.] A medicine which promotes the secretion of milk.—**galactose,** ga•lak′tōz, *n.* [Gr. *gala*, *galaktos*, milk.] A sweet substance derived from milk sugar.

galangal, ga•lang′gal, *n.* [Fr. *galanga*, O.Fr. *garingal*; of Eastern origin.] A dried rhizome brought from China and used in medicine, being an aromatic stimulant of the nature of ginger.

galantine, gal•an•tēn′, *n.* [Fr.] A dish of veal, chickens, or other white meat, freed from bones and served cold.

galaxy, gal′ak•si, *n.* [Fr. *galaxie*, from Gr. *galaxias* (*kyklos*, circle, being understood), from *gala*, *galaktos*, milk.] A multitude of stars, such as the Milky Way; a system of stars, including star clusters, nebulae, etc.; a brilliant or splendid assemblage of persons.

galbanum, gal′ba•num, *n.* [L., from Heb. *chelbnah*, galbanum, from *chelev*, fat.] A fetid gum resin brought from the Levant, Persia, and India, used in the arts, as in the manufacture of varnish, and also as a medicine.

gale, gāl, *n.* [Gael. and Ir. *gal*, a gale or puff of wind; or connected with Icel. *gol*, *gola*, a breeze.] A wind; a breeze; a wind between a breeze and a storm or tempest.

gale, gāl, *n.* [O.E. *gawl*, A.Sax. D. and G. *gagel*, wild-myrtle.] A small shrub with a pleasant aromatic odor found in bogs and wet heaths.

galea, gā′li•a, *n.* [L., a helmet.] *Bot.* parts of a calyx or corolla when with the form of a helmet.—**galeated, galeate,** gā′li•ā•ted, gā′li•āt, *a.* [L. *galeatus*.] Covered as with a helmet; shaped like a helmet.

galena, ga•lē′na, *n.* [Gr. *galēnē*, tranquillity—so named from its supposed effect upon diseases.] The principal ore of lead, of a lead-gray color, with a metallic luster, found massive, or sometimes granular or crystallized.

Galenic, Galenical, ga•len′ik, ga•len′i•kal, *a.* Relating to *Galen*, the celebrated Greek physician of the second century.—**Galenism,** gā′len•izm, *n.* The doctrines of Galen.—**Galenist,** gā′len•ist, *n.* A follower of Galen.

Galilean, gal•i•lē′an, *a.* Of or pertaining to, or invented by *Galileo*, the Italian astronomer.

galilee, gal′i•lē, *n.* [Named after the scriptural *Galilee*]. A portico or chapel annexed to some old churches, and used for various purposes.—**Galilean,** gal•i•lē′an, *n.* A native or inhabitant of Galilee, in Judea.—*a.* Relating to Galilee.

galimatias, gal•i•mā′shi•as, *n.* [Fr., origin doubtful.] Confused talk; nonsense; absurd mixture.

galiot, galliot, gal′i•ot, *n.* [Fr. *galiote*, dim. of *galie*, a galley. GALLEY.] A small galley, or sort of brigantine, moved both by sails and oars; a two-masted Dutch cargo vessel; with very rounded ribs and flattish bottom.

galipot, gal′i•pot, *n.* [Fr., perhaps from being sold in *gallipots*.] The French name for the resin which is obtained by incisions in the stems of the maritime pine.

gall, gąl, *n.* [A.Sax. *gealla*=acel. *gall*. D. *gal*, G. *galle*; cog. with Gr. *cholē*, L. *fel*, bile.] A bitter fluid secreted in the liver of animals; bile; *fig.* bitterness of mind; rancor; malignity; the gall bladder; nerve, audacity, impudence, brazen assurance. (*Slang.*)—**gall bladder,** *n. Anat.* a small membranous sac shaped like a pear, which receives the gall or bile from the liver.—**gallstone,** *n.* A concretion formed in the gall bladder, or biliary passages.

gall, gąl, *n.* [Fr. *gale*, It. *galla*, from L. *galla*, an oak gall, a gallnut.] A vegetable excrescence produced by the deposit of the egg of an insect in the bark or leaves of a plant, especially the oak, very extensively used in dyeing and in the manufacture of ink.—**gallfly,** *n.* An insect that punctures plants, and occasions galls.—**gallic,** gąl′ik, *a.* Belonging to galls; derived from galls.

gall, gąl, *v.t.* [O.Fr. *galler*, to gall or fret, *galle*, an itching, scurf, perhaps L. *galla*, the diseased vegetable excrescence. Comp. also Armor. *gâl*, eruption.] To make a sore in the skin of by rubbing, fretting, and wearing away; to excoriate; to vex; to chagrin; to cause to have a feeling of bitterness or annoyance; to hurt the feelings of; to harass; to annoy (as by a musketry fire).—*n.* A sore place caused by rubbing.—**galling,** gąl′ing, *a.* Adapted to fret or chagrin; vexing; harassing; annoying.—**gallingly,** gąl′ing•li, *adv.* In a galling manner.

gallant, gal′ant, *a.* [Fr. *galant*, ppr. of O.Fr. verb *galer*, to rejoice, from the Teutonic; comp. G. *geil*, wanton, Goth, *gailjan*, to rejoice, A.Sax. *gál*, merry.] Gay, showy, or splendid in attire or outward appearance; handsome; fine; brave; high-spirited; courageous; magnanimous; noble; chivalrous; (in the following senses pron. also ga•lant′), courtly; polite and attentive to ladies; courteous.—*n.* A gay sprightly man; a high-spirited brave young fellow; a daring spirit; (in the following senses pron. also ga•lant′), a man who is polite and attentive to ladies; a wooer; a suitor.—*v.t.* (ga•lant′). To act the gallant toward; to wait on or be very attentive to (a lady).—**gallantly,** gal′ant•li, *adv.* In a gallant manner; gaily; splendidly; bravely; nobly.—**gallantry,** gal′ant•ri, *n.* [Fr. *galanterie*.] Show; ostentatious finery; bravery; dash; intrepidity; polite attention to ladies; court paid to females for the purpose of winning illicit favors.

galleass, gal′i•as, *n.* [Fr. *galeasse*, It. *galeazza*; akin to *galley*.] A large kind of galley formerly used in the Mediterranean.

galleon, gal′i•un, *n.* [Sp. *galeon*, It. *galeone*, augmentatives from L.L. *galea*, a galley.] A large ship formerly used by the Spaniards in their commerce with America.

gallery, gal′ėr•i, *n.* [Fr. *galerie*, It. *galleria*, L.L. *galeria*, perhaps from L.Gr. *galē*, a gallery.] An apartment of much greater length than breadth, serving as a passage of communication between different rooms of a building; a room or building for the exhibition of paintings, statues, and other works of art; a collection of paintings, statues, etc.; a platform projecting from the walls of a building, and overlooking a ground floor, as in a church, theater, and the like; *fort.* any communication covered in both above and at the sides; *mining*, a narrow passage; *naut.* a frame like a balcony projecting from the stern and quarters of a ship.

galley, gal′i, *n.* [O.Fr. *galie*, It. and L.L. *galea*—probably from Gr. *galē*, a kind of gallery, or *galeos*, *galē*, a sea fish, a kind of shark, which might suggest a swift-sailing vessel. Akin are *galleon*, *galleass*, *galiot*.] A low flat-built vessel with one deck, and navigated with sails and oars, once commonly used in the Mediterranean; a ship of the ancient Greeks and Romans, propelled chiefly by oars; the boat of a warship appropriated for the captain's use; the cook room or kitchen on board ship; *printing*, a movable frame or tray on which the types are placed when composed.—*The galleys*, certain galleys on the Mediterranean which were worked by convicts; hence, a synonym for a place of forced and severe toil.—**galley slave,** *n.* A person condemned for a crime to work at the oar on board of a galley.

gallic, *a.* See GALL.

Gallic, Gallican, gal′ik, gal′i•kan, *a.* [L. *Gallicus*, from *Gallia*, Gaul, France.] Pertaining to Gaul or France (the *Gallican* church or clergy); in the days of Louis XIV and Bossuet, claiming liberty of action denied by the Papal or Ultramontane party.—**Gallicize,** gal′i•sīz, *v.t.*—*gallicized, gallicizing*. To render conformable to the French idiom or language.—**Gallicism,** gal′i•sizm, *n.* [Fr. *gallicisme*.] A mode of speech peculiar to the French nation; a custom or mode of thought peculiar to the French.

galligaskins, gal•i•gas′kinz, *n. pl.* [From Fr. *greguesques*, O.Fr. *guarguesques*, *garguesques*, from It. *grechesco*, Grecian (through such forms as *gleguesques*, *galligasks*).] Large open breeches; wide hose; leather guards worn on the legs by sportsmen.

gallimaufry, gal•i•mą′fri, *n.* [Fr. *galimafrée*, a ragout; of uncertain origin.] A hash; a medley; a hodgepodge.

gallinaceous, gal•i•nā′shus, *a.* [L. *gallinaceus*, from *gallina*, a hen, *gallus*, a cock.] Pertaining to the order of birds which includes the domestic fowls, pheasants, etc.—**gallinacean,** gal•i•nā′shen, *n.* One of the gallinaceous birds.—**gallinule,** gal′i•nūl, *n.* [L. *gallinula*, dim. of *gallina*, a hen.] A grallatorial bird closely allied to the coots; the water hen or moor hen.

gallipot, gal′i•pot, *n.* [Corrupted from O.D. *gleypot*, an earthen pot—*gley*, clay, and *pot*.] A small pot or vessel painted and glazed, used by druggists and apothecaries for containing medicines.

gallium, gal′i•um, *n.* [From *Gallia*, the Latin name for France.] A rare, widely distributed, metallic element of low melting point (29.7°C.). Symbol, Ga; at. no., 31; at. wt., 69.72.

gallivant, gal•i•vant′, *v.i.* [Probably a corrupt form of *gallant*.] To gad or run about; to flirt.

galliwasp, gal′i•wosp, *n.* A species of West Indian lizard, about 1 foot in length.

gallon, gal′un, *n.* [O.Fr. *galon*, *jalon*; Fr. *jale*, a jar, a bowl; origin unknown.] A measure of capacity equal to 4 quarts, dry or liquid, but usually the latter; the U.S. gallon contains 231 cu. in., the English imperial gallon, 277.42 cu. in.

galloon, ga•lön′, *n.* [Fr. and Sp. *galon*; It. *galone*, from *gala*, show.

GALA.] A kind of narrow close lace made of cotton, silk, gold, or silver threads, etc.—**gallooned,** ga•lönd′, *a.* Furnished or adorned with galloon.

gallop, gal′up, *v.i.* [Fr. *galoper,* from O.Flem. *walop,* a galop, an extension of *wallen,* A.Sax. *weallan,* to boil.] To move or run with leaps, as a horse; to run with speed; to ride a horse that is galloping; to ride at a rapid pace; to scamper.—*n.* The movement or pace of a horse, by springs or leaps.—**gallopade,** gal•-up•äd′, *n.* [Fr. *galopade.*] A sidelong or curvetting kind of gallop; a sprightly kind of dance; a galop; the music adapted to it.—*v.i.*—*gallopaded, gallopading.* To gallop; to perform the dance called a gallopade.—**galloper,** gal′up•ėr, *n.* One who or that which gallops.

Galloway, gal′o•wā, *n.* A species of horses of small size but great endurance, first bred in *Galloway* in Scotland.—*Gallovidians, Galwegians,* inhabitants of Galloway.

gallowglass, gallowglas, gal′ō•glas, *n.* [Ir. *galloglach—gall,* a foreigner, an Englishman, and *oglach,* a youth; from being armed after the English model.] An ancient heavy-armed foot soldier of Ireland and the Western Isles.

gallows, gal′ōz, *n. sing.* or *pl.*; also **gallowses** in pl. [A plural form; A.Sax. *galga, gealga* (sing.), a gallows = Dan. and Sw. *galge,* Icel. *gálgi,* Goth. *galga,* G. *galgen,* gallows.] An upright wooden frame with crossbar, on which criminals are executed by hanging; also a pair of suspenders or braces.

galop, gal′op, *n.* [Fr. GALLOP.] A quick, lively kind of dance in 2 = 4 time, somewhat resembling a waltz; the music for this dance.

galore, ga•lōr′, *n.* [Ir. and Gael. *go leòr,* enough—*go,* to, and *leòr,* enough.] Abundance; plenty.—*adv.* In abundance; bountifully. (*Colloq.*)

galosh, galoshe, ga•losh′, *n.* [Fr. *galoche,* from L.L. *calopedia* (through the corruptions *calop'dia, calopdja*), from Gr. *kalopodion,* a wooden shoe—*kalon,* wood, and *pous, podos,* a foot.] A shoe to be worn over another shoe to keep the foot dry; also a kind of gaiter.

galvanic, galvanical,† gal•van′ik, gal•van′i•kal, *a.* [From *Galvani,* an Italian physiologist, an early investigator of galvanism.] Pertaining to galvanism; containing or exhibiting galvanism.—*Galvanic electricity,* electricity arising from chemical action. —*Galvanic pair* or *cell,* a combination of two substances in an exciting liquid which acts chemically upon one more than on the other.—*Galvanic battery,* an association of galvanic pairs for the production of current electricity.—**galvanism,** gal′-van•izm, *n.* That branch of the science of electricity which treats of the electric currents arising from chemical action. *Current electricity, voltaic* are now used instead of *galvanism, galvanic.*—**galvanization,** gal′van•i•zā″shon, *n.* The act of affecting with galvanism; the state of being affected.—**galvanize,** gal′van•-īz, *v.t.*—*galvanized, galvanizing.* To affect with galvanism; to electroplate by galvanism; to coat (sheets of iron) with tin or zinc in this way; to restore to consciousness by galvanic action, as from a state of suspended animation.—**galvanizer,** gal′van•ī•-zėr, *n.* One who or that which galvanizes.—**galvanometer,** gal•van•-om′et•ėr, *n.* An instrument for detecting the existence and determining the strength and direction of an electric current. — **galvanometry,** gal•van•om′et•ri, *n.* The art or process of determining the force of electric or galvanic currents.—**galvanoscope,** gal′van•o•skōp, *n.* An instrument for detecting the existence and direction of an electric current.—**galvanoscopic,** gal′van•o•-skop″ik, *a.* Of or pertaining to a galvanoscope.

gambeson, gam′bi•s'n, *n.* [O.Fr. *gambeson,* from O.H.G. *wamba,* A. Sax. *wambe,* womb, stomach; comp. G. *wams,* doublet.] A stuffed and quilted tunic, fitting the body, and formerly worn under the habergeon.

gambier, gambir, gam′bēr, gam′bir, *n.* [Malayan.] An earthy-looking substance of light-brown hue, procured from the leaves of a Malayan shrub, and used medicinally as an astringent, but far more extensively employed in tanning and dyeing.

gambit, gam′bit, *n.* [Fr., from It. *gambetto,* a tripping up of one's legs, from *gamba,* the leg.] *Chess,* the sacrifice of a pawn early in the game, for the purpose of taking up an attacking position.

gamble, gam′bl, *v.i.*—*gambled, gambling.* [Freq. of *game,* with *b* inserted, as in *number, humble.*] To play or game for money or other stake, especially to be in the habit of doing so.—*v.t.* To lose or squander by gaming: with *away.*—**gambler,** gam′-bler, *n.* One who gambles.

gamboge, gam•bōj′, *n.* [From *Camboja, Cambodia,* a portion of the empire of Anam, in Asia.] The hardened juice or sap yielded by several species of trees, and used as a purgative in medicine, and also in the arts, chiefly in water-color painting.

gambol, gam′bol, *v.i.*—*gambolled, gambolling.* [O.E. *gambolde, gambaude,* from Fr. *gambade,* gambol, *gambiller,* to wag the leg or kick, O.Fr. *gambe,* It. *gamba,* the leg, Fr. *jambe.*] To dance and skip about in sport; to frisk; to leap; to play in frolic.—*n.* A skipping or leaping about in frolic; a skip, frisk, leap, prank.

gambrel, gam′brel, *n.* [From It. *gamba,* the leg.] The hind leg of a horse; a stick crooked like a horse's leg, used by butchers for suspending animals.—*Gambrel roof,* a hipped roof; a mansard roof.

game, gām, *n.* [A.Sax. *gamen,* joy, pleasure; Icel. *gaman,* Dan. *gammen,* delight, gratification; O.G. *gaman,* jest, sport. *Gamble* is a derivative, and *gammon,* humbug, is of same origin.] Sport of any kind; jest; play; some contrivance or arrangement for sport, recreation, testing skill, and the like (as baseball or football); a single contest in any such game; specifically (*pl.*), diversions or contests, as in wrestling, running, and other athletic exercises; a scheme pursued or measures planned; such animals, collectively, as are usually pursued or taken in the chase or in the sports of the field: in this sense without a plural; the animals enumerated in the game laws.—*To make game of,* to turn into ridicule; to delude or humbug.—*v.i.*—*gamed, gaming.* [A.Sax. *gamenian.*] To gamble; to play at cards, dice, billiards, etc., for money; to be in the habit of so doing.—*a.* Having the courageous spirit of a gamecock; courageous. (*Colloq.*)—*To die game,* to maintain a bold, resolute, courageous spirit to the last.—**gamebag,** *n.* A bag for holding the game killed by a sportsman.—**gamecock,** *n.* A cock bred or used to fight; a cock of a good fighting breed.—**gamekeeper,** *n.* One who has the care of game; one who is employed to look after animals kept for sport.—**game laws,** *n. pl.* Laws enacted with regard to, or for the preservation of, the animals called game.—**game** *n.* Cricket. *To play* the *game,* to play according to rule; to act straightforwardly.— —**gamely,** gām′li, *adv.* In a game or courageous manner.—**gameness,** gām′nes, *n.*—**gamy,** gā′mi, *a.* Having the flavor of game.

gamete, ga•mēt′, *n.* [Gr. *gameō,* I marry.] *Biol.* a matured sex cell or germ cell; in lower plants, the similar sex cells of thallophytes, which unite to form a zygote; in animals and higher plants, the dissimilar cells, called sperm and egg, which unite to form an embryo.

gamin, gam′in, ga•man′, *n.* [Fr.] A neglected street boy; an Arab of the streets.

gamma, gam′mä, *n.* [M.E. from L.L. from Gr. of Sem. origin, akin to Heb. *gamel, gimel.*] The third letter of the Greek alphabet, equivalent to the English *g,* as in *go.*—**gamma rays,** *n. Phys.* rays similar to X-rays, emitted from radioactive materials and used in radiotherapy.

gammer, gam′ėr, *n.* [Contr. for *goodmother* or *grandmother.* Comp. *gaffer.*] An old wife; the correlative of *gaffer.*

gammon, gam′un, *n.* [O.Fr. *gambon,* It. *gambone,* a big leg, a gammon, from *gamba,* a leg.] The thigh of a hog, pickled and smoked or dried; a smoked ham.—*v.t.* To make into bacon; to pickle and dry in smoke.

gammon, gam′un, *n.* [Connected with *game*; comp. Dan. *gammen,* sport.] An imposition or hoax; humbug. (*Colloq.*)

gamogenesis, gam•o•jen′e•sis, *n.* [Gr. *gamos,* marriage, and *genesis.*] Generation by copulation of the sexes; sexual generation. —**gamogenetic,** gam′o•je•net″ik, *a.* Of or relating to gamogenesis.—**gamopetalous,** gam•-o•pet′a•lus, *a.* [Gr. *gamos,* and *petalon,* a flower leaf.] *Bot.* monopetalous.

—**gamophyllous,** ga•mof′i•lus or gam•o•fil′lus, *a.* [Gr. *gamos*, and *phyllon*, a leaf.] *Bot.* having a single perianth whorl with coherent leaves. —**gamosepalous,** gam•o•sep′a•lus, *a.* [Gr. *gamos*, and E. *sepal.*] *Bot.* monosepalous.

gamp, gamp, *n.* A clumsy umbrella, as carried by Mrs. Sairey Gamp, in Dickens. Fr. *Robinson*, from the umbrella of Robinson Crusoe.

gamut, gam′ut, *n.* [Gr. *gamma*, the letter G and *gamma* plus *ut*, the first note of Guido's music scale.] The series of recognized musical notes in a scale; an entire range or series; the compass of a voice or instrument.

gander, gan′dėr, *n.* [A.Sax. *gandra*, for *ganra*, from the root *gan* seen in G. *gans*, a goose, *gänserich*, a gander. GOOSE.] The male of the goose.

gang, gang, *n.* [A.Sax. *gang*, a way, a passage, *genge*, a gang, a company, from *gangan*, to go. GO.] A number going in company, hence, a company or number of persons associated for a particular purpose; contemptuous or disreputable persons.—*v.i.* To act in concert; to form a group.—*v.t.* To assemble or operate mechanical parts simultaneously; to attack in a gang.—**gangster,** gang′stėr, *n.* One of a gang of toughs.—**gangway,** gang′-wā, *n.* A temporary means of access to some position, formed of planks or boards; a narrow framework or platform leading into or out of a ship, or from one part of a ship to another.—*interj.* Clear the way!

gangling, gan′gling, *adj.* [From Scottish, *gang*, to go.] Loosely built; lanky; spindly or awkwardly long.

ganglion, gang′gli•on, *n.* pl. **ganglia,** or **ganglions,** [Gr. *ganglion*, a sort of swelling or excrescence, a tumor under the skin.] *Anat.* an enlargement occurring somewhere in the course of a nerve; a mass of nervous matter containing nerve cells, and giving origin to nerve fibers; *surg.* an encysted tumor situated somewhere on a tendon.—**gangliated,** gang′gli•āt•ed, *a.* Having ganglions. —**ganglionic,** gang•gli•on′ik, *a.* Pertaining to a ganglion.

gangrene, gang′grēn, *n.* [L. *gangræna*, from Gr. *gangraina*, from *graino*, to gnaw.] The first stage of mortification of living flesh; *bot.* a disease ending in putrid decay.—*v.t.*—*gangrened*, *gangrening*. To produce a gangrene in; to mortify.—*v.i.* To become mortified.—**gangrenous,** gang′grē•nus, *a.* Attacked by gangrene; mortified; indicating mortification of living flesh.

gangue, gang, *n.* [G. *gang*, a vein.] The stony matrix of metallic ores.

gangway. See GANG.

ganister, gan′is•tėr, *n.* A close-grained hard sandstone or grit found under certain coal beds in England.

gannet, gan′et, *n.* [A.Sax. *ganet*, *ganot*, a sea fowl, a gannet; allied to *gander*, *goose*.] The solan goose, an aquatic bird of the pelican family, 3 feet in length, common on insular rocks in the northern seas.

ganoid, gan′oid, *a.* [Gr. *ganos*, splendor, and *eidos*, appearance.] Belonging to an order of fishes, the majority of them extinct, characterized by scales composed of horny or bony plates, covered with glossy enamel.—*n.* One of these fishes.

gantlet, gant′let, *n.* Same as *Gauntlet*.

gantlet, gant′let, *n.* [From Sw. *gatlopp*, from *gata*, a street, a line of soldiers, and *lopp*, a course, akin to E. *leap*, D. *loopen*, to run.] A punishment in which the culprit was compelled to run between two ranks of men armed with rods, etc., receiving a blow from each; *rail.* a stretch of track where two lines overlap (as in a tunnel), eliminating the need for switching.

gantry, gan′tri, *n.* [O.F. *gantier*, *chantier*, from L. *cantherius*, from G. *kanthelios*, pack ass.] A framework raised on side supports and extended over something; a frame supporting a cask or barrel.

gap, gap, *n.* [Icel. and Sw. *gap*, a gap or hiatus; akin *gape*, *gaby*.] A break or opening, as in a fence, wall, or the like; a breach; a chasm; a hiatus. —*v.t.* To make a gap or gaps in; to notch or jag; to cut into teeth.

gape, gāp, *v.i.*—*gaped*, *gaping*. [A. Sax. *geápan*, to gape or open wide, from *geáp*, wide; Dan. *gabe*, Icel. *gapa*, to gaze with open mouth; D. *gapen*, G. *gaffen*, to gape; akin *gap*, *gaby*.] To open the mouth wide, as indicative of drowsiness, dullness, surprise, expectation, etc.; to stand open; to present a gap; to show a fissure or chasm.—*To gape for or after*, to crave; to desire or covet earnestly.—*n.* The act of gaping; *zool.* the width of the mouth when opened, as of birds, fishes, etc.; *pl.* a disease of young poultry attended with much gaping.—**gaper,** gā′pėr, *n.* One who gapes; a bivalve mollusk with a shell permanently open at the posterior end.

garage, ga•räzh, *n.* [Fr.] A place for receiving or repairing motor vehicles.

garb, gärb, *n.* [O.Fr. *garbe*, a garb, appearance, comeliness, from O.H. G. *garawi*, *garwi*, attire; akin to A.Sax. *gearwa*, clothing; E. *gear* and *yare*.] Clothing; vesture; costume; habit; an official or other distinguishing dress; fashion or mode. —*v.t.* To dress; to clothe. (*Tenn.*)

garbage, gär′bij, *n.* [O.E. *garbash*, probably from *garble*, to sift; being thus what is sifted out, refuse.] Refuse or offal; refuse animal or vegetable matter; any worthless, offensive matter.

garble, gär′bl, *v.t.*—*garbled*, *garbling*. [O.Fr. *garbeller*, from Sp. *garbillar*, to sift *garbillo*, a coarse sieve; from Ar. *gharbil*, a sieve.] To sift or bolt‡; to examine for the purpose of separating the good from the bad‡; to falsify by leaving out parts; to mutilate so as to give a false impression (to *garble* historical documents); to sophisticate; to corrupt.—**garbler,** gär′blėr, *n.* One who garbles; formerly an official in London who looked after the purity of drugs and spices.

garden, gär′dn, *n.* [O.Fr. *gardin*, Mod.Fr. *jardin*, a word of Teutonic origin; comp. L.G. *garden*, G. *garten*, a garden; Goth. *gards*, A.Sax. *geard*, O.E. *garth*, an inclosed place, a yard. YARD.] A piece of ground appropriated to the cultivation of plants, fruits, flowers, or vegetables; a rich well-cultivated spot or tract of country.—*v.i.* To lay out or cultivate a garden.—**gardener,** gär′dn•ėr, *n.* One whose occupation is to keep a garden.—*Garden city*, a town laid out with many gardens and open spaces.—*Garden party*, a party held out of doors on the lawn or in the garden of a private residence.

gardenia, gär•dē′ni•a, *n.* [After Dr. *Garden*, an American botanist.] A name of certain plants of Asia and Africa with large white or yellowish fragrant flowers.

garfish, gär′fish, *n.* [A.Sax. *gár*, a dart.] A fish with a remarkably elongated body and a long, narrow, beaklike snout; seapike or sea needle.

Gargantua, gar•gan′tu•a, *n.* A gigantic hero of a satirical romance by Rabelais; **Gargantuan,** *a.* Gigantic; coarse.

gargle, gär′gl, *v.t.*—*gargled*, *gargling*. [A word akin to *gargle*, *gorge*, *gargoil*; Fr. *gargouiller*, to gargle; L. *gurgulio*, the gullet; Gr. *gargarizō*, to rinse the mouth; G. *gurgel*, the throat, *gurgeln*, to gargle.] To wash or rinse (the mouth or throat) with a liquid preparation.—*n.* Any liquid preparation for washing the mouth and throat.

gargoyle, gär′goil, *n.* [Fr. *gargouille*, a gargoil or spout. GARGLE.] *Arch.* a projecting spout for throwing the water from the gutters of a building, generally carved into a grotesque figure from whose mouth the water gushes.

garibaldi, gar•i•bold′i, *n.* A loose red blouse worn by women, named from the red-shirt troops of the Italian patriot *Garibaldi*.

garish, gâ′rish, *a.* [From O.E. *gare*, to stare, probably a form of *gaze* with change from *z*-sound to *r*, as in *snore*, *snooze*; *frore*, *freeze*, etc.] Gaudy; showy; staring; overbright; dazzling.—**garishly,** gâ′rish•ly, *adv.* In a garish manner.—**garishness,** gâ′rish•nes, *n.* The state or quality of being garish.

garland, gär′land, *n.* [O.E. *girlond*, *gerlond*, from Fr. *guirlande*, a garland, from O.H.G. *wiera*, a coronet, through a verb *wierelen*, to plait.] A wreath or chaplet made of leaves, twigs, flowers, or the like; a collection of little printed pieces; an anthology.—*v.t.* To deck with a garland or garlands.

garlic, gär′lik, *n.* [A.Sax. *gárleác*, from *gár*, a dart or lance—from the spear-shaped leaves—and *leác*, a leek, as in hem*lock*, char*lock*, etc.] A plant allied to the onion, leek, etc., having an acrid pungent taste and very strong odor, indigenous to the south of Europe, where it forms a favorite condiment.

garment, gär′ment, *n.* [Fr. *garnement*; O.Fr. *garniment*, from *garnir*, to garnish, to deck. GARNISH.] Any article of clothing or piece of dress, as a coat, a gown, etc.; a vestment.

garner, gär′nėr, *n.* [Fr. *grenier*, O.Fr. *gernier*, a cornloft, from L. *granaria*, a granary, from *granum*, grain. GRANARY.] A granary; a building or place where grain is stored for preservation.—*v.t.* To store in, or as in, a granary.

garnet, gär′net, *n.* [Fr. *grenat*, It. *granata*, from L. *granum*, grain, seed, and in later times the cochineal insect and the scarlet dye obtained from it, the stone being so called on account of its fine crimson color.] The name common to a group or family of precious stones, varying considerably in composition, the prevailing color being red of various shades, but often brown, and sometimes green, yellow, or black; *naut.* a sort of tackle fixed to a stay, and used to hoist in and out cargo.

garnish, gär′nish, *v.t.* [Fr. *garnir*, to provide or equip; It. *guarnire*, *guernire*, O.Sp. *guarnir*; from the German—comp. O.H.G. *warnôn*, G. *warnen*, A.Sax. *warnian*, to take care, to warn. WARN. Akin *garment*, *garrison.*] To adorn; to decorate with appendages; to set off; *cookery*, to ornament (a dish) with colorful trimming; *law*, to warn, or bring into court, by garnishment.—*n.* Something added for embellishment; ornament; decoration; *cookery*, something added to food as an embellishment.—**garnishee,** *v.t.* To obtain legal attachment on property or money.—*n.* The person subject to garnishment.—**garnisher,** gär′nish•ėr, *n.*—**garnishment,** gär′nish•ment, *n.* Ornament; *law*, a legal notice commanding one to appear in court; the legal attachment of money for debt.

garotte, garotter. See GARROTE, GARROTTER.

garret, gar′et, *n.* [O.Fr. *garite*, a place of refuge or outlook, from *garer*, to beware, from O.H.G. *werjan*, Goth. *varjan*, to defend. Akin *ward*, *guard*, *wary*, *warn.*] That part of a house which is on the uppermost floor, immediately under the roof; a loft.

garrison, gar′i•sn, *n.* [Fr. *garnison*, from *garnir*, to garnish. GARNISH.] A body of troops stationed in a fort or fortified town; a fort, castle, or fortified town furnished with troops. —*v.t.* To place a garrison in; to secure or defend by garrisons.

garrote, garrotte, ga•rōt′, ga•rot′, *n.* [Fr. *garrotte*, from Sp. *garrote.*] A mode of capital punishment in Spain by strangling the prisoner by means of an iron collar attached to a post; the instrument of this punishment.—**garrote, garrotte,** ga•rōt′, ga•rot′, *v.t.*—*garroted, garrotted*; *garroting, garrotting*. To strangle by means of the garrote; to rob by suddenly seizing a person and compressing his windpipe until he becomes insensible, or at least helpless, usually carried out by two or three accomplices.—**garroter,** ga•rōt′ėr, *n.* One who commits the act of garroting.

garrulous, ga′rū•lus, *a.* [L. *garrulus*, from *garrio*, to prate, to chatter; allied to Gr. *gēryō*, *garyō*, to cry; Ir. *gairim*, to bawl.] Talkative; prating; characterized by long prosy talk, with minuteness and frequent repetition in recording details.—**garrulity,** ga•rū′li•ti, *n.* The quality of being garrulous; talkativeness; loquacity.—**garrulously,** ga′rū•lus•li, *adv.* In a garrulous or talkative manner.—**garrulousness,** ga′rū•lus•nes, *n.* Talkativeness; garrulity.

garter, gär′tėr, *n.* [From O.Fr. *gartier*=Fr. *jarretière*, from *jarret*. O.Fr. *garret*, ham, hough, from the Celtic; Armor. *gar* or *garr*, W. *gar*, the leg, Gael. *gar*, in *gartan*, a garter.] A band or strip of elastic worn to hold up a stocking; [*usually cap.*] the badge of the highest order of knighthood in Great Britain, called *the Order of the Garter*; hence, also, the order itself, and the name given to the principal king-of-arms in England.—*v.t.* To bind with a garter.

gas, gas, *n.* [A word formed by the Dutch chemist Van Helmont, who died in 1644.] An elastic, airlike fluid; a substance, such as air, the particles of which tend to fly apart from each other, thus causing it to expand indefinitely; in common usage, any gaseous substance except air, as *acetylene gas*, which in combination with oxygen is used in welding; *coal gas*, distilled from coal and used for heating, cooking, and less frequently, lighting; *laughing gas* or nitrous oxide, employed in dentistry or surgery as an anesthetic; *natural gas*, found under the earth's crust and used as a fuel and illuminant; *poison gas*, such as chlorine, employed in warfare. Fuel gases, poison gases, and firedamp are often referred to simply as *gas*. Gasoline is colloquially termed *gas*.—*v.t.* To treat with gas, as in industrial processes; to poison with gas.—**gas burner,** a jet or series or jets where gas is burned as it issues out.—**gaselier,** gas′e•lēr, *n.* A chandelier adapted for burning gas.—**gaseous,** gas′ē•us, *a.* In the form of gas; of the nature of gas.—**gas fitter,** a workman who fixes pipes and fits burners and other appliances for gas. —**gasiform,** gas′i•form, *a.* Gaseous; aeriform.—**gasify,** gas′i•fī, *v.t.*—*gasified, gasifying*. To convert into gas.—**gaslight,** light produced by the combustion of coal gas; a gas jet. —**gas mask,** *n.* Covering for the face, worn as a protection against poison gas.—**gasoline,** gas′o•lēn, *n.* Refined petroleum, a volatile liquid hydrocarbon, highly flammable and, when vaporized and mixed with air, explosive, used as a solvent and as a fuel in engines.—**gasometer,** gas•om′e•tėr, *n.* An instrument or apparatus intended to measure, collect, or mix gases.—**gas station,** *n.* Place where gasoline and oil are sold, chiefly for use in automobiles. —**gas turbine,** gas tėr′bin, *n.* An engine in which curved turbine blades are propelled by the forcing of compressed hot gases introduced from the combustion chamber through the blades, creating a rotary work force.

Gascon, gas′kon, *n.* [Fr.; akin to *Basque.*] A native of Gascony in France; hence, a boaster, the Gascons being noted for boasting.—**gasconade,** gas•ko•nād′, *n.* [Fr.] A boast or boasting; a vaunt; a bravado; a bragging.—*v.i.*—*gasconaded, gasconading*. To boast; to brag, to vaunt; to bluster.

gash, gash, *n.* [Perhaps from O.Fr. *garser*, to scarify, to pierce with a lancet; L.L. *garsa*, scarification.] A deep and long cut, particularly in flesh.—*v.t.* To make a gash in.

gasket, gas′ket, *n.* [Fr. *garcette*, Sp. *garceta*, a gasket.] Anything used as a packing, such as a metal or rubber ring; a line used to bind a furled sail to the yard of a boat.

gasp, gasp, *v.i.* [Icel. *geispa*, to yawn; Dan. *gispe*, to gasp; L.G. *japen*, *japsen*; akin to E. *gape*.] To open the mouth wide in laborious respiration; to labor for breath; to respire convulsively; to pant violently.—*v.t.* To emit or utter with gaspings or pantings; with *away*, *forth*, *out*, etc. —*n.* A labored respiration; a short painful catching of the breath.

gastralgia, gas•tral′ji•a, *n.* [Gr. *gastēr*, *gastros*, the belly, and *algos*, pain.] Pain in the stomach or belly.

gastric, gas′trik, *a.* [From Gr. *gastēr*, *gastros*, the belly or stomach.] Of or pertaining to the belly or stomach. —*Gastric juice*, the digestive fluid containing enzymes and hydrochloric acid and secreted by stomach glands. —**gastritis,** gas•trī′tis, *n.* Chronic inflammation of the stomach.—**gastroenteritis,** gas•trō•en•te•rīt′is, *n.* Inflammation of the stomach and intestines.—**gastrointestinal,** gas•trō•in•tes′ti•nul, *n.* Something that involves both stomach and intestines.—**gastronomy,** gas•tron′o•mi, *n.* The art or science of good living; the pleasures of the table; epicurism.—**gastronomic, gastronomical,** gas•tro•nom′ik, gas•tro•nom′i•kal, *a.* Pertaining to gastronomy.—**gastronome, gastronomist,** gas′tro•nōm, gas•tron′o•mist, *n.* One versed in gastronomy; a judge of the art of cookery; a gourmet; an epicure.—**gastroscopy,** gas•tros′ko•pi, *n.* [Gr. *skopeō*, to view.] *Med.* an examination of the abdomen in order to detect disease.—**gastrovascular,** *a.* Belonging to digestion and circulation (the *gastrovascular* body cavity of certain animals).

gastropod, gasteropod, gas′tro•pod, gas′tėr•o•pod, *n.* [Gr. *gastēr*, the belly, and *pous*, *podos*, a foot.] One of a class of mollusks, consisting of snails, periwinkles, and other animals inhabiting a univalve shell (although some of them are destitute of a shell), the distinguishing characteristic being the *foot*, a broad muscular organ attached to the ventral surface.—**gastropodous,** gas•trop′o•dus, *a.* Belonging to the gastropods.

gastrula, gas′tru•la, *n.* [A dim. of *gaster*, Gr. *gastēr*, belly.] A germ or embryonic form developed by invagination from a morula or blastula, and having the character of a double-walled sac with an orifice leading into it.—**gastrulation,** *n.* The process by which a gastrula is produced.

gate, gāt, *n.* [A.Sax. *geat*, a gate or door.] A door or frame opening into an enclosing fence or wall; a movable barrier, often grated, that is raised or lowered to permit passage into an enclosure; a wooden barrier that is let down to block passage at a railroad crossing; the frame which shuts or stops a passage for water, as at the entrance to a dock.—**gate-leg table,** *n.* A table with folding leaves and movable legs.—**gateway,** gāt'wā, *n.* An opening which is or may be closed with a gate.

gather, gaTH'ėr, *v.t.* [A.Sax. *gaderian*, *gadrian*, from *gador*, *geador*, together, seen also in *together*; comp. D. *gadern*, to gather, *te gader*, L.G. *to gader*, together.] To bring together; to collect into one place or one aggregate; to assemble; to congregate; to pick; to pluck; to accumulate; to amass; to draw together; to bring together in folds or plaits, as a garment; hence, to plait; to pucker; to acquire or gain, with or without effort (to *gather* strength); to deduce by inference; to conclude.—*To gather one's self together*, to collect all one's powers for a strong effort.—*To be gathered to one's fathers*, to be interred along with one's ancestors, or simply to die.—*v.i.* To collect; to become assembled; to congregate; to take origin and grow; to come to a head (as a boil).—*n.* A plait or fold in cloth held in position by a thread drawn through it; a pucker.—**gatherer,** gaTH'ėr•ėr, *n.* One who or that which gathers.—**gathering,** gaTH'ėr•ing, *n.* The act of collecting or assembling; that which is gathered; a crowd; an assembly; a collection of pus; an abscess.

Gatling gun, gat'ling gun, *n.* A form of the mitrailleuse or repeating machine gun, so named from the inventor.

gauche, gōsh, *adj.* [Fr.] Tactless; lacking in the social graces.

gaucherie, gōsh•rē', *n.* [Fr., from *gauche*, left-handed, awkward.] An awkward action; awkwardness.

Gaucho, gou'chō, *n.* A cowboy of the South American pampas, of mixed Spanish and Indian blood.

gaud, ga̤d, *n.* [L. *gaudium*, joy, gladness; in later times something showy; akin *joy*, *jewel*.] Something worn for adorning the person; a piece of showy finery (*Shak.*).—**gaudery,**† ga̤'dėr•i, *n.* Finery; fine things.—**gaudily,** ga̤'di•li, *adv.* In a gaudy manner.—**gaudiness,** ga̤'di•nes, *n.* The quality or condition of being gaudy.—**gaudy,** ga̤'di, *a.* Gay beyond the simplicity of nature or good taste; showy; tastelessly or glaringly adorned.

gauge, gage, gāj, *v.t.*—*gauged, gaged, gauging, gaging.* [O.Fr. *gauger*, perhaps of the same origin with *gallon*, and signifying to find the number of measures in a vessel.] To measure or to ascertain the contents or capacity of; to measure in respect to capability, power, character, etc.; to appraise; to estimate.—*n.* A standard of measure; an instrument to determine dimensions or capacity; a measure; means of estimating; the distance between the lines of rails of a railway, the standard distance being 4 feet 8½ inches; this is called *standard gauge*; *broad* or *wide gauge* and *narrow gauge* are respectively larger and smaller; *joinery*, a simple instrument made to strike a line parallel to the straight side of a board, etc.—**gauger,** gāj'ėr, *n.* One who gauges; an officer whose business is to ascertain the contents of casks.

Gaul, ga̤l, *n.* [L. *Gallus*, a Gaul, an inhabitant of *Gallia*, the country now called France.] An inhabitant of Gaul.—**Gaulish,** ga̤'lish, *a.* Pertaining to Gaul.

gaultheria, ga̤l•thē'ri•a, *n.* [After M. Gaulthier, Canadian botanist.] A shrub of a large genus of plants of the heath family that includes the American wintergreen.—*gaultheria oil*, oil of wintergreen.

gaunt, ga̤nt, *a.* [Comp. N. *gand*, a slender stick, a thin man.] Attenuated, as with fasting or suffering; lean; meager; haggard; slender; forbidding; desolate, as of an abandoned and dilapidated building.—**gauntly,** ga̤nt'li, *adv.* Leanly; meagerly.—**gauntness,** *n.*

gauntlet, ga̤nt'let, *n.* [Fr. *gantelet*, dim. from *gant*, a glove, from the Teut.; D. *want*, Dan. *vante*, Icel. *vöttr* (for *vantr*), a glove.] A large iron glove with fingers covered with small plates, formerly worn as armor; a long glove for a lady, which envelops the hand and wrist. The gauntlet used to be thrown down in token of challenge; hence, *to throw down the gauntlet*, to challenge; *to take up the gauntlet*, to accept the challenge.—**gauntleted,** ga̤nt'let•ed, *a.* Wearing a gauntlet.

gauss, gous, *n.* [After the mathematician *Gauss*.] The unit of intensity of magnetic field, equal to the intensity produced by unit magnetic pole at a distance of one centimeter.

gauze, ga̤z, *n.* [Fr. *gaze*, Sp. *gasa*, from the town *Gaza*, whence it was first brought.] A very thin, slight, transparent stuff, of silk, linen, or cotton; any slight open material resembling this (wire *gauze*).—**gauzy,** ga̤'zi, *a.* Like gauze; thin as gauze.

gavel, gav'el, *n.* [Origin unknown.] The small mallet used by a presiding officer to rap for order or attention. —*v.t.* To force, through use of the gavel.

gavelkind, ga'vel•kind, *n.* [A.Sax. *gafol*, payment, *cynd*, kind, offspring.] An old land tenure in England, still prevailing in Kent, by which land descends to all the sons in equal shares.

gavial, gā'vi•al, *n.* [Indian name.] A crocodile found in India, with an extremely lengthened muzzle.

gavotte, ga•vot', *n.* [Fr., from *Gavot*, a native of the Pays de *Gap* in the Hautes Alpes, where the dance originated.] A sort of French dance; the music to which the dance was performed, or a similar instrumental movement.

gawk, ga̤k, *n.* [A.Sax. *geác*, Icel. *gaukr*, Sc. *gowk*, cuckoo, simpleton.] A clumsy, awkward person.—*v.i.* To stare; to act like a gawk.—**gawky,** ga̤'ki, *a.* Awkward; clownish.

gay, gā, *a.* [Fr. *gai*, of Teutonic origin; comp. O.H.G. *gâhi*, swift, excellent, G. *gähe*, *jähe*, quick. *Jay*, the bird, is akin.] Excited with merriment or delight; merry; sportive; frolicsome; fine; showy (a *gay* dress); given to pleasure, often to vicious pleasure; dissipated.—**gaiety,** gā'e•ti, *n.* The state of being gay; merriment; mirth; show.—**gaily, gayly,** gā'li, *adv.* In a gay manner.—**gayness,** gā'nes, *n.* The state or quality of being gay.

gaze, gāz, *v.i.*—*gazed, gazing.* [Sw. *gasa*, to gaze; allied to E. *agast*, Goth. *usgaisjan*, to terrify.] To fix the eyes and look steadily and earnestly; to look with eagerness or curiosity.—*v.t.* To view with fixed attention (*Mil.*).—*n.* A fixed look; a look of eagerness, wonder, or admiration.—**gazer,** gā'zėr, *n.* One who gazes.

gazelle, ga•zel', *n.* [Fr. *gazelle*, from Sp. *gazela*, from Ar. *ghazal*.] An antelope of Africa, central and southwest Asia, and India, about the size of a roebuck, of a graceful form, and with long slender limbs.

gazette, ga•zet', *n.* [It. *gazzetta*, a gazette, from *gazzetta*, a small Venetian coin (from L. or rather Per. *gaza*, treasure), the price of the newspaper; or the name may have been equivalent to 'The Chatterer,' *gazzetta* being a dim. of *gazza*, a magpie.] A newspaper; especially an official or government newspaper containing public announcements, such as appointments to civil or military posts, the names of persons who have been declared bankrupt, etc.; hence, *to appear in the gazette* often means to be publicly announced there as a bankrupt.—*v.t.*—*gazetted, gazetting.* To insert or publish in a gazette; hence, *to be gazetted*, to have one's name announced in the gazette as appointed to some post or promoted to some rank.—**gazetteer,** gaz•et•tēr', *n.* A manager of a gazette; more commonly a book containing geographical and topographical information alphabetically arranged; a geographical dictionary.

gean, gēn, *n.* [Fr. *guigne*, O.Fr. *guisne*, a word of Teutonic origin.] A kind of wild cherry tree common in England and Scotland, with fruit of an excellent flavor.

gear, gēr, *n.* [A.Sax. *gearwe*, habiliments, equipments, from *gearu*, *gearo*, prepared, ready, whence also *yare*, ready; akin *garb*, dress.] Whatever is prepared for use or wear; hence, dress; ornaments; the harness or furniture of domestic animals;

naut. the ropes, blocks, etc., belonging to any particular sail or spar; *mach.* a mechanism of toothed wheels and shafts that transmits or changes motion.—*v.t.* To put gear on; to harness; to put into gear.—*v.i.* To come into or be in gear; to fit exactly.—**gearing,** gē′ring, *n.* Harness; the parts by which motion is communicated from one portion of a machine to another.—**gearshift,** gēr′shift, *n.* A device by which transmission gears, as in an automobile, are engaged and disengaged.

geck, gek, *n.* [Comp. D. *gek,* G. *geck,* a silly person; also E. *gawk,* a simpleton.] A dupe; a gull. (*Shak.*)

gecko, gek′o, *n.* A name of various nocturnal lizards of the warm parts of both hemispheres.

geese, gēs, *n.* pl. of *goose.*

Gehenna, gi•hen′na, *n.* [L. *gehenna,* Gr. *geenna,* from the Heb. *gehinom,* the valley of Hinom at Jerusalem, where children were 'passed through the fire' to Moloch.] A term used in the New Testament as typical of the place of future punishment and translated hell, hell-fire.

Geiger counter, [After Hans *Geiger,* German physicist.] *Phys.* an instrument for detecting ionized particles, consisting of a metallic tube containing a gas into which projects a needle-like electrode.

geisha, gā′sha, *n.* One of the Japanese dancing and singing girls who perform at private parties and elsewhere.

gelatin, gelatine, jel′a•tin, *n.* [Fr. *gelatine,* It. and Sp. *gelatina,* from L. *gelo,* to congeal. GELID.] A substance obtained from various animal tissues, and employed in the arts and as human food, being known in its coarser forms as *glue, size,* and *isinglass*;a transparent color sheet stretched over a stage light to create a color spotlight. —**gelatination,** je•lat′i•nā″shon, *n.* The act or process of converting into gelatine.—**gelatinize,** je•lat′i•nīz, *v.t.* and *i.* To convert or be converted into gelatine. Also **gelatinate,** je•lat′i•nāt.—**gelatinous,** je•lat′i•nus, *a.* Of or pertaining to, or consisting of gelatine; resembling jelly; viscous.

geld, geld, *v.t.* [From Icel. *gelda,* Dan. *gilde,* G. *gelten,* to geld.] To castrate; to emasculate; to deprive of anything essential (*Shak.*).— —**gelder,** gel′dėr, *n.* One who castrates.—**gelding,** gel′ding, *n.* A castrated animal; especially a castrated horse.

gelid, jel′id, *a.* [L. *gelidus,* from *gelo,* to freeze, seen also in *gelatine, congeal, jelly,* the root being that of *cool.*] Cold; very cold; icy or frosty.—**gelidity,** je•lid′i•ti, *n.* The state of being gelid; extreme cold.—**gelidly,** jel′id•li, *adv.* In a gelid manner.

gelsemium, jel•sē′mi•um, *n.* [It. *gelsomino,* jasmine.] A twining shrub, the yellow jasmine of the United States; a dangerous drug derived from this plant.

gem, jem, *n.* [L. *gemma,* a bud, a precious stone.] A precious stone of any kind, especially when cut or polished; a jewel; anything resembling a gem, or remarkable for beauty, rarity, or costliness.—*v.t.*—*gemmed, gemming.* To adorn with gems or what resembles gems; to bespangle.

GEM. See AIR-CUSHION VEHICLE.

Gemara, ge•mä′ra, *n.* [Aramaic, completion.] A part of the Talmud, a commentary on the Mishna.

geminate,† jem′i•nāt, *v.t.* [L. *gemino, geminatum,* to double, from *geminus,* twin.] To double.—*a. Bot.* twin; combined in pairs; binate.—**gemination,** jem•i•nā′•shon, *n.* A doubling; duplication; repetition.—**Gemini,** jem′i•nī, *n. pl.* [L., twin brothers, Castor and Pollux.] *Astron.* the third sign of the zodiac, so named from its two brightest stars, Castor and Pollux.

gemma, jem′a, *n.* pl. **gemmae,** jem′ē, [L., a bud. GEM.] *Bot.* a leaf bud as distinguished from a flower bud.—**gemmate,** jem′āt, *a.* [L. *gemmatus.*] *Bot.* having buds; reproducing by buds.—**gemmation,** jem•ā′shon, *n.* [L. *gemmatio.*] *Zool.* the process of reproduction by buds; the formation of a new individual by budding; *bot.* the act of budding; vernation.—**gemmiparous,** jem•ip′a•rus, *a.* [L. *pario,* to produce.] Producing buds; *zool.* reproducing by buds.—**gemmule,** jem′ūl, *n.* [L. *gemmula.*] *Bot.* the growing point of the embryo in plants; one of the buds of mosses; a reproductive spore of algae; *zool.* the ciliated embryo or reproductive body of some of the lowest animals.

gemsbok, gemz′bok, *n.* [D. *gemsbok,* G. *gemsbock,* the male chamois, from *gemse,* chamois, and *bock,* buck.] A fine large antelope inhabiting South Africa.

gendarme, zhäṅ′därm, *n.* [Fr., from the pl. *gens d'armes,* men at arms.] A private in the armed police of France.—**gendarmery,** zhäṅ•därm•rē′, *n.* [Fr. *gendarmerie.*] The body of gendarmes.

gender, jen′dėr, *n.* [Fr. *genre,* from L. *genus, generis,* kind or sort, gender; with *d* inserted as in tender, adj. GENUS.] Kind or sort‡; a sex, male or female; *gram.* one of those classes or categories into which words are divided according to the sex, natural or metaphorical, of the beings or things they denote; a grammatical category in which words of similar termination are classed together; such a distinction in words. [In English grammar words expressing males are all said to be of the *masculine gender*; those expressing females, of the *feminine gender*; and words expressing things having no sex are of the *neuter gender*; but in other languages gender has a different basis, thus in French it has comparatively little to do with sex, all nouns being either masculine or feminine.]—*v.t.*† To beget; to engender.—*v.i.* To copulate.

gene, jēn, *n.* [From the Gr. root *genos,* born, of a certain kind.] A unit of a chromosome that determines the character and activities of cells and transmits inherited traits.

genealogy• jē•ni•al′o•ji or jen•i•al′o•ji, *n.* [L. and Gr. *genealogia*—Gr. *genea,* family (root *gen,* to beget), and *logos,* discourse. GENUS.] An account or synopsis tracing the descent of a person or family from an ancestor; an enumeration or table of ancestors and their children in the order of succession; pedigree; lineage; the study of pedigrees or family history.—**genealogical,** jē′ni•a•loj″•i•kal, *a.* Pertaining to genealogy; exhibiting or tracing genealogies.—*Genealogical tree,* the genealogy or lineage of a family drawn out under the form of a tree.—**genealogically,** jē′ni•a•loj″i•kal•li, *adv.* In a genealogical manner.—**genealogist,** jē•ni•al′o•jist, *n.* One who traces descents of persons or families.

genera, jen′ėr•a, *n.* pl. of *genus.*

general, jen′ėr•al, *a.* [Fr. *général,* from L. *generalis,* belonging to a genus, generic, general, from *genus, generis,* a kind. GENUS.] Relating to a whole genus, kind, class, or order; relating to, affecting, or comprehending the whole community; public; common to many or the greatest number; extensive, though not universal; common; usual; ordinary (a *general* opinion); not restrained or limited to a particular import; not specific (a *general* term); not directed to a single object; taken as a whole; regarded in the gross. ∴ This word affixed to another word is common in names expressive of rank or office, as *adjutant-general, attorney-general,* etc.—*General Assembly,* under ASSEMBLY. —*n.* The whole community‡; a general or comprehensive notion; a military officer of the highest rank; the commander of an army or of a division or brigade; the chief of an order of monks.—*In general,* in the main; for the most part; not always or universally; also in the aggregate, or as a whole.—**generalissimo,** jen′ėr•a•lis″i•mō, *n.* [It.] The chief commander of an army or military force which consists of two or more grand divisions under separate commanders.—**generality,** jen•ėr•al′i•ti, *n.* The state of being general; the quality of including species or particulars; a statement which is general or not specific, or which lacks application to any one case.—*The generality,* the main body; the bulk; the greatest part.—**generalization,** jen′ėr•al•i•zā″shon, *n.* The act or process of generalizing; a general inference.—**generalize,** jen′ėr•al•īz, *v.t.*—*generalized; generalizing.* To reduce or bring under a general law, rule, or statement; to bring into relation with a wider circle of facts; to deduce from the consideration of many particulars.—*v.i.* To form objects into classes; to bring or classify particulars under general heads or rules. **generally,** jen′ėr•al•li, *adv.* In general; commonly; ordinarily; extensively, though not universally; most frequently, but not without exceptions; without detail; leaving particular facts out of account; in the whole taken together.—**generalship,** jen′-ėr•al•ship. *n.* The office of a general; the discharge of the functions of a general; military skill exhibited in the judicious handling of troops; management or judicious tactics generally.

generate, jen′ėr•āt, *v.t.—generated, generating.* [L. *genero, generatum,* to beget. GENUS.] To procreate (young); to produce; to cause to be; to bring into existence; to cause (heat, vibrations).—**generable,** jen′-ėr•a•bl, *a.* Capable of being generated.—**generation,** jen•ėr•ā′shon, *n.* The act of generating; production formation; a single succession of the human race in natural descent, calculated at thirty years; the average period of time between one succession of children and the next following; people who are contemporary or living at the same time; a race; progeny; offspring.—*Equivocal* or *spontaneous generation,* in *biol.* the production of animals and plants without previously existing parents; abiogenesis.—*Alternate generation,* under ALTERNATE.—**generative,** jen′-ėr•ā•tiv, *a.* Having the power of generating; belonging to generation or the act of procreating.—**generator,** jen′ėr•ā•tėr, *n.* One who or that which begets, causes, or produces; *elec.* a device that changes mechanical energy into electrical energy; *chem.* an apparatus that causes vapor or gas to form.

generic, je•ner′ik, *a.* [Fr. *générique,* from L. *genus, generis,* kind. GENUS.] Pertaining to a genus; descriptive of, belonging to, or comprehending the genus, as distinct from the species or from another genus; referring to a large class.—**generically,** je•ner′i•kal•li, *adv.*

generous, jen′ėr•us, *a.* [L. *generosus,* of honorable birth, generous, from *genus, generis,* birth, extraction, family. GENUS.] Noble; honorable; magnanimous (of persons or things); liberal; bountiful; munificent; free in giving; strong; full of spirit (*generous* wine).—**generously,** jen′-ėr•us•li, *adv.* In a generous manner. —**generosity,** jen•ėr•os′i•ti, *n.* [L. *generositas.*] The quality of being generous; nobleness of soul; liberality of sentiment; a disposition to give liberally.—**generousness,** jen′-ėr•us•nes, *n.* The quality of being generous; generosity.

genesis, jen′e•sis, *n.* [Gr. *genesis,* from root *gen,* to beget. GENUS.] The act of producing or giving origin; a taking origin; generation; origination; [*cap.*] the first book of the Old Testament, containing the history of the creation of the world and of the human race.

genet, jen′et, *n.* [Fr. *genette,* Sp. *ginete,* from the name of a Berber tribe who supplied the Moorish sultans of Grenada with cavalry.] A small-sized, well-proportioned Spanish horse: spelled also *Jennet.*

genet, genette, jen′et, je•net′, *n.* [Sp. *gineta,* from Ar. *jarnait.*] A carnivorous animal belonging to the civet family, a native of western Asia; the fur of the genet.

genetic, genetical, je•net′ik, je•net′-i•kal, *a.* [From Gr. *genetēs,* a begetter, or *genesis,* generation.] Relating to genetics; pertaining to the origin of a thing or its mode of production. —**genetically,** je•net′i•kal•li, *adv.*— **genetics,** je•net′iks, *n.* The scientific study of heredity.

geneva, je•nē′va, *n.* [From L. *juniperus,* juniper; *gin* is a contraction of this.] A spirit distilled from grain or malt, with the addition of juniper berries; gin.

Genevan, je•nē′van, *a.* Pertaining to Geneva.—*n.* An inhabitant of Geneva; a Genevese; a Calvinist.

genial, jē′ni•al, *a.* [L. *genialis,* from *genius,* social disposition, genius, from root *gen.* GENUS.] Characterized by kindly warmth of disposition and manners such as promotes cheerfulness on the part of others; cordial; kindly; sympathetically cheerful; enlivening; warming; contributing to life and cheerfulness (the *genial* sun).—**geniality, genialness,** jē•ni•al′i•ti, je′ni•al•nes, *n.* The state or quality of being genial; sympathetic cheerfulness or cordiality.—**genially,** jē′ni•al•li, *adv.* In a genial manner.

geniculate, je•nik′ū•lāt, *a.* [L. *geniculatus,* from *geniculum,* a knot or joint, from *genu,* the knee.] *Bot.* knee-jointed; having knots like knees. —**geniculation,** je•nik′ū•lā•shon, *n.* Knottiness; a knot or joint like a knee.

genie, jē′nē, *n.* pl. **genii,** je′nē•ī. [A form due to the influence of the word *genius.*] Same as *Jinni.*

genipap, jen′i•pap, *n.* [From *genipapo,* the name in Guiana.] The fruit of a South American and West Indian tree of the Madder family, about the size of an orange.

genital, jen′i•tal, *a.* [L. *genitalis,* from *gigno, genitum,* to beget. GENUS.] Relating to generation; of, or pertaining to, the sexual organs.— **genitals,** jen′i•talz, *n.* pl. The reproductive organs, especially the external sexual organs.—**genitalia,** jen•i•tāl′ia, *n.* pl. The genitals.

genitive, jen′i•tiv, *a.* [L. *genitivus,* relating to birth or origin, from *gigno, genitum,* to beget.] *Gram.* a term applied to a case in the declension of nouns, adjectives, pronouns, etc., in English called the possessive case.—*n. Gram.* the genitive case.— **genitival,** jen•i•ti′val, *a.* Relating to the genitive.

genius, jē′ni•us, *n.* [L., a genius or tutelary spirit, social disposition, wit or genius, from the root *gen,* to beget. GENUS.] A tutelary deity; an imaginary being ruling or protecting men, places, or things; a good or evil spirit supposed to be attached to a person; that disposition or bent of mind which is peculiar to every man, and which qualifies him for a particular employment; intellectual endowment of the highest kind, particularly, the power of invention or of producing original combinations; a man thus intellectually endowed; peculiar character or constitution; pervading spirit or influence from associations or otherwise (the special *genius* of a language). [Plural *Genii* meaning spirits, *Geniuses* meaning men.]

Genoese, jen′o•ēz, *a.* Relating to Genoa.—*n.* An inhabitant or the people of Genoa in Italy.

genocide, jen′o•sīd, *n.* [Gr. *genos,* race, plus *cide.*] The use of calculated, systematic means to bring about the extermination of a racial, cultural, or political group.

genre, zhäṅr, *n.* [Fr., from L. *genus, generis,* kind.] *Painting,* a term applied to paintings which depict scenes of ordinary life, as domestic, rural, or village scenes.

gent, jent. A vulgar abbreviation for *Gentleman.*

genteel, jen•tēl′, *a.* [Fr. *gentil,* from L. *gentilis,* belonging to the same family or nation, not foreign, latterly also gentile or pagan, from *gens, gentis,* race, stock, family. GENUS. *Gentle* and *gentile* are doublets of this.] Having the manners of well-bred people; well-bred; refined; free from anything low or vulgar; of a station above the common people; furnishing a competence (a *genteel* allowance).—**genteelly,** jen•tēl′li, *adv.* In a genteel manner.—**genteelness,** jen•tēl′nes, *n.* The state or quality of being genteel.—**gentility,** jen•til′i•ti, *n.* The state or character of being genteel; the manners or circumstances of genteel people.

gentian, jen′shi•an, *n.* [L. *gentiana*— said to be named after *Gentius,* king of Illyria, who first experienced the virtue of gentian.] The name of certain bitter herbaceous plants with beautiful blue or yellow flowers, the roots of some species being highly valued as a tonic.

gentile, jen′tīl, *n.* [L. *gentilis,* from *gens, gentis,* nation, race. GENTEEL.] *Scrip.* any one belonging to the non-Jewish nations; any person not a Jew or a Christian; a heathen; applied by Mormons to those outside their sect.—*a.* Belonging to the non-Jewish nations; *gram.* denoting one's race or country (a *gentile* noun).— **gentilism,** jen′tīl•ism, *n.* Heathenism; paganism.

gentility. See GENTEEL.

gentle, jen′tl, *a.* [Fr. *gentil.* GENTEEL.] Well-born; of a good family; soft and refined in manners; mild; meek; not rough, harsh, or severe; not wild, turbulent, or refractory; placid; bland; not rude or violent.— *n.* A person of good birth; a gentleman.—**gentleness,** jen′tl•nes, *n.* The state or quality of being gentle.— **gently,** jen′tli, *adv.* In a gentle manner; mildly; meekly; placidly.— **gentlefolk,** jen′tl•fōk, *n.* Persons of good breeding and family: generally in plural, *gentlefolks.*—**gentleman,** jen′tl•man, *n.* [*Gentle,* that is, well-born, and *man*; Fr. *gentilhomme.* GENTEEL.] A man of good family or good social position; in a somewhat narrow and technical sense, any man above the rank of yeomen, including noblemen; in a more limited sense, a man who without a title bears a coat of arms; as commonly applied, any man whose education, occupation, or income raises him above menial service or an ordinary trade; a man of good breeding and politeness, as distinguished from the vulgar and clownish; a man of the highest honor, courtesy, and morality, often used almost as a polite equivalent for 'man': in the plural the appellation by which men are addressed in popular assemblies, whatever may be their condition or character.—**gentlemanly, gentlemanlike,** jen′tl•men•li, jen′tl•men•līk, *a.* Pertaining to or becoming a gentleman; like a gentleman.—**gentleman-at-arms,** *n.* One of forty gentlemen attached to the English court whose office it is to attend the sovereign to and from the chapel-royal, etc.—**gentlewoman,** jen′tl•wụm•an, *n.* A woman of good family or of good breeding; a woman above the vulgar; a woman who waits about the person of one of high rank.

gentry, jen′tri, *n.* [O.Fr. *genterise,* for *gentilise,* high birth, from *gentil,* L. *gentilis.* GENTEEL.] Rank or good birth (*Shak.*)‡; courtesy (*Shak.*)‡; *pl.* people of good position; wealthy or well-born people in general, of a rank below the nobility; also ironically applied to disreputable characters.

genuflect, jen′ū•flekt, *v.i.* [L. *genu,* the knee, and *flecto,* to bend, as in *inflect, reflect,* etc.] To kneel, as in worship, to make a genuflection or genuflections.—**genuflection, genuflexion,** jen•ū•flek′shon, *n.* The act of bending the knee, particularly in worship.

genuine, jen′ū•in, *a.* [L. *genuinus,* from root of *gigno,* to beget. GENUS.] Belonging to the original stock; hence, real; natural; true; pure; not spurious, false, or adulterated. ∴ Syn. under AUTHENTIC.—**genuinely,** jen′ū•in•li, *adv.* In a genuine manner.—**genuineness,** jen′ū•in•nes, *n.* The state of being genuine.

genus, jē′nus, *n.* pl. **genera** or **genuses,** jen′ėr•a, jē′nus•ez. [L. *genus, generis,* a kind, class = Gr. *genos,* race, family; from root *gen,* Skr. *jan,* to beget, the same as in E. *kin, kind.* This root is seen in a great many words: *generous, genesis, genial, genital, genuine, indigenous, ingenious, progeny,* etc.] A kind, class, or sort; *logic,* a class of a greater extent than a species; a word which may be predicated of several things of different species; in *scientific classifications,* an assemblage of species possessing certain characters in common, by which they are distinguished: subordinate to *phylum, class, order, family.*

geocentric, geocentrical, jē•ō•sen′trik, jē•ō•sen′tri•kal, *a.* [Gr. *gē,* earth, and *kentron,* center.] *Astron.* having reference to the earth for its center; seen from the earth: applied to the place of a planet as seen from the center of the earth.

geochemistry, jē•ō•kem′ist-ri, *n.* [Gr. *ge,* earth, and E. chemistry (which see).] The chemical study of the earth; combining parts of geology and chemistry, a study of the elements in the earth, in its waters, and in its atmosphere.

geode, jē′ōd, *n.* [Gr. *geōdes,* earthy, from *gē,* earth.] *Mineral,* a roundish hollow lump of agate or other mineral, having the cavity frequently lined with crystals.

geodesy, jē•od′e•si, *n.* [Gr. *geōdaisia*—*gē,* the earth, and *daiō,* to divide.] That branch of applied mathematics which determines the figures and areas of large portions of the earth's surface, the general figure of the earth, and the variations of the intensity of gravity in different regions.—**geodesic,** jē•o•des′ik, *a.* Shaped like a dome from a basic framework of polygonal sections in tension.—*n.* The shortest line between any two points on a mathematically defined surface.—**geodesical,** jē•o•des′i•kal, *a.*—**geodetic, geodetical,** jē•o•det′ik, jē•o•det′i•kal, *a.* Of or pertaining to geodesy.

geognosy, jē•og′no•si, *n.* [Gr. *gē,* the earth, and *gnōsis,* knowledge.] That part of natural science which treats of the structure of the earth—a term nearly equivalent to *geology,* but having less to do with scientific reasoning and theory.

geography, jē•og′ra•fi, *n.* [Gr. *geōgraphia*—*gē,* the earth, and *graphē,* description.] The science or branch of knowledge which treats of the world and its inhabitants, describing more especially the external features of the world, and in its widest scope embracing *mathematical geography,* which deals with the figure and measurement of the earth, latitude and longitude, etc.; *physical geography,* which describes the earth's features and explains their relations to each other, treating also of climate, animals, and plants, and their distribution; the ocean and its phenomena, etc.; and *political geography,* which treats of the states and peoples of the earth and their political and social characteristics; a description of the earth or a certain portion of it; a book containing such a description.—**geographer,** jē•og′ra•fėr, *n.* One who is versed in, or compiles a treatise on, geography.—**geographic, geographical,** jē•o•graf′ik, jē•o•graf′i•kal, *a.* Relating to geography; containing information regarding geography.—**geographically,** jē•o•graf′i•kal•li, *adv.* In a geographical manner.

geology, jē•ol′o•ji, *n.* [Gr. *gē,* the earth, and *logos,* discourse.] The science which deals with the structure, especially the internal structure, of the crust of the globe, and of the substances which compose it; the science which treats of the minerals, rocks, earths, or other substances composing the globe, the relations which the several constituent masses bear to each other, their formation, structure, position, and history, together with the successive changes that have taken place in the organic and inorganic kingdoms of nature as illustrated by fossils or otherwise.—**geologic, geological,** jē•o•loj′ik, jē•o•loj′i•kal, *a.* Pertaining to geology.—**geologically,** jē•o•loj′i•kal•li, *adv.* In a geological manner.—**geologist,** jē•ol′o•jist, *n.* One versed in geology.—**geologize,** jē•ol′o•jīz, *v.i.* To study geology; to make geological investigations.

geomancy, jē′o•man•si, *n.* [Gr. *gē,* the earth, and *manteia,* divination.] A kind of divination by means of figures or lines formed by little dots or points, originally on the earth and afterward on paper.—**geomancer,** jē′o•man•sėr, *n.* One versed in or who practices geomancy.—**geomantic,** jē•o•man′tik, *a.* Of or pertaining to geomancy.

geometry, jē•om′e•tri, *n.* [Gr. *geōmetria, gē,* the earth, and *metron,* measure—the term being originally equivalent to landmeasuring or surveying.] The science of magnitude; that science which treats of the properties of lines, angles, surfaces, and solids; that branch of mathematics which treats of the properties and relations of magnitudes.—**geometric, geometrical,** jē•ō•met′rik, jē•ō•met′ri•kal, *a.* [Gr. *geōmetrikos.*] Pertaining to geometry; according to the rules or principles of geometry; done or determined by geometry.—*Geometrical elevation,* a design for the front or side of a building drawn according to the rules of geometry, as opposed to *perspective* or *natural elevation.*—*Geometrical progression,* progression in which the terms increase or decrease by a common ratio, as 2, 4, 8, 16, etc.—*Geometrical proportion,* proportion involving equal ratios in the two parts—1:3::4:12.—**geometrically,** jē•o•met′ri•kal•li, *adv.* In a geometrical manner.—**geometrician, geometer,** jē•om′e•trish•an, jē•om′e•tėr, *n.* One skilled in geometry.

geophagism, jē•of′a•jizm, *n.* [Gr. *gē,* the earth, and *phagō,* to eat.] The act or practice of eating earth, as clay, chalk, etc.—**geophagist,** jē•of′a•jist, *n.* One who eats earth.

geophysics, jē′o•fiz″iks, *n.* The physics of the earth, particularly the use of instruments such as the seismograph and magnetometer to study the inaccessible portions of the earth.

geoponic, jē•o•pon′ik, *a.* [Gr. *gē,* the earth, and *ponos,* labor.] Pertaining to tillage or agriculture.—**geoponics,** jē•o•pon′iks, *n.* The art or science of cultivation.

George, jorj, *n.* [This proper name is from Gr. *geōrgos,* a husbandman—*gē,* the earth, and *ergon,* labor.] A figure of St. George on horseback encountering the dragon, worn pendent from the collar by knights of the Garter.—*St. George,* the patron saint of England, supposed to be martyred in A.D. 303 under Diocletian.—*St. George's Cross,* the English flag, a red cross on a white ground, opposed to the St. Andrew's Cross of Scotland, a silver saltire on a blue ground.—**Georgian,** jor′ji•an, *a.* Belonging or relating to the reigns of the four *Georges*, kings of Great Britain; a native of Georgia in the United States, or of Georgia in the Caucasus.—**georgic,** jor′jik, *n.* [Gr. *geōrgikos*, rustic.] A rural poem; a poetical composition on the subject of husbandry.—**Georgics,** *n.* Poem in four books by Virgil.

geothermal, jē•o•thėr′mal, *a.* [Gr. *gē* plus *thermal.*] Of, or relating to, the heat of the earth's interior.

geotropism, jē•ot′ro•pizm, *n.* [Gr. *gē*, the earth, and *tropos*, a turning.] Disposition or tendency to turn or incline toward the earth, the characteristic exhibited in a young plant when deprived of light.—**geotropic,** jē•ō•trop′ik, *a.* Pertaining to or exhibiting geotropism.

gerah, gē′ra, *n.* [Heb.] The smallest piece of money among the ancient Jews, equal to about three halfpennies.

geranium, je•rā′ni•um, *n.* [L. *geranium*, Gr. *geranion*, from *geranos*, a crane—on account of the long projecting spike of the seed capsule.] The crane's-bill genus, a genus of herbaceous plants (rarely undershrubs), natives of the temperate regions of the world, having flowers which are usually blue or red, and often handsome; the geraniums of gardens belong, however, to a different genus (*Pelargonium*).

gerbil, jėr′bil, *n.* [Fr. *gerbille*, from *gerbo*, the Arabic name.] A small burrowing rodent found in the sandy parts of Africa and Asia, one species, inhabiting Egypt, being about the size of a mouse.

gerfalcon, jėr′fa̤•kn, *n.* See GYRFALCON.

geriatrics, jer•i•at′riks, *n.* [Gr. *geras*, old age, and *iatrics.*] A field of medicine concerned with old age and its health problems.

germ, jėrm, *n.* [Fr. *germe*, L. *germen*, an offshoot, a sprout.] A microorganism causing disease; *physiol.* the earliest form under which any organism appears; the rudimentary or embryonic form of an organism; hence, that from which anything springs; origin; first principle.—**germ cell,** *n. Animal physiol.* the cell which results from the union of the spermatozoon with the germinal vesicle or its nucleus.—**germinal,** jėr′mi•nal, *a.* Pertaining to a germ or seed bud.—*Germinal vesicle, animal physiol.* a cell which floats in the yoke of an egg; *bot.* a cell contained in the embryo sac, from which the embryo is developed.—**germinal disk,** jėr′min•al disk, *n.* In large eggs full of nutritive matter (e.g., those of birds), the part which develops into the body of the embryo.—**germinate,** jėr′mi•nāt, *v.i.*—*germinated, germinating.* To sprout; to bud; to shoot; to begin to vegetate, as a plant or its seed.—*v.t.* To cause to sprout or bud.—**germination,** jėr•mi•nā′shon, *n.*—**germinative,** jėr′mi•nā•tiv, *a.*

german, jėr′man, *a.* [L. *germanus*, a brother, for *germinanus*, from *germen*, an offshoot. GERM.] Sprung from the same father and mother or from members of the same family; germane‡.—**germane,** jėr′mān, *a.* Closely akin; nearly related; allied; relevant; pertinent.

German, jėr′man, *n.* [L. *Germanus*, German, *Germani*, the Germans, not a native German appellation, but probably borrowed by the Romans from the Celts; of doubtful origin.] A native or inhabitant of Germany; the language of the higher and more southern districts of Germany, and the literary language of all Germany, called by the people themselves *Deutsch* (=*Dutch*), and also known as *High German*, to distinguish it from the *Low German*, or vernacular of the lowland or northern parts of Germany. See also DUTCH.—*a.* Belonging to Germany.—**Germanic,** jėr•man′ik, *a.* Pertaining to Germany; a name of certain languages otherwise called *Teutonic.*—**Germanism,** jėr′man•izm, *n.* An idiom or phrase of the German language.—**German silver,** *n.* A white alloy of nickel, formed by fusing together 100 parts of copper, 60 of zinc, and 40 of nickel.—**German tinder,** *n.* Amadou.

germander, jėr•man′dėr, *n.* [Fr. *germandrée*, corrupted from L. *chamædrys*, Gr. *chamaidrys*, germander—*chamai*, on the ground, and *drys*, an oak.] The common name of certain labiate plants, a few species of which are common in Britain.—*Germander speedwell.* SPEEDWELL.

germanium, jur•mā′ni•um, *n.* [From *Germany.*] A rare grayish-white metallic element. Symbol, Ge; at. no., 32; at. wt., 72.59.

germicide, jėr′mi•sīd, *n.* [E. *germ*, L. *cædo*, I kill.] A substance that destroys germs, especially disease germs.

germ plasm, jėrm′plazm, *n.* [From *germ* and Gr. *plasma*, anything formed.] A hypothetical constituent of the nucleus in a sex cell, by which hereditary characters are supposed to be transmitted.

gerontocracy, jer•on•tok′ra•si, *n.* [Gr. *gerōn, gerontos*, an old man, and *kratos*, power.] Government by old men.

gerrymander, ger′i•man″dėr, *v.i.* [From *Gerry*, governor of Massachusetts.] To divide a state into election districts in an unfair way.

gerund, jer′und, *n.* [L. *gerundium*, from *gero*, to carry on or perform, the gerund expressing the doing or the necessity of doing something.] A part of the Latin verb, or a kind of verbal noun, used to express the meaning of the present infinitive active; a term adopted into other languages to indicate various forms or modifications of the verb, in English being applied to verbal nouns such as *teaching* in expressions like *fit for teaching boys.*—**gerundial,** je•run′di•al, *a.*—**gerundive,** je•run′div, *n.* A name given originally by Latin grammarians to the future participle passive, a form similar to the gerund, sometimes used in regard to other languages.

gestalt, ge•shta̤lt′, *n.* [G. *gestalt*, form.] An organized pattern of experiences or acts; *psychol.* the theory that acts or experiences do not occur through the summation of separate elements, such as reflexes, but rather through the formed patterns or configurations of these called *Gestalten*, which operate individually or interact.

gestation, jes•tā′shon, *n.* [L. *gestatio*, from *gesto, gestatum*, freq. from *gero*, *gestum*, to carry, seen also in *gesture, gesticulate, congest, digest, suggestion*, etc.] The act of carrying young in the womb from conception to delivery; pregnancy.—**gestic,**† jes′tik, *a.* [From old *gest*, a deed or exploit; L. *gestum*, from *gero.*] Pertaining to deeds or exploits. (*Goldsmith.*)

gesticulate, jes•tik′ū•lāt, *v.i.*—*gesticulated, gesticulating.* [L. *gesticulor, gesticulatus*, from *gero, gestum*, to bear or carry. GESTATION.] To make gestures or motions, as in speaking; to use postures.—*v.t.*† To represent by gesture.—**gesticulation,** jes•tik′-ū•lā″shon, *n.* [L. *gesticulatio.*] The act of gesticulating or making gestures; a gesture.—**gesticulator,** jes•tik′ū•lā•tėr, *n.* One that gesticulates.—**gesticulatory,** jes•tik′ū•la•to•ri, *a.* Pertaining to gesticulation.

gesture, jes′chėr, *n.* [L.L. *gestura*, mode of acting, from L. *gestus*, posture, motion, from *gero, gestum*, to bear, to carry. GESTATION.] A motion or action intended to express an idea or feeling, or to enforce an argument or opinion; movement of the body or limbs.—*v.t. gestured, gesturing.* To express by gesture.—*v.i.* To make gestures.

get, get, *v.t.* pret. *got* (*gat*, obs.), pp. *got, gotten*, ppr. *getting.* [A.Sax. *gitan*, to obtain; Icel. *geta*, O.H.G. *gezan*, Goth. *gitan*; probably of same root as Gr. *chandanō*, to contain, L. (*pre*)*hendo*, to catch, as in *comprehend*. Hence *beget, forget.*] To procure; to obtain; to gain possession of by any means; to beget; to procreate; to commit to memory; to learn; to prevail on; to induce; to persuade; to procure or cause to be or occur (to *get* a letter sent, to *get* things together); *refl.* to carry or betake one's self.—*To get in*, to collect and bring under cover.—*To get off*, to put or be able to put off; to take off.—*To get on*, to be able to put on; to draw or pull on.—*To get out*, to draw or be able to draw forth.—*v.i.* To make acquisition; to gain; to arrive at any place or state; to become, followed by some modifying word, and sometimes implying difficulty or labor.—*To get above*, to surmount; to surpass.—*To get along*, to proceed; to advance.—*To get at*, to reach; to make way to; to come to.—*To get away*, to depart; to leave; to disengage one's self.—*To get back*, to arrive at the place from which one departed; to return.—*To get before*, to advance to the front or so as to be before.—*To get behind*, to fall in the rear; to lag.—*To get clear*, to disengage one's self; to be released.—*To get down*, to descend; to come from an elevation.—*To get* *drunk*, to become intoxicated.—*To get forward*, to proceed; to advance; also, to prosper.—*To get home*, to arrive at one's dwelling.—*To get in*, to obtain admission; to insinuate one's self.—*To get loose* or *free*, to disengage one's self; to be released from confinement.—*To get off*, to escape; to depart; to get clear; to alight or come down from a thing.—*To get on*, to proceed; to advance; to succeed; to prosper; to mount.—*To get out*, to depart from an enclosed place or from confinement; to escape; to free one's self from embarrassment.—*To get over*, to pass over; to surmount; to conquer; to recover from.—*To get quit of, to get rid of*, to shift off, or to disengage one's self from.—*To get through*, to pass through and reach a point beyond; also, to finish; to accomplish.—*To get to*, to reach; to arrive at.—*To get up*, to rise from a bed or a seat; to ascend; to climb; to originate and prepare or bring forward (to *get up* a concert); to dress; to equip (the actor was well *got up*).—**getter,** get′ėr, *n.* One who gets; one who begets†.—**getting,** get′ing, *n.* The act of obtaining; acquisition.—**getup,** *n.* Equipment; dress and other accessories (an actor's *getup*); initiative.

gewgaw, gū′ga, *n.* [Origin unknown.] A showy trifle; a bauble.

geyser, gī′zėr, *n.* [Icel. *geysir*, lit. the gusher, from *geysa*, to gush; allied to E. *gush*.] The name given to springs or fountains of hot water characterized by periodic eruptions, the water rising up in a column.

g-force, jē′fors, *n.* [*Gravity* and *force*.] *Phys.* gravitational pull equal to the force exerted on a body at rest, used to indicate the pull acting on a body when the body is accelerated.

ghastly, gast′li, *a.* [A.Sax. *gaestlic*, terrible, *gaest* being the same as *ghast* in *aghast*. AGHAST.] Terrible of countenance; deathlike; dismal; horrible; shocking; dreadful.—*adv.* In a ghastly manner; hideously.

ghat, ghaut, gät, gạt, *n.* [Hind.] In the East Indies, a pass through a mountain; a range or chain of hills; a landing place or stairway to the rivers of India.—**ghat.** As at Cal*cutta*, Cali*cut*, to the shrines of the goddess *Kali*.

Gheber, Ghebre, gā′bėr, *n.* The name given by the Mohammedans to one belonging to the Persian fire worshipers, called in India, Parsees.

ghee, gē, *n.* [Hind.] In India, the butter made from the milk of the buffalo converted into a kind of oil.

gherkin, gėr′kin, *n.* [G. *gurke*, D. *agurkje*, Dan. *agurke*, from Ar. *al-khiyâr*, Per. *khiyâr*, cucumber.] A small-fruited variety of the cucumber used for pickling.

ghetto, get′to, *n.* [It. *borghetto*, *borgo*, borough.] Jewish pen or quarter, a Jewry; the quarter, closed and locked at night, in Italian and Rhine-valley towns, in which Jews lived.

ghost, gōst, *n.* [A.Sax. *gást*, a spirit, a ghost; D. *geest*, G. *geist*, a spirit; from a root seen in Icel. *geisa*, to chafe, to rage as fire; Sw. *gasa*, to ferment; E. *yeast*.] The soul or spiritual part of man‡; the visible spirit of a dead person; a disembodied spirit; an apparition; shadow (not the *ghost* of a chance).—*To give up the ghost*, to yield up the spirit; to die.—*The Holy Ghost*, the third person in the Trinity.—**ghostlike,** gōst′līk, *a.* Like a ghost; spectral.—**ghostliness,** gōst′li•nes, *n.* The state or quality of being ghostly.—**ghostly,** gost′li, *a.* Having to do with the soul or spirit; spiritual; not carnal or secular; pertaining to apparitions (a *ghostly* visitant); suggestive of ghosts (*ghostly* gloom).

ghoul, göl, *n.* [Per. *ghûl*, a kind of demon supposed to devour men.] An imaginary evil being among eastern nations, which is supposed to prey upon human bodies.

ghyll, gil, *n.* Same as *Gill*, a ravine.

giant, jī′ant, *n.* [O.E. *geant*, Fr. *géant*, from L. *gigas*, *gigantis*, from Gr. *gigas*, *gigantos*, a giant, formed by reduplication of root *gan*, *gen*, to produce.] A man of extraordinary bulk and stature; a person of extraordinary strength or powers, bodily or intellectual.—*a.* Like a giant; extraordinary in size or strength.—**giantess.** jī′an•tes, *n.* A female giant.

gibber, jib′ėr, *v.i.* [Akin to *jabber* and *gabble*, perhaps also to *gibe*.] To speak rapidly and inarticulately; to gabble or jabber.—**gibberish,** jib′ėr•ish, *n.* Rapid and inarticulate talk; unintelligible language.

gibberellin, jib•er•el′in, *n.* [From *Gibberella*, genus name of *Gibberella fujikuroi* plus *in*.] A substance obtained from the fungus *Gibberella fujikuroi* and having plant growth-stimulating hormones.

gibbet, jib′et, *n.* [Fr. *gibet*, O.Fr. *gibbet*; comp. O.Fr. *gibet*, a large stick.] A kind of gallows; a gallows with a crossbeam or an arm projecting from the top, on which notorious malefactors were hanged; the projecting beam or jib of a crane.—*v.t.* To hang on a gibbet or gallows; to hold up to ridicule, scorn, infamy, etc.

gibbon, gib′on, *n.* A name of various apes of the Indian Archipelago, slender in form and with very long arms.

gibbous, gib′us, *a.* [L. *gibbosus*, from *gibbus*, humped, a hump.] Swelling out or protuberant; exhibiting a sort of hump or convex swelling; hunched: applied to the moon when more than half and less than full; *bot.* more convex or tumid in one place than another.—**gibbose,** gib•ōs′, *a.* Humped; having humps; gibbous.—**gibbosity,** gib•os′i•ti, *n.* The state of being gibbous or gibbose; a protuberance or round swelling prominence; convexity. — **gibbousness,** gib′us•nes, *n.*

gibe, jīb, *v.i.*—*gibed*, *gibing*. [From the same root as *gab*, the mouth, *gabble*, *jabber*, etc.; comp. Sw. *gipa*, to wry the mouth.] To utter taunting sarcastic words; to flout; to fleer.—*v.t.* To assail with contemptuous words; to mock; to flout; to treat with sarcastic reflections; to taunt.—*n.* A taunt or sarcastic remark; a mocking jest; a scoff.—**giber,** jī′bėr, *n.* One who gibes.

giblets, jib′lets, *n. pl.* [O.Fr. *gibelet*, a dish of game.] The entrails of a goose or other fowl removed before roasting; rags or tatters†.

giddy, gid′i, *a.* [A.Sax. *gydig*, insane, from *god*, a god, a heathen deity.] Having in the head a sensation of a whirling or reeling about; affected with vertigo; dizzy, reeling; rendering giddy; inducing giddiness (a *giddy* height); suggestive of giddiness from its motion; whirling; inconstant; changeable; flighty; thoughtless; rendered wild by excitement; having the head turned.—*v.t.*—*giddied*, *giddying*. To make giddy.—*v.i.* To turn quickly; to reel.—**giddily,** gid′i•li, *adv.* In a giddy manner.—**giddiness,** gid′i•nes, *n.* The state of being giddy.

gier-eagle, gēr′ē•gl, *a.* [D. *gier*, G. *geier*, a vulture.] A kind of eagle. (O.T.)

gift, gift, *n.* [A.Sax. *gift*, from *gifan*, to give. GIVE.] That which is given or bestowed; a present; a donation; the act, right, or power of giving (it is not in his *gift*); a natural quality or endowment regarded as conferred; power; faculty; talent. *v.t.* To confer as a gift; to make a gift or present to; to endow.—**gifted,** gif′ted, *pp.* or *a.* Endowed by nature with any power or faculty; largely endowed with intellect or genius; talented.

gig, gig, *n.* [Origin doubtful; comp. *jig*.] Any little thing that is whirled round in play; a whirligig (*Shak.*); a light one-horse carriage with two wheels; a long narrow rowing boat; a ship's boat suited for rowing expeditiously, and generally furnished with sails; a machine for teazling woolen cloth; a kind of harpoon.

gigantic, jī•gan′tik, *a.* [L. *giganticus*, from *gigas*, a giant. GIANT.] Of the size or proportions of a giant; colossal; huge; enormous; immense.—**gigantically,** jī•gan′tik•a•li, *adv.*—**gigantism,** jī•gan′tizm, *n.* The state of being a giant; excessive largeness.

giggle, gig′l, *n.* [Imitative, like *cackle*; D. *gicken*, *gickelen*, to cackle; Swiss *gigelen*, to giggle.] A kind of laugh, with short catches of the voice or breath; a titter.—*v.i.*—*giggled*, *giggling*. To laugh with short catches of the breath or voice; to titter.—**giggler,** gig′lėr, *n.* One that giggles.—**giggling,** gig′ling, *a.* Characterized by giggles; tittering.—**giglet, giglot,** gig′let, gig′lot, *n.* [From *giggle*, or from *gig* with a diminutive termination.] A light giddy girl; a wanton.—*a.* Giddy; inconstant; wanton (*Shak.*).

gigot, jig′ot, *n.* [Fr., from O.Fr. *gigue*, the thigh, a fiddle, from O.G. *gîge*, G. *geige*, a violin, from its shape.] A leg of mutton.

gilbert, gil′bert, *n.* [After the natural philosopher *Gilbert*.] The C.G.S. unit of magnetomotive force.

gild, gild, *v.t.*—pret. and pp. *gilded* or *gilt*. [A.Sax. *gyldan*, from *gold*.] To overlay with gold, either in leaf or powder, or in amalgam with quicksilver; to give a golden hue to;

to illuminate; to brighten; to render bright; to give a fair and agreeable external appearance to.—**gilded,** *a.* *Gilded chamber*, the House of Lords. —*Gilded youth*, wealthy young people; fashionables. [Fr. *jeunesse dorée.*] **gilder,** gil′dėr, *n.* One who gilds.—**gilding,** gil′ding, *n.* The art of a gilder; what is laid on by the gilder; a thin coating of gold leaf; *fig.* fair superficial show.

gild, gild, *n.* Same as *Guild.*

gilder, gil′dėr, *n.* A Dutch coin; a guilder.

gill, gil, *n.* [Not in A.Sax. or German; a Scandinavian word: Dan. *giaelle*, Sw. *gäl*, *fisk-gel*, a fish gill; comp. Gael. *gial*, a jaw, a gill.] The respiratory organ of fishes and other animals which breathe the air that is mixed in water.—*Gill arches and clefts*, in fishes, etc., those visceral arches and clefts (which see) related to gills; *pl.* the flap that hangs below the beak of a fowl; the flesh under or about a person's chin; the radiating plates on the under side of a fungus.

gill, jil, *n.* [O.Fr. *gelle*, a wine measure; akin to *gallon.*] A measure of capacity containing the fourth part of a pint.

gill, gil, *n.* [Icel. *gil*, a ravine.] A ravine or chasm in a hill; a brook.

gillie, gil′i, *n.* [Gael. *gillie*, a boy, a gillie. In the Highlands an outdoor male servant, especially one who attends a person while hunting.

gillyflower, jil′i•flou•ėr, *n.* [Formerly *gilofer*, from Fr. *giroflée*, from L. *caryophyllus*, Gr. *karyophyllon*, the clove tree—*karyon*, a nut, and *phyllon*, a leaf.] The popular name given to certain plants, as the pink or clove pink. CLOVE.

gilt, gilt, pp. of *gild.* Overlaid with gold.—*n.* Gold laid on the surface of a thing; gilding.—**gilt-edged securities.** Favored as safe by trustees, brokers, and bankers.—**gilthead,** *n.* The name of two fishes.

gimbals, jim′bals, *n. pl.* [Formerly *gemmal*, *gimmal-ring*, from Fr. *gemelle*, from L. *gemellus*, twin, paired, double, from *geminus*, twin.] A contrivance consisting usually of two movable hoops or rings, supported upon horizontal pivots, the one moving within the other about two axes at right angles to each other and in the same plane; a contrivance such as supports the mariner's compass and causes it to assume a constantly vertical position.

gimcrack, jim′krak, *n.* [Probably from Prov.E. *gimp*, *gim*, neat, spruce, and old *crack*, a pert boy; originally applied to a boy.] A trivial piece of mechanism; a toy; a pretty thing.

gimlet, gim′let, *n.* [O.Fr. *guimbelet*, a bore.] A small instrument with a pointed screw at the end, for boring holes in wood by turning.—*v.t.* To use a gimlet upon.

gimmick, gim′ik, *n.* A device which can secretly and dishonestly be used to control a gambling apparatus; a novel idea or unconventional approach to a problem.—*v.t.* To alter by means of a gimmick.

gimp, gimp, *n.* [Origin unknown.] A narrow, ornamental twist of silk used for trimming dresses, furniture, etc.; a limping walk; a cripple.

gin, jin, *n.* [A contr. of *Geneva.*] Spirits distilled with juniper berries, etc.

gin, jin, *n.* [A contr. of *engine.*] A trap or snare; a contrivance for raising weights, consisting of three upright poles meeting at top with block and tackle; a machine for separating the seeds from cotton; a machine for driving piles.—*v.t.*—*ginned*, *ginning*. To catch in a gin; to clear of seeds by the cotton gin.

ginger, jin′jėr, *n.* [O.Fr. *gengibre*, Fr. *gingembre*, from L. *zingiber*, ultimately from Skr. *cringa-vêra*—*cringa*, horn, *vêra*, shape.] The rhizome or underground stem of a perennial herb cultivated in most tropical countries, used in medicine and largely as a condiment.—*v.t.* To put life and vigor into.—**ginger ale,** *n.* A carbonated beverage, amber colored, flavored with ginger.—**ginger beer,** *n.* A white carbonated, nonalcoholic beverage differing from ginger ale principally in that bitters are used in the brewing of it.—**gingerbread,** *n.* A plain cake flavored with ginger, and usually sweetened with molasses; gaudy ornamentation.—**gingersnap,** *n.* A small, thin cooky flavored with ginger and molasses.

gingerly, jin′jėr•li, *adv.* [Connected with prov. *ging*, *gang*, to go.] Cautiously; daintily (to walk, to handle a thing *gingerly*).

gingham, ging′am, *n.* [From Malay *ginggang*, checkered cloth.] A kind of printed cotton cloth.

ginkgo, gingk′ō, *n.* [From Jap. *gingko.*] A tree with fan-shaped leaves and yellow fruit, native to eastern China and used as a temple tree.

ginseng, jin′seng, *n.* [Chinese name.] A name of two plants, the root of which is considered by the Chinese a panacea or remedy for all ailments.

gipsy, jip′si, *n.* See GYPSY.

giraffe, ji•raf′, *n.* [Fr. *girafe*, *giraffe*, Sp. *girafa*, from Ar. *zurafa*, said to mean longnecked.] The camelopard, a ruminant animal inhabiting Africa, the tallest of all animals (owing to the extraordinary length of the neck), a full-grown male reaching the height of 18 or 20 feet.

girandole, jir′an•dōl, *n.* [Fr., from It. *girandola*, from *girare*, to turn, from L. *gyrus*, a turn.] A chandelier; a kind of revolving firework.

girasole, jir′a•sōl, *n.* [Fr., from It. *girasole*—*girare*, to turn, L. *gyrus*, a turn, and *sole*, L. *sol*, the sun.] ARTICHOKE. *Jerusalem.* A plant, the European heliotrope or turnsole; a variety of opal showing a reddish color when turned toward the sun or any bright light.

gird, gėrd, *n.* [A.Sax. *gyrd*, a rod (whence also E. *yard*, a measure); D. *garde*, G. *gerte*, a twig, a switch.] A stroke with a switch or whip; a jibe.—*v.t.* To gibe; to lash.—*v.i.* To gibe; to utter severe sarcasms: with *at*.

gird, gėrd, *v.t.* pret. & pp. *girded* or *girt*. [A.Sax. *gyrdan*=Goth. *gairdan*, Icel. *gyrtha*, Dan. *giorde*, G. *gûrten*, to gird; akin *garth*, *girth*, *yard*, an enclosure.] To bind by surrounding with any flexible substance; to make fast by binding; to tie round; usually with *on*; to clothe, invest, or surround; to encircle; to encompass.—**girder,** gėr′dėr, *n.* One who girds; a main beam, either of wood or iron, resting upon a wall or pier at each end, employed for supporting a superstructure or a superincumbent weight.—**girdle,** gėr′dl, *n.* [A.Sax. *gyrdel*, from *gyrdan*, to gird; Sw. *gördel*, G. *gürtel.*] A band or belt for the waist; what girds or encloses. See GRIDDLE. (*Scottish.*)—*v.t.*—*girdled*, *girdling*. To bind with a girdle; to enclose or environ.

girl, gėrl, *n.* [Formerly applied to both sexes, and probably connected with L.G. *gör*, *göre*, a child; Swiss *gurre*, *gurrli*, depreciatory term for girl.] A female child; a female not arrived at puberty; sweetheart (*colloq.*); a young woman.—**girlhood,** gėrl′hụd, *n.* The state of being a girl; the earlier stage of maidenhood. —**girlish,** gėr′lish, *a.* Like or pertaining to a girl; befitting a girl.—**girlishly,** *adv.*—**girlishness,** *n.*—**Girl Scouts,** an organization for girls.

Girondist, ji•ron′dist, *n.* [Fr.] Member of the moderate Republican party formed in the French Legislative Assembly of 1791, and consisting of the Deputies for the Gironde district and their adherents.

girt, gėrt, pret. & pp. of *gird.*

girth, gėrth, *n.* [From *gird*, *v.t.*, or rather directly from Icel. *gerth*, *gjörth*, girth.] The band fastening the saddle on a horse's back; the measure round a person's body or anything cylindrical.—*v.t.* To bind with a girth.

gist, jist, *n.* [O.Fr. *giste*, a lying place, lodging, from *gesir*, L. *jacere*, to lie (as in *adjacent*).] The main point of a question or that on which it rests; the substance or pith of a matter.

gittern, git′ėrn, *n.* [O.D. *ghiterne*, from L. *cithara*, Gr. *kithari*, a kind of lyre.] An instrument of the guitar kind strung with wire; a cittern.

give, giv, *v.t.*—*gave* (pret.), *given* (pp.), *giving* (ppr.). [A.Sax. *gifan*= Dan. *give*, Icel. *gefa*, D. *geven*, G. *geben*, Goth. *giban*, to give; probably causative from same root as L. *habeo*, to have (whence *habit*, etc.)=to make to have.] To convey to another; to bestow; to communicate (an opinion, advice); to utter; to pronounce (a cry, the word of command); to grant; to cause or enable (he *gave* me to understand); to addict; often with *up*; to excite (to *give* offense); to pledge (one's word); to propose, as a toast; to ascribe; to pay; to yield, as a result or product.—*To give away*, to make over to another; to transfer.—*To give back*, to return; to restore.—*To give birth to*, to bring forth, as a child; to be the origin of.—*To give chase*, to pursue.—*To give ear*, to listen; to pay attention; to give heed.

—*To give forth*, to publish; to report publicly,—*To give ground*, to retire before an enemy; to yield.—*To give in*, to yield; to declare; to make known; to tender.—*To give the lie*, to charge with falsehood.—*To give over*, to leave; to cease; to abandon; to regard as past recovery.—*To give out*, to report; to decide, give the decision that the batsman is out; to proclaim; to publish; to issue; to declare or pretend to be; to emit; to distribute.—*To give place*, to retire so as to make room.—*To give tongue*, said of dogs, to bark.—*To give up*, to resign; to yield as hopeless; to surrender; to cede; to deliver or hand over.—*To give way*, to yield; to withdraw; to yield to force; to break or break down; *naut.* to row after ceasing, or to increase exertions.—*v.i.* To make gifts; to be liberal; to yield, as to pressure; to recede; to afford entrance or view; to face or be turned (as a house).—*To give in*, to give way; to yield; to confess one's self beaten.—*To give in to*, to yield assent to.—*To give out*, to cease from exertion; to yield.—*To give over*, to cease; to act no more.—**given,** giv'n, *p.* and *a.* Bestowed; conferred; admitted or supposed; addicted; disposed (much *given* to carping); *math.* supposed or held to be known.—**giver,** giv'ėr, *n.* One who gives.

gizzard, giz'ėrd, *n.* [Fr. *gésier*, O.Fr. *gezier*, from L. *gigeria*, entrails of poultry.] The second stomach of birds, having a thick, horny lining in which to grind food.

glabrous, glā'brus, *a.* [L. *glaber*, smooth.] Smooth; having a surface devoid of hair or pubescence.

glacial, glā'shi•al, *a.* [Fr., from L. *glacialis*, from *glacies*, ice.] Pertaining to ice or to the action of ice; pertaining to glaciers; icy; frozen; having a cold glassy look.—*Glacial period* or *epoch*, in *geol*, that interval of time in the later tertiary period during which both the arctic regions and a great part of the temperate regions were covered with a sheet of ice.—**glacialist,** glā'shi•al•ist, *n.* One who studies or writes on glacial phenomena.—**glaciate,** glā'shi•āt, *v.i.* To be converted into ice.—*v.t.* To convert into or cover with ice; to act upon by glaciers.—**glaciation,** glā'shi•ā'shon, *n.* The act of freezing; the process or result of glacial action on the earth's surface; the striation and smoothing of rock surfaces by glacial action.—**glacier,** glā'shi•ėr, *n.* [Fr., from *glace*, ice.] An immense accumulation of ice, or ice and snow, formed in lofty valleys above the line of perpetual congelation, and slowly moving downward into the lower valleys, reaching frequently to the borders of cultivation.—*Glacier snow*, the coarsely granular snow from which glaciers are formed; névé.—*Glacier tables*, large stones found on glaciers supported on pedestals of ice, formed by the melting away of the ice where it is not shaded from the sun by the stone.—*Glacier theory*, a theory in regard to glaciers; the theory attributing important geological changes (as the erosion of valleys) to the action of glaciers.

glacis, glā'sis, *n.* [Fr., from *glace*, ice—from the smoothness of its surface.] *Fort.* a sloping bank so raised as to bring the enemy advancing over it into the most direct line of fire from the fort.

glad, glad, *a.* [A.Sax. *glaed*, glad= Dan. *glad*, glad, D. *glad*, Icel. *glathr*, smooth. polished, cheerful; G. *glatt*, smooth. Allied to *glide* and to *glow*.] Affected with pleasure or satisfaction; pleased; joyful; gratified; well contented: often followed by *of* or *at*; cheerful; bright; wearing the appearance of joy (a *glad* countenance).—*v.t.*—*gladded, gladding.* To make glad; to gladden. (*Poet.*)—**gladden,** glad'n, *v.t.* To make glad; to cheer; to please; to exhilarate.—*v.i.* To become glad; to rejoice.—**gladly,** glad'li, *adv.* With pleasure; joyfully; cheerfully.—**gladness,** glad'nes, *n.* The state or quality of being glad.—**gladsome,** glad'sum, *a.* Glad; cheerful; causing joy, pleasure, or cheerfulness. (*Poet.*)

glade, glād, *n.* [Lit. a light or bright place, a glad place; Icel. *glathr*, bright, glad. GLAD.] An opening or passage through a wood; a kind of avenue in a wood or forest covered with grass.

gladiate, glad'i•āt, *a.* [L. *gladius*, a sword.] Sword-shaped.—**gladiator,** glad'i•ā•tėr, *n.* [L., from *gladius*, a sword.] Among the ancient Romans one who fought with deadly weapons in the amphitheater and other places for the entertainment of the people; hence, a combatant in general; a prizefighter; a disputant.—**gladiatorial,** glad'i•a•tō"ri•al, *a.* Pertaining to gladiators; pertaining to combatants in general who fight singly, as to disputants.—**gladiolus,** gla•dī'o•lus, glad•i•ō'lus, *n.* pl. **gladioli,** gla•dī'o•li, glad•i•ō'li, [L. *gladiolus* dim. of *gladius*, a sword, from their leaves.] An extensive and very beautiful genus of bulbous-rooted plants, found most abundantly in South Africa; sword lily.

glair, glâr, *n.* [Fr. *glaire*, from L. *clarus*, clear, the glair of an egg being the clear portion. CLEAR.] The white of an egg used as varnish to preserve paintings, and as a size in gilding; any similar substance.—*v.t.* To varnish or smear with glair.—**glairy,** glâ'ri, *a.*

glamour, glam'ėr, *n.* [A modified form of *glammar*—*grammar*—*gramarye*, having formerly meant learning, deep learning, magic.] A charm, as of manner, appearance and poise, endowing its owner with a mysterious, often illusory, fascination; a stirring attractiveness as of a person or a place.

glance, glans, *n.* [Same word as Sw. *glans*, Dan. *glands*, D. *glans*, G. *glanz*, luster, splendor; *glint. glitter, glisten, gleam*, etc., are connected.] A sudden dart or flash of light or splendor; a sudden look or darting of sight; a rapid or momentary casting of the eye; a name given to some minerals which possess a metallic luster.—*v.i.*—*glanced, glancing.* To shoot or dart rays of light or splendor; to emit flashes or coruscations of light; to flash; to fly off in an oblique direction; to strike or graze; to dart aside; to look with a sudden cast of the eye.—*v.t.* To shoot or dart suddenly, to cast for a moment (to *glance* the eye).

gland, gland, *n.* [L. *glans, glandis*, an acorn.] *Anat.* a distinct soft body, formed by the convolution of a great number of vessels, different glands having specialized secretions; *bot.* a secreting organ occurring on the epidermis of plants; also, a kind of one-celled fruit, with a dry pericarp.—**glanders,** glan'dėrz, *n.* A very dangerous and highly contagious disease, chiefly seen in horses, but capable of being transmitted to man, which especially affects the glands (whence the name), the mucous membrane of the nose, the lungs, etc.—**glandered,** glan'dėrd, *p.* and *a.* Affected with glanders.—**glandular,** glan'dū•lėr, *a.* Consisting of a gland or glands; pertaining to glands.—**glaudulous,** glan'dū•lus, *a.* [L. *glandulosus*.] Glandular.

glare, glâr, *n.* [Akin to A.Sax. *glaer*, amber; Dan. *glar*, Icel. *gler*, glass; L.G. *glaren*, to glow; E. *glass, glance, gleam*, etc.] A bright dazzling light; splendor that dazzles the eyes; a confusing and bewildering light; a fierce, piercing look.—*v.i.*—*glared, glaring.* To shine with a bright dazzling light; to look with fierce; piercing eyes; to have a dazzling effect; to be ostentatiously splendid.—*v.t.* To shoot out or emit, as a dazzling light.—**glaringness,** glâr'ing•nes, *n.* The state or quality of having a glaring appearance.—**glaring,** glâr'ing, *p.* and *a.* Shining with dazzling luster; excessively bright; vulgarly splendid; forcing one's notice; notorious; open; barefaced (a *glaring* crime).—**glaringly,** glâr'ing•li, *adv.* In a glaring manner.

glass, glas, *n.* [A.Sax. *glaes*; L.G. D.G. Sw. and Icel. *glas*: Icel. also *gler*; akin *glisten, glance, glare*, etc.] A hard, brittle, transparent artificial substance, formed by the fusion of siliceous matter (as powdered flint or fine sand) with some alkali; something made of glass; especially, a mirror or looking glass; a glass vessel filled with running sand for measuring time; a drinking vessel made of glass; the quantity which such a vessel holds (hence, *the glass*= strong drink); an optical instrument, such as a lens or a telescope; a barometer or thermometer; *pl.* spectacles.—*a.* Made of glass.—*v.t.* To reflect; to mirror; to cover with glass.—**glassful,** glas'fụl, *n.* As much as a glass will hold.—**glassily,** glas'i•li, *adv.* So as to resemble glass.—**glassiness,** glas'i•nes, *n.* The quality of being glassy.—**glassy,** glas'i, *a.* Made of glass; vitreous; resembling glass; having a luster or surface like glass.—**glass blower,** *n.* One whose business it is to blow and fashion vessels of glass.—**glasshouse,** *n.* A manufactory of glass; a house built largely of glass, as a conservatory or greenhouse.—**glass snake,** *n.* A North American lizard, so called from its brittleness.—**glassware,** *n.* Articles made of glass.—**glasswork,** *n.* Articles of or in glass; an establishment where glass is made.—**glasswort,** glas′wėrt, *n.* A name of various plants common on the Mediterranean coasts.

Glauber salt, gla̧′bėr sa̧lt, *n.* [After *Glauber* (died 1688), a German chemist, who first prepared it.] Sulfate of soda, a well-known cathartic.

glaucous, gla̧′kus, *a.* [L. *glaucus,* from Gr. *glaukos,* bluish-green or sea-green.] Of a sea-green color; of a light green or bluish green; *bot.* covered with a fine bluish or greenish powder or bloom.—**glaucoma,** gla̧•kō′ma, *n.* [Gr. *glaukōma,* from *glaukos,* sea-green.] A disease of the eye characterized by increased intraocular pressure and sudden or progressive loss of vision.—**glaucomatous,** gla̧•kō′ma•tus, *a.* Pertaining to or resembling glaucoma.

glaze, glāz, *v.t.*—*glazed, glazing.* [From *glass.*] To furnish with glass or panes of glass; to encrust or overlay with glass or a vitreous coating; to give a glossy, or smooth, shining surface to.—*v.i.* To assume a dim, glassy luster; said of the eye.—*n.* That which is used in glazing.—**glazer,** glā′zėr, *n.* One who or that which glazes.—**glazier,** glā′zhėr, *n.* One whose business is to fix panes of glass in windows, etc.—**glazing,** glā′zing, *n.* The act or art of one who glazes; the substance with which anything is overlaid to give it a glassy appearance; enamel; glaze; *paint.* transparent or semitransparent colors passed thinly over other colors, to modify the effect.

gleam, glēm, *n.* [A.Sax. *glaem,* a glittering; comp. O.Sax. *glimo,* splendor, Sw. *glimma,* to flash; allied to *glimmer, glow, glance,* etc.] A beam or flash of light; a ray; a small stream of light; brightness.—*v.i.* To dart or throw rays of light; to glimmer.—**gleamy,** glē′mi, *a.*

glean, glēn, *v.t.* [Fr. *glaner,* from L.L. *glenare,* to glean, from W. *glain, glân,* clean; comp. A.Sax. *gilm,* a handful.] To gather after a reaper, or on a reaped cornfield, the ears of grain left ungathered, hence, to collect in scattered portions; to gather slowly and assiduously.—*v.i.* To gather ears of grain left by reapers; to go through carefully, as a book or written speech, in order to extract bits of information.—**gleaner,** glē′nėr, *n.*

glebe, glēb, *n.* [Fr. *glèbe,* from L. *gleba,* a clod or lump of earth.] Soil; ground; earth; the land belonging to a parish church or ecclesiastical benefice.

glede, glēd, *n.* [A.Sax. *glida,* the kite, lit. glider, from its gliding flight. GLIDE.] A bird of prey.

glee, glē, *n.* [A.Sax. *gleō, gliw, glig,* music, sport; Icel. *gly,* laughter.] Joy; merriment; mirth; gaiety; a musical composition consisting of two or more contrasted movements, with the parts forming as it were a series of interwoven melodies.—**glee club.** A group organized for singing songs.—**gleeman,** glē′man, *n.* [A.Sax. *gleóman.*] A minstrel or musician of former days.—**gleeful, gleesome,** glē′fu̧l, glē′sum, *a.* Full of glee; merry; gay; joyous.

gleet, glēt, *n.* [O.Fr. *glette,* slime, phlegm; Sc. *glet, glit,* phlegm.] A transparent mucous discharge from the urethra, an effect of gonorrhea; a thin ichor running from a sore.

glen, glen, *n.* [Ir. and Gael. *gleann,* W. *glyn,* a glen.] A secluded narrow valley; a dale; a depression or space between hills.

Glengarry, *n.* Highland bonnet.

glenoid, glē′noid, *a.* [Gr. *glēnē,* the pupil, the eyeball.] *Anat.* a term applied to any shallow, articular cavity which receives the head of a bone.

glib, glib, *a.* [Comp. D. *glibberig,* smooth, slippery; *glibberen,* L.G. *glippen,* to slide; akin to *glide.*] Smooth; slippery; more commonly voluble; fluent; having words always ready.—**glibly,** glib′li, *adv.* In a glib manner; smoothly; volubly.—**glibness,** glib′nes, *n.*

glide, glīd, *v.i.*—*glided, gliding.* [A. Sax. *glidan*=Dan. *glide,* D. *glijden,* G. *gleiten,* to slide; allied to *glad.*] To flow gently; to move along silently and smoothly; to pass along without apparent effort (a river, a bird, a skater *glides*)—*v.i.* To fly on a descending path, when the aircraft is not under power.—*n.* A smooth, gliding step, as in dancing; act of moving smoothly or gliding.—**glider,** glī′dėr, *n.* One who glides; a form of aircraft similar to an airplane but lacking an engine.—**glidingly,** glī′ding•li, *adv.* In a gliding manner.

glimmer, glim′ėr, *v.i.* [A. freq. of *gleam*=Dan. *glimre,* to glitter, from *glimme,* to gleam; comp. G. *glimmer,* a faint light; *glimmen,* to shine.] To emit feeble or scattered rays of light; to shine faintly; to give a feeble light; to flicker.—*n.* A faint and unsteady light; feeble, scattered rays of light; glitter; twinkle; also, a name of mica.—**glimmering,** glim•-ėr•ing, *n.* A glimmer; a gleam; a faint indication; an inkling; a glimpse.

glimpse, glimps, *n.* [Formerly *glimse,* from the stem of *gleam, glimmer,* etc., the *p* being inserted as in *empty, sempstress,* etc. Comp. Swiss *glumsen,* to glow; D. *glimpen, glinsen,* to sparkle.] A gleam; a momentary flash; a short transitory view; a glance; a faint resemblance; a slight tinge.—*v.i.* —*glimpsed, glimpsing.* To appear by glimpses.—*v.t.* To see by a glimpse or glimpses.

glint, glint, *v.i.* [Of kindred origin with *glimpse, glimmer, glance,* etc.; comp. Dan. *glimt,* a gleam, *glimte,* to flash.] To glance; to gleam; to give a flash of light.—*n.* A glance; a flash; a gleam.

glissade, glis•äd′, *n.* [Fr. *glissade;* from *glisser,* to glide or slide.] A sliding or gliding down a slope.

glisten, glis′n, *v.i.* [A.Sax. *glisnian,* akin to G. *gleissen,* Icel. *glyssa,* O.G. *glizan,* to shine; same root as *glitter, gleam,* etc.] To shine; to sparkle with light; to shine with a scintillating light.—*n.*† Glitter; sparkle.—**glister,** glis′tėr, *v.i.* To shine; to glitter.—*n.* Luster; glitter.

glitter, glit′ėr, *v.i.* [A. freq. from stem *glit,* seen in A.Sax. *glitnian,* to glitter=Sw. *glittra,* Icel. *glitra* (from *glita,* to shine), G. *glitzern,* to shine; akin to *gleam, glance,* etc.] To shine with a broken and scattered light; to emit rapid flashes of light; to gleam; to sparkle; to glisten; to be showy or brilliant.—*n.* Bright sparkling light; brilliancy; splendor; luster.

gloaming, glōm′ing, *n.* [A.Sax. *glóm-ung,* twilight, from *glóm,* E. *gloom.*] Fall of the evening; the twilight; closing period; decline. [Scotch, but adopted by English writers.]

gloat, glot, *v.i.* [Allied to Sw. *glutta, glōtta,* to look at with prying eyes; G. *glotzen,* to stare.] To gaze with admiration, eagerness, or desire; to contemplate with evil satisfaction.

globe, glōb, *n.* [L. *globus,* a ball; Fr. *globe,* Sp. and It. *globo.*] A round or spherical solid body; a ball; a sphere; the earth; an artificial sphere on whose convex surface is drawn a map or representation of the earth (*a terrestrial globe*) or of the heavens (*a celestial globe*).—*v.t.* To gather into a round mass; to conglobate.—**globate, globated,** glō′bāt, glō′bā•ted, *a.* [L. *globatus.*] Shaped like a globe; spherical.—**globose, globous,** glō•bōs, glō′bus, *a.* [L. *globosus.*] Spherical; globular.—**globosity,** glō•bos′i•ti, *n.* The quality of being globose.—**globular,** glob′-ū•lėr, *a.* Globe-shaped; having the form of a ball; world-wide.—**globule,** glob′ūl, *n.* A small particle of matter in spherical form; a round body or corpuscle found in the blood.

globe-trotter, glōb′trot•ėr, *n.* One who travels to all parts of the globe.

globulin, glob′yä•lin, *n.* [Fr. from L. *globulus,* dimin. of *globus,* globe.] Proteins such as gamma globulin, characterized by their insolubility in water and solubility in a dilute salt solution.—**globefish,** *n.* The name of several fishes able to inflate themselves into a globular form.

glochidate, glō′kī•dāt, *a.* [Gr. *glōchis,* a point.] *Bot.* barbed at the point like a fishhook.

glomerate, glom′ėr•āt, *v.t.* [L. *glomero, glomeratum,* from *glomus, glomeris,* a ball, as in *conglomerate.*] To gather or wind into a ball; to collect into a spherical form or mass.—*a.* Congregated; gathered into a round mass or dense cluster.—**glomeration,** glom•ėr•ā′shon, *n.* The act of glomerating; conglomeration; an aggregate.—**glomerule,** glom′ėr·ūl, *n. Bot.* a cluster of flower heads enclosed in a common involucre.

gloom, glöm, *n.* [A.Sax. *glóm,* gloom, twilight, *glómung,* gloaming; allied to *glum, glow, gleam, glimmer,* etc.] Obscurity; partial darkness; thick shade; dusk; cloudiness or heaviness of mind; heaviness, dejection, anger, sullenness; a depressing state of affairs; a dismal prospect.—*v.t.* To appear dimly; to be seen in an imperfect or waning light; to look gloomy, sad, or dismal; to frown; to lower,—*v.t.* To make gloomy or dark; to fill with gloom or sadness.—**gloomily,** glö′mi·li, *adv.* In a gloomy manner.—**gloominess,** glö′mi·nes, *n.* The condition or quality of being gloomy.—**gloomy,** glö′mi, *a.* Involved in gloom; imperfectly illuminated; dusky or dark; characterized by gloom; wearing the aspect of sorrow; dejected; heavy of heart; dismal; doleful.

glory, glō′ri, *n.* [L. *gloria,* fame, glory; allied to Gr. *kleos,* fame, *kleō,* to celebrate, *klyō,* to hear.] Praise, honor, admiration, or distinction, accorded by common consent to a person or thing; honorable fame; renown; celebrity; a state of greatness or renown; pomp; magnificence; brightness; luster; splendor; brilliancy; the happiness of heaven; celestial bliss; distinguished honor or ornament; an object of which one is or may be proud; *painting,* the radiation round the head or figure of a deity, saint, angel, etc.—*v.i.*—*gloried, glorying.* To exult with joy; to rejoice; to be boastful; to have pride.—**glorification,** glō′ri·fi·kā″shon, *n.* The act of glorifying or the state of being glorified.—**glorify,** glō′ri·fī, *v.t.*—*glorified, glorifying.* [Fr. *glorifier,* L. *gloria,* glory, and *facio,* to make.] To give or ascribe glory to; to praise; to magnify and honor; to honor; to extol; to make glorious; to exalt to glory.—**gloriole,** glō′ri·ōl, *n.* [Formed on type of *aureole.*] A circle, as of rays, in ancient paintings surrounding the heads of saints.—**glorious,** glō′ri·us, *a.* [Fr. *glorieux,* L. *gloriosus,* from *gloria.*] Characterized by attributes, qualities, or acts that are worthy of glory; of exalted excellence and splendor; noble; illustrious; renowned; celebrated; magnificent; grand; splendid; hilarious or elated (*colloq.*).—**gloriously,** glō′ri·us·li, *adv.* In a glorious manner.—**gloriousness,** glō·ri·us·nes, *n.*

gloss, glos, *n.* [Akin to Icel. *glossi,* flame, brightness, *glys,* finery, whence *glysligr,* showy or specious; Sw. *glossa,* to glow; G. *glotzen,* to shine, to glance; allied to *glass, glow, gloom, gleam,* etc.] Brightness or luster of a body proceeding from a smooth and generally a soft surface; polish; sheen (the *gloss* of silk); a specious appearance or representation; external show that may mislead. —*v.t.* To give gloss to; to give a superficial luster to; to make smooth and shining; hence, to give a specious appearance to; to render specious and plausible; to palliate by specious representation.—**glosser,** glos′ėr, *n.* One who glosses; one who palliates.—**glossily,** glos′i·li, *adv.* In a glossy manner.—**glossiness,** glos′i·nes, *n.* The state or character of being glossy; polish or luster of a surface.—**glossy,** glos′i, *a.* Having a gloss; having a soft, smooth, and shining surface; lustrous with softness to the touch; specious or plausible.

gloss, glos, *n.* [L. *glossa,* an obsolete or foreign word that requires explanation, from Gr. *glōssa,* the tongue, latterly also an obsolete or foreign word.] A marginal note or interlineation explaining the meaning of some word in a text; a remark intended to illustrate some point of difficulty in an author; comment; annotation; explanation.—*v.t.* To render clear by comments; to annotate; to illustrate.—**glossarial,** glos·sâ′ri·al, *a.* Connected with, or consisting in a glossary.—**glossarist,** glos′a·rist, *n.* One who compiles a glossary.—**glossary,** glos′a·ri, *n.* [L. L. *glossarium.*] A vocabulary of words used by any author, especially by an old author, or one writing in a provincial dialect, or of words occurring in a special class of works, of technical terms, etc.—**glosser,** glos′ėr, *n.* One who writes glosses.—**glossographer,** glos·og′ra·fėr, *n.* A writer of glosses; a scholiast.—**glossological,** glos·o·loj′i·kal, *a.* Pertaining to glossology.—**glossologist,** glos·ol′o·jist, *n.* One who is versed in glossology.—**glossology,** glos·ol′o·ji, *n.* The definition and explanation of terms, as of a science; terminology; universal; grammar; glottology.—**glossotomy,** glos·ot′o·mi, *n. Anat.* dissection of the tongue.

glottis, glot′is, *n.* [Gr. *glōttis,* from *glōtta, glōssa,* the tongue, whence also *glossary,* etc.] The opening at the upper part of the windpipe, and between the vocal chords, which, by its dilatation and contraction, contributes to the modulation of the voice.—**glottal,** glot′al, *a.* Relating to the glottis.—**glottology,** glot·ol′o·ji, *n.* [Gr. *glōtta,* language, and *logos,* discourse.] The science of language; comparative philology; glossology.—**glottological, glottic,** glot·o·loj′i·kal, glot′ik, *a.* Pertaining to glottology.—**glottologist,** glot·ol′o·jist, *n.* One versed in glottology.

glove, gluv, *n.* [A.Sax. *glóf*; probably from prefix *ge,* and Goth. *lofa,* Sc. *loof,* Icel. *lófi,* the palm of the hand.] A cover for the hand, or for the hand and wrist, with a separate sheath for each finger.—*To throw down the glove.* Same as *to throw down the gantlet,* under GANTLET.—*v.t.*—*gloved, gloving.* To cover with or as with a glove.—**glover,** gluv′ėr, *n.* One whose occupation is to make or sell gloves.

glow, glō, *v.i.* [A.Sax. *glówan,* to glow=D. *gloeijen,* G. *glühen,* to glow; Icel. *glóa,* to glitter; Sw. *gloa,* to sparkle; allied to *gloat, gleam, gloom, gloaming, gloss,* etc.] To burn with an intense or white heat, and especially without flame; to give forth bright light and heat; to feel great heat of body; to be hot or flushed in person; to be bright or red, as with animation, blushes, or the like; to exhibit brightness of color; to feel the heat of passion; to be ardent; to burn or be vehement; to rage.—*n.* Shining heat, or white heat; incandescence; brightness of color; redness; vehemence of color; ardor; animation.—**glowing,** glō′ing, *p.* and *a.* Shining with intense heat; bright in color; red; ardent; vehement; fervid; heated; fiery.—**glowingly,** glō′ing·li, *adv.* In a glowing manner.—**glowworm,** glō′wėrm, *n.* The wingless female of a kind of beetle, emitting a shining green light to attract the male.

glower, glou′ėr, *v.i.* [M.L.G. *gluren* to watch, D. *glaren* to peep, Nor. dial. *glyra.*] To look intently; to stare angrily or with a scowling intentness.

gloxinia, glok·sin′i·a, *n.* [*Gloksin,* a German botanist.] A genus of almost stemless plants with fine bell-shaped flowers, natives of tropical America.

gloze, glōz, *v.i.*—*glozed, glozing.* [O.E. *glose,* a gloss or interpretation; the meaning being influenced by *gloss,* luster. GLOSS.] To comment or expound‡; to use specious words; to talk smoothly or flatteringly.—*v.t.* To gloss over; to extenuate.—*n.* Flattery; specious words.

glucose, glö′kōs, *n.* [From Gr. *glykys* or *glukus,* sweet, from its salts having a sweet taste.] Grape sugar, a variety of sugar, less sweet than cane sugar, produced from grapes, cane sugar, starch, etc.—**glucoside,** glö′kō·sīd, *n.* One of those substances that yield glucose.

glue, glö, *n.* [O.Fr. *glu,* from L.L. *glutis,* L. *gluten, glutinis,* glue; comp. W. *glyd,* viscous matter.] Common or impure gelatin, obtained by boiling animal substances, as the skins, hoofs, etc., of animals, with water; used for uniting pieces of wood or other materials.—*v.t.*—*glued, gluing.* To join with glue or other viscous substance; to hold together, as if by glue; to fix; to rivet.—**gluey,** glö′i, *a.*

glum, glum, *a.* [Akin to *gloom,* and Sc. *gloum,* a frown.] Frowning; sullen.—**glumly,** glum′li, *adv.*—**glumness,** glum′nes, *n.*

glume, glöm, *n.* [L. *gluma,* a husk, from *glubo,* to peel, akin to Gr. *glyphō,* to hollow out.] The husk or chaff of grain; the palea or pale.—**glumaceous,** glö·mā′shus, *a.* Having or bearing glumes; of or pertaining to the glumales.

glut, glut, *v.t.*—*glutted, glutting.* [L. *glutio, gluttio,* to swallow; whence also *englut, glutton.*] To swallow, or to swallow greedily (*Shak.*); to cloy, sate, or disgust; to feast or delight to satiety.—*To glut the market,* to furnish an oversupply of any article, so that there is no sale for it all.—*n.* Plenty even to loathing; superabundance; an oversupply of any commodity in the market.

gluteal, glö′ti•al, *a.* [Gr. *gloutos*, the buttock.] *Anat.* of or pertaining to certain parts connected with the buttocks.—**gluteus,** glö′tē•us, *n. Anat.* the three muscles of the buttocks.

gluten, glö′ten, *n.* [L. See GLUE.] A tough elastic substance of a grayish color, which becomes brown and brittle by drying, found in the flour of wheat and other grain.—**glutinous,** glö•ti•nus, *a.* [L. *glutinosus.*] Gluey; viscous; viscid; tenacious; resembling glue; *bot.* besmeared with a slippery moisture.—**glutinousness,** glö′ti•nus•nes, *n.* The quality of being glutinous.

glutton, glut′n, *n.* [Fr. *glouton*, from L. *gluto*, *glutto*, a glutton, from *glutio*, to swallow. GLUT.] One who indulges to excess in eating, or eating and drinking; a gormandizer; a carnivorous quadruped, 2½ feet long, yielding a valuable fur, and inhabiting Northern Europe and America, known also as the *Wolverine.*—**gluttonize,**† glut′n•iz, *v.i.* To eat gluttonously.—**gluttonous,** glut′n•us, *a.* Characterized by gluttony; given to excessive eating; insatiable.—**gluttonously,** glut′n•us•li, *adv.* In a gluttonous manner.—**gluttony,** glut′n•i, *n.* The act or practice of a glutton; excess in eating, or eating and drinking.

glycerin, glis′ėr•in, *n.* [From Gr. *glykeros*, sweet.] A transparent, sirupy trihydric alcohol used as a solvent in cosmetics, explosives, etc., obtained from fatty acids and as a by-product in soapmaking.—**glycerol,** glis′ėr•ōl, *n.* The same as glycerin.

glycogen, glī′ko•jen, *n.* [Gr. *glykys*, sweet, and root *gen*, to produce.] Animal starch, $(C_6H_{10}O_5)x$, a carbohydrate that serves as a sugar reserve for animals, formed in the liver and other organs.

glyph, glif, *n.* [Gr. *glyphē*, carving, from *glyphō*, to carve.] *Sculp.* and *arch.* a channel or cavity, usually vertical, intended as an ornament —**glyphic,** glif′ik, *a.* Of or pertaining to carving or sculpture.—**glyphograph,** glif′o•graf, *n.* A plate formed by glyphography.—**glyptic,** glip′tik, *a.* [Gr.*glyptikos.*] Pertaining to the art of sculpture or engraving.—**glyptographer,** glip•tog′ra•fėr, *n.* An engraver on precious stones.— **glyptographic,** glip•to•graf′ik, *a.* Of or pertaining to glyptography.—**glyptography,** glip•tog′ra•fi, *n.* The art or process of engraving on precious stones.

gnarl, närl, *n.* [From old *gnar*, a knot, also *knarr*, *knurr*; akin to D. *knorre*, a knot, G. *knorren*, a lump.] A protuberance on the outside of a tree; a knot.— **gnarled,** närld, *a.* Having many knots or knotty protuberances; cross-grained; perverse.—**gnarly,** när′li, *a.* Having knots; knotty.

gnarl, närl, *v.i.* [O.E. *gnerr*, found in similar forms in the other Teut. languages, and probably imitative of snarling.] To growl; to murmur; to snarl.

gnash, nash, *v.t.* [O.E. *gnaste*, *gnayste*, akin to Dan. *knaske*, D. *knarsen*, G. *knirschen*, Sw. *knastra*, *gnissta*, to gnash.] To strike together (the teeth), as in anger or pain.—*v.i.* To strike or dash the teeth together, as in rage or pain.

gnat, nat, *n.* [A.Sax. *gnaet*, L.G. *gnid*, a gnat; perhaps akin to G. *gnatze*, the itch.] A small two-winged fly whose mouth is furnished with bristly stings which inflict irritating wounds.

gnathic, nath′ik, *a.* [Gr. *gnathos*, jaw.] Pertaining to the jaw or jaws.

gnaw, na̦, *v.t.* [A.Sax. *gnagan*=D. *knagen*, G. *gnagen*, Dan. *gnave*, *nage*, Icel. and Sw. *gnaga*, *naga*, to gnaw; akin verb to *nag.*] To bite by little and little; to wear away by biting; to nibble at; to bite in agony or rage; to fret; to corrode.—*v.i.* To use the teeth in biting; to bite with repeated efforts; to cause or be affected with steady annoying pain.—**gnawer,** na̦′ėr, *n.* One who or that which gnaws; a rodent.

gneiss, nīs, *n.* [G. *gneiss*, gneiss.] A kind of hard tough crystalline rock, having a structure exhibiting layers either straight or curved, and like granite composed in the main of quartz, feldspar, and mica.—**gneissoid,** nīs′oid, *a.* Resembling gneiss; having the characteristics of gneiss. Also **gneissic,** nīs′ik.

gnome, nōm, *n.* [Gr. *gnome*, formed from Gr. *gnōmē*, intelligence; see next art.] An imaginary being, fabled to inhabit the inner parts of the earth, and to be the guardian of mines, quarries, etc.; a goblin; a small misshapen person.

gnome, nōm, *n.* [Gr. *gnōmē*, a maxim, from stem of *gnōnai*, to know. KNOW.] A brief reflection or maxim; a saw; an aphorism.—**gnomic, gnomical,** nō′mik, nō′mi•kal, *a.* [Gr. *gnōmikos.*] Containing or dealing in maxims (the ancient Greek *gnomic* poets).

gnomon, nō′mon, *n.* [Gr. *gnōmōn*, an index, from stem of *gnōnai*, to know; whence also *gnome*, *Gnostic.*] The style or pin of a sun dial, which by its shadow shows the hour of the day; a style consisting of a pillar, pyramid, etc., erected perpendicular to the horizon, in order to find the altitudes, declinations, etc., of the sun and stars; the index of the hour circle of a globe.—**gnomonic, gnomonical,** nō•mon′ik, nō•mon′i•kal, *a.* Pertaining to the art of dialing; *bot.* bent at right angles.—*Gnomonic projection*, a projection of the surface of the sphere, in which the point of sight is taken at the center of the sphere.

Gnostic, nos′tik, *n.* [L. *gnosticus*, Gr. *gnōstikos*, from stem of *gnōnai*, to know, cog. with E. *know.*] One of several sects arising in the 2d century whose members claimed to have the only true knowledge of Christianity, actually basing their beliefs on a blend of several Christian and non-Christian doctrines.—**Gnosticism,** nos′ti•sizm, *n.* The doctrines or principles of the Gnostics.

gnu, nū, *n.* [Hottentot *gnu* or *nju.*] A ruminant quadruped, partaking of the form of the antelope, ox, and horse, inhabiting South Africa.

go, gō, *v.i.*—pret. *went*, pp. *gone.* [A.Sax. *gán*, *gangan*, O. and Prov. E. and Sc. *gang*, to go; Dan. *gaae*, D. *gaan*, G. *gehen*, Goth. *gaggan* (that is *gangan*), Icel. *ganga*, O.H.G. *gangan. Went* though now used as the pret., is really the past tense of *wend*, A.Sax. *wendan*, to turn, to go.] To walk; to pass, proceed, move, or be in motion; to depart or move from a place; opposed to *come*; to have currency or use; to circulate (the story *goes*); to be reckoned or esteemed; to proceed or happen in a given manner; to have course; to turn out (the case *went* against him); to have recourse (to *go* to law); to be about to (in this usage a kind of auxiliary and usually in ppr.—*going* to say, *going* to begin); to be guided or regulated (to *go* by some rule); to be with young; to be pregnant; to be alienated, sold, or disposed of (it *went* for a trifle); to extend, reach, lead (this road *goes* to London); to extend in effect, meaning, or purport; to be of force or value; to proceed or tend toward a result or consequence; to contribute, conduce, concur (frequently with *to*, *towards*, etc.); to perish; to sink or die; to become (she has *gone* mad).—*To go about*, *naut.* to tack; to turn the head of a ship.—*To go about to*, to set one's self to; to take a circuitous way to.—*To go against*, to march to attack; to be in opposition; to be disagreeable.—*To go ahead*, to make rapid progress; to be enterprising. (*Colloq.*)—*To go between*, to interpose or mediate between; to attempt to reconcile.—*To go beyond*, to overreach.—*To go by*, to pass near and beyond (*by* being a prep.); to pass away unnoticed or disregarded (*by* adv.).—*To go down*, to descend; to come to nothing; to be received as true or correct.—*To go for nothing*, to have no value, weight, or efficacy. —*To go hard with*, to bring danger of a fatal issue to; to be all but ruinous for: used impersonally.—*To go in for*, to be in favor of; to make the object of acquirement or of attainment.—*To go in to* (*Scrip.*), to have sexual commerce with.—*To go off*, to leave a place; to die; to decease; to be discharged, as firearms; to explode; to be sold.—*To go on*, to proceed; to advance forward; to be put on, as a garment.—*To go out*, to issue forth; to go on an expedition; to become extinct, as light or life.—*To go over*, to read; to peruse; to examine; to view or review (*over* being the prep.); to change sides; to pass from one party to another (*over* adv.).—*To go through*, to pass or penetrate through; to accomplish; to perform thoroughly; to undergo; to sustain to the end.—*To go through with*, to execute effectually.—*To go upon*, to proceed as on a foundation; to take as a principle supposed or settled.—*To go with*, to accompany; to side with; to be in party or design with; to agree with; to suit.—*It goes ill* or *well with* a person, he has ill or good fortune.—*To go without*, to be or remain destitute.—*To go wrong*, to become unsound, as meat, fruit; to leave the paths of virtue; to take a wrong way.—*Go to!* come; move; begin; a phrase of exhortation; also a phrase of rebuke or reproof; tush; nonsense.—[In the following usages the verb may be construed as transitive.] To undertake (to *go* a journey, to *go* equal risks).—*To go one's way*, to set forth; to depart; to move on.—*To go an errand, to go a drive, to go circuit*, to go on an errand; to go upon or for a drive; to go upon circuit.—*n.* [As a noun the word is colloq. or slang.] The fashion or mode; a glass or other measure of liquor called in when drinking; stamina, bottom, or power of endurance; spirit; animation; fire.—*Great go, little go*, university cant terms for the examination for degrees and the previous or preliminary examination.—**goer,** gō′ėr, *n.* One who or that which goes; one that has a gait good or bad; often applied to a horse, and to a watch or clock.—**going,** gō′ing, *n.* The act of moving in any manner; departure; procedure; behavior, or course of life: chiefly in the *pl.*—*Goings-on*, actions; conduct; used mostly in a bad sense. —**gone,** gon, *pp.* Passed; vanished away; consumed; finished; dead; lost or destroyed; worn out, exhausted, or overpowered.—**go-ahead,** *a.* Characterized by or disposed to progress; enterprising. (*Colloq.*)—**go-between,** *n.* An intermediary: often an agent in disreputable negotiations.—**gocart,** *n.* A framework on casters, to support children while learning to walk; a baby carriage with front wheels smaller than the rear.

goad, gōd, *n.* [A.Sax. *gád*, a point of a weapon, a goad. GAD.] A pointed instrument used to stimulate a beast to move faster; hence, anything that urges or stimulates.—*v.t.* To drive with a goad; hence, to incite; to stimulate; to instigate; to urge forward.

goal, gōl, *n.* [Fr. *gaule*, a pole, a word of Germanic origin, from Goth. *walus*, Fris. *walu*, Icel. *völr*, staff, rod.] The point set to bound a race; the space between the two upright posts in the game of football; also the act of driving the ball through between the posts; the end to which a design tends, or which a person aims to reach or accomplish.

goat, gōt, *n.* [A.Sax. *gát*=Icel. L.G., D., and Fris. *geit*, G. *geiss*, goat; cog. with L. *haedus*, a kid.] A well-known horned ruminant quadruped, nearly of the size of a sheep, but stronger, less timid, and more agile. —**goatee,** gō•tē′, *n.* A beard that hangs down from the chin without whiskers.—**goatherd,** gōt′hėrd, *n.* One whose occupation is to tend goats.—**goatish,** gōt′ish, *a.* Resembling a goat in any quality, especially in smell or lustfulness.—**goatishly,** gōt′ish•li, *adv.* In a goatish manner; lustfully.—**goatishness,** gōt′ish•nes, *n.* The quality of being goatish; lustfulness.—**goat pepper,** *n.* A species of capsicum or Cayenne pepper.—**goatsbeard,** *n.* The name of herbaceous perennials, one species of which (*salsify*) is cultivated in gardens for its root.

gob, gob, *n.* [Origin unknown.] A sailor of the U.S. Navy.

gob, gob, *n.* [O.Fr. *gobe.*] A mass or lump.

gobbet, gob′et, *n.* [Fr. *gobet*, from O.Fr. *gob*, a mouthful.] A mouthful; a morsel; a lump.—**gobble,** gob′l, *v.t.* and *i.*—*gobbled, gobbling.* To swallow in large pieces; to swallow hastily.

gobble, gob′l, *v.i.* [Imitative.] To make a sound in the throat, as a turkey *gobbles.*—*n.* A noise made in the throat, as that made by the turkey cock.—**gobbler,** gob′lėr, *n.* A turkey.

Gobelin, gob′e•lin, *a.* [From the *Gobelins* establishment in Paris, where tapestry, etc., is made, named from, and originally belonging to a family of dyers called *Gobelin.*] A term applied to a species of rich tapestry, also to a printed worsted cloth for covering chairs, sofas, etc., in imitation of tapestry.

goblet, gob′let, *n.* [Fr. *gobelet*, dim. of O.Fr. *gobel*, a drinking glass, from L.L. *gobellus*, from L. *cupa*, a tub, a cask. CUP.] A kind of cup or drinking vessel without a handle.

goblin, gob′lin, *n.* [Fr. *gobelin*, from L. *cobalus*, Gr. *kobalos*, a kind of malignant being or goblin; whence also G. *kobold.*] An evil or mischievous sprite; a gnome; an elf; a malicious fairy.

goby, gō′bi, *n.* [L. *gobius*, Gr. *kōbios*, the gudgeon.] A name given to various rather small fishes.

god, god, *n.* [A.Sax. *god*=D. *god*, Icel. *goth, guth*, Dan. and Sw. *gud*, Goth. *guth*, G. *gott*, God; root unknown; not connected with *good.*] A being conceived of a possessing divine power, and therefore to be propitiated by sacrifice, worship, and the like; a divinity; [*cap.*] the Supreme Being; Jehovah; the eternal Spirit, the Creator, and the Sovereign of the universe; any person or thing exalted too much in estimation, or deified and honored as the chief good.—**godchild,** god′child, *n.* A godson or goddaughter.—**goddaughter,** god′dạ•tėr, *n.* A female for whom one becomes sponsor at baptism.—**goddess,** god′es, *n.* A female deity; a woman of superior charms or excellence.—**godfather,** god′fä•THėr, *n.* In the Anglican, Roman Catholic, and several other churches, a man who at the baptism of a child makes a profession of the Christian faith in its name, and guarantees its religious education; a male sponsor.—*v.t.* To act as godfather to; to take under one's fostering care.—**godhead,** god′-hed, *n.* [*God*, and suffix *-head*, same as *-hood.*] Godship; deity; divinity; divine nature or essence.—*The Godhead*, the Deity; God; the Supreme Being.—**godless,** god′les, *a.* Having or acknowledging no God; impious; ungodly; irreligious; wicked.—**godlessness,** god′les•nes, *n.* The state or quality of being godless.—**godlike,** god′līk, *a.* Resembling a god or God; divine; of superior excellence.—**godlikeness,** god′līk•nes, *n.* The state of being godlike.—**godlily,** god′li•li, *adv.* In a godly manner; piously; righteously.—**godliness,** god′li•nes, *n.* The condition or quality of being godly.—**godly,** god′li, *a.* Pious; reverencing God and his character and laws; devout; religious; righteous; conformed to or influenced by God's law.—*adv.* Piously; righteously.—**godmother,** god′muTH•ėr, *n.* A woman who becomes sponsor for a child in baptism.—**godsend,** god′send, *n.* Something sent by God; an unlooked-for acquisition or piece of good fortune.—**godship,** god′ship, *n.* Deity; divinity; the rank or character of a god.—**godson,** god′sun, *n.* A male for whom one has been sponsor at baptism.—**Godspeed,** god′spēd, *n.* [A contraction of 'I wish that *God* may *speed* you.'] Success; prosperity; a prosperous journey: usually in phrase *to bid* a person *godspeed.*—**Godward, Godwards,** god′wėrd, god′wėrdz, *adv.* Toward God.—**God's acre,** *n.* The churchyard.

godwit, god′wit, *n.* [A.Sax. *god*, good, and *wiht*, creature, *wight*, from the excellence of their flesh.] A name of several grallatorial birds of no great size, the flesh of which is highly esteemed.

goffer, gof′ėr, *v.t.* [GAUFFER.] To plait or flute; to gauffer.—**goffer,** gof′ėr, *n.* An ornamental plaiting, used for the frills and borders of women's caps, etc.

goggle, gog′l, *v.t.* and *i.* [M.E. *gogelen*, to squint.] To stare or roll the eyes. —*a.* Prominent and rolling or staring: said of the eyes.—*n.* A strained or affected rolling of the eye; pl. a kind of spectacles with fixed plain glasses surrounded by leather for protecting the eyes from wind, debris, intense light.

goiter, goitre, goi′tėr, *n.* [Fr. *goître*, from L. *guttur*, the throat.] An enlargement of the thyroid gland, forming a tumor or protuberance on the front part of the neck.—**goitrous,** goi′trus, *a.* Pertaining to goiter; affected with goiter.

gold, gōld, *n.* [A.Sax. *gold*=D. *goud*, Sc. *gowd*, Sw. *guld*, Icel. *gull*, Goth. *gulth*; from root of *yellow.* Hence *gild.*] A heavy yellow metallic element, the most malleable and ductile of all metals—symbol, Au (Latin, *aurum*); at. no., 79; at. wt., 196.967; sp. gr., 19.3—money; riches; wealth; a symbol of what is valuable or much prized; a bright yellow color, like that of the metal; *archery*, the exact center of the target, marked with gold, or of a gold color.—*a.* Made of gold; consisting of gold.—**goldbeater,** *n.* One whose occupation is to beat gold into thin leaves for gilding.—*Goldbeater's skin*, the prepared outside membrane of the large intestine of the ox, used by goldbeaters to lay between the leaves of the metal while they beat it.—**gold digger,** *n.* One who digs for gold; a woman whose relations with men are for selfish mercenary advantages.—**golden,** gōl'dn, *a.* Made of gold; of the color or luster of gold; yellow; shining; splendid; excellent; most valuable; precious; happy; marked by the happiness of mankind; pre-eminently favorable or auspicious (a *golden* opportunity).—*Golden age,* an early period in the history of the human race, fabled to have been one of primeval innocence and enjoyment; any period of great brilliancy or prosperity.—*Golden balls,* the three gilt balls placed in front of a pawnbroker's place of business; the arms of Lombardy, and the bankers settled in Lombard Street.—*Golden bull,* the edict issued in 1356, at Nuremberg, regulating the special form for election to the Holy Roman Empire.—*Golden calf* (*Exodus,* xxxii), money and its worship.—*Golden fleece,* an order of knighthood, the *toison d'or*; the order of Flanders and Spain, commemorating the wool trade of the Flemish towns; in *Greek myth.* the fleece of gold in quest of which Jason undertook the Argonautic expedition.—*Golden Horn,* the inlet of the Bosporus in European Turkey forming the harbor of Istanbul.—*Golden legend,* a collection of lives and legends of saints in high repute in the Middle Ages.—*Golden-mouthed,* eloquent, applied to John *Chrysostom* of Antioch, A.D. 347-407.—*Golden number,* in *chron.* a number showing the year of the moon's cycle.—*Golden wedding,* the fiftieth anniversary of a marriage, the seventy-fifth being the diamond wedding.—**goldeneye,** *n.* A species of duck; the garrot.—**golden pheasant,** *n.* A beautiful species of pheasant belonging to China.—**goldenrod,** *n.* A name of certain composite plants with rodlike stems and terminal spikes or racemes of small yellow flowers.—**goldfinch,** gōld'finsh, *n.* [A.Sax. *goldfinc.*] A songbird belonging to the finches, so named from the yellow markings on its wings.—**goldfish,** *n.* A species of carp, so named from its color, now largely bred in ponds, tanks, or glass vessels.—**gold leaf,** *n.* Gold beaten into an exceedingly thin sheet or leaf.—**goldsmith,** gōld'smith, *n.* An artisan who manufactures vessels and ornaments of gold.—**gold standard,** *n.* Monetary standard, in which the basic currency standard equals a specified amount of gold.—**goldthread,** *n.* A thread formed of flattened gold laid over a thread of silk by twisting it.

golf, golf, *n.* [D. *kolf,* a club to drive balls with; Dan. and G. *kolbe,* a club.] A game played with clubs and balls, generally over large commons, downs, or links; the object being to drive the ball, with as few strokes as possible, into holes placed at considerable distances apart.—**golfer,** gol'fėr, *n.* One who plays golf.

Golgotha, gol'go•tha, *n.* [Heb.] A charnel house; scene of the Lord's crucifixion.

gollywog, go'li•wog, *n.* A black-faced, staring-eyed doll of hideous or whimsical appearance.

golosh, gō•losh', *n.* See GALOSH.

gomphosis, gom•fō'sis, *n.* [Gr., from *gomphos,* a nail.] *Anat.* an immovable articulation, as in the insertion of the teeth in their sockets.

gomuti, gō•mū'ti, *n.* The Malayan name for the sago palm, which yields a bristly useful fiber resembling black horsehair, known by the same name.

gonad, gōn'ad, *n.* [Gr. *gonē,* that which generates.] *Anat.* a primary sex gland; ovary; testis.

gondola, gon'do•la, *n.* [It., origin unknown.] A flat-bottomed boat, very long and narrow, and having toward the center a curtained chamber for the passengers, used chiefly at Venice; a freight car, having sides and ends but no top, for carrying bulk loads.—**gondolier,** gon•do•lēr', *n.*

gone, gon, pp. of *go.*

gonfalon, gonfanon, gon'fa•lon, gon'fa•non, *n.* [Fr. *gonfalon,* O.Fr. *gonfanon,* from O.G. *guntfano*—*gunt,* a combat (=A.Sax. *gūth*), and *fano,* a banner.] An ensign or standard, the bearer of which in many of the medieval republican cities of Italy was often the chief personage in the state.—**gonfalonier,** gon'fal•o•nēr", *n.* One entrusted with a gonfalon; a chief magistrate in medieval Italian cities.

gong, gong, *n.* [Malay.] A Chinese percussion instrument, made of a mixed metal and shaped like a large round flat dish.

gonidia, go•nid'i•a, *n. pl.* [Gr. *gonē,* generation, and *eidos,* appearance.] *Bot.* the secondary, reproductive, green, spherical cells in the thallus of lichens.

goniometer, gō•ni•om'et•ėr, *n.* [Gr. *gōnia,* angle, and *metron,* measure.] An instrument for measuring solid angles, particularly the angles formed by the faces of mineral crystals.—**goniometric, goniometrical,** gō'ni•o•met"rik, gō'ni•o•met"ri•kal, *a.* Pertaining to or determined by a goniometer.—**goniometry,** gō•ni•om'et•ri, *n.* The art of measuring solid angles.

gonophore, gon'o•fōr, *n.* [Gr. *gonos,* seed, and *phoreō,* to bear.] *Bot.* the short stalk which bears the stamens and carpels in some plants; *zool.* one of the generative buds or receptacles of the reproductive elements in the Hydrozoa.

gonorrhea, gon•o•rē'a, *n.* [Gr. *gonorrhoia*—*gonos,* semen, and *rheō,* to flow.] An inflammatory infection of the male urethra or the female vagina, attended with secretion of mucus intermingled with pus.

good, gu̦d, *a.* [A.Sax. *gód,* good=D. *goed,* Dan. and Sw. *uod,* Icel. *gothr,* Goth. *gods,* G. *gut*; not connected with *god.*] The opposite of bad; conducive, in general, to any useful end or purpose; serviceable; advantageous; beneficial; wholesome; suitable; useful; fit; proper; right; possessing desirable or valuable physical or moral qualities; virtuous, righteous, dutiful, pious, or religious; excellent, valuable; precious; kind, benevolent, humane, merciful, or friendly; clever, skillful, or dexterous; adequate, sufficient, or competent; valid; of unimpaired credit; able to fulfill engagements; real, actual, serious (*good* earnest); considerable; more than a little; not deficient; full or complete; not blemished; unsullied; immaculate; honorable.—*Good Friday,* a feast of the Christian Church, in memory of the Saviour's crucifixion, kept on the Friday before Easter.—*In good time,* opportunely; not too soon nor too late; in proper time.—*To make good,* to perform; to fulfill; to verify or establish (an accusation); to supply deficiency in; to make up for defect; to maintain or carry out successfully.—*To stand good,* to be firm or valid.—*To think good, to see good,* to be pleased or satisfied; to think to be expedient.—*As good as his word,* equaling in fulfillment what was promised.—*n.* What is good, especially a result that is so (no *good* can come of it); what is serviceable, fit, excellent, kind, benevolent, or the like (to do *good*); benefit; advantage: opposed to *evil, ill, harm,* etc.; welfare or prosperity (the *good* of the state); a valuable possession or piece of property: almost always in the plural in this sense, and equivalent to wares, commodities, movables, household furniture, chattels, effects.—*For good, for good and all,* to close the whole business; for the last time; finally.—**good-by,** gu̦d•bī'. [Corruption of *God be with you.*] A form of salutation at parting; farewell.—**Good Conduct Medal,** gu̦d kon'dukt med'al, *n.* A medal given to a soldier as a reward for 'long service with irreproachable character and conduct'.—**good fellow,** *n.* A man esteemed for his companionable or social qualities; a good-natured pleasant person.—**good-fellowship,** *n.* Merry society; companionableness; friendliness.—**good humor,** *n.* A cheerful temper or state of mind.—**good-humored,** *a.* Characterized by good humor. — **good-humoredly,** *adv.* In a good-humored manner; in a cheerful way.—**goodish,** gu̦d'ish, *a.* Pretty good; tolerable; fair.—**goodliness,** gu̦d'li•nes, *n.* The quality of being goodly.—**goodly,** gu̦d'li, *a.* Being of a handsome form; fair to look on; beautiful; graceful; well-favored; pleasant; agreeable; large; considerable.—**goodman,** gu̦d'man, *n. Archaic.* A familiar appellation of civility; a husband; the head of a family.—**goodwife,** gu̦d'wif, *n.* The mistress of a household: correlative to *goodman.*—**good nature,** *n.* Natural mildness and kindness of disposition. — **good-natured,** *a.* Having good-nature; naturally mild in temper.—**good-naturedly,** *adv.* In a good-natured manner. — **good-naturedness,** *n.* The quality of being good-natured.—**goodness,** gu̇d'nes, *n.* The state or quality of being good; a euphemism for God (thank *Goodness*).—**good-tempered,** *a.* Having a good temper; not easily irritated or annoyed.—**good will,** *n.* Benevolence; kindly feelings; heartiness; earnestness; zeal; *com.* the custom of any trade or business; the right to take up a trade or business connection, purchased of one who gives it up.—**goody,** gu̇d'i, *n.* [Probably contr. from *goodwife*, as *housewife*, *hussy*.] A term of civility applied to women in humble life.—**goody,** gu̇d'i, **goody-goody,** *a.* Affected with mawkish morality; excessively squeamish in morals.

goosander, gös'an•dėr, *n.* [Lit. goose-duck, from *goose*, and Icel. *andar*, genit. of *ōnd*, A.Sax. *ened*, a duck. DRAKE.] A swimming bird allied to the ducks and divers; the merganser. MERGANSER.

goose, gös, *n.* pl. **geese,** gēs. [A.Sax. *gós* (pl. *gés*, *gees*), a goose=Icel. *gás*, Dan. *gaas*, D. and G. *gans*, Rus. *gus*; cog. with L. *anser*, Gr. *chēn*, Skr. *hunsa*; from a root meaning to gape, seen in E. *yawn*.] The name of several well-known swimming birds larger than ducks; a silly, stupid person, from the popular notion as to the stupidity of the goose; a tailor's smoothing iron; a game formerly common in England, played with dice on a card divided into small compartments, on certain of which a goose was figured.—*To cook one's goose*, to do for one; to finish a person (*slang*).—*v.t.* To hiss out; to condemn by hissing. (*Slang.*)—**goose flesh, goose skin,** *n.* A peculiar roughness of the human skin produced by cold, fear, and other depressing causes, as dyspepsia.—**gooseneck,** *n.* A pipe shaped like the letter S.—**goose-step,** *n.* The act of a soldier marking time by raising the feet alternately without advancing; the stiff German parade step.

gooseberry, gös'be•ri, *n.* [A corruption of *gossberry* for *gorseberry*, from prickles on the bush giving it a resemblance to gorse; or for *groseberry*, from Fr. *groseille*, a gooseberry, from G. *kräusbeere*, *kräuselbeere*, a gooseberry—*kraus*, frizzled, curled, crisp, and *beere*, a berry.] The fruit of a prickly shrub either red, yellow, or green in color, and hairy or smooth on the surface, well known and much esteemed; also the shrub itself; a small ball of barbed wire.

gopher, gō'fėr, *n.* [Fr. *gaufre*, honey-comb.] The name given in America to several burrowing animals from their honeycombing the earth; also a species of burrowing tortoise of the Southern States.

gopherwood, gof'ėr, *n.* [Heb. *gopher.*] A species of wood used in the construction of Noah's ark, perhaps cypress.

gorbelly, gor'bel•li, *n.* [A.Sax. *gor*, dirt, dung, E. *gore*, and *belly*.] A prominent belly; a person having a big belly.—**gorbellied,** *a.* Big-bellied.—**gorcock,** gor'kok, *n.* [From its red color; or from *gorse*, furze.] The red grouse.—**gorhen,** *n.* The female of the red grouse.

Gordian, gōr'di•an, *a.* Pertaining to *Gordius*, king of Phrygia, or the knot tied by him, and which could not be untied, but which was ultimately cut by Alexander the Great; hence, the term *Gordian knot* is applied to any inextricable difficulty; and to *cut the Gordian knot* is to remove a difficulty by bold or unusual measures.

gore, gōr, *n.* [A.Sax. *gor*, gore, filth, Icel. and Dan. *gor*, Sw. *gorr.*] Blood that is shed; thick or clotted blood.—**gory,** gō'ri, *a.* Covered with gore; bloody.

gore, gōr, *n.* [A.Sax. *gára*, a point or corner of land, from *gár*, a spear; like Icel. *geiri*, a triangular piece, from *geirr*, a spear.] A triangular-shaped piece, as of cloth, let into or regarded as let into a larger piece; a gusset.—*v.t.* To cut a gore in; to piece with a gore.

gore, gōr, *v.t.*—*gored*, *goring*. [Directly from A.Sax. *gár*, a spear or dart; Icel. *geirr.*] To stab; to pierce with a pointed instrument, as a spear, or with the horns (as an ox).

gorge, gorj, *n.* [Fr. *gorge*, from It. *gorgia*, L. *gurges*, a whirlpool; akin *gargle*, *gurgle*, etc.] The throat or gullet; that which is swallowed; food caused to regurgitate through nausea or disgust; a narrow passage between hills or mountains; the entrance into a bastion or other outwork of a fort; *arch.* the narrowest part of the Tuscan and Doric capital; also, a cavetto.—*v.t.*—*gorged*, *gorging*. To swallow, especially with greediness or in large quantities; to fill the stomach of; to satiate: often *refl.*—*v.i.* To feed greedily; to stuff one's self.

gorgeous, gor'jus, *a.* [O.Fr. *gorgias*, gaudy, flaunting, from *gorgias*, a ruff for the neck, from *gorge*, the throat (which see).] Exceedingly showy; splendid; magnificent; glittering with gay colors.—**gorgeously,** gor'jus•li, *adv.* In a gorgeous manner.—**gorgeousness,** gor'jus•nes, *n.*

gorget, gor'jet, *n.* [Fr. *gorgette*, from *gorge*, the throat. GORGE.] A piece of armor for defending the throat or neck; a small crescent-shaped metallic ornament formerly worn by officers on the breast.

Gorgon, gor'gon, *n.* [Gr. *gorgō*, *gorgon*, from *gorgos*, fierce, grim.] *Greek myth.* one of several monsters of terrific aspect, the sight of which turned the beholder to stone; hence, some one like a Gorgon.—*a.* Very ugly or terrific.—**Gorgonian,** gor•-

Gorgonian, gor•gō'ni•an, *a.* [From Gr. *gorgas*, fierce, grim, and *Gorgon*, a Greek mythological monster.] Like a Gorgon; pertaining to Gorgons or monsters.—*a.* Very ugly.—**gorgonize,** gor'gō•nīz, *v.t.* To turn into stone; to petrify.

Gorgonzola, gor•gon•zō'la, *n.* A kind of Italian ewe-milk cheese made at Gorgonzola, a village near Milan.

gorilla, go•ril'la, *n.* [Originally an African name, found in use by the Phoenician navigator Hanno in the fifth century B.C.] The largest of the apes, very strong and fierce, found chiefly in the woody equatorial regions of Africa, sometimes living in trees, and feeding on vegetable substances.

gormand, gor'mand, *n.* [Fr. *gourmand.*] A gourmand.—**gormandism,** gor'man•dizm, *n.* Gluttony.—**gormandize,** gor'man•dīz, *v.i.*—*gormandized*, *gormandizing*. To eat greedily; to swallow voraciously.—**gormandizer,** gor'man•dī•zėr, *n.* A voracious eater.

goshawk, gos'ha̤k, *n.* [A.Sax. *góshafoc*, goose-hawk—so called from being flown at geese.] A kind of large hawk, formerly much used in falconry.

gosling, goz'ling, *n.* [A.Sax. *gós*, goose, and the dim. term. *-ling*.] A young goose; a kind of catkin.

Gospel, gos'pel, *n.* [A.Sax. *godspell*—*gód*, good, and *spell*, history, narration—answering to the Gr. *euangelion*, L. *evangelium*; a good or joyful message, evangel; or compounded of A.Sax. *god*, God, and *spell*—lit. God's word.] The history of Jesus Christ; any of the four records of Christ's life left by his apostles; the whole scheme of salvation as revealed by Christ and his apostles; some portion of one of the Four Gospels appointed to be read in the service of the Anglican Church.—*a.* Accordant with the Gospel; relating to the Gospel; evangelical; [*not. cap.*] system of gospel doctrine or of religious truth; any general doctrine (a political *gospel*).—**gospeler,** gos'pel•ėr, *n.* An evangelist; the priest or minister who reads the gospel in the church service.

gossamer, gos'a•mėr, *n.* [A name apparently applied originally to the period at which gossamer is commonly observed, and equivalent to *goose-summer*, the term having perhaps arisen from geese being then driven out to the stubble and from their well-known connection with Michaelmas; comp. the German names for gossamer, 'our lady's summer', 'flying summer', 'old wives summer'.] A fine filmy substance, a kind of delicate cobwebs, floating in the air in calm clear weather, especially in autumn, formed by small species of spiders.—**gossamery,** gos'a•mėr•i, *a.* Like gossamer; flimsy; unsubstantial.

gossan, gos'an, *n.* *Mining*, an oxide of iron and quartz, a sure indication of ore at greater depth.

gossip, gos'sip, *n.* [From *God* and prov. E. *sib*, relation, related, lit. related in the service of God.] An idle tattler or carrier of tales; mere tattle; groundless rumor.—*v.i.* To prate; to chat; to tell idle tales.—**gossiper,** gos'sip•ėr, *n.* One who gossips; a gossip.—**gossipry,** gos'sip•ri, *n.* Idle talk or gossip.—**gossipy,** gos'sip•i, *a.* Full of gossip.

got, got, pret. of *get*.—**got, gotten,** got'n, pp. of *get*.

Goth, goth, *n.* [L. *Gothi*, Goths.] One of an ancient Teutonic race of people, first heard of as inhabiting the shores of the Baltic, and who afterward overran and took an important part in subverting the Roman empire; a barbarian; a rude ignorant person; one defective in taste.—**Gothic,** goth′ik, *a.* Pertaining to the Goths; rude; barbarous; the term applied to that style of architecture, the characteristic feature of which is the pointed arch and the subserviency of the other parts to this feature: originally used in a depreciatory sense.—*n.* The language of the Goths; *printing*, the name of a boldfaced type, used for titling and jobbing work; the Gothic style or order of architecture.—**Gothicism,** goth′i•sizm, *n.* A Gothic idiom; conformity to the Gothic style of architecture; rudeness of manners; barbarousness. —**Gothicize,** goth′i•sīz, *v.t.*—*Gothicized, Gothicizing.* To make Gothic; to bring back to barbarism.

gothamite, gōt′am•īt, *n.* A person deficient in wisdom, so called from *Gotham*, in Nottinghamshire, noted for some pleasant blunders; a term sportively applied to the inhabitants of New York, then pron. gō′tham•īt.

gouge, gouj, *n.* [Fr. *gouge*, LL. *guvia*, a gouge; origin uncertain.] A chisel with a hollow or grooved blade, used to cut holes, channels, or grooves.—*v.t.*—*gouged, gouging.* To scoop out or turn with or as with a gouge.

gourd, görd, *n.* [Fr. *gourde*, O.Fr. *gouorde, gougorde*, from L. *cucurbita*, a gourd.] The popular name of the family of plants represented by the melon, cucumber, pumpkin, vegetable marrow, etc., or for their fruits.

gourmand, gör′mand, *n.* [Fr., of Celtic origin; comp. W. *gormant*, that which tends to overfill; *gormodd*, excess, from *gor*, excess.] A glutton; a greedy feeder; a dainty feeder; an epicure; a gourmet.

gourmet, gör′mā or gör′met, *n.* [Fr., a wine taster, for *groumet*, from the O.D. word=E. *groom.*] A man of keen palate; a connoisseur in wines and meats; a nice feeder; an epicure.

gout, gout, *n.* [Fr. *goutte*, L. *gutta*, a drop, from the old medical theory that diseases were due to the deposition of drops of morbid humor in the part.] A disease giving rise to paroxysms of acute pain with inflammation, affecting the small joints, and generally the first joint of the great toe, and often accompanied by calculi or concretions at the joints; a drop; a clot or coagulation (*Shak.*). —**goutily,** gout′i•li, *adv.* In a gouty manner.—**goutiness,** gout′i•nes, *n.* The state of being gouty; gouty affections.—**gouty,** gout′i, *a.* Diseased with or subject to the gout; pertaining to the gout.

govern, guv′ėrn, *v.t.* [Fr. *gouverner*, from L. *gubernare*, to govern, a form of Gr. *kybernaō*, to govern.] To direct and control; to regulate by authority; to keep within the limits prescribed by law or sovereign will; to influence; to direct; to restrain; to keep in due subjection; to steer or regulate the course of; *gram.* to cause to be in a particular case, or to require a particular case.—*v.i.* To exercise authority; to administer the laws; to maintain the superiority; to have the control.—**governable,** guv′ėr•na•bl, *a.* Capable of being governed; submissive to law or rule.—**governance,** guv′ėr•nans, *n.* Government; exercise of authority; control; management.—**governess,** guv′ėr•nes, *n.* A female that governs; a lady who has the care of educating or teaching children in their homes.—**government,** guv′ėrn•ment, *n.* The act of governing; regulation; control; restraint; the exercise of authority; direction and restraint exercised over the actions of men in communities, societies, or states; the administration of public affairs; the system of polity in a state; the mode or system according to which the sovereign powers of a nation, the legislative, executive, and judicial powers, are vested and exercised; a body politic governed by one authority; a province or division of territory ruled by a governor; the persons or council who administer the laws of a kingdom or state; the administration; the executive power; *gram.* the influence of a word in regard to construction.—**governmental,** guv′ėrn•men•tal, *a.* Pertaining to government; made by government.—**governor,** guv′ėr•nėr, *n.* One who governs; the supreme executive magistrate of a state, community, corporation, etc.; a tutor to a boy at home; a contrivance in mills and machinery for maintaining a uniform velocity with a varying resistance; a contrivance in a steam engine which automatically regulates the admission of steam to the cylinder.—**governor general,** *n.* A governor who has under him subordinate or deputy governors; a viceroy.—**governorship,** guv′ėr•nėr•ship, *n.* The office of a governor.

gown, goun, *n.* [O.Fr. *goune*, L.L. *gunna*, furred robe, fur.] A woman's outer garment; a dress; a dressing gown or a nightgown; the official dress worn by members of certain professions, as divinity, medicine, law, by magistrates, university professors and students, etc.; sometimes used as the emblem of civil life, as the sword of military. 'Gowns not arms' (*Milton*, Sonnets, xvii); collectively, the students of a university or college (the town and *gown*).—*v.t. Gowned, gowning.* To put a gown on; to clothe or dress in a gown.—*v.i.* To put on a gown; to wear a gown or robe.—**gownsman,** gounz′man, *n.* One whose professional habit is a gown, as a lawyer, professor, or student of a university.

Graafian, grä′fi•an, *a.* [From Regnier de *Graaf*, a Dutch physician.] Applied to certain vesicles developed in the ovaries of mammals for the special purpose of expelling the ovum.

Graal, grāl, *n.* Same as *Grail.*

grab, grab, *v.t.*—*grabbed, grabbing.* [Sw. *grabba*, to grasp; D. *grabbelen*, to snatch; akin *grapple, gripe, graip, grope*, etc.] To seize; to snatch; to grip suddenly. (*Colloq.*)—*n.* A sudden grasp or seizure; a catch; an advantage (*colloq.*); an implement for clutching objects.—**grabber,** grab′ėr, *n.* One who or that which grabs.

grace, grās, *n.* [Fr., from L. *gratia*, favor, from *gratus*, pleasant (seen also in *grateful, gratitude, agree, ingrate*, etc.); from a root seen in Gr. *chairō*, to rejoice, Gael. *gradh*, love, and E. *yearn.*] Favor, goodwill, or kindness; disposition to oblige another; the love and favor of God; divine influence renewing the heart and restraining from sin; a state of reconciliation to God; virtuous or religious affection or disposition proceeding from divine influence; mercy; pardon; favor conferred; a license, dispensation, or peculiar privilege; a short prayer before or after meals acknowledging the grace or goodness of God; [*usually cap.*] (with possessive pronouns) a title used in addressing or speaking of a duke or duchess; that external element in acting or speaking which renders it appropriate and agreeable; elegance with appropriate dignity; a beauty or element in what pleases the eye; an embellishment; an affectation of elegance, dignity, or refinement (a person's airs and *graces*); dispensation by university authorities to take a degree; [*cap.*] *Greek myth.* beauty or elegance deified; one of three goddesses in whose gift were grace, loveliness, and favor; *mus.* a turn, trill, shake, etc., introduced for embellishment.—*Days of grace, com.* three days immediately following the day when a bill becomes due, which days are allowed to the debtor or payer to make payment in. —*A person's good graces*, a person's favor or friendly regard.—*With a good grace*, graciously; with at least an air of graciousness.—*With a bad grace*, ungracefully; ungraciously.—*v.t.*—*graced, gracing.* To lend or add grace to; to adorn; to serve to embellish or dignify; to honor.—**grace cup,** *n.* A final parting cup, after grace has been said.—**graceful,** grās′fụl, *a.* Displaying grace in form or action; possessing a peculiar elegance or attraction in mien or appearance: used particularly of motion, looks, and speech.—**gracefully,** grās′fụl•li, *adv.* In a graceful manner. —**gracefulness,** grās′fụl•nes, *n.* The condition or quality of being graceful.—**graceless,** grās′les, *a.* Void of grace; somewhat careless in regard to religious matters; not at all devout; unregenerate; unsanctified.—**gracelessly,** grās′les•li, *adv.* In a graceless manner.—**gracelessness,** grās les•nes, *n.*—**grace note,** *n. Mus.* a note added by way of ornament, and printed or written in smaller characters; an appoggiatura.—**gracious,** grā′shus, *a.* [Fr. *gracieux*, L. *gratiosus.*] Favorable; benevolent; merciful; benign; kind; friendly; proceeding from, produced by, or associated with divine grace, virtuous; good; polite.—**graciously,** grā′shus•li, *adv.* In a gracious manner. —**graciousness,** grā′shus•nes, *n.*

gracile,† gräs′il, *a.* [L. *gracilis*, slender.] Slender.—**gracility,** gra•sil′i•ti, *n.* Slenderness.

grackle, grak′l, *n.* [L. *graculus*, a jackdaw, imitative of the cry.] Any of various birds of Asia and Africa of the starling family; any of certain blackbirds of the U.S., as the purple grackle.

grade, grād, *n.* [Fr. *grade*, from L. *gradus*, a step, from *gradior*, *gressus*, to go, seen also in *congress*, *degrade*, *degree*, *egress*, *ingredient*, *progress*, *retrograde*, etc.] A degree in any series, rank, or order, relative position or standing; one of the sections of a school system, as divided into years of work; the group of pupils in one of these sections; a mark rating a pupil's work; the rate of ascent or descent; the part of a road which slopes.—*v.t.*—*graded*, *grading*. To arrange in order according to size, quality, rank, degree of advancement, and the like; to reduce (the line of a railway, etc.) to such levels or degrees of inclination as may make it suitable for being used. —**gradation,** gra•dā′shon, *n.* [L. *gradatio*.] The act of grading; the state of being graded; arrangement by grades or ranks; a regular advance from step to step; a degree or relative position in any order or series; the gradual blending of one tint into another.—**gradational,** gra•dā′shon•al, *a.* Of or pertaining to, or according to gradation.—**gradient,** grā′di•ent, *a.* [L. *gradiens*, *gradientis*, ppr. of *gradior*.] Moving by steps†; walking†; rising or descending by regular degrees of inclination.—*n.* The degree of slope or inclination of the ground over which a railway, road, or canal passes; the rate of ascent or descent; the part of a road which slopes.—**gradual,** grad′ū•al, *a.* [Fr. *graduel*.] Proceeding by steps or degrees; advancing step by step; regular and slow; progressive.—*n.* An ancient servicebook of the church: also called *Grail*; [*cap.*] song sung between epistle and Gospel at the steps of the altar.—**gradually,** grad′ū•al•li, *adv.* In a gradual manner; by degrees; step by step; regularly.—**graduate,** grad′ū•āt, *v.t.* —*graduated*, *graduating*. [Fr. *graduer*, from L. *gradus*.] To mark with degrees, regular intervals, or divisions; to divide into small regular distances (to *graduate* a thermometer); to temper or modify by degrees; to characterize or mark with degrees or grades, as of intensity; to confer a university degree on; to reduce to a certain consistency by evaporation.—*v.i.* To receive a degree from a college or university; to pass by degrees; to change gradually; to shade off.—*n.* One who has been admitted to a degree in a college or university, or by some incorporated society; a vessel with graduated measurement marks.—*a.* Arranged by successive steps or degrees. — **graduation,** grad•ū•ā′shon, *n.* The act of graduating, or state of being graduated; the marks or lines made on an instrument to indicate degrees or other divisions.—**graduator,** grad′ū•ā•tėr, *n.* One who or that which graduates; an instrument for graduating; a contrivance for accelerating evaporation.

graffiti, grä•fē′tē, *n. pl.* [Pl. of It. *graffito*, a scribbling, from *graffiare*, to scribble.] A class of rude scribblings or figures on the walls of Pompeii, the Catacombs etc., dating from ancient Roman times.

graft, graft, *n.* [O.Fr. *graffe*, Fr. *greffe*, a slip or shoot of a tree for grafting, originally a pointed instrument, from L. *graphium*, a style for writing on waxen tablets, from Gr. *graphō*, to write.] A small shoot or scion of a tree, inserted in another tree and becoming part of it, but retaining the characters of its own parent; *surg.* living tissue implanted, as in a lesion, to become an organic part; the act of grafting; corrupt gains or practices in politics.—*v.t.* To insert a graft on; to propagate by a graft; to incorporate after the manner of a graft.—*v.i.* To practice grafting or engage in corrupt but profitable pursuits.—**grafter,** graf′tėr, *n.* One who grafts; one who gains money or material profit by graft.

graham flour, grā′am, wheat flour made from the whole kernel.

grail, grāl, *n.* [O.Fr. *graal*, *greal*, L.L. *gradalis*, *gradale*, etc., perhaps from *cratella*, dim. of L. *crater*, Gr. *kratēr*, a cup.] The holy vessel used by Christ in the Last Supper (called the Holy Grail), said to have been found by Joseph of Arimathea, who had caught the last drops of Christ's blood in it.

grain, grān, *n.* [Fr. *grain*, from L. *granum*, a grain, seed, kernel. Of same origin are *granite*, *grange*, *garner*, etc.] A single seed of a plant, particularly of those plants whose seeds are used for food of man or beast; used collectively for edible seeds in general, or the fruits of cereal plants, as wheat, rye, oats, etc., as also for the plants themselves; *pl.* the husks or remains of grain used in brewing or distilling; any small hard particle, as of sand, sugar, salt, etc.; a minute particle; a small amount (not a *grain* of sense); the twentieth part of the scruple in apothecaries' weight, and the twenty-fourth part of a pennyweight troy; the substance of a thing regarded with respect to the size, form, or direction of the constituent particles; the fibers of wood or other fibrous substance, with regard to their arrangement or direction; texture (stone or wood of a fine *grain*); formerly the scarlet dye made from the kermes or cochineal insects, from their round, seedlike form; hence, a red-colored dye; also, a permanent color of any kind.—*To dye in grain*, originally, to dye with kermes; then, to dye deeply or permanently; now usually to dye in the fiber or raw material.—*Grain side of leather*, the side from which the hair has been removed.—*Against the grain*, against the fibers of wood; hence, against the natural temper; unwillingly; unpleasantly; reluctantly.—*Grains of Paradise*, the pungent, somewhat aromatic seeds of a plant of the ginger family, a native of tropical Western Africa.—*v.t.* To form into grains, as powder, sugar, and the like; to paint so as to give the appearance of grains or fibers; *tan.* to give a granular appearance to the surface; to prepare the hairy side as the outer side.—*v.i.* To form grains or to assume a granular form, as the result of crystallization.—**grainer,** grā′nėr, *n.* One who or that which grains; a peculiar brush or a toothed instrument used by painters.—**grainy,** grā′ni, *n.* Full of grains or corn; full of kernels.—**granary,** gran′a•ri, *n.* [L. *granarium*, from *granum*.] A storehouse for grain after it is threshed.—**graniform,** gran′i•form, *a. Bot.* formed like grains of corn.—**granivorous,** gra•niv′o•rus, *a.* [L. *granum*, and *voro*, to eat.] Eating grain; feeding or subsisting on seeds.

grain, grān, *n.* [Same word as Dan. *green*, a branch, a prong; Icel. *grein*, a branch; akin *groin*.] A tine, prong, or spike; *pl.* a kind of harpoon with four or more barbed points.

Grallatores, Grallae, gral•a•tō′rēz, gral′ē, *n. pl.* [L. *grallæ*, stilts, *grallator* (pl. *grallatores*), one who goes on stilts, from *gradior*, to go. GRADE.] An order of birds generally characterized by very long legs, long necks, and long bills, including the cranes, plovers, snipes, rails, coots, etc., etc.; the waders.—**grallatorial,** gral•a•tō′ri•al, *a.* Pertaining to the Grallatores.

gram, gram, *n.* The name of a chickpea extensively cultivated in the East Indies.

gram, gram, *n.* [Fr., from Gr. *gramma*, a letter, also the weight of a scruple, from *grapho*, to write.] The unit of weight in the metric system equivalent to a cubic centimeter of water.—**gram molecule,** gram mol′e•kūl, *n.* The quantity of a substance having a weight in grams numerically equal to its molecular weight; also **gram-molecular weight.**

gramineous, gra•min′i•us, *a.* [L. *gramineus*, from *gramen*, *graminis*, grass.] Like or pertaining to grass or to the tribe of grasses.

grammar, gram′mar, *n.* [Fr. *grammaire*, from a hypothetical L.L. form *grammaria*, from Gr. *gramma*, a letter, from *graphō*, to write (whence *graphic*, etc.). GRAVE, *v.t.*] The exposition of the principles which underlie the use of language; a system of general principles and of particular rules for speaking or writing a language; a book containing such principles and rules; language as regulated by rules or usage; propriety of speech (to violate *grammar*; *good* grammar, *bad* grammar, correct or incorrect language); a treatise on the elements or principles of any science; an outline of the principles of any subject.—*a.* Belonging to or contained in grammar.—**grammarian,** gram•mâ′ri•an, *n.* One versed in grammar.—**grammatical,** gram•-

mat′i•kal, *a.* Belonging to grammar; according to the rules of grammar.—**grammatically,** gram•mat′i•kal•li, *adv.* In a grammatical manner; according to the rules of grammar.—**grammar school,** *n.* A grade school; a school including the intermediate grades between the primary grades and high school; a school in which Latin and Greek are more especially taught.

grampus, gram′pus, *n.* [Sp. *gran pez,* from L. *grandis,* great, and *piscis,* a fish; comp. *porpoise, porpus.*] A marine mammal of the dolphin family, which grows to the length of 25 feet, and preys on fish; in secondary sense, a person who snores.

granadilla, gran•a•dil′la, *n.* [Sp., dim. of *granada,* a pomegranate.] The fruit of a species of passion flower much esteemed in tropical countries; also the plant.

granary. See GRAIN.

grand, grand, *a.* [Fr. *grand,* from L. *grandis,* great, grand, seen also in *aggrandize.*] Great; illustrious; high in power or dignity; noble; splendid; magnificent; principal or chief: used largely in composition (*grand* juror, *grand* master); conceived or expressed with great dignity; implying an additional or second generation, as in *grand*father, *grand*child, etc.—**grandam,** gran′dam, *n.* [*Grand* and *dame*] An old woman; a grandmother.—**grandaunt,** *n.* The aunt of one's father or mother.—**grandchild,** grand′child, *n.* A son's or daughter's child or offspring —**granddaughter,** grand′da̤•tėr, *n.* The daughter of a son or daughter.—**grandfather,** grand′fä•THėr, *n.* A father's or mother's father.—**grandmother,** grand′-muTH•ėr, *n.* A father's or mother's mother.—**grandnephew,** *n.* The grandson of a brother or sister.—**grandniece,** *n.* The granddaughter of a brother or sister.—**grandparent,** grand′pâ•rent, *n.* The parent of a parent.—**grandsire,** grand′sīr, *n.* A grandfather; any ancestor preceding a father.—**grandson,** grand′sun, *n.* The son of a son or daughter.—**granduncle,** *n.* The uncle of one's father or mother.—**grand duke,** the title of former sovereigns of certain German states; also applied to members of the former imperial family of Russia.—**grandee,** gran•dē′, *n.* [Sp. *grande,* a nobleman.] A Spanish nobleman of the first rank; hence a nobleman or man of high rank in general.—**grandeur,** grand′yėr, *a.* [Fr.] The state or quality of being grand.—**grandiloquence,** gran•dil′o•-kwens, *n.* The quality of being grandiloquent. — **grandiloquent,** gran•dil′o•kwent, *a.* [L. *grandiloquens* —*grandis,* and *loquor,* to speak.] Speaking in a lofty style; expressed in high-sounding words; bombastic; pompous.—**grandiose,** gran′di•ōs, *a.* [Fr.] Impressive from inherent grandeur; imposing; commonly, aiming at or affecting grandeur; grandiloquent; bombastic; turgid.—**grandiosity,** gran•di•os′i•ti, *n.* The quality of being grandiose.—**grand jury,** a jury whose duty is to examine into the grounds of accusation against offenders, and if they see just cause, to find a true bill against them.—**grandly,** grand′li, *adv.* In a grand or lofty manner.—**grandness,** grand′-nes, *n.* Grandeur; greatness with beauty; magnificence.—**grand opera,** opera that compares with serious drama in characterization and plot and has a completely sung text.—**grandstand,** *n.* An elevated system of seats arranged one row above another at a racecourse or athletic field, usually with a roof, whence a good view can be obtained —**grand vizier,** the chief minister of the former Turkish Empire.

grange, grānj, *n.* [Fr. *grange,* a barn, from L.L. *granea, granica,* a barn, from L. *granum,* grain. GRAIN.] A farm, with the dwelling house, stables, barns, etc.; one of the local lodges of the secret farmers' organization called "The Patrons of Husbandry." Nationally, the Grange dates from 1867, and includes both men and women. Its social, fraternal, and educational aims were later expanded to become an effective influence in political and legislative matters, both state and national, in the interest of the farm population.

granite, gran′it, *n.* [Fr. *granit,* from It. *granito,* lit. grained stone, from L. *granum,* a grain. GRAIN.] An unstratified rock, one of the most abundant in the earth's crust, composed generally of grains or crystals of quartz, feldspar, and mica, united without regular arrangement.—**granitic,** gra•nit′ik, *a.* Of or pertaining to granite; having the nature of granite; consisting of granite.—**granitoid,** gran′i•toid, *a.* Resembling granite.—**graniteware,** *n.* Articles made of iron coated with vitreous enamel.

grant, grant, *v.t.* [From O.Fr. *graanter, graunter, craanter, creanter,* to promise, to agree, to guarantee, from (hypothetical) L.L. *credentare,* to make to believe or trust, from L. *credens,* pp. of *credo,* to believe. CREED.] To transfer the title or possession of; to convey, give, or make over; to bestow or confer, particularly in answer to prayer or request; to admit as true though not proved; to allow; to yield; to concede.—*v.i.* To make a grant; to consent (*Shak.*). —*n.* The act of granting, bestowing, or conferring; the thing granted or bestowed.—**grantable,** gran′ta•bl, *a.* Capable of being granted or conveyed.—**grantee,** gran•tē′, *n.* The person to whom a grant or conveyance is made.—**granter,** gran′tėr, *n.* One who grants —**grantor,** gran′tor, *n.* *Law,* the person who makes a grant or conveyance.

granular, gran′ū•lėr, *a.* [From L. *granum,* grain. GRAIN.] Consisting of or resembling granules or grains. —**granulate,** gran′ū•lāt, *v.t.*—*granulated, granulating.* [Fr. *granuler.*] To form into grains or small masses; to raise in granules or small asperities; to make rough on the surface.—*v.i.* To collect or be formed into grains; to become granular.—**granulation,** gran•ū•lā′shon, *n.* The act of granulating; a reducing to the form of small grains; *surg.* a process by which little granular fleshy bodies form on sores when healing; the fleshy grains themselves —**granule,** gran′ūl, *n.* [Fr., dim. from L. *granum,* a grain.] A little grain; a small particle; a minute round body of vegetable or animal matter.

grape, grāp, *n.* [O.Fr. *grape,* grape, Mod.Fr. *grappe,* a bunch or cluster, originally a hook, from O.G. *krapfe,* a hook.] A smooth-skinned berry from a vine of the Vitaceae family, ranging in color from white to deep red and blue-black, eaten fresh or dried, as raisins, and used for making wine; *milit.* grapeshot. —*Sour grapes,* things professedly despised because they are beyond our reach: from Aesop's fable of 'The Fox and the Grapes'.—**grapery,** grā′pėr•i, *n.* A place where grapes are grown; a vinery.—**grapefruit,** *n.* A large, yellow citrus fruit developed from the shaddock; the tree bearing this fruit.—**grapeshot,** *n.* Iron balls held in a frame and fired from a cannon.—**grapestone,** *n.* The stone or seed of the grape.—**grape sugar,** a variety of sugar from grapes; glucose.—**grapevine,** *n.* The vine that bears grapes; also some secret means of communicating rumor.

graph, graf, *n.* [Gr. *graphō,* I write.] A diagram representing the relation between two varying magnitudes by means of a curve referred to fixed axes.—**graphic, graphical,** graf′ik, graf′i•kal, *a.* Pertaining to the art of writing, engraving, or delineating; written; pictorial; describing with accuracy or vividly; vivid; portraying in vivid and expressive language. —*Graphic granite,* a variety of granite which when cut in one direction exhibits markings resembling Hebrew characters.—**graphically,** graf′-i•kal•li, *adv.* In a graphic manner.—**graphite, graf′īt,** *n.* [Gr. *graphein,* to write.] One of the forms under which carbon occurs, made into pencils, and used as a moderator in atomic reactors.

grapnel, grap′nel, *n.* [Dim. from Fr. *grappin,* a grapnel; of same origin as *grape.*] A small anchor with four or five flukes or claws, used to hold boats or small vessels; a grappling iron.

grapple, grap′l, *v.t.*—*grappled, grappling.* [Directly from O.Fr. *grappil,* a grapnel; or from *grab* or *gripe.*] To lay fast hold on, either with the hands or with hooks; to seize and hold.—*v.i.* To contend in close fight, as wrestlers.—*To grapple with,* to contend with; to struggle with; to confront boldly.—*n.* A close seizure or hug; the wrestler's hold; close fight or encounter; a hook by which one ship fastens on another.—**grappling iron.** *n.* An instrument consisting of four or more iron claws for grappling and holding fast.

grasp, grasp, *v.t.* [From stem of *grope, gripe,* or *grab*; comp. G.

grapsen, to snatch, from O.G. *grappen, grabben.*] To seize and hold by the fingers or arms; to lay hold of; to take possession of; to seize by the intellect; to comprehend.—*v.i.* To make a clutch or catch; to gripe.—*To grasp at*, to catch at; to try to seize.—*n.* The grip or seizure of the hand; reach of the arms; hence, the power of seizing and holding; forcible possession; power of the intellect to seize and comprehend; wide-reaching power of intellect.—**grasper,** gras′pėr, *n.* One who or that which grasps.
grasping, gras′ping, *a.* Covetous; rapacious; avaricious; greedy; miserly.—**graspingly,** gras′ping•li, *adv.* In a grasping manner.
grass, gras, *n.* [A.Sax. *græs, gæs*=Goth. Icel. D. and G. *gras*, Dan. *græs*, Sw. *gräs*; probably akin to *grow* and *green.*] In common usage (and without a plural), herbage; the verdurous covering of the soil; also any plant of the family to which belong the grain-yielding and pasture plants.—*China grass*, a Chinese plant, of the nettle family, from the fiber of which grass cloth is made.—*Esparto grass.* ESPARTO.—*v.t.* To cover with grass; to furnish with grass; to bleach on the grass.—**grasshopper,** gras′hop•ėr, *n.* A leaping orthopterous insect allied to the locusts, commonly living among grass.—**grassiness,** gras′i•nes, *n.* The condition of being grassy.—**grassland,** *n.* Land kept under grass.—**grass roots, gras rọts,** *n.* The rural and farming districts regarded as a source of independent popular opinion.—*To get down to grass roots*, to get down to the fundamental part, close to, or emerging from, the people.—**grass widow,** *n.* Formerly, an unmarried woman who had a child: now applied to a wife separated from her husband.—**grassy,** gras′i, *a.*
grate, grāt, *n.* [It. *grata*, a grate, lattice, hurdle, from L.L. *grata, crata*, L. *crates*, a hurdle. CRATE.] A series of parallel or cross bars, with interstices; a kind of latticework; a grating; a metallic receptacle for holding burning fuel, and formed to a greater or less extent of bars.—*v.t.* To furnish with a grate or grates; to fill in or cover with crossbars.—**grating,** grā′ting, *n.* A partition or frame of parallel or cross bars.—**gratelike,** grāt′līk, *a.*
grate, grāt, *v.t.*—*grated, grating.* [O.Fr. *grater*, Fr. *gratter*, to scratch, to rub; from the Teutonic; comp. O.H.G. *chrazón*, G. *kratzen*, to scratch; Dan. *kratte, kradse*, to scratch; E. *scratch.*] To rub hard or roughly together, as a body with a rough surface against another body; to wear away in small particles by rubbing with anything rough or indented; to offend or irritate.—*v.i.* To rub roughly with the surface in contact (a body *grates* upon another); to have a galling or annoying effect (to *grate* upon the feelings); to make a harsh sound by friction; to sound disagreeably.—**grater,** grā′tėr, *n.* One who or that which grates.—**grating,** gra′ting, *p.* and *a.* Irritating; harsh.—*n.* The harsh sound or the feeling caused by strong attrition or rubbing.—**gratingly,** *adv.* In a grating manner.
grateful, grāt′fụl, *a.* [From O.Fr. *grat.* L. *gratus*, pleasing, and E. adjectival term, *ful.* GRACE.] Having a due sense of benefits; having kind feelings and thankfulness toward one from whom a favor has been received; expressing gratitude; indicative of gratitude; affording pleasure; agreeable; pleasing to the taste or the intellect; gratifying.—**gratefully,** grāt′fụl•li, *adv* In a grateful manner.—**gratefulness,** grāt′fụl•nes, *n.* The state or quality of being grateful.—**gratitude,** grat′i•tūd, *n.* [L.L. *gratitudo.*] The feeling of one who is grateful; a warm and friendly emotion awakened by a favor received; thankfulness.
gratify, grat′i•fī, *v.t.*—*gratified, gratifying.* [Fr. *gratifier*, L. *gratificor*—*gratus*, pleasant, agreeable, and *facio*, to make. GRATEFUL.] To please; to give pleasure to; to indulge, delight, humor, satisfy.—**gratification,** grat′i•fi•kā″shon, *n.* [L. *gratificatio.*] The act of gratifying or pleasing; that which affords pleasure; enjoyment; satisfaction; delight.—**gratifier,** grat′i•fī•ėr, *n.* One who gratifies.
gratis, grā′tis, *adv.* [L., from *gratia*, favor. GRACE.] For nothing; freely; without recompense (to give a thing *gratis*).—*a.* Given or done for nothing.
gratitude. See GRATEFUL.
gratuitous, gra•tū′i•tus, *a.* [L. *gratuitus*, from *gratus*, pleasing, agreeable. GRATEFUL, GRACE.] Given without an equivalent or recompense; free; voluntary; not required, called for, or warranted by the circumstances; adopted or asserted without any good ground (a *gratuitous* assumption).—**gratuitously,** gra•tū′i•tus•li, *adv.* In a gratuitous manner.—**gratuitousness,** gra•tū′i•tus•nes, *n.*—**gratuity,** gra•tū′i•ti, *n.* A free gift; a present; a donation.
gratulate,† grat′ū•lāt, *v.t. gratulated, gratulating.* [L. *gratulor, gratulatus*, from *gratus*, pleasing, agreeable. GRACE.] To salute with declarations of joy; to congratulate.—**gratulant,** grat′ū•lant, *a.* Congratulatory.—**gratulation,** grat•ū•lā′shon, *n.* [L. *gratulatio.*] Congratulation.—**gratulatory,** grat′ū•la•to•ri, *a.* Congratulatory.—*n.* A congratulation.
gravamen, gra•vā′men, *n.* [L., from *gravo*, to weigh down, from *gravis*, heavy. GRAVE, *a.*] That part of an accusation which weighs most heavily against the accused; ground or burden of complaint in general.
grave, grāv, *v.t.*—*graved* (pret.), *graven* or *graved* (pp,), *graving* (ppr.). [A.Sax. *grafan*, to dig, to grave or carve=D. *graven* Dan. *grave*, Icel. *grafa*, G. *graben*, to dig, to engrave; cog. Ir. *grafaim*, to engrave, to scrape; Gr. *graphō*, to grave, to write.] To carve or cut; to form or shape by cutting with a tool; to delineate by cutting; to engrave; hence, to impress deeply.—**graver,** grā′vėr, *n.* One who carves or engraves; an engraving tool; a burin.
grave, grāv, *n.* [A.Sax. *græf*, a grave, a trench, from stem of *grafan*, to dig or grave=Dan. *graf*, Icel. *gröf*, D. *graf*, G. *grab*, Rus. *grob*, a grave. GRAVE, to carve.] An excavation in the earth in which a dead human body is deposited; hence, any place of interment; a tomb; a sepulcher.—**graveclothes,** *n. pl.* The clothes in which the dead are interred.—**gravestone,** *n.* A stone placed at a grave as a monument to the dead.—**graveyard,** *n.* A yard or enclosure for the interment of the dead.
grave, grāv, *v.t.* [From the *graves* or dregs of melted tallow with which ships' hulls were formerly smeared.] To clean a ship's bottom of seaweeds, etc., and pay it over with pitch or tar.—**graving dock,** *n.* See DOCK.
grave, grāv, *a.* [Fr. *grave*, from L. *gravis*, heavy (whence also *grief, aggravate, gravid, gravitate*); allied to Gr. *barys*, heavy, *baros*, weight (in *barometer*); Skr. *guru*, heavy.] Solemn; serious; opposed to *light* or *jovial*; plain; not showy; important; momentous; having a serious and interesting import; *mus.* low; depressed; opposed to *sharp, acute*, or *high.*—**gravely,** grāv′li, *adv.* In a grave manner.—**graveness,** grāv′nes, *n.* The state or quality of being grave; gravity.
gravel, grav′el, *n.* [Fr. *gravele*, from O.Fr. *grave*, sand or gravel, from the Celtic; Armor. *grouan*, sand; W. *grou*, pebbles, coarse gravel.] Small stones or very small pebbles collectively; small stones, sand, etc., combined; *pathol.* small concretions or calculi in the kidneys or bladder; the disease occasioned by such concretions.—*v.t.*—*graveled, graveling*, or *gravelled, gravelling.* To cover with gravel; to cause to stick in the sand or gravel; hence, to perplex and bring to an intellectual standstill; to puzzle; to hurt the foot of (a horse) by gravel lodged under the shoe.—**gravel-blind,** *a.* [A mistaken coinage, as in Shak., *Merchant of Venice*, ii, 2, 38, on the supposed analogy of *sand-blind.*] More blind than sand-blind and less than stoneblind.—**gravelly,** grav′el•i, *a.* Abounding with gravel; consisting of gravel.
graven, grā′vn, pp. of *grave*, to carve.
gravid, grav′id, *a.* [L. *gravidus*, from *gravis*, heavy. GRAVE. *a.*] Being with child, pregnant.—**gravidity,** gra•vid′i•ti, *n.* pregnancy; impregnation.
gravimeter, gra•vim′et•ėr, *n.* [L. *gravis*, heavy, and Gr. *metron*, a measure.] An instrument for determining the specific gravities of bodies, whether liquid or solid, as a hydrometer.
graving dock, See GRAVE (to clean a ship's bottom) and DOCK.
gravitate, grav′i•tāt, *v.i.*—*gravitated, gravitating.* [Fr. *graviter*, from L.

gravitas, from *gravis*, heavy. GRAVE, *a*]. To be affected by gravitation; to move under the influence of gravitation; *fig.* to have a tendency toward some attracting influence.—**gravitation,** grav•i•tā'shon, *n.* The act of gravitating or tending to a center of attraction; the force by which bodies are drawn, or by which they tend toward the center of the earth or other center or the effect of that force.—**gravitative,** grav'i•tā•tiv, *a.* Causing to gravitate or tend to a center.—**gravity,** grav'i•ti, *n.* The state or character of being grave; solemnity of deportment, character, or demeanor; seriousness; weight or weightiness; enormity (the *gravity* of an offense); the force which causes a mass of matter to tend toward a center of attraction, especially toward the center of the earth; the force by which the planets mutually attract each other and are attracted toward the sun; centripetal force.—*Specific gravity*, the relative gravity or weight of any body or substance considered with regard to the weight of an equal bulk of pure distilled water at a specific temperature.

gravy, grā'vi, *n.* [From *graves*, *greaves*, the dregs of melted tallow.] A sauce for meat, made chiefly from the juice that drips from meat in cooking, seasoned and thickened; (slang) something valuable offered or received over and above expectations.

gray, grey, grā, *a.* [A.Sax. *graeg*=D. *graauw*, Icel. *grār*, Dan. *graa*, G. *grau*, gray; other connections are unknown.] Of the color of hair whitened by age; hoary; white with a mixture of black; of the color of ashes; having gray hairs; old; mature (*gray* experience).—*n.* A gray color; a dull or neutral tint; an animal of a gray color, as a horse. —**grayback, greyback,** a whalebone whale.—**graybeard, greybeard,** *n.* A man with a gray beard; an old man; a large earthen jar or bottle for holding liquor.—**grayish,** grā'ish, *a.* Somewhat gray; gray in a moderate degree.—**grayling,** grā'ling, *n.* [From the silvery gray of its back and sides.] A game fish of the salmon family, 16 to 18 inches long, found in cold, swift streams.—**gray matter,** nerve tissue made up of both nerve cells and nerve fiber; hence, brains; intelligence.—**grayness, greyness,** grā'nes, *n.* The state or quality of being gray.—**gray owl,** the tawny owl; a large, arctic owl.—**gray squirrel,** a large, grayish-colored squirrel of the eastern U.S.—**graywacke, grauwacke,** grā•wak'e, grou•wak'e, *n.* [G. *grauwacke*—*grau*, gray, and *wacke*, a kind of rock.] A kind of sandstone in which grains or fragments of various minerals or rocks are embedded in an indurated matrix, which may be siliceous or argillaceous.

grayhound. See GREYHOUND.

graze, grāz, *v.t.*—*grazed, grazing.* [Perhaps from the combined influence of *grate*, to rub, and *rase*; or perhaps originally meaning to skim along the grass, from *grass*, like *graze*, to pasture.] To rub or touch lightly in passing, as a missile does; to brush lightly the surface of.—*v.i.* To pass so as to touch or rub lightly.—*n.* The act of grazing; a slight rub or brush.

graze, grāz, *v.t.*—*grazed, grazing.* [A.Sax. *grasian*, to graze or feed, from *græs*, grass; comp. D. *grazen*, to graze, and *gras*, grass, G. *grasen*, and *gras*.] To feed or supply with growing grass; to furnish pasture for; to feed on; to eat from the ground.—*v.i.* To eat grass; to feed on growing herbage.—*n.* The act of grazing or feeding on grass.—**grazer,** grā'zėr, *n.* One that grazes.—**grazier,** grā'zhėr, *n.* One who grazes or pastures cattle for the market; a farmer who raises and deals in cattle.—**grazing,** grā'zing, *n.* The act of feeding on grass; a pasture.

grease, grēs, *n.* [Fr. *graisse*, O.Fr. *gresse*, from L. *crassus*, fat, gross, whence E. *crass*; akin Gael. *creis*, fat.] Animal fat in a soft state; particularly the fatty matter of land animals, as distinguished from the oily matter of marine animals; *farriery*, a swelling and inflammation in a horse's legs attended with the secretion of oily matter and cracks in the skin.—*v.t.* (grēz or grēs).—*greased, greasing*. To smear, anoint or daub with grease or fat.—**greasily,** grē'zi•li, *adv.* In a greasy manner.—**greasiness,** grē'zi•nes, *n.* The quality or state of being greasy.—**greasy,** grē'zi, *a.* Composed of or characterized by grease; fatty; unctuous; having the appearance of fat or grease; seemingly unctuous to the touch, as some minerals; gross; indecent.

great, grāt, *a.* [A.Sax. *great*=L.G. and D. *groot*, G. *gross*, great; perhaps allied to L. *grandis*.] Large in bulk, surface, or linear dimensions; of wide extent; big; large in number; numerous; large, extensive, or unusual in degree; long continued; of long duration; important; weighty; involving important interests; holding an eminent or prominent position in respect of mental endowments or acquirements, virtue, or vice, rank, office, power, or the like; eminent; distinguished; celebrated; notorious; of elevated sentiments; generous; noble; on an extensive scale; sumptuous; magnificent; wonderful; sublime; grand; pregnant; teeming; filled; denoting a degree of consanguinity in the ascending or descending line (*great* grandfather).—*Great circle*, a circle formed on the surface of a sphere by its plane cutting through the center of the sphere.—*The great*, pl., the rich, the distinguished, persons of rank and position.—**Great Dane,** a dog of a breed noted for its great size and strength.—**Great Divide,** the Rocky Mountains, dividing continental drainage east and west.—**greathearted,** *a.* High-spirited; magnanimous.—**greatly,** grāt'li, *adv.* In a great manner or degree.—**greatness,** grāt'nes, *n.* The state or quality of being great; magnitude; dignity; eminence; distinguished rank or position.

greave, grēv, *n.* [Fr. *grève*, armor for the leg; Sp. and Pg. *greba*, probably of Ar. origin.] Armor worn on the front of the lower part of the leg, across the back of which it was buckled.

grebe, grēb, *n.* [Fr. *grèbe*, from Armor. *krib*, W. *crib*, a comb, a crest, one variety having a crest.] An aquatic bird of various species, having no tail, toes separate, but broadly fringed by a membrane, and legs set so far back that on land it assumes the upright position of the penguin.

Grecian, grē'shan, *a.* [GREEK.] Pertaining to Greece; Greek.—*n.* A native of Greece; or a person of the Greek race; one versed in the Greek language.—**Grecism,** grē'sizm, *n.* An idiom of the Greek language.—**Grecize,** grē'siz, *v.t.*—*Grecized, Grecizing*. To render Grecian: to translate into Greek.—*v.i.* To speak the Greek language.

greedy, grē'di, *a.* [A.Sax. *grédig*, *graedig*=Goth. *gredags*, Icel. *gráthugr*, Dan. *graadig*, D. *gretig*, greedy. Hence *greed*, which is quite a modern word in English=Icel. *gráthr*, Goth *gredus*, hunger.] Having a keen appetite for food or drink; ravenous; voracious; very fond of eating; gluttonous; having a keen desire for anything; covetous (*greedy* of gain).—**greed,** grēd, *n.* An eager desire or longing; greediness.—**greedily,** grē'di•li, *adv.* In a greedy manner; voraciously; eagerly.—**greediness,** grē'di•nes, *n.* The quality of being greedy.

Greek, grēk, *a.* [Fr. *grec*, L. *græcus*, Greek, from the *Graikoi*, an insignificant tribe of ancient northwestern Greece.] Pertaining to Greece.—*n.* A native of Greece; the language of Greece.—*Greek calends*, a supposed date, that never occurs, for payment, etc., there being calends only in the Roman calendar.—*Greek Church*, the established church in Greece; that part of the Christian church, more properly known as the Eastern Orthodox Church, that separated from the Roman (Western) Church in the eleventh century.—*Greek fire*, a combustible preparation, the constituents of which are supposed to have been asphalt, niter, and sulfur.—*Greek gift*, a gift presented in order to betray one.—*Greek-letter fraternity*, an organization, as in a university, designated by Greek letters.

green, grēn, *a.* [A.Sax. *gréne*=Dan. and Sw. *grön*, Icel. *grænn*, G. *grün*; akin to *grow*; L. *holus*, *olus*, green vegetables; Gr. *chloē*, a young shoot, *chlōros*, pale green; Skr. *hari*, green.] Of the color of grass or herbage and plants when growing; emerald; verdant; new; fresh; recent; fresh and vigorous; flourishing; undecayed (a *green* old age); containing its natural juices; not dry; not seasoned;

unripe, immature (*green* fruit); immature in age; young; raw; inexperienced; easily imposed upon.—*Green corn*, sweet Indian corn, grown for the table.—*Green tea*, tea of a greenish color from the mode in which the leaves are treated and having a peculiar flavor.—*Green turtle*, the turtle of which the soup is made.—*Green vitriol*, a name of sulfate of iron in a crystallized form. —*n.* A green color; a grassy plain or plat; a piece of ground covered with verdant herbage; a name of several pigments; *pl.* the leaves and stems of young plants used in cookery, especially certain plants of the cabbage kind.—*v.t.* To make green.—*v.i.* To grow green.—**greenback,** grēn′back, *n.* A note belonging to the paper money of the United States, first issued in 1862, from the back of the notes being of a green color.—**greenery,** grē′nėr•i, *n.* A mass of green foliage; the green hue of such a mass.—**green-eyed,** *a.* Having green eyes; seeing all things discolored or distorted; jaundiced.—**greenfinch,** *n.* A common European finch of a greenish color; the green linnet or grosbeak.—**greengage,** *n.* [After a person named *Gage*, who introduced it into England.] A species of plum having a juicy greenish pulp of an exquisite flavor.—**greengrocer,** *n.* A retailer of greens and other vegetables.—**greenheart,** *n.* See BEBEERU.—**greenhorn,** grēn′horn, *n.* A person easily imposed upon; a raw, inexperienced person.—**greenhouse,** grēn′hous, *n.* A building principally consisting of glazed frames or sashes for the purpose of cultivating exotic plants which are too tender to endure the open air: often artificially heated up.—**greening,** grēn′ing, *n.* A name given to certain varieties of apples green when ripe.—**greenish,** grēn′ish, *a.* Somewhat green; having a tinge of green; somewhat raw and inexperienced.—**greenness,** grēn′nes, *n.* The quality of being green.—**greenroom,** *n.* A room near the stage in a theater, to which actors retire during the intervals of their parts in the play.—**greensand,** *n.* A name given (from the color of some of the beds) to two groups of strata, the one (lower greensand) belonging to the lower cretaceous series, the other (upper greensand) to the upper cretaceous series.—**greenshank,** *n.* A well-known species of sandpiper with greenish legs.—**greensickness,** *n.* See CHLOROSIS.—**greenstone,** grēn′stōn, *n.* [From a tinge of green in the color.] A general designation for the hard granular crystalline varieties of trap.—**greensward,** *n.* Turf green with grass.—**greenth,** grēnth, *n.* The quality of being green; greenness.—**greenwood,** grēn′wud, *n.* A wood or forest when green, as in summer.—*a.* Pertaining to a greenwood.

greet, grēt, *v.t.* [A.Sax. *grétan*, to salute, hail, bid farewell = G. *grüssen*, D. *groeten*, to greet; comp. A.Sax. *grétan*, Prov. E. and Sc. *greet*, Goth. *gretan*, Icel. *gráta*, to weep.] To address with salutations or expressions of kind wishes; to pay respects or compliments to; to salute; to hail.—*v.i.* To meet and salute each other.—**greeter,** grēt′ėr, *n.* One who greets.—**greeting,** grēt′ing, *n.* Expression of kindness or joy; salutation at meeting; compliment sent by one absent.

greet, grēt, *v.i.* [GREET, to salute.] To weep. *(Old English* and *Scotch.)*

gregarious, gri•gâ′ri•us, *a.* [L. *gregarius*, from *grex*, *gregis*, a flock or herd; seen also in *aggregate*, *congregate*, *egregious*.] Having the habit of assembling or living in a flock or herd; not habitually solitary or living alone.—**gregariously,** gri•gâ′ri•us•li, *adv.* In a gregarious manner. —**gregariousness,** gri•gâ′ri•us•nes, *n.* The state or quality of being gregarious.—**gregarine,** greg′a•rin, *n.* A name of certain minute animals of a low type, having no definite organs observable, found inhabiting the intestines of various animals.

Gregorian, gri•gō′ri•an, *a.* [From *Gregory*.] Relating to any pope named Gregory.—*Gregorian calendar*, the calendar as reformed by Pope Gregory XIII in 1582.—*Gregorian chant*, a choral melody introduced into the service of the Christian church by Pope Gregory I about the end of the sixth century.

gremlin, grem′lin, *n.* [Perhaps from E. *goblin*, Irish-Gaelic *gruaimin*, ill-humored little fellow.] A tiny mischievous gnome, whimsically said to be responsible for disordering equipment.

grenade, gre•nād′, *n.* [Fr. *grenade*, Sp. *granada*, a pomegranate, a grenade (the missile somewhat resembling the fruit), from L. *granatum*, a pomegranate. GRAIN.] A hollow ball or shell of iron or other metal, or of annealed glass, filled with powder, fired by means of a fuse, and thrown among enemies.—**grenadier,** gren•a•dēr′, *n.* Originally a soldier who threw hand grenades; a tall soldier.

grenadine, gren′a•dēn, *n.* [From *Granada*.] A thin gauzy fabric.

grenadine, gren′a•dēn, *n.* [GRENADE.] A red syrup used in mixed drinks.

gressorial, gres•sō′ri•al, *a.* [L. *gressus*, a going, step. GRADE.] *Ornith.* having three toes forward (two of them connected) and one behind.

grew, grö, pret. of *grow*.

grewsome. See GRUESOME.

grey, grā. See GRAY.

greyhound, grā′hound, *n.* [Icel. *greyhundr*, from *grey*, a greyhound, a bitch; Sc. *grew*, a greyhound; Ir. *grech*, a hound; the name has no reference to the color.] A dog kept for the chase, remarkable for its beauty of form and its great fleetness.

griddle, grid′l, *n.* [W. *greidell*, from *greidiaw*, to heat, to scorch; Ir. *greidell*, *greidaim*, to scorch.] A broad metal disk used for frying griddle cakes.—**griddlecake,** *n.* A batter cake browned on both sides.

gride, grīd, *v.i.* [Partly from O.E. *girden*, to strike, pierce, cut, from *gerde*, a rod=*yard*; partly from O.E. *grede*, A.Sax. *graedan*, to cry.] To pierce; to cut through; to cut (*Mil.*); to give out a harsh creaking sound; to jar harshly (*Tenn.*)—*n.* A grating or harsh sound.

gridiron, grid′ī•ėrn, *n.* [From *grid*- of *griddle*, and *iron*.] A grated utensil for broiling flesh and fish over coals; anything likened to such a frame, a football field.

grief, grēf, *n.* [Fr. *grief*, grievance, what oppresses, from L. *gravis*, heavy. GRAVE. *a.*] Pain of mind, arising from any cause; sorrow; sadness; cause of sorrow or pain; that which afflicts; trial; grievance; bodily pain (*Shak.*)†.—*To come to grief*, to come to a bad end; to come to ruin; to meet with an accident. ∴ Syn. under AFFLICTION. —**grievance,** grē′vans, *n.* That which causes grief or uneasiness; wrong done and suffered; injury.—**grieve,** grēv, *v.t.*—*grieved*, *grieving*. [O.Fr. *griever*.] To cause to feel grief; to give pain of mind to; to make sorrowful; to afflict; to sorrow over; to deplore.—*v.i.* To feel grief; to sorrow; to mourn; followed by *at*, *for*, and *over*.—**griever,** grē′vėr, *n.* One who or that which grieves.—**grievingly,** grē′ving•li, *adv.* In a grieving manner.—**grievous,** grē′vus, *a.* Causing grief or sorrow; afflictive; hard to bear; heavy; severe; harmful; great; atrocious; aggravated; full of grief; indicating great grief or affliction.—**grievously,** grē′vus•li, *adv.* In a grievous manner.—**grievousness,** grē′vus•nes, *n.*

griffin, griffon, grif′in, grif′on, *n.* [Fr. *griffon*, It. *grifone*, from L. *gryps*, *gryphus*, griffin, from Gr. *gryps*, a griffon, from *grypos*, hook-beaked.] A mythical animal, in the fore part represented as an eagle, in the hinder part as a lion; a species of vulture found in the mountainous parts of Europe and in North Africa.

grig, grig, *n.* [Connected with *cricket*; in second sense with Sw. *kråka*, to creep.] A cricket; a grasshopper; the sand eel; a small eel of lively and incessant motion.

grill, gril, *v.t.* [From Fr. *griller*, to broil, from *gril*, a gridiron, *grille*, a grate; O.Fr. *graille*, from L.L. *graticula*, corrupted for L. *craticula*, a small gridiron, dim. of *crates*, a hurdle. GRATE, CRATE.] To broil on a gridiron or similar instrument. —*n.* A grated utensil for broiling meat, etc., over a fire; a gridiron.—**grillage,** gril′ij, *n.* [Fr., from *grille*, a grate, a railing.] A heavy framework of beams used to sustain foundations in soils of unequal compressibility.—**grille,** gril, *n.* [Fr.] A lattice or grating; a piece of grated work.

grilse, grils, *n.* [Probably a corruption of Sw. *græ-lax*, gray salmon.] The young of the salmon on its first return from the sea to fresh water.

grim, grim, *a.* [A.Sax. *grim*, fierce, ferocious; akin to *grama*, fury; Icel. *grimmr*, savage, angry, *gramr*, wrath; Dan. *grim*, ugly; D. *gram*, angry, *grimmen*, to growl; Gr *grimm*, furious, *grimmen*, to rage; comp. W. *grem*, a snarl, *gremiaw*, to snarl.] Of a forbidding or fear-inspiring aspect; fierce; stern; sullen; sour; surly.—*v.t.* To make grim; to give a forbidding or fear-inspiring aspect to (*Carl.*).—**grimly,** grim′li, *a.* Having a grim, hideous, or stern look.—*adv.* In a grim manner.—**grimness,** grim′nes, *n.* The state or quality of being grim.

grimace, gri•mās′, *n.* [Fr., a wry face, from the Teutonic; comp. D. *grimmen*, to snarl, to make faces. GRIM.] A distortion of the countenance expressive of affectation, scorn, disapprobation, self-satisfaction, or the like; a smirk; a wry face.—*v.i.*—*grimaced, grimacing*. To make grimaces.

grimalkin, gri•mal′kin, *n.* [For *graymalkin—gray*, and *malkin*, that is *Mollkin*, dim. from *Mary*; comp. *Tom-cat*.] An old cat, especially a female cat.

grime, grīm, *n.* [Same as Dan. *grime*, a spot or streak, *grim*, soot, lampblack.] Foul matter; dirt; dirt deeply ingrained.—*v.t.*—*grimed, griming*. To sully or soil deeply; to dirt.—**grimily,** grī′mi•li, *adv.* In a grimy manner or condition; foully.—**griminess,** grī′mi•nes, *n.* The state or quality of being grimy.—**grimy,** grī′mi, *a.* Full of grime; foul; dirty.

grin, grin, *v.i.*—*grinned, grinning*. [A.Sax. *grinnian, grennian*, to grin = Dan. *grine*, D. *grijnen*, G. *greinen*, to grin, to cry, to weep; perhaps allied to *groan*.] To snarl and show the teeth, as a dog; to set the teeth together and open the lips; to show the teeth as in laughter, scorn, or pain.—*v.t.* To show, set, or snap (the teeth), in grinning; to express by grinning.—*n.* The act of withdrawing the lips and showing the teeth; a forced or sneering smile.—**grinner,** grin′ėr, *n.* One who grins.—**grinningly,** grin′ing•li, *adv.* In a grinning manner.

grind, grīnd, *v.t.*—*ground* (pret. & pp.), very rarely *grinded*. [A.Sax. *grindan*, to grind; same root as Gr. *chriō*, to graze or touch lightly; Skr. *ghrish*, to grind. *Grist* and *ground* (*n.*) are from this word.] To break and reduce to fine particles or powder by friction, as in a mill; to comminute by attrition; to triturate; to wear down, smooth, or sharpen by friction; to whet; to oppress by severe exactions; to harrass; to prepare for examination in some subject of study, or to study (in these senses university slang).—*v.i.* To grind corn or other matter; to be rubbed together, as in the operation of grinding; to be ground or pulverized; to drudge or perform hard work; to study hard, especially for an examination (*slang*).—*n.* The act of one who grinds; a spell of work.—**grinder,** grin′dėr, *n.* One who or that which grinds; a molar tooth.—**grindstone,** grīnd′stōn, *n.* A revolving stone used for grinding or sharpening tools.—*To bring or hold a person's nose to the grindstone*, to oppress him; to punish him.

grip, grip, *n.* [Directly from Fr. *gripper*, to grasp, which itself is from a Germanic word = E. *gripe*.] The act of grasping by the hand; grasp; the grasp peculiar to any secret fraternity as a means of recognition; a fast hold; a hilt or handle.—*v.t.*—*gripped, gripping*. To grasp by the hand; to gripe; to seize forcibly; to hold fast.—*v.i.* To take hold; to hold fast.

gripe, grīp, *v.t.*—*griped, griping*. [A.Sax. *grīpan*, to gripe, to grasp = Icel. *gripa*, D. *grijpen*, Goth. *greipan*, G. *greifen*, to seize; same root as *grab, grope, grasp*.] To catch with the hand and clasp closely with the fingers; to hold tight or close; to clutch; to seize and hold fast; to clench; to tighten; to give pain in the bowels, as if by pressure or contraction; to straiten or distress.—*v.i.* To take fast hold with the hand; to clasp closely with the fingers.—*n.* Grasp; seizure; grip; oppression; affliction; pinching distress; a kind of brake to act on a wheel; *pl.* a pinching intermittent pain in the intestines, of the character of that which accompanies diarrhea or colic.—**griper,** grī′pėr, *n.* One who gripes.—**griping,** grī′ping, *a.* Grasping; greedy; extortionate, causing a pinching feeling in the bowels.

grippe, grip, *n.* [Fr.] The influenza.

grisaille, gri•zāl′, *n.* [Fr., from *gris*, gray.] A style of painting in various gray tints employed to represent solid bodies in relief, as friezes, moldings, bas-reliefs, etc.

grisette, gri•zet′, *n.* [Fr. Originally, a gray woolen fabric, much used for dresses by women of the inferior classes, from *gris*, gray.] A young woman of the working class in France; a belle of the working class given to gaiety and gallantry.

grisly, griz′li, *a.* Gray; of a mixed color; grizzled.

grisly, griz′li, *a.* [A.Sax. *grislic*, from *grisan* or *ágrisan*, to dread, to fear greatly; allied to G. *grässlich*, horrible, *grausen*, horror; *grieseln*, to shudder; E. *grewsome*.] Frightful; horrible; terrible; grim.—**grisliness,** griz′li•nes, *n.* Quality of being grisly.

grist, grist, *n.* [A.Sax. *grist*, a grinding, from *grindan*, to grind. GRIND.] Corn ground in the mill or to be ground; the grain carried to the mill at one time, or the meal it produces.—*To bring grist to the mill*, to be a source of profit; to bring profitable business into one's hands.—**grist-mill,** *n.* A mill for grinding grain.

gristle, gris′l, *n.* [A.Sax. *gristel*, gristle; akin to *grist*, being named from the grinding or crunching it requires; comp. A.Sax. *gristlung*, a gnashing.] Cartilage.—**gristly,** gris′li, *a.* Consisting of or like gristle; cartilaginous.

grit, grit, *n.* [A.Sax. *greót*, sand; akin to E. *grits, grout, groats*; comp. Icel. *grjót*, stones, rubble; G. *gries*, grit.] Any hard sandstone; firmness of character; structure of a stone in regard to fineness and closeness of texture.—*v.i.* To give forth a grating sound, as sand beneath the shoes.—*v.t.* To spread with grit or abrasive, as marble before polishing; to clamp one's teeth together, causing them to grind.—**grittiness,** grit′i•nes, *n.*—**gritty,** grit′i, *a.*

grits, grits, *n. pl.* [A.Sax. *grytta, gryttan*, grits or groats.] Coarse hominy (*U.S.*); grain hulled or coarsely ground.

grivet, griv′et, *n.* A small green-gray Abyssinian monkey.

grizzle, griz′l, *n.* [From Fr. *gris*, gray, from O.G. *gris*, gray.] A gray color; a mixture of white and black; a mixture of white among dark hairs.—*v.i.* To grow gray or grizzly; to become gray-haired.—**grizzled,** griz′ld, *a.* Of a grayish color.—**grizzly,** griz′li, *a.* Somewhat gray; grayish.—*Grizzly* or *grisly bear*, a large and ferocious bear of Western North America.

groan, grōn, *v.i.* [A.Sax. *gránian*, to groan; perhaps imitative of the sound made in groaning; comp. A.Sax. *grunan*, to grunt; W. *grwn*, a groan.] To utter a mournful voice, as in pain or sorrow; to utter a deep, low-toned, moaning sound.—*n.* A deep, mournful sound uttered in pain, sorrow, or anguish; a deep sound uttered in disapprobation or derision.—**groaner,** grō′nėr, *n.* One who groans.

groat, grōt, *n.* [D. *groot*, G. *grot*, that is, *great*, a great piece or coin: so called because before this piece was coined by Edward III (1351) the English had no silver coin larger than a penny.] An old English coin and money of account, equal to fourpence; hence, colloquially, in England, fourpence, or a fourpenny piece.

groats, grōts, *n. pl.* [A.Sax. *grátan*, groats; akin *grits, grout*.] Oats or wheat with the husks taken off.

grocer, grō′sėr, *n.* [Properly a *grosser*, or one who sells things in the *gross*; O.Fr. *grossier*, one who sells by wholesale, from *gros*, great. GROSS.] A merchant who deals in tea, sugar, spices, coffee, fruits; a retail purveyor of foodstuffs.—**grocery,** grō′sėr•i, *n.* A grocer's shop; *pl.* the commodities sold by grocers.

grog, grog, *n.* [From 'Old *Grog*', a nickname given to Admiral Vernon, who introduced the beverage, from his wearing a *grogram* cloak in rough weather.] A mixture of spirit and water not sweetened; also used as a general term for strong drink.—**grogginess,** grog′i•nes, *n.* The state of being groggy.—**groggy,** grog′i, *a.* Overcome with grog; tipsy; *farriery*, moving in an uneasy, hobbling manner, owing to tenderness of the feet: said of a horse.—**grogshop,** *n.* A dramshop.

grogram, grog′ram, *n.* [Fr. *grosgrain*, coarse grain, of a coarse texture. GROSS, GRAIN.] A kind of coarse stuff made of silk and mohair; also, a kind of strong, coarse silk.

groin, groin, *n.* [Icel. *grein*, a branch, an arm of the sea, *greina*, to branch off or separate; Sw. *gren*, a branch, *grena*, to divide; Sc. *grain*, a branch, a prong of a fork.] The hollow of the human body in front at the junction of the thigh with the trunk; *arch.* the angular projecting curve made by the intersection of simple vaults crossing each other at any angle.—*v.t. Arch.* to form into groins; to ornament with groins.—**groined,** groind, *a. Arch.* having a groin or groins; formed of groins meeting in a point.—**groining,** groi'ning, *n. Arch.* the arrangement of groins; groins collectively.

grommet, grum'et, *n.* [Armor. *grom*, a curb.] *Naut.* a ring of rope; a metal eyelet, such as is used on canvas mailbags or the edge of a sail.

groom, gröm, *n.* [From A.Sax. *guma*, O.E. *gome*, man, with an inserted *r*; comp. O.D. *grom*, Icel. *gromr*, a youth. *Guma* (Goth. *guma*, O.H.G. *homo*) is the Teutonic word equivalent to L. *homo*, a man. Hence *bridegroom* (A.Sax. *brydguma*).] A man or boy who has the charge of horses; one who takes care of horses or the stable; one of several officers in the English royal household; a bridegroom.—*v.t.* To curry or care for a horse.—**groomsman,** grömz'-man, *n.* One who acts as attendant on a bridegroom at his marriage.

groove, gröv, *n.* [From D. *groeve*, *groef*, a furrow, a ditch, a channel = G. *grube*, a pit, hole, grave; the stem being same as in E. *grave, v.t.*] A furrow or long hollow, such as is cut by a tool; a channel, usually an elongated narrow channel; the fixed routine of one's life.—*v.t.*—*grooved, grooving*. To cut a groove or channel in; to furrow.—**groover,** grö'vėr, *n.* One who or that which grooves.

grope, grōp, *v.i.*—*groped, groping*. [A.Sax. *grápian*; closely allied to *gripe*, *grab*, and *grasp*.] To search or attempt to find something in the dark, or as a blind person, by feeling; to feel one's way; to attempt anything blindly.—*v.t.* To search out by feeling in or as in the dark (to *grope* our way).—**groper,** grō'pėr, *n.* One who gropes.—**gropingly,** grō'-ping•li, *adv.* In a groping manner.

grosbeak, *n.* See GROSS.

groschen, grō'shen, *n.* (*pl.* the same). [From L.L. *grossus*, thick—in opposition to ancient thin lead coins.] An old German coin; the ten-pfennig piece. (*Colloq.*)

gross, grōs, *a.* [Fr. *gros*, big, thick, coarse; L.L. *grossus*, thick, crass; of doubtful origin. Hence *grocer*.] Coarse or rough; indelicate, obscene, or impure; sensual; great, palpable or enormous; shameful; flagrant (a *gross* mistake, *gross* injustice); dense; not attenuated; whole; entire; total‡; bulky‡; of some size‡.—*Gross weight*, the weight of merchandise or goods, with the bag, cask, chest, etc., in which they are contained.—*n.* Main body; chief part; bulk; the number of twelve dozen (being the *gross* or great hundred): has no plural form. —*A great gross*, twelve gross or 144 dozen.—*In the gross, in gross*, in the bulk, or the undivided whole; all parts taken together.—**grosbeak,** grōs'bēk, *n.* A name common to a group of finches distinguished by the thickness and strength of the bill.—**grossly,** grōs'li, *adv.* In a gross manner.—**grossness,** grōs'nes, *n.* The quality of being gross; obscenity; greatness.

grot, grot, *n.* See GROTTO. [Poet.]

grotesque, grō•tesk', *a.* [Fr., from *grotte*, a grotto, from the style of the paintings found in the ancient crypts and grottos. GROTTO.] Having a wild, extraordinary, or extravagant form; of the utmost oddness; whimsical; extravagant.—*n.* A capricious variety of arabesque ornamentation; a whimsical figure or scenery.—**grotesquely,** grō•tesk'li, *adv.* In a grotesque manner.—**grotesqueness,** grō•tesk'nes, *n.*—**grotesquerie,** grō•tes'kėr•i, *n.* Grotesque whims or antics; grotesque conduct.

grotto, grot'tō, *n.* pl. **grottos,** or **grottoes,** grot'tōz. [Fr. *grotte*, It. *grotta*, from L. *crypta*, Gr. *kryptē*, a cave, a vault, from *kryptō*, to conceal. CRYPT.] A cave or natural cavity in the earth, as in a mountain or rock; an artificial cavern decorated with rock work, shells, etc., constructed for coolness and pleasure.

grouch, grouch, *n.* [O.F. *groucher*, grumble.] (U.S. colloq.) A sulky or grumbling person.—*v.i.* To be morose; to grumble or sulk.

ground, ground, *n.* [A.Sax. *grund*, ground; G. Dan. and Sw. *grund*, D. *grond*, Icel. *grunnr*, ground.] The surface of the earth; the earth we tread on and subject to tillage, etc.; the soil; the soil of a particular country or person; land; estate; that on which anything may rest, rise, or originate; basis; foundation; support; *elect.*, a general term for the connection of an electrical conductor to the earth; *painting*, the first layer of color on which the others are wrought; the primary or predominating color; a foil or background that sets off anything; *etching*, a composition spread over the surface of the plate to be etched, to prevent the acid from eating into the plate, except where an opening is made with the point of the etching needle; *pl.* sediment at the bottom of liquors; dregs; lees.—*To break ground*, to penetrate the soil for the first time, as in cutting the first turf of a railway; hence, *fig.* to take the first step; to enter upon an undertaking.—*To fall to the ground*, to come to nought. —*To gain ground*, to advance; to obtain an advantage; to gain credit; to become more general or extensive. —*To lose ground*, to withdraw from the position taken; to lose advantage; to decline; to become less in force or extent.—*To give ground*, to recede; to yield advantage.—*To stand one's ground*, to stand firm; not to recede or yield.—*v.t.* To lay or set on or in the ground; to cause to run (a ship) aground; to settle or establish, as on a foundation or basis; to fix or settle firmly; to found; to base; to thoroughly instruct in elements or first principles; *elect.*, to connect an electrical conductor to the earth.—*v.i.* To run aground; to strike the ground and remain fixed (the ship *grounded* in two fathoms of water).—**groundless,** ground'les, *a.* Wanting ground or foundation; wanting cause or reason; baseless; false.—**groundlessly,** ground'les•li, *adv.* In a groundless manner.—**groundling,** ‡ground'ling, *n.* A spectator who stood in the pit of the theater (*Shak.*) —**ground floor,** *n.* The floor of a house on a level, or nearly so, with the exterior ground.—**ground hog,** the woodchuck.—**ground-hog day,** February 2, when the woodchuck is supposed to rouse from its sleep to see if winter is over.—**ground ivy,** a trailing plant with purplish flowers and oval leaves; English ivy.—**groundnut,** *n.* The peanut; also see EARTHNUT.—**ground plan,** *n.* A plan showing the divisions of a building on the same level as the surface of the ground.—**ground rent,** *n.* Rent paid for the privilege of building on another man's land.—**ground squirrel,** *n.* The name of several animals allied to the true squirrels, but having cheek pouches, and living in holes.—**ground swell,** *n.* A drop swell or rolling of the sea, occasioned along the shore by a distant storm or gale. —**groundwork,** ground'wėrk, *n.* The work which forms the foundation of anything; that to which the rest is additional; the basis.

ground, ground, pret. & pp. of *grind*.

groundsel, ground'sel, *n.* [O.E. *groundswell*, Sc. *groundie-swallow*, A.Sax. *grundeswelge*, *grundswelige*, groundsel, lit. ground-swallowing, that is, entirely covering.] A common annual weed, much used as food for caged birds. Also *grunsel-edge* (Mil.).

group, gröp, *n.* [Fr. *groupe*, a group; allied to *croupe*, the buttocks of a horse; Icel. *croppr*, a hump or bunch. CROUP (rump) and CROP (craw of a bird.)] An assemblage, either of persons or things; a number collected; a cluster; an artistic combination of figures; in scientific classifications a number of individuals having some resemblance or common characteristic.—*v.t.* To form into a group; to arrange in a group or in groups.

grouper, gröp'ėr, *n.* [Akin to Pg. *garoupa*, Sp. of Central America, *garopa*, the grouper.] A fish of warm seas of the genus *Epinephelus*, found chiefly off the Florida and West Indies coasts; also, the California rockfish.

grouse, grous, *n.* [Etym. doubtful.] The common name of a number of rasorial game birds with mottled plumage, more particularly applied to the red grouse and the ruffed grouse.

grout, grout, *n.* [A.Sax. *grút*, barley or wheat meal; Icel. *grautr*, porridge; akin to *groats*, *grits* (which see).] Coarse meal; pollard; a thin mortar used for pouring into the joints of masonry and brickwork; a kind of thick ale; lees; grounds; dregs.

grove, grōv, *n.* [A.Sax. *gróf*, a grove, from *grafan*, to dig, a grove being originally an alley cut out in a wood; akin *grave* (*v.* and *n.*).] A cluster of trees shading an avenue or walk;

an assemblage of growing trees of no great extent; a small wood.

grovel, grov′el, *v.i.*—*groveled, groveling,* or *grovelled, grovelling.* [Akin to O.E. *grof, gruf,* flat, with the face toward the earth; Icel. *grufla,* to grovel, *grufl,* a groveling; Sw. *grufa,* prone, with the face toward the earth.] To lie prone or move with the body prostrate on the earth; to have a tendency toward, or take pleasure in low or base things; to be low, abject, or mean.—**groveler,** grov′el•ėr, *n.* One who grovels.—**groveling,** grov′el•ing, *p.* and *a.* Indulging by preference in what is low or base.

grow, grō, *v.i.*—*grew* (pret.), *grown* (pp.). [A.Sax. *grówan,* past *greów,* pp. *grówen*=D. *groeijen,* Icel. *gróa,* Dan. *groe,* Sw. *gro,* to grow; allied to *green.*] To become enlarged in bulk or stature, by a natural and organic process: said of animals and vegetables; to increase in any way; to become larger and stronger; to be augmented; to wax; to advance; to extend; to swell (the wind *grew* to a hurricane); to be changed from one state to another; to result, as from a cause or reason; to become (to *grow* pale).—*To grow out of,* to issue from by growth; to result from, as an effect from a cause.—*To grow up,* to advance to full stature or maturity.—*To grow together,* to become united by growth.—*v.t.* To cause to grow; to cultivate; to produce; to raise.—**grower,** grō′ėr, *n.* One who or that which grows or increases; one who grows, raises, or produces; a cultivator.—**grown,** grōn, pp. of *grow.* Increased in growth; having arrived at full size or stature.—*Grown over,* covered by the growth of anything; overgrown.—*Grown-up,* full-grown; having attained man's or woman's estate.—**growth,** grōth, *n.* The process of growing; increase of bulk in animals and plants; gradual increase in any way, as in number, bulk, etc.; that which has grown; something produced by growing.

growl, groul, *v.i.* [Comp. D. *grollen,* to growl or grumble; G. *grollen,* to roar; perhaps imitative of sound.] To murmur or snarl, as a dog; to utter an angry, grumbling sound.—*v.t.* To express by growling; to utter in an angry or grumbling tone.—*n.* The angry snarl of a dog; the inarticulate grumble of a discontented or angry person.—**growler,** grou′lėr, *n.* One who growls.

grub, grub, *v.i. grubbed, grubbing.* [O.E. *grubbe, grobbe*; akin to *grope*; comp. G. *gruben,* to dig.] To dig in or under the ground; to be occupied in digging.—*v.t.* To dig; to dig up by the roots; to root up by digging; generally followed by *up* or *out.*—*n.* [From grubbing in the ground, dirt, etc.] The larva of an insect, especially of beetles; food (*slang*).—**grubber,** grub′ėr, *n.* One who grubs; an instrument for grubbing out roots, weeds, etc.—**grub hoe,** an instrument for digging up trees, shrubs, etc., by the roots; a mattock.—**grubstake,** *n.* Food or equipment given to a prospector in return for a share of what he may find.

grudge, gruj, *v.t.*—*grudged, grudging.* [Formerly *grucche, grutche, groche,* etc., from O.Fr. *groucher, grouchier, groucer,* to grumble; of doubtful origin.] To permit or grant with reluctance; to begrudge.—*v.i.* To be envious; to cherish ill will.—*n.* Unwillingness to benefit; reluctance felt in giving; ill will from envy or sense of injury.—**grudger,** gruj′ėr, *n.* One that grudges. — **grudgingly,** gruj′ing•li, *adv.* With reluctance or discontent.

gruel, grū′el, *n.* [O.Fr. *gruel,* for *grutel,* from D. or L.G. *grut*=E. *grout* (which see).] A kind of broth made by boiling ingredients in water: usually made of the meal of oats.—**grueling,** grū′el•ing, *a.* Very tiring; wearisome to the point of exhaustion.

gruesome, grewsome, grö′sum, *a.* [D. *gruwen,* Dan. *grue,* G. *grauen,* to shudder.] Causing one to shudder; frightful; horrible.

gruff, gruf, *a.* [Same word as D. *grof,* Dan. *grov,* G. *grob,* coarse, blunt, rude.] Of a rough or stern manner, voice, or countenance; sour; surly.—**gruffly,** gruf′li, *adv.*—**gruffness,** *n.*

grum, grum, *a.* [Comp. A.Sax. *grom, gram,* severe.] Morose; severe of countenance; sour; surly; glum.

grumble, grum′bl, *v.i.*—*grumbled, grumbling.* [Perhaps same as D. *grommelen, grommen,* Fr. *grommeler,* to grumble; akin to A.Sax. *grimman,* to murmur, to rage; E. *grim, grum.* This, like other words such as *grunt, growl,* may have been partly affected by sound imitation.] To murmur with discontent; to utter in a low voice by way of complaint; to give vent to discontented expressions; to growl; to snarl; to rumble; to roar; to make a harsh and heavy sound.—*v.t.* To express or utter by grumbling.—**grumbler,** grum′blėr, *n.* One who grumbles; a discontented man.—**grumblingly,** grum′bling•li, *adv.* With grumbling or complaint.

grume, gröm, *n.* [O.Fr. *grume,* Fr. *grumeau,* a clot; from L. *grumus,* a little heap.] A fluid of a thick, viscid consistence; a clot, as of blood.—**grumose,** grö′mōs, *a. Bot.* grumous.—**grumous,** grö′mus, *a.* Resembling or containing grume; thick; clotted; *bot.* formed of coarse grains, as some clustered tubercular roots.

grumpy, grum′pi, *a.* [Connected with *grum, grumble.*] Surly; angry; gruff.—**grumpily,** grum′pi•li, *adv.*

grunt, grunt, *v.i.* [Probably from an imitative root seen in A.Sax. *grunan,* E. *groan,* Dan. *grynte,* G. *grunzen,* to grunt; comp. also L. *grunnio,* Fr. *grogner,* to grunt; Gr. *gru,* the cry of a pig.] To snort or make a noise like a hog; to utter a short groan or a deep guttural sound, as of a hog.—*n.* A deep guttural sound, as of a hog.—**grunter,** grun′tėr, *n.* One that grunts; a fish that makes a grunting sound.

Gruyère, gru•yār′, *n.* A kind of cheese made from a mixture of goats' and ewes' milk, from Gruyère in Switzerland.

guacharo, gwa•chä′rō, *n.* [Sp.] A South American bird of the goatsucker family, valued for its fat.

guaiacum, gwā′ya•kum, *n.* [Native name.] A South American tree and the resin obtained from it, the latter, as well as the bark and wood, being of medicinal value.

guan, gwän, *n.* A South American gallinaceous bird, allied to the curassows.

guanaco, gwa•nä′kō, *n.* [Sp., Peruv. *huanacu.*] A quadruped closely allied to the llama and alpaca.

guano, gwä′nō, *n.* [Sp. *guano, huano,* from Peruv. *huanu,* dung.] A substance found on many small islands, especially in the Pacific Ocean and on the west coast of South America, chiefly composed of the excrement of sea fowl in a decomposed state, much used as a manure.—**guanine,** gū•ä′nēn, *n.* [From *guano.*] A nitrogenous waste product formed in the animal body.

guarantee, gar•an•tē′, *v.t.*—*guaranteed, guaranteeing.* [O.Fr. *guarantie,* a form of *warranty.* WARRANT, etc.] To warrant; to pledge one's self for; to become bound that an article shall be as good or useful as it is represented; to secure the performance of; to undertake to secure to another (claims, rights, possessions); to undertake to uphold or maintain.—*n.* An undertaking that the engagement or promise of another shall be performed; a pledging of one's self as surety; one who binds himself to see the stipulations of another performed; a guarantor.—**guarantor,** gar•an•tor′, *n.* A warrantor; one who gives a guarantee.—**guaranty,** same as *Guarantee.*

guard, gärd, *v.t.* [The form in which the Germanic equivalent of E. *ward* passed into English through the Norman; O.Fr. *guarder,* Fr. *garder,* to guard. WARD.] To secure against injury, loss, or attack; to defend; to keep in safety; to accompany for protection; to provide or secure against objections or attacks.—*To guard one's self against,* to be on one's guard against; to take pains to avoid doing or saying.—*v.i.* To watch by way of caution or defense; to be cautious; to be in a state of caution or defense (to *guard* against mistake).—*n.* A state of caution or vigilance, or the act of observing what passes in order to prevent surprise or attack; defense; attention; watch; heed; *fencing* or *boxing,* a posture of defense; the arms or weapon in such a posture; one who guards or keeps watch; one whose business is to defend or prevent attack or surprise; a brakeman or gateman on a railway; *football,* one of two players in the line on either side of center; in England, the body of troops that guards the king; that which guards or protects; any appliance or attachment designed to protect or secure against injury; an ornamental border on one's dress.—*On guard,* acting as a guard or sentinel.—*To be on our* (*your, my,* etc.) *guard,* to be in a watchful state.—**guarded,** gär′ded, *p.* and *a.* Protected; defended; cautious; circumspect (*guarded* in language); framed or uttered with caution.—**guardedly,** gär′ded•li, *adv.* In a guarded or cautious manner.—**guardedness,** gär′ded•nes, *n.*—**guardian,** gär′di•an, *n.* [Fr. *gardien.*] One who guards; one to whom anything is committed for preservation from injury; one who has the charge or custody of any person or thing.—*a.* Protecting; performing the office of a protector.—**guardianship,** gär′di•an•ship, *n.* The office of a guardian; protection; care; watch.—**guardhouse, guardroom,** *n.* A house or room for the accommodation of a guard of soldiers, and where military defaulters are confined.—**guardsman,** gärdz′man, *n.* A watchman; an officer or private in a regiment of guards.

guava, gwä′va, *n.* [The native name in Guiana.] A small tropical tree of the myrtle family, the fruit of which is made into a delicious jelly.

gubernatorial, gū′bėr•na•tō″ri•al, *a.* [L. *gubernator*, a governor. GOVERN.] Pertaining to government or to a governor.

gudgeon, guj′on, *n.* [Fr. *goujon*, from L. *gobio*, *gobius*, Gr. *kōbios*, a gudgeon.] A small fresh-water fish which is very easily caught; hence, a person easily cheated or ensnared.—*v.t.* To cheat; to impose on.

gudgeon, guj′on, *n.* [Fr. *goujon*; origin doubtful.] A metallic piece let into the end of a wooden shaft and forming a sort of axle to it; the bearing portion of a shaft.

guelder-rose, gel′dėr, *n.* [Brought from *Guelder*land in Holland.] A shrub of the woodbine family with handsome flowers.

Guelphs, Ghibellines, gwelfs, gib′el•ēns, *n.* The Welfs and Waiblings, names of German-Italian political parties in the early medieval times, favoring respectively the Pope and the Emperor; Papalists and Imperialists.

guerdon, gėr′don, *n.* [O.Fr. *guerdon*, It. *guiderdone*, from L.L. *widerdonum*, corrupted from O.G. *widarlon* (A.Sax. *witherleán*), a recompense, through the influence of the L. *donum*, a gift—from *widar* (G. *wider*), against, and *lón*, reward (=E. *loan*).] A reward; requital; recompense: used both in a good and bad sense (*poet.* or *rhet.*).—*v.t.* To give a guerdon to; to reward.

guernsey, gėrn′se, *n.* A sort of close-fitting woolen knitted shirt; [*cap.*] a breed of dairy cattle.

guerrilla, guerilla, ge•ril′lä: Sp. pron. ger•rēl′yä, *n.* [Sp. *guerrilla*, dim. of *guerra*, Fr. *guerre*, war, from O.H.G. *werra*, war.] One who engages in irregular warfare as a member of a small group, frequently harassing the regular army and committing other acts of sabotage.

guess, ges, *v.t.* [O.E. *gesse*=L.G. and D. *gissen*, Dan. *gisse*, Icel. *giska*, *gizka*, to guess, lit. to try to *get*. GET.] To form an opinion without good means of knowledge or sufficient evidence; to judge of at random; to suppose; to imagine; often followed by a clause. [This verb is much used colloquially in the sense of to believe, to be sure.]—*v.i.* To form a conjecture; to judge at random, or without any strong evidence: with *at*.—*n.* A conjecture.—**guesser,** ges′ėr, *n.* One who guesses.—**guesswork,** ges′wėrk, *n.* Mere conjecture; the act of working by hazard.

guest, gest, *n.* [A.Sax. *gaest*, *gest*= Icel. *gestr*, Dan. *giest*, D. and G. *gast*, Goth. *gasts*, a guest, a stranger; cog. Armor. *hostiz*, Rus. *gosty*, a guest; L. *hostis*, an enemy (whence E, *host*, *hostile*).] A visitor or friend entertained in the house or at the table of another; a lodger at a hotel or lodginghouse.

guffaw, guf′fa̤, *n.* [Imitative.] A loud or sudden burst of laughter.—*v.i.* To burst into a loud or sudden laugh.

guggle, gug′l, *v.i.* [Imitative, suggested by *gurgle.*] To make a sound like that of a liquid passing through a narrow aperture; to gurgle.—*n.* A sound of this kind; a gurgle.

guide, gīd, *v.t.*—*guided*, *guiding*. [Fr. *guider*, It. *guidare*, Sp. *guiar*—of Teutonic origin, and akin to G. *weisen*, to show, to lead, Goth. *witan*, to watch over; A.Sax. *witan*, to know, to *wit*, with change of *w* to *gu* as in *guile*, *guard*. WIT.] To lead or direct in a way; to conduct in a course or path; to direct; to regulate; to influence in conduct or actions; to give direction to; to instruct and direct; to superintend.—*n.* [Fr. *guide*, It. *guida*, Sp. *guia.*] A person who guides; a leader or conductor; one who conducts travelers or tourists in particular localities; one who or that which directs another in his conduct or course of life; a director; a regulator; a guidebook; *technology*, applied to various contrivances intended to direct or keep to a fixed course or motion.—**guidable,** gī′da•bl, *a.* Capable of being guided.—**guidance,** gī′dans, *n.* The act of guiding; direction; government.—**guidebook,** *n.* A book for giving travelers or tourists information about the places they visit.—**guided missile.** A rocket or other missile (ballistic or air-breathing, solid or liquid-fueled) whose course is determined by self-contained instruments or radio signals.—**guidepost,** *n.* A post for directing travelers.

guidon, gī′don, *n.* [Fr., lit. a *guiding* flag.] The flag of a troop of cavalry; a flag used to signal with at sea, etc.

guild, gild, *n.* [A. Sax. *gild*, a payment, hence a society where payment was made for its protection and support, from *gildan*, to pay; D. *gild*, a guild. GUILT, YIELD.] An association or incorporation of men belonging to the same class or engaged in similar pursuits, formed for mutual aid and protection.

guile, gīl, *n.* [French form of E. *wile* (which see); O.Fr. *guile*, guile, from a Germanic form, with regular change of G. *w* into Romance *gu* (as in *guide*).] Craft; cunning; artifice; duplicity; deceit—**guileful,** gīl′fu̧l, *a.* Full of guile; intended to deceive; crafty; wily; deceitful; insidious; treacherous. — **guilefully,** gīl′fu̧l•li, *adv.* In a guileful manner.—**guilefulness,** gīl′fu̧l•nes, *n.* The state or quality of being guileful.—**guileless,** gīl′les, *a.* Free from guile.—**guilelessness,** gīl′les•nes, *n.*

guillemot, gil′li•mot, *n.* [Fr. *guillemot*, perhaps from Armor. *gwéla*, to weep, and O.Fr. *moëtte*, a gull.] A marine swimming bird allied to the auks and divers.

guillotine, gil•o•tēn′, *n.* [From Dr. *Guillotin* who introduced in the French Convention the motion for the use of the machine, first called *Louisette*, from inventor, Dr. Louis.] An engine for beheading persons by means of a steel blade loaded with a mass of lead, and sliding between two upright posts; a machine which consists of a knife descending between grooved posts, much used for cutting paper, straw, etc.—*v.t.*—*guillotined*, *guillotining*. To behead by the guillotine.

guilt, gilt, *n.* [A.Sax. *gylt*, a crime, from *gildan*, *gyldan*, to pay, to requite; akin Icel. *gjald*, payment, retribution, *gjalda*, to pay, to yield; E. *yield*, *guild.*] Criminality; that state of a moral agent which results from his wilful or intentional commission of a crime or offense, knowing it to be a crime or violation of law—**guiltily,** gil′ti•li, *adv.* In a guilty manner.—**guiltiness,** gil′ti•nes, *n.* The state of being guilty; wickedness; criminality; guilt.—**guiltless,** gilt′les, *a.* Free from guilt, crime, or offense; innocent; not having experience; ignorant (with *of*; *poet.*)—**guiltlessly,** gilt′les•li, *adv.* In a guiltless manner.—**guiltlessness,** gilt′les•nes, *n.* State or quality of being guiltless.—**guilty,** gil′ti, *a.* Having incurred guilt; not innocent; criminal; morally delinquent: with *of* before the crime; pertaining to guilt; indicating guilt (a *guilty* look).

guinea, gin′ē, *n.* [Because first coined of gold brought from *Guinea*, in Africa.] A gold coin formerly current in Great Britain of the value of 21 shillings sterling; a sum of money of the same amount; also abbreviated form of *guinea* fowl.—**Guinea corn,** *n.* A kind of millet cultivated in Guinea and elsewhere.—**guinea fowl,** *n.* A fowl of the rasorial order, closely allied to the peacocks and pheasants, common in Guinea.—**Guinea pepper,** *n.* A kind of capsicum; a name of various kinds of pepper.—**guinea pig,** *n.* [Perhaps for *Guianapig.*] A tailless rodent mammal, about 7 inches in length, belonging to South America, and often used for medical experimentation.—**Guinea worm,** *n.* A worm common in hot countries, which often insinuates itself under the human skin, causing intense pain.

guipure, gē•pūr′, *n.* [Fr.] An imitation of antique lace; a kind of gimp.

guise, gīz, *n.* [Fr. *guise*, the equivalent of E. *wise*, mode, fashion, O.H.G. *wisa*, G. *weise*, with common change from *w* to *gu-* in words borrowed into French from the German; comp.

guile, wile.] External appearance: dress; garb; manner; mien; cast or behavior; custom; mode; practice.

guitar, gi•tär′, *n.* [Fr. *guitare,* It. *chitarra,* from L. *cithara,* Gr. *kithara,* a kind of lyre.] A musical stringed instrument having six strings, which are played by twitching with the fingers of the right hand, while the notes are stopped by the fingers of the left.

gular, gū′lėr, *a.* [From L. *gula,* the throat or gullet.] Pertaining to the gullet.

gulch, gulch, *n.* [Allied to Sw. *gölka,* to swallow, D. *gulzig,* greedy.] A deep, abrupt ravine caused by the action of water; the dry bed of a torrent; a gully.

gulden, gu̦l′den, *n.* The unit of the Netherlands coinage.

gules, gūlz, *n.* [Fr. *gueules,* from Per. *gul,* a rose.] *Her.* vertical, parallel lines in a shield indicating the color red.

gulf, gulf, *n.* [Fr. *golfe,* It. *golfo,* Mod.Gr. *kolphos,* from Gr. *kolpos,* a gulf or bay.] A large indentation on the coast line of a country and the sea embraced in it; a bay; a bight; an abyss, chasm, or deep opening in the earth; what gulfs or swallows; a wide interval, as in station, education, and the like.—*v.t.* To swallow up; to engulf; to refuse a degree with honors, but concede a pass.—**gulfweed,** *n.* A seaweed found abundantly in the Atlantic Ocean, where it covers vast areas; drift weed.

gull, gul, *n.* [In Old and Prov.E., a young unfledged bird, lit. a yellow bird, from the yellowness of the beak and plumage of young birds, from O.E. *gul,* yellow=Icel. *gulr,* Dan. *gul,* *gaul,* yellow. YELLOW. Comp. Fr. *béjaune,* yellow-beak, novice.] A young unfledged bird (*Shak.*); one easily cheated; a simpleton; a trick (*Shak.*).—*v.t.* To make a fool of; to mislead by deception; to trick.—**gullibility,** gul•i•bil′i•ti, *n.* The quality of being gullible.—**gullible,** gul′i•bl, *a.* Easily gulled or cheated.

gull, gul, *n.* [From the Celtic; W. *gwylan,* Armor. *gwelan,* Corn. *gullan,* a gull.] A name for many marine swimming birds found on the shores of all latitudes, and having large wings, slender legs, webbed feet, and a small or no hind toe.

gullet, gul′et, *n.* [Fr. *goulet,* from L. *gula,* the throat.] The passage in the neck of an animal by which food and liquid are taken into the stomach; the esophagus; something resembling this.

gully, gul′i, *n.* [Fr. *goulet,* a gullet, a channel for water. GULLET.] A channel or hollow worn in the earth by a current of water; a ravine; a ditch; a gutter; a large knife.—*v.t.* To wear into a gully or channel.

gulp, gulp, *v.t.* [M.E. *gulpen,* from Dan. *gulpen,* to drink heartily.] To swallow eagerly or in large draughts. —*v.i.* To catch the breath between swallows.—*n.* The act of taking a large swallow.

gum, gum, *n.* [A.Sax. *góma,* Icel. *gómr,* G. *gaum,* palate, gum.] The fleshy substance on the jaws which envelops the neck of the teeth.—**gumboil,** *n.* A boil or small abscess on the gum.

gum, gum, *n.* [Fr. *gomme,* from L. *gummi,* Gr. *kommi,* gum.] A resinous substance extracted from trees or plants, soluble in water but hard when dry; chewing gum; the adhesive substance on the back of postage stamps.—*v.t.*—*gummed, gumming.* To smear with gum; to unite or stiffen by gum or a gumlike substance.—*v.i.* To exude or form gum.—**gum arabic,** *n.* The juice of various species of acacia.—**gumminess,** gum′i•nes, *n.* The state or quality of being gummy; viscousness. —**gummous,** gum′us, *a.* Of the nature or quality of gum; gummy.—**gummy,** gum′i, *a.* Consisting of gum; of the nature of gum; giving out gum; covered with gum or viscous matter.

gumbo, gum′bō, *n.* A soup thickened with the mucilaginous seed pods of the okra; the plant okra or its seed pods; rich, black soil that becomes soapy or sticky when wet.

gumption, gump′shon, *n.* [Origin unknown.] Enterprise; initiative; shrewd common sense.

gun, gun, *n.* [From the name *Gunnhildr,* of fourteenth century. So Mons *Meg,* Brown *Bess,* Fat *Bertha* (Krupp), 1917.] A name applied to every species of firearm for throwing projectiles by the explosion of gunpowder or other explosive; any portable firearm, such as a rifle, pistol, shotgun, etc.; a discharge of a gun in signal or salute, as a *21-gun* salute.—*v.i.* To hunt with a gun.—**gunboat,** *n.* A boat or small vessel fitted to carry one or more guns of heavy caliber, and from its light draught capable of running close inshore or up rivers.—**guncotton,** *n.* A highly explosive substance produced by soaking cotton or similar vegetable fiber in nitric and sulfuric acids, and then leaving it to dry.—**gunfire,** *n. Milit.* the hour at which the morning or evening gun is fired.—**gunflint,** *n.* A piece of shaped flint, fixed in the lock of a musket or pistol to fire the charge before the introduction of percussion caps. —**gun metal,** *n.* An alloy, generally of nine parts of copper and one part of tin, used for the manufacture of cannon, etc.—**gunner,** gun′ėr, *n.* One who works a gun or cannon, either on land or sea; a warrant officer in the navy connected with the charge of the ordnance.—**gunnery,** gun′ėr•i, *n.* The art of firing or managing guns; the science of artillery.—**gunpowder,** gun′pou•dėr, *n.* An explosive mixture of saltpeter, sulfur, and charcoal, reduced to a fine powder, then granulated and dried.—*Gunpowder tea,* a fine species of green tea with a granular appearance.—**gunrunner,** *n.* One who runs or secretly conveys guns into a district.—**gunshot,** gun′shot, *n.* The firing of a gun; the distance to which shot can be thrown so as to be effective.—*a.* Made by the shot of a gun (*gunshot* wounds).—**gunsmith,** gun′smith, *n.* One whose occupation is to make or repair small firearms.

gunny, gun′i, *n.* [Bengalee.] A strong coarse cloth manufactured of jute in Bengal, for making into bags, sacks, etc.

gunwale, gunnel, gun′el, *n.* [*Gun* and *wale.*] *Naut.* the upper edge of a ship's or boat's side.

guppy, gup′i, *n.* [After R. J. L. *Guppy* of Trinidad who first gave specimens of them to the British Museum.] The small minnow (*Lebistes reticulatus*) of Trinidad, Barbados and Venezuela, kept as an aquarium fish.

gurge,† gerj, *n.* [L. *gurges,* a whirlpool.] A whirlpool (*Mil.*).

gurgle, gėr′gl, *v.i.*—*gurgled, gurgling.* [Probably imitative or connected with *gorge;* comp. G. *gurgeln,* It. *gorgogliare,* to gurgle. GARGLE.] To run or flow in an irregular, noisy current, as water from a bottle; to flow with a purling sound.—*n.* The sound made by a liquid flowing from the narrow mouth of a vessel, or generally through any narrow opening.

Gurkha, gu̦r•ka, *n.* A native of Nepal, in Hindustan. There are Gurkha regiments in the Indian army.

gurnard, gėr′närd, *n.* [O.Fr. *grougnaut,* probably from *grogner,* L. *grunnire,* to grunt or grumble, from the sound these fishes make when taken from the water.] The name of certain marine fishes, having an angular head wholly covered with bony plates.

gush, gush, *v.i.* [Icel. *gjosa,* to gush, *gusa,* a gush, to gush; a Scandinavian word, allied to A.Sax. *geótan,* Goth. *giutan,* G. *giessen,* to pour; E. *gut, gust* (of wind), *geyser.*] To rush forth as a fluid from confinement; to flow suddenly or copiously; to be extravagantly and effusively sentimental.—*v.t.* To emit suddenly, copiously, or with violence.—*n.* A sudden and violent issue of a fluid; an emission of liquid in a large quantity and with force; an outpour; an effusive display of sentiment.—**gusher, gush′ėr,** *n.* **One that gushes;** an oil well from which oil spurts freely.—**gushingly,** gush′ing•li, *adv.* In a gushing manner.

gusset, gus′et, *n.* [Fr. *gousset,* a gusset, from *gousse,* a husk or shell.] A triangular piece of cloth inserted in a garment for the purpose of strengthening or enlarging some part; something resembling such a piece of cloth in shape or function.

gust, gust, *n.* [L. *gustus,* taste; *gusto,* to taste (as in *disgust*); from root seen in *choose.*] The sense or pleasure of tasting; gratification of the appetite; relish; gusto; taste.—**gustable,** gus′ta•bl, *a.* Capable of being tasted; having a pleasant relish†.—**gustation,**† gus•tā′shon, *n.* [L. *gustatio.*] The act of tasting.—**gustatory,** gus′ta•to•ri, *a.* Pertaining to gust or taste.—**gusto,** gus′tō, *n.* [It.] Nice appreciation or enjoyment; keen relish; taste; fancy.

gust, gust, *n.* [Icel. *gustr*, a blast of wind; allied to E. *gush.*] A violent blast of wind; a sudden rushing or driving of the wind, of short duration; a sudden violent burst of passion.—**gusty,** gus′ti, *a.* Subject to gusts or sudden blasts of wind; tempestuous; given to sudden bursts of passion.

gut, gut, *n.* [A.Sax. *gut*, *gutt*, gut, *guttas*, entrails; comp. Prov. E. *gut*, a water channel, a drain; O.E. *gote*, a drain; from stem of A.Sax. *geótan*, Goth. *giutan*, to pour out. GUSH.] The intestinal canal of an animal from the stomach to the anus; an intestine; *pl.* the stomach and digestive apparatus generally, the viscera or entrails; a preparation of the intestines of an animal used for various purposes, as for the strings of a fiddle; a channel or passage.—*v.t.*—*gutted*, *gutting*. To take out the entrails of; to eviscerate; to plunder of contents; to destroy or take out the interior of.

gutta, gut′ta, *n.* pl. **guttae,** gut′tē, [L.] A drop; specifically, *arch.* one of a series of pendent ornaments attached to the under side of the mutules and under the triglyphs of the Doric order.—**guttate,** gut′āt, *a. Bot.* spotted, as if discolored by drops.

gutta-percha, gut′ta pėr′cha, *n.* [Malay *gutta*, gum, and *percha*, the tree.] The hardened milky juice of a large tree which grows in the Malayan Peninsula and in some of the islands of the Eastern Archipelago, resembling caoutchouc in many of its properties, but stronger, more soluble, and less elastic.

gutter, gut′ėr, *n.* [Fr. *gouttière*, from *goutte*, L. *gutta*, a drop.] A channel at the side of a road, street, or the like, also at the eaves of, or on, a roof of a building for conveying away water.—*v.t.* To cut or form gutters in.—*v.i.* To become channeled.

guttle, gut′l, *v.i.* [A form of *guzzle.*] To swallow greedily; to gormandize.—**guttler,** gut′lėr, *n.* A gormandizer.

guttural, gut′ėr•al, *a.* [From L. *guttur*, the throat, whence also *goitre.*] Pertaining to the throat; uttered from the throat.—*n.* A letter or combination of letters pronounced in the throat; any guttural sound.—**gutturalize,** gut′ėr•al•īz, *v.t.* To speak or enunciate gutturally.—**gutturally,** gut′ėr•al•li, *adv.* In a guttural manner.—**gutturalness, gutturality,**†, gut′ėr•al•nes, gut•ėr•al′i•ti, *n.* The quality of being guttural.

guy, gī, *n.* [Sp. *guia*, a guide, a small rope used on board ship. GUIDE.] A rope used to steady anything; a rope to steady an object which is being hoisted; a rope or rod to steady a suspension bridge.—*v.t.* To steady or direct by means of a guy.

guy, gī, *n.* A fright; a person of queer looks or dress: from the effigy of *Guy* Fawkes burned on November 5.

guzzle, guz′l, *v.i.* and *v.t.*—*guzzled*, *guzzling*. [O.Fr. *goziller*, to gulp down; connected with Fr. *gosier*, the throat.] To swallow liquor greedily; to swill; to drink much. *n.* A debauch, especially on drink. **guzzler,** guz′lėr, *n.* One who guzzles.

gymkhana, jim•kä′na, *n.* [Of Anglo-Indian origin.] A meeting for athletic or other sport contests.

gymnasium, jim•nā′zi•um, *n.* pl. **gymnasiums, gymnasia.** [Gr. *gymnasion*, from *gymnos*, naked.] A place where athletic exercises are performed; in Europe, a school for the higher branches of education; a school preparatory to the universities.—**gymnast,** jim′nast, *n.* One who teaches or practices gymnastic exercises.—**gymnastic, gymnastical,** jim•nas′tik, jim•nas′ti•kal, *a.* [L. *gymnasticus*; Gr. *gymnastikos.*] Pertaining to athletic exercises.—**gymnastically,** jim•nas′ti•kal•li, *adv.* In a gymnastic manner.—**gymnastics,** jim•nas′tiks, *n.* The art of performing athletic exercises; athletic exercises; feats of skill or address.

gymnocarpous, jim•no•kär′pus, *a.* [Gr. *gymnos*, naked, and *karpos*, fruit.] *Bot.* having a naked fruit.—**gymnogynous,** jim•noj′i•nus, *a.* [Gr. *gynē*, female.] *Bot.* having a naked ovary.—**gymnosophist,** jim•nos′o•fist, *n.* [Gr. *sophistēs*, a philosopher.] One of a sect of ancient Hindu ascetics who lived solitarily, and wore little or no clothing.

gymnosperm, jim′no•spėrm, *n.* [Gr. *gymnos*, and *sperma*, seed.] A plant that produces seeds not enclosed in an ovary.—**gymnospermous,** jim•no•spėr′mus, *a.*

gynarchy, jin′är•ki, *n.* [Gr. *gynē*, woman, and *archē*, rule.] Government by a female or females.

gynecocracy, gynaecocracy, jin•e•kok′ra•si, *n.* [Gr. *gynē*, *gynaikos*, a woman, and *kratos*, power.] Government by a woman; female rule.—**gyneolatry,** jin•e•ol′a•tri, *n.* [Gr. *latreia*, worship.] The extravagant adoration or worship of woman.—**gynecology,** jin•e•kol′o•ji, *n.* The branch of medical science dealing with functions, diseases, and hygiene of women.—**gynecologist,** jin•e•kol′o•jist, *n.*

gynophore, jin′o•fōr, *n.* [Gr. *phoros*, bearing.] The stalk on which the ovary stands in certain flowers; *zool.* the generative bud of a hydrozoon containing ova.

gyp, jip, *n.* [Said to be a sportive application of Gr. *gyps*, a vulture, from their alleged rapacity.] A college servant (English usage).—*n.*, *v.t.* and *i. U.S. slang*, to cheat; to swindle.

gypsum, jip′sum, *n.* [L. *gypsum*, from Gr. *gypsos*, chalk.] A mineral which is found in a compact and crystallized state, as alabaster, or in the form of a soft chalky stone which by heat becomes a fine white powder, extensively used under the name of plaster of Paris.—**gypseous,** jip′si•us, *a.* Of the nature of gypsum; resembling gypsum.—**gypsiferous,** jip•sif′ėr•us, *a.* Producing gypsum.

gypsy, gipsy, jip′si, *n.* [For *Egyptian*, from the belief that the race are descendants of the ancient people of Egypt. Called by themselves *Romany*, perhaps indicative of their first reaching Europe by *Rumania.*] One of a peculiar wandering race deriving their origin from India; a name of slight or humorous reproach to a young woman; the language of the gypsies.—*a.* Pertaining to the gypsies.

gypsy moth, *n.* A European tussock moth, now found in the East, the caterpillars of which do much damage to trees.

gyrate, jī′rāt, *v.i.* [L. *gyro*, *gyratum*, from *gyrus*, Gr. *gyros*, a circle.] To turn round circularly; to revolve round a central point; to move spirally.—*a.* Winding or going round, as in a circle.—**gyration,** jī•rā′shon, *n.* A turning or whirling round; a circular motion.—**gyratory,** jī′ra•to•ri, *a.* Moving in a circle or spirally.—**gyre,** jīr, *n.* A circular motion, or a circle described by a moving body; a turn.—**gyrose,** jī′rōs, *a. Bot.* bent round like a crook.

gyrfalcon, jėr′fą•kn, *n.* [L.L. *gyrofalco*, from *gyrus*, a circle, so called from its flight.] A species of falcon, one of the boldest and most beautiful of the tribe.

gyrocompass, jī″rō•kum′pas, *n.* [From Gr. *gyros*, ring, and *compass.*] A compass which uses a steadily rotating gyroscope, instead of a magnetic needle, to determine the geographic north.

gyroscope, jī′ro•skōp, *n.* [Gr. *skopeō*, to view.] An apparatus, consisting of a pivoted disk rotating in different ways, for illustrating peculiarities of rotation; also used to increase steadiness of ships and airplanes.—**gyroplane,** jī′ro•plān, *n.* An airplane propelled by windmill-like wings revolving about a vertical axis.—**gyrostat,** jī′ro•stat, *n.* A kind of spinning top.

gyrus, jī′rus, pl. **gyri,** jī′ri, *n.* [Gr. *gyros*, a circle.] *Anat.* a name given to the ridges or raised convolutions on the surface of the brain.

gyve, jīv, *n.* [W. *gevyn*; Ir. *geibion*, from *geibhim*, to get, to hold; same root as L. *capio*, to take.] A shackle, usually for the legs; a fetter; commonly in the plural.—*v.t.*—*gyved*, *gyving*. To fetter; to shackle; to chain.

H

H, h, āch, the eighth letter of the English alphabet, a consonant often called the *aspirate*, as being a mere aspiration or breathing.

ha, hä. An exclamation, denoting surprise, wonder, joy, or other sudden emotion.

haaf, häf, *n.* [N. *haf*, high sea.] Deep-sea fishing ground.

habeas corpus, hā′bi•as kor′pus, [L., you may have the body.] *Law*, a common-law writ designed to safeguard citizens from unjust imprisonment, directed to any person who detains another in custody and commanding him to produce the body of this person with a statement of the day and cause of his apprehension and detention that the court may deal with him.

haberdasher, hab′ėr•dash•er, *n.* [Lit. a seller of *hapertas*, from O.Fr. *hapertas*, a kind of cloth.] The proprietor of a store which deals principally in men's furnishings; formerly a dealer in drapery goods, woolens, linens, silks, ribbons, etc.—**haberdashery,** hab′ėr•dash•ėr•i, *n.*

habergeon, ha•bėr′jon, *n.* [Fr. *haubergeon*, from *heuberc*, a hauberk. HAUBERK.] A short coat of mail or armor consisting of a jacket without sleeves.

habiliment, ha•bil′i•ment, *n.* [Fr. *habillement*, from *habiller*, to dress, from L. *habilis*, fit, proper. HABIT.] A garment; clothing: usually plural. —**habilitate,** ha•bil′i•tāt, *v.t.* To equip for operation, as a mine.

habit, hab′it, *n.* [Fr. *habit*, from L. *habitus*, state, dress, manner, condition, etc., from *habeo*, *habitum*, to have, to hold; of similar origin are *habiliment*, *habitation*, *inhabit*, *exhibit*, *prohibit*, also *able*, *debt*, *duty*, etc.] The ordinary state or condition of the body, either natural or acquired; tendency or capacity resulting from frequent repetition of the same acts; practice; usage; a way of acting; a peculiar practice or custom; a characteristic item of behavior; dress; garb; the outer dress worn by ladies while on horseback. ∴ *Syn.* under CUSTOM.—*v.t.* To dress; to clothe; to array.—**habited,** hab′it•ed, *a.* Clothed, as with a habit.—**habitual,** ha•bit′ū•al, *a.* [Fr. *habituel.*] Formed or acquired by habit, frequent use, or custom; constantly practiced; customary; regular; as a matter of course.—**habitually,** ha•bit′ū•al•li, *adv.* In a habitual manner. —**habitualness,** ha•bit′ū•al•nes, *n.* **habituate,** ha•bit′ū•āt, *v.t.*—*habituated*, *habituating*. [L. *habituo*, *habituatum.*] To accustom; to make familiar by frequent use or practice; to familiarize.—*a.* Formed by habit. —**habituation,** ha•bit′ū•ā″shon, *n.* The act of habituating, or state of being habituated.—**habitude,** hab′i•tūd, *n.* [Fr. *habitude*, from L. *habitudo.*] Customary manner or mode of living, feeling, or acting; long custom; habit.—**habitué,** ha•bi′tū•ā, *n.* [Fr., pp. of *habituer*, to accustom.] A habitual frequenter of any place, especially one of amusement, recreation, and the like.

habitable, hab′i•ta•bl, *a.* [Fr., from L. *habitabilis*, from *habito*, to dwell, a freq. of *habeo*, to have.] Capable of being inhabited or dwelt in; capable of sustaining human beings. —**habitability, habitableness,** hab′i•ta•bil″i•ti, hab′i•ta•bl•nes, *n.* State of being habitable; capacity of being inhabited.—**habitably,** hab′i•ta•bli, *adv.* So as to be habitable.—**habitant,** hab′i•tant, *n.* [L. *habitans*, *habitantis*, ppr. of *habito.*] An inhabitant; a dweller; a resident.—**habitat,** hab′i•tat, *n.* [L. *habitat*, 'it dwells'.] The natural abode or locality of a plant or animal.—**habitation,** hab•i•tā′shon, *n.* [L. *habitatio.*] Act of inhabiting; occupancy; place of abode; a settled dwelling; a house or other place in which man or any animal dwells.

habitude, habitué. See HABIT.

hachure, hä•shör′, *n.* [Fr., from *hacher*, to hack. HACK, *v.t.*] Short lines which mark half-tints and shadows in designing and engraving. —*v.t.* To cover with hachures.

hacienda, hä•sē•en′dä, *n.* [Sp.] In Spain, Spanish America, etc., a farmhouse; a farm.

hack, hak, *v.t.* and *i.* [A.Sax. *haccan* or *haccian*=E. *hatch* (in engraving), *hatchet*, *hash*.] To cut irregularly and into small pieces; to notch; to mangle; to chop; to cough in a short, dry manner.—*n.* A notch; a cut; a hacking cough.—**hack saw,** *n.* A fine-toothed saw fixed in a frame, used to cut metal.—**hacking,** hak′ing, *a.* Short and interrupted (a *hacking* cough).

hack, hak, *n.* [Short for *hackney.*] A horse kept for hire; a horse much worked; a worn-out horse; a person overworked; a writer employed in the drudgery and details of bookmaking.—*a.* Much used or worn, like a hired horse; hired.—*v.t.* To use as a hack; to let out for hire.

hackberry, hak′be•ri, *n.* [Same as Prov. E. *hag-berry*, bird-cherry= *haw*-berry, *hedge*-berry.] A North American tree bearing sweet edible fruits as large as bird cherries.

hackbut, hak′but, *n.* Same as *arquebus*.

hackle, hak′l, *n.* [D. *hekel*, G. *hechel*, Dan. *hegle*, a hackle for flax or hemp; akin to *hook*. The secondary senses are from similarity to tufts of hackled fibers.] A hatchel, heckle, or comb for dressing flax; raw silk; any flimsy substance unspun; a long pointed feather on the neck of a fowl, or any similar feather.—*v.t.* To comb (flax or hemp); to hatchel or heckle.—**hackler,** hak′lėr, *n.* One who hackles.

hackmatack, hak′ma•tak, *n.* [Amer. Indian.] The American black larch.

hackney, hak′ni, *n.* [O.Fr. *haquenee*, a pacing horse, Sp. *hacanea*, a nag; probably from O.D. *heckeneye*, *hakkenei*, a hackney; lit. perhaps a hacked or dock-tailed nag.] A horse kept for riding or driving; a pad; a nag; a horse kept for hire; a hack; a person accustomed to drudgery, often literary drudgery.—*a.* Let out for hire; much used; common; trite.—*v.t.* To use as a hackney; to devote to common or vulgar use.—**hackney coach,** *n.* A coach kept for hire.—**hackneyed,** hak′nid, *p.* and *a.* Discussed or talked of without end; in everybody's mouth; trite; commonplace.

had, had, pret. & pp. of *have*.

haddock, had′ok, *n.* [Comp. O.Fr. *hadot*, *hadou*, Ir. *codog*, a haddock.] A well-known fish of the cod family, smaller than the cod, and having a dark spot on each side just behind the head.

hade, hād, *n.* [A.Sax. *heald*, inclined, bent; G. *halde*, declivity.] *Mining*, a slope or inclination; inclination of a vein or bed from a vertical direction. —*v.i.* To slope or incline from the vertical.

Hades, hā′dēz, *n.* [Gr. *Hadēs*, i.e. *aidēs*, invisible, unseen, from *a* not, and *idein*, to see.] The invisible abode of the dead; the place or state of departed souls; the world of spirits.

hadj, haj, *n.* [Ar.] The Mohammedan pilgrimage to Mecca and Medina.—**hadji,** haj′ē, *n.* A Mussulman who has performed his pilgrimage to Mecca.

haemal, hē′mal, *a.* [Gr. *haima*, *haimatos*, blood. Some of the words in which this forms part are spelled indifferently *he-* or *hæ-*; in others there is a preference. See also under HE.] Pertaining to the blood; connected with the blood vessels or circulation.—**haematite,** hē′ma•tīt, *n.* HEMATITE.—**haematocryal,** hē•ma•tok′ri•al, *a.* [Gr. *cryos*, cold.] *Zool.* applied to the cold-blooded vertebrates.—**haematothermal,** hē′ma•to•ther″mal, *a.* [Gr. *thermos*, warm.] Of or pertaining to the warm-blooded vertebrates.—**haematoxylin,** hē•ma•tok′si•lin, HEMATOXYLIN.—**haematozoa,** hē′ma•to•zō″a, *n. pl.* [Gr. *zōon*, an animal.] The entozoa which exist in the blood of mammals, birds, reptiles, etc.

hafnium, haf′ni•um, *n.* [From *Hafnia*, L. for Copenhagen.] A metallic element found in zirconium ores. Symbol, Hf; at. no., 72; at. wt., 178.49.

haft, haft, *n.* [A.Sax. *hæft*, a haft=D. and G. *heft*, a handle; Icel. *hepti* (=*hefti*), a haft, from the stem of *have* or *heave.*] A handle; that part of an instrument which is taken into the hand, and by which it is held and used.—*v.t.* To set in a haft; to furnish with a handle.

hag, hag, *n.* [Shortened from A.Sax. *hægtesse*; akin to G. *hexe*, D. *heks*, a witch; probably from A.Sax. *haga*, a hedge, G. *hag*, a wood (the meaning being woman of the woods).] An ugly old woman; a witch; a sorceress; a she-monster; an eel-shaped fish which eats into and devours other fishes.—**haggish,** hag′ish, *a.* Pertaining to or resembling a hag; ugly; horrid.

hagbut, hag′but, *n.* Same as *Arquebus*.

haggard, hag′ärd, *a.* [Fr. *haggard*, originally a wild falcon, from G. *hag*, a wood, and afflix *-ard*. In secondary sense perhaps for *hagged*, that is *hag*-like. HEDGE, HAW.] Wild; intractable (a *haggard* hawk); having the expression of one wasted by want or suffering; having the face worn and pale; lean-faced; gaunt.—*n.* An untrained or refractory hawk. —**haggardly,** hag′ärd•li, *adv.* In a haggard manner.

haggis, hag′is, *n.* [From *hag*, to chop, a form of *hack*; comp. Fr. *hachis*, a hash.] A Scotch dish, commonly made in a sheep's stomach, of the heart, lungs, and liver of the animal minced with suet, onions, oatmeal, and seasoned with salt and pepper.

haggle, hag′l, *v.t.*—*haggled, haggling.* [Freq. of *hag,* for *hack,* to hack.] To cut into small pieces; to notch or cut in an unskillful manner; to mangle.—*v.i.* To be difficult in bargaining; to hesitate and cavil; to stick at small matters; to higgle.—**haggler,** hag′l•ėr, *n.* One who haggles.

Hagiographa, hā•gi•og′ra•fa, *n. pl.* [Gr. *hagios,* holy, and *graphē,* a writing.] The last of the three Jewish divisions of the Old Testament, comprehending Psalms, Proverbs, Job, Daniel, Ezra, Nehemiah, Ruth, Esther, Chronicles, Canticles, Lamentations, and Ecclesiastes.—**hagiography,** hā•gi•og′ra•fi, *n.* Sacred writing; the lives of the saints or holy men.—**hagiographic,** hā′gi•o•graf″ik, *a.* Pertaining to hagiography.—**hagiographer,** hā•gi•og′ra•fėr, *n.* One of the writers of the hagiography; a writer of lives of the saints.—**hagiologist,** hā•gi•ol′o•jist, *n.* One who writes or treats of the sacred writings; a writer of lives of the saints.—**hagiology,** hā•gi•ol′o•ji, *n.* [Gr. *hagios,* and *logos.*] Sacred literature; that branch of literature which has to do with the lives and legends of the saints.

ha-ha, hä′hä, *n.* [Reduplicated form of *haw,* a hedge.] A sunk fence or ditch; a hawhaw.

haiku, hī′kö, *n.* pl. **haiku.** [Japanese.] A 3-line unrhymed Japanese poem of 5, 7 and 5 syllables, respectively, containing a seasonal reference.

hail, hāl, *n.* [A.Sax. *hagal, hagol*= G., D., Dan. and Sw. *hagel,* Icel. *hagl,* hail; root doubtful.] The small masses of ice or frozen vapor falling from the clouds in showers or storms; frozen rain.—*v.t.* and *i.* To pour down hail.—**hailstone,** hāl′stōn, *n.* A single ball or pellet of hail.—**hailstorm,** *n.* A storm of hail.

hail, hāl, *interj.* [Same as *hale,* adj.; Icel. *heill,* Dan. *heel,* hale. HALE, HEALTH.] A term of greeting or salutation expressive of well-wishing.—*v.t.* To call to; to greet from a distance; to call to in order to arrest attention; to designate as; to salute or address as.—*v.i.* Used only in the phrase *to hail from,* originally used of a ship, which is said *to hail from* the port whence she comes; hence, to have as one's residence or birthplace; to belong to.—*n.* Call.—*Within hail,* within call; within reach of the sound of the voice.

hair, hâr, *n.* [A.Sax. *haer, hér*=Icel. *hár,* O.D. *hair,* D. Dan. and G. *haar,* hair; perhaps akin to Icel. *hörr,* flax, E. *hards* (which see).] A small filament issuing from the skin of an animal, and from a bulbous root; the collection or mass of filaments growing from the skin of an animal and forming an integument or covering; such filaments in the mass; a filament resembling a hair; *bot.* a species of down or pubescence.—*To a hair,* to a nicety.—*To split hairs,* to be unduly nice in making distinctions.—**hairbreadth, hairsbreadth,** *n.* The diameter or breadth of a hair; a minute distance.—*a.* Of the breadth of a hair; very narrow (a *hairbreadth* escape).—**hairbrush,** *n.* A brush for dressing and smoothing the hair.—**haircloth,** *n.* A kind of cloth made of hair or in part of hair.—**hairdresser,** *n.* One who dresses or cuts people's hair; a barber.—**hairiness,** hā′ri•nes, *n.* The state of being hairy.—**hairless,** hâr′les, *a.* Destitute of hair; bald.—**hairline,** *n.* A line made of hair; a very slender line made in writing or drawing; a hair stroke.—**hairpin,** *n.* A pin used to keep the hair in a certain position; especially, a doubled pin or bent wire used by women.—**hair shirt,** *n.* Shirt or belt made of horsehair and worn by way of self-mortification.—**hair space,** *n.* The thinnest space used by printers.—**hairsplitting,** *n.* The act or practice of making minute distinctions in reasoning.—**hairsplitter,** *n.* One given to hair-splitting.—**hairspring,** *n.* The fine hairlike spring giving motion to the balance wheel of a watch.—**hair stroke,** *n.* The fine up-stroke in penmanship.—**hair trigger,** *n.* A trigger to a gunlock, so delicately adjusted that the slightest touch will discharge the piece.—**hairy,** hâ′ri, *a.* Overgrown with hair; covered with hair.

hake, hāk, *n.* [Prov. E. *hake,* a hook, from the hook-shaped jaw of the fish.] A fish of the cod family, one species of which is known as king of herrings, on which it preys.

hakim, hä•kēm′ *n.* [Ar.] An Oriental name for a physician.

halberd, halbert, hal′bėrd, hal′bėrt, *n.* [Fr. *hallebarde,* from O.G. *helmparte, helmbarte,* a halberd—*helm,* a handle, a helm, and *parte, barte,* an ax.] An ancient military weapon, a kind of combination of a spear and battle-ax, with a shaft about 6 feet long.—**halberdier,** hal•bėr•dēr′, *n.* One who is armed with a halberd.

halcyon, hal′si•on, *n.* [L. *halcyon,* from Gr. *halkyōn,* a kingfisher, said to be from *hals,* the sea, and *kyō,* to conceive.] An old or poetical name of the kingfisher, which was fabled to have the power of charming the winds and waves during the period of its incubation, so that the weather was then calm.—*a.* Pertaining to or connected with the halcyon; calm; quiet; peaceful.—*Halcyon days,* the seven days before and as many after the winter solstice, when the halcyon was believed to brood, and the weather was calm; hence, days of peace and tranquillity.

hale, hāl, *a.* [Same as Icel. *heill,* Dan. *heel,* Goth. *hails,* in good health, sound, etc. (hence, *hail* in salutations); closely akin to A.Sax. *hál,* whole, sound, whence E. *whole;* cog. with Gr. *kalos,* beautiful. Akin *heal, health, hollow, holy.*] Sound; healthy; robust; not impaired in health.

hale, hāl, *v.t.*—*haled, haling.* [HAUL.] To pull or draw with force; to haul.—*n.* A violent pull; a haul.

half, häf, *n.* pl. **halves,** hävz, [A.Sax. *half* or *healf*=O.Fris., D., and Sw. *half,* Icel. *halfr,* Goth. *halbs,* G. *halb,* half.] One part of a thing which is divided into two equal parts, either in fact or in contemplation; a moiety (we usually say *half* a pound, *half* a mile, etc., omitting *of*).—*To cry halves,* to claim an equal share.—*To go halves,* to agree with another for the division of anything into equal parts.—*adv.* In an equal part or degree; by half; to some extent; much used in composition and often indefinite (*half*-learned, *half*-hatched).—*a.* Consisting of a moiety or half.—**half-and-half,** *n.* A mixture of two malt liquors, especially porter and sweet or bitter ale.—**halfback,** *n.* Player in football, immediately behind the forwards.—**half binding,** *n.* A style of binding books in which the back and corners are in leather and the sides in paper or cloth.—**half blood,** *n.* One born of the same mother but not the same father as another, or *vice versâ;* a half-breed.—**half-bound,** *a.* A term applied to a book in half binding.—**half-bred,** *a.* Imperfectly bred; mixed; mongrel; partially or imperfectly acquainted with the rules of good breeding.—**half-breed,** *n.* One born of parents of different races; specifically applied to the offspring of American Indians and whites.—**half brother,** *n.* A brother by one parent, but not by both.—**half-caste,** *n.* One born of a Hindu and a European; a halfblood or half-breed.—**half cock,** *n.* The position of the hammer of a gun when it is elevated only halfway and retained by the first notch.—**half crown,** *n.* A silver coin of Britain valued at 2*s,* 6*d.*—**half dollar,** *n.* A silver coin of the United States, value fifty cents.—**halfhearted,** *a.* Devoid of eagerness or enthusiasm; indifferent; lukewarm.—**half-hourly,** *a.* Occurring at intervals of half an hour.—**half life,** *n.* The time it takes one-half the atoms of a radioactive substance to disintegrate.—**half-moon,** *n.* The moon at the quarters, when half its disk appears illuminated; anything in the shape of a half-moon.—**half note,** *n.* *Mus.* a minim, being half a semibreve; a semitone.—**half pay,** *n.* Half wages or salary; a reduced allowance paid to an officer in the army or navy when not in actual service.—*a.* Receiving or entitled to half pay.—**halfpenny,** hā′pen•i, *n.* pl. **halfpence,** häf′pens or hā′pens. A British copper coin of the value of half a penny or one cent.—*a.* Of the price or value of a halfpenny.—**half sister,** *n.* A sister by the father's side only, or by the mother's side only.—**half sovereign,** *n.* A British gold coin, value 10*s.*—**half tide,** *n.* The tide when halfway between the ebb and flood.—**half-timbered,** *a.* Built half of timber, as a dwelling.—**half tone,** *n.* A tone intermediate between the extreme lights and shades of a picture; a kind of photoengraving.—**halfway,** *adv.* In the middle; at half the distance.—*a.*

Midway; equidistant from the extremes.—**halfwitted,** *a.* Weak in intellect; silly; foolish.

halibut, holibut, hal′i•but, hol′i•but, *n.* [From *hali*, that is, holy, and *but* or *butt*, a flounder=D. *heilbot*, G. *heilbutt*, *heiligbutt*.] One of the largest of the flat-fish family, allied to the turbot, but much less broad comparatively, valuable as food.

halite, hal′īt, hā′līt, *n.* [Gr. *hals*, salt.] *Mineral.* native salt.

halitosis, hal•i•tō′sis, *n.* [L. *habitus*, breath, and *osis*.] Condition of having foul or offensive breath.

halitus, hal′i•tus, *n.* [L. from *halo*, to breathe out (in *exhale*).] *Physiol.* the breath or moisture of the breath; vapor exhaled from the body.

hall, hạl, *n.* [A.Sax. *heal*, *heall*=Icel. *höll*, *hall*, Sw. *hall*, D. *hal*, from root signifying to cover, seen also in E. *hell*.] A large room, especially a large public room; a room or building devoted to public business, or in which meetings of the public or corporate bodies are held; a large room at the entrance of a house; lobby; a manor house.—**hallmark,** *n.* The official stamp affixed to articles of gold and silver; a distinguishing mark or characteristic.

hallelujah, halleluiah, hal•lē•lö′yä, *n.* and *interj.* See ALLELUIA.

halliard, hal′yärd, *n.* See HALYARD.

halloo, hal•lö′, *interj.* and *n.* [Comp. G. *halloh!* and Fr. *halle*, an exclamation used to cheer on dogs; *haller*, to encourage dogs.] An exclamation, used as a call to invite attention; also, a hunting cry to set a dog on the chase.—*v.i.* To call *halloo*; to shout; to cry, as after dogs.—*v.t.* To shout to.

hallow, hal′lō, *v.t.* [A.Sax. *hálgian*, to hallow, from *hálig*, holy. HOLY.] To make holy; to consecrate; to set apart for holy or religious use; to reverence; to honor as sacred.—**Halloween,** *n.* The eve or vigil of Allhallows or All Saints' Day. [Sc.]—**hallowmas,** hal′lō•mas, *n.* [A.Sax. *hálga*, a saint, and *mæsse*, mass, festival.] The feast of All Saints or the time at which it is held.

hallucination, hal•lū′si•nā″shon, *n.* [L. *hallucinatio*, from *hallucinor*, to wander in mind, to talk idly.] An unfounded and mistaken notion; an entire misconception; a mere dream or fancy; *med.* a morbid condition of the brain or nerves, in which objects are believed to be seen and sensations experienced; the object or sensation thus erroneously perceived.—**hallucinatory,** hal•lū′si•na•to•ri, *a.* Partaking of hallucination.

hallux, hal′uks, *n.* [Erroneous form, for L. *hallex*, the thumb or great toe.] The great toe or corresponding digit of an animal; the hind toe of a bird.

halm, hạm, *n.* Same as *Haulm.*

halo, hā′lō, *n.* pl. **halos, haloes,** hā′lōz, [Gr. *halōs*, a round floor, the sun's disk, a halo.] A luminous ring, either white or colored, appearing round the sun or moon; any circle of light, as the glory round the head of saints; a colored circle round the nipple; an ideal glory investing an object (a *halo* of romance).—*v.i.*, To form itself into a halo.—*v.t.* To surround with a halo.

halogen, hal′o•jen, *n.* [Gr. *hals*, salt, and root *gen*, to produce.] *Chem.* a name given to substances (such as chlorine or iodine) which form compounds of a saline nature by their union with metals.—**halogenous,** ha•loj′e•nus, *a.* Having the nature of halogens.

haloid, hal′oid, *a.* [Gr. *hals*, sea-salt, and *eidos*, resemblance.] *Chem.* resembling common salt in composition; formed by the combination of a halogen and a metal; common salt is a *haloid salt.*—*n.* A haloid salt.

halophyte, hal′o•fīt, *n.* [Gr. *hals*, *halos*, the sea, salt, and *phyton*, a plant.] One of the plants which inhabit salt marshes, and by combustion yield barilla or Spanish soda.

halt, hạlt, *v.i.* [A.Sax. *healtian*, to be lame, *healt*, lame, from Icel. *haltr*, Dan. and Sw. *halt*, Goth. *halts*, lame; Dan. and Sw. *halte*, to limp. In sense of to stop in marching, probably of German origin, from *halten*, E. to *hold*.] To limp; to be lame; to limp or be defective in regard to meter, versification, or connection of ideas; to stop in marching or walking; to cease to advance; to stand in doubt whether to proceed or what to do; to hesitate.—*v.t.* To stop; to cause to cease marching.—*a.* Lame; not able to walk without limping.—*n.* Lameness; a limp; a stopping; a stop in walking or marching.—**halter,** hạl′tėr, *n.* One who halts or limps.—**haltingly,** hạl′ting•li, *adv.* In a halting manner.

halter, hạl′tėr, *n.* [A.Sax. *hælfter*, headstall, noose=D.L.G. and G. *halfter*; origin doubtful.] A cord or strap forming a headstall for leading or confining a horse or other animal; a rope specially intended for hanging malefactors.—*v.t.* To put a halter on.

halteres, hal•tē′rēz, *n. pl.* [Gr. *haltēres*, weights held while leaping, from *hallomai*, to leap.] The balancers of insects; the aborted second pair of wings.

halve, häv, *v.t.*—*halved*, *halving*. [From *half*.] To divide into two halves or equal parts; to join (timbers) by lapping or letting into each other.—**halves,** hävz, *n. pl.* of *half*.

halyard, hal′yärd, *n.* [*Hale* or *haul*, and *yard*.] *Naut.* a rope or tackle for hoisting and lowering sails, yards, gaffs, etc.; halliard.

ham, ham, *n.* [A.Sax. *ham*, *hamm*, the ham=D. *ham*, Icel. *höm*, G. *hamme*, a ham.] The inner bend or hind part of the knee; the thigh of an animal, particularly of a hog, salted and cured; an unskilled actor; a showoff.—*v.t.* To overplay a scene in a play; overact (to *ham* it up.)—**hamstring,** ham′string, *n.* One of the tendons of the ham.—*v.t.* To lame or disable by cutting the tendons of the ham; to make ineffective.—**hamburger,** ham′bėr•gėr, *n.* [From *Hamburg steak*.] Ground beef; a sandwich of cooked ground beef placed between halves of a bun.

hamadryad, ham′a•drī•ad, *n.* [Gr. *hamadryas*, from *hama*, together, and *drys*, a tree.] In classical mythology a wood nymph, fabled to live and die with the tree to which she was attached.

hamal, ham′al, *n.* A porter in the Orient.

hame, hām, *n.* [Same as D. *haam*, a hame.] One of two curved pieces of wood or metal in the harness of a draft horse, to which the traces are fastened, and which lie upon the collar or have pads attached to them fitting the horse's neck.

hamite, ham′īt, *n.* A descendant of *Ham*; an Ethiopian.—**hamitic,** ham•it′ik, *a.* Relating to *Ham* or his descendants; appellative of a class of African tongues, comprising Coptic, Ethiopian or Abyssinian, etc.

hamlet, ham′let, *n.* [Dim. of A.Sax. *ham*, dwelling, enclosure; akin *home*.] A small village; a little cluster of houses in the country.

hammer, ham′ėr, *n.* [A.Sax. *hamor*=D. *hamer*, G. and Dan. *hammer*, Icel. *hamarr*; root doubtful.] An instrument for driving nails, beating metals, and the like, consisting usually of an iron head, fixed crosswise to a handle; a striking piece in the mechanism of a clock and a piano; that part in the lock of a gun, rifle, etc., which when the trigger is pulled falls with a smart blow, and causes the explosion of the detonating substance in connection with the powder.—*To bring to the hammer*, to sell by auction.—*v.t.* To beat, form, or forge, with a hammer; to contrive by intellectual labor; to excogitate: usually with *out*; to declare bankrupt or defaulting a member of the Stock Exchange.—*v.i.* To strike anything repeatedly, as with a hammer; to work; to labor in contrivance.—**hammerer,** ham′ėr•ėr, *n.* One who works with a hammer.—**hammerhead,** *n.* The iron head of a hammer; a genus of sharks with a head like a double-headed hammer.

hammock, ham′ok, *n.* [Sp. *hamaca*, a word of West Indian origin.] A kind of hanging bed, consisting of a piece of cloth suspended by cords and hooks.

hamper, ham′pėr, *n.* [Contr. from *hanaper* (which see).] A kind of rude basket or wickerwork receptacle, chiefly used as a case for packing articles.—*v.t.* To put into a hamper.

hamper, ham′pėr, *v.t.* [A nasalized form corresponding to D. *haperen*, to stammer, falter, stick fast; comp. Sc. *hamp*, to stammer; Goth. *hamfs*, *hanfs*, mutilated.] To impede in motion or progress, or to render progress difficult to; to shackle; to embarrass; to encumber.—*n.* Something that hampers or encumbers; a clog.

hamster, ham′stėr, *n.* [G.] A burrowing animal of the rat family common in Germany, having a short tail and large cheek pouches.

hamstring, *n.* and *v.t.* See HAM.

hamulus, ham′ū•lus, *n.* [L., a little hook, dim. of *hamus*, a hook.] A little hook; a hooklike process in animals and plants.

hanaper, han′a•pėr, *n.* [L.L. *hanaperium*, lit. a receptacle for cups, from L.L. *hanapus*, a cup, from O.H.G. *hnap*, A. Sax. *hnaep*, a cup; hence *hamper, n.*] A kind of basket used in early days by the kings of England for holding and carrying with them their money; the king's treasury.—*Clerk of the hanaper.*

hand, hand, *n.* [Common in similar forms, to all the Teutonic tongues; allied to Goth. *hinthan*, to capture; O.E. *hent*, to seize; perhaps also *hunt*. *Handsel, handle, handy, handsome* are derivatives.] The extremity of the arm, consisting of the palm and fingers, connected with the arm at the wrist; the corresponding member in certain of the lower animals; a measure of 4 inches; a palm; applied chiefly to horses; side or direction, either right or left (on the one *hand* or the other); handiwork; style of penmanship; power of performance; skill; agency; part in performing (to have a *hand* in mischief); possession; power (in the *hands* of the owner); that which performs the office of the hand or of a finger in pointing (the *hands* of a clock); a male or female in relation to an employer; a person employed on board ship or in factories; a person with some special faculty or ability (a good *hand* at a speech); in *card playing*, the cards held by a single player; one of the players.—*At hand*, near in time or place; within reach or not far distant.—*At first hand*, from the producer or seller directly; *at second hand*, or simply *second hand*, from an intermediate purchaser; old or used.—*By hand*, with the hands and not by the instrumentality of tools, etc.—*For one's own hand*, on one's own account; for one's self.—*From hand to hand*, from one person to another.—*In hand*, in ready money; in possession; in the state of preparation or execution.—*Off hand*, without hesitation or difficulty; without previous preparation.—*Off one's hands*, out of one's care or attention; ended.—*On hand*, in present possession.—*On one's hands*, under one's care or management; as a burden upon one.—*Out of hand*, at once; directly; without delay or hesitation; off one's hands.—*To one's hand*, already prepared; ready to be received.—*Under one's hand*, with the proper writing or signature of the name.—*Hand in hand*, with hands mutually clasped: hence, in union; conjointly; unitedly.—*Hand to hand*, in close union; close fight.—*Hand to mouth*, as want requires; without making previous provision or having an abundant previous supply.—*Hands off!* keep off; forbear; refrain from blows.—*Clean hands*, innocence; freedom from guilt.—*To ask the hand of*, to ask in marriage.—*To be hand and glove with*, to be intimate and familiar, as friends or associates.—*To bear a hand* (*naut.*), to give assistance quickly; to hasten.—*To change hands*, to change owners.—*To come to hand*, to be received; to come within one's reach.—*To have one's hands full*, to be fully occupied; to have a great deal to do.—*To lay hands on*, to seize; to assault.—*Laying on of hands*, a ceremony used in consecrating one to office.—*To lend a hand*, to give assistance.—*To set the hand to*, to engage in; to undertake.—*To shake hands*, to clasp the right hand mutually (with or without a shake), as a greeting or in token of friendship or reconciliation.—*To strike hands*, to make a contract or to become surety for another's debt or good behavior (O.T.).—*To take by the hand*, to take under one's protection.—*To take in hand*, to attempt; to undertake; to seize and deal with (a person).—*To wash one's hands of*, to have nothing more to do with; to renounce all connection with or interest in.—*v.t.* To give or transmit with the hand (*hand* me a book); to lead, guide, and lift with the hand; to conduct.—*To hand down*, to transmit in succession, as from father to son, or from predecessor to successor.—*a.* Belonging to or used by the hand: much used in composition for that which is manageable or wrought by the hand.—**handbarrow,** *n.* A kind of litter or stretcher, with handles at each end, carried between two persons.—**handbill,** *n.* A printed paper or sheet to be circulated for the purpose of making some public announcement.—**handbook,** *n.* A small book or treatise such as may be easily held in the hand; an establishment where bets are accepted on horse races.—**handbreadth,** *n.* A space equal to the breadth of the hand; a palm.—**handcart,** *n.* A cart drawn or pushed by hand.—**handcuff,** hand′kuf, *n.* [Modified from A.Sax. *handcops*—*hand*, the hand, *cops*, a fetter.] A manacle or fastening for the hand.—*v.t.* To put a handcuff on; to manacle.—**handed,** han′ded, *a.* Having a hand possessed of any peculiar property: used especially in compounds (right-*handed*, left-*handed*, empty-*handed*, full-*handed*, etc.).—**handfasting,** *n.* An irregular marriage by agreement or mutual pledge.—**handful,** hand′ful, *n.* As much as the hand will grasp or contain; a small quantity or number.—**hand glass,** *n.* *Hort.* a glass used for placing over plants to protect them or forward growth.—**hand grenade,** *n.* A grenade to be thrown by the hand.—**handmade,** *a.* Manufactured by the hand and not by a machine.—**hand organ,** *n.* A portable or barrel organ.—**handrail,** hand′rāl, *n.* A rail or railing to hold by.—**handsaw,** *n.* A saw to be used with the hand.—**handspike,** hand′-spīk, *n.* A bar used as a lever for various purposes, as in raising weights, heaving about a windlass, etc.—**handwork,** *n.* Work done by the hands.—**handwrite,**† hand′rīt, *v.t.* To express in handwriting; to write out.—**handwriting,** hand′rīt•ing, *n.* The cast of writing peculiar to each person; chirography; writing.

handicap, han′di•kap, *n.* [For *hand i' cap, hand in the cap*, the allusion being to drawing a lot out of a cap, from the fairness of both principles.] In sports, an advantage given to inferior competitors, or a disadvantage placed upon superior competitors, to equalize the chances of winning; a disadvantage that makes success more difficult.—*v.t.*—*handicapped, handicapping.* To place at a disadvantage; to assign handicaps to; put a handicap on; to equalize by a handicap.—**handicapper,** han′di•kap•ėr, *n.* One who handicaps.

handicraft, han′di•kraft, *n.* [Equivalent to *hand-craft*, the *i* representing old prefix *ge*, as in *handiwork*.] Manual occupation; work performed by the hand.—**handicraftsman,** han′-di•krafts•man, *n.* A man employed in manual occupation; an artisan.

handiwork, han′di•wėrk, *n.* [A.Sax. *handgeweorc*, from *hand*, the hand, and *geweorc*=*weorc*, work, with prefix *ge*.] Work done by the hands; hence, the work or deed of any person.

handkerchief, hang′kėr•chēf, *n.* [*Hand* and *kerchief*. KERCHIEF.] A piece of cloth, usually silk, linen, or cotton, carried about the person for wiping the face, hands, etc.; a similar piece worn round the neck.

handle, han′dl, *v.t.*—*handled, handling.* [A.Sax. *handlian*, to handle, a kind of freq. from *hand*=D. *handelen*, Dan. *handle*, Icel. *hōndla*, G. *handeln*.] To bring the hand or hands in frequent contact with; to finger; to touch; to feel; to manage, ply, or wield; to treat of or deal with, as a person or a topic.—*v.i.* To use the hands; to feel with the hands.—*n.* That part of a thing which is intended to be grasped by the hand in using or moving it; the instrument or means of effecting a purpose.—*To give a handle*, to furnish an occasion.—*A handle to one's name*, a title (*colloq.*).—**handler,** han′dlėr, *n.* One who handles.—**handling,** han′dling, *n.* A touching or using by the hand; a treating in discussion; dealing; action.

handsel, hansel, hand′sel, han′sel, *n.* [From *hand*, and stem *sell, sale*; Icel. *handsal* (from *hand*, and *sal*, sale), a bargain by shaking hands; Dan. *handsel*, hansel, earnest.] An earnest, or earnest penny; a sale, gift, or using, which is regarded as the first of a series; the first money received for the sale of goods.—*v.t.* To give a handsel to; to use or do for the first time.

handsome, hand′sum, *a.* [From *hand*, and term. *-some*=D. *handzaam*, tractable, serviceable, mild; G. *handsam*, convenient, favorable.] Possessing a form agreeable to the eye or to correct taste; having a certain share of beauty along with dignity; having symmetry of parts; well formed; shapely; becoming; appropriate; ample or large (a *handsome* fortune); characterized by or expressive of liberality or generosity.—**handsomely,** hand′sum•li, *adv.* In a handsome manner. — **handsomeness,** hand′-sum•nes, *n.*

handy, han′di, *a.* [From *hand*; comp. the D. and L.G. *handig*, handy.] Skilled to use the hands with ease; dexterous; ready; adroit; ready to the hand; near; convenient.—**handily,** han′di•li, *adv.* In a handy manner.—**handiness,** han′di•nes, *n.*

hang, hang, *v.t.* pret. & pp. *hung* or *hanged* (the latter being obsolete except in sense to put to death by the rope). [A.Sax. *hangian*, to hang or be suspended, and *hón* (contracted for *hahan*), pret. *heng*, pp. *hangen*, to suspend; O.H.G. *hahan*, G. *hangen*, *hangen*, Dan. *hænge*, Icel. *hanga*, *hengja*. Goth. *hahan*, to suspend, to hang. Akin *hank*, *hanker*, *hinge*.] To suspend; to fasten to some elevated point without support from below: often with *up*; to put to death by suspending by the neck; to fit up so as to allow of free motion (a door, a gate, etc.); to cover, furnish, or decorate by anything suspended (to *hang* an apartment with curtains); to cause or suffer to assume a drooping attitude (to *hang* the head).—*To hang fire*, to be slow in communicating fire through the vent to the charge: said of a gun; hence, to hesitate or be slow in acting; to be slow in execution.—*To hang out*, to suspend in open view; to display; to suspend in the open air.—*To hang up*, to suspend; to keep or suffer to remain undecided.—*v.i.* To be suspended; to be sustained wholly or partly by something above; to dangle; to depend; to bend forward or downward; to lean or incline; to be attached to or connected with in various ways; to hover; to impend (dangers *hang* over us); to linger, lounge, loiter; to incline; to have a steep declivity; to be put to death by suspension from the neck.—*To hang back*, to halt; to incline to retire; to go reluctantly forward.—*To hang on* or *upon*, to weigh upon; to drag; to rest; to continue (sleep *hung on* his eyelids); to be dependent on; to regard with the closest attention (he *hung* upon the speaker's words). —*To hang together*, to be closely united; to be self-consistent.—*n.* The way a thing hangs; slope or declivity; inclination, bent, or tendency.—**hangdog,** *n.* A base and degraded character, fit only to be the hangman of dogs.—*a.* Of or pertaining to a hangdog; having a low, degraded, or blackguard-like appearance.—**hanger,** hang′ėr, *n.* One who hangs; a short broad sword, incurvated at the point, which was suspended from the girdle; that from which something is hung.—**hanger-on,** *n.* pl. **hangers-on**. One who hangs on or sticks to a person, a place, society, etc.; a parasite; a dependent.—**hanging,** hang′ing, *a.* Such as to incur punishment by the halter (a *hanging* matter).—*n.* Death by suspension; what is hung up to drape a room, as tapestry or the like: used chiefly in the plural.—**hangman,** hang′man, *n.* One who hangs another.

hangar, hang′ar, *n.* [Fr. *hangar*, a shed.] A shed for housing airplanes.

hangnail, hang′nāl, *n.* [Corruption of *agnail*.] A tiny strip of skin peeling loose at the fingernail base.

hank, hangk, *n.* [Same as Icel. *hönk*, a hank or skein; Dan. *hank*, a hook, a clasp; Sw. *hank*, a band; akin to *hang*.] A parcel consisting of two or more skeins of yarn or thread tied together; *naut.* a ring of wood, rope, or iron, fixed to a stay to confine the staysails.

hanker, hang′kėr, *v.i.* [Allied to D. *hunkeren*, to desire, to long after; probably to *hang*.] To long for; to be uneasily desirous.—**hankering,** hang′-kėr•ing, *n.*

hanky-panky, hang′ki pang′ki, *n.* [From *hocus-pocus*, pretended incantation of jugglers.] Trickery; mischief; questionable activity.

Hansard, han′sėrd, *n.* The published debates of the British Parliament, originally issued by the Messrs. *Hansard.*

hanse, hans, *n.* [G. *hanse*, *hansa*, league.] A league; a confederacy.—**Hanse, Hanseatic,** han•sē•at′ik, *a.* Of or pertaining to a confederacy of commercial cities, associated together as early as the twelfth century; the name *Hanse towns* is still applied to Lübeck, Hamburg, and Bremen.

hansom, hansom cab, han′sum, *n.* A two-wheeled cab, so named after the inventor.

hap, hap, *n.* [Icel. *happ*, good fortune, luck; comp. A.Sax. *gehæp*, fit; D. *happen*, to snatch at; seen also in *mishap*, *perhaps*.] Chance; accident; casual event; vicissitude.—*v.i.* To happen; to befall; to come by chance. —**haphazard,** *n.* Chance; accident. —**hapless,** hap′les, *a.*—**happen,** hap′-n, *v.i.* [From *hap*.] To be or be brought about unexpectedly or by chance; to chance; to take place; to occur.—*To happen on*, to meet with; to fall or light upon.—**happily,** hap′-i•li, *adv.* In a happy manner, state, or circumstance.—**happiness,** hap′-i•nes, *n.* The state or quality of being happy; felicity; contentedness along with actual pleasure; good fortune.—**happy,** hap′i, *a.* [From *hap*.] Contented in mind; highly pleased; satisfied; fortunate; successful; secure of good; bringing or attended with good fortune; prosperous; favorable; well suited for a purpose or occasion; well devised; felicitous; living in concord.

hara-kiri, hä′ra-kē′ri, *n.* [Jap. *hara*, belly, and *kiri*, cutting.] A traditional Japanese method of suicide, ceremonially performed by slashing across the abdomen with a dagger and then twisting it upward; simultaneously, the second, previously selected by the suicide, swings a sword on his friend's neck. Originally it was voluntarily practiced by nobles defeated in battle, by men as a mark of loyalty to a deceased noble, by men who had lost face or prestige; and obligatorily practiced, as an honorable way out, by men guilty of treachery or disloyalty to the mikado. It is now practiced chiefly as a mark of protest against a national policy.

harangue, ha•rang′, *n.* [Fr. *harangue* =Pr. *arengua*, It. *aringa*, a harangue, lit. a speech made to a ring, or crowd, of people.] A loud address to a multitude; a popular oration; a bombastic or pompous address; a tirade or declamation.—*v.i. harangued*, *haranguing*. To make a harangue; to make a bombastic or pretentious speech.—*v.t.* To address by a harangue.—**haranguer,** ha•-rang′ėr, *n.* One who harangues.

harass, har′as, *v.t.* [Fr. *harasser*; probably connected with Fr. *harier*, to harry; vex; *harer*, to set a dog on.] To weary, fatigue, or tire with bodily labor; to weary with importunity, care, or perplexity; to perplex; to annoy by repeated attacks.—*n.*† Distress; devastation.—**harasser,** har′-as•ėr, *n.* One who harasses.—**harassment,** har′as•ment, *n.* The act of harassing or state of being harassed.

harbinger, här′bin•jėr, *n.* [O.E. *harbegier*, *harbergeour*, *harbesher*, etc., one who provides harborage or lodging, a harbinger; for the insertion of the *n* compare *messenger*, *passenger*. HARBOR.] One who went before to provide lodgings and other accommodations; hence, a forerunner; a precursor; that which precedes and gives notice of the expected arrival of something else.—*v.t.* To precede as harbinger; to presage or predetermine, as a harbinger.

harbor, här′bėr, *n.* [Same as L.G. *harbarge*, D. *herberg*, Icel. *herbergi*, lit. army-shelter, the elements being the same as A.Sax. *here*, an army, and *beorgan*, *bergan*, to shelter or protect. BOROUGH.] A place of shelter, protection, or refuge; a port or haven for ships.—*v.t.* To shelter or take under protection; to protect; to entertain or cherish in the mind (to *harbor* malice).—*v.i.* To lodge or abide for a time for shelter or protection; to take shelter.—**harborage,** här′bėr•āj, *n.* State of being harbored; shelter; lodgment.—**harborer,** här′bėr•ėr, *a.* One who harbors.—**harborless,** här′bėr•les, *a.* Without a harbor; destitute of shelter.—**harbor master,** *n.* An officer who attends to the berthing, etc., of ships in a harbor.

hard, härd, *a.* [A.Sax. *heard*=Goth. *hardus*, Icel. *hardr*, Dan. *haard*, D. *hard*, G. *hart*; cog. Gr. *kratos*, *kartos*, strength (as in *aristocrat*, *democrat*, etc.). Hence *hardy*.] Not easily penetrated or separated into parts; not yielding to pressure; applied to material bodies, and opposed to *soft*; difficult to the understanding; not easy to the intellect; difficult of accomplishment; not easy to be done or executed; laborious; fatiguing; difficult to endure; oppressive; severe; cruel; distressing; painful; unfeeling; insensible; harsh; obdurate; exacting; avaricious; grasping; harsh or abusive (*hard* words); pinching with cold; rigorous (a *hard* winter); austere; rough; acid or sour (*hard* cider); forced; constrained; unnatural; coarse; unpalatable, or scanty (*hard* fare); *gram.* applied to the consonants (also called *surd*) *f*, *k*, *p*, *s*, *t*, and the sound of *th* in *thin*, and also to the sound of *c* as in *corn* and *g* as in *get*, as distinguished from the sounds in *city* and *gin*; applied to water not very suitable for washing from holding salts of lime or magnesia in solution.—*Hard cash*, gold or silver coin, as distinguished from paper money. (*Colloq.*)—*adv.* Close; near (*hard by*); with urgency; vehemently; vigorously; energetically; violently; with great force; with difficulty or labor.—*To die hard*, to die, as it were, reluctantly, and after a struggle for life; to die unrepentant. —*Hard up*, in want of money; needy; without resources.—*Hard up for*, having difficulty in getting anything; at a loss how to find.—*Hard a-weather! hard a-port!* etc., *naut.* a direction for the helm to be turned as much as possible to the weather-side, the port-side, etc.—**harden,** här′dn, *v.t.* To make hard or more hard; to confirm in effrontery, obstinacy, wickedness, opposition, or enmity; to make insensible or unfeeling; to make firm; to inure.—*v.i.* To become hard or more hard; to acquire solidity or mere compactness; to become unfeeling; to become inured.—**hardener,** här′dn•ėr, *n.* One who or that which hardens.—**hard-featured,** *a.* Having a hard or stern face.—**hard-favored,** *a.* Having coarse features; harsh of countenance.—**hardfisted, hardhanded,** *a.* Having hard hands; closefisted; covetous. — **hardheaded,** *a.* Shrewd; clearheaded and firm.—**hardhearted,** *a.* Pitiless; unfeeling; inhuman; inexorable.—**hard landing,** *n.* The deliberate destruction of an experimental space capsule upon impact with a predetermined target.—**hardly,** härd′li, *adv.* Not easily; severely; harshly; scarcely; barely; not quite. —**hardness,** härd′nes, *n.* The state or quality of being hard; *mineral*, the capacity of a substance to scratch another or be scratched by another. —**hardpan,** *n. Agri.* the name given to a hard stratum of earth below the soil proper.—**hardship,** härd′ship, *n.* Something hard, oppressive, toilsome, distressing; want or privation; grievance.—**hardtack,** härd′tak, *n.* A saltless biscuit made of flour and water.—**hardware,** härd•wâr, *n.* Articles of iron or other metal, as pots, kettles, saws, knives, etc.—**hardwood,** härd′wụd, *n.* Any wood of a close and solid texture, as beech, oak, ash, maple, ebony, etc.

hards, härdz, *n. pl.* [Also written *hurds*; from A.Sax. *heordan* (pl.), hards, tow; Icel. *hörr*, flax; same root as L. *caro*, to card, *carduus*, thistle, *coma*, hair; perhaps E. *hair*.] The refuse or coarse part of flax or wool.

hardy, här′di, *a.* [Fr. *hardi*, bold, daring, properly the pp. of the old verb *hardir*, to make bold, from O.H.G. *hartjan*, from *hart* (E. *hard*), hard, bold. HARD.] Bold; brave; stout; daring; resolute; intrepid; confident; full of assurance; inured to fatigue; proof against hardship; capable of bearing exposure to cold weather (a *hardy* plant).—**hardihood,** här′di•hụd, *n.* Boldness; bravery; intrepidity; venturesomeness; audacity.—**hardily,** här′di•li, *adv.* In a hardy manner.—**hardiness,** här′di•nes, *n.* The state or quality of being hardy.

hare, hâr, *n.* [A.Sax. *hara*=Dan. and Sw. *hare*, Icel. *héri*, D. *haas*, G. *hase*; probably allied to Skr. *çaça*, a hare, from *çaç*, to jump.] A mammal of the genus *Lepus*, with long ears, a short tail, soft hair, a divided upper lip, and long hind legs, often hunted for sport or for its flesh, which is excellent food.—**harebell,** hâr′bel, *n.* A species of the campanula or bellflower, also termed the common bellflower and Scottish bluebell; also applied in many districts to the wild hyacinth.—**harebrained,** *a.* [Comp. ‘mad as a March *hare*’.] Giddy; volatile; heedless.—**harelip,** *n.* A malformation of the lip consisting of a fissure or vertical division of one or both lips, sometimes extending also to the palate.

harem, hâ′rem, *n.* [Ar. *harām*, anything prohibited, from *hharram*, to prohibit.] In a Muslim household, a group of women who are the wives and concubines of one man; the apartments occupied by these women.

haricot, har′i•kō, *n.* [Fr., a ragout; O.Fr. *harigoter*, to mince, *harigote*, a morsel; *haricot*-bean=ragout-bean.] A kind of ragout of meat and roots; the kidney bean or French bean (in this sense short for haricot bean).

hark, härk, *v.i.* [Contr. from *hearken*.] To listen; to hearken: now only used in the imperative.—*Hark!* a hunting cry used with various adjuncts to stimulate or direct the hounds.—

harken, HEARKEN.

harl, härl, *n.* [Probably=*hardle*, from *hards*.] A filament, as of flax or hemp; a barb of one of the feathers from a peacock's tail, used in dressing fly hooks.

Harlequin, här′le•kwin, *n.* [Fr. *harlequin*, *arlequin*; O.Fr. *hellequin*, *hierlekin*, etc.; origin quite uncertain.] A performer in a pantomime, masked, dressed in tight particolored clothes, covered with spangles, and armed with a magic wand or sword; [*not. cap.*] a buffoon in general.—**harlequinade,** här′le•kwin•äd″, *n.* The portion of a pantomime in which the harlequin and clown play the principal parts.

harlot, här′lot, *n.* [O.Fr. *harlot*, *herlot*, Pr. *arlot*, Sp. *arlote*, It. *arlotto*, a glutton, a lazy good-for-nothing, a word of uncertain origin; comp. W. *herlawd*, a stripling, *herlodes*, a damsel.] A woman who prostitutes her body for hire; a prostitute.—**harlotry,** här′lot•ri, *n.* A trade or practice of prostitution.

harm, härm, *n.* [A.Sax. *hearm*, harm, evil, grief=Dan., Sw., and G. *harm*, grief, offense; Icel. *harmr*; comp. Skr. *çram*, to weary.] Physical or material injury; hurt; damage; detriment; moral wrong; evil; mischief; wickedness.—*v.t.* To hurt; to injure; to damage.—**harmful,** härm′fụl, *a.* Full of harm; hurtful; injurious; noxious. — **harmfully,** härm′fụl•li, *adv.* In a harmful manner.—**harmfulness,** härm′fụl•nes, *n.*—**harmless,** härm′les, *a.* Free from harm; uninjured; free from power or disposition to harm; not injurious; innocuous; inoffensive.—**harmlessly,** härm′les•li, *adv.* In a harmless manner.—**harmlessness,** härm′les•nes, *n.*

harmattan, här•mat′tan, *n.* [Arabic name.] An extremely dry and hot wind which blows periodically from the interior parts of Africa toward the Atlantic Ocean.

harmony, här′mo•ni, *n.* [L. and Gr. *harmonia*, from Gr. *harmos*, a suiting or fitting together a joint, from *arō*, to fit, to adapt, the same root being seen in E. *ărm*.] The just adaptation of parts to each other, in any system or combination of things, or in things intended to form a connected whole; concord; consonance; concord or agreement in facts, views, sentiments, manners, interests, and the like; peace and friendship; *mus.* musical concord; the accordance of two or more sounds, or that union of different sounds which pleases the ear, or a succession of such sounds called chords; the science which treats of such sounds; the agreement or consistency of the accounts of the first three (synoptic) Gospels with the fourth by St. John.—**harmonic,** här•mon′ik, *a.* Relating to harmony or music; concordant; musical; harmonious.—*Acoustics*, a secondary tone heard along with a fundamental tone, produced by secondary or partial vibrations.—*Harmonical proportion*, *math.* the relation between four quantities when the first is to the fourth as the difference between the first and second is to the difference between the third and fourth; also a similar relation between three quantities.—*Harmonical series*, a series of numbers in continued harmonical proportion.—*Harmonic triad*, *mus.* the chord of a note consisting of its third and perfect fifth, or in other words, the common chord.—*n. Mus.* a secondary and less distinct tone which accompanies any principal and apparently simple tone.—**harmonica,** här•mon′i•ka, *n.* A collection of musical glass goblets; also an instrument, the tones of which are produced by striking rods or plates of glass or metal with hammers; a mouth organ.—**harmonically,** här•mon′i•kal•li, *adv.* In a harmonic manner.—**harmonicon,** här•mon′i•kon, *n.* A large barrel organ, containing, in addition to the common pipes, others to imitate the different wind instruments, and an apparatus to produce the effects of drums, triangles, cymbals, etc.; also, a toy musical instrument with free reeds blown by the mouth.—**harmonics,** här•mon′iks, *n.* The doctrine or science of musical sounds.—**harmonious,** här•mō′ni•us. *a.* Exhibiting or characterized by harmony.—**harmoniously,** här•mō′ni•us•li, *adv.* In a harmonious manner.—**harmoniousness,** här•mō′ni•us•nes, *n.*—**harmonist,** här′mon•ist *n.* One who harmonizes; one skilled in the principles of harmony; a writer of harmony.—**harmonium,** här•mō′ni•um, *n.* A musical instrument resembling a small organ, and much used as a substitute for it, the tones of which are produced by the forcing of air through free reeds.—**harmonization,** här′mon•i•zā″shon, *n.* The act of harmonizing. — **harmonize,** här′-mon•ız, *v.i.*—*harmonized, harmonizing.* To unite harmoniously or in harmony; to be in peace and friendship; to agree in action, effect, sense, or purport; to be musically harmonious.—*v.t.* To bring to be harmonious; to cause to agree; to show the harmony or agreement of; to reconcile the contradictions between; *mus.* to combine according to the laws of counterpoint; to set accompanying parts to, as to an air or melody.—**harmonizer,** här′mon•ī•zėr, *n.* One who harmonizes; a harmonist.

harness, här′nes, *n.* [W. *harnais, haiarnaez,* harness, from *haiarn,* iron. IRON.] A person's armor and military furniture; the gear or tackle by which a horse or other animal is yoked and made to work; the apparatus in a loom by which the sets of warp thread are shifted alternately.

harp, härp, *n.* [A.Sax. *hearpe*=D. *harp,* Icel. *harpa,* Dan. *harpe,* Gr. *harfe,* a harp; perhaps same root as L. *carpo,* to pluck or twitch.] A stringed musical instrument of great antiquity, now usually nearly triangular in form, with wire strings stretched from the upper part to one of the sides, played with both hands while standing upright, the strings being struck or pulled by fingers and thumb.—*v.i.* To play on the harp; to dwell on a subject tiresomely and vexatiously: usually with *on* or *upon.* —*To harp on one string,* to dwell too exclusively upon one subject, so as to weary or annoy the hearers.—**harper, harpist,** här′pėr, här′pist, *n.*

harpoon, här•pön′, *n.* [Fr. *harpon,* a harpoon, from *harper,* to clutch, from *harpe,* a claw, a hook, from Gr. *harpagē,* a hook, *harpazō,* to seize.] A spear or javelin used to strike and kill whales and large fish.—*v.t.* To strike with a harpoon.—**harpooner,** här•pö′nėr, *n.* One who uses a harpoon.

harpsichord, härp′si•kord, *n.* [From O.Fr. *harpechorde,* It. *arpicordo*—*harp* and *chord.*] A keyboard stringed instrument of the 15th century still used in concert, having strings which are plucked with quills.

harpy, här′pi, *n.* [Fr. *harpie,* from L. *harpyia,* Gr. *harpuia,* from root of *harpazō,* to seize.] [*cap.*] *Class. mythol.,* the name given to three foul monsters having the face of a woman and the body of a bird, with feet and fingers armed with sharp claws, who were sent to punish Phineus for his cruelty to his children.—**harpy eagle,** *n.* A large and very powerful raptorial bird of Mexico and South America.

harquebus, harquebuse, harquebuss, här′kwē•bus. See ARQUEBUS.

harridan, har′i•dan, *n.* [Akin to Fr. *haridelle,* Prov. Fr. *hardele, harin,* a wornout horse, a jade.] A hag; an odious old woman; a vixenish woman; a trollop.

harrier, har′i•ėr, *n.* [From *hare.*] A small kind of dog of the hound species employed in hunting the hare; also, a cross-country runner.

harrier, har′i•ėr, *n.* [A.Sax. *hergian,* to afflict with an army, to ravage.] One who pillages; name for several species of hawks which strike their prey upon the ground and generally fly very low.

Harrovian, ha•rō′vi•an, *a.* Of or pertaining to Harrow, an exclusive boys' school in England.—*n.* One who attends, or is a graduate of, Harrow.

harrow, har′ō, *n.* [Same word as Dan. *harve,* Sw. *harf,* a harrow; akin to D. *hark,* G. *harke,* a rake.] An agricultural implement, usually formed of pieces of timber or metal crossing each other, and set with iron teeth, called tines, used for covering seed when sown, etc.—*v.t.* To draw a harrow over; *fig.* to lacerate (the feelings); to torment; to harass.—**harrower,** har′ō•ėr, *n.* One who harrows.—**harrowing,** har′ō•ing, *a.* Causing acute distress to the mind.

harry, har′i, *v.t.*—*harried, harrying.* [A.Sax. *hergian,* to ravage, from *here* (genit. *herges*), an army; Icel. *herja,* to lay waste, to oppress; Dan. *hærge, hærje,* G. (*ver*) *heeren,* to ravage. Akin *herring, herald.*] To pillage; to plunder; to rob; to harass‡.

harsh, härsh, *a.* [O.E. and Sc. *harsk,* harsh, acid; same as Dan. and O.Sw. *harsk,* rancid; G. *harsch,* harsh, rough; root doubtful; perhaps akin to *hard.*] Grating, either to the touch, to the taste, or to the ear; austere; crabbed; morose; rough; rude; rigorous; severe.—**harshen,** har′shn, *v.t.* To render harsh.—**harshly,** härsh′li, *adv.* In a harsh manner.—**harshness,** härsh′nes, *n.*

harslet, härs′let, *n.* See HASLET.

hart, härt, *n.* [A.Sax. *heort*=L.G. and D. *hert,* Dan. *hiort,* Sw. *kjort,* Icel. *hjörtr,* G. *hirsch,* stag; lit. horned animal; allied to Gr. *keras,* L. *cornu,* a horn. HORN.] A stag or male deer, especially when he has passed his fifth year, and the sur-royal or crown antler is formed.—**hartshorn,** harts′horn, *n.* The horn of the hart or stag; an ammoniacal preparation obtained from the horn, and used medicinally; solution of ammonia.

hartal, här′täl, *n.* [Hindi, var. of hattāl.] An organized cessation of business to protest against government policy or action; noncooperation.

hartebeest, här′te•bēst, härt′bēst, *n.* [Dutch.] An antelope common in South Africa.

harum-scarum, hâ′rum•skâ′rum, *a.* [Perhaps from O.E. *hare,* to fright, or from *hare,* the animal, and *scare.*] Harebrained; unsettled; giddy; rash. —*n.* A giddy, harebrained, or rash person. (*Colloq.*)

haruspice, haruspicy. See ARUSPEX.

harvest, här′vest, *n.* [A.Sax. *haerfest* =O.Fris. *harvest,* G. *herbst,* D. *herfst,* Icel. *haust,* Sw. and Dan. *höst,* autumn, harvest; cognate with Gr. *karpos,* fruit, L. *carpo,* to pluck.] The season of gathering a crop of any kind; the time of reaping and gathering corn and other grain; that which is reaped and gathered in; the product of any labor; gain; result; effect; consequence.—*v.t.* To reap or gather (corn and fruits).—**harvest bug,** *n.* A species of tick which infests the skin in the autumn.—**harvester,** här′ves•tėr, *n.* One who or that which harvests; a mower; a reaper.—**harvest home,** *n.* The bringing home of the harvest; the harvest feast.—**harvest moon,** *n.* The full moon at the time of harvest, or about the autumnal equinox, when it rises nearly at the same hour for several days.

has, haz. The 3rd pers. sing. pres. of the verb *have.*—**has-been,** haz′-bin, *n.* One who has had his day; that which has passed its usefulness. (*Colloq.*)

hash, hash, *v.t.* [Fr. *hacher,* E. to *hack.* HACK.] To chop into small pieces; to talk over again a previous conversation (to *hash it over*).—*n.* Food previously cooked, as meat and potatoes, chopped up and cooked again; a restating of facts already well discussed (making a *hash* of them); a jumble; a hodgepodge.

hashish, hash′ēsh, *n.* A narcotic plant of Asia, similar to marijuana, the dried leaves of which are smoked in cigarettes.

haslet, has′let, *n.* [For *hastelet,* from Fr. *hastille,* the pluck of an animal, lit. a little roast, from *haste,* a spit, L. *hasta,* a spear.] The cooked heart, liver, etc., of a hog.

hasp, hasp, *n.* [A.Sax. *hæpse,* the hook of a hinge=Icel. *hespa,* G. *haspe, häspe,* a fastening; Dan. *haspe,* a hasp, a reel.] A clasp that passes over a staple to be fastened by a padlock; a metal hook for fastening a door; the fourth part of a spindle (of yarn).—*v.t.* To shut or fasten with a hasp.

hassle, has′l, *n.* An argument; a mix-up. (Slang)

hassock, has′ok, *n.* [Origin doubtful; comp. W. *hesg,* sedge, also Sw. *hwass,* rushes.] A thick mat or hard cushion on which persons kneel in church; a footstool stuffed with flock or other material.

hastate, has′tāt, *a.* [L. *hastatus,* from *hasta,* a spear.] Spear-shaped; resembling the head of a spear; triangular.

haste, hāst, *n.* [Same word as G.Sw. and Dan. *hast,* haste, whence O.Fr. *haste,* Mod. Fr. *hâte,* haste; akin to *hate.*] Celerity of motion; speed; swiftness; dispatch; expedition; applied only to voluntary beings, as men and animals; sudden excitement of passion; quickness; precipitance; the state of being pressed by business; hurry; urgency.—*To make haste,* to hasten; to proceed rapidly.—**haste, hasten,** hāst, hā'sn, *v.t.* [Sw. *hasta,* Dan. *haste,* G. *hasten,* to haste.] To drive or urge forward; to push on; to hurry; to expedite; with *me, him,* etc., to make haste; to be speedy or quick.—*v.i.* To move with celerity; to hurry.—**hastener,** hā'sn•ėr, *n.* One that hastens; a metal kitchen stand for keeping in the heat of the fire to a roast while cooking.—**hastily,** hās'-ti•li, *adv.* In a hasty manner.—**hastiness,** hās'ti•nes, *n.* The state or quality of being hasty.—**hasty,** hās'ti, *a.* Moving or acting with haste; quick; speedy: opposed to *slow*; precipitate; rash; inconsiderate; opposed to *deliberate*; irritable; easily excited to wrath; passionate; arising from or indicating passion (*hasty* words); early ripe (O.T.).—**hasty pudding,** *n.* A pudding made of milk and flour boiled quickly together; also, oatmeal and water boiled together; porridge.

hat, hat, *n.* [A.Sax. *hæt*=Dan. *hat* Sw. *hett,* Icel. *hattr*—hat, from a root meaning to cover.] A covering for the head; a headdress with a crown, sides, and continuous brim, made of different materials, and worn by men and women; the dignity of a cardinal: from the broad-brimmed scarlet hat which forms part of a cardinal's dress.—*To give one a hat,* to lift the hat to one.—**hatband,** *n.* A band round a hat.—**hatbox,** *n.* A box for a hat.—**hat tree,** *n.* A rack or stand of various forms furnished with pegs for hanging hats on.—**hatter,** hat'ėr, *n.*

hatch, hach, *v.t.* [Same word as Dan. *hække,* to hatch, or nidificate, from *hæk,* a hatching; Sw. *hächa,* to hatch; G. *hecken,* to hatch, *hecke,* the pairing of birds, a brood; connected with *hack,* from the chipping of the shell.] To produce young from eggs by incubation, or by artificial heat; to contrive or plot; to originate and produce (a scheme, mischief, etc.).—*v.i.* To perform or undergo the process of incubation.—*n.* A brood; as many young birds as are produced at once; the act of hatching.—**hatcher,** hach'ėr, *n.*—**hatchery,** hach'ėr•i, *n.* A place for hatching eggs, especially those of poultry and fish.

hatch, hach, *v.t.* [Fr. *hacher,* to hack, to shade by lines. HACK.] To shade by lines crossing each other in drawing and engraving.—**hatching,** hach'ing, *n.*

hatch, hach, *n.* [A.Sax. *hæc,* a grating; Dan. *hæk,* D. *hek,* a grating; G. *heck,* a fence of laths.] The frame of crossbars laid over the opening in a ship's deck; the cover or a hatchway; the opening in a ship's deck; the hatchway; a similar opening in a floor; a trap door; a half door or a door with an opening over it; a floodgate; a frame or weir in a river for catching fish.—*To be under hatches,* to be in the interior of a ship with the hatches down.—*Naut.* dead, gone below, opposed to *gone aloft.*—*v.t.* To close with a hatch or hatches.—**hatchway,** hach'wā, *n.* A square or oblong opening in a ship's deck for communication with the interior.

hatchel, hach'el, *n.* [A form of *hackle* or *heckle.*] A hackle or heckle for flax.—*v.t.* To clean by drawing through the teeth of a hatchel; to hackle or heckle.

hatchet, hach'et, *n.* [Fr. *hachette,* from *hacher,* to cut, from G. *hacken,* to cut. HACK.] A small ax with a short handle, used with one hand.—*To take up the hatchet,* to make war; *to bury the hatchet,* to make peace; phrases derived from the customs of the American Indians.—**hatchet-faced,** *a.* Having a thin face with prominent features.

hatchment, hach'ment, *n.* [Corrupted from *achievement.*] The coat of arms of a dead person, placed on the front of a house, in a church, or elsewhere at funerals, notifying the death and the rank of the deceased. Also called *Achievement.*

hatchway, *n.* See HATCH, *n.*

hate, hāt, *v.t.*—*hated, hating.* [A.Sax. *hate, hete,* hate, hatred, *hatian,* to hate; D. *haat,* Sw. *hat,* Icel. *hatr,* Goth. *hatis,* hate; Goth. *hatan,* Icel. and Sw. *hata,* D. *haten,* G. *hassen,* to hate.] To dislike greatly or intensely; to have a great aversion to; to detest.—*n.* Great dislike or aversion; hatred.—**hatable, hateable,** hā'ta•bl, *a.* Capable or worthy of being hated; odious.—**hateful,** hāt'ful, *a.* Causing hate; exciting great dislike; odious; detestable; feeling hatred; malevolent.—**hatefully,** hāt'fu̧l•li, *adv.* In a hateful manner.—**hatefulness,** hāt'fu̧l•nes, *n.* The quality of being hateful.—**hater,** hā'tėr, *n.* One that hates.—**hatred,** hā'tred, *a.* [*Hate,* and suffix *-red,* as in *kindred*=A.Sax. *-raeden,* condition, state.] Great dislike or aversion; hate; detestation; active antipathy.

hauberk, ha̧'bėrk, *n.* [O.Fr. *hauberc,* from O.H.G. *halsberg*—*hals,* the throat, and *bergen,* to defend; A.Sax. *healsbeorga,* Icel. *hálsbjörg,* a gorget. *Habergeon* is a diminutive. HAWSE, BOROUGH.] A coat of mail without sleeves, formed of steel rings interwoven.

haughty, ha̧'ti, *a.* [O.Fr, *hautain,* haughty, from *haut, hault,* from L. *altus,* high (whence *altitude, exalt*); *gh* was inserted through influence of *high.*] Proud and disdainful; having a high opinion of one's self, with some contempt for others; lofty and arrogant; disdainful; supercilious.—**haughtily,** ha̧'ti•li, *adv.* In a haughty manner.—**haughtiness,** ha̧'ti•nes, *n.* The quality of being haughty.

haul, ha̧l, *v.t.* [Same as D. *halen,* Icel. and Sw. *hala,* Dan. *hale,* to haul; G. holen, to fetch, to tow (whence Fr. *haler,* to haul); hence *halliard, halyard.*] To pull or draw with force; to transport by drawing; to drag; to tug.—*To haul over the coals,* to bring to a reckoning; to take to task; to reprimand.—*v.i. Naut.* to change the direction of sailing: with *off, up,* etc.—*n.* A pulling with force; a violent pull; a draught of fish in a net; that which is caught by one haul; hence, that which is taken, gained, or received at once.—**haulage,** ha̧'lij, *n.* The act of hauling or drawing; the force expended in hauling; dues or charges for hauling or towing.—**hauler,** ha̧'-lėr, *n.* One who pulls or hauls.

haulm, ha̧lm, *n.* [A.Sax. *healm*=D. Dan. and Sw. *halm,* Icel. *hálmr*; cog. L. *calamus,* Gr. *kalamos,* a reed.] The stem or stalk of grain of all kinds, or of peas, beans, hops, etc.; dry stalks in general.

haunch, ha̧nsh, *n.* [Fr. *hanche,* the haunch, from the Teutonic; Fris. *hancke, hencke,* haunch; G. *hanke,* the haunch of a horse.] The hip; the bend of the thigh; part of the body of a man and of quadrupeds between the last ribs and the thigh; *arch.* the middle part between the vertex or crown and the springing of an arch; the flank.

haunt, ha̧nt, *v.t.* [Fr. *hanter,* to frequent, from Armor. *hent,* a way, *henti,* to frequent.] To frequent; to resort to much or often, or to be much about; to visit customarily; to appear in or about, as a specter; to be a frequent spectral visitant of.—*v.i.* To be much about a place; to make frequent resort.—*n.* A place to which one frequently resorts; a favorite resort; a common abiding place.

haustellum, ha̧s•tel'lum, *n.* [L., from *haurio, haustum,* to draw up.] The suctorial organ of certain insects, otherwise called the proboscis or antlia.—**haustellate,** ha̧s'tel•lāt, *a.* Provided with a haustellum or sucker; suctorial.

hautboy, hō'boi, *n.* [Fr. *hautbois*—*haut* (in E. *haughty*), high, and *bois* (E. *bush*), wood, from the high tone of the instrument.] An oboe; a wind instrument of wood, sounded through a double-reed.

hauteur, ō'tėr, *n.* [Fr. HAUGHTY.] Pride; haughtiness; insolent manner or spirit.

Havana, ha•van'a, *n.* A kind of cigar largely manufactured at *Havana,* the capital of Cuba.

have, hav, *v.t.*—pret. & pp. *had,* ppr. *having.* Ind. pres. I *have,* thou *hast,* he *has*; we, ye, they *have.* [A.Sax. *habban,* from *hafian* (*fi* becoming regularly *bb* between vowels)=Dan. *have,* Icel. *hafa,* Goth. *haban,* G. *haben,* to have; cog. L. *capio,* to take (whence *capable,* etc.). *Behave, haft, haven* are connected.] To possess; to hold; to be in close relation to (to *have* a son, a master, a servant); to accept; to take as husband or wife; to hold or regard (to *have* in honor); to maintain or hold in opinion; to be under necessity, or impelled by duty (to *have* to do it); to procure or make to be; to cause (he *had* him murdered); to gain, procure, receive, obtain; to bring forth (a child); to experience in any way, as to enjoy, to participate in, to suffer from; to understand.—*I had as good*, it would be as well for me; *I had better*, it would be better for me; *I had best*, it would be best for me; *I had as lief* or *lieve*, I would as willingly; *I had rather*, I should prefer.—*Have after!* pursue! let us pursue!—*Have at!* go at! assail! encounter! as *have* at him!—*Have with you!* come on! agreed!—*To have away*, to remove; to take away.—*To have in*, to contain.—*To have on*, to wear; to carry, as apparel or weapons.—*To have a care*, to take care; to be on guard, or to guard.—*To have a person out*, to meet him in a duel.—*To have it out of a person*, to punish him; to retaliate on him; to take him to task. [*Have* is used as an auxiliary verb to form certain compound tenses, as the perfect and pluperfect of both transitive and intransitive verbs.]

haven, hā´vn, *n.* [A.Sax. *hæfen*=D. and L.G. *haven*, Icel. *hōfn*, Dan. *havn*, G. *hafen*; connected with *have*.] A harbor; a port; a bay, recess, or inlet which affords anchorage and a station for ships; a shelter, asylum, or place of safety.—*v.i.* To shelter, as in a haven.

haversack, hav´ėr•sak, *n.* [Fr. *havresac*, from D. *haverzak*, G. *hafersack*, a haversack, literally a sack for oats, from D. *haver*, G. *hafer*, Dan. *havre*, oats.] A bag of strong cloth worn over the shoulder by soldiers in marching order for carrying their provisions.

havoc, hav´ok, *n.* [From O.Fr. *havot*, pillage, plunder.] Devastation; wide and general destruction.—*v.t.* To destroy; to lay waste (*Mil.*).

haw, hạ, *n.* [A.Sax. *haga*, an enclosure, a yard=Icel. *hagi*, Sw. *hage*, an enclosure, akin *hedge*, *haggard*.] A hedge; an enclosure; the hawthorn and its berry or seed.

haw, hạ, *n.* [Origin unknown.] The nictitating membrane in the eye of a dog, horse, etc.

haw, hạ, *v.i.* [Imitative.] To equivocate (to hem and *haw*).

hawk, hạk, *n.* [A.Sax. *hafoc*=D. *havik*, G. *habicht*, Icel. *haukr*, a hawk.] A rapacious bird of the falcon family; a falcon.—*v.t.* and *i.* To hunt by means of trained hawks or falcons; to practice falconry; to fly in the manner of the hawk.—**hawker,** hạ´kėr, *n.* One who hawks; a falconer.—**hawk moth,** *n.* A moth, so called from its hovering motion.—**hawksbill,** *n.* A turtle with a mouth like the beak of a hawk.

hawk, hạk, *v.i.* [Probably imitative, Comp. D. *harke*, and W. *hochi*, to hawk.] To make an effort to force up phlegm with noise.—*v.t.* To raise by hawking.—*n.* An effort to force up phlegm by coughing.

hawk, hạk, *v.t.* [From D. *heukeren*, to retail, to huckster, *heuker*, a retailer; akin to G. *hōken*, *höcken*, to retail, *höker*, *hōcker*, a hawker, from *hocken*, *hucken*, to take upon the back, to squat. Akin *huckster*.] To sell, or try to sell, by offering the goods at people's doors; to convey through town or country for sale.—**hawker,** hạ´kėr, *n.* [D. *heuker*, a retailer.] One who travels selling wares; a peddler; a packman.

hawse, hạs, *n.* [O. and Prov. E. *halse*, the neck.] *Naut.* that part of a vessel's bow where the hawseholes are cut; the hole in the vessel's bow; the distance between a ship's head and her anchors.—**hawsehole,** *n.* A hole in a vessel's bow through which a cable passes.

hawser, hạ´sėr, *n.* [M.E. *haucer*, from O.Fr. *haucier*, raise, from L. *altus*, high.] A large rope used in making a ship secure.

hawthorn, hạ´thorn, *n.* [A.Sax. *hagathorn*, *hæg-thorn*, haw-thorn, lit. hedgethorn; like G. *hagedorn*, D. *haagedoorn*. HAW, HEDGE.] A kind of small tree, one species of which is an excellent hedge plant, while some of its varieties are very beautiful when in full blossom.

hay, hā, *n.* [A.Sax. *hig*=O.Fris. *hai*, Dan. *hō*, Icel. *hey*, Goth. *havi*, G. *heu*, hay; connected with verb to *hew*. HEW.] Grass cut and dried for fodder; a small sum of money; a reward.—**haycock,** *n.* A conical pile or heap of hay.—**hay fever,** *n.* A summer ailment caused by allergy to pollen and marked by sneezing and other symptoms of a cold.—**hayfork,** *n.* A two-pronged fork for turning or lifting hay, etc.—**haystack,** *n.* A large pile of hay in the open air, laid up for preservation.—**haywire,** *a.* Tangled; confused.

hazard, haz´ėrd, *n.* [Fr. *hasard*, from Sp. *azar*, an unlucky throw of the dice, from Ar. *az-zahr*, a die.] A fortuitous event; chance; danger; peril; risk; a game played with dice.—*v.t.* To expose to chance; to put in danger of loss or injury; to risk.—**hazardous,** haz´ėr•dus, *a.* Exposing to peril or danger of loss or evil; dangerous; risky.—**hazardously,** haz´ėr•dus•li, *adv.* In a hazardous manner.—**hazardousness,** haz´ėr•dus•nes.

haze, hāz, *n.* [Allied to A.Sax. *haso*, dusky, dark; Icel. *hōss*, gray, dusky.] Fog; a grayish or dusky vapor in the air, hence, obscurity; dimness; mental fog.—**haze,** hāz, *v.t.* To make hazy.—*v.i.* To be hazy.—**hazy,** hā´zi, *a.* Foggy; misty; thick with haze; mentally obscure.

haze, hāz, *v.t.* [M.Fr. *haser*, to irritate, to vex.] To harass or annoy by practical jokes.

hazel, hā´zl, *n.* [A.Sax. *hæsel*, *hæsl*=Icel. *hasl*, Dan. *hassel*, G. *hasel*, hazel; cog. with L. *corylus*, for *cosylus*, a hazel.] A tree growing wild and yielding edible nuts, while the wood is employed for hoops, fishing rods, walking sticks, etc.—*a.* Of a light-brown color like the hazelnut.—**hazelly,** hā´zl•li, *a.*—**hazelnut,** *n.* The nut of the hazel.

H-bomb. See HYDROGEN BOMB.

he, hē, *pron.* possessive *his*, objective *him* (also dative). [A.Sax. *hé*, *heó*, *hit*, he, she, it; D. *hij*, Dan. and Sw. *han*, Icel. *haan*, he; akin *hence*, *her*, *here*, *hither*. *She* is of different origin.] The masc. sing. form of the pronoun of the 3rd person. It is sometimes used as a noun, being equivalent to man or male person, and is often prefixed to the names of animals to designate the male kind (a *he-goat*).—*n.* Male person or animal.

head, hed, *n.* [A.Sax. *heafod*=Dan. *hoved*, Icel. *hōfuth*, G. *haupt*, Goth. *houbith*, head; cog. L. *caput* (whence *chief*), Gr. *kephalē*, head.] The name applied generally to the anterior part or extremity of animals; the part which forms the seat of the brain and mental faculties; hence, understanding, intellect, will or resolution, mind, an individual; a unit (a thousand *head* of sheep: used only in *sing.*); a chief; a leader; a commander; what gives a striking appearance to the head, as the hair, antlers of a deer, etc.; part of a thing resembling in position or otherwise the human head (the *head* of a spear, of a nail); the main point or part; the forepart (the *head* of a ship); the upper part (of a bed, etc.); the top; the principal source of a stream; the part most remote from the mouth or opening; a headland; promontory; the foremost place; crisis; height; pitch; division of discourse; title of a subdivision.—*Hydraulics*, the height of water or other fluid above a given level, regarded as producing pressure.—*Head and ears*, deeply; wholly; completely.—*Head and shoulders*, by force; violently (to drag in a topic *head and shoulders*); by as much as the height of the head and shoulders.—*A broken head*, a flesh wound in the head.—*To make head against*, to resist with success.—*To give*, *to get*, etc., *the head*, used literally of a horse that is not held in by the reins, and hence figuratively *head* means license, freedom from check, control, or restraint.—*v.t.* To be or put one's self at the head of; to lead; to direct; to behead; to decapitate; to form a head to; to fit or furnish with a head; to go in front of, so as to keep from advancing (to *head* a drove of cattle).—*a.* Belonging to the head; chief; principal: often used in composition (*head* workman, a *head* master, etc.).—**headache,** hed´āk, *n.* Pain in the head.—**headband,** hed´band, *n.* A band for the head; the band at each end of a bound book.—**headcheese,** hed´chēz, *n.* A jellied mass or loaf consisting of parts of the head and feet of hogs, cut up, seasoned, cooked and cooled.—**headdress,** *n.* The dress of the head; the covering or ornaments of a woman's head.—**headed,** hed´ed, *p.* and *a.* Furnished with a head; used chiefly in composition (clear*headed*, long*headed*, etc.).—**header,** hed´ėr, *n.* One who puts a head on anything; one who stands at the head of anything; a leader; a plunge or dive into water headforemost.—**headforemost,** *adv.* With the head first; rashly; precipitately.—**headily,** hed´i•li, *adv.* In a heady manner.—**headiness,** hed´i•nes, *n.* The quality of being heady.—**heading,** hed'ing, *n.* The act of one who heads; what stands at the head; a title of a section in a book; a compass direction used by ships or airplanes in aiming at a destination.—**headland,** hed'land, *n.* A cape; a promontory.—**headless,** hed'les, *a.* Having no head; destitute of a chief or leader.—**headline,** hed'-line, *n.* Title above a news story, summarizing its contents; *print.* the line at the top of the page that gives title, page number, etc.—*v.t.* To provide a headline for a news story.—**headlong,** hed'long, *adv.* With the head foremost; rashly; precipitately; without deliberation. —*a.* Precipitous; rash.—**headmaster,** *n.* The principal master of a school. —**headmost,** hed'most, *a.* Most advanced; first.—**headpiece,** *n.* A helmet; a morion; the head, especially the head as the seat of the understanding.—**headquarters,** *n. pl.* The quarters of the commander of an army; a center of authority or order; the place where one chiefly resides.—**headship,** hed'ship, *n.* The state or position of being a head or chief; authority; supreme power; government.—**headsman,** hedz'man, *n.* One that cuts off heads; an executioner.—**headstall,** *n.* That part of a bridle which encompasses the head.—**headstone,** *n.* The chief or corner stone; the keystone of an arch; the stone at the head of a grave.—**headstrong,** hed'-strong, *a.* Obstinate; ungovernable; bent on pursuing one's own course. —**headwater,** *n.* The part of a river near its source, or one of the streams that contribute to form it.—**headway,** hed'wā, *n.* The progress made by a ship in motion; hence, progress or success of any kind.—**headwind,** *n.* A wind directly opposed to a ship's course.—**headwork,** *n.* Mental or intellectual labor.—**heady,** hed'i, *a.* Rash; hasty; precipitate; headstrong; apt to affect the mental faculties; intoxicating; strong.

heal, hēl, *v.t.* [A.Sax. *haelan*, to heal, from *hál*, whole, sound (=E. *whole*); comp. the related words *hale, hail, whole, holy, health.*] To make hale, sound, or whole; to cure of a disease or wound and restore to soundness; to reconcile, as a breach or difference.—*v.i.* To grow sound; to return to a sound state; sometimes with *up* or *over.*—**healer,** he'lėr, *n.* One who or that which heals.—**healingly,** hē'ling•li, *adv.* In a healing manner.

health, helth, *n.* [A.Sax. *haelth*, from *haelan*, to heal.] That state of a being in which all the parts and organs are sound and in proper condition; moral or intellectual soundness; salvation or divine favor or grace (O.T.). [It is often used in toasts, and hence sometimes means toast.]—**healthful,** helth'fụl, *a.* Full of health; free from disease; promoting health; wholesome.—**healthfully,** helth'fụl•li, *adv.* In a healthful manner.—**healthfulness,** helth'fụl•nes, *n.* The state of being healthful or healthy.—**healthily,** hel'thi•li, *adv.* In a healthy manner or condition.—**healthy,** hel'thi, *a.* Being in health; enjoying health; hale; sound; conducive to health; wholesome; salubrious.—**healthiness,** hel'thi•nes, *n.* State of being healthy.

heap, hēp, *n.* [A.Sax. *heáp*, a pile, a crowd=D. *hoop*, Dan. *hob*, Icel. *hópr*, G. *haufe*. Akin *hip.*] A pile or mass; a collection of things piled up; a large quantity; a great number. —*v.t.* To lay in a heap; to pile; to amass; often with *up* or with *on*; to round or form into a heap.

hear, hēr *v.t.*—pret. & pp. *heard.* [A.Sax. *hýran, héran*, to hear= O.Fris. *hera, hora*, Icel. *heyra*, D. *hooren*, G. *hören*, Goth. *hausjan*; hence *hearken, hark.*] To perceive by the auditory sense; to take cognizance of by the ear; to give audience or allowance to speak; to listen to; to heed; to obey; to try judicially (a cause) in a court of justice; to listen to one repeating or going over, as a task or the like.—*v.i.* To enjoy the sense or faculty of perceiving sound; to listen; to hearken; to attend, to be told; to receive by report.—**hearer,** hē'rėr, *n.* One who hears; an auditor; one who sits under the ministry of another.—**hearing,** hē'ring, *n.* The act of perceiving sound; the faculty or sense by which sound is perceived; audience; an opportunity to be heard; a judicial investigation before a court; reach of the ear; extent within which sound may be heard.—**hearsay,** hēr'sā, *n.* Report; rumor; common talk.—*Hearsay evidence*, evidence repeated at second hand by one who heard the actual witness relate or admit what he knew of the transaction or fact in question.

hearken, här'kn, *v.i.* [A.Sax. *heorcnian, hýrcnian*, from *hyran*, to hear. HEAR.] To listen; to lend the ear; to give heed to what is uttered; to hear with obedience or compliance. —*v.t.* To hear by listening; to hear with attention; to regard.

hearse, hėrs, *n.* [O.Fr. *herce*, a harrow, a kind or portcullis, a *herse*, from L. *hirpex, hirpicis*, a harrow; hence *rehearse* (which see).] A bier; a bier with a coffin; a carriage for conveying the dead to the grave.—*v.t.* To put on or in a hearse.

heart, härt, *n.* [A.Sax. *heorte*=Goth. *hairto*, D. *hart*, Icel. *hjarta*, Dan. *hjerte*, G. *herz*; cog. Gael. *cridhe*, L. *cor, cordis*, Gr. *kardia*, Skr. *hrid*, heart; from a root meaning to leap.] A muscular organ, which is the propelling agent of the blood in the animal body, situated in the thorax of vertebrated animals; the mind, the soul, the consciousness; the thinking faculty; the seat of the affections and passions; the moral side of our nature in contradistinction to the intellectual; courage; spirit; the seat of the will or inclination; hence, disposition of mind; tendency; conscience, or sense of good and ill; the inner part of anything; the part nearest the middle or center; the vital or most essential part; the core; the very essence; that which has the shape or form of a heart or is regarded as representing the figure of a heart; one of a suit of playing cards marked with such a figure.—*At heart*, in real character or disposition; at bottom; substantially; really (he is good *at heart*).—*To break the heart of*, to cause the deepest grief to; to kill by grief.—*To find in the heart*, to be willing or disposed.—*To get* or *learn by heart*, to commit to memory.—*To have in the heart*, to purpose; to have design or intention. —*To have the heart in the mouth*, to be terrified.—*To lay* or *take to heart*, to be much affected by; to be zealous, ardent, or solicitous about.—*To wear the heart upon the sleeve*, to expose one's feelings, wishes, or intentions to every one.—*v.i.* To form a close compact head, as a plant.—**heartache,** härt'āk, *n.* Anguish of mind.—**heartbreak,** *n.* Overwhelming sorrow or grief.—**heartbroken,** *a.* Deeply grieved; in despair.—**heartburn,** *n.* An uneasy burning sensation in the stomach from indigestion and excess of acidity.—**heartburning,** *a.* Causing discontent.—*n.* Discontent; secret enmity.—**hearted,** här'ted, *a.* Having a heart; frequently used in composition (hard-*hearted*, faint-*hearted*, etc.) —**hearten,** här'tn, *v.t.* To encourage; to incite or stimulate the courage of. —**heartfelt,** *a.* Deeply felt; deeply affecting.—**heartily,** här'ti•li, *adv.* In a hearty manner.—**heartiness,** här'ti•nes, *n.* The state of being hearty.—**heartless,** härt'les, *a.* Without a heart; destitute of feeling or affection; cruel.—**heartlessly,** härt'-les•li, *adv.* In a heartless manner.—**heartlessness,** härt'les•nes. *n.* The quality of being heartless.—**heart-rending,** *a.* Breaking the heart; overpowering with anguish; very distressing.—**heartsease,** *n.* Ease of heart; a plant of the violet genus; the pansy.—**heartsick,** *a.* Sick at heart; pained in mind; deeply depressed.—**heartsome,** härt'sum, *a.* Inspiring with heart or courage; exhilarating; cheerful; lively.—**heartsore,** *a.* Sore at heart.—**heartstring,** *n.* A hypothetical nerve or tendon, supposed to brace and sustain the heart.—**heart-whole,** *a.* Not affected with love; having unbroken spirits or good courage.—**heartwood,** *n.* The central part of the wood of exogens; the duramen.—**hearty,** här'-ti, *a.* Having the heart engaged in anything; proceeding from the heart; sincere; warm; zealous; cordial; sound and healthy; large to satisfaction (a *hearty* meal); loud and unrestrained (a *hearty* laugh).

hearth, härth, *n.* [A.Sax. *heorth*, hearth=D. *haard*, G. *heerd, herd*, area, floor, hearth; root doubtful.] That portion of the floor of a room on which the fire stands, generally a pavement or floor of brick or stone below a chimney; the fireside; the domestic circle.—**hearthstone,** *n.* The stone forming the hearth.

heat, hēt, *n.* [A.Sax. *haetu, haete*, from *hát*, hot; root in Gr. *kaiō*, to burn (whence *caustic*).] A form of energy consisting of waves measuring 1 inch to 81/1,000,000 of an inch; the sensation produced by bodies that are hot; the bodily feeling when one is exposed to fire, the sun's rays, etc.; the reverse of cold; high temperature, as distinguished from low; hot weather; a hot period; a single effort, as in a race; utmost ardor or violence; rage; vehemence; agitation of mind; inflammation or excitement; exasperation; animation in thought or discourse; fervency; sexual excitement in animals; fermentation.—*v.t.* To make hot; to communicate heat to; to cause to grow warm; to make feverish; to excite; to warm with passion or desire; to animate.—*v.i.* To grow warm or hot.—**heater,** hē'tėr, *n.* One who or that which heats.

heath, hēth, *n.* [A.Sax. *haeth*=L.G., D., Fris., and G. *heide*, the plant, also a moor; Goth. *haithi*, a field; Icel. *heithi*, *heithr*, a waste, a fell. Hence *heathen*, *heather*.] A name of numerous shrubby plants, many of them having beautiful flowers, and three species being common in Britain; a place overgrown with heath; a waste tract of land.—**heathberry,** *n.* The crowberry.—**heath cock,** *n.* The blackcock (under BLACK).—**heathy,** hē'thi, *a.* Of, pertaining to, or resembling heath; covered or abounding with heath.

heathen, hē'THen, *n.* [A.Sax. *haethen*, lit. one inhabiting a heath, from *haeth*, a heath, so that it is similar in meaning to the L. *paganus*, a pagan, originally a countryman.] One who worships idols or does not acknowledge the true God; a pagan; an idolater; a rude, barbarous, or irreligious person.—*a.* Gentile; pagan.—**heathendom,** hē'THen•dum, *n.* Those parts of the world in which heathenism prevails.—**heathenish,** hē'THen•ish, *a.* Belonging to heathens or their religions; barbarous; uncivilized; irreligious.—**heathenishness,** hē'THen•ish•nes, *n.* —**heathenism,** hē'THen•izm, *n.* The system of religion or the manners and morals of a heathen nation; paganism; barbarism.—**heathenize,** hē'THen•īz, *v.t.* To render heathenish —**heathenry,** hē'THen•ri, *n.* Heathenism; heathens collectively.

heather, heTH'ėr, *n.* [Formerly *hadder*; comp. G. *heiter*, gay.] Common heath, a low shrub with clusters of rose-colored flowers, covering immense tracts of waste land in Britain. —**heathery,** heTH'ėr•i, *a.* Abounding in heather; heathy.

heave, hēv, *v.t.*—*heaved* or *hove* (pret. and pp.), *heaving*. [A.Sax. *hebban*, pret. *hof*, pp. *hafen*=Goth. *hafjan*, O.Fris. *heva*, D. *heffen*, *heven*, Dan. *hæve*, Icel. *hefja*, G. *heben*, to lift; akin *heavy*, *heaven*.] To lift; to raise; to elevate; to raise or force from the breast (to *heave* a sigh); to throw; to cast; *naut.* to apply power to, as by means of a windlass, in order to pull or force in any direction.—*To heave to*, to bring a ship's head to the wind and stop her motion.—*v.i.* To be thrown or raised up; to rise; to rise and fall with alternate motions; to swell up; to pant, as after severe labor or exertion; to make an effort to vomit; to retch.—*To heave in sight*, to appear; to make its first appearance, as a ship at sea. *n.* An upward motion; swell, as of the waves of the sea; an effort of the lungs, etc.; an effort to raise something; *pl.* a disease of horses, characterized by difficult and laborious respiration.—**heaver,** hē'vėr, *n.* One who or that which heaves.

heaven, hev'n, *n.* [A.Sax. *heofon*, heaven; O.Sax. *hevan*, L.G. *heben*, Icel. *hifinn*; from root of *heave*.] The blue expanse which surrounds the earth, and in which the sun, moon, and stars seem to be set; the sky; the upper regions; often in the plural; the final abode of the blessed; the place where God manifests himself to the blessed; [*cap.*] often used as equivalent to God or Providence; supreme felicity; bliss; a sublime or exalted condition.—**heavenliness,** hev'n•li•nes, *n.* The condition or quality of being heavenly.—**heavenly,** hev'n•li, *a.* Pertaining to heaven; inhabiting heaven; celestial; supremely blessed; supremely excellent.—*adv.* In a heavenly manner.—**heavenward,** hev'n•wėrd, *adv.* Toward heaven.

heavy, hev'i, *a.* [A.Sax. *hefig*, heavy, from the stem of *hebban*, to heave= Icel. *hōfigr*. HEAVE.] That can be lifted only with labor; ponderous; weighty: the opposite of *light*; large in amount or quantity (a *heavy* rain, a *heavy* crop); not easily borne; hard to endure; burdensome; oppressive; severe; hard to accomplish; weighed or bowed down; burdened with sorrow, sleep, weariness, or the like; slow; sluggish; inactive; dull; lifeless; inanimate; impeding motion or action (*heavy* roads); acting or moving with violence (a *heavy* sea; cannonade; dark; gloomy; threatening; lowering (a *heavy* sky); not easily digested (food); deep and voluminous (sound).—**heavily,** hev'i•li, *adv.* In a heavy manner.—**heaviness,** hev'i•nes, *n.* The state or quality of being heavy; weight; severity; sadness; dullness or lifelessness.—**heavy spar,** *n.* The sulfate of barium, occurring in veins massive, fibrous, lamellar, and in prismatic crystals.—**heavyweight,** *n.* A boxer or wrestler, etc., of what is usually the heaviest class; one weighing not less than 175 pounds.

hebdomadal, heb•dom'a•dal, *a.* [Gr. *hebdomas*, the number seven, seven days, from *hepta*, seven.] Weekly; consisting of seven days, or occurring every seven days.

Hebe, hē'bē, *n.* The goddess of youth among the Greeks; hence, a beautiful young woman.

hebetate, heb'ē•tāt, *v.t.*—*hebetated*, *hebetating*. [L. *hebeto*, *hebetatum*, from *hebes*, dull.] To dull; to blunt; to stupefy.—**hebetude,** heb'ē•tūd, *n.* [L. *hebetudo*.] Dullness; stupidity.

Hebrew, hē'brö, *n.* [Fr. *hébreu*, L. *hebræus*, Gr. *hebraios*, from Heb.: supposed to mean a person *from beyond* (the Euphrates).] One of the descendants of Jacob; an Israelite; a Jew; the language of the Jews, one of the Semitic tongues.—*a.* Pertaining to the Hebrews.—**Hebraic** hē'-brā'ik, *a.* Pertaining to the Hebrews or their language.—**Hebraism,** hē'-brā•izm, *n.* A peculiarity of Hebrew or the Hebrews.—**Hebraist,** hē'brā•-ist, *n.* One versed in the Hebrew language.—**Hebraize,** hē'brā•iz, *v.t.* —*hebraized*, *hebraizing*. To convert into the Hebrew idiom; to make Hebrew.—*v.i.* To conform to the Hebrew idiom, manners, etc.

hecatomb, hek'a•tom, *n.* [Gr. *hekatombē*—*hekaton*, a hundred, and *bous*, an ox.] A sacrifice of a hundred oxen or other beasts; hence, any great sacrifice of victims; a great number of persons or animals slaughtered.

heckle, hek'l, *n.* [Same as *hackle*.] A sort of comb for flax or hemp; a hackle or hatchel.—*v.t.* To dress with a heckle; *fig.* to tease or vex; to catechise severely.—**heckler,** hek'lėr, *n.* One who heckles.

hectare, hek'tār, *n.* [Fr.] A French measure containing 100 ares, or= 2.47 acres.

hectic, hek'tik, *a.* [Gr. *hektikos*, habitual, hectic or consumptive, from *hexis*, habit of body, from *echō*, future *hexō*, to have.] Relating to or affected with a fluctuating, but persistent, fever; characterized by excitement or feverish activity; restless. —*n.* A hectic fever.—**hectically,** hek'ti•kal•li, *adv.* In a hectic manner.

hectocotylus, hek•to•kot'i•lus, *n.* [Gr. *hekaton*, a hundred, and *kotylē*, a small cup, a sucker.] The reproductive arm of certain of the male cuttlefishes.

hectogram, hek'to•gram, *n.* [Fr., from Gr. *hekaton*, a hundred, and *gramma*, a gram.] A metric measure of weight containing 100 grams, or 3.527 ounces avoirdupois.—**hectoliter,** hek'to•lē•tėr, *n.* A metric measure for liquids, containing 100 liters, or 26.418 gallons.—**hectometer,** hec'to•mē•tėr, *n.* A metric measure of length containing 100 meters, or 109.36 yards.

hector, hek'tėr, *n.* [From *Hector*, the son of Priam, a brave Trojan warrior.] A bully; a blustering, turbulent, noisy fellow.—*v.t.* To treat with insolence; to bully.—*v.i.* To play the bully; to bluster; to be turbulent or insolent.

heddle, hed'l, *n.* [By metathesis for *heald*; perhaps from A.Sax. *heald*, hold.] *Weav.* one of the parallel double threads with a center loop or eye which raises the warp threads to form the shed and allow the shuttle to pass; a heald.

hedge, hej, *n.* [A.Sax. *hecg*, a hedge, closely akin to *haga*, an enclosure; Icel. *hagi*, an enclosed field; D. *hegge*, a hedge, *haag*, a hedge (whence the *Hague*); E. *hawthorn*, that is *hedgethorn*.] A fence formed by bushes or small trees growing close together; any line of shrubbery closely planted.

—*v.t. hedged, hedging.* To enclose or fence with a hedge; to obstruct with a barrier; to stop by any means; to surround for defense; to hem in.—*To hedge a bet,* to bet upon both sides, thus guarding one's self against great loss, whatever may be the result.—*v.i.* To hide in a hedge; to skulk (*Shak.*); to protect one's self from loss by cross bets.—**hedgehog,** hej'hog, *n.* An Old World insectivorous quadruped about 9 inches long, the upper part of whose body is covered with prickles or spines; in America, the porcupine; *elec.* a kind of transformer; *milit.* a kind of barbed wire entanglement.—**hedgehop,** hej'hop, *v.t.* & *i.* To fly an airplane at a very low altitude, just skimming the ground. (*Slang.*)—**hedge hyssop,** any of a number of herbs, as the goldenpert.—**hedger,** hej'ėr, *n.* One who makes or repairs hedges; one who hedges bets; one who evades.—**hedgerow,** hej'rō, *n.* A row or series of shrubs or trees forming a hedge between fields.—**hedge sparrow,** a red-brown European warbler.

hedonic, hē•don'ik, *a.* [Gr. *hēdonikos,* from *hēdonē,* pleasure.] Pertaining to pleasure; pursuing, or placing the chief good in, sensual pleasure.—**hedonics,** hē•don'iks, *n.* That branch of ethics which treats of active or positive pleasure or enjoyment.—**hedonism,** hē'don•izm, *n.* The doctrine that the chief good of man lies in the pursuit of pleasure.—**hedonist,** hē'don•ist, *n.* One who professes hedonism.

heed, hēd, *v.t.* [A.Sax. *hédan,* to heed; D. *hoeden,* to care for, *hoede,* care; G. *hüten,* to look after, from *hut,* protection; akin *hood.*] To regard with care; to take notice of; to attend to; to observe.—*n.* Care; attention; notice; observation; regard; usually with *give* or *take.*—**heedful,** hēd'fu̧l, *a.* Full of heed; attentive; watchful; cautious; wary.—**heedfully,** hēd'fu̧l•li, *adv.* In a heedful manner.—**heedfulness,** hēd'fu̧l•nes, *n.* The quality of being heedful; attention; caution.—**heedless,** hēd'les, *a.* Without heed; inattentive; careless.—**heedlessly,** hēd'les•li, *adv.* In a heedless manner.—**heedlessness,** hēd'les•nes, *n.*

heel, hēl, *n.* [A.Sax. *hél*=Icel. *haell,* D. *hiel,* the heel; radically akin to L. *calx,* the heel (seen in *inculcate*).] The hinder part of the foot in man or quadrupeds; the hinder part of a covering for the foot; something shaped like the human heel, or that occupies a position corresponding to the heel; the latter or concluding part.—*To be at the heels,* to pursue closely; to follow hard; also, to attend closely.—*To be down at heel,* to be slipshod; hence, to be in decayed circumstances.—*To lay by the heels,* to fetter; to shackle; to confine.—*To show the heels,* to flee; to run away.—*To take to the heels,* to betake one's self to flight.—*v.t.* To perform by the use of the heels, as a dance (*Shak.*); to add a heel to.—**heelpiece,** *n.* A piece of leather on the heel of a shoe; armor for the heel.—**heeltap,** *n.* A small piece of leather for the heel of a shoe; the small portion of liquor left in a glass when the main portion has been drunk.

heel, hēl, *v.i.* [Same as A.Sax. *heldan,* D. *hellen,* Dan. *helde,* Sw. *hälla,* to tilt.] To incline or cant over from a vertical position, as a ship.—*n.* The act of so inclining; a cant.

heft, heft, *n.* [From *heave,* to lift.] The act of heaving; violent strain or exertion; effort (*Shak.*).—**heft, hefty,** *a.* Vigorous, strong. (*Colloq.*)

Hegelian, he•gē'li•an, *a.* Pertaining to Hegel (hā'gl) or his system of philosophy.—*n.* A follower of Hegel.—**Hegelianism,** he•gē'li•an•izm, *n.* The system of philosophy of Hegel.

hegemony, hej'e•mo•ni or he•jem'o•ni, *n.* [Gr. *hēgemonia,* from *hegemōn,* guide, leader, from *hēgeomai,* to lead.] Leadership; predominance; preponderance of one state among others.—**hegemonic,** hej•e•mon'ik, *a.* Ruling; predominant; principal.

hegira, hej'i•ra, *n.* [Ar. *hijrah,* departure, from *hajara,* to remove.] [*Often cap.*] The flight of Mohammed from Mecca, adopted by the Mohammedans in reckoning their time, their era beginning July 16, 622, hence, [*not cap.*] any similar flight.

heifer, hef'ėr, *n.* [A.Sax. *heahfore;* origin doubtful.] A young cow.

heigh-ho! hī'hō. An exclamation usually expressing some degree of languor or uneasiness.

height, hīt, *n.* [For *highth,* as in *Milton;* A.Sax. *heáhtho, hyhtho,* from *heáh,* high. HIGH.] The condition of being high; the distance which anything rises above its foot, basis, or foundation, or above the earth; altitude; an eminence; a summit; a hill or mountain; elevation or preeminence among other persons; elevation in excellence of any kind; elevation or dignity, as of sentiment, expression, or the like; extent; degree; stage in progress or advancement: *the height,* the utmost degree in extent or violence.—**heighten,** hī'tn, *v.t.* To make high; to raise higher; to elevate; to increase; to augment; to intensify.—**heightener,** hī'tn•ėr, *n.* One who or that which heightens.

heinous, hā'nus, *a.* [Fr. *haineux,* from *haine,* malice, hate, from *haïr,* O.Fr. *hadir,* to hate, from Teut. verb=E. to hate.] Hateful; odious; hence, notorious; enormous; aggravated (sin or crime, sinner).—**heinously,** hā'nus•li, *adv.* In a heinous manner.—**heinousness,** hā'nus•nes, *n.* The condition or quality of being heinous.

heir, âr, *n.* [O.Fr. *heir,* L. *hæres,* an heir; whence *hereditary, heritage, inherit.*] One who succeeds or is to succeed another in the possession of property; an inheritor; one who receives any endowment from an ancestor.—*Heir apparent,* one whose right to inherit is unforfeitable, if he survives the ancestor.—*Heir presumptive,* one who will be the heir if the ancestor should die, but whose rights may be cut off by the birth of a nearer relative or some other contingency.—**heiress,** âr'es, *n.* A female heir.—**heirloom,** âr'löm, *n.* [*Heir* and *loom* in old sense of tool, implement, article.] A personal chattel that descends to an heir; any piece of personal property which has belonged to a family for a long time.—**heirship,** âr'ship, *n.* The state of an heir; right of inheriting.

hejira, hej'i•ra, *n.* Same as *Hegira.*

held, held, pret. & pp. of *hold.*

heliac, heliacal, hē'li•ak, hē•lī'a•kal, *a.* [L. *heliacus,* from Gr. *hēlios,* the sun; akin L. *sol,* and W. *haul,* sun.] *Astron.* emerging from the light of the sun or passing into it; rising or setting at the same time, or nearly the same time, as the sun.—**heliacally,** hē•lī'a•kal•li, *adv.* In a heliacal manner.

helianthus, hē•li•an'thus, *n.* [Gr. *hēlios,* the sun, and *anthos,* a flower.] The sunflower; the Jerusalem artichoke genus.

helical, helicoid, helicoidal, etc. See HELIX.

Heliconian, hel•i•kō'ni•an, *a.* Pertaining to *Helicon,* the famous Grecian mountain, the residence of the muses.

helicopter, hel'i•kop•ter, *n.* [From Fr. hélicoptère, from Gr. *helix, -ikos,* spiral, plus *pteron,* wing.] A heavier-than-air craft, sustained in the air solely by propellers revolving around a vertical axis.—**heliport,** hel'i•port, *n.* A take-off and landing place for helicopters.

heliocentric, heliocentrical, hē'li•o•sen"trik, hē'li•o•sen"tri•kal, *a.* [Gr. *hēlios* (akin L. *sol,* W. *haul*), the sun, and *kentron,* center.] *Astron.* relating to the sun as a center; appearing as if seen from the sun's center.—**heliochrome,** hē'li•o•krōm, *n.* [Gr. *chrōma,* color.] A colored photograph.—**heliochromic,** hē'li•o•krōm"ik, *a.* Pertaining to heliochromy.—**heliograph,** hē'li•o•graf, *n.* [Gr. *graphō,* to write.] A photograph; an instrument for taking photographs of the sun; a sun telegraph; a heliostat.—*v.t.* and *i.* To convey or communicate by means of a heliostat or similar instrument.—**heliographic,** hē'li•o•graf"ik, *a.* Of or pertaining to heliography.—**heliography,** hē•li•og'ra•fi, *n.* Photography; also, the art or process of signaling by reflecting the sun's rays.—**heliogravure,** hē•li•o•grāv"ūr, *n.* [Gr. *helios,* sun, Fr. *gravure,* engraving.] A process by which a photographic print is mechanically etched on a copper plate, from which impressions are then taken.—**heliolater,** hē•li•ol'a•tėr, *n.* [Gr. *latrueō,* to worship.] A worshiper of the sun.—**heliolatry,** hē•li•ol'a•tri, *n.* The worship of the sun.

heliometer, hel•i•om'eter, *n.* [F. *heliometre.*] A double image micrometer used for measuring any short arc of the celestial sphere, but originally invented to measure the sun's diameter.

heliostat, hē'li•o•stat, *n.* [Gr. *statos,* fixed.] A name of various contrivances for reflecting the sun's light temporarily or continuously to an observer at a distance.

heliotrope, hē'li•o•trōp, *n.* [Gr. *tropē,*

a turning, *trepō*, to turn.] A heliostat; a variety of quartz, of a deep green color, with bright red spots; bloodstone; a name of plants, mostly natives of warm regions, one species of which is a favorite garden plant from the fragrance of its flowers.—**heliotropic,** hē'li•o•trop"-ik, *a.*—**heliotropism,** hē•li•ot'ro•-pizm, *n.* The tendency of a plant to direct its growth toward the sun or toward light; a phototropism.—**helium,** hē'li•um, *n.* A nonflammable gaseous element, inert and colorless, the lightest gas next to hydrogen. Symbol, He; at. no., 2; at. wt., 4.0026.

helix, hē'liks, *n.* pl. **helices,** hel'i•sēz. [Gr. a winding, a spiral.] A spiral line, as of wire in a coil; something that is spiral; a circumvolution; *geom.* such a curve as is described by every point of a screw that is turned round in a fixed nut; *arch.* a small volute or twist under the abacus of the Corinthian capital; *anat.* the whole circuit of the external body of the ear; *zool.* a genus of mollusks, comprising the land shell snails.—**helical,** hel'i•kal, *a.* Of or pertaining to a helix; spiral.—**helically,** hel'i•kal•li, *adv.* In a helical manner.—**helicoid, helicoidal,** hel'-i•koid, hel'i•koi•dal, *a.* Spirally curved like the spire of a univalve shell.—**helicoid,** hel'i•koid, *n.* *Geom.* a spirally curved surface.

hell, hel, *n.* [A.Sax. *hel,* from *helan,* to cover, conceal, lit. a place of concealment=D. and Icel. *hel,* G. *hölle,* hell; same root as L. *celo,* to conceal. Akin *helmet,* perhaps *hole.*] The place of the dead, or of souls after death; the place or state of punishment for the wicked after death; the infernal powers; the domain of the devil; verbal castigation; unrestrained sportiveness (they raised *hell*); haunt of the vicious or depraved.—**hellish,** hel'ish, *a.* Pertaining to hell; infernal; malignant; wicked; detestable.—**hellishly,** hel'-ish•li, *adv.* In a hellish manner.—**hellishness,** hel'ish•nes, *n.* The state or quality of being hellish.—**hell-fire,** *n.* The fire of hell; the torments of hell.—**hellhound,** *n.* A dog of hell; an agent of hell; a miscreant.

hellebore, hel'le•bōr, *n.* [L. *helleborus,* Gr. *helleboros.*] A name applied to plants of two very different genera, the black hellebore or Christmas rose, and the white hellebore; the powdered root of white hellebore used by gardeners for killing caterpillars.—**helleborin,** hel'le•bō•rin, *n.* A resin obtained from the root of black hellebore.

Hellenes, hel•lē'nez, *n. pl.* [Gr.] The inhabitants of Greece; the Greeks.—**Hellenic,** hel'len'ik, *a.* [Gr. *hellēnikos.*] Pertaining to the Hellenes; Greek; Grecian.—**Hellenism,** hel'-len•izm, *n.* A Greek idiom; the type of character usually considered peculiar to the Greeks.—**Hellenist,** hel'len•ist, *n.* One who affiliates with Greeks; one skilled in the Greek language.—**Hellenistic, Hellenistical,** hel•len•is'tik, hel•len•is'ti•kal, *a.* Pertaining to Hellenists.—**Hellenization,** hel'len•ī•zā"shon, *n.* Act of Hellenizing.—**Hellenize,** hel'len•īz, *v.i.* To use the Greek language or adopt Greek manners.

hello, he•lo', *interj.* [Apparently, a form of *hollo,* an exclamation.] A greeting or exclamation to call attention or show surprise, etc.

helm, helm, *n.* [A.Sax. *helma,* a helm; D. *helm,* a tiller; G. *helm,* a helve, a tiller; akin to *helve.*] The instrument by which a ship is steered, consisting of a rudder, a tiller, and in large vessels a wheel; in a narrower sense, the tiller; *fig.* the place or post of direction or management. —*v.t.*† To steer; to guide.—**helmsman,** helmz'man, *n.* The man at the helm or wheel who steers a ship.

helm, helm, *n.* [A.Sax. *helm,* what covers, a helmet, from *helan,* to cover; D. and G. *helm,* Goth. *hilms,* Icel. *hjálmr,* Dan. *hjelm*; *helmet* is a dim. form. HELL.] [*obs.*] A helmet. (*Poet.*)—*v.t.* To cover with a helmet. —**helmeted,** hel'met•ed, *a.* Furnished with a helmet.—**helmet,** hel'met, *n.* A defensive covering for the head; head armor composed of metal, leather, etc.; *bot.* the upper part of a ringent corolla.

helminthagogue, hel•min'tha•gog, *n.* [Gr. *helmins, helminthos,* a worm, and *agō,* to expel.] *Med.* a remedy against worms; an anthelmintic.—**helminthiasis,** hel•min•thī'a•sis, *n.* *Med.* the disease of worms in any part of the body.—**helminthic,** hel•-min'thik, *a.* Relating to worms; expelling worms.—*n.* A medicine for expelling worms; a vermifuge.—**helminthology,** hel•min•thol'o•ji, *n.* The knowledge or natural history of worms.

Helot, he'lot, *n.* [Gr. *heilōtēs.*] A slave in ancient Sparta; [*often not cap.*] hence, a slave in general.—**helotism,** he'lot•izm, *n.* The condition of a Helot; slavery.—**helotry,** he'lot•ri, *n.* Helots collectively; bondsmen.

help, help, *v.t.* [A.Sax. *helpan*=Goth. *hilpan,* D. *helpen,* Icel. *hjálpa,* Dan. *hjelpe,* G. *helfen,* to help—from same root as Skr. *kalp,* to suit, to be of service.] To give assistance or aid to; to aid; to assist; to succor, to relieve; to cure or mitigate (pain or disease); to avail against; to prevent; to remedy; to forbear; to avoid (to *help* doing something).—*To help forward,* to advance by assistance; to assist in making progress.—*To help on,* to forward; to aid.—*To help out,* to aid in delivering from difficulty, or to aid in completing a design.—*To help over,* to enable to surmount.—*To help* (a person) *to,* to supply with; to furnish with.—*v.i.* To lend aid; to be of use; to avail.—*n.* [A.Sax. *helpe,* Icel. *hjálp.*] Aid furnished; deliverance from difficulty or distress; assistance; that which gives assistance; one who or that which contributes to advance a purpose; remedy; relief; a domestic servant (U.S.).—**helper,** hel'pėr, *n.* One that helps, aids, or assists; an assistant; an auxiliary.—**helpful,** help'fu̧l, *a.* Furnishing help; useful.—**helpfulness,** help'fu̧l•nes, *n.* The quality of being helpful.—**helpless,** help'les, *a.* Destitute of help or strength; needing help; feeble; weak; affording no help; beyond help.—**helplessly,** help'les•li, *adv.* In a helpless manner. —**helplessness,** help'les•nes, *n.* The state of being helpless.—**helpmate,** help'māt, *n.* An assistant; a helper; a partner; a consort; a wife.—**helpmeet,** help'mēt, *n.* A helpmate.

helter-skelter, hel'tėr•skel'tėr, *adv.* [A term formed to express hustle; comp. G. *holter-polter,* D. *hulter de bulter,* Sw. *huller om buller,* etc.] An expression denoting hurry and confusion.

helve, helv, *n.* [A.Sax. *helfe,* O.H.G. *halbe, helbe*; same root as *helm* (of a ship), *hilt.*] The handle of an ax or hatchet.—*v.t.*—*helved, helving.* To furnish with a helve, as an ax.

Helvetic, hel•vet'ik, *a.* [L. *Helveticus,* from *Helvetii,* the ancient inhabitants of Switzerland.] Of or pertaining to Switzerland.

hem, hem, *n.* [A.Sax. *hem,* a hem; akin to Icel. *hemja,* Dan. *hemme,* O.Fris. *hemma,* D. and G. *hemmen,* to stop, check, restrain.] The border of a garment, doubled and sewed to strengthen it; edge, border, margin. —*v.t. hemmed, hemming.* To form a hem or border on; to border; to edge.—*To hem in,* to enclose and confine; to surround closely; to environ.

hem, hem, *interj.* [Imitative and more correctly *hm.*] An exclamation consisting in a sort of half-cough, loud or subdued as the emotion may suggest; sometimes used as a noun.—*v.i.* To make the sound *hem*; hence, to hesitate or stammer in speaking.

hemachrome, hē'ma•krōm, *n.* Same as *Haemachrome,* some words of which Gr. *haima,* blood, forms the first part, being written *He* or *Hae.*—**hemastatics,** hē•ma•stat'iks, *n.* The doctrine as to the circulation of the blood.—**hemathermal,** hē•ma•thėr'-mal, *a.* Warm-blooded.—**hematoxylin,** hē•ma•tok'si•lin, *n.* [Gr. *haima, haimatos,* and *xylon,* wood.] The coloring principle of logwood.

hematite, hē'ma•tīt, *n.* [Gr. *haimatitēs,* from *haima,* blood.] A name of two ores of iron, red hematite and brown hematite.—**hematitic,** hē•-ma•tit'ik, *a.*

hematosis, hē•ma•tō'sis, *n.* [N.L. from Gr. *haimatōsis,* from *haimatoein,* to change into blood.] Arterialization of blood in the lungs; the formation of the blood.—**hematology,** hem•a•tol'o•gy, *n.* The science that deals with the blood.

hemicrania, hem•i•krā'ni•a, *n.* [Gr. *hēmi,* half, *cranion,* the skull.] A pain that affects only one side of the head.

hemicycle, hem'i•sī•kl, *n.* [Gr. *hēmi,* half, and *kyklos,* a circle.] A half circle; a semicircle; a semicircular area.

hemihedral, hem•i•hē'dral, *a.* [Gr. *hēmi,* half, and *hedra,* a face.] *Mineral,* applied to a crystal having only half the normal number of faces. —**hemihedrally,** hem•i•hē'dral•li, *adv.* In a hemihedral manner.

hemiplegia, hemiplegy, hem•i•plē′ji•a, hem′i•plej•i, *n.* [Gr. *hēmi*, half, and *plēgē*, a stroke.] Paralysis of one half of the body.—**hemiplegic,** hem•i•plej′ik, *a.* Relating to hemiplegia.

hemipter, he•mip′tėr, *n.* [Gr. *hēmi*, half, and *pteron*, a wing.] One of an order of four-winged insects, so named because many of them have the outer wings leathery at the base and transparent toward the tips, including the locusts, bugs, plant lice, etc.—**hemipterous,** he•mip′tėr•us, *a.* Pertaining to the hemipters.

hemisphere, hem′i•sfēr, *n.* [Gr. *hēmisphairion—hēmi*, half, and *sphaira*, a globe.] A half sphere; one half of a sphere or globe; half the terrestrial or the celestial globe.—*Hemispheres of the brain*, the two parts, one on each side, which constitute great part of the brain.—**hemispheric, hemispherical,** hem•i•sfer′ik, hem•i•sfer′i•kal, *a.* Pertaining to a hemisphere.—**hemispheroid,** hem•i•sfer′oid, *n.* The half of a spheroid.

hemistich, hem′i•stik, *n.* [Gr. *hēmistichion—hēmi*, half, and *stichos*, a verse.] Half a poetic verse, or a verse not completed.—**hemistichal,** he•mis′ti•kal, *a.* Pertaining to or written in hemistichs.

hemlock, hem′lok, *n.* [A.Sax. *hemleác.*] A poisonous plant of the carrot family, with small white flowers; various evergreen trees native to North America.—*Ground hemlock*, the American yew.

hemoglobin, hē′mo•glō•bin, *n.* [Gr. *haima*, blood, and L. *globus*, globe.] Protein pigment of the red corpuscles of vertebrates, which contains iron and carries oxygen from the lungs to the body tissues.

hemophilia, hē•mo•fil′i•a, *n. Med.* A constitutional tendency, usually hereditary, to excessive bleeding.—**hemophiliac,** hē•mo•fil′i•ac, *n.* One afflicted with hemophilia.

hemoptysis, hē•mop′tis•is, *n.* [Gr. *ptysis*, a spitting.] The coughing up of blood.

hemorrhage, he′mor•ij, *n.* [Gr. *haimorrhagia—haima*, blood, and *rhēgnymi*, to break, to burst.] A discharge of blood from the blood vessels.—**hemorrhagic,** hē•mo•raj′ik, *a.* Pertaining to hemorrhage.

hemorrhoids, he′mor•oidz, *n. pl.* [Gr. *haimorrhoïs, haimorrhoïdos*, a gushing of blood—*haima*, blood, and *rhoos*, a flowing, from *rheō*, to flow.] Piles.

hemostat, hē′mo•stat, *n.* [Gr. *haima*, blood, and *stat*, from Gr. *statikos*, causing to stand.] An instrument that checks the flow of blood by compressing a bleeding blood vessel.

hemp, hemp, *n.* [A.Sax. *henep, hanep*; cog. L. *cannabis*, Gr. *kannabis*, Skr. *cana*, hemp.] An annual herbaceous plant, the prepared fiber of which, also called hemp, is made into sailcloth, ropes, etc.; the hangman's rope.—**hempen,** hem′pn, *a.*

hen, hen, *n.* [A.Sax. *hen, henn*=D. *hen*, Icel. *haena*, G. *henne*, hen—the feminines corresponding to A.Sax. and Goth. *hana*, D. *haan*, G. *hahn*, Icel. *hani*, a cock, the root being same as in L. *cano*, to sing.] The female of any kind of bird; especially, the female of the domestic or barnyard fowl.—**henbane,** hen′bān, *n.* A poisonous Old World plant found in waste ground, and sometimes fatal to domestic fowls, but yielding a juice that is used as a sedative and narcotic.—**hennery,** hen′ėr•i, *n.* An enclosed place for hens.—**henpeck,** hen′pek, *v.t.* To govern or rule: said of a wife who has the upper hand of her husband.

hence, hens, *adv.* [O.E. *hennes*, a genit. form from older *henne*; A.Sax. *heonan*, hence; G. *hin*, Goth. *hina*, hence.] From this place; from this time (a week *hence*); as a consequence, inference, or deduction.—**henceforth, henceforward,** hens′forth, hens•for′wėrd, *adv.* From this time forward.

henchman, hensh′man, *n.* [M.E. *henchemanne, henxtman*, probably meaning groom, apparently from O.E. *hengest*, stallion, and E. *mann*, man.] A trusted follower; a political follower, particularly one who desires personal gain.

hendecagon, hen•dek′a•gon, *n.* [Gr. *hendeka*, eleven, and *gōnia*, an angle.] *Geom.* a plane figure of eleven sides and as many angles.

hendecasyllable, hen•dek′a•sil•la•bl, *n.* [Gr. *hendeka*, eleven, and *syllabē*, a syllable.] A metrical line of eleven syllables.—**hendecasyllabic,** hen•dek′a•sil•lab″ik, *a.*

hendiadys, hen•dī′a•dis, *n.* [Gr. *hen dia dyoin*, one by two.] A figure of speech by which two nouns are used instead of one, or one and an adjective.

henna, hen′a, *n.* [Ar. *hinnâ-a.*] A tropical plant of the Old World, the leaves of which yield a rich reddish-orange dye; the color henna, a rich, brownish red.—*v.t.* To color with henna dye or paste.

henotheism, hen′o•thē•izm, *n.* [Gr. *heis, henos*, one, and *theos*, god.] The worship of one deity as supreme among others.

henry, *n.* The practical electrical unit of self-induction and mutual induction.

hepatic, hi•pat′ik, *a.* [L. *hepaticus*, Gr. *hepatikos*, from *hēpar, hēpatos*, the liver.] Pertaining to the liver.—*n.* A medicine that acts on the liver.—**hepatica,** hi•pat′i•ka, *n.* A species of anemone with trilobed leaves; any one of the genus of plants (*Hepatica*) allied to the mosses, and called liverworts.—**hepatitis,** hep•a•tī′tis, *n.* Inflammation of the liver.—**hepatization,** hep′a•tī•zā″shon, *n.* The state of being hepatized; the condensation of a texture so as to resemble the liver.—**hepatotomy,** hep′a•to″to•mi, *n.* [Gr. *tomē*, cutting.] The operation of cutting into the liver.

heptachord, hep′ta•kord, *n.* [Gr. *hepta*, seven, and *chordē*, chord.] *Anc. mus.* a diatonic octave without the upper note; an instrument with seven strings.

heptad, hep′tad, *n.* [Gr. *heptas, heptados*, from *hepta*, seven.] A sum of seven.

heptagon, hep′ta•gon, *n.* [Gr. *hepta*, seven, and *gōnia*, an angle.] *Geom.* a plane figure having seven sides and as many angles.—**heptagonal,** hep•tag′on•al, *a.* Having seven angles or sides.

heptamerous, hep•tam′ėr•us, *a.* [Gr. *hepta*, seven, and *meros*, a part.] *Bot.* consisting of seven parts; having its parts in sevens.

heptarchy, hep′tär•ki, *n.* [Gr. *hepta*, seven, and *archē*, rule.] A government by seven persons, or the country governed by seven persons: usually applied to the seven Anglo-Saxon kingdoms into which England was once divided.

Heptateuch, hep′ta•tūk, *n.* [Gr. *hepta*, seven, and *teuchos*, book.] The first seven books of the Old Testament.

heptose, hep′tōs, *n.* [*Hept* and *ose.*] Any of several monosaccharides obtainable from lower sugars, containing 7 carbon atoms in the molecule.

her, hėr, *pron.*, a form answering to several cases of *she.* [O.E. *hire*, A.Sax. *hire, heore*, genit. and dat. case of the pronoun *heó*, she, the feminine of *hé*, he. HE.] The possessive case of *she* (*her* face); the dative case of *she* (give *her* that book); the objective case of *she* (I love *her*).—**hers,** hėrz, *pron.* [From *her*, with *s* of the possessive case.] A possessive pronoun used instead of *her* and a noun, as subject, object, or predicate.—**herself,** hėr•self′, *pron.* An emphasized or reflexive form of the third pers. pron. fem., used in the same way as *himself* (which see).

herald, her′ald, *n.* [O.Fr. *herault, herald*, Fr. *héraut*, from O.H.G. *hariwalt* (G. *herold*), an officer of an army—*hari, heri*, an army (akin E. *harry*), and *waltan*, to rule (E. *wield*).] An officer whose business was to denounce or proclaim war, to challenge to battle, to proclaim peace, to bear messages, etc.; an officer who marshals processions; a proclaimer; a forerunner.—*v.t.* To introduce or to give tidings of, as by a herald; to proclaim.—**heraldic,** he•ral′dik, *a.*—**heraldry,** her′ald•ri, *n.* The art or office of a herald; the art of blazoning arms or ensigns armorial, or the knowledge pertaining thereto.

herb, ėrb or hėrb, *n.* [Fr. *herbe*, L. *herba, herb*, from a root meaning to eat or nourish, seen in Gr. *phorbē*, pasture, fodder.] Any plant with a soft or succulent stem which dies to the root every year, as distinguished from a *tree* and a *shrub*, which have woody stems.—**herbaceous,** hėr•bā′shus, *a.* [L. *herbaceus.*] Pertaining to herbs.—*Herbaceous plants*, plants which perish annually down to the root; soft, succulent vegetables.—**herbage,** ėrb′ij or hėrb′ij, *n.* Herbs collectively; green food for beasts; grass; pasture.—**herbal,** hėr′bal, *n.* A book containing the names and descriptions of plants; a collection of plants dried and preserved; a herbarium.—*a.* Pertaining to herbs.—**herbalist,** hėr′bal•ist, *n.* A person who makes collections of plants;

a dealer in medicinal plants.—**herbarium,** hėr•bā′ri•um, *n.* A collection of dried plants systematically arranged; a book or other contrivance for preserving dried specimens of plants.—**herbary,** hėr′ba•ri, *n.* A garden of plants.—**herb bennet,** *n.* Common avens, an aromatic, tonic, and astringent plant.—**herbivore,** hėr′bi•vōr, *n.* A herbivorous animal. —**herbivorous,** hėr•biv′o•rus, *a.* [L. *herba*, and *voro*, to eat.] Eating herbs; subsisting on plants (a *herbivorous* animal).

herculean, hėr•kū′li•an, *a.* Pertaining to *Hercules*; resembling Hercules in strength; very difficult or dangerous (a *Herculean* task).

herd, hėrd, *n.* [A.Sax. *heord, herd*= Goth. *hairda*, D. *herde*, Dan. *hjord*, Icel. *hjōrth*, G. *herde*, a herd, flock, drove, etc.] A number of beasts feeding or driven together; a company of men or people, in contempt or detestation; a crowd; a rabble.—*v.t.* and *i.* To form in a herd; to feed or run in herds; to associate; to unite in companies.—**herdsman,** hėrdz′man, *n.* A man attending a herd.

herd, hėrd, *n.* [A.Sax. *hirde*, a herdsman or shepherd, from *heord*, a flock or herd; Goth. *hairdeis*, Icel. *hirdi*, Dan. *hyrde*, G. *hirt*; same origin as the preceding.] A keeper of cattle or sheep: now mostly in composition, as shep*herd*, goat*herd*, swine*herd*.

here, hēr, *adv.* [A.Sax. *hér*=Dan. and Goth. *her*, Icel. *hér*, G. and D. *hier*, here; based on the pronominal element seen in *he*.] In this place; in the place where the speaker is present: opposed to *there*; in the present life or state; to this place, hither (come *here*). *Here* in *Here's* for you, *Here* goes, etc., is a sort of exclamation to attract attention to something about to be done, the subject in familiar phrases having been dropped out.—*Neither here nor there*, neither in this place nor in that; hence, unconnected with the matter in hand; irrelevant; unimportant.—*Here and there*, in one place and another; thinly or irregularly dispersed.—**hereabout, hereabouts,** hēr′a•bout, hēr′a•bouts, *adv.* About this place; in this vicinity or neighborhood.—**hereafter,** hēr•af′tėr, *adv.* In time to come; in some future time or state.—*n.* A future state.—**hereat,** hēr•at′, *adv.* At or by reason of this.—**hereby,** hēr•bī′, *adv.* By this; by means of this; close by; very near.—**herein,** hēr•in′, *adv.* In this.—**hereinafter,** hēr•in•af′tėr, *adv.* In this afterwards: applied to something afterwards to be named or described in a writing.—**hereinto,** hēr•in′tö, *adv.* Into this.—**hereof,** hēr•ov′, *adv.* Of this; concerning this; from this.—**hereon,** hēr•on′, *adv.* On this.—**hereto,** hēr•tö′, *adv.* To this. —**heretofore,** hēr•tö•fōr′, *adv.* Before or up to this time; formerly.—**hereunto,** hēr•un•tö′, *adv.* Unto this or this time; hereto.—**hereupon,** hēr•up•on′, *adv.* Upon this; hereon. —**herewith,** hēr•with′, *adv.* With this; by means of this.

hereditable, he•red′i•ta•bl, *a.*—[L.L. *hereditabilis*, from L. *hereditas, hereditatis*, the act of inheriting, from *heres, heredis*, an heir. HEIR.] Capable of being inherited.—**hereditability,** he•red′i•ta•bil″i•ti, *n.* State of being hereditable.—**hereditament,** he•re•dit′a•ment, *n.* [L.L. *hereditamentum.*] Any species of property that may be inherited.—**hereditarily,** he•red′i•te•ri•li, *adv.* By inheritance.—**hereditary,** he•red′i•te•ri, *a.* [L. *hereditarius.*] Descended by inheritance; descending from an ancestor to an heir; descendible to an heir-at-law; that is or may be transmitted from a parent to a child.—**heredity,** he•red′i•ti, *n.* [L. *hereditas.*] Hereditary transmission of qualities of like kind with those of the parent; the doctrine that the offspring inherits the characteristics of the parent or parents.

heresy, her′e•si, *n.* [Fr. *hérésie*, L. *hæresis*, from Gr. *hairesis*, a taking, a principle or set of principles, from *haireō*, to take.] A doctrine, principle, or set of principles at variance with established or generally received principles; especially an opinion or opinions contrary to the established religious faith, or what is regarded as the true faith; heterodoxy.—**heresiarch,** he•rē′si•ärk, *n.* [Gr. *hairesiarchos, hairesis*, heresy, and *archē*, rule.] A leader in heresy; a prominent or arch heretic.—**heretic,** her′e•tik, *n.* [L. *hæreticus.*] A person who holds heretical opinions; one who maintains heresy —**heretical,** he•ret′i•kal, *a.* Containing or pertaining to heresy.—**heretically,** he•ret′i•kal•li, *adv.* In a heretical manner.

heriot, her′i•ot, *n.* [A.Sax. *heregeatu*, military equipment, a heriot—*here*, an army, and *geatu*, equipment.] *Eng. law*, a chattel or payment given to the lord of a fee on the decease of the tenant or vassal.

heritable, her′i•ta•bl, *a.* [O.Fr. *héritable*, abbrev. from L.L. *hereditábilis.* HEREDITABLE.] Capable of being inherited; inheritable.—*Heritable property*, the name in Scotland for *real property.*—*Heritable security*, security constituted by heritable property.—**heritage,** her′i•tij, *n.* [Fr., from L. *hereditas*, heritage.] That which is inherited; inheritance; *Scots law*, heritable estate or realty.—**heritor,** her′i•tėr, *n.* An inheritor; in Scotland, a proprietor or landholder in a parish.

hermaphrodite, hėr•maf′ro•dīt, *n.* [From *Hermaphroditos* of Greek mythology, son of *Hermes* and *Aphrodite*, who became united into one body with a nymph.] An animal in which the characteristics of both sexes are either really or apparently combined; *bot.* a flower that contains both the stamen and the pistil, or the male and female organs. —*a.* Including or being of both sexes.—*Hermaphrodite brig*, a brig that is square-rigged forward and schooner-rigged aft.—**hermaphroditic, hermaphroditical,** hėr•maf′ro•dit″ik, hėr•maf′ro•dit″i•kal, *a.* Of or pertaining to a hermaphrodite.—**hermaphroditically,** hėr•maf′ro•dit″i•kal•li, *adv.* After the manner of hermaphrodites.—**hermaphroditism,** hėr•maf′rod•it•izm, *n.* The state of being hermaphrodite.

hermeneutics, hėr•mi•nū′tiks, *n.* [Gr. *hermēneutikos*, from *hermēneus*, an interpreter, from *Hermēs*, Mercury.] The art or science of interpretation; especially applied to the interpretation of the Scriptures; exegesis.—**hermeneutic, hermeneutical,** hėr•mi•nū′tik, hėr•mi•nū′ti•kal, *a.* Interpreting; explaining; exegetical; unfolding the signification.

hermetic, hermetical, hėr•met′ik, hėr•met′i•kal, *a.* [Fr. *hermétique*, from the ancient *Hermes Trismegistus*, who was regarded as skilled in alchemy and occult science.] Appellative of or pertaining to alchemy or the doctrines of the alchemists; effected by fusing together the edges of the mouth or aperture, as of a bottle or tube, so that no air, gas, or spirit can escape (the *hermetic* method of sealing).—**hermetically,** hėr′met′i•kal•li, *adv.* In a hermetic manner; by fusing the edges together.

hermit, hėrmit, *n.* [Fr. *ermite*, O.Fr. *hermite*, Gr. *erēmitēs*, from *erēmos*, lonely, solitary, desert.] A person who retires from society and lives in solitude; a recluse; an anchorite.—**hermitage,** hėr′mi•tij, *n.* The habitation of a hermit; a kind of French wine.—**hermit crab,** *n.* A species of crab which takes possession of and occupies the cast-off shells of various mollusks, carrying this habitation about with it, and changing it for a larger one as it increases in size.—**hermitical,** hėr•mit′i•kal, *a.* Pertaining or suited to a hermit or to retired life.

hernia, hėr′ni•a, *n.* [L.] *Surg.* a protrusion of some part from its natural cavity by an abnormal aperture; commonly the protrusion of viscera through an aperture in the wall of the abdomen; rupture.—**hernial,** hėr′ni•al, *a.* Pertaining to hernia.

hero, hē′rō, *n.* pl. **heroes,** hē′rōz. [L. *heros*, from Gr. *hērōs*; akin to L. *vir* (seen in *virile, virtue*), A.Sax. *wer*, a man; Skr. *vira*, a hero.] A kind of demigod in ancient Greek mythology; hence, a man of distinguished valor or intrepidity; a prominent or central personage in any remarkable action or event; the principal personage in a poem, play, novel, etc.—**heroic,** he•rō′ik, *a.* [L. *heroicus.*] Pertaining to a hero; becoming a hero; characteristic of a hero; brave; magnanimous; intrepid and noble; reciting the achievements of heroes; epic.—*Heroic treatment, remedies, med.* treatment or remedies of a violent character.—*Heroic verse*, in English poetry, the iambic verse of ten syllables, in French the iambic of twelve, and in classical poetry the hexameter.—**heroically,** he•rō′i•kal•li, *adv.* In a heroic manner.—**heroine,** her′ō•in, *n.* [Fr. *héroïne.*] A female hero.—**heroism,**

he′rō•izm, *n.* The qualities of a hero; bravery; courage; intrepidity.
heroin, her′ō•in, *n.* [From *Heroin*, a trademark.] Diacetyl-morphine, a white crystalline drug used as a sedative, limited in distribution by law because it is habit-forming.
heron, her′un, *n.* [Fr. *heron*, O.Fr. *hairon*, from O.H.G. *heigro*, *heigero*, Icel. *hegri*, Sw. *häger*, a heron; hence also Fr. *aigre*, dim. *aigrette*, E. *egret.*] A grallatorial bird with a long bill cleft beneath the eyes, long slender legs and neck, formerly the special game pursued in falconry.—**heronry,** her′un•ri, *n.* A place where herons breed.
herpes, hėr′pēz, *n.* [Gr. *herpēs*, from *herpō*, to creep.] A skin disease characterized by the eruption of inflamed vesicles, such as shingles.—**herpetic,** hėr•pet′ik, *a.* Pertaining to or resembling herpes.
herpetology, hėr•pe•tol′o•ji, *n.* [Gr. *herpeton*, a reptile, from *herpō*, to creep, and *logos*, discourse.] A description of reptiles; the natural history of reptiles. **herpetological,** hėr•pet′o•loj″i•kal, *a.* Pertaining to herpetology.—**herpetologist,** hėr•-pe•tol′o•jist, *n.*
herring, her′ing, *n.* [A.Sax. *haering* = D. *haring*, G. *häring*, Icel. *haeringr*, herring; from A.Sax. *here*, G. *heer*, an army. HERALD.] A common fish, which is found in incredible numbers in the North Sea, the northern parts of the Atlantic, etc., of great importance as an article of food or commerce.—**herringbone,** *n.* A pattern made of rows of parallel lines, each with a reverse slant from the next, as in the spinal bones of the herring.—*v.t.* To produce a herringbone pattern, as in a fabric.—*v.i.* To climb a slope on skis, imprinting a *herringbone* pattern on the snow.
hers, hėrz, *pron.* See HER.
herse, hėrs, *n.* [Fr. *herse*, O.Fr. *herce*, a harrow, a portcullis; same as *hearse.*] A portcullis in the form of a harrow, set with iron spikes; a similar structure used for a cheval-de-frise; a framework whereon lighted candles were placed in some of the ceremonies of the church, and at the obsequies of distinguished persons; sometimes a hearse.
herself. See HER.
hertzian waves, hert′si•an wavz, *n.* [From Heinrich *Hertz*, G. physicist.] Long electromagnetic waves.
hesitate, hez′i•tāt, *v.i.*—*hesitated*, *hesitating.* [L. *hæsito*, *hæsitatum*, intens. from *hæreo*, *hæsum*, to stick, as in *adhere*, *cohere*, *inherent.*] To stop or pause respecting decision or action; to be doubtful as to fact, principle, or determination; to stammer; to stop in speaking.—**hesitatingly,** hez′i•tā•ting•li, *adv.*—**hesitation,** hez•i•tā′shon, *n.* The act of hesitating; stammering.—**hesitative,** hez′i•tā•tiv, *a.*—**hesitancy,** hez′i•tan•-si, *n.*—**hesitant,** hez′i•tant, *a.*
Hesperian, hes•pē′ri•an, *a.* [L. *hesperius*, western, from Gr. *hesperos* (=L. *vesper*), the evening.] Western; situated at the west. (*Poet.*)—**Hesperides,** hes•per′i•dēz, *n. pl. Greek myth.* the daughters of Hesperus, possessors of the garden of golden fruit, watched over by a dragon, at the western extremities of the earth.
Hessian, hesh′n, *a.* Relating to *Hesse* in Germany.—*Hessian boot*, a kind of long boot originally worn by the Hessian troops.—*n.* A native of Hesse; a Hessian boot.—**Hessian-fly,** *n.* A small two-winged fly nearly black, the larva of which is very destructive to young wheat.
hetaera, hetaira, he•tē′ra, he•tī′rā, *n.* [Gr. *hetarē*, *hetaira.*] A courtesan of the superior class.—**hetaerism, hetairism,** he•tēr′izm, he•tī′rizm, *n.* Concubinage; a supposed primitive social state, in which women of a tribe were held in common.
heterocercal, het′e•ro•sėr•kal, *a.* [Gr. *heteros*, other, *kerkos*, a tail.] Having the vertebral column running to a point in the upper lobe of the tail, as in the sharks and sturgeons; contrasted with *homocercal.*
heteroclite, het′e•ro•klīt, *n.* [Gr. *heteroklitōn*—*heteros*, other, and *klinō*, to incline, to lean away from the normal form.] A word which is irregular or anomalous either in declension or conjugation; something abnormal.
heterodox, het′e•ro•doks, *a.* [Gr. *heteros*, other, and *doxa*, opinion.] Contrary to established or generally received opinions; contrary to some recognized standard of opinion.—**heterodoxy,** het′e•ro•dok•si, *n.* The holding of heterodox opinions.
heterodyne, het′er•o•dīn, *n.* [Gr. *heteros*, other, and *dyne*, from Gr. *dynamis*, power.] The beating together in an electrical circuit of two frequencies, one of a signal-carrying current, and one of an uninterrupted current, to produce new frequencies.
heteroecism, het′er•ēs″ism, *n.* [Gr. *heteros*, different, *oikos*, a house.] In fungi, living on more than one kind of host in the course of the life history.
heterogamous, het•e•rog′a•mus, *a.* [Gr. *heteros*, other, *gamos*, marriage.] *Bot.* irregular in regard to the arrangement of the sexes; having florets of different sexes in the same flower head.—**heterogamy,** het•e•-rog′a•mi, *n.*
heterogeneous, het′e•ro•jē″ni•us, *a.* [Gr. *heteros*, other, and *genos*, kind.] Differing in kind; composed of dissimilar or incongruous parts or elements: opposed to *homogeneous.*—**heterogeneously,** het′e•ro•jē″ni•us•li, *adv.*—**heterogeneousness, heterogeneity,** het′e•ro•jē″ni•us•nes, het′e•ro•-ji″nē•i•ty, *n.*
heterogenesis, heterogeny, het′e•-ro•jen″e•sis, het′e•roj′e•ni, *n.* [Gr. *heteros*, other, and *genesis*, generation.] *Biol.* spontaneous generation; also, same as *alternate generation.*
heterologous, het•e•rol′o•gus, *a.* [Gr. *heteros*, other, and *logos*, analogy, proportion.] Different; not analogous or homologous.—**heterology,** het•e•rol′o•ji, *n.* The state or quality of being heterologous; *biol.* want or absence of relation or analogy between parts.
heteromorphic, heteromorphous, het′e•ro•mor″fik, het′e•ro•mor″fus, *a.* [Gr. *heteros*, other, *morphē*, form.] Of an irregular or unusual form; having two or more diverse shapes.—**heteromorphism,** het′e•ro•mor″-fizm, *n.* The state or quality of being heteromorphic; existence under different forms at different stages of development.
heteronomy, het•er•on′o•mi, *n.* [Gr. *heteronomie*, from Gr. *heteros*, and *nomos*, law.] Subjection to another's rule; not self-governed.
heteronym, het′ėr•o•nim, *n.* [Gr. *heteros*, other, *onoma*, name.] A word with the same spelling as another but a different pronunciation; a different name for the same thing.
heterophyllous, het•e•rof′i•lus or het•e•ro•fil′lus, *a.* [Gr. *heteros*, other, *phyllon*, leaf.] *Bot.* having two different kinds of leaves on the same stem.
heterosexual, het•er•o•seks′shu•al, *adj.* [Gr. *heteros*, other, and *sexual.*] Of or relating to relationships between persons of the opposite sex.
heterosphere, het′er•o•sphere, *n.* [Gr. *heteros*, other, and *sphere.*] A layer of the atmosphere stretching about 22,000 miles.
heterosporous, het′er•o•spōr″us, *a.* [Gr. *heteros*, different, *sporos*, seed.] With spores of different kinds.
heterotaxy, het′e•ro•tak″si, *n.* [Gr. *heteros*, other, and *taxis*, arrangement.] Arrangement other than normal; confused or abnormal arrangement or structure.
hetman, het′man, *n.* [Pol., from G. *hauptman*, head-man, chieftain.] The title of the head (general) of the Cossacks.
heuristic, hū•ris′tik, *a.* [Gr. *heuriskein*, to find out.] Aiding or leading on toward discovery or finding out.
hew, hū, *v.t.*—pret. *hewed*, pp. *hewed* or *hewn.* [A.Sax. *heáwan*, D. *houwen*, G. *hauen*, Icel. *höggva*, Dan. *hugge*, to hew; akin *hoe*, *hay.*] To cut or fell with an ax or other like instrument; to shape with a sharp instrument: often with *out.*—**hewer,** hū′ėr, *n.* One who hews.
hex, heks, *n.* [Gr. *hexe*, witch.] A spell or curse.—*v.t.* To put a curse on.
hexacord, hek′sa•kord, *n.* [Gr. *hex*, six, and *chordē*, a chord.] *Mus.* a series of six notes, each rising one degree over the other.
hexagon, hek′sa•gon, *n.* [Gr. *hex*, *six*, and *gōnia*, an angle.] *Geom.* a figure of six sides and six angles.—**hexagonal,** hek•sag′on•al, *a.*—**hexagonally,** hek•sag′on•al•li, *adv.*
hexahedron, hek•sa•hē′dron, *n.* [Gr. *hex*, six, and *hedra*, a base or seat.] A regular solid body of six sides; a cube.—**hexahedral,** hek•sa•hē′dral, *a.* Of the figure of a hexahedron.
hexameter, hek•sam′e•tėr, *n.* [Gr. *hex*, six, and *metron*, measure.] *Pros.* a verse of six feet, the first four of which may be either dactyls or spondees, the fifth normally a dactyl, though sometimes a spondee, and the sixth always a spondee.

—*a.* Having six metrical feet.—**hexametric, hexametral,** hek•sa•met′rik, hek•sam′et•ral, *a.* Consisting of six metrical feet; forming a hexameter.

hexangular, hek•sang′gū•lėr, *a.* [Gr. *hex,* six, and E. *angular.*] Having six angles.

hexapla, hek′sa•pla, *n. pl.* [Gr. *hexaplous,* sixfold—*hex,* six, and term. as in *double.*] An edition of the Holy Scriptures in six languages or six versions in parallel columns.—**hexaplar,** hek′sa•plėr, *a.* Pertaining to a hexapla.

hexapod, hek′sa•pod, *a.* [Gr. *hex,* six, and *pous, podos,* a foot.] Having six feet.—*n.* An animal having six feet.

hexastich, hexastichon, hek′sa•stik, hek•sas′ti•kon, *n.* [Gr. *hex,* six, *stichos,* a verse.] A poem consisting of six lines or verses.

hey, hā. [Comp. G. and D. *hei.*] An exclamation of joy or to call attention.

heyday, hā′dā, *interj.* [Comp. G. *heyda, heidi, heia,* huzzah! heyday!] An exclamation of cheerfulness and sometimes of wonder.

heyday, hā′dā, *n.* [Equivalent to *highday.*] A frolic; the wildness, or frolicsome period of youth.

hiatus, hī•ā′tus, *n.* [L., from *hio,* to open or gape.] An opening; a gap; a space from which something is wanting; a lacuna; *pros.* the coming together of two vowels in two successive syllables or words.

hibernal, hī•bėr′nal, *a.* [L. *hibernalis,* from *hibernus,* wintry, akin to *hiems,* winter; Gr. *chiōn,* Skr. *hima,* snow.] Belonging or relating to winter; wintry.—**hibernate,** hī′bėr•nāt, *v.i.* —*hibernated, hibernating.* [L. *hiberno, hibernatum.*] To winter; to pass the winter in sleep or seclusion, as some animals.—**hibernation,** hī•bėr•nā′shon, *n.* The act of hibernating.—**hibernaculum,** hī•bėr•nak′ū•lum, *n.* The winter retreat of an animal.

Hibernian, hī•bėr′ni•an, *a.* [L. *Hibernia,* Ireland.] Pertaining to Hibernia, now Ireland; Irish.—*n.* A native or inhabitant of Ireland.—**Hibernianism, Hibernicism,** hī•bėr′ni•an•izm, hī•bėr′ni•sizm, *n.* An idiom or mode of speech peculiar to the Irish.

hibiscus, hī•bis′kus, *n.* [Gr. *hibiskos.*] Any of a large genus *(Hibiscus)* of herbs, shrubs or small trees of the mallow family, having showy flowers.

hiccup, hiccough, hik′up, *n.* [Imitative.] A spasmodic catching in the breath with a sudden sound; a convulsive catch of the respiratory muscles repeated at short intervals.—*v.t.* and *i.* To have, or say with, hiccups.

hickory, hik′o•ri, *n.* [North Amer. Indian.] A North American tree of the walnut family with pinnate leaves, growing from 70 to 80 feet high, the wood of which is heavy, strong, tenacious, and very valuable.

hidalgo, hi•dal′gō, Sp. pron. ē•däl′gō, *n.* [Sp., contr. for *hijodalgo, hijo de algo,* son of somebody—*hijo,* from L. *filius,* son, and *algo,* from L. *aliquod,* something, somewhat.] In Spain, a man belonging to the lower nobility; a gentleman by birth.

hide, hīd, *v.t.*—*hid* (pret.), *hid, hidden* (pp.), *hiding* (ppr.). [A.Sax. *hydan,* to hide; cog. W. *cuddiaw,* to cover, *cudd,* darkness, Gr. *keuthō,* to hide; akin *hide,* skin.] To withhold or withdraw from sight or knowledge; to keep secret; to conceal.—*v.i.* To conceal one's self; to lie concealed.—**hid, hidden,** hid, hid′n, *p.* and *a.* Concealed; placed in secrecy; secret; unseen; mysterious.—**hider,** hī′dėr, *n.* One who hides or conceals.

hide, hīd, *n.* [A.Sax. *hýd*=D. *huid,* Icel, *huth,* Dan. and Sw. *hud,* G. *haut,* hide; cog. L. *cutis,* Gr. *skutos,* the skin of a beast, from root meaning to cover, as in *hide, v.t.*] The skin of an animal; especially, the undressed skin of the larger domestic animals, as oxen, horses, etc.; the human skin, in contempt.—*v.t.* To beat; to flog. (*Colloq.*)—**hiding,** hī′ding, *n.* A flogging or beating. (*Colloq.*)—**hidebound,** hīd′-bound, *a.* Having the skin tight on the body, said of horses or cattle; narrowminded; unyielding in opinion.

hide, hīd, *n.* [A.Sax. *hid,* contr. from *higid,* a hide; same root as *hive.*] An old measure of land variously estimated at 60, 80, and 100 acres.

hideous, hid′ē•us, *a.* [Fr. *hideux,* O.Fr. *hisdous,* rough, shaggy, hideous, from L. *hispidosus,* for *hispidus,* rough, shaggy.] Frightful to the sight; dreadful; shocking to the eye; shocking in any way; detestable; horrible.—**hideously,** hid′ē•us•li, *adv.* In a hideous manner.—**hideousness,** hid′ē•us•nes, *n.*

hideout, hīd′out, *n.* A place of refuge and concealment.

hie, hī, *v.i.*—*hied, hieing.* [A.Sax. *higian,* to endeavor, to hasten; perhaps from *hyge, hige,* the mind, thought; comp. D. *hijgen,* Dan. *hige,* to covet.] To move or run with haste; to go in haste (often with *him, me,* etc., reflexively; as, he *hied him* home).

hierarch, hī′ėr•ärk, *n.* [Gr. *hieros,* sacred, and *archē,* rule.] One who rules or has authority in sacred things.—**hierarchic, hierarchical,** hī•ėr•är′kik, hī•ėr•är′ki•kal, *a.* Pertaining to a hierarch or hierarchy.—**hierarchically,** hī•ėr•är′ki•kal•li, *adv.* In a hierarchic manner.—**hierarchy,** hī′ėr•är•ki, *n.* Authority in sacred things; a ranking of individuals, as of officials according to their power in government or in the church; arrangement of scientific items according to their logical relationships.

hieratic, hieratical, hī•ėr•at′ik, hī•ėr•at′i•kal, *a.* [Gr. *hieratikos,* from *hieros,* holy.] Consecrated to sacred uses; pertaining to priests; sacred; sacerdotal; especially applied to the characters or mode of writing used by the ancient Egyptian priests, a development from the hieroglyphics.

hierocracy, hī•ėr•ok′ra•si, *n.* [Gr. *hieros,* holy, and *kratos,* power.] Government by ecclesiastics; hierarchy.

hieroglyph, hieroglyphic, hī′ėr•o•glif, hī′ėr•o•glif″ik, *n.* [Gr. *hieros,* sacred, and *glyphō,* to carve.] The figure of an animal, plant, or other object intended to convey a meaning or stand for an alphabetical character; a figure implying a word, an idea, or a sound, such as those in use among the ancient Egyptians; a figure having a hidden or enigmatical significance; a character difficult to decipher.—**hieroglyphical,** hī′ėr•o•glif″i•kal, *a.* Forming a hieroglyphic; consisting of hieroglyphics; expressive of meaning by hieroglyphics.—**hieroglyphically,** hī′ėr•o•glif″i•kal•li, *adv.* In a hieroglyphic manner.—**hieroglyphist,** hī′ėr•o•glif•ist, *n.* One versed in hieroglyphics.

hierology, hī•ėr•ol′o•ji, *n.* [Gr. *hieros,* sacred, and *logos,* discourse.] Sacred lore; knowledge of hieroglyphics or sacred writing.

hierophant, hī′ėr•o•fant, *n.* [Gr. *hierophantēs — hieros,* sacred, and *phainō,* to show.] A priest; one who teaches the mysteries and duties of religion.—**hierophantic,** hī′ėr•o•fan″tik, *a.* Belonging to hierophants.

hi-fi, hī′fī, *n.* [Abbrev. for *high fidelity.*] Life-like sound reproduction or *high fidelity;* the radio or phonographic equipment that reproduces sound with comparatively slight distortion.

higgle, hig′l, *v.i.*—*higgled, higgling.* [A weaker form of *haggle,* to chaffer.] To haggle.—**higgler,** hig′l•ėr, *n.*

high, hī, *a.* [A.Sax. *heáh, héh*=Goth. *hauhs,* Icel. *hár,* Dan. *hoi,* D. *hoog,* G. *hoch,* high; hence *height.*] Having a great extent from base to summit; rising much above the ground or some other object; elevated, lofty, tall; exalted, excellent, superior (mind, attainments, art); elevated in rank, condition, or office; difficult to comprehend; abstruse; arrogant, boastful, proud; loud, boisterous, threatening, or angry (*high* words); extreme, intense, strong, forcible; exceeding the common measure or degree (a *high* wind; *high* color); full or complete (*high* time); dear; of a great price, or greater price than usual; remote from the equator north or south (a *high* latitude); *mus.* acute or elevated in tone; capital; committed against the king, sovereign, or state (*high* treason); *cook.* tending towards putrefaction; strong-scented (venison kept till it is *high*). Used substantively for people of rank or high station (*high* and low).—*On high,* aloft; in a lofty position.—*High and dry,* out of the water; out of reach of the current or waves.—*High altar,* the chief altar in a church.—*High Church,* that branch of the Church of England known as the Anglo-Catholic Church, in contradistinction to the Protestant Episcopal Church.—*High day,* a festival or gala day.—*High day, high noon,* the time when the sun is in the meridian.—*High Dutch, High German.* DUTCH, GERMAN.—*High life,* the style of living of the upper classes.—*High* *living*, indulgence in rich or costly food and drink.—*High Mass*, principal Mass, a solemn ceremony in which the priest is assisted by a deacon and subdeacon.—*High place*, in Scrip. an eminence or mound on which sacrifices were offered, especially to heathen deities.—*High school*, the school next above a grammar or elementary school, usually public and offering a four-year course.—*To be on the high horse, to mount one's high horse*, to stand on one's dignity; to assume a lofty tone or manner; to take offense.—*adv.* In a high manner; to a great altitude; highly; richly; luxuriously.—**highball,** hī'bąl, *n.* An iced alcoholic drink, made of spirits mixed with soda or ginger ale, etc., and served in a tall glass.—**highborn,** *a.* Being of noble birth.—**highbrow,** *n.* An intellectual. (*Slang*)—**high explosives,** *n.* Explosives of extremely powerful class, especially such as are based on nitroglycerine.—**high fidelity.** Sound reproduction by radio or phonograph to closely approximate the original; shortened form, hi-fi.—**highflier,** *n.* One who is extravagant in pretensions or manners. (*Colloq.*)—**high-flown,** *a.* Elevated; proud; turgid; extravagant.—**high frequency,** *adj.* Any frequency above the audible range, particularly a radio frequency.—**highhanded,** *a.* Oppressive; violent; arbitrary.—**highland,** hī'land, *n.* An elevated or mountainous region: [cap.] generally in plural (the *Highlands* of Scotland).—*a.* Pertaining to highlands, [cap.] especially the Highlands of Scotland.—**highlander,** hī'land•ėr, *n.* An inhabitant of highlands, [cap.] particularly the Highlands of Scotland.—**Highland fling,** *n.* A sort of dance peculiar to the Scottish Highlanders, danced by one person.—**high-hat,** *n.* A snob.—*v.t.* To snub someone.—**highly,** hī'li, *adv.* In a high manner or to a high degree; greatly; decidedly; markedly.—**high-minded,** *a.* Characterized by, or pertaining to, elevated principles and feelings.—**high-mindedness,** *n.*—**highness,** hī'nes, *n.* [cap.] A title of honor given to princes or other persons of rank: used with poss. pron. *his, her*, etc.—**high-pressure,** *a.* Having a pressure much greater than that of the normal pressure of the atmosphere; pressing, intense, urgent.—**high priest,** *n.* A chief priest.—**highroad,** *n.* A highway, hence, an easy way.—**high seas,** *n.* pl. The open sea or ocean; the ocean beyond the limit of 3 miles from the shore.—**high-sounding,** *a.* Pompous; ostentatious; bombastic.—**high-spirited,** *a.* Having a high spirit; bold; manly.—**high-strung,** *a.* Having some intense emotion.—**high tension,** *adj.* Having a high voltage; capable of operating under a voltage of 1,000 volts or more.—**high tide,** *n.* High water.—**high-toned,** *a.* High in tone or pitch; high-principled; dignified; chic.—**highway,** hī'wā, *n.* A public road; a way open to all travelers.—**highwayman,** hī'wā•man, *n.* One who robs on the public road or highway.—**high-wrought,** *a.* Agitated to a high degree.

hike, hīk, *v.i.* [Perhaps from *hitch.*] To walk or tramp for some distance, usually in the country; to march, as a soldier; to raise, as a price.—*v.t.* To lift up with a jerk; to increase an amount suddenly.—*n.* A walk or tramp; a march.

hilarity, hi•lar'i•ti, *n.* [Fr. *hilarité*, from L. *hilaritas*, from *hilaris, hilarus*, Gr. *hilaros*, cheerful; hence *exhilarate.*] A pleasurable excitement of the animal spirits; mirth; merriment; gaiety.—*Hilary term*, a law term beginning near the festival of St. *Hilary*, which is January 13.—**hilarious,** hi•lâ'ri•us, *a.* Mirthful; merry.

hill, hil, *n.* [A.Sax. *hill, hyll*, a hill; O.D. *hille, hil*; same root as L. *collis*, a hill, *columna*, a column.] A natural elevation less than a mountain; an eminence rising above the level of the surrounding land; a heap (a mole*hill*),—**hillbilly,** *n.* One who lives in a rough, hilly region, such as the southern Appalachians or the Ozarks. (*Colloq.*)—**hilliness,** hil'i•nes, *n.*—**hillside,** hil'sīd, *n.* The side or declivity of a hill.—**hilltop,** hil'-top, *n.* The top or summit of a hill.—**hilly,** hil'i, *a.* Consisting of hills.—**hillock,** hil'ok, *n.* [Dim. of *hill.*] A small hill.

hilt, hilt, *n.* [A.Sax. *hilt*, hilt=Icel. *hjalt*, Dan. *hjalte*, O.H.G. *helza*; same root as *helve.*] The handle of a sword, dagger, etc.

hilum, hī'lum, *n.* [L.] The mark or scar on a seed (as the black patch on a bean) produced by its separation from the placenta.

him, him, *pron.* [In A.Sax. the dative and instrumental of *he* and *hit*, he and it, afterwards used instead of *hine*, the real accusative sing. masc.; *m* is properly a dative suffix, as in *them, whom.*] The dative and objective case of *he.*—**himself,** him•self', *pron.* An emphatic and reflexive form of the 3rd pers. pron. masc.; as, *himself*, he *himself*, the man *himself*, told me; it was *himself*, or he *himself*; he struck *himself*. It often implies that the person has command of himself, or is possessed of his natural frame or temper; as, he is not *himself* at all; he soon came to *himself*.—*By himself*, alone; unaccompanied.

Himyaritic, him•ya•rit'ik, *a.* [From *Himyar*, an ancient king of Yemen.] Pertaining to the ancient Arabic of Southeast Arabia.—*n.* The language of Southeast Arabia.

hin, hin, *n.* [Heb.] A Hebrew measure containing about 5 quarts.

hind, hīnd, *n.* [A.Sax. *hind*=G. and D. *hinde*, Icel., Dan., and Sw. *hind.*] The female of the red deer, the stag being the male.

hind, hīnd, *n.* [A.Sax. *hine, hina*, with *d* affixed, as in *lend, sound*; akin *hive.*] In England an agricultural laborer.

hind, hīnd, *a.* [A.Sax. *hind*, hind, *hindan*, behind; Goth. *hindana, hindar*, O.H.G. *hintar*, G. *hinten*, behind, *hinter*, hind; hence to *hinder.*] Backward; pertaining to the part which follows or is behind; opposite of *fore.*—**hinder,** hīn'dėr, *a.* In the rear; following; after.—**hindmost,** hīnd'mōst, *a.* [A.Sax. *hindema*, hindmost; the *-most* is a corruption as in *foremost* (which see).] Farthest behind; behind all others; last.—**hindsight,** hīnd'sīt, *n.* Rear sight on a gun; judgment of an incident after it has passed; opposite of *foresight*.

hinder, hin'dėr, *v.t.* [A.Sax. *hindrian*, to hinder, from *hinder*, compar. of *hind, a.* (which see).] To prevent from proceeding or from starting; to stop; to interrupt; to obstruct; to impede; to check or retard in progression or motion; to debar; to shut out; to balk; often with *from* and a verbal noun (to *hinder* him *from* going; the *from* is sometimes omitted).—*v.i.* To interpose obstacles or impediments.—**hinderer,** hin'dėr•ėr, *n.* One who hinders.—**hindrance,** hin'drans, *n.* The act of hindering, that which hinders; impediment; obstruction; obstacle.

Hindu, Hindoo, hin•dö' or hin'dö, *n.* A disciple of Hinduism; an Asiatic Indian.—**Hinduism, hindooism,** hin'dö•izm, *n.* The doctrines and rites of the Hindus; Brahmanism.—**Hindustani,** hin•dö•stan'i, *n.* A language of Hindustan, akin to Sanskrit, but having a large admixture of Persian and Arabic words, spoken more or less throughout nearly the whole Peninsula.—**Hindi,** hin'di, *n.* A language of Northern India akin to Hindustani, but much more purely Sanskrit.

hinge, hinj, *n.* [Probably from *hang*, O. and Prov. E. and Sc. *hing*; comp. Prov. E. *hingle*, a small hinge; D. *hengsel*, a hinge.] The hook or joint on which a door, lid, gate, or shutter, and the like turns; the joint of a bivalve shell; *fig.* that on which anything depends or turns; a governing principle, rule, or point.—*v.t.* To furnish with hinges.—*v.i.*—*hinged, hinging*. To stand, depend, or turn, as on a hinge.

hint, hint, *n.* [Perhaps from O.E. *hente*, A.Sax. *hentan*, to seize; comp. also Icel. *ymtr*, a muttering.] A motive or occasion (*Shak.*); a distant allusion or slight mention; a word or two suggesting or insinuating something; a suggestion.—*v.t.* To bring to notice by a hint; to suggest indirectly. ∴ To *hint* is merely to make some reference or allusion that may or may not be apprehended; to *suggest* is to offer something definite for consideration.—*v.i.* To make or utter a hint.—*To hint at*, to allude to.—**hinter,** hin'tėr, *n.* One who hints.—**hintingly,** hin'-ting•li, *adv.* In a hinting manner.

hinterland, hin'tėr•land, *n.* [G.] The outlying region, remote from any towns.

hip, hip, *n.* [A.Sax. *hype*=Icel. *huppr*, Dan. *hofte*, Goth. *hups*, D. *heup*, G. *hufte*; akin to *heap*, perhaps to *hump.*] The fleshy projecting part of the thigh; the haunch; *arch.* the external angle at the junction of two sloping roofs or sides of a roof.—*To have a person on the hip*, to have the advantage over him; to have got some catch on him.—*To smite hip and thigh*, to overthrow completely with great slaughter (O.T.).—*v.t.*—*hipped, hipping*. To sprain or dislocate the hip.—**hip joint,** *n.* The joint of the hip, a ball-and-socket joint.—**hip roof,** *n.* A roof, the ends of which slope inwards with the same inclination to the horizon as its two other sides.—**hipshot,** *a.* Having the hip dislocated; lame; awkward.

hip, hip, *n.* [A.Sax. *heope.*] The fruit of the dog rose or wild brier.

hip, hip, *n.* [Contr. of *hypochondria.*] Hypochondria.—*v.t.* To render hypochondriac or melancholy.—**hipped,** hipt, *p.* and *a.* Rendered melancholy; characterized by melancholy.—**hippish,** hip′ish, *a.* Somewhat melancholy or hypochondriac.

hip, hip, *interj.* An exclamation expressive of a call to any one or to arouse attention (*hip, hip, hip,* hurrah!).

hippocras, hip′o•kras, *n.* [Fr., lit. wine of *Hippocrates.*] A medicinal drink, composed of wine with an infusion of spices and other ingredients, used as a cordial.—**Hippocratic,** hip•o•krat′ik, *a.* Pertaining to Hippocrates, a Greek physician, born 460 B.C.—*Hippocratic oath*, pledge to a code of ethics taken by those entering upon medical practice.

Hippocrene, hip′o•krēn, *n.* [Gr. horse fount.] Fountain on Mount Helicon, the seat of the Muses in Boeotia, produced by the stamp of the foot of the winged horse Pegasus; source of poetic inspiration.

hippodrome, hip′o•drōm, *n.* [Gr. *hippodromos*—*hippos*, a horse, *dromos*, a course.] Anciently, a place in which horse races and chariot races were performed; a circus.

hippogriff, hippogryph, hip′o•grif, *n.* [Gr. *hippos*, a horse, and *gryps*, a griffon.] A fabulous monster, half horse and half griffon.

hippophagy, hip•pof′a•ji, *n.* [Gr. *hippos*, a horse, and *phagō*, to eat.] The act or practice of feeding on horse-flesh.—**hippophagous,** hip•pof′a•gus, *a.* Feeding on horse flesh.

hippopotamus, hip•o•pot′a•mus, *n.* pl. **hippopotamuses** or **hippopotami,** hip•o•pot′a•mus•ez, hip•o•pot′a•mi. [Gr. *hippos*, a horse, and *potamos*, a river.] A hoofed quadruped of great bulk inhabiting lakes and rivers in Africa, being an excellent swimmer and diver, and feeding on herbage.

hircine, hėr′sīn, *a.* [L. *hircinus*, from *hircus*, a goat.] Pertaining to or resembling a goat; having a strong, rank smell like a goat; goatish.

hire, hīr, *v.t.*—*hired, hiring.* [A.Sax. *hýrian*, from *hýr*, hire; Dan. *hyre*, to hire, *hyre*, wages, Sw. *hyra*, G. *heuer*, hire.] To procure from another person and for temporary use at a certain price or equivalent; to engage in service for a stipulated reward; to grant the temporary use or service of for compensation; to let: in this sense usually with *out*, and often reflexively.—*n.* The compensation given for the temporary use of anything; the reward or recompense paid for personal service; wages.—**hireling,** hīr′ling, *n.* [A.Sax. *hýreling.*] One who is hired or who serves for wages; a venal or mercenary person.—*a.* Venal; mercenary.—**hirer,** hī′rėr, *n.* One that hires.

hirsute, hėr•sūt′, *a.* [L. *hirsutus*, shaggy, from *hirtus*, hairy, connected with *horrid.*] Rough with hair; hairy; shaggy.—**hirsuteness,** hėr•sūt′nes, *n.*

hirundine, hi•run′dīn, *a.* and *n.* [L. *hirundo*, a swallow.] Swallow-like; a swallow.

his, hiz, *pron.* [In A.Sax. the genit. sing. of *hé*, he, and of *hit*, it.] The possessive case singular of the personal pronoun *he*; of or belonging to him; formerly also used for *its*.

hispid, his′pid, *a.* [L. *hispidus*, rough, hairy. HIDEOUS.] Rough; shaggy; bristly; *bot.* beset with stiff bristles.—**hispidity,** his•pid′i•ti, *n.* The state of being hispid.—**hispidulous,** his•pid′ū•lus, *a. Bot.* having short stiff hairs.

hiss, his, *v.i.* [A.Sax. *hysian*, O.D. *hissen*, imitative of sound.] To make a sound like that of the letter *s*, in contempt or disapprobation; to emit a similar sound; said of serpents, of water thrown on hot metal, etc,—*v.t.* To condemn by hissing; to express disapproval of by hissing.—*n.* The sound made by propelling the breath between the tongue and upper teeth, as in pronouncing the letter *s*, especially as expressive of disapprobation; any similar sound.

hist, hist, *exclam.* [Origin unknown.] A word commanding silence, equivalent to *hush*, be silent.

histamine, his′tä•mēn, *n.* [*His*tadine and *amine.*] A substance occurring in animal and vegetable tissues, used to dilate blood vessels and stimulate gastric secretions in treating certain diseases.

histological, his•to•loj′i•kal, *a.* [Gr. *histos*, tissue.] Pertaining to histology.—**histologist,** his•tol′o•jist, *n.*—**histology,** his•tol′o•ji, *n.* The science which deals with the microscopic structure of the tissues and organs.

history, his′to•ri, *n.* [L. *historia*, a history, from Gr. *historia*, a learning by inquiry, from G. *histor*, knowing, learned.] That branch of knowledge which deals with events that have taken place in the world's existence; the study or investigation of the past; a narrative or account of an event or series of events in the life of a nation, or that have marked the progress or existence of any community or institution; a verbal relation of facts or events; a narrative; an account of things that exist; a description; an account of an individual person.—**historian,** his•tō′ri•an, *n.* A writer or compiler of history; a historical writer.—**historic, historical,** his•tor′ik, his•tor′i•kal, *a.* [L. *historicus.*] Pertaining to or connected with history; containing or contained in, deduced from, suitable to, representing, etc., history.—**historically,** his•tor′i•kal•li, *adv.* In a historic manner.—**historied,**† his′to•rid, *a.* Recorded in history.—**historiographer,** his•tō′ri•og″ra•fėr, *n.* A historian; particularly, a professed or official historian.—**historiography,** his•tō′ri•og″ra•fi, *n.* The art or employment of a historian; the writing of history.

histrionic, histrionical, his•tri•on′ik, his•tri•on′i•kal, *a.* [L. *histrionicus*, from *histrio*, an actor; same root as Skr. *has*, to laugh at.] Pertaining to an actor or stage player; belonging to stage playing; theatrical; stagey; feigned for purposes of effect.—**histrionic,**† his•tri•on′ik, *n.* A dramatic performer.—**histrionically,** his•tri•on′i•kal•li, *adv.* In a histrionic manner.—**histrionics,** his•tri•on′iks, *n.* The art of theatrical representation.—**histrionism, histrionicism,** his′tri•on•izm, his•tri•on′i•sizm, *n.* Stage playing; theatrical or artificial manners or deportment.

hit, hit, *v.t.*—*hit, hitting.* [Same as Icel. *hitta*, Dan. *hitte*, to hit, to meet with.] To strike or touch with some degree of force; not to miss; to give a blow to; to reach or attain to an object desired; to light upon; to get hold of or come at (to *hit* a likeness); to suit; to agree with.—*v.i.* To strike; to meet; to clash: followed by *against* or *on*; to agree; suit.—*n.* The act of hitting; the blow which successfully strikes the target aimed at; a person or thing that is a noted success; *baseball*, a blow by which the ball is knocked, permitting the batter to get on base; an effective phrase or remark.—**hit-and-miss,** *a.* Sometimes effective, sometimes not; careless.—**hit-and-run,** *a. Baseball*, a play in which a runner starts for the next base, as the pitcher starts to pitch and the batter tries to hit the ball behind the runner; a term for motor vehicle drivers who leave the scene of an accident in which they are involved.—**hitter,** hit′er, *n.*

hitch, hich, *v.i.* [Comp. Prov. E. *hick*, to hop or spring; G. dial. *hiksen*, to limp; Sc. *hotch*, to move by jerks, to hobble; Prov. E. *huck*, to shrug.] To move by jerks or with stops; to become entangled; to be caught or hooked (the cord *hitched* on a branch); to be linked or yoked.—*v.t.* To fasten; to yoke; to make fast; to hook; to raise or pull up; to raise by jerks (to *hitch up* one's trousers).—*n.* A catch; an impediment; a breakdown, especially of a casual and temporary nature; a heave or pull up; temporary help or assistance (to give one a *hitch*); *naut.* a kind of knot or noose in a rope for fastening it to an object.—**hitchhike,** hich′hīk, *v.i.* To travel by getting free rides, especially in passing automobiles.—**hitchhiker,** hich′hīk•er, *n.*

hither, hiᴛʜ′ėr, *adv.* [A.Sax. *hider*,

hither, Goth. *hídre*, Icel. *hethra*, hither, from stem of *he* with comparative suffix.] To this place; here: with verbs signifying motion.—*Hither and thither*, to this place and that.—*a.* On this side or in this direction; nearer.—**hitherto,** hiTH'ėr•tö, *adv.* To this time or place; until now.—**hitherward,** *adv.* Toward this place.

hive, hīv, *n.* [A.Sax. *hýf*, *hýfe*, *hýfi*, a hive; probably of same root as L. *cupa*, a cup, whence E. *cup*, *cupola*, *goblet*, etc.] A box or kind of basket for the reception and habitation of a swarm of honeybees; the bees inhabiting a hive; a place swarming with busy occupants.—*v.t.*—*hived*, *hiving*. To collect into a hive; to cause to enter a hive; to lay up in store for future use.—*v.i.* To take shelter together; to reside in a collective body.

hives, hīvz, *n.* [Perhaps akin to *heave.*] The eruption of urticaria.

ho, hoa, hō' hō'a, *interj.* [Fr. *ho*, Icel. *hó.*] A cry or call to arrest attention.

hoar, hōr, *a.* [A.Sax. *hár*, hoary, grayhaired; Icel. *hárr*, hoar, *hæra*, gray hair, hoariness; comp. Sc. *haar*, a whitish mist.] White (*hoarfrost*); gray or grayish white; white with age; hoary.—*n.* Hoariness; antiquity.—*v.i.* To become moldy or musty.—**hoarfrost,** *n.* The white particles of frozen dew, rime.—**hoariness,** hō'ri•nes, *n.* The state of being hoary.—**hoary,** hō'ri, *a.* White or gray with age; hence, *fig.* remote in time past; *bot.* covered with short, dense, grayish-white hairs; canescent.

hoard, hōrd, *n.* [A.Sax. *hord*=O.Sax. and G. *hort*, Icel. *hood*, Goth. *huzd*, hoard, treasure; from root of *house*, and of L. *custos*, a guardian.] A store, stock, or large quantity of anything accumulated or laid up; a hidden stock.—*v.t.* To collect and lay up in a hoard; to amass and deposit in secret: often followed by *up.*—*v.i.* To collect and form a hoard; to lay up store of money.—**hoarder,** hōr'dėr, *n.* One who hoards.

hoarding, hōr'ding, *n.* [O.Fr. *horde*, a barrier. HURDLE.] A timber enclosure round a building when the latter is in the course of erection or undergoing alteration or repair.

hoarse, hōrs, *a.* [A.Sax. *hás*, hoarse, husky=Icel. *háss*, Dan. *haes*, D. *heesch*, G. *heiser*, hoarse: the *r* is intrusive.] Having a harsh, rough, grating voice, as when affected with a cold; giving out a harsh, rough cry or sound.—**hoarsely,** hōrs'li, *adv.* In a hoarse manner.—**hoarsen,** hōr'sn, *v.t.* and *i.* To make or to grow hoarse.—**hoarseness,** hōrs'nes, *n.* The state or quality of being hoarse.

hoax, hōks, *n.* [For *hocus.*] Something done for deception or mockery; a trick played off in sport; a practical joke.—*v.t.* To play a trick upon for sport or without malice.—**hoaxer,** hōk'sėr, *n.* One that hoaxes.

hob, hob, *n.* [Same as *hub*; comp. Dan. *hob*, a heap; *hump* is akin, and *hobnail* is a compound.] The part of a grate or fireplace on which things are placed in order to be kept warm.

hobble, hob'l, *v.i.*—*hobbled*, *hobbling*. [From or connected with *hop*; comp. D. *hobbelen*, to hobble, to stammer.] To walk lamely, bearing chiefly on one leg; to limp; to walk awkwardly; to wabble or wobble; *fig.* to halt or move irregularly in versification.—*v.t.* To hopple.—*n.* A halting gait; a difficulty; a scrape; a clog; a fetter.—**hobbler,** hob'lėr, *n.* One that hobbles.—**hobblingly,** hob'ling•li, *adv.*

hobbledehoy, hob'l•di•hoi, *n.* [Of uncertain origin.] A raw gawky youth approaching manhood.

hobby, hob'i, *n.* [Comp. Fr. *hoberau*, dim. of O.Fr. *hobe*, a little bird of prey.] A small but strong-winged Old World falcon.

hobby, hob'i, *n.* [M.E. *hoby*, *hobyn*, perhaps for *Hobbin*, nickname of Robert or Robin.] A favorite pursuit; an interest apart from one's regular work, as painting or gardening, enjoyed as a relaxation.

hobbyhorse, hob'i•hors, *n.* [Comp. D. *hoppe*, a mare.] A figure of a horse on which children ride.

hobgoblin, hob•gob'lin, *n.* [From *hob*, formerly a rustic, a clown, an elf; corruption of *Robin*, *Robert.*] A goblin; an elf; an imp.

hobnail, hob'nāl, *n.* [*Hob*, a projection, and *nail.*] A nail with a thick strong head used for shoeing horses, or for the soles of heavy boots.—**hobnailed,** hob'nāld, *a.* Set with hobnails; rough.

hobnob, hob'nob, *v.i.* [Lit., have or not have, drink if it please you—A.Sax. *habban*, to have, and *nabban*, for *ne habban*, not to have.] To drink familiarly; to clink glasses; to be boon or intimate companions.

hobo, hō'bō, *n.* [From *hey* and *beau.*] A migratory worker; a tramp.

hock, hok, *n.* [A.Sax. *hóh*, the heel; Icel. *ha*, D. *hak.*] The joint of an animal between the knee and the fetlock.

hock, hok, *v.t.* [D. *hok*, hovel, prison.] To hamstring; to pawn; to pledge.

hock, hok, *n.* [G. *Hochheimer*, from *Hochheim*, in Nassau, where it is produced.] A light sort of Rhenish wine which is either sparkling or still.

hockey, hok'i, *n.* [From *hook.*] A game played on ice (ice hockey) or in a field (field hockey) in which opposing teams try to send a rubber disk or a ball into each other's goal.—**hockey stick,** a club curved at the lower end, used in the game of hockey.

hocus, hō'kus, *v.t.*—*hocussed*, *hocussing*. [The *hocus* of *hocus-pocus.*] To impose upon; to cheat; to hoax; to stupefy with drugged liquor for the purpose of cheating or robbing; to drug for this purpose.—**hocus-pocus,** hō'kus•pō'kus, *n.* [An invented word imitative of Latin.] A juggler's trick; trickery used by conjurers.—*v.t.* and *i.* To cheat; to trick.

hod, hod, *n.* [Northern English for *hold.*] A kind of trough for carrying mortar and bricks to masons and bricklayers, fixed to the end of a a pole, and borne on the shoulder.—**hod carrier, hodman,** a worker who carries bricks or mortar in a hod.

hodgepodge, hoj'poj, *n.* [Corruption of *hotchpot.*] A mixed mass; a medley of ingredients, in Scotland, a thick soup of vegetables boiled with beef or mutton (in this sense always *hotch-potch*).

hoe, hō, *n.* [O.Fr. *hoe*, Fr. *houe*, from the German; O.H.G. *houwa*, G. *haue*. HEW.] An instrument for cutting up weeds and loosening the earth in fields and gardens.—*v.t.*—*hoed*, *hoeing*. To cut, dig, scrape, or clean with a hoe.—*v.i.* To use a hoe.

hog, hog, *n.* [W. *hwch*, Corn. *hoch*, Armor. *houch hoch*, a sow, swine, hog.] A swine; a pig, or any animal of that species; a castrated boar; a sheep of a year old; a brutal fellow; one who is mean and filthy.—**hoggish,** hog'ish, *a.* Having the qualities of a hog; brutish; filthy.—**hoggishly,** hog'ish•li, *adv.* In a hoggish manner.—**hoggishness,** hog'ish•nes, *n.*—**hogwash,** *n.* The refuse of a kitchen or a brewery, or like matter given to swine; swill.

hogan, hō'gan, *n.* [From Navaho *qoghan*, a hut.] The dwelling of the Navaho Indian, a hut made of earth and branches.

hogmanay, hog'ma•nā, *n.* [Of French origin, and same as Norman *hoguinané*, O.Fr. *aguillanneuf*, a cry used in connection with New Year's gifts, and the last day of December, meaning perhaps 'to the mistletoe the New Year'.] The name given in Scotland to the last day of the year.

hogshead, hogz'hed, *n.* [Corrupted from D. *okshoofd*, Dan. *oxehoved*, the measure called a hogshead, and lit. ox's head; probably modified from some term of quite other meaning.] A large cask, especially a cask containing from 63 to 140 gallons; a liquid measure of 63 gallons or 238.5 liters; abbreviated to *hhd.*

hoiden, hoi'dn. See HOYDEN.

hoist, hoist, *v.t.* [O.E. *hoise*, Sc. *heese*=D. *hijsschen*, *hysen*, L.G. *hissen*, Dan. *heise*, *hisse*, to hoist; the *t* was added as in *against*, *amongst.*] To heave or raise; especially to raise by means of block and tackle.—*n.* The act of hoisting; that by which anything is hoisted; a machine for elevating goods, passengers, etc., in a warehouse, hotel, and the like; an elevator.—*pp.* Hoisted.

hoity-toity, hoi'ti•toi'ti. An exclamation denoting surprise or disapprobation, with some degree of contempt; equivalent to pshaw!—*a.* Elated; flighty; petulant.

hokum, hō'kum, *n.* [HOCUS-POCUS.] Material, especially speech, given a deliberate simulation of significance in order to excite interest and emotion; pleasing and effective nonsense; bunk; empty talk: claptrap.

hold, hōld, *v.t.* pret. & pp. *held.* [A.Sax. *healdan*=Dan. *holde,* D. *houden,* Icel. *halda,* Goth. *haldan,* G. *halten,* to hold; hence *behold.*] To have or grasp in the hand; to grasp and retain (to *hold* a sword, a pen, a candle); to bear, put, or keep in a certain position (to *hold* the hands up); to consider; to regard (I *hold* him in honor); to account (I *hold* it true); to contain, or to have capacity to receive and contain; to retain within itself; to keep from running or flowing out; to keep possession of; to maintain, uphold, preserve; not to lose; to be in possession of; to possess, occupy, own, keep; to have or to entertain (to *hold* enmity); to derive or deduce title to (he *held* lands of the king); to stop, restrain, withhold; to keep fixed, as to a certain line of action; to bind or oblige (to *hold* one to his promise); to keep in continuance or practice (to *hold* intercourse); to prosecute or carry on, observe, pursue (a course, an argument); to celebrate, solemnize, carry out (a feast, a meeting); to occupy or keep employed; to engage the attention of.—*To hold in play,* to keep occupied so as to withdraw from something else.—*To hold water* (*fig.*), to be logically sound or capable of standing investigation,—*To hold in,* to guide with a tight rein; hence, to restrain, check, repress.—*To hold off,* to keep off; to keep from touching.—*To hold out,* to extend; to stretch forth; hence, to propose; to offer.—*To hold up,* to raise; to keep in an erect position; to sustain, support, uphold; to show, exhibit, put prominently forward.—*To hold one's own,* to keep good one's present condition; not to lose ground.—*To hold one's peace,* to keep silence.—*To hold the plow,* to guide it in plowing.—*v.i.* To take or keep a thing in one's grasp; to maintain an attachment; to continue firm; not to give way or break; to adhere; to stand, be valid, apply (the argument *holds* good, this *holds* true); to stand one's ground; generally with *out* (the garrison *held out*); to refrain; to be dependent on for possessions, to derive right or title: with *of,* sometimes *from;* to stop, stay, or wait; to cease or give over: chiefly in the imperative. —*To hold forth,* to speak in public.—*To hold off,* to keep at a distance; to avoid connection.—*To hold on,* to continue; to keep fast hold; to cling; to proceed in a course.—*To hold to,* to cling or cleave to; to adhere.—*To hold with,* to side with; to stand up for.—*To hold together,* not to separate; to remain in union.—*Hold on! hold hard!* stop; cease.—*n.* A grasp, gripe, clutch (often in to *take hold,* to *lay hold*); *fig.* mental grasp; grasp on or influence working on the mind; something which may be seized for support; power of keeping; authority to seize or keep; claim; a place of confinement; a position of strength, a keep, stronghold; the whole interior cavity of a ship between the bottom and deck or lowest deck (in this sense seems modified from D. *hol,* a hole, a ship's hold).—**holder,** hōl′dėr, *n.* One who or that which holds; a payee of a bill of exchange or a promissory note.—**holdfast,** hōld′-fast, *n.* Something used to secure and hold in place something else.—**holding,** hōl′ding, *n.* A tenure; a farm held of a superior; that which holds, binds, or influences.

hole, hōl, *n.* [A.Sax. *hol,* hollow, hole; D. *hol,* Icel. *hol, hola,* a hollow, a cavity; G. *hohl,* hollow; of same root as A.Sax. *helan,* to cover, whence *hell;* or as Gr. *koilos,* hollow.] A hollow place or cavity in any solid body; a perforation, orifice, aperture, pit, rent, fissure, crevice, etc.; the excavated habitation of certain wild beasts; a mean habitation; a wretched abode.—*v.i.*—*holed, holing.* To go into a hole.—*v.t.* To make a hole or holes in; to drive into a hole; *mining,* to undercut a coal seam.

holily, holiness. See HOLY.

holiday, hol′i•dā, *n.* [M.E. from O.E. *haligdaeg,* holy day.] Any day in which, by custom or law, ordinary business is suspended; a religious feast day; a day or several days exempt from labor.

holla, hollo, holloa, hol•lä′, hol•lō′. [Fr. *holà—ho!* ho! and *là,* there.] An exclamation to some one at a distance, in order to call attention or in answer to one that hails.—*v.i.* To call, shout, or cry aloud.

holland, hol′and, *n.* A kind of fine linen originally manufactured in *Holland;* also a coarser linen fabric used for covering furniture, carpets, etc.—**Hollander,** hol′an•dėr, *n.* A native of Holland.—**Hollands,** hol′-andz, *n.* A sort of gin imported from Holland.

hollow, hol′ō, *a.* [A.Sax. *holg, holh,* a hollow space, from *hol,* a hole. HOLE.] Containing an empty space within; having a vacant space within; not solid; concave; sunken (eye, cheek); sounding as if reverberated from a cavity; deep or low; not sincere or faithful; false; deceitful.—*n.* A depression or excavation below the general level or in the substance of anything; a cavity.—*v.t.* To make a hollow or cavity in, to excavate.—*adv.* Utterly; completely (in certain phrases, as he beat him *hollow*).—**hollowhearted,** *a.* Insincere; deceitful; not true.—**hollowly,** hol′ō•li, *adv.* In a hollow manner.—**hollowness,** hol′ō•nes, *n.* The state or quality of being hollow.

holly, hol′i, *n.* [O.E. *holin,* A.Sax. *holegn, holen,* holly, allied to W. *celyn,* Gael. *cuilionn,* holly.] An evergreen tree or shrub with indented thorny leaves, and which produces clusters of beautiful red berries; also a name sometimes given to the holm oak, an evergreen oak.—*kneeholly,* butcher's-broom.

hollyhock, hol′i•hok, *n.* [Lit. holy hock—*hock* being A.Sax. *hoc,* W. *hocys,* mallow; so called because brought from the Holy Land.] A tall single-stemmed biennial plant of the mallow family, a frequent ornament of gardens.

holm, hōlm or hōm, *n.* [A.Sax. L.G., G., and Dan. *holm,* a small island in a river; Sw. *holme,* Icel. *hólmr,* an island.] A river island; a low flat tract of rich land by the side of a river.

holmium, hōl′mi•um, *n.* [From *Stockholm,* Sweden.] A metallic element, one of the rare-earth series. Symbol, Ho; at. no., 67; at. wt., 164.930.

holm oak, hōlm or hōm, *n.* [Lit. hollyoak, *holm* being from A.Sax. *holen,* holly, the leaves resembling those of the holly. HOLLY.] The evergreen oak.

holoblast, hol′o•blast, *n.* [Gr. *holos,* whole, and *blastos,* a bud or germ.] *Zool.* an ovum consisting entirely of germinal matter. MEROBLAST.—**holoblastic,** hol′o•blas•tik, *a.* Pertaining to a holoblast; of fertilized ova from which the embryo is formed by complete division or cleavage.

holocaust, hol′o•kąst, *n.* [Gr. *holos,* whole, and *kaustos,* burned.] A burnt sacrifice or offering, the whole of which was consumed by fire; a great slaughter or sacrifice of life.

holograph, hol′o•graf, *n.* [Gr. *holos,* whole, and *graphein,* to write.] Any document, as a letter, deed, etc., wholly written by the person in whose name it appears. Used also as an adj.—**holographic, holographical,** hol•o•graf′ik, hol•o•graf′i•kal, *a.* Being holograph; written by the grantor or testator himself.

holophotal, hol•o•fō′tal, *a.* [Gr. *holos,* whole, and *phōs, phōtos,* light.] *Optics,* reflecting the rays of light in one unbroken mass without perceptible loss.

holothurian, hol•o•thū′ri•an, *n.* [Gr. *holothourion,* a sea animal; origin doubtful.] One of the sea cucumbers or sea slugs.

Holstein, hōl′stīn, *n.* [From *Holstein,* a region in northwest Germany.] A breed of black and white dairy cattle that produces low-fat milk.

holster, hōl′stėr, *n.* [D. *holster,* a pistolcase=A.Sax. *hoolster,* a cover, a recess; Icel. *hulster,* Dan. *hulster,* a case; root seen in A.Sax. *helad,* to cover, whence also *hell.*] A leather case for a pistol, usually hung on a belt or saddle.

holus-bolus, hō′lus-bō′lus, *adv.* [From *whole,* and *bolus,* a pill.] All at a gulp; altogether; all at once. (*Vulgar.*)

holy, hō′li, *a.* [A.Sax. *hálig,* holy, from *hál,* whole; similarly D. and G. *heilig,* Icel. *heilagr,* Dan. *hellig,* holy; akin *hale, heal, hallow, whole,* etc., same root also in Gr. *kalos,* beautiful.] Free from sin and sinful affections; pure in heart; pious; godly; hallowed; consecrated or set apart to a sacred use.—**holily,** hō′li•li, *adv.* In a holy manner.—**holiness,** hō′li•nes, *n.* The state or quality of being holy or sinless; sanctity; godliness; sacredness; *his holiness,* a title of the pope.—*Holy* *of holies*, the innermost apartment of the Jewish tabernacle or temple, where the ark was kept.—*Holy Ghost* or *Holy Spirit*, the Divine Spirit; the third person in the Trinity.—*Holy Office*, the Inquisition.—*Holy Thursday*, Ascension Day; also Thursday in Holy Week. —*Holy Saturday*, Saturday in Holy Week.—*Holy water*, in the *Roman Catholic Church*, water consecrated by the priest, and used in various rites and ceremonies.—*Holy week*, the week before Easter (the last week of Lent). —*Holy Writ*, the sacred Scriptures. —**holystone,** *n.* A soft sandstone used by seamen for cleaning the decks of ships.—*v.t.* To scrub with holystone.

homage, hom′ij, *n.* [Fr. *hommage*, O.Fr. *homenage*, L.L. *hominaticum*, homage, from L. *homo*, *hominis*, a man, in late times a vassal. HUMAN.] Acknowledgment of vassalage made by a feudal tenant to his lord on receiving investiture of a fee; hence, obeisance; respect paid by external action; reverence directed to the Supreme Being; reverential worship; devout affection.—*v.t.* To pay homage to.—**homager,** hom′ij•ėr, *n.* One who does or is bound to do homage.

home, hōm, *n.* [A.Sax. *hám*, home, house, dwelling=L.G. and Fris. *ham*, D. and G. *heim*, Icel. *heimr*, Goth. *haims*, abode, village, etc.; cog. Gr. *kōmē*, a village, *keimai*, I rest; probably L. *quies*, quiet, etc.] One's own abode or dwelling; the abode of the family or household of which one forms a member; abiding place; one's own country; the seat (the *home* of war); an institute or establishment affording to the homeless, sick, or destitute the comforts of a home (a sailors' *home*, an orphan's *home*, etc.).—*At home*, in or about one's own house or abode; in one's own country.—*At home in* or *on a subject*, conversant, familiar, thoroughly acquainted with it.—*To make one's self at home*, to conduct one's self in another's house as unrestrainedly as if at home. —*a.* Connected with one's home; domestic; often opposed to *foreign*.—*Home economics*, the domestic science of making and caring for a home.—*adv.* To one's home or one's native country; often opposed to *abroad*; to one's self; to the point; to the mark aimed at; so as to produce an intended effect; effectively; thoroughly (to strike *home*).—**home-bred,** hōm′bred, *a.* Bred at home; originating at home; not foreign; not polished by travel.—**homeless,** hōm′les, *a.* Destitute of a home.—**homelessness,** hōm′les•nes, *n.* The state of being homeless.—**homeliness,** hōm′li•nes, *n.* The state or quality of being homely.—**homely,** hōm′li, *a.* Pertaining to home; domestic‡; of plain features; not handsome; like that which is made for common domestic use; plain; coarse; not fine or elegant.—**home-made,** *a.* Made at home; of domestic manufacture.—**home plate,** a five-sided plate of rubber, set in the ground, beside which the batter stands (*Baseball*).—**homer,** hō′mer, *n.* A *home run* (*Colloq.*)—**home rule,** government of a district, colony, territory, etc., by the inhabitants themselves, particularly with regard to local matters.—**home run,** a hit which, unaided by error, allows the batter to circle the bases and return to the home plate (*Baseball*).—**homesick,** *a.* Ill from being absent from home; affected with homesickness.—**homesickness,** *n.* Intense and uncontrolled grief at a separation from one's home or native land; nostalgia; longing for home.—**homespun,** hōm′spun, *a.* Spun or wrought at home; hence, plain; coarse; homely.—*n.* Cloth made at home.—**homestead,** hōm′sted, *n.* A house or mansion with the grounds and buildings immediately contiguous; a home.—**home stretch,** the section of a racecourse between the last curve and the finish.—**homeward, homewards,** hōm′wėrd, hōm′werdz, *adv.* Toward home, toward one's abode or native country.—*a.* Being in the direction of home.—**homework,** work to be done at home, especially that assigned by a teacher to students.—**homing,** hōm′ing, *a.* Coming home; a term applied to birds, such as the carrier pigeon.

homeopathy, hō•mē•op′a•thi, *n.* [Gr. *homoios*, like, *pathos*, feeling, suffering.] The system of treating disease by administering in minute quantities drugs which would, if given in larger doses, to a healthy person, produce symptoms similar to those of the disease.—**homeopathist,** hō•mē•op′a•thist, *n.* One who practices or supports homeopathy.

homer, hō′mėr, *n.* [Heb.] A Hebrew measure equivalent to about 75 gallons or to 11 bushels.

Homeric, hō•mer′ik, *a.* Pertaining to *Homer*, the great poet of Greece; resembling Homer's verse or style.

homicide, hom′i•sīd, *n.* [L. *homicidium*, the crime, *homicida*, the perpetrator—*homo*, man, and *cædo*, to strike, to kill.] The killing of one man or human being by another; a person who kills another; a manslayer.—**homicidal,** hom•i•sī′dal, *n.* Pertaining to homicide; murderous.

homily, hom′i•li, *n.* [Gr. *homilia*, intercourse or converse, instruction, a sermon, from *homilos*, a throng—*homos*, same (cog. with E. *same*), and *ilē*, a throng.] A discourse or sermon read or pronounced to an audience; a sermon; a serious discourse.—**homiletic, homiletical,** hom•i•let′ik, hom•i•let′i•kal, *a.* [Gr. *homilētikos.*] Relating to homilies or homiletics; hortatory.—*Homiletic theology*, homiletics.—**homiletics,** hom•i•let′iks, *n.* The art of preaching; that branch of practical theology which treats of sermons and the best mode of composing and delivering them.—**homilist,** hom′i•list, *n.* One that composes homilies; a preacher.

hominy, hom′i•ni, *n.* [Amer.-Indian *auhuminea*, parched corn.] Corn hulled and coarsely ground, prepared for food by being boiled with water.

homocentric, ho•mo•sen′trik, *a.* [Gr. *homos*, same, *kentron*, a center.] Having the same center; concentric.

homocercal, hō•mo•sėr′kal, *a.* [Gr. *homos*, same, *kerkos*, tail.] *Ichthyol.* having the lobes of the tail diverging symmetrically from the backbone, as in the cod, herring, etc. HETEROCERCAL.

homochromous, hō•mok′ro•mus, *a.* [Gr. *homos*, same, *chrōma*, color.] *Bot.* having all the florets of the same color.

homogamous, hō•mog′a•mus, *a.* [Gr. *homos*, same, *gamos*, marriage.] *Bot.* having all the florets of a flower head, or the florets of the spikelets in grasses, hermaphrodite. —**homogamy,** hō•mog′a•mi, *n.* The state of being homogamous.

homogeneous, ho•mō•jē′nē•us, *a.* [Gr. *homogenēs*—*homos*, like, and *genos*, kind; root *gen*, cog. with E. *kin.*] Of the same kind or nature; consisting of similar parts, or of elements of the like nature; opposite of *heterogeneous.*—**homogeneousness,** hō•mo•jē′nē•us•nes, *n.* The state or character of being homogeneous.—**homogenize,** ho•moj′e•nīz, *v.t.* To make homogeneous; to pass milk, cream, etc., through an apparatus that breaks up the fat globules to make the product the same throughout.

homogenesis, hō•mo•jen′e•sis, *n.* [Gr. *homos*, same, *genesis*, birth.] Sameness of origin; reproduction of offspring similar to their parents.

homograph, hō′mo•graf, *n.* [Gr. *homos*, same, *graphō*, to write.] A word which has exactly the same form as another, though of a different origin and signification; a homonym.—**homographic,** hō•mo•graf′ik, *a.* Relating to homographs.

Homoiousian, ho•moi•ö′si•an, *n.* [Gr. *homoios*, similar, and *ousia*, being.] A person holding the belief that the nature of Christ is not the same with, but only similar to, that of the Father. HOMOOUSIAN.

homologate, hō•mol′o•gāt, *v.t.*—*homologated*, *homologating*. [L.L. *homologo*, *homologatum*, from Gr. *homos*, same, and *logos*, discourse, from *legō*, to speak.] To approve; to express approval of or assent to; to ratify.

homologous, hō•mol′o•gus, *a.* [Gr. *homos*, same, and *logos*, proportion.] Having the same relative position, proportion, or structure; corresponding in use or general character; of similar type.—**homologue,** hō′mo•log, *n.* That which is homologous; an organ of an animal homologous with another organ.—**homology,** hō•mol′o•ji, *n.* The quality of being homologous; correspondence in character or relation; sameness or correspondence in organs of animals as regards general structure and type, thus the human arm corresponds to the foreleg of a quadruped and the wing of a bird.—**homological,** hō•mō•loj'i•kal, *a.* Pertaining to homology; having a structural affinity.—**homologically,** hō•mo•loj'i•kal•li, *adv.* In a homological manner.

homomorphous, homomorphic, hō•mo•mor'fus, hō•mo•mor'fik, *a.* [Gr. *homos,* same, *morphē,* shape.] Having the same external appearance or form.—**homomorphism,** hō•mo•mor'fizm, *n.* The condition of being homomorphous.

homonym, hō'mo•nim, *n.* [Gr. *homos,* same, *onoma,* name.] A word which agrees with another in sound, and perhaps in spelling, but differs from it in signification; a homograph; as *fair, a.* and *fair, n.*—**homonymic,** ho•mo•nim'ik, *a.* Relating to homonymy or to homonyms.—**homonymous,** hō•mon'i•mus, *a.* Having the same sound or spelling.—**homonymy,** hō•mon'i•mi, *n.* Sameness of name with a difference of meaning; ambiguity; equivocation.

Homoousian, hō•mō•ö'si•an, *n.* [Gr. *homos,* same, and *ousia,* being.] A person who maintains that the nature of the Father and the Son is the same, in opposition to the *Homoiousians.*

homophone, hō'mo•fōn, *n.* [Gr. *homos,* same, *phōnē,* sound.] A letter or character expressing a like sound with another; a word having the same sound as another; a homonym.—**homophonous,** hō•mof'o•nus, *a.* Of like sound; agreeing in sound but differing in sense.—**homophony,** hō•mof'o•ni, *n.* Sameness of sound.

homoplasmy, hō'mo•plas•mi, *n.* [Gr. *homos,* same, *plassō,* to form.] *Biol.* resemblance in form or structure with difference in origin.—**homoplastic,** *a.* Similar in form or structure.

Homo sapiens, hō'mō sā'pi•ens. [From O.L. *hĕmo,* man, and *sapio,* wise.] Modern man, the surviving species of the genus *Homo.*

homosexual, hō'mō•sek"shụ•al, *a.* [*Homo* and *sexual.*] Sexual attraction toward those of the same sex.—*n.* One who is attracted toward someone of the same sex.

homotaxis, hō•mo•tak'sis, *n.* [Gr. *homos,* same, *taxis,* arrangement.] Agreement in arrangement; *geol.,* agreement in the arrangement of strata in different localities.

homuncule, homunculus, hō•mung'kūl, hō•mung'kū•lus, *n.* [L., dim. of *homo,* a man.] A manikin; a dwarf.

hone, hōn, *n.* [A.Sax. *hán,* Icel. *hein,* Sw. *hen,* a hone, a whetstone; root seen in Skr. *co,* to sharpen, and in L. *conus,* a hone.] A stone of a fine grit, used for sharpening instruments that require a fine edge.—*v.t.* To sharpen on a hone.

honest, on'est, *a.* [O.Fr. *honeste* (Fr. *honnête*), from L. *honestus,* from *honor, honos,* honor. HONOR.] Fair in dealing with others; free from trickishness, fraud, or theft; upright; just; equitable; sincere, candid, or unreserved; honorable; reputable; chaste or virtuous; pleasant-looking in features.—**honestly,** on'est•li, *adv.* In an honest manner.—**honesty,** on'es•ti, *n.* The state or quality of being honest; integrity; uprightness; fairness; candor.

honey, hun'i, *n.* [A.Sax. *hunig*=D. and G. *honig,* Icel. *hunang,* honey.] A sweet, viscid juice, collected from flowers by several kinds of insects, especially bees; *fig.* sweetness or pleasantness; as a word of endearment, sweet one, darling.—*v.t.* To become sweet; to become complimentary or fawning.—*v.i.* To become tender and coaxing, also, to fawn (to *honey* up a person).—**honeybee,** *n.* A bee that produces honey; the hive bee.—**honeycomb,** *n.* The waxy structure formed by bees for the reception of honey, and for the eggs which produce their young.—**honeydew,** *n.* A sweet saccharine substance found on the leaves of trees and other plants in small drops like dew.—**honeydew melon,** a very sweet muskmelon with a white, smooth skin.—**honeyed, honied,** hun'id, *p.* and *a.* Covered with or as with honey; hence, sweet; full of compliments or tender words.—**honeymoon,** hun'i•mön, *n.* The first month after marriage; the interval spent by a newly married pair before settling down in a home of their own.—**honeysuckle,** hun'i•suk•l, *n.* [From children sucking the honey out of the nectary.] The popular name for a genus of upright or climbing shrubs with fragrant flowers of a tubular shape.

hong, hong, *n.* [Chinese *hong, hang.*] The Chinese name for foreign factories or mercantile houses.

honor, on'ėr, *n.* [O.Fr. *honor, honeur,* Fr. *honneur,* from L. *honor, honos,* honor, whence *honestus,* honest.] Esteem paid to worth; high estimation; reverence; veneration; any mark of respect or estimation by words or actions; dignity; exalted rank or place; distinction; reputation; good name; a nice sense of what is right, just, and true; scorn of meanness; a particular virtue, as bravery or integrity in men and chastity in females; one who or that which is a source of glory or esteem; he who or that which confers dignity (an *honor* to his country); title or privilege of rank or birth; one of the highest trump cards, as the ace, king, queen, or knave, and, in bridge, ten; a title of address or respect now restricted, except among the vulgar, to the holders of certain offices (e.g. judges): with *his, your,* etc.; (*pl.*) civilities paid, as at an entertainment; (*pl.*) academic and university distinction or pre-eminence.—*Honors of war,* distinctions granted to a vanquished enemy, as of marching out of a camp or intrenchments armed and with colors flying.—*An affair of honor,* a dispute to be decided by a duel.—*Word of honor,* a verbal promise or engagement which cannot be violated without disgrace.—*Debt of honor,* a debt, as a bet, for which no security is required or given except that implied by honorable dealing.—*Maid of honor,* a lady whose duty it is to attend a queen in public; chief attendant, if unmarried, of a bride at a wedding; if married, *matron of honor.*—*v.t.* To regard or treat with honor; to revere; to respect; to reverence; to bestow honor upon; to elevate in rank or station; to exalt; to render illustrious; *com.* to accept and pay when due (to *honor* a bill of exchange).—**honorarium,** on•ė•râ'ri•um, or hon', *n.* [L. *honorarium* (*donum,* gift).] A fee to a professional man for professional services.—**honorary,** on'ėr•e•ri, *a.* [L. *honorarius.*] Done or made in honor; indicative of honor; intended merely to confer honor (an *honorary* degree); possessing a title or post without performing services, or without receiving benefit or reward (an *honorary* secretary or treasurer).—**honorable,** on'ėr•a•bl, *a.* Worthy of being honored; estimable; illustrious or noble; actuated by principles of honor; conferring honor; consistent with honor or reputation; regarded with esteem; accompanied with marks of honor or testimonies of esteem; upright and laudable; directed to a just and proper end; not base; a title of distinction applied to certain members of noble families, persons in high position, etc., *right honorable* being a higher grade.—**honorableness,** on'ėr•a•bl•nes, *n.* The state of being honorable.—**honorably,** on'ėr•a•bli, *adv.* In an honorable manner.

hood, hụd, *n.* [A.Sax. *hód*=D. *hoed,* G. *hut,* a hat; allied to D. *heed*; G. *hüten,* D. *hoeden,* to protect; Skr. *chad,* to cover.] A soft covering for the head worn by females and children; the part of a monk's outer garment with which he covers his head; a cowl; a similar appendage to a cloak or overcoat; an ornamental fold at the back of an academic gown; a covering for a hawk's head or eyes, used in falconry; anything that resembles a hood in form or use.—*v.t.* To dress in a hood or cowl; to put a hood on; to cover or hide.—**hooded,** hụd'ed, *p.* and *a.* —**hoodwink,** hụd'wingk, *v.t.* To blind by covering the eyes; to blindfold; to deceive by external appearances.

hoodlum, höd'lum, *n.* A rowdy; a rough. (*Colloq.*)

hoodoo, hö'dö, *n.* VOODOO. Something which brings misfortune.—*v.t.* To bring bad luck. (*Colloq.*)

hooey, hö'i, *n.* and *interj.* Nonsense. (*Slang.*)

hoof, höf, *n.* pl. **hoofs,** rarely **hooves,** hövz. [A.Sax. *hóf,* Icel. *hófr.* D. *hoef,* Dan. *hov,* G. *huf,* a hoof.] The horny substance that covers the feet or the digits of the feet of certain animals, as horses, oxen, sheep, deer, etc.—**hoofbound,** *a. Farriery,* having a dryness and contraction of the hoof, which occasions pain and lameness.—**hoofed,** höft, *a.* Furnished with hoofs.

hook, hụk, *n.* [A.Sax. *hóc,* a hook, a crook=D. *hoek,* Icel. *haki,* G. *haken,* O.H.G. *hako,* a hook: same root as *hang*.] A piece of iron or other metal bent into a curve for catching, holding, or sustaining anything; any similar appliance; *baseball*, a curve; *boxing*, a short, swinging blow delivered with elbow bent but rigid.—*By hook or by crook*, by some means or other.—*v.t.* To catch or fasten with a hook or hooks; to bend into the form of a hook; to furnish with hooks; to catch by artifice; to entrap.—*v.i.* To bend; to be curving; to catch into something.—**hookedness,** hụk′ed•nes, *n.* —**hooker,** hụk′ėr, *n.*

hookah, hö′kä, *n.* [Ar.] A tobacco pipe with a long pliable tube and water vase so constructed that the smoke passes through the water before being inhaled.

hooker, hụk′ėr, *n.* [D. *hoeker, hoekboot*.] An Irish fishing smack.

hooky, hụk′i, *n.* [Probably from M.E. *haken*, from *hak*, hook.] A word used in the phrase *to play hooky*, to play truant.

hooligan, hö′li•gan, *n.* [Irish personal name.] A street rough or rowdy.

hoop, höp, *n.* [A.Sax. *hóp*, Fris. *hop*, D. *hoop*; akin *hump*.] A band of wood or metal used to confine the staves of casks, tubs, etc., or for other similar purposes; a combination of circles of thin whalebone or other elastic material used to expand the skirts of ladies' dresses; a farthingale; a crinoline.—*v.t.* To bind or fasten with hoops.—**hooper,** hö′pėr, *n.*

hoopoe, hö′pö, *n.* [Fr. *huppe*, L. *upupa*, Gr. *epops*, hoopoe: names given from its cry.] A beautiful bird with a crest, which it can erect or depress at pleasure, and a long, sharp, curved bill, found in Europe and North Africa and named for its whooping cry.

hoosegow, hoosgow, hös′gou, *n.* [Sp. *juzgado*, a court.] A place of confinement; a jail. (Slang)

Hoosier, hö′zhėr, *n.* A person from the state of Indiana, which is nicknamed the *Hoosier State*.

hoot, höt, *v.i.* [From the sound; comp. Fr. *houter*, to call, to cry.] To cry out or shout in contempt; to cry as an owl.—*v.t.* To utter cries or shouts in contempt of; to utter contemptuous cries or shouts at.—*n.* A cry or shout in contempt; the cry of an owl.

hootenanny, höt′nan•i, *n.* [Origin unknown.] An informal folksinging party, sometimes with dancing.

hop, hop, *v.i.*—*hopped, hopping*. [A. Sax. *hoppian*=Icel. and Sw. *hoppa*, D. *huppen*, G. *hüpfen*, to hop; akin *hobble, hobby*.] To hop or leap; to leap or spring on one foot.—*v.t.* To move by successive leaps, as a frog.—*n.* A leap on one leg; a short trip; an informal dance.—**hopper,** hop′ėr, *n.* One who hops; a wooden trough through which grain, coal, etc., pass into a mill, so named from its moving or shaking; any similar contrivance; a box that holds legislative bills.—**hopscotch,** *n.* A children's game which consists in hopping over scores or scotches on the ground.

hop, hop, *n.* [D. *hop, hoppe*, G. *hopfen*, hop.] A climbing plant of the hemp family, whose female flowers are used to flavor malt liquors and make them keep.—*v.t.*—*hopped, hopping*. To mix hops with.—*v.i.* To pick or gather hops.

hope, hōp, *n.* [A.Sax. *hopa*=D. *hoop*, Sw. *hopp*, Dan. *haab*, hope; G. *hoffen*, to hope; possibly akin to L. *cupio*, to desire.] A desire of some good, accompanied with at least a slight expectation of obtaining it, or a belief that it is obtainable; expectation of something desirable; confidence in a future event; trust; that which gives hope; one in whom trust or confidence is placed; the object of hope; the thing hoped for.—*Forlorn hope*. Under FORLORN. —*v.i.*—*hoped, hoping*. [A.Sax. *hopian*. D. *hopen*, to hope.] To entertain or indulge hope; to have confidence; to trust.—*v.t.* To entertain hope for; to desire with expectation. —**hopeful,** hōp′fụl, *a.* Full of or entertaining hope; having qualities which excite hope; promising.—*n.* A young person whose prospects are promising; one in whom another places hope.—**hopefully,** hōp′fụl•li, *adv.*—**hopefulness,** hōp′fụl•nes, *n.*—**hopeless,** hōp′les, *a.* Destitute of hope; giving no ground of hope.—**hopelessly,** hōp′les•li, *adv.*—**hopelessness,** hōp′les•nes, *n.*

hoplite, hop′līt, *n.* [Gr. *hoplitēs*, from *hoplon*, a weapon.] A heavy-armed soldier of ancient Greece.

hopple, hop′l, *v.t.* [From *hop*, to leap; also in form *hobble*.] To tie the feet of (a horse) near together to prevent leaping or running; to hobble.—*n.* A fetter for the legs of grazing horses or other animals.

horary, horal, hō′ra•ri, hō′ral, *a.* [L. *hora*, an hour.] Pertaining to the hours; occurring once an hour; hourly.

Horatian, ho•rā′shan, *a.* Relating to or resembling the Latin poet *Horace* (Horatius) or his poetry.

horde, hōrd, *n.* [Fr. *horde*, from Turk. and Per. *ordû*, court, camp, horde.] A tribe, clan, or race of Asiatic or other nomads; a wandering tribe; hence, a gang; a migratory crew; rabble.—*v.i.* To live in hordes; to huddle together.

horehound, hōr′hound, *a.* [A.Sax. *hárahune*—*hár*, hoar, and *hune*, the generic name of these plants.] The popular name of several plants of the mint family, one of which, white horehound, has an aromatic smell and bitter taste, and has been much in use for coughs and asthma. Written also *Hoarhound*.

horizon, ho•rī′zon, *n.* [Gr. *horizōn*, from *horizō*, to bound from *horos*, a limit; lit. that which bounds.] The circle which bounds that part of the earth's surface visible to a spectator from a given point; the apparent junction of the earth and sky; called the *visible* or *apparent horizon*; an imaginary great circle parallel to this whose plane passes through the center of the earth; called the *celestial horizon*.—*On the same horizon, geol.* said of fossils or strata which appear to be of the same age.—**horizontal,** hor•i•zon′tal, *a.* Pertaining to the horizon; on the same or a parallel plane with the horizon; on a level; measured or contained in the plane of the horizon (*horizontal* distance)—**horizontally,** hor•i•zon′tal•li, *adv.* In a horizontal direction or position.

hormone, hor′mōn, *n.* [Gr. *hormaō*, I excite.] An internal secretion of the endocrine glands, such as insulin, epinephrine, etc., carried by the blood to other organs, where it stimulates them to physiological activity; *bot.* similar substances operating in like manner in plants.—**hormonal,** hor•mōn′al, *a.*

horn, horn, *n.* [A.Sax. *horn*, a horn, a trumpet=Icel., Sw., Dan., and G. *horn*, D. *horen*, Goth. *haurn*; cog. W. and Armor. *corn*, L. *cornu*, Gr. *keras*—horn. *Hornet* is a derivative, and *hart* is akin.] A hard projecting appendage growing on the heads of certain animals, and particularly on cloven-hoofed quadrupeds; the material of which such horns are composed; a wind instrument of music, originally made of horn; a drinking cup of horn; a utensil for holding powder for immediate use, originally made of horn; a powder flask; something similar to a horn; the feeler of an insect, snail, etc.; an extremity of the moon when waxing or waning.—*Put to the horn*, to outlaw by three blasts on a horn at the Cross of Edinburgh for refusal to answer summons (in Scots law).—*To draw in the horns*, to repress one's ardor, or to restrain pride, in allusion to the habit of the snail withdrawing its feelers when startled.—**hornbeam,** horn′bēm, *n.* A small bushy tree of the oak family, with a hard white wood.—**hornbill,** horn′bil, *n.* A name of certain birds with very large bills surmounted by an extraordinary horny protuberance. —**hornblende,** horn′-blend, *n.* [G. *horn*, horn, and *blende*, blende (from *blenden*, to dazzle), from its horny and glittering appearance.] A dark green or black lustrous mineral of several varieties, an important constituent of several rocks.—**hornblendic,** horn•blen′dik, *a.* Containing hornblende; resembling hornblende.—**hornbook,** horn′-bụk, *n.* In former times a child's alphabet book or primer, with a transparent sheet of horn placed over the single page of which it usually consisted, the whole being fixed to a wooden frame.—**horned,** hornd, *a.* Having horns or projections resembling them (the *horned* moon); wearing horns; made a cuckold.—**hornless,** horn′les, *a.* Having no horns.—**hornmad,** *a.* Outrageous; stark mad: in allusion to a mad bull.—**hornpipe,** horn′pīp, *n.* A musical instrument formerly popular in Wales; a lively dance tune; a sprightly dance, usually performed by one person.—**hornstone,** horn′-stōn, *n.* A siliceous stone, a variety of quartz.—**horny,** hor′ni, *a.* Consisting or composed of horn; resembling horn in appearance or composition; exhibiting hardened skin.—**horned toad,** horn'd töd, *n.* A small, harmless North American lizard of the genus *Phrynosoma,* having hornlike spikes.

hornet, hor'net, *n.* [A.Sax. *hyrnet,* from *horn,* a horn, from its antennae or horns, or because its buzzing is compared to the blowing of a horn; G. *horniss,* a hornet.] A large, powerful wasp, the sting of which is very painful; hence, anyone who gives particular annoyance.

horography, ho•rog'ra•fi, *n.* [Gr. *hōra,* hour, and *graphō,* to write.] An account of the art of constructing instruments for showing the hours; horology.—**horologe,** hō'ro•lōj, *n.* [Fr. *horologe,* L. *horologium,* Gr. *hōrologion*—*hōra,* hour, and *legō,* to tell.] A piece of mechanism for indicating the hours of the day; a timepiece of any kind.—**horologer, horologist,** hō•rol'o•jėr, hō•rol'o•jist, *n.* A maker or vender of clocks and watches; one versed in or who writes on horology. — **horologic, horological,** hō•ro•loj'ik, hō•ro•loj'i•kal, *a.* Pertaining to horology; *bot.* opening and closing at certain hours: said of flowers.—**horology,** hō•rol'o•ji, *n.* The science of measuring time; the art of constructing machines for measuring time, as clocks, watches, dials.—**horoscope,** hō'ro•skōp, *n.* [Gr. *hōroskopos*—*hōra,* hour, and *skopeō,* to view.] A scheme or figure of the heavens at a given time, used by astrologers to foretell future events and the fortunes of persons, according to the position of the stars at the time of their birth.—**horoscopy,** hō•ros'ko•pi, *n.* The predicting of future events by the disposition of the stars and planets.

horrible, hor'ri•bl, *a.* [L. *horribilis,* from *horreo,* to bristle or stand on end, to be terrified; akin to *hirtus,* shaggy, *hirsutus,* hirsute.] Exciting or tending to excite horror; dreadful; terrible; shocking; hideous.—**horrent,** hor'ent, *a.* [L. *horrens, horrentis.*] Bristling.—**horribleness,** hor'ri•bl•nes, *n.* The state or quality of being horrible.—**horribly,** hor'ri•bli, *adv.* In a horrible manner; excessively; very much.—**horrid,** hor'rid, *a.* [L. *horridus,* from *horreo.*] Fitted to excite horror; dreadful; hideous; shocking; very offensive (*colloq.*).—**horridly,** hor'rid•li, *adv.* In a horrid manner.—**horridness,** hor'rid•nes, *n.* The quality of being horrid.—**horrific,** hor•rif'ik, *a.* [L. *horrificus.*] Causing horror.—**horrify,** hor'ri•fī, *v.t.*—*horrified, horrifying.* [L. *horror,* and *facio,* to make.] To strike or impress with horror.—**horripilation,** hor'ri•pi•lā"shon, *n.* [L. *horreo,* to bristle, *pilus,* hair.] The bristling or standing on end of the hair.—**horror,** hor'ėr, *n.* [L., from *horreo.*] A powerful feeling of fear, dread, and abhorrence; a shuddering with terror and loathing; that which excites horror.

hors d'oeuvre, ạr•dė'vr. [Fr.] An appetizer or relish (usually in pl.).

horse, hors, *n.* [A.Sax. *hors*=Icel. *hross, hors,* O.H.G. *hros,* G. *ross,* D. *ros,* allied to Skr. *hreca,* neighing, or to L. *curro,* to run.] A well-known quadruped, the most important to man of all animals that are used as beasts of burden and of draft; the male animal, in distinction from the female called a *mare*; cavalry; troops serving on horseback (in this sense no plural termination); a wooden frame with legs for supporting something; *naut.* a rope attached to a yard to support the sailors while they loose, reef, or furl the sails.—[*Horse,* in compounds, often implies largeness or coarseness; as *horse* chestnut, *horse*play.]—*To take horse,* to mount or set out on horseback.—*v.t.*—*horsed, horsing.* To provide with a horse; to supply a horse or horses for; to sit astride; to bestride (*Shak.*).—**horseback,** hors'bak, *n.* The back of a horse; that part on which the rider sits: generally in the phrase *on horseback,* that is, mounted or riding on a horse.—**horse chestnut,** *n.* A well-known tree with beautiful flowers, often planted for ornament, the nuts of which have been used as food for animals.—**horsecloth,** *n.* A cloth to cover a horse.—**horseflesh,** hors'flesh, *n.* The flesh of a horse; horses generally; a species of mahogany.—**horsefly,** hors'flī, *n.* A large fly that sucks the blood of horses.—**Horse Guards,** *n. pl.* A body of cavalry for guards.—**horsefly,** hors'flī, *n.* A large fly that sucks the blood of horses.—**horsehair,** *n.* sing. and pl. The hair of horses, more particularly of the mane and tail.—**horse latitudes,** hors lat'i•tūdes, *n.* *Naut.* either of two belts of calms and light winds, 35° north and 35° south of the Equator.—**horselaugh,** *n.* A loud, coarse, boisterous laugh.—**horse mackerel,** *n.* A fish about the size of a mackerel, with oily rank flesh.—**horseman,** hors'man, *n.* A man who rides on horseback; one who uses and manages a horse; a soldier who serves on horseback.—**horsemanship,** hors'man•ship, *n.* The art of riding and managing horses; equestrian skill.—**horseplay,** *n.* Rough or rude practical jokes or the like; rude pranks.—**horsepower,** *n.* The power of a horse or its equivalent; the force with which a horse acts when drawing; the standard for estimating the power of a steam engine, each horsepower being estimated as equivalent to 33,000 lb. raised one foot high per minute.—**horse-radish,** *n.* A perennial plant of the cabbage family, the white cylindrical root of which has a pungent taste, and is used as a condiment with roast beef.—**horseshoe,** *n.* A shoe for horses, commonly a piece of iron, in shape resembling the letter U, nailed to the horse's foot; anything shaped like a horseshoe.—*Horseshoe magnet,* an artificial steel magnet nearly in the form of a horseshoe.—**horsetail,** *n.* The tail of a horse; a standard of rank and honor among the Turks, consisting of one or more tails of horses mounted on a lance; an equisetum (which see).—**horsewhip,** hors'hwip, *n.* A whip for driving or striking horses.—*v.t.*—*horsewhipped, horsewhipping.* To lash or strike with a horsewhip.—**horsewoman,** hors'wụm•an, *n.* A woman who rides on horseback; an equestrienne.—**horsy,** hor'si, *a.* Connected with, fond of, or much taken up with horses.—**horsiness,** hor'si•nes, *n.* The quality of being horsy.

hortation, hor•tā'shon, *n.* [L. *hortatio,* from *hortor,* to exhort.] The act of exhorting; exhortation.—**hortative,** hor'ta•tiv, *a.* Giving exhortation.—*n.* A precept given to incite or encourage; exhortation.—**hortatory,** hor'ta•to•ri, *a.* Exhortative.

horticulture, hor'ti•kul•tūr, *n.* [L. *hortus,* a garden (same root as *garden, yard*), and *cultura,* culture.] The cultivation of a garden; the art of cultivating or managing gardens.—**horticultural,** hor•ti•kul'tūr•al, *a.* Pertaining to horticulture.—**horticulturist,** hor•ti•kul'tūr•ist, *n.* One who practices horticulture.—**hortus siccus,** hor'tus sik'kus, *n.* [L.] *Lit.* a dry garden; a collection of specimens of plants carefully dried and preserved; a herbarium.

hosanna, ho•zan'na, *n.* [Heb., save, I beseech you.] An exclamation of praise to God, or an invocation of blessings.

hose, hōz, *n.* [A.Sax. *hosa* (pl. *hosan*), a leg covering=D. *hoos,* Icel. *hosa,* G. and Dan. *hose*; comp. A.Sax. *hose,* Dan. *hase,* a husk; perhaps allied to *house.*] Stockings; socks (in these senses now used as a plural); close-fitting trousers or breeches reaching to the knee; covering for the lower part of the legs, including the feet; a flexible tube or pipe for conveying water or other fluid to any required point.—*v.t.* To apply water, etc., by means of a hose, as to *hose* a garden.—**hosiery,** hō'zhi•ėr•i, *n.* Stockings, or goods similarly knitted; also a place where knit goods are made or sold.

hospice, hos'pis, *n.* [Fr., from L. *hospitium,* hospitality, a lodging, an inn.] A place of refuge and entertainment for travelers on some difficult road or pass, as among the Alps.

hospitable, hos'pi•ta•bl, *a.* [Fr. *hospitable,* L. *hospitalis,* from *hospes, hospitis,* a host, a guest. HOST.] Receiving and entertaining strangers with kindness and without reward; kind to strangers and guests; pertaining to the liberal entertainment of guests.—**hospitably,** hos'pi•ta•bli, *adv.* In a hospitable manner.—**hospital,** hos'pi•tal, *n.* [O.Fr. *hospital,* L.L. *hospitale. Hotel, hostel* doublets of this.] An institution for the reception and treatment of the old, sick, etc., for the education and support of orphans, or for the benefit of any class of persons who are more or less dependent upon public help; an institution of medical service for the sick and injured, where medical and surgical treatment are given.—**hospitality,** hos•pi•tal'i•ti, *n.* The kind and generous reception of strangers or guests; hospitable treatment or disposition.—**hospitalization,** hos•pi•tal•i•zā′shon, *n.*—**hospitalize,** hos′pi•tal•īz, *v.t.* To place in a hospital for medical care.—**hospitaler,** hos′pi•tal•ėr, *n.* A member of a religious body whose office it was to relieve the poor, the stranger, and the sick; one of an order of knights who built a hospital at Jerusalem in A.D. 1042 for pilgrims, called *Knights of St. John*, and, after their removal to Malta, *Knights of Malta.*

hospodar, hos•pō•där′, *n.* A Slavonic title formerly borne by the princes of Moldavia and Wallachia, etc.

host, hōst, *n.* [O.Fr. *hoste*, Fr. *hôte*; from L. *hospes, hospitis*, a host, for *hostipes*, from *hostis*, an enemy, a stranger (akin E. *guest*), and root *pa*, to protect, as in L. *pater*, a father, *potens*, powerful. From *hospes* are also derived *hospital, hostler, hotel*, etc.] One who receives and entertains another at his own house; a landlord: the correlative of *guest*; an animal or organism in or on whose organs a parasite exists.—**hostess,** hōs′tes, *n.* A female host.

host, hōst, *n.* [O.Fr. *host*, from L. *hostis*, a stranger, an enemy, in later usage an army; *guest* is cog, with *hostis*. See also HOST, above.] An army; a number of men embodied for war; any greater number or multitude.

host, hōst, *n.* [L. *hostia*, a sacrificial victim, from *hostire*, to strike.] The altar bread or wafer in the Eucharist, or in the Roman Catholic sacrament of the Mass.

hostage, hos′tij, *n.* [O.Fr. *hostage*, Fr. *otage*. L.L. *hostagius, obstagius, obsidaticus*, from L. *obses, obsidis*, hostage—*ob*, at, near, *sedeo*, to sit.] A person handed over to an enemy as a pledge for the performance of certain conditions.

hostel, hos′tel, *n.* [HOTEL.] An inn; a lodginghouse.

hostile, hos′tīl, *a.* [L. *hostilis*, from *hostis*, an enemy. See HOST, army.] Belonging to an enemy; holding the position of an enemy or enemies; showing ill will and malevolence.—**hostilely,** hos′til•li, *adv.* In a hostile manner.—**hostility,** hos•til′i•ti, *n.* [L. *hostilitas.*] State of being hostile; an act of an open enemy; an act of warfare (in this sense generally *pl.*).

hostler, hos′lėr, *n.* [O.Fr. *hostelier*, from *hostel*, Mod. Fr. *hôtel*, an inn, from L.L. *hospitale*, a hospital. HOTEL.] The person who has the care of horses at an inn, formerly the innkeeper; a stableboy.

hot, hot, *a.* [A.Sax. *hát*=Sc. *het*. D. *heet*, Sw. *het*, Dan. *hed, heed*, Icel. *heitr*, G. *heiss*. HEAT.] Having much sensible heat; exciting the feeling of warmth in a great or powerful degree; very warm; ardent in temper; easily excited or exasperated; vehement; violent; furious; animated; brisk; keen; lustful; lewd; acrid; biting; stimulating; pungent; wanted by the police; *phys. and chem.* radioactive; electrically energized (*hot* wire).—**hotbed,** hot′bed, *n. Hort.* a bed of earth heated by fermenting substances, and covered with glass, used for growing early or exotic plants; a place which favors rapid growth or development.—**hot-blooded,** *a.* Having hot blood; having warm passions; irritable.—**hot dog,** a hot frankfurter, usually served in a roll.—**hotheaded,** *a.* Violent; rash; impetuous.—**hothouse,** hot′hous, *n.* A greenhouse or house to shelter tender plants, artificially heated; a conservatory.—**hot war,** *n.* A shooting war.—**hotly,** hot′li, *adv.*—**hotness,** hot′nes, *n.* The condition or quality of being hot.

hotchpot, hoch′pot, *n.* [Fr. *hochepot*—*hocker*, to shake (from D. or Flem. *hotsen*), and *pot*, a pot or dish.] A hodgepodge or mixture; *law*, a commixture of property for equality of division.—**hotchpotch,** *n.* HODGEPODGE.

hotel, hō•tel′, *n.* [Fr. *hôtel*, O.Fr. *hostel*, an inn; same word as *hospital, hostel.*] A house for entertaining strangers or travelers; an inn; especially, one of some style and pretensions; a large town mansion (*French usage*).

Hottentot, hot′n•tot, *n.* [From D. *hot en tot, hot* and *tot*, syllables intended to imitate sounds frequent in their language.] A member of a primitive tribe or race of South Africa; the language of this people, characterized by curious clicking or clucking sounds.

hough, hok, *n.* [Written also *hock*, which see.] The hock of a horse; the back part of the human knee joint; the ham.—*v.t.* To hamstring; to disable by cutting the sinews of the ham. (O.T.)

hound, hound, *n.* [A.Sax. *hund*, a dog or hound=G. Dan. and Sw. *hund*, D. *hond*, Icel. *hundr*, Goth. *hunds*; cog. W. *cun*, Gael. *cù*, L. *canis*, Gr. *kyōn*, Skr. *çvan*, a dog.] A term restricted to particular breeds or varieties of dogs used in the chase, as in hunting the deer, the fox, the hare; sometimes used as a term of contempt for a man.—*v.t.* To set on the chase; to incite to pursuit of animals; hence, to urge, incite, or spur to action: usually with *on.*

hour, our, *n.* [O.Fr. *hore, houre*, from L. *hora*, from Gr. *hōra*, a season, an hour; seen also in *horologe, horoscope.*] The twenty-fourth part of a day; sixty minutes; the particular time of the day; a fixed or appointed time; a time, period, or season; *pl.* certain prayers in the Roman Catholic Church, to be repeated at stated times of the day.—*To keep good hours*, to be at home regularly in good season, or not after the usual hours of retiring to rest; *to keep bad hours*, the opposite.—*The small hours*, the early hours of the morning, as one, two, etc.—**hourglass,** *n.* A glass in two compartments connected by a narrow neck, for measuring time by the running of a quantity of sand from one compartment to the other.—**hourly,** our′li, *a.* Happening or done every hour; frequent; often repeated; continual.—*adv.* Every hour; frequently; continually.

houri, hou′ri or hö′ri, *n.* [Ar.] Among the Mohammedans, a nymph of paradise.

house, hous, *n.* pl. **houses,** hou′zez. [A.Sax. *hús*=Icel. *hús*, Dan. Sw. and Goth. *hus*, D. *huis*, G. *haus*; from root meaning to cover, as in *hide, hose, sky*, etc. Akin *husband, hussy.*] A building serving or intended to serve as an abode; a building for the habitation of man, or for his use or accommodation; a dwelling; an abode; a household; a family; a family regarded as consisting of ancestors, descendants, and kindred; especially a noble or illustrious family; a legislative body of men (the *House* of Representatives); a legislative quorum; the audience at a place of entertainment; a firm or commercial establishment; a twelfth part of the astrological heavens.—*House of Representatives*, the lower branch of the United States Congress.—*House organ*, a publication brought out by a business concern, etc., for its members.—*House party*, a social gathering, lasting one or more nights, usually at a country house.—*To bring down the house*, to draw forth a universal burst of applause, as in a theater.—*To keep house*, to maintain an independent family establishment.—*v.t.*—*housed, housing* (houz). To put or receive into a house; to provide with a dwelling or residence; to shelter; to cause to take shelter.—*v.i.* To take shelter or lodgings; to take up abode.—**houseboat,** *n.* A boat with a wooden house, for lodgings by river in summer.—**housebreaker,** *n.* One who breaks into a house with a felonious intent; a burglar.—**housebreaking,** *n.* Burglary.—**housecarl,** *n.* [*Hus-carl.*] A member of the bodyguard of king or nobleman, e.g., of Harold at Hastings.—**housefly,** *n.* A well-known two-winged fly common in dwelling houses.—**household,** hous′hōld, *n.* Those who dwell under the same roof and compose a family; those under the same domestic government; house; family.—*a.* Pertaining to the house and family; domestic.—*Household gods*, gods presiding over the house or family among the ancient Romans; hence, objects endeared to one from being associated with home.—*Household troops, Household brigade*, troops whose special duty it is to attend the sovereign and guard the metropolis.—**householder,** hous′hōl•dėr, *n.* The chief of a household; the occupier of a house.—**housekeeper,** hous′kē•pėr, *n.* A householder; a head female servant in a household; a female who looks after a person's household.—**housekeeping,** hous′kē•ping, *n.* The management of domestic concerns; the maintenance of a household.—**houseleek,** *n.* A well-known plant which grows on the tops of houses and on walls, and the fleshy leaves of which are applied to bruises and other sores.—**houseless,** hous′les, *a.* Destitute of a house or habitation; without shelter.—**housemaid,** hous′mād, *n.* A female servant employed to keep a house clean, etc.—**houseroom,** hous′röm, *n.* Room or accommodation in a house.—**housewarming,** *n.* A merrymaking at the time a family enters a new house.—**housewife,** hous′wīf, *n.* The mistress of a family; the wife of a householder; a female manager of domestic affairs; a little case for needles, thread, scissors, etc.—**housewifely,** hous′wīf•li, *a.* Pertaining to or like a housewife; thrifty.—**housewifery,** hous′wīf•ri, *n.* The business or management of a housewife.

housing, hou′zing, *n.* [HOUSE.] Act of sheltering; the providing of houses and other dwelling quarters, as by a government; a frame to support machinery, etc., or parts of a machine.

housing, hou′zing, *n.* [From Fr. *housse,* a covering, a horsecloth; from D. *hulse,* a husk or shell; akin *holster, hull, husk.*] A cloth laid over a saddle; a saddlecloth; a horsecloth.

hove, hōv, pret. of *heave.*

hovel, huv′el, *n.* [Dim. of A.Sax. *hof,* a house, a dwelling = Icel. *hof,* a hall, G. *hof,* a court, a farm.] A poor cottage; a small mean house.

hover, huv′ėr, *v.i.* [Perhaps from O.E. *hove,* to abide, to linger, same origin as *hovel.*] To hang fluttering in the air or upon the wing; to be in doubt or hesitation; to be irresolute; to move to and fro threateningly or watchingly (an army *hovering* on our borders).—**hoveringly,** huv′ėr•ing•li, *adv.* In a hovering manner.

how, hou, *adv.* [A.Sax. *hú, hwú, hwý,* instrumental case of *hwá, hwæt,* who, what; really the same word as *why.*] In what manner; by what means or method; to what degree or extent; by what measure or quantity (*how* long, *how* much better); in what state, condition, or plight. Besides being used as an interrogative, direct or indirect, it is sometimes used interjectionally, or even substantively (the *how* and why of it).—**howbeit,** hou•bē′it, *adv.* [*How, be,* and *it.*] However it be; be it as it may; nevertheless; however.—**however,** hou•ev′ėr, *adv.* In whatever manner or degree; in whatever state.—*conj.* Nevertheless; notwithstanding; yet; still; though.—**howsoever,** hou•sō•ev′ėr, *adj.* or *conj.* In what manner soever; however.

howdah, hou′da, *n.* [Hind. and Ar. *haudah.*] A seat erected on the back of an elephant for two or more persons to ride in: usually covered overhead.

howitzer, hou′it•sėr, *n.* [From G. *haubitze,* from Bohem. *haufnice,* originally a sling.] A short gun firing a heavy shell with a low velocity, fired at a high angle, reaching objects not to be reached with direct fire; it represents the old *mortar.*

howl, houl, *v.i.* [An imitative word = D. *huilen,* G. *heulen,* Dan. *hyle,* to howl; comp. L. *ululo,* Gr. *ololyzō,* to wail, to howl; akin *owl,* L. *ulula,* an owl.] To utter a loud, protracted, mournful cry, as that of a dog or wolf; to produce any similar sound, as the wind; to wail or lament (N.T.).—*v.t.* To utter in a loud or mournful tone.—*n.* The cry of a dog or wolf or other like sound; a cry of distress.—**howler,** hou′lėr, *n.* One who howls; a name given to a monkey of South America from its cry; an error that cries aloud for correction.

hoy, hoi, *n.* [D. and G. *heu* (pron. hoi); Dan. *höy.*] A heavy barge; † a small coasting vessel.

hoyden, hoiden, hoi′dn, *n.* [O.D. *heyden,* a heathen, a gypsy, a vagabond. HEATHEN.] A rude, bold girl.—*a.* Romping, roistering.—*v.i.* To romp rudely; to act like a hoyden.

hub, hub, *n.* [HOB.] The central cylindrical part of a wheel in which the spokes are set; the nave; a block of wood for stopping a carriage wheel; a mark at which quoits, etc., are cast; the hilt of a weapon.

hubble-bubble, hub′l•bub′l, *n.* A kind of tobacco pipe so arranged that the smoke passes through water, making a bubbling noise—hence its name; a hookah.

hubbub, hub′ub, *n.* [Imitative of confused noise.] A noise of many confused voices; a tumult; uproar.

huckaback, huk′a•bak, *n.* [Originally linen *hawked* or *huckstered* by being carried on the *back.*] A kind of linen cloth with raised figures on it, used principally for towels.

huckle, huk′l, *n.* [Connected with *hook;* lit. a thing bent or hooked; akin *huckster.*] The hip; a bunch or part projecting like the hip.—**huckleberry,** huk′l•be•ri, *n.* [Corruption of *whortleberry.*] A name for North American plants allied to the whortleberry.—**hucklebone,** *n.* The hipbone.

huckster, huk′stėr, *n.* [Akin to *hawker;* the name was given from the bending of the back in carrying a pack; comp. D. *hukken,* to squat, *heuker,* a hawker; G. *hocken,* to take on the back; Dan. *hökre,* to huckster; *huckle, hook,* are also akin.] A retailer of small articles; a hawker; one who higgles.—*v.i.* To deal in small articles or in petty bargains; to higgle.—*v.t.* To hawk or peddle; to make a matter of bargain.

huddle, hud′l, *v.i.*—*huddled, huddling.* [Same word as G. *hudeln,* Dan. *hutle,* D. *hoetelen,* to bungle; akin *hustle.*] To crowd or press together without order or regularity; to hustle.—*v.t.* To crowd together without order; to produce in a hurried manner; to hunch one's body together, often with *up.*—*n.* A crowd or confused mass; a gathering of football players behind the line of scrimmage to receive instructions, etc.

hue, hū, *n.* [A.Sax. *hiw, heow,* appearance; Sw. *hy,* color: Goth. *hiwi,* shape, show.] Color, or shade of color; dye; tint; *painting,* a compound of one or more colors forming an intervenient shade.—**hued,** hūd, *a.* Having a hue or color.

hue, hū, *n.* [Fr. *huer,* to hoot, to shout; akin *hoot.*] A shouting or clamor: used only in the phrase *hue and cry,* which is the outcry raised, or public warning at once given, by a person who has been robbed, or who knows that a felony has been committed.

huff, huf, *n.* [An imitative word meaning lit. to blow, to puff; comp. *whiff.*] A fit of peevishness or petulance; anger at some offense, real or fancied; one filled with a false opinion of his own importance.—*To take huff,* to take offense.—*v.t.* To swell or puff up‡; to treat with insolence; to bully; to make angry.—*v.i.* To swell up; to bluster; to take offense.—**huffiness,** huf′i•nes, *n.* The state of being huffy.—**huffish,** huf′ish, *a.* Inclined to huff; insolent.—**huffishly,** huf′ish•li, *adv.* In a huffish manner.—**huffishness,** huf′ish•nes, *n.*—**huffy,** huf′i, *a.* Puffed up; swelled; arrogant or insolent; easily offended.

hug, hug, *v.t.*—*hugged, hugging.* [Origin doubtful; comp. Icel. *hugga,* to soothe, to comfort; D. *hugen,* to coax; Dan. *huge,* to squat.] To press closely with the arms; to embrace closely; to clasp to the breast; to grasp or gripe, as in wrestling; to cherish in the mind (to *hug* delusions); to keep close to (to *hug* the land in sailing); *refl.* to congratulate one's self.—*v.i.* To lie close; to crowd together (*Shak.*).—*n.* A close embrace; a clasp or gripe.—**hugger,** hug′ėr, *n.* One who hugs.

huge, hūj, *a.* [O.E. *huge,* also *hogge;* comp. O.Fr. *ahuge,* huge; origin unknown.] Having an immense bulk; very large or great; enormous; very great in any respect (a *huge* difference).—**hugely,** hūj′li, *adv.* In a huge manner.—**hugeness,** hūj′nes, *n.* The state of being huge.

huggermugger, hug′ėr•mug′ėr, *n.* [Comp. *hug,* to lie close; obsolete *hugger,* to lurk; N. *mugg,* secrecy.] †Concealment; privacy; secrecy.—*a.* Clandestine; sly; confused; slovenly.

Huguenot, hū′ge•not, *n.* [Fr.; probably corrupted from G. *eidgenoss,* a confederate, there being found various early forms, such as *higuenot, eidguenot, enguenot, anguenot,* etc.] A French Protestant of the period of the religious wars in France in the sixteenth century.—**Huguenotism,** hū′ge•not•izm, *n.* The religion of the Huguenots.

hulk, hulk, *n.* [Same word as D. *hulk,* G. *hulk, holk,* Sw. *holk,* a kind of ship, from L.L. *hulca, olca,* from Gr. *holkas,* a ship of burden, from *helkō,* to draw.] A heavy ship‡; the body of a ship; the body of an old ship laid by as unfit for service; something bulky or unwieldy.—*The hulks,* old or dismasted ships, formerly used as prisons.—**hulking, hulky,** hul′king, hul′ki, *a.* Large and clumsy of body; unwieldy; loutish.

hull, hul, *n.* [A.Sax. *hulu,* a hull or husk; akin G. *hülle,* a covering, Goth. *huljan,* to cover; same root as in *hell, holster.*] The outer covering of something, particularly of fruits, grain, etc.; the husk; the body of a ship, exclusive of her masts, yards, and rigging.—*Hull down,* said of a ship when so distant that her hull is below the horizon.—*v.t.* To deprive of the hull or hulls; to pierce the hull of, as with a cannon ball.—'To hull on the flood', of the ark; drifting, or sinking in the flood (*Mil.*).—**huller,** hul'ėr, *n.* One who hulls; a machine for separating seeds from their hulls.

hullabaloo, hul'a•ba•lö", *n.* [Imitative of confused noise; comp. *hurly-burly.*] Uproar; noisy confusion.

hullo, hul•lō', *interj.* [Same as *Halloo.*] An exclamation to call attention.

hum, hum, *v.i.—hummed, humming.* [Imitative of sound; comp. G. *hummen, summen,* D. *hommelen,* to hum. *Humble-bee, humbug, humdrum* are connected.] To make a dull, prolonged sound, like that of a bee in flight; to drone; to murmur; to buzz; to give utterance to a similar sound with the mouth; to mumble; to make a drawling, inarticulate sound in speaking.—*v.t.* To sing in a low voice; to murmur without articulation.—*n.* The noise made by bees or any similar sound; a buzz; any inarticulate, low, murmuring, or buzzing sound; a murmur of applause; a low inarticulate sound uttered by a speaker.—*interj.* A sound with a pause, implying doubt and deliberation; ahem.—**humming,** hum'ing, *n.* The sound of that which hums; a buzzing; a low murmuring sound.—**hummingbird,** *n.* A name given to the individuals of a family of minute and beautiful birds, from the sound of their wings in flight.

human, hū'man, *a.* [Fr. *humain,* L. *humanus,* from *homo, hominis,* a man (whence also *homage*); akin to *humus,* the ground (whence *humilis,* E. *humble*); also to A.Sax. *guma,* a man (seen in *bridegroom*).] Belonging to a man or mankind; having the qualities or attributes of man.—*n.* A human being.—**humane,** hū•mān', *a.* [Same word as *human.*] Human‡; having the feelings and dispositions proper to man; kind; benevolent; tender; merciful; tending to humanize or refine.—**humanely,** hū•mān'li, *adv.* In a humane manner.—**humaneness,** hū•mān'nes, *n.* The quality of being humane.—**humanism,** hū'man•izm, *n.* Classical learning; a philosophical system.—**humanist,** hū'man•ist, *n.* One who studies the humanities; one versed in the knowledge of human nature; one at the revival of letters devoted to the study of the ancient classics. So *Literæ Humaniores,* not rendering more humane, but as opposed to sacred studies.—**humanistic,** hū•man•is'tik, *a.* Of or pertaining to humanity.—**humanitarian,** hū•man'i•tâ"ri•an, *n.* One who has a great regard or love for humanity; a philanthropist; one who denies the divinity of Christ, and believes him to have been a mere man; one who maintains the perfectibility of human nature without the aid of grace.—**humanitarianism,** hū•man'i•tâ"ri•an•izm, *n.* The practices or beliefs of a humanitarian.—**humanity,** hū•man'i•ti, *n.* [Fr. *humanité,* L. *humanitas,* from *humanus.*] The quality of being human; humanness; mankind collectively; the human race; the quality of being humane; tenderness and kindness toward all created beings: opposed to *cruelty*; classical and polite literature or a branch of such literature: in this sense generally plural and with the definite article—'*the humanities*': but in the Scottish universities used in the singular and applied to Latin and Latin literature alone.—**humanization,** hū'man•i•zā"shon, *n.* The act of humanizing.—**humanize,** hū'man•īz, *v.t.—humanized, humanizing.* To render human or humane.—*v.i.* To become more humane; to become more civilized.—**humanizer,** hū'man•i•zėr, *n.* One who humanizes.—**humankind,** hū'man•kīnd, *n.* The race of man; mankind; the human species.—**humanly,** hū'man•li, *adv.* In a human manner; after the manner of men.

humble, hum'bl, *a.* [Fr. *humble,* from L. *humilis,* from *humus,* the earth (seen also in *exhume*). HUMILIATE, HUMAN.] Of a low, mean, or unpretending character; not grand, lofty, noble, or splendid; having a low estimate of one's self; not proud, arrogant, or assuming; lowly; modest; meek; submissive.—*v.t.—humbled, humbling.* To render humble; to reduce the power, independence, or state of; to bring down; to abase; to lower; to bring down the pride or vanity of: often *refl.*—**humbleness,** hum'bl•nes, *n.* The state of being humble or low.—**humbler,** hum'blėr, *n.* One who or that which humbles.—**humbly,** hum'bli, *adv.* In a humble manner; meekly; submissively.

humblebee, hum'bl•bē, *n.* [From old *humble,* to hum, from *hum*; comp. G. *hummel,* Dan. *humle-bi,* Sw. *humla,* humblebee; from the humming sound it makes; whence also *bumblebee.* HUM.] The common name of various large wild bees; the bumblebee.

humble pie, *n.* A pie made of the *humbles,* or heart, liver, kidneys, etc., of the deer.—*To eat humble pie,* to have to take a humble tone; to come down from an assumed position; to apologize, or humiliate one's self, abjectly: the phrase arose from the humbles being allotted to the huntsmen and servants, the meaning being influenced by the adj. *humble.*

humbug, hum'bug, *n.* [From *hum* and *bug, hum* having its old sense of to deceive, and *bug* its old meaning of *bugbear*; hence = false alarm.] An imposition played off under fair pretenses; a hoax; spirit of deception or imposition; falseness; hollowness; a cheat; a trickish fellow. *v.t. humbugged, humbugging.* To impose on; to cajole or trick; to hoax.—**humbugger,** hum•bug'ėr, *n.* One who humbugs.—**humbuggery,** hum'bug•ėr•i, *n.* The practice of humbugging; quackery.

humdrum, hum'drum, *a.* [From *hum* and *drum*; originally droning, monotonous.] Commonplace; homely; dull; heavy.—*n.* A droning tone of voice; dull monotony.

humeral, hū'mėr•al, *a.* [L. *humerus,* the shoulder.] Belonging to the shoulder.—**humerus,** hū'mėr•us, *n. Anat.* the long cylindrical bone of the arm, situated between the shoulder blade and the forearm; also the shoulder.

humid, hū'mid, *a.* [L. *humidus, umidus,* from *humeo, umeo,* to be moist.] Moist; damp; wet or watery.—**humidify,** hū•mid'i•fi, *v.t.* To moisten; to make humid, especially the atmosphere.—**humidity, humidness,** hū•mid'i•ti, hū'mid•nes, *n.* Moisture or dampness in the atmosphere.—**humidifier,** hū•mid'i•fī•ėr, *n.* A machine that keeps a specific amount of moisture in the air.—**relative humidity,** the ratio of the amount of aqueous vapor in the air to the amount that would saturate it at the same temperature, expressed as a percentage.—**humidor,** hū'mi•dōr, *n.* A box in which a suitable humidity is maintained, especially one for storing tobacco.

humiliate, hū•mil'i•āt, *v.t.—humiliated, humiliating.* [L. *humilio, humiliatum,* from *humilis,* humble. HUMBLE.] To reduce to a lower position in one's own estimation or the estimation of others; to humble; to depress.—**humiliating,** hū•mil'i•āt•ing, *p.* and *a.* Humbling; reducing self-confidence; mortifying. — **humiliation,** hū•mil'i•ā"shon, *n.* The act of humiliating; the state of being humiliated, humbled, or mortified.—**humility,** hū•mil'i•ti, *n.* [L. *humilitas.*] The state or quality of being humble; humbleness; lowliness of mind; a feeling of one's own insignificance.

hummock, hum'ok, *n.* [Probably a dim. form of *hump.*] A rounded knoll; a mound; a hillock; a protuberance on an ice field.—**hummocky,** hum'ok•i, *a.* Abounding in hummocks.

humor, humour, hū'mėr, ū'mėr, *n.* [Fr. *humeur*; L. *humor,* moisture, liquid, from *humeo,* to be moist. HUMID.] Moisture or moist matter; fluid matter in the human or an animal body, not blood (the vitreous *humor* of the eye); a morbid fluid collected; *old med.* a fluid, of which there were four—blood, phlegm, yellow bile, and black bile—on the conditions and proportions of which the bodily and mental health was supposed to depend; hence, turn or frame of mind; disposition, or a peculiarity of disposition, often temporary (not in the *humor* for reading); a caprice, whim, or fancy (*Shak.*); temper (as regards anger or annoyance or the opposite); that mental quality which gives to ideas a ludicrous or fantastic turn, and tends to excite laughter or mirth; a quality or faculty akin to wit, but depending for its effect rather on kindly human feeling than on point or brilliancy of expression.—*Bad humor,* feeling of irritation, annoyance, or displeasure.—*Good humor,* feeling of cheerfulness; good temper.—*Out of humor,* out of temper; displeased; annoyed.—*v.t.* To comply with the humor or inclination of; to soothe by compliance; to gratify; to indulge, to adapt one's self to.—**humoral,** hū'-

mėr•al, *a.* Pertaining to or proceeding from the humors of the body (*humoral* pathology).—**humorist,** hū′mėr•ist, *n.* Formerly; a person who exhibited certain strong peculiarities of disposition or manner; one who indulged in whims or eccentricities; now, one that makes use of a humorous style in speaking or writing; one whose conversation or writings are full of humor; one who has a playful fancy or genius; a wag; also, one who attributes all diseases to a depraved state of the humors.—**humoristic,** hū•mėr•is′tik, *a.* Pertaining to or like a humorist.—**humorous,** hū′mėr•us, *a.* Moist or humid‡; full of humor; exciting laughter; jocular; governed by humor or caprice; capricious; whimsical. —**humorously,** hū′mėr•us•li, *adv.* In a humorous manner; pleasantly; jocosely.—**humorousness,** hū′mėr•us•nes, *n.* The state or quality of being humorous.

hump, hump, *n.* [A nasalized form of *hub* or *hob*=L.G. *hump,* heap; D. *homp,* a lump; akin *hunch, heap.*] A protuberance; especially the protuberance formed by a crooked back; a hunch.—**humpback,** hump′bak, *n.* A back with a hump; a person who has such a back; a whale that has a hump on the back.—**humpbacked,** hump′bakt, *a.* Having a crooked back.—**humped,** humpt, *a.* Having a hump.—**humpy,** hump′i, *a.* Full of humps.

humph, humf, *interj.* An exclamation expressive of disbelief, doubt, dissatisfaction, or the like.

humus, hū′mus, *n.* [L. *humus,* soil.] Vegetable mold; a dark-brown or blackish matter from decayed vegetable substances.—**humic,** hū′mik, *a.* Obtained from or pertaining to humus.

hunch, hunsh, *n.* [A form of *hump.*] A hump; a lump; a thick piece; a push or jerk with the fist or elbow. —*v.t.* To make a hunch on; to push with the elbow.—**hunchback,** hunsh′bak, *n.* A humpback; a humpbacked person. —**hunchbacked,** hunsh′bakt, *a.* Humpbacked.—**hunched,** hunsht, *a.* Having a hunch or hump.

hundred, hun′dred, *a.* [A.Sax. *hundred*=Icel. *hundrath,* Dan. *hundrede,* D. *honderd,* G. *hundert*; from *hund,* cog. with L. *centum,* Skr. *catam,* a hundred, and a termination akin to E. *read,* and to Goth. *garathjan,* to reckon.] Ten times ten; ninety and ten added.—*n.* The product of ten multiplied by ten; a collection of ten times ten individuals or units; a division of a county in England, supposed to have originally contained a *hundred* families or freemen.—**hundredfold,** *n.* A hundred times as much.—**hundredth,** hun′dredth, *a.* The ordinal of a hundred; one portion of a hundred equal parts into which anything is divided.—*n.* The one after the ninety-ninth; one of a hundred equal parts of a thing.—**hundredweight,** hun′dred•wāt, *n.* A weight, usually denoted by *cwt.,* containing 100 pounds in the United States; in England, 112 pounds.

hung, hung, pret. & pp. of *hang.*

Hungarian, hung•gâ′ri•an, *n.* A native of Hungary; a Magyar; the language of the Hungarians; Magyar.—*a.* Pertaining to Hungary.

hunger, hung′gėr, *n.* [A.Sax. *hunger, hungor*=G. Dan. and Sw. *hunger,* Icel. *hungr.* Goth. *huhrus,* hunger.] An uneasy sensation occasioned by the want of food; a craving for food; craving appetite; strong or eager desire.—*v.i.* To feel hunger; to crave food; to desire eagerly; to long.—**hungrily,** hung′gri•li, *adv.* In a hungry manner.—**hungry,** hung′gri, *a.* [A.Sax. *hungrig.*] Feeling hunger; having a keen appetite; eagerly desirous; proceeding from hunger.

hunk, hungk, *n.* [A form of *hunch.*] A large lump; a hunch.

hunky, hunky-dory, *a.* All right; satisfactory; comfortable. (*Slang.*)

hunt, hunt, *v.t.* [A.Sax. *huntian,* to hunt, akin to *hentan,* to seize; O.G. *hundjan,* Goth. (*fra*)*hinthan,* to catch; allied to E. *hand,* and to *hind* (female deer).] To chase, search for, or follow after (wild animals, particularly quadrupeds), for the purpose of catching or killing; to search after, pursue, follow closely; to pursue game or wild animals over (to *hunt* a district).—*To hunt up* or *out,* to seek for; to search for.—*To hunt down,* to pursue and kill or capture; to exterminate in a locality.—*v.i.* To follow the chase; to go in pursuit of game or other wild animals; to seek by close pursuit; to search: with *after* or for. —*n.* The chasing of wild animals; a pursuit; a chase; a pack of hounds; an association of huntsmen in a district.—**hunter,** hun′tėr, *n.* One who hunts; a huntsman; a horse used in the chase; a watch whose glass is protected by a metal cover.—**hunting box, hunting lodge,** *n.* A residence occupied for the purpose of hunting.—**hunting watch,** *n.* See HUNTER.—**huntress,** hunt′res, *n.* A female that hunts or follows the chase.—**huntsman,** hunts′man, *n.* One who hunts or who practices hunting; a person whose office it is to manage the chase.—**hunt's-up,** *n.* The tune formerly played on the horn under the windows of sportsmen to awaken them, to show that the game was roused by the hounds, and the hunt was to begin.

hurdle, hėr′dl, *n.* [A.Sax. *hyrdel,* a dim. corresponding to G. *horde, hürde,* a hurdle; Icel. *hurth,* Goth. *haurds,* a door; akin E. *hoarding.*] A movable frame made of interlaced twigs or sticks, or of bars or rods crossing each other, varying in form according to its use.—*v.t.*—*hurdled, hurdling.* To fence or provide with hurdles.—**hurdle race,** *n.* A race of men or horses over hurdles or fences.

hurds, hėrdz, *n. pl.* [HARDS.] The coarse part of flax or hemp; hards.

hurdy-gurdy, hėr′di•gėr′di, *n.* [Intended to suggest its sound.] A stringed instrument, whose tones are produced by the friction of a wheel acting the part of a bow against four strings; various instruments, usually playing street music, operated by turning a handle.

hurl, hėrl, *v.t.* [A contracted form of *hurtle,* influenced by *whirl.*] To send whirling or flying through the air; to throw or dash with violence; to emit or utter with vehemence.—*v.i.*† To move rapidly; to whirl.—*n.* The act of throwing with violence.—**hurler,** hėr′lėr, *n.* One who hurls.—**hurling,** hėrl′ing, *n.* An old game of ball.

hurly, hurly-burly, hėr′li, hėr′li•bėr′li, *n.* [Intended to express by its sound noise or confusion, suggested by *hurl* or *hurry*; comp. Dan. *hurlumhei,* hurry-scurry; Fr. *hurluberlu,* a hare-brained person.] Tumult; bustle; confusion.

hurrah, hurray, hu•rä′, hu•rā′ *interj.* [Comp. E. *huzza,* G. *hurrah,* Dan. and Sw. *hurra,* Pol. *hura.*] An exclamation expressive of joy, applause, or encouragement; also used as a noun.—*v.i.* To utter a hurrah.—*v.t.* To receive with hurrahs; to encourage by cheering.

hurricane, hur′i•kān, *n.* [Sp. *huracan,* Fr. *ouragan,* D. *orkaan,* G. *orkan,* all from a native American word.] An extremely violent tempest or storm of wind; anything resembling a violent tempest.—*Hurricane deck,* an elevated deck in steamboats, especially the deck above a saloon.

hurry, hur′i, *v.t.*—*hurried, hurrying.* [Akin to G. *hurren,* to move hastily; Icel. *hurr,* a confused noise; Dan. *hurre,* to buzz; Sw. *hurra,* to whirl; imitative like *whirr, hurlyburly,* etc.] To impel to greater speed or haste; to urge to act or proceed with precipitance; to cause to be performed with great or undue rapidity; to impel to violent or thoughtless action.—*v.i.* To move or act with haste; to proceed with precipitation; to make great haste in going.—*n.* The act of hurrying; urgency; bustle; confusion,—**hurried,** hur′id, *p.* and *a.* Done in a hurry; evidencing hurry.—**hurriedly,** hur′id•li, *adv.* In a hurried manner.—**hurriedness,** hur′id•nes, *n.* State of being hurried. —**hurry-skurry,** hur′i•skur′i, *adv.* [*Hurry* and *scurry.*] Confusedly; in a bustle.—*n.* Fluttering haste; great confusion.

hurt, hėrt, *v.t.* pret. & pp. *hurt.* [O.Fr. *hurter,* Mod. Fr. *heurter,* to knock against; perhaps of Celtic origin; comp. W. *hwyrdd,* a push, a thrust, a blow. Hence *hurtle, hurl.*] To cause physical pain to; to wound or bruise painfully; to cause mental pain; to wound the feelings of; to cause injury, loss, or diminution to; to impair; to damage; to harm.—*n.* A wound, a bruise, or the like; injury; loss; damage; detriment.—**hurtful,** hėrt′fu̧l, *a.* Causing hurt; harmful; injurious; mischievous; detrimental.—**hurtfully,** hėrt′fu̧l•li, *adv.* In a hurtful manner.—**hurtfulness,** hėrt′fu̧l•nes, *n.* The quality of being hurtful.—**hurtless,** hėrt′les, *a.* Inflicting no injury; harmless; receiving no injury.—**hurtlessness,** hėrt′les•nes, *n.*

hurtle, hėr′tl, *v.i.*—*hurtled, hurtling.* [From *hurt.*] To clash or meet in shock; to make a sound suggestive of hostile clash; to clash; to sound threateningly; to resound.

hurtleberry, hėr′tl•be•ri, *n.* See WHORTLEBERRY.

husband, huz′band, *n.* [A.Sax. *hús-bonda,* the master of the house, from Icel. *húsbóndi* (*hús,* house, and *búandi,* dwelling in), Dan. *huusbond,* Sw. *husbonde,* the master of the house; A.Sax. *búan,* Icel. *búa,* G. *bauen,* to inhabit, to cultivate. HOUSE, BOOR.] A man joined to a woman by marriage; the correlative of *wife.*—*Ship's husband,* an agent of the owners who sees that a ship is supplied with stores and properly repaired before she proceeds to sea.—*v.t.* To spend, apply, or use with economy; to keep from spending in view of an effort required.—**husbandman,** huz′band•man, *n.* A farmer; a cultivator; one engaged in agriculture.—**husbandry,** huz′band•ri, *n.* Domestic economy; good management; frugality; thrift; the business of a husbandman; agriculture.

hush, hush, *a.* [Akin to *hist, whist, hiss;* G. *hush,* Dan. *hys, hyst,* a sound made to enjoin silence.] Silent; still; quiet.—*v.t.* To still; to silence; to make quiet; to repress the noise or clamor of.—*To hush up,* to suppress; to procure silence concerning; to keep concealed.—*v.i.* To be still; to be silent; used chiefly in the imperative; be still; make no noise.—*n.* Stillness; quiet.—**hush money,** *n.* A bribe to secure silence; money paid to prevent disclosure of facts.

husk, husk, *n.* [Akin to D. *hulze,* G. *hülse,* a husk; equivalent to E. *hull,* a husk, with *sk* as a termination. HULL.] The external covering of certain fruits or seeds of plants; glume; hull; rind; chaff.—*v.t.* To deprive of the husk.—**husker,** hus′kėr, *n.* One who or that which husks.—**husky,** hus′ki, *a.* Abounding with husks; consisting of husks; resembling husks.

husky, hus′ki, *a.* [Allied to *hoarse;* A. Sax. *hwósta,* Sc. *hoast,* a cough.] Rough in tone, as the voice; powerful; burly.—**huskily,** hus′ki•li, *adv.* In a husky manner.—**huskiness,** hus′ki•nes, *n.* The state of being husky; hoarseness; burliness.

hussar, hụ•zär′, *n.* [Hung. *huszar,* from *husz,* twenty, because in the wars against the Turks every twenty families were bound to furnish one cavalry soldier.] Originally one of the national cavalry of Hungary; now a light cavalry soldier of European armies.

Hussite, hus′īt, *n.* A follower of John *Huss,* the Bohemian religious reformer, burned in 1415.

hussy, huz′i, *n.* [Contr. from *huswife, housewife.*] A bad or worthless woman or girl; a jade; a jilt; a forward girl; a pert, frolicsome wench; also a hussif. See HUSWIFE.

hustings, hus′tingz, *n. pl.* [A.Sax. *hústing,* from acel. *hús-thing.* an assembly, a council—*hús,* house, and *thing,* cause, council. THING.] *Eng.* the platform on which parliamentary candidates stood when addressing the electors; now, any such place; election campaign proceedings. *Hustings court,* a local court in Virginia.

hustle, hus′l, *v.t.* [From D. *hutselen, hutsen,* to jumble or shake together; Sw. *hutla,* to shuffle; akin *hotch*-pot.] To crowd upon so as to shove about roughly; to push or elbow out or about rudely; to jostle.—*v.i. hustled, hustling.* To push or crowd; to move in a confused crowd; to shamble hurriedly.

huswife, huz′if, *n.* A housewife.

hut, hut, *n.* [Same word as D. *hut,* G. *hütte,* Dan. *hytte,* Sw. *hydda,* a hut; comp. W. *cwt,* a hovel.] A small house, hovel, or cabin; a mean dwelling; a wooden house for troops in camp or for settlers in a wild country.—*v.t.*—*hutted, hutting.* To place in huts, as troops encamped in winter quarters.—*v.i.* To take lodgings in huts.

hutch, huch, *n.* [Fr. *huche,* a chest, from L.L. *hutica,* a chest; probably of Teutonic origin and akin to *hut.*] A chest, box, coffer, bin, or other receptable in which things may be stored or animals confined; a low wagon in which coal is drawn up out of the pit; a measure of two bushels.—*v.t.* To place in a hutch.

huzza, hu•zä′, *interj.* A form of *Hurrah.*

hyacinth, hī′a•sinth, *n.* [Gr. *Hyakinthos,* the name of a youth said to have been slain by Apollo, and changed into the flower.] A liliaceous bulbous plant, of which there are many varieties cultivated; a mineral; a variety of zircon, transparent or translucent, of a red color tinged with yellow or brown: the name is also given to varieties of the garnet, the sapphire, and the topaz.—**hyacinthine,** hī•a•sin′thīn, *a.* Made of hyacinth; resembling hyacinth.

Hyades, Hyads, hī′a•dēz, hī′adz, *n. pl.* [Gr. *hyades,* from *hyō,* to rain.] A cluster of seven stars supposed by the ancients to indicate the approach of rainy weather when they rose with the sun.

hyaline, hī′a•lēn, *n.* [L. *hyalinus,* from Gr. *hyalinos,* of glass.] Glassy, transparent, horny substance like that which forms the shell of insects (chitin), found in hydatid cysts.—**hyaline cartilage,** *n.* The horny substance covering the bone ends at the joint.—*a.* Glassy; crystalline; transparent.—**hyalite,** hī′al•īt, *n.* A pellucid variety of opal, resembling colorless gum or resin.—**hyaloid,** hī′al•oid, *a.* Resembling glass; vitriform; transparent.

hybrid, hī′brid or hib′rid, *n.* [From L. *hybrida, hibrida,* a hybrid; origin doubtful.] A crossbred animal or plant; an offspring of two different breeds, genera or varieties.—*a.* Derived or bred from heterogeneous sources.—**hybridism, hybridity,** hī′brid•izm, hib•rid′i•ti, *n.*—**hybridization,** hī′brid•i•zā″shon, *n.*—**hybridize,** hī′brid•īz, *v.t.* To bring into the condition of producing a hybrid; to render hybrid.—**hybridizer,** hī′brid•īz•ėr, *n.*

hydatid, hīd′a•tid, *n.* [Gr. *hydatis,* a vesicle, from *hydōr,* water.] A term applied to larval forms of tapeworms, found in the bodies of men and certain animals, or to similar vesicular or cystlike bodies.

Hydra, hī′dra, *n.* [L. *hydra;* Gr. *hydra,* from *hydōr,* water.] A monster of Greek mythology destroyed by Hercules, and represented as having many heads, one of which, being cut off, was immediately succeeded by another, unless the wound was cauterized; [*not cap.*] hence, evil or misfortune arising from many sources and not easily to be surmounted; a genus of fresh-water polyps of a very low type of structure.—**hydroid,** hī′droid, *a.* Resembling the hydra polyp in character.

hydrangea, hī•dran′jē•a, *n.* [Gr. *hydōr,* water, and *angeion,* a vessel, from the shape of its capsules.] An Asiatic shrub cultivated in gardens for the beauty of its flowers.

hydrant, hī′drant, *n.* [Gr. *hydrainō,* to irrigate, from *hydōr,* water.] A pipe with suitable valves and a spout by which water is raised and discharged from a main pipe.

hydrargyrum, hī•drär′ji•rum, *n.* [L., from Gr. *hydōr,* water, and *argyros,* silver.] Quicksilver or mercury.

hydrate, hī′drāt, *n.* [Gr. *hydōr,* water.] A chemical compound in which water is a characteristic ingredient.—**hydrated,** hī′drā•ted, *a.* Formed into a hydrate.

hydraulic, hī•drạ′lik, *a.* [Fr. *hydraulique,* L. *hydraulicus,* Gr. *hydraulikos,* from *hydraulis,* an instrument played by water—*hydōr,* water, and *aulos,* a pipe.] Pertaining to fluids in motion, or the action of water utilized for mechanical purposes.—*Hydraulic cement,* a cement having the property of becoming hard under water.—*Hydraulic press,* a machine for the application of great power by means of water.—*Hydraulic ram,* a machine by which descending water can be made to raise a portion of itself to a considerable height.—**hydraulics,** hī•drạ′liks, *n.* That branch of science which treats of the motion of liquids, and deals with the application of water in machinery.

hydric, hī′drik, *a.* [Gr. *hydōr,* water.] Of or pertaining to hydrogen.

hydride, hī′drīd, *n.* [Gr. *hydōr,* water and *ide.*] *Chem.* a chemical compound of hydrogen and a metal, or some base.

hydrocarbon, hī•drō•kär′bon, *n.* A chemical compound of hydrogen and carbon.—*Hydrocarbon furnace, hydrocarbon stove,* one in which liquid fuel is used.

hydrocele, hī′dro•sēl, *n.* [Gr. *hydōr,* water, and *kēlē,* a tumor.] *Med.* a morbid collection of serous fluid in the scrotum or testicle.

hydrocephalus, hī′drō•sef″a•lus, *n.* [L. from Gr. *hydrokephalon,* from *hy-*

dōr, water, and *kephatē*, head.] *Med.* a condition in which an abnormal amount of cerebrospinal fluid accumulates in the brain's cavities (ventricles), exerting excessive pressure.

hydrochloric, hī·drō·klō′rik, *a. Chem.* pertaining to, or compounded of, chlorine and hydrogen.

hydrochloric acid, hī′drō·klō″rik as′id, *n.* [*Hydrogen* and *chlorine.*] A concentrated aqueous solution of hydrogen chloride, HCl, that is a strong corrosive acid.

hydrocyanic, hī′drō·sī·an″ik, *a.* [*Hydrogen* and *cyanogen.*] Derived from the combination of hydrogen and cyanogen.

hydrocyanic acid, hī′drō·sī·an″ik as′id, *n.* [*Hydrogen* and *cyanogen.*] An aqueous solution of hydrogen cyanide, HCN, that is a poisonous weak acid used in fumigating.

hydrodynamic, hī′drō·di·nam″ik, *a.* [Gr. *hydōr*, water, and *dynamis*, power.] Pertaining to the force or pressure of water.—**hydrodynamics,** hī′drō·di·nam″iks, *n.* That branch of science which treats of the application of forces to fluids, especially when producing motion in fluids.

hydroelectric, hī′drō·i·lek″trik, *a.* Pertaining to the production of electric current by water power; of a frictional electric machine worked by steam.

hydrofluoric, hī′drō·flū·or″ik, *a.* Consisting of fluorine and hydrogen (*hydrofluoric* acid, a most powerful corrosive.)

hydrofoil, hī″drō·foil′, *n.* [Gr. *hydōr*, water, and *foil.*] A surface, similar to an airfoil, that develops lift as it moves in water; a finlike submerged body, which, at high speeds, lifts a craft's hull above the surface of the water.

hydrogen, hī′dro·jen, *n.* [Gr. *hydōr*, water, and root *gen*, to generate.] A gaseous element, colorless, odorless, flammable, and lighter than any other element. Symbol, H; at. no., 1; at. wt., 1.00797.—**hydrogenate,** hi·droj′e·nate, *v.t.* To treat with, or expose to, hydrogen; to combine with hydrogen.—**hydrogenous,** hī·droj′e·nus, *a.*—**hydrogen bomb,** *n.* A bomb which releases large quantities of atomic energy through the fusion of nuclei at high temperature and pressure.

hydrography, hī·drog′ra·fi, *n.* [Gr. *hydōr*, water, and *graphō*, to describe.] That branch of science which has for its object the measurement and description of the sea, lakes, rivers, and other waters, and includes marine surveying, the drawing of charts, etc.—**hydrographer,** hī·drog′ra·fėr, *n.* One who is proficient in hydrography.—**hydrographic, hydrographical,** hī·dro·graf′ik, hī·dro·graf′i·kal, *a.* Relating to or treating of hydrography.

hydroid. See HYDRA.

hydrokinetics, hī′drō·ki·net″iks, *n.* [Gr. *hydōr*, water, and *kinetics.*] Study of the effect of forces on fluids.

hydrology, hī·drol′o·ji, *n.* [Gr. *hydōr*, water, and *logos*, discourse.] The science that treats of water, its properties, laws, distribution, etc.—**hydrological,** hī·dro·loj′i·kal, *a.* Pertaining to hydrology.—**hydrologist,** hi·drol′o·jist, *n.* One skilled in hydrology.

hydrolysis, hī·drol′i·sis, *n.* [*Hydro* and *lysis*, N.L. from Gr., a loosing.] The chemical decomposition of organic compounds by water.

hydromancy, hī′dro·man·si, *n.* [Gr *hydōr*, water, and *manteia*, divination.] A method of divination by water.

hydromel, hī′dro·mel, *n.* [Fr., from Gr. *hydōr*, water, and *meli*, honey.] A liquor consisting of honey diluted in water; when fermented it forms mead.

hydrometallurgy, hī·dro·met′al·ėr·ji, *n.* The process of assaying or reducing ores by liquid reagents.

hydrometeorology, hī·dro·mē′tē·ėr·ol″o·ji, *n.* The branch of meteorology which concerns itself with water in the atmosphere in the form of rain, clouds, snow, etc.—**hydrometeorological,** hī·dro·mē′tē·ėr·o·loj″i·kal, *a.* Pertaining to this.

hydrometer, hī·drom′et·ėr, *n.* [Gr. *hydōr*, water, *metron*, a measure.] An instrument to measure the specific gravity or density of water and other fluids, and hence the strength of spirituous liquors and of various solutions.—**hydrometric, hydrometrical,** hī·dro·met′rik, hī·drō·met′ri·kal, *a.* Pertaining to a hydrometer or hydrometry.—**hydrometry,** hī·drom′et·ri, *n.* The art or operation of determining the specific gravity, density, force, etc., of fluids.

hydropathy, hī·drop′a·thi, *n.* [Gr. *hydōr*, water, and *pathos*, affection.] The treatment of disease by the use of cold water externally or internally; the water cure.—**hydropathic,** hī·dro·path′ik, *a.* Relating to hydropathy.—*n.* An establishment in which persons are boarded and receive the hydropathic treatment if they wish.—**hydropathist,** hī·drop′a·thist, *n.* One who practices or advocates hydropathy.

hydrophane, hī′dro·fān, *n.* [Gr. *hydōr*, water, and *phainō*, to show.] A variety of opal made transparent by immersion in water.

hydrophobia, hī·dro·fō′bi·a, *n.* [Gr. *hydōr*, water, *phobos*, fear.] A morbid unnatural dread of water; rabies. —**hydrophobic,** hī·dro·fob′ik, *a.*

hydrophone, hī′dro·fōn, *n.* [Gr. *hydōr*, water, and *phōnē*, sound.] An instrument used on ships for the detection of submarines.

hydrophyte, hī′dro·fīt, *n.* [Gr. *hydōr*, water, and *phyton*, a plant.] A plant which lives and grows in water.

hydropic, hydropical, hī·drop′ik, hī·drop′i·kal, *a.* [L. *hydropicus*, Gr. *hydrōpikos*, from *hydrōps*, dropsy—*hydōr*, water, and *ōps*, the face.] Dropsical; pertaining to dropsy.

hydroplane, hī′dro·plān, *n.* [Gr. *hydōr*, water, and *plane.*] An airplane that can take off and land on water; a speedboat with hydrofoils.

hydroscope, hī′dro·skōp, *n.* [Gr. *hydōr*, water, and *skopeō*, to view.] An instrument to mark the presence of water in the air; a kind of ancient water clock.

hydrosoma, hydrosome, hī·dro·sō′ma, hī′dro·sōm, *n.* [*Hydra*, and Gr. *sōma*, body.] The entire organism of any hydrozoan.

hydrostatics, hī·dro·stat′iks, *n.* [Gr. *hydōr*, water, and *statics.*] The science which treats of the weight and equilibrium of fluids, particularly of water; that branch of science which treats of the properties of fluids at rest.

hydrotherapy, hī·drō·ther′a·pi, *n.* [*Hydro* and *therapy.*] The treatment of disease or injury with water, by immersion, etc.

hydrothermal, hī·dro·thėr′mal, *a.* [Gr. *hydōr*, water, and *thermos*, hot.] Of or relating to heated water.

hydrothorax, hī·dro·thō′raks, *n. Med.* dropsy in the thorax or chest.

hydrotropism, hīd′ro·tro̅p″ism, *n.* [Gr. *hydōr*, water, *trepō*, I turn.] *Bot.* curving toward or away from moisture.

hydrous, hī′drus, *a.* Containing water; watery.

hydroxide, hīd·roks′īd, *n.* [Gr. *hydōr*, water, *oxys*, acid.] A compound formed by the union of a metallic or basic radical with one or more hydroxyl groups.

hydroxyl, hīd·roks′il, *n.* [Gr. *hydōr*, water, and *oxys*, acid.] The univalent radical OH, consisting of an oxygen atom and a hydrogen atom linked together.

hydrozoan, hī·dro·zō′an, *n.* pl. **hydrozoa,** hī·dro·zō′a. [Gr. *hydra*, a hydra, and *zōon*, a living creature.] *Zool.* any one of a class of animals that belong to the phylum Coelenterata, consisting mostly of marine animals and including the jellyfish (or nettlefish), the sea anemone, the hydra (or fresh-water polyp), etc.

hyena, hī·ē′na, *n.* [L. *hyæna*, from Gr. *hyaina*, a hyena, from *hys*, a hog, from its hoglike back.] A digitigrade carnivorous animal of several species, belonging to Asia and Africa, strong and fierce, feeding chiefly on carrion, and of nocturnal habits.

hyetal, hī′e·tal, *a.* [Gr. *hyetos*, rain, from *hyō*, to rain.] Relating to rain, or its distribution with reference to different regions.—**hyetograph,** hī′e·to·graf, *n.* A chart showing the rainfall in different regions.—**hyetographic, hyetographical,** hī′e·to·graf″ik, hī′e·to·graf″i·kal, *a.* Pertaining to hyetography.—**hyetography,** hī·e·tog′ra·fi, *n.* The science of the distribution of rain.—**hyetology,** hī·e·tol′o·ji, *n.* That branch of meteorology which treats of the phenomena connected with rain.

hygeian, hī·jē′yan, *a.* [From Gr. *hygieia*, *hygeia*, health, from *hygiēs*, healthy.] Pertaining to health or its preservation.—**hygeist,** hī′jē·ist, *n.* One versed in hygiene.—**hygiene,** hī′ji·ēn, [Fr. *hygiène*, from Gr. *hygieinos*, healthy, wholesome.] A system of principles or rules designed for the promotion of health, especially the health of households or communities; sanitary science.—**hygienic,** hī•ji•en′ik, *a.* Relating to hygienic or sanitary matters.—**hygienically,** hī•ji•en′i•kal•li, *adv.* In a hygienic manner.—**hygienics,** hī•ji•en′iks, *n.* The science of health; hygiene; sanitary science.

hygrograph, hī′grō•graf, *n.* [Gr. *hygros,* moist, and *graphō,* I write.] An instrument which registers automatically the variations of the atmosphere as regards moistness.—**hygrometer,** hī•grom′et•ėr, *n.* An instrument for measuring the degree of moisture of the atmosphere.—**hygrometric,** hī•gro•met′rik, *a.* Pertaining to hygrometry; readily absorbing and retaining moisture.—**hygrometry,** hī•grom′et•ri, *n.* The determination of humidity, or of the moisture of the atmosphere.—**hygrophyte,** hī′gro•fīt, *n.* [Gr. *hygros,* moisture, *phyton,* a plant.] A land plant adapted to moist surroundings.—**hygroscope,** hī′gro•skōp, *n.* An instrument for indicating the presence of moisture in the atmosphere.—**hygroscopic,** hī•gro•skop′ik, *a.* Pertaining to the hygroscope; imbibing moisture from the atmosphere.

hylism, hī′lizm, *n.* [Gr. *hylē,* a wood, timber, matter.] A theory which regarded matter as the original principle of evil, in opposition to the good spirit.—**hylozoism,** hī•lo•zō′izm, *n.* [Gr. *zōe,* life.] The doctrine that matter possesses a species of life, or that life and matter are inseparably connected.—**hylozoist,** hī•lo•zō′ist, *n.* A believer in hylozoism.—**hylozoic,** hī•lo•zō′ik, *a.* Pertaining to hylozoism.

hymen, hī′men, *n.* [Gr. *hymēn,* a skin, a membrane; *Hymēn,* the God of marriage.] *Anat.* the virginal membrane, situated at the entrance of the vagina; *bot.* the fine pellicle which encloses a flower in the bud.

hymeneal, hymenean, hī•men•ē′al, hī•men•ē′an, *a.* Pertaining to marriage.—*n.* A marriage song.

hymenopter, hymenopteran, hī•men•op′tėr, hī•men•op′tėr•an, *n.* [Gr. *hymēn,* a membrane, and *pteron,* a wing.] A member of an order of insects, having four membranous wings, and including the bees, wasps, ants, etc.—**hymenopterous,** hī•men•op′tėr•us, *a.* Belonging or pertaining to the hymenopters.

hymn, him, *n.* [L. *hymnus,* from Gr. *hymnos,* a song, a song of praise.] A song or ode in honor of God, or in honor of some deity; a sacred lyric; a song of praise, adoration, or thanksgiving.—*v.t.* To praise or celebrate in hymn or song; to sing.—*v.i.* To sing in praise or adoration.—**hymnal, hymnbook,** him′nal, *n.* A collection of hymns, generally for use in public worship.—**hymnologist,** him•nol′o•jist, *n.* A composer of hymns.—**hymnology, hymnody,** him•nol′o•ji, him′no•di, *n.* A body of sacred lyrics composed by several authors of a particular period or country; hymns collectively.

hyoid, hī′oid, *a.* [Gr. *hyoeidēs,* shaped like the letter *u* or *y.*] Applied to a movable bone having somewhat the shape of the letter U, between the root of the tongue and the larynx.

hyoscyamine, hī•o•sī′am•in, *n.* [From *hyoscyamus.*] Alkaloid poisons occurring in henbane (*Hyoscyamus*).

hypaethral, hypethral, hī•pē′thral, *a.* [Gr. *hypaithros,* under the sky—*hypo* under, and *aithēr,* ether.] *Arch.* applied to a building not covered by a roof.

hypanthium, hī•pan′thi•um, *n.* [Gr. *hypo,* under, *anthos,* flower.] *Bot.* the fleshy enlarged hollow of the end of a flowerstalk, as in the rose.

hyperaemia, hī•per•ē′mi•a, *n.* [Gr. *hyper,* over or above, and *haima,* blood.] An excessive accumulation of blood in a part of the body.—**hyperaemic,** hī•pėr•ē′mik, *a.* Pertaining to or affected with hyperaemia.

hyperaesthesis, hyperaesthesia, hī′pėr•es•thē″sis, hī′pėr•es•thē″zi•a, *n.* [Gr. *over,* and *aisthēsis,* sensation.] Morbid excess of sensibility.

hyperbola, hī•pėr′bo•la, *n.* [Gr. *hyperbolē.* HYPERBOLE.] *Geom.* a curve formed by a plane that cuts a cone in a direction parallel to its axis, or so that the plane makes a greater angle with the base than the side of the cone makes.—**hyperbolic,** hī•pėr•bol′ik, *a.* Having the properties of the hyperbola.

hyperbole, hī•pėr′bo•lē, *n.* [Gr. *hyperbolē,* excess—*hyper,* beyond, *ballō,* to throw.] A figure of speech which expresses much more or less than the truth; an exaggerated statement; exaggeration.—**hyperbolic, hyperbolical,** hī•pėr•bol′ik, hī•pėr•bol′i•kal, *a.*—**hyperbolically,** hī•pėr•bol′i•kal•li, *adv.*—**hyperbolism,** hī•pėr′bol•izm, *n.*—**hyperbolize,** hī•pėr′bol•īz, *v.t.* and *i.* To speak or write with exaggeration; to exaggerate.

Hyperborean, hī•pėr•bō′rē•an, *a.* [Gr. *hyper,* beyond, *boreas,* the north.] Belonging to a region very far north; northern; arctic; frigid.—*n.* An inhabitant of the most northern region of the earth.

hypercatalectic, hī•pėr•kat′a•lek″tik, *a.* [Gr. *hyper,* beyond, and *katalēxis,* termination.] *Pros.* having a syllable or two beyond the regular measure.

hypercritic, hī•pėr•krit′ik, *n.* [Gr. *hyper,* beyond, and *kritikos,* critical. CRITIC.] One who is critical beyond measure or reason.—**hypercritical,** hī•pėr•krit′i•kal, *a.* Overcritical; critical beyond use or reason.—**hypercritically,** hī•pėr•krit′i•kal•li, *adv.* In a hypercritical manner.

hyperdulia, hī•pėr•dū′li•a, *n.* [Gr. *hyper,* beyond, and *douleia,* service.] The worship offered by Roman Catholics to the Virgin Mary, so called because higher than that given to saints (which is known as *dulia*).

hypergolic, hī•pėr•gol′ik, *adj.* [*Hypergol* and *ic.*] Capable of igniting itself on contact with an oxidizer, said of rocket fuel.

hyperkinesis, hī′pėr•ki•nē″sis, *n.* [Gr. *hyper,* beyond, and *kinēsis,* motion.] Abnormal increase of muscular movement; spasmodic action.—**hyperkinetic,** hī′pėr•ki•net″ik, *a.*

hypermeter, hī•pėr′me•tėr, *n.* [Gr. *hyper,* beyond, and *metron,* measure.] A hypercatalectic verse; something beyond ordinary measure.—**hypermetrical,** hī•pėr•met′ri•kal, *a.*

hypermetropia, hypermetropy, hī′pėr•me•trō″pi•a, hī•pėr•met′ro•pi, *n.* [Gr. *hyper,* over, *metron,* measure, *ops,* the eye.] A defect of the eyesight in which the focus for all objects falls behind the retina, and which is corrected by convex glasses; long-sightedness.

hyperplasia, hī•pėr•plā′si•a, *n.* [Gr. *hyper,* beyond, *plassō,* to form.] *Pathol.* excessive growth of a part by multiplication of cells.

hyperpyrexia, hī′pėr•pi•rek″si•a, *n.* [Prefix *hyper* and *pyrexia.*] An excessive degree of fever.

hypersonic, hī•pėr•son′ik, *a.* [*Hyper* and *sonic,* from L. *sonus,* sound.] Of a speed five times or more faster than that of sound in air; capable of moving or using air currents that move at hypersonic speed.

hypersthene, hī′pėr•sthēn, *n.* [Gr. *hyper,* beyond, *sthenos,* strength; from its difficult frangibility as compared with hornblende.] A mineral of the hornblende group, a constituent of some rocks; also called *Labrador hornblende.*

hypertension, hī•pėr•ten′shon, *n.* [*Hyper* and *tension.*] Abnormally high arterial blood pressure.

hyperthyroidism, hī•pėr•thī′roid•ism, *n.* [*Hyper* and *thyroidism.*] *Med.* excessive activity of the thyroid gland.—**hyperthyroid,** hī•pėr•thī′roid, *n.* and *a.*

hypertrophy, hī•pėr′tro•fi, *n.* [Gr. *hyper,* above, and *trophē,* nutrition.] A morbid enlargement of a part of the body; excessive growth.—**hypertrophic,** hī•pėr•trof′ik, *a.*

hypha, hī′fa, *n.*; pl. **hyphae,** hī′fē. [Gr. *hypē,* a web.] The thready or filamentous matter forming the mycelium of a fungus.—**hyphal,** hī′fal, *a.* Pertaining to a hypha.

hyphen, hī′fen, *n.* [Gr. *hyphen,* strictly *hyph'hen,* into or in one, together—*hypo,* under, and *hen,* one.] A mark or short line made between two words to show that they form a compound word, or used to connect the syllables of a divided word.—*v.t.* To join by a hyphen.

hypnosis, hip•nō′sis, *n.* The hypnotic state; a sort of sleep artificially induced, often by the person fixing his attention upon some bright object, being accompanied by more or less unconsciousness.—**hypnotist,** hip′no•tist, *n.* One who hypnotizes.

hypnotic, hip•not′ik, *a.* [Gr. *hypnos,* sleep; akin L. *sopor,* sleep, A.Sax. *swefen,* a dream.] Having the quality of producing sleep; tending to produce sleep; soporific.—*n.* A medicine that produces sleep; a soporific.—**hypnotism,** hip′no•tizm, *n.* A sleeplike condition brought on by artificial means.—**hypnotize,** hip′no•tīz, *v.t.* To affect with hypnotism.—**hypnologist,** hip•nol′o•jist, *n.* One versed in hypnology.—**hypnology,** hip•nol′o•ji, *n.* Facts relating to the phenomena of sleep.

hypoblast, hī′po•blast, *n.* [Gr. *hypo,* under, and *blastos,* a bud.] *Bot.* the flat dorsal cotyledon of a grass; *anat.* the lower of the two layers of cells forming the blastoderm, the upper being the epiblast.

hypocaust, hī′po•kąst, *n.* [Gr. *hypokauston—hypo,* under, and *kaiō,* to burn.] *Anc. arch.* an arched chamber in which a fire was kindled for the purpose of giving heat to the rooms above it; also a compartment of some modern stoves.

hypochondria, hī•po•kon′dri•a, *n.* [From the *hypochondrium* being regarded as the seat of the disease. See below.] *Med.* a disease characterized by exaggerated uneasiness and anxiety, mainly as to what concerns the health, etc.; spleen; vapors; low spirits.—**hypochondriac, hypochondriacal,** hī•po•kon′dri•ak, hī′po•kon•drī″a•kal, *a.* Pertaining to hypochondria or to the hypochondrium: affected with hypochondria.—**hypochondriac,** *n.* A person affected with hypochondria.—**hypochondriacally,** hī′po•kon•drī″a•kal•li, *adv.* In a hypochondriac manner.—**hypochondriasis,** hī′po•kon•drī″a•sis, *n.* Hypochondria.—**hypochondrium,** hī•po•kon′dri•um, *n.* pl. **hypochondria.** [Gr. *hypochondrion,* from *hypo,* under, and *chondros,* cartilage—from its situation.] *Anat.* the name of the two regions of the abdomen under the cartilages of the false ribs on the right and left side.

hypocotyl, hī′po•kot″il, *n.* [Gr. *hypo,* under, *cotyl*(edon).] In seedlings, that part of the stem below the seed leaves (cotyledons).

hypocrisy, hi•pok′ri•si, *n.* [Fr. *hypocrisie,* L. *hypocrisis,* Gr. *hypokrisis,* a playing a part on the stage, simulation, from *hypokrinomai,* to play a part, to feign—*hypo,* and *krinō,* to separate, discern. CRITIC.] The act or practice of simulating or feigning to be what one is not; especially, the assuming of a false appearance of piety and virtue; dissimulation; insincerity.—**hypocrite,** hip′o•krit, *n.* [Fr. *hypocrite,* Gr. *hypokritēs.*] One who practices hypocrisy.—**hypocritical,** hip•o•krit′i•kal, *a.* Pertaining to, or proceeding from, hypocrisy; characterized by hypocrisy; pretending goodness or religion; insincere.—**hypocritically,** hip•o•krit′i•kal•li, *adv.*

hypocycloid, hī•po•sī′kloid, *n.* [Gr. *hypo,* under, and E. *cycloid.*] A curve generated by the movement of a curve upon the concave side of a fixed curve.

hypodermic, hī•po•dėr′mik, *a.* [Gr. *hypo,* under, *derma,* the skin.] Pertaining to or relating to parts under the skin or to the introduction of medicines under the skin.—**hypodermic injection,** hī•po•dėr′mik in•jek′shon, *n. Med.* an injection made into the subcutaneous tissues.

hypogastrium, hī•po•gas′tri•um, *n.* [Gr. *hypo,* under, and *gastēr,* the belly.] *Anat.* the lower anterior region of the abdomen.—**hypogastric,** hī•po•gas′trik, *a.*

hypogeal, hypogeous, hī•po•jē′al, hī•po•jē′us, *a.* [Gr. *hypo,* beneath, *gē,* the earth.] *Lit.* subterranean; *bot.* a term applied to parts of plants which grow beneath the surface of the earth.

hypogene, hī′po•jēn, *a.* [Gr. *hypo,* under, and root *gen,* to produce.] *Geol.* formed or originating under the surface of the earth (as crystalline rocks).

hypoglossal, hī•po•glos′al, *a.* [Gr. *hypo,* under, *glōssa,* the tongue.] *Anat.* pertaining to the under side of the tongue.

hypogynous, hī•poj′i•nus, *a.* [Gr. *hypo,* under, *gynē,* a female.] *Bot.* placed below the ovary or seed vessel; having the corolla and stamens inserted below the ovary.

hyponasty, hī′po•nas•ti, *n.* [Gr. *hypo,* under, *nastos,* pressed.] *Bot.* excessive growth of the under surface of an organ, causing it to bend upward: as opposed to *epinasty.*

hypophosphite, hī′po•fos′fit, *n.* The name of certain bodies containing phosphorus, some of which are used medicinally.

hypostasis, hī•pos′ta•sis, *n.* pl. **hypostases,** hī•pos′ta•sēz. [Gr. *hypostasis,* substance, nature, essence, also sediment.] The sediment or deposit that settles at the bottom of a fluid; the essential nature of any thing or any person; the accumulation of blood in the lower parts of the body; *theol.* the distinct substance or subsistence of the Father, Son, and Holy Spirit in the Godhead.—**hypostatic, hypostatical,** hī•po•stat′ik, hī•po•stat′i•kal, *a.* Relating to hypostasis.—*Hypostatic union,* the union of the three persons in the Godhead, or the union of the divine and human nature in the person of Christ.—**hypostatize,** hī•pos′ta•tīz, *v.t.* To regard as a distinct substance.

hypostyle, hī′po•stīl, *n.* [Gr. *hypo,* under, *stylos,* a pillar.] *Arch.* a covered colonnade; a pillared hall.—*a.* Having the roof supported by pillars.

hyposulfite, hī•po•sul′fīt, *n.* The name of certain substances containing sulfur, of which the hyposulfite of sodium is used in medicine and the arts.

hypotenuse, hypothenuse, hī•pot′e•nūs, *n.* [Gr. *hypoteinousa—hypo,* under, and *teinō,* to stretch.] *Geom.* the longest side of a right-angled triangle; the line that subtends the right angle.

hypothec, hī•poth′ek, *n.* [L. *hypotheca,* Gr. *hypothēkē,* a pledge, from *hypotithēmi,* to put under, to pledge.] *Scots law,* a lien such as that which a landlord has over the furniture or crops of his tenant in respect of the current rent.—**hypothecary,** hī•poth′e•ke•ri, *a.* Of or pertaining to hypothecation.—**hypothecate,** hī•poth′e•kāt, *v.t.—hypothecated, hypothecating.* To pledge in security for a debt, but without transfer; to mortgage.—**hypothecation,** hī•poth′e•kā″shon, *n.* The act of hypothecating.—**hypothecator,** hī•poth′e•kā•tėr, *n.* One who hypothecates.

hypothesis, hī•poth′e•sis, *n.* pl. **hypotheses,** hī•poth′e•sēz. [Gr. *hypothesis,* a supposition, from *hypo,* under, and *tithēmi,* to place.] A supposition; something not proved, but assumed for the purpose of argument; a theory imagined or assumed to account for what is not understood.—**hypothesize,** hi•poth′e•sīz, *v.i.* To form hypotheses.—**hypothetical,** hī•po•thet′i•kal, *a.*—**hypothetically,** hī•po•thet′i•kal•li, *adv.*

hypothyroid, hī•po•thī′roid, *n.* [*Hypo* and *thyroid,* Gr. *thyreos,* a shield, *eidos,* form.] One affected by a deficient thyroid gland.—**hypothyroidism,** hī•pō•thī′roid•izm, *n. Med.* the deficient activity of the thyroid gland; the resulting condition.

hypsometer, hip•som′et•ėr, *n.* [Gr. *hypsos,* height, *metron,* measure.] A special kind of barometer for measuring altitudes; an apparatus used for measuring heights by noting the boiling point of water.—**hypsometric, hypsometrical,** hip•so•met′rik, hip•so•met′ri•kal, *a.* Pertaining to hypsometry.—**hypsometrically,** hip•so•met′ri•kal•li, *adv.* According to hypsometry.—**hypsometry,** hip•som′et•ri, *n.* The art of measuring the heights of places upon the surface of the earth.

Hyrcanian, hėr•kā′ni•an, *a.* Pertaining to Hyrcania, which was an ancient province of the Persian Empire in Asia, somewhere southwest of the Caspian Sea. The Caspian Sea in literature is sometimes called the "Hyrcanian Sea."

hyrax, hī′raks, *n.* [Gr., a shrew mouse.] A small rabbit-like animal of Syria, believed to be the 'coney' of Scripture; a kindred species of South Africa.

hyson, hī′son, *n.* [Chinese *hi-tshun,* lit. first crop.] A species of green tea from China.

hyssop, his′op, *n.* [Gr. *hyssōpos,* hyssop.] The name of small bushy herbs of the mint family, the plants being aromatic and stimulating.

hysterectomy, his•tėr•ek′to•mē, *n.* [Gr. *hystera,* the uterus, *ektomē,* a cutting out or off.] In surgery, the excision, or removal, of the uterus.

hysteresis, his′te•rē″sis, *n.* [N.L. from Gr. *hysterein,* to be behind, to lag.] Any of several lagging effects resembling an internal friction which result when the forces acting on a body (such as magnetism, electricity and physical strain) are changed.

hysteria, hysterics, his•tē′ri•a, his•ter′iks, *n.* [L.L. *hysteria,* from Gr. *hystera,* the womb.] A nervous illness, marked by fits of laughing and crying.—**hysterical,** his•ter′i•kal, *a.*—**hysterically,** his•ter′i•kal•li, *adv.*

hysteron proteron, his′tėr•on prot″ėr•on, *n.* [Gr. *hysteron,* last, and *proteron,* first.] An inversion of the natural order in words; a putting first what should be last.

hysterotomy, his•tėr•ot′o•mi, *n.* [Gr. *hystera,* the uterus, *tomē,* a cutting.] The operation of cutting into the uterus to take out a fetus which cannot be expelled by the usual means.

I

I, i, ī, the ninth letter and the third vowel of the English alphabet, in which it represents not only several vowel sounds but also the consonantal sound of *y*.

I, ī, *pron.* pos. *my* or *mine*, dat. and obj. *me*; pl. nom. *we*, pos. *our* or *ours*, dat. and obj. *us*. [A.Sax. *ic*, D. *ik*, Goth. *ik*, G. *ich*, Icel. *ek*, Dan. *jeg*, L. *ego*, Gr. *egō*, Skr. *aham*, W. *ym*, Armor. *em*—I.] The nominative case of the pronoun of the first person; the word by which a speaker or writer denotes himself: sometimes used as a noun; the ego.

iamb, iambus, ī′amb, ī•am′bus, *n.* pl.—**iambs, iambi,** ī′ambs, ī•am′bī. [Gr. *iambos*, from *iapto*, to assail.] *Pros.* a foot consisting of two syllables, the first short and the last long, or the first unaccented and the last accented, as in *delight*.—**iambic,** ī•am′bik, *a.* Pertaining to the iambus; composed of iambi.—*n.* An iambic foot; a verse consisting of iambi.

Iberian, ī•bē′ri•an, *n.* One of the primitive inhabitants of Spain; the language of the ancient Iberians, of which Basque is supposed to be the representative.

ibex, ī′beks, *n.* [L., a kind of goat.] An animal of the goat family found in the Alps and Pyrenees, with large horns directed backward and marked with transverse ridges in front.

ibis, ī′bis, *n.* [Gr. and L.] A name of certain grallatorial birds allied to the storks, the most remarkable species of which, the sacred ibis, was revered by the ancient Egyptians.

Icarian, ī•kā′ri•an, *a.* [From *Icarus*, in Greek mythol., who, flying with a pair of artificial wings, soared so high that the sun melted the wax that cemented his wings, and caused him to fall into the sea.] Adventurous in flight; soaring too high for safety.

ICBM. See INTERCONTINENTAL.

ice, īs, *n.* [A.Sax. *īs*=D. *ijs*, Dan. and Sw. *is*, Icel. *iss*, G. *eis*, referred along with *iron*, G. *eisen*, to a root meaning to shine or glance.] Water or other fluid congealed or in a solid state in consequence of the abstraction of the heat necessary to preserve its fluidity.—*To break the ice*, to make the first opening to any attempt; to open the way.—*v.t.*—*iced, icing*. To cover with ice; to convert into ice; to cool with ice; to freeze; to cover with concreted sugar.—**iceberg,** īs′bėrg, *n.* [D. *ijsberg*—*ijs*, ice, and *berg*, a mountain.] A vast body of ice floating on the ocean.—**iceboat,** *n.* A strong boat that can break a passage through ice; a boat for sailing with runners on the surface of ice.—**icebound,** īs′bound, *a.* Surrounded with ice so as to be immovable, or inaccessible.—**icebreaker,** *n.* A massive and powerful steamer that smashes and forces a way through ice.—**ice cream,** *n.* Cream variously flavored, and congealed by means of a freezing mixture.—**iced,** īst, *p.* Covered with ice; cooled with ice; frosted.—**ice field,** *n.* A large sheet of sea ice whose limits cannot be seen.—**ice foot,** īs′fụt, *n.* A belt or fringe of ice that forms round the shores in arctic regions.—**icehouse,** īs′hous, *n.* A repository for the preservation of ice during warm weather.—**ice plant,** *n.* A plant belonging to Greece, the Canaries, and the Cape, so called from being studded with pellucid watery vesicles which shine like pieces of ice.—**ice sheet,** *n.* A thick sheet of ice covering a land area and not limited to valleys.—**icicle,** ī′si•kl, *n.* [A.Sax. *is-gicel*, from *is*, and *gicel*, an icicle; akin to Icel. *jökull*, icicle, *jaki*, a piece of ice.] A pendent conical mass of ice formed by the freezing of water or other fluid as it drops from something.—**icily,** ī′si•li, *adv.* In an icy manner.—**iciness,** ī′si•nes, *n.* The state of being icy or very cold.—**icy,** ī′si, *a.* Pertaining to, composed of, produced by, resembling or abounding with ice; *fig.* characterized by coldness or coolness, as of manner, etc.; frigid; chilling; indifferent.

Icelander, īs′lan•dėr, *n.* A native of Iceland.—**Icelandic,** īs•lan′dik, *a.* Pertaining to Iceland.—*n.* The language of the Icelanders or of their literature, the oldest of the Scandinavian group of tongues.—**Iceland moss,** *n.* A species of lichen found in the arctic regions and on lofty mountains, used in medicine and as a nutritious article of diet.—**Iceland spar,** *n.* A transparent variety of calcareous spar, or carbonate of lime, valuable for experiments on the double refraction and polarization of light.

ichneumon, ik•nū′mon, *n.* [Gr., from *ichneuō*, to track out, from *ichnos*, a footstep—the animal searches out crocodiles' eggs.] A digitigrade carnivorous animal of Egypt, resembling a weasel, and feeding on crocodiles' eggs, snakes, etc.; a mongoose; a hymenopterous insect whose larvae are parasitic on other insects (called also *ichneumon fly*).

ichnite, ik′nīt, *n.* [Gr. *ichnos*, a footprint.] *Geol.* a fossil footprint; the footprint of an extinct animal marked on rocks.—**ichnology,** ik•nol′o•ji, *n.* The fossil footmarks of animals.

ichnography, ik•nog′ra•fi, *n.* [Gr. *ichnos*, a footstep, and *grapho*, to describe.] The horizontal section of a building or other object, showing its true dimensions according to a geometric scale; a ground plan.

ichor, ī′kor, *n.* [Gr.] An ethereal fluid that supplied the place of blood in the veins of the gods of the Greeks and Romans; *med.* a thin watery humor, like serum or whey; a thin watery acrid discharge from an ulcer, wound, etc.—**ichorous,** ī′ko•rus, *a.* Like ichor; thin; watery; serous.

ichthyic, ik′thi•ik, *a.* [Gr. *ichthys*, a fish.] Pertaining to fishes; fishlike.—**ichthyography,** ik•thi•og′ra•fi, *n.* The description of fishes.—**ichthyoid, ichthyoidal,** ik′thi•oid, ik•thi•oi′dal, *a.* More or less fishlike.—**ichthyologic, ichthyological,** ik′thi•o•loj″ik, ik′thi•o•loj″i•kal, *a.* Pertaining to ichthyology.—**ichthyologist,** ik•thi•ol′o•jist, *n.* One versed in ichthyology.—**ichthyology,** ik•thi•ol′o•ji, *n.* The science of fishes; that branch of zoology which treats of fishes.—**ichthyophagous,** ik•thi•of′a•gus, *a.* Eating or subsisting on fish.—**ichthyophagy,** ik•thi•of′a•ji, *n.* The practice of eating fish.—**ichthyornis,** ik•thi•or′nis, *n.* [Gr. *ornis*, a bird.] A fossil bird with vertebrae like those of fishes, and with teeth set in sockets.—**ichthyosaurus, ichthyosaur,** ik′thi•o•sạ″rus, ik″thi•o•sạr′, *n.* [Gr. *sauros*, a lizard.] A fishlike lizard; an immense fossil marine reptile, combining many of the characters of lizards and fishes.—**ichthyosis,** ik•thi•ō′sis, *n.* A disease of the skin, portions of which become hard and scaly, with a tendency to excrescences.

icon, ī′kon, *n.* [Gr. *eikōn*, an image, from *eikō*, to resemble.] An image or representation; a portrait; the holy picture or emblem regarded as sacred in the Greek and Russian Church.—**iconoclasm,** ī•kon′o•klazm, *n.* The act, principles, or proceedings of an iconoclast.—**iconoclast,** ī•kon′o•klast, *n.* [Gr. *eikōn*, and *klastēs*, a breaker, from *klaō*, to break.] A breaker of images; any destroyer or exposer of shams or superstitions; one who makes attacks upon cherished beliefs.—**iconoclastic,** ī•kon′o•klas″tik, *a.* Pertaining to an iconoclast.—**iconography,** ī•ko•nog′ra•fi, *n.* [Gr. *eikōn*, and *graphō*, to describe.] That branch of knowledge which treats of ancient statues, busts, paintings in fresco, mosaic works, engraving on gems or metals, and the like.—**iconographic,** ī•kon′o•graf″ik, *a.* Relating to iconography; representing by diagrams or pictures.—**iconolater,** ī•ko•nol′at•ėr, *n.* [Gr. *eikōn*, and *latreia*, service.] One that worships images.—**iconolatry,** ī•ko•nol′at•ri, *n.* The worship or adoration of images.—**iconology,** ī•ko•nol′o•ji, *n.* The doctrine of images or emblematical representations; iconography.

icosahedral, ī′kos•a•hē″dral, *a.* [Gr. *eikosi*, twenty, and *hedra*, seat, side.] Having twenty equal sides.—**icosahedron,** ī′kos•a•hē″dron, *n.* A solid of twenty equal sides.

icteric, icterical, ik•ter′ik, ik•ter′i•kal, *a.* [L. *icterus*, jaundice.] Affected with jaundice; curative of jaundice.

ictus, ik′tus, *n.* [L., from *ico*, to strike.] A stroke; the stress laid on an accented syllable.

id, id, *n.* [Gr. *idios*, distinct.] *Psych.* that part of the unconscious that harbors instinctive impulses and seeks pleasure.

idea, ī•dē′a, *n.* [L. *idea*, from Gr. *idea*, the form or appearance of a thing, kind or species, from *idein*, to see; same root as E. *wit*.] The form, image, or model of anything in the mind; that which is held or comprehended by the understanding or intellectual faculties; as a philosophical term, now generally used to designate subjective notions and representations, with or without objective validity; popularly it signifies notion, conception, thought, opinion, belief.—**ideal,** ī•dē′al, *a.* Existing in idea; existing in fancy or imagination only; visionary.—*n.* An imaginary model of perfection; a standard of perfection or beauty.—*Beau Ideal.* See BEAU.—**idealism,** ī•dē′al•izm, *n.* That system of philosophy according to which nothing exists but the mind itself and ideas perceived by the mind, or which maintains that we have no rational grounds for believing in the reality of anything but percipient minds and ideas.—**idealist,** ī•dē′al•ist, *n.* One who holds the doctrine of idealism; one who idealizes; one who indulges in flights of fancy or imagination; a visionary.—**idealistic,** ī•dē′al•is″tik, *a.* Pertaining to idealism or idealists.—**ideality,** ī•di•al′i•ti, *n.* The condition or quality of being ideal; capacity to form ideals of beauty and perfection.—**idealization,** ī•dē′al•i•zā″shon, *n.* The act of idealizing.—**idealize,** ī•dē′al•īz, *v.t.*—*idealized, idealizing.* To make ideal; to give form to in accordance with any preconceived ideal; to embody in an ideal form.—*v.i.* To form ideals.—**idealizer,** ī•dē′al•ī•zėr, *n.* One who idealizes; an idealist.—**ideally,** ī•dē′al•li, *adv.* In an ideal manner.—**ideation,** ī•di•ā′shon, *n.* The faculty of the mind for forming ideas; the establishment of a distinct mental representation or idea of an object.—**ideational,** ī•di•ā′shon•al, *a.* Pertaining to ideation.—**ideograph, ideogram,** id′i•o•graf, id′i•ō•gram, *n.* In some systems of writing, a character, symbol, or figure which suggests the idea of an object without expressing its name; a hieroglyphic.—**ideographic, ideographical,** id′i•o•graf″ik, id′i•o•graf″i•kal, *a.* Representing ideas independently of sounds; pertaining to that mode of writing which, by means of symbols, figures, or hieroglyphics, suggests the ideas of objects.—**ideographically,** id′i•o•graf″i•kal•li, *adv.* In an ideographic manner.—**ideography,** id•i•og′ra•fi, *n.* Writing in ideographic characters or symbols.—**ideology,** id′i•ol″o•ji, *n.* The science of ideas or of their understanding; that system of mental philosophy which exclusively derives our knowledge from sensation.—**ideological,** id′i•o•loj″i•kal, *a.* Pertaining to ideology.—**ideologist,** id•i•ol′o•jist, *n.* One who treats of ideas; one who indulges in ideas or theories; a supporter of ideology.

identical, identic, ī•den′ti•kal, ī•den′tik, *a.* [L.L. *identicus,* from L. *idem,* the same.] The same; not another or different.—*Identical proposition,* a proposition in which the terms of the subject and the predicate comprise the same idea, as that the whole is equal to its parts.—**identically,** ī•den′ti•kal•li, *adv.* In an identical manner.—**identicalness,** ī•den′ti•kal•nes, *n.* Sameness.—**identification,** ī•den′ti•fi•kā″shon, *n.* The act of identifying.—*Identification tag.* A disk worn around the neck by both officers and men in active military service, showing name, number, unit, etc.—**identify,** ī•den′ti•fī, *v.t.*—*identified, identifying.* [From *identi-,* in *identity,* and L. *facio,* to make.] To make to be the same; to unite or combine in such a manner as to make one; to determine or establish the identity of; to ascertain or prove to be the same with something described or claimed.—*v.i.* To become the same.—**identity,** ī•den′ti•ti, *n.* [L.L. *identitas,* from L. *idem,* same.] The state or fact of being identical; sameness, as distinguished from similitude and diversity.—*Personal identity,* our being the same persons from the commencement to the end of life while the matter of the body, the dispositions, habits, thoughts, etc., are continually changing.—*Principle of identity, philos.* the principle that a thing is what it is and not another.

ideograph, ideology, etc. See IDEA.

ides, īdz, *n. pl.* [L. *idus,* the ides, from *iduo,* to divide.] In the ancient Roman calendar the 13th of January, February, April, June, August, September, November, and December, and the 15th of March, May, July, and October.

idiocrasy, id•i•ok′ra•si, *n.* [Gr. *idios,* peculiar, and *krasis,* mixture, temperament.] Peculiarity of constitution; temperament or constitution peculiar to a person; idiosyncrasy.

idiocy. See IDIOT.

idioelectric, id′i•ō•i•lek″trik, *a.* [Gr. *idios,* one's own, and E. *electric.*] Electric by virtue of its own peculiar properties.

idiom, id′i•om, *n.* [Fr. *idiome,* L. *idioma,* from Gr. *idiōma,* from *idios,* proper, or peculiar to one's self.] A mode of expression peculiar to a language or to a person; a phrase or expression having a special meaning from usage, or a special grammatical character; the genius or peculiar cast of a language; a peculiar form or variety of language; a dialect.—**idiomatic, idiomatical,** id′i•o•mat″ik, id′i•o•mat″i•kal, *a.* Having the character of an idiom; pertaining to the particular modes of expression which belong to a language.—**idiomatically,** id′i•o•mat″i•kal•li, *adv.* In an idiomatic manner.

idiomorphic, id′i•o•mor″fik, *a.* [Gr. *idios,* one's own, *morphē,* form.] Having a peculiar or distinctive form.

idiopathy, id•i•op′a•thi, *n.* [Gr. *idios,* proper, peculiar, and *pathos,* suffering.] A morbid state or condition not preceded and occasioned by any other disease.—**idiopathic,** id′i•o•path″ik, *a.* Pertaining to idiopathy; not symptomatic.

idiosyncrasy, id′i•o•sin″kra•si, *n.* [Gr. *idios,* proper, *syn,* with, and *krasis,* temperament.] A personal peculiarity of constitution or temperament; a mental or moral characteristic belonging to and distinguishing an individual; peculiar way of thinking or feeling.—**idiosyncratic,** id′i•ō•sin•krat″ik, *a.* Relating to idiosyncrasy.

idiot, id′i•ot, *n.* [L. *idiota,* from Gr. *idiōtēs,* a private, vulgar, unskilled person, from *idios,* private, peculiar to one's self.] The lowest level of feeblemindedness in which an individual is possessed of a maximum mental age of two years, or an IQ of 25; a silly, foolish person.—*a.* Pertaining to an idiot; afflicted with idiocy.—**idiocy,** id′i•o•si, *n.*—**idiotic, idiotical,** id•i•ot′ik, id•i•ot′i•kal, *a.* Like or relating to an idiot; foolish; utterly absurd.—**idiotically,** id•i•ot′i•kal•li, *adv.* In an idiotic manner.

idle, ī′dl, *a.* [A.Sax., *idel,* vain, empty, idle = D. *ijdel,* G. *eitel,* idle; Dan. *idel,* mere; from root meaning to shine (Skr. *idh,* Gr. *aithō,* to burn).] Not engaged in any occupation; unoccupied; doing nothing; slothful; averse to labor or employment; lazy; vacant, or not spent in work (*idle* hours); remaining unused; producing no effect; useless, vain, ineffectual, or fruitless (*idle* rage); trifling or irrelevant (an *idle* story).—*v.i.*—*idled, idling.* To lose or spend time in inaction or without being employed.—*v.t.* To spend in idleness: generally followed by *away.*—**idleness,** ī′dl•nes, *n.* The condition or quality of being idle.—**idler,** īd′lėr, *n.* One who idles.—**idle wheel,** *n.* In machinery, a wheel placed between two others for the purpose simply of transferring the motion from one axis to the other without change of direction.—**idly,** īd′li, *adv.* In an idle manner.

idocrase, ī′dō•krās, *n.* [Gr. *eidos,* form, and *krasis,* mixture, from the mixture of forms its crystals display.] A mineral differing from garnet chiefly in form, occurring, variously colored, in the lavas of Vesuvius and elsewhere; pyramidal garnet or Vesuvian.

idol, ī′dol, *n.* [Fr. *idole,* L. *idolum,* from Gr. *eidōlon,* an image, form, phantom, idol, from *eidos,* form; same root as in *idea.*] An image, representation, or symbol of a deity made or consecrated as an object of worship; any person or thing on which we strongly set our affections; that to which we are excessively, often improperly, attached.—**idolater,** ī•dol′a•tėr, *n.* [Fr. *idolatre,* L. *idololatre,* Gr. *eidōlolatrēs,* an idolworshiper. IDOLATRY.] A worshiper of idols; one who worships as a deity that which is not God; a pagan; an adorer; a great admirer.—**idolatress,** ī•dol′at•res, *n.* A female worshiper of idols.—**idolatrize,** ī•dol′at•rīz, *v.i.* To worship idols.—*v.t.* To adore; to worship.—**idolatrous,** ī•dol′at•rus, *a.* Pertaining to idolatry; partaking of the nature of idolatry; worshiping false gods; consisting in or partaking of an excessive attachment or reverence.—**idolatrously,** ī•dol′at•rus•li, *adv.* In an idolatrous manner.—**idolatry,** ī•dol′at•ri, *n.* [Fr. *idolatrie,* L. *idololatria,* from Gr. *eidōlolatreia*—*eidōlon,* idol, and *latreuō,* to worship.] The worship of idols, images, or anything made by hands, or which is not God; excessive attachment to or veneration for any person or thing.—**idolism,**† ī′dol•izm, *n.* The worship of idols.—**idolize,** ī′-dol•īz, *v.t.*—*idolized, idolizing.* To worship as an idol; to make an idol of; to love to excess; to love or reverence to adoration.—**idolizer,** ī′-dol•ī•zėr, *n.* One who idolizes.

idyl, idyll, ī′dil, *n.* [L. *idyllium,* Gr. *eidyllion,* from *eidos,* form.] A short highly wrought descriptive poem, consisting generally of scenes or events of pastoral life.—**idyllic,** ī•dil′ik, *a.* Of or belonging to idyls or pastoral poetry; pastoral.

if, if, *conj.* [A.Sax. *gif,* if; Icel. *ef, if,* if; akin O.G. *ibu,* G. *ob,* if, whether; Goth. *iba,* whether, *jabai,* if.] A particle used to introduce a conditional sentence, equal to—in case that, granting that, supposing that, allowing that; also, whether: in dependent clauses (I know not *if* he will).

igloo, ig′lö, *n.* [Eastern Eskimo *igdlu,* snow house.] A dome-shaped Eskimo dwelling made of square blocks of packed snow.

igneous, ig′ni•us, *a.* [L. *igneus,* from *ignis,* fire, allied to Skr. *agni,* fire.] Pertaining to, consisting of, or resembling fire; produced by or resulting from the action of fire.—**ignescent,** ig•nes′ent, *a.* [L. *ignescens.*] Emitting sparks of fire when struck, especially with steel.—*n.* A mineral that gives out sparks when struck.—**ignite,** ig•nīt′, *v.t.*—*ignited, igniting.* To kindle or set on fire; to communicate fire to.—*v.i.* To take fire; to become red with heat.—**ignition,** ig•nish′on, *n.* The act of igniting, or state of being ignited; the act or means of exploding the charge of gases in the cylinder of an internal-combustion engine.

ignoble, ig•nō′bl, *a.* [L. *ignobilis*—*in,* not, and *gnobilis,* or *nobilis,* noble. NOBLE.] Of low birth or family; not noble; not illustrious; mean; worthless; not honorable; base.—**ignobleness,** ig•nō′bl•nes, *n.* The condition or quality of being ignoble.—**ignobly,** ig•nō′bli, *adv.* In an ignoble manner.

ignominy, ig′no•min•i, *n.* [L. *ignominia*—*in,* not, and *gnomen, nomen,* name, from root seen in E. *know.*] Public disgrace; shame; dishonor; infamy.—**ignominious,** ig•no•min′i•us, *a.* [L. *ignominiosus.*] Marked with ignominy; shameful; dishonorable; infamous; despicable.—**ignominiously,** ig•no•min′i•us•ly, *adv.* In an ignominious manner.

ignoramus, ig•no•rā′mus, *n.* pl. **ignoramuses,** ig•no•rā′mus•ez. [1st pers. pl. pres. ind. of L. *ignoro*—lit. we are ignorant. IGNORE.] An ignorant person; a vain pretender to knowledge.

ignorant, ig′nė•rant, *a.* [L. *ignorans, ignorantis,* ppr. of *ignoro,* to be ignorant. IGNORE.] Destitute of knowledge; uninstructed or uninformed; untaught; unenlightened; unacquainted; unconscious.—**ignorantly,** ig′nė•rant•li, *adv.* In an ignorant manner.—**ignorance,** ig′nė•rans, *n.* [L. *ignorantia.*] The state of being ignorant; want of knowledge.

ignore, ig•nōr′, *v.t.*—*ignored, ignoring.* [L. *ignoro,* to be ignorant of, from *ignarus,* not knowing—*in,* not, and *gnarus,* knowing, from root of *gnosco,* to know, and E. *know.*] To pass over or by without notice; to act as if one were unacquainted with; to shut the eyes to; to leave out of account; to disregard; to reject.

iguana, ig•wä′na, *n.* [Sp., from the Haytian language.] A reptile of the lizard family, with pendulous dewlaps, native of tropical America, some species of which are much esteemed as food.

iguanodon, ig•wä′no•don, *n.* [*Iguana* and Gr. *odous, odontos,* a tooth, from the character of its teeth.] A colossal fossil lizard found in the Wealden strata.

ileum, il′ē•um, *n.* [From Gr. *eilō,* to roll, from its convolutions; or from L. *ilia,* intestines. ILIAC.] *Anat.* the lower three-fifths of the small intestine in man.

ileus, ī′lē•us, *n.* [Gr. *ileos, eileos,* a severe pain in the intestines.] *Med.* colic; iliac passion.

iliac, il′i•ak, *a.* [L. *iliacus,* from *ilia,* the flank, the groin, the intestines.] Pertaining to the bowels, especially the lower bowels, or to the part of the abdomen containing them.—*Iliac region,* the side of the abdomen between the ribs and the hips.—*Iliac arteries,* the arteries formed by the bifurcation of the aorta near the last lumbar vertebra.—*Iliac passion,* a dangerous ailment, consisting in obstruction of the bowels, accompanied with severe griping pain, and often vomiting of fecal matter.—**ilium,** il′i•um, *n.* [Properly *os ilium,* bone of the ilia or flank.] *Anat.* a bone that forms the outer portion of the pelvis on either side; the hipbone.

ilk, ilk, *a.* [A.Sax. *ilc, ylc,* same.] Same. [Old E.]—*Of that ilk,* in Scot., a phrase sometimes used after the name of a landed gentleman to denote that his surname and the title of his estate are the same.

ill, il, *a.* [From the Scandinavian; Icel. *illr,* adj. ill; Icel. and Sw. *illa,* adv. *ill;* a contracted form of *evil.* Its comparative and superlative, *worse* and *worst,* are from a different root.] Bad or evil; the opposite of good; wicked; wrong: used of things rather than persons; producing evil or misfortune; calamitous or unfortunate (an *ill* end); cross, crabbed, surly, or peevish (*ill* nature, *ill* temper); suffering from disease or sickness; sick or indisposed; unwell (*ill* of a fever); not proper; rude or unpolished (*ill* manners, *ill* breeding).—*Ill turn,* an unkind or injurious act.—*n.* Wickedness; evil; misfortune; calamity; whatever annoys or impairs happiness or prevents success.—*adv.* Not well; not rightly or perfectly (*ill* at ease); not easily; with pain or difficulty (he is *ill* able to sustain the burden). [*Ill,* prefixed to participles, or adjectives having the form of participles, forms a great number of compound words the meaning of which is generally obvious.]—**illness,** il′nes, *n.* The state or condition of being ill; an ailment or sickness.—**ill-advised,** *a.* Badly advised; resulting from bad advice or the want of good; injudicious.—**ill-bred,** *a.* Not well bred; badly educated or brought up; impolite.—**ill-fated,** *a.* Having an ill or evil fate; ill-starred; unfortunate.—**ill-favored,** *a.* Having ill features; ugly.—**ill-gotten,** *a.* Gained by unfair or improper means; dishonestly come by.—**ill-humor,** *n.* Ill temper, fretfulness.—**ill-judged,** *a.* Not well judged; injudicious; unwise.—**ill-mannered,** *a.* Uncivil; rude; impolite.—**ill-matched,** *a.* Badly assorted; not well suited.—**ill-nature,** *n.* Evil nature or disposition; bad temper; crossness; crabbedness.—**ill-natured,** *a.* Having ill-nature; of habitual bad temper; bad tempered.—**ill-naturedly,** *adv.* In an ill-natured manner; crossly.—**ill-omened,** *a.* Having unlucky omens; unfortunate.—**ill-starred,** *a.* Having an evil star presiding over one's destiny; hence, fated to be unfortunate; ill-fated.—**ill-tempered,** *a.* Of bad temper.—**ill will,** *n.* A desire that evil will befall a person; enmity.

illation, il•lā′shon, *n.* [L. *illatio*—*il* for *in,* in, on, and *latio,* a bearing, from *fero, latum,* to bear.] The act of inferring from premises or reasons; inference; an inference, deduction, or conclusion.—**illative,** il′la•tiv, *a.* Relating to illation; capable of being inferred or of inferring; denoting an inference (*then* or *therefore* is an *illative* word).—*n.* An illative word.

illaudable, il•lạ′da•bl, *a.* [Prefix *il* for *in,* not, and *laudable.*] Not laudable.

illegal, il•lē′gal, *a.* [Prefix *il* for *in,* not, and *legal.*] Not legal; contrary to law; unlawful; illicit.—**illegality,** il•lē•gal′i•ti, *n.* The condition or quality of being illegal.—**illegally,** il•lē′gal•li, *adv.* In an illegal manner.

illegible, il•lej′i•bl, *a.* [Prefix *il* for *in,* not, and *legible.*] Incapable of being read; obscure or defaced so that the words cannot be known.—**illegibility, illegibleness,** il•lej′i•bil″-i•ti, il•lej′i•bl•nes, *n.* The state or quality of being illegible.—**illegibly,** il•lej′i•bli, *adv.* In an illegible manner.

illegitimate, il•li•jit′i•mit, *a.* [Prefix *il* for *in,* not, and *legitimate.*] Not legitimate; born out of wedlock; not in conformity with law; not authorized; not legitimately inferred or deduced; not warranted (an *illegitimate* inference).—*v.t.*—*illegitimated, illegitimating.* To render illegitimate; to bastardize.—**illegitimacy,** il•li•jit′i•me•si, *n.* The state of being illegitimate, bastardy.—**illegitimately,** il•li•jit′i•mit•li, *adv.* In an illegitimate manner.

illiberal, il•lib′ėr•al, *a.* [Prefix *il* for *in,* not, and *liberal.*] Not liberal; not free or generous; of narrow or contracted mind or opinions.—**illiberality, illiberalness,** il•lib′ėr•al″i•ti, il•lib′ėr•al•nes, *n.* The quality of being illiberal.—**illiberally,** il•lib′ėr•al•li, *adv.* In an illiberal manner.

illicit, il•lis′it, *a.* [L. *illicitus*—*il,* not, and *licitus,* lawful, from *liceo,* to be allowed.] Not permitted, sanctioned, or allowed by law, rule or tradition; prohibited; unlawful.—**illicitly,** il•lis′it•li, *adv.* In an illicit manner.—**illicitness,** il•lis′it•nes, *n.* The state or quality of being illicit.

illimitable, il•lim′it•a•bl, *a.* [Prefix *il* for *in*, not, and *limitable.*] Incapable of being limited or bounded; boundless; immeasurable.—**illimitably,** il•lim′it•a•bli, *adv.* Without possibility of being bounded; without limits.—**illimitableness,** il•lim′it•a•bl•nes, *n.*

illiterate, il•lit′er•it, *a.* [L. *illiteratus*—*il* for *in*, not, and *literatus*, lettered, learned, from *litera*, a letter. LETTER.] Ignorant of letters or books; untaught; unlearned; ignorant.—**illiteracy,** il•lit′er•e•si, *n.* The state of being illiterate; a literary error†. — **illiterately,** il•lit′er•it•li, *adv.* In an illiterate manner.

illness. See ILL.

illogical, il•loj′i•kal, *a.* [Prefix *il* for *in*, not, and *logical.*] Ignorant or negligent of the rules of logic or correct reasoning; contrary to logic or sound reasoning.—**illogically,** il•loj′i•kal•li, *adv.* In an illogical manner.—**illogicalness,** il•loj′i•kal•nes, *n.* The quality of being illogical.

illuminate, il•lū′mi•nāt, *v.t.*—*illuminated, illuminating.* [L. *illumino, illuminatum*—prefix *il* for *in*, in, and *lumen, luminis*, light. LUMINARY, LUCID.] To enlighten; to throw light on; to supply with light; to light up with festal lamps, bonfires, or the like; to adorn (a manuscript) with gilded and colored decorations or illustrations.—**illume,** il•lūm′, *v.t.*—*illumed, illuming.* To illumine or illuminate. (*Poet.*)—**illuminable,** il•lū′mi•na•bl, *a.* Capable of being illuminated.—**illuminant,** il•lū′mi•nant, *n.* That which illuminates or affords light.—**illuminati,** il•lū′mi•nä″tī, *n. pl.* A term formerly applied to certain sects and secret societies, now applied to persons who affect to possess extraordinary knowledge whether justly or otherwise.—**illumination,** il•lū′mi•nā″shon, *n.* [L. *illuminatio, illuminationis.*] The act of illuminating, or state of being illuminated; a festive display of lights, etc.; an ornament or illustration in colors and gilding, such as those with which ancient manuscripts or books were embellished.—**illuminative,** il•lū′mi•nā•tiv, *a.* Having the power of illuminating; tending to throw light; illustrative.—**illuminator,** il•lū′mi•nā•tėr, *n.* One who or that which illuminates.—**illumine,** il•lū′min, *v.t.* To illuminate. (*Poet.*)

illusion, il•lū′zhon, *n.* [L. *illusio, illusionis*, from *illudo.* ILLUDE.] The act of deceiving or imposing upon; deception; mockery; a deceptive appearance; an unreal vision presented to the bodily or mental eye; hallucination.—**illusionist,** il•lū′zhon•ist, *n.* One given to illusion.—**illusive,** il•lū′siv, *a.* Deceiving by false show; illusory.—**illusively,** il•lū′siv•li, *adv.* In an illusive manner.—**illusiveness,** il•lū′siv•nes, *n.*—**illusory,** il•lū′so•ri, *a.* [Fr. *illusoire*, from L. *illudo, illusum.*] Causing illusion; deceiving or tending to deceive by false appearances; false and deceptive; fallacious.

illustrate, il′us•trāt, *v.t.*—*illustrated, illustrating.* [L. *illustro, illustratum*, to light up, to illuminate—*il* for *in*, and *lustro*, to make light. LUSTER.] To illuminate‡; to glorify‡; to make bright or conspicuous‡; to make clear, intelligible, or obvious; to throw light on by examples, by comparisons, and the like; to ornament and elucidate by means of pictures, drawings, etc.—**illustration,** il•lus•trā′shon, *n.* The act of illustrating; that which illustrates; a particular case or example intended to throw light on one's meaning; a picture accompanying and illustrating the text of a book.—**illustrative,** il•lus′tra•tiv, *a.* Tending to illustrate.—**illustratively,** il•lus′tra•tiv•li, *adv.* By way of illustration or elucidation.—**illustrator,** il′lus•trā•tėr, *n.* One who illustrates.

illustrious, il•lus′tri•us, *a.* [From L. *illustris*, lighted up, clear, distinguished; probably contr. for *illucestris*—*il* for *in*, into, and *lux, lucis*, light. LUCID.] Distinguished by greatness, nobleness, or eminence among men; conspicuous for praiseworthy qualities; renowned; eminent; glorious; brilliant (an *illustrious* man, an *illustrious* action).—**illustriously,** il•lus′tri•us•li, *adv.* In an illustrious manner.—**illustriousness,** il•lus′tri•us•nes, *n.*

ilmenite, il′men•īt, *n.* A black ore of iron found in the *Ilmen* Mountains in Russia.

image, im′ij, *n.* [Fr., from L. *imago*, an image, likeness, apparition, etc., from stem of *imitor*, to imitate.] A representation of any person or thing, sculptured, painted, or otherwise made visible; a statue, picture, or stamped representation; an effigy; an idol; what forms a counterpart or likeness of something else; likeness; embodiment; a picture drawn by fancy; semblance; show; appearance; *optics*, the figure or appearance of an object made by reflection or refraction.—*v.t.*—*imaged, imaging.* To represent by an image; to reflect the image or likeness of; to mirror; to represent to the mental vision; to form a likeness of in the mind.—**imagery,** im′a•jėr•i, *n.* Images in general or collectively; forms of the fancy; imaginary phantasms; rhetorical figures collectively; comparisons, similes, etc., in discourse.

imagine, i•maj′in, *v.t.*—*imagined, imagining.* [Fr. *imaginer*, L. *imaginor, imaginatum*, to imagine, from *imago*, image. IMAGE.] To form a notion or idea of in the mind; to bring before the mind's eye; to produce by the imagination; to conceive in thought; to think, scheme, or devise (O.T.).—*v.i.* To conceive; to suppose; to fancy; to think.—**imaginable,** i•maj′i•na•bl, *a.* Capable of being imagined or conceived.—**imaginably,** i•maj′i•na•bli, *adv.* In an imaginable manner.—**imaginal,**† i•maj′i•nal, *a.* Characterized by imagination; imaginative.—**imaginary,** i•maj′i•ne•ri, *a.* [L. *imaginarius.*] Existing only in imagination or fancy; conceived by the imagination, not real; fancied.—**imagination,** i•maj″i•nā′shon, n. [L. *imaginatio, imaginationis.*] The power or faculty of the mind by which it conceives and forms ideas of things from knowledge communicated to it by the organs of sense; the faculty by which we can bring absent objects and perceptions forcibly before the mind; the power or faculty which enables a person to produce a new, impressive, and artistic whole by selecting and working up ideas derived through observation and memory, and which thus includes a certain share of invention; an image or conception in the mind; idea; an unsolid or fanciful opinion.—**imaginative,** i•maj′i•nā•tiv, *a.* Endowed with imagination.—**imaginativeness,** i•maj′i•nā″tiv•nes. *n.*

imago, i•mā′gō, *n.* [L., an image.] The last or perfect state of an insect, usually that in which it has wings; *Psychoanalysis*, the childhood conception of the parent retained in the unconscious.

imam, imaum, i•mäm′, i•mạm′, *n.* [Ar. *imâm*, from *amma*, to walk before, to preside.] A minister or priest who performs the regular service of the mosque among the Mohammedans; a title given to the successors of Mohammed; one who has followers in law or theology.

imamate, i•mam′āt, *n.* The region that is ruled by an imam.

imbalance, im•bal′ans, *n.* [Prefix *im*, not, and *balance.*] A lack of balance; an unequal distribution; a disproportion; poor muscular or glandular functioning.

imbecile, imbecilic, im′be•sil, im•be•sil′ic, *a.* [L. *imbecillis, imbecillus*, feeble in body or mind—origin doubtful.] Having a mental capacity between idiocy and feeblemindedness, or a mental age of 2 to 7 years, or an IQ of 25 to 50.—*n.* One that is imbecile or impotent either in body or mind.—**imbecility,** im•be•sil′i•ti, *n.*

imbed, im-bed′, *v.t.* To embed.

imbibe, im•bīb′, *v.t.*—*imbibed, imbibing.* [L. *imbibo*—*im* for *in*, in, into, and *bibo*, to drink, whence also *beverage.*] To drink in; to absorb; to receive or admit into the mind and retain.—**imbiber,** im•bī′bėr, *n.* One who or that which imbibes.—**imbibition,** im•bi•bish′on, *n.* The act of imbibing.

imbitter, imbody, imbolden, imbosom, imbower. See EMBITTER, etc.

imbricate, imbricated, im′bri•kāt, im′bri•kā•ted, *a.* [L. *imbricatus*, from *imbrex, imbricis*, a hollow tile for a roof, from *imber*, a shower=Gr. *ombros*, rain.] Formed like a bent or hollow tile; lapping over each other, like tiles on a roof, scales of fishes, and reptiles. or leaves in a bud—**imbrication,** im•bri•kā′shon, *n.* State of being imbricate; a hollow like that of a roof tile.

imbroglio, im•brōʹlyō, *n.* [It., from prefix *im* for *in*, and *brogliare*, to confound or mix together; akin *broil.*] An intricate and perplexing state of affairs; a misunderstanding between persons or nations of a complicated nature.

imbrown, im•brounʹ, *v.t.* To make brown, to embrown.

imbrue, im•bröʹ, *v.t.—imbrued, imbruing.* [O.Fr. *embruer, s'embruer*, to dabble one's self, from prefix *im* for *in*, in, and L. *bibere*, to drink; comp. Fr. *breuvage*, beverage, also from *bibere.*] To soak or drench in a fluid, as in blood.

imbrute, im•brötʹ, *v.t.—imbruted, imbruting.* To degrade to the state of a brute.—*v.i.* To sink to the state of a brute. (*Mil.*)

imbue, im•būʹ, *v.t.—imbued, imbuing.* [L. *imbuo*, allied to *imber*, a shower; Skr. *ambu*, water. IMBRICATE.] To soak, steep, or tinge deeply; *fig.* to inspire, impress, or impregnate (the mind); to cause to become impressed or penetrated.

imitate, imʹi•tāt, *v.t.—imitated, imitating.* [L. *imitor, imitatus*, from a root which gives also *imago*, image.] To follow as a model, pattern, or example, to copy or endeavor to copy in acts, manners, or otherwise; to produce a likeness of in form, color, qualities, conduct, manners, and the like; to counterfeit.—**imitable,** imʹi•ta•bl, *a.* Capable of being imitated or copied.—**imitation,** im•i•tāʹshon, *n.* [L. *imitatio, imitationis.*] The act of imitating; that which is made or produced as a copy; a likeness; a copy; a counterfeit; *mus.* the repetition of the same melodic idea by different parts or voices in a composition.—**imitative,** imʹi•tā•tiv, *a.* Inclined to imitate or copy; aiming at imitation; exhibiting an imitation of a pattern or model; formed after a model or original; intended to represent an actual sound by the sound of the letters (an *imitative* word).—**imitatively,** imʹi•tā•tiv•li, *adv.* In an imitative manner.—**imitativeness,** imʹi•tā•tiv•nes, *n.* Quality of being imitative.—**imitator,** imʹi•tā•tėr, *n.* One who imitates.

immaculate, im•makʹū•lit, *a.* [L. *immaculatus—im* for *in*, not, and *maculatus*, from *macula*, a spot.] Spotless, pure; unstained; undefiled; without blemish.—*Immaculate Conception*, the dogma of the Roman Catholic Church (settled in 1854), that the Virgin Mary was conceived and born without original sin.—**immaculately,** im•makʹū•lit•li, *adv.* In an immaculate manner.—**immaculateness,** im•makʹū•lit•nes, *n.* The condition or quality of being immaculate.

immanent, imʹma•nent, *a.* [L. *immanens, immanentis*, ppr. of *immaneo—im* for *in*, in, and *maneo*, to remain (as in *remain, mansion*).] Remaining in or within; hence, not passing out of the subject; inherent and indwelling; internal or subjective; opposed to *transitive.*—**immanence, immanency,** imʹma•nens, imʹma•nen•si, *n.* The condition of being immanent.

Immanuel, im•manʹū•el, *n.* [Heb.—*im*, with, *anu*, us, and *El*, God.] God with us: an appellation of the Saviour.

immaterial, im•ma•tēʹri•al, *a.* [Prefix *im* for *in*, not, and *material.*] Not consisting of matter; incorporeal; spiritual; of no essential consequence; unimportant.—**immaterialism,** im•ma•tēʹri•al•izm, *n.* The doctrine that immaterial substances or spiritual beings exist or are possible; the doctrine that there is no material world, but that all exists only in the mind.—**immaterialist,** im•ma•tēʹri•al•ist, *n.* One who professes immaterialism.—**immateriality, immaterialness,** im•ma•tēʺri•alʹi•ti, im•ma•tēʹri•al•nes, *n.* The quality of being immaterial or not consisting of matter; absence of matter.—**immaterialize,** im•ma•tēʹri•al•īz, *v.t.* To make immaterial or incorporeal.—**immaterially,** im•ma•tēʹri•al•li, *adv.* In an immaterial manner.

immature, im•ma•tūrʹ, *a.* [L. *immaturus*, unripe—*im* for *in*, not, and *maturus*, ripe.] Not mature or ripe; unripe; not brought to a complete state; too early; premature.—**immaturely,** im•ma•tūrʹli, *adv.* In an immature manner.—**immatureness, immaturity,** im•ma•turʹnes, im•ma•tūʹri•ti, *n.* The state or quality of being immature; unripeness.

immeasurable, im•mezhʹe•ra•bl, *a.* [Prefix *im* for *in*, not, and *measurable.*] Incapable of being measured.—**immeasurably,** im•mezhʹe•ra•bli, *adv.* In an immeasurable manner; immensely; beyond all measure.

immediate, im•mēʹdi•it, *a.* [Prefix *im* for *in*, not, and *mediate.*] Not separated by anything intervening; placed in the closest relation; not separated by an interval of time; instant; acting without a medium, or without the intervention of another object as a cause, means, or condition; produced, acquired, or obtained without the intervention of a medium; direct.—**immediacy,** im•mēʹdi•e•si, *n.* The relation of being immediate; immediateness; proximity.—**immediately,** im•mēʹdi•it•li, *adv.* In an immediate manner; without the intervention of anything; directly; without delay; instantly; forthwith.—**immediateness,** im•mēʹdi•it•nes, *n.*

immemorial, im•me•mōʹri•al, *a.* [L. *im* for *in*, not, and *memoria*, memory.] Beyond memory; extending beyond the reach of record or tradition.—**immemorially,** im•me•mōʹri•al•li, *adv.* Beyond memory; from time out of mind.

immense, im•mensʹ, *a.* [L. *immensus—im* for *in*, not, and *mensus*, measured, pp. of *metior, mensus*, to measure. MEASURE.] Vast in extent or bulk; very great; very large; boundless; huge; enormous. ∴ Syn. under ENORMOUS.—**immensely,** im•mensʹli, *adv.* In an immense manner; vastly.—**immenseness,** im•mensʹnes, *n.* The condition or quality of being immense.—**immensity,** im•menʹsi•ti, *n.* [L. *immensitas,*] The condition or quality of being immense; that which is immense.

immensurable, im•menʹsū•ra•bl, *a.* [L. *im* for *in*, not, and *mensurabilis*, from *mensura*, measure. MEASURE.] Not to be measured; immeasurable.

immerge, im•mėrjʹ, *v.t.—immerged, immerging.* [L. *immergo—im* for *in*, into, and *mergo*, to plunge.] To plunge into or under anything, especially into or under a fluid.—*v.i.* To disappear by entering into any medium.

immerse, im•mėrsʹ, *v.t.—immersed, immersing.* [L. *immergo, immersum—im* for *in*, into, and *mergo*, to plunge. MERGE.] To plunge into anything that covers or surrounds, as into a fluid; to dip; *fig.* to engage deeply; to involve (to be *immersed* in business).—**immersion,** im•mėrʹshon, *n.* A baptism by total submersion in water; *astron.* the disappearance of a celestial body by passing either behind another or into its shadow: opposed to *emersion.*—**immersionist,** im•mėrʹshon•ist, *n.* One who holds that immersion is essential to Christian baptism.

immethodical, im•me•thodʹi•kal, *a.* [Prefix *im* for *in*, not, and *methodical.*] Not methodical; without system, order, or regularity.

immigrate, imʹmi•grāt, *v.i.* [L. *immigro—im* for *in*, into, and *migro*, to migrate.] To remove into a country of which one is not a native for the purpose of permanent residence.—**immigrant,** the correlative of *emigrant.*—**immigration,** im•mi•grāʹshon, *n.* The act of immigrating; the number of immigrants arriving in a certain country in a specific time.

imminent, imʹmi•nent, *a.* [L. *imminens, imminentis*, ppr. of *immineo*, to hang over—*im* for *in*, on, and *mineo*, as in *eminent.*] Hanging over; threatening to fall or occur; impending; near at hand.—**imminence,** imʹmi•nens, *n.*—**imminently,** imʹmi•nent•li, *adv.*

immiscible, im•misʹi•bl, *a.* [Prefix *im*, not, and *miscible* from L. *miscere*, to mix.] Not capable of being intermingled.—**immiscibility,** im•misʹi•bilʺi•ti, *n.*—**immiscibly,** im•misʹi•bli, *adv.*

immix, im•miksʹ, *v.t.* [Prefix *im* for *in*, and *mix.*] To mix; to mingle.

immobile, im•mōʹbil, *a.* [Prefix *im* for *in*, not, and *mobile*; L. *immobilis.*] Not mobile; immovable; fixed; stable.—**immobility,** im•mō•bilʹi•ti, *n.*—**immobilize,** im•mōʹbil•īz, *v.t.*—*immobilized, immobilizing.*—To make incapable of moving; to fix in place; *finance*, to employ currency as reserve by withholding it from circulation.—**immobilization,** im•mōʹbi•li•zaʺshon, *n.*

immoderate, im•modʹe•rit, *a.* [Prefix *im*, not, and *moderate*; L. *immoderatus.*] Not moderate; exceeding just or usual bounds; excessive; extravagant; unreasonable. — **immoderately,** im•modʹe•rit•li, *adv.* In an immoderate manner.—**immod-**

erateness, immoderacy, immoderation, im•mod′e•rit•nes, im•mod′e•re•si, im•mod′e•rā″shon, *n.* The condition or quality of being immoderate.

immodest, im•mod′est, *a.* [Prefix *im* for *in*, not, and *modest.*] Not modest; wanting in the reserve or restraint which decency requires; indelicate; unchaste.—**immodestly,** im•mod′est•li, *adv.* In an immodest manner. —**immodesty,** im•mod′es•ti. *n.* The quality of being immodest.

immolate, im′mo•lāt, *v.t.*—*immolated, immolating.* [L. *immolo, immolatum*, to sacrifice—*im* for *in*, on, and *mola*, meal, which was thrown on the head of the victim.] To sacrifice; to kill, as a victim offered in sacrifice; to offer in sacrifice.—**immolation,** im•mo•lā′shon, *n.* The act of immolating; a sacrifice offered.—**immolator,** im′mo•lā•tėr, *n.* One who immolates.

immoral, im•mor′al, *a.* [Prefix *im* for *in*, not, and *moral.*] Not moral; inconsistent with morality or rectitude; contrary to morals; wicked; unjust.—**immorality,** im•mo•ral′i•ti, *n.* The quality of being immoral; an immoral act or practice.—**immorally,** im•mor′al•li, *adv.* In an immoral manner.

immortal, im•mor′tal, *a.* [L. *immortalis*—*im*, for *in*, not, and *mortalis*, mortal.] Not mortal; having life that shall never end; undying; connected with immortality (*immortal* hopes); imperishable (*immortal* fame).—*n.* One who is immortal; often applied to the gods of classical mythology.—**immortality,** im•mor•tal′i•ti, *n.* [L. *immortalitas.*] The condition or quality of being immortal; exemption from death and annihilation; unending existence.—**immortalize,** im•mor′tal•īz, *v.t.*—*immortalized, immortalizing.* To render immortal; to make famous for ever.—**immortally,** im•mor′tal•li, *adv.* In an immortal manner.—**immortelle,** im•mor•tel′, *n.* A flower of the sort called *Everlasting*, or a wreath made of such flowers.

immovable, im•mö′va•bl, *a.* [Prefix *im* for *in*, not, and *movable.*] Not movable; incapable of being moved in place; firmly fixed; fast; not to be moved from a purpose; steadfast; unalterable; unchangeable; not impressible; unfeeling.—**immovability, immovableness,** im•mö′va•bil″i•ti, im•mö′va•bl•nes, *n.* The condition or quality of being immovable.—**immovably,** im•mö′va•bli, *adv.*

immunity, im•mū′ni•ti, *n.* [L. *immunitas*, from *immunis*, exempt—*im* for *in*, not, and *munis*, office, duty.] Exemption from obligation, duty, office, tax, etc.; a particular privilege; freedom or exemption in general. In medicine, the ability of the body to resist the growth and products of microörganisms.—**immune,** im•mūn′, *a.* Proof against disease or poison.

immunize, im′ū•nīz, *v.t.* To produce immunity.

immure, im•mūr′, *v.t.*—*immured, immuring.* [O.Fr. *emmurer*—L. *in*, and *murus*, a wall. MURAL.] To enclose or imprison within walls; to shut up; to confine.—**immurement,** im•mūr′ment, *n.* The act of immuring or state of being immured.

immutable, im•mū′ta•bl, *a.* [Prefix *im* for *in*, not, and *mutable.*] Not mutable; not subject to mutation; unchangeable; invariable; unalterable.

imp, imp, *n.* [Originally a shoot or scion; from L.L. *impotus*, a graft or scion, from Gr. *emphytos*, engrafted—*en*, in, and *phyō*, to grow, to produce; similarly Sw. *ymp*, Dan. *ympe*, twig, shoot, scion.] A scion or graft‡; a son, offspring, or progeny (*Shak.*)‡; a young or little devil; a little malignant spirit; hence, a mischievous child; also something added or united to another to repair or lengthen it out.—*v.t.* To graft; to strengthen or enlarge by something inserted or added; to mend a deficient wing by the insertion of a feather; to strengthen.—**impish,** imp′ish, *a.* Having the qualities of an imp; fiendish.—**impishly,** imp′ish•li, *adv.* After the manner of an imp.

impact, im′pakt, *n.* [From L. *impingo, impactum*, to drive or strike. IMPINGE.] A forcible touch; a collision; a stroke; communicated force; *mech.* the shock or collision occasioned by the meeting of two bodies.

impair, im•pâr′, *v.t.* [Fr. *empirer*, from prefix, *em*, intens., *pire*, worse, from L. *pejor*, worse.] To make worse; to lessen in some good quality, as in quantity, value, excellence, strength; to deteriorate.—*v.i.* To become worse; to deteriorate.—**impairer,** im•pâ′rėr, *n.* One who or that which impairs.—**impairment,** im•pâr′ment, *n.* The act of impairing.

impale, im•pāl′, *v.t.*—*impaled, impaling.* [L. *im* for *in*, on, and *palus*, a pole, stake, pale.] To put to death by fixing on an upright sharp stake; to empale; *her.* to join, as two coats of arms, by an upright line.—**impalement,** im•pāl′ment, *n.* The act of impaling.

impalpable, im•pal′pa•bl, *a.* [Prefix *im* for *in*, not, and *palpable.*] Not to be felt; incapable of having its individual particles distinguished by the touch (an *impalpable* powder); not easily or readily apprehended or grasped by the mind.—**impalpably,** im•pal′pa•bli, *adv.* In an impalpable manner.—**impalpability,** im•pal′pa•bil″i•ti, *n.* The quality or state of being impalpable.

impanate, im•pā′nāt, *a.* [L. *in*, in, into, and *panis*, bread.] Embodied in the bread used in the Eucharist.—**impanation,** im•pa•nā′shon, *n.* The supposed real presence in, and union of the body and blood of Christ with the bread and wine, after consecration, in the Eucharist; consubstantiation: distinct from *transubstantiation*, which holds that there is a change of the elements into the real body and blood of Christ.

impanel, im•pan′el, *v.t.*—*impanelled, impanelling.* [Prefix *im* for *in*, and *panel.*] To form, complete, or enroll, the list of jurors in a court of justice.

imparidigitate, im•par′i•dij″i•tāt, *a.* [L. *impar*, unequal (*im*, not, *par*, equal), and *digitus*, a finger.] *Zool.* having an uneven number of fingers or toes.—**imparipinnate,** im•par′i•pin″āt, *a. Bot.* applied to a pinnate leaf when there is a terminal or odd leaflet at the end.

imparity, im•par′i•ti, *n.* [From L. *impar*, unequal—*im*, not, and *par*, equal. PAIR, PEER.] Inequality; disproportion; want of equality; disparity.

impart, im•pärt′, *v.t.* [O.Fr. *impartir*, from L. *impartio*, *impertio*—*im* for *in*, and *partio*, to divide, from *pars, partis*, a part.] To bestow a part, share, or portion of; to give, grant, confer, or communicate; to communicate the knowledge of; to make known; to show by words or tokens.—*v.i.* To give a part or share.—**impartation,** im•pär•tā′shon, *n.* The act of imparting.—**imparter,** im•pär′tėr, *n.* One who imparts.—**impartibility,** im•pär′ti•bil″i•ti, *n.* The quality of being impartible.—**impartible,** im•pär′ti•bl, *a.* Capable of being imparted.—**impartment,** im•pärt′ment, *n.* The act of imparting.

impartial, im•pär′shal, *a.* [Prefix *im* for *in*, not, and *partial.*] Not partial; not favoring one party more than another; unprejudiced; equitable; just.—**impartiality, impartialness,** im•pär′shi•al″i•ti, im•pär′shal•nes, *n.* The quality of being impartial.—**impartially,** im•pär′shal•li, *adv.* In an impartial manner; without bias; fairly.

impartible, im•pär′ti•bl, *a.* [Prefix *im* for *in*, not, and *partible.*] Not partible or subject to partition.—**impartibility,** im•pär′ti•bil″i•ti, *n.* The quality of being impartible.

impassable, im•pas′a•bl, *a.* [Prefix *im* for *in*, not, and *passable.*] Not passable; incapable of being passed. —**impassableness,** im•pas′a•bl•nes, *n.*

impasse, im•päs′, *n.* A blind alley; a cul-de-sac; a road having no way out; *fig.* a position from which there is no escape; a deadlock.

impassible, im•pas′i•bl, *a.* [L. *impassibilis*—*im* for *in*, not, and *passibilis*, capable of feeling, from *patior, passus*, to suffer. PATIENT.] Incapable of pain, passion, or suffering; not to be moved to passion or sympathy; without or not exhibiting feeling.—**impassibility, impassibleness,** im•pas′i•bil″i•ti, im•pas′i•bl•nes, *n.* The quality or condition of being impassible.

impassion, im•pash′on, *v.t.* [Prefix *im* for *in*, intens., and *passion.*] To move or affect strongly with passion.—**impassionate,** im•pash′on•it, *a.* Strongly affected.—**impassioned,** im•pash′ond, *a.* Actuated or animated by passion, ardor, or warmth of feeling; animated; excited (an *impassioned* orator or discourse).

impassive, im•pas′iv, *a.* [Prefix *im* for *in*, intens., and *passive.*] Not susceptible of pain or suffering; impassible; not exhibiting feeling or sensibility.—**impassively,** im•pas′iv•li, *adv.* In an impassive manner.—**impassiveness, impassivity,** im•pas′iv•nes, im•pa•siv′i•ti, *n.* The state or quality of being impassive.

impaste, im•pāst′, *v.t.* [Prefix *im* for *in*, and *paste*.] To knead or make into paste; *painting*, to lay on (colors) thickly and boldly; *engrav.* to intermix lines and points on (a plate) so as to represent thickness of coloring.—**impastation,** im•pas•tā′shon, *n.* The act of impasting; a combination of materials of different colors and consistencies united by a cement and hardened.—**impasto,** im•pas′to, *n.* [It.] *Painting*, the thickness of the layer of pigment applied by the painter.

impatient, im•pā′shent, *a.* [Prefix *im* for *in*, not, and *patient*.] Not patient; uneasy under given conditions and eager for change; followed by *of*, *at*, *for*, *under*; prompted by impatience; exhibiting or expressing impatience (an *impatient* gesture).—**impatiently,** im•pā′shent•li, *adv.* In an impatient manner.—**impatience,** im•pā′shens, *n.* The condition or quality of being impatient.

impeach, im•pēch′, *v.t.* [Fr. *empêcher*, O.Fr. *empeechier*, Pr. *empedigar*; from L. *impedicare*, to entangle—*in*, and *pedica*, a snare, from *pes*, *pedis*, the foot. IMPEDE.] To charge with a crime or misdemeanor; to accuse; specifically, to exhibit charges of maladministration against, as against a minister of state or other high official, before a competent tribunal; to call in question (motives, sincerity); to disparage or detract from.—**impeachable,** im•pēch′a•bl, *a.* Liable to impeachment.—**impeacher,** im•pēch′ėr, *n.* One who impeaches.—**impeachment,** im•pēch′ment, *n.* Impediment or obstruction‡; the act of impeaching, or state of being impeached.

impeccable, impeccant, im•pek′a•bl, im•pek′ant, *a.* [L. *impeccabilis*—prefix *im* for *in*, not, and *pecco*, to sin.] Not liable or subject to sin; exempt from the possibility of doing wrong.—*n.* A person exempt from the possibility of sinning.—**impeccability, impeccance, impeccancy,** im•pek′a•bil″i•ti, im•pek′ans, im•pek′an•si, *n.* The condition or quality of being impeccant or impeccable.

impecunious, im•pi•kū′ni•us, *a.* [Prefix *im* for *in*, not, and *pecunia*, money.] Not having money; hard-up; without funds.—**impecuniosity,** im•pi•kū′ni•os″i•ti, *n.* State of being impecunious.

impedance, im•pēd′ans, *n. Elect.* virtual resistance due to self-induction; opposed to true or ohmic resistance.

impede, im•pēd′, *v.t.*—*impeded*, *impeding*. [L. *impedio*, to entangle the feet of—*im* for *in*, and *pes*, *pedis*, the foot; seen also in *pedestrian*, *expedite*, *biped*, *pedestal*, *impeach*, etc.] To hinder; to stop or delay the progress of; to obstruct.—**impediment,** im•ped′i•ment, *n.* [L. *impedimentum*.] That which impedes; obstruction; a voice defect.—**impedimenta,** [L.] Baggage.—**impedimental,** im•ped′i•men″tal, *a.* Of the nature of an impediment.—**impeditive,** im•ped′i•tiv, *a.* Impeding.

impel, im•pel′, *v.t.*—*impelled*, *impelling*. [L. *impello*—*im* for *in*, on, and *pello*, to drive (as in *compel*, *dispel*, *repel*, *pulse*).] To drive or urge forward; to press on; to excite to motion or action in any way.—**impellent,** im•pel′ent, *a.* Having the quality of impelling.—*n.* A power or force that impels.—**impeller,** im•pel′ėr, *n.* One who or that which impels.

impend, im•pend′, *v.i.* [L. *impendeo*—*im* for *in*, in, on, over, and *pendeo*, to hang (as in *depend*, *pendant*, etc.).] To hang over; to threaten from near at hand; to be imminent.—**impendence, impendency,** im•pen′dens, im•pen′den•si, *n.* The state of being impendent.—**impendent,** im•pen′dent, *a.* Impending; imminent.

impenetrable, im•pen′i•tra•bl, *a.* [Prefix *im* for *in*, not, and *penetrable*.] Not penetrable; incapable of being penetrated or pierced; hence, incapable of intellectual or emotional impression; obtuse or unsympathetic; *phys.* preventing any other substance from occupying the same place at the same time.—**impenetrably,** im•pen′ē•tra•bli, *adv.* In an impenetrable manner.—**impenetrability, impenetrableness,** im•pen′i•tra•bil″i•ti, im•pen′i•tra•bl•nes, *n.* The quality of being impenetrable.

impenitent, im•pen′i•tent, *a.* [Prefix *im* for *in*, not, and *penitent*.] Not penitent; not repenting of sin; obdurate; of a hard heart.—*n.* One who does not repent; a hardened sinner.—**impenitence, impenitency,** im•pen′i•tens, im•pen′i•ten•si, *n.* The condition of being impenitent.—**impenitently,** im•pen′i•tent•li, *adv.*

impennate, im•pen′āt, *a.* [L. *im* for *in*, not, and *penna*, a feather.] *Ornithol.* having short wings covered with feathers resembling scales, as the penguins.

imperative, im•per′a•tiv, *a.* [L. *imperativus*, from *impero*, to command. EMPEROR.] Expressive of command; containing positive command; authoritative; not to be avoided or evaded; obligatory (*imperative* duty); *gram.* applied to the mood or form of a verb which expresses command, entreaty, advice, or exhortation (*go*, *write*, *attend*); in this sense often used *substantively*.—**imperatively,** im•per′a•tiv•li, *adv.* In an imperative manner; also, by way of, or as, the imperative mood.—**imperatorial,** im•per•a•tō′ri•al, *a.* [From L. *imperator*, a commander.] Pertaining to a commander or emperor; commanding; imperial.

imperceptible, im•pėr•sep′ti•bl, *a.* [Prefix *im* for *in*, not, and *perceptible*.] Not perceptible; not to be perceived; not discernible; not easily apprehended. —**imperceptibility, imperceptibleness,** im•pėr•sep′ti•bil″i•ti, im•pėr•sep′ti•bl•nes, *n.* The state or quality of being imperceptible.—**imperceptibly,** im•pėr•sep′ti•bli, *adv.* In an imperceptible manner.—**imperceptive,** im•pėr•sep′tiv, *a.* Not perceiving.

imperfect, im•pėr′fekt, *a.* [Prefix *im* for *in*, not, and *perfect*; L. *imperfectus*.] Not perfect; not complete in all parts; wanting something necessary to completeness; defective; not reaching a certain standard or ideal; morally deficient or defective; not completely good.—*Imperfect tense*, *gram.* a tense expressing an uncompleted action or state, especially in time past.—*n.* An imperfect tense.—**imperfection,** im•pėr•fek′shon, *n.* The condition or quality of being imperfect; defect; flaw; blemish.—**imperfectly,** im•pėr′fekt•li, *adv.* In an imperfect manner or degree; defectively; faultily.—**imperfectness,** im•pėr′fekt•nes, *n.* The state or quality of being imperfect.

imperforate, im•pėr′fo•rit, *a.* [Prefix *im* for *in*, not, and *perforate*.] Not perforated or pierced; having no opening or pores.

imperial, im•pēr′i•al, *a.* [L. *imperialis*, from *imperium*, empire, supreme command, from *impero*, to command. EMPEROR.] Pertaining to an empire or to an emperor; pertaining to supreme authority or to one who wields it; sovereign; supreme; suitable for an emperor; of superior excellence.—*n.* A tuft of hair on a man's lower lip (the style of beard made fashionable by Napoleon III); a trade term for an article of unusual size or excellence, as a large decanter, etc.; a size of paper measuring 23 by 31 inches.—**imperialism,** im•pēr′i•al•izm, *n.* Imperial state or authority; the spirit of empire.—**imperialist,** im•pēr′i•al•ist, *n.* A subject or soldier of an emperor; one favorable to empire or imperial government.—**imperially,** im•pē′ri•al•li, *adv.* In an imperial manner.

imperil, im•per′il, *v.t.*—*imperilled*, *imperilling*. [Prefix *im* for *in*, into, and *peril*.] To bring into peril; to endanger.

imperious, im•pēr′i•us, *a.* [L. *imperiosus*, from *imperium*, empire. IMPERIAL.] Giving orders or commands in an arbitrary or absolute manner; dictatorial; haughty; arrogant; domineering; urgent, pressing, or overmastering (*imperious* necessity).—**imperiously,** im•pēr′i•us•li, *adv.* In an imperious manner.—**imperiousness,** im•pēr′i•us•nes, *n.*

imperishable, im•per′ish•a•bl, *a.* [Prefix *im* for *in*, not, and *perishable*.] Not perishable; not subject to decay; indestructible; enduring permanently.—**imperishableness, imperishability,** im•per′ish•a•bl•nes, im•per′ish•a•bil″i•ti, *n.* The quality of being imperishable.—**imperishably,** im•per′ish•a•bli, *adv.*

impermeable, im•pėr′mi•a•bl, *a.* [Prefix *im* for *in*, not, and *permeable*.] Not permeable; impervious.—**impermeability, impermeableness,** im•pėr′mi•a•bil″i•ti, im•pėr′mi•a•bl-nes, *n.*—**impermeably,** im•pėr′mi•a•bli, *adv.*

impersonal, im•pėr′son•al, *a.* [Prefix *im* for *in*, not, and *personal.*] Not having personal existence; not endued with personality.—*Impersonal verb, gram.* a verb (such as *it rains*, *it becomes* us to be modest) which is used only with an impersonal nominative or subject.—*n.* That which wants personality; an impersonal verb.—**impersonality,** im•pėr′so•nal″i•ti, *n.* The condition of being impersonal.—**impersonally,** im•pėr′son•al•li, *adv.* In an impersonal manner.

impersonate, im•pėr′son•āt, *v.t.*—*impersonated, impersonating.* [Prefix *im* for *in*, in (or *in* intens.), and *personate.*] To invest with personality; to assume the person or character of; to represent in character (as on the stage).—**impersonation,** im•pėr′so•nā″shon, *n.* The act of impersonating.—**impersonator,** im•pėr′son•ā•tėr, *n.* One who impersonates.

impertinent, im•pėr′ti•nent, *a.* [Prefix *im* for *in*, not, and *pertinent.*] Not pertinent or pertaining to the matter in hand; having no bearing on the subject; not to the point; irrelevant; unbecoming in speech or action; meddling with matters in which one has no concern; petulant and rude; uncivil.—*n.* One who acts impertinently.—**impertinently,** im•pėr′ti•nent•li, *adv.* In an impertinent manner; irrelevantly; in a rude, saucy manner.—**impertinence, impertinency,** im•pėr′ti•nens, im•pėr′ti•nen•si, *n.* The quality of being impertinent; that which is impertinent; impertinent conduct or language.

imperturbable, im•pėr•tėr′ba•bl, *a.* [Prefix *im* for *in*, not, and *perturb.*] Incapable of being perturbed or agitated; unmoved; calm; cool.—**imperturbability,** im•pėr•tėr′ba•bil″i•ti, *n.* Quality of being imperturbable.—**imperturbation,** im•pėr′tėr•bā″shon, *n.* Freedom from agitation of mind.

impervious, im•pėr′vi•us, *a.* [Prefix *im* for *in*, not, and *pervious.*] Not pervious; not admitting entrance or passage; incapable of being passed through.—**imperviously,** im•pėr′vi•us•li, *adv.* In an impervious manner. —**imperviousness,** im•pėr′vi•us•nes, *n.*

impetigo, im•pe•tī′gō, *n.* [L., from *impeto*, to assail. IMPETUOUS.] *Med.* an eruption of itching pustules in clusters on the skin.—**impetiginous,** im•pe•tij′i•nus, *a.* Pertaining to impetigo.

impetrate, im′pe•trāt, *v.t.*—*impetrated, impetrating.* [L. *impetro, impetratum*, to obtain—prefix *im* for *in*, intens., and *patro*, to bring to pass.] To obtain by prayer or petition.—**impetration,** im•pe•trā′shon, *n.* The act of impetrating; formerly specifically applied to the obtaining from the Roman see of benefices belonging to lay patrons.—**impetrative,** im′pe•trā•tiv, *a.* Containing or expressing entreaty.

impetuous, im•pet′ū•us, *a.* [L. *impetuosus*, from *impetus*, an attack—*im*, in, and *peto*, to assail (whence *petition, compete*).] Rushing with force and violence; furious in motion; forcible; fierce; raging; vehement in feeling; passionate; violent.—**impetuously,** im•pet′ū•us•li, *adv.* In an impetuous manner.—**impetuosity, impetuousness,** im•pet′ū•os″i•ti, im•pet′ū•us•nes, *n.* The quality of being impetuous; fury; vehemence. —**impetus,** im′pe•tus, *n.* [L.] Force of motion; the force with which any body is driven or impelled; momentum.

impi, im′pi, *n.* A brigade or large body of Kaffir soldiers.

impignorate,† im•pig′no•rāt, *v.t.* [L. *in*, in, and *pignus, pignoris*, a pledge.] To pledge or pawn, to transfer as security.

impinge, im•pinj′, *v.i.* [L. *impingo, impactum*—*im* for *in*, on, and *pango*, to strike. PACT.] To strike, knock, or dash against; to clash upon; to strike; to hit.—**impingement,** im•pinj′ment, *n.* Act of impinging.

impious, im′pi•us, *a.* [L. *impius*—*im* for *in*, not, and *pius*, pious.] The reverse of pious; irreverent toward the Supreme Being; wanting in veneration for God and His authority; irreligious; irreverent; profane (*impious* men, deeds, words).—**impiously,** im′pi•us•li, *adv.* In an impious manner.—**impiousness,** im′pi•us•nes, *n.* Impiety.—**impiety,** im•pī′e•ti, *n.* [L. *impietas.*] The condition or quality of being impious; an act of wickedness or irreligion: in this latter sense with a plural.

impish, impishly. See IMP.

implacable, im•plā′ka•bl, *a.* [Prefix *im* for *in*, not, and *placable.*] Not placable; not to be appeased or pacified; inexorable; stubborn or constant in enmity.—**implacability, implacableness,** im•plā′ka•bil″i•ti, im•plā′ka•bl•nes, *n.* The quality of being implacable.—**implacably,** im•plā′ka•bli, *adv.* In an implacable manner.

implacental, im′pla•sen″tal, *a.* [Prefix *im* for *in*, not, and *placental.*] Destitute of a placenta, as marsupials and monotremes.—n. A mammal destitute of a placenta.

implant, im•plant′, *v.t.* [Prefix *im* for *in*, in, into, and *plant.*] To plant; to set in soil (lit. or fig.); to insert; to sow (to *implant* truths, principles, virtue, etc.).—**implantation,** im•plan•tā′shon, *n.* The act of implanting.

implead, im•plēd′, *v.t.* [Prefix *im* for *in*, and *plead.*] To institute and prosecute a suit against in court; to sue at law.—**impleader,** im•plē′dėr, *n.* One who impleads; an accuser.

implement, im′ple•ment, *n.* [L.L. *implementum*, lit. what accomplishes, from L. *impleo*, to fill up—*im* for *in*, and *pleo*, to fill, as in *complete, replete*, etc., the root being in E. *full.*] An instrument, tool, or utensil; an article assisting in carrying on manual labors. ∴ Syn. under TOOL. —*v.t.* To fulfill or satisfy the conditions of; to fulfill or perform; to carry into effect (to *implement* a bargain). —**implemental,** im•ple•men′tal, *a.* Pertaining to implements; characterized by the use of implements (*implemental* stage in civilization).

implicate, im′pli•kāt, *v.t.*—*implicated, implicating.* [L. *implico, implicatum*—*im* for *in*, in, into, and *plico*, to fold. PLY.] To entangle to a certain extent in some affair; to show or prove to be connected or concerned; to involve (*implicated* in a conspiracy. ∴ *Implicate* is a less strong word than *involve*, a person who is *implicated* being connected only to a small extent, while one who is *involved* is deeply concerned or entangled.—**implication,** im•pli•kā′shon, *n.* The act of implicating or state of being implicated; an implying, or that which is implied but not expressed; an inference, or something which may fairly be understood though not expressed in words.—**implicative,** im′pli•kā•tiv, *a.* Tending to implicate.—**implicatively,** im′pli•kā•tiv•li, *adv.* By implication.

implicit, im•plis′it, *a.* [L. *implicitus*, from *implico, implicitum*, and *implicatum*, to infold. IMPLICATE.] Fairly to be understood, though not expressed in words; implied (an *implicit* promise); entirely depending or resting on something or someone else; hence, free from doubt or questioning; settled; deep rooted (*implicit* faith in one's word).—**implicitly,** im•plis′it•li, *adv.* In an implicit manner.—**implicitness,** im•plis′it•nes, *n.*

implore, im•plōr′, *v.t.*—*implored, imploring.* [L. *imploro*—*im* for *in*, on, upon, and *ploro*, to cry out (as in *deplore, explore*).] To call upon or for, in supplication; to beseech; to pray earnestly; to entreat; to beg (to *implore* forgiveness, to *implore* a person to forgive).—*v.i.* To entreat; to beg.—**imploration,** im•plo•rā′shon, *n.* The act of imploring; earnest supplication.—**imploratory,** im•plōr′a•to•ri, *a.* Earnestly supplicating; imploring; entreating.—**implorer,** im•plōr′ėr, *n.* One who implores.—**imploringly,** im•plōr′ing•li, *adv.* In an imploring manner.

imply, im•plī′, *v.t.*—*implied, implying.* [From L. *implico*—*in*, and *plico*, to fold, whence also *implicate* (which see); comp. *apply, reply, ply.*] To involve or contain by fair inference; to contain by implication or as a consequence; to include virtually (words *imply* a promise; an effect *implies* a cause).—**impliedly,** im•plīd′li, *adv.* In an implied manner; by implication.

impolite, im•po•līt′, *a.* [Prefix *im* for *in*, not, and *polite.*] Not polite; unpolite; uncivil; rude.—**impolitely,** im•po•līt′li, *adv.* In an impolite manner.—**impoliteness,** im•po•līt′nes, *n.*

impolitic, im•pol′i•tik, *a.* [Prefix *im* for *in*, not, and *politic.*] Not politic; wanting policy or prudent management; unwise; imprudent; indiscreet; injudicious.—**impolicy,** im•pol′i•si, *n.* The quality of being impolitic; inadvisability. —**impoliticly,** im•pol′i•tik•li, *adv.*—**impoliticness,** im•pol′i•tik•nes, *n.*

imponderable, im•pon′dėr•a•bl, *a.* Not ponderable; without sensible weight.—*n.* A thing which has no appreciable weight.—**imponderability, imponderableness,** im•pon′dėr•a•bil″i•ti, im•pon′dėr•a•bl•nes, *n.* The quality of being imponderable.

import, im•pōrt′, *v.t.* [Fr. *importer,* to bring from abroad, to matter or be of consequence, L. *importo,* to bring in, to cause—*im* for *in,* and *porto,* to bring or carry, whence *port,* a person's bearing, *porter.* PORT.] To bring into a place from abroad; to bring into one's own country: opposed to *export;* to bear or carry as a signification; to mean; to signify; to imply; to be of importance, moment, or consequence to; to matter to.—*n.* (im′pōrt). That which is imported or brought into a country from abroad; that which a word bears as its signification; purport; meaning; the application or interpretation of an action, of events, etc.; bearing; importance, weight, or consequence.—**importable,** im•pōr′ta•bl, *a.* Capable of being imported.—**importation,** im•pōr•tā′shon, *n.* The act or practice of importing; a quantity imported.—**importer,** im•pōr′tėr, *n.* One who imports.

important, im•por′tant, *a.* [Fr. *important,* lit. being of great import or moment. IMPORT.] Full of or bearing import, weight, or consequence; momentous; weighty; material; influential; grave.—**importantly,** im•por′tant•li, *adv.* In an important manner.—**importance,** im•por′tans, *n.* The quality of being important; weight; consequence; moment.

importune, im•por•tūn′, sometimes im•por′tūn, *v.t.*—*importuned, importuning.* [Fr. *importuner,* to importune, pester, from L. *importunus,* distressing, rude—*im* for *in,* not, and *portus,* a port or harbor, access.] To press with solicitation; to solicit or urge with frequent or unceasing application; to annoy with unremitting demands.—*v.i.* To solicit earnestly and repeatedly.—**importunate,** im•por′tū•nit, *a.* Troublesome by frequent demands; incessant in solicitation; urgent; unreasonable.—**importunately,** im•por′tū•nit•li, *adv.* In an importunate manner.—**importuner,** im•por•tū′nėr, *n.* One who importunes.—**importunity, importunacy, importunateness,** im•por•tū′ni•ti, im•por′tū•ni•si, im•por′tū•net•nes, *n.* The quality of being importunate; application urged with troublesome pertinacity.

impose, im•pōz′, *v.t.*—*imposed, imposing.* [Fr. *imposer*—*im* for *in,* on, upon, and *poser,* to place. COMPOSE, POSE.] To lay, set, or place on (to *impose* the hands); to lay or enjoin as a burden, tax, penalty, command, law, etc.; to palm or pass off; *printing,* to arrange and adjust (pages) and fasten into a chase.—*v.i.* Used in phrase *to impose on* or *upon,* to pass or put a trick or deceit on; to deceive; to victimize.—**imposer,** im•pō′zėr, *n.* One who imposes; one who enjoins.—**imposing,** im•pō′zing, *a.* Impressive in appearance; commanding; stately; majestic.—**imposingly,** im•pō′zing•li, *adv.* In an imposing manner.—**imposing stone, imposing table,** *n. Printing,* a table of stone or metal on which the pages or columns of type are imposed or made into forms.—**imposition,** im•po•zish′on, *n.* The act of imposing or laying on; that which is imposed, levied, inflicted, enjoined, and the like; the act of tricking or deceiving; a trick or deception; a fraud; an imposture; an exercise enjoined on students as a punishment.

impossible, im•pos′i•bl, *a.* [L. *impossibilis*—*im* for *in,* not, and *possibilis,* possible. POSSIBLE.] Not possible; not capable of being or being done; incapable of being accomplished, thought, endured, etc.—**impossibly,** im•pos′i•bli, *adv.* Not possibly.—**impossibility,** im•pos′i•bil″i•ti, *n.* The state or quality of being impossible; that which is impossible.

impost, im′pōst, *n.* [O.Fr. *impost,* Fr. *impôt,* L. *impositum,* from *impono, impositum,* to lay upon—*in,* on, and *pono,* to place.] That which is imposed or levied; a tax, tribute, or duty; *arch.* the point where an arch rests on a wall or column.

impostor, im•pos′tėr, *n.* [L. *impostor,* from *impono*—*in,* on, and *pono,* to place.] One who imposes on others; a person who assumes a character for the purpose of deception; a deceiver under a false character.—**imposture,** im•pos′chėr, *n.* [L. *impostura,* from *impono, impositum.*] The act or conduct of an impostor; fraud or imposition.

impotent, im′po•tent, *a.* [L. *impotens, impotentis*—*im* for *in,* not, and *potens,* able, *potent.*] Entirely wanting power, strength, or vigor of body or mind; deficient in capacity; weak; feeble; destitute of the power of sexual intercourse or of begetting children.—**impotently,** im′po•tent•li, *adv.* In an impotent manner.—**impotence, impotency,** im′po•tens, im′po•ten•si, *n.* The condition or quality of being impotent.

impound, im•pound′, *v.t.* [Prefix *im* for *in,* and *pound.*] To put in a pound (as a straying animal); to confine; to take possession of, as of a document, for use when necessary.—**impoundage,** im•poun′dij, *n.* The act of impounding.—**impounder,** im•poun′dėr, *n.* One who impounds.

impoverish, im•pov′ėr•ish, *v.t.* [Prefix *im,* intens., and Fr. *pauvre,* poor. POOR.] To make poor; to reduce to poverty or indigence; to exhaust the strength, richness, or fertility of (to *impoverish* land).—**impoverisher,** im•pov′ėr•ish•ėr, *n.* One who or that which impoverishes.—**impoverishment,** im•pov′ėr•ish•ment, *n.* The act of impoverishing.

impower, im•pou′ėr, *v.t.* To empower.

impracticable, im•prak′ti•ka•bl, *a.* Not practicable; not to be performed or effected by human means or by the means at command; not to be dealt with or managed; unmanageable; incapable of being passed or traveled (an *impracticable* road).—**impracticably,** im•prak′ti•ka•bli, *adv.* In an impracticable manner.—**impracticability, impracticableness,** im•prak′ti•ka•bil″i•ti, im•prak′ti•ka•bl•nes, *n.* The state or quality of being impracticable.—**impractical,** im•prak′ti•kal, *a.* Not practical; not taking a common-sense view of things; full of theories.

imprecate, im′pri•kāt, *v.t.*—*imprecated, imprecating.* [L. *imprecor, imprecatus*—*im* for *in,* on, and *precor,* to pray. PRAY.] To call down, as a curse, calamity, or punishment, by prayer; to invoke (a curse or some evil).—**imprecation,** im•pri•kā′shon, *n.* [L. *imprecatio.*] The act of imprecating; a prayer that a curse or calamity may fall on anyone; a curse.—**imprecatory,** im′pri•kā•to•ri, *a.* Of the nature of or containing an imprecation.

impregnable, im•preg′na•bl, *a.* [O. Fr. *imprenable* (the *g* being inserted as in *pregnable*)—*im* for *in,* not, and *prendre,* to take.] Not to be taken; incapable of being reduced by force (an *impregnable* fortress); not to be moved, impressed, or shaken.—**impregnability, impregnableness,** im•preg′na•bil″i•ti, im•preg′na•bl•nes, *n.* State of being impregnable.—**impregnably,** im•preg′na•bli, *adv.*

impregnate, im•preg′nāt, *v.t.*—*impregnated, impregnating.* [L.L. *imprægno, imprægnatum*—L. *im* for *in,* in, and *prægnans,* pregnant. PREGNANT.] To make pregnant or with young; to cause to conceive; to transmit or infuse an active principle into; to imbue; to communicate qualities to by mixture.—**impregnation,** im•preg•nā′shon, *n.* The act of impregnating.

impresario, im•pres•ä′ri•o, *n.* [It.] One who organizes, manages, or conducts a company of concert or opera performers.

imprescriptible, im•pri•skrip′ti•bl, *a.* [Prefix *im* for *in,* not, and *prescriptible.*] Incapable of being lost by neglect to use, or by the claims of another founded on prescription.—**imprescriptibility,** im•pri•skrip′ti•bil″i•ti, *n.* State of being imprescriptible.

impress, im•pres′, *v.t.* [L. *imprimo, impressum*—*im* for *in,* on, upon, and *premo,* to press. PRESS.] To press or stamp in or upon; to mark by pressure; to make a mark or figure upon; to stamp (to *impress* a design on; to *impress* with a design); to stamp on the mind; to inculcate (truth, facts, etc.); to affect deeply the feelings or sentiments.—*n.* (im′pres). A mark or figure made by pressure, or as by pressure; stamp; impression.—**impressibility,** im•pres′i•bil″i•ti, *n.* The quality of being impressible.—**impressible,** im•pres′i•bl, *a.* Capable of being impressed; susceptible of impression; easily affected; susceptive.—**impression,** im•presh′on, *n.* [L. *impressio, impressionis.*] The act of impressing; that which is impressed, printed, or stamped; a copy taken by pressure from type, from an engraved plate, and the like; the aggregate of copies taken at one time; edition; effect or influence on the senses, on the mind, feelings, or sentiments; an indistinct notion, remembrance or belief.—**impressionability, impressionableness,** im•presh′on•a•bil″i•ti, im•presh′on•a•bl•nes, *n.*—**impressionable,** im•presh′on•a•bl, *a.* Having the mind or feelings easily affected.—**impressionist,** im•presh′-on•ist, *n.*—**impressionism,** im•presh′-on•izm, *n.* A type of art which strives to create a sensation or evoke a mood; *paint.* a 19th-century French school of painting that emphasized quick visual impression and painting directly from nature; *mus.* a style of orchestral composition that invokes mood through associations.—**impressionistic,** im•presh′on•ist″ic, *a.*—**impressive,** im•pres′iv, *a.* Making or tending to make an impression; having the power of affecting or of exciting attention and feeling.—**impressively,** im•pres′iv•li, *adv.* In an impressive manner.—**impressiveness,** im•pres′iv•nes, *a.*

impress, im•pres′, *v.t.* [Influenced by *press*, but originally meaning to hire by ready money, from O.E. *prest*, ready money; O.Fr. *prester*, to give, to lend; L. *præsto*, in readiness (*præ*, before, and *sto*, to stand).] To compel to enter into public service, as a seaman; to seize and take into service by compulsion; to take for public use.—*n.* The act of impressing; compulsion to serve.—**impressment,** im•pres′ment, *n.* The act of impressing.

imprimatur, im•pri•mā′tėr, *n.* [L., let it be printed.] A license to print a book, etc.; hence, a mark of approval in general.

imprint, im•print′, *v.t.* [O.E. *emprent*, Fr. *empreint*, pp. of *empreindre*, to imprint, L. *imprimere*, to impress. PRINT.] To mark by pressure; to stamp; to print; to fix indelibly or permanently, as on the mind or memory; to impress.—*n.* (im′print). Whatever is impressed or printed; especially, the name of the printer or publisher of a book, with the place and often the time of publication.

imprison, im•priz′on, *v.t.* [Prefix *im* for *in*, in, and *prison*.] To put into a prison; to incarcerate; to confine.—**imprisoner,** im•priz′on•ėr, *n.* One who imprisons.—**imprisonment,** im•priz′on•ment, *n.* The act of imprisoning or state of being imprisoned.

improbable, im•prob′a•bl, *a.* [Prefix *im* for *in*, not, and *probable*.] Not probable; not likely to be true; unlikely.—**improbability, improbableness,** im•prob′a•bil″i•ti, im•prob′-a•bl•nes, *n.* The quality of being improbable.—**improbably,** im•prob′-a•bli, *adv.* In an improbable manner.

improbity, im•prōb′i•ti, *n.* [L. *improbitas*—*im* for *in*, not, and *probitas*, probity.] Want of probity; want of integrity or rectitude of principle; dishonesty.

impromptu, im•promp′tū, *adv.* [L. *in promptu*, in readiness, from *promptus*, readiness. PROMPT.] Off hand; without previous study.—*n.* A saying, poem, epigram, or the like made offhand, or without previous study; an extemporaneous effusion.—*a.* Offhand; extempore.

improper, im•prop′ėr, *a.* [Prefix *im* for *in*, not, and *proper*.] Not proper; not suitable, adapted, or suited; unbecoming; indecent.—*Improper fraction*, a fraction whose numerator is equal to or greater than its denominator.—**improperly,** im•prop′ėr•li, *adv.* In an improper manner.—**impropriety,** im•prō•prī′e•ti, *n.* [Fr. *impropriété*, from L. *improprius*, improper.] The quality of being improper; that which is improper; an unsuitable act, expression, and the like.

impropriate, im•prō′pri•āt, *v.t.*—*impropriated*, *impropriating*. [L. *im* for *in*, and *proprio*, *propriatum*, to appropriate, from *proprius*, one's own. PROPER.] To appropriate; *eccles.* to place the profits or revenue of in the hands of a layman; to put in the possession of a layman or lay corporation.—*a.* Devolved into the hands of a layman.—**impropriation,** im•prō′pri•ā″shon, *n.* The act of impropriating; that which is impropriated.—**impropriator,** im•prō′-pri•ā•tėr, *n.* One who impropriates.

impropriety. See IMPROPER.

improve, im•pröv′, *v.t.*—*improved*, *improving*. [Prefix *im* for *in*, intens., and O.Fr. *prover*, to test, to show to be sufficient. PROVE.] To make better; to increase the value, worth, or good qualities of; to use or employ to good purpose; to turn to profitable account (to *improve* the time).—*v.i.* To grow or become better; to advance in goodness, knowledge, wisdom, or anything else desirable.—*To improve on* or *upon*, to make additions or amendments to; to make an advance in; to bring nearer to perfection. ∴ Syn. under AMEND.—**improvability, improvableness,** im•prö′va•bil″i•ti, im•prö′-va•bl•nes, *n.* The state or quality of being improvable.—**improvable,** im•prö′va•bl, *a.* Capable of being improved.—**improvement,** im•pröv′-ment, *n.* The act of improving, or state of being improved; that which improves; that by which the value of anything is increased, its excellence enhanced, and the like; a beneficial or valuable addition or alteration.—**improver,** im•prö′vėr, *n.* One who improves.—**improvingly,** im•prö′ving•li, *adv.* In an improving manner.

improvident, im•prov′i•dent, *a.* [Prefix *im* for *in*, not, and *provident*.] Not provident; wanting forecast; wanting care to make provision for future exigencies; thriftless; thoughtless.—**improvidence,** im•prov′i•dens, *n.* The quality of being improvident.—**improvidently,** im•prov′i•dent•li, *adv.* In an improvident manner; thriftlessly.

improvise, im′pro•vīz, *v.t.*—*improvised*, *improvising*. [Fr. *improviser*, It. *improvvisare*, to sing in extempore rhymes, from L. *in*, not, *pro*, before, and *visus*, seen.] To compose and recite or sing without premeditation; to speak extempore, especially in verse; to do or form on the spur of the moment for a special occasion; to bring about in an offhand way.—*v.i.* To recite or sing compositions without previous preparation.—**improvisation,** im•prov′i•zā″shon, *n.* The act or faculty of improvising; a song or other poem which is improvised.—**improviser, improvisator,** im•pro•vī′zėr, im•prov′i•zā•tėr, *n.* One who improvisates or improvises.—**improvisatory,** im•pro•viz′a•tō•ri, *a.* Relating to improvisation or improvisers.

imprudent, im•prö′dent, *a.* [L. *imprudens*—*im* for *in*, not, and *prudent*.] Not prudent; wanting prudence or discretion; indiscreet; injudicious; rash; heedless.—**imprudence,** im•prö′dens, *n.* The quality of being imprudent; an imprudent act or course of conduct.—**imprudently,** im•prö′dent•li, *adv.* In an imprudent manner.

impudent, im′pū•dent, *a.* [L. *impudens*, *impudentis*, without shame—*in*, not, and *pudens*, from *pudeo*, to be ashamed.] Offensively forward in behavior; intentionally treating others without due respect; wanting modesty; shameless; impertinent.—**impudently,** im′pū•dent•li, *adv.* In an impudent manner.—**impudence,** im′pū•dens, *n.* The quality of being impudent; impudent language or behavior; offensive forwardness.

impugn, im•pūn′, *v.t.* [Fr. *impugner*; L. *impugno*—*im* for *in*, against, and *pugno*, to fight or resist (akin *pugnacious*, *repugnant*, *pugilism*.] To attack (a statement, truthfulness, etc.) by words or arguments; to contradict; to call in question; to gainsay.—**impugnable,** im•pū′na•bl, *a.* Capable of being impugned.—**impugner,** im•pū′nėr, *n.* One who impugns.

impulse, im′puls, *n.* [L. *impulsus*, from *impello*, *impulsum*, to drive on. IMPEL.] Force communicated suddenly; motion produced by suddenly communicated force; thrust; push; influence acting on the mind suddenly or unexpectedly; sudden thought or determination; a force of infinitely large magnitude acting for an infinitely short time so as to produce a finite change of momentum.—**impulsion,** im•pul′shon, *n.* [L. *impulsio*, *impulsionis*.] The act of impelling or state of being impelled; instigation; impulse.—**impulsive,** im•pul′siv, *a.* [Fr. *impulsif*.] Having the power of impelling; impellant; actuated or liable to be actuated by impulses; under the sway of one's emotions.—**impulsively,** im•pul′siv•li, *adv.* In an impulsive manner.—**impulsiveness,** im•pul′siv•nes, *n.*

impunity, im•pū′ni•ti, *n.* [Fr. *impunité*, from L. *impunitas*, from *impunis*, unpunished—*im* for *in*, not, and *punio*, to punish. PUNISH.] Exemption from punishment or penalty; freedom or exemption from injury, suffering, or loss.

impure, im•pur′, *a.* [Fr. *impur*, from

L. *impurus*—*im* for *in*, not, and *purus*, pure.] Not pure; mixed or impregnated with foul or extraneous substance; foul; obscene; unchaste; lewd; unclean; defiled by sin or guilt; unhallowed or unholy.—**impurely**, im•pūr′li, *adv*. In an impure manner. —**impureness**, im•pūr′nes, *n*. The quality or condition of being impure. —**impurity**, im•pū′ri•ti, *n*. [L. *impuritas*.] The condition or quality of being impure; foulness; that which is impure; foul matter.

impute, im•pūt′, *v.t.* [L. *imputo*—*in* into, and *puto*, think, consider, reckon (as in *compute*, *repute*, *putative*).] To charge, attribute, or ascribe; to set to the account of; *theol.* to reckon or set down to the account of one what does not belong to him. —**imputability, imputableness**, im•pū′ta•bil″i•ti, im•pū′ta•bl•nes, *n*. The quality of being imputable.—**imputable**, im•pū′ta•bl, *a*. Capable of being imputed.—**imputation**, im•pū•tā′shon, *n*. [L. *imputatio*, *imputationis*.] The act of imputing; that which is imputed or charged; charge, as of evil; censure; reproach; *theol.* the charging or reckoning to the account of one, something which properly attaches to another.—**imputative**, im•pū′ta•tiv, *a*. Coming by imputation; imputed.—**imputatively**, im•pū′ta•tiv•li, *adv*. By imputation.—**imputer**, im•pū′tėr, *n*. One that imputes.

in, in, *prep*. [A.Sax. *in*=D. and Goth. *in*, Icel. *inn*, *i*, Dan. *ind*, *i*, G. *in*, *ein*, forms corresponding to L. *in*, Gr. *en*, W. *yn*, Armor. *enn*; akin to *on*.] Within; inside of; surrounded by; indicating presence or situation within limits, whether of place, time, or circumstances (*in* the house, *in* the year, *in* sickness); or existence as a part, constituent, or quality of (evil *in* a man's disposition); or a certain state (a vehicle *in* motion, to put *in* operation).—*In as much as*, or *inasmuch as*, seeing that; considering that; since.—*In that*, because; for the reason that.—*In name of*, by way of; as (a sum paid *in name of* damages).—*In the name of*, in behalf of; on the part of; by the authority of.—*adv*. In or within some place; in some state, affair, or circumstances; not out (he is *in*, that is, in the house; the party is *in*, that is, in office; the ship is *in*, that is, in port); into some place or state, implying motion or change (come *in*, that is, into the house).—*To breed in and in*, to breed among members of the same family.—*To keep one's hand in*, to keep up one's acquirements; to maintain one's skill by practice.—Sometimes used substantively, as in the phrase '*ins* and outs', nooks and corners; all the details and intricacies of a matter.

inability, in•a•bil′i•ti, *n*. [Prefix *in*, not, and *ability*.] The state of being unable; want of the necessary power or ability.

inaccessible, in•ak•ses′i•bl, *n*. [Prefix *in*, not, and *accessible*.] Not accessible; not to be reached, obtained, or approached.—**inaccessibly**, in•ak•ses′i•bli, *adv*. In an inaccessible manner.—**inaccessibility, inaccessibleness**, in•ak•ses′i•bil″i•ti, in•ak•ses′i•bl•nes, *n*. The quality or state of being inaccessible.

inaccurate, in•ak′kū•rāt, *a*. [Prefix *in*, not, and *accurate*.] Not accurate, exact, or correct; making or containing incorrect statements; not according to truth; erroneous.—**inaccurately**, in•ak′kū•rāt•li, *adv*. In an inaccurate manner.—**inaccuracy**, in•ak′kū•ra•si, *n*. The state of being inaccurate; an inaccurate statement; a mistake in a statement; an error.

inaction, in•ak′shon, *n*. [Prefix *in*, not, and *action*.] Want of action; state of being inactive; idleness; rest. —**inactive**, in•ak′tiv, *a*. [Prefix *in*, not, and *active*.] Not active; inert; having no power to move; not engaged in action or effort; idle; indolent; sluggish; *chem.* and *med.* inoperative.—Syn. see INERT. **inactively**, in•ak′tiv•li, *adv*. In an inactive manner.—**inactivity**, in•ak•tiv′i•ti, *n*. The quality or condition of being inactive.

inadequate, in•ad′i•kwit, *a*. [Prefix *in*, not, and *adequate*.] Not adequate; not equal to the purpose; insufficient; defective.—**inadequacy, inadequateness** in•ad′i•kwi•si, in•ad′i•kwit•nes, *n*. The state or quality of being inadequate.—**inadequately** in•ad′i•kwit•li, *adv*.

inadmissible, in•ad•mis′i•bl, *a*. [Prefix *in*, not, and *admissible*.] Not admissible; not proper to be admitted, allowed, or received.—**inadmissibly**, in•ad•mis′i•bli, *adv*. In a manner not admissible.—**inadmissibility**, in•ad•mis′i•bil″i•ti, *n*. The quality of being inadmissible.

inadvertent, in•ad•vėr′tent, *a*. [L. prefix *in*, not, and *advertens*, *advertentis*, ppr. of *adverto*, to attend to. ADVERT.] Not paying strict attention; failing to notice or observe; heedless; unwary.—**inadvertently**, in•ad•vėr′tent•li, *adv*. In an inadvertent manner.—**inadvertence, inadvertency**, in•ad•vėr′tens, in•ad•vėr′ten•si, *n*. The quality of being inadvertent; an oversight, mistake, or fault which proceeds from some degree of heedlessness.

inalienable, in•āl′yen•a•bl, *a*. [Prefix *in*, not, and *alienable*.] Incapable of being alienated or transferred to another.—**inalienability**, in•āl′yen•a•bil″i•ti, *n*. The state or quality of being inalienable.—**inalienably**, in•āl′yen•a•bli, *adv*. In a manner that forbids alienation.

inalterable, in•ạl′tėr•a•bl, *n*. [Prefix *in*, not, and *alterable*.] Not alterable; unalterable.

inamorato, in•ä′mō•rä″tō, *n*. [It. *innamorato*, fem. *innamorata*, from L. *in*, in, *amor*, love.] A male lover.—**inamorata**, in•ä′mō•rä″ta, *n*. A female in love; a mistress.

inane, in•ān′, *a*. [L. *inanis*, empty.] Empty; void; frivolous; worthless; void of sense or intelligence. *n*. That which is void or empty; infinite void space. (*Tenn.*)—**inanition**, in•a•nish′on, *n*. The condition of being inane; exhaustion from want of food. —**inanity**, in•an′i•ti, *n*. The state of being inane; mental vacuity; silliness.

inanimate, in•an′i•mit, *a*. [Prefix *in*, not, and *animate*.] Not animate; destitute of life or animation; without vivacity or briskness; dull; inactive; sluggish. — **inanimateness**, in•an′i•mit•nes, *n*.

inappetence, inappetency, in•ap′pe•tens, in•ap′pe•ten•si, *n*. [Prefix *in*, not, and *appetence*, *appetency*.] Want of appetence, desire, or inclination.

inapplicable, in•ap′pli•ka•bl, *a*. [Prefix *in*, not, and *applicable*.] Not applicable; incapable of being applied; not suited or suitable to the purpose. —**inapplicability, inapplicableness**, in•ap′pli•ka•bil″i•ti, in•ap′pli•ka•bl•nes, *n*.—**inapplicably**, in•ap′pli•ka•bli, *adv*.

inapposite, in•ap′po•zit, *a*. [Prefix *in*, not, and *apposite*.] Not apposite, fit, or suitable; not pertinent.

inappreciable, in•ap•prē′shi•a•bl, *a*. [Prefix *in*, not, and *appreciable*.] Not appreciable; so small as hardly to be noticed or estimated.

inapproachable, in•ap•prōch′a•bl, *a*. [Prefix *in*, not, and *approachable*.] Not approachable; inaccessible; that cannot be equaled; unrivaled.

inappropriate, in•ap•prō′pri•it, *a*. [Prefix *in*, not, and *appropriate*.] Not appropriate; unsuited; unsuitable; not proper.—**inappropriately**, in•ap•prō′pri•it•li, *adv*. In an inappropriate manner.—**inappropriateness**, in•ap•prō′pri•it•nes, *n*.

inapt, in•apt′, *a*. [Prefix, *in*, not, and *apt*.] Unapt; not apt; unsuitable; unfit.—**inaptitude, inaptness**, in•ap′ti•tūd, in•apt′nes, *n*. Unfitness; unsuitableness.—**inaptly**, in•apt′li, *adv*. Unfitly; unsuitably.

inarch, in•ärch′, *v.t.* [Prefix *in*, into, and *arch*.] To graft by uniting to the stock without separating (for a time) the scion from its parent tree.

inarticulate, in•är•tik′ū•lit, *a*. [Prefix *in*, not, and *articulate*.] Not articulate; not uttered with distinctness of sounds or syllables; *zool.* not jointed or articulated.—**inarticulately**, in•är•tik′ū•lit•li, *adv*. In an inarticulate manner.—**inarticulateness**, in•är•tik′ū•lit•nes, *n*. The state or quality of being inarticulate.

inartificial, in•är′ti•fish″al, *a*. [Prefix *in*, not, and *artificial*.] Not artificial; formed without art; simple; artless. —**inartificially**, in•är′ti•fish″al•li, *adv*. In an inartificial manner.

inasmuch, in•az•much′, *adv*. See IN.

inattention, in•at•ten′shon, *n*. [Prefix *in*, not, and *attention*.] Want of attention; heedlessness.—**inattentive**, in•at•ten′tiv, *a*. Not attentive; not fixing the mind on an object; heedless.—**inattentively**, in•at•ten′tiv•li, *adv*. Carelessly; heedlessly.—**inattentiveness**, in•at•ten′tiv•nes, *n*.

inaudible, in•ạ′di•bl, *a*. [Prefix *in*, not, and *audible*.] Not audible; incapable of being heard.—**inaudibly**, in•ạ′di•bli, *adv*. In an inaudible manner.—**inaudibility, inaudibleness**, in•ạ′di•bil″i•ti, in•ạ′di•bl•nes, *n*. The quality of being inaudible.

inaugurate, in•ạ′gū•rāt, *v.t.*—*inaugurated*, *inaugurating*. [L. *inauguro*, *inauguratum*, to inaugurate, to install —*in*, into, and *augur*, an augur.] To introduce or induct into an office with solemnity or suitable ceremonies; to invest in a formal manner; to begin or set in progress with formality or some degree of solemnity, pomp, or ceremony; to initiate; to perform in public initiatory ceremonies in connection with; to celebrate the completion of.—**inaugural,** in•a̤′gū•ral, *a.* Having to do with an inauguration.—*n.* An address given at the inception of a term of office. —**inauguration,** in•a̤′gū•rā″shon, *n.* —**inaugurator,** in•a̤′gū•rā•tėr, *n.*

inauspicious, in•a̤•spish′us, *a.* [Prefix *in*, not, and *auspicious*.] Not auspicious; ill-omened; unlucky; unfavorable.—**inauspiciously,** in•a̤•spish′us•li, *adv.* In an inauspicious manner. —**inauspiciousness,** in•a̤•spish′us•nes, *n.*

inboard, in′bōrd, *a.* Within a ship or other vessel (an *inboard* cargo).—*adv.* Within the hold of a vessel; on board of a vessel.

inborn, in′born, *a.* Innate; implanted by nature.

inbreathe, in•brēTH′, *v.t.* To breathe in, or infuse by breathing.

inbred, in′bred, *a.* Bred within; innate; natural.—**inbreed,** in•brēd′, *v.t.* To produce or generate within; to cross or mate closely related individuals.

Inca, ing′ka, *n.* A king or prince of Peru before the Spanish conquest; the dominant group of Indians in Peru at that time.

incalculable, in•kal′kū•la•bl, *a.* [Prefix *in*, not, and *calculable*.] Not calculable; beyond calculation; very great.—**incalculableness,** in•kal′kū•la•bl•nes, *n.*—**incalculably,** in•kal′kū•la•bli, *adv.*

incalescent, in•ka•les′ent, *a.* [L. *incalesco*, to grow warm—*in*, and *calesco*, to grow warm, *caleo*, to be warm. CALID.] Growing warm; increasing in heat.—**incalescence,** in•ka•les′ens, *n.* The state of being incalescent.

incandescent, in•kan•des′ent, *a.* [L. *incandesco*, to become warm—*in*, intens., and *candesco*, to begin to glow.] White or glowing with heat; luminous; radiant.—**incandescent lamp,** *n.* A lamp whose light is produced by the action of electric current on some specially prepared material.—**incandescence,** in•kan•des′ens, *n.*

incantation, in•kan•tā′shon, *n.* [L. *incantatio, incantationis*, from *incanto*, to chant a magic formula over one—*in*, on, and *canto*, to sing. CHANT.] The act of using certain words and ceremonies for the purpose of raising spirits or performing magical actions; the form of words so used; a magical spell, charm, or ceremony.

incapable, in•kā′pa•bl, *a.* [Prefix *in*, not, and *capable*.] Not capable; possessing inadequate power; not admitting; not susceptible; not equal to anything; unable; unqualified or disqualified: generally followed by *of*. ∴ *Incapable* properly denotes a want of passive power, and is applicable particularly to the mind, or said of something inanimate; *unable* denotes the want of active power or power of performing, and is applicable to the body or mind.—*n.* One physically or mentally unable to act with effect; an inefficient or silly person.—**incapability, incapableness,** in•kā′pa•bil″i•ti, in•kā′pa•bl•nes, *n.* The quality of being incapable.—**incapably,** in•kā′pa•bli, *adv.* In an incapable manner.

incapacitate, in•ka•pas′i•tāt, *v.t.*—*incapacitated, incapacitating*. [Prefix *in*, not, and *capacitate*.] To deprive of capacity or natural power; to render or make unable or unfit; to disqualify or render incompetent.—**incapacitation,** in•ka•pas′i•tā″shon, *n.* The act of incapacitating.—**incapacity,** in•ka•pas′i•ti, *n.* Want of capacity, power, or ability; inability; incompetency.

incarcerate, in•kär′sėr•āt, *v.t.*—*incarcerated, incarcerating*. [L. *in*, in, into, and *carcer*, a prison.] To imprison; to confine in a jail; to shut up or enclose.—**incarceration,** in•kär′sėr•ā″shon, *n.* The act of incarcerating; imprisonment.—**incarcerator,** in•kär′sėr•ā•tėr, *n.* One who incarcerates.

incarnadine, in•kär′na•din, *v.t.* [Fr. *incarnadin*, flesh-colored—L. *in*, in, and *caro, carnis*, flesh.] To tinge with the color of flesh; to dye red.

incarnate, in•kär′nāt, *v.t.*—*incarnated, incarnating*. [L.L. *incarno, incarnatum*—L. *in*, into, and *caro, carnis*, flesh (whence also *carnage, carnal, carnation*).] To clothe with flesh; to embody in flesh.—*a.* Invested with flesh; embodied in flesh or a human body.—**incarnation,** in•kär•nā′shon, *n.* The act of assuming flesh or taking a human body and the nature of man; the state of being incarnated; a visible embodiment; a vivid exemplification in person or act (he is the *incarnation* of wickedness).

incase, in•kās′, *v.t.*—*incased, incasing*. To enclose in, or as in, a case.

incautious, in•ka̤′shus, *a.* [Prefix *in*, not, and *cautious*.] Not cautious; unwary; heedless.—**incautiously,** in•ka̤′shus•li, *adv.* In an incautious manner. — **incautiousness,** in•ka̤′shus•nes, *n.*

incendiary, in•sen′di•e•ri, *n.* [L. *incendiarius*, from *incendo*, to burn—*in*, and *candeo*, to shine or be on fire. CANDID.] A person who willfully and maliciously sets fire to a building, etc.; one who sets fire to another's property; one who is guilty of arson; one who excites or inflames factions and promotes quarrels.—*a.* Pertaining to willful and malicious fire raising; tending to excite or inflame factions, sedition, or quarrel.—**incendiarism,** in•sen′di•er•izm, *n.* The act or practice of an incendiary.

incense, in′sens, *n.* [Fr. *encens*, from L. *incensum*, what is set on fire, from *incensus*, pp. of *incendo*, to burn. INCENDIARY.] The odors of spices and gums, burned in religious rites, or as an offering to some deity; the materials burned for making perfumes.—*v.t.*—*incensed, incensing*. To perfume with incense.

incense, in•sens′, *v.t.*—*incensed, incensing*. [L. *incensus*, provoked, inflamed; same word as *Incense*, above.] To enkindle or inflame to violent anger; to excite to angry passions; to provoke, irritate, exasperate.

incentive, in•sen′tiv, *a.* [L. *incentivus*, striking up or leading a melody —*in*, on, and *cano*, to sing. CHANT.] Inciting; encouraging or stirring up. —*n.* That which incites or has a tendency to incite to determination or action; what prompts to good or ill; motive; spur.

inception, in•sep′shon, *n.* [L. *inceptio, inceptionis*, from *incipio*, to begin—prefix *in*, and *capio*, to take. CAPABLE.] The act of beginning; a beginning; commencement; first stage.—**inceptive,** in•sep′tiv, *a.* [L. *inceptivus*.] Pertaining to inception; beginning; applied to a verb which expresses the beginning of an action. —*n.* An inceptive verb.—**inceptor,** in•sep′tėr, *n.* A beginner; one who is on the point of taking the degree of Master of Arts at an English university.

incertitude, in•sėr′ti•tūd, *n.* [Prefix *in*, not, and *certitude*.] Uncertainty; doubtfulness; doubt.

incessant, in•ses′ant, *a.* [L. prefix *in*, not, and *cessans, cessantis*, ppr. of *cesso*, to cease. CEASE.] Continuing without interruption; unceasing; unintermitted; uninterrupted; continual; ceaseless.—**incessantly,** in•ses′ant•li, *adv.* In an incessant manner; continually.

incest, in′sest, *n.* [Fr. *inceste*, L. *incestum*, unchastity, incest, from *incestus*, unchaste—*in*, not, and *castus*, chaste (whence *chaste*).] The offense of sexual commerce between persons related within the degrees wherein marriage is prohibited by law.—**incestuous,** in•ses′tū•us, *a.* Guilty of incest; involving the crime of incest. —**incestuously,** in•ses′tū•us•li, *adv.* In an incestuous manner.

inch, insh, *n.* [A.Sax. *ince, ynce*, an inch, the twelfth part of a foot; from L. *uncia*, a twelfth part. *Ounce* is the same word.] A lineal measure, being the twelfth part of a foot; proverbially, a small quantity or degree.—*By inches*, by slow degrees; gradually.—*a.* Measuring an inch: used in composition (two-*inch*, four-*inch*).

inchoate,† in′kō•āt, *v.t.* [L. *inchoa, inchoatum*, to begin.] To begin.—*a.* Recently or just begun; incipient; rudimentary; incomplete.—**inchoately,** in′kō•āt•li, *adv.* In an inchoate state.—**inchoation,** in•kō•ā′shon, *n.* The act of beginning; inception.—**inchoative,** in′kō•ā•tiv, *a.* Expressing or indicating beginning; inceptive.—*n.* That which serves to begin; *gram.* an inceptive verb.

incidence, in′si•dens, *n.* [L.L. *incidentia*, from E. *incido*, to fall upon—*in*, into, upon, and *cado*, to fall (whence *cadence, chance, case*, etc.).] A falling or occurring; the manner of falling (the *incidence* of taxation in a state); *physics*, the direction in which a body, or a ray of light, heat, etc., falls upon any surface, this direction, as regards the surface on which the body or ray falls, being called the *line of incidence.*—*Angle of incidence,* the angle formed by the line of incidence, and a line drawn from the point of contact, perpendicular to the surface.—*Point of incidence,* the point where an incident ray meets a surface.—**incident,** in′si•dent, *a.* [L. *incidens, incidentis,* ppr. of *incido.*] Falling or striking, as a ray of light upon a surface; liable to happen; apt to occur; hence, naturally happening or appertaining (ills *incident to* human life).—*n.* What falls out, happens, or takes place; an event; an appertaining fact; *law,* a thing appertaining to, or passing with another or principal thing.—**incidental,** in•si•den′tal, *a.* Happening as an occasional event forming an incident; casual; not necessary to the chief purpose; appertaining and subsidiary.—**incidentally,** in•si•den′tal•li, *adv.* In an incidental manner.

incinerate, in•sin′ėr•āt, *v.t.* [L. *in,* into, and *cinis, cineris,* ashes.] To burn to ashes.—**incineration,** in•sin′ėr•ā″shon, *n.* The act of incinerating.

incipient, in•sip′i•ent, *a.* [L. *incipiens, incipientis,* ppr. of *incipio,* to begin—*in,* and *capio,* to take. CAPABLE.] Beginning; commencing; beginning to show itself.—**incipience, incipiency,** in•sip′i•ens, in•sip′i•en•si, *n.* The condition of being incipient.—**incipiently,** in•sip′i•ent•li, *adv.* In an incipient manner.

incise, in•sīz′, *v.t.*—*incised, incising.* [Fr. *inciser,* from L. *incido, incisum*—*in,* into, and *cædo,* to cut, as in *concise, decide, excision,* etc.] To cut into; to make a deep cut in; to carve.—**incised,** in•sīzd′, *p.* and *a.* Cut; made by cutting.—**incision,** in•sizh′on, *n.* The act of cutting into a substance; that which is produced by incising; a cut; a gash; *fig.* sharpness; trenchancy.—**incisive,** in•sī′siv, *a.* [Fr. *incisif,* incisive.] Cutting in; sharply and clearly expressive; trenchant (*incisive* language or style).—**incisor,** in•sī′zėr, *n. Zool.* a fore-tooth; one of those teeth, the special task of which is to cut or separate.—**incisory,** in•sī′ze•ri, *a.* Having the quality of cutting.

incite, in•sīt′, *v.t.*—*incited, inciting.* [L. *incito*—*in,* on, and *cito,* to urge, to rouse. CITE.] To move to action; to stir up; to stimulate, urge, provoke, spur on.—**incitement, incitation,** in•sīt′ment, in•si•tā′shon, *n.* The act of inciting; that which incites or moves to action; incentive; impulse; spur; stimulus.—**inciter,** in•sī′tėr, *n.* One who incites.

incivil, in•siv′il, *a.* [Prefix *in,* not, and *civil.*] [*obs.*] Not civil; rude; unpolite.—**incivility,** in•si•vil′i•ti, *n.* Want of courtesy; rudeness; impoliteness.

incivism, in•siv′izm, *n.* In French Revolution the charge of lack of patriotism, of bad performance of civic duties; disaffection.

inclement, in•klem′ent, *a.* [Prefix *in,* not, and *clement.*] Not clement; unmerciful, severe, or harsh; tempestuous, rough, stormy, boisterous, or otherwise hard to bear (weather).—**inclemency,** in•klem′en•si, *n.* The condition or quality of being inclement.

incline, in•klīn′, *v.i.*—*inclined, inclining.* [L. *inclino,* to incline—*in,* in, on, and *clino,* Gr. *klinō,* to bend. DECLINE.] To deviate from a direction which is regarded as normal; to bend, lean, tend; to tend, as toward an opinion, course of action, etc.—*v.t.* To cause to deviate from a line, position, or direction; to give a leaning to; to give a tendency or propensity to; to dispose; to bend, stoop, or bow (the body, the head).—*n.* (in′klīn). An ascent or descent, as in a road; a slope.—**inclinable,** in•klī′na•bl, *a.* [L. *inclinabilis,* from *inclino.*] Tending; inclined; somewhat disposed.—**inclination,** in•kli•nā′shon, *n.* [L. *inclinatio, inclinationis.*] The act of inclining, leaning, or bending; deviation from a direction regarded as the normal one; *geom.* the approach or leaning of two lines or planes toward each other, so as to make an angle at the point where they meet, or where their lines of direction meet; a disposition more favorable to one thing or person than to another; leaning; feeling in favor; propensity.—*Inclination of an orbit, astron.* the angle which the plane of an orbit makes with the ecliptic. DIP.—**inclinatory,** in•klī′na•to•ri, *a.* Having the quality of inclining.—**inclined,** in•klīnd′, *p.* and *a.* Having a leaning or tendency; disposed.—*Inclined plane,* a plane inclined to the horizon, or forming with a horizontal plane any angle whatever excepting a right angle: it is one of the mechanical powers.

include, in•klūd′, *v.t.*—*included, including.* [L. *includo*—*in,* in, and *claudo,* to shut up, as in *conclude, exclude,* etc. CLOSE.] To confine, hold, or contain; to comprise; to comprehend; to embrace or involve.—*Included style, included stamens, bot.* a style or stamens which do not project beyond the mouth of the corolla.—**includible,** in•klu′di•bl, *a.* Capable of being included.—**inclusion,** in•klū′zhon, *n.* [L. *inclusio.*] The act of including.—**inclusive,** in•klū′siv, *a.* [Fr. *inclusif,* from L. *includo.*] Enclosing; encircling; comprehended in the number or sum; comprehending the stated limit or extremes.—**inclusively,** in•klū′siv•li, *adv.* In an inclusive manner.

incogitable, in•koj′i•ta•bl, *a.* [Prefix *in,* not, and *cogitable.* COGITATE.] Not cogitable; incapable of being made the object of thought.—**incogitant,** in•koj′i•tant, *a.* Not thinking; thoughtless.

incognito, in•kog′ni•tō, *a.* or *adv.* [It., Sp., and Fr., from L. *incognitus,* unknown—*in,* not, and *cognitus,* known. COGNITION.] In disguise; in an assumed character and under an assumed name.—*n.,* the fem. being **incognita,** in•kog′ni•ta. One unknown, or in disguise, or passing under an assumed name; assumption of a disguised or feigned character.—**incog,** in•kog′, *a., adv.* & *n.* Incognito. (*Colloq.*)

incognizable, in•kog′ni•za•bl or in•kon′i•za•bl, *a.* [Prefix *in,* not, and *cognizable.*] Not cognizable; incapable of being recognized, known, or distinguished.—**incognizance,** in•kog′ni•zans or in•kon′i•zans, *n.* Failure to recognize, know, or apprehend.—**incognizant,** in•kog′ni•zant or in•kon′i•zant, *a.* Not cognizant; unacquainted with.

incoherent, in•kō•hē′rent, *a.* [Prefix *in,* not, and *coherent.*] Not coherent; not cohering or attached together; unconnected (*incoherent* particles); wanting coherence or rational connection (ideas, language, etc.); rambling and unintelligible.—**incoherence, incoherency,** in•kō•hē′rens, in•kō•hē′ren•si, *n.* The quality of being incoherent.—**incoherently,** in•kō•hē′rent•li, *adv.* In an incoherent manner.

incombustible, in•kom•bus′ti•bl, *a.* [Prefix *in,* not, and *combustible.*] Not combustible; incapable of being burned or consumed by fire.—**incombustibility, incombustibleness,** in•com•bus′ti•bil″i•ti, in•kom•bus′ti•bl•nes, *n.* The quality of being incombustible.—**incombustibly,** in•kom•bus′ti•bli, *adv.* So as to resist combustion.

income, in′kum, *n.* [From *in* and *come,* lit. that which comes in: comp. *outcome.*] Receipts or benefits (usually in the form of money) regularly accruing from labor, business, or property (as, his annual *income* is $1,000); revenue.—**income tax,** *n.* A tax levied on incomes according to their amount.—**incomer,** in′kum•ėr, *n.* One who comes in; a stranger, not a native.—**incoming,** in′kum•ing, *a.* Coming in, as an occupant (an *incoming* tenant).—*n.* The act of coming in.

incommensurable, in•kom•men′shū•ra•bl, *a.* [Prefix *in,* not, and *commensurable.*] Not commensurable; having no common measure.—*n.* One of two or more quantities which have no common measure.—**incommensurability, incommensurableness,** in•kom•men′shū•ra•bil″i•ti, in•kom•men′shū•ra•bl•nes, *n.*—**incommensurably,** in•kom•men′shū•ra•bli, *adv.*—**incommensurate,** in•kom•men′shū•rāt, *a.* [Prefix *in,* not, and *commensurate.*] Not commensurate; incommensurable; not adequate or of sufficient amount.—**incommensurately,** in•kom•men′shū•rāt•li, *adv.* Not in due measure or proportion; inadequately.

incommode, in•kom•mōd′, *v.t.*—*incommoded, incommoding.* [Fr. *incommoder,* from L. *incommodo,* to be troublesome to—*in,* not, *commodus,* convenient.—COMMODIOUS.] To give inconvenience to; to inconvenience; to put about; to trouble.—**incommodious,** in•kom•mō′di•us, *a.* [Prefix *in,* not, and *commodious.*] Not commodious; inconvenient; tending to incommode.—**incommodiously,** in•kom•mō′di•us•li, *adv.* In an incommodious manner.—**incommodiousness,** in•kom•mō′di•us•nes, *n.*

incommunicable, in•kom•mū′ni•ka•bl, *a.* [Prefix *in,* not, and *communicable.*] Not communicable; incapable of being communicated, told, or imparted to others.—**incommunicability, incommunicableness,** in•kom•mū′ni•ka•bil″i•ti, in•kom•mū′ni•ka•bl•nes, *n.*—**incommunicably,** in•kom•mū′ni•ka•bli, *adv.*—**incommunicative,** in•kom•mū′ni•kā•tiv, *a.* [Prefix *in,* not, and *communicative.*] Not communicative; not inclined to impart information to others; not disposed to hold communion or intercourse. —**incommunicativeness,** in•kom•mū′ni•kā•tiv•nes, *n.*

incommunicado, in•ko•mū′ni•kä″dō, *a.* [Sp. *in,* in, and *comunicar,* to communicate.] Held without communication with others; in solitary confinement.

incommutable, in•kom•mū′ta•bl, *a.* [Prefix *in,* not, and *commutable.*] Not commutable; incapable of being exchanged.—**incommutability, incommutableness,** in•kom•mū′ta•bil″i•ti, in•kom•mū′ta•bl•nes, *n.*

incomparable, in•kom′pa•ra•bl, *a.* [Prefix *in,* not, and *comparable.*] Not comparable; without a match, rival, or peer; unequaled; transcendent.—**incomparableness,** in•kom′pa•ra•bl•nes, *n.*—**incomparably,** in•kom′pa•ra•bli, *adv.*

incompatible, in•kom•pat′i•bl, *a.* [Prefix *in,* not, and *compatible.*] Not compatible; incapable of subsisting, being possessed, or being made to accord with something else; incapable of harmonizing (feelings or tempers *incompatible with* each other). —*n.* A thing that is incompatible.—**incompatibility, incompatibleness,** in•kom•pat′i•bil″i•ti, in•kom•pat′i•bl•nes, *n.* The quality or condition of being incompatible.—**incompatibly,** in•kom•pat′i•bli, *adv.*

incompetent, in•kom′pe•tent, *a.* [Prefix *in,* not, and *competent.*] Not competent; wanting adequate strength, power, capacity, means, qualifications, etc.; unable; incapable; inadequate; wanting necessary legal or constitutional qualifications (an *incompetent* witness in a court); not permissible or admissible (an *incompetent* defense).—**incompetence, incompetency,** in•kom′pe•tens, in•kom′pe•ten•si, *n.* The condition or quality of being incompetent.—**incompetently,** in•kom′pe•tent•li, *adv.* In an incompetent manner.

incomplete, in•kom•plēt′, *a.* [Prefix *in,* not, and *complete.*] Not complete; not finished; imperfect; defective.—**incompletely,** in•kom•plēt′li, *adv.* In an incomplete manner.—**incompleteness, incompletion,** in•kom•plēt′nes, in•kom•plē′shon, *n.* The state of being incomplete.

incompliant, in•kom•plī′ant, *a.* [Prefix *in,* not, and *compliant.*] Not compliant; not disposed to comply.—**incompliance,** in•com•plī′ans, *n.* The quality of being incompliant.—**incompliantly,** in•kom•plī•ant•li, *adv.* In an incompliant manner.

incomprehensible, in•kom′pri•hen″si•bl, *a.* [Prefix *in,* not, and *comprehensible.*] Not comprehensible; incapable of being comprehended or understood; beyond the reach of human intellect; inconceivable; *theol.* as in Athanasian Creed; illimitable; infinite; not comprehended in or bounded by space.—**incomprehensibility, incomprehensibleness,** in•kom′pri•hen′si•bil″i•ti, in•kom′pri•hen″si•bl•nes, *n.* The quality of being incomprehensible. — **incomprehensibly,** in•kom′pri•hen″si•bli, *adv.* In an incomprehensible manner.—**incomprehensive,** in•kom′pri•hen″siv, *a.* Not comprehensive; not extensive; limited.—**incomprehensiveness,** in•kom′pri•hen″siv•nes, *n.*

incompressible, in•kom•pres′i•bl, *a.* [Prefix *in,* not, and *compressible.*] Not compressible; resisting compression. —**incompressibility, incompressibleness,** in•kom•pres′i•bil″i•ti, in•kom•pres′i•bl•nes, *n.* The quality of being incompressible.

incomputable, in•kom•pū′ta•bl, *a.* [Prefix *in,* not, and *computable.*] Not computable; incapable of being computed or reckoned.

inconceivable, in•kon•sē′va•bl, *a.* [Prefix *in,* not, and *conceivable.*] Not conceivable; incapable of being conceived or thought of; incomprehensible.—**inconceivability, inconceivableness,** in•kon•sē′va•bil″i•ti, in•kon•sē′va•bl•nes, *n.* The quality of being inconceivable.—**inconceivably,** in•kon•sē′va•bli, *adv.* In an inconceivable manner; beyond conception.

inconclusive, in•kon•klū′siv, *a.* [Prefix *in,* not, and *conclusive.*] Not conclusive; not producing a conclusion; not settling a point in debate or a doubtful question.—**inconclusively,** in•kon•klū′siv•li, *adv.* In an inconclusive manner.—**inconclusiveness,** in•kon•klū′siv•nes, *n.* The quality of being inconclusive.

incondensable, incondensible, in•kon•den′sa•bl, in•kon•den′si•bl, *a.* [Prefix *in,* not, and *condensable.*] Not condensable; incapable of being condensed.—**incondensability, incondensibility,** in•kon•den′sa•bil″i•ti, in•kon•den′si•bil″i•ti, *n.*

incondite, in•kon′dit, *a.* [L. *inconditus,* confused, rude—*in,* not, and *conditus,* pp. of *condo,* to put together, to join.] Rude; unpolished: said of literary compositions.

inconformity, in•kon•for′mi•ti, *n.* [Prefix *in,* not, and *conformity.*] Nonconformity; lack of conformity.

incongruous, incongruent, in•kong′gru̥•us, in•kong′gru̥•ent, *a.* [L. *incongruus*—*in,* not, and *congruus,* congruous.] Not congruous; not of a kind or character to mingle well together; not such as to make a harmonious whole; not suiting each other; inharmonious; inconsistent (*incongruous* parts, elements, mixtures).—**incongruity, incongruence,** in•kon•gru̥′i•ti, in•kong′gru̥•ens, *n.* The quality of being incongruous; that which is incongruent; something exhibiting a want of congruity. —**incongruously,** in•kong′gru̥•us•li, *adv.* In an incongruous manner.—**incongruousness,** in•kong′gru̥•us•nes, *n.* The state or quality of being incongruous.

inconsequent, in•kon′si•kwent, *a.* [Prefix *in,* not, and *consequent;* L. *inconsequens.*] Not following from the premises; not in accordance with logical method; inconclusive.—**inconsequence,** in•kon′si•kwens, *n.* [L. *inconsequentia.*] The condition or quality of being inconsequent; want of logical sequence.—**inconsequential,** in•kon′si•kwen″shal, *a.* [Prefix *in,* not, and *consequential.*] Not consequential; inconsequent; not of consequence or importance; of little moment.—**inconsequentiality,** in•kon′si•kwen″shi•al″i•ti, *n.* State of being inconsequential.—**inconsequentially,** in•kon′si•kwen″shal•li, *adv.* In an inconsequential manner.

inconsiderable, in•kon•sid′ėr•a•bl, *a.* [Prefix *in,* not, and *considerable.*] Not worthy of consideration or notice; unimportant; small; trivial; insignificant.—**inconsiderably,** in•kon•sid′ėr•a•bli, *adv.* In an inconsiderable manner or degree.

inconsiderate, in•kon•sid′ėr•it, *a.* [Prefix *in,* not, and *considerate;* L. *inconsideratus.*] Not considerate; not acting with due consideration; hasty; imprudent; thoughtless; heedless.—**inconsiderately,** in•kon•sid′ėr•it•li, *adv.* In an inconsiderate manner.—**inconsiderateness,** in•kon•sid′ėr•it•nes, *n.* The condition or quality of being inconsiderate.—**inconsideration,** in•kon•sid′ėr•ā″shon, *n.* Want of due consideration.

inconsistent, in•kon•sis′tent, *a.* [Prefix *in,* not, and *consistent.*] Not consistent; irreconcilable in conception or in fact; contrary; contradictory; incompatible; incongruous; not exhibiting uniformity of sentiment or conduct, steadiness to principle or the like.—**inconsistently,** in•kon•sis′tent•li, *adv.* In an inconsistent manner.—**inconsistency, inconsistence,** in•kon•sis′ten•si, in•kon•sis′tens, *n.* The condition or quality of being inconsistent; opposition or disagreement of particulars; self-contradiction; incongruity in action or conduct.

inconsolable, in•kon•sōl′a•bl, *a.* [Prefix *in,* not, and *consolable.*] Incapable of being consoled; grieved beyond consolation.—**inconsolableness,** in•kon•sōl′a•bl•nes, *n.* State of being inconsolable. — **inconsolably,** in•kon•sōl′a•bli, *adv.* So as to be inconsolable.

inconsonant, in•kon′so•nant, *a.* [Prefix *in,* not, and *consonant.*] Not consonant or agreeing; inconsistent; discordant.—**inconsonantly,** in•kon′so•nant•li, *adv.* In an inconsonant manner.—**inconsonance,** in•kon′so•nans, *n.* Want of harmony; discordance.

inconspicuous, in•kon•spik′ū•us, *a.* [Prefix *in,* not, and *conspicuous.*] Not conspicuous or readily noticed; not to be easily perceived.—**inconspicuously,** in•kon•spik′ū•us•li, *adv.* In an inconspicuous manner.—**inconspicuousness,** in•kon•spik′ū•us•nes, *n.* Want of conspicuousness.

inconstant, in•kon′stant, *a.* [Prefix *in,* not, and *constant;* L. *inconstans,* Fr. *inconstant.*] Not constant; subject to change of opinion, inclination, or purpose; not firm in resolution; unsteady; fickle; capricious: said of persons; mutable, changeable, or variable: said of things.—*n.* A thing which is not constant; a variable. —**inconstantly,** in•kon′stant•li, *adv.* In an inconstant manner.—**inconstancy,** in•kon′stan•si, *n.* [L. *inconstantia.*] The quality of being inconstant.

inconsumable, in•kon•sū′ma•bl, *a.* [Prefix *in,* not, and *consumable.*] Not consumable; incapable of being consumed.

incontestable, in•kon•tes′ta•bl, *a.* [Prefix *in,* not and *contestable.*] Not contestable; not to be disputed; too clear to be controverted; incontrovertible. —**incontestability,** in•kon•tes′ta•bil″i•ti, *n.* The state or quality of being incontestable.—**incontestably,** in•con•tes′ta•bli, *adv.* In an incontestable manner; incontrovertibly; indubitably.

incontinent, in•kon′ti•nent, *a.* [Prefix *in,* not, and *continent*; L. *incontinens*; Fr. *incontinent,* incontinent, and (as adv.) forthwith, immediately.] Not continent; not restraining the passions or appetites, particularly the sexual appetite; unchaste; lewd; *med.* unable to restrain natural discharges or evacuations.—**incontinence,** in•kon′ti•nens, *n.* [L. *incontinentia,* Fr. *incontinence.*] The condition or quality of being incontinent.—**incontinently,** in•kon′ti•nent•li, *adv.* In an incontinent manner; immediately; instantly; forthwith; at once.

incontrovertible, in•kon′tro•vėr″ti•bl, *a.* [Prefix *in,* not, and *controvertible.*] Not controvertible; too clear or certain to admit of dispute or controversy. —**incontrovertibility, incontrovertibleness,** in•kon′tro•vėr″ti•bil″i•ti, in•kon′tro•vėr″ti•bl•nes, *n.* State of being incontrovertible.—**incontrovertibly,** in•kon′trō•vėr″ti•bli, *adv.* In an incontrovertible manner; incontestably.

inconvenient, in•kon•vē′ni•ent, *a.* [Prefix *in,* not, and *convenient.*] Not convenient; incommodious; giving some trouble; wanting due facilities; causing embarrassment; inopportune.—**inconveniently,** in•kon•vē′ni•ent•li, *adv.* In an inconvenient manner.—**inconvenience, inconveniency,** in•kon•vē′ni•ens, in•kon•vē′ni•en•si, *n.* The quality of being inconvenient; something that incommodes or gives trouble or uneasiness.—**inconvenience,** in•kon•vē′ni•ens, *v.t.—inconvenienced, inconveniencing.* To put to inconvenience; to incommode.

inconvertible, in•kon•vėr′ti•bl, *a.* [Prefix *in,* not, and *convertible.*] Not convertible; incapable of being converted into or exchanged for something else.—**inconvertibility, inconvertibleness,** in•kon•vėr′ti•bil″i•ti, in•kon•vėr′ti•bl•nes, *n.* The quality of being inconvertible.

inconvincible, in•kon•vin′si•bl, *a.* [Prefix *in,* not, and *convincible.*] Incapable of being convinced.

incorporate, in•kor′po•rāt, *v.t.—incorporated, incorporating.* [L. *incorporo, incorporatum—in,* into, and *corpus, corporis,* a body.] To form into one body; to combine or mix into one mass; to unite with another body or substance; to combine or unite intimately (to *incorporate* things together or one thing *with* another); to embody or give material form to; to form into a corporation or body of individuals that can act as one.—*v.i.* To unite so as to form a part of another body; to be mixed or blended; to grow into; usually followed by *with.*—*a.* Incorporated; united in one body.—**incorporated,** in•kor′po•rā•ted, *p.* and *a.* Mixed or united in one body; associated so as to form a corporation; united in a legal body.—**incorporation,** in•kor′po•rā″shon, *n.* The act of incorporating or state of being incorporated; that which is incorporated; a society or body formed by the union of individuals and authorized by law to act as a single person.—**incorporative,** in•kor′po•rā•tiv, *a.* Tending to incorporate; incorporating; *philol.* tending to combine many elements into one long word.

incorporeal, in•kor•pō′ri•al, *a.* [Prefix *in,* not, and *corporeal.*] Not corporeal; not consisting of matter; not having a material body; immaterial; intangible.—**incorporeally,** in•kor•pō′ri•al•li, *adv.* In an incorporeal manner; immaterially.—**incorporeity,** in•kor′pō•rē″i•ti, *n.* The quality of being incorporeal.

incorrect, in•ko•rekt′, *a.* [Prefix *in,* not, and *correct.*] Not correct; not exact; inexact; erroneous; faulty; not according to fact.—**incorrectly,** in•ko•rekt′li, *adv.* In an incorrect manner.—**incorrectness,** in•ko•rekt′nes, *n.*

incorrigible, in•kor′i•ji•bl, *a.* [Prefix *in,* not, and *corrigible.*] Incapable of being corrected or amended; bad beyond correction or reform.—*n.* One who is bad beyond correction or reform.—**incorrigibility, incorrigibleness,** in•kor′i•ji•bil″i•ti, in•kor′i•ji•bl•nes, *n.* The condition or quality of being incorrigible.—**incorrigibly,** in•kor′i•ji•bli, *adv.* In an incorrigible manner.

incorrupt, in•ko•rupt′, *a.* [Prefix *in,* not, and *corrupt*; L. *incorruptus.*] Not corrupt or corrupted; not suffering from corruption or decay; not depraved; pure; untainted; above the influence of corruption or bribery.—**incorruptibility, incorruptibleness,** in•ko•rup′ti•bil″i•ti, in•ko•rup′ti•bl•nes, *n.* The condition of being incorruptible.—**incorruptible,** in•ko•rup′ti•bl, *a.* Incapable of corruption, decay, or dissolution; incapable of being corrupted or bribed; inflexibly upright.—**incorruptibly,** in•ko•rup′ti•bli, *adv.* In an incorruptible manner.—**incorruption,** in•ko•rup′shon, *n.* Absence of or exemption from corruption or decay.—**incorruptly,** in•ko•rupt′li, *adv.* In an incorrupt manner; without corruption.—**incorruptness,** in•ko•rupt′nes, *n.* The condition or quality of being incorrupt; probity; integrity.

incrassate, in•kras′āt, *v.t.—incrassated, incrassating.* [L. *incrasso, incrassatum—in,* intens., and *crassus,* thick, crass.] To make thick or thicker; to make less fluid; to inspissate; to thicken.—**incrassation,** in•kras•ā′shon, *n.* The act of thickening; inspissation.

increase, in•krēs′, *v.i.—increased, increasing.* [Prefix *in* or *en,* and O.Fr. *creser,* L. *crescere,* to grow, allied to *creare,* to create—similarly *decrease.*] To become greater; to grow; to augment; to advance; to multiply by the production of young; *astron.* to show a gradually enlarging luminous surface; to wax (the moon *increases*).—*v.t.* To make greater or larger; to augment in bulk, quantity, amount, or degree; to add to.—*n.* (in′krēs). Augmentation; a growing greater or larger; enlargement; extension; the amount by which anything is augmented; increment; interest of money; produce; issue or offspring (O.T.); *astron.* the period of waxing, as of the moon.—**increasable,** in•krēs′a•bl, *a.* Capable of being increased.—**increaser,** in•krēs′ėr, *n.* One who or that which increases.—**increasingly,** in•krēs′ing•li, *adv.* In the way of increase; by continual increase.

incredible, in•kred′i•bl, *a.* [Prefix *in,* not, and *credible.*] Not credible; impossible to be believed; too extraordinary and improbable to admit of belief.—**incredibility,** in•kred′i•bil″i•ti, *n.* The quality of being incredible; that which is incredible.—**incredibleness,** in•kred′i•bl•nes, *n.* The quality of being incredible.—**incredibly,** in•kred′i•bli, *adv.* In an incredible manner.

incredulous, in•kred′ū•lus, *a.* [Prefix *in,* not, and *credulous.*] Not credulous; not given to believe readily; refusing or withholding belief; skeptical.—**incredulity, incredulousness,** in•krė•dū′li•ti, in•kred′ū•lus•nes, *n.* The quality of being incredulous.—**incredulously,** in•kred′ū•lus•li, *adv.* In an incredulous manner.

increment, in′kre•ment, *n.* [L. *incrementum,* from *incresco,* to increase. INCREASE.] Act or process of increasing; augmentation or growth; something added; increase; *math.* the increase of a quantity from its present value to its next ascending value; *rhet.* an amplification without necessarily involving a true climax.

increscent, in•kres′ent, *a.* [L. *increscens, increscentis,* ppr. of *incresco,* to increase.] Increasing; growing; augmenting; swelling.

incriminate, in•krim′i•nāt, *v.t.—incriminated, incriminating.* [L.L. *incrimino, incriminatum*—L. *in,* and *crimino,* to accuse one of a crime, from *crimen, criminis,* a charge.] To charge with a crime or fault; to accuse; to criminate.—**incriminatory,** in•krim′i•na•to•ri, *a.* Accusatory; tending to criminate.

incrust, in•krust′, *v.t.* [L. *incrusto—in,* in, on, and *crusta,* crust.] To cover with a crust or with a hard coat; to form a crust on the surface of.—**incrustation,** in•krus•tā′shon, *n.* The act of incrusting; a crust or hard coating on the surface of a body; a covering or inlaying.

incubate, in′kū•bāt, *v.i.* [L. *incubo, incubatum,* to lie in or upon—prefix *in,* in, on, and *cubo,* to lie, seen also in *incubus, incumbent, covey.*] To care for in such a way as to induce hatching (of eggs) or promote development (of embryos, etc.)—*v.i.* To be incubated; to brood.—**incubation,** in•kū•bā′shon, *n.* Act of incubating; *pathol.* the period of maturation, without visible symptoms, of a contagious disease.—**incubative,** in″-kū•bā′tiv, *a.*—**incubator,** in″kū•bā′-tėr, *n.* An apparatus for hatching eggs by artificial heat; an apparatus for maintaining proper body temperature in babies born prematurely or otherwise physically subnormal; an apparatus for incubating bacteriological cultures, etc.

incubus, in′kū•bus, *n.* pl. **incubuses, incubi,** in′kū•bus•ez, in′kū•bī. [L., from *incubo,* to lie on. INCUBATE.] Nightmare; an imaginary being or demon, formerly supposed to be the cause of nightmare; hence something that weighs heavily on the mind or feelings; an encumbrance of any kind; a dead weight.

inculcate, in•kul′kāt, *v.t.*—*inculcated, inculcating.* [L. *inculco, inculcatum*—*in,* in, and *calco,* to tread; akin *calx,* the heel.] To impress by frequent admonitions; to teach and enforce by frequent repetitions; to urge on the mind.—**inculcation,** in•kul•kā′-shon, *n.* The act of inculcating.—**inculcator,** in•kul′kā•tėr, *n.* One who inculcates.

inculpable, in•kul′pa•bl, *a.* [Prefix *in,* not, and *culpable.*] Not culpable; not to be accused; blameless.

inculpate, in•kul′pāt, *v.t.*—*inculpated, inculpating.* [L.L. *inculpo, inculpatum*—L. *in,* into, and *culpa,* a fault; akin *culpable, culprit.*] To show to be in fault; to accuse of crime; to impute guilt to; to incriminate: opposed to *exculpate.*—**inculpation,** in•kul•pā′shon, *n.* The act of inculpating.—**inculpatory,** in•kul′pa•to•-ri, *a.* Tending to inculpate or criminate.

incult, in•kult′, *a.* [L. *incultus*—prefix *in,* not, and *cultus,* pp. of *colo,* to cultivate.] Uncultivated; rude; not polished or refined.

incumbent, in•kum′bent, *a.* [L. *incumbens, incumbentis,* ppr. of *incumbo,* to lie—*in,* on, and *cumbo,* to lie down. INCUBATE.] Lying or resting upon; resting upon a person as a duty or obligation to be performed; imposed and calling for performance.—*n.* A person in possession of an ecclesiastical benefice or other office.—**incumbently,** in•kum′bent•li, *adv.* In an incumbent manner.—**incumbency,** in•kum′ben•si, *n.* The state of being incumbent; what is incumbent; *eccles.* the state of holding or being in possession of a benefice.

incumber, in•kum′bėr, *v.t.* Same as *Encumber.*

incunabulum, in•kū•nab′ū•lum, *n.* pl. **incunabula,** in•kū•nab′ū•la. [L. *incunabula,* swaddling clothes, birthplace, origin—prefix *in,* and *cunabula,* from *cunæ,* a cradle.] A book printed in the early times of printing; generally, a book printed before the year 1500.

incur, in•kėr′, *v.t.*—*incurred, incurring.* [L. *incurro,* to run against—*in,* and *curro,* to run. CURRENT.] To run in danger of or liability to; to expose one's self to; to become liable to; to become subject to (to *incur* danger, inconvenience, etc.); to contract (to *incur* a debt).—**incurrence,** in•kėr′ens, *n.* The act of incurring.

incurable, in•kū′ra•bl, *a.* [Prefix *in,* not, and *curable.*] Not curable; beyond the power of skill and medicine; not admitting remedy.—*n.* A person diseased beyond the reach of cure.—**incurability, incurableness,** in•kū′ra•bil″i•ti, in•kū′ra•bl•nes, *n.* The state of being incurable.—**incurably,** in•kū′ra•bli, *adv.* In an incurable manner.

incurious, in•kū′ri•us, *a.* [Prefix *in,* not, and *curious.*] Not curious or inquisitive; destitute of curiosity.—**incuriously,** in•kū′ri•us•li, *adv.* In an incurious manner.—**incuriosity, incuriousness,** in•kū′ri•os″i•ti, in•-kū′ri•us•nes, *n.* The quality of being incurious.

incursion, in•kėr′zhon, *n.* [L. *incursio, incursionis,* from *incurro.* INCUR.] An entering into a territory with hostile intention; an invasion not followed by continued occupation; an inroad.—**incursive,** in•kėr′-siv, *a.* Making an attack or incursion; aggressive.

incurvate, incurve, in•kėr′vāt, in•-kėrv′, *v.t.*—*incurvated, incurvating; incurved, incurving.* [L. *incurvo, incurvation*—*in,* in, and *curvo,* to bend. CURVE.] To curve inward; to make curved; to bend; to crook.—**incurvate,** *a.* Curved inward or upward.—**incurvation,** in•kėr•vā′shon, *n.* The act of incurvating; a bending or bend.

incus, ing′kus, *n.* [L., an anvil.] A bone of the internal ear, so called from its shape.

incuse,† in•kūz′, *v.t.* [L. *incudo, incusum,* to forge.] To impress by striking or stamping.

indagate,† in′da•gāt, *v.t.* [L. *indago, indagaium.*] To seek or search out.

indebted, in•det′ed, *a.* [Prefix *in,* in, and *debt.*] Being under a debt; having incurred a debt; held to payment or requital; obliged by something received, for which restitution or gratitude is due.—**indebtedness,** in•-det′ed•nes, *n.* The state of being indebted; the amount of debt owed.

indecent, in•dē′sent, *a.* [Prefix *in,* not, and *decent;* L. *indecens,* unseemly.] Offending against decency; unfit to be seen or heard; offensive to modesty and delicacy; immodest; unseemly.—**indecently,** in•dē′sent•li, *adv.* In an indecent manner.—**indecency,** in•dē′sen•si, *n.* The quality of being indecent; what is indecent in language, actions, or manners; grossness in speech or behavior; immodesty.

indeciduate, in•di•sid′u•āt, *a.* [Prefix *in,* not, and *deciduate.*] Not deciduate; not having a decidua.

indeciduous, in•di•sid′ū•us, *a.* [Prefix *in,* not, and *deciduous.*] Not deciduous; evergreen.

indecipherable, in•di•sī′fėr•a•bl, *a.* [Prefix *in,* not, and *decipherable.*] Not decipherable; incapable of being deciphered.

indecision, in•di•sizh′on, *n.* [Prefix *in,* not, and *decision.*] Want of decision or settled purpose; a wavering of mind; irresolution.—**indecisive,** in•di•sī′siv, *a.* [Prefix *in,* not, and *decisive.*] Not decisive; not bringing to a final close or ultimate issue; not having come to a decision; irresolute; vacillating; hesitating.—**indecisively,** in•di•sī′siv•li, *adv.* In an indecisive manner.—**indecisiveness,** in•di•sī′-siv•nes, *n.*

indeclinable, in•di•klī′na•bl, *a.* [Prefix *in,* not, and *declinable.*] *Gram.* not declinable; not varied by terminations.—*n. Gram.* a word that is not declined.

indecomposable, in•dē′kom•pō″za•-bl, *a.* [Prefix *in,* not, and *decomposable.*] Not decomposable; incapable of decomposition.—**indecomposableness,** in•dē′kom•pō″za•bl•-nes, *n.*

indecorous, in•dek′o•rus, *a.* [Prefix *in,* not, and *decorous.*] Not decorous; violating decorum or propriety; unseemly; unbecoming.—**indecorously,** in•dek′o•rus•li, *adv.* In an indecorous manner.—**indecorousness,** in•dek′o•-rus•nes, *n.* The quality of being indecorous.—**indecorum,** in•de•kō′-rum, *n.* Want of decorum; impropriety of behavior.

indeed, in•dēd′, *adv.* [Prep. *in,* and *deed.*] In reality; in truth; in fact: sometimes used as intimating a concession or admission; sometimes interjectionally, as an expression of surprise, or for the purpose of obtaining confirmation.

indefatigable, in•di•fat′i•ga•bl, *a.* [L. *indefatigabilis,* from *in,* not, and *defatigo,* to tire completely—*de,* intens., and *fatigo,* to fatigue.] Incapable of being fatigued; not yielding to fatigue; unremitting in labor or effort; unwearied; untiring.—**indefatigably,** in•di•fat′i•ga•bli, *adv.* In an indefatigable manner; unremittingly; sedulously.—**indefatigability, indefatigableness,** in•di•fat′i•ga•bil″-i•ti, in•di•fat′i•ga•bl•nes, *n.* The quality of being indefatigable.

indefeasible, in•di•fē′zi•bl, *a.* [Prefix *in,* not, and *defeasible.*] Not defeasible; not to be defeated or made void (right, claim, or title).—**indefeasibly,** in•di•fē′zi•bli, *adv.* In an indefeasible manner.—**indefeasibility,** in•di•fē′zi•bil″i•ti, *n.* The quality of being indefeasible.

indefensible, in•di•fen′si•bl, *a.* [Prefix *in,* not, and *defensible.*] Not defensible; incapable of being defended, vindicated, or justified.—**indefensibility,** in•di•fen′si•bil″i•ti, *n.* The quality or state of being indefensible.—**indefensibly,** in•di•-fen′si•bli, *adv.* In an indefensible manner.

indefinable, in•di•fī′na•bl, *a.* [Prefix *in,* not, and *definable.*] Incapable of being defined; unsusceptible of definition; not to be clearly explained by words.—**indefinably,** in•di•fī′na•bli, *adv.* In an indefinable manner.

indefinite, in•def′i•nit, *a.* [Prefix *in,* not, and *definite.*] Not definite; not limited or defined; not precise or certain; having no determinate or certain limits; *bot.* too numerous or various to make a particular enumeration important: said of the parts of a flower.—*Indefinite inflorescence, bot.* one in which the flowers all arise from axiliary buds, the stem growing indefinitely.—**indefinite article,** *Gram., a* or *an.*—**indefinitely,** in•def′i•nit•li, *adv.*—**indefiniteness,** in•def′i•nit•nes, *n.*

indehiscent, in•di•his′ent, *a.* [Prefix *in,* not, and *dehiscent.*] *Bot.* not dehiscent; not opening spontaneously when ripe, as a capsule.—**indehiscence,** in•di•his′ens, *n. Bot.* the property of being indehiscent.

indelible, in•del′i•bl, *a.* [L. *indelebilis*—*in,* not, and *deleo,* to delete.] Not to be blotted out; incapable of being effaced, canceled, or obliterated.—**indelibility, indelibleness,** in•del′i•bil″i•ti, in•del′i•bl•nes, *n.* Quality of being indelible.—**indelibly,** in•del′i•bli, *adv.* In an indelible manner; ineffaceably.

indelicate, in•del′i•kit, *a.* [Prefix *in,* not, and *delicate.*] Wanting delicacy; offensive to modesty or purity of mind; tending toward indecency or grossness; somewhat immodest.—**indelicately,** in•del′i•kit•li, *adv.* In an indelicate manner.—**indelicacy,** in•del′i•ka•si, *n.* The condition or quality of being indelicate; a certain want of modesty or purity of mind.

indemnify, in•dem′ni•fī, *v.t.*—*indemnified, indemnifying.* [L. *indemnis,* free from loss or injury, and *facio,* to make. INDEMNITY.] To save harmless; to secure against loss, damage, or penalty; to reimburse for expenditure made.—**indemnification,** in•dem′ni•fi•kā″shon, *n.* The act of indemnifying; that which indemnifies.

indemnity, in•dem′ni•ti, *n.* [Fr. *indemnité,* from L. *indemnitas,* from *indemnis,* uninjured—prefix *in,* not, and *damnum,* loss, damage. DAMN.] Security or exemption from damage, loss, injury, or punishment; compensation or equivalent for loss, damage, or injury sustained.

indent, in•dent′, *v.t.* [L.L. *indenture,* O.Fr. *endenter,* from L. *in,* in, and *dens, dentis,* a tooth. DENTAL.] To notch, jag, or cut into points or inequalities, like a row of teeth; to indenture; *printing,* to begin (a line) farther in from the margin than the rest of the paragraph.—*n.* A notch in a margin; an indentation; *printing,* the blank space at the beginning of a paragraph; *com.,* an order for goods.—**indentation,** in•den•tā′shon, *n.* The act of indenting; a cut or notch in a margin; an angular recess or depression like a notch in any border.—**indented,** in•den′ted, *p.* and *a.* Having notches or points like teeth on the margin; toothed; bound by indenture.—**indenture,** in•den′chėr, *n.* The act of indenting; an indentation; *law,* a deed under seal, entered into between two or more parties, each party having a duplicate: so called from the duplicates having originally been written on one skin, which was divided by a jagged cut, so that the correspondence of the two halves was at once manifest.—*v.i.*—*indentured, indenturing.* To indent; to bind by indentures, as in apprenticeship.

independent, in•di•pen′dent, *a.* [Prefix *in,* not, and *dependent.*] Not dependent; not subject to the control of others; not relying on others; with *of* before an object; not subordinate; moderately wealthy, as an *independent* fortune; acting and thinking for one's self; not swayed by bias or influence; self-directing; proceeding from or expressive of a spirit of independence in air or manner; [*cap.*] in England, pertaining to the Independents or Congregationalists.—*adv.* Irrespective; without taking note or regard; not to make mention: with *of.*—*n.* In politics, one not bound by party; *eccles.* one who maintains that every congregation forms a church or independent religious society in itself.—*Independent clause, gram.,* a clause not dependent on other words of a sentence.—**independence, independency,**† in•di•pen′dens, in•di•pen′den•si, *n.* The state of being independent; that which renders one independent; property or income sufficient to make one independent of others or of his own exertions.—**Independence Day,** the 4th of July, an annual holiday in the United States, commemorative of the adoption of the Declaration of Independence in 1776.—**independently,** in•di•pen′dent•li, *adv.* In an independent manner; leaving out of consideration (he is richer *independently of* that).

indescribable, in•di•skrī′ba•bl, *a.* [Prefix *in,* not, and *describable.*] Not describable; incapable of being described.

indestructible, in•di•struk′ti•bl, *a.* [Prefix *in,* not, and *destructible.*] Not destructible; incapable of being destroyed.—**indestructibility,** in•di•struk′ti•bil″i•ti, *n.* The quality of being indestructible. — **indestructibly,** in•di•struk′ti•bli, *adv.* In an indestructible manner.

indeterminate, in•di•tėr′mi•nāt, *a.* [Prefix *in,* not, and *determinate.*] Not determinate; not settled or fixed; not definite; uncertain; not precise; *math.* applied to problems which have an indefinite number of solutions, not arbitrary but correlated; of a sentence, one making the imprisonment or release of the prisoner dependent on his conduct and amendment.—*Indeterminate inflorescence.* Same as *indefinite inflorescence.*—**indeterminable,** in•di•tėr′mi•na•bl, *a.* [Prefix *in,* not, and *determinable.*] Incapable of being determined, ascertained, or fixed; not to be determined or ended; interminable.—**indeterminately,** in•di•tėr′mi•nāt•li, *adv.* In an indeterminate manner.—**indeterminateness,** in•di•tėr′mi•nāt•nes, *n.* The state or quality of being indeterminate.—**indetermination,** in•di•tėr′mi•nā″shon, *n.* Want of determination; an unsettled or wavering state, as of the mind.—**indeterminism,** *n.* The philosophic theory maintaining that not all our actions are determined or conditioned by motives; the opposite of rigid determinism.

indevout, in•di•vout′, *a.* [Prefix *in,* not, and *devout.*] Not devout; not having devout affections.

index, in′deks, *n.* pl. **indexes,** in′dek•sez, or **indices,** in′di•sez. [L., one who or that which points out, a table of contents—*in,* in, and stem of *dico,* to say (DICTION); seen in Skr. *diç,* Gr. *deiknymi,* to show.] Something that points out, shows, indicates, or manifests; a pointer or hand that points or directs to anything; the hand ☞ used by printers, etc., to call attention; a table of the contents of a book in alphabetical order; *anat.* the forefinger; *math.* the figure or letter which shows to what power any quantity is evolved; the exponent.—*Index of refraction, optics,* the ratio of the sine of the angle of incidence to the sine of the angle of refraction when a ray passes from one medium into another (*relative index*), or from a vacuum into a medium (*absolute index*).—*Index Expurgatorius* (Index Expurgatory), *Index Prohibitorius* (Index Prohibitory), or more fully *Index Librorum Prohibitorum* (Index of Prohibited Books), a catalogue of books which are forbidden by the Roman Catholic Church to be read by the faithful.—*v.t.* To provide with an index; to place in an index.—**indexer,** in′dek•sėr, *n.* One who makes an index.—**index finger,** *n.* The forefinger.—**indexical,** in•dek′si•kal, *a.* Having the form of an index; pertaining to an index.

India, in′di•a, *n.* [From *Indus,* the name of a river in Asia; akin Skr. *sindhu,* a river, *syand,* to flow.] A republic in Asia, formerly part of the British Empire; a color darker than cream and lighter than tan.—*India ink,* a black writing fluid used chiefly by draftsmen.—*Indiaman,* a large ship formerly employed in the India trade.—*India paper,* a thin opaque paper used in printing.—*India rubber,* caoutchouc; a soft variety of rubber.—**Indian,** *a.* Of or pertaining to either of the Indies, East or West, or to the aborigines of America, so called by Columbus who mistook his discovery of America for the finding of a new route to India; made of maize or India corn.—*Department of Indian Affairs,* a division of the Department of the Interior with jurisdiction over affairs between the Indians and the Federal government.—*Indian club,* a wooden club used in calisthenics.—*Indian corn,* a native American plant and its ripened ears.—*Indian file,* single file.—*Indian red,* a species of ocher; a very fine purple earth used in both oil and watercolor painting.—

Indian summer, summer-like weather, with calm and absence of rain, occurring in autumn.—*Indian turnip*, Jack-in-the-pulpit.—*Indian yellow*, a bright yellow pigment.—*n.* An East Indian, West Indian or Anglo-Indian; one of the aborigines of America; a Red Indian.—**Indic,** in′dik, *a.* Applied to that branch of the Indo-European languages of India which includes Hindustani, Prakrit, Pali, and Sanskrit.

indican, in′di•kan, *n.* [From *indigo.*] A substance which is present in the indigo plant, and is the source of indigo blue.

indicate, in′di•kāt, *v.t.*—*indicated, indicating.* [L. *indico, indicatum,* from *index, indicis.* INDEX.] To point out; to direct the mind to a knowledge of; to show; to intimate. —**indicant,** in′di•kant, *a.* [L. *indicans, indicantis.*] Serving to point out; indicating.—**indication,** in•di•kā′shon, *n.* The act of indicating or pointing out; what serves to indicate or point out; intimation; mark; token; sign; symptom.—**indicative,** in•dik′a•tiv, *a.* [L. *indicativus.*] Pointing out or indicating; serving as an indication; giving intimation or knowledge of (movements *indicative of* uneasiness); *gram.* applied to that mood of the verb that declares directly or that asks questions.—*n. Gram.* the indicative mood.—**indicatively,** in•dik′a•tiv•li, *adv.* In an indicative manner. —**indicator,** in′di•kā•tėr, *n.* One who or that which indicates, an instrument for ascertaining and recording the pressure of steam in the cylinder of a steam engine; a recording instrument of various kinds; a South African cuckoo that by its movements indicates the presence of the nests of wild bees.—*Indicator diagram*, the diagram traced by the indicator in a steam engine. It represents the pressures at all stages of the piston stroke, and its area gives the work done by the piston during the stroke.—**indicatory,** in′di•ka•to•ri, *a.* Serving to indicate.

indict, in•dīt′, *v.t.* [O.Fr. *inditer, indicter,* from L. *indico, indictum,* to declare publicly—*in,* and *dico,* to say, to speak. INDEX.] To accuse or charge with a crime or misdemeanor in due form of law.—**indictable,** in•dī′ta•bl, *a.* Capable of being or liable to be indicted; that may bring an indictment on one (an *indictable* offense).—**indictment,** in•dīt′ment, *n.* The act of indicting; a formal accusation or charge against a person; a written accusation.—**indicter, indictor,** in•dī′tėr, *n.* One who indicts.—**indiction,** in•dik′shon, *n. Chron.* a cycle of fifteen years.

indifferent, in•dif′ėr•ent, *a.* [L. *indifferens, indifferentis*—*in,* not, and *differens,* ppr. of *differo,* to differ. DIFFER.] Impartial; unbiased; uninterested; unconcerned; careless; having no preference; of no account or moment; neither very good nor very bad, but rather bad than good; middling; tolerable.—Formerly used adverbially (*indifferent* honest).—**indifference,** in•dif′ėr•ens, *n.* The state or quality of being indifferent; absence of feeling or interest; unconcern; apathy; mediocrity or some degree of badness.—**indifferentism,** in•dif′er•ent•izm, *n.* Systematic indifference; reasoned disregard; want of zeal.—**indifferently,** in•dif′ėr•ent•li, *adv.* In an indifferent manner; impartially; no more than passably.

indigene, in′di•jēn, *n.* [L. *indigena*—*indu,* old form of *in,* and *gen,* root of *gigno,* to beget. GENUS.] One born in a country; a native animal or plant.—**indigenous,** in•dij′en•us, *a.* Originating or produced naturally in a country or climate; native, not foreign or exotic.

indigent, in′di•jent, *a.* [L. *indigens, indigentis,* from *indigeo,* to want—*ind,* a form of *in,* and *egeo,* to be in want.] Destitute of the means of comfortable subsistence; needy; poor.—**indigence,** in′di•jens, *n.* The condition of being indigent; penury; poverty.

indigested, in•di•jes′ted, *a.* [Prefix *in,* not, and *digested.*] Not digested; undigested; not reduced to due form; not methodized; crude; not prepared or softened by heat, as chemical substances.—**indigestibility, indigestibleness,** in•di•jes′ti•bil″i•ti, in•di•jes′ti•bl•nes, *n.* The quality of being indigestible.—**indigestible,** in•di•jes′ti•bl, *a.* [Prefix *in,* not, and *digestible.*] Not digestible; digested with difficulty.—**indigestion,** in•di•jest′yon, *n.* [Prefix *in,* not, and *digestion.*] Incapability of or difficulty in digesting food; dyspepsia.

indignant, in•dig′nant, *a.* [L. *indignans, indignantis,* ppr. of *indignor,* to consider as unworthy, to disdain—*in,* not, and *dignor,* to deem worthy, from *dignus,* worthy (whence *dignity, deign*).] Displeased at what is unworthy or base; affected with indignation.—**indignantly,** in•dig′nant•li, *adv.* In an indignant manner. —**indignation,** in•dig•nā′shon, *n.* [L. *indignatio, indignationis.*] A feeling of displeasure at what is unworthy or base; anger, mingled with contempt, disgust, or abhorrence; violent displeasure.—**indignity,** in•dig′ni•ti, *n.* [L. *indignitas.*] Any action toward another which manifests contempt for him or design to lower his dignity; an insult; an affront; an outrage.

indigo, in′di•gō, *n.* [Sp. and It. *indigo,* from L. *indicum,* indigo, from *Indicus,* Indian, from *India.*] A deep, slightly reddish blue, one of the seven chief colors of the spectrum, as named by Newton; a blue dye, extensively employed, now usually synthesized from amino compounds, but originally obtained from various plants native to the East and West Indies.—**indigo blue,** the color indigo; the substance indigotin.—**indigo bunting,** a small bird of the eastern United States.—**indigoid,** in′di•goid, *a.* Referring to a class of dyes, similar in structure to indigo.—**indigo plant,** a plant yielding indigo.—**indigotin,** in•dig′o•tin, *n.* A powder, the coloring principle of indigo.

indirect, in•di•rekt′, *a.* [Prefix *in,* not, and *direct.*] Not direct; deviating from a direct line or course; circuitous; not tending directly to an aim or end; roundabout; not open and straightforward; not resulting directly; having something mediate or interposed.—**indirection,** *n.* Roundabout methods; deceit. (*Shak.*) —**indirectly,** in•di•rekt′li, *adv.* In an indirect manner.—**indirectness,** in•di•rekt′nes, *n.*

indiscernible, in•diz•zėr′ni•bl, *a.* [Prefix *in,* not, and *discernible.*] Incapable of being discerned; undiscernible.

indiscoverable, in•dis•kuv′ėr•a•bl, *a.* [Prefix *in,* not, and *discoverable.*] Incapable of being discovered; undiscoverable.

indiscreet, in•dis•krēt′, *a.* [Prefix *in,* not, and *discreet.*] Not discreet; wanting in discretion or sound judgment; injudicious; inconsiderate.—**indiscreetly,** in•dis•krēt′li, *adv.* In an indiscreet manner.—**indiscreetness,** in•dis•krēt′nes, *n.* The quality of being indiscreet.—**indiscretion,** *n.* The condition or quality of being indiscreet; want of discretion; an indiscreet act; an ill-judged act.

indiscriminate, in•dis•krim′i•nit, *a.* [Prefix *in,* not, and *discriminate.*] Without discrimination or distinction; not making any distinction; confused; promiscuous.—**indiscriminately,** in•dis•krim′i•nit•li, *adv.* In an indiscriminate manner.—**indiscriminating,** in•dis•krim′i•nāt•ing, *p.* and *a.* Not discriminating; not making any distinction.—**indiscrimination,** in•dis•krim′i•nā″shon, *n.* Want of discrimination.

indispensable, in•dis•pen′sa•bl, *a.* [Prefix *in,* not, and *dispensable.*] Incapable of being dispensed with; absolutely necessary or requisite.—**indispensability, indispensableness,** in•dis•pen′sa•bil″i•ti, in•dis•pen′sa•bl•nes, *n.* The quality of being indispensable.—**indispensably,** in•dis•pen′sa•bli, *adv.* In an indispensable manner; absolutely.

indispose, in•dis•pōz′, *v.t.*—*indisposed, indisposing.* [Fr. *indisposer*—prefix *in,* not, and *disposer,* to dispose. DISPOSE.] To disincline; to render averse or unfavorable; to render unfit or unsuited; to disqualify; to affect with indisposition.—**indisposed,** in•dis•pōzd′, *p.* and *a.* Not disposed; disinclined; averse; slightly disordered in health, somewhat ill.—**indisposition,** in•dis′po•zish″on, *n.* The state of being indisposed; disinclination; want of tendency; slight ailment or disorder of the health.

indisputable, in•dis•pū′ta•bl, *a.* [Prefix *in,* not, and *disputable.*] Incapable of being disputed; incontrovertible; incontestable.—**indisputability, indisputableness,** in•dis•pū′ta•bil″i•ti, in•dis•pū′ta•bl•nes, *n.* The state or quality of being indisputable.—**indisputably,** in•dis•pū′ta•bli, *adv.*

In an indisputable manner; incontrovertibly.

indissoluble, in•dis•sol'ū•bl, *a.* [Prefix *in*, not, and *dissoluble*; L. *indissolubilis.*] Not capable of being dissolved; not capable of being broken or rightfully violated; perpetually binding or obligatory (agreement, ties, etc.); firm; stable.—**indissolubility, indissolubleness,** in•dis•sol'ū•bil"i•ti, in•dis•sol'ū•bl•nes, *n.* The quality of being indissoluble.—**indissolubly,** in•dis•sol'ū•bli, *adv.* In an indissoluble manner.

indistinct, in•dis•tingkt', *a.* [Prefix *in*, not, and *distinct*; L. *indistinctus.*] Not distinct; not readily distinguishable; faint to the sight; obscure to the mind; not clear; confused; imperfect or dim (*indistinct* vision).—**indistinctly,** in•dis•tingkt'li, *adv.* In an indistinct manner; not clearly; dimly or obscurely.—**indistinctness,** in•dis•tingkt'nes, *n.* The quality or condition of being indistinct.

indistinguishable, in•dis•ting'gwish•a•bl, *a.* [Prefix *in*, not, and *distinguishable.*] Incapable of being distinguished; undistinguishable.—**indistinguishably,** in•dis•ting'gwish•a•bli, *adv.* So as not to be distinguishable.

indite, in•dīt', *v.t.*—*indited, inditing.* [O.Fr. *inditer.* INDICT.] To compose or write; to direct, prompt, or dictate.—*v.i.* To compose; to write; to pen.—**inditement,** in•dīt'ment, *n.* The act of inditing.—**inditer,** in•dī'tėr, *n.* One who indites.

indium, in'di•um, *n.* [From the *indigo* lines in its spectrum.] A rare metallic element, white, malleable, and easily fusible, found in various ores. Symbol, In; at. no., 49; at. wt., 114.82.

individual, in•di•vid'ū•al, *a.* [Fr. *individuel*, from L. *individuus*, indivisible—*in*, not, and *dividuus*, divisible. DIVIDE.] Subsisting as one indivisible entity or distinct being; single; one; pertaining to one only; peculiar to or characteristic of a single person or thing.—*n.* A being or thing forming one of its kind; a single person, animal, or thing; especially, a human being; a person.—**individualism,** in•di•vid'ū•al•izm, *n.* The quality of being individual; individuality; self-interest; a system or condition in which each individual works for his own ends, in either social, political, or religious matters.—**individualistic,** in•di•vid'ū•al•is"tik, *a.* Pertaining to or characterized by individualism.—**individuality,** in•di•vid'ū•al"i•ti, *n.* The condition of being individual; existence as an individual; oneness; the sum of the characteristics or traits peculiar to an individual.—**individualization,** in•di•vid'ū•al•i•zā"shon, *n.* The act of individualizing.—**individualize,** in•di•vid'ū•al•īz, *v.t.*—*individualized, individualizing.* To mark as an individual; to distinguish by peculiar or distinctive characters.—**individually,** in•di•vid'ū•al•li, *adv.* In an individual manner; separately; each by itself.—**individuate,** in•di•vid'ū•āt, *v.t.*—*individuated, individuating.* To give the character of individuality to; to individualize.—*v.i.* To become individual.—**individuation,** in'di•vid•ū•ā"shon, *a.* The act of individuating, or state of being.

indivisible, in•di•viz'i•bl, *a.* [Prefix *in*, not, and *divisible.*] Not divisible; not separable into parts.—*n.* That which is indivisible.—**indivisibility, indivisibleness,** in•di•viz'i•bil"i•ti, in•di•viz'i•bl•nes, *n.* The state or property of being indivisible.—**indivisibly,** in•di•viz'i•bli, *adv.* In an indivisible manner.

indocile, in•dos'il or in•dō'sīl, *a.* [Prefix *in*, not, and *docile*; L. *indocilis*, unteachable.] Not docile or teachable; intractable.—**indocility,** in•dō•sil'i•ti, *n.* The quality of being indocile.

indoctrinate, in•dok'tri•nāt, *v.t.*—*indoctrinated, indoctrinating.* [L. *in*, in, and *doctrina*, learning. DOCTRINE.] To instruct in any doctrine; to imbue or cause to imbibe certain principles; to instruct.—**indoctrination,** in•dok'tri•nā"shon, *n.* The act of indoctrinating; instruction.

Indo-European, *a.* A term applied to that family of languages which includes the Sanskrit and the kindred tongues of India and Persia, Greek, Latin, and the Romance tongues, the Teutonic, Celtic, and Slavonic tongues.—*n.* An Aryan.

Indo-Germanic, *a.* A term sometimes used as equivalent to *Indo-European* or *Aryan.*

indolent, in'do•lent, *a.* [Fr. *indolent*—L. *in*, not, and *dolens, dolentis*, ppr. of *doleo*, to feel pain (whence *dolor, dole*).] Habitually idle or indisposed to labor; lazy; slothful; sluggish; idle (person, life); *med.* causing little or no pain (an *indolent* tumor)—**indolently,** in'do•lent•li, *adv.* In an indolent manner.—**indolence,** in•do'lens, *n.* The condition or quality of being indolent; laziness; sloth.

indomitable, in•dom'i•ta•bl, *a.* [L. prefix *in*, not, and *domito*, freq. of *domo, domitum*, to tame. DAUNT, TAME.] Not to be tamed or subdued; unconquerable; untamable.—**indomitably,** in•dom'i•ta•bli, *adv.* In an indomitable manner.

indoor, in'dōr, *a.* Being within doors; domestic (an *indoor* servant).—**indoors,** in'dōrz, *adv.* Within doors; inside a house.

indorse, in•dors', *v.t.* Same as *Endorse.*

indri, in'dri, *n.* [Native name, signifying 'man of the woods'.] A tailless quadrumanous animal of the lemur family, a native of Madagascar, about the size of a cat.

indubitable, in•dū'bi•ta•bl, *a.* Prefix *in*, not, and *dubitable*; L. *indubitabilis.*] Not dubitable; too plain to admit of doubt; incontestable; unquestionable. —**indubitableness,** in•dū'bi•ta•bl•nes, *n.* State of being indubitable.—**indubitably,** in•dū'bi•ta•bli, *adv.* In an indubitable manner; undoubtedly; unquestionably.

induce, in•dūs', *v.t.*—*induced, inducing.* [L. *induco, inductum*—*in*, in, and *duco*, to lead. DUKE.] To lead by persuasion or argument; to prevail on; to draw by motives; to impel; to bring on, produce, cause (an ailment *induced* by overstudy); to establish a theory from observation of situations or given facts. —*Induced current*, an electric current excited by the presence of a primary current.—*Induced magnetism*, magnetism produced in soft iron when a magnet is held near, or a wire through which an electric current is passing is coiled round it.—**inducement,** in•dūs'ment, *n.* The act of inducing; that which induces or leads one to act; a motive; a consideration that leads to action.—**inducer,** in•dū'sėr, *n.* One who or that which induces.—**inducible,** in•dū'si•bl, *a.* Capable of being induced; capable of being inferred.

induct, in•dukt', *v.t.* [L. *inductus*, pp. of *inducere*, to lead in, introduce, induce.] To bring into; to introduce; to install in office; to call into military service.—**inductance,** in•duk'tans, *n.* That in a circuit or circuit element that resists changes in the flow of current, therefore causing changes in current to lag behind changes in voltage.—**inductee,** in•duk•tee', *n.* One called into military service.—**induction,** in•duk'shon, *n.* The act of inducting; introduction; installation in office or benefice; *logic*, the method of reasoning from particulars to generals; the deriving of a general principle or conclusion from particular facts; the conclusion or inference thus drawn or arrived at; *phys.* the property by which one body, having electrical, galvanic, or magnetic polarity, causes or induces it in another body without direct contact.—*Induction coil*, an apparatus for producing electric currents by induction and for utilizing them.—**inductive,** in•duk'tiv, *a.* Proceeding by induction; employed in drawing conclusions by induction; *elect.* able to produce electricity by induction; operating by induction; facilitating induction.—**inductively,** in•duk'tiv•li, *adv.*—**inductor,** in•duk'tėr, *n.* A device possessing inductance.

inductile, in•duk'til, *a.* [Prefix *in*, not and *ductile.*] Not ductile.—**inductility,** in•duk•til'i•ti, *n.* The quality of being inductile.

indue, in•dū', *v.t.*—*indued, induing.* [L. *induo*, from *indu*, old form of *in*, in, and verbal stem seen also in *exuo*, to put off (whence *exuviæ*).] To put on, as clothes; to clothe or invest; hence, to furnish; to supply; to endow.

indulge, in•dulj', *v.t.*—*indulged, indulging.* [L. *indulgeo*, to indulge or give one's self up to; origin doubtful.] To give one's self up to; not to restrain or oppose; to give free course to (to *indulge* the passions); to gratify by compliance; to humor to excess (to *indulge* children).—*v.i.* To indulge one's self; to practice indulgence; to be self-indulgent (to *indulge* in pleasure).—**indulgence,** in•dul'jens, *n.* [L. *indulgentia.*] The act or practice of indulging; an indulgent act; favor granted; intemperance in eating and drinking; readiness to forgive faults; tolerance; *R. Cath. Ch.* remission, by church authority, to a repentant sinner, of the penance attached to certain sins.—*The Declaration of Indulgence*, illegal declarations or proclamations by Charles II in 1672, and by James II in 1687, dispensing with penal laws against Roman Catholics and Dissenters.—**indulgent,** in•dul′jent, *a.* [L. *indulgens, indulgentis*, ppr. of *indulgeo.*] Prone to indulge or humor; overcompliant; not strict.—**indulgently,** in•dul′jent-li, *adv.* In an indulgent manner.—**indulger,** in•dul′jėr, *n.* One who indulges.

induplicate, in•dū′pli•kāt, *a.* [L. *in*, in, and *duplicatus*, doubled.] *Bot.* having the edges bent or rolled inward, as petals or leaves in the bud.

indurate, in′dū•rāt, *v.i.* [L. *induro, induratum*—prefix *in*, intens., and *duro*, to harden, from *durus*, hard, whence also *durable, durance*, etc.] To grow hard; to harden or become hard.—*v.t.*—*indurated, indurating.* To make hard; to harden; to make unfeeling; to render obdurate.—**induration,** in•dū•rā′shon, *n.* The act of hardening or process of growing hard; the state of being indurated.

indusium, in•dū′zi•um, *n.* pl. **indusia,** in•dū′zi•a. [L., a woman's undergarment, from *induo*, to put on. INDUE.] *Bot.* United hairs forming a sort of cup enclosing the stigma of a flower; the covering of the capsules or spore cases in ferns; *zool.* the case or covering of a larva; *anat.* the amnion.—**indusial,** in•dū′zi•al, *a.* Pertaining to an indusium; composed of or containing indusia or the cases of larvae (*indusial* limestone).

industrious, in•dus′tri•us, *a.* [L. *industrius*, from *indu*, old form of *in*, and *struo*, to fabricate. STRUCTURE.] Given to or characterized by industry; diligent in business or study; always working at something.—**industriously,** in•dus′tri•us•li, *adv.* In an industrious manner.—**industrial,** in•dus′tri•al, *a.* Pertaining to, involving, or characterized by industry (arts, establishment, capacity).—*Industrial exhibition, industrial museum*, an exhibition, museum of industrial products. — *Industrial school*, a school for training youth in the industrial arts and in habits of industry.—**industrialism,** in•dus′-tri•al•izm, *n.* Devotion to or employment in industrial pursuits.—**industrialist,** in•dus′tri•al•ist, *n.* One engaged in industry, usually as promoter or director.—**industrialize,** in•dus′tri•al•ize, *v.t.* To make industrial.—**industrially,** in•dus′tri•al•li, *adv.* In an industrial manner.—**industry,** in′dus•tri, *n.* [L. *industria*, from *industrius.*] Diligence in employment; steady attention to work or business; assiduity; the industrial arts generally, or any one of them; any productive occupation, especially one in which numbers of people are employed.

indwell, in•dwel′, *v.t.* To abide within; to occupy.—*v.i.* To dwell or exist in or within some place.—**indweller,** in′dwel•ėr, *n.* One who dwells in a place; an inhabitant.

inebriate, in•ē′bri•āt, *v.t.*—*inebriated, inebriating.* [L. *inebrio, inebriatum*—*in*, intens., and *ebrio*, to intoxicate, from *ebrius*, drunk, whence also *ebriety*: akin *sober.*] To make drunk; to intoxicate; to disorder the senses of; to turn the head of.—*n.* An habitual drunkard.—**inebriation,** in′-ē•bri•ā″shon, *n.* The act of inebriating or state of being inebriated.—**inebriety,** in•ē•brī′e•ti, *n.* Drunkenness; intoxication.—**inebriant,** in•ē′bri•ant, *a.* [L. *inebrians, inebriantis*, ppr. of *inebrio.*] Intoxicating.—*n.* Anything that intoxicates.

inedible, in•ed′i•bl, *a.* Not edible.

inedited, in•ed′it•ed, *a.* [Prefix *in*, not, and *edited.*] Not edited; unpublished.

ineffable, in•ef′a•bl, *a.* [L. *ineffabilis*—prefix *in*, not, and *effabilis*, speakable, from *effor*, to speak—*ef* for *ex*, out, and *for, fari*, to speak. FATE.] Incapable of being expressed in words.—**ineffability, ineffableness,** in•ef′a•bil″i•ti, in•ef′a•bl•nes, *n.* The quality of being ineffable or unutterable.—**ineffably,** in•ef′a•bli, *adv.* In an ineffable manner; unutterably.

ineffaceable, in•ef•fā′sa•bl, *a.* [Prefix *in*, not, and *effaceable.*] Incapable of being effaced.—**ineffaceably,** in•-ef•fā′sa•bli, *adv.* So as not to be effaceable; indelibly.

ineffective, in•ef•fek′tiv, *a.* [Prefix *in*, not and *effective.*] Incapable of producing any effect, or the effect intended; inefficient; useless; impotent; wanting energy.—**ineffectively,** in•ef•fek′tiv•li, *adv.* In an ineffective manner.—**ineffectiveness,** in•ef•fek′tiv•nes, *n.* Quality of being ineffective.—**ineffectual,** in•-ef•fek′chū•al, *a.* [Prefix *in*, not, and *effectual.*] Not effectual; inefficient; weak.—**ineffectually,** in•ef•fek′chū•-al•li, *adv.* In an ineffectual manner.—**ineffectualness,** in•ef•fek′chū•al•-nes, *n.*

inefficacious, in•ef′fi•kā″shus, *a.* [Prefix *in*, not, and *efficacious.*] Not efficacious; not producing the effect desired; of inadequate power.—**inefficaciously,** in•ef′fi•kā″shus•li, *adv.* In an inefficacious manner.—**inefficaciousness, inefficacy,** in•-ef′fi•kā″shus•nes, in•ef′fi•ka•si, *n.* Want of efficacy; ineffectualness; failure of effect.

inefficient, in•if•fish′ent, *a.* [Prefix *in*, not, and *efficient.*] Not efficient; not producing the required effect; incapable of effective action; incompetent.—*n.* One who is incompetent to perform the duties of a service.—**inefficiency,** in•if•fish′en•-si, *n.* The condition or quality of being inefficient.—**inefficiently** in•-if•fish′ent•li, *adv.* In an inefficient manner.

inelastic, in•ē•las′tik, *a.* [Prefix *in*, not, and *elastic.*] Not elastic; wanting elasticity; unelastic.—**inelasticity,** in•i′las•tis″i•ti, *n.* Want of elasticity.

inelegant, in•el′e•gant, *a.* [Prefix *in*, not, and *elegant*; L. *inelegans, inelegantis*, inelegant.] Not elegant; wanting in elegance; wanting in anything which correct taste requires.—**inelegance, inelegancy,** in•el′e•gans, in•el′e•gan•si, *n.* [L. *inelegantia*; Fr. *inélégance.*] The condition or quality of being inelegant; an inelegant point or feature.—**inelegantly,** in•-el′e•gant•li, *adv.* In an inelegant manner.

ineligible, in•el′i•ji•bl, *a.* [Prefix *in*, not, and *eligible.*] Not eligible; not capable of or fit for being elected or adopted; not worthy to be chosen or preferred.—**ineligibility,** in•el′i•ji•bil″i•ti, *n.* Condition of being ineligible.—**ineligibly,** in•el′i•ji•bli, *adv.* In an ineligible manner.

ineloquent, in•el′o•kwent, *a.* [Prefix *in*, not, and *eloquent.*] Not eloquent; wanting in eloquence; not eloquently written or delivered.—**ineloquently,** in•el′o•kwent•li, *adv.* In an ineloquent manner.—**ineloquence,** in•-el′o•kwens, *n.* The quality of being ineloquent.

inept, in•ept′, *a.* [L. *ineptus*—prefix *in*, not, and *aptus*, fit, apt. APT.] Unsuitable; improper; foolish; silly; nonsensical.—**ineptitude, ineptness,** in•ep′ti•tūd, in•ept′nes, *n.* [L. *ineptitudo.*] The condition or quality of being inept; unfitness; inaptitude; foolishness.—**ineptly,** in•-ept′li, *adv.* In an inept manner.

inequal, in•ē′kwal, *a.* [Prefix *in*, not, and *equal*; L. *inæqualis.*] Not equal; unequal; uneven; varying.—**inequality,** in•ē•kwol′i•ti, *n.* [L. *inæqualitas.*] The condition or quality of being inequal or unequal; disparity; unevenness; want of levelness; an elevation or a depression of a surface.

inequitable, in•ek′wi•ta•bl, *a.* [Prefix *in*, not, and *equitable.*] Not equitable; not just or fair.—**inequity,** in•ek′-wi•ti, *n.* Unfairness; injustice.

ineradicable, in•i•rad′i•ka•bl, *a.* [Prefix *in*, not, and *eradicable.*] Incapable of being eradicated.—**ineradicably,** in•i•rad′i•ka•bli, *adv.* So as not to be eradicated.

inert, in•ėrt′, *a.* [L. *iners, inertis*, unskilled, inactive—*in*, not, and *ars*, acquired skill, art. ART.] Destitute of the power of moving itself; not moving or acting; indisposed to move or act; sluggish; inactive. ∴ *Inert* refers rather to the external manifestation of a habit which may be either natural or induced; *inactive*, not exhibiting activity, often refers to a temporary, perhaps voluntary, state.—**inertia,** in•ėr′shi•a, *n.* Passiveness; inactivity; inertness; sluggishness; *phys.* the property of matter by which it retains its state of rest or of uniform rectilinear motion so long as no foreign cause occurs to change that state.—*Inertial guidance*, navigation of a missile or other aircraft through self-contained governors which respond to inertial forces.—**inertly,** in•ėrt′li, *adv.*—**inertness,** in•ėrt′nes, *n.*

inessential, in•es•sen′shal, *a.* [Prefix *in*, not, and *essential*,] Not essential; unessential.

inestimable, in•es′ti•ma•bl, *a.* [Prefix *in*, not, and *estimable*; L. *inæstimabilis*.] Incapable of being estimated or computed; too valuable or excellent to be rated or fully appreciated; incalculable.—**inestimably**, in•es′ti•ma•bli, *adv.* In a manner not to be estimated.

inevitable, in•ev′i•ta•bl, *a.* [L. *inevitabilis*, from *in*, not, and *evito*, to avoid—*e*, out, and *vito*, to shun.] Incapable of being avoided; unavoidable; admitting of no escape or evasion; certain to befall.—**inevitability, inevitableness**, in•ev′i•ta•bil″i•ti, in•ev′i•ta•bl•nes, *n.* Unavoidableness; certainty.—**inevitably**, in•ev′i•ta•bli, *adv.* Unavoidably; certainly.

inexact, in•ig•zakt′, *a.* [Prefix *in*, not, and *exact*.] Not exact; not precisely correct or true.—**inexactness**, in•ig•zakt′nes, *n.* The state of being inexact; incorrectness.

inexcusable, in•iks•kū′za•bl, *a.* [Prefix *in*, not, and *excusable*.] Incapable of being excused or justified; unpardonable; indefensible.—**inexcusableness**, in•iks•kū′za•bl•nes, *n.* The condition or quality of being inexcusable.—**inexcusably**, in•eks•kū′za•bli, *adv.* In an inexcusable manner; without excuse.

inexhaustible, in•igz•a̤s′ti•bl, *a.* [Prefix *in*, not, and *exhaustible*.] Not exhaustible; incapable of being exhausted or spent; unfailing.—**inexhaustibility**, in•igz•a̤s′ti•bil″i•ti, *n.* The state of being inexhaustible.—**inexhaustibly**, in•igz•a̤s′ti•bli, *adv.* In an inexhaustible manner or degree.

inexorable, in•ek′so•ra•bl, *a.* [Prefix *in*, not, and *exorable*.] Incapable of being moved by entreaty or prayer; too firm and determined to yield to supplication; unyielding; unbending; implacable.—**inexorability, inexorableness**, in•ek′so•ra•bil″i•ti, in•ek′so•ra•bl•nes, *n.* The state or quality of being inexorable.—**inexorably**, in•ek′so•ra•bli, *adv.* In an inexorable manner.

inexpedient, in•eks•pē′di•ent, *a.* [Prefix *in*, not, and *expedient*.] Not expedient; inappropriate; unsuitable to time and place; not advisable. —**inexpedience, inexpediency**, in•eks•pē′di•ens, in•eks•pē′di•en•si, *n.* The condition or quality of being inexpedient.—**inexpediently**, in•eks•pē′di•ent•li, *adv.* In an inexpedient manner.

inexpensive, in•iks•pen′siv, *a.* [Prefix *in*, not, and *expensive*.] Not expensive.

inexperience, in•iks•pē′ri•ens, *n.* [Prefix *in*, not, and *experience*.] Want of experience.—**inexperienced**, in•iks•pē′ri•enst, *a.* Not having experience.

inexpert, in•iks•pėrt′, *a.* [Prefix *in*, not, and *expert*.] Not expert; not skilled.—**inexpertness**, in•iks•pėrt′nes, *n.*

inexpiable, in•eks′pi•a•bl, *a.* [Prefix *in*, not, and *expiable*; L. *inexpiabilis*.] Incapable of being expiated; not to be atoned for; unpardonable.—**inexpiableness**, in•eks′pi•a•bl•nes, *n.*—**inexpiably**, in•eks′pi•a•bli, *adv.*

inexplicable, in•eks′pli•ka•bl, *a.* [Prefix *in*, not, and *explicable*; L. *inexplicabilis*,] Incapable of being explained or interpreted; unaccountable; mysterious.—**inexplicability, inexplicableness**, in•eks′pli•ka•bil″i•ti, in•eks′pli•ka•bl•nes, *n.* The quality of being inexplicable.—**inexplicably**, in•eks′pli•ka•bli, *adv.* In an inexplicable manner; unaccountably.

inexplicit, in•iks•plis′it, *a.* [Prefix *in*, not, and *explicit*.] Not explicit; not clear in statement; not clearly stated.

inexpressible, in•iks•pres′i•bl, *a.* [Prefix *in*, not, and *expressible*.] Not expressible; not to be uttered; unspeakable; unutterable. — **inexpressibles**, in•iks•pres′i•blz, *n. pl.* A colloquial euphemism for trousers.—**inexpressibly**, in•iks•pres′i•bli, *adv.* In an inexpressible manner.—**inexpressive**, in•iks•pres′iv, *a.* Not expressive; wanting in expression; inexpressible; ineffable.—**inexpressiveness**, in•iks•pres′iv•nes, *n.*

inextinguishable, in•iks•ting′gwish•a•bl, *a.* [Prefix *in*, not, and *extinguishable*.] Incapable of being extinguished; unquenchable (flame, thirst, desire).—**inextinguishably**, in•iks•ting′gwish•a•bli, *adv.* In an inextinguishable manner.

inextricable, in•eks′tri•ka•bl, *a.* [Prefix *in*, not, and *extricable*; L. *inextricabilis*.] Incapable of being extricated or disentangled; not permitting extrication.—**inextricableness**, in•eks′tri•ka•bl•nes, *n.*—**inextricably**, in•eks′tri•ka•bli, *adv.*

infallible, in•fal′i•bl, *a.* [Prefix *in*, not, and *fallible*.] Not fallible; not capable of erring or falling into error; not leading into error; perfectly reliable; certain (*infallible* testimony).—**infallibly**, in•fal′i•bli, *adv.* In an infallible manner.—**infallibility**, in•fal′i•bil″i•ti, *n.* The quality of being infallible.—*Infallibility of the pope*, the dogma established as an article of faith in 1870, that the pope, when speaking as pope upon matters of faith or morals, is infallible.

infamy, in′fa•mi, *n.* [L. *infamia*, ill fame, ill report, from *infamis*, infamous—*in*, not, and *fama*, fame.] Total loss of reputation; public disgrace; bad or disgraceful repute; shamefulness; disgracefulness; scandalousness; extreme baseness or vileness.—**infamous**, in′fa•mus, *a.* Having a reputation of the worst kind; scandalous; notoriously vile; shameful; branded with infamy.—**infamously**, in′fa•mus•li, *adv.* Scandalously; disgracefully; shamefully.

infant, in′fant, *n.* [L. *infans, infantis*, that cannot speak, an infant—prefix *in*, not, and *fari*, to speak. FAME.] A child in the first two or three years of life; *law*, a person not of legal age.—*a.* Pertaining to infancy. —**infancy**, in′fan•si, *n.* [L. *infantia*.] The state of being an infant; earliest period of life; *law*, the period from birth to twenty-one; nonage; minority; the first age of anything.—**infanta**, in•fan′tä, *n.*, *fem.*; **infante**, in•fan′tā, *n.*, *m.* Formerly in Spain and Portugal, children of the king except the eldest son.—**infanticide**, in•fan′ti•sīd, *n.* [L. *infanticidium*, the crime, *infanticida*, the perpetrator—*infans*, and *cædo*, to kill.] The murder and murderer of an infant; child murder.—**infantile**, in′fan•til, *a.* Pertaining to or characteristic of infancy or an infant.—**infantile paralysis**, *n.* Poliomyelitis.—**infantilism**, in•fan′ti•lizm, *n.* Childlike speech patterns; retarded anatomical, physiological, and psychological development in adults.

infantry, in′fant•ri, *n.* [Fr. *infanterie*, It. *infanteria*, infantry (lit. a band of youths), from *infante*, a young person, originally an infant.] The soldiers or troops that serve on foot, as distinguished from *cavalry*.

infatuate, in•fat′ū•āt, *v.t.*—*infatuated, infatuating*. [L. *infatuo, infatuatum*, to make foolish—prefix *in*, intens., and *fatuus*, foolish (whence *fatuous*).] To make foolish; to inspire with folly; to inspire with an extravagant passion that cannot be controlled.—**infatuated**, in•fat′ū•ā•ted, *p.* and *a.* Affected with folly; besotted; inspired with foolish passion.—**infatuation**, in•fat′ū•ā″shon, *n.* The act of infatuating or state of being infatuated; extreme folly; foolish passion.

infeasible, in•fē′zi•bl, *a.* [Prefix *in*, not, and *feasible*.] Not feasible; impracticable.

infect, in•fekt′, *v.t.* [Fr. *infecter*, from L. *inficio, infectum*, to put in, to stain—*in*, into, and *facio*, to do. FACT.] To communicate disease to; to contaminate with germs or bacteria; to affect with one's mood, opinion, or beliefs; to impart qualities to (usually unfavorable); *law*, to place in danger of penalty or forfeiture.—**infector**, in•fek′tėr, *n.* —**infection**, in•fek′shon, *n.* The act or process of infecting; the state of being infected; a disease communicated from one organism to another; the imparting of qualities or mood or belief by means of example, teaching, etc.—**infectious, infective**, in•fek′shus, in•fek′tiv, *a.*—**infectiously**, in•fek′shus•li, *adv.*—**infectiousness**, in•fek′shus•nes, *n.*

infecund, in•fē′kund, *a.* [Prefix *in*, not, and *fecund*: L. *infecundus*.] Not fecund; unfruitful; barren.—**infecundity**, in•fi•kun′di•ti, *n.* State of being infecund.

infelicity, in•fē•lis′i•ti, *n.* [Prefix *in*, not, and *felicity*; L. *infelicitas*.] The state of being unhappy; unhappiness; misery; unfavorableness.—**infelicitous**, in•fē•lis′i•tus, *a.* Not felicitous; unhappy; unfortunate.

infelt, in′felt, *a.* [Prefix *in*, within, and *felt*.] Felt within or deeply; heartfelt.

infer, in•fėr′, *v.t.*—*inferred, inferring*. [L. *infero*, to bring in or on, to conclude—*in*, upon, and *fero*, to bear. FERTILE.] To gather or derive either by induction or deduction; to deduce, as a fact or consequence; to conclude or arrive at by reasoning. —**inferable,** in•fėr′a•bl, *a.* Capable of being inferred; inferrible.—**inference,** in′fėr•ens, *n.* The act of inferring; conclusion drawn or inferred; deduction; consequence.—**inferential,** in•fėr•en′shal, *a.* Of or pertaining to an inference.—**inferentially,** in•fėr•en′shal•li, *adv.* In an inferential manner; by way of inference.—**inferrible,** in•fėr′i•bl, *a.* Such as may be inferred; to be gathered or concluded by reasoning.

inferior, in•fē′ri•ėr, *a.* [L. compar. from *inferus,* low; akin *infernal.*] Lower in place, station, rank, value, importance; subordinate; *bot.* growing below some other organ; *astron.* situated between earth and sun (the *inferior* planets).—*n.* One lower in station, rank, intellect, than others.—**inferiority,** in•fē′ri•or″i•ti, *n.* The state of being inferior.—*Inferiority complex,* a feeling of personal inferiority (real or imaginary).—**inferiorly,** in•fē′ri•ėr•li, *adv.* In an inferior manner.

infernal, in•fėr′nal, *a.* [L. *infernalis,* from *infernus,* infernal; akin *inferior.*] Pertaining to the lower regions, or regions of the dead; pertaining to hell; inhabiting hell; characteristic or worthy of hell or the inhabitants of hell; hellish; diabolical; wicked and detestable.—*Infernal machine,* a machine or apparatus of an explosive nature, contrived for the purposes of assassination or other mischief.—**infernally,** in•fėr′nal•li, *adv.* In an infernal manner.—**inferno,** *n.* A hell upon earth, with general reference to the poem of Dante, the first part of his *Divine Comedy.*

infertile, in•fėr′tīl or in•fėr′til, *a.* [Prefix *in,* not, and *fertile.*] Not fertile; not fruitful or productive; barren.—**infertility,** in•fėr•til′i•ti, *n.* Unproductiveness; barrenness.

infest, in•fest′, *v.t.* [Fr. *infester;* L. *infestare,* to attack, to molest, from *infestus,* hostile—*in,* in, and same root as *fendo* in *offendo, defendo,* to offend, defend.] To make hostile attacks or depredations on; to harass, torment, disturb, annoy.—**infestation,** in•fes•tā′shon, *n.* [L. *infestatio.*] The act of infesting.—**infester,** in•fes′tėr, *n.* One who infests.

infidel, in′fi•del, *n.* [L. *infidelis,* faithless, unbelieving—prefix *in,* not, and *fidelis,* faithful. FIDELITY.] A disbeliever; one who has no religious faith; an atheist; not holding the true faith.—*a.* Unbelieving.—**infidelity,** in•fi•del′i•ti, *n.* [Fr. *infidélité;* L. *infidelitas.*] Want of faith or belief; atheism or disbelief in God or religion; skepticism; unfaithfulness in married persons; adultery; unfaithfulness to a charge or moral obligation; treachery; deceit.

infield, in′fēld, *n. Baseball,* the square or diamond portion of a playing field marked off by four bases; collectively, the shortstop and three basemen.—**infielder,** in″fēl′dėr, *n.* One member of the infield; a baseman or the shortstop.

infiltrate, in•fil′trāt, *v.t.* and *i.* [Prefix *in,* and *filtrate.*] To enter by penetrating the pores or interstices of a substance; to pass through or pervade, as by filtering; to enter inconspicuously or secretly in small groups (troops *infiltrating* enemy territory).—**infiltration,** in•fil•trā′shon, *n.*

infinite, in′fi•nit, *a.* [Prefix *in,* not, and *finite;* L. *infinitus.*] Not finite; without limits; not limited or circumscribed: applied to time, space, and the Supreme Being and his attributes; exceedingly great in excellence, degree, capacity, and the like; boundless; limitless; immeasurable.—*n.* That which is infinite; an infinite space or extent; the infinite being; the Almighty.—**infinitely,** in′fi•nit•li, *adv.* In an infinite manner.—**infiniteness,** in′fi•nit•nes, *n.* The state of being infinite.—**infinitesimal,** in′fin•i•tes″i•mal, *a.* [Fr. *infinitésimal.*] Infinitely or indefinitely small; less than any assignable quantity.—*n. Math.* an infinitely small quantity, or one less than any assignable quantity.—**infinitesimally,** in′fin•i•tes″i•mal•li, *adv.* To an infinitesimal extent or in an infinitesimal degree.—**infinitive,** in•fin′i•tiv, *a.* [L. *infinitivus,* unlimited, indefinite.] Not limiting or restricting: a grammatical term applied to that mood of a verb which expresses the action of the verb, without limitation of person or number.—*n.* The infinitive mood.—**infinitival,** in•fin′i•ti•val, *a. Gram.* of or belonging to the infinitive mood.—**infinitude,** in•fin′i•tūd, *n.* The quality or state of being infinite; infinite extent; infinity; immensity; boundless number.—**infinity,** in•fin′i•ti, *n.* [L. *infinitas.*] Unlimited extent of time, space, quantity, excellence.

infirm, in•fėrm′, *a.* [Prefix *in,* not, and *firm;* L. *infirmus,* not strong, weak, feeble.] Not firm or sound; weak as regards the body; feeble; not steadfast; irresolute; not solid or stable.—**infirmary,** in•fėr′ma•ri, *n.* A place where the infirm or sick, or those suffering from accidents, are lodged and nursed, or have their ailments attended to.—**infirmity,** in•fėr′mi•ti, *n.* [L. *infirmitas.*] The state of being infirm; an unsound or unhealthy state of the body; a disease; a malady; an ailment, weakness, failing, defect, foible.

infix, in•fiks′, *v.t.* [L. *infigo, infixum*—*in,* in, into, and *figo,* to fix.] To fix or fasten in; to cause to remain or adhere, as in the mind; to implant or fix, as principles, thoughts, etc.—*n.* A part of a word similar to a prefix or suffix, but inserted in the body of a word.

inflame, in•flām′, *v.t.*—*inflamed, inflaming.* [L. *inflammo*—*in,* and *flammo,* to inflame, from *flamma,* flame. FLAME.] To set on fire; to kindle; to redden or make fiery (the eyes, the face); to excite or increase, as passion or appetite; to enkindle into violent action; to enrage or exasperate; *med.* to make morbidly red and swollen.—*v.i.* To take fire; to grow angry; to grow hot and painful.—**inflamer,** in•flā′mėr, *n.* One who or that which inflames.—**inflammability, inflammableness,** in•flam′a•bil″i•ti, in•flam′a•bl•nes, *n.* The state or quality of being inflammable.—**inflammable,** in•flam′a•bl, *a.* Capable of being set on fire; easily kindled; combustible. —**inflammably,** in•flam′a•bli, *adv.* In an inflammable manner.—**inflammation,** in•fla•mā′shon, *n.* [L. *inflammatio.*] The act of inflaming; *med.* a redness and swelling of any part of an animal body, attended with heat, pain, and febrile symptoms.—**inflammatory,** in•flam′a•to•ri, *a.* Tending to inflame; tending to excite inflammation; accompanied with great heat and excitement of arterial action; tending to excite anger, animosity, or the like.

inflate, in•flāt′, *v.t.*—*inflated, inflating.* [L. *inflo, inflatum*—*in,* into, and *flo,* to blow. FLATULENT.] To swell or distend by injecting air; to puff up; to elate, as with pride; to raise above the real value or value according to sound commercial principles (*inflated prices*).—**inflatable,** in•flā′ta•bl, *a.* Capable of being inflated.—**inflated,** in•flā′ted, *p.* and *a.* Distended with air; puffed up; turgid; tumid; bombastic (an *inflated* style of writing.)—**inflation,** in•flā′shon, *n.* [L. *inflatio, inflationis.*] The act of inflating; the state of being inflated; sharp increase in amount of money and credit causing advances in the price level.—**inflationist,** in•flā′shon•ist, *n.* One who causes or believes in manipulated expansion of prices.

inflect, in•flekt′, *v.t.* [L. *inflecto*—*in,* intens., and *flecto,* to bend. FLEX.] To bend; to turn from a direct line or course; to modulate (the voice); *gram.,* to go over the inflections of; to decline or conjugate.—**inflection, inflexion,** in•flek′shon, *n.* [L. *inflexio, inflexionis.*] The act of inflecting, or the state of being inflected; modulation or rise and fall of the voice; *optics,* deflection or diffraction; *gram.* the variation of nouns, etc., by declension, and of verbs by conjugation.—**inflectional,** in•flek′shon•al, *a.* Pertaining to or having inflection.—**inflective,** in•flek′tiv, *a.* Having the power of inflecting.—**inflexed,** in•flekst′, *a.* [L. *inflexus,* pp. of *inflecto.*] Curved; bent.—*Inflexed leaf, bot.* a leaf curved or bent upward and inward at the apex. —**inflexibility,** in•flek′si•bil″i•ti, *n.* The quality of being inflexible.—**inflexible,** in•flex′si•bl, *a.* [L. *inflexibilis,* that cannot be bent.] Incapable of being bent; firm in purpose; not to be prevailed on; incapable of being turned from a purpose; inexorable; unalterable.—**inflexibleness,** in•flek′si•bl•nes, *n.* Inflexibility. —**inflexibly,** in•flek′si•bli, *adv.* In an inflexible manner; firmly; inexorably.

inflict, in•flikt′, *v.t.* [L. *infligo, inflictum*—*in,* upon, and *fligo,* to strike, as in *afflict, conflict.*] To cause to bear or suffer from; to cause to feel or experience; to impose (pain, disgrace, punishment).—**inflicter,** in•flik′tėr, *n.* One who inflicts.—**infliction,** in•flik′shon, *n.* [L. *inflictio, inflictionis.*] The act of inflicting or imposing; that which is inflicted.—**inflictive,** in•flik′tiv, *a.* Tending to inflict.

inflorescence, in•flō•res′ens, *n.* [From L. *inflorescens,* ppr. of *infloresco,* to begin to blossom—*in,* intens., and *floresco,* to begin to blossom. FLOURISH.] A flowering; the unfolding of blossoms; *bot.* a mode of flowering or the manner in which blossoms are arranged and supported on their footstalks or peduncles.

influence, in′flu̦•ens, *n.* [Fr. *influence,* from L. *influens, influentis,* ppr. of *influo,* to flow in—*in,* in, *fluo,* to flow. FLUENT.] Agency or power serving to affect, modify, or sway in some way; ability or power sufficient to produce some effect; sway; effect; power or authority arising from elevated station, wealth, and the like; acknowledged ascendancy with people in power.—*v.t.*—*influenced, influencing.* To exercise influence on, to modify or affect in some way; to act on; to bias; to sway.—**influent,** in′flu̦•ent, *a.* [L. *influens, influentis.*] Flowing in.—**influential,** in•flu̦•en′shal, *a.* Exerting influence.

influenza, in•flū•en′za, *n.* [It. *influenza,* lit. influence. INFLUENCE.] An acute, infectious, and highly contagious disease affecting the respiratory tract, and producing symptoms not unlike a severe cold; pneumonia is a frequent complication, particularly when the disease is epidemic; intestinal, or abdominal, influenza attacks the digestive system

influx, in′fluks, *n.* [L. *influxus,* a flowing in, from *influo.* INFLUENCE.] The act of flowing in; infusion; inflow; a coming in; introduction; importation in abundance (an *influx* of money); the point at which one stream runs into another or into the sea.

infold, in•fold′, *v.i.* To fold in; to wrap up or inwrap; to clasp with the arms; to embrace.

inform, in•form′, *v.t.* [Fr. *informer,* to apprise, L. *informo,* to shape, to describe—*in,* intens., and *formo,* to form, from *forma,* form.] To give form or shape to; to inspire and give life to; to actuate with vitality; to animate; to communicate knowledge to; to instruct, to tell, acquaint, apprise (to *inform* a person *of* something).—*v.i.* To give information.—*To inform against,* to communicate facts by way of accusation against.—**informant,** in•for′mant, *n.* One who informs; an informer.—**information,** in•for•mā′shon, *n.* [L. *informatio.*] The act of informing; news or intelligence communicated by word or writing; intelligence; knowledge derived from reading or instruction, or gathered in any way; a statement of facts laid before a court of justice.—**informative,** in•for′ma•tiv, *a.* Affording knowledge or information; instructive.—**informer,** in•for′mėr, *n.* One who informs; an accomplice who in order to escape punishment gives evidence against another or others; one who makes a business of informing against others.

informal, in•for′mal, *a.* [Prefix *in,* not, and *formal.*] Not in the regular or usual form; not in accordance with official, conventional, or customary forms; without ceremony.—**informality,** in•for•mal′i•ti, *n.* The state of being informal; want of formality.—**informally,** in•for′mal•li, *adv.* In an informal manner.

infraction, in•frak′shon, *n.* [L. *infractio, infractionis,* a breaking in pieces, from *infringo, infractum.* INFRINGE.] The act of infringing; breach; violation; infringement.

infralapsarian, in′fra•lap•sâ″ri•an, *a.* and *n.* The doctrine of the sect holding that God's election or predestination of some was consequent on his prescience of the fall, and contemplated man as already fallen. Modifications are *sublapsarian, supralapsarian.*

infrangible, in•fran′ji•bl, *a.* [Prefix *in,* not, and *frangible.*] Not capable of being broken; not to be violated or infringed.—**infrangibility, infrangibleness,** in•fran′ji•bil″i•ti, in•fran′ji•bl•nes, *n.* State or quality of being infrangible.

infrared, in•fra•red′, *a.* Pertaining to rays beyond the visible red of the spectrum.

infrasonic, in•fra•so′nik, *a.* [Prefix, *infra,* below, and *sonic,* from L. *sonus,* sound.] Beneath the range of human hearing.

infrequent, in•frē′kwent, *a.* [L. *infrequens*—*in,* not, and *frequens,* frequent.] Not frequent; seldom; rare.—**infrequency,** in•frē′kwen•si, *n.*—**infrequently,** in•frē′kwent•li, *adv.* Not frequently; seldom.

infringe, in•frinj′, *v.t.*—*infringed, infringing.* [L. *infringo*—*in,* intens., and *frango,* to break. FRACTION.] To break, as laws or contracts; to violate; to contravene; to impair or encroach on.—*v.i.* To encroach: followed by *on* or *upon.*—**infringement,** in•frinj′ment, *n.* Act of infringing or violating.—**infringer,** in•frin′jėr, *n.* One who infringes; a violator.

infundibular, infundibulate, infundibuliform, in•fun•dib′ū•lėr, in•fun•dib′ū•lāt, in•fun•dib′ū•li•form, *a.* [From *infundibulum,* a funnel—*in,* in, and *fundo,* to pour. FUSE.] Having the form of a funnel.

infuriate, in•fū′ri•āt, *v.t.*—*infuriated, infuriating.* [L.L. *infurio, infuriatum*—L. *in,* intens., and *furia,* rage, madness.] To render furious or mad; to enrage.—*a.* Enraged; mad; raging.

infuse, in•fūz′, *v.t.*—*infused, infusing.* [Fr. *infuser,* from L. *infundo, infusum,* to pour into—*in,* into, and *fundo,* to pour. FUSE.] To pour in, as a liquid; to pour; to shed; to instill, as principles or qualities; to introduce; to diffuse; to steep in liquor without boiling, in order to extract medicinal or other qualities.—**infuser,** in•fū′zėr, *n.* One who infuses.—**infusibility,** in•fū′zi•bil″i•ti, *n.* The capability of being infused.—**infusible,** in•fū′zi•bl, *a.* Capable of being infused.—**infusion,** in•fū′zhon, *n.* The act or process of infusing; that which is infused or instilled; liquor obtained by infusing or steeping.—**infusive,** in•fū′siv, *a.* Having the power of infusion.

infusorian, in•fū•sō′ri•an, *n.* [L.] One of a group of minute, mostly microscopic animals, belonging to the class Infusoria of the protozoa.—**infusorial,** in•fū•sō′ri•al, *a.*

infusible, in•fū′zi•bl, *a.* [Prefix *in,* not, and *fusible.*] Not fusible; incapable of fusion.—**infusibility,** in•fū′zi•bil″i•ti, *n.* Absence of fusibility.

ingeminate, in•jem′i•nāt, *v.t.* [L. *ingemino, ingeminatum*—*in,* intens., and *gemino,* to double. GEMINATE.] To double or repeat.—*a.* Redoubled; repeated.—**ingemination,** in•jem′i•nā″shon, *n.* Repetition; reduplication.

ingenerate, in•jen′ėr•āt, *v.t.* [L. *ingenero, ingeneratum*—*in,* and *genero,* to generate.] To generate or produce within.—*a.* Generated within; inborn; innate; inbred.

ingenious, in•jē′ni•us, *a.* [L. *ingeniosus,* able, ingenious, from *ingenium,* ability, cleverness—*in,* in, and root *gen,* to beget. GENUS.] Possessed of cleverness or ability†; having the faculty of invention; skillful or prompt to invent; apt in contriving or forming new combinations of ideas; contrived with ingenuity; of curious design, structure, or mechanism; witty or well conceived (an *ingenious* compliment).—**ingeniously,** in•jē′ni•us•li, *adv.* In an ingenious manner.—**ingeniousness,** in•jē′ni•us•nes, *n.* Ingenuity.—**ingenuity,** in•jen•ū′i•ti, *n.* [Fr. *ingénuité,* L. *ingenuitas,* from *ingenuus.* INGENUOUS.] Ingenuousness‡; the quality or power of being ingenious; ready invention; skill in contrivance. [In form, though not in meaning, this word belongs to the next entry.]

ingenuous, in•jen′ū•us, *a.* [L. *ingenuus,* inborn, freeborn, ingenuous—*in,* and root *gen,* to produce. GENUS.] Honorable, noble, or generous‡; open, frank, or candid; free from reserve, disguise, equivocation, or dissimulation; of persons or things.—**ingenuously,** in•jen′ū•us•li, *adv.* In an ingenuous manner; openly; candidly.—**ingenuousness,** in•jen′ū•us•nes, *n.* The condition or quality of being ingenuous; openness of heart; frankness.—**ingénue,** an̍•zhā•nū′, *n.* An ingenuous, artless, naïve girl or young woman: used often of female parts in plays; also, an actress who plays such parts.

ingest, in•jest′, *v.t.* [L. *ingero, ingestum*—*in,* into, and *gero,* to bear. GESTURE.] To take into the stomach.—**ingestion,** in•jest′shon, *n.* The act of taking into the stomach.—**ingesta,** in•jes′ta, *n. pl.* [*Lit.* things carried in. INGEST.] Substances absorbed by an organism, or entering the alimentary canal; things taken into the mind.

inglorious, in•glō′ri•us, *a.* [Prefix *in,* not, and *glorious;* L. *inglorius.*] Not glorious; without renown; obscure; bringing disgrace rather than glory; disgraceful; ignominious.—**ingloriously,** in•glō′ri•us•li, *adv.* In an inglorious manner. — **ingloriousness,** in•glō′ri•us•nes, *n.*

ingoing, in′gō•ing, *n.* The act of entering; entrance.—*a.* Going in; entering, as on an office.

ingot, in′got, *n.* [From *in*, and A.Sax. *geótan*, D. *gieten*, to pour; originally meaning a mass of molten metal. GUSH.] A mass or wedge of gold or silver cast in a mold; a mass of unwrought metal.

ingraft, in•graft′, *v.t.* [*In* and *graft.*] To graft; to attach by grafting; hence, to insert; to introduce; to set or fix deeply and firmly.

ingrain, in•grān′, *v.t.* To dye with grain or kermes; hence, from the permanence and excellence of this dye, to dye in any deep, permanent, or enduring color; to dye deep; to incorporate with the grain or texture of anything; to paint in imitation of the grain of wood; to grain.

ingrate, in′grāt, *n.* [Fr. *ingrat*, from L. *ingratus*, ungrateful—*in*, not, and *gratus*, grateful.] An ungrateful person.

ingratiate, in•grā′shi•āt, *v.t.*—*ingratiated, ingratiating.* [L. *in*, into, and *gratia*, favor. GRACE.] To introduce or commend to another's good will, confidence, or kindness: always *refl.*

ingratitude, in•grat′i•tūd, *n.* [Prefix *in*, not, and *gratitude.*] Want of gratitude; insensibility to favors, and want of a disposition to repay them; unthankfulness.

ingredient, in•grē′di•ent, *n.* [L. *ingrediens, ingredientis*, ppr. of *ingredior*, to go in—*in*, into, and *gradior*, to go. GRADE.] That which enters into a compound or is a component part of any compound or mixture; an element, component, or constituent.

ingress, in′gres, *n.* [L. *ingressus*, a going into, from *ingredior.* INGREDIENT.] Entrance; *astron.* the entrance of the moon into the shadow of the earth in eclipses, the sun's entrance into a sign, etc.; power or liberty of entrance; means of entering.—*v.i.* (in•gres′). To go in or enter.—**ingression,** in•gresh′on, *n.* [L. *ingressio.*] The act of entering; entrance.

inguinal, in′gwi•nal, *a.* [L. *inguinalis*, from *inguen, inguinis*, the groin.] Pertaining to the groin.

ingulf, in•gulf′, *v.t.* Same as *Engulf.*

ingurgitate, in•gėr′ji•tāt, *v.t.*—*ingurgitated, ingurgitating.* [L. *ingurgito, ingurgitatum*, to gorge—*in*, into, and *gurges*, a gulf. GORGE.] To swallow eagerly or in great quantity.—*v.i.* To drink largely; to swill.—**ingurgitation,** in•gėr′ji•tā″shon, *n.* The act of ingurgitating.

inhabit, in•hab′it, *v.t.* [L. *inhabito—in*, and *habito*, to dwell. HABIT.] To live or dwell in; to occupy as a place of settled residence.—*v.i.* To dwell; to live; to abide.—**inhabitable,** in•hab′i•ta•bl, *a.* Capable of being inhabited; habitable.—**inhabitancy,** in•hab′i•tan•si, *n.* The condition of an inhabitant; habitancy.—**inhabitant,** in•hab′i•tant, *n.* [L. *inhabitans, inhabitantis*, ppr. of *inhabita.*] One who inhabits; one who dwells or resides permanently in a place, as distinguished from an occasional visitor.—**inhabitation,** in•hab′i•tā″shon, *n.* The act of inhabiting; an abode.—**inhabiter,** in•hab′i•tėr, *n.* One who inhabits; an inhabitant (N.T.).

inhale, in•hāl′, *v.t.*—*inhaled, inhaling.* [L. *inhalo—in*, in, into, and *halo*, to breathe, as in *exhale.*] To draw into the lungs; to inspire; to suck in.—**inhaler,** in•hā′lėr, *n.* One who inhales; *med.* an apparatus for inhaling vapors and volatile substances, as steam of hot water, vapor of chloroform, iodine, etc.; a respirator.—**inhalant,** in•hā′lant, *a.* Inhaling.—**inhalation,** in•ha•lā′shon, *n.* The act of inhaling.

inharmonic, inharmonical, in•här•mon′ik, in•här•mon′i•kal, *a.* Not harmonic; inharmonious; discordant.—**inharmonious,** in•här•mō′ni•us, *a.* Not harmonious; discordant.—**inharmoniously,** in•här•mō′ni•us•li, *adv.* In an inharmonious manner.—**inharmoniousness,** in•här•mō′ni•us•nes, *n.* Want of harmony; discord.

inhere, in•hēr′, *v.i.*—*inhered, inhering.* [L. *inhæreo, inhæsum—in*, and *hæreo*, to stick, as in *adhere, cohere, hesitate.*] To exist or be fixed in; to belong, as attributes or qualities, to a subject; to be innate.—**inherence, inherency,** in•hē′rens, in•hē′ren•si, *n.* The state of inhering; existence in something.—**inherent,** in•hē′rent, *a.* [L. *inhærens, inhærentis*, ppr. of *inhæreo.*] Inhering; inseparable; naturally pertaining; inborn; innate.—**inherently,** in•hē′rent•li, *adv.* In an inherent manner.

inherit, in•her′it, *v.t.* [O.Fr. *enheriter*, L. *inhæredito*, to inherit, from *hæres, hæredis*, an heir. HEIR.] To receive or obtain by descent from an ancestor; to take by being the heir; to receive from a progenitor as part of one's nature; to come into possession of; to hold as belonging to one's lot.—*v.i.* To take an inheritance; to take the position of heir or heirs.—**inheritability,** in•her′i•ta•bil″i•ti, *n.* The quality of being inheritable.—**inheritable,** in•her′i•ta•bl, *a.* Capable of being inherited; capable of being transmitted from parent to child.—**inheritance,** in•her′i•tans, *n.* That which is or may be inherited; an estate derived or to be derived from an ancestor to his heir; a possession received by gift or without purchase.—**inheritor,** in•her′i•tėr, *n.* One who inherits or may inherit; an heir.—**inheritress, inheritrix,** in•her′it•res, in•her′it•riks, *n.* An heiress.

inhibit, in•hib′it, *v.t.* [L. *inhibeo, inhibitum*, to restrain—*in*, in, and *habeo*, to have. HABIT.] To restrain by command or interdict; to hinder; to forbid, prohibit, or interdict.—**inhibiter,** in•hib′i•tėr, *n.*—**inhibition,** in•hi•bish′on, *n.* The act of inhibiting; *physiol.* the restraining of an action by stimulating an antagonistic action; *psych.* restraint of spontaneous activity by psychological impediments or social or cultural controls; suppressive interaction between two or more processes.—**inhibitory,** in•hib′i•to•ri, *a.*

inhospitable, in•hos′pi•ta•bl, *a.* [Prefix *in*, not, and *hospitable.*] Not hospitable; wanting in hospitality; hence, affording no subsistence or shelter to strangers (*inhospitable* shores).—**inhospitality, inhospitableness,** in•hos′pi•tal″i•ti, in•hos′pi•ta•bl•nes, *n.* The quality of being inhospitable.—**inhospitably,** in•hos′pi•ta•bli, *adv.* In an inhospitable manner.

inhuman, in•hū′man, *a.* [Prefix *in*, not, and *human*; L. *inhumanus.*] Destitute of the kindness and tenderness that belong to human beings; cruel; barbarous; savage; unfeeling.—**inhumanity,** in•hū•man′i•ti, *n.*—**inhumanly,** in•hū′man•li, *adv.*

inhume, in•hūm′, *v.t.*—*inhumed, inhuming.* [Fr. *inhumer*, L. *inhumo, inhumatum—in*, in, and *humus*, the ground. HUMBLE.] To deposit in the earth; to bury; to inter (a dead body).—**inhumation,** in•hū•mā′shon, *n.* The act of burying; interment.

inimical, in•im′i•kal, *a.* [L. *inimicus—in*, not, and *amicus*, friendly. AMICABLE.] Unfriendly; hostile; adverse; hurtful (*inimical* to commerce).—**inimically,** in•im′i•kal•li, *adv.* In an inimical manner.

inimitable, in•im′i•ta•bl, *a.* [Prefix *in*, not, and *imitable.*] Incapable of being imitated or copied; surpassing imitation.—**inimitability, inimitableness,** in•im′i•ta•bil″i•ti, in•im′i•ta•bl•nes, *n.* The quality of being inimitable.—**inimitably,** in•im′i•ta•bli, *adv.* In an inimitable manner.

inion, in′i•on, *n.* [Gr. *inion*, the nape.] *Anat.* the ridge of the occiput; the nape.

iniquity, in•ik′wi•ti, *n.* [L. *iniquitas*, from *iniquus*, unequal, from *in*, not, and *æquus*, equal. EQUAL.] Want of equity; a deviation from rectitude; unrighteousness; a sin or crime; wickedness; an act of injustice.—**iniquitous,** in•ik′wi•tus, *a.* Characterized by iniquity; unjust; wicked; unrighteous.—**iniquitously,** in•ik′wi•tus•li, *adv.* In an iniquitous manner.

initial, in•ish′al, *a.* [L. *initialis*, from *initium*, beginning, from *ineo, initum*, to go in—*in*, in, and *eo, itum*, to go, present also in *ambition, exit, circuit, issue, transient*, etc. AMBITION.] Placed at the beginning (an *initial* letter); of or pertaining to the beginning; beginning; incipient.—*n.* The first letter of a word: a person's *initials* are the first letters in proper order of the words composing his name.—*v.t.*—*initialed, initialing.* To put one's initials on or to; to sign or mark by initials.—**initially,** in•ish′al•li, *adv.* In an initial manner; by way of beginning.—**initiate,** in•ish′i•āt, *v.t.*—*initiated, initiating.* [L. *initio, initiatum*, from *initium.*] To begin or enter upon; to set afoot; to be the first to practice or bring in; to guide or direct by instruction in rudiments or principles; to let into secrets; to indoctrinate; to introduce into a society or organization; to admit.—*a.* Initiated; introduced to the knowledge of something.—**initiation,** in•ish′i•ā″shon, *n.* The act or process of initiating.—**initiative,** in•ish′i•a•tiv, *a.* Serving to initiate; initiatory.—*n.* An introductory act or step; the first active procedure in any enterprise; power of taking the lead or of originating.—**initiatory,** in•ish′i•a•to•ri, *a.* Pertaining to initiation or introduction; introductory; initiating or serving to initiate.

inject, in•jekt′, *v.t.* [L. *injicio, injectum—in,* into, and *jacio,* to throw, as in *abject, eject, reject,* etc. DEJECT, JET.] To throw in; to cast in or into. —**injection,** in•jek′shon, *n.* The act of injecting; the throwing of a liquid medicine into a cavity of the body by a syringe or pipe; that which is injected.—**injector,** in•jek′tėr, *n.* One who or that which injects; an apparatus for supplying the boilers of steam engines with water.

injudicious, in•jū•dish′us, *a.* [Prefix *in,* not, and *judicious.*] Not judicious; acting without judgment; not according to sound judgment or discretion; unwise; indiscreet; inconsiderate.—**injudiciously,** in•jū•dish′us•li, *adv.* In an injudicious manner.—**injudiciousness,** in•jū•dish′us•nes, *n.*

injunction, in•jungk′shon, *n.* [L. *injunctio, injunctionis,* from *injungo,* to enjoin—*in,* and *jungo,* to join. JOIN.] The act of enjoining or directing; that which is enjoined; a command, order, precept; *law,* a writ requiring a person to do or refrain from doing certain acts.

injure, in′jụr, *v.t.—injured, injuring.* [Fr. *injurier,* L. *injurior, injuriari,* from *injuria,* injury, *injurius,* injurious, from *in,* not, and *jus, juris,* right, justice. JURY.] To do harm or injury to; to impair the excellence, value, strength, etc., of; to hurt; to damage.—**injurer,** in′jụr•ėr, *n.* One who or that which injures.—**injurious,** in•jū′ri•us, *a.* [L. *injurius.*] Tending to injure; hurtful; harmful; prejudicial.—**injuriously,** in•jū′ri•us•li, *adv.* In an injurious or hurtful manner.—**injuriousness,** in•jū′ri•us•nes, *n.* The quality of being injurious.—**injury,** in′jụ•ri, *n.* [L. *injuria,* from *injurius.*] The doing of harm; harm or damage occasioned; a wrong or loss received; mischief; detriment.

injustice, in•jus′tis, *n.* [L. *injustitia—in,* not, and *justitia,* justice.] Want of justice or equity; any violation of another's rights; iniquity; wrong.

ink, ingk, *n.* [O.E. *enke, inke,* O.Fr. *enque,* Fr. *encre* , Pr. *encaut,* from L. *encaustum,* purple ink used by the Roman emperors, from Gr. *enkaustos,* burned in—*en,* in, and *kaiō,* to burn (whence *caustic, encaustic, calm*).] A colored liquid, usually black, used for writing, printing, and the like; a pigment, as China or India *ink* (under INDIAN).—*v.t.* To blacken, color, or daub with ink.—**inkhorn,** ingk′horn, *n.* [From horns being formerly used for holding ink.] A small vessel used to hold ink on a writing table or desk, or for carrying it about the person.—**inkstand,** ingk′stand, *n.* A vessel for holding ink and other writing utensils.—**inkwell,** *n.* An ink bottle fitted into a hole in the top of a writing-desk.—**inky,** ingk′i, *a.* Consisting of ink; containing ink; smeared with ink; resembling ink; black.

inkle, ingk′l, *n.* [Formerly *lingle,* then, by loss of *l, ingle, inkle,* from Fr. *ligneul, lignol,* strong thread used by shoemakers, L. *linum,* flax (whence *linen*).] Formerly, a kind of crewel or worsted; afterward a sort of broad linen tape.

inkling, ingk′ling, *n.* [M. E. *inclen,* to hint.] A hint or whisper; an intimation; inclination; desire.

inlaid, in•lād′, pp. of *inlay.*

inland, in′land, *a.* [That is, *in the land* or interior as opposed to the coast.] Interior; remote from the sea; carried on within a country; domestic, not foreign; confined to a country; drawn and payable in the same country (an *inland* bill of exchange).—*adv.* In or toward the interior of a country.—*n.* The interior part of a country.—**inlander,** in′lan•dėr, *n.* One who lives in the interior of a country.

inlay, in•lā′, *v.t.*—pret. & pp. *inlaid.* [*In* and *lay.*] To lay or insert in; to ornament or diversify by inserting precious stones, metals, fine woods, ivory, etc., in a groundwork of some other material.—*n.* Pieces inlaid and forming a pattern.—**inlayer,** in•lā′ėr, *n.* One who inlays.

inlet, in′let, *n.* [Something *let in.*] A passage or opening by which an enclosed place may be entered; place of ingress; entrance; a creek or narrow recess in a shore.

inlier, in•lī′ėr, *n. Geol.* a portion of one formation lying in and completely surrounded by another formation: opposed to *outlier.*

inly, in′li, *adv.* [Adv. *in,* and suffix *-ly.*] Internally; in the heart; secretly.

inmate, in′māt, *n.* [*In* or *inn,* and *mate.*] A person who lodges or dwells in the same house with another; one of the occupants of hospitals, asylums, prisons, etc.

inmesh, in•mesh′, *v.t.* Same as *Enmesh.* To involve in meshes, as of a net; to entangle or ensnare.

inmost, in′mōst, *a.* [A.Sax. *innemest,* a double superlative of the prep. or adv. *in,* altered erroneously like *foremost.* FOREMOST.] Farthest within; remotest from the surface or external part.

inn, in, *n.* [A.Sax. *inn,* a chamber, a house, an inn; Icel. *inni,* a house; from the prep. *in.*] A house for the lodging and entertainment of travelers; a college of law professors and students.—*Inns of Court,* certain colleges or corporate societies in London; they are now four, the Inner Temple, the Middle Temple, Lincoln's Inn, and Gray's Inn.—**innkeeper,** in′kē•pėr, *n.* The keeper of an inn.

innate, in•nāt′, *a.* [L. *innatus—in,* in, and *natus,* born. NATAL.] Inborn; belonging to the body or mind by nature; natural; derived from the constitution of the mind, as opposed to being derived from experience (*innate* ideas).—**innately,** in•nāt′li, *adv.* In an innate manner.—**innateness,** in•nāt′nes, *n.* The quality of being innate.

inner, in′ėr, *a.* [A.Sax. *innera,* compar. of *in.*] Interior; farther inward than something else; internal; not outward (the *inner* man); not obvious; esoteric.—*n.* The center, or that part of a rifle target next to the bull's-eye; a shot that strikes the center.—**innermost,** in′ėr•mōst, *a.* Farthest inward.

innerve, in•nėrv′, *v.t.* [Prefix *in,* in, and *nerve.*] To give nerve to; to invigorate; to strengthen.—**innervation,** in•nėr•vā′shon, *n.* Act of innerving or strengthening; *physiol.* the properties or functions of the nervous system; a special activity in any part of the nervous system.

inning, in′ing, *n.* [Lit. the state of being *in;* a sort of verbal noun.] *Baseball, Cricket,* etc. A team's turn at bat and to score; opposing teams each having innings in a game of baseball; a turn or opportunity in other ways.

innocent, in′no•sent, *a.* [L. *innocens, innocentis,* harmless—*in,* not, and *nocens,* ppr. of *noceo,* to hurt. NOXIOUS.] Not noxious or hurtful; free from guilt; not having done wrong or violated any law; guiltless; sinless; pure; upright; free from the guilt of a particular crime or evil action.—*n.* One free from guilt or harm; an innocent person; a natural or simpleton.—**innocently,** in′no•sent•li, *adv.* In an innocent manner. —**innocence, innocency,** in′no•sens, in′no•sen•si, *n.* [L. *innocentia.*] The quality of being innocent; harmlessness; freedom from crime, guilt, or sin; freedom from the guilt of a particular crime.

innocuous, in•nok′ū•us, *a.* [L. *innocuus—in,* not, and *nocuus,* hurtful, from *noceo,* to hurt. INNOCENT.] Harmless; producing no ill effect.—**innocuously,** in•nok′ū•us•li, *adv.* In an innocuous manner.—**innocuousness,** in•nok′ū•us•nes, *n.*

innominable, in•nom′i•na•bl, *a.* [L. *innominabilis—in,* not, and *nomen,* a name.] Not to be named.—**innominate,** in•nom′i•nāt, *a.* [L. *innominatus.*] Having no name.—*Innominate bone,* the bony mass forming either side of the pelvis and consisting of three bones that have grown together.

innovate, in′no•vāt, *v.t.*‡—*innovated, innovating.* [L. *innovo, innovatum,* to renew—*in,* intens., and *novus,* new (whence *novel*). NEW.] To change or alter by introducing something new.—*v.i.* To introduce novelties; to make changes in anything established: with *on* or *in* (to *innovate on* established customs). —**innovation,** in•no•vā′shon, *n.* The act of innovating; change made in established laws, customs, rites, and practices by the introduction of something new.—**innovator,** in′no•vā•tėr, *n.* One who innovates.—

innovationist, in•no•vā′shon•ist, *n.* One who favors or introduces innovations.—**innovative,** in′no•vā•tiv, *a.* Introducing or tending to introduce innovations.

innuendo, in•nū•en′dō, *n.* [L. *innuendo* (ablative of gerund), by giving a nod, *innuo,* to give a nod—*in,* and *nuo,* Gr. *neuō,* to nod.] An oblique hint; a remote intimation; an insinuation.

innumerable, in•nū′mėr•a•bl, *a.* [L. *innumerabilis—in,* not, and *numerabilis,* from *numero,* to number.] Incapable of being enumerated or numbered for multitude; hence, extremely numerous; countless.—**innumerably,** in•nū′mėr•a•bli, *adv.* Without number.—**innumerous,**† in•nū′mėr•us, *a.* [L. *innumerus.*] Innumerable. [*Mil.*]—**innumerableness,** in•nū′mėr•a•bl•nes, *n.*

innutrition, in•nu•trish′on, *n.* [Prefix *in,* not, and *nutrition.*] Want of nutrition or nourishment.—**innutritious,** in•nū•trish′us, *a.* Not nutritious; not nourishing.

inobservable, in•ob•zėr′va•bl, *a.* [Prefix *in,* not, and *observable.*] Incapable of being seen, perceived, or observed.—**inobservance,** in•ob•zėr′vans, *n.* Want of observance; disobedience.—**inobservant,** in•ob•zėr′vant, *a.* [Prefix *in,* not, and *observant.*] Not taking notice; not quick or keen in observation; heedless; disobedient.

inoculate, in•ok′ū•lāt, *v.t.—inoculated, inoculating.* [L. *inoculo, inoculatum,* to ingraft an eye or bud of one tree into another—*in,* into, and *oculus,* an eye (whence *ocular).*] To graft by inserting a bud; to bud; *med.* to communicate a disease to by introducing its germs or virus into the tissues; to communicate a disease to a healthy body in order to produce immunity through a mild form of the disease.—*v.i.* To practice inoculation.—**inoculation,** in•ok′ū•lā″shon, *n.* The act or practice of inoculating.—**inoculator,** in•ok′ū•lā•tėr, *n.* One who inoculates.

inoffensive, in•of•fen′siv, *a.* [Prefix *in,* and *offensive.*] Giving no offense or provocation; harmless; doing no injury or mischief.—**inoffensively,** in•of•fen′siv•li, *adv.* In an inoffensive manner.—**inoffensiveness,** in•of•fen′siv•nes, *n.*

inoperative, in•op′e•rā•tiv, *a.* [Prefix *in,* not, and *operative.*] Not operative; producing no effect.

inopportune, in•op′por•tūn, *a.* [Prefix *in,* not, and *opportune;* L. *inopportunus.*] Not opportune; inconvenient; unseasonable.—**inopportunely,** in•op′por•tūn•li, *adv.* In an inopportune manner.

inordinate, in•or′di•nāt, *a.* [L. *inordinatus—in,* not, and *ordinatus,* well-ordered. ORDER.] Excessive; immoderate; not limited by rules prescribed or to usual bounds.—**inordinateness,** in•or′di•nāt•nes, *n.* The state or quality of being inordinate.—**inordinately,** in•or′di•nāt•li, *adv.* In an inordinate manner; excessively.

inorganic, in•or•gan′ik, *a.* [Prefix *in,* not, and *organic.*] Having no organs; devoid of an organized structure, or the structure of a living being; pertaining to or embracing the department of unorganized substances (*inorganic* chemistry).

inosculate, in•os′kū•lāt, *v.i.—inosculated, inosculating.* [L. *in,* and *osculor, osculatus,* to kiss. OSCULATION.] To unite by apposition or contact, as arteries, nerves, geometrical curves, etc.; to anastomose; to run into one another.—*v.t.—inosculated, inosculating.* To cause to unite in this way.—**inosculation,** in•os′kū•lā″shon, *n.*

inosite, ī′no•sit, *n.* [Gr. *is, inos,* strength, nerve.] A saccharine substance found in the human body and also in plants.

inpatient, *n.* A patient who is lodged, fed, and treated in hospital or infirmary.

inphase, in′fāz, *a. Elec.* In the same phase.

input, in′put, *n.* Something put in; power or energy introduced into a machine or circuit to operate it or be converted; the terminal for such power or energy; data supplied to a computer; an ingredient in production.

inquest, in′kwest, *n.* [O.Fr. *enquesis,* from L. *inquiro,* to seek after. INQUIRE.] Act of inquiring; inquiry; search; *law,* a judicial inquiry, especially one before a jury; the jury itself.—*Coroner's inquest,* an inquest held by a coroner on bodies of such as die a violent death.

inquietude, in•kwī′e•tūd, *n.* [L. *inquietudo—in,* not, and *quietudo,* quietude.] Want of quiet; restlessness; uneasiness, either of body or mind.

inquire, in•kwīr′, *v.i.—inquired, inquiring.* [L. *inquiro,* to seek after—*in,* into, and *quæro,* to seek. QUERY, QUEST.] To ask a question or questions; to seek for information by asking questions; to seek for truth by argument or the discussion of questions, or by investigation (to *inquire* of a person, *after, concerning, into,* etc., a thing).—*v.t.* To ask about; to seek by asking (to *inquire* the way of a person).—**inquirer,** in•kwī′rėr, *n.* One who inquires; an investigator.—**inquiringly,** in•kwī′ring•li, *adv.* In an inquiring manner; by way of inquiry.—**inquiry,** in•kwī′ri, *n.* [From *inquire,* like *expiry* from *expire.*] The act of inquiring; a question or interrogation; search for information or knowledge; research; investigation.

inquisition, in•kwi•zish′on, *n.* [L. *inquisitio, inquisitionis,* from *inquiro, inquisitum,* to seek after. INQUIRE.] The act of inquiring; inquiry; investigation; a judicial inquiry; an inquest; [cap.] a former Roman Catholic court or tribunal established for the examination and punishment of heretics; any attempt to suppress nonconformity.—**inquisitional,** in•kwi•zish′on•al, *a.* Relating to inquisition or inquiry; relating to the Inquisition.—**inquisitive,** in•kwiz′i•tiv, *a.* Addicted to inquiry; inclined to seek information; given to pry into anything; troublesomely curious; prying.—**inquisitively,** in•kwiz′i•tiv•li, *adv.* In an inquisitive manner.—**inquisitiveness,** in•kwiz′i•tiv•nes, *n.* The quality of being inquisitive.—**inquisitor,** in•kwiz′i•tėr, *n.* One whose official duty it is to inquire and examine; a member of the Inquisition.—**inquisitorial,** in•kwiz′i•tō″ri•al, *a.* Pertaining to inquisition, especially to the Court of Inquisition; making strict or searching inquiry.—**inquisitorially,** in•kwiz′i•tō″ri•al•li, *adv.* In an inquisitorial manner.

inroad, in′rōd, *n.* [A *road* or rather a *raid* or riding into a country.] The hostile entrance of an enemy into a country; a sudden incursion or invasion; an encroachment; loss or impairment (to make *inroads* on one's health).

insalivation, in•sal′i•vā″shon, *n.* The blending of the saliva with the food in eating.

insalubrious, in•sa•lū′bri•us, *a.* [Prefix *in,* not, and *salubrious.*] Not salubrious; unfavorable to health; unhealthy.—**insalubrity,** in•sa•lū′bri•ti, *n.* The state or quality of being insalubrious; unhealthiness.

insane, in•sān′, *a.* [Prefix *in,* not, and *sane;* L. *insanus.*] Not sane; unsound or deranged in mind or intellect; mad; crazy; delirious; distracted; intended for insane persons.—**insanely,** in•sān′li, *adv.* In an insane manner.—**insanity, insaneness,** in•san′i•ti, in•sān′nes, *n.* The state of being insane or of unsound mind; madness; lunacy.

insanitary, in•san′i•ta•ri, *n.* [Prefix *in,* not, and *sanitary.*] Not sanitary; injurious to health.

insatiable, in•sā′shi•a•bl, *a.* [Prefix *in,* not, and *satiable;* L. *insatiabilis.*] Incapable of being satiated, satisfied, or appeased.—**insatiability, insatiableness,** in•sā′shi•a•bil″i•ti, in•sā′shi•a•bl•nes, *n.* The quality of being insatiable.—**insatiably,** in•sā′shi•a•bli, *adv.* In an insatiable manner.—**insatiate,** in•sā′shi•āt, *a.* [L. *insatiatus.*] Not satisfied; insatiable.

inscribe, in•skrīb′, *v.t.—inscribed, inscribing.* [L. *inscribo, inscriptum—in,* and *scribo,* to write. DESCRIBE.] To write down or engrave; to mark down (to *inscribe* a motto); to mark with characters or words (to *inscribe* a monument); to assign, address, or dedicate (to *inscribe* a poem to a person); to imprint deeply; to impress; *geom.* to draw or delineate within another figure so that the boundaries of the two are in contact at certain points.—**inscriber,** in•skrī′bėr, *n.* One who inscribes.—**inscription,** in•skrip′shon, *n.* [L. *inscriptio, inscriptionis.*] The act of inscribing; any words or writing engraved on stone, metal, or other hard substance for public inspection; an address of a book, poem, etc., to a person as a mark of respect, less formal than a dedication; *numis.* the words placed in the middle of the reverse side of some coins and medals.—**inscriptive,** in•skrip′tiv, *a.*

Of the character of an inscription.
inscrutable, in•skrö′ta•bl, *a.* [Fr. *inscrutable,* L. *inscrutabilis—in,* not, and *scrutor,* to search. SCRUTINY.] Incapable of being searched into and understood; incapable of being penetrated or understood by human reason; not to be satisfactorily accounted for or explained. **inscrutably,** in•skrö′ta•bli, *adv.* In an inscrutable manner.—**inscrutability, inscrutableness,** in•skrö′ta•bil″i•ti, in•skrö′ta•bl•nes, *n.*
insculp,† in•skulp′, *v.t.* [L. *insculpo—in,* and *sculpo,* to engrave.] To engrave; to carve.
insect, in′sekt, *n.* [L. *insectum,* something cut in (from their shape), from *inseco, insectum,* to cut into—*in,* into, and *seco,* to cut. DISSECT.] One of a class of small animals that in their mature state have the three divisions of the body—the head, thorax, and abdomen—always distinct from one another, and usually have three pairs of legs and two pairs of wings, as the numerous creatures known as flies, beetles, bees, etc.; a puny contemptible person.—*a.* Pertaining to insects; resembling an insect.—**insecticide,** in•sek′ti•sīd, *n.* That which kills insects.—**insectivore,** in•sek′ti•vōr, *n.* A member of the Insectivora, nocturnal terrestrial mammals which feed on insects; an insect-eating animal or plant.—**insectivorous,** in•sek•tiv′ō•rus, *a.* Feeding or subsisting on insects.
insecure, in•si•kūr′, *a.* [Prefix *in.* not, and *secure.*] Not secure; not confident of safety; not sufficiently strong or guarded; unsafe.—**insecurity,** in•si•kū′ri•ti, *n.* The state of being insecure; want of security.
inseminate, in•sem′i•nāt, *v.t.—inseminated, inseminating.* [L. *inseminatus,* pp. of *inseminare,* to sow.] To implant seed; to inject (the female genital tract) with sperm; to imbed ideas, etc.—**insemination,** in•sem′i•nā″shon, *n.—Artificial insemination,* injection of semen into the female by artificial means, used in animal breeding.
insensate, in•sen′sāt, *a.* [L.L. *insensatus*—L. *in,* not, and *sensus,* sensation, sense. SENSE.] Destitute of sense or sensation; wanting sensibility; stupid.—**insensateness,** in•sen′sāt•nes, *n.* The state of being insensate.
insensible, in•sen′si•bl, *a.* [L. *insensibilis*—prefix *in,* not, and *sensibilis,* sensible.] Not apprehended by the senses; imperceptible; incapable of being felt or perceived; so slow or gradual that the stages are not noted; destitute of the power of feeling or perceiving; numb or dead to pain; not susceptible of emotion or passion; void of feeling; unfeeling; callous; apathetic; indifferent.—**insensibly,** in•sen′si•bli, *adv.* In an insensible manner; imperceptibly; by slow degrees.—**insensibility,** in•sen′si•bil″i•ti, *n.* The condition or quality of being insensible; dullness; apathy; numbness; torpor.—**insensitive,** in•sen′si•tiv, *a.* Not sensitive; having little sensibility.—**insentient,** in•sen′shi•ent, *a.* Not sentient; inanimate.
inseparable, in•sep′a•ra•bl, *a.* [Prefix *in,* not, and *separable;* L. *inseparabilis.*] Incapable of being separated or disjoined; not to be parted; always together.—**inseparably,** in•sep′a•ra•bli, *adv.* In an inseparable manner.—**inseparability,** in•sep′a•ra•bil″i•ti, *n.*
insert, in•sėrt′, *v.t.* [L. *insero, insertum—in,* and *sero,* to put (as in *assert, exert, concert*). SERIES.] To set in or among; to put or thrust in; to introduce.—**insertion,** in•sėr′shon, *n.* [L. *insertio.*] The act of inserting; something inserted; *bot.* the place or mode of attachment of an organ to its support; of a muscle, the end attached to a relatively movable part.
Insessores, in•ses•sō′rēz, *n. pl.* [Pl. of L. *insessor,* one that sits—*in,* and *sedeo,* to sit.] In old classifications an order of perchers or passerine birds, comprehending all those which live habitually among trees, with the exception of the birds of prey and climbing birds.—**insessorial,** in•ses•sō′ri•al, *a.* Belonging to the Insessores or perching birds.
inset, in•set′, *v.t.* To set in; to infix or implant.—*n.* (in′set). That which is set in; insertion.
insheathe, in•shēTH′, *v.t.* To hide or cover in a sheath.
inshore, in′shōr, *a.* or *adv.* Near the shore.
inside, in′sīd, *a.* [Lit., within the sides.] Being within; interior; internal.—*n.* That which is within; specifically, the entrails or bowels; an inside passenger in a vehicle.—*prep.* In the interior of; within.
insidious, in•sid′i•us, *a.* [L. *insidiosus,* from *insidiæ,* an ambush, from *insideo,* to sit upon—*in,* in, upon, and *sedeo,* to sit. SIT.] Characterized by treachery or stealthy and guileful acts; treacherous; guileful; working evil secretly (an *insidious* person, plot, disease).—**insidiously,** in•sid′i•us•li, *adv.* In an insidious manner.—**insidiousness,** in•sid′i•us•nes, *n.*
insight, in′sīt, *n.* [Prefix *in,* and *sight.*] Deep inspection or view; thorough knowledge; power of observation; discernment; penetration.
insignia, in•sig′ni•a, *n. pl.* [L., pl. of *insigne,* a mark, neut. of *insignis,* remarkable—*in,* intens., and *signum,* a mark. SIGN.] Badges or distinguishing marks of office or honor; any characteristic marks or signs.
insignificant, in•sig•nif′i•kant, *a.* [Prefix *in,* not, and *significant.*] Void of signification; having no weight or effect; unimportant; trivial or trifling; without weight of character; mean; contemptible.—**insignificantly,** in•sig•nif′i•kant•li, *adv.* In an insignificant manner. —**insignificance, insignificancy,** in•sig•nif′i•kans, in•sig•nif′i•kan•si, *n.* The condition or quality of being insignificant.
insincere, in•sin•sēr′, *a.* [Prefix *in,* not, and *sincere;* L. *insincerus.*] Not sincere; dissembling; hypocritical; false; deceitful; of persons, statements, etc.—**insincerely,** in•sin•sēr′li, *adv.* In an insincere manner.—**insincerity,** in•sin•ser′i•ti, *n.* The quality of being insincere.
insinuate, in•sin′ū•āt, *v.t.—insinuated, insinuating.* [L. *insinuo, insinuatum—in,* and *sinuo,* to wind, from *sinus,* a bending, curve, bosom.] To introduce gently, or as by a winding or narrow passage; hence, *refl.* to push or work gradually into favor; to introduce one's self by slow or artful means; to infuse gently or artfully; to instill (to *insinuate* a doubt); to hint or suggest. —*v.i.* To creep or wind; to act by insinuation; to make an insinuation; to wheedle.—**insinuating,** in•sin′ū•āt•ing, *p.* and *a.* Given to or characterized by insinuation; wheedling; insensibly winning favor and confidence.—**insinuatingly,** in•sin′ū•āt•ing•li, *adv.* In an insinuating manner.—**insinuation,** in•sin′ū•ā″shon, *n.* [L. *insinuatio, insinuationis.*] The act of insinuating; a wheedling manner; a suggestion, hint, or innuendo.—**insinuative,** in•sin′ū•ā•tiv, *a.* Insinuating; stealing on the affections.—**insinuator,** in•sin′ū•ā•tėr, *n.* One who insinuates.
insipid, in•sip′id, *a.* [L. *insipidus—in,* not, and *sapidus,* savory, from *sapio,* to taste. SAVOR.] Tasteless; destitute of taste; vapid; wanting interest, spirit, life, or animation; dull, heavy, or uninteresting.—**insipidity, insipidness,** in•si•pid′i•ti, in•sip′id•nes, *n.* The quality of being insipid.—**insipidly,** in•sip′id•li, *adv.* In an insipid manner.
insist, in•sist′, *v.i.* [L. *insisto—in,* and *sisto,* to stand, as in *consist, desist, persist, resist,* etc. STATE.] To rest, dwell, or dilate upon as a matter of special moment; to be persistent, urgent, peremptory, or pressing: usually with *on* or *upon.*—**insistence,** in•sis′tens, *n.* Act of insisting; persistency; urgency.
insociable, in•sō′shi•a•bl, *a.* [Prefix *in,* not, and *sociable.*] Not sociable; unsociable; taciturn.—**insociably,** in•sō′shi•a•bli, *adv.* In an unsociable manner; unsociably.—**insociability,** in•sō′shi•a•bil″i•ti, *a.* The quality of being insociable.
insolate, in′so•lāt, *v.t.—insolated, insolating.* [L. *insolo, insolatum—in,* and *sol,* the sun (whence *solar*).] To dry or prepare in the sun's rays; to expose to the heat of the sun.—**insolation,** in•so•lā′shon, *n.* [L. *insolatio, insolationis.*] The act of exposing, or condition of being exposed, to the rays of the sun; sunstroke.
insolent, in′so•lent, *a.* [L. *insolens, insolentis,* contrary to custom, immoderate, haughty, insolent—*in,* not, and *solens,* ppr. of *soleo,* to be wont.] Showing haughty disregard of others; using rude and haughty or defiant language; overbearing; saucy; proceeding from insolence.—**insolently,** in′so•lent•li, *adv.* In an insolent manner.—**insolence,** in′so•lens, *n.* [L. *insolentia,* from *insolens.*] Haugh-

tiness manifested in contemptuous and overbearing treatment of others; insolent language.

insoluble, in•sol'ū•bl, *a.* [Prefix *in*, not, and *soluble.*] Incapable of being dissolved, particularly by a liquid; not to be solved or explained.—**insolubility, insolubleness,** in•sol'ū•bil"i•ti, in•sol'ū•bl•nes, *n.* The quality of being insoluble.

insolvable, in•sol'va•bl, *a.* [Prefix *in*, not, and *solvable.*] Not solvable; not to be solved or explained; not admitting solution.

insolvent, in•sol'vent, *a.* [Prefix *in*, not, and *solvent.*] Not solvent; not having money, goods, or estate sufficient to pay all debts.—*n.* A debtor unable to pay his debts.—**insolvency,** in•sol'ven•si, *n.* The condition of being insolvent; inability of a person to pay all his debts.

insomnious, in•som'ni•us, *a.* [L. *insomniosus*, from *insomnia*, sleeplessness—*in*, not, and *somnus*, sleep.] Restless in sleep, or being without sleep.—**insomnia,** in•som'ni•a, *n.* [L.] Want of sleep; morbid or unnatural sleeplessness.

insomuch, in•sō•much', *adv.* [*In*, *so*, and *much.*] To such a degree; in such wise; so: followed by *that*, sometimes *as*.

insouciant, an•sö•syän', *a.* [Fr.—*in*, not, and *soucier*, to care, *souci*, care, from L. *sollicitus*, uneasy, solicitous.] Careless; heedless; regardless; unconcerned.—**insouciance,** an•sö•syäns', *n.* The quality of being insouciant.

inspan, in•span', *v.t.* [D. *inspannen*—*in*, in, and *spannen*, to yoke.] To yoke, as draft oxen: correlative of *outspan*. [South African.]

inspect, in•spekt', *v.t.* [L. *inspicio*, *inspectum*—*in*, and *specio*, to view. SPECIES.] To view or examine for the purpose of ascertaining the quality or condition, discovering errors, etc.; to examine officially.—**inspection,** in•spek'shon, *n.* [L. *inspectio.*] The act of inspecting; official view or examination.—**inspector,** in•spek'tėr, *n.* One who inspects or oversees. —**inspectorate,** in•spek'tėr•at, *n.* A body of inspectors or overseers; inspectorship.

inspire, in•spīr', *v.i.*—*inspired*, *inspiring*. [L. *inspiro*—*in*, and *spiro*, to breathe, whence *spirit*, *expire*, *respire.*] To draw in breath; to inhale air into the lungs.—*v.t.* To breathe in; to draw into the lungs; to infuse by or as if by breathing; to instill; to communicate divine instructions to the mind of; to animate by supernatural infusion; to rouse or animate in general.—**inspirer,** in•spī'rėr, *n.* One who inspires.—**inspirable,** in•spī'ra•bl, *a.* Capable of being inspired; inhalable. —**inspiration,** in•spi•rā'shon, *n.* [L. *inspiratio.*] The act of inspiring; the divine influence by which the sacred writers were instructed; influence emanating from any object, giving rise to new and elevated thoughts or emotions; the state of being inspired; something conveyed to the mind when under extraordinary influence.—*Verbal*, *plenary inspiration*, the doctrine maintaining that the very words were inspired, as opposed to general inspiration by the Spirit; textual inerrancy.—**inspirational,** in•spi•rā'shon•al, *a.* Pertaining to inspiration.—**inspiratory,** in•spīr'a•to•ri, *a.* Pertaining to or assisting in inspiration (the *inspiratory* muscles).

inspirit, in•spir'it, *v.i.* [Prefix *in*, and *spirit.*] To infuse or excite spirit in; to enliven, animate, encourage, invigorate.

inspissate, in•spis'āt, *v.t.*—*inspissated*, *inspissating*. [L. *inspisso*, *inspissatum*—*in*, intens., and *spissus*, thick.] To thicken by boiling so as to evaporate the water; to bring to greater thickness by evaporation.—*a.* Thick; inspissated.—**inspissation,** in•spis•ā'shon, *n.* The act or operation of inspissating.

instable, in•stā'bl, *a.* [L. *instabilis*—*in*, not, and *stabilis*, stable.] Not stable; unstable.—**instability,** in•sta•bil'i•ti, *n.* Want of stability; inconstancy; want of firmness in construction.

install, in•stal', *v.t.* [Fr. *installer*—*in*, in, and O.H.G. *stal*, a place, E. *stall*. STALL.] To place in an office or post; to invest formally with a charge, office, or rank; to set up or establish for use (as a heating system).—**installation,** in•sta•lā'shon, *n.* Act of installing; something installed. —**installment,** in•stal'ment, *n.* Installation; a part of a whole (especially a novel) produced at stated periods; one part of a sum to be paid at stated intervals.

instance, in'stans, *n.* [L. *instantia*, a standing near, importunity, urgency —*in*, on, and *sto*, to stand. STATE.] The act or state of being instant or urgent; urgency; a case occurring; a case offered as an exemplification or precedent; an example; an occurrence.—*v.t.*—*instanced*, *instancing*. To mention as an instance, example, or case in point.—**instant,** in'stant, *a.* [E. *instans*, *instantis.*] Pressing, urgent, importunate, or earnest (N.T.); immediate; without intervening time (send him to *instant* execution); quick; making no delay; present or current: usually abbreviated to *inst.*, as 10th *inst.*, that is, 10th day of the present month.—*n.* A point in duration; a moment; a part of duration that occupies the time of a single thought.—**instantaneousness,** in•stan•tā'ni•us•nes, *n.* The quality of being instantaneous.—**instantaneous,** in•stan•tā'ni•us, *a.* [Made on the model of *contemporaneous.*] Done in an instant; occurring without any perceptible lapse of time.—**instantaneously,** in•stan•tā'ni•us•li, *adv.* In an instant; in a moment.—**instanter,** in•stan'tėr, *adv.* [L., from *instans.*] Immediately; forthwith; on the moment.—**instantly,** in'stant•li, *adv.* With urgency; earnestly; immediately; forthwith; at once.

instate, in•stāt', *v.t.*—*instated*, *instating*. [Prefix *in*, and *state.*] To establish, as in a rank or condition; to install.

instead, in•sted', *adv.* [From *in*, and *stead*, place; *stead* retaining its character of a noun, and being followed by *of.*] In the place or room. [When *instead* is used without *of* following, there is an ellipsis of a word or words that would otherwise follow the *of.*]

instep, in'step, *n.* [Formerly *instop*, *instup*, perhaps from *in* and *stoop*, lit. the bend in.] The forepart of the upper side of the human foot, near its junction with the leg; part of the hind leg of a horse from the ham to the pastern joint.

instigate, in'sti•gāt, *v.t.*—*instigated*, *instigating*. [L. *instigo*, *instigatum*—*in*, on, and root *stig*, to prick. INSTINCT, STIGMA.] To incite; to set on; to provoke; to urge; used chiefly or wholly in a bad sense.—**instigation,** in•sti•gā'shon, *n.* [L. *instigatio.*] act of instigating; incitement, as to evil or wickedness.—**instigator,** in'sti•gā•tėr, *n.* One who instigates.

instill, instil, in•stil', *v.t.*—*instilled*, *instilling*. [L. *instillo*—*in*, and *stillo*, to drop. DISTILL.] To pour in by drops; hence, to infuse slowly or by degrees into the mind; to cause to be imbibed; to insinuate imperceptibly.—**instillation,** in•stil•ā'shon, *n.* The act of instilling.—**instillatory,** in•stil'a•to•ri, *a.* Relating to instillation.—**instiller,** in•stil'ėr, *n.* One who instills.—**instillment,** in•stil'ment, *n.* The act of instilling.

instinct, in'stingkt, *n.* [L. *instinctus*, instigation, impulse, from *instinguo*, *instinctum*, to impel—*in*, on, and root meaning to prick, as in *stimulus*, *sting.*] An impulse to a particular kind of action which the being needs to perform as an individual, but which it could not possibly learn to perform before it needs to act; as a general term it includes all original impulses and that apparent knowledge and skill which animals have without experience; hence, natural feeling or sense of what is correct or effective in artistic matters or the like.—*a.* (in-stingkt'). Animated or stimulated from within; inspired; fully suffused and breathing out (a portrait *instinct* with life).—**instinctive,** in•stingk'tiv, *a.* Prompted by or proceeding from instinct; determined by natural impulse or propensity; spontaneous.—**instinctively,** in•stingk'tiv•li, *adv.* In an instinctive manner.

institute, in'sti•tūt, *v.t.*—*instituted*, *instituting*. [L. *instituo*, *institutum*—*in*, and *statuo*, to set, place, from *sto*, *statum*, to stand. STATE.] To set up or establish; to ordain; to originate; to found; to set in operation; to begin (an investigation, etc.). —*n.* That which is instituted or formally established; an established law, precept, or principle; a society established according to certain laws or regulations for the furtherance of some particular object (a philosophic *institute*, a literary *institute*, a mechanics *institute*); *pl.* a book of elements or principles, particularly a work containing the principles of a system of jurisprudence.—**institution,** in•sti•tū'shon, *n.* [L. *institutio.*] The act of instituting; something instituted or established; a permanent rule of conduct or of government; something forming a prominent or established feature in social or national life; a society established or body organized for promoting any object, public or social.—**institutional,** in•sti•tū'shon•al, *a.* Relating to institutions; instituted by authority; relating to elementary knowledge.—**institutionary,** in•sti•tū'shon•e•ri, *a.* Relating to an institution or to institutions.—**institutive,** in'sti•tū•tiv, *a.* Tending or intended to institute or establish.—**institutor,** in'sti•tū•tėr, *n.* [L.] One who institutes.

instruct, in•strukt', *v.t.* [L. *instruo, instructum—in,* and *struo,* to join together, to pile up. STRUCTURE.] To teach; to educate; to impart knowledge or information to; to enlighten; to direct or command; to furnish with orders; to order or enjoin.—**instruction,** in•struk'shon, *n.* [L. *instructio.*] The act of instructing; that which is communicated for instructing; that with which one is instructed; information; order, mandate, or direction.—**instructional,** in•struk'shon•al, *a.* Relating to instruction; educational.—**instructive,** in•struk'tiv, *a.* Conveying knowledge; serving to instruct or inform.—**instructively,** in•struk'tiv•li, *adv.* In an instructive manner.—**instructiveness,** in•struk'tiv•nes, *n.*—**instructor,** in•struk'tėr, *n.* [L.] One who instructs; a teacher.

instrument, in'stru̧•ment, *n.* [L. *instrumentum,* from *instruo,* to prepare. INSTRUCT.] That by which work is performed or anything is effected; a tool; a utensil; an implement; one who or that which is subservient to the execution of a plan or purpose; means used or contributing to an effect; any contrivance from which music is produced, as an organ, harp, violin, flute, etc.; *law,* a writing instructing one in regard to something that has been agreed upon.—**instrumental,** in•stru̧•men'tal, *a.* Conducive as an instrument or means to some end; pertaining to instruments, especially musical instruments.—**instrumentalist,** in•stru̧•men'tal•ist, *n.* One who plays upon a musical instrument.—**instrumentality,** in'stru̧•men•tal"i•ti, *n.* The condition of being instrumental; subordinate or auxiliary agency; agency as means to an end.—**instrumentally,** in•stru̧•men'tal•li, *adv.* By way of an instrument; as means to an end; with instruments of music.—**instrumentation,** in'stru̧•men•tā"shon, *n.* The art of arranging music for a number of instruments; the music for a number of instruments; execution of music on an instrument.

insubordinate, in•sub•or'di•nāt, *a.* [Prefix *in,* not, and *subordinate.*] Not submitting to authority; mutinous; riotous.—*n.* One who is unruly.—**insubordination,** in•sub•or'di•nā"shon, *n.* The quality of being insubordinate.

insubstantial, in•sub•stan'shal, *a.* [Prefix *in,* not, and *substantial.*] Unsubstantial.

insufferable, in•suf'fėr•a•bl, *a.* [Prefix *in,* not, and *sufferable.*] Not to be suffered, borne, or endured; intolerable; unendurable.—**insufferably,** in•suf'fėr•a•bli, *adv.*

insufficient, in•suf•fish'ent, *a.* [Prefix *in,* not, and *sufficient.*] Not sufficient; inadequate to any need, use, or purpose.—**insufficiency,** in•suf•fish'en•si, *n.* The condition or quality of being insufficient.—**insufficiently,** in•suf•fish'ent•li, *adv.* In an insufficient manner.

insular, in'sū•lėr, *a.* [L. *insularis,* from *insula,* an island.] Of or pertaining to an island or the opinions or views of islanders; hence, narrow-minded (*insular* prejudices); contracted.—**insularity,** in•sū•lar'i•ti, *n.* The state of being insular.—**insulate,** in'sū•lāt, *v.t.—insulated, insulating.* To make an island of; to isolate; to separate, as an electrified or heated body, from other bodies by inserting nonconductors; to free from combination with other substances, as a chemical substance.—**insulation,** in•sū•lā'shon, *n.* The act of insulating, or state of being insulated; materials for insulating.—**insulator,** in'sū•lā•tėr, *n.* One who or that which insulates; *elec.* a nonconducting piece, as of glass, used to insulate wires, etc.

insulin, in'sū•lin, *n.* [L. *insula,* island, and *in.*] A secretion of the islands of Langerhans in the pancreas which controls the use of sugar in the body; a trademark for a similar hormone extracted from the pancreas of some animals.

insult, in'sult, *n.* [Fr. *insulte;* L. *insultus,* from *insilio, insultum,* to leap on—*in,* and *salio,* to leap.] Any gross affront offered to another, either by words or actions; act or speech of insolence or contempt.—*v.t.* (in-sult'). To treat with insult, gross abuse, insolence, or contempt.—*v.i.* To behave with insolent triumph.—**insulter,** in•sult'ėr, *n.* One who insults.—**insulting,** in•sult'ing, *a.* Containing or conveying insult.—**insultingly,** in•sult'ing•li, *adv.* In an insulting manner; so as to insult.

insuperable, in•sū'pėr•a•bl, *a.* [L. *insuperabilis—in,* not, and *supero,* to overcome. SUPERIOR.] Incapable of being overcome or surmounted; insurmountable (difficulties, objections, obstacles, etc.).—**insuperability,** in•sū'pėr•a•bil"i•ti, *n.* The quality of being insuperable.—**insuperably,** in•sū'pėr•a•bli, *adv.* In an insuperable manner.

insupportable, in•sup•pōr'ta•bl, *a.* [Prefix *in,* not, and *supportable.*] Not to be supported or borne; insufferable; intolerable.—**insupportably,** in•sup•pōr'ta•bli, *adv.*

insuppressible, in•sup•pres'i•bl, *a.* [Prefix *in,* not, and *suppressible.*] Incapable of being suppressed or concealed.—**insuppressibly,** in•sup•pres'i•bli, *adv.* So as not to be suppressed.

insure, in•shör', *v.t.—insured, insuring.* [Prefix *in,* intens., and *sure.*] To make sure; to ensure (which is the word now commonly used in this general sense); to contract for the payment of a certain sum in the event of loss or damage happening to, or at the death or termination of (to *insure* a house against fire, a ship against damage, to *insure* one's life); to make a subject of insurance.—**insurer,** in•shö'rer, *n.* One who insures.—**insurable,** in•shö'ra•bl, *a.* Capable of being insured.—**insurance,** in•shö'rans, *n.* The act of insuring; a contract by which a person or company, in consideration of a sum of money or percentage (technically called a *premium*), becomes bound to indemnify the insured or his representatives against loss by certain risks; the premium paid for insuring property or life.—*Marine insurance* is the term used for the insurance on ships, goods, etc., at sea.—*Fire insurance* is for the insuring of property on shore from fire.—*Life insurance* is for securing the payment of a certain sum at the death of the individual insured, or when he reaches a given age, or of an annuity.—*Social insurance,* a type of insurance which provides benefits for unemployment, sickness, old age, etc., obtained from funds into which usually the worker, employer, and government contribute.—*Insurance policy,* the document by which the insurance is ratified.

insurgent, in•sėr'jent, *a.* [L. *insurgens, insurgentis,* ppr. of *insurgo,* to rise against—*in,* on, and *surgo,* to rise, whence *surge, source,* etc.] Rising in opposition to lawful civil or political authority; rebellious.—*n.* A person who rises in opposition to civil or political authority. ∴ An *insurgent* differs from a *rebel* in holding a less pronounced position of antagonism, and may or may not develop into a rebel. INSURRECTION.—**insurgency,** in•sėr'jen•si, *n.* The condition of being insurgent.

insurmountable, in•sėr•moun'ta•bl, *a.* [Prefix *in,* not, and *surmountable.*] Incapable of being surmounted, passed over, or overcome.—**insurmountably,** in•sėr•moun'ta•bli, *adv.*

insurrection, in•sėr•rek'shon, *n.* [L. *insurrectio, insurrectionis,* from *insurgo, insurrectum.* INSURGENT.] The open and active opposition of a number of persons to the civil or political authorities of a city or country, in defiance of law and order; a revolt by a number of persons against constituted authorities. ∴ An *insurrection* is less serious than a *rebellion,* for the latter attempts to overthrow the government, to establish a different one, or to place the country under another jurisdiction; a *mutiny* is a movement of revolt against minor institutions, or against the authorities in the army or navy;

a *revolt* is a less strong form of a rebellion.—**insurrectional, insurrectionary,** in•sėr•rek′shon•al, in•-sėr•rek′shon•a•ri, *a.* Pertaining to insurrection.—**insurrectionist,** in•sėr•-rek′shon•ist, *n.* One who favors insurrection.

insusceptible, in•sus•sep′ti•bl, *a.* [Prefix *in,* not, and *susceptible.*] Not susceptible; not capable of being affected or impressed (a heart *insusceptible of* pity).—**insusceptibility,** in•sus•sep′ti•bil″i•ti, *n.* The quality of being insusceptible.

intact, in•takt′, *a.* [L. *intactus*—prefix *in,* not, and *tactus,* touched, pp. of *tango,* to touch; whence also *tangent, tact,* etc.] Untouched by anything that harms or defiles; uninjured; unimpaired; left complete, whole, or unharmed.

intaglio, in•tal′yō, *n.* [It., from *intagliare,* to carve—*in,* and *tagliare,* to cut, Fr. *tailler* (whence *tailor*).] Any figure engraved or cut into a substance so as to form a hollow; a gem with a figure or design that is sunk below the surface; the reverse of *cameo,* which has the figure in relief.

intake, in′tāk, *n.* A point where a water supply is diverted from a main stream; amount taken in (hourly *intake*).

intangible, in•tan′ji•bl, *a.* [Prefix *in,* not, and *tangible.*] Not tangible; incapable of being touched; not perceptible to the touch.—**intangibleness, intangibility,** in•tan′ij•bl•-nes, in•tan′ji•bil″i•ti, *n.*—**intangibly,** in•tan′ji•bli, *adv.*

integer, in′te•jėr, *n.* [L. *integer,* whole, entire—*in,* not, and *tag,* root of *tango,* to touch. ENTIRE, TANGENT.] *Arith.* a whole number, in contradistinction to a fraction.—**integral,** in′te•gral, *a.* Whole; entire; complete; belonging to, or forming a necessary part of, a whole; *math.* pertaining to a whole number or undivided quantity; not fractional; pertaining to integration.—*n.* A whole; an entire thing.—**integrally,** in′ti•gral•li, *adv.*—**integrant,** in′ti•-grant, *a.*

integrate, in′ti•grāt, *v.t.*—*integrated, integrating.* [L. *integratus,* pp. of *integrare,* to make whole.] To make entire; to form into one whole; to perfect; to give the sum or total of.—**integration,** in•ti•grā′shon, *n.* The act of integrating; incorporation of diverse groups or individuals into a well-ordered community or society whose behavior is based on similar standards; *math.* the determination of a function from its differential or its differential coefficient.—**integrationist,** in•ti•grā′shon•ist, *n.*—**integrator,** in′ti•grā•tėr, *n.*

integrity, in•teg′ri•ti, *n.* [F. *integrité,* from L. *integritas,* from *integer,* entire.] Behavior in accordance with a strict code of values, moral, artistic, etc.; honesty; entirety; the quality of wholeness; something without mark or stain; soundness.

integument, in•teg′ū•ment, *n.* [L. *integumentum, intego,* to cover—*in,* intens., and *tego,* to cover (same root as E. *thatch*).] *Anat.* the skin, membrane, or shell which covers any part; *bot.* the cellular skin of seed, leaf, or stem.—**integumentary,** in•-teg′ū•men″te•ri, *a.* Belonging to or composed of integument.

intellect, in′tel•lekt, *n.* [L. *intellectus,* from *intelligo,* to understand—*inter,* between, and *lego,* to choose or pick, to read; seen also in *collect, elect, select, legend, lesson, lecture,* etc.] That faculty of the human mind which receives or comprehends ideas, as distinguished from the power to feel and to will; the understanding faculty; also, the capacity for higher forms of knowledge.—**intellection,** in•tel•lek′shon, *n.* The act of understanding; simple apprehension.—**intellective,** in•tel•lek′tiv, *a.* Pertaining to the intellect; perceivable by the understanding only, not by the senses.—**intellectively,** in•tel•-lek′tiv•li, *adv.* In an intellective manner.—**intellectual,** in•tel•lek′chū•al, *a.* Relating to the intellect or understanding; appealing to or perceived by the intellect; existing in the understanding; ideal; having or characterized by intellect.—**intellectualism,** in•tel•lek′chū•al•izm, *n.* Intellectuality; the doctrine that knowledge is derived from pure reason.—**intellectualist,** in•tel•lek′chū•al•ist, *n.* One who overrates intellectualism.—**intellectuality,** in•tel•lek′chū•al″li•ti, *n.* The state of being intellectual; intellectual power.—**intellectualize,** in•tel•lek′chū•al•īz, *v.t.* To endow with intellect; to give an intellectual or ideal character to.—**intellectually,** in•tel•lek′chū•al•li, *adv.* In an intellectual manner.—**intelligence,** in•-tel′i•jens, *n.* [L. *intelligentia.*] Intellectual power; knowledge imparted or acquired; general information; information communicated; news or notice; an intelligent or spiritual being.—*Intelligence quotient, Abbr. I. Q.,* mental rating found by test. (Divide age into mental age shown.) *Intelligence test,* a psychological test used to show comparative mental capacity.—**intelligencer,** in•tel′i•jen•-sėr, *n.* One who conveys intelligence; a messenger or spy.—**intelligent,** in•-tel′i•jent, *a.* [L. *intelligens, intelligentis,* ppr. of *intelligo.*] Endowed with the faculty of understanding or reason; endowed with a good intellect; having superior intellectual capacities; well informed.—**intelligently,** in•tel′i•jent•li, *adv.* In an intelligent manner. — **intelligibility,** in•tel′i•ji•bil″i•ti, *n.* The quality or state of being intelligible.—**intelligible,** in•tel′i•ji•bl, *a.* [L. *intelligibilis.*] Capable of being understood or comprehended; comprehensible; clear.—**intelligibly,** in•tel′i•gi•bli, *adv.*

intelligentsia, in•tel•li•jen′si•a, *n. pl.* Intellectuals; the broadly educated.

intemperance, in•tem′pėr•ans, *n.* [Prefix *in,* not, and *temperance;* L. *intemperantia,* want of moderation. TEMPER.] Want of moderation or due restraint; excess of any kind; specifically, habitual indulgence in the use of alcoholic liquors, especially with intoxication.—**intemperate,** in•-tem′pėr•it, *a.* [L. *intemperatus,* immoderate.] Not exercising due moderation or restraint; addicted to an excessive or habitual use of alcoholic liquors; excessive, immoderate, or inordinate (*intemperate* language).—*n.* One who is not temperate.—**intemperately,** in•-tem′pėr•it•-li, *adv.* In an intemperate manner.—**intemperateness,** in•tem′pėr•-it•nes, *n.* State of being intemperate.

intend, in•tend′, *v.t.* [L. *intendo,* to stretch forth, to intend—*in,* and *tendo,* to stretch (as in *attend, contend,* etc.). TEND.] To fix the mind upon, as the object to be effected or attained; to mean; to design; to purpose.—**intendancy,** in•ten′dan•si, *n.* The office, employment, or district committed to the charge of an intendant.—**intendant,** in•ten′dant, *n.* [Fr., from L. *intendo.*] One who has the charge or management of some public business; a superintendent.—**intended,** in•ten′ded, *p.* and *a.* Betrothed; engaged.—*n.* A person engaged to be married to another; an affianced lover.

intense, in•tens′, *a.* [L. *intensus,* stretched, tight, pp. of *intendo,* to stretch. INTEND.] Closely strained; kept on the stretch (study, thought, etc.); extreme in degree; vehement; violent; severe (pain, cold, etc.).—**intensely,** in•tens′li, *adv.* In an intense manner.—**intenseness,** in•tens′nes, *n.* The state of being intense.—**intensification,†** in•ten′si•fi•kā″shon, *n.* The act of intensifying or making more intense.—**intensifier,** in•ten′-si•fī•ėr, *n.* One who or that which intensifies.—**intensify,** in•ten′si•fī, *v.t.*—*intensified, intensifying.* To render intense or more intense.—*v.i.* To become intense or more intense.—**intension,** in•ten′shon, *n.* [L. *intensio, intensionis.*] Act of straining or intensifying; the state of being strained: opposed to *remission* or *relaxation.*—**intensity,** in•ten′si•ti, *n.* The state of being intense; relative degree, vigor, or activity; keenness (of feeling, etc.); *phys.,* the amount of energy with which a force operates or a cause acts.—*Intensity of field,* the force experienced by a unit pole when placed in a field of magnetic force.—*Intensity of magnetization,* in a uniformly magnetized mass, is the quotient of the moment (q.v.) of the magnet by its volume.—*Intensity of pressure,* where the pressure is uniform over an area, is the total pressure divided by the area; measured in dynes or grams per square centimeter or pounds per square inch.—**intensive,** in•ten′siv, *a.* Serving to give force or emphasis (an *intensive* particle or prefix.)—*Intensive cultivation,* thorough cultivation of the soil by free use of stimulating manures, etc.—*Intensive drill,* a method of drill especially adopted for particular purposes of attack by shock or storm troops in war. (*Recent.*)—**intensively,** in•ten′siv•li, *adv.* In an intensive manner.—**intensiveness,** in•ten′siv•nes, *n.* The quality of being intensive.—**intent,** in•tent′, *a.* [L.

intentus, pp. of *intendo*.] Having the mind strained or bent on an object; sedulously applied; eager in pursuit of an object; anxiously diligent: with *on* before a noun.—*n*. Design, purpose, or intention; meaning; drift; aim.—*To all intents and purposes*, in all applications or senses; practically; really.—**intention,** in•ten′shon, *n*. [L. *intentio*, attention, design.] Determination to act in a particular manner; purpose, design; end; aim; the state of being strained or intensified; intension; *logic*, any mental apprehension of an object.—**intentional,** in•ten′shon•al, *a*. Done with intention, design, or purpose; intended; designed. —**intentionally,** in•ten′shon•al•li, *adv*. With intention; by design; of purpose.—**intently,** in•tent′li, *adv*. In an intent manner.—**intentness,** in•tent′nes, *n*. The state of being intent.

inter, in•tėr′, *v.t.*—*interred, interring*. [Fr. *enterrer*—*en*, and *terre*, L. *terra*, the earth (whence *terrace, terrestrial*, etc.).] To bury; to inhume.—**interment,** in•tėr′ment, *n*. The act of interring; burial.

interact, in′tėr•akt, *n*. [Prefix *inter*, and *act*.] The interval between two acts of a drama; an interlude; any intermediate employment of time.—*v.i.* To act reciprocally; to act on each other.—**interaction,** in•tėr•ak′shon, *n*. Intermediate action; mutual or reciprocal action.

interblend, in•tėr•blend′, *v.t.* and *i*. [Prefix *inter*, and *blend*.] To blend or mingle together.

interbreed, in•tėr•brēd′, *v.t.* and *i*. [Prefix *inter*, and *breed*.] To breed by crossing one kind of animal or plant with another.

intercalary, in•tėr′ka•le•ri, *a*. [L. *intercalarius*—*inter*, between, and *calo*, to call or proclaim, seen also in *calendar, council*.] Inserted or introduced among others, as the odd day (February 29th) inserted in leap year.—**intercalate,** in•tėr′ka•lāt, *v.t.* —*intercalated, intercalating*. [L. *intercalo*.] To insert between others; *chron*. to insert between other days or other portions of time; *geol*. to insert, as a layer or series of layers, between the regular series of the strata.—**intercalation,** in•tėr′ka•lā″shon, *n*. [L. *intercalatio*.] The act of intercalating.—**intercalative,** in•tėr′ka•lā•tiv, *a*. Tending to intercalate; intercalating.

intercede, in•tėr•sēd′, *v.i.*—*interceded, interceding*. [L. *intercedo*—*inter*, between, and *cedo*, to go; *lit*. to pass between. CEDE.] To act between parties with a view to reconcile those who differ or contend; to plead in favor of another; to interpose; to mediate or make intercession.—**interceder,** in•tėr•sē′dėr, *n*. One who intercedes.—**intercession,** in•tėr•sesh′on, *n*. [L. *intercessio*.] The act of interceding; mediation.—**intercessional,** in•tėr•sesh′on•al, *a*. Pertaining to or containing intercession. —**intercessor,** in′tėr•ses•sėr, *n*. One who intercedes.—**intercessory,** in•tėr•ses′se•ri, *a*. Containing intercession; interceding.

intercellular, in•tėr•sel′lū•lėr, *a*. [Prefix *inter*, between, and *cellular*.] *Bot*. and *zool*. lying between cells or cellules.

intercept, in•tėr•sept′, *v.t.* [Fr. *intercepter*; L. *intercipio, interceptum*, to intercept—*inter*, between, and *capio*, to take. CAPABLE.] To stop or interrupt the journey or the progress of.—**interceptor,** in•tėr•sep′tėr, *n*. A fighter plane equipped for fast climb and high speeds, used for intercepting enemy aircraft.—**interception,** in•tėr•sep′shon, *n*.—**interceptive,** in•tėr•sep′tiv, *n*.

interchange, in•tėr•chānj′, *v.t.*—*interchanged, interchanging*. [Prefix *inter*, and *change*.] To change reciprocally; to put each in the place of the other.—*v.i.* To change reciprocally; to succeed alternately.—*n*. in′tėr•chānj. The act or process of mutually giving and receiving; a junction of highways where bridges and underpasses separate the roads in levels so as to accommodate change from one roadway to another without stopping traffic.—**interchangeable,** in•tėr•chān′ja•bl, *a*.—**interchangeability, interchangeableness,** in•tėr•chān′ja•bil″i•ti, in•tėr•chān′ja•bl•nes, *n*.—**interchangeably,** in•tėr•chān′ja•bli, *adv*.

interclavicle, in•tėr•klav′i•kl, *n*. [Prefix *inter*, and *clavicle*.] A bone between the clavicles or in front of the breastbone in many vertebrates.

intercolonial, in•tėr•ko•lō′ni•al, *a*. [Prefix *inter*, between, among, and *colonial*.] Subsisting between different colonies.

intercolumniation, in′tėr•ko•lum′ni•ā″shon, *n*. [Prefix *inter*, between, and *column*.] *Arch*. the space between two columns measured at the lowest part of their shafts.

intercom, in′tėr•kom, *n*. [INTERCOMMUNICATE.] An intercommunication system with a microphone and speaker at each end for local communication.

intercommunicate, in′tėr•kom•mū″ni•kāt, *v.i.* and *t*. [Prefix *inter*, and *communicate*.] To communicate mutually; to hold mutual communication.—**intercommunication,** in′tėr•kom•mū′ni•kā″shon, *n*.

intercommunion, in′tėr•kom•mūn″yon, *n*. [Prefix *inter*, and *communion*.] Mutual communion; mutual intercourse.—**intercommunity,** in′tėr•kom•mū″ni•ti, *n*. A mutual communication or community.

interconnect, in′tėr•kon•nekt″, *v.t.* [Prefix *inter*, and *connect*.] To connect or unite closely or by various bonds.—**interconnection,** in′tėr•kon•nek″shon, *n*.

intercontinental, in′tėr•kon•ti•nen″tal, *a*. [Prefix *inter*, and *continent*.] Subsisting between different continents.—*Intercontinental ballistic missile*, a ballistic missile capable of traveling from one continent to another, its minimum range being 5,000 miles. Abbrev. ICBM.

intercostal, in•tėr•kos′tal, *a*. [L. *inter*, between, and *costa*, a rib.] *Anat*. placed or lying between the ribs.

intercourse, in′tėr•kōrs, *n*. [Prefix *inter*, between, and *course*; L. *intercursus*.] Reciprocal dealings between persons or nations; interchange of thought and feeling; copulation.

intercross, in•tėr•kros′, *v.t.* and *i*. [Prefix *inter*, and *cross*.] To cross mutually; to cross one another, as lines; to interbreed.

intercurrent, in•tėr•kur′ent, *a*. [Prefix *inter*, between, and *current*; L. *intercurrens, intercurrentis*.] Running between or among; intervening; *med*. applied to diseases which occur sporadically during the prevalence of other diseases.

interdenominational, in′tėr•di•nom′i•nā″shon•al, *a*. [Prefix *inter*, and *denomination*.] Between or among diverse religious denominations.

interdependence, interdependency, in′tėr•dē•pen″dens, in′tėr•dē•pen″den•si, *n*. [Prefix *inter*, and *depend*.] Reciprocal dependence; dependence each upon the others reciprocally.—**interdependent,** in′tėr•dē•pen″dent, *a*. Reciprocally dependent.

interdict, in•tėr•dikt′, *v.t.* [L. *interdico, interdictum*—*inter*, between, and *dico*, to speak. DICTION.] To debar, forbid, or prohibit; to restrain by an interdict.—*n*. in′tėr•dikt. A prohibition; a prohibiting order or decree; a papal prohibition of the performance of divine service and the administration of religious rites.—**interdiction,** in•tėr•dik′shon, *n*.—**interdictive, interdictory,** in•tėr•dik′tiv, in•tėr•dik′te•ri, *a*.

interest, in′tėr•est, *n*. [O.Fr. *interest*, Fr. *intérêt*, from L. *interest*, it concerns, it is of importance, from L. *interesse*—*inter*, between, and *esse*, to be (whence also *essence, entity*).] The profit per cent derived from money lent or invested; a share of an investment or business or other value; heed or curiosity paid to something; advantage; benefit; the situation in which one is or is not affected by something; something in addition to a mere equivalent (to repay injury with *interest*); influence with a person, especially with persons in power (to get a post by *interest*); a collective name for those interested in any particular business (the landed *interest*, the shipping *interest*).—*Simple interest* is that which arises from the principal sum only.—*Compound interest* is that which arises from the principal with the interest of one year added together to form a new principal for the next year, and so on successively.—*v.t.* To engage the attention of; to awaken interest or concern in.—**interested,** in′tėr•es•ted, *p*. and *a*. Having an interest or share; affected; moved; having attention roused; concerned in a cause or in consequences; liable to be biased by personal considerations; chiefly concerned for one's own private advantage.—**interestedness,** in′tėr•es•ted•nes, *n*.—**interesting,** in′tėr•es•ting, *a*. Engaging the attention or curiosity; exciting or adapted to excite attention and sympathy.—**interestingly,** in′tėr•es•ting•li, *adv*. In an interesting manner.—**interestingness,** in′tėr•es•ting•nes, *n*.

interface, in′tėr•fās, *n*. [Prefix *inter*,

and *face.*) The line or surface between two facing bodies.—**interfacial,** in•tėr•fā′shi•al, *a.*

interfere, in•tėr•fēr′, *v.i.*—*interfered, interfering.* [O.Fr. *entreferir,* to exchange blows—L. *inter,* between, and *ferio,* to strike (whence *ferule*).] To interpose; to intermeddle; to enter into or take a part in the concerns of others; to clash, come in collision, or be in opposition; *phys.* to act reciprocally upon each other so as to modify the effect of each; *sports,* to prevent an opposing player's movement by some illegal means.—**interference,** in•tėr•fē′rens, *n.* The act of interfering or intermeddling; *phys.* the mutual action of waves of any kind (water, sound, heat, or light) upon each other, by which the vibrations and their effects are increased, diminished, or neutralized; *sports,* illegal prevention of the opposition's action; defense of one's team members by blocking of the opposition.—**interferer,** in•tėr•fē′rėr, *n.*—**interferingly,** in•tėr•fēr′ing•li, *adv.*

interfuse, in•tėr•fūz′, *v.t.*—*interfused, interfusing.* [L. *interfusus,* pp. of *interfundo—inter,* between, and *fundo,* to pour. FUSE.] To pour or spread between or among; to mix up together; to make interdependent.—**interfusion,** in•tėr•fū′zhon, *n.*

intergalactic, in•tėr•gė•lăk′tik, *a.* [Prefix *inter,* and *galactic.*] Existing or happening in the large areas between galaxies.

interglacial, in•tėr•glā′shi•al, *a.* [Prefix *inter,* and *glacial.*] *Geol.* formed or occurring between two periods of glacial action.

interim, in′tėr•im, *n.* [L., in the meantime.] The meantime; time intervening.—*a.* Belonging to an intervening time; belonging to the meantime; temporary.

interior, in•tē′ri•ėr, *a.* [L., inner, interior, compar. of *interus,* internal, itself a compar. from *in.* Akin *entrails, internal, intestine.*] Internal; being within any limits, enclosure, or substance: opposed to *exterior* or *superficial;* inland; remote from the frontiers or shore.—*Interior angles, geom.* the angles made within any figure by the sides of it.—*Interior planets, astron.* the planets between the earth's orbit and the sun; inferior planets.—*Interior screw,* a screw cut on the interior surface of anything hollow.—*n.* The internal part of a thing; the inside; the inland part of a country; the department of a government having charge of home affairs.—**interiority,** in•tē′ri•or″i•ti, *n.* The quality of being interior.—**interiorly,** in•tē′ri•or•li, *adv.* Internally; inwardly.

interjacent, in•tėr•jā′sent, *a.* [L. *interjacens,* ppr. of *interjaceo—inter,* between, and *jaceo,* to lie, as in *adjacent, subjacent,* etc.] Lying or being between; intervening.

interject, in•tėr•jekt′, *v.t.* [L. *interjicio, interjectum—inter,* between, and *jacio,* to throw. JET.] To throw between; to throw in between other words.—**interjection,** in•tėr•jek′shon, *n.* [L. *interjectio.*] The act of throwing between; a word thrown in between words connected in construction, to express some emotion or passion, as exclamations of joy, grief, astonishment, etc.—**interjectional,** in•tėr•jek′shon•al, *a.* Thrown in between other words; partaking of the character of an interjection.—**interjectionally,** in•tėr•jek′shon•al•li, *adv.* In an interjectional manner.

interknit, in•tėr•nit′, *v.t.* [Prefix *inter,* and *knit.*] To knit together closely.

interlace, in•tėr•lās′, *v.t.*—*interlaced, interlacing.* [Prefix *inter,* and *lace;* Fr. *entrelacer.*] To weave or twine together; to entangle or interweave one thing with another.—*v.i.* To be intertwined or interwoven; to have parts crossing or intersecting.—**interlacement,** in•tėr•lās′ment, *n.* The act or state of interlacing.

interlard, in•tėr•lärd′, *v.t.* [Prefix *inter,* and *lard.*] Primarily, to mix fat with lean; hence, to mix by something frequently occurring; to diversify by mixture (talk *interlarded* with oaths).

interleave, in•tėr•lēv′, *v.t.*—*interleaved, interleaving.* [Prefix *inter,* and *leaf.*] To insert a blank leaf or blank leaves in; to insert between the other leaves of (a book).

interline, in•tėr•līn′, *v.t.*—*interlined, interlining.* [Prefix *inter,* and *line.*] To write or print in alternate lines; to write or print between the lines of.—**interlineal, interlinear,** in•tėr•lin′i•al, in•tėr•lin′i•ėr, *a.* Written or printed between lines before written or printed.—**interlineation,** in•tėr•lin′i•ā″shon, *n.* The act of interlining; that which is interlined.

interlock, in•tėr•lok′, *v.i.* [Prefix *inter,* and *lock.*] To unite or be locked together by a series of connections.—*v.t.* To lock one in another firmly.

interlocution, in′tėr•lō•kū″shon, *n.* [L. *interlocutio,* from *interloquor—inter,* between, and *loquor,* to speak (in *loquacious, elocution,* etc.).] Dialogue; interchange of speech; *law,* an intermediate act or decree before final decision.—**interlocutor,** in•tėr•lok′ū•tėr, *n.* One who speaks in a dialogue or conversation; *Scots law,* the term, judgment, or order of any court of record.—**interlocutory,** in•tėr•lok′ū•to•ri, *a.* Consisting of dialogue or conversation.

interlope, in•tėr•lōp′, *v.i.*—*interloped, interloping.* [From the noun, which is from D. *enterlooper,* a smuggler or smuggling vessel—Fr. *entre,* between, and D. *loopen,* to leap, to run=E. to *leap.* LEAP.] To traffic without a proper license; to run into a matter in which one has no right.—**interloper,** in•tėr•lō′pėr, *n.* One who unwarrantably intrudes or thrusts himself into a business, position, or matter.

interlude, in′tėr•lūd, *n.* [L.L. *interludium,* an interlude—L. *inter,* between, and *ludus,* a play. DELUDE.] A short lively entertainment performed between the acts of a play, or between the play and the afterpiece; a piece of music played between the verses of a canticle or hymn, or between certain portions of a church service.

interlunar, in•tėr•lū′nėr, *a.* [L. *inter,* between, and *luna,* the moon.] Belonging to the time when the moon is invisible.

intermarry, in•tėr•mar′i, *v.i.*—*intermarried, intermarrying.* [Prefix *inter,* and *marry.*] To marry together; to become connected by marriage, as two families, ranks, tribes, or the like.—**intermarriage,** in•tėr•mar′ij, *n.* Marriage between two families, tribes, or nations.

intermeddle, in•tėr•med′l, *v.i.*—*intermeddled, intermeddling.* [Prefix *inter,* and *meddle.*] To meddle in affairs in which one has no concern; to meddle officiously; to interfere.—**intermeddler,** in•tėr•med′lėr, *n.* One who intermeddles.

intermediate, in•tėr•mē′di•it, *a.* [Fr. *intermédiat,* L. *intermedius—inter,* between, and *medius,* middle (whence *medium, mediate,* etc.).] Lying or being between; in the middle place or degree between two extremes; intervening; interposed. Also **intermediary,** in•tėr•mē′di•a•ri, in same sense.—**intermediately,** in•tėr•mē′di•it•li, *adv.* In an intermediate position.—**intermediation,** in•tėr•mē′di•ā″shon, *n.* Intervention; interposition.—**intermediary,** in•tėr•mē′di•e•ri, *n.* One who or that which interposes or is intermediate; an intervening agent.—**intermediator,** in•tėr•mē′di•ā•tėr, *n.* A mediator between parties.

interment. See INTER.

intermezzo, in•tėr•met′zō, *n.* [It.] *Mus.* a short composition, generally of a light sparkling character, played between more important pieces; an interlude.

intermigration, in′tėr•mī•grā″shon, *n.* [Prefix *inter,* and *migration.*] Reciprocal migration.

interminable, in•tėr′mi•na•bl, *a.* [L. *interminabilis—in,* not, and *terminus,* a bound or limit. TERM.] Boundless; endless; admitting no limit; wearisomely spun out or protracted.—**interminably,** in•tėr′mi•na•bli, *adv.* In an interminable manner; endlessly.

intermingle, in•tėr•ming′gl, *v.t.*—*intermingled, intermingling.* [Prefix *inter,* and *mingle.*] To mingle or mix together; to mix up; to intermix.—*v.i.* To be mixed or incorporated.

intermission. See INTERMIT.

intermit, in•tėr•mit′, *v.t.*—*intermitted, intermitting.* [L. *intermitto,* to let go between, to interrupt—*inter,* and *mitto,* to send. MISSION.] To cause to cease for a time; to interrupt; to suspend or delay.—*v.i.* To cease for a time; to cease or relax at intervals, as a fever.—**intermittence,** in•tėr•mit′ens, *n.* The act or state of intermitting; intermission.—**intermittent,** in•tėr•mit′ent, *a.* Ceasing at intervals.—*Intermittent* or *intermitting spring,* a spring which flows for some time and then ceases, again flows and again ceases, and so on, usually having a siphon-shaped channel of outflow.—*n.* A fever which entirely subsides or ceases at certain intervals.

—**intermission,** in•tėr•mish′on, *n.* [L. *intermissio.*] The act or state of intermitting; cessation for a time; pause; the temporary subsidence of a fever.—**intermissive,** in•tėr•mis′iv, *a.* Intermittent.

intermix, in•tėr•miks′, *v.t.* [Prefix *inter,* and *mix.*] To mix together; to intermingle.—*v.i.* To be mixed or intermingled.—**intermixture,** in•tėr•miks′chėr, *n.* A mass formed by mixture; a mass of ingredients mixed; admixture.

intermundane, in•tėr•mun′dān, *a.* [L. *inter,* between, *mundus,* a world.] Being between worlds or between orb and orb (*intermundane* spaces).

intermural, in•tėr•mū′ral, *a.* [L. *inter,* between, *murus,* a wall.] Between walls.

intern, interne, in′tėrn, *n.* [Fr. *interne.*] A graduated physician serving in a hospital for experience.—**internship,** in′tėrn•ship, *n.* A period of service for the purpose of gaining experience.

intern, in•tėrn′, *v.t.* [Fr. *interner,* from L. *internus,* internal.] To send to or cause to remain in the interior of a country without permission to leave it; to disarm and quarter in some place, as a defeated body of troops.—**internment,** in•tėrn′ment, *n.* The act of interning; the state of being interned.

internal, in•tėr′nal, *a.* [L. *internus,* internal. INTERIOR.] Inward; interior; being within any limit or surface; not external; pertaining to the mind or thoughts, or to one's inner being; pertaining to itself, its own affairs, or home interests: said of a country; domestic; not foreign.—*Internal-combustion engine,* an engine which is propelled into motion by the combustion of a fuel-air mixture within the cylinders.—*Internal revenue,* taxes derived from levies on certain domestic transactions.—**internality,** in•tėr•nal′i•ti, *n.*—**internally,** in•tėr′nal•li, *adv.*

international, in•tėr•nash′on•al, *a.* [Prefix *inter,* and *national.*] Pertaining to or reciprocally affecting nations; regulating the mutual intercourse between different nations.—*International law,* the law of nations; those maxims or rules that regulate states in their conduct toward one another.—[*cap.*] **International,** *n.* The International Congress of Socialistic Workers.—**internationalism,** in•tėr•na′shon•al•izm, *n.* The principle of cooperation among nations for their common good; an international as opposed to a national policy.—**internationally,** in•tėr•nash′on•al•li, *adv.*

internecine, in•tėr•nē′sin, *a.* [L. *internecinus,* deadly, murderous—*inter,* between, among, and *neco,* to kill.] Marked by destructive hostilities or much slaughter; causing great slaughter, as between fellow citizens (*internecine* war).

internode, in′tėr•nōd, *n.* [L. *inter,* between, and *nodus,* knot.] *Bot.* the space which intervenes between two nodes or leafbuds.

internuncio, in•tėr•nun′shi•ō, *n.* [L. *internuncius*—*inter,* between, and *nuncius,* a messenger.] A messenger between two parties; an envoy of the pope, sent to small states and republics while a nuncio is sent to emperors and kings.

interoceanic, in•tėr•ō′shē•an″ik, *a.* [Prefix *inter,* and *ocean.*] Between oceans (*interoceanic* railway, canal, etc.).

interosculate, in•tėr•os′kū•lāt, *v.i.* [Prefix *inter,* and *osculate.*] To touch or run into one another at various points; to form a connecting link between objects or groups by having characters in common.

interpellate, in•tėr′pel•lāt, *v.t.*—*interpellated, interpellating.* [L. *interpello, interpellatum,* to interrupt in speaking—*inter,* between, and *pello,* to drive (seen in *appeal, compel, pulse,* etc.).] To question, especially to question imperatively; to interrupt by a question.—**interpellation,** in′tėr•pel•lā″shon, *n.* [L. *interpellatio.*] The act of interrupting; an interruption by speaking; a question put by a member of a legislative assembly to a minister or member of the government.

interpenetrate, in•tėr•pen′e•trāt, *v.t.* and *i.*—*interpenetrated, interpenetrating.* [Prefix, *inter,* and *penetrate.*] To penetrate between or within; to penetrate mutually.—**interpenetration,** in•tėr•pen′e•trā″shon, *n.* The act of interpenetrating.

interplanetary, in•tėr•plan′e•te•ri, *a.* [Prefix *inter,* and *planetary.*] Situated or existing between the planets; carried on between planets.

interplead, in•tėr•plēd′, *v.i.* [Prefix *inter,* and *plead.*] *Law,* to proceed by interpleader.—**interpleader,** in•tėr•plē′dėr, *n. Law,* one who interpleads; a legal process by which a person threatened with a suit in which he has no real interest gets the proper parties to plead in the matter.

interpolate, in•tėr′po•lāt, *v.t.*—*interpolated, interpolating.* [L. *interpolo, interpolatum,* to interpolate or falsify, from *interpolus,* vamped up, falsified —*inter,* between, and *polio,* to polish.] To foist in; to insert, as a spurious word or passage in a manuscript or book; to corrupt or vitiate by the insertion of new matter; *math.* and *phys.,* to fill up intermediate terms of, as of a series, according to the law of the series.—**interpolation,** in•tėr′po•lā″shon, *n.* [L. *interpolatio.*] The act of interpolating; that which is interpolated or inserted; a spurious word or passage inserted.—**interpolater,** in•tėr′po•lā•tėr, *n.* One who interpolates.

interpose, in•tėr•pōz′, *v.t.*—*interposed, interposing.* [Fr. *interposer*—*inter,* between, and *poser,* to place. POSE, COMPOSE.] To place between; *fig.* or *lit.* to present or bring forward by way of interruption or for some service (to *interpose* one's hand, one's self, one's aid or services).—*v.i.* To step in between parties at variance; to mediate; to interfere; to put in or make a remark by way of interruption.—**interposer,** in•tėr•pō′zėr, *n.* One who interposes.—**interposition,** in•tėr′po•zish″on or in′tėr•po•zish″on, *n.* The act of interposing; a coming between; mediation; intervention.

interpret, in•tėr′pret, *v.t.* [L. *interpretor,* from *interpres, interpretis,* an interpreter—*inter,* between, and root seen in (*pre*)*paro,* to prepare.] To explain the meaning of; to expound; to translate from an unknown to a known language, or into intelligible or familiar words; to free from mystery or obscurity; to make clear; to unravel; to represent artistically.—**interpretable,** in•tėr′pre•ta•bl, *a.*—**interpretation,** in•tėr′pre•tā″shon, *n.* [L. *interpretatio.*] The act of interpreting; translation; explanation; the sense given by an interpreter; conception and representation of a character on the stage.—**interpretative,** in•tėr′pre•tā•tiv, *a.* Designed or fitted to explain; explanatory.—**interpretatively,** in•tėr′pre•tā•tiv•li, *adv.* In an interpretative manner.—**interpreter,** in•tėr′pre•tėr, *n.* One who or that which interprets.

interracial, in•tėr•rā′shi•al, *a.* [Prefix *inter,* and *racial.*] Concerning two or more races; intended for members of two or more races.

interregnum, in•tėr•reg′num, *n.* [L. from *inter,* between, and *regnum,* reign.] The time between the death or abdication of a king and the accession of his successor; the interval between the cessation of one government and the establishment of another.

interrelation, in′tėr•ri•lā″shon, *n.* [Prefix *inter,* and *relation.*] Mutual; reciprocal, or corresponding relation; correlation.

interrogate, in•tėr′o•gāt, *v.t.* [L. *interrogo, interrogatum*—*inter,* between, and *rogo,* to ask (as in *abrogate, arrogant, derogate, prorogue,* etc.).] To question; to examine by asking questions.—**interrogation,** in•ter′o•gā″shon, *n.* [L. *interrogatio.*] The act of questioning; a question put; the sign ?, indicating that the sentence immediately preceding it is a question, or used to express doubt or to mark a query.—**interrogative,** in•te•rog′a•tiv, *a.* [L. *interrogativus.*] Denoting a question; expressed in the form of a question.—*n. gram.* a word used in asking questions; as *who? what? which?*—**interrogatively,** in•te•rog′a•tiv•li, *adv.* In an interrogative manner.—**interrogator,** inter′o•gā•tėr, *n.* One who interrogates or asks questions.—**interrogatory,** in•ter•rog′a•to•ri, *n.* [L. *interrogatorius.*] A question; an interrogation. —*a.* Containing a question; expressing a question.

interrupt, in•tėr•rupt′, *v.t.* [L. *interrumpo, interruptum*—*inter,* between, and *rumpo,* to break. RUPTURE.] To stop or hinder by breaking in upon the course or progress of; to break the current or motion of; to cause to stop in speaking; to cause to be delayed or given over; to break the uniformity of.—**interrupter,** in•tėr•rup′tėr, *n.* One that interrupts.—**interruption,** in•tėr•rup′shon, *n.* [L.

interruptio.] The act of interrupting or breaking in upon; a break or breach; intervention; interposition; obstruction or hindrance; cause of stoppage.—**interruptive,** in•tėr•rup′tiv, *a.* Tending to interrupt; interrupting.

intersect, in•tėr•sekt′, *v.t.* [L. *interseco, intersectum—inter,* between, and *seco,* to cut. SECTION.] To cut into or between; to cut or cross mutually; to divide into parts by crossing or cutting.—*v.i.* To cut into one another; to meet and cross each other.—**intersection,** in•tėr•sek′shon, *n.* [L. *intersectio.*] The act or state of intersecting; the point or line in which two lines or two surfaces cut each other.—**intersectional,** in•tėr•sek′shon•al, *a.* Relating to or formed by an intersection.

intersperse, in•tėr•spėrs′, *v.t.—interspersed, interspersing.* [L. *interspergo, interspersum—inter,* between, and *spargo,* to scatter.] To scatter or set here and there among other things; to diversify by scattering objects.—**interspersion,** in•tėr•spėr′zhon, *n.* The act of interspersing.

interspinal, interspinous, in•tėr•spī′nal, in•tėr•spī′nus, *a.* [Prefix *inter,* and *spine.*] *Anat.* lying between the processes of the spine, as muscles, nerves, etc.

interstate, in•tėr•stāt′, *a.* Relations of or between states, as *interstate* commerce. *Interstate Commerce Commission* (*I.C.C.*), established by the U.S. in 1887 to regulate commerce between the states, especially railroads and express companies, or rail and water transport when combined. It passes on rates, financing, building and abandonment of railroads.

interstellar, in•tėr•stel′ėr, *a.* [Prefix *inter,* and *stellar.*] Situated among the stars.

interstice, in•tėr′stis, *n.* [Fr., from L. *interstitium—inter,* between, and *sto,* to stand. STATE.] A narrow or small space between things close together, or between the component parts of a body; a chink, crevice, or cranny.—**interstitial,** in•tėr•stish′al, *a.* Of or containing interstices.

interstratify, in•tėr•strat′i•fī, *v.t.* [Prefix *inter,* and *stratify.*] *Geol.* to cause to occupy a position between other strata; to intermix as to strata. —*v.i.* To assume a position between other strata.—**interstratification,** in•tėr•strat′i•fi•kā″shon, *n.* The condition of being interstratified.

intertexture, in•tėr•teks′chėr, *n.* [Prefix *inter,* and *texture.*] The act of interweaving; state of things interwoven; what is interwoven.

intertropical, in•tėr•trop′i•kal, *a.* [Prefix *inter,* and *tropic.*] Situated between or within the tropics.

intertwine, in•tėr•twīn′, *v.t.—intertwined, intertwining.* [Prefix *inter,* and *twine.*] To unite by twining or twisting one with another; to interlace.—*v.i.* To be mutually interwoven.

intertwist, in•tėr•twist′, *v.t.* [Prefix *inter,* and *twist.*] To twist one with another; to interweave or interlace.

interurban, in•tėr•ėr′ban, *a.* [Prefix *inter,* and *urban.*] Between cities.—*n.* A train or car which commutes between two cities.

interval, in′tėr•val, *n.* [L. *intervallum,* the space between the rampart—*inter,* between and *vallum,* an earthen rampart. WALL.] A space or distance between things; space of time between two definite points or events; the lateral space between units having the same alignment or frontage; *mus.* the difference in pitch between two sounds, sounded successively (melodic) or simultaneously (harmonic).

intervene, in•tėr•vēn′, *v.i.—intervened, intervening.* [L. *intervenio—inter,* between, and *venio,* to come, as in *advene, convene,* etc. VENTURE.] To come or be between persons or things; to be situated between; to occur, fall, or come between points of time or events; to come in the way.—**intervener, interventionist,** in•tėr•vē′nėr, in•tėr•ven′shon•ist, *n.* One who intervenes or advocates intervention.—**intervention,** in•tėr•ven′shon, *n.* [L. *interventio.*] Act of intervening; a coming between.

interview, in′tėr•vū, *n.* [Prefix *inter,* and *view;* Fr. *entrevue.*] A meeting between two or more persons face to face for the purpose of obtaining information as to aptitude, skills, etc.; the conversation, published or aired over television or radio, between a writer or reporter and a person of importance or notoriety from whom he is seeking information.—*v.t.* To have an interview with.—**interviewer,** in′tėr•vū•ėr, *n.*

interweave, in•tėr•wēv′, *v.t.—interwove* (pret.); *interwoven* (pp.); *interweaving* (ppr.). To weave together; to intermingle as if by weaving; to unite intimately; to interlace.

intestate, in•tes′tāt, *a.* [L. *intestatus—in,* not, and *testatus,* having made a will, pp. of *testor,* to make a will. TESTAMENT.] Dying without having made a will; not disposed of by will; not devised or bequeathed.—*n.* A person who dies without making a will, or a valid will.—**intestacy,** in•tes′ta•si, *n.* The state of being intestate.

intestine, in•tes′tin, *a.* [L. *intestinus,* inward, *intestinum,* an intestine, from *intus,* within, from *in,* in; akin *interior.*] Internal with regard to a state or country; domestic; not foreign.—*n.* The canal or tube that extends with convolutions from the stomach to the anus; *pl.* entrails or viscera in general.—**intestinal,** in•tes′ti•nal, *a.* Pertaining to the intestines of an animal body.—*Intestinal canal,* the intestine or tube through which food passes in being digested.

inthrall, inthral, in•thrąl′, *v.t.* To enthral.

inthrone, in•thrōn′, *v.t.* To enthrone.

intimate, in′ti•mit, *a.* [Fr. *intime,* L. *intimus,* inmost, superl. of obs. *interus,* internal. INTERIOR.] Inward or internal‡; close in friendship; on very familiar terms (also refers to illicit sex relationship); very close as regards connection or relation (an *intimate* union).—*n.* An intimate friend; a close associate.—**intimacy,** in′ti•ma•si, *n.* The state of being intimate.—**intimately,** in′ti•mit•li, *adv.* In an intimate manner.

intimate, in′ti•māt, *v.t.—intimated, intimating.* [L. *intimo, intimatum,* to publish or make known, from *intimus,* inmost. INTIMATE.] *a.* To hint, indicate, or suggest‡; to announce; to make known.—**intimation,** in•ti•mā′shon, *n.* [L. *intimatio.*] The act of intimating; a hint; an explicit announcement or notification.

intimidate, in•tim′i•dāt, *v.t.—intimidated, intimidating.* [L.L. *intimido, intimidatum*—L. *in,* intens., and *timidus,* timid.] To inspire with fear; to dishearten; to cow; to deter by threats.—**intimidation,** in•tim′i•dā″shon, *n.* The act of intimidating; the deterring of a person by threats or otherwise.

intitle, in•tī′tl. See ENTITLE.

into, in′tö, *prep.* [A.Sax. *in tó, in* being the adv. and *tó* the prep.] A compound preposition expressing motion or direction toward the inside of, whether literally or figuratively; or expressing a change of condition (to go *into* a house, to fall *into* a fever).

intolerable, in•tol′ėr•a•bl, *a.* [L. *intolerabilis—in,* not, and *tolerabilis,* bearable, from *tolero,* to bear. TOLERATE.] Not to be borne or endured; unendurable; insufferable.—**intolerableness, intolerability,** in•tol′ėr•a•bl•nes, in•tol′ėr•a•bil″i•ti, *n.* The state or quality of being intolerable. —**intolerably,** in•tol′ėr•a•bli, *adv.* In an intolerable manner; unendurably.—**intolerant,** in•tol′ėr•ant, *a.* [L. *intolerans, intolerantis—in,* not, and *tolero,* to bear.] Not enduring; not able to endure (an animal *intolerant* of cold); refusing to tolerate others in the enjoyment of their opinions, rights, or worship; unduly impatient of difference of opinion on the part of others.—**intolerantly,** in•tol′ėr•ant•li, *adv.* In an intolerant manner.—**intolerance,** in•tol′ėr•ans, *n.* The quality of being intolerant; want of toleration; want of capacity to endure.

intomb, in•töm′, *v.t.* To entomb.

intonate, in′to•nāt, *v.i.* [L. *in,* in, and *tonus,* tone.] To modulate the voice; to sound the notes of the musical scale.—*v.t.* to pronounce with a certain tone or modulation.—**intonation,** in•to•ná′shon, *n.* The act or manner of intonating; modulation of the voice musically as in reading; the act of intoning; utterance with a special tone.—**intone,** in•tōn′, *v.i.* To use a musical monotone in pronouncing or repeating; to chant. —*v.t.* To pronounce with a musical tone; to chant.

intort, in•tort′, *v.t.* [L. *intorqueo, intortum—in,* and *torqueo,* to twist. TORTURE.] To twist inward; to wreathe.—**intortion,** in•tor′shon, *n.* A winding or twisting inward.

intoxicate, in•tok′si•kāt, *v.t.—intoxicated, intoxicating.* [L.L. *intoxico, intoxicatum*—L. *in,* and *toxicum,* poison = Gr. *toxikon,* a poison in which arrows were dipped, from *toxon*, a bow.] To inebriate; to make drunk, as with spirituous liquor; *fig.* to excite the spirits of to a very high pitch; to elate to enthusiasm, frenzy, or madness. *v.i.* To have the power of intoxicating, or making drunk.—**intoxicant,** in•tok′si•kant, *n.* That which intoxicates; an intoxicating liquor or substance.—**intoxication,** in•tok′si•kā″shon, *n.* The act of intoxicating; the state of being intoxicated; inebriation; drunkenness.

intracellular, in•tra•sel′lū•ler, [L. *intra*, within, *cellula*, a little cell.] Within a cell.

intractable, in•trak′ta•bl, *a.* [Prefix *in*, not, and *tractable*; L. *intractabilis.*] Not tractable; not to be governed or managed; perverse; refractory; indocile.—**intractableness, intractability,** in•trak′ta•bl•nes, in•trak′ta•bil″i•ti, *n.* The quality of being intractable.—**intractably,** in•trak′ta•bli, *adv.* In an intractable manner.

intrados, in•trā′dos, *n.* [Fr., from L. *intra*, within, and *dorsum*, back.] *Arch.* the interior and lower line or curve of an arch. EXTRADOS.

intramundane, in•tra•mun′dān, *a.* [Prefix *intra*, and *mundane.*] Being within the world; belonging to the material world.

intramural, in•tra•mū′ral, *a.* [Prefix *intra*, and *mural.*] Being within the walls or boundaries, as of a university, city, or town; of activities carried on within the confines of a college, company, etc.; *athletics*, games between various teams formed within a university, company, etc.

intransigent, in•tran′si•jent, *a.* [Fr. *intransigeant*, from L. *in*, not, and *transigo*, to transact, to come to a settlement.] Refusing to agree or come to a settlement; irreconcilable. —*n.* An irreconcilable person.

intransitive, in•tran′si•tiv, *a.* [Prefix *in*, not, and *transitive.*] *Gram.* expressing an action or state that is limited to the subject; not having an object (an *intransitive* verb).—**intransitively,** in•tran′si•tiv•li, *adv.* In an intransitive manner.

intrant, in′trant, *a.* [L. *intrans, intrantis*, ppr. of *intro*, to go into, to enter.] Entering.—*n.* One who makes an entrance; one who enters upon public duty or office.

intrastate, in′tra•stāte, *a.* Within a state, as intrastate shipping of goods.

intravenous, in′tra•vē″nus, *a.* [Prefix *intra*, and *venous.*] Introduced within the veins.

intrepid, in•trep′id, *a.* [L. *intrepidus* —*in*, not, and *trepidus*, alarmed. TREPIDATION.] Fearless; bold; brave; undaunted. —**intrepidity,** in•tre•pid′i•ti, *n.* Fearlessness; fearless bravery in danger; undaunted courage. —**intrepidly,** in•trep′id•li, *adv.* In an intrepid manner.

intricacy. See INTRICATE.

intricate, in′tri•kit, *a.* [L. *intricatus*, pp. of *intrico*, to entangle—*in*, into, and *tricoe*, trifles, hindrances, as in *extricate*; akin *intrigue.*] Entangled; involved; difficult to unravel or follow out in all the windings; complicated.—**intricately,** in′tri•kit•li, *adv.* In an intricate manner.—**intricacy,** in′tri•ka•si, *n.* The state of being intricate or entangled; a winding or complicated arrangement; entanglement; complication.

intrigue, in•trēg′ or in′trēg, *n.* [Fr. *intriguer*, from L. *intrico*, to entangle. INTRICATE.] A plot or scheme of a complicated nature, and especially political in character; the plot of a play, poem, or romance; an illicit intimacy between two persons of different sexes; a liaison.—*v.i.*—*intrigued, intriguing.* To form an intrigue; to engage in an intrigue; to carry on a liaison.—**intriguer,** in•trē′gėr, *n.* One who intrigues.—**intriguing,** in•trēg′ing, *p.* and *a.* Addicted to intrigue.—**intriguingly,** in•trēg′ing•li, *adv.* In an intriguing manner.

intrinsic, intrinsical, in•trin′sik, in•trin′si•kal, *a.* [L. *intrinsecus—intra*, inward, *in*, in, and *secus*, beside, from root of *sequor*, to follow (whence *sequence*).] Inherent; essential; belonging to the thing in itself; not extrinsic or accidental (the *intrinsic* value of gold or silver, *intrinsic* merit). —**intrinsically,** in•trin′si•kal•li, *adv.* By intrinsic character; in its nature; essentially; inherently.

introduce, in•tro•dūs′, *v.t.*—*introduced, introducing.* [L. *introduco*—*intro*, within, and *duco*, to lead. DUKE.] To lead or bring in; to conduct or usher in; to pass in; to put in; to insert; to make known by stating one's name; often used of the action of a third party with regard to two others; to bring to be acquainted; to present (to *introduce* one person, one's self, to another); to bring into use or practice (a fashion, custom, etc.); to bring before the public; to bring into a country; to bring forward (a topic) with preliminary or preparatory matter.—**introducer,** in•tro•dū′sėr, *n.* One who introduces.—**introduction,** in•tro•duk′shon, *n.* [L. *introductio.*] The act of introducing, bringing in, making persons acquainted, etc.; the part of a book or discourse which precedes the main work, and which gives some general account of its design and subject; a preface or preliminary discourse; a treatise introductory to more elaborate works on the same subject.—**introductive,** in•tro•duk′tiv, *a.* Serving to introduce.—**introductory,** in•tro•duk′to•ri, *a.* Serving to introduce something else; serving as or given by way of an introduction; prefatory; preliminary.

introit, in•trō′it, *n.* [L. *introitus*, an entrance, from *intro*, within, and *eo*, to go. INITIAL.] *R. Cath. Ch.* the beginning of the mass; a piece sung or chanted while the priest proceeds to the altar to celebrate mass; a musical composition designed for opening the church service.

intromit, in•tro•mit′, *v.t.*—*intromitted, intromitting.* [L. *intromitto*—*intro*, within, and *mitto, missum*, to send.] To send in, put in, or let in.—*v.i.* *Scots law*, to intermeddle with the effects, of another.—**intromittent,** in•tro•mit′ent, *a.* Letting or conveying into or within.—**intromitter,** in•tro•mit′ėr, *n.* One who intromits.—**intromission,** in•tro•mish′on, *n.* The act of sending or letting in; admission; *Scots law*, the transactions of an agent or subordinate with the money of his superior.

introrse, in•trors′, *a.* [L. *introrsum*, inward—*intro*, within, and *versus*, pp. of *verto*, to turn.] Turned or facing inward; turned toward the axis to which they appertain, as the anthers in plants.

introspect, in•tro•spekt′, *v.t.* [L. *introspicio, introspectum—intro*, within, and *specio*, to look.] To examine in depth; to look inside of.—*v.i.* To look inward; to contemplate one's thoughts or feeling.—**introspection,** in•trō•spek′shun, *n.*—**introspective,** in•trō•spek′tiv, *a.*

introvert, in•tro•vėrt′, *v.f.* [L. *intro*, within, and *verto*, to turn.] To turn inward; to turn thought on oneself.—*n.* in′tro•vėrt. That which can be introverted; *psych.* one inclined to introversion.—**introversion,** in′tro•ver″shon, *n.* Turning inward; *psych.* interest directed inward.

intrude, in•tröd′, *v.i.*—*intruded, intruding.* [L. *intrudo—in*, in, into, and *trudo*, to thrust, as in *detrude, obtrude, protrude, abstruse.*] To thrust one's self forwardly or unwarrantably into any place or position; to force one's self upon others; to encroach; to enter unwelcome or uninvited into company; *geol.* to penetrate, as into fissures or between the layers of rocks.—*v.t.* To thrust in, or cause to enter without right or welcome: often with the reflexive pronoun.—**intruder,** in•trö′dėr, *n.* One who intrudes.—**intrusion,** in•trö′zhon, *n.* The act of intruding; unwarrantable entrance; *law*, an unlawful entry into lands and tenements void of a possessor by a person who has no right to the same; *geol.* the penetrating of one rock, while in a melted state, into fissures, etc., of other rocks.—**intrusive,** in•trö′siv, *a.* Characterized by intrusion; apt to intrude; of the nature of an intrusion.—**intrusively,** in•trö′siv•li, *adv.* In an intrusive manner.—**intrusiveness,** *n.*

intrust, in•trust′, *n.* See ENTRUST.

intubation, in•tūb•ā′shon, *n.* [L. *in*, in, *tuba*, tube.] The process of inserting a tube into a body organ to keep it open.

intuition, in•tū•ish′on, *n.* [From L. *intueor, intuitus*, to look upon, to contemplate—*in*, in, upon, and *tueor*, to look (whence *tutor, tuition*).] *Philos.* the act by which the mind perceives the agreement or disagreement of two ideas, or the truth of things immediately, and without reasoning and deduction; a truth discerned by the mind directly and necessarily as so; a truth that cannot be acquired by, but is assumed in experience.—**intuitional,** in•tū•ish′on•al, *a.* Pertaining to, derived from, or characterized by intuition; intuitive.—**intuitionalism,** in•tū•ish′on•al•izm, *n.* The doctrine that the perception of truth is from intuition.—**intuitive,** in•tū′i•tiv, *a.* Perceived by the mind immediately without the intervention of reasoning; based on intuition; received or obtained by intuition; having the power of discovering truth without reasoning.—**intuitively,** in•tū′i•tiv•li, *adv.* In an intuitive manner; by intuition.

intumesce, in•tū•mes′, *v.i.*—*intumesced, intumescing.* [L. *intumesco*—*in,* and *tumesco,* to begin to swell, incept. of *tumeo,* to swell. TUMID.] To enlarge or expand with heat; to swell out in bulk.—**intumescence,** in•tū•mes′ens, *n.* The state or process of intumescing.

intussuscept, in′tus•su•sept″ *v.t.* [L. *intus,* within, and *suscipio,* to take or receive. SUSCEPTIBLE.] To take into the interior; to receive by intussusception. — **intussusception,** in′tus•sus•sep″shon, *n.* The reception of one part within another; the descent or doubling in of a higher portion of intestine into a lower one; the act of taking foreign matter into the substance of a living body; the process by which nutriment is absorbed into and goes to form part of the system.

intwine, in•twīn′, *v.t.*—*intwined, intwining.* To twine or twist in or together; to wreathe; to entwine.

inunction, in•ungk′shon, *n.* [L. *inunctio, inunctionis,* from *inungo, inunctum,* to anoint.] The action of anointing; unction.

inundate, in′un•dāt or in•un′dāt, *v.t. inundated, inundating.* [L. *inundo, inundatum*—*in,* and *undo,* to overflow (also in *abound*), from *unda,* a wave. UNDULATE.] To spread or flow over; to overflow; to deluge; to flood; to submerge; to fill with an overflowing abundance or superfluity.—**inundation,** in•un•dā′shon, *n.* [L. *inundatio.*] The act of inundating or state of being inundated; a flood; a rising and spreading of waters over low grounds.—**inundant,** in•un′dant, *a.* Overflowing; inundating.

inure, in•ūr′, *v.t.*—*inured, inuring.* [Prefix *in,* in, and obsol. *ure,* operation, work, from O.Fr. *eure,* Mod. Fr. *œuvre,* from L. *opera,* work. The *-ure* of this word therefore = *ure* of *manure.* OPERATE.] To apply or expose in use or practice till use gives little or no pain or inconvenience, or makes little impression; to habituate; to accustom (to toil or hardships).—**inurement,** in•ūr′ment, *n.* The act or process of inuring.

inurn, in•ėrn′, *v.t.* [Prefix *in,* and *urn.*] To put in an urn, especially a funeral urn; hence, to bury; to entomb. (*Poet.*)

inutility, in•ū•til′i•ti, *n.* [Prefix *in,* not, and *utility;* L. *inutilitas.*] The quality of being useless or unprofitable; uselessness; unprofitableness.

invade, in•vād′, *v.t.*—*invaded, invading.* [L. *invado*—*in,* into, and *vado,* to go, seen also in *evade, pervade;* akin *wade.*] To enter with hostile intentions; to enter as an enemy, with a view to conquest or plunder; to enter by force; to make an inroad or incursion on; to intrude upon; to infringe, encroach on, or violate (rights or privileges).—*v.i.* To make an invasion.—**invader,** in•vā′dėr, *n.* One who invades.—**invasion,** in•vā′zhon, *n.* [L. *invasio,* from *invado.*] The act of invading; a hostile entrance into the country or possessions of another; an attack on the rights of another.—**invasive,** in•vā′siv, *a.* Tending to invade; aggressive.

invaginate, in•vaj′i•nāt, *v.i.* [L. *in,* in, into, and *vagino,* a sheath.] To enter as into a sheath; to enter by intussusception into another part.—**invagination,** in•vaj′i•nā″shon, *n. Anat.* the reception of one part within another by being doubled backward; intussusception.

invalid, in•val′id, *a.* [Prefix *in,* not, and *valid;* L. *invalidus.*] Not valid; of no force, weight, or cogency; weak (an *invalid* argument); *law,* having no force, effect, or efficacy; void; null.—*n.* (in′va•lid). [Directly from Fr. *invalide.*] A person who is weak and infirm; a sufferer from ill health; one who is disabled for active service, especially a soldier or seaman worn out in service.—*a.* In ill health; infirm; disabled for active service.—*v.t.* To render an invalid; to enroll on the list of invalids in the military or naval service.—**invalidate,** in•val′i•dāt, *v.t.* —*invalidated, invalidating.* To render invalid or not valid; to render of no legal force or effect.—**invalidation,** in•val′i•dā″shon, *n.* Act of invalidating.—**invalidism,** in′va•lid•izm, *n.* The condition of being an invalid.—**invalidity,** in•va•lid′i•ti, *n.* Want of validity; want of cogency; want of legal force or efficacy.

invaluable, in•val′ū•a•bl, *a.* [Prefix *in,* not, and *valuable.*] Precious above estimation; so valuable that its worth cannot be estimated; inestimable.—**invaluably,** in•val′ū•a•bli, *adv.* Inestimably.

invar, in′var, *n.* [From *inva*riable.] An alloy of nickel and steel which is practically unaffected by extremes of temperature.

invariable, in•vâ′ri•a•bl, *a.* [Prefix *in,* not, and *variable.*] Not variable; constant in the same state; always uniform; never varying.—*n. Math.* an invariable quantity; a constant.—**invariableness, invariability,** in•vâ′ri•a•bl•nes, in•vâ′ri•a•bil″i•ti, *n.* State of not varying.—**invariably,** in•vâ′ri•a•bli, *adv.* Constantly; uniformly; always.

invasion, invasive. See INVADE.

invective, in•vek′tiv, *n.* [Fr., from L. *invectivus,* abusive, from *inveho,* to inveigh. INVEIGH.] A severe or violent utterance of censure or reproach; something uttered or written intended to cast opprobrium, censure, or reproach on another; railing language; vituperation.—*a.* Containing invectives; abusive; vituperative. —**invectively,** in•vek′tiv•li, *adv.* In an invective manner; abusively.—**invectiveness,** in•vek′tiv•nes, *n.* The quality of being invective or vituperative.

inveigh, in•vā′, *v.i.* [L. *invehor,* to attack with words, to inveigh against —*in,* into, against, and *veho,* to carry. VEHICLE.] To utter invectives; to exclaim or rail against a person or thing; to utter censorious or opprobrious words; with *against.* —**inveigher,** in•vā′ėr, *n.* One who inveighs or rails; a railer.

inveigle, in•vē′gl, *v.t.* [Norm. *enveogler,* to inveigle, to blind, for Fr. *aveugler,* to blind, from *aveugle,* blind—L. *ab,* not, and *oculus,* the eye. OCULAR.] To persuade to something evil by deceptive arts or flattery; to cajole into wrongdoing; to entice; to seduce.—**inveiglement,** in•vē′gl•ment, *n.* The act of inveigling.—**inveigler,** in•vē′gl•ėr, *n.* One who inveigles.

invent, in•vent′, *v.t.* [Fr. *inventer,* from L. *invenio, inventum,* to come upon, to find—*in,* upon, and *venio,* to come, as in *advent, convent, convene, prevent,* etc. VENTURE.] To contrive and produce; to devise, make, or construct as the originator of something that did not before exist; to frame by the imagination; to excogitate; to concoct; to fabricate. ∴ Syn. under DISCOVER.—**inventible,** in•ven′ti•bl, *a.* Capable of being invented.—**invention,** in•ven′shon, *n.* [L. *inventio, inventionis.*] The act of inventing; the contrivance of that which did not before exist; origination; something invented or contrived; a contrivance; the power of inventing; that skill or ingenuity which is or may be employed in contriving anything new; that faculty by which a poet or novelist produces plots, incidents, and characters, etc.—**inventive,** in•ven′tiv, *a.* Able to invent; quick at invention or contrivance; ready at expedients.—**inventively,** in•ven′tiv•li, *adv.* By the power of invention. —**inventiveness,** in•ven′tiv•nes, *n.* The faculty of inventing.—**inventor, inventer,** in•ven′tor, in•vent′ėr, *n.* One who invents or creates some new contrivance or device.

inventory, in′ven•tō•ri, *n.* [L. *inventarium,* an inventory, lit. a list of goods *found* in a place, from *invenio.* INVENT.] A list containing a description, with the values, of goods and chattels, made on various occasions, as on the sale of goods, or at decease of a person; any catalogue of goods or wares; a catalogue or account of particular things.—*v.t.*—*inventoried, inventorying.* To make an inventory, list, catalogue, or schedule of; to insert or register in an account of goods.—**inventorial,** in•ven•tō′ri•al, *a.* Of or pertaining to an inventory.—**inventorially,** in•ven•tō′ri•al•li, *adv.* In the manner of an inventory.

inverse, in•vėrs′, *a.* [L. *inversus,* pp. of *inverto*—*in,* on, to, and *verto,* to turn, as in *advert, convert, revert,* *subvert*, etc. VERSE.] Opposite in order or relation; inverted; having what usually is or should be after placed before; proceeding the backward or reverse way; *math.* opposite in nature and effect; thus, subtraction is *inverse* to addition, division to multiplication.—*Inverse proportion*, proportion such that one thing is greater or less as another is less or greater.—**inversely,** in•vėrs'li, *adv.* In an inverse order or manner; in inverse proportion.—**inversion,** in•vėr'zhon, *n.* [L. *inversio, inversionis*, from *inverto, inversum.*] The act of inverting or the state of being inverted; a change of order or position so that what was after is now before, and *vice versa*; a making inverse in order; *gram.* and *rhet.* transposition of words so that they are out of their natural order ('wise was Solomon' for 'Solomon was wise'); *mus.* change of position, as of an interval or a chord; *math.* a change in the order of the terms of a proportion, so that the second takes the place of the first, and the fourth of the third.

invert, in•vėrt', *v.t.* [L. *invertere, inversum*, from *in*, in, and *vertere*, to turn.] To turn upside down; to place in a contrary order or position; to put in inverse order or position.—*n.* in'vėrt. A homosexual; something inverted.—**inverted,** in•vėr'ted, *p.* and *a.* Turned to a contrary direction; turned upside down; changed in order; *bot.* having the apex in an opposite direction to that which is normal.—*Inverted arch*, an arch with its curve turned downward, as in a sewer, in foundations, etc.—*Inverted commas*, commas turned upside down to mark the beginning of a quotation, the end being indicated by apostrophes.—**invertible,** in•vėr'ti•bl, *a.*

invertebrate, in•vėr'te•brit, *a.* [Prefix *in*, not, and *vertebrate.* VERTEBRA.] Destitute of a backbone or vertebral column; morally or mentally without stamina or backbone.—**invertebrate,** in•vėr'te•brāt, *n.* An animal belonging to a major division of the animal kingdom, including all animals that have no vertebral column or spine.

invest, in•vest', *v.t.* [L. *investio—in*, and *vestio*, to clothe, from *vestis*, a garment. VEST.] To put garments on; to clothe, to dress, to array: usually followed by *with*, sometimes by *in*, before the thing put on; to clothe, as with office or authority; to place in possession of an office, rank, or dignity; *milit.* to enclose or surround for the purpose of besieging; to lay siege to; to lay out (money or capital) on some species of property, usually of a permanent nature, and with the purpose of getting a return (to *invest* money *in* bank shares).—*v.i.* To make an investment.—**investiture,** in•ves'ti•chėr, *n.* The act of investing; the act or right of giving possession of an office, dignity, etc.; that which invests or clothes; clothing; covering (*poet.* in this sense); the long medieval contest between Kings and the Papacy for the right of investing bishops and others with ecclesiastical or feudal dignities and rights.—**investment,** in•vest'ment, *n.* The act of investing; the act of besieging by an armed force; the laying out of money in the purchase of some species of property; money laid out for profit; that in which money is invested.—**investor,** in•ves'tėr, *n.* One who invests.

investigate, in•ves'ti•gāt, *v.t.—investigated, investigating.* [L. *investigo, investigatum—in*, and *vestigo*, to follow a track, to search, from *vestigium*, a track. VESTIGE.] To search into; to inquire and examine into with care and accuracy; to make careful research or examination into.—**investigable,** in•ves'ti•ga•bl, *a.* Capable of being investigated.—**investigation,** in•ves'ti•gā"shon, *n.* [L. *investigatio, investigationis.*] The act of investigating; the process of inquiring into a subject; research; inquiry.—**investigative,** in•ves'ti•gā•tiv, *a.* Given to or concerned with investigation.—**investigator,** in•ves'ti•gā•tėr, *n.* One who investigates.

inveterate, in•vet'ėr•it, *a.* [L. *inveteratus*, pp. of *invetero*, to render old—*in*, in, and *vetus, veteris*, old. VETERAN.] Firmly established by long continuance; deep-rooted or ingrained in a person's nature or constitution; firmly fixed by time or habit (*inveterate* disease, custom); confirmed in any habit by practice (an *inveterate* liar).—**inveterately,** in•vet'ėr•it•li, *adv.* In an inveterate manner.—**inveteracy,** in•vet'ėr•a•si, *n.* The state or quality of being inveterate; obstinacy confirmed by time.

invidious, in•vid'i•us, *a.* [L. *invidiosus*, from *invidia*, envy, *invidus*, envious. ENVY.] Envious‡; likely to bring on envy, ill will, or hatred; likely to provoke envy; entailing odium (*invidious* distinctions, preference, position).—**invidiously,** in•vid'i•us•li, *adv.* In an invidious manner.—**invidiousness,** in•vid'i•us•nes, *n.* The quality of being invidious.

invigorate, in•vig'or•āt, *v.t.—invigorated, invigorating.* [L. *in*, intens., and *vigor*, strength. VIGOR.] To give vigor to; to cause to feel fresh and vigorous; to strengthen; to give life and energy to.—**invigoration,** in•vig'o•rā"shon, *n.* Act of invigorating; state of being invigorated.

invincible, in•vin'si•bl, *a.* [L. *invincibilis—in*, not, and *vincibilis*, conquerable, from *vinco*, to conquer. VICTOR.] Incapable of being conquered or subdued; incapable of being overcome; unconquerable; insuperable.—*n.* One who is invincible.—**invincibility, invincibleness,** in•vin'si•bil"i•ti, in•vin'si•bl•nes, *n.* The quality of being invincible.—**invincibly,** in•vin'si•bli, *adv.* In an invincible manner; unconquerably; insuperably.

inviolable, in•vī'o•la•bl, *a.* [L. *inviolabilis—in*, not, and *violabilis*, that may be violated, from *violo*, to violate. VIOLATE.] Not to be violated or profaned; not to be polluted or treated with irreverence; not to be broken or infringed (agreement, secrecy); not to be injured or tarnished (chastity, honor); not susceptible of hurt or wound (*Mil.*).—**inviolably,** in•vī'o•la•bli, *adv.* In an inviolable manner; without violation or profanation.—**inviolability, inviolableness,** in•vī'o•la•bil"i•ti, in•vī'o•la•bl•nes, *n.* The state or quality of being inviolable.—**inviolate,** in•vī'o•lāt, *a.* [L. *inviolatus.*] Not violated; unprofaned; unpolluted; unbroken; inviolable.—**inviolately,** in•vī'o•lāt•li, *adv.* In an inviolate manner.—**inviolateness,** in•vī'o•lāt•nes, *n.*

invisible, in•viz'i•bl, *a.* [Prefix *in*, not, and *visible*; L. *invisibilis.*] Incapable of being seen; imperceptible by the sight.—*Invisible green*, a shade of green so dark as scarcely to be distinguishable from black.—**invisibleness, invisibility,** in•viz'i•bl•nes, in•viz'i•bil"i•ti, *n.* The state of being invisible; imperceptibleness to the sight.—**invisibly,** in•viz'i•bli, *adv.* In an invisible manner; imperceptibly to the eye.

invite, in•vīt', *v.t.—invited, inviting.* [L. *invito*, to invite, perhaps for *invicto, invecto—in*, and root of *vox*, voice.] To ask, request, bid, or call upon to do something; to summon; to ask to an entertainment or to pay a visit; to allure or attract; to tempt to come.—*v.i.* To give invitation; to allure or entice.—*n.* An invitation. (*Genteel slang.*)—**invitation,** in•vi•tā'shon, *n.* [L. *invitatio, invitationis.*] The act of inviting; solicitation; the requesting of a person's company as to an entertainment, on a visit, or the like.—**invitatory,** in•vī'ta•to•ri, *a.* Using or containing invitations.—**inviter,** in•vī'tėr, *n.* One who invites.—**inviting,** in•vī'ting, *p.* and *a.* Alluring; tempting; attractive (an *inviting* prospect).—**invitingly,** in•vī'ting•li, *adv.* In an inviting manner; attractively.—**invitingness,** in•vī'ting•nes, *n.* Attractiveness.

invocate, in'vō•kāt, *v.i.—invocated, invocating.* [L. *invoco, invocatum—in*, and *voco*, to call, *vox*, voice. VOICE, VOCAL.] To invoke; to call on in supplication; to implore; to address in prayer.—**invocation,** in•vo•kā'shon, *n.* [L. *invocatio, invocationis.*] The act of invoking or addressing in prayer; the form or act of calling for the assistance or presence of any being, particularly of some divinity.—**invocatory,** in•vō'ka•to•ri, *a.* Making invocation; invoking.

invoice, in'vois, *n.* [Fr. *envois*, things sent, goods forwarded, pl. of *envoi*, a sending, a thing sent, from *envoyer*, to send—L. *in*, and *via*, a way. ENVOY.] A written account of the particulars of merchandise sent to a purchaser, consignee, factor, etc., with the value or prices and charges annexed.—*v.t.—invoiced, invoicing.* To write or enter in an invoice.

invoke, in•vōk', *v.t.—invoked, invoking.* [Fr. *invoquer*, L. *invocare.* INVOCATE.] To address in prayer; to call on for assistance and protection; to call for solemnly or with earnestness.

involucre, involucrum, in•vo•lū′-kėr, in•vo•lū′krum, *n.* [L. *involucrum*, a wrapper or envelope, from *involvo*, to involve or wrap round—*in*, and *volvo*, to roll. INVOLVE.] *Bot.* any collection of bracts round a cluster of flowers; *anat.* a membrane which surrounds or encloses a part, as the pericardium.—**involucral,** in•vo•lū′-kral, *a.* Pertaining to or having an involucre.—**involucrate,** in•vo•lū′-krāt, *a. Bot.* having an involucre, as umbels, etc.—**involucel,** in•vol′ū•sel, *n.* [Dim. of *involucre, involucrum.*] *Bot.* the secondary involucrum or small bracts surrounding an umbellule of an umbelliferous flower.

involuntary, in•vol′un•te•ri, *n.* [Prefix *in*, not, and *voluntary.*] Not voluntary; not able to act or not acting according to will or choice (an *involuntary* agent); independent of will or choice (an *involuntary* movement); not proceeding from choice; not done willingly; unwilling.—**involuntarily,** in•vol′un•te•ri•li, *adv.* In an involuntary manner. —**involuntariness,** in•vol′un•te•ri•nes, *n.*

involute, involuted, in′vo•lūt, in′-vo•lū•ted, *a.* [L. *involutus*, pp. of *involvo.* INVOLVE.] Involved; twisted; confusedly mingled; *bot.* rolled inward from the edges: said of leaves and petals in vernation and estivation; *zool.* turned inward at the margin: said of the shells of mollusks.—*n.* A curve traced by any point of a tense string when it is unwrapped from a given curve.—*v.i.*, in•vo•lūt′—*involuted, involuting.* To curl up; return to normal.—**involution,** in•vo•lū′shon, *n.* The action of infolding; the state of being entangled or of being folded in; complication; *arith.* and *alg.* the raising of a quantity from its root to any power assigned; *biol.*, the reverse growing process; degeneration; *physiol.* the aging process.

involve, in•volv′, *v.t.*—*involved, involving.* [L. *involvo*—*in*, into, and *volvo*, to roll, as in *convolve, devolve, evolve, revolve, voluble*, etc. WALLOW.] To roll or wrap up; to envelop in folds; to entwine; to envelop; to cover with surrounding matter (*involved* in darkness); to imply or comprise, as a logical consequence (a statement that *involves* a contradiction); to connect by way of natural result or consequence; to entangle; to implicate; to complicate; to blend; to mingle confusedly; *arith.* and *alg.* to raise to any assigned power. ∴ Syn. under IMPLICATE.—**involved,** in•volvd′, *p.* and *a.* Complicated; entangled; intricate.—**involvement,** in•volv′ment, *n.* Act of involving.

invulnerable, in•vul′nėr•a•bl, *a.* [Prefix *in*, not, and *vulnerable*; L. *invulnerabilis.*] Not vulnerable; incapable of being wounded or of receiving injury; unassailable, as an argument; able to reply to all arguments.—**invulnerability, invulnerableness,** in•vul′nėr•a•bil″i•ti, in•vul′nėr•a•bl•nes, *n.* The quality or state of being invulnerable.—**invulnerably,** in•vul′-nėr•a•bli, *adv.* In an invulnerable manner.

inward, in′wėrd, *a.* [A.Sax. *inneweard*—prep. *in*, and suffix *-ward*, as in *backward, toward*, etc.] Internal; interior; placed or being within; in or connected with the mind, thoughts, soul, or feelings.—*adv.* also **inwards** (in′wėrdz). Toward the inside; toward the center or interior; into the mind or thoughts.—*n. pl.* the inner parts of an animal; the viscera.—**inwardly,** in′wėrd•li, *adv.* In an inward manner; internally; mentally; privately.—**inwardness,** in′wėrd•nes, *n.* The state of being inward or internal.

inweave, in•wēv′, *v.t.*—*inwove* (pret.), *inwoven* (pp.), *inweaving* (ppr.). To weave together.

inwreathe, in•rēTH′, *v.t.*—*inwreathed, inwreathing.* [Prefix *in*, and *wreathe.*] To surround or twine, as with a wreath; to infold or involve.

inwrought, in′ra̤t, *p.* and *a.* [Prefix *in*, and *wrought.*] Wrought or worked in or among other things.

iodine, ī′o•dīn, *n.* [Gr. *iōdēs*, resembling a violet (from its color)—*ion*, a violet, and *eidos*, resemblance.] A nonmetallic element occurring as a grayish-black crystalline solid; used in medicine. Symbol, I; at. no., 53; at. wt., 126.9044.—**iodic,** ī•od′ik, *a.* Pertaining to or containing iodine (*iodic* silver).—*Iodic acid*, an acid formed by the action of oxidizing agents on iodine in presence of water or alkalies.—**iodide,** ī′o•dīd, *n.* A compound of iodine and another element; a salt of hydriodic acid.—**iodism,** ī′o•dīzm, *n. Pathol.* a peculiar morbid state produced by the use of iodine.—**iodize,** ī′o•dīz, *v.t.*—*iodized, iodizing.* To treat with iodine; to impregnate or affect with iodine.—**iodoform,** ī•od′o•form, *n.* A compound of carbon, hydrogen, and iodine, analogous to chloroform.

iodol, ī′od•ōl. [From *iodine.*] An antiseptic derived from coal tar.

iolite, ī′o•līt, *n.* [Gr. *ion*, a violet, and *lithos*, stone.] A mineral of a violet blue color; dichroite.

ion, ī′on, *n.* [Gr. *ion*, from *eimi*, go.] An atom or group of atoms having either a positive or a negative charge from having lost or gained one or more electrons.—*Ion exchange*, a reversible transfer of ions between a solid and a solution without a substantial change in the make-up of the solid.—**ionize,** ī′on•īz, *v.t.*—*ionized, ionizing.* To convert into ions; to cause ions in.—*v.i.* To become conductors, by being changed into the form of ions.—**ionization,** ī′on•i•zā″shon, *n.* The conversion into ions.—*Ionization chamber*, an enclosure where ionized gases are studied; a device for the calculation of the radioactivity of a substance by measuring the current resulting from the ionization of its escaping vapor.—**ionosphere,** ī•on′o•sfēr, *n.* That part of the earth's atmosphere which lies beyond the stratosphere, approximately 65 miles up.

Ionic, ī•on′ik, *a.* Relating to *Ionia*, or to the Ionian Greeks.—*Ionic order*, one of the five orders of architecture, the distinguishing characteristic of which consists in the volutes of its capital.—*Ionic dialect*, a dialect of the ancient Greek language.

iota, ī•ō′ta, *n.* [Gr. *iōta*; hence *jot.*] Primarily the name of the Greek letter *i*, which in certain cases is indicated by a sort of dot under another letter (as ῳ); hence, a very small quantity; a tittle; a jot.

I O U, ī′ ō ū, *n.* [A phonetic equivalent of *I owe you.*] A paper addressed to a person having on it these letters, followed by a sum, and duly signed; serving as an acknowledgment of a debt.

ipecac, ipecacuanha, ip′i•kak, i′pi•kak•ū•an″a, *n.* [Tupi, *ipekaaguene*, from *ipeh* low *kaa*, leaves, and *guene*, vomit.] A South American shrub from whose root a powerful emetic or expectorant is extracted; the drug itself.

iracund,† ī′ra•kund, *a.* [L. *iracundus*, angry, from *ira*, anger; whence *ire, irate*, etc.] Angry; passionate. (*Carl.*)

irade, i•rä′di, *n.* [Turk.] A decree or proclamation of the Sultan of Turkey.

Iranian, ī•rā′ni•an, *a.* Pertaining to *Iran*, the native name of Persia; applied to certain languages, including Persian, Zend, and cognate tongues.

irascible, i•ras′i•bl, *a.* [L. *irascibilis*, from *irascor*, to be angry, from *ira*, anger, whence also *ire, irate.*] Readily made angry; easily provoked; apt to get into a passion; irritable.—**irascibility, irascibleness,** i•ras′i•bil″i•ti, i•ras′i•bl•nes, *n.* The quality of being irascible.—**irascibly,** i•ras′-i•bli, *adv.* In an irascible manner.

irate, ī•rāt′, *a.* [L. *iratus*, angry, from *irascor*, to be angry. IRASCIBLE.] Angry; enraged; incensed.

ire, īr, *n.* [O.Fr., from L. *ira*, wrath.] Anger; wrath; keen resentment.—**ireful,** īr′fu̥l, *a.* Full of ire; angry; wroth.—**irefully,** īr′fu̥l•li, *adv.*

iridescent, ir•i•des′ent, *a.* [L. *iris*, *iridis*, the rainbow.] Giving out colors like those of the rainbow; gleaming or shimmering with rainbow colors.—**iridescence,** ir•i•des′-ens, *n.*

iridium, i•rid′i•um, *n.* [L. *iris*, the rainbow.] A metallic element resembling platinum; one of the heaviest substances known. Symbol, Ir; at. no., 77; at. wt., 192.2.—**iridosmine, iridosmium,** ir•i•dos′-min, ir•i•dos′mi•um, *n.* A native compound of iridium and osmium used for pointing gold pens.

iris, ī′ris, *n.* pl. **irises,** ī′ris•ez, **irides,** ī′ri•dēz (especially of the eye). [L. *iris, iridis*, Gr. *iris, iridos*, the rainbow, the plant iris, the iris of the eye.] The rainbow; an appearance resembling the rainbow; a kind of muscular curtain stretched vertically in the anterior part of the eye, forming its colored part, and perforated by the pupil for the transmission of light; the fleur-de-lis, or flag flower, a plant of various species.

Irish, ī′rish, *a.* Pertaining to Ireland or its inhabitants; Erse.—*n.* The Irish language; with plural signification, the people of Ireland.—*Irish moss*, a seaweed of the Atlantic Ocean which, when dried and bleached, is used to keep solids in suspension, and as a thickening in some cooking.—*Irish setter*, a russet-colored hunting dog taught to stand rigid and point upon finding game.

irk, ėrk, *v.t.* [The same word as Sw. *yrka*, to urge, enforce, press, from root of *work*, *wreak*, and *urge*.] To weary; to give annoyance or uneasiness to; to be distressingly tiresome to; to annoy: used chiefly or only impersonally (it *irks* me).—**irksome,** ėrk′sum, *a.* Wearisome; burdensome; vexatious; giving uneasiness (*irksome* labor, delay, etc.).—**irksomely,** ėrk′sum•li, *adv.* In an irksome manner.—**irksomeness,** ėrk′sum•nes, *n.*

iron, ī′ėrn, *n.* [A.Sax. *iren*, *isen*, Goth. *eisarn*, D. *ijzer*; comp. Skr. *ayas*, W. *haiarn*.] A metallic element, silver white, malleable, and ductile, widely found in combination, strongly attracted by magnets, and easily oxidized. Symbol, Fe (Latin *ferrum*); at. no., 26; at. wt., 55.847.—An instrument or utensil made of iron; an instrument that when heated is used for smoothing cloth; *pl.* fetters; chains; manacles; handcuffs.—*To have many irons in the fire*, to be engaged in many undertakings. [*Cast iron* is iron direct from the smelting furnace (blast furnace), also called *pig iron*; *wrought* or *malleable iron* has to undergo the further process of puddling; *steel* is a variety of iron containing more carbon than malleable iron and less than cast iron.]—*a.* Made of iron; consisting of iron; resembling iron, either really or metaphorically; hence, harsh, rude, severe; capable of great endurance; firm; robust; inflexible.—*v.t.* To smooth with an iron; to fetter or handcuff; to furnish or arm with iron. —**Iron Age,** that cultural epoch chiefly distinguished by the use of iron; roughly, the last thousand years B. C.—**ironbark,** ī′ėrn•bärk, *n.* Certain Australian eucalypti with hard bark.—**ironbound,** *a.* Bound with iron; faced or surrounded with rocks; rugged (an *ironbound* coast).—**ironclad,** *a.* Covered or clothed with iron plates; armor-plated.—*n.* A vessel prepared for naval warfare by being cased or covered, wholly or partially, with thick iron plates. —**iron curtain,** *n.* A barrier of strict censorship and restriction of freedom, as the boundary between Soviet-held territory and the free world.—**ironer,** ī′ėn•ėr, *n.*—**iron horse,** a locomotive. (Colloq.)—**iron lung,** *n.* A device for forcing air into and out of the lungs by means of rhythmically changing pressure in a chamber surrounding the lungs.—**iron pyrites.** PYRITES.—**ironsmith,** ī′ėrn•smith, *n.* A worker in iron, as a blacksmith, locksmith, etc.—**ironstone,** *n.* A general name applied to the ores of iron containing oxygen and silica.—**ironware,** ī′ėrn•wãr, *n.* Utensils, tools, and various light articles of iron.—**ironweed,** ī•ėrn•wēd, *n.* A plant of the genus *Vernonia* found in the eastern U.S.—**ironwood,** *n.* The popular name given to several very hard and very heavy woods in different countries.—**ironwork,** ī′ėrn•wėrk, *n.* A general name of the parts of a building, vessel, bridge, etc., which consist of iron; a work or establishment where iron is manufactured. **irony,** ī′ėrn•i, *a.* Pertaining to or resembling iron in any qualities.

irony, ī′ron•i, *n.* [Fr. *ironie*, L. *ironia*, from Gr. *eirōneia*, from *eirōn*, a dissembler in speech, from *eirō*, to speak.] A mode of speech by which words express a sense contrary to that really intended; sarcasm, in which apparent praise really conveys disapprobation.—**ironical, ironic,** ī•ron′i•kal, ī•ron′ik, *a.* Relating to or containing irony; addicted to irony; using irony.—**ironically,** ī•ron′i•kal•li, *adv.* In an ironical manner.—**ironicalness,** *n.*

Iroquois, ir′o•kwoi, *n.* sing., pl. An early Indian confederation of New York state, composed of Cayugas, Mohawks, Oneidas, Onondagas, Senecas and later the Tuscaroras, referred to as the Five Nations; a member of one of these tribes.

irradiate, ir•rā′di•āt, *v.t.*—*irradiated, irradiating.* [L. *irradio*, *irradiatum*—*in*, in or on, and *radius*, a ray.] To illuminate or shed a light upon; to cast splendor or brilliancy upon; to illuminate; to penetrate by radiation; to treat for healing by radiation, as by that of X rays or ultraviolet rays. —*v.i.* To emit rays; to shine.—**irradiance, irradiancy,** ir•rā′di•ans, ir•rā′di•an•si, *n.* Emission of rays of light on an object; luster; splendor. —**irradiant,** ir•rā′di•ant, *a.*—**irradiation,** ir•rā′di•ā″shon, *n.* Exposure to rays of all types; use of X-rays in therapy; emission of radiant energy; use of radiation to induce chemical change.

irrational, ir•rash′on•al, *a.* [Prefix *ir* for *in*, not, and *rational*.] Not rational; void of reason or understanding; contrary to reason; absurd; *math.* not capable of being exactly expressed by an integral number or by a vulgar fraction; surd.—**irrationality, irrationalness,** ir•rash′on•al″i•ti, ir•rash′on•al•nes, *n.* The condition or quality of being irrational.—**irrationally,** ir•rash′on•al•li, *adv.* In an irrational manner.

irreclaimable, ir•ri•klā′ma•bl, *a.* [Prefix *ir* for *in*, not, and *reclaimable*.] Incapable of being reclaimed or recalled from error or vice; incapable of being reformed; incorrigible.—**irreclaimably,** ir•ri•klā′ma•bli, *adv.*

irreconcilable, ir•rek′on•sī″la•bl, *a.* [Prefix *ir* for *in*, not, and *reconcilable*.] Not reconcilable; not to be reconciled; implacable (an enemy, enmity); incapable of being made to agree or be consistent; inconsistent. —*n.* One who is not to be reconciled; especially, a member of a political body who will not work in harmony with his co-members.—**irreconcilability, irreconcilableness,** ir•rek′on•sī′la•bil″i•ti, ir•rek′on•sī″la•bl•nes, *n.* The quality of being irreconcilable.—**irreconcilably,** ir•rek′on•sī″la•bli, *adv.* So as to preclude reconciliation.

irrecoverable, ir•ri•kuv′ėr•a•bl, *a.* [Prefix *ir* for *in*, not, and *recoverable*.] Incapable of being recovered or regained; not capable of being restored, remedied, or made good.—**irrecoverableness,** ir•ri•kuv′ėr•a•bl•nes, *n.* The state of being irrecoverable.—**irrecoverably,** ir•ri•kuv′ėr•a•bli, *adv.* In an irrecoverable manner; beyond recovery.

irredeemable, ir•ri•dē′ma•bl, *a.* [Prefix *ir* for *in*, not, and *redeemable*.] Not redeemable; not subject to be paid at its nominal value: specifically applied to a depreciated paper currency.—**irredeemably,** ir•ri•dē′ma•bli, *adv.* So as not to be redeemed.

irreducible, ir•ri•dū′si•bl, *a.* [Prefix *ir* for *in*, not, and *reducible*.] Not reducible; incapable of being reduced.

irrefragable, ir•ref′ra•ga•bl, *a.* [Prefix *ir* for *in*, not, and L. *refragor*, to withstand or gainsay—*re*, back, and root of *frango*, to break. FRACTION.] Incapable of being refuted or overthrown; incontestable; undeniable; incontrovertible. —**irrefragability,** ir•ref′ra•ga•bil″i•ti, *n.* The quality of being irrefragable.—**irrefragably,** ir•ref′ra•ga•bli, *adv.* In an irrefragable manner; incontestably.

irrefutable, ir•ref′ū•ta•bl or ir•ri•fū′ta•bl, *a.* [Prefix *ir* for *in*, not, and *refutable*.] Not refutable; incapable of being refuted or disproved.—**irrefutably,** ir•ri•fū′ta•bli or ir•ref′ū•ta•bli, *adv.* In an irrefutable manner.

irregular, ir•reg′ū•lėr, *a.* [Prefix *ir* for *in*, and *regular*.] Not regular; not according to rules, established principles, or customs; not conformable to the usual operation of natural laws; deviating from the rules of moral rectitude; vicious; not straight or uniform; *gram.* deviating from the common form in respect to the inflectional terminations; *geom.* applied to a figure whose sides as well as angles are not all equal and similar among themselves; *bot.* not having the parts of the same size or form, or arranged with symmetry.—*n.* One not conforming to settled rule; especially, a soldier not in regular service. —**irregularity,** ir•reg′ū•lar″i•ti, *n.* State or character of being irregular; want of regularity; that which is irregular; a part exhibiting or causing something to be irregular or impairing uniformity; an action or behavior constituting a breach of morality; vicious conduct.—**irregularly,** ir•reg′ū•lėr•li, *adv.* In an irregular manner.

irrelative, ir•rel′a•tiv, *a.* [Prefix *ir* for *in*, not, and *relative*.] Not relative; without mutual relations.—**irrelatively,** ir•rel′a•tiv•li, *adv.*

irrelevant, ir•rel′e•vant, *a.* [Prefix *ir* for *in*, not, and *relevant*.] Not relevant; not applicable or pertinent; not bearing on the case in point or matter in hand.—**irrelevantly,** ir•-

rel′e•vant•li, *adv.* In an irrelevant manner.—**irrelevance, irrelevancy,** ir•rel′e•vans, ir•rel′e•van•si, *n.* The quality of being irrelevant.

irreligion, ir•ri•lij′on, *n.* [Prefix *ir* for *in*, not, and *religion.*] Want of religion or contempt of it; impiety.—**irreligious,** ir•ri•lij′us, *a.* Characterized by irreligion; disregarding or contemning religion; contrary to religion; profane; impious; ungodly. —**irreligiously,** ir•ri•lij′us•li, *adv.* In an irreligious manner.

irremeable,† ir•re•mi′a•bl, *a.* [L. *irremeabilis*—*ir* for *in*, not, *re*, back, and *meo*, to go.] Not permitting of a person's return.

irremediable, ir•ri•mē′di•a•bl, *a.* [Prefix *ir* for *in*, not, and *remediable.*] Incapable of being remedied or cured; not to be corrected or redressed; incurable; irreparable.—**irremediableness,** ir•ri•mē′di•a•bl•nes, *n.*—**irremediably,** ir•ri•mē′di•a•bli, *adv.*

irremissible, ir•ri•mis′i•bl, *a.* [Prefix *ir* for *in*, not, and *remissible.*] Not remissible; unpardonable; not capable of being remitted.—**irremissibly,** ir•ri•mis′i•bli, *adv.*

irremovable, ir•ri•mö′va•bl, *a.* [Prefix *ir* for *in*, not, and *removable.*] Not removable; immovable; inflexible. —**irremovably,** ir•ri•mö′va•bli, *adv.* In an irremovable manner.—**irremovability,** ir•ri•mö′va•bil″i•ti, *n.* The quality or state of being irremovable.

irreparable, ir•rep′a•ra•bl, *a.* [Prefix *ir* for *in*, not, and *reparable.*] Not reparable; incapable of being repaired; irremediable.—**irreparability, irreparableness,** ir•rep′a•ra•bil″i•ti, ir•rep′a•ra•bl•nes, *n.* State of being irreparable.—**irreparably,** ir•rep′a•ra•bli, *adv.* In an irreparable manner; irrecoverably.

irrepressible, ir•ri•pres′i•bl, *a.* [Prefix *ir* for *in*, not, and *repressible.*] Not repressible; incapable of being repressed, restrained, or kept under control.—**irrepressibly,** ir•ri•pres′i•bli, *adv.* In a manner or degree precluding repression.

irreproachable, ir•ri•prōch′a•bl, *a.* [Prefix *ir* for *in*, not, and *reproachable.*] Incapable of being reproached; not occasioning reproach; upright; innocent; faultless; unblemished.—**irreproachableness,** ir•ri•prōch′a•bl•nes, *n.* The quality or state of being irreproachable.—**irreproachably,** ir•ri•prōch′a•bli, *adv.* In an irreproachable manner; faultlessly; blamelessly.

irresistance, ir•ri•zis′tans, *n.* [Prefix *ir* for *in*, not, and *resist.*] Forbearance to resist; nonresistance.—**irresistible,** ir•ri•zis′ti•bl, *a.* Not resistible; incapable of being successfully resisted or opposed; resistless; invincible.—**irresistibility,** ir•ri•zis′ti•bil″i•ti, *n.* The quality of being irresistible.—**irresistibly,** ir•ri•zis′ti•bli, *adv.* In an irresistible manner; resistlessly.

irresoluble,† ir•rez′o•lū•bl, *a.* [Prefix *ir* for *in*, not, and *resoluble.*] Incapable of resolution into parts; indissoluble. —**irresolubleness,** ir•rez′o•lū•bl•nes, *n.*

irresolute, ir•rez′o•lūt, *a.* [Prefix *ir* for *in*, not, and *resolute.*] Not resolute; not firm or constant in purpose; undecided; wavering; given to doubt or hesitation; vacillating.—**irresolutely,** ir•rez′o•lūt•li, *adv.* In an irresolute manner.—**irresoluteness,** ir•rez′o•lūt•nes, *n.* The quality of being irresolute.—**irresolution,** ir•rez′o•lū″shon, *n.* Want of resolution or decision; a fluctuation of mind; vacillation.

irresolvable, ir•ri•zol′va•bl, *a.* [Prefix *ir* for *in*, not, and *resolvable.*] Incapable of being resolved.

irrespective, ir•ri•spek′tiv, *a.* [Prefix *ir* for *in*, not, and *respective.*] Having no respect to particular circumstances: generally used in the prepositional phrase *irrespective of*, that is, leaving out of account.—**irrespectively,** ir•ri•spek′tiv•li, *adv.* Without regard to certain circumstances (*irrespectively of* these matters).

irrespirable, ir•ri•spī′ra•bl, *a.* [Prefix *ir* for *in*, not, and *respirable.*] Not respirable; unfit for respiration.

irresponsible, ir•ri•spon′si•bl, *a.* [Prefix *ir* for *in*, not, and *responsible.*] Not responsible; not liable to answer for consequences. —**irresponsibly,** ir•ri•spon′si•bli, *adv.* In an irresponsible manner.—**irresponsibility,** ir•ri•spon′si•bil″i•ti, *n.* Want of responsibility.

irresponsive, ir•ri•spon′siv, *a.* [Prefix *ir* for *in*, not, and *responsive.*] Not responsive.

irretraceable, ir•ri•trā′sa•bl, *a.* [Prefix *ir* for *in*, not, and *retraceable.*] Not retraceable.

irretrievable, ir•ri•trē′va•bl, *a.* [Prefix *ir* for *in*, not, and *retrievable.*] Not retrievable; irrecoverable; irreparable.—**irretrievably,** ir•ri•trē′va•bli, *adv.* In an irretrievable manner; irrecoverably.

irreverence, ir•rev′er•ens, *n.* [Prefix *ir* for *in*, not, and *reverence*; L. *irreverentia.*] Want of reverence or veneration; want of a due regard to the authority and character of a superior; irreverent conduct or an irreverent action.—**irreverent,** ir•rev′er•ent, *a.* [L. *irreverens.*] Exhibiting or marked by irreverence (person, conduct, words); wanting in respect to superiors.—**irreverently,** ir•rev′er•ent•li, *adv.* In an irreverent manner; with want of reverence; disrespectfully.

irreversible, ir•ri•vėr′si•bl, *a.* [Prefix *ir* for *in*, not, and *reversible.*] Not reversible; incapable of being reversed.—**irreversibly,** ir•ri•vėr′si•bli, *adv.* In an irreversible manner; so as not to be reversed; immutably.

irrevocable, ir•rev′o•ka•bl, *a.* [Prefix *ir* for *in*, not, and *revocable.*] Not to be recalled or revoked; incapable of being reversed, repealed, or annulled; irreversible (fate, decree, etc.). —**irrevocability, irrevocableness,** ir•rev′o•ka•bil″i•ti, ir•rev′o•ka•bl•nes, *n.* State of being irrevocable.—**irrevocably,** ir•rev′o•ka•bli, *adv.* In an irrevocable manner; irreversibly; immutably.

irrigate, ir′ri•gāt, *v.t.*—*irrigated, irrigating.* [L. *irrigo, irrigatum*—*ir* for *in*, and *rigo*, to water. RAIN.] To bedew or sprinkle; to water (land) by causing a stream to flow upon it and spread over it; to water by various artificial channels for water.—**irrigation,** ir•ri•gā′shon, *n.* [L. *irrigatio.*] The act or operation of irrigating.—**irriguous,** ir•rig′ū•us, *a.* [L. *irriguus.*] Having many streams; well watered. (*Mil.*)

irritant, ir′ri•tant, *a.* [L. *irrito*, to make void, from *in*, not, and *ratus*, ratified.] *Scots law*, rendering null and void.—**irritancy,** ir′ri•tan•si, *n.* The state of being irritant or null and void.

irritate, ir′ri•tāt, *v.t.* [L. *irrito*, *irritatum*, to incite, stir up, provoke; perhaps from *hirrire*, to snarl.] To excite anger in; to provoke; to tease; to exasperate; to excite heat and redness in, as in the skin or flesh; to inflame; to fret; *physiol.* to excite by certain stimuli; to cause to exhibit irritation.—**irritation,** ir•ri•tā′shon, *n.* [L. *irritatio*, *irritationis.*] The act of irritating or state of being irritated; provocation; exasperation; angry feeling; feeling of heat and pain in a part of the body; *physiol.* the change or action which takes place in muscles or organs when a nerve or nerves are affected by the application of external bodies.—**irritative,** ir′ri•tā•tiv, *a.* Serving to excite or irritate.—**irritable,** ir′ri•ta•bl, *a.* [L. *irritabilis.*] Capable or susceptible of being irritated; readily provoked or exasperated; of a fiery temper; *physiol.* susceptible of responding to or being acted upon by stimuli.—**irritability, irritableness,** ir′ri•ta•bil″i•ti, ir′ri•ta•bl•nes, *n.* The state or quality of being irritable.—**irritably,** ir′ri•ta•bli, *adv.* In an irritable manner.—**irritant,** ir′ri•tant, *a.* [L. *irritans*, *irritantis*, ppr. of *irrito.*] Irritating; producing pain, heat, or tension; producing inflammation (an *irritant* poison).—*n.* That which excites or irritates; a medical application that causes pain or heat (as a fly blister); an irritant poison.

irruption, ir•rup′shon, *n.* [L. *irruptio*, *irruptionis*, from *irrumpo*, *irruptum*—*in*, in, and *rumpo*, to break. RUPTURE.] A bursting in; a breaking, or sudden, violent rushing into a place; a sudden invasion or incursion. —**irruptive,** ir•rup′tiv, *a.* Rushing in or upon.

is, iz, [A.Sax. is = Goth. *ist*, L. *est*, Gr. *esti*, Skr. *asti*, is. AM.] The 3rd, pers. sing. of the verb *to be.* BE.

isagogic, ī•sa•goj′ik, *a.* [Gr. *eisagōgikos*, from *eisagó*, to introduce—*eis*, in, into, and *agó*, to lead.] Introductory; especially, introductory to the study of theology.—**isagogics,** ī•sa•goj′iks, *n.* The department of theological study introductory to exegesis.

ischiadic, is•ki•ad′ik, *a.* [L. *ischiadicus*, from *ischias*, sciatica, from *ischium*, Gr. *ischion*, the hip.] Pertaining to sciatica.—*Ischiadic passion* or *disease*, sciatica.—**ischial,** is′ki•al, *a.* Belonging to the ischium or hipbone.—**ischiatic,** is•ki•at′ik, *a.* Pertaining to the ischium of the hip.—**ischium,** is′ki•um, *n.* [Gr. *ischion.*] *Anat.* the posterior and inferior part of the pelvic arch at the hip joint.

Ishmaelite, ish′mi•el•it, *n.* [From *Ishmael*: Gen. xvi. 12.] A descendant of Ishmael; one resembling Ishmael, whose hand was against every man and every man's hand against him; one at war with society. **Ishmaelitish,** ish′mi•el•īt•ish, *a.* Like Ishmael or an Ishmaelite.

isinglass, ī′zing•glas, *n.* [Corrupted from D. *huizenblas—huizen,* a sturgeon, and *blas,* a vesicle, a bladder (akin to *blow, bladder*).] A gelatinous substance from air bladders of certain fishes, particularly species of sturgeon found in the rivers of Russia, used in clarifying liquors, as a cement, etc.; also thin sheets of mica.

Isis, ī′sis, *n.* One of the chief deities in the Egyptian mythology, regarded as the sister or sister-wife of Osiris.

Islam, iz′lam, *n.* [Ar., from *salama,* to be free, safe, or devoted to God.] The religion of Mohammed, and also the whole body of those who profess it throughout the world.—**Islamic,** iz•lam′ik, *a.*—**Islamism,** iz′-lam•izm, *n.*—**Islamite,** iz′lam•it, *n.* A Mohammedan.—**Islamize,** iz′lam•-īz, *v.t.* or *i.* To conform to Islamism; to Mohammedanize.

island, ī′land, *n.* [From A.Sax. *igland,* lit. island-land, from *ig,* an island, and *land,* land; the *s* is due to erroneous connection with L. *insula,* O.Fr. *isle.* ISLE.] A tract of land surrounded by water, whether of the sea, a river, or a lake; anything resembling an island; a safety zone in the middle of a street; the raised area located next to the flight deck on the starboard side of an aircraft carrier.—*v.t.* To cause to become or appear like an island; to isolate; to dot, as with islands.—**islander,** ī′lan•dėr, *n.*

isle, īl, *n.* [O.Fr. *isle,* Fr. *ile,* Prov. *isla,* from L. *insula,* an island. INSULATE.] An island. [Chiefly poet.] —*v.t.*—*isled, isling.* To cause to become or appear like an isle; to isolate; to island.—**islet,** īl′et, *n.* [Dim. of *isle.*] A little isle or something similar.

isobar, ī′so•bär, *n.* [Gr. *isos,* equal, and *baros,* weight.] A line drawn on a map connecting places at which the mean height of the barometer at sea level is the same; isotopes of different chemical elements which have equal atomic masses but different atomic numbers.—**isobaric,** ī•so•bar′ik, *a.*

isocheim, ī′so•kīm, *n.* [Gr. *isos,* equal, and *cheima, cheimōn,* winter.] A line drawn on a map through places which have the same mean winter temperature.—**isocheimal, isochimal,** ī•so•kī′mal, *a.* Of the same mean winter temperature; marking places with the same mean winter temperature.—*Isocheimal line.* Same as *Isocheim.*

isochromatic, ī′so•krō•mat″ik, *a.* [Gr. *isos,* equal, and *chrōma,* color.] Having the same color; marking correspondence in tint as colored light passes through biaxial crystals.

isochronal, isochronous, ī•sok′ron•-al, ī•sok′ron•us, *a.* [Gr. *isos,* equal, and *chronos,* time.] Uniform in time; of equal time; performed in equal times (as oscillations of pendulums). —**isochronally,** ī•sok′ron•al•li, *adv.* So as to be isochronal.—**isochronism,** ī•sok′ron•izm, *n.* State or quality of being isochronous.

isoclinal, isoclinic, ī•so•kli′nal, ī•so-klin′ik, *a.* [Gr. *isos,* equal, and *klinō,* to incline.] Of equal inclination or dip.

isodynamic, ī′so•di•nam″ik, *a.* [Gr. *isos,* equal, and *dynamis,* power.] Having equal power or force.

isogeotherm, ī•so•jē′o•thėrm, *n.* [Gr. *isos,* equal, *gē,* the earth, and *thermē,* heat.] An imaginary line or plane under the earth's surface passing through points having the same mean temperature.—**isogeothermal,** ī•so•jē′o•thėr″mal, *a.* Pertaining to isogeotherms.

isogonic, ī•so•gon′ik, *a.* [Gr. *isos,* equal, and *gōnia,* an angle.] Having equal angles.—*Isogonic lines,* lines connecting those places where the deviation of the magnetic needle from the true north is the same.

isohel, ī′so•hel, *n.* [Gr. *helios,* sun.] A line drawn on a map through places having the same amount of bright sunshine.

isolate, ī′so•lāt or is′o•lāt, *v.t.*—*isolated, isolating.* [Fr. *isoler,* It. *isolare,* from *isola*=L. *insula,* an island. INSULATE.] To place or leave in a detached situation; to place apart; *elect.* to insulate; *chem.* to obtain (a substance) free from all its combinations.—**isolation,** ī•so•lā′shon, *n.* State of being isolated or alone.—**isolable,** ī′so•la•bl, *a.*

isomerism, ī•som′ėr•izm, *n.* [Gr. *isos,* equal, and *meros,* a part.] *Chem.* identity or close similarity of elements in weight, but with differences in structure, and therefore in properties; *phys.* and *chem.* elements of the same atomic number and mass number but having different properties.—**isomeric,** ī•so•-mėr′ik, *a.*—**isomerous,** ī•som′ėr•us, *a. Bot.* having organs composed each of an equal number of parts.

isometric, isometrical, ī•so•met′-rik, ī•so•met′ri•kal, *a.* [Gr. *isos,* equal, *metron,* measure.] Pertaining to, or characterized by, equality of measure.—*Isometrical perspective* or *projection,* a method of drawing plans whereby the elevation and ground plan are represented in one view.—**isometrics,** ī•so•met′riks, *n. Physiol.* a series of physical exercises, employing opposing forces, such as in pushing against the body itself or against an immovable object.

isomorphism, ī•so•mor′fizm, *n.* [Gr. *isos,* like, and *morphē,* form.] A similarity of crystalline form in minerals.—**isomorphous,** ī•so•mor′-fus, *a.* Exhibiting the property of isomorphism.

isonomy, ī•son′o•mi, *n.* [Gr. *isos,* equal, and *nomos,* law.] Equal law; equal distribution of rights and privileges.

isopod, ī′so•pod, *n.* [Gr. *isos,* equal, and *pous, podos,* the foot.] One of an order of crustaceans, comprehending those whose feet are of equal size and move in the same direction; the wood lice, and slaters are examples.

isopyre, ī′so•pīr, *n.* [Gr. *isos,* like, and *pyr,* fire.] A variety of opal mixed with impurities.

isosceles, ī•sos′se•lēz, *a.* [Gr. *isoskelēs—isos,* equal, and *skelos,* leg.] Having two legs or sides only that are equal (an *isosceles* triangle).

isoseismal, isoseismic, ī•so•sīs′-mal, ī•so•sīs′mik, *a.* [Gr. *isos,* equal, and *seismos,* an earthquake, from *seiō,* to shake.] Marking equal earthquake disturbance on the earth's surface.

isothere, ī′so•thēr, *n.* [Gr. *isos,* equal, and *theros,* summer.] An imaginary line on the earth's surface passing through points having the same mean summer temperature.—**isotheral,** ī•soth′ėr•al, *a.* Pertaining to or marked by isotheres.

isotherm, ī′so•thėrm, *n.* [Gr. *isos,* equal, proper, and *therme,* heat.] An imaginary line on the earth's surface passing through places having a corresponding temperature either throughout the year or at any particular period.—**isothermal,** ī•so•-thėr′mal, *a.* Pertaining to an isotherm or isotherms; marking correspondence in temperature.—*Isothermal line,* an isotherm.

isotonic, ī•so•ton′ik, *a.* [Gr. *isos,* equal, and *tonos,* tone.] Having or indicating equal tones.

isotope, ī′so•tōp, *n.* [Gr. *isos,* equal, and *topos,* place.] Any of two or more forms of a chemical element having the same atomic number but different atomic weights.

isotropic, ī•so•trop′ik, *a.* [Gr. *isos,* equal, and *tropē,* a turning, from *trepō,* to turn.] *Phys.* pertaining to bodies whose properties are the same in all directions; *biol.* without predetermined axes, as some eggs.

Israelite, iz′ri•el•īt, *n.* A descendant of *Israel,* or Jacob; a Jew.—**Israelitic, Israelitish,** iz′ri•el•it″ik, iz′ri•el•īt″-ish, *a.* Pertaining to Israel; Jewish; Hebrew.

issue, ish′ū, *n.* [Fr. *issue,* issue, outlet, event, from O.Fr. *issir,* to go out, to flow forth, and that from L. *exeo, exire,* to go out—*ex,* out, and *eo,* to go (in *circuit, exit, initial,* etc). ITINERANT.] The act of passing or flowing out; a moving out of any enclosed place; the act of sending out; delivery (of commands, money, etc.); the whole quantity sent forth or issued at one time (an *issue* of paper money; yesterday's *issue* of the *Times*); what happens or turns out; event; consequence; progeny; a child or children; offspring; all persons descended from a common ancestor; a flux of blood (*N.T.*); *surg.* an artificial ulcer made in some part of the body to promote a secretion of pus; *law,* the close or result of pleadings; the point or matter depending in a suit on which two parties join and put their cause to trial; hence, a material point turning up in any argument or debate, when one party takes the negative, the other the positive side on an important point.—*At issue*, in controversy; disputed; opposing or contesting.—*To join issue, to take issue*, said of two parties who take up a positive and negative position respectively on a point in debate.—*v.i.*—*issued, issuing.* To pass, flow, or run out, as from any enclosed place; to proceed, as from a source; to rush out; to proceed, as progeny; to be produced, as an effect or result; to close, end, terminate.—*v.t.* To send out; to deliver for use; to deliver authoritatively (orders, etc.); to put (notes, coin, newspapers) into circulation.—**issuable,** ish′ū•a•bl, *a.* Capable of being issued; admitting of issue being taken upon it.—**issuance,** ish′ū•ans, *n.* The act of issuing or giving out.—**issuer,** ish′ū•er, *n.* One who issues or emits.

isthmus, is′mus, *n.* [L., from Gr. *isthmos*, a neck of land or narrow passage.] A neck or narrow slip of land by which two continents are connected, or by which a peninsula is united to the mainland.—**isthmian,** is′mi•an, *a.* Of or pertaining to an isthmus.—*Isthmian games*, ancient Greek games celebrated at the Isthmus of Corinth, in the first and third year of each olympiad, in honor of Poseidon.

it, it, *pron*, [A.Sax. nom. *hit*, neut. corresponding to *hé*, he, genit. or pos. *his*, dat. and instrumental *him*; Goth. *ita*, D. *het*, O.H.G. *iz*, G. *es*. HE.] A pronoun of the neuter gender corresponding with the masculine *he* and the feminine *she*, having the same plural *they*. Besides standing in place of neuter nouns *it* is used (1) as the nominative to impersonal verbs (*it* rains; *it* snows); (2) to introduce a sentence, preceding a verb as a nominative, but referring to a clause or distinct member of the sentence following (*it* is well ascertained that the figure of the earth is an oblate spheroid); (3) for a preceding clause of a sentence (we have been defeated for the present, *it* is true); (4) to begin a sentence when a personal pronoun, or the name of a person, or a masculine or feminine noun follows, where it may represent any one of the three persons or of the three genders (as, *it* is I; *it* was they); (5) for state of matters, condition of affairs, or the like (has *it* come to this?); (6) after intransitive verbs very indefinitely (to walk *it*, to run *it*). ∴ The possessive case *its* does not appear till a year or two before 1600, *his* being used both for the masculine and the neuter possessive.

Italian, i•tal′yan, *a.* Pertaining to *Italy*.—*n.* A native of Italy; the language used in Italy or by the Italians.—*Italian iron*, a smoothing iron, consisting essentially of a metal tube with a closed rounded end heated by a metal bolt; used for fluting or gauffering.—*Italian warehouse*, a name in England for shops where groceries, including some Italian products, are sold.—*Italian handwriting*, the method of penmanship, practically the copperplate hand of clear lettering, adopted from Italy, opposed to the old Gothic script.—**Italianism, Italicism,** i•tal′yan•izm, i•tal′i•sism, *n.* An Italian expression, manner, or custom.—**Italianize,** i•tal′yan•īz, *v.t.* To give an Italian color or character to.—**Italic,** i•tal′ik, *a.* Pertaining to Italy; [*not cap.*] the name of a printing type sloping toward the right, invented about A.D. 1500 by Aldus Manutius, a Venetian printer.—*n.* [*not cap.*] An italic letter or type.—**italicize,** i•tal′i•sīz, *v.t.*—*italicized, italicizing.* To write or print in italic characters; to distinguish by italics.

itch, ich, *n.* [O.E. *ichyn*, *gykin*, A.Sax. *giccan*, to itch; G. *jucken*, to itch; D. *jeuking*, *jeukte*, Sc. *yuik*, itch.] A sensation in the skin causing a great desire to scratch or rub; a cutaneous disease due to a minute species of mite; a constant teasing desire (an *itch* for praise).—*v.i.* To feel an itch; to have an uneasy or teasing sensation impelling to something.—**itch mite,** *n.* The microscopic animal which produces itch.—**itchy,** ich′i, *a.* Infected with or having the sensation as if suffering from itch.

item, ī′tem, *n.* [L. *item*, also.] A separate article; a particular; a piece of information; one thing in a list; a scrap of news.—**itemize,** ī′tem•īz, *v.t.* To list or state the items, to particularize.

iterate, it′ėr•āt, *v.t.*—*iterated, iterating.* [L. *itero*, *iteratum*, to do again, to repeat, from *iterum*, again, from *id*, it, with the comparative suffix; akin Skr. *itara*, another.] To utter or do a second time; to repeat.—**iteration,** it•ėr•ā′shon, *n.* [L. *iteratio*, *iterationis*.] Repetition; recital or performance a second time.—**iterative,** it′ėr•ā•tiv, *a.* Repeating.

itinerant, ī•tin′ėr•ant, *a.* [L.L. *itinerans*, *itinerantis*, traveling, from L. *iter*, *itineris*, a way or journey; from root *i*, to go, seen also in *circuit*, *exit*, *transit*, *ambition*, *initial*, *issue*, *perish*, etc.] Passing or traveling about a country or district; wandering; not settled; strolling.—*n.* One who travels from place to place.—**itineracy,** ī•tin′ėr•a•si, *n.* Practice of itinerating.—**itinerancy,** ī•tin′ėr•an•si, *n.* A passing from place to place; the passing from place to place in the discharge of official duty.—**itinerantly,** ī•tin′ėr•ant•li, *adv.* In an itinerant, unsettled, or wandering manner.—**itinerary,** ī•tin′ėr•a•ri, *n.* [L.L. *itinerarium*.] A work containing notices of the places and stations; route of a journey or trip; the outline of a prospective route to be taken in making a journey; the course of an official tour of royal or distinguished visitors.—*a.* Pertaining to a travel route.—**itinerate,** ī•tin′ėr•āt, *v.i.*—*itinerated, itinerating.* To travel from place to place, particularly for the purpose of preaching.

its, its. Possessive case of the pronoun it.—**itself,** it•self′, *pron.* The neuter pronoun corresponding to *himself*, *herself*.

ivory, ī′vo•ri, *n.* [O.Fr. *ivurie*, Fr. *ivoire*, from L. *eboreus*, made of ivory, from *ebur*, ivory; akin Skr. *ibha*, an elephant.] The substance of elephant tusks; a similar substance obtained from the tusks of the walrus, the hippopotamus, the narwhal, etc.; a color, like ivory. *pl.* Articles made of ivory, such as piano keys or dice.—*a.* Consisting or made of ivory.—**ivory black,** *n.* A fine black pigment, prepared from ivory dust by calcination.—**ivory nut,** *n.* The seed of a South American palm, about as large as a hen's egg, and resembling ivory in texture and color; vegetable ivory.—**ivory palm,** *n.* The tree which bears the ivory nut.

ivy, ī′vi, *n.* [A.Sax. *ifig*; akin to G. *epheu*. O.G. *ebeheu*, *ebah*, ivy.] An evergreen climbing plant, growing in hedges, woods, on old buildings, rocks, and trunks of trees.

ixtle, iks′tle, *n.* A name for a kind of fiber obtained in Mexico from a species of agave.

J

J, j, jā, Tenth letter in the English alphabet, the seventh consonant, sounding like *g* in *genius*.

jab, jab, *v.t.* and *i.* [Imitative.] To stab, as with a sharp stick.—*n.* A poke or quick thrust with something sharp.

jabber, jab′ėr, *v.i.* [A form equivalent to *gabble*, Sc. *gabber*, freq. of *gab*, to talk much or pertly, GAB.] To talk rapidly, indistinctly, or nonsensically; to chatter.—*v.t.* To utter rapidly (to *jabber* French).—*n.* Rapid, indistinct utterance.—**jabberer,** jab′ėr•ėr, *n.* One who jabbers.

jabiru, jab′i•rö, *n.* [Brazilian name.] A tall wading bird resembling the stork, a native of Africa and America.

jaborandi, jab•o•ran′di, *n.* [Brazilian.] A drug obtained from a Brazilian plant of the rue family, causing increase of saliva and profuse perspiration.

jaçana, zhä′se•nä″, *n.* The name of sundry tropical grallatorial birds, having very long toes, so that they can easily walk on the leaves of aquatic plants.

jacaranda, jak•a•ran′da, *n.* The name of several Brazilian trees yielding fancy woods.

jacinth, ja′sinth, *n.* The gem also called *Hyacinth*.

jack, jak, *n.* [From Fr. *Jacques*, L. *Jacobus*, James; it came to be used as a familiar substitute for the common name *John*, instead of for *James*.] [cap.] A sailor; a name of various contrivances or implements; an implement to assist a person in pulling off his boots; a bootjack; a contrivance for raising great weights by the action of screws; a contrivance for turning a spit; a blackjack; a small bowl thrown out for a mark to the players in the game of bowls; a flag displayed from a staff on the end of a bowsprit; male of certain animals, as the ass; the fish more commonly called the pike; a young pike; any of the knaves in a pack of cards; pl. a game played with a half dozen small six-pointed metal pieces and a rubber ball; the metal pieces themselves; a receptacle with connections to electric circuits, into which a plug can be inserted.—**jackanapes,** jak′a•nāpes, *n.* An impertinent or presumptuous fellow.—**jack-in-the-box,** *n.*—A toy made of a box, out of which, when the lid is opened, a figure springs.—**jack-o'-lantern,** *n.* A lantern made from a hollowed pumpkin carved to resemble a face.—**jackass,** jak′ass, *n.* The male of the ass; an ignorant or stupid person.—**jack boot,** *n.* A kind of large boot reaching up over the knee.—**jackdaw,** jak′dą, *n.* A small species of crow.—**jack-of-all-trades,** *n.* A man handy with tools; a man possessing a superficial skill in several trades, hence, *Jack-of-all-trades, and master of none.*—**jackknife,** *n.* A large strong clasp knife for the pocket.—**jack-in-the-pulpit,** *n.* An American flowering herb of the Arum family (*Arisaema atrorubens*), its upright spadix arched over by a green and purple spathe.—**jackpot,** *n. Poker,* the pool which is opened when one player has a pair of jacks or something higher; unexpected success or winnings.—**jack rabbit,** *n.* One of the large hares, several species of which have long ears and long hind legs, destructive to crops in the middle west and west.—**jackscrew,** *n.* A jack for lifting heavy objects.—**jacksnipe,** *n.* A small species of snipe.—**jackstone,** *n.* A children's game, played with small stones or metal pieces.—**jackstraw,** *n.* A figure of a man made of straw; pl. a game played with straws or strips of wood, etc.—**jack towel,** *n.* A coarse towel for general use, hanging from a roller.

jackal, jak′ąl, *n.* [Fr. *chacal*, Turk, *chakal*, Per. *shaghál*, *shagál*, a jackal.] A carnivorous animal closely allied to the dog and the wolf; from an erroneous notion that the jackal hunted up prey for the king of beasts, he was often called the lion's provider, hence, a person who performs a similar office for another.

jacket, jak′et, *n.* [Fr. *jaquette*, dim. of *jaque*, a coat of mail, a jacket.] A short outer garment extending downward to the hips; an outer casing of cloth, felt, wood, etc.; a general term for an outside covering (a potato *jacket*); the outside covering of a book.—*v.t.* To cover or furnish with a jacket.

Jacobean, ja•ko′bē•an, *a.* [L. *Jacobus*, James, from Heb. *Jacob.*] *Arch.* the term sometimes applied to the later style of Elizabethan architecture prevailing in the age of James I.—**Jacobin,** jak′o•bin, *n.* [Fr., from L. *Jacobus*, James.] A Gray or Dominican Friar, from these friars having first established themselves in Paris in the Rue St. Jacques (Saint James Street); a member of a club of violent republicans in France during the revolution of 1789; a politician of similar character; [*not cap.*] a variety of pigeon whose neck feathers form a hood.—**Jacobinic, Jacobinical,** jak•o•bin′ik, jak•o•bin′i•kal, *a.* Pertaining to or resembling the Jacobins of France.—**Jacobinism,** jak′o•bin•izm, *n.* The principles of Jacobins.—**Jacobinize,** jak′o•bin•īz, *v.t.*—*jacobinized, jacobinizing.* To taint with Jacobinism.—**Jacobite,** jak′o•bīt, *n.* [From L. *Jacobus*, James.] A partisan or adherent of James II of England after he abdicated the throne, and of his descendants.—*a.* Pertaining to the Jacobites.—**Jacobitical,** jak•o•bit′i•kal, *a.* Pertaining to the Jacobites.—**Jacobitism,** jak′o•bit•ism, *n.* The principles of the Jacobites.—**Jacob's-ladder,** *n.* A garden plant with handsome blue (sometimes white) flowers; *naut.* a rope ladder with wooden steps or spokes.

Jacquard loom, jak•kärd′, *n.* [From *Jacquard* of Lyons, who died in 1834.] An ingenious loom for weaving figured goods.

jactitation, jak•ti•tā′shon, *n.* [L. *jactito*, freq. from *jacto*, freq. of *jacio*, to throw. JET.] A frequent tossing of the body; restlessness; also, vain boasting; bragging.

jaculate, jak′ū•lāt, *v.t.* [L. *jaculor*, *jaculatus*, to throw the javelin, from *jaculum*, javelin, *jacio*, to throw.] To dart; to throw out.

jade, jād, *n.* [Sc. *yaud*, *jaud*, an old mare; Icel. *jalda*, Prov. Sw. *jälda*, a mare.] A mean or poor horse; a worthless nag; a mean or vile woman; a hussy, used opprobriously; a young woman, used in humor or slight contempt.—*v.t.*—*jaded, jading.* To ride or drive severely; to overdrive; to weary or fatigue.—*v.i.* To become weary; to lose spirit.—**jaded,** jā′ded, *p.* and *a.* Wearied out; fatigued; harassed.—**jadish,** jā′dish, *a.* Like or pertaining to a jade.

jade, jād, *n.* [Fr. *jade* from Sp. *ijada*, colic stone.] A kind of hard, tenacious gem or stone of a color more or less green, of a resinous or oily aspect when polished, capable of being carved, and used, especially by the Chinese, for ornaments.

jag, jag, *v.t.*—*jagged, jagging.* [Origin doubtful; comp. W. and Gael. *gag*, a cleft or chink; Gael. *gag*, to notch.] To notch; to cut into notches or teeth like those of a saw.—*n.* A notch or denticulation; a sharp protuberance or indentation; state of inebriation (*slang*).—**jagged,** jag′ed, *p.* and *a.* Having notches or teeth; cleft; divided; laciniate.—**jaggedness,** jag′ed•nes, *n.*—**jagger,** jag′ėr, *n.* One who or that which jags.

jaggery, jag′ėr•i, *n.* [Hind *jâgri.*] In the East Indies sugar in its coarse state; imperfectly granulated sugar; also, the inspissated juice of the palmyra tree.

jaguar, jag•wär′, *n.* [Brazilian *jaguara.*] The American tiger; a powerful, spotted member of the cat family found mostly in South America.

Jahve, yä′ve, *n.* [Heb.] Jehovah.

jail, jāl, *n.* [Fr. *geole*, O.Fr. *gaiole*, a prison; L.L. *gabiola*, from L. *cavea*, a cage, coop, den, from *cavus*, hollow. CAVE.] A prison; a building or place for the confinement of persons arrested for crime; a lockup.—*v.t.* To put in prison; to imprison.—**jailbird,** jāl′bėrd, *n.* One who has been confined in jail.

Jain, Jaina, jān, jā′na, *n.* One of a Hindu religious sect believing doctrines similar to those of Buddhism.—**Jainism,** jān′izm, *n.* The doctrines of the Jains.

jalap, jal′ap, *n.* [Fr. *jalap*; Sp. *jalapa*, from *Jalapa* in Mexico.] A purgative medicine, principally obtained from the tuberous roots of a climbing plant of the convolvulus family, a native of Mexico.

jalopy, ja•lop′i, *n.* [Origin unknown.] A neglected or run-down automobile or airplane. (Slang)

jalousie, zhäl•ö•zē′, *n.* [Fr., from *jaloux*, jealous. JEALOUS.] A wooden frame or blind for shading from the sunshine, much used in hot countries; a venetian blind.

jam, jam, *n.* [Probably from *jam*, *v.t.*; related to *champ.*] A conserve of fruits boiled with sugar and water.

jam, jam, *v.t.*—*jammed, jamming.* [Perhaps from *jamb*, pressing between two uprights or jambs.] To squeeze or press into a close or tight position; to become unworkable, as a machine, because parts are wedged together; to apply suddenly with force (*jam* on the brakes).—*n.* Act of jamming; a crush of people.—**jamming,** jam′ing, *n. Radio,* blocking radio messages by broadcasting noises, etc. on the same wavelength.—**jam session,** *n.* A meeting of jazz musicians for the purpose of improvising together.

jamb, jam, *n.* [Fr. *jambe*, a leg, a jamb.] The side or vertical piece of any opening in a wall, such as a door or window.

jamboree, jam•bo•rē′, *n.* A boy scout assembly; a noisy gathering.

jangle, jang′gl, *v.i.*—*jangled, jangling.* [O.Fr. *jangler*, *gangler*, from L.G. and D. *jangelen*, to brawl; imitative of sound.] To sound discordantly or harshly; to quarrel in words; to altercate; to bicker; to wrangle.—*v.t.* To cause to sound harshly or inharmoniously; to utter in a discordant manner.—*n.* Discordant sound; prate; babble.

janitor, jan′i•tėr, *n.* [L., from *janua*, a door.] A caretaker of a building.

Janizary, jan′i•ze•ri, *n.* [Turk. *yeni*, new, and *tcheri*, militia, soldiers.] [*often not cap.*] A soldier of the Turkish footguards, a body originally composed of Christian slaves, but suppressed after a terrible struggle in 1826.

Jansenist, jan′sen•ist, *n.* A follower of *Jansen,* R. Catholic bishop of Ypres in Flanders, who leaned to the doctrine of irresistible grace as maintained by Calvin.—**Jansenism,** jan′sen•izm, *n.* The doctrine of the Jansenists.

January, jan′ū•e•ri, *n.* [L. *januarius,* the month consecrated to the god *Janus,* a deity represented with two faces looking opposite ways.] The first month of the year according to the present computation.—**Janus-faced,** *a.* Having two faces; double-dealing; deceitful.

japan, ja•pan′, *n.* [From the country so called.] Work varnished and figured in the manner practiced by the natives of Japan; the varnish employed in japanning articles; Japan lacquer.—*v.t.*—*japanned, japanning.* To varnish or cover with Japan lacquer.—*Japanned leather,* a species of enameled or varnished leather.—**Japanese,** jap′a•nēz, *a.* Pertaining to Japan or its inhabitants.—*n.* A native or natives of Japan; the language of the inhabitants of Japan.—**Japan lacquer,** *n.* A valuable black hard varnish used in japanning.

jape, jāp, *n.* A merry jest, or joke.

Japhetic, ja•fet′ik, *a.* Pertaining to *Japheth,* one of the sons of Noah (the *Japhetic* nations).

japonica, ja•pon′i•ka, *n.* [From *Japan.*] Japanese species of pear or quince.

jar, jär, *v.i.*—*jarred, jarring.* [Also found in forms *chur, jur,* and imitative of sound.] To strike together with a short rattle or tremulous sound; to give out a harsh sound; to sound discordantly; to be inconsistent; to clash or interfere; to quarrel; to dispute.—*v.t.* To cause a short tremulous motion to; to cause to shake or tremble.—*n.* A rattling vibration of sound; a harsh sound; clash of interest or opinions; collision; discord.

jar, jär, *n.* [Fr. *jarre,* Sp. *jarra,* a jar, from Ar. *jarra,* a water-pot.] A vessel of earthenware or glass, of various shapes and dimensions; the contents of a jar.

jardiniere, zhär•dēn•yâr′, *n.* [Fr., a female gardener, a gardener's wife.] An ornamental stand for plants and flowers.

jargon, jär′gon, *n.* [Fr.; origin doubtful. JAR. *v.i.*] Confused; unintelligible talk or language; gabble; gibberish; phraseology peculiar to a sect, profession, or the like; professional slang.—*v.i.* To utter unintelligible sounds.—**jargonize,** jär′gon•īz, *v.i.* To utter jargon.

jargon, jargoon, jär′gon, jär•gön′, *n.* [Fr. *jargon,* from It. *giargone,* properly a yellow stone, from Pers. *zargun,* gold-colored.] A variety of zircon, colorless or colored, the colorless forms resembling the diamond.—**jargonelle,** jär•go•nel′, *n.* [Fr., from *jargon,* the mineral.] A variety of early pear.

jasmine, jasmin, jas′min, *n.* [Fr. *jāsmin*; Ar. and ultimately Pers. *yāsemin,* jasmine.] The name of several elegant erect or climbing shrubs, with white or yellow flowers, from some of which delicious perfumes are extracted.

jasper, jas′pėr, *n.* [O.Fr. *jaspre,* Fr. *jaspe,* L., Gr. *iaspis,* Ar. *yashb,* Heb. *yashpheh*; hence *diaper.*] An impure opaque colored quartz, which admits of an elegant polish, and is used for vases, seals, etc.

jaundice, jąn′dis, *n.* [O.E. *jaunes, jaunis,* Fr. *jaunisse,* from *jaune,* O.Fr. *jalne,* L. *galbanus, galbinus,* yellowish, *galbus,* yellow; same root as *yellow.*] A disease characterized by suppression and alteration of the liver functions, yellowness of the eyes and skin, with loss of appetite and general languor and lassitude; any feeling or emotion disordering the judgment.—*v.t.*—*jaundiced, jaundicing.* To affect with jaundice; to affect with prejudice.

jaunt, jąnt, *v.i.* [Formerly *jaunce,* from O.Fr. *jancer*; of doubtful origin.] To wander here and there; to make an excursion or trip; to ramble.—*n.* An excursion; a ramble; a short journey.—**jaunting car,** *n.* A light car used in Ireland in which the passengers ride back to back on folding-down seats placed at right angles to the axle.

jaunty, jąn′ti, *a.* [O.E. *gent,* Sc. *genty* elegant, pretty; from *gentle,* genteel, but modified by *jaunt.*] Gay and easy in manner or actions; airy; sprightly.—**jauntily,** jąn′ti•li, *adv.*—**jauntiness,** jän′ti•nes, *n.*

Java, ją′va, *n.* Indonesian island; a variety of coffee; slang for coffee.—**Javanese,** jäv′a•nēz, *a.* Relating to Java.—*n.* A native of, or the language of Java.

javelin, jav′lin, *n.* [Fr. *javeline,* It. *giavelina,* Sp. *jabalina.*] A light spear of wood, 8½ feet long, thrown by hand as a weapon in war; a wooden spear thrown for distance in athletic competition.—*v.t.* To strike or wound with a javelin.

jaw, ją, *n.* [O.E. *chaw,* that which *chaws* or *chews.* CHEW.] The bones of the mouth in which the teeth are fixed; the upper or lower bony portion of the mouth; anything resembling a jaw in form or use (the *jaws* of a vise); loquacity or talk (a vulgar usage).—*v.i.* To talk or gossip; also, to scold (vulgar).—*v.t.* To use impudent language toward (vulgar).—**jawbone,** *n.* The bone of the jaw in which the teeth are fixed.

jay, jā, *n.* [Fr. *geai,* O.Fr. *gai,* Pr. *gai, jai,* Sp. *gayo*; same origin as adjective *gay*; lit. the gay or lively bird.] A bird allied to the crows, and one species of which, a beautiful bird with a crest of erectile feathers, is a native of Britain, another (the blue jay) is a native of North America.

jaywalk, jā′wąk, *v.i.* To cross a street carelessly amid traffic and away from a regular crossing place.

jazz, jaz, *n.* [Originally from Creole *jazz,* for *jass,* to speed things up.] *Mus.* American music derived from Negro spirituals and ragtime, characterized by syncopated dance rhythms and spontaneous and inventive harmonies improvised on melodic themes.—*v.t.* To play a musical instrument in jazz style.—*v.i.* To dance to jazz.—(Slang) To enliven or speed up a performance.—**jazzy,** jaz′ē, *a.* Something lively or suggestive of jazz.

jealous, jel′us, *a.* [O.Fr. *jalous,* Fr. *jaloux,* It. *geloso,* from L.L. *zelosus*—L. *zelus,* Gr. *zēlos,* zeal. Another form of *zealous.*] Uneasy through fear of, or on account of, preference given to another; suspicious in love; apprehensive of rivalry; zealous.—**jealously,** jel′us•li, *adv.*—**jealousness,** jel′us•nes, *n.*—**jealousy,** jel′us•i, *n.*

jean, jēn, *n.* [Probably from *Genoa.*] A twilled cotton cloth; pl. trousers of this material.

jeep, jēp, *n.* [After *G.P.,* for *General Purpose* (Vehicle).] A multipurpose motor vehicle of ¼ ton capacity used by the U.S. military.

jeer, jēr, *v.i.* [Perhaps from O.Fr. *girer.*] To utter severe sarcastic reflections; to scoff; to make a mock of some person or thing (to *jeer at* a person).—*v.t.* To treat with scoffs or derision.—*n.* A scoff; a taunt.—**jeerer,** jē′rėr, *n.*—**jeeringly,** jē′ring•li, *adv.*

Jeffersonian, jef•fer•sō′ni•an, *a.* Of Thomas Jefferson (third U. S. president, 1801-9) or his political teachings, advocating broad rights of the states.

Jehovah, ji•hō′va, *n.* A Scripture name of the Supreme Being, the proper form of which, according to most scholars, should be *Yahveh* or *Yahweh.*—**Jehovist,** ji•hō′vist, *n.* The supposed author or authors of the *Jehovistic* portions of the Old Testament. ELOHIST.—**Jehovistic,** ji•hō•vis′tik, *a.* Pertaining to those passages in the Old Testament, especially of the Pentateuch, in which the Supreme Being is spoken of under the name *Jehovah.*

jehu, jē′hū, *n.* [From *Jehu,* the son of Nimshi, 2 Ki. ix. 20.] A slang name for a coachman or one fond of driving.

jejune, ji•jūn′, *a.* [L. *jejunus,* hungry, dry, barren.] Devoid of interesting matter, or attractiveness of any kind: said especially of literary productions; bare; meager; barren; unprofitable.—**jejunely,** ji•jūn′li, *adv.*

jejunum, ji•jū′num, *n.* [L., from *jejunus,* hungry or empty.] *Anat.* the second portion of the small intestine comprised between the duodenum and ileum.

jelly, jel′i, *n.* [Fr. *gelée,* from *geler,* L. *gelo,* to freeze; so *gelatine, congeal.*] A food preparation of fruit juice boiled down with sugar, which achieves its soft elasticity through the presence of pectin.—*v.t.* To bring to the consistency of jelly.—*v.i.* To become jelly.—**jellyfish,** *n.* Popular name for various marine coelenterates having a soft, gelatinous body and long tentacles; a medusa.

jemadar, jem•a•där′, *n.* [Hind. *jamadâr,* from *jama,* a number or body, and *dâr,* a holder.] In India, a native officer in a sepoy government corresponding in rank to a lieutenant.

jenny, jen′i, *n.* [For *ginny*, from *gin*, short for *engine*, influenced by its resemblance to a common female name.] A machine for spinning, moved by water or steam.

jeopardy, jep′ėr•di, *n.* [O.E. *jupartie*, from Fr. *jeu parti*, lit. a divided game; L.L. *jocus partitus*, an even chance. JOKE, PART.] Exposure to death, loss, or injury; hazard; danger; peril.—*v.t.*†—*jeopardied, jeopardying.* To jeopardize.—**jeopard,** jep′ėrd, *v.t.* To put in danger; to hazard.—**jeopardize,** jep′ėr•dīz, *v.t.* To expose to loss or injury; to jeopard.—**jeopardous,** jep′ėr•dus, *a.* Perilous; hazardous.

jerboa, jėr•bō′a, *n.* [Ar. *yerbôa, yerbûa.*] A name of certain small rodents mainly characterized by the disproportionate length of the hind limbs.

jereed, jerid, je•rēd′, *n.* A wooden javelin used in Persia and Turkey, especially in mock fights.

jerk, jėrk, *v.t.* [Comp. O.E. and Sc. *yerk*, a quick, smart lash or blow; prov. *girk*, a rod; perhaps same as *gird* (*n.*).] To thrust with a sudden effort; to give a sudden pull, twitch, thrust, or push to; to throw with a quick smart motion.—*v.i.* To make a sudden motion; to give a start.—*n.* A short sudden thrust, push, or twitch; a jolt; a sudden spring; a start; a leap or bound.—**jerky,** jėr′ki, *a.* Moving by or exhibiting jerks.

jerk, jėrk, *v.t.* [Chilian, *charqui.*] To cut (beef) into long thin pieces, and dry in the sun, as is done in S. America. CHARQUI.

jerkin, jėr′kin, *n.* [Dim. of D. *jurk*, a frock.] A jacket; a short coat; a close waistcoat.

jeroboam, jer•ạ•bō′am, *n.* [After *Jeroboam*, first King of Israel.] A large wine bottle that holds ⅘ of a gallon; a large bowl.

jerry-builder, je′ri•bil″dėr, *n.* [Origin dubious.] One who builds with cheap, flimsy materials.

jersey, jėr′zi, *n.* [From the island so called.] Fine yarn of wool; a kind of close-fitting knitted woolen upper shirt or similar article of dress; [*cap.*] a species of dairy cow developed on the island and noted for its rich milk.

Jerusalem artichoke, ji•rū′sa•lem, *n.* [*Jerusalem* is here a corruption of the Italian *girasole.* GIRASOLE.] A well-known plant, the tubers of which are of a sweetish farinaceous nature, somewhat akin to the potato.

jess, jes, *n.* [O.Fr. *ges, gest, get*, etc., from L.L. *jactus*, a jess, from L. *jacio, jactum*, to throw. JET.] A short strap of leather fastened round each of the legs of a hawk, to which the leash tied round the falconer's hand was attached.—**jessed,** jest, *a.* Having jesses.

jessamine, jes′a•min, *n.* Jasmine.

jesse, jes′sē, *n.* [From its resemblance to the genealogical tree of *Jesse*, the father of David, of which a picture used to be hung up in churches.] A large brass candlestick branched into many sconces, used in churches.—*Jesse tree*, alluding to Isaiah. xi. 1: 'A rod out of the stem of Jesse'.

jest, jest, *n.* [O.E. *geste*, a jest, a tale, from L. *gestum*, something done, a deed, a feat, from *gero*, to do, whence *gesture*, etc.] A joke; something ludicrous uttered and meant only to excite laughter; the object of laughter; a laughingstock.—*In jest*, for mere sport or diversion; not in truth and reality; not in earnest.—*v.i.* To make merriment by words or actions; to utter jests, to talk jokingly; to joke.—**jester,** jes′tėr, *n.* One who jests; a person given to jesting; a buffoon; a merry-andrew; a person formerly retained by persons of rank to make sport for them.—**jestingly,** jes′ting•li, *adv.* In a jesting manner; not in earnest.

Jesuit, jez′ū•it, *n.* [One of the order or Society of *Jesus.*] One of a religious order belonging to the Roman Catholic church, founded by Saint Ignatius of Loyola in 1534, and approved by Pope Paul III in 1540.—**Jesuitic, Jesuitical,** jez•ū•it′ik, jez•ū•it′i•kal, *a.*—**Jesuitically,** jez•ū•it′i•kal•li, *adv.*—**Jesuitism,** jez′ū•it•izm, *n.*

Jesus, jē′zus, *n.* [Gr. *Iesous*, from Heb. *Jeshuah, Jehosuah*, 'help of Jehovah'.] The Son of God; the Saviour of men; frequently conjoined with Christ (which see).

jet, jet, *n.* [Old forms *jeat, jayet*, O.Fr. *jayet, gayet*, from Gr. *gagatēs*, from *Gagæ*, a town and river in Lycia, where it was obtained.] A highly compact species of coal susceptible of a good polish, deep black and glossy, wrought into buttons and ornaments of various kinds.—**jet-black,** *a.* Of the deepest black, the color of jet.

jet, jet, *n.* [Fr. *jet*, a throw, a jet, a fountain, from L. *jactus*, a throwing, from *jacio*, to throw.] A shooting forth or spouting; what issues or streams forth from an orifice, as water or other fluid, gas or flame.—*v.i.*—*jetted, jetting.* To issue in a jet.—*v.t.* To emit; to spout forth.—**jet airplane,** *n.* An airplane propelled by one or more jet engines.—**jet engine,** *n.* A reaction engine driven by jet propulsion, having one or more combustion chambers and exhaust nozzles for discharging a mixture of hot, gaseous air.—**jet-propelled,** *a.* Propelled by one or more jet engines; high-powered and suggestive of speed and force (a *jet-propelled* career).—**jet propulsion,** A method of producing forward motion of a vehicle by the rearward discharge of a high-speed jet, usually of hot gases.

jetsam, jet′sam, *n.* [See JETTISON.] Goods cast overboard to lighten a ship in distress.

jettison, jet′i•sun, *n.* [O.Fr. *getaison*, L. *jactatio*, a throwing, from *jacio*, to throw.] The throwing of goods overboard to lighten a ship in distress.—*v.t.* To throw overboard.

jetty, jet′i, *n.* [O.Fr. *jettée*, Fr. *jetée*, from O.Fr. *jetter*, to throw. JET.] A projecting portion of a building; a projecting structure (generally of piles), affording a convenient landing place for vessels or boats; a kind of small pier.

Jewish, jū′ish, *a.* [O. Fr. *Juis;* L. *Judaeus*, from *Judaea*, so named from *Judah.*] Pertaining to the Jews or Hebrews.—**Jewry,** jū′ri, *n.* Judaea; also a city quarter inhabited by Jews.—**jew's-harp,** *n.* An instrument of music which is held between the teeth and by means of a thin bent metal tongue, struck by the finger, gives out a sound.

jewel, jū′el, *n.* [O.Fr. *jouel, joiel, joel* (Fr. *joyau*), either from L.L. *jocale*, a jewel, from L. *jocare*, to jest, *jocus*, a jest (whence *joke*), or from L.L. *gaudiale*, from L. *gaudium*, joy (whence *joy*).] A personal ornament in which precious stones form a principal part; a precious stone; anything of exceeding value or excellence.—*v.t.*—*jeweled, jeweling.* To dress or adorn with jewels; to fit or provide with a jewel (as a watch); to deck or adorn as with jewels.—**jeweler,** jū′el•ėr, *n.* One who makes or deals in jewels and other ornaments.—**jewelry,** jū′el•ri, *n.* The trade or occupation of a jeweler; jewels in general.

Jezebel, jez′e•bel, *n.* [From *Jezebel*, the infamous wife of Ahab, king of Israel.] An unscrupulous, daring, vicious woman.

jib, jib, *n.* [From Dan. *gibbe*, D. *gijpen*, to turn suddenly, said of sails.] The foremost sail of a ship, triangular in shape and extended from the outer end of a jib boom toward the foretopmast-head; in sloops, a sail on the bowsprit.—**jibe,** jīb, *v.t.*—*jibed, jibing. Naut.* to shift (a fore-and-aft sail) from one side to the other.—**jib boom,** *n.* A spar run out from the extremity of the bowsprit, and which serves as a continuation of it.

jib, jib, *v.i.*—*jibbed, jibbing.* [O.Fr. *giber*, to struggle; *regibber*, to kick.] To balk, as a horse; to move restively sideways or backward.—**jibber,** jib′-er, *n.*

jibe, jīb, *v.t.* To jeer. GIBE.

jibe, jīb, *v.i.* [Origin unknown.] To be in accord. (Colloq.)

jiffy, jif′i, *n.* [Prov.E. *jiffle*, to be restless; comp. *jib*, to turn suddenly.] A moment; an instant. (Colloq.)

jig, jig, *n.* [O.Fr. *gigue, gige*, a stringed instrument; the same word as *gig.*] A lively step dance in triple rhythm; a hook or group of hooks which can be jerked up and down through water, as in ice fishing.—*mech.* a device for guiding a drill, etc., so that machined pieces will be uniform.—**jigsaw,** *n.* A saw with a vertical motion, moved by a vibrating lever or crank rod.—*v.i.*—*jigged, jigging.* To dance a jig; to move with a light jolting motion; to fish with a jig.—*v.t.* To sing in the style of a jig, or in *jig* time; to work with the mechanical aid of a *jig.*—**jigger,** jig′ėr, *n. Mining*, a man who cleans ores by means of a wirebottom sieve; the sieve itself; a kind of light tackle used in ships; a potter's wheel by which earthenware vessels are shaped; 1½-ounce glass measure.

jigger, jig′ėr, *n.* [CHIGOE.] The chigoe.

jiggle, jig′l, *v.t.*—*jiggled, jiggling.*

[From *jig*.] To move up and down or back and forth in quick little jerks. —*n*. The motion of jiggling.

jilt, jilt, *n*. [Contr. from *jillet*, a dim. of *jill*, *gill*, a young woman, a giddy girl. GILL.] A woman who gives her lover hopes and capriciously disappoints him.—*v.t.* To treat as a jilt does her lover.

jimmy, jim'i, *n*. [Nickname for *James*.] A short crowbar used by burglars.—*v.t.* To force open with a jimmy.

Jimson weed, *n*. [From *Jamestown weed*, for Jamestown, Va.] A poisonous datura (*Datura stramonium*) with large white flowers and rank-smelling foliage.

jingle, jing'gl, *v.i.*—*jingled*, *jingling*. [Probably imitative, like *jangle*, *chink*, *tinkle*, G. *klingeln*.] To sound with a tinkling metallic sound.—*v.t.* To cause to give a tinkling metallic sound.—*n*. A rattling or clinking sound, as of metal; something that jingles; a brief musical advertisement on television or radio.

jingo, jing'gō, *n*. An expletive used as a mild oath (*By jingo!*); a person exaggeratedly patriotic and clamorous for war.—**jingoism**, jing'gō•izm, *n*. Exaggerated and bellicose patriotism.—**jingoist**, jing'gō•ist, *n*. & *a*. —**jingoistic**, jing'gō•is"tic, *a*.

jinks, jingks, *n*. [Chiefly in *high jinks*.] Frolics; pranks.

jinni, jinnee, ji•nē', *n*. pl. **jinn**, jin. [From Ar. *jinn*, a demon.] *Mohammedan mythology*, one of a class of good or evil spirits (angels or demons) inhabiting the earth, capable of assuming various forms and of exercising magical powers.

jinrikisha, jin•rik'shä, *n*. [Japanese.] A small, two-wheeled vehicle, drawn by one or more men.

jinx, jingks, *n*. & *v*. [From *jynx*, bird, the wryneck used in witchcraft.] Some thing which brings bad luck; a hoodoo. (Slang)

jitney, jit'ni, *n*. [Origin doubtful.] A nickel; five cents; a bus or taxicab having a low fare. (Slang)

jitter, jit'ėr, *v.i.* [CHATTER.] To behave nervously.—**jitterbug**, jit'ėr•bug, *n*. A dance to swing music; a dancer who does the jitterbug.—**jitters**, jit'ėrz, *n*. pl. Nervousness. (Slang)

jiujitsu, jiujutsu. See JUJITSU.

job, job, *n*. [A form of Prov.E. *gob*, a lump, a portion; akin *gobbet*.] A piece of work undertaken; employment; position; a public transaction made for private profit; a task; something that has to be done with great labor; a robbery. (Slang)—*v.t.* *jobbed*, *jobbing*. To sublet work (*job* a contract); to buy in large quantities and sell in smaller lots.—*v.i.* To work at chance jobs; to deal in the public stocks; to buy and sell as a broker; to put some public undertaking to private advantage.—*a*. Applied to goods bought and sold under special circumstances, and generally under the ordinary trade price.—**jobber**, job'ėr, *n*. One who deals in goods as middle man; one who deals or dabbles in stocks; a stockjobber.—**jobbery**, job'ėr•i, *n*.—**jobless**, job'les, *a*.—**job lot**, *n*. A miscellaneous collection sold.—**job printer**, *n*. A printer who does miscellaneous work, as bills, circulars, etc.

Job's comforter, jōb, *n*. [From *Job* of Scripture.] One who pretends to sympathize with you, but attributes your misfortunes to your own misconduct.

jockey, jok'i, *n*. [For *Jackey*, dim. of *Jack*, for *John*; *Jockey* and *Jock* being Northern English forms. JACK.] A man whose profession it is to ride horses in horse races.—*v.t.* *jockeyed* or *jockied*, *jockeying*. To ride in a race; to maneuver (to *jockey* for position); to jostle by riding against; to cheat; to trick; to deceive in trade.

jocose, jō•kōs', *a*. [L. *jocosus*, from *jocus*, a joke. JOKE.] Given to jokes and jesting; merry; waggish; containing a joke; sportive; merry.—**jocosely**, jō•kōs'li, *adv*. In a jocose manner.—**jocoseness**, jō•kōs'nes. *n*. The quality of being jocose.—**jocosity**, jō•kos'i•ti, *n*. Jocularity; merriment; waggery; a jocose act or saying.—**jocular**, jok'ū•lėr, *a*. [L. *jocularis*, from *jocus*.] Given to jesting; jocose; merry; waggish; containing jokes; facetious.—**jocularity**, jok•ū•lar'i•ti, *n*. The quality of being jocular.—**jocularly**, jok'ū•lėr•li, *adv*. In a jocular manner.

jocund, jok'und, *a*. [L. *jocundus*, *jucundus*, connected with *juvenis*, a young man, *juvare*, to assist (as in *adjutant*, *coadjutor*); E. *young*.] Merry; cheerful; blithe; gleeful; gay; sprightly; sportive; lighthearted.—**jocundity**, jo•kun'di•ti, *n*. State of being jocund.—**jocundly**, jok'und•li, *adv*.

jodhpurs, jōd'pörs, *n. pl.* [From Jodhpur, India.] Riding breeches that fit tightly from the knees to the ankles.

jog, jog, *v.t.*—*jogged*, *jogging*. [Perhaps a form of *jag*, or allied to W. *gogi*, to shake.] To push or shake with the elbow or hand; to give notice or excite attention by a slight push.—*v.i.* To move at a slow trot; to walk or travel idly or slowly; to move along with but little progress: generally followed by *on*—*n*. A push; a slight shake; a shake or push intended to give notice or awaken attention; *carp.* and *masonry*, a square notch.—**joggle**, jog'l, *v.t.*—*joggled*, *joggling*. [Freq. of *jog*.] To shake slightly; to give a sudden but slight push; *carp.* to join or match by jogs or notches so as to prevent sliding apart.—*v.i.* To push; to shake; to totter.—*n*. A joint made by means of jogs or notches; a joint held in place by means of pieces of stone or metal introduced into it; the piece of metal or stone used in such a joint.—**jog trot**, *n*. A slow, easy trot; hence, a slow routine of daily duty to which one pertinaciously adheres. —*a*. Monotonous; easygoing; humdrum.

John, jon, *n*. [L. *Johannes*, *Joannes*, Gr. *Ioannēs*, from Heb.] A proper name of men.—*John Bull*, a humorous designation of the English people, first used in Arbuthnot's satire *The History of John Bull*.—**John Doe**, *n*. *Law*. Name used for an unknown person.—**John Dory**, *n*. DORY.—**John Hancock**, han'kok, *n*. One's signature, from the exceptionally legible writing of John Hancock. —**johnnycake**, jon'i, *n*. Bread or cake made of corn meal, salt, water, and shortening.—**Johnny-jump-up**, *n*. The wild pansy.

Johnsonese, jon•son•ēz', *n*. The style or language of Dr. Johnson, or an imitation of it; a pompous inflated style.

join, join, *v.t.* [Fr. *joindre*, from L. *jungere*, *junctum*, to join, seen in many E. words, as *junction*, *juncture*, *adjoin*, *conjoin*, *enjoin*, *rejoin*, *conjugal*, *conjugate*, etc.; same root as Skr. *yuj*, to join; E. *yoke*.] To connect or bring together, physically or otherwise; to place in contiguity; to couple; to combine; to associate; to engage in (to *join* the fray); to make one's self a party in; to become connected with; to unite with; to enter or become a member of; to merge in (to *join* the army, one river joins another).—*To join battle*, to engage in battle.—*To join issue*. Under ISSUE.—*v.i.* To be contiguous or in contact; to form a physical union; to coalesce; to unite or become associated, as in marriage, league, partnership, society; to confederate; to associate; to league.—**joiner**, joi'nėr, *n*. One who joins; a mechanic who does the woodwork of houses; a carpenter.—**joinery**, joi'nėr•i, *n*. The art of a joiner; carpentry.

joint, joint, *n*. [Fr. *joint*, from *joindre*, pp. *joint*, to join. JOIN.] The place or part at which two separate things are joined or united; the mode of connection of two things; junction; articulation; *anat.* the joining of two or more bones, as in the elbow, the knee, or the knuckle; *bot.* a node or knot; also, the part between two nodes; an internode; *geol.* a fissure or line of parting in rocks at any angle to the plane of stratification; *building*, the surface of contact between two bodies that are held firmly together by means of cement, mortar, etc., or by a superincumbent weight; the place where or the mode in which one piece of timber is connected with another. DOVETAIL, SCARF, MITER, MORTISE, TENON.—*Universal joint*, a mechanical arrangement by which one part may be made to move freely in all directions in relation to another connected part. —*Out of joint*, dislocated, as when the head of a bone is displaced from its socket; hence, figuratively, confused; disordered.—*a*. Shared by two or more (*joint* property); having an interest in the same thing (*joint* owner); united; combined; acting in concert (a *joint* force, *joint* efforts).—*v.t.* To form with a joint or joints; to articulate; to unite by a joint or joints; to fit together; to cut or divide into joints or pieces.—*v.i.* To coalesce by joints.—**jointed**, join'ted, *p.* and *a*. Provided with joints; formed with knots or nodes.—**jointer**, join'tėr, *n*. One who or that which joints.

—**jointly,** joint′li, *adv.* In a joint manner; together; unitedly; in concert.—**joint stock,** *n.* Stock held in common.—*Joint stock company,* an association of a number of individuals who jointly contribute funds for the purpose of carrying on a specified business or undertaking, of which the shares are transferable by each owner without the consent of the other partners.—**jointure,** join′chėr, *n.* Property settled on a woman in consideration of marriage, and which she is to enjoy after her husband's decease.

joist, joist, *n.* [O.Fr. *giste,* Fr. *gîte,* a bed, a place to lie on, L.L. *gista,* from L. *jacitum,* pp. of *jacere,* to lie. JET, GIST.] One of the stout pieces of timber to which the boards of a floor or the laths of a ceiling are nailed, and which are supported by the walls or on girders.—*v.t.* To fit or furnish with joists.

joke, jōk, *n.* [L. *jocus,* Fr. *jeu,* It. *giuoco, gioca,* a jest; same root as *jacio,* to throw (JET). Akin *jocose, jocular, juggler, jeopardy.*] Something said for the sake of exciting a laugh; something witty or sportive; a jest; what is not in earnest or actually meant.—*A practical joke,* a trick played on one, usually to the injury or annoyance of his person.—*In joke,* in jest; with no serious intention.—*v.i.*—*joked, joking.* To jest; to utter jokes; to jest in words or actions.—*v.t.* To cast jokes at; to make merry with; to rally.—**joker,** jō′kėr, *n.* A jester; a merry fellow; in a legal document, a seemingly harmless clause which greatly alters the apparent meaning; an extra playing card which, when used, as in poker or euchre, has special privileges.—**jokingly,** *adv.*

jole, jōl, *n.*† [JOWL, Hence *jolt.*] The jowl; the head.

jolly, jol′i, *a.* [O.Fr. *joli, jolif,* Fr. *joli,* gay, merry, from the Scand., and originally referring to the festivities of Christmas; from Icel. *jól,* Sw. and Dan. *jul,* E. *yule,* Christmas. YULE.] Merry; gay; lively; full of life and mirth; jovial; expressing mirth; exciting mirth or gaiety; plump; in excellent condition of body.—**jollification,** jol′i•fi•kā″shon, *n.* A scene of merriment, mirth, or festivity; a carouse; merrymaking.—**jollily,** jol′i•li, *adv.* In a jolly manner.—**jolliness,** jol′i•nes, *n.* The quality or condition of being jolly.—**jollity,** jol′i•ti, *n.* The quality of being jolly; mirth; gaiety; festivity; joviality.

jolly boat, *n.* [*Jolly* here is same as Dan. *jolli,* D. *jol,* a yawl, a jolly-boat.] One of a ship's boats, about 12 feet in length, with a bluff bow; a yawl.

jolt, jolt, *v.i.* [From *joll,* obs. of *jowl,* and obs. *jot,* to bump.] To jar or jounce with light bumping motions, as a car traveling on a rough road; to shock by speech (a remark to *jolt* you); to jar with a hard blow, as in boxing.—*n.* A sudden sharp blow; a jar or shock.—**jolter,** jol′ter, *n.*

Jonathan, jo′na•than, *n.* Son of Saul, friend of David; a variety of apple.

jongleur, jong′glėr, *n.* [Fr.] A juggler; a medieval wandering minstrel; akin to *juggler, jingler.*

jonquil, jon′kwil, *a.* [Fr. *jonquille;* It. *giunchiglia,* dim. from L. *juncus,* a rush.] A species of narcissus or daffodil, with rush-like leaves and flowers that yield a fine perfume.

jorum, jō′rum, *n.* [Perhaps a corruption of *jordan,* a vessel in which pilgrims brought home water from the *Jordan.*] A colloquial term for a bowl or drinking vessel with liquor in it.

joseph, jō′zef, *n.* [Probably in allusion to *Joseph's* coat of many colors.] A riding coat or habit for women, formerly much in use.

josh, josh, *v.t.* [Origin unknown.] To tease or make fun of lightly.—*v.i.* To banter good-naturedly.—*n.* A good-humored joking.

joss, jos, *n.* [Chin. *joss,* a deity, from Pg. *deos,* from L. *deus,* a god.] A Chinese idol.—**joss house,** *n.* A Chinese temple. **joss stick,** *n.* In China, a small reed covered with the dust of odoriferous woods, and burned before an idol.

jostle, jos′l, *v.t.*—*jostled, jostling.* [A dim. from *joust.*] To push against; to crowd against; to elbow; to hustle.—*v.i.* To hustle; to shove about as in a crowd.—*n.* A crowding or pushing together.

jot, jot, *n.* [From *iōta,* the smallest letter in the Greek alphabet. IOTA.] An iota; the least quantity assignable.—*v.t.*—*jotted, jotting.* To make a memorandum of.—**jotting,** jot′ing, *n.*

joule, jöl, *n.* [*Joule,* scientist.] The unit of electric energy, equal to the work done in maintaining for one second a current of 1 ampere against a resistance of 1 ohm; equal to 10^7 ergs.

journal, jėr′nal, *n.* [Fr., from L. *diurnalis,* diurnal, from *dies,* a day. DIURNAL, DIAL, DIARY.] A diary; an account of daily transactions and events, or the book containing such account; a newspaper or other periodical published daily; a periodical; *bookkeeping,* a book in which every particular article or charge is entered under each day's date, or in groups at longer periods; *naut.* a daily register of the ship's course and distance, the winds, weather, and other occurrences; a log book; *mach.* that part of an axle or shaft which rests and moves in the bearings.—**journalism,** jėr′nal•izm, *n.* The trade or occupation of publishing, writing in, or conducting a journal.—**journalist,** jėr′nal•ist, *n.* The conductor of or writer in a public journal; a newspaper editor or regular contributor.—**journalistic,** jėr•nal•is′tik, *a.* Pertaining to journalism.—**journalize,** jėr′nal•īz, *v.t.*—*journalized, journalizing.* To enter in a journal; to give the form of a journal to.—**journalese,** jėr•nal•ēs′, *n.* Choice of language considered to be typical of newspapers. (Colloq.)

journey, jėr′ni, *n.* [Fr. *journée,* a day, a day's work, a day's journey, from L. *diurnus,* daily, from *dies,* a day. JOURNAL.] Travel from one place to another; a passage made between places; a distance traveled at a time.—*v.i.* To travel from place to place; to pass from home to a distance.—**journeyer,** jėr′ni•ėr, *n.*—**journeyman,** jėr′ni•man, *n.* Strictly, a man hired to work by the day, but in fact, any experienced mechanic or workman.

joust, joust, just, *n.* [O.Fr. *juste, jouste, joste,* jousting, from O.Fr. *juster, jouster, joster,* to tilt; from L. *juxta,* near to, nigh.] An encounter with spears on horseback for trial of skill; a combat between two knights at a tournament for sport or for exercise.—*v.i.* To engage in a mock fight on horseback; to tilt.—**jouster,** joust′ėr, jus′tėr, *n.* One who jousts.

Jove, jōv, *n.* [L. *Jovis, Diovis,* the old name of *Jupiter* (that is Jove-father), latterly appearing only in the oblique cases; same root as *deus,* a god. See DEITY.] The chief divinity of the Romans; Jupiter; the planet Jupiter.—**jovial,** jō′vi•al, *a.* [L.L. *Jovialis,* because the planet Jupiter was believed to make those born under it of a jovial temperament.] Gay; merry; joyous; jolly.—**joviality, jovialness,** jō•vi•al′i•ti, jō′vi•al•nes, *n.* The state or quality of being jovial.—**jovially,** jō′vi•al•li, *adv.*—**Jovian,** jō′vi•an, *a.* Pertaining to Jupiter.

jowl, jōl, *n.* [Also in forms *jole, joll, chowl,* from A.Sax. *ceafl,* jaw, snout. Akin *jolt.*] The hanging flesh of the jaw, as in a fat person; the wattle of a fowl; the dewlap of cattle.

joy, joi, *n.* [O.Fr. *joye, joie, goie,* Fr. *joie,* It. *gioja,* from L. *gaudium,* joy, *gaudere,* to rejoice; seen also in *gaudy, rejoice, jewel.*] Excitement of pleasurable feeling caused by the acquisition or expectation of good; gladness; pleasure; delight; exultation; exhilaration of spirits; the cause of joy or happiness.—*v.i.* To rejoice; to be glad; to exult.—*v.t.* To give joy to; to gladden. (*Shak.*)—**joyance,** joi′ans, *n.* [O.Fr. *joiant,* joyful.] Enjoyment; happiness; delight. (*Poet.*)—**joyful,** joi′fụl, *a.* Full of joy; very glad; exulting; joyous; gleeful.—**joyfully,** joi′fụl•li, *adv.* In a joyful manner.—**joyfulness,** joi′fụl•nes, *n.* The state of being joyful.—**joyless,** joi′les, *a.* Destitute of joy; wanting joy; giving no joy or pleasure.—**joylessly,** joi′les•li, *adv.* In a joyless manner.—**joylessness,** joi′les•nes, *n.* State of being joyless.—**joyous,** joi′us, *a.* [O.Fr. *joyous;* Fr. *joyeux;* from L. *gaudiosus,* from *gaudium.*] Glad; gay; merry; joyful; giving joy.—**joyously,** joi′us•li, *adv.* In a joyous manner.—**joyousness,** joi′us•nes, *n.* The state of being joyous.

jubilant, jū′bi•lant, *a.* [L. *jubilans,* ppr. of *jubilo,* to shout for joy, from *jubilum,* a shout of joy; not connected with *jubilee.*] Uttering songs of triumph; rejoicing; shouting or singing with joy.—**jubilate,** jū′bi•lāt, *v.i.* To rejoice; to exult; to triumph.

jubilation, jū•bi•lā′shon, *n.* [L. *jubilatio.*] A rejoicing; a triumph; exultation; a joyful or festive celebration.

jubilee, jū′bi•li, *n.* [Fr. *jubilé,* L. *jubilæus,* jubilee, from Heb. *yôbēl,* a ram's horn.] Among the Jews, every fiftieth year, at which time there was a general release of all debtors and slaves, hence, a season of great public joy and festivity; any occasion of rejoicing or joy; a celebration of a marriage, pastorate, or the like, after it has lasted fifty years; Negro spiritual saluting a future happy time; the sound of jubilation.

Judaic, Judaical, jū•dā′ik, jū•dā′i•kal, *a.* [L. *Judaicus,* from *Judæa.* JEW.] Pertaining to the Jews.—**Judaism,** jū′dä•izm, *n.* The religious doctrines and rites of the Jews, as enjoined in the laws of Moses; conformity to the Jewish rites and ceremonies.—**Judaist,** jū′dä•ist, *n.* An adherent to Judaism.—**Judaistic,** jū•dä•is′tik, *a.* Relating or pertaining to Judaism.—**Judaize,** jū′dä•īz, *v.i.—judaized, judaizing.* To conform to the religious doctrines and rites of the Jews; to assume the manners or customs of the Jews.—*v.t.* To bring into conformity with what is Jewish.—**Judaizer,** jū′dä•ī•zėr, *n.* One who judaizes.—**Judean,** jū•dē′an, *n.* A native or inhabitant of Judaea.—*a.* Relating to Judaea.

Judas, jö′das, *n.* [After the false apostle.] A treacherous person; one who betrays under the semblance of friendship.

judge, juj, *n.* [Fr. *juge,* from L. *judex, judicis,* a judge, from *jus, juris,* law or right, and *dico,* to pronounce (JURY, DICTION). This word appears in *adjudge, judicature, judicial, judicious,* etc.] A civil officer invested with power to hear and determine causes, civil and criminal, and to administer justice between parties in courts held for the purpose; one who has skill to decide on the merits of a question or on the value of anything; a critic; a connoisseur; *Jewish hist.* a chief magistrate with civil and military powers; hence, *pl.* the name of the seventh book of the Old Testament.—*v.i.—judged, judging.* [Fr. *juger,* L. *judicare,* to judge.] To hear and determine, as in causes on trial; to pass judgment upon any matter; to sit in judgment; to compare facts, ideas, or propositions, and perceive their agreement or disagreement; to form an opinion; to express censorious opinions; to determine; to estimate; to discern.—*v.t.* To hear and determine authoritatively, as a cause or controversy; to examine into and decide; to examine and pass sentence on; to try; to be censorious toward; to esteem, think, reckon.—**judgeship,** juj′ship, *n.* The office of a judge.—**judgment,** juj′ment, *n.* [Fr. *jugement.*] The act of judging; the act of deciding or passing decision on something; the act or faculty of judging truly, wisely, or skillfully; good sense; discernment; understanding; opinion or notion formed by judging or considering; the act or mental faculty by which man compares ideas and ascertains the relations of terms and propositions; a determination of the mind so formed, producing when expressed in words a proposition; *law,* the sentence pronounced in a cause by the judge or court by which it is tried; hence, a calamity regarded as inflicted by God for the punishment of sinners; the final trial of the human race.—*Judgment of God,* a term formerly applied to trials of crimes by single combat, by ordeal, etc.—**judgment day,** *n.* The last day, when final judgment will be pronounced on men.

judicable, jū′di•ka•bl, *a.* [L. *judicabilis,* from *judico,* to judge, from *judex,* a judge. JUDGE.] Capable of being tried or decided.—**judicative,** jū′di•kā•tiv, *a.* Having power to judge.—**judicatory,** jū′di•ka•to•ri, *a.* [L. *judicatorius.*] Pertaining to the passing of judgment; belonging to the administration of justice; dispensing justice.—*n.* A court of justice.—**judicature,** jū′di•kā•chėr, *n.* The power of distributing justice; a court of justice; a judicatory; extent of jurisdiction of a judge or court.

judicial, jū•dish′al, *a.* [L. *judicialis,* from *judicium,* a trial, a judicial inquiry, judgment, discernment, from *judex, judicis,* a judge. JUDGE.] Pertaining or appropriate to courts of justice or to a judge thereof; proceeding from, issued or ordered by, a court of justice; inflicted as a penalty or in judgment; enacted by law or statute.—**judicially,** jū•dish′al•li, *adv.* In a judicial manner.—**judiciary,** jū•dish′i•a•ri, *a.* [L. *judiciarius.*] Pertaining to the courts of judicature or legal tribunals; judicial.—*n.* The system of courts of justice in a government; the judges taken collectively.—**judicious,** jū•dish′us, *a.* [Fr. *judicieux,* from L. *judicium,* judgment.] According to sound judgment; adapted to obtain a good end by the best means; well considered; said of things; acting according to sound judgment; possessing sound judgment; directed by reason and wisdom: said of persons.—**judiciously,** jū•dish′us•li, *adv.* In a judicious manner.—**judiciousness,** jū•dish′us•nes, *n.* The quality of being judicious.

judo, jū′dō, *n.* [Japanese *jūdō.*] A modern form of jujitsu.

jug, jug, *n.* [From *Jug* or *Judge,* an old familiar form or *Joan* or *Jenny,* the name being jocularly given to the vessel, like *jack, black-jack.*] A vessel, usually of earthenware, metal, or glass, of various sizes and shapes, and generally with a handle or ear, used for holding and conveying liquors; a drinking vessel; a mug.

jugate, jugated, jū′gāt, jū′gā•ted, *a.* [L. *jugum,* a yoke, a ridge or summit.] *Bot.* coupled together, as the pairs of leaflets in compound leaves.

Juggernaut, jug′ėr•nat, *n.* [Properly *Jagannātha,* lord of the world.] The famous idol to which people in India used to sacrifice themselves at festivals. [*not cap.*] Any idea, custom, fashion, or the like, to which one either devotes himself or is blindly or ruthlessly sacrificed.

juggle, jug′l, *v.i.—juggled, juggling.* [O.Fr. *jogler,* Fr. *jongler,* It. *giocolare,* from L. *joculor,* to jest or joke, from L. *jocus,* a jest. JOKE.] To play tricks by sleight of hand; to practice artifice or imposture; to toss and catch articles, keeping several continuously in the air.—**juggler,** jug′lėr, *n.* [O.Fr. *jugleor, jogleor,* from L. *joculator,* one who jokes.] One who juggles.—**jugglery,** jug′lėr•i, *n.* The art or performances of a juggler; legerdemain; trickery; imposture.

jugular, ju′gū•lėr, *a.* [L. *jugulum,* the collarbone, the neck, from root of *jungo,* to join. JOIN.] *Anat.* pertaining to the neck or throat.—*Jugular vein,* one of the large trunks (two on each side) by which the greater part of the blood that has circulated in the head, face, and neck is returned to the heart.

juice, jūs, *n.* [O.E. *jows,* Fr. *jus,* from L. *jus,* broth, soup; cog. Skr. *yûsha,* broth.] The sap or watery part of vegetables, especially of fruits; also, the fluid part of animal substances; electricity. (*Slang.*)—**juiceless,** jūs′les, *a.*—**juiciness,** jū′si•nes, *n.* The state of being juicy—**juicy,** jū′si, *a.* Abounding with juice; succulent; also, interesting, amusing.

jujitsu, jö•jit′sö, *n.* [Japan.] A style of Japanese wrestling resting on a knowledge of muscular action.

jujube, jö′jöb, *n.* [Fr. *jujube,* a jujube, from L. *zizyphum,* Gr. *zizyphon,* Ar. *zizuf,* the jujube tree.] The fruit of a spiny shrub or small tree of lands about the Mediterranean sea; the tree itself; a confection made of gelatin, sweetened and flavored to resemble the jujube fruit.

julep, jū′lep, *n.* [Fr. *julep,* Ar. *julâb,* from Per. *gulâb,* rose-water—*gul,* rose, and *âb,* water.] A sweet drink; a sweetened mixture serving as a vehicle to some form of medicine; a drink composed of spirituous liquor, as bourbon whisky, sugar, crushed ice, and mint leaves.

Julian, jū′li•an, *a.* Pertaining to or derived from *Julius* Caesar.—*Julian calendar,* the calendar as adjusted by Julius Caesar.

julienne, jö•li•en′, *n.* [Fr.] A kind of soup made with various herbs or vegetables cut in very small pieces.

July, jū•lī′, *n.* The seventh month of the year, during which the sun enters the sign Leo; so called from *Julius* Caesar, who was born in this month, and by whom the calendar was reformed.

jumble, jum′bl, *v.t.—jumbled, jumbling.* [O.E. *jombre, jumbre, jumpre,* to agitate, to shake together; akin to *jump,* and to Dan. *gumpe,* to jolt.] To mix in a confused mass; to put or throw together without order; often followed by *together* or *up.*—*v.i.* To meet, mix, or unite in a confused manner.—*n.* Confused mixture, mass, or collection without order; disorder; confusion; medley.

jump, jump, *v.i.* [Akin Dan. *gumpe,* Prov. G. *gumpen,* to jolt or jump; Icel. *goppa,* to jump or skip; also *jumble.*] To throw one's self in any direction by lifting the feet wholly from the ground and again alighting upon them; to leap; to spring; to cause a price to rise swiftly; to make a sudden verbal attack on (to *jump on* someone).—*To jump at,* to embrace or accept (an offer) with eagerness (colloq.).—*v.t.* To increase sharply, as an admission price; to pounce upon; to seize another's rights, as a mining claim; to pass by a leap; to pass over eagerly or hastily; to skip over; to leap.—*n.* The act of jumping; a leap; a spring; a bound; an advantage, as in time (he got the *jump* on me); one in a series of moves (a *jump* ahead).—**jumper,** jump'ėr, *n.* One who or that which jumps; a horse trained to jump, as for a horse show; a woman's sleeveless, one-piece dress, worn with a blouse; *elec.* a piece of wire across a broken circuit.—**jumpy,** jump'i, *a.*

juncaceous, jung'kā'shus, *a.* [L. *juncus,* a rush.] *Bot.* pertaining to or resembling the order of plants of which the rush is the type.

junco, jun'kō, *n.* A snowbird; a genus of American finches.

junction, jungk'shon, *n.* [From L. *junctio,* from *jungo,* to join. JOIN.] The act or operation of joining; the state of being joined; the place or point of union; joint; juncture; the place where two or more railroads meet.—**juncture,** jung'chėr, *n.* [L. *junctura.*] The line or point at which two bodies are joined; a point of time; particularly, a point rendered critical or important by a concurrence of circumstances.

June, jūn, *n.* [L. *Junius,* perhaps after L. *Junius* Brutus.] The sixth month of the Gregorian calendar, having 30 days.—**June bug** or **beetle,** *n.* Any of the large, brown, winged beetles that appear about June and feed on grass and plant roots.

jungle, jung'gl, *n.* [Hind. *jangal,* forest, jungle.] Land covered with forest trees, thick, impenetrable brushwood, or any coarse, rank vegetation; any tangled mass of seemingly impenetrable material, as objects, words, etc.—**jungle fowl,** *n.* A name given to two birds, the one a native of Australia, the other of India.

junior, jū'ni•ėr, *a.* [L., contracted from *juvenior,* comp. of *juvenis,* young. JUVENILE, YOUNG.] Younger; not as old as another; applied to distinguish the younger of two persons bearing the same name: opposed to *senior;* lower or younger in standing, as in a profession.—*n.* A person younger than another; one of inferior standing in his profession to another.—**junior college,** *n.* An educational institution offering the first two years of college study.—**junior high school,** *n.* A school offering the upper elementary grades and one or more years of high school.

juniper, jū'ni•pėr, *n.* [L. *juniperus*—akin to L. *juncus,* a rush or reed. JONQUIL.] A coniferous shrub whose berries are used in the preparation of gin, varnish, etc., and in medicine as a powerful diuretic.

junk, jungk, *n.* [Fr. *jonc,* L. *juncus,* a bulrush, of which ropes were made in early ages. JUNKET.] Pieces of old cable or old cordage; waste material; salt beef supplied to vessels for long voyages.

junk, jungk, *n.* [Fr. *jonque,* Sp. and Pg. *junco,* from Malay *ajong,* a large ship.] A flat-bottomed ship used in China and Japan, often of large dimensions.

junket, jung'ket, *n.* [Formerly written *juncate,* from It. *giuncata,* cream cheese brought to market in rushes, from L. *juncus,* a rush. JUNK (rope).] Curds mixed with cream, sweetened and flavored; a gay entertainment of any kind; a trip taken for pleasure; a business trip. —*v.i.* To go on a junket; to feast; to banquet; to take part in a gay entertainment.—*v.t.* To entertain; to feast.

Juno, jū'nō, *n.* [L.; the root is the same as that of *Jove.*] The highest divinity of the Latin races in Italy, next to Jupiter, of whom she was the sister and wife, the equivalent of the Greek Hera.

junta, jun'tä, hụn'tä, *n.* [Sp. *junta,* a meeting or council, *junto,* united, from L. *junctus,* joined. JOIN.] A meeting; a council; persons controlling a government after a revolutionary seizure.—**junto,** jun'to, hön'to, *n.* A select council or assembly which deliberates in secret on any affair of government; a faction; a cabal.

Jupiter, jū'pi•tėr, *n.* [L., equivalent to *Jovis pater,* lit. Jove-father. JOVE.] The supreme deity among the Latin races in Italy, the equivalent of the Greek Zeus; one of the superior planets, remarkable for its size and brightness.

jupon, ju•pon', *n.* [Fr. from Sp. *jupon,* from Ar. *jubbah,* an outer garment.] A tight-fitting military garment without sleeves, formerly worn over the armor; a petticoat.

Jurassic, jū•ras'ik, *a. Geol.* of or belonging to the formation of the *Jura* mountains between France and Switzerland.—*Jura limestone,* the limestone rocks of the Jura corresponding to the oölite formation.—*Jurassic system,* the system of rocks of the Mesozoic era between the Triassic and the Cretaceous.

jurat, jū'rat, *n.* [Fr., from L. *juratus,* sworn, from *juro,* to swear. JURY.] A person under oath; specifically, a magistrate in some corporations; an alderman, or an assistant to a bailiff.

juridical, juridic, jū•rid'i•kal, jū•rid'ik, *a.* [L. *juridicus*—*jus, juris,* law, and *dico,* to pronounce. JURISDICTION.] Acting in the distribution of justice; pertaining to a judge, or the administration of justice; used in courts of law or tribunals of justice.—**juridically,** jū•rid'i•kal•li, *adv.* In a juridical manner.

jurisconsult, jū'ris•kon•sult, *n.* [L. *juris consultus*—*jus, juris,* law, and *consultus,* from *consulo,* to consult.] One who gives his opinion in cases of law; anyone learned in jurisprudence; a jurist.

jurisdiction, jū•ris•dik'shon, *n.* [L. *jurisdictio*—*jus, juris,* law, and *dictio,* from *dico,* to pronounce. JURY, DICTION.] The extent of the authority which a court has to decide matters tried before it; the right of exercising authority; the extent of the authority of a government, an officer, etc., to execute justice; the district or limit within which power may be exercised. —**jurisdictional,** jū•ris•dik'shon•al, *a.* Pertaining to jurisdiction.

jurisprudence, jū•ris•prö'dens, *n.* [L. *jurisprudentia*—*jus, juris,* law, and *prudentia,* skill. JURY, PRUDENT.] The science of law; the knowledge of the laws, customs, and rights of men in a state or community, necessary for the due administration of justice.—**jurisprudent,** jū•ris•prö'dent, *n.* A jurist.—**jurisprudential,** jū'ris•prö•den"shal, *a.*

jurist, jū'rist, *n.* [Fr. *juriste;* from L. *jus, juris,* law. JURY.] A man who professes the science of law.—**juristic, juristical,** jū•ris'tik, jū•ris'ti•kal, *a.*

juror, jū'rėr, *n.* [O.Fr. *jureur,* a sworn witness, from *jurer,* to swear. JURY.] One that serves on a jury; a member of a jury; a juryman.

jury, jū'ri, *n.* [O.Fr. *jurie,* an assize, from Fr. *jurer,* L. *jurare,* to swear; same origin as *jus, juris,* right, law (whence *jurist,* etc.), *justus,* just, from root meaning to bind, seen in *jungo,* to join (see JOIN), and in E. *yoke.*] A certain number of men selected according to law and sworn to inquire into or to determine facts, and to declare the truth according to the evidence legally adduced; a body of men selected to adjudge prizes, etc., at a public exhibition.—**juryman,** jū'ri•man, *n.* One who is impaneled on a jury, or who serves as a juror.

jury, jū'ri, *a.* [The origin of this term is quite uncertain; perhaps from Pg. *ajuda,* help.] *Naut.* a term applied to a thing employed to serve temporarily in room of something lost, as a *jury* mast, a *jury* rudder.

jussive, jus'iv, *a.* [From L. *jussum,* an order, from *jubeo, jussi,* to command.] Conveying or containing a command or order.

just, just, *a.* [Fr. *juste,* L. *justus,* what is according to *jus,* the rights of man. JURY.] Acting or disposed to act conformably to what is right; rendering or disposed to render to each one his due; equitable in the distribution of justice; upright; impartial; fair; blameless; righteous; conformed to rules or principles of justice; equitable; due; merited (*just* reward or punishment); rightful; proper; conformed to fact; exact.—*adv.* Exactly or nearly in time (*just* at that moment, *just* now); closely in place (*just* by, *just* behind him); exactly; nicely; accurately (*just* as they were);

narrowly; barely; only.—**justly,** just′li, *adv.* In a just manner.—**justness,** just′nes, *n.* The quality of being just.—**justice,** jus′tis, *n.* [L. *justitia,* from *justus,* just.] The quality of being just; justness; propriety; correctness; rightfulness; just treatment; vindication of right; requital of desert; merited reward or punishment; a judge holding a special office; used as an element in various titles, as Chief-*Justice* and the eight associate *justices* of the U. S. Supreme Court.—*Justices of the peace,* local judges or magistrates appointed to keep the peace, to inquire into felonies and misdemeanors, and to discharge numerous other functions. —**justiciable,** jus•tish′a•bl, *a.* Proper to be brought before a court of justice.—**justiciary, justiciar,** jus•tish′i•a•ri, jus•tish′i•ėr, *n.* [L. *justiciarius.*] An administrator of justice; in England, a lord chief-justice.—*High Court of Justiciary,* the supreme criminal tribunal of Scotland.

justify, jus′ti•fī, *v.t.*—*justified, justifying.* [Fr. *justifier;* L. *justus,* just, and *facio,* to make.] To prove or show to be just or comformable to law, right, justice, propriety, or duty; to defend or maintain; to vindicate as right; to absolve or clear from guilt or blame; to prove by evidence; to verify; to make exact; to cause to fit, as the parts of a complex object; to adjust, as lines and words in printing; *theol.* to pardon and clear from guilt; to treat as just, though guilty and deserving punishment.—*v.i.* To form an even surface or true line with something else.—**justifiable,** jus′ti•fī•a•bl, *a.* Capable of being justified; defensible; vindicable; warrantable; excusable.—**justifiableness,** jus′ti•fī•a•bl•ness. *n.* The quality of being justifiable.—**justifiably,** jus′ti•fī•a•bli, *adv.* In a manner that admits of justification; defensibly; excusably.—**justification,** jus′ti•fi•kā″shon, *n.* The act of justifying or state of being justified; *theol.* acceptance of a sinner as righteous through the merits of Christ.—**justificative,** jus′ti•fi•kā•tiv, *a.* Justifying; justificatory.—**justificatory,** jus•tif′i•ka•to•ri, *a.* Vindicatory; defensory.—**justifier,** jus′ti•fī•ėr, *n.* One who justifies.

justle, jus′l, *v.i.* See JOSTLE.

jut, jut, *v.i.*—*jutted, jutting.* [A different spelling of *jet.*] To shoot out or to project beyond the main body.—*n.* That which juts; a projection.—**jutty,** jut′i, *n.* A jetty.

jute, jūt, *n.* [Hind. *jût.*] A fibrous substance resembling hemp, obtained from an Indian plant of the linden family, and used in the manufacture of carpets, bagging, etc.; the plant itself.

juvenile, jū′ve•nīl, *a.* [L. *juvenilis,* from *juvenis,* young; cog. Skr. *yuvan,* young, E. *young.*] Young; youthful; pertaining or suited to youth.—*n.* A young person or youth.—*Juvenile delinquent,* a youth who violates a U.S. law not punishable by death; a youth guilty of antisocial behavior (truancy, etc.) outside the range of parental control.—**juvenility,** jū•ve•nil′i•ti, *n.*—**juvenescent,** jū•ve•nes′ent, *a.* Becoming young.—**juvenescence,** jū•ve•nes′ens, *n.*

juxtapose, juks•ta•pōz′, *v.t.* [L. *juxta,* near, and E. *pose.*] To place near or next; place side by side.—**juxtaposition,** juks′ta•po•zish″on, *n.* The act of juxtaposing, or state of being juxtaposed; proximity.

K

K, k, kā, the eleventh letter and the eighth consonant of the English alphabet; in Anglo-Saxon represented by *c.*

Kaaba, kä′a•ba, *n.* See CAABA.

kab, kab, *n.* A Hebrew measure. CAB.

kabala, kab′a•la, *n.* Cabala.

Kabyle, ka•bēl′, *n.* [Ar. *k'bila,* a league.] One belonging to a race of Berbers inhabiting Algeria and Tunis.

kadi, käd′i or kā′di, *n.* See CADI.

Kaffir, Kafir, kaf′ėr, *n.* [Ar. *Kâfir,* an unbeliever, an infidel.] One of a group of Bantu people; the language of the Kafirs.—*a.* Of or belonging to the Kafirs.—**kafir corn,** *n.* A kind of millet (sorghum) cultivated in parts of Africa.

kaftan, kaf′tan, *n.* [Per.] A garment worn in Turkey, Egypt, etc., consisting of a kind of long vest tied round at the waist with a girdle and having sleeves longer than the arms.

kainite, kī′nīt, *n.* [Gr. *kainos,* recent.] A mineral (hydrated magnesium sulfate and potassium chloride) occurring in the upper layers of Stassfurt salt deposits in Germany and used as a fertilizer and a source of potassium and magnesium.

kaiser, kī′zer, *n.* [G.] An emperor. CAESAR.

kaka, kä′kä, *n.* [From its cry.] A New Zealand parrot of the same genus as the kea, which latter attacks sheep and tears out portions of flesh from their backs.

kakapo, kak′a•po, *n.* [Native name.] The owl parrot, a New Zealand parrot resembling an owl.

kale, kāl, *n.* [Icel. *kal,* Dan. *kaal.* COLE.] Cabbage having curled or wrinkled leaves, but not a close head; colewort.

kaleidoscope, ka•lī′do•skōp, *n.* [Gr. *kalos,* beautiful, *eidos,* form, and *skopeō,* to view.] An optical instrument which exhibits, by reflection, a variety of beautiful colors and symmetrical forms, consisting in its simplest form of a tube containing two reflecting surfaces inclined to each other at a suitable angle, with loose pieces of colored glass, etc., inside. —**kaleidoscopic, kaleidoscopical,** ka•lī′do•skop″ik, ka•lī′do•skop″i•kal, *a.* Relating to the kaleidoscope.

kalendar, kal′en•dėr. See CALENDAR.

kali, kā′li, *n.* [Ar. *qali.* ALKALI.] Glasswort, a plant, the ashes of which are used in making glass.

kalif, kā′lif. See CALIPH.

kalmia, kal′mi•a, *n.* [From Peter *Kalm,* a botanist.] A genus of American evergreen shrubs of the heath family, with showy flowers in corymbs.

Kalmuk, Kalmuck, kal′muk, *n.* Calmuck.

kalong, kā′long, *n.* [Native name.] A name given to several species of fox bats.

kamala, kam′a•la, *n.* [Of Asiatic origin.] A drug obtained from an Asiatic tree, used as a vermifuge and a dyestuff.

kangaroo, kang′ga•rö, *n.* The native name of certain marsupials of Australia, with long and powerful hind legs for leaping, and small and short forelegs.—**kangaroo rat,** *n.* A small jumping rodent.—**kangaroo court,** *n.* An unauthorized court which mocks or disregards legal procedure.

Kantianism, kant′i•a•nizm, *n.* The philosophic system of Immanuel Kant.

kaolin, kā′o•lin, *n.* [Chinese *kau-ling,* high ridge, the name of a hill where it is found.] A fine variety of clay, resulting from the decomposition of the feldspar of a granitic rock under the influence of the weather; porcelain or China clay.

kappa, kap′ä, *n.* [Gr.] The tenth letter of the Greek alphabet, *k.*

kaput, kä•pụt′, *a.* [G. *kaput,* broken.] Finished; done for; ruined.

karma, kär′ma, *n.* [Skr., act, fate.] In the Buddhist religion, the quality belonging to actions in virtue of which they entail on the actor a certain fate or condition in a future state of existence; a term also used in theosophy.

karroo, karoo, ka•rö′, *n.* [Hottentot *karusa,* hard, from the hardness of their soil under drought.] The name given to the immense arid tracts of clayey tablelands of South Africa, which are covered with verdure only in the wet season.

karyokinesis, kar′i•ō•ki•nē″sis, *n.* [Gr. *karyon,* a nut, *kinēsis,* movement.] Indirect cell division.

katabolism, ka•tab′ol•ism, *n.* [Gr. *katabolē,* a casting down.] Downbreaking chemical changes in living bodies.

katalysis. See CATALYSIS.

kathode, kath′ōd, *n.* See CATHODE.

kation, kat′i•on, *n.* See CATION.

katydid, kā′ti•did, *n.* A species of grasshopper found in the United States: it gives out a loud sound which its name is intended to imitate.

kauri, kou′ri, *n.* [Native name.] A coniferous tree of New Zealand, yielding gum-damar, damar-resin, or kauri-gum, and having a tall straight stem, rising to a height of 150 to 200 ft., yielding valuable timber.

kava, kä′vä, *n.* A Polynesian shrub of the pepper family, and beverage made from it.

kayak, kī′ak, *n.* [Eskimo name.] A light boat, made of sealskins stretched round a wooden frame, with an opening in the middle.

kea, kē′a, *n.* See KAKA.

keck, kek, *v.i.* To vomit.

kedge, kej, *n.* [Softened form of *keg*; Icel. *kaggi*, a keg, a cask fastened as a float to an anchor, hence, the anchor itself.] A small anchor used to keep a ship steady when riding in a harbor or river, or to assist in warping her.—*v.t. kedged, kedging.* To warp (a ship) by means of a rope attached to a kedge.

keel, kēl, *n.* [From Icel. *kjolr*, Dan. *kjöl*, Sw. *kôl*, a keel of a vessel; D. *kiel*, a keel; in sense of barge, from Icel. *kjóll*, a barge=A.Sax. *ceól*, barge, O.H.G. *kiol*, a ship.] The principal timber in a ship, extending from stem to stern at the bottom, and supporting the whole frame; the corresponding part in iron vessels; *fig.* the whole ship; a projecting ridge on a surface; a low, flat-bottomed vessel used in the river Tyne for loading the colliers; a coal barge; *bot.* the lower petal of a papilionaceous corolla, enclosing the stamens and pistil.—*v.i.* To turn up the keel; to capsize.—**keelhaul,** kēl′hal, *v.t.* To punish by dropping into the sea on one side of a ship and hauling up on the other.—**keelson,** kēl′sun or kel′sun, *n.* [Dan. *kjölsviin*, Sw. *kölsvin*, G. *kielschwein*, lit. *keelswine*; comp. *pig* of lead.] An internal keel laid on the middle of the floor timbers over the keel.

keen, kēn, *a.* [A.Sax. *céne*, *cén*=Icel. *kœnn*, wise, clever; D. *koen*, G. *kühn*, keen, bold; same root as *ken*.] Acute of mind; penetrating; quick-witted; eager; vehement; full of relish or zest; sharp (a *keen* appetite); having a very fine edge (a *keen* razor); piercing; penetrating; severe (cold or wind); bitter, acrimonious (*keen* satire).—**keenly,** kēn′li, *adv.* In a keen manner.—**keenness,** kēn′nes, *n.* The state or quality of being keen; acuteness; eagerness.

keen, kēn, *v.i.* [Ir. *caoinim*.] To lament in a wailing tone.

keep, kēp, *v.t.* pret. & pp. *kept.* [A.Sax. *cépan*, to keep, observe, regard; Fris. *kijpen*, to look.] To hold; to retain in one's power or possession; not to lose or part with; to have in custody for security or preservation; to preserve; to protect; to guard; to restrain; to detain or delay; to tend or have the care of; to maintain, as an establishment, institution, etc.; to manage; to hold in any state; to continue or maintain, as a state, course, or action (to *keep* silence; to *keep* the same pace; to *keep* step); to remain confined to; not to quit (the house, one's bed); to observe in practice; not to neglect or violate; to fulfill; to observe or solemnize; to board, maintain, supply with necessaries of life; to have in the house; to entertain (to *keep* lodgers, company); to be in the habit of selling; to have a supply of for sale.—*To keep back*, to reserve; to withhold; not to disclose or communicate; to restrain; to prevent from advancing; not to deliver.—*To keep down*, to prevent from rising; to hold in subjection; to restrain.—*To keep house*, to maintain a separate residence for one's self, or for one's self and family; to remain in the house; to be confined to the house.—*To keep in*, to prevent from escape; to hold in confinement; not to tell or disclose; to restrain; to curb, as a horse.—*To keep off*, to hinder from approach or attack.—*To keep on foot*, to maintain, as a standing army.—*To keep one's self to one's self*, to shun society; to keep one's own counsel; to keep aloof from others.—*To keep out*, to hinder from entering or taking possession.—*To keep under*, to hold in subjection.—*To keep up*, to maintain; to prevent from falling or diminution; to continue; to hinder from ceasing.—*v.i.* To remain in any position or state; to continue; to abide; to stay; not to be impaired; to continue fresh or wholesome; not to become spoiled.—*To keep at it*, to continue hard at work. (*Colloq.*)—*To keep from*, to abstain from; to refrain from.—*To keep on*, to proceed; to continue to advance.—*To keep to*, to adhere strictly to; not to neglect or deviate from.—*To keep up*, to retain one's spirits; to be yet active or not to be confined to one's bed.—*n.* Guard, care, or heed; the state of being kept; the means by which one is kept; subsistence; provisions; the stronghold of an ancient castle; a donjon.—**keeper,** kēp′ėr, *n.* One who keeps; one who has the care of a prison and the custody of prisoners; one who has the charge of animals in a zoological garden; one who has the care, custody, or superintendence of anything; something that keeps or holds safe.—**keeping,** kēp′ing, *n.* A holding; custody; guard; maintenance; support; food; just proportion; consistency; harmony.—*To be in keeping with*, to accord or harmonize with; to be consistent with.—**keepsake,** kēp′sāk, *n.* Anything kept or given to be kept for the sake of the giver; a token of friendship.

keg, keg, *n.* [Formerly *kag*; Icel. *kaggi*, Sw. *kagge*, a keg. KEDGE.] A small cask or barrel.

kelp, kelp, *n.* [Origin unknown.] The alkaline substance yielded by seaweeds when burned, containing soda and iodine; any member of the order or large brown seaweed called Laminariaceae and Fucaceae.

kelpie, kelpy, kel′pi, *n.* [Perhaps connected with *yelp*, from his bellowing.] In Scotland, a malignant spirit of the waters, generally seen in the form of a horse.

kelson, kel′son, *n.* Same as *Keelson.*

kelt, keltic, kelt, kel′tik. See CELT, CELTIC.

kelter, kilter, kel′tėr, kil′tėr, *n.* [Comp. *kilt*, to tuck up the clothes.] Regular or proper state. (*Colloq.*)

ken, ken, *v.t.*—*kenned, kenning.* [Icel. *kenna*, D. and G. *kennen*, A.Sax. *cunnan*, to ken, to know; allied are *can, cunning, known.* KNOW.] To know; to take cognizance of; to see at a distance; to descry; to recognize. (Now only provincial and poetical.)—*n.* Cognizance; reach of sight or knowledge.

kennel, ken′el, *n.* [Norm. Fr., from *ken*, Fr. *chien*, a dog, from L. *canis*, a dog.] A shelter for dogs; a doghouse; a place where dogs are bred; a pack of dogs.—*v.i.*—*kenneled, kenneling*, or *kennelled, kennelling.* To live in, as a dog.—*v.t.* To keep or confine in a kennel.

kennel, ken′el, *n.* [A form of *channel, canal.*] The watercourse of a street; a gutter.

kenosis, ken′ō•sis, *n.* [Gr. *kenōsis*, emptying.] The renunciation for a time of the divine nature by Christ during the incarnation.

kentledge, kent′lej, *n.* Pig iron for ballast laid on the floor of a ship.

Kentucky bluegrass, ken•tuk′i, *n.* [From its jointed, bluish-green stem.] A perennial, rough-stalked pasture grass of the U. S., Europe, and Asia, grown in its finest state in the limestone regions of Kentucky and Tennessee. Kentucky is called the *Bluegrass State.*

kepi, kep′i, *n.* A military cap.

kept, kept, pret. & pp. of *keep.*

keramic. ke•ram′ik, *a.* Ceramic.

keratin, ker′a•tin, *n.* [Gr. *keras, keratos*, horn.] The complex compound of which horny substances (*e.g.* hair and nails) are mainly composed.

keratode, keratose, ker′a•tōd, ker′a•tōs, *n.* [Gr. *keras, keratos*, horn.] The horny substance of which the skeleton of many sponges is composed.

kerbstone. See CURB.

kerchief, kėr′chēf, *n.* [O.E. *coverchief*, O.Fr. *couvrechief, couvrechef*—Fr. *couvrir*, to cover, and *chef*, the head. COVER, CHIEF.] A cloth to dress or cover the head; hence, any loose cloth used in dress.—**kerchiefed, kerchieft,** kėr′chēft, *a.* Dressed or covered with a kerchief.

kerf, kėrf, *n.* [A.Sax. *cyrf*, a cutting off, from *ceorfan, cearfan*, to cut, to carve. CARVE.] The cut or way made through wood by a saw or other cutting instrument.

kermes, kėr′mēz, *n.* [Ar. and Per. *kermes, kirmis*, from Skr. *krimi*, a worm; *crimson, carmine*, are derivatives.] A scarlet dyestuff consisting of the dried bodies of the females of certain insects found on various species of oak round the Mediterranean.

kern, kerne, kėrn, *n.* [O.Gael. and Ir. *cearn*, a man.] A light-armed foot soldier of ancient Ireland and the Highlands of Scotland: opposed to *gallowglass.*

kern, kėrn, *n.* [Probably from L. *crena*, notch.] *Printing*, that part of a type which hangs over the body or shank.

kernel, kėr′nel, *n.* [A.Sax. *cyrnel*, a little corn, a kernel, dim. of *corn*, a grain. CORN, GRAIN.] The edible substance contained in the shell of a nut or the stone of a fruit; anything enclosed in a shell, husk, or integument; a grain of corn; the seed of pulpy fruit; a small mass around which other matter is concreted; a nucleus; *fig.* the main or essential point, as opposed to matters of less import; the core; the gist.—*v.i.* To harden or ripen into kernels, as the seeds of plants.

kerosene, ker'o•sēn, *n.* [Gr. *kēros,* wax.] A liquid hydrocarbon distilled from coals, bitumen, petroleum, etc., extensively used in lamps, stoves, etc.

kersey, kėr'zi, *n.* [Said to be from *Kersey,* in Suffolk.] A species of coarse woolen cloth, usually ribbed, made from long wool.—*a.* Consisting of kersey; hence, homespun; homely.

kerseymere, kėr'zi•mēr, *n.* [CASSIMERE.] A thin twilled stuff woven from the finest wools, used for men's garments; cassimere.

kestrel, kes'trel, *n.* [Fr. *quercerelle, cresserelle,* kestrel; L. *querquedula,* a teal.] A common British species of falcon, 13 to 15 inches in length, capable of hovering against the wind.

ketch, kech, *n.* [Perhaps akin to *catch.*] A fore-and-aft rigged vessel with a mainmast and a mizzenmast, the latter being forward of the rudder post.

ketchup, catchup, catsup, kech'up, *n.* [Malay *kechap,* a kind of East Indian pickles.] A sauce for meat and fish, made from mushrooms, unripe walnuts, tomatoes, etc.; usually, a thick, seasoned tomato sauce.

ketone, kē'tōn, [G. *keton,* from F. *acétone.*] An organic compound of the general formula R-CO-R′, in which the radicals (R and R′) may be identical or different alkyl or aryl groups, as in CH_3COCH_3, acetone.

kettle, ket'l, n. [A. Sax. *cetel*=D. *ketel,* Icel. *ketill,* kettle; from L. *catillus,* dim. of *catinus,* a deep bowl, a vessel for cooking food.] A vessel of iron or other metal, of various shapes and dimensions, used for heating and boiling water or other liquor.—**kettledrum,** *n.* A drum consisting of a copper vessel, usually hemispherical, covered with parchment.

kevel, kev'el, *n.* [Dan. *kievle,* a peg, a rolling-pin.] *Naut.* a piece of timber serving to belay great ropes to.—**kevelhead,** *n. Naut.* the end of one of the top timbers used as a kevel.

key, kē, *n.* [A.Sax. *caeg, caege,* Fris. *kai, kei,* a key; affinities doubtful.] An instrument for shutting or opening a lock; that whereby any mystery is disclosed or anything difficult explained; a guide; a solution; an explanation; a tone or pitch; a legend, as on a map or a puzzle; something that fastens, keeps tight, prevents movement, or the like; a binding or connecting piece; a movable piece in a musical instrument, struck or pressed by the fingers in playing to produce the notes; the keynote.—*a.* Of basic importance; main.—*v.t.* To furnish or fasten with a key; to fasten or secure firmly; to make a legend to aid understanding; to make nervous, with *up.*—**keyboard,** *n.* The series of levers in a keyed musical instrument, as a pianoforte, organ, or in a typewriter or typesetting machine, on which the fingers press.—**keyhole,** *n.* A hole in a door or lock for receiving a key.—**keynote,** *n.* The main idea; *mus.,* the first note, or "do" tone, of a scale.—*Keynote address,* a speech, as at a political convention, to arouse enthusiasm and present the basic issues.—**keystone,** kē'stōn, *n.* The stone at the apex of an arch which, when put in, keys or locks the whole.

key, kē, *n.* CAY.

khaki, kä•kē, *n.* [Hind., from *khâk;* dust.] A light-brown thin material used for uniforms.

khalif, kā'lif, *n.* Calif.

khamsin, kam'sin, *n.* [Ar. *khamsin,* fifty, because it blows about fifty days.] A hot southerly wind in Egypt; the simoom.

khan, kän, *n.* [Tartar and Turk. *khân.*] In Asia, a governor; a king; a prince; a chief.—**khanate,** kan'āt, *n.* The dominion or jurisdiction of a khan.

khan, kän, *n.* [Per. *khân,* a house, a tent.] An eastern inn; a caravansary.

khedive, ke•dēv', *n.* A Turkish title formerly applied to the Pasha or governor of Egypt, implying a rank or authority superior to a prince or viceroy, but inferior to an independent sovereign.

khitmutgar, kit•mut'gär, *n.* [Hind. *khidmat-gâr—khidmat,* service, duty, and *gâr,* a doer.] In India, a waiter at table; an under butler.

kibe, kīb, *n.* [W. *cibwst—cib,* cup, and *gwst,* moist, fluid.] A chilblain.

kibitzer, kib'it•sėr, *n.* [Yiddish, from G. *kiebitzen,* to look on, from *kiebitz,* a bothersome spectator.] One who gives unwanted advice, especially such a one looking on at a card game.—**kibitz,** kib'its, *v.i.* To behave as a kibitzer; to meddle.

kibosh, ki•bosh', kī'bosh, *n.* [Origin doubtful.] Nonsense.—*Put the kibosh on,* squelch; stop. (Slang)

kick, kik, *v.t.* [W. *ciciaw,* to kick, *cic,* the foot.] To strike with the foot; to strike in recoiling, as a gun; *football,* to win a goal by kicking.—*To kick up a row or a dust,* to create a disturbance. (Colloq.)—*v.i.* To strike with the foot or feet; to be in the habit of so striking; to manifest repugnance to restraint; to be recalcitrant; to recoil, as a firearm.—*n.* A blow with the foot or feet; a striking or thrust of the foot; the recoil of a firearm; a measurable feeling; a thrill.—**kicker,** kik'ėr, *n.*—**kickback,** kik'bak, *n.* An unofficial and sometimes illegal return of a portion of wages or dividends, etc., to the payer.—**kickoff,** kik'ąf, *n. Football,* a place kick at or near the center of the field to begin play; the opening or beginning of a campaign or event.—**kickup,** kik'up, *n.* A disturbance; a row.

kickshaw, kik'shą, *n.* [Originally *kickshaws,* as a singular noun, from Fr. *quelque chose,* something.] Something fantastical or uncommon; a light, unsubstantial dish.

kid, kid, *n.* [Dan. and Sw. *kid,* Icel. *kith,* G. *kitz, kitze,* a kid; akin *chit, child.*] A young goat; leather made from the skin of a kid, or in imitation of it; a child or youngster.—*v.t.* and *i.*—*kidded, kidding.* To bring forth a young goat; to tease; to joke.

kid, kid, *n.* [A form of *kit.*] A small wooden tub or vessel.

Kidderminster, kid'ėr•min•stėr, *n.* A carpeting, so named from the town where formerly it was principally manufactured.

kidnap, kid'nap, *v.t.*—*kidnaped, kidnaping.* [Slang E *kid* a child, and *nap* for *nab,* to steal.] To forcibly abduct or steal a human being, to seize and forcibly carry away.—**kidnaper,** kid'nap•ėr, *n.*

kidney, kid'ni, *n.* [O.E. *kidnere*=Sc. *kite,* A.Sax. *cwith,* Icel. *kvithr,* Sw. *qued,* the belly, and Sc. *neer,* Icel. *nyra,* G. *niere,* a kidney.] Either of the two oblong, flattened, bean-shaped glands which secrete the urine, situated in the belly on either side of the backbone; constitution, character, or temper.—**kidney bean,** *n.* The English term for the common string bean; in France the haricot bean.

kilderkin, kil'der•kin, *n.* [O.D. *kindeken, kinneken.*] A small barrel; an old liquid measure containing the eighth part of a hogshead or 18 gallons.

kill, kil, *v.t.* [O.E. *kylle, kulle, culle,* to strike.] To deprive of life by any means; to render inanimate; to put to death; to slay; to deprive of active qualities; to deaden (pain); to overpower; to stop; to cause to waste (to *kill* time).—*n.* The act of killing; the game killed in a hunt.—**killer,** kil'ėr, *n.* A murderer; that which kills, as a beast of prey.—**killjoy,** kil'joi, *n.* One who ruins the fun or enjoyment for others.—**killingly,** kil'ing•li, *adv.*

killdeer, kil'dēr, *n.* [From its clear, plaintive cry.] An American plover, a shore bird with a grayish-brown back and a white breast.

kiln, kil, *n.* [A.Sax. *cylene, cyln,* perhaps from L. *culina,* a kitchen (whence *culinary*).] An oven of brick or stone which may be heated for the purpose of hardening, burning, or drying anything placed in it.

kilocycle, kil'o•sī•kl, *n.* A thousand cycles; *radio,* a thousand cycles per second.

kilogram, kil'o•gram, *n.* [Fr. *kilogramme* from Gr. *chilioi,* a thousand, and Fr. *gramme.*] A measure of weight, being 1,000 grams.—**kilogram-meter,** *n.* A unit of work, or the amount taken to raise one kilogram one meter (almost 7¼ foot-pounds).—**kiloliter,** kil'o•lē•tėr, *n.* 1,000 liters.

kilometer, ki•lom'e•tėr, *n.* 1,000 meters.—**kilowatt,** kil'o•wot, *n.* An electric unit of power, equivalent to 1,000 watts, or to 1.34 horsepower.—**kilowatt hour,** *n.* A unit of energy equal to that expended by one kilowatt acting for one hour.

kilt, kilt, *n.* [A Scandinavian word; comp. Icel. *kilting,* a skirt, *kjalta,* a person's lap; Dan. *kilte*, to tuck up or kilt.] A kind of short petticoat worn by men as an article of dress in lieu of trousers; regarded as peculiarly the national dress of the Highlanders of Scotland; the filibeg. —*v.t.* To tuck up like a kilt for greater freedom of movement.

kimono, ki•mo'no, *n.* [Jap.] A loose, robe-like garment, usually made of silk, worn by both Japanese men and women; a similar garment worn indoors by occidental women; a dressing gown.

kin, kin, *n.* [A.Sax. *cynn, cyn,* Icel. *kyn,* Goth. *kuni,* O.H.G. *chunni,* kin, kind, family, race; akin are *kind, n.* and *a., king*; D. and G. *kind,* a child; L. *genus,* Gr. *genos,* race, offspring. GENUS.] Relationship; consanguinity or affinity; connection by blood; relatives collectively; kindred; used in this sense with a verb in the plural.—*a.* Of the same nature or kind; kindred; congenial.—**kinsfolk,** kinz'fōk, *n. pl.* Relations kindred.—**kinship,** kin'ship, *n.* Relationship; consanguinity.—**kinsman,** kinz'man, *n.* A man of the same race or family, one related by blood.—**kinswoman,** kinz'wum•an, *n.* A female relation.

kind, kīnd, *n.* [A.Sax. *cynde, gecynde,* nature, kind, race, generation, from same root as *cyn,* offspring. KIN.] Race genus; generic class; sort; variety; nature; style; manner; character.—*In kind,* with produce or commodities, as opposed to *in money* (to pay one *in kind*).

kind, kīnd, *a.* [A.Sax. *cynde, gecynde,* natural harmonious; closely akin to *kind, n.* KIN.] Disposed to do good to others, and to make them happy; having tenderness or goodness of nature; benevolent; benignant; friendly; proceeding from or dictated by tenderness or goodness of heart.—**kindhearted,** *a.* Having much kindness of nature; characterized by kindness of heart.—**kindheartedness,** *n.* Kindness of heart.—**kindliness,** kīnd'li•nes, *n.* The quality of being kindly.—**kindly,** kīnd'li, *adv.* In a kind manner.—*a.* Of a kind disposition or character; sympathetic; congenial; benevolent favorable; refreshing (*kindly* showers).—**kindness,** kīnd'nes, *n.* The state or quality of being kind; good will; benevolence; a kind act; an act of good will.

kindergarten, kin'dėr•gär•ten, *n.* [G.; lit. children's garden. CHILD, GARDEN.] A kind of infants' school, intermediate between the nursery and the primary school, in which systematically arranged amusements are combined with a certain amount of instruction.

kindle, kin'dl, *v.t.*—*kindled, kindling.* [Allied to or derived from Icel. *kynda,* to kindle, *kyndill,* a torch or candle; perhaps from L. *candela,* E. *candle.*] To set on fire; to cause to burn with flame; to light; to inflame, as the passions; to rouse; to provoke; to excite to action.—*v.i.* To take fire; to grow warm or animated; to be roused or exasperated.—**kindling,** kind'ling, *n.* The act of one who kindles; materials for lighting a fire.

kindred, kind'red, *n.* [O.E. *kinrede,* kindred, from *kin,* and term. *-red,* as in hat*red* (which see): the *d* is inserted, as in gen*der*, thun*der*. KIN.] Relationship by birth or marriage; consanguinity; kin; in plural sense, relatives by blood or marriage, more properly the former; relations or relatives.—*a.* Related; congenial; allied.

kinematics, ki•ne•mat'iks, *n.* [Gr. *kinēma,* movement, from *kineō,* to move.] That branch of the science of mechanics which treats of motion, without reference to the forces producing it.—**kinematic, kinematical,** ki•ne•mat'ik, ki•ne•mat'i•kal, *a.* Of or belonging to kinematics.—*Kinematic viscosity,* the relation of absolute viscosity to density; air being fourteen times as kinematically viscous as water.—**kinetic,** ki•net'ik, *a.* Causing motion; motory: applied to force actually exerted.—*Kinetic energy,* energy of motion, equal (in absolute measure) to $\frac{1}{2}\ mv^2$, where *m* represents the mass and *v* the velocity of the moving body; in gravitational measure it is $mv^2/2\ g$.—**kinetics,** ki•net'iks, *n.* That branch of the science of dynamics which treats of forces causing or changing motion in bodies. DYNAMICS.—**kinematograph,** ki•ne•mat'o•graf (popularly, sin•e•mat'o•graf), *n.* A method of casting upon a screen a series of instantaneous photographs, producing the effect of motion.

king, king, *n.* [A.Sax. *cyning,* from *cyn,* kin, race, and term. *-ing,* one of, descendant (as in *atheling*); D. *koning,* Icel. *konungr,* Dan. *konge,* G. *kōnig,* king. KIN.] The sovereign of a nation; a man invested with supreme authority over a nation, tribe, or country; a monarch; a prince; a ruler; a playing card having the picture of a king; the chief piece in the game of chess; a crowned man in the game of checkers; [*cap.*] *pl.* title of two books in the Old Testament, relating particularly to the Jewish kings.—*v.t.* To rule over as king.—*v.i.* To act like a king.—*a.* Most important; main: often in combination (*king* post).—**kingbird,** *n.* Certain of the various birds of the flycatcher family.—**kingcrab,** *n.* A kind of crustacean with a carapace of horseshoe shape, and a long tail spine.—**kingcraft,** king'kraft, *n.* The art of governing; royal polity or policy.—**kingdom,** king'dum, *n.* The power or authority of a king (*Shak.*); the territory or country subject to a king; the dominion of a king or monarch; domain or realm in a general sense; *nat. hist.* one of the most extensive divisions into which natural objects are classified (the animal, vegetable, and mineral *kingdoms*).—**kingfisher,** king'fish•ėr, *n.* A crested and bright-colored bird with a short tail and long sharp-pointed bill. It frequents the banks of rivers and dives for fish.—**kinglet,** king'let, *n.* A little king; a tiny bird, similar to the warbler, the golden-crowned or ruby-crowned kinglet.—**kingliness,** king'li•nes, *n.* State of being kingly.—**kingly,** king'li, *a.* Belonging or pertaining to a king or to kings; royal; monarchical; becoming a king; august; splendid. ∴ Syn. under ROYAL.—*adv.* With an air of royalty; as becoming a king.—**kingpin,** *n. Bowling,* the number-one pin; the leader; the chief person.—**king post,** *n.* The middle post standing at the apex of a pair of rafters, and having its lower end fastened to the middle of the tie beam.—**king's evil,** *n.* A disease of the scrofulous kind, formerly believed curable by the touch of a king.—**kingship,** king'ship, *n.* Royalty; the state, office, or dignity of a king; royal government.—**king truss,** *n.* A truss for a roof framed with a king post.—**kingwood,** *n.* A Brazilian wood beautifully streaked with violet tints, and used in cabinetwork.

kink, kingk, *n.* [D., G., and Sw. *kink,* a twist or coil in a cable.] A twist in a rope or thread such as prevents it running freely; an unreasonable and obstinate notion; a crotchet.—*v.i.* To get into a kink; to twist or run into knots.

kinkajou, king'ka•jö, *n.* A plantigrade carnivorous mammal of South America, resembling the lemurs in structure and aspect, but allied to the bear.

kino, kī'nō, *n.* [An East Indian word.] An astringent extract resembling catechu, obtained from various tropical trees.

kinsfolk, kinship, kinsman, kinswoman. See KIN.

kiosk, ki•osk', *n.* A Turkish word signifying a kind of open pavilion or summer house; a similar lightweight structure used as an open-air newsstand, bandstand, etc.; a roadside telephone booth.

kipper, kip'ėr, *n.* [O.E. *cypera,* spawning salmon, prob. from *coper,* copper, the color.] A salmon at, or directly after, the spawning season; a fish, as a salmon or herring, split open, salted, and dried or smoked. —*v.t.* To cure (salmon) by splitting open, salting, and drying.

kirk, kirk, *n.* [The old form of *church*; A.Sax. *cyrc.* CHURCH.] A church: still in common use in Scotland.

kirsch, kērsh, *n.* [G., from *kirsche,* cherry.] An alcoholic liquor distilled from the fermented juice of the small black cherry.

kirtle, kėr'tl, *n.* [A.Sax. *cyrtel,* Icel. *kyrtill,* Dan. *kjortel*; akin to *short.*] A kind of short gown; a petticoat.—*v.t.* To tuck up so as to give the appearance of a kirtle to.—**kirtled,** kėr'tld, *a.* Wearing a kirtle.

kismet, kis'met, *n.* [Per. *kusmut.*] A Mohammedan expression for fate or destiny.

kiss, kis, *v.t.* [A.Sax. *cyssan,* from *coss,* a kiss; Icel. and Sw. *kyssa,* Dan. *kysse,* G. *kussen,* to kiss; the corresponding nouns being Icel. *koss,* Dan, *kys,* G. *kuss.*] To touch with the lips in salutation or as a mark of affection; to caress by joining lips; to touch gently, as if with fondness.—*v.i.* To join lips in love or respect; to meet or come in contact (as curved lines, etc.).—*n.* A salute given with the lips; a kind of confection.—**kisser,** kis′ėr, *n.* (Slang) The mouth or face.

kit, kit, *n.* [D. *kit*, a large bottle; O.D. *kitte*, a beaker, decanter.] A large bottle; a kind of wooden tub for holding fish, butter, etc.; that which contains necessaries or tools, and hence the necessaries and tools themselves; something to be assembled (airplane *kit*); a collection of related materials (a convention *kit*).

kit, kit, *n.* [Probably an abbreviated form of *guitar*, *gittern*, *cittern*.] A diminutive fiddle, used generally by dancing masters.

kitchen, kich′en, *n.* [A.Sax. *cycene*, from L. *coquina*, kitchen, from *coquo*, to cook. COOK.] The room of a house appropriated to cookery; style of cooking or of food prepared.—**kitchener,** kich′en•ėr, *n.* A servant in the kitchen; a cookstove.—**kitchenette, kitchenet,** *n.* A small room or recess compactly furnished as a kitchen.—**kitchen garden,** a garden in which vegetables are grown for the table.—**kitchenmidden,** *n.* [Dan. *kjokkenmodding*.] A refuse heap of a prehistoric people.—**kitchenware,** *n.* Utensils used in a kitchen.

kite, kīt, *n.* [A.Sax. *cyta*, a kite.] A bird of the falcon family having a somewhat long forked tail, long wings, and comparatively weak bill and talons; a light frame of wood and paper constructed for flying in the air for amusement.

kith, kith, *n.* [A.Sax. *cytth*, knowledge, relationship, native country, from *cúth*, known, pp. of *cunnan*, to know. CAN.] Acquaintances or friends collectively.—*Kith and kin*, friends and relatives.

kitten, kit′n, *n.* [Dim. of *cat*.] A young cat.—*v.i.* To bring forth young, as a cat.—**kittenish,** kit′n•ish, *a.* Like a kitten; fond of playing.—**kitty,** kit′i, *n.* A kitten.

kittiwake, kit′i•wāk, *n.* [From its cry.] A species of gull found in great abundance in the northern parts of the world.

kitty, kit′i, *n.* [From *kit*.] A pool or common fund into which participants contribute for a particular purpose.

kiwi, kē′wē, *n.* [Maori.] An apteryx, a flightless bird of New Zealand.

kleptomania, klep•to•mā′ni•a, *n.* [Gr. *kleptō*, to steal, and *mania*, madness.] A form of neurosis marked by an irresistible impluse to steal, usually for no economic reason.—**kleptomaniac,** klep•to•mā′ni•ak, *n.* One affected with kleptomania.

knack, nak, *n.* [Imitative of sound, like D. *knak*, Dan. *knaek*, G. *knack*, a crack, a snap; originally a snap of the fingers, then a trick or way of doing a thing as if with a snap.] Readiness; habitual facility of performance; dexterity; adroitness; a knickknack or toy (*Shak.*).

knacker, nak′ėr, *n.* [From Icel. *hnakkr*, a saddle: originally it meant a saddler and harness maker.] One whose occupation is to slaughter diseased or useless horses.

knap, nap, *v.t.*—*knapped*, *knapping*. [Same as D. *knappen*, to crack, to munch, to lay hold of; G. *knappen*, to crack, to snap.] To bite; to bite off; to break short; to snap; to make a short sharp sound.—*n.* A short sharp noise; a snap.

knapsack, nap′sak, *n.* [L.G. *knappsack*, D. *knapzak*, G. and D. *knappen*, to snap, to eat, and *sack*—lit. a provision sack.] A bag of leather or strong cloth for carrying a soldier's necessaries, strapped to the back between the shoulders; any similar bag, such as those used by tourists and others for carrying light personal luggage.

knar, när, *n.* [GNARL.] A knot in wood.—**knarred,** närd, a Gnarled; knotty.—**knarry,** när′i, *a.* Knotty; stubby.

knave, nāv, *n.* [A.Sax *cnapa*. or *cnafa*, a boy, a youth, a son; D. *knaap*, G. *knabe*, a boy or young man, Icel. *knapi*, a servant boy; root doubtful; comp. *knight*.] A boy‡; a male servant‡; a false deceitful fellow; a dishonest man or boy; a rascal; in a pack of playing cards, a card with a soldier or servant painted on it: a jack.—**knavery,** nā′vėr•i, *n.* The conduct of a knave; dishonesty; deception in traffic; trickery; petty villainy; fraud.—**knavish,** nā′vish, *a.* Acting like or belonging to a knave; dishonest; fraudulent; mischievous‡.—**knavishly,** nā′vish•li, *adv.* In a knavish manner.—**knavishness,** nā′vish•nes, *n.* The quality or habit of being knavish.

knead, nēd, *v.t.* [A.Sax. *cnedan*, *cnaedan*; D. *knedan*, G. *kneten*, Icel. *knotha*, to knead; akin Slav. *gneta*, *gnesti*, to press, to knead.] To work and press into a mass; particularly, to work into a well-mixed mass, as the materials of bread, cake, or paste; to beat or pommel.—**kneader,** nē′dėr, *n.* One who kneads.

knee, nē, *n.* [A.Sax. *cneó*, *cneów* = Icel. *kné*, Dan. *knae*, D. and G. *knie*, Goth. *kniu*; cognate with L. *genu*, Gr. *gonu*, Skr. *jânu*, knee.] The joint connecting the two principal parts of the leg; the articulation of the thigh and bones of the lower leg; something resembling or suggestive of this; a piece of bent timber or iron used to connect the beams of a ship with her sides or timbers.—**knee action,** *n.* In an automobile, independent front wheel suspension.—**kneecap,** *n.* The movable bone covering the knee joint in front; the kneepan; the patella; a leather cap or covering for the knee of a horse.—**kneed,** nēd, *a.* Having knees: chiefly in composition (in-*kneed*, out-*kneed*); *bot.* geniculated.—**knee-deep,** *a.* as deep as would come to the knee.—*adv.* so as to be up to the knees in something.—**kneepan,** *n.* The bone covering the knee joint; the kneecap.

kneel, nēl, *v.i.*—pret. & pp. *kneeled*, *knelt*. [O.E. *kneole*, *kneoli*, from *knee*; corresponding to D. *knielen*, Dan. *knaele*, to kneel. Comp. *handle*, from *hand*.] To bend the knee; to fall on the knees.—**kneeler,** nēl′ėr, *n.* One who kneels or worships by kneeling.

knell, nel, *n.* [A.Sax. *cnyll*, a sound of a bell; *cnyallan*, to sound a bell; comp. G. *knellen*, *knallen*, to make a loud noise; G. and D. *knal*, Sw. *knall*, a loud sound; Icel. *knylla*, to beat, *gnella*, to scream; imitative of sound; *knoll* is akin.] The sound of a bell rung at a funeral; a passing bell; a death signal in general.—*v.i.* To sound as a funeral knell; to sound as an omen or warning of coming evil.—*v.t.* To summon by, or as by, a knell.

knelt, nelt, pret. & pp. of *kneel*.

knew, nū, pret. of *know*.

knickerbockers, nik′ėr•bok•ėrz, *n. pl.* [Properly Dutch breeches, after Washington Irving's character Diedrich *Knickerbocker*, as representative of a Dutchman.] A kind of loose breeches reaching just below the knee, where they are gathered in so as to clasp the leg.—**knickers,** *n. pl.* A short form for *Knickerbockers*.

knickknack, nik′nak, *n.* [A reduplication of *knack*; comp. *click-clack*, *tip-top*, *ding-dong*, etc.] A trifle or toy; any small article more for ornament than use.

knife, nīf, *n.* pl. **knives,** nīvz. [A.Sax. *cníf* = D. *knijf*, Icel. *knífr*, Dan. *kniv*, Sw. *knif*; akin to *nip*. NIP.] A cutting instrument consisting of a sharp-edged blade of small or moderate size attached to a handle.—*War to the knife*, a war carried on to the utmost extremity; mortal combat.—**knife-edge,** *n.* A piece of steel with a fine edge, serving to support with the least friction an oscillating body, as the beam of a pair of scales.

knight, nīt, *n.* [A.Sax. *cniht*, a boy, a servant, a military follower; D. and G. *knecht*, a male servant, Dan. *knegt*, a fellow, the knave at cards: perhaps from root of *kin* or of *knave*.] In feudal times, a man admitted to a certain military rank, with special ceremonies; in the British Empire, one holding a dignity conferred by the sovereign and entitling the possessor to have the title of *Sir* prefixed to his Christian name, but not hereditary like the dignity of baronet; a member of an order of chivalry; a champion; one of the pieces in the game of chess, usually the figure of a horse's head.—*Knight of the shire*, a county member of the British Parliament.—*v.t.* To dub or create a knight; to confer the honor of knighthood upon, the accolade or blow of a sword being commonly a part of the ceremony.—**knight-errant,** *n.* A knight who traveled in search of adventures and to exhibit his prowess.—**knight-errantry,** *n.* The role, character, or practice of a knight-errant.—**knighthood,** nīt′hu̇d *n.* The character or dignity of a knight; the rank or honor accompanying the title of knight; knights collectively.—*Order of Knighthood*, in

England, an organized and duly constituted body of knights, as those of the Garter or the Bath.—**knightliness,** nīt′li•nes, *n.* The character or quality of being knightly.—**knightly,** nīt′li, *a.* Pertaining to a knight; becoming a knight; chivalrous.—*adv.* In a manner becoming a knight.—**Knights of Columbus,** a Roman Catholic society.—**Knight Templar,** member of a branch of Freemasonry.

knit, nit, *v.t.*—*knit* or *knitted, knitting.* [A.Sax. *cnyattan,* to knit, to tie, from *cnotta,* a knot; Icel. *knyta,* from *knutr,* a knot; Dan. *knytte,* to knit, to knot. KNOT.] To tie together; to tie with a knot; to fasten by tying; to weave or form by looping or knotting a continuous thread by means of wires or needles; to cause to grow together; to join closely; to contract into folds or wrinkles (to *knit* the brows).—*v.i.* To make a fabric by interlooping yarn or thread by means of needles, etc.; to unite closely; to grow together.—**knitter,** nit′ėr, *n.* One that knits; a knitting machine.

knives, nīvz, *n.* pl. of *knife.*

knob, nob, *n.* [Older form *knop*; comp. A.Sax. *cnœp,* a top, a knob, D. *knop, knoop,* G. *knopf,* Icel. *knappr,* Dan. *knop, knap,* a knob, button, bud, etc.; also W., Ir., and Gael. *cnap,* a knob.] A hard protuberance; a hard swelling or rising; a round ball at the end of anything; the more or less ball-shaped handle for a door, drawer, or the like; a boss; a knot; a bunch of foliage carved or cast for ornament,—*v.i.*—*knobbed, knobbing.* To grow into knobs; to bunch.—**knobbed,** nobd, *a.* Containing knobs; full of knobs.—**knobby,** nob′i, *a.* Full of knobs or hard protuberances.

knock, nok, *v.i.* [A.Sax. *cnocian, cnucian,* to knock; to beat; Icel. *knoka,* Sw. *knacka,* to knock; also seen in Gael. and Ir. *cnag,* a knock; W. *cnociaw,* to knock; akin *knack, knag, knuckle,* etc.] To strike or beat with something thick, hard, or heavy; to drive or be driven so as to come in collision with something; to strike against; to clash; to criticize, belittle, or disparage. *(Colloq.)* —*To knock about,* to wander here and there; to move about in the world. (*Colloq.*)— *To knock off,* to cease from labor; to stop work. (*Colloq.*)—*To knock under,* to yield; to submit; to acknowledge one's self conquered. (*Colloq.*)—*v.t.* To dash; to drive; to cause to collide; to drive or force by a succession of blows.—*To knock down,* to strike down; to fell; to prostrate by a blow; at *auctions,* to assign to a bidder, generally by a blow with a hammer.—*To knock on the head,* to stun or kill by a blow or blows on the head; hence, to frustrate, as a project or scheme; to render abortive. (*Colloq.*)—*n.* A blow; a stroke with something thick, hard, or heavy; a stroke on a door, intended as a request for admittance; a rap.—**knocker,** nok′ėr, *n.* One that knocks; a contrivance fastened to a door to knock for admittance.—**knock-kneed,** *a.* Having the legs so much curved inward that they touch or knock together in walking; hence, feeble (a *knock-kneed* argument).—**knockout,** *n.* A person or thing strikingly attractive (*slang*); *boxing,* a blow which fells an opponent for a minimum period of ten seconds.

knoll, nol, *n.* [A.Sax. *cnoll,* a knoll, a summit; N. *knoll,* Dan. *knold,* a knoll; G. *knolle, knollen,* a lump; comp. W. *cnol,* the top, a round hillock.] The top or crown of a hill; a small or low round hill; a small elevation of earth.

knop, nop, *n.* [KNOB.] A knob; a boss; a bunch. (O.T.)

knot, not, *n.* [A.Sax. *cnotta,* a knot= D. *knot,* Icel. *knútr,* Sw. *knut,* G. *knoten,* a knot; cog. L. *nodus,* that is, *gnodus* (whence *node*). KNIT.] A complication of a thread, cord, or rope, or of two or more, by tying, knitting, or entangling; a fastening made by looping a cord or thread on itself; a tie; a figure with interlaced lines; a bond of association; a union (the nuptial *knot*); a cluster, collection, group; a difficulty or perplexity; something not easily solved; a hard part in timber caused by the shooting out of a branch; a protuberance; a nodule; a bunch; a knob; *naut.* a division of the log line, forming the same fraction of a mile as half a minute is of an hour, that is, the hundred and twentieth part of a nautical mile; so that the number of knots run off the reel in half a minute shows the vessel's speed per hour in miles; hence, a nautical mile or 6080 feet.—*v.t.*—*knotted, knotting.* To tie in a knot or knots; to form a knot on; to entangle; to unite closely.—*v.i.* To become knotted; to form knots or joints, as in plants.—**knotgrass,** *n.* A common, low weed, with branched trailing stems and knotted joints.—**knotted,** not′ed, *a.* Full of knots; having knots; *bot.* having knobs or enlargements as on a stem.—**knottiness,** not′i•nes, *n.* The quality of being knotty.—**knotty,** not′i, *a.* Full of knots; having many knots; difficult; intricate; involved; hard to unravel (a *knotty* question or point).—**knotweed,** *n.* Knotgrass.

knot, not, *n.* [Said to be named after king *Canute* (*Cnut*), who was very fond of it.] A small grallatorial bird, closely allied to the snipe.

knout, nout, *n.* [Russ. *knute.*] An instrument of punishment used in Russia consisting of a handle 2 feet long, a leather thong 4 feet, with a metal ring at the end to which the striking part, a flat tongue of hardened hide 2 feet long is attached; the punishment inflicted with the knout.—*v.i.* To punish with the knout.

know, nō, *v.t.*—*knew* (pret.), *known* (pp.). [A.Sax. *cnáwan,* pret. *cneów,* pp. *cnáwen,* to know; Icel. *kná,* to be able; comp. the allied words E. *can,* to be able, *ken,* to know, Icel. *kunna,* used in both senses; G. *können,* to be able (*ich kann,* I can), *kennen,* to know; from a root *gna, gan,* to know, seen also in *name, noble, narrate* (these words have lost *g* before the *n,* as in *ignoble, ignorant*), *uncouth*; L. *gnosco, nosco,* Gr. *gignōskō,* to know.] To perceive with certainty; to understand clearly; to be convinced or satisfied regarding the truth or reality of; to be assured of; to be aware of; to distinguish (to *know* a star from a planet); to be familiar or acquainted with (a person, a topic, etc.); to have experience of.—*v.i.* To have clear and certain perception; not to be doubtful; to be informed.—**knowable,** nō′a•bl, *a.* Capable of being known.—**knower,** nō′ėr, *n.* One who knows.—**knowing,** nō′ing, *a.* Well-informed; well-instructed; intelligent; sagacious; conscious; expressive of knowledge or cunning (a *knowing* look).—**knowingly,** nō′ing•li, *adv.* In a knowing manner.—**knowingness,** nō′ing•nes, *n.*—**knowledge,** nol′ij, *n.* [O.E. *knowleche,* from *know,* and term. seen in Icel. *kunnleikr,* knowledge, and in E. *wedlock,* and which is derived from A.Sax. *lác,* Icel. *leikr,* Goth. *laiks,* sport, play, gift.] The clear and certain perception of that which exists, or of truth and fact; indubitable apprehension; cognizance; learning; erudition; information; skill in anything; familiarity gained by actual experience; acquaintance with any fact or person.—**known,** nōn, *p.* and *a.* Perceived; understood; recognized; familiar.

knuckle, nuk′l, *n.* [A.Sax. *cnucel,* D. *knokkel, kneukel,* Dan. *knokkel,* G. *knöchel,* a knuckle, *knochen,* a bone; comp. W. *cnwc,* a knob or knot; allied are probably *knock, knag, knack.*] The joint of a finger, particularly when protuberant by the closing of the fingers; the knee joint of a calf or pig (a *knuckle* of veal).—*v.t.*—*knuckled, knuckling.* To strike with the knuckles; to pommel. —*v.i.* Only used in the colloquial phrases *to knuckle down, to knuckle under,* to yield; to submit; to acknowledge one's self beaten; phrases of doubtful origin.—**knuckle-duster,** *n.* An iron instrument with knobs or points projecting, contrived to cover the knuckles, and which renders a blow struck more powerful.—**knuckle joint,** *n. Mach.* any flexible joint formed by two abutting links.

knur, knurl, nėr, nėrl, *n.* Same as GNARL.

koala, kō•ä′la, *n.* [Native name.] A marsupial animal of Australia, arboreal in habit.

kobold, kō′bold, *n.* [GOBLIN.] A domestic spirit or elf in German mythology; a kind of goblin.

Kodak, kō′dak, *n.* Trade name of a photographic camera.

Kohinoor, kō′i•nör, *n.* [Per. *koh-i-nur,* mountain of light.] The great Indian diamond of the Deccan, owned first by the Mogul kings, and finally, in 1849, the property of the British Crown; anything of supreme excellence.

kohl, kōl, *n.* A black pigment used by Eastern women as a cosmetic.
kohlrabi, kōl•rä'bē, *n.* [G., from *kohl*, kale, and L. *rapa*, a turnip; kale or cabbage turnip.] A variety of cabbage distinguished by a globular swelling immediately above the ground, which is the part used.
koodoo, kö'dö, *n.* See KUDU.
kopeck, kopek, kö'pek, *n.* A small Russian coin, one hundredth part of a ruble, worth about half a cent.
Koran, kō'ran or ko•rän', *n.* See ALKORAN.
kos, kos, *n.* A Jewish measure of capacity equal to about 4 cubic inches.
kosher, kōsh'ėr, *a.* [Heb. *kasher*, right.] Designating food prepared in the way prescribed by Jewish ceremonial rites; right; proper.
kowtow, kou•tou', *n.* [Chinese.] Prostrating one's self and touching the ground with the forehead; showing deference and submissiveness.—*v.i.* To perform the kowtow; to show honor and respect.
kraal, kräl, *n.* [Pg. *curral*, a pen for animals, akin *corral*.] A native village or collection of huts in South Africa; a pen for livestock in Africa.
kraken, krä'ken, *n.* A supposed enormous sea monster, said to have been seen at different times off the coast of Norway.
Kremlin, krem'lin. [Rus. *kreml.*] The citadel of Moscow, including within it the Soviet government.
kreutzer, kreuzer, kroit'sėr, *n.* [G. *kreuzer*, from *kreuz*, a cross, because formerly stamped with a cross.] An old South German copper coin, the sixtieth part of the gulden or florin; an Austrian coin equal to the hundredth part of a florin.
kriegspiel, krēg'spēl, *n.* [G., game of war—*krieg*, war, and *spiel*, game.] A game of German origin, played by means of pieces representing troops on a map exhibiting all the features of a country.
kris, krēs, *n.* A Malay dagger; a creese.
krone, krō'ne, *n.* [Dan., a crown.] A Scandinavian monetary unit.
kruller, krul'ėr, *n.* [O.E. *crult*, curled; D. *krullen*, to curl.] See CRULLER.
krypton, krip'ton, *n.* A rare gaseous element. Symbol, Kr; at. no., 36; at. wt., 83.80.
Kshatriya, kshat'ri•a, *n.* A member of the second or military caste in the social system of the Brahmanical Hindus.
kudos, kū'dos, *n.* [Gr.] Glory; fame; renown.
kudu, kö'dö, *n.* [Native name.] A striped antelope of South Africa, the male having long and twisted horn.
Kufic, *a.* See CUFIC.
kumiss, kö'mis, *n.* [Of Tartar origin.] A liquor made from mare's milk fermented and distilled; fermented milk used by the Tartars.
kümmel, kụm'l or kim'l, *n.* [G. *kümmel*, caraway.] A liqueur, flavored with caraway seeds.
kumquat, kum'kwot, *n.* [Chinese (Cantonese) *kam*, golden, and *kwat*, orange.] A small citrus fruit, used chiefly in preserves.
Kurd, kėrd, *n.* An inhabitant of Kurdistan.—**Kurdish,** kėr'dish, *a.* Of or relating to Kurdistan or the Kurds.
kyanite, kī'an•īt, *n.* [Gr. *kyanos*, blue.] A gem of the garnet family of a blue color, somewhat resembling sapphire.
kymograph, kī'mo•graf, *n.* [Gr. *kyma*, a wave, *graphō*, I write.] An instrument for graphically recording variations in blood pressure.
Kyrie eleison, kir"ē•e' e•lā"i•s'n, *n.* [Gr. *kyrie*, Lord, *eleēson*, have mercy.] A form of invocation in ancient Greek, liturgies and still used in the Roman Catholic service.

L

L, l, el, the twelfth letter and ninth consonant of the English alphabet.
la, lä, *Mus.* the sixth of the seven syllables that represent the seven sounds in the diatonic scale.
laager, lä'gėr, *n.* [D., a camp.] In South Africa, an encampment; a temporary defensive enclosure, formed of wagons.—*v.i.* To encamp; to form a temporary defense by means of wagons.
labarum, lab'a•rum, *n.* [L. *labarum*, *labōrum*, Gr. *labaron*, *labōron*; etym. doubtful.] The standard adopted by Constantine the Great after his conversion to Christianity; a banner bearing the Greek letters X P (that is, *Chr*), conjoined so as to form a monogram of the name of Christ.
labdanum, lab'da•num. See LADANUM.
labefaction, lab•e•fak'shon, *n.* [L. *labefactio*, from *labefacio*—*labo*, to totter, and *facio*, to make.] A weakening; decay; downfall.
label, lā'bl, *n.* [O.Fr. *label*, *lambel*, a rag, a tatter, a shred; of Germanic or Celtic origin.] A slip of paper, parchment, or other material, containing a name, title, address, statement of contents, nature, or the like, affixed to anything; a narrow slip affixed to diplomas, deeds, or writings to hold the appended seal; *arch.* a projecting tablet or molding over doors, windows, etc.—*v.t.*—*labeled*, *labeling*. To affix a label to; to classify and name.—**labeler, labeller,** lā'bl•ėr, *n.* One who labels.
labellum, la•bel'lum, *n.* [L., a little lip, dim. of *labrum*, a lip.] *Bot.* one of the three pieces forming the corolla in orchidaceous plants, usually turned downward.
labial, lā'bi•al, *a.* [From L. *labium*, a lip. LIP.] Pertaining to the lips; uttered by the lips; owing its special character to the lips (a *labial* consonant).—*n.* A vowel or consonant formed chiefly by the lips, as *b*, *m*, *p*, *o*.—**labialize,** lā'bi•al•īz, *v.t.* To give a labial sound or character to; to utter labially.—**labiate,** lā'bi•āt, *a.* [L.L. *labiatus*, from L. *labium*, lip.] *Bot.* applied to an irregular gamopetalous corolla, the limb or expanded portion cleft so as to present an upper and lower lip.—**labiodental,** lā'bi•o•den•tal, *a.* and *n.* [L. *labium*, a lip, and *dens*, a tooth.] Formed or pronounced by the cooperation of the lips and teeth; a sound thus formed (*f* and *v*).—**labium,** lā'bi•um, *n.* [L.] One of the lip-like folds of the vulva, *Labia majora*, the two outer folds, and *Labia minora*, the two inner folds; the lower lip of insects.
labor, labour, lā'bėr, *n.* [O.Fr. *labour*, Fr. *labeur*, L. *labor*, *laboris*, labor.] Exertion, physical or mental, or both, undergone in the performance of some task or work; particularly, the exertion of the body in occupations by which subsistence is obtained; the performance of work; toil; work done or to be done; laborers or producers in the aggregate (the claims or rights of *labor*); travail; the pangs and efforts of childbirth.—*v.i.* To engage in labor; to work; to toil; to exert the body or mind, or both, in the prosecution of any design; to proceed or act with difficulty; to be burdened; to suffer (to *labor* under a disease); *naut.* to pitch and roll heavily, as a ship in a turbulent sea.—*v.t.* To till; to cultivate; to prosecute with effort.—*Labor Day*, in the U.S., the first Monday in September, observed as a legal holiday in honor of the working classes.—*Labor Party*, a party claiming to represent the interests of the working classes. *Labor union*, a trade union; an organization of wage earners designed to advance the economic interests and general working conditions of its members.—**labored,** lā'bėrd, *p.* and *a.* Produced with labor; bearing the marks of constraint and effort; opposed to *easy* or *natural* (a *labored* speech).—**laborer,** lā'bėr•ėr, *n.* One who labors; a man who does work that requires little skill or special training, as distinguished from an artisan.—**laborsaving,** *a.* Saving labor; adapted to supersede or diminish the labor of men.—**laborious,** la•bō'ri•us, *a.* [L. *laboriosus*.] Requiring labor; toilsome; not easy; diligent in work or service; industrious; assiduous.—**laboriously,** la•bō'ri•us•li, *adv.* In a laborious manner.—**laboriousness,** la•bō'ri•us•nes, *n.*
laboratory, lab'o•ra•to•ri, *n.* [L.L. *laboratorium*, from L. *labor*, labor. LABOR.] A building or room designed for investigation and experiment in chemistry, physics, or other subject; a chemist's workroom; the shop of a druggist.
laborite, lā'bėr•īte, *n.* One who upholds the theories and practices of labor organizations.
labradorite, lab'ra•dor•īt, *n.* A mineral, a kind of feldspar, found on the coast of Labrador, distinguished by its splendent changeability of color; called also *Labrador feldspar*.
labret, lab'ret, *n.* [L. *labrum*, lip.] A lip ornament worn by certain

savage peoples, consisting of a piece of bone, wood, or the like, inserted in an artificial opening.

labrum, lā′brum, *n.* [L.] An upper or outer lip, LABIUM.—**labrose,** lā′-brōs, *a.* Having thick lips.

laburnum, la•bėr′num, *n.* [L.] A leguminose tree, well known for the beauty of its pendulous racemes of yellow pea-shaped flowers, and having wood which is much valued for turnery work.

labyrinth, lab′i•rinth, *n.* [L. *labyrinthus*; Gr. *labyrinthos.*] A structure having numerous intricate winding passages; a place full of inextricable windings; an ornamental maze or wilderness in gardens; an intricate arrangement of bands or lines used for ornamentation; any intricate matter or business; *anat.* that part of the internal ear which lies behind the tympanum; *metal.* a series of troughs attached to a stamping mill, through which a current of water passes so as to carry off and deposit in certain places the ground ore.—**labyrinthian,** lab•i•rinth′i•an, *a.* Labyrinthine.—Also **labyrinthic,** lab•i•rinth′ik, **labyrinthical,** lab•i•rinth′i•kal.—**labyrinthine,** lab•i•rinth′in, *a.* Pertaining to or like a labyrinth; full of windings; intricate; mazy.

lac, lak, *n.* [Per. *lak*, Skr. *lâkshâ*, and *râkshâ*, the lac insect, from *ranj*, to dye; hence *lacquer*, *lake* (color).] A resinous substance produced mainly upon the banyan tree, by the puncture of a small insect, and used in preparing lacquers, varnishes, etc.—*Stick lac* is the substance in its natural state, incrusting small twigs; when broken off and washed with water it is called *seed lac*; when melted and reduced to a thin crust it is called *shell-lac, shellac.*—*Lac dye* and *lac lake*, scarlet coloring matters obtained from stick lac.

lac, lakh, lak, *n.* [Hind. *lakh*, Skr. *laksha.*] In the East Indies a word used to denote 100,000.

LACE. See LIQUID.

lace, lās, *n.* [O.Fr. *las*, from L. *laqueus*, a noose, a snare; akin *lasso*, *latchet.*] A string or cord used for fastening boots or some other part of the dress, or plaited and otherwise ornamented and used for decoration; a delicate kind of network, used for the ornamenting of female dresses, etc.—*v.t.*—*laced, lacing.* To fasten with a lace or string through eyelet holes; to adorn with lace, or as with a lace; to strengthen *beer, tea,* with some alcoholic flavoring.—*v.i.* To be fastened or tied by a lace; to have a lace.—**lacing,** lās′ing, *n.* The act of fastening with a lace; a cord used in drawing tight or fastening.

lacerate, las′ėr•āt, *v.t.*—*lacerated, lacerating.* [L. *lacero, laceratum*, to tear, from *lacer*, mangled, torn.] To tear; to rend; to make a ragged wound or gash in by violence or tearing; *fig.* to torture; to harrow.—**lacerate, lacerated,** las′ėr•āt, las′-ėr•ā•ted, *p.* and *a.* Rent; torn; *bot.* having the appearance of being torn.—**laceration** las•ėr•ā′shon, *n.* The act of lacerating; the breach made by rending.

lacertian, lacertilian, la•sėr′shi•an, las•ėr•til′i•an, *a.* [L. *lacerta*, a lizard.] Belonging to the family of lizards.

laches, lach′es or lash′ez, *n.* [Norm. Fr. *lachesse*, remissness, lit. looseness, from O.Fr. *lasche*, from L. *laxus*, lax, slow.] *Law*, neglect; negligence; remissness; inexcusable delay.

lachrymal, lak′ri•mal, *a.* [L. *lachryma, lacryma, lacrima*, a tear; cog. with Gr. *dakry*, a tear, and E. *tear.*] Pertaining to tears; generating or secreting tears (the *lachrymal* gland); conveying tears (*lachrymal* canal).—**lachrymatory,** lak′ri•ma•to•ri, *n.* A vessel found in sepulchres of the ancients, in which it has been supposed the tears of a deceased person's friends were collected and preserved with the ashes and urn. Also called *Lachrymal.*—**lachrymose,** lak′ri•mōs, *a.* Generating or shedding tears; appearing as if shedding or given to shed tears; tears; tearful.—**lachrymosely,** lak′ri•mōs•li, *adv.* In a lachrymose manner.

lacing. See LACE.

laciniate, laciniated, la•sin′i•āt, la•sin′i•ā•ted, *a.* [L. *lacinia*, a lappet, fringe, or border.] Adorned with fringes; *bot.* jagged; applied to leaves or petals which are divided by deep tapering incisions.

lack, lak, *v.t.* [Same as D. *laken*, to blame, O.D. *laecken*, to fail, to decrease; Dan. *lak*, fault, want; Icel. *lakr*, defective; perhaps connected with *leak.*] To be destitute of; not to have or possess; to want; to need; to require.—*v.i.* To be in want; to be wanting.—*n.* Want; destitution; need; failure.—**lack-luster,** *a.* Wanting luster or brightness.

lackaday, lak•a•dā′, [Contr. for *alack, the-day.*] Exclamation of sorrow or regret; alas!—alas! the day.—**lackadaisical,** lak•a•dā′zi•kal, *a.* Affectedly pensive; listless; maudlinly sentimental.

lackey, lak′i, *n.* [Fr. *laquais*, from Sp. and Pg. *lacayo, alacay*, possibly from Ar. *lakiyy*, attached to some one.] An attending male servant; a footboy or footman; any servile follower.—*v.t.* To wait on as a lackey; to attend servilely.—*v.i.* To act as a lackey; to pay servile attendance on some person.

laconic, la•kon′ik, *a.* [Fr. *laconique*, L. *laconicus*, from *Lacones*, the Spartans.] Short; brief; pithy; sententious; expressing much in few words, after the manner of the Spartans, who were Laconians.—**laconically,** la•kon′i•kal•li, *adv.* In a laconic manner; concisely; in few words.—**laconism,** lak′on•izm, *n.* [L. *laconismus.*] A concise style; a brief sententious phrase or expression.

lacquer, lak′ėr, *n.* [Pg. *lacre*, from *laca*, lac. LAC.] A solution of shell-lac (sometimes sandarach, mastic, etc.) in alcohol; sap of the Japanese or Chinese sumac or any of the synthetic varnishes used to give a highly lustrous coating to wood or metals; an item coated with lacquer.—*v.t.* To varnish with lacquer.

lacrosse, la•kros′, *n.* [Fr.] A game which originated with the North American Indians, played with two opposing teams of twelve men each, the object of the game being to score by throwing a hard-rubber ball about the size of a baseball into the opponents' goal with a crosse or lacrosse stick.

lactarene, lactarine, lak′ta•rēn, lak′-ta•rin, *n.* [L. *lac, lactis*, milk; cog. with Gr. *gala, galaktos*, Ir. *laith*, milk.] A preparation of the casein of milk, extensively used by calico printers.—**lactary,** lak′ta•ri, *a.* [L. *lacterius*, milky.] Milky; full of white juice like milk.—**lactate,** lak′tāt, *n.* *Chem.* a salt or ester of lactic acid.—*v.i.* To produce milk.—**lactation,** lak•tā′shon, *n.* The function of secreting and excreting milk.—**lactase,** lak′tās, *n.* An enzyme capable of reducing lactose to dextrose and galactose.—**lacteal,** lak′ti•al, *a.* Pertaining to or resembling milk; milky; conveying chyle.—*n.* *Anat.* one of numerous minute tubes which absorb or take up the chyle or milk-like fluid from the alimentary canal and convey it to the thoracic duct.—**lacteous,** lak′ti•us, *a.* [L. *lacteus.*] Milky; lacteal.—**lactescence,** lak•tes′ens, *n.* The state of being lactescent; milkiness or milky color; the milky liquor which flows from a plant when wounded.—**lactescent,** lak•tes′ent, *a.* [L. *lactescens*, ppr. of *lactesco*, to become milky.] Becoming milky; having a milky appearance or consistence.—**lactic,** lak′tik, *a.* [Fr. *lactique.*] Pertaining to milk or produced from sour milk or whey *(lactic acid)*.—*Lactic acid*, a sirupy acid, $CH_3CH(OH)CO_2H$.—**lactiferous,** lak•tif′ėr•us, *a.* Producing or conveying milk or milky juice.—**lactose,** lak′tōs, *n.* Sugar of milk, a crystalline deposit, $C_{12}H_{22}O_{11}$, left after milk has been evaporated.

lacuna, la•kū′na, *n.* pl. **lacunae,** la•kū′nē. [L., a hollow.] A pit or depression on a surface; a small blank space; a gap; a hiatus; one of the spaces left among the tissues of the lower animals, serving in place of vessels for the circulation of the fluids.—**lacunal,** la•cū′nal, *a.* Pertaining to or having lacunae.—**lacunar,** la•kū′nėr, *n.* pl. **lacunars, lacunaria,** la•kū′nėrz, lak•u•nâ′ri•a. [L.] *Arch.* one of the sunk compartments or panels in ceilings, etc.—**lacunose,** la•kū′nōs, *a.* [L. *lacunosus.*] Having lacunae; furrowed or pitted.

lacustrine, lacustral, la•kus′trin, la•kus′tral, *a.* [From L. *lacus*, a lake.] Pertaining to a lake.—*Lacustrine* or *lake dwellings*, the name given to ancient habitations built on small islands in lakes, or on platforms supported by piles near the shores of lakes.

lad, lad, *n.* [Of doubtful origin; comp. W. *llawd*, Ir. *lath*, a lad, a youth; *lass* is the feminine corresponding.] A young man or boy; a stripling; a familiar term applied to grown men; fellow; comrade.

ladanum, lad′a•num, *n.* [Gr. *ladanon*, from Per. *lâdan*, the shrub.] The resinous juice which exudes from several species of cistus growing in Spain and Portugal, Crete, Syria, etc., formerly used in plasters, etc.

ladder, lad′ėr, *n.* [A.Sax. *hlaedder*= O.Fris. *hladder*, D. *ladder*, O.H.G. *hleitra, hleitara*, Mod.G. *leiter*, a ladder; cog. L. *clathri*, a trellis or grate.] An article of wood, metal, or rope, consisting of two long sidepieces connected by crosspieces at suitable distances, forming steps by which persons may ascend a building etc.; *fig.* a means of rising to eminence.

lade, lād, *v.t.*—pret. *laded*, pp. *laded laden* (the former always in second sense), ppr. *lading*. [A.Sax. *hladan*, to load, to lade water; O.Sax. and O.H.G. *hladan*, Icel. *hlatha*, Goth. *hlathan*, D. *laden*, G. (*be*)*laden*, to load. *Load* is almost the same word, and *ladle* is a derivative.] To load; to put a load or cargo on or in; to lift or throw in or out (a fluid) with some utensil; to lave.—**laden,** lā′dn, *p.* and *a.* [Pp. of *lade* in first sense.] Loaded; charged with a burden or freight; *fig.* oppressed; burdened.—**lading,** lā′ding, *n.* That which constitutes a load or cargo; freight; burden.—*Bill of lading*. See BILL.

ladle, lā′dl, *n.* [A.Sax. *hlaedel*, from *hladan*, to draw water. LADE, *v.*] A sort of dish with a long handle, used for lifting or serving out liquids from a vessel; the receptacle of a mill wheel which receives the water that moves it; *founding*, an iron vessel in which liquid metal is carried from the furnace to the mold.—*v.t.*—*ladled, ladling*. To lift or deal out with a ladle; to lade.

lady, lā′di, *n.* [A.Sax. *hlaefdige, hlaefdie*, lit. bread kneader, from *hlâf*, bread, loaf, and *-dige*, kneader. LORD.] A woman of rank or distinction; correlative to *lord*; in the British Empire, the proper title of any woman whose husband is above the rank of a baronet or knight, or who is the daughter of a nobleman not lower than an earl, though often the wife of a baronet or a knight is called by this title; a term applied by courtesy to any woman; one of the fair sex; specifically, a woman of good breeding, education, and refinement of mind: the correlative to *gentleman*; the wife of a gentleman or man in good position; the mistress or possessor of an estate; an apparatus in the stomach of a lobster for grinding its food.—*Our Lady*, the Virgin Mary.—**ladies' man, lady's man,** *n.* One who much affects the society of ladies; a beau.—**ladybird, ladybug, ladybeetle,** *n.* A small beetle, the larva of which feeds on aphids or plant lice.—**Lady chapel,** *n.* A chapel dedicated to the Virgin Mary, frequently attached to large churches.—**Lady Day,** *n.* The day of the annunciation of the Virgin Mary, March 25.—**ladyfinger,** *n.* A kind of finger-shaped spongecake.—**lady-killer,** *n.* A man whose fascinations are irresistible among the ladies; a general lover.—**lady-killing,** *n.* Act or practice of a lady-killer; gallantry.—**ladylike,** lā′di•līk, *a.* Like a lady in any respect.—**ladylove,** *n.* A female sweetheart; a lady who is loved.—**ladyship,** lā′di•ship, *n.* The condition or rank of a lady; employed as a title (with *her, your*, etc.)—**lady's maid,** *n.* A female attendant upon a lady.—**lady's-slipper,** *n.* An orchid having flowers resembling a slipper; in the U. S., the garden balsam.

lag, lag, *a.* [Of Celtic origin; W. *llag*, weak; akin L. *laxus*, loose; lax, *languidus*, languid.] Coming after or behind (*lag* end of my life).—*n.* The quantity of retardation of some movement (the *lag* of the valve of a steam engine, the *lag* of the tide); a comparative retardation of movement or progress (a cultural *lag*).—*v.i.*—*lagged, lagging*. To walk or move slowly; to loiter; to stay behind.—**laggard,** lag′ėrd, *a.* [*Lag.* and suffix *-ard*.] Slow; sluggish; backward.—*n.* One who lags; a loiterer; a lazy, slack fellow.—**lagger,** lag′ėr, *n.* One who lags or loiters.—**laggingly,** lag′ing•li, *adv.* Loiteringly.

lagan, lag′an, *n.* Same as *Ligan*.

lager beer, lä′gėr bēr, *n.* [G. *lagerbier*—*lager*, a storehouse, and *bier*, beer.] A beer, so called from its being stored for some months before use.

lagniappe, lagnappe, lan•yap′, *n.* [Creole, *la*, the, Sp. *ñapa, llapa*, lagniappe.] A small present given by a storekeeper to a customer.

lagoon, lagune, la•gön′, la•gūn′, *n.* [It. and Sp. *laguna*, from L. *lacuna*, from *lacus*, a lake. LAKE.] A shallow lake or sheet of water connected with the sea or a river.

laic, laical, lā′ik, lā′i•kal, *a.* [L. *laicus*, from Gr. *laikos*, from *laos*, people. LAY, *a.*] Belonging to the laity or people, in distinction from the clergy.—*n.* A layman.—**laically,** lā′i•kal•li, *adv.* In a laic manner.

laid, lād, pret. & pp. of *lay*; so written for *Layed*.—*Laid paper*, writing paper with a slightly ribbed surface, called *cream-laid, blue-laid*, etc., according to color.

lain, lān, pp. of *lie*.

lair, lâr, *n.* [A.Sax. *leger*, a bed, a couch, a grave, from the root of *lay, lie*=D. *leger*, G. *lager*. LAY.] A place to lie or rest; especially the resting place of a wild beast, etc.; in Scotland, a portion of a burying-ground sufficient for one grave.

laird, lârd, *n.* [A form of *lord*.] In Scotland, a land owner or house proprietor.

laissez-faire, laisser-faire, les′ā•fâr″, *n.* [Fr. *laisser*, leave, let, *faire*, to do.] A letting alone; non-interference; a term especially used in regard to the interference of a government with social, commercial or other matters.

laity. See LAY, *a.*

lake, lāk, *n.* [Fr. *lac*, from L. *lacus*, lake; cog. *loch*.] A sheet or body of water wholly surrounded by land, and having no direct communication with the sea, or having so only by means of rivers.—**lake dwelling,** *n.* See LACUSTRINE.—**laky,** lā′ki, *a.* Pertaining to a lake or lakes.

lake, lāk, *n.* [Fr. *laque*. LAC.] A pigment consisting of an earthy substance impregnated with red coloring matter of certain animal and vegetable substances, there being thus cochineal and lac lakes, madder lake, etc.

lallation, lal•lā′shon, *n.* [Fr. *lallation*, from the letter *l*.] The imperfect pronunciation of the letter *r*, which is made to sound like *l*.

lama, lä′mä, *n.* [Tibetan.] A priest or ecclesiastic belonging to that variety of Buddhism which is known as Lamaism, and prevails in Tibet and Mongolia.—**Lamaism,** lä′mä•izm, *n.* A variety of Buddhism chiefly prevailing in Tibet and Mongolia.—**Lamaist,** lä′mä•ist, *n.* One belonging to the religion of Lamaism.—**Lamaistic,** lä•mä•is′tik, *a.* Pertaining to lamaism.—**lamasery,** lä′mä•sėr•i, *n.* A monastery of lamas.

Lamarckian, la•mark′i•an, *a.* [*Lamark*, French zoologist.] The theory of organic evolution by inherited modifications of the individual through habit or other causes.

lamb, lam, *n.* [A.Sax., O.Sax., Goth., Icel., and O.H.G. *lamb*; D. and Dan. *lam*, G. *lamm*, lamb.] The young of sheep; a person as gentle or innocent as a lamb.—*The Lamb, The Lamb of God*, the Saviour Jesus Christ.—*v.i.* To bring forth a lamb or lambs.—**lambkin,** lam′kin, *n.* A small lamb; one fondly cherished.—**lamblike,** lam′līk, *a.*—**lambskin,** lam′skin, *n.* The skin of a lamb dressed with the fleece on, or made into leather.

lambda, lam′dä, *n.* [Gr.] The eleventh letter of the Greek alphabet, corresponding to the English letter *L, l*.

lambdoidal, lam′doi•dal, *a.* [Gr. *lambdoeidēs*—*lambda* (Λ), and *eidos*, resemblance.] In the form of the Greek letter lambda (Λ).

lambent, lam′bent, *a.* [L. *lambens, lambentis*, ppr. of *lambo*, to lick, a nasalized form akin to *lap*.] Licking; playing about; touching lightly; gliding over (a *lambent* flame); gleaming; twinkling; flickering.

lame, lām, *a.* [A.Sax. *lama*=D. Dan. and Sw. *lam*, G. *lahm*, lame; Icel. *lama*, a lame person; akin prov. E. *lam*, to beat.] Crippled or disabled in one or more of the limbs; crippled; disabled (a *lame* arm); imperfect, defective, not sound or unassailable (a *lame* excuse).—*v.t.*—*lamed, laming*. To make lame; to cripple or disable; to render imperfect.—**lame duck,** *n.* A slang term for a defaulter on the stock exchange; a Congressman not reelected and serving the last session of his term.—**lamely,** lām′li, *adv.* In a lame or imperfect manner.—**lameness,** lām′nes, *n.* The condition of being lame, crippled or disabled.

lamella, la•mel′la, *n.* pl. **lamellae,** la•mel′lē. [Dim. of *lamina.*] A thin plate or scale; one of an aggregate of thin plates; one of the thin plates which compose the gills of certain mollusks; one of the gills forming the hymenium of an agaric.—**lamellar,** la•mel′lėr, *a.* Composed of thin plates or lamellae; disposed in thin plates or scales.—**lamellate, lamellated,** lam′el•lāt, lam′el•lā•ted, *a.* Formed in thin plates or lamellae, or covered with them; furnished with lamellae.—**lamellibranchiate,** la•mel′li•brang″ki•āt, *a.* [L. *lamella,* a thin plate, and *branchiae,* gills.] Having lamellar gills, especially having lamellar gills and bivalve shells as the mollusks of the class or order (Lamellibranchiata) of which mussels, cockles, and oysters are familiar examples. Also used as a noun.—**lamellicorn,** la•mel′li•korn, *a.* [L. *lamella,* a plate, and *cornu,* a horn.] Having lamellar antennae; having antennae the three last joints of which are plate-like and disposed somewhat like the teeth of a comb: said of beetles, such as the cockchafers, etc. Used also as *n.*—**lamellirostral,** la•mel′li•ros″tral, *a.* [L. *rostrum,* a beak.] Having a beak furnished along its margins with numerous lamellae or dental plates as the ducks, geese, swans, etc.—**lamellose,** la•mel′lōs, *a.* Covered with or in the form of lamellae.

lament, la•ment′, *v.i.* [L. *lamentor,* to wail, from *lamentum,* a wail; same root as *latrare,* to bark, an onomatopoetic word.] To mourn; to weep or wail; to express sorrow; to regret deeply; to grieve.—*v.t.* To bewail; to mourn for; to bemoan; to deplore. —*n.* Lamentation; an elegy or mournful ballad or air.—**lamentable,** lam′en•ta•bl, *a.* [L. *lamentabilis.*] To be lamented; exciting or calling for sorrow; grievous; mournful; miserable; pitiful; wretched.—**lamentably,** lam′en•ta•bli, *adv.* In a lamentable manner.—**lamentation,** lam•en•tā′shon, *n.* [L. *lamentatio.*] The act of lamenting; a wailing; expression of sorrow; cries or words expressive of grief; [*cap.*] *pl.* a book of Scripture containing the Lamentations of Jeremiah.

lamia, lā′mi•a, *n.* [Gr.] *Greek myth.* A female monster sucking the blood of infants.

lamina, lam′i•na, *n.* pl. **laminae,** lam′i•nē. [L., a thin plate or lamina.] A thin plate or scale; a layer or coat lying over another: applied to the plates of minerals, bones, etc.; *bot.* the upper broad part of the petal in a polypetalous corolla; the blade of a leaf.—**laminable,** lam′i•na•bl, *a.* Capable of being formed into thin plates.—**laminar,** lam′i•nėr, *a.* Formed of laminae or plates; consisting of thin plates or layers.—**laminate,** lam′i•nāt, *a.*—**laminate,** lam′i•nāt, *v.i.*—*laminated, laminating.* To separate or split up into thin plates or layers.—*v.t.* To divide in thin sheets; to form into thin layers by beating or rolling; to compress layers of material into a hard, durable substance by means of heat and chemicals; to overlay with laminae. —**lamination,** lam•i•nā′shon, *n.*

Lammas, lam′as, *n.* [A.Sax. *hláf-mæsse,* that is *loaf mass,* bread feast, so called because on this day offerings were formerly made of the first fruits of harvest.] The first day of August.—**Lammastide,** *n.* The time of Lammas.

lammergeier, laemmergeyer, lam′-mėr•gī•ėr, lem′mėr•gī•ėr, *n.* [G. *lämmergeier*—*lämmer,* pl. of *lamm,* a lamb, and *geier,* a vulture.] The bearded vulture, the largest European bird of prey, inhabiting the Alps, as well as Asia and Africa.

lamp, lamp, *n.* [Fr. *lampe,* L. and Gr. *lampas,* from Gr. *lampō,* to shine; akin *lantern.*] A vessel for containing oil or other liquid inflammable substance, to be burned by means of a wick; any contrivance adapted to contain an artificial light; something metaphorically communicating light.—**lampblack,** lamp′-blak, *n.* A fine soot formed by the condensation of the smoke of burning oil, pitch, or resinous substances, used as a pigment.—**lamplighter,** *n.* A man employed to light street or other public lamps.

lampas, lam′pas, *n.* [Fr. *lampas.*] A swelling in the roof of a horse's mouth immediately behind the foreteeth.

lampoon, lam•pön′, *n.* [Fr. *lampon,* a drinking or scurrilous song, from *lamper,* to drink, to guzzle; akin *lap,* to lick.] A personal satire in writing; a satiric or abusive attack in prose or verse.—*v.t.* To write a lampoon against; to assail in a lampoon.—**lampooner,** lam•pön′ėr, *n.* The writer of a lampoon.—**lampoonry,** lam•pön′ri, *n.* The act of lampooning; the matter in a lampoon.

lamprey, lam′pri, *n.* [Fr. *lamproie,* It. *lampreda,* from L.L. *lampetra*—L. *lambo,* to lick, and *petra,* a stone, from their habit of attaching themselves to stones by their mouths.] The name of several marsipobranchiate, eel-like, scaleless fishes, with suctorial mouths, inhabiting both fresh and salt water.

lanate, lā′nāt, *a.* [L. *lanatus.*] Woolly; covered with a growth or substance resembling wool.

lance, lans, *n.* [Fr. *lance,* from L. *lancea,* a lance.] An offensive weapon consisting of a long wooden shaft with a sharp-pointed head of steel or other metal, used in war by both ancient and modern nations; a spear.—*v.t.*—*lanced, lancing.* To pierce with a lance or other pointed instrument; to open with a lancet or other sharp instrument.—**lance corporal,** *n.* A private soldier performing the duties of a corporal with a temporary rank as such.—**lancelet,** lans′let, *n.* A small wormlike transparent fish of very anomalous structure.—**lanceolate,** lan′-sē•o•lāt, *a.* [L. *lanceola,* dim. of *lancea,* a lance.] Shaped like a lance head.—**lancer,** lan′sėr, *n.* One who lances; one who carries a lance; a cavalry soldier armed with a lance.—**lancet,** lan′set, *n.* [Fr. *lancette,* dim. of *lance.*] A small surgical instrument, sharp-pointed and generally two-edged, used in opening veins, tumors, abscesses, etc.—**lancet window,** *n.* A high and narrow window pointed like a lancet.—**lancet arch,** *n.* An arch whose head is shaped like the point of a lancet: generally used in lancet windows.—**lancewood,** *n.* [So named from its being suitable for making the shafts of lances.] The wood of several trees of the custard-apple family, natives of Guiana and the West Indies, which possesses great toughness and elasticity, and is much used for rods, etc.

lancinate, lan′si•nāt, *v.t.* [L. *lancino, lancinatum;* akin to *lance, lacerate.*] To tear; to lacerate.—**lancinating,** lan′si•nā•ting, *a.* Piercing: applied to a sudden sharp shooting pain, as in cancer.—**lancination,** lan•si•nā′-shon, *n.* A sudden, sharp, shooting pain; laceration; wounding.

land, land, *n.* [A.Sax. D. Dan. Icel. Sw. Goth. and G. *land;* connections very doubtful.] The solid or fixed part of the surface of the globe, in distinction from the sea or other waters, which constitute the fluid or movable part; a definite portion of the solid surface of the globe as set apart or belonging to an individual or a people, as a country, estate, or farm (to travel in all *lands,* his *land* adjoins mine); the people of a country or region; ground or soil (good *land,* poor *land*); in Scotland, a building including houses occupied by different families.—*To make the land,* or *to make land* (*naut.*), to discover land from the sea as the ship approaches it.—*v.t.* To set on shore; to disembark; to bring to or put in a certain place or condition; to catch, as a fish.—*v.i.* To bring an aircraft to rest on the ground or on water; to go on shore from a ship or boat; to disembark; to arrive; to reach.—**landed,** lan′ded, *a.* Having an estate in land; consisting in real estate or land (*landed* property).—**landfall,** land′fa̤l, *n.* The first land discovered after a voyage; a landslide.—**landgrant school,** in the U. S., a college or university which received federal aid by the Morrill Act of 1862 for teaching vocational subjects, as agriculture, etc.— **landholder,** *n.* A holder, owner, or proprietor of land.—**landing,** land′-ing, *n.* The level part of anything, especially on a staircase, used for resting; the act of going or setting on land; a place where persons land or where goods are set on shore; the act of alighting, as an aircraft on a field.—*Landing gear,* the understructure of an aircraft, consisting of wheels, or of floats, and their supporting frame.—*Landing net,* a small bag-shaped net used to take the fish from the water after being hooked.—*Landing stage,* a stage or platform, frequently so constructed as to rise and fall with the tide, for the convenience of landing or shipping passengers and goods.—**landlady** land′-lā′di, *n.* A woman who has tenants under her; the mistress of an inn or of a lodginghouse; correlative to *landlord.*—**landless,** land′les, *a.* Destitute of land; having no property in land. —**landlocked,** land′lokt, *pp.* Enclosed or encompassed by land.—**landloper,** land′lō•pėr (Scottish land *louper*), *n.* [*Land,* and *loper,* as in *interloper.*] A vagabond or vagrant; one who has no settled habitation.—**landlord,** land′lord, *n.* The owner of land or of houses who has tenants under him; the master of an inn, tavern, lodginghouse; a host.—**landlubber,** land′lub•ėr, *n.* A contemptuous term among seamen for a landsman.—**landmark,** land′märk, *n.* A mark to designate the boundary of land; any mark or fixed object by which the limits of a portion of territory may be known and preserved; any prominent and distinguishing feature of a locality; some elevated object on land that serves as a guide to seamen; what marks a stage in any course of development; any striking historical event to which others may be referred.—**land measure,** *n.* The system of quantities used in computing the area of pieces of land.—**land office,** *n.* A government office in which the sales of public lands are recorded.—**land-office business,** a rushing, profitable business (*colloq.*).—**land-owner,** *n.* A proprietor of land.—**land-poor,** *a.* Financially embarrassed by having too much money invested in land, or by too much expense for upkeep of land.—**landscape,** land′skāp, *n.* [D. *landschap,* Dan. *landskab,* equivalent to *land-shape.*] A picture representing a tract of country with the various objects it contains; such pictures in general, or the painting of such pictures; a natural scene that might form the subject of such a picture.—**landslide,** land′slīd, *n.* The slipping or sliding down of a considerable portion of land or earth from a higher to a lower level; the earth which so slides or slips.—**landsman,** landz′man, *n.* One who lives on the land: opposed to *seaman.* —**Landsturm,** länt′sturm, *n.* [G., lit. land-storm.] A former local militia of Germany, called in case of actual invasion.—**landward,** land′-wėrd, *adv.* Toward the land.—*a.* Lying toward the land, or toward the interior, or away from the seacoast; situated in or forming part of the country, as opposed to the town; rural.—**Landwehr,** länt′vâr, *n.* [G.—*land,* country, and *wehr,* defense (E. *ware, beware*).] Formerly that portion of the military forces of some European nations who in time of peace followed their occupations, excepting when called out to complete compulsory training.

landau, lan•da′, *n.* [From *Landau,* a town in Germany, where first made.] A kind of carriage with an openable top; an automobile of similar design.

landgrave, land′grāv, *n.* [G. *landgraf,* D. *landgraaf—land,* land, and *graf, graaf,* an earl or count.] In Germany, originally, the title of district or provincial governors; later, the title of three princes of the empire, whose territories were called landgravates. —**landgravate,** land′gra•vāt, *n.* The territory or office of a landgrave.—**landgravine,** land′gra•vēn, *n.* The wife of a landgrave.

lane, lān, *n.* [A.Sax. *lane,* a lane; D. *laan,* alley; Fris. *lona, lana,* a lane.] A narrow way or passage, as between hedges or buildings; a narrow street; an alley; a narrow pass; one division of a road used for a single line of traffic; prescribed routes for shipping or air traffic so as to avoid collisions.

langrage, langrel, lang′grij, lang′-grel, *n.* Old bolts, nails, and pieces of iron bound together and fired from a ship's guns.

langsyne, lang•sīn′, *n.* [Sc. *lang,* long, and *syne,* since.] The time long ago. (*Scotch.*)

language, lang′gwij, *n.* [Fr. *langage,* from *langue,* L. *lingua,* the tongue; which is cog. with E. *tongue* (*l* corresponding to *t,* as in L. *lacrima,* E. *tear*).] Human speech; the expression of thoughts by words or articulate sounds; the aggregate of the words employed by any community for intercommunication; the speech peculiar to a nation; words appropriate to or especially employed in any branch of knowledge (the *language* of chemistry); general style or manner of expression; the expression of thought in any way articulate or inarticulate (the *language* of the eyes, of flowers, etc.).

languid, lang′gwid, *a.* [L. *languidus,* from *langueo,* to droop or flag. LANGUISH.] Flagging; drooping; weak; heavy; dull; indisposed to exertion; slow; tardy; without animation.—**languidly,** lang′gwid•li, *adv.* In a languid manner.—**languidness,** lang′gwid•nes, *n.* The state or quality of being languid.

languish, lang′gwish, *v.i.* [Fr. *languir,* ppr. *languissant,* from L. *langueo,* to languish; akin to *lax, lag, slack.*] To lose strength or animation; to be or become dull, feeble, or spiritless; to pine; to be or to grow heavy; to droop; to wither; to fade; to be no longer active and vigorous.—*n.* Act of pining; also, a soft and tender look or appearance.—**languisher,** lang′gwish•ėr, *n.* One who languishes.—**languishing,** lang′gwish•ing, *p.* and *a.* Losing strength; becoming feeble; pining; having a soft and tender expression (a *languishing* eye).—**languishingly,** lang′-gwish•ing•li, *adv.* In a languishing manner. —**languishment,** lang′-gwish•ment, *n.* The state of languishing or pining; softness of look or mien.—**languor,** lang′gwėr, *n.* [L. *languor.*] The state of body induced by exhaustion of strength; feebleness; faintness; lassitude of body; dullness of intellect; listlessness; an agreeable listless or dreamy state.—**languorous,** lang′gwėr•us, *a.* Characterized by languor.

laniard, lan′yerd, *n.* See LANYARD.

laniary, lan′i•e•ri, *n.* [L. *laniarius,* pertaining to a butcher, from *lanius,* a butcher.] Shambles‡; a place of slaughter‡; one of the canine teeth of the carnivorous animals.—*a.* Used for lacerating or tearing flesh (*laniary* teeth).

lank, langk, *a.* [A.Sax. *hlanc;* connections doubtful.] Loose or lax and easily yielding to pressure‡; languid or drooping‡; not distended; not plump; of a thin or slender habit of body.—**lankly,** langk′li, *adv.* In a lank manner; loosely; laxly.—**lankness,** langk′nes, *n.* The state or quality of being lank.—**lanky,** lang′-ki, *a.* Lank.

lanner, lan′ėr, *n.* [Fr. *lanier,* L. *laniarius, lanius,* a butcher.] A species of hawk, especially the female of the species, found in the south and east of Europe.—**lanneret,** lan′ėr•et, *n.* The male of the lanner.

lanolin, lan′o•lin, *n.* [L. *lana,* wool, *oleum,* oil.] An oily or greasy substance obtained from unwashed wool, used as a basis of many ointments, lotions, etc.

lansquenet, lans′ke•net, *n.* [Originally a foot soldier, from G. *landsknecht,* a foot soldier—*land,* country, *knecht,* a servant, a *knight.*] An old game at cards.

lantern, lan′tėrn, *n.* [Fr. *lanterne,* L. *lanterna,* from Gr. *lamptēr,* a light, a beacon, from *lampō,* to shine, whence also *lamp.*] A case enclosing a light and protecting it from wind and rain, sometimes portable and sometimes fixed; *arch.* an erection on the top of a dome, the roof of an apartment, etc., to give light, for ventilation, or for ornament; a tower which has the whole or a considerable portion of the interior open to view; a light open erection on the top of a tower; the upper part of a lighthouse where the light is shown.—*Chinese lantern.* See CHINESE.—*Dark lantern,* one with a single opening, which may be closed so as to conceal the light.—*Magic lantern.* See MAGIC. —**lantern fly,** *n.* A hemipterous insect of South America which emits a strong light in the dark.—**lantern-jawed,** *n.* Having lantern-jaws; having a long thin visage. (*Colloq.*)

lanthanum, lan′tha•num, *n.* [Gr. *lanthanō,* I lie hid, because its existence long remained unknown.] A metallic element of the rare-earth series, allied to aluminum. Symbol, La; at. no., 57; at. wt., 138.91.

lanthorn, lan′tėrn, *n.* An old and erroneous spelling of *Lantern,* due to the fact that lanterns used to have *horn* sides.

lanuginous, lanuginose, la•nū′ji•-nus, la•nū′ji•nōs, *a.* [L. *lanuginosus,* from *lanugo,* down, from *lana,* wool.] Downy; covered with down or fine soft hair.

lanyard, lan′yerd, *n.* [Also written *lanier, laniard,* from Fr. *lanière,* a thong, strap, originally a woolen band, from L. *lana,* wool.] *Naut.* a short piece of rope or line used for fastening something in ships; *milit.* a piece of strong twine with an iron hook at one end, used in firing cannon with a friction tube.

Laodicean, la·od′i·sē″an, *a.* Like the Christians of Laodicea; lukewarm in religion.

lap, lap, *n.* [A.Sax. *læppa*; D. and Dan. *lap*, Sw. *lapp*, G. *lappen*, a lap, a loose flap, *lappen*, to hang loose; akin to *label*, *lobe*, *limp* (*a.*), *lapse*; *lapel*, *lappet*, are derivatives.] The lower part of a garment that hangs loosely; the part of clothes that lies on the knees when a person sits down; hence, the upper part of the legs in this position; the part of one body which lies on and covers a part of another (as a slate in roofing); the last part or round in a race.—**lapboard,** *n.* A board resting on the lap, employed by tailors for cutting out or ironing work upon.—**lap dog,** lap′dog, *n.* A small dog fondled in the lap, a pet dog.—**lapful,** lap′ful, *n.* As much as the lap can contain.

lap, lap, *v.t.*—*lapped*, *lapping*. [From O.E. *wlap*, to wrap, a form of *wrap* (which see).] To wrap or twist round; to fold; to double over; to lay partly above; to overlap ideas; *racing*, to win or be ahead of by at least one circuit of the racetrack; to cuddle.—*v.i.* To be spread or laid; to be turned over; to lie over something in part (as slates on a roof).—**lapper,** lap′ėr, *n.*

lap, lap, *v.i.*—*lapped*, *lapping*. [A.Sax. *lapian*, *lappian*, acel. *lepja*, O.D. *lappen*, *lapen*, L.G. *lappen*, to lap or lick up; allied to L. *lambo*, Gr. *laptō*—to lap or lick.] To take up liquor or food with the tongue; to feed or drink by licking up; to make a sound like that produced by taking up water by the tongue.—*v.t.* To take into the mouth with the tongue; to lick up.—*n.* A lick, as with the tongue; a sound made in this way; a sound as of water rippling against the beach.—**lapper,** lap′ėr, *n.* One who laps or takes up with the tongue.

lap, lap, *n.* [Short for *lapidary* wheel.] A wheel or revolving disk of soft metal, which by means of a polishing powder is used in cutting glass, gems, etc.

laparectomy, lap′ar·ek″to·mi, *n.* [Gr. *lapara*, flanks, *ektomē*, cutting out.] The excision of intestines at the side.

laparotomy, lap′ar·ot″o·mi, *n.* Cutting of the abdominal walls.

lapel, la·pel′, *n.* [Dim. from *lap*, part of a garment.] That part of a garment which is made to lap or fold over; the part in the front of a coat or waistcoat that is folded back.

lapidary, lap′i·de·ri, *n.* [L. *lapidarius*, from *lapsis*, *lapidis*, a stone; akin Gr. *lepas*, a rock.] An artificer who cuts, polishes, and engraves gems or precious stones; a dealer in precious stones.—*a.* Of or pertaining to the art of polishing and engraving precious stones.—*Lapidary style*, pompous style of language adopted on monuments; sonorous Latinity.—**lapidification,** la·pid′i·fi·kā″shon, *n.* The act of lapidifying or converting into stone; the state of being lapidified.—**lapidify,** la·pid′i·fī, *v.t.*—*lapidified*, *lapidifying*. To form into stone.—*v.i.* To turn into stone; to become stone.

lapilli, la·pil′lī, *n. pl.* [L. *lapillus*, a little stone, contr. of *lapidulus*, dim. of *lapis*, a stone. LAPIDARY.] Volcanic ashes which consist of small angular fragments or particles.

lapis lazuli, la′pis laz′ū·li, *n.* [L. *lapis*, a stone, and L.L. *lazulum*, this mineral; same origin as *azure*.] An aluminous mineral of a rich blue color, used in mosaic work and other kinds of ornament, and when powdered yielding ultramarine.

lappet, lap′et, *n.* [Dim. of *lap*, a loose part, etc.] A little lap or flap, as on a dress, especially on a headdress; a cotton fabric with imitation of embroidery on surface.

Lapps, *n.* The natives of Lapland, in northern Scandinavia.

lapse, laps, *n.* [L. *lapsus*, from *labi*, *lapsus*, to slide, to fall (as in *collapse*, *elapse*, *relapse*, etc.); akin *lap* (*n.*), *lobe*, etc. LAP.] A gliding, slipping, or gradually falling; an unobserved or very gradual advance; an unnoticed passing away (of time); a slip or error; a failing in duty; a deviation from truth or rectitude; *eccles. law*, the omission of a patron to present a clerk to a benefice within six months after it becomes void.—*v.i.*—*lapsed*, *lapsing*. To pass slowly, silently, or by degrees; to glide away; to fall gradually; to slip in moral conduct; to fail in duty; to commit a fault; to fall or pass from one person to another, through some omission or negligence; *law*, to become ineffectual or void.

lapwing, lap′wing, *n.* [O.E. *lapwinke*, A.Sax. *hleápewince*, equivalent to *leapwink*; from its leaping or jerking mode of flight.] A well-known and handsome bird belonging to the plover family, about the size of a pigeon, often called the *pee-wit* from its cry.

lar, lär, *n.* pl. **lares,** lâ′rēz. [Related to L. *larva*, a specter.] A household deity among the ancient Romans, regarded as the spirit of a deceased ancestor.

larboard, lär′bōrd, *n.* [Perhaps from M.E. *ladeborde*, the loading side.] *Naut.* the left-hand or port side of a ship, a term now given up in favor of *port*, the latter being shorter and more distinctive in sound: opposite of *starboard*.

larceny, lär′se·ni, *n.* [Contr. for *latrociny*, from L. *latrocinium*, from *latro*, a robber.] The unlawful taking and carrying away of any article or piece of goods with intent to deprive the right owner of the same; theft.—**larcener, larcenist,** lär′sen·ėr, lär′sen·ist, *n.* One who commits larceny; a thief.—**larcenous,** lär′sen·us, *a.* Pertaining to or having the character of larceny; guilty of or inclined to larceny.

larch, lärch, *n.* [L. and G. *larix*, the larch.] A well-known coniferous tree remarkable for the elegance of its form and the durability and value of its wood.

lard, lärd, *n.* [Fr. *lard*, L. *lardum*, *laridum*, allied to Gr. *larinos*, fat, from *laros*, dainty.] The fat of swine after being melted and separated from the flesh.—*v.t.* To mix with lard or bacon; to stuff with pieces of bacon (as in cooking a fowl); to fatten; to mix with something by way of improvement.—*v.i.* To grow fat.—**larder,** lär′dėr, *n.* A room, house, box, or the like, where meat and other food are kept.—**lardon,** lär-don, *n.* A strip of pork or bacon used to lard meat.

lares, *n.* pl. of *Lar*.

large, lärj, *a.* [Fr. *large*, L. *largus*, abundant, large.] Being of great size; having great dimensions; big; bulky; great; containing or consisting of a great quantity or number; abundant; plentiful; numerous; liberal, many-sided, comprehensive (a *large* mind); generous, noble, sympathetic (a *large* heart).—*At large*, without restraint or confinement; diffusely; fully; with all details; elected at large (by the whole state), as congressman-*at-large*.—**largehearted,** *a.* Having a large heart; generous; magnanimous; sympathetic.—**largeheartedness,** *n.* Largeness of heart.—**largely,** lärj′li, *adv.* In a large manner; to a large or great degree or extent; widely; extensively.

largess, lär′jes, *n.* [Fr. *largesse*, from L. *largitio*, a bounty, from *largiri*, to bestow, from *largus*, large.] A present; a gift or donation; a bounty bestowed.

larghetto, lär·get′to. [It.] *Mus.* somewhat slowly, but not so slowly as *largo*.—**largo,** lär′gō. [It.] *Mus.* slowly; slowly, with breadth and dignity.

lariat, la′ri·at, *n.* [Sp. *lariata*.] The lasso; a long cord or thong of leather with a noose used in catching wild horses, etc.

lark, lärk, *n.* [A.Sax. *láwerce*, *láferce*, O. and Prov.E. *lavrock*, *laverock* = D. *leeuwerik*, *leeuwrik*, Dan. *lærke*, Icel. *lævirki*, G. *lerche*—a lark; the Icel. *lævirki* seems to literally mean *craft-worker*.] One of a genus of perching birds characterized by having a long straight hind claw, and of which there are various species, as the skylark, wood lark, shore lark, etc., the skylark being celebrated for its song.—**larkspur,** lärk′spėr, *n.* [From the long spur of one of the sepals.] The common name of a genus of plants, several species of which are common in gardens.

lark, lärk, *n.* [From A.Sax. *lác*, Icel. *leikr*, Goth. *laiks*, sport, play.] Sport; frolic; a piece of merriment. (*Slang* or *colloq.*)—*v.i.* and *t.* To sport; to make sport. (*Slang* or *colloq.*)

larrikin, lar′i·kin, *n.* Australian hooligan; street-corner rough.

larrup, lar′up, *v.t.* To whip or flog.

larva, lär′va, *n.* pl. **larvae,** lär′vē. [L. *larva*, a mask, a specter.] The early form of any animal which during its development is unlike its parent; an insect in the caterpillar or grub state, that is, the first stage after the egg, preceding the chrysalis and the perfect insect.—**larval,** lär′val, *a.* Pertaining to a larva.

larynx, lar′ingks, *n.* [Gr.] *Anat.* the upper part of the windpipe or trachea, a cartilaginous cavity which plays an important part in the utterance of articulate sounds.—**laryngeal,** lar•in•ji′al, *a.* Pertaining to the larynx.—**laryngitis,** la•rin•ji′tis, *n.* [Term. *-itis* denotes inflammation.] An inflammation of the larynx of any sort.—**laryngoscope,** la•ring′go•skōp, *n.* A reflecting contrivance for examining the larynx and commencement of the trachea.—**laryngoscopic,** la•ring′go•skop″ik, *a.* Pertaining to the inspection of the larynx.—**laryngotomy,** lar•in•got′o•mi, *n.* [Gr. *tomē,* a cutting.] The making of an incision into the larynx for assisting respiration when obstructed, for removing foreign bodies, or for other reasons.

lascar, las′kar, *n.* In the East Indies, properly, a camp follower; but by Europeans applied to a native sailor.

lascivious, las•siv′i•us, *a.* [L. *lascivia,* lewdness, *lascivus,* wanton, allied to Skr. *las,* to embrace, *lash,* to desire, Gr. *lilaiomai,* to desire.] Wanton; lewd; lustful; exciting voluptuous emotions.—**lasciviously,** las•siv′i•us•li, *adv.* In a lascivious manner.—**lasciviousness,** las•siv′i•us•nes, *n.* The state or quality of being lascivious.

laser, lā′zėr, *n.* [*l*ight *a*mplification by *s*timulated *e*mission of *r*adiation.] A microwave amplifier that produces an intense beam of light by the stimulation of high-energy atoms in the visible spectrum.

lash, lash, *n.* [Akin to G. *lasche,* a flap, a thong, a latchet, also a scarf joint; D. *lasch,* a piece joined on, a joining; Dan. *laske,* Sw. *laska,* to scarf.] The thong or cord at the point of a whip; any thong, cord, or the like for flogging; a whip; a scourge; a stroke with a whip or anything pliant and tough; a stroke of satire; a sarcasm or cutting remark.—*v.t.* To strike with a lash or anything pliant; to scourge; to beat, as with something loose; to dash against (as waves); to satirize; to censure with severity.—*v.i.* To ply the whip; to aim sarcasms; to hit.—*To lash out,* to make a sharp verbal attack; to kick.

lash, lash, *v.t.* [O.Fr. *lachier,* form of *lacier,* to lace.] To bind, lace, or tie with a rope.—**lashing,** lash′ing, *n.* A piece of rope binding or making fast one thing to another.

lass, las, *n.* [A contr. for *ladess,* fem. of *lad,* or a contr. of W. *llodes,* a lass. LAD.] A young woman; a girl: in familiar language often applied to a woman of any age.—**lassie,** las′i, *n.* [Dim. of *lass.*] A young girl; a term of endearment for a young woman. (*Colloq.*)

lassitude, las′i•tūd, *n.* [L. *lassitudo,* from *lassus,* weary; same root as *late.*] The state of having the energies weakened; weakness; weariness; languor of body or mind; enervation.

lasso, las′sō, *n.* [Sp. *lazo,* Pg. *laço,* from *laqueus,* a noose. LACE.] A lariat, rope or cord, with a noose, used for catching wild horses and other animals.—*v.t.* To catch with a lasso.

last, last, *a.* [A.Sax. *last,* a contr. for *latost,* latest; comp. *best* for *betst.* LATE.] Coming after all the others; latest; hindmost; closing; final; next before the present; most recent; utmost; extreme; lowest; meanest; farthest of all from possessing a given quality, character, use, or the like; most unlikely (you are the *last* man I should consult).—*At last,* formerly *at the last,* at the end; in the conclusion.—*To the last,* to the end; till the conclusion.—*adv.* On the last occasion; the time before the present; after all others; lastly; finally.

last, last, *v.i.* [A.Sax. *laestan,* to follow, to observe or perform, to last, to endure; Goth. *laistjan,* to trace footsteps, to follow, from A. Sax. *last,* Goth. *laists,* a footstep. See LAST, for shoes.] To continue in time; to endure; to remain in existence; to hold out and be sufficient in quantity (provisions to *last* a week); to continue unimpaired; not to decay or perish.—**lasting,** las′ting, *p.* and *a.* Such as will or can continue or endure; durable; of long continuance (*lasting* good, evil, impression).—*n.* A species of stiff and very durable woolen stuff, used for making shoes and other purposes.—**lastingly,** las′ting•li, *adv.* In a lasting manner.—**lastingness,** las′ting•nes, *n.* The state or quality of being lasting.—**lastly,** last′li, *adv.* In the last place; at last; finally.

last, last, *n.* [A.Sax. *hlæst,* from *hladan,* to lade; D., Dan., and G. *last,* Icel. *lest,* a load. LADE.] A load; hence, a certain weight or measure, which varies in different articles, but is generally estimated at 4000 lb.; the burden of a ship.

last, last, *n.* [A.Sax. *lást, laest,* D. *leest,* Dan. *læst,* a last; Goth. *laists,* footstep; Icel. *leistr,* the foot below the ankle, a short sock. LAST, *v.i.*] A mold or form of the human foot, made of wood, on which boots and shoes are formed.—*v.t.* To form on or by a last.

Latakia, lät•ä•kē′a, *n.* A fine variety of Turkish tobacco, so named from *Latakia* (anciently *Laodicea*), near which it is produced.

latch, lach, *n.* [From O.E. *lacche, latche,* A.Sax. *læccan,* to seize, to take hold of.] A simple contrivance or catch for fastening a door.—*v.t.* To fasten with a latch; to catch hold of; to attach oneself to.—**latchkey,** *n.* A key used to raise the latch of a door.

latchet, lach′et, *n.* [Fr. *lacet,* a lace or string. LACE.] The string or thong that fastens a shoe or sandal.

late, lāt, *a.* [A.Sax. *læt,* D. *laat,* Icel. *latr,* Dan. *lad,* Sw. *lat,* late, slow, tardy; Goth. *lats,* sluggish; G. *lass,* wearied; akin L. *lassus* (for *ladtus*); the root is that of *let.* This adjective is compared by *later, latter, latest* or *last.*] Coming after the usual time; slow; tardy; long delayed; far advanced toward the end or close (a *late* hour of the day); existing not long ago, but not now; deceased; departed; last or recently in any place, office, or character.—*adv.* After the usual time, or the time appointed; after delay; not long ago; lately; far in the night, day, week, or other particular period.—*Of late,* lately, in time not long past, or near the present.—**lately,** lāt′li, *adv.* Not long ago; recently.—**lateness,** lāt′nes, *n.* The state of being late; tardiness; far advanced period.—**latish,** lāt′ish, *a.* Somewhat late.

lateen, la•tēn′, *a.* [Fr. *voile latine,* lit. Latin sail.] A term applied to a triangular sail having its foremost edge fastened to a yard which hoists obliquely to the mast: used in xebecs, feluccas, etc., in the Mediterranean.

latent, lā′tent, *a.* [L. *latens, latentis,* from *lateo,* to lurk; allied to Gr. *lanthanō, lathein,* to escape notice.] Not visible or apparent; not seen; not manifested; under the surface of what outwardly appears.—*Latent heat,* that portion of heat which exists in any body without producing any effect upon another, or upon the thermometer.—**latently,** lā′tent•li, *adv.* In a latent manner.—**latency,** lā′ten•si, *n.* The state of being latent.

lateral, lat′ėr•al, *a.* [L. *lateralis,* from *latus, lateris,* a side, as in *collateral, equilateral.*] Pertaining to the side; directed to the side; proceeding from the side; situated on the side.—**laterally,** lat′ėr•al•li, *adv.*

laterite, lat′ėr•it, *n.* [L. *later,* a brick or tile.] An argillaceous sandstone of a reddish color.

latescent,† la•tes′ent, *a.* [L. *latesco,* to hide one's self. LATENT.] Lying hid; latent.—**latescence,**† la•tes′ens, *n.* The quality or condition of being latescent.

latex, lā′teks, *n.* [L., a fluid juice.] *Bot.* the white milky sap of some seed plants which coagulates on exposure to air and from which rubber, gutta-percha, chicle, etc., are produced.

lath, lath, *n.* [A.Sax. *lætta,* D. and G. *latte,* whence Fr. *latte,* It. *latta,* a lath, a pole, etc. Akin *lattice, latten.*] A thin narrow board or slip of wood that is nailed to the rafters of a building to support the tiles or covering; a thin narrow slip of wood, perforated metal, or wire mesh that is nailed to a wall to support the plastering; such materials collectively; any similar piece of wood.—*v.t.* To cover or line with laths.—**lather,** *n.* One who applies laths.—**lathing,** *n.* Lath materials; lath work on a wall; work of putting on lath materials.

lathe, lāᴛʜ, *n.* [Icel. *löth,* Dan. *lad,* a lathe, *dreielad,* a turning lathe; in second sense it corresponds with Sw. and G. *lade,* a lay or lathe in a loom.] An apparatus for turning and polishing wood, ivory, metals, etc., by supporting and causing the article to revolve while being operated on; the part of a loom to which the reed is fixed, and by the movements of which the weft-threads are driven home in weaving; called also *lay.*

lather, laᴛʜ′ėr, *n.* [A.Sax. *leáthor;* akin to Icel. *lauthr, löthr,* froth of sea water, also a kind of soap; Sw. *lodder*, soap; from root meaning to wash, seen also in *lave*.] Foam or froth made by soap and water; foam or froth from profuse sweat, as of a horse.—*v.i.* To form a foam with soap and water; to become frothy.—*v.t.* To spread over with lather.

laticiferous, lat•i•sif′ėr•us, *a.* [L. *latex*, sap, and *fero*, to bear.] *Bot.* bearing or containing latex or elaborated sap.

latifoliate, latifolious, lā•ti•fō′li•āt, lā•ti•fō′li•us, *a.* [L. *latus*, broad, and *folium*, a leaf.] Broad-leaved, as a plant.

Latin, lat′in, *a.* [L. *Latinus*, from *Latium*, the district of Italy in which Rome was built.] Pertaining to the Latins, a people of Latium in Italy; Roman; pertaining to or composed in the language spoken by the Latins or Romans.—*Latin Church*, the Western Church; the Church of Rome, as distinct from the Greek or Eastern Church.—*Latin races*, the Italian, French, Spanish, etc., whose language is based on the Latin, and among whose ancestors were Roman colonists.—*n.* The language of the ancient Romans.—*v.t.* To turn into Latin.—**Latinism,** lat′in•izm, *n.* A Latin idiom; a mode of speech peculiar to the Latins.—**Latinist,** lat′in•ist, *n.* One skilled in Latin.—**Latinity,** la•tin′i•ti, *n.* Latin style or idiom; purity of Latin style.—**Latinization,** lat′in•i•zā″shon, *n.* The act of rendering into Latin.—**Latinize,** lat′in•īz, *v.t.*—*latinized, latinizing.* To translate into Latin; to give Latin terminations or forms to, as to foreign words.—*v.i.* To use words or phrases borrowed from the Latin.

latitude, lat′i•tūd, *n.* [L. *latitudo*, lit. breadth, from *latus*, broad, wide; as applied in geography this term was adopted because ancient geographers thought the breadth (latitude) of the earth from north to south was much less than its length (longitude) from east to west.] Extent from side to side; breadth; width; room or scope; comprehensiveness or looseness of application; extent of deviation from a standard; freedom from rules or limits; laxity; extent; amplitude; distance north or south of the equator, measured on a meridian and expressed in degrees, minutes, and seconds, the greatest possible latitude being 90° north or south, and any latitude approaching this being a *high* latitude, the opposite being a *low* latitude; *astron.* the distance of a star north or south of the ecliptic, measured on a circle at right angles to the ecliptic and passing through the body.—*Parallels of latitude*, circles parallel to the equator, used in measuring latitude.—**latitudinal,** lat•i•tū′di•nal, *a.* Pertaining to latitude; in the direction of latitude.—**latitudinarian,** lat′i•tū•di•nâ″ri•an, *a.* Embracing a wide circle or range; having a wide scope; characterized by freedom, independence, or want of respect for the usual standards of belief or opinion; lax in religious principles or views; freethinking; liberal.—*n.* One who is liberal or loose in his notions; one who has no respect for commonly accepted doctrines or opinions; one who indulges a latitude of thinking and is careless of orthodoxy.—**latitudinarianism,** lat′i•tū•di•nâ″ri•an•izm, *n.* The principles of latitudinarians; freedom of opinion, particularly in theology.

latria, la•trī′a, *n.* [L., from Gr. *latreia*, service.] The highest kind of worship, or that paid to God, distinguished by Roman Catholics from *dulia*, or the inferior worship paid to saints.

latrine, la•trēn′, *n.* [L. *latrina*, a bath, a water closet, from *lavo*, to wash.] A privy; a water closet.

latten, lat′en, *n.* [O.Fr. *laton*, Fr. *laiton*, brass; It. *latta*, tin-plate; akin to *lath*; so called from the material being used in flat pieces or plates. LATH.] A fine kind of brass or bronze anciently used for crosses, candlesticks, brasses of sepulchral monuments, etc.; as a modern commercial term, metal in sheets or strips, especially sheet or plate brass or thin plates of mixed metal.

latter, lat′ėr, *a.* [An irregular comparative of *late*. LATE.] More late or recent; the second of two; opposed to *former*; mentioned the last of two; modern; lately past (in these *latter* ages).—**Latter-day Saint,** *n.* MORMON.—**latterly,** lat′ėr•li, *adv.* Of late; in time not long past; lately; ultimately; at last.

lattice, lat′is, *n.* [Fr. *lattis*, from *latte*, lath. LATH.] A structure of wood or iron made by crossing laths, rods, or bars, and forming open checkered or reticulated work; a window made of laths or strips of iron which cross one another like network, so as to leave open interstices.—*v.t.*—*latticed, latticing.* To give the form or appearance of a lattice to; to furnish with a lattice.—**lattice girder,** *n.* A girder of which the side consists of diagonal pieces arranged like lattice work.

laud, lạd, *v.t.* [L. *laudo*, to praise, from *laus, laudis*, praise; *allow* is a derivative.] To praise in words alone, or with words and singing; to extol; to celebrate.—*n.* Praise; a song or hymn of praise; *pl.* a service of the church comprising psalms of praise, and generally included in matins.—**laudability,**† **laudableness,** lạ•da•bil′i•ti, lạ′da•bl•nes, *n.* The quality of being laudable.—**laudable,** lạ′da•bl, *a.* [L. *laudabilis*.] Praiseworthy; commendable.—**laudably,** lạ′da•bli, *adv.* In a laudable or commendable manner.—**laudation,** lạ•dā′shon, *n.* Praise; commendation.—**laudatory,** lạ′da•to•ri, *a.* Containing or expressing praise; tending to praise.—*n.* That which contains or expresses praise.—**lauder,** lạ′dėr, *n.* One who lauds or praises.

laudanum, lạ′da•num, *n.* [From L. *ladanum*, a resinous juice. LADANUM.] Opium prepared in spirit of wine by maceration, straining, and filtering; tincture of opium.

laugh, läf, *v.i.* [A.Sax. *hlehhan, hlihhan*, to laugh; comp. Goth. *hlahjan*, O.H.G. *hlahhan*, Icel. *hlæja*, D. *lagchen*, G. *lachen*, to laugh; imitative of sound made in laughing.] To make that convulsive or chuckling noise which sudden merriment excites; when said of things, to appear gay, bright, or brilliant.—*To laugh at*, to ridicule; to treat with some degree of contempt.—*To laugh in the sleeve*, to laugh to one's self or so as not to be observed, especially when apparently maintaining a demure countenance.—*To laugh on the wrong side of the mouth*, to weep or cry; to be made to feel vexation or disappointment after exhibiting a boastful or exultant spirit.—*n.* The inarticulate expression of sudden mirth peculiar to man.—*v.t.* To express by laughing; to ridicule or deride; with *out* or *down*.—*To laugh to scorn*, to deride; to treat with mockery, contempt, and scorn.—**laughable,** läf′a•bl, *a.* That may justly excite laughter; comical; ludicrous.—**laughableness,** läf′a•bl•nes, *n.* The quality of being laughable.—**laughably,** läf′a•bli, *adv.* In a manner to excite laughter.—**laugher,** läf′ėr, *n.* One who laughs or is fond of merriment.—**laughing gas,** *n.* Nitrous oxide, or protoxide of nitrogen: so called because, when inhaled, it usually produces exhilaration.—**laughingly,** läf′ing•li, *adv.* In a laughing or merry way; with laughter.—**laughingstock,** *n.* A person or thing that is an object of ridicule; a butt for laughter or jokes.—**laughter,** läf′tėr, *n.* [A.Sax. *hleahtor*, Icel. *hlair*, O.H.G. *hlahtar*.] The act or sound of laughing; an expression of mirth, manifested chiefly in certain convulsive and partly involuntary actions of the muscles of respiration, which produce a succession of short abrupt sounds, with certain movements of the muscles of the face, and often of other parts of the body.

launce, läns, *n.* A name of two species of sand eels, from their lancelike form.

launch, länsh, *v.t.* [Fr. *lancer*, O.Fr. *lanchier*, to throw or dart.] To throw, as a lance; to dart; to let fly; to set afloat (to *launch* a ship); to catapult or send off (to *launch* a rocket); *fig.* to put out into another sphere of duty, another field of activity, or the like.—*v.i.* To glide forward, as a ship into the water; to enter upon a new field of activity; to enter upon a new topic (to *launch* into a discussion).—*n.* The setting afloat of a ship or boat.—**launcher,** län′shėr, *n.*—**launching pad,** *n.* A nonflammable platform from which a rocket or missile can be launched.

launch, länsh, *n.* [Sp. and Pg. *lancha*, boat.] A kind of boat, longer, lower, and more flat-bottomed than a long boat; the largest boat carried by a man-of-war.

launder, län′dėr, *n.* [Contr. from

O.E. *lavander*, from Fr. *lavandier*, *lavandière*, from *laver*, L. *lavo*, to wash. LAVE.] A washerwoman; a long trough used by miners for washing ore.—*v.t.*‡ To wash; to wet.—**launderer,** län′dėr•ėr, *n.* A man who follows the business of washing clothes.—**laundress,** län′-dres, *n.* A female whose employment is the washing and the ironing of underclothing, table linen, etc.—**laundry,** län′dri, *n.* [Contr. for *lavendery*.] The place or room where clothes are washed.

laureate, ląʹri•āt, *a.* [L. *laureatus*, from *laurea*, a laurel, from *laurus*, a laurel. LAUREL.] Decked or invested with laurel.—*Poet laureate*, in Great Britain, an officer belonging in virtue of his office to the royal household, who was formerly required to compose an ode annually for the sovereign's birthday, for a great national victory, and the like—a requirement discontinued since the reign of George III, the post being now a sinecure.—*n.* One crowned with laurel; a poet laureate.—*v.t.*—*laureated, laureating.* To honor with a wreath of laurel; to invest with the office of poet laureate.—**laureateship,** ląʹri•āt•ship, *n.* Office of a laureate; the post of a poet laureate.

laurel, ląʹrel, *n.* [O.E. *laurer*, *lorer*, Fr. *laurier*, Sp. Pr. *laurel*, from L. *laurus*, a laurel, for *daurus*, being akin to Gr. *drys*, W. *derw*, an oak, E. *tree*.] The sweet bay, a native of the North of Africa and south of Europe, cultivated in gardens from its elegant appearance and the aromatic fragrance of its evergreen leaves; a name also given to several other shrubs botanically very different, but somewhat similar in their evergreen foliage, as the cherry laurel and Portugal laurel, both of the cherry genus; *pl.* a crown of laurel, formerly bestowed as a distinction on poets, heroes, etc.; hence, honor, fame, distinction.—**laureled,** ląʹreld, *a.* Crowned or decorated with laurel, or with a laurel wreath; laureate.

laurustine, ląʹrus•tīn, *n.* [L. *laurus*, laurel, and *tinus*, this plant.] A popular garden evergreen shrub or tree, native of the south of Europe, with pinkish or white flowers.

lava, läʹva, *n.* [It., from L. *lavo*, to wash. LAVE.] The general term for all rock-matter that flows in a molten state from volcanoes.—*Lava ware*, a kind of coarse ware resembling lava made from iron slag.

lavaliere, lavalier, lav′ä•lēr″, *n.* [Fr. *la valliere*, *lavalliere*, a kind of necktie with a bow, prob. from Louise de *La Valliere*, mistress of Louis XIV.] A pendant necklace, usually jeweled.

lave, lāv, *v.t.*—*laved, laving.* [Fr. *laver*, L. *lavo*, to wash; to bathe; akin to *luo*, Gr. *louō*, to wash; connected are *laundress*, *lavender*, *lava*, *ablution*, *alluvial*, *deluge*, *lotion*.] To wash; to bathe.—*v.i.* To wash one's self; to bathe; to wash, as the sea on the beach.—**lavation,** la•vāʹshon, *n.* [L. *lavatio*.] A washing or cleansing.—**lavatory,** lavʹa•to•ri, *a.* Washing or cleansing by washing.—*n.* A room or place for washing or personal ablutions; a wash or lotion.—**laver,** lāʹvėr, *n.* A vessel for washing; a large basin; in *Script. hist.* a basin placed in the court of the Jewish tabernacle, where the officiating priests washed their hands and feet.

lavender, lavʹen•dėr, *n.* [L.L. *lavendula*, *lavandula*, It. *lavandola*, *lavanda*, Fr. *lavande*, G. *lavandel*, lavender.] An aromatic plant of the mint family, the flower spikes of which are used to perfume clothes, and afford by distillation a valuable essential oil; a pale blue color with a slight mixture of red.

lavish, lavʹish, *v.t.* [Irregularly formed from E. *lave*, to pour out.] To expend or bestow with profusion; to expend without necessity or use; to waste; to squander.—*a.* Expending or bestowing with profusion; profuse; liberal to a fault; wasteful; being overflowing or in profusion; superabundant; superfluous.—**lavisher,** lavʹish•ėr, *n.* One who lavishes.—**lavishly,** lavʹish•li, *adv.* In a lavish manner.—**lavishness,** lavʹish•nes, *n.*

law, lą, *n.* [A.Sax. *lagu*, from same root as *lie*, *lay*, *low*; cog. Sw. *lag*. Icel. *lag*, *lög*, Dan. *lov*, a law; the root is also in L. *lex*, a law (whence *legal*). LIE.] A rule of action or conduct laid down or prescribed by authority; an edict or decree of a ruler or a government; a general command or order expressly laid down; such rules, edicts, or decrees collectively; the whole body of rules regulating and controlling the individuals of a state or community (to break the *law*, a violation of *law*, a father-in-*law*); legal procedure; litigation; the science dealing with legal enactments and procedure; jurisprudence; rights established by law; justice; one of the rules or principles by which any matter or proceeding is regulated (the *laws* of versification, of horse racing); an allowance in distance or time granted to a weaker competitor in a race or the like; a theoretical principle deduced from practice or observation; a formal statement of facts invariably observed in natural phenomena (the *law* of gravitation).—*The law, theol.* the code of Moses, or the books containing it; the preceptive part of revelation in contradistinction to the doctrinal, that is, to *the gospel*.—*Law French*, the Norman dialect or old French, still employed in certain formal state proceedings.—*Law language*, the language used in legal writings and forms.—*Law Latin*, corrupt Latin used in law and legal documents.—*Law merchant*, mercantile or commercial law; international law regulating commerce. See also under CIVIL, COMMERCIAL, COMMON, CRIMINAL, ECCLESIASTICAL, etc.—**law-abiding,** *a.* Observant of the law; obeying the law.—**lawbreaker,** *n.* One who violates the law.—**lawful,** ląʹfụl, *a.* Agreeable or conformable to law; allowed by law; legitimate; permissible (*lawful* but not expedient); competent; free from objection; rightful (*lawful* owner).—**lawfully,** ląʹfụl•li, *adv.* In a lawful manner; legitimately; legally.—**lawfulness,** ląʹfụl•nes, *n.* The quality of being lawful.—**lawless,** ląʹles, *a.* Not obedient or conforming to law; unrestrained by the law of morality or of society; contrary to or unauthorized by law; illegal; apparently uncontrolled by any law; capricious.—**lawlessly,** ląʹles•li, *adv.* In a lawless manner.—**lawlessness,** ląʹles•nes, *n.* Illegality; disregard of law; arbitrariness; violence.—**lawmaker,** *n.* A legislator; a lawgiver.—**law of nations,** international law.—**lawsuit,** ląʹsūt, *n.* A suit in law for the recovery of a supposed right; an action before a court instituted by a party to compel another to do him justice.—**lawyer,** ląʹyėr, *n.* [From *law*; comp. *bowyer*, *sawyer*.] One versed in the laws; or a practitioner of law; one whose profession is to institute suits in courts of law, or to prosecute or defend the cause of clients.

lawn, ląn, *n.* [O.E. *laund*, *lawnde*, a clear space in a forest, a wild shrubby or woody tract, from W. *llan*, an enclosed space, or from Fr. *lande*, a heath or wild tract.] A glade in a forest; a vista through trees; a space of ground covered with grass, and kept smoothly mown, generally in front of or around a mansion.—**lawn mower,** *n.* machine for mowing lawns.

lawn, ląn, *n.* [Perhaps same as preceding word, and so called from its transparency, being seen through as we see through a lawn or vista, but more probably, derived from the earlier term *laune lynen*, i. e., lawn linen, from *Laon*, a town in France.] A fabric of linen or cotton, sheer, fine, and plain woven, thinner than cambric, employed in handkerchiefs, dresses, etc.—**lawny,** ląnʹi, *a.*

lawrencium, ą•renʹsē•um, *n.* [After Ernest Lawrence.] A radioactive metallic element of the actinoid series; symbol Lw; at. no. 103.

lax, laks, *a.* [L. *laxus*, loose, from same root as *langueo*, to languish, and probably E. *slack*; hence *relax*, *lease*, *leash*, *release*.] Loose; flabby; soft; not tense, firm, or rigid; not tightly stretched or drawn; not rigidly exact or precise; vague; equivocal; not sufficiently strict or rigorous; remiss; having too frequent discharges from the bowels.—**laxation,** lak•sāʹshon, *n.* [L. *laxatio*.] The act of loosening or slackening.—**laxative,** lakʹsa•tiv, *a.* [Fr. *laxatif*.] Having the power or quality of loosening or opening the intestines and relieving from constipation.—*n.* A medicine that acts as a gentle purgative.—**laxity,** lakʹsi•ti, *n.* [L. *laxitas*.] The state or quality of being lax; looseness; want of strictness; remissness.—**laxly,** laksʹli, *adv.* In a lax manner; loosely; with-

out exactness; remissly; flabbily.
lay, lā, pret. of *lie*.
lay, lā, *v.t.*—pret. & pp. *laid*; ppr. *laying*. [A.Sax. *lecgan* (pret. *legde, léde*, pp. *gelegd, geled*), a causal corresponding to *lie*, A.Sax. *licgan*; similarly Goth. *lagjan*, Icel. *laggja*, Dan. *lægga*, D. *leggen*, G. *legen*, to lay, from corresponding intrans. verbs. [LIE.] To place in a lying position; to cause to lie; to prostrate; to put, set, or place in general; to impose (taxes, commands, blame, etc.); to bring into a certain state; with various adjectives (to *lay* bare; to *lay* open, etc.); to settle (dust); to still (the wind); to allay (pain); to dispose with regularity in building or in other technical operations; to place at hazard; to wager; to stake; to contrive, scheme, plan (a plot); to place before a court of justice (an indictment, damages).—*To lay aside*, to put off or away; not to retain; to abandon.—*To lay away*, to reposit in store; to put aside for preservation.—*To lay before*, to exhibit or show to; to present to the view of.—*To lay by*, to reserve for future use; to put off.—*To lay by the heels*, to put in the stocks; to confine; to put in prison.—*To lay claim*, to claim; to advance or bring forward a claim.—*To lay down*, to give up or resign; to declare (to *lay down* a proposition or principle); to delineate on paper; to stake, or deposit as a pledge, equivalent, or satisfaction.—*To lay down the law*, to assert dictatorially what the speaker holds to be right.—*To lay eggs*, to produce them naturally from the body, as a bird or reptile.—*To lay hold of, to lay hold on*, to seize; to catch; to apprehend.—*To lay in*, to collect and store; to provide previously.—*To lay it on*, to do something to excess, as to charge an exorbitant price.—*To lay on*, to apply with force; to supply, as water, gas, etc., to houses by means of pipes leading from a main reservoir.—*To lay one's self open to*, to expose one's self to.—*To lay one's self out for*, to be ready to take part in; to put one's self in the way of.—*To lay one's hand on a thing*, to find it when wanted.—*To lay open*, to open; to make bare; to uncover; also, to show; to expose; to reveal.—*To lay out*, to expend; to plan or dispose in order the several parts of (to *lay out* a garden); to dress in graveclothes and place in a decent posture (to *lay out* a corpse).—*To lay to heart*, to consider seriously and intently; to feel deeply or keenly.—*To lay to one's charge*, to accuse him of.—*To lay up*, to store; to treasure; to reposit for future use; to confine to the bed or chamber; *naut.* to dismantle (a ship) and put in a dock or other place of security.—*To lay siege to*, to besiege; to importune; to annoy with constant solicitations.—*To lay wait*, to lie in ambush.—*To lay waste*, to devastate; to desolate.—*v.i.* To bring forth or produce eggs; *betting*, to wager; to bet; to stake money.—*To lay about one*, to strike on all sides; to act with vigor.—*To lay at*, to endeavor to strike.—*To lay on*, to deal blows with vehemence. [*To lay* is sometimes erroneously used, even by good writers, for *to lie*, but this should be carefully avoided. See under LIE.]—*n.* A stratum; the direction or lie in which the different strands of a rope are twisted.—**layoff,** lā'af, *n.* Discharge, as of workmen; a period of closing down; the act of laying off.—**layout,** lā'out, *n.* Floor plan, such as of a house; the equipment, as of an office or shop; a rough sketch to show how a proposed arrangement of photographs and type will look in print (an artist's *layout*).—**layover,** lā'ō•vėr, *n.* A wait between stages of a journey; a stopover in a place.
lay, lā, *a.* [Fr. *lai*, from L. *laicus*, Gr. *laikos*, from *laos*, people.] Pertaining to the people, as distinct from the clergy; not clerical; not professional; not appertaining to one who has professional knowledge.—*Lay brother*, a person received into a convent of monks, under vows, but not in holy orders.—*Lay clerk*, in the *English Ch.* a person not in orders who leads the people in their responses.—*Lay sister*, one received into a convent of nuns, under vows, but who does not perform any sacred office.—**laity,** lā'i•ti, *n.* Collectively all people who do not belong to the clergy; people outside of any profession as distinguished from those in it.—**layman,** lā'man, *n.* Any man not a clergyman; one of the laity; a man not professionally or specially devoted to a pursuit.
lay, lā, *n.* [O.Fr. *lai*, from the Celtic; Ir. and Gael. *laoi*, a verse, hymn, poem; same root as in G. *lied*, a song.] A song; a ballad; a narrative poem.
layer, lā'ėr, *n.* [From the verb *lay*.] One who or that which lays; a stratum; a coat, as of paint; a row or course of masonry, brickwork, or the like; a shoot or twig of a plant, not detached from the stock, partly laid under ground for growth or propagation.—*v.t. Gardening*, to propagate by bending the shoot of a living stem into the soil, the shoot striking root while being fed by the parent plant.
layette, lā•et', *n.* [Fr.] Clothing, blankets, etc., for a new-born child.
lay figure, layman, lā'fig•ūr, lā'man, *n.* [D. *leeman*, lit. joint-man, *lee* being for *lede*, from *leden*, pl. of *lid* (A.Sax. *lith*, Dan. *lid*. Goth. *lithus*), a joint.] A jointed figure used by painters in imitation of the human body, and which can be placed in any attitude so as to serve when clothed as a model for draperies, etc.
lazar, lā'zėr, *n.* [O.Fr. *lazare*, from *Lazarus* of the New Testament (Luke, xvi. 20).] A leper; any person infected with a nauseous and pestilential disease.—**lazaretto, lazaret,** laz•a•ret'tō, laz'a•ret, *n.* A hospital for the reception of diseased persons, particularly those affected with contagious diseases; at seaports often a vessel used for this purpose; a hospital for quarantine.
lazuli, laz'ū•lī, *n.* Lapis lazuli.—**lazulite,** laz'ū•līt, *n.* Blue spar, a phosphate of aluminum, magnesium and iron.
lazy, lā'zi, *a.* [Origin doubtful; perhaps for *late-sy* (from *late*), with term, as in *tricksy, tipsy*; or O.Fr. *lasche*, lax, slow, remiss, from L. *laxus*.] Disinclined to action or exertion; sluggish; indolent; averse to labor; heavy in motion; moving slowly or apparently with labor.—**lazily,** lā'zi•li, *adv.* In a lazy manner. —**laziness,** lā'zi•nes, *n.* The state or quality of being lazy; indolence; sloth.—**lazybones,** lā'zi•bōnz, *n.* A lazy fellow; an idler.
lea, lē, *n.* [Also written *lay*, from A.Sax. *leáh*, untilled land, pasture; Dan. dialect *lei*, fallow; D. *leeg*, empty, fallow.] A meadow or grassy plain; land under grass or pasturage.
leach, lēch, *n. Naut.* the side edge of a sail. LEECH.
leach, lēch, *v.t.* and *i.* To remove soluble parts by percolating a liquid through something.
lead, led, *n.* [A.Sax. *leád*; akin D. *lood*, Sw. and Dan. *lod*, G. *loth*, a plummet, the lead for taking soundings.] A heavy metallic element, pliable and soft and of a grayish-blue color, its chief ore being sulfide galena—symbol, Pb (Latin *plumbum*); at. no., 82; at. wt., 207.19; a plummet or mass of lead used in sounding at sea; *print.* a thin plate of metal used to give space between lines; a neutral gray color of medium brilliance; bullets (a shower of *lead*); a small piece of black lead, or plumbago, used in pencils.—*Black lead*, a name of graphite or plumbago. See GRAPHIC.—*White lead*, carbonate of lead, forming a white, quick-drying substance much used in painting. —*v.t.* To cover or line with lead; to fit with lead; *print.* to widen the space between (lines) by inserting a lead or thin plate of type metal.—**leaden,** led'n, *a.* Made of lead; resembling lead (a *leaden* sky); dull; gloomy.—**lead pencil,** *n.* An instrument for drawing or writing, usually made by enclosing a slip of plumbago, or graphite (black lead), in a casing of wood.—**leadsman,** ledz'man, *n. Naut.* the man who heaves the lead.
lead, lēd, *v.t.* pret. & pp. *led*. [A.Sax. *laeden*, to lead, from *lad*, a course, from *lithan*, to go or travel; D. *leiden*; akin *lode, lodestone*.] To guide by the hand; to guide or conduct by showing the way; to direct; to conduct, as a chief or commander; to head; to direct and govern; to precede; to hold the first place in rank or dignity among; to show the method of attaining an object; to direct, as in an investigation; to draw, entice, allure; to induce; to prevail on; to influence; to pass or spend (to *lead* a life of gaiety); to cause to spend or endure (he *led* his wife a sad life); *card playing*, to commence a round or trick with.—*To lead captive*, to carry into captivity.—*To lead one a dance* or *a fine dance*, to cause one more exertion

or trouble than necessary or expected.—*To lead the way*, to go before and show the way.—*v.i.* To go before and show the way; to have precedence or pre-eminence; to take the first place; to have a position of authority; to be chief, commander, or director; to conduct, bring, draw, induce (gambling *leads* to other evils); *card playing*, to play the first card of a round or trick.—*To lead off* or *out*, to begin.—*n.* A going before; guidance; act of leading; precedence; the right of playing the first card in a round or trick.—**leader,** lē′dėr, *n.* One that leads or conducts; a guide; a conductor; a chief; a commander; the chief of a party, faction, or any body of people; a musical performer who leads a band or choir; one of the front horses in a team.—**leadership,** lē′dėr•ship, *n.* The office of a leader; guidance.—**leading,** lē′-ding, *p.* and *a.* Guiding; conducting; chief; principal; most influential.—*Leading question*, a question which suggests the answer.—**leading strings,** *n. pl.* Strings by which children are supported when beginning to walk; hence, *to be in leading strings*, to be a mere puppet in the hands of others.

leaf, lēf, *n.* pl. **leaves,** lēvz. [A.Sax. *leáf*=O.Sax. *lôf*, Goth. *laufs*, Icel. *lauf*, Dan. *lōv*, D. *loof*, G. *laub*, a leaf; allied to Lith. *lapas*, a leaf; Gr. *lepis*, a scale.] One of the external parts of a plant, usually shooting from the sides of the stem and branches, and ordinarily green in color; something resembling a leaf; the part of a book or folded sheet containing two pages; a side, division, or part of a flat body, the parts of which move on hinges, as folding doors, window shutters, a fire screen, etc.; the part of a table which can be raised or lowered at pleasure; a very thin plate of metal (gold-*leaf*); the brim of a soft hat.—*To turn over a new leaf*, to adopt a different and better line of conduct. —*v.i.* To shoot out leaves; to produce leaves.—**leafage,** lēf′ij, *n.* Leaves collectively; abundance of leaves; foliage.—**leafless,** lēf′les, *a.* Destitute of leaves.—**leaflet,** lēf′let, *n.* A little leaf; a small printed folder; *bot.* one of the divisions of a compound leaf; a foliole.—**leafstalk,** *n.* The petiole or stalk which supports a leaf.—**leafy,** lē′fi, *a.* Full of leaves; abounding with leaves.—**leave,** lēv, *v.i.* To produce leaves; to leaf.—**leaved,** lēvd, *a.* With leaves; and compounded, as two-*leaved.*

league, lēg, *n.* [Fr. *ligue*, It. *lega*, L.L. *liga*, from L. *ligo*, to bind (in *ligament*, *ligature*, *ally*, etc.).] A combination of parties for promotion of their mutual interests, or for executing any design in concert, as of states for military aid or defense.—*League of Nations*, a group of nations formed after the World War (1920) to cooperate in world affairs. It assigned mandates of surrendered territories and planned arbitration in disputes between nations.—*Baseball*, *National League* (organized 1876), *American League* (1900), of ten teams each in major cities.

league, lēg, *n.* [O.Fr. *legue*, Fr. *lieue*, from L.L. *leuca*, *leuga*, etc., and that from the Celtic.] A measure of length varying in different countries, the English land league being 3 statute miles, the nautical league nearly 3½.

leaguer, lē′gėr, *n.* [D. *leger*, G. *lager*, a bed, a couch, a camp; allied to *lair*, *lie*, *lay*.] A camp; the camp of a besieging army; a siege.

leak, lēk, *n.* [Icel. *leki*, a leak; *lekr*, leaky; D. *lek*, Dan. *laek*, G. *leck*, a leak, leaky. See the verb.] A crack, fissure, or hole in a vessel that admits water, or permits a fluid to escape; the passing of liquid through such a crack or aperture.—*To spring a leak*, to open or crack so as to let in water; to begin to let in water.—*v.i.* [Icel. *leka*, Dan. *laekke*, D. *lekken*, to leak; allied to A.Sax. *leccan*, to wet, to moisten, and to E. *lack*.] To let water or other liquor in or out through a hole or crevice (the vessel *leaks*); to ooze or pass, as water or other fluid, through a crack, fissure, or aperture in a vessel.—*To leak out*, to find vent; to find publicity in a clandestine or irregular way.—**leakage,** lēk′ij, *n.* A leaking; the quantity of a liquor that enters or issues by leaking; *com.* a certain allowance for the leaking of casks, or the waste of liquors by leaking.—**leakiness,** lēk′i•nes, *n.* State of being leaky.—**leaky,** lēk′i, *a.* Letting water or other liquid pass in or out.

lean, lēn, *v.i.*—pret. & pp. *leaned* or *leant* (lent). [A.Sax. *hlinian*, to lean; O.H.G. *hlinen*, cog. with Gr. *klinō*, to make to bend, and L. *clino*, *inclino*, to bend, to *incline*.] To slope or incline from a straight or perpendicular position or line; to slant; to incline in feeling or opinion; to tend toward; to rest as for support, hence, to depend for consolation, comfort, and the like, usually with *against*, *on*, or *upon*.—*v.t.* To cause to lean; to incline; to support or rest.—**lean-to,** lēn′tö, *a.* Having rafters pitched against or leaning on another building or a wall.—*n.*, *n.* pl. **lean-tos,** lēn′töz, *Arch.* a building addition having a lean-to roof; a shed built against trees or posts or another building.

lean, lēn, *a.* [A.Sax. *hlaene*, L.G. *leen*, lean; allied to *lean*, v.] Wanting flesh or fat on the body; meager; not fat; not rich, fertile, or productive; barren of thought; jejune.—*n.* That part of flesh which consists of muscle without fat.—*Lean mixture*, a compound of air and gas or vapor without a combustible component.

leap, lēp, *v.i.*—*leaped*, pret. & pp., rarely *leapt* (lept). [A.Sax. *hleápan* to leap, to run, pret. *hleóp*; Sc. *loup*, Goth. *hlaupan*, G. *laufen*; allied to Gr. *kraipnos*, *karpalimos*, swift.] To spring or rise from the ground with feet in the air; to move with springs or bounds; to jump, vault, bound, skip; to make a sudden transition.—*v.t.* To pass over by leaping; to spring or bound from one side to the other of; to cause (one's horse) to take a leap; to make to pass by leaping.—*n.* The act of leaping; the space passed over or cleared in leaping; a jump; a spring; a bound; a sudden transition.—**leapfrog,** *n.* A game in which one player, by placing his hands on the back or shoulders of another in a stooping posture, leaps over his head.—**leap year,** *n.* Bissextile; every fourth year, in which February has an additional day, and there are thus 366 days in all: so called because after February the days of the week *leap* an extra day as compared with other years.

learn, lėrn, *v.t.*—*learned*, *learnt* (lėrnd, lėrnt), pret. & pp. [A.Sax. *leornian*, to learn, to teach; akin to *laeran*, to teach, *lár*, learning, lore; comp. G. *lernen*, to learn, *lehren*, to teach; D. *leeren*, Icel. *laera*, to teach, to learn; Goth. *laisjan*, to teach; allied to A.Sax. *lesan*, Icel. *lesa*, to gather.] To gain or acquire knowledge of or skill in; to acquire by study; to teach (*Shak.*).—*v.i.* To gain or receive knowledge, information, or intelligence; to receive instruction; to be taught.—**learned,** lėr′ned, *a.* Possessing knowledge; having a great store of information obtained by study; erudite; well acquainted; having much experience; skillful; often with *in* (*learned in* martial arts); containing or indicative of learning (a *learned* book).—**learnedly,** lėr′ned•li, *adv.* In a learned manner.—**learner,** lėr′nėr, *n.* A person who learns; one who is taught; a scholar; a pupil.—**learning,** lėr′ning, *n.* Acquired knowledge in any branch of science or literature; knowledge acquired by the study of literary productions; erudition.

lease, lēs, *n.* [Norm. *lees*, *leez*, a lease, L.L. *lessa*; from L. *laxare*, to loosen, relax, from *laxus*, lax. LAX.] A letting of lands, tenements, etc., to a person for a specified rent or compensation; the written contract for such letting; any tenure by grant or permission; the time for which such a tenure holds good.—*v.t.*—*leased*, *leasing*. To grant by lease; to let for a specified rent; to let; to occupy in terms of a lease.—**leasehold,** lēs′hōld, *a.* Held by lease. —*n.* A tenure by lease.—**leaseholder,** lēs′hōl•dėr, *n.* A tenant under a lease.

leash, lēsh, *n.* [Fr. *laisse*, O.Fr. *lesse*, a leash, from L.L. *laxa*, a loose cord, from L. *laxus*, loose. LAX.] A thong or line by which a dog (or two or three dogs) is held in hunting; a line holding in a hawk; three creatures of any kind, especially greyhounds, foxes, bucks, and hares; hence, three things in general.—*v.t.* To hold or fasten by a leash.

least, lēst, *a.* [A.Sax. *laest*, *laesast*, superl. of *læssa*, less.] Smallest; little beyond others, either in size, degree, value, worth, importance, or the like.—*adv.* In the smallest or lowest degree.—*At least*, *at the least*, to say no more; at the lowest degree; on the lowest estimate.—**leastways, leastwise,** lēst′wāz, lēst′wīz, *adv.* At least; however. (*Vulgar.*)

leather, leᴛʜ′ėr, *n.* [A.Sax. *lether*= L.G. *ledder, lier,* Icel. *lethr,* Dan. *læder, lær,* G. and D. *leder*; root unknown.] The skin of animals dressed and prepared for use by tanning, tawing, or other processes; tanned hide.—*a.* Consisting of leather.—*v.i.* To furnish with leather; to beat as with a thong of leather. (*Vulgar*)—**leatherneck,** *n.* A marine, from the stock once worn around the neck. **leatherette,** leᴛʜ•ėr•et′, *n.* A kind of imitation leather.—**leathery,** leᴛʜ′-ėr•i, *a.* Pertaining to or resembling leather; tough.

leave, lēv, *n.* [A.Sax. *leáf, geleaf,* leave, permission; same as the *-lieve* in *believe*; akin D. *-lof* in *oorlof,* permission; Icel. *leyfi,* permission, *lof,* praise, permission; G. (*er*)*lauben,* to permit; allied also to E. *love, lief*; L. *libet,* it is pleasing.] Liberty granted to act; permission; allowance; a formal parting of friends or acquaintances; farewell: used chiefly in the phrase to *take leave.* ∴ *Leave* is usually employed on familiar or unimportant occasions; *liberty* in relation to more important matters. —**leave-taking,** *n.* The act of taking leave; a bidding good-bye.

leave, lēv, *v.t.*—*left* (pret. & pp.), *leaving.* [A.Sax. *laefan,* to leave, to cause to remain, from *lifian,* to remain; Icel. *leifa,* O.Fris. *leva,* O.H.G. *bi-liban,* Mod.G. *b-leiben,* to remain; same stem as *live.*] To suffer to remain; not to take or remove; to have remaining at death; to commit or trust to, as a deposit; to bequeath; to give by will; to withdraw or depart from; to forsake, desert, abandon; to relinquish, resign, renounce; to refer; to commit for decision; to let remain without further discussion.—*To be left to one's self,* to be left alone; to be permitted to follow one's own opinions or desires.—*To leave off,* to desist from; to forbear; to cease wearing or practicing.—*To leave out,* to omit.—*v.i.* To set out; to take one's departure; to desist.—*To leave off,* to cease; to desist; to stop.—**leavings,** lēv′ings, *n.* Residue; that which is left; remains.

leaven, lev′n, *n.* [Fr. *levain,* from *lever,* L. *levare,* to raise; akin *levity, lever, relieve,* etc.] A substance that produces fermentation, as in dough; fermenting dough; what resembles leaven in its effects.—*v.t.* To mix with leaven; to impregnate or imbue with a modifing influence.—**leavening,** lev′en•ing, *n.*

lebensraum, lā′bens•roum, *n.* [G. *leben,* life, living, and *raum,* space.] A term used by Germans to indicate area in Europe which they considered vital to their national existence.

lecher, lech′ėr, *n.* [O.Fr. *lecheor,* gourmand, parasite, libertine; Fr. *lécher,* to lick; from G. *lecken,* O.H. G. *leccôn,* to lick. LICK, LICKERISH.] A man given to lewdness.—*v.i.* To practice lewdness.—**lecherous,** lech′-ėr•us, *a.* Addicted to lewdness; prone to indulge lust; lustful; lewd. —**lecherously,** lech′ėr•us•li, *adv.* In a lecherous manner.—**lecherousness,** lech′ėr•us•nes, *n.*—**lechery,** lech′ėr•i, *n.* [O.Fr. *lecherie.*] Lewdness; free indulgence or practice of lust.

lecithin, les′ith•in, *n.* [Gr. *lekithos,* egg yolk.] A complex fatty compound containing nitrogen and phosphates, and widely distributed through the animal body.

lectern, lek′tėrn, *n.* [O.Fr. *lectrin*; L.L. *lectrinum,* from *lectrum,* pulpit, Gr. *lektron,* a couch.] A desk or reading stand, especially in churches, from which scripture is read.

lection, lek′shon, *n.* [L. *lectio,* from *lego,* to read. LECTURE.] The act of reading; a difference or variety in copies of a manuscript or book; a reading; a lesson or portion of Scripture read in divine service.—**lectionary,** lek′shon•e•ri, *n.* A book containing portions of Scripture to be read for particular days.—**lector,** lek′tėr, *n.* [L.] A person in the Church of Rome whose office it is to read the lessons in church.

lecture, lek′chėr, *n.* [Fr. *lecture,* from L. *lectura,* a reading, from *lego,* to read, whence also *legend, lesson, legible,* etc. LEGEND.] A discourse on some subject read or delivered before an audience; a formal or methodical discourse intended for instruction; a reprimand, as from a superior; a formal reproof.—*v.t.*—*lectured, lecturing.* To give a lecture to; to speak to dogmatically or authoritatively; to reprimand; to reprove.—*v.i.* To read or deliver a formal discourse; to deliver lectures for instruction.—**lecturer,** lek′chėr•ėr, *n.* One who lectures; a professor or instructor who delivers formal discourses to students.—**lectureship,** lek′chėr•-ship, *n.* The office of a lecturer.

led, led, pret. and pp. of *lead.*

ledge, lej, *n.* [From stem of *lie*; comp. Sc. *leggin,* Icel. *lögg,* the ledge or rim at the bottom of a cask.] A shelf on which articles may be placed; anything which resembles such a shelf; a part rising or projecting beyond the rest; a ridge or shelf of rocks; *arch.* a small molding; also, a string course; *joinery,* a piece against which something rests.

ledger, lej′ėr, *n.* [Perhaps lit. a book that rests on a *ledge* or shelf; in any case from the same stem; comp. old *leger, ledger,* resting in a place; D. *legger,* one that lies; akin *lie* (to rest).] The principal book of accounts among merchants and others, so arranged as to exhibit on one side all the sum at the debit of the accounts and on the other all those at the credit; *arch.* a flat slab of stone, such as is laid horizontally over a grave; the covering slab of an altar tomb.—**ledger line,** *n. Mus.* a short line added above or below the staff for the reception of a note too high or too low to be placed on the staff.

lee, lē, *n.* [Icel. *hlé,* Dan. *lae*; D. *lij,* G. *lee,* lee; akin A.Sax. *hleó,* a shade, a shelter, Goth. *hlija,* a tent.] The quarter toward which the wind blows, as opposed to that from which it proceeds; the shelter caused by an object interposed, and keeping off the wind: almost exclusively a nautical term.—*Under the lee of,* on that side of which is sheltered from the wind; protected from the wind by; opposed to on the *weather* side of.—*a. Naut.* of or pertaining to the part or side toward which the wind blows; opposite to *weather.*—*Lee shore,* the shore under the lee of a ship, or that toward which the wind blows.—*Lee tide,* a tide running in the same direction as the wind is blowing.—**leeboard,** *n.* A long flat piece of wood attached to each side of a flat-bottomed vessel (as a Dutch galiot), intended to prevent her from drifting fast to leeward.—**leeward,** lē′wėrd or lū′wėrd, *a.* Pertaining to the part toward which the wind blows.—*n.* The quarter or direction toward the lee.—**leeway,** lē′wā, *n.* The drifting of a ship to the leeward of her course; the deviation from her true course which a vessel makes by drifting to leeward; extra time, space, etc.; a degree of freedom or choice; tolerance.

leech, lēch, *n.* [A.Sax. *laece,* a physician; Goth. *leikeis,* Icel. *lœknari,* Sw. *läkare,* a physician.] The common name of several bloodsucking wormlike animals, some of which are used in medicine; a hanger-on; a parasite.—*v.t.* To bleed by the use of leeches; to exhaust.—*v.i.* To attach like a leech.

leech, lēch, *n.* [L.G. *leik,* Icel. *lik,* Sw. *lik,* Dan. *lig,* leech-line, boltrope.] *Naut.* the border or edge of a sail which is sloping or perpendicular.

leek, lēk, *n.* [A.Sax. *leác,* an herb, a leek=L.G. and D. *look,* Icel. *laukr,* Sw. *lök,* Dan. *lōg,* G. *lauch,* Rus. *luk*; this gives the term. in *garlic, hemlock.*] A plant of the lily family, *Allium Porrum,* similar to the onion in form and use, but having flat, succulent leaves.

leer, lēr, *n.* [A.Sax. *hleór,* O.E. *lere, lire,* O.Sax. *hlear,* Icel. *hlyr,* face, cheek.] A side glance expressive of malignity, amorousness, or some unworthy feeling; an arch or affected glance or cast of countenance.—*v.i.* To cast a look expressive of contempt, malignity, or amorousness; to cast a sly or amorous look.—*v.t.* To allure with a leer.—**leeringly,** lē′ring•li, *adv.* In a leering manner.

leery, lēr′i, *a.* [E. dial. *lear,* from E. *lore,* learning.] Suspicious, knowing, wary.

lees, lēz, *n. pl.* [Fr. *lie,* Walloon *lizi,* L.L. *liœ*; origin unknown.] The grosser parts of any liquor which have settled on the bottom of a vessel; dregs; sediment.

leet, lēt, *n.* [Icel. *leiti,* a share or part.] In Scotland, a list of candidates for any office.

leeward, leeway. See LEE.

left, left, pret. & pp. of *leave.*—**left-off,** *a.* Laid aside; no longer worn (*left-off* clothes).

left, left, *a.* [A.Sax. *left,* worthless; O.E. *lift, luft,* O.D. *lucht, luft,* left; probably allied to A.Sax. *lef,* O.Sax. *lef,* weak, infirm.] Denoting the part opposed to the *right* of the body; belonging to the side next which the heart is situated (the *left* hand, arm, or side); in a political sense, a party or individuals opposed to conservatism; espousing progressive and advanced liberal policies and legislation.—*The left bank of a river,* that which would be on the left hand of a person whose face is turned down stream.—*n.* The side opposite to the right; that part which is on the left side; a liberal or radical political group.—**left-handed,** *a.* Having the left hand more capable of being used than the right; clumsy; turned toward the left hand.—*Left-handed marriage.* MORGANATIC.—**left-handedness,** *a.*—**leftist,** lef'tist, *n.* A member of the left; a radical.—*a.* Of or pertaining to the left.—**leftover,** *n.* The part remaining, as of a meal.—**left wing,** *n.* The most liberal or radical elements of a political or social group.—*a.* Of or pertaining to the left wing.—**left-winger,** *n.*

leg, leg, *n.* [A Scandinavian word: Icel. *leggr,* a leg, hollow bone, stem or trunk; Dan. *laeg,* Sw. *lägg,* the calf or shin.] The limb of an animal, used in supporting the body and in walking and running; in a narrower sense, that part of the limb from the knee to the foot; a long slender support, as the *leg* of a chair or table; one of the sides of a triangle as opposed to the base; the part of a stocking or other article of dress that covers the leg; *cricket,* the part of the field that lies to the left and behind the batsman as he faces the bowler; the fielder who acts in that part of the field.—*To put one's best leg foremost,* to do one's utmost endeavor.—*To have not a leg to stand on,* to have exhausted all one's strength or resources.—*On one's legs,* standing, especially to speak.—**legged,** legd, *a.* Having legs: used in composition (bandy-*legged,* two-*legged*).—**legging,** leg'ing, *n.* A covering for the leg, usually worn over the trousers and reaching to the knees; a long gaiter.—**legless,** leg'les, *a.*

legacy, leg'a•si, *n.* [From L. *legatum,* a legacy, from *lego,* to bequeath, to appoint. LEGATE.] A bequest; a particular thing or certain sum of money given by last will or testament; anything handed down by an ancestor or predecessor.

legal, lē'gal, *a.* [Fr. *légal,* from L. *legalis,* from *lex, legis,* law (also in *alloy, legitimate, legislator,* etc.); akin to *legare,* to delegate (as in *legate*); root same as in E. *lay, lie. Loyal* is the same word.] According to law; in conformity with law; permitted by law; pertaining to law; created by law.—**legalism,** lē'gal•izm, *n.* Strict adherence to law; a legal doctrine; inclination to the doctrine of works as opposed to grace.—**legalist,** lē'gal•ist, *n.* A stickler for adherence to law.—**legality,** li•gal'i•ti, *n.* The state or quality of being legal.—**legalization,** lē'gal•iz•ā"shon, *n.* The act of legalizing.—**legalize,** lē'gal•iz, *v.t.*—*legalized, legalizing.* To make legal or lawful; to render conformable to law.—**legally,** lē'gal•li, *adv.* In a legal manner; by permission of or in conformity with law.

legate, leg'it, *n.* [L. *legatus,* from *lego,* to send, to delegate. LEGAL.] An ambassador; especially, the pope's ambassador to a foreign prince or state.—**legateship,** leg'it•ship, *n.* The office of a legate.—**legatine,** leg'a•tin, *a.* Pertaining to a legate; made by or proceeding from a legate.—**legation,** li•gā'shon, *n.* [L. *legatio.*] A person or persons sent as envoys or ambassadors to a foreign court; an embassy; a diplomatic minister and his suite; a district ruled by a papal legate.

legatee, leg•a•tē', *n.* [From L. *legatum,* a legacy. LEGACY.] One to whom a legacy is bequeathed.

legato, li•gä'tō. [It., tied, from L. *ligare,* to tie.] *Mus.* played or sung in an even, smooth, gliding manner.

legend, lej'end, *n.* [Fr. *légende,* from L. *legenda,* lit. things to be read from *lego,* to read; originally applied to lives of the saints that had to be read as a religious duty. *Lego,* to read, originally to gather, appears in a great many English words, as in *lecture, lesson, coil, cull, collect, intellect, neglect, diligent, elegant,* etc.] A story generally of a marvelous character told respecting a saint; hence, any marvelous story handed down from early times; a tradition; a nonhistorical narrative; an inscription; *numismatics,* the words arranged circularly on a medal or coin, as distinguished from the inscription, which is across it.—**legendary,** lej'en•de•ri, *a.* Consisting of legends; like a legend; fabulous.

legerdemain, lej'ėr•di•mān", *n.* [Fr. *léger de main,* light of hand—*léger,* L.L. *leviarius,* from L. *levis,* light (whence *levity*), and *main,* L. *manus,* hand.] Sleight of hand; a deceptive performance which depends on dexterity of hand; trickery or deception generally.—**legerdemainist,** lej'ėr•di•mān"ist, *n.* One who practices legerdemain; a juggler.

leghorn, leg'orn, *n.* A kind of straw plait for bonnets and hats imported from Leghorn; a hat made of that material. [*cap.*] A Mediterranean breed of domesticated fowl.

legible, lej'i•bl, *a.* [L. *legibilis,* from *lego,* to read. LEGEND.] Capable of being read; consisting of letters or figures that may be distinguished by the eye.—**legibility,** lej•i•bil'i•ti, *n.* The quality of being legible.—**legibly,** lej'i•bli, *adv.* In a legible manner.

legion, lē'jon, *n.* [L. *legio,* from *lego,* to collect. LEGEND.] A body of ancient Roman infantry consisting at different periods of from 3000 to above 6000, often with a complement of cavalry; hence, a body of troops in general; a great number.—*Legion of honor,* an order instituted in France by Napoleon I, as a reward for merit, both civil and military, now greatly altered in character.—*American Legion,* veterans of World War I and World War II, organized Nov. 8, 1919, in the interests of fellowship, world peace, justice, freedom, democracy. Has state and national bodies.—*v.t.* To enroll or form into a legion.—**legionary,** lē'jon•a•ri, *a.* Belonging to a legion or legions.—*n.* One of a legion; a Roman soldier belonging to a legion.

legislate, lej'is•lāt, *v.i.*—*legislated, legislating.* [L. *lex, legis,* law, and *fero, latum,* to give, pass, or enact. LEGAL.] To make or enact a law or laws.—**legislation,** lej•is•lā'shon, *n.* The act of legislating or enacting laws; laws when enacted.—**legislative,** lej'is•lā•tiv, *a.* Enacting laws; having power or authority to enact laws; pertaining to the enacting of laws.—*n.* The branch of government which makes and repeals laws.—**legislatively,** lej'is•lā•tiv•li, *adv.* In a legislative manner.—**legislator,** lej'is•lā•tėr, *n.* A law giver; one who frames or establishes the laws and polity of a state or kingdom; a member of a national or supreme legislative assembly.—**legislature,** lej'is•lā•chėr, *n.* The body of men in a state or kingdom invested with power to make and repeal laws; the supreme legislating power of a state.—**legist,** lē'jist, *n.* One skilled in the laws.

legitimate, li•jit'i•mit, *a.* [L.L. *legitimatus,* from *legitimare,* to legitimate, from L. *legitimus,* lawful, from *lex,* law. LEGAL.] Lawfully begotten or born; born in wedlock; genuine; not false or spurious; following by logical or natural sequence; allowable (a *legitimate* argument or influence); rightful; *politics,* according to law or established usage; in a narrower sense, according to the doctrine of divine right.—*Legitimate drama,* drama or plays performed on the stage, as opposed to motion picture, vaudeville, or radio performances.—*v.t.*—*legitimated, legitimating.* To make lawful (*Mil.*); to render legitimate.—**legitimately,** li•jit'i•mit•li, *adv.* In a legitimate manner.—**legitimacy,** li•jit'i•ma•si, *n.* The state or quality of being legitimate.—**legitimation,** li•jit'i•mā"shon, *n.* The act of making or rendering legitimate.—**legitimatize,** li•jit'i•ma•tīz, *v.t.* To make legitimate.—**legitimism,** li•jit'im•izm, *n.* The principles of the legitimists.—**legitimist,** li•jit'i•mist, *n.* One who supports legitimate authority; one who believes in the sacredness of hereditary monarchies or the doctrine of divine right.—**legitimize,** li•jit'i•mīz, *v.t.*—*legitimized, legitimizing.* To legitimate.

legume, leg'ūm, *n.* [L. *legumen,* pulse—said to be from *lego,* to gather, because gathered and not cut. LEGEND.] *Bot.* a seed vessel of two valves, like the pod of a pea, in which the seeds are fixed to the ventral suture only; *pl.* the fruit of leguminous plants of the pea kind;

pulse.—**legumin,** leg'ū•min, *n.* A nitrogenous substance obtained from peas; vegetable casein.—**leguminous,** le•gū'mi•nus, *a. bot.*, bearing legumes.

lei, lā'i, lā, *n.* pl. **leis,** lā'ėz. [Hawaiian.] A wreath of leaves and flowers, etc., worn about the neck or head.

leister, lēs'tėr, *n.* [Icel. *ljóstr*, Sw. *ljustra*, a leister.] A pronged and barbed instrument for striking and taking fish; a salmon spear. (Scotch.)

leisure, lē'zhėr or lezh'ėr, *n.* [O.E. *leisere, leiser*, etc., Fr. *loisir*, from O.Fr. *leisir, loisir* (infin.), from L. *licere*, to be allowed, to be lawful; comp. *pleasure*, which is similarly formed. Akin *license*.] Freedom from occupation or business; vacant time; time free from employment; time which may be appropriated to any specific object.—*At leisure*, free from occupation; not engaged.—*At one's leisure*, at one's ease or convenience. —*a.* Not used or spent in labor or business; vacant: said of time.—**leisurely,** lē'zhėr•li or lezh'ėr•li, *adv.* Not in haste or hurry; slowly; at leisure.—*a.* Done at leisure; not hasty; deliberate.

leitmotiv, leitmotif, līt"mō•tēf', *n.* [G. *leitmotiv*, leading motive.] *Musical drama*, a theme or musical passage which signifies a particular character and recurs with his every appearance.

lemma, lem'ma, *n.* [Gr. *lemma*, from *lambanō*, to receive.] *Math.* a preliminary or preparatory proposition laid down and demonstrated for the purpose of facilitating something more important that follows.

lemming, lem'ing, *n.* [Dan.] A rodent mammal found in Norway, Lapland, Siberia, etc., vast hordes of which periodically migrate toward the sea, destroying all vegetation in their path.

lemon, lem'on, *n.* [Sp. *limon*, It. *limone*, Ar. *laymum*, Hind. *limu, limbu*.] A fruit resembling the orange, but having a much more acid pulp, and furnishing a cooling acid juice; the tree that produces lemons; a failure or dud.—*a.* Possessing the color of a lemon.—**lemonade,** lem•on•ād', *n.* A liquid consisting of lemon juice mixed with water and sweetened.—**lemon yellow,** *n.* A beautiful, vivid, light yellow color.

lemur, lē'mėr, *n.* [L., a spectre: so called from its nocturnal habits and stealthy step.] A name of certain small, arboreal, nocturnal mammals, family Lemuroidea, inhabiting Madagascar, allied to monkeys, insectivores, and rodents.—**lemures,** lem'ū•rēz, *n.* The ghosts or spirits of the dead, regarded as mischievous. —**lemuroid,** lem'ū•roid, *a.* Resembling the lemurs; belonging to the family or group of the lemurs.

lend, lend, *v.t.*—pret. & pp. *lent*. [A.Sax. *laenan*, to lend, from *laen*, a loan; Icel. *lana*, to lend. LOAN.] To grant to another for temporary use on condition of the thing or its equivalent in kind being returned; to afford, grant, or furnish in general (assistance, an ear to a discourse, etc.); *refl.* to accommodate; to give up so as to be of assistance (he *lent himself* to the scheme); to make a loan to be returned with interest over a period of time.—*v.i.* To make a loan or loans.—**lender,** len'dėr, *n.*

length, length, *n.* [A.Sax. *length*, from *lang*, long; comp. *strength*, from *strong*. LONG.] The longest measure of any object, in distinction from *depth, thickness, breadth*, or *width*, extent from end to end; one of the three dimensions of space; distance to a place; a portion of space considered as measured longwise; some definite long measure (to cut a rope into *lengths*); long continuance; duration of any extent in time; detail or amplification in language; extent, degree, height, as in conduct or action (to go to great *lengths*); extent of progress; one of the three fundamental conceptions (corresponding to space) represented by a fundamental unit. United States and British scientific unit, the foot; French, the centimeter.—*At length*, at or in the fullest extent; with amplitude of detail; at last; after a long period; at the end or conclusion. —**lengthen,** leng'thn, *v.t.* To make long or longer; to extend in length (often followed by *out*).—*v.i.* To grow longer.—**lengthily,** leng'thi•li, *adv.* In a lengthy manner.—**lengthiness,** leng'thi•nes, *n.* The state of being lengthy.—**lengthwise,** length•wīz, *adv.* In the direction of the length; in a longitudinal direction.—**lengthy,** leng'thi, *a.* Long or moderately long; protracted, as a *lengthy* discourse.

lenient, lē'ni•ent, *a.* [L. *leniens*, from *lenio*, to soften, from *lenis*, soft, mild; akin *lentus*, slow (in *relent*).] Softening‡; mitigating‡; acting without rigor or severity; gentle; merciful; clement.—**leniently,** lē'ni•ent•li, *adv.* In a lenient manner.—**lenience, leniency,** lē'ni•ens, lē'ni•en•si, *n.* The quality of being lenient; clemency.—**lenitive,** len'i•tiv, *a.* Having the quality of softening or mitigating, as pain; assuasive; emollient.—*n.* A medicine or application of this kind.—**lenity,** len'i•ti, *n.* [L. *lenitas*.] Gentleness; clemency; tenderness; mercy.

lens, lenz, *n.* pl. **lenses,** len'zez. [L. *lens*, a lentil—a convex lens somewhat resembles a lentil seed.] A transparent substance, usually glass, with one or both sides curved so that rays of light passing through it are made to change their direction, and thus cause objects to appear magnified or diminished in size; one of the glasses of a telescope, microscope, etc.; a part of the eye which focuses light rays.

lent, lent, pret. and pp. of *lend*.

Lent, lent, *n.* [A.Sax. *lencten*, spring, *lencten-faesten*, spring fast, Lent; D. *lente*, G. *lenz*, spring; perhaps connected with *long*, the days becoming longer in spring.] A fast of forty days, beginning at Ash Wednesday and continuing till Easter, observed in the Christian Church in commemoration of the forty days' fast of Christ.—**Lenten,** len'ten, *a.* Pertaining to Lent; as meager as the fasting diet of Lent; hence, spare; plain (*lenten* fare).

lenticel, len'ti•sel, *n.* [Fr. *lenticelle*, L. *lenticula*, dim. of *lens, lentis*, a lentil. LENS.] *Bot.* one of the small oval spots found on the surface of young stems; a small lens-shaped gland on the under side of some leaves.—**lenticular,** len•tik'ū•lėr, *a.* [L. *lenticularis*.] Resembling a lentil in size or form; having the form of a double-convex lens.—**lentoid,** len'toid, *a.* Of the form of a lens; lenticular.

lentigo, len•tī'gō, *n.* [L. *lentigo*, a freckle, from L. *lens, lentis*, a lentil.] *Med.* a freckly eruption on the skin. —**lentiginous,** len•tij'i•nus, *a.* Pertaining to lentigo; freckly; scurfy.

lentil, len'til, *n.* [Fr. *lentille*, from L. *lens, lentil*, a lentil. LENS.] An annual pea-like leguminous plant cultivated in Egypt and Palestine from remote antiquity, having seeds used in soups, etc., and forming a very nutritious diet.

lento, len'tō. [It., from L. *lentus*, slow.] *Mus.* a direction that the music is to be performed slowly.

l'envoi, l'envoy, len'voi, *n.* [Fr. ENVOY.] A sort of postscript appended to literary compositions.

Leo, lē'ō, *n.* [L., a lion.] The Lion, the fifth sign of the zodiac.—**Leonides,** lē•on'i•dēz, *n. pl.* A name for the group of meteors observed annually in November, which seem to radiate from the constellation *Leo*.—**leonine,** lē'o•nīn, *a.* [L. *leoninus*.] Belonging to a lion; resembling a lion or partaking of his qualities.—**leoninely,** lē'o•nīn•li, *adv.* In a leonine manner; like a lion.

Leonine, lē'o•nīn, *a.* [From *Leon* or *Leoninus*, an ecclesiastic of the twelfth century, who wrote largely in this measure.] A term applied to a certain Latin measure popular in the middle ages, consisting of hexameter and pentameter verses, rhyming at the middle and end.

leopard, lep'ėrd, *n.* [L. *leo*, lion, and *pardus*, a panther.] A carnivorous animal of the cat genus, inhabiting Africa, Iran, China, and India, of a yellowish-fawn color variegated with dark spots.

leotard, lē'o•tärd, *n.* [From *Léotard*, a French aerial gymnast.] A close-fitting garment with or without sleeves worn by acrobats, dancers, etc.; tights.

leper, lep'ėr, *n.* [Fr. *lepre*, L. *lepra*, from Gr. *lepra*, leprosy, from *lepros*, scaly, connected with *lepos*, a husk.] A person affected with leprosy; a social outcast.—**leprosy,** lep'ro•si, *n.* An infectious disease characterized by dusky red or livid tubercules on the face, ears, and extremities, thickened or rugose state of the skin, loss of fingers and toes, etc., eventually causing death.—**leprous,** lep'rus, *a.*

lepidolite, lep'i•do•līt, *n.* [Gr. *lepis, lepidos*, a scale, and *lithos*, a stone.] A mineral found in scaly masses, ordinarily of a violet or lilac color, allied to mica.

lepidopterous, lepidopteral, lep•-

i•dop'tėr•us, lep•i•dop'tėr•al, *a.* [Gr. *lepis*, a scale, and *pteron*, a wing.] Of or belonging to the order of insects called Lepidoptera (lep•i•dop'tėr•a), comprising the butterflies and moths.

lepidosiren, lep'i•do•sī"ren, *n.* [Gr. *lepis*, *lepidos*, a scale, and *seirēn*, a siren.] A fish found in western Africa and South America, having both gills and lungs, and being thus enabled to lie packed in the mud of their native rivers during the dry season. Called also *mudfish*.

lepidote, lep'i•dōt, *a.* [Gr. *lepidōtos*, scaly, from *lepis*, a scale.] *Bot.* covered with scurfy scaly spots.

leporine, lep'o•rīn, *a.* [L. *leporinus*, from *lepus*, *leporis*, a hare.] Pertaining to a hare; having the qualities of the hare.

lepra, lep'ra, *n.* [L., leprosy.] *Med.* a non-contagious skin disease, in which scales occur, generally on the limbs.—**leprose,** lep'rōs, *a. Bot.* having a scurfy appearance.

leprechaun, lep'ri•kon, *n.* [Ir. *luprecān*, *lugharcān*, from Ir. *luchrupān*, from *lu*, little, and *corpān*, dim. of *corp*, body, from L. *corpus*.] *Irish folklore*, a small fairy, thought of as a sly tricky old man who, if caught, will point out a treasure.

leprosy, leprous, etc. See LEPER.

leptodactylous, lep•tō•dak'ti•lus, *a.* [Gr. *leptos*, slender, *daktylos*, a digit.] Having slender toes.

Lesbian, lez'bi•an, *a.* [Gr. Island of Lesbos.] Addicted to the unnatural vice attributed to Sappho.

lese-majesty, lēz'maj•is•ti, *n.* [Fr. *lèsemajesté*, high treason, from L. *laesa majestas*, *laedo*, *laesum*, to injure, and *majestas*, majesty.] Any crime committed against the sovereign power in a state; treason.

lesion, lē'zhon, *n.* [L. *læsio*, from *lædo*, to hurt; seen also in *collide*, *elide*.] *Med.* injury; a morbid change in the texture or substance of organs.

less, les, *a.* serving as the comparative of *little*. [A.Sax. *læs*, *læssa*; O.Fris. *lessa*; allied to Goth. *lasiws*, weak, Icel. *lasinn*, feeble; the superl. *least*. *Little* is from a different root. Hence *lest*.] Smaller; not so large or great.—*adv*. In a smaller or lower degree.—*n*. Not so much; a quantity not so great as another quantity; what is below a certain standard.—*No less*, nothing of inferior consequence or moment; nothing else.—**lessen,** les'n, *v.t.* To make less or smaller; to diminish; to reduce; to reduce in dignity; to depreciate; to disparage.—*v.i.* To become less or smaller; to decrease or diminish.—**lesser,** les'ėr, *a.* [A double compar. from *less*.] Less; smaller; especially common with the definite article, and where there is opposition to *greater*: not used in comparisons with *than*.—*adv*. Less. (*Shak.*)

lessee, les•sē', *n.* [LEASE.] The person to whom a lease is given.—**lessor,** les•sor', *n.* One who leases or lets to a tenant for a term of years.

lesson, les'n, *n.* [Fr. *leçon*, from L. *lectio*, *lectionis*, from L. *lego*, *lectum*, to read. LEGEND.] Anything read or recited to a teacher by a pupil or learner; what is assigned by a preceptor to a pupil to be learned at one time; something to be learned; piece of instruction conveyed; what is learned or may be learned from experience; a portion of Scripture read in divine service; a doctrine or notion inculcated; a precept; a reproof or rebuke.

lessor. See LESSEE.

lest, lest, *conj.* [O.E. *leste*, for *les the*, shortened from A.Sax. *thý*, *læs the*, the, less that, lest—*thý*, by that (=*the* in *the* more, etc.), *læs*=*less*, *the*, indeclinable relative.] For fear that; in case; that . . . not.

let, let, *v.t.*—*let* (pret. & pp.), *letting*. [A.Sax. *laetan*, *lǽtan*=D. *laten*, Icel. *láta*, Goth. *letan*, G. *lassen*; allied to E. *late*, and L. *lassus*, weary.] To permit; to allow; to suffer; to give leave; not to prevent; to lease; to grant possession and use of for a compensation.—In such phrases as *let us* go, *let* often expresses merely a suggestion for mutual action, in *let him* go, etc., it often has the force of a command. (When *let* governs an infinitive the latter never takes *to*.)—*To let alone*, to leave untouched; to suffer to remain without intermeddling.—*To let be*, to suffer to be as at present; to let alone.—*To let blood*, to open a vein and suffer the blood to flow.—*To let down*, to permit to sink or fall; to lower.—*To let drive* or *let fly*, to send forth or discharge with violence, as an arrow, stone, etc.—*To let go*, to allow or suffer to go; to relax hold of anything.—*To let in* or *into*, to permit or suffer to enter; to admit; to place in as an insertion.—*To let loose*, to free from restraint; to permit to wander at large.—*To let off*, to allow to escape; to release, as from a penalty or an engagement; to discharge, as an arrow; to fire, as a gun.—*To let out*, to allow to issue; to suffer to escape; to extend; to lease or let on hire.—*To let slip*, to let go from one's hold; to let loose; to lose (an opportunity) by negligence.—*To let well alone*, to forbear trying to improve what is already satisfactory.—*v.i.* To yield a certain rent by being hired out; to be taken on hire.—*To let in*, to leak; to admit water.

lethal, lē'thal, *a.* [L. *lethalis*, *letalis*, mortal, from *letum*, death.] Deadly; mortal; fatal.

lethargy, leth'är•ji, *n.* [L. *lethargia*, from Gr. *lēthargia*, oblivion, *lēthargos*, forgetful, from *lēthē*, oblivion.] Unnatural sleepiness; morbid drowsiness; profound sleep, from which a person can scarcely be awaked; dullness; inaction; inattention.—**lethargic, lethargical,** le•thär'jik, le•thär'ji•kal, *a.* Affected with lethargy; morbidly inclined to sleep; dull; heavy; pertaining to lethargy.—**lethargically,** le•thär'ji•kal•li, *adv.* In a lethargic manner.—**lethargize,** leth'ėr•jīz, *v.t.* To render lethargic.

Lethe, lē'thē, *n.* [Gr. *lethē*, forgetfulness; akin L. *lateo*, to lie hid.] *Greek myth.* the river of oblivion; one of the streams of the infernal regions; hence, oblivion; a draft of oblivion.—**Lethean,** lē•thē'an, *a.* Pertaining to the river Lethe; inducing forgetfulness or oblivion.

Lett, let, *n.* A member of a race inhabiting the Baltic provinces of Russia.—**Lettish, Lettic,** let'ish, let'ik, *a.* Pertaining to the Letts.—*n.* The language spoken by the Letts, one of the Aryan tongues.

letter, let'ėr, *n.* [Fr. *lettre*, from L. *litera*, a letter.] A mark or character used as the representative of a sound; a character standing for a vowel or a consonant; a written or printed message; an epistle; *printing*, a single type or character; also types collectively; *pl.* learning; erudition (a man of *letters*).—*The letter*, neither more nor less than what words literally express; the literal or verbal meaning.—*v.t.* To impress or form letters on (to *letter* a book).—**letter carrier,** *n.* A man who carries about and delivers letters; a postman.—**letterhead,** *n.* A heading engraved on stationery; paper having such engraving.—**lettering,** let'ėr•ing, *n.* The act of impressing letters; the letters impressed.—**letterpress,** *n.* Words impressed by types; print.

Lettish, Lettic, *a.* and *n.* See LETT.

lettuce, let'is, *n.* [From L. *lactuca*, a lettuce; from *lac*, *lactis*, milk (as in *lacteal*).] The popular name of several species of annual composite plants, the leaves of some of which are used as salads.

leucine, leucin, lū'sin, *n.* [Gr. *leukos*, white.] A white pulverulent substance obtained by treating muscular fiber with sulfuric acid, and afterward with alcohol.—**leucite,** lū'sīt, *n.* A mineral, so called from its whiteness, found among volcanic products.

leucocyte, lūk'o•sīt, *n.* [Gr. *leukos*, white, *kytos*, a cell.] A white or colorless blood corpuscle.—**leucocytosis,** lūk'o•sīt•ō"sis, *n.* [Gr. *leukos*, *kytos*.] An increase in the number of leucocytes in the blood, esp. as in certain pathologic conditions: fevers, anemia, etc.—**leukemia,** lū•kē'mia, *n.* [Gr. *leukos*, white, *kytos*, a cell, and *haima*, blood.] *Med.* A fatal disease in which there is a pronounced increase in the number of leucocytes, attended by progressive anemia and complications.

leucoma, lū•kō'ma, *n.* [Gr. *leukōma*, from *leukos*, white.] A white opacity of the cornea of the eye, the result of acute inflammation.

leucorrhea, lū•ko•rē'a, *n.* [Gr. *leukos*, and *rheo*, to flow.] *Med.* a morbid discharge of a white or yellowish mucus from the female genital organs; the whites.

Levant, le•vant', *n.* [It. *levante*, the east, the direction of sunrise, from L. *levare*, to raise, *se levare*, to rise. LEVITY.] The eastern portion of the Mediterranean and its seaboard or the contiguous countries, as Syria, Asia Minor, Egypt, etc.—**Levanter,** le•van'tėr, *n.* A wind in the Mediterranean from the direction of the

Levant.—**Levantine,** le•van′tin or lev′an•tīn, *a.* Pertaining to the Levant.—*n.* A native of the Levant; [*not cap.*] a particular kind of silk cloth.

levant, le•vant′, *v.i.* [Sp. *levantar,* to raise, to remove; *levantar la casa,* to break up house—from L. *levare,* to raise. See above.] To run away; to decamp; to run away without paying debts.—**levanter,** le•van′tėr, *n.* One who levants.

levator, le•vā′tėr, *n.* [L., what raises, from *levo,* to raise.] *Anat.* a name applied to many muscles, such as raise the lips, eyelids, etc.; a surgical instrument used to raise a depressed part of the skull.

levee, lev′ē, *n.* [Fr. *lever,* a rising, a levee or reception; *levée,* a levy, an embankment. from *lever,* L. *levare,* to raise, from *levis,* light. LEVITY.] A morning reception of visitors held by a prince or great personage; any similar assemblage; in America, an embankment on the margin of a river, to confine it within its natural channel.

level, lev′el, *n.* [O.Fr. *level, livel* (now *niveau*), from L. *libella,* dim. of *libra,* a level, a balance; akin *deliberate, equilibrium.*] An instrument by which to find or draw a straight line parallel to the plane of the horizon; a line or surface which coincides with the plane of the horizon; a surface without inequalities; usual elevation; customary height; equal elevation with something else; a state of equality; natural position; position to which anything is entitled; *mining,* a horizontal gallery in a mine.—*a.* Horizontal; coinciding with the plane of the horizon, or parallel to it; not having one part higher than another; even; flat; on the same line or plane; equal in rank or degree; having no degree of superiority; well-balanced; steady; honest; fair in dealings; trustworthy.—*v.t.*—*leveled, leveling.* To make level; to remove inequalities of surface in; to bring to ground level; to reduce to equality of condition, state, or degree; to point, in taking aim; to aim; to direct or point at.—*v.i.* To bring to a level; to deal frankly with.—*v.i.* To point a gun or the like at the mark; to aim.—**leveler,** lev′el•ėr, *n.* One who levels; one who would destroy social and political distinctions, in advocating equality.—**level-headed,** *a.* Of sound judgment.—**leveling,** lev′el•ing, *n.* The act of one who levels; the art or operation of ascertaining the different elevations of objects on the surface of the earth, as in surveying.—**leveling pole, leveling rod, leveling staff,** *n.* An instrument used in leveling in conjunction with a spirit level and telescope.—**levelly,** lev′el•li, *adv.* In a level manner; evenly.—**levelness,** lev′el•nes, *n.* The condition of being level; evenness.

lever, lē′vėr, *n.* [Fr. *levier,* from *lever,* L. *levare,* to raise. LEVITY.] A bar of metal, wood, or other substance turning on a support called the fulcrum or prop, and used to overcome a certain resistance (called the weight), encountered at one part of the bar, by means of a force (called the power) applied at another part; a watch having a vibrating lever to connect the action of the escape wheel with that of the balance.—**leverage,** lē′vėr•ij, *n.* The action of a lever; lever power; the mechanical advantage or power gained by using a lever.

leveret, lev′ėr•et, *n.* [Fr. *levrette,* dim. of O.Fr. *levre* (now *lièvre*), a hare, from L. *lepus, leporis,* a hare.] A hare in the first year of its age.

leviable. See LEVY.

leviathan, le•vī′a•than, *n.* [Heb. *livyāthān,* a long jointed monster.] An aquatic animal described in the book of Job, ch. xli; a fabulous sea monster of immense size; a large political state run by a totalitarian bureaucracy and the machinery of coercion; something large and formidable.

levigate, lev′i•gāt, *v.t.*—*levigated, levigating.* [L. *lævigo,* from *lævis,* smooth.] To make smooth; to polish; to rub or grind to a fine impalpable powder, especially with the use of a liquid.—**levigation,** lev•i•gā′shon, *n.* The operation of grinding or rubbing a solid substance to a fine impalpable powder.

levirate, leviratical, lev′i•rāt, lev•i•rat′i•kal, *a.* [L. *levir,* a husband's brother; akin Gr. *daēr.*] Pertaining to marriage with a husband's brother; applied to the Jewish law according to which a woman whose husband died without issue was to be married to the husband's brother.—**leviration,** lev•i•rā′shon, *n.* Marriage according to the levirate law.

levitate, lev′i•tāt, *v.t.* [L. *levitas,* lightness, from *levis,* light.] To cause to become buoyant in the atmosphere; to cause to float in the air.—**levitation,** lev•i•tā′shon, *n.* The act of making light or buoyant; lightness; buoyancy.

Levite, lē′vīt, *n.* [From *Levi,* one of the sons of Jacob.] In *Jewish history,* one of the tribe or family of Levi; a descendant of Levi; more particularly, an inferior or subordinate priest.—**Levitical,** le•vit′i•kal, *a.* Belonging to or connected with the Levites; priestly.—*Levitical degrees,* degrees of kindred within which persons are prohibited (in the book of Leviticus) to marry.—**Leviticus,** le•vit′i•kus, *n.* A book of the Old Testament containing the ceremonial law or the laws and regulations relating to the priests and Levites and to offerings.

levity, lev′i•ti, *n.* [L. *levitas,* from *levis,* light; akin to E. *light,* G. *leicht,* easy, slight, Gr. *elachys,* small. L. *levis* gives *lever, levy, elevate, alleviate, relieve,* etc.] Lightness; especially lightness of temper or conduct; want of seriousness; disposition to trifle; fickleness; capriciousness; volatility.

levogyrate, lē•vo•jī′rāt, *a.* [L. *lævus,* left, *gyro,* to turn. GYRE.] Turning rays to the left in the polarization of light: said of crystals; opposite of *dextrogyrate.*

levulose, lev′ū•lōs, *n.* [L. *lævus,* left, and *ule* and *ose.*] Fructose; fruit sugar, $C_6H_{12}O_6$, obtained from honey and most sweet fruits.

levy, lev′i, *n.* [Fr. *levée,* from *lever,* L. *levare,* to raise. LEVITY, LEVEE.] The act of raising, collecting, or enlisting troops; the raising of taxes; that which is levied; a body of troops raised.—*v.t.*—*levied, levying.* To raise or enlist (troops); to collect (taxes).—*To levy war,* to raise or begin war; to raise troops for attack.—**leviable,** lev′i•a•bl, *a.* Capable of being levied.—**levier,** lev′i•ėr, *a.* One who levies.

lewd, lūd, *a.* [O.E. *lewed,* A.Sax. *laewed,* lay, ignorant, pp. of *laewan,* to weaken, to betray; akin Icel. *læ,* Goth. *lew,* craft.] Vile, despicable, profligate, or wicked (*N.T.*); given or pertaining to the unlawful indulgence of lust; lustful; libidinous; lascivious.—**lewdly,** lūd′li, *adv.* In a lewd manner.—**lewdness,** lūd′nes, *n.* The state or quality of being lewd; lechery; lasciviousness.

Lewis machine gun, lū′is ma•shēn′ gun, *n.* An automatic rifle, gas-operated and air-cooled, capable of firing forty-seven rounds without reloading.

lexicon, lek′si•kon, *n.* [Gr. *lexicon,* from *lexis,* a speaking, speech, a word, from *legō,* to speak. LEGEND.] A dictionary; a book containing an alphabetical arrangement of the words in a language, with the definition or an explanation of the meaning of each; usually applied to dictionaries of the Greek or Hebrew tongues.—**lexical,** lek′si•kal, *a.* Pertaining to a lexicon.—**lexicographer,** lek•si•kog′ra•fėr, *n.* The author or compiler of a lexicon or dictionary.—**lexicographic, lexicographical,** lek′-si•ko•graf″ik, lek′si•ko•graf″i•kal, *a.* Pertaining to lexicons or lexicography.—**lexicography,** lek•si•kog′ra•fi, *n.* The act or art of compiling a lexicon or dictionary; the occupation of composing dictionaries.—**lexigraphic, lexigraphical,** lek•si•graf′ik, lek•si•graf′i•kal, *a.* Pertaining to lexicography.

Leyden jar, lī′dn, *n.* [So named from having been invented at *Leyden,* Holland.] A glass phial or jar coated inside and outside, usually with tinfoil, to within a third of the top, that it may be readily charged with electricity.

leze majesty, lez′maj•is•ti, *n.* See LESE-MAJESTY.

liable, lī′a•bl, *a.* [Either from the verb to *lie,* with the sense of lying open or subject to, or from Fr. *lier,* to bind, and hence akin to *ally, lien.* Comp. *rely* and *reliable.*] Answerable for consequences; bound to make good a loss; responsible; apt or not unlikely to incur something undesirable; subject; exposed; with *to.* ∴*Liable* is used chiefly with regard to what may befall; *subject* to what is likely to do so, and does so customarily.—**liability,** lī•a•bil′i•ti, *n.* The state of being liable; that for which one is liable; *pl.* sums or amounts which one is under obligation to pay; debts.—*Limited Liability*.—See LIMITED.

liaison, lē•ā•zoṅ′, *n.* [Fr., from L. *ligatio*, a binding, from L. *ligare*, to bind. LIGAMENT.] A bond of union; an entanglement; commonly, an illicit intimacy between a man and a woman.—*Liaison officer*, an officer employed in linking up troops under different commands.

liana, li•ä′na, *n.* [Fr. *liane*, from *lier*, L. *ligare*, to bind; akin *lien*. LIAISON.] A term applied to the larger climbing and twining plants in tropical forests.

liar, lī′ėr, *n.* See LIE.

Lias, lī′as, *n.* [Fr. *liais*, O.Fr. *liois*, Arm. *liach*, Gael. *leac*, a stone.] *Geol.* that series of strata, consisting principally of thin layers of limestone embedded in thick masses of blue argillaceous clay, lying at the basis of the oölitic series, and above the triassic or new red sandstone.

libation, li•bā′shon, *n.* [L. *libatio*, *libationis*, from *libō*, to taste, to make libation; Gr. *leibō*; same root as *liquid*.] The act of pouring a liquid, usually wine, either on the ground or on a victim in sacrifice, in honor of some deity; a portion of wine or other liquor poured out in honor of a deity by the person who is to drink.

libel, lī′bel, *n.* [Fr. *libelle*, L. *libellus*, a libel or lampoon, lit. a little book, dim. of *liber*, the inner bark or rind of a tree used for paper, and hence a book; akin *library*.] A defamatory writing; a malicious publication containing representations tending to bring a person into contempt, or expose him to public hatred or derision; *law*, the writ commencing a suit and containing the plaintiff's allegations.—*v.t.*—*libeled*, *libeling*. To publish a libel against; to defame by libel; to lampoon.—**libelant,** lī′bel•ant, *n.* One who brings a libel in a court.—**libeler,** lī′bel•ėr, *n.* One who libels; a lampooner.—**libelous,** lī′bel•us, *a.* Containing matter of the nature of a libel; defamatory.—**libelously,** lī′bel•us•li. *adv.* In a libelous manner.

liberal, lib′ėr•al, *a.* [L. *liberalis*, from *liber*, free; akin to *libet*, *lubet*, it pleases, it is agreeable, Skr. *lubh*, to desire. L. *liber* gives also *liberate*, *liberty*, *libertine*, *livery*, *deliver*.] Befitting a freeman or one wellborn (the *liberal* arts, a *liberal* education); of a free heart; bountiful; generous; giving largely, ample, large, abundant, profuse (donation, supply, etc.); not characterized by selfish, narrow, or contracted ideas or feelings; favorable to civil, political, and religious liberty; favorable to reform or progress, and in politics often opposed to *conservative*; not too literal or strict; free. It is used in various self-explanatory compounds; as, *liberal*-hearted; *liberal*-minded; *liberal*-souled.—*n.* An advocate of freedom from restraint, especially in politics and religion; a member of that party which advocates progressive reform.—*Liberal Arts*, the modern curriculum of an undergraduate academic or collegiate education, as distinguished from professional training; the languages, science, history and philosophy which are the requisites for a baccalaureate degree.—**liberalism,** lib′ėr•al•izm, *n.* Liberal principles; the principles or practice of Liberals.—**liberality,** lib•ėr•al′i•ti, *n.* [L. *liberalitas*; Fr. *liberalité*.] The quality of being liberal; largeness of mind or view; disposition to give largely; munificence; generosity; a particular act of generosity (in this sense with a plural).—**liberalize,** lib′ėr•al•īz, *v.t.*—*liberalized*, *liberalizing*. To render liberal; to free from narrow views or prejudices.—**liberally,** lib′ėr•al•li, *adv.* In a liberal manner.

liberate, lib′ėr•āt, *v.t.*—*liberated*, *liberating*. [L. *libero*, *liberatum*, from *liber*, free. LIBERAL.] To release from restraint or bondage; to set at liberty; to free; to deliver; to disengage.—**liberation,** lib•ėr•ā•shon, *n.* [L. *liberatio*.] The act of liberating.—**liberator,** lib′er•ā•tėr, *n.* One who liberates.

libertarian. See LIBERTY.

liberticide, lib′ėr•ti•sīd, *n.* [*Liberty*, and L. *cædo*, to kill.] Destruction of liberty; a destroyer of liberty.

libertine, lib′ėr•tēn, *n.* [L. *libertinus*, a freedman, from *liber*, free. LIBERAL.] A freedman or manumitted slave (N.T.); one unconfined; one free from restraint (*Shak.*); one who indulges his lust without restraint; one who leads a dissolute, licentious life; a rake.—*a.* Licentious; dissolute.—**libertinism,** lib′ėr•tin•izm, *n.* The conduct of a libertine or rake.

liberty, lib′ėr•ti, *n.* [Fr. *liberté*, L. *libertas*, from *liber*, free. LIBERAL.] The state or condition of one who is free; exemption from restraint; power of acting as one pleases; freedom; permission granted to do something; leave; immunity enjoyed; a special privilege or exemption; a place or district within which certain exclusive privileges may be exercised; freedom of action or speech beyond the ordinary bounds of civility or decorum; freedom from occupation or engagements; state of being disengaged.—*Liberty of the press*, the free power of publishing what one pleases, subject only to punishment for publishing what is mischievous to the public or injurious to individuals.—*Cap of liberty*, a cap or hat used as a symbol of liberty; a red cap worn by French revolutionaries. ∴ Syn. See LEAVE.—**libertarian,** lib•ėr•tâ′ri•an, *a.* Pertaining to the doctrine of free will, as opposed to the doctrine of necessity.—*n.* One who holds the doctrine of the freedom of the will.—**libertarianism,** lib•ėr•tâ′ri•an•izm, *n.* The principles or doctrines of libertarians.

libidinous, li•bid′i•nus, *a.* [L. *libidinosus*, from *libido*, *lubido*, lust, from *libet*, *lubet*, it pleases. LIBERAL.] Characterized by lust or lewdness; having an eager appetite for sexual indulgence; fitted to excite lustful desire; lustful; lewd.—**libidinously,** li•bid′i•nus•li, *adv.* In a libidinous manner.—**libidinousness,** li•bid′i•nus•nes, *n.* The quality of being libidinous; lustfulness.

Libra, lī′bra, *n.* [L., a balance.] The Balance, the seventh sign in the zodiac, which the sun enters at the autumnal equinox in September.

library, lī′bra•ri, *n.* [L. *librarium*, a bookcase, *libraria*, a bookseller's shop, from *liber*, a book. LIBEL.] A collection of books belonging to a private person or to a public institution, etc.; an apartment, suite of apartments, or a whole building appropriated to the keeping of a collection of books.—**librarian,** lī•brâ′ri•an, *n.* The keeper of a library.

librate, lī′brāt, *v.t.*—*librated*, *librating*. [L. *libro*, *libratum*, from *libra*, a balance, a level. LEVEL.] To hold in equipoise; to poise; to balance.—*v.i.* To balance; to be poised.—**libration,** lī•brā′shon, *n.* The act of balancing; a state of equipoise; *astron.* a real or apparent motion like that of a balance before coming to rest; an apparent irregularity of the moon's motion, whereby those parts very near the border of the lunar disk alternately become visible and invisible.—**libratory,** lī′bra•to•ri, *a.*

libretto, lē•bret′tō, *n.* [It., a little book. LIBEL, LIBRARY.] A book containing the words of an extended musical composition, as an opera; the musical text itself.—**librettist,** li•bret′ist, *n.*

lice, līs, *n.* pl. of *louse*.

license, lī′sens, *n.* [Fr. *license*, from L. *licentia*, from *licet*, it is permitted (seen also in *illicit*, *leisure*); akin to *linquo*, to leave.] Authority given to act in a particular way; power conferred upon a person by proper authority, to do particular acts, practice in professions, conduct certain trades, etc.; the document containing such authority; excess of liberty; undue freedom; freedom abused or used in contempt of law or decorum; deviation from an artistic standard.—**license,** *v.t.*—*licensed*, *licensing*. To permit or empower by license; to grant a license to.—**licensee,** lī•sen•sē′, *n.* One to whom a license is granted.—**licenser,** lī′sen•sėr, *n.* One who licenses.—**licentiate,** lī•sen′shi•āt, *n.* One who has a license to practice some profession; a person licensed in medicine or theology; in Scottish church, one licensed but not ordained to a charge; a probationer; corresponding largely to the French *abbé*.—**licentious,** lī•sen′shus, *a.* [L. *licentiosus*.] Characterized by license; overpassing due bounds; loose in behavior; profligate; dissolute; libidinous.—**licentiously,** lī•sen′shus•li, *adv.* In a licentious manner.—**licentiousness,** lī•sen′shus•nes, *n.*

lichen, lī′ken, *n.* [Gr. *leichēn*, the plant, the disease, from *leichō*, to lick.] *Bot.* one of the group of thallophyte plants, a fungus and alga in symbiotic association, growing on the bark of trees, etc., and including rock moss, tree moss, etc.; *med.* an eruption of small pimples, of a red or white color, clustered together or spread over the surface of the skin.—**lichenous,** lī′ken•us or lich′-en•us, *a.* Relating to or covered with lichens; pertaining to the disease called lichen.

lich gate, lich′gāt, *n.* [Lit. corpse-gate, from A.Sax. *lic,* Icel. *lik,* Goth, *leik,* form, body; G. *leiche,* a corpse. Akin *like.*] A church-yard gate, with a porch under which a bier might stand while the introductory part of the service was read.

licit,† lis′it, *a.* [L. *licitus,* lawful, from *liceo,* to be permitted. LICENSE.] Lawful.—**licitly,**† lis′it•li, *adv.* Lawfully.

lick, lik, *v.t.* [A.Sax. *liccian*=D. *likken,* Dan. *likke,* G. *lecken,* Goth. *laigon* (in *bilaigon*); cog. Ir. *lighim,* L. *lingo,* Gr. *leichō,* Skr. *lih,* to lick. Akin *lecher, lickerish.*] To pass or draw the tongue over the surface of; to lap; to take in by the tongue; to flog, beat, or conquer (*colloq.*).—*To lick up,* to devour; to consume entirely (O.T.).—*To lick the dust,* to be slain; to perish in battle; to act abjectly and servilely.—*To lick into shape,* to give form or method to, from the old notion that the young bear is born shapeless and its mother licks it into shape.—*n.* A rubbing or drawing of the tongue over anything; a slight smear or coat, as of paint; a blow or stroke (*colloq.*).—**lickspit,** lik′spit, *n.* A flatterer or parasite of the most abject character.

lickerish, lik′ėr•ish, *a.* [From the stem *lick,* and akin to *lecher, lecherous;* comp. G. *lecker,* lickerish, dainty, delicate.] Nice in the choice of food; dainty; eager to taste or enjoy; appetizing.—**lickerishness,** lik′ėr•ish•nes, *n.* The quality of being lickerish.

licorice, lik′or•is, *n.* [Fr. *liquerice,* [L.L. *liquiritia,* from Gr. *glykyrrhiza—glykys,* sweet, and *rhiza,* root.] A perennial plant of the bean family, the roots of which supply a sweet juice.

lictor, lik′tor, *n.* [L., from *ligare,* to bind.] A Roman officer whose ensigns of office were an ax and fasces, and who attended the chief magistrates in public.

lid, lid, *n.* [A.Sax. *hlid,* lid, cover, protection; D. *lid,* O.Fris. *hlid, lid,* G. *lied,* as in *augen-lied,* an eyelid; Icel. *hlith,* a gate, gateway, interval; allied to L. *claudo,* to shut.] A movable cover for the opening of a vessel, box, etc.; the cover of the eye; the eyelid.—**lidless,** lid′les, *a.* Having no lid.

lie, lī, *v.i.*—*lied, lying.* [A.Sax. *leógan* =D. *liegen,* Goth. *liugan,* Icel. *ljúga,* G. *lügen,* to lie; comp. Gael. *leog,* idle talk.] To utter falsehood with an intention to deceive; to knowingly utter untruth.—*n.* [A. Sax. *lige, lyge,* a lie, from *leógan,* to lie; acel. *lygi,* D. *logen,* G. *lüge,* a lie.] A falsehood uttered for the purpose of deception; an intentional violation of truth.—*To give the lie to,* to charge with falsehood; to prove to be false; to belie.—**liar,** lī′ėr, *n.* One who lies or tells lies; a person who knowingly utters falsehood; one who declares to be a fact what he knows is not.

lie, lī, *v.i.*—pret. *lay;* pp. *lain* (*lien,* obsolete); ppr. *lying.* [A.Sax. *licgan,* to lie (of which *lecgan,* to lay, is a causative)=Goth. *ligan,* D. *liggen,* Dan. *ligge,* acel. *liggja,* G. *liegen,* to lie; same root as L. *lectus,* Gr. *lechos,* a bed, also seen in L. *lex,* E. *law; ledge, layer, lair,* etc., being also akin.] To occupy a horizontal or nearly horizontal position; to rest lengthwise, or be flat upon the surface of anything; to be placed and remain without motion; to lay or place one's self in a horizontal or nearly horizontal position: often with *down;* to be in bed; to sleep or pass the night; to lean or recline; to be situated; to have place or position (Ireland *lies* west of England); to be posted or encamped, as an army; to remain or be in some condition: with words denoting the particular condition (to *lie* waste, to *lie* fallow, to *lie* open, to *lie* hid, etc.); to be present or contained; to be found; to exist; to depend (it does not *lie in* my power; success *lies* in vigilance); to weigh or press; to be sustainable in law; to be capable of being maintained (an action will not *lie*).—*To lie at one's heart,* to be an object of affection, desire, or anxiety.—*To lie by,* to rest untouched or unnoticed.—*To lie hard* or *heavy,* to press; to oppress; to burden.—*To lie in,* to be in childbed.—*To lie in the way,* to be an obstacle or impediment.—*To lie in wait,* to wait in ambush or concealment.—*To lie on* or *upon,* to be incumbent on; to be a matter of obligation or duty; to depend on.—*To lie on hand, to lie on one's hands,* to be or remain unsold or undisposed of.—*To lie over,* to remain for future attention; to be deferred to some future occasion, as a motion or resolution in a deliberate assembly.—*To lie to, naut.* to stop in her course and remain stationary, as a ship.—*To lie under,* to be subject to; to suffer; to be oppressed by.—*To lie with,* to lodge or sleep with; to have carnal knowledge of; to belong to (it *lies with* you to make amends). [The trans. verb *to lay* is often erroneously used for *to lie.* This is a gross blunder which should be carefully avoided, and may easily be so by attending to the meaning and conjugation of the two verbs. *To lay* is always transitive, and has for its preterit *laid;* as, he told me to *lay* it down, and I *laid* it down. Hence it is utterly wrong to say, we must know how the land *lays;* I went and *laid* down for a little.]—*n.* The relative position of one object with regard to another or to a point of the compass; general bearing or direction; position or state of an affair; *geol.* the manner in which strata are disposed.

lied, lēt, lēd, *n.* pl. **lieder,** lē′dėr. [G.] A German song, lyric, or lay.

liege, lēj, *a.* [Fr. *lige,* Pr. *litje,* It. *ligio,* L.L. *ligius, legius;* origin uncertain; perhaps O.G. *lidic* (G. *ledig*), free.] Connected by loyalty or duty; bound by or resting on feudal ties (a *liege* lord, *liege* vassalage).—*n.* A vassal or person owing duties to his feudal lord; a lord or superior; a sovereign; a law-abiding citizen or citizen in general (in this sense usually in the *pl.*).—**liege man,** lēj′man, *n.* A vassal; a liege.

lien, lē′en, *n.* [Fr. *lien,* from L. *ligamen,* from *ligo,* to bind. LIGAMENT.] *Law,* a legal claim; a right in one man to retain the property of another until some claim of the former is paid or satisfied.

lientery, lī′en•tėr•i, *n.* [Gr. *leienteria—leios,* smooth, and *enteron,* an intestine.] *Med.* a species of diarrhea, in which the food is discharged undigested.—**lienteric,** lī•en•tėr′ik, *a.* Pertaining to a lientery.

lieu, lū, *n.* [Fr., from L. *locus,* place.] Place; room; stead; preceded by *in* (to give goods *in lieu* of wages).

lieutenant, lū•ten′ant, *n.* [Fr., composed of *lieu,* L. *locus,* place, and *tenant,* L. *tenens,* holding.] An officer, civil or military, who supplies the place of a superior in his absence; a commissioned officer in the army, ranking next below a captain; in the navy the ranking is: ensign, lieutenant junior grade, lieutenant, lieutenant commander, commander.—**lieutenancy,** lū•ten′an•si, *n.* The office or commission of a lieutenant.—**lieutenant colonel,** *n.* An army officer next in rank below a colonel.—**lieutenant general,** *n.* An army officer next in rank below a general.—**lieutenant governor,** *n.* An officer ranking next below a governor.

life, līf, *n.* pl. **lives,** līvz. [A.Sax. *lif,* acel. *lif,* Dan. *liv,* D. *lijf,* Goth. *libains,* life. LIVE.] That state of an animal or a plant in which its organs are capable of performing their functions, or in which the performance of functions has not permanently ceased; animate existence; vitality; the time during which such a state continues; the period during which anything continues to exist; outward manifestation of life; a person's condition or circumstances; mode, manner, or course of living, as morally good or bad; social surroundings and characteristics (high or low *life*); that which makes alive; animating or inspiring principle; animation; vivacity; energy; the living form, or nature itself, in opposition to a copy or imitation; a living person (many *lives* were sacrificed); collectively, human beings in any number (a great loss of *life*); animated beings in the aggregate (the abundance of *life* on the globe); narrative of a person's life; a biography or memoir; human affairs; course of things in the world; happiness in the favor of God; eternal felicity; phase or aspect of a creature's existence (adult *life,* sex *life*); the period of existence of a thing (*life* of a car); one inspiring animation and vigor (the *life* of the party).—*For life,* for the whole term of one's existence. —**lifeblood,** *n.* The blood necessary to life; vital blood; that which is essential to existence or strength.—**lifeboat,** *n.* A boat for saving shipwrecked people; a small boat carried by ships for emergency use.—**life buoy,** *n.* See BUOY.—**life cycle,** *n.* A series of activities including development, changes of environment, dormancy and return to original status, experienced by various organisms.—**life expectancy,** *n.* The probable life span of an individual or class of persons, determined by a study of their heredity and environment.—**lifeguard,** *n.* A skilled swimmer employed at a beach to save bathers from drowning.—**life history,** *n.* Account of the activity and environment of an individual from birth to death.—**lifeless,** līf′les, *a.* Deprived of life; dead; inanimate; inorganic; destitute of life or spirit; spiritless; dull; heavy; inactive.—**lifelessly,** līf′les•li, *adv.*—**lifelessness,** līf′les•nes, *n.*—**lifelike,** līf′līk, *a.* Like a living person; true to the life.—**lifeline,** *n.* A rope projected to a foundering ship, or to a drowning person; a line by which a diver is kept in touch with the surface; an indispensable sea, land, or air transportation route.—**lifelong,** līf′long, *a.* Lasting or continuing through life. —**life preserver,** *n.* A buoyant jacket, belt, or similar device worn to prevent drowning.—**lifesaver,** *n.* One who saves a life; a lifeguard; a life preserver.—**lifesaving,** *n.*—**lifetime,** līf′tīm, *n.* The time that life continues; duration of life; *phys.* the average time between the appearance and disappearance of an ion or subatomic particle.

lift, lift, *v.t.* [From O.E. *lift,* A.Sax. *lyft,* air, sky; comp. Icel. *lypta* (pron. *lifta*), from *lopt* (pron. *loft*), air; Sw. *lyfta,* Dan. *löfte,* G. *lüften,* to lift, from Sw. Dan. and G. *luft,* air, atmosphere. LURE.] To bring from a lower to a higher position or place; to raise, elevate, upheave; to elevate, exalt, or improve, as in fortune, estimation, dignity, or rank; to elate; often with *up*; to take and carry away; to remove by stealing (to *lift* cattle).—*To lift up the eyes,* to look; to raise the eyes in order to look.—*To lift the hand,* to raise the hand for the purpose of striking; to strike or threaten to strike.—*To lift the hand against,* to strike; to assail; to injure; to oppress.—*To lift up the voice,* to cry aloud; to call out, either in grief or joy.—*v.i.* To raise or try to raise; to rise, or to be raised or elevated (the fog *lifts*).—*n.* The act or manner of raising or lifting; elevation; the act of stealing; *aeronautics,* the component of the force exerted by the air on an airfoil, being opposite the force of gravity and causing an aircraft to stay in the air; a conveyor that carries people up a mountain (a ski *lift*); an elevating influence.—**lifter,** lif′tėr, *n.*—**lift-off,** *n.* A take-off by an aircraft or a missile.

ligament, lig′a•ment, *n.* [L. *ligamentum,* from *ligo,* to bind (whence also *ligation, ligature, lien, league, -ly* in *ally,* etc.).] What ties or unites one thing or part to another; a band; a bond; a strong flexible fastening; *anat.* a strong, compact, tendinous substance, serving to bind one bone to another.—**ligamentous,** lig•a•men′tus, *a.* Of the nature of a ligament.

ligan, lī′gan, *n.* [Contr. for *ligamen,* a band, from *ligo,* to bind.] Goods sunk in the sea, but having something buoyant attached to mark their position.

ligation, lī′gā′shon, *n.* [L. *ligatio, ligationis.* LIGAMENT.] The act of binding; a bond; a ligature.—**ligature,** lig′a•chėr, *n.* [L. *ligatura.*] Something that binds; a cord, thong, band, or bandage; a ligament; the act of binding; *mus.* a line connecting notes; *printing,* a type consisting of two or more letters or characters cast on the same body, as *fi, fl*; *surg.* a cord or string for tying blood vessels to prevent hemorrhage.

light, līt, *n.* [A.Sax. *leóht,* bright, shining, *leóht, líht,* a light; D. and G. *licht,* Icel. *ljos,* Dan. *lys,* Goth. *liuhath*; allied to L. *lux, lumen,* light, *luceo,* to shine, *luna,* the moon; Gr. *leukos,* white, *leassō,* to see; W. *llug,* Gael. *leus,* light. LUCID.] That agent or force by the action of which upon the organs of sight objects from which it proceeds are rendered visible; that phenomenon which makes vision possible, traveling 186,326 miles per second; a radiant body, as the sun, the moon, a candle, etc.; mental or spiritual illumination; knowledge; information; a person who is conspicuous or eminent in any study; a model or example; the phenomenon constituting day, hence, open view, public observation, publicity; a compartment of a window; the illuminated part of an object or picture; the point of view or position in which or from which anything is looked at or considered; aspect.—*Northern lights,* the aurora borealis. See AURORA.—*To stand in one's own light,* to be the means of preventing one's own good, or frustrating one's own purposes.—*To bring to light,* to bring to knowledge, detection, or discovery.—*To come to light,* to be detected; to be discovered or found. —*a.* Bright; clear; not dark or obscure; white or whitish; not intense or deep, as a color; not dark in hue.—*v.t.*—pret. & pp. *lighted,* sometimes *lit.* To set fire to; to kindle; to ignite; to set burning; to give light to; to fill or spread over with light; to show the way to by means of a light; to illuminate.—**lighten,** lī′tn, *v.i.* To exhibit the phenomenon of lightning; to give out flashes; to flash; to become lighter; to become less dark or gloomy; to clear.—*v.t.* To make light or clear; to dissipate darkness from; to illuminate; to enlighten; to flash forth.†—**lighter,** lī′tėr, *n.* One who or that which lights.—**lighthouse,** līt′hous, *n.* A tower or other lofty structure with a powerful light at top, erected as a guide or warning of danger to navigators at night.—**lighting,** līt′ing, *n.* Illumination; the disposition of light in a work of art, as a painting or a play; artificial light, either direct or indirect; the fixture supplying light. —**lightless,** līt′les, *a.*—**lightness,** līt′-nes, *n.*—**lightning,** līt′ning, *n.* A flash of light, the result of a discharge of atmospheric electricity.—**lightning bug,** *n.* A firefly.—**lightning rod,** *n.* A metallic rod attached to buildings or vessels to protect them from lightning by conducting it into the earth or water.—**lightship,** *n.* A ship anchored and hoisting a strong light to serve as a lighthouse.—**lightsome,** līt′sum, *a.* Bright; light; gay; cheering.—**lightsomely,** līt′sum•li, *adv.*—**lightsomeness,** līt′sum•nes, *n.*—**light year,** *n.* The distance light can travel in a year, about 5,880,000,000,000 miles, used to measure stellar distances.

light, līt, *a.* [A.Sax. *leóht,* D. *ligt,* G. *leicht,* Icel. *léttr,* Dan. *let,* light; allied to L. *levis* (whence *levity*), Gr. *elachys,* Skr. *laghu,* light. Hence *alight, lighter* (boat), *lights.*] Not heavy; having little weight; not burdensome; easy to be lifted, borne, or carried; not oppressive; easy to be suffered or endured; easy to be performed; not difficult; easy to be digested; not oppressive to the stomach; not heavily armed, or armed with light weapons; swift; nimble; not dense or gross; not strong; not copious or vehement (a *light* rain); inconsiderable; easily influenced by trifling considerations; unsteady; volatile; trifling; gay; airy; wanton; unchaste; not of legal weight (*light* coin); loose; sandy; easily pulverized (a *light* soil); having a sensation of giddiness; employed in light work (a *light* porter).—*To set light by,* to slight; to treat as of no importance.—*To make light of,* to treat as of little consequence; to slight; to disregard.—**lighten,** lī′tn, *v.t.* To make lighter or less heavy; to relieve of a certain amount of weight; to make less burdensome or oppressive; to alleviate.—**lighter,** lī′-tėr, *n.* A large open flat-bottomed barge, often used in lightening or unloading and loading ships.—**light-fingered,** *a.* Thievish; addicted to petty thefts; often applied to pickpockets.—**light-footed,** *a.* Nimble in running or dancing; active.—**lightheaded,** *a.* Having dizziness or giddiness in the head; dizzy; delirious; thoughtless; heedless; weak; volatile; unsteady,—**lightheadedness,** *n.*—**lighthearted,** *a.* Free from grief or anxiety; gay; cheerful; merry.—**lightheartedness,** *n.*—**lightly,** līt′li, *adv.*—**lightness,** līt′nes, *n.*—**light opera,** *n.* An opera with a gay, popular musical score and trivial, entertaining plot.—**lightweight,** *n.*

Sporting, a man weighing not more than 135 pounds.

light, līt, *v.i.*—pret. & pp. *lighted*, sometimes *lit.* [A.Sax. *lihtan*, to descend, alight, from *leóht*, light, not heavy: to *alight* from horseback or a vehicle is to make it lighter by relieving it of weight.] To descend, as from a horse or carriage (with *down, off, from*); to fly or fall and settle; to come to rest; to fall or come by chance; to happen to find: with *on* or *upon*.

ligneous, lig′ni•us, *a.* [L. *ligneus*, from *lignum*, wood.] Made of wood; consisting of wood; resembling wood; woody; wooden.—**lignification,** lig′ni•fi•kā″shon, *n.* The act of lignifying, or the state of being lignified.—**ligniform,** lig′ni•form, a. Like wood; resembling wood.—**lignify,** lig′ni•fī, *v.t.*—*lignified, lignifying.* [L. *lignum*, and *facio*, to make.] To convert into wood.—*v.i.* To become wood.—**lignin,** lig′nin, *n.* A modification of cellulose; vegetable fiber.—**lignite,** lig′nīt, *n.* Fossil wood, wood coal, or brown coal, a combustible substance mineralized to a certain degree, but retaining distinctly its woody texture.—**lignitic,** lig•nit′ik, *a.* Containing lignite; resembling lignite.—**lignose,** lig′nōs, *a.* Ligneous.—**lignum vitae,** lig•num vī′tē, *n.* [L., wood of life, from its hardness and durability.] The popular name of a small West Indian and South American tree, the wood of which is valued for its extreme hardness.

ligroine, lig′rō•in, *n.* An oil of medium density distilled from crude petroleum.

ligula, ligule, lig′ū•la, lig′ūl, *n.* [L. *ligula*, a strap, from *ligo*, to bind. LIGAMENT.] *Bot.* a strap-shaped petal of composite flowers; the membrane at the base of a grass leaf.—**ligulate,** lig′ū•lāt, *a.* Like a bandage or strap; *bot.* having the form of a ligula: applied especially to the ray florets of composite flowers.

ligure, lig′ūr, *n.* [Gr. *linggourion, ligurion.*] A kind of precious stone (O.T.).

like, līk, *a.* [A.Sax. *lic, gelic*=D. *lijk, gelijk*, Icel. *likr, glikr*, G. *gleich*, Goth. *leiks, galeiks*, like. From A.Sax. *lic*, form, body (see LICH GATE). Hence the termination in *each, such, which*, and the *-ly* of adjectives and adverbs, as also the verb *to like.*] Equal; exactly corresponding; of the same kind; similar; resembling (*like* passions); probable; likely (it is *like* he will); feeling equal or disposed to.—*Had like*, was like; had nearly; came little short of. *Like* is frequently suffixed to nouns to form adjectives denoting resemblance, as child*like*, etc.—*n.* Some person or thing resembling another; an exact counterpart.—*adv.* In the same or a similar manner; similarly; likely; probably.—**likelihood,** līk′li•hụd, *n.* Likeliness; probability.—**likely,** līk′-li, *a.* Like the truth; credible; probable (a *likely* story); giving a probability of something (I am *likely* to be away from home tonight); suitable, well adapted, or convenient for some purpose.—*adv.* Probably; as may be expected or reasonably thought.—**liken,** lī′kn, *v.t.* To make like; to cause to resemble; to compare; to represent as resembling.—**likeness,** līk′nes, *n.* The condition or quality of being like; similarity; what exactly resembles something else, especially, a portrait.—**likewise,** līk′wīz, *conj.* and *adv.* In like manner; also; moreover; too.

like, līk, *v.t.*—*liked, liking.* [A.Sax. *lícian, gelícian*, to please, to suit, lit. to be *like* one's tastes; originally impersonal; D. *lijken*, to suit; Icel. *líka*, to please, to like; from the adjective (which see).] To please or suit: used impersonally‡; to be pleased with in a moderate degree; to approve; to take satisfaction in; to enjoy.—*v.i.* To be pleased; to choose.—*n.* A liking; a fancy: used chiefly in the phrase *likes and dislikes*.—**likeable,** līk′a•bl, *a.* Such as to attract liking; lovable.—**likeableness,** līk′a•bl•nes, *n.* Quality of being likeable.—**liking,** līk′ing, *n.* Inclination; desire; satisfaction: often with *for* or *to* (an amusement to your *liking*).

lilac, lī′lak, *n.* [Sp. *lilac*, Ar. *līlak*, lilac; Per. *līlaj*; from a word meaning blue.] A beautiful flowering shrub of the genus *Syringa* with flowers generally pink, white, bluish, or lavender.

Lilliputian, lil•i•pū′shan, *n.* A member of the diminutive race of beings described in Swift's imaginary kingdom of *Lilliput* in *Gulliver's Travels*; a person of very small size.—*a.* Very small.

lilt, lilt, *v.t.* and *i.* [Akin to *lull.*] To sing, especially in a cheerful manner; to give musical or harmonious utterance. (*Tenn.*)—*n.* A song; a tune.

lily, lil′i, *n* [A.Sax. *lilie*, from L. *lilium*, Gr. *leirion.*] The popular name of many bulbous plants with showy and fragant flowers, as the white lily, orange lily, tiger lily, scarlet lily, etc.—*Lily of the valley*, a perennial plant with small white bell-shaped flowers.—**liliaceous,** lil•-i•ā′shus, *a* Pertaining to the order of lilies; lilylike.—**lily-livered,** *a.* White-livered; cowardly. (*Shak.*)

limb, lim, *n.* [A.Sax. *lim*, Icel. *limr*, Dan. and Sw. *lem*, a limb. The *b* is added as in crum*b*, thum*b*, etc.] One of the jointed members of the human body or of any animal; an arm or leg, more especially the latter; a pretty large or main branch of a tree.—*v.t.* To supply with limbs; to dismember; to tear the limbs from.—**limbed,** limd, *a.* Having limbs: mostly in composition (large-*limbed*, short-*limbed*).

limb, lim, *n.* [L. *limbus*, a border, edging, or fringe.] *Astron.* the border or outermost edge of the sun or moon; the graduated edge of a circle or other astronomical or surveying instrument, etc.; *bot.* the border or upper spreading part of a monopetalous corolla, or of a petal or sepal.—**limbate,** lim′bat, *a. Bot.* bordered, as when one color is surrounded by an edging of another.

limber, lim′bėr, *a.* [Closely allied to *limp*, pliant, flaccid.] Easily bent; flexible; pliant.—*v.t.* To render limber or pliant.—**limberness,** lim′bėr•-nes, *n.* The quality of being limber.

limber, lim′bėr, *n.* [Really a plural form from Icel. *limar*, limbs, branches of a tree; akin to *limb.*] *Artill.* a carriage on two wheels with the ammunition boxes and shafts for the horses, attached to the gun carriage, properly so called, of a field gun or cannon; *pl.* thills; shafts of a carriage (*local*).—*v.t.* To attach the limber to.

limbo, lim′bō, *n.* [It., from L. *limbus*, a hem or edge.] A supposed region where souls of the innocent are detained till the final judgment; any similar region apart from this world; a prison or other place of confinement (*colloq.*).

Limburger, lim′bėrg•ėr, *n.* A soft cheese with a characteristic odor.

lime, līm, *n.* [A.Sax. *lim*, glue, cement =D. *lijm*, acel. *lim*, G. *leim*, glue; allied to *loam*, L. *limus*, slime, Skr. *li*, to be viscous.] A viscous substance for catching birds; birdlime; calcium oxide, prepared by heating limestone or shells; quicklime, as used in mortar, in industry, and to counteract acidity in soil.—*v.t.*—*limed, liming.* To smear with birdlime; to entangle; to ensnare; to manure with lime; to cement or glue (*Shak.*).—**limekiln,** līm′kil, *n.* A kiln in which limestone is exposed to a strong heat and reduced to lime.—**limelight,** *n.* A powerful light produced by an oxyhydrogen flame on a piece of lime; on the stage, a spotlight; *fig.* center of public interest.—**limestone,** līm′stōn, *n.* A kind of stone consisting of varieties of carbonate of lime.—**limewater,** *n.* A water solution of calcium hydroxide, used in medicine as an antacid, and in the chemical industry; natural water containing calcium carbonate or calcium sulfate.—**limy,** lī′mi, *a.*

lime, līm, *n.* [Formerly *line*, from A.Sax. *lind*, D. and G. *linde*, Dan. Sw. Icel. *lind*, the tree.] The linden tree.

lime, līm, *n.* [Fr. *lime*, from Per. *limû, limûn*, whence also *lemon.*] A species of tree cultivated in southern Europe, the U. S., etc., and producing small, greenish-yellow fruit used for flavoring punch, sherbet, etc.

limerick, lim′ėr•ik, *n.* A jingling verse form of five lines, with lines 1, 2, and 5 rhyming, as do lines 3 and 4, popularized by Edward Lear (1812-88) in his *Book of Nonsense*, 1846.

liminal, lim′in•al, *a.* [L. *limen*, threshold.] Belonging to the lowest limit (or threshold) of perception.

limit, lim′it, *n.* [Fr. *limite*, from L. *limes, limitis*, a bound or limit; allied to *limen*, a threshold; akin *lintel, eliminate.*] That which terminates, circumscribes, or confines; bound, border, utmost extent; *math.* a determinate quantity to which a variable one continually approaches, but can never exceed.—*v.t.* To set limits or bounds to; to bound; to confine within certain bounds; to circumscribe; to restrain; to narrow or confine the signification of; to apply exclusively (words or conceptions).—**limitable,** lim′i•ta•bl, *a.* Capable of being limited.—**limitary,** lim′i•te•ri, *a.* Circumscribed or bounded in power or authority.—**limitation,** lim•i•tā′shon, *n.* The act of limiting, bounding, or circumscribing; the condition of being so limited; that which limits; limiting circumstance; restriction; qualification.—**limited,** lim′i•ted, *p.* and *a.* Confined within limits; narrow; circumscribed.—*Limited monarchy,* a monarchy in which the monarch shares the supreme power with a class of nobles, with a popular body, or with both.—**limitedly,** lim′i•ted•li, *adv.* In a limited manner or degree.—**limiter,** lim′i•tėr, *n.* One who limits.—**limitless,** lim′it•les, *a.* Having no limits; unbounded; boundless; infinite.

limn, lim, *v.t.* [Fr. *enluminer,* from L. *illumino,* to illuminate.] To draw or paint; to make a portrait or likeness of.—**limner,** lim′nėr, *n.* One who limns; a painter of portraits or miniatures.

limonene, li′mo•nēn, *n.* [Fr. *limon,* a lemon.] A hydrocarbon in oil of lemon.

limonite, lī′mon•īt, *n.* [Gr. *leimōn,* meadow.] An important ore of iron, a variety of which is brown hematite.

limousine, lim′o•zēn″, *n.* [From *Limousin,* an old French province.] A closed automobile with the driver partitioned off from the passengers.

limp, limp, *v.i.* [A.Sax. *limp-halt, lemp-healt,* limping-halt, lame; comp. L.G. *lumpen,* to limp; Icel. *limpa,* weakness; allied to *limp, limber,* and probably to *lame.*] To halt or walk lamely.—*n.* The act of limping; a halt in one's gait; the Jacobite toast, with a limping motion, from the initial letters of Louis XIV, James, Mary (of Modena, wife of James II), Prince (the old Pretender).

limp, limp, *a.* [Akin to *limp,* the verb, and to *limber*; comp. Skr. *lamb,* to hang.] Easily bent; flexible; pliant; lacking stiffness; flaccid.

limpet, lim′pet, *n.* [O.Fr. *limpine,* a limpet.] A univalve mollusk with a conical shell, found adhering to rocks; a person who clings to something; an explosive designed to adhere to the side of a ship.

limpid, lim′pid, *a.* [L. *limpidus*; allied to Gr. *lampō,* to shine, hence akin to *lamp.*] Characterized by clearness or transparency; clear and bright; translucent; transparent: said of water.—**limpidity, limpidness,** lim•pid′i•ti, lim′pid•nes, *n.* The state of being limpid.

limy, *a.* See LIME.

linage, līn′ij, *n.* The number of printed lines on a page; measure of space sold for advertising; alignment.

linchpin, linsh′pin, *n.* [Lit. axle-pin, from A.Sax. *lynis,* an axletree; D. *luns, lens,* G. *lünse,* a linchpin.] A pin used to prevent the wheel of a carriage or other vehicle from sliding off the axletree; an axle pin.

linden, lin′den, *n.* [An adj. form from A.Sax. *lind,* the linden.] The basswood tree.

line, līn, *n.* [A.Sax. *line,* a cord or line, from L. *linea,* a linen thread, a string, a line or stroke, from *lineus,* flaxen, *linum,* flax; Fr. *ligne,* a line. LINEN.] A small rope or cord; a thread-like marking, as with a pen, pencil, etc.; a stroke or score; a marking or furrow upon the hands or face; a mark traced or imagined to show latitude, longitude, temperature, or the like on a map or the globe; a row of things; a straight row of soldiers drawn up with an extended front; a similar disposition of ships in preparation for an engagement; a straight row of words or figures between two margins (a page of thirty *lines*); the words which form a certain number of poetical feet; a verse; an outline, contour, lineament (a statue of fine *lines*); a short epistle; course of thought, conduct, occupation, policy, or the like; a continuous or connected series, as of descendants from a common progenitor; a series of public conveyances, as buses, steamships, airplanes, etc., passing between places with regularity; *fort.* (pl.) works made to cover extended positions; (pl.) words of a character in a drama; *football,* offensive or defensive players that take their positions near the scrimmage; a source of communication.—*Line engraving, photoengraving,* an engraving, usually on zinc, without a screen (*line cut*).—*Line of defense, mil.* fortifications or trenches used as protective barriers; the standing army.—*Line drive,* in baseball, a low-hit ball which approximately parallels the ground the greater part of its course.—*Meridian line,* a line drawn at any station to show the directions of true north and south.—*Fraunhofer's lines,* the dark lines observed crossing a spectrum at right angles to its length.—**streamline,** *n.* The design of form which permits passage through the air or water with a minimum of resistance, as in the shape of an airplane or boat.—*v.t.*—*lined, lining.* To draw lines upon; to mark with lines or thread-like strokes; cross out; form in lines; place at intervals.—**linage,** līn′ij, *n.* The number of printed lines on a page; measure of space sold for advertising.—**liner,** lī′nėr, *n.* One of a line of ocean-going ships.—**lineman,** *n.* A repair man who works on electric light, power, telephone or telegraph lines; *football,* one who plays forward.—**linesman,** *n.* A referee in football or tennis.—**line-up,** *n.* Arrangement of players in football or baseball; a line of persons to be inspected (a police *line-up*).

line, līn, *v.t.*—*lined, lining.* [O.E. *line,* to double a garment with *linen.*] To cover on the inside; to protect by a layer on the inside (to *line* a garment).—**lining,** līn′ing, *n.* The covering of the inner surface of anything, as a coat lining.—**liner,** lī′nėr, *n.* Something used as a lining; one who lines.

lineage, lin′i•ij, *n.* [Fr. *lignage,* from *ligne,* L. *linea,* a line. LINE.] Descendants in a line from a common progenitor; line of descent from an ancestor; race; progeny.—**lineal,** lin′i•al, *a.* [L. *linealis.*] Composed of lines; in a direct line from an ancestor; hereditary; pertaining to or ascertained by a line or lines (*lineal* measure).—**lineally,** lin′i•al•li, *adv.* In a lineal manner; in a direct line of descent.—**lineament,** lin′i•a•ment, *n.* [L. *lineamentum.*] The outline or contour of a body or figure, particularly of the face; a line of form or feature.—**linear,** lin′i•ėr, *a.* [L. *linearis.*] Pertaining to a line; consisting of lines; lineal; in *bot.* like a line in form; long and slender.—*Linear perspective,* that which regards only the positions, magnitudes, and forms of the objects delineated.—**lineate, lineated, lineolate,** lin′i•āt, lin′i•ā•ted, lin′i•o•lāt, *a. Bot.* marked longitudinally with depressed parallel lines.

linen, lin′en, *n.* [Properly an adj. signifying made of flax, from A.Sax. *lin,* flax, L. *linum,* Gr. *linon,* flax; comp. Armor. *lin,* W. *llin,* flax.] Cloth made of flax; a flaxen fabric or material; underclothing in general, because chiefly made of linen or similar materials.—*a.* Made of flax, or yarn from flax.

ling, ling, *n.* [D. *ling*; Dan. and N. *lange*; G. *leng, langfisch,* so named from being *long.*] A fish of the cod family, rather long in proportion to its thickness, found in the North Atlantic Ocean, and when salted and dried, is used as food.

ling, ling, *n.* [Icel. and Dan. *lyng,* heather.] Common heather.

linger, ling′gėr, *v.i.* [From A.Sax. *lengra,* compar. of *lang,* long; comp. the verb *lower,* from compar. of *low.*] To delay; to loiter; to lag or hang behind; to be slow to move or act; to hesitate; to remain long (the disease *lingers*).—*v.t.* To spend in a wearisome manner: with *out* or *away.*—**lingerer,** ling′gėr•ėr, *n.* One who lingers.

lingerie, län′zhe•rē, *n.* [Fr.] Linen articles, especially women's underwear. Now used for feminine intimate apparel.

lingo, ling′gō, *n.* [L. *lingua,* the tongue.] Language; speech; a contemptuous term for language one does not understand. (*Vulgar.*)

lingua franca. A compound or mongrel language in the Levant, made up of words from French, Italian, Spanish, and modern Greek, serving as a common medium of communication.

lingual, ling′gwal, *a.* [L. *lingua,* the tongue, originally *dingua*; cog. with E. *tongue* (comp. L. *lacrima,* E. *tear*).] Pertaining to the tongue; pronounced chiefly by means of the tongue.—*n.* A letter pronounced chiefly by means of the tongue as *l, r.*—**linguiform,** ling′gwi•form, *n.* Having the form or shape of a tongue.—**linguist,** ling′gwist, *n.* A person skilled in languages; one who knows several languages.—**linguistic,** ling•gwis′tik, *a.* Relating to language or to the affinities of language; philological.—**linguistics,** ling′gwis′tiks, *n.* The science of language, or of the origin, significations, affinities, and application of words; comparative philology.—**lingulate,** ling′gū•lāt, *a.* Shaped like the tongue or a strap; ligulate.

liniment, lin′i•ment, *n.* [L. *linimentum,* from *lino,* to anoint.] *Med.* a species of soft ointment, of a stimulating or soothing character, to be rubbed into the skin.

lining, *n.* See LINE.

link, lingk, *n.* [A.Sax. *hlence,* Sw. *länk,* Dan. *lænke,* Icel. *hlekkr,* a link; G. *gelenk,* a joint, a link (from *lenken,* to bend).] A single ring or division of a chain; anything doubled and closed like a link; something that serves to connect one thing or part with another; any constituent part of a connected series; *land measuring,* a division of Gunter's chain, having a length of 7.92 inches; *mach.* any straight rod connecting two rotating pieces by flexible joints.—*v.t.* To connect by, or as if by, a link or links; to unite or join.—*v.i.* To be joined or connected: with *together* or *in.*—**linkage,** lingk′ij, *n.* The act of linking; the state of being linked; *biol.* the inclination of certain genes to remain correlated in inheritance; *elec.* the product of the magnetic flux through a coil by its number of turns; *mech.* a combination of bars or pieces linked so as to pivot about each other in parallel planes.

link, lingk, *n.* [Origin uncertain; perhaps equivalent to *lint,* the first part of *linstock.*] A torch made of tow or other materials, with tar or pitch.—**linkboy,** *n.* A boy or man that carries a link.

links, lingks, *n.* pl. [A.Sax. *hlinc,* rising ground; same root as L. *clivus,* sloping. DECLINE.] A golf course.

Linnaean, Linnean, lin•nē′an, *a.* Pertaining to Linnaeus, the celebrated botanist.

linnet, lin′et, *n.* [A.Sax. *linet;* Fr. *linot, linotte,* from L. *linum,* flax.] One of the commonest of Old World singing birds, frequenting open places.

linoleum, li•nō′li•um, *n.* [L. *linum,* flax, and *oleum,* oil.] A preparation of linseed oil with chloride of sulfur, which when mixed with ground cork and pressed upon canvas forms floor-cloth; the floor-cloth thus produced.

Linotype, *n.* [A 'line o'type'.] In printing, a machine for setting and casting lines of type by the operation of a keyboard.

linseed, lin′sēd, *n.* [O.E. *lin,* flax. LINE.] The seed of flax.—**linseed oil,** *n.* An oil procured by pressure from the seed of flax.—**linsey-woolsey,** lin′si•wul•si, *n.* A fabric made of linen and wool; an incongruous mixture (*Shak.*)—*a.* Made of linen and wool mixed; of different and unsuitable ingredients.

linstock, lin′stok, *n.* [For *lintstock, luntstock,* from D. *lont,* Dan. *lunte,* a match, and *stock,* a stick.] A staff with a crotch or fork at one end to hold a lighted match, used in firing cannon.

lint, lint, *n.* [A.Sax. *linet,* L. *linteum, linteus,* from *linum,* flax. LINE.] Flax; linen scraped into a soft substance; bits of thread or fuzz from yarn or fabrics; cottonseed wool.

lintel, lin′tel, *n.* [O.Fr. *lintel,* Fr. *linteau,* from L.L. *limitellus,* dim. from L. *limes, limitis,* a limit. LIMIT.] The horizontal piece of timber or stone supporting the load above a window, door, or other opening.

lion, lī′on, *n.* [Fr. *lion,* from L. *leo, leonis,* a lion; Gr. *leōn.*] A well-known carnivorous animal, of a tawny color, having a full-flowing mane in the male, and a tufted tail; a sign of the zodiac; Leo; an object of interest and curiosity (the *lion* of the day; to visit the *lions* of the place), a usage derived from the time when the lions kept in the Tower of London were one of the chief sights to which strangers were taken.—*Lion's provider,* a popular name for the jackal.—*Lion's share,* the whole or a very disproportionate share in advantages.—**lionel, lionet,** lī′on•el, lī′on•et, *n.* A lion's whelp; a young lion.—**lioness,** lī′on•es, *n.* The female of the lion.—**lionism,** lī′on•izm, *n.* The attracting of notice as a lion; the treating of a person as an object of curiosity.—**lionize,** lī′on•īz, *v.t.* To visit, as the objects of curiosity in a place; to treat as a lion or object of curiosity and interest.

lip, lip, *n.* [A.Sax. *lippe* = D. *lip,* Dan. and G. *lippe;* allied to verb to *lap;* Lith. *lupa,* Per. *lab,* Hind. *lub,* L. *labium,* lip; *lambo,* to lap.] The name of the two fleshy or muscular parts (upper and lower) covering the front teeth in man and many other animals; something similar; the edge or border of something hollow (as a vessel, a wound); brink or margin; back talk (slang).—*v.t.* and *i.* To touch, as with the lip; to kiss.—**lipreading,** *n.* Understanding what one says from the movement of his lips: used in communicating with the deaf.—**lip service,** *n.* A mere verbal profession of service.

lipase, lī′pās, lip′ās, *n.* [Gr. *lipos,* fat, and *ase.*] A fat-digesting enzyme; an enzyme secreted by the pancreas and other organs of the digestive system which converts fats to fatty acids and glycerol.

lipoma, lip•ō′ma, *n.* [Gr. *lipos,* fat, *oma,* a tumor.] A fatty tumor.

liquate, lī′kwāt, *v.i.* and *t.*—*liquated, liquating.* [L. *liquo, liquatum.* LIQUID.] To melt; to liquefy; *metal.* to separate from a less fusible metal, by applying just sufficient heat to melt the more easily liquefiable.—**liquation,** lī′kwā′shon, *n.* The act or operation of liquating.—**liquefacient,** lik•wi•fā′shi•ent, *n.* That which causes to melt.—**liquefaction,** lik•wi•fak′shon, *n.* [L. *liqueo,* to be fluid, and *facio,* to make.] The act or operation of melting or dissolving; a becoming liquid; the state of being melted.—**liquefiable,** lik′wi•fī•a•bl, *a.* Capable of being liquefied.—**liquefy,** lik′wi•fī, *v.t.*—*liquefied, liquefying.* To convert from a solid form to that of a liquid; to melt by heat.—*v.i.* To be melted; to become liquid.—**liquescency,** li•kwes′en•si, *n.* The condition of being liquescent.—**liquescent,** li•kwes′ent, *a.* [L. *liquesco,* to melt.] Melting; becoming fluid.

liqueur, li•kėr′ or li•kūr′, *n.* [Fr. lit. liquor.] A sweet, alcoholic beverage with some infusion or extract from fruits, spices, or various aromatic substances, usually served after dinner.

liquid, lik′wid, *a.* [L. *liquidus,* from *liqueo,* to melt, from root seen also in *lino,* to smear (whence *liniment*).] Composed of particles that move freely among each other on the slightest pressure and do not separate as in a gas; fluid; not solid; flowing smoothly or easily to the ear; devoid of harshness; pronounced with a slight contraction of the organs of articulation.—*n.* Fluid; investments that may be quickly be converted to cash; a letter pronounced with a smooth flowing sound, as *l* and *r.*—**liquid air,** *n.* Air in its liquid state, prepared by subjection to great pressure and cooling.—**liquid-air-cycle-engine** (LACE), *n.* A bi-propellant rocket engine that produces its own oxidizer.—**liquidambar,** lik′wid•am•bėr, *n.* A kind of fragrant gum or resin from several trees.—**liquidate,** lik′wi•dāt, *v.t.*—*liquidated, liquidating.* To make liquid; to decide the precise amount of something by agreement; to adjust, dissolve or clear off debts; to distribute the assets and liabilities and clear up the accounts of a business or estate when terminating it; to dispose of secretly; to do away with.—*v.i.* To close out one's debts or accounts.—**liquidation,** lik•wi•dā′shon, *n.*—**liquidator,** lik•wi•dā′tėr, *n.*—**liquidity,** lik•wid′i•ti, *n.*—**liquidly,** lik′wid•li, *adv.*—**liquidness,** lik′wid•nes, *n.*—**liquor,** lik′ėr, *n.* A liquid or fluid substance, often specifically an intoxicating beverage; drink.—*v.t.* To moisten; to drench.—*v.i.* To drink, especially intoxicating liquor. (Colloq.)

liquorice, lik′ėr•is, *n.* See LICORICE.

lira, lē′ra, *n.* pl. **lire,** lē′rā. [From L. *libra,* a pound, whence also Fr. *livre.*] An Italian silver coin.

lisle, līl, *n.* A kind of thread made of linen, or linen and cotton; material made of lisle.

lisp, lisp, *v.i.* [A.Sax. *wlisp, wlips,* lisping; D. *lispen,* Dan. *laespe,* Sw. *läspa,* to lisp; G. *lispeln,* to whisper, to lisp.] To pronounce the sibilant letters *s* and *z* imperfectly, as by giving the sound of *th* or *dh;* to speak imperfectly, as a child.—*v.t.* To pronounce with a lisp or imperfectly.—*n.* The habit or act of lisping; the habitual utterance of *th* for *s.*—**lisper,** lis′pėr, *n.* One who lisps.

lissom, lissome, lis′um, *a.* [Fr. *lithesome.* LITHE.] Supple; flexible; lithe; nimble; active.—**lissomeness,** lis′um•nes, *n.* State of being lissome.

list, list, *n.* [A.Sax. *list,* selvedge =

Icel. *listi*, Sw. *list*, Dan. *liste*, a fillet, a selvedge; G. *leiste*, a strip, a border; D. *lijst*, border, margin, catalogue.] The edge or selvage woven on cloth; a strip of cloth; a fillet; a record or register of names or items; pl. the ground or field enclosed for a combat or competition.—**list price,** *n. Bus.* a price given in a catalogue; the common or retail price of an item.—*v.t.* To enroll; to enlist; to fit or cover with list; to put an edge or border on.—*v.i.* To enlist, as in the army.

list, list, *v.i.* [A.Sax. *lystan*, to wish (used impers.), from *lust*, pleasure; so Icel. *lysta*. LUST.] To desire or choose; to be disposed; to please.

list, list, *n.* [Origin unknown.] *Naut.* an inclination to one side (the ship has a *list* to port).—*v.t.* To cause to list.—*v.i.* To lean to one side (said of a ship); to careen.

listen, lis'n, *v.i.* [A.Sax. *hlystan*, from *hlyst*, hearing.] To pay attention with the ear; to hear and attend to; to take advice.—**listener,** lis'n•ėr, *n.*

listless, list'les, *a.* [O.E. *list*, A.Sax. *lyst*, desire, pleasure. See LIST, to desire.] Indifferent to or taking no pleasure in what is passing; languid and indifferent; uninterested; vacant.—**listlessly,** list'les•li, *adv.* In a listless manner.—**listlessness,** list'les•nes, *n.* The state of being listless.

lit, lit, pret. & pp. of *light*, to kindle; also sometimes of *light*, to alight, to chance.

litany, lit'a•ni, *n.* [Fr. *litanie*; Gr. *litaneia*, from *litaneuō*, to pray, *litē*, a prayer.] A solemn supplication used in public worship; [*cap.*, with *The*] a collection of short supplications in the *Book of Common Prayer*, uttered by the priest and people alternately.

litchi, lēch'ē, *n.* A delicious fruit yielded by a tree belonging to China and the Malayan Archipelago.

liter, lē'tėr, *n.* [From Gr. *litra*, a pound.] Metric measure of capacity, a cubic decimeter, or 61.025 cu. in., or 1.0567 U. S. liquid quarts.

literal, lit'ėr•al, *a.* [L. *literalis*, from *litera*, a letter. LETTER.] According to the letter or verbal expression; not figurative or metaphorical; following the letter or exact words; not free (a *literal* translation); consisting of or expressed by letters.—**literalism,** lit'ėr•al•izm, *n.* The act of adhering to the letter; a mode of interpreting literally.—**literalist,** lit'ėr•al•ist, *n.* One who practices literalism; an interpreter according to the letter.—**literally,** lit'ėr•al•li, *adv.* In a literal manner or sense; according to the primary and natural import of words; not figuratively.—**literalness,** lit'ėr•al•nes, *n.* The state or quality of being literal.—**literary,** lit'er•e•ri, *a.* [L. *literarius*.] Pertaining to letters or literature; treating of or dealing with learning or learned men; engaged in literature; consisting in written or printed compositions (*literary* property).—**literate,** lit'ėr•it, *a.* [L. *literatus*.] Instructed; learned; lettered.—*n.* One who has received a certain university education, but was not graduated; a literary man.—**literati,** lit•ėr•ä'tī. [It. *litterato*] Literary men.—**literator.**† lit'ėr•ā•tėr, *n.* [L.] A literary man; a litterateur.—**literature,** lit'ėr•a•chėr, *n.* [L. *litteratura*.] Learning; literary knowledge; literary productions collectively; the literary productions upon a given subject, or a particular branch of knowledge; the collective writings of a country or period; the class of writings in which beauty of style is a characteristic feature; the calling of authors of books, etc.

lith, lith, *n.* [A.Sax. *lith*=D. *lid*, Dan. *led*, Icel. *lithr*, Goth. *lithus*, limb, joint.] A limb; a joint; a symmetrical part or division; a member.

litharge, lith'ärj, *n.* [Gr. *lithargyros*—*lithos*, stone, *argyros*, silver.] An oxide of lead, much used in assaying as a flux, and entering into the composition of the glaze of common earthenware.

lithe, līTH, *a.* [A.Sax. *lithe*, gentle; G. *linde*, *gelind*, Dan. *lind*, Icel. *linr*, soft, mild; allied to L. *lentus*, pliant, *lenis*, mild (whence *lenity*). Hence *lissome*.] That may be easily bent; pliant; flexible; limber.—**litheness,** līTH'nes, *n.* Pliancy; flexibility; limberness.—**lithesome,** līTH'sum, *a.* Pliant; lissome.

lithia, lith'i•a, *n.* [From Gr. *lithos*, a stone.] The oxide of the metal lithium, of a white color, acrid and caustic; *med.* the formation of stone or concretions in the human body.—**lithic,** lith'ik, *a.* Pertaining to or consisting of stone; pertaining to stone in the bladder.

lithium, lith'i•um, *n.* [N.L. from Gr. *lithos*, stone.] A metallic element, soft and silver white, the lightest metal known. Symbol, Li; at. no., 3; at. wt., 6.939.—**lithia water,** *n.* A mineral water containing lithium salts.

lithograph, lith'o•graf, *v.t.* [Gr. *lithos*, a stone, and *grapho*, to write.] To engrave or trace on stone and transfer to paper, etc., by printing.—*n.* A print from a drawing on stone.—**lithographer,** li•thog'ra•fėr, *n.* One who practices lithography.—**lithographic, lithographical,** lith•o•graf'ik, lith•o•graf'i•kal, *a.* Pertaining to lithography; engraved upon or printed from stone.—*Lithographic stone, lithographic slate*, a slaty compact limestone, of a yellowish color and fine grain, used for receiving the designs in lithography.—**lithographically,** lith•o•graf'i•kal•li, *adv.* By the lithographic art.—**lithography,** li•thog'ra•fi, *n.* The art of writing or drawing with special pigments on a peculiar kind of stone, and of producing impressions from it on paper.

lithoid, lithoidal, lith'oid, li•thoi'dal, *a.* [Gr. *lithos*, a stone.] Resembling a stone; of a stony structure.

lithologic, lithological, lith•o•loj'ik, lith•o•loj'i•kal, *a.* [Gr. *lithos*, a stone, and *logos*, discourse.] Of or pertaining to lithology or the science of stones.—**lithologist,** li•thol'o•jist, *n.* A person skilled in the science of stones.—**lithology,** li•thol'o•ji, *n.* The science or natural history of stones; the study of the mineral structure of rocks.

lithomarge, lith'o•märj, *n.* [Gr. *lithos*, stone, L. *marga*, marl.] A term applied to varieties of clay of great fineness and capable of being fused into a soft slag.

lithophyte, lith'o•fīt, *n.* [Gr. *lithos*, stone, *phyton*, a plant.] A polyp whose substance is stony or horny.

lithosphere, lith'o•sfēr, *n.* [Prefix *litho*, and *sphere*.] The solid part of the earth.

lithotome, lith'o•tōm, *n.* [Gr. *lithos*, stone, and *temnō*, to cut.] A surgical instrument for cutting into the bladder in operations for the stone.—**lithotomic, lithotomical,** lith•o•tom'ik, lith•o•tom'i•kal, *a.* Pertaining to or performed by lithotomy.—**lithotomy,** li•thot'o•mi, *n.* The operation, art, or practice of cutting for the stone in the bladder.

lithotrity, li•thot'ri•ti, *n.* [Gr. *lithos*, a stone, and L. *tero*, *tritum*, to grind.] The operation of crushing to pieces a stone in the bladder by means of an instrument called a lithotritor.

litigate, lit'i•gāt, *v.t.*—*litigated, litigating*. [L. *litigo*, *litigatum*—*lis*, *litis*, strife, dispute, and *ago*, to carry on.] To make the subject of a lawsuit; to bring before a court of law for decision.—*v.i.* To carry on a suit by judicial process.—**litigable,** lit'i•ga•bl, *a.* Capable of being litigated or defended at law.—**litigant,** lit'i•gant, *a.* Disposed to litigate; contending in law; engaged in a lawsuit.—*n.* A person engaged in a lawsuit.—**litigation,** lit•i•gā'shon, *n.* The act or process of litigating; the proceedings in a suit at law; a lawsuit.—**litigator,** lit'i•gā•tėr, *n.* One who litigates.—**litigious,** li•tij'us, *a.* [L. *litigiosus*, from *litigium*, a dispute.] Inclined to go to law; fond of litigation; given to bringing lawsuits; contentious.—**litigiously,** li•tij'us•li, *adv.* In a litigious manner.—**litigiousness,** li•tij'us•nes, *n.*

litmus, lit'mus, *n.* [From G. *lackmus*, D. *lakmoes*—*lack*, lacker, and *mus*, *moes*, pulp, pap.] A coloring matter procured from certain lichens, used as a test for acids, paper tinged blue with it turning red with acids, and blue again with alkalies.

litotes, lī'to•tēz, *n.* [Gr. *litotēs*, plainness, simplicity.] *Rhet.* a figure which expresses less than what is intended to be conveyed. Thus. 'a citizen of no mean city,' means of an illustrious or important city.

litter, lit'ėr, *n.* [Fr. *litière*, from L.L. *lectaria*, from L. *lectus*, a bed; same root as *lie*, *lay*.] A kind of frame for supporting a bed, in which a person may be borne by men or by a horse; straw, hay, or other soft substance, used as a bed for horses and other animals; articles scattered in a slovenly manner; scattered rubbish; a condition of disorder.—*v.t.* To furnish (animals) with litter or bedding; to spread straw, etc., for; to scatter in a careless or slovenly manner.—*v.i.* To lie or sleep in litter.

litter, lit′ėr, *n.* [Comp. Icel. *látr*, the place where animals lay their young, from *lag*, a laying; Sc. *lachter*, the quantity of eggs a hen lays.] The young produced at a birth by a quadruped which brings forth several at a birth; a birth or bringing forth, as of pigs, kittens, rabbits, puppies, etc.—*v.t.* To bring forth or give birth to: said of such quadrupeds as the sow, cat, rabbit.—*v.i.* To bring forth a litter.

litterateur, lit′ėr•a•tėr, *n.* [Fr. *littérateur.* LITERAL.] A literary man; one who adopts literature as a profession.

little, lit′l, *a.*—comparative *less*, superlative *least* (both from a different root); superlative very rarely *littlest.* [A.Sax. *lytel*, D. *luttel*, Icel. *litill*, Sw. *liten*, Dan. *liden*, *lille*, Goth. *leitile*, little; same root as *lout.*] Small in size or extent; not great or large; short in duration; small dignity, power, or importance; of small force or weight; slight; inconsiderable; small in mind; petty; mean; narrow.—*n.* That which is little; a small quantity, space, etc; small degree or scale; miniature.—*A little*, somewhat; to or in a small degree; to a limited extent.—*Little by little*, by slow degrees; gradually.—*adv.* In a small quantity or degree.—**littleness,** lit′l•nes, *n.* The state or quality of being little.

littoral, lit′o•ral, *a.* [L. *littoralis*, from *littus*, *littoris*, the shore.] Pertaining to a shore; inhabiting the seashore.—*n.* The shore of a sea, or other water, and the country lying near it.—*Littoral zone*, the interval or zone on a seacoast between high and low water mark; a coast strip or district (the Red Sea *littoral*).

liturgy, lit′ėr•ji, *n.* [Gr. *leitourgia*—*leitos*, public, from *laos*, *leōs*, the people, and *ergon*, work.] The ritual or established formulas for public worship in those churches which use prescribed forms.—**liturgic, liturgical,** li•tėr′jik, li•tėr′ji•kal, *a.* Pertaining to a liturgy or to public prayer and worship.—**liturgics,** li•tėr′jiks, *n.* The doctrine or theory of liturgies.

live, liv, *v.i.*—*lived, living.* [A.Sax. *lifian*, to live or dwell; L.G. and D. *leven*, Icel. *lifa*, Dan. *leve*, G. *leben*, Goth. *liban*, to live; akin *life*; same root as *leave*, the original meaning being to be left, to survive.] To have life; to be capable of performing the vital functions; to continue; to remain still effective; not to perish; to pass or spend life in a particular manner; to conduct one's self in life; to regulate one's life; to abide, dwell, reside; to feed; subsist; be nourished and supported (to *live* on grass or insects); to acquire a livelihood; *Scrip.* to be exempt from spiritual death.—*v.t.* To pass or spend (to *live* a life of ease).—*To live down*, to live so as to subdue or give the lie to; to prove false by the course of one's life (to *live down* a calumny).—**liver,** liv′ėr, *n.* One who lives; one who resides; a resident; one who lives in a certain manner (the manner being expressed by an adjective).—**living,** liv′ing, *p.* and *a.* Having life; not dead; producing action, animation, and vigor; quickening.—*Living force*, in *physics*, the force of a body in motion.—*Living rock*, rock in its natural place and condition.—*The living*, those who are alive.—*Living wage*, sufficient to live by, enough for bare life.—*n.* Means of subsistence; livelihood; power of continuing life; manner of life.—**living room,** *n.* The parlor; a centralized, general room.

live, līv, *a.* [Short for *alive*, that is, 'in life'.] Having life; alive; not dead; exhibiting or containing force (a *live* wire, a *live* ball, or a *live* bomb); of, involving, or before real people at the time of production (*live* audience, *live* broadcast); ignited; not extinct (a *live* coal), vivid, as color.—*Live salesman*, a person whose business it is to sell livestock.—*Livestock*, the quadrupeds and other animals employed or reared on a farm.—**lived,** livd, *a.* Having a life; existing; used in composition (long-*lived*, short-*lived*).—**livelihood,** līv′li•hụd, *n.* [Corrupted from O.E. *liflode*, *livelode*, A. Sax. *lif-láde*, lit. life-leading, lead or course of life; from *lif*, life, and *lád*, a leading, as in *lode*, *lode*stone.] Means of maintaining life; support of life; maintenance.—**livelily,** līv′li•li, *adv.* In a lively manner.—**liveliness,** līv′li•nes, *n.* The quality or state of being lively or animated.—**livelong,** liv′long, *a.* That endures long; lasting; durable.—*Livelong day*, day throughout its whole length; entire day; with undercurrent of joy or lassitude; originally *lefe* (LIEF) *long*.—**lively,** līv′li, *a.* Brisk; vivacious; active; animated; spirited; living; strong, energetic, keen (a *lively* faith or hope); fresh; bright: said of colors.—*adv.* In a lively manner.—**live oak,** *n.* An evergreen oak of the Southern United States yielding valuable timber.—**live wire,** *n.* A fun-loving, energetic person.

liver, liv′ėr, *n.* [A.Sax. *lifer*, D. and Dan. *lever*, Icel. *lifr*, G. *leber*; root doubtful.] The glandular organ which in animals secretes the bile, in man placed in the right upper side and toward the front of the abdominal cavity.—**liverwort,** liv′ėr•wėrt, *n.* [From the appearance of the plants.] The Hepaticae, a class of the byrophytes allied to the scale mosses.

livery, liv′ėr•i, *n.* [Fr. *livrée*, a giving out, something given out or delivered over, from *livré*, pp. of *livrer*, to deliver, from L. *libero*, to liberate. LIBERAL.] Release‡; deliverance (*Mil.*)‡; an allowance of food statedly given out, as to a family, to servants, to horses, etc.‡; hence, the state of a horse that is kept and fed at a certain rate (to keep horses at *livery*); a distinctive dress in which the male servants of some person of position are clad; a distinctive garb worn by any body or association of persons; the body or association of persons wearing such a garb; characteristic covering or outward appearance (the *livery* of May, of grief).—*v.t.* To clothe in, or as in, livery.—**livery company,** *n.* A company of London liverymen,—**liveryman,** liv′ėr•i•man, *n.* One who wears a livery; one who keeps horses for hire; keeper of a livery stable.—**livery stable,** *n.* A stable where horses are kept for hire.

livid, liv′id, *a.* [L. *lividus*, from *liveo*, to be black and blue.] Black and blue; of a lead color; discolored, as flesh by contusion.—**lividity, lividness,** li•vid′i•ti, liv′id•nes, *n.* The state of being livid.

livre, lē•vr, *n.* [Fr., from L. *libra*, a pound.] An old French money of account, superseded by the franc.

lixivial, lixivious, lik•siv′i•al, lik•siv′i•us, *a.* [L. *lixivius*, made into lye, *lixivium*, lye, from *lix*, ashes.] Pertaining to lye or the water impregnated with alkaline salt extracted from wood ashes; of the nature of lye; obtained by lixiviation.—**lixiviate,** lik•siv′i•āt, *v.t.* To subject to the process of lixiviation.—**lixiviation,** lik•siv′i•ā″shon, *n.* The process of extracting alkaline salts from ashes by pouring water on them, the water passing through them taking up the salts and thus forming lye.—**lixivium,** lik•siv′i•um, *n.* Lye, that is, water impregnated with alkaline salts taken up from wood ashes.

lizard, liz′ėrd, *n.* [Fr. *lézard*, from L. *lacerta*, a lizard.] The popular name of many four-footed, tailed reptiles; *naut.* a piece of rope with one or more iron thimbles in it for ropes to lead through.

llama, lä′mä or lyä′mä, *n.* [A Peruvian word.] A hoofed ruminating quadruped of South America, allied to the camel, but smaller and not having a hump.

llanos, lan′ōz or lyä′nōz, *n. pl.* [Sp., from L. *planus*, level.] Vast and almost entirely level grassy plains in the northern part of South America.

Lloyd's, loidz, *n.* [Because the headquarters of the underwriters were originally (from 1716) *Lloyd's* coffeehouse.] A society of underwriters and others in London, Eng., for the collection and diffusion of maritime intelligence, the insurance, classification, and certification of vessels, and the transaction of business of various kinds connected with shipping.—*Lloyd's numbers*, numbers selected to designate the size of various parts of ships.—*Lloyd's Register*, an annual register of ships, their size, classification, etc.

lo, lō, *interj.* [A.Sax. *lá.*] Look; see; behold; observe.

loach, lōch, *n.* [Fr. *loche*, a loach, origin unknown.] A small, freshwater fish of the Old World, related to the carp family.

load, lōd, *n.* [O.E. *lode*, a load, from A.Sax. *hladan*, to load, pret. *hlód.* LADE.] What is laid on or put in anything for conveyance; a burden; as much as can be carried at one time by any conveyance; a grievous weight; an encumbrance; something that burdens or oppresses the mind or spirits; in building construction, the external forces acting upon a structure and the weight of the structure itself.—*Dead load*, one gradually applied and remaining steady.—*Live load*, one suddenly applied and accompanied by shock or vibration.—*Load line*, a line drawn on the side of a vessel to show the depth to which she may safely sink in the water.—*v.t.* To charge with a load; to lay a burden on; to weigh down, oppress, encumber; to bestow or confer in great abundance; to fill; to stuff; to make heavier for some purpose by adding special weight; to charge; as a gun with powder, or with powder and ball or shot.—*To load a cane* or *a whip*, to make it serve as a weapon by weighting it with lead or iron.—*To load dice*, to make one side heavier than the other, so as to cause the opposite to come regularly up.—*To load wine*, to drug or hocus wine.—**loader,** lō′dėr, *n.* One who loads.

loadstar, lodestar, lōd′stär, *n.* [*Lode*, *load*, is from A.Sax. *lád*, course, way (the termination of *livelihood*), from *lithan*, to go (akin to lead).] A star that leads or serves to guide; especially the pole star.—**loadstone, lodestone,** lōd′stōn, *n.* An ore of iron; the magnetic oxide of iron, which possesses the property of attracting iron, and the power of communicating this property to iron and steel, thus forming artificial magnets; hence, a magnet.

loaf, lōf, *n.* pl. **loaves,** lōvz. [A.Sax. *hláf*; Icel. *hleifr*, Goth. *hlaibs*, *hlaifs*, O.H.G. *hlaib*, G. *laib*, *leib*, allied to Rus. *chljeb*, Pol. *chleb*, bread, loaf. This word forms part of *lord*, *lady*, and *lammas*.] A regularly shaped or molded mass of bread of some size; a conical lump of sugar.

loaf, lōf, *v.i.* [The verb is from the noun *loafer*, G. *läufer*, D. *looper*, one that runs or gads about. Akin *leap*.] To lounge; to idle away one's time.—*v.t.* To pass or spend in idleness, as time; to spend lazily.—**loafer,** lō′fėr, *n.* A lazy or disreputable lounger; a lazy fellow who picks up a living anyhow.

loam, lōm, *n.* [A.Sax. *lám*; D. *leem*, G. *lehm*, loam, clay, allied to E. *lime*, and probably L. *limus*, slime, mud.] A rich soil compounded of sand, clay, vegetable mold, etc.; a mixture of sand, clay, etc., used for molding in iron founding.—*v.t.* To cover with loam; to clay.—**loamy,** lō′mi, *a.* Consisting of loam; partaking of the nature of loam.

loan, lōn, *n.* [A.Sax. *lan* (?), *laen*, a loan, from *lihan*, to lend; Icel. *lán*, Dan. *laan*, D. *leen*, a loan; same root as L. *linguo*, to leave (whence *relinquish*). LEND.] The act of lending or condition of being lent; a lending; that which is lent; especially a sum of money lent at interest.—*v.t.* and *i.* To lend.—**loan shark,** *n.* One who lends money at an excessive rate of interest.

loath, lōth, *a.* [A.Sax. *lath*, hateful, odious; O.H.G. *leit*, odious.] Filled with disgust or aversion; unwilling; reluctant; averse.—**loathe,** lōTH, *v.t.* —*loathed*, *loathing*. To feel disgust at; to have an extreme aversion of the appetite toward; to dislike greatly; to abhor.—**loathful,** lōTH′fụl, *a.*—**loathing,** lōTH′ing, *n.* Extreme disgust.—**loathly,** lōTH′li, *a.*—**loathsome,** lōTH′sum, *a.* Causing to loathe; exciting disgust.—**loathsomely,** lōTH′-sum•li, *adv.*—**loathsomeness,** lōTH′-sum•nes, *n.*

lob, lob, *v.t.*—*lobbed*, *lobbing*. [M.L.G., *lobbe*, short, fat person, akin Fris. *lob*, *lobbe*, hanging mass of flesh.] To throw or toss slowly and heavily. —*n.* An unhurried toss.

lobar, lō′ber, *a.* Pertaining to a lobe, as of the liver or brain.—*Lobar pneumonia*, inflammation of a whole lobe of the lungs, as distinguished from *lobular pneumonia*, which attacks the lungs in patches.

lobate, lobated. See LOBE.

lobby, lob′i, *n.* [L.L. *lobia*, *lobium*, etc., a portico, from O.H.G. *laubja*, G. *laube*, an arbor, from *laub*, a leaf, foliage. LEAF. *Lodge* is another form of this word.] An entrance hall, especially one used as a waiting room; a large public room in a hotel, where guests register and check out, etc.; a foyer, an open room or hallway at a theater entrance; in politics, a group of people who endeavor by personal persuasion to influence legislators.—*v.i.* To persuade by lobbying.—*v.t.* To accomplish by lobbying.

lobe, lōb, *n.* [Fr. *lobe*, L.L. *lobus*, from Fr. *lobos*, a lobe.] A round projecting part of an organ, as of the liver, lungs, brain, etc., the lower soft part of the ear; *bot.* a rounded projection or division of a leaf.—**lobate, lobated,** lō′bāt, lō′bā•ted, *a.* Consisting of or having lobes; applied to the foot of a bird furnished at the side with a broad-lobed membrane.—**lobed,** lōbd, *a.* Lobate.—**lobular,** lob′ū•lėr, *a.* Having the character of a lobule.—**lobule,** lob′ūl, *n.* [Dim. of *lobe*.] A small lobe.

lobelia, lō•bē′li•a, *n.* [From Matthew *Lobel*, physician and botanist to James I.] A genus of beautiful plants belonging to the bell-flower family, a blue species being common in gardens.

lobscouse, lob′skous, *n.* [For *lobscourse*, from *lob* and *course*, that is, course or dish for lubbers.] *Naut.* a hash of meat, biscuit, etc., baked.

lobster, lob′stėr, *n.* [A.Sax. *loppestere*, *lopystre*, corrupted from L. *locusta*, a lobster, a locust.] The name of certain long-tailed (macrurous), ten-footed crustaceans with large claws, allied to the crabs, and used for food.

lobular, lobule. See LOBE.

lobworm, lob′wėrm, *n.* The lugworm.

local, lō′kal, *a.* [L. *localis*, from *locus*, a place, seen also in *lieu*, *lieutenant*, *allocate*, *collocate*, *couch*, *allow*, etc.] Pertaining to a particular place; limited or confined to a spot, place, or definite district, *med.* confined to a particular part or organ.—*Local option* the principle by which the inhabitants of a locality vote directly on the sale there of intoxicants.—*n.* A local item of news; a local railroad train. (*Colloq.*)—**local color,** *n. Lit.* the distinctive features and peculiarities of a people or an area, used for interest and realism in writing.—**locale,** lō•kal′, *n.* A locality.—**localism,** lō′kal•izm, *n.* The state of being local; a local idiom or peculiarity of speech.—**locality,** lō•kal′i•ti, *n.* Position, situation, place, district; geographical place or situation.—**localization,** lo′kal•i•zā″shon, *n.* The act of localizing.—**localize,** lō′kal•īz, *v.t.*—*localized*, *localizing*. To fix in or assign to a particular place to discover or detect the place of.—**locally,** lō′kal•li, *adv.* With respect to place; in place.—**locate,** lō′kāt, *v.t.*—*located*, *locating*. [L. *loco*, *locatum*.] To set in a particular spot or position; to place; to settle.—*v.i.* To reside; to adopt a fixed residence. —**location,** lō•kā′shon, *n.* The act of locating; situation with respect to place; place.—**locative,** lō′ka•tiv, *a. Gram.* indicating place (a *locative* adjective; a *locative* case).—*n.* The locative case; a case expressing position.

loch, loch, *n.* [Gael.; allied to *lake*.] A lake; an arm of the sea running into the land, especially if narrow or to some extent landlocked.

lock, lok, *n.* [A.Sax. *loca*, *loc*, a lock; Icel. *lok*, a cover, shutter; *luka*, to shut; Dan. *lukke*, a lock, *lukke*, to lock; D. *luiken*, to shut.] An appliance used for fastening doors, chests, drawers, etc., its main feature being a bolt moved with a key; the mechanism by which a firearm is discharged; a fastening together; a state of being closely entangled; a grapple in wrestling; an enclosure in a canal, with gates at each end, used in raising or lowering boats as they pass from one level to another. —*v.t.* To fasten with a lock and key; to fasten so as to impede motion (to *lock* a wheel); to shut up or confine with, or as with, a lock, or in an enclosed place; to close fast; to seal; to join or unite firmly, as by intertwining or infolding; to embrace closely.—*To lock out*, to close the doors of an industrial establishment against the operatives; to throw out of employment, so as to bring workmen to the master's terms.—*To lock up*, to close or fasten with a lock; to confine; to restrain.—*v.i.* To become fast; to unite closely by mutual insertion of parts.—**lockage,** lok′ij, *n.* Works which form the locks on a canal; toll paid for passing the locks.—**locker,** lok′ėr, *n.* A closed receptacle, as a drawer or small cupboard in a ship, that may be closed with a lock.—**locket,** lok′et, *n.* [Dim. from *lock*.] A little case worn as an ornament, often pendent to a necklace.—**lock nut,** *n.* A nut, usually of metal, so constructed that it cannot work itself loose when properly applied.—**lockjaw,** *n. Med.* a form of tetanus consisting in spasmodic rigidity of the under jaw, so that the mouth cannot be opened.—**lockout,** *n.* The closing of a place of work against the workmen on the part of the employers, in order to bring the men to their terms as to hours, wages, etc.—**locksmith,** lok′smith, *n.* A mechanic whose occupation is to make or repair locks.—**lock step,** step used by a file of men keeping as close as possible to one another.—**lock stitch,** stitch formed by the locking of two threads.—**lockup,** *n.* A room or place in which persons under arrest are temporarily confined.

lock, lok, *n.* [A.Sax. *locc*=D. and Dan. *lok,* Icel. *lokkr,* G. *locke,* a curl or ringlet.] A tuft of hair or wool; a tress; a ringlet; a tuft of hay or other like substance.

locomotion, lō•ko•mō′shon, *n.* [L. *locus,* place, and *motio,* motion. LOCAL.] The act or power of moving from place to place.—**locomotive,** lō•ko•mō′tiv, *a.* Pertaining to locomotion; moving from place to place. —*n.* A self-driven vehicle, used for hauling passenger or freight cars, that runs on rails.

locomotor ataxia, lō•ko•mō′tėr ä•-tak′si•ä, *n.* [L.] *Med.* difficulty in walking and coordination caused by the effects of syphilis on the nervous system.

locoweed, lō′kō•wēd, *n.* [Prefix Sp. *loco,* crazy, and *weed.*] Any of the herbs of the genera *Astragalus* and *Oxytropis,* common in the southwestern U.S.

locum tenens, lō′kum tē′nenz, *n.* [L.] One who temporarily acts for another; a deputy or substitute.

locus, lō′kus, *n.* pl. **loci,** lō′sī. [L. LOCAL.] A place; specifically, *geom.* the line traversed by a point which is constrained to move in accordance with certain determinate conditions. —*Locus classicus,* the classical or all-important passage in an author or book dealing with a specific point.—*Locus standi,* recognized place or position; the right of a party to appear and be heard on the question before any tribunal.

locust, lō′kust, *n.* [L. *locusta* (whence *lobster*).] The name of several large insects allied to the grasshoppers and crickets, and some of which appear in immense multitudes and eat up every green thing; the locust tree.

locution, lō•kū′shon, *n.* [L. *locutio, locutionis,* from *loquor,* to speak. LOQUACIOUS.] A mode of speech; a phrase.

lode, lōd, *n.* [A.Sax. *lád,* a way, a course, same as *load* in *loadstar, loadstone.*] An open ditch; a straight water channel; *mining,* a metallic vein, or any regular mineral vein.

lodestar, *n.* Same as *Loadstar.*

lodestone, *n.* Same as *Loadstone.*

lodge, loj, *n.* [Fr. *loge,* It. *loggia,* from L.L. *lobia.* LOBBY.] A small house in a park, forest, or domain; a small country residence; a temporary habitation; a hut; a small house connected with a larger (a porter's *lodge*); a place where a society or branch of a society, as freemasons, holds its meetings; the body of members who meet at such a place.—*v.t.*—*lodged, lodging.* To furnish with temporary house accommodation; to provide with a temporary place of abode; to set, lay, or deposit for keeping (to *lodge* money in a bank); to plant, fix, or settle (to *lodge* an arrow in one's breast); to beat down or lay flat (growing crops).—*v.i.* To have a temporary abode; to dwell at someone else's house; to be deposited or fixed; to settle; to reside; to dwell or have a fixed position.—**lodging,** loj′ing, *n.* A place of temporary rest or residence; a room or rooms hired for residence by a person in the house of another: often in this sense spoken of as plural.—**lodginghouse,** *n.* A house in which lodgers are accommodated. —**lodgment,** loj′ment, *n.* The act of lodging; accumulation of something deposited; deposition; *milit.* the occupation of a position, as in a siege, by the besieging party.

lodicule, lō′di•kūl, *n.* [L. *lodicula,* a coverlet.] *Bot.* one of the scales which occur at the base of the fruit of grasses.

loess, lės, *n.* [G. *löss,* from *lösen,* to pour or dissolve.] An unstratified yellowish-brown loam or alluvial deposit found in North America, Europe and Asia.

loft, loft, *n.* [Dan. *loft,* a ceiling, loft; Icel. *lopt,* air, sky.] The room or space below the rafters; also a gallery in a church, hall, etc.; upper rooms in a factory or barn; the act of lofting.—*v.t.*—*lofted, lofting.* To furnish with a loft; to place in a loft (to *loft* hay); *golf,* to slant the face of the club; to hit the ball so it rises well; to clear an obstacle.—*v.i. Golf,* to loft the ball.—**loftily,** lof′-ti•li, *adv.*—**loftiness,** lof′ti•nes, *n.*—**lofty,** lof′ti, *a.* [From *loft, aloft.*] Much elevated in place; high; tall; elevated in condition or character; dignified; indicative of pride or haughtiness; proud; haughty; elevated in language or style; sublime; stately.

log, log, *n.* [Icel. *lág,* a felled tree; D. Dan. and G. *log,* the nautical log; akin *lie, lay.*] A bulky piece of timber unhewed; a large lump or piece of wood not shaped for any purpose; *naut.* a contrivance for measuring the rate of a ship's velocity through the water, consisting essentially in a piece of board in form of a quadrant of a circle, loaded so as to float upright, which, being thrown from a ship, drags on the line to which it is attached and causes it to unwind at a rate corresponding to the ship's velocity; the record of a ship's progress; a logbook.—**logbook,** *n. Naut.* a book in which are entered all particulars relating to the weather, winds, courses, etc., with any other matters relating to the vessel's voyage that are considered worthy of being registered; a book for memoranda kept by a public teacher.—**log chip, log ship,** *n.* The log or board attached to the log line.—**log line,** *n.* —**logrolling,** *n.* The lumbermen's water sport of treading floating logs; the political practice of legislators' combining forces to aid one another.—**logroller,** *n.*

log, log, *n.* A Hebrew measure of liquids, containing three-quarters or five-sixths of a pint.

loganberry, *n.* A cross between a blackberry and a raspberry.

logarithm, log′a•riTHm, *n.* [Gr. *logos,* ratio, and *arithmos,* number.] *Math.* the exponent of the power to which a given invariable number (or base) must be raised in order to produce another given number. Thus, in the common system of logarithms, in which the base is 10, the logarithm of 1000 is 3, because 10 raised to the third power is 1000. Many calculations are greatly facilitated by the use of logarithms, but for this special tables are required.—**logarithmic, logarithmical,** log•a•riTH′-mik, log•a•riTH′mi•kal, *a.* Pertaining to logarithms; consisting of logarithms.—**logarithmically,** log•a•-riTH′mi•kal•li, *adv.* By the use or aid of logarithms.

loggerhead, log′ėr•hed, *n.* [From *log* and *head*; comp. *blockhead.*] A blockhead; a dunce; a dolt; a species of turtle found in the south seas.—*To be at loggerheads,* to be engaged in a fight; to be involved in a dispute.—*To come to loggerheads,* to come to a quarrel.

loggia, loj′a, *n.* pl. **loggias,** loj′az [It. LODGE.] *Italian arch.* a term applied to a gallery or arcade in a building running along the front or part of the front and open on one side to the air, on which side are a series of pillars or slender piers.

logic, loj′ik, *n.* [Fr. *logique*; L. *logica*; Gr. *logikē* (*technē,* art, understood), from *logos,* reason.] The science of reasoning; the science of the operations of the understanding subservient to the estimation of evidence; the science whose chief end is to ascertain the principles on which all valid reasoning depends, and which may be applied to test the legitimacy of every conclusion that is drawn from premises; the art or practice of reasoning.—**logical,** loj′i•kal, *a.* Pertaining to logic; used in logic; according to the rules or principles of logic; skilled in logic; discriminating.—**logicality,** loj•i•-kal′i•ti, *n.* The state or quality of being logical.—**logically,** loj′i•kal•li, *adv.* In a logical manner.—**logician,** lō•jish′an, *n.* A person skilled in logic.—**logistic, logistical,** lō′jis•tik, lō•jis′ti•kal, *a.* [Gr. *logistikos,* from *logizomai,* to calculate or reckon.] Pertaining to judging, estimating, or calculating.

logogram, log′o•gram, *n.* [Gr. *logos,* a word, and *gramma,* a letter.] A single printing type that forms a word; a phonogramic symbol that, for the sake of brevity, represents a word.—**logographic, logo-**

graphical, lo•go•graf'ik, lo•go•graf'i•kal, *a.* Pertaining to logography.—**logography,** lō•gog'ra•fi, *n.* A method of printing, in which a type forms a word, instead of forming a letter.

logomachy, lō•gom'a•ki, *n.* [Gr. *logos,* word, and *machē,* contest.] A contention about words; a war of words.—**logomachist,** lō•gom'a•kist, *n.* One who contends about words.

Logos, lōg'os, *n.* [Gr., word, speech, reason, from *legō,* to speak.] The Word; the Divine Word; Christ.

logotype, log'o•tīp, *n.* A word or group of words cast together, as the name of a magazine, or the masthead of a paper, as opposed to a *ligature,* two or three letters united and cast together, as *æ, ffl.*

logwood, log'wụd, *n.* [From being imported in *logs.*] A dark-red dyewood, imported from Central America and the West Indies, much employed in dyeing and in calico printing to give a black or brown color.

loin, loin, *n.* [O.Fr. *logne* (Fr. *longe*), from L. *lumbus,* the loin.] The part of an animal on either side between the false ribs and the haunch bone; the part on either side of the trunk from the ribs to the lower limbs.

loiter, loi'tėr, *v.i.* [Allied to D. *leuteren,* to waggle or waver; perhaps to *late,* like Icel. *lötra,* to linger, from *latr,* late; comp. E. *linger,* from *long.*] To be slow in moving; to delay; to spend time idly; to hang about.—*v.t.* To consume in trifles; to waste carelessly; used with *away.*—**loiterer,** loi'tėr•ėr, *n.* One who loiters.

Loki, lō'ki, *n.* [Icel. *loki.*] *Scandinavian myth.* the evil deity, the author of all calamities.

loll, lol, *v.i.* [Akin to Icel. *lulla,* to loll, *lalla,* to toddle as a child.] To lie at ease; to lie in a careless attitude; to recline; to hang extended from the mouth, as the tongue of a dog when heated from exertion; to move in a lax, lazy manner.—*v.t.* To suffer to hang out, as the tongue.

Lollard, lol'ėrd, *n.* [L.G. and D. *lollen, lullen,* to sing, from the practice of the original Lollards of singing dirges at funerals.] A member of a society for the care of the sick and the burial of the dead, originating at Antwerp about 1300, and blamed for holding heretical opinions; one of the followers of Wickliffe in England.

lollipop, lol'i•pop, *n.* [From *loll,* to protrude the tongue, and *pop,* probably same as *pap,* infants' food.] Candy; usually a hard candy that is sucked rather than chewed, and so each piece is on a short stick, for easy handling; a sucker. (*Colloq.*)

Lombard, lom'bärd, *n.* [L.L. *Longobardi,* lit. 'long beards', being a latinized form of the German words for *long* and *beard.*] A native of Lombardy in Italy; an old name for a banker or money lender. Hence—*Lombard Street,* in London, where a large number of the principal bankers, moneybrokers, and bullion dealers have their offices.—*a.* Of or pertaining to Lombardy or the Lombards.—**Lombardic,** *a.*

Lombardy poplar, lom'bär•di, *n.* A variety of *Populus nigra italicus,* or black poplar, whose branches lie close to the upright, tapering tree trunk, used for beauty in landscaping rather than for shade.

loment, lomentum, lō'ment, lō•men'tum, *n. Bot.* an indehiscent legume which separates spontaneously by a transverse division between every two seeds.—**lomentaceous,** lō•men•tā'shus, *a.* Bearing loments; pertaining to a loment.

lone, lōn, *a.* [A contr. from *alone.*] Solitary; retired; unfrequented; without any companion or fellow; not having others near; single; unmarried, or in widowhood.—**loneliness,** lōn'li•nes, *n.* The condition of being lonely.—**lonely,** lōn'li, *a.* Unfrequented by man; retired; sequestered; not having others near; apart from fellows or companions; sad from want of companionship or sympathy.—**lonesome,** lōn'sum, *a.* Dreary from want of company or animation.

long, long, *a.* [A.Sax. *lang, long*= D., Dan., and G. *lang,* Icel. *langr,* Goth. *laggs* (*langs*); same as (but not borrowed from) L. *longus,* long. Hence verb to *long, along, belong, length, ling, linger,* etc.] Drawn out in a line or in the direction of length: opposed to *short,* and contradistinguished from *broad* or *wide*; drawn out or extended in time; lasting during a considerable time; continued or protracted; extended to any specified measure; having certain linear extent (a yard *long*; a mile *long*); occurring after a protracted interval; late; containing much verbal matter (a *long* speech or book). *Long home,* the grave or death. (O.T.)—*In the long run,* in the ultimate result.—*Long cloth,* a kind of fine cotton or calico fabric.—*Long clothes,* a baby's dress, which stretches much below the feet.—*Long firm,* a fictitious or pretended firm, consisting of swindlers who order goods without any intention of paying.—*Long ton,* the weight of 2240 pounds avoirdupois.—*n.* Something that is long.—*The long and the short,* or *the short and the long,* the sum of a matter in a few words; the whole.—*adv.* To a great extent in time; at a time far distant, either prior or posterior (not *long* before or after); throughout; without intermission (in such phrases as all my life *long,* forty years *long*).—**longboat,** *n.* The largest and strongest boat carried by a ship.—**longbow,** *n.* The old English archer's weapon, measuring about 6 feet long.—**long distance,** *a.* Being far away; placed at a great distance; over a great distance (*long-distance* running).—*n.* Telephone communication between two points widely separated.—**long dozen,** *n.* Thirteen.—**longhair,** *n.* One seriously interested in the arts; a lover of classical music.—**longhand,** long'hand, *n.* Ordinary written characters; handwriting.—**longheaded,** *a.* Having a long head; dolichocephalic; shrewd; far-seeing; discerning.—**longhorn,** *n.* A type of cattle so called because of their very long horns and, in the U. S., found mostly in Texas.—**long-lived,** long'līvd, *n.* Having a long life or existence; lasting long.—**long-range,** *a.* Involving a long period of time; at a great distance; designed to cover a long distance.—**long shot,** *n.* Something involving great risk but promising equally great rewards if successful; an entry (in a horse race) having little chance of winning.—**longshoreman,** *n.* A stevedore; a dock laborer employed at loading cargo, etc.—**long-suffering,** *a.* Bearing injuries or provocation for a long time; patient; not easily provoked.—*n.* Long endurance; patience of offense.—**longways, longwise,** long'wāz, long'wīz, *adv.* Lengthwise.—**long-winded,** *a.* Tedious in speaking, argument, or narration.

long, long, *v.i.* [A.Sax. *langian,* to lengthen, to long, from *lang,* long; similarly Icel. *langa,* G. *verlangen,* to wish for.] To desire earnestly or eagerly; usually followed by the infinitive, or *for* or *after*; to have an eager appetite; to have a morbid craving; usually followed by *for.*—**longing,** long'ing, *n.* An eager desire; a craving or morbid appetite.—**longingly,** long'ing•li, *adv.*

longevous, lon•jē'vus, *a.* [L. *longus,* long, and *ævum,* age.] Long-lived.—**longevity,** lon•jev'i•ti, *n.* [L. *longævitas.*] Length or duration of life; more generally, great length of life.

longing, longingly. See LONG, *v.i.*

longitude, lon'ji•tūd, *n.* [L. *longitudo,* from *longus,* long. LONG.] Length; measure along the longest line; *geog.* distance (in degrees, minutes, and seconds, or in miles) on the surface of the globe measured on an arc of the Equator or parallel of latitude, the meridian of Greenwich being selected as a starting point, and called the first meridian, and longitude being called *east* or *west* accordingly; *astron.* distance measured on the ecliptic from the first point of Aries.—**longitudinal,** lon•ji•tū'di•nal, *a.* Pertaining to longitude; running lengthwise, as distinguished from *transverse* or across.—*Longitudinal vibrations,* vibrations executed in the same line as that in which the undulation advances, as in the transmission of sound waves through air.—**longitudinally,** lon•ji•tū'di•nal•li, *adv.*

loo, lö *n.* [Originally called *lanterloo,* Fr. *lanturlu,* the meaningless refrain of a famous song.] A game at cards, formerly played with five cards, now commonly with three.

looby, lö'bi, *n.* [Allied to *lob, lubber*; W. *llabi,* a looby; *llab,* a blockhead.] An awkward, clumsy fellow; a lubber.

look, lụk, *v.i.* [A.Sax. *lócian,* to look; akin Prov. G. *lugen,* O.H.G. *luogen, luoken,* to look, G. *loch,* a hole.] To direct the eye toward an object; to gaze; to apply the mind or understanding; to consider; to have expectation or anticipation; to expect; to take heed or care; to mind; to have a particular direction or situation; to face; to front; to appear; to have a particular aspect; to give certain indications; to have or assume any air or manner.—*To look about*, to look on all sides or in different directions.—*To look after*, to tend; to take care of; to seek; to search for.—*To look down on* or *upon*, to regard as an inferior; to regard with contempt; to despise.—*To look for*, to expect (*to look for* news); to seek or search for.—*To look into*, to inspect closely; to examine.—*To look on*, to regard; to consider; to think or judge.—*To look over*, to examine one by one.—*To look out*, to be on the watch.—*To look to*, to watch; to take care of; to depend on for fulfilling some expectation.—*To look through*, to see through; to penetrate with the eye or with the understanding; to take a view of the contents of.—*v.t.* To express or manifest by a look.—*To look out*, to search for and discover.—*To look up*, to search for till found; to pay a visit to. (*Colloq.*)—*n.* Cast of countenance; air of the face; aspect; the act of looking or seeing.—**looker,** lu̦k'ėr, *n.* One who looks.—*A looker on*, a mere spectator.—**looking glass,** *n.* A glass silvered on the back and intended to show by reflection the person looking on it; a mirror.—**lookout,** *n.* A careful looking or watching for any object or event; a place from which such observation is made; the person or party watching.

loom, löm, *n.* [O.E. *lome*, A.Sax. *lóma*, tool, utensil, vessel; connections unknown. Hence *heir-loom*.] A frame or machine by means of which thread is worked into cloth being either driven by the person weaving (a *hand loom*) or driven and worked by steam or other motive power (a *power loom*); that part of an oar which is within the boat when used in rowing.

loom, löm, *v.i.* [Icel. *ljóma*, to shine, *ljómi*, a ray; A.Sax. *leómian*, *leóma*, a ray or beam.] To appear larger than the real dimensions and indistinctly; to show large in darkness or fog: said of distant objects; to appear to the mind faintly or as at a distance.—*n.* The indistinct and magnified appearance of objects in darkness, fog, mist, etc.

loon, lön, *n.* [Same word as O.D. *loen*, a stupid man.] A crazy person; an idler.

loon, lön, *n.* [O.E. *loom*, Dan. *loom*, Icel. *lómr*, G. *lohme*, *lomme*, a loon.] A bird, the great northern diver.

loony, lö'ni, *a.* [From *lunatic*.] Crazy; daft.—*n.* One who is crazy.

loop, löp, *n.* [Ir. *lup*, Gael. *lub*, *luib*, loop, noose, thong, etc.] The doubled part of a string, rope, chain, etc.; a noose; a bight; anything resembling a loop, as the bend of a river; *elec.* a complete electric or magnetic circuit; *phys.* the part of a string or column between two nodes.—*v.t.* To form into a loop or loops; *avi.* to make a complete circle vertically in the air.

loop, löp, *n.* [G. *luppe*, a loop, akin *lupp*, rennet; same root as E. *leap*, D. *loopen*, to run; comp. *run*, in sense of melting.] A mass of half-melted iron taken from the furnace in a pasty state for the forge or hammer.

loophole, löp'hōl, *n.* [D. *luipen*, to peep.] A small aperture in the wall of a fortification through which small arms are fired at an enemy; a hole that gives a passage or the means of escape; *fig.* an underhand or unfair opportunity of escape or evasion.

loose, lös, *a.* [A.Sax. *leás*, D. and G. *los*, Dan. Sw. *lös*, Icel. *laus*, loose; Goth. *laus*, empty; same as term. *-less*. *Lose*, *loss*, are closely allied.] Not attached together or to something fixed; untied; not fastened or confined; *fig.* free from ties; not tight or close (a *loose* garment); not dense, close, or compact (*loose* texture); not precise or exact; vague; indeterminate; lax; careless; unconnected; rambling; having lax bowels; dissolute; unchaste.—*To break loose*, to escape from confinement; to gain liberty by violence; *fig.* to cast off moral restraint.—*To let* or *set loose*, to free from restraint or confinement. Used substantively in the phrases.—*On the loose*, escaped from restraint; leading a loose life.—*To give a loose*, to give free vent. (*Thack.*)—*v.t.*—*loosed*, *loosing*. [Partly from the adj., partly from the allied A.Sax. *losian*, to set free.] To untie or unbind; to free from any fastening; to set free; to liberate; to relax; to loosen; to free from obligation, burden, or the like.—**loosely,** lös'li, *adv.* In a loose manner; laxly; slackly; carelessly; negligently; dissolutely.—**loosen,** lös'n, *v.t.* To make loose; to untie; to unfix or unsettle; to free from restraint, tightness, tension, firmness, or fixedness.—*v.i.* To become loose.—**loosener,** lös'n•ėr, *n.* One who or that which loosens.—**looseness,** lös'nes, *n.* The state of being loose or relaxed; slackness; laxity; dissoluteness.

loot, löt, *n.* [Hind. *lūt*, plunder.] Booty; plunder, especially such as is taken in a sacked city.—*v.t.* and *i.* To plunder, as a sacked city; to ransack.—**looter,** lö'tėr, *n.*

lop, lop, *v.t.* and *i.*—*lopped*, *lopping*. [Akin O.D. *luppen*, to maim.] To cut off, as the top or extreme part of anything or superfluous parts; to trim by cutting.—*n.* That which is lopped off.—**lopper,** lop'ėr, *n.*

lop, lop, *v.t.* and *i.* [Allied to *lap*.] To be pendulous.—**lop-eared,** *a.* Having pendulous ears.—**loppy,** lop'i, *a.*—**lopsided,** *a.* Heavier at one side than the other; lying to one side.

lope, lōp, *v.i.* [O.N. *hlaupa*, to leap.] To move or run with a long, easy stride.—*v.t.* To cause to lope.—*n.* An easy gait which may be maintained a long while.

lophobranchiate, lō•fo•brang'ki•āt, *a.* [Gr. *lophos*, a crest or tuft, and *branchia*, gills.] Having the gills disposed in tufts along the branchial arches, as in the pipefish and hippocampus.

loquacious, lo•kwā'shus, *a.* [L. *loquax*, *loquacis*, from *loquor*, to speak; Skr. *lap*, to speak, to talk; seen also in *locution*, *colloquy*, *eloquent*, *obloquy*, etc.] Talkative; given to continual talking; prating.—**loquaciously,** lo•kwā'shus•li, *adv.* In a loquacious manner.—**loquacity,** lo•kwas'i•ti, *n.* The quality of being loquacious; talkativeness.

loquat, lō'kwät, *n.* A Chinese and Japanese evergreen tree of the apple family, yielding a fruit the size of a large gooseberry, with the flavor of an apple.

loran, lō'ran, la̦'ran, *n.* [*Lo*ng-*ra*nge *n*avigation.] A device for determining a ship's position by means of pulsed signals sent out by two known radio stations.

lord, lord, *n.* [O.E. *laverd*, *lowerd*, etc., A.Sax. *hlaford*, a lord, from *hláf*, bread, a loaf, and *weard*, E. *ward*, that is, breadward.] A master; a person possessing supreme power and authority; a lady's husband; a ruler, governor, monarch; the proprietor of a manor; a nobleman; a title in Britain given to those who are noble by birth or creation, being thus applied to peers of the realm (dukes, marquises, earls, viscounts, and barons), and by courtesy to the sons of dukes and marquises, and to the eldest sons of earls; an honorary title of certain official personages, generally as part of a designation (*Lord* chancellor, *Lord*-mayor, *Lord*-provost); [cap.] the Supreme Being; Jehovah; Christ.—to Christ, especially in the expression *our Lord*.—*The Lord's Supper*, the sacrament of the Eucharist.—*Lords of Session*, the judges of the Court of Session in Scotland.—*Lords temporal*, those lay peers who have seats in the House of Lords.—*Lords spiritual*, the archbishops and bishops who have seats in the House of Lords.—*House of Lords*, that branch of the British legislature which consists of the lords spiritual and temporal assembled in one house.—*v.i.* To domineer; to rule with arbitrary or despotic sway: often followed by *over* and an indefinite *it* (to *lord it over* us).—**lordliness,** lord'li•nes, *n.* The state or quality of being lordly.—**lordly,** lord'li, *a.* Pertaining to, befitting, or suitable for a lord; large; liberal; haughty; imperious.—*adv.* Proudly; imperiously; despotically.—**Lord's day, the,** *n.* The first day of the week; Sunday.—**lordship,** lord'ship, *n.* The state or quality of being a lord; (with *his*, *your*, *their*) a title given to a lord; the territory over which a lord holds jurisdiction.

lordosis, lor•dō'sis, *n.* [N.L., from Gr. *lordōsis*, from *lordos*, bent so as to be convex in front.] *Med.* forward curvature of the spine.

lore, lōr, *n.* [A.Sax. *lár*, from stem of

laeran, to teach; D. *leer*, Dan. *laere*, G. *lehre*, lore. LEARN.] The store of knowledge which exists regarding anything; learning; erudition.—*Folklore*, the study of customs and legendary institutions.

lore, lōr, *n.* [L. *lorum*, a strap.] *Ornith.* the space between the bill and the eye of a bird; *entom.* a horny process observed in the mouth of some insects.

lorgnette, lorn•yet′, *n.* [Fr., from *lorgner*, to spy or peep.] An opera glass with folding handle; eyeglasses with hollow handle, into which they fold.

lorica, lo•rī′ka, *n.* [L., originally a corselet of leather thongs, from *lorum*, a thong.] An ancient Roman cuirass or corselet; a kind of lute or clay with which vessels are coated before they are exposed to the fire, as in chemical processes; *zool.* the protective case with which certain infusoria are provided.—**loricate,** lor′i•kāt, *v.t.*—*loricated, loricating.* To cover with some protective coating or crust.—**loricate, loricated,** lor′i•kā•ted, *pp.* Covered or plated over; covered as with plates of mail.

lorikeet, lor′i•kēt, *n.* [A dim. of *lory*, formed on the type of *parrakeet.*] The name of certain small Australian birds belonging to the parrot tribe.

loris, lō′ris, *n.* [Native name.] A quadrumanous mammal allied to the lemurs.

lorn, lorn, *a.* [An old or poetic pp. of *loss.* FORLORN.] Undone; forsaken; forlorn.

lorry, lor′i, *n.* [Comp. Prov. E. *lurry*, to pull or drag.] A four-wheeled truck or railroad car for heavy or bulky loads, with or without sides; a low, flat, motor-driven or horse-drawn truck.

lory, lō′ri, *n.* [Malay *luri.*] A name of certain Oriental birds of the parrot family with brilliant plumage.

lose, löz, *v.t.*—*lost* (pret. & pp.), *losing.* [A.Sax. *losian*, to become loose, to lose, from *los*, loss, also *leósan*, to lose, usually in the compound form *forleósan*, like Goth. *fraliusan*, Dan. *forlise*, D. *verliezen*, G. *verlieren.* The old pp. was *loren*, hence E. *lorn.*] To cease to have in possession, as through accident; to become dispossessed or rid of unintentionally; to cease to possess; to forfeit, as by unsuccessful contest; not to gain or win; to wander from and not be able to find; to miss; to cease to perceive, as from distance or darkness; to cease or fail to see or hear.—*To lose one's self*, to lose one's way; to be bewildered.—*To lose one's temper*, to become angry.—*To lose sight of*, to cease to see; to overlook; to omit to take into calculation.—*v.i.* To forfeit anything in contest; to fail in a competition; not to win; to suffer by comparison.—**loser,** lö′zėr, *n.* One who loses, or is deprived of anything by defeat, forfeiture, or the like.—**losing,** lö′zing, *a.* Causing or incurring loss.—**loss,** los, *n.* [A.Sax. *los*, damage.] The act of losing something; privation from something being lost; deprivation; forfeiture; failure to win or gain; that which is lost; quantity or amount lost; defeat; overthrow; ruin; misuse; failure to utilize (*loss* of time).—*To bear a loss*, to make it good; also, to sustain it without sinking under it.—*To be at a loss*, to be puzzled; to be unable to determine; to be in a state of uncertainty.—**lost,** lost, *p.* and *a.* Parted with; not to be found; no longer held or possessed; missing (a *lost* book or sheep); forfeited, as in an unsuccessful contest; not gained (a *lost* prize, a *lost* battle); not employed or enjoyed; misspent; squandered; wasted; having wandered from the way, bewildered; perplexed; ruined; quite undone; wrecked or drowned at sea; hardened beyond sensibility or recovery (*lost* to shame); no longer perceptible to the senses; not visible (a person *lost* in a crowd).—*The lost*, those who are doomed to misery in a future state.

lot, lot, *n.* [A.Sax. *hlot*, from *hleótan*, to get by lot; D. *lot*, Dan. *lod*, Icel. *hlutr*, G. *loos*, Goth. *hlauts*, lot. Hence *allot*; akin *lottery.*] Something selected by or falling to a person by chance, and adopted to determine his fate, portion, or conduct; the part, fate, or fortune which falls to one by chance; part in life allotted to a person; a distinct portion or parcel (a *lot* of goods); a large or considerable quantity or number (a *lot* of people): often in plural in same sense (he has *lots* of money).—*To cast in one's lot with*, to connect one's fortunes with.—*To cast lots*, to throw dice or use similarly some other contrivance to settle a matter as by previous agreement determined.—*To draw lots*, to determine an event by drawing so many lots from a number whose marks are concealed from the drawers.—*v.t.*—*lotted, lotting.* To allot; to assign; to distribute; to sort; to catalogue; to portion.

loth, lōth, *a.* [See LOATH.] Unwilling; not inclined; reluctant; loath.

Lothario, lō•thā′ri•ō, *n.* [From *Lothario*, one of the characters in Rowe's *Fair Penitent.*] A gay libertine; a sėducer of female virtue; a gay deceiver: as *Lovelace*, the character in Richardson's *Clarissa.*

lotion, lō′shon, *n.* [L. *lotio*, from *lavo*, to wash. LAVE.] A wash or fluid preparation for improving the complexion, etc.; a fluid applied externally in cutaneous diseases to relieve pain, and the like.

lottery, lot′ėr•i, *n.* [Fr. *loterie.* LOT.] Allotment or distribution by lots or chance; a procedure or scheme for the distribution of prizes by lot; the drawing of lots.

lotto, lot′ō, *n.* [It. *lotto*, lottery.] A game of chance, played with a series of balls or knobs, numbering from one to ninety, with a set of cards or counters having corresponding numbers.

lotus, lō′tus, *n.* [Gr. *lōtos.*] A name vaguely applied to a number of different plants famous in mythology and tradition; especially, a tree, the fruit of which was fabled among the ancient Greeks to have the property of making people forget their country and friends and to remain idle in the lotus-land; a name also applied to the Egyptian water lily and other plants.—**lotus-eater,** *n.* in the *Odyssey*, one of a fabulous people who ate lotus fruit, which induced languor and forgetfulness of home.

loud, loud, *a.* [A.Sax. *hlud*, loud; O.Sax. O.Fris. *hlud*, D. *luid*, G. *laut*, loud; Icel. *hljóth*, G. *laut*, sound; akin *listen*; cog. Gr. *klyó*, to hear, *klytos*, famous; L. (*in*)*clytus*, famous; *laus*, praise, whence E. *laud.*] Strong or powerful in sound; high-sounding; making use of high words; clamorous; vehement; flashy; showy: colloquially applied to dress or manner.—*adv.* Loudly.—**loudly,** loud′li, *adv.* In a loud manner; with great sound or noise; noisily; clamorously; vehemently.—**loudness,** loud′nes, *n.* The quality of being loud; noise; clamor.

louis d'or, lö•i•dor, *n.* [Fr., a Louis of gold, as *Napoleon*, *Daric* (Darius), *Philip*, *Jacobus.*] A gold coin of France, first struck in 1640, in the reign of *Louis* XIII.

lounge, lounj, *v.i.*—*lounged, lounging.* [O.E. *lungis*, an awkward, slow-moving fellow, from O.Fr. *lóngis*, *longin*, a lout, from *long*, L. *longus*, long.] To dawdle or loiter; to spend the time in idly moving about; to recline in a lazy manner; to loll.—*n.* A sauntering or strolling; the act of reclining at ease or lolling; a place which idlers frequent; a kind of couch or sofa.—**lounger,** loun′jėr, *n.* One who lounges.

louse, lous, *n.* pl. **lice,** līs, [A.Sax. *lús*, pl. *lys*=D. *luis*, Dan. *lus*, Icel. *lús*, G. *laus*, perhaps from root of *lose.*] The common name of various wingless insects, parasitic on man and other animals.—*v.t.* (louz)—*loused, lousing.* To clean from lice.—**lousily,** lou′zi•li, *adv.* In a lousy manner.—**lousiness,** lou′zi•nes, *n.* The state of being lousy.—**lousy,** lou′zi, *a.* Swarming with lice; infested with lice.

lout, lout, *v.i.* [A.Sax. *lútan*, to bow or stoop; Icel. *lúta*, Dan. *lude*, to stoop; same root as *little.*] To bend, bow, or stoop down.—*n.* A mean awkward fellow; a bumpkin; a clown.—**loutish,** lout′ish, *a.* Clownish; rude; awkward.—**loutishly,** lout′ish•li, *adv.* In a loutish manner.—**loutishness,** lout′ish•nes, *n.*

louver, lö′vėr, *n.* [Fr. *lover*, *lovier*, a louver; a word of which the origin is unknown.] A dome or turret rising out of the roof of a hall or other apartment, formerly open at the sides, and intended to allow the smoke to escape.—*Louver window*, a window partially closed by sloping boards or bars called *louver boards* (corrupted into *luffer* or *lever boards*), placed across so as to admit air, but exclude rain.

lovage, luv′ij, *n.* [By corruption from L. *ligusticum*, lovage, from *Ligusticus*, Ligurian.] A name of certain stout, umbelliferous plants of Europe, one of them specially known as Scottish lovage.

love, luv, *v.t.—loved, loving.* [A.Sax. *lufian*, from *lufu*, love; D. *lieven*, G. *lieben*, to love, *liebe*, love; allied to *lief*, dear, *leave*, permission, be-*lieve*; L. *libido*, desire, *liber*, free (whence *liberal*); *libeo*, *lubeo*, to please; Skr. *lubh*, to desire.] To regard with a strong feeling of affection; to have a devoted attachment to; to regard with the characteristic feelings of one sex toward the other; to like; to be pleased with; to delight in.—*v.i.* To be in love; to love each other; to be tenderly attached.—*n.* A strong feeling of affection; devoted attachment to a person; especially, devoted attachment to a person of the opposite sex; courtship (as in the phrase to *make love to*, that is, to court, to woo); fondness; strong liking (*love* of home, of art, etc.); the object beloved; a sweetheart; a representation or personification of love; a Cupid.—*Love* is the first element in a great number of compound words of obvious signification.—**lovable, loveable,** luv′a•bl, *a.* Worthy of love; amiable.—**love apple,** *n.* The tomato.—**lovebird,** *n.* A name of a diminutive bird belonging to the parrot family, so called from the great attachment shown to each other by the male and female.—**love feast,** *n.* AGAPE.—**Love-in-idleness,** *n.* A plant, the heart's-ease.—**love knot,** *n.* A complicated knot, or a figure representing such; so called from being symbolic of love.—**loveless,** luv′les, *a.* Void of love.—**lovelily,**† luv′li•li, *adv.* In a lovely manner.—**loveliness,** luv′li•nes, *n.* The state or quality of being lovely; great beauty.—**lovelock,** *n.* A particular curl or lock of hair hanging by itself or so as to appear prominently.—**lovelorn,** *a.* Forsaken by one's love; pining or suffering from love.—**lovely,** luv′li, *a.* Fitted to attract or excite love; exciting admiration through beauty; extremely beautiful.—**love-making,** *n.* Courtship; paying one's addresses to a lady.—**lover,** luv′ėr, *n.* One who loves or is attached to another; a person in love; a man who loves a woman; one who likes or has a fondness for anything (a *lover* of books).—**lovesick,** *a.* Sick or languishing with love; expressive of languishing love.—**loving,** luv′ing, *p.* and *a.* Fond; affectionate; expressing love or kindness.—**loving cup,** *n.* A large cup containing liquor passed from guest to guest at banquets, especially those of a ceremonious character.—**loving-kindness,** luv′ing•kīnd′nes, *n.* Tender regard; mercy; favor: a scriptural word.—**lovingly,** luv′ing•li, *adv.* In a loving manner; affectionately.—**lovingness,** luv′ing•nes, *n.*

low, lō, *a.* [O.E. *law*, *lagh*, etc.; not in A.Sax. = Icel. *lágr*, Dan. *lav*. D. *laag*; akin to *lie*, and to *law*.] Not rising to any great elevation; of little height: the opposite of *high*; not of the usual height; much below the adjacent ground; not much above sea level; below the usual rate or amount (*low* wages; a *low* estimate); not loud; grave; depressed in the scale of sounds; indicative of a numerical smallness (a *low* number); near or not very distant from the Equator (a *low* latitude, as opposed to a *high* latitude); dejected; depressed; humble in rank; groveling; base; dishonorable; feeble; having little vital energy (a *low* pulse, a *low* state of health); not excessive or intense; not violent (a *low* temperature); plain; not rich, high-seasoned, or nourishing (a *low* diet); in a prone position.—*Low Church*, the party in the *Ch.* of *Eng.* which believes in evangelical doctrine.—*Low Countries*, *n.* The land region near the North Sea corresponding to the Netherlands, Belgium and Luxembourg.—*Low Sunday*, the Sunday next after Easter.—*Low water, low tide*, the lowest point of the ebb or receding tide.—*adv.* Not aloft or on high; near the ground; under the usual price; in a mean condition.—**low-born,** *a.* Of mean or lowly birth.—**lowbrow,** *a.* Pertaining to those of uncultivated tastes.—*n.* One who is unable to appreciate intellectual influences.—**lower case,** *n. Print.* the case of boxes that contains the small letters of printing type, hence, small letters of printing type.—**low-down,** *a.* Mean; sneaking; treacherous.—*n.* The facts in the case; the truth of the matter.—**lowland,** lō′land, *n.* Land which is low with respect to the neighboring country; a low or level country.—*The Lowlands*, applies to the southern parts of Scotland.—**lowliness,** lō′li•nes, *n.*—**lowly,** lō′li, *a.* Low or humble in position of life; not lofty or exalted; meek; free from pride.—*adv.* In a low manner or condition.—**lowness,** lō′nes, *n.* Want of elevation; depression; dejection; meanness.—**low-pressure,** *a.* Having a low degree of expansive force, and consequently exerting a low degree of pressure; applied to steam or steam engines.—**low-spirited,** *a.* Cast down in spirit; dejected; depressed.

low, lō, *v.i.* [A.Sax. *hlówan* = D. *loeijen*, Icel. *hlóa*, O.H.G. *hlojan*, to low.] To bellow, as an ox or cow.—*n.* The sound uttered by a bovine animal, as a bull, ox, cow; a moo.—**lowing,** lō′ing, *n.* The bellowing or cry of cattle.

lower, lō′ėr, *v.t.* [From *lower*, compar. of *low*; comp. *linger*, from *long*, adj.] To make lower in position; to let down; to take or bring down; to reduce or humble; to make less high or haughty; to reduce, as value or amount.

lower, lou′ėr, *v.i.* [Same word as D. *loeren*, to frown; L.G. *luren*, to look sullen; akin to *leer*.] To frown; to look sullen; to appear dark or gloomy; to be clouded; to threaten a storm.—**lowering,** lou′ėr•ing, *p.* and *a.* Threatening a storm; cloudy; overcast.—**loweringly,** lou′ėr•ing•li, *adv.* In a lowering manner.—**lowery,** lou′ėr•i, *a.* Cloudy; gloomy.

lown, loun, *n.* A low fellow; a loon. (*Shak.*)

lox, loks, *n.* [Yiddish, *laks*, from M.H.G. *lahs*, salmon.] A kind of smoked salmon.

lox, loks, *n.* Liquid oxygen, a colloq. abbreviation.

loxodromic, lok•so•drom′ik, *a.* [Gr. *loxos*, oblique, and *dromos*, a course.] Pertaining to oblique sailing, or sailing by the rhumb.—*Loxodromic curve*, or *line*, or *spiral*, the path of a ship when her course is directed constantly toward the same point of the compass, so as to cut all the meridians at equal angles.—**loxodromics, loxodromy,** lok•so•drom′iks, lok•sod′ro•mi, *n.*

loyal, loi′al, *a.* [Fr. *loyal*, O.Fr. *loial*, *leial*, *leal*, from L. *legalis*, legal, from *lex*, *legis*, a law. *Leal* is another form. LEGAL.] True or faithful in allegiance; faithful to the lawful government, to a prince or superior; true to plighted faith, duty, or love; not treacherous; constant.—**loyalist,** loi′al•ist, *n.* A person who adheres to his sovereign or to constituted authority.—**loyally,** loi′al•li, *adv.* In a loyal manner; faithfully.—**loyalism,** loi′al•izm, *n.* Loyalty.—**loyalty,** loi′al•ti, *n.* The state or quality of being loyal; fidelity; constancy.

lozenge, loz′enj, *n.* [Fr. *losange*, probably from Sp. *losa*, a slate or flat stone for paving.] A rectilineal figure with four equal sides, having two acute and two obtuse angles: called also a *diamond*; a small medicated candy in the form of a lozenge.

LSD-25. See LYSERGIC ACID DIETHYLAMIDE.

luau, lū′ou, *n.* [Hawaiian.] A Hawaiian dinner of many courses served outdoors.

lubber, lub′ėr, *n.* [Allied to *looby*, *lob*, W. *llob*, *llabi*, a lubber.] A clumsy or awkward fellow; a term applied by sailors to one who does not know seamanship.—*Lubber's point*, a black vertical mark drawn on the inside of the case of the mariner's compass in a line with the ship's head, as a guide to show the vessel's course.—*Lubber's hole*, the hole in the top or platform at the head of a lower mast through which sailors may mount without going over the rim by the futtock shrouds.—**lubberly,** lub′ėr•li, *a.* Like a lubber; clumsy; clownish.

lubricate, lū′bri•kāt, *v.t.—lubricated, lubricating.* [L. *lubrico*, from *lubricus*, slippery.] To soften with an emollient or mucilaginous substance; to rub or supply with an oily or greasy substance, for diminishing friction.—**lubricant,** lū′bri•kant, *a.* Lubricating.—*n.* That which lubricates.—**lubrication,** lū•bri•kā′shon, *n.* The act of lubricating.—**lubricator,** lū′bri•kā•tėr, *n.* One who or that which lubricates; an oil cup attached to a machine.—**lubricity,** lū•bris′i•ti, *n.* Smoothness or slipperiness; instability; shiftiness; lasciviousness.

lucarne, lū′kärn, *n.* [Fr. *lucarne*, L.

lucerna, a lamp, from *luceo*, to shine.] A dormer or garret window.

luce, lūs, *n.* [L. *lucius.*] The fish called the pike.

lucent, lū′sent, *a.* [L. *lucens, lucentis*, ppr. of *luceo*, to shine. LUCID.] Shining; bright; resplendent.—**lucency**, lū′sen•si, *n.* The state or quality of being lucent.

lucerne, lucern, lū′sėrn, *n.* [Fr. *luzerne, luserne*; origin unknown.] A leguminous plant cultivated for fodder in the U. S. and Europe; also called alfalfa.

lucid, lū′sid, *a.* [L. *lucidus*, akin to L. *lucere*, to shine.] Bright; clear; easily understandable; rational or sane.—**lucidity**, lū•sid′i•ti, *n.*

Lucifer, lū′si•fėr, *n.* [L. *lux, lucis*, light, and *fero*, to bring.] The morning star; Satan (from an erroneous interpretation of the term as applied by Isaiah); a person of Satanic attributes; [*not cap.*] a match ignitible by friction; called also *lucifer-match.* —**luciferous**, lū•cif′ėr•us, *a.* Light-giving.

luciferin, lū•cif′ėr•in, *n.* A substance generated by luminescent fishes and insects which causes their luminosity.

luck, luk, *n.* [O.Fris. *luk*, D. *luk*, *geluk*, G. *glück*, fortune, prosperity; allied to D. *lokken*, Dan. *lokke*, G. *locken*, to entice.] What is regarded as happening by chance; what chance or fortune sends; fortune; chance; accident; hap; good fortune; success.—**luckily**, luk′i•li, *adv.* In a lucky manner.—**luckiness**, luk′i•nes, *n.* The state or quality of being lucky. —**luckless**, luk′les, *a.* Without luck; ill-fated; unfortunate.—**lucklessly**, luk′les•li, *adv.* In a luckless manner. —**lucky**, luk′i, *a.* Favored by luck; fortunate; meeting with good success; sent by good luck; favorable; auspicious.

lucrative, lū′kra•tiv, *a.* [Fr. *lucratif*, from L. *lucrativus*, from *lucror*, to profit, from *lucrum*, gain; same root as G. *lohn*, reward.] Yielding lucre or gain; gainful; profitable.—**lucratively**, lū′kra•tiv•li, *adv.* In a lucrative manner.—**lucre**, lū′kėr, *n.* [Fr. *lucre*, L. *lucrum.*] Gain in money; profit; pelf: often in sense of base or unworthy gain.

lucubrate, lū′kū•brāt, *v.i.* [L. *lucubro*, *lucubratum*, to study by candlelight, from obs. adj. *lucuber*, bringing light, from *lux*, light.] To study by candlelight or a lamp; to study by night.—*v.t.* To elaborate, as by laborious night study.—**lucubration**, lū•kū•brā′shon, *n.* Nocturnal study; what is composed, or supposed to be composed, by night; a literary composition of any kind.—**lucubrator**, lū′kū•brā•tėr, *n.* One who makes lucubrations.

luculent, lū′kū•lent, *a.* [L. *luculentus*, from *luceo*, to shine.] Lucid; bright; evident; unmistakable.

Lucullan, lū•kul′len, *a.* [From the Roman consul *Lucullus*, who was famous for luxurious living.] Bountiful; voluptuous.

Luddite, lud′īt, *n.* In 18th Century England, one of the rioters against the displacement of factory workers by machinery. (From a leader, Ned Lud.)

ludicrous, lū′dik•rus, *a.* [L. *ludicrus*, from *ludus*, sport or game; seen also in *allude, delude, elude, illusion, prelude.*] Adapted to raise good-humored laughter; very ridiculous; comical; droll.—**ludicrously**, lū′dik•rus•li, *adv.* In a ludicrous manner.—**ludicrousness**, lū′dik•rus•nes, *n.*

lues, lū′ēz, *n.* [L.] A poison or pestilence; a plague.—*Lues venerea*, the venereal disease.

luff, luf, *n.* [Formerly *loof*, from D. *loef*, Dan. *luv*, G. *luf*, weather gauge.] *Naut.* the weather gauge; the weather part of a fore-and-aft sail.—*v.t.* and *i.* To turn the head of a ship toward the wind.

lug, lug, *v.t.*—*lugged, lugging.* [A.Sax. *geluggian*, to lug; N. *lugga*, to haul by the hair.] To haul; to drag; to pull along or carry, as something heavy and moved with difficulty; to introduce laboriously (to *lug* a story into the conversation).—*v.i.* To pull or tug.—*n.* The ear; a projecting part of an object resembling the human ear, as the handle of a vessel. —**luggage**, lug′ij, *n.* That which is lugged; baggage; collectively, the containers for a traveler's belongings. —**lugger**, lug′ėr, *n.* A vessel carrying either two or three lugsails.—**lugsail**, *n.* A square sail bent upon a yard that hangs obliquely to the mast at one-third of its length.

lugubrious, lū•gū′bri•us, *a.* [L. *lugubris*, mournful, from *lugeo*, to weep; akin Gr. *lygros*, sad.] Mournful; indicating or expressive of sorrow; doleful.—**lugubriously**, lū•gū′bri•us•li, *adv.* In a lugubrious manner.—**lugubriousness**, lū•gū′bri•us•nes, *n.* The quality of being lugubrious.

lugworm, lug′wėrm, *n.* [Sw. *lugg*, tuft of hair, the forelock; it has tufts and bristles along its sides.] An annelid or worm which burrows in the muddy sand of the shore, and is much esteemed for bait. Also called *Lobworm.*

lukewarm, lūk′wa̤rm, *a.* [O.E. *luke*, lukewarm, D. *leuk*, G. *lau*, lukewarm.] Moderately warm; tepid; not ardent; not zealous; cool; indifferent.—**lukewarmly**, lūk′wa̤rm•li, *adv.*—**lukewarmness**, lūk′wa̤rm•nes, *n.*

lull, lul, *v.t.* [Dan. *lulle*, Sw. *lulla*, G. *lullen*; probably an imitation of the sound.] To sing to in order to induce to sleep; to cause to rest by gentle, soothing means; to quiet; to compose.—*v.i.* To subside; to cease; to become calm (the wind *lulls*).—*n.* A season of temporary quiet after storm, tumult, or confusion.—**lullaby**, lul′a•bī, *n.* A song to lull or quiet babes.

lumbago, lum•bā′gō, *n.* [L., from *lumbus*, loin.] Rheumatism or rheumatic pains affecting the lumbar region.—**lumbar**, lum′bėr, *a.* [L. *lumbus*, a loin. LOIN.] Pertaining to the loins.—*Lumbar region*, the portion of the body between the false ribs and the upper part of the hip bone; the small of the back.

lumber, lum′bėr, *n.* [Originally a pawnbroking establishment, from the *Lombards*, who were famed as pawnbrokers or moneylenders.] Things bulky and thrown aside as of no use; old furniture, discarded utensils, or the like; timber sawed or split for use as beams, boards, planks, etc.—*v.t.* To heap together in disorder; to fill with lumber.—*v.i.* To move heavily, as a vehicle; to cut timber in the forest and prepare it for the market.—**lumbering**, *n.* Logging; cutting and removing timber for commercial purposes.—*a.* Clumsy; awkward.—**lumberjack**, *n.* A timber cutter. (*Colloq.*)

lumbrical, lum′bri•kal, *a.* [L. *lumbricus*, a worm.] Pertaining to or resembling a worm.—*n.* A wormlike muscle of the fingers and toes.

lumen, lö′men, *n.* [L. for *light.*] The cavity of a blood vessel or other tube; a unit of light, being the light emitted by a source of one international candle intensity per unit space angle in a second.

luminary, lū′mi•na•ri, *n.* [Fr. *luminaire*, L. *luminare*, from *lumen, luminis*, light, for *lucmen*, from *luceo*, to shine. LUCID.] Any body that gives light, but chiefly one of the heavenly bodies; a person who enlightens mankind.—**luminescence**, *n.* The emission of light by certain bodies that have been exposed to light or radiant energy, or self-generated light, as in fireflies and certain deep-sea fishes.—**luminiferous**, lū•mi•nif′ėr•us, *a.* Producing light; yielding light; serving as the medium for conveying light (the *luminiferous* ether).—**luminosity, luminousness**, lū•mi•nos′i•ti, lū•mi•nus•nes, *n.* The quality of being luminous; brightness; clearness.—**luminous**, lū′mi•nus, *a.* [L. *luminosus.*] Shining; emitting light; bright; brilliant; giving mental light; clear (a *luminous* essay or argument).

lummox, lum′uks, *n.* A dull-witted, awkward person.

lump, lump, *n.* [O.D. *lompe*, Sw. *lump*, N. *lump*, piece, mass; allied to *lubber, lunch.*] A small mass of matter, of no definite shape; a mass of things blended or thrown together without order or distinction.—*In the lump*, the whole together; in gross.—*v.t.* To throw into a mass; to take in the gross.—**lumpfish**, lump′fish, *n.* A fish of the northern seas, having the ventral fins modified into a sucker, by means of which it adheres to bodies.—**lumpy**, lump′i, *a.* Full of lumps or small compact masses.

lump, lump, *v.t.* [Origin unknown.] To put up with (something disagreeable) (like it or *lump* it).

lunacy, lū′na•si, *n.* [From L. *lunaticus*, lunatic, moon-struck, from *luna*, the moon (lunatics being at one time supposed to be affected by the moon), for *lucna*, from root of *luceo*, to shine. LUCID.] The state or quality of being lunatic; insanity; properly the kind of insanity which is broken by intervals of reason; the height of folly.—**lunatic**, lū′na•tik, *a.* Affected by lunacy; mad; insane.—

n. A person affected by lunacy; an insane person.—*Lunatic asylum,* a house or hospital established for the reception of lunatics.

luna moth, *n.* A large American moth (*Tropaea luna*) having long tails on the hind wings and greenish coloring.

lunar, lū'nėr, *a.* [L. *lunaris,* from *luna,* the moon. LUNACY.] Pertaining to the moon; measured by the revolutions of the moon (*lunar* days or years).—*Lunar caustic,* nitrate of silver (silver being called *Luna* by the alchemists).—*Lunar month,* the period of a complete revolution of the moon, 29½ days.—**lunate, lunated,** lū'nāt, lū'nā•ted. *a.* Crescent-shaped.—**lunation,** lū•nā'shon, *n.* The time from one new moon to the following.

lunch, lunsh, *n.* [A form of *lump,* as *hunch* of *hump, bunch* of *bump.*] A luncheon.—*v.i.* To eat a lunch.—**luncheon,** lunsh'on, *n.* [A longer form of *lunch,* perhaps for *lunching.*] A slight repast or meal between breakfast and dinner.—**luncheonette,** lunsh•on•et', *n.* A lunchroom where light lunches are served.—**lunchroom,** u. A restaurant where quick meals are served.

lune, lūn, *n.* [L. *luna,* the moon. LUNACY.] Anything in the shape of a crescent or half-moon; a geometrical figure in shape of a crescent.—**lunette,** lū•net', *n.* [Fr. *lunette,* dim. from L. *luna.*] *Fort.* a work in the form of a redan with flanks, used as an advanced work; *arch.* an aperture for the admission of light in a concave ceiling; *archaeol.* a crescent-shaped ornament for the neck.—**luniform,** lū'ni•form, *a.* Resembling the moon.

lung, lung, *n.* [A.Sax. *lunge,* pl. *lungan,* Icel. *lunga,* D. *long,* D. and G. *lunge,* a lung; same root as *light,* from their lightness (comp. the name *lights*).] One of the two organs of respiration in air-breathing animals, light and spongy and full of air cells; a similar saclike respiratory organ found in certain air-breathing invertebrates; an underwater device that enables persons leaving a submarine to rise to the surface; a device used to introduce, mechanically, fresh air into the lungs.—**lungwort,** lung'wėrt, *n.* A common garden flower, having leaves speckled like lungs.—**lungfish,** *n.* One of a group of fishes (Dipnoi) breathing by means of lungs as well as gills.

lunge, lunj, *n.* [Formerly *longe, allonge,* from Fr. *allonger,* to lengthen, to thrust—L. *ad,* to, *longus,* long.] A sudden thrust or pass, as with a sword.—*v.i.*—*lunged, lunging.* To make a thrust or pass, as with a sword or rapier.—*v.t.* To exercise (a horse) by making him run round in a ring while held by a *long* rein.

lunisolar, lū•ni•sō'lėr, *a.* [L. *luna,* moon, and *sol,* sun.] Compounded of the revolutions of the sun and moon; resulting from the united action of the sun and moon.—**lunula, lunule,** lū'nū•la, lū'nūl, *n.* [Dim. of L. *luna,* the moon.] Something in the shape of a little moon or crescent.—**lunulate, lunulated,** lū'nū•lāt, lū'nū•lā•ted, *a.* Resembling a small crescent.

Lupercal, lū•pėr'kal or lū'pėr•kal, *a.* Pertaining to the Lupercalia, or feasts of the Romans in honor of Lupercus or Pan.—*n.* pl. **Lupercalia,** lū•pėr•kā'li•a. An ancient Roman feast in honor of Pan.

lupine, lū'pin, *a.* [L. *lupus,* a wolf; cog. with E. *wolf.*] Like a wolf; wolfish; ravenous.—**lupine,** lū'pin, *n.* [Fr. *lupin;* L. *lupinus,* in allusion to its destroying or exhausting land.] The name of various leguminous plants, some of which are commonly cultivated in gardens for the sake of their gaily-colored flowers.

lupulin, lupuline, lū'pū•lin, *n.* [L. *lupulus,* hops.] The peculiar bitter aromatic principle of the hop; the fine yellow powder of hops, which contains the bitter principle, largely used in medicine.

lupus, lū'pus, *n.* [L., a wolf.] A disease which eats away the flesh, producing ragged ulcerations of the nose, cheeks, forehead, eyelids, and lips.

lurch, lėrch, *n.* [O.Fr. *lourche,* It. *lurcio,* G. *lurz, lurtsch,* a lurch at cribbage.] A term in the game of cribbage, denoting the position of a player who has not made his thirty-first hole when his opponent has pegged his sixty-first. Hence, *to leave in the lurch,* to leave in a difficult situation or in embarrassment; to leave in a forlorn state or without help.

lurch, lėrch, *v.i.* [A form of *lurk,* as *church* of *kirk, birch* of *birk,* etc. LURK.] To lie in ambush or in secret; to lie close; to lurk; to shift or to play tricks (*Shak.*); to roll suddenly to one side, as a ship in a heavy sea; to stagger to one side, as a tipsy man.—*n.* A sudden roll of a ship; a roll or stagger of a person.—**lurcher,** lėrch'ėr, *n.* One that lies in wait or lurks; a dog that lies in wait for game.

lurdan, lurdane, lėr'dan, lėr'dān, *a.* [O.Fr. *lourdin, lourdein,* from *lourd,* heavy, dull.] Blockish; stupid; clownish; lazy and useless. (*Tenn.*)

lure, lūr, *n.* [Fr. *leurre,* from M.H.G., *luodar,* a lure, G. *luder,* carrion, a bait for wild beasts.] Any artificial bait, usually imitating the appearance of insects or small fish, used in angling; any enticement; that which invites by the prospect of advantage or pleasure.—*v.t.*—*lured, luring.* To attract by a lure or to a lure; to entice; to attract; to invite.

lurid, lū'rid, *a.* [L. *luridus.*] Pale yellow, as flame; ghastly pale. Also vivid; violent; harshly terrible; as a *lurid* crime or *lurid* story.

lurk, lėrk, *v.i.* [Akin to N. *luska,* Dan. *luske,* to lurk, to skulk; Dan. *lur,* G. *lauer,* an ambush or watching.] To lie hid; to lie in wait; to lie concealed or unperceived.—**lurker,** lėr'kėr, *n.* One that lurks.

luscious, lush'us, *a.* [Perhaps for *lustious,* from *lusty.*] Very sweet; delicious; delightful; sweet to excess, hence, unctuous; fulsome.—**lusciously,** lush'us•li, *adv.* In a luscious manner. —**lusciousness,** lush'us•nes, *n.* The state or quality of being luscious.

lush, lush, *a.* [Shortened from *luscious.*] Fresh, luxuriant, and juicy; succulent.

lush, lush, *n.* [Origin unknown.] A habitual drunkard; liquor.

lust, lust, *n.* [A.Sax., D., G., and Sw. *lust,* Icel. and Dan. *lyst,* desire.] Longing desire; eagerness to possess or enjoy; depraved affection or desire; more especially, sexual appetite; unlawful desire of sexual pleasure; concupiscence.—*v.i.* To desire eagerly; to long; to have carnal desire: with *after.*—**lustful,** lust'ful, *a.* Inspired by lust or the sexual appetite; provoking to sensuality.—**lustfully,** lust'ful•li, *adv.* In a lustful manner.—**lustfulness,** lust'ful•nes, *n.* The state of being lustful.

luster, lustre, lus'tėr, *n.* [Fr. *lustre,* from L. *lustrum,* purificatory sacrifice (see LUSTRAL), or from stem of *luceo,* to shine (see LUCID).] Brightness; splendor; brilliance; sheen; *mineral.* a variation in the nature of the reflecting surface of minerals; the splendor of birth, of deeds, or of fame; renown; distinction; a branched chandelier ornamented with drops or pendants of cut glass; a fabric for ladies' dresses, consisting of cotton warp and woolen weft.—**lustring,** lūs'tring, *n.* A species of glossy silk cloth.—**lustrous,** lus'trus, *a.* Characterized by luster; bright; shining; luminous.—**lustrously,** lus'trus•li, *adv.* Brilliantly; luminously.

lustily, lustiness. See LUSTY.

lustral, lus'tral, *a.* [L. *lustralis,* from *lustro,* to purify, from *lustrum,* a purificatory sacrifice, from stem of *luo, lavo,* to wash. LAVE.] Used in purification; pertaining to purification.—**lustrate,** lus'trāt, *v.t.* [L. *lustro, lustratum,* to cleanse.] To purify as by water.—**lustration,** lus•trā'shon, *n.* A cleansing or purifying.—**lustrum,** lus'trum, *n.* pl. **lustrums** or **lustra,** lus'trumz, lus'tra. [L.] In ancient Rome, the purification of the whole people performed at the end of every five years; hence a period of five years.

lusty, lus'ti, *a.* [From *lust*=D. and G. *lustig,* D. *lystig,* merry, jovial.] Characterized by life, spirit, vigor, health, or the like; stout; vigorous; robust; healthful; bulky; large; lustful; hot-blooded.—**lustihood,** lus'ti•hud, *n.* The quality of being lusty; vigor of body. (*Tenn.*)—**lustily,** lus'ti•li, *adv.* In a lusty manner; vigorously; stoutly.—**lustiness,** lus'ti•nes, *n.* The state of being lusty.

lute, lūt, *n.* [Fr. *luth, lut,* Sp. *laud,* from Ar. *al ûd,* the wood (*al* being the definite article).] A stringed musical instrument of the guitar kind, formerly very popular in Europe.—*v.t.* To play on a lute.—**lutanist, lutist,** lū'tan•ist, lū'ten•ist, lūt'ist, *n.* A performer on the lute.

lute, luting, lūt, lūt'ing, *n.* [L. *lutum,* mud, clay, from *luo,* to wash.] *Chem.* a composition of clay or other substance used for stopping the juncture of vessels so closely as to prevent the escape or entrance of air, or applied as a coating to glass retorts in order that they may support a high temperature.—**lute,** *v.t.*—*luted, luting.* To close or coat with lute.

lutetium, lu•te'shi•um, *n.* [L. *Lutetia,* Paris.] A metallic element of the rare-earth series. Symbol, Lu; at. no., 71; at. wt., 174.97.

Lutheran, lū'ther•an, *a.* Pertaining to Martin *Luther,* the reformer.—*n.* A disciple or follower of Luther; one who adheres to the doctrines of Luther.—**lutheranism,** lū'thėr•an•-izm, *n.* The doctrines of religion as taught by Luther.

luxate, luk'sāt, *v.t.*—*luxated, luxating.* [L. *luxo, luxatum,* from *luxus,* dislocated, Gr. *loxos,* slanting.] To put out of joint, as a limb; to dislocate.—**luxation,** luk'sā•shon, *n.* The act of luxating; a dislocation.

luxuriant, lug•zhū'ri•ant, *a.* [L. *luxurians,* from *luxurio,* to luxuriate, from *luxuria,* luxury, *luxus,* excess.] Exuberant in growth; rank; abundant; growing to excess; excessive or superfluous.—**luxuriantly,** lug•zhū'-ri•ant•li, *adv.* In a luxuriant manner or degree.—**luxuriance, luxuriancy,** lug•zhū'ri•ans, lug•zhū'ri•an•si, *n.* The state of being luxuriant.—**luxuriate,** lug•zhū'ri•āt, *v.i.*—*luxuriated, luxuriating.* [L. *luxurio,* to be rank or luxurious, to be wanton.] To grow rankly or exuberantly; to feed or live luxuriously; *fig.* to indulge or revel without restraint.—**luxuriation,** lug•zhū'ri•ā″shon, *n.* The act of luxuriating.—**luxurious,** lug•zhū'ri•us, *a.* [L. *luxuriosus.*] Characterized by indulgence in luxury; given to luxury; voluptuous; administering to luxury; furnished with luxuries.—**luxuriously,** lug•zhū'ri•us•li, *adv.* In a luxurious manner.—**luxuriousness,** lug•-zhū'ri•us•nes, *n.* The state or quality of being luxurious.—**luxury,** lug'-zhū•ri, *n.* [L. *luxuria.*] A free or extravagant indulgence in the pleasures of the table, or in costly dress and equipage; that which is delightful to the senses, the feelings, etc.; that which gratifies a nice and fastidious appetite; anything not necessary, but used for personal gratification.

lycanthrope, lī'kan•thrōp, *n.* [Gr. *lykos,* a wolf, and *anthrōpos,* a man.] Formerly a man believed to be transformed into a wolf; a werwolf; now, a person affected with lycanthropy.—**lycanthropy,** lī•kan'thro•pi, *n.* A kind of insanity in which the patient supposes himself to be a wolf.

lyceum, lī•sē'um, *n.* [L. *Lyceum,* Gr. *Lykeion,* from a temple dedicated to Apollo *lykeios.* Apollo the wolf-slayer, from *lykos,* a wolf.] A building at ancient Athens where Aristotle taught; hence a building appropriated to instruction by lectures; a literary institute; a cultural association which provides lectures, concerts, etc.

lycopod, lī'kō•pod, *n.* [Gr. *lykos,* a wolf, and *pous, podos,* a foot.] A plant belonging to an order intermediate between mosses and ferns, and in some respects allied to the conifers.—**lycopodium,** lī•kō•pō'di•-um, *n.* A genus of lycopods.

lyddite, lid'īt, *n.* [From *Lydd,* in Kent.] An explosive prepared from picric acid.

Lydian, lid'i•an, *a.* Pertaining to ancient *Lydia* in Asia Minor; a term applied to one of the ancient Greek modes of music of a soft pleasing character.—*Lydian stone,* a jasper-like siliceous rock used by the ancients as a touchstone.

lye, lī, *n.* [A.Sax. *leáh,* G. *lauge,* D. *loog,* lye; allied to L. *lavo,* to wash.] Water impregnated with alkaline salt imbibed from the ashes of wood; a solution of an alkali used for cleaning purposes.

lymph, limf, *n.* [Fr. *lymphe,* L. *lympha,* water.] A fluid in animal bodies contained in certain vessels called *lymphatics,* which differs from the blood in its corpuscles being all of the colorless kind.—**lymphatic,** lim•fat'ik, *a.* Pertaining to lymph; phlegmatic; sluggish.—*n.* A vessel or duct in an animal body containing lymph.—**lymph gland,** *n.* Gland-like bodies occurring in the lymphatic vessels from which come lymphocytes.—**lymphocyte,** lim'fō•cīt, *n.* A white or colorless blood cell derived from lymphoid tissue.—**lymphoid,** lim'foid, *a.* Of, pertaining to, or resembling lymph; of or pertaining to tissue characteristic of the lymph glands.

lynch, linsh, *v.t.* [Said to be from a Virginian farmer of the name of *Lynch,* noted for taking the law into his own hand.] To inflict punishment upon, without the forms of law, as by a mob or by unauthorized persons.—**lynch law,** *n.* The practice of punishing men by unauthorized persons without a legal trial.

lynx, lingks, *n.* [L. and G. *lynx*; same root as in L. *lux,* light, from its bright eyes.] A name given to several carnivorous mammals of the cat family, long famed for their sharp sight.—**lynx-eyed,** *a.* Having extremely acute sight.

lyonnaise, lī•o•nāz', *a.* [From French *Lyonnais,* Lyon.] Prepared with onions (*lyonnaise* potatoes).

lyre, līr, *n.* [Fr. *lyre,* L. and Gr. *lyra*; etymology uncertain.] One of the most ancient stringed musical instruments of the harp family, used by the Greeks.—**lyrate, lyrated,** lī'rāt, lī'rā•ted, *a.* Shaped like a lyre.—**lyrebird,** *n.* An Australian bird somewhat smaller than a pheasant, having erect tail feathers in form resembling an ancient lyre.—**lyric, lyrical,** lir'ik, lir'i•kal, *a.* Pertaining to a lyre or harp; *poetry,* exhibiting the poet's own thoughts and feelings.—**lyric,** *n.* A lyric poem; pl. the words of a song.—*a.* Suitable to be set to music or sung.—**lyricism,** lir'i•sizm, *n.* Lyric composition; a lyrical form of language.—**lyricist,** lir'i•sist, *n.*—**lyrist,** lir'ist, *n.* A musician who plays on the lyre.

lysis, lī'sis, *n.* [Gr., a solution, from *lyō,* to dissolve.] *Med.* the gradual ending of a disease, without critical symptoms.

lysergic acid diethylamide, lī'sėr•-jik as'id dī'ethl•a•mīd, *n.* A drug causing hallucinations and other simulated mental disorders, used in psychological experimentation. Abbrev. LSD-25.

M

M, m, em, is the thirteenth letter and tenth consonant of the English alphabet, representing a labial and nasal articulation.

ma'am, mam, *n.* A colloquial contraction for *Madam.*

macabre, macaber, ma•kä'bėr, *a.* [Fr. *Danse macabre,* dance of death.] Ghastly; hideous; gruesome; representing death.

macadamize, mak•ad'am•īz, *v.i.*—*macadamized, macadamizing.* [From J. L. McAdam, the inventor.] To cover, as a road, with small broken stones, which, when consolidated, form a firm surface.—**macadamization,** mak•ad'am•ī•zā″shon, *n.*—**macadam,** mak•ad'am, *n.* Macadamized pavement or roadway; the broken stone used in the process.

macaque, ma•käk', *n.* [Fr.] An Old World monkey with short tail and prominent eyebrows.

macaroni, mak•a•rō'ni, *n.* pl. [Fr. and Prov. It. *macaroni,* It. *maccheroni,* originally a mixture of flour, cheese, and butter.] A dough of fine wheaten flour made into a tubular or pipe form, a favorite food among the Italians; a medley; a sort of droll or fool; a name formerly given to fops or dandies; a confused mixture of things; a macaronic verse or poem.

macaroon, mak•a•rön', *n.* A small sweet cake, with egg white and sugar basis, containing almond meal or shredded coconut.

macaw, ma•ka̤', *n.* [Native name in the Antilles.] One of a genus of beautiful birds of the parrot family, having cheeks destitute of feathers, and long tail feathers.

Maccabean, mak•ka•bē'an, *a.* Pertaining to the Jewish princes called *Maccabees.*—**Maccabees,** mak'ka•-bēz, *n. pl.* Two books treating of Jewish history under the Maccabean princes, included in the Apocrypha.

mace, mās, *n.* [O.Fr. *mace,* Fr. *masse,* It. *mazza,* a club; from L. *matea* (only found in the dim. *mateola*), a kind of mallet.] A weapon of war consisting of a staff with a heavy metal head frequently in the form of a spiked ball, used for breaking armor; an ornamental staff of metal borne before a dignitary as a symbol of his authority.—**mace-bearer,** *n.* A person who carries a mace before public functionaries.—**macer,** mās'-ėr, *n.* A mace-bearer; an officer attending several Scottish courts.

mace, mās, *n.* [Fr. *macis,* It. *mace,* L. *macis, macir,* Gr. *maker,* an Indian spice.] A spice, the dried aril or covering of the seed of the nutmeg, chiefly used in cooking or in pickles.

macédoine, mas•e•dwän′, *n.* [Fr., early meaning, Macedonian parsley.] A combination or mixture; used to designate a sauce or jellied salad containing mixed small or diced vegetables.

macerate, mas′ėr•āt, *v.t.*—*macerated, macerating.* [L. *macero, maceratum,* to make soft: same root as *mass,* a lump.] To steep almost to solution; to soften and separate the parts of by steeping in a fluid, or by the digestive process; to mortify‡.—*v.i.* To become macerated; to waste away.—**maceration,** mas•ėr•ā′shon, *n.* The act of macerating.

machete, mä•chā′tā, *n.* [Sp.] A kind of large knife or cutlass used in South America and the West Indies as a tool or a weapon.

Machiavelian, mak′i•a•vel′yan, *a.* Pertaining to *Machiavelli,* an Italian writer, secretary and historiographer to the Republic of Florence (died 1527); in conformity with Machiavelli's principles; cunning in political management; crafty.—*n.* One who adopts the principles of Machiavelli.

machicolation, ma•chik′o•lā″shon, *n.* [Fr. *mâchicoulis, mâchecoulis*; origin doubtful.] *Milit. arch.* a vertical opening in the floor of a projecting gallery, parapet, etc., for hurling missiles or pouring boiling lead, pitch, etc., upon the enemy; a part thus projecting, as at the top of a tower, without any such opening.—**machicolate,** ma•chik′o•lāt, *v.t.* To form with machicolations.

machinate, mak′i•nāt, *v.t.* and *i.*—*machinated, machinating.* [L. *machinor, machinatus,* from *machina.* MACHINE.] To plan; to contrive; to form, as a plot or scheme.—**machination,** mak•i•nā″shon, *n.* The act of machinating; a plot; an artful design or scheme formed with deliberation.—**machinator,** mak′i•nā•tėr, *n.* One who machinates or plots with evil designs.

machine, ma•shēn′, *n.* [Fr. *machine,* L. *machina,* from Gr. *mēchanē,* machine, device, contrivance, from *mechos,* means, expedient.] Any appliance which serves to increase or regulate the effect of a given force or to produce motion (*simple machines* or mechanical powers being such as the lever, pulley, etc.); a complex structure, consisting of a combination or peculiar modification of the mechanical powers; a term of contempt applied to a person whose actions do not appear to be under his own control, but to be directed by some external agency; a mere tool or creature; a term formerly applied to a coach or cart, now particularly to an automobile, airplane, etc.—*v.t.* To apply machinery to; to produce by machinery.—**machine gun,** *n.* A piece of ordnance that is loaded and fired mechanically, and can discharge a number of projectiles in rapid succession, having usually two or more barrels, as in the case of the Gatling gun, the mitrailleuse, etc.—**machinery,** ma•shēn′ėr•i, *n.* A complicated apparatus, or combination of mechanical powers, designed to increase, regulate, or apply motion and force; machines in general; any complex system of means and appliances designed to carry on any particular work or effect a specific purpose.—**machine shop,** *n.* A workshop in which machines are made.—**machine tool,** *n.* An adjustable machine for cutting metals into any required shape.—**machinist,** ma•shēn′ist, *n.* A constructor of machines; one who tends or works a machine.

Mach number, mäk, *n.* [After Ernest *Mach,* an Austrian physicist.] A number indicating the ratio of the air speed of an object to the speed of sound in the atmosphere.

mackerel, mak′ėr•el, *n.* [O.Fr. *maquerel,* Fr. *maquereau,* from L.L. *macarellus.*] A well-known food fish (*Scomber scombrus*) of the North Atlantic, a spiny-finned swift swimmer 18 inches long sporting blue bars on his back, and silver bars below.—*Mackerel sky,* a sky in which the clouds have the form called *cirrocumulus.*

macle, mak′l, *n.* [Fr.; L. *macula,* a spot, the mesh of a net.] A double crystal, particularly a flat, double crystal of diamond.

macramé, mak•ra•mā′, *n.* [Ar. *miqramah,* emboidered veil, Turk, *maqramah,* kerchief.] Fringe or heavy lace of knotted thread, usually in geometrical patterns.

macrobiotic, mak′ro•bī•ot″ik, *a.* [Gr. *makros,* long, and *bios,* life.] Long-lived.—**macrocosm,** mak′ro•kozm, *n.* [Gr. *kosmos,* world.] The great world; the universe, regarded as analogous to the *microcosm,* or little world constituted by man.—**macron,** mak′ron, *n.* [Gr. *makros,* long.] A mark placed over a vowel to show that it is long, as fāte, mē, nōte, tūbe.—**macroscopic,** mak•ro•skop′ik, *a.* [Gr. *makros* long, *skopeo,* I see.] Visible to the naked eye; opposed to *microscopic.*—**macrospore,** mak′ro•spōr, *n.* [Gr. *makros,* long, *sporos,* seed.] *Bot.* a large (female) spore.

Macrura, mak•rụ′ra, [Gr. *makros,* long, and *oura,* a tail.] A family of stalk-eyed decapod crustaceans, including the lobster, prawn, shrimp, so called in contrast to the Brachyura (crabs), because their flexible abdomen extends straight backward, and is used in swimming.—**macrural, macrurous,** mak•rụ′ral, mak•rụ′rus, *a.* Belonging to the Macrura.—**macruran,** mak•rụ′ran, *n.* One of the Macrura.

macula, mak′ū•la, *n.* pl. **maculae,** mak′ū•lē. [L. *macula,* a spot; hence, *mackerel, mail* (armour).] A spot, as on the skin.—**maculate,** mak′ū•lāt, *v.t.* [L. *maculo.*] To spot; to stain; to blur.—*a.* Marked with spots; blotted; hence, defiled; impure.—**maculation,** mak•ū•lā′shon, *n.* The act of spotting; a spot; a stain.—**macule,** mak′ūl, *n.* A spot; *printing,* a blur causing the impression of a page to appear double.

mad, mad, *a.* [O.E. *maad,* A.Sax. *mǽd, gemaed,* mad; allied to Goth. *gamaids,* injured; O.H.G. *gameit,* blunt, dull; Icel. *meitha,* to hurt.] Disordered in intellect; deprived of reason; distracted; crazy; insane; beside one's self; frantic; furious; wildly frolicsome; infatuated; furious from disease or otherwise; said of animals.—*Like mad,* madly; furiously. (*Colloq.*)—*v.t.*—*madded, madding.* To make mad; to madden.—*Madding crowd,* distracting (*v.t.*) or raving madly (*v.i.*) (?) Gray's 'madding crowd's ignoble strife', taken by him from Drummond of Hawthornden's 'madding worldling's hoarse discords', apparently *v.i.*—**madcap,** mad′kap, *n.* A person of wild or eccentric behavior; a flighty or hare-brained person; one who indulges in frolics.—*a.* Pertaining to a madcap.—**madden,** mad′n, *v.t.* To make mad; to craze; to excite with violent passion; to enrage.—*v.i.* To become mad; to act as if mad.—**madding,** mad′ing, *a.* Raging; furious; wild.—**madhouse,** mad′hous, *n.* A house where insane persons are confined; a lunatic asylum.—**madly,** mad′li, *adv.* In a mad or frenzied manner; frantically; furiously.—**madman,** mad′-man, *n.* A lunatic; a crazy person; one inflamed with extravagant passion, and acting contrary to reason.—**madness,** mad′nes, *n.* The state or quality of being mad; lunacy; insanity; frenzy; extreme folly.

madam, mad′am, *n.* [Fr. *ma,* my, and *dame,* lady, from L. *mea domina,* in same sense.] *Lit.* my lady; a term of compliment used in address to ladies, chiefly to married and elderly ladies; sometimes used with a slight shade of disrespect (a proud *madam*). Pl. **mesdames,** mā′damz.

madder, mad′ėr, *n.* [A.Sax. *maeddere,* madder.] A climbing perennial plant, largely cultivated in Southern Europe, the root of which furnishes several valuable dyes and pigments, such as *madder-red, madder-lake, madder-yellow.*—*v.t.* and *i.* To dye with madder.

made, mād, *pret. and pp.* of *make.* The pp. besides being used in the senses of the verb is often equivalent to destined, fitted, suitable ('a place *made* for murders', *Shak.*).

Madeira, ma•dē′ra, *n.* A rich wine made in the island of Madeira.

Madonna, ma•don′a, *n.* [It. *madonna,* from L. *mea domina,* my lady. MADAM.] An Italian form of address equivalent to *Madam*; the Virgin Mary, pictures of whom are called *madonnas.*

madras, ma•dras′, *n.* A cotton cloth of fine thread and close weave much used for men's shirts; a large cotton kerchief.

madrepore, mad′ri•pōr, *n.* [Fr. *madrépore,* from It. *madrepora,* from *madre,* mother, and Gr. *pōros,* a kind of stone.] A common variety of reef coral, of a stony hardness and of a spreading or branching form; the coral-building polyp itself.

madrigal, mad′ri•gal, *n.* [Fr. *madrigal*; It. *madrigale*, older It. *mandriale*, from L. and Gr. *mandra*, a sheepfold; originally a shepherd's song.] A little amorous poem, consisting of not less than three or four stanzas, and containing some tender and delicate, though simple thought, suitably expressed; a vocal composition, now commonly of two or more movements, and in five or six parts.

Maecenas, me•sē′nas, *n.* A munificent patron of art or literature, after Horace's friend.

Maelstrom, māl′strom, *n.* [Dutch *malen*, to grind, *stroom*, a stream.] A great whirlpool off the coast of Norway. Hence, [*not cap.*] a vortex or gulf; some dangerous movement or current in social life.

maenad, mē′nad, *n.* [Gr. *mainas*, *mainados*, from *mainomai*, to rave.] A votaress of Bacchus; hence, a raving, frenzied woman.

maestro, mīs′trō, *n.* [It. from L. *magister*, a master.] A master of any art; specifically, a master in music; a musical composer.—**maestoso,** mī•stō′sō, *a.* Majestic; stately, a direction in music.

Maffia, Mafia, mäf′fē•ä, *n.* A secret organization in Sicily which disregards or flouts laws and legal restrictions; branch organizations in other countries where the members are lawless and defiant toward all government.

magazine, mag′a•zēn′, *n.* [Fr. *magasin*, a storehouse, Sp. *magacen*, *almagacen*, from Ar. *al-makhzen*, a warehouse, from *khazana*, to store.] A receptacle in which anything is stored; a warehouse; a storehouse; a building or chamber constructed for storing in security large quantities of gunpowder or other explosive substances; a publication issued in a series of numbers or parts and containing papers of an entertaining or instructive character; a lighttight chamber for storing motion picture film.—**magazinist,** mag•ä•zēn′ist, *n.* One who writes for a magazine.

magdalen, mag′da•len, *n.* [From Mary *Magdalene*, erroneously supposed to be the woman mentioned in St. Luke vii. 36-50.] A reformed prostitute; a house into which prostitutes are received with a view to their reformation.

Magellanic, maj•el•lan′ik, *a.* Pertaining to *Magellan*, the celebrated navigator.—*Magellanic clouds*, two conspicuous whitish nebulae, of a cloud-like appearance, near the South Pole.

magenta, ma•jen′ta, *n.* [Discovered in 1859, the year of the battle of *Magenta*.] A brilliant blue-red color derived from coal tar.

maggot, mag′ot, *n.* [W. *magiad*, a maggot or grub, from *magu*, to breed.] The larva of a fly or other insect; a grub; a whim; an odd fancy; a crotchet.—**maggotiness,** mag′ot•i•nes, *n.* The state of being maggoty.—**maggoty,** mag′o•ti, *a.* Full of or infested with maggots; capricious; whimsical.

Magi, mā′jī, *n. pl.* [L. *magus*, from Gr. *magos*, a Magian, from Per. *mag*, a priest, same root as L. *magnus*, great.] The caste of priests among the ancient Medes and Persians; hence holy men or sages of the East.—**Magian,** mā′ji•an, *a.* Pertaining to the Magi.—*n.* One of the Magi; a priest of the Zoroastrian religion.

magic, maj′ik, *n.* [L. *magicus*, pertaining to sorcery, from *magia*, Gr. *mageia*, the theology of the Magians, magic. MAGI.] The art of producing effects by superhuman means, as by spiritual beings or the occult powers of nature; sorcery; enchantment; necromancy; power or influence similar to that of enchantment.—*Natural magic*, the art of applying natural causes, whose operation is secret, to produce surprising effects. —*a.* Pertaining to magic; used in magic; working or worked by or as if by magic.—*Magic square*, a square figure formed by a series of numbers disposed in parallel and equal ranks, and such that the sums of each row or line taken perpendicularly, horizontally, or diagonally are equal. *Magic lantern*, a kind of lantern by means of which small pictures are represented on the wall of a dark room, or on a white sheet, magnified to any size at pleasure.—**magical,** maj′i•kal, *a.* Pertaining to magic; proceeding from magic; having supernatural qualities; acting or produced as if by magic. ∴ *Magical* differs from *magic*, chiefly in the fact that the latter is not used predicatively; thus we do not say 'the effect was *magic*'.—**magically,** maj′i•kal•li, *adv.* In a magical manner.—**magician,** ma•jish′an, *n.* One skilled in magic; an enchanter; a necromancer.

magilp, magilph, ma•gilp′, ma•gilf′, *n.* See MEGILP.

magisterial, maj′is•tē′ri•al, *a.* [L. *magisterius*, from *magister*, a master. MASTER.] Belonging to a master or ruler; pertaining to a magistrate or his office; authoritative; arrogant; imperious; domineering.—**magisterially,** maj•is•tē′ri•al•li, *adv.* In a magisterial manner.—**magistral,** maj′is•tral, *a.* Imperious; authoritative; *phar.* specially prepared.

magistrate, maj′is•trāt, *n.* [L. *magistratus*, a magistrate, from *magister*, a master.] A public civil officer invested with the executive government or some branch of it; a justice of the peace; a person who dispenses justice in police courts, etc.—**magistracy,** maj′is•tra•si, *n.* The office or dignity of a magistrate; the body of magistrates.

magma, mag′ma, *n.* [Gr., a mass, dregs, from *massō*, to knead. MASS.] A mixture of mineral or other matters in a pasty state; a thick residuum separated from a fluid.

magna cum laude, mag′na cum lou′dā, *a.* [L.] With great praise, the second highest honors awarded at graduation.

magnanimous, mag•nan′i•mus, *a.* [L. *magnanimus*—*magnus*, great (MAGNITUDE), and *animus*, mind (ANIMAL).] Great of mind; elevated in soul or in sentiment; raised above what is low, mean, or ungenerous: said of persons; exhibiting nobleness of soul: said of actions, etc.—**magnanimously,** mag•nan′i•mus•li, *adv.* In a magnanimous manner.—**magnanimity,** mag•na•nim′i•ti, *n.* The quality of being magnanimous; greatness of mind; elevation, nobility, or dignity of soul; lofty generosity.

magnate, mag′nāt, *n.* [L. *magnates* (pl.), powerful persons, the great, from *magnus*, great. MAGNITUDE.] A person of rank; a noble or grandee; a person of note or distinction in any sphere.

magnesia, mag•nē′shi•a, *n.* [From *Magnesia* in Asia Minor, whence also *magnet*.] Oxide of magnesium, a white tasteless earthy substance, possessing alkaline properties.—*Sulfate of magnesia*, Epsom salts.—**magnesian,** mag•nē′shi•an, *a.* Pertaining to magnesia; containing or resembling magnesia.—*Magnesian limestone*, a rock composed of carbonates of lime and magnesia, more or less useful for building or ornamental purposes; dolomite.—**magnesium,** mag•nē′shi•um, *n.* A light, malleable, ductile, silver-white metallic element that burns with a dazzling light, used in lightweight alloys. Symbol, Mg; at. no., 12; at. wt., 24.312.—*Magnesium light*, a dazzlingly bright light produced by burning magnesium.

magnet, mag′net, *n.* [L. *magnes*, *magnetis*, from Gr. *magnēs*, from *Magnesia* in Asia Minor, whence the stone was first brought.] The loadstone; also a bar or mass of iron or steel to which the peculiar properties of the loadstone have been imparted, either by contact or by other means. ELECTROMAGNET, HORSESHOE MAGNET.—**magnetic,** mag•net′ik, *a.* Pertaining to the magnet or magnetism; possessing the properties of the magnet, or corresponding properties; pertaining to the earth's magnetism; attractive, as if magnetic.—*Magnetic amplitude, azimuth*, etc., *navig.* the amplitude, azimuth, etc., indicated by the compass.—*Magnetic battery*, a kind of battery formed of several magnets (usually horseshoe magnets) combined together with all their poles similarly disposed.—*Magnetic compensator*, a contrivance connected with a ship's compass for compensating or neutralizing the effects upon the needle of the iron of the ship.—*Magnetic dip*. See DIP.—*Magnetic elements*, for any place, are the intensity of the earth's attraction, the DIP (which see), and the DECLINATION (which see).—*Magnetic equator*, a line passing round the globe near its equator, in every part of which the dip of the needle is nothing.—*Magnetic field*, the space in the vicinity of a magnet through which magnetic forces act. —*Magnetic meridian*, a great circle, the plane of which at any place corresponds with the direction of the magnetic needle at that place.—*Magnetic needle*, any small magnetized iron or steel rod turning on a pivot, such as the needle of the mariner's compass.—*Magnetic north*, that point of the horizon which is indicated by the direction of the magnetic needle.—*Magnetic oxide of iron*, magnetite.—*Magnetic poles*, nearly opposite points on the earth's surface where the dip of the needle is 90°, at some distance from the earth's poles.—*Magnetic reluctance*. See RELUCTANCE.—*Magnetic susceptibility*. See SUSCEPTIBILITY.—*Magnetic storm*, a violent disturbance in the earth's magnetism; a sudden alteration in the magnetic elements of a place.—**magnetical,** mag•net′i•kal, *a*. Magnetic.—**magnetically,** mag•net′-i•kal•li, *adv*. In a magnetic manner; by magnetism.—**magnetism,** mag′net•izm, *n*. A peculiar property possessed by certain bodies, whereby, under certain circumstances, they naturally attract or repel one another according to determinate laws; that branch of science which treats of the properties of the magnet, and magnetic phenomena in general; power of attraction.—*Animal magnetism*. MESMERISM.—*Terrestrial magnetism*, the magnetic force exerted by the earth.—**magnetite,** mag′net•īt, *n*. A black oxide of iron, which sometimes possesses polarity, and is highly magnetic; magnetic iron ore.—**magnetizable,** mag•net•ī′za•bl, *a*. Capable of being magnetized.—**magnetization,** mag′-net•i•zā″shon, *n*. The act of magnetizing, or state of being magnetized.—**magnetize,** mag′net•īz, *v.t.*—*magnetized, magnetizing*. To communicate magnetic properties to; to attract or repel one another according to determinate laws.—**magneto,** mag•nē′tō, *n*. A small machine or generator having permanent magnets for poles, used to generate current.—**magnetoelectric, magnetoelectrical,** *a*. Pertaining to magnetoelectricity.—**magnetoelectricity,** *n*. Electricity evolved by the action of magnets; the science which treats of phenomena connected with both magnetism and electricity.—**magnetometer,** mag•net•om′et•ėr, *n*. An instrument for measuring any of the terrestrial magnetic elements, as the dip, inclination, and intensity, especially the latter.—*Magnetomotive force*, the magnetizing influence to which a magnetic substance is subjected in a magnetic field; its unit is the GILBERT (which see).—**magnetron,** mag′ne•tron, *n*. A vacuum tube in which the flow of electrons from cathode to a heated anode is under the influence of an external magnetic field; used for generation of ultrashort radio waves.—**magnetosphere,** mag•nē′tō•sfēr, *n*. A belt of highly charged particles, trapped in the earth's magnetic field, which extends to an altitude of over 40,000 miles at the Equator.

Magnificat, mag•nif′i•kat, *n*. Canticle of the Virgin Mary in Luke, i. 46-55: 'My soul doth magnify (L. *magnificat*) the Lord'.

magnificent, mag•nif′i•sent, *a*. [L. *magnificens*—*magnus*, great, *facio*, to make. MAGNITUDE.] Grand in appearance; splendid; fond of splendor; showy; stately.—**magnificently,** mag•nif′i•sent•li, *adv*. In a magnificent manner.—**magnific, magnifical,** mag•nif′ik, mag•nif′i•kal, *a*. [L. *magnificus*, noble, splendid.] Grand; splendid; illustrious.—**magnificence,** mag•nif′i•sens, *n*. [L. *magnificentia*.] The condition or quality of being magnificent.—**magnifico,** mag•nif′-i•kō, *n*. pl. **magnificoes,** A grandee; a magnate.—**magnifier,** mag′ni•fī•-ėr, *n*. One who or that which magnifies.—**magnify,** mag′ni•fī, *v.t.*—*magnified, magnifying*. [Fr. *magnifier*, L. *magnificare*.] To make great or greater; to increase the apparent dimensions of; to enlarge; to augment; to exalt; to represent as greater than reality; to exaggerate.—*v.i.* To possess the quality of causing objects to appear larger than reality.—*Magnifying glass*, a plano-convex or double-convex lens.—**magnification,** mag′ni•fi•kā″shon, *n*. Exaltation; praise; the seeming enlargement of an object by means of optics.

magniloquence, mag•nil′o•kwens, *n*. [L. *magniloquentia*—*magnus*, great (MAGNITUDE), and *loquens*, speaking (LOCUTION).] A lofty manner of speaking or writing; tumidity; pompous words or style; grandiloquence; bombast.—**magniloquent,** mag•nil′o•kwent, *a*. Big in words; speaking loftily or pompously; tumid; grandiloquent.—**magniloquently,** mag•nil′o•kwent•li, *adv*. In a magniloquent manner.

magnitude, mag′ni•tūd, *n*. [L. *magnitudo*, from *magnus*, great; same root as Gr. *megas*, great, E. *may*, *might*, *much*, *more*, etc. More or less akin are *magnate*, *majesty*, *master*, etc.] Greatness; the comparative extent, bulk, size, quantity, or amount of anything that can be measured; any quantity that can be expressed in terms of a quantity of the same kind taken as a unit; *geom*. that which has one or more of the three dimensions, length, breadth, and thickness; consequence (an affair of *magnitude*); a star's brightness according to a 100 logarithmic numbering system, as *first* magnitude, etc.

magnolia, mag•nō′li•a, *n*. [After Pierre *Magnol*, professor of botany at Montpellier.] A genus of trees and shrubs, chiefly natives of North America, India, China, Japan, etc., much admired for their flowers and foliage.

magnum, mag′num, *n*. [L., a large thing. MAGNITUDE.] A bottle holding two quarts.—**magnum opus,** *n*. [L.] Literally, a great work; the major production of an author or artist.

magpie; mag′pī, *n*. [*Mag*, for *Margaret*, and *pie*, a magpie, from L. *pica*, a pie or magpie; comp. *Jenny*-wren, *Robin*-red-breast, etc.] A well-known bird of the crow family, about 18 inches in length, plumage black and white, tail very long; a person who chats like a magpie.

Magyar, mag′yär; Hung. pron. mod′-yor, *n*. A Hungarian of Asiatic race, allied to the Turks and Finns; the language of the Hungarians, belonging to the Turanian class of tongues.

maharajah, mä′ha•rä″ja, *n*. [Skr. *mahä*, great, and *räjā*, a prince or king.] The title assumed by some Indian princes ruling over a considerable extent of territory.—**maharani, maharanee,** mä′ha•rä″nē, *n*. [Skr., great queen or princess.] A female Indian ruler.

mahatma, ma•hät′ma, *n*. [Skr. *maha*, great, *âtmâ*, mind, soul.] A name among theosophists for certain Asiatic chiefs of their faith, said to be able to communicate by occult or nonmaterial means with other persons at any distance.

Mahdi, mä′di, *n*. [Ar., the director.] A name assumed by some of the successors of Mohammed; a descendant of Mohammed who is to arise and at the head of the faithful spread Mohammedanism over the world.

mahlstick, mal′stik *n*. See MAULSTICK.

mahogany, ma•hog′an•i, *n*. [*Mahagoni*, native American name.] A valuable timber tree, the wood of which is of a reddish color, very hard, and susceptible of a fine polish; a dinner table or table in general (over the *mahogany*).

Mahometan, ma•hom′e•tan. See MOHAMMEDAN, etc.

Mahound, ma•hound′, *n*. An old corruption of Mohammed; also applied to the devil or other evil spirit.

mahout, ma•hout′, *n*. [Hind.] In the East Indies, an elephant driver or keeper.

Mahratta, ma•rat′ta, *n*. One of a race of Hindus inhabiting central India.

maid, mād, *n*. [Short for *maiden*, A.Sax. *mægden*, dim of *mægeth*, a maiden, Goth. *magaths*, G. *magd*, maid; akin A.Sax. *magu*, Goth. *magus*, Icel. *mōgr*, a boy, a son; allied to Gael. *mac*, a son.] A young unmarried woman; a virgin; an unmarried woman who has preserved her chastity; a female servant; a female skate.—*Maid of all work*, a female servant who does housework of every kind.—**maid of honor,** an unmarried woman who accompanies a bride to the altar.—**maiden,** mā′dn, *n*. A young unmarried woman; a virgin or maid; an instrument of capital punishment; a race horse that has not yet won a race.—*a*. Pertaining to a maiden or virgin; consisting of virgins; like a maiden; fresh; unpolluted; unused.—*Maiden fortress*, one hitherto impregnable to assaults from the enemy; uncaptured.—*Maiden over* (*cricket*), one during whose delivery no runs are made.—*Maiden speech*, a person's first public speech.—*Maiden sword*, a sword hitherto unused and unstained with blood.—**maidenhair,** mā′dn•hãr, *n.* An elegant fern found growing on rocks and walls.—**maidenhead,** mā′dn•hed, *n.* [*Maiden,* and term. *-head.*] Virgin purity; virginity.—**maidenhood,** mā′dn•hụd, *n.* The state of being a maid or maiden; the state of an unmarried female; virginity.—**maidenliness,** mā′dn•li•nes, *n.* Behavior that becomes a maid; modesty.—**maidenly,** mā′dn•li, *a.* and *adv.* Like a maid; modest.—**maidhood,** mād′hụd, *n.* Virginity.—**maidservant,** *n.* A female servant; a female domestic.

maieutic, mā•ū′tik, *a.* [Gr. *maieutikos,* pertaining to midwifery, from *maia,* a midwife.] Serving to assist or accelerate childbirth; pertaining to the obstetric art; aiding in bringing forth, in a metaphorical sense.

maigre, mā′gr, *a.* [Fr., lean, spare, meager.] *Cookery,* a term applied to a preparation cooked merely with butter.—*Maigre dishes, maigre food,* dishes used by Roman Catholics on the days when their church forbids flesh-meats.

mail, māl, *n.* [Fr. *maille,* the mesh of a net, a link of mail; from L. *macula,* a spot, a mesh. MACULA.] Armor; a defensive covering for warriors, and sometimes their steeds; any defensive covering, as the shell of a lobster.—*v.t.* To put on mail or armor; to arm defensively.—**mail-clad,** *a.* Clad with a coat of mail.—**mailed,** māld, *p.* and *a.* Covered with mail or armor; *zool.* protected by an external covering of scales or hard substance.

mail, māl, *n.* [Fr. *malle,* O.Fr. *male,* a bag, a mail; either from Armor. *mal,* Ir. and Gael. *mala,* a bag. or from O.H.G. *malaha,* a wallet; Icel. *malr,* a knapsack.] Originally a bag; hence, a bag for the conveyance of letters and papers; the letters, papers, etc., conveyed in such a bag; the person or conveyance by which the mail is conveyed.—*v.t.* To put in the mail.—**mailable,** māl′a•bl, *a.* Capable of being carried in the mail.—**mailbag,** *n.* A bag in which the public mail is carried.—**mailer,** *n.* A machine for addressing mail.—**mailman,** *n.* A postman.—**mail order,** *n.* An order sent by mail for goods to be shipped to the buyer.

maim, mām, *v.t.* [O.E. *main,* to hurt or maim; from O.Fr. *mechaigner,* Pr. *maganhar,* at. *magagnare,* to maim; origin doubtful.] To deprive of the use of a limb; to mutilate; to cripple; to disable.—*n.* An injury by which a person is maimed or mutilated.

main, mān, *a.* [Icel. *megn, meginn,* main, strong, mighty; *megin,* might, main, main part; A.Sax. *maegn, maegen,* power, strength; same root as *may, might.*] Principal, chief, or most important among other things; most to be regarded or considered; first in size, rank, importance, etc. (the *main* branch of a river, the *main* timbers of an edifice, the *main* consideration); mighty; vast (the *main* ocean); directly applied; used with all one's might (*main* strength).—*Main body,* the corps of an army which marches between the advance and rear guard. —*The main chance,* the chance of making gain; one's own interests generally.—*n.* All one's strength; violent effort (in the phrase 'with might and *main*'); the chief or main portion; the gross, bulk, greater part; the ocean, the great sea, the high sea; a principal gas or water pipe in a street, as distinguished from the smaller ones supplied by it.—*In the main,* for the most part; speaking generally.—**mainland,** mān′land, *n.* The continent; territory of great extent as compared with an island near it.—**mainly,** mān′li, *adv.* In the main; chiefly; principally.—**mainmast,** *n. Naut.* the principal mast in a ship or other vessel; the middle lower mast of a ship.—**mainsail,** *n. Naut.* the principal sail in a ship; the chief sail on the mainmast bent on the main yard.—**mainsheet,** *n. Naut.* a rope at one or both of the lower corners of a mainsail to keep it properly extended. —**mainspring,** mān′spring, *n.* The principal spring of any piece of mechanism, as in a watch; *fig.* the main cause of any action.—**mainstay,** *n. Naut.* the stay extending from the top of the mainmast to the deck; hence, *fig.* chief support.—**maintop,** *n. Naut.* a platform placed at the head of the main mast.—**mainyard,** *n. Naut.* the yard on which the mainsail is extended.

maintain, mān•tān′, *v.t.* [Fr. *maintenir—main,* L. *manus,* the hand, and Fr. *tenir,* L. *teneo,* to hold.] To preserve or keep in any particular state or condition; to support; to keep possession of; not to lose or surrender; to continue (a conversation); to support with food, clothing, etc.; to uphold; to vindicate or justify (one's right or cause); to assert.—**maintainable,** mān•tā′na•bl, *a.*—**maintainer,** mān•tā′nėr, *n.*—**maintenance,** mān′ten•ans, *n.* The act of maintaining, upholding, or keeping up; that which maintains or supports; *law,* intermeddling in a suit in which the person has no interest, by assisting either party with money or means to prosecute or defend it.

maître d'hôtel, mā′tre dō•tel′, *n.* [Fr. master of the house.] The chief steward or servant of a house or hotel; a kind of sauce prepared with melted butter, chopped parsley, and vinegar or lemon juice.

maize, māz, *n.* [Sp. *maiz,* from Taino *mahiz, mayz.*] Indian corn.

majesty, maj′es•ti, *n.* [L. *majestas,* from *majus,* compar. form of *magnus,* great. MAGNITUDE.] Grandeur or dignity of rank, character, or manner; imposing loftiness of person or mien; stateliness; sublimity; a title of emperors, kings, and queens; generally with a possessive pronoun (may it please your *majesty*).—**majestic,** ma•jes′tik, *a.* Possessing majesty; having dignity of appearance; august; splendid; grand; sublime; stately.—**majestical,** ma•jes′ti•kal, *a.* Majestic.—**majestically,** ma•jes′ti•kal•li, *adv.* In a majestic manner.

majolica, ma•jol′i•ka, *n.* [It. *Maiolica* or *Maiorica,* for *Majorca.*] A kind of earth used for making dishes, vases, etc., afterward applied to the ware itself.

major, mā′jėr, *a.* [L., compar. of *magnus,* great. MAGNITUDE.] The greater in number, quantity, extent, or dignity; the more important; *mus.* applied to the modes in which the third is four semitones above the tonic, or keynote, and to intervals consisting of four semitones; pertaining to a subject in one's special field of study or research.—*Major tone* or *interval,* an interval represented by the ratio of 8 to 9, while a minor tone is represented by the ratio of 9 to 10.—*Major term* of a syllogism, in *logic,* the predicate of the conclusion; the *major premise* is that which contains the major term.—*n.* An officer in the army next in rank above a captain and below a lieutenant-colonel; the lowest field officer; *law,* a person of full age to manage his own concerns; *logic,* the first proposition of a regular syllogism, containing the major term.—**major-domo,** mā•jėr•dō′mō, *n.* [It. *maggiordomo*—L. *major,* greater, and *domus,* a house.] A man who takes charge of the management of a large household; a steward; a chief minister or great officer of a palace.—

major general, *n.* A military officer the next in rank below a lieutenant-general.—**major-generalship,** *n.* The office of a major general.—**majority,** ma•jor′i•ti, *n.* [Fr. *majorité.*] The state of being major or greater; the greater number; more than half; the number by which one quantity which can be counted exceeds another; full age; the age at which the law permits a young person to manage his own affairs; the office, rank, or commission of a major.—*To join the majority,* to pass over to the dead.

majuscule, ma•jus′kūl, *n.* [L. *majuscala* (*litera,* letter, understood), from *majusculus,* somewhat great, dim. from *major, majus,* greater.] A capital letter; opposed to *minuscule.*—*Majuscule writing,* writing composed entirely of capital letters, as in ancient manuscripts.

make, māk, *v.t.* pret. & pp. *made;* ppr. *making.* [A.Sax. *macian,* L.G. and D. *maken,* G. *machen,* to make: same root as *may,* and L. *magnus,* great.] To cause to exist as a distinct thing; to create, frame, fashion, fabricate; to produce or effect, as agent or cause (money *makes* friends); to cause to be or become: with words expressive of the result or condition of the object (to *make* a matter public; to *make* a man king); to constrain, compel, cause, occasion, with infinitives after the object (to *make* a person laugh: *to* the sign of the infinitive, being omitted); to gain, acquire (money, profit, etc.); to get or ascertain, as the result of computation or calculation; to pass over in sailing or traveling; to put in a desired or desirable position or condition; to prepare for use (a bed, a fire); to compose, as parts united in a whole; to constitute; to serve or answer for (she *makes* a good wife); to complete, as by being added to a sum; *naut.* to arrive at; to have within sight (to *make* a port, land).—*Make* is often used periphrastically with substantives, the two together being thus equal to a single verb; thus to *make complaint*=to complain; to *make answer*=to answer; to *make haste*=to hasten, etc.—*To make believe*, to pretend.—*To make good*, to maintain; to establish (to *make good* one's footing); to accomplish (to *make good* one's word); to supply an equivalent for (to *make good* a loss).—*To make love to*, to court.—*To make out*, to discover; to decipher; to prove or establish by evidence or argument; to find to the full; as, he was not able to *make out* the whole sum.—*To make over*, to transfer the title of; to convey; as, he *made over* his estate in trust.—*To make sail* (*naut.*), to increase the quantity of sail already set.—*To make shift*, to contrive or manage with such means or appliances as are available.—*To make up*, to make full or complete; to collect into a sum or mass; to compose, as ingredients or parts; to constitute; to compensate for or make good (to *make up* a loss); to reconcile, settle, adjust (quarrels, etc.); to bring to a definite conclusion (to *make up* one's mind).—*To make water*, to leak, as a ship; to void the urine.—*To make way*, to make progress; to open a passage; to clear the way.—*v.i.* To act or do: often with adjectives to express the manner of acting (to *make bold*, etc.); to interfere; to proceed, move, direct one's course (he *made* toward home; he *made* after the boy); to rise or flow toward land: said of the tide.—*To make against*, to tend to injure; to be adverse to; to form an argument against; to tend to disprove.—*To make as if*, to act as if; to pretend that.—*To make at*, to make a hostile movement against.—*To make away with*, to take away and put out of reach; to remove by killing; to murder secretly.—*To make bold*, to venture; to take leave or liberty (to *make bold*, to say).—*To make for*, to contribute toward; to be of service to; to favor (this *makes for* the argument).—*To make free with*, to treat with freedom or without ceremony; to make free use of.—*To make light of*, to regard as trifling or of no consequence; to belittle.—*To make out*, to succeed and no more.—*To make sure*, to ascertain with certainty.—*To make sure of*, to consider as certain; to secure to one's self.—*To make up*, to dress, etc., as an actor.—*To make up to*, to approach; to court.—*To make up for*, to serve as compensation for.—*n.* Structure; construction; shape; form (a man of slender *make*).—**make-believe,** *n.* Making believe or pretending; pretense; pretext; sham.—*a.* Unreal; sham.—**maker,** mā'kėr, *n.* One who makes: [*cap.*] the Creator;—**makeshift,** *n.* Something to serve a present purpose; a temporary substitute.—**make up,** *v.t.* To compose something; to settle in one's mind; to shuffle (a deck) for dealing; to bring up to; to concoct (a story); to arrange, prepare, adjust, assume a guise, compensate or reconcile; in printing, to arrange the type in columns or pages; in the theater and motion pictures, to apply cosmetics, dress, or accessories for a part; in education, to remove a deficiency.—*v.i.* To put on cosmetics for a performance; to resume friendship after an argument; to compensate.—**make-up,** *n.* The ingredients of a thing; cosmetics used to accentuate and highlight facial features; the mental or physical constitution of a person.

Malacca, ma•lak'ka, *a.* Pertaining to Malacca, in the Malay Peninsula.—*Malacca cane*, a cane made of the brown mottled or clouded stem of a kind of palm.

malachite, mal'a•kīt, *n.* [Fr. *malachite*, from Gr. *malachē*, a mallow, from its color resembling that of the leaves of mallow.] A mineral; a carbonate of copper found in solid masses of a beautiful green color, the green carbonate of copper, used for many ornamental purposes.

malacology, mal•a•kol'o•ji, *n.* [Gr. *malakos*, soft, and *logos*, discourse.] The branch of zoology that treats of the Mollusca or soft-bodied animals.—**malacologist,** mal•a•kol'o•jist, *n.* One versed in malacology.

malacopterygian, mal•a•kop'tėr•ij"-i•an, *a.* [Gr. *malakos*, soft, and *pterygion*, a fin, a little wing, from *pteryx*, a wing.] A term applied to those osseous fishes that have all the rays of the fins soft.—**malacostracan,** mal•a•kos'tra•kan, *n.* [Gr. *ostrakon*, a shell.] A division of crustaceans, including the shrimps, lobsters, etc.—**malacostracan, malacostracous,** mal•a•kos'tra•kus, *a.*

maladjustment, mal•ad•just'ment, *n.* [Prefix *mal*, bad.] A bad or wrong adjustment: *psychology*, a lack of harmony between an individual's desires or capacities and his mode of living.

maladministration, mal•ad•min'is•-trā"shon, *n.* [Prefix *mal*, bad.] Faulty administration; bad management of public affairs.

maladroit, mal•a•droit', *a.* [Prefix *mal*, bad.] Not adroit or dexterous; awkward.—**maladroitly,** mal•a•-droit'li, *adv.* Clumsily; awkwardly.—**maladroitness,** mal•a•droit'nes, *n.* Clumsiness; awkwardness.

malady, mal'a•di, *n.* [Fr. *maladie*, from *malade*, O.Fr. *malabde*, ill, from L. *male*, *habitus*, in bad condition. HABIT.] Any disease of the human body; an ailment; an indisposition; moral or mental disorder.

Malaga, mal'a•ga, *n.* A wine imported from Malaga in Spain; the white grape from which the wine is made, grown also in California.

Malagasy, mal'a•gas•i, *a.* and *n.* The language of Madagascar.

malaise, mal•āz', *n.* [Fr., from *mal*, bad, and *aise*, ease.] State of being ill at ease; morbid and indefinite feeling of uneasiness.

malanders, mal'an•dėrz, *n.* [Fr. *malandres*, L. *malandria*.] A dry scab or scurfy eruption on the hock of a horse or at the bend of the knee.

malapert, mal'a•pėrt, *a.* [O.Fr. *malappert*, over-ready—prefix *mal*, badly, and O.Fr. *appert*, ready, prompt, from L. *apertus*, open. PERT.] Pert; saucy; impudent; forward.—*n.* A pert, saucy person.—**malapertly,** mal'a•pėrt•li, *adv.* Saucily; with impudence.—**malapertness,** mal'a•-pėrt•nes, *n.* Sauciness; impudent pertness.

malapropos, mal•ap'rō•pō", *a.* and *adv.* [Prefix *mal*, badly, and *apropos*.] The opposite of apropos; ill to the purpose.—**malapropism,** mal'a•-prop•izm, *n.* The blundering use of words characteristic of Mrs. *Malaprop* in Sheridan's *Rivals*, e.g. 'an allegory on the banks of the Nile'.

malar, mā'lėr, *a.* [From L. *mala*, the cheek bone, the jaw.] Pertaining to the cheek or cheek bone.—*n. Anat.* the cheek bone.

malaria, ma•lâ'ri•a, *n.* [It. *mala aria*, bad air, from L. *malus*, bad, and *aer*, air.] An infectious febrile disease formerly believed contracted from air tainted by deleterious emanations from animal or vegetable matter, but now known to be caused by a blood parasite transmitted by the bite of certain mosquitoes.—**malarial, malarian, malarious,** *a.*

malassimilation, mal'as•sim•i•lā"-shon, *n.* [Prefix *mal*, bad.] Imperfect or morbid assimilation or nutrition; faulty digestion.

Malay, Malayan, ma•lā', ma•lā'yan, *n.* A native of the Malay Peninsula; the language of the Malays.—*a.* Belonging to the Malays or to their country.

malcontent, mal'kon•tent, *n.* [Prefix *mal*, ill.] A discontented person; a discontented subject of a government.—**malcontent,** *a.* Discontented with the government.

mal de mer, mal• dä• mâr', *n.* [Fr.] Seasickness.

male, māl, *a.* [Fr. *mâle*, O.Fr. *masle*, from L. *masculus*, male, from *mas*, *maris*, a male. MASCULINE.] Pertaining to the sex that begets young, as distinguished from the *female*; masculine; *bot.* having fecundating organs, but not fruit-bearing.—*Male rhymes*, rhymes in which only the final syllables correspond.—*Male screw*, the screw whose threads enter the grooves of the female screw.—*n.* One of the sex which begets young; *bot.* a plant which bears stamens.

malediction, mal•e•dik'shon, *n.* [L. *maledictio*, *maledictionis*—*male*, evil, and *dico*, to speak. DICTION.] Evil speaking; a curse or execration; an imprecation; the act of slandering.

malefactor, mal•e•fak′tėr, *n.* [L., evildoer—*male,* ill, and *facio,* to do.] One who commits a crime; a criminal. —**malefaction,** mal•e•fak′shon, *n.* An offense; an evil or criminal deed.

malefic, ma•lef′ik, *a.* [L. *maleficus,* that does ill—*male,* ill, and *facio,* to do.] Doing mischief.—**maleficence,** ma•lef′i•sens, *n.*—**maleficent,** ma•lef′i•sent, *a.* Doing evil; harmful.

malevolent, ma•lev′o•lent, *a.* [L. *malevolens, malevolentis—male,* ill, and *volens,* willing or disposed. VOLITION.] Having an evil disposition toward another or others; malicious; spiteful.—**malevolently,** ma•lev′o•lent•li, *adv.*—**malevolence,** ma•lev′o•lens, *n.*

malfeasance, mal•fē′zans, *n.* [Fr. *malfaisance—mal,* ill, and *faire,* L. *facere,* to do.] *Law,* doing what a person ought not to do; illegal deed.

malformation, mal•for•mā′shon, *n.* Ill or wrong formation; a deviation from the normal structure of an organ.

malfunction, mal•funk′shon, *v.t.* (Prefix *mal,* bad, and *function.*) To operate or function badly; to misfire. —*n.* The act or state of functioning badly.

malic, mā′lik, *a.* [L. *malum,* an apple.] Pertaining to apples; obtained from the juice of apples.—*Malic acid,* an acid found in many fruits, particularly in the apple.

malice, mal′is, *n.* [Fr. *malice,* L. *malitia,* from *malus,* evil; cog. Gr. *melas,* black; Skr. *malam,* filth; Ir. *maile,* evil. *Malus* is seen also in *malady, malign, malignant,* etc.] Enmity of heart; a disposition to injure others for mere personal gratification, or from a spirit of revenge; spite; ill-will; *law,* a formed design of doing mischief to another; called also *malice prepense* or *aforethought.* ∴ *Malice* is a deeper and more abiding feeling than *malevolence, malevolence* being of a more casual and temporary character. *Malignity* is malice intensified, proceeding from an innate love of doing harm to others.—**malicious,** ma•lish′us, *a.* [L. *malitiosus.*] Indulging malice; harboring ill-will without provocation; proceeding from ill-will; dictated by malice.—*Malicious mischief,* an injury to property from sheer malice, in some instances a felony, in others a misdemeanor.—*Malicious prosecution,* a prosecution preferred without reasonable cause.—**maliciously,** ma•lish′us•li, *adv.* In a malicious manner.—**maliciousness,** ma•lish′us•nes, *n.*

malign, ma•līn′, *a.* [L. *malignus* for *maligenus,* of an evil nature—*malus,* bad, and *genus,* kind (MALICE, GENUS). Comp. *benign,* with exactly the opposite sense.] Of an evil nature, disposition, or character; malicious; pernicious; tending to injure or produce evil effects.—*v.t.* To speak evil of; to traduce, defame, vilify.—**malignance, malignancy,** ma•lig′nans, ma•lig′nan•si, *n.* The quality of being malignant; extreme malevolence; bitter enmity; *med.* virulence.—**malignant,** ma•lig′nant, *a.* [L. *malignans,* from *maligno,* to act maliciously.] Having extreme malevolence or enmity; virulently inimical; malicious; exerting pernicious influence; *med.* threatening a fatal issue; virulent (a *malignant* ulcer); extremely heinous. ∴ Syn. under MALICE.—*n. English history,* one of the adherents of Charles I and his son: so called by the Roundheads.—**malignantly,** ma•lig′nant•li, *adv.* In a malignant manner.—**maligner,** ma•līn′ėr, *n.* One who maligns.—**malignity,** ma•lig′ni•ti, *n.* [L. *malignitas.*] The state or quality of being malignant; evil disposition of heart toward another; malice without provocation; rancor; virulence.

malinger, ma•ling′gėr, *v.i.* [Fr. *malingre,* sickly, weakly; from *mal,* ill, and O.Fr. *hingre, heingre,* feeble, nasalized form of L. *aeger,* sick.] *Milit.* to feign illness in order to avoid duty.—**malingerer,** ma•ling′gėr•ėr, *n.* A soldier who feigns himself ill.

malison, mal′i•zn, *n.* [O.Fr. *malison, maleïcon,* contr. from *malediction.* Comp. *benison,* for *benediction.*] A malediction; curse; execration.

mall, mal, *n.* [Fr. *mail,* It. *maglio, malleo,* L. *malleus,* a hammer. MALLEABLE.] A heavy wooden beetle or hammer; (originally an alley where the game of *pall-mall* was played with *malls* and balls) a public walk; a level shaded walk.

mallard, mal′erd, *n.* [O.Fr. *malard,* Prov. Fr. *maillard,* from *maille* (L. *macula*), a spot on a bird's feather, from the iridescent spot on the wing.] The common wild duck.

malleable, mal′lē•a•bl, *a.* [Fr. *malléable,* from L.L. *malleo,* to beat with a hammer, from L. *malleus,* a hammer (akin *mallet, maul*).] Capable of being shaped or extended by beating with the hammer: said of metals.—**malleability, malleableness,** mal′lē•a•bil″i•ti, mal′lē•a•bl•nes, *n.* The quality of being malleable.

mallee, mal′lē, *n.* Kind of dwarf eucalyptus.

malleolus, mal′lē•ō•lus, *n.* [L., dim. of *malleus,* a hammer.] One of the two projections of the leg bones at the ankle.—**malleolar,** mal′lē•ō•lėr, *a. Anat.* pertaining to the ankle.

mallet, mal′et, *n.* [Dim. of *mall.*] A wooden hammer, used chiefly by stonecutters, joiners, etc.

malleus, mal′ē•us, *n.* [L., a mallet.] *Anat.* one of the chain of small bones in the ear; *zool.* a hammer-shaped body forming part of the masticatory apparatus in some microscopic animals.

mallow, mal′ō, *n.* [A.Sax. *malwe,* G. *malve,* from L. *malva,* mallow, allied to Gr. *malachē,* mallow, *malakos,* soft—from its emollient properties.] The common name of a number of plants, chiefly herbaceous or annual, some of them valuable for medicinal properties. Also called *mallows,* as a singular.

malm, mäm, *n.* [A.Sax. *mealm,* Goth. *malma,* sand; akin to *meal,* from root meaning to grind.] A soft, grayish limestone, easily crumbled; *Eng.* marl; a soil containing clay and chalk.

malmsey, mäm′zi, *n.* [O.E. *malvesie,* Fr. *malvoisie*; from Napoli di *Malvasia,* in the Morea; the white and red wines produced there first received the name.] A kind of grape; a strong sweet white wine made in Madeira.

malnutrition, mal′nū•trish″un, *n.* Insufficient or otherwise faulty nutrition.

malodor, malodour, mal•ō′dėr, *n.* [Prefix *mal,* bad.] An offensive odor. —**malodorous,** mal•ō′dėr•us, *a.* Having a bad or offensive odor.

Malpighian, mal•pig′i•an, *a.* [After *Malpighi,* an eminent Italian anatomist and botanist.] *Anat.* applied to certain small round bodies in the cortical substance of the kidney, and to corpuscles in the spleen.

malposition, mal•po•zish′on, *n.* [Prefix *mal,* bad.] A wrong position.

malpractice, mal•prak′tis, *n.* [*Mal* and *practice.*] Professional malfeasance or improper and careless performance of duty, as of a physician or lawyer.

malt, mạlt, *n.* [A.Sax. *mealt* G. *malz,* malt, from *meltan,* to melt.] Grain, usually barley, steeped in water and made to germinate and used in brewing and distilling; liquor produced from malt; beer.—*v.t.* To make into malt.—*v.i.* To be converted into malt.—**malted milk,** *n.* A beverage prepared by whipping a combination of flavored malt, ice cream, and milk.— **maltster,** mạlt′stėr, *n.* A man who makes malt.

maltase, mal′tās, *n.* [*Malt* and *ase.*] *Chem.* an enzyme found in plants, animals, bacteria, yeast, etc., which speeds the hydrolysis of maltose to glucose.

Maltese, mạl′tēz, *n. sing.* and *pl.* A native or natives of Malta.—*a.* Belonging to Malta.

maltha, mal′tha, *n.* [Gr., a mixture for caulking ships.] A variety of bitumen like pitch, intermediate between liquid petroleum and solid asphalt.

Malthusian, mal•thū′zi•an, *a.* Relating to the theory of the Rev. T. R. *Malthus,* that population, when unchecked, goes on increasing in a higher ratio than the means of subsistence can be made to increase. —*n.* One who holds the doctrines of Malthus.

maltose, mạlt′ōz, *n.* [From *malt.*] Malt sugar; a white crystalline sugar, $C_{12}H_{22}O_{11}$-H_2O, formed by the action of amylase on starch.

maltreat, mal•trēt′, *v.t.* [*Mal* and *treat.*] To treat ill.—**maltreatment,** mal•trēt′ment, *n.*

malvaceous, mal•vā′shus, *a.* [L. *malva,* mallow.] Pertaining to the plants of the mallow family.

malversation, mal•vėr•sā′shon, *n.* [Fr. *malversation*—L. *male,* badly, and *versor,* to occupy one's self, from *verto, versum,* to turn. VERSE.] Evil conduct; fraudulent tricks; misbehavior in an office or employment, as fraud, breach of trust, etc.

Mameluke, mam′e•lūk, mam′a•lūk,

n. [Ar. *mamlúk*, that which is possessed, a slave, from *malak*, to possess.] One of the former mounted soldiery of Egypt, a powerful body broken up and massacred in 1811.

mamma, mama, mä′mä, *n.* [A repetition of the infantile utterance *ma, ma.*] Mother; a word of tenderness and familiarity, used chiefly by young persons in addressing, or reference to, mother.

mamma, mam′ma, *n.* pl. **mammae,** mam′mē. [L., the female breast, from root meaning to swell, to swell with juice.] The breast; the organ in females that secretes the milk.—**mammal,** mam′mal, *n.* An animal of the class Mammalia.—**Mammalia,** mam•mā′li•a, *n. pl.* [Lit. breast-animals.] The highest class in the animal kingdom, whose distinctive characteristic is that the female suckles the young.—**mammalian,** mam•-mā′li•an, *a.* Pertaining to the mammals.—**mammalogy,** mam•mal′o•ji, *n.* The science of mammals.—**mammary,** mam′ma•ri, *a.* Pertaining to the female breasts or paps.—**mammiferous,** mam•mif′ėr•us, *a.* Having the distinguishing characteristics of a mammifer.—**mammilla,** mam•mil′la, *n.* [L. *mamilla*, a little breast.] A little breast; something of this form.—**mammillary,** mam′-mil•a•ri, *a.* Pertaining to or resembling a nipple or pap; *anat.* applied to two small protuberances like nipples in the brain; *mineral.* studded with mammiform protuberances.—**mammillate, mammillated,** mam′-mil•āt, mam′mil•ā•ted, *a.* In the form of a pap or nipple; having small protuberances like nipples.

mammee, mam•mē′, *n.* An American tree yielding a large and nourishing fruit.—**mammee sapota,** mam•-mē′sa•pō′ta, *n.* A large tree of the West Indies and tropical America, yielding a fruit which is called natural marmalade.

mammon, mam′mon, *n.* [L. *mammona*, Gr. *mammōnas*, mammon, riches, from Chal. *mammōn, māmōn.*] The Syrian god of riches, mentioned in the New Testament as a personification of worldliness; hence, riches; [*cap.*] wealth.—**mammonism,** mam′mon•izm, *n.* Devotion to the service of Mammon or the pursuit of wealth.—**mammonist, mammonite,** mam′mon•ist, mam′mon•it, *n.* A person entirely devoted to the acquisition of wealth.

mammoth, mam′moth, *n.* [Rus. *mamant, mamont*, from Tart. *mamma*, the earth, because their remains being found in the earth the natives believed that they burrowed like moles.] An extinct species of elephant with long tusks and covered with dense, shaggy hair, the remains of which are found in Siberia and elsewhere.—*a.* Resembling the mammoth in size; very large; gigantic.—**mammoth tree,** *n.* The giant sequoia tree of California, specimens having reached more than 325 feet with a diameter of 25 feet.

man, man, *n.* pl. **men,** men. [A.Sax. *man, mann*, man, person = D., O. H.G., and Sw. *man*, G. *mann*, Icel. *mathr, mannr*, Dan. *mand*, Goth. *manna*; from root *man*, to think, seen in Skr. *man*, to think, *manas*, mind, *manushya*, man, and also in E. *mean*, to intend, *mind*, L. *mens*, the mind (whence *mental*).] A human being; a person; particularly, a male adult of the human race; the human race; mankind: in this sense without article or plural (*man* is born to trouble); a male servant; an adult male in some person's employment or under his direction; a piece with which a game, as chess or checkers, is played.—*Man of straw*, a man of no substantial character, influence, or means; in commercial language, a person destitute of capital put forward by way of decoy.—*v.t. manned, manning.* To supply with men; to furnish with a sufficient force or complement of men; to infuse courage into.—**man-at-arms,** *n.* A term applied to a fully equipped or heavily armed soldier of the Middle Ages.—**man-eater,** *n.* A cannibal; one of those tigers which have acquired a special preference for human flesh.—**manful,** man′fụl, *a.* Manly; bold; brave.—**manfully,** man′fụl•li, *adv.* In a manful manner.—**manfulness,** man′fụl•nes, *n.* The quality of being manful.—**manhole,** man′hōl, *n.* A hole through which a man may creep into a drain, cesspool, steam boiler, etc., for cleaning or repairing.—**manhood,** man′hụd, *n.* The state of being a man; the qualities of or becoming a man.—**manikin,** man′i•-kin, *n.* A little man; a dwarf; an anatomic model of the human body.—**mankind,** man•kīnd′ or man′kīnd, *n.* The human race; man taken collectively; the males of the human race.—**manlike,** man′līk, *a.* Resembling a man; having the qualities proper to a man.—**manliness,** man′-li•nes, *n.* The quality of being manly.—**manly,** man′li, *a.* Pertaining to or becoming a man; having the nobler attributes of a man; self-reliant; brave.—**mannish,** man′ish, *a.* Characteristic of or resembling a man; as applied to a woman, masculine; unwomanly.—**mannishly,** man′-ish•li, *adv.* In a mannish manner.—**mannishness,** man′ish•nes, *n.*—**manpower,** *n.* The amount of power provided by human effort; a nation's strength as determined by the number of men and women available for the armed services and civil defense.—**man-of-war,** *n.* A government vessel employed for the purposes of war.—**manservant,** *n.* A male servant.—**manslaughter,** *n.* The unlawful killing of a man, without malice.

manacle, man′a•kl, *n.* [Fr. *manicle*, L. *manicula*, dim. of *manica*, a manacle, from *manus*, the hand. MANAGE.] An instrument of iron for fastening the hands; handcuff; shackle: generally in plural.—*v.t.—manacled, manacling.* To put handcuffs or other fastening upon; to shackle.

manage, man′ij, *v.t.—managed, managing.* [Fr. *manège*, the management of a horse; It. *maneggiare*, to handle, to manage; from L. *manus*, the hand, whence also *manacle, manual*, etc. MANUAL.] To have under control and direction; to conduct, carry on, guide, administer; to make tractable, or get under due control; to wield; to move or use in the manner desired (tools or the like); to treat (a person) with caution or judgment; to govern with address.—*v.i.* To direct or conduct affairs; to carry on concerns or business.—**manageability,** man′-ij•a•bil″i•ti, *n.* State of being manageable.—**manageable,** man′ij•a•bl, *a.* Capable of being managed; easily made subservient to one's views or designs.—**manageableness,** man′ij•-a•bl•nes, *n.* The quality of being manageable.—**manageably,** man′ij•-a•bli, *adv.* In a manageable manner.—**management,** man′ij•ment, *n.* The act of managing; the manner of treating, directing, carrying on, or using for a purpose; conduct; administration; cautious handling or treatment; the body of directors or managers of any undertaking, concern, or interest collectively.—**manager,** man′ij•ėr, *n.* One who manages; one who has the guidance or direction of anything; one who is directly at the head of an undertaking.—**managerial,** man•a•jē′ri•al, *a.* Of or belonging to a manager.—**managership,** man′ij•ėr•ship, *n.* The office of a manager.

manakin, man′a•kin, *n.* [Dim. of *man*, as applied to birds, originally the name of a species with a beard-like tuft of feathers on the chin.] A manikin; a name for certain small tropical American birds.

manatee, man•a•tē′, *n.* [Haitian.] The sea cow, an aquatic herbivorous mammal allied to the cetaceans, and found on the coasts of South America, Africa, and Australia.

manchet, man′shet, *n.* [Comp. Fr. *miche, michette*, a manchet or small loaf.] A small loaf of fine bread; fine white bread.—*a.* Fine and white: said of bread or flour.

manchineel, man•chi•nēl′, *n.* [It. *mancinello*, Fr. *manzanille*, Sp. *manzanillo*, from *manzana*, an apple, from L. *malum Matianum*, a kind of apple, from *Matius*, a Roman name.] A tree of the West Indies and Central America, abounding in acrid and highly poisonous juice, the wood being valuable for cabinet work.

Manchu, man•chö′, *n.* A native of Manchuria, or one of the same race; one of the reigning dynasty in China; the language of the Manchus; the court language of China.

manciple, man′si•pl, *n.* [O.Fr. *mancipe*, L. *manceps*, one who purchases anything at a public sale—*mānus*, the hand, and *capio*, to take.] A steward; a purveyor, particularly of a college or inn of court.

mandamus, man•dā′mus, *n.* [L., lit. we command.] *Law*, a command or writ issuing from a superior court, directed to any person, corporation, or inferior court, requiring them to do some specified act.

mandarin, man•da•rin′, *n.* [Pg. *man-*

darim, from Skr. *mantrin*, a counsellor, a minister, from *mantra*, counsel.] The general name given by Europeans to Chinese magistrates or public officials, whether civil or military; a northern dialect of China; a miniature orange tree from which our mandarin orange comes.

mandate, man′dāt, *n.* [L. *mandatum*, an order, from *mando*, to command (from *manus*, the hand, and *do*, to give), seen also in *command*, *commend*, *demand*, *remand*, *recommend*, etc.] A command; an order, precept, or injunction; written authority by one person to another to act for him.—**mandatory**, man′da•to•ri, *n.* [Fr. *mandataire*.] One to whom a mandate or charge is given; one who receives special written authority to act for another.—**mandatory**, *a.* Containing a command; directory.

mandible, man′di•bl, *n.* [L. *mandibulum*, the jaw, from *mando*, to chew.] An animal's jaw, particularly the under jaw of a mammal; the upper or lower jaw of a bird; one of the upper or anterior pair of jaws of an insect or other articulate animal.—**mandibular**, man•dib′ū•lėr, *a.* Belonging to a mandible.—**mandibulate**, man•dib′ū•lāt, *a.* Provided with mandibles, as many insects.

mandolin, man′do•lin, *n.* [Fr. *mandoline*, from It. *mandola*, *mandora*, *pandora*, a species of lute. BANDORE.] A musical instrument of the guitar kind.

mandragora, man•drag′o•ra, *n.* [L. and Gr. *mandragoras*, the mandrake.] Mandrakes.—**mandrake**, man′drāk, *n.* A plant of the Mediterranean region, with large thick roots, and possessing strong purgative and narcotic properties, formerly the subject of various superstitions.

mandrel, mandril, man′drel, man′dril, *n.* [Fr. *mandrin*, from Gr. *mandra*, an enclosed space, the bed in which the stone of a ring is set.] A bar of iron on which an article is fitted to be turned on a lathe; any straight bar upon which a tube or ring is welded.

mandrill, man′dril, *n.* [Fr. *mandrille*, from the West African name.] The great blue-faced or rib-nosed baboon, the largest and most hideous of the baboons.

manducate, man′dū•kāt, *v.t.*—*manducated*, *manducating*. [L. *manduco*, *manducatum*, from *mando*, to chew; akin *mandible*, *manger*.] To masticate; to chew.

mane, mān, *n.* [O.D. *mane*, D. *manen*, Dan. *man*, Icel. *mōn*, O.H.G. *mana*, G. *mähne*; allied to W. *mwng*, a mane, *mwn*, the neck.] The long hair on the upper side of the neck of some animals, as the horse, lion, etc., usually hanging down on one side.—**maned**, mānd, *a.* Having a mane.

manège, ma•nezh′, *n.* [Fr. *manège*, from It. *maneggio*, management. MANAGE.] A school for training horses and teaching horsemanship; the art of breaking, training, and riding horses; the art of horsemanship.

manes, mā′nēz, *n. pl.* [L., from O.L. *manus*, good, benevolent.] [*often cap.*] Among the Romans the ghosts, shades, or souls of deceased persons; the deified shades of the dead.

maneuver, manoeuvre, ma•nö′vėr, or ma•nū′vėr, *n.* [Fr. *manœuvre*—*main*, L. *manus*, the hand, and *œuvre*, L. *opera*, work. *Manure* is the same word.] A regulated dexterous movement, particularly in an army or navy; any movement of troops, ships, etc., for attack on or defense against an enemy; management with address or artful design; an adroit procedure; intrigue; stratagem.—*v.i.*—*maneuvered*, *maneuvering*. To perform maneuvers, especially military or naval maneuvers; to employ intrigue or stratagem to effect a purpose.—*v.t.* To make to perform maneuvers or evolutions.—**maneuverer**, ma•nö′vėr•ėr, or ma•nū′vėr•ėr, *n.* One who maneuvers.

manful, etc. See MAN.

manganese, man′ga•nēz, *n.* [By metathesis from *magnesium*, the name first given to it.] A grayish-white metallic element used as an alloying agent to give steel toughness. Symbol, Mn; at. no., 25; at. wt., 54.9380.—**manganic**, man•gan′ik, *a.*—**manganite**, man′gan•it, *n.* One of the ores of manganese, used in the manufacture of glass.

mange, mānj, *n.* [O.Fr. *mangeson*, Fr. *démangeaison*, an itching, from *manger*, L. *manduco*, to eat. MANDUCATE.] A cutaneous disease very similar to itch, and to which horses, cattle, dogs, and other beasts are subject.—**mangily**, mān′ji•li, *adv.* In a mangy manner.—**manginess**, mān′ji•nes, *n.* The quality or condition of being mangy.—**mangy**, mān′ji, *a.* Infected with the mange; scabby; mean.

mangel-wurzel, mang′gl•wėr′zl, *n.* [G., lit. want-root, but the proper form is *mangold-wurzel*—G. *mangold*, beet, and *wurzel*, root = beetroot.] A variety of beet, extensively cultivated as food for cattle.

manger, mān′jėr, *n.* [Fr. *mangeoire*, from *manger*, from L. *manducare*, to eat. MANDUCATE.] A trough or box in which fodder is laid for horses or cattle; the receptacle from which horses or cattle eat in a stable or cow house.

mangle, mang′gl, *v.t.*—*mangled*, *mangling*. [Perhaps from L. *mancus*, maimed, through L.L. *mangulare*, to mangle; comp. A.Sax. *bemancian*, to maim; L.G. *mank*, mutilated; D. *mank*, lame; G. *mangel*, a defect; *mangeln*, to be wanting.] To cut by repeated blows, making a ragged or torn wound, or covering with wounds; to cut in a bungling manner; to hack; to lacerate; applied chiefly to the cutting of flesh; *fig.* to destroy the symmetry or completeness of; to mutilate.—**mangler**, mang′glėr, *n.* One who mangles; one who mutilates.

mangle, mang′gl, *n.* [D. and G. *mangel*, from O.Fr. *mangonel*, Gr. *manganon*, a war engine, the axis of a pulley.] A well-known machine for smoothing tablecloths, sheets, and other articles of linen or cotton.—*v.t.* To smooth cloth with a mangle.—**mangler**, mang′glėr, *n.* One who uses a mangle.

mango, mang′gō, *n.* [Malay.] The fruit of the mango tree, a native of tropical Asia, but widely cultivated throughout the tropics; a fruit highly valued for dessert.

mangonel, man′go•nel, *n.* [O.Fr. *mangonel*, It. *manganello*, *mangano*, from Gr. *manganon*. MANGLE, *n.*] An engine formerly used for throwing stones and battering walls.

mangosteen, mang′go•stēn, *n.* [Malay *mangusta*.] A tree of the East Indies, the fruit of which is about the size of an orange, and most delicious.

mangrove, man′grōv, *n.* [Malay *manggi-manggi*.] A tropical tree growing on the banks of rivers and on the seacoast, remarkable for giving off adventitious roots from the stem and branches.

mania, mā′ni•a, *n.* [L., from Gr.; allied to Gr. *menos*, the mind; E. *mind* and *man*.] Madness; also rage or eager desire for anything; insane or morbid craving; mental disorder characterized by high, uncontrolled excitement; excitement and frenzy.—**maniac**, mā′ni•ak, *a.* Raving with madness; proceeding from disordered intellect; mad; excited; frenzied.—*n.* A madman; one who has an ungovernable enthusiasm for something.—**maniacal**, ma•nī′a•kal, *a.*—**manic depressive**, *n.* One who has a type of mental disorder alternating between periods of acute excitement and periods of acute depression.

Manichaean, Manichean, man•i•kē′an, *n.* [From the founder *Manes* or *Manichaeus*, who lived in the third century.] One of a sect in Persia who maintained that there are two supreme principles, the one good, the other evil, which produce all the happiness and calamities of the world.—**Manichaean**, *a.* Pertaining to the Manichaeans or their doctrines.—**Manichaeanism**, *n.*

manicure, man′i•kūr, *n.* [L. *manus*, hand, *cura*, care.] The care of the nails and the hands; a person whose occupation is to trim the nails and improve the condition of the hands.—*v.t.* & *i.* To trim or care for the nails.—**manicurist**, *n.*

manifest, man′i•fest, *a.* [L. *manifestus*, lit. that may be laid hold of by the hand—*manus*, the hand, and root seen in obs. *fendo*, to dash against (as in *offend*).] Clearly visible to the eye or obvious to the understanding; not obscure or difficult to be seen or understood; evident; plain.—*n.* A document signed by the master of a vessel at the place of lading, to be exhibited at the customhouse, containing a description of the ship and her cargo, the destination of the ship and the goods, etc.—*v.t.* To disclose to the eye or to the understanding; to show plainly; to display; to exhibit.—**manifestation**, man′i•fes•tā″shon, *n.* The act of manifesting; a making evident to the eye or to the understanding; the exhibition of anything by clear evidence; display; what is the means of displaying.—**manifestly,** man′i•fest•li, *adv.* In a manifest manner; clearly; evidently; plainly.—**manifesto,** man•i•fes′to, *n.* [It.] A public declaration, usually of a sovereign or government.

manifold, man′i•fōld, *a.* [*Many* and *fold.*] Numerous and various in kind or quality; exhibiting or embracing many points, features, or characteristics (the *manifold* wisdom of God); operating several parts at once.—*v.t.* To multiply impressions of, as of a letter.—*n.* A copy made by manifolding; a whole having many different parts; *mech.* that part of an internal-combustion engine which distributes a fuel-air mixture to the various cylinders; a pipe to which several other pipes are attached.—**manifoldly,** man′i•fōld•li, *adv.*—**manifoldness,** man′i•fōld•nes, *n.*

manikin, man′i•kin, *n.* [D. *manneken,* dim. of *man,* man.] A little man; a dwarf; an anatomic model of the human body.

Manila hemp, *n.* A fibrous material from a plant which grows in the Philippine Islands, etc.—**Manila paper,** *n.* A paper of strong fiber made from Manila hemp.

manioc, man′i•ok, *n.* [Pg. and Brazil *mandioca.*] A plant cultivated in tropical America and the West Indies, from the large fleshy root of which tapioca and cassava are prepared.

maniple, man′i•pl, *n.* [L. *manipulus, maniplus,* a handful, a company of soldiers—*manus,* the hand, and root of *plenus,* full (as in *plenary,* etc.).] *Rom. antiq.* a company of soldiers consisting of sixty common soldiers, two centurions, and a standard-bearer; in the Latin Ch., originally a handkerchief, now only a symbolical ornament attached to the left arm of the celebrant at mass.—**manipular,** ma•nip′ū•lėr, *a.* Pertaining to a maniple.—**manipulate,** ma•nip′ū•lāt, *v.t.*—*manipulated, manipulating.* [L.L. *manipulo, manipulatum.*] To handle or operate on with the hands, as in artistic or mechanical operations; to subject to certain processes; to operate upon for the purpose of giving a false appearance to (to *manipulate* accounts).—*v.i.* To use the hands, as in artistic processes, mechanical operations, or the like.—**manipulation,** ma•nip′ū•lā″shon, *n.* The art or mode of manipulating or working by hand; the act of operating upon skillfully, for the purpose of giving a false appearance to.—**manipulative, manipulatory,** ma•nip′ū•lā•tiv, ma•nip′ū•lā•to•ri, *a.* Pertaining to or performed by manipulation.—**manipulator,** ma•nip′ū•lā•ter, *n.* One who manipulates.

manito, manitou, man′i•tō, man′i•tö, *n.* Among North American Indians, a good or evil spirit or a fetish.

mankind, manly, etc. See MAN.

manna, man′na, *n.* [Generally derived from the Heb. *man hu,* what is it?] A substance miraculously furnished as food for the Israelites in their journey through the wilderness of Arabia; the sweet solidified juice which is obtained by incisions made in the stem of a species of ash.—**mannite,** man′īt, *n.* A peculiar variety of sugar obtained from manna.

mannequin, man′e•kin, *n.* [A corruption of *manikin.*] An artist's model fashioned of wood or wax; a woman who serves as a model by wearing clothes for display.

manner, man′ėr, *n.* [From Fr. *manière,* manner, O.Fr. *manier,* belonging to the hand, from L. *manus* the hand—properly, the method of handling a thing. MANAGE, MANUAL.] The mode in which anything is done; the way of performing or effecting anything; a person's peculiar or habitual way of carriage; bearing or conduct; deportment; *pl.* carriage or behavior, considered as decorous or indecorous, polite or impolite, pleasing or displeasing; ceremonious behavior; polite or becoming deportment (he has no *manners*); sort; kind; in this use having often the sense of a plural = sorts, kinds (all *manner* of things).—*In a manner,* in a certain degree or measure: to a certain extent (it is *in a manner* done already.)—**mannered,** man′ėrd, *a.* Having manners of this or that kind; exhibiting the peculiar style of an author or artist, more particularly in its objectionable form.—**mannerism,** man′ėr•izm, *n.* Excessive adherence to a characteristic, mode or manner of action or treatment; a personal and prominent peculiarity of style, as in a writer or an artist.—**mannerist,** man′ėr•ist, *n.* One addicted to mannerism.—**mannerliness,** man′ėr•li•nes, *n.* The quality of being mannerly.—**mannerly,** man′ėr•li, *a.* Showing good manners; correct in deportment; polite; not rude or vulgar.—*adv.* With good manners; without rudeness.

mannish, etc. See MAN.

mannite. See MANNA.

mannose, man′ōs, *n.* [From *manna.*] A kind of sugar related to glucose.

man-of-war. See MAN.

manometer, ma•nom′e•ter, *n.* An instrument for measuring the pressure of gases and vapors.—**manometric, manometrical,** man′o•met′rik, man•o•met′ri•kal, *a.* Pertaining to the manometer.

manor, man′or, *n.* [O.Fr. *manoir, maneir, maner,* L.L. *manerium,* a dwelling-place, a mansion, from L. *maneo,* to stay, to dwell. MANSION.] The land belonging to a lord or nobleman, or so much land as a lord formerly kept in his own hands for the use and subsistence of his family; a residence with a certain portion of land annexed to it.—**manor house,** *n.* The mansion belonging to a manor.—**manorial,** ma•nō′ri•al, *a.* Pertaining to a manor.

mansard roof, *n.* [From Francois *Mansard,* a French architect, the inventor, who died in 1666.] A curb roof, or roof of two slopes, the lower being steeper than the upper slope.

manse, mans, *n.* [L.L. *mansus, mansum,* a residence, from L. *mansum,* to stay, to dwell. MANSION.] The dwelling-house of a clergyman.

manservant. See MAN.

mansion, man′shon, *n.* [L. *mansio, mansionis,* from *maneo, mansum,* to dwell (seen also in *manor, menial, remain, remnant,* etc.).] A dwelling or residence, especially one of considerable size and pretension; a habitation; an abode.

mantel, man′tel, *n.* [O.Fr. *mantel,* Fr. *manteau,* mantle.] The supporting beam for the masonry above a fireplace.—**mantelpiece,** *n.* The shelf of a mantel.

mantelet, mantlet, man′tel•et, mant′let, *n.* [Dim. of *mantle.*] A small cloak worn by women; *fort.* a kind of movable parapet or penthouse set on wheels for protecting sappers from musketry fire.

mantic,† man′tik, *a.* [Gr. *mantikos,* from *mantis,* a prophet.] Relating to prophecy or divination; prophetic.

mantilla, man•til′la, *n.* [Sp.; same origin as *mantle.*] A hood; a Spanish head covering for women, which falls down upon the shoulders and may be used as a veil; a light cloak thrown over the dress of a lady.

mantis, man′tis, *n.* [Gr., a prophet, the mantis.] A genus of orthopterous insects, frequently resembling twigs and leaves, the praying mantis being so called from the position of the anterior legs resembling that of a person's hands at prayer.

mantissa, man•tis′a, *n.* [L., addition, increase.] The decimal part of a logarithm following the integral part.

mantle, man′tl, *n.* [O.Fr. *mantel,* Fr. *manteau,* It. *mantello,* from L. *mantellum, mantelum,* a mantle, a napkin.] Hence *mantel.*] A kind of cloak or loose garment to be worn over other garments; a covering; something that covers and conceals; *zool.* the external fold of the skin in most mollusks. Sometimes used in same sense as *mantel.*—*v.t.*—*mantled, mantling.* To cloak or cover.—*v.i.* To be expanded or spread out like a mantle; to become covered with a coating, as a liquid; to send up froth or scum; to cream; to display superficial changes of hue.

mantlet, *n.* See MANTELET.

mantua, man′tū•a, *n.* [Either a corruption of Fr. *manteau,* a mantle, or from *Mantua* in Italy (comp. *milliner,* from *Milan*).] A lady's gown.

manual, man′ū•al, *a.* [L. *manualis,* pertaining to the hand, from *manus,* the hand (root *ma,* to measure), seen also in *manacle, manage, manifest, manner, manure, maintain,* etc.] Performed or done by the hand; such as to require bodily exertion (*manual* labor); used or made by the hand.—*Manual training,* training in handicraft, as the work of carpenters, plumbers, or machinists.—*n.* A small book, such as may be carried in the hand or conveniently handled; any book of instructions or orders; the keyboard of an organ or the like.—**manually,** *adv.*

manubrium, ma•nū′bri•um, *n.* [L., a handle, from *manus,* the hand.] *Anat.* the upper bone of the sternum.

manufactory, man•ū•fak′to•ri, *n.* [L. *manus,* the hand, and *factura,* a making, from *facio,* to make.] A building in which goods are manufactured; a factory.—**manufacture,** man•ū•fak′chėr, *n.* The operation of making wares of any kind; the operation of reducing raw materials into a form suitable for use, by more or less complicated operations; an article made from raw materials.—*v.t.—manufactured,manufacturing.*To make or fabricate from raw materials, and work into forms convenient for use, especially by more or less complicated processes.—*v.i.*—To be occupied in manufactures.—**manufacturer,** man•ū•fak′chėr•ėr *n.* One who manufactures; one who employs workmen for manufacturing; the owner of a manufactory.—**manufacturing,** man•ū•fak′chėr•ing, *pp.* and *a.* Employed in making goods; pertaining to manufactures.

manumit, man•ū•mit′, *v.t.—manumitted, manumitting.* [L. *manumitto*—*manus,* hand, and *mitto,* to send.] To release from slavery; to free, as a slave; to emancipate.—**manumission,** man•ū•mish′on, *n.* [L. *manumissio.*] The act of manumitting; emancipation.

manure, ma•nūr′, *v.t.—manured, manuring.* [Originally to work by manual labor or by the hand, the same word as *manœuvre.*] To cultivate by manual labor;‡ to enrich (soils) with fertilizing substances; to treat with manure.—*n.* Any matter or substance added to the soil with the view of fertilizing it, or of accelerating vegetation and increasing the production of the crops, such as guano, dung, bone dust, the drainage from a dung heap (liquid *manure*), etc.—**manurer,** ma•nū′rėr, *n.* One that manures lands.

manus, mā′nus, *n.* [L., the hand.] The hand; the part of an animal's fore limb corresponding to the hand in man.

manuscript, man′ū•skript, *n.* [L. *manuscriptum,* written with the hand —*manus,* the hand, and *scribo, scriptum,* to write.] A book or paper written with the hand or pen; a writing of any kind, in contradistinction to what is printed; often contracted to *MS.,* pl. *MSS.*—*a.* Written with the hand; not printed.

Manx, mangks, *n.* The native language of the inhabitants of the Isle of Man; *pl.* the natives of Man.—*a.* Belonging to the Isle of Man or its language.

many, men′i, *a.* [A.Sax. *manig, maenig, monig;* D. *menig,* Dan. *mange,* Goth. *manags,* O.H.G. *manac,* G. *manch,* many.] Numerous; forming or comprising a great number (*many* men); always followed by *an* or *a* before a noun in the singular number (*many* a man), and then with more of a distributive force.—*The many,* the great majority of people; the crowd; the common herd.—*So many,* the same number of; a certain number indefinitely.—*Too many,* too strong; too powerful; too able (*colloq.*). [*Many* is prefixed to a great number of adjectives forming compounds which explain themselves (*many*-colored, *many*-cornered, *many*-eyed, etc.).]—**many-sided,** *a.* Having many sides; showing mental or moral activity in many different directions; exhibiting many phases.

Maori, mä′o•ri, *n.* [A New Zealand word signifying native or indigenous.] One of the native inhabitants of New Zealand.—*a.* Of or belonging to the native inhabitants of New Zealand.

map, map, *n.* [L. *mappa,* a napkin—*mappa mundi,* a map of the world; akin are *apron, napery.*] A representation of the surface of the earth or of any part of it, or of the whole or any part of the celestial sphere, usually on paper or other material.—*v.t.—mapped, mapping.* To delineate in a map, as the figure of any portion of land; to represent in detail.

maple, mā′pl, *n.* [A.Sax. *maepel.*] The name given to any tree of the genus *Acer,* the wood of which is valuable.—*Sugar maple,* a maple of North America, the juice of which, obtained in early spring by tapping, is converted into sugar.

mar, mär, *v.t.—marred, marring.* [A.Sax. *myrran, merran, amyrran, amerran,* to hinder, to spoil; D. *marren,* to retard; Icel. *merja,* to crush; O.H.G. *marrjan,* to hinder. Akin to *moor* (verb).] To injure in any way; to spoil, impair, deface, deform.—**marplot,** mär′plot, *n.* One who, by his officious interference, mars or defeats a design or plot.

marabou, mar′a•bö, *n.* [Fr. *marabout,* orig. a Mohammedan hermit.] The name of two large storks, the delicate white feathers beneath the wing and tail of which form the marabou feathers, used in millinery.

maraschino, mar•as•kē′nō, *n.* [It., from *marasca, amarasca,* a kind of sour cherry, from L. *amarus,* bitter.] A kind of liqueur made in Dalmatia from cherries.

marasmus, ma•ras′mus, *n.* [Gr. *marasmos,* from *marainō,* to cause to pine or waste away.] A wasting of flesh without fever or apparent disease; atrophy.

marathon, mar′a•thon, *n.* [From the Battle of *Marathon,* 490 B.C.] A long-distance race; a 26-mile foot race; an endurance test.

maraud, ma•rąd′, *v.i.* [Fr. *marauder.*] To rove in quest of plunder.—*v.t.* To raid for plunder.—**marauder,** ma•rą′dėr, *n.*

maravedi, mar•a•vā′di, *n.* [Sp., from *Márabitin,* an Arabian dynasty which reigned in Spain.] A very small copper coin formerly used in Spain.

marble, mär′bl, *n.* [Fr. *marbre,* from L. *marmor,* marble, Gr. *marmaros,* any stone or rock which sparkles in the light, from *marmairō,* to flash, to gleam.] The popular name of any species of calcareous stone, of a compact texture and of a beautiful appearance, susceptible of a good polish; a column, tablet, or the like, of marble, remarkable for some inscription or sculpture; a little ball of marble, of other stone, or of baked clay, used by children in play.—*a.* Composed of marble; stained or veined like marble; *fig.* hard or insensible like marble (*marble*-hearted, *marble*-breasted).—*v.t.—marbled, marbling.* To give an appearance of marble to; to stain or vein like marble.—**marbling,** mär′bling, *n.* Imitation of marble; any marking resembling that of veined marble.

marc, märk, *n.* [Fr.] The refuse matter which remains after the pressure of fruit, as of grapes, olives, etc.

marcasite, mär′ka•sīt, *n.* [Fr. *marcassite,* a word of Arabic origin.] Iron pyrites or bisulfide of iron, nearly of the color of tin, used for industrial or ornamental purposes.

marcescent, mär•ses′ent, *a.* [L. *marcescens, marcescentis,* ppr. of *marcesco,* to fade.] Withering; fading; decaying; specifically, *bot.* withering, but not falling off till the part bearing it is perfected.

march, märch, *n.* [A.Sax. *mearc,* a mark, sign, boundary; Icel. *mark,* O.H.G. *marcha* (whence Fr. *marche,* boundary). MARK.] A frontier or boundary of a territory; most common in pl., and especially applied to the boundaries or confines of political divisions; in Scotland the boundary line of conterminous estates or lands, whether large or small.—*v.i.* To be contiguous; to be situated next, with a boundary line between.

march, märch, *v.i.* [Fr. *marcher;* It. *marciare;* either from Fr. *marche,* a boundary (MARCH, a frontier), through such usages as in 'aller de *marche* en *marche*', to wander from boundary to boundary; or from L. *marcus,* a hammer, through L.L. *marcare,* to beat the ground with the feet, to march.] To move by steps and in order, as soldiers; to move in a military manner; to walk with a steady, regular tread.—*Marching regiment,* a colloquial term for an infantry regiment of the line.—*v.t.* To cause to march.—*n.* The measured and uniform walk of a body of men, as soldiers, moving simultaneously and in order; stately and deliberate walk; steady or labored progression; an advance of soldiers from one halting place to another; the distance passed over; progressive advancement; progress (the *march* of intellect); a musical composition designed to accompany and regulate the movement of troops or other bodies of men.—*March past,* a march past the reviewing officer or some high dignitary on parade.

March, märch, *n.* [O.Fr. *march,* from L. *Martius,* pertaining to Mars, the god of war; *Martius· mensis,* Mars' month.] The third month of the year.—*Mad as a March hare,* quite mad or crazy, from March being the rutting month of hares, during which they are in an excited state.

marchioness, mär′shun•es, *n.* [A fem. from L.L. *marchio*, a marquis. MARQUIS.] The wife or widow of a marquis; a female having the rank of a marquis.

marchpane, märch′pān, *n.* [O.Fr. *marcepain*, It. *marzapane*, L.Gr. *maza*, a barleycake, and L. *panis*, bread.] A kind of sweet bread or cracker containing almonds.

marconigram, mär•kō′ni•gram, *n.* A message sent by Marconi's system of wireless telegraphy.

mare, mâr, *n.* [A.Sax. *mere, miere*, a mare, fem. of *mear, mearh*, a horse; Icel. *mar*, a horse, *merr*, a mare, G. *māhre*, a mare, O.H.G. *marah, march*, a horse; allied to Ir. *marc*, W. *march*, a horse.] The female of the horse.—*Mare's nest*, a discovery that is no discovery, and that a person merely fancies he has made.—**mare's-tail,** *n.* A common marsh plant somewhat resembling in appearance the equisetum or horse-tail, but quite distinct.

mare, mâr, *n.* pl. **maria,** ma•rē′ä, [N.L. from L. *mare*, sea.] Any of the dark sections of the surface of the moon or Mars.

maremma, ma•rem′ma, *n.* pl. **maremme,** ma•rem′me. [It.] Marshy and malarious tracts of country in middle Italy.

margaric, mär•gar′ik, *a.* [L. *margarita*, Gr. *margaritēs*, pearl, from Per. *mervarid*, a pearl.] Pertaining to pearl; having a pearly appearance.—*Margaric acid*, a so-called acid, a mixture of palmitic and stearic acid obtained from oils and fats, and often in the form of pearly scales.

margarine, mär′je•rin, *n.* [Fr. from Gr. *margaron* and *ine*.] A mixture of artificially prepared edible fats, extracted from animal fats and vegetable oils, sold as a substitute for butter.

margay, mär′gā, *n.* A Brazilian carnivorous animal about the size of a cat.

margin, mär′jin, *n.*; poetically **marge,** märj. [Formerly *margine*, or *margent*, Fr. *marge*, It. *margine*, from L. *margo, marginis*, a brink, a margin.] A border; edge; brink; verge (of a river, etc.); the edge of the leaf or page of a book, left blank or partly occupied by notes; a sum or quantity reserved to meet contingencies in addition to what is known to be necessary; the difference between the cost of an article and its selling price; *bot.* the edge or border of a leaf or other organ of a plant; *fig.* a certain latitude to go and come upon.—**marginal,** mär′ji•nal, *a.* Pertaining to a margin; written or printed in the margin of a page.—**marginalia,** mär•ji•nā′li•a, *n. pl.* Notes written on the margins of books.—**marginally,** mär′ji•nal•li, *adv.* In the margin of a book.—**marginated, marginate,** mär′ji•nā•ted, mär′ji•nāt, *a.* Having a margin.

margrave, mär′grāv, *n.* [Fr. *margrave*, from D. *markgraaf*, G. *markgraf*—*mark*, a march or border, and *graf*, an earl or count.] Originally, like marquis, a lord or keeper of the marches or borders; a title of nobility in Germany, etc.—**margravate, margraviate,** mär′gra•vāt, mär•grā′vi•āt, *n.* The territory or jurisdiction of a margrave.—**margravine,** mär′gra•vēn, *n.* [Fr. *margravine*, G. *markgräfin*.] The wife of a margrave.

marigold, mar′i•gōld, *n.* [*Mary*, that is, the Virgin Mary, and *gold*.] The popular name applied to several composite plants bearing bright yellow flowers.

marijuana, marihuana, mâ•ri•wä′nä, *n.* [Am. Sp., native word, from *María Juana*, Mary Jane.] Indian hemp (*Cannabis sativa*); a narcotic derived from the dried leaves and flowers of the hemp.

marinade, mar•i•nād′, *n.* [Fr., from *marin*, marine, L. *mare*, the sea.] A compound liquor, generally of wine and vinegar, with herbs and spices, in which fish or meats are steeped before dressing to improve their flavor.—*v.t.* To salt or pickle (fish); to let stand in oil and vinegar. Also **marinate.**

marine, ma•rēn′, *a.* [L. *marinus*, from *mare*, the sea; allied to W. *mór*, the sea, A.Sax. *mere*, a lake, and E. *marsh*; the root being same as in L. *mors*, death (dead or stagnant water).] Pertaining to or in some way connected with the sea; found or formed in the sea; inhabiting the sea (*marine* forms of life); used at sea; suited for use at sea (a *marine* engine); naval; maritime (a *marine* officer; *marine* forces).—*n.* The entire navy of a kingdom or state; the collective shipping of a country.—*Marines*, troops serving on a war vessel or at shore-stations, as a separate unit of the Navy to supplement naval activities. They are used primarily as landing forces in wartime, and to guard American lives and property abroad.—**mariner,** mar′i•nėr, *n.* [Fr. *marinier*.] A seaman or sailor; one whose occupation is to assist in navigating ships.—*Mariner's compass*, a navigator's device consisting of a magnetic needle and a card marking directions.

Mariolatry, mâ•ri•ol′a•tri, *n.* [L. *Maria*, Mary, the Virgin Mary, and Gr. *latreia*, service, worship.] The adoration of the Virgin Mary.

marionette, mar′i•o•net″, *n.* [Fr., for *Mariolette*, a dim. of *Mariole*, a little figure of the Virgin *Mary*.] A puppet moved by strings.

marish,† mar′ish, *n.* A fen; a marsh.

marital, mar′i•tal, *a.* [L. *maritalis*, from *maritus*, marriage.] Of or pertaining to a marriage.

maritime, mar′i•tīm, *a.* [L. *maritimus*, from *mare*, the sea. MARINE.] Relating or pertaining to navigation or commerce by sea; connected or belonging to shipping; naval; having a navy and commerce by sea (*maritime* powers); bordering on the sea; situated near the sea (a *maritime* town).

marjoram, mär′jo•ram, *n.* [G. *marjoran*, It. *marjorana*, L.L. *marjoraca*, from L. *amaracus*, Gr. *amarakos*, marjoram.] A perennial plant of the mint family, of several species; the sweet marjoram is aromatic and fragrant, and used in cookery.

mark, märk, *n.* [A.Sax. *mearc*, mark, sign, limit, boundary=Goth. *marka*, a boundary; L. *margo*, edge or border; G. *mark*, a boundary, a district.] A visible sign or impression on something, as a dot, line, streak, stamp, figure, or the like; any sign by which a thing can be distinguished; a certain sign which a merchant puts upon his goods in order to distinguish them from others; a trademark; pre-eminence, distinction, importance, eminent position (a man of *mark*); respectful attention or regard; heed; anything to which a missile may be directed; the point to be reached; the proper standard; the extreme estimate or allowance (below or within the *mark*); a character, generally in the form of a cross, made by a person who cannot write his name, and intended as a substitute for it; a mark in paper (a water *mark*); a target or focal point (hit the *mark*); the point at which one begins a race (on your *mark*...); a postmark; a grade given a student.—*To make one's mark*, to gain a place of influence and distinction.—*v.t.* To make a mark on; to single out, point out, stamp, or characterize; to denote; often with *out*, to take particular observation of; to take note of; to trace or chart a route; to set off boundaries (used with *off*); to indicate; to register, as an instrument; to trace with marks.—*To mark time, milit.* to lift and bring down the feet alternately at the same rate as in marching; to stall progress for a time.—*v.i.* To note; to observe critically; to remark.—**markdown,** märk′doun, *n.* A reduction in price.—**marker,** mär′kėr, *n.* One who marks; something used to make a mark.—**marking,** mär′king, *n.* The act of impressing a mark; a mark or series of marks upon something; characteristic arrangement of natural coloring (the *markings* on a bird's egg).—**marksman,** märks′man, *n.* One who is skillful to hit a mark; one who shoots well.—**marksmanship,** märks′man•ship, *n.*

mark, märk, *n.* [A.Sax. *marc*; G. *mark*.] A German monetary unit and coin; formerly a European weight for gold and silver, about 8 oz.

market, mär′ket, *n.* [O.Fr. *markiet*, It. *mercato*, L. *mercatus*, from *mercor*, to buy, from *merx, mercis*, merchandise. MERCANTILE.] An occasion on which goods are publicly exposed for sale and buyers assemble to purchase; a fair; a public place in a city or town where goods are exposed for sale, whether a building or an open space; country or place of sale (the U.S. *market*, the foreign *market*); purchase or sale, or rate of purchase and sale; demand for commodities.—*v.i.* To deal in a market; to make bargains for provisions or goods.—*v.t.* To offer for sale in a market; to vend; to sell.—

marketable, mär′ket•a•bl, *a.* Capable of being sold; salable; fit for the market; current in the market.—**market price,** *n.* The price at which anything is currently sold; current value.

marking, marksman, etc. See MARK.

markka, mär′kä, *n.* [A.Sax. *marc*; G. *mark.*] A monetary unit of Finland.

marl, märl, *n.* [O.Fr. *marle*, D., Dan. Sw., and G. *mergel*, L.L. *margila*, from L. *marga*, marl—a word of Celtic origin.] A mixture of calcareous and argillaceous earth found at various depths under the soil, and extensively used for the improvement of land, there being several varieties of it, as clay marl, shell marl, etc.—*v.t.* To overspread or manure with marl.—**marlite,** mär′līt, *n.* A variety of marl.—**marlitic,** mär•lit′ik, *a.* Partaking of the qualities of marlite.—**marly,** mär′li, *a.* Resembling marl; abounding with marl.

marlin, mär′lin, *n.* [From *marlinspike.*] A large oceanic game fish, having a spiked snout, which appears in the Atlantic and Pacific oceans.

marline, mär′lin, *n.* [D. *marling*, *marlijn*—*marren*, to tie, to moor, and *lijn*, a line, a cord. MOOR, LINE.] *Naut.* a small line composed of two strands loosely twisted, used for winding around ropes to prevent their being chafed.—*v.t. Naut.* to wind marline round, as a rope.—**marlinespike, marlinspike,** mär′lin•spīk, *n.* A sort of iron spike with an eye or hole on one end, used to separate the strands of a rope in splicing.

marmalade, mär′ma•lād, *n.* [Fr. *marmelade*; Pg. *marmēlada*, from *marmelo*, a quince; from L. *melimelum*, Gr. *melimēlon*, lit. a sweet apple—*meli*, honey, and *mēlon*, an apple, peach, orange.] A name applied to preserves made from various fruits, especially bitter and acid fruits, such as the orange, lemon, etc.

marmoreal, marmorean, mär•mō′ri•al, mär•mō′ri•an, *a.* Pertaining to marble; made of marble.

marmoset, mär′mo•zet, *n.* [O.Fr. *marmoset*, Fr. *marmouset*, originally a small grotesque figure, from L.L. *marmoretum*, a small marble figure, from L. *marmor*, marble.] A beautiful American monkey with long tail, long fur, and tufted ears.

marmot, mär′mot, *n.* [Fr. *marmotte*; It. *marmotta*, *marmontana*, from L. *mus* (*muris*) *montanus*, mountain mouse.] A rodent quadruped, an inhabitant of northern latitudes, living in colonies, in extensive burrows, and hibernating in winter.

maroon, ma•rön′, *n.* [Fr. *marron*, runaway, from Sp. *cimarron*, wild, unruly, from *cima*, the top of a hill.] A name once given to fugitive slaves living on the mountains in the West Indies and Guyana.—*v.t.* To put ashore and leave on a desolate island, by way of punishment, as was done by the buccaneers, etc.

maroon, ma•rön′, *a.* [Fr. *marron*, It. *marrone*, a chestnut.] Brownish-crimson; of a color resembling claret.—*n.* A brownish-crimson or claret color.

marque, märk, *n.* [Fr. *marque*, a boundary; letters of marque originally empowered the receivers to cross the boundaries or marches of an enemy. MARK, MARCH (a frontier).] A license granted to a private vessel to make attacks on the ships or belongings of a public enemy, usually in the phrase *letters of marque* or *letters of marque and reprisal*, which constitute a vessel a *privateer*.

marquee, mär•kē′, *n.* [Fr. *marquise*, a marchioness, a marquee.] A large tent erected for a temporary purpose; a roof-like projection above the entrance to a theater or hotel, etc.

marquess, *n.* See MARQUIS.

marquetry, mär′ket•ri, *n.* [Fr. *marqueterie*, from *marqueter*, to spot, to inlay, from *marque*, a mark. MARK.] Inlaid work, often consisting of thin pieces of fine woods of different colors, arranged on a ground so as to form various patterns.

marquis, marquess, mär′kwis, mär′kwes, *n.* [Fr. *marquis*, It. *marchese*, L.L. *marchisus*, *marchensis*, a prefect of the *marches* or border territories. MARK and MARCH, a boundary.] A title of dignity in Britain next in rank to that of duke, and hence the second of the five orders of English nobility.—**marquisate,** mär′kwis•āt, *n.* The seigniory, dignity, or lordship of a marquis.—**marquise,** mär′kēz, *n.* [Fr.] The wife of a marquis; a marchioness.

marriage, mar′ij, *n.* [Fr. *mariage*, L.L. *maritaticum*, marriage, from L. *maritus*, a husband, from *mas*, *maris*, a male. MASCULINE.] The act of marrying; the legal union of a man and woman for life; the ceremony by which they are so united; a wedding.—*Marriage portion*, dower given by a father to his daughter at her marriage. *Marriage settlement*, an arrangement made before marriage whereby a jointure is secured to the wife, and portions to children, in the event of the husband's death. ∴ *Marriage*, the union, or the act of forming or entering into the union; *wedding*, the ceremonies celebrating the union; *nuptials*, a more dignified word for wedding; *matrimony*, the married state; *wedlock*, the vernacular English word for matrimony.—**marriageable,** mar′ij•a•bl, *a.* Of an age suitable for marriage.—**marriageableness,** mar′ij•a•bl•nes, *n.* State of being marriageable.—**married,** mar′id, *p.* and *a.* Formed or constituted by marriage; conjugal; connubial (the *married* state).—**marry,** mar′i, *v.t.*—*married*, *marrying*. [Fr. *marier*, L. *maritare*, to marry, from *maritus*, a husband.] To unite in wedlock or matrimony; to constitute man and wife (the clergyman *marries* a couple); to dispose of in wedlock (as a father his daughter); to take for husband or wife; to wed; *fig.* to unite by some close bond of connection.—*v.i.* To enter into a conjugal state; to take a husband or a wife.

marrow, mar′ō, *n.* [A.Sax. *mearh*, *mearg*=D. *marg*, *merg*, Dan. *marv*, Icel. *mergr*, G. *mark*, marrow; comp. A.Sax. *mearu*, D. *murw*, tender, soft.] The fat contained in the osseous tubes and cells of the bones; *fig.* the essence; the best part; a kind of gourd yielding an oblong fruit used as a vegetable, also called *vegetable marrow*.—*Spinal marrow*, the spinal cord or cord of nervous matter extending through the spine.—**marrowbone,** *n.* A bone containing marrow.—*To go down on one's marrowbones*, to assume a kneeling position. [Humorous.]—**marrowfat,** *n.* A kind of rich pea.—**marrow squash,** *n.* Another name for the vegetable marrow.

marry, mar′i. *interj.* Indeed; forsooth: a term of asserveration derived from the practice of swearing by the Virgin *Mary*.

Mars, märz, *n.* A Latin deity, the god of war, identified at an early period by the Latins themselves with the Greek Ares; the fourth planet from the sun or the first outside of the earth's orbit.

Marseillaise, mär•sā•yāz′, *n.* The national song of the French Republic, dating from the first revolution, being written in 1792, and first sung in Paris by revolutionaries from Marseilles.

marsh, märsh, *n.* [A.Sax. *mersc*, for *merisc* (*mere*, pool, *isc*, ish), a bog; L.G. *marsch*, O.D. *maersche*, *meersch*; allied to L. *mare*, the sea. MARINE.] A tract of low and very wet land; a fen, swamp, morass.—**marsh gas,** Same as METHANE.—**marshiness,** märsh′i•nes, *n.* State of being marshy.—**marsh marigold,** *n.* A marsh plant of the ranunculus family with a bright yellow flower.—**marshy,** märsh′i, *a.* Partaking of the nature of a marsh or swamp; swampy; fenny; produced in marshes.

marshal, mär′shal, *n.* [O.F. *mareschal*, Fr. *maréchal*, L.L. *mariscalcus*, from O.H.G. *marahscalc*—O.G. *marah*, a horse, and *scalc* (Mod.G. *schalk*), a servant. MARE.] Formerly an officer whose duty was to regulate tournaments or combats in the lists; one who regulates rank and order at a feast or any other assembly, directs the order of procession, and the like; in France, the highest rank of military officer; in other countries of Europe, a military officer of high rank, called in full *field-marshal*; in U. S., a civil officer in each judicial district, to execute court orders, and with other duties paralleling those of sheriff.—*v.t.*—*marshaled*, *marshaling*. To dispose in due order (an army, troops); to arrange in a suitable or most effective order (arguments, evidence, etc.).

marshmallow, marsh′mal•ō, *n.* [O.E. *merscmealwe*; see MARSH and MALLOW.] A plant, *Althaea officinalis*, of the hollyhock genus, growing naturally in marshes.—**marshmallow,** marsh″mel′ō, *n.* A soothing confection obtained from marsh mallow, a medicinal root; a corn sirup and gelatin confection, sometimes with beaten egg whites.

marsupial, mär•sū′pi•al, *a.* [L. *marsupium*, Gr. *marsupion*, a pouch.] Having an external abdominal pouch; belonging to the order of marsupials.—*n.* One of an extensive group of mammalia characterized by the absence of a placenta, and the consequent premature production of the fetus, which immediately on its birth is placed by the mother in an external abdominal pouch, in which are the teats, and there nurtured until fully developed.—**marsupium,** mär•sū′pi•um, *n.* The pouch of the marsupials.

mart, märt, *n.* [Contr. from *market.*] A place of sale or traffic, where buying and selling are active; an emporium, a center; as Furniture Mart or Merchandise Mart.

martello tower, mär•tel′lō•tou•ėr, *n.* [From *Mortella* in Corsica, where a tower of this kind made a strong resistance to an English naval force in 1794.] A small circular fort, with very thick walls, built chiefly to defend the seaboard.

marten, mär′ten, *n.* [Older *martern*, Fr. *martre*, from D. *marter*, G. *marder*, a marten.] A carnivorous quadruped of the weasel family, very destructive to game, poultry, and eggs; the pelt of a marten, frequently called *sable* by fur traders.

martial, mär′shal, *a.* [L. *martialis*, from *Mars*, *Martis*, the god of war.] Pertaining to war; suited to war; military; given to war; warlike.—*Martial law*, an arbitrary kind of law, proceeding directly from the military power, and proclaimed in times of war, insurrection, rebellion, or other great emergency.—**martially,** mär′shal•li, *adv.* In a martial manner.

Martian, mär′shan, *a.* Pertaining to Mars, god of war, or to the planet Mars or its supposed inhabitants.

martin, mär′tin, *n.* [From the proper name *Martin*; comp. *robin*-redbreast, etc.] A general name applied to various species of swallows, the best-known being the sand martin and the purple martin.

martinet, mär′ti•net, *n.* [From General *Martinet*, a very strict French officer in the reign of Louis XIV.] A military or naval officer who is an excessively strict disciplinarian; one who lays stress on a rigid adherence to the details of discipline, dress, etc.

martingale, mär′tin•gāl, *n.* [Fr. *martingale*, Sp. *martingala*, a martingale, old kind of breeches; from *Martigal*, an inhabitant of *Martigues*, in Provence.] A strap from a horse's head to the girth under his belly and passing between the forelegs, to prevent him from rearing; *naut.* a short perpendicular spar under the bowsprit.

martini, mar•tē′nē, *n.* [From name *Martini*.] An alcoholic beverage made from gin and dry vermouth.

Martinmas, mär′tin•mas, *n.* [*Martin* and *mass*.] The feast of St. Martin, the 11th of November, a Scotch term-day, on which rents are paid, servants hired, etc.

martlet, märt′let, *n.* [Dim. of *martin.*] The martin, a kind of swallow. (*Shak.*)

martyr, mär′tėr, *n.* [Gr. *martyr*, a martyr, a form of *martys*, a witness.] One who by his death bears witness to the truth; one who suffers death rather than renounce his religious opinions; one who suffers death or persecution in defense of any cause. —*v.t.* To persecute as a martyr; to torment or torture.—**martyrdom,** mär′tėr•dom, *n.* The state of being a martyr; the death of a martyr.—**martyrize,** mär′tėr•īz, *v.t.* To devote to martyrdom. —**martyrological,** mär•tėr•o•loj″i•kal, *a.* Pertaining to martyrology.—**martyrologist,** mär•tėr•ol′o•jist, *n.* A writer of a martyrology.—**martyrology,** mär•tėr•ol′o•ji, *n.* A history or account of martyrs with their sufferings; a register of martyrs.

marvel, mär′vel, *n.* [Fr. *merveille*; It. *maraviglia*; from L. *mirabilia*, wonderful things, from *mirabilis*, wonderful, from *mirur*, to wonder. MIRACLE.] A wonder; an object of great astonishment.—*v.i.*—*marveled, marveling.* To be struck with surprise or astonishment; to wonder.—*v.t.* To wonder at (with clause as object); to be curious about.—**marvelous,** mär′vel•us, *a.* Exciting wonder; astonishing; partaking of the miraculous or supernatural.—**marvelously,** mär′vel•us•li, *adv.*—**marvelousness,** mär′vel•us•nes, *n.*

Marxism, märks′izm, *n.* [After Karl *Marx.*] Communism; the theories of Marx and Engels, in which class struggle is the key to world history and will eventually destroy barriers and cause a classless society.—**Marxist,** märks′ist, *n.* Advocate of the theories of Marx.—**Marxian,** märks′i•an, *a.*

marzipan, mär′zi•pan, *n.* [G.] Same as *marchpane* (which see).

mascara, mas•kâr′ä, *n.* [Sp. *máscara*, a mask.] A coloring for the eyelashes.

mascle, mas′kl, *n.* [O.Fr. *mascle*, Fr. *macle*, from L. *macula*, a spot, the mesh of a net.] *Armor*, a lozenge-shaped plate or scale.

mascot, mas′kot, *n.* [Fr. *mascotte.*] A thing or person supposed to bring good luck.

masculine, mas′kū•lin, *a.* [L. *masculinus*, from *masculus*, male, from *mas*, *maris*, a male.] Of the male sex; strong; robust; powerful; manly; *gram.* denoting or pertaining to the gender of words which are especially applied to male beings or things regarded grammatically as male.—*Masculine rhymes*, rhymes in which only the last, accented syllable agrees, as *contain, domain.*—*n. Gram.* the masculine gender; a word of this gender.—**masculinely,** mas′kū•lin•li, *adv.* — **masculineness, masculinity,** mas′kū•lin•nes, mas•kū•lin′i•ti, *n.*

maser, mā′zėr, *n.* [*m*icrowave *a*mplification by *s*timulated *e*mission of *r*adiation.] A device that produces highly stable electromagnetic waves by harnessing the natural oscillations of an atomic or molecular system.

mash, mash, *n.* [Akin to Dan. *mask*, a mash, Sw. *mäska*, to mash; Sc. *mask*, to infuse, as tea, G. *meisch*, mash (of malt), *meischen*, to mash, mix; E. *mess*, a mixture.] A mixture of ingredients beaten or blended together in a promiscuous manner; especially, a mixture for feeding horses; *brewing*, a mixture of ground malt and warm water yielding wort. —*v.t.* To beat into a confused mass; to crush by beating or pressure; to mix (malt) and steep in warm water for brewing.—**masher,** mash′ėr, *n.* [From being supposed to *mash* the hearts of the fair sex.] An affected fop who dresses in the extremest fashion, and lounges about fashionable resorts; a weak, would-be gallant. (*Slang.*)

mask, mask, *n.* [Fr. *masque*, from Sp. and Pg. *mascara*, a mask, from Ar. *maskharat*, a buffoon, jeer, laugh, from *sakhira*, to ridicule.] A cover for the face, often intended to conceal identity; a disguise, pretense, or subterfuge; a masquerade; a protective covering for the face; a grotesque representation of a face. —*v.t.* To cover the face with a mask; to disguise for concealment; to conceal from an enemy, as by camouflage.—*v.i.* To wear a mask; to disguise oneself.—**masker,** mas′kėr, *n.*

masochism, ma′zō•kizm, *n.* [From Leopold von Sacher-*Masoch*, Austrian novelist who portrayed it.] A pleasure derived from being abused or humiliated; *psych.* the dependence on pain, suffering, and humiliation for sexual gratification.—**masochist,** ma′zō•kist, *n.*—**masochistic,** ma′zō•kis″tic, *a.*

mason, mā′sn, *n.* [Fr. *maçon*; L.L. *macio*, *machio*, *machionis*, from root seen in L. *maceria*, a wall.] A builder in stone or brick; one who constructs the walls of buildings, etc.; [*cap.*] a member of the fraternity of Freemasons.—**Masonic,** ma•son′ik, *a.* Pertaining to the craft or mysteries of Freemasons.—**masonry,** mā′sn•ri, *n.* [Fr. *maçonnerie.*] The art or occupation of a mason; the work produced by a mason; [*cap.*] the mysteries, principles, and practices of Freemasons.

Masonite, mā′sn•īt, *n.* A fiberboard made from steam-exploded wood fiber pressed into sheets.

Mason jar, mā′sn jär, *n.* A preserve glass with porcelain-insert metal top.

Masoretic, mas•o•ret′ik, *a.* Relating to the Jewish interpretation of the Masora, the great traditional body of Biblical information.

masque, mask, *n.* A kind of theatrical spectacle. MASK.—**masquerade,** mas′kėr•ād, *n.* [Fr. *masquerade.*] An assembly of persons wearing masks, and amusing themselves with various diversions, as dancing, walking in procession, etc.; a disguise.—*v.i.* —*masqueraded, masquerading.* To wear a mask; to take part in a masquerade; to go in disguise.—**masquerader,** mas•kėr•ā′dėr, *n.* A person taking part in a masquerade; one that appears in masquerade.

mass, mas, *n.* [Fr. *masse,* L. *massa,* a lump, from Gr. *maza,* a barley-cake, from *massō,* to knead; akin *macerate.*] A body of matter collected into a lump; a lump; a collective body of fluid matter; a great quantity collected; an assemblage (a *mass* of foliage); bulk; magnitude; the main body of things collectively; the generality; the bulk (the *mass* of the people); *phys.* a measure of the amount of matter in a body as determined by comparing the changes in the speeds resulting from impact between the body and a standard body: *mass* is the quotient resulting from dividing the weight of a body by the acceleration due to gravity.—*The masses,* the great body of the people.—*a.* Of, pertaining to, or characteristic of the mass or masses; of a large number.—*v.t.* and *i.* To form a mass; to collect into masses.—**massive,** mas′iv, *a.* Forming or consisting of a large mass; having great size and weight; ponderous; *mineral.* having a crystalline structure, but not a regular form as a whole.—**massively,** mas′iv•li, *adv.*—**massiveness,** mas′iv•nes, *n.*—**mass meeting,** *n.* A large or general meeting called for some specific purpose.—**mass number,** *n. Phys.* and *chem.* an integer most nearly expressive of the mass of an isotope.—**mass production,** *n.* The rapid production by machinery of large quantities of goods.

mass, mas, *n.* [A.Sax. *maesse,* Fr. *messe,* Dan. and G. *messe,* L.L. *missa,* mass, from the proclamation—Ite, *missa* est; 'Go, the assembly is dismissed' (L. *missus,* pp. of *mitto,* to send)—made in the ancient churches when the catechumens were dismissed after a portion of the service, whereupon followed the communion. MISSION.] The service of the Eucharist in the Roman Catholic and Greek Churches; the Roman Catholic communion service; the elaborate musical setting of certain portions of the service of the mass.—*High mass,* a mass performed on solemn occasions, by a priest or prelate, attended by a deacon and subdeacon, with choral music.—*Low mass,* the ordinary mass performed by the priest, assisted by one altar servant only.

massacre, mas′a•kėr, *n.* [Fr. *massacre,* probably from such a German word as L.G. *matsken, matschkern,* to cut in pieces, or G. *metzger,* a butcher, *metzeln,* to cut to pieces; O.G. *meizan,* to cut down.] The indiscriminate killing of human beings, especially without authority or necessity, and without forms civil or military; a great slaughter.—*v.t.*—*massacred, massacring.* To kill with indiscriminate violence; to butcher; to slaughter.—**massacrer,** mas′a•krėr, *n.*

massage, ma•säzh′ or mas′aj, *n.* [Fr., from Gr. *massō,* to knead.] The process of kneading, rubbing, pressing, slapping, etc., parts of the body of a person for remedial or hygienic purposes.—*v.t.* To rub, knead, push, or slap parts of a living body for healthful purposes.—**masseur,** ma•sūr′, *n.* A man who gives massages.—**masseuse,** ma•sėz′, *n.* A woman who practices massage.

masseter, mas′se•tėr, mas•sē′ter, *n.* [Gr. *masētēr, massētēr,* lit. a chewer, from *massaomai,* to chew.] Either of the pair of muscles which raise the under jaw.

massicot, mas′i•kot, *n.* [Fr. *massicot.*] Protoxide of lead or yellow oxide of lead of a deep yellow color and used as a pigment.

mast, mast, *n.* [A.Sax. *maest*=D., G., Sw., and Dan. *mast,* a mast.] A long, round piece of timber or a hollow pillar of iron or steel standing upright in a vessel, and supporting the yards, sails, and rigging in general.—*v.t.* To fix a mast or masts in; to erect the masts of.—**masted,** mas′ted, *a.* Having a mast or masts: chiefly in compounds.—**master,** mas′tėr, *n.* Having a mast or masts: in compounds (a three-*master*).—**masthead,** *v.t.* To send to the top of a mast and cause to remain there for a time by way of punishment.

mast, mast, *n.* (no pl.). [A.Sax. *maest,* G. *mast,* mast; akin to *meat.*] The fruit of the oak and beech or other forest trees; nuts; acorns.

master, mas′ter, *n.* [O.E. *maister, maistre,* O.Fr. *maïstre,* from L. *magister,* master, from root *mag,* seen in L. *magnus,* great (MAGNITUDE): same root as *may, might, much.*] One who rules, governs, or directs; one who has others under his immediate control; an employer; correlative to *slave, servant,* etc. (often in compounds, as, *master*-printer, *master*-builder, etc.); one who has possession and the power of controlling or using at pleasure; the owner; proprietor; a chief, principal, head, leader; the person entrusted with the care and navigation of a merchant ship: otherwise the *captain*; an artist, a sculptor, an architect, whose accomplishments rank far above those of their contemporaries, a Raphael, a Michelangelo, a Brunelleschi; a man so well trained in his profession as to be able to follow it alone; in the *navy,* formerly an officer who navigated the ship under the direction of the captain; the head of, or a teacher in, a school; a man eminently skilled in any pursuit, accomplishment, art, or science; a proficient or adept (a *master* of the violin; a *master* of sarcasm); a civil or respectful title of address used before a person's name, and when the person is grown up always pronounced mis′tėr and written *Mr.* (*Mr.* John Smith); when applied to a boy or young gentleman, however, written in full and pronounced mas′tėr; a title of dignity; a degree in colleges and universities (*Master* of Arts); the title of the head of some societies or corporations; the title of certain high legal or other functionaries (*Master* in chancery).—*The old masters,* ancient painters of eminence.—*To be master of one's self,* to have the command or control of one's own passions.—*v.t.* To become the master of; to overpower; to subdue; to make one's self master of.—*a.* Belonging to a master; chief; principal: often used as the first element in a compound word; as *master*-piece, *master*-mind, etc.—**masterbuilder,** *n.* A chief builder; one who employs workmen in building.—**masterful,** mas′tėr•ful, *a.* Inclined to exercise mastery; imperious; arbitrary; headstrong.—**masterfully,** mas′tėr•ful•li, *adv.* In a masterful manner.—**masterfulness,** mas′tėr•ful•nes, *n.* The quality of being masterful.—**masterless,** mas′tėr•les, *a.* Destitute of a master or owner; ungovernable; beyond control.—**masterliness,** mas′tėr•li•nes, *n.* The quality of being masterly; masterly skill.—**masterly,** mas′tėr•li, *a.* Formed or executed with superior skill; suitable to a master; most able or skillful (a *masterly* design or performance).—*adv.* With the skill of a master.—**masterpiece,** *n.* Something superior to any other performance of the same person; anything done or made with superior skill.—**mastership,** mas′tėr•ship, *n.* The state or office of a master; pre-eminence; mastery.—**mastersinger,** *n.* One of a society of German poets of the fifteenth and sixteenth centuries.—**master stroke,** *n.* A masterly achievement.—**masterwork,** *n.* Principal performance; chef-d'œuvre.—**mastery,** mas′tėr•i, *n.* The act of mastering; dominion or command over something; superiority in competition; pre-eminence; victory in war; eminent skill.

mastic, mas′tik, *n.* [Fr. *mastic,* L. *mastiche, mastichum,* Gr. *mastichē,* from *mastax,* the jaws: so named because chewed in the East.] A resin exuding from a tree of Southern Europe, etc., yielding a varnish; the tree itself; a kind of mortar or cement for plastering walls.

masticate, mas′ti•kāt, *v.t.*—*masticated, masticating.* [L. *mastico, masticatum,* from G. *mastichaō,* to gnash the teeth. MASTIC.] To grind with the teeth and prepare for swallowing and digestion; to chew.—**mastication,** mas•ti•kā′shon, *n.* The act of masticating.—**masticator,** mas′ti•kā•tėr, *n.* One who or that which masticates; a machine for cutting up meat for persons unable to chew properly, also for kneading up raw India rubber or gutta-percha.—**masticatory,** mas′ti•kā•to•ri, *a.* Adapted to perform the office of chewing.—*n. Med.* a substance to be chewed to increase the saliva.

mastiff, mas′tif, *n.* [From a hypothetical Fr. *mastif,* from G. *masten,* to fatten, O.H.G. *mastjan,* to feed, from *mast,* food, mast (acorns, etc.).] A variety of dog of old English breed, large and very stoutly built, and with deep and pendulous lips.

mastitis, mas•tī′tis, *n.* [Gr. *mastos,* the breast, and term. *-itis,* denoting inflammation.] Inflammation of the breast.

mastodon, mas′to•don, *n.* [Gr. *mastos*, breast, and Gr. *odous*, *odontos*, tooth.] A genus of extinct fossil quadrupeds resembling the elephant, but larger.

mastoid, mas′toid, *a.* [Gr. *mastos*, breast, and *oid.*] Resembling a nipple or breast; a process or projection of certain bones behind the ear.—**mastoiditis,** mas′toid•ī″tis, *n.* An inflammation of the mastoid or the mastoid cells.

masturbate, mas′tėr•bāt, *v.t.*—*masturbated*, *masturbating*. [L. *masturbari*, to practice self-gratification.] To artificially stimulate the genitals for sexual self-gratification.—*v.i.* To practice masturbation.—**masturbation,** mas′tėr•bā″shon, *n.*

mat, mat, *n.* [A.Sax. *meatta*, G. *matte*, D. *mat*, Dan. *matte*, Ir. *mata*, all from L. *matta*, a mat made of rushes.] An article of interwoven material to be laid down for cleaning the boots and shoes; some kind of coarse fabric used for covering floors, etc.; an article put below dishes on the table; anything growing thickly or closely interwoven so as to resemble a mat in form or texture (a *mat* of hair).—*v.t.*—*matted*, *matting*. To cover or lay with mats; to interweave like a mat; to entangle.—*v.i.* To grow thick together.—**matting,** mat′-ing, *n.* Materials for mats; matwork.

mat, matte, mat, *a.* [O.Fr. *mat*, downcast, afflicted, from L. *mattus*, a hangover from drinking.] Without luster; dull in surface; lusterless.—*n.* A dull, flat finish; a border of gold, white, or colored paper between the frame and a painting; *print.* a matrix. —*v.t.* To render mat, as glass or metal; to border a picture with a mat.

matador, mat′a•dōr, *n.* [Sp., lit. a killer, from *matar*, L. *mactare*, to kill, to sacrifice.] The man appointed to kill the bull in bullfights.

match, mach, *n.* [Fr. *mèche*, Pr. *mecha*, from L. *myxus*, a wick, Gr. *myxa*, the nozzle of a lamp.] A small slip of wood with a composition on one end that ignites with friction. —**matchlock,** mach′lok, *n.* Originally, the lock of a musket containing a match for firing, hence, a musket fired by means of a match.

match, mach, *n.* [O.E. *make*, a mate, A.S. *maecca*, *maca*, a mate, a wife. MATE.] A person equal to another; one who is able to mate or cope with another; an equal; a mate; the coming together of two parties suited to one another, as for a trial of strength or skill, or the like; a contest; union by marriage; one to be married or gained in marriage.—*v.t.* To be a match or mate for; to be able to compete with; to equal; to show an equal to; to place in competition or comparison with; to oppose as equal; to suit; to make to correspond; to marry; to give in marriage; to join in any way, combine, couple.—*v.i.* To be united in marriage; to be of equal size or quality; to tally, suit, correspond.—**matchless,** mach′les, *a.* Having no match or equal; unequaled; unrivaled.—**matchlessly,** mach′les•li, *adv.* In a matchless manner.—**matchlessness,** mach′les•nes, *n.* The state or quality of being matchless.—**matchmaker,** *n.* One who contrives or effects a union by marriage. —**matchmaking,** *a.* and *n.* Working to bring about marriages.

mate, māt, *n.* [A form of old *make*, a mate, and also of *match* (an equal); O.D. *maet*, D. *maat*, companion, mate; same root as *mete*, to measure.] One who customarily associates with another; a companion; an equal; a match; an officer in a ship whose duty is to assist the master or commander; a husband or wife; one of a pair of animals which associate for propagation and the care of their young.—*v.t.*—*mated*, *mating*. To match; to marry; to match one's self against; to cope with; to equal.

mate, māt, *v.t.* [Fr. *mater*, to enfeeble, from *mat*, worn out or exhausted, from the chess term, Per. *shâh mât*=E. *checkmate.*] To confound; to subdue; to crush; *chess*, to checkmate.—*n.* Same as *Checkmate.*

maté, mä′tā, *n.* [Sp.] Paraguay tea, a shrub whose leaves are used in South America as a substitute for tea.

materfamilias, mā′tėr•fa•mil″i•as, *n.* [L.] The mother of a family: correlative of *paterfamilias.*

material, ma•tē′ri•al, *a.* [L. *materialis*, material, from *materia*, matter. MATTER.] Pertaining to matter; consisting of matter; not spiritual; not mental; pertaining to the physical nature of man, or to the bodily wants, interests, and comforts; important; weighty; momentous; more or less necessary; *logic*, pertaining to the matter of a thing and not to the form.—*n.* What is composed of matter; the substance or matter of which anything is made.—*Raw material*, unmanufactured material; material in its natural state.—**materialism,** ma•tē′ri•al•izm, *n.* The doctrine which denies the existence of spirit or anything but matter; due care of our material nature.—**materialist,** ma•tē′ri•al•ist, *n.* One who holds the doctrine of materialism.—**materialistic,** ma•tē′ri•al•is″tik, *a.* Relating to or partaking of materialism.—**materiality,** ma•tē′ri•al″i•ti, *n.* The quality of being material; material, as opposed to spiritual existence; importance.—**materialization,** ma•tē′ri•al•i•zā″shon, *n.* The act of materializing; among spiritualists, the alleged assumption by a spirit of a material or bodily form.—**materialize,** ma•tē′ri•al•īz, *v.t.*—*materialized*, *materializing*. To invest with matter; to make material; to regard as matter; to explain by the laws appropriate to matter.—**materializing,** ma•tē′ri•al•īz•ing, *a.* Directed toward materialism.—**materially,** ma•tē′ri•al•li, *adv.* In a material manner; in the state of matter; substantially; in an important manner or degree; essentially.—**materia medica,** ma•tē′ri•a med′i•ka, *n.* [L.] That branch of medical science which treats of the drugs, etc., employed in medicine; collectively, all the curative substances employed in medicine.—**matériel,** ma•tā•rē•el, *n.* [Fr.] Material or instruments employed, as the baggage, etc., of an army, in distinction from the *personnel*, or the men; or the buildings, etc., of a college, in distinction from its officers.

maternal, ma•tėr′nal, *a.* [L. *maternus*, from *mater*, mother (which is cog. with E. *mother*); akin *matrimony*, *matriculate*, *matron*, etc.] Pertaining to a mother; becoming a mother; motherly. — **maternally,** ma•tėr′nal•li, *adv.* In a maternal manner.—**maternity,** ma•tėr′ni•ti, *n.* The state, character, or relation of a mother.

mathematics, math•e•mat′iks, *n.* [L. *mathematica*, Gr. *mathematikē* (*technē*, art, understood), from stem of *manthanō*, *mathēsomai*, to learn.] The science that treats of the properties and relations of quantities, comprising *pure mathematics*, which considers quantity abstractly, as arithmetic, geometry, algebra, trigonometry; and *mixed*, which treats of magnitude as subsisting in material bodies, and is consequently interwoven with physical considerations (astronomy, optics, etc.).—**mathematical, mathematic,** math•e•mat′-i•kal, math•e•mat′ik, *a.* [L. *mathematicus.*] Pertaining to mathematics, according to the principles of mathematics.—**mathematically,** math•e•-mat′i•kal•li, *adv.* In a mathematical manner.—**mathematician,** math′e•-ma•tish″an, *n.* One versed in mathematics.

matin, mat′in, *a.* [Fr. *matin*, from L. *matutinus*, pertaining to the morning; same root as *mature.*] Pertaining to the morning; used in the morning. —*n. pl.* Morning worship or service; morning prayers or songs; time of morning service; the first canonical hour in the Roman Church.—**matinal,** mat′in•al, *a.* Relating to the morning or to matins.—**matinee,** mat•i•nā′, *n.* [Fr.] An entertainment or reception held early in the day.

matrass, mat′ras, *n.* [Fr. *matras*, a mattrass.] A chemical vessel with a tapering neck used for digestion, evaporation, etc.

matriarchy, mā′tri•är•ki, *n.* [Gr. *matēr*, mother, *archē*, rule.] The rule or predominance of the mother in a family; the principle of determining descent and inheritance on the mother's side and not on the father's, as is done by certain primitive tribes. —**matriarchal,** mā•tri•är′kal, *a.* Pertaining to matriarchy.

matricide, māt′ri•sīd, *n.* [L. *matricidium*, the crime, *matricida*, the perpetrator—*mater*, *matris*, mother, and *caedo*, to slay.] The killing or murder of one's mother; the killer or murderer of one's mother.—**matricidal,** māt′ri•sī•dal, *a.* Pertaining to matricide.

matriculate, ma•trik′ū•lāt, *v.t.*—*matriculated*, *matriculating*. [L. *matricula*, a public register, dim. of *matrix*, a womb, a parent stem, a register, from *mater*, a mother. MATERNAL.] To enter in a register;

to enroll: especially, to admit to membership in a college or university, by enrolling the name in a register.—*v.i.* To be entered as a member of a society.—*a.* Matriculated; enrolled.—*n.* One who is matriculated.—**matriculation,** ma•trik′ū•lā″shon, *n.* The act of matriculating.

matrimony, mat′ri•mō•ni, *n.* [L. *matrimonium*, from *mater*, *matris*, a mother. MATERNAL.] Marriage; the nuptial state. . Syn. under marriage.—**matrimonial,** mat•ri•mō′ni•al, *a.* [L. *matrimonialis.*] Pertaining to matrimony or marriage; connubial.—**matrimonially,** mat•ri•mō′ni•al•li, *adv.* In a matrimonial manner.

matrix, mā′triks, *n.* pl. **matrices,** mā′tri•sēz. [L. *matrix*, from *mater*, mother.] The womb; that which encloses anything or gives origin to anything, like a womb; the form or mold in which something is shaped; the rock or main substance in which a crystal, mineral, or fossil is embedded; *type founding*, a metal plate engraved to serve as a mold for the type; that part of the cutis which occurs under the nail.

matron, mā′tron, *n.* [Fr. *matrone*, L. *matrona*, from *mater*, mother. MATERNAL.] A married woman, especially an elderly married woman; the mother of a family; a head nurse in a hospital.—**matronage,** mā′tron•ij, *n.* The state of a matron; matrons collectively.—**matronal,** mā′tron•al, *a.* [L. *matronalis.*] Pertaining to a matron.—**matronize,** mā′tron•īz, *v.t.* To render matronlike; to act as a mother to; to chaperon.—**matronly,** mā′tron•li, *a.* Becoming a wife or matron; sedate.

matter, mat′ėr, *n.* [O.Fr. *matere*, Fr. *matière*, from L. *materia*, matter, from root of *mother.*] That which occupies space and which becomes known to us by our senses; that of which the whole sensible universe is composed; body; substance; not mind; the substance of any speech or writing; the ideas or facts as distinct from the words; the meaning; *logic* and *metaph.*, that which forms the subject of any mental operation, as distinguished from the *form*; good sense; substance, as opposed to empty verbosity or frivolous jesting; thing treated; that about which we think, write, or speak; affair or business (thus the *matter* ended); cause or occasion of trouble, disturbance, etc. (as in the phrase, what is the *matter*?); import; consequence; moment (as in 'no *matter* which'); indefinite amount or quantity (a *matter* of 7 miles); substance excreted from living animal bodies; that which is discharged in a tumor, boil, or abscess; pus.—*Matter of fact*, a reality, as distinguished from what is fanciful.—*v.i.* To be of importance; to signify (in such phrases as, it does not *matter*; what does it *matter*?).—**matter-of-fact,** *a.* Treating of facts or realities; not fanciful, imaginative, or ideal; adhering to facts; not given to wandering beyond realities; prosaic.

matting. See MAT.

mattock, mat′ok, *n.* [A.Sax. *mattoc*, a mattock.] A pickax with one or both of its ends broad instead of pointed.

mattoid, mat′oid, *n.* [G. *matt*, dull.] A kind of stupid monomaniac.

mattress, mat′tres, *n.* [O.Fr. *materas*, Fr. *matelas*, It. *materasso*, from Ar. *ma′tra′h*, a quilted cushion.] A manufactured pad stuffed with sponge rubber, cotton matting, etc., and supported on springs and a bedstead.

maturate, mat′ū•rāt, *v.t.*—*maturated*, *maturating.* [L. *maturo*, *maturatum*, to make ripe, from *maturus*, ripe, same root as *mater*, mother.] To bring to ripeness or maturity; to mature; *med.* to promote perfect suppuration in.—*v.i.* To ripen; to come to or toward maturity.—**maturation,** mat•ū•rā′shon, *n.* [L. *maturatio.*] The process of maturing or ripening; *med.* a beginning to suppurate.—**maturative,** ma•tū′ra•tiv, *a.* Ripening; conducing to suppuration.—*n. Med.* anything that promotes suppuration. — **mature,** ma•tūr′, *a.* [L. *maturus*, ripe.] Ripe; perfected by time or natural growth; brought by natural process to a complete state of development; ripe or ready to be put in action; *med.* in a state of perfect suppuration; *com.* become payable; having reached the time fixed for payment.—*v.t.*—*matured*, *maturing.* [L. *maturo.*] To make mature; to ripen; to make ripe or ready for any special use; *med.* to maturate.—*v.i.* To advance toward ripeness, to become mature or ripe; *com.* to reach the time fixed for payment; *med.* to maturate.—**maturely,** ma•tūr′li, *adv.* In a mature manner; with ripeness; with full deliberation.—**matureness,** ma•tūr′nes, *n.* The state of being mature; maturity.—**maturity,** ma•tū′ri•ti, *n.* The state or quality of being mature; ripeness; a state of perfection or completeness; *com.* the time when a note or bill of exchange becomes due.

matutinal, mat•ū′ti•nal, *a.* [L. *matutinus*, pertaining to the morning. MATIN.] Pertaining to the morning; early in the day.

matzo, mät′zō, *n.* pl. **matzoth,** mät′soth. [Heb. *matstsah*, unleavened.] The unleavened bread which the Jews eat at the Feast of Passover.

maud, mąd, *n.* A plaid of undyed brown wool; a gray woolen plaid worn by shepherds in Scotland.

maudlin, mąd′lin, *a.* [From *Maudlin*, Mary *Magdalen*, who is drawn by painters with eyes swollen and red with weeping.] Approaching intoxication; overemotional; sickly sentimental.

maul, mąl, *n.* [Same as *Mall.*] A kind of large hammer or mallet.—*v.t.* To beat with a maul, or as with a maul; to maltreat severely.

maulstick, mąl′stik, *n.* [G. and D. *malen*, to paint, and E. *stick.*] A stick used by painters to steady and support the hand in working.

maund, mąnd, *n.* In the East Indies, a measure of weight, differing according to locality from 25 to about 82 pounds.

maund, mąnd, *n.* [A.Sax. *mand*, *mond*, D. *mand*, a basket.] A handbasket. (*Shak.*)—**maunder,** mąn′dėr, *v.i.* [From old *maunder*, a beggar, one who carries a *maund.*] To speak with a beggar's whine; to grumble; to wander in talking like a drunk or silly old person; to drivel.—**maunderer,** mąn′dėr•ėr, *n.* One who maunders.

Maundy Thursday, mąn′di, *n.* [O.E. *maundee*, a command, Fr. *mandé*, from L. *mandatum*—the first word used in the Vulgate to render the words of the Saviour, when, after supper, he washed his apostles' feet: '*Mandatum* novum do vobis,' a new commandment I give unto you.] The Thursday before Good Friday, on which the sovereign of England distributes alms to a certain number of poor persons at Whitehall.—*Maundy money*, small silver coins (including twopenny and penny pieces) struck for this distribution.

Mauser, mou′zėr, *n.* [Inventor's name.] A kind of rifle.

mausoleum, mą•so•lē′um, *n.* [Gr. *mausōleion*, from *Mausolus*, king of Caria, to whom Artemisia, his widow, erected a stately monument so called.] A magnificent tomb or stately sepulchral monument.

mauve, mōv, *n.* [Fr., mallow, L. *malva*, a mallow—its petals having purple markings.] One of the coal-tar colors, a purple dye obtained from aniline.

maverick, mav′ėr•ik, *n.* [From S.A. *Maverick*, Texas cattle owner who didn't brand his cattle.] An unbranded animal; a calf parted from his mother; one who breaks away from group conformity and forges a new course.

mavis, mā′vis, *n.* [Fr. *mauvis*, Sp. *malvis*, from the Celtic; comp. Armor *milvid*, a mavis.] The throstle or song thrush.

maw, mą, *n.* [A.Sax. *maga*=D. *maag*, Icel. *magi*, O.H.G. *mago*, G. *magen*, the stomach.] The stomach of carnivores; the crop of fowls.

mawkish, mąk′ish, *a.* [From old *mawk*, *mauk*, a maggot; Icel. *mathkr*, N. *makk.*] Apt to cause satiety or loathing; sickly; nauseous.—**mawkishly,** mąk′ish•li, *adv.*—**mawkishness,** mąk′ish•nes, *n.*

maxilla, mak•sil′la, *n.* pl. **maxillae,** mak•sil′lē. [L., a jaw, dim. of *mala*, a jaw, from root of *macerate.*] A term applied to each of the bones supporting the teeth of either jaw: often restricted to the upper jaw of the inferior vertebrates.—**maxillary,** mak′sil•la•ri, *a.*

maxim, mak′sim, *n.* [Fr. *maxime*, from L. *maxima* (*sententia*, opinion, understood), the greatest or chief opinion, *maximus*, superlative of *magnus*, great. MAGNITUDE.] An established principle; a principle or formula embodying a rule of conduct. **maximize,** mak′sim•īz, *v.t.* To make as great as possible; to raise to the maximum.—*v.i.* To give a constitution or duty, etc., the broadest interpretation.—**maximal,** mak′si•mal, *a.* Highest; greatest amount or degree. —**maximum,** mak′si•mum, *n.* The greatest quantity or degree attainable or attained in any given case.—*a.* Greatest.

Maxim gun, mak′sim, *n.* A quick-firing machine gun, single-barreled, with water casing to keep the parts cool, so called from Sir Hiram *Maxim,* the inventor.

may, mā, *n.* [Fr. *mai,* Pr. *mai,* May, from L. *Maius,* from the goddess *Maia,* a goddess of growth or increase, from root of L. *magnus,* great, and E. *may,* the auxiliary.] [*cap.*] The fifth month of the year; *fig.* the early part of life; hawthorn blossom, so named because the hawthorn blooms in this month.—*v.i.* To celebrate the festivities of May Day: used only as a participial noun in such phrases as *to go a Maying,* etc.—**May Day,** *n.* The first day of May, on which various festivities were, and in some places still are, observed.—**Mayflower,** *n.* The trailing arbutus; the name of the ship that brought the Pilgrims to America in 1620.—**may fly,** *n.* A neuropterous insect that appears first in May.—**Maypole,** *n.* A pole wreathed with flowers and set up to be danced round on May Day.—**May queen,** *n.* A young woman honored as queen on May Day.

may, mā, *verb auxiliary*; pret. *might.* Used similarly to *can, could.* [A.Sax. *mugan, magan*=L.G. and D. *mogen,* Goth. and O.H.G. *magan,* G. *mögen,* Icel. *mega,* Dan. *maa,* to be able; from same root are *much, maid,* L. *magnus,* Gr. *megas,* Skr. *mahâ,* great.] Formerly often used in sense of *can,* implying personal power or ability; now to imply possibility with contingency (it *may* be so, the king *may* be killed); opportunity; moral power; permission granted (you *may* now go); desire, as in prayer, aspiration, imprecation, benediction, etc. (*may* he perish miserably!); frequently used to form the compound tenses of the potential mood (you *might* have gone had you pleased).—**maybe,** mā′bē, *adv.* [That is, 'it *may* be'.] Perhaps; possibly; probably. (*Colloq.*)—*n.* A possibility; a probability.—**mayhap,** mā•hap′, *adv.* Peradventure; it may happen; perhaps.

Maya, mä′ya, *n.* An Indian belonging to a great pre-Columbian civilization, whose descendants live in Yucatan and Central America; also, the language spoken by those people. —**Mayan,** mä′yan, *a.*

mayhem, mā′hem, *n. Law,* the act of maiming a man. MAIM.

mayonnaise, mā•on•āz′, *n.* [Fr.] A dish composed of yolks of eggs and salad oil beaten together, used as a sauce for salads, lobster, salmon, etc.

mayor, mā′ėr, *n.* [Fr. *maire,* Sp. *mayor,* from L. *major,* greater, compar. of *magnus,* great. MAGNITUDE.] The chief magistrate of a city or borough; the chief officer of a municipal corporation.—*Mayor of the Palace,* the chief official in the palaces of the Merovingian kings, wielding and controlling all power, rendering the kings *fainéants* or idle puppets in his hands.—**mayoralty,** mā′ėr•al•ti, *n.* The office of a mayor, and the time of his service.—**mayoress,** mā′ėr•es, *n.* The wife of a mayor; a woman mayor.

Mazdean, maz′di•an, *a.* [From *Ahura-Mazda,* the chief deity of the ancient Persians, the Ormuzd of English writers.] Pertaining or relating to Mazdeism.—**Mazdeism,** maz′de•izm, *n.* The religion of the ancient Persians; the worship of Ormuzd.

maze, māz, *n.* [Akin to Prov.E. *mazle,* to wander as if stupefied; Icel. *masa,* to chatter or prattle; Dan. *mase,* to have trouble; comp. also W. *masu,* to swoon. *Amaze* is from this.] A confusing network of paths or passages; a winding and turning; an intricacy; a labyrinth; confusion of thought; perplexity.—*v.t.*—*mazed, mazing.* To confound; to stupefy; to bewilder.—**mazily,** mā′zi•li, *adv.* In a mazy manner.—**maziness,** mā′zi•nes, *n.* The state of being mazy.—**mazy,** mā′zi, *a.* Having the character of a maze; intricate; perplexed.

mazer,‡ mā′zėr, *n.* [Originally a cup made of maple or spotted wood, from O.Fr. *mazre,* spotted wood, or A.Sax. *maser,* a maple (from being spotted); O.H.G. *masar,* G. *maser,* a knur, a spot in wood, G. *mase,* a spot; akin *measles.*] A cup or large goblet, generally of valuable material.

mazurka, ma•zur′ka, *n.* A lively Polish round dance in 3-8 or 3-4 time; the music written for this dance.

me, mē, *pron. pers.* [A.Sax. *mé, mec* (accusative), *mé* (dat.), G. *mich* (acc.), *mir* (dat.), Icel. *mik, mér,* Goth. *mik, mis,* L. *me, mihi,* Gr. *eme, emoi,* Skr. *mâm, mahyam,* me, to me.] The objective or accusative, as also the dative, of *I,* the pronoun of the first person. It stands as a dative in *me*thinks; woe is *me*; give *me* a drink, and the like.

mead, mēd, *n.* [A.Sax. *medu*=D. *mede,* Icel. *mjōthr,* Dan. *miōd,* Sw. *mjōd,* W. *medd,* Ir. *meadh,* mead; Gr. *methy,* wine; Lith. *medus,* Rus. *med,* Skr. *madhu,* honey.] A fermented liquor made from honey and water flavored with spices.

meadow, med′ō, *n.*; poetical, **mead,** mēd. [A.Sax. *maedu,* a meadow, shorter form *maed,* a mead, allied to *math* (after-*math*) and *mow.*] A low, level tract of land under grass, and generally mown annually or oftener for hay; a piece of grassland in general.—*a.* Belonging to or growing in a meadow.—**meadow grass,** *n.* Variety known as June grass or Kentucky blue in U. S.—**meadow lark,** *n.* The American genus *Sturnella* with clear, but melancholy note. It is as large as a robin; its plumage is brown, with yellow breast.—**meadowsweet,** *n.* The plant genus *Spiraea,* containing many beautiful herbs and low deciduous shrubs.

meager, meagre, mē′gėr, *a.* [Fr. *maigre,* from L. *macer,* lean.] Having little flesh; thin; lean; wanting richness, fertility, strength, etc.; small; scanty; *mineral,* dry and harsh to the touch, as chalk.—**meagerly, meagrely,** mē′gėr•li, *adv.* Poorly; thinly; sparely; feebly.—**meagerness, meagreness,** mē′gėr•nes, *n.* The condition of being meager.

meal, mēl, *n.* [A.Sax. *mael,* time, portion, repast; D. and Dan. *maal,* G. *mahl, mal,* Icel. *mál,* part, repast, time; from root seen in *measure, mete, moon.* It is the termination seen in piece*meal,* etc.] A portion of food taken at one of the regular times for eating; occasion of taking food; a repast.—**mealtime,** *n.* The usual time of eating meals.

meal, mēl, *n.* [A.Sax. *melu, melo*= Icel. Sw. *mjöl,* D. Dan. *meel,* G. *mehl,* meal; from the verbal stem seen in Icel. *mala,* Goth. *malan,* G. *mahlen,* L. *molo,* to grind. MILL, MOLAR, MELLOW, MOLLIFY.] The edible part of wheat, oats, rye, barley, etc., ground into flour or a powdery state.—**mealies,** mē′liz, *n. pl.* A name given in South Africa to maize or Indian corn.—**mealiness,** mēl′i•nes, *n.* The quality of being mealy.—**mealy,** mēl′i, *a.* Having the qualities of meal, or resembling meal; powdery like meal; overspread with something that resembles meal.—**mealymouthed,** *a.* Unwilling or hesitating to tell the truth in plain language; inclined to speak of anything in softer terms than the truth will warrant.

mean, mēn, *a.* [A.Sax. *maene,* mean, false, bad, from *mán,* evil, wickedness; Icel. *meinn,* mean; comp. D. and Dan. *gemeen,* Goth. *gamains,* G. *gemein,* common.] Low in rank or birth; ignoble; humble; low-minded; base; spiritless; of little value; contemptible; despicable.—**meanly,** mēn′li, *adv.* In a mean manner; in a low condition; poorly; sordidly.—**meanness,** mēn′nes, *n.* The state or quality of being mean; want of dignity or rank; want of spirit or honor; mean or base conduct or action.

mean, mēn, *a.* [O.Fr. *meien, moien,* Fr. *moyen,* Pr. *meian,* from L. *medianus,* middle, from *medius,* middle. MEDIUM, MID.] Occupying a middle position; middle; midway between extremes; intermediate; *math.* having an intermediate value between two extremes (*mean* distance, *mean* motion).—*Mean proportional,* the second of any three quantities in continued proportion.—*Mean time,* the time according to an ordinary clock, which makes every day of exactly the same length, though if days are measured by the sun they are not so.—*n.* What is midway or intermediate between two extremes; the middle or average rate or degree; medium; *math.* a quantity having an intermediate value between several others, the simple average formed by adding the quantities together and dividing by their number being called an *arithmetical mean,* while a *géometrical mean* is the square root of the product of the quantities; *pl.* the medium or what is used to effect an object; measure or measures adopted; agency; instrumentality (though pl. in form generally used as sing.; by *this means, a means* to an end); income, revenue, resources, estate (his *means* were large).—*By all means,* certainly; on every consideration.—*By no means,* not at all; certainly not.—**meantime,** mēn'tīm, *adv.* During the interval; in the interval between one specified period and another.—*n.* The interval between one specified period and another.—**meanwhile,** mēn'whīl, *adv.* and *n.* Meantime.

mean, mēn, *v.t.*—pret. & pp. *meant* (ment). [A.Sax. *maenan,* to mean, to intend; D. *meenen,* Dan. *mene,* G. *meinen,* to think, to mean; same root as *man, mind, mental,* Skr. *man,* to think.] To have in the mind, view, or contemplation; to intend; to purpose; to design; to signify or be intended to signify (what does the word *mean*?); to import; to denote. —*v.i.* To be minded or disposed; to have such and such intentions (he *means* well).—**meaning,** mēn'ing, *p.* and *a.* Significant; intended to convey some idea (a *meaning* look).—*n.* That which a person means; aim or purpose; intent; what is to be understood, whether by act or language; the sense of words; signification; import; force.—**meaningless,** mēn'ing•les, *a.* Having no meaning.—**meaningly,** mēn'ing•li, *adv.* In a meaning manner; so as to hint at something indirectly; significantly.

meander, mē•an'dėr, *n.* [L. *Maeander,* Gr. *Maiandros,* a river in Phrygia proverbial for its windings.] The winding of a river; a winding course; a maze; a labyrinth; a kind of ornamental or decorative design having a labyrinthine character.—*v.t.* To wind or flow over.—*v.i.* To wind or turn; to have an intricate or winding course.

meanly, meanness, etc. See MEAN (low).

meantime, meanwhile. See MEAN (intermediate).

measles, mē'zlz, *n.* [Lit. the spots or spotted sickness; D. *mazelen,* G. *masern,* pl. of *maser* (also *mase, masel*), O.G. *mása, masar,* a spot. MAZER.] A contagious disease of the human body, usually characterized by a crimson rash upon the skin; rubeola; a disease of swine, characterized by reddish watery pustules on the skin.—**measly, measled,** mēz'li, mē'zld, *a.* Infected with measles or eruptions like measles.

measure, mezh'ėr, *n.* [Fr. *mesure,* from L. *mensura,* from *metior, mensus,* to measure (seen also in *immense, dimension, commensurate*); from root *ma,* to measure, whence also *moon, mete,* etc.] The extent of a thing in length, breadth, and thickness, in circumference, capacity, or in any other respect; a standard of measurement; a fixed unit of capacity or extent; the instrument by which extent or capacity is ascertained; a measuring rod or line; a certain definite quantity (a *measure* of wine); that which is allotted or dealt out to one; moderation; just degree: in such phrases as, *beyond* measure, within *measure*; indefinite quantity or degree (in some *measure* erroneous); action or proceeding directed to an end; something done with a view to the accomplishment of purpose; *music,* that division by which the time of dwelling on each note is regulated; musical time; *poetry,* the metrical arrangement of the syllables in each line with respect to quantity or accent; a grave solemn dance with slow and measured steps, like the minuet; *geol.* beds; strata; used in the term *coal-measures.*—*Measure of a number or quantity, math.* a number or quantity contained in the other a certain number of times exactly.—*Greatest common measure of numbers,* the greatest number which divides them all without a remainder.—*v.t.*—*measured, measuring.* To ascertain the extent, dimensions, or capacity of; to judge of the greatness of; to appreciate; to value; to pass through or over; to proportion; to allot or distribute by measure (often with *out*).—*To measure one's* (own) *length,* to fall or be thrown down.—*To measure strength,* to ascertain by trial which of two parties is the stronger.—*To measure swords,* to fight with swords. —*v.i.* To take a measurement or measurements; to result or turn out on being measured; to be in extent.—**measurable,** mezh'ūr•a•bl, *a.* That may be measured; not beyond measure; moderate.—**measurableness,** mezh'ūr•a•bl•nes, *n.* The quality of being measurable.—**measurably,** mezh'ūr•a•bli, *adv.* In a measurable manner or degree; moderately.—**measured,** mezh'ūrd, *p.* and *a.* Deliberate and uniform; slow and steady; stately; formal; restricted; within bounds; moderate.—**measureless,** mezh'ūr•les, *a.* Without measure; immeasurable.—**measurement,** mezh'ūr•ment, *n.* The act of measuring; the amount ascertained by measuring.—**measurer,** mezh'ūr•ėr, *n.* One who measures; one whose occupation or duty is to measure work or commodities.

meat, mēt, *n.* [A.Sax. *mete*=D. *met,* Icel. *matr.* D. *mad,* Sw. *mat,* Goth. *mats,* food; further connections doubtful.] Food in general; anything eaten as nourishment; the flesh of animals used as food; the edible portion of something (the *meat* of an egg).—*The meat of* a discourse, book or article, its underlying thoughts or argument.—**meaty,** mēt'i, *n.* Abounding in meat; resembling meat.

meatus, mi•ā'tus, *n.* [L., from *meo,* to go.] A passage: applied to various ducts and passages of the body; as, *meatus auditorius,* the passage of the ear.

mechanic, me•kan'ik, *n.* [L. *mēchanicus,* Gr. *mēchanikos,* from *mēchanē,* a machine. MACHINE.] An artisan; an artificer; one who follows a handicraft for his living: sometimes restricted to those employed in making and repairing machinery.—*a.,* Same as *mechanical,* but not so common.—**mechanical,** me•kan'i•kal, *a.* Pertaining to or in accordance with the laws of mechanics; resembling a machine; hence, acting without thought or independence of judgment; done as if by a machine, that is, by the mere force of habit (a *mechanical* motion of the hand); pertaining to artisans or mechanics or their employments; acting by or resulting from weight or momentum (*mechanical* pressure); physical; opposed to *chemical* (a *mechanical* mixture, that is, one in which the ingredients do not lose their identity).—*Mechanical equivalent of heat,* the number of units of mechanical work equivalent to one unit of heat: 778 foot-pounds per pound-degree F., or 1400 foot-pounds per pound-degree C., or 41.9 million ergs per gram-degree C—*Mechanical drawing,* the sketching or drawing of machinery by means of scales, rulers, compasses, etc.—*Mechanical philosophy,* that which explains the phenomena of nature on the principles of mechanics.—*Mechanical powers,* the simple elements of which every machine, however, complicated, must be constructed; they are the lever, the wheel and axle, the pulley, the inclined plane, the wedge, and the screw.—*Mechanical solution of a problem,* a solution by any art or contrivance not strictly geometrical, as by means of the ruler and compasses or other instruments.—**mechanically,** me•kan'i•kal•li, *adv.* In a mechanical manner; by the mere force of habit.—**mechanician,** mek•an•ish'an, *n.*—**mechanics,** me•kan'iks, *n.* The science which treats of motion and force; the technical aspects of something (*mechanics* of poetry).—**mechanism,** mek'an•izm, *n.* The parts, collectively, of a machine or machinery; *phys.* and *biol.* a natural process believed to be mechanically determined and possibly explained by means of physics and chemistry; an automatic natural process; automatic action.—**mechanist,** mek'an•ist, *n.* One skilled in the use of machinery; an adherent of mechanical philosophy.—**mechanistic,** mek'an•is″tik, *a.*—**mechanize,** mek'an•īz, *v.t.*—*mechanized, mechanizing.* To make mechanical or automatic; *milit.* to equip an army with motorized weapons and armored vehicles.—**mechanization,** mek'an•ī•zā″shon, *n.*

Mechlin, mek'lin, *n.* A species of fine lace made at *Mechlin* or Malines in Belgium.

medal, med'al, *n.* [Fr. *médaille,* It. *medaglia,* from L. *metallum,* Gr. *metallon,* metal. METAL.] A coin, or a piece of metal in the form of a coin, stamped with some figure or device, often issued to commemorate a noteworthy event or as a reward of merit.—**medalist, medallist,** med'al•ist, *n.* An engraver, stamper, or molder of medals; a person skilled in medals; one who has gained a medal as a reward of merit; in golf tournament the one who qualifies with the lowest score.—**medallion,** me•dal′yun, *n.* [Fr. *médaillon.*] A large antique medal, usually of gold or silver; anything resembling such a piece of metal, as a circular or oval tablet, bearing on it objects represented in relief.

meddle, med′l, *v.i.*—*meddled, meddling.* [O.E. *medlen,* to mix, from O.Fr. *medler, mesler* (Fr. *méler*), to mix, *se mesler de,* to mix one's self up with; from L.L. *misculare,* from L. *misceo,* to mix. MEDLEY, MIX.] To mix one's self; to deal, treat, tamper (followed by *with*); to interfere; to take part in another person's affairs in an officious, impertinent, or offensive manner (often followed by *with* or *in*).—**meddler,** med′lėr, *n.* One that meddles; a busybody.—**meddlesome,** med′l•sum, *a.* Given to meddling; officiously intrusive.—**meddlesomeness,** med′l•sum•nes, *n.*

Mede, mēd, *n.* A native or inhabitant of *Media,* an ancient kingdom of Asia.

media, *n. pl.* See MEDIUM.

medial, mē′di•al, *a.* [L. *medialis,* from *medius,* middle, (akin to *mid*), seen also in *mediate, medium, medieval, mediocre, meridian, moiety,* etc.] Mean; pertaining to a mean or average.—**median,** mē′di•an, *a.* [L. *medianus.*] Situated in the middle; passing through or along the middle. —*Median line, anat.* a vertical line, supposed to divide the body longitudinally into two equal parts.—**mediant,** mē′di•ant, *n.* [It. *mediante.*] *Mus.* an appellation given to the third above the keynote.

mediastinum, mē′di•as•ti″num, *n.* [L. *mediastinus,* in the middle, from *medius,* middle.] The division of the chest from the sternum backward between the lungs, dividing the cavity into two parts.

mediate, mē′di•it, *a.* [L. *medio, mediatum,* to be in the middle, from *medius,* middle. MEDIAL.] Being between two extremes; middle; acting as a means or medium; not direct or immediately; effected by the intervention of a medium.—*v.i.* mē′-di•āt, *mediated, mediating.* To interpose between parties as the equal friend of each; to negotiate between persons at variance with a view to reconciliation.—*v.t.* To effect by mediation or interposition between parties (to *mediate* a peace).—**mediately,** mē′di•it•li, *adv.* In a mediate manner; indirectly.—**mediation,** mē•di•ā′shon, *n.* The act of mediating; entreaty for another; intercession; interposition; intervention.—**mediative,** mē′di•ā•tiv, *a.* Of or belonging to a mediator; mediatorial.—**mediatize,** mē′di•at•īz, *v.t.* —*mediatized, mediatizing.* To render mediately dependent.—**mediatization,** mē′di•at•i•zā″shon, *n.* The act of mediating; the term applied to the annexation of the smaller German sovereignties to larger contiguous states, when they were made mediately, instead of immediately, dependent on the empire.—**mediator,** mē′di•ā•tėr, *n.* One that mediates or interposes between parties at variance for the purpose of reconciling them: by way of eminence, Christ is called THE MEDIATOR, being our intercessor with God.—**mediatorial,** mē′di•a•tō″ri•al, *a.* Belonging to a mediator.—**mediatress, mediatrix,** mē′di•āt•res, mē′di•āt•riks, *n.* A female mediator.

medic, med′ik, *n.* [Gr. *mēdikē,* lit. a plant of *Media.*] A name of certain leguminous plants yielding fodder and allied to clover; alfalfa.

medical, med′i•kal, *a.* [L.L. *medicalis,* from L. *medicus,* medical, *medeor,* to heal, to cure; allied to *meditor,* to meditate; Gr. *mēdos,* care.] Pertaining to or connected with medicine or the art of healing diseases; medicinal; tending to cure; intended or instituted to teach medical science.—*Medical jurisprudence.* See JURISPRUDENCE.—**medically,** med′i•kal•li, *adv.* In a medical manner; according to the rules of the healing art.—**medicament,** me•dik′-a•ment, *n.* [L. *medicamentum.*] Anything used for healing diseases or wounds; a healing application.—**medicate,** med′i•kāt, *v.t.*—*medicated, medicating.* [L. *medico, medicatum.*] To imbue with healing substances.—**medication,** med•i•kā′shon, *n.* The act or process of medicating.—**medicative,** med′i•kā•tiv, *a.* Tending to cure or heal.—**medicinal,** me•-dis′i•nal, *a.* [L. *medicinalis.*] Having the property of healing or of mitigating disease; containing healing ingredients (*medicinal* springs): pertaining to medicine.—**medicinally,** me•dis′i•nal•li, *adv.* In a medicinal manner.—**medicine,** med′i•sin, *n.* [Fr. *médecine,* L. *medecina,* from *medicus,* healing.] Any substance used as a remedy for disease; a drug; physic; the science and art of preventing, curing, or alleviating disease.—**medicine man,** *n.* Among the American Indians and other savage tribes any man whom they suppose to possess mysterious or supernatural powers.

medieval, mediaeval, med•i•ē′val, *a.* [L. *medius,* middle, and *ævum,* age.] Relating to the Middle Ages or the period between the eighth and the middle of the fifteenth century, A.D.—**medievalism, mediaevalism,** med•i•ē′val•izm, *n.* The spirit or principles of the Middle Ages.—**medievalist, mediaevalist,** med•i•ē′val•ist, *n.* One versed in the history of the Middle Ages.

mediocre, mē′di•ō•kėr, *a.* [Fr. *médiocre,* from L. *mediocris,* middling. MEDIAL.] Of moderate degree or quality; of middle rate; middling.—**mediocrity,** mē•di•ok′ri•ti, *n.* [L. *mediocritas.*] The quality or state of being mediocre; a middle state or degree; a person of mediocre talents or abilities of any kind.

meditate, med′i•tāt, *v.i.*—*meditated, meditating.* [L. *meditor, meditatus,* to meditate. MEDICAL.] To dwell on anything in thought; to cogitate; to turn or revolve any subject in the mind.—*v.t.* To plan by revolving in the mind; to intend; to think on.—**meditation,** med•i•tā′shon, *n.* [L. *meditatio.*] The act of meditating; close or continued thought; the revolving of a subject in the mind.—**meditative,** med′i•tā•tiv, *a.* Addicted to meditation; pertaining to meditation.—**meditatively,** med′i•-tā•tiv•li, *adv.* In a meditative manner.

mediterranean, med′i•te•rā″ni•an, *a.* [L. *mediterraneus*—*medius,* middle, and *terra,* land.] Surrounded by or in the midst of land; inland: now applied exclusively to the *Mediterranean* Sea between Europe and Africa; [*cap.*] pertaining to, situated on or near the Mediterranean Sea.

medium, mē′di•um, *n.* pl. **media** or **mediums,** mē′di•a, mē′di•umz. [L. *medium,* the middle, midst, a means. MEDIAL.] Something placed or ranked between other things; a mean between two extremes; a state of moderation; something serving as a means of transmission of communication, necessary means of motion or action; agency of transmission; that by or through which anything is accomplished, conveyed, or carried on; agency; instrumentality; a person through whom spiritual manifestations are claimed to be made by believers in spiritualism, or who is said to be capable of holding intercourse with the spirits of the deceased; the liquid vehicle with which dry colors are ground and prepared for painting.—*Circulating medium,* coin and bills, or paper convertible into money on demand.—*a.* Middle; middling.

medlar, med′lėr, *n.* [O.Fr. *meslier, mesler, medler,* from L. *mespilus,* Gr. *mespilon,* medlar.] A tree found wild in Central Europe, and cultivated in gardens for its fruit.

medley, med′li, *n.* [O.Fr. *medlée, meslée* (Fr. *mêlee*), from *medler, mesler,* to mix. MEDDLE.] A mingled and confused mass of ingredients; a jumble; a hodge-podge; a kind of song made up of scraps of different songs.

Medoc, mā•dok′, mā′dok, *n.* An excellent red French wine. from *Médoc,* in the department of Gironde.

medulla, mi•dul′a, *n.* [L., marrow, from *medius,* middle.] *Anat.* the fat substance or marrow which fills the cavity of the bones; *bot.* pith.—*Medulla oblongata,* the upper enlarged portion of the spinal cord and the base of the brain.—*Medulla spinalis,* the spinal marrow or cord.—**medullary,** med″u•ler′i, *a.* [L. *medullaris.*] Consisting of or resembling marrow; relating to the pith of plants.—*Medullary sheath, bot.* a thin layer of spiral vessels formed immediately over the pith.—*Medullary rays,* the vertical plates of cellular tissue which connect the pith of exogenous plants with the bark.—*Medullary substance,* that which is the white substance composing the greater part of the brain, spinal marrow, and nerve fibers.

Medusa, me•dū'sa, *n.* [Gr. *Medousa*, originally the fem. of *medōn*, a ruler.] *Myth.* one of the three Gorgons who had her hair changed into serpents by Athene; *zool.* (pl. **medusae**), in zoophytes, a free-swimming sexual stage (jellyfish).—**medusoid,** me•du'soid, *a.* Pertaining to a medusa.

meed, mēd, *n.* [A.Sax. *méd*, *meord*= L.G. *mede*, D. *miede*, G. *miethe*, Goth. *mizdo*, reward, recompense; allied to Gr. *misthos*, pay, hire.] That which is bestowed in consideration of merit; reward; recompense; a gift.

meek, mēk, *a.* [Same as Sw. *miuk*, Icel. *mjúkr*, soft, meek; Dan. *myg*, pliant, supple; Goth. *muks*, soft, meek.] Mild of temper; gentle; submissive; not easily provoked or irritated; marked by meekness.—**meekly,** mēk'li, *adv.* In a meek manner; gently; submissively.—**meekness,** mēk'nes, *n.* The quality of being meek; mildness; gentleness; forbearance under injuries and provocations.

meerschaum, mēr'shum, *n.* [G., lit. seafoam—*meer*, the sea, and *schaum*, foam; from having been found on the seashore in lumps resembling petrified sea foam. MERE (*n.*), SCUM.] A silicate of magnesium occurring as a fine white clay, and largely made into tobacco pipes; a tobacco pipe made of meerschaum.

meet, mēt, *a.* [A.Sax. *gemet*, fit, proper, from *metan*, to measure; Icel. *maetr*, meet, worthy. METE.] Fit; suitable; proper; appropriate.—**meetly,** mēt'li, *adv.* In a meet manner; fitly.

meet, mēt, *v.t.*—pret. & pp. *met.* [A.Sax. *métan*, to meet, from *mót*, a meeting; Dan. *mōde*, Sw. *mōta*, Icel. *maeta*, Goth. *motjan*, *gamotjan*, to meet; akin *moot.*] To come face to face with; to come in contact with; to come to be in company with; to come in hostile contact with; to encounter; to join battle with; to find; to light on; to get, gain, or receive; to satisfy, gratify, answer (to *meet* a demand, one's views or wishes).—*To meet the ear*, to strike the ear; to be heard.—*To meet the eye*, to come into notice; to become visible.—*v.i.* To come together by mutual approach; to come together in hostility; to encounter; to assemble; to come together by being extended; to join.—*To meet with*, to light on; to find; to suffer; to suffer unexpectedly (to *meet with* a loss, an accident).—*n.* A meeting as of huntsmen.—**meeting,** mēt'ing, *n.* A coming together; an interview; an assembly; a hostile encounter; a duel.

megacephalous, meg•a•sef'a•lus, *a.* [Gr. *megas*, great, and *kephalē*, the head.] Large-headed; having a large head.

megacycle, meg"a•sī'kl, *n.* [Gr. *megas*, great, and *kyklos*, circle.] *Phys.* a million cycles.

megalith, meg'a•lith, *n.* [Gr. *megas*, great, *lithos*, stone.] A huge stone, such as those in cromlechs, dolmens, the Cyclopean architecture of the Greeks, etc.—**megalithic,** meg•a•lith'ik, *a.* Pertaining to such stones or structures.

megalomania, meg'a•lo•mā"ni•a, *n.* [Gr. *megalē*, great, and *mania.*] Overestimation of one's importance and abilities; a mania for great things.

megalopolis, meg•a•lop'a•lis, *n.* [Gr. *megal*, large, and *polis*, city.] A large urban region, often consisting of several adjoining cities and suburbs.—**megalopolitan,** meg'a•lō•pol"i•tan, *n.*

megalosaur, meg'a•lō•sar, *n.* [Gr. *megas*, *megalē*, great, and *sauros*, a lizard.] A fossil carnivorous reptile found in the oölite and Wealden strata, 40 to 50 feet long.

megaphone, me'gä•fōn, *n.* [Gr. *megalē*, great, and *phone.*] A funnel-shaped device for magnifying sound.—**megaton,** me'gä•ton, *n.* [Prefix *mega*, and *ton.*] 1,000,000 tons.

megas, megasse, me•gäs'. Same as *Bagasse.*

megilp, megilph, me•gilp', me•gilf', *n.* A mixture of linseed oil and mastic varnish which artists employ as a vehicle for colors.

megrim, mē'grim, *n.* [Fr. *migraine*, corrupted from Gr. *hemicrania*, half the head—*hēmi*, half, and *kranion* the head.] A neuralgic pain in the side of the head, also called *migraine*, *pl.* low spirits; whims or fancies.

meiosis, mī•ō'sis, *n.* [Gr., a lessening, from *meton*, less.] *Biol.* a process in which, through two cell divisions, one cell with the regular (diploid) number of chromosomes becomes four cells, each with half the (haploid) number of chromosomes.

melancholy, mel'an•kol•i, *n.* [Gr. *melancholia*, excess of black bile, melancholy madness—*melas*, *melaina* black, and *cholē*, bile.] Depression of spirits induced by grief; dejection; sadness.—*a.* Gloomy; depressed in spirits; dejected.—**melancholia,** mel•an•kō'li•a, *n.* A variety of mental alienation characterized by excessive depression; a manic-depressive psychosis.—**melancholic,** mel•an•kol'ik, *a.*

mélange, mā•länzh', *n.* [Fr., from *mêler*, to mix. MEDDLE.] A mixture; a medley.

melanic, me•lan'ik, *a.* [Gr. *melas*, *melan*, black.] Of or pertaining to melanism.—**melanism,** mel'an•izm, *n.* An undue development of coloring material in the skin and its appendages: the opposite of *albinism.*—**melanin,** mel•a'nin, *n. Biol.* a dark pigment present in man and some animals, as in dark-skinned peoples, also produced by certain diseases.

melanite, mel'an•īt, *n.* A mineral, a variety of garnet, of a velvet-black or grayish-black color.

melaphyre, mel'a•fīr, *n.* A compact black or blackish-gray trap-rock, consisting of a matrix of labradorite and augite, with embedded crystals of the same minerals.

melee, mā'lā, *n.* [Fr., a participial substantive, from *mêler*, to mix. MEDDLE.] A fight in which the combatants are mingled in confused mass; an affray.

melic, mel'ik, *a.* [Gr. *melikos*, from *melos*, a song.] Relating to song; lyric.

meliceris, mel•i•sē'ris, *n.* [Gr. *melikēris*—*meli*, honey, and *kēros*, wax.] *Pathol.* an encysted tumor, the contents of which resemble wax or honey in consistence.

melilot, mel'i•lot, *n.* [Gr. *melilōton*, *melilōtos*—*meli*, honey, and *lōtos*, lotus.] A leguminous annual or biennial plant allied to the clovers, and cultivated for fodder; hart's-clover.

melinite, mel'in•īt, *n.* A French explosive, the basis or chief ingredient of which is picric acid.

meliorate, mēl'yor•āt, *v.t.*—*meliorated*, *meliorating.* [L. *melioro*, *melioratum*, from *melior*, better, compar. of *bonus*, good.] To make better; to improve; to ameliorate.—*v.i.* To grow better.—**meliorater, meliorator,** mēl'yor•ā•tėr, *n.* One who meliorates.—**melioration,** mēl•yor•ā'shon, *n.* Improvement; amelioration.—**meliorism,** mēl'yor•izm, *n.* The doctrine or opinion that everything in nature is so ordered as to produce a progressive improvement.

meliphagous, me•lif'a•gus, *a.* [Gr. *meli*, honey, *phagein*, to eat.] Feeding upon honey.

mellay, melley, mel'lā, *n.* A melee; a conflict.

melliferous, mel•lif'ėr•us, *a.* [L. *mellifer*—*mel*, *mellis*, honey, and *fero*, to bear.] Producing honey.—**mellification,** mel•lif'i•kā"shon, *n.* [L. *mellifico*—*mel*, and *facio*, to make.] The making or production of honey.—**mellifluence,** mel•lif'lū•ens, *n.* [L. *mel*, and *fluo*, to flow.] The quality of being mellifluent; a flow of sweetness, or a sweet smooth flow.—**mellifluent, mellifluous,** mel•lif'lū•ent, mel•lif'lū•us, *a.* Flowing as with honey; sweetly flowing.—**mellifluently, mellifluously,** *adv.* In a mellifluent manner.

mellow, mel'ō, *a.* [Allied to Prov. G. *möll*, soft, ripe, *mölich*, mellow, *mollig*, soft, L. *mollis*, Gr. *malakos*, Skr. *mridu*, tender, soft, and to E. *meal*, from root *mar*, to grind or crush.] Soft with ripeness; soft to the senses; rich or delicate to the eye, ear, palate, etc., as color, sound, flavor, and the like; toned down by the lapse of time; softened or matured by length of years; rendered good-humored by liquor; half-tipsy.—*v.t.* To render mellow; to soften by ripeness or age; to give richness, flavor, or delicacy; to tone or smooth down; to soften in character; to mature.—*v.i.* To become mellow; to soften in character; to become toned down.—**mellowly,** mel'ō•li, *adv.* In a mellow manner.—**mellowness,** mel'ō•nes, *n.* The state or quality of being mellow.

melodeon, me•lō'di•on, *n.* [From *melody*, Gr. *melōdia.*] A wind instrument furnished with metallic free reeds and a keyboard; a variety of the harmonium.

melodrama, mel•o•drä'ma, *n.* [Gr. *melos*, a song, and *drama*, drama.] A romantic play, generally of a serious character, in which effect is sought by startling incidents, striking situations, and exaggerated sentiment, aided by splendid decoration and music.—**melodramatic,** mel'o•dra•mat"ik, *a.* Pertaining to, suitable for, or having the character of a melodrama.—**melodramatically,** mel'o•dra•mat"i•kal•li, *adv.* In a melodramatic manner; in an affected and exaggerated manner.—**melodramatist,** mel•o•dram'a•tist, *n.* One who acts in melodramas or who writes them.

melody, mel'o•di, *n.* [Gr. *melōdia,* a tune, a choral song—*melos,* a limb, a part, and *ōdē,* a song, an ode.] An agreeable succession of sounds; sweetness of sound; sound highly pleasing to the ear; *mus.* a succession of tones produced by a single voice or instrument, and so arranged as to please the ear or to express some kind of sentiment; the particular air or tune of a musical piece.—**melodic,** me•lod'ik, *a.* Of the nature of melody; relating to melody.—**melodics,** me•lod'iks, *n.* That branch of music which investigates the laws of melody.—**melodious,** me•lō'di•us, *a.* Containing or characterized by melody; musical; agreeable to the ear by a sweet succession of sounds.—**melodiously,** me•lō'di•us•li, *adv.* In a melodious manner.—**melodiousness,** me•lō'di•us•nes, *n.* The quality of being melodious.—**melodist,** mel'o•dist, *n.* A composer or singer of melodies.—**melodize,** mel'o•dīz, *v.t.*—*melodized, melodizing.* To make melodious.

melon, mel'on, *n.* [Fr. *melon,* L. *melo,* an apple-shaped melon, from Gr. *mēlon,* an apple or apple-shaped fruit.] A climbing or trailing annual plant and its fruit, which is large and fleshy, especially the muskmelon or cantaloupe, and the watermelon.

Melpomene, mel•pom'e•nē, *n.* [Gr. *Melpomenē,* from *melpomai,* to sing.] The muse of tragedy; also a small asteroid.

melt, melt, *v.t.* [A.Sax. *meltan,* allied to *malt, mellow,* etc.; Gr. *meldō,* to liquefy; probably also in *smelt.*] To reduce from a solid to a liquid or flowing state by heat; to liquefy; to dissolve; to fuse; *fig.* to soften; to render gentle or susceptible to mild influences.—*v.i.* To become liquid; to dissolve; to pass by imperceptible degrees; to blend; to shade; to become tender, mild, or gentle.—**meltable,** mel'ta•bl, *a.*—**melter,** mel'tėr, *n.*—**melting point,** *n.* The degree of heat at which a solid will melt or fuse.—**melting pot,** *n.* A crucible; a society containing many cultures and races.

melton, mel'tn, *n.* [From *Melton* Mowbray, Eng.] A smooth strong wool having a short nap.

member, mem'bėr, *n.* [L. *membrum,* a limb, a member of the body; comp. Skr. *marman,* a joint.] A part of an animal body capable of performing a distinct office; an organ; a limb; part of an aggregate or a whole; one of the persons composing a society, community, or the like; a representative in a legislative body.—*Member of Congress,* a representative elected by the voters of a congressional district to that branch of Congress called the House of Representatives.—**membership,** mem'bėr•ship, *n.* The state of being a member; the members of a body regarded collectively.

membrane, mem'brān, *n.* [L. *membrana,* a thin skin, parchment, from *membrum,* a limb.] A thin tissue of the animal body which covers organs, lines the interior of cavities, takes part in the formation of the walls of canals, etc.; a similar texture in vegetables.—**membranaceous,** mem•bra•nā'shus, *a.* Membranous; *bot.* thin, like membrane, and translucent.—**membranous,** mem'bra•nus, *a.* Belonging to a membrane; consisting of membranes; resembling a membrane.

memento, mi•men'tō, *n.* [L., remember, be mindful, from *memini,* to remember.] A suggestion, notice, or memorial to awaken memory; something that reminds.

memoir, mem'wär, mem'wąr, *n.* [Fr. *mémoire,* from L. *memoria,* memory, from *memor,* mindful; same root as Skr. *smar,* to remember.] A notice of something remembered or deemed noteworthy; an account of transactions or events written familiarly; a biographical notice; recollections of one's life (in this sense usually in the pl.); a biography or autobiography; a communication to a scientific society on some subject of scientific interest.—**memorabilia,** mem'or•a•bil"i•a, *n. pl.* [L.] Things remarkable and worthy of remembrance or record.—**memorable,** mem'or•a•bl, *a.* [L. *memorabilis.*] Worthy to be remembered; illustrious; remarkable; distinguished.—**memorability,** mem'or•a•bil"i•ti, *n.* The quality of being memorable.—**memorably,** mem'or•a•bli, *adv.* In a manner worthy to be remembered.—**memorandum,** mem•or•an'dum, *n.* pl. **memoranda,** mem•or•an'da, less commonly now **memorandums.** [L., something to be remembered.] A note to help the memory; a brief entry in a diary; *diplomacy,* a summary of the state of a question, or a justification of a decision adopted.—**memorial,** me•mō'ri•al, *a.* [L. *memorialis.*] Preservative of memory; serving as a memorial; contained in the memory.—*n.* That which serves to perpetuate the memory of something; a monument; a written representation of facts made to a legislative or other body or to some person; a species of informal state paper much used in diplomatic negotiations.—**memorialist,** me•mō'ri•al•ist, *n.* One who writes or presents a memorial or memorials.—**memorialize,** me•mō'ri•al•īz, *v.t.*—*memorialized, memorializing.* To present a memorial to; to petition by memorial.—**memorize,** mem'or•īz, *v.t.*—*memorized, memorizing.* To cause to be remembered; to record; to hand down to memory by writing.—**memory,** mem'o•ri, *n.* [L. *memoria,* memory, from *memor,* mindful.] The power, capacity, or faculty of the mind by which it retains the knowledge of past events or ideas; that faculty which enables us to treasure up and preserve for future use the knowledge which we acquire; remembrance; the state of being remembered; that which is remembered about a person or event; the time within which a person may remember what is past. ∴ *Memory* is the faculty or capacity of retaining in the mind and recalling what is past; *recollection* and *remembrance* are exercises of the faculty, the former being a calling to mind, the latter a holding in mind; while *reminiscence* always, and *recollection* often, are used of the thing remembered.

Memphian, mem'fi•an, *a.* [From *Memphis,* the ancient metropolis of Egypt.] Pertaining to Memphis; Egyptian (*Memphian* darkness).

men, men, pl. of *man.*

menace, men'as, *v.t.*—*menaced, menacing.* [Fr. *menacer,* from L. *minax,* threatening, *mina,* a threat, from root *min,* seen in *mineo,* to project (in *prominent, eminent*); akin *mien, demean, amenable,* etc.] To threaten; to show a disposition to inflict punishment or other evil on: followed by *with* before the evil threatened (*threatened* him *with* death); to hold out threats of (to *threaten* revenge).—*n.* A threat or threatening; the indication of a probable evil or catastrophe to come.—**menacingly,** men'as•ing•li, *adv.* In a menacing manner.

ménage, men•äzh', *n.* [Fr. *ménage,* a household; O.Fr. *mesnage,* L.L. *mansionaticum,* from L. *mansio,* a dwelling. MANSION.] A household; housekeeping; household management.—**menagerie,** me•naj'ėr•i, *n.* [Fr. *ménagerie.*] A collection of wild animals, especially of wild or foreign animals kept for exhibition.

mend, mend, *v.t.* [Shorter form of *amend.*] To repair, as something broken, rent, decayed, or the like; to restore to a sound state; to patch up; to alter for the better; to improve (to *mend* one's manners); to better; to improve upon (to *mend* one's pace).—*v.i.* To advance to a better state; to improve; to act or behave better.—**mender,** men'dėr, *n.* One who mends.

mendacious, men•dā'shus, *a.* [L. *mendax, mendacis,* lying, from stem of *mentior,* to lie: same root as *mens,* mind (whence *mental*).] Lying; false; given to telling untruths.—**mendacity,** men•das'i•ti, *n.* The quality of being mendacious; lying; falsehood; a lie.

mendelevium, men'de•lē"vi•um, *n.* A synthetic radioactive element. Symbol, Mv; at. no., 101.

Mendelism, men'del•izm, *n.* [From *Mendel,* an Austrian abbot.] A set of laws of heredity advanced by Mendel, which show that traits are inherited in definite predictable combinations involving dominant and recessive genes.

mendicant, men′di•kant, *a.* [L. *mendicans, mendicantis,* ppr. of *mendico,* to beg, from *mendicus,* a beggar (akin to *menda,* a fault).] Practicing beggary; poor to a state of beggary; begging as part of religious discipline (a *mendicant* friar).—*n.* A beggar; a member of a begging order or fraternity; a begging friar.—**mendicancy,** men′di•kan•si, *n.* Beggary; a state of begging.—**mendicity,** men•dis′i•ti, *n.* [L. *mendicitas.*] The state or practice of begging; the life of a beggar.

menhaden, men•hā′den, *n.* [American Indian.] A salt-water fish of the herring family, abounding on the shores of New England.

menhir, men′hir, *n.* [W. *maen,* a stone, and *hir,* long.] A name for tall, rude, or sculptured stones of unknown antiquity, standing singly or in groups.

menial, mē′ni•al, *a.* [O.E. *meyneal,* etc., O.Fr. *meignial,* from *meignee, maisgnee,* a household, L.L. *masnata*; same origin as *mansion.*] Pertaining to household or domestic servants; servile.—*n.* A domestic servant, especially one of a train of servants, mostly as a term of disparagement.

meninges, me•nin′jēz, *n. pl.* [Gr. *mēningx, mēningos,* a membrane.] *Anat.* the three membranes that envelop the brain, the *dura mater, pia mater,* and *arachnoid membrane.*—**meningeal,** me•nin′jē•al, *a.* Relating to the meninges.—**meningitis,** men•in•jī′tis, *n.* Inflammation of the membranes of the brain or spinal cord.

meniscus, me•nis′kus, *n.* pl. **menisci,** me•nis′si, or **meniscuses.** [Gr. *mēniskos,* a little moon, from *mēn, mēnos,* the moon.] A lens, convex on one side and concave on the other, and in which the two surfaces meet, or would meet if continued, so that it resembles a crescent.

Mennonite, men′non•īt, *n.* [From Simon *Menno,* the founder, 1496-1561.] One of a sect of Anabaptists who do not believe in original sin, and object to taking oaths, making war, or going to law.

menology, mē•nol′o•ji, *n.* [Gr. *mēn,* a month, *logos,* account.] A register or calendar of events according to the days of the months; a calendar of saints and martyrs with their feasts throughout the year.

menopause, men′o•pa̤z, *n.* [Gr. *mēn,* month, *pausis,* a stopping.] The cessation of menstruation at the change of life in woman.

menorrhagia, men•or•rā′ji•a, *n.* [Gr. *mēn, mēnos,* a month, and *rheō,* to flow.] *Med.* an immoderate menstrual discharge; hemorrhage from the uterus.

mensal, men′sal, *a.* [L. *mensis,* a month; same root as Gr. *mēn,* a month. MONTH.] Occurring once a month; monthly.—**menses,** men′sēz, *n. pl.* The catamental or monthly discharge of a woman.—**menstrual,** men′strö•al, *a.* [L. *menstrualis,* monthly; pertaining to the menses of females; menstruous.]—**menstruate,** men′strö•āt, *v.i.*—*menstruated, menstruating.* To discharge the menses.—**menstruation,** men•strö•ā′shon, *n.* The act of menstruating; the period of menstruating.—**menstruous,** men′strö•us, *a.* [L. *menstruus.*] Pertaining to the monthy flow of females.

menstruum, men′strö•um, *n.* pl. **menstrua, menstruums.** [From L. *menstruus,* monthly, from *mensis,* a month; from some old belief of the alchemists about the influence of the moon.] Any fluid which dissolves a solid; a solvent.

mensurable, men′shu̧•ra•bl, *a.* [L. *mensurabilis,* from *mensuro,* to measure, from *mensura,* measure. MEASURE.] Capable of being measured; measurable.—**mensurability,** men′shu̧•ra•bil″i•ti, *n.* Quality of being mensurable.—**mensural,** men′shu̧•ral, *a.* Pertaining to measure.—**mensuration,** men•shu̧•rā′shon, *n.* The act or art of measuring or taking the dimensions of anything; the process of finding any dimension of a figure, or its area or solid content, by means of the most simple measurements possible.

mental, men′tal, *a.* [Fr. *mental,* from L. *mens, mentis,* mind. MENTION.] Pertaining to the mind or intellect; affected with mental disorder (*mental* patient); of or pertaining to telepathic or occult power; performed by or present in the mind.—**mental deficiency,** *n.* A lack of intellectual capacity which sets one apart from his peers, the most extreme form being idiocy, and the mildest form being moronity.—**mentally,** men′ta̧l•li, *adv.*—**mentality,** men•tal′i•ti, *n.* Intellectual capacity and ability.

menthol, men′thol, *n.* [L. *mentha,* mint, *oleum,* oil.] A white crystalline substance obtained from oil of peppermint.—**mentholated,** men′tho•lā•ted, *a.* Treated with menthol.

mention, men′shon, *n.* [L. *mentio, mentionis,* from same root as *mens,* mind, Skr. *man,* to think. MAN.] A brief notice or remark in regard to something; a cursory speaking of anything; often in the phrase *to make mention of,* to name or say something in regard to.—*v.t.* To make mention of.—**mentionable,** men′shon•a•bl, *a.* That can or may be mentioned.

mentor, men′tor, *n.* [From *Mentor,* the counselor of Telemachus, according to Homer.] A wise or faithful adviser or monitor.

menu, men′yū, *n.* [Fr., lit. minute or detailed list, from L. *minutus,* minute.] A list of the dishes, etc., to be served at a dinner, supper, or the like; a bill of fare.

Mephistophelean, mef′i•sto•fē′li•an, *a.* Resembling the character of Mephistopheles, the diabolic spirit of Goethe's Faust and the Faust legend generally; diabolical; sardonic.

mephitis, me•fī′tis, *n.* [L. *mephitis,* a pestilential exhalation.] Noxious exhalations from decomposing substances, filth, or other source.—**mephitic,** me•fit′ik, *a.* Pertaining to mephitis; offensive to the smell; noxious; pestilential.

mercantile, mėr′kan•tīl, *a.* [Fr. *mercantile,* from L. *mercans, mercantis.* MERCHANT.] Pertaining to merchants, or their traffic; pertaining to trade or commerce; commercial.—**mercantilism,** mer′kan•til•izm, *n.* The economic program which superseded that of medieval feudalism and advocated that each nation seek to establish a favorable balance of trade and so accumulate bullion.

Mercator's projection, mėr•kā′tėr. [From Gerard *Mercator,* a Flemish geographer.] A projection or map of the earth's surface, with the meridians and parallels of latitude all straight lines.

mercenary, mėr′se•ne•ri, *a.* [Fr. *mercenaire,* L. *mercenarius,* from *merces,* reward, wages. MERCHANT.] Hired; obtained by hire (services, troops); that may be hired; moved by the love of money; greedy of gain; venal; sordid; entered into from motives of gain (a *mercenary* marriage).—*n.* One who is hired; a soldier that is hired into foreign service.

mercerize, mėr′sėr•īz, *v.t.* [From John *Mercer,* the originator.] To subject to treatment with certain chemical agents, as caustic soda, sulfuric acid, zinc chloride, etc., in order to produce desired results on textile fabrics.

merchant, mėr′chant, *n.* [O.Fr. *marchant,* from L. *mercans, mercantis,* ppr. of *mercor, mercatus,* to barter, to deal, from *merx,* merchandise; akin *mercer, mercenary, mercantile, mercy,* etc.; same root as *merit.*] One who carries on trade on a large scale, especially, a man who exports and imports goods and sells them at wholesale.—*a.* Relating to trade or commerce; commercial.—**merchantable,** mėr′chant•a•bl, *a.* Fit for market; such as is usually sold in market.—**merchantman,** mėr′chant•man, *n.* A ship engaged in commerce, as distinguished from a ship of war; a trading vessel.—**merchant marine,** the commercial vessels belonging to a nation.—**merchandise,** mėr′chan•dīz, *n.* [Fr. *marchandise,* from *marchand,* a merchant.] The objects of commerce; wares; goods.

mercury, mėr′kū•ri, *n.* [L. *Mercurius,* from root of *merces,* wares. MERCHANT.] A heavy silver-white metallic element, the only element that is fluid at ordinary temperatures; quicksilver—symbol, Hg (hydrargyrum); at. no., 80; at. wt., 200.59; [cap.] name of a Roman divinity, identified in later times with the Greek Hermes; [cap.] *astron.* the planet that is closest to the sun.—*Mercury-vapor lamp,* a lamp in which an electric discharge, passing through mercury vapor, produces ultraviolet and actinic radiation.—**mercurial,** mėr•kū′ri•al, *a.* [L. *mercurialis.*] Like the god Mercury or what belongs to him; light-hearted; gay; sprightly; flighty; fickle; pertaining to quicksilver; containing or consisting of quicksilver or mercury.—*n.* A preparation of mercury used as a drug.—**mercurially,** mėr•kū′ri•al•li, *adv.* In a mercurial manner.—**mercuric,**

mercurous, mėr•kū′rik, mėr′kū•rus, *a.* Containing mercury; terms used as part of the name of certain chemical compounds, the former indicating that they contain a smaller proportion of mercury than the latter.

mercy, mėr′si, *n.* [Fr. *merci*, from L. *merces*, *mercedis*, pay, recompense, in L.L. mercy, from stem of *mereo*, to deserve (whence *merit*); akin *mercantile*, *merchant*, *market*, *amerce*, etc.] That benevolence, mildness, or tenderness of heart which disposes a person to overlook injuries; the disposition that tempers justice and leads to the infliction of a lighter punishment than law or justice will warrant; clemency; an act or exercise of mercy or favor; a blessing; compassion; pity; unrestrained exercise of will or authority: often in the phrase *at one's mercy*, that is, completely in one's power.—*To cry mercy*, to beg pardon.—*Sisters of Mercy*, members of female religious communities founded for the purpose of nursing the sick and the performance of similar works of charity and mercy.—**mercy seat**, *n.* The place of mercy or forgiveness; the covering of the ark of the covenant among the Jews.—**merciful**, mėr′si•fụl, *a.* Full of mercy; unwilling to punish for injuries; compassionate; tender; not cruel.—**mercifully**, mėr′si•fụl•li, *adv.* In a merciful manner.—**mercifulness**, mėr′si•fụl•nes, *n.*—**merciless**, mėr′si•les, *a.* Destitute of mercy; pitiless; hard-hearted.—**mercilessly**, mėr′si•les•li, *adv.* In a merciless manner.—**mercilessness**, mėr si•les•nes, *n.*

mere, mēr, *a.* [O.Fr. *mier*, L. *merus*, pure, unmixed.] This or that and nothing else; simple; absolute, entire, utter (*mere* folly).—**merely**, mēr′li, *adv.* Solely; simply; only; for this and no other purpose.

mere, mēr, *n.* [A.Sax. *maere*, *gemaere*, O.D. *meer*, a boundary; Icel. *moerr*, borderland.] A boundary; a boundary stone.

meretricious, mer•e•trish′us, *a.* [L. *meretricius*, from *meretrix*, *meretricis*, a prostitute, from *mereo*, to earn. MERIT, MERCY.] Pertaining to prostitutes; alluring by false show; having a gaudy but deceitful appearance; showy, but in bad taste.—**meretriciously**, mer•e•trish′us•li, *adv.* In a meretricious manner.—**meretriciousness**, mer•e•trish′us•nes, *n.*

merganser, mėr•gan′sėr, *n.* [L. *mergo*, to dive, and *anser*, a goose.] A diving duck having a narrow bill and subsisting on fish.

merge, mėrj, *v.t.*—*merged*, *merging*. [L. *mergo*, to dip, to dive; seen also in *emerge*, *immerge*, *immersion*, *submerge*.] To cause to be swallowed up, absorbed, or incorporated; to sink; to bury; chiefly figurative (the smaller grief was *merged* in the greater).—*v.i.* To be sunk, swallowed, incorporated, or absorbed.—**merger**, mėrj′ėr, *n.* The absorption of one estate, contract, or interest, in another.

meridian, me•rid′i•an, *a.* [L. *meridianus*, from *meridies*, for *medidies*, mid-day—*medius*, middle, and *dies*, day.] Pertaining to midday or noon, when the sun is on the meridian.—*Meridian altitude of the sun* or *stars*, their altitude when on the meridian of the place where they are observed.—*n.* Midday; noon; *fig.* the culmination; the point of greatest splendor; one of the innumerable imaginary circles or lines on the surface of the earth passing through both poles, and through any other given place, and used in denoting the longitudes of places; a similar imaginary line in the heavens passing through the poles of the heavens and the zenith of any place (often called a *celestial meridian*), noon therefore occurring at all places directly under this line when the sun is on it.—*First meridian*, that from which all the others are counted eastward and westward, and from which longitudes are reckoned, usually the meridian of Greenwich.—*Meridian of a globe*, the brazen circle in which it turns, and by which it is supported.—*Magnetic meridian*, one of the great circles which pass through the magnetic poles.—**meridional**, me•rid′i•on•al, *a.* Pertaining to the meridian; hence, southern; having a southern aspect.—*Meridional distance*, *navig.* the distance or departure from the meridian, the easting or westing.—**meridionally**, me•rid′i•on•al•li, *adv.* In the direction of the meridian.

meringue, mė•rang′, *n.* A light delicacy made of powdered sugar and the beaten whites of eggs.

merino, me•rē′nō, *n.* [Sp. *merino*.] A breed of sheep with long, fine wool; a soft, twilled fabric.

meristem, me•ris′tem, *n.* [Gr. *merizō*, I divide.] *Bot.* embryonic plant tissue that reproduces similar cells or differentiates to produce the organs and tissue.

merit, mer′it, *n.* [Fr. *mérite*, L. *meritum*, what is deserved, from *mereo*, to earn or deserve. MERCY.] Desert of good or evil; excellence entitling to honor or reward; worth; reward deserved or merited; pl. the rights of a case or question; the essential points or circumstances.—*v.t.* To deserve, in a good sense; to have a right to claim, as a reward, regard, honor.—**meritorious**, mer•i•tō′ri•us, *a.* Deserving reward or praise; praiseworthy.—**meritoriously**, mer•i•tō′ri•us•li, *adv.*—**meritoriousness**, mer•i•tō′ri•us•nes, *n.*—**merit system**, *n.* The system whereby government employees receive appointment and promotion on the basis of ability rather than by political pressure.

merl, mėrl, *n.* [Fr. *merle*, a blackbird.] The European blackbird.—**merlin**, mėr′lin, *n.* [Fr. *émerillon*, from L. *merula*, a blackbird, meaning blackbird hawk.] A courageous species of hawk about the size of a blackbird.

merlon, mėr′lon, *n.* [Fr. *merlon*; comp. L. *mœrus*, for *murus*, a wall.] *Fort.* the part of an embattled parapet which lies between two embrasures.

mermaid, mėr′mād, *n.* [*Mer* is same as *mere*, a lake.] A fabled marine creature, having the upper part like a woman and the lower like a fish.—**merman**, mėr′man, *n.* The male corresponding to *mermaid*; a man of the sea, with the tail of a fish instead of legs.

meroblast, mer′o•blast, *n.* [Gr. *meros*, a part, and *blastos*, a sprout.] *Biol.* an ovum consisting both of a protoplasmic or germinal portion and an albuminous or nutritive one, as contradistinguished from *holoblast*, an ovum entirely germinal.—**meroblastic**, mer•o•blas′tik, *a.* Pertaining to a meroblast.

Merovingian, mer•o•vinj′i•an, *a.* Of or relating to the Merovingian line of Franks founded by Clovis, and lasting from A.D. 500 to 750.

merry, mer′i, *a.* [O.E. *myrie*, *murie*, A.Sax. *merg*, *mirig*, perhaps from root of *mearo*, tender; comp. Ir. and Gael, *maer*, Gael. *mir*, merry.] Gay and noisy; in overflowing good spirits; hilarious; mirthful; sportive.—*To make merry*, to be jovial; to indulge in hilarity.—**merrily**, mer′i•li, *adv.*—**merriment**, mer′i•ment, *n.* Gaiety with laughter or noise; mirth; hilarity.—**merriness**, mer′i•nes, *n.*—**merry-go-round**, *n.* A circular frame, made to revolve, and on which children are treated to a ride.—**merrymaking**, *n.* A convivial entertainment; a festival.

mesa, mā′sa, *n.* [Sp., from L. *mensa*, a table.] A tableland of small extent rising abruptly from a surrounding plain.

mésalliance, mā•zal′i•ans, *n.* [Fr.] A marriage to a person of an inferior social rank.

mescal, mes•kal′, *n.* [Sp. *mezcal*, from Nahuatl *mexcalli*, a drink.] A cactus (*Lophophora Williamsii* or *L. Lewinii*) of Mexico and Texas, the buttonlike tips of which are dried and used as a stimulant and antispasmodic (by the Indians); a potent liquor distilled from pulque, the fermented juice of the cactus; a cactus yielding such liquor, as the maguey.

meseems, mē•sēmz′, *v. impersonal*—pret. *meseemed*. [Not properly a simple verb, being really an impersonal verb preceded by a pronoun in the dative=it seems to me. Comp. *methinks*.] It seems to me.

mesencephalon, mes•en•sef′a•lon, *n.* [Gr. *mesos*, middle, and *enkephalos*, the brain.] The middle or central portion of the brain.

mesentery, mes′en•ter•i, *n.* [Gr. *mesenterion*—*mesos*, middle, and *enteron*, intestine.] A membrane in the cavity of the abdomen, the use of which is to retain the intestines and their appendages in a proper position.—**mesenteric**, mes•en•ter′ik, *a.* Pertaining to the mesentery.—**mesenteritis**, mes′en•ter•ī″tis, *n.* Inflammation of the mesentery.

mesh, mesh, *n.* [A.Sax. *masc*, *max*, a noose, *mæscre*, a mesh, a net; D. *maas*, Dan. *maske*, Icel. *möskvi*, G. *masche*, a mesh; W. *masg*, a mesh, Lith. *megsti*, to knit, are allied.] The opening or space between the threads of a net; geared wheels.—*v.t.* To catch in a net; to ensnare.—**meshwork,** *n.* Network.

mesial, mē′zi•al, *a.* [Gr. *mesos,* middle.] Middle; median.—*Mesial line, mesial plane,* an imaginary line and plane dividing the body longitudinally into symmetrical halves, one toward the right and the other toward the left.

mesmerism, mez′mėr•izm, *n.* [After *Mesmer,* a German physician, who propounded the doctrine in 1778.] The doctrine that one person can exercise influence over the will and nervous system of another by virtue of a supposed emanation proceeding from him, or simply by the domination of his will over that of the person operated on; the influence itself, now called hypnotism.—**mesmeric,** mez•mer′ik, *a.* Pertaining to mesmerism.—**mesmerist,** mez′mėr•ist, *n.* One who practices or believes in mesmerism.—**mesmerize,** mez′mėr•īz, *v.t.*—*mesmerized, mesmerizing.* To bring into a state of mesmeric sleep.—**mesmerizer,** mez′mėr•īz•ėr, *n.* One who mesmerizes.

mesne, mēn, *a.* [Norm. *mesne,* middle, from L. *medianus,* middle. MEAN, *a.,* middle.] *Law,* middle, intervening; as, a *mesne* lord, *i.e.* a lord who holds land of a superior but grants a part of it to another person.

mesoblast, mes′o•blast, *n.* [Gr. *mesos,* middle, and *blastos,* a bud.] *Physiol.* the layer between the epiblast and hypoblast, the two primary layers of the embryo.

mesocaecum, mes′o•sē•kum, *n.* [Gr. *mesos,* middle, and L. *caecum.*] That part of the peritoneum which embraces the caecum and its appendages.

mesocarp, mes′o•kärp, *n.* [Gr. *mesos,* middle, and *karpos,* fruit.] *Bot.* the middle part or layer of the pericarp, immediately under the epicarp.

mesocephalic, mes′o•se•fal″ik, *a.* [Gr. *mesos,* middle, and *kephalē,* the head.] A term applied to the human skull when it is of medium breadth.

mesoderm, mes′o•dėrm, *n.* [Gr. *mesos,* middle, and *derma,* skin.] *Zool.* the middle layer of tissue between the ectoderm and the endoderm.

mesogastric, mes•o•gas′trik, *a.* [Gr. *mesos,* middle, *gastēr,* the belly.] *Anat.* applied to the membrane which sustains the stomach, and by which it is attached to the abdomen.—**mesogastrium,** mes•o•gas′tri•um, *n. Anat.* the umbilical region of the abdomen.

mesogloea, me•so•glē′a, *n.* [Gr. *mesos,* middle, *gloios,* a jelly.] In zoophytes, a middle layer of the body, often jelly-like.

mesognathous, me•sog′na•thus, *a.* [Gr. *mesos,* middle, *gnathos,* jaw.] *Anthropol.* intermediate between prognathous and orthognathous.

meson, mes′on, *n. Phys.* a particle having a mass of the order of 200 times that of an electron and with a unit positive or negative charge, found in cosmic rays and in high-energy X-rays.

mesonephros, mes′o•nef″ros, *n.* [Gr. *mesos,* middle, *nephros,* a kidney.] In vertebrates, the second of three successive renal organs.

mesosphere, mez′o•sfēr, *n.* [Prefix *meso,* and *sphere.*] An atmospheric layer located above the ionosphere, about 250 miles above the earth's crust.

mesothorax, mes•o•thō′raks, *n.* [Gr. *mesos,* middle, and *thōrax,* the chest.] *Entom.* the middle ring of the thorax.

mesotron, mez′o•tron, *n.* [Prefix *meso,* and *tron.*] A meson.

Mesozoic, mes•o•zō′ik, *a.* [Gr. *mesos,* middle, and *zōē,* life.] *Geol.* pertaining to the secondary age, between the Paleozoic and Cenozoic.

mesquite, mes′kēt, *n.* [Sp. *mezquite,* probably of American origin.] A leguminous shrub of southwestern U. S. and Mexico.

mess, mes, *n.* [O.Fr. *mes,* a dish, a course of dishes at table; It. *messo;* properly that which is sent, from L. *missus,* pp. of *mitto,* to send. MISSION.] A dish or quantity of food set on a table at one time; food for a person at one meal; a number of persons who eat together at the same table, especially in the army or navy.—*v.i.* To take meals in common with others, as one of a mess; to associate at the same table.

mess, mes, *n.* [Formerly *mesh,* which is same as *mash,* lit. a mixture.] A disorderly mixture; a state of dirt and disorder; *fig.* a situation of confusion or embarrassment; a muddle.

message, mes′ij, *n.* [Fr. *message,* It. *messaggio,* L.L. *missaticum,* message, from L. *mitto, missum,* to send. MISSION.] Any communication, written or verbal, sent from one person to another; an official communication delivered by a messenger.—**messenger,** mes′en•jėr, *n.* [O.E. *messager,* Fr. *messager.* The *n* has intruded as in *passenger.*] One who delivers a message or performs an errand; one who conveys dispatches from one government to another; an envoy; an emissary; a harbinger; a herald.

Messiah, mes•sī′a, *n.* [Heb. *mäshiach,* anointed, from *māshach,* to anoint.] The deliverer and savior promised to the Hebrews; Christ, the Anointed; the Saviour of the world.—**Messiahship,** mes•sī′a•ship, *n.* The office of the Saviour.—**Messianic,** mes•si•an′ik, *a.* Relating to the Messiah.

messieurs, mes′ėrz, *n.* [Fr. pl. of *Monsieur* (which see).] Sirs; gentlemen; the plural of *Mr.,* employed in addressing firms or companies of several persons, and generally contracted into *Messrs.*

messuage, mes′wij, *n.* [O.Fr. *messuage, mesnage,* L.L. *messuagium, mansionaticum,* from L. *mansio,* a dwelling. MANSION.] *Law,* a dwelling house, with the adjacent buildings, etc., appropriated to the use of the household; a manor house.

mestizo, mes•tē′zō, *n.* [Sp. *mestizo,* from L. *mixtus, pp.* of *misceo,* to mix.] The offspring of a Caucasian and American Indian; an individual of mixed breed.

metabolic, met•a•bol′ik, *a.* [Gr. *metabolē,* change.] Pertaining to metabolism.—**metabolism,** me•tab′o•lizm, *n. Physiol.* the sum total of the build-up and destruction of cell tissue; the chemical cellular changes providing the energies for the life processes and the elimination of waste materials.—**metabolize,** me•tab′o•līz, *v.t.* To subject to metabolism; transform by metabolism.

metacarpus, met•a•kär′pus, *n.* [Gr. *meta,* beyond, *karpos,* the wrist.] *Anat.* the part of the hand between the wrist and the fingers.—**metacarpal,** met•a•kär′pal, *a.* Pertaining to the metacarpus.

metacenter, met•a•sen′tėr, *n.* [Gr. *meta,* beyond, and *kentron,* center.] *Physics,* that point in a floating body on the position of which its stability depends, and which must be above the center of gravity to prevent the body from turning over.

metage, mēt′ij, *n.* [From *mete.*] Measurement of coal; charge for measuring.

metagenesis, met•a•jen′e•sis, *n.* [Gr. *meta,* after, change, and *genesis.*] *Zool.* the changes of form which the representative of a species undergoes in passing, by a series of successively generated individuals, from the ovum or egg to the perfect state; alternation of generation.—**metagenetic, metagenic,** met′a•je•net″ik, met•a•jen′ik, *a.* Pertaining to metagenesis.

metal, met′al, *n.* [L. *metallum,* from Gr. *metallon,* a mine, a metal—*meta,* after, and root meaning to go or search.] A name given to certain substances of which gold, silver, iron, lead, are examples, having a luster and generally fusible by heat; the name given by workers in glass, pottery, etc., to the material on which they operate when in a state of fusion.—**metallic,** me•tal′ik, *a.* [L. *metallicus.*] Pertaining to metals; consisting of metal; like a metal.—*Metallic oxide,* a compound of metal and oxygen.—*Metallic paper,* paper the surface of which is washed over with a solution of whiting, lime, and size, and which is written on with a pewter pencil.—**metalliferous,** met•al•if′ėr•us, *a.* Producing metal; yielding metal.—**metalline,** met′al•in, *a.* Consisting of or containing metal.—**metallize,** met′al•īz, *v.t.*—*metalized, metalizing.* To form into metal; to give its proper metallic properties to (an ore).—**metallography,** met•al•og′ra•fi, *n.* The science or description of metals; the study of metals by the microscope.—**metalloid,** met′al•oid, *n.* A metallic base of a fixed alkali or alkaline earth; any non-metallic elementary substance.—*a.* Like metal; having the form or appearance of a metal.—**metallurgy,** met′al•ėr•ji, *n.* [Gr. *ergon,* work.] The art of working metals; the process of separating them from other matters in the ore, smelting, refining, etc.—**metallurgic, metallurgical,** met•al•ėr′jik, met•al•ėr′ji•kal, *a.* Pertaining to metallurgy.—**metallurgist,**

met′al·ėr·jist, *n.* One engaged in metallurgy.

metalloid, metallurgy, etc. See METAL.

metamere, met′a·mēr, *n.* [Gr. *meta*, with or among; and *meros*, a part.] *Compar. anat.* one of a series of similar parts; in segmented animals, one of the segments.—**metamerism,** me·tam′ėr·izm, *n. Chem.* the character in certain compound bodies, differing in chemical properties, of having the same elements combined in the same proportion and with the same molecular weight.

metamorphosis, met·a·mor′fō·sis, *n.* [Gr. *metamorphōsis—meta*, denoting change, and *morphē*, form, shape.] Change of form, shape, or structure; transformation; *zool.* the alterations which an animal undergoes after its exclusion from the egg, and which alter extensively the general form and life of the individual; such changes as those from the caterpillar to the perfect butterfly.—**metamorphic,** met·a·mor′fik, *a.* Pertaining to or producing metamorphosis.—*Metamorphic rocks, geol.* stratified rocks of any age whose texture has been rendered less or more crystalline by subterranean heat, pressure, or chemical agency; the lowest and non-fossiliferous stratified rocks, originally deposited from water and crystallized by subsequent agencies.—**metamorphism,** met·a·mor′fizm, *n.* The process of metamorphosing; the change undergone by stratified rocks under the influence of heat and chemical or mechanical agents.—**metamorphose,** met·a·mor′fōz, *v.t.—metamorphosed, metamorphosing.* To change into a different form; to change the shape or character of; to transform.—**Metamorphoses,** *n. pl.* The poem by Ovid dealing with the various changes of human beings and others into different characters.

metanephros, met′a·nef″ros, *n.* [Gr. *meta*, after, *nephros*, a kidney.] In vertebrates, the third of three successive renal organs. The definitive kidney of mammals, birds, and reptiles.

metaphor, met′a·fėr, *n.* [Gr. *metaphora*, from *metapherō*, to transfer—*meta*, over, and *pherō*, to carry.] A figure of speech founded on resemblance, by which a word is transferred from an object to which it properly belongs to another in such a manner that a comparison is implied though not formally expressed. Thus, 'that man is a fox', is a metaphor; but 'that man is like a fox', is a simile or comparison.—**metaphoric, metaphorical,** met·a·for′ik, met·a·for′i·kal, *a.* Pertaining to metaphor; comprising a metaphor; not literal; figurative.—**metaphorically,** met·a·for′i·kal·li, *adv.* In a metaphorical manner; not literally.

metaphrase, met′a·frāz, *n.* [Gr. *metaphrasis—meta*, according to or with, and *phrasis*, phrase.] A verbal translation of one language into another, word for word: opposed to *paraphrase*.—**metaphrast,** met′a·frast, *n.* A literal translator.

metaphysics, met·a·fiz′iks, *n.* [L. *metaphysica*, pl. neut. from Gr. *meta*, after, and *physica*, physics, from *physis*, nature, the science of natural bodies or *physics* being regarded as properly first in the order of studies, and the science of mind or intelligence to be the second.] That science which seeks to trace the branches of human knowledge to their first principles in the constitution of our nature, or to find what is the nature of the human mind and its relations to the external world; the science that seeks to know the ultimate grounds of being or what it is that really exists, embracing both psychology and ontology.—**metaphysic,** met·a·fiz′ik, *n.* Metaphysics.—**metaphysic, metaphysical,** met·a·fiz′i·kal, *a.* Pertaining to metaphysics; according to rules or principles of metaphysics.—**metaphysically,** met·a·fiz′i·kal·li, *adv.* In a metaphysical manner.—**metaphysician,** met·a·fi·zish′an, *n.* One who is versed in metaphysics.

metaplasm, met′a·plazm, *n.* [Gr. *metaplasmos*, transformation—*meta*, over, and *plassō*, to form.] *Gram.* a change in a word by adding, transposing, or retrenching a syllable or letter.

metastasis, me·tas′ta·sis, *n.* [Gr. *metastasis—meta*, over, and *stasis*, position.] *Med.* a translation or removal of a disease from one part to another.—**metastatic,** met·a·stat′ik, *a.* Relating to metastasis.

metatarsus, met·a·tär′sus, *n.* [Gr. *meta*, beyond, and *tarsos*, tarsus.] The middle of the foot, or part between the ankle and the toes.—**metatarsal,** met·a·tär′sal, *a.* Belonging to the metatarsus.—*n.* A bone of the metatarsus.

metathesis, me·tath′e·sis, *n.* [Gr. *metathesis—meta*, over, and *tithēmi*, to set.] *Gram.* transposition of the letters, sounds, or syllables of a word.—**metathetic, metathetical,** met·a·thet′ik, met·a·thet′i·kal, *a.* Relating to metathesis.

metathorax, met·a·thō′raks, *n.* [Gr. *meta*, after, and *thōrax*, the chest.] *Entom.* the third and last segment of the thorax.

métayer, me·tā′yėr, *n.* [Fr. *métayer*, L.L. *medietarius*, from L. *medietas*, middle state, from *medius*, middle.] A cultivator who tills the soil on condition of receiving a share of its produce, the owner furnishing the whole or part of the stock, tools, etc.

Metazoa, met·a·zō′a, *n.* pl. [Gr. *meta*, after, *zoon*, animal.] The subkingdom of animals comprising all except the Protozoa, characterized by two cell layers differentiated into tissues, organs and a digestive cavity.—**metazoan,** met·a·zō′an, *a.* and *n.*

mete, mēt, *v.t.—meted, meting.* [A. Sax. *metan* = D. *meten*, Goth. *mitan*, G. *messen*, to measure; Icel. *meta*, to value; from root of L., *modus* a measure (whence *mode*); Gr. *metron*, a measure; Skr. *mâ*, to measure.] To measure; to ascertain the quantity, dimensions, or capacity of by any rule or standard.

metempirical, met·em·pir′i·kal, *a.* [Gr. *meta*, beyond, and *empeiria*, experience, from *en*, in, and *peira*, trial, experiment.] *Metaph.* beyond or outside of experience; not based on experience; transcendental; a priori: opposed to *empirical* or *experiential*.—**metempiric,** met·em·pir′ik, *n.* One who believes in the transcendental philosophy.

metempsychosis, me·tem′si·kō″sis, *n.* [Gr. *meta*, denoting change, *en*, in, and *psyche*, soul.] Transmigration; the passing of the soul of a man after death into some other animal body.

meteor, mē′tē·ėr, *n.* [From Gr. *meteōros*, raised on high—*meta*, beyond, and *aeirō*, to raise.] A transient celestial body that enters the earth's atmosphere with terrific velocity, white with heat generated by the resistance of the air.—**meteoric,** mē·tē·or′ik, *a.* Pertaining to a meteor or meteors; *fig.* transiently or irregularly brilliant.—*Meteoric iron*, iron as found in meteoric stones.—*Meteoric stones*, those aerolites which fall from the heavens on the surface of the earth, and usually consist of metallic iron and certain silicates.—*Meteoric showers*, showers of shooting stars occurring periodically.—**meteorite,** mē′tē·ėr·īt, *n.* A meteoric stone; an aerolite; especially a meteor which has reached the earth's crust without being completely consumed.—**meteorograph,** mē′tē·ėr·o·graf, *n.* An instrument or apparatus for registering meteorological phenomena.—**meteorology,** mē′tē·ėr·ol″o·ji, *n.* [Gr. *meteorologia.*] The science which treats of atmospheric phenomena, more especially as connected with or in relation to weather and climate.—**meteorologic, meteorological,** mē′tē·ėr·o·loj″ik, mē′tē·ėr·o·loj″i·kal, *a.* Pertaining to meteorology or to the atmosphere and its phenomena.—**meteorologist,** mē′tē·ėr·ol″o·jist, *n.* A person skilled in meteorology.

meter, mē′tėr, *n.* [Fr. *mètre*, L. *metrum*, meter, Gr. *metron*, meter, a measure; same root as in *measure*, *mete*.] Rhythmical arrangement of syllables into verses, stanzas, strophes, etc.; rhythm; measure; verse.—**metric, metrical,** met′rik, met′ri·kal, *a.* Pertaining to rhythm or meter; consisting of verse.—**metrically** met′ri·kal·li, *adv.* In a metrical manner; according to poetic measure.—**metrist,** mē′trist, *n.* A composer of verses.

meter, mē′tėr: Fr. pron. mā·tr, *n.* [Fr. *mètre*, from Gr. *metron*, a measure. See above.] A basic measure of length, equal to 39.37 inches, the standard of linear measure.—**metric,** met′rik, *a.* Pertaining to a system of weights, measures, and moneys, first adopted in France—the decimal system. See DECIMAL.—**metrical,** met′ri·kal, *a.* Pertaining to or employed in measuring.—**metrology,** mi·trol′o·ji, *n.* An account of weights and measures; the art and science of mensuration.—**metronome,** met′ro·nōm, *n.* [Gr.

nomos, a law.] An instrument, consisting of a pendulum set in motion by clockwork, that determines the quickness or slowness of musical compositions.

meter, mē'tėr, *n.* [From *mete.*] One who or that which measures; an instrument that measures and records automatically, as a gas meter, water meter, etc.

methane, me'thān, *n.* Marsh gas (CH_4), the simplest hydrocarbon.

methanol, meth'ä•nol, *n.* [*Methane* and *ol.*] A pungent, flammable, poisonous liquid alcohol (CH_3 OH), formerly distilled from wood, now made synthetically, used as an antifreeze, solvent, etc.

metheglin, mi•theg'lin, *n.* [W. *meddyglyn—medd*, mead, and *llyn*, liquor.] A Welsh variety of the liquor mead.

method, meth'od, *n.* [Fr. *méthode*, L. *methodus*, from Gr. *methodos—meta*, after, and *hodos*, a way.] A way or mode by which we proceed to the attainment of some aim; mode or manner of procedure; logical or scientific arrangement or mode of acting; systematic or orderly procedure; system; *nat. hist.* principle of classification (the Linnaean *method*).—**methodic, methodical,** me•thod'ik, me•thod'i•kal, *a.*—**methodically,** me•thod'i•kal•li, *adv.*—**methodism,** meth'od•izm, *n.* The doctrines and worship of the *Methodists.*—**methodist,** meth'od•ist, *n.* [cap.] One characterized by strict adherence to method; one of a sect of Christians founded by John Wesley, so called from the regularity of their lives and the strictness of their observance of religious duties.—**methodistic,** meth•o•dis'tik, *a.*—**methodize,** meth'od•īz, *v.t.*—*methodized, methodizing.* To reduce to method.—**methodology,** meth•od•ol'o•ji, *n.* The science of methods, rules, procedures, etc., as it is applied by a science or art.

methyl, meth'il, *n.* [Gr. *meta*, after, with, and *hylē*, wood.] A univalent hydrocarbon radical (CH_3).—**methylamine,** me•thil'a•min, *n.* A colorless gas having a strong ammoniacal odor, and resembling ammonia in many of its reactions.—**methylated,** meth'i•lā•ted, *a.* Impregnated or mixed with methyl.—*Methylated spirit*, ordinary, or ethyl, alcohol denatured with wood alcohol, which renders it unfit for drinking.—**methylic,** me•thil'ik, *a.* Pertaining to methyl.

meticulous, me•tik'ū•lus, *a.* [Fr. *méticuleux*, L. *metus*, fear.] Timidly scrupulous; too careful or fastidious.

métier, mā'tyā, *n.* [Fr. *métier*, trade, business.] A calling, business, to which one is peculiarly suited.

metis, mā'tis, *n.* [Fr. on analogy of *mestizo* (q.v.).] A child of white and American Indian parents (*Canada*); an octoroon (*U.S.*).

Metonic cycle, me•ton'ik. [After *Meton*, an ancient astronomer.] The cycle or period of nineteen years, in which the phases of the moon return to the same days of the month.

metonymy, me•ton'i•mi, *n.* [Gr. *metōnymia—meta*, denoting change, and *onoma*, a name.] *Rhet.* a figure by which one word is put for another on account of some actual relation between the things signified, as when we say. 'We read *Virgil*', that is, his *poems* or *writings.*—**metonymic, metonymical,** met•o•nim'ik, met•o•nim'i•kal, *a.*

metope, met'o•pē, *n.* [Gr. *metopē—meta*, between, and *opē*, an aperture.] *Arch.* the space between the triglyphs of the Doric frieze.

metronymic, met•ro•nim'ik, *n.* and *a.* [Gr. *mētrōnymikos—mētēr*, *mētros*, a mother, and *onoma*, a name.] A term applied to a name derived from a mother, as opposed to *patronymic.*

metropolis, me•trop'o•lis, *n.* [Gr. *mētropolis—mētēr*, *mētros*, a mother, and *polis*, a city.] The chief city or capital of a kingdom, state, or country; the see or seat of a metropolitan bishop.—**metropolitan,** met•ro•pol'i•tan, *a.* Belonging to a metropolis; *eccles.* having the authority of a metropolitan; proceeding from a metropolitan.—*n.* A resident of a metropolis or one who is urbane in manners; *eccles.* a bishop having authority over the other bishops of a province.

mettle, met'l, *n.* [Merely an altered spelling of *metal.*] Spirit; constitutional ardor; courage; fire.—*To put a man on* or *to his mettle*, to stimulate a man to do his uttermost.—**mettlesome,** met'l•sum, *a.* Brisk; fiery.

mew, mū, *n.* [A.Sax. *maew*, a gull or mew = Sc. *maw*, D. *meeuw*, G. *möve*, Icel. *már*, a mew.] A sea mew; a gull.

mew, mū, *n.* [Fr. *mue*, a molting, a mew or cage, from L.L. *muta*, a mew, from L. *mutare*, to change. MUTABLE.] The molting of a hawk; a cage for hawks or other birds while molting; a coop for fowls; a place of confinement in general.—*v.t.* To shed or cast; to molt; to shut up, enclose, confine, as in a cage or other enclosure.—*v.i.* To cast the feathers; to molt.—**mews,** mūz, *n. pl.* The royal stables in London, England, so called because built where the king's hawks were once *mewed* or confined; hence (with verbs, etc., in *sing.*), a place where carriage horses are kept in large towns; a lane or alley in which stables or mews are situated.

mew, mū, *v.i.* [Imitative, and also written *meaw*, *miaw*, etc.; comp. W. *mewian*, G. *miauen*, to mew.] To cry as a cat.—*n.* The cry of a cat.—**mewl,** mūl, *v.i.* [Imitative; comp. *miaul*, Fr. *miauler.*] To cry or squall, as a child.

Mexican, mex'i•can, *a.* Of or pertaining to Mexico, a country in North America.

mezereon, mi•zē'ri•on, *n.* [Fr. *mézereon*, Sp. *mezereon*, from Ar. and Per. *māzariyûn*, the camellia.] A common garden shrub whose fragrant pink flowers appear in spring before the leaves expand.

mezzanine, mez'za•nēn, *n.* [It. *mezzanino*, from *mezzo*, middle. MEZZO.] *Arch.* an entresol or low story between two higher ones.

mezzo, med'zō or met'zō, *a.* [It., from L. *medius*, middle.]—*Mus.* middle; mean.—*Mezzo soprano*, a treble voice of medium range, lower than soprano and higher than contralto.—**mezzo-relievo,** med'zō•ri•lē"vō, *n.* Middle relief.—**mezzotint, mezzotinto,** med'zo•tint, med•zo•tin'tō, *n.* [It. *mezzo*, middle, *tinto*, tint.] A manner of engraving on copper or steel in imitation of drawing in India ink, the lights being scraped and burnished out of a prepared dark ground.

mi, mē, *n.* The third note in the musical scale, between *re* and *fa.*

miasma, mī•az'ma, *n.* pl. **miasmata,** mī•az'ma•ta. [Gr. *miasma*, *miasmatos*, from *miainō*, to stain, sully.] Evil-smelling vapor, formerly supposed to be the effluvia or fine particles of any putrefying bodies, rising and floating in the atmosphere, and considered to be noxious to health; noxious emanation.—**miasmal,** mī•az'mal, *a.* Containing miasma; miasmatic.—**miasmatic, miasmatical,** mī•az•mat'ik, mī•az•mat'i•kal, *a.* Pertaining to miasma.

miaul, myạl, *v.i.* [MEW.] To cry as a cat or kitten; to mew.

mica, mī'ka, *n.* [L. *mico*, to glitter.] A mineral of a foliated structure, consisting of thin flexible laminae or scales, having a shining and almost metallic luster.—*Mica schist*, *mica slate*, a metamorphic rock composed of mica and quartz, highly fissile and passing by insensible gradations into clay slate.—**micaceous,** mī•kā'shus, *a.* Pertaining to or containing mica; resembling mica or partaking of its properties.—*Micaceous rocks*, rocks of which mica is the chief ingredient, as mica slate.—*Micaceous schist*, mica schist.

mice, mīs, *n.* pl. of *mouse.*

Michaelmas, mik'el•mas, *n.* [*Michael*, and *mass*, a feast.] The feast of St. *Michael*, the archangel, which falls on the 29th of September.

microanalysis, mī'kro•a•nal"i•sis, *n.* *Chem.* analysis of extremely minute amounts of material.

microbe, mī'krōb, *n.* [Gr. *mikros*, small, *bios*, life.] A microscopic organism such as a bacillus or bacterium.

microbiology, mī'kro•bī•ol"o•ji, *n.* The study and use of microscopic and submicroscopic organisms.

microcephalous, mī•kro•sef'a•lus, *a.* [Gr. *mikros*, small, and *kephalē*, the head.] Having a very small skull.

microchemistry, mī'kro•kem"is•tri, *n.* Chemistry concerned with microscopic objects or amounts.

micrococcus, mī•kro•kok'us, *n.* [Gr. *mikros*, small, and *kokkos*, a berry.] *Zool.* a microscopic organism of a round form.

microcopy, mī'kro•kop•i, *n.* [Gr. *mikros*, small, and *copy.*] A photographic copy of printed matter or photographs, etc., reduced in size and put on film.

microcosm, mī'kro•kozm, *n.* [Gr. *mikros*, small, and *kosmos*, world.] *Lit.* a little world or cosmos, applied to man, as supposed to be an epitome of the universe or great world (the *macrocosm*); a community or unity that epitomizes a larger unit. **microcosmic,** mī•kro•koz′mik, *a.*

microfarad, mī′kro•far•ad, *n.* [Gr. *mikros,* small, and E. *farad.*] The millionth part of a farad.

microfilm, mī′kro•film, *n.* [Gr. *mikros,* small, and E. *film.*] The film of printed matter, etc., that has been reduced in size.—*v.t.* and *i.* To photograph on microfilm.

microgeology, mī′kro•jē•ol″o•ji, *n.* [From *microscope* and *geology.*] That department of the science of geology whose facts are ascertained by the use of the microscope.

micrography, mī•krog′ra•fi, *n.* [Gr. *mikros,* small, and *graphō,* to describe.] The description of objects too small to be discerned without the aid of a microscope.—**micrographic,** mī•kro•graf′ik, *a.* Connected with or relating to micrography.

microhm, mī′krōm, *n.* [Gr. *mikros,* small, and E. *ohm.*] The millionth part of an ohm.

micrology, mī•krol′o•ji, *n.* [Gr. *mikros,* small, and *logos,* description.] That part of science dependent on microscopic investigations; micrography.

micrometer, mī•krom′et•ėr, *n.* [Gr. *mikros,* small, and *metron,* a measure.] An instrument or appliance fitted to a telescope or microscope, for measuring very small distances, or the apparent diameters of objects which subtend very small angles.—**micrometry,** mī•krom′et•ri, *n.* The art of measuring with a micrometer.

micromillimeter (mμ), mī′krō•mil″li•mē•tėr, *n.* [Gr. *mikros,* small, and *millimetre.*] 1/1000000 millimeter; the unit of microscopical measurement.

micron (μ), mī′kron, *n.* [Gr. *mikron,* small.] A unit of length equal to one millionth part of a meter.

micro-organism, mi•krō-or′gan•izm, *n.* [Gr. *mikros,* small, and E. *organism.*] A microscopic organism, as a bacterium or bacillus.

microphone, mī′kro•fōn, *n.* [Gr. *mikros,* small, and *phōnē,* sound.] An instrument for transmitting or intensifying sounds by means of electricity; an instrument for converting sound waves into electrical waves, used especially in radiobroadcasting; often referred to as a *mike.*

microphotography, mī′kro•fo•tog″ra•fi, *n.* [Gr. *mikros,* small, and E. *photography.*] A photographic representation of microscopic size; the photography of microscopic objects.

micropyle, mī′kro•pīl, *n.* [Gr. *mikros,* small, *pylē,* gate.] *Bot.* the opening by which a pollen tube enters the ovule; *zool.* an opening by which the spermatozoa fertilize an ovum.

microscope, mī′kro•skōp, *n.* [Gr. *mikros,* small, and *skopeō,* to view.] An optical instrument consisting of a lens or combination of lenses for rendering minute objects distinctly visible.—**microscopic, microscopical,** mī•kro•skop′ik, mī•kro•skop′i•kal, *a.* Pertaining to the microscope; made by the aid of a microscope (*microscopic* observations); resembling a microscope; capable of seeing small objects; visible only by the aid of a microscope.—**microscopically,** mī•kro•skop′i•kal•li, *adv.* In a microscopic manner; by the microscope.—**microscopist,** mī′kro•skō•pist or mī•kros′ko•pist, *n.* One skilled or versed in microscopy.—**microscopy,** mī•kros′ko•pi, *n.* The use of the microscope; investigation with the microscope.

microspore, mik′ro•spōr, *n.* [Gr. *mikros,* small, *sporos,* seed.] *Bot.* a small (male) spore.

microtome, mī′kro•tōm, *n.* [Gr. *mikros,* small, and *tomos,* a cutting.] An instrument for making very fine sections or slices of objects for the microscope.

microwave, mī′kro•wave, *n.* [Gr. *mikros,* small, and E. *wave.*] Short electromagnetic waves, between 30 centimeters and 1 millimeter in wave length.

micturition, mik•tū•rish′on, *n.* [L. *micturio,* to desire to make water.] The desire of making water; a morbid frequency in the passage of urine.

mid, mid, *a.*; no compar.; superl. *midmost.* [A.Sax. *mid,* mid, in the middle; Goth. *midjis,* Icel. *midr* (*mithr*); cog. L. *medius* (see MEDIAL); Gr. *mesos,* Skr. *madhyas,* middle.] Middle; at equal distance from extremes; intervening.—**mid-channel,** *n.* The middle of a channel.—**midday,** *n.* The middle of the day; noon.—*a.* Pertaining to noon; meridional.—**midland,** mid′land, *a.* Being in the interior country; distant from the coast or seashore; inland.—*n.* The interior of a country.—**midmost,** mid′mōst, *a.* In the very middle; middlemost.—**midnight,** mid′nīt, *n.* The middle of the night; twelve o'clock at night.—*a.* Being or occurring in the middle of the night; dark as midnight; very dark.—**midnoon,** *n.* The middle of the day; noon. (*Tenn.*)—**midrib,** mid′rib, *n. Bot.* a continuation of the petiole extending from the base to the apex of the lamina of a leaf.—**midship,** mid′ship, *a.* Being or belonging to the middle of a ship.—**midshipman,** mid′ship•man, *n.* [From his rank being between that of a superior officer and a common seaman.] An officer in training in the navy, occupying the rank below ensign.—**midsummer,** mid′sum•ėr, *n.* The middle of summer; the summer solstice, about the 21st of June.—**midway,** mid′wā, *n.* A middle way or the middle of the way.—*a.* Being in the middle of the way or distance.—*adv.* In the middle of the way or distance; halfway.—**midwinter,** *n.* The middle of winter, or the winter solstice, December 21.

midden, mid′n, *n.* [A.Sax. *midding,* same word as Dan. *mödding, mögdynge,* from *mög,* dung, and *dynge,* a heap.] A dunghill. [Prov.E. and Scot.]—*Kitchen-midden.* See KITCHEN.

middle, mid′l, *a.*; no compar; superl. *middlemost.* [From *mid*; A.Sax., D., and Dan. *middel,* G. *mittel,* middle. MID.] Equally distant from the extremes; forming a mean; intermediate; intervening.—*Middle Ages,* the period in Europe from the fifth to the middle of the fifteenth century of the Christian era.—*n.* Middle point or part; middle part of the body; an intervening point or part in space, time, or order; something intermediate; a mean.—**middle-aged,** *a.* Being about the middle of the ordinary human life span.—**middle class.** Originally, people having a social position between wage earners and the leisure class; now including many wage earners, such as clerks and office workers.—**middle C,** *n.* The musical note C, represented by the first ledger line below the treble staff, and the first above the bass staff.—**middle ear,** *n. Anat.* the tympanum.—**middleman,** *n.* An intermediary between two parties; a jobber.—**middlemost,** mid′l•mōst, *a.* Midmost.—**middleweight,** mid′l•wāt, *n.* A person of average weight; in boxing, a fighter whose weight lies between that of a welterweight and a light heavyweight, at about 160 pounds.—**middling,** mid′ling, *a.* Of middle state, size, or quality; moderate; mediocre; second-rate.

midge, mij, *n.* [A.Sax. *micge,* a midge=D. *mug,* Dan. *myg,* G. *mücke*; allied to Gr. *myia,* a fly.] The common name of numerous minute species of gnats or flies.—**midget,** mij′et, *n.* [Dim. of *midge.*] A very small creature.

midriff, mid′rif, *n.* [A.Sax. *midhrif*—*mid,* and *hrif,* belly.] The diaphragm; the respiratory muscle dividing the cavity of the thorax from that of the abdomen.

midst, midst, *n.* [From old *middes* (with *t* appended, as in *against, amongst*), the genit. of *mid,* middle.] The middle; in the central part of a place; the position of a thing surrounded by other things.—*In the midst* (*of*), in the middle part of, in the middle stage.—*prep.* Amidst.

midwife, mid′wīf, *n.* [From O.E. and A.Sax. *mid,* with, together with (G. *mit*), and *wife*; comp. Sp. and Pg. *comadre,* a midwife, *co*=L. *cum,* with, and *madre,* a mother.] A practical nurse, as distinguished from a registered nurse, who assists a mother in childbirth.—**midwifery,** mid′wīf•ri, *n.* The art or practice of a midwife; obstetrics.

mien, mēn, *n.* [Fr. *mine,* air, mien; It. *mina,* course, behavior, L.L. *minare,* to lead, conduct, properly to drive with threats, from L. *mina,* a threat. MENACE. Or from Arm. *mîn,* face.] External air or manner of a person; look; bearing; appearance; carriage.

miff, mif, *n.* [Comp. Prov.G. *muff,* sullenness.] A slight quarrel. (*Colloq.*)

might, mīt, *n.* [A.Sax. *miht,* also *meaht,* might, from stem of *may,* to be able; D. Sw. and Dan. *magt,* G. *macht,* might. MAY.] Strength; force; power; often bodily strength or physical power; but also mental power; power of will; political power.—*With might and main*, with the utmost strength or bodily exertion.—**mightily,** mīt′i•li, *adv.* Powerfully; vehemently; greatly; highly.—**mightiness,** mīt′i•nes, *n.* State or attribute of being mighty: also, with possessives, a title of dignity.—**mighty,** mīt′i, *a.* [A.Sax. *mihtig.*] Having great power or dominion; strong; powerful: often an epithet of honor (most *mighty* prince); very great; vast; eminent in intellect or acquirements; displaying great power; performed with great power (*mighty* works).—*adv.* In a great degree; very (*mighty* wise; *mighty* thoughtful). (*Colloq.*)

might, mīt, past tense of *may*.

mignonette, min′yon•et, *n.* [Fr. *mignonnette*, a dim. of *mignon*, darling. MINION.] An annual plant, a native of Egypt, but universally cultivated in gardens on account of the sweet scent of its flowers.

migraine, mī′grān, *n.* [Gr. *hemikrania*, from *hemi*, half, and *kranion*, skull.] A recurring headache, usually on one side of the head, accompanied by nausea and often by sensory disturbances.

migrate, mī′grāt, *v.i.*—*migrated, migrating.* [L. *migro, migratum*, to migrate.] To move from one place of residence to another; changing from one geographic area to another.—**migrant,** mī′grant, *a.* Migratory.—*n.* One who migrates; a migratory bird or other animal.—**migration,** mī•grā′shon, *n.*—**migratory,** mī′gra•to•ri, *a.* Given to migration; migrating at certain seasons (as birds); roving or wandering.

mikado, mi•kä′dō, *n.* [Japanese, lit. the Venerable.] [*often cap.*] The emperor of Japan.

mil, mil, *n.* [From L. *mille*, thousand.] A unit of 0.001 inch, used in measuring the diameter of wire.

milanese, mil•an•ēz′, *n. sing.* and *pl.* A citizen or citizens of *Milan*.—*a.* Of or belonging to Milan or the people of Milan.

milch, milch, *a.* [A.Sax. *melc*, milch, giving milk; comp. L.G. *melke*, Icel. *milkr*, G. *melk*, milch, but L.G. *melk*, *mjólk*, G. *milch*, milk. MILK.] Giving milk; applied only to beasts (a *milch* cow).

mild, mīld, *a.* [A.Sax. *milde* = D. Dan. Sw. and G. *mild*, Icel. *mildr*, Goth. *milds*; from a root meaning to grind or crush, and hence allied to *mellow, meal, mould*, L. *mollis*, soft (whence *mollify*).] Tender and gentle in temper or disposition; not severe or cruel; not fierce, rough, or angry; placid; not stern; not frowning; gently and pleasantly affecting the senses; not violent; soft; bland; gentle (a *mild* temperature); not acrid, pungent, corrosive, or drastic; moderately sweet or pleasant to the taste (*mild* fruit).—**milden,** mīl′den, *v.t.* To render mild; to soften; to make less severe, stringent, or intense.—*v.i.* To become mild; to soften.—**mildly,** mīld′li, *adv.* In a mild manner.—**mildness,** mīld′nes, *n.* The state or quality of being mild; gentleness; softness; clemency; blandness; tenderness.

mildew, mil′dū, *n.* [A.Sax. *mildeáw, meledeáw*; O.H.G. *militou*, G. *mehlthau*; probably = 'honey-dew'; comp. L. *mel*, honey.] Decay produced in living and dead vegetable matter, and in some manufactured products of vegetable matter, by very minute parasitical fungi; a sort of blight; the minute fungi causing this condition.—*v.t.* To affect with mildew.—*v.i.* To become affected with mildew.—**mildewy,** mil′dū•i, *a.* Abounding in mildew; moldy; resembling mildew.

mile, mīl, *n.* [A.Sax. *mil*, like D. *mijl*, Dan. *miil*, G. *meile*, a mile, from L. *mille*, a thousand, used shortly for *mille passus* (or *passuum*), a thousand paces, a Roman mile. Akin *million, milliard*, etc.] A land measure of distance used in the United States and Great Britain, and equal to 1,760 yards, or 5280 feet: the nautical or sea mile, in the United States, is equal to 6,080.20 feet.—*Last mile*, the last walk of a condemned man to the execution chamber. (*Slang.*)—**mileage,** mīl′ij, *n.* A fee or allowance paid for travel by the mile; the aggregate of miles in a railway, canal, etc.; aggregate of miles gone over by vehicles such as automobiles, railroad trains, etc.—**milestone,** mīl′stōn, *n.* A stone or post set up on the side of a road or highway to mark the miles.

milesian, mi•lē′zhi•an, *n.* A native of Ireland, whose inhabitants, according to Irish legend, are descended from *Milesius*, a king of Spain.—*a.* Pertaining to the ancient Irish race.

milfoil, mil′foil, *n.* [Fr. *mille-feuille*, from L. *millefolium*, lit. thousand-leaf.] The yarrow.

miliary, mil′i•e•ri, *a.* [L. *miliarius*, from *milium*, millet.] Resembling millet seeds; accompanied with an eruption like millet seeds (a *miliary* fever).

milieu, mē•lyu′, *n.* [Fr., from Old Fr. *mi*, middle, and *lieu*, place.] Environmental setting.

militant, mil′i•tant, *a.* [L. *militans, militantis*, ppr. of *milito*, to fight, from *miles, militis*, a soldier; perhaps connected with *mille*, a thousand.] Fighting; serving as a soldier.—*Church militant*, the Christian church on earth, which is supposed to be engaged in constant warfare and struggle: as distinguished from the *church triumphant*, or in heaven.—**militantly,** mil′i•tant•li, *adv.* In a militant or warlike manner.—**militancy,** mil′i•tan•si, *n.* Warfare; militarism.—**militarily,** mil′i•te•ri•li, *adv.* In a military or soldierly manner.—**militarism,** mil′i•te•rizm, *n.* [Fr. *militarisme.*] The system that leads a nation to pay excessive attention to military affairs; the keeping up of great armies.—**militarist,** mil′i•te•rist, *n.* A military man; one proficient in the art of war (*Shak.*); one in favor of militarism; one who favors a warlike policy.—**military,** mil′i•te•ri, *a.* [L. *militaris.*] Pertaining to soldiers or the profession of a soldier; becoming the profession of a soldier; pertaining to war; warlike; martial.—*Military attaché*, an army officer, resident abroad with his nation's diplomatic representative, whose duty it is to observe and report on the military developments of a foreign power.—*Military brush*, a hair brush without a handle.—*Military hospital*, a hospital for the treatment of sick and wounded soldiers.—*Military police*, that part of the army which performs police duty among soldiers.—**militate,** mil′i•tāt, *v.i.* [L. *milito, militatum*, to fight.] To stand opposed; to have weight or influence on the opposite side: said of arguments, considerations, etc., and followed by *against* (another fact *militated against* that theory).—**militia,** mi•lish′a, *n.* [L., military service, soldiery.] A body of men enrolled and trained as military reserves for the defense of a nation in time of war; the organized militia of the individual states is called the National Guard.—**militiaman,** *n.* One who belongs to the militia.

milk, milk, *n.* [A.Sax. *meolc, milc*, milk = D. Dan. and L.G. *melk*, Icel. *mjólk*, Sw. *mjölk*, Goth. *miluks*, G. *milch*, milk; also Rus. *moloko*, Pol. and Bohem. *mleko*, milk; root also in L. *mulgeo*, Gr. *amelgō*, to milk.] A whitish fluid secreted by the mammary glands of females of the class Mammalia, including the human species, and drawn from the breasts for the nourishment of their young; the white juice of certain plants; an emulsion of which juice expressed from seeds is one of the constituents (the *milk* of almonds).—*v.t.* To draw milk from the breasts or udder of by the hand (to *milk* a cow).—**milk-and-water,** *a.* Tasteless; insipid; characterless; wishy-washy (*Colloq.*).—**milker,** milk′ėr, *n.* One who or that which milks; a cow or other animal giving milk.—**milk fever,** *n.* A fever which sometimes accompanies the first secretion of milk in females after childbirth.—**milkiness,** milk′i•nes, *n.* State of being milky; qualities like those of milk.—**milk-livered,** *a.* Cowardly; timorous (*Shak.*).—**milkmaid,** milk′-mād, *n.* A woman that milks or is employed in the dairy.—**milkman,** milk′man, *n.* A man that sells milk or carries milk to market.—**milk of magnesia,** *n. Phar.* a solution of magnesium hydroxide, $Mg\ (OH)_2$ suspended in water, used as an antacid or a laxative.—**milk shake,** *n.* A foamy drink made of cold milk, flavoring and, usually, ice cream, shaken together.—**milksop,** *n.* An effeminate man.—**milk sugar,** *n.* Lactose.—**milk tooth,** *n.* One of the first teeth in the temporary set in young animals and children.—**milkweed,** *n.* Any plant of the family Asclepiadaceae, so named for its milky fluid, or latex.—**milky,** milk′i, *a.*—**Milky Way,** *n.* See GALAXY.

mill, mil, *n.* [L. *mille*, a thousand.]

A money of account of the United States, value the thousandth of a dollar, or one-tenth of a cent.

mill, mil, *n.* [O.E. *miln*, A.Sax. *mylen*, *myln*, from L. *molina*, a mill, from *mola*, a mill or millstone, from *molo*, to grind—root same as in *meal*, *mould*, etc.] A machine for grinding and reducing to fine particles grain, fruit, or other substance; applied also to many machines for grinding or polishing by circular motion, or to complicated machinery for working up raw material, etc.; the building where grinding or some process of manufacturing is carried on; *calico printing*, a copper printing cylinder; a pugilistic contest; a fight with the fists (*slang*).—*v.t.* To grind in a mill; to pass through a mill; to stamp in a coining press; especially to stamp so as to make a transversely grooved edge round; to throw, as silk; to full, as cloth.—**millboard,** *n.* A stout kind of pasteboard made in a paper mill.—**milldam,** *n.* A dam crossing a watercourse and raising the water to a height sufficient to turn a mill wheel; in Scotland, a millpond.—**milled,** mild, *p.* and *a.* Having undergone the operation of a mill; having the edge transversely grooved, as a dime or the head of a screw that is to be turned by the fingers; fulled, as cloth.—**miller,** mil′ėr, *n.* One who keeps or attends a mill, especially a flour mill.—**miller's-thumb,** *n.* A small fish found in streams, the bull head.—**millpond,** *n.* A pond or reservoir of water for driving a mill wheel.—**millrace,** *n.* The stream of water that drives a mill wheel, or the channel in which it runs.—**millstone,** mil′stōn, *n.* One of the stones for grinding the grain in a mill; stone or rock from which such stones are made.—*Millstone grit*, a siliceous conglomerate rock used for millstones, building, etc., forming one of the members of the carboniferous group of strata underlying the true coal measures.—*To see into or through a millstone*, to see with acuteness or to penetrate into abstruse subjects.—**mill wheel,** *n.* A wheel used to drive a mill; a water wheel.—**millwright,** *n.* A mechanic or wright whose occupation it is to construct the machinery of mills.

millenarian, mil•le•nâ′ri•an, *a.* [L. *millenarius*, containing a thousand, from *mille*, a thousand. MILE.] Consisting of a thousand; especially consisting of a thousand years; pertaining to the millennium.—*n.* One who believes in the millennium.—**millenary,** mil′le•ne•ri, *a.* Consisting of a thousand.—*Millenary Petition*, the petition presented by the Puritan and Conformist parties to James I in 1603, signed by a thousand ministers, complaining that they were overburdened with the human rites and ceremonies in the Prayer Book.—*n.* The space of a thousand years; a thousandth anniversary.—**millennial,** mil•len′i•al, *a.* Pertaining to the millennium, or to a thousand years.—**millennium,** mil•len′i•um, *n.* [L. *mille*, a thousand, and *annus*, year.] An aggregate of a thousand years; the thousand years mentioned in Rev. xx. 1-5, during which millenarians believe Christ will reign on earth with his saints.

millepede, millipede, mil′e•pēd, mil′i•pēd, *n.* [L. *mille*, a thousand, and *pes*, a foot.] A name common to worm-like articulated animals, from the number of their feet; a myriapod.

millepore, mil′le•pōr, *n.* [L. *mille*, a thousand, and *porus*, a pore.] One of the reef-building corals, so named from their numerous minute cells or pores.

millesimal, mil•les′i•mal, *a.* [L. *millesimus*, from *mille*, a thousand.] Thousandth.

millet, mil′et, *n.* [Fr. *millet*, dim. of *mil*, from L. *milium*, millet; from root meaning to grind as in *mill*.] A common name for various species of small grain cultivated largely in many parts of Europe, Asia, and Africa as food for men; various forage grasses; the seed of any of these grains and grasses.

milliard, mil•yärd, *n.* [Fr.] A thousand millions, usually called a *billion* in America.

milliary, mil′i•e•ri, *a.* [L. *milliarius*, from *mille*, a thousand.] Pertaining to the ancient Roman mile of a thousand paces or five thousand feet; denoting a mile.

millibar, mil′i•bär, *n.* [L. *mille*, thousand, and Gr. *baros*, weight.] *Meteor.* one thousand dynes per square centimeter, used in measuring atmospheric pressure.

milligram, mil′i•gram, *n.* [L. *mille*, thousand, and *gram*, a small weight.] The thousandth part of a gram; equal to a cubic millimeter of water.

milliliter, mil″i•lē′tėr, *n.* [Fr. *millilitre*—L. *mille*, thousand, and Fr. *litre*, an old measure.] A unit of capacity in the metric system equal to 1/1,000 liter.—**millimeter,** mil″i•mē′tėr, *n.* The thousandth part of a meter.—**millimicron,** mil″i•mī′kron, *n.* The millionth part of a millimeter, or thousandth part of a micron.

milliner, mil′i•nėr, *n.* [Supposed to be for *Milaner*, from *Milan*, in Italy, famous for its silks and ribbons.] A person, now usually a woman, who makes and sells hats for females.—**millinery,** mil′i•ner•i, *n.* The business or occupation of a milliner; the articles made or sold by milliners.

million, mil′yon, *n.* [Fr. *million*, from L. *mille*, a thousand. MILE.] The number of ten hundred thousand, or a thousand thousand; with the definite article, the great body of the people; the multitude; the public; the masses.—**millionaire, millionnaire,** mil′yon•âr, *n.* [Fr. *millionnaire*.] A man worth a million of money; a man of great wealth.—**millionth,** mil′yonth, *a.* Ten hundred thousandth; constituting one of a million.—*n.* One of a million parts; a ten hundred thousandth part.

milreis, mil′rās, *n.* [Pg. *mil*, a thousand, and *reis*, pl. of *real*, a small denomination of money.] A Brazilian money of account, written 1$000; an old Portuguese coin.

milt, milt, *n.* [A.Sax. *milte*, Dan. *milt*, Icel. *milti*, G. *milz*, the spleen; D. *milt*, the spleen, the milt of fishes; same root as *melt*.] The soft roe of fishes, or the spermatic organ of the males.—**milter,** milt′ėr, *n.* A male fish, or one having a milt.

mime, mīm, *n.* [L. *mimus*, from Gr. *mimos*, an actor, a mime.] A species of ancient dramatic entertainment in which gestures and mimicry predominated; an actor in such performances.—**mimesis,** mi•mē′sis, *n.* *Rhet.* imitation of the voice or gestures of another; *nat. hist.* same as *Mimicry*.—**mimetic,** mi•met′ik, *a.* Apt to imitate; given to aping or mimicry; *nat. hist.* characterized by mimicry.—**mimic,** mim′ik, *a.* Imitative; inclined to imitate or ape; imitating; consisting of or made in imitation (*mimic* gestures).—*n.* One who imitates or mimics; one who attempts to excite laughter or derision by acting or speaking in the manner of another.—*v.t.*—*mimicked*, *mimicking*. To imitate; to ridicule by imitation.—**mimicker,** mim′ik•ėr, *n.*—**mimicry,** mim′ik•ri, *n.* *Nat. hist.* the close resemblance presented by certain plants and animals to certain other plants or animals, or to the natural objects among which they live, this resemblance serving for protection.

mimeograph, mim″ē•ō•graf′, *n.* [From the former trademark.] A device capable of making many copies of typewritten material by means of a stencil.

mimosa, mi•mō′sa, *n.* [From Gr. *mimos*, a mimic, from their sensitive leaves.] A genus of plants, some of which are remarkable for the irritability of their leaves, hence their name *sensitive-plants*.

mina, mī′na, *n.* Among the Greeks, a weight of 100 drachmae; also, a piece of money valued at 100 drachmae.

minacious, mi•nā′shus, *a.* [L. *minax*, *minacis*, threatening, MENACE.] Threatening; menacing.—**minacity,**† mi•nas′i•ti, *n.* Disposition to threaten.

minaret, min′a•ret, *n.* [Fr. *minaret*, Sp. *minarete*, from Ar. *menâra*, a lighthouse, a minaret, from *nâr*, to shine.] A slender lofty turret rising by different stages or stories, surrounded by one or more projecting balconies, common in mosques in Mohammedan countries, and used for summoning the people to prayers.

minatory, min′a•to•ri, *a.* [L. *minatorius*, from *minator*, a threatener, *mina*, a threat. MENACE.] Threatening; menacing.—**minatorily,** min′a•to•ri•li, *adv.* In a minatory manner.

mince, mins, *v.t.*—*minced*, *mincing*. [A.Sax. *minsian*, from *min*, small; also O.Fr. *mincer*, from *mince*, fine, small; root same as that of *minor*, *minister*.] To cut or chop into very small pieces (to *mince* meat); to diminish in speaking; to extenuate; to palliate (to *mince* the matter, to *mince* matters); to pronounce with affected elegance.—*v.i.* To walk with short steps; to affect delicacy in manner; to speak with affected elegance.—**mincemeat,** *n.* Meat chopped fine; chopped mixture of raisins, apples, other fruit, spices, suet, etc.—**mince pie,** *n.* A pie made of mincemeat.—**mincer,** mins′-ėr, *n.* One who minces; a detractor.—**mincing,** mins′ing, *p.* and *a.* Speaking or walking affectedly.—**mincingly,** mins′ing•li, *adv.* With a mincing manner.

mind, mīnd, *n.* [A.Sax. *mynd, gemynd,* mind, thought, intention; Dan. *minde,* Icel. *minni,* memory; from root *man,* to think, seen also in *mean,* to intend; L. *mens, mentis,* mind (whence *mental*); Gr. *menos,* mind. MAN, MEAN.] The intellectual power in man; the understanding (not in one's right *mind*); cast of thought and feeling; opinion (of the same *mind*); intention; purpose; memory; remembrance (to call to *mind,* to keep in *mind*).—*To be in two minds* about a thing, to be in doubt.—*v.t.* To attend to; to fix the thoughts on; to heed; to notice; to pay attention to; to attend with submission; to obey.—**minder,** mīn′-dėr, *n.* One who minds.—**mindful,** mīnd′fu̧l, *a.* Attentive; bearing in mind; heedful.—**mindfully,** mīnd′-fu̧l•li, *adv.*—**mindfulness,** mīnd′fu̧l•-nes, *n.*—**mindless,** mīnd′les, *a.* Destitute of mind; inattentive; heedless.—**mind reader,** *n.* One who discerns the thoughts of others without the customary means of communication.

mine, mīn, *pronominal adjective.* [A.Sax. *mín,* genit. or adj. corresponding to *me*=Dan. and Sw. *min,* Icel. *minn,* Goth. *meina,* D. *mijn,* G. *mein. My* is a shortened form. Comp. *thy, thine.*] My; belonging to me: once regularly used before nouns beginning with a vowel, now generally used similarly to *thine, hers, ours, yours, theirs,* as equivalent to *my* followed by a noun, and serving either for a nominative or an objective.

mine, mīn, *n.* [Fr. *mine,* a mine, *miner,* to form a mine. Of Celtic origin. Comp. Ir. *meinn,* mine, ore, vein of metal, *mianach,* abounding in ore, W. *Mwn,* mine.] A pit or excavation in the earth, from which coal, metallic ores, or other mineral substances are taken by digging; a contrivance floating on, or near, the surface of the sea to destroy ships by explosion; *milit.* an underground gallery or passage dug under a fortification, in which a quantity of powder or other explosive may be lodged for blowing up the works; *fig.* a rich source or store of wealth or anything highly valued.—*v.i.*—*mined, mining.* To dig a mine; to burrow.—*v.t.* To dig away the foundation from; to undermine; to sap.—**mine sweeping,** *n.* The 'sweeping' of the sea to clear an area of hostile mines.—**mining,** mīn′ing, *p.* and *a.* Of burrowing habits; insidious.—**miner,** mīn′ėr *n.* One who mines; one who digs or works in a mine for metals or other minerals.

mineral, min′ėr•al, *n.* [Fr. *minéral,* from *miner,* to mine. MINE.] Any ingredient in the earth's crust; an inorganic body with a definite chemical composition, and which naturally exists within the earth or at its surface.—*a.* Pertaining to minerals; consisting of minerals; impregnated with minerals or mineral matter (*mineral* waters).—*Mineral acids,* a name given to sulfuric, nitric, and hydrochloric acids.—*Mineral caoutchouc,* a variety of bitumen, much resembling India rubber in its softness and elasticity.—*Mineral charcoal,* a fibrous variety of non-bituminous mineral coal.—*Mineral green,* carbonate of copper.—*Mineral kingdom,* that grand division of natural objects which includes all minerals, and of which mineralogy is the science.—*Mineral oil.* PETROLEUM.—*Mineral pitch,* a solid softish bitumen.—*Mineral tar,* bitumen of a tarry consistence.—*Mineral waters,* a term applied to certain waters, either naturally or artificially impregnated with gases, carbonates, sulfates, iron, etc.—*Mineral wax,* ozocerite.—**mineralization,** min′ėr•-al•i•zā″shon, *n.* The act or process of mineralizing; the process of being converted into a mineral.—**mineralize,** min′ėr•al•īz, *v.t.*—*mineralized, mineralizing.* To convert into a mineral; to impregnate with mineral substance.—**mineralizer,** min′-ėr•al•īz•ėr, *n.* A substance or agent that mineralizes.—**mineralogy,** min-ėr•al′o•ji, *n.* The science which treats of the properties of mineral substances, and teaches us to characterize, distinguish, and classify them according to their properties.—**mineralogical,** min′ėr•a•loj″i•kal, *a.* Pertaining to mineralogy.—**mineralogically,** min′ėr•a•loj″i•kal•li, *adv.* According to the principles of mineralogy.—**mineralogist,** min•ėr•al′o•-jist, *n.*

Minerva, mi•nėr′va, *n.* [L., from root of *mens,* mind. MIND, MENTAL.] One of the chief divinities of the Romans, the goddess of wisdom, of war, and of the liberal arts.

minestrone, min•e•strō′nē, *n.* [From It. *minestra,* soup, from *minestrare,* from L. *ministrāre.*] A thick soup made from meat broth, containing vegetables, herbs, etc.

mingle, ming′gl, *v.t.*—*mingled, mingling.* [From A.Sax. *mengan,* to mix, with freq. term. *-le*; D. *mengen,* G. *mengen,* to mingle.] To mix up together so as to form one whole; to blend; to join in mutual intercourse or in society; to debase by mixture.—*v.i.* To become mixed; to become united in the same whole; to join (to *mingle with* or *in* a crowd).—**mingler,** ming′glėr, *n.* One that mingles.

miniature, min′ye•chėr, *n.* [It. *miniatura,* originally a design such as drawn on the margins of old manuscripts, from *miniare,* to write with *minium* or red lead, this pigment being much used in the ornamenting of old manuscripts.] A painting of very small dimensions, usually executed in watercolors, on ivory, vellum, etc.; anything represented on a greatly reduced scale; a small scale (shown in *miniature*).—*a.* On a small scale.

minify, min′i•fī, *v.t.* [L. *minus,* less, and *facio,* to make.] To make little or less; opposite of magnify; to lessen; to diminish; to slight; to depreciate.

minikin,† min′i•kin, *n.* [O.D. *minneken,* darling, from *minne,* love; akin *minion.*] A darling; a favorite.—*a.* Small; diminutive.

minim, min′im, *n.* [Fr. *minime,* L. *minimus,* least, superlative corresponding to *minor,* small. MINOR.] A note in music, equal in time to half a semibreve or two crotchets; the smallest liquid measure, generally regarded as about equal to one drop, the fluid drachm being divided into sixty minims.—**minimum,** min′i•mum, *n.* [L.] The smallest amount or degree; least quantity assignable in a given case: opposed to *maximum.*—**minimize,** min′i•mīz, *v.t.* To reduce to a minimum.

minion, min′yon, *n.* [Fr. *mignon,* a darling, from O.G. *minne,* love.] An unworthy favorite; a servile dependent.

miniskirt, min′i•skėrt, *n.* [*Miniature* and *skirt.*] A woman's skirt of abbreviated length, usually several inches above the knee.

minister, min′is•tėr, *n.* [L. *minister,* from stem of *minor, minus,* less.] One who acts under the authority of another; a servant; an attendant; one authorized to conduct Christian worship, as a priest or clergyman; one to whom the executive head of a government entrusts the direction of affairs of state; one engaged in the administration of government.—*v.t.* To give; to supply.—*v.i.* To act as a minister or attendant; to perform service; to afford supplies; to give things needful; to supply the means of relief; to furnish (to *minister to* one's necessities).—**ministerial,** min•is•tē′ri•al, *a.* Pertaining to ministry or the performance of service; pertaining to a ministry or to ministers of state; pertaining to ministers of the gospel.—**ministerialist,** min•is•tē′ri•al•ist, *n. Politics,* a supporter of the ministry in office.—**ministerially,** min•is•tē′ri•al•li, *adv.* In a ministerial manner or character.—**ministrant,** min′is•trant, *a.* [L. *ministrans, ministrantis.*] Performing service; acting as minister or attendant; attendant on service.—**ministration,** min•is•trā′shon, *n.* [L. *ministratio.*] The act of ministering or performing service; service or attendance given; ecclesiastical function.—**ministrative,** min′is•trā•tiv, *a.* Affording service; assisting.—**ministry,** min′is•tri, *n.* [L. *ministerium.*] The act of ministering; service; aid; instrumentality; the office or functions of a minister of the gospel; the body of ministers of state or the chief officials of the executive government; duration of the office of a minister, civil or ecclesiastical.

minium, min′i•um, *n.* [L. Hence *miniature.*] Red oxide of lead; red lead.

miniver, min′i•vėr, *n.* [O.Fr. *menuveir, menuvair,* a grayish fur—*menu* [L. *minutus*), small, and *vair,* fur.] The fur of the Siberian squirrel; a fine white fur.

mink, mingk, *n.* An American and European quadruped, allied to the polecat and weasel, yielding a fur of some value.

minnesinger, min′ne•sing•ėr, *n.* [O. G. *minne,* love (MINION), and *singer,* a singer.] One of a class of German lyric poets of the twelfth and thirteenth centuries, so called from love being their chief theme.

minnow, min′ō, *n.* [A.Sax. *myne,* a minnow.] Any of various small fishes of the carp family; loosely, any of several other small fishes.

Minoan, mi•nō′an, *a.* [L. *Minous,* from Gr. *Minōs,* a King of Crete.] Pertaining to the ancient, advanced culture of Crete, existing about 3000 B.C. to 1100 B.C.

minor, mī′nor, *a.* [L. *minor,* smaller (without a positive), from a root *min,* small, seen also in A.Sax. *min,* small; Dan., Sw., *mindre,* Icel. *minni,* G. *minder,* less; Ir. and Gael. *min,* small, fine. Akin *minute, minister, minish,* etc.] Lesser; smaller; used relatively, and opposed to *major;* absolutely small; petty; *music,* less by a lesser semitone, as applied to an interval; having a tone and semitone between the keynote and its third: applied to a scale.—*Minor term, logic,* the subject of the conclusion of a categorical syllogism.—*Minor premise,* that which contains the minor term.—*n.* A person of either sex under full age (not yet twenty-one years); one under the authority of his parents or guardians; *logic,* the minor term or premise; *music,* the minor key.—**Minorite,** mī′nor•īt, *n.* A Franciscan friar.—**minority,** mi•nor′i•ti, *n.* [Fr. *minorité.*] The state of being a minor or not yet come of age; the period or interval before one is of full age, generally the period from birth until twenty-one years of age; the smaller number out of a whole divided into two: opposed to *majority;* a race, religion or political group that is subject to a larger controlling group.

Minotaur, min′o•taur, *n.* [Gr.] Mythical monster, reputed half man, half bull, offspring of Pasiphaë, wife of Minos, the ancient King of Crete, and connected with the legend of Theseus.

minster, min′stėr, *n.* [A.Sax. *mynster,* (like G. *münster,* D. *monster*), from L. *monasterium,* a monastery. MONASTERY.] Originally, a monastery; afterward the church of a monastery; latterly, a cathedral church.

minstrel, min′strel, *n.* [O.Fr. *menestrel,* from L.L. *ministrellus,* a harper, one who ministered to the amusement of the rich by music or jesting; a dim. from L. *minister,* a servant.] A singer or musical performer; in the Middle Ages, one of a class of men who subsisted by the arts of poetry and music.—**minstrel show,** a performance of jokes, melodies, etc., given by comedians usually made up as Negroes.—**minstrelsy,** min′strel•si, *n.* A group of minstrels; the art or occupation of minstrels; music; a body of songs or ballads.

mint, mint, *n.* [A.Sax. *mynet,* from L. *moneta,* the mint, money, from *Moneta,* a surname of *Juno,* in whose temple at Rome money was coined, from *moneo,* to remind (whence *monition, monitor*).] The place where money is coined by public authority; a great supply or store that may be drawn on (a *mint* of reasons).—*v.t.* To coin; to make and stamp into money; to invent; to fabricate.—**mintage,** mint′ij, *n.* That which is coined or stamped; the duty paid for coining.—**minter,** mint′ėr, *n.* A coiner.

mint, mint, *n.* [A.Sax. *minte,* from L. *mentha,* Gr. *mintha, minthē,* mint.] The name of several herbaceous aromatic plants which partake largely of the tonic properties found in all labiate plants; a mint-flavored confection. *Spearmint* and *peppermint* are the popular names of two well-known species.—**mint julep,** *n.* A drink made of whisky, usually Bourbon, with sugar, cracked ice, and mint leaves.

minuend, min′ū•end, *n.* [L. *minuendus,* to be lessened, *minuo,* to lessen. MINOR.] *Arith.* the number from which another number is to be subtracted.

minuet, min′ū•et, *n.* [Fr. *menuet,* from *menu,* small, from L. *minutus,* minute—on account of the small steps of the dance.] A slow graceful dance and the tune or air for it.

minus, mī′nus, *a.* [Neut. of L. *minor,* less. MINOR.] Involving subtraction, as the *minus* sign; not positive, as a *minus* quality.—*prep.* Decreased by the subtraction of (five *minus* three).

minuscule, mi•nus′kūl, *a.* [L. *minusculus,* small, minute.] Very small.

minute, mi•nūt,′ *a.* [L. *minutus,* pp. of *minuo,* to lessen, from root *min,* small. MINOR.] Very small; characterized by attention to small things or details; precise; attentive to the smallest particulars.—**minutely,** mi•nūt′li, *adv.* With minuteness; exactly; nicely.—**minuteness,** mi•nūt′nes, *n.* Extreme smallness; critical exactness.

minute, min′it, *n.* [Fr. *minute,* from L. *minuta,* a minute portion. MINUTE, *a.*] A small portion of time, strictly the sixtieth part of an hour; sixty seconds; *geom.* the sixtieth part of a degree of a circle; *arch.* the sixtieth part of the diameter of a column at the base; a short sketch of any agreement or other subject, taken in writing; a note to preserve the memory of anything.—*v.t.*—*minuted, minuting.* To set down in a short sketch or note.—**minutely,** min′it•li, *adv.* Every minute; with very little time intervening.—**minutebook,** *n.* A book in which minutes are recorded.—**minute gun,** *n.* A gun discharged at intervals of a minute as a signal from a vessel in distress.—**minute hand,** *n.* The hand that points to the minutes on a clock or watch.

minutia, mi•nū′shi•a, *n.*; generally in pl.—**minutiae,** mi•nū′shi•ē. [L. from *minutus,* small. MINUTE, *a.*] Small, minor, or unimportant particulars or details.

minx, mingks, *n.* [Perhaps a sort of abbrev. form of *minikin.*] A pert, wanton girl; a hussy; a she-puppy.

Miocene, mī′o•sēn, *a.* [Gr. *meiōn,* less, and *kainos,* recent.] *Geol.* the name given to the middle subdivision of the tertiary strata, being applied to those strata which overlie the Ocene and are below the Pliocene.—*n. Geol.* the Miocene strata.

miracle, mir′a•kl, *n.* [Fr. *miracle,* from L. *miraculum,* something wonderful, from *miror,* to wonder; akin *marvel, mirror, mirage, admire,* etc.] A wonder or wonderful thing; something that excites astonishment; a sensible deviation from the known laws of nature, held to be wrought by a supernatural being; a supernatural event.—*To a miracle,* wonderfully; astonishingly.—**miracle play,** *n.* Formerly a dramatic representation exhibiting the lives of the saints, or other sacred subjects.—**miraculous,** mi•rak′ū•lus, *a.* Of the nature of a miracle; effected by the direct agency of almighty power; exceedingly surprising or wonderful.—**miraculously,** mi•rak′ū•lus•li, *adv.* In a miraculous manner; by miracle; supernaturally; wonderfully.—**miraculousness,** mi•rak′ū•lus•nes, *n.*

mirage, mi•räzh′, *n.* [Fr., from *mirer,* to look; *se mirer,* to be reflected. MIRACLE, MIRROR.] The name given to a natural optical illusion, consisting in an apparent elevation or approximation of coasts, mountains, ships, etc., accompanied by inverted images; in deserts often causing a plain to assume the appearance of a lake.

mire, mīr, *n.* [Same as Icel. *mýrr, mýri,* Sw. *myra,* N. *myre,* a swamp, fen; same root as *moor, marsh.*] Wet, clayey soil; mud.—*v.t.*—*mired, miring.* To fix or sink in mire (as a carriage); to soil or daub with mud.—*v.i.* To sink in mud, so as to be unable to advance.—**miry,** mī′ri, *a.* Full of or covered with mire or mud.

mirror, mir′ėr, *n.* [Fr. *miroir,* a mirror, from *mirer,* to look at, from L. *miror,* to admire. MIRACLE.] A looking glass; any polished substance that forms images by the reflection of rays of light; a pattern; an exemplar.—*v.t.* To furnish with mirrors; to reflect as in a mirror.

mirth, mėrth, *n.* [A.Sax. *myrgth, mirhth,* etc., from *mirig, merg,* merry. MERRY.] The feeling of being merry; merriment; noisy gaiety; glee; hilarity.—**mirthful,** mėrth′fu̧l, *a.* Merry; jovial; causing or provoking mirth.—**mirthfully,** mėrth′fu̧l•li, *adv.* In a mirthful manner.—**mirthfulness,** mėrth′fu̧l•nes, *n.* Mirth; merriment. —**mirthless,** mėrth′les, *a.* Without mirth; joyless.

mirza, mėr′za, *n.* [Persian, for *emirzadeh,* son of the prince—*emir,* prince, and *zadeh,* son.] A common title of honor in Persia.

misadventure, mis•ad•ven′chėr, *n.* A mischance; ill luck; an unlucky accident.

misadvise, mis•ad•vīz′, *v.t.* To give bad advice to.

misalliance, mis•al•lī′ans, *n.* [MESALLIANCE.] Any improper alliance or association; specifically, an improper connection by marriage.

misanthrope, misanthropist, mis′-an•thrōp, mis•an′thrōp•ist, *n.* [Gr. *misanthrōpos—miseō,* to hate, and *anthrōpos,* man.] A hater of mankind. —**misanthropic, misanthropical,** mis•an•throp′ik, mis•an•throp′i•kal, *a.*—**misanthropy,** mis•an′thro•pi, *n.* Hatred or dislike of mankind.

misapply, mis•ap•plī′, *v.t.* To apply to a wrong purpose.—**misapplication,** mis•ap′pli•kā″shon, *n.* The act of misapplying.

misapprehend, mis•ap′pri•hend″, *v.t.* To misunderstand; to take in a wrong sense.—**misapprehension,** mis•ap′pri•hen″shon, *n.* A mistaking; wrong apprehension of one's meaning or of a fact.

misappropriate, mis•ap•prō′pri•āt, *v.t.* To appropriate wrongly; to put to a wrong purpose.—**misappropriation,** mis•ap•prō′pri•ā″shon, *n.* Wrong appropriation.

misarrange, mis•a•rānj′, *v.t.* To arrange in a wrong order.—**misarrangement,** mis•a•rānj′ment; *n.* Disorderly arrangement.

misbecome, mis•bi•kum′, *v.t.*—pret. *misbecame,* ppr. *misbecoming,* pp. *misbecome* or *misbecomed.* Not to become; to suit ill; not to befit.—**misbecoming,** mis•bi•kum′ing, *p.* and *a.* Unbecoming; unseemly.

misbegot, misbegotten, mis•bi•got′, mis•bi•got′n, *p.* and *a.* Unlawfully or irregularly begotten; used also as a general epithet of opprobrium.

misbehave, mis•bi•hāv′, *v.i.* To behave ill; to conduct one's self improperly; often used with the reflexive pronouns.—**misbehavior,** mis•bi•hāv′yėr, *n.* Improper, rude, or uncivil behavior.

misbelief, mis•bi•lēf′, *n.* Erroneous belief; false religion; unbelief.—**misbeliever,** mis•bi•lē′vėr, *n.* One who holds a false religion.

miscalculate, mis•kal′kū•lāt, *v.t.* To calculate erroneously; to make a wrong guess or estimate of.—**miscalculation,** mis•kal′kū•lā″shon, *n.* Erroneous calculation or estimate.

miscall, mis•ka̧l′, *v.t.* To call by a wrong name; to name improperly; to give a bad name or character to†.

miscarriage, mis•kar′ij, *n.* Unfortunate issue or result of an undertaking; *med.* expulsion of the human fetus prematurely, before it is capable of living outside the womb; abortion.—**miscarry,** mis•kar′i, *v.i.* To fail of the intended effect; to bring forth young before the proper time.

miscast, mis•cast′, *v.t.* [From prefix *mis,* and *cast.*] To place in an unsuitable role.

miscegenation, mis′si•je•nā″shon, *n.* [L. *misceo,* to mix, and *genus,* a race.] Mixture or amalgamation of races.

miscellaneous, mis•sel•lā′ni•us, *a.* [L. *miscellaneus,* from *misceo,* to mix. MEDDLE.] Consisting of several kinds or things mingled; diversified.—**miscellaneously,** mis•sel•lā′ni•us•li, *adv.*—**miscellaneousness,** mis•sel•lā′-ni•us•nes, *n.*—**miscellanist,** mis•sel′-la•nist, *n.*—**miscellany,** mis′sel•a•ni, *n.* A mixture of various kinds; a collection of written compositions on various subjects.

mischance, mis•chans′, *n.* Ill luck; misfortune; mishap; misadventure.

mischief, mis′chif, *n.* [O.Fr. *meschief, meschef,* mischief; from Fr. *mes,* Sp. and Pg. *menos*=L. *minus,* less, and *chef*=L. *caput,* the head. MINOR, CHIEF.] Harm; hurt; injury; damage; evil, whether intended or not; source of vexation, trouble, or annoyance; troublesome or annoying conduct; conduct causing injury; wrong-doing.—**mischief-maker,** *n.* One who makes mischief; one who excites or instigates quarrels or enmity.—**mischief-making,** *a.* Causing harm; exciting enmity or quarrels.—**mischievous,** mis′chi•vus, *a.* Harmful; injurious; fond of mischief; annoying or troublesome in conduct.—**mischievously,** mis′chi•-vus•li, *adv.* In a mischievous manner. —**mischievousness,** mis′chi•vus•-nes, *n.* The quality of being mischievous.

miscible, mis′i•bl, *a.* [Fr. *miscible,* from L. *misceo,* to mix. MEDDLE.] Capable of being mixed.—**miscibility,** mis•i•bil′i•ti, *n.* State of being miscible.

misconceive, mis•kon•sēv′, *v.t.* or *i.* To receive a false notion or opinion of anything; to misjudge; to have an erroneous understanding of anything.—**misconceiver,** mis•kon•sē′-vėr, *n.* One who misconceives.—**misconception,** mis•kon•sep′shon, *n.* Erroneous conception; false opinion; wrong notion or understanding of a thing.

misconduct, mis•kon′dukt, *n.* Wrong or bad conduct; misbehavior.—*v.t.* (mis-kon-dukt′). To conduct amiss; *refl.* to misbehave.

misconstrue, mis•kon′strö, *v.t.* To construe or interpret erroneously; to take in a wrong sense; to misjudge; to misunderstand.—**misconstruction,** mis•kon•struk′shon, *n.* The act of misconstruing.

miscount, mis•kount′, *v.t.* To count erroneously; to misjudge.—*v.i.* To make a wrong reckoning.—*n.* An erroneous counting or numbering.

miscreant, mis′kri•ant, *n.* [O.Fr. *mescreant—mes,* prefix, from L. *minus,* less, and *creant,* believing, from L. *credo,* to believe. MINOR, CREED.] An infidel, or one who embraces a false faith‡; a vile wretch; a scoundrel; a detestable villain.

miscredit, mis•kred′it, *v.t.* To give no credit or belief to; to disbelieve. (*Carl.*)

miscue, mis•kū′, *v.i.* [From prefix *mis,* and *cue.*] *Dram.* to make a mistake on stage because of a missed signal; to miss one's cue.—*n. Billiards,* a stroke in which the cue fails to hit the ball; a slip; a mistake. (Slang)

misdate, mis•dāt′, *v.t.* To date erroneously.

misdeal, mis•dēl′, *n. Card playing,* a wrong deal; a deal in which each player does not receive his proper cards.—*v.t.* or *i.* To divide cards wrongly or unfairly.

misdeed, mis•dēd′, *n.* An evil deed; a wicked action.

misdeem, mis•dēm′, *v.t.* To judge erroneously; to misjudge; to mistake in judging.

misdemean, mis•di•mēn′, *v.t.* To behave ill; used *refl.*—**misdemeanant,** mis•di•mē′nant, *n.* One who commits a misdemeanor.—**misdemeanor,** mis•di•mē′nėr, *n.* Ill behavior; evil conduct; a fault or transgression; *law,* an offense of a less atrocious nature than a crime.

misdirect, mis•di•rekt′, *v.t.* To give a wrong direction to; to direct into a wrong course; to direct to a wrong person or place.—**misdirection,** mis•di•rek′shon, *n.* A wrong direction.

misdo, mis•dö′, *v.t.* or *i.* To do wrong; to do amiss; to commit a crime or fault.—**misdoer,** mis•dö′ėr, *n.* One who does wrong; one who commits a fault or crime.—**misdoing,** mis•dö′ing, *n.* A wrong done; a fault or crime; an offense.

misdoubt, mis•dout′, *n.* Suspicion of crime or danger.—*v.t.* To suspect of deceit or danger.

misemploy, mis•em•ploi′, *v.t.* To employ to no purpose, or to a bad purpose.

miser, mī′zėr, *n.* [L. *miser,* wretched, akin to *mæstus,* sorrowful, and Gr. *misos,* hatred.] One wretched or afflicted (*Shak.*)‡; a sordid wretch; a niggard; one who in wealth makes himself miserable by the fear of poverty.—**miserly,** mī′zėr•li, *a.* Like a miser in habits; pertaining to a miser; penurious; sordid; niggardly.

miserable, miz′ėr•a•bl, *a.* [Fr. *misérable,* L. *miserabilis,* from *miser,* wretched. MISER.] Very unhappy; suffering misery; wretched; filled with misery; abounding in misery; causing misery; very poor or mean; worthless; despicable.—**miserableness,** miz′ėr•a•bl•nes, *n.* The state or quality of being miserable.—**miserably,** miz′ėr•a•bli, *adv.* In a miserable manner.—**Miserere,** miz•-e•re′re, *n.* The name given to the 50th Psalm in the Vulgate, corresponding to the 51st Psalm in the English version, beginning '*Miserere* mei, Domine' ('Pity me, O Lord'); a piece of music composed to this psalm.—**misery,** miz′ėr•i, *n.* [L. *miseria,* from *miser,* wretched.] Great unhappiness; extreme distress;

wretchedness; calamity; misfortune; cause of misery.

misfeasance, mis•fē′zans, *n.* [Fr. *mes*, wrong (L. *minus*), and *faisance*, from *faire*, to do.] *Law*, a trespass; a wrong done.

misfit, mis•fit′, *n.* A wrong or bad fit; a bad match,—*v.t.* To make (a garment, etc.) of a wrong size; to supply with something that does not fit, or is not suitable.

misform, mis•form′, *v.t.* To make of an ill form.—**misformation,** mis•for•mā′shon, *n.* An irregularity of formation.

misfortune, mis•for′chun, *n.* Ill fortune; ill luck; calamity; some accident that prejudicially affects one's condition in life.

misgive, mis•giv′, *v.t.* To fill with doubt; to deprive of confidence; to fail; usually with 'heart' or 'mind', etc., as subject, and a pronoun as object.—**misgiving,** mis•giv′ing, *n.* A failing of confidence; doubt; distrust.

misgovern, mis•guv′ėrn, *v.t.* To govern ill; to administer unfaithfully.—**misgovernment,** mis•guv′ėrn•ment, *n.* The act of misgoverning; bad administration or management of public or private affairs; irregularity in conduct.

misguide, mis•gīd′, *v.t.* To lead or guide into error; to direct ill; to direct to a wrong purpose or end.—**misguidance,** mis•gī′dans, *n.* Wrong direction; guidance into error.

mishap, mis•hap′, *n.* Mischance; evil accident; ill luck; misfortune.

Mishna, mish′na, *n.* [Heb. *shanah*, to repeat.] The collection of precepts that constitute the basis of the Talmud.

misinform, mis•in•form′, *v.t.* To give erroneous information to; to communicate an incorrect statement of facts to.—**misinformation,** mis′in•for•mā″shon, *n.* Wrong information.

misinterpret, mis•in•tėr′pret , *v.t.* To interpret erroneously; to understand or explain in a wrong sense.—**misinterpretation,** mis•in•tėr′pre•tā″shon, *n.* The act of interpreting erroneously.

misjudge, mis•juj′, *v.t.* To mistake in judging of; to judge erroneously.—*v.i.* To err in judgment; to form false opinions or notions.—**misjudgment,** mis•juj′ment, *n.* A wrong or unjust determination.

mislay, mis•lā′, *v.t.* To lay in a wrong place; to lay wrongly; to lay in a place not recollected.

mislead, mis•lēd′, *v.t.* To lead astray; to guide into error; to deceive.—**misleading,** mis•lēd′ing, *p.* and *a.* Leading astray; leading into error; causing mistake.

mislike, mis•līk′, *v.t.* To dislike; to disapprove; to have aversion to.

mismanage, mis•man′ij, *v.t.* To manage ill; to administer improperly.—**mismanagement,** mis•man′ij•ment, *n.* Ill or improper management.

mismate, mis•māt′, *v.t.* To mate or match amiss or unsuitably. [*Tenn.*]

misname, mis•nām′, *v.t.* To call by the wrong name.

misnomer, mis•nō′mėr, *n.* [Prefix *mis*, from Fr. prefix *mes*, wrong (L. *minus*, less), and *nommer*, to name, *nom*, L. *nomen*, a name.] A mistaken or inapplicable name or designation; a misapplied term.

misogamist, mi•sog′am•ist, *n.* [Gr. *miseō*, to hate, and *gamos*, marriage.] A hater of marriage.—**misogamy,** mi•sog′a•mi, *n.* Hatred of marriage.

misogynist, mi•soj′i•nist, *n.* [Gr. *miseō*, to hate, and *gynē*, woman.] A woman-hater.—**misogyny,** mi•soj′i•ni, *n.* Hatred of the female sex.

mispickel, mis′pik•el, *n.* [G.] Arsenical pyrites; an ore of arsenic, containing this metal in combination with iron.

misplace, mis•plās′, *v.t.* To put in a wrong place; to set on an improper object.—**misplacement,** mis•plās′ment, *n.* The act of misplacing or putting in the wrong place.

misprint, mis•print′, *v.t.* To mistake in printing; to print wrong.—*n.* A mistake in printing; a deviation from the copy.

misprision, mis•prizh′on, *n.* [From Fr. prefix *mes* (=L. *minus*, less), and L. *prehensio*, a taking, from *prehendo*, to take.] Mistake; misconception; *law*, any high offense under the degree of capital, but nearly bordering thereon.—*Misprision of treason*, a bare knowledge and concealment of treason, without assenting to it.

misprize, misprise, mis•prīz′, *v.t.* [O.Fr. *mespriser* (Fr. *mépriser*), to despise—prefix *mes*, *mis*=L. *minus*, less, and *priser*=L. *pretiare*, to prize, from *pretium*, price. PRICE.] To slight or undervalue.

mispronounce, mis•pro•nouns′, *v.t.* or *i.* To pronounce erroneously.—**mispronunciation,** mis•pro•nun′si•ā″shon, *n.* A wrong or improper pronunciation.

misproportion, mis•pro•pōr′shon, *v. t.* To err in proportioning one thing to another; to join without due proportion.

misquote, mis•kwōt′, *v.t.* or *i.* To quote erroneously; to cite incorrectly.—**misquotation,** mis•kwō•tā′shon, *n.* An erroneous quotation; the act of quoting wrong.

misread, mis•rēd′, *v.t.* To read amiss; to mistake the sense of.

misreckon, mis•rek′n, *v.t.* To reckon or compute wrong.

misreport, mis•ri•pōrt′, *v.t.* To report erroneously; to give an incorrect account of.—*n.* An erroneous report; a false or incorrect account given.

misrepresent, mis•rep′ri•zent″, *v.t.* To represent falsely or incorrectly; to give a false or erroneous representation of.—**misrepresentation,** mis•rep′ri•zen•tā″shon, *n.* The act of misrepresenting; a false or incorrect representation.

misrule, mis•röl′, *n.* Bad rule; disorder; confusion.—*v.t.* To rule amiss; to govern badly or oppressively.

miss, mis, *n.* [Contr. from *mistress.*] An unmarried female; a young unmarried lady; a girl; a title or address prefixed to the name of an unmarried female; a kept mistress; a concubine.

miss, mis, *v.t.* [A.Sax. *missan*, to miss=D. and G. *missen*, Icel. *missa*, Dan. *miste*, to miss; closely akin to Teut. prefix *mis*; same root as A.Sax. *mīthan*, to conceal, avoid; G. *meiden*, to avoid.] To fail in hitting, reaching, obtaining, finding, seeing, and the like; to discover the absence of, to feel or perceive the want of; to mourn the loss of; to omit; to let slip; to pass over.—*v.i.* To fail to hit or strike what is aimed at.—*n.* A failure to hit, reach, obtain, etc.; loss; want.—**missing link,** *n.* A unit or part needed to complete a series; a hypothetical form of animal connecting the anthropoid apes with man.

missal, mis′al, *n.* [L.L. *missale*, *liber missalis*, from *missa*, the mass. MASS.] The Roman Catholic mass-book or book containing the office of the mass.

missel, missel thrush, mis′el, *n.* [From its feeding on the *mistletoe*; comp. G. *mistel-drossel*, mistletoe thrush.] A common British thrush rather larger than the common thrush.

misshape, mis•shāp′, *v.t.* To shape ill; to give an ill form to; to deform.—**misshapen,** mis•shā′pn, *a.* Ill formed; deformed; malformed; distorted.

missile, mis′il, *a.* [L. *missilis*, from *mitto*, *missum*, to send, to throw. MISSION.] Capable of being thrown or projected from the hand or from any instrument or engine.—*n.* A weapon or projectile thrown or to be thrown; an unmanned, self-propelled projectile, as a rocket.—**missileman,** *n.* One who helps to design, build, or operate a guided missile.—**missilery, missilry,** mis′il•rē, *n.* The science of designing, launching, and controlling guided missiles.

mission, mish′on, *n.* [L. *missio*, a sending, from *mitto*, *missum*, to send, which enters into a great many English words; as *admit*, *commit*, *permit*, *remit*, *dismiss*, *remiss*, *promise*, *message*, *mess*, etc.] A sending or delegating; duty on which one is sent; a commission; an errand; persons sent by authority to perform any service; particularly, persons sent on some political business or to propagate religion; a station of missionaries; the persons connected with such a station.—**missionary,** mish′on•e•ri, *n.* One who is sent upon a religious mission; one who is sent to propagate religion.—*a.* Pertaining to missions.

missive, mis′iv, *n.* [Fr. *missive*, a letter, from L. *missus*, sent. MISSION.] That which is sent; a message; a letter sent.—*a.* Sent or proceeding from some authoritative or official source; intended to be thrown, hurled, or ejected; missile.

misspell, mis•spel′, *v.t.* To spell wrong.

misspend, mis•spend′, *v.t.* To spend amiss, to no purpose, or to a bad one; to waste; to spend for wrong uses.

misstate, mis•stāt′, *v.t.* To state wrongly; to make an erroneous statement of.

mist, mist, *n.* [A.Sax. *mist*, gloom, cloud = L.G., D., and Sw. *mist*, Icel. *mistr*, mist; akin G. *mist*, dung; from root seen in Skr. *mih*, to sprinkle.] Visible watery vapor suspended in the atmosphere at or near the surface of the earth; aqueous vapor falling in numerous but separately almost imperceptible drops; cloudy matter; something which dims or darkens, and obscures or intercepts vision.—*v.t.* To cover with mist; to cloud. (*Shak.*)—*v.i.* To be misty or drizzling.—**mistily,** mis′ti•li, *adv.* In a vague or misty manner; obscurely.—**mistiness,** mis′ti•nes, *n.* The state of being misty.—**misty,** mis′ti, *a.* Accompanied or characterized by mist; overspread with mist; dim; *fig.* obscure; not perspicuous.

mistake, mis•tāk′, *v.t.*—pret. *mistook*, pp. *mistaken*, ppr. *mistaking*. To take in error; to select wrongly; to conceive or understand erroneously; to regard otherwise than as the facts warrant; to misjudge; to take for a certain other person or thing; to regard as one when really another.—*v.i.* To be under a misapprehension or misconception; to be in error.—*To be mistaken*, to be misunderstood or misapprehended; to make or have made a mistake; to be in error.—*n.* An error in opinion or judgment; misapprehension; misunderstanding; a slip; a fault; a wrong act done unintentionally.—**mistakable,** mis•tāk′a•bl, *a.* Capable of being mistaken or misconceived.—**mistaken,** mis•tā′kn, *p.* and *a.* Erroneous; incorrect; having made, or laboring under, a mistake; wrong.—**mistakenly,** mis•tā′kn•li, *adv.* By mistake.

misteach, mis•tēch′, *v.t.* To teach wrongly; to instruct erroneously.

Mister, mis′tėr, *n.* [See MASTER.] The title of respect for a man, usually abbrev. *Mr.*, prefixed to the name, as *Mr.* Jones, prefixed also to certain official designations, as *Mr.* President.

mistime, mis•tīm′, *v.t.* To time wrongly; not to adapt to the time.

mistletoe, mis′l•tō, *n.* [A.Sax. *misteltān*, Icel. *mistel-teinn*; *tān*, *teinn*, meaning a twig or sprout; meaning of *mistel*, doubtful.] A European evergreen plant growing parasitically on trees, with oblong leaves, yellowish-green flowers, and in winter white berries; a similar American plant.

mistral, mis′tral, *n.* [Pr. from L. *magistralis*, lit. the master-wind.] A violent cold northwest wind experienced in Southern France.

mistreat, mis•trēt′, *v.t.* To treat amiss; to maltreat.—**mistreatment,** mis•trēt′ment, *n.* Wrong treatment; abuse.

mistress, mis′tres, *n.* [O.Fr. *maistresse* (Fr. *maîtresse*), fem. corresponding to *maistre*, L. *magister*, a master. MASTER.] The female appellation corresponding to *master*; a woman who is chief or head in a certain sphere; a woman who has authority, command, ownership, etc.; the female head of some establishment, as a family, school, etc.; a female who is well skilled in anything, or has mastered it; a female sweetheart; a woman filling the place but without the rights of a wife; a concubine; a title of address or term of courtesy pretty nearly equivalent to *madam*: now applied only to married or matronly women, and written in the abbreviated form *Mrs.*, which is pronounced mis′is, and used before personal names.

mistrust, mis•trust′, *n.* Want of confidence or trust; suspicion.—*v.t.* To suspect; to doubt; to regard with jealousy or suspicion.—**mistrustful,** mis•trust′fụl, *a.* Suspicious; doubting; wanting confidence.—**mistrustfully,** mis•trust′fụl•li, *adv.* In a mistrustful manner.—**mistrustfulness,** mis•trust′fụl•nes, *n.* The state or quality of being mistrustful.—**mistrustingly,** mis•trust′ing•li, *adv.* With distrust or suspicion.

misty. See MIST.

misunderstand, mis•un′dėr•stand″, *v.t.* To misconceive; to mistake; to take in a wrong sense.—**misunderstanding,** mis•un′dėr•stand″ing, *n.* Misconception; mistake of meaning; error; disagreement; dissension.

misuse, mis•ūz′, *v.t.* To treat or use improperly; to use to a bad purpose; to abuse; to maltreat.—*n.* (mis•ūs′). Improper use; employment in a wrong way or to a bad purpose; abuse; ill-treatment.—**misusage,** mis•ū′zij, *n.* Ill usage; abuse.—**misuser,** mis•ū′zėr, *n.* One who misuses.

mite, mīt, *n.* [A.Sax. *mite* = D. *mijt*, L.G. *mite*, Dan. *mide*, G. *miete*—mite; from root seen in Icel. *meita*, Goth. *maita*, to cut.] A name common to numerous small, in some cases microscopic, animals, of the class Arachnida (cheese-*mite*, sugar-*mite*, itch-*mite*, etc.).

mite, mīt, *n.* [D. *mijt*, a small coin; perhaps lit. something cut small, the origin being same as *mite*, a small insect.] A small coin formerly current; anything proverbially very small; a very little particle or quantity.

miter, mitre, mī′tėr, *n.* [Fr. *mitre*, L. *mitra*, from Gr. *mitra*, headband, turban.] The headdress anciently worn by the inhabitants of Asia Minor; a sort of cap pointed and cleft at the top worn on the head by bishops and archbishops (including the pope), cardinals, and in some instances by abbots, upon solemn occasions, as also by a Jewish high priest.—*v.t.*—*mitered*, *mitred*; *mitering*, *mitring*. To adorn with a miter; to raise to a rank which entitles to a miter; to unite or join by a miter joint.—**mitral,** mī′tral, *a.* Pertaining to a miter; resembling a miter.—**miter joint,** *n. Carp.* and *masonry*, a joint connecting two pieces of wood, stone, etc., at right angles, the line of the joint making an acute angle, or an angle of 45° with both pieces.

mithridate, mith′ri•dāt, *n.* [From *Mithridates*, king of Pontus, who was celebrated for his knowledge of poisons and antidotes.] An antidote against poisons.

mitigate, mit′i•gāt, *v.t.* and *i.*—*mitigated*, *mitigating*. [L. *mitigatum*, to mitigate, from *mitis*, mild.] To alleviate or render less painful, rigorous, intense, or severe; to assuage, lessen, abate, moderate.—**mitigable,** mit′i•ga•bl, *a.*—**mitigant,** mit′i•gant, *a.*—**mitigation,** mit•i•gā′shon, *n.*—**mitigative,** mit′i•gā•tiv, *a.*—**mitigator,** mit″i•gā′tėr, *n.*—**mitigatory,** mit′i•ge•to•ri, *a.*

mitosis, mī•tō′sis, *n.* [Gr. *mitos*, thread.] Ordinary cell division resulting when the chromatin of the nucleus forms into a threadlike segment (chromosomes), which gradually develops, then divides longitudinally into two parts, each having a set of chromosomes similar to that of the original cell.

mitrailleuse, me•trä•yėz′, *n.* [Fr. *mitraille*, small missiles, case shot, as in *mite*.] A breech-loading machine gun discharging small missiles at one time or in quick succession.

mitten, mit′n, *n.* [Fr. *mitaine*, from G. *mitte*, the middle, O.H.G. *mittamo*, half, the mitten being a kind of half or half-divided glove (akin *mid*).] A covering for the hand, differing from a glove in not having a separate cover for each finger, the thumb only being separate.—*To handle without mittens*, to treat roughly.—**mitt,** mit, *n.* [Abbrev. of *mitten*.] A mitten; also a covering for the hand and wrist only, and not for the fingers. In baseball, a glove, heavily padded on the palm side.

mittimus, mit′i•mus, *n.* [L., we send.] *Law*, a warrant of commitment to prison; a writ for removing records from one court to another.

mix, miks, *v.t.* [A.Sax. *miscan*; cog. L. *misceo*, *mixtum* (MEDLEY, MEDDLE), Gr. *mignymi*, *misgō*, to mix.] To unite or blend promiscuously, as various ingredients, into one mass or compound; to mingle; to blend; to join; to associate; to unite with in company; to produce by blending different ingredients.—*v.i.* To become united or blended promiscuously in a mass or compound; to be joined or associated: to mingle.—*n.* The act of mixing; a mixture.—**mixer,** mik′sėr, *n.*—**mixed number,** *n. Math.* the sum of a whole number and a fraction, as 2½.—**mix-up,** miks′-up, *n.* A confused state of affairs; a tangle; a fight. (Colloq.).

mixture, miks′tūr, *n.* [L. *mixtura*, from *misceo*, to mix. MIX.] The act of mixing, or state of being mixed; a mass or compound, consisting of different ingredients blended without order; a liquid medicine formed by mixing several ingredients together.

mizzen, mizen, miz′n, *n.* [Fr. *misaine*, from It. *mezzana*, mizzen, from *mezzano*, middle, from *mezzo*, middle: originally a large lateen sail on a middle mast. MEZZO, MEDIAL.] *Naut.* a fore-and-aft sail on the mast of a ship or barque next the stern; called also *Spanker*.—*a. Naut.*

belonging to the mizzen: applied to the mast supporting the mizzen, and the rigging and shrouds connected with it.

mizzle, miz′l, *v.i.* [For *mistle, misle,* a dim. and freq. from *mist.*] To rain in very fine drops; to drizzle.

mnemonics, ni•mon′iks, *n.* [Gr. *mnēmonikos,* pertaining to memory, from *mnēmōn,* mindful, *mnaomai,* to remember; same root as in E. *mind.*] The art of improving the memory. —**mnemonic,** ni•mon′ik, *a.* Pertaining to mnemonics; assisting or training the memory.

moa, mō′a, *n.* [Maori.] Any of the various extinct New Zealand birds of the family Dinornithidae.

moan, mōn, *v.i.* [O.E. *mone, moone,* etc., A.Sax. *maenan,* to moan.] To utter a low dull sound under the influence of grief or pain; to make lamentations; to utter a groan.—*v.t.* To bemoan or lament.—*n.* A low dull sound due to grief or pain; any sound that resembles a moan.

moat, mōt, *n.* [Fr. *mote,* L.L. *mota,* the mound of earth dug from a trench, a hill or mound on which a castle was built; origin unknown.] A ditch or deep trench round the rampart of a castle or other fortified place to serve as a defense, often filled with water.—*v.t.* To surround with a ditch for defense.

mob, mob, *n.* [Abbreviated from L. *mobile vulgus,* the fickle crowd, from *mobilis,* movable, fickle, from *moveo,* to move. MOVE, VULGAR.] A crowd; a promiscuous multitude of people, rude and disorderly; a rabble; a riotous assembly. — *v.t.* — *mobbed, mobbing.* To crowd round and annoy. —**mobbish,** mob′ish, *a.* Pertaining to a mob; tumultuous.—**mobocracy,** mob•ok′ra•si, *n.* [*Mob,* and Gr. *kratos,* power.] The rule or ascendancy of the mob.

mob, mob, *n.* [Comp. D. *mop,* a pug-dog, *mopmuts,* a mobcap.] A mobcap.—**mobcap,** *n.* A plain cap for females.

mobile, mō′bil, *a.* [Fr. *mobile,* L. *mobilis,* fickle, mobile, movable, from *moveo,* to move. MOVE.] Capable of being easily moved; readily liable to change (*mobile* features); changeable; fickle; readily adaptable.—*n.* mō′bēl. A sculpture of movable parts of wire, paper, etc., which can be set in motion by a current of air.—**mobilize,** mōb′il•iz, *v.t.*—*mobilized, mobilizing. Milit.* to put in a state of readiness for active service.—*v.i.* To be assembled for war.—**mobilization,** mob′il•i•zā″shon, *n.*—**mobility,** mō•bil′i•ti, *n.*

moccasin, mok′a•sin, *n.* [Spelled *mawcahsuns* in old glossary of North American Indian words.] A kind of shoe made of deerskin or other soft leather, without a stiff sole, worn by the North American Indians; a venomous snake, genus *Agkistrodon,* found in North America.

mocha, mō′kä, *n.* [From the seaport, *Mocha,* in Yemen, Arabia.] A choice variety of coffee; coffee flavoring; a fine glove leather.

mock, mok, *v.t.* [Fr. *moquer,* in *se moquer,* to mock, flout; origin doubtful; comp. It. *mocca,* a grimace; also Gr. *mōkos,* mockery.] To imitate or mimic; to deride or flout; to ridicule; to fool, tantalize, disappoint, deceive; to set at naught; to defy.—*v.i.* To use ridicule; to gibe or jeer.—*n.* An object of scorn; an act of ridicule; something jeered at.—*a.* False; counterfeit; assumed: often in compounds.—**mocker,** mok′ėr, *n.*—**mockery,** mok′ėr•i, *n.* The act of mocking; derision; ridicule; sportive insult; sport; subject of laughter; imitation; counterfeit appearance; false show; vain effort.—**mock-heroic,** *a.* Burlesquing the heroic in poetry, action, character, etc.—**mockingly,** mok′ing•li, *adv.*—**mockingbird,** *n.* An American bird of the thrush family remarkable for its wonderful faculty of imitating sounds. —**mock orange,** *n.* A common shrub with creamy white flowers having an odor which at a distance resembles that of orange flowers; the syringa. —**mock turtle,** *n.* A soup prepared from calf's head, in imitation of real turtle soup.—**mock-up,** mok′up, *n.* [From *mock,* imitate, and *up.*] A structural model, built to scale in cardboard, canvas, paper, etc., for use in testing and in study (a *mock-up* of a rocket).

mode, mōd, *n.* [Fr. *mode,* from L. *modus,* mode, manner, measure, etc.: same root as *mete.* Akin are *modify, modest, moderate; mood* (in gram.) is same word.] Manner; method; way (of speaking, acting, etc.); fashion; custom; *the mode,* the prevailing fashion or style; *gram.* and *logic,* same as *mood; mus.* a species of scale of which modern musicians recognize only two, the *major* and the *minor, modes.* MAJOR, MINOR.—**modal,** mō′dal, *a.* Relating to a mode or mood; pertaining to the mode, manner, or form, not to the essence. —*Modal proposition,* in *logic,* one which affirms or denies with a qualification or limitation.—**modality,** mō•dal′i•ti, *n.* The quality of being modal; *philos.* that quality of propositions in respect of which they express possibility or impossibility, existence or non-existence, necessity or contingency.—**modally,** mō′dal•li, *adv.* In a manner or relation expressing or indicating a mode.

model, mod′el, *n.* [Fr. *modèle,* O.Fr. *modelle,* from. It. *modello,* a model, lit. 'a little measure', dim. from L. *modus,* measure. MODE.] A pattern of something to be made; a form in miniature of something to be made on a larger scale; a copy, in miniature, of something already made or existing; an image, copy, facsimile; standard; that by which a thing is to be measured; anything serving or worthy of serving as a pattern; an example; a person, male or female, from whom a painter or sculptor studies his proportions, details, postures, etc.—*v.t.*—*modeled, modelled, modeling, modelling.* To plan or form after some model; to form in order to serve as a model; to mold; to shape.—*v.i.* To make a model; *sculp.* to form a work of some plastic material, as clay.—**modeler, modeller,** mod′el•ėr, *n.* One who models in clay, wax, etc.

moderate, mod′ėr•āt, *v.t.*—*moderated, moderating.* [L. *modero* and *moderor, moderatus,* to limit, moderate, from *modus,* a measure. MODE.] To restrain from excess of any kind; to reduce in intensity (rage, passion, desire, joy, etc.); to qualify; to temper; to lessen; to allay.—*v.i.* To become less violent or intense; to preside as a moderator.—*To moderate in a call,* in Presbyterian churches, to preside at a meeting at which a call is addressed to a minister.—*a.* [L. *moderatus.*] Applied to persons, not going to extremes; temperate in opinions or views; applied to things, not extreme or excessive; not very great; mediocre.—*n.* A member of a party in the Church of Scotland which claimed the character of moderation in doctrine, discipline, and church government.—**moderately,** mod′ėr•it•li, *adv.* In a moderate manner or degree; not excessively.—**moderateness,** mod′ėr•it•nes, *n.* State of being moderate.—**moderation,** mod′ėr•ā′shon, *n.* [L. *moderatio.*] The act of moderating, tempering, or repressing; the state or quality of being moderate; the keeping of a due mean between extremes; freedom from excess; due restraint; the act of presiding as a moderator.—*Moderations,* at Oxford University, the first public examination for degrees.—**moderator,** mod′ėr•ā•tėr, *n.* One who or that which moderates or restrains; the person who presides at a meeting or discussion: now chiefly applied to the chairman of meetings or courts in Presbyterian churches; substance, such as graphite, etc., used to slow down neutrons in a nuclear reactor.—**moderatorship,** mod′ėr•ā•tėr•ship, *n.*

moderato, mod•er•ä′tō, *a.* [It.] *Mus.* moderate; used as a direction indicating *moderate* time.

modern, mod′ėrn, *a.* [Fr. *moderne,* from L.L. *modernus,* modern, belonging to the present mode, from L. *modus,* mode, manner. MODE.] Pertaining to the present time, or time not long past; recent; not ancient.—*n.* A person of modern times: opposed to *ancient.*—**modernism,** mod′ėrn•izm, *n.* The state of being modern; deviation from ancient manner, practice, or mode of expression, notably in literature and the arts; a tendency in churches toward rationalistic interpretation of doctrine.—**modernist,** mod′ėrn•ist, *n.* One who admires what is modern. —**modernistic,** mod•ėrn•is′tic, *a.* Having modern appearance or characteristics.—**modernize,** mod′ėrn•īz, *v.t.*—*modernized, modernizing.* To give a modern character to; to adapt to modern times; to cause to conform to modern ideas or style.—**modernizer,** mod′ėrn•ī•zėr, *n.* One who renders modern or modernizes. —**modernization,** mod′ėrn•i•zā″shon, *n.* The act of modernizing; what is produced by modernizing.

modest, mod′est, *a.* [Fr. *modeste*, L. *modestus*, from *modus*, a limit. MODE.] Restrained by a sense of propriety; not forward or bold; unpretending; bashful; diffident; free from anything suggestive of sexual impurity; pure; moderate; not excessive, extreme, or extravagant.—**modestly,** mod′est•li, *adv.* In a modest manner; with modesty; diffidently; bashfully; not wantonly; not excessively.—**modesty,** mod′es•ti, *n.* [L. *modestia.*] The state or quality of being modest; absence of tendency to forwardness, pretense, or presumption; bashful reserve; absence of anything suggestive of sexual impurity; chastity; moderation; freedom from excess.

modicum, mod′i•kum, *n.* [L., a small or moderate quantity, from *modicus*, moderate, from *modus*, measure. MODE.] A little; a small quantity; a scanty allowance or allotment.

modify, mod′i•fī, *v.t.*—*modified, modifying.* [Fr. *modifier*, from L. *modifico* —*modus*, limit, manner, and *facio*, to make. MODE, FACT.] To change the external qualities of; to give a new form or external character to; to vary; to alter in some respect.—**modifier,** mod′i•fī•ėr, *n.* One who or that which modifies.—**modifiable,** mod′i•fī•a•bl, *a.* Capable of being modified.—**modification,** mod′i•fi•kā″shon, *n.* The act of modifying; the state of being modified; some alteration in form, appearance, or character; a particular form or manner of being; a mode.—**modificatory,** mod′i•fi•kā•to•ri, *a.* Tending to modify or produce change.

modillion, mō•dil′yon, *n.* [Fr. *modillon*, from L. *modulus*, a model, dim. of *modus*, a measure. MODE.] *Arch.* a block carved into the form of an enriched bracket used in cornices of buildings.

modish, mōd′ish, *a.* [From *mode.*] According to the mode or fashion; affectedly fashionable.—**modishly,** mōd′ish•li, *adv.* In a modish manner. —**modishness,** mod′ish•nes, *n.* The quality of being modish; affectation of the fashion.—**modiste,** mō•dēst′, *n.* [Fr. *modiste*, a milliner, from *mode*, fashion.] A female who deals in articles of ladies' dress; particularly, a milliner or dressmaker.

modulate, mod′ū•lāt, *v.t.*—*modulated, modulating.* [L. *modulor, modulatus*, from *modus*, limit, measure, mode. MODE.] To proportion; to adjust; to vary or inflect the sound of in such a manner as to give expressiveness to what is uttered; to vary (the voice) in tone; *music*, to change the key or mode of in the course of composition; to transfer from one key to another.—*v.i. Music*, to pass from one key into another.—**modulation,** mod•ū•lā′shon, *n.* The act of modulating; adjustment; the act of inflecting the voice or any instrument musically; melodious sound; *music*, the change from one scale or mode to another in the course of a composition.—**modulator,** mod′ū•lā•tėr, *n.* One who, or that which modulates; in the tonic sol-fa system of music, a sort of map of musical sounds representing the relative intervals of the notes of a scale, its chromatics, and its more closely related scales.

module, mod′ūl, *n.* [Fr., from L. *modulus*, dim. of *modus*, a measure. MODE.] *Arch.* a measure taken to regulate the proportions of an order or the disposition of the whole building.—**modulus,** mod′ū•lus, *n.* pl. **moduli,** *Math.* and *physics.* a term for some constant multiplier or quantity required to be used in certain calculations.—*Modulus of elasticity*, the quotient of a stress (in units of force per unit area) by the resulting strain.—**modular,** mod′ū•lėr, *a.* Pertaining to a module or modulus.—**modus,** mō′dus, *n.* Mode, manner, or method; *law*, a fixed payment by way of tithe.—*Modus vivendi*, lit. way of living; a temporary arrangement between parties pending the final settlement of matters in dispute.

mogul, moghul, mō•gul′, *n.* [From Ar. and Per. *Mughul*, Mongol.] One of the Mongolian conquerors of India; a person prominent in a particular field or business.

mohair, mō′hâr, *n.* [From Ar. *mokhayyar*, a kind of camlet or haircloth = Fr. *moire.*] The hair of the Angora goat; cloth made of this hair; camlet; a wool-and-cotton cloth made in imitation of real mohair.

Mohammedan, mō•ham′med•an, *a.* Pertaining to Mohammed, or the religion founded by him.—*n.* A follower of Mohammed; one who professes Mohammedanism.—**Mohammedanism,** mō•ham′med•an•izm, *n.* The religion of Mohammed, contained in the Koran.

Mohawk, mō′hąk, *n.* A tribe of North American Indians in what is now New York State, one of the Five Nations confederacy; a member of the tribe; the language of the tribe.

mohole, mō′hōl, *n.* [From moho, or Mohorovicic discontinuity.] A projected hole to the line (moho) between the earth's crust and mantle.

moiety, moi′e•ti, *n.* [Fr. *moitié*, from L. *medietas*, from *medius*, middle. MEDIAL.] The half; one of two equal parts; a portion or share in general.

moil, moil, *v.i.* [From O.Fr. *moiller*, Fr. *mouiller*, to wet, to soften, from L. *mollis*, soft. MOLLIFY.] To labor; to toil; to work with painful efforts.

moire, mwär, mōr, *n.* [Fr. from E. mohair.] A watered mohair or other textile fabric.

moiré, mwä•rā′, mōr′ā, *a.* [Fr. pp. of *moirer*, to water.] Watered; having a watered appearance, as silk, etc. —*n.* A wavelike design on fabrics or metallic surfaces.

moist, moist, *a.* [O.Fr. *moiste*, from L. *musteus*, fresh.] Moderately wet; damp; not dry; humid.—**moisten,** mois′n, *v.i.* To make moist or damp. —*v.i.* To become moist.—**moisture,** mois′chėr, *n.* Diffused wetness.

molar, mō′lėr, *a.* [L. *molaris*, from *mola*, a mill; same root as *meal.* MILL.] Serving to bruise or grind the food in eating; grinding.—*n.* A grinding tooth; a tooth having a flattened, triturating surface.

molar, mō′lėr, *a.* [L. *moles*, a mass.] Pertaining to a mass as a whole.

molasses, mō•las′ez, *n.* [Also *melasses*, a better spelling, being from Fr. *mélasse*, Sp. *melaza*, L. *mellaceus*, resembling honey, from *mel, mellis*, honey.] The uncrystallized sirup produced from sugar in the process of making.

mold, mōld, *n.* [A.Sax. *molde*, mold, earth, from root seen in Goth. *malan.*] Fine, soft earth; dust from incipient decay.—**molder,** mōl′dėr, *v.i.* To turn to dust by natural decay.—*v.t.* To cause to molder.

mold, mōld, *n.* [M.E. *moul*, perhaps confused with *mold*, earth.] A minute fungus, indicative of decay, appearing as a furry growth or film on animal and vegetable tissues, especially where exposed to dampness; a film of fungoid growth.—*v.t.* To cause to contract mold.—*v.i.* To become moldy.—**moldiness,** mōl′di•nes, *n.*—**moldy,** mōl′di, *a.*

mold, mōld, *n.* [Fr. *modle*, from L. *modulus*, dim. of *modus*, a measure. MODE.] The matrix in which anything is cast and receives its form; a hollow tool for producing a form by percussion or compression; cast; form; shape; character.—*v.t.* To form into a particular shape; to shape; to model; to fashion.—**moldboard,** *n.* The curved board or metal plate in a plow, which serves to turn over the furrow.—**molder,** mōl′dėr, *n.*—**molding,** mōl′ding, *n.* Something cast in a mold; *arch.* a general term applied to the varieties of outline or contour given to cornices, bases, door or window jambs, lintels, etc.

molder, mōl′dėr, *v.i.* [From *mold*, earth, mustiness; lit. to turn to *mold.*] To turn to dust by natural decay; to waste away by a gradual separation of the component particles; to crumble; to perish.

moldwarp, mōld′wärp, *n.* The mole.

mole, mōl, *n.* [Same word as *mold*, earth, being abbreviated from the fuller name *moldwarp, mouldwarp*, lit. earth-caster, from *mold*, and *warp*, to cast.] An insectivorous animal which forms burrows just under the surface of the ground, throwing up the excavated soil into little hills; a kind of plow for making drains.—**molehill,** *n.* A heap of earth thrown up by a mole; something insignificant as contrasted with something important.—**moleskin,** mōl′skin, *n.* A strong twilled fustian or cotton cloth, so called from its being soft like the skin of a mole.

mole, mōl, *n.* [A.Sax. *mál*, a blot, a spot = O.D. *mael*, Dan. *maal*, G. *mal*, a spot; cog. L. *macula*, a spot.] A spot, or small discolored protuberance on the human body.

mole, mōl, *n.* [Fr., from L. *moles*, a mass, a dam, a mole; same root as *magnus*, great.] A mound or breakwater formed so as to partially enclose a harbor or anchorage, and protect it from the waves.

molecule, mol′e•kūl, *n.* [Fr. *molécule*, dim. of L. *moles*, a mass. MOLE.] The smallest unit of matter capable of existing independently while retaining its chemical properties.—**molecular,** mo•lek′ū•lėr, *a.* Pertaining to, or consisting of, molecules.—*Molecular attraction*, that force which acts between the molecules or particles of a body, keeping them together in one mass. It is distinct from gravitational attraction and is of much greater magnitude.—**molecular weight,** *n.* The weight of any molecule, obtained by adding the weights of the atoms it contains.

molest, mo•lest′, *v.t.* [Fr. *molester*, from L. *molestus*, troublesome, from *moles*, trouble, a great mass. MOLECULE.] To annoy; to disturb; to vex.—**molestation,** mol•es•tā′shon, *n.* The act of molesting; disturbance; annoyance.

moll, mol, *n.* [Probably from *Moll*, a nickname for Mary.] A gangster's girl friend; a wench; a prostitute.

mollify, mol′i•fī, *v.t.*—*mollified, mollifying*. [O.Fr. *mollifier*, L. *mollificare*—*mollis*, soft, and *facio*, to make. MEAL, MELLOW.] To assuage, as pain or irritation; to pacify; to reduce in harshness; to tone down.—**mollification,** mol′i•fi•kā″shon, *n.* The act of mollifying; mitigation; pacification.—**mollities,** mol•lish′i•ēz, *n.* [L., softness.] *Med.* diseased softening of an organ.

mollusk, mol′usk, *n.* [Fr. *mollusque*, from N.L. *mollusca*, soft, from *mollis*, soft.] One of a large phylum of invertebrates including the snails, mussels, bivalves, cuttlefish, etc., having usually a calcareous shell protecting a soft, unsegmented body, gills, and a muscular foot for digging and creeping.—**molluscan,** mol•lus′kan, *n.*—**molluscous,** mol•lus′kus, *a.* —**molluscoid,** mol•lus′koid, *n.*

mollycoddle, mol′i•kod•l, *n.* [From *Molly*, as general name for a female, and *coddle*.] An effeminate person. (*Slang*.)

Moloch, mō′lok, *n.* [Heb. *molech*, king.] The chief god of the Phoenicians and of the Ammonites, whose worship consisted chiefly of human sacrifices, ordeals by fire, mutilation, etc.; a genus of lizards of repulsive appearance found in Australia.

molt, mōlt, *v.i.* [O.E. *moute*, *mowte* (the *l* having intruded as in *could*), like D. *muiten*, O.L.G. *muton*, from L. *muto*, *mutare*, to change. MEW.] To shed or cast the feathers, hair, skin, horns, etc., as birds and other animals do; most commonly used of birds, but also of crabs, serpents, etc. —*v.t.* To shed or cast, as feathers, hair, skin, etc.—The act of molting; the shedding or changing of feathers.

molten, mōl′tn, *p.* and *a.* Melted.

molto, mōl′tō, *adv.* [It. from L. *multum*, much.] *Mus.* much; very: used in directions.

moly, mō′li, *n.* [Gr. *mōly*.] A fabulous herb of magic power spoken of by Homer.

molybdenum, mol•ib′dē•num, *n.* [N.L. from L. *molybdaena*, from Gr. *molybdaina*, galena (lead ore).] A whitish metallic element mainly used in alloy steel. Symbol, Mo; at. no., 42; at. wt., 95.94.—**molybdic,** mo•lib′dik, *a.*

moment, mō′ment, *n.* [L. *momentum*, movement, impulse, brief space of time, importance, contr. for *movimentum*, from *moveo*, to move. MOVE.] A minute portion of time; an instant; importance; consequence. In *phys.* the moment (or importance) of a force round a point is the product of the magnitude of the force into the perpendicular distance of the point from its line of action.—*The moment of a couple* is the product of either force into the arm.—*The moment of a magnet* is the strength of either pole multiplied by the distance between the poles.—*Moment of inertia*, of a body or system of bodies round an axis, is the sum of the products of each small element of mass by the square of its distance from the axis; similarly with reference to a point and a plane.—*Momentum*, the product of a moving mass into its velocity.—**momentarily,** mō′men•te•ri•li, *adv.* Every moment; from moment to moment.—**momentary,** mō′men•ta•ri, *a.* Lasting but a moment or a very short time; fleeting.—**momently,** mō′ment•li, *adv.* From moment to moment; every moment.—**momentous,** mō•men′tus, *a.* Of moment or importance; weighty; of great consequence.—**momentously,** mō•men′tus•li, *adv.* Weightily; importantly.—**momentum,** mō•men′tum, *n.* The force possessed by a body in motion; the product of the mass and velocity of a body; impetus.

Momus, mō′mus, *n.* [Gr. *mōmos*, derision.] *Greek myth.* the god of raillery and ridicule.

monachal, mon′a•kal, *a.* [L. *monachus*, Gr. *monachos*, a monk, from *monos*, alone. MONK.] Pertaining to monks or a monastic life; monastic.—**monachism,** mon′ak•izm, *n.* [Fr. *monachisme*.] The monastic life or system; monkery; monkishness.

monad, mon′ad, *n.* [Gr. *monas*, *monados*, unity, from *monos*, alone.] An ultimate atom or simple substance without parts; *zool.* a microscopical organism of an extremely simple character developed in organic infusions; *chem.* a univalent element, such as hydrogen, chlorine, etc.; an imaginary entity in the philosophy of Leibnitz.—**monadic, monadical,** mo•nad′ik, mo•nad′i•kal, *a.* Having the nature or character of a monad.

monadelph, mon′a•delf, *n.* [Gr. *monos*, sole, and *adelphos*, brother.] *Bot.* a plant whose stamens are united in one body by the filaments; *zool.* a mammal in which the uterus is single.—**monadelphous,** mon•a•del′fus, *a.* Belonging to the monadelphs.

monander, mon•an′dėr, *n.* [Gr. *monos*, single, and *anēr*, *andros*, a male.] *Bot.* a monoclinous plant having one stamen only.—**monandrous,** mon•an′drus, *a. Bot.* monoclinous, and having one stamen only.—**monandry,** mon•and′ri, *n.* Marriage to one husband only: as opposed to *polyandry*.

monanthous, mon•an′thus, *a.* [Gr. *monos*, single, *anthos*, flower,] *Bot.* producing but one flower.

monarch, mon′ėrk, *n.* [L. *monarcha*, from Gr. *monarchēs*, a monarch, *monarchos*, ruling alone—*monos*, alone, and *archē*, rule.] A sole ruler; the hereditary ruler of a state; a sovereign, as an emperor, king, queen, prince, etc.; one who is superior to others of the same kind (an oak is called the *monarch* of the forest).—**monarchal,** mon•är′kal, *a.* Pertaining to a monarch; sovereign. —**monarchic, monarchical,** mon•är′kik, mon•är′ki•kal, *a.* Vested in a monarch or single ruler; pertaining to a monarchy.—**monarchically,** mon•är′ki•kal•li, *adv.* In a monarchical manner.—**monarchism,** mon′ėrk•īzm, *n.* The principles of monarchy; love or preference of monarchy.—**monarchist,** mon′ėrk•ist, *n.* An advocate of monarchy.—**monarchy,** mon′ėr•ky, *n.* [Gr. *monarchia*.] A state or country in which the supreme power is either actually or nominally lodged in the hands of a single person; the system of government in which the supreme power is vested in a single person; the territory ruled by a monarch; a kingdom; an empire.

monastery, mon′as•tėr•i, *n.* [L.L. *monasterium*, from Gr. *monastērion*, from *monastēs*, a solitary, *monazō*, to be alone, from *monos*, alone, sole.] A house of religious retirement, or of seclusion from ordinary temporal concerns, whether an abbey, a priory, a nunnery, or convent; usually applied to the houses for monks.—**monasterial,** mon•as•tē′ri•al. *a.* Pertaining to a monastery.—**monastic, monastical,** mon•as′tik, mon•as′ti•kal, *a.* [Gr. *monastikos*.] Pertaining to monasteries; pertaining to religious or other seclusion.—**monastic,** *n.* A member of a monastery; a monk.—**monastically,** mon•as′ti•kal•li, *adv.* In a monastic manner; reclusely.—**monasticism,** mon•as′ti•sizm, *n.* Monastic life; the monastic system or condition.

monatomic, mon•a•tom′ik, *a. Chem.* said of an element the molecule of which contains only one atom; in older use = univalent.

monaural. See MONOPHONIC.

Monday, mun′dā, *n.* [A.Sax. *mónandaeg*—*mónan*, genit. of *móna*, the moon, and *daeg*, day.] The second day of the week.

monetary, mon′e•te•ri, *a.* [L. *moneta*, money. MONEY.] Pertaining to money or consisting in money.—*Monetary unit*, the standard of currency.—**monetize,** mon′e•tīz, *v.t.* To form into coin or money.—**monetization,** mon′et•i•zā″shon, *n.* The act of monetizing.

money, mun′i, *n.* pl. **moneys** or **monies,** mun′iz. [O.Fr. *moneie*, *monnoie*, Fr. *monnaie*, from L. *moneta*, the mint, money, originally a surname of Juno (lit. the warner or admonisher, from *moneo*, to admonish), in whose temple at Rome money was coined; whence also *mint.* MONITION.] Coin; gold, silver, or other metal, stamped by public authority and used as the medium of exchange; in a wider sense, any equivalent for commodities, and for which individuals readily exchange their goods or services; a circulating medium; wealth; affluence (a man of *money*); The plural is used in the sense of sums of money or denominations of money.—*A money of account*, a denomination used merely for convenience in keeping accounts, and not represented by any coin.—*To make money*, to gain money; to be in the way of becoming rich.—*Paper money*, bank notes, bills, etc., representing value and passing current as so.—**moneyed,** mun′id, *a.* Rich.—**money-making,** *n.* The process of accumulating money.—*a.* Lucrative; profitable.—**money order,** *n.* An order granted upon payment of a sum and a small commission, by one post office or express or telegraph company, and payable at another.

monger, mung′gėr, *n.* [A.Sax. *mangere*, a dealer, from *mangian*, to traffic; perhaps from L. *mango*, dealer.] A trader; a dealer: now only or chiefly in compounds.

Mongol, Mongolian, mon′gol, mon-gō′li•an, *n.* [*Mongol*, Mongol, from MOGUL.] A native of Mongolia.—*a.* Belonging to Mongolia; one of the great divisions of the human family, having a thick fold of skin over the inner eye, high cheek bones, and straight black hair.—**mongolism,** mon′gol•ism, *n.* A congenital idiocy of unknown cause, producing a broad, flattened skull and slanting eyes.

mongoose, mon′gös, *n.* [East Indian name.] An Indian mammal, quick-eyed and agile, having a long, thick tail, and feeding on snakes, rats, etc.

mongrel, mung′grel, *a.* [From A. Sax. *mang*, mixture, with dim. suffix as in *cockerel*; akin *mingle, among*.] Of a mixed breed; of mingled origins; hybrid.—*n.* A cross between two plants or animals, (breeds, races). Usually fertile, e.g. crosses between varieties of apple or breeds of sheep. Cp. HYBRID.

moniker, monicker, mon′i•kėr, *n.* [Origin unknown.] A name or nickname.

moniliform, mō•nil′i•form, *a.* [L. *monile*, a necklace.] Like a necklace; like a series or string of beads: used especially in natural history.

monism, mon′izm, *n.* [Gr. *monos*, alone, single.] The doctrine which holds that in the universe there is only a single element or principle from which everything is developed, this single principle being either mind (*idealistic monism*) or matter (*materialistic monism*).—**monistic,** mon•is′tik, *a.* Pertaining to monism; pertaining to or derived from a single source.

monition, mo•nish′on, *n.* [L. *monitio*, *monitionis*, from *moneo*, to admonish (hence *moneta*, E. *money*); root in *monstrum*, a monster, *monstrare*, to show (*demonstrate*); *mens*, mind (whence *mental*), E. *mind*.] Admonition; warning; advice by way of caution; indication; intimation.—**monitor,** mon′i•tėr, *n.* One who admonishes or warns of faults and informs of duty; an admonisher; a senior pupil in a school appointed to instruct and look after juniors; a genus of large lizards; something used for monitoring, especially a receiver used to view or pick up what is transmitted; a name for a class of shallow, heavily armed, iron-clad steam vessels sunk deeply in the water: so called from the name of the first vessel of the kind.—*v.t.* and *i.* To tap on to a transmitter of a telephone, television, etc., to be certain it operates properly, without interfering with the transmission; to watch or check for a particular purpose; to keep track of.—**monitory,** mon′i•to•ri, *a.* Giving admonition; admonitory.—**monitress,** mon′i•tres, *n.* A female monitor.

monk, mungk, *n.* [A.Sax. *monec*, *munec*, from L.L. *monachus*, Gr. *monachos*, one who lives alone, from *monos*, alone.] One of a community of males inhabiting a monastery, and bound by vows to celibacy and religious exercises.—**monkhood,** mungk′hu̇d, *n.* Character or condition of a monk.—**monkish,** mungk-ish, *a.* Like a monk, or pertaining to monks; monastic.—**monkishness,** mungk′ish•nes, *n.* The quality of being monkish.

monkey, mung′ki, *n.* [O.Fr. *monne*, a monkey, It. *monna*, a female ape, properly dame, mistress, a contr. of *madonna*, the term *-key* being diminutive, as in *donkey*.] A name used in its wider sense to include all the quadrumana except the lemurs and their allies; but in a more restricted sense designating the long-tailed members of the order as distinguished from the apes and baboons; a term applied to a boy or girl either in real or pretended disapproval; a pile-driving apparatus: a sort of powerhammer; a comical person.—**monkey bread,** *n.* BAOBAB.—**monkey jacket,** *n.* A close-fitting jacket, generally of some stout material.—**monkeypot,** *n.* The fruit of a gigantic Brazilian tree consisting of a capsule furnished with a lid, containing nuts of which monkeys are fond.—**monkey wrench,** *n.* A screw key with a movable jaw, which can be adjusted by a screw.

monobasic, mon•o•bās′ik, *a.* [Gr. *monos*, single, and *basis*, a base.] *Chem.* having only one hydrogen atom replaceable by a basic atom or radical, said of acids.

monocarp, mon′o•kärp, *n.* [Gr. *monos*, single, and *karpos*, fruit.] *Bot.* a plant that perishes after having once borne fruit; an annual plant.—**monacarpous, monocarpic,** mon•o•kär′pus, mon•o•kär′pik, *a. Bot.* a term applied to annual plants.

monochord, mon′o•kord, *n.* [Gr. *monos*, sole, and *chordē*, a chord.] *Mus.* a single string stretched across a soundboard, and having under it a movable bridge, used to show the lengths of string required to produce the notes of the scale, etc.

monochromatic, mon′o•krō•mat″-ik, *a.* [Gr. *monos*, sole, and *chrōma*, color.] Consisting of one color, or presenting rays of light of one color only.—**monochrome,** mon′o•krōm, *n.* A painting in one color, but relieved by light and shade.

monocle, mon′o•kl, *n.* [MONOCULAR.] A single eyeglass.

monoclinal, mon•o•klī′nal, *a.* [Gr. *monos*, single, and *klinō*, to bend.] *Geol.* applied to strata that dip for an indefinite length in one direction.—**monoclinic,** mon•o•klin′ik, *a. Mineral.* having three unequal axes, two intersecting at an oblique angle, and cut by the third at right angles.—**monoclinous,** mon•ok′li•nus, *a. Bot.* having both stamens and pistils in the same flower; *geol.* monoclinal.

monocotyledon, mon′ö•kot•i•lē″-don, *n.* A plant with one cotyledon only; a monocotyledonous plant.—**monocotyledonous,** mon′o•kot•i•lē″do•nus, *a. Bot.* Having only one seed lobe or cotyledon, as endogenous plants have.

monocracy, mon•ok′ra•si, *n.* [Gr. *monos*, sole, and *kratos*, rule.] Government or rule by a single person; autocracy.—**monocrat,** mon′o•krat, *n.* One who governs alone.

monocular, mon•ok′ū•lėr, *a.* [Gr. *monos*, sole, and L. *oculus*, an eye.] Having one eye only; adapted to be used with one eye only, a *monocular* microscope.

monodactylous, mon•o•dak′til•us, *a.* [Gr. *monos*, single, and *daktylos*, finger.] Having one finger or toe only.

monodrama, mon′o•drä•ma, *n.* [Gr. *monos*, single, and *drama*, a drama.] A dramatic performance by a single person.

monody, mon′o•di, *n.* [Gr. *monōdia*—*monos*, single, and *ōdē*, a song.] A mournful kind of song, in which a single mourner is supposed to give vent to his grief.—**monodical,** mon•od′i•kal, *a.* Pertaining to a monody.—**monodist,** mon′od•ist, *n.* One who writes or sings a monody.

monoecious, mo•nē′shus, *a.* [Gr. *monos*, one, and *oikos*, a house.] *Bot.* having male and female flowers on the same plant; *zool.* having male and female organs of reproduction in the same individual.

monogamic, mon•o•gam′ik, *a.* [Gr. *monos*, sole, and *gamos*, marriage.] *Bot.* having flowers distinct from each other, and not collected in a head; monogamous.—**monogamist,** mo•nog′a•mist, *n.* One who practices or upholds monogamy, as opposed to a *bigamist* or *polygamist*.—**monogamous,** mo•nog′a•mus, *a.* Upholding or practicing monogamy; *zool.* having only one mate; *bot.* monogamic.—**monogamy,** mo•nog′a•mi, *n.* The practice or principle of marrying only once; the marrying of only one at a time; *zool.* the pairing with but a single mate at a time.

monogenesis, mon•o•jen′e•sis, *n.* [Gr. *monos,* single, and *genesis,* origin.] *Biol.* direct development of an embryo from a parent similar to itself; descent of an individual from one parent form; development of all the beings in the universe from a single cell.—**monogenetic,** mon′o•je•net″ik, *a.* Of or relating to monogenesis.—**monogenist,** mo•noj′e•nist, *n.* One who maintains the doctrine of monogeny.—**monogeny,** mo•noj′e•ni, *n.* Origin from a single species; the unity of the human species.

monogram, mon′o•gram, *n.* [Gr. *monos,* sole, and *gramma,* letter.] A character or cipher composed of one, two, or more letters interwoven, being an abbreviation of a name, used for instance on seals, letter-paper and envelopes, etc.—**monogrammatic,** mon′o•gram•mat″ik, *a.* In the style or manner of a monogram; pertaining to monograms.

monograph, mon′o•graf, *n.* [Gr. *monos,* single, and *graphē,* description.] An account or description of a single thing or class of things; the only book written by some distinguished writer on a topic.—**monographer,** mon•og′ra•fėr, *n.* A writer of monographs.—**monographic,** mon•o•graf′ik, *a.* Pertaining to a monograph.

monogyny, mo•noj′i•ni, *n.* Marriage to one woman only; the state of having but one wife at a time.

monolith, mon′o•lith, *n.* [Gr. *monos,* single, and *lithos,* a stone.] A pillar, column, and the like formed of a single stone, generally applied to such only as are noted for their magnitude.—**monolithic,** mon•o•lith′ik, *a.* Formed of a single stone; consisting of monoliths.

monologue, mon′o•log, *n.* [Fr. *monologue,* from Gr. *monos,* sole, and *logos,* speech.] That which is spoken by one person alone; a dramatic soliloquy; a long speech or dissertation, uttered by one person in company.—**monologist,** mo•nol′o•jist, *n.* One who soliloquizes; one who monopolizes conversation.

monomania, mon•o•mā′ni•a, *n.* [Gr. *monos,* single, and *mania,* madness.] That form of mania in which the mind of the patient is absorbed by one idea, or is irrational on one subject only.—**monomaniac,** mon•o•mā′ni•ak, *n.* A person affected by monomania.—**monomaniac, monomaniacal,** mon•o•mā′ni•ak, mon•o•mā•nī″a•kal, *a.* Affected with, pertaining to, or resulting from monomania.

monometallism, mon•o•met′al•izm, *n.* [Gr. *monos,* single, E. *metal.*] The fact of having only one metal as a standard in the coinage of a country; the theory of a single metallic standard.—**monometallic,** mon•o•me•tal″ik, *a.* Pertaining to monometallism.

monomial, mo•nō′mi•al, *n.* [Gr. *monos,* sole, and *onoma,* a name.] *Alg.* an expression or quantity consisting of a single term.—*a. Alg.* consisting of only one term or letter.

monomorphic, monomorphous, mon•o•mor′fik, mon•o•mor′fus, *a.* [Gr. *monos,* single, and *morphē,* form.] *Biol.* retaining the same form throughout the various stages of development.

mononucleosis, mon′ō•nū′klē•o″sis, *n.* [N.L. *mono,* one, and *nuclear,* nucleus, and suffix *osis,* condition, state.] A disease in which an abnormally large number of mononuclear leukocytes are present in the blood.

monopetalous, mon•o•pet′al•us, *n.* [Gr. *monos,* single, and *petalon.*] *Bot.* having the petals united together into one piece by their edges; gamopetalous.

monophonic, mon•ō•fon′ik, *a.* [Gr. *monos,* one, and *phōnē,* sound.] Having a single melodic line with little or no accompaniment; in sound transmission, using recording techniques that result in a single transmission path.

monophthong, mon′of•thong, *n.* [Gr. *monos,* sole, and *phthongos,* sound.] A simple vowel sound; two or more written vowels pronounced as one.—**monophthongal,** mon•of•thong′gal, *a.* Consisting of a simple vowel sound.

monophyletic, mon′o•fi•let″ik, *a.* [Gr. *monos,* single, *phylē,* a tribe.] Pertaining to a single family or tribe.

monophyllous, mo•nof′il•us, *a.* [Gr. *monos,* sole, and *phyllon,* leaf.] *Bot.* having one leaf only, or formed of one leaf.

Monophysite, mo•nof′i•sīt, *n.* [Gr. *monos,* single, and *physis,* nature.] One who maintains that Jesus Christ had but one nature. Used also as adj.

monoplane, mon′o•plān, *n.* A flying apparatus with its wings or carrying surfaces arranged in the same plane. AIRPLANE.

monopoly, mo•nop′o•li, *n.* [Fr. *monopole,* L. *monopolium,* Gr. *monopōlion—monos,* single, and *pōleō,* to sell.] An exclusive trading privilege; the sole right or power of selling something, or full command over the sale of it; that which is the subject of a monopoly; the possession or assumption of anything to the exclusion of others.—**monopolist, monopolizer,** mo•nop′o•list, mo•nop′o•lī•zėr, *n.*—**monopolize,** mo•nop′o•līz, *v.t.*—*monopolized, monopolizing.* To obtain a monopoly of; to obtain or engross the whole of.

monorail, mon′o•rāl, *n.* [Gr. *monos,* one, and *rail.*] A system of vehicular propulsion requiring only one rail.

monosepalous, mon•o•sep′al•us, *a.* [Gr. *monos,* one, and E. *sepal.*] *Bot.* composed of sepals which are united by their edges; gamosepalous.

monosperm, mon′o•spėrm, *n.* [Gr. *monos,* single, and *sperma,* seed.] A plant of one seed only.—**monospermous,** mon•o•spėr′mus, *a. Bot.* having one seed only.

monostich, mon′o•stik, *n.* [Gr. *monos,* single, and *stichos,* a verse.] A poem consisting of one verse only.

monostrophe, mo•nos′tro•fi, *n.* [Gr. *monos,* single, and *strophē,* strophe.] A metrical composition having only one strophe.—**monostrophic,** mon•o•strof′ik, *a.* Having one strophe only; written in unvaried measure.

monosyllabic, mon′o•sil•ab″ik, *a.* [Gr. *monos,* single, and *syllabē,* a syllable.] Consisting of one syllable; consisting of words of one syllable.—*Monosyllabic languages,* a class of languages in which each word is a simple uninflected root.—**monosyllable,** mon′o•sil•a•bl, *n.* A word of one syllable.

monotheism, mon′o•thē•izm, *n.* [Gr. *monos,* single, and *theos,* God.] The doctrine or belief of the existence of one God only.—**monotheist,** mon′o•thē•ist, *n.*—**monotheistic,** mon′o•thē•is″tik, *a.*

monotone, mon′o•tōn, *n.* [Gr. *monos,* single, and *tonos,* tone, sound.] A sameness of sound, or the utterance of successive syllables on one unvaried key, without inflection or cadence; sameness of style in writing or speaking.—**monotonous,** mo•not′o•nus, *a.*—**monotonously,** mo•not′o•nus•li, *adv.*—**monotonousness,** mo•not′o•nus•nes, *n.*—**monotony,** mo•not′o•ni, *n.* Uniformity of tone or sound; tiresome sameness; want of variety.

monotrematous, mon•o•trem′a•tus, *a.* [Gr. *monos,* single, *trēma,* aperture.] Characteristic of the Monotremata, the lowest order of mammals, oviparous, and with a single outlet for the feces and the products of the urinary and generative organs, comprising only the ornithorhynchus and echidna.—**monotreme,** mon′o•trēm, *n.* One of the Monotremata.

monotypic, mon•o•tip′ik, *a.* [Gr. *monos,* single and *typos,* a type.] Of one type.—**monotype,** mon′ō•tīp, *n.* In printing, a mechanical method of setting and casting type in single letters.

monovalent, mon′o•vā″lent, *n.* [Gr. *monos,* single, and L. *valens, valentis,* ppr. of *valeo,* to be worth.] *Chem.* having a valence of one, as the cuprous ion (Cu^1).

monoxide, mon•ox′īd, *n.* [Gr. *monos,* one, and Fr. *oxide, oxyde,* from *oxygène,* oxygen, and *acide,* acid.] *Chem.* an oxide containing a single atom of oxygen in the molecule.

Monroe Doctrine. The doctrine formulated by President Monroe of the United States that any attempt at colonizing by a European power within the American area constitutes an unfriendly act, leading to war.

monseigneur, mon•sen•yėr′, *n.* pl. **messeigneurs,** mā•sen•yėr′. [Fr. *mon,* my, and *seigneur,* lord. SENIOR.] A French title of honor given to princes, bishops, and other high dignitaries.—**monsieur,** mos′yė, *n.* pl. **messieurs,** mes′yė. [Fr., contr. of *monseigneur.*] The common title of courtesy and respect in France, answering to the English *Sir* and *Mr.*; abbreviated *Mons., M.*; plural *Messrs., MM.*

monsoon, mon•sön′, *n.* [Fr. *monson,*

mousson, Sp. *monzon*, Pg. *mousão*, from Ar. *mausim*, a time, a season, the favorable season for sailing to India.] The trade wind of the Arabian and Indian seas, for six months (November to March) blowing from about N.E.; and for the next six months (April to October) from about S.W.; an alternating wind in any region.

monster, mon′stėr, *n.* [Fr. *monstre*, from L. *monstrum*, a marvel, a monster, from *moneo*, to admonish. MONITION.] A plant or animal of abnormal structure or greatly different from the usual type; an animal exhibiting malformation in important parts; a person looked upon with horror on account of extraordinary crimes, deformity, or power to do harm; an imaginary creature, such as the sphinx, mermaid, etc.—*a.* Of inordinate size or numbers (a *monster* meeting).—**monstrosity,** mon•stros′i•ti, *n.* The state of being monstrous; that which is monstrous; an unnatural production.—**monstrous,** mon′strus, *a.* [L. *monstrosus*.] Unnatural in form; out of the common course of nature; enormous; huge; extraordinary; shocking; frightful; horrible.—*adv.* Exceedingly; very much (now vulgar or colloquial).—**monstrously,** mon′strus•li, *adv.* In a monstrous manner.—**monstrousness,** mon′strus•nes, *n.*

monstrance, mon′strans, *n.* [L.L. *monstrantia*, from L. *monstro*, to show.] *R. Cath. Ch.* the transparent or glass-faced shrine in which the consecrated host is presented for the adoration of the people.

montage, mon•täj′, *n.* [Fr. *montage*, mounting, putting together.] The art of combining several pictures into one distinct picture; the showing of a series of brief film scenes in rapid succession to present a series of interconnected ideas.

monte, mon′tā, *n.* [Sp., the stock of cards which remain after each player has received his share, from L. *mons*, a mountain.] A Spanish gambling game played with dice or cards.

Montessorian, Mon•tes•so′ri•an, *a.* [After Dr. Maria *Montessori* (1870-1952) of Italy.] A training for children aged three to six, based on methods of scientific pedagogy.

month, munth, *n.* [A.Sax. *mónath*, *mónth*, from *móna*, the moon = Icel. *mánathr*, Dan. *maaned*, D. *maand*, G. *monath*; allied to L. *mensis*, Gr. *mēn*, a month. MOON.] One of the twelve parts of the calendar year, consisting unequally of 30 or 31 days, except February, which has 28, and in leap year 29 days: called distinctively a *calendar month*; the period between change and change of the moon, reckoned as twenty-eight days.—**monthly,** munth′li, *a.* Continued a month or performed in a month; happening once a month, or every month.—*adv.* Once a month; in every month.—*n.* A magazine or other literary periodical published once a month.—**month's mind,** *n.* A celebration in remembrance of a deceased person held a month after the death.

monticule, mon′ti•kūl, *n.* [L. *monticulus*, dim. of *mons*, *montis*, a mountain.] A little mount; a hillock.

monument, mon′ū•ment, *n.* [L. *monumentum*, from *moneo*, to remind, to warn. MONITION.] Anything by which the memory of a person, period, or event is perpetuated; a memorial; especially something built or erected in memory of events, actions, or persons; any enduring evidence or example; a singular or notable instance.—**monumental,** mon•ū•men′tal, *a.* Pertaining to a monument; serving as a monument; memorial; preserving memory.—**monumentally,** mon•ū•men′tal•li, *adv.* By way of monument or memorial; by means of monuments.

moo, mö, *v.i.* [Imitative.] To low, as a cow.—*n.* The low of a cow.

mood, möd, *n.* [Fr. *mode*, L. *modus*; merely a different spelling of *mode*.] *Gram.* a special form of verbs expressive of certainty, contingency, possibility, or the like; *logic*, the determination of propositions according to their quantity and quality, that is, whether universal, affirmative, etc.

mood, möd, *n.* [A.Sax. *mód*, mind, passion, disposition = D. *moed*, Icel. *módr* (*móthr*), Dan. and Sw. *mod*, Goth. *mods*, G. *muth*, mood, spirit, passion, courage, etc.; root doubtful.] Temper of mind; state of the mind in regard to passion or feeling; temporary disposition; humor; a fit of temper or sullenness.—**moodily,** möd′i•li, *adv.* In a moody manner.—**moodiness,** möd′i•nes, *n.* The state or quality of being moody.—**moody,** möd′i, *a.* [A.Sax. *módig*, angry.] Subject to or indulging in moods or humors; fretful; out of humor; gloomy; sullen; melancholy.

moon, mön, *n.* [A.Sax. *móna*, (masc.) = Icel. *máni*, Dan. *maane*, D. *maan*, G. *mond*, Goth. *mena*, Lith. *menu*, Gr. *mēnē*, Skr. *más*; from root *ma*, to measure.] The earth's satellite, revolving around the earth and accompanying it on its annual revolution around the sun, having a diameter of 2,163 miles, and a mean distance from earth of 238,857 miles; a satellite of any planet (the *moons* of Jupiter); the period of a revolution of the moon; a month (poetical); something in the shape of a moon or crescent.—*v.i.* To wander or gaze idly or moodily as if moonstruck (colloq.).—**moonbeam,** *n.* A ray of light from the moon.—**mooncalf,** *n.* A stupid fellow.—**moonish,** mön′ish, *a.* Variable, as the moon; fickle.—**moonlight,** mön′līt, *n.* The light afforded by the moon.—**moonlighter,** mön′līt•ėr, *n.* A person who holds a second job after his day's work is done.—**moonlighting,** mön′līt•ing, *n.* Holding a second job.—**moonlit,** *a.* Lit or illuminated by the moon.—**moonshine,** mön′shīn, *n.* The light of the moon; pretense; empty show; illegal liquor.—**moonstone,** mön′stōn, *n.* A pearly white, translucent fedspar, used as a gem.—**moonstruck,** mön′struk, *a.* Crazed; lunatic.—**moony,** mön′i, *a.* Bewildered or silly.

moor, mör, *n.* [A.Sax. *mór* = Icel. *mór*, a heath; D. *moer*, a morass; Dan. *mor*, a moor, a marsh; G. *moor*, a marsh, a moor; same root as *mire*; *morass* is a derivative.] A tract of waste land, especially when covered with heath; a tract of ground on which game is preserved for sport. (*Brit.*)—**moor cock, moorfowl,** *n.* The red grouse. GROUSE.—**moor hen,** *n.* The gallinule or water hen; also the female of the red grouse.

Moor, mör, *n.* [Fr. *Maure*, from L. *Maurus*, Gr. *Mauros*, a Moor; comp. Gr. *mauros*, black or dark-colored.] A Moslem of the northern coast of Africa.—**moorish,** mö′rish, *a.*

moor, mör, *v.t.* [D. *marren*, *maren*, to tie, to moor; same word as E. *mar*, A.Sax. *merran*, to hinder, to mar, O.H.G. *marrjan*, to stop.] To confine or secure (a ship) in a particular station, as by cables and anchors, or by chains; to fix firmly.—**mooring,** mör′ing, *n.* *Naut.* the act of one who moors; that by which a ship is moored; *pl.* the place where a ship is moored.

moose, mös, *n.* [American Indian name.] A large animal of the deer family, with broadly palmated antlers, found in Canada and northern U. S.

moot, möt, *v.t.* [A.Sax. *mótian*, to meet for deliberation, to discuss, from *mót*, a meeting, whence *métan*, to meet. MEET.] To bring forward and discuss.—*n.* A debate on a hypothetical legal case by way of practice.—*a.* Debatable.

mop, mop, *n.* [A Celtic word: W. *mop*, a mop; Gael. *mob*, a tuft, tassel, mop.] A piece of cloth or coarse yarn fastened to a long handle and used for cleaning floors; something likened to a mop, as a tangle of hair, etc.—*v.t.*—*mopped*, *mopping*. To rub or wipe with a mop.—**mop-up,** *n.* Act of cleaning up or disposing of.—**mop up,** *v.t.* To clear out, especially where enemy resistance still remains.—*v.i.* To complete a project.

mop, mop, *n.* [Comp. D. *moppen*, to pout, to make a sulky face. MOPE.] A wry mouth; a grimace.

mope, mōp, *v.i.*—*moped*, *moping*. [Connected with *mop*, a wry mouth; D. *moppen*, to pout.] To show a dull, downcast, or listless air; to be spiritless or gloomy.—*v.t.* To make listless or dejected.—*n.* One who mopes.—**mopish,** mōp′ish, *a.*

moppet, mop′et, *n.* [Dim. from M.E. *mop*, *moppe*, rag doll, baby.] Young child, youngster. (Colloq.)

moraine, mō•rān′, *n.* [Fr., akin to It. *mora*, a heap of stones.] An accumulation of stones or other debris on the surface of glaciers or in the valleys at their foot, a regular feature in glacier phenomena.

moral, mor′al, *a.* [Fr. *moral*, from L. *moralis*, from *mos, moris*, manner, *mores*, manners, morals (seen also in *demoralize, demure, morose*).] Relating to right and wrong as determined by duty; relating to morality or morals; ethical; capable of distinguishing between right and wrong; governed by the laws of right and wrong; appealing to man as engaged in the practical concerns of life; sufficient for practical purposes (*moral* evidence, certainty); sexually virtuous; conforming to the rules of right conduct.—*Moral law*, the law prescribing moral duties and teaching right and wrong.—*Moral philosophy*, the science which treats of the nature and grounds of moral obligation; ethics.—*Moral sense*, the capacity to perceive what is right and wrong, and to approve or disapprove; conscience.—*n.* The practical lesson inculcated by any story; *pl.* general conduct or behavior as right or wrong; principles and mode of life; also moral philosophy or ethics.—**morale,** mō•räl′, *n.* [An erroneous spelling of Fr. *moral*, used in same sense.] Mental condition of soldiers, etc., as regards courage, good cheer, and determination to do one's duty well, despite privation; the attitude of good will and devotion to duty existing among members of a group for its honor.—**moralist,** mor′al•ist, *n.* One who teaches morals; a writer or lecturer on ethics; one who inculcates or practices moral duties.—**morality,** mō•ral′i•ti, *n.* The doctrine of moral duties; morals; ethics; the practice of the moral duties; the quality of an action, as estimated by a standard of right and wrong.—**morality play,** mō•ral′i•ti plā, *n.* An allegorical dramatic form of the 14th to 18th centuries.—**moralize,** mor′al•īz, *v.t. moralized, moralizing.* To apply to a moral purpose; to draw a moral from.—*v.i.* To make moral reflections; to draw practical lessons from the facts of life.—**moralizer,** mor′al•ī•zėr, *n.*—**morally,** mor′al•li, *adv.*

morass, mō•ras′, *n.* [Same as D. *moeras*, from *moer*, a moor.] A tract of low, soft, wet ground; a marsh.

moratorium, mor•a•tō′ri•um, *n.* [L. *moratorius*, from *mora*, delay.] A special period of delay granted by law to debtors.

Moravian, mō•rā′vi•an, *a.* Pertaining to Moravia or the Moravians.—*n.* A native of Moravia; one of a religious sect, also called United Brethren, tracing its origin to John Huss, and holding evangelical principles.

moray, mo•rā′, mō•rā′, *n.* [Pg. *moreia*, from L. *muraena.*] Any of numerous voracious eels of the family Muraenidae, found in the Mediterranean and other warm seas.

morbid, mor′bid, *a.* [L. *morbidus*, from *morbus*, a disease. MORTAL.] Gloomy; gruesome; not sound and healthful; relating to disease.—**morbidity, morbidness,** mor•bid′i•ti, mor′bid•nes, *n.*—**morbidly,** mor′bid•li, *adv.*

mordacious, mor•dā′shus, *a.* [L. *mordax, mordacis*, from *mordeo*, to bite. MORSEL.] Biting; sarcastic.—**mordacity,** mor•das′i•ti, *n.* [L. *mordacitas.*] The quality of biting; readiness to bite.—**mordant,** mor′dant, *n.* [Fr. *mordant*, from L. *mordeo* to bite.] A substance employed in the process of dyeing which serves to fix the colors; sticky matter by which gold leaf is made to adhere.—*a.* Biting; caustic; severe.

more, mōr, *a.* Serving as the comparative of *much* and *many*, the superlative being *most.* [A.Sax. *mára*; D. *meer*, Dan. *meer, meere*, G. *mehr*, Icel. *meiri, meirr*, Goth. *mais, maiza*, more; from same root as L. *magnus*, great, E. *may.*] With singular nouns (as comparative of *much*): greater in amount, extent, degree, etc. (*more* land, *more* light); with plural nouns (as comparative of *many*): greater in number; in greater numbers (*more* men); added to some former number; additional (one day *more*, or one *more* day).—*adv.* In a greater degree, extent, or quantity; in addition; besides; again (once *more*, no *more*).—*To be no more*, to be destroyed or dead; to have perished. ∴ *More* is used to modify an adjective (or adverb) and form the comparative degree, having the same force and effect as the termination *er* in comparatives; as *more* wise (=*wiser*); *more* wisely; *more* illustrious; *more* illustriously.—*n.* What is more or greater; something farther or in addition.

moreen, mo•rēn′, *n.* [Connected with *mohair*, Fr. *moire.*] A watered woolen, or woolen and cotton fabric used for curtains, heavy dresses, etc.

morel, mo•rel′, *n.* [Fr. *morelle*, nightshade, from L.L. *morellus*, dark-colored, L. *morulus*, dark. So also the morel cherry is a dark-colored cherry.] Garden nightshade; a kind of cherry. MORELLO.

morel, mo•rel′, *n.* [Fr. *morille*, from O.H.G. *morilha*, G. *morchel*, Sw. *murkla.*] A kind of edible fungus.

morello, mo•rel′lō, *n.* [It. *morello*, dark-colored. MOREL.] A kind of cherry with a dark-red skin.

moreover, mōr•ō′vėr, *adv.* [*More* and *over.*] Beyond what has been said; further; besides.

mores, mō′rēz, *n.* pl. [L.] Customs and conventions or folk ways containing the moral views of a people and having the force of law through long use.

Moresque, mō•resk′, *a.* [Fr., from It. *moresco*, from *Moro*, L. *Maurus*, a Moor.] Moorish; after the manner of the Moors.—*n.* A style of ornamentation for flat surfaces; same as *Arabesque.*

morganatic, mor•ga•nat′ik, *a.* [L.L. *morganatica*, a kind of dowry paid on the morning before or after marriage, a dowry accepted in lieu of other claims; corrupted from G. *morgen-gabe*, lit. morning gift (A. Sax. *morgen-gifu*).] Said of a kind of marriage between a monarch, or one of the highest nobility, and a lady of inferior rank; called also a *left-handed marriage*, the offspring of which do not inherit the father's rank or possessions, but are considered legitimate in most other respects.—**morganatically,** mor•ga•nat′i•kal•li, *adv.* In the manner of a morganatic marriage.

morgue, morg, *n.* [Fr. Origin unknown.] A place where the bodies of persons found dead are exposed that they may be claimed by their friends; reference files in a newspaper office.

moribund, mor′i•bund, *a.* [L. *moribundus*, from *morior*, to die. MORTAL.] In a dying state.

morion, mor′i•on, *n.* [Fr. *morion*, from Sp. *morrion*, a morion; origin doubtful.] A kind of helmet of iron, steel, or brass, somewhat like a hat in shape, and without beaver or visor.

Morisco, mo•ris′kō, *n.* [Sp. *morisco*, Moorish, from *Moro*, a Moor.] A name applied to the ancient Moorish population of Spain and to their language; a morris dance.

Mormon, mor′mon, *n.* [From the Book of *Mormon*, accepted by them as of divine origin, and said to have been made known to Joseph Smith by an angel.] A term generally applied to a member of that religious body properly known as the Church of Jesus Christ of Latter-day Saints.—**Mormonism,** mor′mon•izm, *n.* The religion or doctrines of the Mormons.

morn, morn, *n.* [Contr. from O.E. *morwen*, A.Sax. *morgen*, morning, whence also *morrow.*] The first part of the day; the morning: used chiefly in poetry.—**morning,** morn′ing, *n.* [O.E. *morwening*, from A.Sax. *morgen* (D., Dan., and G. *morgen*, Icel. *morginn*, Goth. *maurgins*) by common change of *g* to *w*, with the *-ing* of verbal nouns. (Comp. *even, evening, dawn, dawning.*) The root is seen in Lith. *mirgu*, to glimmer, to gleam.] The first part of the day, beginning at twelve o'clock at night and extending to twelve at noon; in a more limited sense, the time beginning at break of day and extending to the hour of breakfast and of beginning the labors of the day or considerably later; *fig.* the first or early part (as of life). It is often used adjectively.—**morning-glory,** *n.* A name given to several climbing plants of the convolvulus family, with handsome flowers.—**morning star,** *n.* Any of the planets, Venus, Jupiter, Mars, Mercury, Saturn, when it rises before the sun.

morocco, mo•rok′ō, *n.* A fine leather made from the skins of goats, first imported from Morocco, and extensively used in the binding of books, upholstering furniture, making ladies' shoes, etc.

moron, mō′ron, *n.* [Gr. *mōros*, sluggish.] A person having the mental age of 8 to 12 years.

morose, mo•rōs′, *a.* [L. *morosus*, wayward, peevish, morose, from *mos, moris*, a custom, habit. MORAL.] Of a sour temper; severe; sullen and austere.—**morosely,** mo•rōs′li, *adv.* In a morose manner; sourly; with sullen austerity.—**moroseness,** mo•rōs′nes, *n.* The quality of being morose; sourness of temper; sullenness.

morpheme, mor′fēme, *n.* [Fr. *morphème,* from Gr. *morphē.*] A word such as *wait,* or a part of a word, as *ed* in wait*ed,* not further divisible into a meaningful part.—**morphemics,** mor′fē•miks, *n.* The study and analysis of morphemes.

Morpheus, mor′fi•us, *n.* [Gr. from *morphē,* form, from the forms he causes to appear to people in their dreams.] *Greek myth.* the god of sleep and dreams.

morphia, morphine, mor′fi•a, mor′-fēn, *n.* [Gr. *Morpheus,* the god of sleep.] The narcotic principle of opium, a vegetable alkaloid of a bitter taste, of medicinal value as an anodyne.

morphology, mor•fol′o•ji, *n.* [Gr. *morphē,* form, and *logos,* description.] That department of science which treats of the form and arrangement of the structures of plants and animals; the science of form in the organic world.—**morphologic, morphological,** mor•fo•loj′ik, mor•fo•loj′i•kal, *a.* Pertaining to morphology.—**morphologically,** mor•fo•loj′i•kal•li, *adv.* In a morphological manner.—**morphologist,** mor•fol′o•jist, *n.* One versed in morphology.

morris, mor′is, *n.* **morris dance,** [Fr. *moresque,* from Sp. *morisco,* from *Moro,* a Moor.] A dance borrowed from the Moors, or in imitation of their dances; a fantastic dance formerly practiced in England, as in the May games.

Morris chair, a comfortable armchair having an adjustable back.

Morris Plan, a method for making small loans employed by an industrial bank in the United States.

morrow, mor′ō, *n.* [MORNING.] The day next after the present or after any day specified.—*Good morrow,* good morning, a term of salutation. —*To-morrow,* on the morrow; next day.

Morse code. [After its inventor, Professor *Morse,* of Massachusetts.] A system of symbols, consisting of dashes and dots, to be used in transmitting messages either audibly or visually.

morsel, mor′sel, *n.* [O.Fr. *morcel* (Fr. *morceau*), from L.L. *morcellum,* a dim. from L. *morsus,* a bite, from *mordeo,* to bite.] A bite; a mouthful; a small piece of food; a fragment; a little piece in general.

mort, mort, *n.* [Fr. *mort,* death. MORTAL.] A flourish sounded at the death of game.

mortal, mor′tal, *a.* [L. *mortalis,* from *mors, mortis,* death: same root as Skr. *mri,* to die, *mrita,* dead; this root meaning to crush or grind, and being also that of *meal, mild, murder,* etc.] Subject to death; destined to die; deadly; destructive to life; causing death; fatal; incurring the penalty of death or divine condemnation; not venial (*mortal* sin); human; belonging to man, who is mortal. Colloquially applied to periods of time felt to be long or tedious (ten *mortal* hours).—*n.* A being subject to death; a man; a human being.—**mortally,** mor′tal•li, *adv.* In the manner of a mortal; in a deadly manner or manner that must cause death.—**mortality,** mor•tal′i•ti, *n.* [L. *mortalitas.*] The state of being mortal; death; frequency of death; death of numbers in proportion to a population; humanity; human nature; the human race.—*Bills of mortality,* abstracts showing the numbers that have died during certain periods of time.—*Tables of mortality,* tables showing how many out of a certain number of persons of a given age will probably die successively in each year till the whole are dead.

mortar, mor′tėr, *n.* [From L. *mortarium,* a mortar in which things are pounded.] A vessel, usually in form of an inverted bell, in which substances are pulverized or pounded with a pestle; a short piece of ordnance, thick and wide, used for throwing shells, etc., and named from its resemblance to the above utensil; a mixture of lime and sand with water, used as a cement for stones and bricks in walls.—**mortarboard,** mor′tėr•bōrd, *n.* A board for holding mortar; a square-topped academic cap.

mortgage, mor′gij, *n.* [Fr. *mort,* dead, and *gage,* pledge—the estate pledged becomes *dead* or entirely lost by failure to pay.] An assignment or conveyance of land or house property to a person as security for the payment of a debt due to him, and on the condition that if the money shall be paid according to contract the grant shall be void; the deed by which this conveyance is effected.—*v.t.*—*mortgaged, mortgaging.* To grant or assign on mortgage; to pledge; to make liable to the payment of any debt.—**mortgagee,** mor•gi•jē′, *n.* The person to whom an estate is mortgaged.—**mortgagor,** mor′gij•ėr, *n.* The person who mortgages.

mortician, mor•tish′an, *n.* [L. *mors, mortis,* death.] An undertaker.

mortify, mor′ti•fī, *v.t.*—*mortified, mortifying.* [Fr. *mortifier.*—L. *mors, mortis,* death, and *facio,* to make. MORTAL.] To affect with gangrene or mortification; to subdue or bring into subjection by abstinence or rigorous severities; to humiliate.—*v.i.* To practice mortification; to become gangrenous.—**mortification,** mor′ti•fi•ka″shon, *n. Med.* the death of a part of an animal body while the rest is alive; gangrene; the subduing of the passions and appetites by penance, abstinence, etc.; humiliation or slight vexation; chagrin.

mortise, mor′tis, *n.* [Fr. *mortaise,* a mortise; origin unknown.] A hole cut in one piece of material to receive a corresponding projecting piece called a *tenon,* on another piece, in order to fix the two together.—*v.t.*—*mortised, mortising.* To cut a mortise in; to join by tenon and mortise.

mortmain, mort′mān, *n.* [Fr. *mort,* dead, and *main,* hand.] *Law,* possession of lands or tenements in dead hands, or hands that cannot alienate, as those of a corporation; the holding of property more particularly by religious houses, which has been restricted by various statutes.

mortuary, mor′chū•e•ri, *n.* [L.L. *mortuarium,* from L. *mortuus,* dead, from *mori,* to die. MORTAL.] A place for the temporary reception of the dead; a dead-house. *a.* Pertaining to the burial of the dead.

morula, mor′ū•la, *n.* [Dim. of L. *morum,* mulberry, from the appearance of the mass of cells.] *Physiol.* a roundish mass of cells (called blastomeres) resulting from the division or segmentation of an ovum or its yolk in the process of development.

Mosaic, Mosaical, mō•zā′ik, mō•zā′i•kal, *a.* Relating to *Moses,* the Hebrew lawgiver, or his writings and institutions.

mosaic, mō•zā′ik, *a.* [Fr. *mosaïque,* from It. *mosaico, musaico,* from L. Gr. *mousaikos,* belonging to the Muses, from *Mousa,* a Muse.] A term applied to inlaid work formed by little pieces of enamel, glass, marble, precious stones, etc., of various colors, cut and disposed on a ground of cement in such a manner as to form designs, and to imitate the colors and gradations of painting. —*n.* Mosaic or inlaid work.—*Mosaic gold,* an alloy of copper and zinc, called also *ormolu.*—**mosaicist,** mō•zā′i•sist, *n.* One who makes mosaics.

moschatel, mos′ka•tel, *n.* [Fr. *moscatelle,* from L.L. *muscatus,* having the odor of musk. MUSK.] A plant of the temperate regions, with pale green flowers which smell like musk.

Moselle, mo•zel′, *n.* A species of white French and German wine, so named from the river *Moselle.*

Moslem, moz′lem, *n.* [Ar. *moslem, muslim,* a true believer, from *salama,* to resign one's self to God.] A Mussulman or Mohammedan.—*a.* Mohammedan.

mosque, mosk, *n.* [Fr. *mosquée,* It. *moschea,* Sp. *mezquita,* from Ar. *mesjid,* the place of adoration, from *sajad,* to adore.] A Mohammedan temple or place of religious worship.

mosquito, mos•kē′tō, *n.* [Sp. and Pg. *mosquito,* dim. from *mosca,* L. *musca,* a fly.] A name applied to several species of gnatlike flies, common in many regions, and which are very annoying from their severe bites.—*Mosquito nets* or *curtains,* of gauze, are often used to ward off attacks by mosquitoes upon persons reposing or asleep.

moss, mos, *n.* [D., O.G., and Dan. *mos,* Sw. *mossa,* Icel. *mosi,* A.Sax. *meós,* G. *moos,* moss, a bog. Cog. L. *muscus,* moss; Gr. *moschos,* a sprout or tender shoot.] A name common to many cryptogamic plants of small size with simple branching stems and numerous, generally narrow leaves; also a name of various lichens; a bog; a place where peat is found.—*v.t.* To cover with moss. —**mossy,** mos′i, *a.* Overgrown with moss; abounding with moss; like moss.—**mossiness,** mos′i•nes, *n.* The state of being mossy, or overgrown with moss.—**moss agate,** *n.* A kind of agate having internally a moss-like appearance.—**moss-grown,** *a.* Overgrown with moss.—**moss rose,** *n.* A beautiful variety of rose, so named from the calyx being covered with a moss-like growth.—**mosstrooper,** *n.* One of the marauders upon the borders of England and Scotland previous to the union of the crowns, from the mosses so common on the borders.

most, mōst, *a.* superl. of *more.* [A.Sax. *maest*, for *má-est*, superl. of old positive *má*, more; Goth. *maists*, Icel. *mestr*, D. and Dan. *meest*, G. *meist.* MORE.] Greatest in any way: with singular nouns (*most* wisdom, need, etc.); greatest in number; amounting to a considerable majority; with plurals (*most* men; *most* sorts of learning).—*adv.* In the greatest or highest, or in a very great or high degree, quantity, or extent; mostly; chiefly: often used before adjectives and adverbs to form the superlative degree, as *more* is to form the comparative.—*The Most High*, the Almighty.—*n.* The greatest or greater number; the majority: in this case plural; greatest amount or advantage; utmost extent, degree, effect, etc.: often with *the*, and in this sense singular.—*At most* or *at the most*, at furthest; at the utmost extent.—**mostly,** mōst′li, *adv.* For the most part; chiefly; mainly.

mot, mō, *n.* [Fr. *mot*, a word, a motto, L.L. *muttum*, from L. *muttio*, to mutter.] A pithy or witty saying; a bon-mot.

mote, mōt, *n.* [A.Sax. *mot*, a mote; comp. D. *mot*, dust, sweepings.] A small particle; a mere atom; anything proverbially small.

motel, mō•tel′, *n.* [From *mo*torists' *hotel.*] A lodging for motorists along the highway with accommodations for automobiles.

motet, mo•tet′, *n.* [Fr. *motet*, from It. *mottetto*, a dim. of *motto.* MOTTO.] *Mus.* a sacred cantata; a choral composition, usually of a sacred character.

moth, moth, *n.* [A.Sax. *moththe*; D. *mot*, Icel. *motti*, G. *motte*, Sw. *mott*, a moth.] The name of numerous lepidopterous insects allied to the butterflies, but seldom seen on the wing except in the evening or at night; the clothes-moth, the caterpillar of which is notoriously destructive to woolen materials, furs, skins, etc.—**mothy,** moth′i, *a.* Full of moths; eaten by moths.—**moth-eat,** *v.t.* To eat or prey upon, as a moth eats a garment.—**moth-eaten,** *a.* Eaten by moths or rather their larvae.

mother, muTH′ėr, *n.* [A.Sax. *módor*, D. *moeder*, Dan. and Sw. *moder*, Icel. *móthir*, G. *mutter*, Ir. *matair*, Gael. *mathair*, L. *mater*, Gr. *mētēr*, Skr. *mâtâ*, *mâtar*, Per. *mâder*; from root *ma* to bring forth, the term., as in *father*, denoting an agent.] A female parent, especially one of the human race; a woman who has borne a child; that which has produced anything; source of anything; generatrix; a familiar term of address to elderly females; an abbess or other female holding an important position in religious or semi-religious institutions.—*Mother Carey's chicken*, a name given by sailors to the stormy petrel.—*a.* Native; natural (*mother* wit); giving birth or origin; originating (*mother* country).—**motherhood,** muTH′ėr•hụd, *n.* The state of being a mother.—**mother-in-law,** *n.* The mother of one's husband or wife.—**motherless,** muTH′ėr•les, *a.* Destitute of a mother; having lost a mother.—**motherliness,** muTH′ėr•li•nes, *n.* Quality of being motherly.—**motherly,** muTH′ėr•li, *a.* Pertaining to a mother; becoming a mother; tender and affectionate.—**mother-of-pearl,** *n.* The hard silvery brilliant internal layer of several kinds of shells extensively used in the arts. Called also *Nacre.*—**mother tongue,** *n.* One's native language; a language to which other languages owe their origin.—**mother wit,** *n.* Native wit; common sense.

mother, muTH′ėr, *n.* [L.G. *moder*, D. *modder*, Dan. *mudder*, G. *mutter* —dregs, mud, slime, etc.; allied to *mud.*] A thick slimy substance that gathers in liquors, particularly vinegar.—*v.i.* To become mothery.

motif, mō•tēf′, *n.* [Fr.] A passage or theme that reappears in varying form throughout a musical composition; the prevailing idea an artist or writer has endeavored to express.

motific, mō•tif′ik, *a.* [L. *motus*, motion, and *facio*, to make.] Producing motion.—**motile,** mō′til, *a.* Having inherent power of motion, as certain organs of plants.—**motility,** mō•til′i•ti, *n.* Capability of motion.

motion, mō′shon, *n.* [L. *motio*, *motionis*, from *moveo*, *motum*, to move. MOVE.] The act or process of changing place; the passing of a body from one place to another; opposed to *rest*; the power of moving; a single act of motion; a movement; movement of the mind or soul; internal impulse; proposal made; a proposition made in a deliberative assembly; the proposing of any matter for the consideration of an assembly or meeting; *med.*, evacuation of the intestine; alvine discharge. —*v.t.* and *i.* To make a significant motion or gesture for guidance, as with the hand or head.—**motionless,** mō′shon•les, *a.* Wanting motion; being at rest.—**motion picture,** A form of drama produced by means of a series of photographs projected upon a screen to give an illusion of continuous, lifelike motion; any series of pictures photographed and presented in this way.

motivate, mō′ti•vāt, *v.t. Motivated, motivating.* To furnish with a motive; to be the motive of; to impel; to induce.

motive, mō′tiv, *n.* [Fr. *motif*, a motive, L.L. *motivus*, moving, from L. *moveo*, *motum*, to move. MOVE.] That which incites to action; that which determines the choice or moves the will; cause; object; inducement; prevailing design; the theme or leading subject in a piece of music; the prevailing idea in the mind of an artist, to which he endeavors to give expression in his work.—*a.* Causing motion.—*Motive power* or *force*, the power or force acting upon any body or quantity of matter to move it.—*v.t.* To supply a motive to or for; to prompt.—**motivity,** mō•tiv′i•ti, *n.* The power of producing motion.

motley, mot′li, *a.* [W. *mudliw*, a changing color, a motley color—*mud*, change, and *lliw*, a stain, a hue; or akin to *mottle.*] Consisting of different colors; parti-colored (a *motley* coat); exhibiting a combination of discordant elements; heterogeneous (a *motley* style); of a dress of various colors, or the usual dress of a domestic fool.

motor, mō′tėr, *n.* [L., A mover, from *moveo*, to move.] That which imparts motion; a prime mover, especially, a machine which develops power through rotary action, as an electric motor or an internal-combustion engine; an automobile.—*a.* Imparting motion; equipped with a motor; designating or pertaining to a nerve which stimulates the movement of a muscle or the secretory activity of glands.—*v.i.* To travel in, or drive, an automobile or other automotive vehicle.—**motorboat,** *n.* A boat propelled by an internal-combustion engine or by electricity. —**motorbus, motor coach,** *n.* A public vehicle propelled by an internal-combustion engine.—**motorcycle,** *n.* A two-wheeled vehicle propelled by an internal-combustion engine.—**motordrome,** *n.* An enclosed, circular track where motorcycles or automobiles are raced or tested.—**motoring,** *n.* The recreation or act of driving, or traveling in, an automobile.—**motorist,** *n.* A person who drives, or travels in, an automobile.—**motorize,**—*motorized, motorizing, v.t.* To provide with a motor or with motor-powered equipment.—**motorman,** *n.* A man who operates a motor-powered vehicle, as a streetcar or electric locomotive.—**motor ship,** *n.* A ship propelled by internal-combustion (usually Diesel) engines.

mottle, mot′l, *n.* [O.Fr. *mattelé*, clotted, curdled; probably from the German; comp. Prov. G. *matte*, curds.] A blotched or spotted sort of surface as seen in woods employed in cabinet work when polished.—*v.t.* To mark with spots or blotches as if mottled.—**mottled,** mot′ld, *p.* and *a.* Spotted; marked with blotches of color, as some kinds of cabinet wood.

motto, mot′tō, *n.* [It. *motto*, Fr. *mot*, a word, from L.L. *muttum*, a word, from L. *muttio*, to mutter.] A short pithy sentence or phrase, or even a single word, adopted as expressive of one's guiding idea or principle, appended to a coat of arms, or otherwise put prominently forward.

moufflon, mouflon, möf′lon, *n.* [Fr. *mouflon.*] An animal of the sheep kind inhabiting Corsica, Sardinia, and Greece.

mouillé, mü•yā′, *a.* [Fr., wet.] Given a softened, liquid sound, usually caused by a succeeding *y*-sound, as *l* in *William.*

moulin, mö•laṅ, *n.* [Fr. *moulin,* L.L. *molinus,* from L. *mola,* a mill.] A deep cylindrical hole in a glacier, formed by a rill on its surface draining into it.

mound, mound, *n.* [A.Sax. and G. *mund,* a defense; same root as *mount.*] An elevation of earth, generally artificial; a rampart; a hillock or knoll; *baseball,* the slight elevation on which the pitcher stands while pitching.—*v.t.* To heap up in a mound.—**Mound Builder,** *n.* An Indian of any of the various groups that once lived in the Mississippi River and Great Lakes regions and built earthworks.

mount, mount, *n.* [A.Sax. *munt,* Fr. *mont,* from L. *mons, montis,* a hill, from root seen in *eminent, prominent.*] A hill; a mountain; now chiefly poetical, or used in proper names, as *Mount* Vesuvius, *Mount* Sinai; a bulwark for offense or defense (O.T.); the cardboard or other material on which a picture or drawing is mounted or fixed; the setting of a gem or something similar; the opportunity or means of riding on horseback.—*v.i.* [Fr. *monter,* from *mont,* a hill.] To rise on high; to go up; to ascend; to be built to a great altitude; to get on or upon anything, specifically, to get on horseback; to amount; to reach in value.—*v.t.* To raise aloft; to ascend; to climb up to or upon; to place one's self upon (a throne or the like); to furnish with a horse or horses; to put on or cover with something necessary, useful, or ornamental (to *mount* a map on cloth); to prepare for use; to carry or be furnished with (a fort *mounts* a hundred cannon).—*To mount guard,* to take the station and do the duty of a sentinel.—**mountable,** moun′ta•bl, *a.* Capable of being mounted.—**mounter,** moun′tėr, *n.* One that mounts.—**mounting,** moun′ting, *n.* The act of ascending; that with which an article is mounted or set off, or finished for use, as the setting of a gem; the furnishings of a sword, of harness; cardboard on which a picture is pasted, etc.

mountain, moun′tin, *n.* [O.Fr. *muntaine, montaigne,* Fr. *montagne,* from L.L. *montaneus,* mountainous, from L. *mons, montis,* a mountain. MOUNT.] A huge mass of earth and rock rising above the common level of the earth or adjacent land; an elevated mass higher than a hill; something very large or great.—*Chain of mountains,* a group of mountains linked together, thus forming a series, a system, or a chain, as the Allegheny Mountains which range over four states.—*The Mountain,* the extremists of the revolutionary party during the first French Revolution who occupied the highest benches in the National Convention.—*a.* Of, or pertaining to, a mountain.—**mountain ash,** *n.* A genus of trees found in the United States and Europe, having ash-colored leaves, white corymbose flowers and scarlet fruit; in Europe, called the rowan tree.—**mountaineer,** moun′tin•ēr″, *n.* An inhabitant of a mountainous district; a climber of mountains.—*v.i.* To climb mountains.—**mountain goat,** *n.* A goat native to the mountainous regions of the northwestern United States and Canada.—**mountain lion,** *n.* A puma, also called cougar, panther or catamount, largest American species of the cat kind.—**mountainous,** moun′tin•us, *a.* Full of mountains; large as a mountain; huge.

mountebank, moun′ti•bangk, *n.* [It. *montimbanco, montambanco—montare,* to mount, and *banco,* bench.] One who mounts a bench or stage in the market or other public place, and vends medicines which he pretends are infallible remedies; a quack doctor; any boastful and false pretender; a charlatan.—*v.t.* To gull (*Shak.*).

mourn, mōrn, *v.i.* [A.Sax. *murnan*= Icel. *morna,* O.H.G. *mornan,* Goth. *maurnan,* to grieve; root same as *murmur.*] To express grief or sorrow; to grieve; to be sorrowful; to lament; to wear the dress or appearance of grief.—*v.t.* To grieve for; to lament; to deplore; to bewail.—**mourner,** mōr′nėr, *n.* One that mourns; one that follows a funeral in the habit of mourning.—**mournful,** mōrn′fụl, *a.* Expressing sorrow; exhibiting the appearance of grief; doleful; causing sorrow; sad; calamitous; sorrowful; feeling grief.—**mournfully,** mōrn′fụl•li, *adv.* In a mournful manner; dolefully; sorrowfully; sadly.—**mournfulness,** mōrn′fụl•nes, *n.* The state or character of being mournful.—**mourning,** mōr′ning, *n.* The act of expressing grief; lamentation; the dress or customary habit worn by mourners.—*a.* Employed to express grief (a *mourning* ring).—**mourning cloak,** *n.* A handsome purplish brown butterfly with wings bordered with yellow, brown and blue. It is found from the arctic south, in both Europe and America.—**mourning dove,** a small wild dove found in the United States, having a lamenting cry.

mouse, mous, *n.* pl. **mice,** mīs. [A.Sax. *mús,* pl. *mýs* (like *lús, lýs,* louse, lice); Icel. *mús,* Dan. *muus,* D. *muis,* G. *maus;* cog. L. *mus,* Gr. *mys,* Per. *mûsh,* Skr. *mûsha,* mouse.] A well-known small rodent quadruped that infests dwelling-houses, granaries, fields, etc.; a name of various allied animals; a term of endearment.—*v.i.* (mouz)—*moused, mousing.* To hunt for or catch mice.—**mouse-ear,** *n.* Any of various plants, so named from their soft, hairy leaves which seem to resemble in shape the ear of a mouse; the blue or white flowered forget-me-not, symbolic of fidelity.—**mouser,** mou′zer, *n.* A cat good at catching mice; one who snoops about; a detective (*slang*).

mousse, mös, *n.* [Fr. froth, foam.] A frozen dessert of whipped cream, sweetened and flavored, sometimes made firm with gelatin.

mouth, mouth, *n.* pl. **mouths,** mouᴛʜz. [A.Sax. *múth*=Icel. *muthr, munnr,* Sw. *mun,* Dan. and G. *mund,* D. *mond,* Goth. *munths*—mouth. Like *tooth, sooth,* etc., this word has lost an *n* before the *th.*] The aperture in the head of an animal through which food is received and voice uttered; the aperture between the lips or the portion of the face formed by the lips; the cavity within the lips; the opening of anything hollow, as of a pitcher or other vessel; the entrance to a cave, pit, or den, the opening of a well, etc.; the part of a river, creek, etc., by which it joins with the ocean or any large body of water.—*To make a mouth* or *to make mouths,* to distort the mouth; to make a wry face, as in derision.—*Down in the mouth,* chapfallen; dejected; mortified.—*To give mouth to,* to utter, to express.—*v.t.* (mouᴛʜ). To utter with a voice affectedly big or swelling; to seize or shake with the mouth.—*v.i.* To speak with a full, round, or loud, affected voice; to vociferate; to rant; to make wry faces, to grimace (*Tenn.*).—**mouthed,** mouᴛʜd, *a.* Having a mouth of this or that kind: used in composition (foul-*mouthed*).—**mouther,** mou′ᴛʜėr, *n.* One who mouths; an affected declaimer.—**mouthful,** mouth′fụl, *n.* As much as the mouth contains at once; a small quantity.—**mouthpiece,** mouth′pēs, *n.* The part of a musical instrument that is applied to the mouth; a tube by which a cigar is held in the mouth while being smoked; one who speaks on behalf of others.

mouton, mö′ton, *n.* [Fr. sheep, from M.Fr. *mouton,* ram.] A sheepskin that is sheared and dyed and treated to be used as fur similar to otter and sealskin.

move, möv, *v.t.*—*moved, moving.* [O. Fr. *mover, mouver,* Mod.Fr. *mouvoir,* from L. *movere, motum,* to move.] To carry, convey, or draw from one place to another; to cause to change place or posture; to set in motion; to stir; to excite into action; to influence; to prevail on; to rouse or excite the feelings of; to cause the bowels to move; to affect with tender feelings; to touch; to offer formally, as a motion for consideration by a deliberative assembly; *chess, checkers,* etc., to change the position of (a piece) in the regular course of play.—*v.i.* To change place or posture; to stir; to pass or go; to walk; to carry or bear one's self; to change residence; to take action; to begin to act.—*n.* Proceeding; action taken; the moving of a piece in playing chess, etc.; a change of residence; the act of moving; an advance or step.—

To be on the move, to be stirring about.—**movable, moveable,** möv'-a•bl, *a.* Capable of being moved; changing from one date to another. —*n.* Any part of a man's goods capable of being moved.—**movableness, moveableness, movability,** möv'a•bl•nes, möv•a•bil'i•ti, *n.*—**movably, moveably,** möv'a•bli, *adv.* —**movement,** möv'ment, *n.* Act of moving; course or process of change; motion; an individual act of motion; a gesture; an agitation set on foot by one or more persons for the purpose of bringing about some result desired; *mus.* motion or progression in time, also a detached and independent portion of a composition; the train of wheelwork in a watch or clock; *milit.* part of a maneuver; *art*, a trend in style, technique, or subject matter followed by a sufficient number of artists to introduce a significant change.—**mover,** möv'ėr, *n.* One who or that which gives motion.—**moving,** möv'ing, *a.* Causing to move or act; impelling; exciting the feelings; touching; pathetic.—**movingly,** möv'ing•li, *adv.*—**moving picture,** *n.* See MOTION PICTURE.—**movie,** möv'ē, *n.* A motion picture.

mow, mō, *v.t.*—*mowed* (*pret.*) *mowed* or *mown* (*pp.*) [A.Sax. *máwan*; akin. Icel. *múgr*, *múgi*, a swathe; Dan. *meie*, D. *maaijen*, G. *mähen*, to mow; allied to L. *meto*, Gr. *amaō*, to mow. *Meadow* is from this root.] To cut down with a scythe or mowing machine (to *mow* grass); to cut the grass from (to *mow* a meadow); to cut down (men, etc.) indiscriminately, or in great numbers or quantity.—*v.i.* To cut grass; to use the scythe or mowing machine.—**mower,** mō'ėr, *n.* One who mows; a mowing machine.—**mowing machine,** *n.* An agricultural machine employed to cut down grass, clover, grain, etc.

mow, mou, *n.* [A.Sax. *muga*, a heap, a mow, N. *muga*, *mua*, a heap of hay.] A pile of hay or sheaves of grain deposited in a barn; the part of a barn where they are packed.—*v.t.* To put or pile in a mow.

moxa, mok'sa, *n.* [Chinese.] A soft downy substance prepared in China and Japan from the young leaves of certain plants, used for the gout, etc., by burning it on the skin; any substance used in this way as a counterirritant.

mu, mū, mö, *n.* [Gr. *my.*] The twelfth letter of the Greek alphabet, corresponding to the English *M.*

much, much, *a.*; *more* and *most* serve as its comparative and superlative. [Shortened form of old *mochel*, *muchel*, much, from A.Sax. *mycel*, *micel*, much, great, many; akin Icel. *mjōg*, *mjōk*, much, *mikill*, great; Goth. *mikils*, O.H.G. *mihil*; same root as L. *magnus*, great, E. *may.* MAGNITUDE, MAY.] Great in quantity or amount; abundant: used with singular nouns (*much* food, seed, water, money, etc.).—*adv.* In a great degree; to a great amount or extent; greatly: used especially with comparatives and past participles (*much* better, larger, sooner, surprised, etc.); nearly (*much* as it was).—*Much about the same*, nearly equal.—*n.* A great quantity; a great deal; equivalent to an adjective with a noun omitted, and often qualified by *too*, *as*, and *so.*—**muchness,** much'-nes, *n.* State of being much; quantity.

mucilage, mū'si•lij, *n.* [L. *mucilago*, from *mucus*, slime, mucus.] A gummy vegetable matter contained in gum tragacanth, many seeds, roots, etc.; a solution in water of gummy matter of any kind.—**mucilaginous,** mū•si•laj'i•nus, *a.* Pertaining to or secreting mucilage; slimy; ropy; soft, and slightly viscid.

muck, muk, *n.* [From Icel. *myki*, Dan. *mög*, dung (whence *mödding*, midden).] Dung in a moist state, or a mass of dung and rotten vegetable matter; something mean, vile, or filthy.—*v.t.* To manure with muck; to remove muck from.—**mucker,** muk'ėr, *n.* A dishonorable and impolite person; an impudent boor. (*Slang*).—**muck rake,** muk'rāk, *n.* A rake for removing muck.—**muckrake,** *v.i.* To accuse of bad faith or broadcast accusation of corruption, especially if unjustly.

mucous, mucosity. See MUCUS.

mucronate, mū'kro•nāt, *a.* [L. *mucronatus*, from *mucro*, a sharp point.] *Bot.* and *zool.* narrowed to a point; terminating in a sharp point.

mucus, mū'kus, *n.* [L., mucus from the nose; akin *mungo*, to wipe the nose; *mucilage.*] A viscid fluid secreted by the mucous membrane of animals, which it serves to moisten and defend; *bot.* gummy matter soluble in water.—**mucous,** mū'kus, *a.* [L. *mucosus.*] Pertaining to or resembling mucus; slimy; ropy; secreting a slimy substance.—*Mucous membrane*, a membrane that lines all the cavities of the body which open externally (such as the mouth, nose, intestines), and secretes mucus.—**mucosity,** mū•kos'i•ti, *n.* The state of being mucous; sliminess.

mud, mud, *n.* [Allied to L.G. *mod*, *mudde*, D. *modder*, Dan. *mudder*, Sw. *modd*, mud, mire; Icel. *mod*, dust; E. *mother*, slimy sediment. *Muddle* is a derivative.] Wet and soft earth or earthy matter as in a puddle; sediment from turbid waters; mire. —*Mud wall*, a wall built of mud or clay, rendered firm by drying.—*v.t.* —*mudded*, *mudding.* To soil with mud; to muddy.—**muddily,** mud'-i•li, *adv.* In a muddy manner; turbidly; obscurely; confusedly.—**muddiness,** mud'i•nes, *n.* The quality or condition of being muddy.—**muddy,** mud'i, *a.* Abounding in mud; foul with mud; turbid; miry; cloudy in mind; confused; stupid; obscure; wanting in perspicuity.—*v.t.*—*muddied*, *muddying.* To soil with mud; to dirty; to make turbid; to cloud or make dull.—**mudguard,** *n.* A cover over the wheel of a conveyance to stop flying mud.—**mud hen,** *n.* One of several species of waterfowl.—**mud puppy,** *n.* A kind of salamander.—**mudsill,** *n.* The base or lowest sill of a structure, as of a bridge, at the bottom of a river, etc.—**mud turtle,** *n.* A name of the soft tortoises and terrapins.

muddle, mud'l, *v.t.*—*muddled*, *muddling.* [Freq. from *mud.*] To make foul, turbid, or muddy; to intoxicate partially; to cloud or stupefy, particularly with liquor; to bring into a state of confusion; to make a mess of.—*v.i.* To become muddy; to be in a confused state.—*n.* A mess; dirty confusion; intellectual confusion; bewilderment.—**muddled,** mud'ld, *p.* and *a.* Made turbid or muddy; stupefied; confused.—**muddleheaded,** *a.* Having the brains muddled; stupidly confused or dull; doltish.

muezzin, mụ•ez'zin, mö•ez'in, *n.* [A *muezzin*, from *azzana*, to inform, from *azana*, to hear.] A Mohammedan crier attached to a mosque, whose duty it is to proclaim from the balcony of a minaret the summons to prayers five times a day.

muff, muf, *n.* [Dan. *muffe*, D. *mof*, L.G. *muffe*, *muff*, G. *muff*, a muff, akin to O.H.G. *mouwa*, D. *mouw*, a long sleeve; comp. also D. *mof*, a clown, *muf*, musty, silly, doting. Hence *muffle.*] A cylindrical cover, usually made of fur, into which both hands may be thrust in order to keep them warm; a soft, useless fellow; a mean, poor-spirited person (*colloq.*); in various games, an unsuccessful attempt to hold a caught ball.—*v.t.* To bungle; to miss a chance; in games, to fail to hold a caught ball.

muffin, muf'in, *n.* A quick bread baked in individual cup-shaped molds; a drop biscuit.

muffle, muf'l, *v.t.* *muffled*, *muffling.* [O.E. also *muffle*, akin to *muff*; comp. D. *muffel*, a muff; Fr. *moufle*, a mitten.] To enfold or wrap up so as to conceal from view or protect from the weather; to wrap up or cover close, particularly the neck and face; to deaden the sound of (to *muffle* an oar or a drum); to restrain from speaking by wrapping up the head; to put to silence; *fig.* to wrap up or envelop; to involve.—*n.* [Fr. *moufle*, a kind of glove, a chemical vessel.] An arched vessel, resisting the strongest fire, and made to be placed over cupels in the operation of assaying, to preserve them from coming in contact with fuel, smoke, or ashes; a pulley block containing several sheaves.—**muffled,** muf'ld, *p.* and *a.* Wrapped up closely, especially about the face; treated so as to deaden the sound (as when an oar is wrapped with a mat at the rowlock).—**muffler,** muf'ler, *n.* A wrapper for muffling or enveloping the neck; something that deadens noise, especially on a car.

muffle, muf'l, *n.* [Fr. *mufle*, from G. *muffel*, an animal with large hanging lips.] The tumid and naked portion of the upper lip and nose of ruminants and rodents.

mufti, muf'ti, *n.* [Ar. *mufti*, from *āftā*, to judge, to give a decision.] The chief of the ecclesiastical order among the Mohammedans; a doctor of Mohammedan law; an Anglo-Indian term for plain dress worn by officers off duty; civilian dress.

mug, mug, *n.* [N. *mugge*, a ewer, a mug; Sw. *mugg*, an earthen cup; Ir. *mugan*, a mug.] A familiar name for an earthen or metal vessel for drinking from; the face (slang); a tough person (slang).—*v.t.* To photograph, especially a criminal; to assault from behind.—*v.i.* To make faces.—**mugger,** mug′ėr, *n.*

muggy, mug′i, *a.* [Prov. E. *mug*, mist; Icel. *mugga*, mugginess, drizzle; comp. Gael. *mugach*, cloudy; W. *mwg*, smoke.] Damp and close: said of the atmosphere or weather; warm and humid; moist; moldy.

mugwump, mug′wump, *n.* [Algonkin, a great man, a chief.] A person who takes an independent position in politics; a highly superior person in his own eyes.

mukluk, muk′luk, *n.* [Alaskan Eskimo *makliak*, *muklok*, *makluk*, large seal.] A variety of sealskin boot worn by Eskimos.

mulatto, mū•lat′tō, *n.* [Sp. *mulato*, from *mulo*, a mule. MULE.] The offspring of a Caucasian and a Negro; loosely, any individual of mixed Caucasian and Negro blood.

mulberry, mul′be•ri, *n.* [For *murberry*; A.Sax. *múrberie*, a mulberry, also *múr*, *mór*, from L. *morus*, a mulberry tree.] The berry or fruit of a well-known tree, and also the tree itself cultivated from a remote period for silk-worm rearing.—**mulberry-faced,** *a.* Having the face spotted as if with mulberry stains.

mulch, mulsh, *n.* [Akin to *mols* in A.Sax. *molsnian*, to rot, G. *mulsch*, *molsch*, rotten; D. *molsemen*, to molder.] Strawy dung in a somewhat moist state, but not rotten, used for protecting the roots of newly planted shrubs or trees, etc.—*v.t.* To cover with mulch.

mulct, mulkt, *n.* [L. *mulcta*, *multa*, a fine.] A fine or penalty.—*v.t.* To punish by fine or forfeiture; to punish by depriving; to deprive (to *mulct* a person *of* $300).

mule, mūl, *n.* [A.Sax. *múl*, Fr. *mule*, from L. *mulus*, a mule.] A quadruped of a mongrel breed, the offspring of an ass and a mare, or a horse and a she-ass; also any animal produced by a mixture of different species; a hybrid; a hybrid plant; a spinning machine invented by Crompton in 1775, so called from being a combination of the drawing rollers of Arkwright and the jenny of Hargreaves.—**mule skinner,** *n.* A driver of mules. (*Colloq.*)—**muleteer,** mū•le•tēr′, *n.* [Fr. *muletier.*] A muledriver.—**mulish,** mūl′ish, *a.* Like a mule; sullen; stubborn.—**mulishly,** mūl′ish•li, *adv.* In a mulish manner.—**mulishness,** mūl′ish•nes, *n.* Obstinacy or stubbornness.

mule, mūl, *n.* [Fr. from D. *muil*, from L. *mulleus*, a red leather shoe.] A backless slipper.

muliebrity, mū•li•eb′ri•ti, *n.* [L. *muliebritas*, from *muliebris*, womanly. womanish, from *mulier*, a woman.] Womanhood; puberty in a female; womanishness; effeminacy; softness.

mull, mul, *v.t.* [From the spurious participle *mulled* in *mulled ale*, equivalent to *mold-ale*, that is funeral ale, from *mold*, earth, the earth of the grave.] To heat, sweeten, and flavor with spices (to *mull* wine).

mull, mul, *v.i.* & *t.* To cogitate; to contemplate thoughtfully. (*Colloq.*)

mull, mul, *n.* [Hind. *mul-mul*, muslin.] A thin, soft kind of muslin.

mullein, mullen, mul′en, *n.* [A.Sax. *molegn*; comp. Dan. *mól*, a moth: one species is used to drive away moths.] The common name of a genus of wild plants used in domestic medicine.

muller, mul′ėr, *n.* [O.Fr. *moulleur*, from *moulre*, *mouldre* (Fr. *moudre*), L. *molere*, to grind, from *mola*, a millstone.] A sort of flat-bottomed pestle used for grinding pigments, etc.

mullet, mul′et, *n.* [Fr. *mulet*, from L. *mullus*, the surmullet.] A name common to spiny-rayed fishes of two somewhat widely separate families, the gray mullets and the red mullets, or surmullets.

mulligan, mul′i•gan, *n.* A stew of meat and vegetables. (*Slang.*)

mulligatawny, mul′i•ga•ta″ni, *n.* [Tamil *milagutannir*, lit. pepper water.] An East Indian curry soup.

mullion, mul′yon, *n.* [For *munnion*, a word equivalent to Fr. *moignon*, Sp. *muñon*, a stump, the mullion of a window being the stump below the tracery.] *Arch.* a vertical division between the lights of windows, screens, etc., in Gothic architecture; also a division between the panels in wainscoting.

multangular, mul•tang′gū•lėr, *a.* [L. *multus*, many, and *angulus*, angle.] Having many angles; polygonal.

multicostate, mul•ti•kos′tāt, *a.* [L. *multus*, many, *costa*, a rib.] Having many ribs; *bot.* having two or more diverging ribs: said of leaves.

multidentate, mul•ti•den′tāt, *a.* [L. *multus*, many, and *dens*, a tooth.] Having many teeth or teeth-like processes.

multifarious, mul•ti•fâ′ri•us, *a.* [L. *multifarius*, manifold—*multus*, many.] Having great multiplicity; having great diversity or variety; made up of many differing parts.—**multifariously,** mul•ti•fâ′ri•us•li, *adv.* In a multifarious way.—**multifariousness,** mul•ti•fâ′ri•us•nes, *n.*

multifid, mul′ti•fid, *a.* [L. *multifidus* —*multus*, many, and *findo*, to divide.] Cleft or cut by many divisions; *bot.* divided into several parts by clefts extending to about the middle (a *multifid* leaf).

multiflorous, mul•ti•flō′rus, *a.* [L. *multus*, many, *flos*, *floris*, a flower.] Many-flowered; having many flowers.

multiform, mul′ti•form, *a.* [L. *multiformis*—*multus*, many, and *forma*, form.] Having many forms, shapes, or appearances.—**multiformity,** mul•ti•for′mi•ti, *n.* The state of being multiform.

multilateral, mul•ti•lat′ėr•al, *a.* [L. *multus*, many, and *latus*, side.] Having many sides; polygonal; something involving more than two nations (*multilateral* conference).

multilineal, multilinear, mul•ti•lin′ē•al, mul•ti•lin′ē•ėr, *a.* [L. *multus*, many, and *linea*, a line.] Having many lines.

multilocular, mul•ti•lok′ū•lėr, *a.* [L. *multus*, many, *loculus*, a cell.] Having many cells, loculi, or compartments.

multimillionaire, mul•ti•mil•yon•âr′, *n.* [L. *multus*, many, and *millionaire.*] One whose wealth is measured in millions.

multiparous, mul•tip′a•rus, *a.* [L. *multus*, many, *pario*, to bear.] Producing many at a birth.

multipartite, mul′ti•pär•tīt, *a.* [L. *multus*, many, and *partitus*, divided—*pars*, a part.] Divided into several or many parts; *bot.* more deeply cleft than *multifid*.

multipede, multiped, mul′ti•pēd, *n.* [L. *multus*, many, *pes*, *pedis*, a foot.] An animal that has many feet, as a centipede.

multiphase, mul′ti•fās, *a.* [L. *multus*, many, *phasis*, phase.] Showing many phases.

multiple, mul′ti•pl, *a.* [Fr. *multiple*, from L.L. *multiplus*—*multus*, many, and term. as in *triple*.] Manifold; having many parts or divisions.—*n.* A number which contains another an exact number of times without a remainder (thus 24 is a *multiple* of three).—*Multiple sclerosis*, a disease in which tissue of the brain or spinal cord hardens, causing headache, partial paralysis, jerking muscle tremor, etc.

multiplex, mul′ti•pleks, *a.* [L. *multiplex*—*multus*, many, and stem of *plico*, to fold. PLY.] Manifold; complex; *bot.* having petals lying over each other in folds.—**multipliable,** mul′ti•plī•a•bl, *a.* Capable of being multiplied.—**multiplicable,** mul′ti•pli•ka•bl, *a.* Multipliable.—**multiplicand,** mul′ti•pli•kand, *n.* [L. *multiplicandus.*] *Arith.* the number to be multiplied by another, which is called the multiplier.—**multiplicate,** mul′ti•pli•kāt, *a.* [L. *multiplicatus.*] Multiplex.—**multiplication,** mul′ti•pli•kā″shon, *n.* [L. *multiplicatio*, *multiplicationis.*] The act or process of multiplying; the state of being multiplied; *arith.* and *alg.* the operation by which any given number or quantity may be added to itself any number of times proposed.—*Multiplication table*, a table containing the product of all the simple digits multiplied into each other, and onward, to some assumed limit, as to 12 times 12.—**multiplicative,** mul′ti•pli•kā″tiv, *a.* Tending to multiply; having the power to multiply.—**multiplicity,** mul•ti•plis′i•ti, *n.* [L. *multiplicitas*, from *multiplex.*] The state of being multiplex, numerous, or various; an extensive aggregate of individuals of the same kind; a great number.—**multiplier,** mul′ti•plī•ėr, *n.* One who or that which multiplies; the number in arithmetic by which another is multiplied; *teleg.* an instrument for increasing by repetition the strength of an electric current.—**multiply,** mul′ti•plī, *v.t.*—*multiplied, multiplying.* [Fr. *multiplier,* from L. *multiplicare,* from *multiplex.*] To increase in number; to make more by natural reproduction or by addition; to make more numerous; *arith.* to add to itself any given number of times. —*v.i.* To grow or increase in number, or to become more numerous by reproduction; to extend; to spread.

multisonous, mul•tis′ō•nus, *a.* [L. *multus,* many, *sonus,* sound.] Having many sounds, or sounding much.

multispiral, mul•ti•spī′ral, *a.* [L. *multus,* many, *spira,* a coil.] Having many spiral coils or convolutions.

multistriate, mul•ti•strī′āt, *a.* [L. *multus,* many, *stria,* a streak.] Marked with many streaks or striae.

multitubular, mul•ti•tū′bū•lėr, *a.* [L. *multus,* many, and E. *tubular.*] Having many tubes (a *multitubular* boiler).

multitude, mul′ti•tūd, *n.* [L. *multitudo,* from *multus,* much, many.] The state of being many; a great number, collectively; a great many, indefinitely; a crowd or throng; a gathering of people.—*The multitude,* the populace, or the mass of men without reference to an assemblage. —**multitudinous,** mul•ti•tū′di•nus, *a.* Pertaining or belonging to a multitude; consisting of a multitude. —**multitudinously,** mul•ti•tū′di•nus•li, *adv.* In a multitudinous manner.—**multitudinousness,** mul•ti•tū′di•nus•nes, *n.*

multivalent, mul•ti•vā′lent, *a.* [Prefix *multi,* and *valent.*] *Chem.* having a valence of three or more.

multivalve, mul′ti•valv, *a.* [L. *multus,* many, and E. *valve.*] Having many valves (a *multivalve* shell).—*n.* An animal which has a shell of many valves or pieces.

mum, mum, *a.* [Imitative of a low sound made with the lips closed, like L. and Gr. *mu;* akin *mumble.*] Silent; not speaking. Often used as an exclamation = be silent; hush.

mum, mum, *n.* [G. *mumme,* from Christian *Mumme,* who first brewed it at Brunswick in 1492.] A species of malt liquor used in Germany, made of wheat malt.

mum, mumm, mum, *v.i.* [Of Dutch or German origin; comp. G. *mummen,* to mask, *mumme,* a mask, *mummel,* a bugbear; D. *mommen,* to mask, *mom,* a mask, whence O.Fr. *momer,* to mask, *momerie,* mummery; originally perhaps to cover the face and cry *mum,* or similar sound.] To sport or make diversion in a mask or disguise.—**mummer,** mum′ėr, *n.* A masker; a masked buffoon.—**mummery,** mum′ėr•i, *n.* A masking or masquerade; buffoonery; farcical show; hypocritical disguise and parade.

mumble, mum′bl, *v.i.*—*mumbled, mumbling.* [Freq. from *mum;* like D. *mommelen,* Dan. *mumle,* G. *mummeln,* to mumble.] To mutter; to speak so as to render the sounds inarticulate and imperfect; to chew or bite softly; to eat with the lips closed.—*v.t.* To utter with a low inarticulate voice; to chew gently, or to eat with a muttering sound.—**mumbler,** mum′blėr, *n.* One who mumbles.—**mumblingly,** mum′bling•li, *adv.* In a mumbling manner.

mumblety-peg, mumble-the-peg, mum′bl•ti•peg, mum′bl•THi•peg, *n.* [From *mumble the peg,* the phrase said to the game's loser who had to snatch, with his teeth, a peg driven in the ground.] A game in which the players, from several positions, must toss or throw a knife, making it stick in the ground.

Mumbo Jumbo, mum′bō jum•bō, *n.* A god of certain Negro tribes; any senseless object of popular idolatry.

mummy, mum′i, *n.* [Fr. *mumie, momie,* Sp. *momia,* It. *mummia,* from Ar. *mûmia,* from *mûm,* wax.] A dead human body embalmed and dried after the manner of those taken from Egyptian tombs; a human body dried up and preserved, either artificially or by accident; a sort of wax used in grafting and planting trees; a sort of brown bituminous pigment.—*To beat to a mummy,* to beat soundly, or till senseless.—*v.t.* To embalm.—**mummify,** mum′i•fī, *v.t.* To make into a mummy; to embalm and dry, as a mummy.—**mummification,** mum′i•fi•kā″shon, *n.* The act of mummifying; the process of becoming a mummy.

mump, mump, *v.i.* [An imitative word, allied to *mumble* and *munch.*] To mumble or mutter, as in sulkiness; to move the lips with the mouth closed; to nibble; to chew; to munch; to grin or make mouths; to implore alms; to play the beggar. —*v.t.* To munch or chew.

mumps, mumps, *n.* pl. [From *mump,* sullenness.] A disease consisting in an inflammation of the salivary glands, with swelling along the neck; parotitis.

munch, munsh, *v.t.* and *i.* [Imitative of sound; akin *mumble, mump.*] To chew audibly; to mump; to nibble.—**muncher,** munsh′ėr, *n.* One who munches.

mundane, mun′dān, *a.* [L. *mundanus,* from *mundus,* the world.] Belonging to this world; worldly; terrestrial; earthly.—**mundanely,** mun′dān•li, *adv.* In a mundane manner; with reference to worldly things.

mungo, mung′gō, *n.* [Perhaps from some person of this name.] Artificial short-staple wool formed by tearing to pieces and disintegrating old woolen fabrics; akin to shoddy.

municipal, mū•nis′i•pal, *a.* [L. *municipalis,* from *municipium,* a town governed by its own laws—*munia,* official duties, and *capio,* to take.] Pertaining to local self-government; pertaining to the corporation of a town or city, or to the citizens of a state.—*Municipal bond,* a bond issued by a municipal government to provide funds for a public undertaking. —*Municipal law,* the law which pertains to the citizens of a state in their private capacity.—**municipalism,** mū•nis′i•pal•izm, *n.* Municipal state or condition.—**municipality,** mū•nis′i•pal″i•ti, *n.* A town or city possessed of local self-government; a community under municipal jurisdiction.

munificence, mū•nif′i•sens, *n.* [L. *munificentia*—*munus,* a gift or favor, and *facio,* to make.] The quality of being munificent; a giving with great liberality; bounty; liberality. —**munificent,** mū•nif′i•sent, *a.* Liberal in giving or bestowing; bounteous; generous.—**munificently,** mū•nif′i•sent•li, *adv.* In a munificent manner; liberally.

muniment, mū′ni•ment, *n.* [L. *munimentum,* a defense, from *munio,* to fortify, from *mœnia,* walls.] A fortification; a stronghold; support; defense; a writing by which claims and rights are defended or maintained; a title-deed, charter, record, etc.—*Muniment house, Muniment room,* a house or room for keeping deeds, charters, etc.

munition, mū•nish′on, *n.* [L. *munitio, munitionis,* from *munio,* to fortify; hence *ammunition.*] Materials used in war; military stores; ammunition.

mural, mū′ral, *a.* [L. *muralis,* from *murus,* a wall; same root as *munio,* to fortify. MUNITION.] Pertaining to a wall; resembling a wall; perpendicular or steep.—*Mural circle,* an astronomical instrument for measuring angular distances in the meridian, permanently fixed exactly perpendicular in the plane of the meridian.—*Mural crown,* a golden crown bestowed among the ancient Romans on him who mounted the wall of a besieged place and lodged a standard.—*Mural literature,* placards or posters on walls by political parties during elections.—*Mural painting,* a painting upon the surface of a wall.

murder, mėr′dėr, *n.* [A.Sax. *morthor, morther,* from *morth,* death; Goth. *maurthr,* D. *moord,* Dan., Sw., and G. *mord,* Icel. *morth;* L. *mors,* death (E. *mortal*); Skr. *mri,* to die.] The act of unlawfully killing a human being with premeditated malice; something difficult to do.—*v.t.* To kill (a human being) with premeditated malice; to slay feloniously; *fig.* to abuse or violate grossly (to *murder* the king's English).—*v.i.* To commit murder.—**murderer,** mėr′dėr•ėr, *n.* —**murderess,** mėr′dėr•es, *n.* A female who commits murder.—**murderous,** mėr′dėr•us, *a.*—**murderously,** mėr′dėr•us•li, *adv.*

murex, mū′reks, *n.* pl. **murices,** mū′ri•sēz. [L.] A mollusk resembling the whelk, in esteem from the earliest ages on account of the purple dye that some of them yielded; the dye itself.

muriate, mū′ri•āt, *n.* [L. *muria,* brine.] The old name for *Chloride.*—**muriatic,** mū•ri•at′ik, *a.* Pertaining to or obtained from brine or sea salt.—*Muriatic acid,* the older name of *Hydrochloric acid.*

muricate, muricated, mū′ri•kāt, mū′ri•kā•ted, *a.* [L. *muricatus,* from *murex,* the point of a rock.] Full of sharp points; armed with prickles.

murine, mū′rīn, *a.* [L. *murinus*, from *mus, muris*, a mouse.] Pertaining to a mouse or to mice.

murk, mėrk, *n.* [A.Sax *murc, mirce*, dark, Icel. *myrkr*, Dan. and Sw. *mörk*, dark.] Darkness or gloom. (*Shak.*)—**murky,** mėr′ki, *a.* Dark; obscure; gloomy.—**murkily,** mėr′ki•li, *adv.* In a murky manner; darkly.—**murkiness,** mėr′ki•nes, *n.* State of being murky; darkness; gloom.

murmur, mėr′mėr, *n.* [Fr. *murmure*, from L. *murmur*, a reduplication of an imitative syllable *mur*, seen in G. *murren*, D. *morren*, Icel. *murra*, Dan. *murre*, to murmur.] A low sound continued or continually repeated, as that of a stream; a low indistinct sound; a hum; a complaint uttered in a low, muttering voice; a grumble or mutter.—*v i.* To utter or give out a murmur or hum; to grumble; to utter complaints; to mutter.—*v.t.* To utter indistinctly; to mutter. —**murmurer,** mėr′mėr•ėr, *n.* One who murmurs.—**murmuring,** mėr′mėr•ing, *p.* and *a.* Making or consisting in a low continued noise; uttering complaints in a low voice or sullen manner.—*n.* A continued murmur; a low confused noise.—**murmurous,** mėr′mėr•us, *a.* Attended by murmurs; murmuring.—**murmurously,** mėr′mėr•us•li, *adv.*

murrain, mur′in, *n.* [O.Fr. *morine*, from L. *morior*, to die. MORTAL.] A disease that rages among cattle; a cattle plague or epizootic disease of any kind; foot-and-mouth disease. —*Murrain take you, murrain on you*, etc., plague take you, plague upon you.

murre, mėr, *n.* [Etymology doubtful.] A name for the common guillemot.

murrey, mur′i, *n.* [O.Fr. *morée*, a dark-red color, from L. *morum*, a mulberry.] A dark-red or mulberry color.

murrhine, mur′īn, *a.* [L. *murrhinus*, from *murrha*, a material, supposed to be fluorspar.] A name given to a delicate kind of ware anciently brought from the East, and much prized among the Romans. Called also *myrrhine.*

musaceous, mū•zā′shus, *a.* [From *Musa*, the typical genus.] Pertaining to the order of plants to which belong the banana and plantain.

muscadine, mus′ka•din, *n. Muscadinia rotundifolia*, a grape of the southwestern U.S.

muscatel, muscadel, mus′ka•tel, mus′ka•del, *n.* [Fr. *moscatelle*, from L.L. *muscatus*, smelling like musk, L. *muscus*, musk. MUSK.] The name of several sweet and strong Italian and French wines, whether white or red; the grapes which produce these wines.

muscle, mus′l, *n.* [Fr. *muscle*, from L. *musculus*, dim. of *mus*, a mouse.] A band or mass of contractile tissue in an animal organism by means of which bodily movement is effected, the two main kinds of muscles being the *voluntary*, which can be controlled at will, and the *involuntary*, which function without regard to will, such as the muscles of the digestive tract, the heart, the blood vessels, etc.; muscular strength; power.—*v.i.* To push one's way in by force.—**muscular,** mus′kū•lėr, *a.* Pertaining to or consisting of muscles; performed by or dependent on muscles (*muscular* exertion); having well-developed muscles; strong; brawny.—**muscle-bound,** *a.* Having the muscles enlarged, overstrained, and rendered inelastic by overexercise.—**muscularity,** mus•kū•lar′i•ti, *n.*—**muscular dystrophy,** *n. Med.* a hereditary disease marked by a progressive deterioration of the muscles.—**musculature,** mus′kū•la•chėr, *n.* The muscles of all or a part of any animal.

muscovado, mus•ko•vā′dō, *n.* or *a.* [Sp. *mascabado*, from *mas*, more, and *acabado*, finished (further advanced than when in syrup).] A term applied to unrefined sugar, the raw material from which loaf and lump sugar are procured by refining.

muscovite, mus′ko•vīt, *n.* Ordinary mica; [cap.] a native of Muscovy, or Russia.—**muscovy duck,** mus′ko•vi, *n.* The musk duck.

muscular. See MUSCLE.

Muse, mūz, *n.* [Fr. *muse*, L. *musa*, from Gr. *mousa*, a muse. *Music, museum, mosaic* are derivatives.] *Greek myth.* one of the daughters of Zeus and Mnemosyne, who presided over the different kinds of poetry, and the sciences and arts, nine in number, as *Clio*, the muse of history; *Thalia*, the muse of comedy; *Melpomene*, the muse of tragedy; *Calliope*, the muse of epic poetry, etc.; [*not cap.*] hence, poetic inspiration; the inspiring goddess of song.

muse, mūz, *v.i.*—*mused, musing.* [Fr. *muser*, to muse, dawdle, loiter, from O.H.G. *muoza*, idleness, *muozon*, to be idle, G. *musze*, inactivity, leisure. From this comes *amuse* with prefix *a.*] To ponder; to think or meditate in silence; to be absent in mind.—*v.t.* To think or meditate on.—*n.* A fit of abstraction.—**museful,** mūz′fụl, *a.* Musing; thoughtful.—**musing,** mū′zing. *a.* Meditative; absent-minded.—*n.* Meditation; absent-mindedness.—**musingly,** mū′zing•li, *adv.* In a musing way.

museum, mū•zē′um, *n.* [L., from Gr. *mouseion*, originally a temple of the Muses.] A place for the exhibition of objects of interest from history, the arts, or the sciences.

mush, mush, *n.* [G. *mus*, pap.] The meal of corn boiled in water; any mixture of watery consistency; sickening sentimentality.—**mushy,** mush′i, *a.*

mush, mush, *v.i.* [Fr. *marchons*, a starting order.] To journey on foot, particularly over snow, by dog team and sled.—*n.* Such a trip; the call of the driver to start his dogs.

mushroom, mush′röm, *n.* [Fr. *mousseron*, from *mousse*, L. *muscus*, moss. MOSS.] The common name of numerous fungi, especially such as are edible, having a fleshy body and a brownish color.—*v.i.* To grow or expand rapidly, as a mushroom; to spread out on the end as a mushroom.

music, mū′zik, *n.* [Fr. *musique*, L. *musica*, from Gr. *mousikē* (*technē*, art, understood), music, art, culture. MUSE, *n.*] A succession of sounds so modulated as to please the ear; melody or harmony; the art of producing melody or harmony; the written or printed score of a composition.—*Chamber music*, compositions suitable for performance in a private room.—**music box,** *n.* A small instrument, having a toothed barrel operating on vibrating tongues, which plays one or more tunes on being wound up.—**musical,** mū′zi•kal, *a.* Belonging to music; producing music or agreeable sounds; melodious; harmonious.—*Musical glasses*, glass vessels on which music may be played by striking them.—**musical comedy,** a theatrical production with little plot, but with much music and some dancing. —**musicale,** mū•zi•kal′, *n.* A social function with music as the outstanding entertainment.—**musician,** mū•zish′an, *n.* A person skilled in music; one that sings or performs on instruments of music.—**musicology,** mū•zi•kol′o•gi, *n.* The study of musical science or history.

musing. See MUSE (verb).

musk, musk, *n.* [Fr. *musc*, It. and Sp. *musco*, from L. *muscus*, musk, from Per. *mosk*, musk; allied to Skr. *mushka*, a testicle.] A substance obtained from a cyst or bag near the navel of the musk deer, having a strong, peculiar, and highly diffusible odor, used as a perfume; a musky smell; a popular name for one or two plants.—**musky,** mus′ki, *a.* Having the odor of musk.—**musk deer,** *n.* A deer of Central Asia, the male of which has long tusks and yields the well-known perfume musk. —**muskmelon,** *n.* A delicious and fragrant variety of melon.—**musk ox,** *n.* A kind of small hardy ox which inhabits the extreme north of North America, and smells strongly of musk.—**muskrat,** *n.* An American rodent allied to the beaver, which smells of musk in summer: called also *musquash*; the name is also given to two insectivorous animals smelling of musk.—**musk rose,** *n.* A species of rose, so called from its fragrance.

muskallonge, *n.* See MUSKELLUNGE.

muskellunge, mus′kel•lunj, *n.* [American Indian.] A large variety of pike found in the lakes and rivers of northern U. S. and Canada.

musket, mus′ket, *n.* [Fr. *mousquet*, O.Fr. *mousket, moschet*, originally a sparrow hawk, lit. fly-hawk, from L. *musca*, a fly (comp. *falcon, falconet, saker*, etc., as names of firearms).] A general term formerly used to mean any hand gun of smooth bore, but generally conceived of as a shoulder gun; the forerunner of the modern rifle.—**musketeer,** mus•ket•ėr′, *n.* A soldier armed with a musket. —**musketry,** mus′ket•ri, *n.* The fire of muskets; troops armed with muskets; the art or science of firing small arms.

Muslim, muz´lim, *n.* Same as *Moslem.*

muslin, muz´lin, *n.* [Fr. *mousseline,* said to be derived from *Mosul* or *Moussul,* a town in Mesopotamia where first made.] A fine thin cotton fabric, of which there are many different kinds.—*a.* Made of muslin (a *muslin* gown).—**muslin delaine,** muz´lin de•lān´, *n.* [Fr. *mousseline-delaine,* muslin of wool.] A woolen, or cotton and woolen fabric of light texture, used for ladies' dresses, etc.

musquash, mus´kwosh, *n.* A muskrat.

muss, mus, *n.* [Form of *mess.*] Disorder; a dirty mess.—*v.t.* To cause to be untidy; to rumple.—**mussy,** mus´i, *a.*

mussel, mus´el, *n.* [Same as *muscle.*] The common name of various bivalve shellfish, some kinds being largely used for food.

Mussulman, mus´el•man, *n.* pl. **Mussulmans,** mus´el•manz, [Corrupted from *moslemin,* pl. of *moslem.*] A Mohammedan or believer in Mohammed; a Moslem.—**Mussulmanism,** mus´el•man•izm, *n.* Mohammedanism.

must, must, *v.i.*; without inflection and used as a present or a past tense. [A.Sax. *ic móste, wé móston,* I must, we must, a past tense; pres. *ic mót,* I may or must; similar forms in Goth., D., Sw., and G.] A defective or auxiliary verb expressing obligation or necessity, physical or moral; or often merely expressing the conviction of the speaker (you *must* be wrong).

must, must, *n.* [L. *mustum,* new wine, from *mustus,* new, fresh.] Wine or juice pressed from the grape but not fermented.

must, must, *n.* [MUSTY.] Mold or moldiness; fustiness.

mustache, mustachio, mus•täsh´, mus•täsh´i•ō, *n.* [Fr. *moustache,* It. *mostaccio,* from Gr. *mystax,* the upper lip, the beard upon it.] The hair on the upper lip of men; the unshaven hair of the upper lip; often spoken of as plural.

mustang, mus´tang, *n.* [Sp. *mesteno,* belonging to the *mesta,* or body of graziers.] The wild horse of America, a descendant of horses imported.

mustard, mus´tėrd, *n.* [O.Fr. *moustarde,* It. *mostarda,* mustard, from L. *mustum,* must, because it is made with a little must mixed in it. MUST, MOIST.] An annual cruciferous plant extensively cultivated for its pungent seeds, which when ground and properly prepared form the well-known condiment of same name.—**mustard gas,** mus´tėrd, *n.* A poisonous gas with a pungent smell resembling that of mustard.

musteline, mus´te•līn, *a.* [L. *mustelinus,* from *mustela,* a weasel.] Pertaining to the weasel and kindred animals.

muster, mus´tėr, *v.t.* [O.Fr. *moustrer, mostrer, monstrer,* to exhibit, from L. *monstrare,* to show, from *monstrum,* a monster. MONSTER.] To collect, as troops for service, review, parade, or exercise; to assemble or bring together generally; to collect for use or exhibition.—*To muster up,* to gather, collect, or summon up: generally *fig.* (to *muster up* courage). —*v.i.* To assemble or meet in one place, as soldiers.—*n.* An assembling of troops for review or for service; the act of assembling; an assemblage. —*To pass muster,* to pass without censure, as one among a number on inspection; to be allowed to pass.

musty, mus´ti, *a.* [Probably connected with *moist,* or with L. *mucidus,* moldy; comp. Sp. *mustio,* musty.] Moldy; turned sour; fusty; stale; spoiled by age; having an ill flavor; vapid.—**mustily,** mus´ti•li, *adv.* In a musty manner.—**mustiness,** mus´ti•nes, *n.* The state or quality of being musty; staleness.

mutable, mū´ta•bl, *a.* [L. *mutabilis,* from *muto,* to change; akin to *moveo,* to move.] Capable of being altered; subject to change; inconstant.—**mutably,** mū´ta•bli, *adv.*—**mutability, mutableness,** mū•ta•bil´i•ti, mū´ta•bl•nes, *n.*—**mutate,** mū´tāt, *v.t.* To change; to alter.—*v.i.* To undergo change.—**mutation,** mū•tā´shon, *n.* The act or process of changing; change; alteration; modification; *philol.* umlaut; *biol.* a sudden, marked deviation in inherited characteristics; the results of such change.—**mutant,** mū´tent, *a.*

mutchkin, much´kin, *n.* [Comp. D. *mutsje,* a little cap, a quartern; Sc. *mutch,* a kind of cap.] A liquid measure in Scotland containing four gills.

mute, mūt, *a.* [L. *mutus,* silent, dumb; akin to *mutio,* to mumble; Gr. *mu,* a sound with closed lips. MUM, MUTTER.] Silent; not speaking; incapable of utterance; not having the power of speech; dumb; *gram.* and *philol.* silent, not pronounced, or having its sound suddenly and completely checked by closure of the vocal organs; applied to certain consonants (as *t, p*).—*n.* A dumb person; one unable to use articulate speech; a hired attendant at a funeral; *gram.* and *philol.* a mute letter; *mus.* a utensil applied to a musical instrument to deaden or soften the sounds.—**mutely,** mūt´li, *adv.* In a mute manner; silently; dumbly.—**muteness, mutism,** mūt´nes, mūt´izm, *n.* The state of being mute.

mutilate, mū´ti•lāt, *v.t.*—*mutilated, mutilating.* [L. *mutilo, mutilatum,* to lop, from *mutilus,* maimed; akin Gr. *mitylos,* docked.] To cut off a limb or essential part of; to maim; to remove any material part from so as to render the thing imperfect.—**mutilation,** mū•ti•lā´shon, *n.* The act of mutilating or state of being mutilated.—**mutilator,** mū´ti•lā•tėr, *n.* One who mutilates.

mutiny, mū´ti•ni, *n.* [From Fr. *mutin,* O.Fr. *meutin,* mutinous, riotous, *meute,* a revolt, an *emeute,* from L.L. *mota,* a body of men raised for an expedition, from L. *moveo, motus,* to move. MOVE.] A resistance to or revolt against constituted authority; specifically an insurrection of soldiers or seamen against the authority of their commanders; open resistance to officers or opposition to their authority.—*v.i.*—*mutinied, mutinying.* To engage in mutiny; to rise against military or naval officers; to be guilty of mutinous conduct.—**mutineer,** mū•ti•nēr´, *n.* One guilty of mutiny.—**mutinous,** mū´ti•nus, *a.* Engaged in or disposed to mutiny.—**mutinously,** mū´ti•nus•li, *adv.* In a mutinous manner.—**mutinousness,** mū´ti•nus•nes, *n.* The state or quality of being rebellious or of inciting mutiny.

mutt, mut, *n.* [From *muttonhead,* a stupid person.] A mongrel dog; a stupid person.

mutter, mut´ėr, *v.i.* [An imitative word; comp. G. *muttern,* L. *muttire,* to mutter. MUMBLE.] To utter words with a low voice and compressed lips; to grumble; to murmur.—*v.t.* To utter with a low murmuring voice.—*n.* Murmur.—**mutterer,** mut´ėr•ėr, *n.*—**mutteringly,** mut´ėr•ing•li, *adv.*

mutton, mut´n, *n.* [Fr. *mouton,* It. *moltone,* a sheep; supposed to be from L. *mutilus,* mutilated, through L.L. *multo, mutilo,* a wether, a castrated ram.] The flesh of sheep, raw, or dressed for food.—**mutton-chop,** *n.* A rib-piece of mutton for broiling, having the bone cut, or *chopped* off at the small end.

mutual, mū´chu•al, *a.* [Fr. *mutuel,* from a L.L. *mutualis,* from L. *mutuus,* mutual, from *muto,* to change. MUTABLE.] Reciprocally given and received; pertaining alike or reciprocally to both sides; interchanged; equally relating to, affecting, proceeding from two or more together; common to two or more combined; shared alike.—**mutuality,** mū•chu•al´i•ti, *n.* The state or quality of being mutual.—**mutually,** mū´chu•al•li, *adv.* In a mutual manner; reciprocally; conjointly; in common.

mutule, mū´tūl, *n.* [L. *mutulus.*] *Arch.* a projecting block under the corona of the Doric cornice.

muzzle, muz´l, *n.* [O.Fr. *musel* (Mod. Fr. *museau*), dim. of O.Fr. *muse,* L.L. *musus,* a mouth, from L. *morsus,* a bite, from *mordeo, morsum,* to bite. MORSEL.] The projecting mouth and nose of an animal, as of a horse, dog, etc.; the open end of a gun or pistol, etc.; a fastening for the mouth which hinders an animal from biting.—*v.t.*—*muzzled, muzzling.* To put a muzzle on; to bind the mouth of, to prevent biting or eating; to put to silence.—**muzzle-loader,** *n.* A gun loaded by the muzzle; opposed to *breechloader.*

muzzy, muz´i, *a.* [Akin to *muse,* to be absent-minded.] Absent in mind; bewildered; tipsy.

my, mī, *pronom. adj.* [Contr. from *mine,* A.Sax. *min.* MINE.] Belonging to me (this is *my* book): always used before a noun or attributively, *mine* being used predicatively (this book is *mine*).—*interj.* An exclamation of surprise (Oh *my*!).

myalgia, mī•al′ji•a, *n.* [Gr. *mys*, muscle, and *algos*, pain.] Cramp.

mycelium, mī•sē′li•um, *n.* pl. **mycelia,** mī•sē′li•a. [Gr. *mykēs*, a fungus.] The cellular filamentous spawn of fungi, consisting of whitish filaments spreading like a network.—**mycelioid,** mī•sē′li•oid, *a. Bot.* resembling a mycelium.

mycology, mī•kol′o•ji, *n.* [Gr. *mykēs*, fungus, and *logos*.] That department of botany which investigates fungi.—**mycologist,** mī•kol′o•jist, *n.*

Mycoplasma, mī″kō•plaz′ma, *n.* [Gr. *mykēs*, and *plasma*, anything molded.] The sole genus of the family Mycoplasmataceae, which are parasitic organisms intermediate between viruses and bacteria and have complex life cycles, reportedly involving the breaking of filaments into nondivisible spherical organisms.

mycorrhiza, mī′ko•rī″za, *n.* [Gr. *mykēs*, a fungus, *rhiza*, a root.] A sheath of fungal threads surrounding a root. Probably a case of SYMBIOSIS (which see).

mydriatic, mid′ri•at″ik, *n.* [Gr. *mydriasis*, undue dilation of the pupil.] Causing dilation of the pupil; a drug for effecting this.

myelencephalous, mī′el•en•sef″al•us, *a.* [Gr. *myelos*, marrow, and *enkephalon*, the brain.] Exhibiting a nervous system concentrated in a brain and spinal cord, as the higher animals.

myelin, myeline, mī′e•lin, *n.* [Gr. *myelos*, marrow.] A white, soft, fatty material forming a thick sheath around the axis cylinder of certain nerve fibers.—**myelitis,** mī′e•lī″tis, *n. Med.* inflammation of the spinal cord or bone marrow.

myna, mī′na, *n.* [Ind. name.] An Indian bird of the starling family that can be taught to speak, and is often kept in cages in Europe and America.

myology, mī•ol′o•ji, *n.* [Gr. *mys*, *myos*, muscle, and *logos*, discourse.] The scientific knowledge or description of the muscles of the human body.—**myologist,** mī•ol′o•jist, *n.* One who is versed in myology.

myope, mī′ōp, *n.* [Gr. *myōps*—*myō*, to shut, and *ōps*, the eye.] A shortsighted person.—**myopia,** mī•ō′pi•a, *n.* Shortsightedness; nearsightedness; a condition in which the image is focused before reaching the retina.—**myopic,** mī•op′ik, *a.* Pertaining to or affected with myopia.

myosin, mī′o•sin, *n.* [Gr. *mys*, *myos*, a muscle.] A peculiar constituent of muscle.

myosis, mī•ō′sis, *n.* [Gr. *myō*, to close the eye.] *Pathol.* an abnormal contraction of the pupil of the eye.—**myotic,** mī•ot′ik, *a.* and *n.* Causing such contraction, or a drug that causes it.

myosotis, mī•o•sō′tis, *n.* [Gr. *mys*, *myos*, a mouse, and *ous*, *ōtos*, an ear.] The plant forget-me-not.

myriad, mir′i•ad, *n.* [Gr. *myrias*, *myriados*, from *myria*, ten thousand, innumerable.] The number of ten thousand collectively; an immense number indefinitely.—*a.* Innumerable; multitudinous but indefinite.

myriagram, mir′i•a•gram, *n.* [Gr. *myria*, ten thousand, and Fr. *gramme*, a gram.] A French weight of 10,000 grams, or 22 lbs. avoirdupois.—**myrialiter,** mir′i•a•lē•tėr, *n.* A French measure of capacity containing 10,000 liters, or 610,280 cubic inches.—**myriameter,** mir′i•a•mē•tėr, *n.* A French measure of length equal to 10 kilometers or 6.21 miles.

myriapod, mir′i•a•pod, *n.* [Gr. *myria*, ten thousand, and *pous*, *podos*, a foot.] An individual belonging to the class of animals that includes the centipedes and millipedes, having bodies of a lengthened form and in numerous segments, the segments being provided with pairs of feet.

Myrmidon, mėr′mi•don, *n.* One of an ancient Greek race in Thessaly, whom Achilles ruled, and who accompanied him to Troy; [*not cap.*] hence, a soldier of a rough character; one of a ruffianly band under a daring or unscrupulous leader; an unscrupulous follower.—*myrmidons of the law*, bailiffs, sheriffs' officers, policemen, and other law menials.

myrobalan, mī•rob′a•lan, *n.* [L. *myrobalanum*, Gr. *myrobalanos*—*myron*, unguent, and *balanus*, a nut.] A dried fruit of different species of the plum kind, brought from the East Indies, and used by dyers and tanners.

myrrh, mėr, *n.* [L. *myrrha*, Gr. *myrrha*, Ar. *murr*, bitter.] The gummy resinous exudation of a spiny shrub long in use as an aromatic in perfume, incense, and medicine.

myrtle, mėr′tl, *n.* [L. *myrtus*, Gr. *myrtos*, from *myron*, perfume.] An evergreen shrub of the south of Europe having buds and berries that yield a volatile oil, while the distilled flowers yield a perfume.—**myrtaceous,** mėr•tā′shus, *a.* Of or pertaining to the myrtles.

myself, mī•self′, *pron.* pl. **ourselves,** our•selvz′. As a nominative it is used, generally after I, to express emphasis and mark distinction; I, and not another: in the objective often used reflexively and without any emphasis.

mystagogue, mis′ta•gog, *n.* [Gr. *mystagōgos*—*mystēs*, one initiated in mysteries, and *agōgos*, a leader.] One who instructs in or interprets mysteries.—**mystagogy,** mis′ta•gō•ji, *n.* The practice or doctrines of a mystagogue; the interpretation of mysteries.

mystery, mis′tėr•i, *n.* [L. *mysterium*, from Gr. *mysterion*, from *mystēs*, one initiated, from *myō*, to close, to shut.] Something hidden from human knowledge and fitted to inspire a sense of awe; something incomprehensible through being above human intelligence; something intentionally kept hidden; a secret; a species of dramatic performance in the Middle Ages; divine revelation; a mystery novel; a sacramental rite; pl. rites and ceremonies in ancient, chiefly Greek and Roman, religions, only known to, and practiced by, those who had been initiated; the Eucharist.—**mysterious,** mis•tē′ri•us, *a.* Partaking of, or containing, mystery; occult; enigmatical.—**mysteriously,** mis•tē′ri•us•li, *adv.*—**mysteriousness,** mis•tē′ri•us•nes, *n.*—**mysterium,** mis•tē′ri•um, *n.* A space phenomenon that cannot be explained in terms of any known scientific principle.

mystic, mystical, mis′tik, mis′ti•kal, *a.* [L. *mysticus*, Gr. *mystikos*, from *mystēs*, one initiated. MYSTERY.] Hidden from or obscure to human knowledge or comprehension; involving some secret meaning or import; mysterious; occult; pertaining to the ancient mysteries; pertaining to mystics or mysticism.—**mystic,** *n.* One who is addicted to mysticism.—**mystically,** mis′ti•kal•li, *adv.* In a mystic manner.—**mysticalness,** mis′ti•kal•nes, *n.*—**mysticism,** mis′ti•sizm, *n.* Views or tendencies in religion which aspire toward a communication between man and his Maker through the inward perception of the mind, more direct than that which is afforded us through revelation; a seeking to solve the mysteries of existence by internal illumination or special revelation; a dreamy contemplation on ideas that have no foundation in human experience.

mystify, mis′ti•fī, *v.t.*—*mystified*, *mystifying*. [Coined from *mystic*, and *-fy*, Fr. *-fier*, L. *facere*, to make.] To perplex purposely; to play on the credulity of; to bewilder; to befog.—**mystification,** mis′ti•fi•kā″shon, *n.* The act of mystifying or state of being mystified.

myth, mith, *n.* [Gr. *mythos*, a word, a fable, a legend.] A fable or legend of natural upgrowth, embodying the convictions of a people as to their gods or other divine personages, their own origin and early history and the heroes connected with it, the origin of the world, etc.; in a looser sense, an invented story; something purely fabulous or having no existence in fact.—**mythical, mythic,** mith′i•kal, mith′ik, *a.* Relating to myths; described in a myth; fabulous; fabled.—**mythically,** mith′i•kal•li, *adv.* In a mythical manner.—**mythographer,** mi•thog′ra•fėr, *n.* A framer or writer of myths.—**mythological, mythologic,** mith•o•loj′i•kal, mith•o•loj′ik, *a.* Relating to mythology; proceeding from mythology; of the nature of a myth; fabulous.—**mythologically,** mith•o•loj′i•kal•li, *adv.* In a mythological manner.—**mythologist,** mi•thol′o•jist, *n.* One versed in mythology.—**mythologize,** mi•thol′o•jīz, *v.i.*—*mythologized*, *mythologizing*. To relate or explain myths.—**mythology,** mi•thol′o•ji, *n.* The science or doctrine of myths; the myths of a people or nation collectively.—*Comparative mythology*, the science which investigates the relationship between myths of different peoples.

myxedema, miks•i•dē′ma. [Gr. *myxa*, mucus, *oidēma*, a swelling.] A disease due to deficient secretion of the THYROID GLAND (which see).

N

N, n, en, the fourteenth letter and the eleventh consonant of the English alphabet.

nab, nab, *v.t.* [Same as Dan. *knappe,* Sw. *knappa,* to snatch; comp. D. and G. *knappen,* to snap.] To catch or seize suddenly or unexpectedly. (*Colloq.*)

nabob, nā′bob, *n.* [Corruption of Hind. *nawwâb,* from Ar. *nuwwâb,* pl. of *nâyib,* a deputy, from Ar. *nâba,* to take one's turn.] A governor of a province or commander of an army in India under the Mogul empire: a person who has acquired great wealth in the East and uses it ostentatiously.

nacelle, nä•sel′, *n.* [Fr.] An enclosed part of an aircraft which houses the engine or passengers.

nacre, nā′kėr, *n.* [Fr. *nacre,* Sp. *nacar,* from Per. *nakar,* an ornament of different colors.] Mother-of-pearl.—**nacreous,** nā′krē•us, *a.* Consisting of or resembling nacre or mother-of-pearl.

nadir, nā′dėr, *n.* [Fr. *nadir,* Ar. and Per. *nadir, nazir,* the nadir, from *nazara,* to correspond, to be opposite.] That point of the heavens or lower hemisphere directly opposite to the zenith; the point directly under the place where we stand; *fig.* the lowest point; the point or time of extreme depression.

nag, nag, *n.* [Same as Sc. *naig,* D. *negge,* a pony; perhaps akin to *neigh*:] A small horse, or in familiar language any horse.

nag, nag, *v.t.* and *i.* [N. and Sw. *nagga,* to gnaw, irritate, scold=G. *nagen,* E. to *gnaw.* NAIL, GNAW.] To scold pertinaciously; to find fault constantly.

nagana, na•gä′na. [Native word.] 'Fly disease' of horses in tropical Africa. Due to a microscopic parasite introduced by the bite of the tsetse fly.

naiad, nā′yad, *n.* [Gr. *naias, naiados,* a naiad, from *naō,* to flow.] A water nymph; a female deity that presides over rivers and springs.

naïf, nä•ēf, *a.* [Fr. See NAIVE.] Ingenuous; artless; having a natural luster without being cut: said of jewels.

nail, nāl, *n.* [A.Sax. *naegel,* D. and G. *nagel,* the human or a metallic nail; Icel. *nagl,* Dan. *negl,* a human nail, *nagli* and *nagle,* a metallic nail; cog. Lith. *nagas,* L. *unguis,* Skr. *nakha,* a human nail; allied to *nag* (verb).] The horny scale growing at the end of the human fingers and toes; a similar appendage in the lower animals; a claw; a small pointed piece of metal, with some sort of a head, used for driving through or into timber or other material for the purpose of holding separate pieces together, or left projecting that things may be hung on it; a stud or boss; a measure of length, being $2\frac{1}{4}$ inches, or 1-16th of a yard.—*To hit the nail on the head,* to hit or touch the exact point, in a figurative sense.—*v.t.* To fasten with nails; to drive nails into; to stud with nails.—**nailer,** nāl′ėr, *n.* One that nails; one whose occupation is to make nails.

nail file, a small file for the fingernails.

nail set, a steel rod used to drive a nailhead below the surface.

nainsook, nān′sụk, *n.* [Hind.] A kind of muslin, plain and striped, originally made in India.

naïve, nä•ēv′, *a.* [Fr. *naïf,* fem. *naïve,* from L. *nativus,* native, latterly also rustic, simple.] Ingenuous; artless; showing candor or simplicity; unsophisticated.—**naïvely,** nä•ēv′li, *adv.* In a naïve manner.—**naïveté,** nä•ēv′te, *n.* [Fr.] Native simplicity of soul; unaffected ingenuousness.

naked, nā′ked, *a.* [A.Sax. *nacod,* naked, a participial form; D. *naakt,* Icel. *naktr, nakinn,* Dan. *nögen,* Goth. *naqviths,* G. *nackt*; same root as L. *nudus,* nude; Skr. *nagna,* naked.] Not having clothes on; bare; nude; not having a covering, especially a customary covering (a *naked* sword); *bot.* not having a calyx; not enclosed in a pod, or the like; *zool.* not having a calcareous shell; *fig.* open to view; not concealed; manifest; mere, bare, simple; unarmed; defenseless; unprovided; destitute.—*The naked eye,* the eye unassisted by any instrument, as spectacles, telescope, or microscope.—**nakedly,** nā′ked•li, *adv.* In a naked manner; without covering.—**nakedness,** nā′ked•nes, *n.* The state of being naked; nudity; bareness; plainness.

namaycush, na•mā′kush, *n.* A large North American species of fish.

namby-pamby, nam′bi-pam′bi, *a.* [Contemptuously formed from the name of *Ambrose* Phillips, a rather weak poet of Addison's time.] Affectedly pretty; weakly sentimental; insipid; vapid (*namby-pamby* sentiment, rhymes).

name, nām, *n.* [A.Sax. *nama,* a name; D. *naam,* G. *name,* Goth. *namo,* Icel. *nafn,* Dan. *navn* (for *namn*), Sw. *namn,* all cog. with L. *nomen,* for *gnomen* (whence E. *noun*), Skr. *nâman,* for *jnâman* or *gnâman,* a name; from same root as *know.*] That by which a person or thing is called or designated, in distinction from other persons or things; appellation; reputation; character (one's good or bad *name*); renown; fame; eminence; the mere word by which anything is called; sound only; not reality; authority; behalf; persons having a certain name; a family; *gram.* a noun‡.—*To call names,* to apply opprobrious names.—*Christian name,* a personal name preceding the family name, and usually bestowed at baptism: as distinguished from a *surname.*—*v.t.*—*named, naming.* To give a name or distinctive appellation to; to denominate; to mention by name; to nominate; to designate for any purpose by name; to pronounce to be; to speak of or mention as.—*To name a day,* to fix a day for anything; *to name the day,* said of a lady's fixing her marriage day.—**namable, nameable,** nām′a•bl, *a.* Capable or worthy of being named.—**nameless,** nām′les, *a.* Without a name or appellation; not known to fame; obscure; without family or pedigree; that cannot or ought not to be named; inexpressible.—**namelessly,** nām′les•li, *adv.* In a nameless manner.—**namelessness,** nām′les•nes, *n.* The state of being nameless.—**namely,** nām′li, *adv.* To mention by name; to particularize; that is to say.—**namer,** nām′ėr, *n.* One that names or calls by name.—**namesake,** nām′sāk, *n.* One that has the same name as another; one named after another.

nankeen, nankin, nan•kēn′, *n.* [*Nankin* in China.] A sort of cotton cloth, usually of a yellow color; pl. trousers or breeches made of this material.

nanny goat, a female goat.

naos, nā′os, *n.* [Gr. *naos,* a temple.] *Arch.* the body of an ancient temple.

nap, nap, *v.i.*—*napped, napping.* [A. Sax. *hnappian, hnaeppian,* to take a nap, to doze.] To have a short sleep; to drowse; to be in a careless, secure state.—*n.* A short sleep or slumber; a game at cards. (Contraction of *Napoleon.*)

nap, nap, *n.* [A.Sax. *hnoppa,* the nap of cloth=D. *nop, noppe,* Dan. *noppe,* L.G. *nobbe,* nap; allied to *knob* or *knop,* from the little tufts on coarse cloth.] The woolly substance on the surface of cloth, etc.; the pile, as of a hat; what resembles this, as the downy substance on some plants.—*v.t.*—*napped, napping.* To raise or put a nap on.

napalm, nā′päm, *n.* [From *na*phthenic and *palm*itic acids.] A jellied gasoline used in incendiary bombs, flamethrowers, etc.

nape, nāp, *n.* [Same as A.Sax. *cnaep,* a top; akin *nap, knob, knop.*] The back part of the neck; the prominent part of the neck behind.

napery, nā′per•i, *n.* [Fr. *napperie,* from *nappe,* a towel, from L. *mappa,* a towel, whence also *map*; akin *napkin, apron.*] A collective term for linen cloths used for domestic purposes, especially for the table.

naphtha, nap′tha or naf′tha, *n.* [Gr. Chal., Syr., and Ar. *naphtha,* Per. *naft,* naphtha.] A variety of bitumen, fluid, inflammable, emitting a strong odor, and generally of a yellow color, used as a source of light, as a solvent for caoutchouc, etc.—*Native naphtha,* petroleum or rock oil.—**naphthalene,** nap′tha•lēn, *n.* A white crystallizable solid formed during the distillation of coal for gas, or obtained by re-distilling coal tar.

napiform, nā′pi•form, *a.* [L. *napus,* a turnip, and *forma,* form.] Having the general shape of a turnip (a *napiform* root).

napkin, nap′kin, *n.* [Dim. of Fr. *nappe,* a cloth, a tablecloth, from L. *mappa,* a napkin. NAPERY.] A cloth used for wiping the hands; a towel; a handkerchief‡.

napoleon, na•pō′lē•on, *n.* [After *Napoleon* I.] Formerly, a French gold coin, worth 20 francs; a card game.

naprapathy, nä•prap′a•thi, *n.* [From Czech *napravа*, correction.] A system of treatment of disease or illness by manipulation and adjustment of joints and muscles.

narceine, när′sē•in, *n.* [Gr. *narkē*, torpor.] An alkaloid contained in opium.

narcissism, när•cis′sizm, *n.* (*Psychoanalysis.*) A morbid love and admiration of self.—**narcissist,** *n.*—**narcissistic,** *a.*

narcissus, när•sis′us, *n.* [L., from Gr. *narkissos*, from *narkē*, torpor; from the narcotic properties of the plants.] An extensive genus of bulbous plants, including the daffodil, the jonquil, etc.; [*cap.*] in Gr. mythology a handsome youth who died from hopeless love of his own reflection in water, and was transformed into a narcissus.

narcosis, när•kō′sis, *n.* [Gr. See below.] The effect of a narcotic; the state produced by narcotics.

narcotic, när•kot′ik, *n.* [Gr. *narkōtikos*, from *narkoō*, to render torpid, from *narkē*, torpor.] A substance which relieves pain, produces sleep, and in large doses brings on stupor, coma, and even death, as opium, hemlock, alcohol, etc.—*a.* Having the properties of a narcotic. —**narcotism,** när′ko•tizm, *n.* Narcosis.—**narcotize,** när′ko•tīz, *v.t.* To bring under the influence of a narcotic; to affect with stupor.

nard, närd, *n.* [L. *nardus*, from Gr. *nardos*, Heb. and Per. *nard*, nard.] A plant, same as *Spikenard*; an unguent prepared from the plant.

narghile, nargileh, när′gi•le, *n.* [Persian and Turkish name.] A kind of tobacco pipe or smoking apparatus used by the Orientals in which the smoke is passed through water. Spelled also *Nargile.*

narrate, nar•rāt′, *v.t.*—*narrated, narrating.* [L. *narro, narratum*, to relate, for *gnarro*, from root *gna*, seen also in E. *know*; comp. *gnarus*, knowing. KNOW.] To tell or recite, as a story; to relate the particulars of in speech or writing.—**narration,** nar•rā′shon, *n.* The act of narrating; that which is related; a narrative; *rhet.* that part of a discourse which recites the time, manner or consequences of an action.—**narrative,** nar′a•tiv, *a.* Pertaining to narration.—*n.* That which is narrated or related; a relation or narration; a relation in words or writing of the particulars of any transaction or event.—**narratively,** nar′a•tiv•li, *adv.* By way of narration. —**narrator,** nar•rā′tėr, *n.* One who narrates or produces a narrative.

narrow, nar′ō, *a.* [A.Sax. *nearu, nearo*, narrow, troublesome or painful; cog. O.Sax. *naru*, Fris. *naar*;] Of little breadth; having little distance from side to side; of little extent; limited or contracted; limited as to means; straitened; contracted in mind; of confined views; bigoted; not liberal or bountiful; niggardly; near; within but a little; hence, barely sufficient to avoid evil, etc. (a *narrow* escape, majority); close; scrutinizing.—*Narrow gauge*, in railways, a gauge or distance between the rails of less than 4 feet 8½ inches, which is considered the standard gauge and is the most common.—*n.* A narrow channel of water between one sea or lake and another; a strait or sound: usually in the plural.—*v.t.* To make narrow or contracted, literally or figuratively.—*v.i.* To become narrow or narrower.—**narrowly,** nar′ō•li, *adv.* In a narrow manner; contractedly; sparingly; closely; rigorously; nearly; within a little.—**narrowminded,** *a.* Of confined views or sentiments; illiberal.—**narrowness,** nar′ō•nes, *n.* The quality or condition of being narrow, illiberality; want of enlarged views.

narthex, när′theks, *n.* [Gr.] A kind of vestibule in the afterpart of a church.

narwhal, narwal, när′hwal, när′wal, *n.* [Dan. *narhval*, Icel. *na-hvalr*, 'corpsewhale', Icel. *na, nár*, a corpse, from the animal's pale color.] A cetaceous mammal of northern seas, with no teeth except two canines in the upper jaw, of which one is frequently developed into a long projecting tusk; the sea unicorn.

nasal, nā′zal, *a.* [Fr. *nasal*, from L. *nasus*, the nose. NOSE.] Pertaining to the nose; uttered through the nose or through both the nose and mouth simultaneously (as *m* in English, *en* in French).—*Nasal fossae, anat.* the two cavities which constitute the internal part of the nose.—*n.* An elementary sound uttered through or partly through the nose; a medicine that operates through the nose; an errhine; the noseguard of an ancient helmet.—**nasality,** nā•zal′i•ti, *n.* The state or quality of being nasal. — **nasalization,** nā′zal•i•zā″-shon, *n.* The act of nasalizing or uttering with a nasal sound.—**nasalize,** nā′zal•īz, *v.t.*—*nasalized, nasalizing.* To render nasal, as the sound of a letter; to insert a nasal letter in, especially *n* or *m* (L. *tundo*, is a *nasalized* form from the root *tud*, to strike).—**nasally,** nā′zal•li, *adv.* In a nasal manner; by or through the nose.

nascent, nas′ent, *a.* [L. *nascens, nascentis*, ppr. of *nascor*, to be born. NATAL.] Beginning to exist or to grow; coming into being; arising.—**nascency,** nas′en•si, *n.* The state of being nascent.

naseberry, nāz′ber•i, *n.* [Sp. *nispero*, medlar, from L. *mespilus*, medlar; modified so as to have an English form, like *barberry.*] The fruit of the sapodilla.

nasturtium, nas•tėr′shi•um, *n.* [L., from *nasus*, the nose, and *torqueo, tortum*, to twist, from the acridity of its smell.] A genus of herbs, including the common watercress; also a name given to the Indian cress, an American annual with pungent fruit.

nasty, nas′ti, *a.* [O.E. *nasky*, connected with L.G. *nask*, Sw. *naskug, nasket*, unclean, dirty.] Filthy; dirty; indecent; obscene; disgusting to taste or smell; disagreeable; troublesome; extremely unpleasant (*nasty* weather). —**nastily,** nas′ti•li, *adv.* In a nasty manner; filthily; obscenely.—**nastiness,** nas′ti•nes, *n.* The quality of being nasty, or what is nasty; filthiness; filthy matter; obscenity.

natal, nā′tal, *a.* [L. *natalis*, from *nascor, natus*, to be born (whence also *nature, native, nation*); from same root as *genus, kind.* NATURE, GENUS.] Pertaining to one's birth; dating from one's birth.

natant, nā′tant, *a.* [L. *natans, natantis*, ppr. of *nato*, to swim, freq. of *no, natum*, to swim; same root as *navis*, a ship. NAVAL.] Floating on the surface of water; swimming, as the leaf of an aquatic plant.—**natation,** na•tā′shon, *n.* [L. *natatio.*] The art or act of swimming.—**natatorial,** nā•ta•tō′ri•al, *a.* Swimming or adapted to swimming; belonging to the Natatores.—**natatorium,** nā•ta•tō′ri•um, *n.* A swimming pool, particularly, one indoors.

nation, nā′shon, *n.* [L. *natio*, from *natus*, born, *nascor*, to be born. NATAL.] A people inhabiting a certain extent of territory, and united by common political institutions; an aggregation of persons speaking the same or a cognate language; a federation of Indian tribes; a division of students in some universities according to their place of birth; a great number; a great deal, by way of emphasis.—*Law of nations.* Same as *International Law.*—**national,** nash′on•al, *a.* Pertaining to a nation; common to a whole people or race; public; general.—*n.* A member of a particular nation, entitled to its protection.—*National air*, a popular tune peculiar to a particular nation; a tune by national consent sung or played on certain public occasions. —*National Church*, the established church of a country or nation.—*National debt*, the sum which is owing by a government to individuals who have advanced money to it for public purposes.—*National Guard*, in the U. S., organizations of militia in the several states, subject to both state and federal government.—**nationalism,** nash′on•al•izm, *n.* Nationality; a national idiom or trait; advocacy of making one's own nation distinct, and separate from others in social, cultural, and political matters; a socialist program for national control or ownership of industries and resources.—**nationalist,** nash′on•al•ist, *n.* and *a.*—**nationality,** nash′on•al″i•ti, *n.* The qualities that distinguish a nation; national character; strong attachment to one's own nation or countrymen; the people constituting a nation; a nation; a race of people; separate existence as a nation; national unity and integrity.—**nationalize,** nash′on•al•īz, *v.t.*—*nationalized, nationalizing.* To make national; to make the common property of the nation as a whole; to give the character of a distinct nation; to give control of properties to the government.—**nationalization,** nash•on•al•ī•zā′shon, *n.*—**nationally,** nash′on•al•li, *adv.* In a national manner; as a whole nation.—**nationwide,** *a.* Extending throughout the whole of a nation.

native, nā'tiv, *a.* [L. *nativus,* born, innate, natural, native, from *nascor, natus,* to be born. NATAL.] Pertaining to the place or circumstances of one's birth; being the scene of one's origin (our *native* land); conferred by birth; belonging to one's nature or constitution; not artificial or acquired; occurring in nature pure or unmixed with other substances: said of mineral bodies (as iron or silver when found almost pure).—*n.* One born in a place or country, and not a foreigner or immigrant; an oyster raised in an artificial bed.—**natively,** nā'tiv•li, *adv.* By birth; naturally; originally.—**nativeness,** nā'tiv•nes, *n.* State of being native.—**nativity,** na•tiv'i•ti, *n.* [L. *nativitas.*] A coming into life or the world; birth; the circumstances attending birth; a picture representing the birth of Christ; *astrol.* same as *Horoscope.*—*To cast a nativity,* to draw out one's horoscope, and calculate the future influence of the predominant stars.—*The Nativity,* the birth of the Saviour.

natron, nā'tron, *n.* [Fr. and Sp. *natron,* from Ar. *natrun,* native carbonate of soda: same word as *niter.*] Native carbonate of soda, or mineral alkali, found in the ashes of several marine plants, in some lakes, and mineral springs.—**natrolite,** nā'tro•līt, *n.* [Gr. *lithos,* a stone.] A mineral substance occurring in traprocks, and containing a great quantity of soda.

natty, nat'i, *a.* [Akin to *neat.*] Neat; tidy; spruce.—**nattily,** nat'i•li, *adv.* In a natty manner; sprucely; tidily.—**nattiness,** nat'i•nes, *n.* State of being natty.

nature, nā'chėr, *n.* [Fr. *nature,* from L. *natura,* from *natus* (for *gnatus*), born, produced, from root *gna* or *gan,* seen in E. *know, kind, kin;* Skr. *jan,* to produce. GENUS.] The universe; the system of things of which ourselves are a part; the world of matter or of matter and mind; the creation, especially that part of it by which man is more immediately surrounded; often also the agent, author, or producer of things, or the powers that carry on the processes of the creation; the total of all agencies and forces in the creation; the inherent qualities of anything; the essential qualities which constitute it what it is; disposition of mind; personal character; individual constitution; quality; sort; natural affection; life or reality as distinguished from that which is artificial.—*To go the way of nature, to pay the debt of nature,* and similar phrases, to die.—*Laws of nature,* those generalizations which express the order observed in the phenomena of nature.—*In a state of nature,* naked as when born; in a state of sin; unregenerated.—**natural,** na'chėr•al, *a.* [L. *naturalis.*] Pertaining to nature; produced by nature; not artificial, acquired, or assumed (*natural* color, strength, heat), in conformity with the laws of nature; regulated by the laws which govern events, actions, sentiments, etc. (a *natural* enemy, supposition); happening in the ordinary course of things (the *natural* consequence); connected with the existing physical system of things, or creation at large (*natural* philosophy, laws, etc.); according to life and reality; without affectation or artificiality (he was always *natural*); born out of wedlock; bastard; in a state of nature; unregenerated; *mus.* a term applied to the scale of C.—*Natural gas,* a gas issuing from fissures in the earth's crust.—*Natural history,* the study or description of nature in its widest sense, usually for the general public.—*Natural resources,* a country's wealth in terms of land, water power, minerals, etc.—*Natural science,* any of the areas of knowledge dealing with natural objects or phenomena and based on experiment, as *biology.*—*n.* One born without the usual powers of reason or understanding; an idiot; a fool; *mus.* a character marked thus ♮, the use of which is to make void a preceding sharp or flat; one who has natural talents, skills, etc.—**naturalism,** na'chėr•al•izm, *n.* Natural religion; the doctrine that there is no interference of any supernatural power in the universe; a natural mode of acting; reality in art, but usually concerned with the seamy side of life.—**naturalist,** na'chėr•al•ist, *n.* One who is versed in natural science or natural history; one who holds the doctrine of naturalism.—**naturalistic,** na'chėr•al•is"tik, *a.* Pertaining to naturalism; in accordance with nature; based on natural objects.—**naturalization,** na'chėr•al•i•zā"shon, *n.* The act of naturalizing; the act of investing an alien with the rights and privileges of a natural subject.—**naturalize,** na'chėr•al•īz, *v.t.*—*naturalized, naturalizing.* To make natural; to confer the rights and privileges of a native subject upon; to accustom to a climate; to acclimatize; to adopt as native or vernacular (to *naturalize* foreign words).—**naturally,** na'chėr•al•li, *adv.* In a natural manner; according to nature; not by art or habit; without affectation; according to the usual course of things; spontaneously; without cultivation.—**naturalness,** na'chėr•al•nes, *n.* The state of being natural; conformity to nature; absence of affectation.

naught, nạt, *n.* [A.Sax. *náht, nóht, náwiht,* lit. *no whit,* not a whit (see AUGHT). *Naught* is the same and *not* is an abbreviated form.] Nought; nothing.—*To set at naught,* to slight, disregard, or despise.—*a.* Worthless; of no value or account; bad; vile.—**naughty,** nạ'ti, *a.* [From *naught.*] Bad: mischievous; ill-behaved; very wrong (a *naughty* child).—**naughtily,** nạ'ti•li, *adv.* In a naughty manner; mischievously.—**naughtiness,** nạ'ti•nes, *n.* The state of being naughty; misbehavior, as of children.

naumachia, naumachy, nạ•mā'ki•a, nạ'ma•ki, *n.* [Gr. *naumachia*—*naus,* a ship, and *machē,* fight.] *Rom. antiq.* a show or spectacle representing a sea fight; the place where these shows were exhibited.

nauplius, nạ'pli•us, *n.* [Gr. *Nauplios,* a son of Neptune.] In lower Crustacea, an ovoid unsegmented larva, possessing only the three first pairs of head limbs, which are used as swimming organs

nausea, nạ'shi•a, *n.* [L., from Gr. *nausia,* from *naus,* a ship. NAVAL.] Seasickness; any similar sickness of the stomach, accompanied with a propensity to vomit; loathing.—**nauseate,** nạ'shi•āt, *v.i.*—*nauseated, nauseating.* [L. *nauseo.*] To feel nausea; to be inclined to vomit.—*v.t.* To loathe; to reject with disgust; to affect with disgust.—**nauseous,** nạ'shus, *a.* Exciting or fitted to excite nausea; loathsome; disgusting.—**nauseously,** na'shus•li, *adv.* In a nauseous manner.—**nauseousness,** na'shus•nes, *n.* The quality of being nauseous; loathsomeness.

nautch girl, nạch, *n.* In the East Indies, a native professional dancing girl.

nautical, nạ'ti•kal, *a.* [L. *nauticus* from *nauta,* a seaman, for *navita,* from *navis,* a ship. NAVAL.] Pertaining to seamanship or navigation; maritime; naval.—**nautically,** nạ'ti•kal•li, *adv.* In a nautical manner.

nautilus, nạ'ti•lus, *n.* [Gr. *nautilos,* a sailor, a nautilus, from *naus,* a ship. NAVAL.] A genus of cephalopods with many-chambered shells in the form of a flat spiral, the animal residing in the external chamber, and the others being separated by partitions; also a name for the argonaut or paper nautilus; a form of diving bell which requires no suspension, sinking and rising by means of condensed air.—*Nautilus propeller,* a hydraulic device for propelling ships.

Navaho, Navajo, na'vä•hō, *n.* [Sp. Apaches de *Navajó.*] One of a tribe of Indians living in Arizona, New Mexico and Utah.

naval, nā'val, *a.* [L. *navalis,* from *navis,* a ship (whence also *nautical, navigate, navy*); cog. Gr. *naus,* Skr. *naus;* from a root *nu* for *snu,* meaning to float or flow.] Consisting of ships, or of forces fighting in ships; pertaining to a navy or to ships of war; maritime.—*Naval officer,* one belonging to the navy of a country.—*Naval crown,* among the ancient Romans, a crown conferred for bravery at sea.—*Naval decorations,* specifically, three awards presented by the naval authorities to men in the service who perform acts of bravery beyond the call of duty: Medal of Honor, Distinguished Service Medal, and Navy Cross.

nave, nāv, *n.* [A.Sax. *nafu, nafa* = D. *nave, naaf,* Dan. *nav,* Icel. *nöf,* G. *nabe,* a nave; cog. Skr. *nâbhi,* a nave, a navel. *Navel* is a dim. from this, and *auger* is partly derived from it.] The thick piece in the center of a wheel in which the spokes and axle are inserted; the hub.

nave, nāv, *n.* [Lit. ship, from O.Fr. *nave* (Mod.Fr. *nef*), It. *nave*, from L. *navis*, a ship. NAVAL.] The middle part, lengthwise, of a church; the part between the aisles and extending from the entrance.

navel, nā'vl, *n.* [A.Sax. *nafel*, *nafol*=D. *navel*, Dan. *navle*, Icel. *nafle*, G. *nabel*—navel; dim. forms from words signifying nave of a wheel. NAVE.] A depression in the center of the abdomen, the point where the umbilical cord passes out of the fetus. —**navel orange,** *n.* A large, juicy orange, usually seedless, which has a navel-like indentation in its rind.

navicular, na•vik'ū•lėr, *a.* [L. *navicula*, a little ship, from *navis*, a ship. NAVAL.] Shaped like a boat (the *navicular* bone of the wrist or ankle).

navigate, nav'i•gāt, *v.i.*—*navigated, navigating.* [L. *navigo*, *navigatum*, from *navis*, a ship, *ago*, to do. NAVAL.] To pass on water in ships; to manage a ship; to sail.—*v.t.* To pass over in ships; to sail on; to steer or manage in sailing.—**navigation,** nav•i•gā'shon, *n.* [L. *navigatio.*] The act of navigating; the science or art of managing ships.—*Aerial navigation*, the art and science of operation through the air of lighter- and heavier-than-air machines; the setting of a course along a known route; the application of directional knowledge gained by the use of landmark maps, previous flying experience, and the extensive use of various instruments for dead reckoning and position finding, such as radio compass, direction finders, altimeters, artificial horizon gauges, drift indicators, barometers, and the radio telephone.—**navigator,** nav'i•gā•tėr, *n.* One that navigates; one who directs the course of a ship.—**navigable,** nav'i•ga•bl, *a.* Capable of being navigated; affording passage to ships.—**navigableness, navigability,** nav'i•ga•bl•nes, nav'i•ga•bil"i•ti, *n.* The quality or state of being navigable.

navy, nā'vi, *n.* [O.Fr. *navie*, from L. *navis*, a ship. NAVAL.] The collective name for such vessels as are built and maintained for war or for other purposes pertaining to national defense; the institutions and equipment, such as navy yards, stores, fueling stations, naval academies, etc., for the maintenance of sea defenses and vessels of war.—**navy bean,** *n.* A strain of the kidney bean. —**navy yard,** *n.* A shipyard where government vessels are built and repaired.

nawab, na•wab', *n.* [See NABOB.] A viceroy; a deputy.

nay, nā, *adv.* [Equivalent to *ne aye* (A.Sax. *ne*, not), that is, not ever; from Icel. and Dan. *nei*, Sw. *nej*, no, nay; comp. *nor* for *ne or*, not or; *neither*, for *ne either*, not either, etc. NO.] No; a word that expresses negation or refusal; also used to intimate that something is to be added to an expression; not only so; not this alone.—*To say nay*, to deny; to refuse.—*n.* Denial; refusal.

Nazarene, naz•a•rēn', *n.* An inhabitant of *Nazareth*; a name given to Christ and the early converts to Christianity, in contempt.

Nazarite, naz'a•rīt, *n.* [Heb. *nazir*, separated.] A Jew who by certain vows and acts devoted himself to the peculiar service of Jehovah for a certain time or for life. Num. vi. 2-21.

Nazi, nä'tsē, *a.* Of or pertaining to, or embodying the principles of, Naziism.—*n.* A member of the German National Socialist Workers' Party.—**Naziism,** nä'tsē•izm, *n.* A totalitarian form of government administered by the Nazi Party (the German National Socialist Workers' Party) which advocated the building of a highly nationalistic Aryan state, with the revival and substitution of Germanic Hero Worship for Christianity, and recognized private ownership except when the state determined otherwise.

Neanderthal, ni•an'dėr•tal, *a.* [From the Neanderthal Valley in Germany, its place of discovery.] Of or pertaining to the skeletal remains of a paleolithic man discovered in 1856. —*n.* A European paleolithic man.

neap, nēp, *a.* [A.Sax. *nep*, neap; akin to Dan. *knap*, Icel. *hneppr*, narrow, scanty, and probably to *nip*.] Low, or not rising high: applied to the lowest tides, being those that happen in the middle of the second and fourth quarters of the moon, taking place about four or five days before the new and full moons.—**neap, neap tide,** *n.* One of the lowest tides or the time of one; opposite to *spring* tide.

near, nēr, *a.* [A.Sax. *neár*, compar. of *neáh*, nigh=Icel. *nær*, *nærri*, Dan. *nær*, near; nearer. NEXT, NIGH.] Nigh; not far distant in place, time, or degree; closely connected by blood (*near* relations); intimate; familiar (a *near* friend); close or literal; narrow (a *near* escape); on the left of a horse (the *near* foreleg); short, or not circuitous; niggardly; approximately like the original (*near*beer).—*prep.* Close to.—*adv.* Almost; within a little; closely.—*v.t.* and *i.* To approach; to come near.—**nearby,** nēr•bī', *a.* and *adv.* Close at hand.—**nearly,** nēr'li, *adv.* Almost; intimately; in a parsimonious or niggardly manner.—**nearness,** nēr'nes, *n.*—**nearsighted,** *a.* Shortsighted; seeing at a small distance only.

neat, nēt, *n.* [A.Sax. *neát* (sing. and pl.); Sc. *nowt*, Icel. *naut*. Sw. *nót*, Dan. *nód*, cattle, an ox; from verbal stem Icel. *njóta*, A.Sax. *neótan*, to use, to enjoy; Goth. *niutan*, to take.] Cattle of the bovine type, as oxen or cows: used either collectively or of one individual.—*Neat's-foot oil*, an oil obtained from the feet of *neat* cattle.

neat, nēt, *a.* [Fr. *net*, *nette*, from L. *nitidus*, shining, from *niteo*, to shine.] Having everything in perfect order; tidy; trim; expressed in few and well-chosen words; chaste; said of style; with all deductions made (usually written *Net* or *Nett*).—**neatly,** nēt'li, *adv.* In a neat manner; tidily; with good taste.—**neatness,** nēt'nes, *n.* The state or quality of being neat; tidiness; simple elegance.

nebula, neb'ū•la, *n.* pl. **nebulae, nebulas,** neb'ū•lē, neb'ū•läz. [L. *nebula*, a cloud; allied to Gr. *nephēlē*, a cloud; G. *nebel*, mist.] The name for celestial objects resembling white clouds, in many cases resolved by the telescope into clusters of stars, though many nebulae consist of masses of incandescent gas; a white spot or a slight opacity of the cornea of the eye.—**nebular,** neb'ū•lėr, *a.* Pertaining to nebulae.—*Nebular hypothesis*, a hypothesis that the bodies composing the solar system once existed in the form of a nebula, from which, when condensed by refrigeration, the planets were constituted, the main body forming the sun.—**nebulosity,** neb•ū•los'i•ti, *n.* The state of being nebulous; the faint misty appearances surrounding certain stars.—**nebulous,** neb'ū•lus, *a.* [L. *nebulosus.*] Cloudy; hazy; literally or figuratively; *astron.* pertaining to or having the appearance of a nebula; nebular.—**nebulousness,** neb'ū•lus•nes, *n.*

necessary, nes'es•se•ri, *a.* [L. *necessarius*, from *necesse*, necessary, unavoidable; origin doubtful.] Such as must be; inevitable; unavoidable; indispensable; essential; that cannot be absent; acting from necessity; opposed to *free* (as regards the will).—*Necessary truths*, those truths which cannot from their very nature but be true.—*n.* Anything necessary or indispensably requisite.—**necessarily,** nes'es•se•ri•li, *adv.* In a necessary manner; by necessity; indispensably.—**necessitarian,** ne•ses'i•tâ"ri•an, *n.* One who maintains the doctrine of philosophical necessity in opposition to the freedom of the will.—**necessitarianism,** ne•ses'i•tâ"ri•an•izm, *n.* The doctrine of philosophical necessity.—**necessitate,** ne•ses'i•tāt, *v.t.*—*necessitated, necessitating.* To make necessary or indispensable; to render necessary; to compel; to force.—**necessitous,** ne•ses'i•tus, *a.* Exhibiting indigence; pressed with poverty; indigent; destitute.—**necessitously,** ne•ses'i•tus•li, *adv.* In a necessitous manner. —**necessitousness,** ne•ses'i•tus•nes, *n.* Extreme poverty; pressing want. —**necessity,** ne•ses'i•ti, *n.* [L. *necessitas.*] The state of being necessary; condition demanding that something must be; unavoidableness; indispensableness; need; irresistible compulsion; compulsion of circumstances; the absolute determination of the will by motives; that which is requisite; a necessary; extreme indigence; pinching poverty.

neck, nek, *n.* [A.Sax. *hnecca*, the neck=D. *nek*, Dan. *nakke*, Icel. *hnakki*, the nape; G. *nacken*, the neck; connections doubtful.] The part of an animal's body between the head and the trunk and connecting them; part of a thing corresponding to the neck of animals; a narrow tract of land connecting two larger tracts; an isthmus; the slender part of a vessel, as a bottle; that part of a violin or similar instrument which connects the scroll or head and body.—*Neck and crop.* Under CROP.—*Neck or nothing*, at every risk.—*A stiff neck*, in *Scrip.* obstinacy in sin.—*To break the neck of an affair*, to destroy the main force of it; to get over the worst part of it.—*To tread on the neck of* (*fig.*), to subdue utterly.—*Neck and neck*, close, as in a race.—To *get it in the neck*, to get the worst of it.—*On the neck of*, adhering to, or immediately following.—**neckband,** *n.* The band of a shirt round the neck, to which the collar is attached.—**neckcloth,** nek'kloth, *n.* A piece of linen or cotton cloth worn round the neck as part of a gentlemen's dress.—**neckerchief,** nek'ėr•chif, *n.* A kerchief for the neck.—**necklace,** nek'-lis, *n.* A string of beads, precious stones, or other ornamental objects worn on the neck.—**necktie,** *n.* A band of cloth worn round the neck under the collar and knotted in front; a cravat; a scarf or tie.

necrobiosis, nek'rō•bī•ō"sis, *n.* [Gr. *nekros*, dead, and *bios*, life.] *Med.* the degeneration or wearing away of living tissue.—**necrolatry,** nek•-rol'a•tri, *n.* [Gr. *latreia*, worship.] Excessive veneration for or worship of the dead.—**necrology,** nek•rol'-o•ji, *n.* A register of deaths; a collection of obituary notices.—**necrological,** nek•ro•loj'i•kal, *a.* Pertaining to a necrology.—**necrologist,** nek•-rol'o•jist, *n.* One who writes obituary notices.—**necromancy,** nek'-ro•man•si, *n.* [Gr. *manteia*, divination.] Divination by means of a pretended communication with the dead; the black art; the art of magic or sorcery.—**necromancer,** nek'ro•-man•sėr, *n.* One who practices necromancy; a sorcerer; a wizard.—**necromantic,** nek•ro•man'tik, *a.* Pertaining to necromancy.—**necrophagous,** nek•rof'a•gus, *a.* [Gr. *phagein*, to eat.] Feeding on the dead, or putrescent substances.—**necrophobia,** nek•ro•fō'bi•a, *n.* [Gr. *phobos*, fear.] A horror of dead bodies; exaggerated fear of death.—**necropolis,** nek•rop'o•lis, *n.* [Gr. *polis*, a city; the city of the dead.] A cemetery, especially one that is extensive and ornamentally laid out.—**necroscopy,** nek•ros'ko•pi, *n.* Examination of the dead; a post-mortem examination.—**necrosis,** ne-krō'sis, *n.* [Gr. *nekrōsis*, deadness.] *Pathol.* death of the bone substance, a condition corresponding to what gangrene is to the flesh; *bot.* a disease of plants chiefly found upon the leaves and soft parts.

necrosis, ne•krō'sis, *n.* [Gr. *nekrosis*, deadness.] *Pathol.* death in a local area of the tissues.

nectar, nek'tėr, *n.* [Gr.] *Greek myth.* the drink of the gods, ambrosia being their solid food; hence, any delicious drink; *bot.* the honey of a flower.—**nectarean,** nek•tâ'rē•an, *a.* Resembling nectar; very delicious.—**nectareous,** nek•tâ'rē•us, *a.* Nectarean.—**nectarine,** nek'tėr•īn,—*n.* A variety of the common peach, having a smoother rind and firmer pulp.—**nectarous,** nek'tėr•us, *a.* Sweet as nectar.—**nectary,** nek'te•ri, *n.* The part of a flower that contains or secretes the nectar.

nee, nā, *pp.* [Fr., from L. *natus*, born. NATAL.] Born; a term placed before a married woman's maiden name to indicate her parentage; as, Madame de Staël, *nee* Necker, that is, whose family name was Necker.

need, nēd, *n.* [A.Sax. *nēd*=D. *nood*, Icel. *nauth*, Dan *nöd*, G. *noth*, Goth. *nauths*, need, necessity.] A state that requires supply or relief; pressing occasion for something; urgent want; necessity; want of the means of subsistence; poverty; indigence.—*v.t.* To have necessity or need for; to want, lack, require.—*v.i.* To be wanted; to be necessary.—*verb. aux.* To be under obligation, or necessity (it *needs* to be that way).—**needful,** nēd'fu̥l, *a.* Needy; necessitous; necessary; requisite.—**needfully,** nēd'fu̥l•li, *adv.*—**needfulness,** nēd'fu̥l•nes, *n.*—**neediness,** nē'di•nes, *n.*—**needless,** nēd'les, *a.* Not wanted; unnecessary; not requisite.—**needlessly,** nēd'les•li, *adv.*—**needlessness,** nēd'les•nes, *n.*—**needs,** nēdz, *adv.* Of necessity; necessarily; indispensably: generally with *must*.—**needy,** nē'di, *a.* Necessitous; indigent; very poor.

needle, nē'dl, *n.* [A.Sax. *naedl*, a needle; G. *nähen*, to sew, L. *neo*, Gr. *neō*, to spin.] A small instrument of steel pointed at one end, and having an eye or hole through which is passed a thread, used for sewing; a similar instrument used for interlacing a thread or twine in knitting, netting, embroidery, etc.; a name of sundry long and sharp-pointed surgical instruments; a magnetized bar of steel in a compass; a sharp pinnacle of rock; a needle-shaped crystal; a slender piece of steel or other material used to transmit vibrations, as from a phonograph record; *bot.* the needle-shaped leaf of a conifer.—*v.t.* To sew or pierce with a needle; to heckle; to goad into action.—*v.i.* To work with a needle; to form needle-like protuberances in crystallization.—**needlefish,** *n.* The pipefish, also the gar.—**needle point,** *n.* A kind of lace; a kind of embroidery done on canvas.—**needlewoman,** *n.* A seamstress.—**needlework,** *n.* Work executed with a needle; sewed work; embroidery; the business of a seamstress.

needless, needs, needy, etc. See NEED.

ne'er, nār. A contraction of *never*.

nefarious, ni•fâ'ri•us, *a.* [L. *nefarius*, from *nefas*, impious, unlawful, from *ne*, not, and *fas*, law, from *for*, *fari*, to utter. FATE.] Wicked in the extreme; impious.—**nefariously,** ni•-fâ'ri•us•li, *adv.*—**nefariousness,** ni•-fâ'ri•us•nes, *n.*

negation, ni•gā'shon, *n.* [L. *negatio*, a denying, from *nego*, to deny—*ne*, not, and verbal affix, *-go*, *-igo*. Akin *deny*, *renegade*.] Denial; a declaration that something is not, has not been, or will not be; contradiction or contradictory condition: opposed to *affirmation*.—**negate,** ne•gāt', *v.t.* To deny; to disprove or prove nonexistent.—**negative,** neg'a•tiv, *a.* Implying or containing denial or negation: opposed to *affirmative*; tending in the direction of denial without directly denying or controverting: opposed to *positive* (a *negative* result); *photog.* applied to a picture in which the lights and shades are the opposites of those in nature; *bacteriol.* not affirming the presence of an organism; *biol.* moving away from a source of stimulation.—*Negative electricity*, electricity associated with an excess of electrons.—*Negative pole*, the metal, or equivalent, placed in opposition to the *positive*, in the voltaic battery.—*Negative quantities*, *alg.* quantities which have the sign— (minus) prefixed to them.—*n.* A proposition by which something is denied; an opposite or contradictory term or conception; a negative proposition; a word that denies (*not*, *no*); that side of a question which denies or refuses; a decision or answer expressive of negation; *photog.* a photographic picture on glass or sensitized film, in which the lights and shades are the opposite of those in nature, used as a plate from which to print positive impressions; a veto or negative vote; *elec.* the negative plate of a battery.—*v.t.*—*negatived*, *negativing*. To disprove; to prove the contrary; to say *no* to; to reject; to refuse to enact or sanction.—**negatively,** neg'a•tiv•li, *adv.*—**negativeness, negativity,** neg'a•tiv•nes, neg•-a•tiv'i•ti, *n.*—**negativism,** neg'a•tiv•-izm, *n.* Atheism or agnosticism; any of the philosophies of denial; negativistic behavior.

negatron, neg'a•tron, *n.* [*Negat*ive and elec*tron*.] *Chem.* and *phys.* an electron.

neglect, neg•lekt', *v.t.* [L. *negligo*, *neglectum*, lit. not to pick up—*neg*, not, nor, and *lego*, to pick up. LEGEND.] To treat with no regard or attention or with too little; to slight; to set at naught; to omit to do; to leave undone; to forbear; often with an infinitive as object (to *neglect* to pay a visit).—*n.* Omission; forbearance to do anything that should be done; carelessness; omission of due attention or civilities; negligence; habitual want of regard; state of being disregarded.—**neglecter,** neg•lek'tėr, *n.* One that neglects.—**neglectful,** neg•lekt'fu̥l, *a.* Apt to neglect; treating with neglect; negligent; careless; inattentive.—**neglectfully,** neg•lekt'fu̥l•li, *adv.* In a neglectful manner.—**neglectfulness,** neg•lekt'fu̥l•nes, *n.*

negligee, neg'le•zhā", *n.* [Fr. *negligē*, from *negliger*, to neglect.] An informal dressing gown or wrapper worn by women.

negligent, neg'li•jent, *a.* [L. *negligens*, *negligentis*, ppr. of *negligo*, to neglect. NEGLECT.] Characterized by neglect; apt to neglect; careless; heedless; neglectful.—**negligently,** neg′li•jent•li, *adv.* In a negligent manner.—**negligence,** neg′li•jens, *n.* [L. *negligentia.*] The quality of being negligent; neglect; remissness; an act of negligence.—**negligible,** neg′-li•ji•bl, *a.* That may be neglected.

negotiate, ni•gō′shi•āt, *v.i.* [L. *negotior, negotiatus,* from *negotium,* want of leisure, business—*neg,* not, and *otium,* leisure.] To treat with another respecting purchase and sale; to hold intercourse in bargaining or trade; to hold diplomatic intercourse with another, as respecting a treaty, league, or other matter; to treat; to conduct communications in general. —*v.t.*—*negotiated, negotiating.* To procure or bring about by negotiation (a treaty, a loan); to pass in the way of business; to put into circulation (to *negotiate* a bill of exchange); to *negotiate* a corner, said of a motor car or other vehicle, taking an obstacle carefully in order to overcome it.—**negotiable,** ni•-gō′shi•a•bl, *a.* Capable of being negotiated; transferable by assignment from one person to another, as a bill or promissory note.—**negotiability,** ni•gō′shi•a•bil″i•ti, *n.* The quality of being negotiable.—**negotiation,** ni•gō′shi•ā″shon, *n.* The act of negotiating; the treating with another respecting sale or purchase; the intercourse of governments by their agents, in making treaties and the like.—**negotiator, negotiant,** † ni•go′shi•ā•tėr, ni•gō′shi•ant, *n.* One that negotiates.

Negro, nē′grō, *n.* pl. **Negroes,** nē′-grōz. [It. and Sp. *negro,* black, from L. *niger,* black.] A member of the African branch of the black race, formerly called the Ethiopian, which is characterized by the black or very dark color of the skin and the possession of hair of a woolly or crisp nature.—*a.* Relating to Negroes; black.—**Negroid,** nē′groid, *a.* Resembling Negroes; having Negro characteristics.—**Negrito, Negrillo,** ne•grē′tō, ne•gril′lō, *n.* and *a.* [Dim. of *Negro.*] A name given to the diminutive Negro-like tribes inhabiting the Philippines and the Eastern Archipelago.

negus, nē′gus, *n.* [From the inventor Col. *Negus* of Queen Anne's time.] A beverage made of wine, hot water, sugar, nutmeg, and lemon juice, or only of wine, water, and sugar; [*cap.*] the former ruler of Ethiopia.

neigh, nā, *v.i.* [A.Sax. *hnaegan,* Icel. *hneggja, gneggja,* Sw. *gnägga,* probably an imitative word; comp. L. *hinnio.*] To utter the cry of a horse; to whinny.—*n.* The cry of a horse; a whinnying.—**neighing,** nā′ing, *n.* A whinnying.

neighbor, nā′bėr, *n.* [A.Sax. *neáh-búr, néh-búr,* lit. a near-dweller, from *néah,* near (NIGH), and *búr, gebúr,* a dweller, a boor (BOOR).] One who lives near another; one who lives in a neighborhood; one in close proximity; one who lives on friendly terms with another; often used as a familiar term of address.—*a.* Being in the vicinity; adjoining; next.—*v.t.* To adjoin; to border on or be near to.—**neighborhood,** nā′-bėr•hụd, *n.* A place or district the inhabitants of which may be called neighbors; vicinity; the adjoining district or locality; neighbors collectively; a district or locality in general (a low *neighborhood*)—**neighboring,** nā′bėr•ing, *a.* Living as neighbors; being situated near.—**neighborliness,** nā′bėr•li•nes, *n.* State or quality of being neighborly. —**neighborly,** nā′bėr•li, *a.* Becoming a neighbor; acting as a good neighbor; social.

neither, nē′THėr or nī′THėr, *pron.* and *pronominal adjective.* [Used as negative of either; earlier forms *nather, naither, nouther,* A.Sax. *náuther, náhwæther=nowhether.*] Not one of two; not either; not the one or the other; used either alone or with a noun following.—*conj.* Not either: generally prefixed to the first of two or more co-ordinate negative propositions or clauses, the others being introduced by *nor*: sometimes used instead of *nor* in the second of two clauses, the former containing *not.*

nelumbo, ni•lum′bō, *n.* The Hindu and Chinese lotus, a beautiful water plant with rose-colored flowers.

nematocyst, nem′a•to•sist, *n.* [Gr. *nēma, nēmatos,* a thread, and *kystis,* a bag.] *Physiol.* a thread cell or stinging apparatus of coelenterate animals.

nematode, nem′ä•tōd, *n.* [Gr. *nēma, nēmatos,* a thread, from *neō,* to spin.] A parasitic worm of the class Nematoda, having a long cylindrical, and often filiform, body; a roundworm.

Nemean, nē′mē•an or ne•mē′an, *a,* Of or belonging to *Nemea* in Argolis. Greece.—*Nemean games,* ancient games or festivals celebrated at Nemea every second year.

Nemesis, nem′e•sis, *n.* [Gr., from *nemesis,* distribution of what is due.] A Greek goddess personifying retributive justice; one who takes vengeance; [*often not cap.*] act of retribution.

neodymium, nē′o•dim″i•um, *n.* [*Neo,* and *didymium.*] A metallic element of the rare-earth series. Symbol, Nd; at. no., 60; at. wt., 144.24.

Neo-Lamarckism, nē′ō•la•mark″-ism, *n.* [Gr. *neos,* new, and *Lamarck,* an eminent French naturalist.] A theory of evolution postulating the existence of definite laws of growth.

Neolithic, nē•ō•lith′ik, *a.* [Gr. *neos,* new, *lithos,* a stone.] *Archeol,* applied to the more recent of the two periods into which the Stone Age has been subdivided, as opposed to *Paleolithic.* During the Neolithic age, stone implements were polished, domesticated animals became common, cereals and fruit trees were grown, pottery made, linen woven, and boats used.

neology, ni•ol′o•ji, *n.* [Gr. *neos,* new, and *logos,* a word.] The introduction of a new word or of new words into a language; novel doctrines; rationalistic views in theology.—**neological,** nē•o•loj′i•kal, *a.* Pertaining to neology.—**neologism, neologianism,** ni•ol′o•jizm, nē•o•-lō′ji•an•izm, *n.* A new word or phrase, or new use of a word; the use of new words or of old words in a new sense; new doctrines.—**neologist,** ni•ol′o•jist, *n.* One who introduces new words or phrases; an innovator in doctrines or beliefs.

neon, nē′on, *n.* [Gr. *neon,* new.] A colorless inert gaseous element occurring in the atmosphere. Symbol, Ne; at. no., 10; at. wt., 20.183.—**neon lamp,** neon contained in a vacuum tube, through which an electric current passes, producing a reddish-orange glow, valuable in electric advertising signs (*neon signs*), and in aeronautics for beacons.

neophyte, nē′o•fīt, *n.* [Gr. *neos,* new, and *phyton,* a plant, from *phyō,* I grow.] A new convert or proselyte; a novice; one newly admitted to the order of priest; a tyro; a beginner in learning.

neoplasm, nē′o•plasm, *n.* [*Neo,* and *plasm.*] Any new and abnormal body tissue, such as a tumor.

Neoplatonism, nē•o•plā′ton•izm, *n.* [Gr. *neos,* new, and E. *Platonism.*] A philosophical system growing up in Alexandria, and prevailing chiefly from the 3rd to the 5th century after Christ, deriving elements from the philosophy of Plato, and from Christianity, Gnosticism, and Oriental beliefs.

neoprene, nē′o•prēn, *n.* [*Neo,* and chloro*prene.*] A rubber-like plastic acquired through the polymerization of chloroprene.

neoteric, nē•o•ter′ik, *a.* [Gr. *neōterikos,* young, from *neos,* new.] New; recent in origin; modern.

Neotropical, nē•o•trop′i•kal, *a.* [Gr. *neos,* new, and E. *tropical.*] Applied to a region of the earth in reference to its characteristic fauna, including all America south of the isthmus of Tehuantepec.

Neozoic, nē•ō•zō′ik, *a.* [Gr. *neos,* new, recent, and *zōē,* life.] *Geol.* a name given to strata from the beginning of the trias up to the most recent deposits, including the Mesozoic and Cenozoic divisions.

nepenthe, nepenthes, nē•pen′thē, nē•pen′thēz, *n.* [Gr. *nēpenthēs*—*nē,* not, and *penthos,* grief.] A kind of magic potion, supposed to make persons forget their sorrows and misfortunes; any draught or drug capable of removing pain or care.

nephew, nef′ū, *n.* [Fr. *neveu,* from L. *nepos, nepotis,* a nephew; cog. A.Sax. *nefa,* Icel. *nefi,* G. *neffe,* Skr. *napat,* a nephew. Akin *niece.*] The son of a brother or sister.

nephralgia, ne•fral′ji•a, *n.* [Gr. *nephros,* a kidney, and *algos,* pain.] Pain in the kidneys.—**nephrite,** nef′-rīt, *n.* [Gr. *nephritēs.*] The mineral otherwise called jade.—**nephritic,** ne•frit′ik, *a.* Pertaining to the kidneys; relieving disorders of the kidneys.—**nephritis,** ni•frī′tis, *n.* [Gr. term. *-itis,* signifying inflammation.] Inflammation of the kidneys.—**nephrology,** ne•frol′o•ji, *n.* A description of the kidneys.—**nephrotomy,** ne•frot′o•mi, *n.* [Gr. *tomē*, a cutting.] *Surg.* the operation of cutting for stone in the kidney.

nephridium, pl. **-ia,** nef•rid′i•um, *n.* [Gr. dim. of *nephros*, a kidney.] In animals, an excretory tube placing the COELOM (which see) in communication with the interior.

nepotism, nep′o•tism, *n.* [Fr. *nepotisme*, from L. *nepos*, nephew. NEPHEW.] Favoritism shown to nephews and other relations; patronage bestowed in consideration of family relationship and not of merit.—**nepotist,** nep′o•tist, *n.* One who practices nepotism.

Neptune, nep′tūn, *n.* [L. *Neptunus.*] The chief marine divinity of the Romans, identified by them with the Greek Poseidon; a planet beyond the orbit of Uranus, the third largest and second remotest from the sun.—**Neptunian,** nep•tū′ni•an, *a.* Pertaining to the ocean or sea; formed by water or aqueous solution (as rocks).—*Neptunian theory*, in *geol.* the theory of Werner, which refers the formation of all rocks and strata to the agency of water: opposed to the *Plutonic* theory.

neptunium, nep•tū′ni•um, *n.* [From *Neptune.*] A radioactive element produced artificially by neutron bombardment of uranium-238. Symbol, Np; at. no., 93; at. wt., 237.

Nereid, ni′ri•id, *n.* [Gr. *nērēis, nērēidos*, from *Nēreus*, a marine deity.] *Myth.* one of the daughters of Nereus, the constant attendants of Neptune; a sea nymph; a marine annelid; a sea centipede.

neroli, ner′ō•li, *n.* [The name of an Italian princess, its discoverer.] The fragrant essential oil from the flowers of the bitter orange.

nerve, nėrv, *n.* [L. *nervus*, a sinew, strength, vigor, from root *snar* (with initial *s*), seen in E. *snare.*] A sinew or tendon‡; strength; muscular power; self-command or steadiness, especially under trying circumstances; firmness of mind; courage; one of the whitish fibers which proceed from the brain and spinal cord, or from the central ganglia, of animals, and ramify through all parts of the body, and whose function is to convey sensation and originate motion; *pl.* the general tone of one's system as an indicator (*nerves* of steel); nervousness; hysteria; *bot.* one of the ribs or principal veins in a leaf.—*v.t.*—*nerved, nerving.* To give nerve, strength, or vigor to.—**nervation,** nėr•vā′shon, *n.* Venation.—**nerve cell,** *n. Anat.* and *physiol.* any cell containing the cellular components of nerve tissue.—**nerve-fiber,** *n.* An axon, dendrite, or process of a nerve cell.—**nerveless,** nėrv′les, *a.* Without nerve; without fear.—**nervewracking,** *a.* Very trying on the nerves; irritating; jarring.—**nervous,** nėr′vus, *a.* Pertaining to the nerves; affecting the nerves; having the nerves affected; having weak or diseased nerves; easily agitated; strong; vigorous; sinewy; characterized by force or strength in sentiment or style.—*Nerve centers*, the organs whence the nerves originate, as the brain.—*Nervous system* the nerves and nervous centers collectively which control movement and condition behavior and consciousness, in higher animals consisting of two parts, the cerebrospinal and autonomic systems.—*Nervous temperament*, that in which the predominating characteristic is a great excitability of the nervous system, and an undue predominance of the emotional impulses.—**nervously,** nėr′vus•li, *adv.*—**nervousness,** nėr′vus•nes, *n.* The state or quality of being nervous.—**nervure,** nėr′vūr, *n. Bot.* the vein or nerve of a leaf; *entom*, one of the corneous tubes which help to expand the wing and keep it tense.—**nervy,** nėr′vi, *a.* Sinewy; vigorous; cocky, bold, nervous.

nescience, nē′shi•ens, *n.* [L. *nescientia*, from *nescio*, not to know—*ne*, not, and *scio*, to know. SCIENCE.] The state of not knowing; want of knowledge; ignorance.

ness, nes, *n.* [A.Sax. *naes*, Icel. *nes*, Dan. *naes*, a ness; probably a form of *nose.*] A promontory; a cape; a headland.

nest, nest, *n.* [A.Sax., L.G., D., and G. *nest*; allied to L. *nidus*, a nest, for *nisdus*, from root *nas*, to dwell, seen in Greek *nostos*, return.] The place or bed formed or used by a bird for incubation and rearing the young; a place where the eggs of insects, turtles, etc., are produced; a place in which the young of various small animals (as mice) are reared; a number of persons frequenting the same haunt: generally in a bad sense; a set of articles of diminishing sizes, each enveloping the one next smaller (a *nest* of boxes); a set of small drawers.—*v.i.* To build a nest; to nestle.—**nestegg,** *n.* An egg left in the nest to prevent the hen from forsaking it; something laid up as a beginning or nucleus.—**nestle,** nes′l, *v.i.*—*nestled, nestling.* [Freq. from *nest.*] To make or occupy a nest; to take shelter; to lie close and snug.—*v.t.* To house or shelter, as in a nest; to cherish and fondle closely.—**nestling,** nest′ling, *n.* [A dim. from *nest.*] A young bird in the nest, or just taken from the nest.

Nestor, nest′or, *n.* The type of an old and faithful counselor, from Nestor in Homer, King of Pylos in Messenia.

Nestorian, nes•tō′ri•an, *n.* An adherent of Nestorius, patriarch of Constantinople in the fifth century, who maintained that the two natures in Christ were separate.

net, net, *n.* [A.Sax. *net, nett*, a net=Icel., Dan., and D. *net*, Sw. *nät*, Goth. *nati*, G. *netz*, a net; cog. L. *nassa*, a basket for catching fish; from root seen in Skr. *nada*, a stream.] An instrument formed of thread, twine, or other fibrous materials, wrought or woven into meshes, used for catching fish, birds, etc., and also for securing or containing articles of various kinds; a fabric of fine open texture.—*v.t.*—*netted, netting.* To make into a net or network; to take in a net; hence, to capture by wile or stratagem; to enclose in a net or network.—*v.i.* To form network.—**netted,** net′ed, *p.* and *a.* Made into a net or network; reticulated.—**netting,** net′ing, *n.* The process of making nets; a piece of network; a net of small ropes, to be stretched along the upper part of a ship's quarter to contain hammocks.—**network,** *n.* Work formed in the same manner as a net; any net-like fabric; an interlacement into a fabric or web; a complicated intermingling of lines as of a railroad system; a political undercover group, whose members are separated, but in indirect communication; in radio, a series of stations or broadcasting units called a hookup.

net, net, *n.* [M.E. Clean, clear, akin to *neat.*] A final amount remaining after all deductions.—*a.* Final; clear; remaining after all deductions have been made.—*v.t.* To make or gain as clear profit.

nether, neTH′ėr, *a.* [A.Sax. *nither, nithor, neothra*, compar. of *nithe*, under, downward (whence *neothan, beneothan, beneath*); cog. L.G., D., and Dan. *neder*, Icel. *netharr*, G. *nieder*; root seen in Skr. *ni*, downward.] Lower; lying or being beneath or in the lower part; opposed to *upper*.—**nethermost,** neTH′ėr•mōst, *a.* [A double superlative, like *hindmost.*] Lowest.

nettle, net′l, *n.* [A.Sax. *netele*=D. *netel*, Dan. *naelde, nelde*, G. *nessel*, a nettle; root doubtful.] A plant with stinging hairs, usually of the genus *Urtica.*—*v.t.*—*nettled, nettling.* To irritate or vex.—**nettle rash,** *n.* An eruption upon the skin much resembling the effects of the sting of a nettle; urticaria.

neural, nū′ral, *a.* [Gr. *neuron*, a nerve; akin to L. *nervus.* NERVE.] Pertaining to the nerve or nervous system.—*Neural arch*, the arch or projection posteriorly inclosing and protecting the spinal cord of the vertebra.—*Neural axis*, the central trunk of the nervous system, also called the *cerebro-spinal axis.*—**neuralgia,** nū•ral′ji•a, *n.* [Gr. *algos*, pain.] Pain in a nerve; an ailment the chief symptom of which is acute pain, apparently seated in a nerve or nerves.—**neuralgic,** nū•ral′jik, *a.* Pertaining to neuralgia.—**neurasthenia,** nū′ras•thē″ni•a, *n.* [Gr. *neuron*, nerve, *astheneia*, weakness. ASTHENIA.] *Med.* nervous debility or exhaustion; *psychol.* a form of mental disturbance characterized by excessive irritability, fatigue, and worry.—**neuration,** nū•ra′shon, *n.* The arrangement of the veins or nervures in the wings of insects; nervation.—**neuritis,** nū•rī′tis, *n. Med.* inflammation of a nerve.—**neurological,** nū•ro•loj′i•kal, *a.* Pertaining to neurology.—**neurologist,** nū•rol′o•jist, *n.* One versed in neurology.—**neurology,** nū•rol′o•ji, *n.* That branch of science which treats of the nerves.—**neuron,** nū´ron, *n.* The fundamental part of a nerve cell.—**neuropteran,** nū•rop´tėr•an, *n.* An individual belonging to an order of insects (Neuroptera) having four membranous, transparent, naked wings, reticulated with veins, or nervures, as the dragonflies. —**neuropterous,** nu•rop´ter•us, *a.* Belonging to the Neuropters.—**neurosis,** nū•rō´sis, *n.* A functional disorder of the nervous system without any apparent physical counterpart.—**neurotic,** nū•rot´ik, *a.* Of the nerves; relating to or acting on the nerves; affected by neurosis.—*n.* A disease of the nerves; a medicine for nervous affections; a neurotic person.

neuter, nū´tėr, *a.* [L., not either, not one nor the other—compounded of *ne* and *uter,* either of two.] Neutral‡; *gram.* of neither gender; neither masculine nor feminine (in *Eng. gram.* applied to all names of things without life); neither active nor passive; intransitive (a *neuter* verb); *bot.* having neither stamens nor pistils; *zool.* having no fully developed sex (*neuter* bees.)—*n.* An animal of neither sex, or incapable of propagation; one of the imperfectly developed females of certain social insects, as ants and bees; *bot.* a plant which has neither stamens nor pistils; *gram.* a noun of the neuter gender.—**neutral,** nū´tral, *a.* [L. *neutralis.*] Not taking an active part with one of certain contending parties; not interested one way or another; indifferent.—*Neutral colors,* those in which the hue is broken by partaking of the reflected colors of the objects which surround them.—*Neutral salts, chem.* salts which do not exhibit any acid or alkaline properties.—*Neutral tint,* a dull, grayish hue, partaking of the character of none of the brilliant colors.—*n.* A person or nation that takes no part in a contest between others.—**neutrality,** nū•tral´i•ti, *n.* The state of being neutral; the state of taking no part on either side.—**neutralization,** nū´tral•i•zā″shon, *n.* The act of neutralizing; *chem.* the process by which an acid and an alkali are so combined as to disguise each other's properties or render them inert.—**neutralize,** nū´tral•īz, *v.t.*—*neutralized, neutralizing.* To render neutral; to destroy the peculiar properties or opposite dispositions of; to render inoperative; to counteract; *chem.* to destroy or render inert or imperceptible the peculiar properties of, by combination with a different substance.—**neutralizer,** nū´tral•ī•zėr, *n.* One who or that which neutralizes.—**neutrally,** nū´tral•li, *adv.* In a neutral manner.

neutrino, nū•trē´nō, *n.* [L. *neutr-,* neither, and *ino.*] *Phys.* and *chem.* a hypothetical neutral particle of smaller mass than the neutron.—**neutron,** nū´tron, *n. Phys.* an uncharged particle in the nucleus of the atom, used for bombardment in atomic-energy reactions.

névé, nā´vā, *n.* [Fr., from L. *nix, nivis,* snow.] The French name for the coarsely granular snow from which glaciers are formed.

never, nev´ėr, *adv.* [The neg. of *ever;* A.Sax. *naefre,* from *ne,* not, and *aefre,* ever; comp. *neither, either,* etc.] Not ever; at no time, whether past, present, or future; in no degree (*never* fear); not at all; none (*never* the better); not, emphatically (he answered *never* a word).—*Never so,* to any or to whatever extent or degree (*never so* much, little, well, etc.; now less common than *ever so*).—*Never* is much used in composition, as in *never*-ending, *never*-failing, *never*-dying, etc.; but in all such compounds it has its usual meaning.—**nevermore,** nev´ėr•mōr, *adv.* Never again; at no future time.

nevertheless, nev´ėr•THe•les″, *conj.* [The *the* is the old instrumental case of the demonstrative used before comparatives; A.Sax. *thý læs,* the or by that less.] Not the less; notwithstanding; in spite of, or without regarding that.

nevus, nē´vus, *n.* [L.] A natural mark, spot, or blemish on the skin of a person; a birthmark.

new, nū, *a.* [A.Sax. *niwe, neówe,* new=D. *nieuw,* Goth. *niujis,* G. *neu;* cog. W. *newydd,* Ir. *nuadh,* L. *novus,* Gr. *neos,* Skr. *navas,* —new; connected with *now.*] Lately made, invented, produced, or come into being; recent in origin; novel: opposed to *old,* and used of things; not before known; recently discovered; recently produced by change; different from a former (to lead a *new* life); not habituated; not familiar; unaccustomed; fresh after any event, never used before, or recently brought into use; not secondhand (a *new* copy of a book); recently commenced; starting afresh (the *new* year, a *new* week).—*New Testament.* See TESTAMENT.—*New World,* a name frequently given to North and South America; the Western Hemisphere.—**newcomer,** *n.* One who has lately come.—**New Deal,** *n.* A term attached to the policies advocated by Franklin Delano Roosevelt and legislation enacted by Congress.—**newfangled,** *a.* New-fashioned.—**new-fashioned,** *a.* Made in a new fashion; lately come into fashion.—**newly,** nū´li, *adv.* Lately; freshly; recently; with a new form; afresh.—**new moon,** *n.* The moon when it is in conjunction with the sun and is totally dark.—**newness,** nū´nes, *n.*—**news,** nūz, *n.* pl. The material reported in a newspaper, magazine, or newscast; a newscast; fresh information of something that has lately taken place, or of something before unknown; tidings; a newspaper.—**newsboy,** *n.* A boy who sells or delivers newspapers.—**newsletter,** *n.* A letter-like report or analysis of a specialized nature, printed for periodic distribution to subscribers.—**newsmonger,** nūz´mung•gėr, *n.* One who deals in news; a gossip; a teller of tales.—**newspaper,** nūz´pā•pėr, *n.* A periodic publication issued daily or weekly, disseminating news, opinions, and reports of immediate significance; the organization that composes, publishes, and distributes newspapers.—**newspaperman,** *n.* One who writes for, edits, or owns a newspaper; a gatherer of news.—**newsprint,** *n.* An inexpensive paper manufactured from woodpulp, machine-finished, used mostly for newspapers.—**newsreel,** nūz´rēl, *n.* A motion picture film depicting current news events.—**newsstand,** *n.* A booth or stand where newspapers and periodicals are sold.—**newsy,** nūz´i, *a.* Full of news.

newel, nū´l, *n.* [O.Fr. *nouel, nouil,* stone of a fruit, der. from L. *nux, nucis,* nut.] The post about which a winding staircase circles, hence, the main or secondary posts of a straight staircase.

Newfoundland dog, nū•found´land, or nū´fėnd•land dag, *n.* [From the island.] A well-known and fine variety of the dog, supposed to be derived from Newfoundland, remarkable for its sagacity, good nature, and swimming powers.

newt, nūt, *n.* [A corruption of *an ewt, ewt, evet* being old forms. EFT.] One of a genus of small-tailed batrachians of lizard-like appearance, living in ponds, ditches, and moist places; an eft.

Newtonian, nū•tō´ni•an, *a.* Pertaining to Sir Isaac *Newton,* or formed or discovered by him.—*Newtonian telescope,* a form of reflecting telescope.

next, nekst, *a.* superl. of *nigh.* [A.Sax. *néhst, néhsta,* superl. of *néh, neáh,* nigh.] Nearest in place, time, rank, or degree. [When *next* stands before an object without *to* after it, it may be regarded as a preposition.]—*Next door to,* close to; allied to; not far removed from.—*adv.* At the time or turn nearest or immediately succeeding (who follows *next?*).

nexus, nek´sus, *n.* [L.] Tie; connection; interdependence existing.

niacin, nī´ä•sin, *n.* [*Ni*cotinic *ac*id and *in.*] One part of the vitamin B complex; nicotinic acid.

nib, nib, *n.* [Same as *neb.*] The bill or beak of a fowl; the point of anything, particularly of a pen; a small pen adapted to be fitted into a holder.—*v.t.*—*nibbed, nibbing.* To furnish with a nib; to mend the nib of, as a pen.

nibble, nib´l, *v.t.*—*nibbled, nibbling.* [A freq. from *nib,* or from *nip.*] To bite by little at a time; to eat in small bits; to bite, as a fish does the bait; just to catch by biting.—*v.i.* To bite gently; *fig.* to carp; to make a petty attack; with *at.*—*n.* A little bite, or the act of seizing with the mouth as if to bite.—**nibbler,** nib´lėr, *n.* One that nibbles.

niblick, nib´lik, *n.* An iron-headed golf club with a wide face at an angle of 45 degrees or more from the vertical, that is used to lift the ball into the air from sandtraps and to approach the green.

nice, nīs, *a.* [O.Fr. *nice, nisce,* simple, from L. *nescius,* from *ne,* not, *scio,* to know. NESCIENCE.] Foolish or silly‡; unimportant‡; over-scrupulous; fastidious; punctilious; distinguishing minutely; made with scrupulous exactness; precise; pleasant to the senses; delicious; dainty; pleasing or agreeable in general: a modern sense.—**nicely,** nīs′li, *adv.* In a nice manner; fastidiously; critically; with delicate perception; accurately; exactly; becomingly; pleasantly.—**niceness,** nīs′nes, *n.* State or quality of being nice; fastidiousness; minute exactness; agreeableness; pleasantness.—**nicety,** nīs′e•ti, *n.* [O.Fr. *niceté.*] State or quality of being nice; excess of delicacy; fastidiousness; delicacy of perception; precision; delicate management; a minute difference or distinction.

Nicene, nī•sēn′, *a.* [*Nicaea,* a town of Asia Minor.] Pertaining to a summary of Christian faith, the *Nicene creed,* composed by the Council of Nice against Arianism, A.D. 325.

niche, nich, *n.* [Fr. *niche,* from It. *nicchia,* from *nicchio,* a shellfish, from L. *mytilus,* a mussel.] A recess in a wall for the reception of a statue, a vase, or some other ornament; a person's place or position.

Nick, nik, *n.* [A name among the Teutonic nations for a water-goblin; A.Sax. *nicor,* Dan. *nök,* Icel. *nykr,* N. *nykk, nök,* G. *nix, nixe.*] Originally, a goblin or spirit of the waters, but now applied only to the Evil One, generally with the addition of *Old.*

nick, nik, *n.* [Same as D. *knik,* Sw. *nick,* a nod, a wink; G *nicken,* to nod; or connected with *nick,* a notch.] The exact point of time required by necessity or convenience; the critical time.—*v.t.* To strike at the lucky time; to hit; to make a hit at by some trick (*Shak.*).

nick, nik, *n.* [Comp. G. *knick,* a flaw; also E. *notch,* O.D. *nocke,* a notch.] A notch; a notch in the shank of a type to guide the hand of the compositor in setting.—*v.t.* To make a nick or notch in; to cut in nicks or notches.

nickel, nik′el, *n.* [Sw. *nickel,* nickel; a name connected with *nick,* the evil spirit, and given to this metal because its copper-colored ore deceived the miners by giving no copper.] A hard silver-white metallic element, malleable and ductile, much used in alloys. Symbol, Ni; at. no., 28; at. wt., 58.71. The five-cent coin composed of copper and nickel. (*U.S.*)—**nickelic,** ni•kel′ik, *a.* Pertaining to or containing nickel.—**nickeliferous,** nik•el•if′ėr•us, *a.* Containing nickel.—**nickel-plating,** *n.* The plating of metals with nickel.—**nickel silver,** *n.* An alloy composed of copper, zinc, and nickel.

nicknack, nik′nak, *n.* [KNICKKNACK.] A trinket; a gimcrack; a trifle. Spelled also *knickknack.*

nickname, nik′nām, *n.* [Probably for *ekename* (Icel. *auk-nefni*), the initial *n* being that of *an,* the indef. art., like *newt* for *ewt.*] A name given to a person in contempt or derision; a familiar or contemptuous name or appellation; a familiar form of a proper name, such as "Bill," for William.

nicotine, nik′o•tin, *n.* A volatile alkaloid from tobacco, highly poisonous.

nicotinic acid, nik•o•tin′ik a′sid, *n.* [From *nicotine.*] An acid resulting from the oxidation of nicotine, (C_5H_4 N) COOH, and one of the members of the vitamin B complex; niacin.

nictitate, nictate, nik′ti•tāt, nik′tāt, *v.i.*—*nictitated, nictated; nictitating, nictating.* [From L. *nicto, nictatum,* to wink.] To wink with the eyes.—*Nictitating membrane,* a thin movable membrane, most largely developed in birds, which covers and protects the eyes from dust or too much light.—**nictitation, nictation,** nik•ti•tā′shon, nik•tā′shon, *n.* The act of winking.

nidificate, nid′i•fi•kāt, *v.i.* [L. *nidifico,* from *nidus,* a nest, *facio,* to make. NIDULANT.] To make a nest.—**nidification,** nid′i•fi•kā″shon, *n.* The act of building a nest.

nidus, nī′dus, *n.* [L., a nest.] Any part of a living organism where a parasite finds nourishment; *med.* the bodily seat of a zymotic disease; the part of the organism where such a disease is developed.

niece, nēs, *n.* [Fr. *nièce,* O.Fr. *niepce,* from L. *neptis,* a granddaughter; allied to *nepos, nepotis,* a nephew. NEPHEW.] The daughter of a brother or sister; also, the daughter of a brother or sister in law.

nielio, ni•el′i•ō, *n.* [It., from L.L. *nigellum,* from L. *nigellus,* dim. of *niger,* black.] A method of ornamenting metal plates by cutting lines in the metal and filling them up with a black or colored composition.

nifty, nif′ti, *a.* [Slang] Very good; attractive and stylish.

niggard, nig′ėrd, *n.* [From Icel. *knöggr,* Sw. *njugg,* niggardly, with term. *-ard.*] A miser; a person meanly covetous; a sordid, parsimonious wretch.—**niggard, niggardly,** nig′ėrd•li, *a.* Miserly; meanly covetous; sordidly parsimonious.—**niggardly,** *adv.* In a niggard manner.—**niggardliness,** nig′ėrd•li•nes, *n.* The quality of being niggardly; sordid parsimony.

niggle, nig′l, *v.i.*—*niggled, niggling.* [N. *nigla.*] To trifle; to putter around.

nigh, nī, *a.* compar, *nigher,* superl. *next,* [A.Sax. *neáh, néh,* nigh, near; D. *na,* Icel. *ná-,* G. *nah, nahe,* near, prep. *nach,* to, Goth. *nehwa*—nigh. NEAR, NEIGHBOR.] Near; not distant or remote in place or time; closely at hand; ready to aid.—*adv.* Near; close; almost; nearly.—*prep.* Near to; at no great distance from.

night, nīt, *n.* [A.Sax. *niht, neaht*= Icel. *nátt,* Sw. *natt,* Dan. *nat,* Goth. *nahts,* D. and G. *nacht;* cog. Ir. *nochd,* W. *nos,* Armor. *noz,* Lith. *naktis,* L. *nox, noctis,* Gr. *nyx, nyktos,* Skr. *nakti, nakta*—night; from root *nak,* to vanish, to perish.] That part of the natural day when the sun is beneath the horizon, or the time from sunset to sunrise; *fig.* a state or time of darkness, depression, misfortune, and the like; a state of ignorance or intellectual darkness; obscurity; the darkness of death or the grave; a time of sadness or sorrow.—**nightly,** nīt′li, *a.* Done by night; happening in the night; done every night.—*adv.* By night; every night.—**nightward,** nīt′wėrd, *a.* Approaching toward night. *Night* is much used as a first element in compounds, many of them self-explanatory.—**night blindness,** *n.* A disease in which the eyes can see only by day or bright light.—**nightcap,** *n.* A cap worn in bed; toddy or other potation taken before going to bed.—**night clothes,** *n.* pl. Clothes worn in bed.—**night club,** *n.* A café or restaurant, serving liquors and presenting entertainment for the enjoyment of night pleasure-seekers.—**nightcrawler,** *n.* A large angleworm which crawls about by night.—**nightfall,** nīt′fa̤l, *n.* The fall of night; the close of the day; evening.—**nightgown,** *n.* A loose gown worn in bed; a nightdress.—**nighthawk,** *n.* Any of the North American longwinged goatsuckers (genus *Chordeiles*) related to the whippoorwill; a person up and about during the night.—**night letter,** *n.* A telegram sent at night at a per-word rate lower than a straight telegram.—**nightlong,** *a.* Lasting a night.—**nightmare,** nīt′mār, *a.* A dream causing a state of oppression or feeling of suffocation, hence, some overpowering, oppressive, or stupefying influence.—**night rider,** *n.* A member of a band of terrorists who go about at night performing acts of violence and destruction to punish or scare.—**nightshade,** nīt′shād, *n.* [A.Sax. *nihtscada,* lit. the shade or shadow of night; so D. *nachtschade,* G. *nachtschatten,* the nightshade.] The popular name of various plants of the potato genus which possess narcotic or poisonous properties; also applied to plants of different genera.—*Deadly nightshade,* belladonna.—**nightshirt,** *n.* A pull-over sleeping garment for men and boys.—**nightwalker,** *n.* One that walks in his sleep; a somnambulist; one that roams in the night for evil purposes.—**night watch,** *n.* A watch or period of the night; a watch or guard in the night.

nightingale, nīt′in•gāl, *n.* [A.Sax. *nihtegale,* lit. the night-singer, from *niht,* night, *galan,* to sing; so D. *nachtegaal,* Dan. *nattergal,* G. *nachtigall.* The *n* medial is intrusive, as in *passenger, messenger.*] A well-known migratory bird that sings at night, often called in poetry Philomela or Philomel.

nigrescent, nī•gres′ent, *a.* [L. *nigresco,* to grow black, from *niger,* black.] Growing black; approaching to blackness.—**nigritude,** nig′ri•tūd, *n.* [L. *nigritudo.*] Blackness.

nihilism, nī'hil•izm, *n.* [L. *nihil*, nothing.] Nothingness; *metaph.* the denial of the basis of all knowledge; the doctrine that existence is meaningless and life has little value. —**nihilist,** nī'hil•ist, *n.* One who holds the doctrine or principles of nihilism; a member of a Russian secret society, the adherents of which maintained the need for an entire reconstruction of society and held revolutionary ideas generally.—**nihilistic,** nī•hil•is'tik, *a.*—**nihility,** nī•hil'i•ti, *n.* A state of being nothing; nothingness.

nil, nil, *n.* [L. NIHIL.] Nothing; as, his liabilities were over $5000 and his assets *nil*.

Nilometer, nī•lom'et•ėr, *n.* [Gr. *Neilos*, Nile, and *mētron*, measure.] An instrument for measuring the rise of water in the Nile during its periodical floods.—**Nilotic,** nī•lot'ik, *a.* Pertaining to the Nile.

nimble, nim'bl, *a.* [O.E. *nemel*, capable, A.Sax. *numol*, capable, catching, from *niman*, to take=Icel. *nema*, D. *nemen*, G. *nehmen*, Goth. *niman*, to take; akin *numb*, *benumb*.] Light and quick in motion; moving with ease and celerity; agile; prompt; swift.—**nimbleness,** nim'bl•nes, *n.* Agility; quickness; celerity.—**nimbly,** nim'bli, *adv.* In a nimble manner; with agility.

nimbus, nim'bus, *n.* [L., a cloud.] A cloud; a rain cloud; a kind of halo or disc surrounding the head in representations of divine or sacred personages.

nincompoop, nin'kom•pöp, *n.* [A corruption of L. *non compos*, not of sound mind.] A fool; a blockhead; a simpleton.

nine, nīn, *a.* [A.Sax. *nigon*=L.G. and D. *negen*, G. *neun*, Goth. *niun*, Icel. *niu*, Sw. *niu*, Dan. *ni*; cog. W. *naw*, Ir. *naov*, L. *novem*, Gr. *ennea*, Skr. *navam*—nine. NOON.] One more than eight, or one less than ten.—*Nine days' wonder*, a subject of astonishment and gossip for a short time.—*The nine worthies*, certain famous personages, often alluded to by old writers, like the seven wonders of the world, etc.—*n.* The number composed of eight and one. —*The Nine*, among English poets, the nine Muses.—**ninefold,** nīn'fōld, *a.* Nine times repeated.—**ninepins,** *n. pl.* A game with nine pins of wood set on end, at which a ball is rolled.—**nineteen,** nīn'tēn, *a.* and *n.* [A.Sax. *nigontyne*, i.e. *nine ten*.] Nine and ten.—**nineteenth,** nīn'tēnth, *a.* The ordinal of nineteen.—*n.* A nineteenth part.—**ninety,** nīn'ti, *a.* and *n.* [A.Sax. *nigontig*—*nigon*, nine, and *tig*, ten.] Nine times ten.—**ninetieth,** nīn'ti•eth, *a.* The ordinal of ninety.—*n.* A ninetieth part.—**ninth,** nīnth, *a.* The ordinal of nine; the next preceding ten.—*n.* A ninth part; *mus.* an interval containing an octave and a tone.—**ninthly,** nīnth'li, *adv.* In the ninth place.

ninny, nin'i, *n.* [A contr. for *nincompoop*, or from It. *ninno*, Sp. *niño*, a child.] A fool; a simpleton.—**ninnyhammer,** nin'i•ham•ėr, *n.* A simpleton.

niobium, nī•ō'bi•um, *n.* [From *Niobe*.] A gray metallic element, formerly called columbium. Symbol, Nb; at. no., 41; at. wt., 92.906.

nip, nip, *v.t.*—*nipped* or *nipt*, *nipping*. [Not found in A.Sax.; akin to Dan. *nippe*, to twitch, *knibe*, to nip, to pinch; D. *knippen*, to nip, *nijpen*, to pinch; Icel. *kneif*, pincers; G. *kneipen*, *kneifen*, to pinch, *knippen*, to fillip; akin *knife*, *neap*.] To catch and compress sharply between two surfaces or points, as of the fingers; to pinch; to cut, bite, or pinch off the end of; to blast, as by frost; to benumb; to chill.—*To nip in the bud*, to destroy in the first stage of growth.—*n.* A pinch, as with the points of the fingers, nails, etc.; a blast by frost.—**nip and tuck.** Uncertainty as to the probable success of alternate element.—**nipper,** nip'ėr, *n.* One who or that which nips; a foretooth of a horse.—**nippingly,** nip'ing•li, *adv.* In a nipping manner; sarcastically.—**nippy,** *a.* Brisk or tangy, as of the air or of a cheese.

nip, nip, *n.* [Dan. *nip*, a sip, *nippe*, D. and G. *nippen*, to nip; akin *nipple*.] A sip or small draught, especially of some strong spirituous beverage.

nipper, nip'ėr, *n.* In the plural, pincers; a tool.

nipple, nip'l, *n.* [A.Sax. *nipele*; probably connected with *nip*, a sip, L.G. *nippen*, Dan. *nippe*, to sip.] The spongy protuberance by which milk is drawn from the breasts of females; a pap; a teat; something like a nipple, as that part of a gun over which the cap is placed; a connecting piece of pipe.

nirvana, nir•vä'na, *n.* [Skr. *nir*, out, and *vāna*, blown; lit. blown out.] *Buddhism* the final beatitude attained through the extinguishing of desire and human consciousness; a state of oblivion to human reality, as pain, concern, etc.

Nisan, nī'san, *n.* A month of the Jewish calendar, originally called Abib.

nisei, nē'sā, *n.* [Jap. *ni*, second, and *sei*, generation.] An American-born child of Japanese immigrant parents.

Nissen hut, nis'n hut, *n.* A fairly portable wooden hut with iron roof. It was said to be warm in winter and cool in summer; actually it was the reverse.

nit, nit, *n.* [A.Sax. *hnitu*; D. *neet*, Icel. *nitr*, Dan. *gnid*, Sw. *gnet*, G. *niss*, a nit; cog. Gr. *konis*, a nit.] The egg of a louse or other small insect.

niter, nī'tėr, *n.* [Fr. *nitre*, L. *nitrum*, Gr. *nitron*, from some oriental source.] A substance called also saltpeter; potassium nitrate or sodium nitrate used for making gunpowder, in dyeing, metallurgy, medicine, etc. —**nitrate,** nī'trāt, *n.* A salt of nitric acid; potassium nitrate or sodium nitrate used as a fertilizer.—*v.t.* To join or treat with nitric acid or a nitrate; *chem.* to convert to a nitro compound or a nitrate.—**nitric,** nī'trik, *a.* A term in the nomenclature of the oxygen compounds of nitrogen, indicating more nitrogen content, especially of higher valence than nitrous substances.—*Nitric acid*, an important acid, HNO_3, employed in etching, explosives, etc.—**nitrification,** nīt'rif•i•kā"shon, *n.* Formation of nitrates as plant food by the action of certain bacteria on organic substances.—**nitrify,** nī'tri•fī, *v.t.* *Chem.* to infuse or join with nitrogen or a nitrogen compound; to change, by oxidation, into nitrous or nitric acid or their salts.—**nitrite,** nī'trīt, *n.* A salt of nitrous acid.—**nitrogen,** nī'tro•jen, *n.* That element which is the principal ingredient of atmospheric air, of which it constitutes about four-fifths, possessing neither taste nor smell. Symbol, N; at. no., 7; at. wt., 14.0067.—*Nitrogen cycle*, a revolving course of natural fertilizing processes involving the passing of nitrogen through air, soil, and organisms.—**nitrogenize,** nī'tro•jen•īz, *v.t.* To impregnate or imbue with nitrogen.—**nitrogenous,** nī•troj'e•nus, *a.*—**nitroglycerin,** *n.* A compound produced by the action of a mixture of strong nitric and sulfuric acids on glycerin at low temperatures, a most powerful explosive.—**nitrometer,** nī•trom'et•ėr, *n.* An instrument for ascertaining the quality or value of niter. —**nitrous,** nī'trus, *a. Chem.* applied to compounds containing less oxygen than those called *nitric*.—*Nitrous oxide gas*, a combination of nitrogen and oxygen which, when inhaled, causes insensibility, and hence is used as an anaesthetic during surgical operations; diluted with air it produces an exhilarating effect, hence the name of *laughing gas*.

nitid, nī'tid, *a.* [L. *nitidus*.] Bright; shining; gay; spruce; *bot.* having a smooth polished surface.

nitwit, nit'wit, *n.* [G. *nix*, not, and E. *wit*.] A dull-witted or stupid person.

nix, niks, *n.* [G. *nichts*, nothing.] Nothing; no one; no.

Nizam, ni•zäm', *n.* [Hind. and Ar. from Ar. *nazama*, to govern.] Formerly the title of the ruler of Hyderabad in India.

no, nō, *adv.* [A.Sax. *ná*, *nó*, no, from the negative particle, *ne*, *no* and *á*, ever; this negative particle=Icel. *ne*, Goth. *ni*, Bohem, and Russ. *ne*, Armor. and Gael. *na*, L. *ne*, Zend. *na*, Skr. *na*; akin *nor*, *not*, *nay*, *non*.] A word of denial or refusal, expressing a negative, and opposed to *yes*. When repeated or when used with another negative it is specially emphatic. It may be used as the correlative of *whether* (*whether* or *no*), though now less common than *not*.—*n.* A negative vote, or a person who votes in the negative (the *noes* have it).—**noway, noways, nowise,** nō'wā, nō'wāz, nō'wīz, *adv.* In no way, manner, or degree.—**nowhere,** no'hwâr, *adv.* Not in or to any place.—**nowhither,** nō'hwiтн•ėr, *adv.* Not in any direction or to any place.

no, nō, *adv.* [A.Sax. *ná, nó,* no, from the negative particle, *ne, no* and *á,* ever; Goth. *ni,* L. *ne,* Skr. *na;* akin *nay.*] A word of denial or refusal, expressing a negative, and opposed to *yes;* a word used to emphasize or qualify a previous negative statement; not any; not at all.—*a.* Not at all; not a (I have *no* great love for him).—*n.* A negative vote; pl. persons who vote in the negative (the *noes* have it).—**noway, noways, nowise,** nō′wā, nō′wāz, nō′wīz, *adv.* In no way, manner, or degree.—**nowhere,** no′-hwâr, *adv.* Not in or to any place.

Noachian, nō•ā′ki•an, *a.* Relating to *Noah,* the patriarch, or his time.

nob, nob, *n.* [From *knob.*] The head: in humor or contempt.

nob, nob, *n.* [An abbreviation of *nobleman.*] A member of the aristocracy; a swell. (*Slang.*)—**nobby,** nob′i, *a.* Showy; stylish; smart. (*Slang.*)

nobelium, nō•bē′li•um, *n.* [From *Nobel* Institute.] A radio-active element produced artificially. Symbol, No; at. no., 102.

noble, nō′bl, *a.* [Fr. *noble,* from L. *nobilis,* high-born, noble; for *gnobilis,* from stem of *gnosco, nosco,* to know, seen also in E. *note.*] High in excellence or worth; lofty in character; magnanimous (a *noble* mind); proceeding from or characteristic of greatness of mind (*noble* sentiments); of the best kind; choice; pertaining to the nobility or peerage; magnificent; stately (a *noble* edifice). —*Noble metals,* those which have high value, superior qualities, and do not easily corrode: gold, silver, platinum, etc.—*n.* A nobleman.—**nobility,** nō•bil′i•ti, *n.* The quality of being noble; nobleness; the state of being of noble birth or rank; the peerage.—**nobly,** nō′bli, *adv.*—**nobleman,** nō′bl•man, *n.* One of the nobility.—**noblewoman,** nō′bl•wu̧•man, *n.*—**nobleness,** nō′bl•nes, *n.* —**noblesse,** nō•bles′, *n.* [Fr.] The nobility.—*Noblesse oblige,* the idea that noble birth or rank necessitates honorable and beneficent behavior.

nobody, nō′bod•i, *n.* [*No* and *body.*] No person; no one; an insignificant or contemptible person; a person of no standing or position.

nock, nok, *n.* [M.E. *nocke,* prob. from Sw. *nock, nocka,* akin M.D. *nocke,* D. *nok,* L.G. *nokk,* tip or projection.] *Archery,* the notch at either end of the bow for holding the string, or the notch in the arrow for fitting it to the bow.—*v.t.* To notch the bow or arrow.

noctambulation, noctambulism, nok•tam′bū•lā″shon, nok•tam′bū•lizm, *n.* [L. *nox, noctis,* night, and *ambulo,* to walk.] Somnambulism; sleepwalking.—**noctambulist,** nok•-tam′bū•list, *n.* A somnambulist.—**nocturne,** nok′tėrn, *n.* [F.] In music, a serenade concerning the night; a light, dreamy composition, variable in form; the musical piece of that name made famous by Chopin. —**nocturnal,** nok•tėr′nal, *a.* Pertaining or belonging to the night; done or occurring at night; *zool.* active by night; *bot.* closing during the day and expanding during the night; said of flowers.—**nocturnally,** nok•tėr′nal•li, *adv.* By night; nightly.

nod, nod, *v.i.*—*nodded, nodding.* [Allied to O.H.G. *nuoton, knoton,* to shake; Dan. *noder,* gestures; or perhaps to W. and Ir. *nod,* a mark, a notice; Gael. *nodadh,* a wink or nod.] To incline the head with a quick motion; either forward or sidewise; to let the head sink from sleep; to make an inclination of the head, as in assent or in beckoning; to bend or incline the top with a quick motion (*nodding* plumes).—*v.t.* To incline, as the head or top; to signify by a nod; to beckon by a nod.—*n.* A quick downward motion of the head as a sign of assent, salutation, from drowsiness, etc.—**nodder,** nod′ėr, *n.* One who nods.

noddle, nod′l, *n.* [A dim. corresponding to D. *knod, knodde,* a knob, a knot; Dan. *knude,* a knot; akin to *knot.*] The head: used humorously.

noddy, nod′i, *n.* [Probably from *nod,* and equivalent to sleepy-head; comp. *noodle.*] A simpleton; a fool; a seafowl; so called from its being easily taken.

node, nōd, *n.* [L. *nodus* (for *gnodus*), a knot; cog. *knot, noddle.*] A knot; a knob; a protuberance; *bot.* a sort of knot on a stem where leaves arise; *mus.* a nodal point; *astron.* one of the two points in which two great circles of the celestial sphere (as the ecliptic and equator) intersect each other; one of the points in which the orbit of a satellite intersects the plane of the orbit of its primary.—*Lunar nodes,* the points at which the orbit of the moon cuts the ecliptic.—**nodal,** nō′dal, *a.* Pertaining to a node or to nodes; nodated.—*Nodal points* and *nodal lines,* the points or lines of a vibrating body which remain at rest during the vibration.—**nodical,** nod′i•kal, *a.* *Astron.* relating to nodes.—**nodose,** nō•dōs′, *a.* [L. *nodosus.*] Knotted; jointed.—**nodosity,** nō•dos′i•ti, *n.* The state or quality of being nodose; knottiness; a knotty protuberance.—**nodular,** nod′ū•lėr, *a.* Pertaining to or in the form of a nodule.—**nodule,** nod′ūl, *n.* [L. *nodulus,* dim. from *nodus,* a knot.] A little knot or lump; *bot.* a small woody body found in bark; *geol.* a rounded irregular-shaped mineral mass.—**nodulose, nodulous,** nod′ū•lōs, nod′ū•lus, *a.* Having little knots; knotty.

noel, no′el, *n.* [Fr. from L. *dies natalis,* birthday of Christ.] Christmas carols; [cap.] Christmas.

nog, nog, *n.* [Same as Dan. *knag, knage,* a wooden peg; D. *knog,* a yardarm; akin *knag.*] A wooden pin; a treenail or pin used in shipbuilding; a brick-shaped piece of wood inserted in a wall; a timber-brick; a square piece of wood used to prop up the roof of a mine.—*Eggnog,* a drink containing an egg beaten with sugar, milk, flavoring, and usually liquors, served hot or cold.—**nogging pieces,** horizontal pieces of timber in brick work.

noggin, nog′in, *n.* [Ir. *noigin,* Gael. *noigean,* a noggin.] A small mug or wooden cup; a measure equivalent to a gill; the head.

noils, noilz, *n.* [Origin doubtful.] The knots and short wool separated out from the long wool in combing.

noise, noiz, *n.* [Fr. *noise,* strife, quarrel, noise, probably through a form *noxia,* for L. *noxa,* injury, hurt. NOXIOUS.] A sound of any kind or proceeding from any cause; more especially a din, a confused mixture of sounds; outcry; clamor; frequent talk; much public conversation or discussion.—*v.i. noised, noising.* To sound loud.—*v.t.*—*noised, noising.* To spread by rumor or report; to report.—**noiseless,** noiz′-les, *a.* Making no noise; silent.—**noiselessly,** noiz′les•li, *adv.* In a noiseless manner; silently.—**noiselessness,** noiz′les•nes, *n.* The state of being noiseless; silence.—**noisy,** noi′-zi, *a.* Making a loud noise; clamorous; full of noise.—**noisily,** noi′zi•li, *adv.* In a noisy manner; with noise.—**noisiness,** noi′zi•nes, *n.* The state of being noisy.

noisome, noi′sum, *a.* [From obsol. *noye,* annoyance, to annoy, shortened from *annoy,* with term. *-some.*] Noxious to health; morally noxious or injurious; offensive to the smell or other senses; fetid.—**noisomely,** noi′sum•li, *adv.* In a noisome manner.—**noisomeness,** noi′sum•nes, *n.*

nolle prosequi, nol′i pros′e•kwī, *n.* [L. to be unwilling to prosecute.] *Law,* the refusal of a plaintiff in an action to proceed any further.

nomad, nō′mad, *n.* [Gr. *nomas, nomados,* living on pasturage, from *nemō,* to feed, to pasture.] One of those people whose chief occupation consists in feeding their flocks, and who shift their residence according to the state of the pasture.—*a.* Nomadic.—**nomadic,** nō•mad′ik, *a.* [Gr. *nomadikos.*] Pertaining to nomads; subsisting by the tending of cattle, and wandering for the sake of pasturage; pastoral.—**nomadically,** nō•mad′i•kal•li, *adv.* In a nomadic manner.—**nomadism,** nō′-mad•izm, *n.* The state of being a nomad.

no man's land. The ground between hostile trenches, as belonging to neither side; unclaimed or uninhabited land.

nom de plume, nom′ de plöm, *n.* Pen name.

nome, nōm, *n.* [Gr. *nomos,* a district.] A province or other political division of a country, especially of modern Greece.—**nomarch,** nom′ärk, *n.* [Gr. *archō,* to rule.] The governor or chief magistrate of a nome.—**nomarchy,** nom′är•ki, *n.* The jurisdiction of a nomarch.

nomenclator, nō′men•klā•tėr, *n.* [L., from *nomen,* name, and *calo,* to call (seen in *calendar*).] A person who gives names to things; one who settles and adjusts the names of things in any art or science.—

nomenclature, nō′men•klā•tūr, *n.* A system of names; the systematic naming of things; the vocabulary of names or technical terms which are appropriated to any branch of science. ∴ As distinguished from *terminology* it is applied to the names for individual things, while the latter is generally applied to the technical terms describing the characteristics of things.

nominal, nom′i•nal, *a.* [L. *nominalis*, from *nomen*, *nominis*, a name. NAME.] Pertaining to a name or term; nounal; existing in name only; not real; merely so called.—**nominalism,** nom′i•nal•izm, *n.* The principles of the nominalists.—**nominalist,** nom′i•nal•ist, *n.* One of a sect of scholastic philosophers who maintained that general notions (such as the notion of a tree) have no realities corresponding to them, and have no existence but as names (*nomina*) or words: opposed to *realist*.—**nominalistic,** nom′i•nal•-is″tik, *a.* Relating to nominalism.—**nominally,** nom′i•nal•li, *adv.* In a nominal manner; in name only, not really (*nominally* king).—**nominate,** nom′i•nāt, *v.t.*—*nominated, nominating*. [L. *nomino*, *nominatum*.] To name; to mention by name; to designate by name for an office or place; to propose by name, or offer the name of, as a candidate for an office or place; to set down in express terms (*Shak.*).—**nomination,** nom•i•nā′shon, *n.* The act of nominating; the act of proposing by name for an office; the state of being nominated; the power of nominating or appointing to office.—**nominative,** nom′i•na•tiv, *a.* [L. *nominatus*, naming.] A term applied to that form of a noun or pronoun which is used when the noun or pronoun is the subject of a sentence.—*n.* The nominative case; a nominative word.—**nominator,** nom′i•nā•tėr, *n.* One that nominates.—**nominee,** nom•-i•nē′, *n.* A person nominated; one proposed to fill a place or office.

nomography, nō•mog′ra•fi, *n.* [Gr. *nomos*, a law, and *graphō*, to write.] Exposition of the proper manner of drawing up laws.—**nomology,** nō•mol′o•ji, *n.* [Gr. *nomos*, and *logos*.] The science or knowledge of law, legislation, and government.

nonacceptance, *n.* A refusal to accept.

nonage, non′ij, *n.* [L. *non*, not, and E. *age*.] The time of life before a person becomes legally of age; minority; period of immaturity in general.

nonagenarian, non′a•je•nâ″ri•an, *n.* [L. *nonagenarius*, from *nonageni*, ninety each, *nonaginta*, ninety, *novem*, nine.] A person ninety or between ninety and a hundred years old.

nonagon, non′a•gon, *n.* [L. *nonus*, ninth, and Gr. *gonia*, an angle.] A figure having nine sides and nine angles.

nonappearance, *n.* A failure to appear; default or appearance.

nonattendance, *n.* A failure to attend; personal absence.

nonce, nons, *n.* [Same as *once*, with an initial *n* belonging to the old dative of the article, seen in the phrases *for then anes*, *for then ones*, for the nonce, *anes*, *ones*, being an adverbial genitive from A.Sax. *án*, one, used substantively; comp. *the tother*, for *that other*.] Present occasion or purpose: used only in the phrase *for the nonce*.

nonchalant, non′sha•lant or noṅ•-sha•laṅ′, *a.* [Fr., from *non*, not, *chaloir*, to care for, from L. *calere*, to be warm.] Indifferent.—**nonchalantly,** non•sha•lant′li, *adv.*—**nonchalance,** non′sha•lans or non•-sha•lans′, *n.*

noncombatant, *n.* Anyone connected with a military or naval force whose duty it is not to fight; civilians in a place occupied by troops.

noncommissioned, *n.* Not having a commission.—*Noncommissioned officers*, subordinate officers below the rank of lieutenant, as sergeants and corporals in the army, and quartermasters and gunners mates in the navy.

noncommittal, *a.* Indicating a refusal to commit oneself; revealing no preference.

noncompliance, *n.* Neglect or failure of compliance.

non compos mentis, non kom′pos men′tis [L.] *Law*, not of sound mind; referring to any mental disorder.

nonconcurrence, *n.* A refusal to concur.

nonconductor, *n.* A substance which resists or conducts with difficulty such a force as heat or electricity.

nonconformist, non•kon•for′mist, *n.* One who does not conform; especially one who refuses to conform to an established church.—**nonconformity,** non•kon•for′mi•ti, *n.* Neglect or failure of conformity; the neglect or refusal to unite with an established church.

noncooperation, non•kō•op′ėr•ā″-shon, *n.* Failure or refusal to cooperate or comply.

nondescript, non′di•skript, *a.* [L. *non*, not, and *descriptus*, described.] Not hitherto described or classed; not easily described; odd; indescribable.—*n.* A person or thing not easily classed.

none, nun, *n.* or *pron.* [A.Sax. *nán*—*ne*, not, and *án*, one.] Not one; not any; not a part; not the least portion.—*None the less*, nevertheless.—**nonesuch,** nun′such, *n.* A person or thing such as to have no parallel.

noneffective, *a.* Having no power to produce an effect; causing no effect.

nonefficient, *a.* Not efficient; specifically, *milit.* a term applied to a volunteer who has not attended a prescribed number of drills and passed a certain standard in shooting.—*n.* One who is not efficient.

nonego, *n.* [L., not I.] *Metaph.* all beyond or outside of the *ego* or conscious thinking subject; the object as opposed to the subject.

nonelastic, *a.* Not elastic; destitute of the property of elasticity.

nonelect, *n. sing.* and *pl.* One who is or those who are not elect; those who are not chosen to salvation.—**nonelection,** *n.* Failure of election.

nonelectric, nonelectrical, *a.* Not electric; not conducting electricity.—*n.* A nonelectric substance.

nonentity, non•en′ti•ti, *n.* [L.L. *nonentitas*. ENTITY.] Nonexistence; a thing not existing; a person utterly without consequence or importance.

nones, nōnz, *n. pl.* [L. *nonae*, from *nonus*, for *novenus*, ninth, from *novem*, nine. NINE.] In the *Rom. calendar*, the fifth day of the months January, February, April, June, August, September, November, and December, and the seventh day of March, May, July, and October: so called as falling on the *ninth* day before the ides, both days included; the office for the ninth hour, one of the breviary offices of the Roman Catholic Church.

nonessential, *a.* Not essential or necessary; not absolutely necessary.—*n.* A thing that is not absolutely necessary.

nonexistence, *n.* Absence of existence; the negation of being.—**nonexistent,** *a.* Not having existence.

nonextensile, *a.* Not extensile; incapable of being stretched.

nonfeasance, *n. Law.* Omission of performance of legal duty.

nonfulfillment, *n.* Absence of fulfillment; neglect or failure to fulfill.

nonillion, nō•nil′yun, *n.* [L. *nonus*, nine, and E. *million*.] In the U.S. and France a unit with 30 ciphers annexed; in Great Britain and Germany a unit with 54 ciphers.

nonintervention, *n.* Abstention from intervening; a policy of not interfering in foreign politics excepting where a country's own interests are distinctly involved.

nonjuring, non•jūr′ing, *a.* [L. *non*, not, and *juro*, to swear.] Not swearing allegiance: an epithet applied to those who would not swear allegiance to the English government after the Revolution of 1688.—**nonjuror,** non•jū′rėr, *n.* One who refused to take the oath of allegiance to the government of England at the Revolution of 1688.

nonluminous, *a.* Not luminous; not giving out light.

nonmetal, non•me′tal, *n. Chem.* an element that is not a metal, as carbon, oxygen, nitrogen, etc., none of which forms basic oxides or hydroxides.

nonobjective, non•ob•jek′tiv, *a. Art*, abstract or nonrepresentational art, involving forms that are not related to objects of the real world.

nonobservance, *n.* Neglect or failure to observe or fulfill.

nonpareil, non•pa•rel′, *n.* [Fr. *non*, not or no, and *pareil*, equal, from L. *par*. equal (whence *pair*).] A person or thing of peerless excellence; a small printing type.

nonpartisan, *n.* One not bound by party ties or obligations.

nonpayment, *n.* Neglect of payment; failure of payment.

nonperformance, *n.* A failure or neglect to perform.

nonplus, non′plus, *n.* [L. *non*, not, and *plus*, more, further (whence *plural*).] A state in which one is unable to proceed or decide; inability to say or do more; puzzle: usually in the phrase *at a nonplus*.—*v.t.*—*nonplussed, nonplussing*. To puzzle; to confound; to stop by embarrassment.

nonproductive, non•pro•duk′tiv, *a.* Unproductive; not directly productive.

nonprofessional, *a.* Not belonging to a profession; not done by or proceeding from professional men.

nonproficiency, *n.* Failure of proficiency.—**nonproficient,** *n.* One who has failed to improve or make progress in any study or pursuit.

nonresidence, *n.* Failure or neglect of residing where official duties require one to reside, or on one's own lands; residence by clergymen away from their cures.—**nonresident,** *a.* Not residing in a particular place, on one's own estate, or in one's proper place.—*n.* One who is nonresident.

nonresistance, *n.* The omission of resistance; submission to authority, power, or usurpation without opposition.—**nonresistant,** *a.* Making no resistance to power or oppression.—*n.* One who is nonresistant.

nonrestrictive, non•rē•strik′tiv, *a.* Not restrictive; without bounds.

nonruminant, *a.* Not ruminating or chewing the cud.

nonsectarian, non•sek•târ′ē•an, *a.* Not limited to one sect or group; open to those of all faiths.

nonsense, non′sens, *n.* Words or language conveying no just ideas; absurdity; things of no importance.—**nonsensical,** non•sen′si•kal, *a.* Having no sense; unmeaning; absurd.—**nonsensically,** non•sen′si•kal•li, *adv.* In a nonsensical manner.

nonsensitive, *a.* Not sensitive; not keenly alive to impression.

non sequitur, non sek′wi•tėr, [L., it does not follow.] *Logic*, a conclusion which does not follow the premises upon which it is based.

nonskid, *a.* Corrugated or with special tread to resist skidding.

nonsolvent, *a.* Not able to pay debts.

nonstriated, *a.* Not striated.—*Nonstriated fiber*, the fiber constituting the involuntary muscles.

nonsuit, non′sūt, *n.* A stoppage of a suit at law ordered by a judge when the plaintiff fails to make out a legal cause of action.—*v.t.* To subject to a nonsuit.

noodle, nö′dl, *n.* [G. *nudel.*] A ribbon-like flour-and-egg paste.

noodle, nö′dl, *n.* [From obsolete *noddle*, head.] (Slang) The head.

nook, nök, *n.* [Comp. Sc. *neuk*, Ir. *niuc*, a nook.] A corner; a recess; a secluded retreat.

noon, nön, *n.* [A.Sax. *nón*, L. *nona* (*hora*), the ninth hour; originally 3 p.m., the time of eating the chief meal, but afterward the term became applied to the midday hour, the chief meal being no doubt also shifted correspondingly.] The middle of the day; the time when the sun is in the meridian; twelve o'clock; the time of greatest brilliancy or power; the prime.—**noonday,** nön′dā, *n.* Midday; twelve o'clock in the day.—*a.* Pertaining to midday; meridional.—**noontide,** nön′tīd, *n.* The time of noon; midday.

noose, nös or nöz, *n.* [Probably from O. or Prov. Fr. *nous*, a knot, from L. *nodus*, a knot. NODE.] A running knot, which binds the closer the more it is drawn.—*v.t.* (nöz)—*noosed, noosing*. To catch in a noose; to entrap; to ensnare.

nopal, nō′pal, *n.* [Mexican *nopalli.*] A name of several cactaceous plants cultivated for the cochineal insect.

nor, nor, *conj.* [*Or* with the neg. particle *ne*, *n-* prefixed: old forms were *nother*, *nouther*. OR, NO.] A word used to render negative the second or a subsequent member of a clause or sentence: correlative to *neither* or other negative; also equivalent to *and not*, and in this case not always corresponding to a foregoing negative.

Nordic, nor′dik, *a.* One of the three divisions of the Caucasian race; the blond peoples from northern Europe.—*n.* An individual with Nordic characteristics.

noria, nō′ri•a, *n.* [Sp.] A hydraulic machine used for raising water.

norm, norm, *n.* [L. *norma*, a carpenter's square, a rule, for *gnorima*, from root *gno*, to know (see NOBLE); hence *enormous.*] A rule; a pattern; a model; an authoritative standard; a type.—**normal,** nor′mal, *a.* [L. *normalis.*] According to a rule, principle, or norm; conforming with a certain type or standard; not abnormal; regular; *geom.* perpendicular.—*Normal pressure*, perpendicular; a *pressure* is said to be *normal* to a surface when it acts at right angles to it or perpendicularly thereon.—*Normal school* (from Fr. *école normale*, lit. a school that serves as a model), a school in which teachers are instructed in the principles of their profession and trained in the practice of it; a training college.—*n. Geom.* a straight line at right angles to the tangent or tangent plane at any point of a curve or curved surface.—**normalization,** nor′mal•i•zā″shon, *n.* Reduction to a standard or type.—**normalize,** nor′mal•īz, *v.t.*—*normalized, normalizing*. To make normal; to reduce to a standard or type.—**normally,** nor′mal•li, *adv.* In a normal manner or state.

Norman, nor′man, *n.* A native or inhabitant of Normandy.—*a.* Pertaining to Normandy, or the Normans.—*Norman architecture*, the round-arched style of architecture, a variety of the Romanesque.—*Norman-French*, the language of the Normans at the English Conquest, and still to a small extent made use of in several formal proceedings of state in England.

Norse, nors, *n.* The language of Norway.—*Old Norse*, the ancient language of Scandinavia, represented by the classical Icelandic and still with wonderful purity by modern Icelandic.—*a.* Belonging to ancient Scandinavia or its language.—**Norseman,** nors′man, *n.* A native of ancient Scandinavia.

north, north, *n.* [A.Sax. *north* = Icel. *northr*, G., Sw., and Dan. *nord*, north; origin unknown.] One of the cardinal points, being that point of the horizon which is directly opposite to the sun in the meridian; the opposite of *south*; a region, tract, or country lying opposite to the south.—*a.* Northern; being in the north.—**northeast,** *n.* The point midway between the north and east.—*a.* Pertaining to, proceeding from, or directed toward that point; northeastern.—**northeaster,** *n.* A wind from the northeast.—**northeasterly,** *a.* Toward or from the northeast.—**northeastern,** *a.* Pertaining to or being in the northeast, or in a direction to the northeast.—**northeastward,** *adv.* Toward the northeast.—**northerliness,** nor′THėr•li•nes, *n.* The state of being northerly.—**northerly,** nor′THėr•li, *a.* Pertaining to or being in or toward the north; northern; proceeding from the north.—**northern,** nor′THėrn, *a.* Pertaining to or being in the north; in a direction toward the north; proceeding from the north (the *northern* wind).—*Northern diver*, a marine swimming bird. DIVER.—*Northern Hemisphere*, that half of the earth north of the equator.—*Northern lights*, the popular name of the aurora borealis.—**northern, northerner,** nor′THėr•ner, *n.* A native or inhabitant of the north, of a northern country or part.—**northernmost,** nor′THėrn•mōst, *a.* Situated at the point farthest north.—**northing,** north′ing, *n. Navig.* and *surv.* the difference of latitude northward from the last point of reckoning: opposed to *southing*.—**Northman,** north′man, *n.* Norseman.—**North Pole,** *n.* That point of the heavens toward the north which is 90° distant from the equinoctial; the northern extremity of the earth's axis.—**North Star,** *n.* The north polar star, of the constellation Ursa Minor, toward which the earth's axis points.—**northward,** north′wėrd, *adv.* and *a.* Toward the north.—*n.* The northern part.—**northward,** north′wėrdz, *adv.* Toward the north; northward.—**northwest,** *n.* The point midway between the north and west; [cap.] that part of the United States which lies in the northwest part of the country.—*a.* Pertaining to, or being between, the north and the west; northwesterly; proceeding from the northwest (a *northwest* wind).—*adv.* Toward the northwest.—**northwester,** *n.* A wind from the northwest.—**northwesterly,** *a.* Toward the northwest; from the northwest.—**northwestern,** *a.* Pertaining to or being in the northwest; from the northwest.—**northwestward,** *adv.* Toward the northwest.

Norwegian, nor•wē′ji•an, *a.* Belonging to Norway.—*n.* A native of Norway.

nose, nōz, *n.* [A.Sax. *nosu*, *nasu* = Icel. *nös*, Dan. *näse*; cog., L. *nasus*, Skr.

nâsâ, nasâ—nose. *Ness* is akin.] The part of the face where the nostrils are located; the sense of smell; the olfactory organ; the forward or projecting part of anything (the *nose* of a boat).—*To thrust one's nose into*, to meddle.—*To turn up the nose*, to show contempt.—*v.t.*—*nosed, nosing*. To smell; to defeat by a narrow margin; to touch with the nose.—*v.i.* To smell; to pry officiously; to move forward slowly.—**nose bag,** *n.* A bag which may be fastened to a horse's head while he eats the provender in it.—**nose bleed,** *n.* Bleeding or hemorrhage from the nose; epistaxis. —**nose dive,** *n.* The sudden plunge of an aircraft downward; any sudden drop (the stock market took a *nose dive*).—**nosegay,** nōz′gā, *n.* A bunch of flowers; a posy.—**nosepiece,** *n.* A piece on a helmet coming down in front of the nose; a bridge on a pair of glasses.—**nosy, nosey,** nō′zē, *a.* Inquisitive; prying; meddlesome.

nosography, nō•sog′ra•fi, *n.* [Gr. *nosos*, disease, and *graphō*, to write.] The science of the description of diseases.—**nosology,** nō•sol′o•ji, *n.* [Gr. *nosos* and *logos*.] A systematic arrangement or classification of diseases; that branch of medical science which treats of the classification of diseases.—**nosological,** nos•o•loj′i•kal, *a.* Pertaining to nosology.—**nosologist,** nō•sol′o•jist, *n.* One versed in nosology.

nostalgia, nos•tal′ji•a, *n.* [Gr. *nostos*, return, and *algos*, pain.] A longing desire to revisit one's native country; homesickness.—**nostalgic,** nos•tal′-jik, *a.* Relating to nostalgia; homesick.

nostoc, nos′tok, *n.* [G. *nostok, nostoch*.] A sort of gelatinous algae often found after wet weather, especially on sandy soils.

nostril, nos′tril, *n.* [O.E. *nosethril, nosethirl*, A.Sax. *nósthyrl*, lit. nose hole, *thyrl* or *thyrel* meaning a hole, whence *thyrlian*, to bore (same word as *thrill*).] One of the two apertures of the nose which give passage to air.

nostrum, nos′trum, *n.* [L. *nostrum*, ours, that is, a medicine belonging to us alone.] A medicine, the ingredients of which are kept secret; a quack medicine; any scheme or device proposed by a quack or charlatan in any department.

not, not, *adv.* [Older *nat*, contr. from *naught*, nought, and equivalent to *ne aught*. NAUGHT.] A word that expresses negation, denial, refusal, or prohibition.

notable, nō′ta•bl, *a.* [Fr. *notable*, L. *notabilis*, from *noto*, to mark or note, from *nota*, a mark, for *gnota*, from *notus, gnotus*, known. NOTE, NOBLE.] Worthy of notice; remarkable; memorable; noted or distinguished; conspicuous; manifest; observable. —*n.* A person or thing of note or distinction; *French hist.* one of the nobles or notable men selected by the king to form a parliament, before the revolution.—**notableness,** nō′ta•bl•nes, *n.* The quality of being notable.—**notably,** nō′ta•bli, *adv.* In a notable manner; remarkably; eminently; especially.—**notability,** nō•ta•bil′i•ti, *n.* The quality of being notable; a notable person or thing; a person of note.

notary, nō′te•ri, *n.* [L. *notarius*, from *nota*, a note. NOTE.] An officer authorized to attest written documents, to authenticate deeds, contracts, etc., and to administer oaths; called also *Notary Public*.—**notarial,** nō•tâ′ri•al, *a.* Pertaining to a notary; done or taken by a notary.

notation, nō•tā′shon, *n.* [L. *notatio*, from *noto*, to mark. NOTE.] The act or practice of noting; the art of recording by marks or characters; a system of signs or characters used for expressing briefly facts connected with an art or science, as in arithmetic, algebra, music, etc.

notch, noch, *n.* [Softened form of old *nock*, a notch=O.D. *nock*, O.Sw. *nocka*, a notch; akin *nick*.] A hollow cut in anything; a nick; what resembles such a cutting; a gap in a mountain or hill.—*v.t.* To cut a notch or notches in; to nick; to indent; to fit to a string by the notch, as an arrow.

note, nōt, *n.* [Fr. *note*, from L. *nota*, a mark, sign, character, from *notus*, known, for *gnotus*, from *gnosco, nosco*, to know. NOBLE, KNOW.] A mark on the margin of a book‡; a mark, character, or symbol‡; a statement subsidiary to the text of a book elucidating or adding something; an explanatory or critical comment; an annotation; a memorandum or short writing intended to assist the memory or for after use or reference; a list of items; a reckoning, bill, account; a written or printed paper acknowledging a debt and promising payment (a promissory *note*; a bank-*note*); a diplomatic or official communication in writing; a short letter; a billet; notice; heed; observation; reputation; consequence; distinction; *pl.* a newspaper reporter's or shorthand writer's report; *mus.* a character which represents a sound; a musical sound; voice; harmonious or melodious sound.—*v.t.*—*noted, noting*. To observe carefully; to heed; to attend to; to set down in writing; to make a memorandum of; to mark (a bill) as being dishonored—a proceeding done by a notary.—**notebook,** *n.* A book in which notes or memoranda are written.—**noted,** nō′-ted, *a.* Being of note; much known by reputation or report; celebrated. —**notedness,** nō′ted•nes, *n.* The state or quality of being noted.—**noteless,** nōt′les, *a.* Not attracting notice; not conspicuous.—**note paper,** *n.* Paper of a small size for writing notes or letters on.—**noteworthy,** nōt′wėr•thi, *a.* Worthy of note; worthy of observation or notice.

nothing, nu′thing, *n.* [*No thing*.] Not anything: opposed to *anything* and *something*; nonexistence; nothingness; a trifle; a thing of no consideration or importance; *arith.* a cipher.—*adv.* In no degree; not at all.—**nothingness,** nu′thing•nes, *n.* Nihility; nonexistence; insignificance.

notice, nō′tis, *n.* [Fr. *notice*, from L. *notitia*, notice, from *nosco, notum*, to know. NOTE.] The act of noting, observing, or remarking; heed; regard; cognizance; note; information; intelligence; direction; order; premonition; warning; intimation beforehand; a paper that communicates information; attention; respectful treatment; civility; a short statement; a brief critical review.—*v.t.*—*noticed, noticing*. To take cognizance or notice of; to perceive; to become aware of; to observe; to mention or make observations on; to treat with attention and civilities.—**noticeable,** nō′tis•a•bl, *a.* Worthy of being noticed or observed; observable; likely to attract attention.—**noticeably,** nō′-tis•a•bli, *adv.* In a noticeable manner; evidently; distinctly.

notify, nō′ti•fī, *v.t.*—*notified, notifying*. [Fr. *notifier*, L. *notificare*, from *notus*, known, and *facio*, to make. NOTE.] To make known; to declare; to publish; to give notice to; to inform by words or writing.—**notification,** nō′ti•fi•kā″shon, *n.* The act of notifying or giving notice; notice given in words or writing, or by signs; intimation; the writing which communicates information; an advertisement, citation, etc.

notion, nō′shon, *n.* [L. *notio*, from *notus*, known. NOTE.] A mental conception; mental apprehension of whatever may be known or imagined; idea; an opinion; a belief or view entertained; a fancy article; an article of smallware; chiefly in the plural, needles, thread, pins, etc.; a gadget. —**notional,** nō′shon•al, *a.* Pertaining to a notion or conception; imaginary; ideal; existing in idea only; visionary; whimsical; fanciful.—*Notional words*, those words which express *notions* or objects of the understanding, as verbs and nouns, in distinction from *relational* words or words expressing relation, as prepositions.

notochord, nō′to•kord, *n.* [Gr. *nōtos*, the back, and *chordē*, a string.] A fibrocellular rod in the embryo of vertebrates, usually replaced in the adult by the vertebral column.

notorious, nō•tō′ri•us, *a.* [L.L. *notorius*, from L. *notoria, notorium*, an indictment, *notor*, a voucher, *notare*, to mark. NOTE.] Publicly or generally known and spoken of; manifest to the world; known to disadvantage; publicly known from something discreditable.—**notoriety,** nō•to•rī′-e•ti, *n.* The state or attribute of being notorious; the state of being publicly known to disadvantage; discreditable publicity.—**notoriously,** nō•tō′ri•us•li, *adv.* In a notorious manner.—**notoriousness,** nō•tō′ri•us•nes, *n.* The state of being notorious; notoriety.

notornis, nō•tor′nis, *n.* [Gr. *notos*, the south wind, the south, and *ornis*, a bird.] A genus of rare or extinct grallatorial birds of New Zealand, allied to the coots, but of larger size and with rudimentary wings.

no-trump, *n. Bridge*, and some other card games, play declared in which no suit is designated as trumps.

notwithstanding, not•with•stan′ding,

a participial compound passing into a *prep.* and a *conj.* [*Not with*, in the old sense of against, and *standing*.] In spite of; without hindrance or obstruction from; despite; nevertheless; however.

nougat, nö′gä, nö′gat, *n.* [Fr.] Candy made of egg white, sugar, corn sirup, or honey, with chopped nuts or fruits.

nought, nąt, *n.* [A.Sax. *náwiht*, i.e. no whit. NAUGHT.] Not anything; nothing; a cipher.

noumenon, nou′men•on, *n.* pl. **noumena,** nou′men•a. [Gr., the thing perceived, from *noeō*, to perceive, from *nous*, the mind.] *Metaph.* an object conceived by the understanding or thought of by the reason, as opposed to a *phenomenon*.

noun, noun, *n.* [O.Fr. *noun*, *non*, *nom*, Mod. Fr. *nom*, from L. *nomen*, name. NAME.] *Gram.* a word that denotes any object of which we speak, whether that object be animate or inanimate, material or immaterial.—**nounal,** noun′al, *a.* Pertaining to a noun; having the character of a noun.

nourish, nur′ish, *v.t.* [O.Fr. *nurrir*, *norrir*, Mod.Fr. *nourrir*, from L. *nutrire*, to nourish.] To feed and cause to grow; to supply with nutriment; *fig.* to supply the means of support and increase to; to encourage; to foster; to cherish; to comfort.—**nourisher,** nur′ish•ėr, *n.* —**nourishing,** nur′ish•ing, *a.*—**nourishingly,** nur′ish•ing•li, *adv.*—**nourishment,** nur′ish•ment, *n.* The act of nourishing; sustenance; nutriment.

nouveau riche, nö•vō rēsh′, *n.* [Fr. —*nouveau*, new, and *riche*, rich.] A person of newly acquired riches.

nova, nō′va, *n.* [L. fem. sing. of *novus*, new.] A star which suddenly increases its brightness and energy enormously, then fades into its former obscurity.

novel, nov′el, *a.* [O.Fr. *novel*, Fr. *nouvelle*, novel, a novel, from L. *novellus*, a dim. from *novus*, new. NEW.] Of recent origin or introduction; new; unusual; strange.—*n.* A lengthy fictitious prose narrative having an almost unlimited range of subject matter and varied techniques containing one or more plots. —**novella,** nō•vel′la, *n.* A short narrative with a compact and pointed plot. —**novelette,** nov•el•et′, *n.* A short novel.—**novelist,** nov′el•ist, *n.*—**novelize,** nov′el•īz, *v.t.* To put into the form of a novel.—**novelty,** nov′el•ti, *n.* The quality of being novel; something new or strange; pl. small articles used as decoration or adornment.

November, nō•vem′bėr, *n.* [L., from *novem*, nine.] The eleventh month of the year, containing 30 days.

novena, nō•vē′na, *n.* [L. *novem*, nine.] *R. Cath. Ch.* A special nine days' devotion.

novice, nov′is, *n.* [Fr., from L. *novitius*, new, fresh, from *novus*, new. NOVEL.] One who is new to the circumstances in which he or she is placed; one newly converted to the Christian faith; one that has entered a religious house, but has not taken the vow; a probationer; one who is new in any business; a beginner.—**novitiate, noviciate,** nō•vish′i•āt, *n.* The state or time of being a novice; apprenticeship; a year or other time of probation.

novocain, nō′vo•kān″, *n.* [L. *novus*, new, and *cocaine*.] A local anesthetic.

now, nou, *adv.* [A.Sax. *nú*, a word common to all the Teutonic tongues; cog. L. *nunc*; Gr. *nun*, now; perhaps allied to *new*.] At the present time; at a particular past time (he was *now* king); at that time; after this had happened. It often implies a connection between a subsequent and a preceding proposition, or it introduces an inference or an explanation of what precedes ('*now* Barabbas was a robber').—*But now*, only a little while ago; very lately.—*Now and then*, at one time and another; indefinitely; occasionally; at intervals.—*Now . . now*, at one time—at another time; alternately. Similarly *now . . then*.—*n.* Present time or moment.—**nowadays,** nou′a•dāz, *adv.* At the present time; in these days.

noway, noways. See NO.

nowhere, nowhither, nowise, *adv.* See NO.

noxious, nok′shus, *a.* [L. *noxius*, from *noxa*, injury, from root of *noceo*, to hurt (as in *innocent*, *innocuous*), same as that of *night*; akin *noise*, *nuisance*.] Hurtful; harmful; pernicious; unwholesome; injurious, in a moral sense.—**noxiously,** nok′shus•li, *adv.* In a noxious manner; hurtfully.—**noxiousness,** nok′shus•nes, *n.*

noyade, nwä•yäd, *n.* [Fr., from *noyer*, to drown.] A putting to death by drowning: a mode of executing victims during the reign of terror in France, practiced by Carrier at Nantes.

nozzle, noz′l, *n.* [For *nosle*, a dim. of *nose*.] The projecting spout of something; a terminal pipe or terminal part of a pipe.

nu, nū, nö, *n.* The 13th letter of the Greek alphabet.

nuance, nū′äns, *n.* [From Fr. *nuer*, to make shades of color, from L. *mutare*, to change, and Fr. *nuage*, cloud.] A delicate gradation in feeling, color, meaning, etc.

nub, nub, *n.* [From Dan. *knub*, black, L.G. *knubbe*, knot, E. *knub*, knob.] A knob; a lump; the point of a story (colloq.)—**nubbin,** nub′bin, *n.* Any small bit that projects; a small, undeveloped ear of Indian corn.—**nubby,** nub′bi, *a.*

nubile, nū′bil, *a.* [L. *nubilis*, from *nubo*, to marry. NUPTIAL.] Of an age suitable for marriage; marriageable.

nubilous, nū′bil•us, *a.* [L. *nubilus*, from *nubes*, a cloud.] Cloudy.

nucellus, nū•sel′lus. [Dim. of L. for a *kernel*.] The central part of an ovule, containing the EMBRYO SAC (which see).

nuchal, nū′kal, *a.* [L.L. *nucha*, from Ar.] Pertaining to the nape of the neck.

nuciferous, nū•sif′ėr•us, *a.* [L. *nux*, *nucis*, a nut, and *fero*, to bear.] Bearing or producing nuts.—**nuciform,** nū′si•form, *a.* *Bot.* resembling a nut; nut shaped.

nucleon, nū′kli•on, *n.* *Phys.* an elementary particle in the atomic nucleus; either a proton or a neutron.

nucleoprotein, nūk′li•ō•prō″tē•in. [From *nucleus* and *protein*.] A conjugated protein, combining a protein and a nucleic acid and occurring in living cells; an essential constituent of genes.

nucleus, nū′kli•us, *n.* pl. **nuclei,** nū′kli•ī. [L., a kernel, from *nux*, *nucis*, a nut.] A central mass about which matter is collected; *bot.* the central succulent part of an ovule in which the embryo plant is generated; *physiol.* the solid or vesicular body found in many cells; the germ of a cell; *astron.* the body of a comet, called also its head; *phys.* the central or mass part of an atom, its positive charge equal to the atomic number of the element.—**nuclear,** nū′kli•ar, *a.* Pertaining to, or having the character of, a nucleus; constituted by a nucleus; *phys.* pertaining to the atomic nucleus (*nuclear* physics).—**nucleate,** nū′kli•āt, *a.* Having a nucleus.—**nucleolus,** nū•klē′ō•lus, *n.* pl. **nucleoli,** nū•klē′ō•lī. The spherical particle found in the center of a cell nucleus.—**nucleic acid,** a complex organic compound important in the heredity and the control of the metabolism of all living cells, the groups of nucleic acids being distinguished as DNA and RNA.

nude, nūd, *a.* [L. *nudus*, naked (seen also in *denude*); same root as *naked*.] Naked; not covered with clothes or drapery.—*n.* A nude or naked figure or statue; generally the *nude*, that is, the undraped human figure.—**nudely,** nūd′li, *adv.* In a nude or naked manner; nakedly.—**nudeness,** nūd′nes, *n.* The state or quality of being nude or naked.—**nudity,** nū′di•ti, *n.* The state of being naked; nakedness.

nudge, nuj, *n.* [Allied to Prov.G. *knütschen*, Dan. *knuge*, to squeeze; E. to *knock*.] A jog with the elbow, or a poke in the ribs.—*v.t.*—*nudged*, *nudging*. To give a hint or signal by a private touch with the hand, elbow, or foot.

nudity. See NUDE.

nugatory, nū′ga•to•ri, *a.* [L. *nugatorius*, from *nugor*, *nugatus*, to trifle, from *nugae*, trifles.] Trifling; futile; worthless; of no force; inoperative.

nugget, nug′et, *n.* [Formerly *nigot*, *niggot*, an ingot; perhaps a corruption of *ingot* (*an ingot*, a *ningot*, a *nigot*).] A lump, especially, one of the larger lumps of native gold found in the diggings.

nuisance, nū′sans, *n.* [O.Fr. *nuisance*, *noisance*, from *nuisir*, *noisir* (Mod.Fr. *nuire*), L. *nocere*, to annoy. NOXIOUS.] Something that annoys or gives trouble; that which is offensive or irritating; an annoyance; a plague or pest; a bore.

null, nul, *a.* [L. *nullus*, not any, none —*ne*, not, and *ullus*, any.] Of no legal or binding force or validity; void; invalid (as in *null and void*);

having no character or expression (as the features).—**nullify,** nul′i•fī, *v.t.*—*nullified, nullifying.* [L. *nullus,* and *facio,* to make.] To annul; to render invalid; to deprive of legal force or efficacy.—**nullification,** nul′-i•fi•kā″shon, *n.* The act of nullifying; a rendering void and of no effect.—**nullity,** nul′i•ti, *n.* The state or quality of being null; want of validity.

nullah, nul′la, *n.* In British India, a bed of a rivulet; a rivulet.

numb, num, *a.* [Lit. taken, being from A.Sax. *numen,* pp. of *niman,* O.E. *nim,* Goth. *niman,* to seize; hence also *benumb* (with prefix *be*); *nimble.* The final *b* is excrescent.] Torpid, benumbed, or deadened; having lost the power of sensation and motion.—*v.t.* To make numb or torpid.—**numbness,** num′nes, *n.* The state of being numb; torpidity; torpor.

number, num′bėr, *n.* [O.Fr. *numbre,* Fr. *nombre,* from L. *numerus,* number (whence also *numeral, numerous, enumerate*), same root as *nomad,* Gr. *nemō,* to distribute. (As to inserted *b* comp. *humble, nimble.*)] That which may be counted; an aggregate of units, or a single unit considered as part of a series; an aggregate of several individuals; not a few; many; one of a numbered series of things, as a division of a book published in parts; a part of a periodical; metrical arrangement of syllables; poetical rhythm or measure; *gram.* that distinction in the form which a word assumes according as it is spoken of or expresses one individual or several individuals; the form that denotes one individual being the *singular number,* that set apart for two the *dual number,* that which refers to two or more the *plural number.*—*Number one,* self.—*v.t.* To count; to reckon; to enumerate; to reckon, rank, or consider; to put a number or numbers on; to amount to; to reach the number of.—**numberer,** num′bėr•ėr, *n.* One that numbers.—**numberless,** num′bėr•les, *a.* That cannot be counted; innumerable.—**Numbers,** num′bėrz, *n.* The fourth book of the Pentateuch.

numen, nū′men, *n.,* pl. **numina,** nū′-mi•na. A divine or leading spirit, as in the Roman Catholic Church.

numerable, nū′mėr•a•bl, *a.* [L. *numerabilis,* from *numerus,* number. NUMBER.] Capable of being numbered or counted.—**numeral,** nū′mėr•al, *a.* [L. *numeralis.*] Pertaining to number; consisting of number; expressing number; representing number.—*n.* A figure or character used to express a number; *gram.* a word expressing a number (one, two, three, etc.).—**numerary,** nū′mėr•e•-ri, *a.* Belonging to a certain number.—**numerate,** nū′mėr•āt, *v.t.* and *i.* [L. *numero, numeratum.*] To count.—**numeration,** nū•mėr•ā′shon, *n.* [L. *numeratio.*] The act or art of numbering; *arith.* the art of expressing in figures any number proposed in words, or of expressing in words any number proposed in figures.—**numerator,** nū′mėr•ā•tėr, *n.* One that numbers; *arith.* the number in fractions which shows how many parts of a unit are taken—the number above the line.—**numerical,** nū•-mer′i•kal, *a.* Belonging to number; denoting number; consisting in numbers.—**numerically,** nū•mer′i•kal•li, *adv.* In numbers; with respect to numerical quantity.—**numerology,** nū′mėr•ol″o•ji, *n.* Belief in the occult influence of numbers upon the life of an individual.—**numerous,** nū′-mėr•us, *a.* [L. *numerosus.*] Consisting of many individuals.

numismatic, numismatical, nū•-mis•mat′ik, nū•mis•mat′i•kal, *a.* [L. *numisma,* coin, from Gr. *nomisma,* coin, lit. what is sanctioned by law, from *nomizō,* to sanction, from *nomos,* law.] Pertaining to coins or medals.—**numismatics,** nū•mis•mat′iks, *n.* The science of coins and medals.—**numismatist,** nū•mis′mat•ist, *n.* One versed in numismatics.—**numismatology,** nū•mis′ma•tol″o•ji, *n.* Numismatics.

numskull, num′skul, *n.* [*Numb* and *skull.*] A dunce; a stupid fellow.

nun, nun, *n.* [A.Sax. *nunne,* from Eccles. L. *nonna,* a nun, *nonnus,* a monk, L.Gr. *nonna, nonnos,* from Coptic or Egypt. *nane, nanu,* good, beautiful, monasteries and convents having first arisen in Egypt.] A woman devoted to a religious life who lives in a convent or nunnery, under a vow of perpetual chastity; the blue titmouse; a kind of pigeon having its head almost covered with a veil of feathers.—**nunnery,** nun′-ėr•i, *n.* A convent in which nuns reside.

Nunc Dimittis, nungk di•mit′tis, *n.* [L., now thou lettest depart.] The canticle of Simeon (Luke, ii. 29-32).

nuncio, nun′shi•ō, *n.* [Sp. *nuncio,* It. *nunzio,* from L. *nuncius,* a messenger, for *noventius,* from *novus,* new; akin *announce, renounce, pronounce, enunciate,* etc.] An ambassador of the first rank (not a cardinal) representing the pope at the seat of a foreign government (an ambassador of the first rank who is a cardinal being styled a *legate*).—**nunciature,** nun′-shi•a•chėr, *n.*

nunnery. See NUN.

nuptial, nup′shal, *a.* [L. *nuptialis,* from *nuptiæ,* marriage, from *nubo, nuptum,* to marry; akin *nubes, nimbus,* a cloud (from the veiling of the bride).] Pertaining to marriage; used or done at a wedding.—**nuptials,** nup′shalz, *n. pl.* [L. *nuptiæ* (pl.), a wedding.] A wedding or marriage. ∴ Syn. under MARRIAGE.

nurl, nėrl, *v.t.* [Same as *knurl, knarl, gnarl.*] To mill or indent on the edge.

nurse, nėrs, *n.* [Fr. *nourrice,* from L. *nutrix, nutricis,* a nurse, from *nutrio,* to nourish. NOURISH.] One who tends or takes care of the young, sick, or infirm; a female who has the care of a child or children; a female attendant in a hospital; one who or that which nurtures, cherishes, or protects; *hort.* a shrub or tree which protects a young plant.—*v.t.*—*nursed, nursing.* To feed and tend generally in infancy; to suckle; to rear; to nurture; to tend in sickness or infirmity; to promote growth or vigor in; to foment; to foster; to manage with care and economy, with a view to increase.—**nursemaid,** *n.* A maidservant employed in nursing children.—**nursery,** nėr′sėr•i, *n.* A place or apartment in a house set apart for children; a place where trees, shrubs, flowering plants, etc., are raised from seed or otherwise in order to be transplanted, or sold; a place where anything is fostered and the growth promoted.—**nursery rhyme,** *n.* A tale for children, usually written in rhyming verse.—**nurseryman,** *n.* One who has a nursery of plants, or is employed in one.—**nursery school,** *n.* A school for children usually under age 5.—**nursling,** nėrs′ling, *n.* One who or that which is nursed; a child; a fondling.

nurture, nėr′chėr, *n.* [Fr. *nourriture,* from *nourrir,* to nourish. NOURISH, NURSE.] The act of nursing or nourishing; education; that which nourishes; food; diet.—*v.t.*—*nurtured, nurturing.* To nourish; to educate; to bring or train up.

nut, nut, *n.* [A.Sax. *hnutu* = Icel. *hnot,* O.H.G. *hnuz,* Dan. *nöd,* G. *nuss,* Gael. *cnudh.*] The fruit of certain trees and shrubs which have the seed enclosed in a bony, woody, or leathery covering, not opening when ripe; *bot.* a bony pericarp containing a single seed, to which it is not closely attached; a small block of metal or wood, with an internal or female screw put upon the end of a screw bolt to keep it firmly in its place.—*A nut to crack,* a difficult problem to solve; a puzzle to be explained.—*v.i.*—*nutted, nutting.* To gather nuts.—**nutty,** nut′i, *a.* Abounding in nuts; having the flavor of nuts; enthusiastic; mentally unbalanced; crazy. (*Slang*)—**nutcracker,** *n.* An instrument for cracking hard-shelled nuts; a brown spotted bird of Europe and a related greyish-white bird of North America.—**nuthatch,** *n.* [*Hatch* is a softened form of *hack.*] Various small creeping birds of Europe and America, related to the titmice.—**nutshell,** *n.* The hard shell of a nut.—*To be* or *lie in a nutshell,* to be in small compass; to admit of a very simple explanation or statement.

nutant, nū′tant, *a.* [L. *nutans, nutantis,* ppr. of *nuto,* to nod, freq. of *nuo,* to nod. INNUENDO.] *Bot.* drooping or nodding.—**nutation,** nū•tā′shon, *n.* [L. *nutatio.*] A nodding; *astron.* a slight gyratory movement of the earth's axis tending to make the pole describe a minute ellipse, due to the attraction of the sun and moon and connected with *precession.*

nutmeg, nut′meg, *n.* [From *nut,* and O.Fr. *muguette,* nutmeg, from L. *muscus,* musk; lit. the scented nut.] The kernel of the fruit of a tree of the Malayan Archipelago agreeably aromatic, and much used in cookery.—

Nutmeg butter, a solid oil extracted from the nutmeg.

nutria, nū´tri•a, *n.* [Sp. *nutria*, *lutria*, from L. *lutra*, an otter.] The commercial name for the skins or fur of the coypou.

nutrient, nū´tri•ent, *a.* [L. *nutrio*, to nourish. NURSE.] Nourishing; nutritious.—*n.* Any substance which nourishes.—**nutriment,** nū´tri•ment, *n.* [L. *nutrimentum*.] That which nourishes; nourishment; food; aliment.—**nutrition,** nū•trish´on, *n.* [L. *nutritio*, from *nutrio*.] The act or process by which organisms, whether vegetable or animal, absorb into their system their proper food; the process of assimilating food; that which nourishes; nutriment.—**nutritious,** nū•trish´us, *a.* Containing or serving as nutriment; promoting the growth or repairing the waste of organic bodies; nourishing.—**nutritiously,** nū•trish´us•li, *adv.* In a nutritious manner.—**nutritiousness,** nū•trish´us•nes, *n.* The quality of being nutritious.—**nutritive,** nū´tri•tiv, *a.* Having the quality of nourishing; nutritious; pertaining to nutrition.—**nutritively,** nū´tri•tiv•li, *adv.* In a nutritive manner.—**nutritiveness,** nū´tri•tiv•nes, *n.*

nuts, nuts, *interj.* (Slang) A term of anger, defiance, etc.—*a.* Insane; crazy.

nux vomica, nuks vom´i•ka, *n.* [From L. *nux*, a nut, and *vomeo*, to vomit.] The fruit of an East Indian tree, containing the virulent poison strychnine; a drug containing strychnine.

nuzzle, nuz´l, *v.t.*—*nuzzled*, *nuzzling*. [A form of *nozzle*.] To put a ring into the nose of; to root up with the nose.—*v.i.* To work with the nose, as a pig; to hide the head, as a child in its mother's bosom.

nyctalopia, nik•ta•lō´pi•a, *n.* [Gr. *nyktalōpia*, from *nyktalōps*, seeing by night only —*nyx*, *nyktos*, night, and *ōps*, the eye.] The faculty or defect of seeing in darkness or in faint light, with privation of sight in daylight; also applied to night blindness, the exactly opposite defect of vision.

nyctitropic, nik•ti•trop´ik, *a.* [Gr. *nyx*, *nyktos*, night, *tropos*, a turn.] *Bot.* said of certain plants, the leaves of which assume certain positions at night.

nylon, nī´lon, *n.* A synthetic material, formed when molten into fibers, sheets, or bristles of extreme toughness, strength, and elasticity, made mainly from coal, water, and air.

nymph, nimf, *n.* [L. *nympha*, Gr. *nymphē*, a nymph.] One of a numerous class of inferior divinities, imagined among the Greeks and Romans as beautiful maidens, not immortal, but always young; those who presided over rivers, brooks, and springs being called *Naiads*; over mountains *Oreads*; over woods and trees, *Dryads* and *Hamadryads*; over the sea, *Nereids*; hence, a young and attractive woman; a maiden; a damsel. Also same as *Nympha*.—**nympha,** nim´fa, *n.* The pupa or chrysalis of an insect.—**nymphal, nymphean,** nim´fal, nim•fē´an, *a.* Pertaining to nymphs.

nymphomania, nim•fo•mā´ni•a, *n.* [Gr. *nymphē*, a bride, and *mania*, madness.] Morbid and uncontrollable sexual desire in females.

nystagmus, nis•tag´mus, *n.* [Gr. *nystagmos*, a nodding.] *Med.* an involuntary rolling motion of the eyes.

O

O, o, ō, the fifteenth letter and the fourth vowel in the English alphabet.

O, *interj.* An exclamation used in earnest or solemn address, appeal, or invocation, and prefixed to the noun of address; the sign of the vocative: often confounded with *Oh*, which is strictly a particle expressive of emotion prefixed to a sentence or clause. When *O* is the word, the mark of exclamation, if used, should follow the noun of address ('Hear, O Israel!'); when *oh* is the word, the mark should follow it, or the exclamatory clause of which it is a part, thus: *Oh! Oh, dear! Oh, dear me!* exclamations of surprise, uneasiness, fear, pain, etc., regarded as corruptions of Fr. *O Dieu!* It. *O Dio!* O God! It. *O Dio mio!* O my God!

oaf, ōf, *n.* [From Icel. *álfr*, an elf. ELF.] A fairy changeling; a dolt; a blockhead.—**oafish,** ōf´ish, *a.*—**oafishness,** ōf´ish•nes, *n.*

oak, ōk, *n.* [A.Sax. *āc*=Sc. *aik*, Icel. *eik*, D. *eik*, L.G. *eeke*, Dan. *eeg*, Sw. *ek*, G. *eiche*; root unknown.] A well-known and valuable timber tree, or its wood, which is hard, tough, and strong; a member of the beech family (Fagaceae).—**oak apple,** *n.* An oak gall.—**oaken,** ō´kn, *a.* Made of oak or consisting of oak.

oakum, ō´kum, *n.* [A.Sax. *ácumba*, tow, oakum, lit. matter combed out, from prefix *á*, away, out, and *camb*, a comb. COMB.] The substance of old ropes untwisted and pulled into loose fibers; used for caulking the seams of ships, stopping leaks, etc.

oar, ōr, *n.* [A.Sax. *ár*; Icel. *ár*, Dan. *aare*, Sw. *àra*; perhaps from root *ar*, seen in A.Sax. *erian*, Goth. *arjan*, L. *aro*, to plow; or allied to *rudder*, *row*.] A long piece of timber, flat at one end and round at the other, used to propel a boat, barge, or galley through the water.—*To feather the oars.* See FEATHER, *v.t.*—*To lie on the oars*, to suspend rowing; hence, *fig.* to cease from work; to rest.—*To muffle the oars*, to wrap some soft substance round the part that lies in the rowlock.—*To put one's oar in*, to interfere in the business or concerns of others.—*v.i.* To row.—*v.t.* To impel by rowing.—**oarlock,** *n.* A rowlock.—**oarsman,** ōrz´man, *n.* One who rows with an oar; a boatman.

oasis, ō•ā´sis, *n.* pl. **oases,** ō•ā´sēz. [L. and Gr., from Coptic *oueh*, to dwell, and *saa*, to drink.] A fertile tract where there is water, in the midst of a desert or waste; a green spot in the midst of barrenness; often used figuratively.

oast, ōst, *n.* [D. *ast*, *eest*, *eijst*, a kiln.] A kiln to dry hops or malt.

oat, ōt, *n.* [O.E. *ote*, *ate*, *oote*, A.Sax. *áta*, the oat; Icel. *œti*, an eatable, oats; perhaps akin to *eat*.] A cereal plant valuable for the grain it produces; an oaten pipe, typical of pastoral poetry (*Mil.*); *pl.* a quantity of the plant in cultivation or of the grain (field of *oats*).—*Wild oats*, youthful excesses: generally in the phrase *to sow one's wild oats*, to indulge in youthful excesses, dissipations, or follies; *to have sown one's wild oats*, to have given up youthful follies.—**oatcake,** *n.* A cake made of the meal of oats.—**oaten,** ō´tn, *a.* Pertaining to or made of oats or oatmeal.—**oatmeal,** ōt´mēl, *n.* Meal made from oats.

oath, ōth, *n.* pl. **oaths,** ōTHz. [A.Sax. *áth*=Sc. *aith*, Icel. *eithr*, Dan. and Sw. *ed*, Goth. *aiths*, D. *eed*, G. *eid*, oath.] A solemn affirmation or declaration, made with an appeal to God for the truth of what is affirmed; a solemn swearing; a blasphemous use of the name of the Divine Being; an imprecation.

obbligato, ob´li•gä•tō, *n.* [It. OBLIGATE.] An instrumental part or accompaniment of such importance that it cannot be dispensed with.

obcordate, ob•kor´dāt, *a.* [Prefix *ob*, and *cordate*.] *Bot.* shaped like a heart, with the apex downward.

obdurate, ob´dū•rit, *a.* [L. *obduratus*, from *obduro*, to harden—*ob*, intensive, *duro*, to harden, from *durus*, hard (seen in *indurate*, *endure*, *duration*).] Hardened in heart; persisting obstinately in sin; stubborn; inflexible; inexorable; harsh or rough†.—**obduracy,** ob´dū•re•si, *n.* The state or quality of being obdurate; invincible hardness of heart; obstinacy in wickedness.—**obdurately,** ob´dū•rit•li, *adv.* In an obdurate manner; inflexibly.—**obdurateness,** *n.* Obduracy; stubbornness.

obeah, ō´bi•a, *n.* A species of sorcery or witchcraft among the African Negroes.

obedience, ō•bē´di•ens, *n.* [Fr. *obédience*, from L. *obedientia*, obedience. OBEY.] The act or habit of obeying; compliance with a command, prohibition, or known law and rule prescribed; submission to authority. —*Passive obedience*, unqualified obedience to authority, whether the commands be reasonable or unreasonable, lawful or unlawful.—**obedient,** ō•bē´di•ent, *a.* [L. *obediens*, ppr. of *obedio*.] Submission to authority; complying with all commands; yielding compliance; dutiful. —**obediently,** ō•bē´di•ent•li, *adv.* In an obedient manner; dutifully; submissively.

obeisance, ō•bā´sans, *n.* [Fr. *obéissance*, from L. *obedientia*.—OBEDIENCE.] A bow or courtesy; an act of reverence, deference, or respect.

obelisk, ob′e•lisk, *n.* [Gr. *obeliskos,* dim. of *obelos,* a spit.] A column or monumental structure of rectangular form, diminishing toward the top, and generally finishing with a low pyramid; a mark (thus †) referring the reader to a note in the margin or at the foot of the page: called also a *dagger.*

obelus, ob′e•lus, *n.* [Gr. *obelos,* a spit.] A mark in ancient MSS. or old editions of the classics, indicating a suspected passage or reading.—**obelize,** ob′e•līz, *v.t.* To mark as spurious or suspicious.

Oberon, ōb′ėr•on, *n.* [Fr. *Auberon, Alberon,* G. *Alberich.*] King of the fairies, married to Titania.

obese, ō•bēs′, *a.* [L. *obesus,* fat—*ob,* intens., and *edo, esum,* to eat. EAT.] Excessively corpulent; fat; fleshy.—**obesity,** ō•bes′i•ti, *n.* [L. *obesitas.*] The state or quality of being obese; excessive corpulency.

obey, ō•bā′, *v.t.* [Fr. *obéir,* from L. *obedio, obedire,* to obey, O.L. *obœdire*—prefix *ob,* and *audio,* to hear. AUDIBLE.] To give ear to; to comply with the commands of; to be under the government of; to be ruled by; to submit to the direction or control of.—*v.i.* To submit to commands or authority; to do as one is bid.—**obeyer,** ō•bā′ėr, *n.* One who yields obedience.

obfuscate, ob•fus′kāt, *v.t.*—*obfuscated, obfuscating.* [L. *obfusco, obfuscatum*—prefix *ob,* and *fusco,* to obscure, from *fuscus,* dark.] To darken; to obscure; to bewilder; to confuse; to muddle.—**obfuscation,** ob•fus•kā′shon, *n.* The act of obfuscating; confusion or bewilderment of mind.

obi, ō′bē, *n.* [Jap.] A broad sash worn with a kimono and fastened in the back.

obit, ōb′it, *n.* [L. *obitus,* death, from *obeo, obitum,* to die—*ob,* against, and *eo,* to go. ITINERANT.] A person's decease; an obituary.—**obituary,** o•bich′ū•a•ri, *n.* A list of the dead; an account of a person's death.—*a.* Relating to, or written about, a person at his death (an *obituary* notice.)

obiter dictum [L.] A remark by the way; an off-hand aphorism or statement.

object, ob′jekt, *n.* [L. *objectum,* lit. something thrown before or against—*ob,* against, and *jacio,* to throw (as in *deject, eject, reject,* etc.). JET (of water).] That toward which the mind is directed in any of its states or activities; what is thought about, believed, or seen; some visible and tangible thing; a concrete reality (*objects* of interest in a museum); that to which efforts are directed; aim; end; ultimate purpose; a deformed person; *gram.* the word, clause, or member of a sentence expressing that on which the action expressed by a transitive verb is exercised, or the word or member governed by a preposition.—*v.t.* (ob•jekt′). [Fr. *objecter,* L. *objicio, objectum.*] To place before or in the way‡; to bring forward as a matter of reproach, or as an adverse ground or reason; to state or urge in opposition; to state as an objection (I have nothing to *object against* him).—*v.i.* To make opposition in words or arguments; to offer adverse reasons.—**object glass,** *n.* In a telescope or microscope, the lens or combination of lenses directed upon the object and producing an image of it, which is viewed through the eyepiece.—**objectify,** ob•jek′ti•fī, *v.t.* To form into an object; to give the character of an object to.—**objection,** ob•jek′shon, *n.* The act of objecting; that which is or may be objected; adverse reason, argument, or charge; fault found.—**objectionable,** ob•jek′shon•a•bl, *a.* Such as might reasonably be objected to; justly liable to objection; calling for disapproval; reprehensible (as actions, language, etc.).—**objective,** ob•jek′tiv, *a.* [Fr. *objectif.*] Belonging to what is external to the mind; hence, when used of *literature* or *art,* containing no trace of the writer's or artist's own feelings or individuality: opposed to *subjective*; *gram.* belonging to the object of a transitive verb or a preposition (the *objective* case, an *objective* clause).—*n.* The objective case; an object glass; the aim of a military maneuver or operation.—**objectively,** ob•jek′tiv•li, *adv.* In an objective manner.—**objectiveness,** ob•jek′tiv•nes, *n.* The state or relation of being objective.—**objectivity,** ob•jek•tiv′i•ti, *n.* The quality or state of being objective.—**objectless,** ob′jekt•les, *a.*—**object lesson,** *n.* A lesson to the young by means of articles themselves or pictures of them.—**objector,** ob•jek′tėr, *n.*

objet d'art, ob′zhe′dâr, *n.* [Fr.] Something of artistic value.

objurgate, ob′jėr•gāt, *v.t.* and *i.*—*objurgated, objurgating.* [L. *objurgo, objurgatum*—prefix *ob,* and *jurgo,* to chide.] To chide, reprove, or reprehend.—**objurgation,** ob•jėr•gā′shon, *n.* The act of objurgating; a reproof.—**objurgatory,** ob•jėr′ga•to•ri, *a.*

oblate, ob′lāt, *a.* [L. *oblatus,* thrust forward (i.e. at the equator), also offered, devoted—*ob,* against, before, and *latus,* carried, borne.] *Geom.* flattened or depressed at the poles.—*Oblate spheroid,* a spherical body flattened at the poles, that is, having the shape of the earth.—*n. Eccles.* a secular person who offered or devoted himself and his property to some monastery, into which he was admitted as a kind of lay brother; a member of a congregation of secular priests who live in community.—**oblation,** ob•lā′shon, *n.* [L. *oblatio,* an offering.] Anything offered or presented in worship or sacred service.

obligate, ob′li•gāt, *v.t.*—*obligated, obligating.* [L. *obligo, obligatum,* to bind, to bring under an obligation—prefix *ob,* and *ligo,* to bind. LIGAMENT.] To bring or place under some obligation; to hold to some duty; a word not much used by good writers.—**obligate,** *a.* Of bacteria and parasites, bound to particular conditions of life.—**obligation,** ob•li•gā′shon, *n.* [L. *obligatio,* from *obligo,* to bind, oblige.] That which binds or obliges to do something; binding or constraining power or effect; an external act or duty imposed by the relations of society; a claim upon one; the position in which one is bound or indebted to another for a favor received; a favor bestowed and binding to gratitude.—**obligatorily,** ob•li′ga•to•ri•li, *adv.* In an obligatory manner.—**obligatory,** ob•li′ga•to•ri, *a.* Imposing obligation or duty; binding in law or conscience; requiring performance or forbearance of some act (*obligatory on* a person).

obligato, ob•li•gä′tō. See OBBLIGATO.

oblige, o•blīj′, *v.t.*—*obliged, obliging.* [Fr. *obliger,* from L. *obligo,* to bind, to oblige—*ob,* and *ligo,* to bind. OBLIGATION.] To constrain by any force, physical, moral, or legal; to compel; to bind by any restraint; to bind by some favor done; to lay under obligation of gratitude.—**obliged,** o•blījd′, *p.* and *a.* Having received some obligement or favor; laid under obligation; indebted.—**obligee,** ob•li•jē′, *n. Law,* the person to whom another is bound.—**obliger,** o•blī′jėr, *n.* One that obliges.—**obliging,** o•blī′jing, *a.* Having the disposition to do favors; conferring favors or kindnesses; complaisant; kind.—**obligingly,** o•blī′jing•li, *adv.* In an obliging manner.—**obligingness,** o•blī′jing•nes, *n.* The state or quality of being obliging.—**obligor,** ob•li•gor′, *n. Law,* the person who binds himself to another.

oblique, ob•lēk′ or ob•līk′, *a.* [Fr. *oblique,* L. *obliquus*—prefix *ob,* and *liquis,* awry.] Having a direction neither perpendicular nor parallel to some line or surface which is made the standard of reference; not direct; aslant; slanting; *fig.* indirect or by allusion; not direct in descent; collateral.—*Oblique angle,* any angle except a right angle.—*Oblique arch,* a skew arch.—*Oblique bridge,* a skewbridge.—*Oblique case, gram.* any case except the nominative.—*Oblique cone* or *cylinder,* one whose axis is oblique to the plane of its base.—*Oblique speech, oblique narration, rhet.* that which is quoted indirectly, or in a different person from that employed by the original speaker.—**obliquely,** ob•lēk′li or ob•līk′li, *adv.* In an oblique manner or direction; indirectly; by a side glance; by an allusion; not in the direct or plain meaning.—**obliqueness, obliquity,** ob•lēk′nes or ob•līk′nes, ob•lik′wi•ti, *n.* [L. *obliquitas.*] The state of being oblique; deviation from parallelism or a perpendicular; deviation from moral rectitude; a mental or moral twist.—*Obliquity of the ecliptic,* the angle which the plane of the ecliptic makes with that of the equator.

obliterate, ob•lit′ėr•āt, *v.t.* [L. *oblitero,* to blot out, to cause to be forgotten—prefix *ob,* and *litera,* a letter. LETTER.] To efface; to erase or blot out; to make undecipherable; to cause to be forgotten.—**obliteration,** ob•lit′ėr•ā″shon, *n.* The act of obliterating or effacing.

oblivion, ob•liv′i•on, *n.* [L. *oblivio, oblivionis,* from *obliviscor,* to forget—prefix *ob,* and *liveo,* to become black. LIVID.] The state of being blotted out from the memory; a being forgotten; forgetfulness; the act of forgetting; a forgetting of offenses, or remission of punishment.—**oblivious,** ob•liv′i•us, *a.* [L. *obliviosus.*] Causing forgetfulness (*Shak.*); forgetful; mentally absent. —**obliviously,** ob•liv′i•us•li, *adv.* In an oblivious manner.—**obliviousness,** ob•liv′i•us•nes, *n.* State of being oblivious.

oblong, ob′long, *a.* [L. *oblongus,* oblong—*ob,* against, inversely, and *longus,* long.] Rectangular, and having the length greater than the breadth; longer than broad.—*n.* An oblong figure.—**oblongness,** ob′-long•nes, *n.*

obloquy, ob′lo•kwi, *n.* [L. *obloquium,* from *obloquor*—*ob,* against, and *loquor,* to speak. LOQUACIOUS.] Censorious speech; reproachful language; language that causes reproach and odium to rest on men or their actions; odium.

obnoxious, ob•nok′shus, *a.* [L. *obnoxius*—*ob,* and *noxa,* harm, hurt. NOXIOUS.] Reprehensible; censurable; odious; hateful; offensive; unpopular.—**obnoxiously,** ob•nok′shus•li, *adv.*—**obnoxiousness,** ob•nok′shus•-nes, *n.*

oboe, ō′bō, *n.* [It. *oboe,* from Fr. *hautbois,* an oboe.] A hautboy; a wood-wind instrument made from a slender, conical tube that produces a thin, penetrating, plaintive tone by means of a double reed.—**oboist,** ō′bō•ist, *n.*

obolus, ob′o•lus, *n.* [Gr. *obolos.*] A small coin of ancient Greece.

obovate, ob•ō′vāt, *a.* [Prefix *ob,* implying inversion.] *Bot.* inversely ovate; having the narrow end downward.—**obovoid,** ob•ō′void, *a. Bot.* approaching the obovate form.

obscene, ob•sēn′, *a.* [L. *obscenus, obscaenus,* filthy, repulsive, obscene: etymol. doubtful.] Impure in language or action; indecent; offensive to chastity and delicacy; inauspicious; ill-omened.—**obscenely,** ob•-sēn′li, *adv.* In an obscene manner.—**obsceneness, obscenity,** ob•sēn′nes, ob•sen′i•ti, *n.* The state or quality of being obscene; impurity; ribaldry; lewdness.

obscure, ob•skūr′, *a.* [Fr. *obscur,* from L. *obscurus*—prefix *ob,* and root seen in *scutum,* a shield, Skr. *sku,* to cover.] Imperfectly illuminated; gloomy; not clear or distinct to view; dim; not easily understood; not obviously intelligible; abstruse; indistinct; not much known or observed; unknown to fame; unnoticed.—*v.t.*—*obscured, obscuring.* To darken; to make dark or dim; to make less intelligible, legible, or visible; to hide; to prevent from being seen or known. **obscurely,** ob•skūr′li, *adv.* In an obscure manner; darkly; dimly; not clearly; in retirement; not conspicuously.—**obscureness,** ob•skūr′nes, *n.* State of being obscure; obscurity.—**obscurity,** ob•skū′ri•ti, *n.* [L. *obscuritas.*] The quality or state of being obscure; darkness; dimness; darkness of meaning; a state of being unknown to fame.—**obscurant, obscurantist,** ob•skū′rant, ob•skū′rant•-ist, *n.* One who obscures; one who opposes the progress of knowledge, or labors to prevent enlightenment, inquiry, or reform.—**obscurantism,** ob•skū′rant•izm, *n.* The system or principles of an obscurant.—**obscuration,** ob•skū•rā′shon, *n.* The act of obscuring or darkening; the state of being darkened or obscured.

obsecrate, ob′si•krāt, *v.t.* [L. *obsecro,* to entreat—prefix *ob,* and *sacer,* sacred. SACRED.] To beseech; to entreat; to supplicate.—**obsecration,** ob•si•krā′shon, *n.* The act of obsecrating; entreaty; supplication.

obsequious, ob•sē′kwi•us, *a.* [From L. *obsequiosus,* obsequious, from *obsequium,* compliance, from *obsequor,* to follow—prefix *ob,* and *sequor,* to follow. SEQUENCE.] Promptly obedient or submissive to the will of another; compliant; officious; devoted; servilely condescending; compliant to excess; cringing; fawning.—**obsequiously,** ob•sē′kwi•us•li, *adv.* In an obsequious manner; servilely; cringingly.—**obsequiousness,** ob•-sē′kwi•us•nes, *n.* The quality of being obsequious.

obsequy, ob′se•kwē, *n.* pl. **obsequies,** ob′se•kwēz, [O.Fr. from L. *obsequiae,* pl. funeral rites.] A funeral rite or ceremony (commonly used only in the plural).

observe, ob•zėrv′, *v.t.*—*observed, observing.* [L. *observo*—*ob,* before, in front, and *servo,* to keep or hold. SERVE.] To look on with attention; to regard attentively; to watch; to notice; to perceive; to detect; to discover; to remark in words; to mention; to keep with due ceremonies; to celebrate; to keep or adhere to in practice; to comply with; to obey. ∴ Syn. under SEE.—*v.i.* To be attentive; to remark; to comment.—**observer,** ob•zėr′vėr, *n.* One who observes.—**observingly,** ob•zėr′-ving•li, *adv.* In an observing manner. —**observable,** ob•zėr′va•bl, *a.* Capable of being observed; worthy of observation.—**observably,** ob•zėr′-va•bli, *adv.*—**observance,** ob•zėr′-vans, *n.* The act of observing; performance; a rite or ceremony; an act of respect, worship, and the like; obedient regard or attention; respectful or servile attention; homage.—**observant,** ob•zėr′vant, *a.* Characterized by observation; taking notice; attentively noticing; attentive to duties or commands; obedient; adhering to in practice (*observant of* duties).—**observantly,** ob•zėr′vant•-li, *adv.* In an observant manner.—**observation,** ob•zėr•vā′shon, *n.* [L. *observatio.*] The act, power, or habit of observing; a taking notice or paying attention; *science,* the act of taking notice of particular phenomena as they occur in the course of nature; the observing of some phenomenon, often by the assistance of an instrument; information gained by such an act; a remark based or professing to be based on what has been observed; notice; observance†.—*Observation officer,* an artillery officer placed so as to command a view of enemy positions, and in communication by telephone with those in charge of the guns to which he is attached. He directs the laying of the guns so as to bring selected objects under fire, the objects being commonly invisible to the gunners.—*Observation post,* the position occupied by an observation officer.—**observational,** ob•zėr•vā′shon•al, *a.* Relating to or based on observations.—**observatory,** ob•zėr′va•to•ri, *n.* A place used for making observations of natural phenomena; a building constructed for astronomical observations; a place of outlook.

obsess, ob•ses′, *v.t.* [L. *obsideo,* to besiege—*ob,* before, *sedeo,* to sit.] To beset or besiege; to vex or harass, as an evil spirit.—**obsession,** ob•se′shon, *n.* Act of obsessing.

obsidian, ob•sid′i•an, *n.* [L. *Obsidianus,* from *Obsidius* or *Obsius,* its alleged discover.] Vitreous lava, or volcanic glass, a glassy mineral of several varieties.

obsolete, ob′so•lēt, *a.* [L. *obsoletus,* pp. of *obsolesco,* to go out of use—prefix *ob,* and *soleo,* to use, to be wont.] Gone into disuse; disused; neglected; out of fashion; *biol.* imperfectly developed or abortive. —**obsoleteness,** ob′so•lēt•nes, *n.* The state of being obsolete.—**obsolescence,** ob•so•les′ens, *n.* The state or process of becoming obsolete—**obsolescent,** ob•so•les′ent, *a.* [L. *obsolescens.*] Becoming obsolete; going out of use, passing into desuetude.

obstacle, ob′sta•kl, *n.* [Fr. *obstacle,* from L. *obstaculum,* from *obsto,* to withstand—*ob,* against, and *sto,* to stand. STATE, STAND.] Anything that stands in the way and hinders progress; a hindrance; an obstruction or impediment, either physical or moral.

obstetric, obstetrical, ob•stet′rik, ob•stet′ri•kal, *a.* [L. *obstetrix,* a midwife—*ob,* before, and *sto,* to stand. OBSTACLE.] Pertaining to midwifery, or care of a woman in pregnancy and labor.—**obstetrician,** ob•ste•trish′an, *n.* One skilled in obstetrics.—**obstetrics,** ob•stet′-riks, *n.* That branch of medical science which includes prenatal care, as well as childbirth and any complications arising therefrom.

obstinate, ob′sti•nit, *a.* [L. *obstinatus,* pp. of *obstino, obstinatum,* to resolve, from *obsto,* to stand against—*ob,* against, and *sto,* to stand. OBSTACLE.] Pertinaciously adhering to an opinion or purpose; fixed firmly in resolution; not yielding to reason, arguments, or other means; stubborn: said of persons; not yielding or not easily subdued or removed (an *obstinate* fever; an *obstinate* cough). ∴ To be *obstinate* implies the doing what we ourselves choose; to be *stubborn* denotes, rather, determination not to do what others advise or desire.—**obstinacy, obstinateness,** ob′sti•na•si, ob′sti•nit•nes, *n.* The state or quality of being obstinate.—**obstinately,** ob′sti•nit•li, *adv.* In an obstinate manner.

obstreperous, ob•strep′ėr•us, *a.* [L. *obstreperus,* from *obstrepo,* to roar—*ob,* intens., and *strepo,* to make a noise.] Making a tumultuous noise; clamorous; vociferous; noisy; loud. —**obstreperously,** ob•strep′ėr•us•li, *adv.* In an obstreperous manner.—**obstreperousness,** ob•strep′ėr•us•nes, *n.* Clamor; noisy turbulence.

obstruct, ob•strukt′, *v.t.* [L. *obstruo, obstructum*—*ob,* against, and *struo,* to pile up. STRUCTURE.] To block up, stop up, or close, as a passage; to fill with obstacles or impediments that prevent passing; to hinder from passing; to impede; to stand in the way of; to retard, interrupt, render slow.—**obstructer,** ob•struk′tėr, *n.* One that obstructs or hinders.—**obstruction,** ob•struk′shon, *n.* The act of obstructing; anything that stops or closes a way, passage, or channel; obstacle; impediment; that which impedes progress; check; hindrance; the state of having the vital functions obstructed†.—**obstructionist,** ob•struk′shon•ist, *n.* One who practices obstruction; an obstructive.—**obstructive,** ob•struk′tiv, *a.* Obstructing or tending to obstruct.—*n.* One who obstructs; one who hinders the transaction of business.—**obstruent,** ob′stru•ent, *a.* [L. *obstruens,* ppr. of *obstruo.*] Blocking up; obstructing; hindering.—*n.* Anything that obstructs; something that blocks up the natural passages of the body.

obtain, ob•tān′, *v.t.* [L. *obtineo*—prefix *ob,* and *teneo,* to hold. TENANT.] To gain possession of; to gain, procure, receive, get, acquire.—*v.i.* To be received in customary or common use; to be established in practice; to hold good; to subsist (the custom still *obtains*).—**obtainable,** ob•tā′na•bl, *a.* Capable of being obtained.—**obtainer,** ob•tā′nėr, *n.* One who obtains.

obtected, ob•tek′ted, *a.* [L. *obtectus*—prefix *ob,* and *tego, tectus,* to cover.] Covered; *zool.* covered with a hard shelly case.

obtest, ob•test′, *v.t.* [L. *obtestor*—prefix *ob,* and *testor,* to witness. TESTAMENT.] To call upon earnestly; to entreat, implore, conjure; to supplicate.—**obtestation,** ob•tes•tā′shon, *n.* The act of obtesting.

obtrude, ob•tröd′, *v.t.*—*obtruded, obtruding.* [L. *obtrudo*—prefix *ob,* and *trudo,* to thrust. INTRUDE.] To thrust prominently forward; to force into any place or state unduly or without solicitation; often *refl.* (to *obtrude* one's self upon a person's notice); to offer with unreasonable importunity.—*v.i.* To obtrude one's self; to enter when not invited.—**obtruder,** ob•trö′dėr, *n.* One who obtrudes.—**obtrusion,** ob•trö′zhon, *n.* The act of obtruding.—**obtrusive,** ob•trö′siv, *a.* Disposed to obtrude; forward; intrusive.—**obtrusively,** ob•trö′siv•li, *adv.* In an obtrusive, manner.—**obtrusiveness,** ob•trö′siv•nes, *n.*

obtuse, ob•tūs′, *a.* [L. *obtusus*—prefix *ob,* and *tundo, tudi* (Skr. *tud*), to beat. CONTUSE.] Not pointed or acute; blunt; not having acute sensibility; stupid; dull.—*Obtuse angle,* an angle greater than 90° but less than 180°.—**obtusely,** ob•tūs′li, *adv.*—**obtuseness,** ob•tūs′nes, *n.*

obverse, ob′vėrs, *a.* [L. prefix *ob,* and *versus,* turned.] Pertaining to the one of two possible sides or theories; *numis.* bearing the face or head.—*n.* The one of two possible ways of looking at a thing; *numis.* that side of a coin or medal which has the face or head on it, the other being the *reverse.*—**obversely,** ob′vėrs•li, *adv.* In an obverse form or manner.—**obversion,** ob•vėr′shon, *n.* The act of obverting.—**obvert,** ob•vėrt′, *v.t.* To turn toward.—*In logic,* to infer another proposition with a contradictory predicate by changing the quality of the proposition.

obviate, ob′vi•āt, *v.t.*—*obviated, obviating.* [L. *obvio, obviatum,* to meet —*ob,* against, and *via,* a way. VOYAGE, WAY.] To meet, as difficulties or objections; to overcome; to clear out of the way.—**obviation,** ob•vi•ā′shon, *n.*

obvious, ob′vi•us, *a.* [L. *obvius,* in the way.] Easily discovered, seen, or understood; perfectly plain, manifest, or evident.—**obviously,** ob′vi•us•li, *adv.* In an obvious manner. —**obviousness,** ob′vi•us•nes, *n.* State of being obvious.

obvolute, ob′vo•lūt, *a.* [L. *ob,* against, and *volutus,* rolled.] Rolled or turned in; *bot.* having the margins of opposite leaves alternately overlapping.

ocarina, ō•ka•rē′na, *n.* [It.] A small musical instrument of terra cotta pierced with holes, there being seven instruments in a set.

occasion, ok•kā′zhon, *n.* [L. *occasio, occasionis,* from *occido, occasum,* to fall—*ob,* and *cado,* to fall. ACCIDENT.] Time of an occurrence, incident, or event; opportunity; favorable time, season, or circumstances; incidental cause; a cause acting on the will; a motive or reason; incidental need; casual exigency; requirement (*to have occasion* or *no occasion* for a thing); peculiar position of affairs; juncture; exigency.—*v.t.* To cause incidentally; to produce; to induce.—**occasional,** ok•kā′zhon•al, *a.* Incidental; occurring at times, but not regular or systematic; made or happening as opportunity requires or admits.—**occasionally,** ok•kā′zhon•al•li, *adv.* In an occasional manner; at times; sometimes but not often.

occident, ok′si•dent, *n.* [Fr. *occident,* L. *occidens, occidentis,* ppr. of *occido,* to fall, to set, as the sun. OCCASION.] The west: the opposite of *orient;* [cap.] the Western Hemisphere and Europe.—**occidental,** ok•si•den′tal, *a.* Western; [cap.] pertaining to the Occident or Occidentals.—*n.* [cap.] A native of the Occident.

occipital, ok•sip′i•tal, *a.* [From L. *occiput,* the back part of the head—prefix *ob,* and *caput,* the head.] Pertaining to the back part of the head. —**occiput,** ok′si•put, *n.* [L.] The hinder part of the head.

occlude, ok•klūd′, *v.t.* —*occluded, occluding.* [L. *occludo*—*ob,* and *claudo,* to shut.] To obstruct; to shut in or out; to cut off by closing a passage. —*v.i.* To close with the cusps fitting snugly: said of teeth.—**occlusion,** ok•klū′zhon, *n.*—**occlusive,** ok•klū′siv, *a.*

occult, ok•kult′, *a.* [L. *occultus,* pp. of *occulo,* to cover over—prefix *ob,* and root of *celo,* to conceal, and E. *hell.*] Hidden from the eye or understanding; invisible and mysterious; unknown.—*Occult sciences,* certain so-called sciences of the Middle Ages, as alchemy, necromancy or magic, astrology.—**occultation,** ok•kul•tā′shon, *n. Astron.* the hiding of a star or planet from our sight by passing behind some other of the heavenly bodies; the time of a planet or star being so hidden; hence, *fig.* disappearance from view; withdrawal from public notice.—**occultism,** ok′ult•izm, *n.* A system of occult or mysterious doctrines; the beliefs of the theosophists, typified in such works as Bulwer-Lytton's *Zanoni, A Strange Story; The Coming Race.*

occupy, ok′kū•pī, *v.t.*—*occupied, occupying.* [L. *occupo,* to take possession of, possess—prefix *ob,* and *capio,* to take. CAPABLE.] To take possession of; to possess; to hold and use; to take up, as room or space; to cover or fill; to employ or use (one's time); to engage; to busy: often *refl.*—*v.i.* To be an occupant; to hold possession.—**occupancy,** ok′kū•pan•si, *n.* The act of occupying; a holding in possession; term during which one is occupant.—**occupant,** ok′kū•pant, *n.* [L. *occupans, occupantis,* ppr. of *occupo,* to occupy.] An occupier.—**occupation,** ok•kū•pā′shon, *n.* [L. *occupatio.*] The act of occupying or taking possession; what engages one's time and attention; a vocation; calling; trade.—*Army of Occupation,* army provisionally occupying territory that has been overrun, until a form of government is established. —**occupational,** ok•kū•pā′shon•al, *a.* Of or pertaining to a particular occupation (an *occupational* disease). —*Occupational therapy,* mental and physical therapy by means of creative activity, such as carpentry, designed to develop confidence, muscular control, etc.

occur, ok•kėr′, *v.i.*—*occurred, occurring.* [L. *occurro*—*ob,* against, and *curro,* to run. CURRENT.] To meet or come to the mind, imagination, or memory; to befall; to happen; to take place; to exist so as to be capable of being found or seen; to be found; to be met with.—**occurrence,** ok•kėr′ens, *n.* The act of occurring or taking place; any incident or accidental event; an observed instance.

ocean, ō'shen, *n.* [L. *oceanus*, from Gr. *ōkeanos*, the ocean, the deity of the ocean.] The vast body of water which covers more than three-fifths of the surface of the globe; the sea; also, one of the great basins or areas into which it has been divided; any immense expanse (the boundless *ocean* of eternity).—*a.* Pertaining to the main or great sea (the *ocean* wave).—**oceanic,** ō•shi•an'ik, *a.* Pertaining to the ocean; occurring in or produced by the ocean, as distinguished from smaller seas; pertaining to Oceania (the islands lying between Asia and America) or its inhabitants. —*Oceanic island,* an island that has never formed part of a continent, e.g. Azores.—**oceanography,** ō•shen•og'ra•fi, *n.* The department of knowledge that deals with oceanic phenomena.

ocellus, ō•sel'lus, *n.* pl. **ocelli,** ō•sel'lī. [L. *ocellus*, dim. of *oculus*, an eye. OCULAR.] One of the minute simple eyes of insects, many spiders, crustaceans, mollusks, etc.—**ocellate, ocellated,** ō•sel'lāt, ō•sel'lā•ted, *a.* [L. *ocellatus*.] Resembling an eye; studded with the figures of little eyes.

ocelot, o'se•lot, *n.* [Nahuatl, abbrev. of *thalocelotl*, field jaguar.] A leopard-like American cat (*Felis pardalis*) about three feet long.

ocher, ochre, ō'kėr, *n.* [L. *ochra*, Gr. *ochra*, from *ochros*, pale, pale yellow.] A name applied to clays colored with the oxides of iron in various proportions, and varying in color from pale yellow to brownish red; the color of ocher.—**ocherous, ochreous,** ō'kėr•us, *a.*

ochlocracy, ok•lok're•si, *n.* [Gr. *ochlos*, the multitude, and *kratos*, power.] The rule or ascendency of the multitude or common people; a mobocracy.—**ochlocratic, ochlocratical,** ok•lō•krat'ik, ok•lō•krat'i•kal, *a.* Relating to ochlocracy.

o'clock, o•klok', *contr.* Of the clock.

ocrea, ok'rē•a, *n. pl.* **ocreae,** [L. *ocrea*, a greave or legging.] *Bot.* the union of two stipules around the stem in a kind of sheath.—**ocreate,** ok'rē•āt, *a. Bot.* furnished with ocreae.

octachord, ok'ta•kord, *n.* [Gr. *oktō*, eight, and *chorde*, a string.] A musical instrument having eight strings.

octagon, ok'ta•gon, *n.* [Gr. *oktō*, eight, and *gōnia*, angle.] *Geom.* a figure of eight sides and eight angles. —**octagonal,** ok•tag'on•al, *a.* Having eight sides and eight angles.

octahedron, ok•ta•hē'dron, *n.* [Gr. *oktō*, eight, *hedra*, a base.] *Geom.* a solid contained by eight faces, which take the form of equal and equilateral triangles.—**octahedral,** ok•ta•hē'dral, *a.* Having eight equal surfaces.

octameter, ok•tam'et•ėr, *n.* [Gr. *oktō*, eight, *metron*, a measure.] A verse of eight feet.

octane, ok•tān', *n.* [Prefix *oct-* and *-ane*.] *Chem.* any of a group of 18 isomeric hydrocarbons, C_8H_{18}, of the methane series.—**octane number, octane rating,** *n.* The numerical statement of the anti-knock qualities of a motor fuel.

octangular, ok•tang'gū•lėr, *a.* [L. *octo*, eight, and E. *angular*.] Having eight angles.

octant, ok'tant, *n.* [L. *octans*, an eighth part, from *octo*, eight.] The eighth part of a circle; an instrument resembling a sextant or quadrant in principle, but having an arc the eighth of a circle, or 45°.

octave, ok'tiv, *n.* [L. *octavus*, eighth, from *octo*, eight.] The eighth day after a church festival, the festival itself being counted; the week immediately following a church festival; the first two stanzas in the sonnet of four verses each; a stanza of eight lines; *mus.* an eighth, or an interval of seven degrees or twelve semitones; one sound eight tones higher than another.—*a.* Consisting of eight.—**octavo,** ok•tā'vō, *n.* and *a.* The size of a leaf of a sheet of paper folded so as to make eight leaves: usually written *8vo*; a book of this size.

octennial, ok•ten'i•al, *a.* [L. *octo*, eight, and *annus*, a year.] Happening every eighth year; lasting eight years. —**octennially,** ok•ten'i•al•li, *adv.* Once in eight years.

octet, ok'tet, *n.* [L. *octo*, eight.] *Mus.* a musical composition for eight parts; the eight performers of such a composition; a group of eight; the first eight lines of a sonnet.

octillion, ok•til'yon, *n.* [L. *octo*, eight, and term of *million*.] The figure 1 followed by 27 zeros (*American and French*), or 1 followed by 48 zeros (*English and German*).

October, ok•tō'bėr, *n.* [L., from *octo*, eight: the eighth month of the primitive Roman year, which began in March.] The tenth month of the year; ale or cider brewed in October. —*October club,* a political club of squires in Queen Anne's day, devoted to the consumption of October ale and to the policy of enforcing strong anti-Whig measures on the Government.

octodecimo, ok•tō•des'i•mō, *n.* [L. *octodecim*, eighteen—*octo*, eight, and *decem*, ten.] The size of one leaf of a sheet of paper folded so as to make eighteen leaves; a book in which each sheet is folded into eighteen leaves: usually written *18mo*. Also used as an adjective.

octogenarian, ok'tō•je•nâ"ri•an, *n.* [L. *octogenarius*, from *octogeni*, eighty, *octo*, eight.] A person eighty years of age; any one whose age is between eighty and ninety.—*a.* Of eighty years of age; between eighty and ninety years of age.

octopus, ok'to•pus, *n.* [N.L. from Gr. *oktōpous*, eight-footed, from *okto*, eight, and *pous*, *podus*, foot.] Any animal of the genus (*Octopus*) that has eight arms with suckers.

octoroon, ok•to•rön', *n.* [L. *octo*, eight.] The offspring of a quadroon and a white person.

octosyllabic, ok'to•sil•lab"ik, *a.* [Gr. *oktō*, eight, and *syllabē*, a syllable.] Consisting of eight syllables.—*n.* A word of eight syllables.

octroi, ok•trwạ', *n.* [Fr., from L. *auctor*, an author.] A duty levied at the gates of French cities on articles brought in.

octuple, ok'tū•pl, *a.* [L. *octuplus*—*oktō*, eight.] Eightfold.

ocular, ok'ū•lėr, *a.* [L. *ocularis*, from *oculus*, the eye, a word cognate with E. *eye*. EYE.] Pertaining to the eye; depending on the eye; received by actual sight.—*n.* The eyepiece of an optical instrument. **oculist,** ok'ū•list, *n.* One skilled in diseases of the eyes.

od, od, *n.* The name invented by Reichenbach for a peculiar force which he fancied he had discovered associated with magnetism, and which was said to explain the phenomena of mesmerism or animal magnetism. Called also *Odic force.*—**odic,** od'ik, *a.* Pertaining to od.

odalisque, odalisk, ō'dä•lisk, *n.* [Fr. *odalisque*, from Turk., *ōdahliq*, chambermaid, from *ōdah*, chamber.] A slave in a harem, especially a Turkish sultan's harem.

odd, od, *a.* [From Icel. *oddi*, a triangle, an odd number, a tongue of land.] Not even; not exactly divisible by 2; left over; additional to a whole; not included with others: hence, unheeded; of little value or account (*odd* times, *odd* trifles); incidental; casual; forming one of a pair of which the other is wanting; belonging to a broken set; singular; strange; peculiar; eccentric; queer.—**Odd Fellow,** od'fel•ō, *n.* A member of an extensively ramified friendly society, originally modeled on freemasonry.—**oddity,** od'i•ti, *n.* The state or quality of being odd; singularity; something odd or singular; a singular person.—**oddly,** od'li, *adv.* In an odd manner; not evenly; strangely; whimsically; singularly.—**oddment,** od'ment, *n.* An odd article or one left over.—**oddness,** od'nes, *n.* The state of being odd; state of not being even; singularity; strangeness. —**odds,** odz, *n. sing.* or *pl.* Excess of one amount or quantity compared with another; difference in favor of one and against another; amount by which the bet of one party exceeds that of the other.—*At odds,* at variance; in controversy or quarrel. —*Odds and ends,* small miscellaneous articles.

ode, ōd, *n.* [L. *ode*, Gr. *ōdē*, song or poem, from *aoidē*, a song; seen in *parody*, *prosody*.] A short poem or song; a poem to be set to music or sung; a lyric poem of a lofty cast.

odeum, ō•dē'um, *n.* [Gr. *ōdeion*, from *ōdē*, a song.] A theater for musical or dramatic performances.

odic. See OD.

Odin, Woden, ō'din, wō'den, *n.* [Former from Scandinavian, latter Anglo-Saxon and German.] The chief god of Northern mythology, after whom is named Wednesday.

odious, ō'di•us, *a.* [L. *odiosus*, from *odium*, hatred, *odi*, I hate; same root as A.Sax. *atol*, hateful, horrible. ANNOY, NOISOME.] Of such a character as to be hated or greatly disliked; hateful; causing disgust or repugnance; offensive.—**odiously,**

ō′di•us•li, *adv.* In an odious manner; hatefully.—**odiousness,** ō′di•us•nes, *n.* The quality of being odious.—**odium,** ō′di•um, *n.* [L.] Hatred; dislike; the quality that provokes hatred.—*Odium theologicum,* theological hatred; the hatred of contending divines toward each other.

odometer, ō•dom′e•tėr, *n.* [Gr. *hodometron*—*hodos,* way, and *metron,* measure.] A device which measures the distance traveled by a vehicle.

odontalgia, ō•don•tal′ji•a, *n.* [Gr. *odous, odontos,* tooth, *algos,* pain.] Pain in the teeth; toothache.—**odontalgic,** ō•don•tal′jik, *a.* Pertaining to the toothache.—*n.* A remedy for the toothache.—**odonto,** ō•don′tō, *n.* [Gr. *odous, odontos.*] A dentifrice; a toothwash.—**odontoglossum,** ō•don•to•glos′um, *n.* [Gr. *odous, odontos,* a tooth, and *glōssa,* a tongue.] A genus of tropical American orchids, with magnificent flowers.—**odontoid,** ō•don′toid, *a.* Tooth-like. —*Odontoid process,* the part of the first vertebra of the neck, forming a pivot for the head.—**odontological,** ō•don′to•loj″i•kal, *a.* Belonging to odontology.—**odontology,** ō•don•tol′o•ji, *n.* That branch of anatomical science which treats of the teeth.—**odontophore,** ō•don′to•fōr, *n.* [Gr. *phoros,* bearing.] The so-called tongue or lingual ribbon of certain mollusks, covered with minute teeth.

odor, ō′dėr, *n.* [L. *odor,* a smell; allied to Gr. *ozō,* to smell; akin *olfactory.*] Any scent or smell, whether pleasant or offensive: when used alone most commonly a sweet smell; fragrance.—*In bad odor,* in bad repute; in disfavor.—*Odor of sanctity,* the reputation of being a saint.—**odoriferous,** ō•dėr•if′ėr•us, *a.* [L. *odoriferus.*] Giving odor or scent; diffusing fragrance; fragrant.—**odoriferously,** ō•dėr•if′ėr•us•li, *adv.* In an odoriferous manner.—**odoriferousness,** ō•dėr•if′ėr•us•nes, *n.*—**odorous,** ō′dėr•us, *a.* Having or emitting an odor; sweet of scent; fragrant.—**odorously,** ō′dėr•us•li, *adv.* In an odorous manner; fragrantly.—**odorousness,** ō′dėr•us•nes, *n.* The quality of being odorous.—**odorless,** ō′dėr•les, *a.* Having no odor.

odyssey, od′i•si, *n.* [From Homer's epic, *The Odyssey,* recounting Odysseus' years of wandering.] A long wandering or journey.

Oedipus complex, ed′i•pus kom′plex, *n.* [From Gr. *Oidipous,* son of Laius and Jocasta, who, in accordance with a prophecy, unknowingly, killed his father and married his mother.] The unconscious sexual feelings of a child (especially a male) for the parent of the opposite sex, which, if unresolved in adult life, can be a source of an emotional disorder.

oenanthic, ē•nan′thik, *a.* [Gr. *oinos,* wine, and *anthos,* a flower.] Having or imparting the characteristic odor of wine.—*Oenanthic acid,* an acid obtained from oenanthic ether.—*Oenanthic ether,* an oily liquid which gives to wine its characteristic odor. —**oenology,** ē•nol′o•ji, *n.* That branch of knowledge which deals with wine.

o'er, ōr. A contraction (generally poetical) of *over.*

oersted, er′sted, *n.* [After *Oersted,* the physicist.] The C.G.S. unit of magnetic reluctance, equal to the reluctance of a magnetic circuit of unit length, unit area, and unit permeability.

oestrus, ēs′trūs, *n.* [Gr. *oistros,* gadfly.] Irresistible impulse; passion; sexual impulse of animals.

of, ov, *prep.* [A.Sax. *of.*=Icel., Sw., Dan., and D. *af,* Goth. *af,* G. *ab;* cog. L. *ab,* Gr. *apo,* Skr. *apa,* from, away from. *Off* is the same word.] A word used in regard to source, cause, origin, motive, etc.; possession or ownership; attribute, quality, or condition (his state *of* mind); an aggregate or whole with a partitive reference (all, some, *of* us); the relation of object to a verbal notion (a desire *of* fame); to express concerning, relating to, about; distance or time (within a mile *of*); identity, equivalence, or apposition—appositive use of *of* (the city *of* London); on or in; with indefinite expressions of time, as a quarter *of* (an hour); so *of* late, in recent times.

off, of, *adv.* [OF.] Away; distant (a mile *off*); from or away by removal or separation (to cut *off*); not on; from, in the way of departure, abatement, remission (the fever goes *off*); so as to be less (attendance fell *off*); away from, as daily work (to take a day *off*).—*Off and on, on and off,* with interruptions and resumptions; at intervals.—*a.* Distant; as applied to horses, right hand: opposed to *near;* not on (his shoe is *off*); on the way (he is *off* to work); inaccurate (the sum is *off*); below standards; in a certain specified circumstance.—*prep.* Not on; away from; from or out of (a lane leading *off* a street); to seaward from; at the expense of (live *off* the land); relieved, or released, from (to be *off* duty); abstaining from (to be *off* liquor); below a certain level or standard.—*interj.* A command to depart: away! begone!—**offcast,** of′kast, *n.* That which is rejected as useless.—**offing,** of′ing, *n.* The portion of the sea seen from land; the near future.—**off-color,** *a.* Defective in color, as a gem; in poor taste; risque′, etc.—**offhand,** *adv.* Readily; with ease.—*a.* Done without study or hesitation; unpremeditated.—**offish,** of′ish, *a.* Tending to be aloof.—**offset,** of′set, *n.* A sum set off against another as an equivalent; *print.* a printing process involving the transfer of ink from a rubber covered roller to the paper; an accidental transfer of ink.—*v.t.* of•set′. To compensate for.—**offshoot,** of′shöt, *n.* A branch from a main stem, stream, mountain range, etc.—**offspring,** of′spring, *n.* sing. or pl. Progeny; a child or children; what arises or is produced from something.

offal, of′al, *n.* [Lit. *off-fall;* so D. *afval,* Icel. *affall,* G. *abfall,* with similar meanings.] Waste meat; a trade term for kidneys, heart, tongue, liver, and other parts of a carcass; carrion; refuse; rubbish.

offense, of•fens′, *n.* [Fr. *offense,* from L. *offensa,* an offense, from *offendo, offensum,* to strike against — *ob,* against, and old *fendo,* to strike, seen in *defend,* also in *manifest.*] A striking against or assailing (arms of *offense*); hurt; injury; an affront, insult, or wrong; the state of being offended; displeasure; any transgression of law, divine or human; a crime or sin; a misdemeanor.—*To take offense,* to become angry or displeased at something said or done.—**offend,** of•fend′, *v.t.* [L. *offendo.*] To displease; to make angry; to affront; to mortify; to shock, annoy, or pain (the taste or smell); to sin against; to disobey (*Shak.*).—*v.i.* To transgress the moral or divine law; to sin; to cause dislike or anger; to take offense (N.T.).—**offender,** of•fen′dėr, *n.* One who offends; a criminal; a transgressor.—**offensive,** of•fen′siv, *a.* [Fr. *offensif.*] Causing offense; giving provocation; irritating; disgusting; disagreeable (as to the senses); pertaining to offense; used in attack: opposed to *defensive;* consisting in attack; proceeding by attack.—*Alliance offensive and defensive,* one that requires the parties to make war together, and each party to defend the other in case of being attacked.—*n.* With the definite article: the act of attacking (to act on the *offensive*).—**offensively,** of•fen′siv•li, *adv.* In an offensive manner.—**offensiveness,** of•fen′siv•nes, *n.* The quality of being offensive; unpleasantness.

offer, of′ėr, *v.t.* [A.Sax. *offrian,* and Fr. *offrir* (*j'offre,* I offer), from L. *offerre,* to offer—*ob,* towards, and *fero,* to bring. FERTILE.] To present for acceptance or rejection; to tender; to present to notice; to proffer; to present, as an act of worship; to sacrifice (often with *up*); to attempt or do with evil intent (to *offer* violence, an insult); to bid, as a price or wages.—*v.i.* To present itself (an opportunity *offers*); to declare a willingness.—*n.* The act of offering; a proposal to be accepted or rejected; the act of bidding a price, or the sum bid.—**offerer,** of′ėr•ėr, *n.* —**offering,** of′ėr•ing, *n.* That which is offered; a gift, as an oblation.—**offertory,** of′ėr•to•ri, *n.* The oblation of the unconsecrated bread and wine to God during the Eucharist; the prayers recited and hymns sung at this time; the point at which money is offered during a religious service; the money offered.

office, of′is, *n.* [Fr. *office,* from L. *officium,* duty, office, from prefix *ob,* and *facio,* to do, or from *opem,* aid (OPULENCE), and *facio* (FACT).] Employment or business; duty or duties falling on or entrusted to a person; that which is performed or assigned to be done by a particular thing; function; act of good or ill voluntarily tendered: usually in a good sense; service; *eccles.* a formulary of devotion, or a service appointed for a particular occasion; a house or apartment in which persons transact business; a place where official acts are done; a body of persons entrusted with certain duties; persons who transact business in an office (often applied to an insurance company); *pl.* kitchens, outhouses, etc., of a mansion, dwelling house, or farm.—*Holy Office,* the Inquisition, or the authorities at Rome who direct it.—*Office hours,* the hours during which offices are open for the transaction of business.—**officer,** of′is•ėr, *n.* A person who holds an office; a person commissioned or authorized to fill a public situation or to perform any public duty; one who holds a commission in the army or navy.—*v.t.* To furnish with officers; to appoint officers over.—**official,** of•fish′al, *a.* [L. *officialis.*] Pertaining to an office or public duty; derived from the proper office or officer, or from the proper authority (an *official* permission); communicated by virtue of authority.—*n.* One invested with an office of a public nature; *eccles.* a deputy appointed by a bishop, chapter, archdeacon, etc.—**officialism,** of•fish′al•izm, *n.* A system of official government; a system of excessive official routine; red-tapism.—**officially,** of•fish′al•li, *adv.* In an official manner; by virtue of the proper authority.—**officiate,** of•fish′i•āt, *v.i.* —*officiated, officiating.* To perform official duties.—**officiator,** of•fish′i•ā•tėr, *n.* One who officiates.

officinal, of•fis′i•nal, *a.* [From L. *officina,* a shop; same origin as *office.*] Used in a shop, or belonging to it; *phar.* used in the preparation of recognized medical recipes (an *officinal* plant).—*n.* A drug sold in an apothecary's shop.

officious, of•fish′us, *a.* [L. *officiosus,* dutiful, obliging, from *officium,* an office. OFFICE.] Obliging‡; doing kind offices‡; excessively forward in kindness; interposing services not wanted; annoyingly eager to oblige or assist; meddling.—**officiously,** of•fish′us•li, *adv.* In an officious manner; with forward zeal; meddlesomely.—**officiousness,** of•fish′us•nes, *n.* Improper forwardness; meddlesomeness.

offing, offscouring, offset, offshoot, offspring, etc. See OFF.

oft, oft, *adv.* [A.Sax., Icel., and G. *oft,* Dan. *ofte,* Sw. *ofta,* Goth. *ufta,* oft, often; *often* is a later form; akin to *over.*] Often; frequently. (*Poet.*)—**often,** of′n, *adv.* Frequently; many times; not seldom.—*a.* Frequent.—**oftentimes,** of′n•tīmz, *adv.* Frequently; often; many times.—**ofttimes,** oft′tīmz, *adv.* Frequently; often.

ogam, og′am, *n.* See OGHAM.

ogee, ō•jē′, *n.* [Fr. *ogive, augive*; etymology doubtful.] *Arch.* a molding consisting of two members, the one concave, the other convex, the outline thus resembling the letter S (sometimes expressed by O G).

ogham, og′ham, *n.* A kind of writing practiced by the ancient Irish, the characters of which also were called *oghams.*

ogive, ō′jīv, *n.* [Fr. OGEE.] *Arch.* a French term for the Gothic or pointed arch.—**ogival,** ō•jī′val, *a. Arch.* of or pertaining to an ogive or ogee.

ogle, ō′gl, *v.t.*—*ogled, ogling.* [Same as L.G. *oegeln,* to eye, G. *äugeln,* to ogle, from *auge,* D. *oog,* the eye. EYE.] To view with side glances, as in fondness or with a design to attract notice.—*v.i.* To cast side glances.—*n.* A side glance or look.—**ogler,** ō′glėr, *n.* One that ogles.

ogre, ō′gėr, *n.* [Fr. *ogre,* from L. *Orcus,* the god of the infernal regions, hell.] A monster of popular legends who lived on human flesh; a person likened to an ogre.—**ogress,** ō′gres, *n.* [Fr. *ogresse.*] A female ogre.—**ogreish,** ō′gėr•ish, *a.* Resembling or suggestive of an ogre.

oh, ō, *interj.* Expression of surprise.

ohm, ōm, *n.* [From *Ohm,* the propounder of the law known by his name.] The practical unit of electrical resistance, equal to 10^9 absolute electromagnetic units of resistance. The international ohm adopted in 1893 is the resistance of a column of mercury at 0° C., of 14.4521 gm. mass, of uniform cross section, and of 106.3 cm. height.—*Ohm's Law,* an important law referring to the causes that tend to impede the action of a voltaic battery.

oil, oil, *n.* [O.Fr. *oile, oille,* from L. *oleum,* oil; akin *olive.*] A substance of animal and vegetable origin, liquid at ordinary temperatures, insoluble in water, and burning with a more or less luminous flame; a substance of somewhat similar character of mineral origin (as petroleum). Oils are divided into *fixed* and *volatile* or *essential oils,* the latter being diffusible in vapor by heat.—*v.t.* To smear or rub over with oil.—*Oiled silk,* silk prepared with oil, etc., so as to be impervious to moisture and air.—*Oiled paper,* paper besmeared with oil so as to render it transparent, used for tracing designs.—**oily,** oi′li, *a.* Consisting of or containing oil; resembling oil; fat; greasy; *fig.* unctuous; sanctimonious; hypocritically pious.—**oiliness,** oi′li•ness, *n.* The quality of being oily; unctuousness.—**oil cake,** *n.* A cake or mass of compressed linseed, rape, or other seed from which oil has been extracted, linseed cake being much used as food for cattle.—**oilcloth,** *n.* Cloth treated with oil or paint, used for shelf covering, etc.—**oil color,** *n.* A pigment made by grinding a coloring substance in oil.—**oiler,** oil′ėr, *n.* One who oils.—**oil painting,** *n.* The art of painting with oil colors, the highest branch of the painter's art; a picture painted in oil colors.—**oil palm,** *n.* A West African palm whose fruit yields palm oil.—**oilskin,** *n.* Waterproof cloth; prepared linen for making garments to keep out the rain.—**oilstone,** *n.* A fine-grained stone on which tools receive a fine edge by the aid of oil.—**oil well,** *n.* A well sunk into an oil-bearing mineral bed.

ointment, oint′ment, *n.* [From Fr. *oindre,* pp. *oint,* to anoint, from L. *ungere.* UNCTION.] Any soft unctuous substance used for smearing, particularly the body or a diseased part; an unguent.

Ojibwa, Ojibway, o•jib′wā, *n.* [Amer. Ind. *ojibway,* from *ojib, ub-way,* a kind of moccasin.] A member of a large tribe of Algonquin Indians of the Lake Superior area; the tribe itself.

OK, okay, ō•kā′, *n.* [From Democratic *O.K.* Club, supporters of van Buren, from his birthplace *O*ld *K*inderhook, N.Y.] Approval; endorsement.—*a.* and *adv.* All right; correct.—*v.t.*—*OK'd, okayed, OK'-ing, okaying.* To approve; to authorize (to *OK* the bill).

okapi, ō•kä′pi, *n.* An African animal akin to the giraffe, but smaller and striped.

oke, ōk, *n.* An Egyptian and Turkish weight equal to about 2 ¾ lb.

okra, ō′kra, *n.* A plant of the mallow family (genus *Abelmoschus*) cultivated as a vegetable in tropical countries.

old, ōld, *a.* [A.Sax. *ald, eald*; D. *oud,* G. *alt,* Goth. *altheis*; cog. with L. *alo,* to nourish, *altus,* lofty.] Advanced far in years or life (an *old* man or tree); not new or fresh; long made or produced (*old* clothes, wine); not modern; ancient; of any duration whatever (a year *old*); former (*old* habits); long practiced; experienced (*old* offender); having the feelings of an old person; crafty or cunning (colloq.); a familiar term of affection or cordiality; worn or used.—*The old country,* an immigrant's country of origin.—*Old glory,* the flag of the United States (colloq.).—*Old Guard,* Napoleon's original bodyguard (1804).—*Old maid,* an unmarried woman no longer young; one manifesting characteristics of an old maid, primness, prudishness, etc.; a simple game of cards.—*Old school,* persons having the character, manner, or opinions of a past age (of the *old school*).—*Old Testament.* See TESTAMENT.—*Old World,* the Eastern Hemisphere, or Europe, Asia, and Africa.—*n.* An ancient or past time (days of *old*).—**olden,** ol′dn, *a.* Ancient.—**old-fashioned,** *a.* Formed according to obsolete fashion or custom; characterized by antiquated fashions or customs.—**oldness,** old′-nes, *n.*—**oldster,** *n.* An older or elderly person.—**old style,** *n. Print.* a type distinguished from modern style by having rather irregular strokes in size and thickness and slanted serifs.—**old-world,** *a.* Belonging to a far bygone age.

oleaginous, ō•li•aj′i•nus, *a.* [L. *oleaginus,* from *oleum,* oil. OIL.] Having the qualities of oil; unctuous; *fig.* (applied to persons, manners, etc.) smoothly sanctimonious; unwholesomely fawning.—**oleaginousness,** ō•li•aj′i•nus•nes, *n.* Oiliness.

oleander, ō•li•an′dėr, *n.* [Fr. *oléandre,* from L.L. *arodandrum,* by corruption for *rhododendron.*] A beautiful evergreen flowering shrub.

oleaster, ō•li•as′tėr, *n.* [L., from

olea, the olive tree.] The so-called wild olive, a plant resembling the olive.

olefiant, ō•lē′fi•ant, *a.* [L. *oleum*, oil, and *facio*, to make.] Forming or producing oil.—*Olefiant gas*, a gas obtained from a mixture of sulfuric acid and alcohol forming with chlorine an oily compound.—**oleic,** ō•lē′ik, *a.* Pertaining to or derived from oil. —**olein,** ōl′ē•in, *n.* [L. *oleum*, oil.] One of the chief constituents of animal fat.—**oleograph,** ō′li•o•graf, *n.* A picture produced in oils by a process analogous to that of lithographic printing.

oleomargarine, ō′li•ō•mar″ja•rēn, *n.* [L. *oleum*, and E. *margarin.*] Margarine.

oleoresin, ō′li•ō•rez″in, *n.* [Prefix *oleo*, and *resin.*] A natural combination of an essential oil and a resin, as turpentine.

olfactory, ol•fak′te•ri, *a.* [L. *olfacio*, *olfactum*, to smell—*oleo*, to smell, and *facio*, to make. ODOR.] Pertaining to smelling; connected with the sense of smelling.—*n.* An organ of smelling (usually pl.).—**olfaction,** ōl•fak′shon, *n.* The sense of smell; the act or process of smelling.

olibanum, o•lib′a•num, *n.* [L.L. *olibanum*, from L. *oleum*, oil, and *libanus*, frankincense.] A kind of incense; frankincense.

oligarchy, ol′i•gär•ki, *n.* [Gr. *oligarchia*—*oligos*, few, and *archē*, rule.] A form of government in which the supreme power is placed in the hands of a small exclusive class; those who form such a class or body. —**oligarch,** ol′i•gärk, *n.* A member of an oligarchy.—**oligarchic, oligarchical,** ol•i•gär′kik, ol•i•gär′ki•kal, *a.*

Oligocene, ol′ig•o•sēn, *a.* [Gr. *oligos*, little, and *kainos*, recent.] *Geol.* slightly recent; somewhat more recent than *eocene*.

oligoclase, ol′i•gō•klās, *n.* [Gr. *oligos*, small, and *klasis*, a fracture.] A kind of feldspar, occurring in granite, porphyry, and other metamorphic and volcanic rocks.

olio, ō′li•o, *n.* [From Sp. *olla* (pron. *olya*), a dish of meat, from L. *olla*, a pot.] A dish of stewed meat; a mixture; a medley; a miscellany.

olive, ol′iv, *n.* [Fr. *olive*, L. *oliva*, an olive, akin to Gr. *elaia*, an olive; same root as *oleum*, oil.] An evergreen tree much cultivated in Southern Europe, etc., for the valuable oil contained in its berries, formerly sacred to Minerva, furnishing wreaths used by the Greeks and Romans to crown the brows of victors, and still universally regarded as an emblem of peace; the berry or drupe of the olive; the color of the olive, a brownish-green color or one composed of violet and green mixed in nearly equal proportions.—*a.* Relating to the olive; of the color of the olive; brown, tending to a yellowish-green.—**olivaceous,** ol•i•vā′shus, *a.* Of the color of the olive; having the qualities of olives.—**olivary,** ol′i•va•ri, *a.* Resembling an olive.—**olive branch,** *n.* A branch of the olive tree: the emblem of peace; *fig.* a child.—**olivenite,** ol′iv•en•īt, *n.* A mineral of an olive-green color, containing copper and arsenic. Called also *Olive-ore*.—**olive oil,** *n.* An oil obtained from the fruit of the olive, and much used in cookery and for medicinal and manufacturing purposes.—**olivine,** ol′iv•in, *n.* An olive-green variety of chrysolite.

olla, ol′la, *n.* [Sp. *olla*, a jar or pot, L. *olla.*] A jar or urn.—*Olla podrida*, po•drē′da. [Sp., lit. rotten or putrid pot], a favorite dish in Spain, consisting of a mixture of various kinds of meat stewed with vegetables; hence, a mixture or miscellaneous collection.

Olympiad, ō•lim′pi•ad, *n.* [Gr. *olympias*, *olympiados*, from *Olympia*, where the Olympic games were held.] A period of four years reckoned from one celebration of the Olympic games to another, by which the ancient Greeks computed time, from 776 B.C.—**Olympian, Olympic,** ō•lim′pi•an, ō•lim′pik, *a.* Pertaining to Olympus or to Olympia in Greece.—*Olympic games*, a great national festival of the ancient Greeks, celebrated at intervals of four years on the plain of Olympia in Peloponnesus; a modern revival (Athens, Greece, 1896) in which athletes of the world meet quadrennially in various countries.

omasum, o•mā′sum, *n.* [L.] The third stomach of ruminating animals: the manyplies.

omber, ombre, om′bėr, *n.* [Fr., from Sp. *hombre*, man, L. *homo.*] An old game at cards, usually played by three persons.

omega, o•mē′ga, o•mā′ga, ō′me•ga, *n.* [Gr. *o*, and *mega*, great, lit. the great or long *o.*] The name of the last letter of the Greek alphabet, hence in Scripture *Omega* denotes the last, the ending.

omelet, om′e•let, *n.* [Fr. *aumelette*, *omelette.*] Beaten eggs fried, at times with cheese, chopped meat, fruit, etc.

omen, ō′men, *n.* [L. *omen*, older *osmen*, from *os*, *oris*, the mouth, or connected with *auris*, the ear; hence *abominate.*] A casual event or occurrence thought to portend good or evil; a prognostic; an augury.—*v.i.* To prognosticate as an omen; to augur; to betoken.—*v.t.* To divine; to predict.—**omened,** ō′mend, *a.* Containing an omen or prognostic.—**omening,** ō′men•ing, *n.* An augury; a prognostication.—**ominous,** om′i•nus, *a.* [L. *ominosus.*] Containing an ill omen; foreboding or betokening evil; inauspicious.—**ominously,** om′i•nus•li, *adv.* In an ominous manner; with ill omen.—**ominousness,** om′i•nus•nes, *n.*

omentum, ō•men′tum, *n.* [L.] *Anat.* the caul or epiploön.—**omental,** ō•men′tal, *a.* Relating to the omentum.

omicron, ō•mī′kron, *n.* [Gr. *o mikron*, *lit.* little *o.*] The short *o*, the 15th letter (*O*, *o*) of the Greek alphabet.

omit, ō•mit′, *v.t.*—*omitted, omitting.* [L. *omitto*, to neglect, disregard, say nothing of—prefix *ob*, and *mitto*, to send. MISSION.] To pass over or neglect; to let slip; to fail to do or to use; to leave out; not to insert.—**omission,** ō•mish′on, *n.* [L. *omissio.*] The act of omitting; a neglect or failure to do something that should have been done; the act of leaving out; something omitted or left out.—**omissible,** ō•mis′i•bl, *a.* Capable of being omitted.—**omissive,** ō•mis′iv, *a.* Leaving out; neglectful.

omnibus, om′ni•bus, *n.* [L., for all.] A bus; a collection in one volume of an author's works.

omnific, om•nif′ik, *a.* [L. *omnis*, all, and *facio*, to make.] All-creating.

omnipotence, om•nip′o•tens, *n.* [L. *omnipotens*, omnipotent—*omnis*, all, and *potens*, powerful. POTENT.] Unlimited or infinite power; almighty power; an attribute of God; hence sometimes used for God (being then written with a capital).—**omnipotent,** om•nip′o•tent, *a.* Almighty; all-powerful.—*The Omnipotent*, the Almighty.—**omnipotently,** om•nip′o•tent•li, *adv.* In an omnipotent manner.

omnipresence, om•ni•prez′ens, *n.* [L. *omnis*, all, and *praesens*, present.] The faculty or power of being present in every place at the same time, an attribute peculiar to God.—**omnipresent,** om•ni•prez′ent, *a.* Present in all places at the same time; ubiquitous.

omniscience, om•nish′ens, *n.* [L. *omnis*, all, and *scientia*, knowledge. SCIENCE.] The faculty of knowing everything; knowledge unbounded or infinite; an attribute of God.—**omniscient,** om•nish′ent, *a.* Having knowledge of all things; infinitely knowing.—**omnisciently,** om•nish′ent•li, *adv.* In an omniscient manner.

omnium, om′ni•um, *n.* [L., of all (things).] A term used on the Stock Exchange to express the aggregate value of the different stocks in which a loan is funded.—**omnium-gatherum,** om′ni•um•gaTH″ėr•um, *n.* A miscellaneous collection of things or persons. (*Colloq.*)

omnivorous, om•niv′o•rus, *a.* [L. *omnivorus*—*omnis*, all, and *voro*, to eat.] All-devouring; eating food of every kind indiscriminately (*omnivorous* animals); having an insatiable appetite for anything (an *omnivorous* reader).

omphalic, om•fal′ik, *a.* [Gr. *omphalos*, the navel.] Pertaining to the navel.

on, on, *prep.* [A.Sax. *on*, *an*, on, in; D. *aan*, G. *an*, Goth. *ana*, Skr. *anu*, in; akin to *in* and *under.*] Above and so as to touch; not off; performing by means of (to play *on* a harp, a violin); in addition to (loss *on* loss); at or near (*on* the coast); expressing reliance, dependence, basis, etc. (a statement founded *on* error); at or in the time of (we say *on* the day, *at* the hour, *in* the week, month, year); at the time of or during (*on* public occasions); immediately after and as a result (he retired *on* the ratification of the treaty); in reference or relation to (*on* our part); toward or so as to affect (mercy *on* him); denoting a pledge, engagement, or affirmation (*on* my word, *on* his honor); *betting*, in support of the chances of; among the staff of or contributors to: with names of periodicals; pointing to a state, condition, occupation, etc. (*on* fire, *on* duty).—*On a sudden*, suddenly.—*On fire*, in a state of burning; in a passion or eager state. —*On hand*, in present possession (goods *on hand*).—*On high*, in an elevated place.—*On the way*, *on the road*, proceeding, journeying, or making progress.—*On the wing*, in flight; flying; *fig*. departing.—*adv*. Forward, in progression (move *on*); forward, in succession (and so *on*); without interruption or ceasing (sleep *on*, say *on*); attached to the body (his clothes are not *on*). Also used elliptically as an imperative = go on, advance.—**oncoming,** *a*. Approaching; nearing.—*n*. A coming or drawing near; approach.—**onlooker,** on′lu̦k•ėr, *n*. A looker on; a spectator.—**onrush,** on′rush, *n*. A rush or dash onward; a rapid or violent onset.—**onset,** on′set, *n*. A violent attack; an assault; an assault by an army or body of troops.—**onslaught,** on′sla̦t, *n*. [From *on*, and A.Sax. *sleaht*, a blow, from *slagan*, *sleán*, to strike (to *slay*).] An attack or onset; an assault.

onager, on′a•jėr, *n*. [L., from Gr. *onagros*—*onos*, ass, and *agrios*, wild.] The wild ass of Central Asia.

once, wuns, *adv*. [O.E. *ones*, *onis*, an adverbial genit. of *one*; comp. *twice* and *thrice*. NONCE.] One time; on one occasion; at a former time.—*At once*, at the same time; immediately.—*n*. Only time; one time (at *once*, this *once*).—*conj*. As soon as; whenever.—**once-over,** *n*. A quick appraisal.

one, wun, *a*. [O.E. *oon*, A.Sax. *án* = D., L.G., and Dan. *een*, Sw. *en*, Icel. *einn*, G. *ein*, Goth. *ains*; cog. L. *unus*, W. *un*, Gael. *aon*, *an*, Armor. *unan*—one. The indefinite article *an*, *a* is the same word; *once* and *only* are derivatives, and *atone* = *at one*.] Being but a single thing or a unit; not two or more; indicating a contrast or opposition to some other thing; closely united; forming a whole; undivided; single in kind. *One* occurs in many compound words of obvious meaning, etc.—*One day*, on a certain or particular day; at an indefinite time, either past or future.—*All one*, just the same; of no consequence; no matter. —*n*. The first of the simple units; the symbol representing this (= 1); a particular individual, whether thing or person (in this sense with a plural).—*At one*, in union; in concord or agreement.—*pron*. Any single person; any man, any person (*one* may speak *one's* mind).—*One another*, one or each the other.—**one-horse,** *n*. Drawn by a single horse.—**oneness,** wun′nes, *n*. The state of being one; singleness; unity.—**oneself,** wun•self′, *pron*. One's self; himself or herself.—**one-sided,** *a*. Related to, or having but one side; partial; unjust; unfair. —**onetime,** *a*. Former; past; quondam.—*adv*. Formerly.—**one-track,** *a*. Possessed of only one track, as a railroad, hence, narrow, unchanging. —**one-way,** *a*. Traffic or motion in one direction only.

oneirocritic, o•nī′ro•krit″ik, *n*. [Gr. *oneiron*, a dream, *kritikos*, discerning.] An interpreter of dreams.—**oneirocritical,** o•nī′ro•krit″i•kal, *a*. Having the power of interpreting dreams.—**oneiromancy,** o•nī′ro•man•si, *n*. [Gr. *manteia*, divination.] Divination by dreams.

onerous, on′ėr•us, *a*. [O.Fr. *onereus*, from L. *onerosus*, from *onus*, *oneris*, a load.] Burdensome; troublesome in the performance.—**onerously,** on′ėr•us•li, *adv*. Oppressively.

onion, un′yun, *n*. [Fr. *oignon*, *ognon*, from L. *unio*, *unionis*, unity, an onion.] A biennial cultivated plant of the lily family, and particularly its bulbous root, much used as an article of food.

onlooker. See ON.

only, ōn′li, *a*. [*One*, with its old pronounciation, and term. *-ly*; A. Sax. *ánlic*.] Single; alone in its class; solitary.—*adv*. For one purpose alone; simply; merely; barely; solely; singly.—*conj*. But; excepting that.

onomatopoeia, on′o•ma•to•pē″a, *n*. [Gr. *onomatopoiia*—*onoma*, *onomatos*, a name, and *poieō*, to make.] The formation of words by imitation of sounds; the expressing by sound of the thing signified; thus *buzz*, *hum*, *pewit*, *whippoorwill*, etc., are produced by *onomatopoeia*.—**onomatopoetic,** on′o•ma•to•pō•et″ik, *a*. Pertaining to or formed by onomatopoeia.

onset, onslaught. See ON.

ontogenesis, ontogeny, on•to•jen′e•sis, on•toj′e•ni, *n*. [Gr. *on*, *ontos*, being, and *genesis*—root *gen*, to produce.] *Biol*. the history of the individual development of an organized being.—**ontogenetic,** on′to•je•net″ik, *a*. Pertaining to ontogenesis.

ontology, on•tol′o•ji, *n*. [Gr. *on*, *ontos*, being, and *logos*, discourse.] The doctrine of being; that part of metaphysics which investigates and explains the nature of all things or existences, treating of whatever does or can exist: sometimes equivalent to *metaphysics*.—**ontological,** on•to•loj′i•kal, *a*. Pertaining to ontology, or the science of being.—**ontologist,** on•tol′o•jist, *n*. One versed in ontology.

onus, ō′nus, *n*. [L.] A burden; often used for *onus probandi*, the burden of proof; the burden of proving what has been alleged.

onward, on′wėrd, *adv*. [*On* and *ward*, denoting direction, similar to *toward*; A.Sax. *onweard*.] Toward the point before or in front; forward; on; in advance.—*a*. Advanced or advancing (an *onward* course); carried so far toward an end; forward; advanced.—**onwards,** on′wėrdz, *adv*. Same as *Onward*.

onyx, on′iks, *n*. [Gr. *onyx*, the nail; the color of the gem resembles that of the nail.] A semi-pellucid gem with variously colored zones or veins; an agate with layers of chalcedony, one of which is flesh-colored: used for cameos.

oöcyte, ō′o•sīt, *n*. [Gr. *ōon*, an egg, *kytos*, a cell.] *Zool*. an egg before formation of the polar bodies.

oodles, ö′dlz, *n*. pl. (colloq.) A lot; an abundance.

oögonium, ō′o•gōn″i•um, *n*. [Gr. *ōon*, an egg, *gonos*, offspring.] In lower plants, the female organ, producing one or more egg cells.

oölite, ō′ol•īt, *n*. [Gr. *oon*, an egg, and *lithos*, stone, from its resemblance to the roes of fish.] *Geol*. a species of limestone composed of globules clustered together, commonly without any visible cement or base; the oölitic formation or system.—**oölitic,** ō-o•lit′ik, *a*. Pertaining to oölite; composed of oölite; resembling oölite.—*Oölitic system*, a series of strata comprehending limestones, calcareous sandstones, marls, shales, and clays which underlie the chalk formation and rest on the Trias, the Jurassic system.

oölogy, ō•ol′o•ji, *n*. [Gr. *ōon*, an egg, and *logos*, a treatise.] The branch of knowledge that deals with bird's eggs.—**oölogist,** ō•ol′o•jist, *n*. One versed in oölogy.

oolong, ö′long, *n*. [Cant. pron. of Chin. (Pek.) *wu-lung*, *lit*. a black dragon.] A tea made from leaves partly oxidized before firing.

oöphyte, ō′o•fīt, *n*. [Gr. *ōon*, an egg, *phyton*, a plant.] *Bot*. the GAMETOPHYTE (which see).

oösperm, ō′o•sperm, *n*. [Gr. *ōon*, an egg, *sperma*, seed.] A fertilized ovum; a zygote.

oöspore, ō′o•spōr, *n*. [Gr. *ōon*, an egg, and E. *spore*.] *Bot*. a spore that receives impregnation before germination.

oötheca, ō•o•thē′ka, *n*. [Gr. *ōon*, an egg, and *théca*, a case.] An eggcase, as that for the eggs of some insects.

ooze, öz, *v.i.*—*oozed*, *oozing*. [A.Sax. *wōs*, juice, liquor, *wáse*, mire, mud; Icel. *vás*, wetness; same root as *water*.] To percolate, as a liquid, through the pores of a substance, or through small openings; to flow in small quantities from the pores of a body: often used figuratively (the secret *oozed* out).—*v.t.* To emit in the shape of moisture.—*n*. Soft mud or slime, as at the bottom of any sheet of water; *tanning*, a solution of tannin; the liquor of a tan-vat.

opacity. See OPAQUE.

opah, ō′pa, *n*. A large and beautiful seafish of the Eastern Seas.

opal, ō′pal, *n*. [L. *opalus*, Gr. *opallios*, an opal; comp. Skr. *upala*, a precious stone.] A precious stone of various colors and varieties, the finest characterized by its iridescent reflection of light, and formerly believed to possess magical virtues.—**opalescence,** ō•pal•es′ens, *n*. A play of colors like that of the opal; the reflection of a milky and iridescent light.—**opalescent,** ō•pal•es′ent, *a*. Resembling opal; having the iridescent tints of opal.—**opaline,** ō′-

pal•īn, *a.* Pertaining to or like opal.

opaque, o•pāk′, *a.* [Fr. *opaque,* from L. *opacus,* shady, dark, obscure.] Impervious to the rays of light; not transparent.—*n.* Opacity (*Young*).—**opaquely,** o•pāk′li, *adv.* In an opaque manner.—**opaqueness,** o•pāk′nes, *n.* The quality of being opaque.—**opacity,** o•pas′i•ti, *n.* [L. *opacitas.*] State or quality of being opaque; want of transparency.

ope, ōp, *v.t.* and *i.*—*oped, oping.* To open: used only in poetry.

open, ō′pn, *a.* [A.Sax. *open,* open=D. *open,* Icel. *opinn,* Dan. *áaben,* G. *offen,* open; akin to *up.*] Not shut; not closed; not covered; not stopped (as a bottle); unsealed (as a letter); free to be used or enjoyed; not restricted; affording free ingress; accessible; public; spread; expanded; not drawn together or contracted (an *open* hand; *open* arms); hence, free, liberal, bounteous; free from dissimulation; candid; not secret or concealed; clear; unobstructed (an *open view;* an *open* country); not frosty; free from frost and snow (an *open* winter); exposed to view; laid bare; exposed or liable to be assailed; fully prepared; attentive; not yet decided (an *open* question); not settled, balanced, or closed (an *open* account); enunciated without closing the mouth, or with a full utterance (an *open* vowel); *mus.* produced without stopping by the finger or without using a slide, key, piston, etc.—*Open verdict,* a verdict upon an inquest finding that a crime has been committed, but without specifying the criminal; or which finds that a sudden or violent death has occurred, but does not decide on the cause.—*n.* An open or clear space.—*The open,* the open country; a place or space clear of obstructions.—*v.t.* [A.Sax. *openian.*] To make open; to unclose; to remove any fastening or obstruction from, so as to afford an entrance, passage, or view of the inner parts; to spread; to expand (the fingers, the arms); to enter upon; to commence (to *open* a negotiation or correspondence); to declare open; to set in operation with some ceremony; to reveal; to disclose (to *open* one's mind).—*To open fire,* to begin to fire or discharge firearms.—*v.i.* To unclose itself; to be unclosed; to be parted; to begin to be seen from a distance; to commence; to begin; to begin to fire, as a battery.—**open and shut,** *a.* Obvious; very simple.—**open door,** *n.* An opportunity for exchange of trade and goods with equal opportunities for all; open or free admission to all.—**opener,** ō′pen•ėr, *n.*—**open-eyed,** *a.* Having the eyes open, hence, watchful; vigilant.—**open-handed,** *a.* Generous; liberal; munificent.—**openhearted,** *a.* Candid; frank; sincere; not sly.—**openheartedly,** *adv.*—**opening,** ō′pen•ing, *n.* A break or breach in something; a hole or perforation; an aperture; beginning; commencement; a vacancy; an opportunity of commencing a business or profession; a thinly wooded space without underbrush, as in a forest.—**open letter,** *n.* A communication of protest or appeal addressed to one person but meant for public view.—**openly,** o′pen•li, *adv.*—**openmouthed,** *a.* Having the mouth open; gaping, as with astonishment.—**open shop,** *n.* An establishment where union and nonunion workers are employed without discrimination.—**openwork,** *n.* Ornamental work, with openings through its substance.

opera, op′e•ra, *n.* [It. *opera,* work, from L. *opera,* work.] A musical drama; a dramatic composition set to music and sung and acted on the stage, accompanied with musical instruments; the score or words of a musical drama.—**opera glass,** *n.* A small binocular telescope of low magnifying power, used in theaters, etc.—**opera house,** *n.* A theater for the performance of operas.—**operatic,** op•e•rat′ik, *a.*

operate, op′e•rāt, *v.i.*—*operated, operating.* [L. *operor, operatum,* to work, from *opus, operis,* a work.] To exert power or strength, physical or mechanical; to work; to act; to have agency; to produce an effect; to issue in a designed result; *med.* to take appropriate effect on the human system; *surg.* to perform some manual act in a methodical manner upon a human body.—*v.t.* To effect; to accomplish; to put into operation; to work; to drive (a machine).—**operant,** op′e•rant, *a.* Having power to produce an effect; operative.—*n.* One who operates; an operator.—**operation,** op•e•rā′shon, *n.* [L. *operatio.*] The act or process of operating; a working or proceeding; process; manipulation; the carrying out of preconcerted measures by regular movements (military or naval *operations*); a surgical proceeding to which the human body is subjected for curative ends.—**operative,** op′e•ra•tiv, *a.* Operating; exerting force; active in the production of effects; efficacious; producing the effect; having to do with manual or other operations.—*n.* A skilled workman; an artisan.—**operator,** op′e•rā•tėr, *n.* One who operates; one who operates a machine (to be an IBM *operator*); one who owns, leases, or manages a mining property; (slang) one who cleverly manages people and situations to his own advantage.

operculum, ō•pėr′kū•lum, *n.* [L., from *operio,* to close or shut.] A little lid or cover; the cover or lid of the spore cases of mosses; the lid of a pitcher-form leaf; a horny or shelly plate serving to close the aperture of the shell of many mollusks when the animal is retracted within it; the bony apparatus which protects the gills of fishes.—**operculated, operculate,** ō•pėr′kū•lā•ted, ō•pėr′kū•lāt, *a.* Pertaining to or having an operculum.

operetta, op•e•ret′ta, *n.* [It. dim. of *opera.*] A short musical drama of a light character.

operose, op′e•rōs, *a.* [L. *operosus,* from *opera,* work. OPERA.] Laborious; attended with labor; tedious.—**operosely,** op′e•rōs•li, *adv.* In an operose manner.—**operoseness,** op′e•rōs•nes, *n.* Laboriousness.

ophidian, ō•fid′i•an, *a.* [Gr. *ophis,* a serpent.] Pertaining to serpents; having the characters of the serpents; serpentine.—*n.* One of an order of reptiles which comprises all the snakes or serpents.

ophiolatry, of•i•ol′a•tri, *n.* [Gr. *ophis, ophios,* a serpent, and *latreia,* worship.] Serpent worship.—**ophiological,** of′i•o•loj″i•kal, *a.* Pertaining to ophiology.—**ophiologist,** of•i•ol′o•jist, *n.* One versed in ophiology.—**ophiology,** of•i•ol′o•ji, *n.* That branch of zoology which treats of serpents; the natural history of serpents.

ophite, of′īt, *n.* [Gr. *ophis,* a serpent.] Green porphyry or serpentine, a metamorphic rock; [*cap.*] also a name for certain Gnostics of the second century, who held that the serpent by which Eve was tempted was Christ, and hence regarded the serpent as sacred.

ophthalmia, of•thal′mi•a, *n.* [Gr., from *ophthalmos,* the eye, from root *op,* to see, as in *optic.*] Inflammation of the eye or its appendages.—**ophthalmic,** of•thal′mik, *a.* Pertaining to the eye.—**ophthalmitis,** of•thal•mī′tis, *n.* Inflammation of the eye.—**ophthalmology,** of•thal•mol′o•ji, *n.* That branch of science which deals with the eye.—**ophthalmologist,** of•thal•mol′o•jist, *n.* A person versed in ophthalmology.—**ophthalmoscope,** of•thal′mo•skōp, *n.* An instrument for viewing the interior of the eye by means of a mirror.—**ophthalmoscopy,** of•thal•mos′ko•pi, *n.* The art of using the ophthalmoscope.

opiate, ō′pi•āt, *n.* [From *opium.*] Any medicine that contains opium and has the quality of inducing sleep or repose; a narcotic; anything that dulls sensation; mental or physical.—*a.* Inducing sleep; soporific; narcotic.

opine, ō•pīn′, *v.i.* and *t.*—*opined, opining.* [Fr. *opiner,* from L. *opinor,* to think. OPINION.] To think; to suppose; to be of opinion.

opinion, o•pin′yun, *n.* [L. *opinio, opinionis,* from *opinor,* to think; same root as *opto,* to wish, *optimus,* best. OPTATIVE.] A judgment or belief formed without certain evidence; belief stronger than impression, less strong than positive knowledge; judgment or sentiments on persons or things as regards their character or qualities; settled judgment or persuasion; belief (religious *opinions*).—**opinionated,** o•pin′yun•ā•ted, *a.* Obstinate in opinion; opinionative; conceited.—**opinionative,** o•pin′yun•ā•tiv, *a.* Unduly attached to one's own opinions; dogmatic; obstinate in beliefs.—**opinionatively,** o•pin′yun•ā•tiv•li, *adv.* In an opinionative manner.—**opinionativeness,** o•pin′yun•ā•tiv•nes, *n.*

opium, ō′pium, *n.* [L. *opium,* Gr.

opion, from *opos*, vegetable juice.] A drug derived from dried juice of the unripe seed pod of the poppy; a narcotic or medicinal sedative.—**opium eating,** the practice of taking opium by mouth.—**opium smoking,** the habit of smoking opium.

opodeldoc, op•ō•del′dok, *n.* [Probably an arbitrary name coined by Paracelsus.] A saponaceous camphorated liniment; a solution of soap in alcohol, with the addition of camphor and essential oils.

opossum, o•pos′um, *n.* [From *opassom*, its native American name.] The name of several marsupial mammals of America.

oppidan, op′i•dan, *n.* [L. *oppidanus*, from *oppidum*, a city or town.] An inhabitant of a town‡; at Eton College a student not on the foundation, and who lives in a boarding house.

opponent, op•pō′nent, *a.* [L. *opponens, opponentis*, ppr. of *oppono*, to oppose—*ob*, against, and *pono*, to place. POSITION.] Opposing; antagonistic; opposite.—*n.* One that opposes; an adversary; an antagonist; one that supports the opposite side in controversy, disputation, or argument.

opportune, op•or•tūn′, *a.* [Fr. *opportun*, from L. *opportunis*, lit. offering a port or harbor—prefix *op*, for *ob*, and *portus*, a port, harbor, haven. PORT.] Seasonable; timely; well timed; convenient.—**opportunely,** op•or•tūn′li, *adv.* In an opportune manner.—**opportuneness,** op•or•tūn′nes, *n.* Quality of being opportune or seasonable.—**opportunism,** op•or•tūn′izm, *n.* The practice of seizing or turning opportunities to advantage; a political attitude dispensing with a fixed and moral program, but merely waiting for something to turn up to be utilized for immediate service.—**opportunity,** op•or•tū′ni•ti, *n.* [L. *opportunitas*.] Fit or convenient time or occasion; a time favorable for the purpose; a suitable time, combined with other favorable circumstances.

oppose, op•pōz′, *v.t.*—*opposed*, *opposing*. [Fr. *opposer*—prefix *op*, and *poser*, to place. POSE, COMPOSE.] To place in front; to set opposite; to place as an obstacle; to put with a view to hinder, defeat, destroy, or prevent effect; to act against; to resist, either by physical or other means; to act as an opponent to; to confront; to check; to withstand; to resist effectually.—*v.i.* To make objections; to act obstructively.—**opposability,** op•pō′za•bil″i•ti, *n.* The capability of being placed so as to act in opposition.—**opposable,** op•pō′za•bl, *a.* Capable of being opposed or resisted; capable of being opposed to something else.—**opposer,** op•pō′zėr, *n.* One that opposes.

opposite, op′po•zit, *a.* [L. *oppositus*—*ob*, before, and *positus*, placed. POSITION, COMPOSE.] Standing or situated in front; facing; adverse; opposed; hostile; different in nature or quality; mutually antagonistic; contrary; inconsistent; repugnant; *bot.* growing in pairs; each pair crosswise to that above or below it.—*n.* One who or that which opposes; one who or that which is opposite or adverse.—**oppositely,** op′po•zit•li, *adv.* In an opposite or adverse manner.—**oppositeness,** op′po•zit•nes, *n.* The state of being opposite or adverse.—**opposition,** op•pō•zish′on, *n.* [Partly from *oppose*, partly from *opposite*.] Situation so as to front something; a standing over against; the state of being opposed or contrasted; the state of being adverse; the act of opposing; attempt to check, restrain, or defeat resistance; that which opposes; the collective body of opposers; the party in either house of Congress or a state legislature opposed to the administration or the party in power; *astron.* the situation of two heavenly bodies when diametrically opposite to each other, or when their longitudes differ by 180°. Also used adjectively (an *opposition* scheme).

oppress, op•pres′, *v.t.* [Fr. *oppresser*, from L. *oppressus*, from *opprimo*—*ob*, and *premo, pressum*, to press. PRESS.] To load or burden with cruel, unjust, or unreasonable impositions; to treat with unjust severity, rigor, or hardship; to overburden; to overwhelm; to subdue; to sit or lie heavy on (as food in the stomach).—**oppression,** op•presh′on, *n.* The act of oppressing; excessively rigorous government; severity; hardship; calamity; depression; a sense of heaviness or weight in the mind or body.—**oppressive,** op•pres′iv, *a.* Unreasonably burdensome; unjustly severe; given to oppression; tyrannical; overpowering; overwhelming.—**oppressively,** op•pres′iv•li, *adv.* In an oppressive manner.—**oppressiveness,** op•pres′iv•nes, *n.* The quality of being oppressive.—**oppressor,** op•pres′ėr, *n.* One that oppresses or harasses.

opprobrium, op•prō′bri•um, *n.* [L., from *ob*, against, and *probrum*, a shameful or disgraceful act.] Scurrilous or abusive language; contemptuous reproaches; scurrility; disgrace; infamy.—**opprobrious,** op•prō′bri•us, *a.* Containing or expressive of opprobrium; scurrilous; abusive; infamous.—**opprobriously,** op•prō′bri•us•li, *adv.* Scurrilously.—**opprobriousness,** op•prō′bri•us•nes, *n.*

oppugn, op•pūn′, *v.t.* [L. *oppugno*—*ob*, against, and *pugno*, to fight, from *pugnus*, the fist. PUGNACIOUS.] To attack by arguments or the like, not by weapons; to oppose; to resist; to exercise hostile reasoning against.—**oppugnancy,** op•pug′nan•si, *n.* Opposition; resistance; contention.—**oppugnant,** op•pug′nant, *a.* Resisting; opposing; hostile.—**oppugner,** op•pūn′ėr, *n.* One who oppugns.

opsonic, op•son′ik, *a.* [Gr. *opson*, cooked meat.] Having the effect on bacteria of making them easier of consumption by phagocytes.—**opsonin,** op′so•nin, *n.* The substance in a patient's blood produced by the injection of dead cultures of the bacteria of his disease.

opt, opt, *v.i.* [Fr. *opter*, from L. *optare*, to choose.] To make a choice; to choose.

optative, op′te•tiv, *a.* [L. *optativus*, from *opto*, to desire or wish (as in *adopt, option*); root same as in *opinion, opulence, optimism*.] Expressing desire or wish; *gram.* applied to that mood of the verb in which wish or desire is expressed.—*n. Gram.* the optative mood of a verb.

optic, op′tik, *a.* [Fr. *optique*, from Gr. *optikos*, from root *op*, to see—L. *oculus*, E. *eye*, being from same root.] Relating or pertaining to vision or sight; pertaining to the organ of vision; subservient to vision; relating to the science of optics.—*Optic axis*, the axis of the eye, or a line going through the middle of the pupil and the center of the eye.—*n.* An organ of sight; an eye.—**optic nerve,** the nerve of sight which connects the eye with the optic centers of the brain.—**optical,** op′ti•kal, *a.* Relating to or connected with the science of optics.—**optically,** op′ti•kal•li, *adv.*—**optician,** op•tish′an, *n.* A person skilled in the science of optics; one who makes or sells optic glasses and instruments.—**optics,** op′tiks, *n.* That branch of physical science which treats of the nature and properties of light and vision, optical instruments, etc.—**optigraph,** op′ti•graf, *n.* A telescope used in drawing landscapes.

optimates, op•ti•mā′tēz, *n. pl.* [L., aristocrats, from *optimus*, best. OPTIMISM.] The Roman aristocracy; hence, an aristocracy or nobility in general.—**optime,** op′ti•mē, *n.* In the University of Cambridge, a student in the second rank of honors, next to the wranglers.

optimism, op′ti•mizm, *n.* [From L. *optimus*, best. OPTATIVE.] The doctrine that everything in nature is ordered for the best; the tendency always to take the most hopeful view of matters social or political.—**optimist,** op′ti•mist, *n.*—**optimistic,** op•ti•mis′tik, *a.*

optimum, op′ti•mum, *n.* [L. *optimus*, best.] The greatest number or degree; the most favorable of conditions, as for plant growth.

option, op′shon, *n.* [L. *optio*, option, from *opto*, to wish or desire. OPTATIVE.] The power or liberty of choosing; right of choice; the power of deciding on any course of action; choice; election; preference; *stock exchange*, a right to effect a certain transaction or not at a certain date, at the desire of the person bargaining, who pays for the right.—*Local option*, the principle by which the people of a certain locality may decide as to the sale of intoxicating liquors there.—**optional,** op′shon•al, *a.* Left to one's option or choice; depending on choice or preference.—**optionally,** op′shon•al•li, *adv.* In an optional manner; at pleasure.

optometer, op•tom′et•ėr, *n.* [From

opt- of *optic*, and Gr. *metron*, a measure. OPTIC.] An instrument for testing and measuring the visual adjustment of the eye, used to determine the focal lengths of lenses needed to correct defects of vision.

optometry, op•tom′e•tri, *n.* [From Gr. *optikos*, optic, and *metron*, measuring.] Scientific measurement of the range of vision; the fitting of lenses to effect needed adjustments. — **optometrist,** op•tom′e•trist, *n.*

opulence, opulency, op′ū•lens, op′ū•len•si, *n.* [L. *opulentia*, from *opes*, wealth. OPTATIVE.] Wealth; riches; affluence.—**opulent,** op′ū•lent, *a.* [L. *opulentus.*] Wealthy; rich; affluent; having large means.

opuntia, ō•pun′shi•a, *n.* A kind of cactus largely cultivated in Mexico for raising the cochineal insect.

opus, ō′pus, *n.* [L. *pl.* OPERA.] A work; especially a musical composition.

opuscule, ō•pus′kūl, *n.* [L. *opusculum*, dim. from *opus*, work. OPERATE.] A small work; a little book.

or, or, *conj.* [Contr. from the older *other*, formerly used both for 'either' and 'or', the same word as *either*.] A particle that marks, or seems to mark, an alternative, frequently corresponding to a preceding *either*, and also to *whether*, with which words it is sometimes interchangeable in poetry; it often connects a series of words or propositions, presenting a choice between any two of them (he may study law *or* medicine *or* divinity, *or* he may enter into trade); beginning a sentence it expresses an alternative with the foregoing sentence.

or, or, *n.* [Fr. *or*, L. *aurum*, gold.] *Her.* gold, expressed in engraving by numerous small points or dots.

orach, orache, or′ach, *n.* [Formerly *arrach*, from Fr. *arroche*, orache; origin unknown.] A name of several plants of which a garden species is used like spinach.

oracle, or′a•kl, *n.* [L. *oraculum*, from *oro*, to speak, to pray, from *os*, *oris*, the mouth; akin *oral*, *orifice*, *orator*, *adore*, etc.] The answer of a god or the inspired priest or priestess of a god, to an inquiry made respecting some affair; the deity who gave or was supposed to give answers to inquiries; the place where the answers were given; the sanctuary (O.T.); a divine communication, revelation, or message; any person reputed uncommonly wise, and whose opinions have great weight.—**oracular,** o•rak′ū•lėr, *a.* Pertaining to an oracle or oracles; uttering oracles; resembling the utterance of an oracle; authoritative; sententious; ambiguous, like the ancient oracles.—**oracularly,** o•rak′ū•lėr•li, *adv.* In the manner of an oracle.

oral, ō′ral, *a.* [Fr., from L. *or*, *oris*, the mouth. ORACLE.] Uttered by the mouth or in words; spoken, not written; *zool.* pertaining to the mouth of animals.—**orally,** ō′ral•li, *adv.* In an oral manner; by word of mouth; verbally.

orange, or′anj, *n.* [Fr. *orange*, It. *arancia*, *arancio*, Sp. *naranja*, from Ar. *nâranj*, an orange, the form of the word being influenced by Fr. *or*, gold.] A tree cultivated abundantly in the south of Europe, the Azores, America, etc., and also its fruit, which is imported into other countries in great quantities.—*a.* Belonging to an orange; colored as an orange.—**orangeade,** or•anj•ād′, *n.* Drink made from orange juice or flavored with orange peel.—**orange pekoe,** *n.* An Indian or Ceylon black tea.—**orangery,** or′an•jėr•i, *n.* [Fr. *orangerie.*] A place where oranges are cultivated; a house for orange trees.

Orangeman, or′anj•man, *n.* [From William III of England, Prince of *Orange*, a place now in France.] A member of a secret society instituted in Ireland in 1795, to uphold Protestant ascendency, and to oppose the Catholic religion and influence.—**Orangeism,** or′anj•izm, *n.* The tenets or principles of the Orangemen.

orangutan, orangoutang, o•rang′ö•tan, o•rang′ö•tang, *n.* [Malay *orangutan*, lit. man of the woods.] One of the largest of the anthropoid apes, a native of Sumatra and Borneo.

oration, o•rā′shon, *n.* [L. *oratio*, from *oro*, *oratum*, to pray. ORACLE.] A speech or discourse composed according to the rules of oratory, and spoken in public; a set speech; a formal discourse pronounced on a special occasion.—**orate,** or•āt′, *v.i.* To deliver an oration, with undercurrent idea of pomposity.—**orator,** or′a•tėr, *n.* [L.] A public speaker; one who delivers an oration; one who is skilled as a speaker; an eloquent man.—**oratorical,** or•a•tor′i•kal, *a.* Pertaining to an orator or to oratory; rhetorical.—**oratorically,** or•a•tor′i•kal•li, *adv.* In an oratorical manner.—**oratorio,** or•a•tō′ri•ō, *n.* [It.] A sacred musical composition, consisting of airs, recitatives, duets, trios, choruses, etc., the subject of which is generally taken from Scripture.—**oratory,** or′a•to•ri, *n.* [Partly from *orator*, partly from L. *oratorium*, a place of prayer.] The art of public speaking; the art of an orator; exercise of eloquence; eloquence; a place for prayer; a small apartment for private devotions.—*Priests of the Oratory*, a religious order, the members of which are not bound by any special vow.

orb, orb, *n.* [Fr. *orbe*, from L. *orbis*, a circle, a ring, a disk; seen also in *orbit*, *exorbitant.*] A spherical body; a sphere or globe; also a circular body or disk; *anc. astron.* a hollow globe or sphere forming part of the solar or sidereal system; *arch.* a plain circular boss. BOSS.—*v.i.*† To exhibit or assume the appearance of an orb.—*v.t.* To encircle; to enclose.—**orbed,** orbd, *a.* Having the form of an orb; round; circular.—**orbicular,** or•bik′ū•lėr, *a.* [L. *orbicularis.*] In the form of an orb; spherical; circular.—*Orbicular leaf*, a circular leaf with the stalk attached to the center of it.—*Orbicular muscles*, muscles with circular fibers surrounding some natural opening of the body.—**orbicularly,** or•bik′ū•lėr•li, *adv.* Spherically; circularly.—**orbiculate, orbiculated,** or•bik′ū•lāt, or•bik′ū•lā•ted, *a.* [L. *orbiculatus.*] In the form of an orb; orbicular.

orbit, or′bit, *n.* [L. *orbita*, a wheel-track, a circuit, from *orbis*, an orb. ORB.] The path of a planet or comet through space; the curved line which a planet describes in its periodical revolution round its central body (the *orbit* of Jupiter or Mercury); *anat.* the bony cavity in which the eye is situated; *ornith.* the skin which surrounds the eye of a bird.—**orbital,** or′bi•tal, *a.* Pertaining to an orbit.—**orbitary,** or′bi•ta•ri, *a.* Connected with or surrounding the orbit (*orbitary* feathers).

orcein, or′sē•in, *n.* The chief ingredient of archil, a purple dyestuff obtained from orcinol (which see).

orchard, or′chėrd, *n.* [A.Sax. *ortgeard*, *wyrtgeard*, lit. a wort-yard; so Dan. *urtgaard*, Goth. *aurti-gards*, a garden. WORT, YARD.] A garden‡; an enclosure devoted to the culture of fruit growing or nut-bearing trees.—**orchardist,** or′chėrd•ist, *n.* One that cultivates orchards; a fruit grower.

orchestra, or′kes•tra, *n.* [Gr. *orchēstra*, from *orcheomai*, to dance.] The part of a theater appropriated to the musicians; in the Grecian theaters a part of the stage allotted to the chorus; the whole instrumental band performing together in public places of amusement.—**orchestral,** or•kes′tral, *a.* Pertaining to an orchestra.—**orchestration,** or•kes•trā′shon, *n.* The arrangement of music for an orchestra; instrumentation.

orchid, orchis, or′kid, or′kis, *n.* [Gr. *orchis*, a testicle, hence an orchid, from the form of the root.] The name of a family of perennial plants, with tuberous fleshy roots, and beautiful flowers of remarkable form, found almost everywhere and prized by florists; a light reddish-blue color.—**orchidaceous,** or•ki•dā′shus, *a.* Pertaining to the orchids.

orcinol, orcin, or′si•nōl, or′sin, *n.* [Fr. *orcine*, from *orchella.*] A colorless phenol obtained from lichens celebrated as dyeweeds (orchella-weed).

ordain, or•dān′, *v.t.* [O.E. *ordeyne*, *ordeine*, O.Fr. *ordener* (Fr. *ordonner*), from L. *ordino*, to order, from *ordo*, *ordinis*, order. ORDER.] To set in order or arrange‡; to decree, appoint, establish, institute; to set apart for an office; to invest with ministerial or sacerdotal functions.—**ordainer,** or•dā′nėr, *n.* One who ordains.—*Ordainers*, the Committee of Regency, composed of twenty-one members, named by Parliament in 1310, to draw up a scheme for the better management of the realm, in opposition to Edward II and Piers Gaveston.—**ordainment,** or•dān′ment, *n.* The act of ordaining; *eccles.* an appointment to a church.

ordeal, or•dē′al, *n.* [A.Sax. *ordél, ordál*, decision, ordeal, lit. *out-deal* (like D. *oordeel*, G. *urtheil*, a decision), from A.Sax. prefix *or*, Goth. *us*, out, and verb meaning to *deal*. DEAL.] An ancient form of trial to determine guilt or innocence, as by causing the accused to handle red-hot iron or put the hand into boiling water, escape from injury being considered a proof of innocence; hence, any severe trial or strict test.

order, or′dėr, *n.* [Fr. *ordre*, from L. *ordo, ordinis*, a row, a regular series, from root *or*, seen in *orient, origin*; connected are *ordain, ordinary, ordinance, extraordinary, subordinate*, etc.] Regular disposition or methodical arrangement; established succession; a proper state or condition; the established usage or settled method; regularity; public tranquillity; absence of confusion or disturbance; a mandate, precept, or authoritative direction; a rule or regulation, oral or written; a direction, demand, or commission to supply goods; a written direction to pay money; a free pass for admission to a theater or other place of entertainment; a rank or class of men; a body of men of the same rank or profession constituting a separate class in the community; a religious fraternity; a body of men having had a common honorary distinction conferred on them; the distinction, rank, or dignity itself (the *order* of the Garter); a large division in the classification of natural objects, as plants or animals; *arch.* a column entire, with a superincumbent entablature, viewed as forming an architectural whole, there being five architectural orders, viz. Doric, Ionic, Tuscan, Corinthian, and Composite.—*Close order*, said of the ranks of soldiers when drawn up at the distance of a pace between each other.—*General orders*, the commands or notices which military headquarters issue on routine matters of general importance. *Holy orders*, the clerical or ecclesiastical character conferred on a person by ordination or consecration to the ministry in the church; often used without the word 'holy' (*to be in orders, to take orders*).—*In order*, for the purpose; with a view; to the end; as means to an end.—*Religious orders*, religious brotherhoods or communities, as monastic, military, and mendicant *orders*.—*Standing orders*, certain general rules and instructions in force until specifically changed, as in a military post or legislative body.—*Order in council*, an order issued by the British sovereign, by and with the advice of the privy-council.—*Order of battle*, the arrangement and disposition of the different parts of an army for the purpose of engaging an enemy.—*Order of the day*, a parliamentary phrase denoting the business regularly set down for consideration on the minutes or votes; *milit.* specific directions issued by a superior officer to the troops under his command.—*v.t.* To put in order; to dispose or arrange; to manage or conduct; to command; to give an order to; to give an order or commission for.—*v.i.* To give command or direction.—**orderliness,** or′dėr•li•nes, *n.* The state or quality of being orderly; regularity.—**orderly,** or′dėr•li, *a.* In accordance with good order; well ordered; methodical; regular; *milit.* being on duty (an *orderly* officer).—*n.* A private soldier or noncommissioned officer who attends on a superior officer to carry orders or messages.—*adv.* According to due order.

ordinal, or′di•nal, *a.* [L. *ordinalis*, from *ordo, ordinis*, a row. ORDER.] Applied to a number which expresses order or succession (the *ordinal* numbers, *first, second, third*, etc.); *nat. hist.* pertaining to an order.—*n.* A number denoting order (as *first*); a book containing the ordination service.

ordinance, or′di•nans, *n.* [O.Fr. *ordenance* (Fr. *ordonnance*), from *ordener*, to ordain. ORDAIN.] A rule established by authority; a law, edict, decree, or the like; an established rite or ceremony; a law or provision enacted by a municipal government for local application.

ordinary, or′di•ne•ri, *a.* [L. *ordinarius*, from *ordo, ordinis*, order. ORDER.] Established; regular; customary; common; usual; frequent; habitual; met with at any time; hence, somewhat inferior; of little merit.—*Ordinary seaman*, a seaman capable of the common duties, but not considered fit to be rated as an able seaman.—*n.* A person who has ordinary or immediate jurisdiction in matters ecclesiastical; an ecclesiastical judge (usually a bishop); a meal prepared for all comers, as distinguished from one specially ordered; an eating house where there is a fixed price for the meal; one of the common heraldic figures formed with straight lines (as the bend, cross, saltire).—*In ordinary*, in actual and constant service; statedly attending and serving (a physician or chaplain *in ordinary*). An ambassador *in ordinary* is one constantly resident at a foreign court.—*Lord Ordinary*, one of the five judges of the Scottish Court of Session constituting the Outer House.—A ship *in ordinary* is one not in actual service, but laid up under the direction of a competent person.—**ordinarily,** or′di•ne•ri•li, *adv.* In an ordinary manner; usually; generally; in most cases.

ordinate, or′di•nāt, *a.* [L. *ordinatus*, well-ordered. ORDINARY.] Regular; methodical.—*n. Geom.* one of those lines of reference which determine the position of a point; a straight line drawn from a point in the abscissa. The abscissa and ordinate, when spoken of together, are called *coordinates*. See CO-ORDINATE.

ordination, or•di•nā′shon, *n.* [L. *ordinatio*, regulation, from *ordino*, to ordain.] The act of ordaining; the act of settling or establishing; appointment; settled order of things; the act of conferring holy orders.

ordnance, ord′nans, *n.* [Same as *ordinance*, Fr. *ordonnance*, arrangement, equipment; originally it had reference to guns of a particular size or equipment.] Cannon, mortars and howitzers collectively; artillery and small arms, ammunition and supplies, equipment for manufacture and repair of ordnance; equipment and supplies for naval warfare.—*Ordnance Department*, U.S., the department in charge of arsenals and depots and the purchase, manufacture and distribution of ordnance to the army and militia.

Ordovician, or′dō•vish″an, *n.* [L. *Ordovices*, a North Welsh tribe.] A series of strata succeeding the CAMBRIAN (which see).

ordure, or′dūr, *n.* [Fr. *ordure*, from O.Fr. *ord*, at. *ordo*, filthy, from L. *horridus*, horrid.] Dung; excrement; feces.

ore, ōr, *n.* [A.Sax. *âr*, brass, copper = Icel. *eir*, brass, O.G. *êr*, Goth. *aiz*, ore; cog. L. *aes, aeris*, ore, brass; Skr. *ayas*, iron.] A mineral consisting of a metal and some other substance, as oxygen, sulfur, or carbon, in combination, being the source from which metals are usually obtained by smelting (metals found free from such combination being called *native metals*); metal, sometimes gold (*poetical*).

oread, ō′ri•ad, *n.* [Gr. *oreias, oreiados*; from *oros*, mountain.] A mountain nymph.

organ, or′gan, *n.* [L. *organum*, from Gr. *organon*, an instrument, implement, from *ergō*, to work; same root as E. *work*.] An instrument or means; that which performs some office, duty, or function; more commonly, a part of an animal or vegetable by which some function is carried on (as the heart, the eye); a means of communication between one person or body of persons and another; a medium of conveying certain opinions; specifically, a newspaper; the largest and most harmonious of wind instruments of music, consisting of a great number of pipes and with keys similar to those of the piano.—**organic,** or•gan′ik, *a.* [L. *organicus*.] Pertaining to an organ or to organs of animals and plants; pertaining to objects that have organs, hence to the animal and vegetable worlds; exhibiting animal or vegetable life and functions (*organic* bodies, tissues, etc.); forming a whole with a systematic arrangement of parts; organized; systematized.—*Organic chemistry*. CHEMISTRY.—*Organic disease*, a disease in which the structure of an organ is morbidly altered; opposed to *functional disease*.—*Organic laws*, laws directly concerning the fundamental parts of the constitution of a state.—*Organic remains*, those organized bodies, whether animals or vegetables, found in a fossil state.—*Organic selection*, the co-operation of ACCOMMODATION and ADAPTATION (which see) in the production of new species.—**organically,** or•gan′i•kal•li, *adv.* In an organic manner; by or with organs.—

organism, or′gan•izm, *n.* Organic structure; a body exhibiting organization and organic life; member of the animal or the vegetable kingdom. —**organist,** or′gan•ist, *n.* One who plays on the organ.—**organizable,** or•gan•īz′a•bl, *a.* Capable of being organized.—**organization,** or•gan•i•zā″shon, *n.* The act or process of organizing; the act of systematizing or arranging; a whole or aggregate that is organized; organic structure; arrangement of parts or organs for the performance of vital functions.—**organize,** or′gan•īz, *v.t.—organized, organizing.* To give an organic structure to; to arrange the several parts of for action or work; to establish and systematize.—**organizer,** or′gan•īz•ėr, *n.* One who organizes, establishes, or systematizes.—**organogenesis,** or′gan•ō•jen″•e•sis, *n.* [Gr. *organon,* an organ, and *genesis,* birth.] The development of an organ or of organs in plants or animals.—**organography,** or•gan•og′ra•fi, *n.* A description of the organs of plants or animals.—**organology,** or•gan•ol′o•ji, *n.* The physiology of the different organs of animals or plants.—**organon, organum,** or′ga•non, or′ga•num, *n.* A body of rules and canons for the direction of the scientific faculty. The *Novum Organum* of Bacon is the new, in relation to the old or Aristotelian method or instrument of logical thought.—**organotherapy,** or•gan′ō•thėr″a•pi, *n.* [Gr. *organon,* and *therapeuō,* I heal.] *Med.* the use of animal extracts for curative and other purposes.

organdy, organdie, or′gan•di, *n.* [Fr. *organdi.*] A fine muslin, plain or figured.

organzine, or′gan•zin, *n.* [Fr. *organsin,* It. *organzino.*] A silk thread of several threads twisted together; a fabric made of such thread.

orgasm, or′gazm, *n.* [Gr. *orgasmos,* from *orgaō,* to swell.] Extreme excitement or action, especially in coition. —**orgasmic,** or′gaz•mik, *a.*

orgeat, or′zhat, *n.* [Fr., from *orge,* barley.] A preparation extracted from barley and almonds, used to mix in certain drinks, or medicinally as a mild demulcent.

orgy, or′ji, *n.* [Gr. *orgia,* secret rites, from *orgē,* violent passion, anger.] Secret rites or ceremonies connected with the worship of some of the Greek deities, hence, a wild or frantic revel; drunken revelry.—**orgiastic,** or′jē•as″tik, *a.*

oriel, ō′ri•el, *n.* [O.Fr. *oriol,* L.L. *oriolum,* a porch, a hall; origin doubtful.] A large window projecting from a wall, and forming a bay or recess inside; a bay window.

orient, ō′ri•ent, *a.* [L. *oriens,* rising, ppr. of *orior, ortus,* to arise; whence also *origin, (ab)ortion*; root also in *order.*] Rising, as the sun or moon; eastern; oriental; bright; shining.—*The Orient,* the East; oriental countries.—*v.t.* [Fr. *orienter.*] *Surv.* to define the position of, in respect to the east or other points of the compass.—**oriental,** o•ri•en′tal, *a.* Eastern; situated in the east; proceeding from the east; applied to gems as a mark of excellence; precious: opposed to *occidental.*—*Oriental region,* southern Asia, together with the western part of the East Indies, the Philippines, and Formosa.—*n.* [*cap.*] A native of some eastern part of the world; an Asiatic.—**orientalism,** ō•ri•en′tal•izm, *n.* An eastern mode of thought or expression; erudition in oriental languages or literature.—**orientalist,** ō•ri•en′tal•ist, *n.* An oriental; one versed in the eastern languages and literature.—**orientalize,** ō•ri•en′tal•īz, *v.t.* To render oriental or conformed to oriental manners.—**orientate,** ō′ri•en•tāt, *v.t.* To cause to assume an easterly direction.—**orientation,** ō′ri•en•tā″shon, *n.* A turning toward the east; position east and west; as applied to churches, such a position as that the chancel shall point to the east; the determining of one′s position with reference to new ideas, etc.

orifice, or′i•fis, *n.* [Fr. *orifice,* from L. *orificium—os, oris,* the mouth, and *facio,* to make. ORAL.] The mouth or aperture of a tube, pipe, or other similar object; a perforation; an opening; a vent.

oriflamme, or′i•flam, *n.* [Fr., from L. *aurum,* gold, *flamma,* flame.] The ancient royal standard of France; a piece of red silk fixed on a gilt spear with the anterior edge cut into points.

origami, o•ri•gam′ē, *n.* [Jap.] The Japanese art of folding paper into various shapes.

origin, or′i•jin, *n.* [Fr. *origine,* from L. *origo, originis,* from *orior,* to rise. ORIENT.] The first existence or beginning of anything; the commencement; fountain; source; that from which anything primarily proceeds; of a muscle, the end attached to a relatively fixed part.—**original,** o•rij′i•nal, *a.* [L. *originalis.*] Pertaining or belonging to the origin or early state of something; primitive; pristine; having the power to originate new thoughts or combinations of thought; produced by an author; not copied.—*Original sin, theol.* the first sin of Adam, namely, the eating of the forbidden fruit; hence, either the imputation of Adam's sin to his posterity, or that corruption of nature and tendency to sin inherited from him.—*n.* Origin; source; first copy; archetype; that from which anything is copied; a work not copied from another, but the work of an artist himself; the language in which any work is composed as distinguished from a translation; a person of marked individuality of character; a primary stock or type from which varieties have been developed.—**originality,** o•rij′i•nal″i•ti, *n.* The quality or state of being original; the power of originating new thoughts, or uncommon combinations of thought. — **originally,** o•rij′i•nal•li, *adv.* In an original manner; at the very beginning; from the first.—**originate,** o•rij′i•nāt, *v.t.—originated, originating.* To give origin or beginning to; to cause to be; to produce.—*v.i.* To take first existence; to have origin.—**origination,** o•rij′i•nā″shon, *n.* The act or mode of originating; production.—**originative,** o•rij′i•nā•tiv, *a.* Having power to originate.—**originatively,** o•rij′i•nā•tiv•li, *adv.* In an originative manner.—**originator,** o•rij′i•nā•tėr, *n.* A person who originates.

oriole, ō′ri•ōl, *n.* [O.Fr. *oriol,* from L. *aureolus,* dim. of *aureus,* golden, from *aurum,* gold.] Any of the species of the genus *Icterus,* family Icteridae, an American song bird of brilliant color, chiefly orange and black.

Orion, ō•rī′on, *n.* [A celebrated hunter of Greek mythology.] A constellation represented by the figure of a man with a sword by his side, three stars on a line forming his *belt.*

orison, or′i•zon, *n.* [O.Fr. *orison, oreison,* from L. *oratio,* a prayer, from *oro,* to pray. *Oration* is a doublet of this.] A prayer or supplication. (*Poet.*)

orle, orl, *n.* [Fr. *orle,* dim. from L. *ora,* a border.] *Her.* a figure on an escutcheon resembling a smaller escutcheon with the interior cut out; *arch.* a fillet under the ovolo of a capital (also called *orlet*).

orlon, or′lon, *n.* [From the trademark *Orlon.*] An acrylic fiber used in knitted goods; a fabric made of orlon fiber.

orlop, or′lop, *n.* [D. *overloop—over,* over, and *loopen,* to run. OVER, LEAP.] *Naut.* the lowest deck in a ship of war or merchant vessel that has three decks; sometimes a temporary deck.

ormer, or′mėr, *n.* [Fr. *ormier,* L. *auris maris,* ear of the sea.] An edible univalve shellfish.

ormolu, or′mo•lū, *n.* [Fr. *or-moulu—or,* gold, and *moulu,* pp. of *moudre,* L. *molere,* to grind.] A variety of brass containing 25 per cent zinc and 75 per cent copper, made to imitate gold.

ornament, or′na•ment, *n.* [Fr. *ornement,* L. *ornamentum,* from *orno, ornatum,* to adorn.] That which embellishes or adorns; something which, added to another thing, renders it more beautiful to the eye; decoration; fair outward show; that which adds beauty to the mind or character.—*v.t.* To adorn; to embellish.—**ornamental,** or•na•men′tal, *a.* Serving to ornament; pertaining to ornament.—**ornamentally,** or•na•men′tal•li, *adv.* In an ornamental manner.—**ornamentation,** or′na•men•tā″shon, *n.* The act of ornamenting; the ornaments or decorations produced.

ornate, or′nāt, *a.* [L. *ornatus,* pp. of *orno,* to adorn. ORNAMENT.] Adorned; decorated; ornamental; richly and artistically finished; much embellished.—**ornately,** or′nāt•li, *adv.* In an ornate manner.—**ornateness,** or′nāt•nes, *n.*

ornery, or′nėr•i, *a.* [Corruption of *ordinary.*] Cross in disposition or temper.—**orneriness,** or′nėr•i•nes, *n.*

ornis, or′nis, *n.* [Gr. *ornis,* a bird.] The birds of a region, or its avifauna.

ornithic, or•nith′ik, *a.* [Gr. *ornis,*

ornithos, a bird.] Of or pertaining to birds.—**ornithological,** or′ni•tho•loj″i•kal, *a.* Pertaining to ornithology. —**ornithologist,** or•ni•thol′o•jist, *n.* A person skilled in ornithology.—**ornithology,** or•ni•thol′o•ji, *n.* That branch of zoology which treats of the form, structure, classification, and habits of birds.—**ornithopter,** or•ni•thop′tėr, *n.* [Gr. *pteron*, wing.] A form of aircraft deriving its support and propelling force from flapping surfaces.—**ornithorhynchus,** or′ni•thō•ring″kus, *n.* [Gr. *rhynchos*, a beak.] An oviparous mammal of Australia and Tasmania, one of the monotremata, with a body like that of an otter, a horny beak resembling that of a duck, and webbed feet; the duckbill, duck-mole, or water-mole.

orogeny, o•roj′e•ni, *n.* [Gr. *oros*, mountain, and root *gen.* GENUS.] The origin and formation of mountains.

orography, o•rog′ra•fi, *n.* [Gr. *oros*, a mountain, and *graphō*, to describe.] The science which describes or treats of the mountains and mountain systems of the globe; orology.—**orographic, orographical,** or•o•graf′ik, or•o•graf′i•kal, *a.* Relating to orography.

oroide, o′rō•id, *n.* [Fr. *or*, gold, and Gr. *eidos*, resemblance.] An alloy resembling gold in appearance, and used in the manufacture of cheap watchcases, trinkets, etc.—**orology,** o•rol′o•ji, *n.* [Gr. *oros*, a mountain, and *logos*, discourse.] A description of mountains; orography.—**orological,** or•o•loj′i•kal, *a.* Pertaining to orology.—**orologist,** o•rol′o•jist, *n.* A describer of mountains; one versed in orology.

orotund, or′o•tund, *a.* [L. *os*, *oris*, the mouth, and *rotundus*, round, rotund.] *Rhet.* characterized by fullness, richness, and clearness; rich and musical: applied to the voice or manner of utterance.

orphan, or′fan, *n.* [Gr. *orphanos*, orphaned; allied to L. *orbus*, bereaved.] A child bereft of both parents.—*a.* Being an orphan; bereaved of parents.—*v.t.* To reduce to the state of an orphan; to bereave of parents, children, or friends.—**orphanage,** or′fan•ij, *n.* The state of an orphan; a home or institution for the care of orphans.

orphean, or•fē′an, *a.* Pertaining to *Orpheus*, the legendary poet and musician of ancient Greece; hence melodious.—**orpheon,** or′fe•on, *n.* A kind of musical instrument.—**orphic,** or′fik, *a.* Orphean.

orpiment, or′pi•ment, *n.* [Fr. *orpiment*, from L. *auripigmentum—aurum*, gold, and *pigmentum*, a pigment.] A mineral substance, a compound of sulfur and arsenic, of a brilliant yellow color, forming the basis of the yellow paint called *king's-yellow.*—*Red orpiment*, a name of *realgar*.

orpine, or′pīn, *n.* [Fr. *orpin.*] An herb of the stonecrop species, or sedum.

orrery, or′e•ri, *n.* A machine that represents, by the movements of its parts, the motions and phases of the planets in their orbits, named after an Earl of *Orrery*.

orris, or′is, *n.* [Fr. *or*, gold.] A sort of gold or silver lace; a pattern in which gold and silver lace is worked.

orris, or′is, *n.* [Corruption of *iris.*] A plant from which is obtained orrisroot.—**orrisroot,** *n.* The root of three species of iris which, in its dried state, is used in perfume.

ort, ort, *n.* [L.G. *ort*, O.D. *oorete*, remnants of food; from *or*, as in *ordeal*, and verb to *eat* (D. *eten*).] A scrap of food left; a fragment; a piece of refuse, commonly in the plural.

orthoclase, or′tho•klāz, *n.* [Gr. *orthos*, straight, and *klasis*, fracture.] A kind of feldspar with a straight flat fracture.

orthodontia, or•tho•don′ti•a, *n.* [Gr. *orthos*, straight, and Gr. *odontos*, teeth.] Dentistry dealing with the prevention and correction of irregularities of the teeth.—**orthodontic,** or•tho•don′tik, *a.*

orthodox, or′tho•doks, *a.* [Gr. *orthodoxos*, sound in the faith—*orthos*, right, and *doxa*, opinion (akin *dogma*).] Sound in opinion or doctrine; particularly, sound in religious opinions or doctrines: opposed to *heterodox*; in accordance with sound doctrine; sound; correct (an *orthodox* faith or proceeding).—**orthodoxly,** or′tho•doks•li, *adv.* In an orthodox way; with soundness of faith.—**orthodoxy,** or′tho•dok•si, *n.* [Gr. *orthodoxia.*] Soundness of faith; correctness of opinion or doctrine, especially in religious matters.

orthoëpy, or′thō•e•pi or or•thō′e•pi, *n.* [Gr. *orthoepeia—orthos*, right, *epos*, a word.] The art of uttering words with propriety; a correct pronunciation of words.—**orthoëpic,** or•thō•ep′ik, *a.* Pertaining to orthoëpy.—**orthoëpist,** or′thō•ep•ist or or•thō′•ep•ist, *n.* One who is skilled in orthoëpy; one who writes on orthoëpy.

orthogamy, or•thog′a•mi, *n.* [Gr. *orthos*, straight, and *gamos*, marriage.] *Bot.* direct or immediate fertilization without the intervention of any mediate agency.

orthogenesis, or′tho•jen″e•sis, *n.* [Gr. *genesis*, origin.] The view of evolution by which all variations follow a defined direction, and are not simply accidental.

orthognathic, orthognathous, or•thōg•nath′ik, or•thog′na•thus, *a.* [Gr. *orthos*, straight, and *gnathos*, a jaw.] Having jaws that do not protrude; having a skull in which the forehead does not recede and the jaws project. See PROGNATHIC.

orthogonal, or•thog′on•al, *a.* Right-angled.—**orthogonally,** or•thog′on•al•li, *adv.* With or at right angles.

orthography, or•thog′ra•fi, *n.* [Gr. *orthographia—orthos*, right, and *graphē*, writing.] The art of writing words with the proper letters; spelling; the part of grammar which treats of letters and spellings.—**orthographer,** or•thog′ra•fėr, *n.*—**orthographic, orthographical,** or•tho•graf′ik, or•tho•graf′i•kal, *a.* Pertaining to orthography.—*Orthographic projection*, a projection used in drawing maps, etc., the eye being supposed to be at an infinite distance from the object.—**orthographically,** or•tho•graf′i•kal•li, *adv.* According to the rules of proper spelling; in the manner of the orthographic projection.

orthopedic, or•tho•pe′dik, *a.* [Gr. *orthos*, straight, and *pais*, a child.] Referring to the remedying of deformities; pertaining to orthopedics. —**orthopedics,** or•tho•pē′diks, *n.* A branch of surgery dealing with the correction or deformities and with the treatment of chronic diseases of the joints and spine.—**orthopedist,** *n.* A surgeon who practices orthopedics.

orthopter, orthopteran, or•thop′•tėr, or•thop′tėr•an, *n.* [Gr. *orthos*, straight, and *pteron*, a wing.] One of an order of insects which have four wings, the anterior pair being semi-coriaceous or leathery, the posterior pair folding longitudinally like a fan, such as the cockroaches, grasshoppers, and locusts.—**orthopterous,** or•thop′tėr•us, *a.* Pertaining to the orthopterans.

orthoscopic, or•tho•skop′ik, *a.* [Gr. *orthos*, straight, and *skopeō*, to see.] Pertaining to or giving correct vision.

orthostichy, or•thos′ti•ki, *n.* [Gr. *orthos*, straight, *stichos*, a row.] A vertical row of leaves.

orthotropous, or•thot′ro•pus, *a.* [Gr. *orthos*, straight, and *trepō*, to turn.] *Bot.* having an ovule with the foramen opposite the hilum, or an embryo with radicle next the hilum.

ortolan, or′to•lan, *n.* [It. *ortolano*, from L. *hortulanus*, from *hortus*, a garden; it frequents the hedges of gardens.] A European bird of the bunting family, much esteemed for the delicacy of its flesh; in the United States, the bobolink.

oryx, o′riks, *n.* [L. and Gr.] A name for a species of antelope, a native of the countries on both sides of the Red Sea; also the gemsbok of South Africa.

Osage orange, ō′sāj, *n.* A North American tree of the mulberry family, producing large yellow fruits resembling an orange, but not edible.

Oscan, os′kan, *n.* An ancient Italian language, of which a few fragments remain; allied to the Latin.

oscillate, os′sil•lāt, *v.i.*—*oscillated*, *oscillating.* [L. *oscillo*, *oscillatum*, from *oscillum*, a little face or mask hung to a tree and swaying with the wind, dim. of *os*, the mouth, the face. ORACLE.] To swing; to move backward and forward; to vibrate; to vary or fluctuate between fixed limits. —**oscillation,** os•sil•lā′shon, *n.* [L. *oscillatio.*] The act or state of oscillating or swinging backward and forward; vibration.—**oscillator,** os′•sil•lā•tėr, *n.* One who or that which oscillates.—**oscillatory,** os′sil•la•to•ri, *a.* Moving backward and forward like a pendulum.—**oscillograph,** os•sil′lo•graf, *n.* [Gr. *graphein*, to write.]

An instrument for indicating alternating-current wave forms.

oscitancy, os´si•tan•si, *n.* [L. *oscito*, to yawn, from *os*, the mouth.] The act of gaping or yawning; sleepiness; drowsiness.

osculate, os´kū•lāt, *v.t.—osculated, osculating.* [L. *osculor*, to kiss, from *osculum*, a kiss, dim. of *os*, the mouth. ORACLE.] To salute with a kiss; to kiss; *geom.* to touch, as one curve another.—*v.i.* To kiss one another; to kiss; *geom.* to touch at a point, as two curves coming in contact.—**osculation,** os•kū•lā´shon, *n.* The act of osculating; a kissing; specifically, *geom.* the contact between any given curve and another curve.—*Point of osculation*, the point where the osculation takes place, and where the two curves have the same curvature.—**osculatory,** os´kū•la•to•ri, *a.* Pertaining to osculation or kissing.—**osculum,** os´kū•lum, *n.* pl. **oscula,** os´kū•la. *Lit.* a little mouth; *zool.* one of the large exhalant apertures by which a sponge is perforated; one of the suckers of the tapeworms, etc.

osier, ō´zhi•ėr, *n.* [Fr. *osier*, Fr. dial. *oisis*, Armor. *ozil*, *aozil*, an osier; comp. Gr. *oisos*, an osier.] The name of various species of willow, chiefly employed in basket making.—*a.* Made of osier or twigs; like osier.

Osiris, ō•sī´ris, *n.* The great Egyptian deity, the husband of Isis, and the personification of all physical and moral good.

osmium, os´mi•um, *n.* [Gr. *osmē*, odor.] A bluish-white metal, very hard, and more infusible than any other metal. Symbol, Os; at. no., 76; at. wt., 190.2.

osmose, os´mōs, *v.t.* [Gr. *ōsmos*, an impulse, a pushing, from *ōtheō*, to push.] *Chem.* to subject to diffusion through a membrane.—**osmosis,** os•mō´sis, *n.* The tendency of two solutions of different concentration, separated by a membrane with very fine pores, to pass through the membrane, mix with each other, and equalize their concentration. (The living cells of plant and animal tissues have such membranes and many of their activities depend upon osmosis.)—**osmotic,** os•mot´ik, *a.* Pertaining to osmosis.—*Osmotic pressure*, pressure exerted on a membrane through which solutions of different density are diffusing, the pressure being in the direction of the less dense solution.—**osmotically,** os•mot´i•ka•li, *adv.*

osmund, os´mund, *n.* [Fr. *osmonde.*] Any fern of the genus *Osmunda*; especially the royal fern.

osprey, os´prā, *n.* [Corrupted from *ossifrage*, L. *ossifraga*, lit. the bone-breaker—*os*, a bone, and *frango*, to break.] A well-known rapacious bird which feeds almost entirely on fish captured by suddenly darting upon them when near the surface.

ossein, os´sē•in, *n.* [From L. *osseus*, bony, from *os*, *ossis*, a bone; akin Gr. *osteon*, Skr. *asthi*, a bone.] Bone tissue; the soft glue-like substance of bone left after the removal of the earths.—**osseous,** os´si•us, *a.* [L. *osseus.*] Bony; resembling bone.—**ossicle,** os´i•kl, *n.* [L. *ossiculum*, dim. from *os*, a bone.] A small bone; some of the small bones of the human skeleton, as those of the internal ear; a small hard structure in starfishes, etc.—**ossification,** os´si•fi•kā″shon, *n.* The act of ossifying; the change or process of changing into a bony substance.—**ossifrage,** os´si•frāj, *n.* [L. *ossifraga.* OSPREY.] A name formerly given to the osprey or its young.—**ossify,** os´si•fī, *v.t.—ossified, ossifying.* [L. *os*, *ossis*, bone, and *facio*, to form.] To form into bone; to change from a soft animal substance into bone, or a substance of the hardness of bones.—*v.i.* To become bone or bony.—**ossuary,** os´sū•a•ri, *n.* [L. *ossuarium.*] A charnel house; a place where the bones of the dead are deposited.

osteal, os´ti•al, *a.* [Gr. *osteon*, a bone. OSSEIN.] Consisting of or pertaining to bone.

ostensible, os•ten´si•bl, *a.* [Fr. *ostensible*, from L. *ostendo*, *ostensum*, to show—*ob*, toward, and *tendo*, to hold out. TEND, TENT.] Put forth as having a certain character, whether worthy of it or not; hence, frequently, apparent and not real; having something of sham or pretense; pretended; professed. ∴ Syn. under COLORABLE.—**ostensibly,** os•ten´si•bli, *adv.* In an ostensible manner; professedly.—**ostensive,** os•ten´siv, *a.* [Fr. *ostensif*, from L. *ostendo*, to show.] Showing; exhibiting.—**ostensively,** os•ten´siv•li, *adv.* In an ostensive manner.—**ostentation,** os•ten•tā´shon, *n.* [L. *ostentatio*, from *ostento*, to show off, to display, intens. of *ostendo.*] Ambitious display; pretentious parade; display dictated by vanity, or to invite praise or flattery.—**ostentatious,** os•ten•tā´shus, *a.* Characterized by ostentation; showy; intended for vain display.—**ostentatiously,** os•ten•tā´shus•li, *adv.* In an ostentatious manner.

osteological, os´ti•o•loj″i•kal, *a.* Pertaining to osteology.—**osteologist,** os•ti•ol´o•jist, *n.* One versed in osteology; one who describes the bones of animals.—**osteology,** os•ti•ol´o•ji, *n.* [Gr. *logos*, discourse.] That branch of anatomy which treats of bones and bone tissue.—**osteopath, osteopathist,** os´ti•o•path, os•ti•op´a•thist, *n.* One who practices osteopathy.—**osteopathy,** os•ti•op´a•thi, *n.* That system of the healing art which places the chief emphasis on the structural integrity of the body mechanism as the most important factor to maintain the organism in health.—**osteoplasty,** os´ti•o•plas•ti, *n.* [Gr. *plassō*, to form.] An operation by which the total or partial loss of a bone is remedied.—**osteotomy,** os•ti•ot´o•mi, *n.* [Gr. *tomē*, a cutting.] The dissection of bones.

osteomyelitis, os´tē•ō•mī•e•līt″is, *n.* [Gr. *osteo*, *oste*, from *osteon*, bone, and Gr. *myelitis*, from *myelos*, marrow, and Gr. suffix, *itis.*] Inflammation of the bone marrow.

ostiole, os´ti•ōl, *n.* [L. *ostiolum*, dim. of *ostium*, door.] A small orifice or opening, as in certain sacs or cells in plants.—**ostiolar,** *a.* Of or pertaining to an ostiole.

ostler, os´lėr, *n.* [HOSTEL.] Stableman.

ostracism, os´tra•sizm, *n.* [Gr. *ostrakismos*, from *ostrakon*, a shell, a voting tablet.] A political measure among the ancient Athenians by which persons considered dangerous to the state were banished by public vote for a term of years: so called because the votes were given on shells; banishment from society; expulsion.—**ostracize,** os´tra•sīz, *v.t.—ostracized, ostracizing.* To exile by ostracism; to banish from society; to exclude from public or private favor.

ostrich, os´trich, *n.* [O.Fr. *ostruche*, *ostruce*, Fr. *autruche*, from L. *avis*, a bird, and *struthio*, Gr. *struthiōn*, an ostrich.] A large running bird inhabiting the sandy plains of Africa and Arabia, the largest of all existing birds, and whose wing and tail feathers form plumes of great beauty and value; an allied bird of S. America.

Ostrogoth, os´tro•goth, *n.* [L.L. *ostrogothus*, from *ostrus*, eastern (G. *ost*, easti, and *Gothus*, a Goth.] One of the eastern Goths, as distinguished from the Visigoths or western Goths.—**ostrogothic,** os•tro•goth´ik, *a.* Pertaining to the Ostrogoths.

otalgia, ō•tal´ji•a, *n.* [Gr. *ous*, *ōtos*, the ear, and *algos*, pain.] A pain in the ear; earache.

other, ᴜᴛʜ´ėr, *a.* and *pron.* [A.Sax. *ōther*,=D. and G. *ander*, Icel. *annar*, Dan. *anden*, Goth. *anthar*; cog. Lith. *antras*, L. *alter*, Skr. *anyatara* (compar. of *anya*)—other; all comparative forms.] Not the same; different; second of two; additional (get *other* knowledge as well); not this; opposite (the *other* side of the street); often used reciprocally with *each*, and applicable to any number of individuals (help *each other*). It is also used substantively, and may take the plural number and the sign of the possessive case, and frequently is opposed to *some, one, I*, or the like (*some* were right, *others* were wrong; the *one* and the *other*).—*The other day*, a day just past; quite recently.—*Every other*, every second (*every other* day, *every other* week).—**otherness,** ᴜᴛʜ´ėr•nes, *n.*—**otherwhere,** ᴜᴛʜ´ėr•hwâr, *n.* In some other place; elsewhere.—**otherwise,** ᴜᴛʜ´ėr•wīz, *adv.* In a different manner; differently; not so; by other causes; in other respects.—**other world,** *n.* Pertaining to a world beyond the actual world.—**otherworldly,** ᴜᴛʜ″er•world´li, *a.* Concerned with a world to come.—**otherworldliness,** ᴜᴛʜ´er•world″li•nes, *n.*

otic, ō´tik, *a.* [Fr. *otique*, from Gr. *ous*, *otos*, the ear.] Belonging or relating to the ear.

otiose, ō´shi•ōs, *a.* [L. *otiosus*, from *otium*, leisure.] Idle; unemployed; useless; futile; needless; being at leisure.—**otiosity,** ō•shi•os´i•ti, *n.* The state or quality of being otiose.

otitis, ō•tī′tis, *n.* [Gr. *ous*, *ōtos*, the ear, and term. *-itis*, signifying inflammation.] Inflammation of the tympanic cavity of the ear, accompanied with intense pain.—**otocyst**, ō′to•sist, *n.* [Gr. *kystis*, a bladder.] In animals, a sense organ in the form of a minute sac containing calcareous particles suspended in fluid. Probably concerned with space perception and maintenance of equilibrium.—**otolith**, ō′to•lith, *n.* [Gr. *lithos*, a stone.] A name of small calcareous bodies contained in the ear cavities of some of the lower animals.—**otology**, ō•tol′o•ji, *n.* That branch of anatomy which concerns itself with the ear.—**otorrhea**, ō•tor•rē′a, *n.* [Gr. *rheō*, to flow.] A purulent discharge from the ears.—**otoscope**, ō′to•skōp, *n.* *Surg.* an instrument for examining the interior of the ear.

ottar, ot′tär, *n.* See ATTAR.

ottava rima, ot•tä′va rē′ma, *n.* [It., eighth or octuple rhyme.] An Italian form of versification consisting of eight lines, of which the first six rhyme alternately and the last two form a couplet.

G. *otter*, Dan. *odder*, Icel. *otr*; cog. Lith. *udra*, Rus. and Pol. *wydra*, same root as *water*.] A digitigrade carnivorous mammal of amphibious habits, there being several species; they feed on fish, and their fur is much prized.

otto, ot′tō. See ATTAR.

Ottoman, ot′to•man, *a.* [From *Othoman* or *Osman*, the sultan who laid the foundation of the Turkish Empire in Asia.] Pertaining to or derived from the Turks.—*n.* A Turk; [not cap.] a kind of couch or sofa introduced from Turkey; a footstool.

oubliette, ö•bli•et′, *n.* [Fr., from *oublier*, L. *obliviscor*, to forget. OBLIVION.] A dungeon with an opening only at the top for the admission of air, used for persons condemned to perpetual imprisonment, or to perish secretly, and existing in some old castles or other buildings.

ouch, ouch, *n.* [For *nouch*, from O.Fr. *nouche*, *nosche*, O.H.G. *nusca*, a brooch.] The setting of a precious stone (O.T.); a jewel; a brooch.

ouch, ouch, *interj.* [Echoic.] An exclamation of pain.

ought, ąt, *v. auxil.* [Originally the preterite of the verb *to owe*, A.Sax. *ágan*, to possess, but now used indifferently as a present and a past; *I ought, thou oughtest, he ought, we, ye, they ought*, to do or to have done. OWE.] To be held or bound in duty or moral obligation.

ought, ąt, *n.* See AUGHT.

ought, ąt, *n.* [A corruption of *nought*.] A cipher.

Ouija, wē′ja, *n.* [Fr. *oui*, yes, and G. *ja*, *yes*.] A trademark for a board, marked with symbols and the alphabet, used with a smaller board that is moved over it with the fingertips to obtain answers and messages.

ounce, ouns, *n.* [From L. *uncia*, the twelfth part of anything; whence also *inch*.] A weight, the twelfth part of a pound troy, and the sixteenth of a pound avoirdupois.

ounce, ouns. [Fr. *once*, Sp. *onza*, It. *lonza*, probably from L.L. *luncea*, a lynx.] A carnivorous animal resembling a small panther inhabiting the warmer parts of Asia; a name sometimes given to the American jaguar.

our, our, *a.* [A.Sax. *úre*, our, contr. for *úser*, our, from *ús*, us = G. *unser*, Goth. *unsar*, our. US.] Pertaining or belonging to us (*our* country; *our* rights). *Ours* is a later possessive form and is used in place of *our* and a noun (the book is *ours*).—**ourself**, our′self, *pron.* Myself: used like *we* and *us* in the regal or formal style.—**ourselves**, our′selvz, pl. of *ourself*. We or us, not others: often when used as a nominative added to *we* by way of emphasis or opposition; when in the objective often without emphasis and simply serving as the reflexive pronoun corresponding to *us*.

ourari, ö•rä′ri, *n.* See CURARI.

ousel, ouzel, ö′zl, *n.* [A.Sax. *ósle*, an ousel, akin to O.H.G. *amisala*, G. *amsel*, an ousel.] A European blackbird.

oust, oust, *v.t.* [O.Fr. *ouster*, Mod. Fr. *ôter*, supposed to be from L.L. *hausto*, *haustare*, to remove, a freq. from L. *haurio*, to draw out (as in *exhaust*).] To eject; to turn out; to dispossess.—**ouster**, ous′tėr, *n.* *Law*, dispossession or ejection.

out, out, *adv.* [A.Sax., O.Sax., O. Fris., Icel., and Goth. *út*, Sw. *ut*, Dan. *ud*, D. *uit*, G. *aus*, out; seen in *but*, *about*, *utter*, *utmost*.] On or toward the outside; not in or within; without: opposed to *in*, *into*, or *within*; not indoors; abroad; beyond usual limits (he was *out* when I called); no longer concealed or kept secret; not in a state of obscurity; public (the secret is *out*); finished; exhausted; used up; deficient; having expended (*out* of money; extinguished; no longer burning (the candle or fire is *out*); not in employment; not in office; to an end or settlement (hear me *out*); loudly; in an open and free manner (to laugh *out*); not in the hands of the owner (*out* on loan); in an error; at a loss; in a puzzle; having taken her place as a woman in society (said of a young lady); away from one's own control (parceled *out* the land); in a direction away from the inside or center; from among others (picked *out* a hat); *baseball*, so as to be retired (he struck *out*).—*interj.* Begone! Away!—*Out* forms a prefix in many words, especially verbs, in which it usually expresses a greater measure or degree in doing something.—*n.* One who is out; especially one out of office, politically; retiring of an offensive player from the game.—*prep.* Out through (came *out* the window); outward, along, or on (ride *out* the river road).—*a.* Situated at a distance; not in power (the *out* group).—*v.t.* To put out; to eject.—*v.i.* To become public (good news will *out*).—**out of**, *prep.* Proceeding from as source or origin; in consequence of; taken, extracted, or quoted from; from or proceeding from a place or the interior of a place; beyond (*out of* the power of fortune); not in; excluded from (*out of* favor; *out of* use); denoting deviation from what is common, regular, or proper (*out of* order); from, by way of rescue or liberation (to be delivered *out of* afflictions); not within the limits or scope of (*out of* hearing, *out of* sight, *out of* reach); denoting loss or exhaustion (*out of* breath).—*Out-of-door, a.*, out of the house; open-air (*out-of-door* exercise).—*Out-of-doors, adv.*, out of the house.—*Out of hand*, immediately; without delay.—*Out of print* denotes that a book is not on sale or to be purchased, the copies printed having been all sold.—*Out of sorts*, out of order; unwell.—*Out of temper*, in bad temper; irritated.—*Out-of-the-way, a.*, remote from populous districts; secluded; unfrequented; unusual; uncommon.—*Out of trim*, not in good order.—*Out of one's time*, having finished one's apprenticeship.—*Out of tune*, discordant; not harmonious.—**out-and-out**, *adv.* Completely; thoroughly; without reservation. (*Colloq.*)—*a.* Thorough; thoroughpaced; absolute; complete.

outbid, out•bid′, *v.t.* To bid more than; to go beyond in the offer of a price.—**outboard**, out′bōrd, *a.* *Naut.* applied to anything that is on the outside of the ship (the *outboard* works, etc.).—**outbrag**, out•brag′, *v.t.* To surpass in bragging, bravado, or ostentation.—**outbrave**, out•brāv′, *v.t.* To surpass in braving; to bear down by more daring or insolent conduct.—**outbreak**, out′brāk, *n.* A breaking out; a bursting forth; a sudden and violent manifestation (as of fever, anger, disease).—**outburst**, out′bėrst, *n.* A breaking or bursting out; an outbreak (an *outburst* of wrath).

outcast, out′kast, *n.* One who is cast out or expelled; an exile; one driven from home or country.—*a.* Cast out; thrown away; rejected as useless.—**outcome**, out′kum, *n.* That which comes out of or results from something; the issue; the result; the consequence.—**outcrop**, out′krop, *v.i.* *Geol.* to crop out or appear above the surface of the ground: said of strata.—*n.* *Geol.* the exposure of an inclined stratum at the surface of the ground; the part so exposed; the basset.—**outcry**, out′krī, *n.* A vehement or loud cry; cry of distress; clamor; noisy opposition; sale at public auction.—*v.t.* (out•krī′). To surpass or get the better of by crying; to cry louder than.

outdare, out•dâr′, *v.t.* To dare or venture beyond.—**outdistance**, out•dis′tans, *v.t.* To excel or leave far behind in any competition or career.—**outdo**, out•dö′, *v.t.* To excel; to surpass; to perform beyond another.—**outdoor**, out′dōr, *a.* Being without the house; exterior; in the open air.—**outdoors,** out•dōrz′, *adv.* Abroad; out of the house; in the open air.—**outdoor theater,** one situated in the open air without a roof.

outer, out′ėr, *a.* [Compar. of *out.*] Being on the outside; farther removed from a person or fixed point. —**outer-directed,**out′ėr-di•rek″ted,*a.* Directed by the rules and values of one's society.—**outermost,** out′-ėr•mōst, *a.* Being on the extreme external part remotest from the midst; most distant.

outer space, out•ėr spās′, *n.* The region outside the earth's atmosphere.

outface, out•fās′, *v.t.* To brave; to bear down with an imposing front or with effrontery; to stare down.—**outfall,** out′fal, *n.* The mouth of a river; the lower end of a water-course; the point of discharge for, or the embouchure of a drain, culvert, or sewer.—**outfit,** out′fit, *n.* The act of fitting out for a voyage, journey, or expedition; articles for fitting out; the equipment of one going abroad.—**outfitter,** out′fit•ėr, *n.* One who furnishes or makes outfits.—**outflank,** out•flangk′, *v.t.* To go or extend beyond the flank or wing of; hence, to outmaneuver; to get the better of.—**outflow,** out′-flō, *n.* The act of flowing out; efflux.—*v.i.* (out•flō′). To flow out.—**outfly,** out•flī′, *v.t.* To fly faster than.

outgeneral, out•jen′ėr•al, *v.t.* To exceed in generalship; to gain advantage over by superior military skill.—**outgo,** out•gō′, *v.t.* To advance before in going; to go faster than; to surpass; to excel.—*n.* (out′gō). That which goes out; specifically, expenditure.—**outgoing,** out′gō•ing, *p.* or *a.* Going out; removing (an *outgoing* tenant).—*n.* The act of going out; outlay; expenditure.—**outgrow,** out•grō′, *v.t.* To surpass in growth; to grow too great or too old for.—**outgrowth,** out′grōth, *n.* That which grows out or proceeds from any body; an excrescence; *fig.* that which grows out of a moral cause; a result.

out-Herod, out•her′od, *v.t.* To excel in resembling Herod; to go beyond in any excess of evil or enormity.

outhouse, out′hous, *n.* An out-building, especially a privy.

outing, out′ing, *n.* The act of going out; an excursion; an airing.

outlandish, out•land′ish, *a.* [A.Sax. *útlændisc*, foreign, from *ut*, out, and *land*, land.] Belonging to or characteristic of a foreign country; foreign; not native; hence, strange, barbarous; uncouth; bizarre.—**outlast,** out-last′, *v.i.* To last longer than; to exceed in duration; to outlive.—**outlaw,** out′la, *n.* [From *out* and *law*; A.Sax. *útlag*, *útlaga.*] A fugitive from justice, as a bandit, a murderer, etc.—*v.t.* To declare illegal; to taboo, as to outlaw war; to proscribe a person or a thing.—**outlawry,** out′la•ri, *n.* The putting of a person out of the protection of law by legal means, or the process by which a man is deprived of that protection, being the punishment of a man who, when called into court, contemptuously refuses to appear.—**outlay,** out′lā, *n.* A laying out or expending; that which is laid out or expended; expenditure.—*v.t.* (out•lā′). To lay or spread out; to expose; to display. —**outlet,** out′let, *n.* The place or opening by which anything is let out, escapes, or is discharged; a means of egress; a place of exit; a vent.—*v.t.* To let forth; to emit.—**outlier,** out′lī•ėr, *n.* A part lying without, or beyond the main body; *geol.* a portion of a rock, stratum, or formation detached, and at some distance from the principal mass.—**outline,** out′līn, *n.* The line by which a figure is defined; the exterior line; contour; a drawing in which an object or scene is represented merely by lines of contour without shading; first general sketch of any scheme or design.—*v.t.* To draw in outline; to delineate.—**outlive,** out•liv′, *v.t.* To live beyond; to survive,—**outlook,** out′lök, *n.* A looking out or watching; vigilant watch (to bc on the *outlook* for something); the place of watch; what lies before the eye; prospect; survey.—**outlying,** out•lī′ing, *a.* Lying away from the main body or design; remote; being on the exterior or frontier.

outmaneuver, out•ma•nö′vėr or out•-ma•nū′vėr, *v.t.* To surpass in maneuvering.—**outmarch,** out•märch′, *v.t.* To mareh faster than; to march so as to leave behind.—**outmost,** out′mōst, *a.* [A superlative of *out.*] Farthest outward; most remote from the middle; outermost.

outnumber, out•num′bėr, *v.t.* To exceed in number.

outpatient, *n.* A patient not residing in a hospital, but who receives medical advice, etc., from the institution.—**outpost,** out′pōst, *n.* A post or station without the limits of a camp, or at a distance from the main body of an army; the troops placed at such a station.—**outpour,** out•pōr′, *v.t.* To pour out; to send forth in a stream; to effuse.—*n.* (out′pōr). An outflow.—**output,** out′-put, *n.* The quantity of material put out or produced within a specified time, as coal from a pit or iron from a furnace, etc.

outquarters, out′kwar•tėrz, *n. pl. Milit.* quarters away from the head-quarters.

outrage, out′rāj, *n.* [Fr. *outrage*, O.Fr. *oultrage*, from L.L. *ultragium*, L. *ultra*, beyond. ULTRA.] Rude or injurious violence offered to persons or things; excessive abuse; an act of wanton mischief; an audacious transgression of law or decency.—*v.t.*—*outraged, outraging.* [Fr. *outrager.*] To treat with violence and wrong; to do violence to; to abuse; to maltreat; to commit a rape or indecent assault upon.—**outrageous,** out•rā′jus, *a.* Characterized by outrage; violent; furious; turbulent; excessive; exceeding reason or decency; enormous; atrocious.—**outrageously,** out•rā′jus•li, *adv.* In an outrageous manner.—**outrageousness,** out•rā′jus•nes, *n.* The quality of being outrageous.—**outride,** out•-rīd′, *v.t.* To pass by riding; to ride faster than.—**outrider,** out′-rī•dėr, *n.* A servant on horseback who precedes or accompanies a carriage.—**outrigger,** out′rig•ėr, *n.* A structure of spars, etc., rigged out from the side of a sailing boat to steady it; an iron bracket on the outside of a boat, with the rowlock at the extremity; a light boat provided with such apparatus.—**outright,** out•rīt′, *adv.* Completely; wholly; altogether (to kill him *outright.*)—**outroot,** out•röt′, *v.t.* To eradicate; to extirpate.—**outrun,** out-run′, *v.t.* To excel in running; to leave behind; to exceed or go beyond.—**outrush,** out•rush′, *v.i.* To rush or issue out rapidly or forcibly. —*n.* (out′rush). A gushing or rushing out; an outflow.

outre, ö•trā′, ö′trā, *a.* [Fr. pp. of *outrer*, to exaggerate.] Beyond the limits of what is considered correct; bizarre; extravagant.

outsail, out•sāl′, *v.t.* To leave behind in sailing.—**outset,** out′set, *n.* A setting out; beginning; start.—**outsettlement,** out′set•l•ment, *n.* A settlement away from the main settlement.—**outsettler,** out′set•lėr, *n.* One who settles at a distance from the main body.—**outshine,** out•shīn′, *v.t.* To excel in luster or excellence.—*v.i.* To shine out or forth.—**outshoot,** out•shöt′, *v.t.* To excel in shooting; to shoot beyond.—**outside,** out′sīd, *n.* The external outer or exposed parts or surface; superficial appearance; external aspect or features; space immediately without or beyond an enclosure; the farthest limit; the utmost; extreme estimate (with *the*). —*a.* Being on the outside; external; superficial.—*Outside broker*, a broker outside of the regular Stock Exchange.—**outsider,** out′sī•dėr, *n.* One not belonging to a party, association, or set; unconnected or not admitted. —**outsit,** out•sit′, *v.t.* To sit beyond the time of anything; to sit longer than.—**outskirt,** out′skėrt, *n.* Part near the edge or boundary of an area; border; purlieu. — **outspan,** out•span′, *v.t.* and *i.*—*outspanned, outspanning.* [E. *out*, and D. *spannen*, to yoke.] To unyoke (a team of oxen) from a wagon; correlative of *inspan.* (*South Africa.*)—**outspeak,** out•spēk′, *v.t.* To exceed in speaking; to say more than.—*v.i.* To speak out or aloud.—**outspoken,** out′spō•-kn, *a.* Free or bold of speech; candid; frank.—**outspokenness,** out•-spō′kn•nes, *n.* The character of being outspoken.—**outspread,** out•-spred′, *v.t.* To spread out; to extend. —**outstanding,** out•stand′ing, *a.* Not collected; unpaid; prominent. —**outstare,** out•stâr′, *v.t.* To stare out of countenance; to face down; to outface.—**outstay,** out•stā′, *v.t.* To stay longer than; to overstay.—**outstretch,** out•strech′, *v.t.* To extend; to stretch or spread out;

to expand.—**outstrip,** out•strip′, *v.t.* To outrun; to advance beyond; to exceed.—**outswear,** out•swâr′, *v.t.* To exceed in swearing.

outtalk, out•tąk′, *v.t.* To overpower by talking; to exceed in talking.

outvote, out•vōt′, *v.t.* To exceed in the number of votes given; to defeat by plurality of votes.

outwalk, out•wąk′, *v.t.* To walk farther, longer, or faster than; to leave behind in walking.—**outward,** out′wėrd, *a.* [A.Sax. *úteweard—úte*, out, and *weard*, denoting direction.] Forming the superficial part; exterior; external; visible; appearing; tending to the exterior; derived from without; not properly belonging; adventitious.—*adv.* Outward; from a port or country.—**outwardly,** out′wėrd•li, *adv.* Externally; on the outside; in appearance only.—**outward,** out′wėrd, *adv.* Toward the outer parts.—**outwatch,** out•woch′, *v.t.* To surpass in watching; to watch longer than.—**outwear,** out•wâr′, *v.t.* To wear out; to last longer than.—**outweigh,** out•wā′, *v.t.* To exceed in weight or in value, influence, or importance.—**outwit,** out•wit′, *v.t.*—*outwitted, outwitting.* To defeat or frustrate by superior ingenuity; to prove too clever for; to overreach.—**outwork,** out′wėrk, *n.* Part of a fortification distant from the main fortress or citadel.

ouzel, *n.* See OUSEL.

ova, ō′va, *n.* Plural of *ovum.*

oval, ō′val, *a.* [Fr. *ovale*, from L. *ovum*, an egg; cog. Gr. *ōon*, an egg.] Of the shape of the outline of an egg; resembling the longitudinal section of an egg; elliptical.—*n.* A figure in the shape of the outline of an egg; an elliptical figure.—**ovally,** ō′val•li, *adv.* In an oval form; so as to be oval.

ovary, ō′ve•ri, *n.* [Mod. L. *ovarium*, from L. *ovum*, an egg. OVAL.] The female organ in which ova, reproductive germs or eggs, are formed and developed; *bot.* a case enclosing ovules or young seeds, and ultimately becoming the fruit.—**ovariotomy,** ō•vâ′ri•ot″o•mi, *n.* The operation for removing a tumor in the ovary or the ovary itself.

ovate, ō′vāt, *a.* [L. *ovatus.* OVAL.] Egg-shaped; oval.

ovation, ō•vā′shon, *n.* [L. *ovatic*, from *ovare*, to exult.] A kind of triumph granted to ancient Roman commanders who could not claim the distinction of a full triumph; hence, any triumphal reception of a person or marks of respect publicly shown.

oven, uv′n, *n.* [A.Sax. *ofen*=D. *oven.* Dan. *ovn*, Icel. *ofn.*] A closely built recess for baking, heating, or drying a substance.—**ovenbird,** uv′en•bėrd, *n.* An American wood warbler (*Seiurus aurocapillus*) known for the oven-shaped nest it builds on the ground.

over, ō′vėr, *prep.* [A.Sax. *ofer*, D. and Dan. *over*; Icel. *ofr*, *yfir*; G. *über*; cog. L. *super*, Gr. *hyper*, Skr. *upari*, above.] Above in place or position; rising to or reaching a height above; across (implying motion); upon the surface of; through the whole extent of; above in eminence or superiority; above in authority; with oversight or watchfulness in respect to (to keep guard *over*); denoting motive or occasion (to rejoice *over*); denoting superiority as the result of a struggle or contest; upward of; more than; beyond the comprehension of (talked *over* their heads); by a certain means of communication (broadcast *over* the radio).—*adv.* Above; so as to turn the underside up; from side to side; in width; across; from one side to the other or to another (to roll *over*); on all the surface; above the top, brim, or edge; more than the quantity assigned; in excess; throughout; completely; having come to an end; past (till this heat be *over*); excessively; in a great degree.—**overly,** ō′vėr•li, *adv.* Overmuch; too; excessively (colloq.)—*Over again*, once more; with repetition.—*Over and above*, besides; beyond what is supposed or limited.—*Over against*, opposite; in front of.—*All over*, so as to affect the whole surface; complete.—*a.* Upper; superior; covering; outer (*overshoes*).—*Over* forms the first element in many compounds. Of these we can only give the principal.

overact, ō•vėr•akt′, *v.t.* To act or perform to excess.—*v.i.* To act more than is necessary.

overall, ō″vėr•all′, *a.* From one end to the other (the *overall* length of a room); covering or including everything.

overalls, ō′vėr•ąlz, *n. pl.* Loose trousers worn over others to protect them from being soiled.

overanxious, *a.* Anxious to excess.

overarch, ō•vėr•ärch′, *v.t.* and *i.* To arch over; to cover with an arch.

overawe, ō•vėr•ą′, *v.t.* To restrain by awe, fear, or superior influence.

overbalance, ō•vėr•bal′ans, *v.t.* To more than balance; to exceed in weight, value, etc.; to surpass; to destroy the balance or equilibrium of (used *refl.*).—*n.* Excess; something more than an equivalent.

overbear, ō•vėr•bâr′, *v.t.* To bear down; to overpower; to overcome by argument, effrontery, or the like.—**overbearing,** ō•vėr•bâr′ing, *p.* and *a.* Haughty and dogmatical; given to effrontery.

overblown, ō•vėr•blōn′, *a.* Blown to excess; marked by larger size or proportions than is usual.

overboard, ō′ver•bōrd, *adv.* Over the side of a ship; out of a ship or from on board.—*Thrown overboard* (*fig.*), discarded; deserted; betrayed.

overbold, ō′vėr•bōld, *a.* Unduly bold; forward; impudent.

overbuild, ō•vėr•bild′, *v.t.* To build over; to build more than the area properly admits of, or than the population requires.—*v.i.* To build beyond the demand.

overburden, ō•vėr•bėr′dn, *v.t.* To load with too great weight; to overload.

overcast, ō•vėr•kast′, *v.t.* To cloud; to obscure with clouds; to cover with gloom; to sew by running the thread over a rough edge.—*a.* Clouded over.

overcharge, ō•vėr•chärj′, *v.t.* To charge or burden to excess; to fill too numerously; to make an excessive charge against; to charge at too high a sum or price; to exaggerate.—*n.* ō′vėr•chärj. An excessive charge; a charge of more than is just in an account.

overcloud, ō•vėr•kloud′, *v.t.* To cover or overspread with clouds.

overcoat, ō′vėr•kōt, *n.* A coat worn over all the other dress; a topcoat.

overcome, ō•vėr•kum′, *v.t.* To conquer; to vanquish; to surmount; to get the better of.—*v.i.* To gain the superiority; to be victorious.

overconfidence, ō•vėr•kon′fi•dens, *n.* Too great or excessive confidence.—**overconfident,** ō•vėr•kon′fi•dent, *a.* Confident to excess.

overcrowd, ō•vėr•kroud′, *v.t.* To fill or crowd to excess, especially with human beings.

overdo, ō•vėr•dö′, *v.t.* To do to excess; to overact; to surpass or exceed in performance; to boil, roast, or otherwise cook too much.

overdose, ō′vėr•dōs, *n.* Too great a dose.—*v.t.* (ō•vėr•dōs′). To dose excessively.

overdraw, ō•vėr•drą′, *v.t.* To draw upon for a larger sum than is standing at one's credit in the books of a bank, etc.; to exaggerate either in writing, speech, or a picture.

overdress, ō•vėr•dres′, *v.t.* and *i.* To dress to excess.

overdrive, ō′vėr•drīv, *n.* *Mach.* an automotive transmission gear set to provide driving speed greater than the engine crankshaft speed.

overdue, ō′vėr•dū, *a.* Not arrived at the proper date or assigned limit (an *overdue* ship); past the time of payment (an *overdue* bill).

overeager, ō•vėr•ē′gėr, *a.* Too eager; too vehement in desire.

overeat, ō•vėr•ēt′, *v.t.* To surfeit with eating; used *refl.* (to *overeat oneself*).

overestimate, ō•vėr•es′ti•māt, *n.* An estimate or calculation that is too high.—*v.t.* To estimate too high; to overvalue.

overexcitement, ō•vėr•ek•sīt′ment, *n.* The state of being overexcited.

overexpose, o′vėr•ex•pōs″, *v.t.* *Photog.* to subject film too long to light.

overfatigue, ō•vėr•fa•tēg′, *n.* Excessive fatigue.—*v.t.* To fatigue to excess.

overfeed, ō•vėr•fēd′, *v.t.* and *i.* To feed to excess.

overflow, ō•vėr•flō′, *v.t.* To run over the brim of; to deluge; to overwhelm.—*v.i.* To run over the brim or banks; to abound.—*n.* ō′vėr•flō. An inundation; a flowing over; superabundance.

overgrow, ō•vėr•grō′, *v.t.* To cover with growth or herbage; generally in *pp.* (a ruin *overgrown* with ivy).—*v.i.* To grow beyond the fit or natural size.—**overgrowth,** ō′vėr•grōth, *n.* Exuberant or excessive growth.

overhand, ō′vėr•hand, *a.* Made with the hand brought above the shoulder (*overhand* throw); with the hand approaching over the object (*overhand* stroke).—*adv.* In an overhand manner.—*n.* Something done in an overhand manner.
overhang, ō′vėr•hang, *v.t.* To impend over; to be suspended over.—*v.i.* To project far enough to be over something.—*n.* Something that overhangs; the amount of overhang; the part of a roof extending beyond the walls of a building.
overhardy, ō•vėr•här′di, *a.* Excessively or unduly hardy or daring; foolhardy.
overhasty, ō•vėr•hās′ti, *a.* Too hasty; rash; precipitate.
overhaul, ō•vėr•hal′, *v.t.* To turn over for examination; to examine thoroughly with a view to repairs; to re-examine (as accounts); to gain upon or overtake.—*To overhaul a ship,* to gain upon her in following; to search for contraband goods.—**overhaul, overhauling,** ō′vėr•hal, ō′vėr•hal•ing, *n.* Examination; inspection; repair.
overhead, ō•vėr•hed′, *adv.* Aloft; in the zenith; above one's head.—*n.* ō′vėr•hed. Expenses of a business, as rent, office expenses, taxes, depreciation, etc.—*a.* Situated above.
overhear, ō•vėr•hēr′, *v.t.* To hear though not intended or expected to hear.
overissue, ō′vėr•ish•ū, *n.* An excessive issue; an issue (as of coin or bills) in excess of the conditions which should regulate or control it.—*v.t.* To issue in excess, as bank notes or bills of exchange; to issue contrary to prudence or honesty.
overjoy, ō•ver•joi′, *v.t.* To give great or excessive joy to; generally in *pp.*
overland, ō′vėr•land, *a.* Passing by land; made upon or across the land (an *overland* journey).
overlap, ō•vėr•lap′, *v.t.* To lap or fold over; to extend so as to lie or rest upon.—*n.* The lapping of one thing over another; *geol.* the extension of a superior stratum over an inferior so as to cover and conceal it.
overlay, ō•vėr•lā′, *v.t.*—pret. & pp. *overlaid.* To lay too much upon; to overwhelm; to cover or spread over the surface of; to coat or cover; to smother with close covering, or by lying upon; to obscure by covering.
overleap, ō•vėr•lēp′, *v.t.* To leap over; to pass by leaping; *refl.* to leap too far.
overlie, ō•vėr•lī′, *v.t.* pret. *overlay,* pp. *overlain.* To lie over or upon; to smother by lying on (to *overlie* a child; comp. OVERLAY).
overlive, ō•vėr•liv′, *v.t.* To outlive; to survive.
overload, ō•vėr•lōd′, *v.t.* To load with too heavy a burden or cargo; to overburden.
overlook, ō•vėr•luk′, *v.t.* To view from a higher place; to rise or be elevated above; to see from behind or over the shoulder of another; to inspect or superintend; to pass over indulgently; to omit to censure or punish (a fault); to slight.
overlord, ō′vėr•lord, *n.* One who is lord over another; a feudal superior.
overmaster, ō•vėr•mas′tėr, *v.t.* To overpower; to subdue; to vanquish.
overmatch, ō•vėr•mach′, *v.t.* To be too powerful for.—*n.* One superior in power; one able to overcome.
overmodest, ō•vėr•mod′est, *a.* Modest to excess; bashful.
overmuch, ō′vėr•much, *a.* Too much; exceeding what is necessary or proper.—*adv.* In too great a degree.—*n.* More than sufficient.
overnight, ō′vėr•nīt, *adv.* Through or during the night; in the course of the night or evening; in the evening before.
overpass, ō′vėr•pas, *n.* A section of a highway, etc., crossing over another road, railroad, etc.—*v.t.* (ō•vėr•pas′). To pass over; to cross.
overpay, ō•vėr•pā′, *v.t.* To pay in excess; to reward beyond the price or merit.
overpeople, ō•vėr•pē′pl, *v.t.* To overstock with inhabitants.
overplay, ō•vėr•plā′, *v.t.* To play a part on stage in an exaggerated fashion; to overemphasize; *golf,* to strike a golf ball beyond the putting green.
overplus, ō′vėr•plus, *n.* [*Over,* and L. *plus,* more.] Surplus; that which remains after a supply, or beyond a quantity proposed.
overpower, ō•vėr•pou′ėr, *v.t.* To vanquish by power or force; to subdue; to be too intense or violent for (his emotions *overpowered* him).—**overpowering,** ō•vėr•pou′ėr•ing, *p.* and *a.* Bearing down by superior power; irresistible.—**overpoweringly,** ō•vėr•pou′ėr•ing•li, *adv.* In an overpowering manner.
overprize, ō•vėr•prīz′, *v.t.* To value or prize at too high a rate.
overproduction, ō•vēr•prō•duk′shon, *n.* Production of commodities in excess of demand.
overrate, ō•vėr•rāt′, *v.t.* To rate at too much; to regard as having greater talents, abilities, or more valuable qualities than is really the case.
overreach, ō•vėr•rēch′, *v.t.* To reach beyond; to rise above; to deceive by cunning, artifice, or sagacity; to cheat; to outwit.
overrefinement, ō•vėr•rē•fīn′ment, *n.* Excessive refinement; refinement with excess of subtlety or affectation of nicety.
override, ō•vėr•rīd′, *v.t.* To ride over; hence, to trample down; to supersede; to annul—*To override one's commission,* to discharge one's office in too arbitrary a manner or with too high a hand.
overripe, ō′vėr•rīp, *a.* Ripe or matured to excess.—**overripen,** ō•vėr•rī′pn, *v.t.* To make too ripe.
overrule, ō•vėr•röl′, *v.t.* To influence or control by predominant power; to set aside (objections); *law,* to rule against or reject.
overrun, ō•vėr•run′, *v.t.* To run or spread over; to grow over; to overcome and take possession by an invasion; to outrun.—*v.i.* To run over; to defeat and occupy the conquered area.—*n.* o′vėr•run. Act of overrunning; *print.* a run in excess of the quantity ordered.
overscrupulous, ō•vėr•skrö′pū•lus, *a.* Scrupulous to excess.
oversea, ō′vėr•sē, *a.* Foreign; from beyond sea.—**overseas,** ō′vėr•sēz, *adv.* Beyond or across the sea; abroad.
oversee, ō•vėr•sē′, *v.t.* To superintend; to overlook; to take charge of.—**overseer,** ō′vėr•sēr, *n.* One who supervises; a superintendent; an officer who has the care or superintendence of any matter.—*Overseers of the poor,* officers in England who are concerned with relief of the poor.
overset, ō•vėr•set′, *n.* An upsetting; an overturn.—*v.t.* To turn from the proper position; to turn upon the side, or to turn bottom upward (as a vehicle); to subvert; to overthrow.—*v.i.* To turn or be turned over.
overshadow, ō•vėr•shad′ō, *v.t.* To throw a shadow over; to shelter or cover with protecting influence.
overshoe, ō′vėr•shö, *n.* A shoe worn over another; an outer waterproof shoe.
overshoot, ō•vėr•shöt′, *v.t.* To shoot beyond (a mark); to venture too far.—**overshot,** ō″vėr•shot′, *a.* Having the upper jaw extend beyond the lower.
oversight, ō′vėr•sīt, *n.* A mistake or inadvertence; an overlooking; omission.
oversimplify, ō′vėr•sim″pli•fī, *v.t.* To simplify to the point where meaning is distorted.—*v.i.* To engage in excessive simplification.
oversleep, ō•vėr•slēp′, *v.t.* To sleep beyond or too long.
overspread, ō•vėr•spred′, *v.t.* To spread over; to cover completely; to scatter over.—*v.i.* To be spread or scattered over.
overstate, ō•vėr•stāt′, *v.t.* To exaggerate in statement; to state in too strong terms.—**overstatement,** ō′vėr•stāt•ment, *n.* An exaggerated statement.
overstay, ō•vėr•stā′, *v.t.* To stay too long for; to stay beyond the limits or duration of.
overstep, ō•vėr•step′, *v.t.* To step over or beyond; to exceed.
overstock, ō•vėr•stok′, *v.t.* To stock to too great an extent; to fill too full; to supply with more than is wanted (the market with goods; a farm with cattle).
overstrain, ō•vėr•strān′, *v.i.* and *t.* To strain to excess; to stretch too far; to exert too much.
oversupply, ō′vėr•sup•plī, *n.* An excessive supply; a supply in excess of demand.
overt, ō′vėrt, *a.* [O.Fr. *overt,* Fr. *ouvert,* O.Fr. *ovrir,* to open, from L. *aperire,* to open.] Open to view; public; apparent; *law,* not covert or secret; manifest.—**overtly,** ō′vėrt•li, *adv.* In an overt manner; openly; publicly; in a manifest manner.

overtake, ō•vėr•tāk′, *v.t.* To come up with in following; to follow and reach or catch; to come upon; to take by surprise.
overtask, ō•vėr•task′, *v.t.* To impose too heavy a task or duty on.
overtax, ō•vėr•taks′, *v.t.* To tax too heavily.
overthrow, ō•vėr•thrō′, *v.t.* To overset; to turn upside down; to throw down; to demolish; to defeat, conquer, vanquish; to subvert or destroy.—*n.* (ō′vėr•thrō). The act of overthrowing; ruin; subversion; defeat.
overtime, ō′vėr•tīm, *n.* Time during which one works beyond the regular hours.
overtone, ō′vėr•tōn, *n. Mus.* a higher, less distinct tone which, with the fundamental, makes up a complex musical tone; a secondary effect.
overtop, ō•vėr•top′, *v.t.* To rise above the top of; to excel; to surpass.
overtrade, ō•vėr•trād′, *v.i.* To trade beyond capital or too rashly.
overture, ō′vėr•chėr, *n.* [O.Fr. *overture,* Fr. *ouverture,* an opening, an overture. OVERT.] A proposal; something offered for consideration; a musical introduction to precede important compositions, as oratorios, operas, etc., written for a full orchestra.
overturn, ō•vėr•tėrn′, *v.t.* To overset or overthrow; to turn or throw from a foundation; to subvert; to ruin.—*n.* (ō′vėr•tėrn). State of being overturned; overthrow.
overvaluation, ō′vėr•val•ū•ā″shon, *n.* Too high valuation; an overestimate.
overween, ō•vėr•wēn′, *v.i.* To think too highly, arrogantly, or conceitedly. —**overweening,** ō•vėr•wēn′ing, *p.* and *a.* Haughty; arrogant; proud; conceited.—**overweeningly,** ō•vėr•wēn′ing•li, *adv.*
overweigh, ō•vėr•wā′, *v.t.* To exceed in weight; to outweigh.
overwhelm, ō•vėr•hwelm′, *v.t.* To whelm entirely; to swallow up; *fig.* to bear down; to crush.—**overwhelmingly,** ō•vėr•hwel′ming•li, *adv.*
overwind, ō•vėr•wīnd′, *v.t.* To wind too far (to *overwind* a watch).
overwise, ō′vėr•wīz, *a.* Wise to affectation.
overwork, ō•vėr•wėrk′, *v.t.* To work beyond strength; to cause to labor too much; often *refl.* (to *overwork one's self*).—*n.* (ō′vėr•wėrk). Excessive work or labor; work done beyond the amount required by stipulation.
overwrought, ō•vėr•rąt′, *p.* and *a.* Labored to excess; worked all over; affected or excited to excess; tasked beyond strength.
overzealous, ō′vėr•zel•us, *a.* Too zealous; eager to excess.
oviduct, ō′vi•dukt, *n.* [L. *ductus,* a duct.] A passage for the ovum or egg from the ovary of animals.—**oviform,** ō′vi•form, *a.* Having the form or figure of an egg.
ovine, ō′vīn, *a.* [L. *ovinus,* from *ovis,* a sheep.] Pertaining to sheep; consisting of sheep.
oviparous, ō•vip′a•rus, *a.* [L. *ovum,* an egg, *pario,* to produce.] Producing eggs, especially eggs that are hatched after exclusion from the body (as opposed to *ovoviviparous*).
oviposit, ō•vi•poz′it, *v.i.* [L. *ovum,* an egg; and E. *posit.*] To deposit eggs: said of insects.—**oviposition,** ō′vi•po•zish″on, *n.* The depositing of eggs by insects.—**ovipositor,** ō•vi•poz′it•ėr, *n.* An organ at the extremity of the abdomen of many insects for depositing their eggs.
ovisac, ō′vi•sak, *n.* [L. *ovum,* an egg, *saccus,* a sack.] The cavity in the ovary which immediately contains the ovum.
ovoid, ō′void, *a.* [L. *ovum,* and Gr. *eidos,* form. OVAL.] Having a shape of an egg.
ovoviviparous, ō′vō•vī•vip″a•rus, *a.* [L. *ovoviviparus*—*ovo,* ovum, and *viviparous.*] Producing eggs which are hatched within the body (as is the case with vipers). OVIPAROUS.
ovulate, ō′vū•lāt, *v.i.* [From *ovule,* L. *ovulum,* dim. of *ovum.*] To produce eggs; to discharge eggs from an ovary.—**ovulation,** ō′vū•la″shon, *n.*—**ovule,** ō′vūl, *n.* A small, immature ovum; a small pellucid body borne by the placenta of a plant, and changing into a seed.
ovum, ō′vum, *n.* pl. **ova,** ō′va. [L.] A small egg within the ovary of a female animal, when impregnated becoming the embryo; an egg.
owe, ō, *v.t.*—*owed, owing.* [From A.Sax. *ágan,* to own, to have (pret. *áhte,* whence *ought*; pp. *ágen,* whence *own*); Icel. *eiga,* Sw. *äga, ega,* O.H.G. *eigan,* Goth. *aigan,* to possess.] To possess or own‡; to be indebted in; to be bound to pay; to be obliged to ascribe; to be obliged for (he *owes* his safety to me); to be due or owing. —**owing,** ō′ing, *ppr.* [Pres. part. used in passive sense of *owed, being due.*] Required by obligation to be paid; remaining as a debt; ascribable, as to a cause; due; imputable, as to an agent.
owl, oul, *n.* [A.Sax. *úle*=D. *uil,* Icel. *ugla,* Dan. *ugle,* Sw. *uggla,* G. *eule,* names imitative of its cry; comp. L. *ululo,* to lament, E. *howl.*] One of the nocturnal birds of prey, well known for their somewhat catlike heads and their harsh and screeching note.—**owlet,** oul′et, *n.* [Dim. of *owl.*] An owl; a young owl.—**owlish,** oul′ish, *a.* Resembling an owl.
own, ōn, *a.* [A.Sax. *ágen,* pp. of *ágan,* to possess, like Dan. and Sw. *egen,* Icel. *eiginn,* D. and G. *eigen,* own. OWE.] Belonging to me, him, us, you, etc., distinctly and emphatically: always following a possessive pronoun, or a noun in the possessive, as *my own, his own, John's own*: sometimes used to impart tenderness to an expression (thine *own* true knight). —*To hold one's own,* to maintain one's own cause; not to lose ground. —*v.t.* [A.Sax. *ágnian* (from *ágen*= *own, a.*), Icel. *eigna,* Dan. *egne,* G. *eignen,* to own.] To have the right of property in; to hold or possess by right; to acknowledge or avow (*owned* him as his son); to concede; to admit to be true.—**owner,** ō′nėr, *n.* One who owns; the rightful proprietor.—**ownership,** ō′nėr•ship, *n.*
ox, oks, *n.* pl. **oxen,** ok′sn. [A.Sax. *oxa,* pl. *oxan*=Icel. *oxi,* Sw. and Dan. *oxe,* D. *os,* G. *ochs, ochse,* Goth. *auhsa, auhsus,* an ox; cog. L. *vacca,* a cow, Skr. *ukshâ,* an ox.] The general name for any animal of the cow or bovine kind; especially, a male castrated, and full grown, or nearly so.—**oxbow,** *n.* A curved piece of wood encircling an ox's neck when yoked; *arch.* an oval dormer window.—**oxlip,** oks′lip, *n.* A species of primrose.
oxalate, ok′sa•lāt, *n.* [Gr. *oxalis,* sorrel, from *oxys,* sharp, acid.] *Chem.* a salt or ester of oxalic acid.
oxalic acid, oks•al′ik as′id, *n.* A white, crystalline, poisonous solid, obtained from wood sorrel and other plants, used in dyeing, bleaching, etc.
oxeye, oks′ī, *n.* [*Ox* and *eye.*] Any of various plants whose flowers are formed of a disk with marginal rays (*oxeye* daisy).
oxford, oks′ford, *n.* [From the city of *Oxford,* England.] A low shoe laced over the instep.
Oxford clay, oks′ford, *n. Geol.* a bed of dark-blue clay between the lower and middle oölites, abounding in ammonites and belemnites.—**Oxford movement,** *n.* The Neo-Catholic movement of Newman, Keble, and Pusey, propagated by the *Tracts for the Times.*
oxide, ok′sīd, *n.* [Gr. *oxys,* acid, sharp.] *Chem.* a compound of oxygen with another element (thus rust is *oxide* of iron).—**oxidation,** ok•si•dā′shon, *n.* The operation or process of converting into an oxide.—**oxidize,** ok′si•dīz, *v.t.* To convert into an oxide (which see); to change an element or ion from a lower to a higher positive valence.—**oxidizer,** ok′si•dīz•ėr, *n.* That which oxidizes. —**oxidizable,** ok′si•dī•za•bl, *a.*
Oxonian, ok•sō′ni•an, *n.* A native or inhabitant of Oxford; a member or a graduate of the University of Oxford.
oxyacetylene, oks′i•a•set″i•len, *a.* [From *oxy,* oxygen, and *acetylene.*] Pertaining to a mixture of oxygen and acetylene (an *oxyacetylene* torch).
oxygen, ok′si•jen, *n.* [Gr. *oxys,* acid, and root *gen,* to generate: so named because supposed to be present in all acids.] A colorless, odorless, tasteless gas essential to respiration in most living cells, which constitutes about $\frac{1}{5}$ of the atmosphere and supports combustion in air. Symbol, O; at. no., 8; at. wt., 15.9994.—**oxygenate,** ok′si•jen•āt, *v.t.* To unite or cause to combine with oxygen.—**oxygenation,** ok′si•jen•ā″shon, *n.*
oxyhemoglobin, oks′i•hē″mo•glō•bin, *n.* [From *oxy,* oxygen, and *hemoglobin.*] The bright red substance created when hemoglobin and oxygen unite loosely in the blood.
oxymoron, ok•si•mō′ron, *n.* [Gr. *oxymóron,* a smart saying which at first view appears foolish, from *oxys,* sharp, and *móros,* foolish.] *Rhet.* a figure in which an epithet of a quite contrary signification is added to a word: as *cruel kindness; foolish wisdom.*

oxytone, ok′si•tōn, *a.* [Gr. *oxys,* sharp, *tonos,* tone.] Having an acute sound; *Greek gram.* having the acute accent on the last syllable.

oyer, ō′yėr, *n.* [Norm. *oyer,* Fr. *ouir,* L. *audire,* to hear.] *Law,* a hearing or trial of causes.—*Court of oyer and terminer* (to hear and determine), a court constituted to hear and determine felonies and misdemeanors. —**oyes, oyez,** ō′yes. ['Hear ye.'] The introduction to a proclamation made by a public crier, in order to secure silence and attention, and repeated three times.

oyster, ois′tėr, *n.* [O.Fr. *oistre,* from L. *ostrea, ostreum,* from Gr. *ostreon,* an oyster, akin to *osteon,* a bone.] A well-known edible mollusk with a shell composed of two irregular valves, living in the sea and adhering to other objects.—**oyster bed,** *n.* A breeding place of oysters; a place where they are artificially or naturally reared.—**oyster catcher,** *n.* A British shore bird which feeds on small Mollusca.

ozocerite, o•zō′se•rīt, *n.* [Gr. *ozō,* to smell, and *kēros,* wax.] A mineral wax or paraffin of a brown or brownish-yellow color, made into candles.

ozone, ō′zōn, *n.* [From Gr. *ozō,* to smell.] A bluish gas (a form of oxygen, O_3) with an odor like chlorine, used as a bleaching agent.

P

P, p, pē, the sixteenth letter of the English alphabet.—*To mind one's P's and Q's,* to be very careful in behavior—a colloquial phrase of unknown origin.

pabular, pab′ū•lėr, *a.* [L. *pabulum,* food, from *pasco,* to feed. PASTOR.] Pertaining to food or pabulum.

pabulum, pab′ū•lum, *n.* [L. *pabulum,* food, from *pasco,* to feed. PASTOR.] Food; aliment; *fig.* food for the mind or intellect.

paca, pä′ka, *n.* [Pg. *paca,* from *pak,* the native name.] A large rodent animal of South America and the West Indies, much esteemed for food.

pace, pās, *n.* [Fr. *pas,* from L. *passus,* a step, from *pateo,* to lie open (whence *patent*), or from *pando, passum,* to stretch out. *Pass* has the same origin.] A step, or the space between the feet in walking (about 2½ feet); sometimes the distance from the place where either foot is taken up to that where the same foot is set down (this being the Roman pace); manner of walking; walk; gait (heavy, quick, or slow *pace*); degree of celerity; rate of progress (events followed at a great *pace*); a mode of stepping among horses.—*To keep* or *hold pace with,* to keep up with; to go or move as fast as: literally or figuratively.—*v.i.*—*paced, pacing.* To step; to walk; to step slowly or with measured tread; to stride.—*v.t.* To measure by steps; to walk over with measured paces.—**paced,** pāst, *p.* and *a.* Having a particular gait (slow-*paced*); trained in paces, as a horse; broken in. —*Thorough-paced* (*lit.* thoroughly trained), perfect in something bad; out-and-out (a *thorough-paced* scoundrel, etc.).—**pacer,** pā′sėr, *n.* One that paces; a horse well-trained in pacing.

pacha, pa•shä′, *n.* [French spelling.] PASHA.

pachymeter, pa•kim′et•ėr, *n.* [Gr. *pachys,* thick, and *metron,* a measure.] An instrument for measuring small thicknesses, as of glass or paper.—**pachyderm,** pak′i•dėrm, *n.* [Gr. *derma,* skin.] A nonruminant hoofed animal; a member of an old mammalian order including the elephant, hippopotamus, horse, hog, etc.—**pachydermatous,** pak•i•dėr′ma•tus, *a.* Belonging to the pachyderms; thickskinned; hence *fig.* not sensitive to ridicule, sarcasm, or the like.

pacify, pas′i•fī, *v.t.*—*pacified, pacifying.* [Fr. *pacifier,* L. *pacificare.*] To appease; to cause to give up anger or excited feeling; to allay the agitation or excitement of; to calm; to restore peace to; to tranquilize.—**pacifiable,** pas•i•fī′a•bl, *a.* Capable of being pacified.—**pacific,** pa•sif′ik, *a.* [L. *pacificus,* from *pacifico,* to make peace—*pax, pacis,* peace, and *facio,* to make. PEACE.] Suited to make or restore peace; conciliatory; appeasing; pacifying; calm, peaceful, tranquil; not warlike (*pacific* disposition).—*Pacific Ocean, Pacific,* the ocean situated between the west coast of America and the shores of Asia and Australia.—**pacifically,** pa•sif′i•kal•li, *adv.* In a pacific manner. —**pacification,** pa•sif′i•kā″shon, *n.* The act of pacifying; state or condition of being pacified; appeasement; reconciliation.—**pacificatory,** pa•sif′i•ka•to•ri, *a.* Tending to make peace; conciliatory.—**pacifier,** pas′i•fī•ėr, *n.* One who pacifies; a device resembling a nipple, for a baby to suck.—**pacifism,** pas′i•fizm, *n.* Opposition to war or the unrestricted use of military force; belief that all international disputes should be settled by arbitration.—**pacifist,** pas′i•fist, *n.* One who favors or supports a policy of pacifism (also used as *a.*).

pack, pak, *n.* [Either from D. *pak,* Dan. *pak, pakke,* G. *pack,* a pack or bundle; or from Armor., Ir., and Gael. *pac,* a pack.] A bundle made up to be carried; a bale; a budget; a collection; a complete set of playing cards; a number of hounds or dogs hunting or kept together; a number of persons united in a bad design or practice (a *pack* of rascals).—*v.t.* To put together for transportation or storage; to make up into a package, bundle, or bale; to stow; to fill methodically with contents (to *pack* a trunk); to assemble or bring together iniquitously and with a view to favor some particular side (to *pack* a jury; to *pack* a meeting); to dismiss without ceremony; to make begone; to make airtight by stuffing, as the piston of an engine; to stuff; to preserve in close vessels (to *pack* meat or fish).—*v.i.* To make up bundles or packs; to put up things for transportation; to depart in haste (with *off* or *away*); to gather together into flocks or bands (the grouse begin to *pack*).—**package,** pak′ij, *n.* A bundle or bale; a packet; a parcel.—*v.t.* To place in a package or packages; to make up into a package or packages (to *package* sugar).—**pack animal,** *n.* A beast of burden used on mountain and wilderness trails for transport of supplies and equipment.—**packer,** pak′ėr, *n.* One who packs; one who owns a meatpacking house; one who works in a meatpacking house.—**packet,** pak′et, *n.* [Fr. *paquet.*] A small pack or package; a little bundle or parcel; a parcel of letters; a vessel employed in carrying mails, goods, and passengers on regular days of starting; also called *packet boat, packet vessel.* —**packing,** pak′ing, *n.* Any material used for filling up empty spaces; stuffing; filling.—**packinghouse,** *n.* An establishment where meats are packed for the market.—**packman,** pak′man, *n.* One who carries a pack; a peddler.—**packsaddle,** *n.* A saddle on which burdens are laid for conveyance by pack animals.—**pack thread,** pak′thred, *n.* Strong thread or twine used in tying up parcels.

pact, pakt, *n.* [Fr. *pacte,* L. *pactum,* a bargain (as in *compact*), from *paciscor, pactus,* to fix, bargain, covenant; same root as *pax,* peace. PEACE.] A contract; an agreement or covenant.

pad, pad, *n.* [Origin uncertain; perhaps akin to *pod.*] A cushion, soft saddle, bolster, part of a garment, etc., stuffed with some soft material; a quantity of blotting paper used for blotting or writing upon (a blotting or writing *pad*).—*v.t.*—*padded, padding.* To stuff so as to make a pad; to furnish with a pad.—**padding,** pad′ing, *n.* The act of stuffing; the materials used for stuffing a saddle, bolster, etc.; literary matter inserted in a book, periodical, etc., merely to increase the bulk.

pad, pad, *n.* [A form of *path*; comp. Prov. E. *pad,* Sc. *paad,* a path.] A robber that infests the road on foot; a footpad; an easy-paced horse.

paddle, pad′l, *v.i.*—*paddled, paddling.* [A freq. and dim. from *pad,* to go = L.G. *paddeln,* to go with short steps, to paddle.] To play in the water with the hands or feet in swimming or sport; to use a paddle; to row with a paddle.—*v.t.* To propel by an oar or paddle.—*n.* A sort of short broad oar used in propelling and steering canoes and boats by a vertical motion; one of the floatboards placed on the circumference of the wheel of a steam vessel; *zool.* the swimming apparatus of the turtles and certain other animals.—**paddle box,** *n.* The wooden covering of the paddle wheel of a steamer.—**paddler,** pad′l•ėr, *n.* One that paddles.—**paddle wheel,** *n.* A wheel with boards or floats on its circumference, driven by steam and propelling a vessel over water.

paddock, pad′ok, *n.* [A.Sax. *pada,* a frog or toad (with dim. suffix *-ock*) = Icel. and Sw. *padda,* Dan. *padde,* D. *pad, padde,* a frog or toad.] A toad or frog.

paddock, pad′ok, *n.* [For *parrok,* A.Sax. *pearroc.* PARK.] A small field enclosed for pasture; ground adjacent to racecourse stables, used for the exercising of horses.

paddy, pad′i, *n.* [Malay *padi.*] Rice in the husk whether in the field or gathered; a rice field.

padishah, pä′di•shä, *n.* [Per. *pádishâh,* from *pâd,* protector, master, and *shâh,* a king.] A title of the Turkish sultan and Persian shah.

padlock, pad′lok, *n.* [Either from *pad,* a path, lit. a lock for a gate on a path, or from *pad* in the local sense of a pannier.] A movable lock with a bow or semicircular link to be fastened through a staple.—*v.t.* To fasten or provide with a padlock or padlocks.

padre, pä′drā, *n.* [It. *padre,* L. *pater,* father.] A title applied in Latin countries to a minister of religion and by sailors and soldiers to a chaplain.

paduasoy, pad′ū•a•soi, *n.* [From *Padua,* in Italy, and Fr. *soie,* silk.] A particular kind of silk stuff.

paean, pē′an, *n.* [Gr.] An ancient Greek hymn in honor of Apollo, who was also called Paean; a war song before or after a battle; hence, a song of triumph generally; a loud and joyous song.

paedogenesis, pē′do•jen″e•sis, *n.* [Gr. *pais, paidos,* a child, *genesis,* descent.] In animals, precocious sexual reproduction by immature individuals.

paeon, pē′on, *n.* [Gr. *paeon.*] A metrical foot, consisting of four syllables, one long and three short.

pagan, pā′gan, *n.* [L. *paganus,* a peasant, from *pagus,* a village or country district; comp. origin of *heathen.* Akin *peasant.*] One who worships false gods; one who is neither a Christian, a Jew, nor a Mohammedan; a heathen; an idolater.—*a.* Pertaining to pagans or heathens; heathenish; idolatrous.—**paganish,** pā′gan•ish, *a.* Heathenish.—**paganism,** pā′gan•izm, *n.* The worship of false gods; the religious opinions and worship of pagans; heathenism. — **paganize,** pa′gan•īz, *v.t.—paganized, paganizing.* To render heathenish; to convert to heathenism.

page, pāj, *n.* [Fr. *page,* It. *paggio,* a page, from L.L. *pagius,* perhaps from Gr. *padion,* or *pais,* child]. A young male attendant on kings, nobles, or other persons of distinction; a lad in the service of people of rank or wealth, whose duty it is to run errands, attend to the door, etc.—*v.t.—paged, paging.* To attend as a page.

page, pāj, *n.* [Fr. *page,* from L. *pagina,* a page, from stem *pag,* seen in L. *pango,* Gr. *pēgnymi,* to fix; akin *compact* (*a.*), *pageant.*] One side of the leaf of a book; a writing or record (the *page* of history); *printing,* types set up for one side of a leaf.—*v.t. paged, paging.* To mark or number the pages of.—**paginal,** paj′i•nal, *a.* Consisting of pages.—**paginate,** paj′i•nāt, *v.t.—paginated, paginating.* To number the pages of; to page.—**pagination,** paj•i•nā′shon, *n.* The act of paging; the marks or figures which indicate the number of pages.

pageant, paj′ent or pā′jent, *n.* [Old forms *pagyn, pagen,* originally a scaffold or stage, from L. *pagina,* a slab, a page (of a book). PAGE.] A spectacle or entertainment; a great display or show, as at some public rejoicing; a theatrical exhibition; anything showy, without stability or duration.—**pageantry,** paj′ent•ri, *n.* Pageants collectively; a showy exhibition or spectacle; splendid or ostentatious show.

paginal, pagination. See PAGE.

pagoda, pa•gō′da, *n.* [Fr. *pagode,* from Per. and Hind, *but-gadah—but,* an idol, and *gadah,* a house.] A Hindu temple in which idols are worshiped; a Buddhist temple.

Pagurus, pa•gū′rus, *n.* [Gr. *pagouros* —root *pag,* to fix, and *oura,* tail.] A genus of crabs which includes the hermit crabs, etc.—**pagurian,** pa•gū′ri•an, *n.* A crab of this genus or of the same family.

paid, pād, pret. and pp. of *pay.*

pail, pāl, *n.* [O.Fr. *paile, paele,* from L. *patella,* a pan, from *pateo,* to lie open. PATENT.] A vessel of wood, or of tin or other metal, in which milk or water is commonly carried.—**pailful,** pāl′ful, *n.* The quantity that a pail will hold.

paillasse, pal•yas′, *n.* [Fr., from *paille,* straw, L. *palea,* chaff.] An under bed of straw; an under mattress.

pain, pān, *n.* [Fr. *peine,* O.Fr. *peine, paine,* etc., from L. *pœna,* punishment, and latterly pain, torment; akin *penal, penitence, pine* (verb), *punish,* etc.] Penalty; suffering annexed to the commission of a crime (under *pain* of death); an uneasy sensation in animal bodies; bodily distress; suffering; the throes of travail or childbirth (generally in plural); mental distress; careful labor; close application in working; trouble (chiefly in plural).—*v.t.* To give pain to; to cause to endure physical or mental suffering; to afflict; to distress.—**painful,** pān′fụl, *a.* Full of pain; giving or accompanied by pain; distressing; requiring labor or toil; difficult; executed with pains; attended with close and careful application or attention.—**painfully,** pān′fụl•li, *adv.* In a painful manner.—**painfulness,** pān′fụl•nes, *n.* The state or quality of being painful.—**painless,** pān′les, *a.* Free from pain.—**painstaking,** pānz′tā•king, *a.* Taking or given to taking pains; giving close application; laborious and careful.—*n.* The taking of pains; careful labor.

paint, pānt, *v.t.* [O.Fr. *paindre,* pp. *paint* (Fr. *peindre*), from L. *pingere, pictum,* to paint. PICTURE.] To lay color or colors on with a brush or otherwise; to diversify with hues; to color; to produce (a representation) in colors; to form a likeness or representation of in colors; to represent or exhibit to the mind; to describe vividly; to delineate; to depict.—*v.i.* To practice painting; to lay artificial color on the face.—*n.* A substance used in painting; a pigment; color laid on the face; rouge.—**painter,** pān′tėr, *n.* One whose occupation is to paint; an artist who represents objects by means of colors or pigments.—*Painter's colic,* a disease to which painters and others who work with poisonous preparations of lead are liable.—**painting,** pān′ting, *n.* The act, art, or employment of laying on colors; the art of representing objects by means of figures and colors on a plane surface so as to produce the appearance of relief; a painted picture.

painter, pān′tėr, *n.* [Ir. *painteir,* a snare, a net.] A rope used to fasten a boat to a ship or other object.—*To cut the painter,* to assert one's independence by severing a connection with a person or thing.

pair, pâr, *n.* [Fr. *paire,* from L. *par,* equal, whence also *parity, peer, compeer, disparage,* etc.] Two things similar in form and suited to each other or used together (a *pair* of gloves or stockings); a single thing composed of two pieces suiting each other (a *pair* of scissors or of trousers); two of a sort; a couple; a brace; distinctively, a man and his wife; in *parliament,* and similar bodies, two members who would vote on opposite sides and agree not to vote for a specified time.—*Pair* formerly often meant a set of things; hence, we speak of a *pair* of stairs for a flight of stairs or steps.—*v.i.* To join in pairs; to couple; to mate (as birds).—*To pair, to pair off,* to depart from a company in pairs or couples; to form a pair in the parliamentary sense.—*v.t.* To unite in pairs or couples; to assort in twos.

paisley, pāz′lē, *n.* [For the town in Scotland.] A woolen fabric patterned in geometric designs of various colors.—*a.* Of a paisley pattern.

pajamas, pa•jä′mas, *n. pl.* [Hind.] A loose garment, usually including jacket and trousers, worn for sleeping, lounging, etc. (Seldom used in singular except attributively, as in *pajama* coat.)

pal, pal, *n.* [Of Gypsy origin.] Mate; partner; accomplice; chum. (*Slang.*)

palace, pal′is, *n.* [Fr. *palais,* from L. *Palatium,* the house of Augustus, on the hill at Rome, called by this name.] The house in which an emperor, a king, or other distinguished person resides; a splendid residence; a stately mansion.

paladin, pal′a•din, *n.* [Fr. *paladin,* from L. *palatinus,* attached to the palace, from *palatium.* PALACE.] A knight attached to a sovereign's court; a knight-errant; a heroic champion; an eminent hero.

palanquin, palankeen, pal•an•kēn′, *n.* [Fr. and Pg. *palanquin,* from Pali, *pâlangki.*] A covered conveyance used in India, China, etc., borne by poles on the shoulder, and carrying a single person; a covered litter.

palate, pal′at, *n.* [L. *palatum*, the palate.] The roof or upper part of the mouth; taste; relish; sometimes intellectual taste.—**palatable,** pal′at•a•bl, *a.* Agreeable to the taste or palate; savory.—**palatableness,** pal′at•a•bl•nes, *n.* The quality of being palatable to the taste.—**palatably,** pal′at•a•bli, *adv.* In a palatable manner.—**palatal,** pal′at•al, *a.* Pertaining to the palate; uttered by the aid of the palate, as certain sounds.—*n.* A sound pronounced by the aid of the palate; as that of *ch* in *church*, and that of *j*.—**palatalize,** pal′a•tal•īz, *v.t.* To give a palatal sound to; to convert from guttural to palatal (*church* is palatalized compared with *kirk*).

palatial, pa•lā′shal, *a.* [From L. *palatium*, palace. PALACE.] Pertaining to a palace; becoming a palace; magnificent.—**palatine,** pal′a•tīn, *a.* [Fr. *palatin*, L. *palatinus*, from *palatium*, palace.] Pertaining to a palace; holding office in the king's palace; possessing royal privileges.—*County palatine* is a county over which an earl, bishop, or duke had a royal jurisdiction.—*n.* One invested with royal privileges and rights; a count palatine.—**palatinate,** pa•lat′i•nāt, *n.* The province or seignory of a palatine.

palaver, pa•lä′vėr, *n.* [Pg. *palavra*, Sp. *palabra*, a word, from L. *parabola*, a parable, in late times a word. PARABLE.] A talk or conference among some barbaric races; a conversation; superfluous or idle talk.—*v.t.* To flatter; to humbug by words.—*v.i.* To talk idly; to indulge in a palaver or palavers.

pale, pāl, *a.* [O.Fr. *pale* (Fr. *pâle*), from L. *pallidus*, pale. PALLID.] White or whitish; wan; not ruddy or fresh of color; not bright; of a faint luster; dim.—*v.t.—paled, paling.* To make pale; to diminish the brightness of.—*v.i.* To turn pale.—**paleface,** *n.* A name among the North American Indians for a white person.—**palely,** pāl′li, *adv.* In a pale manner; wanly; not ruddily.—**paleness,** pāl′nes, *n.* The quality or condition of being pale.—**palish,** pāl′ish, *a.* Somewhat pale or wan.—**paly,** pāl′i, *a.* Pale; wanting color. (*Poet.*)

pale, pāl, *n.* [A.Sax. *pal*, Fr. *pal*, from L. *palus*, a stake, from root seen in *page* (of a book), *pageant, pact.*] A pointed stake used in fencing or enclosing, fixed upright in the ground, or joined above and below to a rail; a picket; what surrounds and encloses; the space enclosed; an enclosure; an instrument for trying the quality of a cheese; in *her.* when a shield is divided into halves by a perpendicular line, it is said to be *palewise* or *per pale.*—*The Pale*, that portion of Ireland within which English rule was for some centuries confined after the conquests of Henry II.—*v.t.* To enclose with pales or stakes; to encompass.—**paling,** pāl′ing, *n.* Pales in general, or a fence formed with pales.—**paly,** pāl′i, *n.* The division of a shield into perpendicular bars of alternate tinctures and an even number of divisions.

palea, pā′li•a, *n.* pl. **paleae,** pā′li•ē. [L. *palea*, chaff.] *Bot.* one of the bracts upon the receptacle of composite plants between the florets; one of the interior bracts of the flowers of grasses.—**paleaceous,** pā•li•ā′shus, *a. Bot.* consisting of chaff-like scales; covered with paleae.

Palearctic, pā•lē•ärk′tik, *a.* [Gr. *palaios*, ancient, and E. *arctic.*] Said of a region of the earth marked by a characteristic fauna, and embracing Europe, Africa north of the Atlas, and Northern Asia.

paleobotany, pā′li•ō•bot″a•ni, *n.* [Gr. *palaios*, and E. *botany.*] The study of the plants that are found in a fossil state.

paleography, pā′li•og″ra•fi, *n.* [Gr. *palaios*, ancient, and *graphō*, to write.] An ancient manner or form of writing; ancient writings collectively; the art of deciphering ancient documents or inscriptions.—**paleographer,** pā•li•og′ra•fėr, *n.*—**paleographic,** pā•li•o•graf′ik, *a.*

paleolithic, pā•li•o•lith′ik, *a.* [Gr. lithos, stone.] Of the second period of the Stone Age, characterized by stone implements.

paleontography, pā′li•on•tog″ra•fi, *n.* [Gr. *onta*, beings.] The description of fossil remains.—**paleontographical,** pā•li•on′to•graf″i•kal, *a.* Relating to paleontography.—**paleontology,** pā′-li•on•tol″o•ji, *n.* The science of the ancient life of the earth; that branch of biological science which treats of fossil organic remains.—**paleontological,** pā′li•on•to•loj″i•kal, *a.* Relating to paleontology.—**paleontologically,** pā′li•on•to•loj″i•kal•li, *adv.* In a paleontological sense or point of view.—**paleozoology,** pā′li•ō•zō•ol″o•ji, *n.* [Gr. *zoon*, an animal.] That branch of biology which concerns itself with the fossil remains of animals.

Paleozoic, pa′li•o•zō″ik, *a.* [Gr. *zōē*, life.] A geological era that extends from the beginning of the Cambrian to the end of the Permian.

palestra, pa•les′tra, *n.* [Gr. *palaistra*, from *palē*, wrestling.] A place appropriated to the exercise of wrestling or other athletic exercises; exercises of wrestling.

paletot, pal′e•tō, *n.* [Fr. *paletot*, *paletoque*, a paletot, an overcoat, from D. *paltsrok*, a pilgrim's coat.] A loose sort of man's coat or woman's long jacket; an overcoat.

palette, pal′et, *n.* [Fr. *palette*, from L.L. *paleta*, dim. from L. *pala*, a spade or shovel.] A thin oval board or tablet, with a thumb hole at one end, on which a painter lays the pigments with which he paints his pictures; a pallet.—**palette knife,** *n.* A sort of knife used by painters for mixing colors, and by druggists to mix salves.

palfrey, pal′fri, *n.* [O.Fr. *palefrei*, from L.L. *parafredus*, L. *paraveredus*, an extra post horse, from Gr. *para*, beside, and L. *veredus*, a post horse (from *veho*, to carry, and *rheda*, a carriage).] An ordinary riding horse, or a horse used by noblemen and others for state, distinguished from a war horse; a small horse fit for ladies.

Pali, pä′li, *n.* The sacred language of the Buddhists, a descendant of the Sanskrit, now used only in religious works.

palimpsest, pa′limp•sest, *n.* [Gr. *palimpsestos*, rubbed again—*palin*, again, and *psaō*, to rub.] A parchment or other piece of writing material from which one writing has been erased to make room for another, often leaving the first faintly visible, a process to which many ancient manuscripts were subjected.

palindrome, pal′in•drōm, *n.* [Gr. *palindromos*, running back—*palin*, again, and *dromos*, a running.] A word, verse, or sentence that is the same when read backward or forward.

paling. See PALE.

palingenesis, pal•in•jen′e•sis, *n.* [Gr. *palin*, again, and *genesis*, birth.] A transformation from one state to another; a metamorphosis as of insects; a great geological change on the earth.

palinode, pal′i•nōd, *n.* [Gr. *palinōdia*—*palin*, again, and *ōdē*, a song.] Originally a poetical recantation; a piece in which a poet retracts the invectives contained in a former piece; hence, a recantation in general.

palisade, pal•i•sād′, *n.* [Fr. *palissade*, from *palisser*, to pale, from *palis*, a pale. PALE (a stake).] A fence or fortification consisting of a row of strong stakes or posts set firmly in the ground; also applied to one of the stakes; a mass of rock, as the denuded face of a mountain.

palish. See PALE.

pall, pal, *n.* [A.Sax. *paell*, from L. *pallium*, a cloak, a pall.] An outer mantle of dignity; *eccles.* a vestment sent from Rome to patriarchs, primates, and metropolitans as an ensign of jurisdiction, and sometimes, as a mark of honor, to bishops; consisting of a band made of white lamb's wool, passing round the shoulders, and having a strip hanging down before and behind; a large black cloth thrown over a coffin at a funeral, or over a tomb; rich cloth of any kind, 'in purple and pall'.—*v.t.* To cover with a pall; to cover or invest; to shroud.—**pallbearer,** *n.* One of those who attend the coffin at a funeral.

pall, pal, *v.i.* [W. *pallu*, to fail; *pall*, loss of energy, failure; the verb *appal* was probably to some extent affected by this word.] To become vapid; to become insipid; to become devoid of agreeableness or attraction (pleasures begin to *pall*).—*v.t.* To make vapid or insipid; to cloy; to dispirit or depress‡.

Palladian, pal•lā′di•an, *a.* Pertaining to Andrea *Palladio*, a celebrated Italian architect (1518-80).—*Palladian architecture*, a species of Italian architecture founded upon the Roman antique.

Palladium, pal•lā′di•um, *n.* [From Pallas or Athene, equivalent to the Latin *Minerva.*] A sacred statue or image of *Pallas*, the Greek goddess, on the preservation of which, according to ancient legend, was said to have depended the safety of Troy.

palladium, pal•lā′di•um, *n.* [N.L., from the asteroid *Pallas*, from Gr. *Pallas*, the goddess.] *Chem.* a silver-white, malleable and ductile, metallic element of the platinum group. Symbol, Pd; at. no., 46; at. wt. 106.4.

pallet, pal′et, *n.* [Fr. *palette*, from L.L. *paletta*, dim. from L. *pala*, a spade or shovel.] A palette; a wooden instrument used by potters, etc., for forming and rounding their wares; an instrument to take up and apply goldleaf; pieces which receive the impulse from a pendulum or balance wheel.

pallet, pal′et, *n.* [From Fr. *paille*, straw; L. *palea*, chaff.] A small or rude bed; a bed or mattress of straw.

palliate, pal′i•āt, *v.t.*—*palliated, palliating.* [Fr. *pallier*, to cloak, palliate; from L. *pallium*, a cloak, whence also *pall* (*n.*).] To conceal the enormity of by excuses and apologies; to extenuate; to soften or tone down by favorable representations; to mitigate, lessen, or abate (to *palliate* a disease).—**palliation,** pal•i•ā′shon, *n.* The act of palliating; what palliates or serves to excuse; extenuation; mitigating; alleviation.—**palliative,** pal′i•ā•tiv, *a.* [Fr. *palliatif.*] Serving to palliate or extenuate; extenuating; mitigating.—*n.* That which palliates.

pallid, pal′id, *a.* [L. *pallidus*, from *palleo*, to become pale. PALE, FALLOW.] Pale; wan; deficient in color; not high colored.—**pallidly,** pal′id•li, *adv.* Palely; wanly.—**pallidness,** pal′id•nes, *n.* Paleness.

pallium, pal′li•um, *n.* [L. *pallium*, whence *pall* (*n.*).] An ecclesiastical or other pall; *zool.* an outgrowth of the dorsal body-wall of many mollusks, forming folds or processes which represent the foot and other parts.

pall-mall, pel-mel′, *n.* [O.Fr. *palemail*, from It. *pallamaglio*, from *palla*, a ball (akin E. *ball*), and *maglio*, L. *malleus*, a mallet.] An ancient game in which a ball was struck with a mallet or club through a ring elevated upon a pole; the alley or walk where the game was played (hence the street in London called *Pall Mall*).

pallor, pal′or, *n.* [L. PALLID.] Paleness.

palm, päm, *n.* [L. *palma*, the palm of the hand, a palm tree (so named from the shape of its branches); cog. Gr. *palamē*, A.Sax. *folm*, O.H.G. *folma*, the palm of the hand.] The inner part of the hand; a lineal measure equal to 3 or 4 inches; a broad flat part, as of an anchor fluke; any of the plants of a well-known order of arborescent or tree-like endogens, chiefly inhabiting the tropics, of great value to man as affording food, etc.; a branch or leaf of the palm tree anciently borne as a symbol of victory or triumph; hence, superiority, victory, triumph (to carry off the *palm*); a popular name for the bloom or a branch of the willow, carried on Palm Sunday as a substitute for the Eastern palm branches.—*v.t.*—*palmed, palming.* To conceal in the palm of the hand, as jugglers or cheaters; to impose by fraud (to *palm off* trash *upon* the public).—*Palma Christi* (palm of Christ), a name for the castor-oil plant.—**palmaceous,** pal•mā′shus, *a.* Belonging to the palm tribe.—**palmar,** pal′mėr, *a.* [L. *palmaris.*] Pertaining to the palm of the hand; of the breadth of the hand.—**palmate, palmated,** pal′māt, pal′mā•ted, *a.* [L. *palmatus.*] Having the shape of the hand (*palmated* leaves); having the toes webbed (the *palmate* feet of aquatic birds).—**palmately,** pal′māt•li, *adv.* In a palmate manner.—**palmer,** päm′ėr, *n.* A pilgrim that returned from the Holy Land with a branch of palm; one who palms or cheats, as at cards or dice.—**palmerworm,** *n.* A name for certain hairy caterpillars.—**palmetto,** pal•met′tō, *n.* [Sp. *palmito.*] A name of several palms; the cabbage palm of the West Indies and southern United States.—**palmistry,** pä′mis•tri, *n.* The art of telling fortunes by the lines and marks in the palm of the hand; manual dexterity (humorous).—**palmitic,** pal•mit′ik, *a.* Pertaining to or obtained from palm oil (*palmitic* acid).—**palmitin,** pal′mi•tin, *n.* The principal solid ingredient of palm oil.—**palm oil,** *n.* A fatty substance resembling butter obtained from palms, chiefly from the fruit of the African oil palm, employed in the manufacture of soap and candles, for lubricating.—**Palm Sunday,** *n.* The Sunday next before Easter, commemorative of the Saviour's triumphal entry into Jerusalem, when the multitude strewed palm branches in the way.—**palmy,** pä′mi, *a.* Abounding in palms; flourishing; prosperous.—**palmyra, palmyra palm,** pal•mī′ra, *n.* The most common palm of India, the wood, leaves, fruit, and juice of which are all of great value and use.

palomino, pal′ō•mi″nō, *n.* [Amer. Sp. from Sp. *palomilla.*] A tan or cream-colored horse with slender legs and white mane and tail; a color like that of the horse.

palp, palpus, palp, pal′pus, *n.* (pl. **palpi,** pal′pī). [Mod. L. *palpus*, from L. *palpare*, to stroke, to feel.] A jointed sensitive organ on the head of an insect; a feeler.

palpable, pal′pa•bl, *a.* [Fr. *palpable*, from L. *palpabilis*, from *palpo*, to touch; akin *palpitate.*] Perceptible by the touch; capable of being felt; easily perceived and detected; plain; obvious; easily perceptible.—*Palpable obscure*, darkness that may be felt. (*Mil.*)—**palpability,** pal•pa•bil′i•ti, *n.* Plainness; obviousness.—**palpably,** pal′pa•bli, *adv.* Plainly; obviously.—**palpation,** pal•pā′shon, *n.* [L. *palpatio.*] The act of feeling; *pathol.* manual examination.

palpebral, pal′pe•bral, *a.* [L. *palpebra*, an eyelid.] Pertaining to the eyelid or eyebrow.

palpi. See PALP.

palpitate, pal′pi•tāt, *v.i.*—*palpitated, palpitating.* [L. *palpito, palpitatum*, freq. of *palpo*, to feel. PALPABLE.] To flutter or move with slight throbs; to throb; to pulsate violently: applied particularly to an abnormal movement of the heart, as from fright or disease; hence, to tremble; to quiver.—**palpitation,** pal•pi•tā′shon, *n.* A violent and unnatural beating or pulsation of the heart, as from violent action, fright, or disease.

palsgrave, pąlz′grāv, *n.* [G. *pfalzgraf*, from *pfalz* (contr. from L. *palatium*, palace), and *graf*, an earl.] A count palatine; a count with the superintendence of the king's palace.—**palsgravine,** pąlz′gra•vin, *n.* The consort of a palsgrave.

palsy, pąl′zi, *n.* [A contr. of *paralysis*, Fr. *paralysie.*] Paralysis, especially in a limb or some of the superficial muscles.—*v.t.*—*palsied, palsying.* To affect with palsy or as with palsy; to paralyze.—**palsied,** pąl′zid, *p.* and *a.* Affected with palsy.

palter, pąl′tėr, *v.i.* [Of same origin as *paltry*, and originally having reference to the haggling of dealers in old clothes.] To act insincerely; to equivocate; to haggle; to shift; to dodge; to play tricks.

paltry, pąl′tri, *a.* [Same as L.G. *paltrig, palterig*, ragged, from *palte*, Fris. *palt*, G. *palte*, Sw. *palta* (plur. *paltor*), Dan. *pialt*, a rag; akin *palter.*] Mean; vile; worthless; despicable. ∴ Syn. under CONTEMPTIBLE.—**paltrily,** pąl′tri•li, *adv.* In a paltry manner.—**paltriness,** pąl′tri•nes, *n.* The state of being paltry, vile, or worthless.

paludal, pal′ū•dal, *a.* [L. *palus, paludis*, a marsh.] Pertaining to marshes; generated by marshes (*paludal* fever).

paludine, pal′ū•dīn, *a.* [L. *palus, paludis*, a pool, a marsh.] Pertaining to marshes; marshy.

paly. See PALE.

pam, pam, *n.* In five-card loo, the knave of clubs.

pampas, pam′pas, *n. pl.* [Sp.-Amer.] The grassy treeless plains of South America, resembling the prairies of North America; especially the immense plains in the southern portion of South America east of the Andes.—**pampas grass,** *n.* A variety of grass with flower stems 10 to 14 feet high growing on the pampas, introduced as an ornamental grass into Britain.—**pampean,** pam•pē′an, *a.* Pertaining to the pampas.

pamper, pam′pėr, *v.t.* [Probably akin to *pap* (with *m* inserted); comp. G. *pampen*, Bav. *pampfen*, to stuff, to cram with food.] To indulge with rich food; to feed luxuriously; to gratify to the full; to indulge to excess.—**pamperer,** pam′pėr•ėr, *n.* One who pampers.

pampero, pam•pâ′ro, *n.* [Sp.-Amer. *pampas.*] The cold wind blowing from the Andes to the Atlantic.

pamphlet, pam′flet, *n.* [Formerly

paunflet, pamfilet, pamflet: from Med. L. *Pamphilet*, name of a popular poem.] A small book consisting of a sheet of paper, or of a few sheets stitched together but not bound; a short treatise or essay published by itself.—**pamphleteer,** pam•flet•ēr′, *n.* A writer of pamphlets; a scribbler.—*v.i.* To write and issue pamphlets.

pan, pan, *n.* [A.Sax. *panne*, D. *pan*, G. *pfanne*, all from L.L. *panna*, for *patna*, L. *patina*, a pan, from *pateo*, to be wide. PATENT.] A vessel of tin, iron, or other metal, often rather shallow; a vessel of various kinds used for domestic purposes; an open vessel for boiling or evaporating or other operations (a sugar *pan*, a salt *pan*, etc.); a pond for evaporating salt water to make salt; the part of a flintlock which holds the priming; the skull or cranium (the brain*pan*).—*Pan out*, to yield a good return='to cut-up' well: from the phrase of miners washing out the gravel of the gold in pans; to succeed; *agri.* HARDPAN.—**pancake,** *n.* A thin cake of batter fried or baked in a pan.

Pan, pan, *n.* [Hence *panic.*] *Greek myth.* the chief god of pastures, forests, and flocks.—**Pandean,** pan•dē′an, *a.* Pertaining to Pan.—*Pandean pipes*, *Pan's pipes*, a musical wind instrument composed of reeds of different lengths tied together; a syrinx.

panacea, pan•a•sē′a, *n.* [L., from Gr. *panakeia*, a universal remedy—*pan*, all, and *akeomai*, to cure.] A remedy for all diseases; a universal medicine or remedy.

panada, pa•nä′da, *n.* [Fr. *panade*, from L. *panis*, bread.] A food made by boiling bread in water to the consistence of pulp.

panama, pa′na•mä, *n.* [From Panama City.] A soft straw hat made from young jipijapa leaves.

panatela, pa•na•tel′a, *n.* [Sp.] A short slender cigar.

pancake. See PAN.

panchromatic, pan•krō•mat′ik, *a.* [Prefix *pan*, and *chromatic*, color.] *Photog.* sensitive to all colors.

pancratium, pan•krā′shi•um, *n.* [Gr. *pangkration*—*pan*, all, and *kratos*, strength.] A gymnastic contest of ancient Greece consisting of boxing and wrestling.

pancreas, pan′kri•as, *n.* [Gr. *pan*, all, and *kreas*, flesh.] A large gland which secretes a digestive fluid into the intestine; the pancreas of cattle, used as food, called sweetbread.—**pancreatic,** pan•kri•at′ik, *a.*

panda, pan′da, *n.* A carnivorous quadruped of the genus *Ailurus*, found in the Himalayas and Tibet, belonging to the raccoon family, whose fur is reddish-brown on the back and sides, and black on the underside and legs.—*Giant panda*, an animal of the genus *Ailuropoda*.

pandect, pan′dekt, *n.* [Gr. *pandektēs*—*pan*, all, and *dechomai*, to contain.] A treatise which contains the whole of any science; *pl.* the digest or collection of Roman civil law, made by order of the emperor Justinian, and consisting of fifty books.

pandemic, pan•dem′ik, *a.* [Gr. *pan*, all, and *demos*, people.] Incident to a whole people; epidemic.

pandemonium, pan•di•mō′ni•um, *n.* [Gr. *pan*, all, and *daimōn*, a demon.] The place or abode of demons or evil spirits—a name invented by Milton; hence, any lawless, disorderly place or assemblage.

pander, pan′dėr, *n.* [From *Pandarus*, who performs the part of a pimp in the story of Troilus and Cressida.] A pimp; a procurer; a male bawd; hence, one who ministers to the gratification of any of the baser passions.—*v.i.* To act as agent for the lusts of others.

Pandora, pan•dō′ra, *n.* [Gr., from *pan*, all, and *dōron*, a gift.] *Class. myth.* the name of the first woman on earth, on whom all the gods and goddesses bestowed gifts.—*Pandora's box*, a box Pandora received, containing all human ills, from which all escaped and spread over the earth, hope alone remaining.

pandour, pan′dör, *n.* [Croatian *bandur*, under a banner, later *pandur*, mounted policeman.] One of a body of Croatian foot soldiers, formerly dreaded for their savage mode of warfare.

pandurate, panduriform, pan′dū•rāt, pan•dū′ri•form, *a. Bot.* shaped like a violin; fiddle-shaped; applied to a leaf.

pane, pān, *n.* [Fr. *pan*, a panel or definite portion of a surface, from L. *pannus*, a piece of cloth, a patch (whence also *panel, pawn.*)] A distinct part of a flat surface‡; a plate of glass inserted in a window, door, etc.; a panel or division of a work; a sunken portion surrounded by a border.

panegyric, pan•e•jir′ik, *n.* [Gr. *panēgyrikos*, fit for a public assembly, from *panēgyris*, a public assembly—*pas, pan*, all, and *agyris*, an assembly.] A laudatory oration; a formal eulogy; an elaborate encomium; praise bestowed; laudation.—**panegyrical,** pan•e•jir′i•kal, *a.* Containing praise or eulogy; encomiastic,—**panegyrically,** pan•e•jir′i•kal•li, *adv.* By way of panegyric.—**panegyrist,** pan•e•jir′ist, *n.* One who bestows praise; a eulogist.—**panegyrize,** pan′e•ji•rīz, *v.t.*—*panegyrized, panegyrizing*. To write or pronounce a panegyric or eulogy on.—*v.i.* To indulge in panegyric; to bestow praises.

panel, pan′el, *n.* [O.Fr. *panel*, dim. of *pan*, a pane, a panel. PANE.] A surface or compartment of a surface more or less distinct from others; an area on a wall sunk from the general surface; a similar portion fixed in the framing of a door, shutter, etc.; a piece of wood upon which a picture is painted; *law*, a document containing the names of persons summoned to serve upon a jury; the jury; *Scots law*, the accused person in a criminal action.—*v.t.*—*paneled, paneling*. To form with panels.—**paneling,** pan′el•ing, *n.* Paneled work.

pang, pang, *n.* [Comp. W. *pang*, a pang, a convulsion.] A sudden paroxysm of extreme pain; a sudden spasm or throe.

pangenesis, pan•jen′e•sis, *n.* [Gr. *pan*, *genesis*, descent.] A provisional theory, now abandoned, attributing the transmission of hereditary characters to living particles migrating into the sex cells from all parts of the body.—**pangenetic,** pan•je•net′ik, *a.* Pertaining to or relating to pangenesis.

Pan-Germanism, pan•jėr′man•ism, *n.* A movement aimed at keeping Germans, resident in any part of the world, conscious of their common cultural heritage.

panhandle, pan′han•dl, *n.* A projection of land resembling a handle of a pan, as in the northwest section of Texas.—*v.t.* and *i.* To approach one on the street and beg.

Panhellenic, pan•hel•len′ik, *a.* [Gr. *pan*, all, and *Hellēnikos*, Greek, from *Hellēnes*, the Greeks.] Pertaining to all Greece.—**Panhellenism,** pan•hel′len•izm, *n.* The proposed union of all the Greeks into one political body.—**Panhellenist,** pan•hel′len•ist, *n.* One who favors Panhellenism.

panic, pan′ik, *n.* [From Gr. *panikos*, of or belonging to *Pan*, the god who was believed to inspire sudden fear, fear arising among people without visible cause.] A sudden fright, particularly without real cause; terror inspired by a trifling cause.—*a.* Extreme or causeless; applied to fright.—**panicky,** pan′ik•i, *a.* Showing or inspired by panic.—**panic-stricken, panic-struck,** *a.* Struck with a panic or sudden fear.

panic grass, pan′ik, *n.* [L. *panicum*, a kind of grass.] The name of several species of grass.

panicle, pan′i•kl, *n.* [L. *panicula*, a panicle, dim. of *panus*, thread on the bobbin in a shuttle.] A branching form of inflorescence, as in the lilac or the oat.—**Paniculate, paniculated,** pa•nik′ū•lāt, pa•nik′ū•lā•ted, *a. Bot.* furnished with or arranged in a panicle; like a panicle.

panic switch, pan′ik swich [E. panic and switch (which see).] The control on the ejector mechanism that throws a jet pilot from his plane in case of emergency.

pannier, pan′i•ėr, *n.* [Fr. *panier*, from L. *panarium*, a breadbasket, from *panis*, bread. PANTRY.] A wicker-basket, primarily a breadbasket, but now one of two baskets slung across a beast of burden, in which things are carried; a part of a lady's dress attached to the back of the skirt; *arch.* a corbel.

pannikin, pan′i•kin, *n.* A small pan or cup.

panoply, pan′o•pli, *n.* [Gr. *panoplia*—*pan*, all, and *hopla*, arms.] Complete armor of defense; an elaborate covering.—**panoplied,** pan′o•plid, *a.* Having a panoply or full suit of armor.

panorama, pan•o•ra′ma, *n.* [Gr. *pan*, all, and *horama*, view, from *horaō*, to see.] A picture in which all the objects of nature that are visible from a single point are represented on the interior surface of a round or cylindrical wall, the point of view being in the axis of the cylinder.—**panoramic,** pan•ō•ram′ik, *a.* Pertaining to or like a panorama, or complete view.

Pan-Slavic, pan•slav′ik, *a.* [Gr. *pan,* all, and E. *Slavic.*] Pertaining to all the Slavic races.—**Pan-Slavism,** pan•slav′izm, *n.* The proposed amalgamation of all the Slavic races into one confederacy.

pansy, pan′zi, *n.* [Fr. *pensée,* thought, heart's-ease, from *penser,* to think. PENSIVE.] A name applied to the garden varieties of violet; heart's-ease.

pant, pant, *v.i.* [From or connected with O.Fr. *pantoier,* to pant, to gasp, *pantois,* a panting; Pr. *panteiar,* to be breathless.] To breathe quickly, as after exertion or from excited eagerness; to gasp; to throb or heave with unusual violence, as the heart or the breast after hard labor; to desire ardently.—*v.t.* To breathe forth; to gasp out.—*n.* A quick, short respiration; a gasp; a throb or palpitation.—**pantingly,** pan′ting•li, *adv.* In a panting manner; with gasping or rapid breathing.

pantalets, pan′ta•lets, *n. pl.* [From *pantaloon.*] Loose drawers worn by females and children.

pantaloon, pan•ta•lön′, *n.* [Fr. *pantalon,* lit. a Venetian, after their patron saint *Pantalone* or *Pantaleon.*] A character in the Italian comedy: so called from his dress; in modern pantomimes, a character usually represented as the butt of the clown; pl. a pair of trousers.

pantheism, pan′thē•izm, *n.* [Gr. *pan,* all, and *Theos,* God.] The doctrine that the universe, taken or conceived of as a whole, is God, or that all things are simply modes or manifestations of God.—**pantheist,** pan′thē•ist, *n.* One that believes in pantheism.—**pantheistic, pantheistical,** pan•thē•is′tik, pan•thē•is′ti•kal, *a.* Pertaining to pantheism.—**pantheistically,** pan•thē•is′ti•kal•li, *adv.* In the manner or from the point of view of a pantheist.

pantheon, pan′thē•on or pan•thē′on, *n.* [Gr. *pantheon, pantheion—pan,* all, and *theos,* a god.] A temple dedicated to all the gods, especially [*cap.*] the building so called at Rome, now converted into a church; all the divinities collectively worshiped by a people.

panther, pan′thėr, *n.* [L. *panthera,* Gr. *panthēr*; compr. Skr. *pundarika,* a leopard.] A carnivorous animal of Asia and Africa, identical with or a variety of the leopard.

pantile, pan′tīl, *n.* [*Pan* and *tile.*] A tile with a cross section resembling the letter S, overlapping the tile by its side as well as the one beneath.

pantofle, pantoffle, pan′tofl, pan•tof′l, *n.* [Fr. *pantoufle.*] A lounging slipper.

pantograph, pan′to•graf, *n.* [Gr. *pan, pantos,* all, and *graphō,* to write.] An instrument by means of which drawings, maps, plans, etc., can be copied mechanically on the original scale, or on one reduced or enlarged.—**pantographic,** pan•to•graf′ik, *a.* Pertaining to a pantograph.

pantology, pan•tol′o•ji, *n.* [Gr. *pas, pantos,* all, and *logos,* discourse.] Universal knowledge; a systematic view of all branches of human knowledge.—**pantological,** pan•to•loj′i•kal, *a.* Relating to pantology.

pantomime, pan′to•mīm, *n.* [L. *pantomimus,* Gr. *pantomimos—pan, pantos,* all, and *mimos,* a mimic.] A player who acted, not by speaking, but wholly by gesticulations; a theatrical entertainment in dumbshow; hence, dumb show generally; a popular stage entertainment usually produced about the Christmas season, the effects being heightened by gorgeous scenery and catching music.—**pantomimic,** pan•to•mim′ik, *a.* Pertaining to pantomime.—**pantomimist,** pan′to•mīm•ist, *n.* One who acts in pantomime.

pantry, pan′tri, *n.* [Fr. *paneterie,* a pantry, from L. *panis* (Fr. *pain*), bread, whence also *pannier.*] A room or closet, generally entered from the kitchen, for provisions, silverware, china, and glassware.

pants, pants, *n. pl.* Shortened form of pantaloons; trousers.

panzer, pan′zėr, *a.* [G.] Armored.—*n.* A tank.

pap, pap, *n.* [D. and Dan. *pap,* G.; *pappe,* probable from an infantile cry. PAPA.] A kind of soft food for infants; the pulp of fruit.

pap, pap, *n.* [Of similar origin to *pap,* food; comp. L. *papilla,* the nipple.] A nipple of the breast; a teat; a round hill resembling a pap.

papa, pä•pa, *n.* [A reduplication of one of the earliest cries uttered by infants—Fr., G., D., and Dan. *papa,* L. *papa, pappa,* Gr. *pappa*; comp. *mama, mamma.*] Father: a word used by children.

papacy, pā′pa•si, *n.* [L.L. *papatia,* the papacy, from L. *papa,* the pope, lit. father. PAPA, POPE.] The office and dignity of the pope; papal authority and jurisdiction; the popedom; the popes collectively.—**papal,** pā′pal, *a.* Belonging to the pope or to popedom; proceeding from the pope.

papaw, pạ′pạ, *n.* A small North American tree and its pulpy fruit. (Not the same as *papaya,* which see.)

papaya, pa•pä′yä, *n.* [Sp. and Pg. *papaya,* of Malabar origin.] A tropical American tree and its edible melonlike fruit. Source of papain, a digestive ferment used in tenderizing tough meat.

paper, pā′pėr, *n.* [Fr. *papier,* It. *papiro,* from L. *papyrus,* Gr. *papyros,* the papyrus, PAPYRUS.] A well-known substance used for writing and printing on, and for various other purposes, manufactured principally of vegetable fiber reduced to a pulp; a piece, leaf, or sheet of paper; a single sheet appearing periodically; a newspaper; a journal; an essay or article on some subject; any written or printed document; collectively, such documents as promissory notes, bills of exchange, etc.—*a.* Made of paper; appearing merely in certain documents without really existing (a *paper* army); thin; slight.—*v.t.* To cover with paper; to furnish with paper hangings; to fold or enclose in paper.—**papery,** pā′pėr•i, *a.* Like paper; having the thinness and consistency of paper.—**paper cutter,** *n.* A paper knife; a machine for cutting paper in piles, or for trimming the edges of books, etc.—**paper hanger,** *n.* One whose employment is to hang wallpaper.—**paper hangings,** *n. pl.* Paper for covering and adorning the walls of rooms; wallpaper.—**paper knife,** *n.* An instrument of bone, ivory, etc., with an edge like a blunt knife used in cutting open the leaves of books, etc., or for folding paper.—**paper money,** *n.* Banknotes or the like circulated as the representative of coin.—**paper nautilus** *n.* The paper sailor or argonaut.—**paperweight,** *n.* A small weight laid on loose papers to keep them in place.

papeterie, päp•trē′, *n.* [Fr., stationery or writing materials.] An ornamented case or box containing papers and other materials for writing.

Paphian, pā′fi•an, *a.* Pertaining to *Paphos,* a city of Cyprus sacred to Venus; hence, pertaining to Venus or her rites.

papier-mâché, päp•yā-mä•shā′, *n.* [Fr., lit masticated paper.] A material prepared by pulping different kinds of paper into a mass, which is molded into various articles, dried, and japanned.

papilionaceous, pa•pil′i•o•nā″shus, *a.* [L. *papilio,* a butterfly.] Resembling the butterfly; *bot.* having the corolla shaped like a butterfly, such as the flower of the pea.

papilla, pa•pil′la, *n.* pl. **papillae,** pa•pil′lē, [L.] A small pap or nipple; a little eminence on the surface of the skin, as on the tongue.—**papillary,** pap′il•le•ri, *a.* Pertaining to or resembling the nipple; papillose.—**papilloma,** pap′il•ō″ma, *n.* [Gr. *oma,* a tumor.] A benign tumor shaped like a papilla.—**papillose,** pap′il•lōs, *a.* Papillary.—**papillote,** pap′il•lōt, *n.* [Fr.] A curl paper.

papist, pā′pist, *n.* [Fr. *papiste,* from Fr. *pape,* L. *papa,* pope.] A Roman Catholic.—**papistic, papistical,** pa•pis′tik, pa•pis′ti•kal, *a.* Popish, pertaining to popery. (Usually in disparagement.)

papoose, pa•pös′, *n.* Among the native Indians of North America, a babe or young child.

pappus, pap′us, *n.* [L., from Gr. *pappos,* the down of plants.] *Bot.* the feathery appendage that crowns many single-seeded seed vessels; a form of calyx in composite plants of a downy or hairy character.—**pappose, pappous,** pap′ōs, pap′us, *a.* Downy; furnished with pappus.

paprika, pap•ri′ka, *n.* [Hung. *paprika.*] The ripe fruit of a pepper of the *Capscium* genus; a spice from the fruit.

papule, pap′ūl, *n.* [L.] A pimple. —**papular,** pap′ū•lėr, *a.*

papyrus, pa•pī′rus, *n.* pl. **papyri,** pa•pī′ri. [Gr. *papyros*, of Egyptian origin. Hence *paper*.] A tall sedge abundant in the valley of the Nile, the stems of which afforded the most ancient material for writing; a written scroll made of the papyrus.

par, pär, *n.* [L. *par*, equal, whence *pair* and *peer*.] Equality in circumstances or in value; the state of the shares of a public undertaking when they may be purchased at the original price; established value of coin or the standard value of one country expressed in the coin or standard value of another; *golf*, the number of strokes required to play a hole or a round perfectly.—*a.* Average or normal; *bus.* at or pertaining to par.—*Above par*, above the original price; at a premium.—*Below par*, below the original price, at a discount.

para- par′a. [Gr. *para-*, par, from *para*, beside.] A prefix meaning beside, with its variations; alongside, aside from, amiss, beyond, as in parallel, paragraph, etc.

para-, par′a [F. fr. Ital. imper. of *parare*, to shield or defend.] To protect from, or that which shields, as in *parasol* and *parachute*.

parable, par′a•bl, *n.* [Fr. *parabole*, from L. *parabola*, Gr. *parabolē*, from *paraballō*, to throw beside, to compare—*para*, beside, and *ballō*, to throw. Of same origin are *parley*, *parlor*, *parole*.] Originally, a comparison or similitude; now a fable or allegorical representation of something real in life or nature, from which a moral is drawn for instruction; *Scrip.* a proverbial or notable saying; a thing darkly or figuratively expressed.—*v.t.*—*parabled*, *parabling*. To represent by a parable.—**parabola,** pa•rab′o•la, *n.* [Gr. *parabolē*, so called from its axis being parallel to the side of the cone.] A geometrical figure, one of the conic sections, shown when a cone is cut by a plane parallel to one of its sides; the curve which a projectile theoretically describes.—**parabolic,** par•a•bol′ik, *a.* Having the form of a parabola; pertaining to a parabola, pertaining to a parable. —**parabolical,** par•a•bol′i•kal, *a.* Parabolic, of the nature of or having the character of a parable.—**parabolically,** par•a•bol′i•kal•li, *adv.* By way of parable; in the form of a parabola.—**paraboloid,** pa•rab′ol•oid, *n.* The solid generated by the revolution of a parabola about its axis; a parabolic conoid.

parachute, par′a•shöt, *n.* [Fr., from *parer*, to ward off, and *chute*, a fall.] *Avi.* an apparatus of an umbrella shape with which aircraft are provided, for the purpose of enabling safe descent by crew or troops.—*v.t.* and *i.* To descend or drop by means of a parachute.—**parachutist,** par′a•shö•tist, *n.*

paraclete, par′a•klēt, *n.* [Gr. *paraklētos*, from *parakaleō*—*para*, to, and *kaleō*, to call.] One called to aid or support; hence, [*cap.*] a term applied to the Holy Spirit.

parade, pa•rād′, *n.* [Fr. *parade*, from Sp. *parada*, a parade, a place for the exercise of troops, from L. *paro*, *paratus*, to prepare. PARE, PREPARE.] Show; ostentation; display; a showy or pompous procession; a military display; the collection of troops for inspection or the like; the place where such display is held; a public walk or promenade.—*v.t.*—*paraded*, *parading*. To exhibit in a showy manner; to make a show of; to assemble and march in military order.—*v.i.* To assemble in military order; to go about in military procession; to walk about for show.

paradigm, par′a•dim, *n.* [Gr. *paradeigma*—*para*, beside, and *deigma*, example, from *deiknumi*, to show.] An example; a model; *gram.* an example of a word, as a noun, adjective, or verb, in its various inflections.—**paradigmatic, paradigmatical,** par′a•dig•mat″ik, par′a•dig•mat″i•kal, *a.* Pertaining to a paradigm; suited for being an example; exemplary.—**paradigmatically,** par′a•dig•mat″i•kal•li, *adv.* In the way of paradigm or example.

paradise, par′a•dīs, *n.* [L. *paradisus*, from Gr. *paradeisos*, a garden—properly a Persian word.] The garden of Eden, in which Adam and Eve were at first placed; hence, a place of bliss; a region of supreme felicity; the abode of sanctified souls after death.—*Bird-of-paradise*. See BIRD.—**paradisaic, paradisaical,** par′a•di•sā″ik, par′a•di•sā″i•kal, *a.* Pertaining to paradise.

paradox, par′a•doks, *n.* [Gr. *paradoxon*, from *para*, beyond, and *doxa*, opinion. ORTHODOX.] A tenet or proposition contrary to received opinion; a statement which seems to be at variance with common sense, or to contradict some previously ascertained truth, though when properly investigated it may be perfectly well founded,—*Hydrostatic paradox*. HYDROSTATIC.—**paradoxical,** par•a•dok′si•kal, *a.* Having the nature of a paradox; inclined to paradox.—**paradoxically,** par•a•dok′si•kal•li, *adv.* In a paradoxical manner.—**paradoxicalness,** par•a•dok′si•kal•nes, *n.*

paraffin, par′a•fin, *n.* [L. *parum*, little, and *affinis*, akin, from its resistance to chemical reagents.] A fatty substance obtained from the dry distillation of wood, bituminous coal, wax, etc., largely used in the manufacture of candles; *chem.* any member of the methane series.—*v.t.* To saturate with paraffin.

paragenesis, par•a•jen′e•sis, *n.* [Gr. *para*, side by side with, and *genesis*, generation.] Origin of two things side by side; that state of minerals when they are made up of an aggregate of interblended crystals or crystals which have not assumed their normal structure (as in granite, etc.).—**paragenetic,** par•a•je•net′ik, *a.* Characterized by or pertaining to paragenesis.

paragoge, par′a•gō•ji, *n.* [Gr. *paragōgē*—*para*, beside, and *agō*, to lead.] The addition of a letter or syllable to the end of a word.—**paragogic,** par•a•goj′ik, *a.* Pertaining to paragoge; lengthening a word by being affixed.

paragon, par′a•gon, *n.* [Fr. *parangon*, from Sp. *paragon*, *parangon*, model, from the prepositions *para*, beside, and *con*, in comparison with.] A model or pattern, especially a model or pattern of superior excellence or perfection.—*v.t.* To compare; to rival; to form a rival or equal to.

paragraph, par′a•graf, *n.* [Gr. *paragraphē*, a marginal note—*para*, beside, and *graphō*, to write.] Originally a marginal note; hence the character ¶ used as a reference, or to mark a division in a written composition; a distinct part of a discourse or writing, consisting of one or several sentences; a portion or section which relates to a particular point, and is generally distinguished by a break.—*v.t.* To express within a paragraph; to divide into paragraphs. —*v.i.* To work as a paragrapher.—**paragraphic,** par•a•graf′ik, *a.*—**paragrapher,** par′a•graf•ėr, *n.*

Paraguay tea, par′a•gwā, *n.* See MATÉ.

parakeet, par′a•kēt, *n.* [Fr. *parroquet*, *perroquet*, a parakeet. PARROT.] The name given to various parrots of the Eastern Hemisphere, generally of small size and having very long tail feathers.

paraleipsis, paralepsis, paralipsis, par•a•līp′sis, par•a•lep′sis, par•a•lip′sis, *n.* [Gr. *paraleipsis*, omission—*para*, beside, and *leipō*, to leave.] *Rhet.* a pretended omission; a figure by which a speaker pretends to pass by what at the same time he really mentions.

parallax, par′al•laks, *n.* [Gr. *parallaxis*, from *parallassō*, to vary, decline, or wander—*para*, beyond, and *allasō*, to change.] The apparent change of position of an object relatively to other objects when viewed from different places; *astron.* the difference between the position of any celestial object as viewed from the surface of the earth, and that which it would have when viewed from the center of either the earth or the sun; *optics*, the noncoincidence of the cross fibers of a telescope with the focus of the eyeglass.—**parallactic,** par•al•lak′tik, *a.* Pertaining to parallax.

parallel, par′al•lel, *a.* [Gr. *parallēlos* —*para*, side by side, and *allēlōn*, of one another.] Extended in the same direction, and in all parts equally distant; being exactly at an equal distance throughout their length or breadth (said of lines or surfaces); hence, having the same direction or tendency; running in accordance with something; equal in all essential parts, points, or features; exactly similar (a *parallel* passage or incident).—*Parallel forces*, forces which act in directions parallel to each other.—*Parallel lines*, *geom.* straight lines which are in the same plane, and being produced ever so far both ways, do not meet.—*Parallel motion*, a contrivance invented by Watt for converting a reciprocating circular motion into an alternating rectilinear motion, and applied in the steam engine.—*Parallel roads*, a phenomenon observed in some valleys of the Scottish Highlands, consisting in a series of parallel and nearly horizontal lines running along the sides of the hills, supposed to have been formed by the action of a lake. —*Parallel rod*, in locomotive engines, a rod that connects the crankpins of the driving wheels.—*Parallel ruler*, a mathematical instrument for drawing parallel lines, formed of two equal rulers, connected by two crossbars of equal length and movable about joints.—*Parallel sailing*, sailing on a parallel of latitude.—*n.* A line which throughout its whole extent is equidistant from another line; one of the circles on a sphere parallel to its equator; a line on a map marking latitude (called also a *parallel of latitude*); resemblance or conformity in essential points; likeness; comparison (to draw a *parallel* between two historians); one who corresponds essentially to another; a counterpart; *milit.* a trench cut before a fortress, parallel to its defenses, for covering the besiegers from the guns of the place; *printing*, a mark of reference (thus ||) used to direct attention to notes.—*v.t.*—*paralleled, paralleling* (also with *ll* in the second place); to make parallel; to form or serve as a parallel to; to match; to correspond to; to show or furnish an equal to; to compare.—**parallelepiped, parallelepipedon,** par•a•lel′e•pī″ped, par•a•lel′e•pī″ped•on, *n.* [Gr. *parallēlepipedon*—*parallēlos*, parallel, and *epipedos*, plane, superficial—*epi*, upon, and *pedon*, the ground.] A solid body with six sides forming parallelograms; a solid in the shape of a brick.—**parallelism,** par′a•lel•izm, *n.* State of being parallel; resemblance in a number of important particulars; correspondence; a comparison.—*Parallelism of the earth's axis*, that feature according to which the axis is always inclined at exactly the same slope.—**parallelogram,** par•a•lel′o•gram, *n.* A four-sided figure composed of straight lines, and having its opposite sides parallel and equal; popularly, a quadrilateral figure of greater length than breadth.

paralogism, pa•ral′o•jizm, *n.* [Gr. *paralogismos*—*para*, beyond, and *logismos*, reasoning. LOGIC.] A fallacious argument; an instance of false reasoning.—**paralogize,** pa•ral′o•jīz, *v.i.*—*paralogized, paralogizing*. To reason falsely.

paralysis, pa•ral′i•sis, *n.* [G. *paralysis*, from *paralyō*, to loosen—*para*, beside, and *lyō*, to loose.] A loss or diminution of the power of motion in some part of the body, arising from disease of the nerves; a loss of sensation in any part of the body; palsy.—**paralyze,** par′a•līz, *v.t.*—*paralyzed, paralyzing*. To affect with *paralysis*; to destroy physical or mental energy in.—**paralytic,** par•a•lit′ik, *a.* Pertaining to paralysis; affected with paralysis. —*n.* A person affected with paralysis.

paramagnetic, par′a•mag•net″ik, *a.* A term proposed by Faraday as a substitute for *magnetic* in contradistinction to *diamagnetic*.—**paramagnetism,** par•a•mag′net•izm, *n.* Magnetism as opposed to *diamagnetism*.

paramatta, par•a•mat′ta, *n.* A light twilled dress fabric, the weft of merino wool and the warp cotton: said to have been made originally with wool from *Paramatta* in Australia.

paramecium, par•a•mē′shi•um *n.* [N.L. from Gr. *paramēkēs*, oblong, from *para* and *mēkos*, length.] *Zool.* a ciliate infusorian (*Paramecium*) having an elongated body with a large oral opening at the anterior end.

parameter, pa•ram′et•ėr, *n.* [Gr. *para*, beside, and *metron*, measure.] *Geom.* a constant straight line belonging to each of the three conic sections; the constant quantity which enters into the equation of a curve.

paramo, pä′rä•mō, *n.* In South America a mountainous district covered with stunted trees, and in which a damp cold perpetually prevails.

paramount, par′a•mount, *a.* [O.Fr. *par* (L. *per*), through, completely, and *amont*, above. AMOUNT.] Superior in power or jurisdiction (lord *paramount*, the supreme lord of a fee or of lands, etc.); eminent; of the highest order; superior to all others.—*n.* Chief; highest in rank or order.—**paramountcy,** par′a•mount•si, *n.* The condition of being paramount.

paramour, par′a•mör, *n.* [Fr. *par amour*, with love—*par* = L. *per*, by, *amour*, L. *amor*, love.] A lover‡; a wooer‡; one who takes the place of a husband or wife without possessing the rights.

paranoia, par•a•noi′a, *n.* [Gr. *para*, beside, *nous*, mind.] A mental disease marked by delusions of one's importance and of being persecuted.—**paranoiac,** par•a•noi′ak, *n.* A person affected by paranoia.—*a.* Pertaining to or affected by paranoia.

paranymph, par′a•nimf, *n.* [Gr. *paranymphos*—*para*, by and *nymphē*, a bride.] In ancient Greece, a bridesman.

parapet, par′a•pet, *n.* [Fr. *parapet*, It. *parapetto*—*parare* (Fr. *parer*, E. *parry*), to ward off, to guard, and *petto* (L. *pectus*), the breast.] *Lit.* a wall or rampart breasthigh; *milit.* a wall or rampart to cover the soldiers from the attacks of the enemy in front; a breastwork; *arch.* a wall placed at the edges of platforms, sides of bridges, etc., to prevent people from falling over.—**parapeted,** par′a•pet•ed, *a.* Furnished with a parapet.

paraph, par′af, *n.* [Fr. *parafe*, *paraphe*, an abbreviation of *paragraph*.] The figure formed by the flourish of a pen at the conclusion of a signature.—*v.t.* To add a paraph to; to sign.

paraphernalia, par′a•fėr•nā″li•a, *n. pl.* [L.L. *paraphernalia*, from Gr. *parapherna*, what a bride has besides her dower—*para*, beyond, and *phernē*, a dowry.] The belongings of a wife over and above her dower or portion, as apparel and ornaments; personal attire of a showy or accessory description; also, fittings, etc., of an apartment or house; appendages; ornaments; trappings.

paraphrase, par′a•frāz, *n.* [Gr. *paraphrasis*—*para*, beside, and *phrasis*, phrase.] A restatement of a text, passage, or work, giving the sense of the original in other words; the setting forth in clearer and ampler terms of the signification of a passage or work; a sacred song or hymn based on a selected portion of Scripture.—*v.t.*—*paraphrased, paraphrasing*. To make a paraphrase of; to explain or translate with latitude. —*v.i.* To interpret or explain amply. —**paraphrast,** par′a•frast, *n.* [Gr. *paraphrastēs*.] One who paraphrases. —**paraphrastic,** par•a•fras′tik, *a.* Having the character of a paraphrase; explaining in words more clear and ample than those of the author.

parapsychology, par′a•sī•kol″o•ji, *n.* [Prefix *para*, and *psychology*.] A branch of psychology dealing with the investigation of psychic phenomena, as clairvoyance, extrasensory perception, etc.

paraplegia, par•a•plē′ji•a, *n.* [Gr. *paraplēgia*, paralysis—*para*, beyond, and *plēgē*, stroke.] That kind of paralysis which affects the lower part of the body.

parasang, par′a•sang, *n.* [Gr. *parasangēs*, from Per. *farsang*, a parasang.] An ancient Persian measure of length equal to 3¾ miles.

paraselene, par′a•se•lē″nē, *n.* pl. **paraselenae,** par′a•se•lē″nē. [Gr. *para*, about, or near, and *selēnē*, the moon.] A mock moon; a luminous ring encompassing the moon, in which sometimes are other bright spots bearing some resemblance to the moon.

parasite, par′a•sīt, *n.* [Fr. *parasite*, from L. *parasitus*, Gr. *parasitos*, one who eats at the table of another, a parasite, a toady—*para*, beside, and *sitos*, food.] One that frequents the tables of the rich and earns his welcome by flattery; a hanger-on; a sycophant; an animal that lives upon or in, and at the expense of, other animals; a plant which grows upon another plant, and feeds upon its juices.—**parasitic, parasitical,** par•a•sit′ik, par•a•sit′i•kal, *a.* Of the nature of a parasite; meanly dependent on others for support; *bot.* and *zool.* growing or living as a parasite.—**parasitically,** par•a•sit′i•kal•li, *adv.* In the manner of a parasite.—**parasiticide,** par•a•sit′i•sīd, *n.* [E. *parasite*, and L. *caedo*, to kill.] Any agent for destroying animal or vegetable parasites.—**parasitism,** par′a•sīt•izm, *n.* The behavior or manners of a parasite; the state of being a parasite.

parasol, par′a•sol, *n.* [Fr. *parasol*,

from It. *parasole—parare* (L. *parare*, to prepare), to ward off, and *sole* (L. *sol*), the sun. PARRY.] A small umbrella used by ladies to defend their faces from the sun's rays.

parataxis, par•a•tak′sis, *n.* [Gr. *para*, beside, and *taxis*, arrangement.] *Gram.* the mere ranging of propositions one after another, without marking their dependence on each other by way of consequence or the like.—**paratactic,** par•a•tak′tik, *a.* Pertaining to parataxis.

parathyroid, par•a•thī′roid, *a.* [Prefix *para* and *thyroid.*] Situated beside the thyroid gland.—*Parathyroid glands*, four small glands that control the calcium content of the blood and body.

paratroop, par′a•tröp, *n.* pl. **paratroops** [Prefix *para*, and *troop.*] A military unit trained to drop by parachute from an aircraft into a specific area.—**paratrooper,** *n.*

paratyphoid, par′a•tī″foid, *n.* [Gr. *para*, beyond, *typhoid.*] A bacterial disease with symptoms resembling typhoid fever.

paravane, pa•ra•vān′, *n.* A torpedo-shaped machine fitted with an apparatus for severing the moorings of sea mines.

parboil, pär′boil, *v.t.* [Fr. *parbouillir—part*, part, and *bouiller*, to boil; lit. to partboil.] To boil in part; to boil in a moderate degree.

parbuckle, pär′buk•l, *n.* A purchase formed by a single rope round a heavy object for hoisting or lowering, the object itself acting as a movable pulley.—*v.t.* To hoist or lower by means of a parbuckle.

parcel, pär′sel, *n.* [Fr. *parcelle*, from a L.L. *particella*, equivalent to L. *particula*, dim. of *pars, partis*, a part. PART.] A portion of anything taken separately; a particle; a collection; a group; a lot; a quantity or number of things put up together; a bundle; a package: now the common meaning.—*v.t. parceled, parcelled, parceling, parcelling.* To divide or put up into parts or portions; to make up into a mass.—**parceling, parcelling,** pär′sel•ing, *n.* A dividing into small parts, as a *parceling* of land; *naut.* long narrow slips of canvas daubed with tar and bound about a rope like a bandage.—**parcel post,** *n.* The department of a post-office system by which parcels are sent.

parcener, pär′sen•ėr, *n.* [O.Fr. *parçonnier*, from *parcon*, L. *partitio, partitionis*, a portion. PARTITION.] A coheir or coparcener.

parch, pärch, *v.t.* [Perhaps from Fr. *percer*, Fr. dial. *percher*, to pierce, as if to pierce or penetrate with heat; or a corruption of L. *peratesco*, to grow very dry.] To burn the surface of; to scorch; to dry to extremity.—*v.i.* To become scorched or very dry.

parcheesi, parchisi, pär•chē′zē, *n.* [Hind. *pachisi*, from *pachis*, twenty-five, the highest throw in the game.] A game somewhat resembling backgammon.

parchment, pärch′ment, *n.* [Fr. *parchemin*, from L. *pergamena, pergamina*, paper of Pergamus, from *Pergamus* in Asia Minor.] The skin of a very young calf, sheep, or goat dressed or prepared and rendered fit for writing on; ordinary paper with the appearance of parchment.

pardon, pär′dn, *v.t.* [O.Fr. *pardoner*, (Fr. *pardonner*), from L.L. *perdonare*, to pardon—L. *per*, through, quite, and *dono*, to give. DONATION.] To release from liability to suffer punishment for a crime or a fault; to forgive (an offender); to remit the penalty or punishment of; to forgive (the offense).—*Pardon me*, forgive me; excuse me: a phrase often used when a person means civilly to deny or contradict what another affirms. ∴ *Pardon* means strictly to remit the punishment or retaliation we were entitled to inflict; *forgive* implies that the party who has suffered injury entirely overlooks the offense, and cherishes no ill-feeling whatever against the offender.—*n.* Forgiveness of an offender or of his offense; a passing over without, or not visiting with, punishment; remission of penalty; forgiveness; an official warrant of penalty remitted.—**pardonable,** pär′dn•a•bl, *a.* Capable of being pardoned or forgiven; excusable; venial.—**pardonably,** pär′dn•a•bli, *adv.* In a manner admitting of pardon; excusably.—**pardoner,** pär′dn•ėr, *n.* One who pardons; one licensed to sell the pope's indulgences‡.

pare, pâr, *v.t.—pared, paring.* [Fr. *parer*, to pare, to dress, to curry, from L. *parare*, to prepare, seen in a number of words, as *parade, parry, prepare, repair, separate*, etc.] To cut off, as the superficial substance or extremities of a thing; to shave off with a sharp instrument; to trim by shaving the surface; to diminish by little and little.—**paring,** pâr″ing, *n.* What is pared off; a piece clipped off; the rind.

paregoric, par•e•gor′ik, *a.* [Gr. *parēgorikos*, soothing, from *parēgoreō*, to exhort, console, soothe—*para*, beside, and *agoreuō*, to speak in an assembly.] *Med.* mitigating or assuaging pain.—*Paregoric elixir*, a camphorated tincture of opium, flavored by aromatics.—*n.* A medicine that mitigates pain; an anodyne.

pareira brava, pa•rā′ra brä′va, brā′va, or **pareira,** *n.* [Portuguese *parreira brava*, wild brier.] The roots of certain plants of Brazil employed in medical practice, as tonics and diuretics.

parenchyma, pa•ren′ki•ma, *n.* [Gr. *para*, beside, and *enchyma*, an infusion—*en*, in, and *cheō*, to pour.] *Anat.* the essential, functional tissue of the glands or other solid organs as distinct from the framework or supporting tissue, or stroma; *bot.* the pith or pulp of plants; the spongy and cellular tissue.—**parenchymatous,** par•en•kim′a•tus, *a.* Pertaining to or of the nature of parenchyma.

parent, pâr′ent, *n.* [L. *parens, parentis*, from *pario, parere*, to bring forth; to beget; akin to *parere*, to appear (APPEAR), *parare*, to prepare (PARE).] A father or mother; he or she that produces young: used of animals and plants as well as of man; one who or that which produces; cause; source.—**parentage,** pâr′en•tij, *n.* Extraction; birth; origin; condition with respect to the rank or character of parents.—**parental,** pa•ren′tal, *a.* Pertaining to parents; suited to or characteristic of parents.—**parentally,** pa•ren′tal•li, *adv.* In a fatherly or parental manner.—**parenthood,** pâr′ent•hụd, *n.* The state of being a parent; the condition of a parent.

parenthesis, pa•ren′the•sis, *n.* pl. **parentheses,** pa•ren′the•sēz. [Gr. *parenthesis—para*, beside, *en*, in, and *thesis*, a placing, from *tithēmi*, to place.] An explanatory or qualifying sentence, or part of a sentence, inserted into the midst of another sentence, without being grammatically connected with it, generally marked off by upright curves ( ); *printing*, the parenthetical sign ( ).—**parenthetic, parenthetical,** par•en•thet′ik, par•en•thet′i•kal, *a.*—**parenthetically,** par•en•thet′i•kal•li, *adv.*

paresis, pä•rē′sis, par′e•sis, *n.* [Gr., from *pariēmi*, to relax.] *Pathol.* a slight incomplete paralysis, affecting motion but not sensation.

par excellence, pär ek′se•läns, *a.* or *adv.* [Fr.] Above all others; preeminent.

parfait, pär•fā′, *n.* A dessert made of beaten eggs and whipped cream, sweetened, flavored, and frozen without stirring.

parget, pär′jet, *n.* [O.E. *pariet*, O.Fr. *pariette*, from L. *paries, parietis*, a wall.] Plaster laid on roofs or walls.—*v.t.* To cover with plaster or parget; to ornament with parge work.—*v.i.* To plaster.—**pargeting,** pär′jet•ing, *n.* Plasterwork; plasterwork with patterns and ornaments raised or indented upon it, whether inside or outside a house.

parhelion, pär•hē′li•on, *n.* pl. **parhelia,** pär•hē′li•a, [Gr. *para*, near, and *hēlios*, the sun.] A mock sun, having the appearance of the sun itself, sometimes white and sometimes tinted with prismatic colors.—**parhelic,** pär•hel′ik, *a.* Relating to parhelia.

pariah, pa•rī′a, *n.* [A Tamil word.] One of a low caste of people in southern India; hence, one despised and contemned by society; an outcast.

Parian, pâ′ri•an, *a.* Pertaining to *Paros*, an isle in the Aegean Sea.—*Parian marble*, a marble of Paros, chosen by the ancients for their choicest works.—*n.* A fine variety of porcelain or porcelain clay, of which statuettes, etc., are made, resembling Parian marble.

parietal, pa•rī′et•al, *a.* [L. *parietalis*, from *paries, parietis*, a wall.] Pertaining to a wall; *anat.* pertaining to the walls of a cavity of the body, or to the bones which form the sides and upper part of the skull; *bot.* growing from the side of another organ.

pari-mutuel, par′i mū′tu•el, *n.* [Fr.] A plan of race-horse betting in which the total amount wagered on all of the horses in a race, less a small fee, is shared in proportion to amounts wagered by the betters who selected the win, place, and show horses.

paripinnate, par•i•pin′āt, *a.* [L. *par,* equal, and *pinnatus, pinnate.*] *Bot.* equally pinnate; abruptly pinnate; said of a compound pinnate leaf ending in two leaflets.

Paris green, *n.* A poisonous, green-colored arsenic compound used as an insecticide.

parish, par′ish, *n.* [Fr. *paroisse,* L.L. *paroecia,* from Gr. *paroikia,* a parish, a neighborhood, from *para,* beside, and *oikos,* a house (whence *economy*).] The district under the charge of a priest or minister; the congregation of a church; a subdivision of the state of Louisiana, equivalent to a county.—**parishioner,** pa•rish′on•ėr, *n.*

parity, par′i•ti, *n.* [Fr. *parité,* L. *paritas,* from *par,* equal. PAIR.] The condition of being equal or equivalent; like state or degree; equality; *finance,* equal purchasing power at a given ratio of currency of different kinds; equal value in foreign currency.

park, pärk, *n.* [Either from Fr. *parc,* or L.L. *parcus,* a park.] A large piece of ground enclosed and set apart for beasts of chase; a piece of public ground in or near a large town, laid out and kept for the sole purpose of pleasure and recreation; a stadium for sports events, as a baseball *park*; *milit.* a place occupied by military equipment, supplies, etc., hence the objects themselves (a *park* of jeeps). —*v.t.* To put or keep temporarily in a place (to *park* a car); to leave in a place (he *parked* his hat); to enclose in a park.—*v.i.* To place or station a vehicle.—**parker,** pär′kėr, *n.*—**parkway,** pärk′wā, *n.* A wide street or thoroughfare lined with trees, shrubs and turf.

parka, pär′ka, *n.* [Rus.] A fur outer garment or coat cut like a shirt with an attached hood.

parlance, pär′lans, *n.* [O.Fr., from *parlant,* ppr. of *parler,* to speak. PARLEY.] Conversation; talk.

parlay, pär′lā, *v.t.* and *i.* [Fr. *paroli,* from It. *paroli,* from *paro,* equal.] To place a bet on one horse, the proceeds of which are to be applied as a wager on a second horse; to so act in any similar venture.—*n.* Such a venture.

parley, pär′li, *v.i.* [Fr. *parler,* to speak, O.Fr. *paroler,* from L.L. *parabolare,* to speak, from L. *parabola,* a comparison, later, a word. PARABLE.] To confer or speak with a person on some point of mutual concern; especially to confer with an enemy.—*n.* Mutual conversation; a conference with an enemy in war.

parliament, pär′li•ment, *n.* [Fr. *parlement—parler,* to speak, and term. *-ment,* as in *complement,* etc. PARLEY.] A meeting or assembly of persons for conference or deliberation; a supreme national or general council; the legislature of the three estates of the United Kingdom of Great Britain, the lords spiritual, lords temporal, and the commons; the general council of Great Britain constituting the legislature, summoned by the sovereign's authority to consult on the affairs of the nation, and to enact and repeal laws.—*Act of parliament,* a statute or law made by the sovereign, with the advice and consent of the lords temporal and spiritual and the commons in parliament assembled.—**Parliamentarian,** pär′li•men•tâ″ri•an, *n.* One of those who adhered to the parliament in the time of Charles I; [*not cap.*] one thoroughly acquainted with the rules of order for group meetings, as public assemblies, clubs, or conventions.—**parliamentary,** pär•li•men′ta•ri, *a.* Pertaining to parliament; enacted or done by parliament; according to the rules and usages of parliament, or similar legislative bodies.—*Parliamentary government,* a government whose legislature has complete power to make laws and control the administration of their enforcement.—*Parliamentary procedure,* the generally accepted rules and practices followed in conducting the business of a deliberative body.

parlor, pär′lėr, *n.* [Fr. *parloir,* from *parler,* to speak. PARLEY.] A room for familiar intercourse; the room commonly used by a family; an ordinary sitting room; also applied to a certain type of business, trade or amusement place.—**parlor car,** a chair-fitted railroad car on which travelers pay extra fare.

parlous, pär′lus, *a.* [For *perilous.*] Dangerous; risky; extreme or shocking *(colloq.).*

Parmesan, pär•me•zan′, *n.* [*Parma,* in Italy.] Name of a sharp, dry type of cheese made there.

Parnassian, pär•nas′i•an, *a.* Pertaining to *Parnassus,* the celebrated mountain in Greece sacred to Apollo and the Muses.

parochial, pa•rō′ki•al, *a.* [L. *parochia,* corruption from *paroecia,* a parish. PARISH.] Belonging to a parish; restricted to a parish; hence, limited in range or scope; narrow.— —*Parochial school,* an elementary school maintained by a parish, usually adding religious instruction to secular subjects.—**parochialism,** pa•rō′ki•al•izm, *n.* The state of being parochial; narrowness or contractedness of mind resulting from confining one's attention or interest to the affairs of one's parish or neighborhood.—**parochially,** pa•rō′ki•al•li, *adv.* In a parochial manner; in a parish; by parishes.

parody, par′o•di, *n.* [Fr. *parodie,* from Gr. *parōdia—para,* beside, and *ōdē,* an ode.] A literary composition in which the form and expression of serious writings are closely imitated but adapted to a ridiculous subject or a humorous method of treatment; a burlesque imitation of a serious poem.—*v.t.*—*parodied, parodying.* To turn into a parody; to write a parody upon.

parole, pa•rōl′, *n.* [Fr. *parole,* from L.L. *parabola,* a word, a parable. PARABLE.] Word of promise; word of honor; a promise given by a prisoner of war that he will not try to escape if allowed to go about at liberty, or not to bear arms against his captors for a certain period, or the like; *milit.* a sort of countersign given out every day; *penology,* release of a convict under supervision before he has served his full sentence and on promise of good conduct; a state or condition of one on parole.—*v.t.* To free for a parole period.—*To break parole,* to conduct one's self contrary to conditions of the parole.—**parolee,** pa′rōl•ē′, *n.* A person released on parole.

paronymous, pa•ron′i•mus, *a.* [Gr. *parōnymos—para,* beside, and *onoma,* a name, a word.] Having the same or a like sound, but differing in orthography and signification, as *all, awl*; *ball, bawl*; having the same derivation, as *wise, wisely, wisdom.*—**paronym,** par′o•nim, *n.* A paronymous word.

paroquet, par′o•ket, *n.* See PARAKEET.

parotid, pa•rot′id, *a.* [Gr. *parōtis, parōtidos—para,* beside, and *ous, ōtos,* the ear.] *Anat.* a salivary gland on either side of the face, in front of the ear, and communicating with the mouth by a duct.—**parotitis,** par•o•tī′tis, *n.* Inflammation of the parotid gland; mumps.

paroxysm, par′ok•sizm, *n.* [Gr. *paroxysmos—para,* in excess, and *oxynō,* to sharpen, from *oxys,* sharp.] A fit or period of great intensity of a disease; a sudden and violent access of feeling (as of rage); convulsion; fit; *geol.* any sudden and violent effect of natural agency.—**paroxysmal,** par•ok•siz′mal, *a.* Pertaining to or marked by a paroxysm.

paroxytone, pa•rok′si•tōn, *a.* and *n.* [Gr.] *Gram.* said of a word having the acute accent on the penultimate syllable.

parquet, pär•kā′, *n.* [Fr. *parquet,* dim. of *parc,* a park.] First floor in a theater or music hall, frequently known as orchestra section.—*Parquet circle,* mezzanine balcony seats at rear of orchestra section.—*v.t.*—*parqueted, parqueting.* To form or ornament with parquetry.—**parquetry,** pär′ket•ri, *n.* [Fr. *parqueterie.*] Inlaid woodwork in geometric or other patterns, and generally of different colors.

parr, pär, *n.* A small fish now known to be a young salmon at a certain stage.

parrakeet, par′a•kēt, *n.* See PARAKEET.

parrel, parral, par′el, par′al, *n.* [Abbrev. from *apparel.*] *Naut.* a band of rope, or now, more generally, an iron collar which confines a yard to the mast at the center.—*v.t.* and *i.* To make fast with a parrel.

parricide, par′ri•sīd, *n.* [L. *parricida,* the criminal, *parricidium,* the crime, from *pater,* father, and *caedo,* to kill.] A person who murders his father or mother; the murder of a parent.—**parricidal,** par•ri•sī′dal, *a.* Pertaining to parricide; committing parricide.

parrot, par′ot, *n.* [From Fr. *Perrot,* or *Perrette,* personal names from *Pierre,* Peter (like Fr. *pierrot,* a sparrow, from *Pierre*); comp. Sp. *Perico,* a dim. for *Pedro,* Peter, also a small parrot, *periquito,* a small parrot. Comp. such names as *Magpie, Jackdaw, Robin-redbreast,* etc.] A name common to a family of scansorial or climbing birds, including the parakeets, macaws, lories, cockatoos, etc., or restricted to certain members of the family, all of which have hooked and rounded bills and fleshy tongues, some of them having the faculty of imitating the human voice in a high degree.—*v.t.* To repeat as a parrot; to repeat by rote.—**parrot fever,** *n. Med.* psittacosis.—**parrot fish,** *n.* A fish of the wrasse family, remarkable for the beak-like plates into which the teeth of either jaw are united.

parry, par′i, *v.t.—parried, parrying.* [Fr. *parer,* It. *parare,* to ward off, from L. *parare,* to prepare, keep off. PARE.] To ward off (a blow, a thrust); to stop or to put or turn aside; to prevent taking effect.—*v.i.* To put aside thrusts or strokes; to fence.

parse, pärs, *v.t.* [L. *pars orationis,* a part of a speech.] *Gram.* to analyze or describe grammatically; to show the several parts of speech composing (a sentence) and their relation to each other by government or agreement.

parsec, pär′sek, *n.* [*Par*allax and *sec*ond.] *Astron.* an interstellar distance unit of a heliocentric parallax of one second of arc, equal to 206,265 times the distance between the earth and the sun, or 3.26 light years.

Parsee, pär•sē′, *n.* [Per. and Hind. *pârsi,* a Persian, a fire-worshiper.] One of the adherents of the Zoroastrian or ancient Persian religion in India, originally from Persia.—**Parseeism,** pär•sē′izm, *n.* The religion and customs of the Parsees.

parsimony, pär′si•mo•ni, *a.* [Fr. *parsimonie,* from L. *parsimonia, parcimonia,* from *parco, parsum,* to spare.] Closeness or sparingness in the use or expenditure of money; niggardliness; miserliness.—*Law of parsimony,* in *logic,* also called 'Occam's Razor', the principle laid down by the Nominalist leader, William of Ockham (1270-1347), the Invincible Doctor, that entities or supposed existences must not be multiplied in a theory beyond what is strictly necessary.—**parsimonious,** pär•si•mō′ni•us, *a.* Exhibiting or characterized by parsimony; niggardly; closefisted.—**parsimoniously,** pär•si•mō′ni•us•li, *adv.* In a parsimonious manner.

parsley, pärs′li, *n.* [O.E. *persely, persylle,* etc., Fr. *persil,* from L. *petroselinum,* Gr. *petroselinon,* rock parsley—*petra,* a rock, and *selinon,* parsley.] A well-known garden herb, the leaves of which are used for seasoning and also as a garnish.

parsnip, pärs′nip, *n.* [Corrupted from Fr. *pastinaque,* L. *pastinaca,* a parsnip, from *pastinum,* a kind of two-pronged dibble, and *nip, nep,* L. *napus,* a turnip.] An umbelliferous plant much cultivated for its edible roots.

parson, pär′sn, *n.* [O.Fr. *persone,* from L.L. *persona ecclesiæ,* the person of the church, L. *persona,* a person.] The priest or incumbent of a parish; one who has the parochial charge or cure of souls; a clergyman; a man that is in orders or has been licensed to preach.—**parsonage,** pär′sn•ij, *n.* The official dwelling of a parson.

part, pärt, *n.* [L. *pars, partis,* a part (whence also *particle, parcel, partial, party, partner, participate, apart,* etc.); same root as *parare,* to prepare, *portio,* a portion. PARE.] Any portion of a thing less than the whole; a piece or fragment separated from a whole thing; a portion or quantity not separated in fact, but considered as by itself; one of a number of equal portions or quantities that make up a whole; a constituent portion of a whole; a member of a whole; that which falls to each in division; share, portion, lot; concern or interest; side or party (to take one's *part*); allotted duty; particular office or business (to perform one's *part*); character assigned to an actor in a play or other like performance; *mus.* one of the different melodies of a concerted composition, which, heard in union, compose its harmony (the treble, tenor, or bass *part*); *pl.* qualities; powers; faculties; often excellent or superior endowments (a man of *parts*); *pl.* regions; districts; locality (well-known in these *parts*).—*For my* (*his, her,* etc.) *part,* so far as concerns me (him, her).—*For the most part,* commonly; oftener than otherwise.—*In part,* in some degree or extent; partly.—*In good part,* favorably; acceptably; in a friendly manner; not in displeasure.—*In ill part,* unfavorably; with displeasure.—*Part and parcel,* an essential portion; a part.—*Part of speech, gram.* a sort or class of words of a particular character as regards their meaning or relations to other words in a sentence.—*v.t.* [Fr. *partir,* to part, separate.] To divide; to separate or break into two or more pieces; to distribute; to share; to cause to sunder or go apart; to intervene betwixt; to interpose between; to separate, as combatants; *naut.* to break; to suffer the breaking of (the ship *parted* her cables).—*v.i.* To become separate or detached; to divide; to move apart; to go away from another or others; to quit each other; to take leave (to *part with* or *from* a person); to have a share; to share (O.T.); to break; to be torn asunder (the rope *parted*).—*To part with* a thing, to let it leave us; to resign it.—*adv.* Partly; in some measure.—**partible,** pär′ti•bl, *a.* Capable of being parted; divisible.—**parted,** pär′ted, *p.* and *a.* Divided; separated; *bot.* cleft into divisions.—**parting,** pär′ting, *p.* and *a.* Serving to part; dividing; separating; given at separation (a *parting* kiss).—*n.* The act of dividing or separating; a division; a separation; leave-taking; *geol.* a fissure in strata.—**partly,** pärt′li, *adv.* In part; in some measure or degree; not wholly; used in stating particulars that make up a whole.—**part song,** *n.* A song adapted to be sung in two or more distinct vocal parts.—**part-time,** *a.* Involving or working less than the amount of time considered standard.

partake, pär•tāk′, *v.i.—partook* (pret.), *partaken* (pp.), *partaking* (ppr.). [*Part* and *take.*] To take a part, portion, or share in common with others; to have a share or part; to participate (to *partake* of a repast, *in* festivities); to have something of the character or nature of; to have features in common with: followed by *of.*—*v.t.* To have a part in; to share.—**partaker,** pär•tā′kėr, *n.* One who partakes; a sharer, a participator; usually followed by *of* or *in.*

parterre, pär•târ′, *n.* [Fr., from *par,* on, by, and *terre,* earth, ground.] *Hort.* a system of flower beds, connected together with intervening spaces of gravel or turf for walking on; the pit of a French theater.

parthenogenesis, pär′the•nō•jen″e•sis, *n.* [Gr. *parthenos,* a virgin, and *genesis,* production.] Reproduction by development of an unfertilized egg, as in certain plants and insects.—**parthenogenetic,** pär′the•nō•je•net″ik, *a.*

Parthian, pär′thi•an, *a.* Pertaining to *Parthia* or its inhabitants.—*Parthian arrow,* a shaft aimed at an adversary while flying from or avoiding him; a parting shot; from the habit of the ancient Parthians in war.

partial, pär′shal, *a.* [Fr. *partial,* from L. *pars, partis,* a part. PART.] Affecting a part only; not general or universal; not total; inclined to favor one party in a cause, or one side of a question more than the other; not indifferent; inclined to favor without principle or reason (a fond and *partial* parent); having a predilection; inclined or favorable; with *to*; *bot.* being one of several subordinates (a *partial* umbel, a *partial* peduncle).—**partiality,** pär•shal′i•ti, *n.* The state or quality of being partial; unfair or undue bias; undue favor shown; a special liking or fondness.—**partially,** pär′shal•li, *adv.* In a partial manner; with undue bias; in part; not totally; to some extent.

partible. See PART.

participate, pär•tis′i•pāt, *v.i.—participated, participating.* [L. *participo, participatum—pars, partis,* a part, and *capio,* to take. PART, CAPABLE.] To partake; to take a part; to have a share in common with others; generally followed by *of* or *in.*—*v.t.*

To partake, share, receive a part of.—**participation,** pär•tis′i•pā″shon, *n.* The state of participating or sharing in common with others.—**participator,** pär•tis′i•pā•tėr, *n.* One who participates.—**participant,** pär•tis′-i•pant, *a.* Sharing; having a share or part.—*n.* One participating; a partaker.

participle, pär′ti•si•pl, *n.* [L. *participium*, from *particeps*, partaking—*pars*, *partis*, a part, and *capio*, to take; comp. *principle*, from L. *principium.* PARTICIPATE.] *Gram.* a part of speech, so called because it partakes of the character both of a verb and an adjective, though it differs from the adjective chiefly in that it implies time, and therefore applies to a specific act, while the adjective designates a habitual quality or characteristic, without regard to time.—**participial,** pär•ti•sip′i•al, *a.* Having the nature and use of a particle; formed from a participle (a *participial* noun).—*n.* A word formed from a verb, and having the nature of a participle.—**participially,** pär•ti•sip′i•al•li, *adv.* In the sense or manner of a participle.

particle, pär′ti•kl, *n.* [Fr. *particule*, L. *particula*, dim. of *pars*, *partis*, part. PART.] A minute part or portion of matter, the aggregation of which parts constitutes a whole mass; any very small portion or part; an atom; a jot; *gram.* a word that is not varied or inflected, as the preposition, conjunction, etc.; *physics*, a mass of matter conceived as a point, but yet possessing inertia and other properties of matter.

particolored, pär′ti•kul•ėrd, *a.* Colored differently in different parts; of many colors.

particular, pär•tik′ū•lėr, *a.* [Fr. *particulier*, L.L. *particularis*, from L. *particula.* PARTICLE.] Pertaining to one and not to more; special; not general; individual; considered separately; peculiar; personal; private (our own *particular* wrongs); not ordinary; notable (of no *particular* importance); minute; circumstantial (a full and *particular* account); singularly nice in taste; precise; fastidious.—*n.* A single instance; a single point; a distinct, separate, or minute part; a detail.—*In particular*, specially; particularly; to particularize.—**particularity,** pär•tik′ū-lar″i•ti, *n.*—**particularization,** pär-tik′ū•lėr•i•zā″shon, *n.*—**particularize,** pär•tik′ū•lėr•īz, *v.t.* To state in detail.—*v.i.* To mention or attend to particulars; to be circumstantial.—**particularly,** pär•tik′ū•lėr•li, *adv.* In a particular or especial manner; especially; chiefly.

partisan, pär′ti•zan, *n.* [Fr., from *parti*, a party, from L. *pars, partis*, a part.] An adherent of a party or faction; one who is violently and passionately devoted to a party or interest; a guerrilla fighter.—*a.* Pertaining to a party or faction; biased in favor of a party or interest.—**partisanship,** pär′ti•zan•ship, *n.*

partisan, pär′ti•zan, *n.* [Fr. *pertuisane*, Sp. *partesana*, It. *partigiana*; origin doubtful.] A kind of halberd or pike formerly in use; a baton; a truncheon; a quarterstaff.

partite, pär′tīt, *a.* [L. *partitus*, pp. of *partio*, to divide. PART.] *Bot.* divided to the base (as a leaf).—**partition,** pär•tish′on, *n.* [L. *partitio.*] The act of parting, dividing, or separating into portions and distributing; division; separation; that by which different parts are separated; a wall separating apartments in a building; a division between the chambers or cells of a thing; *music*, SCORE.—*v.t.* To divide by walls or partitions; to divide into shares.—**partitive,** pär′ti•tiv, *a. Gram.* denoting a part; expressing the relation of a part to a whole (a *partitive* genitive, 'the mountain's brow').—*n. Gram.* a word expressing partition.—**partitively,** pär′ti•tiv•li, *adv.* In a partitive manner.

partlet, part′let, *n.* [Fr. *Pertelote*, female proper name.] A hen.

partly. See PART.

partner, pärt′nėr, *n.* [In part directly from *part*, partly from old *parcener*, O.Fr. *parçonor*, from L. *partitio*, a sharing. PARTITION.] One who partakes or shares with another; a partaker; an associate; one who has a share with another or others in some commercial, manufacturing, or other undertaking; a member of a partnership; one who dances with another, either male or female; a husband or wife.—**partnership,** pärt′nėr•ship, *n.* The state or condition of being a partner; the association of two or more persons for the purpose of undertaking and prosecuting conjointly any business, occupation, or calling.

partridge, pär′trij, *n.* [O.E. *partryke*, *partriche*, from O.Fr. *pertrix*, Fr. *perdrix*, from L. and Gr. *perdix*, a partridge.] Any of a number of rasorial birds similar to the grouse, especially game birds; in America, has particular reference to the ruffed grouse and the quail.

part song. See PART.

parturient, pär•tū′ri•ent, *a.* [L. *parturiens, parturientis*, ppr. of *parturio*, from *partus*, birth, from *pario*, to bear. PARENT.] Bringing forth or about to bring forth young.—**parturition,** pär•tū•rish′on, *n.* [L. *parturitio.*] The act of bringing forth or being delivered of young.

party, pär′ti, *n.* [Fr. *partie*, a party, side, faction, a suitor or litigant, etc., from Fr. *partir*, L. *partio*, to divide, from *pars, partis*, a part. PART.] A number of persons united in opinion or design, in opposition to others in the community; persons in a state united by certain political views; a faction; persons collected for a particular purpose, often an armed force; a detached portion of a larger body or company; a detachment; a select company invited to an entertainment (a tea *party*, an evening *party*); one of two litigants; one concerned or interested in an affair (a *party* to a scheme or plot); a single person distinct from or opposed to another; a person under special consideration; hence, a person in general; an individual (in this sense vulgar).—**party-colored,** See PARTICOLORED.—**party line,** *n.* A single telephone circuit connecting several subscribers with the exchange; a boundary line.—**party wall,** *n.* A wall between buildings to separate them from each other; a wall separating adjoining tenements.

parvenu, pär′ve•nū, *n.* [Fr. *parvenu*, lit. one who has arrived, from *parvenir*, L. *pervenire*, to arrive.] An upstart, or one newly risen into notice.

parvis, pär′vis, *n.* [Fr. *parvis*, from L.L. *parvisius*, *paravisus*, from L. *paradisus*, paradise.] A name formerly given to the porch of a church, now applied to the area round a church.

Pasch, pask, *n.* [L. and Gr. *pascha*, from Heb. *pascha*, passage, from *pâsach*, to pass over.] The Passover; the feast of Easter.—**paschal,** pas′kal, *a.* Pertaining to the Passover or to Easter.

pash,‡ pash, *v.t.* [Same as Sw. *paska*, Prov. G. *paschen*, to strike.] To strike violently; to dash or smash. (*Shak.*)

pasha, pa•shä′ or pash′a, *n.* [Per. *pâshâh*, contr. from *pâdishâh*, protector or great king. PADISHAH.] In Turkey, a title formerly conferred upon military commanders and governors of provinces.—**pashalic, pachalic,** pa•shä′lik, pash′a•lik, *n.* The jurisdiction of a pasha.

pasqueflower, pask, *n.* [O.Fr. *pasque*, Easter. PASCH.] A species of anemone with large handsome purple flowers, so named in consequence of its flowering about Easter.

pasquil, pasquinade, pas′kwil, pas′-kwi•nād, *n.* [From *Pasquino*, a witty and satirical tailor (or barber) of Rome, whose name after his death was bestowed upon a statue that had been dug up near his shop, and to which satirical placards were affixed at night.] A lampoon or short satirical publication.—*v.t.* and *i.*—*pasquilled, pasquilling*; *pasquinaded, pasquinading.* To lampoon; to satirize in writing.

pass, pas, *v.i.* pret. & pp. *passed* or sometimes *past.* [Fr. *passer*, It. *passare*, from L. *passus*, a step, a pace. PACE.] To go; to proceed (to *pass* away, from, into, over, under, etc.); to go past a certain person or place (we saw him *pass*); to alter or change condition or circumstances; to undergo transition; to vanish, disappear, be lost: hence, to depart from life; to die; to elapse; to be spent; to receive the sanction of a legislative house or body by a majority of votes (the bill has *passed*); to be current; to gain reception or be generally received (bills *pass* as a substitute for coin); to be regarded, held, or considered; to occur; to take place (what *passes* within one's own mind); to thrust; to make a push in fencing or fighting; to throw a ball, as a football or basketball; *Baseball*, four balls pitched wide of the plate entitling the batter to proceed to first base; *Cards*, to decline a privilege, as of making a bid; to go unheeded or neglected; to be transferred from an owner; to go successfully through an inspection or examination.—*To come to pass*, to happen; to occur.—*To pass away*, to move from sight; to vanish; hence, to die; to be spent (as time, life).—*To pass by*, to move near and beyond a certain person or place.—*To pass into*, to unite and blend gradually.—*To pass on*, to continue to go forward; to proceed.—*To pass over*, to go or move to another side; to cross.—*To pass through*, to undergo; to experience.—*v.t.* To move near and go beyond; to move from side to side of; to live through; to spend (to *pass* the summer); to let go by without care or notice; to take no notice of; to transcend, exceed, excel, surpass; to transfer; to make to change hands; to hand over; to send; to circulate; to undergo successfully, as an examination, ordeal, or the like; to obtain the legislative or official sanction of; to be enacted by (the bill has *passed* the house); to give legal or official sanction to; to enact or ratify; to allow as valid or just; to give forth officially; to pronounce (to *pass* a sentence of death); to void, as feces or other matter; *baseball*, to go to first base after four balls; *football*, to throw the ball to another player.—*To pass off*, to impose by fraud; to palm off.—*To pass over*, to let go by unnoticed; to disregard.—*n.* A passage; a narrow road or defile between two mountains; permission to pass, or to go or come; a ticket of free transit or admission; a thrust or push in fencing; a movement of the hand over or along anything; a manipulation of a mesmerist; state or condition of things; an embarrassing situation; the successful or satisfactory standing or going through an examination.—**passable,** pas′a•bl, *a.* Capable of being passed, traveled, traversed, penetrated, etc.; capable of being passed from person to person; current; receivable; tolerable; allowable; admissible; mediocre.—**passably,** pas′a•bli, *adv.* Tolerably; moderately.—**passbook,** *n.* A book in which a shopkeeper makes an entry of goods sold on credit to a customer, for the information of the customer; also, a bankbook.—**passer,** pas′ėr, *n.* One who passes; a passenger.—**passer-by,** *n.* One who goes by or near.—**passing,** pas′ing, *adv.* Surpassingly; wonderfully; exceedingly (*passing* fair, *passing* strange).—*prep.* Exceeding; beyond; over.—**passing note,** *n. Music,* a note introduced between two others to form a transition, but not constituting an essential part of the harmony.—**password,** *n.* A secret parole or countersign by which a friend may be distinguished from a stranger, and allowed to pass.

passage, pas′ij, *n.* [Fr. *passage*, from *passer*, to pass. PASS.] The act of passing; transit from one place to another; a going by, through, over, or the like; transit by means of a conveyance; a journey by a conveyance, especially a ship; liberty of passing; access; entry or exit; way by which a person or thing may pass; avenue; way of entrance or exit; a gallery or corridor leading to the various divisions of a building; a part or portion quoted or referred to in a book, poem, etc.; the act of carrying through all the steps necessary to render valid (the *passage* of a bill or of a law); an encounter (a *passage* at arms, a *passage* of love).—*Birds of passage*, birds which migrate with the season from a colder to a warmer or from a warmer to a colder climate.

passant, pas′ant, *a.* [Fr. *passant*, ppr. of *passer*, to pass. PASS.] *Her.* a term applied to an animal which appears to walk.

passé, pas•ā′, *a.* [Fr.] Past; faded: as applied to persons, past the heyday of life.

passenger, pas′en•jėr, *n.* [O.E. *passager*, one who makes a passage; the *n* being an intrusive element, as in *messenger*.] One who passes or is on his way; a wayfarer; a traveler; one who travels, for payment, on a railroad, steamboat, coach, or other conveyance.—**passenger pigeon,** *n.* A North American wild pigeon, great flocks of which once abounded, especially in the Mississippi valley. It was widely hunted and is now extinct.

Passeres, pas′ėr•ēz, *n. pl.* [L., sparrows, so called because the bulk of them are small birds.] A name given to the extensive order of birds also called Insessores or perchers.—**passerine,** pas′ėr•īn, *a.* Pertaining to the order Passeres.—*n.* A passerine bird.

passible, pas′i•bl, *a.* [L. *passibilis*, from *patior*, *passus*, to suffer. PASSION.] Capable of feeling or suffering; susceptible of impressions from external agents.—**passibility,** pas•i•bil′i•ti, *n.* The quality of being passible.

passion, pash′on, *n.* [L. *passio*, *passionis*, from *patior*, *passus*, to bear, to suffer; allied to Gr. *pathos*, suffering; akin *patient, passive, compatible*, etc.] The suffering of bodily pangs; [*usually cap.*] specifically, the last suffering of the Saviour. A strong feeling or emotion by which the mind is swayed, as ambition, avarice, revenge, fear, hope, joy, grief, love, hatred, etc.; a strong deep feeling; violent agitation or excitement of mind; violent anger; zeal, ardor, vehement desire (a *passion* for fame); love; ardent affection; amorous desire; a passionate display; an exhibition of deep feeling (a *passion* of tears); a pursuit to which one is devoted.—*v.i.* To bewail; to cry out in a passionate way or lament. (*Shak.*)—**passional,** pash′on•al, *n.* A book in which are described the sufferings of saints and martyrs.—**passionate,** pash′on•it, *a.* Characterized by passion; exhibiting or expressing passion; readily moved to anger; fiery; showing strong emotion; vehement; warm (*passionate* affection).—**passionately,** pash′on•it•li, *adv.* In a passionate manner; ardently; vehemently; angrily.—**passionateness,** pash′on•it•nes, *n.* State of being passionate.—**passion-flower,** *n.* A genus of plants with showy flowers, chiefly natives of tropical South America, so called because in the anthers, styles, etc., was seen a resemblance to the symbols of the Lord's passion.—**passionless,** pash′on•les, *a.* Void of passion.—**Passion play,** *n.* A mystery or miracle play representing the different scenes in the Passion of Christ.—**Passion Sunday,** the fifth Sunday in Lent.—**Passion Week,** the week before Holy Week, beginning with Passion Sunday.

passive, pas′iv, *a.* [L. *passivus*, from *patior*, *passus*, to suffer. PASSION.] Not active; inert; not acting, receiving, or capable of receiving impressions from external objects; unresisting; not opposing; receiving or suffering without resistance; *gram.* expressive of suffering or being affected by some action; expressing that the nominative is the object of some action or feeling (the *passive* voice, a *passive* verb or inflection).—**passively,** pas′iv•li, *adv.* In a passive manner; without action; unresistingly; as a passive verb; in the passive voice.—**passiveness,** pas′iv•nes, *n.* Quality of being passive.—**passivity,** pas•iv′i•ti, *n.* Passiveness; the tendency of a body to continue in a given state till disturbed by another body.—**passive resistance,** *n.* Resistance to authority (especially that of government) without violence or active fighting, but rather by civil disobediance.—**passivist,** pas′iv•ist, *n.*

Passover, pas′ō•vėr, *n.* A feast of the Jews, instituted to commemorate the providential escape of the Hebrews in Egypt, when God, smiting the first born of the Egyptians, *passed over* the houses of the Israelites, which were marked with the blood of the paschal lamb; the sacrifice offered at the feast of the passover; the paschal lamb.

passport, pas′pōrt, *n.* [Fr. *passeport*, a safe-conduct, originally a permission to enter or leave a port. PASS, PORT.] A warrant of protection and authority to travel, granted to persons moving from place to place, by a competent authority; especially granted to persons traveling in a foreign country; something that enables one to pass with safety or certainty, or to attain any object or reach any end (the favor of the great was his *passport*); in *diplomacy*, *to demand a passport* is the request by an ambassador to leave a foreign country as a preliminary to war.—*To receive his passports*, is to be dismissed from an enemy country at the commencement of hostilities.

past, past, *p.* and *a.* [A form of *passed*.] Gone by; belonging to a time previous to this; not present nor future; spent; ended; over; existing no more.—*n.* A past or former time or state; a bygone time;

a state of matters no longer present.—*prep*. Beyond in time; after; having lost; no longer possessing (*past* sense of feeling); beyond; out of reach of; out of the scope or influence of (*past* help), beyond in position; further than.—*adv*. By.—**past master,** *n*. One who has occupied the office or dignity of master, especially in such bodies as Freemasons, etc.; *fig*. one who has experience in his particular craft or business. **past participle,** *n*. A participle having a past or perfect meaning.—**past perfect,** *n*. A verb form describing action or state as terminated at or before a past time referred to (she *had left* before I arrived).

paste, pāst, *n*. [O.Fr. *paste*, Fr. *pâte*; from L. *pasta*, paste, from Gr. *pastē*, a mess of barley-porridge, from *passō*, to sprinkle.] A composition in which there is just sufficient moisture to soften without liquefying the mass; a mixture of flour with milk, water, etc., used in cookery, as for pies, pastry, etc.; a kind of cement variously compounded; a composition of pounded rock crystal melted with alkaline salts, and colored with metallic oxides, used for making imitation gems; *mineral*, the mineral substance in which other minerals are embedded.—*v.t.*—*pasted, pasting*. To unite or cement with paste; to fasten with paste.—**pasteboard,** pāst′bōrd, *n*. A species of thick paper formed of several single sheets pasted one upon another, or by macerating paper and casting it in molds, etc.; cardboard.—*a*. Made of pasteboard.—**pastry,** pās′tri, *n*. Viands made of paste, or of which paste constitutes the principal ingredient; the crust or cover of a pie, tart, or the like.—**pasty,** pās′ti, *a*. Like paste; of the consistence of paste.—*n*. A meat pie covered with a crust.

pastel, pas•tel′, *n*. [Fr. *pastel*, a pastel, woad, from L. *pastillus*, a little roll. PASTIL.] A colored crayon; also, any of a number of pale or faint colors.

pastern, pas′tėrn, *n*. [O.Fr. *pasturon*, from *pasture*, a shackle for cattle at pasture, from L. *pasco*, *pastum*, to feed. PASTURE.] The part of a horse's leg between the joint next the foot and the coronet of the hoof; a shackle for horses while pasturing.

pasteurize, pas′tėr•īz, pas′tūr•īz, *v.t.* [After *Louis Pasteur*, Fr. scientist.] To sterilize liquids by heating (to *pasteurize* milk).—**pasteurization,** pas•tėr•ī•zā′shon, *n*.

pastil, pastille, pas•til′, pas•tēl′, *n*. [Fr. *pastille*, L. *pastillus*, a little roll, from *pastus*, food, *pasco*, *pastum*, to feed. PASTOR.] A small roll of aromatic paste, composed of gum benzoin, sandalwood, spices, etc., for burning as a fumigator or disinfectant; a lozenge.

pastime, pas′tīm, *n*. [*Pass* and *time*.] That which amuses and serves to make time pass agreeably; sport; amusement.

pastor, pas′tor, *n*. [L. *pastor*, a shepherd, from *pasco*, *pastum*, to feed; same root as W. *pasg*, a feeding, Armor. *paska*, to feed, Skr. *pâ*, to guard.] A shepherd‡; a minister of the gospel having the charge of a church and congregation.—**pastoral,** pas′tor•al, *a*. [L. *pastoralis*.] Pertaining to shepherds; rustic; rural; descriptive of the life of shepherds or of a country life (a *pastoral* poem); relating to the cure of souls, or to the pastor of a church.—*Pastoral epistles*, epistles of St. Paul to Titus and Timothy dealing with the pastoral organization of their various spheres.—*Pastoral letter*, a letter or circular addressed by a bishop to the clergy and people of his diocese.—*Pastoral theology*, that part of theology which treats of the obligations of pastors and their relations toward their flocks.—*n*. A poem describing the life and manners of shepherds; a bucolic poem; a pastoral letter or address; *mus*. a simple melody in six-eight time in a rustic style; a symphony whose simple movements are designed to suggest pastoral scenes.—**pastorale,** pas•tō•rä′le, *n*. [It.] *Mus*. a pastoral.—**pastoralism,** pas′tor•al•izm, *n*. Pastoral character.—**pastorally,** pas′tor•al•li, *adv*. In a pastoral or rural manner; in the manner of a pastor.—**pastoral staff,** *n*. The official staff of a bishop or abbot, with a curved head. See CROZIER.—**pastorate,** pas′tor•it, *n*. The office or jurisdiction of a pastor; a body of pastors.

pastry. See PASTE.

pasture, pas′chėr, *n*. [O.Fr. *pasture* (Fr. *pâture*), from L. *pastura*, from *pasco*, to feed. PASTOR.] Grass for the food of cattle or other animals; ground covered with grass for the food of animals; a grazing ground.—*v.t.*—*pastured, pasturing*. To feed on growing grass, or to supply pasture for.—*v.i.* To graze.—**pasturable,** pas′chėr•a•bl, *a*. Fit for pasture.—**pasturage,** pas′chėr•ij, *n*. [O.Fr. *pasturage*.] The business of feeding or grazing cattle; grazing ground; growing grass on which cattle feed.

pasty. See PASTE.

pat, pat, *v.t.*—*patted, patting*. [Imitative of the sound of a slight sharp blow; comp. W. *ffat*, a blow, and E. *tap*. *Patter* is a frequentative from this.] To strike gently with the fingers or hand; to tap.—*n*. A light quick blow with the fingers or hand; a small lump of butter molded or cut into shape.—*a*. Hitting the mark; apt; fit; convenient.—*adv*. Fitly; conveniently; just in the nick; also unmoved, as to stand *pat*.

patagium, pa•tā′ji•um, *n*. [L., the border of a dress.] The flying appendage or expansion of bats, flying squirrels, etc.

patch, pach, *n*. [Connected with Swiss *patschen*, to patch, to clap on a piece, *batsch*, a patch; also It. *pezza*, a patch, a piece.] A piece of cloth sewed on a garment to repair it; any similar piece; a small piece of silk formerly stuck on the face by way of adornment; a small piece of ground; a plot; the name of the clown in patchwork or motley; the medieval fool; any sorry or poor creature.—*v.t.* To mend with patches or pieces; to repair clumsily; to adorn (the face) with a patch or with patches; to make up of pieces and shreds; *fig*. to make hastily or without regard to forms: usually with *up* (to *patch up* a quarrel).—**patcher,** pach′ėr, *n*. One that patches.—**patchwork,** pach′wėrk, *n*. Work composed of various figures or colors sewed together; anything formed of ill-assorted parts.—**patchy,** pach′i, *a*. Full of patches.

patchouli, patchouly, pa•chö′li, *n*. [An Indian name.] A plant of India and China, the leaves of which furnish an odorous oil; the perfume itself.

pate, pāt, *n*. [Perhaps from Ir. *pata*, *pota*, Sc. *pat*, a pot, the radical meaning being the brainpan or skull.] The head of a person; the top of the head.—**pated,** pā′ted, *a*. Having a pate: in composition (shallow-*pated*).

patella, pa•tel′la, *n*. [L. dim. of *patera*, a cup, from *pateo*, to lie open. PATENT.] A small pan, vase, or dish; *anat*. the kneepan.—**patelliform,** pa•tel′li•form, *a*. Like the patella; of the form of a saucer.

paten, pat′en, *n*. [L. *patina*, a pan, from *pateo*, to lie open. PATENT.] A metallic plate or flat dish; the round metallic plate on which the bread is placed in the sacrifice of the Lord's supper.

patent, pat′ent, *a*. [From L. *patens*, *patentis*, ppr. of *pateo*, to lie open; same root as Gr. *petannymi*, to spread; *petalon*, a leaf; akin *pan*, *paten*, *patella*.] Open; spreading; expanded; open to the perusal of all (letters *patent*); secured by law as an exclusive privilege; patented (*patent* medicines); manifest to all; evident.—*n*. A document conferring a right; a privilege or license; a writing conveying to the individual or individuals specified therein the sole right to make, use, or dispose of some new invention or discovery for a certain limited period.—*v.t.* To make the subject of a patent; to secure by patent right.—**patentable,** pat′ent•a•bl, *a*. Capable of being patented.—**patentee,** pat′en•tē″, *n*. One who holds a patent; one by whom a patent is secured.—**patent leather,** *n*. A kind of leather to which a permanent polish is given by a process of japanning.—**patent right,** *n*. An exclusive privilege in an invention, etc., granted by patent.

paterfamilias, pā′tėr•fa•mil″i•as, *n*. [L., from *pater*, father, and *familia*, a family.] The father or head of a family.

paternal, pa•tėr′nal, *a*. [Fr. *paternel*, from L. *paternus*, from *pater*, father (FATHER); akin *parricide*, *patriarch*, *patrimony*, *patriot*, *patron*, *pattern*.] Pertaining to a father; fatherly; derived from the father; hereditary.—**paternally,** pa•tėr′nal•li, *adv*. In a paternal manner.—**paternity,** pa•tėr′ni•ti, *n*. [Fr. *paternité*.] Fatherhood; the relation of a father to his offspring; derivation from a father (the child's *paternity*); hence, origin; authorship.

paternoster, pa′tėr•nos•tėr, *n*. [L.,

our Father, the first two words of the Lord's prayer in Latin.] [*often capped.*] The Lord's prayer; every tenth large bead in the Rosary; the Rosary itself.

path, päth, *n.* pl. **paths,** päTHZ. [A. Sax. *paeth*=D. and L.G. *pad,* G. *pfad,* a path; perhaps from Gr. *patos,* a trodden way, *patein,* to walk.] A way beaten or trodden by the feet of man or beast, or made hard by wheels; a narrow or unimportant road; a footway; a way or route in general; the way or course which an animal or any object follows in the air, in water, or in space; *fig.* course of life; course of conduct or procedure.—**pathless,** päth'les, *a.* Having no beaten way; untrodden.—**pathway,** päth'wā, *n.* A path; a narrow way to be passed on foot; a way; a course of life.

Pathan, pat•hän', *n.* A person of Afghan race settled in Hindustan; an Afghan.

pathetic. See PATHOS.

pathogen, path'o•jen, *n.* [Gr. *pathos,* suffering, disease, and *gen,* born.] A disease-causing organism or virus. —**pathogenic,** path'o•jen"ik, *a.* Causing disease.

pathogeny, pa•thoj'e•ni, *n.* [Gr. *pathos,* suffering, and root *gen,* to produce.] The doctrine or science of the generation and development of disease.

pathology, pa•thol'o•ji, *n.* [Gr. *pathos,* suffering, and *logos,* discourse.] That part of medicine which explains the nature of diseases, their causes, and symptoms.—**pathologic, pathological,** path•o•loj'ik, path•o•loj'i•kal, *a.*—**pathologically,** path•o•loj'i•kal•li, *adv.*—**pathologist,** pa•thol'o•jist, *n.*

pathos, pā'thos, *n.* [Gr. *pathos,* passion, suffering, from stem of *pathein,* to suffer.] That quality, attribute, or element which awakens such tender emotions as pity, compassion, or sympathy.—**pathetic,** pa•thet'ik, *a.* Moving the feelings; exciting pity, sorrow, or other tender emotion; affecting.—**pathetical,** pa•thet'i•kal, *a.*—**pathetically,** pa•thet'i•kal•li, *adv.*

patience, pā'shens, *n.* [Fr. *patience,* from L. *patientia,* from *patiens,* patient. PASSION.] The quality of being patient; the power or capacity of physical endurance; the character or habit of mind that enables one to suffer afflictions, provocation, or other evil, with a calm unruffled temper; calmness; composure; quietness or calmness in waiting for something to happen; forbearance; long-suffering; constancy in labor or exertion; perseverance; a card game played by one person alone.—**patient,** pā'shent, *a.* [L. *patiens, patientis.*] Physically able to support or endure; proof against (*patient of* labor or pain, heat, or cold); bearing pain or trial without murmuring; sustaining afflictions with fortitude, calmness, or submission; waiting with calmness; not hasty; long-suffering; persevering; calmly diligent.—*n.* One who or that which is passively affected; a sufferer from an ailment; a person who is under medical treatment.—**patiently,** pā'shent•li, *adv.* In a patient manner; with patience; submissively; uncomplainingly.

patina, pat'i•na, *n.* [L. *patina,* a dish, a kind of cake, from *pateo,* to be open. PATENT, PAN.] The fine green rust with which bronze and copper become covered by oxidization; a weathered surface, in general, of aesthetic value.

patio, pa'ti•ō, *n.* [Sp.] A courtyard; a paved area adjoining a dwelling and used for recreation.

patois, pat•wä', *n.* [Fr.] A dialect peculiar to the peasantry or uneducated classes; a provincial form of speech, the survival of a once literary dialect.

patriarch, pā'tri•ärk, *n.* [L. *patriarcha,* from Gr. *patriarchēs*—*patria,* a family, from *patēr,* father, and *archē,* rule. PATERNAL.] The father and ruler of a family; generally applied to Abraham, Isaac, Jacob, and the sons of Jacob, or to the heads of families before the flood; hence, an aged venerable man; in the *Greek Church,* a dignitary superior to an archbishop.—**patriarchal,** pā•tri•är'kal, *a.* Belonging to patriarchs; subject to a patriarch.—**patriarchate,** pā'tri•är•kāt, *n.* The office or jurisdiction of a patriarch.—**patriarchy,** pā'tri•är•ki, *n.* An ecclesiastical patriarchate.

patrician, pa•trish'an, *a.* [Fr. *patricien,* from L. *patricius,* pertaining to the *patres,* senators or patricians, from *pater,* father. PATERNAL.] Pertaining to the senatorial order in ancient Rome; hence, of noble birth; not plebeian.—*n.* A person of patrician or noble birth; a nobleman.—**patriciate,** pa•trish'i•āt, *n.* The aristocracy collectively.

patricide, pat'ri•sīd, *n.* [L. *pater, patris,* father, and *caedo,* to kill.] The murder or murderer of one's father; parricide —**patricidal,** pat•ri•sī'dal, *a* Relating to patricide; parricidal.

patrimony, pat'ri•mo•ni, *n.* [L. *patrimonium,* from *pater, patris,* father. PATERNAL.] A right or estate inherited from one's father or ancestors; heritage; a church estate or revenue.—**patrimonial,** pat•ri•mō'ni•al, *a.* Pertaining to a patrimony; inherited from ancestors.

patriot, pā'tri•ot, *n.* [Fr. *patriote,* from L. *patria,* one's native country, from *pater,* father. PATERNAL.] A person who loves his country, and zealously supports and defends it and its interests.—*a.* Patriotic.—**patriotic,** pā•tri•ot'ik, *a.* Having the feelings of a patriot; inspired by the love of one's country; directed by zeal for the public safety and welfare. —**patriotically,** pā•tri•ot'i•kal•li, *adv.* In a patriotic manner.—**patriotism,** pā'tri•ot•izm, *n.* Love of one's country; the passion which leads a person to serve his country with zeal.

patrist, pā'trist, *n.* [From L. *patres,* fathers.] One versed in the writings of the fathers of the Christian church. —**patristic, patristical,** pa•tris'tik, pa•tris'ti•kal, *a.* Pertaining to the ancient fathers of the Christian church. — **patristically,** pa•tris'ti•kal•li, *adv.* In a patristic manner.

patrol, pa•trōl', *n.* [Fr. *patrouille,* from *patrouiller,* to patrol, also to paddle with the feet, from *patte,* O.Fr. *pate,* a paw=G. *pfote,* D. *poot,* a paw.] *Milit.* the marching round of a guard in the night to secure the peace and safety of a camp or other place; the persons who go the rounds; a policeman who goes round a regular beat.—*v.i. patrolled, patrolling.* To go the rounds as a guard in a camp or garrison; to go the rounds in a city, as is done by a body of police.—*Patrol flotilla,* a flotilla or fleet of vessels acting by way of patrol, that is moving about and keeping guard against the approach of hostile craft and against attempts to break a blockade.—*v.t.* To pass through or perambulate in the capacity of a patrol.

patron, pā'tron, *n.* [L. *patronus,* a protector or patron, from *pater,* a father. PATERNAL.] Among the ancient Romans, a master who had freed his slave, and still retained some rights over him; a man of distinction under whose protection another placed himself; hence, one who countenances, supports, or protects either a person or a work; a man of rank or standing who assists a person in an inferior position; a patron saint; one who has the gift and disposition of an ecclesiastical benefice.—*Patron saint,* any saint under whose special protection a church, a society, or a person is regarded as placed.—**patronage,** pāt'ron•ij, *n.* The act of patronizing; protection; encouragement; guardianship, as of a saint; the right of presentation to a church or ecclesiastical benefice.—**patroness,** pā'tron•es, *n.* A female patron.—**patronize,** pāt'ron•īz, *v.t.*—*patronized, patronizing.* To act as patron toward; to give support or countenance to; to favor; to assist; to assume the air of a patron or superior toward.—**patronizer,** pāt'ron•īz•ėr, *n.* One who patronizes.—**patronizingly,** pāt'ron•īz•ing•li, *adv.*

patronymic, pat•ro•nim'ik, *n.* [L. *patronymicus,* from Gr. *patēr, patros,* a father, and *onoma,* a name. PATERNAL.] A personal name derived from that of parent or ancestor (*Tydides,* the son of Tydeus; *Williamson,* the son of William).

patroon, pa•trön', *n.* [D. *patroon,* a patron.] The proprietor of land and manorial privileges granted by the old Dutch governments of New York and New Jersey.

patten, pat'en, *n.* [Fr. *patin,* a clog, patten, from *patte,* the foot. PATROL.] A wooden shoe or sole, standing on an iron ring, worn to keep the shoes from the dirt or mud; *masonry,* the base of a column or pillar; the sole for the foundation of a wall.

patter, pat'ėr, *v.i.* [Freq. from *pat,* to give a slight blow. PAT.] To strike, as falling drops of water or hail, with a quick succession of small sounds; to move with quick steps, making a succession of small sounds.—*n.* A quick succession of small sounds.

patter, pat′ėr, *v.t.* [Perhaps from the *Paternoster*, or Lord's prayer, repeated in churches in a low tone of voice. Comp. also Icel. *pata*, to prattle, *pati*, a rumor.] To repeat in a muttering way; to mutter.—*n.* Rapid, routine talk used by magicians, comedians, etc.

pattern, pat′ėrn, *n.* [Same word as *patron*, which has also the sense of *pattern* in French and Spanish, as has L.L. *patronus*.] An original or model proposed for imitation; that which is to be copied or imitated; a piece or part exhibited as a specimen of the whole; a design or figure corresponding in outline to an object that is to be fabricated, and serving as a guide for determining its shape and dimensions; an ornamental design on some woven fabric: the counterpart in wood of something that is to be cast in metal.

patty, pat′i, *n.* [Fr. *pâté*, pie, pasty.] A little pie; a pasty.—**pattypan,** *n.* A pan to bake patties in.

patulous, pat′ū•lus, *a.* [L. *patulus*, from *pateo*, to be open. PATENT.] Spreading slightly; expanded; opening widely; with a spreading aperture.

paucity, pa̤′si•ti, *n.* [L. *paucitas*, from *paucus*, few; cog. with E. *few*.] Fewness; smallness of number; smallness or scantness of quantity.

Pauline, pa̤l′ēn, *a.* Pertaining to St. *Paul*, or to his writings; a member of St. Paul's School in London.

paunch, pa̤nsh, *n.* [O.Fr. *panche* (Fr. *panse*), from L. *pantex*, *panticis*, the belly.] The belly and its contents; the abdomen; the first and largest stomach in ruminating quadrupeds, into which the food is received before rumination.—**paunchy,** pa̤n′shi, *a.* Having a prominent paunch; big-bellied.

pauper, pa̤′pėr, *n.* [L. *pauper*, poor (whence *poverty*, *poor*, *impoverish*); akin *paucus*, few. PAUCITY.] A poor person; one in a state of indigence; particularly, one who, on account of poverty, becomes chargeable to a parish.—**pauperism,** pa̤′pėr•izm, *n.* The state of being a pauper; a state of indigence in a community.—**pauperize,** pa̤′pėr•īz, *v.t.*—*pauperized*, *pauperizing*. To reduce to pauperism.

pause, pa̤z, *n.* [Fr., from L. *pausa*, Gr. *pausis*, a stopping, from *pauō*, to stop; *pose* (seen in *compose*, *impose*, etc.) is of same origin.] A temporary cessation; an intermission of action, of speaking, singing, or the like; a short stop; cessation proceeding from doubt; suspense; a mark of suspension of the voice; a character marking a halt in music.—*v.i.*—*paused*, *pausing*. To make a pause or short stop; to intermit speaking or action; to wait; to forbear for a time; to hesitate; to hold back; to be intermitted (the music *pauses*).—**pauser,** pa̤′zėr, *n.* One who pauses.

pave, pāv, *v.t.*—*paved*, (pp. sometimes *paven*), *paving*. [Fr. *paver*, L.L. *pavare*, from L. *pavire*, to ram, to pave.] To make a hard level surface upon by laying with stones, bricks, etc.; to floor with brick, stone, or other material.—*To pave a way* (*fig.*), to prepare a way; to remove difficulties or obstacles beforehand.—**pavement,** pāv′ment, *n.* [L. *pavimentum*.] A paved path or road; a floor or surface that is trodden on, consisting of stones, bricks, etc.; the stones or other material with which anything is paved.—**paver,** pā′vėr, *n.* One who paves; a pavior.—**paving,** pāv′ing, *n.* Pavement; the laying of floors, streets, etc., with pavement.—*Paving stones*, large prepared stones or slabs for paving.—**pavior, paviour,** pā′vi•ėr, *n.* One whose occupation is to pave; a slab or brick used for paving; a rammer for driving paving stones.

pavid, pav′id, *a.* [L. *pavidus*, from *paveo*, to fear.] Timid; fearful.

pavilion, pa•vil′yon, *n.* [Fr. *pavillon*, L. *papilio*, *papilionis*, a butterfly, also a tent, from shape of latter.] A tent; particularly, a large tent raised on posts; a canopy; *arch.* a small building or a part of a building having a tent-formed roof.—*Pavilion roof*, a roof sloping or hipped equally on all sides.—*v.t.* To furnish with tents; to shelter with a tent.

pavonine, pav′o•nīn, *a.* [L. *pavoninus*, from *pavo*, a peacock.] Belonging to a peacock; resembling a peacock; exhibiting the brilliant hues of the tail of a peacock; iridescent; applied to ores, etc.—*n.* The iridescent luster found on some ores and metallic products.

paw, pa̤, *n.* [From the Celtic: W. *pawen*, Armor. *pav*, *pao*; comp. D. *poot*, G. *pfote*, a paw.] The foot of quadrupeds having claws.—*v.i.* To draw the forefoot along the ground; to scrape with the forefoot (as a horse does).—*v.t.* To scrape or strike with the forefoot; to handle roughly.

pawky, pa̤′ki, *a.* Humorous, dry and satiric in tone.

pawl, pa̤l, *n.* [W. *pawl*, akin to L. *palus*, a stake. POLE.] A short bar pivoted at one end, so as to catch in a notch of a revolving body and stop its motion; a click or detent which falls into the teeth of a ratchet wheel.—*v.t.* To stop with a pawl.

pawn, pa̤n, *n.* [Fr. *pan*, a piece of a garment, formerly also a pawn or pledge, from L. *pannus*, a cloth, a rag. PANE.] Some article or chattel given or deposited as security for money borrowed; a pledge.—*In pawn*, *at pawn*, in the state of being pawned or pledged.—*v.t.* To give or deposit in pledge; to pledge with a pawnbroker; to pledge for the fulfillment of a promise.—**pawnbroker,** pa̤n′brō•kėr, *n.* A person licensed to lend money at a legally fixed rate of interest on goods deposited with him.—**pawnbroking,** pa̤n′brō•king, *n.* The business of a pawnbroker.—**pawnee,** pa̤•nē′, *n.* The person to whom a pawn is delivered as security.—**pawner,** *n.* One that pawns.

pawn, pa̤n, *n.* [O.Fr. *paon*, *poon*, *peon*, properly a foot soldier. PEON.] A piece of the lowest rank at chess; an insignificant factor or person used as a tool by another.

pawpaw, pa̤′pa̤, *n.* See PAPAW.

pax, paks, *n.* [L. *pax*, peace.] In the Roman Catholic Church a small tablet engraved with sacred figures or emblems, which, having been kissed by the priest, was then kissed by others.

paxwax, paks′waks, *n.* [Also called *faxwax*, from A.Sax. *feax*, hair, and *weaxan*, to wax or grow.] A strong tendinous ligament strengthening the neck of the ox, sheep, etc.

pay, pā, *v.t.*—pret. and pp. *paid*, [O.Fr. *paier*, *paer* (Fr. *payer*), to pay, originally to please, being from L. *pacare*, to pacify—*pax*, *pacis*, peace. PEACE.] To recompense for goods received or for service rendered; to discharge one's obligation to; to compensate, remunerate, reward, requite; to discharge (as a debt) by giving or doing that which is due; to give; to render or offer; without any sense of obligation (to *pay* attention, respect, court, a visit); *naut.* to cover or coat, as the bottom of a vessel, a mast, etc.—*To pay out*, *naut.* to slacken or cause to run out (a rope).—*v.i.* To make payment or requital; to be worth the pains or efforts spent; to be remunerative.—*To pay for*, to make amends for; to atone for.—*To pay off*, to pay wages and discharge.—*n.* An equivalent given for money due, goods purchased, or services performed.—**payable,** pā′a•bl, *a.*—**pay dirt,** *n.* *Mining*, earth, ore, rock, etc., which yields a profit to the miner.—**payee,** pā•ē′, *n.* The person to whom money is to be paid.—**payer,** pā′ėr, *n.* One that pays; the person named in a bill or note who has to pay the holder.—**payload,** pā′lōd, *n.* Any useful cargo in a transport vehicle; in military rockets, the warhead.—**paymaster,** pā′mas•tėr, *n.* One from whom wages or reward are received.—**payment,** pā′ment, *n.* The act of paying; the thing given in discharge of a debt; requital.—**payola,** pā•ō′lä, *n.* An illegal payment for commercial favors, as to a disc jockey for promoting a song.—**payroll,** pa′rōl, *n.* A list of employees and of their wages; money needed for payment of wages.

paynim, pā′nim, *n.* [O.Fr. *apienime*, *paienisme*, paganism, from *paien*, L. *paganus*, a pagan. PAGAN.] A pagan; a heathen.

pea, pē, *n.* [O.E. *pese*, *pees*, a pea, pl. *pesen*, *peses*, A.Sax. *pise*, from L. *pisum*, Gr. *pisos*, a pea. *Pea* is a false form, the *s* of the root being mistaken for the sign of the plural. In the plural we always write *peas* for the individual seeds, but often *pease* for an indefinite quantity (this form being the old singular): three or four *peas*, a bushel of *pease* (or *peas*).] A well-known plant with papilionaceous flowers, one of the most valuable of vegetables, cultivated in the garden and in the field; one of the seeds of the plant.—**peanut,** *n.* An American plant, whose pods grow first above and then below ground; the nutlike seed of this plant.—**peanut butter,** *n.* A paste made from crushed peanuts.

peace, pēs, *n.* [From O.Fr. *pais* (Fr. *paix*), from L. *pax, pacis,* peace—root *pac,* seen in *paciscor,* to agree (whence *pact*); of same origin as *pay, appease.*] A state of quiet or tranquility; calm, quietness, repose; especially freedom from war; a cessation of hostilities; absence of strife; tranquility of mind; quiet of conscience; harmony; concord; public tranquility.—*At peace,* in a peaceful state.—*Breach of the peace,* a violation of public tranquility by riotous or other conduct.—*To hold one's peace,* to be silent; to suppress one's thoughts; not to speak.—*To make* a person's *peace,* with another, to reconcile the other to him.—*Peace establishment,* the reduced number of effective men in the army during time of peace.—*Commission of the peace,* a commission appointing justices of the peace, and by virtue of which the judges sit upon circuit.—*Justices of the peace.* JUSTICE.—**peaceable,** pēs′a•bl, *a.* Tranquil; peaceful; disposed to peace; not quarrelsome. ∴ *Peaceable* usually refers to the character and disposition of men; *pacific* to designs and intentions; while *peaceful* refers to the state or condition of men or things.—**peaceableness,** pēs′a•bl•nes, *n.* The state or quality of being peaceable.—**peaceably,** pēs′a•bli, *adv.* In a peaceable manner.—**peaceful,** pēs′-fu̱l, *a.* Full of, possessing, or enjoying peace; tranquil; quiet; removed from noise or tumult; pacific.—**peacefully,** pēs′fu̱l•li, *adv.* In a peaceful manner; quietly; tranquilly.—**peacefulness,** pēs′fu̱l•nes, *n.* The state or quality of being peaceful.—**peacemaker,** pēs′mā•kėr, *n.* One who reconciles parties at variance.—**peace offering,** *n.* Something offered to procure peace.—**peace pipe,** *n.* The ceremonial, long-stemmed pipe of the North American Indians, also called the *calumet,* smoked by the members to signify peace.

peach, pēch, *n.* [Fr. *pêche,* It. *pesca, persica,* from L. *persica. Persicum* (*malum*), the Persian apple.] A fruit tree of many varieties, grown in temperate climates; the fruit of the tree, a sweet, juicy drupe a little smaller than an apple, containing a stone; also, that which resembles a peach, as in beauty or goodness.—**peach blossom,** *n.* The delicate pink flower of the peach, which appears in early spring.

peacock, pē′kok, *n.* [*Pea*=A.Sax. *pawa,* from L. *pavo,* a peacock, the name being perhaps from the bird's cry.] A large and beautiful gallinaceous bird remarkable for the beauty of its plumage, properly the male of the species, the female being, for distinction's sake, called a *peahen.*—**peafowl,** *n.* The peacock or peahen.

pea jacket, pē′jak•et, *n.* [*Pea* is from D. and L.G. *pije,* coarse, thick cloth, a warm jacket; akin to Goth. *paida,* a garment.] A thick loose woolen jacket worn by seamen, fishermen, etc.

peak, pēk, *n.* [Fr. *pic,* a mountain peak, a pick, *pique,* a pike, from Armor. *pic,* W. *pig.* a point, a pike, a beak; akin *beak, pike, pick, peck.*] The top of a hill or mountain, ending in a point; a projecting point; a projecting portion on a head covering (the *peak* of a cap); *naut.* the upper corner of a sail which is extended by a gaff or yard; the highest point; the point of greatest development.—*v.t.* To cause to come to a peak.—*v.i.* To reach the peak of.—**peaked,** pēkt, *a.* Pointed; having a peak.

peak, pēk, *v.i.* [Perhaps from *peak, n.,* from the sharpened features of sickly persons.] To look sickly or thin; to be or become emaciated.—**peakish,** pēk′ish, *a.* Of a thin and sickly cast or face.

peal, pēl, *n.* [A mutilated form of *appeal.*] A succession of loud sounds, as of bells, thunder, cannon, shouts of a multitude, etc.; a set of bells tuned to each other; the changes rung on such bells.—*v.i.* To utter or give out a peal.—*v.t.* To cause to ring or sound; to utter loudly and sonorously.

pean. See PAEAN.

pear, pâr, *n.* [A.Sax. *peru,* Fr. *poire,* from L. *pirum,* a pear.] A fruit tree of the genus *Pyrus,* grown in temperate climates; the fruit itself, a sweet, fleshy pome.

pearl, pėrl, *n.* [Fr. *perle,* from L.L. *perula, perla,* a pearl, either for *pirula,* from L. *pirum,* a pear, or for *pilula,* a pill, a globule.] A silvery or bluish-white, hard, smooth, lustrous body, of a roundish, oval, or pear-shaped form, produced by certain mollusks; anything very valuable; what is best.—*a.* Relating to, made of pearl.—*v.t.* To set or adorn with pearls.—**pearlash,** pėrl′-ash, *n.* Commercial carbonate of potash.—**pearl barley,** *n.* The seed of barley ground into small round grains.—**pearl nautilus,** *n.* The true nautilus as distinguished from the argonaut or paper nautilus.—**pearly,** pėr′li, *a.* Containing pearls; resembling pearls; nacreous.

peasant, pez′ant, *n.* [O.Fr. *païsant* (Fr. *paysan*), from *pais, pays,* L. *pagus,* a district of country (with *t* affixed as in *tyrant*). PAGAN, PAGE (boy).] A rustic or countryman; one occupied in rural labor.—*a.* Rustic; rural.—**peasantry,** pez′ant•-ri, *n.* Peasants collectively; the body of country people.

pease, pēz, *n.* See PEA.

peat, pēt, *n.* [For *beat, bete,* from old *bete,* to mend a fire; A.Sax. *bétan,* to make better; akin *bette boot.*] A kind of turf used as fuel; the natural accumulation of vegetable matter, more or less decomposed, cut and dried for fuel.—**peat moss,** pēt mos, *n.* Any moss, especially of the genus *Sphagnum,* from which peat has formed or may form.—**peaty,** pēt′i, *n.*

pebble, peb′l, *n.* [A.Sax. *papolstán,* lit. pebble-stone; etym. unknown.] A small round stone worn and rounded by the action of water; a transparent, colorless rock crystal.—*v.t.* To pelt or pave with pebbles; to grain leather, paper, etc., for a rough surface.—**pebbly,** peb′li, *a.*

pecan, pē•kan′, *n.* [Fr. *pacane,* Sp. *pacana.*] A species of hickory and its fruit.

peccable, pek′a•bl, *a.* [L.L. *peccabilis,* peccable, from L. *pecco,* to sin.] Liable to sin; subject to transgress the divine law.—**peccability,** pek•a•bil′i•ti, *n.* State of being peccable.—**peccadillo,** pek•a•-dil′ō, *n.* [Sp. *pecadillo,* dim. of *pecado,* L. *peccatum,* a sin, from *pecco.*] A slight trespass or offense; a petty crime or fault.—**peccancy,** pek′an•si, *n.* State or quality of being peccant.—**peccant,** pek′ant, *a.* [L. *peccans, peccantis,* ppr. of *pecco.*] Sinning; criminal; morbid; corrupt (*peccant* humors).—**peccantly,** pek′-ant•li, *adv.*

peccary, pek′a•ri, *n.* [South American name.] A pachydermatous quadruped of America, representing the swine of the Old World, to which it is allied.

peccavi, pek•kä′vi, [L., I have sinned, from *pecco,* to sin.] A word used to express confession or acknowledgment of an offense.

peck, pek, *n.* [Perhaps a form of *pack;* but comp. Fr. *picotin,* a peck; L.L. *picotus,* a liquid measure.] The fourth part of a bushel; a dry measure of 8 quarts.

peck, pek, *v.t.* [A slightly different form of *pick.*] To strike with the beak; to pick up with the beak; to make by striking with the beak, or a pointed instrument (to *peck* a hole).—*v.i.* To make strokes with a beak, or a pointed instrument; to attack with petty criticism.—*n.* A quick, light stroke with a beak; a quick, light kiss (colloq.).—**pecker,** pek′ėr, *n.*

pecten, pek′ten, *n.* [L. *pecten,* a comb, a kind of shellfish, from *pecto, pexum,* to comb; root *pek,* also in Gr. *pekō,* to comb.] A genus of marine bivalves having a shell marked with diverging ribs and furrows.

pectic, pek′tik, *a.* [Gr. *pēktikos,* curdling, from *pēgnymi,* to fix.] Having the property of forming a jelly; said of an acid found in fruits.

pectin, pek′tin, *n.* [Gr. *pektos,* curdled, congealed.] A carbohydrate which forms the basis of vegetable jelly.

pectinal, pek′ti•nal, *a.* [L. *pecten,* a comb. PECTEN.] Pertaining to a comb; resembling a comb.—**pectinate, pectinated,** pek′ti•nāt, pek′ti•-nā•ted, *a.* [L. *pectinatus.*] Having resemblance to the teeth of a comb; toothed like a comb; serrated.—**pectination,** pek•ti•nā′shon, *n.* The state of being pectinated; what is pectinated.

pectoral, pek′to•ral, *a.* [L. *pectoralis*, from *pectus, pectoris*, the breast.] Pertaining to the breast.—*Pectoral fins*, the two fore fins of a fish, situated near the gills.—*Pectoral theology*, heartfelt, unctuous belief.—*Pectus theologum facit* (Augustine).—*n.* A covering or protection for the breast; a breastplate; the breastplate of the Jewish high priest; a medicine for complaints of the chest; a pectoral fin.

peculate, pek′ū•lāt, *v.i.*—*peculated, peculating.* [L. *peculor, peculatus*, to steal, from *peculium*, private property, from *pecu*, cattle, in which wealth originally consisted; cog. E. *fee.* PECULIAR, PECUNIARY.] To appropriate public money, or goods entrusted to one's care; to embezzle. —**peculation,** pek•ū•lā′shon, *n.* The act of peculating; embezzlement.—**peculator,** pek′ū•lā•tėr, *n.* One who peculates.

peculiar, pi•kūl′yėr, *a.* [L. *peculiaris*, one's own, peculiar, extraordinary, from *peculium*, one's own property. PECULATE.] One's own; of private, personal, or characteristic possession and use; specially belonging (*peculiar* to that part of the country); singular; striking; unusual; eccentric.—*n. England.* A parish or church which has ecclesiastical jurisdiction within itself.—**peculiarity,** pi•kū′li•ar″i•ti, *n.* The quality of being peculiar; that which is peculiar to a person or thing; a special characteristic or feature.—**peculiarize,** pi•kū′li•ėr•iz, *v.t.*—*peculiarized, peculiarizing.* To make peculiar; to set apart; to appropriate.—**peculiarly,** pi•kū′li•ėr•li, *adv.* In a peculiar manner; especially; in a manner not common to others.

pecuniary, pi•kū′ni•a•ri, *a.* [Fr. *pecuniaire*, L. *pecuniarius*, from *pecunia*, money, from *pecu*, cattle. PECULATE.] Relating to or connected with money; consisting of money.

pedagogue, ped′a•gog, *n.* [Gr. *paidagōgos*—*pais, paidos*, a child, and *agō*, to lead.] A teacher of children; a schoolmaster; now generally by way of contempt.—**pedagogic, pedagogical,** ped•a•goj′ik, ped•a•goj′i•kal, *a.* Resembling or belonging to a pedagogue.—**pedagogics,** ped•a•goj′iks, *n.* The science or art of teaching. —**pedagogism,** ped′a•gog•izm, *n.* The business or manners of a pedagogue.—**pedagogy,** ped′a•go•ji, *n.* The art or office of a pedagogue.

pedal, ped′al, *a.* [L. *pedalis*, belonging to the foot, from *pes, pedis*, the foot, seen also in *pedestal, pedestrian, biped, quadruped, centipede, expedite, impede, dispatch*, etc. FOOT.] Pertaining to a foot (*pedal* digits); *mus.* relating to a pedal.—*n.* A lever to be pressed down by the foot; a sort of treadle; a part of a musical instrument acted on by the feet, as in the piano for strengthening or softening the sound; on the organ for opening additional sets of pipes; on the harmonium for working the bellows, etc.—*v.t.* To work the pedal of a bicycle, to increase or decrease the speed.—*v.i.* To advance or slow down on a bicycle.

pedant, ped′ant, *n.* [Fr. *pédant*, It. Sp., and Pg. *pedante*, for *pedagogante*, from L. *paedagogans, paedagogantis*, ppr. of *paedagogo*, to educate. PEDAGOGUE.] A person who makes a vain display of his learning, or who prides himself on his book learning but is devoid of taste; one devoted to a system of rules.—**pedantic, pedantical,** pi•dan′tik, pi•dan′ti•kal, *a.* Pertaining to a pedant or to pedantry.—**pedantically,** pi•dan′ti•kal•li, *adv.* In a pedantic manner.—**pedantry,** ped′ant•ri, *n.* The manners or character of a pedant; ostentation or boastful display of learning; obstinate adherence to rules or established forms.

pedate, ped′āt, *a.* [L. *pedatus*, from *pes, pedis*, the foot. PEDAL.] Having divisions like toes; divided into distinct lobes; *bot.* applied to certain palmate leaves.—**pedatifid,** pi•dat′i•fid, *a.* [L. *findo, fidi*, to divide.] *Bot.* divided in a pedate manner.

peddle, ped′l, *v.i.*—*peddle, peddling.* [From Prov. E. *ped* or *pad*, a wicker basket, a pannier, akin to *pod.* Hence *pedlar.*] To travel about and retail small wares; to trifle.—*v.t.* To sell or retail in small quantities while traveling about.—**peddler,** ped′lėr, *n.*

pederasty, ped′ėr•as•ti, *n.* [Gr. *paiderastia*, from *pais, paidos*, boy, and *eraō*, to long for.] Unnatural sex relations between males.—**pederast,** ped′e•rast, *n.* One who practices pederasty.

pedestal, ped′es•tal, *n.* [Sp. *pedestal*, Fr. *piedestal*, It. *piedestallo*, from L. *pes, pedis*, the foot, and G. and E. *stall.*] A basement or support for a column, a statue, a vase, etc.

pedestrian, pe•des′tri•an, *a.* [L. *pedestris*, from *pes, pedis*, the foot. PEDAL.] Going on foot; performed on foot; walking; in literary criticism, prosaic in tone.—*n.* One that walks or journeys on foot; a remarkable walker.—**pedestrianism,** pe•des′tri•an•izm, *n.* The practice of walking; the art of a professional walker.

pediatrician, pē′di•a•trish″an, *n.* [Gr. *pais*, child, and *iatreia*, medical treatment.] A physician specializing in pediatrics.—**pediatrics,** pē•di•at′riks, *n.* The medical care of children.

pedicel, ped′i•sel, *n.* [From *pedicellus*, a form equivalent to L. *pediculus*, dim. of *pes, pedis*, the foot. PEDAL.] *Bot.* the stalk that supports a single flower, leaf, etc.; any short small footstalk; *zool.* a footstalk by which certain animals of the lower orders, as zoophytes, etc., are attached.—**pedicellate,** ped′i•sel•āt, *a.* Having a pedicel.—**pedicle,** ped′i•kl, *n.* See PEDICEL.

pedicular, pediculous, pe•dik′ū•lėr, pe•dik′ū•lus, *a.* [L. *pediculus*, a louse.] Lousy; being infested with lice.

pediculosis, pe•dik′ū•lō″sis, *n.* [N.L. from L. *pediculus*, louse, and Gr. suffix *osis*, signifying a condition, state.] *Med.* infestation with lice.

pedicure, ped′i•kūr, *n.* [L. *pes, pedis*, foot, *cura, care.*] Care and grooming of the feet; one whose business is foot care; a chiropodist.

pedigree, ped′i•grē, *n.* [O.Fr. *pedegru*, Fr. *pie de grue*, crane's foot; L. *pes*, foot, *de*, of, *grus*, crane.] A line of ancestors; lineage; a genealogy; a genealogical or family tree.

pediment, ped′i•ment, *n.* [From L. *pes, pedis*, the foot.] *Arch.* the low triangular mass resembling a gable at the end of buildings in the Greek style, surrounded with a cornice, and often ornamented with sculptures; a small gable or triangular decoration like a gable over a window, a door, etc.—**pedimental,** ped′i•men•tal, *a.* Relating to a pediment.

pedobaptism, pē•do•bap′tizm, *n.* [Gr. *pais, paidos*, a child.] The baptism of infants or children.

pedometer, pi•dom′et•ėr, *n.* [L. *pes, pedis*, the foot, and Gr. *metron*, a measure.] An instrument (often resembling a watch) by which paces are numbered as a person walks, and the distance thus ascertained.

peduncle, pi•dung′kl, *n.* [From L. *pes, pedis*, a foot.] *Bot.* the stalk that supports the fructification of a plant, *i.e.*, the flower and fruit; *zool.* the stem or stalk by which certain brachiopods, etc., are attached.—**peduncular,** pi•dung′kū•lėr, *a.* Pertaining to a peduncle, growing from a peduncle.—**pedunculate, pedunculated,** pi•dung′kū•lāt, pi•dung′kū•lā•ted, *a.* Having a peduncle; growing on a peduncle.

peek, pēk, *v.i.* To peep; to look or spy through half closed eyes.—*n.* A quick, secret glance.

peel, pēl, *n.* [W. *pill*, a tower, a fortress.] A name of certain strong square towers or strongholds common on the Scottish borders.

peel, pēl, *v.t.* [O.Fr. *peiler* (Fr. *peler*), to peel, from L. *pellis*, the skin (cog. with E. *fell*, a skin), whence also *pellicle, peltry, pelisse*, etc.] To strip the skin, bark, or rind from; to strip by drawing or tearing off the skin; to decorticate; to strip (bark) from the surface.—*v.i.* To lose the skin or rind; to fall off (as bark or skin).—*n.* The skin or rind of anything.—**peeler,** pēl′ėr, *n.* One that peels.

peel, pēl, *n.* [Fr. *pelle*, from L. *pala*, a spade.] A wooden shovel used by bakers to put their bread in and take it out of the oven.

peen, pēn, *n.* [Scand.] The head of a hammer opposite the face.—*v.t.* To shape an object by striking it with the peen.

peep, pēp, *v.i.* [Imitative of sound, like D. and G. *piepen*, Dan. *pippe*, L. *pipio*, Gr. *pippizō*, to chirp; the other meaning is supposed to have been suggested from the chicken's peep or chirp closely accompanying its peeping from the shell.] To cry, as chickens; to cheep; to chirp; to begin to appear; to look through a crevice; to look narrowly, closely, or slyly.—*n.* The cry of a chicken;

a sly look, or a look through a crevice.—*Peep of day*, the dawn or daybreak.—**peeper**, pēp′ėr, *n.* One that peeps.—**peephole**, *n.* A hole through which one may peep without being discovered.—**peep show**, *n.* A show of small pictures viewed through a hole fitted with a magnifying lens.

peer, pēr, *n.* [Lit. an equal; O.Fr. *peer*, *per*, *par* (Fr. *pair*), from L. *par*. equal. PAIR.] One of the same rank, qualities, or the like; an equal; a match; a companion; a member of one of the five degrees of British nobility (duke, marquis, earl, viscount, baron); a nobleman.—*House of Peers*. the House of Lords.—**peerage**, pēr′ij, *n.* The rank or dignity of a peer; the body of peers.—**peeress**, pēr′es, *n.* The consort of a peer; a woman ennobled by descent, by creation, or by marriage.—**peerless**, pēr′les, *a.* Unequaled; having no peer or equal.—**peerlessly**, pēr′les•li, *adv.* In a peerless manner.—**peerlessness**, pēr′les•nes, *n.*

peer, pēr, *v.i.* [O.Fr. *perer*, *pareir* from L. *pareo*, to appear; same as *-pear* in *appear*; or from L.G. *piren*, to peer.] To come just in sight; to appear (*Shak.*); to look narrowly; to pry; to peep.

peevish, pē′vish, *a.* [Comp. Dan. *piaeve*, to cry like a child; Sc. *pew*, *pyow*, a sound of complaint.] Apt to mutter and complain; easily vexed or fretted; fretful; querulous; self-willed.—**peevishly**, pē′vish•li, *adv.*—**peevishness**, pē′vish•nes, *n.*

peg, peg, *n.* [Comp. Dan. *pig*; a spike; W. *pig*, something sharp; allied probably to E. *peak*, *pick*.] A wooden pin used in fastening things, as a mark, or otherwise; one of the pins on a musical instrument for stretching the strings; a pin on which to hang anything.—*To take one down a peg*, to humiliate him.—*v.t.*—*pegged*, *pegging*. To put pegs into for fastening, etc.; to fasten on the sole of (a shoe) with pegs; to mark off by pegs.—*v.i.* To work diligently; generally followed by *away* or *on*. (Colloq.)—**peg top**, *n.* A child's toy, a variety of top made to spin by a string.—*a.* Tapering in shape like a top (*peg-top* pants).

Pegasus, peg′a•sus, *n.* The winged horse of Greek mythology, often regarded as the horse of the Muses, and hence connected with poets and poetry.

peignoir, pān•wär′, pān′wär, *n.* [Fr. from *peigner*, to comb, from L. *pectinare*.] A woman's loose negligee.

pejorative, pē′jor•ā•tiv, *a.* [L. *pejor*, worse.] Conveying a depreciatory meaning.—*n.* A word conveying such a meaning (*poetaster* being a *pejorative* of *poet*).

Pekingese, Pekinese, pē′king•ēz″, *n.* [From *Peking*.] A native of Peking; a small pet dog, originally from China, having a flat face and short legs.

pekoe, pē′kō, *n.* [Chinese, lit. white down.] A fine black tea.

pelage, pel′ij, *n.* [Fr. *pelage*, hair of the hide, from L. *pilus*, hair. PILE.] *Zool.* the hairy covering of an animal.

Pelagian, pe•lā′ji•an, *n.* A follower of *Pelagius*, a British monk of the fourth century, who denied original sin, and asserted the doctrine of free will and the merit of good works.—**Pelagianism**, pe•lā′ji•an•izm, *n.* The doctrines of Pelagius.

pelagic, pe•laj′ik, *a.* [Gr. *pelagos*, the ocean.] Belonging to the ocean; inhabiting the open ocean.

pelargonium, pel•är•gō′ni•um, *n.* [From Gr. *pelargos*, a stork—from the shape of the capsules.] Stork's-bill, an extensive genus of highly ornamental plants, usually called *Geraniums*. See GERANIUM.

Pelasgian, Pelasgic, pe•las′ji•an, pe•las′jik, *a.* Pertaining to the Pelasgians or Pelasgi, prehistoric inhabitants of Greece, etc.

pelerine, pel′ėr•in, *n.* [Fr., from *pelerin*, a pilgrim. PILGRIM.] A lady's long cape or fur tippet.

pelf, pelf, *n.* [O.Fr. *pelfre*, spoil, booty, from L. *pilare*, to rob, and *facere*, to make. PILFER.] Money; riches; filthy lucre: a contemptuous term.

pelican, pel′i•kan, *n.* [From L. *pelicanus*, Gr. *pelekanos*, a pelican, from *pelekys*, a hatchet—from shape of bill.] A web-footed bird, larger than the swan, with a very large bill, and beneath the under mandible a huge pouch for holding fish.

pelisse, pe•lēs′, *n.* [Fr. *pelisse*, from L. *pelliceus*, made of skins, from *pellis*, a skin. PEEL, *v.t.*] Originally a garment lined or trimmed with fur; now a robe of silk or other material worn by ladies.

pellagra, pe•lā′gra, *n.* [It. *pellagra*, L. *pellis*, skin, and Gr. *agra*, seizure.] A disease affecting the skin, digestive system, and nervous system caused by vitamin B deficiency.—**pellagrous**, pel•lā′grus, *a.*

pellet, pel′et, *n.* [Fr. *pelote*, from L.L. *pilota*, *pelota*, dim. of L. *pila*, a ball. PILE (heap).] A little ball; one of the globules of small shot.—*v.t.* To form into pellets.

pellicle, pel′i•kl, *n.* [L. *pellicula*, dim. of *pellis*, skin. PEEL, *v.t.*] A thin skin or film on a surface; *bot.* the outer cuticular covering of plants.—**pellicular**, pel•lik′ū•lėr, *a.* Pertaining to a pellicle.

pellitory, pel′i•to•ri, *n.* [A corruption of L. *parietaria*, lit. the wall plant, from *paries*, *parietis*, a wall.] A name of several plants of the nettle family; also, a number of European plants which are similar to yarrow.

pellmell, pel′mel, *adv.* [Fr. *pêle-mêle*, from *pelle* (L. *pala*), a shovel, and *mêler*, to mix (MEDLEY).] With confused violence; in a disorderly body; in utter confusion; at a wild speed.—*a.* Tumultuous; disorderly; helter-skelter.—*n.* A violent disorder; an indiscriminate mingling.—*v.t.* To throw together or execute pellmell.

pellucid, pel•lū′sid, *a.* [L. *pellucidus*—*pel*, for *per*, through, and *lucidus*, bright. LUCID.] Transparent; admitting the passage of light; translucent; not opaque.—**pellucidity, pellucidness**, pel•lū•sid′i•ti, pel•lū′sid•nes, *n.* The state or quality of being pellucid.—**pellucidly**, pel•lū′sid•li, *adv.* In a pellucid manner.

Peloponnesian, pel′ō•pon•nē″si•an, *a.* Belonging to *Peloponnesus*, or the southern peninsula of Greece.

peloria, pi•lō′ri•a, *n.* [Gr. *pelōr*, a monster.] *Bot.* regularity of structure in the flowers of plants which normally bear irregular flowers.—**peloric**, pi•lor′ik, *a.* Characterized by peloria.

pelt, pelt, *n.* [Shortened from *peltry*, from L. *pellis*, a skin. PEEL, *v.t.*] The skin of a beast with the hair on it; a raw hide.—**peltry**, pel′tri, *n.* [Fr. *pelletrie*.] Pelts collectively; usually applied to the skins of fur-bearing animals in the raw state.

pelt, pelt, *v.t.* [O.E. *pulten*, probably from L. *pultare*, to strike or knock, from *pello*, to drive. PULSE.] To strike or assail with something thrown or driven; to drive by throwing something.—*v.i.* To throw missiles.—*n.* A blow or stroke from something thrown.—**pelter**, pel′tėr, *n.* One who or that which pelts.

peltate, pel′tāt, *a.* [L. *pelta*, a target.] Shield-shaped; *bot.* fixed to the stalk by the center or by some point distinctly within the margin.—**peltately**, pel′tāt•li, *adv.*

pelvis, pel′vis, *n.* [L. *pelvis*, a basin.] *Anat.* the bony cavity of the body constituting a framework for the lower part of the abdomen.—**pelvic**, pel′vik, *a.* Pertaining to the pelvis.

pemmican, pem′i•kan, *n.* [North Amer. Indian.] A North American Indian preparation consisting of the lean of venison dried, pounded into a paste, and pressed into cakes so that it will keep long; beef dried and similarly preserved.

pemphigus, pem′fi•gus, *n.* [Gr. *pemphix*, *pemphigos*, a bubble.] A disease of the skin, consisting in an eruption of vesicles or pustules.

pen, pen, *n.* [O.Fr. *penne*, a pen, a feather, from L. *penna*, a feather, for *pesna*, from root seen in Gr. *petomai*, to fly, and in E. *feather*. FEATHER.] A quill or large feather‡; an instrument used for writing by means of a fluid ink; formerly almost always made of the quill of some large bird, but now commonly of metal; a writer; a penman; style or quality of writing; the internal bone of some cuttlefishes.—*v.t.*—*penned*, *penning*. To write; to compose and commit to paper.—**penknife**, pen′nīf, *n.* A small pocketknife, so called from its former use in making and mending quill pens.—**penman**, pen′man, *n.* pl. **penmen**, pen′men. A calligrapher; an author; a writer.—**penmanship**, pen′man•ship, *n.* The use of the pen; the art of writing; manner of writing.—**pen name**, *n.* An author's pseudonym.

pen, pen, *v.t.*—*penned* or *pent*, *penning*. [Lit. to fasten with a *pin*; O.E. *pinne*, to bolt; A.Sax. *onpinnian*, to bolt in; L.G. *pinnen*, *pennen*, to shut, to bolt.] To shut in a small enclosure; to coop up; to encage. —*n.* A small enclosure, as for cows, sheep, fowls, etc.; a fold; a coop.

penal, pē′nal, *a.* [Fr. *pénal,* from L. *pœnalis,* from *pœna,* pain, punishment. PAIN.] Pertaining to punishment; enacting punishment; inflicting punishment; incurring or entailing punishment.—*Penal code,* a code of laws relating to the punishment of crimes.—*Penal law,* a law prohibiting an act and imposing a penalty for commission of it.—*Penal servitude,* a punishment consisting in imprisonment, often with hard labor at some special establishment. —**penalize,** pē′nal•īz, *v.t.* To make penal or subject to a penalty.—**penalty,** pen′al•ti, *n.* The punishment annexed to the commission of a crime, offense, or trespass; the suffering to which a person subjects himself by agreement, in case of nonfulfillment of stipulations; the sum forfeited for breaking an agreement.

penance, pen′ans, *n.* [O.Fr. *penance, peneance,* from L. *pœnitentia,* repentance, from *pœnitens,* penitent; it is a doublet of *penitence.* PAIN.] An ecclesiastical punishment imposed for sin; the suffering to which a person subjects himself as an expression of repentance; a sacrament of the Roman Catholic Church for remission of sin.

penates, pi•nā′tēz, *n. pl.* [L.] The household gods of the ancient Romans including the lares.

pence, pens, *n.* The plural of *penny.*

penchant, pen′shent, *n.* [Fr., from *pencher,* to incline.] Strong inclination; decided taste; liking; bias.

pencil, pen′sil, *n.* [O.Fr. *pincel,* a hair pencil, a brush; from L. *penicellus,* dim. of *penis,* a tail.] A small delicate brush used by painters for laying on their pigments; an instrument for marking, drawing, or writing, formed of graphite, colored chalk, or the like; often a lead pencil; *optics,* an aggregate of rays of light which converge to or diverge from the same point.—*v.t.*—*pencilled, pencilling.* To write or mark with a pencil.

pendant, pen′dant, *n.* [Fr. *pendant,* hanging, what hangs, a counterpart, from *pendre,* L. *pendere,* to hang, which with the allied *pendere,* to weigh, appears in *pensile, pendulum, depend, impend, expend, compensation, compendium,* etc.] Anything hanging down by way of ornament, but particularly from the neck; *naut.* a flag borne at the masthead of certain ships, of two kinds—the *long pendant,* and the *broad pendant;* an apparatus hanging from a roof or ceiling for giving light by gas; one of a pair of companion pictures, statues, etc.; an appendix or addition; *arch.* a hanging ornament used in the vaults and timber roofs of Gothic architecture.—**pendency,** pen′den•si, *n.* State of being pendent or suspended; the state of being continued as not yet decided.—**pendent,** pen′dent, *a.* [L. *pendens, pendentis,* hanging, ppr. of *pendere,* to hang.] Hanging; suspended; depending; overhanging; projecting.—*n.* Something pendent or hanging.—**pendentive,** pen•den′tiv, *n.* [Fr. *pendentif.*] *Arch.* the part of a groined ceiling springing from one pillar or impost.—**pendently,** pen′dent•li, *adv.* In a pendent or projecting manner.—**pending,** pen′ding, *p.* and *a.* Depending; remaining undecided; not terminated.—*prep.* [A participle converted into a preposition, like *during.*] For the time of the continuance of; during.

pendragon, pen•drag′on, *n.* [W. *pen,* a head, and *dragon,* a leader.] A chief leader, a title among the ancient British.

pendulous, pen′dū•lus, *a.* [L. *pendulus,* from *pendeo,* to hang. PENDANT.] Hanging so as to swing freely; loosely pendent; swinging.—**pendulousness,** pen′dū•lus•nes, *n.* The state of being pendulous.—**pendulum,** pen′dū•lum, *n.* [Lit. what hangs down, from L. *pendulus.*] A body so suspended from a fixed point as to swing to and fro by the alternate action of gravity and momentum; the swinging piece in a clock serving as the regulating power, the wheelwork being attached to register the number of vibrations, and the weight or spring serving to counteract the effects of friction and resistance of the air.—*Compensation pendulum.* See COMPENSATION.

peneplain, pēn′i•plān, *n.* [L. *paene,* almost.] A denuded area approximating to a plain.

penetrate, pen′e•trāt, *v.t.*—*penetrated, penetrating.* [L. *penetro, penetratum,* to penetrate; root *pen,* denoting internality, and *tra,* to go.] To enter or pierce; to make way into the interior of; to pass into or affect the mind of; to touch; to pierce into by the intellect; to arrive at the inner meaning of; to understand.—*v.i.* To enter into or pierce anything; to pass or make way in.—**penetrating,** pen′e•trāt•ing, *p.* and *a.* Having the power of entering or piercing; sharp; acute; discerning.—**penetratingly,** pen′e•trāt•ing•li, *adv.* In a penetrating manner.—**penetration,** pen•e•trā′shon, *n.* The act of penetrating; a seeing into something obscure or difficult; discernment; mental acuteness.—**penetrative,** pen′e•trā•tiv, *a.* Sharp; subtle; acute; discerning.—**penetrable,** pen′e•tra•bl, *a.* [L. *penetrabilis.*] Capable of being penetrated, entered, or pierced by another body; susceptible of moral or intellectual impression.—**penetrability,** pen′e•tra•bil″i•ti, *n.* State of being penetrable. — **penetrably,** pen′e•tra•bli, *adv.* In a penetrable manner; so as to be penetrable.—**penetralia,** pen′e•trā″li•a, *n. pl.* [L., from *penetralis,* internal.] The inner parts of a building, as of a temple or palace; a sanctuary; hidden things.—**penetrant,** pen′e•trant, *a.* Having the power to penetrate or pierce.

penguin, pen′gwin, *n.* [Probably from W. *pen,* head, and *gwyn,* white, a name formerly given to certain white-headed birds and transferred to penguins.] A name of swimming birds allied to the auks and guillemots, having rudimentary wings useless for flight, but effective in swimming.

penicillate, pen•i•sil′āt, *a. Bot.* consisting of a bundle of short, compact fibers or hairs; *zool.* supporting bundles of diverging hairs.

penicillin, pen′i•sil″in, *n.* An antibiotic produced from molds of the genus *Penicillium* and effective against a number of disease-producing micro-organisms.

peninsula, pe•nin′sū•la, *n.* [L., from *pene,* almost, and *insula,* an island.] A portion of land almost surrounded by water, and connected with the mainland by an isthmus.—*The Peninsula,* Spain and Portugal together. —**peninsular,** pe•nin′sū•lėr, *a.* In the form of a peninsula; pertaining to a peninsula.

penis, pē′nis, *n.* [L.] The male organ of generation.

penitence, pen′i•tens, *n.* [Fr. *pénitence,* from L. *pœnitentia,* repentance. *Penance* is the same word. PENAL.] Sorrow for the commission of sin or offenses; repentance; contrition.—**penitent,** pen′i•tent, *a.* [L. *pœnitens,* repentant.] Suffering sorrow of heart on account of sins or offenses; contrite; sorry for wrongdoing and resolved on amendment.—*n.* One who is penitent; one under church censure, but admitted to penance.—**penitential,** pen•i•ten′shal, *a.* Pertaining to, proceeding from, or expressing penitence.—*Penitential psalms,* the psalms numbered vi., xxxii., xxxviii., li., cii., cxxx., cxliii. of the authorized version of the Bible.—*n.* In the *R. Cath. Ch.* a book containing the rules which relate to penance.—**penitentially,** pen•i•ten′shal•li, *adv.* In a penitential manner.—**penitentiary,** pen•i•ten′sha•ri, *a.* Relating to penance.—*n.* A penitent; an official or office of the Roman Catholic Church connected with the granting of dispensations, etc.; a house of correction in which offenders are confined for punishment and reformation, and compelled to labor.—**penitently,** pen′i•tent•li, *adv.* In a penitent manner.

penknife, penman, etc. See PEN.

pennant, pen′ant, *n.* [From *pennon,* but influenced by *pendant.*] A small flag; a pennon; a pendant.

pennate, pen′āt, *a.* [L. *pennatus,* winged, from *penna,* a feather.] *Bot.* same as *Pinnate.*—**penniform,** pen′i•form, *a.* Having the appearance of the barbs of a feather.—**pennigerous,** pe•nij′ėr•us, *a.* Bearing feathers or quills.

pennon, pen′on, *n.* [Fr. *pennon,* from L. *penna,* a feather, a plume. PEN.] A small pointed flag or streamer formerly carried by knights attached to their spear or lance, and generally bearing a badge or device; a pennant. —**pennoncel, pennoncelle,** pen′on•sel, *n.* A small pennon.

penny, pen′i, *n.* pl. **pennies** or **pence,** pen′iz, pens. *Pennies* denotes the number of coins; *pence* the amount in value. [A.Sax. *penig*, *pening*, *pending*=D. *penning*, Dan. *penge*, Icel. *penningr*, O.H.G. *pfenting*, G. *pfennig*; perhaps of same origin as *pawn*, a pledge. PAWN.] A British coin, bronze, worth about one cent in U. S. money, twelve make a shilling; a cent in U. S. money, *Colloq.* Any small sum of money, as, to make an honest *penny*.—**penniless,** pen'i•les, *a.* Moneyless; destitute of money; poor.—**penny-a-liner,** *n.* A person who furnishes matter for public journals at a penny a line, or some such small price; any poor writer for hire.—**pennyroyal,** pen'i•roi•al, *n.* An aromatic plant of the mint family.—**pennyweight,** pen'i•wāt, *n.* A troy weight containing 24 grains—anciently, the weight of a silver penny.—**pennywise,** *a.* Saving small sums at the hazard of larger; niggardly on unimportant occasions: generally in the phrase '*pennywise* and pound foolish'.—**pennyworth,** pen'i•wėrth, *n.* As much as is bought for a penny; a purchase; a bargain.

penology, pē•nol'o•ji, *n.* [Gr. *poinē*, punishment, and *logos*, discourse.] The science which treats of public punishments.

pensile, pen'sil, *a.* [L. *pensilis*, from *pendeo*, to hang. PENDANT.] Hanging; suspended; pendulous.

pension, pen'shon, *n.* [Fr. *pension*, from L. *pensio*, *pensionis*, a paying, from *pendo*, *pensum*, to weigh, to pay (whence *expend*, etc.). PENDANT.] A stated allowance to a person in consideration of past services; a yearly sum granted by government to retired public officers, to soldiers or sailors who have served a certain number of years or have been wounded, or others; a boardinghouse or boarding school on the Continent (in this sense pronounced pän̈•sē•on̈, being French.)—*Old Age Pension.* A regular payment made by a government or institution to persons who have attained a certain age, usually 65 or over.—*v.t.* To grant a pension to.—**pensionary,** pen'shon•e•ri, *a.* Receiving a pension; consisting in a pension.—*n.* A person who receives a pension; a pensioner.—*The Grand Pensionary of Holland*, the first minister of Holland: title from 1619 to 1794.—**pensioner,** pen'shon•ėr, *n.* One in receipt of a pension; a dependent on the bounty of another; in the University of Cambridge, England, one who pays for his commons out of his own income, the same as a commoner at Oxford.

pensive, pen'siv, *a.* [Fr. *pensif*, from *penser*, to think or reflect, from L. *pensare*, to weigh, to consider, a freq. from *pendo*, *pensum*, to weigh. PENDANT.] Thoughtful; employed in serious thought or reflection; thoughtful and somewhat melancholy; expressing thoughtfulness with sadness.—**pensively,** pen'siv•li, *adv.* In a pensive manner.—**pensiveness,** pen'siv•nes, *n.* The state or quality of being pensive.

penstock, pen'stok, *n.* [*Pen*, an enclosure, and *stock*.] A trough, tube, or conduit of boards for conducting water; a sluice above a water wheel.

pent, pent, pp. of *pen.* Penned or shut up; closely confined.

pentacle, pen'ta•kl, *n.* [L.L. *pentaculum*, from Gr. *pente*, five.] A figure consisting of five straight lines so joined and intersecting as to form a five-pointed star: formerly a mystic sign in astrology or necromancy.

pentad, pent'ad, *n.* [Gr. *pente*, five.] An aggregate of five; a period of five years.

pentagon, pen'ta•gon, *n.* [Gr. *pente*, five, and *gōnia*, an angle.] *Geom.* a figure of five sides and five angles; [cap.] a building in Arlington, Va., housing most of the U. S. Defense Department offices.—**pentagonal,** pen•tag'on•al, *a.*—**pentagonally,** pen•tag'on•al•li, *adv.*

pentagram, pen'ta•gram, *n.* [Gr. *pente*, five, and *grammē*, a line.] A pentacle.

pentahedron, pen•ta•hē'dron, *n.* [Gr. *pente*, five, and *hedra*, a side or base.] A solid having five equal sides.—**pentahedral,** pen•ta•hē'dral, *a.* Having five equal sides.

pentamerous, pen•tam'ėr•us, *a.* [Gr. *pente*, five, and *meros*, a part.] Having or divided into five parts; *zool.* having five joints to the tarsus of each leg, a term applied to a family (Pentamera) of beetles.

pentameter, pen•tam'et•ėr, *n.* [Gr. *pente*, five, and *metron*, measure.] *Pros.* a verse of five feet, belonging more especially to Greek and Latin poetry, the first two feet being either dactyls or spondees; the Greek line whose first two feet may consist of either a dactyl or a spondee, followed by a caesura, and followed in turn by two dactyls closed by a second caesura.—*a.* Having five metrical feet.

pentane, pent'ān, *n.* [Gr. *pente*, five.] Paraffin hydrocarbon occurring as a colorless fluid in petroleum and other oils.

pentarchy, pen'tär•ki, *n.* [Gr. *pente*, five, *archē*, rule.] A government in the hands of five persons.

pentastich, pen'ta•stik, *n.* [Gr. *pente*, five, and *stichos*, a verse.] A composition consisting of five verses.

Pentateuch, pen'ta•tūk, *n.* [Gr. *pente*, five, and *teuchos*, a book.] A collective term for the first five books of the Old Testament.

pentavalent, pen•ta•vā'lent, *a.* [Prefix *penta*, and *valent.*] *Chem.* having a valence of 5.

Pentecost, pen'ti•kost, *n.* [Gr. *pentēkoste* (*hēmera*), the fiftieth (day), from *pentēkonta*, fifty, from *pente*, five.] A solemn festival of the Jews, so called because celebrated on the fiftieth day after the Passover; Whitsuntide, which is fifty days after Easter.—**Pentecostal,** pen•ti•kos'tal, *a.* Pertaining to Pentecost.

penthouse, pent'hous, *n.* [Formerly *pentice*, from Fr. *appentis*, a penthouse.—L. *ad*, to, and *pendeo*, to hang. PENDANT.] A roof sloping up against a wall; a shed standing aslope from a building; a dwelling or apartment situated on the roof of a larger building.

penult, penultima, pē'nult, pi•nul'ti•ma, *n.* [L. *penultimus*—*pene*, almost, and *ultimus*, last.] The last syllable of a word except one.—**penultimate,** pi•nul'ti•māt, *a.* The last but one.—*n.* The last syllable but one of a word.

penumbra, pi•num'bra, *n.* [L. *pene*, almost, and *umbra*, shade.] The partial shadow outside of the total shadow caused by an opaque body intercepting the light from a luminous body, as in eclipses; *painting*, the boundary of shade and light, where the one blends with the other.—**penumbral,** pi•num'bral, *a.* Pertaining to a penumbra.

penury, pen'ū•ri, *n.* [Fr. *pénurie*, L. *penuria*, akin to Gr. *penia*, poverty.] Want of pecuniary means; indigence; extreme poverty.—**penurious,** pe•nū'ri•us, *a.* Pertaining to penury; niggardly; parsimonious; sordid.—**penuriously,** pe•nū'ri•us•li, *adv.* In a penurious manner.—**penuriousness,** pe•nū'ri•us•nes, *n.* The quality of being penurious.

peon, pē'on, *n.* [Sp. *peon*, a foot soldier, a day laborer, from L. *pes*, *pedis*, the foot. PAWN (at chess), PEDAL.] In Hindustan, a foot soldier; a native constable; in Spanish America, a day laborer; a farmer of Spanish descent; a kind of serf.—**peonage, peonism,** pē'on•ij, pē'on•izm, *n.* The state or condition of a peon.

peony, pē'o•ni, *n.* [L. *paeonia*, from Gr. *paiōnia*, from *Paiōn*, Apollo, who used this flower to cure the wounds of the gods.] A ranunculaceous genus of plants cultivated in gardens for their large gaudy flowers.

people, pē'pl, *n.* [O.E. *peple*, *puple*, etc., O.Fr. *pople*, *pueple*, Fr. *peuple*, from L. *populus*, people. POPULAR.] The body of persons who compose a community, race, or nation; a community; a body social (in this sense it admits the plural *peoples*); persons indefinitely; men (*people* may say what they please); with possessives, those who are closely connected with a person, as attendants, domestics, relatives, etc.—*v.t.*—*peopled*, *peopling.* To stock with people or inhabitants; to populate.

pep, pep, *n.* [Abbrev. of *pepper.*] (Slang) Energy; exuberance; initiative.—*v.t.* To stimulate; to give energy to (usually with *up*).

pepo, pē'pō, *n.* [L., a melon.] Any fruit of the type of the melon or gourd.

pepper, pep'ėr, *n.* [A.Sax. *pipor*, *peppor*, from L. *piper*, Gr. *piperi*, *peperic* a word of Oriental origin.] A pepper plant, *Capsicum*, and its pod, which may be sweet or hot and yields a red pepper; a pepper plant, *Piper*, and its seed, which yields the table condiment black pepper.—*Cayenne pepper*, the produce of different species of capsicum.—*v.t.* To sprinkle with pepper; to pelt with shot or missiles; to cover thoroughly.—**pepperbox,** *n.* A small box with a perforated lid, for sprinkling pepper on food.—**peppercorn,** pep'ėr•korn, *n.* The dried berry of the black pepper.—**peppermint,** pep′ėr•mint, *n.* A plant of the mint genus having a strong pungent taste, glowing like pepper, and followed by a sense of coolness; a liqueur; a candy flavored with peppermint.—**pepper pot,** *n.* A West Indian dish, the principal ingredient of which is cassareep, with meat or dried fish and vegetables; a pepperbox.—**peppery,** pep′ėr•i, *a.* Having the qualities of pepper; choleric; irritable.

pepsin, pep′sin, *n.* [Gr. *pepsis*, digestion, from *peptō*, to digest.] A digestive enzyme of the gastric juices; a preparation containing this enzyme.—**peptic,** pep′tik, *a.* Digestive.—**peptone,** pep′tōn, *n.* The substance into which the nitrogenous elements of the food are converted by the action of the gastric juice.

per, pėr. A Latin preposition, denoting through, by, by means of, etc.; for each.

peradventure, pėr•ad•ven′chėr, *adv.* [Prefix *per*, by, and *adventure*, Fr. *par aventure.*] Perchance; perhaps; it may be. Sometimes used as a noun = doubt; question.

perambulate, pėr•am′bū•lāt, *v.t.*—*perambulated, perambulating.* [L. *perambulo*—*per*, and *ambulo*, to walk. AMBLE.] To walk through or over; to survey the boundaries of (to *perambulate* a parish).—**perambulation,** pėr•am′bū•lā″shon, *n.* The act of perambulating; a traveling survey or inspection; a walking through or over ground for the purpose of settling boundaries.—**perambulator,** pėr•am′bū•lā•tėr, *n.* One who perambulates; a small carriage for a child, propelled from behind.

percale, pėr•kāl′, *n.* [Fr. from *pargālah.*] A closely woven, fine cotton fabric, printed or plain.

per capita, pėr kap′i•tä, *adv.* [L.] For each individual.

perceive, pėr•sēv′, *v.t.*—*perceived, perceiving.* [Fr. *percevoir*, L. *percipio*, to perceive, to comprehend—*per*, and *capio*, to take. CAPABLE.] To have or obtain knowledge of by the senses; to apprehend or take cognizance of by the organs of sense; to apprehend by the mind; to discern, know, understand. ∴ Syn. under SEE.—**perceivable,** pėr•sē′va•bl, *a.* Capable of being perceived; perceptible.—**perceivably,** pėr•sē′va•bli, *adv.* In a perceivable manner.—**percept,** pėr′sept, *n.* That which is perceived.—**perceptible,** pėr•sep′ti•bl, *a.* Capable of being perceived.—**perceptibly,** pėr•sep′ti•bli, *adv.* In a perceptible manner; so as to be perceived.—**perception,** pėr•sep′shon, *n.* [L. *perceptio, perceptionis.*] The act of perceiving; that act or process of the mind which makes known an external object; the faculty by which man holds communication with the external world or takes cognizance of objects outside the mind.—**perceptive,** pėr•sep′tiv, *a.* Relating to the act or power of perceiving; having the faculty of perceiving.

percent, pėr•sent′, *n.* [Abbrev. of L. *per centum*, by the hundred.] By the hundred; units or parts to the hundred (used in expressing rates of interest, proportions, etc.).—**percentage,** pėr•sen′taj, *n.* Interest, a part of a whole, a proportion, etc., expressed in hundreds; a share, portion, or part.—**percentile,** pėr•sen′til, *n.* A value of a statistical variable which divides its distribution into 100 groups having equal frequencies.

perch, pėrch, *n.* [Fr. *perche*, L. *perca*, from Gr. *perkē*, the perch, from *perkos*, dark-colored.] The popular name of certain spiny-finned fishes, one species of which is found in rivers and lakes throughout the temperate parts of the United States.

perch, pėrch, *n.* [Fr. *perche*, from L. *pertica*, a pole, a staff.] A measure of length containing 5½ yards; a pole or rod; a roost for birds; anything on which they light; hence, an elevated seat or position.—*v.i.* To sit or roost; to light or settle as a bird.—*v.t.* To place on a perch.—*Perched blocks*, blocks of stone that have been left by ancient glaciers high up on mountains.—**percher,** pėrch′ėr, *n.* One that perches; a bird belonging to the order of Insessores.

perchance, pėr•chans′, *adv.* [L. *per*, by, and E. *chance.*] Perhaps; peradventure.

perchloric, pėr•klo′rik, *a.* Applied to an acid forming a syrupy liquid very explosive.—**perchlorate,** pėr•klō′rāt, *n.* A salt of perchloric acid.

percipient, pėr•sip′i•ent, *a.* [L. *percipiens*, ppr. of *percipio.* PERCEIVE.] Perceiving; having the faculty of perception.—*n.* One who perceives.—**percipience, percipiency,** pėr•sip′i•ens, pėr•sip′i•en•si, *n.* Act or power of perceiving; perception.

percoid, pėr′koid, *a.* [Gr. *perke*, perch, and *eidos*, form.] Resembling the perch; belonging to the perch family.

percolate, pėr′ko•lāt, *v.t.*—*percolated, percolating.* [L. *percolo*—*per*, and *colo*, to strain, from *colum*, a sieve (whence *colander*).] To strain or filter.—*v.i.* To pass through small interstices or pores; to filter.—**percolator,** pėr′ko•lā•tėr, *n.* One who or that which filters.—A kind of coffeepot in which boiling water is forced upward and filters down through the coffee.

percuss,† pėr•kus′, *v.t.* [L. *percussus*, from *percutio*, *percussum* — *per*, through, and *quatio*, to strike (as in *concuss*). QUASH.] To strike against; to give a shock to.—**percussion,** pėr•kush′on, *n.* [L. *percussio.*] The act of striking one body against another with some violence; forcible collision, the shock produced by the collision of bodies; the impression or effect of sound on the ear; *med.* the method of eliciting sounds by striking the surface of the body, for the purpose of determining the condition of the organs subjacent (as the lungs or heart).—**percussion cap,** *n.* A small copper cap or cup containing fulminating powder, used in a percussion lock to explode gunpowder.—**percussion lock,** *n.* A lock for a gun, causing the ignition of the charge by the impact of a hammer or striker.—**percussive,** pėr•kus′iv, *a.* Acting by percussion; striking against.

per diem, pėr dī′em, *adv.* [M.L.] By the day; for each day.

perdition, pėr•dish′on, *n.* [L.L. *perditio*, from L. *perdo*, *perditus*, to destroy, to ruin—*per*, thoroughly, and *do*, a verb cog. with E. *do.*] Entire ruin; utter destruction; loss of final happiness in a future state; future misery or eternal death.

perdu, perdue, pėr′dū or per•dū′, *a.* [Fr. *perdu*, lost, from *perdre*, to lose, L. *perdo.*] Hid; in concealment: generally in the phrase *to lie* or *to be perdu.*

perdurable, pėr′dū•ra•bl, *a.* [Fr., from L. *perduro*—*per*, intens., and *duro*, to last. DURABLE.] Very durable; lasting; continuing long.—**perdurably,** pėr′dū•ra•bli, *adv.* In a perdurable manner; lastingly.

peregrinate, per′e•gri•nāt, *v.i.*—*peregrinated, peregrinating.* [L. *peregrinor*, from *peregrinus*, a traveler or stranger—*per*, through, and *ager*, land. PILGRIM.] To travel from place to place; to wander.—**peregrination,** per′e•gri•nā″shon, *n.* A traveling, roaming, or wandering about; a journey.—**peregrinator,** per′e•gri•nā•tėr, *n.* A traveler.—**peregrine,** per′e•grin, *a.* [L. *peregrinus.*] Foreign; not native.—*Peregrine falcon*, a handsome species of European falcon.—*n.* A peregrine falcon.

peremptory, per•emp′tė•ri, *a.* [L. *peremptorius*, from *perimo*, *peremptus*, to destroy—*per*, thoroughly, and *emo*, to take, to buy (seen also in *exempt*, *example*, *prompt*).] Precluding debate or expostulation; decisive; authoritative; fully resolved; determined; positive in opinion or judgment; dogmatical; *law*, final; determinate.—**peremptorily,** per•emp′tė•ri•li, *adv.* In a peremptory manner.—**peremptoriness,** per•emp′tė•ri•nes, *n.*

perennial, per•en′i•al, *a.* [L. *perennis*—*per*, through, and *annus*, a year.] Lasting or continuing without cessation through the year; continuing without stop or intermission; unceasing; never-failing; *bot.* continuing more than two years (a *perennial* plant).—*n.* A plant whose root remains alive more years than two.—**perennially,** per•en′i•al•li, *adv.*

perfect, pėr′fekt, *a.* [L. *perfectus*, pp. of *perficio*, to complete or finish—*per*. thoroughly, and *facio*, to do. FACT.] Brought to a consummation or completion; having received and possessing all its parts; finished; completed; of the best, highest, or completest type; without blemish or defect; faultless; completely skilled (*perfect* in discipline).—*Perfect gas*, a theoretical gas which satisfies several conditions, and follows exactly the law of Boyle, that the volume varies inversely as the pressure when the temperature is constant. Actual gases at best only approximate to this perfectness.—*Perfect tense, gram.* a tense which expresses an act completed.—*v.t.* To finish or complete so as to leave nothing wanting; to make perfect; to instruct fully; to make fully skillful (often *refl.*).—**perfecter,** pėr′fek•tėr, *n.* One that makes perfect.—**perfectibility,** pėr•fek′ti•bil″i•ti, *n.* The quality of being perfectible; the capacity of becoming or being made morally perfect.—**perfectible,** pėr•fek′ti•bl, *a.* Capable of becoming or being made perfect.—**perfection,** pėr•fek′shon, *n.* [L. *perfectio, perfectionis.*] The state of being perfect or complete; supreme degree of moral or other excellence; a quality of the highest worth.—**perfectionism,** pėr•fek′shon•izm, *n.* The doctrine of the Perfectionists.—**perfectionist,** pėr•fek′shon•ist, *n.* One who believes that some persons actually attain to moral perfection in the present life; [*cap.*] one of an American sect of Christians founded on socialist principles.—**perfective,** pėr•fek′tiv, *a.* Conducing to bring to perfection.—**perfectively,** pėr•fek′tiv•li, *adv.*—**perfectly,** pėr′fekt•li, *adv.*

perfecto, pėr•fek′to, *n.* [Sp. perfect.] A large cigar, tapering to both ends from a thick center.

perfervid, pėr•fėr′vid, *a.* [L. *perfervidus—per*, intens., and *fervidus*, fervid.] Very fervid; very hot or ardent.

perfidy, pėr′fi•di, *n.* [L. *perfidia*, from *perfidus*, faithless—prefix *per*, and *fidus*, faithful; *per* having the same force as in *perjure*, *pervert*. FAITH.] The act of violating faith or allegiance; breach of faith; treachery; faithlessness.—**perfidious,** pėr•fid′i•us, *a.* Guilty of or involving perfidy or treachery; treacherous; consisting in breach of faith; traitorous.—**perfidiously,** pėr•fid′i•us•li, *adv.* In a perfidious manner.—**perfidiousness,** pėr•fid′i•us•nes, *n.*

perfoliate, pėr•fō′li•āt, *a.* [L. *per*, through, and *folium*, a leaf.] *Bot.* applied to a leaf that has the base surrounding the stem, as if the stem ran through it.

perforate, pėr′fo•rāt, *v.t.*—*perforated*, *perforating*. [L. *perforo*, *perforatus*—prefix *per*, through, and *foro*, to bore. BORE.] To bore through; to pierce with a pointed instrument; to make a hole or holes through by boring.—**perforate, perforated,** pėr′fo•rāt, pėr′fo•rā•ted, *a.* Bored or pierced through. — **perforation,** pėr•fo•rā′shon, *n.* The act of perforating, boring, or piercing; a hole bored; a hole passing through anything.—**perforator,** pėr′for•ā•tėr, *n.* One who or that which perforates.

perforce, pėr•fōrs′, *adv.* [Prefix *per*, through, by, and *force.*] By force or compulsion; of necessity.

perform, pėr•form′, *v.t.* [O.E. *parforme*, *parfourne*, from O.Fr. *parfournir*, to perform—prefix *par*, and *fournir*, to accomplish, to furnish. FURNISH.] To do; to execute; to accomplish; to fulfill, act up to, discharge (a duty); to act or represent as on the stage.—*v.i.* To act a part; to play on a musical instrument, represent a character on the stage, or the like.—**performable,** pėr•for′ma•bl, *a.* Capable of being performed.—**performance,** pėr•for′mans, *n.* The act of performing or condition of being performed; an action, deed, or thing done; a literary work; a composition; the acting or exhibition of character on the stage; an exhibition of skill and capacity; an entertainment provided at any place of amusement.—**performer,** pėr•for′mėr, *n.* One who performs; an actor, musician, etc., who exhibits his skill.

perfume, pėr′fūm or pėr•fūm′, *n.* [Fr. *parfum*, from L. *per*, through, and *fumus*, smoke; lit. smoke or vapor that disseminates itself.] A substance that emits a scent or odor which affects agreeably the organs of smelling; the scent or odor emitted from sweet-smelling substances.—*v.t.* (pėr•fūm′)—*perfumed*, *perfuming*. To fill or impregnate with a grateful odor; to scent.—**perfumer,** pėr•fūm′ėr, *n.* One who perfumes; one whose trade is to sell perfumes.—**perfumery,** pėr•fūm′ėr•i, *n.* Perfumes collectively; the art of preparing perfumes.

perfunctory, pėr•fungk′to•ri, *a.* [L. L. *perfunctorius*—L. *per*, and *fungor*, *functus*, to perform, execute. FUNCTION.] Done in a half-hearted or careless manner, and merely for the sake of getting rid of the duty; careless, slight, or not thorough; negligent. — **perfunctorily,** pėr•fungk′to•ri•li, *adv.* In a perfunctory manner. — **perfunctoriness,** pėr•fungk′to•ri•nes, *n.*

pergola, per′go•la, *n.* [It.] A kind of arbor or bower on which plants may grow.

perhaps, pėr•haps′, *adv.* [L. *per*, by (as in *perchance*), and E. *hap.*] Peradventure; perchance; it may be; possibly.

peri, pâ′ri, *n.* [Per. *pari*, a fairy.] *Per. myth.* a sort of spiritual being or fairy, represented as a descendant of fallen angels, excluded from paradise till the accomplishment of a task imposed as a penance.

perianth, per′i•anth, *n.* [Gr. *peri*, about, and *anthos*, a flower.] *Bot.* a term for the floral envelope when the calyx and corolla are so combined that they cannot be satisfactorily distinguished from each other.

periapt, per′i•apt, *n.* [Gr. *periapton*, *peri*, around, *haptō*, to fasten.] An armlet or necklet worn as a charm. (*Shak.*)

pericardium, per•i•kär′di•um, *n.* [Gr. *perikardion*—*peri*, around, and *kardia*, the heart.] The membranous sac that encloses the heart.—**pericardial, pericardiac,** per•i•kär′di•al, per•i•kär′di•ak, *a.* Relating to the pericardium.—**pericarditis,** per′i•kär•dī″tis, *n.* [Term. *-itis*, signifying inflammation.] Inflammation of the pericardium.

pericarp, per′i•kärp, *n.* [Gr. *peri*, about, and *karpos*, fruit.] The seed vessel of a plant, or the shell of the seed vessel; the part enclosing the seed.—**pericarpial,** per•i•kär′pi•al, *a.* Belonging to a pericarp.

perichondrium, per•i•kon′dri•um, *n.* [Gr. *peri*, around, and *chondros*, cartilage.] *Anat.* a synovial membrane which covers certain cartilages.

pericranium, per•i•krā′ni•um, *n.* [Gr. *peri*, about, and *kranion*, the skull.] The membrane that invests the skull.

periderm, per′i•dėrm, *n.* [Gr. *peri*, around, and *derma*, skin.] A sort of outer layer or skin; *bot.* the outer layer of bark.

peridot, per′i•dot, *n.* A precious stone of a yellowish-green color.

perigee, per′i•jē, *n.* [Gr. *peri*, about, and *gē*, the earth.] That point of the moon's orbit which is nearest to the earth; formerly also this point in the orbit of any heavenly body. APOGEE.—**perigean,** per•i•jē′an, *a.* Pertaining to the perigee.

perigynous, pe•rij′i•nus, *a.* [Gr. *peri*, around, and *gynē*, a female.] *Bot.* having the ovary free, but the petals and stamens borne on the calyx.

perihelion, per•i•hē′li•on, *n.* [Gr. *peri*, about, and *hēlios*, the sun.] That part of the orbit of a planet or comet in which it is at its least distance from the sun: opposed to *aphelion.*

peril, per′il, *n.* [Fr. *péril*, from L. *periculum*, danger, from root seen in *perior*, *experior*, to try (whence *experiment*); same ultimate root as E. *fare*, *ferry.*] Danger; risk; hazard; jeopardy; exposure of person or property to injury, loss, or destruction.—*v.t.*—*periled*, *periling*. To hazard; to risk; to expose to danger.—**perilous,** per′i•lus, *a.* Full of peril; dangerous; hazardous.—**perilously,** per′i•lus•li, *adv.* In a perilous manner.—**perilousness,** per′i•lus•nes, *n.*

perimeter, pe•rim′et•ėr, *n.* [Gr. *peri*, about, and *metron*, measure.] *Geom.* the boundary of a body or figure, or the sum of all the sides.—**perimetrical,** per•i•met′ri•kal, *a.* Pertaining to the perimeter.

perimorph, per′i•morf, *n.* [Gr. *peri*, about, and *morphē*, form.] *Mineral.* a mineral or crystal enclosing other minerals or crystals. ENDOMORPH.

perineum, per•i•nē′um, *n.* [Gr. *perinaion*, *perineon.*] *Anat.* the inferior surface of the trunk of the body, from the anus to the external organ of generation.—**perineal,** per•i•nē′al, *a. Anat.* pertaining to the perineum.

period, pē′ri•od, *n.* [L. *periodus*, from Gr. *periodos*—*peri*, about, and *hodos*, way.] Originally a circuit; hence, the time taken up by the revolution of a heavenly body, or the time till it returns to the point of its orbit where it began; any round of time or series of years, days, etc., in which a revolution is completed, and the same course is to be begun; an indefinite portion of any continued state, existence, or series of events (the early *period* of life); the time in which anything is performed; termination or point of completion of any cycle or series of events; end; conclusion; limit; a complete sentence from one full stop to another; the point that marks the end of a complete sentence, or indicates an abbreviation, etc.; a full stop, thus (.).—**periodic, periodical,** pē•ri•od′ik, pē•ri•od′i•kal, *a.* Pertaining to a period or to periods; performed in a period or regular revolution; happening or returning regularly in a certain period of time; recurring; published at regular intervals, as a newspaper, magazine, etc. (in this sense *periodical* is the only form).—*Periodical diseases*, those of which the symptoms recur at stated intervals.—*Periodic law*, *chem.* the law determining the classification of elements into groups with comparable characters.—*Periodic system*, a classification of chemical elements according to their atomic weights, whereby they fall into groups having similar characters.—**periodical,** *n.* A publication which appears in successive numbers at regular intervals, as a newspaper or magazine.—**periodically,** pē•ri•od′i•kal•li, *adv.* In a periodical manner; at stated periods.—**periodicity,** pē′ri•o•dis″i•ti, *n.* The state or quality of being periodical.

periosteum, per•i•os′ti•um, *n.* [Gr. *peri*, about, and *osteon*, bone.] *Anat.* a vascular membrane immediately investing the bones of animals, and conducting the vessels by which the bone is nourished.—**periosteal,** per•i•os′ti•al, *a.* Belonging to the periosteum.—**periostitis,** per′i•os•tī″tis, *n.* Inflammation of the periosteum.

peripatetic, per′i•pa•tet″ik, *a.* [Gr. *peripatētikos*, from *peripateō*, to walk about—*peri*, about, and *pateō*, to walk. Aristotle taught his system of philosophy, and his followers disputed questions, *walking* in the Lyceum at Athens.] Walking about; itinerant; pertaining to Aristotle's system of philosophy; Aristotelian —**peripatetic,** *n.* One who walks; one who walks much; [*cap.*] a follower of Aristotle.

periphery, pe•rif′ėr•i, *n.* [Gr. *peri*, around, and *pherō*, to bear.] The outside or surface of a body; *geom.* the boundary line of a closed figure; the perimeter; in a circle, the circumference.—**peripheral,** pe•rif′ėr•al, *a.* Pertaining to or constituting a periphery.

periphrasis, pe•rif′ra•sis, *n.* pl. **periphrases,** pe•rif′ra•sēz. [Gr. *periphrasis*—*peri*, about, and *phrazō*, to speak.] A roundabout phrase or expression; circumlocution; the use of more words than are necessary to express the idea.—**periphrase,** per′i•frāz, *n.* A periphrasis.—*v.t.*—*periphrased*, *periphrasing*. To express by periphrasis or circumlocution.—*v.i.* To use circumlocution.—**periphrastic,** per•i•fras′tik, *a.* Having the character of or characterized by periphrasis —**periphrastically,** per•i•fras′ti•kal•li, *adv.* In a periphrastic manner.

peripteral, pe•rip′ter•al, *a.* [Gr. *peripteros*, from *peri*, around, and *pteron*, a wing, a row of columns.] *Greek arch.* surrounded by a single row of insulated columns.—**periptery,** pe•rip′ter•i, *n.* A surrounding row of columns.

periscope, per′i•skōp, *n.* [Gr. *peri*, round, *skopeō*, to look.] An apparatus or structure rising above the deck of a submarine vessel, giving by means of mirrors, etc., a view of outside surroundings, though the vessel itself remains submerged, and enabling the crew to see how to direct torpedoes. A device of a similar kind is used on land in trenches or elsewhere.—**periscopic, periscopical,** per•i•skop′ik, per•i•skop′i•kal, *a.* Viewing on all sides: applied to spectacles having concavo-convex lenses for increasing the distinctness of objects when viewed obliquely; also to a kind of lens in microscopes.

perish, per′ish, *v.i.* [Fr. *périr*, ppr. *périssant*, to perish, from L. *perio*, to perish—*per*, through, and *eo*, to go. ITINERANT.] To lose life or vitality in any manner; to die; to be destroyed; to pass away, come to nothing, be ruined or lost.—*v.t.* To cause to perish; to destroy.—**perishable,** per′ish•a•bl, *a.* Liable to perish; subject to decay and destruction.—*Perishable goods*, goods which decay and lose their value if not consumed soon, such as fish, fruit, and the like.—**perishability, perishableness,** per′ish•a•bil″i•ti, per′ish•a•bl•nes, *n.* The state of being perishable.

perissodactyl, perissodactylous, pe•ris′o•dak″til, pe•ris′o•dak″ti•lus, *a.* [Gr. *perissos*, uneven, and *daktylos*, a finger or toe.] Having feet with toes odd in number; odd-toed: applied to a section of the ungulate or hoofed animals, including the rhinoceros, tapir, horse, etc.

peristalsis, per′i•stal″sis, *n.* [N.L. from Gr. *peristaltikos*, compressing.] *Physiol.* the wavelike constriction and release of cylindrical muscular structures in an organism (as in animal intestines) so as to push their contents forward.—**peristaltic,** per′i•stal″tik, *a.*

peristome, per′i•stōm, *n.* [Gr. *peri*, around, and *stome*, a mouth.] *Bot.* a ring or fringe of bristles or teeth that close up the orifice of the seed vessel in mosses; *zool.* a term used for the similar parts in sea urchins, etc.

peristyle, per′i•stīl, *n.* [Gr. *peri*, about, and *stylos*, a column.] *Arch.* a range of surrounding columns.

perithecium, per•i•thē′si•um, *n.* [Gr. *peri*, around, and *thēkē*, a theca or case.] *Bot.* the envelope surrounding the masses of fructification in some fungi and lichens.

peritoneum, peritonaeum, per′i•to•nē″um, *n.* [Gr. *peritonaion*—*peri*, about, and *teinō*, to stretch.] A thin, smooth, serous membrane investing the whole internal surface of the abdomen, and more or less all the viscera contained in it.—**peritoneal, peritonaeal,** per′i•to•nē″al, *a.* Pertaining to the peritoneum.—**peritonitis,** per′i•to•nī″tis, *n.* Inflammation of the peritoneum.

perivisceral, per•i•vis′ėr•al, *a.* [Gr. *peri*, about, and L. *viscera*.] *Anat.* applied to the space surrounding the viscera.

periwig, per′i•wig, *n.* [O.E. *perriwig*, *perewake*, *perwicke*, etc., corrupted from Fr. *perruque*. (PERUKE.) *Wig* is simply the final syllable of this word.] A small wig; a peruke.—*v.t.*—*periwigged*, *periwigging*. To dress with a periwig.

periwinkle, per•i•wing′kl, *n.* [From A.Sax. *pinewincle*, from L. *pinna*, *pina*, a mussel, and A.Sax. *wincle*, a winkle or whelk.] A kind of edible sea snail abounding on the shores of the North Atlantic; the shell of this snail.

periwinkle, per•i•wing′kl, *n.* [O.E. *pervinke*, *pervenke*, Fr. *pervenche*, from L. *pervinca*, the periwinkle.] The myrtle, a trailing herb with evergreen leaves and white, blue, or purple flowers; a related species, called the *large periwinkle*.

perjure, pėr′jėr, *v.t.*—*perjured*, *perjuring*. [L. *perjuro*—*per*, and *juro*, to swear, *per* here conveying a bad sense as in *perfidia*, perfidy.] To cause to be false to oaths or vows; to swear falsely to an oath in judicial proceedings; to forswear: generally used *refl.* (the witness *perjured himself*).—**perjurer,** pėr′jėr•ėr, *n.* One that willfully takes a false oath.—**perjury,** pėr′jė•ri, *n.* The act of willfully making a false oath; knowingly making a false oath in a judicial proceeding in a matter material to the issue or cause in question; the act of violating an oath or solemn promise.

perk, pėrk, *a.* [W. *perc*, neat, trim, smart; comp. also *pert*, spruce, dapper.] Trim; smart; vain; pert.—*v.i.* To hold up the head pertly; to look narrowly or sharply.—*v.t.* To make trim or smart; to prank; to hold up (the head) pertly.—**perky,** pėr′ki, *a.* Perk; trim; saucy.

perlite, pėr′līt, *n.* A form of vitreous rock, usually occurring as a mass of enamel-like globules.

permanent, pėr′ma•nent, *a.* [L. *permanens*, permanent, from *permaneo*, to continue—*per*, through, and *maneo*, to remain. MANSION.] Continuing in the same state, or without any change that destroys the form or nature of the thing; remaining unaltered or unremoved; durable; lasting; abiding; fixed.—*Permanent way*, *rail*, the finished roadbed and track, including bridges, viaducts, crossings, and switches.—**permanently,** pėr′ma•nent•li, *adv.* In a permanent manner.—**permanence, permanency,** pėr′ma•nens, pėr′ma•nen•si, *n.* The state or quality of being permanent; continuance; fixedness.

permanganate, per•mang′ga•nāt, *n.* [L. *per*, intensive, and *manganese*.] A dark, purple, crystalline substance, containing potassium, manganese, and oxygen: used in solution as an oxidizer and disinfectant.

permeate, pėr′mi•āt, *v.t.*—*permeated*, *permeating*. [L. *permeo*, *permeatum*—*per*, through, and *meo*, to flow or pass.] To pass through the pores or interstices of; to penetrate and pass through without rupture or displacement of parts: applied particularly to fluids which pass through substances of loose texture; also used *fig.*—**permeable,** pėr′mi•a•bl, *a.* [L. *permeabilis.*] Capable of being permeated.—**permeability,** pėr′mi•a•bil″i•ti, *n.* The quality or state of being permeable; in *magnetics,* the capacity or power of being traversed by magnetic lines of force; the unit of permeability is that of air.—**permeation,** pėr•mi•ā′shon, *n.* The act of permeating.

Permian, pėr′mi•an, *a.* [From *Perm,* in Russia, or that part of Russia which formed the ancient kingdom of *Permia,* where the series is largely developed.] *Geol.* a term applied to a system of rocks lying beneath the Triassic rocks, and immediately above the Carboniferous system, and forming the uppermost of the Paleozoic strata.

permission, etc. See PERMIT.

permit, pėr•mit′, *v.t.—permitted, permitting.* [L. *permitto*—prefix *per,* and *mitto,* to send. MISSION.] To allow by silent consent or by not prohibiting; to suffer without giving express authority; to grant leave or liberty to by express consent; to allow expressly; to give leave to do or be done.—*v.i.* To grant leave or permission; to allow (if circumstances *permit*).—*n.* (pėr′mit). A permission; a written permission given by officers of customs or excise, or other competent authority, for conveying spirits, wine, etc., from one place to another.—**permissibility,** pėr•mis′i•bil″i•ti, *n.* The quality of being permissible.—**permissible,** pėr•mis′i•bl, *a.* Proper to being permitted or allowed; allowable.—**permissibly,** pėr•mis′i•bli, *adv.* In a permissible manner.—**permission,** pėr•mish′on, *n.* [L. *permissio.*] The act of permitting or allowing; authorization; allowance; license or liberty granted; leave.—**permissive,** pėr•mis′iv, *a.* Permitting; granting liberty; allowing.—*Permissive laws,* laws that permit certain persons to have or enjoy the use of certain things, or to do certain acts without enforcing anything.—**permissively,** pėr•mis′iv•li, *adv.* By allowance; without prohibition or hindrance.—**permitter,** pėr•mit′ėr, *n.* One who permits.

permute, pėr•mūt′, *v.t.—permuted, permuting.* [L. *permuto*—prefix *per,* and *muto,* to change. MUTABLE.] To interchange; to change as regards order or arrangement.—**permutable,** pėr•mū′ta•bl, *a.* Capable of being permuted; exchangeable.—**permutation,** pėr•mū•tā′shon, *n.* [L. *permutatio.*] Interchange; change among various things at once; *math.* change or combination in different order of any number of quantities; any of the different ways in which a set of quantities can be arranged.

pernicious, pėr•nish′us, *a.* [L. *perniciosus,* from *pernicies,* destruction—*per,* thoroughly, and stem of *nex, necis,* death (as in *internecine*).] Having the effect of destroying; very injurious or destructive.—**perniciously,** pėr•nish′us•li, *adv.*—**pernicious anemia,** a severe form of anemia in which the red blood corpuscles become progressively fewer and larger.

peroneal, per•o•nē′al, *a.* [Gr. *peronē,* a brooch, also a name of the fibula.] Pertaining to the fibula.

peroration, per•o•rā′shon, *n.* [L. *peroratio,* from *peroro,* to speak from beginning to end—*per,* through, and *oro,* to speak, to pray. ORATION.] The concluding part of an oration, in which the speaker recapitulates the principal points of his discourse or argument, and urges them with greater earnestness; a rhetorical passage at the conclusion of a speech.—**perorate,** per′o•rāt, *v.i.* To make a peroration; also, to speechify; to spout.

peroxide, pėr•ok′sīd, *n.* [Prefix *per,* and *oxide.*] *Chem.* an oxide containing a large proportion of oxygen.—*v.t.* To bleach the hair with peroxide.

perpend, pėr•pend′, *v.t.* [L. *perpendo,* to weigh carefully—*per,* intens., and *pendo,* to weigh. PENDANT.] To weigh in the mind; to consider attentively.

perpend, pėr′pend, *n.* [Fr. *parpaing, parpain,* from *par,* through, and *pan,* the side of a wall.] A long stone reaching through the thickness of a wall so as to be visible on both sides; a bonder.

perpendicular, per•pen•dik′ū•lėr, *a.* [L. *perpendicularis,* from *perpendiculum,* a plumb line—*per,* intens., and *pendeo,* to hang. PENDANT.] Perfectly upright or vertical; extending in a straight line from any point toward the center of the earth, or at right angles with the plane of the horizon; *geom.* falling directly on a line or surface at right angles; at right angles to a given line or surface or making a normal with a curved surface.—*Perpendicular style, arch.* the florid or Tudor style of Gothic; the latest style of purely English architecture.—*n.* A line at right angles to the plane of the horizon; a vertical line; *geom.* a line falling at right angles on another line or on a plane.—**perpendicularity,** pėr•pen•dik′ū•lar•i•ti, *n.* The state of being perpendicular.—**perpendicularly,** pėr•pen•dik′ū•lėr•li, *adv.* In a perpendicular manner; vertically.

perpetrate, pėr′pe•trāt, *v.t.—perpetrated, perpetrating.* [L. *perpetro*—*per,* through, and *patro,* to finish or perform; same root as *pater,* father. PATERNAL.] To do, execute, or perform, generally in a bad sense; to be guilty of; to commit; also used humorously for to produce something execrable or shocking (to *perpetrate* a pun).—**perpetration,** pėr•pe•trā′shon, *n.* The act of perpetrating; commission.—**perpetrator,** pėr′pe•trā•tėr, *n.* One that perpetrates.

perpetual, pėr•pet′ū•al, *a.* [Fr. *perpétuel,* L. *perpetualis,* from *perpetuus,* perpetual—*per,* through, and *peto,* to seek. PETITION.] Continuing or lasting for ever in future time; destined to be eternal; continuing or continued without intermission; uninterrupted. ∴ Syn. under CONTINUOUS.—*Perpetual curate,* a permanent holder of a curacy in which all the tithes are appropriated and no vicarage endowed.—*Perpetual motion,* motion that once originated, generates a power of continuing itself forever or indefinitely, by means of mechanism or some application of the force of gravity—such a motion being, however, impossible.—*Perpetual screw,* an endless screw. See ENDLESS.—**perpetually,** pėr•pet′ū•al•li, *adv.* In a perpetual manner; constantly; forever.—**perpetuate,** pėr•pet′ū•āt, *v.t.—perpetuated, perpetuating.* [L. *perpetuo, perpetuatum.*] To make perpetual; to cause to endure or to be continued indefinitely; to preserve from extinction or oblivion.—**perpetuation,** pėr•pet′ū•ā″shon, *n.* The act of perpetuating or making perpetual.—**perpetuity,** pėr•pe•tū′i•ti, *n.* [L. *perpetuitas.*] The state or quality of being perpetual; something of which there will be no end; duration of which there will be no end; duration to all futurity; exemption from intermission or ceasing.

perplex, pėr•pleks′, *v.t.* [From L. *perplexus,* entangled, intricate, involved—*per,* intens., and *plecto, plexum,* to twist; akin to Gr. *plekō,* L. *plico,* to fold. PLY.] To involve, entangle, make complicated or intricate; to puzzle; to tease with suspense, anxiety, or ambiguity.—**perplexedly,** pėr•plek′sed•li, *adv.* In a perplexed or perplexing manner.—**perplexing,** pėr•plek′sing, *p.* and *a.* Embarrassing; difficult; intricate.—**perplexity,** pėr•plek′si•ti, *n.* The state of being perplexed, puzzled, or at a loss; the state of being intricate or involved.

perquisite, pėr′kwi•zit, *n.* [L. *perquisitum,* something sought out, from *perquiro*—*per,* intens., and *quæro,* to seek. QUERY.] Something obtained from a place or office over and above the settled wages or emoluments; something in addition to regular wages or salary.

perron, per′on, *n.* [Fr., from L.L. *petronus,* a perron, from L. and Gr. *petra,* a stone.] *Arch.* an external stair by which access is given to the entrance door of a building.

perry, per′i, *n.* [Fr. *poiré,* perry, from *poire,* L. *pirum,* a pear.] A fermented liquor made from the juice of pears and resembling cider.

per se, pėr•sā′. [L.] By or of itself; as such.

persecute, pėr′se•kūt, *v.t.—persecuted, persecuting.* [Fr. *persecuter,* from L. *persequor, persecutus,* to persecute—*per,* intens., and *sequor,* to follow. SEQUENCE.] To harass or afflict with repeated acts of cruelty or annoyance; to afflict persistently; specifically, to afflict or punish on account of holding particular opinions or adhering to a particular creed or mode of worship.—**persecution,** pėr•se•kū′shon, *n.* The act or practice of persecuting; the state of being persecuted.—**persecutor,** pėr′se•kū•tėr, *n.* One who persecutes.

Perseides, pėr•sē′i•dēz, *n. pl.* A name given to the August meteors because they seem to radiate from the constellation *Perseus.*

persevere, pėr•se•vēr′, *v.i.—persevered, persevering.* [L. *persevero,* from *perseverus,* very severe or strict—*per,* intens., and *severus,* severe, strict. SEVERE.] To continue resolutely in any business or enterprise undertaken; to pursue steadily any design or course commenced; not to give over or abandon what is undertaken. ∴ Syn. under PERSIST. —**persevering,** pėr•se•vē′ring, *p.* and *a.* Steadfast in purpose; persisting in any business or course begun.—**perseveringly,** pėr•se•vē′ring•li, *adv.* In a persevering manner.—**perseverance,** pėr•se•vē′rans, *n.* [L. *perseverantia.*] The act or habit of persevering; persistence in anything undertaken.

Persian, pėr′zhan, *a.* Pertaining to ancient Persia, the Persians or their language.—*n.* A native of Persia; the language spoken in Persia (now Iran); a silk formerly used for lining.—*Persian lamb,* the karakul lamb, the pelts of which are used in the making of outer clothing.

persiflage, pėr′si•fläzh, *n.* [Fr., from *persifler* to quiz—L. *per,* and *sibilare,* to hiss.] Idle bantering talk; a frivolous or jeering talk regarding any subject, serious or otherwise.—**persifleur,** pėr′si•flėr, *n.* One who indulges in persiflage.

persimmon, pėr•sim′on, *n.* [Virginia Indian.] An American tree of the ebony family, and also its fruit, which is about the size of a small plum and has a very sweet pulp.

persist, pėr•sist′, *v.i.* [Fr. *persister,* L. *persisto—per,* through, and *sisto,* to stand. STATE, STAND.] To continue steadily and firmly in the pursuit of any business or course commenced; to continue in the face of some amount of opposition; to persevere; (of things) to continue in a certain state. ∴ *Persist* is nearly synonymous with *persevere;* but *persist* frequently implies more obstinacy than *persevere,* particularly in that which is evil or injurious to others.—**persistence, persistency,** pėr•sis′tens, pėr•sis′ten•si, *n.* The state of persisting, or of being persistent; steady continuance in a course; perseverance, often in evil; *physics,* the continuance of an effect after the cause which first gave rise to it is removed, as the *persistence* of the impression of light on the retina after the luminous object is withdrawn.—**persistent,** pėr•sis′tent, *a.* Inclined to persist; persevering; tenacious of purpose; *bot.* continuing without withering or falling off.—**persistently,** pėr′sis•tent•li, *adv.* In a persistent manner.

person, pėr′son, *n.* [L. *persona,* primarily a mask used by actors, hence, a character, a person, from *personare,* to sound through—*per,* through, and *sonare,* to sound.] An individual human being; a man, woman, or child; bodily form; human frame, with its characteristic appearance (to appear in *person;* cleanly in *person*); a human being, indefinitely; one; a man (a *person* would think so); a term applied to each of the three beings of the Godhead; *gram.* one of three relations in which nouns and pronouns are regarded as standing to the act of speaking, a pronoun of the *first person* denoting the speaker, the *second person* one who is spoken to and the *third person* one who or that which is spoken of (thus including all nouns); one of the three corresponding inflections of a verb singular and plural.—*In person,* by one's self, not by representative.—**personable,** pėr′son•a•bl, *a.* Having a well-formed body or person; of good appearance.—**personage,** pėr′son•ij, *n.* A person; a man or woman of distinction (an illustrious *personage*); a being regarded as having an individuality like that of a human being (a divine or a mythological *personage*).—**personal,** pėr′son•al, *a.* [L. *personalis.*] Pertaining to a person as distinct from a thing; relating to or affecting some individual person; peculiar or proper to him or her, or to private actions or character; applying to the person, character, or conduct of an individual, generally in a disparaging manner (*personal* reflections or remarks); belonging to face and figure (*personal* charms); done in person, not by representative (a *personal* interview); *gram.* denoting or pointing to the person (a *personal* pronoun, as *I, we, thou, you, he, she, it, they*); having the modifications of the three persons.—*Personal identity, metaph.* sameness of being at every stage of life, of which consciousness is the evidence.—*Personal property, personal estate,* movables; chattels; things belonging to the person, as money, jewels, furniture, etc., as distinguished from *real* estate in land and houses.—**personality,** pėr•son•al′i•ti, *n.* The state of being personal; what constitutes an individual; a distinct person; the state of existing as a thinking intelligent being; application or applicability to a person; an application of remarks to the conduct, character, or appearance of some person; traits that characterize a nation, a group, or an individual; reference to personal traits (to indulge in *personalities*); a noted person; *law,* personal estate; personality.—**personalize,** pėr′son•al•īz, *v.t.—personalized, personalizing.* To make personal.—**personally,** pėr′son•al•li, *adv.* In a personal manner; in person; with respect to an individual; as regards one's personal existence or individuality.—**personalty,** pėr′son•al•ti, *n. Law,* personal property, in distinction from *realty* or real property.—**personate,** pėr′son•āt, *v.t.—personated, personating.* To assume the character or appearance of, whether in real life or on the stage; to represent by an assumed appearance; to act the part of; to assume or put on.—*a.* [L. *personatus,* masked.] *Bot.* a term applied to a gamopetalous corolla somewhat resembling an animal's mouth, as in the snapdragon.—**personation,** pėr•son•ā′shon, *n.* The act of counterfeiting the person or character of another.—*False personation,* the offense of personating another for the purpose of fraud.—**personator,** pėr′son•ā•tėr, *n.* One who personates; one who assumes the character of another.—**personification,** pėr•son′i•fi•kā″shon, *n.* The act of personifying; an embodiment; an impersonation; *rhet.* a species of metaphor, which consists in representing inanimate objects or abstract notions as endued with life and action, or possessing the attributes of living beings.—**personify,** pėr•son′i•fī, *v.t.* —*personified, personifying.* [L. *persona,* and *facio,* to make.] To treat or regard as a person; to treat for literary purposes as if endowed with the characters of a rational being or person; to impersonate—**personnel,** pėr•son•el′, *n.* [Fr., from *personne,* a person.] The body of persons employed in any occupation; often opposed to *matériel.*

perspective, pėr•spek′tiv, *a.* [Fr. *perspectif,* from L. *perspicio, perspectum—per,* through, and *specio,* to view. SPECIES.] Producing certain optical effects when looked through; optical (a *perspective* glass); pertaining to the art of perspective.—*n.* A telescope‡; the art or science which teaches how to draw or paint objects or scenes so that they appear to have their natural dimensions, positions, and relations—*aerial* perspective dealing with light, shade, and color, *linear* perspective with form and magnitude; a representation of objects in perspective; quality of a picture as regards perspective; view; vista.—**perspectively,** pėr•spek′tiv•li, *adv.* According to the rules of perspective.

perspicacious, pėr•spi•kā′shus, *a.* [L. *perspicax, perspicācis,* from *perspicio,* to look through. PERSPECTIVE.] Quick-sighted; quickly seeing through or understanding anything; of acute discernment.—**perspicaciously,** pėr•spi•kā′shus•li, *adv.* In a perspicacious manner.—**perspicacity,** pėr•spi•kas′i•ti, *n.* The state or quality of being perspicacious; acuteness of discernment; penetration; sagacity.—**perspicuity,** pėr•spi•kū′i•ti, *n.* [L. *perspicuitas.*] The quality of being perspicuous; easiness to be understood; freedom from obscurity or ambiguity.—**perspicuous,** pėr•spik′ū•us, *a.* [L. *perspicuus.*] Clear to the understanding; not obscure or ambiguous; lucid.—**perspicuously,** pėr•spik′ū•us•li, *adv.* In a perspicuous manner.—**perspicuousness,** pėr•spik′ū•us•nes, *n.* Perspicuity; intelligibility; lucidity.

perspire, pėr•spīr′, *v.i.—perspired, perspiring.* [L. *perspiro—per,* through, and *spiro,* to breathe. SPIRIT.] To give out watery matter through the pores of the skin; to sweat; to exude. —*v.t.* To emit through the excretories of the skin; to give out through pores.—**perspiration,** pėr-spi•rā'shon, *n.* The act of perspiring; excretion of watery fluid (sweat) from the surface of the body (whether visibly or in the form of invisible vapor);—**perspiratory,** pėr•spī'ra•to•ri, *a.* Pertaining to perspiration; causing perspiration; perspirative.

persuade, pėr•swād', *v.t.*—*persuaded, persuading.* [L. *persuadeo*—*per*, effectively, and *suadeo*, to advise, urge. SUASION.] To influence by argument, advice, or expostulation; to argue or reason into a certain course of action; to advise; to try to influence; to convince by argument or reasons offered.—*v.i.* To use persuasion.—**persuadable,** pėr•swā'da•bl, *a.* Capable of being persuaded.—**persuader,** pėr•swā'dėr, *n.* One who persuades.—**persuasible,** pėr•swā'zi•bl, *a.* [L. *persuasibilis.*] Capable of being persuaded.—**persuasion,** pėr-swā'zhon, *n.* [L. *persuasio, persuasionis.*] The act of persuading; the state of being persuaded or convinced; settled opinion or conviction; a creed or belief; a sect or party adhering to a creed or system of opinions. ∴ Syn. under CONVICTION.—**persuasive,** pėr•swā'ziv, *a.* Having the power of persuading; influencing to a course of action.—*n.* That which persuades; an incitement; an exhortation.—**persuasively,** pėr•swā'ziv•li, *adv.* In a persuasive manner.—**persuasiveness,** pėr•swā'ziv•nes, *n.* The quality of being persuasive.

pert, pėrt, *a.* [Partly from O.Fr. *apert, appert* (as in *malapert*), from L. *apertus*, open (APERIENT); partly from W. *pert, perc*, trim, spruce (PERK).] Lively; brisk; dapper; smart; forward; saucy; indecorously free.—**pertly,** pėrt'li, *adv.* In a pert manner; briskly; smartly; with indecorous boldness. —**pertness,** pėrt'nes, *n.* The state or quality of being pert; smartness; sauciness; forward boldness.

pertain, pėr•tān', *v.i.* [L. *pertineo*—*per*, intens., and *teneo*, to hold, whence also *tenant, contain, obtain, retain*, etc. TENANT.] To belong; to be the property, right, duty of; to appertain; to have relation or bearing; always followed by *to*.

pertinaceous, pėr•ti•nā'shus, *a.* [L. *pertinax*—*per*, intens., and *teneo*, to hold; PERTAIN.] Holding or adhering to any opinion, purpose, or design with obstinacy; obstinate; perversely persistent; resolute; constant.—**pertinaciously,** pėr•ti•nā'shus•li, *adv.* In a pertinacious manner; persistently; obstinately.—**pertinacity, pertinaciousness,** pėr-ti•nas'i•ti, pėr•ti•nā'shus•nes *n.* Firm or unyielding adherence to opinion or purpose; obstinacy; resolution; constancy.

pertinent, pėr'ti•nent, *a.* [L. *pertinens*, ppr. of *pertineo*, to pertain. PERTAIN.] Related to the subject or matter in hand; just to the purpose; apposite; not foreign to the question.—**pertinence, pertinency,** pėr'ti•nens, pėr'ti•nen•si, *n.* The quality of being pertinent; justness of relation to the subject or matter in hand; fitness; appositeness.—**pertinently,** pėr'ti•nent•li, *adv.* In a pertinent manner; appositely; to the purpose.

perturb, pėr•tėrb', *v.t.* [L. *perturbo*—*per*, intens., and *turbo*, to disturb, from *turba*, a crowd. DISTURB, TURBID.] To disturb; to agitate; to disorder; to confuse.—**perturbable,** pėr•tėr'ba•bl, *a.* Capable of being perturbed or agitated.—**perturbation,** pėr•tėr•bā'shon, *n.* [L. *perturbatio.*] The act of perturbing or state of being perturbed; disorder; especially, disquiet of mind; commotion of the passions; agitation; cause of disquiet.—*Perturbations of the planets*, their orbital irregularities or deviations from their regular elliptic orbits, arising from their attraction for one another.

pertussis, pėr•tus'is, *n.* [L. *per*, intens., and *tussis*, a cough.] *Med.* the whooping cough.

peruke, pe•rūk', *n.* [Fr. *perruque*, It. *perucca*, It. dial. *pilucca*, peruke, from L. *pilus*, hair. *Periwig* is a corruption of *perruque*, and its final syllable has become *wig*.] An artificial cap of hair; a periwig; a perruque.

peruse, pe•rūz', *v.t.*—*perused, perusing.* [From prefix *per*, intens., and *use*.] To read through; to read with attention; to observe; to examine with careful survey.—**peruser,** pe•rū'zėr, *n.* One who peruses.—**perusal,** pe•rū'zal, *n.* The act of perusing or reading.

Peruvian, pe•rū'vi•an, *a.* Pertaining to *Peru* in South America.—*n.* A native of Peru.—**Peruvian bark,** *n.* The bark of several species of *Cinchona*, trees of Peru, yielding quinine. See CINCHONA, QUININE.

pervade, pėr•vād', *v.t.*—*pervaded, pervading.* [L. *pervado*, to go through—*per*, through, and *vado*, to go (as in *invade*); cog. A.Sax. *wadan*, E. *wade.*] To pass or flow through; to extend through; to spread or be diffused through the whole extent of.—**pervasion,** pėr•vā'zhon, *n.* The act of pervading.—**pervasive,** pėr-vā'siv, *a.* Tending or having power to pervade.

perverse, pėr•vėrs', *a.* [L. *perversus*, from *perverto*, to pervert, corrupt, overthrow—*per*, and *verto*, to turn. VERSE.] Turned aside from the right; turned to evil; obstinate in the wrong; froward; stubborn; intractable; cross; petulant; untoward.—**perversely,** pėr•vėrs'li, *adv.* In a perverse manner; stubbornly; obstinately in the wrong.—**perverseness,** pėr•vėrs'nes, *n.* The quality of being perverse; disposition to thwart or cross.—**perversion,** pėr-vėr'shon, *n.* [L. *perversio.*] The act of perverting; a diverting from the true intent or object; sexual aberration.—**perversity,** pėr•vėr'si•ti, *n.* [L. *perversitas.*] State or quality of being perverse; perverseness.—**perversive,** pėr•vėr'siv, *a.* Tending or having power to pervert. —**pervert,** pėr•vėrt', *v.t.* [L. *perverto.*] To turn from truth, propriety, or from its proper purpose; to distort from its true use or end; to misinterpret willfully; to turn from the right; to corrupt.—**pervert,** pėr'vėrt, *n.* One who has been perverted; an apostate; a degenerate; one who is sexually perverted; an invert.—**perverter,** pėr•vėr'tėr, *n.* One that perverts; one that distorts, misinterprets, or misapplies.—**pervertible,** pėr•vėr'ti•bl, *a.* Capable of being perverted.

pervicacious, pėr•vi•kā'shus, *a.* [L. *pervicax*, headstrong.] Very obstinate; stubborn; willfully contrary or refractory.

pervious, pėr'vi•us, *a.* [L. *pervius*—*per*, through, and *via*, a way. VOYAGE, WAY.] Capable of being penetrated by another body or substance; penetrable; allowing an entrance or a passage through; capable of being penetrated by the mental sight.—**perviousness,** pėr'vi•us•nes, *n.* The quality of being pervious.

peseta, pe•sā'te, *n.* [Sp.] A Spanish gold monetary unit of 100 centimes; a silver coin of nominally equal value.

Peshito, pesh•ē'tō, *a.* and *n.* [Syriac, single or true.] The Syrian translation of the Old and New Testaments (incomplete) made by a Christian in the second century.

pesky, pes'ki, *a.* [Variant of *pest* and *risky*.] Troublesome; vexatious.

peso, pā'sō, *n.* [Sp.] A dollar; a term used in certain of the Central and South American countries.

pessary, pes'a•ri, *n.* [Med. L. *pessarium*, from L. *pessum*, Gr. *pessos*, a small oval stone, a medicated plug.] A device introduced into the vagina to correct uterine displacement, to prevent conception, etc.

pessimism, pes'im•izm, *n.* [L. *pessimus*, the worst.] The belief or doctrine that man is imperfectible and that his life is essentially unhappy; the tendency to take the most unfavorable view of situations or actions: opposed to *optimism*.—**pessimist,** pes'im•ist, *n.* One who believes in pessimism, also one who is inclined to take a despondent view of things.—**pessimistic,** pes-si•mis'tik, *a.* Pertaining to pessimism.

pest, pest, *n.* [Fr. *peste*, from L. *pestis*, a plague, a pest (whence *pestilent, pestiferous*); same root as *perdo*, to destroy (PERDITION).] A plague, pestilence, or deadly epidemic disease; anything very noxious, mischievous, or destructive; a mischievous or destructive person.—**pesthouse,** *n.* A hospital for persons infected with the plague or other pestilential disease.

Pestalozzian, pes•ta•lot'si•an, *a.* Pertaining to the system of elementary education instituted by a Swiss philanthropist named *Pestalozzi*, which is substantially the system now followed.

pester, pes'tėr, *v.t.* [O.Fr. *empestrer*, originally to shackle the feet of a horse at pasture, from L.L. *pasto-*

rium, foot shackles, from L. *pastor*, a shepherd. PASTERN, PASTOR.] To encumber‡; to crowd or cram‡; to trouble; to disturb; to annoy with little vexations.

pestiferous, pes•tif′ėr•us, *a.* [L. *pestis*, plague, and *fero*, to produce. PEST.] Pestilential; noxious to health; infectious; noxious in any manner; malignant.—**pestiferously,** pes•tif′ėr•us•li, *adv.* In a pestiferous manner; pestilentially.

pestilence, pes′ti•lens, *n.* [L. *pestilentia*, from *pestilens*, pestilent, from *pestis*, plague. PEST.] The disease called the plague or pest; any contagious and malignant disease that is epidemic and mortal; what is pestilential or pestiferous; something morally evil or destructive.—**pestilent,** pes′ti•lent, *a.* [L. *pestilens.*] Pestilential; mischievous; noxious to morals or society; troublesome; corrupt.—**pestilential,** pes•ti•len′shal, *a.* Having the nature of the plague or other infectious and deadly disease; producing or tending to produce infectious disease; destructive.—**pestilently,** pes′ti•lent•li, *adv.* In a pestilent manner.

pestle, pes′l, *n.* [O.Fr. *pesteil*, from L. *pistillum*, a pestle, from *pinso, pistum*, to bray, to pound; akin *pistil, piston.*] An instrument for pounding and breaking substances in a mortar. —*v.t.*—*pestled, pestling.* To break or pulverize with a pestle.

pet, pet, *n.* [Possibly an abbreviated form of *petulant* or *petulance.*] A slight fit of peevishness or fretful discontent.—**pettish,** pet′ish, *a.* Proceeding from or pertaining to a pet or peevish humor.—**pettishly,** pet′ish•li, *adv.* In a pettish manner.—**pettishness,** pet′ish•nes, *n.* Fretfulness; peevishness.

pet, pet, *n.* [From Ir. *peat*, Gael. *peata*, a pet, or perhaps from *petty*, Fr. *petit*, little.] A fondling; a darling; a favorite child; an animal fondled and indulged.—*v.t.*—*petted, petting.* To treat as a pet; to fondle; to indulge.—*a.* Petted; favorite (a *pet* lamb, a *pet* theory).

petal, pet′al, *n.* [From Gr. *petalon*, a leaf, from *petalos*, spread out, expanded; same root as in *patent.*] *Bot.* a flower leaf; one of the separate parts of a corolla.—**petaled,** pet′ald, *a.* Having petals.—**petaline,** pet′al•īn, *a. Bot.* pertaining to a petal.—**petaloid,** pet′al•oid, *a.* Having the form of a petal; resembling petals.—**petalous,** pet′al•us, *a. Bot.* having petals; petaled.

petard, pe•tärd′, *n.* [Fr. *pétard*, from *péter*, to break wind, to bounce, from L. *pedo, peditum*, with same sense.] An engine of war made of metal, to be loaded with powder and fixed on a gate, barricade, etc., in order to break it down by explosion.—*Hoist with his own petard*, (*fig.*) caught in his own trap; involved in the danger he meant for others.

petasos, petasus, pet′a•sos, pet′a•sus, *n.* [Gr. *petasos.*] A broad-brimmed hat; the winged cap of Mercury.

Peter, *n.*—*The Blue Peter*, the flag hoisted by a merchantman on the eve of leaving the docks.

peter out, pē•tėr•out′, *v.i.* Said of a mine or vein of ore when it is exhausted and yields no return. (*Colloq.*)

Peter pence, Peter's pence, pē•tėr pens′, *n. pl.* A tribute that used to be regularly offered to the popes (as the successors of St. Peter); a similar contribution still voluntarily given by some Roman Catholics.

petersham, pē′tėr•sham, *n.* [After Lord *Petersham*, who set the fashion of wearing it.] A style of overcoat formerly fashionable; the heavy, rough-napped woolen cloth of which such overcoats were made.

petiole, pet′i•ōl, *n.* [Fr., from L. *petiolus*, a dim. from *pes, pedis*, a foot.] *Bot.* a leafstalk; the stalk connecting the blade of the leaf with the branch or stem.—**petiolar,** pet′i•ō•lėr, *a. Bot.* pertaining to a petiole, or proceeding from it.—**petiolate,** pet′i•ō•lāt, *a.* Having a petiole.—**petiolule,** pet′i•ōl•ūl, *n.* [A dim. of *petiole.*] *Bot.* a little or partial petiole, such as belongs to the leaflets of compound leaves.

petit, pet′i or pė•tē′; **petite** (feminine form), pė•tēt′, *a.* [Fr.] Little; petty; small in figure.—*Petit juror*, a person serving on a petit jury.—*Petit jury*, a group of twelve persons impaneled as a jury to decide a case tried in a law court; distinguished from *grand jury*.

petite, pe•tēt′, *a.* [Fr.] Small; tiny and delicate, usually said of a woman.

petition, pe•tish′on, *n.* [L. *petitio, petitionis*, from *peto, petitum*, to seek.] An entreaty, supplication, or prayer; a formal written request; a document containing such a request, usually signed by persons supporting the request.—*v.t.* To make a petition or request to.—*v.i.* To present a petition.—**petitionary,** pe•tish′on•e•ri, *a.*—**petitioner,** pe•tish′on•ėr, *n.*

petrel, pet′rel, *n.* [Dim. of *Peter*, in allusion to St. Peter's walking on the sea, as the birds often seem to do.] The name of web-footed oceanic birds of several species, found at great distances from land, and generally in stormy weather: hence the name *stormy petrels.*

petri dish, pet′ri, *n.* [For R. J. *Petri.*] A shallow dish of thin glass with a cover, used in growing bacteriological cultures.

petrify, pet′ri•fī, *v.t.*—*petrified, petrifying.* [L. *petra* (from Gr. *petra*), a stone or rock (seen also in *petroleum, pier*), and *facio*, to make.] To convert to stone or stony substance, as by the infiltration and deposition of mineral matter; to turn into a fossil; *fig.* to make callous or obdurate; to paralyze or stupefy with fear or amazement.—*v.i.* To become stone or of a stony hardness.—**petrifaction,** pet•ri•fak′shon, *n.* The process of changing into stone; an organized body rendered hard by deposition of a stony substance in its cavities; a fossil; a state of being paralyzed as with astonishment.—**petrifactive,** pet•ri•fak′tiv, *a.* Having power to petrify or convert into stone.

Petrine, pē′trīn, *a.* Relating to St. *Peter* (the *Petrine* epistles).

petrography, pe•trog′ra•fi, *n.* [Gr. *petros*, a stone, and *graphō*, to write.] The study of rocks; a scientific description of rocks; petrology.—**petrographer,** pe•trog′ra•fėr, *n.*—**petrographic, petrographical,** pet•ro•graf′ik, pet•ro•graf′i•kal, *a.*

petrol, pet′rol, *n.* [From *petroleum.*] *British*, gasoline.

petrolatum, pet•ro•lā′tum, *n.* [From *petroleum.*] A colorless, odorless, tasteless substance derived from petroleum and used in ointments and as a protective dressing.

petroleum, pe•trō′li•um, *n.* [L. *petra*, rock, and *oleum*, oil.] A natural, oily liquid consisting chiefly of hydrocarbons which, by fractional distillation, yields such products as gasoline, kerosene, lubricating oils, fuel oils, etc.

petrology, pe•trol′o•ji, *n.* [Gr. *petros*, a rock, and *logos*, a treatise.] The study of rocks; that branch of geology which determines the constitution of rocks by investigating the chemical composition of the separate mineral ingredients of which they consist. Spelled also *Petralogy.*—**petrological,** pet•ro•loj′i•kal, *a.* Of or pertaining to petrology.—**petrologist,** pe•trol′o•jist, *n.* One versed in petrology.

petronel, pet′ro•nel, *n.* [O.Fr. *petrinal, poictrinal*, from L. *pectus, pectoris*, the breast, being discharged with the stock placed against the breast.] A kind of carbine or large horseman's pistol.

petrosal, pi•trō′sal, *a.* and *n.* [L. *petrosus.*] Applied to the petrous portion of the temporal bone or to a homologous bone. See PETROUS.

petrosilex, pet•ro•si′leks, *n.* [L. *petra*, a stone, and *silex*, flint.] Rock stone; rock flint or compact feldspar.

petrous, pē′trus, *a.* [L. *petrosus*, from *petra*, a stone.] Like stone; hard; stony; *anat.* applied to that portion of the temporal bone in which the internal organs of hearing are situated, from its hardness (known as the *petrosal portion*).

petticoat, pet′i•kōt, *n.* [From *petty*, short, small, and *coat.*] A loose undergarment worn by females; hence, a woman.—*Petticoat government*, female government, either political or domestic.

pettifog, pet′i•fog, *v.i.*—*pettifogged, pettifogging.* [*Petty* and Prov.E, *fog*, to seek gain by mean practices.] To act in mean or petty cases, as a lawyer.—**pettifogger,** pet•i•fog′ėr, *n.* An inferior attorney or lawyer who is employed in mean business.—**pettifoggery,** pet•i•fog′ėr•i, *n.* The practice of a pettifogger; tricks; quibbles.

pettiness. See PETTY.

pettish. See PET.

pettitoes, pet′i•tōz, *n. pl.* [*Petty* and *toes.*] The toes or feet of a pig: sometimes used humorously for the human feet, as those of a child.

petty, pet′i, *a.* [Fr. *petit,* little; small, akin to W. *pitw,* small, *pid,* a point.] Small; little; trifling; inconsiderable; having little power or possessions; having little importance; inferior (a *petty* prince).—*Petty averages,* the accustomed duties of anchorage, pilotage, etc., which are paid by a vessel.—*Petty cash,* money kept on hand from which change is made and small bills are paid.—*Petty-cash book,* a book in which small receipts and payments are entered.—*Petty jury,* same as PETIT JURY.—*Petty officer,* an officer in the navy whose rank corresponds with that of a noncommissioned officer in the army. —**pettily,** pet′i•li, *adv.* In a petty manner.—**pettiness,** pet′i•nes, *n.*

petulant, pet′ū•lant, *a.* [L. *petulans, petulantis,* petulant, from *peto,* to attack. PETITION.] Manifesting pique, perversity, fretfulness; saucy; pert; capricious.—**petulance, petulancy,** pet′ū•lans, pet′ū•lan•si, *n.* [L. *petulantia.*] Freakish passion; peevishness; pettishness; sauciness.—**petulantly,** pet′ū•lant•li, *adv.* In a petulant manner; with saucy pertness.

petunia, pe•tū′ni•a, *n.* [Brazil, *petun,* tobacco.] A genus of American herbaceous plants, nearly allied to the tobacco plant, and much prized by horticulturists for the beauty of their flowers.

pew, pū, *n.* [O.Fr. *pui,* a raised place, from L. *podium,* a balcony, from Gr. *podion,* from *pous, podos,* the foot.] A fixed seat in a church, enclosed and separated from those adjoining by partitions.

pewee, pē′wē, *n.* [From its call.] One of the North American fly-catchers; the phoebe.

pewit, pē′wit, *n.* [From its call.] The lapwing; a small European black-headed gull.

pewter, pū′tėr, *n.* [O.Fr. *peutre, piautre,* D. *peauter,* also, *speauter,* same as *spelter.*] An alloy of tin and lead, or of tin with such proportions of lead, zinc, bismuth, antimony, or copper as experience has shown to be most conducive to the improvement of its hardness and color; a vessel, or vessels collectively, made of pewter.—*a.* Made of pewter.—**pewterer,** pū′tėr•ėr, *n.* One whose occupation is to make articles of pewter.

pfennig, pfen′ig, *n.* In Germany, the reichspfennig, a bronze coin worth 1/100 mark.

phaeton, fā′e•ton, *n.* [From Gr. *Phaethōn,* who obtained leave from his father Helios (the Sun) to drive the chariot of the sun, but as he was unable to restrain the horses Zeus dashed him with a thunderbolt headlong into the River Po.] An open four-wheeled carriage usually drawn by two horses.

phagedena, phagedaena, faj•e•dē′na, *n.* [Gr. *phagedaina,* from *phagein,* to eat.] A spreading obstinate ulcer.

phagocyte, fag′o•sīt, *n.* [Gr. *phagein,* to eat, *kytos,* cell.] A white blood corpuscle that absorbs and destroys disease germs.—**phagocytosis,** fag′o•sit•ō″sis, *n.* The destruction of disease germs and diseased products by phagocytes.

phalange, fa•lanj′, *n.* [Gr. *phalanx, phalangos,* battle array, a phalanx of soldiers, a bone of the fingers or toes.] *Anat.* one of the small bones of the fingers and toes; *bot.* a collection of several stamens joined more or less by their filaments.—**phalangal, phalangeal,** fa•lang′gal, fa•lan′ji•al, *a.* Belonging to the phalanges of the fingers and toes.—**phalanger,** fa•lan′jėr, *n.* [From two of the toes being joined as far as the last *phalanges.*] An Australian marsupial animal of several species, nocturnal in habits and living in trees.—**phalanx,** fal′angks, *n.* pl. **phalanges,** fa•lan′jēz, also, except in anatomy, **phalanxes,** fal′angk•sēz. *Greek antiq.* the heavy-armed infantry of an army, especially when formed in ranks and files close and deep; a body of troops or men in close array; *anat.* one of the small bones of the fingers or the toes.

phalanstery, fal′an•ste•ri, *n.* [Fr. *phalanstère,* from Gr. *phalanx,* a phalanx.] A socialistic community living together according to the system proposed by Fourier; the dwelling of such a community.

phalarope, fal′a•rōp, *n.* [From Gr. *phalaros,* white, and *pous, podos,* a foot.] A lobe-footed grallatorial bird resembling the sandpiper.

phallus, fal′lus, *n.* [Gr. *phallos,* the virile organ.] Image of the male organ of generation, symbolizing the power of fertility and reproductiveness in nature, as worshiped in some primitive systems of religion; in anatomy, the penis or clitoris.—**phallic,** fal′lik, *a.* Pertaining to the phallus, or to the worship of the generative principle in nature.

phanerogam, fan′ėr•o•gam, *n.* [Gr. *phaneros,* evident, and *gamos,* marriage.] *Bot.* a flowering plant or a plant with conspicuous flowers containing stamens and pistils: opposed to a *cryptogam.*—**phanerogamic, phanerogamous,** fan′ėr•o•gam″ik, fan•ėr•og′a•mus, *a. Bot.* belonging to the flowering plants, in contradistinction to *cryptogamic, cryptogamous.*

phantasm, fan′tazm, *n.* [Gr. *phantasma,* from *phantazein,* to show, from the stem of *phainein,* to show. PHENOMENON.] A creation of the fancy; an imaginary existence which seems to be real; an apparition; a phantom; an idea; a notion; a fancy. —**phantasmagoria,** fan•tas′ma•gō″ri•a, *n.* [Gr. *phantasma,* and *agora,* an assembly.] Any exhibition of images by means of shadows, as by the magic lantern; the apparatus used in such an exhibition; any mixed gathering of figures; illusive images. —**phantasmagorial, phantasmagoric,** fan•tas′ma•gō″ri•al, fan•tas′ma•gor″ik, *a.* Relating to a phantasmagoria.—**phantasmal,** fan′taz•mal, *a.* Pertaining to or resembling a phantasm; spectral; illusive.

phantasy, fan′ta•si, *n.* See FANTASY.

phantom, fan′tom, *n.* [Fr. *fantôme,* from L. *phantasma;* same word as *phantasm.* PHANTASM.] An apparition or specter; a ghost; a fancied vision; a phantasm; something unreal.

Pharaoh, fâ′rō, *n.* A name given by the Hebrews to the ancient monarchs of Egypt; a game at cards. FARO.—*Pharaoh's chicken,* the Egyptian vulture.—*Pharaoh's rat,* the ichneumon. —**Pharaonic,** fâ•rā•on′ik, *a.* Pertaining to the Pharaohs, or to the old Egyptians.

Pharisee, far′i•sē, *n.* [Gr. *pharisaios,* from Heb. *pârûsh,* separated.] One of a sect among the Jews distinguished by their strict observance of rites and ceremonies and of the traditions of the elders, and who considered themselves as more righteous than other Jews; hence, a strict observer of the outward forms or ceremonies in religion without the spirit of it; a hypocrite.—**pharisaic, pharisaical,** far•i•sā′ik, far•i•sā′i•kal, *a.* Pertaining to the Pharisees; resembling the Pharisees; addicted to external forms and ceremonies; making a show of religion without the spirit of it; hypocritical.—**pharisaically,** far•i•sā′i•kal•li, *adv.* In a pharisaical manner, hypocritically. —**pharisaicalness,** far•i•sā′i•kal•nes, *n.*—**Pharisaism,** far′i•sā•izm, *n.* The doctrines and conduct of the Pharisees, as a sect; rigid observance of external rites and forms of religion without genuine piety; hypocrisy in religion.

pharmaceutic, pharmaceutical, fär•ma•sū′tik, fär•ma•sū′ti•kal, *a.* [Gr. *pharmakeutikos,* from *pharmakeuein,* to administer medicine, from *pharmakon,* a drug.] Pertaining to the knowledge or art of pharmacy or preparing medicines.—*Pharmaceutical chemistry,* chemistry applied to those substances which are employed for the cure of diseases.—**pharmaceutically,** fär•ma•sū′ti•kal•li, *adv.* In the manner of pharmacy.—**pharmaceutics,** fär•ma•sū′tiks, *n.* The science of preparing medicines; pharmacy. —**pharmaceutist,** fär•ma•sū′tist, *n.* One who prepares medicines; one who practices pharmacy; an apothecary.—**pharmacist,** fär′ma•sist, *n.* One skilled in pharmacy; a druggist.—**pharmacologist,** fär•ma•kol′o•jist, *n.* One who is skilled in pharmacology.—**pharmacology,** fär•ma•kol′o•ji, *n.* [Gr. *pharmakon* and *logos.*] The science or knowledge of drugs, or the art of preparing medicines: a branch of materia medica; a treatise on preparing medicines.—**pharmacopoeia,** fär′ma•kō•pē″a, *n.* [Gr. *pharmakon,* and *poiein,* to make.] A book of directions for the preparation, etc., of medicines, generally published by authority.—**pharmacy,** fär′ma•si, *n.* [Fr. *pharmacie,* from Gr. *pharmakeia,* from *pharmakon.*] The art of preparing and compounding medicines, and of dispensing them according to the prescriptions of medical practitioners; the occupation of an apothecary; the place where medicines are compounded or dispensed.

pharos, fâ′ros, *n.* A lighthouse or

tower which anciently stood on the isle of Pharos, at the entrance to the Port of Alexandria; hence, any lighthouse for the direction of seamen; a beacon.

pharynx, far'ingks, *n.* [Gr. *pharynx, pharyngos*; akin to *pharanx*, a chasm.] The muscular sac which intervenes between the cavity of the mouth and the esophagus, its contraction aiding in swallowing the food.—**pharyngeal,** fa•rin'ji•al, *a.* Belonging to or affecting the pharynx.—**pharyngitis,** far•in•jī'tis, *n.* Inflammation of the pharynx.—**pharyngotomy,** far•in•got'o•mi, *n.* [Gr. *pharynx*, and *tomē*, a cutting.] The operation of making an incision into the pharynx to remove anything that obstructs the passage.

phase, fāz, *n.* [Fr. *phase*, from Gr. *phasis*, from *phainomai*, to appear. PHENOMENON.] One of the recurring appearances or states of the moon or a planet in respect to quantity of illumination or figure of enlightened disk; the particular state, at a given instant, of a continuously varying and periodic phenomenon (the *phases* of a tide, etc.); an aspect or appearance of that which presents various aspects; one of the various aspects in which a question presents itself to the mind; a turn or chance.—*Phase rule*, an equation ($c+2-p=F$) expressing the relation between the solid, liquid, and gaseous states (phases) of substances in solution (c=components; p=number of phases; F=degrees of freedom).

phasis, fā'sis, *n.* pl. **phases,** fā'sēz. *Astron.* a phase.

pheasant, fez'ant, *n.* [L. *phasianus*, from Gr. *phasianos*, from *Phasis*, a river of Asia, near the mouth of which these birds are said to have been numerous.] A well-known and beautiful gallinaceous bird bred as a game bird.

phenacetin, fē•nas'e•tin, *n.* [*Phen* (indicating a benzene derivative) and *acetin.*] A drug of coal-tar origin, used to relieve pain and fever.

phenix, fē'niks, *n.* See PHOENIX.

phenobarbital, fē'nō•bar"bi•tal, *n.* [*Pheno* and *barbital.*] A barbiturate $C_{12}H_{12}N_2O_3$ used as a sedative and hypnotic; luminal.

phenol, fē'nol, *n.* A name for *Carbolic Acid.*

phenology, fin•ol'o•jē, *n.* [Gr. *phaino*, I appear, *logos*, a discourse.] The study of times and seasons in relation to plants and animals as embodied in nature calendars.

phenolphthalein, fē'nol•thăl"ēn, *n.* [*Phenol* and *phthlein.*] An off-white crystalline compound $C_{20}H_{14}O_4$ used as a laxative and as an indicator for acids and bases.

phenomenon, fi•nom'e•non, *n.* pl. **phenomena,** fi•nom'e•na. [Gr. *phainomenon*, what appears, from *phainomai*, I appear.] An observable fact or event; a remarkable thing or person.—**phenomenal,** fi•nom'e•nal, *a.* Connected with, relating to, or constituted by phenomena; remarkable or extraordinary; astounding.—**phenomenalism,** fi•nom'e•nal•izm, *n.* That system of philosophy which inquires only into the causes of existing phenomena.—**phenomenally,** fi•nom'e•nal•li, *adv.*

phial, fī'al, *n.* [L. *phiala*, from Gr. *phialē*, a phial. *Vial* is another form.] A glass vessel or bottle; especially, a small glass bottle used for holding liquors, and particularly liquid medicines.—*Leyden-phial*, a vessel used in electrical experiments. LEYDEN-JAR.—*v.t.*—*phialed, phialing.* To put or keep in a phial, or as in a phial.

philander, fi•lan'dėr, *v.i.* [From *Philander*, a virtuous youth in Ariosto's *Orlando Furioso*, between whom and a married lady there were certain tender passages.] To make love sentimentally to a lady; to flirt; to pretend admiration.

philanthropy, fi•lan'thro•pi, *n.* [Gr. *philanthropia*, from *philos*, loving, and *anthrōpos*, a man.] Love toward mankind; benevolence toward the whole human family. —**philanthropic, philanthropical,** fil•an•throp'ik, fil•an•throp'i•kal, *a.* [Gr. *philanthrōpikos.*] Pertaining to philanthropy; possessing general benevolence; entertaining good will toward all men.—**philanthropically,** fil•an•throp'i•kal•li, *adv.* In a philanthropic manner. — **philanthropist,** fi•lan'throp•ist, *n.* One who evinces philanthropy; a person of general benevolence; one who exerts himself in doing good to his fellow men.

philately, fi•lat'e•li, *n.* [Fr. *philatélie*, a ridiculous compound of Gr. *philos*, loving, and *ateleia*, exemption from taxation.] The practice of collecting all sorts of postage stamps.—**philatelist,** fi•lat'e•list, *n.*

philharmonic, fil•här•mon'ik, *a.* [Gr. *philos*, loving, and *harmonia*, harmony.] Loving music, hence, referring to musical societies and their concerts. —*n.* A musical organization.

philhellenist, fil•hel'len•ist, *n.* [Fr. *philhellène*, from Gr. *philos*, loving, and *Hellen*, a Greek.] A friend of Greece; one who supports the cause and interests of the Greeks (Hellenes); one who supported them in their successful struggle with the Turks for independence.—**philhellenic,** fil•hel•len'ik, *a.* Loving the Greeks.—**philhellenism,** fil•hel'len•izm, *n.* The principles of the philhellenists.

Philippian, fi•lip'i•an, *n.* A native or inhabitant of Philippi, a city of ancient Macedonia ('the Epistle of Paul to the *Philippians*').

Philippic, fi•lip'ik, *n.* One of a series of orations delivered by Demosthenes, the Grecian orator, against *Philip*, king of Macedon; [*not cap.*] any discourse full of acrimonious invective.

Philippine, fil'i•pēn, *a.* [Sp. *Filipino.*] Of the Philippine Islands.

Philistine, fi•lis'tin or fil'is•tin, *n.* An inhabitant of *Philistia*, now a portion of Syria; the English form of *Philister*, a term applied by German students to any one who has not been trained in a university; hence, a matter-of-fact, commonplace person deficient in liberal culture and large intelligence, and so wanting in sentiment and taste; a person of narrow views; a prosaic, practical man.—**Philistinism,** fil'is•tin•izm, *n.* Manners or modes of thinking of Philistines.

philodendron, fil•o•den'dron, *n.* [N.L. from Gr. *philodendros*, loving trees.] A climbing plant cultivated for its showy heart-shaped leaves.

philogyny, fi•loj'i•ni, *n.* [Gr. *philos*, loving, and *gynē*, a woman.] Fondness for women; uxoriousness.

philology, fi•lol'o•ji, *n.* [Gr. *philologia*, from *phileō*, to love, and *logos*, a word.] The study of language and literature; the study of languages in connection with the whole moral and intellectual action of the peoples using them; the study of the classical languages, literature, and history; but the most common meaning now is the science of language; linguistic science; linguistics: often expressed by the qualified title of *comparative philology.*—**philologist, philologer, philologian,** fi•lol'o•jist, fi•lol'o•jėr, fil•o•lō'ji•an, *n.* One versed in philology, or the study of language in a scientific manner.—**philological, philologic,** fil•o•loj'i•kal, fil•o•loj'ik, *a.* Pertaining to philology.

philomel, fil'o•mel, *n.* [From *Philomela*, daughter of Pandion, king of Athens, who was changed into a nightingale.] The poetic name of the nightingale.

philoprogenitiveness, fil'o•prō•jen"i•tiv•nes, *n.* [Gr. *philos*, fond, and E. *progeny.*] The love of offspring, a term used chiefly by phrenologists.

philosopher, fi•los'o•fėr, *n.* [Gr. *philosophos*—*philos*, loving, and *sophos*, wise.] A person versed in or devoted to philosophy; one who devotes himself to the study of moral or intellectual science; one who conforms his life to the principles of philosophy; one who lives according to reason or the rules of practical wisdom.—*Philosophers' stone*, a stone or preparation which the alchemists formerly sought, as the instrument of converting the baser metals into pure gold.—**philosophical, philosophic,** fil•o•sof'i•kal, fil•o•sof'ik, *a.* Pertaining, suitable, or according to philosophy; characterized or constituted by philosophy; proceeding from philosophy; characteristic of a practical philosopher; based on the rules of practical wisdom; calm; cool; temperate.—**philosophically,** fil•o•sof'i•kal•li, *adv.* In a philosophical manner. —**philosophism,** fi•los'of•izm, *n.* [Fr. *philosophisme.*] Spurious or would-be philosophy; the affectation of philosophy.—**philosophize,** fi•los'o•fīz, *v.i.*—*philosophized, philosophizing.* To reason like a philosopher; to form or attempt to form a philosophical system or theory.—**philosophizer,** fi•los'o•fī•zėr, *n.* One who philosophizes.—**philosophy,** fi•los'o•fi, *n.* [Gr. *philosophia*, lit. love of wisdom, from *philos*, love, and *sophia*, wisdom.] The science which aims at an explanation of all the phenomena of the universe by ultimate causes; the knowledge of phenomena as explained by, and resolved into, causes and reasons, powers and laws; a particular philosophical system or theory; the calm and unexcitable state of mind of the wise man; practical wisdom; course of studies for the degree of 'Doctor of Philosophy' in Germany or elsewhere.—*Moral philosophy*. See ETHICS.—*Mental philosophy*. See METAPHYSICS.—*Natural philosophy*. See PHYSICS.

philter, philtre, fil'tėr, *n.* [Fr. *philtre*, L. *philtrum*, from Gr. *philtron*, from *philos*, loving.] A potion supposed by the ancients, and even by the ignorant of the present day, to have the power of exciting love.—*v.t.*—*philtered, philtred*; *philtering, philtring*. To impregnate with a love potion; to administer a potion to.

phiz, fiz, *n.* [A contr. of *physiognomy*.] The face or visage. (*Humorous.*)

phlebitis, fle•bī'tis, *n.* [Gr. *phleps, phlebos*, a vein, and *-itis*, implying inflammation.] Inflammation of the inner membrane of a vein.—**phlebotomy,** fli•bot'o•mi, *n.* [Gr. *phlebotomia—phleps, phlebos*, and *tomē*, a cutting.] The act or practice of opening a vein for letting blood.—**phlebotomist,** fli•bot'o•mist, *n.* One that opens a vein for letting blood; a bloodletter. — **phlebotomize,** fli•bot'o•mīz, *v.t.*—*phlebotomized, phlebotomizing*. To let blood from; to bleed by opening a vein.

phlegm, flem, *n.* [Gr. *phlegma, phlegmatos*, a slimy humor, from *phlegō*, to burn. FLAME.] The thick viscid matter secreted in the digestive and respiratory passages, and discharged by coughing or vomiting; bronchial mucus; *fig.* coldness; sluggishness; indifference.—**phlegmatic, phlegmatical,** fleg•mat'ik, fleg•mat'i•kal, *a.* [Gr. *phlegmatikos*.] Abounding in phlegm; generating phlegm; cold or sluggish in temperament; not easily excited into action or passion; not mercurial or lively.—**phlegmatically,** fleg•mat'i•kal•li, *adv.* In a phlegmatic manner; coldly; heavily.

phloem, flō'em, *n.* [Gr. *phloios*, bark.] *Bot.* the liber or bast tissue in plants.

phlogiston, flo•jis'ton, *n.* [Gr. *phlogistos*, burnt, from *phlogizō*, to burn, from *phlegō*, to burn.] According to an obsolete theory, the supposed principle of inflammability; a hypothetical element which was thought to be pure fire fixed in combustible bodies.—**phlogistic,** flo•jis'tik, *a.* Pertaining to phlogiston; *med.* inflammatory.

phlox, floks, *n.* [Gr. *phlox*, a flame, from the appearance of the flowers.] A North American genus of plants, with red, purple, or white flowers, cultivated in gardens.

phlyctena, phlyctaena, flik•tē'na, *n.* [Gr. *phlyktaina*.] A kind of watery pustule on the skin.

phobia, fō'bi•a, *n.* [Gr. *phobos*, fear.] Any persistent, morbid fear or dread. —**phobic,** fō'bic, *a.*

phocine, fō'sīn, *a.* Pertaining to the seals.

phoebe, fē'bē, *n.* [Imitative.] Any of the small American flycatchers (genus *Sayornis*).

Phoebus, fē'bus, *n.* [Gr. *Phoibos*, lit. the brilliant one.] A name of Apollo, often used in the same sense as Sol, the sun.

Phoenician, fē•nish'i•an, *a.* Pertaining to Phoenicia.—*n.* A native of ancient Phoenicia, the region between Lebanon and the Mediterranean; the language of the Phoenicians, an extinct Semitic tongue, akin to Hebrew.

phoenix, fē'niks, *n.* [Gr. *phoinix*.] A bird of ancient legend said to be the only one of its kind and to live 500 or 600 years, at the end of which it built for itself a funeral pile, lighted it with the fanning of its wings, and rose again from its ashes; hence, an emblem of immortality; a paragon; a person of singular distinction or beauty.

phonation, fō•nā'shon, *n.* [Gr. *phōnē*, voice.] The act of uttering vocal sounds.

phonautograph, fō•nạ'to•graf, *n.* [Gr. *phōnē*, sound, *auto*, self, and *graphō*, to write.] An instrument for automatically showing sound vibrations by waved lines.

phone, fōn. Short for *Telephone*: used as noun and verb.

phoneme, fō'nēm, *n.* **[Fr. *phonème*, from Gr. *phōnēma*, sound.] In a language, the smallest sound unit that distinguishes one utterance from another.—phonemic,** fō•nē'mik, ***a.*—phonemics,** fō•nē'miks, ***n.* The analysis of a language by a study of its phonemes.**

phonetic, phonetical, fo•net'ik, fo•net'i•kal, *a.* [Gr. *phōnetikos*, from *phōnē*, voice, sound.] Pertaining to the voice; pertaining to the representation of sounds; representing sounds.—*Phonetic spelling*, a system which aims at spelling words precisely according to their sound, and not in the loose manner in which English is spelled.—**phonetically,** fo•net'i•kal•li, *adv.* In a phonetic manner.—**phonetics,** fo•net'iks, *n.* The doctrine of sounds; the science which treats of the sounds of the human voice, and the art of representing them by writing.—**phonic,** fō'nik, *a.* Pertaining to sound.—**phonics,** fō'niks, *n.* The doctrine or science of sounds; phonetics.

phonograph, fō'no•graf, *n.* [Gr. *phōnē*, sound, and *graphō*, to write.] A type or character for expressing a sound; a character used in phonography; an instrument by means of which sounds can be permanently registered, and afterward mechanically reproduced almost in the original tones from the register.—**phonogram,** fō'no•gram, *n.* A sound as reproduced by the phonograph.—**phonographer,** fō•nog'raf•ėr, *n.* One versed in phonography; one who uses or is skilled in the use of the phonograph.—**phonographic,** fō•no•graf'ik, *a.* Pertaining to or based upon phonography; pertaining to the phonograph. —**phonographically,** fō•no•graf'i•kal•li, *adv.* In a phonographic manner.—**phonography,** fō•nog'ra•fi, *n.* The description of sounds; the representation of sounds by characters, each of which represents one sound, and always the same sound; phonetic shorthand; the art of using the phonograph.

phonolite, fō'no•līt, *n.* [Gr. *phōnē*, sound, and *lithos*, stone.] Same as *Clinkstone*.

phonology, fō•nol'o•ji, *n.* [Gr. *phōnē*, sound, voice, and *logos*, discourse.] The science or doctrine of the elementary sounds uttered by the human voice; phonetics.—**phonologic, phonological,** fō•no•loj'ik, fō•no•loj'i•kal, *a.* Pertaining to phonology.—**phonologist,** fō•nol'o•jist, *n.* One versed in phonology.

phonometer, fō•nom'et•ėr, *n.* [Gr. *phōnē*, sound, *metron*, a measure.] An instrument for ascertaining the number of vibrations of a given sound in a given time.

phonoscope, fō'no•skōp, *n.* [Gr. *phōnē*, a voice, a sound, and *skopeō*, to view.] An instrument for producing figures of light from vibrations of sound by means of an electric current.

phonotypy, fō•no•tī'pi, *n.* [Gr. *phōnē*, sound, and *typos*, type.] A method of representing each of the sounds of speech by a distinct printed character or letter; phonetic printing.—**phonotype,** fō'no•tīp, *n.* A type or character used in phonetic printing. —**phonotypic,** fō•no•tip'ik, *a.*

phony, fō'nē, ***a.* [Origin unknown.] Not genuine; pretentious.**

phosgene, fos'jēn, ***n.* [Gr. *phōs*, light, and root *gen*, to produce.] A heavy, poisonous gas with a nauseating, choking smell.**

phosphorus, fos'for•us, ***n.* [L. from Gr. *phosophoros*, light-bearing.] A solid, nonmetallic, glowing material. Symbol, P; at. no., 15; at. wt., 30.9738.—phosphate,** fos'fāt, ***n.* A salt of phosphoric acid; a carbonated drink.—phosphoresce,** fos•fo•res', ***v.i.*—*phosphoresced, phosphorescing*. To emit a faint, heatless light. —phosphorescence,** fos•fo•res'ens, ***n.* The state or quality of being phosphorescent; the property which certain bodies possess of becoming luminous.—phosphorescent,** fos•fo•res'ent, ***a.* Shining by phosphorescence.—phosphoric,** fos•for'ik, ***a.* Pertaining to, obtained from, or resembling phosphorus.—phosphoric acid, *n.* An oxygen acid of phosphorus.—phosphorous,** fos'for•us, ***a.* Of phosphorus.—phosphorous acid, *n.* A crystalline acid H_3PO_3 from which phosphates are derived.**

photics, fō'tiks, *n.* [Gr. *phōs*, *phōtos*, light.] That department of science which treats of light.

photo, fō'to, ***n.* Short for *photograph*** (colloq.).

photochemistry, fō•to•kem'ist•ri, *n.* [Gr. *phōs*, *phōtos*, light, and E. *chemistry*.] That branch of chemistry which treats of the chemical action of light, especially of solar light.—**photochemical,** fō•to•kem'i•kal, *a.* Pertaining to the chemical action of light.

photochromy, fō•to•krō'mi, *n.* [Gr. *phōs*, *phōtos*, light, and *chrōma*, color.]

The art or operation of reproducing colors by photography.

photoelectric cell, fō'tō•i•lek"trik sel, *n.* A vacuum tube in which the action of light produces, or changes the strength of, electric current.

photoelectrotype, *n.* A process in which a photographic picture is produced in relief so as to afford, by electric deposition, a matrix for a cast, from which impressions in ink may be obtained.

photoengraving, fō'tō•en•grā"ving, *n.* [Combining form *photo* and *engraving.*] A photographic engraving process in which the printing surface is in relief; a print made by this process.

photoflash, fō"tō•flash', *n.* [Combining form *photo* and *flash.*] An electrically operated flash lamp.

photoflood, fō"tō•flood', *n.* [Combining form *photo* and *flood.*] A high-voltage electric lamp of intense sustained brilliance used in photography.

photogene, fō'to•jēn, *n.* [Gr. *phōs, phōtos,* light, and root *gen,* to produce.] A more or less continued impression or picture on the retina.

photogenic, fō'tō•gen"ik, *a.* [Gr. *phōs, phōtos,* light, and combining form *genic,* meaning suitable for reproduction.] Suitable for photographing; producing or generating light; *biol.* phosphorescent.

photography, fo•tog'ra•fi, *n.* [Gr. *phōs, phōtos,* light, and *graphō,* to describe.] The art of obtaining accurate representations of scenes and objects by means of the action of light on substances treated with certain chemicals.—**photograph,** fō'-to•graf, *n.* A picture obtained by means of photography.—*v.t.* To take a picture with a camera.—*v.i.* To practice photography.—**photographer,** fo•tog'raf•ėr, *n.*—**photographic,** fō•to•graf'ik,—**photographically,** fō•to•graf'i•kal•li, *adv.*

photogravure, fō'to•grav•ūr", *n.* [Gr. *phōs, phōtos,* light, Fr. *gravure,* engraving.] A process by which an engraving is produced on a metal plate by photographic methods.

photolithograph, fō'to•lith"o•graf, *n.* [Combining form *photo* and *lithograph.*] A print reproduced by any photolithography process.—**photolithography,** fō'to•li•thog"ra•fi, *n.* A mode of lithographing in which a photograph is transferred to a thin metal plate.

photometer, fō•tom'et•ėr, *n.* [Gr. *phōs, phōtos,* light, and *metron,* measure.] An instrument intended to measure the comparative intensity of different lights.—**photometric, photometrical,** fo•to•met'rik, fō•to•-met'ri•kal, *a.* Pertaining to or made by a photometer.—**photometry,** fō•-tom'et•ri, *n.* The measurement of the relative amounts of light emitted by different sources.

photomicrography, *n.* [Gr. *phōs, phōtos,* light, *mikros,* small, and *graphō,* to write.] The art or process of photographing minute objects when magnified by means of the microscope.

photon, fō'ton, *n.* [Combining form *photo* and Gr. suffix *on.*] *Phys.* a quantum of light energy.

photo-offset, fō'tō-of"set, *n.* [Combining form *photo* and *offset.*] A printing process in which a photographic image of design or type is used in the preparation of a plate for offset printing.

photophobia, fō•to•fō'bi•a, *n.* [Gr. *phōs, phōtos,* light, and *phobia,* dread.] An intolerance or dread of light.

photoplay, fō'to•plā, *n.* A play reproduced by motion pictures; a motion picture.

photosensitive, fō•to•sen'si•tiv, *a.* Readily affected or changed by light or other radiant energy.

photospectroscope, fō•to•spek'tro•-skōp, *n.* An instrument for photographing spectra.

photosphere, fō'to•sfēr, *n.* [Gr. *phōs, phōtos,* light, and E. *sphere.*] An envelope of light; the luminous envelope, supposed to consist of incandescent matter, surrounding the sun.

photosynthesis, fō'to•sin"the•sis, *n.* [Gr. *phōs, phōtos,* light, *synthĕsis,* a putting together.] In green plants, the utilization by protoplasm of the energy of light, aided by the green pigment chlorophyll, for building up organic matter from water and carbonic acid gas.

phototropism, fō•tot'rō•pizm, *n.* [Combining form *photo* and *tropism,* from Gr. *tropē,* a turning.] A tropism in which light is the stimulant.

phototype, fō'to•tīp, *n.* [Gr. *phōs, phōtos,* light, and *typos,* a type.] A plate produced from a photograph by a peculiar process, as by photolithography, and from which copies can be printed.—**phototypy,** fō•to•-tī'pi, *n.* The art or process of producing phototypes.

photozincography, *n.* The process of printing from a prepared zinc plate on which a photograph has been taken.

phrase, frāz, *n.* [Gr. *phrasis,* a phrase (seen also in *periphrasis, paraphrase*), from *phrazō,* I speak.] A brief expression; two or more words forming a complete expression by themselves or being a portion of a sentence; a peculiar or characteristic expression; an idiom; the manner or style in which a person expresses himself; diction; *music,* a short part of a composition usually occupying a distinct rhythmical period of from two to four bars.—*v.t.*—*phrased, phrasing.* To call; to style; to express.—**phraseogram,** frā'zē•-o•gram, *n.* A combination of shorthand characters to represent a phrase or sentence.—**phraseological,** frā'zē•o•loj"i•kal, *a.* Pertaining to phraseology; exhibiting idiomatic phrases.—**phraseologist,** frā•zē•ol'-o•jist, *n.* A stickler for a particular form of words or phraseology; a coiner of phrases. — **phraseology,** frā•zē•ol'o•ji, *n.* Manner of expression; peculiar words or phrases used in a sentence; diction; a collection of phrases in a language. ∴ Syn. under DICTION.

phrenetic, fre•net'ik, *a.* [L. *phreneticus,* from Gr. *phrenetikos,* suffering from *phrenitis* or inflammation of the brain, from *phrēn,* the mind, the midriff. FRANTIC.] Having the mind disordered; frantic; frenetic.—*n.* A frantic or frenzied person; one whose mind is disordered.—**phrenetically,** fre•net'i•kal•li, *adv.* In a phrenetic manner.—**phrenic,** fren'ik, *a.* [From Gr. *phrēn,* in sense of diaphragm.] *Anat.* belonging to the diaphragm.—**phrenitis,** fre•nī'tis, *n.* [Gr., from *phrēn,* the mind, and *-itis,* term. denoting inflammation.] *Med.* an inflammation of the brain; delirium; frenzy.

phrenology, fre•nol'o•ji, *n.* [Gr. *phrēn, phrenos,* the mind, and *logos,* discourse.] A doctrine which professes to found a philosophy of the human mind upon a presumed knowledge of the functions of different portions of the brain obtained by comparing their relative forms and magnitudes in different individuals with the propensities and intellectual powers which these individuals are found respectively to possess.—**phrenologic, phrenological,** fren•o•loj'ik, fren•o•loj'i•kal, *a.* Pertaining to phrenology.—**phrenologist,** fre•nol'o•jist, *n.* One versed in phrenology.

Phrygian, frij'i•an, *a.* [From *Phrygia,* in Asia Minor.] Pertaining to Phrygia or to the Phrygians.—*Phrygian cap,* the red cap of liberty worn by the leaders during the first French Republic.—*Phrygian mode,* one of the modes in ancient music.

phthalic acid, thal'ik, fthal'ik, one of three isomeric benzene-dicarboxylic acids, the most important of which is used in making synthetic dyes, resins, etc.

phthisis, thī'sis, fthī'sis, *n.* [L. from Gr. *phthinō,* decay.] *Med.* a wasting away; pulmonary tuberculosis.

phycology, fī•kol'o•ji, *n.* [Gr. *phykos,* and *logos.*] That department of botany which treats of the algae or seaweeds.

phylactery, fi•lak'tėr•i, *n.* [Gr. *phylaktērion,* from *phylassō,* to defend or guard.] An amulet worn as a preservative from danger or disease among the Jews; a strip of parchment inscribed with certain texts from the Old Testament, enclosed within a small leather case, and fastened on the forehead or on the left arm near the region of the heart.

phyletic, fī•let'ik, *a.* [Gr. *phylē,* a tribe or race.] Pertaining to a race or tribe: applied especially in connection with the development of animal tribes.

phylloclade, fil'lō•klād, *n.* [Gr. *phyllon,* a leaf, *klados,* a branch.] A CLADODE (which see).

phyllode, fil'ōd, *n.* [Gr. *phyllon,* a leaf.] A flattened leaf stalk which performs the functions of a leaf blade.

phyllodium, fil•ō'di•um, *n.* [Gr. *phyllon,* a leaf, and *eidos,* likeness.] *Bot.* a leafstalk developed into a flattened expansion like a leaf.—**phylloid,** fil'oid, *a.* Leaf-like; shaped like a leaf.—**phyllopod,** fil'o•pod, *n.* [Gr. *phyllon,* and *pous, podos,* a foot.] One of those crustaceans that have limbs of leaf-like form for swimming.—**phyllotaxis, phyllotaxy,** fil'o•tak•sis, fil'o•tak•si, *n.* [Gr. *taxis,* order.] *Bot.* the arrangement of the leaves on the axis or stem.—**phylloxera,** fil•ok•sē'ra, *n.* [Gr. *phyllon,* a leaf, and *xēros,* parched.] An insect which infests the leaves and roots of the oak, vine, etc., one species of which has caused immense damage in some wine-producing countries.

phylogenesis, phylogeny, fī•lo•jen'e•sis, fī•loj'e•ni, *n.* [Gr. *phylē,* a tribe, and *genesis,* root *gen,* to produce.] *Biol.* the origin and history of races or types of animal forms.—**phylogenetic,** fī'lo•je•net''ik, *a.* Pertaining to phylogenesis or phylogeny, or the race history of an animal.

phylum, fī'lum, *n.* pl. **phyla.** [Gr. *phylon,* a tribe.] One of the grand subdivisions of the animal or vegetable kingdom.

physic, fiz'ik, *n.* [Gr. *physikos,* pertaining to nature, natural, from *physis,* nature, from *phyō,* to bring forth, to spring up; cog. with Skr. *bhû,* to be; E. to *be.* BE.] The science or knowledge of medicine; the art of healing; a medicine, popularly a medicine that purges; a purge; a cathartic.—*Physic garden,* an old name for a botanic garden.—*Physic nut,* the seed of one or two tropical plants (genus *Jatropha*), having strong purgative and emetic properties.—*v.t.*—*physicked, physicking.* To treat with physic; to purge with a cathartic; to remedy.—**physical,** fiz'i•kal, *a.* Pertaining to nature; relating to what is material and perceived by the senses; pertaining to the material part or structure of an organized being, as opposed to what is mental or moral (*physical* force); material (the *physical* world); pertaining to physics or natural philosophy.—*Physical geography.* See GEOGRAPHY.—*Physical science.* PHYSICS.—**physically,** fiz'i•kal•li, *adv.* In a physical manner; as regards the material world; as regards the bodily constitution.—**physician,** fi•zish'an, *n.* A person skilled in the art of healing; one whose profession is to prescribe remedies for diseases.—**physicist,** fiz'i•sist, *n.* One skilled in physics; a natural philosopher.—**physics,** fiz'iks, *n.* That branch of science which treats of the laws and properties of matter; the department of science that deals with mechanics, dynamics, light, heat, sound, electricity, and magnetism; natural philosophy.

physiognomy, fiz•i•og'no•mi, *n.* [Properly *physiognomony,* from Gr. *physiognōmonia*—*physis,* nature, and *gnōmōn,* one who knows, from stem of *gignōskō,* to know.] The art of discerning the character of the mind from the features of the face; the face or countenance as an index of the mind; particular cast or expression of countenance.—**physiognomic, physiognomical,** fiz'i•og•nom''ik, fiz'i•og•nom''i•kal, *a.* Pertaining to physiognomy.—**physiognomist,** fiz•i•og'no•mist, *n.* One skilled in physiognomy.

physiography, fiz•i•og'ra•fi, *n.* [Gr. *physis,* nature, and *graphō,* to describe.] The science which treats of the earth's physical features, and the causes by which they have been modified, as well as of the climates, life, etc., of the globe; physical geography.—**physiographical,** fiz'i•ō•graf''i•kal, *a.* Pertaining to physiography.

physiology, fiz•i•ol'o•ji, *n.* [Fr. *physiologie,* Gr. *physiologia*—*physics,* nature, and *logos,* discourse.] That science which has for its aim the study and elucidation of the phenomena of life in animals and plants.—**physiologic, physiological,** fiz'i•o•loj''ik, fiz'i•o•loj''i•kal, *a.*Pertaining to physiology.—*Physiological selection,* partial or complete sterility of varying forms with the parent stock; a suggested cause of the isolation necessary for evolution of new species.—**physiologically,** fiz'i•o•loj''i•kal•li, *adv.* According to the principles of physiology.—**physiologist,** fiz•i•ol'o•jist, *n.* One who is versed in or who treats of physiology.

physique, fi•zēk', *n.* [Fr.] A person's physical or bodily structure or constitution.

phytogenesis, phytogeny, fī•to•jen'ē•sis, fī•toj'e•ni, *n.* [Gr. *phyton,* a plant, and *genesis.*] The doctrine of the generation of plants.

phytogeography, fī'to•jē•og''ra•fi, *n.* [Gr. *phyton,* a plant, and E. *geography.*] The geography or geographical distribution of plants.

phytography, fī•tog'ra•fi, *n.* [Gr. *phyton,* a plant, and *graphē,* description.] That branch of botany which concerns itself with the rules to be observed in describing and naming plants.

phytology, fī•tol'o•ji, *n.* [Gr. *phyton,* a plant, *logos,* discourse.] The science of plants, a name sometimes used as equivalent to botany.—**phytological,** fī•to•loj'i•kal, *a.* Relating to phytology.

phytophagous, fī•tof'a•gus, *a.* [Gr. *phyton,* a plant, *phagō,* to eat.] Eating or subsisting on plants.

pi, pī, pē, *n.* [Gr.] The 16th letter of the Greek alphabet; the symbol used to denote the ratio of the circumference of a circle to its diameter, approximate value 3.14159265.

pi, pī, *n* [Origin unknown.] *Print.* disarranged or mixed type.—*v.t.* To disarrange or mix type; to throw into confusion.

piacular, pī•ak'ū•lėr, *a.* [L. *piacularis,* from *piaculum,* expiation, from *pio,* to expiate, from *pius,* pious.] Expiatory; pertaining to expiation.

pia mater, pī'a mā'tėr, *n.* [L., lit. pious mother.] *Anat.* a vascular membrane investing the whole surface of the brain. See DURA MATER.

piano, pi•ä'nō, *a.* [It., soft, smooth, from L. *planus,* plain.] *Mus.* soft; a direction to execute a passage softly or with diminished volume of tone.—*n.* (pi•an'ō). A musical metal-stringed instrument with a keyboard, by means of which the metal strings are struck by hammers.—**pianoforte,** pi•an'ō•fort, *n.* [It. *piano,* soft, smooth, and *forte* (L. *fortis*), strong.] A piano.—**pianissimo,** pi•a•nis'i•mō, [It. superl. of *piano,* soft.] *Mus.* very soft; a direction to execute a passage in the softest manner.—**pianist,** pi•an'ist, pi'an•ist, *n.* A performer on the piano.

piassava, pi•a•sä'vä, *n.* [Pg. *piaçaba.*] The fiber of a Brazilian palm tree, extensively used in making brooms and brushes for street sweeping.

piaster, piastre, pi•as'tėr, *n.* [Fr. *piastre,* It. and Sp. *piastra,* a thin plate of metal, a dollar, from L.L. *plastra,* L. *emplastrum,* Gr. *emplastron,* a plaster. PLASTER.] A denomination of money of various countries, especially Egypt and Turkey.

piazza, pi•az'za, *n.* [It. *piazza,* open place, square, market place. PLACE.] A rectangular open space surrounded by buildings or colonnades.

pibroch, pē'broch, *n.* [Gael. *piobaireachd,* from *piobair,* a piper, *piob,* a pipe.] Martial variations performed on the bagpipe, in the Highlands of Scotland.

pica, pī'ka, *n.* [L. *litera picata,* pitch-black letter.] Printing type 12 points in size; a standard printing measure, about $\frac{1}{6}$ inch.

picador, pik'a•dor, *n.* [Sp., from *pica,* a pike or lance.] One of the horsemen armed with a lance who excites and irritates the bull in a bullfight.

picaroon, pik•a•rön', *n.* [Sp. *picaron,* augmentative of *picaro,* a rogue.] A rogue or cheat; one that lives by his wits; an adventurer.—**picaresque,** pik•a•resk', *a.* [Fr.] Pertaining to rogues or picaroons; describing the fortunes of rogues.

picayune, pik•a•yūn', *n.* [Fr. *picaillon.*] A coin of small value, formerly used in Louisiana; anything of little value.

piccalilli, pik'a•lil•li, *n.* An imitation Indian pickle of various vegetables, with pungent spices.

piccolo, pik'ko•lō, *n.* [It. *piccolo,* small.] A small flute, the tones of which range an octave higher than those of the ordinary orchestral flute; an octave flute.

pice, pīs, *n. sing.* and *pl.* Small East Indian coin.

piceous, pis'i•us, *a.* [L. *piceus,* from *pix, picis,* pitch.] Of or belonging to pitch; black as pitch.

pick, pik, *v.t.* [Allied to W. *pig,* a point, a pike; Gael. *pioc, piocaid,* a pick, a pickax; *pike, peak, peck, beak;* same root also in *spike.*] To strike at with anything pointed; to peck at, as a bird, with its bill; to pierce; to clean by removing with the teeth, fingers, claws, or a small instrument, something that adheres (to *pick* a bone, the teeth); to separate from other things; to select; to choose (to *pick* the best men); to pluck; to gather, as fruit or things growing; to gather up here and there; to collect (often with *up*); to snatch thievishly (a purse); to steal the contents of (to *pick* a pocket).—*To pick off*, to separate by the fingers or a small instrument; to separate by a sharp sudden movement (to *pick off* a leaf); to aim at and kill.—*To pick out*, to draw out by anything pointed; to select from a number or quantity; to relieve with figures or lines of a different color.—*To pick up*, to take up with the fingers, or otherwise to snatch; to obtain by repeated effort or casually (to *pick up* a livelihood).—*To pick a hole in one's coat*, to find fault with one.—*To pick a lock*, to open it with some instrument other than the key.—*To pick oakum*, to make oakum by untwisting old ropes.—*To pick a quarrel*, to quarrel intentionally with a person.—*v.i.* To eat slowly or by morsels; to nibble; to pilfer.—*To pick up*, to acquire fresh strength, vigor, or the like. (*Colloq.*)—*n.* A heavy sharp-pointed iron tool, with a wooden handle, used for loosening hard earth, stones, etc., in digging, ditching, etc.; a sharp hammer used in dressing stones.—**pickax,** pik′aks, *n.* A tool with a point at one end and a blade at the other; also, simply a pick.—**picker,** pik′ėr, *n.*—**pickpocket,** pik′pok•et, *n.* One who steals from others' pockets.—**pickup,** pik′up, *n.* The act of picking up; a small truck.—**pick up,** *v.t.* To lift; to gain by occasional opportunity; to take something into a vehicle; to grasp (meaning); to bring into range of reception (*pick up* a radio signal).

pickaback, pik′a•bak, *a.* or *adv.* [From the older form *pickapack*, a reduplication of *pack.*] On the back or shoulders like a pack. (*Colloq.*)

pickaninny, pik′a•nin•i, *n.* [Sp. *pequeño niño*, little infant.] A Negro or mulatto infant.

pickerel, pik′ėr•el, *n.* [From *pike.*] A name applied to several small fresh-water fishes of the pike family.

picket, pik′et, *n.* [Fr. *piquet*, a dim. of *pique*, a pike. PICK.] A stake sharpened or pointed, used in fortification and encampments; a narrow pointed board; *milit.* a detachment of troops in a camp kept equipped to protect the camp from surprise; a person posted, as by a labor union, before or near a place of business where the workers are on strike; a game at cards.—*v.t.*—*picketed, picketing.* To fortify with pickets or pointed stakes; to fence with narrow pointed boards or pales; to fasten to a picket or stake; to place or post as a guard of observation.

pickle, pik′l, *n.* [D. and L.G. *pekel*, G. *pōkel, bōkel*, brine.] A solution of salt and water in which flesh, fish, or other substance is preserved; brine; vinegar, in which vegetables, fish, oysters, etc., are preserved; a thing preserved in pickle; a state of difficulty; a chemical cleaning solution.—*v.t.*—*pickled, pickling.* To preserve in brine or pickle; to treat with pickle.

picnic, pik′nik, *n.* [Fr. *piquenique.*] A pleasure party, the members of which carry provisions along with them on an excursion to some place in the country; used also adjectively (a *picnic* party).—*v.i.*—*picnicked, picnicking.* To attend or take part in a picnic party.

picot, pē′kō, *n.* [Fr.] One of a series of ornamental loops on a border of lace, ribbon, etc.

picotee, pik•o•tē′, *n.* [Fr. *picotie*, from *Picot de la Perousse*, a French botanist.] A variety of carnation or clove pink, having the dark color only on the edge of the petals.

picric acid, pik′rik as′id, *n. Chem.* a bitter, toxic acid $(NO_2)_3\ C_6H_2OH$ used as a dye and an explosive.

Pict, pikt, *n.* [From *Picti*, the name given them by Latin writers; of uncertain origin.] One of a race of people (probably Celts) who anciently inhabited the northeast of Scotland.—**Pictish,** pik′tish, *a.* Pertaining to the Picts.

pictograph, pik′to•graf, *n.* [L. *pictura*, and *graph.*] An ancient or prehistoric drawing; a record made with pictorial symbols; a symbol in a pictographic system.

picture, pik′chėr, *n.* [L. *pictura*, from *pingo, pictum*, to paint. PAINT.] A painting, drawing, or engraving exhibiting the resemblance of anything; any resemblance or representation, either to the eye or to the mind; a likeness; an image; a representation or description in words.—*Picture hat*, a large-sized hat of the Duchess of Devonshire style; the style seen in the portraits by Sir Joshua Reynolds and Gainsborough.—*Picture house*, the place of entertainment devoted to moving pictures.—*v.t.*—*pictured, picturing.* To draw or paint a resemblance of; to represent pictorially; to bring before the mind's eye; to form an ideal likeness of; to describe in a vivid manner.—**pictorial,** pik•tō′ri•al, *a.* [L. *pictor*, a painter.] Pertaining to pictures; illustrated by pictures; constituting a picture.—**pictorially,** pik•tō′ri•al•li, *adv.* In a pictorial manner; with pictures or engravings.—**picturesque,** pik•chėr•esk′, *a.* Forming or fitted to form a pleasing picture; expressing that peculiar kind of beauty which is agreeable in a picture; abounding with vivid and striking imagery; graphic in style of writing.—*The picturesque*, the quality that renders a scene suitable for making into a good picture.—**picturesquely,** pik•chėr•esk′li, *adv.* In a picturesque manner.—**picturesqueness,** pik•chėr•esk′nes, *n.*

picul, pi′kul, *n.* In China, a weight of 133½ lbs.

piddle, pid′l, *v.i.* [A form of *peddle.*] To deal in trifles; to attend to trivial concerns.

pidgin, pij′in, *n.* [Chin. pronunciation of *business.*] A simplified speech used by persons with different languages; a jargon; originally, an English-based jargon used in Chinese commercial ports.

pie, pī, *n.* [From the Celtic; comp. Ir. *pighe*, a pie.] An article of food consisting of dough baked with something in it or under it.

pie, pī, *n.* [Fr. *pie*, from L. *pica*, a magpie.] The magpie.

piebald, pī′bąld, *a.* [From *pie*, a magpie, and *bald*, spotted with white. BALD.] Having spots or patches of white and black or other color; having patches of various colors; pied; diversified; mongrel.

piece, pēs, *n.* [Fr. *pièce*, Pr. *peza*, It. *pezza*, from L.L. *petium*, a piece, probably from the Celtic: W. *peth*, Armor. *pez*, a piece.] A fragment or part of anything separated from the whole, in any manner (to tear in *pieces*); a part of anything, though not separated or separated only in idea; a portion; a definite quantity or portion of certain things (a *piece* of muslin, a *piece* of work); an artistic or literary composition (a *piece* of poetry or sculpture); a coin (a fourpenny *piece*); a gun or single firearm (a fowling *piece*).—*To work by the piece*, to work by the measure of quantity, and not by the measure of time.—*Of a piece*, of the same sort, as if taken from the same whole; alike.—*A piece of one's mind*, a colloquial phrase for blunt and uncomplimentary statements.—*v.t.*—*pieced, piecing.* To mend by the addition of a piece; to patch; to unite; to join; to cement.—*To piece out*, to extend or enlarge by addition of a piece or pieces.—**piece goods,** *n. pl.* Goods generally sold by the piece, as cottons, shirtings, etc.—**piecemeal,** pēs′mēl, *adv.* [*Piece*, and suffix *-meal*, A.Sax. *maelum*, by parts.] In pieces; by pieces; by little and little in succession.—**piecer,** pēs′ėr, *n.* One that pieces; a boy or girl employed in a spinning factory to join broken threads.—**piecework,** pēs′wėrk, *n.* Work done and paid for by the measure of quantity.

pied, pīd, *a.* [From *pie*, magpie.] Particolored; variegated with spots of different colors; spotted with larger spots than if speckled.

pie plant, pī′plant, *n.* [From its use in pie.] Garden rhubarb.

pier, pēr, *n.* [O.Fr. *pere, piere*, a stone (Fr. *pierre*), from L. and Gr. *petra*, a stone.] *Arch.* the solid parts between openings in a wall, as between doors or windows; the square or other mass or post to which a gate is hung; the solid support from which an arch springs; a large pillar or shaft; one of the supports of the arches of a bridge; a mole or jetty carried out into the sea, serving to protect vessels from the open sea, to form a harbor, etc.; a projecting quay, wharf, or landing-place.—**pier glass,** *n.* A mirror or glass hanging between windows.—**pier table,** *n.* A table placed between windows.

pierce, pērs, *v.t.*—*pierced, piercing.* [Fr. *percer*, to pierce; origin uncertain.] To stab or transfix with a pointed instrument; to penetrate; to force a way into; to affect keenly; to move deeply; to penetrate into, as into a secret or purpose.—*v.i.* To enter, as a pointed instrument; to penetrate.—**piercer,** pēr′sėr, *n.* An instrument that pierces; a person that pierces or perforates; that organ of an insect with which it pierces bodies; the ovipositor.—**piercingly,** pēr′sing•li, *adv.* In a piercing manner.

Pierides, pī•er′i•dēz, *n. pl.* [L.] A name of the Muses, from *Pieria,* where they were first worshiped among the Thracians.—**Pierian,** pī•ē′ri•an, *a.* Belonging to the Pierides.

Pierrot, pē′er•ō, *n.* [Fr. dim. of *Pierre,* Peter.] Itinerant minstrel or vocalist, generally at seaside places, with the dress of a clown in French pantomime.

piety, pī′e•ti, *n.* [L. *pietas,* from *pius,* pious. *Pity* is the same word.] Veneration or reverence of the Supreme Being and love of His character; the exercise of these affections in obedience to His will and devotion to His service; filial reverence; reverence toward parents or friends, with affection and devotion to them.—**pietism,** pī′et•izm, *n.* The principles or practice of the pietists.—**Pietists,** pī′et•ists, *n. pl.* A religious party in Germany who proposed to revive declining piety in the Reformed churches; hence, applied to one who makes a display of strong religious feelings.—**pietistic,** pī•et•is′tik, *a.*

piezoelectricity, pī•ē′zo•e•lek′tris″i•ti, *n.* Electricity created by pressure as from compression along a certain axis of a crystal such as quartz.

piezometer, pī•e•zom′et•ėr, *n.* [Gr. *piezō,* to press, *metron,* measure.] An instrument for measuring compressibility.

piffle, pif′l, *n.* [Origin doubtful.] Silly spoken or written matter; trash.

pig, pig, *n.* [A.Sax. *pecga,* akin to D. *big, bigge,* L.G. *bigge,* a pig.] A young swine, male or female; a swine in general; an oblong mass of unforged iron, lead, or other metal. ∴ In the process of smelting, the principal channel along which the metal in a state of fusion runs, when let out of the furnace, is called the *sow,* and the lateral channels or molds are denominated *pigs,* whence the iron in this state is called *pig iron.*—*v.t.* or *i.*—*pigged, pigging.* To bring forth pigs; to act as pigs; to live or huddle as pigs.—**piggery,** pig′ėr•i, *n.* A place with sties and other accompaniments allotted to pigs.—**piggish,** pig′ish, *a.* Relating to or like pigs; swinish.——**pigheaded,** pig′hed•ed, *a.* Obstinate.—**pig iron,** *n.* Iron, direct from a furnace, that is to be refined.—**pigskin,** pig′skin, *n. Sports,* a football. —**pigsty,** *n.* A sty or pen for pigs.—**pigtail,** pig′tāl, *n.* The tail of a pig; the hair of the head tied behind in a tail; tobacco twisted into a long rope.

pigeon, pij′on, *n.* [Fr. *pigeon,* from L. *pipio, pipionis,* a chirping bird, from *pipio*; to peep, to chirp.] A common bird of the family Columbidae; a young woman; an easy mark or a dupe.—**pigeonhole,** *n.* One of the holes in a dovecot where the pigeons go in and out; a little compartment or division in a case for papers.—*v.t.* To lay aside; to classify.—**pigeon-toed,** *a.* Having the toes turned inward.

piggin, pig′in, *n.* [Gael. *pigean,* Ir. *pigin,* an earthen pitcher.] A small wooden vessel with an erect handle.

pigment, pig′ment, *n.* [L. *pigmentum,* from the stem of *pingo,* to paint. PAINT.] Paint; any substance used by painters, dyers, etc., to impart colors to bodies; the coloring matter found in animal and plant bodies.—*v.t.* and *i.* To color or tint; to become colored or tinted.—**pigmentation,** pig•men•tā′shon, *n.* A deposit of pigment; coloration.

Pigmy, pig′mi, *n.* and *a.* See PYGMY.

pika, pī′ka, *n.* A species of rodent allied to the hares that has a voice like that of a quail.

pike, pīk, *n.* [Fr. *pique,* a pike; closely allied to *pick, peck.* PICK.] A military weapon, consisting of a long wooden shaft or staff with a flat pointed steel head; a pointed peak, hill, or mountain summit; a fresh-water fish, so named from its long shape or from the form of its snout; a turnpike, or road on which a toll is charged; also, the toll; any main highway.—**pikeman,** pīk′man, *n.* A soldier armed with a pike.—**pikestaff,** *n.* The shaft of a pike; a lòng staff with a sharp pike in the lower end of it.

piker, pī′ker, *n.* One who gambles, speculates, etc., in a small, cautious way.

pilaster, pi•las′tėr, *n.* [Fr. *pilastre,* It. *pilastro,* from L. *pila,* a pile.] A square pillar projecting from a pier or from a wall to a short distance.

pilau, pilaw, pi′la̤, *n.* [Per. and Turk.] An oriental dish consisting of rice cooked with fat, butter, or meat.

pilchard, pil′chėrd, *n.* [Probably a Cornish word; comp. Ir. *pilseir,* a pilchard; W. *pilcod,* a minnow.] A fish resembling the herring, but smaller.

pile, pīl, *n.* [Partly A.Sax. *pil,* a heap, a stake, partly from Fr. *pile,* a heap, a pier, a voltaic pile; both from L. *pila,* a pier or mole.] A heap; a mass or collection of things in an elevated form; a collection of combustibles arranged for burning a dead body; a large building or mass of buildings; an edifice; *elect.* a series of plates of two dissimilar metals, such as copper and zinc, laid one above the other alternately, with cloth between each pair, moistened with an acid solution, for producing a current of electricity; a galvanic or voltaic battery; a large amount of money; a fortune; an atomic reactor; a large amount; a heraldic figure resembling a wedge. —*v.t.*—*piled, piling.* To lay or throw into a heap; to heap up; to accumulate; to drive piles into; to furnish or support with piles.—*To pile arms,* to place three muskets so that the butts remain firm upon the ground, and the muzzles close together.—**pile driver,** *n.* A workman whose occupation is to drive piles; a machine or contrivance worked by steam for driving in piles.

pile, pīl, *n.* [A.S. *pil,* stake.] A supporting beam; a post driven into the ground to support a structure.

pile, pīl, *n.* [O.Fr. *peil,* from L. *pilus,* hair.] A hair; a fiber of wool, cotton, etc.; the nap or fine hairy or woolly surface of cloth; also, the shag or hair on the skins of animals.—**pileous,** pil′ē•us, *a.* Pertaining to the hair; covered by or consisting of hair; pilose.

pileate, pileated, pī′lē•āt, pī′lē•ā•ted, *a.* [From L. *pileus,* a cap.] Having the form of a cap or cover for the head; *bot.* having a cap or lid like the cap of a mushroom.

pileous, pī′lē•us, *a.* See PILE (nap).

piles, pīlz, *n. pl.* [L. *pila,* a ball.] The dilatation of veins of the lower part of the rectum near the anus, the veins often forming bleeding enlargement and tumors; hemorrhoids.

pileus, pī′lē•us, *n.* [L., a cap.] *Bot.* the cap or top of a mushroom, supported by the stalk.

pilfer, pil′fėr, *v.i.* [O.Fr. *pelfrer,* to plunder, from *pelfre,* goods, spoil, booty. PELF.] To steal in small quantities; to practice petty theft.—*v.t.* To steal or gain by petty theft; to filch.—**pilferer,** pil′fėr•ėr, *n.* One who pilfers.

pilgarlic, pil•gär′lik, *n.* [*Peeled garlic.*] A poor bald-headed creature.

pilgrim, pil′grim, *n.* [Same as D. *pelgrim,* Dan. *pilegrim,* Icel. *pilagrimr,* Fr. *pelegrin,* from L. *peregrinus,* a traveler, a foreigner—*per,* through, and *ager,* land (as in *agriculture*).] A wanderer; a traveler; one that travels to a distance from his own country to visit a shrine or holy place, or to pay his devotion to the remains of dead saints; [cap.] one of the colonists from England who founded the colony at Plymouth, Massachusetts, in 1620, which was the first permanent New England settlement of Europeans.—**pilgrimage,** pil′gri•mij, *n.* A journey by a pilgrim; a journey to some place deemed sacred for a devotional purpose; the journey of human life. —**Pilgrim Fathers,** *n.* The Puritans who landed at Plymouth Rock, Massachusetts, in 1620, founding the first New England settlement.

pili, pī′li, *n. pl.* [L. *pilus,* a hair.] *Bot.* fine slender bodies, like hair, covering some plants.—**piliferous,** pī•lif′ėr•us, *a.* Bearing or producing hairs, as a leaf.—**piliform,** pī′li•form, *a.* Formed like or resembling down or hairs.

pill, pil, *n.* [Abbrev. of L. *pilula,* a dim. of *pila,* a ball (whence *pile,* a heap.] A little ball or small round mass of medicinal substance to be swallowed whole; something unpleasant that has to be metaphorically swallowed or accepted.—*v.t.* To dose with pills; to form into pills.

—**pillbox,** *n.* A box for holding pills; in military slang, a small concrete blockhouse, used in Europe as a machine gun emplacement.

pillage, pil′ij, *n.* [Fr. *pillage,* from *piller,* to rob.] Plunder; spoil; that which is taken by open force, particularly from enemies in war; the act of plundering.—*v.t.*—*pillaged, pillaging.* To strip of money or goods by open violence, and usually by a number of persons; to plunder; to spoil.—**pillager,** pil′-ij•ėr, *n.* One who pillages.

pillar, pil′ėr, *n.* [Fr. *pilier,* a pillar, from L.L. *pilare,* from L. *pila,* a column. PILE.] A column; a columnar mass or upright body; *fig.* a supporter; one who or that which sustains or upholds.

pillion, pil′yon, *n.* [From the Celtic; W. *pilyn,* Ir. *pillin,* Gael. *pillean,* a pillion, a packsaddle, from root of L. *pilus,* hair (whence *pile,* of cloth).] A cushion for a woman to ride on behind a person on horseback; a pad; a low saddle; the pad of a saddle that rests on the horse's back.

pillory, pil′o•ri, *n.* [Fr. *pilori,* a pillory, Pr. *espitlori,* L.L. *pilorium, spilorium,* a pillory; origin uncertain.] A frame of wood erected on a post or pole, with movable boards resembling those in the stocks, and holes through which were put the head and hands of an offender, who had to stand there by way of public punishment.—*v.t.*—*pilloried, pillorying.* To punish with the pillory; *fig.* to expose to ridicule, contempt, abuse, and the like.

pillow, pil′ō, *n.* [O.E. *pilwe, pulwe,* from L. *pulvinus,* a cushion.] A long cushion to support the head of a person when reposing, filled with feathers, down, or other soft material; a supporting piece for an axle or shaft; a bearing.—*v.t.* To rest or lay on for support.—**pillowcase, pillow slip,** *n.* The movable sack or case which is drawn over a pillow.—**pillow lace,** *n.* Handmade lace worked on a small pillow or cushion.

pilose, pī′lōs, *a.* [L. *pilosus,* from *pilus,* hair (whence *pile,* of cloth).] Covered with, abounding in, or full of hairs; hairy.—**pilosity,** pī•los′i•ti, *n.* Hairiness.

pilot, pī′lot, *n.* [From It. *pilota,* from Gr. *pēdon,* oar.] A helmsman; one who conducts ships into harbors, through channels, etc.; a guide; *avi.* the one who controls a spacecraft or aircraft; a test operation.—*v.t.* To act as a pilot; to guide.—**pilotage,** pī′lot•ij, *n.* The act of piloting.—**pilot fish,** *n.* A fish that often swims with sharks.—**pilot house,** *n.* A deckhouse for a ship's steering gear and pilot.—**pilot light,** *n.* A small permanent flame from which the burners of a stove are lit; a pilot lamp.

pilous, pī′lus, *a.* See PILOSE.

pilular, pil′ū•lėr, *a.* [L. *pilula,* a pill.] Pertaining to pills.—**pilule,** pil′ūl, *n.* A little pill.

pimento, pi•men′to, *n.* [Pg. *pimenta,* It. *pimento,* from L. *pigmentum,* paint, juice of plants. PIGMENT.] Allspice, the berry of a tree of the West Indies; Jamaica pepper. See ALL.

pimp, pimp, *n.* [A nasalized form of *pipe* (Pr. *pimpa,* a pipe), a pimp being as it were one who whistles for females like a callbird.] One who provides gratifications for the lust of others; a procurer; a pander.—*v.i.* To pander; to procure lewd women for the gratification of others.

pimpernel, pim′pėr•nel, *n.* [Fr. *pimprenelle,* It. *pimpinella.*] A little red-flowered prostrate annual found in cornfields.

pimple, pim′pl, *n.* [A nasalized form of L. *papula,* a pimple; or from W. *pwmp, pwmpl,* a knob.] A small elevation of the skin, with an inflamed base, seldom containing a fluid or suppurating, and commonly terminating in scurf.—**pimpled,** pim′pld, *a.* Having pimples on the skin; full of pimples.—**pimply,** pim′pli, *a.* Full of pimples.

pin, pin, *n.* [Same as D. *pin,* Dan. *pind,* G. *pinn,* W. *pin.* a pin, a peg, etc., from L. *penna* or *pinna,* a feather, a pen. PEN.] A piece of metal, wood, or the like, used for fastening separate articles together, or as a support from which a thing may be hung; a peg; a bolt; a small piece of wire pointed at one end and with a rounded head at the other, much used as a cheap and ready means of fastening clothes, etc.; a peg in stringed musical instruments for increasing or diminishing the tension of the strings; the center of a target; a central part.—*v.t.*—*pinned, pinning.* To fasten with a pin or pins of any kind; to clutch; to hold fast.—*v.t.* To enclose; to confine; to pen or pound. —**pincushion,** *n.* A small cushion or pad in which pins are stuck for preservation.—**pinfeather,** pin′feTH-ėr, *n.* A small or short feather; a feather not fully grown.—**pinhole,** pin′hōl, *n.* A small hole made by the puncture of a pin; a very small aperture.—**pin money,** *n.* An allowance made by a husband to his wife for her separate use, originally *to buy pins.*—**pintail,** *n.* A variety of duck with a sharp-pointed tail.—**pinwheel,** *n.* A wheel of which the cogs are pins projecting outward.

piña cloth, pēn′ya or pī′na, *n.* [Sp. *piña,* the pineapple.] A delicate, soft, transparent cloth made from the fibers of the pineapple leaf.

pinafore, pin′a•fōr, *n.* [Because it is or was *pinned* on *before.*] A sort of apron worn by children to protect the front part of their dress; a child's apron.

pinaster, pi•nas′tėr, *n.* [L., from *pinus,* pine.] A species of pine growing in the south of Europe.

pincers, pin′sėrz, *n. pl.* [From Fr. *pincer,* to pinch (whence *pince,* pincers). PINCH.] An instrument by which anything is gripped in order to be drawn out, as a nail, or kept fast for some operation; the nippers of certain animals; prehensile claws.

pinch, pinsh, *v.t.* [Fr. *pincer,* It. *pizzare,* Sp. *pizcar, pinchar,* to pinch; of doubtful origin.] To press hard or squeeze between the ends of the fingers, the teeth, claws, or with an instrument, etc.; to nip; to distress; to afflict; to nip with frost.—*v.i.* To act with pressing force; to press painfully; to be sparing or niggardly.—*To know* or *feel where the shoe pinches,* to have practical and personal experience as to where the cause of trouble in any matter lies.—*n.* A close compression, as with the ends of the fingers; a nip; a gripe; a pang; distress inflicted or suffered; straits; difficulty; a strong iron lever; a crowbar; as much as is taken by the finger and thumb; a small quantity generally of snuff.—**pincher,** pinsh′ėr, *n.* One who or that which pinches.—**pinchers,** pinsh′ėrz, *n. pl.* See PINCERS.

pinchbeck, pinsh′bek, *n.* [From the name of the inventor, a London watchmaker of the last century.] An alloy of copper and zinc, somewhat like gold in color, and formerly much used for cheap jewelry. Hence, when used adjectively, sham; not genuine.

Pindaric, pin•dar′ik, *a.* After the style and manner of *Pindar.*—*n.* An ode in imitation of the odes of Pindar the Grecian lyric poet; an irregular ode.

pine, pīn, *n.* [From L. *pinus,* a pine-tree; same root as *pix, picis,* pitch.] The name of a valuable genus of evergreen coniferous trees, of which about seventy species are known, furnishing timber, turpentine, pitch, and resin; the pineapple, also the plant that produces it.—**pineal,** pin′-ē•al, *a.* [Fr. *pinéale,* from L. *pinea,* the cone of a pine, from *pinus,* a pine.] Resembling a pine cone in shape.—*Pineal gland,* an internal part of the brain, about the size of a pea, considered by Descartes as the seat of the soul.—**pineapple,** *n.* A tropical fruit so called from its resemblance to the cone of the pine tree; the plant itself.—*Pineapple rum,* rum flavored with sliced pineapples. —**pine cone,** *n.* The crown or strobilus of a pine tree.—**pinery,** pī′nėr•i, *n.* A hothouse in which pineapples are raised; a place where pine trees grow.—**pinetum,** pī•nē′-tum, *n.* [L., a pine plantation.] A plantation or collection of growing pine trees of different kinds, especially for ornamental or scientific purposes.

pine, pīn, *v.i.*—*pined, pining.* [A.Sax. *pinian,* to pain, to pine; same word as *pain.*] To languish; to lose flesh or grow weakly under any distress or anxiety of mind; to languish with desire (to *pine for* a thing).—*v.t.* To pain or torment; to grieve for.—*n.* Pain; anguish; misery.

pinfold, pin′fōld, *n.* [A.Sax. *pyndan,* to pound, to shut in, and *fold.* POUND.] A place in which cattle straying and doing damage are temporarily confined; a pound.

ping, ping, *n.* [Imitative.] The sound made by a bullet, as from a rifle, in passing through the air.—**Ping-pong,** *n.* A trademark for a kind of tennis played on a table.

pinion, pin'yon, *n.* [Fr. *pignon,* a pinion or small wheel; Sp. *piñon,* a joint of a bird's wing; from L. *pinna, penna,* a feather. PEN.] The joint of a fowl's wing remotest from the body; a wing; a small wheel which plays in the teeth of a larger.—*v.t.* To confine by binding the wings; to disable by cutting off the first joint of the wing; to bind the arms of; to shackle; to fetter.

pink, pingk, *n.* [Comp. D. *pinken,* to twinkle with the eyes, to wink—some of them are marked with eyelike spots.] A name of various garden flowers, as the clove pink or carnation and garden pink; a light red color or pigment resembling that of the common garden pink; anything supremely excellent (the *pink* of perfection); a fish, the minnow: so called from the color of its abdomen in summer.—*a.* Resembling in color the most frequent hue of the pink.—**pinkeye,** *n.* A contagious disease of the eye; contagious conjunctivitis.

pink, pingk, *v.t.* [A nasalized form of *pick.*] To work in eyelet-holes; to ornament with holes, scallops, etc.; to stab; to wound with a sword or rapier.—**pinkroot,** *n.* The root of the Indian pink used as a vermifuge.

pink, pingk, *n.* [D. and Dan.] A ship with a very narrow stern, a build now obsolete.

pinna, pin'a, *n.* pl. **pinnae,** pin'ē. [L. *pinna, penna,* a feather, a wing, a fin.] *Zool.* the wing or feather of a bird; the fin of a fish; *anat.* the pavilion of the ear, that part which projects beyond the head; *bot.* a leaflet of a pinnate leaf.

pinnace, pin'is, *n.* [Fr. *pinasse,* Sp. *pinaza,* Pg. *pinaça,* It. *pinaccia, pinazza,* a pinnace, from L. *pinus,* a pine tree.] A small vessel propelled by oars and sails, and having generally two masts rigged like those of a schooner; a boat usually rowed with eight oars.

pinnacle, pin'a•kl, *n.* [Fr. *pinacle,* L.L. *pinnaculum,* from L. *pinna,* a feather. PINION.] A rocky peak; a sharp or pointed summit; *arch.* any lesser structure, whatever be its form, that rises above the roof of a building, or that caps and terminates the higher parts of other buildings.—*v.t.*—*pinnacled, pinnacling.* To put a pinnacle or pinnacles on; to furnish with pinnacles.

pinnate, pin'āt, *a.* [L. *pinnatus,* from *pinna,* a feather or fin. PEN.] *Bot.* shaped or branching like a feather; formed like a feather.—*Pinnate leaf, bot.* a compound leaf wherein a single petiole has several leaflets attached to each side of it; *zool.* having fins or processes resembling fins.—**pinnately,** pin'āt•li, *adv.* In a pinnate manner.—**pinnatifid,** pin•nat'i•fid, *a.* [L. *pinna,* and *findo,* to cleave.] *Bot.* said of a simple leaf divided transversely into irregular lobes. —**pinnatipartite,** pin•nat'i•pär"tīt, *a.* [L. *partitus,* divided.] *Bot.* having the lobes of the leaf separated beyond the middle.—**pinnatiped,** pin•nat'i•ped, *a.* [L. *pinna,* and *pes, pedis,* a foot.] Fin-footed; having the toes bordered by membranes, as certain birds.—*n.* A bird which has the toes bordered by membranes.—**pinnatisect,** pin•nat'i•sekt, *a.* [L. *seco, sectum,* to cut.] *Bot.* having the lobes divided down to the midrib.

pinners, pin'ėrz, *n. pl.* A female headdress, having long flaps hanging down the sides of the cheeks, worn during the early part of the eighteenth century.

pinniped, pin'i•ped, *n.* [L. *pinna,* and *pes, pedis,* a foot.] A fin-footed animal.

pinnula, pin'ū•la, *n.* [L. *pinnula,* dim. of *pinna,* a feather.] *Zool.* one of the lateral processes of the arms of crinoids; the barb of a feather; *bot.* a leaflet.—**pinnulate,** pin'ū•lāt, *a.* *Bot.* applied to a leaf in which each pinna is subdivided.—**pinnule,** pin'ūl, *n.* A pinnula.

pinochle, pē'nuk•ėl, *n.* [Origin unknown.] A card game for two, three, or four persons played with a special 48–card pack; in the game, the combination of the queen of spades and the jack of diamonds.

pint, pīnt, *n.* [D. *pint,* Fr. and G. *pinte,* a pint, Sp. *pinta,* a mark, also a pint (a quantity marked), from L. *pingo, pinctum,* to paint. PICTURE.] A measure of capacity containing the eighth part of a gallon.

pintle, pin'tl, *n.* [Dim. of *pin.*] A pin or bolt; *artillery,* a long iron bolt to prevent the recoil of a cannon; *naut.* an iron bolt by which the rudder is hung to the sternpost; a pin passing through an axle to hold on a wheel.

pioneer, pī•o•nēr', *n.* [Fr. *pionnier,* O.Fr. *peonier,* from *peon,* It. *pedone,* a foot soldier. PEON.] One whose business is to march with or before an army to repair the road or clear it of obstructions, work at intrenchments, etc.; anyone that goes before to prepare the way for another (*pioneers* of civilization).—*v.t.* To go before and prepare a way for.—*v.i.* To act as pioneer; to clear the way.

pious, pī'us, *a.* [L. *pius,* pious, devout, kind, whence also *piety, pity.*] Having due respect and affection for parents or other relatives; more commonly, duly reverencing the Supreme Being; godly; devout; dictated by reverence to God; proceeding from piety; practiced under the pretense of religion (*pious* frauds).—*Pious belief,* a Catholic opinion not of the importance of a dogma.—**piously,** pī'us•li, *adv.* In a pious manner.

pip, pip, *n.* [D. *pip,* L.G. *pipp,* Fr. *pipie,* from L.L. *pipita,* for L. *pituita,* phlegm, the pip.] A disease of fowls, consisting in a secretion of thick mucus in the mouth by which the nostrils are stopped.

pip, pip, *n.* [Fr. *pipin,* a kernel; derivation uncertain.] The kernel or seed of fruit; a spot on cards.

pip, pip, *v.i.* [An imitative word, slightly differing in form from *peep* = Dan. *pipe,* Sw. *pipa,* G. *pipen,* to pip. PEEP, PIPE.] To cry or chirp, as a chicken.

pipe, pīp, *n.* [A.Sax. *pipe,* a pipe; D. *pijp,* Icel. *pipa,* Dan. *pibe,* G. *pfeife;* of imitative origin; comp. L. *pipo, pipio,* to cheep, chirp.] A wind instrument of music, consisting of a tube of wood or metal; a long tube or hollow body made of various materials, such as are used for the conveyance of water, gas, steam, etc.; a tube of clay or other material with a bowl at one end, used in smoking tobacco, etc.; the windpipe; the sound of the voice; a whistle or call of a bird; a roll in the exchequer, so named from resembling a pipe; a wine measure, usually containing about 105 imperial or 126 wine gallons; *naut.* the boatswain's whistle used to call the men to their duties.—*v.i.*—*piped, piping.* To sound or play on a pipe; to have a shrill sound; to whistle.—*v.t.* To play on a pipe or other wind instrument; to utter in a sharp or high tone; *naut.* to call by means of the boatswain's pipe or whistle.—**pipe clay,** *n.* The purest kind of potter's clay, manufactured into tobacco pipes, and used by soldiers for cleaning belts, jackets, trousers, etc.—*v.t.* To whiten with pipe clay.—**pipefish,** *n.* A long and slender fish, the thickest part of whose body is only equal to a swan's quill.—**piper,** pī'pėr, *n.* One who plays on a pipe; a bagpiper; a sea urchin common in the northern seas.—*To pay the piper,* to be at the expense; to suffer or make good the loss.—**pipette,** pi•pet', *n.* [Fr., a small pipe.] A small tube terminating in a perforated point, used by chemists for transferring liquids.—**piping,** pī'ping, *p.* and *a.* Playing on a pipe; having or giving out a shrill whistling sound; accompanied by the music of the peaceful pipe (this *piping* time of peace); boiling; hissing with heat (*piping* hot).—*n.* Pipes, as for gas, water, etc., collectively; *hort.* a jointed stem used for propagating plants.

piperaceous, pī•pėr•ā'shus, *a.* [L. *piper,* pepper.] Belonging to the pepper tribe of plants.—**piperin, piperine,** pī'pėr•in, *n.* A crystalline substance extracted from black pepper.

pipette. See PIPE.

pipit, pip'it, *n.* [Probably imitative of its cry.] A name of birds allied to the lark.

pipkin, pip'kin, *n.* [Dim. of *pipe.*] A small earthen boiler.

pippin, pip'in, *n.* [Perhaps because grown from the *pips* or seeds.] The name given to several kinds of apples.

piquant, pē'kant, *a.* [Ppr. of Fr. *piquer,* to prick, to be sharp, to pique; of same origin as *pick, pike, peak,* etc.] Making a lively, half-pleasing, half-painful impression on the organs of sense; sharp; racy; lively; sparkling; interesting; sharp or cutting to the feelings; pungent; severe.—**piquantly,** pē'kant•li, *adv.* In a piquant manner; tartly.—**piquancy,** pē'kan•si, *n.* The state or quality of being piquant; sharpness; pungency.

pique, pēk, *n.* [Fr. PIQUANT.] An offense taken; slight anger at persons; feeling arising from wounded pride, vanity, or self-love.—*v.t.*—*piqued, piquing.* [Fr. *piquer.*] To nettle; to irritate; to sting (less strong than *exasperate*); to stimulate; to touch with envy, jealousy, or other passion; *refl.* to pride or value one's self.—*v.i.* To cause irritation.—**piquet,** pik′et, *n.* [From Fr. *pique,* a pike, a lance, a spade at cards.] *Milit.* a picket; a game at cards played between two persons with thirty-two cards, the ace of spades being highest card.

piracy. See PIRATE.

piragua, pi•rä′gwa, *n.* A rude canoe. See PIROGUE.

piranha, pi•rän′yä, *n.* [Pg. from Tupi.] A small, voracious South American fresh-water fish of the genus *Serrasalmo.*

pirate, pī′rat, *n.* [Fr. *pirate,* L. *pirata,* from Gr. *peiratēs,* from *peiraō,* to attempt, *peira,* a trial.] A robber on the high seas; one that by open violence takes the property of another on the high seas; an armed ship or vessel engaged in piracy; a publisher or compiler who appropriates the literary labors of an author without compensation or permission.—*v.i.*—*pirated, pirating.* To play the pirate; to rob on the high seas.—*v.t.* To publish without right or permission.—**piratic, piratical,** pī•rat′ik, pī•rat′i•kal, *a.* [L. *piraticus.*] Having the character of a pirate; robbing or plundering by open violence on the high seas; pertaining to or consisting in piracy.—**piratically,** pī•rat′i•kal•li, *adv.* In a piratical manner; by piracy.—**piracy,** pī′ra•si, *n.* The act, practice, or crime of robbing on the high seas; the profession of pirate; literary theft; any infringement on the law of copyright.

pirogue, pi•rōg′, *n.* [Fr. *pirogue,* Sp. *piragua;* originally a W. Indian word.] A kind of canoe made from a single trunk of a tree hollowed out.

pirouette, pi•rö•et′, *n.* [Fr.; origin unknown.] A rapid whirling on the point of one foot; the short turn of a horse so as to bring his head suddenly in the opposite direction to where it was before.—*v.i.*—*pirouetted, pirouetting.* To perform a pirouette, as in dancing.

piscator, pis•kā′tor, *n.* [L., from *piscis,* a fish.] A fisherman; an angler.—**piscatorial, piscatory,** pis•ka•tō′ri•al, pis′ka•tō•ri, *a.* [L. *piscatorius.*] Relating to fishermen or to fishing; pertaining to angling.—**Pisces,** pis′sēz, *n. pl.* [L. *piscis,* a fish.] *Astron.* the Fishes, the twelfth sign or constellation in the zodiac, next to Aries; the vertebrate animals of the class fishes.—**pisciculture,** pis•i•kul′chėr, *n.* [L. *piscis,* a fish, and *cultura,* culture.] The breeding, rearing, preservation, feeding, and fattening of fish by artificial means; fish culture.—**pisciform,** pis′i•form, *a.* Having the shape of a fish. **piscina,** pis•sī′na, *n.* [L., a cistern, a fishpond.] A niche on the south side of the altar in churches, with a small basin and water drain connected, into which the priest empties any water used.—**piscine,** pis′sīn, *a.* Pertaining to fish or fishes.—**piscivorous,** pis•siv′o•rus, *a.* [L. *piscis,* and *voro,* to eat.] Feeding or subsisting on fishes.

pisiform, pī′si•form, *a.* [L. *pisum,* a pea, and *forma,* form.] Having the form of a pea; having a structure resembling peas.

pismire, pis′mīr, *n.* [E. *piss,* and *mire*=D. *mier,* Sw. *myra,* Icel. *maurr,* an ant; it discharges an irritant fluid vulgarly regarded as urine.] The ant or emmet.

pisolite, pī′sō•līt, *n.* [Gr. *pison,* a pea, and *lithos,* a stone.] A carbonate of lime slightly colored by the oxide of iron, occurring in little globular concretions of the size of a pea or larger, which usually contain each a grain of sand as a nucleus.—**pisolitic,** pī•sō•lit′ik, *a.* Composed of, containing, or resembling pisolite.

pistachio, pistachio nut, pis•tä′shi•ō, *n.* [Sp. *pistacho,* L. *pistacium,* the fruit; *pistacia,* Gr. *pistakia,* the tree, from Per. *pista,* the pistachio tree.] The nut of the pistachio tree, a member of the sumac family; a yellowish-green color.

pistil, pis′til, *n.* [L. *pistillum,* a pestle, a dim. from *pinso, pistum,* to pound, to beat in a mortar; akin *pestle, piston.*] *Bot.* the seed-bearing organ of a flower, consisting of the ovary, the stigma, and often also of a style.—**pistillate,** pis′til•lāt, *a.* Having a pistil.

pistol, pis′tol, *n.* [Fr. *pistole,* from It. *pistola,* a pistol; originally a dagger made at *Pistola* or *Pistoia,* near Florence. From diminutive poniards the name came to be given to miniature firearms.] A small firearm, the smallest used, designed to be fired with one hand only.—*v.t.*—*pistoled, pistoling.* To shoot with a pistol.

pistole, pis•tōl′, *n.* [Fr. *pistole,* same as *pistol,* so named as being originally a halfcrown, a diminutive of the crown.] An old gold coin in Spain, France, etc.

piston, pis′ton, *n.* [Fr., from L. *pinso, pistum,* to beat, to pound. PISTIL.] *Mach.* a movable piece of a cylindrical form, which exactly fits a hollow cylinder, such as the barrel of a pump or the cylinder of a steam engine, and capable of being driven alternately in two directions.—**piston rod,** *n.* A rod which connects a piston to a point outside the cylinder, and either moved by the piston or moving it.

pit, pit, *n.* [A.Sax. *pyt,* pit=D. *put,* Icel. *pyttr,* a well; from L. *puteus,* a well.] A hollow or cavity more or less deep, either natural or made by digging in the earth; the shaft of a mine; a vat in tanning, bleaching, dyeing, etc.; *hort.* an excavation in the soil covered by a glazed frame, for protecting plants; a concealed hole in the ground for snaring wild beasts; any hollow, cavity, or depression in the flesh (the arm*pits*); a place or area where cocks or dogs are brought to fight, or where dogs are trained to kill rats; part of a theater on the floor of the house, and somewhat below the level of the stage.—*The pit* (*Scrip.*), the place of the dead or the abode of evil spirits.—The *bottomless pit,* hell (N.T.).—*v.t.*—*pitted, pitting.* To lay in a pit or hole; to mark with little hollows, as by the smallpox; to set in competition; to set against one another, as in combat (*lit.* like cocks in a *pit*).—**pitfall,** pit′fal, *n.* A pit slightly covered over, forming a kind of trap.—**pitman,** pit′man, *n.* One who works in a pit.—**pit saw,** *n.* A large saw worked by two men, one of whom stands in a pit below.

pitapat, pit′a•pat, *adv.* [A reduplication of *pat,* a slight blow.] In a flutter; with palpitation or quick succession of beats.—*n.* A light quick step.

pitch, pich, *n.* [A softened form of O.E. *pik,* A.Sax. *pic,* from L. *pix, picis,* pitch, akin to *pinus,* a pine (tree).] A thick, tenacious oily substance, commonly obtained from tar, and extensively used for closing up the seams of ships, for preserving wood from the effects of water, for coating ironwork, etc.; in *acoustics,* the quality of a sound which depends upon the number of vibrations per second.—*Jew's pitch, mineral pitch,* bitumen.—*v.t.* To smear or cover over with pitch.—**pitchblende,** *n.* A mineral which constitutes one of the most important sources of the metal uranium and its compounds.—**pitch-dark,** *a.* Dark as pitch; very dark.—**pitchiness,** pich′i•nes, *n.* State or quality of being pitchy.—**pitchstone,** *n.* The glassy form of felstone; retinite.—**pitchy,** pich′i, *a.* Partaking of the qualities of pitch; like pitch; smeared with pitch; dark; dismal.

pitch, pich, *v.t.* [O.E. *picche,* to pierce, to peck, to dart or throw, a softened form of *pick, pike.* PICK.] To fix or plant, as stakes or pointed instruments; to fix by means of such; hence, to set in array; to marshal or arrange in order (to *pitch* a tent, to *pitch* a camp); to fling or throw; to cast forward; to hurl; to toss, as *pitch* a baseball; to regulate or set the keynote of; to pave or face with stones, as an embankment.—*Pitched battle,* one in which the armies are previously drawn up in form, with a regular disposition of the forces.—*v.i.* To light; to settle; to come to rest from flight; to plunge or fall headlong; to fix choice: with *on* or *upon;* to fix a tent or temporary habitation; to encamp; *naut.* to rise and fall, as the head and stern of a ship passing over waves.—*n.* A point or degree of elevation or depression; height or depth; degree; rate; loftiness; the degree of slope or inclination (the *pitch* of a hill or roof); the rise of an arch; a throw; a toss; that part of a cricket field where the wickets are put up; a cast or jerk of something from the hand; *music,* the relative height of a sound; in certain technical senses, a distance between two points (as the *pitch* of a screw, that is, the distance between its threads).—**pitcher,** pichėr′, *n.* One who or that which pitches.—**pitchfork,** pich′fork, *n.* A fork used in lifting or throwing hay or sheaves of grain; a tuning fork.—*v.t.* To lift or throw with a pitchfork; hence, to put suddenly or accidentally into any position.—**pitch pipe,** *n.* A small flute or free-reed pipe used in regulating the *pitch* or elevation of the key or leading note of a tune.

pitcher, pich′ėr, *n.* [O.Fr. *picher, pichier, pechier,* O.It. *pecchero,* from O.H.G. *pechar, behhar,* a beaker. BEAKER.] A vessel with a spout for holding liquors; an earthen or metallic vessel for holding water for domestic purposes; a water pot, jug, or jar with ears.—**pitcher plant,** *n.* A name given to several plants from their pitcher-shaped leaves.

piteous, etc. See PITY.

pitfall. See PIT.

pith, pith, *n.* [A.Sax. *pitha,* D. *pit,* marrow, pith, kernel.] A soft cellular substance occupying the center of the root, stem, and branches of exogenous plants; the spinal cord or marrow of an animal; strength, vigor, or force; closeness and vigor of thought and style; cogency; condensed substance or matter; quintessence.—**pithily,** pith′i•li, *adv.* In a pithy manner.—**pithiness,** pith′i•nes, *n.* The state or quality of being pithy.—**pithy,** pith′i, *a.* Consisting of pith; containing pith; abounding with pith; terse and striking; forcible; energetic; uttering energetic words or expressions.

pitiable, pitiful, pitiless, etc. See PITY.

pittance, pit′ans, *n.* [Fr. *pitance,* a monk's mess, from L.L. *pietantia, pitantia,* a monk's allowance, from L. *pietas,* piety.] An allowance of food bestowed in charity; a charity gift; a very small portion allowed or assigned.

pituitary, pi•tū′i•te•ri, *n.* [L. *pituitarius,* pertaining to phlegm.] *Anat.* the pituitary gland; *med.* an extract obtained from the pituitary gland.—**pituitary gland,** *n.* A two-lobed endocrine gland at the base of the brain; the hypophysis.

pity, pit′i, *n.* [Fr. *pitié,* O.Fr. *pité,* from L. *pietas,* piety, from *pius,* pious. (PIOUS.) *Piety* is the same word.] The suffering of one person excited by the distresses of another: commiseration; compassion; mercy; the ground or subject of pity; cause of grief; thing to be regretted; in this sense it has a plural (it is a thousand *pities* he should fail).—*To have pity upon, to take pity upon,* generally to show one's pity toward by some benevolent act.—*v.t.*—*pitied, pitying.* [O.Fr. *pitoyer,* to pity.] To feel pity or compassion toward; to feel pain or grief for; to have sympathy for; to commiserate; to compassionate.—*v.i.* To be compassionate; to exercise pity.—**pityingly,** pit′i•ing•li, *adv.* So as to show pity; compassionately.—**piteous,** pit′i•us, *a.* Fitted to excite pity; moving pity or compassion; mournful; affecting; lamentable.—**piteously,** pit′i•us•li, *adv.* In a piteous manner.—**piteousness,** pit′i•us•nes, *n.* The state of being piteous.—**pitiable,** pit′i•a•bl, *a.* Deserving or exciting pity.—**pitiableness,** pit′i•a•bl•nes, *n.* State of being pitiable.—**pitiably,** pit′i•a•bli, *adv.* In a pitiable manner.—**pitiful,** pit′i•fu̦l, *a.* Full of pity; tender; compassionate; miserable; moving compassion; paltry; insignificant; contemptible. ∴ Syn. under CONTEMPTIBLE.—**pitifully,** pit′i•fu̦l•li, *adv.* In a pitiful manner.—**pitifulness,** pit′i•fu̦l•nes, *n.* The state or quality of being pitiful.—**pitiless,** pit′i•les, *a.* Destitute of pity; hardhearted; relentless; exciting no pity.—**pitilessly,** pit′i•les•li, *adv.* In a pitiless manner.—**pitilessness,** pit′i•les•ness, *n.* The state of being pitiless.

pityriasis, pit•i•rī′a•sis, *n.* [Gr. *pityron,* bran.] A cutaneous disease consisting of irregular branlike scaly patches.

pivot, piv′ot, *n.* [Fr. *pivot,* a pivot, from It. *piva,* a pipe (=Fr. and E. *pipe*).] A pin on which anything turns; a short shaft or point on which a wheel or other body revolves; *milit.* the officer or soldier upon whom the different wheelings are made in the various evolutions of the drill, etc.; that on which important results depend; a turning point.—*v.t.* To place on a pivot; to furnish with a pivot.—**pivotal,** piv′ot•al, *a.* Belonging to a pivot.

pix, piks, *n.* See PYX.

pixy, pixie, pik′si, *n.* [Perhaps for *pucksy,* from *Puck.*] A sort of fairy.

pizza, pēt′sä, *n.* [It.] A flat open pie baked with cheese, meat, spices, etc.—**pizzeria,** pēt′sä•rē″ä, *n.* A place where pizza is made or sold.

pizzicato, pit•si•kä′tō, *a.* [It., twitched.] *Mus.* to be plucked by the finger, and not played with the bow of the violin.

placable, plak′a•bl or plā′ka•bl, *a.* [L. *placabilis,* from *placo,* to soothe, pacify; akin to *placeo,* to please. PLEASE.] Capable of being appeased or pacified; appeasable.—**placability,** plak•a•bil′i•ti or plā•, *n.* The quality of being placable.—**placate,** plā′kāt, *v.t.*—*placated, placating.* To appease, pacify, or conciliate.

placard, plak′ärd or pla•kärd′, *n.* [Fr., from *plaque,* a plate, from the Teutonic; comp. D. *plak,* a flat piece of wood, a slice, *plakbriefje,* a placard; L.G. *plakke,* a piece of turf.] A written or printed paper posted in a public place; a bill posted up to draw public attention; a poster.—*v.t.* To post placards on; to make known by placard.

place, plās, *n.* [Fr. *place,* a place, post, position, an open space in a town; from L. *platea,* a street, an area, from Gr. *plateia,* from *platys,* flat, broad. PLATE.] A broad way or open space in a city; an area; a particular portion of space marked off by its use or character; a locality, spot, or site; position; a town or village; a fortified post; a passage in a book; point or degree in order of proceeding (in the first *place*); rank; order of priority, dignity, or importance; office; employment; official station; ground or occasion; room; station in life; calling; occupation; condition; room or stead, with the sense of substitution (to act in *place* of another); the position in the heavens of a heavenly body.—*To give place,* to make room or way; to retire in favor of another; to yield.—*To have place,* to have a station, room, or seat; to have actual existence.—*To take place,* to come to pass; to happen; to occur; to take the precedence or priority.—*v.t.*—*placed, placing.* To put or set in a particular place or spot; to set or put in a certain relative position; to locate; to appoint, set, induct, or establish in an office; to put or set in any particular rank, state, or condition; to set; to fix (to *place* confidence in a friend); to invest; to lend (to *place* money in the funds).—**place kick,** *n.* In football, the act of kicking the ball after it has been placed on the ground.—**placement,** plās′ment, *n.* The act of placing or of putting in a certain spot or position.

placebo, plā•sē′bō, *n.* [L. I shall please.] *R. Cath. Ch.* vespers for the dead; a harmless medicine given to please a patient; something intended to soothe.

placenta, pla•sen′ta, *n.* [L., a cake.] The afterbirth; a temporary organ developed in mammals during pregnancy, and forming a connection between the mother and the fetus; *bot.* that part of a seed vessel on which the ovules or seeds are placed.—**placental,** pla•sen′tal, *a.* Pertaining to the placenta; possessing a placenta.—*n.* An animal that possesses a placenta.—**placentary,** pla′sen•te•ri, *n. Bot.* a placenta bearing numerous ovules.—*a.* Having reference to the placenta.—**placentation,** pla•sen•tā′shon, *n.* The disposition of the placenta, more especially in plants.

placer, plas′ėr, *n.* [Sp.] A glacial or alluvial deposit that contains particles of gold or other valuable mineral.—**placer mining,** *n.*

placid, plas′id, *a.* [L. *placidus,* from *placeo,* to please. PLEASE.] Gentle; quiet; unruffled.—**placidity, placidness,** pla•sid′i•ti, plas′id•nes, *n.*—**placidly,** plas′id•li, *adv.*

placket, plak′et, *n.* [From the Fr. *plaquer,* to lay or clap on. PLACARD.] A petticoat; the opening or slit in a petticoat or skirt.

placoid, plak′oid, *a.* [Gr. *plax, plakos,* something flat.] Applied to a certain class of fishes' scales, consisting of detached bony grains, tubercles, or plates.—*n.* A fish with such scales.

plagal, plā′gal, *a.* [Gr. *plagios,* oblique.] *Music,* applied to a cadence in which the chord of the subdominant is followed by that of the tonic.

plagiary, plā′ji•e•ri, *n.* [L. *plagiarius,* a plagiary, a kidnaper, from *plagium,* manstealing, kidnaping, from *plaga,* a snare.] One that steals or purloins the words or ideas of another and passes them off as his own; a literary thief; plagiarism.—**plagiarism,** plā′ji•a•rizm, *n.* The act of plagiarizing; the crime of literary theft; that which is plagiarized.—**plagiarist,** plā′ji•a•rist, *n.* One who plagiarizes.—**plagiarize,** plā′ji•a•rīz, *v.t.* and *i.*—*plagiarized, plagiarizing.* To steal or purloin the thoughts or words of another in literary composition.

plagioclase, plā′ji•o•klāz, *n.* [Gr. *plagios,* oblique, and *klasis,* fracture.] A name of triclinic feldspars, the two prominent cleavage directions in which are oblique to one another.—**plagioclastic,** plā′ji•o•klas″tik, *a.* Of the nature of or containing plagioclase.

plague, plāg, *n.* [Same as D. *plaag,* Dan. and G. *plage,* Icel. *plaga,* Pr. *plaga,* O.Sp. *plaga,* the plague; all from L. *plaga,* a blow, stroke, calamity. PLAINT.] A blow or calamity; severe trouble or vexation; a pestilential disease; a malignant fever of the East eminently contagious, and attended by excessive debility, as also with carbuncles or buboes.—*Plague on* or *upon,* a kind of denunciation expressive of weariness or petty annoyance. — *v.t.* — *plagued, plaguing.* To vex; to tease; to harass; to trouble; to embarrass; to scourge with disease, calamity, or natural evil of any kind.—**plaguer,** plā′gėr, *n.* One who plagues or vexes.—**plaguily,** plā′gi•li, *adv.* Vexatiously; in a manner to vex, harass, or embarrass. (*Colloq.*)—**plaguy,** plā′gi, *a.* Vexatious; troublesome; tormenting; annoying; wearisome. (*Colloq.*)—*adv.* Vexatiously; deucedly. (*Colloq.*)

plaice, plās, *n.* [From L. *platessa,* a flatfish, from Gr. *platys,* flat.] A well-known species of the flatfish family, more flat and square than the halibut.

plaid, plād or plad, *n.* [Gael. *plaide,* from *peallaid,* a sheepskin, from *peall,* a skin or hide. PELT.] A large rectangular outer garment or wrap, frequently of tartan, worn by the Highlanders and others in Scotland.—**plaided,** plā′ded, *a.* Of the cloths of which plaids are made; tartan; wearing a plaid.

plain, plān, *a.* [Fr. *plain,* Pr. *plan,* It. *piano,* from L. *planus,* plain (same root as *plango,* to beat). *Plan* and *plane* are the same word.] Without elevations and depressions; level; flat; even; smooth; void of ornament; without embellishment; simple; unadorned; without beauty; homely; sometimes used as a euphemism for *ugly;* artless; simple; unlearned; without disguise, cunning, or affectation; without refinement; unsophisticated; honestly undisguised; open; unreserved; mere; absolute; unmistakable; without difficulties or intricacies; evident to the understanding; clear; manifest; not obscure; not highly seasoned; not rich or luxurious (a *plain* diet).—*Plain clothes,* the ordinary dress of society; nonofficial dress; opposed to *uniform.*—*adv.* In a plain manner; plainly; frankly; bluntly.—*n.* A piece of level land; a piece of ground with an even surface, or a surface little varied by inequalities; *geog.* the general term for all those parts of the dry land which cannot properly be called hilly or mountainous.—**plainly,** plān′li, *adv.* In a plain manner.—**plainness,** plān′nes, *n.* The state or quality of being plain; evenness of surface; openness; candor; intelligibility.—**plain song,** *n. Music,* the simple, grave, and unadorned chant in which the services of the Roman Catholic Church have been rendered from a very early age; the simple notes of an air without ornament or variation; hence, a plain unexaggerated statement.

plaint, plānt, *n.* [Fr. *plainte,* a complaint, from *plaindre,* to complain, from L. *plango, planctum,* to beat the breast, to lament, akin to *plaga,* a blow, Gr. *plēssō,* to strike. PLAGUE.] Lamentation; complaint; audible expression of sorrow; representation made of injury or wrong done.—**plaintiff,** plān′tif, *n. Law,* the person who commences a suit before a tribunal for the recovery of a claim; opposed to *defendant.*—**plaintive,** plān′tiv, *a.* Expressive of sorrow or melancholy; mournful; sad.—**plaintively,** plān′tiv•li, *adv.* In a plaintive manner.—**plaintiveness,** plān′tiv•nes, *n.* The quality or state of being plaintive.

plait, plāt, plat, *n.* [O.Fr. *ploit, pleit,* from L. *plicatus,* folded, from *plicare,* to twist, whence *ply.*] A flattened gather or fold; a doubling of cloth or any similar tissue or fabric; a braid, as of hair, straw, etc.—*v.t.* To fold; to double in narrow strips; to braid; to interweave the locks or strands of (to *plait* the hair).

plan, plan, *n.* [Fr. *plan,* from L. *planus,* plain, flat, level. PLAIN.] The representation of anything drawn on a plane, and forming a map or chart (the *plan* of a town); the representation of a horizontal section of a building, showing the extent, division, and distribution of its area into apartments, passages, etc.; a scheme devised; a project; disposition of parts according to a certain design; a method or process; a way; a mode.—*v.t.*—*planned, planning.* To invent or contrive for construction; to scheme; to devise; to form in design.—**planner,** plan′ėr, *n.* One who plans.

planchette, plan•shet′, *n.* [Fr. *planchette.* PLANK.] A small board, usually heartshaped, resting on two castors and the point of a pencil; when the board is touched by the fingers, the pencil is said to trace words.

plane, plān, *a.* [From L. *planus.* PLAIN.] Without elevations or depressions; even; level; flat.—*n.* A smooth or perfectly level surface; a part of something having a level surface; the supporting surface of an airplane; a surface such that if any two points whatever in it be joined by a straight line, the whole of the straight line will be in the surface; an ideal surface, supposed to cut and pass through solid bodies or in various directions; frequently used in astronomy (the *plane* of the ecliptic, the *plane* of a planet's orbit); a joiner's tool, consisting of a smooth-soled stock, through which passes obliquely a piece of edged steel or a chisel, used in paring or smoothing boards or wood of any kind.—*v.t.*—*planed, planing.* To make smooth, especially by the use of a plane; to travel by airplane.—*Plane angle,* an angle contained between two straight lines meeting in a plane.—*Plane geometry,* the geometry of plane figures, in contradistinction to *solid geometry,* or the geometry of solids.—*Plane sailing,* the art of determining a ship's place, on the supposition that she is moving on a plane, or that the surface of the ocean is plane instead of being spherical.—*Plane trigonometry,* that branch of trigonometry which treats of triangles described on a plane.—**plane iron,** *n.* The cutting iron of a plane.—**planer,** plā′nėr, *n.* One who planes; a wooden block used to smooth the face of a form of type before printing; a planing machine.

planet, plan′et, *n.* [L. *planeta,* a planet, from Gr. *planētēs,* a wanderer, from *planaō,* to wander.] A celestial body (such as the earth) which revolves about the sun; the nine major planets, Mercury, Venus, Earth, Mars, Jupiter, Saturn, Uranus, Neptune, and Pluto.—*Primary planets,* those which revolve about the sun as their center.—*Secondary planets,* those which revolve about other planets; satellites or moons.—**planetarium,** plan•e•tâ′ri•um, *n.* An astronomical machine which, by the movement of its parts, represents the motions and orbits of the planets.—**planetary,** plan′e•ta•ri, *a.* Pertaining to the planets; having the nature of a planet.—*Planetary years,* the periods of time in which the several planets make their revolutions round the sun.—**planetoid,** plan′et•oid, *n.* One of a numerous group of very small planets revolving round the sun between the orbits of Mars and Jupiter; an asteroid.—**planetoidal,** plan′et•oi•dal, *a.* Pertaining to the planetoids; relating to a planetoid.—**planet-stricken, planet-struck,** *a.* Affected by the influence of planets; blasted.—**planet wheel,** *n.* The exterior revolving wheel of the 'sun-and-planet' motion.

plangent,† plan′jent, *a.* [L. *plangens, plangentis,* ppr. of *plango,* to beat.] Beating; dashing, as a wave.—**plangency,**† plan′jen•si, *n.* The state or quality of being plangent.

planifolious, planipetalous, plā•ni•fō′li•us, plā•ni•pet′a•lus, *a.* [L. *planus,* plain, and *folium, petalon,* a leaf.] Applied to a flower made up of plane leaves or petals, set together in circular rows round the center.

planimeter, pla•nim′et•ėr, *n.* [L. *planus,* plain, and Gr. *metron,* a measure.] An instrument for measuring the area of any plane figure.—**planimetry,** pla•nim′et•ri, *n.* The mensuration of plane surfaces.

planish, plan′ish, *v.t.* [From *plane.*] To make smooth or plain, as wood; to condense, smooth, and toughen, as a metallic plate, by light blows of a hammer; to polish.

planisphere, plan′i•sfēr, *n.* [L. *planus,* plain, and E. *sphere.*] A sphere projected on a plane; a map exhibiting the circles of the sphere.

plank, plangk, *n.* [Fr. dial. *planke,* Pr. *planca, plancha,* Fr. *planche,* from L. *planca* (for *planica*), a board, slab, from L. *planus,* plain.] A broad piece of sawed timber, differing from a board only in being thicker; in political slang, one of the principles in the system adopted by a party. See PLATFORM.—*v.t.* To cover or lay with planks.

plankton, plangk′ton, *n.* [Gr. *plagkton,* wandering.] The mass of small organisms, plant or animal, floating or drifting in the ocean.

planner. See PLAN.

plano-concave, plā′nō, *a.* Plane on one side and concave on the other.—**plano-convex,** *a.* Plane or flat on one side and convex on the other.

planometer, plā•nom′et•ėr, *n.* A plane, hard surface used in machine making as a gauge for plane surfaces.—**planometry,** plā•nom′et•ri, *n.* The act of measuring or gauging plane surfaces; the art or act of using a planometer.

plant, plant, *n.* [Fr. *plante,* a plant, from L. *planta,* a plant, a twig, the sole of the foot, from root of *planus,* plain.] One of the organisms which form the vegetable kingdom; a vegetable; an organized living body deriving its sustenance from the inorganic world, generally adhering to another body, and drawing from it some of its nourishment, and having the power of propagating itself by seeds or similar reproductive bodies; popularly the word is generally applied to the smaller species of vegetables; a collective term for the fixtures, machinery, tools, apparatus, etc., necessary to carry on any trade or mechanical business; a put-up game; a swindle. (*Colloq.*)—*v.t.* To put in the ground and cover, as seed for growth; to set in the ground for growth; to furnish with plants; to lay out and prepare with plants; to set upright; to set firmly; to fix; to set and direct or point (to *plant* cannon against a fort); to furnish the first inhabitants of; to settle (to *plant* a colony); to introduce and establish (to *plant* Christianity).—*v.i.* To perform the act of planting.—**plantation,** plan•tā′shon, *n.* [L. *plantatio.*] The act of planting or setting in the earth for growth; the place planted; a small wood; a grove; in the Southern states, a large estate cultivated chiefly by share croppers.—**planter,** plan′tėr, *n.* One who plants, sets, introduces, or establishes; one who owns a plantation.—**plant louse,** *n.* An aphis.

plantain, plan′tin, *n.* [Fr. *plantain,* from L. *plantago,* from *planta,* the sole of the foot, from a vague resemblance of the leaves to the foot.] A genus of perennial or annual herbs, found in all temperate regions. They are mostly roadside weeds with elliptic ribbed leaves and spikes of small greenish flowers.

plantain, plan′tān, *n.* [Sp. *plantano, platano,* from L. *platanus,* a plane-tree.] A large herbaceous plant, with a soft succulent stem, sometimes attaining the height of 20 feet, the fruit of which is of great importance as an article of food in tropical climates.

plantar, plan′tar, *a.* [L. *planta,* the sole of the foot.] *Anat.* relating or belonging to the sole of the foot.

plantigrade, plan′ti•grād, *a.* [L. *planta,* the sole of the foot, and *gradior,* to walk.] Walking on the sole of the foot and not on the toes (digitigrade): applied to a section of carnivorous animals, including the bears.

planula, plan′ū•la, *n.* [L. dim. of *planus,* a wanderer.] In sponges and zoophytes, an oval ciliated larva.

plaque, plak, *n.* [Fr.] An ornamental plate; a brooch; the plate of a clasp; a flat plate of metal upon which enamels are painted.

plash, plash, *n.* [D. *plasch, plas,* a puddle, perhaps from sound of splashing; comp. D. *plassen,* G. *platschen, platschern,* to paddle in water; L.G. *plasken,* E. to *splash.*] A small collection of standing water; a puddle; a pond; a splash.—*v.i.* To dabble in water; to fall with a dabbling sound; to splash.—**plashy,** plash′i, *a.* Watery; abounding with puddles.

plash, plash, *v.t.* [O.Fr. *plassier, plessier,* from L. *plexus,* pp. of *plecto,* to weave, to twist (as in *complex*). *Pleach* is a collateral form.] To bend down and interweave the branches or twigs of (to *plash* a hedge).

plasma, plaz′ma, *n.* [Gr. *plasma,* something formed or molded, from *plassō,* to form, whence *plastic.*] A siliceous mineral of a color between grass green and leek green, used by the ancients for engraving upon; formless elementary matter; the liquid part of blood and lymph; specifically, *biol.* the simplest form of organized matter in the vegetable and animal body, out of which the several tissues are formed; the nearly colorless fluid in which the corpuscles of the blood are suspended.—**plasmic, plasmatic,** plaz′mik, plaz•mat′ik, *a.* Pertaining to plasma; having the character of a plasma.

plasmodium, plaz•mōd′i•um, *n.* In slime fungi (Myxomycetes), a stage in the life history consisting of a creeping mass of naked protoplasm.

plaster, plas′tėr, *n.* [O.Fr. *plaster* (Fr. *plâtre*), from L. *emplastrum,* Gr. *emplastron,* plaster, from *emplassō,* to daub over —*en,* on, in, and *plassō,* to form, to shape (whence also *plastic, plasma*).] A composition of lime, water, and sand, with or without hair for binding, used for coating walls and partitions of houses; calcined gypsum, used, when mixed with water, for finishing walls, for casts, cement, etc.; *phar.* an external application of a harder consistence than an ointment, spread on linen, silk, etc.—*Plaster* of *Paris,* a composition of several species of gypsum, originally obtained from Montmartre near Paris, used for various purposes.—*Plaster cast,* a copy of an object obtained by pouring plaster of Paris mixed with water into a mold which forms a copy of the object in reverse.—*v.t.* To overlay or cover with plaster; to lay coarsely on; to bedaub.—**plasterer,** plas′tėr•ėr, *n.* One that overlays with plaster.—**plastery,** plas′tėr•i, *a.* Resembling plaster; containing plaster.

plastic, plas′tik, *a.* [Gr. *plastikos,* from *plassō,* to form. PLASTER.] Having the power to give form or fashion to a mass of matter; capable of being molded into various forms; capable of change or modification; capable of receiving a new bent or direction (as the mind); applied to sculpture and the kindred arts, as distinguished from painting and the graphic arts; any of a group of synthetic or natural organic materials that when soft may be molded or cast to make an infinite number of articles.—*Plastic clay,* a name given to one of the beds of the Eocene period, from its being used in the manufacture of pottery.—**plasticity,** plas•tis′i•ti, *n.* The state or quality of being plastic.

plastron, plas′tron, *n.* [Fr. *plastron,* a breastplate, same origin as *plaster.*] A piece of leather stuffed, used by fencers to defend the breast against pushes; *zool.* the lower or ventral portion of the bony case of tortoises and turtles.

plat, plat, *v.t.*—*platted, platting.* [Same as *plait.*] To interweave; to plait.—**platter,** plat′ėr, *n.* One who plats or forms by weaving.

plat, plat, *n.* [Same word as *plot;* but probably affected by Fr. *plat, plate,* flat. PLATE.] A small piece of ground marked out and devoted to some special purpose; a plot of ground; a map or chart.

platan, plat′an, *n.* [L. *platanus.*] The plane tree.

plate, plāt, *n.* [From Fr. *plate,* a metal plate, a piece of plate armor, and *plat,* a dish; from *plat, plate,* flat; perhaps (like *place*) from Gr. *platys,* broad, cog. with Skr. *prithu,* broad.] A flattened piece of metal with a uniform thickness; armor composed of broad pieces or plates; domestic vessels or utensils made of gold or silver; a small shallow vessel of metal, porcelain, or earthenware, from which food is eaten at table; a piece of timber laid horizontally in a wall to receive the ends of other timbers; a piece of metal on which anything is engraved for the purpose of being printed off on paper; a page of stereotype for printing.—*v.t.*—*plated, plating.* To cover with a plate or plates; to overlay with a thin coating of silver or other metal: used particularly of silver (*plated* vessels).—**plate**

armor, *n.* Defensive armor consisting of plates of metal.—**plate glass,** *n.* A superior kind of thick glass used for mirrors, etc.—**plater,** plā′tėr, *n.* One who coats articles with gold or silver; horse of a poor quality competing for cups of gold or silver plate.—**plating,** plā′ting, *n.* The art of covering articles with a thin coating of metal, especially of overlaying articles made of the baser metals with a thin coating of gold or silver; a thin coating of one metal laid upon another metal.

plateau, pla•tō′, *n.* pl. **plateaus, plateaux,** pla•tōz′, *n.* [Fr., from *plat*, flat; akin to *plate.*] A broad, flat area of land in an elevated position; a tableland.

platen, plat′en, *n.* [From Fr. *plat*, flat.] *Printing*, the flat part of a press by which the impression is made; the roller of a typewriter.

platform, plat′form, *n.* [Fr. *plateforme*—*plate*, flat, and *forme*, a form. PLATE.] Any flat or horizontal structure, especially if raised above some particular level; the flat roof of a building on the outside; the place where guns are mounted on a fortress or battery; the raised walk at a railroad station for landing passengers and goods; a place raised above the floor of a hall set apart for the speakers at public meetings; the aggregate of principles adopted or avowed by any body of men, such as a political party; a declared system of policy (a political *platform*).

platina, plat′i•na, *n.* [Sp. *platina*, from *plata*, silver; akin to *plate.*] The old name of platinum; twisted silver wire.

platinum, plat′i•num, *n.* [From *platina.*] A heavy, grayish-white metallic element, malleable and ductile and resistant to most chemicals; used for jewelry and scientific apparatus. Symbol, Pt; at no., 78; at. wt., 195.09.—**platinic,** pla•tin′ik, *a.* Pertaining to platinum.—**platinize,** plat′i•nīz, *v.t.* To combine or cover with platinum.—**platinoid,** plat′i•noid, *n.* [From *platinum.*] A metal of similar composition to German silver (which see), with an essential addition of 1 to 2 per cent of tungsten; any one of a series of metals allied to platinum.—**platinotype,** plat′i•nō•tīp, *n.* [*Platinum* and *type.*] A permanent photographic print produced by a process in which platinum is used.—**platinous,** plat′i•nus, *a.* Containing or consisting of platinum.

platitude, plat′i•tūd, *n.* [Fr., from *plat*, flat.] Flatness; dullness; insipidity; a trite, dull, or stupid remark; a truism.—**platitudinize,** plat•i•tū′di•nīz, *v.i.* To utter platitudes; to make stale or insipid remarks.

Platonic, Platonical, pla•ton′ik, pla•ton′i•kal, *a.* Pertaining to Plato the philosopher, or to his philosophy, his school, or his opinions.—*Platonic bodies*, the five regular geometrical solids.—*Platonic love*, a pure spiritual affection subsisting between the sexes, unmixed with carnal desires.—*Platonic year*, a period of time determined by the revolution of the equinoxes, which is accomplished in about 26,000 years.—*n.* A follower of Plato.—**Platonically,** pla•ton′i•kal•li, *adv.* In a Platonic manner.—**Platonism,** plā′ton•izm, *n.* The doctrines, opinions, or philosophy of Plato.—**Platonist,** plā′ton•ist, *n.* One who adheres to the philosophy of Plato.—**Platonize,** plā′ton•īz, *v.i.*—*platonized, platonizing.* To adopt the opinions or philosophy of Plato.

platoon, pla•tön′, *n.* [Fr. *peloton*, a ball of thread, a platoon, from *pelote*, a ball of thread, from L.L. *pelota, pilota*, from L. *pila*, a ball.] A military unit of two or more squads or sections; a group of persons with a common characteristic.

platter, plat′ėr, *n.* [From O.Fr. *platel*, dim. of *plat*, a plate. PLATE.] A plate; a large shallow dish for holding eatables.

platter. See PLAT.

platycephalic, platycephalous, plat′i•se•fal″ik, plat•i•sef′a•lus, *a.* [Gr. *platys*, broad, and *kephalē*, head.] Broadheaded; flatheaded.

platypus, plat′i•pus, *n.* [Gr. *platys*, broad, and *pous*, a foot.] A small aquatic mammal of Australia and Tasmania that has a fleshy bill similar to that of a duck.

plaudit, plą′dit, *n.* [L. *plaudite*, do you applaud, imper. of *plaudo, plausum*, to applaud, seen in *plausible, applause, explode.*] Applause; praise bestowed: usually in plural.

plausible, plą′zi•bl, *a.* [L. *plausibilis*, from *plaudo.* PLAUDIT.] Praiseworthy‡; apparently worthy of praise; apparently right; specious; using specious arguments or discourse; fair-spoken. ∴ Syn. under COLORABLE.—**plausibility, plausibleness,** plą•zi•bil′i•ti, plą′zi•bl•nes, *n.* The state or quality of being plausible; speciousness; superficial appearance of right.—**plausibly,** plą′zi•bli, *adv.* In a plausible manner; speciously.—**plausive,** plą′ziv, *a.* Applauding; manifesting praise.

play, plā, *v.i.* [A.Sax. *plegian*, to play, from *plega*, play, pastime; connections doubtful.] To do something not as a task or for profit, but for amusement; to act wantonly or thoughtlessly; to dally, trifle, toy; to move irregularly; to flutter; to contend in a game; to gamble; to perform on an instrument of music; to act with free motion; to work freely (the lungs *play*); to act; to behave; to act a part on the stage; to personate a character.—*To play on* or *upon*, to make sport of; to trifle with; to delude; to give a humorous or fanciful turn to (to *play upon* words).—*v.t.* To perform in sport or for sport or for a prize; to make use of in a game (to *play* a trump card); to enter into a game with; to perform music on; to perform on a musical instrument (a tune); to act on the stage; to act or represent in general; to act like; to behave in the manner of (to *play* the fool); to perform; to execute (to *play* a trick).—*n.* Any exercise intended for pleasure, amusement, or diversion, as baseball, quoits, etc.; a game; amusement; sport; frolic; jest; not earnest; gaming; practice in any contest (sword-*play*); action; use; employment; practice; manner of acting or dealing (fair *play*); a dramatic composition; a comedy or tragedy; a dramatic performance; motion; movement, regular or irregular (the *play* of a wheel); hence, power or space for motion; liberty of action; scope; swing.—*To hold in play*, to keep occupied.—*Play of colors*, an appearance of several prismatic colors in rapid succession on turning an object, as a diamond.—*A play on words*, the giving of words a double signification; a pun.—**playbill,** plā′bil, *n.* A bill exhibited as an advertisement of a play, with the parts assigned to the actors.—**playbook,** plā′bu̧k, *n.* A book of dramatic compositions.—**played out,** *pp.* or *a.* Exhausted, from a game at cards which has been played to the last extremity or deal.—**player,** plā′ėr, *n.* One who plays; an actor; a musician.—**playfellow,** plā′fel•ō, *n.* A companion in amusements or sports.—**playful,** plā′fu̧l, *a.* Sportive; frolicsome; frisky; indulging in gambols; full of sprightly humor; pleasantly jocular or amusing.—**playfully,** plā′fu̧l•li, *adv.* In a playful manner; sportively.—**playfulness,** plā′fu̧l•nes, *n.* The state of being playful; sportiveness.—**playgoer,** plā′gō•ėr, *n.* One who frequents plays.—**playgoing,** plā′gō•ing, *a.* Frequenting the exhibitions of the stage.—**playground,** plā′ground, *n.* A piece of ground set apart for open-air recreation, especially connected with a school, etc., for the pupils.—**playhouse,** plā′hous, *n.* A theater.—**playmate,** plā′māt, *n.* A playfellow; a companion in diversions.—**plaything,** plā′thing, *n.* A toy; anything that serves to amuse.—**playwright,** plā′rīt, *n.* A maker of plays.

plaza, plä′zä, plaz′ä, *n.* [Sp.] A public square in a city or town.

plea, plē, *n.* [O.Fr. *plai, plaid, plait*, a suit, a plea; from L. *placitum*, an opinion, a determination, from *placeo*, to please. PLEASE.] That which is alleged by a party to a legal action in support of his demand; the answer of a defendant to the plaintiff's declaration; a suit or action; a cause in court; that which is alleged in support, justification, or defense; an excuse; a pleading.

pleach,‡ plēch, *v.t.* [Akin to *plash*, to interweave.] To plash; to interweave.

plead, plēd, *v.i.*—pret. and pp. *pleaded*, sometimes *pled.* [Fr. *plaider*, to plead, from L.L. *placitare*, from L. *placitum.* PLEA.] To argue in support of a claim, or in defense against the claim of another; to urge reasons for or against; to attempt to persuade one by argument or supplication; *law*, to present a plea; to present an answer to the declaration of a plaintiff; to deny the plaintiff's declaration and demand.—*To plead guilty* or *not guilty*, to admit or deny guilt.—*v.t.* To discuss, defend, and attempt to maintain by arguments or reasons (to *plead* one's cause); to allege or adduce in proof, support, or vindication; to offer in excuse (to *plead* poverty); to allege and offer in a legal plea or defense, or for repelling a demand in law.—**pleadable,** plē'da•bl, *a.* Capable of being alleged in proof, defense, or vindication.—**pleader,** plē'dėr, *n.* One who pleads; a lawyer who argues in a court of justice; one that forms pleas or pleadings (a special *pleader*).—**pleading,** plē'ding, *n.* The act of advocating any cause; the act or practice of advocating client's causes in courts of law; one of the written statements containing the subject matter of a litigant's demand or claim, or of his defense or answer.

pleasant, etc. See PLEASE.

please, plēz, *v.t.*—*pleased, pleasing.* [O.Fr. *plaisir, pleisir,* etc., Mod.Fr. *plaire,* from L. *placere,* to please; of similar origin are *placid, placable, plea, plead.*] To excite agreeable sensations or emotions in; to delight; to gratify; to satisfy; to content; to seem good to: in this sense used impersonally.—*To be pleased* to do a thing, to take pleasure in doing it; to think fit or condescend to do it.—*v.i.* To give pleasure; to gain approbation; to like; to choose; to prefer; to condescend; to be pleased; to be kind enough (do it, if you *please*).—**pleasing,** plē'zing, *a.* Giving pleasure or satisfaction; agreeable; gratifying; delightful.—**pleasingly,** plē'zing•li, *adv.* In a pleasing manner; in such a way as to give pleasure.—**pleasant,** plez'ant, *a.* [Fr. *plaisant,* ppr. of *plaire.*] Pleasing; agreeable; grateful to the mind or to the senses; cheerful; gay; lively; jocular.—**pleasantly,** plez'ant•li, *adv.* In a pleasant manner; gaily; merrily; cheerfully.—**pleasantness,** plez'ant•nes, *n.* State or quality of being pleasant or agreeable; cheerfulness; gaiety.—**pleasantry,** plez'ant•ri, *n.* [Fr. *plaisanterie.*] Gaiety; merriment; a sprightly or humorous saying; a jest; raillery; lively talk; a laughable trick; a frolic.—**pleasance,** plez'ans, *n.* [Fr. *plaisance.*] Pleasure; delight; a part of a garden or pleasure-grounds secluded by trees or hedges. (*Archaic.*)—**pleasure,** plezh'ėr, *n.* [O.Fr. *plaisir, pleisir,* Mod.Fr. *plaisir,* from L. *placere,* to please; properly an infinitive but as in *leisure* the final syllable has been assimilated to that of nouns in *-ure,* L. *-ura.* PLEASE.] The gratification of the senses or of the mind; agreeable sensations or emotions; the feeling produced by enjoyment or the expectation of good; delight; opposed to *pain*; sensual or sexual gratification; vicious indulgence of the appetite; what the will dictates or prefers; choice; wish; desire; a favor; arbitrary will or choice (to go or stay at *pleasure*).—*To take pleasure in,* to have pleasure or enjoyment in.—*v.t.*—*pleasured, pleasuring.* To give or afford pleasure to; to please; to gratify.—**pleasurable,** plezh'ėr•a•bl, *a.* Pleasing; giving pleasure.—**pleasurableness,** plezh'ėr•a•bl•nes, *n.*—**pleasurably,** plez'ėr•a•bli, *adv.*

pleat, plēt, *n.* [Var. of plait.] A fold of cloth or other material; a plait.—*v.t.* To fold cloth, etc.

plebe, plēb, *n.* [From *plebian.*] A freshman at a military academy.

plebeian, ple•bē'an, *a.* [L. *plebeius,* from *plebes, plebs,* the common people; same root as in PLENTY.] Pertaining to the common people; vulgar; common; belonging to the lower ranks.—*n.* One of the common people or lower ranks of men; originally applied to the common people of ancient Rome, or those free citizens who did not come under the class of the patricians.—**plebeianism,** plē•bē'an•izm, *n.* The state or quality of being plebeian; vulgarity.

plebiscite, pleb'i•sit or pleb'i•sīt, *n.* [Fr., from L. *plebiscitum*—*plebis,* the people, and *scitum,* a decree.] A vote of a whole people or community; a decree of a country obtained by an appeal to universal suffrage.

plectrum, plek'trum, *n.* [L. *plectrum,* from Gr. *plēktron,* from *plēssō,* to strike.] The small instrument of ivory, horn, or metal used for striking the strings of the lyre, or other stringed instrument.

pledge, plej, *n.* [Fr. *pleige,* L.L. *plegius, plegium, plivium, pluvium,* pledge; origin uncertain.] *Law,* the transfer of a chattel by a debtor to a creditor in security of a debt; the thing pawned as security for the repayment of money borrowed or for the performance of some agreement or obligation; a pawn; anything given or considered as a security for the performance of an act; a guarantee; a promise; a surety; a hostage; the drinking of another's health; a health.—*To put in pledge,* to pawn.—*To hold in pledge,* to keep in security.—*To take the pledge,* a popular method of binding one's self to observe principles of total abstinence from intoxicating drink.—*v.t.*—*pledged, pledging.* To give as a pledge or pawn; to deposit in possession of a person as a security; to gage (to *pledge* one's word or honor) to engage solemnly (to *pledge* one's self); to drink a health to; to drink to one's welfare.—**pledgee,** plej'ē', *n.* The person to whom anything is pledged or pawn, promise, etc., is given.—**pledger,** plej'ėr, *n.* One who pledges or offers a pledge; one who drinks a health.

pledget, plej'et, *n.* A compress or small flat mass of lint, laid over a wound to imbibe the matter discharged and keep it clean.

Pleiad, plē'ad, *n. pl.* **Pleiades,** plē'a•dēz, [Gr. *Pleiades,* the Pleiads, from *pleo,* to sail, as the rising of the seven stars indicated the time of safe navigation.] The Pleiads are a cluster of seven stars in the neck of the constellation Taurus; in *poetry,* a group of seven contemporaries in the reign of Ptolemy Philadelphus at Alexandria; seven poets in the reign of Henry III of France modeling their style on Latin and Greek work; seven poets in the reign of Louis XIII.

Pleiocene, plī'i•sēn. See PLIOCENE.

Pleistocene, plīs'to•sēn, *n.* [Gr. *pleistos,* most, and *kainos,* recent.] *Geol.* a division of the Quaternary period of which the fossil remains belong almost wholly to existing species.

plenary, ple'na•ri, *a.* [L.L. *plenarius,* from L. *plenus,* full. PLENTY.] Full; entire; complete.—*Plenary inspiration,* in *theol.* that kind or degree of inspiration which excludes all mixture of error.—**plenarily,** ple'na•ri•li, *adv.* In a plenary manner.

plenipotence, ple•nip'o•tens, *n.* [L. *plenus,* full, and *potentia,* power. PLENTY, POTENT.] Fullness or completeness of power.—**plenipotent,** ple•nip'o•tent, *a.* [L. *plenipotens.*] Possessing full power.—**plenipotentiary,** plen'i•pō•ten"shi•a•ri, *n.* A person invested with full power to transact any business; particularly, an ambassador or envoy to a foreign court, furnished with full power to negotiate a treaty or to transact other business.—*a.* Invested with or containing full power.

plenish, plen'ish, *v.t.* [L. *plenus,* full. REPLENISH.] To replenish.

plenitude, plen'i•tūd, *n.* [L. *plenitudo,* from *plenus,* full.] The state of being full or complete; plenty; abundance; repletion.

plenty, plen'ti, *n.* [O.Fr. *plentē,* from L.L. *plenitas,* fullness, abundance, from L. *plenus,* full, from root of *pleo,* to fill, which is seen also in Gr. *plērēs, pleos,* full, and also in E. *full, fill.*] Abundance; copiousness; a full or adequate supply; sufficiency; abundance of things necessary for man (a time of *plenty*).—*a.* Plentiful; being in abundance. (*Colloq.*)—**plenteous,** plen'tē•us, *a.* Abundant; copious; sufficient for every purpose; yielding abundance; having an abundance.—**plenteously,** plen'tē•us•li, *adv.* In a plenteous manner; plentifully.—**plenteousness,** plen'tē•us•nes, *n.* The state of being plenteous.—**plentiful,** plen'ti•fụl, *a.* Existing in great plenty; copious; abundant; ample; yielding abundant crops; fruitful.—**plentifully,** plen'ti•fụl•li, *adv.* In a plentiful manner.—**plentifulness,** plen'ti•fụl•nes, *n.*

plenum, plē'num, *n.* [L. *plenus,* full.] That state of things in which every part of space is supposed to be full of matter; in opposition to a *vacuum.*

pleomorphism, plē'o•morf"ism, *n.* [Gr. *pleōn,* more, *mōrphē,* form.] In fungi, etc., the occurrence of more than one independent form in the life history.

pleonasm, plē'o•nazm, *n.* [Gr. *pleonasmos,* from *pleon, pleion,* more. PLENTY.] Redundancy of words in speaking or writing; the use of more words to express ideas than are necessary.—**pleonastic,** plē•o•nas'-

tik, *a.* Pertaining to pleonasm; redundant.—**pleonastically,** plē•o•nas′ti•kal•li, *adv.* In a pleonastic manner.

plesiosaur, plesiosaurus, plē′si•ō•sạr, plē′si•ō•sạ″rus, *n.* [Gr. *plēsios,* near, and *sauros,* a lizard.] An extinct marine saurian, chiefly remarkable for its length of neck, nearly allied to the ichthyosaurus.

plethora, pleth′e•ra, *n.* [Gr. *plēthōra,* from *plēthō,* to be full, from *pleos,* full. PLENTY.] *Med.* overfullness of blood; a redundant fullness of the blood vessels; hence, overfullness in any respect; a superabundance.—**plethoric,** ple•thor′ik, *a.* Characterized by plethora; having a full habit of body.—**plethorically,** ple•thor′i•kal•li, *adv.* In a plethoric manner.

pleura, plụ′ra, *n.* [Gr. *pleuron,* a rib, pl. *pleura,* the side.] *Anat.* a thin membrane which covers the inside of the thorax, and also invests the lungs.—**pleural,** plụ′ral, *a.* Pertaining to the pleura.—**pleurisy,** plụ′ri•si, *n.* An inflammation of the pleura.—**pleuritic,** plụ•rit′ik, *a.* Pertaining to pleurisy; diseased with pleurisy.—**pleuropneumonia,** plụ′rō•nū•mō″ni•a, *n.* [Gr. *pleura,* and *pneumōn,* the lungs.] An inflammation of the pleura and substance of the lungs; a combination of pleurisy and pneumonia.

plexiform, plek′si•form, *a.* [L. *plexus,* a fold, and *forma,* form.] In the form of network; complicated.

pleximeter, plek•sim′et•ėr, *n.* [Gr. *plēxis,* percussion, and *metron,* a measure.] *Med.* a small circular or ovoid plate, composed of ivory, india rubber, or the like, placed in contact with the body in diagnosis of disease by percussion.

plexure, plek′sūr, *n.* [L. *plexus,* an interweaving, from *plecto, plexum,* to interweave.] An interweaving; a texture; that which is woven together.—**plexus,** plek′sus, *n.* [L.] *Anat.* a network of vessels, nerves, or fibers.

pliable, plī′a•bl, *a.* [Fr. *pliable,* from *plier,* to bend, to fold, from L. *plico,* to fold, to bend.] Easy to be bent; flexible; pliant; flexible in disposition; easy to be persuaded.—**pliability, pliableness,** plī•a•bil′i•ti, plī′a•bl•nes, *n.* The quality of being pliable; flexibility; a yielding to force or to moral influence.—**pliably,** plī′a•bli, *adv.* In a pliable manner.—**pliant,** plī′ant, *a.* [Fr. ppr. of *plier,* to bend. PLY.] Capable of being easily bent; readily yielding to force or pressure without breaking; flexible; lithe; limber; plastic; easily yielding to moral influence; easy to be persuaded.—**pliantly,** plī′ant•li, *adv.* In a pliant manner.—**pliancy,** plī′an•si, *n.* The state or quality of being pliant; easiness to be bent; readiness to be influenced.

plica, plī′ka, *n.* [L., a fold. PLY.] *Med.* a disease of the hair, in which the hair is vascularly thickened, matted, or clotted; *bot.* a diseased state in plants in which the buds, instead of developing true branches, become short twigs, the whole forming an entangled mass.—**plicate, plicated,** plī′kāt, plī′kā•ted, *a.* [L. *plicatus,* from *plico,* to fold, *plica,* a fold.] *Bot.* plaited; folded like a fan.—**plicately,** plī′kāt•li, *adv.* In a plicate or folded manner.—**plication,** plī•kā′shon, *n.* A folding or fold; *geol.* a bending back of strata on themselves.—**plicature,** plī•kā′chėr, *n.* [L. *plicatura.*] A plication; a folding.

pliers, plī′ėrz, *n. pl.* [Fr. *plier,* to bend. PLY.] A small pair of pincers adapted to handle small articles, and also for bending and shaping wire.

plight, plīt, *v.t.* [A.Sax. *plihtan,* to pledge, to expose to danger, from *pliht,* a pledge, danger; D. *verpligten,* Dan. *forpligte,* G. *verpflichten,* to bind, oblige, or engage. See the noun.] To pledge, as one's word, hand, faith, honor; to give as a security for the performance of some act: never applied to property or goods, and therefore differing from *pledge,* which is applied to property as well as to word, honor, etc.—*n.* [A.Sax. *pliht,* a pledge, obligation, danger; D. and Dan. *pligt,* Sw. *pligt, plikt,* G. *pflicht,* duty.] A pledge or security‡; condition; state; predicament; generally, a risky or dangerous state; a distressed condition (to be in a wretched *plight*).—**plighter,** plī′tėr, *n.* One who plights.

Plimsoll mark, plim′sol, the line on the hull of a British merchant ship, regulating the load carried, first proposed in the Merchant Shipping Act of 1876 by Samuel Plimsoll; since 1930, ships registered in the United States have been required to carry a similar line.

plinth, plinth, *n.* [Gr. *plinthos,* a brick or tile; L. *plinthus.*] *Arch.* a flat square member, in form of a slab, which serves as the foundation of a column; the flat square table under the molding of the base and pedestal, at the bottom of the order.

Pliocene, plī′ō•sēn, *a.* and *n.* [Gr. *pleiōn,* more, and *kainos,* recent.] A geological term applied to the most modern of the divisions of the Tertiary epoch.

plod, plod, *v.i.—plodded, plodding.* [Akin to Prov. E. *plowd,* to wade, *plodge,* to walk through mud or water; Ir. and Gael. *plod, plodach,* a puddle; the primary sense being to walk laboriously, as through mire.] To travel or work slowly, or with steady laborious diligence; to study dully but with steady diligence; to toil; to trudge; to moil.—*v.t.* To go or walk over in a heavy laboring manner; to accomplish by toilsome exertion.—**plodder,** plod′ėr, *n.* A dull, heavy, laborious person.—**plodding,** plod′ing, *p.* and *a.* Given to plod or work with slow and patient diligence; patiently laborious.—**ploddingly,** plod′ing•li, *adv.* In a plodding manner.

plop, plop, *v.t.* and *i.* [Imitative.] To make a sound like that of an object striking water.—*n.* The act of plopping.

plot, plot, *n.* [A.Sax. *plot,* a spot of ground, a spot; Goth. *plats,* a patch. *Plat* is another form. *Plot* in sense of scheme is related to *plot,* piece of ground, as *plan,* a scheme, to *plan,* a design on a flat surface, only *plot* has generally the sense of ill design.] A plat or small extent of ground of a well-defined shape; *surv.* a plan or draft of a field, farm, estate, etc., on paper; a scheme, stratagem, or plan, usually a mischievous one; an intrigue; a conspiracy; the story of a play, poem, novel, or romance, comprising a complication of incidents; the intrigue.—*v.t.—plotted, plotting.* To make a plan of; to plan; to devise; to contrive; to trace a curve on a graph.—*v.i.* To formulate a scheme of mischief against another, or against a government or those who administer it; to conspire; to contrive a plan.—**plotter,** plot′ėr, *n.* One who plots; a conspirator.

plover, pluv′ėr, *n.* [O.Fr. *plovier,* Fr. *pluvier,* lit. the rain bird, from L. *pluvia,* rain, from *pluo,* to rain.] The common name of several species of shore birds of the family Charadriidae generally.

plow, plou, *n.* [Same as Icel. *plogr,* Dan. *ploug, plov,* O.Fris. *ploch,* D. *ploeg,* G. *pflug,* a plough.] An agricultural implement for breaking and turning soil preparatory to planting seed, originally operated by hand, later drawn by oxen or horses, but in modern times generally drawn by a tractor; any of a variety of implements, tools, or instruments for cutting grooves; a carpenter's or joiner's tool for grooving; *astron.* Charles's Wain, otherwise known as the Dipper or the constellation Ursa Major.—*Ice plow,* a plow for cutting grooves in ice preparatory to its removal; an ice breaker.—*Rotary snow plow,* a snow plow equipped with a large rotary fan or propeller, which plows into the snow and clears the highway by blowing the snow to one side.—*Snow plow,* a device attached to the front of a locomotive, street car, automobile, or motor truck to remove snow from sidewalks, streets, highways—*v.t.* To turn the soil; to turn the soil with a plow; to make furrows, grooves, or ridges; to *plow* under;, to cut through water with a yacht, speedboat, or any other type of craft; to *plow* through water.—*v.i.* To do work with a plow; to admit of plowing, as dry snow *plows* easily.—**plowboy, plowman,** *n.* A boy or man who operates or guides a plow; a rustic person; a farmer.—**plowshare,** *n.* That part of the plow which cuts and turns the soil.

pluck, pluk, *v.t.* [A.Sax. *pluccian,* to pluck=D. and L.G. *plukken,* Dan. *plukke,* Icel. *plokka, plukka,* G. *pflụcken.*] To gather; to pick; to cull, as berries or flowers; to pull with sudden force or effort; to twitch; by a similar action to cause the string of a musical instrument to vibrate and produce a sound;

to strip by plucking; to strip feathers from (to *pluck* a fowl); to rob (*slang*); to pull or draw, literally or figuratively.—*To pluck up courage*, to assume or resume courage.—**plucker,** pluk′er, *n.*

pluck, pluk, *n.* [Comp. Gael. and Ir. *pluc*, a lump, a knot, a bunch; as to the figurative sense compare a bold *heart*, a lily-*livered* rascal, a man of another *kidney*, *bowels* of compassion, etc.] The heart, liver, and lungs of a sheep, ox, or other animal of the butcher's market; courage or spirit (*colloq.*).—**pluckily,** pluk′i·li, *adv.* In a plucky manner; spiritedly. (*Colloq.*)—**plucky,** pluk′i, *a.* Spirited; courageous. (*Colloq.*)

plug, plug, *n.* [Same as D. *plug*, L.G. *pluck*, a block.] Any piece of wood or other material used to stop a hole; a stopper; a fitting in various electrical connections; a spark plug; a cake of tobacco, usually for chewing; that part of a cylindrical lock which is rotated by the key; a discharge pipe or hydrant for drawing water from a water main (a *water* plug); something wornout or inferior; especially a wornout horse (*slang*).—*v.t.* To insert a plug; to make tight by stopping a hole; to shoot (*slang*); to work steadily; to plod (*slang*).—**plugger,** plug′ėr, *n.* One who works doggedly. (*Slang.*)

plum, plum, *n.* [A.Sax. *plume*, L.G. *plumme*, G. *pflaume*, from L.L. *pruna* (Fr. *prune*), from L. *prunum*, a plum, from *prunus*=Gr. *prounos*, the plum tree.] A well-known fleshy fruit containing a stone or kernel, and when dried being called a prune; also the tree producing it; a choice or lucrative thing.—**plum pudding,** *n.* Pudding containing raisins or currants.

plumb, plum, *n.* [Fr. *plomb*, from L. *plumbum*, lead.] A plummet.—*a.* Standing according to a plumb line; perpendicular.—*adv.* In a perpendicular direction.—*v.t.* To adjust by a plumb line; to set in a perpendicular direction; to sound with a plummet; hence to ascertain the capacity of; to test.—**plumbago,** plum·bā′gō, *n.* [L., from *plumbum*, lead.] Another name for *Graphite*.—**plumbaginous,** plum·baj′i·nus, *a.* Resembling or consisting of plumbago.—**plumbeous,** plum·bē′us, *a.* [L. *plumbum*, lead.] Consisting of lead; leaden.—**plumber,** plum′ėr, *n.* One who fits and repairs water and gas pipes; originally a worker in lead.—**plumbic,** plum′bik, *a.* Pertaining to lead; derived from lead.—**plumbiferous,** plum·bif′ėr·us, *a.* Producing lead.—**plumbing,** plum′ing, *n.* Plumber's trade or work; that which is installed by a plumber; the act of using a plumb.—**plumbism,** plum′bizm, *n.* Poisoning by lead taken into the system.—**plumb line,** *n.* A line having a metal weight attached to one end, used to determine a perpendicular; a line perpendicular to the plane of the horizon.—**plumb rule,** *n.* A narrow board with a plumb line attached, used by masons, bricklayers, etc., for determining a perpendicular.

plume, plöm, *n.* [Fr., from L. *pluma*, the downy part of a feather, a small soft feather; cog. W. *pluf*, plumage; Skr. *plu*, to swim, to fly.] The feather of a bird, particularly a large or conspicuous feather; a feather or collection of feathers worn as an ornament; token of honor; prize of contest. *v.t.*—*plumed*, *pluming*. To pick and adjust the feathers of; to dress the feathers; to adorn with feathers or plumes; to pride; to boast: in this sense used reflexively.—**plumage,** plö′mij, *n.* [Fr., from *plume*, a feather.] The feathers that cover a bird.—**plumelet,** plöm′let. *n.* A small plume.—**plumose,** plö′mōs, *a.* [L. *plumosus*.] Feathery; resembling feathers; *bot.* consisting of long hairs which are themselves hairy (*plumose* bristle).—**plumosity,** plö·mos′i·ti, *n.* The state of being plumose.

plummet, plum′et, *n.* [Fr. *plumbet*, from *plumb*; O.Fr. *plummet*, Fr. *plomet*. PLUMB.] A piece of lead or other metal attached to a line, used in sounding the depth of water.—*v.i.* To drop or plunge down.

plump, plump, *a.* [Allied to D. *plomp*, unwieldy, bulky; G., Dan., and Sw. *plump*, clumsy, massive, coarse; from a verbal root seen in E. *plim*, to swell.] Swelled with fat or flesh to the full size; fat or stout in person; fleshy; having a full skin; distended.—*v.t.* To make plump; to dilate; to fatten; to cause to fall suddenly and heavily.—*v.i.* [Perhaps an imitative word in first sense; as also in last sense above.] To plunge or fall like a heavy mass or lump of dead matter; to fall suddenly or at once; to grow plump.—*adv.* At once or with a sudden heavy fall; suddenly; heavily.—**plumper,** plump′ėr, *n.* One who or that which plumps; a vote given to one candidate when more than one are to be elected, which might have been divided among the number to be elected; a person who gives such a vote.—**plumply,** plump′li, *adv.* Fully; roundly; without reserve.—**plumpness,** plump′nes, *n.* The state or quality of being plump; fullness of skin.—**plumpy,** plump′i, *a.* Plump; fat; jolly.

plumule, plö′mūl, *n.* [L. *plumula*, dim. of *pluma*, a feather. PLUME.] *Bot.* the growing point of the embryo, situated at the apex of the radicle, and at the base of the cotyledons, by which it is protected when young; the rudiment of the future stem of a plant.

plunder, plun′dėr, *v.t.* [G. *plündern* (from *plunder*, baggage.)=D. *plunderen*, Sw. *plondra*, Dan. *plyndre*, to plunder. The word entered the English and other tongues about the time of the Thirty Years' War.] To take goods or valuables forcibly from; to pillage; to spoil; to rob in a hostile way; to take by pillage or open force.—*n.* The act of plundering; robbery; that which is taken from an enemy by force; pillage; spoil; that which is taken by theft; robbery, or fraud.—**plunderer,** plun′dėr·ėr, *n.* One who plunders.

plunge, plunj, *v.t.*—*plunged*, *plunging*. [From Fr. *plonger*, from hypothetical Latin *plumbicare*, from *plumbum*, lead; lit. to fall like lead or to fall plumb.] To thrust into water or other fluid substance, or into any substance easily penetrable; to immerse; to thrust; to thrust or drive into any state or condition (to *plunge* a nation into war); to baptize by immersion.—*v.t.* To thrust or drive one's self into water or other fluid; to drive or to rush in; to fall or rush into distress or any state or circumstances in which the person or thing is enveloped, enclosed, or overwhelmed (to *plunge* into war); to throw the body forward and the hind legs up, as an unruly horse; to bet heavily and recklessly (*slang*).—*n.* A dive, rush, or leap into something; the act of pitching or throwing the body forward and the hind legs up, as an unruly horse; a place for diving, as a swimming tank or deep pool; a reckless speculation (*slang*).—**plunger,** plun′jėr, *n.*

plunk, plungk, *v.t.* and *i.* [Imitative.] To make a hollow metallic sound; to drop or put down suddenly.—*n.* The act or sound of plunking; a blow.—*adv.* With a plunking sound.

pluperfect, plö′pėr·fekt, *a.* and *n.* [L. *plus quam perfectum*, more than perfect.] *Gram.* applied to that tense of a verb which denotes that an action was finished at a certain period in the past; past or preterite perfect (he *had done* it).

plural, plö′ral, *a.* [L. *pluralis*, from *plus*, *pluris*, more.] Containing more than one; consisting of two or more, or designating two or more; *gram.* the *plural number* is that number or form of a word which designates more than one.—*n.* A form of a word expressing more than one; the plural number.—**pluralism,** plö′ral·izm, *n.* The quality of being plural; a philosophic doctrine which maintains that there are more than one (usually more than two) fundamental substances.—**pluralist,** plö′ral·ist, *n.*—**plurality,** plö·ral′i·ti, *n.* The state of being plural; an aggregate of two or more of the same kind; the greater number; the majority; in an election, the excess of votes of one candidate over those of any other candidate for the same office.—**pluralize,** plö′ral·īz, *v.t.*—*pluralized*, *pluralizing*. To make plural by using the termination of the plural number.—**plurally,** plö′ral·li, *adv.* In a plural manner; in a sense implying more than one.

plus, plus. [L., more.] *Alg.* or *arith.* the name of a character marked thus +, which being placed between two numbers or quantities, signifies that they are to be added together; frequently used prepositionally, with the signification of in addition to (ability *plus* impudence.)

plush, plush, *n.* [Fr. *pluche*, *peluche*, It. *peluzzo*, from L. *pilus*, hair.

PILE.] A textile fabric with a sort of velvet nap or shag on one side resembling short hairs.

pluteus, plö'tē•us, *n.* [L.] A balustrade; a parapet; among the Romans a sort of wheeled shed covered with raw hides in which a besieging party made their approaches.

Pluto, plö'tō, *n.* In Greek mythology, the chief divinity of the lower regions; a planet of the solar system, the remotest known from the sun, visible only by telescope.

plutocracy, plö•tok'ra•si, *n.* [Gr. *Ploutos*, the god of wealth, and *krateia*, rule, *archē*, power.] The power or rule of wealth,—**plutocrat,** plö'to•krat, *n.* A person possessing power or influence solely or mainly owing to his riches.—**plutocratic,** plö•to•krat'ik, *a.* Pertaining to or characteristic of a plutocracy or a plutocrat.

Plutonic, Plutonian, plö•ton'ik, plö•tō'ni•an, *a.* [From *Pluto*, the king of the infernal regions among the ancient Greeks.] Of or relating to Pluto or to the regions of fire; subterranean, dark.—*Plutonic action*, the influence of volcanic heat and other subterranean causes under pressure.—*Plutonic rocks*, unstratified crystalline rocks formed at great depth beneath the earth's surface.—*Plutonic theory*, that which ascribes the changes on the earth's surface to the agency of fire. See NEPTUNIAN.

plutonium, plö•tō'ni•um, *n.* A radioactive element formed in the disintegration of neptunium. Symbol, Pu; at. no., 94.

pluvial, plö'vi•al, *a.* [L. *pluvialis*, from *pluvia*, rain, from *pluo*, to rain; same root as in *flow*.] Rainy; humid; relating to rain; *geol.* applied to results and operations which depend on or arise from the action of rain.—**pluvious,** plö'vi•us, *a.* [L. *pluviosus*.] Rainy; pluvial.

pluviometer, plö•vi•om'et•ėr, *n.* [L. *pluvia*, rain, and Gr. *metron*, measure.] A rain gauge; an instrument for measuring rainfall.—**pluviometrical,** plö'vi•o•met"ri•kal, *a.*

ply, plī, *v.t.*—*plied, plying.* [From Fr. *plier* (also *ployer*), to fold or bend, from L. *plicare*, to fold.] To fold.—*n.* A fold; a thickness; a unit of yarn, as two-ply.—**plywood,** plī'wụd, *n.* Wood made from several thin sheets, which are glued together.

ply, plī, *v.t.* [From *apply*.] To use or wield diligently or steadily; to employ with diligence (to *ply* a needle or an oar); to keep busy; to practice or perform with diligence; to busy one's self in; to press hard, with blows or missiles; to assail briskly; to beset; to urge; to solicit, as for a favor.—*To ply with*, to present or offer to urgently and repeatedly; to press upon, especially with some ulterior object (to *ply* one *with* flattery).—*v.i.* To be steadily employed; to work steadily; to offer service; to run regularly between any two ports or places, as a vessel or vehicle; *naut.* to endeavor to make way against the wind.—*n.* A fold; a plait; a twist: often used in composition to designate the number of twists, etc. (a three-*ply* carpet); bent; turn; direction; bias.—**plyer,** plī'ėr, *n.* One who or that which plies; *pl.* same as *Pliers*.

Plymouth Brethren, plim'uth, breTH'ren, *n. pl.* A sect of Christians who first appeared at Plymouth, England, in 1830.—**Plymouth Rock,** the spot in Plymouth harbor, Mass., where the Pilgrims landed, Dec. 21, 1620; an American breed of chicken.

pneumatic, nū•mat'ik, *a.* [Gr. *pneumatikos*, from *pneuma*, *pneumatos*, breath, spirit, from *pneō*, to breathe or blow.] Consisting of or resembling air; having the properties of an elastic fluid; pertaining to air, or to elastic fluids or their properties; moved or played by means of air; filled with or fitted to contain air; applied to numerous instruments, machines, apparatus, etc., for experimenting on elastic fluids, or for working by means of the compression or exhaustion of air (*pneumatic conveyors* and *pneumatic tools*, such as drills, hammers, grinders, rammers, diggers, pavement breakers, and hoists).—*Pneumatic philosophy*, a name formerly applied to the science of metaphysics.—**pneumatics,** nū•mat'iks, *n.* That branch of physics which treats of the mechanical properties of elastic fluids and particularly of atmospheric air.—**pneumatology,** nū•ma•tol'o•ji, *n.* The branch of philosophy which treats of the nature and operations of mind or spirit; psychology.—**pneumatometer,** nū•ma•tom'et•ėr, *n.* An instrument for measuring the quantity of air inhaled into the lungs at each inspiration and given out at each respiration; a spirometer.

pneumogastric, nū•mō•gas'trik, *a.* [Gr. *pneumōn*, a lung, and *gastēr*, the belly.] *Anat.* pertaining to the lungs and stomach.—*Pneumogastric nerves*, a pair of nerves extending over the viscera of the chest and abdomen.

pneumonia, nū•mō'ni•a, *n.* [Gr. *pneumōn*, a lung, from *pneō*, to breathe.] *Med.* an inflammation of the lungs.—**pneumonic,** nū•mon'ik, *a.* Pertaining to the lungs; pulmonic.

poach, pōch, *v.t.* [From Fr. *pocher*, to poach eggs, from *poche* a pouch or pocket, the white of the egg forming a sort of pocket for the yolk. POUCH.] To cook (eggs) by breaking and pouring into boiling water; to cook with butter after breaking in a vessel.

poach, pōch, *v.i.* [Either from the above word, meaning originally to pouch or pocket thievishly, or a softened form of *poke*, to push, to intrude.] To intrude or encroach on the property of another to steal or plunder; to steal game or carry it away privately; to kill or destroy game contrary to law.—**poacher,** pōch'ėr, *n.* One who poaches or steals game; one who kills game unlawfully.

poach, pōch, *v.t.* [A later and softened form of *poke*, to thrust. POKE.] To stab; to pierce; to spear (to *poach* fish); to force or drive into so as to penetrate; to tread, as snow or soft ground, so as to render it broken and slushy.—*v.i.* To become soft and slushy or miry; to be swampy.

pochard, pōch'ėrd, *n.* [Lit. the *poacher*, one that poaches or pokes.] The name of a genus of oceanic ducks, natives of the Arctic Seas.

pock, pok, *n.* [A.Sax. *poc* or *pocc*, D. *pok*, G. *pok*, a vesicle or pustule; perhaps akin to *poke*, a bag. *Pox*=*pocks*.] A pustule raised on the surface of the body in an eruptive disease, as the small pox.—**pockmark,** pok'märk, *n.* Mark or scar made by the small pox.

pocket, pok'et, *n.* [A dim. of *poke*, a pouch or bag.] A small bag inserted in a garment for carrying small articles; a small bag or net to receive the balls in billiards; a certain quantity, from 1½ to 2 cwt. (a *pocket* of hops); *mineral.* a small cavity in a rock, or on its surface, containing gold; a mass of rich ore.—*To be in pocket*, to have gain or profit from some transaction.—*To be out of pocket*, to expend or lose money.—*v.t.* To put or conceal in the pocket; to take clandestinely.—*To pocket an insult*, *affront*, *wrong*, or the like, to receive it without resenting it, or at least without seeking redress.—**air pocket,** *n.* A condition of the atmosphere met with by aviators in which the machine tends to drop as if into a 'pocket' empty of air, supposed to be due to a downward current at the point.—**pocketbook,** *n.* A case used for carrying papers in the pocket; a handbag or purse.—**pocket book,** *n.* A small paperbound book.—**pocket knife,** *n.* A knife that has one or more blades which fold into the handle.—**pocket money,** *n.* Money for small expenses.—**pocket veto,** *n.* An indirect veto by which an executive holds a legislative bill, without signing it, until the legislature adjourns.

pockmark, etc. See POCK.

pococurante, pō'kō•kö•ran"tā, *n.* [It. *poco*, little, and *curo*, to care.] One who cares little; an apathetic, careless, indifferent person.—**pococurantism,** pō'kō•kö•rant"izm, *n.* The character, disposition, or habits of a pococurante; extreme indifference, apathy, or carelessness.

pod, pod, *n.* [Probably connected with Dan. *pude*, Sw. *puta*, a pillow or cushion, as also with E. *pad*, a cushion.] A term applied to a number of different pericarps or seed vessels of plants, such as the legume, the loment, the siliqua, the silicle, the follicle, etc.—*v.i.*—*podded, podding.* To swell and assume the appearance of a pod; to produce pods.

podagra, pō•dag'ra, *n.* [Gr., from *pous*, *podos*, the foot, and *agra*, a taking or seizure.] Gout in the foot.

podesta, pō•des'ta, *n.* [It. *podesta*, a

governor, from L. *potestas*, power.] A chief magistrate of the Italian republics of the Middle Ages.

podgy, poj'i, *a.* Pudgy; fat and short.

podiatry, pō·dī'a·tri, *n.* [Gr. *pous, podos*, foot, and the suffix *iatry*.] *Med.* the study and treatment of foot disorders.

podium, pō'di·um, *n.* [L. *podium*, Gr. *pous, podos*, foot.] The low enclosure running all round the amphitheater; *arch.* a continuous pedestal or low wall on which columns rest.

podophyllin, pod·o·fil'in, *n.* [Gr. *pous, podos*, a foot, and *phyllon*, a leaf.] A resin obtained from the root stock of the mayapple, used in medicine as a purgative.

poem, pō'em, *n.* [Fr. *poème*, from L. *poema*, from Gr. *poiēma*, lit. the thing made, from *poieō*, to make. POET.] A metrical composition; a composition in which the verses consist of certain measures, whether in blank verse or in rhyme; a composition in which the language is that of excited imagination.—**poesy,** pō'e·si, *n.* [Fr. *poésie*, L. *poesis*, from Gr. *poiēsis*, the art of writing poems.] The art of or skill in composing poems; poetry; metrical composition; a short conceit engraved on a ring or other thing (*Shak.*). POSY.—**poet,** pō'et, *n.* [Fr. *poète*, from L. *poeta*, Gr. *poiētēs*, lit. a maker, from *poieō*, to make. So in England poets were formerly often called 'makers'.] The author of a poem; the composer of a metrical composition; one skilled in making poetry, or who has a particular genius for metrical composition; one distinguished for poetic talents. —**poetaster,** pō'et·as·tėr, *n.* [From *poet*, and the pejorative *-aster*; comp. *criticaster*, etc.] A petty poet; a pitiful rhymer or writer of verses.—**poetess,** pō'et·es, *n.* A female poet.—**poetic, poetical,** pō·et'ik, pō·et'i·kal, *a.* [L. *poeticus*, Gr. *poiētikos*.] Pertaining to poetry; suitable to poetry; expressed in poetry; having a metrical form; possessing the peculiar beauties of poetry.—*Poetical justice*, a distribution of rewards and punishments such as is common in poetry and works of fiction, but hardly in accordance with the realities of life.—*Poetic license*, a liberty or license taken by a poet with regard to matters of fact or language in order to produce a desired effect.—**poetically,** pō·et'i·kal·li, *adv.* In a poetical manner.—**poetics,** pō·et'iks, *n.* That branch of criticism which treats of the nature and laws of poetry.—**poetize,** pō'et·īz, *v.i.* [Fr. *poétiser*.] To write as a poet; to compose verse.—**poet laureate,** *n.* See LAUREATE.—**poetry,** pō'et·ri, *n.* [O.Fr. *poeterie*, from *poete*, a poet.] That one of the fine arts which exhibits its special character and powers by means of language; the art which has for its object the creation of intellectual pleasure by means of imaginative and passionate language, generally in verse; the language of the imagination or emotions rhythmically expressed, or such language expressed in an elevated style of prose; especially that creative writing which is divided into lines, each containing a determined number of sounds, the sounds being accented according to a regular and determined rhythmical pattern; similar creative writing, of looser structure, in which the phrases flow in a cadenced pattern; in a wide sense whatever appeals to the emotions or the sense of beauty; verse; poems.

pogrom, pō·grom', *n.* [Russian.] An organized massacre or attack on a party, e.g., Jews.

poignant, poi'nant, *a.* [Fr. *poignant*, part. of *poindre*, from L. *pungere*, *pungo*, to prick. POINT.] Stimulating the organs of taste; piquant; pointed; keen; bitter; irritating; satirical; severe; piercing; very painful or acute.—**poignantly,** poi'nant·li, *adv.* In a poignant manner.—**poignancy,** poi'nan·si, *n.* The state or quality of being poignant.

poilu, pwa·lü', *a.* [Fr. 'hairy'.] A slang term, equivalent to the English 'Tommy', and applied to a soldier in French army; from the custom of letting the beard grow when on active service.

poinsettia, poin·set'i·a, *n.* [N.L. after J. R. Poinsett (1779-1851).] A tropical plant (genus *Poinsettia*) with lobed leaves and bright red bracts.

point, point, *n.* [Fr. *point*, a point, a spot, a matter, moment, etc., *pointe*, something sharp or pointed, from L. *punctum*, a puncture, from *pungo, punctum*, to puncture, the latter the fem. part of Fr. *poindre*, to prick.] The mark made by the end of a sharp piercing instrument; *geom.* an element which has neither length, breadth, nor thickness; a mark of punctuation; a division of the card of the mariner's compass, the card of which has its circumference divided into 32 equal spaces; north, south, east, and west, or any intermediate direction; any place marked in the heavens of importance in astronomical calculations; that which pricks, pierces, or punctures; particularly the sharp end of a thorn, pin, needle, knife, sword, and the like; a tool or instrument which pricks or pierces; a small cape or promontory; a lace, string, or the like, with a tag, formerly used for fastening articles of dress; lace worked by the needle; a lively turn of thought or expression which strikes with force or agreeable surprise; the sting of an epigram; hence, force or expression generally (his action gave *point* to his words); a salient trait of character; a peculiarity; a characteristic (the good or bad *points* of a man); a certain external peculiarity of an animal (the *points* of a horse or a dog); single thing or subject; matter (right in every *point*); particular thing desired or required; aim; purpose (to gain one's *point*); a single part of a complicated question, or of a whole; an indivisible part of time or space; the eve or verge (at the *point* of death); a fielder in the game of cricket who stands a little to the off side of the batter's wicket, or the spot where he stands; a mark to denote the degree of success or progress one has attained in certain trials of skill and games, as in rifle shooting, billiards, cards, and the like, a single point counting one.—*Acting point*, in *physics*, the exact point at which any impulse is given.—*Physical point*, the smallest or least sensible object of sight.—*Point of incidence*, that point upon the surface of a medium at which a ray of light falls.—*Point of reflection*, the point from which a ray is reflected.—*Point of sight*, that point of a picture which is determined by a line from the eye of the artist perpendicular to the perspective plane.—*Point of war*, a martial note on a trumpet or bugle.—*Vowel points*, in Hebrew, etc., certain marks representing the vowels, which precede or follow the consonant sounds.—*To stand upon points*, to be punctilious; to be nice or overscrupulous.—*v.t.* To give a point to; to cut, forge, grind, or file to a point; to add to the force or expression of; to direct toward an object or place; to aim; to direct the eye or notice to; to indicate the purpose or point of; to punctuate; *masonry*, to fill the joints of with mortar, and smooth them with the point of a trowel.—*To point out*, to show by the finger or by other means.—*v.i.* To direct the finger for designating an object and exciting attention to it: with *at*; to indicate the presence of game by standing and turning the nose in its direction, as dogs do to sportsmen; to show distinctly by any means.—**point-blank,** *a.* [This phrase has its origin in the directness with which an arrow is aimed at the white mark or blank in the center of a butt.] In *gun.* having a horizontal direction; *fig.* direct; plain; explicit; express. As an adverb, horizontally; directly. —**point-device,**† *a.* [From *point*, condition, and *devise*, to imagine; lit. in as fine a condition as could be imagined.] Precise, nice, or finical to excess. (*Shak.*)—**pointed,** poin'ted, *p.* and *a.* Having a sharp point. aimed at or expressly referring to some particular person (a *pointed* remark); epigrammatical; abounding in conceits or lively turns.—*Pointed style*, in *arch.* a name applied to several styles usually called *Gothic*. —**pointedly,** poin'ted·li, *adv.* In a pointed manner.—**pointedness,** poin'ted·nes, *n.* The state or quality of being pointed.—**pointer,** poin'tėr, *n.* One who or that which points; a variety of dog remarkable for its habit of pointing at game.—**Pointers,** *n.* Two stars in the Great Bear, through which a straight line points to the polestar.—**point lace,** *n.* A fine kind of lace wrought with a needle.—**pointless,** point'les, *a.* Having no point; blunt; obtuse; having no smartness or keenness.—

point of view, *n.* The position from which something is observed or considered; personal standpoint; attitude.

poise, poiz, *v.t.—poised, poising.* [O. Fr. *poiser, peiser,* Fr. *peser,* from L. *penso,* to weigh out, from *pensus,* weighed, pp. of *pendo,* to weigh. PENDANT.] To balance in weight; to make of equal weight; to hold or place in equilibrium or equiponderance; to load with weight for balancing.—*v.i.* To be balanced or suspended; *fig.* to hang in suspense; to depend.—*n.* Weight; gravity; a thing suspended or attached as a counterweight; a counterpoise; hence, regulating power; that which balances; the weight used in weighing with steelyards, to balance the substance weighed; equipoise; balance; equilibrium.

poison, poi′zn, *n.* [Fr. *poison,* from L. *potio, potionis,* a drink, a draught, from *poto,* to drink. POTION.] Any agent capable of producing a morbid, noxious, dangerous, or deadly effect upon the animal economy, when introduced either by cutaneous absorption, respiration, or the digestive canal; that which taints or destroys moral purity or health.—*v.t.* To infect with poison; to put poison in or on; to add poison to; to attack, injure, or kill by poison; to taint; to mar, impair, vitiate, corrupt.—**poisoner,** poi′zn•ėr, *n.*—**poison gas,** *n.* A noxious gas used (as in warfare) to kill, injure, or disable.—**poison ivy,** *n.* A three-leafed, vinelike ivy having white berries, poisonous to the touch.—**poison oak,** *n.* A species of poison ivy.—**poison sumac,** *n.* A poisonous swamp shrub, related to poison ivy, having seven to thirteen leaves and greenish-white berries.—**poisonous,** poi′zn•us, *a.*—**poisonously,** poi′zn•us•li, *adv.*

poke, pōk, *n.* [O.D. a *poke,* a sack or bag; Icel. *poki,* a sack, a bag; *pouch* is a softened form of this, and *pocket* a diminutive.] A pouch; a bag; a sack.—**poke bonnet,** *n.* A long, straight, projecting bonnet formerly worn by women.

poke, pōk, *v.t.—poked, poking.* [D. and L.G. *poken,* to poke; Sw. *pak,* a stick; comp. Ir. *poc,* a blow; Gael. *puc,* to push.] To thrust something long or pointed against, as the hand or a stick, hence, to feel or search, as in the dark or in a hole —*To poke fun at,* to ridicule.—*v.i.* To grope; to search; to feel or push one's way, as in the dark; to busy one's self without a definite object: followed by *about.*—*n.* A gentle thrust; a jog; a sudden push.—**poker,** pō′kėr, *n.* One who pokes; a metal rod for stirring fire.

poker, pō′kėr, *n.* [Origin unknown.] A gambling game played with cards. —**poker face,** *n.* An inscrutable facial expression.

pokeweed, pōk′wēd, *n.* [Of American Indian origin.] A North American plant (genus *Phytolacca*) whose berries and roots have emetic and purgative qualities.

polar. See POLE.

polder, pōl′dėr, *n.* [D.] In the Netherlands, a tract of land below the level of the sea or nearest river, which, being originally a morass or lake, has been drained and brought under cultivation.

pole, pōl, *n.* [A.Sax. *pal,* a pole, a stake; collateral form of *pale,* L.G. and D. *paal,* from L. *palus,* a stake. PALE.] A long slender piece of wood; a tall piece of timber: frequently used in composition (a carriage-*pole,* a May-*pole*); a perch or rod, a measure of length containing 5½ yards. *Under bare poles,* said of a ship when her sails are all furled.—*v.t.—poled, poling.* To furnish with poles for support; to bear or convey on poles; to impel by poles; to push forward by the use of poles; as to *pole* a skiff.

pole, pōl, *n.* [Fr. *pôle,* L. *polus,* the pole of the heavens, the heavens, from Gr. *polos,* the axis of the sphere, the firmament, from *pelō,* to turn or move.] One of the two points in which the axis of the earth is supposed to meet the sphere of the heavens; the fixed point about which the stars appear to revolve; one of the extremities of the earth's axis; a point on the surface of any sphere equally distant from every part of the circumference of a great circle of the sphere; the polestar; one of the points of a body at which its attractive or repulsive energy is concentrated, or in which a polar force is exerted; in *magnetism,* one of the two points at which the magnetic strength of a magnet is principally concentrated.—*Unit strength of pole,* or unit pole, is that pole which will attract or repel a pole of equal strength at a distance of one centimeter with unit force.—*The strength of a pole* is the force exerted between it and a unit pole at unit distance.—*Magnetic pole,* one of the points on the earth at which the dipping needle is vertical, or the magnetic intensity greatest.—*Poles of a voltaic cell* or *battery,* the connections at which the current passes from the battery to the external circuit, and *vice versa*; the current leaving the battery at the *positive* pole, and entering it at the *negative* pole.—**polestar,** *n.* A star of the second magnitude, situated about 1° from the North Pole, round which it describes a small circle; *fig.* that which serves as a guide or director; a lodestar.—**polar,** pō′lėr, *a.* [L.L. *polaris,* from L. *polus,* a pole.] Pertaining to a pole or the poles of a sphere; pertaining to one of the poles of the earth or of the heavens; proceeding from the poles of the earth; pertaining to a magnetic pole or poles; pertaining to the points of a body at which its attractive or repulsive energy is concentrated.—*Polar angle,* the angle at a pole formed by two meridians.—*Polar axis,* that axis of an equatorial which is parallel to the earth's axis.—*Polar bear.* See BEAR.—**polar bodies,** *n.* Two minute cells resulting from the last stages of the cell divisions, which end in the production of an ovum (egg cell).—*Polar circles,* the arctic and antarctic circles.—*Polar clock,* an apparatus whereby the hour of the day is found by means of the polarization of the scattered sunlight from the polar regions.—*Polar distance,* the angular distance of a heavenly body from the elevated pole of the heavens.—*Polar forces,* physical forces that are developed and act in pairs, with opposite tendencies, as in magnetism, electricity, etc.—*Polar lights,* the aurora borealis or australis.—*Polar star,* the polestar.—**polarimeter, polariscope,** pō•lar•im′et•ėr, pō•lar′i•skōp, *n.* An optical instrument, various kinds of which have been contrived, for exhibiting the polarization of light.—**polarity,** pō•lar′i•ti, *n.* That quality of a body in virtue of which peculiar properties reside in certain points called poles.—**polarization,** pō′lėr•i•zā″-shon, *n.* The act of polarizing or giving polarity to a body; the state of being polarized or of having polarity; in a voltaic cell, the setting up of a back electromotive force owing to the deposition of gases on the electrodes.—*Polarization of light,* a change produced upon light by the action of certain media, by which it exhibits the appearance of having polarity or poles possessing different properties.—**polarize,** pō′lėr•īz, *v.t. —polarized, polarizing.* To develop polarity in.—**polarizer,** pō•lėr•ī′zėr, *n.* That part of a polariscope by which light is polarized.

Pole, pōl, *n.* A native of Poland.

poleax, *n.* [*Pole* may here be the long stick; but perhaps it is for *poll,* the head.] A kind of ax or hatchet.

polecat, pōl′kat, *n.* [Supposed to be for *poult-cat,* that is, chicken or poultry cat, or abbrev. from *Polish cat.*] An animal of the weasel family, about 17 inches in length excluding the tail, very destructive to poultry; also, a skunk.

polemic, polemical, pō•lem′ik, pō•lem′i•kal, *a.* [Gr. *polemikos,* from *polemos,* war.] Pertaining to polemics; given to controversy; engaged in supporting an opinion or system by controversy.—**polemic,** *n.* A disputant; one who carries on a controversy; one who writes in support of an opinion or system in opposition to another.—**polemics,** pō•lem′iks, *n.* The art or practice of disputation; controversy; controversial writings.

police, po•lēs′, *n.* [Fr. *police,* from L. *politia,* from Gr. *politeia,* government, administration, from *polis,* a city.] The means instituted by a government or community to maintain public order, liberty, property, and individual security; the body of men by whom the municipal laws and regulations are enforced and public order maintained.—*Police commissioner,* one of a body of men, elected or appointed, whose duty it is to manage police affairs.—*Police court,* a court for the trial of offenders brought up on charges preferred by the police.—*Police mag-*

istrate, a judge who presides at a police court.—*Police squad,* a group of policemen operating together.—*Police squad car,* an automobile, equipped with one-way or two-way shortwave radio, in which police patrol.—*Police station,* the headquarters of the police or of a section of them.—**policeman,** po•lēs′man, *n.* An ordinary member of the police force, (if assigned to a beat, a *patrolman*).

policy, pol′i•si, *n.* [L. *politia,* Gr. *politeia,* polity. POLICE.] The art or manner of governing a nation; the line of conduct which the rulers of a nation adopt on particular questions, especially with regard to foreign countries; the principles on which any measure or course of action is based; prudence or wisdom of governments or individuals in the management of their affairs public or private; dexterity of management; in Scotland, the pleasure grounds around a gentleman's country residence. ∴ *Policy* is the course of conduct pursued, or the management of an affair, in certain circumstances; *polity,* the general principles on which such course of conduct is based.

policy, pol′i•si, *n.* [Fr. *police,* from L.L. *poleticum,* a register, from L. *polyptychum,* Gr. *polyptychon,* an account book—*polys,* many, and *ptychē,* a fold.] A written contract by which a corporation or other persons engage to pay a certain sum on certain contingencies, as in the case of fire or shipwreck, in the event of death, etc., on the condition of receiving a fixed sum or percentage on the amount of the risk, or certain periodical payments.—*Insurance policy.* See INSURE.—**policyholder,** *n.* One who holds a policy or contract of insurance.

poliomyelitis, pō′li•ō•mī′e•lī″tis, *n.* [N.L. from Gr. *polios,* gray and *myelitis,* inflammation of the spinal cord.] An acute virus disease marked by fever, motor paralysis, and atrophy of skeletal muscles, often permanently disabling; also called *infantile paralysis.*

Polish, pō′lish, *a.* Pertaining to Poland or to its inhabitants.—*n.* The language of the Poles.

polish, pol′ish, *v.t.* [Fr. *polir, polissant,* from L. *polio,* to smooth, whence also *polite.*] To make smooth and glossy, usually by friction; to burnish; to deprive of rudeness, rusticity, or coarseness; to make elegant and polite (to *polish* life or manners).—*v.i.* To become smooth; to take a smooth and glossy surface; to become refined.—*n.* A substance used to impart a gloss; a smooth glossy surface produced by friction; artificial gloss; refinement; elegance of manners.—**polisher,** pol′ish•ėr, *n.* One who or that which polishes.

polite, po•līt′, *a.* [L. *politus,* from *polio,* to polish. POLISH.] Polished or elegant in manners; refined in behavior; well bred; courteous; complaisant.—**politely,** po•līt′li, *adv.* In a polite manner.—**politeness,** po•līt′nes, *n.*

politic, pol′i•tik, *a.* [L. *politicus,* Gr. *politikos,* from *polis,* a city. POLICE.] Consisting of citizens; constituting the state (the body *politic*); prudent and sagacious in devising and pursuing measures adapted to promote the public welfare; well devised and adapted to the public prosperity; ingenious in devising and pursuing any scheme of personal or national aggrandizement; cunning; artful; sagacious in adapting means to an end; well devised; adapted to its end, right or wrong.—**political,** po•lit′i•kal, *a.* Having a fixed or regular system or administration of government; relating to civil government and its administration; concerned in state affairs or national measures; pertaining to a nation or state, or to nations or states, as distinguished from *civil* or *municipal;* treating of politics or government.—*Political economy,* the science of the laws which regulate the production, distribution, and consumption of the products, necessary, useful, or agreeable to man, which it requires some portion of voluntary labor to produce, procure, or preserve.—*Political geography.* See GEOGRAPHY.—*Political science,* that science which deals with the structure, organization and government or nations and their component parts.—**politically,** po•lit′i•kal•li, *adv.* In a political manner.—**politician,** pol•i•tish′an, *n.* One versed in the science of government and the art of governing; one skilled in politics; one who occupies himself with politics.—**politicly,** pol′i•tik•li, *adv.* In a politic manner.—**politics,** pol′i•tiks, *n.* [Fr. *politique,* Gr. *politikē.*] The science of government; that part of ethics which relates to the regulation and government of a nation or state for the preservation of its safety, peace, and prosperity; political affairs, or the conduct and contests of political parties.—**polity,** pol′i•ti, *n.* A form of political organization.

polka, pōl′ka, *n.* [Pol. *polka,* Polish woman.] A lively dance of Bohemian origin, in duple time with three steps and a hop to each bar.—*v.i.* To dance the polka.

poll, pōl, *n.* [O.D. *pol, bol,* a ball, the head; L.G. *polle,* the head, the top of a tree; allied to *ball, bowl*: *pollard* is a derivative.] The head of a person, or the back part of the head; a catalogue or register of heads, that is, of persons; the voting or registering of votes for candidates in elections (the close of the *poll*); the fish called a chub; the blunt end of a hammer, or the butt of an ax.—*v.t.* To remove the top or head of; to lop, clip, shear; to cut closely; to mow; to register or give a vote; to bring to the poll; to receive or elicit, as a number of votes or voters.—*v.i.* To vote at a poll; to record a vote, as an elector.—**polled,** pōld, *p.* and *a.* Deprived of the poll; lopped, as a tree having the top cut; having the hair cut; cropped; bald; having cast the horns, as a stag; hence, wanting horns (*polled* cattle).—**poll tax,** *n.* A tax levied per head or person, usually on all males of mature years without regard to wealth or station.

pollack, pol′ak, *n.* [D. and G. *pollack.*] A species of marine fish belonging to the cod family.

pollard, pol′ėrd, *n.* [From *poll,* the head, and affix *-ard.*] A tree with the head cut off at some height from the ground, for the purpose of inducing it to throw out branches all round the section where amputation has taken place; a stag that has cast his horns; also, a hornless ox; a coarse product of wheat, but finer than bran.—*v.t.* To make a pollard of; to convert into a pollard by cutting off the head.

pollen, pol′en, *n.* [L. *pollen* and *pollis,* fine flour or dust.] The male element in flowering plants; the fine dust or powder which by contact with the stigma effects the fecundation of the seeds.—**polliniferous,** pol•i•nif′ėr•us, *a.* Producing pollen.—**pollenize,** pol′en•īz, *v.t.* To pollinate.—**pollinate,** pol′i•nāt, *v.t. Bot.* to convey pollen from the anther to the stigma of.—**pollination,** pol•i•nā′shon, *n. Bot.* the conveyance of the pollen from the anther to the stigma.

pollex, pol′leks, *n.* [L.] The thumb in man; a corresponding digit of other animals.

pollinium, pol•lin′i•um, *n.*; pl. **-ia.** [L. for *dust.*] An agglutinated mass of pollen grains, as in orchids.

pollute, pol•lūt′, *v.t.*—*polluted, polluting.* [L. *polluo, pollutum,* from prep. *pol, por,* used in composition, and *luō,* to wash. LAVE.] To make foul or unclean; to render impure; to defile; to soil; to taint; to corrupt or defile in a moral sense; to impair; to profane.—**pollution,** pol•lū′shon, *n.* [L. *pollutio.*] The act of polluting; the state of being polluted.

polo, pō′lō, *n.* [Balti, ball.] A game similar to hockey, played on horseback.

polonaise, pol•o•nāz′, *n.* [Fr.] A robe or dress worn by ladies and adopted from the fashion of the Poles; a courtly Polish dance.

polonium, pol•ō′ni•um, *n.* [From *Poland.*] A radioactive element (radium F) discovered in pitchblende by M. and Mme. Curie. Symbol, Po; at. no., 84.

poltroon, pol•trōn′, *n.* [Fr. and Sp. *poltron,* from It. *poltrone,* from *poltro,* lazy, dastardly, from O.H.G. *polstar,* a pillow. BOLSTER.] An arrant coward; a dastard; a wretch; without spirit or courage.—*a.* Base; vile; contemptible.—**poltroonery,** pol•trōn′ėr•i, *n.* Cowardice; want of spirit.

polyandrous, pol•i•an′drus, *a.* [Gr. *polys,* many, *anēr, andros,* a male.] *Bot.* having many stamens, that is, any number above twenty, inserted in the receptacle.

polyandry, pol•i•an′dri, *n.* [Gr. *polys,* many, *anēr, andros,* a man.] The practice of females having more husbands than one at the same time; plurality of husbands.

polyanthus, pol•i•an′thus, *n.* [Gr.

polys, many, *anthos*, a flower.] A garden variety of the oxlip primrose which has long been a favorite.

polyarchy, pol′i•är•ki, *n.* [Gr. *polys*, many, and *arche*, rule.] The government of many, whether a privileged class (aristocracy) or the people at large (democracy).

polyatomic, pol′i•a•tom″ik, *a.* [Gr. *polys*, many, E. *atomic*.] *Chem.* a term applied to elements or radicals which have an equivalency greater than one; polybasic.

polybasic, pol•i•bā′sik, *a.* [Gr. *polys* many, and E. *basic*.] *Chem.* of acids with more than one replaceable hydrogen atom.

polychromy, pol′i•krō•mi, *n.* [Gr. *polys*, many, and *chrōma*, color.] The practice of coloring statues and the exteriors and interiors of buildings; architectural ornamentation in colors. — **polychromatic, polychromic,** pol′i•krō•mat″ik, pol′i•krō•mik, *a.* Exhibiting a play of colors.—**polychrome,** pol′i•krōm, *a.* Having several or many colors; executed in the manner of polychromy.—*Polychrome printing*, the art of printing in one or more colors at the same time.

polycotyledon, pol′i•kot•i•lē″don, *n.* [Gr. *polys*, many, *kotylēdon*.] *Bot.* a plant that has many or more than two cotyledons or lobes to the seed.—**polycotyledonous,** pol′i•kot•i•lē″do•nus, *a.* Having more than two cotyledons.

polydactylism, pol•i•dak′til•izm, *n.* [Gr. *polys*, many, *daktylos*, a finger.] The condition of having several or many fingers or digits.—**polydactylous,** pol•i•dak′ti•lus, *a.* Having many fingers or toes.

polyester, pol•ē•es′ter, *n.* [Gr. *polys*, many, and *ester*.] An ester formed by condensation, used in clothing fibers.

polyethylene, pol′i•eth″i•lēn, *n.* [Gr. *polys*, many, and *ethylene*.] A polymer of ethylene; a plastic material.

polygamy, po•lig′a•mi, *n.* [Gr. *polys*, many, and *gamos*, marriage.] A plurality of wives or husbands at the same time, or the having of such plurality.—**polygamous,** po•lig′a•mus, *a.*—**polygamist,** po•lig′a•mist, *n.*

polygenesis, pol•i•jen′e•sis, *n.* [Gr. *polys*, many, and *genesis*.] The doctrine that beings have their origin in many cells or embryos of different kinds: opposed to *monogenesis*.—**polygenetic,** pol′i•je•net″ik, *a.* Relating to polygenesis. See MONOGENETIC.

polyglot, pol′i•glot, *n.* [Gr. *polys*, many, *glōtta*, a language.] A book containing many languages, particularly a Bible that presents the Scriptures in several languages. Also used as an adjective.

polygon, pol′i•gon, *n.* [Gr. *polys*, many, *gōnia*, an angle.] *Geom.* a plane figure of many angles and sides, or at least of more than four sides.—*Similar polygons* have their several angles equal each to each, and the sides about their equal angles proportional.—**polygonal,** po•lig′o•nal, *a.* Having the form of a polygon; having many angles. *Polygonal numbers*, the successive sums of a series of numbers in arithmetical progression.

polygraph, pol′i•graf, *n.* [Gr. *polys*, many, *graphē*, a writing.] An instrument for multiplying copies of a writing.—**polygraphic,** pol•i•graf′ik, *a.* Pertaining to polygraphy; done with a polygraph.

polygynous, po•lij′i•nus, *a.* Having many pistils or styles; polygynic.—**polygyny,** po•lij′i•ni, *n.* The practice of having more wives than one at the same time.

polyhedron, pol•i•hē′dron, *n.* [Gr. *polys*, many, *hedra*, a side.] *Geom.* a solid bounded by many faces or planes, and when all the faces are regular polygons the solid becomes a regular body; a multiplying glass with several plane surfaces; a polyscope. —**polyhedral,** pol•i•hē′dral, *a.*

polymer, pol′i•mėr, *n.* [Gr. *polys*, many, and *meros*, part.] A compound of high molecular weight formed by polymerization.—**polymeric,** pol•i•mer′ik, *a.* Of or relating to a polymer.—**polymerous,** po•lim′ėr•us, *a.* Containing many parts.—**polymerize,** pol′i•mėr•īz, *v.t.*—*polymerized*, *polymerizing*. To subject to polymerization.—*v.i.* To undergo polymerization.—**polymerization,** pol′i•mėr•i•zā″shon, *n.* The formation of large molecules from two or more smaller ones.

polymorphism, pol•i•mor′fizm, *n.* [Gr. *polys*, many, *morphe*, form.] The property of existing in different forms; the property of crystallizing in two or more fundamental forms.—**polymorphous, polymorphic,** pol•i•mor′fus, pol•i•mor′fik, *a.* Having many forms; assuming many forms.

Polynesian, pol•i•nē′zhi•an, *a.* [Gr. *polys*, many, *nēsos*, an island.] Pertaining to *Polynesia*, the region of many islands in the Pacific.—*n.* A native or inhabitant of Polynesia.

polynomial, pol•i•nō′mi•al, *n.* [Gr. *polys*, many and *nomen*, name.] An algebraic expression of two or more terms.—**polynomial,** *a.*

polyp, pol′ip, *n.* [L. *polypus*, a polyp, a growth or tumor, from Gr. *polypous*—*polys*, many, *pous*, a foot.] A name loosely applied to what were once known as *radiate* animals, having the mouth surrounded by more or less numerous arms or tentacles, now commonly applied to the hydra or the sea anemone; a zoophyte.—**polypary,** pol′i•pa•ri, *n.* The horny envelope or case of polyps (Hydrozoa, Polyzoa, etc.).—**polypidom,** po•lip′i•dom, *n.* [L. *polypus*, and *domus*, a house.] A stem or permanent fabric in which are the cells constituting the abodes of the polyps which fabricate it.

polypetalous, pol•i•pet′a•lus, *a.* [Gr. *polys*, many, *petalon*, a petal.] *Bot.* having or consisting of many petals (a *polypetalous* corolla).

polyphagous, po•lif′a•gus, *a.* [Gr. *polys*, many, *phagein*, to eat.] Eating or subsisting on many things or kinds of food.

polyphase, pol′i•fāz″, *a.* [Gr. *polys*, many, and *phasis*, appearance.] Of a combination of electric currents differing in their phases by constant amounts.

polyphonic, pol•i•fon′ik, *a.* [Gr. *polys*, many, *phōne*, sound.] Having or consisting of many voices or sounds; *music*, consisting of several parts progressing simultaneously according to the rules of counterpoint; contrapuntal.—**polyphony,** po•lif′o•ni, *n.* Multiplicity of sounds or voices.

polyphyllous, po•lif′i•lus, *a.* [Gr. *polys*, many, *phyllon*, a leaf.] *Bot.* many leaved.

polypody, pol′i•pō•di, *n.* [Gr. *polypodion*, from its spreading rootstock.] A name of various ferns, one of them common to Britain and North America.

polypous. See POLYPUS.

polypus, pol′i•pus, *n.* pl. **polypi,** pol′i•pī. [POLYP.] A polyp; *pathol.* a pedunculated tumor in the mucous membrane, especially that of the nostrils and uterus.—**polypous,** pol′i•pus, *a.* Pertaining to a polypus.

polysepalous, pol•i•sep′a•lus, *a.* [Gr. *polys*, many, and E. *sepal*.] *Bot.* a term applied to a calyx which has its sepals separate from each other.

polysyllable, pol′i•sil•la•bl, *n.* [Gr. *polys*, many, *syllabē*, a syllable.] A word of many syllables, that is, consisting of four or more syllables. —**polysyllabic, polysyllabical,** pol′i•sil•lab″ik, pol′i•sil•lab″i•kal, *a.* Consisting of many syllables or of more than three.

polysyndeton, pol•i•sin′de•ton, *n.* [Gr., from *polys*, many, *syn*, together, *deō*, I bind.] A figure of rhetoric by which the copulative conjunction is often repeated.

polytechnic, pol•i•tek′nik, *a.* [Gr. *polys*, many, and *technē*, art.] Of or designating an educational institution in which instruction is given in many technical arts and applied sciences.—*n.* A school of instruction in applied sciences; an exhibition of objects belonging to the industrial arts.

polytheism, pol•i•thē′izm, *n.* [Gr. *polys*, many, *theos*, god.] The doctrine of a plurality of gods.—**polytheist,** pol•i•thē′ist, *n.* A person who believes in a plurality of gods.—**polytheistic, polytheistical,** pol′i•thē•is″tik, pol′i•thē•is″ti•kal, *a.* Pertaining to polytheism; holding a plurality of gods.

Polyzoa, pol•i•zō′a, *n. pl.* [Gr. *polys*, many, *zōon*, an animal.] A class of animals, chiefly marine, forming compound groups or colonies, being the lowest members of the Mollusca, and generally known by the popular names of 'sea-mosses' and 'sea-mats'. —**polyzoarium,** pol′i•zō•â″ri•um, *n.* A polyzoan colony or its dermal system.

polyzonal, pol•i•zō′nal, *a.* [Gr. *polys*, many, *zōnē*, a zone.] Composed of many zones or belts; a term applied to burning lenses composed of pieces united in rings.

pomace, pom′is, *n.* [From L. *pomum*, an apple.] The substance of apples or of similar fruit crushed by grinding.—**pomaceous,** pō•mā′shus, *a.* Like pomace; pertaining to the apple family of trees.

pomade, pō•mād′, *n.* [Fr. *pommade*,

It. *pomada*, *pomata*, from L. *pomum*, an apple. Originally it was prepared from apples.] Perfumed ointment, especially ointment for the hair; pomatum.

pomander, pō′man•dėr, *n.* [Fr. *pomme d'ambre*, apple or ball of amber.] A perfume ball, or a mixture of perfumes, formerly carried in the pocket or suspended from the neck or the girdle.

pomatum, pō•mā′tum, *n.* [From L. *pomum*, an apple. POMADE.] A perfumed unguent used in dressing the hair; pomade.

pome, pōm, *n.* [L. *pomum*, an apple.] *Bot.* a fleshy or pulpy pericarp without valves, containing a capsule or capsules, as the apple, pear, etc.

pomegranate, pom′gra•nit, *n.* [L. *pomum*, an apple, and *granatum*, grained, having many grains or seeds. GRAIN, GARNET.] A fruit as large as an orange, having a hard rind filled with a soft pulp and numerous grains or seeds; the fruit that produces pomegranates, supposed to be a native of Persia; an ornament on the robe and ephod of the Jewish high priest.

pomelo, pom′e•lō, *n.* The shaddock; the grapefruit.

Pomeranian, pom′er•ā″ni•an, *n.* A small dog from Pomerania in Prussia.

pomiferous, pō•mif′ėr•us, *a.* [L. *pomum*, an apple, and *fero*, I produce.] Apple bearing; an epithet applied to plants which bear the larger fruits (as melons, gourds, cucumbers, etc.).

pommel, pum′mel, *n.* [O.Fr. *pommel*, from L. *pomum*, an apple or similar fruit.] A knob or ball; the knob on the hilt of a sword; the protuberant part of a saddlebow; a round knob on the frame of a chair.—*v.t.*—*pommeled*, *pommeling*. To beat; to bruise. Spelled also *Pummel*.

pomology, pō•mol′o•ji, *n.* [L. *pomum*, an apple, Gr. *logos*, discourse.] The branch of knowledge that deals with fruits; the cultivation of fruit trees.—**pomological,** pō•mo•loj′i•kal, *a.* Pertaining to pomology.—**pomologist,** pō•mol′o•jist, *n.* One who is versed in pomology.

pomp, pomp, *n.* [Fr. *pompe*, L. *pompa*, from Gr. *pompē*, a procession, from *pempō*, to send.] A procession distinguished by splendor or magnificence; a pageant; magnificence; parade; splendor; display.—**pompous,** pom′pus, *a.* [Fr. *pompeux.*] Displaying pomp; splendid; showing self-importance; exhibiting an exaggerated sense of dignity; ostentatious.—**pompously,** pom′pus•li, *adv.* In a pompous manner; ostentatiously.—**pompousness, pomposity,** pom′pus•nes, pom•pos′i•ti, *n.* Pompous display; show; ostentation.

pompom, *n.* [From sound.] An automatic gun firing small shells.

pompon, pom′pon, *n.* [Fr.] An ornament of feathers, artificial flowers, etc., for a bonnet or hat; a ball on a soldier's shako.

pompous, pompously, etc. See POMP.

poncho, pon′chō, *n.* [Sp.] In Spanish America a garment like a narrow blanket with a slit in the middle for the head to pass through.

pond, pond, *n.* [A slightly different form of *pound*, A.Sax. *pund*, an enclosure.] A body of still water of less extent than a lake, either artificial or natural.—**pond lily,** *n.* The water lily.—**pondweed,** *n.* A name of several British water weeds.

ponder, pon′dėr, *v.t.* [Fr. *ponderer*, from L. *pondero*, to weigh, from *pondus*, *ponderis*, weight.] To weigh carefully in the mind; to think about; to reflect upon; to examine carefully.—*v.i.* To think; to muse; to deliberate: with *on* or *over*.—**ponderable,** pon′dėr•a•bl, *a.* [L. *ponderabilis.*] Capable of being weighed; having weight.—**ponderability,** pon′-dėr•a•bil″i•ti, *n.* That property of bodies by which they possess sensible weight.—**ponderous,** pon′dėr•-us, *a.* [L. *ponderosus.*] Very heavy; of great weight; massive; weighty; forcible.—**ponderously,** pon′dėr•us•-li, *adv.* In a ponderous manner.—**ponderousness, ponderosity,** pon′-dėr•us•nes, pon•dėr•os′i•ti, *n.* The state or quality of being ponderous; gravity; heaviness.

pongee, pon′ji, *n.* [Chinese.] Soft unbleached Chinese silk employed in the construction of balloons.

poniard, pon′yėrd, *n.* [Fr. *poignard*, from *poing*, L. *pugnus*, the fist.] A small dagger; a pointed weapon for stabbing.—*v.t.* To pierce with a poniard; to stab.

pontifex, pon′ti•feks, *n.* pl. **pontifices,** pon•tif′i•sēz. [L. *pontifex*, *pontificis*, a high priest, from *pons*, *pontis*, a bridge, and *facio*, to make.] The name by which the Romans designated the highest members of their great colleges of priests, the chief being termed *Pontifex Maximus*.—**pontiff,** pon′tif, *n.* A high priest; a designation of the pope.—**pontifical,** pon•tif′i•kal, *a.* Relating to pontiffs or priests; relating to a pope; belonging to the pope; in a lofty manner, expressive of infallibility of speaker.—*n.* A book containing rites and ceremonies ecclesiastical; *pl.* the dress and ornaments of a pope, priest, or bishop.—**pontificate,** pon•-tif′i•kāt, *n.* [L. *pontificatus.*] The state or dignity of a high-priest; the office or dignity of the pope; the papacy; the reign of a pope.

pontoon, pon•tön′, *n.* [Fr. *ponton*, from L. *pons*, *pontis*, a bridge.] A flat-bottomed boat, or any light framework or floating body used in the construction of a temporary military bridge over a river; a lighter, a low flat vessel resembling a barge, used in careening ships; a water-tight structure placed beneath a submerged vessel and then filled with air, to assist in refloating the vessel.—**pontonier,** pon•to•nēr′, *n.* [Fr.] A soldier having charge of pontoons; one who constructs pontoon bridges.—**pontoon bridge,** *n.* A temporary military bridge supported on pontoons.

pony, pō′ni, *n.* [Gael. *ponaidh*, Ir. *poni*, a pony.] A small variety of horse; a small liqueur glass; a printed or written translation used by students to avoid work.

pood, pöd, *n.* A Russian weight, equal to 36.113 lbs.

poodle, pö′dl, *n.* [Same as G. and Dan. *pudel*, D. *poedel*, L.G. *budel*, a poodle; akin to L.G. *pudeln*, to waddle.] A small variety of dog covered with long curling hair.

pooh, pö, *interj.* Pshaw! pish! an expression of dislike, scorn, or contempt.—**pooh-pooh,** *v.t.* To turn aside with a pooh; to express scorn or contempt for; to sneer at.

pool, pöl, *n.* [A.Sax. *pól*=L.G. *pohl*, *pool*, Icel. *pollr*, D. *poll*, G. *pfuhl*, pool, fen; the word is also Celtic; W. *pwll*, a pool, a pit; perhaps akin to L. *palus*, a marsh.] A small collection of water or other liquid in a hollow place; a small piece of stagnant water; a hole in the course of a stream deeper than the ordinary bed.

pool, pöl, *n.* [Fr. *poule*, a hen.] The receptacle for the stakes at certain games of cards, billiards, etc.; the stakes themselves; games played on a table similar to a billiard table but having six pockets, usually with fifteen object balls and one cue ball; a common fund or combination of properties and interests, often arranged for speculation in grain or commodity markets.—*v.t.* to combine interests or properties.

poon, pön, *n.* [Indian name.] The name of several valuable trees of India (genus *Calophyllum*).

poop, pöp, *n.* [Fr. *poupe*, from L. *puppis*, the poop.] The highest and aftermost part of a ship's deck above the complete deck of the vessel.—*v.t. Naut.* to break heavily over the stern or quarter of; to drive in the stern of.

poor, pör, *a.* [O.E. *poure*, O.Fr. *poure*, *povre*, Mod.Fr. *pauvre*, from L. *pauper*, poor, from *paucus*, few, and *pario*, to produce.] Destitute of riches; not having property sufficient for a comfortable subsistence; needy; wanting good or desirable qualities; having little value or importance; trifling; insignificant; paltry; mean; destitute of fertility; barren; destitute of intellectual or artistic merit (a *poor* discourse); wanting in spirit or vigor; weak; impotent; worthy of pity; ill-fated; a word of tenderness or endearment (*poor* thing); a word of slight contempt; wretched.—*The poor*, collectively, the indigent; the needy: opposed to the rich; those unable to support themselves, and who have to depend for support on the contributions of others.—*Poor in spirit*, humble; contrite. (N.T.)—**poorhouse,** pör′hous, *n.* A residence for persons receiving public charity.—**poor law,** *n.* A law or the laws collectively established for the management of the funds for the maintenance of the poor.—**poorly,** pör′li, *adv.* In a poor manner or condition; in indigence; with little or no success; in an inferior manner; insufficiently; defectively.—*a.* Somewhat ill; indisposed; not in health. (*Colloq.*)—**poorness,** pör′nes, *n.* The state or quality of being poor; poverty.—**poor-spirited,** *a.* Of a mean spirit; cowardly.—**poor-spiritedness,** *n.*

pop, pop, *n.* [From the sound.] A small smart sound or report; a blow with a hatchet.—*v.i.*—*popped, popping.* To appear to the eye suddenly; to enter or issue forth with a quick, sudden motion; to dart; to start from a place suddenly.—*v.t.* To thrust forward, or offer suddenly; to thrust or push suddenly with a quick motion; to protrude (his eyes *popped*); to burst open.—*To pop corn,* to parch or roast Indian corn until it expands and 'pops' open.—*To pop the question,* in familiar language, to make an offer of marriage to a lady—*adv.* Suddenly; unexpectedly.—**popcorn,** *n.* Corn for parching; popped corn.—**popgun,** *n.* A small gun or tube used by children for shooting pellets, which makes a 'pop' when the pellet is expelled.

pope, pōp, *n.* [A.Sax. *pápa,* from L.L. *papa,* the pope, lit. father, same word as *papa,* the childish name for father. PAPA.] The Bishop of Rome, the head of the Roman Catholic Church; in the *Greek Church,* a priest or chaplain; the ruffe, a small fish closely allied to the perch.—*Pope's eye,* the gland surrounded with fat in the middle of the thigh of an ox or sheep, much prized for its delicacy.—**popedom,** pōp′dum, *n.* The place, office, dignity, or jurisdiction of the pope.—**pope joan,** *n.* A game of cards.—**popery,** po′pėr•i, *n.* The religion of the Church of Rome, comprehending doctrines and practice: a term offensive to Catholics.—**popish,** pō′pish, *a.* Pertaining to the pope or the Roman Catholic Church: used with a shade of contempt.—**popishly,** pō′pish•li, *adv.* In a popish manner; with a tendency to popery.

popinjay, pop′in•jā, *n.* [O.E. *popingay,* Fr. *papegai,* Sp. and Pg. *papagayo,* L.Gr. *papagas,* from Ar. *babaghâ, babbagâ,* a parrakeet.] A parrot‡; a gay, trifling young man; a fop or coxcomb.

poplar, pop′lėr, *n.* [O.Fr. *pōplier,* Mod.Fr. *peuplier,* from L. *populus,* a poplar.] A common name of sundry well-known trees, of which there are numerous species, as the white poplar, gray poplar, trembling poplar or aspen, black poplar, etc.

poplin, pop′lin, *n.* [Fr. *Popeline.*] Corded fabric of silk or worsted, originally made in the *papal* city of Avignon, and used especially for women's clothing.

poppet, pop′et, *n.* [M.E. *popet,* doll, puppet.] A valve that rises perpendicularly from its seat; an upright support fastened at the bottom of a machine; a doll.

popple, pop′l, *v.i.* [Dim. and freq. of *pop.*] To move quickly up and down, as a cork dropped on water.

poppy, pop′i, *n.* [A.Sax. *papig, popig,* from L. *papaver,* a poppy.] A gay flowering plant of many species, including *Papaver californicum,* a red annual, and *P. somniferum,* the opium poppy.

populace, pop′ū•lis, *n.* [Fr. *populace,* It. *popolazzo,* from L. *populus,* the people (whence *popular, people*); the root is doubtful.] The common people; the vulgar; the multitude, comprehending all persons not distinguished by rank, education, office, or profession: usually with the definite article.—**popular,** pop′ū•lėr, *a.* [L. *popularis.*] Pertaining to the common people; constituted by or depending on the people; suitable to common people; easy to be comprehended; plain; familiar; beloved by the people; pleasing to people in general.—**popularity,** pop•ū•lar′i•ti, *n.* The state or quality of being popular, or esteemed by the people at large; good will or favor proceeding from the people.—**popularization,** pop′ū•lėr•i•zā″shon, *n.* The act of making popular.—**popularize,** pop′ū•lėr•iz, *v.t.*—*popularized, popularizing.* To make popular; to treat in a popular manner, or so as to be generally intelligible; to spread among the people.—**popularly,** pop′ū•lėr•li, *adv.* In a popular manner; so as to please the populace; among the people at large; currently; commonly.—**populate,** pop′ū•lāt, *v.t.*—*populated, populating.* To furnish with inhabitants; to people.—**population,** pop•ū•lā′shon, *n.* The act or process of populating or peopling; the whole number of people in a country, town, etc.; populousness.—**Populist,** pop′ū•list, *n.* Member of a political party, formed in 1891, advocating an advanced program of national control and proprietorship of all natural means of production.—**populous,** pop′ū•lus, *a.* [L. *populosus.*] Full of inhabitants; thickly peopled.—**populously,** pop′ū•lus•li, *adv.* With many inhabitants in proportion to extent.—**populousness,** pop′ū•lus•nes, *n.* The state of being populous.

porbeagle, por′bē•gl, *n.* [Lit. hog-beagle—Fr. *porc,* a hog, and E. *beagle,* the latter term, like *dog* and *hound,* being applied to several sharks; comp. *porpoise.*] A species of shark.

porcelain, pōr′se•lan, *n.* [Fr. *porcelaine,* from It. *porcellana,* first a certain shell, then the nacre of the shell, and last porcelain, from L. *porcus,* a hog, from some fancied resemblance in the shell to a hog. PORK.] The finest species of pottery ware, originally manufactured in China and Japan, formed from the finest clays united with siliceous earths, which communicate a certain degree of translucency by means of their vitrification.—*a.* Belonging to or consisting of porcelain.—**porcelaneous,** pōr•se•lā′nē•us, *a.* Pertaining to or resembling porcelain.—*Porcelaneous shells* are those which have a compact texture, an enameled surface, and are generally beautifully variegated.

porch, pōrch, *n.* [Fr. *porche,* It. *portico,* from L. *porticus,* a porch, from *porta,* a gate, entrance. PORT.] *Arch.* an exterior appendage to a building forming a covered approach or vestibule to a doorway; a covered walk or portico.—*The Porch,* a public portico in Athens, where Zeno, the philosopher, taught his disciples; hence, *the Porch* is equivalent to the *school of the Stoics.*

porcine, pōr′sīn, *a.* [L. *porcinus,* from *porcus,* a hog. PORK.] Pertaining to swine; like a swine; hoglike.

porcupine, por′kū•pīn, *n.* [O.Fr. *porcespin,* lit. spine-hog; from L. *porcus,* a pig, and *spina,* a spine or thorn. PORK, SPINE.] A rodent quadruped covered with long spines mixed with bristly hairs, which the animal can erect at pleasure, and which serve for his defense.

pore, pōr, *n.* [Fr. *pore,* from L. *porus,* Gr. *poros,* a passage, a pore. PORT (a gate).] A small opening in a solid body, especially one of the minute openings on the surface of organized bodies through which fluids and minute substances are excreted or exhaled or by which they are absorbed; one of the small interstices between the molecules of matter which compose bodies.—**porous,** pō′rus, *a.* Having many pores or minute openings or interstices; having the molecules separated by intervals or pores.—**porousness, porosity,** pō′rus•nes, pō•ros′i•ti, *n.* The state or quality of being porous or of having pores.

pore, pōr, *v.i.*—*pored, poring.* [O.E. *poure;* origin uncertain; possibly same as *pour.*] To look with steady continued attention or application; to read or examine anything with steady perseverance: generally followed by *on* (*upon*) or *over.*

porgy, por′gi, *n.* [Origin doubtful.] The name given to a number of fishes, some of them used as food.

porism, pōr′izm, *n.* [Gr. *porisma,* a corollary, from *porizō,* I gain.] *Geom.* a corollary; a proposition affirming the possibility of finding such conditions as will render a certain problem indeterminate or capable of innumerable solutions.

pork, pōrk, *n.* [Fr. *porc,* from L. *porcus,* a swine, a pig. FARROW.] The flesh of swine, fresh or salted, used for food.—**porker,** pōr′kėr, *n.* A hog; a pig, especially one fed for pork.—**pork barrel,** *n.* Government appropriations or projects that are designed to give patronage benefits for political advantage.

pornography, por•nog′ra•fi, *n.* [Gr. *pornē,* prostitute, *graphō,* I write.] Literature in which prostitutes figure; obscene writing.—**pornographic,** por•no•graf′ik, *a.* Pertaining to the literary treatment of such subjects.

porosity, porous, etc. See PORE.

porphyry, por′fi•ri, *n.* [Fr. *porphyre,* Pr. *porfiri,* from Gr. *porphyritēs,* lit. a purple-colored rock, from *porphyra,* purple. PURPLE.] Originally, the name given to a very hard Egyptian stone containing crystals of rose-colored feldspar, partaking of the nature of granite, susceptible of a fine polish, and consequently much used for sculpture; also applied generally to any unstratified or igneous rock in which detached crystals of feldspar or some other mineral are diffused through a compact base. —**porphyritic,** por•fi•rit′ik, *a.* Composed of, resembling, or containing porphyry.

porpoise, por′pus, *n.* [O.E. *porcpisce, porpesse,* etc., lit. swine fish, from L. *porcus,* a swine, and *piscis,* a fish. PORK.] A cetaceous mammal, rarely exceeding 5 feet in length, frequenting the northern seas, and frequently seen off the shores pursuing shoals of herring, mackerel, etc.

porridge, por′ij, *n.* [Perhaps from L. *porrum, porrus,* a leek, and meaning originally leek soup or broth; or a corruption of *pottage.*] A kind of food made by slowly stirring oatmeal, or other similar substance, into water or milk while boiling till a thickened mass is formed.—**porringer,** por′in•jėr, *n.* [From *porridge.* The *n* has intruded as in *messenger.*] A porridge dish; a small earthenware or tin vessel out of which children eat their food.

port, pōrt, *n.* [A.Sax. *port,* a port, haven, harbor, from L. *portus,* a haven; akin to *porta,* a gate; same root as *fare.* It enters into many place names, as *Port*land, *Ports*mouth, Brid*port.*] A natural or artificial harbor; a haven; any bay, cove, inlet, or recess of the sea, or of a lake, or the mouth of a river, which vessels can enter, and where they can lie safe from injury by storms.

port, pōrt, *n.* [Fr. *porte,* L. *porta,* a gate, from same root as Gr. *poros,* a passage, and E. to *fare.* See above.] A gate; an entrance; a passageway in the side of a ship; an opening in the side of a ship of war, through which cannon are discharged: called also a porthole; an aperture for the passage of steam or a fluid.—**portal,** pōr′tal, *n.* [O.Fr. *portal,* L.L. *portale,* from L. *porta,* a gate.] A door or gate: a poetical or dignified term; *arch.* the lesser gate when there are two of different dimensions at the entrance of a building; a kind of arch over a door or gate, or the framework of the gate.—*a. Anat.* belonging to a vein forming a sort of entrance (*port*) to the liver. —*Portal circulation,* a special circulation of venous blood from the intestines, etc., through the liver.—**porter,** pōr′tėr, *n.* [Fr. *portier.*] One who has charge of a door or gate; a doorkeeper; a waiter in a hall.—**porteress, portress,** pōr′tėr•es, pōr′tres, *n.* A female porter.—**porthole,** *n.* The port of a ship.

port, pōrt, *v.t.* [Fr. *porter,* from L. *porto,* to carry (seen in *export, import, report, transport, sport,* etc.); same root as *portus,* a harbor, a port.] To carry in military fashion; to carry a weapon, such as a rifle, in a slanting direction, upward toward the left, and across the body in front, as in the military command 'to *port* arms'.—*n.* [Fr. *port,* carriage, demeanor, from *porter,* L. *porto,* to carry.] Carriage; air; mien; manner of movement or walk; demeanor; external appearance (the *port* of a gentleman).—**portability,** pōr•ta•bil′i•ti, *n.* The state of being portable.—**portable,** pōr′ta•bl, *a.* [L. *portabilis.*] Capable of being carried by the hand or about the person; capable of being carried or transported from place to place; easily carried; not bulky or heavy.—**portage,** pōr′tij, *n.* The act of carrying; the price of carriage; a break in a chain of water communication over which goods, boats, etc., have to be carried, as from one lake, river, or canal to another, or along the banks of rivers round waterfalls, rapids, etc.—**porter,** pōr′tėr, *n.* [Fr. *porteur,* from *porter,* to carry.] A carrier; a person who carries or conveys burdens, parcels, or messages for hire; a dark-colored malt liquor made wholly or partially with high-dried malt; so called from its having been originally the favorite beverage of *porters.*—**porterage,** pōr′tėr•ij, *n.* Money charged or paid for the carriage of burdens or parcels by a porter.

port, pōrt, *n.* [Etym. uncertain.] *Naut.* the larboard or left side of a ship.—*v.t.* and *i. Naut.* to turn or put to the left.

port, pōrt, *n.* [From *Oporto,* Portuguese city.] A rich, sweet wine, dark red in color.

portage, pōr′tij, *n.* [From Fr. *porter,* to carry.] The work of carrying; the carrying of something overland from one body of water to another.

portal. See PORT (gate).

portamento, por•ta•men′tō, *n.* [It.] *Mus.* the gliding from one note to another without a break.

portcullis, pōrt•kul′is, *n.* [Fr. *porte,* a gate, and *coulisse,* groove, from *couler,* to slip or slide.] *Fort.* a strong grating of timber or iron, resembling a harrow, made to slide in vertical grooves in the jambs of the entrance gate of a fortified place, to protect the gate in case of assault.

Porte, pōrt, *n.* [The chief office of the Ottoman Empire is styled *Babi Ali,* lit. the High Gate, from the gate (*bab*) of the palace at which justice was administered; and the French translation of this term being *Sublime Porte,* hence the use of this word.] The Ottoman court; the government of the Turkish Empire.

portend, por•tend′, *v.t.* [L. *portendo,* to stretch forth, point out, portend—*por, pro,* forth or forward, and *tendo,* to stretch. TEND.] To foreshow ominously; to foretoken; to indicate something future by previous signs.—**portent,** por′tent or por•tent′, *n.* [L. *portentum.*] That which portends or foretokens; especially, an omen of ill.—**portentous,** por•ten′tus, *a.* Of the nature of a portent; ominous; foreshowing ill; monstrous; prodigious; wonderful. —**portentously,** por•ten′tus•li, *adv.* In a portentous manner.—**portentousness,** por•ten′tus•nes, *n.*

porter. See PORT, a gate, and PORT, to carry.

portfolio, pōrt•fō′li•ō, *n.* [In imitation of Fr. *porte-feuille,* a portfolio, the office of a minister—*porter,* to carry (L. *portare*), and *feuille,* a leaf, L. *folium.*] A portable case of the form of a large book, for holding loose drawings, prints, papers, etc.; the office and functions of a minister of state or cabinet member.

portico, pōr′ti•kō, *n.* pl. **porticoes,** pōr′ti•kōs. [It. and Sp. *portico,* from L. *porticus.* PORCH.] *Arch.* a kind of porch before the entrance of a building fronted with columns.

portion, pōr′shon, *n.* [L. *portio, portionis,* a portion; akin to *pars, partis,* a part. PART.] A part of anything separated from it; that which is divided off, as a part from a whole; a part, though not actually divided, but considered by itself; a part assigned; an allotment; fate; final state (N.T.).—*v.t.* To divide or distribute into portions or shares; to parcel out; to allot in shares; to endow with a portion or an inheritance.—**portionless,** pōr′shon•les, *a.* Having no portion.

portland cement, pōrt′land se•ment′. [Called so because of its resemblance, when set, to a stone found on the Isle of Portland, in England.] A cement of superior quality, consisting of a mixture of clay and limestone, or two similar substances, which are first ground, then heated until they form clinker, then powdered, after which they harden into stone upon the addition of water or even when immersed in water.

portly, pōrt′li, *a.* [From *port,* carriage, mien, demeanor.] Grand or dignified in mien; stately; of a noble appearance and carriage; rather tall, and inclining to stoutness.—**portliness,** pōrt′li•nes, *n.* The state or quality of being portly.

portmanteau, pōrt•man′tō, *n.* [Fr. *portemanteau,* from *porter,* to carry, and *manteau,* a cloak or mantle.] A case or trunk, usually made of leather, for carrying apparel, etc., on journeys; a leather case attached to a saddle behind the rider.

portrait, pōr′trāt, *n.* [Fr. *portrait,* pp. of *portraire,* to portray. PORTRAY.] A painted picture or representation of a person, and especially of a face drawn from the life: also used generally for engravings, photographs, crayon drawings, etc., of this character; a vivid description or delineation in words.—**portraiture,** pōr′trā•chėr, *n.* [Fr.] A portrait; the art or practice of drawing portraits, or of vividly describing in words.

portray, pōr•trā′, *v.t.* [Fr. *portraire,* to portray, to depict, from L. *portraho,* to draw forth—L. *por, pro,* forward, and *trahere,* to draw, whence *traction, abstract,* etc.] To paint or draw the likeness of; to depict; to describe in words.—**portrayal,** pōr•trā′al, *n.* The act of portraying; delineation; representation.—**portrayer,** pōr•trā′ėr, *n.*

Portuguese, por′tū•gēz, *a.* Of or pertaining to Portugal.—*n.* The language of Portugal; the people of Portugal.

portulaca, pōr′tu•lak″ä, *n.* [L. *purslane.*] Any of the plants of the genus *Portulaca*, herbs of thick succulent leaves, sporting variously colored flowers.

pose, pōz, *v.t.—posed, posing.* [Fr. *poser*, to place, to put a question, from L. *pauso*, to halt, to stop, from *pausa*, a pause; but the meaning, as well as that of the compounds, has been influenced by *pono, positum*, to put, place, set, which gives *position*, etc. This word is seen in com*pose*, de*pose*, dis*pose*, re*pose*, etc. PAUSE.] To embarrass by a difficult question; to cause to be at a loss; to puzzle.—**poser,** pō′zėr, *n.* One that poses or puzzles by asking difficult questions; something that puzzles, as a difficult question.

pose, pōz, *n.* [Fr. *pose*, an attitude, from L. *pausa*, See above.] Attitude or position taken naturally, or assumed for effect; an artistic posture or attitude.—*v.i.—posed, posing.* [Fr. *poser.*] To attitudinize; to assume characteristic airs.—*v.t.* To cause to assume a certain posture; to place so as to have a striking effect.

posit, poz′it, *v.t.* [L. *pono, positum*, to place. POSITION.] To lay down as a position or principle; to present to the consciousness as an absolute fact.

position, po•zish′on, *n.* [Fr. *position*, L. *positio*, from *pono, positum*, to place, set, which appears as *-pound* in com*pound*, etc., as *-pone* in post*pone*, and is seen also in *deposit, opposite, positive, post, posture*, etc.] State of being placed; situation; generally with reference to other objects, or to different parts of the same object; relation with regard to other persons, or to some subject; manner of standing or being placed; attitude; that on which one takes one's stand; hence, principle laid down; predication; affirmation; place or standing in society; social rank; state; condition of affairs; *arith.* a mode of solving a question by one or two suppositions.

positive, poz′i•tiv, *a.* [Fr. *positif*; L.L. *positivus*, from L. *pono, positum.* POSITION.] Definitely laid down or expressed; direct; explicit; absolute; real; existing in fact; not negative; direct (*positive* proof); confident; fully assured; dogmatic; overconfident; distinctly ascertained or ascertainable; *photog.* having the lights and shades rendered as they are in nature: opposed to *negative*; the form of an adjective which denotes simple or absolute quality; having a real force or position (a *positive* influence); *elect.* electricity produced by rubbing glass with silk; electricity arising from a deficiency of electrons in a body; *math.* greater than zero; tending to increase; indicating affirmation, lack of doubt; *pathol.* indicating the presence of a disease.—*Positive philosophy*, a philosophical system founded by Auguste Comte (1798-1857), which limits itself strictly to human experience, denies all metaphysics and all search for first or for final causes.—*Positive pole*, one of the terminals in an electric generator, battery, or circuit: opposed to *negative.*—*n. Gram.* the positive degree; *photog.* a picture in which the lights and shades are rendered as they are in nature: opposed to *negative.*—**positively,** poz′i•tiv•li, *adv.*—**positiveness,** poz′i•tiv•nes, *n.*—**positivism,** poz′i•tiv•izm, *n.* The positive philosophy.—**positivist,** poz′i•tiv•ist, *n.*

positron, poz′i•tron, *n.* [*Posi*tive and elec*tron.*] A charged particle with a mass equal to that of an electron.

posse, pos′sē. [L., to be able.] A number of people; a small body of men.—*Posse comitatus, lit.* the power of a county; *law*, the body of men which the sheriff is empowered to raise in case of riot, etc.

possess, poz•zes′, *v.t.* [L. *possideo, possessum*, to occupy, to possess—*pos* for *por*, before, near, and *sedeo*, to sit (as in *reside, preside*, etc.).] To occupy in person; to have and hold; to have as a piece of property or as a personal belonging; to be owner of; to own; to affect strongly (fear *possessed* them); to pervade; to fill or take up entirely; to have full power or mastery over; as, an evil spirit, evil influence, violent passion, etc. (*possessed* with a fury); to put in possession; to make master or owner: with *of* before the thing, and now generally in the passive or with reflexive pronouns (to be *possessed of* a large fortune; to *possess one's self* of another's property); to furnish or fill; to imbue or instill into: with *with* before the thing.—**possession,** poz•zesh′on, *n.* The having or holding of property; the state of owning or having in one's hands or power; the thing possessed; land, estate, or goods owned; the state of being mastered by some evil spirit or influence.—*To take possession*, to enter on the possession of property; to assume ownership.—*To give possession*, to put in another's power or occupancy.—**possessive,** poz•zes′iv, *a.* [L. *possessivus.*] Pertaining to possession; expressing possession.—*Possessive case*, the genitive case, or case of nouns and pronouns which expresses possession, ownership (*John's* book), or some relation of one thing to another (*Homer's* admirers).—*Possessive pronoun*, a pronoun denoting possession or property, as *my, thy*, etc.—*n.* A pronoun or other word denoting possession.—**possessively,** poz•zes′iv•li, *adv.* In a manner denoting possession.—**possessor,** poz•zes′ėr, *n.* One who possesses.—**possessory,** poz•zes′o•ri, *a.* Pertaining to possession.

posset, pos′et, *n.* [Comp. W. *posel*, curdled milk, a posset, from *posiaw*, to gather.] A drink composed of hot milk curdled by some infusion, as wine or other liquor.—*v.t.* To curdle; to coagulate. (*Shak.*)

possible, pos′i•bl, *a.* [L. *possibilis*, from *posse*, to be able, from *potis*, able, and *esse*, to be; akin *power.*] That may be or exist; that may be now, or may happen or come to pass; that may be done; not contrary to the nature of things; capable of coming to pass, but improbable.—**possibly,** pos′i•bli, *adv.* In a possible manner; perhaps; perchance.—**possibility,** pos•i•bil′i•ti, *n.* The state or condition of being possible; a chance of happening; a thing possible; that which may take place or come into being.

post, pōst, *n.* [A.Sax. *post*, from L. *postis*, post, a doorpost, from *pono, positum*, to place, set. POSITION.] A piece of timber, metal, or other solid substance set upright, and often intended to support something else.

post, pōst, *n.* [From Fr. *poste*, (masc.), a military post or station, an office, and *poste* (fem.), a letter carrier, a post-house, a post office, etc., both from L.L. *posta*, for *posita*, from L. *positum*, placed. POST, above.] The place at which some person or thing is stationed or fixed; a station or position occupied, especially a military station; the place where a single soldier or a body of troops is stationed; a bugle call giving notice to soldiers to retire to their quarters for the night, sounded at tattoo, there being a first post and a last post, the latter sounded also at military funerals; an office or employment; an appointment; a berth; a messenger or a carrier of letters and papers; one that goes at stated times to convey the mails or dispatches; a postman; an established system for the public conveyance of letters; a post office; a size of writing and printing paper, measuring about 18¾ inches by 15¼.—*To ride post*, to be employed to carry dispatches and papers; and as such carriers rode in haste, hence the phrase signifies to ride in haste, to pass with expedition. *Post* is thus used adverbially for swiftly, expeditiously, or expressly (to travel *post*).—*v.i.* [Fr. *poster*, to post.] To travel with post horses; to travel with speed; to rise and sink on the saddle in accordance with the motion of the horse, especially when trotting.—*v.t.* To fix up in a public place, as a notice or advertisement; to expose to public reproach; to expose to opprobrium by some public action; to place; to station (to *post* troops on a hill); *bookkeeping*, to carry (accounts or items) from the journal to the ledger; to make the requisite entries in, for showing a true state of affairs; to place in the post office; to transmit by post (to *post* letters).—*To post up, in bookkeeping*, to make the requisite entries in up to date; hence, to make one master of all the details of a subject.—**postage,** pōs′tij, *n.* The charge levied on letters or other articles conveyed by post.—**postage stamp,** *n.* An adhesive stamp of various values issued by the Post Office Department for affixing to letters, packets, etc., as payment of cost of transmission.—**postal,** pōst′al, *a.* Relating to a post office or the carrying of mails.—**post card,** *n.* Any card, to which a stamp may be affixed, transmitted through the mail; also, officially *Postal card*, a similar card, on which a stamp has been printed, issued by the government.—**post chaise,** *n.* A chaise for conveying travelers from one station to another. (*Historical.*)—**poster,** pōst′ėr, *n.* One who posts; a courier; a post horse; a large printed bill or placard posted for advertising.—**post-free,** *a.* Franked; paying no postage.—**posthaste,** *n.* Haste or speed in travelling, like that of a post or courier.—*adv.* With speed or expedition.—**postman,** pōst′man, *n.* A post or courier; a letter carrier.—**postmark,** pōst′märk, *n.* The mark or stamp of a post office on a letter.—**postmaster,** pōst′mas•tėr, *n.* The officer who has the superintendence and direction of a post office.—**postmaster general,** *n.* The chief executive head of a postal system; one of the members of the cabinet of the President of the United States of America, having charge of the Post Office Department.—**post office,** *n.* An office or house where letters are received for transmission to various parts, and from which letters are delivered that have been received from places at home and abroad; a department of the government charged with the conveyance of letters, etc., by post.—*General post office.* See GENERAL.—*Post-office order. Money order,* see MONEY.—**postpaid,** *a.* Having the postage prepaid.—**postroad,** *n.* A road along which the mail is carried.

postbellum, pōst•bel′um, *a.* [L.] After the war, especially the American Civil War.

postdate, pōst′dāt, *v.t.*—*postdated, postdating.* [Prefix *post*, after, and *date*.] To date a check, letter, or other document later than the current date.

postdiluvial, postdiluvian, pōst•di•lū′vi•al, pōst•di•lū′vi•an, *a.* [L. *post*, after, and *diluvium*, the deluge.] Being or happening posterior to the Flood in Noah's days.—**postdiluvian,** *n.* A person who lived or has lived since the Flood.

posterior, pos•tē′ri•ėr, *a.* [L. *posterior*, compar. of *posterus*, from *post*, after.] Later or subsequent in time; opposed to *prior*; later in order; coming after; situated behind; hinder (the *posterior* portion of the skull): opposed to *anterior*.—*A posteriori.* A PRIORI.—**posteriority,** pos•tē′ri•or″i•ti, *n.* The state of being later or subsequent.—**posteriorly,** pos•tē′ri•ėr•li, *adv.* Subsequently in time; behind.—**posteriors,** pos•tē′ri•ėrz, *n. pl.* The hinder part of an animal's body.—**posterity,** pos•ter′i•ti, *n.* [L. *posteritas*, from *posterus*, later.] Descendants; the race that proceeds from a progenitor; succeeding generations.

postern, pōs′tėrn, *n.* [O.Fr. *posterne*, from L.L. *posterna, posterula*, a secret means of exit, from L. *posterus*, behind, posterior, from *post*, behind.] Primarily, a back door or gate; a private entrance; hence, any small door or gate; *fort.* a covered passage leading under a rampart to the ditch in front.

postfix, pōst′fix, *n.* [Prefix *post*, after and *fix*.] *Gram.* an affix or suffix.—*v.t.* To add or annex to the end of a word.

postglacial, pōst•glā′shi•al, *a. Geol.* belonging to a section of the post-tertiary deposits. See GLACIAL.

postgraduate, pōst•grad′ū•āt, *n.* One who engages in advanced academic studies after receiving a degree, usually bachelor's.—*a.* Pertaining to such a student or to such studies.

posthumous, pos′tū•mus, *n.* [L. *postumus*, last, superl. of *posterus*, coming after, from *post*, behind.] Born after the death of the father; published after the death of the author (*posthumous* works); being or continuing after one's decease (*posthumous* fame).—**posthumously,** pos′tū•mus•li, *adv.* After one's decease.

postillon, postillion, pōs•til′yon, *n.* [Fr. *postillon*, from *poste*, a post.] The rider of the near lead horse of a traveling or other carriage.

postimpressionism, pōst•im•pre′shon•izm, *n.* [*Post* and *impressionism*.] *Art*, a reaction from impressionism that emphasized the individual artist's reaction to objects rather than representation of purely visual impressions.

postliminium, postliminy, pōst•li•min′i•um, pōst•lim′i•ni, *n.* [L., from *post*, after, and *limen*, end, limit.] That right by virtue of which persons and things taken by an enemy in war are restored to their former state.

postmeridian, pōst•me•rid′i•an, *a.* [L. *postmeridianus.* MERIDIAN.] Coming after the sun has passed the meridian; being or belonging to the afternoon.—*n.* The afternoon.

post-mortem, pōst•mor′tem, *a.* [L. *post*, after, *mors*, death.] After death.—*Post-mortem examination*, an examination of a body made after death.

postnatal, pōst•nā′tal, *a.* Subsequent to birth.

postnuptial, pōst•nup′shal, *a.* Being or happening after marriage.

post-obit, pōst•ob′it, *n.* [L. *post*, *obitum*, after death.] A bond given for the purpose of securing to a lender a sum of money on the death of some specified individual from whom the borrower has expectations.

postoperative, pōst•op′ėr•ä•tiv, *a.* [*Post* and *operative*.] Of, or pertaining to, the care of a patient after an operation, or the results of the operation.

postpone, pōst•pōn′, *v.t.*—*postponed, postponing.* [L. *postpono*—*post*, after, and *pono*, to put. POSITION.] To put off; to defer to a future or later time.—**postponement,** pōst•pōn′ment, *n.* The act of postponing or deferring to a future time.—**postponer,** pōst•pō′nėr, *n.* One who postpones.

postposition, pōst•pō•zish′on, *n.* The act of placing after; the state of being put behind; *gram.* a word or particle placed after or at the end of a word.—**postpositive,** pōst•poz′i•tiv, *a.* Placed after something else as a word.

postprandial, pōst•pran′di•al, *a.* [L. *post*, after, and *prandium*, a dinner.] Happening after dinner.

postscript, pōst′skript, *n.* [L. *post*, after, and *scriptum*, written.] A paragraph added to a letter after it is concluded and signed by the writer; any addition made to a book or composition after it had been supposed to be finished; something appended.

postulate, pos′tū•lāt, *n.* [L. *postulatum*, a demand, from *postulo*, to demand, from *posco*, to ask.] A position or supposition of which the truth is demanded or assumed for the purpose of future reasoning; a necessary assumption; *geom.* something of the nature of a problem assumed or taken for granted; the enunciation of a self-evident problem.—*v.t.*—*postulated, postulating.* To beg or assume without proof; to regard as self-evident, or as too obvious to require further proof.—**postulant,** pos′tū•lant, *n.* One who demands or requests; a candidate.—**postulation,** pos•tū•lā′shon, *n.* The act of postulating or supposing without proof; supplication; intercession.

posture, pos′chėr, *n.* [Fr. *posture*, from L. *positura* a placing, from *pono, positum*, to place. POSITION.] The disposition of the several parts of the body with respect to each other, or with respect to a particular purpose; pose of a model or figure used by an artist; attitude; situation; condition; particular state with regard to something else (the *posture* of affairs).—*v.t.*—*postured, posturing.* To place in a particular posture.—*v.i.* To dispose the body in particular postures; to contort the body into artificial attitudes; to behave in an artificial manner.—**posturer,** pos′chėr•ėr, *n.* One who postures; especially one who behaves and comports himself in a highly artificial manner.—**postural,** pos′chėr•al, *a.* Pertaining or relating to posture.

postwar, pōst•wạr′, *a.* Belonging to the period after a war, especially one of the World Wars.

posy, pō′zi, *n.* [Corrupted from *poesy*, being originally a piece of poetry.] A poetical quotation or motto attached to or inscribed on something, as on a ring; a motto or verse sent with a nosegay; hence, a bunch of flowers; sometimes a single flower, as for a buttonhole.

pot, pot, *n.* [A widely spread word, the origin of which is not clear = Fr. *pot*, D. *pot*, Dan. *potte*, Icel. *pottr*, W. *pot*, Ir. *pota*, a pot.] A hollow vessel more deep than broad, used for various domestic and other purposes (an iron *pot* for boiling meat or vegetables; an earthern *pot* for plants, called a *flowerpot*, etc.); a mug; a jug containing a specified quantity of liquor; the quantity contained in a pot; definitely, a quart (a *pot* of porter); a size of paper, 12½ inches by 15 inches the sheet: said to have had originally a pot as watermark; the metal or earthenware top of a chimney.—*To go to pot*, to be destroyed or ruined; to come to an ill end; the pot being here probably that in which old metal is melted down. (*Colloq.*)—*v.t.*—*potted, potting*. To put into pots; to preserve seasoned in pots (*potted* fowl and fish); to plant or cover in pots of earth.—**potbellied,** *a.* Having a prominent belly.—**potbelly,** *n.* A protuberant belly.—**potboy,** pot′boi, *n.* A boy or man who carries pots of ale or beer for sale; a menial in a public house.—**potherb,** *n.* A herb for the pot and for cookery; a culinary plant.—**pothole,** *n.* A circular cavity in the rocky beds of rivers formed by stones being whirled round by the action of the current.—**pothook,** *n.* A hook on which pots and kettles are hung over the fire; a letter or character like a pothook, written by children in learning to write.—**pothouse,** *n.* An alehouse; a tavern.—**pothunter,** *n.* A sportsman who has more regard to winning prizes than to mere sport.—**potluck,** *n.* What may chance to be in the pot or provided for a meal.—*To take potluck*, is for an unexpected visitor to partake of the family meal, whatever it may chance to be. (*Colloq.*)—**potpourri,** pō•pö•rē′, *n.* [Fr. *pot*, pot, and *pourrir*, to putrefy, to boil very much; from L. *putere*, to rot.] A dish of different kinds of meat and vegetables cooked together; hence, a miscellaneous collection; a medley.—**potsherd,** pot′shėrd, *n.* [*Pot.* and *sherd*=*shard, shred*, a fragment.] A piece or fragment of an earthenware pot.—**potstone,** pot′stōn, *n.* A coarsely granular variety of steatite or soapstone, sometimes manufactured into kitchen vessels (hence the name).—**potter,** pot′ėr, *n.* [From *pot.*] One whose occupation is to make earthenware vessels or crockery of any kind; one who pots viands.—*Potter's clay*, a variety of clay of a reddish or gray color which becomes red when heated.—*Potter's wheel*, an apparatus consisting of a vertical iron axis, on which is a horizontal disk made to revolve by treadles, the clay being placed on the disk.—**pottery,** pot′ėr•i, *n.* The ware or vessels made by potters; earthenware glazed and baked; the place where earthen vessels are manufactured; the business of a potter.—**pot-valiant,** *a.* Courageous over drink; heated to valor by strong drink.—**pot-walloper,** pot•wol′lop•ėr, *n.* [*Pot*, and *wallop*, to boil; akin to *gallop.*] A parliamentary voter in some English boroughs before 1832, who was admitted to vote on proof that he had boiled a pot within the borough bounds during the six months preceding the election.

potable, pō′ta•bl, *a.* [L.L. *potabilis*, from L. *poto*, to drink, whence *potion, poison.*] Drinkable; suitable for drinking; capable of being drunk. —*n.* Something that may be drunk. —**potation,** pō•tā′shon, *n.* The act of drinking; a drinking bout; a a draught; a drink.

potash, pot′ash, *n.* [*Pot*, and *ash*, from being prepared by evaporating the lixivium of wood ashes in iron pots.] Alkali in an impure state, procured from the ashes of plants by lixiviation and evaporation, largely employed in the manufacture of flint glass and soap, bleaching, making alum, etc.—*Potash water*, an aerated beverage consisting of carbonic acid water, to which is added bicarbonate of potash.

potassa, po•tas′sa, *n.* The older name for *Potash.*

potassium, po•tas′si•um, *n.* [A Latinized term from *potash.*] A soft white metallic element occurring in combination; compounds used as fertilizer, etc. Symbol, K (Latin, *kalium*); at. no., 19; at. wt., 39.102.—**potassic,** po•tas′ik, *a.*—**potassium nitrate,** *n.* A crystalline compound, KNO_3, used as a preservative and in gunpowder; saltpeter.—**potassium cyanide.** See CYANIDE.

potation. See POTABLE.

potato, po•tā′tō, *n.* pl. **potatoes,** po•tā′tōz. [Sp. *patata, batata*; said to be a Haitian word.] Originally the sweet potato; now the edible starchy tuber of a plant, *Solanum tuberosum*; the plant itself.—**potato beetle,** *n.* A leaf beetle, *Leptinotarsa decemlineata*, causing damage to potato crops.

poteen, potheen, po•tēn′, *n.* [From Ir. *poitir*, little pot.] Whisky illicitly distilled by the Irish peasantry; whisky generally. (*Irish.*)

potent, pō′tent, *a.* [L. *potens*, powerful, pres. part. of *posse*, to be able, from *potis*, able (same root as E. *father*, L. *pater*), and *esse*, to be. *Potent* is seen in *impotent, omnipotent.* POWER.] Powerful, in a physical or moral sense; efficacious; having great authority, interest, or the like. —**potency, potentness,** pō′ten•si, pō′tent•nes, *n.* The state or quality of being potent.—**potentate,** pō′ten•tāt, *n.* [Fr. *potentat.*] A person who possesses great power or sway; a prince; a sovereign; an emperor, king, or monarch.—**potential,** pō•ten′shal, *a.* [L. *potentia*, power.] Being in possibility, not in actuality; latent; that may be manifested; in *electrostatics*, at a given point, the work required to bring a unit of positive electricity from an infinite distance to that point under given conditions of electrification.—*Potential energy*, energy of position, the energy of a system which is due only to the positions of its particles; the difference between total energy and kinetic energy.—*Potential mood*, that form of the verb which is used to express the power, possibility, liberty, or necessity of an action or of being (I *may go*; he *can write*).—*n.* Anything that may be possible; a possibility.—**potentiality,** pō•ten′shi•al″i•ti, *n.* State of being potential; possibility, but not actuality; inherent power or quality not actually exhibited.—**potentially,** pō•ten′shal•li, *adv.* In a potential manner; in possibility, not in act.—**potentiometer,** pō•ten′shi•om″et•ėr, *n.* [From *potential*, and *meter.*] An electrical instrument which can be used to measure pressure, current, or resistance.—**potently,** po′tent•li, *adv.* In a potent manner; powerfully.

potentilla, pō•ten•til′la, *n.* [From L. *potens*, powerful, from the supposed medicinal qualities of some of the species.] An extensive genus of herbaceous perennials, of which one species is used in Lapland and the Orkney Islands to tan and dye leather.

pother, POTH′ėr, *n.* [A different form of *bother* or of *potter.*] Bustle; confusion; tumult; flutter.—*v.i.* To make a pother or bustle; to make a stir.—*v.t.* To bother; to puzzle; to tease.

potion, pō′shon, *n.* [L. *potio*, a drinking, a draught, from *poto*, to drink. *Poison* is the same word.] A draught; a liquid medicine; a dose to be drunk.

potpourri, potsherd. See POT.

pott, pot, *n.* See POT.

pottage, pot′ij *n.* [Fr. *potage*, lit. what one puts in the *pot.*] A species of food made of meat boiled to softness in water, usually with some vegetables; also, oatmeal or other porridge.

potter, pottery, etc. See POT.

potter, pot′ėr, *v.i.* [Comp. Sw. *pota*, D. *poteren, peuteren*, to poke or search with the finger or a stick; W. *pwtio*, to poke or thrust. PUT.] To busy or perplex one's self about trifles; to work with little energy or effect; to trifle.

pottle, pot′l, *n.* [Fr. *potel*, a dim. of *pot.*] Originally a liquid measure of two quarts; hence, any large tankard; a vessel or small basket for holding fruit.

pouch, pouch, *n.* [A softened form of *poke*, a bag, a pouch.] A small bag; a pocket; a bag or sac belonging to or forming an appendage of certain animals, as that of a marsupial animal.—*v.t.* To put into a pouch or pocket.—**pouched,** poucht, *a.* Having a pouch; furnished with a pouch for carrying the young, as the marsupials.

poult, pōlt, *n.* [Fr. *poulet*, a dim. of *poule*, a hen. POULTRY.] A young chicken, partridge, grouse, etc.

poultice, pōl′tis, *n.* [From L. *puls, pultis*, pottage, gruel, pap.] A soft composition of meal, bread, or the like mollifying substance, to be applied to sores, inflamed parts of the body, etc.; a cataplasm.—*v.t.* —*poulticed, poulticing*. To cover with a poultice; to apply a poultice to.

poultry, pōl′tri, *n.* [A collective from *poult*, pullet, from Fr. *poulet*, a chicken, from *poule*, a hen, L. *pullus*, a young animal, a chicken; akin to Gr. *polōs*, E. *foal.*] Domestic fowls which are reared for their flesh as an article of food, for their eggs, feathers, etc., such as cocks and hens, turkeys, ducks, and geese. —**poulterer,** pōl'tėr•ėr, *n.* One who makes it his business to sell fowls for the table.

pounce, pouns, *n.* [Fr. *ponce,* It. *pomice*; from L. *pumex, pumicis,* a pumice stone.] A fine powder, such as pulverized cuttlefish bone, used to prevent ink from spreading on paper, but now almost entirely superseded by blotting paper.—*v.t.* —*pounced, pouncing.* To sprinkle or rub with pounce.

pounce, pouns, *n.* [Ultimately from L. *pungo, punctum,* to prick or pierce; comp. Fr. *poinçon,* a bodkin; Sp. *punzar,* to prick, to pierce. PUNCTURE, PUNCH, POINT.] The claw or talon of a bird of prey.—*v.t.*—*pounced, pouncing.* To seize or strike suddenly with the claws or talons: said of birds of prey.—*v.i.* To fall on and seize with the claws or talons; to dart or dash on: with *on* or *upon.*

pound, pound, *n.* [A.Sax., Dan., Sw., Icel., and Goth. *pund*; G. *pfund*; from L. *pondo,* a pound, akin to L. *pondus,* a weight. PONDEROUS, PENDANT.] A standard weight consisting of 12 ounces troy, or 16 ounces avoirdupois; the British monetary unit consisting of 20 shillings. The *pound Scots* was only equal to a twelfth of the pound sterling, that is 1*s.* 8*d.*—**poundage,** poun'dij, *n.* A sum deducted from a pound, or a certain sum or rate per pound; payment rated by the weight of a commodity.—**poundal,** poun'dal, *n.* In *physics,* the unit of force, equal to the force which in one second produces in one pound a velocity of one foot per second.—**pounder,** poun'dėr, *n.* A person or thing denominated from a certain number of pounds; often applied to pieces of ordnance along with a number to express the weight of the shell they fire (a 64-*pounder,* a cannon firing shells weighing 64 lbs.).

pound, pound, *n.* [A.Sax. *pund,* an enclosure; a different form of *pond.*] An enclosure in which cattle are confined when taken in trespassing, or going at large in violation of law; a penfold or pinfold.—*v.t.* To shut up as in a pound; to confine in a public penfold; to impound.—**poundage,** poun'dij, *n.* Confinement of cattle in a pound; a mulct levied upon the owners of cattle impounded.

pound, pound, *v.t.* [A.Sax. *punian,* to beat, bray; the *d* has become attached, as in *sound, compound.* Hence *pun.*] To beat; to strike repeatedly with some heavy instrument; to comminute and pulverize by beating; to bruise or break into fine parts by a heavy instrument.—**pounder,** poun'dėr, *n.* One who or that which pounds.

pour, pōr, *v.t.* [Perhaps from W. *bwrw,* to cast, to shed, as in *bwrw dagrau,* to shed tears; *bwrw gwlaw,* to rain.] To cause to flow, as a liquid, either out of a vessel or into it; to send forth in a stream or continued succession; to emit; to give vent to, as under the influence of strong feeling; to throw in profusion.—*v.i.* To flow; to issue forth in a stream; to gush; to rush in continued procession.—**pourer,** pō'rėr, *n.* One who or that which pours.

poussette, pö•set', *n.* [Comp. Fr. *poussette,* a child's game with pins, from *pousser,* to push.] A figure executed by a couple who swing together in a country-dance.—*v.i.*—*poussetted, poussetting.* To swing round in couples, as in a country-dance.

pout, pout, *v.i.* [From W. *pwtiaw,* to push, or from dial. Fr. *pout, potte,* Pr. *pot,* the lip.] To thrust out the lips, as in sullenness, contempt, or displeasure; hence, to look sullen; to swell out, as the lips; to be prominent.—*n.* A protrusion of the lips as in sullenness; a fit of sullenness.—**pouter,** pout'ėr, *n.* One who pouts; a variety of pigeon, so called from its inflated breast.

poverty, pov'ėr•ti, *n.* [Fr. *pauvreté,* L. *paupertas,* from *pauper,* poor. POOR.] The state of being poor or indigent; indigence; a deficiency of necessary or desirable elements; barrenness (*poverty* of soil); poorness; want of ideas or information; want or defect of words (*poverty* of language).

poverty-stricken, *a.* Reduced to a state of poverty; indigent.

powder, pou'dėr, *n.* [Fr. *poudre,* O.Fr. *pouldre,* It. *polvēre,* from L. *pulvis, pulveris,* dust, powder.] Any dry substance composed of minute particles; a substance comminuted or triturated to fine particles; gunpowder; face powder.—*v.t.* To reduce to fine particles; to pulverize; to sprinkle with powder or as with powder; to sprinkle with salt, as meat.—*v.i.* To fall to dust; to become like powder; to pat or rub powder on the face.—**powder blue,** *n.* Powdered smalt, as generally used in laundering; pale blue blended with gray.—**powder flask,** *n.* A flask in which gunpowder is carried.—**powder horn,** *n.* A horn in which gunpowder used to be carried by sportsmen before the introduction of cartridges.—**powder mill,** *n.* A mill in which gunpowder is made.—**powder room,** *n.* The apartment in a ship where gunpowder is kept.—**powdery,** pou'dėr•i, *a.* Sprinkled or covered with powder; resembling powder; *bot.* having a surface covered with fine powder.

power, pou'ėr, *n.* [O.Fr. *pooir* (Mod. Fr. *pouvoir*), from old infinitive *podir,* from L.L. *potēre,* to be able, used for L. *posse,* to be able, from *potis,* able, and *esse,* to be; akin *possible, potent,* etc. POTENT.] Ability to act; the faculty of doing or performing something; that in virtue of which one can; capability of producing an effect; strength, force, or energy manifested in action; capacity; susceptibility (great *power* of resistance); natural strength; animal strength; influence; predominance (as of the mind, imagination); faculty of the mind as manifested by a particular mode of operation (the *power* of thinking); ability; capability; the employment of strength or influence among men; command; the right of governing or actual government; dominion; rule; authority; one who or that which exercises authority or control (the *powers* that be); a sovereign, or the sovereign authority of a state; a state (the great *powers* of Europe); a spirit or superhuman agent having a certain sway (celestial *powers*); legal authority; warrant; *mech.* that which produces motion or force, or that which may be applied to produce it; a mechanical agent; the moving force applied to produce the required effect; mechanical advantage or effect; force or effect considered as resulting from the action of a machine; rate of doing work; the unit for practical purposes in the U. S. is HORSEPOWER (which see); *arith.* and *alg.* the product arising from the multiplication of a number or quantity into itself; *optics,* the degree to which an optical instrument magnifies the apparent dimensions of an object.—*Power of attorney,* authority given to a person to act for another. See ATTORNEY.—*European powers,* a term in modern diplomacy by which are usually meant Great Britain, France, Germany, Russia, and Italy.—**powerful,** pou'ėr•fụl, *a.* Having great power; able to produce great effects; strong; potent; energetic; efficacious.—**powerfully,** pou'ėr•fụl•li, *adv.* In a powerful manner; with great effect; forcibly.—**powerless,** pou'ėr•les, *a.* Destitute of power; weak; impotent. —**powerlessly,** pou'ėr•les•li, *adv.* In a powerless manner.—**powerlessness,** pou'ėr•les•nes, *n.*—**power plant,** *n.* A plant, including buildings and machines, for the generation of power; a device for supplying power for a mechanical operation or process; a powerhouse.

powwow, pou'wou, *n.* [Algonquian.] A medicine-man among the North American Indians; also, a public feast, festival, or conference.—*v.i.* To confer.

pox, poks, *n.* [A peculiar spelling of *pocks,* pl. of *pock.*] A disease characterized by pustules, as the smallpox, chicken pox; syphillis.

pozzuolana, pozzolana, pot'zụ•o•lä"na, pot•zo•lä'na, *n.* A volcanic product occurring near *Pozzuoli,* on the Gulf of Naples, largely employed in the manufacture of Roman or hydraulic cement.

practicable, prak'ti•ka•bl, *a.* [From L.L. *practicare,* to transact, from L. *practicus,* active; Gr. *praktikos,* active, practical, from *prassō,* to do, to work.] Capable of being effected or performed by human means, or by powers that can be applied; feasible; capable of being passed or traveled over; passable; assailable. —**practicability, practicableness,** prak'ti•ka•bil"i•ti, prak'ti•ka•bl•nes, *n.* The quality of being practicable; feasibility.—**practicably,** prak'ti•ka•bli, *adv.* In a practicable manner.—**practical,** prak'ti•kal, *a.* [L. *practicus.*] Relating to practice, use, or employment: opposed to *speculative, ideal,* or *theoretical*; that may be turned to use; reducible to use in the conduct of life; given to or concerned with action or practice; capable of reducing knowledge or theories to actual use; educated by practice or experience; skilled in actual work (a *practical* gardener); derived from practice or experience. —*Practical joke*. See JOKE.—**practically,** prak'ti•kal•li, *adv.* In a practical manner; not merely theoretically; so far as actual results or effects are concerned; in effect.—**practicality,** prak•ti•kal'i•ti, *n.* The quality of being practical.—**practice,** prak'tis, *n.* [Formerly *practicke*, *practike*, from O.Fr. *practique*, from Gr. *praktikē*, practical knowledge.] A piece of conduct; a proceeding; a customary action; custom or habit; use or usage; state of being used; customary use; method or art of doing anything; actual performance (as opposed to *theory*); exercise of any profession (the *practice* of law); application of remedies; medical treatment of diseases; drill; exercise for instruction or discipline; skillful or artful management; stratagem; artifice: usually in a bad sense; a rule in arithmetic for expeditiously multiplying quantities expressed in different denominations.—**practice,** prak'tis, *v.t.*—*practiced, practicing.* [From the noun.] To do or perform frequently, customarily, or habitually; to use for instruction or discipline, or as a profession or art (to *practice* law or medicine); to put into practice; to perform; to do; to teach by practice; to accustom; to train.—*v.i.*—*practiced, practicing.* To perform certain acts frequently or customarily, for instruction, profit, or amusement; to form a habit of acting in any manner; to use artifices or stratagems; to exercise some profession, as that of medicine or of law. —**practiced,** prak'tist, *p.* and *a.* Skilled through practice.—**practicer,** prak'tis•ėr, *n.* One that practices.—**practitioner,** prak•tish'on•ėr, *n.* One who is engaged in the exercise of any art or profession, particularly in law or medicine.—*A general practitioner*, one who practices both medicine and surgery.

praedial, prē'di•al, *a.* See PREDIAL.

praemunire, prē•mū•nī'rē, *n.* [A corruption of L. *praemonere*, to preadmonish, from the words of the writ.] *Law*, a name given to a species of writ, to the offense for which it is granted, and also to the penalty it incurs, this penalty being forfeiture of goods and imprisonment, and being attached in former times to the offenses of asserting the jurisdiction of the pope, denying the sovereign's supremacy, etc.

praetexta, prē•teks'ta, *n.* [L., from *prae*, before, on the edge, and *textus*, woven.] Among the ancient Romans, a white robe with a narrow scarlet border worn by a youth; the white outer garment bordered with purple of the higher magistrates.

praetor, prē'tor, *n.* [L., from *prae*, before, and *eo*, I go.] In ancient Rome, a title originally of the consuls, in later times of two important magistrates of the city, and lastly of a number of magistrates who administered justice in the state.—**praetorial, praetorian,** prē•tō'ri•al, prē•tō'ri•an, *a.* Belonging to a praetor.—*Praetorian bands* or *guards*, bodies of troops originally formed by the emperor Augustus to protect his person and his power, and afterward long maintained by successive Roman emperors; the household troops or bodyguards of the emperors.—*n.* A soldier of the Praetorian guard.

pragmatic, pragmatical, prag•mat'-ik, prag•mat'i•kal, *a.* [L. *pragmaticus*, Gr. *pragmatikos*, from *pragma*, business, from *prassō*, I do. PRACTICE.] Skilled in business‡; active or diligent‡; forward to intermeddle; impertinently busy or officious in the concerns of others.—*The pragmatic sanction*, the instrument by which the German emperor Charles VI, being without male issue, endeavored to secure the succession for his female descendants.—**pragmatically,** prag•mat'i•kal•li, *adv.* In a pragmatic manner; impertinently. —**pragmatism,** prag'ma•tizm, *n.* A nonspeculative system of philosophy, which regards the practical consequences and useful results of ideas as the test of their truthfulness, and which considers truth itself to be a process; especially the modern form of this philosophy, introduced by C. S. Pierce and William James.—**pragmatist,** prag'ma•tist, *n.*

prairie, prâ'ri, *n.* [Fr., from L.L. *prataria*, from L. *pratum*, a meadow.] The extensive, mostly level tracts of land of the Middle West, including the Great Plains from the Mississippi to the Rockies, usually treeless and covered with coarse grass and flowering plants.—**prairie dog,** *n.* A small burrowing rodent allied to the marmot.—**prairie schooner,** *n.* A long, canvas-topped wagon used by settlers to cross the prairies.—**prairie wolf,** *n.* The coyote.

praise, prāz, *n.* [Formerly *preis*, *preys*, praise, price, value, from O.Fr. *pris*, *preis*, price, honor (Mod.Fr. *prix*), from L. *pretium*, price, value, reward; the same as *price* and to *prize*.] Commendation bestowed on a person; approbation; eulogy; laud; a joyful tribute of gratitude or homage paid to the Divine Being, often expressed in song; the ground or reason of praise; what makes a person worthy of praise. — *v.t.* — *praised, praising.* To commend; to applaud; to express approbation of; to extol in words or song; to laud or magnify, especially applied to the Divine Being.—**praiseless,** prāz'les, *a.* Without praise or commendation.—**praiser,** prā'zėr, *n.* One who praises; a commender.—**praiseworthy,** prāz'-wėr•THi, *a.* Worthy or deserving of praise; commendable.—**praiseworthily,** prāz'wėr•THi•li, *adv.* In a manner deserving of commendation. —**praiseworthiness,** prāz'wėr•THi•-nes, *n.* The quality of being praiseworthy.

Prakrit, prä'krit, *n.* [Skr. *prâkriti*, nature, hence that which is natural or vulgar.] A Hindu language or dialect based on the Sanskrit, and which has been the mother of various modern dialects.

prance, prans, *v.i.*—*pranced, prancing.* [A slightly different form of *prank*.] To spring or bound, as a horse in high mettle; to ride ostentatiously; to strut about in a showy manner or with warlike parade.—**prancer,** prans'ėr, *n.* A prancing horse.

prandial, pran'di•al, *a.* [L. *prandium*, dinner.] Relating to a dinner, or meal in general.

prank, prangk, *v.t.* [Allied to D. *pronk*, finery, *pronken*, to strut; Dan. *prange*, G. *prangen*, *prunken*, to make a show; comp. also G. *pracht*, D. and Dan. *pragt*, pomp.] To adorn in a showy manner; to dress up.—*v.i.* To have a showy or gaudy appearance.—*n.* A gambol or caper; a playful or sportive action; a merry trick; a mischievous act, generally rather for sport than injury.—**prankish,** prangk'ish, *a.* Full of pranks.

prase, prāz, *n.* [Fr., from Gr. *prason*, a leek.] A species of quartz of a leek-green color.

praseodymium, prā'zi•o•dim"i•um, *n.* [Gr. *prasios*, leek-green, and *didymium*.] A silvery-white metallic element of the rare-earth series. Symbol, Pr; at. no., 59; at. wt., 140.907.

prate, prāt, *v.i.*—*prated, prating.* [Same as L.G. *praten*, Dan. *prate*; probably of imitative origin.] To talk much and without weight; to chatter; to babble.—*v.t.* To utter foolishly.—*n.* Continued talk to little purpose; unmeaning loquacity. —**prater,** prā'tėr, *n.* One that prates. —**prating,** prā'ting, *p.* and *a.* Given to prate; loquacious.—**pratingly,** prā'ting•li, *adv.* In a prating manner.

pratincole, prat'in•kōl, *n.* [From L. *pratum*, a meadow, and *incola*, an inhabitant.] A graceful bird of a genus akin to the plovers, inhabiting the temperate and warmer parts of Europe, Africa, and Asia.

pratique, pra•tēk', *n.* [Fr. *pratique*, practice, intercourse. PRACTICE.] A license to a ship to hold intercourse and trade with the inhabitants of a place, after having performed quarantine: a term used particularly in the European ports of the Mediterranean.

prattle, prat'l, *v.i.*—*prattled, prattling.* [Freq. and dim. of *prate*.] To talk much and idly; to be loquacious on trifling subjects; to talk like a child.—*n.* Puerile or trifling talk.—**prattler,** prat'lėr, *n.* One who prattles.

prawn, pran, *n.* [Etym. unknown.] A small crustaceous animal of the shrimp family, highly prized for food.

praxis, prak'sis, *n.* [Gr., from *prassō*, I do. PRACTICE.] Use; practice; especially, practice or discipline for a specific purpose, as to acquire a specific art; an example or form to teach practice.

pray, prā, *v.i.* [O.Fr. *preier* (Fr. *prier*),

It. *pregare*, to pray, from L. *precari*, to pray (as in *deprecate*, *imprecate*), from *prex*, a prayer (whence also *precarious*); same root as Skr. *prach*, to demand, A.Sax. *frignan*, G. *fragen*, to inquire.] To ask something with earnestness or zeal; to supplicate; to beg (to *pray* for mercy); to make petition to the Supreme Being; to address the Supreme Being with confession of sins and supplication for benefits.—*Pray*, elliptically for *I pray you tell me*, is a common mode of introducing a question.—*v.t.* To make earnest request to; to entreat; to address with a prayer for something such as God may grant; to ask earnestly for; to beseech; to petition. —**prayer**, prā′ėr, *n.* One who prays.

prayer, prā′ėr or prâr, *n.* [Not directly from *pray*, but from O.Fr. *proiere*, Fr. *prière*, a prayer, from L.L. *precaria*, a prayer, from L. *precarius*, obtained by begging. PRAY, PRECARIOUS.] The act of asking for a favor with earnestness; a petition, supplication, entreaty; a solemn petition for benefits addressed to the Supreme Being; the words of a supplication; a formula of church service or of worship, public or private; that part of a petition to a public body which specifies the thing desired to be done or granted.—**prayer book**, *n.* A book containing prayers, used by various churches.—**prayerful**, prâr′•fu̥l or prār′fu̥l, *a.* Devotional; given to prayer.—**prayer meeting**, *n.* A meeting for prayer; usually a mid-week devotional service.—**prayer wheel**, *n. Lamaism.* An apparatus used mainly in Tibet; one of the commoner forms consists of a wheel to which a written prayer is attached, and each revolution of the wheel made by the devotee counts as an utterance of the prayer.

preach, prēch, *v.i.* [O.Fr. *precher* (Fr. *prêcher*), from L. *praedicare*, to declare in public—*prae*, before, and *dico*, *dicatum*, I proclaim; closely akin to *dico*, *dictum*, I say. DICTION.] To pronounce a public discourse on a religious subject, or from a text of Scripture; to deliver a sermon; to give earnest advice; to discourse in the manner of a preacher.—*v.t.* To proclaim; to publish in religious discourses; to inculcate in public discourse; to deliver (a sermon).—**preacher**, prēch′ėr, *n.* One who preaches.—**preachify**, prēch′i•fī, *v.i.* To give a long-winded moral advice. —**preachment**, prēch′ment, *n.* A discourse affectedly solemn: in contempt.

preamble, prē′am•bl, *n.* [Fr. *préambule*, from L. *prae*, before, and *ambulo*, I go about. AMBLE.] The introductory part of a discourse, statute, or written instrument, as the Constitution, usually beginning with *Whereas* and stating the nature and intent of the document.—*v.t.*—*preambled*, *preambling*. To preface; to introduce with previous remarks.

prebend, prē′bend, *n.* [Fr. *prébende*, from L.L. *praebenda*, things to be supplied, from L. *praebeo*, to give, grant, furnish—*prae*, and *habeo*, to have. HABIT.] The stipend granted to a canon of a cathedral or collegiate church out of its estate.—**prebendal**, pri•ben′dal, *a.* Pertaining to a prebend.—**prebendary**, prē′-ben•de•ri, *n.* An ecclesiastic who enjoys a prebend; a canon.

Pre-Cambrian, prē•kam′bri•an, *n.* [L. *pre*, before, *Cambrian.*] The oldest known strata.

precarious, pri•kâ′ri•us, *a.* [L. *precarius*, primarily, depending on request, or on the will of another, from *precor*, I pray. PRAY, PRAYER.] Depending on or held at the will or pleasure of another; hence, held by a doubtful tenure; depending on unknown or unforeseen causes or events.—**precariously**, pri•kâ′ri•us•-li, *adv.* In a precarious manner.—**precariousness**, pri•kâ′ri•us•nes, *n.* The state of being precarious.

precative, precatory, prek′a•tiv, prek′a•to•ri, *a.* [From L. *precor*, I pray. PRAY.] Suppliant; beseeching.

precaution, pri•ka̧′shon, *n.* [L. *praecautio*, from *praecautus*—*prae*, before, and *caveo*, *cautum*, I take care. CAUTION.] Previous caution or care; a measure taken beforehand to ward off evil or secure good.—*v.t.* To warn or advise beforehand, for preventing mischief.—**precautionary**, pri•ka̧′shon•a•ri, *a.* Containing previous caution; proceeding from precaution.

precede, pri•sēd′, *v.t.*—*preceded*, *preceding*. [L. *praecedo*—*prae*, before, and *cedo*, I move. CEDE.] To go before in the order of time; to be previous to; to go before in place, rank, or importance.—**precedence, precedency**, pri•sē′dens, pri•sē′den•si, *n.* The act or state of preceding or going before; priority in time; the state of being before in rank or dignity; the right to a more honorable place; order or adjustment of place according to rank; the foremost place in a ceremony; superior importance or influence.—**precedent**, pri•se′dent, *a.* Going before in time; anterior; antecedent.—**precedent**, pres′e•dent, *n.* Something done or said that may serve or be adduced as an example or rule to be followed in a subsequent act of the like kind; *law*, a judicial decision, which serves as a rule for future decisions in similar or analogous cases.

precentor, pri•sen′tėr, *n.* [L.L. *praecentor*—L. *prae*, before, and *cantor*, a singer, from *cano*, *cantum*, I sing. CHANT.] The leader of the choir in a cathedral, usually a minor canon; a person whose duty it is to lead the psalmody of a Presbyterian or other congregation.—**precentorship**, pri•-sen′tėr•ship, *n.* The office of a precentor.

precept, prē′sept, *n.* [Fr. *précepte*, L. *praeceptum*, from *praecipio*, I teach, instruct—*prae*, before, and *capio*, to take. CAPABLE.] A commandment intended as an authoritative rule of action; a command respecting moral conduct; an injunction; *law*, a mandate in writing sent by a justice of the peace, etc., for bringing a person, record, etc., before him.—**preceptive**, pri•sep′tiv, *a.* [L. *praeceptivus.*] Giving or containing precepts for the regulation of conduct; admonitive; instructive.—**preceptor**, pri•sep′tėr, *n.* [L. *praeceptor.*] A teacher; an instructor; the head of a preceptory among the Knights Templars.—**preceptorial**, pri•sep•tō′ri•al, *a.* Pertaining to a preceptor.—**preceptory**, pri•sep′to•ri, *a.* Giving precepts.—*n.* A subordinate religious house where instruction was given; an establishment of the Knights Templars, the superior of which was called knight preceptor.—**preceptress**, pri•sep′-tres, *n.* A female teacher or preceptor.

precession, pri•sesh′on, *n.* [Fr. *précession*, from L. *praecedo*, *praecessum*, I precede. PRECEDE.] The act of going before or forward.—*Precession of the equinoxes*, an astronomical phenomenon consisting in a slow movement of the equinoctial points around the ecliptic.

precinct, prē′singt, *n.* [From L. *praecingo*, *praecinctum*, I encompass—*prae*, before, and *cingo*, to gird. CINCTURE.] The boundary line encompassing a place; a limit; a part near a border; a district within certain boundaries; a minor territorial division.

precious, presh′us, *a.* [Fr. *précieux*, from L. *pretiosus*, from *pretium*, price PRAISE.] Of great price; costly; of great value or worth; very valuable; much esteemed; highly cherished; ironically, very great; rascally (a *precious* villain).—*Precious metals*, gold and silver.—*Precious stones*, jewels, gems.—**preciously**, presh′-us•li, *adv.* In a precious manner; at a great cost.—**preciousness**, presh′us•-nes, *n.*

precipice, pres′i•pis, *n.* [Fr. *précipice*, from L. *praecipitium*, a falling headlong, a precipice, from *praeceps*, headlong—*prae*, forward, and *caput*, head. CHIEF.] A headlong declivity; a bank or cliff extremely steep, or quite perpendicular or overhanging. —**precipitate**, pri•sip′i•tāt, *v.t.*—*precipitated*, *precipitating*. [L. *praecipito*, from *praeceps*, headlong.] To throw headlong; to cast down from a precipice or height; to urge or press with eagerness or violence; to hasten (to *precipitate* one's flight); to hurry blindly or rashly; to throw or cause to sink to the bottom of a vessel, as a substance in solution.—*v.i.* To fall to the bottom of a vessel, as sediment or any substance in solution.—*a.* Falling, flowing, or rushing with steep descent; headlong; overhasty; rashly hasty; adopted with haste or without due deliberation; hasty; hurried; headlong.—*n.* *Chem.* any matter which, having been dissolved in a fluid, falls to the bottom of the vessel on the addition of some other substance capable of producing a decomposition of the compound. ∴ Substances which fall or settle down, as earthy matter in water, are called *sediments*, the operating cause being mechanical and not chemical.—**precipitately**, pri•-sip′i•tāt•li, *adv.* In a headlong or precipitate manner; too hastily.—**precipitance, precipitancy,** pri•sip′i•tans, pri•sip′i•tan•si, *n.* The quality of being precipitate; rash haste; haste in resolving, forming an opinion, or executing a purpose.—**precipitant,** pri•sip′i•tant, *a.* [L. *praecipitans, praecipitantis,* ppr. of *praecipito.*] Falling or rushing headlong; precipitate.—*n. Chem.* a substance which, when added to a solution, separates what is dissolved and makes it fall to the bottom in a concrete state.—**precipitantly,** pri•sip′i•tant•li, *adv.* In a precipitant manner.—**precipitation,** pri•sip′i•tā″shon, *n.* The act of precipitating, or state of being precipitated; a falling or rushing down with violence and rapidity; rash, tumultuous haste; *chem.* the process by which any substance is made to separate from another or others in a solution, and fall to the bottom.—**precipitin,** pri•sip′it•in, *n.* [From *precipitate.*] A substance formed in the blood that precipitates disease material and renders it harmless.—**precipitous,** pri•sip′i•tus, *a.* [L. *praeceps, praecipitis,* headlong.] Very steep; like or forming a precipice; headlong in descent.—**precipitously,** pri•sip′i•tus•li, *adv.* In a precipitous manner.—**precipitousness,** pri•sip′i•tus•nes, *n.* Steepness of descent.

précis, prā•sē′, *n.* [Fr. *précis,* precise, also an abstract. PRECISE.] A concise or abridged statement; a summary; an abstract.

precise, pri•sīs′, *a.* [L. *praecisus,* from *praecido,* to cut off—*prae,* before, and *caedo,* to cut (as in *concise, excision*).] Sharply or exactly limited or defined as to meaning; exact; definite, not loose, vague, or equivocal; exact in conduct; strict; formal; nice; punctilious.—**precisely,** pri•sīs′li, *adv.* In a precise manner; exactly; accurately; with excess of formality.—**preciseness,** pri•sīs′nes, *n.* Exactness; rigid nicety; excessive regard to forms or rules; rigid formality.—**precisian,** pri•sizh′an, *n.* An over-precise person; one ceremoniously exact in the observance of rules.—**precisianism,** pri•sizh′an•izm, *n.* The conduct of a precisian; excessive exactness.—**precision,** pri•sizh′on, *n.* The state of being precise as to meaning; preciseness; exactness; accuracy.

preclude, pri•klūd′, *v.t.*—*precluded, precluding.* [L. *praecludo*—*prae,* before, and *cludo, claudo,* to shut. CLOSE, *v.t.*] To shut up; to stop; to impede; to hinder; to hinder or render inoperative by anticipative action.—**preclusion,** pri•klū′zhon, *n.* The act of precluding.—**preclusive,** pri•klū′siv, *a.* Tending to preclude; hindering by previous obstacles.—**preclusively,** pri•klū′siv•li, *abv.* In a preclusive manner.

precocious, pri•kō′shus, *a.* [Fr. *précoce,* from L. *praecox, praecocis,* ripe early, precocious—*prae,* before, and *coquo,* to cook, to ripen. COOK.] Ripe before the proper or natural time‡; ripe in understanding at an early period; developed or matured early in life.—**precociously,** pri•kō′shus•li, *adv.* In a precocious manner.—**precociousness, precocity,** pri•kō′shus•nes, pri•kos′i•ti, *n.* The state or quality of being precocious; early development of the mental powers.

precognition, prē•kog•nish′on, *n.* [L. *prae,* before, and *cognitio,* knowledge.] Previous knowledge or cognition; *Scots law,* a preliminary examination of a witness or witnesses to a criminal act, in order to know whether there is ground of trial.

preconceive, prē•kon•sēv′, *v.t.*—*preconceived, preconceiving.* To form a conception or opinion of beforehand; to form a previous notion or idea of.—**preconception,** prē•kon•sep′shon, *n.* The act of preconceiving; conception or opinion previously formed.

preconcert, prē•kon•sėrt′, *v.t.* To concert beforehand; to settle by previous agreement.—*n.* (prē•kon′sėrt). A previous agreement.

preconize, praeconize, prē′kon•īz, *v.t.* [L. *praeco,* a public crier.] To summon or proclaim publicly; to bestow excessive praise.

precontract, prē•kon′trakt, *n.* A contract or agreement previous to another.—*v.t.* and *i.* (prē•kon•trakt′). To contract or stipulate previously.

precursor, pri•kėr′sėr, *n.* [L. *praecursor*—*prae,* before, and *cursor,* a runner, from *curro, cursum,* I run. CURRENT.] A forerunner; a harbinger; one who or that which precedes an event and indicates its approach.—**precursory,** pri•kėr′so•ri, *a.* Preceding as the harbinger; forerunning.—**precursive,** pri•kėr′siv, *a.* Precursory.

predaceous, pri•dā′shus, *a.* [From L. *praeda,* prey, spoil, plunder, etc. PREY.] Living by prey; given to prey on other animals.—**predatory,** pred′a•to•ri, *a.* [L. *praedatorius.*] Plundering; pillaging; practicing rapine.

predate, prē•dāt′, *v.t.*—*predated, predating.* To date by anticipation; to antedate.

predecease, prē•di•sēs′, *v.t.*—*predeceased, predeceasing.* To die before.—*n.* The decease of one before another.

predecessor, pre•di•ses′ėr, *n.* [L. *praedecessor*—*prae,* before, and *decessor,* one who retires, from *decedo, decessum,* I depart—*de,* from, and *cedo,* to go. CEDE.] One who precedes or goes before another in some position; one who has preceded another in any state, position, office, or the like.

predestinate, prē•des′ti•nāt, *v.t.*—*predestinated, predestinating.* [L. *praedestino, prdedestinatum*—*prae,* before, and *destino,* I determine. DESTINE.] To predetermine or foreordain; to appoint or ordain beforehand by an unchangeable purpose.—*a.* Predestinated; foreordained.—**predestinarian,** pri•des′ti•nâ″ri•an, *a.* Belonging to predestination.—*n.* One who believes in the doctrine of predestination.—**predestinarianism,** pri•des′ti•nâ″ri•an•izm, *n.* The system or doctrines of the predestinarians.—**predestination,** prē•des′ti•nā″shon, *n.* The act of decreeing or foreordaining events; especially, *theol.* the doctrine that God has from eternity unchangeably appointed or determined whatever comes to pass; particularly that he has preordained men to everlasting happiness or misery.—**predestine,** pri•des′tin, *v.t.*—*predestined, predestining.* To decree beforehand; to foreordain.

predetermine, prē•di•tėr′min, *v.t.*—*predetermined, predetermining.* To determine beforehand; to doom by previous decree.—*v.i.* To make a determination beforehand.—**predetermination,** pre•di•tėr′mi•nā″shon. *n.* Previous determination; purpose formed beforehand.

predial, prē′di•al, *a.* [Fr. *prédial,* from L. *praedium,* a farm or estate.] Consisting of land or farms; landed; attached to land; derived from land (*predial* tithes).

predicable, pred′i•ka•bl, *a.* [L. *praedicabilis,* from *praedico.* PREDICATE.] Capable of being affirmed of something; that may be attributed to something.—*n.* Anything that may be predicated or affirmed of another; *logic,* one of the five things which can be affirmatively predicated of several others, viz. genus, species, difference, property, and accident.—**predicability,** pred′i•ka•bil″i•ti, *n.* The quality of being predicable.—**predicament,** pri•dik″a•ment, *n.* [L. L. *praedicamentum.*] *Logic,* one of those general heads or most comprehensive terms under one or other of which every other term may be arranged, ten in number, according to Aristotle, viz. substance, quantity, quality, relation, action, passion, time, place, situation, and habit; hence, class or kind described by definite marks; condition; especially, a dangerous or trying condition or state.—**predicant,** pred′i•kant, *n.* [L. *praedicans,* ppr. of *praedico.*] One that affirms anything; a preaching friar; a Dominican.—*a.* Predicating; preaching.

predicate, pred′i•kāt, *v.t.*—*predicated, predicating.* [L. *praedicare, praedicatum,* to affirm, to declare—*prae,* before, and *dicare,* to declare. PREACH.] To affirm as an attribute of something (to *predicate* whiteness of snow); to declare one thing of another.—*v.i.* To make an affirmation.—*n. Logic,* that which, in a proposition, is affirmed or denied of the subject; *gram.* the word or words in a proposition which express what is affirmed or denied of the subject.—**predication,** pred•i•kā′shon, *n.* The act of predicating; affirmation; assertion.—**predicative,** pred′i•kā•tiv, *a.* Expressing affirmation or predication.—**predicatory,** pred′i•ka•to•ri, *a.* Affirmative; positive.

predict pri•dikt′, *v.t,* [L. *praedico, praedictum*—*prae,* before, and *dicere,* to tell. DICTION.] To foretell; to prophesy; to declare to be or happen in the future; to prognosticate.

prediction, pri•dik′shon, *n.* The act of predicting; a foretelling; a prophecy.—**predictive,** pri•dik′tiv, *a.* Foretelling; prophetic.

predigest, prē'di•jest, *v.t.* To assimilate or digest previously.

predilection, prē•di•lek'shon, *n.* [Fr. *prédilection*—L. *prae*, before, and *dilectio*, a choice, from *diligere*, to love. DILIGENT.] A previous liking; a prepossession of mind in favor of something.

predispose, prē•dis•pōz', *v.t.*—*predisposed, predisposing.* To incline beforehand; to give a previous disposition or tendency to; to fit or adapt previously.—**predisposition,** prē•dis'pi•zish″on, *n.* The state of being previously disposed toward something; previous inclination or tendency; previous fitness or adaptation to any change, impression, or purpose.

predominate, pri•dom'i•nāt, *v.i.*—*predominated, predominating.* [Fr. *prédominer*—L. *prae*, before, and *dominari*, to rule, from *dominus*, lord. DOMINATE, DAME.] To have surpassing power, influence, or authority; to have controlling influence among others.—*v.t.* To rule over; to master‡.—**predominance, predominancy,** pri•dom'i•nans, pri•dom'i•nan•si, *n.* Prevalence over others; superiority in power, influence, or authority; ascendency.—**predominant,** pri•dom'i•nant, *a.* Prevalent over others; superior in strength, influence, or authority; ruling; controlling.—**predominantly,** pri•dom'i•nant•li, *adv.* In a predominant manner.

pre-eminence, prē•em'i•nens, *n.* The state or quality of being notably eminent among others; superior or surpassing eminence; undoubted superiority, especially superiority in excellence.—**pre-eminent,** prē•em'i•nent, *a.* Eminent above others; surpassing or highly distinguished in excellence, sometimes also in evil.—**pre-eminently,** prē•em'i•nent•li, *adv.* In a pre-eminent manner or degree.

pre-empt, prē•empt', *v.t.* and *i.* To acquire before others; to claim before others establish rights, as to *pre-empt* public lands.—**pre-emption,** prē•em'shon, *n.* [L. *prae*, before, and *emptio*, a buying, from *emo*, to buy. EXEMPT.] The act or right of purchasing before others; the right of a settler to the first chance of buying land in or near which he has settled.—**pre-emptive,** prē•em'tiv, *a.*

preen, prēn, *v.t.* [O.E. *proine, proigne*, to prune, to preen. PRUNE.] To trim with the beak; to clean and dress: said of birds dressing their feathers.

pre-engage, prē•en•gāj', *v.t.*—*pre-engaged, pre-engaging.* To engage by previous agreement; to engage or attach by previous influence; to preoccupy.

pre-establish, prē•es•tab'lish, *v.t.* To establish or settle beforehand.

pre-exist, prē•eg•zist', *v.i.* To exist beforehand or before something else.—**pre-existence,** prē•eg•zis'tens, *n.* Existence previous to something else; existence in a previous state; existence of the soul before its union with the body.—**pre-existent,** prē•eg•zis'tent, *a.* Existing beforehand; preceding in existence.

prefabricate, prē•fab'ri•kāt, *v.t.* To make and standardize all the parts of a structure (such as a house) at a factory so that it may be rapidly assembled.

preface, pref'is, *n.* [Fr. *préface*, from L. *praefatio*—*prae*, before, and *fari, fatum*, to speak (whence also *fate, fame*).] Something spoken as introductory to a discourse, or written as introductory to a book or other composition.—*v.t.*—*prefaced, prefacing.* To introduce by preliminary remarks.—**prefatory,** pref'a•to•ri, *a.* Having the character of a preface; pertaining to a preface.—**prefatorily,** pref'a•to•ri•li, *adv.* By way of preface.

prefect, prē'fekt, *n.* [L. *praefectus*, from *praeficio*—*prae*, before, and *facio*, I make. FACT.] A governor, commander, chief magistrate, or the like; a name common to several officers, military and civil, in ancient Rome; an important functionary in France; a préfet, that is, an official who presides over and has extensive powers in a department.—**prefecture,** prē'fek•chėr, *n.* The office or jurisdiction of a prefect; *prefecture* is also the official residence of a prefect.

prefer, pri•fėr', *v.t.*—*preferred, preferring.* [L. *praefero*, to carry before, to present, to esteem more highly—*prae*, before, and *ferre*, to bear or carry. FERTILE.] To offer for one's consideration or decision; to present; said especially of petitions, prayers, etc.; to advance, as to an office or dignity; to raise; to exalt; to set above something else in estimation; to hold in greater favor or esteem; to choose rather (to *prefer* one *to* another).—**preferable,** pref'ėr•a•bl, *a.* Worthy to be preferred; more eligible; more desirable.—**preferableness, preferability,** pref'ėr•a•bl•nes, pref'ėr•a•bil″i•ti, *n.* The quality or state of being preferable.—**preferably,** pref'ėr•a•bli, *adv.* In or by preference.—**preference,** pref'ėr•ens, *n.* The preferring of one thing before another; choice of one thing rather than another; higher place in esteem; the object of choice; choice.—**preferred stock,** pri•fėrd', *n.* A form of capital stock given preference in payment of dividends (or other rights) over common stock.—**preferential,** pref•ėr•en'shal, *a.* In a position to which some preference is attached.—**preferment,** pri•fėr'ment, *n.* Advancement to a higher office, dignity, or station; promotion; a superior or valuable place or office, especially in the church.—**preferrer,** pri•fėr'ėr, *n.* One who prefers.

prefigure, prē•fig'yėr, *v.t.*—*prefigured, prefiguring.* To exhibit by antecedent representation or by types and similitudes.—**prefiguration,** prē•fig'ū•rā″shon, *n.* The act of prefiguring; an antecedent similitude.—**prefigurative,** prē•fig'ū•rā•tiv, *a.* Showing by previous figures, types, or similitudes.

prefix, prē•fiks', *v.t.* [Fr. *préfixer*, L. *praefigo, praefixus*—*prae*, before, and *figere*, to fix. FIX.] To put or fix before or at the beginning of another thing (to *prefix* a syllable to a word, an advertisement to a book); to settle, fix, or appoint beforehand (to *prefix* the hour of meeting).—*n.* (prē'fiks.) A letter, syllable, or word put to the beginning of a word, usually to vary its signification.—**prefixion,** prē•fik'shon, *n.* The act of prefixing.

preformation, prē•for•mā'shon, *n.* The obsolete theory that development of an organism simply consists of increase in size. Cp. EPIGENESIS.

pregnable,† preg'na•bl, *a.* [Fr. *prenable* (with inserted *g*), from *prendre*, to take, L. *prehendo, prehensum.* PREHENSILE.] Capable of being taken or won by force; expugnable.

pregnant preg'nant, *a.* [L. *praegnans, praegnantis*—*prae*, before, and *gnans*, ppr. corresponding to *gnatus, natus*, born. NATAL, NATURE.] Being with young; great with child; gravid; full of important matter; abounding with results; full of consequence or significance (a *pregnant* argument).—**pregnancy,** preg'nan•si, *n.* The state of being pregnant; time of going with child; the quality of being full of significance, or the like.—**pregnantly,** preg'nant•li, *adv.* In a pregnant manner.

prehensile, pri•hen'sil, *a.* [L. *prehendere, prehensus*, to lay hold of—*prae*, before, and *hendere*, to seize, as *apprehend, comprehend*, etc. PRIZE, PRISON.] Capable of or adapted to seize or grasp (a monkey's *prehensile* tail).—**prehension,** pri•hen'shon, *n.* A taking hold of; a seizing.

prehistoric, prē•his•tor'ik, *a.* Relating to a period antecedent to that at which history begins.

preinstruct, prē•in•strukt', *v.t.* To instruct previously or beforehand.

prejudge, prē•juj', *v.t.*—*prejudged, prejudging.* [Fr. *préjuger.*] To judge before hearing, or before the arguments and facts are fully known; to decide by anticipation; to condemn beforehand or unheard.—**prejudgment,** prē•juj'ment, *n.* The act of prejudging; judgment without a hearing or full examination.

prejudice, prej'ū•dis, *n.* [Fr. *préjudice*, from L. *praejudicium*, from *prae*, before, and *judicium*, a judgment, from *judex, judicis*, a judge. JUDGE.] A bias or leaning, favorable or unfavorable, without reason, or for some reason other than justice; a prepossession (when used absolutely generally with the unfavorable meaning of wrong or ignorant bias or view); mischief; damage; injury (without *prejudice* to one's interests).—*v.t.*—*prejudiced, prejudicing.* To implant a prejudice in the mind of; to bias by hasty and incorrect notions; to injure by prejudices; to hurt, damage, impair; to injure in general (to *prejudice* one's cause).—**prejudicial,** prej•ū•dish'al, *a.* Hurtful; mischievous; injurious; detrimental.—**prejudicially,** prej•ū•dish'al•li, *adv.* In a prejudicial manner.

prelate, prel'at, *n.* [Fr. *prélat*, from L.L. *praelatus*, from L. *praelatus*, pp.

of *praefero, praelatum—prae*, before and *latus*, borne.] An ecclesiastic of the higher order having authority over the lower clergy, as an archbishop, bishop, or patriarch; a dignitary of the church.—**prelacy,** prel'a•si, *n.* Episcopacy; the system of church government by prelates; prelates collectively.—**prelatic,** pre•-lat'ik, *a.* Pertaining to prelates or prelacy.—**prelatist,** prel'at•ist, *n.* An advocate for prelacy.

prelect, pri•lekt', *v.i.* and *t.* [L. *praelego, praelectus—prae*, before, and *lego*, I read. LEGEND.] To read a lecture or discourse in public.—**prelection,** pri•lek'shon, *n.* A lecture or discourse read in public or to a select company.—**prelector,** pri•-lek'tor, *n.* A reader of discourses; a lecturer.

prelibation, prē•lī•bā'shon, *n.* [L. *prae*, before, and *libo*, to taste. LIBATION.] Foretaste; a tasting beforehand; an effusion or libation previous to tasting.

preliminary, pri•lim'i•ne•ri, *a.* [Fr. *préliminaire*—L. *prae*, before, and *limen*, threshold. LIMIT.] Introductory; preceding the main discourse or business; prefatory.—*n.* Something introductory or preparatory; something to be examined and determined before an affair can be treated of on its own merits; a preparatory act.—**preliminarily,** pri•-lim'i•ne•ri•li, *adv.* In a preliminary manner.

prelude, prē'lūd or prel'ūd, *n.* [Fr. *prélude*, from L. *prae*, before, and *ludus*, play. LUDICROUS.] Something preparatory or leading up to what follows; an introductory performance; *music*, a short introductory strain preceding the principal movement. —*v.t.* (pri•lūd') — *preluded, preluding*. To introduce with a prelude; to serve as prelude to.—*v.i.* To serve as a prelude.—**prelusive, prelusory,** pri•lū'siv, pri•lū'so•ri, *a.* Having the character of a prelude; introductory.—**prelusively, prelusorily,** pri•lū'siv•li, pri•lū'so•ri•li, *adv.* By way of prelude.

premature, prē'ma•tūr, *a.* [L. *praematurus—prae*, before, and *maturus*, ripe.] Happening, arriving, existing, performed, or adopted before the proper time; done, said, or believed too soon; too early; untimely.—**prematurely,** prē•ma•tūr'li, *adv.* In a premature manner. — **prematureness, prematurity,** prē•ma•tūr'-nes, prē•ma•tū'ri•ti, *n.* The state of being premature.

premaxillary, prē•mak'sil•la•ri, *n.* *Anat.* a bone of the upper jaw on either side anterior to the true maxillary bone.

premedical, prē•med'i•kal, *a.* [L. *prae*, before, and *medical*.] Concerning studies preceding the study of medicine.

premeditate, prē•med'i•tāt, *v.t.*—*premeditated, premeditating*. [Fr. *préméditer*, L. *praemeditor—prae*, before, and *meditor*, I meditate.] To think on and revolve in the mind beforehand.—*v.i.* To meditate beforehand.—**premeditation,** prē•med'-i•tā"shon, *n.* The act of premeditating; *law*, preplanning of an act showing intent to commit it.

premier, pri•mir', *a.* [Fr. *premier*, from L. *primarius*, of the first rank, from *primus*, first. PRIME.] First; chief; principal.—*n.* The first or chief minister of state.

première, pre•myär', *n.* [Fr.] A first showing as of a play or movie.—*v.t.* To show a play or movie for the first time.

premise, pri•mīz', *v.t.—premised, premising*. [From L. *praemitto, praemissum—prae*, before, and *mitto*, I send. MISSION.] To set forth or make known beforehand; to lay down as an antecedent proposition.—*v.i.* To make an antecedent statement.—*n.* prem'is. A proposition laid down as a base of argument; *logic*, the name applied to each of the two first propositions of a syllogism, from which the inference or conclusion is drawn; *pl.* the beginning or early portion of a legal deed or document where the subject matter is stated or described in full (lit. 'the things before mentioned'); hence, lands and houses or tenements; a house and the outhouses, etc., belonging to it.

premium, prē'mi•um, *n.* [L. *praemium*, a reward—*prae*, before, and *emo*, to take. PRE-EMPTION.] A reward or prize offered for some specific thing; a bonus; an extra sum paid as an incentive; a bounty; a fee paid for the privilege of being taught a trade or profession; a sum paid periodically to an office for insurance, as against fire or loss of life or property.—*At a premium*, above par, opposed to *at a discount*: said of shares or stock; hence, in high esteem.

premolar, prē•mō'lėr, *n.* *Anat.* a tooth between the canine and the molars.

premonish, pri•mon'ish, *v.t.* [Prefix *pre*, and *-monish*, as in *admonish*.] To forewarn; to admonish beforehand.—**premonition,** prē•mo•nish'-on, *n.* Previous warning, notice, or information.—**premonitory,** pri•-mon'i•to•ri, *a.* Giving previous warning or notice.

premorse, pri•mors', *a.* [L. *praemorsus—prae*, before, and *mordere*, to gnaw. MORDANT.] Bitten off; applied in *bot.* to a root or leaf terminating abruptly, as if bitten off.

prenatal, prē•nā'tl, *a.* [L. *prae*, before, and *natus*, born.] Before, or prior to, birth (*prenatal* care).—**prenatally,** pre•nā'tal•li, *adv.*

prenotion, prē•nō'shon, *n.* A notion which precedes something else in time; previous notion or thought.

prentice, pren'tis. A colloquial contraction of *Apprentice*.

preoccupy, prē•ok'kū•pī, *v.t.—preoccupied, preoccupying*. To occupy or take possession of before another; to engage or occupy the attention of beforehand; to engross beforehand.—**preoccupancy,** prē•ok'kū•-pan•si, *n.* The act or right of taking possession before another.—**preoccupation,** prē•ok'kū•pā"shon, *n.* An occupation or taking possession before another.—**preoccupied,** prē•ok'-kū•pīd, *p.* and *a.* Having the attention taken up previously; absorbed.

preordain, prē•or•dān', *v.t.* To ordain or appoint beforehand; to predetermine.—**preordination,** prē•-or'di•nā"shon, *n.* The act of foreordaining.

prepare, pri•pâr', *v.t.—prepared, preparing*. [Fr. *préparer*, L. *praeparo, praeparatum—prae*, before, and *parare*, to get ready. PARE.] To fit, adapt, or qualify for a particular purpose; to put into such a state as to be fit for use or application; to make ready; often, with a personal object, to make ready for something that is to happen; to give notice to (to *prepare* a person for ill news or calamity); to provide; to procure as suitable (to *prepare* arms, ammunition, etc., for troops).—*v.i.* To make ready; to put things in suitable order; to take the necessary previous measures; to make one's self ready.—**preparation,** pre•pa•-rā'shon, *n.* [L. *praeparatio*.] The act of preparing; that which is prepared for a particular purpose; a substance compounded or made up for a certain use; the state of being prepared or in readiness.—**preparative,** pri•par'a•tiv, *a.* [Fr. *préparatif*.] Tending or serving to prepare or make ready; preparatory. —*n.* That which is preparative or preparatory; that which is done to prepare.—**preparatory,** pri•par'-a•to•ri, *a.* Serving to prepare the way for some proceeding to follow; introductory; preparative.—**preparedly,** pri•pârd'li, *adv.* With suitable previous measures.—**preparedness,** pri•pârd'nes, *n.* The state of being prepared.—**preparer,** pri•pâ'rėr, *n.* One who or that which prepares.

prepay, prē•pā', *v.t.—prepaid, prepaying*. To pay before obtaining possession of; to pay in advance; to pay before the payment falls due.—**prepayment,** prē•pā'ment, *n.* Act of paying beforehand; payment in advance.

prepense, pri•pens', *a.* [L. *praepensus —prae*, before, and *pendere, pensum*, to weigh. POISE.] Deliberated or devised beforehand; premeditated; aforethought; now scarcely used except in the phrase 'malice *prepense*'.

preponderate, pri•pon'dėr•āt, *v.t.*—*preponderated, preponderating*. [L. *praepondero, praeponderatum—prae*, before, and *ponderare*, to weigh, from *pondus, ponderis*, a weight. PONDER.] To outweigh; to have more weight or influence than.—*v.i.* To exceed in weight, influence, or power; to have the greater weight or influence; to have sway or power superior to others.—**preponderance, preponderancy,** pri•pon'dėr•ans, pri•pon'dėr•an•si, *n.* The state or quality of preponderating or being preponderant.—**preponderant,** pri•pon'dėr•ant, *a.* Outweighing; superior in power, influence, or the like.—**preponderantly, preponderatingly,** pri•pon'dėr•ant•li, pri•pon'dėr•ā•-ting•li, *adv.* In a preponderant manner.—**preponderation,** prē•pon′-dėr•ā″shon, *n.* The state of preponderating; preponderance.

preposition, prep•o•zish′on, *n.* [L. *praepositio.* POSITION.] *Gram.* a part of speech which is used to show the relation of one noun or pronoun to another in a sentence, and is usually placed before the word which expresses the object of the relation.—**prepositional,** prep•o•zish′on•al, *a.* Pertaining to or having the nature or function of a preposition.—**prepositionally,** prep•o•zish′on•al•li, *adv.* In a prepositional manner.—**prepositive,** prē•poz′i•tiv, *a.* Put before.—*n.* A word or particle put before another word.

prepossess, prē•poz•zes′, *v.t.* To take previous possession of; to preoccupy the mind or heart of; to fill or imbue beforehand with some opinion or estimate; to prejudice. ∴ *Prepossess* is more frequently used in a good sense than *prejudice.*—**prepossessing,** prē•poz•zes′ing, *a.* Creating an impression favorable to the owner; engaging: said especially of the external characteristics of a person.—**prepossession,** prē•poz•zesh′on, *n.* Prior possession; a preconceived opinion; an impression on the mind in favor or against any person or thing, especially in favor.

preposterous, pri•pos′tėr•us, *a.* [L. *praeposterus—prae,* before, and *posterus,* coming after. POSTERIOR.] Contrary to nature, reason, or common sense; utterly and glaringly foolish; totally opposed to the fitness of things; manifestly absurd.—**preposterously,** pri•pos′tėr•us•li, *adv.* In a preposterous manner.—**preposterousness,** pri•pos′tėr•us•nes, *n.* The state or quality of being preposterous; utter absurdity.

prepotent, prē•pō′tent, *a.* [L. *praepotens—prae,* before, and *potens,* powerful. POTENT.] Very powerful; having a superiority of power or influence.—**prepotency,** prē•pō′ten•-si, *n.* Superior power; predominance.

prepuce, prē′pūs, *n.* [L. *praeputium,* the foreskin.] The foreskin.—**preputial,** pri•pū′shal, *a.* Pertaining to the prepuce.

Pre-Raphaelite, prē•raf′a•el•it, *n.* One who practices or favors the system or style of painting practiced by the early painters before Raphael, or the modern revival of their style or system, said to be a rigidly faithful representation of natural forms and effects.—**Pre-Raphaelitism,** prē•raf′a•el•it•izm, *n.* The style or practice of the pre-Raphaelites.

prerequisite, prē•rek′wi•zit, *a.* Previously requisite; necessary to something subsequent.—*n.* Something that is prerequisite.

prerogative, pri•rog′a•tiv, *n.* [L. *praerogativa,* from *praerogo,* to ask before—*prae,* before, and *rogare,* to ask (as in *interrogate, arrogate, derogate,* etc.).] An exclusive or peculiar privilege; a privilege belonging to one in virtue of his character or position; an official and hereditary right which may be asserted without question; a special right or privilege of a sovereign or other executive of a government; the name given to the century in the Roman Comitia that by lot was empowered to record its vote first, and so was believed to be divinely commissioned to determine the vote of the rest.

presage, pres′ij or pre′sāj, *n.* [Fr. *présage,* L. *praesagium—prae,* before, and *sagire,* to perceive by the senses; allied to *sagacious.*] Something which portends or foreshows a future event; a foreboding.—*v.t.* pris•āj′.—*presaged, presaging.* To forebode; to foreshow; to foretell, predict, prophesy.—*v.i.* To form or utter a prediction.—**presager,** pre•-sā′jėr, *n.* One who predicts.

presbyopia, pres•bi•ō′pi•a, *n.* [Gr. *presbys,* old, and *ōps,* the eye.] An imperfection of vision in which near objects are seen less distinctly than those at a distance, common in old age.—**presbyopic,** pres•bi•-op′ik, *a.* Pertaining to presbyopia.

presbyter, pres′bi•tėr, *n.* [L. *presbyter,* from Gr. *presbyteros,* compar. of *presbys,* old. *Priest* is the same word.] An elder or a person somewhat advanced in age, who had authority in the early Christian church; a priest; a parson.—**presbyterian,** pres•bi•tē′ri•an, *a.* Pertaining to a presbyter; pertaining to ecclesiastical government by presbyteries, or to those who uphold such government.—*n.* [*cap.*] A member of that section of the Christian church who vest church government in presbyteries or associations of ministers and elders, and have no bishops.—**presbyterial,** pres•bi•tē′-ri•al, *a.* Presbyterian.—**presbyterianism,** pres•bi•tē′ri•an•izm, *n.* The doctrines, principles, and discipline or government of presbyterians.—**presbytery,** pres′bi•te•ri, *n.* Presbyterianism; a judicatory consisting of Presbyterian pastors of all the churches of any particular denomination within a given district, along with one ruling elder from each church session.

preschool, prē•sköl′, *a.* [L. *prae,* before, and *school.*] Referring to the period before a child enters school.

prescient, prē′shi•ent, *a.* [L. *praesciens, praescientis,* ppr. of *praescio,* to foreknow—*prae,* before, *scio,* to know. SCIENCE.] Foreknowing; having knowledge of events before they take place.—**prescience,** prē′shi•ens, *n.* [L. *prescientia.*] Foreknowledge; knowledge of events before they take place; foresight.

prescribe, pri•skrīb′, *v.t.*—*prescribed, prescribing.* [L. *praescribo—prae,* before, and *scribere,* to write. SCRIBE.] To lay down authoritatively for direction; to give as a rule of conduct; *med.* to direct to be used as a remedy.—*v.i.* To lay down rules or directions; to dictate; to write or give medical directions; to direct what remedies are to be used; *law,* to become extinguished or of no validity through lapse of time, as a right, debt, obligation, and the like.—**prescriber,** pri•skrī′bėr, *n.* One that prescribes.—**prescript,** prē′-skript, *a.* Directed; set down as a rule; prescribed.—*n.* Direction; precept; model prescribed.—**prescriptible,** pri•skrip′ti•bl, *a.* Suitable for being prescribed; depending or derived from prescription.—**prescription,** pri•skrip′shon, *n.* The act of prescribing; what is prescribed; a direction; prescript; *med.* a written statement of the medicines or remedies to be used by a patient; a claim, right, or title based on long use or custom; the loss of a legal right by lapse of time and neglect.—**prescriptive,** pri•skrip′tiv, *a.* Consisting in or acquired by prescription.

presence. See PRESENT.

present, prez′ent, *a.* [L. *praesens, praesentis,* from *prae,* before, and *sens, esens,* being, an old participle of *sum,* I am; comp. *absent.*] Being in a certain place; opposed to *absent*; being before the face or near; being in company; done on the spot; instant; immediate (*present* death); being now in view or under consideration; now existing, or being at this time; not past or future; ready at hand; quick in emergency.—*The present,* an elliptical expression for *the present time.*—*At present,* elliptically for *at the present time.*—*Present tense, gram.* the tense or modification of a verb which expresses action or being in the present time.—*v.t.* (pri•zent′). [Fr. *présenter,* L. *praesentare,* to present, lit. to make present.] To place or introduce into the presence or before the face of, especially of a superior; to make known; to offer for acquaintance; to exhibit or offer to view or notice (*presented* a wretched appearance); to bestow; to make a gift or donation of; generally to give formally and ceremoniously; to bestow a gift upon; to favor with a donation (to *present* a person *with* a thing); to nominate to an ecclesiastical benefice; to lay before a public body for consideration, as before a legislature, court, etc. (to *present* a memorial or the like); to point, level, aim, as a weapon, particularly some species of firearms.—*To present arms* (*milit.*), to put the arms or guns in a perpendicular position in front of the body, as in saluting a superior officer, or in token of respect.—*n.* (prez′ent). That which is presented or given; a gift; *pl.* (from the adj.), a term used in a legal deed to signify the document itself.—**presence,** prez′-ens, *n.* [L. *praesentia.*] The state of being present; the existence of a person or thing in a certain place; opposed to *absence*; the being in company with; personal attendance; the state of being within sight or call; the state of being in view of a superior; the person of a superior, as a sovereign; mien; air; personal appearance; demeanor.—*Presence of mind,* coolness and readiness of invention or resource in occasions of difficulty; quickness in devising expedients on pressing occasions.—**presence chamber,** *n.* The room in which a great personage receives company.—**presentable,** pri•zen′-ta•bl, *a.* Capable of being presented; in such trim as to be able to present one's self without embarrassment; suitable to be exhibited or offered.—**presentation,** prez•en•tā′shon, *n.* The act of presenting, or state of being presented; the act or right of presenting a clergyman or nominating a minister to a vacant parish.—**presentative,** pri•zen′ta•-tiv, *a.* Serving to present; presenting; *metaph.* applied to what may be apprehended directly, or to the faculty capable of apprehending directly.—**presentee,** prez•en•tē′, *n.* One presented to a benefice.—**presenter,** pri•zen′tėr, *n.* One who presents; one who leads or introduces.—**presentive,** pri•zen′tiv, *a.* *Gram.* applied to words which present a definite conception of an object to the mind; opposed to *symbolic.*—*n.* A presentive word.—**presentiveness,** pri•zen′tiv•nes, *n.*—**presently,** prez′ent•li, *adv.* In a little time; soon; forthwith; immediately.—**presentment,** pri•zent′ment, *n.* The act of presenting or state of being presented; representation or portrait (*Shak.*).

presentiment, pri•zen′ti•ment, *n.* [*Pre,* before, and *sentiment;* O.Fr. *presentiment,* foreboding.] Previous conception, sentiment, or opinion; previous apprehension of something future; anticipation of impending evil; foreboding.

preserve, pri•zėrv′, *v.t.*—*preserved, preserving.* [Fr. *préserver,* L.L. *praeservo*—L. *prae,* before, and *servo,* I keep. SERVE.] To keep or save from injury or destruction; to defend from evil; to save; to keep in the same state; to uphold, sustain, guard; to save from decay; to cause to remain good and wholesome for food by treating with salt, sugar, or otherwise (*preserved* meats or fruits); to prevent being hunted and killed, except at certain seasons or by certain persons, as game, salmon, etc.—*v.i.* To practice the art of seasoning fruits, etc., for preservation; to protect game for purposes of sport.—*n.* That which is preserved; fruit, etc., suitably seasoned, to keep from decay; a place set apart for the shelter and protection of game intended for sport.—**preserver,** pri•-zėr′vėr, *n.* A person or thing that preserves.—**preservable,** pri•zer′va•-bl, *a.* Capable of being preserved.—**preservation,** prez•ėr•vā′shon, *n.* The act of preserving; the state of being preserved; escape from danger; safety.—**preservative,** pri•zėr′va•-tiv, *a.* Having the power of keeping safe from injury, destruction, or decay; tending to preserve.—*n.* That which preserves or has the power of preserving; something that is preventive of injury or decay.

preside, pri•zīd′, *v.i.*—*presided, presiding.* [Fr. *présider,* from L. *praesideo*—*prae,* before, and *sedeo,* I sit. SIT.] To be set over others; to have the place of authority over others, as a chairman or director: usually denoting temporary superintendence and government, as at a public meeting; to exercise superintendence; to watch over as inspector.—**presidency,** prez′i•den•si, *n.* Superintendence; inspection and care; the office of president; the term during which a president holds his office; [*often cap.*] the office of the president of the United States.—**president,** prez′i•-dent, *n.* One who presides; an officer elected or appointed to preside over and control the proceedings of a number of persons; the chief officer of a corporation, company, society, etc.; the chief officer of some colleges or universities; the highest officer of state in a republic.—**presidential,** prez•i•den′shal, *a.* Pertaining to a president.—**presidentship,** prez′i•-dent•ship, *n.* The office of president.

presidio, pri•sid′i•ō, *n.* [Sp.] A fort or fortified station; a garrison town.

presignify, prē•sig′ni•fī, *v.t.*—*presignified, presignifying.* To intimate or signify beforehand; to show previously.

press, pres, *v.t.* [Fr. *presser,* from L. *presso,* a freq. of *premere, pressum,* to press; seen also in *compress, depress, express, impress, repress,* etc.] To act on with force or weight; to squeeze; to crush; to extract the juice of by squeezing; to squeeze for the purpose of making smooth (to *press* cloth or paper); to embrace closely; to constrain or compel; to urge by authority or necessity; to impose importunately (to *press* a gift on one); to straiten or distress (to be *pressed* with want); to urge or solicit with earnestness; to importune; to inculcate with earnestness; to enforce; to bear hard upon; to ply hard.—*v.i.* To exert pressure; to act with compulsive force; to bear heavily; to strain or strive eagerly; to go forward with impulsive eagerness or energetic efforts; to crowd; to throng; to force one's way; to urge.—*To press upon,* to urge with force; to attack closely.—*n.* [Fr. *presse,* a press, a crowd, a throng.] An instrument or machine by which any body is squeezed, crushed, or forced into a more compact form; a machine for printing; a printing press; (with *the*) printed literature in general, often restricted to the literature of newspapers; newspaper reporters; a printing or publishing establishment; also its personnel; a crowd; a throng; multitude of individuals crowded together; a wine vat or cistern (O.T.); an upright cupboard in which clothes or other articles are kept; urgency; urgent demands of affairs.—*Freedom of the press,* the right to publish without political censorship.—*Press of sail* (*naut.*), as much sail as the state of the wind, etc., will permit.—**presser,** pres′ėr, *n.* One who or that which presses.—**pressing,** pres′ing, *p.* and *a.* Urgent; importunate; distressing.—**pressingly,** pres′ing•li, *adv.* In a pressing manner.—**pressman,** pres′-man, *n.* One who works or attends to a printing press.—**pressroom,** *n.* *Print.* the room where the printing presses are worked, as distinguished from a composing room; a room where reporters assemble for a press conference.—**pressure,** presh′ėr, *n.* [O.Fr. *pressure,* L. *pressura.*] The act of pressing; the state of being squeezed or crushed; the force of one body acting on another by weight or the continued application of power; a constraining force or impulse acting on the mind; severity of grievousness, as of personal circumstances; distress, strait, or difficulty; urgency; demand on one's time or energies (the *pressure* of business); force exerted upon a surface.—*v.t.* To bring pressure to bear; to use all one's influence.—**pressurize,** presh′ėr•īz, *v.t.* To cook in a pressure cooker; to hold atmospheric pressure at average level during a high-level flight by plane.—**pressurization,** presh′er•i•zā″shon, *n.*—*Pressure cooker,* an apparatus which may be sealed for cooking or sterilizing under high-pressure superheated steam.

press, pres, *v.t.* [Originally to *impress* or *imprest.* See IMPRESS (in this sense).] To force into service, especially into naval service; to impress.

Prester John, *n.* Priest John, the mythical or legendary Christian king, believed in the Middle Ages to be ruling in Abyssinia.

prestidigitation, pres′ti•dij′i•tā″shon, *n.* [L. *praesto,* at hand, ready, and *digitus,* a finger.] Skill in legerdemain; sleight of hand; juggling.—**prestidigitator,** pres•ti•dij′i•tā•tėr, *n.* One who practices prestidigitation; a juggler.

prestige, pres′tij or pres•tēzh′, *n.* [Fr., from L. *praestigium,* an illusion, a juggler's trick; hence an impression made on spectators.] Weight or influence derived from previous character, achievements, or associations, especially weight or influence derived from past success, on which a confident belief is founded of future triumphs.

presto, pres′to, *adv.* [It. *presto,* quick, quickly, from L. *praesto,* at hand, ready—*prae,* before, and *sto,* to stand.] *Music,* a direction for a quick lively movement or performance; also used interjectionally for quickly, immediately, in haste.

presume, pri•zūm′, *v.t.*—*presumed, presuming.* [Fr. *présumer,* from L. *praesumo,* to presume—*prae,* before, and *sumo,* to take, as in *assume, consume, resume,* etc. SUMPTUOUS.] To take for granted; to suppose on reasonable grounds.—*v.i.* To suppose or believe without examination; to infer; to venture without permission or beyond what is justifiable; to take the liberty; to make bold; to act on overconfident conclusions; to make unwarranted advances (to *presume upon* one's good nature); to act in a forward way; to go beyond the boundaries laid down by reverence, respect, or politeness.—**presumable,** pri•zū′ma•bl, *a.* Capable of being presumed.—**presumably,** pri•zū′-

ma•bli, *adv.* As may be presumed or reasonably supposed.—**presumer,** pri•zū′mėr, *n.* One that presumes.—**presumption,** pri•zum′shon, *n.* [L. *praesumptio.*] A supposition; a ground for presuming; a strong probability; that which is supposed to be true without direct proof; blind or headstrong confidence; unreasonable adventurousness; presumptuousness; arrogance; assurance; *law,* that which comes near to the proof of a fact, in greater or less degree.—**presumptive,** pri•zum′tiv, *a.* Based on presumption or probability; proving circumstantially, not directly (*presumptive* evidence).—*Presumptive heir,* one whose right of inheritance may be defeated by any contingency, as by the birth of a nearer relative.—**presumptively,** pri•zum′tiv•li, *adv.* In a presumptive manner.—**presumptuous,** pri•zum′chū•us, *a.* Imbued with or characterized by presumption; taking undue liberties; given to presume or act in a forward manner; arrogant; overconfident.—**presumptuously,** pri•zum′chū•us•li, *adv.* In a presumptuous manner.—**presumptuousness,** pri•zum′chū•us•nes, *n.* The quality of being presumptuous.

presuppose, prē•sup•pōz′, *v.t.* To suppose or imagine as previous; to cause to be taken for granted; to imply as antecedent; to require to exist previously.—**presupposition,** prē•sup′po•zish″on, *n.* The act of presupposing; that which is presupposed.

presurmise, prē•sėr•mīz′, *n.* A surmise previously formed.

pretend, pri•tend′, *v.t.* [L. *praetendo,* to hold out, pretend—*prae,* before, and *tendere,* to reach or stretch. TEND.] To hold out falsely; to allege falsely; to use as a pretext; to make false appearance or representation of; to feign or affect (to *pretend* zeal); to claim or put in a claim for.—*v.i.* To feign, make believe, or sham; to put in a claim, truly or falsely: usually with *to.*—**pretender,** pri•ten′dėr, *n.* One who pretends; one who lays claim to anything; [*cap.*] *Eng. hist.* a name applied to the son and grandson of James II, the heirs to the house of Stuart, who laid claim to the British crown, from which their house had been excluded by enactment of Parliament.—**pretense,** pri•tens′, *n.* [From L. *praetentum,* later *praetensum,* pp. of *praetendo.*] The act of pretending; the presenting to others, either in words or actions, of a false or hypocritical appearance; false show or statement intended to mislead; a pretext; an excuse; a claim, true or false.—*Escutcheon of pretense* (heraldry), a small shield set in the center of a husband's arms, bearing those of his wife when she is an heiress or co-heiress in blood.—**pretension,** pri•ten′shon, *n.* [Fr. *prétention.*] Claim true or false; a holding out the appearance of possessing a certain character; an alleged or assumed right.—**pretentious,** pri•ten′shus, *a.* Full of pretension; attempting to pass for more than one is worth; pretending to a superiority not real.—**pretentiously,** pri•ten′shus•li, *adv.* In a pretentious manner.

preterit, pret′ėr•it, *a.* [L. *praeteritus,* gone by, pp. of *praetereo—praeter,* beyond, and *ire, itum,* to go. ITINERANT.] *Gram.* expressing past time; applied to the tense expressing action or existence perfectly past or finished; past (he *struck*); also used as equivalent to *perfect.*—*n. Gram.* the preterit tense.—**preterition,** pre•tėr•ish′on, *n.* [L. *praeteritio,* from *praetereo.*] *Rhet.* a figure by which, in pretending to pass over anything, we make a summary mention of it.—**preteritive,** pri•tėr′i•tiv, *a. Gram.* an epithet applied to verbs used only or chiefly in the *preterit* or past tenses.

pretermit, prē•tėr•mit′, *v.t.*—*pretermitted, pretermitting.* [L. *praetermitto—praeter,* beyond, and *mittere,* to send.] To pass by; to omit.—**pretermission,** prē•tėr•mish′on, *n.* A passing by; omission.

preternatural, prē•tėr•nach′ė•ral, *a.* [L. *praeter,* beyond, and E. *natural.*] Beyond what is natural, or different from what is natural, as distinguished from *supernatural,* above nature; and *unnatural,* contrary to nature.—**preternaturally,** prē•tėr•nach′ė•ral•li, *adv.* In a preternatural manner.—**preternaturalism,** prē•tėr•nach′ė•ral•izm, *n.* A state of being preternatural.

pretext, prē′tekst or pri•tekst′, *n.* [Fr. *prétexte,* from L. *praetextum,* from *praetexe—prae,* before, and *texo,* to weave. TEXTURE.] An ostensible reason or motive assigned or assumed as a color or cover for the real reason or motive; a pretense.

pretor, prē′tor. See PRAETOR.

pretty, prit′i, *a.* [O.E. *pretic, praty,* comely, clever; A.Sax. *praetig,* crafty, from *praet,* a trick; Icel. *prettugr,* tricky, *prettr,* a trick.] Having diminutive beauty; of a pleasing and attractive form without the strong lines of beauty, or without gracefulness and dignity; pleasing; neatly arranged; affectedly nice; foppish; ironically, nice; fine; excellent: meaning the opposite.—*adv.* In some degree; moderately; expressing a degree less than *very* (*pretty* well, large, sure, etc.).—**prettily,** prit′i•li, *adv.* In a pretty manner; with prettiness; pleasingly.—**prettiness,** prit′i•nes, *n.* State or quality of being pretty; diminutive beauty; beauty without stateliness or dignity; neatness and taste exhibited on small objects; affected niceness; foppishness.—**prettyish,** prit′i•ish, *a.* Somewhat pretty.

pretzel, pret′sel, *n.* [G. *bretzel.*] A crisp, glazed, salty, knotlike cracker.

prevail, pri•vāl′, *v.i.* [Fr. *prévaloir,* from L. *praevaleo—prae,* before, and *valere,* to be strong. VALID.] To overcome; to gain the victory or superiority: often with *over* or *against*; to be in force; to have extensive power or influence (a disease, a custom *prevails* in a place); to have predominant influence; to succeed; to overcome or gain over by persuasion: with *on* or *upon* (they *prevailed on* him to go).—**prevailing,** pri•vā′ling, *p.* and *a.* Predominant; having superior influence; prevalent; most common or general.—**prevailingly,** pri•vāl′ing•li, *adv.* So as to prevail.—**prevalence,** prev′a•lens, *n.* The state or quality of being prevalent; superiority; general reception or practice; general existence or extension (the *prevalence* of vice or of a fashion).—**prevalent,** prev′a•lent, *a.* Prevailing; predominant; most generally received or current; extensively existing.—**prevalently,** prev′a•lent•li, *adv.* In a prevalent manner.

prevaricate, pri•var′i•kāt, *v.i.*—*prevaricated, prevaricating.* [L. *praevaricor, praevaricatus,* to straddle, to shuffle—*prae,* before, and *varus,* straddling.] To act or speak evasively; to evade or swerve from the truth; to shuffle; to quibble in giving answers.—**prevarication,** pri•var′i•kā″shon, *n.* The act of prevaricating; a shuffling or quibbling to evade the truth or the disclosure of truth; *law,* a collusion between an informer and a defendant, in order to a feigned prosecution; the willful concealment or misrepresentation of truth by giving evasive evidence.—**prevaricator,** pri•var′i•kā•tėr, *n.* One who prevaricates; a shuffler; a quibbler.

prevenient, prē•vē′ni•ent, *a.* [L. *praeveniens.* PREVENT.] Going before; preceding; preventing; preventive.—*Prevenient grace. Theol.* term, the grace that precedes or anticipates repentance, but which disposes the heart of man to seek God.

prevent, pri•vent′, *v.t.* [L. *praevenio, praeventum,* to anticipate, to prevent—*prae,* before, and *venio,* to come (seen also in *advent, convent, circumvent, intervention,* etc.).] To anticipate‡; to forestall‡; to hinder by something done before; to stop or intercept; to impede; to thwart.—**preventable,** pri•ven′ta•bl, *a.* Capable of being prevented or hindered.—**preventer,** pri•ven′tėr, *n.* One who or that which prevents.—**prevention,** pri•ven′shon, *n.* The act of preventing.—**preventive,** pri•ven′tiv, *a.* Tending to prevent or hinder.—*Preventive medicine,* the branch of medical practice which seeks to guard against disease and its spread.—*n.* That which prevents; that which intercepts the access or approach of something; an antidote.—**preventively,** pri•ven′tiv•li, *adv.* By way of prevention.

previous, prē′vi•us, *a.* [L. *praevius—prae,* before, and *via,* a way. VOYAGE, WAY.] Going before in time; being or happening before something else; antecedent; prior.—*Previous question.* See QUESTION.—**previously,** prē′vi•us•li, *adv.* In time preceding; beforehand; antecedently. ∴ Syn. under FORMERLY.—**previousness,** prē′vi•us•nes, *n.* Priority in time.

previse, pri•vīz′, *v.t.*—*prevised, prevising.* [L. *praevisus,* pp. of *praevideo—prae,* before, and *video,* to see. VISION.] To foresee; to forewarn.—**prevision,** pri•vizh′on, *n.* Foresight; foreknowledge; prescience.

prey, prā, *n.* [O.E. *preie, praie,* O.Fr.

preie, *praie* (Fr. *proie*), from L. *praeda*, plunder, whence *predatory*, *depredation*.] Spoil; booty; goods taken from an enemy in war; anything taken by violence and injustice; a victim; that which is seized by carnivorous animals to be devoured.—*Beast of prey*, a carnivorous animal, or one that feeds on the flesh of other animals.—*v.i.* To take prey or booty; to feed by violence: with *on* or *upon* before the object of rapine; to rest heavily, as on the mind; to waste gradually (grief *preyed on* him).

Priapean, prī•a•pē′an, *a.* Pertaining to the Roman deity *Priapus*, the god of procreation; grossly sensual; obscene.

price, prīs, *n.* [O.Fr. *pris*, *preis*, Fr. *prix*, from L. *pretium*, a price; the same word as *praise*, and *prize*, to value.] The sum of money or the value which a seller sets on his goods in market; the current value of a commodity; the equivalent for which something is bought or sold; cost; value; worth (a pearl of great *price*); estimation.—*Price of money*, in *com.* the price of credit, the rate of discount at which capital may be lent or borrowed.—**priced,** prīst, *a.* Set at a value; having a price: mostly in composition (high-*priced*, low-*priced*).—**priceless,** prīs′les, *a.* Invaluable; inestimable; too valuable to admit of a price being fixed.

prick, prik, *n.* [A.Sax. *prica*, *pricu*, a point, a dot=D. *prik*, Dan. *prik*, Sw. *prick*, dot, prick; comp. W. *pric*, a skewer, Ir. *pricadh*, a goad.] A slender pointed thing hard enough to pierce the skin; a thorn; a skewer; a puncture or wound by a prick or prickle; a sting; *fig.* a stinging or tormenting thought; remorse; a dot or small mark (*Shak.*).—*v.t.* To pierce with something sharp pointed; to puncture; to erect (said of the ears, hence, *to prick up the ears*, to listen with eager attention); to fix by a sharp point; to designate or set apart by a puncture or mark (*pricked off* for duty); to spur; to goad; to incite: often with *on*; to sting; to trace by puncturing; to render acid or pungent to the taste (the wine is *pricked*).—*v.i.* To suffer or feel penetration by a point or sharp pain; to be punctured; to become acid; to spur on; to ride rapidly.—**prick-eared,** *a.* Having pointed ears; having ears standing up prominently.—**pricker,** prik′ėr, *n.* That which pricks; a sharp-pointed instrument; one who pricks; a light horseman; one who tested whether women were witches by sticking pins into them.—**prickle,** prik′l, *n.* [Dim. of *prick.*] A little prick; a small sharp point; *bot.* a small pointed shoot or sharp process growing from the *bark*, and thus distinguished from the *thorn*, which grows from the *wood* of a plant; a sharp-pointed process or projection, as from the skin of an animal; a spine; a kind of basket.—*v.t.*—*prickled*, *prickling*. To prick slightly; to pierce with fine sharp points.—**prickly,** prik′li, *a.* Full of sharp points or prickles; armed with prickles; stinging in feeling.—**prickliness,** prik′li•nes, *n.*—**prickly heat,** *n.* The popular name for a heat rash.—**prickly pear,** *n.* A variety of cactus covered with clusters of spines, and producing edible fruit.

pride, prīd, *n.* [A.Sax. *prýte*, pride, from *prút*, proud. PROUD.] The quality or state of being proud; inordinate self-esteem; an unreasonable conceit of one's own superiority over others; generous elation of heart; a noble self-esteem springing from a consciousness of worth; proud behavior; insolence; that which is or may be a cause of pride; that of which men are proud; one who or that which gives rise to pride or glorification; highest pitch; splendid show; ostentation.—*v.t.*—*prided*, *priding*. To indulge in pride; to value one's self: used reflexively.—**prideful,** prīd′fụl, *a.* Full of pride; insolent; scornful.—**pridefully,** prīd′fụl•li, *adv.* In a prideful manner.—**pridefulness,** prīd′fụl•nes, *n.* The state or quality of being prideful.

priest, prēst, *n.* [A.Sax. *preóst*, contr. from L. *presbyter*. PRESBYTER.] A clergyman of the Roman Catholic, Greek Catholic, Orthodox, or Episcopalian church; a person consecrated to the ministry of the gospel; a man who officiates in sacred offices; a minister of public worship; a minister of sacrifice or other mediatorial offices; among many non-Christian sects, the title of men selected and trained to perform sacred functions.—**priestess,** prēs′tes, *n.* A woman who officiates in sacred rites.—**priestly,** prēst′li, *a.* Pertaining to a priest or to priests; sacerdotal; becoming a priest.—**priestliness,** prēst′li•nes, *n.* The quality of being priestly.—**priestcraft,** prēst′kraft, *n.* Priestly policy or system of management based on temporal or material interest; policy of clergy to advance their own order.—**priesthood,** prēst′họd, *n.* The office or character of a priest; the order composed of priests; priests collectively.—**priest-ridden,** *a.* Governed or entirely swayed by priests.

prig, prig, *n.* [From *prick*, in old sense of to trim or dress up.] A pert, conceited, pragmatical fellow.—**priggery, priggism,** prig′ėr•i, prig′izm, *n.* The qualities of a prig; pertness; conceit.—**priggish,** prig′ish, *a.* Conceited; affected.—**priggishly,** prig′ish•li, *adv.* In a priggish manner; pertly.—**priggishness,** prig′ish•nes, *n.* The state or quality of being priggish.

prig, prig, *n.* [O.Fr. *briguer*, to steal, to act the highwayman; akin *brigand.*] A thief; a low or mean thief.—*v.t.*—*prigged*, *prigging*. To filch; to steal.

prim, prim, *a.* [O.Fr. *prim*, prime, first, also thin, slender, neat; from L. *primus*, first. PRIME.] Neat; formal; precise; affectedly nice; demure.—**primly,** prim′li, *adv.* In a prim or precise manner; with primness.—**primness,** prim′nes, *n.* Affected formality; stiffness; preciseness.

primacy. See PRIMATE.

prima donna, prē′ma don′na. [It., first lady.] The first or chief female singer in an opera.—**prima facie,** prī•ma fā′shi•ē. [L. *primus*, first, and *facies*, face.] At first view or appearance.—*Prima facie evidence*, *law*, evidence having such a degree of probability that it must prevail unless the contrary be proved.

primage, prī′mij, *n.* [From verb to *primo.*] A charge paid by the shipper or consigner of goods to the master and sailors for loading the same; the amount of water carried off in steam from the boiler.

primal, prī′mal, *a.* [From L. *primus*, first. PRIME.] Primary; first in time, order, or importance; original.—**primary,** prī′ma•ri, *a.* [L. *primarius.*] First in order of time; original; primitive; first; first in dignity or importance; chief; principal; elementary; preparatory, or lowest in order (*primary* schools); first in intention; radical; original; as the *primary* sense of a word.—*Primary accent*, accent (′) on the stressed syllable of a word. *Primary cell*, *elect.* an ordinary voltaic cell. Comp. SECONDARY CELL, STORAGE BATTERY.—*Primary colors.* COLOR.—*Primary planets.* PLANET.—*Primary election*, *pol. sci.* election held to choose party candidates.—*Primary quills*, the largest feathers of the wings of a bird; primaries.—*Primary rocks*, *geol.* rocks of the paleozoic group; former sense, primitive igneous rocks.—*n.* That which stands highest in rank or importance, as opposed to *secondary*.—**primarily,** prī′ma•ri•li, *adv.* In a primary manner; fundamentally; essentially.

primate, prī′mit, *n.* [Fr. *primat*; L.L. *primas*, *primatis*, from L. *primus*, first. PRIME.] The chief ecclesiastic in certain churches, as the Anglican; an archbishop. The Archbishop of York is entitled *primate* of England; the Archbishop of Canterbury, *primate* of *all* England.—*Primates*, the order of mammals consisting of man and the apes.—**primateship, primacy,** prī′mat•ship, prī′ma•si, *n.* The office or dignity of primate or archbishop.—**primatial,** prī•mā′shi•al, *a.* Pertaining to a primate.

prime, prīm, *a.* [L. *primus*, first; superl. of *prior*, former; same root as Skr. *pra*, Gr. and L. *pro*, before; E. *fore*, *first*, etc. PRINCE, PRIM, PRIMITIVE, etc.] First in order of time; primitive; original (*prime* cost); first in rank, degree, or dignity (*prime* minister); first in excellence, value, or importance; first-rate; capital; early; in the first stage.—*Prime conductor*, *elect.* the metallic conductor opposed to the glass plate or cylinder of an electrical machine.—*Prime cost*, first or original cost; the sum or expenditure for which an article can be made or produced.—*Prime minister*, in Great Britain, the first minister of state; the premier.—*Prime mover*, the initial force which puts a machine in motion; a machine which receives and modifies force as supplied by some natural source, as a waterwheel, a steam engine, etc. —*Prime number*, *arith.* a number not divisible without remainder by any less number than itself except unity. —*Prime vertical*, in *astron.* a celestial great circle passing through the east and west points and the zenith.—*n.* The earliest stage or beginning of anything; the dawn; the morning; the spring of the year; the spring of life; youth; full health, strength, or beauty; the highest or most perfect or most flourishing condition; the best part; that which is best in quality; in *R. Cath. Ch.* the first canonical hour, succeeding to lauds. —*v.t.*—*primed*, *priming*. [Lit. to perform a *prime* or first operation with, to prepare.] To put into a condition for being fired: said of a gun, mine, etc.; to supply with powder for communicating fire to a charge; *painting*, to cover with a ground or first color; to instruct or prepare a person beforehand what he is to say or do; to post up (to *prime* a witness). —**primely**, prīm′li, *adv.* In a prime manner or degree; most excellently. —**primeness**, prīm′nes, *n.* The quality of being prime; supreme excellence.—**primer**, prim′ėr or prī′mėr, *n.* [Fr. *primaire*, elementary, from L. *primarius*, from *primus*, first.] A small elementary book for religious instruction or for teaching children to read; a book of elementary principles; *print.* a name given to two sizes of type, *longprimer* and *great-primer*.—**priming**, prī′ming, *n. Gun.* and *blasting*, the powder used to ignite the charge; *painting*, the first layer of paint or size laid on a surface which is to be painted; *steam engine*, the carrying over of water spray with the steam from the boiler into the cylinder—a troublesome defect.

primero, pri•mâ′ro, *n.* [Sp. *primero*, first.] An old game at cards.

primeval, prī•mē′val, *a.* [L. *primaevus* —*primus*, first, and *aevum*, age. PRIME, AGE.] Original; primitive; belonging to the first ages.—**primevally**, prī•mē′val•li, *adv.* In a primeval manner; in the earliest times.

primigenial, prī•mi•jē′ni•al, *a.* [L. *primigenius*—*primus*, first, and root *gen.* to beget.] First-born; original; primary.

primine, prī′min, *n.* [L. *primus*, first.] *Bot.* the outermost sac or covering of an ovule, the inner being termed *secundine*.

primiparous, prī•mip′a•rus, *a.* [L. *primus*, first, and *pario*, to bring forth.] Bearing young for the first time.

primitive, prim′i•tiv, *a.* [L. *primitivus*, earliest of its kind, from *primus*, first. PRIME.] Pertaining to the beginning or origin; original; first; old-fashioned; characterized by the simplicity of old times; *gram.* applied to a word in its simplest etymological form; not derived; radical; primary; *bot.* original, in opposition to forms resulting from hybridization.—*Primitive colors.* See COLOR.—*n.* A person of simple culture.—**primitively**, prim′i•tiv•li, *adv.*—**primitivism**, prim′i•tiv•izm, *n.* A theory that cultures of primitive or early chronological date are superior to present-day culture.—**primitiveness**, prim′i•tiv•nes, *n.*

primly, primness. See PRIM.

primogeniture, prī•mo•jen′i•chėr, *n.* [Fr. *primogéniture*, from L. *primus*, first, and *genitūra*, a begetting, from *gigno*, *genitum*, to beget. GENDER, GENUS.] The state of being born first of the same parents; seniority by birth among children; the right or principle under which the eldest son of a family succeeds to the father's real estate, in preference to, and in absolute exclusion of the younger sons and daughters.—**primogenitor**, prī•mo•jen′i•tėr, *n.* [L. *primus*, and *genitor*, father.] The first father or forefather; an ancestor.

primordial, prī•mor′di•al, *a.* [L. *primordialis*, from *primordium*, beginning, origin—*primus*, first, and *ordior*, to commence. PRIME, ORDER.] First in order, original, existing from the beginning; *bot.* and *zool.* earliest formed.—*n.* A first principle or element.—**primordially**, prī•mor′di•al•li, *adv.* Under the first order of things; at the beginning.

primp, primp, *v.t.* [From *prim*, or perhaps a form of *prink*.] To deck one's self in a stiff and affected manner.

primrose, prim′rōz, *n.* [O.E. *primerole*. Fr. *primerole*, from L.L. *primula*, the primrose, from *primus*, first (as the first flower of spring); the last syllable was changed to *rose* to give the word an English appearance and a sort of meaning; comp. *barberry*, etc.] The common name for several beautiful herbaceous plants, both cultivated and wild, with flowers colored red, white, and yellow, and with each flower growing on a separate stem or peduncle rather than in clusters; a dye derived from coal tar, pinkish-yellow in color; when referred to as a shade, it signifies a pale greenish-yellow tint.—*a.* Resembling a primrose in color; abounding with primroses; flowery; florid; excessively ornate.—**primrose path**, *n.* The leading of a gay or merry life; indulgence in the showy and sensual pleasures of life.—**primrose yellow**, *n.* A reddish-yellow color.

prince, prins, *n.* [Fr., from L. *princeps*, *principis*, a prince, a chief—*primus*, first, and *capio*, to take. PRIME, CAPABLE.] A man holding the first or highest rank; a sovereign; a sovereign who has the government of a particular territory, but owes certain services to a superior; the son of a sovereign; a male member of a royal family; the chief of any body of men; a man at the head of any class, profession, etc.. (a merchant *prince*).—**princess**, prin′ses, *n.* The daughter of a sovereign; a woman of grandeur, such as a princess; the consort of a prince.—*a.* Denoting a close-fitting, one-piece dress or slip (also **princesse.**).—**princely**, prins′li, *a.* Pertaining to a prince; resembling a prince; noble; grand; august; magnificent.—**princeliness**, prins′li•nes, *n.*—**prince consort**, *n.* The husband of a reigning queen.

principal, prin′si•pal, *a.* [L. *principalis*, from *princeps*, first in time or order, a chief. PRINCE.] Chief; highest in rank, character, authority, or importance; first; main; essential; most considerable.—*n.* A chief or head; one who takes a leading part; the chief executive of an educational institution, particularly, of an elementary or secondary public school; *law*, the actor or absolute perpetrator of a crime, or an abettor; one who engages another person to act as his representative or agent; *com.* a capital sum lent on interest, due as a debt, or used as a fund: so called in distinction to interest; *carp.* a main timber in an assemblage of pieces.—**principality**, prin•si•pal′i•ti, *n.* [Fr. *principalité.*] Sovereignty; supreme power; a prince, or one invested with sovereignty; the territory of a prince, or the country which gives title to a prince.—**principally**, prin′si•pal•li, *adv.* In the chief place; chiefly; above all.

principle, prin′si•pl, *n.* [Fr. *principe*, from L. *principium*, a beginning, origin, element, from *princeps*, *principis*. PRINCE. As to the insertion of the *l* comp. *participle*, *syllable.*] Beginning‡; commencement‡; a source of origin; the primary source from which anything proceeds; element; primordial substance; a general truth; a law comprehending many subordinate truths; a law on which others are founded or from which others are derived; an axiom; a maxim; a tenet; a governing law of conduct; a settled rule of action; a right rule of conduct; uprightness (a man of *principle*); ground of conduct; a motive; *chem.* a component part; an element; a substance on the presence of which certain qualities common to a number of bodies depend.

prink, pringk, *v.i.* [A slightly modified form of *prank.*] To prank; to dress for show; to strut; to put on stately airs.—*v.t.* To deck; to adorn fantastically.

print, print, *v.t.* [Fr. *preinte*, from *preindre*, from L. *primo*, *pressum*, to press. PRESS.] To impress or imprint upon, as to mark or stamp; to impress with or convince of an idea; to apply something with pressure so as to leave a mark; to make an impression or mark with type, engraved plates, etc.; to perform all operations necessary to produce a book, periodical, etc. (to *print* a story); to stamp designs, letters, etc., on (to *print* labels); to produce or publish in print (to *print* a scandal); to form letters or words in characters similar to type, as opposed to writing them; *photog.* to transfer images from negatives or the like to a sensitized surface; to impress a design on cloth.—*v.i.* To use or practice the art of printing.—*n.* A mark made by impression; a stamp; a die, mold, or stamp; that which receives a mark or impression from a die or mold; the state or condition of being printed (it appeared in *print*); that which is produced by printing, especially an engraving; a newspaper or other periodical; printed cloth.—**printable,** print'a•ble, *a.*—**printed circuit,** *n.* A circuit for electronic devices made by depositing conductive material in continuous paths between terminals on an insulating surface.—**printer,** print'ėr, *n.*—**printing,** print'ing, *n.* The combined processes which go into the production of books, periodicals, etc., by impression from movable type, plates, etc.; all the books, etc., printed in one edition; writing in which the letters are similar in form to type; the act of a person or device that prints.—**printing press,** *n.* A press for the printing of books, etc.

prior, prī'or, *a.* [L. *prior*, a compar. to which *primus*, first, is the superl. PRIME.] Preceding, especially in the order of time; earlier; antecedent; anterior.—*adv.* Previously; antecedently (he had never been there *prior* to that time).—*n.* The superior of a priory or a monastery of lower than abbatial rank; a monk next in dignity to an abbot.—*Grand prior*, a title given to the commandants of the priories of the military orders of St. John of Jerusalem, of Malta, and of the Templars.—**priorate, priorship,** prī'or•āt, prī'or•ship, *n.* The dignity or office of a prior.—**prioress,** prī'or•es, *n.* The female head in a convent of nuns, next in rank to an abbess.—**priority,** prī•or'i•ti, *n.* The state of being prior or antecedent in time, or of preceding something else; precedence in place or rank.—**priory,** prī'e•ri, *n.* A religious house of which a prior or prioress is the superior, in dignity below an abbey.

prism, prizm, *n.* [L. and Gr. *prisma*, lit. a sawn piece, from *prizō*, to saw.] A solid whose bases or ends are any similar, equal, and parallel plane figures, and whose sides are parallelograms; a bar of glass with a triangular section, used for decomposing light, as in spectrum analysis.—**prismatic, prismatical,** priz•mat'ik, priz•mat'i•kal, *a.* Resembling or pertaining to a prism; formed or exhibited by a prism.—*Prismatic colors*, the colors into which a ray of light is decomposed in passing through a prism: red, orange, yellow, green, blue, indigo, violet.—**prismatically,** priz•mat'i•kal•li, *adv.* In the form or manner of a prism; by means of a prism.—**prismatoidal,** priz•ma•toi'dal, *a.* Having a prismlike form.—**prismoid,** priz'moid, *n.* A body that approaches to the form of a prism.—**prismoidal,** priz•moi'dal, *a.* Having the form of a prismoid.

prison, priz'on or priz'n, *n.* [Fr. *prison*, from L. *prehensio, prehensionis*, a capture, from *prehendo*, to seize (whence *prehensile*, etc.). APPREHEND.] A place of confinement or involuntary restraint; especially, a public building for the confinement or safe custody of criminals and others committed by process of law; a jail.—*v.t.* To shut up in a prison; to confine; to imprison.—**prisoner,** priz'on•ėr, *n.* One who is confined in a prison; a person under arrest, whether in prison or not; a captive; one taken by an enemy in war; one whose liberty is restrained, as a bird in a cage.—**prisoner's base,** *n.* A game consisting chiefly of running and being pursued from goals or bases.

pristine, pris'tēn, *a.* [L. *pristinus*; same root as *prior, prime*, etc.] Belonging to a primitive or early state or period; original; primitive.

private, prī'vit, *a.* [L. *privatus*, from *privo*, to separate, from *privus*, separate, peculiar (seen also in *deprive, privilege*).] Peculiar to one's self; belonging to or concerning an individual only; personal; opposed to *public* or *national*; not known, open, or accessible to people in general; secret; not invested with public office or employment; not having a public or official character; unconnected with others; solitary; participating in knowledge; privy; *milit.* said of a common soldier.—*Private hospital*, a hospital financed from private sources, rather than public agencies.—*Private nurse*, a nurse caring for one patient.—*In private*, not publicly or openly; secretly.—*n.* A common soldier; one of the lowest rank in the army.—**privacy,** prī'va•si, *n.* A state of being private or in retirement; seclusion; secrecy; solitude; retirement.—**privately,** prī'vit•li, *adv.* In a private or secret manner; not openly or publicly; in a manner affecting an individual; personally.—**privateness,** prī'vit•nes, *n.* The state of being private.—**privateer,** prī•va•tēr', *n.* A vessel of war owned and equipped by one or more private persons, and licensed by a government to seize or plunder the ships of an enemy in war.—*v.i.* To cruise in a privateer.—**privateersman,** prī•va•tērz'man, *n.* An officer or seaman of a privateer.—**privation,** prī•vā'shon, *n.* [L. *privatio*, from *privo*, to bereave.] The state of being deprived; deprivation of what is necessary for comfort; destitution; want; the act of removing something possessed.—**privative,** priv'a•tiv, *a.* Causing deprivation; *gram.* changing the sense from positive to negative.—*n.* A prefix to a word which gives it a contrary sense, as *un* and *in* in *unwise, inhuman*.—**privatively,** priv'a•tiv•li, *adv.* In a private manner.

privet, priv'et, *n.* [Etym. unknown.] A shrub frequently planted to form ornamental hedges in gardens.

privilege, priv'i•lej, *n.* [L. *privilegium*, an exceptional law, from *privus*, separate, peculiar, and *lex, legis*, a law. PRIVATE, LEGAL.] A right or advantage enjoyed by a person or body of persons beyond the common advantages of other individuals; a private or personal favor enjoyed; a peculiar advantage.—*Question of privilege*, in *parliament*, a question affecting the privileges appertaining to the members.—*v.t.* To grant some privilege, right, or exemption to; to invest with a peculiar right or immunity; to authorize; to license.

privy, priv'i, *a.* [Fr. *privé*, from L. *privatus*. PRIVATE.] Private; assigned to private uses; not public; secret; not seen openly; appropriated to retirement; sequestered (O.T.); privately knowing; admitted to the participation of knowledge with another of a secret transaction (*privy to* a thing).—*n.* A latrine or necessary house.—*Gentlemen of the privy chamber*, officers of the royal household of Britain who attend on the sovereign at court, in progresses, etc.—**privily,** priv'i•li, *adv.* In a privy manner; privately; secretly.—**privity,** priv'i•ti, *n.* Privacy‡; private knowledge; joint knowledge with another of a private concern; *pl.* secret parts; the genital organs.—**Privy Council,** *n.* The principal council of the English sovereign, the members of which are chosen at his or her pleasure.—**privy councilor,** *n.* A member of the privy council.—**privy seal,** *n.* In England, the seal appended to grants which are afterward to pass the great seal, and to documents of minor importance; the secretary of state who is entrusted with the privy seal is called *lord privy seal*.

prize, prīz, *n.* [Fr. *prise*, a taking, capture, prize, from *prendre*, to take, from L. *prehendo*, to seize. PRISON.] That which is taken from an enemy in war, particularly a ship, with the property taken in it; that which is deemed a valuable acquisition; any gain or advantage; that which is obtained or offered as the reward of exertion or contest; that which is won in a lottery, or in any similar way.—**prize court,** *n.* A court which adjudicates on captures made at sea.—**prize fight,** *n.* A pugilistic encounter or boxing match for a prize.—**prize fighter,** *n.* A professional pugilist or boxer.—**prize fighting,** *n.* Boxing in public for a reward.—**prize money,** *n.* Money distributed among the captors of a ship or place where booty has been obtained, in certain proportions according to rank, the money being realized from the sale of the prize or booty.—**prize ring,** *n.* A ring or enclosed place for prize fighting; prize fighters collectively (a member of the *prize ring*).

prize, prīz, *v.t.*—*prized, prizing*. [Fr. *priser*, to value, to set a price on, from L. *pretium*, a price. PRICE, PRECIOUS.] To set or estimate the value of; to rate; to value highly; to consider of great worth; to esteem.—*a.* Meriting award of a prize, as *prize* cattle.

pro, prō, *adv.* [L. preposition, for, in favor of.] For, opposed to *con* (against); on the affirmative side.

proa, prō'a, *n.* [Malay *prau, prahu.*]

A kind of Malay vessel with one side flat, and an outrigger adjusted sometimes to the leeward side and sometimes to both sides, remarkable for swiftness.

probable, prob′a•bl, *a.* [Fr. *probable,* from L. *probabilis,* that may be proved, probable, from *probo,* to prove. PROVE.] Supported by or based on evidence which inclines the mind to belief, but leaves some room for doubt; likely; rendering something probable (*probable* evidence).—**probabilism,** prob′a•bil•-izm, *n. R. Cath. theol.* a theory, which, when there are two contrary opinions on a point of morality, considers it lawful to adopt that which is the more in agreement with personal inclination, provided it be supported by some weighty authority.—**probabilist,** prob′a•bil•-ist, *n.* One who maintains the theory of probabilism.—**probability,** prob•-a•bil′i•ti, *n.* [Fr. *probabilité,* L. *probabilitas.*] The state or quality of being probable; likelihood; appearance of truth; anything that has the appearance of reality or truth (in this sense with a plural); *math.* the ratio of the number of chances by which an event may happen, to the number by which it may both happen and fail.—**probably,** prob′a•bli, *adv.* In a probable manner; in all likelihood; as is probable; likely.

probang, prō′bang, *n.* [Probably from *probe.*] *Surg.* a long slender elastic rod of whalebone, with a piece of sponge securely attached to one end, intended to push down anything stuck in the gullet.

probate, prō′bāt, *n.* [L. *probatus,* from *probo,* to prove.] A proceeding before proper authorities by which a person's will or testament is established as such and registered.—**probate court,** *n.* A court concerned with the probate of wills, and all matters relating thereto.

probation, prō•bā′shon, *n.* [L. *probatio, probationis,* an approving. PROBABLE.] The act of proving; proof; any proceeding designed to ascertain character, qualifications, or the like; a preliminary or preparatory trial or examination; a period of time during which a delinquent must report at regular intervals to a probation officer.—**probationer,** prō•bā′shon•ėr, *n.* One who is on probation or trial; a delinquent under the supervision of a probation officer; the designation given to a student nurse during her first year of training.—**probation officer,** *n.* One to whom a probationer must report at regular intervals.—**probative,** prō′ba•tiv, *a.* Serving for trial or proof.—**probatory,** prō′ba•to•ri, *a.* Serving for trial; pertaining to or serving for proof.

probe, prōb, *n.* [From L. *probo,* to test, to try, to prove. PROVE.] A surgeon's instrument for examining the depth or other circumstances of a wound, ulcer, or cavity; an investigation; a device that is launched into outer space in order to gather information.—*v.t.*—*probed, probing.* To apply a probe to; to examine by a probe; *fig.* to search to the bottom; to examine thoroughly into.

probity, prōb′i•ti, *n.* [L. *probitas,* from *probus,* worthy, honest, good.] Tried virtue or integrity; strict honesty; rectitude; uprightness; high principle.

problem, prob′lem, *n.* [Fr. *problème,* L. *problema,* from Gr. *problēma*—*pro,* before, and *ballō,* to throw.] A question proposed for solution, decision, or determination; a knotty point requiring to be cleared up; *geom.* a proposition requiring some operation to be performed, differing from a theorem in that the latter requires something to be proved.—**problematic, problematical,** prob-le•mat′ik, prob•le•mat′i•kal, *a.* Questionable; uncertain; disputable; doubtful.—**problematically,** prob•-le•mat′i•kal•li, *adv.* In a problematical manner.

proboscis, prō•bos′sis, *n.* pl. **proboscides,** prō•bos′si•dēz. [L. *proboscis,* from Gr. *proboskis*—*pro,* before, and *boskō,* to feed.] The snout or trunk projecting from the head of an elephant and other animals; the horny tube formed by the modified jaws of insects, used for sucking blood from animals or juice from plants; the nose; used humorously or in ridicule.—**proboscidian,** prō•-bos•sid′i•an, *a.* Furnished with a proboscis; proboscidean.—**proboscidean,** prō•bos•sid′i•an, *a.* and *n.* Pertaining to, or one of, those mammals which have the nose prolonged into a prehensile trunk, as the elephant, etc.

procaine, prō′cain, *n.* [From prefix *pro* and (co)*caine.*] A basic ester of para-amino benzoic acid used as a local anesthetic, also called novocaine.

procathedral, prō•ka•thē′dral, *n.* A church that serves temporarily as a cathedral.

proceed, prō•sēd′, *v.i.* [Fr. *procéder;* L. *procedo*—*pro,* before, and *cedo,* to go. CEDE.] To move, pass, or go onward; to continue or renew motion or progress; to advance; to go on; to pass from one point, stage, or topic to another; to issue or come, as from an origin, source, or fountain; to set to work and go on in a certain way; to act according to some method; to begin and carry on a legal action.—**procedure,** prō•-sē′dūr, *n.* [Fr. *procédure.*] Manner of proceeding or acting; a course or mode of action; conduct; a step taken; a proceeding.—**proceeding,** prō•sē′ding, *n.* The act of one who proceeds; a measure or step taken; a transaction; a mode of conduct; *pl.* the course of steps in the prosecution of actions at law; the record or account of the transactions of a society.—**proceeds,** prō′sēdz, *n. pl.* The amount accruing from some transaction; the value of goods sold or converted into money.

process, pros′es, *n.* [L. *processus,* from *procedo, processum,* to proceed. PROCEED.] A proceeding or moving forward; progressive course; way in which something goes on; gradual progress; course; series of actions or experiments (a chemical *process*); series of motions or changes going on, as in growth, decay, etc., in physical bodies; course; lapse; a passing or elapsing (the *process* of time); *law,* the whole course of proceedings in a cause; a projecting portion of something; especially, in *anat.* any protuberance or projecting part of a bone or other body; printing done from photoengraved plates.—*Process printing, n.* A method of reproducing objects in natural colors, chiefly pictures, by means of three, four, or more photoengravings, each printing in a different color, and printed one over the other. —**procession,** prō•sesh′on, *n.* [L. *processio.*] The act of proceeding or issuing forth; a train of persons walking, or riding on horseback or in vehicles, in a formal march.—**processional,** prō•sesh′on•al, *n. R. Cath. Ch.* a prayer or hymn used for religious processions.—**process server,** *n.* A bailiff or sheriff's officer.

procès-verbal, prō•sā•vâr•bäl, *n.* In *French law,* a detailed authentic account of an official proceeding; a statement of facts.

proclaim, prō•klām′, *v.t.* [L. *proclamo*—*pro,* before, and *clamo,* to cry out. CLAIM.] To make known by public announcement; to promulgate; to announce; to publish; to outlaw by public denunciation.—**proclaimer,** prō•klā′mėr, *n.* One who proclaims. —**proclamation,** prok•la•mā′shon, *n.* [L. *proclamatio.*] The act of proclaiming; an official public announcement or declaration; a published ordinance.

proclitic, prō•klit′ik, *n.* [From Gr. *pro,* forward, and *klinō,* to lean.] *Greek gram.* a monosyllabic word so closely attached to a following word as to have no independent existence and therefore no accent.

proclivity, prō•kliv′i•ti, *n.* [L. *proclivitas,* from *pro,* before, and *clivus,* a slope. ACCLIVITY.] Inclination; propensity; proneness; tendency; readiness.

proconsul, prō•kon′sul, *n.* [L., from *pro,* for, and *consul.*] In ancient Rome an officer who discharged the duties of a consul without being himself consul; generally one who had been consul.—**proconsular,** prō•-kon′sul•ėr, *a.* Pertaining to a proconsul.—**proconsulate, proconsulship,** prō•kon′sul•āt, prō•kon′sul•-ship, *n.* The office of a proconsul.

procrastinate, prō•kras′ti•nāt, *v.t.* —*procrastinated, procrastinating.* [L. *procrastino, procrastinatus*—*pro,* forward, and *crastinus,* belonging to the morrow, from *cras,* to-morrow.] To put off from day to day; to delay; to defer to a future time.—*v.i.* To delay; to be dilatory.—**procrastination,** prō•kras′ti•nā″shon, *n.* The act or habit of putting off to a future time; dilatoriness.—**procrastinator,** prō•kras′ti•nā′tėr, *n.* One who procrastinates.

procreate, prō′kri•āt, *v.t.*—*procreat-*

ed, procreating. [L. procreo—pro, before, and creo, to create. CREATE.] To beget; to generate and produce; to engender.—**procreation,** prō•kri•ā′shon, n. The act of procreating or begetting.—**procreative,** prō′kri•ā•tiv, a. Having the power or function of procreating.—**procreator,** prō′kri•ā•tėr, n. One that begets; a father or sire.—**procreant,** prō′kri•ant, a. [L. procreans, procreantis, ppr. of procreo.] Procreating; producing young; assisting in producing young†.—n. One who or that which procreates.

Procrustean, prō•krus′ti•an, a. Pertaining to or resembling *Procrustes*, a robber of ancient Greece, who tortured his victims by placing them on a bed, and stretching or lopping off their legs to adapt the body to its length; hence, acting similarly; producing uniformity by deforming or mutilating.

proctor, prok′tėr, n. [Contr. from *procurator*; comp. *proxy*.] A procurator; a person employed to manage another's cause in a court of civil or ecclesiastical law; an official in a university whose function is to see that good order is kept and that obedience is maintained.—**proctorial,** prok•tō′ri•al, a. Pertaining to a proctor.—**proctorship,** n.

procumbent, prō•kum′bent, a. [L. *procumbens*—*pro*, forward, and *cumbere*, to lie.] Lying down; prone; *bot.* trailing; prostrate; lying on the ground, but without putting forth roots (a *procumbent* stem).

procurator, prok′ū•rā•tėr, n. [L., one who manages, an agent, from *procuro*. PROCURE.] The manager of another's affairs; one who undertakes the care of legal proceedings for another; a governor of a province under the Roman emperors.—**procuratorial,** pro•kū′ra•tō″ri•al, a. Pertaining to a procurator or proctor.—**procuracy,** prok′ū•ra•si, n. The office or service of a procurator; the management of an affair for another.—**procuration,** pro•kū•rā′shon, n. Management of another's affairs; the document by which a person is empowered to transact the affairs of another.

procure, prō•kūr′, v.t.—*procured, procuring*. [Fr. *procurer*, from L. *procurare*, to take care of, to attend to—*pro*, for, and *cura*, care. CURE.] To obtain, as by request, loan, effort, labor, or purchase; to get, gain, come into possession of; to bring on; to attract (modesty *procures* respect); to cause, bring about, effect, contrive.—*v.i.* To pimp.—**procurable,** prō•kū′ra•bl, a. Capable of being procured; obtainable.—**procurement,** prō•kūr′ment, n. The act of procuring or obtaining.—**procurer,** prō•kū′rėr, n. One that procures; a pimp; a pander.—**procuress,** prō′kū•res, n. A female pimp; a bawd.

procurvation, prō•kėr•vā′shon, n. [L. *pro*, forward, and *curvatio*, a curving.] A bending forward.

prod, prod, n. [A form of *brod, brad*.] A pointed instrument, as a goad or an awl; a stab.—*v.t.*—*prodded, prodding*. To prick with a pointed instrument; to goad.

prodigal, prod′i•gal, a. [L.L. *prodigalis*, from L. *prodigus*, prodigal, from *pro*, forth, and *ago*, to drive. ACT.] Given to extravagant expenditure; expending wastefully; profuse; lavish; wasteful; lavishly bountiful.—n. One that expends money extravagantly; one that is profuse or lavish; a waster; a spendthrift.

prodigality, prod•i•gal′i•ti, n. Extravagance in expenditure; profusion; waste; excessive or profuse liberality.—**prodigally,** prod′i•gal•li, *adv.* In a prodigal manner; extravagantly; lavishly; wastefully; profusely.

prodigious, prō•dij′us, a. [Fr. *prodigieux*; L. *prodigiosus*, strange, wonderful, from *prodigium*, a prodigy.] Of the nature of a prodigy‡; extraordinary; very great; huge; enormous; excessive; intense.—**prodigiously,** prō•dij′us•li, *adv.* Enormously; astonishingly; excessively.—**prodigiousness,** prō•dij′us•nes, n.—**prodigy,** prod′i•ji, n. [L. *prodigium*.] Something extraordinary from which omens are drawn; a portent; anything very extraordinary; a wonder or miracle (he is a *prodigy* of learning); something out of the ordinary course of nature.

produce, pro•dūs′, v.t.—*produced, producing*. [L. *produco*—*pro*, before, forward, and *ducere*, to lead, bring. DUKE.] To bring forward; to bring or offer to view or notice; to exhibit; to bring forth; to give birth to; to bear, furnish, yield; to cause, effect, bring about; to make; to bring into being or form; to make accrue (money *produces* interest); *geom.* to draw out in length; to extend (to *produce* a line for a certain distance).—*v.i.* To bring forth or yield appropriate offspring, products, or consequences.

produce, prod′ūs, n. A total produced, brought forth, or yielded; the outcome yielded by labor and natural growth; yield or production (the *produce* of a farm or of a country).—**producer,** pro•dū′sėr, n. One who or that which produces; one who finances or supervises the making of motion pictures, plays, etc.—**producers' goods,** n. Instruments of production; tools and raw materials; economic goods that benefit the consumer only indirectly.—**producible,** pro•dū′si•bl, a. Capable of being produced.—**product,** prod′ukt, n. [L. *productum*.] A thing which is produced by nature, as fruit, grain, or vegetables; that which is yielded by the soil; that which is produced by labor or mental application; a production; something resulting as a consequence; result; *math.* the result of, or quantity produced by, the multiplication of two numbers or quantities together.—**production,** pro•duk′shon, n. [L. *productio, productionis*.] The act or process of producing; *pol. econ.* the producing of articles having an exchange value; that which is produced or made (the *productions* of the earth, of art, of intellect).—**productive,** pro•duk′tiv, a. Having the power of producing; fertile; producing good crops; bringing into being; causing to exist (an age *productive* of great men); *pol. econ.* producing commodities of great value; adding to the wealth of the world.—**productively,** pro•duk′tiv•li, *adv.* In a productive manner.—**productiveness,** pro•duk′tiv•nes, n. The quality of being productive.—**productivity,** prō•duk•tiv′i•ti, n. Power of producing; state or quality of being productive.

proem, prō′em, n. [Fr. *proème*, from L. *prœmium*, Gr. *prooimion*—*pro*, before, and *oimos*, way.] Preface; introduction; preliminary observations to a book or writing.—**proemial,** prō•ēm′i•al, a. Having the character of a proem.

profane, prō•fān′, a. [Fr. *profane*, from L. *profanus*, profane, unholy—*pro*, forth from, and *fanum*, a temple. FANE.] Not sacred or devoted to sacred purposes; not possessing any peculiar sanctity; secular; irreverent toward God or holy things; speaking or spoken, acting or acted in contempt of sacred things or implying it; blasphemous; polluted.—*Profane history*, all history other than biblical.—*v.t.*—*profaned, profaning*. To treat as if not sacred or deserving reverence; to treat with irreverence, impiety, or sacrilege; to desecrate (to *profane* the name of God, or the Sabbath); to put to a wrong use; to employ basely or unworthily.—**profanation,** prof•a•nā′shon, n. The act of profaning; the violating of sacred things, or the treating of them with contempt or irreverence; desecration; the act of treating with too little delicacy.—**profanely,** prō•fān′li, *adv.* In a profane manner; impiously; blasphemously.—**profaneness,** prō•fān′nes, n.—**profaner,** prō•fā′nėr, n. One who profanes.—**profanity,** prō•fan′i•ti, n. The quality of being profane; that which is profane; profane language or conduct.

profess, pro•fes′, v.t. [L. *profiteri, professus*, to declare, acknowledge, profess—*pro*, before, and *fateor*, to avow; same root as *fame, fable, fate*.] To make open declaration of; to avow, acknowledge, own; to acknowledge or own publicly to be; to lay claim openly to the character of: used *refl.* (to *profess one's self* a Christian); to make a show of; to make protestations or a pretense of; to pretend (to *profess* great friendship for a person); to declare one's self versed in (he *professes* surgery).—*v.i.* To declare openly; to make any declaration or assertion.—**professedly,** pro•fes′ed•li, *adv.* By profession; avowedly.—**profession,** pro•fesh′on, n. [L. *professio*.] The act of professing; a public avowal or acknowledgment of one's sentiments or belief; a declaration; a representation or protestation (*professions* of friendship or sincerity); a calling superior to a mere trade or handicraft, as that of medicine, law, architecture, etc.; a vocation; the collective body of persons engaged in such calling.—**professional,** pro•fesh′on•al, *a.* Pertaining to a profession; engaged in a profession. —*n.* A member of any profession, but more often applied, in opposition to *amateur,* to persons who make their living by arts, etc., in which nonprofessionals are accustomed to engage.—**professionally,** pro•fesh′-on•al•li, *adv.* In a professional manner; in the way of one's profession or calling.—**professor,** pro•fes′ėr, *n.* [L.] One who professes; one who publicly unites himself to the visible church; one who is visibly or ostensibly religious; one that publicly teaches any art, science, or branch of learning; particularly, an official in a university, college, or other seminary, whose business is to deliver lectures or instruct students.—**professorial,** pro•fes•sō′ri•-al, *a.* Pertaining to a professor in a college, etc.—**professoriate,** pro•fes•-sō′ri•āt, *n.* A body of professors; the teaching staff of professors.—**professorship,** pro•fes′ėr•ship, *n.* The office of a professor.

proffer, prof′ėr, *v.t.* [Fr. *proférer,* from L. *proferre,* to bring forward—*pro,* before, and *ferre,* to bring. FERTILE, BEAR.] To hold out that a person may take; to offer for acceptance.—*n.* An offer made; something proposed for acceptance by another.

proficient, pro•fish′ent, *n.* [L. *proficiens,* from *proficio,* I advance, make progress, improve—*pro,* forward, and *facio,* to make. FACT.] One who has made considerable advances in any business, art, science, or branch of learning; an adept; an expert.—*a.* Well versed in any business or branch of learning; well qualified; competent.—**proficiently,** pro•fish′ent•li, *adv.* In a proficient manner.—**proficiency,** pro•fish′en•-si, *n.* The state of being proficient; skill and knowledge.

profile, prō′fīl, *n.* [Fr. *profil,* from It. *profilo;* from L. *pro,* before, and *filum,* a thread, line.] An outline or contour; especially an outline of the human face seen sideways; the side face or half face; the outline or contour of anything, such as a building, portion of country, etc., as shown by a section. Used also as adj.—*v.t.*—*profiled, profiling.* To draw in profile; to give a profile of.

profit, prof′it, *n.* [Fr. *profit,* from L. *profectus,* progress, increase, from *proficio,* to advance, to improve. PROFICIENT.] Any advantage; an accession of good from labor or exertion; especially, the advantage or gain resulting to the owner of capital from its employment in any undertaking; the difference between the original cost and selling price of anything; pecuniary gain; emolument.—*Rate of profit,* the proportion which the amount of profit bears to the capital employed.—*v.t.* To benefit; to advantage; to be of service to; to advance.—*v.i.* To derive profit; to improve; to make progress intellectually or morally; to gain pecuniarily; to become richer; to be of use or advantage; to bring good.—**profitable,** prof′i•ta•bl, *a.* Yielding or bringing profit or gain; gainful; lucrative; useful; advantageous.—**profitableness,** prof′-i•ta•bl•nes, *n.* The quality of being profitable.—**profitably,** prof′i•ta•bli, *adv.* In a profitable manner; gainfully; advantageously.—**profiteer,** prof•it•ēr′, *n.* A trader who takes advantage of abnormal conditions, such as those of wartime, to make excessive profit.—*v.i.* To make excess profits.—**profitless,** prof′it•les, *a.* Void of profit, gain, or advantage.

profligate, prof′li•git, *a.* [L. *profligatus,* pp. of *profligo,* to rout, to ruin—*pro,* intens., and *fligo,* to strike down; seen also in *conflict, inflict,* etc.] Ruined in morals; abandoned to vice; lost to virtue or decency; vicious; shameless in wickedness.—*n.* An abandoned person; one who has lost all regard to good principles, virtue, or decency.—**profligately,** prof′li•git•li, *adv.* In a profligate manner.—**profligacy, profligateness,** prof′li•ga•si, prof′li•-git•nes, *n.* The quality or condition of being profligate; a profligate or very vicious course of life; abandoned conduct.

profound, pro•found′, *a.* [Fr. *profond,* L. *profundus*—*pro,* forward, far, and *fundus,* bottom. FOUND, FUND.] Deep; descending or being far below the surface, or far below the adjacent places; having great depth; intellectually deep; deep in knowledge or skill (a *profound* scholar); characterized by intensity; far-reaching; deeply felt (*profound* grief); touching; bending low; humble; exhibiting or expressing humility (a *profound* bow, *profound* reverence).—*n.* The deep; the sea; the ocean (with *the*); an abyss; a deep immeasurable space.—**profoundly,** pro•found′li, *adv.* In a profound manner.—**profoundness,** pro•found′-nes, *n.* Profundity; depth.—**profundity,** pro•fun′di•ti, *n.* The quality or condition of being profound; depth of place, of knowledge, etc.

profuse, pro•fūs′, *a.* [L. *profusus,* from *profundo*—*pro,* forth, and *fundere,* to pour. FUSE.] Pouring forth lavishly; extravagant; lavish; liberal to excess; prodigal; poured forth lavishly; exuberant.—**profusely,** pro•-fūs′li, *adv.* In a profuse manner; lavishly; prodigally.—**profuseness,** pro•fūs′nes, *n.* The state or quality of being profuse.—**profusion,** pro•-fū′zhon, *n.* [L. *profusio.*] Profuse or lavish expenditure; rich abundance; lavish supply; exuberant plenty.

progeny, proj′e•ni, *n.* [Fr. *progénie,* L. *progenies,* from *pro,* forth, and root *gen,* to bring forth; seen also in *gender, generation, genus,* etc. GENUS.] Offspring collectively; children; descendants of the human kind, or offspring of other animals.—**progenitor,** pro•jen′i•tėr, *n.* An ancestor in the direct line; a forefather; a parent.

proglottis, prō•glot′is, *n.* pl. **proglottides,** prō•glot′ti•dēz. [Gr., the tip of the tongue.] *Zool.* the generative segment or joint of a tapeworm.

prognathic, prognathous, prog•-nath′ik, prog•nā′thus, *a.* [Gr. *pro,* before, and *gnathos,* the cheek or jawbone.] Characterized by projecting jaws; applied to human skulls when the jaw slants forward, making the lower part of the face very prominent.—**prognathism,** prog•-nā′thizm, *n.* The condition of being prognathic.

prognosis, prog•nō′sis, *n.* [Gr. *prognōsis,* a foreknowing.] Foreknowledge; a forecast, especially of the probable course of a disease.

prognostic, prog•nos′tik, *a.* [Gr. *prognōstikos*—*pro,* before, and *gignōskō,* to know. KNOW.] Foreshowing; indicating something future by signs or symptoms.—*n.* A sign by which a future event may be known or foretold; an omen; a token; a symptom; a foretelling; prediction.—**prognosticate,** prog•-nos′ti•kāt, *v.t.*—*prognosticated, prognosticating.* To foretell by means of present signs; to predict; to foreshow or foretoken; to indicate as to happen in the future.—*v.i.* To judge or pronounce from prognostics.—**prognostication,** prog•nos′ti•kā″-shon, *n.* The act of prognosticating; that which foreshows; a foretoken; previous sign.—**prognosticative,** prog•nos′ti•kā•tiv, *a.* Having the character of a prognostic.—**prognosticator,** prog•nos′ti•kā•tėr, *n.* One who prognosticates.

program, prō′gram, *n.* [Fr. *programme,* from Gr. *programma*—*pro,* before, and *graphō,* to write.] A plan of proceedings sketched out beforehand; an outline or detailed sketch or advertisement of the order of proceedings or subjects embraced in any entertainment, performance, or public ceremony.—*v.t.* To organize data on a problem so it may be solved by an electronic computer.

progress, prog′res, *n.* [L. *progressus,* from *progredior,* I advance—*pro,* before, and *gradior,* to go, whence also *grade, gradual,* etc. GRADE.] A moving or going forward; a proceeding onward; a moving forward in growth; increase; advance in matters of any kind; course; intellectual or moral improvement; a passage from place to place; a journey.—*v.i.* (pro•gres′). To move forward or onward; to advance; to proceed in any course; to advance toward something better; to make improvement.—**progression,** pro•gresh′on, *n.* [L. *progressio.*] The act of progressing, advancing, or moving forward; progress; advance; course; passage; *math.* regular or proportional advance in increase or decrease of numbers; continued proportion, arithmetical or geometrical (thus 2, 4, 6, 8, 10 are numbers in *arithmetical progression;* 2, 4, 8, 16, etc., in *geometrical progression.*—**progressionist,** pro•gresh′on•ist, *n.* One who maintains that society is in a state of progress toward perfection.—**progressive,** pro•gres′iv, *a.* Moving forward; proceeding onward; advancing; improving; in politics, one who advocates the passage of social and economic reform legislation.—**progressively,** pro•gres′iv•li, *adv.*—**progressiveness,** pro•gres′iv•nes, *n.* The state or quality of being progressive.

prohibit, prō•hib′it, *v.t.* [L. *prohibeo, prohibitus—pro,* before, and *habeo,* I have, I hold. HABIT.] To forbid authoritatively; to interdict by authority (to *prohibit* a person from doing a thing; to *prohibit* the thing being done); to prevent; to preclude.—**prohibition,** prō•hi•bish′on, *n.* The act of prohibiting; a declaration to hinder some action; interdict; the Eighteenth Amendment of the United States Constitution, in effect from 1919 to 1933, which forbade the manufacture, sale or transportation of intoxicating liquors for use as beverages.—**prohibitionist,** *n.*—**prohibitive, prohibitory,** prō•hib′i•tiv, prō•hib′i•to•ri, *a.* Serving to prohibit; forbidding; implying prohibition.

project, pro•jekt′, *v.t.* [L. *projicio, projectum,* to cast forth, to cause to jut out—*pro,* forward, and *jacio,* to throw (as in *eject, reject,* etc.). JUT.] To throw out or forth; to cast or shoot forward; to scheme; to contrive; to devise; to exhibit or give a delineation of on a surface; to delineate.—*v.i.* To shoot forward; to extend beyond something else; to jut; to be prominent.—*n.* (proj′ekt). [O.Fr. *project,* Mod.Fr. *projet.*] That which is projected or devised; a plan; a scheme; a design.—**projectile,** pro•jek′til, *a.* Impelling forward (a *projectile* force); caused by impulse (*projectile* motion).—*n.* A body projected or impelled through the air, as a stone thrown from the hand or a sling, a bullet discharged from a cannon.—**projection,** pro•jek′shon, *n.* [L. *projectio.*] The act of projecting, throwing, or shooting forward; the state of projecting or jutting out; a part projecting or jutting out; a prominence; the act of projecting or scheming; the representation of something by means of lines, etc., drawn on a surface; especially the representation of any object on a perspective plane; the delineation of the earth's surface or a portion of it by a map. See GNOMONIC, ORTHOGRAPHIC, STEREOGRAPHIC.—**projector,** pro•jek′tėr, *n.* One who projects; one who forms a scheme or design; an optical device for throwing pictures on a screen; a sort of magic lantern.

prolapse, prolapsus, pro•laps′, pro•lap′sus, *n.* [L. *prolapsus—pro,* forward, and *labor, lapsus,* to slip, fall. LAPSE.] *Med.* a falling down of some internal organ from its proper position; a falling down of the womb.—*v.i.—prolapsed, prolapsing.* To fall down or out; to suffer a prolapse.

prolate, prō′lāt, *a.* [L. *prolatus—pro,* forth, and *latus,* carried.] Extended beyond the line of an exact sphere.—*Prolate spheroid,* a spheroid produced by the revolution of a semi-ellipse about its larger diameter; a sphere that projects too much at the poles. See OBLATE.

proleg, prō′leg, *n.* [L. *pro,* for, and E. *leg.*] One of the leglike organs of certain larvae, used in walking, but which disappear in the perfect insect.

prolegomenon, prō•le•gom′e•non, *n.* pl. **prolegomena,** prō•le•gom′e•na. [Gr., from *pro,* before, and *legō,* to speak.] A preliminary observation: chiefly used in plural, and applied to an introductory discussion or discourse prefixed to a book or treatise.—**prolegomenous,** prō•le•gom′e•nus, *a.* Introductory.

prolepsis, prō•lep′sis, *n.* [Gr. *prolēpsis,* preconception—*pro,* before, and *lambanō,* I take.] Something of the nature of an anticipation; *rhet.* a figure by which a thing is represented as already done, though in reality it is to follow as a consequence of the action which is described ('he washed himself *clean*'); a figure by which objections are anticipated; an anachronism.—**proleptic,** prō•lep′tik, *a.* Pertaining to prolepsis; anticipatory.

proletarian, prō•le•tâ′ri•an, *a.* [L. *proletarius,* a citizen of the lowest class, one useful to the state only by producing children, from *proles,* offspring, from *pro,* before, and *ol,* root of *adolesce.* ADULT.] Pertaining to the proletarians.—*n.* A member of the wage-earning class; a wage earner who does not possess capital; formerly, one of the rabble.—**proletarianism,** prō•le•tâ′ri•an•izm, *n.* The condition or political influence of the lower orders of the community.—**proletariat,** prō•le•tâ′ri•at, *n.* Proletarians collectively; the lower classes.

proliferation, prō•lif′ėr•ā″shon, *n.* [L. *proles, prolis,* offspring, and *ferre,* to bear.] Reproduction by continued cell division or budding; the production of proliferous growths.—**proliferous,** prō•lif′ėr•us, *a. Bot.* bearing or producing something abnormal or adventitious (as a flower within another flower).

prolific, prō•lif′ik, *a.* [Fr. *prolifique;* L. *prolificus—proles,* offspring, and *facio,* to make. PROLETARIAN.] Producing young or fruit, especially in abundance; fruitful; productive; serving to give rise or origin; having the quality of generating abundantly (a topic *prolific* of controversy).—**prolifically,** prō•lif′i•kal•li, *adv.* In a prolific manner.—**prolificness,** prō•lif′ik•nes, *n.*

prolix, prō•liks′, *a.* [L. *prolixus,* extended, prolix—*pro,* forth, and root of *liqueo,* to flow. LIQUID.] Long and wordy; extending to a great length; diffuse; indulging in lengthy discourse; discussing at great length; tedious.—**prolixity, prolixness,** prō•lik′si•ti, prō•liks′nes, *n.* The state or quality of being prolix.—**prolixly,** prō•liks′li, *adv.* In a prolix manner.

prolocutor, prō•lok′ū•tėr, *n.* [L., from *proloquor—pro,* for, and *loquor, locutus,* to speak. LOQUACIOUS.] One who speaks for another†; the speaker or chairman of a convocation.

prologue, prō′log, *n.* [Fr., *prologue,* L. *prologus,* from Gr. *prologos—pro,* before, and *legō,* to speak.] A preface or introduction; the discourse or poem spoken before a dramatic performance or play begins; the speaker of a prologue.—*v.t.—prologued, prologuing.* To introduce with a formal prologue; to preface.—**prologize,** prō′log•īz, *v.i.—prologized, prologizing.* To deliver a prologue.

prolong, pro•long′, *v.t.* [Fr. *prolonger*—L. *pro,* forth, and *longus.* LONG.] To lengthen in time; to extend the duration of; to lengthen out; to put off to a distant time; to extend in space or length (to *prolong* a line).—*v.i.* To put off to a distant time.—**prolongation,** prō•long•gā′shon, *n.* The act of prolonging; a part prolonged; an extension.—**prolonger,** prō•long′ėr, *n.* One who or that which prolongs.

prolusion, pro•lū′zhon, *n.* [L. *prolusio,* a prelude—*pro,* before, and *ludo, lusum,* to play. LUDICROUS.] A prelude or preliminary; a preliminary trial.

prom, prom, *n.* [From *prom*enade.] An American school dance or ball (colloq.)

promenade, prom•e•näd′, *n.* [Fr., from *promener,* from L. *pro,* forward, and *minare,* to drive, from *mina,* a threat. MENACE.] A walk for pleasure and show or exercise; a place for walking in public.—*v.i.—promenaded, promenading.* To walk for amusement, show, or exercise.

Promethean, prō•mē′thē•an, *a.* [From *Prometheus* of Greek mythology, lit. the forethinker, who stole fire from heaven and imparted it to mortals.] Pertaining to Prometheus; pertaining to fire or heat.

promethium, pro•mē′thi•um, *n.* [PROMETHEAN.] A metallic element of the rare-earth series, a fission product of uranium. Symbol, Pm; at. no., 61.

prominence, prom′i•nens, *n.* [L. *prominentia,* from *promineo—pro,* forward, and *minere,* to project. EMINENT.] A standing out from the surface of something; that which juts out; protuberance; state of being distinguished among men; conspicuousness; distinction.—**prominent,** prom′i•nent, *a.* [L. *prominens.*] Standing out beyond the line or surface of something; jutting; protuberant; distinguished above others (a *prominent* character); likely to attract special attention from size, position, etc.; striking; conspicuous.—**prominently,** prom′i•nent•li, *adv.* In a prominent manner.

promiscuous, pro•mis′kū•us, *a.* [L. *promiscuus,* from *promisceo—pro,* and *misceo,* to mix. MIX.] Consisting of individuals united in a body or mass without order; mingled indiscriminately; forming part of a confused crowd or mass; random; indiscriminate; not restricted to an individual.—**promiscuously,** pro•mis′kū•us•li, *adv.* In a promiscuous manner.—**promiscuousness, promiscuity,** prō•mis′kū•us•nes, prō•mis•kū′i•ti, *n.* The state of being promiscuous.

promise, prom'is, *n.* [Fr. *promesse,* from L. *promissus,* put forward—*pro,* before, and *mittere,* to send. MISSION.] A declaration, written or verbal, made by one person to another, which binds the person who makes it to do or forbear a certain act specified; a declaration that something will be done or given for the benefit of another; ground or basis of expectation; earnest; pledge; that which affords a ground for expectation of future distinction (a youth of great *promise*).—*v.t.*—*promised, promising.* To make a promise of; to engage to do, give, grant, or procure for some one; to afford reason to expect (the year *promises* a good harvest).—*v.i.* To make a promise; to assure one by a promise; to afford hopes or expectations.—*I promise you,* I declare to you; I assure you.—**promisee,** prom•is•ē', *n.* The person to whom a promise is made.—**promiser,** prom'is•ėr, *n.* One who promises.—**promising,** prom'-is•ing, *a.* Giving promise; affording reasonable ground of hope for the future; looking as if likely to turn out well.—**promisingly,** prom'is•ing•li, *adv.* In a promising manner.—**promissory,** prom'is•o•ri, *a.* Containing a promise or binding declaration of something to be done or foreborne.—*Promissory note,* a writing which contains a promise of the payment of money to a certain person at a specified date.

promontory, prom'on•tō•ri, *n.* [L. *promontorium*—*pro,* forward, and *mons, montis,* a mountain. MOUNT.] A high point of land or rock projecting into the sea beyond the line of coast; a headland.

promote, pro•mōt', *v.t.*—*promoted, promoting.* [L. *promotus,* pp. of *promovere,* to move forward—*pro,* forward, and *movere,* to move. MOVE.] To contribute to the growth, enlargement, increase, or power of; to forward; to advance; to help onward; to excite; to stir up (as strife); to exalt or raise to a higher post or position; to elevate.—**promoter,** pro•mō'tėr, *n.* One who or that which promotes; an encourager; one that aids in promoting some financial undertaking; one engaged in getting up a joint-stock company.—**promotion,** pro•mō'shon, *n.* The act of promoting; advancement; encouragement; exaltation in rank or honor; preferment.—**promotive,** pro•mō'-tiv, *a.* Tending to advance or promote.

prompt, promt, *a.* [Fr. *prompt,* from L. *promptus,* brought out, ready, quick, from *promo, promptum,* to bring forth—*pro,* forth, and *emo,* to take. EXEMPT.] Ready and quick to act as occasion demands; acting with cheerful alacrity; ready and willing; performed without delay; quick; ready; not delayed.—*v.t.* To move or excite to action or exertion; to incite; to instigate; to assist a speaker when at a loss by pronouncing the words forgotten or next in order (to *prompt* an actor); to dictate; to suggest to the mind.—*n. Com.* an agreement in which one party engages to sell certain goods at a given price, and the other party to take them up and pay at a specified date.—**prompter,** prom'tėr, *n.* One that prompts; specifically, one placed behind the scenes in a theater, whose business is to assist the actors when at a loss by uttering the first words of a sentence or words forgotten.—**promptitude,** prom'ti•tūd, *n.* Readiness; quickness of decision and action when occasion demands; readiness of will; cheerful alacrity.—**promptly,** promt'li, *adv.* In a prompt manner.—**promptness,** promt'nes, *n.* The state or quality of being prompt; promptitude.

promulgate, prō•mul'gāt, *v.t.*—*promulgated, promulgating.* [L. *promulgo, promulgatus;* origin unknown.] To make known by open declaration, as laws, decrees, tidings, etc.; to publish abroad; to announce; to proclaim.—**promulgation,** prō•mul•gā'shon, *n.* The act of promulgating; publication; open declaration.—**promulgator,** prō'mul•gā•tėr or prō•mul'-gā•tėr, *n.* One who promulgates or publishes abroad.—**promulge,** prō•mulj', *v.t.*—*promulged, promulging.* To promulgate.

pronation, prō•nā'shon, *n.* [From L. *pronus,* prone, having the face downward. PRONE.] That motion of the arm whereby the palm of the hand is turned downward; position of the hand with the thumb toward the body and the palm downward.—**pronator,** prō•nā'tėr, *n.* A muscle of the forearm which turns the palm downward.

prone, prōn, *a.* [L. *pronus,* hanging or leaning forwards, prone, from *pro,* before, forward; cog. Gr. *prēnēs,* Skr. *pravana,* prone.] Bending forward; lying with the face downward; rushing or falling headlong or downward; sloping downward; inclined; inclined by disposition or natural tendency; propense; disposed: usually in a bad sense (men *prone* to evil, *prone* to strife).—**pronely,** prōn'li, *adv.* In a prone manner or position.—**proneness,** prōn'nes, *n.* The state of being prone; inclination; propensity; readiness.

pronephros, prō•nef'ros, *n.* [L. *pro,* before, Gr. *nephros,* a kidney.] In vertebrates, the first of three successive renal organs; the 'head' kidney.

prong, prong, *n.* [A nasalized form of prov.E. *prog,* to prod; W. *procio,* to thrust, to poke.] A sharp-pointed instrument; the spike of a fork or of a similar instrument; a pointed projection (the *prongs* of a deer's antlers).—*v.t.* To stab, as with a fork.—**pronghorn,** *n.* A species of hollow-horned antelope which inhabits the western parts of North America.

pronominal, prō•nom'i•nal, *a.* [L. *pronomen,* a pronoun. PRONOUN.] Belonging to or of the nature of a pronoun.—**pronominally,** prō•nom'-i•nal•li, *adv.* With the effect of a pronoun.

pronoun, prō'noun, *n.* [From *pro,* for, and *noun;* L. *pronomen,* a pronoun—*pro,* for, and *nomen,* a name, a noun.] *Gram.* one of a certain class of words or generalized terms often used instead of a noun or name, to prevent the repetition of it: classified under the heads of *personal, relative, interrogative, possessive, demonstrative, distributive,* and *indefinite* pronouns, the last four classes being commonly called *adjective pronouns* or *pronominal adjectives.*

pronounce, pro•nouns', *v.t.*—*pronounced, pronouncing.* [Fr. *prononcer,* from L. *pronuntio, pronuntiatus*—*pro,* before, and *nuntio,* to declare. NUNCIO.] To form or articulate by the organs of speech; to utter; to speak; to utter formally, officially, or solemnly (the court *pronounced* sentence of death); to declare or affirm (he *pronounced* it a forgery).—*v.i.* To speak with confidence or authority; to utter an opinion; to use a certain pronunciation.—**pronounceable,** pro•nouns'a•bl, *a.* Capable of being pronounced.—**pronounced,** pro•-nounst', *a.* [Fr. *prononcé,* pronounced.] Strongly marked or defined; decided (a man of *pronounced* views).—**pronouncement,** pro•nouns'ment, *n.* The act of pronouncing; a formal announcement.—**pronouncer,** prō•-nouns'ėr, *n.* One who pronounces.—**pronunciation,** pro•nun'si•ā"shon, *n.* The act of pronouncing or uttering with articulation; the mode of uttering words or letters.

pronucleus, prō•nū'kli•us, *n.* [L. *pro,* before, *nucleus.*] One of the two nuclei seen in the course of fertilization of an ovum, the *female pronucleus* belonging to the ovum itself, and the *male pronucleus* to the sperm.

pronunciamento, prō•nun'shi•a•-men"to, *n.* [Sp. *pronunciamiento*]. A manifesto or proclamation.

pronto, pron'tō, *a.* and *adv.* [Sp.] Quick; quickly; right away.

proof, pröf, *n.* [O.E. *profe,* Fr. *preuve,* L.L. *proba.* PROVE.] Any effort, process, or operation that ascertains truth or fact; a test; a trial; what serves as evidence; what proves or establishes; that which convinces the mind and produces belief; a test applied to certain manufactured or other articles; the act of testing the strength of alcoholic spirits: hence, also the degree of strength in spirit; *printing,* a rough impression of type, in which errors may be detected and marked for correction; *engr.* an impression taken from an engraving to prove the state of it; an early impression, or one of a limited number taken before the letters to be inserted are engraved on the plate; called a *proof-impression,* and considered the best, because taken before the plate is worn.—*a.* Impenetrable; able to resist, physically or morally (*proof against* shot, *against* temptation).—**proofreader,** *n.* One who reads and marks corrections on printers' proofs.—**proof sheet,** *n.* *Printing,* a rough impression of composed type, taken to see if any errors remain for correction.—**proof spirit,** *n.* Alcoholic liquor, or mixture of alcohol and water, of certain standard strength, in U. S., 50% by volume.

prop, prop, *n.* [Same as Ir. *propa,* Gael. *prop,* a prop.] That which sustains an incumbent weight; a fulcrum; a support; a stay.—*v.t.*—*propped, propping.* To support by placing something under or against; to support by standing under or against; to support or sustain, in a general sense.

propaedeutics, prō•pē•dū′tiks, *n.* [Gr. *propaideuō,* to instruct beforehand, from *pro,* before, and *paideuō,* to educate, from *pais, paidos,* a child.] The preliminary learning connected with any art or science.—**propaedeutic, propaedeutical,** prō•pē•dū′tik, prō•pē•dū′ti•kal, *a.* Pertaining to propaedeutics; instructing beforehand.

propaganda, prop•a•gan′da, *n.* [From the congregatio de *propaganda* fide, at Rome. PROPAGATE.] The dissemination and the defense of beliefs, opinions, or actions deemed salutary to the program of a particular group; the propagation of doctrines and tenets of special interests, as an effort to give credence to information partly or wholly fallacious. [*cap.*] Originally, an institution of the Roman Catholic Church, established as a proselyting agency, now, [*not cap.*] generally an intensive undertaking of political partisans.—**propagandist,** *n.* One who devotes himself to the spread of any system of principles or set of actions; publicity agent.—**propagandize,** *v.t.* To present with propaganda.

propagate, prop′a•gāt, *v.t.*—*propagated, propagating.* [L. *propagare, propagatus,* to peg down, to propagate—*pro,* before, and *pag,* root of *pango,* to fasten, fix, set, plant (seen in *paction, compact, impinge,* etc.).] To continue or multiply by generation or successive reproduction; to cause to reproduce itself: applied to animals and plants; to spread from person to person or from place to place; to diffuse; to generate, beget, produce, originate.—*v.i.* To have young or issue; to be reproduced or multiplied by generation, or by new shoots or plants.—**propagation,** prop•a•gā′shon, *n.* The act of propagating; the multiplication of the kind or species by generation or reproduction; the spreading or extension of anything; diffusion.—**propagator,** prop′a•gā•tėr, *n.* One who propagates.—**propagable,** prop′a•ga•bl, *a.*

propane, prō′pān, *n.* [*Prop*yl and meth*ane*.] *Chem.* a gaseous hydrocarbon, $CH_3CH_2CH_3$, of the methane series, found in crude petroleum.

propel, pro•pel′, *v.t.*—*propelled, propelling.* [L. *propello*—*pro,* forward, and *pello,* to drive, as in *compel, dispel, impel,* etc. PULSATE.] To drive forward; to urge or press onward by force.—**propellant,** pro•pel′ant, *n.* An explosive for projectile propulsion; also rocket-engine fuel. —**propellent,** pro•pel′ent, *a.* Driving forward; propelling. —**propeller,** pro•pel′ėr, *n.* One who or that which propels; a screw for propelling a motor-driven vessel; a rotary fan for propelling an airplane.

propense, pro•pens′, *a.* [L. *propensus,* hanging forwards, projecting, from *propendeo*—*pro,* forward, and *pendeo,* to hang. PENDANT.] Leaning toward, in a moral sense; inclined; disposed, either to good or evil; prone.—**propension,** pro•pen′shon, *n.* The state of being propense; propensity.—**propensity,** pro•pen′si•ti, *n.* Bent of mind, natural or acquired; inclination; natural tendency or disposition, particularly to evil.

proper, prop′ėr, *v.* [Fr. *propre,* from L. *proprius,* one's own, peculiar, proper; allied to *prope,* near. PROPINQUITY.] Peculiar; naturally or essentially belonging to a particular individual or state; natural; particularly suited to or befitting; belonging to as one's own; *gram.* applied to a noun when it is the name of a particular person or thing (Shakespeare, Boston), as opposed to *common;* fit; suitable; adapted; appropriate; correct; just; according to right usage; hence, properly so called; real; actual (the garden *proper*); *bot.* single, or connected with something single.—*Proper motion* (*astron.*), the real motion of the sun, planets, etc., as opposed to their apparent motions.—**properly,** prop′ėr•li, *adv.* In a proper manner; fitly; suitably; rightly; in a strict sense; strictly.—**property,** prop′ėr•ti, *n.* [Fr. *propriété,* L. *proprietas,* from *proprius,* one's own.] A peculiar quality of anything; that which is inherent in a thing, or naturally essential to it; an attribute; the exclusive right of possessing, enjoying, and disposing of a thing; ownership; the subject of such a right; the thing owned; an estate, whether in lands, buildings, goods, money, etc.; in *theaters,* a stage requisite; any article necessary to be produced in some scene.—**propertied,** prop′ėr•tid, *a.* Possessed of property.

prophecy, prof′e•si, *n.* [O.Fr. *prophecie, prophetie,* L. *prophetia,* from Gr. *prophēteia,* from *prophētēs,* a prophet —*pro,* before, and *phēmi,* to tell; same root as *fame.*] A foretelling; a declaration of something to come; especially, a foretelling inspired by God; a book of prophecies; *Scrip.* interpretation of Scripture; exhortation or instruction (O.T.).—**prophesier,** prof′e•sī•ėr, *n.* One who predicts events.—**prophesy,** prof′e•sī, *v.t.*—*prophesied, prophesying.* To foretell; to predict.—*v.i.* To utter predictions; to make declaration of events to come; *Scrip.* to interpret or explain Scripture or religious subjects.—**prophet,** prof′et, *n.* [L. *propheta,* from Gr. *prophētēs.*] One who foretells future events; a predictor; a foreteller; a person inspired or instructed by God to announce future events; *Scrip.* an interpreter. —*Minor prophets,* the authors of the last twelve books of the Old Testament, as opposed to Isaiah, Jeremiah, and Ezekiel.—**prophetess,** prof′et•es, *n.* A female prophet.—**prophetic, prophetical,** pro•fet′ik, pro•fet′i•kal, *a.* Pertaining or relating to a prophet or prophecy; having the character of prophecy; containing prophecy.—**prophetically,** pro•fet′i•kal•li, *adv.* In a prophetic manner; by way of prediction.

prophylactic, prō•fi•lak′tik, *a.* [Gr. *prophylaktikos*—*pro,* before, and *phylassō,* to guard.] *Med.* preventive; defending from or warding off disease.—*n.* A medicine which preserves or defends against disease; a preventive.—**prophylaxis,** prō•fi•lak′sis, *n.* [Gr.] Preventive or preservative treatment.

propinquity, prō•pin′kwi•ti, *n.* [L. *propinquitas,* from *propinquus,* near, from *prope,* near; whence also (ap)-*proach.* PROXIMITY.] Nearness in place; neighborhood; nearness in time; nearness of blood; kindred.

propitiate, pro•pish′i•āt, *v.t.*—*propitiated, propitiating.* [L. *propitio, propitiatum,* to propitiate, from *propitius,* propitious, from *pro,* forward, and *peto,* to seek, primarily referring to a bird whose flight is of happy augury. PETITION.] To appease and render favorable; to make propitious; to conciliate.—**propitiation,** pro•pish′i•ā″shon, *n.* The act of propitiating; *theol.* the atonement or atoning sacrifice offered to God to assuage his wrath and render him propitious to sinners.—**propitiator,** pro•pish′i•ā•tėr, *n.* One who propitiates.—**propitiatory,** pro•pish′i•a•to•ri, *a.* Having the power to make propitious; serving to propitiate.—*n.* *Jewish antiq.* the mercy seat; the lid or cover of the ark of the covenant.—**propitiable,** pro•pish′i•a•bl, *a.* Capable of being propitiated.—**propitious,** prō•pish′us, *a.* Favorably disposed toward a person; disposed to be gracious or merciful; ready to forgive sins and bestow blessings; affording favorable conditions or circumstances (a *propitious* season).—**propitiously,** pro•pish′us•li, *adv.* In a propitious manner.—**propitiousness,** pro•pish′us•nes, *n.*

propolis, prop′o•lis, *n.* [Gr. *pro,* before, and *polis,* city.] A substance having some resemblance to wax, used by bees to stop the holes and crevices in their hives.

propone, pro•pōn′, *v.t.* [L. *propono*—*pro,* before, and *pono,* to place. POSITION.] To propose; to propound.

proponent, prō•pō′nent, *n.* [L. *proponere,* to propose.] One that makes a proposal, or lays down a proposition; *law,* one who propounds something, especially one who propounds a will for probate.

proportion, pro•pōr′shon, *n.* [L. *proportio*—*pro,* before, and *portio,* part or share. PORTION.] The comparative relation of one thing to another in respect to size, quantity, or degree; a quota; symmetrical arrangement; the proper relation of parts in a whole; symmetry; that which falls to one's lot when a whole is divided according to rule; just or equal share; lot; *math.* the quality or similarity of ratios; *arith.* the rule of three, that rule which enables us to find a fourth proportional to three given numbers.—*Simple proportion,* the equality of the ratio of two quantities to that of two other quantities.—*Compound proportion*, the equality of the ratio of two quantities to another ratio, the antecedent and consequent of which are respectively the products of the antecedents and consequents of two or more ratios.—*Continued proportion*, a succession of several equal ratios, as 2, 4, 8, 16, etc.—*Harmonical* or *musical proportion*. See HARMONICAL.—*Reciprocal* or *inverse proportion*. See RECIPROCAL, INVERSE.—*v.t.* To adjust in a suitable proportion; to harmoniously adjust to something else as regards dimensions or extent; to form with symmetry.—**proportionable,** pro•pōr′shon•a•bl, *a.* Capable of being proportioned; being in proportion; having a due comparative relation; corresponding; well proportioned; symmetrical.—**proportional,** pro•pōr′shon•al, *a.* Having a due proportion; being in suitable proportion or degree; *math.* having the same or a constant ratio (*proportional* quantities).—*Proportional parts*, parts of magnitude such that the corresponding ones, taken in their order, are proportional.—*n.* A quantity in proportion; *math.* one of the terms of a proportion.—*Mean proportional.* See MEAN.—**proportionality,** pro•pōr′shon•al″i•ti, *n.* The quality or state of being in proportion.—**proportionally,** pro•pōr′shon•al•li, *adv.* In proportion; in due degree; with suitable comparative relation.—**proportionate,** pro•pōr′shon•it, *a.* Having due proportion or relation; proportional. —*v.t.*—*proportionated, proportionating.* To make proportional; to adjust in due relation.—**proportionately,** pro•pōr′shon•it•li, *adv.* With due proportion.

propose, pro•pōz′, *v.t.*—*proposed, proposing.* [Fr. *proposer*, to purpose, to propose, from *pro* and *poser*. POSE, COMPOSE. *Purpose* is the same word.] To bring forward or offer for consideration or acceptance; to bring forward as something to be done, attained, or striven after: often governing an infinitive.—*v.i.* To form or declare an intention or design; to offer one's self in marriage (to *propose* to a lady).—**proposal,** pro•pō′zal, *n.* That which is proposed or offered for consideration; a scheme or design, terms or conditions proposed (*proposals* of peace, of marriage).—**proposer,** pro•pō′zėr, *n.* One that proposes.—**proposition,** prop′o•zish′on, *n.* [Partly from *propose*, partly from L. *propositio*, from *pro*, before, and *positio*, a placing. POSITION.] That which is proposed or offered for consideration, acceptance, or adoption; a proposal; term or offer advanced; *gram.* and *logic*, a form of speech in which something is affirmed or denied of a subject; *math.* a statement of either a truth to be demonstrated, or an operation to be performed.—**propositional,** prop′o•zish′on•al, *a.* Pertaining to a proposition; considered as a proposition.

propound, pro•pound′, *v.t.* [O.E. *propoune*, from L. *propono*, to put forth—*pro*, before, and *pono*, to place; as to form, comp. *compound*, *expound*. POSITION.] To offer for consideration; to propose; to put or set, as a question.—**propounder,** pro•poun′dėr, *n.* One who propounds.

propraetor, prō•prē′tor, *n.* [L. *propraetor*—*pro*, for, and *praetor*.] A Roman magistrate who, having discharged the office of praetor at home, was sent into a province to command there.

proprietary, prō•prī′e•te•ri, *n.* [Fr. *propriétaire*, a proprietor, from *propriété*, property. PROPERTY.] A proprietor; more commonly a body of proprietors collectively.—*a.* Belonging to a proprietor or owner; belonging to ownership.—**proprietor,** pro•prī′e•tėr, *n.* An owner; the person who has the legal right or exclusive title to anything.—**proprietorship,** pro•prī′e•tėr•ship, *n.* The state or right of a proprietor.—**proprietress,** pro•prī′e•tres, *n.* A female proprietor.—**propriety,** pro•prī′e•ti, *n.* [L. *proprietas*, from *proprius*, one's own.] Property‡; possession‡; suitableness to an acknowledged or correct standard; consonance with established principles, rules, or customs; fitness; justness.—pl. *The proprieties*, conformity with established customs in social life.

propulsion, pro•pul′shon, *n.* [From L. *propello*, *propulsum*. PROPEL.] The act of driving forward.—**propulsive,** pro•pul′siv, *a.* Tending or having power to propel; driving or urging on.

propylaeum, prop′i•le•um, *n.* pl. **propylaea,** prop•i′le•a. [Gr. *propylaion*, from *pro*, before, and *pylē*, a gate.] The porch, vestibule, or entrance of an edifice.

pro rata, prō rā′ta. Proportionately; in accordance with some determined standard, such as a share or liability. —**prorate,** prō•rāt′, *v.t.* and *i.* To distribute proportionately; to make a pro rata assessment.

prorogue, prō•rōg′, *v.t.*—*prorogued, proroguing.* [Fr. *proroger*, from L. *prorogare*, to prolong, continue—*pro*, before, and *rogo*, to ask. ROGATION.] To protract or prolong, to defer or delay‡; to adjourn a parliament for an indefinite period by royal authority. *British parl. practice.*—**prorogation,** prō•rō•gā′shon, *n.* The act of proroguing.

prosaic. See PROSE.

proscenium, prō•sē′ni•um, *n.* [L. *proscenium*, from Gr. *proskēnion*—*pro*, before, and *skēnē*, a scene. SCENE.] *Arch.* the part in a theater from the curtain or drop scene to the orchestra; the curtain and the ornamental framework from which it hangs. In the ancient theater the proscenium comprised the whole stage.

proscribe, prō•skrīb′, *v.t.*—*proscribed, proscribing.* [L. *proscribo*—*pro*, before, in public, and *scribo*, to write. SCRIBE.] Among the Romans, to publish the name of, as doomed to destruction and seizure of property; hence, to put out of the protection of the law; to outlaw; to reject utterly; to interdict, exclude, prohibit.—**proscriber,** prō•skrī′bėr, *n.* One who proscribes.—**proscription,** prō•skrip′shon, *n.* [L. *proscriptio*.] The act of proscribing; outlawry; exclusion; the dooming or denouncing of citizens to death and confiscation of goods, as public enemies. —**proscriptive,** prō•skrip′tiv, *a.* Pertaining to or consisting in proscription; proscribing.—**proscriptively,** prō•skrip′tiv•li, *adv.* In a proscriptive manner.

prose, prōz, *n.* [Fr. *prose*, from L. *prosa* for *prorsa* (*oratio*, speech, understood), from *prorsus*, forward, straight on—*pro*, forward, and *versus*, turned. VERSE.] The ordinary written or spoken language of man; language unconfined to poetical measure, as opposed to *verse* or *metrical composition*; hence, dull and commonplace language or discourse. —*a.* Relating to or consisting of prose; prosaic.—*v.i.*—*prosed, prosing.* To write in prose; to write or speak tediously.—**prosaic,** prō•zā′ik, *a.* In the form of prose; dull; uninteresting; commonplace.—**prosaically,** prō•zā′i•kal•li, *adv.* In a prosaic manner.—**proser,** prō′zėr, *n.* One who proses.—**prosy,** prō′zi, *a.* Like prose; dull; tedious.—**prosily,** prō′zi•li, *adv.* In a prosy manner; tediously.—**prosiness,** prō′zi•nes *n.* State or quality of being prosy.

prosecute, pros′e•kūt, *v.t.*—*prosecuted, prosecuting.* [L. *prosequor*, *prosecutus*—*pro*, before, and *sequor*, to follow. SEQUENCE. *Pursue* is the same word.] To pursue with a view to attain, execute, or accomplish; to apply to with continued purpose; to carry on; to continue; *law*, to seek to obtain by legal process; to pursue for redress or punishment before a legal tribunal.—*v.i.* To carry on a legal prosecution; to act as a prosecutor.—**prosecution,** pros•e•kū′shon, *n.* The act or process of prosecuting; the proceeding with or following up any matter in hand (the *prosecution* of a design, an inquiry, etc.); the carrying on of a suit in a court of law; the process of exhibiting formal charges against an offender before a legal tribunal; the party by whom criminal proceedings are instituted. —**prosecutor,** pros′e•kū•tėr, *n.* One who prosecutes; the person who institutes and carries on proceedings in a court of justice.

proselyte, pros′e•līt, *n.* [Fr. *prosélyte*, from Gr. *prosēlytos*, one newly come —*pros*, towards, and root of *elthein*, to come.] A new convert to some religion or religious sect, or to some particular opinion, system, or party. —**proselytism,** pros′e•līt•izm, *n.* The act or system of making proselytes; conversion to a system or creed.—**proselytize,** pros′e•līt•īz, *v.t.*—*proselytized, proselytizing.* To make a proselyte or convert of.—*v.i.* To engage in making proselytes.

prosencephalon, pros•en•sef′a•lon, *n.* [Prefix *pros*, toward, and Gr. *encephalon*.] The forebrain or anterior part of the brain.

prosenchyma, pros•en′ki•ma, *n.* [Gr. *pros*, near, and *enchyma*, an infusion.] *Bot.* tissue of fusiform or fibriform cells, as of woody tissues.

prosody, pros′o•di, *n.* [L. *prosodia*, from Gr. *prosōdia*, a song sung to music, prosody—*pros*, to, and *odē*, a song, an ode.] That part of grammar which treats of the quantity of syllables, of accent, and of the laws of versification; the rules of rhythm or versification.—**prosodiacal,** pros•-o•dī′a•kal, *a.* Pertaining to prosody. —**prosodial, prosodical,** pro•sō′di•-al, pro•sod′i•kal, *a.* Pertaining to prosody; according to the rules of prosody.—**prosodist,** pros′o•dist, *n.* One skilled in prosody.

prosopopoeia, pros′o•pō•pē″ya, *n.* [Gr. *prosōpopoiia*—*prosōpon*, person, and *poieō* to make.] A figure in rhetoric by which things inanimate are spoken of as animated beings; personification.

prospect, pros′pekt, *n.* [L. *prospectus*, from *prospicio*, to look forward—*pro*, forward, and *specio*, to see. SPECIES.] View of things within the reach of the eye; sight; that which is presented to the eye; the place and the objects seen; a looking forward; anticipation; expectation or ground of expectation (little *prospect* of success).—*v.i.* and *t.* (pros•pekt′). *Mining*, to make a search; to search for metal.—**prospective,** pros•pek′-tiv, *a.* Looking forward; being in prospect or expectation; looked forward to (*prospective* advantages).—**prospectively,** pros•pek′tiv•li, *adv.* In a prospective manner.—**prospector,** pros′pek•tėr, *n.* One who searches for precious stones or metals as preliminary to settled or continuous operations.—**prospectus,** pros•pek′tus, *n.* [L., prospect, sight, view.] A brief sketch issued for the purpose of making known the chief features of some commercial enterprise proposed, as the plan of a literary work, or the proposals of a new company or joint-stock association.

prosper, pros′pėr, *v.i.* [Fr. *prospérer*, L. *prosperare*, from *prosperus*, favorable, fortunate, from *pro*, before, and *spes*, hope.] To be successful; to succeed; to advance in wealth or any good: said of persons; to be in a successful state; to turn out successfully: said of affairs; to be in a healthy growing state; to thrive: said of plants and animals.—*v.t.* To make prosperous; to render successful.—**prosperity,** pros•per′i•ti, *n.* [L. *prosperitas.*] The state of being prosperous; good progress in any business or enterprise; success; attainment of the object desired; good fortune.—**prosperous,** pros′pėr•us, *a.* [L. *prosperus.*] Making good progress in the pursuit of anything desirable; thriving; successful; favorable; favoring success. ∴ Syn. under FORTUNATE.—**prosperously,** pros′pėr•us•li, *adv.* In a prosperous manner; successfully.—**prosperousness,** pros′pėr•us•nes, *n.* Prosperity.

prostate, prostatic, pros′tat, pros•-tat′ik, *a.* [Gr. *prostatēs*, standing before—*pro*, before, and stem *sta*, to stand.] Applied to a gland situated just before the neck of the bladder in males.

prosthesis, pros′the•sis, *n.* [Gr. *pros*, to, and *thesis*, a placing, from *tithēmi*, to place.] *Surg.* the addition of an artificial part to supply a defect of the body; *philol.* the adding of one or more letters to the commencement of a word (*be*loved).—**prosthetic,** pros•thet′ik, *a.* Pertaining to prosthesis.

prostitute, pros′ti•tūt, *v.t.*—*prostituted, prostituting.* [L. *prostituo, prostitutus*—*pro*, before, and *statuo*, to place. STATE.] To offer freely to a lewd use, or to indiscriminate lewdness for hire; to give up to any vile or infamous purpose; to sell to wickedness; to offer or expose upon vile terms or to unworthy persons.—*a.* Openly devoted to lewdness.—*n.* A female given to indiscriminate lewdness; a strumpet; a harlot; a base hireling.—**prostitution,** pros•-ti•tū′shon, *n.* The act or practice of yielding the body to indiscriminate intercourse with men for hire; the act of offering to an infamous employment.—**prostitutor,** pros′ti•tū•-tėr, *n.* One who prostitutes.

prostrate, pros′trāt, *a.* [L. *prostratus*, pp. of *prosterno*, *prostratum*, to lay flat—*pro*, before, and *sterno*, to strew. STRATUM.] Lying at length, or with the body extended on the ground; lying at mercy, as a suppliant; lying in the posture of humility or adoration; *bot.* lying flat and spreading on the ground without taking root.—*v.t.*—*prostrated, prostrating.* To lay flat or prostrate; *refl.* to throw one's self down as in humility or adoration; *fig.* to throw down; to overthrow; to ruin; to reduce to nothing (to *prostrate* one's strength).—**prostration,** pros•trā′shon, *n.* The act of prostrating or laying flat; the act of falling down, or of bowing in humility or adoration; great depression or reduction (as of strength or spirits).

prosy. See PROSE.

protactinium, prō′tak•tin″i•um, *n.* [*Proto*, first, and *actinium.*] A radioactive metallic element yielding actinium upon disintegration. Symbol, Pa; at. no., 91.

protagonist, prō•tag′o•nist, *n.* [Gr. *prōtagōnistes*—*prōtos*, first, and *agōnistēs*, an actor.] The leading character or actor in a literary work.

protasis, prō′ta•sis, *n.* [Gr. *protasis*—*pro*, before, and *teinō*, to stretch.] The first clause of a conditional sentence, being the condition on which the *apodosis* depends, as, if we run (*protasis*) we shall be in time (*apodosis*).

protean. See PROTEUS.

protect, pro•tekt′, *v.t.* [From L. *protectus*, pp. of *protego*, to protect—*pro*, before, and *tego*, to cover, from root seen also in E. *thatch.*] To cover or shield from danger or injury; to serve as a cover or shelter to; to defend; to guard.—**protectingly,** pro•tek′ting•li, *adv.* In a protecting manner.—**protection,** pro•tek′shon, *n.* The act of protecting, or state of being protected; defense; shelter from evil; that which protects or preserves from injury; a passport or other writing which secures from molestation; exemption, as from arrest in civil suits; an artificial advantage conferred by a legislature on articles of home production, usually by duties imposed on the same articles introduced from abroad.—**protectionism,** pro•tek′shon•izm, *n.* The system of protection to commodities of home production.—**protectionist,** pro•tek′shon•ist, *n.* One who favors the protection of some branch of industry by legal enactments; one opposed to free trade; tariff booster.—**protective,** pro•tek′-tiv, *a.* Affording protection; sheltering; defensive.—*Protective duties*, duties imposed on imports to prevent their obtaining an advantage in the market over commodities of home production.—*Protective substance*, an ANTITOXIN (which see).—**protector,** pro•tek′tėr, *n.* One who or that which protects; a defender; a guardian.—*Eng. hist.* one who had the care of the kingdom during the king's minority; a regent; [*cap.*] a title specifically applied to Oliver Cromwell, who assumed the title of *Lord Protector* in 1653.—**protectorate,** pro•tek′tėr•-āt, *n.* Government by a protector; the period in English history during which Cromwell was protector; the protection of a weaker country by a stronger.—**protectorship,** pro•tek′-tėr•ship, *n.* The office of a protector.

protégé, prō•te•zhā′, fem. **protégée,** prō•te•zhā′, *n.* [Fr., one protected.] One under the care and protection of another.

protein, prō′tē•in, *n.* [From Gr. *prōtos*, first.] One of a class of complex chemical compounds which contain carbon, hydrogen, nitrogen, oxygen, and sulfur, are essential constituents of living matter, and on decomposition yield various amino acids.—**proteide,** prō′tē•id, *n.* An older name for PROTEIN.

proteolytic, prō′ti•o•lit″ik, *a.* [*Protein* and Gr. *lysis*, a solution.] Of an enzyme, converting ordinary proteins into peptones.

proteose, prō′ti•ōs, *n.* [Gr. *prōtos*, first.] A class of products derived from proteins by hydrolysis.

protest, pro•test′, *v.i.* [L. *protestor*—*pro*, before, and *testor*, to affirm, from *testis*, a witness. TEST.] To affirm with solemnity; to asseverate; to make a solemn or formal declaration (often in writing) expressive of opposition to something.—*v.t.* To make a solemn declaration or affirmation of; to assert.—*To protest a bill of exchange*, to mark or note it, through a notary public, for non-payment or non-acceptance.—*n.* (prō′test). A solemn declaration of opinion, commonly against some act; a formal statement (usually in writing), by which a person declares that he dissents from an act to which he might otherwise be deemed to have yielded assent; *law*, a formal declaration that acceptance or payment of a bill or promissory note has been refused.—**protestant,** prot′es·tant, *n.* *Lit.* one who protests; [*cap.*] a name given to the party who adhered to Luther at the Reformation in 1529, and protested against a decree of the Emperor Charles V and the diet of Spires; now applied to all those Christian denominations that differ from the Church of Rome, and that sprang from the Reformation.—*a.* Belonging to the religion of the Protestants.—**Protestantism,** prot′-es·tant·izm, *n.* The principles or religion of Protestants.—**protestation,** prot·es·tā′shon, *n.* [L. *protestatio.*] A solemn declaration; an asseveration; a solemn declaration of dissent; a protest.—**protester,** pro·tes′tėr, *n.* One who protests; one who protests a bill of exchange.

Proteus, prō′ti·us, *n.* A marine deity of the ancient Greeks who had the faculty of assuming different shapes; hence, one who easily changes his form or principles; *zool.* a small amphibious animal with both lungs and gills, living in certain subterranean lakes, and having rudimentary eyes.—**protean,** prō′ti·an, *a.* Readily assuming different shapes; exceedingly variable.

prothesis, proth′e·sis, *n.* [Gr. *prothesis—pro,* forth, and *thesis,* a placing.] The place in a church on which the elements for the Eucharist are put previous to their being placed on the altar; a credence.

prothonotary, prō·thon′e·te·ri, *n.* [L.L. *protonotarius*—Gr. *prōtos,* first, and L. *notarius,* a scribe. NOTARY. The insertion of *h* is a mistake.] A chief notary or clerk; in the *R. Cath. Ch.* a sort of registrar; one of twelve constituting a college, who receive the last wills of cardinals, etc.; in the *Eastern Church,* the chief secretary of the patriarch of Constantinople. In some states of the U. S. a chief clerk of a court.

prothorax, prō·thō′raks, *n.* [Gr. *pro,* before, and *thōrax.*] *Entom.* the first or anterior segment of the thorax in insects.

protocol, prō′tō·kol, *n.* [Fr. *protocole,* L.L. *protocollum,* the first leaf, the first sheet of a legal instrument glued to the cylinder round which the document was rolled—Gr. *prōtos,* first, *kolla,* glue.] The minutes or rough draft of some diplomatic document or instrument; a document serving as a preliminary to, or for the opening of, any diplomatic transaction; a record or registry; rules of etiquette and order of preference in diplomatic ceremonies.—*v.t.*—*protocolled, protocolling.* To make a protocol of.

protomartyr, prō′tō·mär″tėr, *n.* [Gr. *prōtos,* first, and *martyr,* martyr.] The first martyr; a term applied to Stephen, the first Christian martyr; the first who suffers or is sacrificed in any cause.

protomorphic, prō·to·mor′fik, *a.* [Gr. *protos,* first, and *morphē,* shape.] In the earliest form or shape.

proton, prō′ton, *n.* A positively charged subatomic particle in the nucleus of an atom, the number of protons in the atomic nucleus of each element being different.

protonema, prō·to·nē′ma, *n.* [Gr. *protōs,* first, *nēma,* a thread.] In mosses, a threadlike structure resulting from germination of a spore.

protonotary, prō·ton′o·ta·ri, *n.* See PROTHONOTARY.

protoplasm, prō′to·plazm, *n.* [Gr. *prōtos,* first, and *plasma,* anything formed or molded, from *plassō,* to mold.] A transparent substance, a complex and unstable mixture of proteins and other compounds, and constituting the basis of living matter in animal and plant structures.—**protoplasmic,** prō·to·plaz′mik, *a.* Pertaining to, resembling, or consisting of protoplasm.—**protoplast,** prō′to·plast, *n.* An original; a thing first formed, as a copy to be imitated. —**protoplastic,** prō·to·plas′tik, *a.* First formed.

prototype, prō′to·tīp, *n.* [Gr. *prōtotypos—prōtos,* first, and *typos,* type.] An original or model after which anything is formed; a pattern; archetype.

protoxide, prō·tok′sīd, *n.* [Gr. *protos,* first, and E. *oxide.*] That member of a series of oxides having the lowest proportion of oxygen.—**protoxidize,** prō·tok′si·dīz, *v.t.*

Protozoa, prō·to·zō′a, *n. pl.* [Gr. *prōtos,* first, and *zōon,* an animal.] A phylum composed of the most lowly organized members of the animal kingdom, and which may be defined to be animals composed of a nearly structureless jelly-like substance without a definite body cavity or trace of a nervous system.

protozoan, prō·to·zō′an, *n.* [Gr. *protos,* first, and *zōon,* animal.] A member of the phylum Protozoa comprised of single-celled, microscopic animals that reproduce by fission.—**protozoic,** prō·to·zō′ik, *a.*

protract, prō·trakt′, *v.t.* [From L. *protractus,* from *protraho—pro,* forward, and *traho,* to draw (whence *trace, traction, extract,* etc.).] To draw out or lengthen in time; to prolong; to lengthen out in space; to delay, defer, put off; *surv.* to draw to a scale.—**protractile,** prō·trak′til, *a.* Capable of being protracted, or thrust forward.—**protraction,** prō·trak′shon, *n.* The act of protracting; *surv.* the act of laying down on paper the dimensions of a field, etc.—**protractive,** prō·trak′tiv, *a.* Prolonging; continuing; delaying.—**protractor,** prō·trak′tėr, *n.* One who protracts; *surv.* an instrument for laying down and measuring angles on paper; *anat.* a muscle which draws forward a part.

protrude, prō·tröd′, *v.t.*—*protruded, protruding.* [L. *protrudo—pro,* forth, forwards, and *trudo,* to thrust (seen in *obtrude, intrude*).] To thrust forward; to shoot forth or project, or cause to project.—*v.i.* To shoot forward; to stand out prominently.—**protrusile,** prō·trö′sīl, *a.* Capable of being protruded and withdrawn.—**protrusion,** prō·trö′zhon, *n.* The act of protruding.—**protrusive,** prō·trö′ziv, *a.* Thrusting or impelling forward.—**protrusively,** prō·trö′ziv·li, *adv.*

protuberate, prō·tū′bėr·āt, *v.t.*—*protuberated, protuberating.* [L.L. *protubero, protuberatus*—L. *pro,* before, and *tuber,* a hump, a swelling, akin to *tumeo,* to swell. TUMID.] To swell or be prominent beyond the adjacent surface; to bulge out —**protuberance,** prō·tū′bėr·ans, *n.* A swelling or tumor; a prominence; a bunch or knob; anything swelled or pushed beyond the surrounding or adjacent surface.—**protuberant,** prō·tū′bėr·ant, *a.* Swelling; prominent beyond the surrounding surface.—**protuberantly,** prō·tū′bėr·ant·li, *adv.*

protyle, prō′tīl, *n.* [Gr. *prōtos,* first.] A hypothetical substance supposed by Crookes to be the basis of all matter.

proud, proud, *a.* [A.Sax. *prút,* proud, whence *prȳte,* pride; cog. Dan. *prud,* stately, magnificent.] Possessing a high and often an unreasonable opinion of one's own excellence; filled with or showing inordinate self-esteem; possessing a praiseworthy self-esteem that deters from anything mean or base; haughty; arrogant; ready to boast; elated; priding one's self (*proud* of one's country); arising from pride; presumptuous; of fearless or untamable character; suggesting or exciting pride; ostentatious; grand; magnificent.—*Proud flesh,* an excessive development of granulations in wounds and ulcers.—**proudly,** proud′li, *adv.*

prove, pröv, *v.t.*—*proved, proving.* [O.Fr. *prover, pruver,* Fr. *prouver,* from L. *probare,* to try, test, prove, lit. to test the good quality of, from *probus,* good (whence *probity*). *Proof* is a derivative.] To try or ascertain by an experiment; to test; to make trial of (to *prove* gunpowder); to establish the truth or reality of by reasoning, induction, or evidence; to demonstrate; to establish the authenticity or validity of; to obtain probate of (to *prove* a will); to gain personal experience of; *arith.* to show or ascertain the correctness of by a further calculation.—*The exception proves the rule,* lit. the exception tests or tries the rule.—*v.i.* To be found or ascertained by experience or trial; to turn out to be (the report *proved* to be false); to attain certainty.—**provable,** prö′va·bl, *a.* Capable of being proved.—**proven,** prö′vn, *pp.* [A strong form for *proved,* the proper pp. Its usage in English is rare.] Proved.—*Not proven, Scots law,* a verdict given by a jury in a criminal case when, although there is a deficiency of evidence to convict the prisoner, there is sufficient to warrant grave suspicion of his guilt.—**prover,** prö′vėr, *n.* One who or that which proves. —**proving ground,** *n.* A place for scientific testing and experiment, hence, a practical test for something.

provenance, prov′e·nans, *n.* [Fr.—L. *pro,* and *venio,* to come.] Source or place of origin; quarter whence something is got.

Provencal, pro·van·säl′, *n.* A native

of Provence, or Southern France; the Romance language of Provence.

provender, prov'en•dėr, *n.* [From Fr. *provende* (with *r* somewhat unaccountably added), from L. *praebenda*, things to be supplied. PREBEND.] Dry food for beasts, as hay, straw, and corn; provisions; food.

proventriculus, prō'ven•trik"ū•lus, *n.* [Gr. *pro*, in front of, L. *ventriculus*, a stomach.] In birds, the first or chemical stomach.

proverb, prov'erb, *n.* [Fr. *proverbe*, L. *proverbium*—*pro*, before, in public, and *verbum*, a word.] A short pithy sentence expressing a truth ascertained by experience or observation; a sentence which briefly and forcibly expresses some practical truth; a wise saw; an adage; a maxim; a short dramatic composition in which some proverb or popular saying is taken as the foundation of the plot; a by-word; a reproach or object of contempt; *Scrip.* a dark saying of the wise that requires interpretation.—**proverbial,** pro•vėr'bi•al, *a.* Comprised in a proverb; used or current as a proverb; resembling a proverb.—**proverbially,** pro•vėr'bi•al•li, *adv.* In a proverbial manner or style; by way of proverb.

provide, pro•vīd', *v.t.*—*provided, providing.* [L. *provideo*, lit. to see before—*pro*, before, and *video, visum*, to see (whence *vision, visible, revise*, etc.).] To procure beforehand; to prepare (to *provide* warm clothing); to furnish; to supply (well *provided* with corn); to lay down as a previous arrangement; to make a previous condition or understanding.—*v.i.* To make provision; to take measures beforehand (we must *provide for* our wants, *against* mishaps).—**provided,** pro•vī'ded, *conj.* [A conjunction only by ellipsis = it being provided that.] On condition; on these terms; this being conceded.—**providence,** prov'i•dens, *n.* [L. *providentia.*] Foresight‡; timely care or preparation‡; prudence; the care of God over his creatures; divine superintendence; [*cap.*] God, regarded as exercising forecast, care, and direction for and over his creatures; the divine being or power; something due to an act of providential intervention; a providential circumstance.—**provident,** prov'i•dent, *a.* [L. *providens*, ppr. of *provideo*, I provide; the same word as *prudent*, as *providence* = *prudence.*] Foreseeing wants and making provision to supply them; prudent in preparing for future exigencies; frugal; economical.—**providential,** prov•i•den'shal, *a.* Effected by the providence of God; referable to divine providence.—**providentially,** prov•i•den'shal•li, *adv.* In a providential manner.—**providently,** *adv.* In a provident manner; with prudent foresight.—**provider,** pro•vī'dėr, *n.* One who provides.

province, prov'ins, *n.* [Fr., from L. *provincia*, a province—*pro*, before, and *vinco*, I conquer.] Originally, a region reduced under Roman dominion and subjected to the command of a governor sent from Rome; hence, a territory at some distance from the metropolis (*the provinces* being often thus used in contradistinction to the metropolis); a large territorial or political division of a state; in England, a division for ecclesiastical purposes under the jurisdiction of an archbishop, there being two *provinces*, that of Canterbury and that of York; *fig.* the proper duty, office, or business of a person; sphere of action; a division in any department of knowledge or speculation; a department.—**provincial,** pro•vin'shal, *a.* Pertaining to a province; forming a province; exhibiting the manners of a province; characteristic of the inhabitants of a province; rustic; not polished; rude; pertaining to an ecclesiastical province or to the jurisdiction of an archbishop.—*n.* A person belonging to a province as distinguished from the metropolis; in some religious orders, a monastic superior in a given district.—**provincialism,** pro•vin'shal•izm, *n.* A peculiar word or manner of speaking in a district of country remote from the principal country or from the metropolis.—**provinciality,** pro•vin'shi•al"i•ti, *n.* The quality of being provincial.—**provincially,** pro•vin'shal•li, *adv.* In a provincial manner.

provision, pro•vizh'on, *n.* [L. *provisio, provisionis*, a foreseeing, foresight, purveying, from *providere, provisum*, to foresee. PROVIDE.] The act of providing or making previous preparation; a measure taken beforehand; provident care; accumulation of stores or materials beforehand; a store or stock; a stock of food provided; hence, victuals; food: usually in the plural; a stipulation or measure proposed in an enactment or the like; a proviso.—*v.t.* To provide with things necessary, especially victuals or food.—**provisional,** pro•vizh'on•al, *a.* Provided for present need or for the occasion; temporarily established; temporary.—**provisionally,** pro•vizh'on•al•li, *adv.* In a provisional manner; for the present exigency; temporarily.—**provisionary,** pro•vizh'on•e•ri, *a.* Provisional; provident.

proviso, pro•vī'zō, *n.* [L. *provisus*, pp. of *provideo*, ablative *proviso*, it being provided. PROVIDE.] An article or clause in any statute, agreement, contract, grant, or other writing, by which a condition is introduced; a conditional stipulation.—**provisory,** pro•vī'zo•ri, *a.* Temporary; provisional; conditional.

provoke, pro•vōk', *v.t.*—*provoked, provoking.* [Fr. *provoquer*, from L. *provoco*, I call forth, challenge, excite—*pro*, forth, and *voco*, to call. VOICE.] To challenge‡; to summon‡; to stimulate to action; to induce by motive; to excite or arouse (as hunger); to call forth; to instigate; to excite to anger or passion; to irritate; to enrage.—*v.i.* To produce anger.—**provoker,** pro•vō'kėr, *n.* One who or that which provokes.—**provoking,** pro•vō'king, *p.* and *a.* Having the power of exciting resentment; annoying; vexatious; exasperating.—**provokingly,** pro•vō'king•li, *adv.* In a provoking manner; annoyingly.—**provocation,** prov•o•kā'shon, *n.* The act of provoking; anything that excites anger; cause of resentment; incitement; stimulus.—**provocative,** pro•vōk'a•tiv, *a.* Serving to provoke; exciting; apt to incense or enrage.—*n.* Anything that tends to excite appetite or passion; a stimulant.

provost, prov'ost, *n.* [O.Fr. *provost* (Fr. *prévôt*), from L. *praepositus*, one who is placed over others, from *praeponere*—*prae*, before, and *ponere*, to place. POSITION.] A superintendent; a university official directing educational activities; *British*, the heads of certain colleges; the chief dignitary of a cathedral or collegiate church; the chief magistrate of a Scotch burgh, corresponding to a mayor.—**provost court,** a military court for the trial of minor offenses.—**provost guard,** soldiers detailed for police duty.—**provost marshal,** *n. Milit.* an officer whose duty it is to attend to offenses committed against military discipline; *navy*, an officer who has the custody of prisoners at a court-martial.

prow, prou, *n.* [Fr. *proue*, Sp. and Pg. *proa*, from L. *prora*, from Gr. *prōra*, a prow; akin to *pro*, before.] The forepart of a ship; the bow; the beak.

prowess, prou'es, *n.* [Fr. *prouesse*, prowess, from O.Fr. *prou* (Fr. *preux*), brave; origin doubtful.] Bravery; valor; military bravery combined with skill; intrepidity and dexterity in war.

prowl, proul, *v.i.* [Origin doubtful; older forms were *proule, prolle.*] To rove or wander stealthily, as a beast in search of prey.—*v.t.* To wander stealthily over.—*n.* The act of prowling (he's on the *prowl*).—**prowler,** prou'lėr, *n.*

proximal, prok'si•mal, *a.* [L. *proximus*, nearest.] Nearest: applied to the extremity of a bone, limb, or organ of animals and plants nearest the point of attachment or insertion; opposed to *distal.*

proximate, prok'si•mit, *a.* [L. *proximatus*, pp. of *proximo*, I come near, from *proximus*, nearest, superl. of *prope*, near. PROPINQUITY.] Nearest; next.—*Proximate cause*, that which immediately precedes and produces the effect, as distinguished from the *remote, mediate*, or *predisposing cause.*—*Proximate principles*, organic compounds which are the constituents of more complex organizations, and which exist ready formed in animals and vegetables, such as albumen, gelatin, gum, starch, etc.—**proximately,** prok'si•mit•li, *adv.*—**proximity,** prok•sim'i•ti, *n.* The state of being proximate or next; immediate nearness, such as in place, time, or alliance.—**proximity fuze,** an electronic mechanism that explodes a projectile within effective range of a target.—**proxi-**

mo, prok′si•mō, *a.* In or of the next month (the 5th *proximo*).

proxy, prok′si, *n.* [Contr. from *procuracy*=L.L. *procuratia.* PROCURATOR.] The agency of a person who acts as a substitute for a principal; authority to act for another; the person deputed to act for another; a deputy; a writing by which one person authorizes another to vote in his place.—*v.i.*—*proxied, proxying.* To act by proxy.

prude, pröd, *n.* [Fr. *prude*; probably from L. *prudens*, prudent.] A person, particularly a woman, affecting great reserve and excessive virtue or delicacy of feeling, or who pretends to great propriety of conduct.—**prudery, prudishness,** prö′dėr•i, prö′dish•nes, *n.* The conduct of a prude; affected delicacy of feeling; coyness.—**prudish,** prö′dish, *a.* Pertaining to a prude; affecting excessive modesty or virtue; coy or reserved.—**prudishly,** prö′dish•li, *adv.* In a prudish manner.

prudent, prö′dent, *a.* [Fr. *prudent*, from L. *prudens, prudentis*, prudent, from *providens, providentis*, ppr. of *providere*, to foresee. PROVIDE.] Cautious or circumspect in determining on any action or line of conduct; careful of the consequences of enterprises, measures, or actions; dictated or directed by prudence (*prudent* behavior); frugal; economical; correct and decorous in manner.—**prudence,** prö′dens, *n.* [L. *prudentia*=*providentia.*] The state or quality of being prudent.—**prudential,** prö•den′shal, *a.* Proceeding from prudence; dictated or prescribed by prudence; exercising prudence.—**prudentially,** prö•den′shalli, *adv.* In conformity with prudence; prudently.—**prudently,** prö′dent•li, *adv.* In a prudent manner; discreetly; cautiously; circumspectly.

pruinose, prö•in′ōs, *a.* [From L. *pruina*, hoar-frost.] Hoary; appearing as if frosted, from a covering of minute dust.

prune, prön, *v.t.*—*pruned, pruning.* [Formerly *proine, proyne*, from Fr. *provigner*, dial. Fr. *preugner, progner*, from L. *propago, propaginis*, a slip or sucker. PROPAGATE.] To lop or cut off, as the superfluous branches of trees; to lop superfluous twigs or branches from; to trim with the knife; to clear from anything superfluous; to preen or trim, as the plumage of a bird.—**pruner,** prö′nėr, *n.* One who prunes.—**pruning hook,** *n.* An instrument for pruning trees, shrubs, etc., with a hooked blade.

prune, prön, *n.* [Fr. *prune*, from L. *prunum*, a plum. PLUM.] A plum; specifically, a dried plum.

prunella, prö•nel′a, *n.* [Fr. *prunelle, prunella*, from its color resembling that of *prunes.* PRUNE.] A kind of woolen stuff of which clergymen's gowns were once made, afterward used for the uppers of shoes; also, a twill.

prurient, prö′ri•ent, *a.* [L. *pruriens*, from *prurire*, to itch or long for a thing, to be lecherous.] Itching after something; eagerly desirous; inclined or inclining to lascivious thoughts; having lecherous imaginations.—**pruriently,** prö′ri•ent•li, *adv.* In a prurient manner; with a longing desire.—**prurience, pruriency,** prö′ri•ens, prö′ri•en•si, *n.* The state of being prurient; lascivious suggestiveness.

prurigo, prö•rī′gō, *n.* [L., an itching, the itch.] An eruption of the skin in which the papules are diffuse and intolerably itchy. — **pruriginous,** prö•rij′i•nus, *a.* Affected by prurigo; caused by prurigo.

Prussian, prush′an, *a.* Pertaining to Prussia.—*Prussian blue*, a cyanide of iron possessed of a deep-blue color, much used as a pigment.—**prussiate,** prus′i•āt or prụs′i•āt, *n.* A compound of cyanogen with iron and potassium; a cyanide.—**prussic acid,** prus′ik or prụs′ik, *a.* [Originally obtained from *Prussian* blue.] The common name for *hydrocyanic acid.*

pry, prī, *v.i.*—*pried, prying.* [A modification of M.E. *prie*, to peer. PEER.] To peep narrowly; to look closely; to attempt to discover something with scrutinizing curiosity; to open with a pry.—*n.* Narrow inspection; impertinent peeping; an instrument used for prying.—**prying,** prī′ing, *p.* and *a.* Inquisitive; curious.—**pryingly,** prī′ing•li, *adv.* In a prying manner.

psalm, säm, *n.* [L. *psalmus*, a psalm, from Gr. *psalmos*, a twitching or twanging with the fingers, from *psallein*, to play a stringed instrument, to sing to the harp.] A sacred song or hymn; [*usually cap.*] especially one of the hymns composed by King David and other Jewish writers, a collection of 150 of which constitutes a book of the Old Testament; also applied to versifications of the scriptural psalms composed for the use of churches.—**psalmist,** säm′ist or säl′mist, *n.* A writer or composer of psalms.—**psalmodist,** säm′od•ist or säl′mod•ist, *n.* One who writes psalms.—**psalmody,** säm′o•di or säl′mo•di, *n.* The singing or writing of psalms; psalms collectively.

Psalter, sạl′tėr, *n.* [L. *psalterium*, Gr. *psaltērion*, a kind of harp, from *psallō.* PSALM.] The Book of Psalms, a book containing the Psalms separately printed; a version of the Psalms used in religious services.—**psalterium,** sạl•tâ′ri•um, *n.* The third stomach of ruminants, called also the *Omasum* or *Manyplies.*—**psaltery,** sạl′tėr•i, *n.* An instrument of music used by the Hebrews, the form of which is not known; a form of dulcimer.

psammite, sam′mīt, *n.* [Gr. *psammos*, sand.] *Geol.* a term used for fine-grained, fissile, clayey sandstones, in contradistinction to those which are more siliceous and gritty.

pseudo-, sū′dō, [Gr. *pseudos*, falsehood.] A Greek prefix, signifying false, counterfeit, or spurious, used in many compound words, often self-explanatory, and occasionally as an independent English word.—**pseudomorph,** sū′do•morf, *n.* [Gr. *morphē*, shape.] A deceptive or irregular form; a mineral having a form belonging, not to the substance of which it consists, but to some other substance which has wholly or partially disappeared.—**pseudomorphism,** sū•do•mor′fizm, *n.* The state of being a pseudomorph.—**pseudomorphous,** sū•do•mor′fus, *a.* Not having the true form; having the character of a pseudomorph.—**pseudonym,** sū′do•nim, *n.* [Gr. *onoma*, a name.] A false or feigned name; a name assumed by a writer.—**pseudonymity,** sū•do•nim′i•ti, *n.* The state of being pseudonymous; writing under an assumed name.—**pseudonymous,** sū•don′i•mus, *a.* [Gr. *pseudonymos*—*pseudos*, and *onoma*, name.] Bearing a false name or signature; applied to an author who publishes a book under a feigned name; also to the book itself.—**pseudopod,** sū′do•pod, *n.* [Gr. *pous, podos*, foot.] An animal with pseudopodia.—**pseudopodia,** sū•do•pō′di•a, *n. pl. Zool.* the organs of locomotion characteristic of the lower Protozoa, consisting of threads or processes projected from any part of the body.

psi, sī, psī, psē, *n.* [Gr.] The twenty-third letter of the Greek alphabet.

psilanthropist, sī•lan′throp•ist, *n.* [Gr. *psilos*, bare, mere, and *anthrōpos*, man.] One who believes that Christ was a mere man; a humanitarian.—**psilanthropism, psilanthropy,** sī•lan′throp•izm, sī•lan′thro•pi, *n.*

psittaceous, sit•tā′shus, *a.* [L. *psittacus*, from Gr. *psittakos*, a parrot.] Belonging to the parrot tribe.

psoas, sō′as, *n.* [From Gr. *psoa*, a muscle of the loin.] The name of two inside muscles of the loins.

psoriasis, sō•rī′a•sis, *n.* [Gr.] A cutaneous affection, consisting of patches of rough, amorphous scales, generally accompanied by chaps and fissures; also, the itch.

psych- or **psycho-,** sīk, sīk′o, *comb. form.* [Gr. *psychē*, breath, principle of life.] Soul; mental activities; brain; psychological methodology.—**psychiatrist,** sī•kī′a•trist, *n.* A physician specializing in psychiatry.—**psychiatry,** sī•kī′a•tri, *n.* That field of scientific thought and practice in medicine and psychology which aims to discover and/or correct mental derangements. —**psychic, psychical,** sī′kik, sī′ki•kal, *a.* [Gr. *psychikos.*] Belonging to the human soul, spirit, or mind; psychological; applied to that force by which spiritualists aver they produce 'spiritual' phenomena.—**psychoanalysis,** sī′kō•a•nal″i•sis, *n.* That process of revealing the subconscious thoughts of an individual by inducing him to relate without restraint the complete details of his life's experiences, in order to detect hidden mental conflicts which may produce disorders of mind and /or body.—**psychoanalyst,** sī′ko•an″a•list, *n.*—**psychoanalyze,** (-līz), *v.t.*—**psychogenesis,** sī•ko•jen′e•sis, *n.* [Gr. *psy-*

chē, and *genesis*, origin.] The origin or generation of the mind as manifested by consciousness.—**psychogenic,** sī•kō•jen′ik, *a.* Originating in the mind.—**psychological,** sī•kō•loj′i•kal, *a.*—*Psychological moment*, the apparently predestined and inevitable moment; the absolute nick of time: by confusion with the 'moment' or momentum impelling the will to act, in a psychological sense.—**psychologically,** sī•ko•loj′i•kal•li, *adv.* In a psychological manner.—**psychologist,** sī•kol′o•jist, *n.* One who studies, writes on, or is versed in psychology.—**psychology,** sī•kol′o•ji, *n.* [Gr. *psychē* and *logos*.] ō•jist, *n.*—**psychology,** sī•kol′o•ji, *n.* The science of the mind; the study of the mental and behavioral characteristics of an individual or group. —**psychoneurosis,** si′kō•nū•ro″sis, *n.* A mental disorder less severe than psychosis but severe enough to impair social adjustment (commonly abbreviated *neurosis*).—**psychopath,** si′kō•path, *n.* One who has a psychopathic disorder.—**psychopathic,** sī′kō•path″ik, *a.* Pertaining to psychopathy.—**psychopathy,** sī•kop′a•thē, *n.* A mental disorder characterized by an inability to restrain antisocial impulses.—**psychopharmacology,** sī′kō•fär′ma•kol″a•ji, *n.* The branch of pharmacology concerned with the effects of drugs on the mind.—**psychosis,** sī•kō′sis, *n.* Mental disorders in which social adjustment is impossible and the patient must be under medical supervision.—**psychosomatic,** si′kō•sō•mat″ik, *a.* Of the interaction of psychic and somatic phenomena.

psyche, sī′kē, *n.* [Gr. *psyche*, the soul.] The soul; [*cap.*] a sort of mythical or allegorical personification of the human soul, as a beautiful maiden, beloved by Cupid.

psychedelic, si′ki•del″ik, *a.* [Gr. *psyche*, the soul, and Gr. *delos*, visible.] Referring to expansion of the senses or mind, especially, to drugs, such as LSD, producing this effect.

psychotherapy, sī•kō•ther′a•pi, *n.* [Gr. *therapeuō*, I attend medically.] That branch of psychiatry which prescribes and administers, methods of treatment to eliminate maladjustments and to correct mental disorders.

psychrometer, sī•krom′et•ėr, *n.* [Gr. *psychros*, cool, and *metron*, measure.] An instrument for measuring the tension of the aqueous vapor in the atmosphere; a form of hygrometer.

ptarmigan, tär′mi•gan, *n.* [Gael. *termachan*, Ir. *tarmochan*, ptarmigan.] A bird of the grouse family, of a white color in winter, frequenting northern regions.

pteridologist, ter•i•dol′o•jist, *n.* [Gr. *pteris*, *pteridos*, a fern, *logos*, discourse.] One versed in the botany of the ferns.—**pteridology,** ter•i•dol′o•ji, *n.* The science of ferns.

pteridophyte, ter′i•dō•fīt, *n.* [Gr. *pteris*, fern; *phuton*, plant.] One of the Pteridophyta, the phylum of plants which includes the ferns and their allies; formerly called a vascular cryptogam.

pterodactyl, ter•o•dak′til, *n.* [Gr. *pteron*, a wing, and *daktylos*, a digit.] An extinct species of flying reptile belonging to the Mesozoic period, and exhibiting affinities to mammals, reptiles, and birds.

pteropod, ter′o•pod, *n.* [Gr. *pteron*, a wing, and *pous*, *podos*, a foot.] One of a class of mollusks which have a swimming expansion on each side of the head.

pterosaur, ter′o•sar, *n.* [Gr. *pteron*, a wing, *sauros*, a lizard.] An extinct flying reptile, such as the pterodactyl.

pterygoid, ter′i•goid, *a.* [Gr. *pteryx*, *pterygos*, a wing.] Wing-shaped; *anat.* applied to processes of the sphenoid bone which complete the osseous palate behind.

ptisan, tī′san, *n.* [L. *ptisana*, from Gr. *ptisanē*, peeled barley, barley water, from *ptissō*, to peel.] A decoction of barley with other ingredients; *med.* a drink containing little or no medicinal agent.

Ptolemaic, tol•e•mā′ik, *a.* [From *Ptolemy*, the geographer and astronomer.] Pertaining to Ptolemy.—*Ptolemaic system*, that maintained by Ptolemy, who supposed the earth to be fixed in the center of the universe, and that the sun and stars revolved around it.—**Ptolemaist,** tol•e•mā′ist, *n.* A believer in the Ptolemaic system.

ptomaine, tō′mān, *n.* [Gr. *ptōma*, a fall, a corpse, from *piptō*, to fall.] One of a class of alkaloids or organic bases which are generated in animal substances during putrefaction.—**ptomaine poisoning,** *n.* A food poisoning caused by bacteria.

ptyalin, tī′al•in, *n.* [Gr. *ptyalon*, saliva.] A ferment in saliva that converts starch into sugar.—**ptyalism,** tī′al•izm, *n.* Salivation; a morbid and copious excretion of saliva.

puberty, pū′bėr•ti, *n.* [L. *pubertas*, from *puber* or *pubes*, *puberis*, of ripe age, adult, same root as *puer*, a boy, *pullus*, a chicken.] The period in both male and female marked by the functional development of the generative system; the age at which persons are capable of begetting or bearing children.—**puberulent,** pū•bėr′ū•lent, *a. Bot.* covered with fine down.—**pubes,** pū′bēz, *n.* [L., the hair which appears on the body at puberty.] *Anat.* the middle part of the hypogastric region, so called because covered with hair at puberty; *bot.* the down or downy substance on plants; pubescence.—**pubescence,** pū•bes′ens, *n.* The state of one who has arrived at puberty; puberty; *bot.* the downy substance on plants. —**pubescent,** pū•bes′ent, *a.* Arriving at puberty; *bot.* covered with pubescence; *zool.* covered with very fine short hairs.—**pubic,** pū′bik, *a.* Pertaining to the pubes.

public, pub′lik, *a.* [Fr. *public* (masc.), *publique* (fem.), from L. *publicus*, for *populicus*, from *populus*, people. PEOPLE.] Not private; pertaining to the whole people; relating to, regarding, or affecting a state, nation, or community (the *public* service); proceeding from many or the many; belonging to people in general (a *public* subscription); open to the knowledge of all; general; common; notorious (*public* report): regarding not private interest, but the good of the community (*public* spirit); open to common use (a *public* road). —*n.* The general body of mankind or of a nation, state, or community. —**publican,** pub′li•kan, *n.* A tax collector in ancient Rome. **publication,** pub•li•kā′shon, *n.* The process of publishing; a published work.—**public defender,** *n.* A lawyer assigned to defend persons who cannot afford legal counsel.—**public domain,** *n.* Land owned by the government; the realm of rights that belong to the community.—**publicist,** pub′li•sist, *n.* An expert on public affairs; one who publicizes. —**publicity,** pub•li′si•tē, *n.* The dissemination of promotional material. —**publicize,** pub′li•sīz, *v.t.*—*publicized*, *publicizing*. To give publicity to.—**public relations,** *n.* The art of developing and maintaining good relations between the public and some person, organization, etc.—**public service,** *n.* The business of supplying a commodity or service to a community.—**public utility,** *n.* An organization that performs some public service.—**public works,** *n.* Works (schools and highways, e.g.) constructed for public use.—**publish,** pub′lish, *v.t.* To make generally known; to produce for publication. —*v.i.* To have a work accepted for publication.—**publishable,** pub′lish•a•bl, *a.* Capable of being published; fit for publication.—**publisher,** pub′lish•ėr, *n.* One who publishes; especially, one who, as the first source of supply, issues books and other literary works, maps, engravings, etc., for sale.

puce, pūs, *a.* [Fr. *puce*, from L. *pulex*, *pulicis*, a flea.] Dark-brown; reddish-brown; of a flea color.

pucka, puk′a, *a.* [Hind. *pakka*, ripe.] Solid; substantial; permanent; genuine; an Anglo-Indian term.

pucker, puk′ėr, *v.t.* [From *poke*, a bag or pocket; comp. to *purse* the lips.] To gather into small folds or wrinkles; to contract into ridges and furrows; to wrinkle.—*v.i.* To become wrinkled; to gather into folds. —*n.* A fold or wrinkle, or a collection of folds.—*To be in a pucker*, to be in a state of flutter or agitation (*colloq.*)—**puckery,** puk′ėr•i, *a.* Full of puckers or wrinkles.

puckish, puk′ish, *a.* [The name *Puck* is from W. *pwca*, Ir. *puca*, a goblin.] [*also cap.*] Resembling the fairy *Puck*; elvish; freakish.

pudding, pụd′ing, *n.* [From the Celtic; same as W. *poten*, Ir. *putag*, Gael. *putog*, a pudding; of the same root as *pod*.] An intestine; a gut of an animal; an intestine stuffed with meat, etc.; a sausage; a compound of flour or other farinaceous substance, with milk and eggs, sometimes enriched with raisins.—

pudding stone, *n.* A term now considered synonymous with conglomerate, but originally applied to a mass of flint pebbles cemented by a siliceous paste.

puddle, pud′l, *n.* [Akin to L.G. *pudel*, pool; D. *poedelen*, to puddle; comp. Ir. and Gael. *plod*, a pool.] A small collection of dirty water; a small muddy pool; clay or earth tempered with water and thoroughly wrought so as to be impervious to water; puddling.—*v.t.*—*puddled, puddling*. To make turbid or muddy; to stir up the mud or sediment in; *fig.* to befoul; to render watertight by means of puddle; to convert into wrought iron by the process of puddling.—*v.i.* To make a dirty stir. —**puddler,** pud′lėr, *n.* One who puddles; one who is employed at the process of turning cast iron into wrought iron.—**puddling,** pud′ling, *n.* The operation of working plastic clay behind piling in a cofferdam, or in other situations, to resist the penetration of water; the clay thus used; the process by which cast iron is converted into malleable iron, consisting in working it in a special furnace, hammering and rolling.—*Puddling furnace*, a kind of reverberatory furnace for puddling iron.

pudency,† pū′den•si, *n.* [L. *pudens, pudentis*; ppr. of *pudere*, to be ashamed (seen also in *impudent*)]. Modesty; shamefacedness.—**pudenda,** pū•den′da, *n. pl.* [L., lit. things to be ashamed of.] The parts of generation.

pudgy, puj′i, *a.* [Also *podgy*, probably akin to *pod, pad*.] Fat and short; thick; fleshy.

pueblo, pweb′lō, *n.* [Sp., a village.] Adobe communal apartment houses constituting the villages of U.S. southwestern Indian tribes; (cap.) any of the Indian tribes living in pueblos.

puerile, pū′ėr•il, *a.* [L. *puerilis*, from *puer*, a boy; same root as *pupus*, a boy, *pullus*, a chicken. PUPIL, PULLET.] Boyish; childish; trifling.—**puerilely,** pū′ėr•il•li, *adv*, In a puerile manner.—**puerility,** pū•ėr•il′i•ti, *n.* [L. *puerilitas*.] The state of being puerile; boyishness; that which is puerile; a childish or silly act, thought or expression; *civil law*, the period of life from the stage of infancy to puberty.

puerperal, pū•ėr′pėr•al, *a.* [L. *puerpera*, a lying-in-woman—*puer*, a boy, and *pario*, to bear.] Pertaining to childbirth.

puff, puf, *n.* [From the sound; comp. G. *puff*, a puff, a thump; Dan. *puff*, W. *pwff*, a puff.] A sudden and single emission of breath from the mouth; a sudden and short blast of wind; a fungous ball filled with dust; a puffball; a substance of loose texture, used to sprinkle powder on the hair or skin; a swelling; a kind of pastry; a loose roll of hair.—*v.i.* To blow with single and quick blasts; to blow, as an expression of scorn or contempt; to breathe with vehemence, as after violent exertion; to be dilated or inflated; to assume importance.—*v.t.* To drive with a blast of wind or air; to inflate or dilate with air; to swell or inflate, as with pride or vanity; often with *up*; to praise with exaggeration.—**puffball,** *n.* A fungus in the form of a ball which bursts when ripe, and discharges its spores in the form of fine powder.—**puffer,** puf′ėr, *n.* One that puffs.—**puffery,** puf′ėr•i, *n.* Act of puffing; extravagant praise.—**puffin,** puf′in, *n.* [In allusion to its puffed-out beak.] The common name for a genus of marine diving birds of the auk family, characterized by a bill resembling that of a parrot.—**puffiness,** puf′i•nes, *n.* State or quality of being puffy.—**puff paste,** *n.* A rich dough for making the light friable covers of tarts, etc.—**puffy,** puf′i•, *a.*

pug, pug, *n.* [A form of *Puck*, the sprite or hobgoblin.] A small, sturdy dog; a small dog which bears a resemblance in miniature to the bulldog.—**pug nose,** *n.* A snub nose.

pugaree, pug′ar•ē, pug′ėr•i, **pugree,** pug′rē, *n.* [Hind. *pagri*, a turban.] A piece of muslin cloth wound round a hat or helmet to ward off the rays of the sun. (*Anglo-Indian*.)

pugilism, pū′jil•izm, *n.* [From L. *pugil*, a pugilist; same stem as *pugnus*, a fist, *pugna*, a fight. PUGNACIOUS.] The practice of boxing or fighting with the fists.—**pugilist,** pū′jil•ist, *n.* A boxer.—**pugilistic,** pū•jil•is′tik, *a.* Pertaining to boxing.

pugnacious, pug•nā′shus, *a.* [L. *pugnax, pugnacis*, from *pugna*, a fight, from stem of *pugnus*, a fist; akin *impugn, oppugn, repugnant*, etc.] Disposed or inclined to fighting; quarrelsome.—**pugnaciously,** pug•nā′shus•li, *adv*. In a pugnacious manner.—**pugnaciousness, pugnacity,** pug•nā′shus•nes, pug•nas′i•ti, *n.* Inclination to fight; quarrelsomeness.

puisne, pū′nē, *a.* [O.Fr. *puisnē*, from *puis*, L. *post*, after, and *nē*, L. *natus*, born. (NATAL.) *Puny* is the same word.] *Law*, younger or inferior in rank; sometimes applied to certain judges.

puissant, pū′is•ant or pū•is′ant, *a.* [Fr. *puissant*, powerful: formed as if from a participle *possens, possentis*, from L. *posse*, to be able. POTENT.] Powerful; strong; mighty; forcible. —**puissantly,** pū′is•ant•li, *adv*. In a puissant manner; powerfully.—**puissance,** pū′is•ans, *n.* Power; strength; might.

puke, pūk, *v.i.*—*puked, puking*. [Akin G. *spucken*, to spit, E. *spew*.] To vomit; to retch; to be disgusted.—*v.t* To vomit or eject from the stomach.

pulchritude, pul′kri•tūd, *n.* [L. *pulchritudo*, from *pulcher*, beautiful.] Beauty; grace; comeliness.

pule, pūl, *v.i.*—*puled, puling*. [Fr. *piauler*, to make the cry represented by the syllable *piau*, to pule; an imitative word; comp. Fr. *miauler*, to mewl, to mew.] To cry like a chicken; to cry as a complaining child; to whimper.—**puler,** pū′lėr, *n.* One that pules.—**puling,** pū′ling, *p.* and *a.* Crying like a chicken; whining; infantine; childish.—*n.* A cry as of a chicken; a whining.—**pulingly,** pū′ling•li, *adv*. In a puling or whining manner.

pull, pu̦l, *v.t.* [A.Sax. *pullian*, to pull; L.G. *pulen*, to pick, to pluck, to pull; connections doubtful.] To draw; to draw toward one or make an effort to draw; to tug; to haul; opposed to *push*; to pluck; to gather by the hand (to *pull* fruit); to tear, rend, draw apart; in this sense followed by some qualifying word or phrase (to *pull in pieces*, to *pull asunder* or *apart*); to impress by a printing press; to move by drawing or pulling (to *pull* a bell, to *pull* a boat).—*To pull down*, to take down by pulling; to demolish (to *pull down* a house); to subvert.—*To pull off*, to separate by pulling; to pluck; also, to take off without force (to *pull off* a coat or hat).— *To pull on*, to draw on (to *pull on* boots).—*To pull out*, to draw out; to extract.—*To pull up*, to pluck up; to tear up by the roots; to apprehend or cause to be apprehended and taken before a court of justice (*colloq*.); to stop by means of the reins (to *pull up* a horse); hence, to stop in any course of conduct.—*To pull the long bow*, to exaggerate; to lie boastingly.—*To pull one through*, to help through a difficulty.—*v.i.* To give a pull; to tug; to exert strength in drawing. —*To pull through*, to get through any undertaking with difficulty.—*To pull up*, to draw the reins; to stop in riding or driving; to halt.—*n.* The act of pulling; an effort to move by drawing toward one; a pluck; a shake; a twitch; the act of rowing a boat.

pullet, pu̦l′et, *n.* [Fr. *poulette* dim. of *poule* a hen L.L. *pulla* from L. *pullus*, a young animal. Of same origin are *poult, poultry*.] A young hen or chicken.

pulley, pu̦l′i, *n.* pl. **pulleys,** pu̦l′iz. [O.E. *poleyne*, a pulley, from Fr. *poulain*, a foal or colt, a slide for letting down casks into a cellar, a pulley rope, from L.L. *pullanus*, from L. *pullus*, the young of an animal. (PULLET.) The names of the horse, ass, goat, and other animals are given in different languages to various mechanical contrivances.] One of the simple machines or mechanical powers, used for raising weights, and consisting of a small wheel movable about an axle, and having a groove cut in its circumference over which a cord passes; used either singly or several in combination; a wheel placed upon a shaft and transmitting power to or from the different parts of machinery, or changing the direction of motion by means of a belt or band which runs over it.

Pullman car, pu̦l′man, *n.* [After G.M. *Pullman*, U.S. inventor.] A passenger railroad car with parlor car fittings, on which additional fare is charged.

pulmonary, pulmonic, pul′mon•e•ri, pul•mon′ik, *a.* [L. *pulmonarius*, from *pulmo, pulmonis*, a lung; akin to Gr. *pleumōn, pneumōn*, a lung.] Pertaining to the lungs; affecting the lungs.—**pulmotor,** pul′mō•tėr, *n.* A respirator that forces air into the lungs.

pulp, pulp, *n.* [Fr. *pulpe,* from L. *pulpa,* fleshy substance, pulp.] Soft undissolved animal or vegetable matter; the soft, succulent part of fruit; material for making paper reduced to a soft uniform mass; the soft vascular substance in the interior of a tooth; pl. magazines dealing with sensational matter (slang).—*v.t.* To make into pulp; to deprive of the pulp.—*v.i.* To be or become as pulp.—**pulpiness,** pul′-pi•nes, *n.*—**pulpy,** pul′pi, *a.*—**pulpwood,** pulp′wụd, *n.* A soft wood used in making paper.

pulpit, pụl′pit, *n.* [L. *pulpitum,* a scaffold, stage, desk.] An elevated place or enclosed stage in a church, in which the preacher stands; frequently used adjectively, and signifying belonging, pertaining, or suitable to the pulpit (*pulpit* eloquence, *pulpit* oratory).—*The pulpit,* preachers generally; the pulpit teaching in churches (the influence of *the pulpit*).—**pulpiteer,** pụl•pi•tēr′, *n.* A preacher, in contempt.

pulque, pụl′kā, *n.* [Sp.] A vinous beverage obtained by fermenting the juice of various species of the agave or American aloe.

pulsate, pul′sāt, *v.i.*—*pulsated, pulsating.* [L. *pulsare, pulsatum,* to beat, from *pellere, pulsum,* to drive (seen also in *expel, compel, impel, impulse, repel,* etc.).] To beat or throb.—**pulsatile,** pul′sa•tīl, *a.* [L. *pulsatilis.*] Played on by beating; intended to be played on by beating; *med.* beating like the pulse; throbbing.—**pulsation,** pul•sā′shon, *n.* The beating or throbbing of the heart or of an artery; a beat of the pulse; a throb; a beat or stroke by which some medium is affected, as in the propagation of sound.—**pulsator,** pul′sā•tėr, *n.* A beater; a striker.—**pulsatory,** pul′sa•to•ri, *a.* Capable of pulsating or beating; throbbing, as the heart and arteries.—**pulse,** puls, *n.* [Fr. *pouls,* L. *pulsus,* a beating, from *pello, pulsum.*] The beating or throbbing of the heart or blood vessels, especially of the arteries; the pulsation of the radial artery at the wrist; pulsation; vibration.—*To feel one's pulse* (*fig.*), to sound one's opinion; to try or to know one's mind.—*v.i.*—*pulsed, pulsing.* To beat, as the arteries or heart.—**pulsimeter,** pul•sim′et•ėr, *n.* [L. *pulsus,* and Gr. *metron,* a measure.] An instrument for measuring the strength or quickness of the pulse.—**pulsometer,** pul•-som′et•ėr, *n.* A sort of pump which acts by the condensation of steam sent into a reservoir, the water rushing up into the vacuum formed by the condensation.

pulse, puls, *n.* [From L. *puls,* pottage made of meal, pulse, etc.] Leguminous plants or their seeds; the plants whose pericarp is a legume, as beans, peas, etc.

pulverize, pul′vėr•īz, *v.t.*—*pulverized, pulverizing.* [Fr. *pulvériser,* from L. *pulvis, pulveris,* powder (whence *powder*).] To reduce to fine powder, as by beating, grinding, etc.—*v.i.* To become reduced to fine powder; to fall to dust.—**pulverizable,** pul•vėr•-ī′za•bl, *a.* Capable of being pulverized.—**pulverizer,** pul′vėr•ī•zėr, *n.* One who or that which pulverizes.—**pulverization,** pul′vėr•i•zā″shon, *n.* The act of pulverizing.—**pulverulent,** pul•ver′ū•lent, *a.* Dusty; consisting of fine powder; powdery.

pulvilli, pul•vil′ī, *n. pl.* [L., little cushions, from *pulvinus,* a cushion.] A name for cushion-like masses on the feet of certain insects.—**pulvinate,** pul′vi•nāt, *a. Bot.* cushion-shaped.—**pulvinated,** pul′vi•-nā•ted, *a. Arch.* a term used to express a swelling in any portion of an order.—**pulvinus,** pul′vin•us, *n.* The thickened base of a leaf stalk.

puma, pū′ma, *n.* [Peruv.] The cougar or mountain lion. See COUGAR.

pumice, pu′mis, *n.* [L. *pumex, pumicis,* originally *spumex,* from *spuma,* foam, from *spuo,* to spit. *Pounce* (powder) is the same word.] A sort of porous stony substance frequently ejected from volcanoes, lighter than water, used for polishing ivory, wood, marble, metals, glass, etc.—**pumiceous,** pu•mish′us, *a.* Pertaining to pumice; consisting of or resembling it.—**pumice stone,** *n.*

pummel, pum′el. See POMMEL.

pump, pump, *n.* [Fr. *pompe,* a pump, from D. and L.G. *pomp,* G. *pumpe,* a pump; origin unknown.] An instrument or machine employed for raising water or other liquid to a higher level, or for exhausting or compressing air or other gases.—*v.i.* To work a pump; to work something as in the motion of pumping; to raise and lower like a pump handle; to try to extract information.—*v.t.* To raise with a pump; to free from water or other fluid by a pump (to *pump* a ship); to put artful questions to for the purpose of extracting information (colloq.); to eject in spurts as by a pumping action.—**pumper,** pump′ėr, *n.*

pump, pump, *n.* [Probably from being worn for *pomp.*] A low shoe holding to the foot only at toe and heel.

pumpernickel, pum′pėr•nik•el, *n.* [G.] A species of coarse bread made from unbolted rye.

pumpkin, pump′kin, *n.* [From Fr. *pompon,* from L. *pepo, peponis,* a pumpkin, from Gr. *pepōn,* a melon, lit. one thoroughly ripened, from root of *peptō* (akin to L. *coquo*), to cook. COOK.] A large, round, yellow-orange, edible gourd (*Cucurbita Pepo*) borne by a vine; the plant bearing the gourd.

pun, pun, *n.* [Origin unknown.] A play on words that agree or resemble in sound but differ in meaning; an expression in which two different applications of a word present an odd or ludicrous idea.—*v.i.*—*punned, punning.* To play on words so as to make puns.—**punning,** pun′ing, *p.* and *a.* Given to making puns.—**punster,** pun′stėr, *n.* One skilled in or given to punning.

punch, punsh, *n.* [Shortened from old *punchon,* a dagger, from O.Fr. *poinson,* a bodkin, from L. *punctio,* a puncturing, from *pungo, punctum,* to prick (whence *point, puncture, pungent,* etc.).] A tool employed for making apertures, as in plates of metal, in impressing dies, etc., usually made of steel, and operated by hammering; a blow, as with the fist, elbow, or knee.—*v.t.* To perforate with a punch; to give a blow or stunning knock to.—**puncher,** punsh′ėr, *n.* One who or that which punches.

Punch, punsh, *n.* [Contr. from *punchinello* (which see).] The chief character in a popular comic exhibition of puppets, who beats to death Judy his wife, belabors a police officer, etc.

punch, punsh, *n.* [From Hind. *panch,* Skr. *panchan,* five.] A beverage introduced from India, and so called from its being composed of the five ingredients, arrack, tea, sugar, water, and lemon juice; in this country, a beverage made from spirits and water, and sweetened and flavored with sugar and lemon juice.—**punch bowl,** *n.* A bowl in which punch is made, or from which it is served to be drunk.

puncheon, punsh′on, *n.* [Fr. *poinçon,* a bodkin, a punch (see PUNCH, the tool); also O.Fr. *poinson,* Fr. *poinçon,* a wine vessel—perhaps one stamped with a punch as of a certain capacity.] A perforating or stamping tool; a punch; *carp.* a short upright piece of timber in framing; a measure of liquids, or a cask containing from 84 to 120 gallons.

punchinello, punsh•i•nel′lo, *n.* [Corrupted from It. *pulcinello,* from L. *pullus,* a chicken=my chicken.] A punch; a buffoon.

punctate, punctated, pungk′tāt, pungk′tā•ted, *a.* [From L. *punctum,* a point. POINT.] Ending in a point; pointed; *bot.* having dots scattered over the surface.

punctilio, pungk•til′i•o, *n.* [From Sp. *puntillo* or It. *puntiglio,* a small point, a punctilio, from L. *punctum,* a point. POINT.] A nice point in conduct, ceremony, or proceeding; particularity or exactness in forms.—**punctilious,** pungk•til′i•us, *a.* Attentive to punctilios; very nice or exact in the forms of behavior; sometimes, exact to excess.—**punctiliously,** pungk•til′i•us•li, *adv.* In a punctilious manner.—**punctiliousness,** pungk•til′i•us•nes, *n.*

punctual, pungk′chö•al, *n.* [Fr. *ponctuel,* from L. *punctum,* a point, from *pungo, punctum,* to prick. POINT, PUNCTURE, etc.] Observant of nice points‡; exact‡; exact in keeping an appointment; exact to the time agreed on; made at the exact time (*punctual* payment).—**punctuality,** pungk•chö•al′i•ti, *n.* The state or quality of being punctual; adherence to the exact time of attendance or appointment.—**punctually,** pungk′-chö•al•li, *adv.* In a punctual manner; with scrupulous regard to time, appointments, promises, etc.—**punc-**

tualness, pungk′chö•al•nes, *n.* Punctuality.

punctuate, pungk′chö•āt, *v.t.—punctuated, punctuating.* [Fr. *ponctuer,* from L. *punctum,* a point. PUNCTUAL, PUNCTURE.] To mark with the points or stops necessary in written or printed compositions; to separate into sentences, clauses, or other divisions by points.—**punctuation,** pungk•chö•ā′shon, *n.* The act or art of punctuating or pointing a writing or discourse.—**punctuator,** pungk′-chö•ā•tėr, *n.* One who punctuates; a punctuist.

puncture, pungk′chėr, *n.* [L. *punctura,* from *pungo, punctum,* to prick (whence *pungent, point,* and a *punch*).] The act of perforating with a pointed instrument, or a small hole thus made; a small wound, as by a needle, prickle, or sting.—*v.t.—punctured, puncturing.* To make a puncture in; to prick.

pundit, pun′dit, *n.* [Skr. *pandita,* a learned man.] A learned Brahmin; one versed in the Sanskrit language, and in the science, laws, and religion of India; sometimes used ironically or contemptuously.

pungent, pun′jent, *a.* [L. *pungens,* ppr. of *pungo, punctum,* to prick, whence also *point, puncture, compunction, expunge,* etc.] Affecting the tongue like small sharp points; biting; acrid; sharply affecting the sense of smell; affecting the mind similarly; caustic; racy; biting.—**pungently,** pun′jent•li, *adv.* In a pungent manner; sharply.—**pungency,** pun′jen•si, *n.* The state or quality of being pungent; tartness; causticity.

Punic, pū′nik, *a.* [L. *punicus,* Carthaginian, from *Puni, Pœni,* the Carthaginians.] Pertaining to the Carthaginians; faithless; deceitful.—*n.* The language of the Carthaginians; Phoenician.

punish, pun′ish, *v.t.* [Fr. *punir, punissant,* from L. *punire,* to punish, from *pœna,* punishment, penalty. PAIN.] To inflict a penalty on; to visit judicially with a penalty; to castigate; to chastise; to visit with pain or suffering inflicted on the offender (to *punish* murder or theft); to inflict pain on in a loose sense (*colloq.*).—**punishable,** pun′ish•a•bl, *a.* Deserving punishment; liable to punishment; capable of being punished.—**punisher,** pun′ish•ėr, *n.* One that punishes.—**punishment,** pun′-ish•ment, *n.* The act of punishing; pain or penalty inflicted on a person for a crime or offense; a penalty imposed in the enforcement of law.—**punitive,** pū′ni•tiv, *a.* Pertaining to or involving punishment; awarding or inflicting punishment.—**punitory,** pū′ni•to•ri, *a.* Punishing or tending to punishment.

punk, pungk, *n.* [Contr. from *spunk.*] Tinder made from a fungus; touchwood; spunk.

punka, punkah, pung′ka, *n.* A large fan slung from the ceilings of rooms in India to produce an artificial current of air.

punster. See PUN.

punt, punt, *v.i.* [Fr. *punter,* It. *puntare,* from L. *punctum,* a point. PUNGENT.] *Football,* to drop and kick the ball before it touches the ground; to gamble for big stakes.—**punter,** punt′ėr, *n.* One who punts; one who plays in games of chance against the banker or dealer.

punt, punt, *n.* [A punt, a pontoon, from *pons, pontis,* a bridge. PONTOON.] A square flat-bottomed vessel without masts, used as a lighter for conveying goods, etc.; a small flat-bottomed boat used in fishing and wild-fowl shooting, etc.—*v.t.* To propel by pushing with a pole against the bed of the water; to convey in a punt.—**punter,** punt′ėr, *n.* One who punts a boat; one who uses a punt.

puny, pū′ni, *a.* [From Fr. *puisné.* PUISNE.] Puisne; imperfectly developed in size and vigor; small and weak; petty; insignificant.—**puniness,** pū′ni•nes, *n.* The state or quality of being puny.

pup, pup, *n.* [Abbrev. of *puppy.*] A puppy; a young seal.—*v.i.—pupped, pupping.* To bring forth whelps.

pupa, pū′pa, *n.* pl. **pupae,** pū′pē. [L. *pupa,* a girl, a doll, fem. of *pupus,* a boy.] The chrysalis form of an insect.—**pupal,** pū′pal, *a.* Pertaining to a pupa.

pupil, pū′pil, *n.* [Fr. *pupille,* L. *pupilla,* a little girl, the apple of the eye, dim. of *pupa,* a girl; also *pupillus,* an orphan boy, dim. of *pupus,* a boy. PUPPET.] The round aperture in the middle of the iris through which the rays of light pass to reach the retina; a young person of either sex under the care of an instructor or tutor; a disciple; a ward; a young person under the care of a guardian.—**pupilage,** pū′pil•ij, *n.* The state of being a pupil; the state or period of being a ward under the care of a guardian.—**pupillary,** pū′pi•ler•i, *a.* [L. *pupillaris.*] Pertaining to a pupil or ward; pertaining to the pupil of the eye.

pupiparous, pu•pip′er•us, *a.* [L. *pupa,* and *pario,* to produce.] Producing pupae from the eggs before they are excluded: said of certain insects.

puppet, pup′et, *n.* [O.E. *popet,* O.Fr. *poupette,* dim. from L. *pupa,* a doll, a puppet. PUPA, PUPIL.] A small figure in the human form, moved by cords or wires, in a mock drama; a marionette; one actuated by the will of another; a person who is a mere tool.—**puppet show,** *n.* A mock drama performed by puppets.

puppy, pup′i, *n.* [Fr. *poupée,* a doll, a puppet, L. *pupa.* PUPA, PUPPET.] A whelp; a young dog not grown up; a conceited and insignificant fellow; a silly fop or coxcomb.

purblind, pėr′blīnd, *a.* [From *pure* in sense of altogether, quite, and *blind.*] Near-sighted or dim-sighted; seeing obscurely. —**purblindness,** pėr′-blīnd•nes, *n.* The state of being purblind; dimness of vision.

purchase, pėr′chas, *v.t.—purchased, purchasing.* [Fr. *pourchasser,* O.Fr. *purchacer,* to pursue, to get—*pour, pur,* for, and *chasser,* to chase. CHASE.] To gain or acquire‡; to obtain by payment of money or its equivalent; to buy; to obtain by labor, danger, or other means.—*n.* Acquisition in general‡; the acquisition of anything by rendering an equivalent in money; buying; that which is purchased; any mechanical advantage (as is gained by a lever) used in the raising or removing of heavy bodies.—*To be worth so many years' purchase,* said of property that would bring in, in the specified time, an amount equal to the sum paid.—**purchasable,** pėr′chas•a•bl, *a.* Capable of being purchased.—**purchaser,** pėr′chas•ėr, *n.* One who purchases; a buyer.

purdah, pur′da, *n.* [Hind. and Per. *pardah,* veil.] A Muslim and Hindi custom of keeping women secluded by the use of screens, face veils, and voluminous clothing.

pure, pūr, *a.* [Fr. *pur,* from L. *purus,* pure (whence *purgo,* E. to *purge*); from root seen also in Skr. *pû,* to purify; and in *fire.*] Free from all heterogeneous or extraneous matter, especially from anything that impairs or pollutes; free from that which defiles or contaminates; innocent; spotless; chaste; stainless; genuine; ceremonially clean; unpolluted; mere; sheer; absolute (*pure* shame, hatred).—*Pure mathematics.* MATHEMATICS.—**purely,** pūr′li, *adv.* In a pure manner; innocently; stainlessly; chastely; merely; absolutely. —**pureness,** pūr′nes, *n.* The state or quality of being pure; purity.—**purify,** pū′ri•fī, *v.t.—purified, purifying.* [Fr. *purifier,* from L. *purificare —purus,* and *facio,* to make.] To make pure or clear; to free from extraneous admixture; to free from guilt or the defilement of sin.—*v.i.* To grow or become pure or clear.—**purification,** pū′ri•fi•kā″shon, *n.* [L. *purificatio.*] The act of purifying or making pure; the act of cleansing ceremonially by removing any pollution or defilement; lustration; a cleansing from guilt or the pollution of sin.—**purificatory,** pū•rif′i•ka•to•ri, *a.* Having power to purify; tending to cleanse.—**purifier,** pū′-ri•fī•ėr, *n.* One who or that which purifies.—**purist,** pū′rist, *n.* [Fr. *puriste,* from *pur,* pure.] One who scrupulously aims at purity, particularly in the choice of language; one who is a rigorous critic of purity in literary style.—**puristic,** pū•ris′tik, *a.* Pertaining or relating to purism.—**purism,** pū′rizm, *n.* Affectation of rigid purity; excessive nicety as to the choice of words.—**purity,** pū′ri•ti, *n.* [L. *puritas.*] The condition of being pure; freedom from foreign matter; cleanness; innocence; chastity.

purée, pū•rā′, *n.* Meat, fish, or vegetables boiled into a pulp and passed through a sieve.

purfle, pėr′fl, *v.t.—purfled, purfling.* [O.Fr. *pourfiler—pour,* L. *pro,* for, before, and *fil,* L. *filum,* a thread. PROFILE.] To decorate with a wrought or flowered border; to border; to broider; to decorate richly.

purge, pėrj, *v.t.—purged, purging.* [L. *purgare,* to cleanse, from *purus,* clean, and *agere,* to do. PURE.] To cleanse or purify by carrying off whatever is impure, foreign, or superfluous; to clear from moral defilement; to clear from accusation or the charge of a crime; to remove from a position of influence, in a political party or nation, persons considered harmful or disloyal; to evacuate the bowels; to operate on by means of a cathartic. —*v.i.* To produce evacuations by a cathartic. *n.* The act of purging; anything that purges; a cathartic medicine; the act of removing from a position of influence, in a political party or nation, persons considered harmful or disloyal.—**purgation,** pėr•gā′shon, *n.* [L. *purgatio.*] The act of purging; the act of carrying away impurities; purification; the act of cleansing from the imputation of guilt.—**purgative,** pėr′ga•tiv, *a.* [Fr. *purgatif.*] Having the power of cleansing; having the power of evacuating the intestines; cathartic.—*n.* A medicine that evacuates the intestines; a cathartic. **purgatory,** pėr′ga•to•ri, *a.* [L. *purgatorius.*] Tending to cleanse; cleansing; expiatory.—*n.* According to R. Catholics and others, a place in which souls after death are purified from venial sins, and suffer punishment for mortal sins not atoned for; colloquially, any place or state of irritating temporary suffering.

purify. See PURE.

Purim, pu′rim, *n.* [Heb. *purim,* lots.] An annual festival among the Jews instituted to commemorate their preservation from the massacre with which they were threatened by the machinations of Haman.

purine, pūr′in, *n.* [Gr. *pyr,* burning.] A nitrogenous excretory substance.

purist. See PURE.

Puritan, pū′ri•tan, *n.* [From L. *puritas,* purity.] The name by which the dissenters from the Church of England were generally known in the reign of Elizabeth and the first two Stuarts; given (probably in derision) on account of the superior purity of doctrine or discipline which they claimed as their own.—*a.* Pertaining to the Puritans.—**puritanic, puritanical,** pū•ri•tan′ik, pū•ri•tan′i•kal, *a.* Pertaining to the Puritans or their doctrines and practice; precise in religious matters; exact; rigid. —**puritanically,** pū•ri•tan′i•kal•li, *adv.* In a puritanical manner.—**Puritanism,** pū′ri•tan•izm, *n.* The doctrines or practices of Puritans.

purity. See PURE.

purl, pėrl, *n.* [Contracted form of *purfle.*] An embroidered border; an inversion of the stitches in knitting, giving a distinctive appearance.

purl, pėrl, *v.i.* [Akin to Sw. *porla,* to purl; probably from the sound; comp. *purr.*] To murmur, as a shallow stream flowing among stones; to flow with a gentle murmur; to ripple.—*n.* A ripple; a murmuring sound, as of a shallow stream among stones; malt liquor flavored with wormwood or aromatic herbs; now a name for beer flavored with gin, sugar, and ginger.

purlieu, pėr′lū, *n.* [From Norm. *purlieu, puraille,* O.Fr. *puralée,* perambulation, from *pur,* L. *per,* through, *alée,* a going. (ALLEY.) Both form and sense have been influenced by Fr. *lieu,* place.] A piece of land set apart from an ancient royal forest by perambulation of its boundaries; a part lying adjacent; the outer portion of any area; the environs.

purloin, pėr′loin, *v.t.* [O.Fr. *porloignier, purloignier,* from L. *prolongare,* to prolong. PROLONG.] To steal; to filch; to take by plagiarism. —*v.i.* To practice theft.—**purloiner,** pėr•loi′nėr, *n.* One who purloins; a thief; a plagiarist.

purple, pėr′pl, *a.* [Old form *purpre,* from L. *purpura,* purple, from Gr. *porphyra,* a kind of shellfish that yielded a purple dye. Akin *porphyry.*] Of a color composed of red and blue blended; imperial; regal—a sense derived from purple robes being formerly distinctive of great personages; bloody; dyed with blood.—*n.* A color compounded by the union of blue and red; a purple robe or dress; hence, from a purple robe having been the distinguishing dress of emperors, etc., used typically of imperial or regal power.—*The purple,* the imperial dignity; also the dignity of a cardinal. *Purple of Cassius,* a pigment used in painting on glass and porcelain.—*v.t.—purpled, purpling.* To dye or color purple; to clothe with purple.—**purplish,** pėr′plish, *a.* Somewhat purple.

purport, pėr′pōrt, *n.* [O.Fr. *purport,* from *pur,* Fr. *pour,* for, and *porter,* to bear. PORT (demeanor).] Meaning; tenor; import.—*v.t.* To convey, as a certain meaning; to import; to signify.—*v.i.* To have a certain purport or tenor.

purpose, pėr′pųs, *n.* [O.Fr. *pourpos,* Fr. *propos,* from L. *propositum,* from *propono—pro,* before, and *ponere, positum,* to place. POSITION.] That which a person sets before himself as an object to be reached or accomplished; end or aim; that which a person intends to do; design; plan; intention.—*Of purpose, on purpose,* with previous design; designedly; intentionally.—*To the purpose,* to the matter in question (to speak *to the purpose*).—*v.t.—purposed, purposing.* To intend; to resolve; to mean; to wish.—*v.i.* To have intention or design; to intend.—**purposeless,** pėr′pųs•les, *a.* Having no object or purpose.—**purposely,** pėr′pųs•li, *adv.* By purpose or design; intentionally.

purpura, pėr′pų•ra, *n.* [PURPLE.] A disease characterized by purple spots on the skin; the purples.

purr, pėr, *v.i.* [Imitative of sound.] To utter a soft murmuring sound, as a cat when pleased.—*v.t.* To signify by purring.—*n.* The sound uttered by a cat when pleased.

purse, pėrs, *n.* [From Fr. *bourse,* L.L. *bursa, byrsa,* a purse, from Gr. *byrsa,* a skin, a hide.] A small bag or case in which money is contained or carried in the pocket; a sum of money collected as a present; a specific sum of money, namely, in Turkey 500 piasters, or about $22.00; *fig.* a treasury; finances.—To have a *long* or *heavy purse,* to have plenty of money; to have a *short* or *light* one, to have little.—*v.t.—pursed, pursing.* To put in a purse; to contract into folds or wrinkles; to pucker.—**purse-proud,** *a.* Proud of wealth; puffed up with the possession of riches.—**purser,** pėr′sėr, *n.* The ticket officer on a steamer.

pursiness, pėr′si•nes, *n.* See PURSY.

purslane, pėrs′lān, *n.* [O.Fr. *porcelaine,* It. *porcellana,* from L. *porcilaca,* purslane.] An annual plant with fleshy succulent leaves, used in salads, as a potherb, in pickles, etc.

pursue, pėr•sū′, *v.t.—pursued, pursuing.* [O.Fr. *poursuir, porsuir* (Fr. *poursuivre*)—*pour*=L. *pro,* forward, and *suir, suivre,* to follow, L. *sequor.* SEQUENCE.] To follow with a view to overtake; to chase; to attend on (misfortune *pursues* him); to seek; to use measures to obtain; to prosecute, continue, or proceed in; to carry on; to follow up; to proceed along, with a view to some end or object; to follow (to *pursue* a course). —*v.i.* To go in pursuit; to proceed; *law,* to act as a prosecutor.—**pursuer,** pėr•sū′ėr, *n.* One who pursues; *Scots law,* the party who institutes an ordinary action; the plaintiff.—**pursuit,** pėr•sūt′, *n.* [Fr. *poursuite.*] The act of pursuing or following with a view to overtake; a following with a view to reach or obtain; endeavor to attain; course of business or occupation; employment (mercantile *pursuits*).—**pursuance,** pėr•sū′ans, *n.* A pursuing or carrying out (of a design); prosecution.—*In pursuance of,* in fulfillment or execution of; in carrying out.—**pursuant,** pėr•sū′ant, *a.* [O.Fr. *porsuiant, poursuiant.*] Done in consequence of anything; agreeable; conformable; with *to.*—*adv.* Conformably; with *to.*—**pursuantly,** pėr•sū′ant•li, *adv.* Pursuant; agreeably; conformably.

pursuivant, pėr′swi•vant, *n.* [Fr. *poursuivant,* from *poursuivre.* PURSUE.] A state messenger; an attendant on heralds; one of the third and lowest order of heraldic officers, of whom there are four in England, named *Rouge Croix, Blue Mantle, Rouge Dragon,* and *Portcullis.*

pursy, pėr′si, *a.* [O.Fr. *pourcif,* also *poulsif,* from *pourcer, poulser* (Mod. Fr. *pousser*), to push, also to breathe or pant, from L. *pulsare,* to beat. PULSE, PUSH.] Short-winded; fat and short-winded; rank; wanton; self-indulgent. '*Pursy* times' (*Hamlet*).—**pursiness,** pėr′si•nes, *n.* A state of being pursy; shortness of breath.

purtenance, pėr′te•nans, *n.* [Shortened from *appurtenance.*] Appurtenance; that which pertains or belongs to anything.

purulent, pū′rų•lent, *a.* [L. *purulentus,* from *pus, puris,* matter. Same root as in *putrid.*] Consisting of pus or matter; full of or resembling pus. —**purulently,** pū′rų•lent•li, *adv.* In a purulent manner.—**purulence, purulency,** pū′ru̦·lens, pū′ru̦·len·si, *n.* The state of being purulent; pus.

purvey, pėr·vā′, *v.t.* [Fr. *pourvoir,* O.Fr. *proveoir, porveoir,* from L. *provideo,* to foresee, to provide. PROVIDE.] To provide, especially to provide provisions or other necessaries for a number of persons.—*v.i.* To purchase provisions, especially for a number.—**purveyance,** pėr·vā′ans, *n.* Act of purveying; in England, the former royal prerogative of preemption of provisions and necessaries for the royal household.—**purveyor,** pėr·vā′ėr, *n.* One who supplies eatables for a number of persons; in England, an officer who formerly exacted provision for the king's household.

purview, pėr′vū, *n.* [O.Fr. *pourveu, purvieu,* Fr. *pourvu,* provided, from *pourvoir,* to provide. PURVEY.] *Law,* the body of a statute as distinguished from the *preamble;* the limit or scope of a statute; limit of sphere of authority; scope.

pus, pus, *n.* [L. *pus, puris,* matter, from same root as in *putrid, putrefy.*] The white or yellowish matter found in abscesses; matter produced in a festering sore.

Puseyism, pū′zi·izm, *n.* The name given collectively to certain doctrines promulgated by Dr. *Pusey,* in conjunction with other divines of Oxford, in a series of pamphlets entitled 'Tracts for the Times'; Tractarianism.—**Puseyite,** pū′zi·īt, *n.* An adherent of Puseyism; a Tractarian.

push, pu̦sh, *v.t.* [O.E. *pusse,* from Fr. *pousser,* O.Fr. *poulser,* from L. *pulsare,* to beat, a freq. from *pello, pulsum,* to drive, whence *expel,* and other verbs in *-pel.* PULSATE.] To press against with force; to impel by pressure; to drive by steady pressure, without striking: opposed to *draw;* to press or urge forward; to advance by exertions (to *push* one's fortune); to enforce, as in argument; to press or ply hard (as an opponent in argument); to urge; to importune; to prosecute energetically (to *push* a trade).—*v.i.* To make a thrust; to make an effort; to press one's self onward; to force one's way.—*To push on,* to drive or urge one's course forward; to hasten.—*n.* The act of pushing; a short pressure or force applied; a thrust; a vigorous effort; an emergency; an extremity (to come to the *push*); persevering energy; enterprise.—**pusher,** push′ėr, *n.* One who pushes.—**pushing,** push′ing, *a.* Pressing forward in business; enterprising; energetic.

Pushtu, push′tö, *n.* The language of the Afghans.

pusillanimous, pū·sil·lan′i·mus, *a.* [L. *pusillanimis,* from *pusillus,* very little, from *pusus,* little (same root as in *puerile*), and *animus,* the mind. PUERILE, ANIMATE.] Destitute of strength and firmness of mind; being of weak courage; faint-hearted; cowardly.—**pusillanimity,** pū′sil·la·nim″i·ti, *n.* Weakness of spirit; cowardliness; timidity.—**pusillanimously,** pū·sil·lan′i·mus·li, *adv.* In a pusillanimous manner.

puss, pu̦s, *n.* [Same as D. *poes,* L.G. *puus,* Gael. and Ir. *pus,* a cat; perhaps imitative of the spitting of a cat. The hare is so called from resembling a cat.] A name for the cat and also for the hare; a sort of pet name sometimes applied to a child or young woman.—**pussy,** pu̦s′i, *n.* Diminutive of *puss.*

pustule, pus′chūl, *n.* [Fr. *pustule,* L. *pustula,* a form of *pusula,* a blister or pimple.] *Med.* an elevation of the cuticle, with an inflamed base, containing pus; *bot.* a pimple or little blister.—**pustular,** pus′chū·lėr, *a.* Having the character of or proceeding from a pustule or pustules.—**pustulate,** pus′chū·lāt, *v.t.*—*pustulated, pustulating.* To form into pustules or blisters.—*a. Bot.* covered with glandular excrescences like pustules.

put, pu̦t, *v.t.*—pret. and pp. *put,* ppr. *putting.* [O.E. *putte,* A.Sax. *potian,* to thrust, to gore; Dan. *putte,* to put or set.] To place, set, or lay in any position or situation; to place in any state or condition (to *put* to shame, to death); to apply (to *put* one's hand, one's mind to a thing); to set before one for consideration; to propose (to *put* a case, a question).—*To put about,* to change the course of (a ship); to put to inconvenience.—*To put an end to,* to stop; to bring to a conclusion.—*To put away,* to renounce or discard; to divorce.—*To put back,* to hinder; to delay; to restore to the original place.—*To put by,* to turn away; to thrust aside; to place in safe-keeping.—*To put down,* to repress; to crush; to confute; to silence; to write down; to subscribe.—*To put forth,* to propose; to offer to notice; to stretch out; to shoot out, as leaves; to exert; to bring into action; to make known, as opinions; to publish, as in a book.—*To put in,* to introduce among others; to insert.—*To put in mind,* to remind.—*To put in practice,* to apply; to make use of.—*To put off,* to take from one's person; to lay aside; to turn aside from a purpose or demand; to delay; to postpone; to push from land.—*To put on,* to invest with as clothes or covering; to impute; to charge with (to *put* blame *on*); to assume (to *put on* a grave face); to impose; to inflict; to turn or let on; to set to work.—*To put out,* to eject; to drive out; to place (money) at interest; to extinguish; to shoot forth (to *put out* leaves); to extend; to reach out; to publish; to make public; to confuse; to disconcert; to dislocate.—*To put over,* to place in authority over; to defer; to postpone.—*To put to,* to add; to unite; to expose; to kill by; to punish by (to *put to* the sword).—*To put to it,* to press hard; to give difficulty to.—*To put the hand to,* to take hold; to begin; to undertake.—*To put this and that together,* to draw a conclusion from certain circumstances; to infer from given premises.—*To put to rights,* to arrange in an orderly condition; to set in proper order.—*To put to trial* or *on trial,* to bring before a court for examination and decision; to bring to a test; to try.—*To put up,* to offer publicly for sale; to hoard; to pack; to hide or lay aside; to put into its ordinary place when not in use; to give entertainment to; to accommodate with lodging.—*v.i.* Used only in certain phrases.—*To put in,* to enter a harbor; to offer a claim.—*To put in for,* to put in a claim for; to stand as a candidate for.—*To put off,* to sail from land.—*To put to sea,* to set sail; to begin a voyage.—*To put up,* to take lodgings; to lodge.—*To put up with,* to suffer without showing resentment; to pocket or swallow (an affront); to accept tamely; to overlook; to endure; to tolerate.—**putter,** pu̦t′ėr, *n.* One who puts.

put, pu̦t, *v.t.*—*putted, putting.* [Akin to above.] To throw upward and forward from the shoulder.

putamen, pū·tā′men, *n.* [L., a shell.] *Bot.* the inner coat or shell of a fruit; the endocarp.

putative, pū′ta·tiv, *a.* [Fr. *putatif,* L. *putativus,* from L. *puto,* to suppose (as in *compute, impute, dispute, repute*).] Supposed; reputed (the *putative* father of a child).

putlog, pu̦t′log, *n.* [From *put* and *log.*] *Carp.* one of the short pieces of timber used in building to carry the floor of a scaffold, having one end inserted in holes in the wall.

putrefy, pū′tre·fī, *v.t.*—*putrefied, putrefying.* [Fr. *putrefier,* L. *putrefacio*—*putris,* putrid, *facio,* to make. PUTRID.] To render putrid; to cause to rot with an offensive smell; to make carious or gangrenous—*v.i.* To become putrid; to rot.—**putrefaction,** pū·tre·fak′shon, *n.* The act or process of putrefying; the decomposition of animal and vegetable substances, attended by the evolution of fetid gases; that which is putrefied.—**putrefactive,** pū·tre·fak′tiv, *a.* Pertaining to putrefaction; tending to cause or causing putrefaction.

putrescent, pū·tres′ent, *a.* [L. *putrescens,* ppr. of *putresco,* to rot. PUTRID.] Becoming putrid; growing rotten; pertaining to the process of putrefaction.—**putrescence,** pū·tres′ens, *n.* The state of being putrescent; a putrid state.—**putrescible,** pū·tres′i·bl, *a.* Capable of being putrefied; liable to become putrid.

putrid, pū′trid, *a.* [Fr. *putride,* L. *putridus,* from *putris,* rotten, *putreo,* to rot, from *puteo,* to stink, from a root seen also in L. *pus,* Gr. *pyon,* matter; the same root producing also E. *foul.* PUS, FOUL.] In a state of decay or putrefaction; corrupt; rotten; proceeding from putrefaction or pertaining to it.—*Putrid fever,* typhus or spotted fever.—**putridity, putridness,** pū·trid′i·ti, pū′trid·nes, *n.* The state of being putrid; corruption; rottenness.

putt, put, *n.* A stroke made on a golf green, the object being to play the ball into the cup.—*v.t.* and *i.*—*putted, putting.* To tap a golf ball while on the golf green in the direction of the cup.—**putter,** *n.* A short-shaft golf club with an almost perpendicular face, used for accurate play near the cup.—**putting green,** *n.* Smooth turf surrounding the putting holes on a golf course.

puttee, put′i, *n.* [Hind. *patti.*] Long roll of cloth wound round soldier's leg from ankle to knee as support and protection.

putty, put′i, *n.* [Fr. *potée,* calcined tin, brass, etc., putty powder, from *pot,* a pot, originally perhaps applied to a solder for pots.] A powder of calcined tin, used in polishing glass and steel; a kind of paste or cement compounded of whiting or soft carbonate of lime and linseed oil, used by glaziers for fixing in the panes or glass in window frames, etc.; a fine cement made of lime and stone dust; the mixture of ground materials in which earthenware is dipped for glazing.—*v.t.*—*puttied, puttying.* To cement with putty; to fill up with putty.

puzzle, puz′l, *v.t.*—*puzzled, puzzling.* [Freq. from *pose,* to perplex with a question; or a form of *puddle;* comp. *muddle,* to make stupid.] To perplex; to nonplus; to put to a stand; to gravel; to make intricate; to entangle; with *out,* to discover or resolve by long cogitation.—*v.i.* To be bewildered; to be awkward.—*n.* Perplexity; embarrassment; a kind of riddle; a toy or contrivance which tries the ingenuity.—**puzzlement,** puz′l•ment, *n.* The state of being puzzled; bewilderment.—**puzzler,** puz′lėr, *n.* One who or that which puzzles.—**puzzling,** puz′ling, *p.* and *a.* Such as to puzzle; perplexing; embarrassing; bewildering.

pyaemia, pī•ē′mi•a, *n.* [Gr. *pyon,* pus (PUTRID), and *haima,* blood.] Blood poisoning, a dangerous disease resulting from the introduction of decaying animal matter, pus, etc., into the system.—**pyaemic,** pī•ē′mik, *a.* Pertaining to pyaemia; characterized by or of the nature of pyaemia.

pygidium, pī•jid′i•um, *n.* [Gr. *pygē,* the posteriors.] The terminal division of the body of a trilobite, also of a flea.

Pygmy, pig′mi, *n.* [Fr. *pygmée;* L. *pygmaeus,* from Gr. *pygmaios,* from *pygmē,* the fist.] One of a Negroid people of small stature; [not cap.] a little or dwarfish person.—*a.* Pygmean; dwarfish; little.—**pygmean,** pig•mē′an, *a.*

pylon, pī′lon, *n.* [Gr. *pylōn,* from *pylē,* a gate.] A lofty massive doorway; a gateway; a large supporting post or tower, as to a bridge; a structure marking an airway.

pylorus, pī•lo′rus, *n.* [Gr. *pylōros,* from *pylē,* a gate, and *ouros,* a guard.] The outlet for the stomach, through which the food passes to the intestines.—**pyloric,** pī•lor′ik, *a.*

pyogenesis, pī•o•jen′e•sis, *n.* [Gr. *pyon,* pus, *genesis,* generation; root *gen,* to produce. PUS.] The generation or formation of pus.—**pyogenic,** pī•o•jen′ik, *a.* Having relation to formation of pus.

pyorrhea, pī′er•rē″a, *n.* [Gr. *pyon,* pus, *rrhea,* a flow.] A suppurative inflammation in and about the sockets of the teeth which results in the loosening of the teeth, abscess formation in the gums, and, unless checked, inflammation of the jawbone.

pyramid, pir′a•mid, *n.* [Fr. *pyramide;* L. *pyramis,* from Gr. *pyramis, pyramidos,* a pyramid; probably an Egyptian word.] A solid structure whose base is a rectilineal figure, and whose sides are triangular and meet at a point; one of the ancient structures of this form erected in different parts of the world, the most noted being those of Egypt, to which the name was originally applied; *geom.* strictly a solid contained by a plane triangular, square, or polygonal base, and by other planes meeting in a point; *pl.* a game at billiards played with fifteen red balls and one white, the red balls being placed together in the form of a triangle or pyramid, and the players trying who will pocket the greatest number of balls.—**pyramidal, pyramidic, pyramidical,** pi•ram′i•dal, pir•a•mid′ik, pir•a•mid′i•kal, *a.* Pertaining to a pyramid; having the form of a pyramid.

pyrargyrite, pīr•ar′ji•rīt, *n.* [Gr. *pyr,* fire, and *argyros,* silver.] An important ore of silver, chiefly sulfide of silver and antimony, with hexagonal crystallization.

pyre, pīr, *n.* [L. *pyra,* from Gr. *pyra,* a pyre, from *pyr,* fire. FIRE.] A heap of combustible materials on which a dead body was laid to be burned; a funeral pile.

pyrene, pī•rēn′, *n.* [Gr. *pyrēn.*] *Bot.* the stone found in the interior of fruits.

pyretic, pī•ret′ik, *n.* [Gr. *pyretos,* burning heat, fever, from *pyr,* fire. PYRE.] A medicine for the cure of fever.—**pyretology,** pir•e•tol′o•ji, *n.* The branch of medical science that treats of fevers.—**pyrexia,** pī•rek′si•a, *n.* [Fr. *pyrexie,* from Gr. *puressō,* to be feverish.] Fever.—**pyrexial,** pī•rek′si•al, *a.* Pertaining to fever; feverish.

pyrex, pī′reks, *n.* A heat-resistant glassware; [cap.] trademark for such glassware.

pyrheliometer, pīr•hē′li•om″et•ėr, *n.* [Gr. *pyr,* fire, *hēlios,* the sun, *metron,* a measure.] An instrument for measuring the intensity of the heat of the sun.

pyridoxin, pir•i•dok′sin, *n.* [*Pyridine* and *oxygen.*] *Biochem.* vitamin B_6 used for the prevention of pellagra.

pyriform, pīr′i•form, *a.* [L. *pyrum,* a pear, and *forma,* shape.] Having the form of a pear.

pyrites, pī•rī′tēz, *n.* [Gr. *pyritēs,* from *pyr,* fire. PYRE.] A term applied to yellow sulfide of iron, because it struck fire with steel; also applied to minerals in which sulfur exists in combination with copper, cobalt, nickel, etc.—*Arsenical pyrites.* See MISPICKEL.—*White iron pyrites.* See MARCASITE.—*Yellow* or *copper pyrites,* the sulfide of copper and iron, the most common ore of copper.—**pyritic, pyritical,** pī•rit′ik, pī•rit′i•kal, *a.* Pertaining to pyrites; consisting of or resembling pyrites.

pyroacid, pīr′ō•as″id, *n.* A product obtained by subjecting certain organic acids to heat.

pyroelectric, pyroelectricity, pīr′ō•i•lek″trik, pīr′ō•i•lek•tris″i•ti. [Gr. *pyr, pyros,* fire, and E. *electric.*] See THERMOELECTRIC, etc.

pyrogenic, pīr•o•jen′ik, *a.* and *n.* [Gr. *pyr, pyros,* fire, and root *gen,* to produce.] Producing or that which tends to produce feverishness.—**pyrogenous,** pi•roj′e•nus, *a.* Produced by fire; igneous.

pyrognostic, pīr•og•nos′tik, *a.* [Gr. *pyr, pyros,* fire, and *gignōskō,* to know.] *Mineral,* pertaining to the phenomena exhibited on the application of the blowpipe.

pyroligneous, pyrolignic, pīr•o•lig′nē•us, pīr•o•lig′nik, *a.* [Gr. *pyr,* fire, and L. *lignum,* wood.] Generated or procured by the distillation of wood.—*Pyroligneous acid,* impure acetic acid obtained by the distillation of wood.

pyrology, pī•rol′o•ji, *n.* [Gr. *pyr,* fire, and *logos,* discourse.] The science of heat.

pyrolusite, pīr•o•lū′sīt, *n.* [Gr. *pyr,* fire, and *louō,* I wash.] A black ore of manganese, much used in chemical processes.

pyromagnetic, pīr′o•mag•net″ik, *a.* [Gr. *pyr, pyros,* fire, and E. *magnetic.*] Having the property of becoming magnetic when heated.

pyromancy, pīr′o•man•si, *n.* [Gr. *pyr, pyros,* fire, and *manteia,* divination.] Divination by fire.

pyromania, pī•rō•mā′ni•a, *n.* [N.L. *pyro,* fire, and *mania.*] *Psych.* an uncontrollable impulse for setting fires.

pyrometer, pī•rom′et•ėr, *n.* [Gr. *pyr, pyros,* fire, and *metron,* a measure.] A term applied to any instrument the object of which is to measure all gradations of temperature above those that can be indicated by the mercurial thermometer.—**pyrometric, pyrometrical,** pīr•o•met′rik, pīr•o•met′ri•kal, *a.* Pertaining to the pyrometer or its use.—**pyrometry,** pī•rom′et•ri, *n.* The use of the pyrometer; the act or art of measuring high degrees of heat.

pyrope, pīr′ōp, *n.* [Gr. *pyr, pyros,* fire, and *ōps,* the face.] Fire garnet or Bohemian garnet, a dark-red variety of garnet.

pyrophoric, pīr•o•for′ik, *a.* Light-producing.

pyrophyllite, pīr•o•fil′līt, *n.* [Gr. *pyr, pyros,* fire, and *phyllon,* a leaf.] A mineral of a foliated structure, resembling talc, and having a white, green, or yellow color and pearly luster.

pyroscope, pīr′o•skōp, *n.* [Gr. *pyr, pyros,* fire, and *skopein,* to view.] An instrument for measuring the intensity of heat radiating from a hot body.

pyrotechnic, pyrotechnical, pīr•o•tek′nik, pir•o•tek′ni•kal, *a.* [Gr. *pyr, pyros,* fire, and *technē,* art.] Pertaining to fireworks or the art of forming them.—**pyrotechnics, pyrotechny,** pīr•o•tek′niks, pir•o•tek′ni, *n.* The art of making fireworks; the use of artificial fireworks; the management and application of fire in various operations.—**pyrotechnist,** pīr•o•tek′nist, *n.* One skilled in pyrotechny; a manufacturer of fireworks.

pyroxene, pīr′ok•sēn, *n.* [Gr. *pyr, pyros,* fire, and *xenos,* a stranger.] Another name for the mineral augite; any of various minerals similar to augite.—**pyroxenic,** pīr•ok•sen′ik, *a.* Pertaining to pyroxene.

pyroxylin, pi•rok′si•lin, *n.* [Gr. *pyr,* fire, and *xylon,* wood.] A nitrocellulose compound, low in nitrogen content, soluble in an ether alcohol solution, and used in the manufacture of plastics, lacquer, etc.

pyrrhic, pir′ik, *n.* [Gr. *pyrrhiche,* a warlike dance.] An ancient Grecian warlike dance; a metrical foot consisting of two short syllables.—*a.* Pertaining to the Greek martial dance; *pros.* consisting of two short syllables, or of feet of two short syllables.—*Pyrrhic victory,* a victory, as of those gained by King Pyrrhus of Epirus over the Romans, costing more to the victor than to the vanquished.

Pyrrhonism, pir′on•izm, *n.* [From *Pyrrho,* the founder of the Skeptics.] Skepticism; universal doubt.

Pythagorean, pi•thag′o•rē″an, *a.* Pertaining to Pythagoras or his system of philosophy, which taught the doctrine of the transmigration of souls, and resolved all philosophy into the relations of numbers.—*Pythagorean system, astron.* the system taught by Pythagoras, afterward revived by Copernicus.—*n.* A follower of Pythagoras.—**pythagoreanism,** pi•thag′o•rē″an•izm, *n.* The doctrines or philosophy of Pythagoras.

Pythian, pith′i•an, *a.* [L. *Pythius,* Gr. *Pythios,* from *Pythō,* the older name of Delphi.] Pertaining to Delphi or to the priestess of Apollo at Delphi.—*Pythian games,* one of the four great national festivals of Greece, celebrated every fifth year in honor of Apollo near Delphi.—**Pythiad,** pith′i•ad, *n.* The period between the celebrations of the Pythian games.

pythogenic, pī•tho•jen′ik, *a.* [Gr. *pythomai,* to rot, and root *gen,* to produce.] Engendered from filth: applied to diseases, as typhus, produced by filth or by a vitiated atmosphere.

python, pī′thon, *n.* [Gr. *pythōn,* a great serpent slain by Apollo.] A genus of large nonvenomous serpents, natives of the East Indies and elsewhere.

pythoness, pī′thon•es, *n.* [Fr. *pythonisse,* from Gr. *Pythō,* old name of Delphi. PYTHIAN.] The priestess of Apollo at Delphi, who gave oracular answers; hence, any woman supposed to have a spirit of divination.—**pythonic,** pī•thon′ik, *a.* Oracular; prophetic.

pyuria, pī•ū′ri•a, *n.* [Gr. *puon,* pus, *ouron,* urine.] *Pathol.* the presence of pus in the urine.

pyx, piks, *n.* [Gr. *pyxis,* a box, especially of boxwood, from *pyxos,* the box tree.] A covered vessel used in the Roman Catholic Church for holding the consecrated host; a box or chest in which specimen coins are deposited at the British mint.—*Trial of the pyx,* the trial by weight and assay of the gold and silver coins of the United Kingdom, prior to their issue from the mint; the assay of gold and silver plate at an assay office. Written also *Pix.*—*v.t.* To test by weight and assay.

pyxidium, pik•sid′i•um, *n.* [Gr. *pyxis,* a box, and *eidos,* resemblance.] *Bot.* a capsule with a lid, as seen in the case of certain fruits; a term also applied to the theca of mosses.

Q

Q, q, kū, the seventeenth letter of the English alphabet, a consonant having the same sound as *k* or hard *c.*

qua, kwä, *adv.* [L.] In the quality or character of; as being; as.

quack, kwak, *v.i.* [Formed from the sound, like D. *kwaaken, kwakken,* G. *quaken,* Dan. *qvakke,* to croak, to quack; comp. Gr. *koax,* the croak of a frog.] To cry like the common domestic duck; to make vain and loud pretensions; to talk noisily and ostentatiously; to play the quack.—*n.* The cry of a duck; one who pretends to skill or knowledge which he does not possess; an empty pretender; a charlatan; especially, a pretender to medical skill.—*a.* Pertaining to or characterized by quackery (*quack* medicines, a *quack* doctor).—**quackery,** kwak′ėr•i, *n.* The boastful pretensions or mean practice of a quack, particularly in medicine; humbug; imposture.—**quackish,** kwak′ish, *a.* Like a quack or charlatan.—**quacksalver,** kwak′sal•vėr, *n.* [D. *kwakzalver,* L.G. *kuaksalver,* G. *quacksalber,* lit. a *quack* that deals in *salves.*] A charlatan; a quack.

quad, kwod, *n.* [Contr. for *quadrangle.*] The quadrangle or court, as of a college or jail; hence, a jail; quod. See QUADRAT.

quadragenarian, kwod′ra•je•nâ″ri•an, *a.* [L. *quadragenarius,* from *quadrageni,* forty each, from *quadraginta,* forty.] Consisting of forty; forty years old.

Quadragesima, kwod•ra•jes′i•ma, *n.* [L. *quadragesimus,* fortieth, from *quadraginta,* forty, from *quatuor,* four.] Lent; so called because it consists of forty days.—*Quadragesima Sunday,* the first Sunday in Lent.—**quadragesimal,** kwod•ra•jes′i•mal, *a.* Connected with the number forty; [*cap.*] belonging to Lent.

quadrangle, kwod′rang•gl, *n.* [L. *quadrus*=*quatuor,* four, and *angulus,* an angle.] A quadrilateral figure; a plain figure having four sides, and consequently four angles; a square or quadrangular court surrounded by buildings.—**quadrangular,** kwod•rang′gū•lėr, *a.* Of a square shape; having four sides and four angles.

quadrant, kwod′rant, *n.* [L. *quadrans, quadrantis,* a fourth.] The quarter of a circle; the arc of a circle containing 90°; the space included between this arc and two radii drawn from the center to each extremity; an instrument for measuring angular altitudes, in principle and application the same as the sextant, by which it is superseded.—**quadrantal,** kwod•ran′tal, *a.* Pertaining to a quadrant.

quadrat, kwod′rat, *n.* [L. *quadratum,* a square, from *quadrus,* square.] *Printing,* a piece of type metal cast lower than a type, used for filling out spaces between letters, words, lines, etc., so as to leave a blank on the paper at the place.

quadrate, kwod′rāt, *a.* [L. *quadratus,* squared, pp. of *quadro, quadratum,* to make square, from *quadrus,* square.] Square in form; square, by being the product of a number multiplied into itself.—*n.* A square surface or figure.—**quadratic,** kwod•rat′ik, *a.* [Fr. *quadratique.*] Pertaining to, denoting, or containing a square, *alg.* involving the square or second power of an unknown quantity (a *quadratic* equation).—*n.* A quadratic equation; *pl.* that branch of algebra which treats of quadratic equations.—**quadrature,** kwod′re•chėr, *n.* [L. *quadratura.*] *Geom.* the act of squaring; the reducing of a figure to a square; thus, the finding of a square which shall contain just as much area as a certain square or triangle, is the *quadrature* of that circle or triangle; *astron.* the position of one heavenly body in respect to another when distant from it 90°.

quadrennial, kwod•ren′i•al, *a.* [From L. *quadriennium,* a space of four years—*quadrus*=*quatuor,* four, and *annus,* year.] Comprising four years; occurring once in four years.—**quadrennially,** kwod•ren′i•al•li, *adv.* Once in four years.

quadriceps, kwod′ri•seps, *n.* [L. *quadrus, quatuor,* four, *caput,* the head.] A large muscle in the front of the thigh.—**quadricipital,** kwod•ri•sip′i•tal, *a.* Four-headed; belonging to the quadriceps.

quadrifid, kwod′ri•fid, *a.* [L. *quadrus*=*quatuor,* four, and *findo, fidi,* to cleave.] Split or deeply cleft into four parts.

quadrifoliate, kwod•ri•fō′li•āt, *a.* [L. *quadrus*=*quatuor,* four, and *folium,* a leaf.] *Bot.* having four leaves attached laterally to a common stalk.

quadriga, kwod•rī′ga, *n.* pl. **quadrigae,** kwod•rī′jē. [L., contr. from *quadrijuga*—prefix *quadrus,* fourfold, and *jugum,* a yoke.] An ancient two-wheeled car or chariot drawn by four horses, harnessed all abreast.

quadrilateral, kwod•ri•lat′ėr•al, *a.* [L. *quadrus*=*quatuor,* four, and *latus, lateris,* side.] Having four sides and consequently four angles.—*n.* A figure having four sides and four angles; the space enclosed between and defended by four fortresses, or the four fortresses collectively.

quadriliteral, kwod•ri•lit′ėr•al, *a.* [L. *quatuor*, *litera*, letter.] Consisting of four letters.

quadrille, kwo•dril′, *n.* [Fr. *quadrille*, Sp. *cuadrilla*, a group of four persons, *cuadrillo*, a small square, from L. *quadra*, *quadrum*, a square, from *quatuor*, four.] A game played by four persons with forty cards; a dance consisting generally of five figures or movements executed by four couples each forming the side of a square; the music for such a dance.

quadrillion, kwod•ril′yon, *n.* [L. *quadrus*=*quatuor*, four, and E. *million*.] According to the United States and French system, a unit followed by 15 zeros; in Gt. Britain and Germany a unit followed by 24 zeros.

quadrinomial, kwod•ri•nō′mi•al, *a.* [L. *quadrus*=*quatuor*, four, and *nomen*, a name.] *Alg.* consisting of four denominations or terms.—*n. Alg.* a quantity consisting of four terms.

quadripartite, kwod•ri•pär′tīt, *a.* [L. *quadrus*=*quatuor*, four, and *partitus*, divided.] Divided into four parts; *bot.* divided to the base into four parts (a *quadripartite* leaf).

quadriphyllous, kwod•ri•fil′lus, *a.* [L. *quadrus*=*quatuor*, and Gr. *phyllon*, a leaf.] *Bot.* having four leaves; four-leaved.

quadrisyllable, kwod•ri•sil′la•bl, *n.* [L. *quadrus*=*quatuor*, four, and E. *syllable*.] A word consisting of four syllables.—**quadrisyllabic,** kwod′-ri•sil•lab″ik, *a.* Consisting of four syllables.

quadrivalent, kwod•riv′a•lent, *a.* [From L. *quadrus*=*quatuor*, four, and *valens*, *valentis*, ppr. of *valeo*, to be worth.] *Chem.* having a valence of four.

quadrivial, kwod•riv′i•al, *a.* [E. *quadrivium*—prefix *quadrus* = *quatuor*, four, and *via*, a way.] Having four roads meeting in a point.—**quadrivium,** kwod•riv′i•um, *n.* [L.L.] A collective term in the Middle Ages for the four lesser arts—arithmetic, music, geometry, and astronomy.

quadroon, kwod•rön′, *n.* [Sp. *cuarteron*, from L. *quartus*, fourth. QUARTER.] The offspring of a mulatto by a white person; a person who is one-fourth Negro.

quadruped, kwod′rṳ•ped, *n.* [L. *quadrupes*, *quadrupedis*=*quadrus*=*quatuor*, four, and *pes*, *pedis*, a foot.] An animal having four legs, usually restricted to four-footed mammals, though many reptiles have also four legs.—**quadrupedal,** kwod•rṳ′-pe•dal, *a.* Belonging to a quadruped, having or walking on four feet.

quadruple, kwod′rṳ•pl, *a.* [L. *quadruplus*—*quadrus*=*quatuor*, four, and term. *-plus*, Gr. *ploos*. DOUBLE.] Fourfold; four times told.—*n.* Four times the sum or number.—*v.t.*—*quadrupled*, *quadrupling*. To make four times as much or as many; to multiply by four.—*v.i.* To become four times as much or as many.—**quadruplet,** kwod•rṳ′plet, *n.* Four children born at one birth; one of these four children.

quadruplicate, kwod•rṳ′pli•kāt, *v.t.* [L. *quadruplico*, *quadruplicatum*—*quadrus*=*quatuor*, four, and *plico*, to fold.] To make fourfold; to double twice.—*a.* Fourfold; four times repeated (a *quadruplicate* ratio or proportion).—**quadruplication,** kwod•rṳ′pli•kā″shon, *n.* The act of making fourfold or four times as great.

quaestor, kwes′tor. See QUESTOR.

quaff, kwäf, *v.t.* [From Ir. and Gael. *cuach*, Sc. *quaich*, *queff*, a drinking cup.] To drink; to swallow in large draughts; to drink copiously.—*v.i.* To drink largely.—**quaffer,** kwäf′ėr, *n.* One who quaffs.

quagga, kwag′a, *n.* [Hottentot; name derived from its cry.] An animal of South Africa closely allied to the zebra.

quagmire, kwag′mīr, *n.* [*Quag* for *quake*, and *mire*; lit. a mire or bog that quakes or shakes.] A piece of soft boggy land that trembles under the foot; a bog; a fen.—**quaggy,** kwag′i, *a.* Trembling under the foot, as soft wet earth; boggy; spongy.

quahog, quahaug, kwä′häg, kwạ•häg′, *n.* [Algonquian origin.] An edible American clam, paricularly the hard-shelled *Venus mercenaria*.

quail, kwāl, *v.i.* [A.Sax. *cwelan*, to die=D. *quelen*, to pine away; O.H.G. *quelan*, to suffer torment. QUELL.] To have the spirits sink or give way, as before danger or difficulty; to shrink; to lose heart; to cower.

quail, kwāl, *n.* [O.Fr. *quaille*, Fr. *caille*, It. *quaglia*, a quail—names derived from its cry. Comp. D. *kwakkel*, G. *wachtel*, and Armor. *coaill*, a quail.] A common name of certain birds nearly allied to the partridges, from which they differ chiefly in being smaller.

quaint, kwānt, *a.* [O.E. *queint*, *coint*, from O.Fr. *coint*, neat, fine, dainty; from L. *cognitus*, known, the meaning having probably been influenced by L. *comptus*, trimmed, adorned. COGNITION, ACQUAINT.] Old and antique; singular; whimsical; curious; fanciful.—**quaintly,** kwānt′li, *adv.* In a quaint manner; oddly; fancifully; singularly; whimsically.—**quaintness,** kwānt′nes, *n.* The quality of being quaint; oddity and antiqueness.

quake, kwāk, *v.i.*—*quaked*, *quaking*. [A.Sax. *cwacian*, same root as *quick*; comp. Prov. G. *quacken*, to waggle, to shake. QUICK.] To shake; to tremble; to shudder (to *quake* with fear); to be shaken with more or less violent convulsions (the earth *quakes*); to shake or tremble, as the earth under the feet, through want of solidity or firmness.—*n.* A shake; a trembling; a tremulous agitation.—**quaker,** kwā′kėr, *n.* One that quakes; [*cap.*] one of the religious sect called the *Society of Friends* (see under FRIEND.)—**Quakeress,** kwā′-kėr•es, *n.* A female Quaker.—**Quakerish,** kwā′kėr•ish, *a.* Relating to or resembling Quakers.—**Quakerism,** kwā′kėr•izm, *n.* The peculiar manners, tenets, or worship of the Quakers.—**Quakerly,** kwā′kėr•li, *a.* Resembling or characteristic of Quakers.

qualify, kwol′i•fī, *v.t.*—*qualified*, *qualifying*. [Fr. *qualifier*, from L.L. *qualificare*, from L. *qualis*, such, of such sort, and *facio*, to make.] To make such as is required; to fit for any place, office, or occupation; to furnish with knowledge, skill, etc., necessary for a purpose; to furnish with legal power or capacity (to *qualify* persons for the franchise); to limit or modify; to restrict; to limit by exceptions (to *qualify* a statement); to moderate, abate, soften; to modify the quality or strength of; to dilute or otherwise fit for taste (to *qualify* spirits with water).—*v.i.* To take the necessary steps for rendering one's self capable of holding any office or enjoying any privilege; to establish a right to exercise any function: followed by *for*.—**qualification,** kwol′i•fi•kā″shon, *n.* The act of qualifying, or the state of being qualified; that which qualifies or fits a person or thing for any use or purpose, as for a place, an office, an employment; legal power; ability; a qualifying or extenuating circumstance; modification; restriction; limitation; an abatement; a diminution.—**qualificative,** kwol′i•fi•kā•tiv, *a.* Serving or having the power to qualify or modify.—*n.* That which serves to qualify; a qualifying term, clause, or statement.—**qualified,** kwol′i•fīd, *p.* and *a.* Having a qualification; furnished with legal power or capacity; accompanied with some limitation or modification; modified; limited (a *qualified* statement).—**qualifiedly,** kwol′i•fīd•li, *adv.* With qualification or limitation.—**qualifier,** kwol′i•fī•ėr, *n.* One who or that which qualifies.

quality, kwol′i•ti, *n.* [Fr. *qualité*, from L. *qualitas*, a quality or property, from *qualis*, such. QUALIFY.] That which makes or helps to make anything such as it is; a distinguishing property, characteristic, or attribute; a property; a trait; moral characteristic, good or bad; comparative rank; condition in relation to others; superior or high rank (ladies of *quality*).—*The quality*, persons of high rank collectively.—**qualitative,** kwol′i•tā•tiv, *a.* Pertaining to quality; estimable according to quality.—*Qualitative analysis*, *chem.* the process of decomposing a compound substance with a view to determine what elements it contains.—**qualitatively,** kwol′i•tā•tiv•li, *adv.* In a qualitative manner; as regards quality.

qualm, kwäm, *n.* [A.Sax. *cwealm*, pestilence, death; D. *kwalm*, Dan. *qvalm*, qualm, vapor; O.H.G. *qualm*, death; from root of *quell*, *quail*.] A throe or throb of pain; a sudden feeling of sickness at the stomach; a sensation of nausea; a scruple or twinge of conscience; compunction.—**qualmish,** kwäm′-ish, *a.* Sick at the stomach; inclined to vomit; affected with nausea.—**qualmishly,** kwäm′ish•li, *adv.* In a qualmish manner.—**qualmishness,** kwäm′ish•nes, *n.* The state of being qualmish.

quamash, kwom′ash, *n.* An American bulbous plant with roots which were much eaten by the Indians; the Camass.

quandary, kwon•da′ri or kwon′da•ri, *n.* [Probably from Fr. *Qu'en dirai-je?* what shall I say of it?] A state of difficulty, perplexity, uncertainty, or hesitation; a pickle; a predicament.—*v.t. quandaried, quandarying.* To put into a quandary.

quantity, kwon′ti•ti, *n.* [Fr. *quantité,* L. *quantitas,* quantity, extent, from *quantus,* how great, from *quam,* to what a degree.] That property in virtue of which a thing is measurable; greatness; extent; measure; size; any amount, bulk, or aggregate (a *quantity* of earth, a *quantity* of water); often a large or considerable amount (wheat shipped in *quantities*); *math.* anything which can be multiplied, divided, or measured; anything to which mathematical processes are applicable; *gram.* the measure of a syllable or the time in which it is pronounced; the metrical value of syllables as regards length or weight in pronunciation; *logic,* the extent in which the subject of a proposition is taken.—*Quantity of electricity,* measured practically in COULOMBS (which see).—*Quantity of heat,* the unit of quantity of heat is the quantity required to raise unit mass of water through one degree of temperature; according to the unit of mass and the scales employed there are the different units known as pound-degree F., pound-degree C., gram-degree C. See CALORIE.—**quantification,** kwon′ti•fi•kā″shon, *n.* The act or process of quantifying; the act of determining the quantity or amount.—**quantify,** kwon′ti•fī, *v.t.—quantified, quantifying.* [L. *quantus,* how much, and *facio,* to make.] To determine the quantity of; to modify or qualify with regard to quantity; more especially a term in logic (to *quantify* the predicate, as by inserting 'all' in 'some men are (all) logicians').—**quantitative,** kwon′ti•tā•tiv, *a.* Estimable according to quantity; relating or having regard to quantity.—*Quantitative analysis, chem.* the process of decomposing a compound substance with a view to determine how much of each element it contains.—**quantitatively,** kwon′ti•tā•tiv•li, *adv.* In a quantitative manner.—**quantum,** kwan′tum, *n.* [L., how much, as much as.] A quantity; an amount; a sufficient amount.—**quantum theory.** *Phys.* a theory that the emission or absorption of energy by atoms or molecules is not continuous but occurs in discrete amounts, each amount being called a quantum.

quarantine, kwor′an•tēn, *n.* [O.Fr. *quarantaine,* It. *quarantana,* a space of forty days, from *quaranta,* from L. *quadraginta,* forty, from *quatuor,* four.] The period, originally of forty days, now of lesser but indeterminate length, during which a ship arriving in port is detained by health officers for investigation of the possible presence of contagious disease; a place where persons with contagious disease are detained; the place where ships are detained for inspection; the edict requiring one to be detained or the time required by health statutes for a person to be detained in his living quarters because of contagion.—*v.t. quarantined, quarantining.* To restrict the entrance to and exit from any place under observation for contagious disease.

quarrel, kwor′el, *n.* [O.Fr. *querele,* Fr. *querelle,* a quarrel, from L. *querela,* a complaint, from *queror,* to complain; akin *querulous,* also *cry.*] A brawl; an angry dispute; a wrangle; an altercation; a breach of friendship or concord; open variance between parties; the basis or ground of being at variance with another; ill-will, or reason to complain; ground of objection.—*v.i.—quarreled, quarreling.* To dispute violently or with loud and angry words; to wrangle; to squabble; to fall out; to pick a quarrel; to get into hostilities; to find fault; to cavil.—**quarreler,** kwor′el•ėr, *n.* One who quarrels.—**quarrelsome,** kwor′el•-sum, *a.* Apt to quarrel; easily irritated or provoked to contest; irascible; choleric.—**quarrelsomely,** kwor′el•sum•li, *adv.* In a quarrelsome manner.

quarrel, kwor′el, *n.* [O.Fr. *quarrel* (Fr. *carreau*), dim. of L. *quadrum,* something square, from *quatuor,* four.] A bolt to be shot from a crossbow, especially with a somewhat square-shaped head; a lozenge-shaped pane of glass in a window; a small paving stone or tile of the square or lozenge form; a glazier's diamond; a kind of graver.

quarry, kwor′i, *n.* [O.Fr. *quarriere* (Fr. *carrière*), lit. a place where stones are squared, from L. *quadro,* to square. QUADRAT, etc.] A place where stones are dug from the earth, or separated, as by blasting with gunpowder, from a large mass of rocks.—*v.t.—quarried, quarrying.* To dig or take from a quarry (to *quarry* marble).—**quarrier,** kwor′i•-ėr, *n.* One who works in a quarry.

quarry, kwor′i, *n.* [Fr. *curée,* the portion given to the dogs, wrapped in the skin of the beast killed, from L. *corium,* a hide, leather.] A part of the entrails of a beast of chase given to the dogs; a heap of game killed; any animal pursued for prey; the game which a hawk or hound pursues; object of chase or pursuit in general.

quart, kwa̤rt, *n.* [Fr. *quarte;* lit. a fourth part, from L. *quartus,* fourth, from *quatuor,* four.] A unit of liquid measure ($^1/_4$ of a gallon) or dry measure ($^1/_8$ of a peck); 2 pints; a container holding a quart.—**quartan,** kwa̤r′tan, *a.* [L. *quartanus,* fourth.] Intermitting so as to occur every fourth day (a *quartan* fever).

quarter, kwa̤r′tėr, *n.* [O.Fr. *quarter, quartier* (Fr. *quartier*), a quarter, from L. *quartarius,* a fourth part, from *quartus,* fourth, from *quatuor,* four.] One of four parts into which anything is divided; a fourth part or portion; the fourth part of a hundredweight, that is, 25 lbs.; the fourth of a dollar, or twenty-five cents (*U.S.*); the fourth part of the moon's period or monthly revolution; one of the four cardinal points; more widely, any region or point of the compass (from what *quarter* does the wind blow?); a particular region of a town, city, or country; a district; a locality (the Latin *quarter* of Paris; the Jews' *quarter* in Florence); the fourth part of the year; in schools, the fourth part of the teaching period of the year; the fourth part of the carcass of a quadruped, including a limb; *her.* one of the divisions of a shield when it is divided into four portions by horizontal and perpendicular lines meeting in the fess point; the piece of leather in a shoe which forms the side from the heel to the vamp; the part of a vessel's side which lies toward the stern; proper position; specific place; assigned or allotted position; the sparing of the life of a vanquished enemy; mercy shown by a conqueror (to give or show *quarter* to a person—perhaps originally to assign a lodging to, or to give a share of one's own quarters); *pl.* (in each of the following senses), temporary residence; shelter (to find *quarters* somewhere); a station or encampment occupied by troops (winter *quarters*); place of lodgment for officers and men; *naut.* the post allotted to the officers and men at the commencement of an engagement.—*On the quarter* (*naut.*), in a direction oblique to the ship's quarter.—*v.t.* To divide into four equal parts; to separate into parts; to cut to pieces; to furnish with lodgings or shelter, to find lodgings and food for (to *quarter* soldiers on the inhabitants); *her.* to add to other arms on the shield by dividing it into four or more compartments.—*v.t.* To be stationed; to lodge; to have temporary residence. —**quarterback,** *n.* In football (*U. S.*) a player who calls signals while standing behind the center from whom he may receive the ball, either carrying it or passing it to another member of the team.—*v. i.* To direct; to make plans and to give instructions for carrying out plans. —**quarter day,** *n.* One of the four days during the year on which payment of rent, interest, etc., is made.—**quarter-deck,** *n. Naut.* that part of the upper deck which is abaft the mainmast.—**quartering,** kwa̤r′tėr•ing, *n. Her.* the conjoining of coats of arms in one shield to denote the alliances of one family with the heiresses of others; one of the compartments on such a shield.—**quarterly,** kwa̤r'tėr•li, *a.* Recurring at the end of each quarter of the year (*quarterly* payments of rent).—*adv.* Once in a quarter of a year.—*n.* A periodical publication issued once every three months.—**quartermaster,** *n. Milit.* an officer who has charge of the quarters, barracks, tents, etc., and supplies all foodstuffs; *naut.* a petty officer who has charge of the stowage of ballast and provisions, and attends to the steering of the ship, etc.—**quarter note,** *n.* In music, the quarter part of a whole note.—**quartersaw,** *v.t.* To saw timber into quarter sections, then into boards, so that when finished, the grain is attractive in appearance.—**quarter section,** *n.* A system of land surveying used by the governments of the U. S. and Canada, whereby farm lands are accurately divided into sections one mile square (640 acres), half sections (320 acres), and quarter sections (160 acres).—**quarterstaff,** *n.* A weapon formed of a stout pole about 6½ feet long, grasped by one hand in the middle, and by the other between the middle and the end.

quartet, kwa̤r•tet', *n.* [It. *quartetto,* from L. *quartus,* fourth.] A piece of music arranged for four voices or four instruments; the persons who execute a quartet; a stanza of four lines.

quartile, kwa̤r'tīl, *n.* [L. *quartus,* fourth.] A point on a distribution curve indicating the division of that distribution into quarters or sections equivalent to 25% of the total number of units.

quarto, kwa̤r'tō, *n.* [L. *quartus,* fourth.] A book of the size of the fourth of a sheet; a size made by twice folding a sheet, which then makes four leaves; abbreviated thus, 4*to.*—*a.* Denoting the size of a book in which a sheet makes four leaves.

quartz, kwa̤rts, *n.* [From G. *quarz, quartz,* quartz, a word of unknown origin.] A name given to varieties of the native oxide of silicon occurring both crystallized and massive, and an important constituent of granite and the older rocks, varieties of it being known as rock crystal, flint, agate, amethyst, etc.—**quartziferous,** kwa̤rt•sif'ėr•us, *a.* [*Quartz,* and L. *fero,* to bear.] Consisting of quartz, or chiefly of quartz; yielding quartz.—**quartzite,** kwa̤rt'sīt, *n.* A rock formed of granular quartz; quartzrock.—**quartz lamp,** *n.* A mercury lamp, used in physical therapy, which emits ultraviolet rays through a quartz lens.

quasar, kwā'sär, *n.* [*Quasi*-stell*ar.*] One of several enormously distant, starlike sources of radio energy.

quash, kwosh, *v.t.* [O.Fr. *quasser,* Fr. *casser,* from L. *quassare,* to shake, shatter, shiver; intens. from *quatio, quassum,* to shake; seen also in *concussion, percussion, discuss.*] To subdue, put down, or quell; to extinguish; to put an end to (to *quash* a rebellion); *law,* to make void from insufficiency, or for other cause.

quasi, kwā'sī. [L.] As if; in a manner; sometimes forming compounds with English words, and generally implying that what it qualifies is in some degree fictitious or unreal, or only has certain features of what it professes to be (a *quasi-argument,* a *quasi-historical* account).

quassia, kwosh'a, *n.* [From *Quassy,* a Negro who first made known the medicinal virtues of one species.] A genus of South American tropical trees containing an extremely bitter principle, having marked tonic properties, and used medicinally.

quatern, kwat'ėrn, *a.* [L. *quaterni,* four each, from *quatuor,* four.] Consisting of four; growing by fours (*quatern* leaves).—**quaternary,** kwa•tėr'ne•ri, *a.* [L. *quaternarius.*] Consisting of four; arranged in fours; *geol.* a term applied to the strata above the tertiary; post-tertiary (which see); *chem.* applied to compounds which contain four elements.—**quaternate,** kwa•tėr'nāt, *a.* Consisting of four.—*Quaternate leaf,* one that consists of four leaflets.

quaternion, kwa•tėr'ni•on, *n.* [L. *quaternio,* a group of four, from *quatuor,* four.] A set or group of four; a term for a quantity employed in a method of mathematical investigation discovered by Sir W. R. Hamilton.

quatrain, kwot'rān, *n.* [Fr., from *quatre,* L. *quatuor,* four.] A stanza of four lines rhyming alternately.

quatrefoil, kä'tėr•foil or kwa̤'tėr•foil, *n.* [Fr. *quatre-feuille*—*quatre* (L. *quatuor*), four, and *feuille* (L. *folium*), a leaf.] *Arch.* an aperture or ornament somewhat resembling four leaves about a common center; an opening showing four radiating cusps.

quaver, kwā'vėr, *v.i.* [From older *quave,* to shake, akin to *quiver*; and to L.G. *quabbeln,* to quiver; perhaps also to *quake.*] To have a tremulous motion; to vibrate; to shake in vocal utterance; to sing with tremulous modulations of voice; to produce a shake on a musical instrument.—*v.t.* To utter with a tremulous sound.—*n.* A shake or rapid vibration of the voice, or a shake on an instrument of music; a note equal to half a crotchet or the eighth of a semibreve.

quay, kē, *n.* [From Fr. *quai,* a quay, a Celtic word=Bret. *cae,* W. *cae,* an enclosure.] A built landing place along a line of coast or a river bank, or forming the side of a harbor, at which vessels are loaded and unloaded; a wharf.—*v.t.* To furnish with quays.—**quayage,** kē'ij, *n.* Quay dues; wharfage.

quean, kwēn, *n.* [A.Sax. *cwene,* a woman, a base woman. QUEEN.] A worthless woman; a slut; a strumpet.

queasy, kwē'zi, *a.* [Allied to Icel. *kveisa,* pain in the stomach; N. *kveis,* sickness after a debauch.] Sick at the stomach; affected with nausea; qualmish; apt to cause nausea.—**queasily,** kwē'zi•li, *adv.* In a queasy manner.—**queasiness,** kwē'zi•nes, *n.* The state of being queasy; qualmishness; disgust.

quebracho, ke•brä'chō, *n.* The name of South American timber trees, the bark of one of which is used in tanning, that of another in medicine.

queen, kwēn, *n.* [A.Sax. *cwén,* a queen, a wife (akin *quean*)=Goth. *qvens, qveins*; a woman; Icel. *kván,* a wife, *kona,* a woman; Dan. *qvinde,* a woman, *kone,* a wife; O.H.G. *quena,* a woman; Ir. and Gael. *coinne,* Gr. *gynē,* Skr. *jani,* a woman. From root *gan* Gr. and L. (*gen*), to produce. KIN, GENUS.] The consort of a king; a woman who is the sovereign of a kingdom; a female sovereign; a woman pre-eminent among others; the sovereign of a swarm of bees, or the female of the hive; a playing card on which a queen is depicted; the most powerful of all the pieces in a set of chessmen; (*slang*) an extraordinarily attractive girl or young woman.—*Queen consort,* the wife of a king. *Queen dowager,* the widow of a deceased king.—*Queen mother,* a queen dowager who is also mother of the reigning sovereign.—**queen bee,** *n.* The only fully developed and prolific female insect in a hive of bees.—**queenly,** kwēn'li, *a.* Like a queen; becoming a queen.—**queenliness,** kwēn'li•nes, *n.* The state of being queenly; queenly quality.—**queen post,** *n. Carp.* one of the two upright posts which connect two opposite rafters of a roof with the horizontal beam between them.

Queen Anne style, *n.* A period of English architecture and furniture design in the reign of Queen Anne, during the 18th century. The buildings were ornamented by modified and simplified classic designs; the characteristic furniture of the time, largely influenced by the Dutch, emphasized comfort, upholstery of simple damask, and simple, curved lines. — **Queen Anne's lace,** *n.* The wild carrot.

queer, kwēr, *a.* [From L.G. *quer, queer,* across=G. *queer, quer,* oblique, athwart, whence *querkopf,* a queer fellow.] Behaving or appearing otherwise than is usual; odd; singular; quaint.—**queerly,** kwēr'li, *adv.* In a queer manner.—**queerness,** kwēr'nes, *n.* The state or quality of being queer; singularity.

quell, kwel, *v.t.* [A.Sax. *cwellan,* to kill=Dan. *quaele,* to stifle, torment; Icel. *kvelja,* Sw. *qvalja,* G. *quälen,* to torment; same root as to *quail.*] To subdue; to cause to cease by using force; to crush (an insurrection or the like); to quiet; to allay.—**queller,** kwel'ėr, *n.* One that quells or crushes.

quench, kwensh, *v.t.* [A.Sax. *cwencan,* to quench, to extinguish; akin to *cwinan,* to dwindle; O.Fris. *kwinka,* to vanish.] To extinguish; to put out (fire); to allay; to slake (thirst); to suppress, stifle, check, repress.—*v.i.* To be extinguished; to go out; to lose zeal (*Shak.*).—**quenchable,** kwensh'a•bl, *a.* Capable of being quenched.—**quencher,** kwensh'ėr, *n.*

One who or that which quenches.—**quenchless,** kwensh′les, *a.* That cannot be quenched; inextinguishable.

quercitron, kwėr′sit•ron, *n.* [L. *quercus,* an oak, and *citrus,* the citron tree.] The black or dyer's oak, a large forest tree of N. America; the bark of this tree yielding a yellow dye; the dyestuff itself.

querist. See QUERY.

quern, kwėrn, *n.* [A.Sax. *cwyrn, cweorn*=D. *kweern,* Icel. *kvern,* Dan. *qvaern,* Goth. *qvairnus,* a millstone, a quern; from root meaning to grind, same as in *corn.*] A stone handmill for grinding grain, still used to some extent by the Highlanders of Scotland.

querulous, kwer′ū•lus, *a.* [L. *querulus,* from *queror,* to complain. QUARREL.] Complaining or habitually complaining; apt to murmur; peevish; expressing complaint.—**querulously,** kwer′ū•lus•li, *adv.* In a querulous manner.—**querulousness,** kwer′ū•lus•nes, *n.* Disposition to complain; peevishness.

query, kwē′ri, *n.* [A modified form of L. *quaere,* imper. of *quaero,* to ask, to inquire, to seek. QUEST.] A question; an inquiry to be answered or resolved; the mark or sign of interrogation (?).—*v.i. queried, querying.* To ask a question or questions.—*v.t.* To seek by questioning; to examine by questions; to doubt of; to mark with a query.—**querist,** kwē′rist, *n.* One who puts a query; one who asks questions.

quest, kwest, *n.* [O.Fr. *queste,* Fr. *quête,* from L. *quaesitus,* pp. of *quaero,* to seek, seen also in *question, query, inquest, request, inquire, require, conquer,* etc.] The act of seeking; search; pursuit; searchers collectively (*Shak.*); inquiry; examination.—*v.i.*† To make search or inquiry.—*v.t.*† To search or seek for.

question, kwes′tyun, *n.* [Fr. *question;* L. *quaestio,* an inquiry, an investigation. QUEST.] An interrogation; something asked; an inquiry; a query; disquisition; discussion; the subject or matter of investigation or discussion; the theme of inquiry (foreign to the *question*); subject of debate; a point of doubt or difficulty; doubt; controversy (true beyond *question*); judicial trial (*Shak.*); *the question,* examination by torture.—*Question!* an exclamation used to recall a speaker to the subject under discussion; also used to express doubt as to the correctness of what a speaker is saying.—*Begging the question,* assuming something without proof; taking for granted what has to be proved.—*In question,* in debate; being at present dealt with (the point in *question*).—*To call in question,* to doubt; to challenge the truth or reality of.—*Out of question,* doubtless; undoubtedly.—*Out of the question,* not worthy of consideration; not to be thought of.—*Leading question.* See LEADING.—*Previous question,* in *parliamentary practice,* the question whether a vote shall be come to on the main issue or not, brought forward before the main or real question is put, and for the purpose of avoiding, if the resolution is in the negative, the putting of this question. The motion is in the form, 'that the question be now put', and the mover and seconder vote against it.—*v.i.* To ask a question or questions; to debate; to doubt.—*v.t.* To inquire of by asking questions; to examine by interrogatories; to doubt of; to have no confidence in; to call in question; to challenge.—**questionable,** kwes′tyun•a•bl, *a.* Capable of being questioned or inquired of; liable to question; suspicious; doubtful; uncertain; disputable.—**questionableness,** kwes′tyun•a•bl•nes, *n.*—**questionably,** kwes′tyun•a•bli, *adv.* In a questionable manner; doubtfully.—**questionnaire,** kwes′-tyun•âr″, *n.* A systematic series of questions prepared for distribution for the purpose of gathering detailed information.—**questioner,** kwes′-tyun•ėr, *n.*—**question mark,** *n.* An interrogation point (?).

questor, kwes′tor, *n.* [L. *quaestor.* QUEST.] The name of certain magistrates of ancient Rome whose chief office was the management of the public treasure; a receiver of taxes, tribute, etc.—**questorship,** kwes′-tor•ship, *n.* The office of questor.

quetzal, ket′zäl, *n.* [Native name.] A magnificent bird of Central America revered by Maya and Aztec.

queue, kū, *n.* [Fr., tail, from L. *cauda,* a tail. CUE.] A pigtail; a line of persons, vehicles, etc.—*v.t.* and *i.* To be or arrange in a line.

quibble, kwib′l, *n.* [A freq. of *quib, quip.*] A turn of language to evade the point in question; an evasion; a prevarication; a pun; a low conceit.—*v.i.*—*quibbled, quibbling.* To evade the point in question by artifice, play upon words, or any conceit; to prevaricate; to pun.—**quibbler,** kwib′lėr, *n.* One who quibbles; a punster.

quick, kwik, *a.* [A.Sax. *cwic,* living, lively=D. *kwik,* Icel. *kvikr,* Dan. *qvik,* Sw. *qvick,* L.G. *quick,* Goth. *qvius;* same root as L. *vivus,* living, Gr. *bios,* life, Skr. *jiv,* to live.] Alive; living (the *quick* and the dead); characterized by liveliness or sprightliness; nimble; brisk; speedy; rapid; swift; perceptive in a high degree (*quick* sight); sensitive; hasty; precipitate; irritable (*quick* of temper); pregnant (*Shak.*).—*adv.* In a quick manner; quickly.—*n.* A growing plant, usually hawthorn, for hedges; with *the,* the living flesh; sensible parts; hence, *fig.* that which is susceptible of or causes keen feeling (stung to the *quick*).—**quicken,** kwik′n, *v.t.* To make alive; to revive or resuscitate; to cheer or refresh; to make quicker; to accelerate; to sharpen; to give keener perception to; to stimulate.—*v.i.* To become alive; to become quicker; to be in that state of pregnancy in which the child gives signs of life.—**quickener,** kwik′n•ėr, *n.*—**quick-freeze,** *v.t.*—pret. *quick-froze,* pp. *quick-frozen,* ppr. *quick-freezing.* To freeze food quickly for storage.—**quickie,** kwik′i, *n.* Anything done or made quickly or shoddily (slang).—**quicklime,** kwik′līm, *n.* Lime burned and not yet slaked with water.—**quickly,** kwik′li, *adv.* Speedily; rapidly; nimbly; soon; without delay.—**quickness,** kwik′nes, *n.* State of being quick or alive; speed; celerity; activity; briskness; acuteness of perception; keenness; sharpness.—**quicksand,** kwik′sand, *n.* A movable sandbank in the sea, a lake, or river, dangerous to vessels or to persons who trust themselves to it; *fig.* something deceptive or treacherous.—**quickset,** kwik′set, *n.* A living plant set to grow, particularly for a hedge; hawthorn planted for a hedge.—*a.* Made of quickset.—*v.t.* To plant with living shrubs for a hedge.—**quicksilver,** kwik′sil•vėr, *n.* [Living silver, so called from its fluidity.] Mercury, metal liquid at all ordinary temperatures. See MERCURY.—**quick-tempered,** *a.* Easily aroused to anger.—**quick time,** *n.* The normal rate of marching, which is 120 paces per minute in the U.S. Army.—**quick-witted,** *a.* Sharp of mind.

quid, kwid, *n.* [A form of *cud.*] A piece of tobacco chewed and rolled about in the mouth.

quiddity, kwid′i•ti, *n.* [Fr. *quiddité,* from L.L. *quidditas,* from L. *quid,* what.] An old philosophical term equivalent to essence, and comprehending both the substance and qualities; a trifling nicety; a quirk or quibble.

quidnunc, kwid′nungk, *n.* [L., what now?] One curious to know everything that passes; one who pretends to know all that goes on.

quiescent, kwī•es′ent, *a.* [L. *quiescens, quiescentis,* ppr. of *quiesco,* to keep quiet. QUIET.] Being in a state of repose; still; not moving; quiet; not excited; tranquil; *gram.* silent; not sounded (a *quiescent* letter).—**quiescence, quiescency,** kwī•es′ens, kwī•es′en•si, *n.* The state or quality of being quiescent; rest; repose.—**quiescently,** kwī•es′ent•li, *adv.* In a quiescent manner.

quiet, kwī′et, *a.* [Fr. *quiet,* L. *quietus,* from *quiesco,* to keep quiet, from *quies, quietus,* rest. *Coy, quit, quite,* have the same origin.] Not in action or motion; still; in a state of rest; free from alarm or disturbance; left at rest; tranquil; peaceable; not turbulent; free from emotion; calm; patient; retired; secluded; free from fuss or bustle; not glaring or showy (*quiet* colors).—*n.* Rest; stillness; tranquillity; repose; freedom from emotion of the mind; calmness.—*v.t.* To make or cause to be quiet; to calm; to pacify; to allay; to tranquillize; to bring to a state of rest.—*v.i.* To become quiet or still‡; to abate.—**quieter,** kwī′et•ėr, *n.* One who or that which quiets.—**quietism,** kwī′et•izm, *n.* The absorption of the feelings or faculties in religious contemplation; the practice of a class of mystics who resigned themselves to mental inactivity in order to bring the soul into direct union with the Godhead.—**quietist,** kwī′et•ist, *n.*

One who believes in or practices quietism; especially applied to one of a sect of mystics originated by Molinos, a Spanish priest, in the latter part of the seventeenth century.—**quietly,** kwī'et•li, *adv.* In a quiet state or manner; peaceably; calmly; patiently; in a manner to attract little or no observation.—**quietness,** kwī'et•nes, *n.* The state of being quiet; tranquillity; calmness.—**quietude,** kwī'e•tūd, *n.* [L. *quietudo.*] Rest; quiet; tranquillity.—**quietus,** kwī•ē'tus, *n.* [L. *quietus*, quiet. *Quietus* or *quietus est* was a formula used in discharging accounts, equivalent to quit, discharged.] A final discharge of an account; a final settlement; a quittance.

quill, kwil, *n.* [O.E. *quylle*, a cane or reed; from Fr. *quille*, a pin, a skittle, from G. *kiel*, a quill, a stalk, a pin, O.G. *kil*, a stalk.] One of the large, strong feathers of geese, swans, turkeys, crows, etc., used for pens, etc.; one of these made into an instrument of writing; the spine of a porcupine; a piece of small reed on which weavers wind the thread of the woof; a piece of quill attached to a slip of wood, by means of which certain stringed musical instruments were played; the fold of a plaited ruff or ruffle, about the size and shape of a goose quill.—*v.t.* To plait with small ridges like quills.—**quilldriver,** *n.* A contemptuous term for one who works with a quill or pen; a clerk.

quilt, kwilt, *n.* [O.Fr. *cuilte*, *coutre*, *coultre*, from L. *culcitra*, *culcita*, a mattress, a pillow, a quilt. This word by corruption or confusion gave the *counter-* of *counterpane.*] A cover or coverlet made by stitching one cloth over another, with some soft substance between; any thick or warm coverlet.—*v.t.* To stitch together, as two pieces of cloth, with some soft substance between; to stuff in the manner of a quilt.—**quilter,** kwilt'ėr, *n.* One who quilts.—**quilting,** kwilt'ing, *n.* The act or operation of forming a quilt; the material used for making quilts; quilted work.

quinary, kwī'na•ri, *a.* [L. *quinarius*, from *quini*, five each, from *quinque*, five.] Consisting of five or a multiple of five; arranged by fives.—**quinate,** kwī'nāt, *a. Bot.* applied to five similar parts arranged together, as five leaflets.

quince, kwins, *n.* [From Fr. *coignasse*, a kind of quince, from L. *cotonium*, *cydonium*, Gr. *kydōnion*, (*mēlon*), a quince, lit. Cydonian fruit, from *Cydonia*, a town in Crete.] A fruit and the tree that bears it, now widely cultivated, the fruit being golden yellow and much used in making preserves.

quincunx, kwin'kungks, *n.* [L., from *quinque*, five, and *uncia*, ounce—a five-ounce weight being marked with five spots.] An arrangement of five objects in a square, one at each corner and one in the middle; an arrangement, as of trees, in such squares continuously.—**quincuncial,** kwin•kun'shal, *a.* Having the form of a quincunx.

quindecagon, kwin•dek'a•gon, *n.* [L. *quinque*, five, Gr. *deka*, ten, and *gōnia*, angle.] *Geom.* a plane figure with fifteen sides and fifteen angles.

quinine, kwī'nīn, *n.* [Peruvian-Indian *kina*, *quina*, bark.] A most important vegetable alkali, obtained from the bark of several trees of the *Cinchona* genus, extensively used in medicine as a febrifuge and tonic.—**quinia, quinina,** kwin'i•a, kwi•nī'na, *n.* Older names for *Quinine.*—**quinidine,** kwin'i•din, *n.* A substance in some cinchona barks, with acids forming salts having febrifugal properties.

quinoline, kwin'o•lēn, *n.* [From *quinine.*] A compound from which quinine is derived.

Quinquagesima, kwin•kwa•jes'i•ma, *n.* [L.] Fiftieth.—*Quinquagesima Sunday*, so called as being about the fiftieth day before Easter; Shrove Sunday.

quinquecapsular, kwin•kwe•kap'sū•lėr, *a.* [L. *quinque*, five, and *capsula*, a little chest.] *Bot.* having five capsules.—**quinquefoliate,** kwin•kwe•fō'li•āt, *a.* [L. *folium*, leaf.] Having five leaves.—**quinquelocular,** kwin•kwe•lok'ū•lėr, *a.* [L. *loculus*, a cell.] *Bot.* five-celled.

quinquennial, kwin•kwen'i•al, *a.* [L. *quinquennium*, a period of five years—*quinque*, five, and *annus*, year.] Occurring once in five years, or lasting five years.—**quinquennium,** kwin•kwen'i•um, *n.* [L.] The space of five years. Also **quinquenniad,**† kwin•kwen'i•ad. (*Tenn.*)

quinquepartite, kwin•kwe•pär'tīt, *a.* [L. *quinque*, five, and *partitus*, divided.] Consisting of five parts; *bot.* divided into five parts almost to the base.

quinquevalent, kwin•kwev'a•lent, *a.* [L. *quinque*, five, and *valens*, *valentis*, ppr. of *valeo*, to be worth.] *Chem.* having a valence of five.

quinsy, kwin'zi, *n.* [From Fr. *esquinancie*, *squinancie*, from L. *cynanche*, Gr. *kynangchē*, a kind of sore throat, from *kyōn*, a dog, and *angchō*, to throttle—'dog' having a pejorative effect. CYNIC.] *Med.* an inflammation of the tonsils; any inflammation of the throat or parts adjacent.

quint, kwint, *n.* [L. *quintus*, fifth.] A set or sequence of five, as in piquet.

quintain, kwin'tin, *n.* [Fr. *quintaine*, L.L. *quintana*, a quintain, from L. *quintana*, a street or broad way in a camp (from *quintus*, fifth), hence a public place, and the exercise practiced in such a place.] A figure or other object to be tilted at, often an upright post, on the top of which was a horizontal bar turning on a pivot, with a sandbag attached to one end, on the other a broad board, it being a trial of skill to tilt at the broad end with a lance, and pass on before the bag of sand could whirl round and strike the tilter.

quintal, kwin'tal, *n.* [Fr. *quintal*, from L. *centum*, a hundred, through the Sp. *quintal*, Ar. *kintâr*, a weight of 100 lb.] A weight of 100 lb.

quintan, kwin'tan, *a.* [L. *quintanus*, from *quintus*, fifth, from *quinque*, five.] Occurring or recurring every fifth day.—*n.* An intermittent fever the paroxysms of which recur every fifth day.

quintessence, kwin•tes'ens, *n.* [L. *quinta*, *essentia*, fifth essence.] According to old notions the fifth or highest essence or most ethereal element of natural bodies; hence, an extract from anything, containing its virtues or most essential part in a small quantity; the best and purest part of a thing.—**quintessential,** kwin•tes•sen'shal, *a.* Consisting of the quintessence.

quintet, quintette, kwin•tet', *n.* [Fr. *quintette*, from It. *quintetto*, from *quinto*, L. *quintus*, fifth.] *Mus.* a vocal or instrumental composition in five parts; those who execute a quintet; a group of five.

quintillion, kwin•til'yon, *n.* [L. *quintus*, fifth, and term. of E. *million.*] In U.S. and France, a unit followed by 18 zeros; in Gt. Britain and Germany a unit followed by 30 zeros.

quintuple, kwin'tū•pl, *a.* [L. *quintuplus*, fivefold—*quintus*, fifth, and term. *-plus*, Gr. *pleon.* DOUBLE.] Fivefold; arranged in five or in fives; *music*, containing five notes of equal value in a bar.—*v.t.*—*quintupled*, *quintupling.* To make fivefold.

quintuplet, kwin'tū•plet, *n.* A collection or mechanism for five of a kind; any one of five offspring born at the same birth.

quip, kwip, *n.* [From L. *quippe*, indeed.] A smart sarcastic turn; a sharp or cutting jest; a jibe.—*v.t.*—*quipped*, *quipping.* To utter quips on; to sneer at.—*v.i.* To use quips; to jibe.

quire, kwīr, *n.* [O.Fr. *quayer*; Fr. *cahier*, from L.L. *quaternum*, a book of four leaves, from L. *quatuor*, four.] A collection of paper consisting of twenty-four sheets of equal size and quality; 1/20 ream.

Quirinal, kwir'i•nal, *n.* The Italian court, as opposed to the Papal court of the Vatican, at Rome.

quirk, kwėrk, *n.* [Prov.E. *quirk*, to turn sharply; comp. W. *chwired*, a sudden start, craft, deceit.] An artful turn for evasion or subterfuge; a shift; a quibble; a quip: *arch.* an acute channel or recess; also, the hollow under the abacus.

quirt, kwėrt, *n.* [Sp. *cuarta.*] A riding whip with a short handle and braided rawhide lash.—*v.t.* To strike with a quirt.

quisling, kwis'ling, *n.* [For Vidkun *Quisling*, a Norwegian leader of the Nazi party.] A traitor, especially one who agrees to govern on behalf of the conquering nation.

quit, kwit, *a.* [From O.Fr. *quite*, Mod.Fr. *quittée*, discharged, freed, quit, from L. *quietus*, quiet. *Quiet* is thus the same word, as is also *quite.*] Discharged or released from a debt, penalty, or obligation; absolved; free; clear (with *of* before an object). It is often used in the form *quits*, as a kind of noun, to be *quits* with one, being to be on even terms, to have got even with him; hence, as an exclamation, *quits!* equivalent to, we are even.—*v.t.*—*quitted, quitting*. [O. Fr. *quiter*, Fr. *quitter*, to leave, to abandon.] To discharge, as an obligation or duty; to meet and satisfy; to repay; to set free, absolve, acquit; to relieve; to rid; to discharge from; to meet expectations entertained of; to acquit: used *refl.* (to *quit one's self* like a man); to depart from; to leave; to resign; to give up; to abandon.—*To quit cost*, to pay expenses.—*To quit scores*, to make even. —**quitclaim,** *n.* The giving up of a claim; a deed or document resigning a claim in favor of another.—**quitrent,** *n.* A small rent once paid by freeholders and copyholders of a manor in discharge of other services. —**quittance,** kwit'ans, *n.* Discharge from a debt or obligation; an acquittance; recompense; repayment. —**quitter,** kwit'ėr, *n.* One who quits; one who withdraws under adverse circumstances.—**quittor,** kwit'or, *n.* An ulcer between the hair and hoof of a horse's foot (for old *quitture*, a discharge of matter).—**quittor-bone,** *n.* A hard round swelling on a horse's coronet.

quitch, quitch grass, kwich, *n.* [A form of *quick grass*—named from its vitality and vigorous growth.] A species of worthless grass; couch grass.

quite, kwīt, *adv.* [Old form of *quit*, that is, primarily, free or clear by complete performance. QUIT.] Completely; wholly; entirely; totally; altogether; to a great extent or degree; very (*quite* warm).

quiver, kwiv'ėr, *v.i.* [Same as D. *quiveren*, to tremble, closely connected with *quaver*, and with old *quiver*, active, nimble, A.Sax. *cwifer*, perhaps also with *quick*.] To shake or tremble; to quake; to shiver; to show a slight tremulous motion; to be agitated.—*n.* The act or state of quivering; a tremulous motion; a shiver.—**quiveringly,** kwiv'er•ing•li, *adv.* In a quivering manner.

quiver, kwiv'ėr, *n.* [O.Fr. *quivre*, *cuivre*, from O.H.G. *kohhar*, *kochar*, G. *köcher*, a quiver; cog. Dan. *koger*, D. *koker*, A.Sax. *cocer*—a case, a quiver.] A case or sheath for arrows. —**quivered,** kwiv'erd, *a.* Furnished with a quiver; sheathed in a quiver.

quixotic, kwik•sot'ik, *a.* [From Don *Quixote*, the hero of Cervantes' celebrated romance, who is painted as a half-crazy reformer and champion, and is a caricature of the ancient knights of chivalry.] Romantic to extravagance; aiming at visionary ends; ideal; high-flown.—**quixotically,** kwik•sot'i•kal•li, *adv.* In a quixotic or absurdly romantic manner.—**quixotism,** kwik'sot•izm, *n.* Romantic and absurd notions.

quiz, kwiz, *n.* [Said to have been originated simply to puzzle people, by Daly, the manager of a Dublin playhouse, who had the letters *q u i z* put on all the walls of Dublin.] Something designed to puzzle; a hoax; a jest; one who quizzes; one liable to be quizzed; a brief, informal examination, as of a class.—*v.t.*—*quizzed, quizzing*. To puzzle; to banter; to make sport of by means of obscure questions; to look at through an eyeglass; to look at inquisitively; to question intensively with a view to obtaining information unwillingly revealed; curious, odd; mocking or teasing, as a *quizzical* remark.—**quizzical,** kwiz'i•kal, *a.* Partaking of the nature of a quiz; addicted to quizzing.

quod, kwod, *n.* [A form of *quad*, a contr. of *quadrangle*.] A jail. (*Slang*.)

quoin, koin, *n.* [A slightly different spelling of *coin*; Fr. *coin*, a corner, a wedge, a quoin, a coin. COIN.] An external solid angle; the external angle of a building; a wedgelike piece of stone, wood, metal, or other material; *printing*, a wedge to wedge the types up within a chase; *gun.*, a wedge to raise a cannon to the desired elevation.

quoit, kwoit, *n.* [Origin doubtful; comp. Prov.E. and Sc. *coit*; *quoit*, to throw; also O.D. *koot*, a die.] A flattish ring of iron, 8 or 9 inches in diameter and of some weight, convex on the upper side and slightly concave on the under side, to be thrown at a fixed mark on the ground at play; *pl.* the game played with such rings.—*v.t.* and *i.* To throw quoits; to play at quoits.

quondam, kwon'dam, *a.* [L., formerly.] Having been formerly; former (one's *quondam* friend).

quorum, kwō'rum, *n.* [Lit. 'of whom', being the genit. pl., of L. *qui*, who—from the phraseology of commissions, etc., written in Latin, certain persons being therein named generally, 'of whom' certain were specially designated as in all cases necessary and therefore constituted a quorum.] A selected group; an absolute majority unless specified to the contrary; such a number of the members of any body (a board of directors, for instance) as is competent to transact business.

quota, kwō'ta, *n.* [From L. *quotus*, which number in the series? QUOTE.] A proportional part or share; share or proportion assigned to each or which each of a number has to contribute.

quote, kwōt, *v.t.*—*quoted, quoting*. [O.Fr. *quoter*, Fr. *coter*, from L.L. *quotare*, to give chapter and verse for, from L. *quotus*, which number in the series? from *quot*, how many?] To adduce from some author or speaker; to adduce by way of authority or illustration; to cite or cite the words of (to *quote* a passage, an author); *com.* to name, as the price of an article.—*n.* A quotation; a quotation mark (colloq.).—**quotable,** kwōt'a•bl, *a.*—**quotation,** kwō•tā'shon, *n.* The act of quoting; the passage quoted or cited; *com.* the current price of commodities or stocks; the statement of commodity prices.

quotidian, kwō•tid'i•an, *a.* [L. *quotidianus*, from *quotidie*, daily—*quot*, how many, every, and *dies*, a day.] Daily; occurring or returning daily. —*n.* Anything that returns every day; a fever whose paroxysms return every day.

quotient, kwō'shent, *n.* [Fr., from L. *quoties*, how often? QUOTE.] *Arith.* the number resulting from the division of one number by another, and showing how often a less number is contained in a greater. —**quotum,**† kwo'tum, *n.* [Neut. of L. *quotus*, how much?] A quota; a share.

R

R, r, är, the eighteenth letter of the English alphabet.—*The three Rs*, a humorous and familiar designation for *Reading*, *(W)riting*, and *(A)rithmetic*.

rabbet, rab'et, *v.t.* [From Fr. *raboter*, to plane—prefix *re*, again, and *abouter*=E. *abut*.] To cut the edge of (as of a board) in a sloping manner, so that it may join by lapping with another piece cut in a similar manner; also, to cut a rectangular groove along the edge of to receive a corresponding projection.—*n.* The cut or groove so made. Sometimes written REBATE.—**rabbet joint,** *n.* A joint formed by rabbeting.

rabbi, rab'bī, *n.* pl. **rabbis, rabbies,** rab'bīz. [Heb. *rabî*, my master, from *rab*, master.] A title of respect given to Jewish doctors or expounders of the law.—**rabbin,** rab'bin, *n.* [A French form.] Same as *Rabbi*.—**rabbinic, rabbinical,** rab•bin'ik, rab•bin'i•kal, *a.* Pertaining to the rabbins, or to their opinions, learning, and language; pertaining to the later and non-canonical Hebrew writings.—**Rabbinic,** rab•bin'ik, *n.* The language or dialect of the rabbins; the later Hebrew.—**rabbinist,** rab'bin•ist, *n.* Among the Jews, one who adhered to the Talmud and the traditions of the rabbins.

rabbit, rab'it, *n.* [O.E. *robbet*, akin to O.D. *robbe*, *robbeken*, a rabbit; connections doubtful.] A well-known lagomorph mammal which feeds on grass or other herbage, and burrows in the earth, characterized by long ears and soft fur.—**rabbit fever,** *n.* *Med.* tularemia.—**rabbit punch,** *n.* A short, sharp blow to the nape of the neck.

rabble, rab'l, *n.* [Comp. D. *rabbelen*, to gabble; G. *rabbeln*, *robbeln*, to chatter; perhaps imitative of noise.] A tumultuous crowd of vulgar, noisy people; a mob; with *the*; the lower class of people; the dregs of the people.—*v.t.*—*rabbled, rabbling*. To assault in a disorderly crowd; to mob.

Rabelaisian, rab'e•lā"zi•en, *a.* [Fr. *Rabelais*.] In the broad, indelicate style of the French author Francois Rabelais.

rabid, rab'id, *a.* [L. *rabidus*, from *rabies*, madness, from *rabo*, to rave. RAGE.] Furious; raging; mad; affected with the distemper called *rabies*; excessively or foolishly enthusiastic; rampant; intolerant (a *rabid* Tory, a *rabid* teetotaler).—**rabidity,** ra•bid'i•ti, *n.* The state of being rabid.—**rabidly,** rab'id•li, *adv.* In a rabid manner; furiously.—**rabidness,** rab'-id•nes, *n.* The state of being rabid.—**rabies,** rā'bēz, *n.* [L.] Hydrophobia; an infectious disease of small animals, particularly dogs, believed to be caused by a virus transmitted to man by the bite of infected animals, and usually proving fatal unless the Pasteur treatment is instituted early in the incubation period.

raccoon, ra•kön', *n.* [Corruption of the American Indian, *arahkunem.*] An American plantigrade carnivorous mammal about the size of a small fox, whose skin is valuable as a fur.

race, rās, *n.* [Fr. *race,* It. *razza,* race, lineage, family.] One of the divisions of mankind; a lineage; a family, tribe, people, or nation believed or presumed to belong to the same stock; a breed or stock; a perpetuated variety of animals or plants.—**racial,** rā'shal, *a.* Of or pertaining to a race or family of man.—**racialism,** rā'shal•izm, *n.* Racial prejudice, hatred, or discrimination. **racism,** rās'izm, *n.* Racialism; the belief in the superiority or dominance of one race over another; the practice of this.—**racist,** rās'ist, *a.* and *n.*

race, rās, *n.* [A.Sax. *rage,* a rush; a rapid course, a stream; same as Icel. *râs,* a race.] A rapid course; career in life; a contest of speed, especially in running, but also in riding, driving, sailing, rowing, etc., in competition; *pl.* horse races (to go to the Santa Anita *races*); a strong or rapid current of water; a powerful current or heavy sea sometimes produced by the meeting of two tides; a canal or watercourse to and from a mill or water wheel; a strong tidal rush of water, as in the Bay of Fundy; the air stream delivered by the propeller of an air machine.—*v.i.*—*raced, racing.* To run swiftly; to run or contend in running.—*v.t.* To cause to run; to cause to contend in running; to drive quickly in a trial of speed.—**race horse,** *n.* A horse bred or kept for racing; a horse that runs in competition.—**race track,** *n.* The place where races of horses, dogs, automobiles, etc., are held.—**racer,** rā'sėr, *n.* One who races; a race horse.

raceme, ra•sēm', *n.* [L. *racemus,* a cluster of grapes.] *Bot.* a species of inflorescence, in which a number of flowers with short and equal pedicels stand on a common slender axis, as in the currant.—**racemose,** ras'e•mos, *a.* [L. *racemosus.*] *Bot.* resembling a raceme; in the form of a raceme; bearing flowers in racemes.

rachis, rā'kis, *n.* [Gr. *rachis,* the spine.] The vertebral column of mammals and birds; something similar to this, as the shaft of a feather, the stalk of the frond in ferns, the common stalk bearing the alternate spikelets in some grasses.—**rachitic,** ra•kit'ik, *a.* Pertaining to rachitis; rickety.—**rachitis,** ra•kī'tis, *n.* [Gr. *rachis,* and term. *-itis,* signifying inflammation.] Formerly inflammation of the spine, now applied to *rickets*; a disease characterized by softening and malformation of the bones.

racily, raciness. See RACY.

rack, rak, *v.t.* [Closely allied to *reach,* Sc. *rax,* to reach; D. *rekken,* Dan. *raekke,* to stretch; G. *recken, racken,* to stretch, to torture, *reckbank,* a rack. See also noun.] To stretch unduly, to strain vehemently (as in 'to *rack* one's brains', to strain or exercise his thoughts to the utmost); to twist; to wrest; to distort; to put a false meaning on; to punish on the rack; to heighten; to exaggerate (*Shak.*); to place on or in a rack or frame (to *rack* bottles).—*n.* [Comp. D. *rak, schotelrak,* a cupboard for dishes; G. *rack,* a rail, *recke,* a trestle, a frame, a rack for supporting things.] An appliance for straining or stretching; an instrument for the judicial torture of criminals and suspected persons, consisting of a framework on which the victim's limbs were strained by cords and levers; hence, torture; extreme pain; anguish; an open wooden framework above a manger to hold hay, grass, straw, etc., as fodder for horses and cattle; a framework on or in which articles are deposited; *mach.* a straight or very slightly curved bar, with teeth on one of its edges, adapted to work into the teeth of a wheel or pinion.

rack, rak, *n.* [A.Sax. *hracca,* O.E. and Sc. *crag,* the neck.] The neck of a carcass of veal or mutton.

rack, rak, *n.* [Icel. *rek, ský-rek,* drift, cloud motion; *reka,* to drive.] Thin flying broken clouds, or any portion of floating vapor in the sky.—*v.i.* To fly, as vapor or clouds.

rack, rak, *v.t.* [From Fr. *raque,* mud, dregs.] To draw off from the lees; to draw off, as pure liquor from its sediments (to *rack* cider or wine).

rack, rak, *n.* [Form of *wreck.*] Wreck; ruin; destruction; in the phrase *to go to rack and ruin.*

racket, rak'et, *n.* [Probably onomatopoetic; comp. Gael. *racaid,* noise.] A confused, clattering noise; noisy talk; clamor; din.—*v.i.* To make a racket; to frolic.—*n.* Any of a number of methods, generally unlawful, for the purpose of exorting money or gaining advantages or control of businesses by violence or threats of physical violence.—**racketeer,** rak•e•tēr', *n.* One who, alone or in company with others, under threats of violence extorts money or business advantages or otherwise controls business enterprises, frequently alleging to grant protection to a victim who subscribes or consents to the racketeer's demands.—**rackety,** rak'et•i, *a.* Making a racket or tumultuous noise.

racket, rak'et, *n.* [Fr. *raquette,* a racket; O.Fr. *rachete, rasquete,* the palm of the hand, from L.L. *racha,* the wrist, from an Arabic word.] The bat with which players at tennis or rackets strike the ball; *pl.* a modern variety of the old game of tennis.—*v.t.* To strike as with a racket; to toss.

raconteur, ra•kon•tėr', *n.* [Fr.] Teller of a good story; conversationalist.

racoon, ra•kön'. See RACCOON.

racquet, rak'et. See RACKET.

racy, rā'si, *a.* [Probably from *race,* lineage, lit. partaking strongly of its race; but comp. O.H.G. *räzer,* racy, *räzer win,* racy wine; Swiss *räss,* sharp, astringent.] Strong and flavorous (*racy* wine); having a strong distinctive character of thought or language; spirited; pungent; piquant (a *racy* style, a *racy* anecdote).—**racily,** rā'si•li, *adv.* In a racy manner.—**raciness,** rā'si•nes, *n.* The quality of being racy.

radar, rā'där, *n.* [Short for *ra*dio *d*etecting *a*nd *r*anging.] An electronic device for determining the presence and location of an object by transmitting radio signals, which are reflected by the object and picked up by a receiving system.

raddle, rad'l, *v.t.*—*raddled, raddling.* [Perhaps a corruption from *hurdle* or *riddle.*] To interweave; to twist or wind together.—*n.* A hedge formed by interweaving the shoots and branches of trees or shrubs; *weaving,* a wooden bar with a row of upright pegs to keep the warp in trim.

raddle, rad'l, *n.* [REDDLE.] A red pigment, chiefly used for marking sheep; reddle or ruddle.—*v.t.*—*raddled, raddling.* To paint, as with ruddle.

radial, rā'di•al, *a.* [From L. *radius,* a ray, a spoke. RADIUS, RAY.] Grouped or appearing like radii or rays; shooting out as from a center; pertaining to the radius, one of the bones of the human forearm (the *radial* artery or nerve).—**radially,** rā'di•al•li, *adv.*—**radiance, radiancy,** rā'di•ans, rā'di•an•si, *n.* [From *radiant.*] Brightness shooting in rays or beams; hence in general, brilliant or sparkling luster.—**radiant,** rā'di•ant, *a.* Shooting or emitting rays of light or heat; shining; beaming with brightness; emitting a vivid light or splendor; *phys.* emitted by radiation.—*Radiant energy,* energy transmitted by a wave, as of light, x-rays, etc.—**radiate,** rā'di•āt, *v.i.*—*radiated, radiating.* To issue and proceed in rays or straight lines from a point or surface, as heat or light; to beam forth; to emit rays.—*v.t.* To emit or send out in direct lines from a point or surface (a body *radiates* heat); to enlighten; to illuminate.—*a.* Having rays; having lines proceeding as from a center like radii.—**radiation,** rā•di•ā'shon, *n.* The act of radiating or state of being radiated; the divergence or shooting forth of anything from any point or surface.—**radiator,** rā'di•ā•tėr, *n.* That which radiates; an appliance for heating a room by means of hot water or steam; in automobiles, the mechanism for cooling circulating water.

radical, rad'i•kal, *a.* [Fr. *radical,* L.

radicalis, from *radix*, *radicis*, a root (whence *radish*, *eradicate*); from root *vrad*, seen in E. *wort*; also in L. *radius*, a ray, *ramus*, a branch.] Pertaining to the root or origin; original; reaching to the principles; fundamental; thorough-going; extreme (a *radical* error, a *radical* cure or reform); implanted by nature; innate; native; *philol.* belonging to or proceeding directly from a root; (the *radical* signification of a word). —**radicalism**, rad′i•kal•izm, *n.* The doctrine or principle of the radicals or advanced liberals.—**radically,** rad′i•kal•li, *adv.* In a radical manner; in root or origin; fundamentally.—**radicate**, rad′i•kāt, *v.t.*—*radicated*, *radicating*. [L. *radicor*, *radicatus*.] To cause to take root; to plant deeply.—**radicle**, rad′i•kl, *n.* [L. *radicula*, dim. of *radix*, a root.] *Bot.* that part of the embryo or seed of a plant which, upon vegetating, becomes the root; the fibrous parts of a root; *chem.* same as RADICAL.

radio, rā′di•ō, *n.* pl. **radios,** rā′di•ōz. [L. *radius*, a ray.] The transmission or reception of electromagnetic waves without conducting wires intervening between transmitter and receiver; the receiving set.—*a.* Of, used in, or transmitted by radio.—*v.t.* and *i.*—*radioed*, *radioing*. To transmit, or communicate with, by radio.—**radioactive,** *a.* Having the property of emitting radiation or particles from an atomic nucleus.—**radioactivity,** *n.*—**radioastronomy,** *n.* A branch of astronomy that uses radio telescopes in the study of radiation emitted by celestial bodies. —**radio beacon,** *n.* A radio station that sends out signals so that a receiver may determine his position by them.—**radiobroadcast,** *n.* The transmission of messages, music, voice, etc., by radio.—**radiocarbon,** *n.* See CARBON-14.—**radiochemistry,** *n.* A certain branch of chemistry which deals with radioactive bodies and radioactivity.—**radio-frequency,** *n.* A frequency higher than 15,000 vibrations per second.—**radiogram,** *n.* A radiotelephonic message.—**radioisotope,** rā′di•ō•ī″so•tōp, *n.* A radioactive isotope.—**radiology,** rā•di•ol′o•ji, *n.* The science of diagnostic medicine by means of radiant energy. —**radiophone,** *n.* A radiotelephone; a device for transmission of sound by means of radiant energy.—**radiotelegraphy,** rā′di•ō•te•leg″ra•fi, *n.* Wireless telegraphy.—**radiotelegraph,** *n.* —**radiotelephony,** rā′di•ō•tel•lef″o•ni, *n.* Wireless telephony; telephoning through the air without wires. —**radiotelescope,** rā′di•ō•tel″e•skōp, *n.* A large reflector, parabolic in shape, that gathers radio signals emitted by celestial bodies.—**radiotherapy,** rā•di•ō•ther″a•pi, *n.* Treatment of diseases by radioactivity, as by the X-ray or by means of a radioactive element such as radium or thorium.—**radiothorium,** rā′di•ō•thōr″i•um, *n.* A radioactive element.—**radio tube,** *n.* An electronic valve generally consisting of an evacuated glass or metal shell, enclosing an electron-generating device, such as a heated filament, from which electrons are propelled by electrical attraction to an anode, or plate. In the valve type of tube a mesh of fine wires is placed in the electronic stream and by suitable charging with a control current, regulates the magnitude of the electrical current flowing between the filament and plate. The tube is used in radio receivers for the amplification and rectification of electromagnetic waves.

radish, rad′ish, *n.* [Fr. *radis*, from L. *radix*, a root. RADICAL.] The name of cruciferous plants with lyre-shaped leaves, the young roots of which are eaten.—*Horse-radish*. See HORSE.

radium, rā′di•um, *n.* [RADIUS.] A radioactive metallic element discovered in pitchblende by M. and Mme. Curie in 1898. Symbol, Ra; at. no., 88; at. wt., 226.—**radium-therapy,** *n.* See RADIOTHERAPY.

radius, rā′di•us, *n.* pl. **radii, radiuses,** rā′di•ī, rā′di•us•ez. [L., a ray, a rod, a beam, a spoke. RADICAL, RAY.] *Geom.* a straight line extending from the center of a circle to its circumference; a circular area limited to the distance of a given radius; *anat.* the shorter, thicker bone of the two bones of the human forearm or of the forelimb of lower animals.

radix, rā′diks, *n.* [L., a root.] A root (of a plant, of a word); *math.* any number which is arbitrarily made the fundamental number or base of any system, as 10 in decimals.

radon, rā′don, *n.* [RADIUM.] A radioactive gaseous element, chemically inert, formed as a disintegration product of radium. Symbol, Rn; at. no., 86.

radula, rad′ū•la, pl. **-ae**, *n.* [L. for a scraper.] In mollusks, a horny tooth-studded ribbon on the floor of the ODONTOPHORE (which see).

raff, raf, *n.* [O.E. *raff*, to sweep; Fr. *raffer*, from G. *raffen*, to sweep, to snatch; akin *raffle*.] Sweepings; refuse; a person of worthless character; the scum of society; the rabble; used chiefly in the reduplicated form *riff-raff*.—**raffish,** raf′ish, *a.* Villainous; scampish; worthless.

raffia, raf′i•a, *n.* [Name in Madagascar.] A fibrous substance obtained from a palm of Madagascar, and another of South America, used for agricultural tie bands.

raffle, raf′l, *n.* [Fr. *rafle*, O.Fr. *raffle*, a kind of game at dice, from G. *raffen*, *raffeln*, to sweep or snatch. RAFF.] A lottery in which several persons deposit a part of the value of something, the winner being determined by chance (as by the drawing of a lucky number)—*v.t.*—*raffled*, *raffling*. To engage in a raffle.—*v.t.* To dispose of by means of a raffle.

Rafflesia, raf•lē′si•a, *n.* [After Sir Stamford *Raffles*, the discover of the first known species.] A genus of parasitical plants, natives of Sumatra and Java, one of which is remarkable for its gigantic flower, about 3 feet in diameter.

raft, raft, *n.* [Properly a float made of beams or rafters; Icel. *raptr* (pron. *raftr*), Dan. *raft*, a rafter. RAFTER.] A float of logs, planks, or other pieces of timber fastened together, for the convenience of transporting them by water; a floating structure used in shipwrecks, often formed of barrels, planks, spars, etc.; a floating mass of trees, branches, etc. —*v.t.* To transport on a raft.—**raftsman,** rafts′man, *n.* A man who manages a raft.

rafter, raf′tėr, *n.* [A.Sax. *raefter*= Icel-*raptr* (pron. *raftr*), Dan. *raft*, a rafter, a beam.] One of the sloping timbers of a roof, which support the outer covering.—*v.t.* To furnish with rafters.

rag, rag, *v.t.*—*ragged*, (ragd), *ragging*. [Origin doubtful.] To torment, tease, or subject to annoyance, often petty or ludicrous.

rag, rag, *n.* [Originally a tuft of rough hair; comp. Sw. and Dan. dial. *ragg*, rough hair; Icel. *rögg*, shagginess, a tuft; allied to *rug*.] Any piece of cloth torn from the rest; a tattered cloth, torn or worn; a fragment of dress; a shred; a tatter; *pl.* tattered garments or mean dress; a term for rock deposits consisting of hard irregular masses (coral-*rag*, Kentish-*rag*, etc.); ragstone.—**ragamuffin,** rag•a•muf′in, *n.* [*Ragamofin* was the name of a demon in some old mystery plays, perhaps from *rag*, and old *mof*, *muff*, a long sleeve, or from *tag*, and D. *muf*, musty.] A poorly dressed youngster.—**ragged,** rag′ed, *a.* Rent or worn into rags or tatters; tattered; having broken or rough edges; jagged; rough with sharp or irregular points; wearing tattered clothes; shabby.—*On the ragged edge*, on the verge of misfortune, failure, or collapse.—**raggedly,** rag′ed•li, *adv.* In a ragged condition. —**raggedness,** rag′ed•nes, *n.* The state of being ragged.—**ragman,** rag′man, *n.* A man who collects or deals in rags.—**ragpicker,** *n.* A collector of rags, bones, etc., from streets, ashpits, etc.; one who makes a living by scavenging.—**ragweed,** rag′wēd, *n.* A coarse, annual weed of the composite family, with some 15 species in North America, its pollen being extremely irritating to hay fever sufferers who are allergic to it.

rage, rāj, *n.* [Fr. *rage*, from L. *rabies*, rage, madness (by a change similar to that seen in *abridge*); from *rabo*, to rave, to be mad; cog. Skr. *rabh*, to desire eagerly. RABID.] Violent anger accompanied with furious words, gestures, or agitation; anger excited to fury; vehemence or violent exacerbation (the *rage* of a fever, of hunger or thirst); fury; extreme violence (the *rage* of a tempest); violent desire.—*The rage*, the object of popular and eager desire; the fashion. (*Colloq.*) ∴ Syn. under

ANGER.—*v.i.*—*raged, raging.* To be furious with anger; to be exasperated to fury; to be in a passion; to act or move furiously, or with mischievous impetuosity (the sea *rages*); to ravage; to prevail with fatal effect (the plague *rages*).

ragee, rag′ē, *n.* [Indian word.] A grain plant of India and elsewhere.

raglan, rag′lan, *n.* A type of coat or overcoat with sleeves (*raglan* sleeves) whose seams extend to the neckline, giving a slanting line to the shoulders.

ragout, ra•gö′, *n.* [Fr. *ragoût*, from L. *re*, again, *ad*, to, and *gustus*, a tasting.] A dish of stewed and highly seasoned meat.

ragtime, rag′tīm, *n.* Syncopated music with a regularly accented accompaniment, being the earliest form of jazz and probably having its origin in Negro melodies.

raid, rād, *n.* [From stem of *ride*; same as Icel. *reith*, a riding, a raid; akin to *road*.] A hostile inroad or incursion, especially one made suddenly by mounted men; a foray; an attack by violence; an unannounced entry or sudden attack by officers of the law in order to make seizures and arrests, etc.—*v.t.* To make a raid.—*v.i.* To take part in a raid.—**raider,** rād′ėr, *n.*

rail, rāl, *n.* [Same as L.G. and Sw. *regel*, G. *riegel*, a bar, a rail; akin G. *reihe*, a row.] A bar of wood or metal extending from one upright post to another, as in fences; a horizontal timber in any piece of framing or paneling; the upper pieces into which the balusters of a stair are mortised; a series of posts or balusters connected by crossbeams, bars, or rods, for enclosure; a railing; one of the parallel iron or steel bars forming a smooth track for the wheels of a locomotive and the cars which it draws, or for a streetcar, elevated, subway, etc.; a railroad (to travel or send goods by *rail*).—*v.t.* To enclose with rails; to send by rail, as goods, etc.—*v.i.* To ride or travel on a railroad.—**railer,** rā′lėr, *n.* One who makes or furnishes with rails.—**railhead,** *n.* The most advanced point of a railroad under construction; the point at which goods are transferred from a railroad to some other means of transport.—**railing,** rā′ling, *n.* A fence or barrier of wood or iron, constructed of posts and rails; rails in general, or the materials for rails.—**railroad,** rāl′rōd, *n.* A permanent roadway consisting of one or more pairs of rails laid parallel to each other and several feet apart, making a track over which locomotives, freight or passenger cars, etc., may run; in an extended sense, the road and all the land, works, buildings, machinery, franchises, and other assets required for the support and use of the road.—*Railroad train*, locomotive and cars running on railroad tracks.—*v.t.* To transport or ship by railroad; to rush through forcefully and without careful consideration, especially a bill through a legislature (*colloq.*); to send a person to prison on a false charge (*slang*).—**railroading,** rāl′rōd•ing, *n.* Construction or operation of railroads; employment on a railroad.

rail, rāl, *n.* [O.Fr. *rasle, raale*, a rail; same origin as *rattle*, being so called from its noisy cry.] The popular name of several grallatorial birds, inhabiting sedgy places, moist herbage, etc., and comprising the land rail or corn crake and the water rail.

rail, rāl, *v.i.* [Fr. *railler*, to banter; from L.L. *radiculare*, from L. *radere*, to scrape. RASE, RASOR.] To utter reproaches; to use insolent and reproachful language; to scold.—**railer,** rā′lėr, *n.* One who rails.—**raillery,** rā′lėr•i, *n.* [Fr. *raillerie*.] Good-humored pleasantry or slight satire; satirical merriment; jesting language; banter.

raiment, rā′ment, *n.* [Contracted from obsolete *arrayment*. ARRAY.] Clothing in general; vestments; vesture; garments; now always in the *sing.*

rain, rān, *n.* [A.Sax. *regn, rén*=Icel., Dan., and Sw. *regn*, D. and G. *regen*, Goth. *rign*; same root as L. *rigare*, to wet, whence *irrigate*. As to the disappearance of *g* compare *hail* and *flail*.] The descent of water in drops from the clouds; the water thus falling; the moisture of the atmosphere condensed and deposited in drops; a shower or pouring down of anything.—*v.i.* To fall in drops from the clouds, as water: used mostly with *it* for a nominative (*it rains, it* will *rain*); to fall or drop like rain (tears *rained* from their eyes).—*v.t.* To pour or shower down, like rain from the clouds; to pour or send down abundantly.—**rainbow,** rān′bō, *n.* A bow or arc of a circle, consisting of all the prismatic colors, formed by the refraction and reflection of rays of light from drops of rain; a wide variety, as of colors.—**raincheck,** rān′chek, *n.* A ticket stub for admission to a later performance in case of a cancellation; a deferred invitation.—**raincoat,** rān′cōt, *n.* A coat of water-repellent or waterproof material.—**raindrop,** *n.* A drop of rain.—**rainfall,** rān′fạl, *n.* A fall of rain; the amount of water that falls as rain.—**rainforest,** *n.* A tropical forest with an annual rainfall of more than 100 inches.—**rainy,** rā′nē, *a.*

raise, rāz, *v.t.*—*raised, raising.* [A caus. of *rise*, but coming directly from a Scandinavian source; Icel. *reisa*, to raise, caus. of *rísa*, to rise. RISE, REAR.] To cause to rise; to put, place, or remove higher; to lift upward; to elevate; to heave; to elevate in social position, rank, dignity, and the like; to increase the value or estimation of; to exalt, enhance, promote, advance; to increase the energy, strength, power, or vigor of; to excite; to heighten (to *raise* the courage, to *raise* the temperature of a room); to cause to appear from the world of spirits; to recall from death (to *raise* the dead); to cause to assume an erect position or posture; to set upright; to awaken; to rouse to action; to incite; to stir up (to *raise* the country, to *raise* a mutiny); to set into commotion (to *raise* the sea); to cause to arise or come into being; to build up; to erect; to construct; to bring or get together; to gather, collect, to levy (to *raise* money, to *raise* an army); to cause to be produced; to breed; to rear; to grow (to *raise* wheat, to *raise* cattle, sheep, etc.); to give rise to; to originate (to *raise* a false report); to give vent or utterance to (to *raise* a cry); to strike up (to *raise* the song of victory); to cause to appear; to call up (to *raise* a smile or a blush); to heighten or elevate in pitch (a sharp *raises* a note half a tone); to increase the loudness of (to *raise* the voice); *law*, to institute or originate (to *raise* an action); to cause to swell, as dough.—*To raise steam*, to produce steam enough to drive an engine.—*To raise a blockade*, to terminate or break it up.—*To raise a siege*, to relinquish the attempt to take a place by besieging it, or to cause the attempt to be relinquished.—*To raise the wind* (*fig.*), to obtain ready money by some shift or other.—*Raised beaches.* See BEACH.

raisin, rā′zn, *n.* [Fr. *raisin*, a grape, from L. *racemus*, a cluster of grapes. RACEME.] A dried grape; a dried fruit of various species of vines.

raja, rajah, rä′jä, *n.* [Skr. and Hind. *râjâ*, a rajah; root in Skr. *râj*, to rule; cog. L. *rex* (for *regs*), a king, *rego*, to rule; Gael. and It. *righ*, a king; A.Sax. *rice*, dominion. REGAL, RICH.] In India, originally a title which belonged to princes of Hindu race who governed a territory; subsequently, a title given to Hindus of rank; a Hindu chief.

rake, rāk, *n.* [A.Sax. *raca*, a rake; cog. Icel. *reka*, a shovel or spade; Sw. *raka*, an oven rake; G. *rechen*, a rake; from root meaning to stretch. REACH.] An implement furnished with wooden or iron teeth, used for collecting hay or straw after mowing or reaping; and in gardening for smoothing the soil, covering the seed, etc.; a small implement like a hoe used for collecting the stakes on a gambling table.—*v.t.*—*raked, raking.* To apply a rake to, or something that serves the same purpose; to gather with a rake; to smooth with a rake; to gather with labor or difficulty (to *rake* together wealth); to ransack; to pass swiftly over; to scour; *milit.* to enfilade; to cannonade so that the balls range the whole length.—*To rake up* (*fig.*), to bring up or revive, as quarrels, grievances, etc.—*v.i.* To use a rake; to seek by raking; to search with minute inspection into every part.—**raker,** rā′kėr, *n.* One who or that which rakes; an implement for raking.

rake, rāk, *n.* [Shortened from M.E. *rakehell*, properly vagabond, wandering; comp. Prov. *rake*, to rove or ramble idly; Sw. *raka*, Icel.

reika, to wander; Dan. *raekel*, a lout.] A loose, disorderly vicious person; one addicted to lewdness; a libertine; a roué.—*v.i.* To play the part of a rake; to lead a dissolute debauched life; to fly wide of game; said of a hawk.—**rakish,** rā′kish, *a.* Given to the practices of a rake; dissolute; debauched.—**rakishly,** rā′kish•li, *adv.* In a rakish or dissolute manner.—**rakishness,** rā′kish•nes, *n.* Dissolute practices.

rake, rāk, *v.i.* [Same as Sw. *raka*, Dan. *rage*, to project, a Scandinavian verb=E. *reach.*] To incline; to slope; *naut.* to incline from a perpendicular direction (a mast *rakes* aft).—*n. Naut.* a slope or inclination; the projection of the stem or stern beyond the extremities of the keel; the inclination of a mast, funnel, etc., from a perpendicular direction.—**rakish,** rā′kish, *a. Naut.* having a rake or inclination of the masts forward or aft.

rallentando, ral•len•tan′dō. [It.] *Music*, a term indicating that the time of the passage over which it is written is to be gradually decreased.

ralline, ral′īn, *a.* [Mod. L. *rallus*, a rail.] *Ornith.* pertaining to the rails.

rally, ral′i, *v.t.*—*rallied, rallying.* [Fr. *rallier*, to rally—prefix *re*, and *allier*, E. *ally*, from L. *alligo*, I bind to—*ad*, to, and *ligo*, I bind. ALLY, LIGAMENT.] To collect and reduce to order, as troops dispersed or thrown into confusion; to bring together as for a fresh effort; to reunite.—*v.i.* To come back quickly to order; to reform themselves into an orderly body for a fresh effort, to resume or recover vigor or strength (the patient begins to *rally*).—*n.* A stand made by retreating troops; return of disordered troops to their ranks; the act of recovering strength; a mass meeting to arouse group enthusiasm.

rally, ral′i, *v.t.*—*rallied, rallying.* [Fr. *railler*, to banter. RAIL (to banter).] To attack with raillery; to treat with good-humor and pleasantry, or with slight contempt or satire; to tease.—*v.i.* To use pleasantry or satirical merriment.

ram, ram, *n.* [A.Sax. *ram, ramm*, D. *ram*, G. *ramm*, a ram. Root uncertain.] The male of the sheep or ovine genus; a battering-ram (under BATTER); a steam ironclad ship-of-war, armed at the prow below the waterline with a heavy iron or steel beak intended to destroy an enemy's ships by the force with which it is driven against them; the loose hammer of a pile-driving machine; the piston of a hydraulic press.—*Hydraulic ram* or *water ram*, an automatic apparatus by which a descending stream of water is made to raise by its own momentum a portion of its mass to a required height.—*The Ram*, Aries, one of the signs of the zodiac.—*v.t.*—*rammed, ramming.* [From the noun, like G. *rammen*, Dan. *ramme*, to strike, to hit.] To strike with a ram; to drive a ram or similar object against; to batter; to force in; to drive down; to fill or compact by pounding or driving; to stuff; to cram.—*v.i.* To use a battering-ram or similar object.—*a.* Strong-scented; stinking (*ram* as a fox).—**rammer,** ram′ėr, *n.* One who or that which rams or drives; a ramrod.—**rammish,** ram′-ish, *a.* Ramlike; hence, lascivious; rank; strong-scented. — **ramrod,** ram′rod, *n.* A rod for ramming down the charge of a gun or other firearm; a rammer.

Ramadan, ra•ma•dän′, *n.* [Ar., the hot month, from *ramida, ramiza*, to be hot.] The ninth month of the Mohammedan year; the great annual Mohammedan fast, kept throughout the entire month from sunrise to sunset.

ramble, ram′bl, *v.i.*—*rambled, rambling.* [A dim. and freq. from *roam*; the *b* has crept in, as in *grumble, nimble, number*, etc.] To rove; to wander; to go from place to place without any determinate object in view; to think or talk in an incoherent manner; to grow without constraint.—*n.* A roving; an excursion or trip in which a person wanders from place to place; an irregular excursion.—**rambler,** ram′-blėr, *n.* One who rambles; a rover; a wanderer.—**rambling,** ram′bling, *p.* and *a.* Roving; wandering; straggling; without method; confused in ideas or language.—*n.* A roving, irregular excursion.

rambunctious, ram•bungk′shus, *a.* [From *ram*, and variant of *bumptious.*] Wild and incorrigible in behavior; unruly; boisterous; impulsive.

ramekin, ramequin, ram′i•kin, *n.* [Fr.] An individual portion of a cheese preparation baked in a small dish; an individual baking dish.

rameous, rā′mē•us, *a.* [From L. *ramus*, a branch. RADIUS.] *Bot.* belonging to a branch; growing on or shooting from a branch.—**ramification,** ram′i•fi•kā″shon, *n.* The act of ramifying; the process of branching out; a small branch or offshoot from a main stock or channel; a subordinate branch; a division or subdivision in a classification, or the like.—**ramiform,** ram′i•form, *a. Bot.* resembling a branch.—**ramify,** ram′i•fī, *v.t.*—*ramified, ramifying.* [Fr. *ramifier*—L. *ramus*, a branch, and *facio*, to make.] To divide into branches or parts.—*v.i.* To shoot into branches, as the stem of a plant; to branch out; to be divided or subdivided; to branch out; as a main subject or scheme.—**ramous, ramose,** rā′mus, rā′mōs, *a.* [L. *ramosus.*] Branchy; full of branches; *bot.* branched, as a stem or root.

ramjet, ram′jet, *n.* [*Ram* and *jet.*] A jet engine that derives thrust from the addition of fuel to, and its combustion by, air compressed solely by forward speed.

rammer, rammish. See RAM.

ramose. See RAMEOUS.

ramp, ramp, *v.i.* [Fr. *ramper*, to creep, to climb=It. *rampare*, to clamber, from the German; comp. Bav. *rampfen*, to snatch; a nasalized form corresponding to L.G. *rappen*, Sw. *rappa*, to snatch. *Romp* is the same word.] To climb, as a plant‡; to rear on the hind legs; to assume a rampant attitude; to spring or move with violence; to rage; to bound; to romp.—*n.* A sloping platform serving as a way between different levels.—**rampage,** ram′pij, *v.i.* [From *ramp.*] To romp or prance about with unrestrained spirits; to rage and storm; to prance about with fury. (*Colloq.*)—*n.* A state of passion or excitement; violent conduct. (*Colloq.*)—**rampageous,** ram•pā′jus, *a.* Boisterous; unruly. (*Colloq.*)—**rampant,** ram′-pant, *a.* [Fr. *rampant*, ppr. of *ramper*, to clamber.] Springing or climbing unchecked; rank in growth; exuberant (*rampant* weeds); overleaping restraint or usual limits; excessively and obtrusively prevalent; predominant (*rampant* vice); *her.* standing upright upon his hind legs (properly on one foot) as if attacking: said of a beast of prey, as the lion.—**rampancy,** ram′pan•si, *n.* The state or quality of being rampant.—**rampantly,** ram′pant•li, *adv.* In a rampant manner.

rampart, ram′pärt, *n.* [Fr. *rempart*, a rampart, from *remparer*, to fortify a place—*re*, again, *em* for L. *in*, in, and *parer*, to defend, from L. *parare*, to prepare. PARE, PREPARE.] A bulwark; a defense; *fort.* an elevation or mound of earth round a place, capable of resisting cannon shot, and on which the parapet is raised; it also may include the parapet.—*v.t.* To fortify with ramparts.

rampion, ram′pi•on, *n.* [A nasalized form from L. *rapum*, a turnip, rape.] A perennial plant of the bellflower order, the root and leaves of which are used in salads.

ramrod. See RAM.

ramshackle, ram′shak•l, *a.* [Perhaps pp. of *ransackle, ransack.*] Ill-adjusted and threatening dissolution; carelessly constructed; rickety.

ramson, ramsons, ram′zon, ram′-zonz, *n.* [A.Sax. *hramsa, hramse*, ramsons (pl. *hramsan*, so that *ramsons* is a double pl.); G. *rams, ramsel, ramsen*, Sw. *rams*, ramsons; allied to Gr. *kromyon*, an onion.] A species of garlic, having broad leaves and a bulbous root, sometimes used in salads.

ramulose, ram′ū•lōs, *a. Bot.* having many small branches.

ran, ran, *pret.* See RUN.

ranch, ranch, *n.* [Sp. *rancho*, a mess, a set of persons who eat and drink together, a messroom.] An establishment and tract of land for raising and grazing horses, cattle, sheep, etc.; the buildings of such an establishment; any farm, as for dairying or fruit growing. (*Colloq.*)—**rancher,** ran′chėr, *n.* One who owns or is employed on a ranch.—**ranchero,** ran•chā′rō, *n.* A person employed on a ranch, or who owns and manages a ranch. (*Spanish Amer.*)—**rancho,** ran′chō, *n.* Rude habitation for ranch or farm workers on a stock farm. (*Spanish Amer.*)

rancid, ran′sid, *a.* [L. *rancidus,* from *ranceo,* to be rank (whence also *rancor*).] Having a rank smell; strong-scented, from turning bad with keeping: said of oils and fats, butter, etc.; musty.—**rancidity, rancidness,** ran•sid′i•ti, ran′sid•nes, *n.* The quality of being rancid.

rancor, rang′kėr, *n.* [L. *rancor,* an ill smell, rancor, from *ranceo,* to be rank or rancid (whence *rancid*).] The deepest malignity, enmity, or spite; deep-seated and implacable malice; inveterate enmity; malignity.—**rancorous,** rang′kėr•us, *a.* Full of rancor; deeply malignant; intensely virulent.—**rancorously,** rang′kėr•us•li, *adv.*

random, ran′dum, *n.* [O.Fr. *randon,* an impetuous course or efflux, vivacity, violence; *à randon,* at random; *randoner, randir,* to run rapidly; from G. *rand,* edge, brim, the word originally having reference to the violence of a stream flowing full to the brim.] A roving motion or course without direction; want of rule or method; chance; used only in the phrase, *at random,* that is, in a haphazard or fortuitous manner; *mining,* the depth below a given plane.—*a.* Done at hazard or without settled aim or purpose; left to chance; fortuitous.—*Random courses, masonry* and *paving,* courses of stones of unequal thickness.—*Random shot,* a shot not directed to a point.—**randomly,** ran′dum•li, *adv.* In a random manner; at hazard.

ranee, rän′ē, *n.* [Hind. *rani,* queen.] The wife of a rajah, or queen in her own right, in native states.

rang, rang, pret. See RING.

range, rānj, *v.t.—ranged, ranging.* [From Fr. *ranger,* to range, from *rang,* O.Fr. *reng,* a rank; from the German. RANK.] To set in a row or in rows; to place in regular lines or ranks; to rank; to arrange systematically; to classify; to class; to rove through or over; to pass over.—*v.i.* To be placed in order; to be ranked; to rank; to rove at large; to wander without restraint; to pass from one point to another; to fluctuate (the price *ranges* between $50 and $60); *gun.* to have range or horizontal direction.—*n.* A series of things in a line; a row; a rank (a *range* of mountains); space or room for excursion; the extent of country over which a plant or animal is naturally spread; compass or extent; discursive power; scope (a wide *range* of thought); the series of sounds belonging to a voice or a musical instrument; a kitchen grate and cooking apparatus; *gun.* the horizontal distance to which a shot or other projectile is carried; a place where gun or rifle practice is carried on.—**range finding,** *n.* The measurement of the distance in yards between a gun and the object of its aim, effected by means of instruments, the rangefinder, the mekometer, etc. The term *range-taking* is used similarly but with wider meaning.—**ranger,** rān′jėr, *n.* One who ranges; a member of a body of mounted, roving troops or police; a government official patrolling forest areas.—**rangership,** rān′jėr•ship, *n.* The office of ranger.—**ranging,** rān′jing, *n.* The process of finding the elevation which should be given to a gun in order that the projectile may hit the object aimed at.

rank, rangk, *n.* [O.E. *ranc, renk,* from Fr. *rang,* O.Fr. *reng, renc,* a rank, row, range (whence also *range*), originally a circular row, from O.H.G. *hring, hrinc,* a ring, a circle. RING.] A row; a line; a tier; a range; *milit.* a line of soldiers; a line of men standing abreast or side by side: often used along with *file* (which see); hence in *pl.* the order of common soldiers (to reduce an officer to the *ranks*); an aggregate of individuals together; a social class; an order; a division; degree of dignity, eminence, or excellence; comparative station; relative place (a writer of the first *rank*); high social position; distinction; eminence (a man of *rank*).—*To fill the ranks,* to complete the whole number.—*To take rank of,* to enjoy precedence over.—*v.t.* To place abreast in a rank or line; to place in a particular class, order, or division; to class or classify; to range.—*v.i.* To be ranged, classed, or included, as in a particular class, order, or division; to have a certain rank; to occupy a certain position as compared with others; to put in a claim against the estate of a bankrupt.

rank, rangk, *a.* [A.Sax. *ranc,* fruitful, rank, proud = Icel. *rakkr,* straight, bold; Dan. *rank,* erect; D. *rank,* slender; Prov. G. *rank,* slender, upright—all nasalized forms from same root as *rack, right, reach.*] Luxuriant in growth; causing vigorous growth; fertile; strong-scented; rancid; strong to the taste; high-tasted; raised to a high degree; excessive; utter (*rank* nonsense); gross; coarse; disgusting.—**rankly,** rangk′li, *adv.* With vigorous growth; rancidly; coarsely; grossly.—**rankness,** rangk′nes, *n.* The state or quality of being rank; vigorous growth; luxuriance; strength and coarseness in smell or taste.

rankle, rang′kl, *v.i.—rankled, rankling.* To fester, as a sore or wound; to produce a painful sensation; *fig.* to produce bitterness or rancor in the mind; to continue to irritate.—*v.t.* To irritate; to inflame.

ransack, ran′sak, *v.t.* [A Scand. word: Icel. *rannsaka,* Sw. *ransaka,* to search, as for stolen goods—Icel. *rann* (Goth. *razns*), a house, and *saekja,* to seek. SEEK.] To search thoroughly; to enter and search every place and part of; to rummage; to plunder; to strip by plundering.

ransom, ran′sum, *n.* [Fr. *rançon,* O.Fr. *raenson, raanson,* etc., from L. *redemptio, redemptionis,* redemption, from *redimo*—*re,* back, and *emo,* I buy. (REDEEM.) The word is therefore *redemption* in another form.] Release from captivity, bondage, or the possession of an enemy by payment; the price paid for such release, or for goods captured by an enemy; price paid for the pardon of sins; redemption of sinners.—*v.t.* To pay a ransom for; to redeem from captivity, bondage, forfeit, or punishment; to deliver.—**ransomer,** ran′sum•ėr, *n.* One who ransoms or redeems.

rant, rant, *v.i.* [Same as O.D. *ranten,* to be enraged, G. *ranten, ranzen,* to move noisily, Prov.G. *rant,* noisy mirth.] To rave in violent or extravagant language; to be noisy and boisterous in words or declamation.—*n.* Boisterous, empty declamation; bombast.—**ranter,** ran′tėr, *n.* One who rants; a noisy talker; a boisterous preacher; [*cap.*] a name given by way of reproach to members of a denomination of Christians which sprang up in 1645; also vulgarly applied to the Primitive Methodists.

Ranunculus, ra•nun′kū•lus, *n.* [L. dim. of *rana,* a frog—a name first given to the aquatic ranunculus because it floats in marshes, ditches, etc.] The crowfoot genus, a genus of flowering plants almost exclusively inhabiting the Northern Hemisphere, possessing acrid properties, and widely distributed over the Temperate Zone.—**ranunculaceous,** ra•nun′kū•lā″shus, *a.* Of the Ranunculaceae or crowfoot family.

rap, rap, *n.* [Same as Sw. *rapp,* a blow, a stroke; Dan. *rap,* a rap; imitative of sound made by a blow; comp. *pat, tap.*] A quick smart blow; a knock.—*v.i.—rapped, rapping.* To strike with a quick sharp blow; to knock.—*v.t.* To strike with a quick blow; to give a knock (to *rap* one's knuckles).—*To rap out,* to utter with sudden violence (to *rap out* an oath).—**rapper,** rap′ėr, *n.* One who raps or knocks; the knocker of a door.

rap, rap, *v.t.—rapped, rapping.* [A Scandinavian word; Sw. *rappa,* Dan. *rappe,* to snatch; comp. Dan. *rap,* Sw. *rapp,* quick, brisk. *Rape* is closely allied; see also RAPT.] To affect with ecstasy or rapture; to snatch or hurry away; to seize by violence.

rap, rap, *v.t.* To criticize or censure.—**rap,** rap, *n.* (*Slang.*) A punishment (to take the *rap*).

rap, rap, *n.* [Possibly derived from the name of a coin of slight value.] Something of trifling worth, chiefly used in such phrases as, *it isn't worth a rap.* (*Colloq.*)

rapacious, ra•pā′shus, *a.* [L. *rapax, rapacis,* from *rapio,* I seize (whence also *rapine, rapture*); same root as *rapid.*] Given to plunder; accustomed to seize or take possession of property by violence; subsisting on prey or animals seized by violence; avaricious; grasping.—**rapaciously,** ra•pā′shus•li, *adv.* In a rapacious manner; by rapine.—**rapaciousness,** ra•pā′shus•nes, *n.* Disposition to plunder or to exact by oppression.—**rapacity,** ra•pas′i•ti, *n.* [L. *rapacitas.*] The quality of being rapacious;

ravenousness; the act or practice of extorting or exacting by oppressive injustice; greediness; insatiability.

rape, rāp, *n.* [From *rap*, to seize, to snatch, the meaning being influenced by L. *rapere, raptum*, to seize. RAP, to seize, RAPTURE.] The act of snatching by force; a seizing and carrying away by force or violence (the *rape* of Proserpine); *law*, the carnal knowledge of a woman forcibly and against her will; something seized and carried away.

rape, rāp, *n.* [Fr. *râpe.*] Refuse stalks and skins of raisins used by vinegar makers after the fruit has been employed in making wine.

rape, rāp, *n.* [From L. *rapa, rapum*, a turnip (whence also *rampion*).] A plant of the mustard family, cultivated for its seeds, from which oil is extracted.

raphe, rā'fē, *n.* [Gr. *raphē*, a seam or suture.] *Bot.* and *zool.* a term applied to parts which look as if they had been sewed or joined together; a suture or line of junction.—**raphides,** raf'i•dēz, *n. pl.* [Pl. of Gr. *raphis*, a needle.] *Bot.* crystals of an acicular or needle-like form occurring in plant cells.

rapid, rap'id, *a.* [Fr. *rapide*, from L. *rapidus*, rapid, from *rapio*, to seize; same root as Gr. *harpazō*, to seize. (HARPY.) *Rapine, rapacious, ravish, rapture*, etc., are from the same L. stem.] Very swift or quick; moving with celerity; advancing with speed; speed in progression (*rapid* growth); quick or swift in performance.—*n.* A swift current in a river, where the channel is descending.—**rapid-fire,** *a.* Firing or adapted to fire in quick succession, hence, proceeding or characterized by sharpness or rapidity; quick.—**rapidity,** ra•pid'i•ti, *n.*—**rapidly,** rap'id•li, *adv.*

rapier, rā'pi•ėr, *n.* [Fr. *rapière*, lit. a rasper, from Sp. *raspar*, to rasp. RASP.] A sword used only in thrusting, and usually having a four-sided blade.

rapine, rap'in, *n.* [Fr., from L. *rapina*, from *rapio*, to seize. RAPID.] The act of plundering; the seizing and carrying away of things by force.

rapparee, rap•a•rē', *n.* [Ir. *rapaire*, a noisy fellow, *rapach*, noisy, slovenly.] A wild Irish plunderer; a worthless fellow. (*Irish.*) Spelled also *Raparee.*

rappee, rap•pē', *n.* [Fr. *râpé*, ppr. of *râper*, to rasp, lit. rasped or powdered tobacco.] A strong kind of snuff made from the darker and ranker kinds of tobacco.

rapper. See RAP.

rapport, rap•pōrt', *n.* [Fr., from L. *re*, again, *ad*, to, and *portare*, to carry. PORTER.] A resemblance; a correspondence; harmony; affinity.

rapscallion, rap•skal'yun, *n.* A good-for-nothing fellow; a rascal.

rapt, rapt, *p.* and *a.* [From *rap*, to snatch, but influenced by L. *raptus*, seized, from *rapio*. RAPTURE.] Snatched away; transported; enraptured; in an ecstasy; entirely absorbed.

raptorial, rap'tō•ri•al, *a.* [L. *raptor*, a plunderer.] Pertaining to the Raptores, or birds of prey; living by rapine or prey; adapted to the seizing of prey.

rapture, rap'chėr, *n.* [From L. *rapere, raptum*, to seize and carry away; whence also *rapine*, etc. RAPID.] A seizing by violence†; a transport of delight; ecstasy; extreme joy or pleasure; enthusiasm.—**rapturous,** rap'chėr•us, *a.* Ecstatic; transporting; ravishing.—**rapturously,** rap'chėr•us•li, *adv.* With rapture; ecstatically.

rare, râr, *a.* [Fr. *rare*, from L. *rarus*, thin, rare.] Thinly scattered; sparse; thin; porous; not dense or compact; uncommon; not frequent; possessing qualities seldom to be met with; excellent or valuable to a degree seldom found.—**rarely,** râr'li, *adv.* In a rare degree or manner; seldom. —**rareness,** râr'nes, *n.*—**rarity,** râ'ri•ti, *n.*—**rarebit,** râr'bit, *n.* Welsh rabbit.—*Rare-earth, chem.* any of the series of similar oxides of the rare-earth metals.—*Rare-earth metals, chem.* a group of trivalent rare metallic elements with the atomic numbers of 57 to 71 inclusive.

rare, râr, *n.* [O.E. *hrere*, boiled lightly.] Not completely cooked; underdone.

rarefy, râ're•fī, *v.t.*—*rarefied, rarefying.* [Fr. *raréfier*; L. *rarefacio*—*rarus*, rare, and *facio*, I make.] To make rare, thin, porous, or less dense; to expand by separation of constituent atoms or particles: opposed to *condense.*—*v.i.* To become rare, that is, not dense or less dense. —**rarefaction,** râ•re•fak'shon, *n.* The act of rarefying or state of being rarefied; expansion or distension by separation of constituent particles: chiefly used in speaking of the aeriform fluids, *dilatation* and *expansion* being used in speaking of solids and liquids: opposed to *condensation.*

rarely, rareness, rarity. See RARE.

rascal, ras'kal, *n.* [Lit. scrapings or refuse; O.E. *rascall, rascayle*, the rabble, also a worthless deer; from a L.L. *rasicare*, from L. *rado, rasum*, to shave or scrape. RASE.] A lean beast, especially a lean deer, not fit to hunt or kill; a mean fellow; a trickish dishonest fellow; a rogue or scoundrel.—*a.* Worthless; mean; paltry; base.—**rascality,** ras•kal'i•ti, *n.* Such qualities as make a rascal; mean trickishness or dishonesty.—**rascally,** ras'kal•li, *a.* Like a rascal; dishonest; vile; base; worthless.

rase, rāz, *v.t.*—*rased, rasing.* [Fr. *raser*, from L.L. *rasare*, freq. of L. *rado, rasum*, to scrape, seen also in *erase, razor, rascal, abrade, rally*, to *rail.*] To touch superficially in passing; to graze; to erase; to level with the ground; to overthrow; to raze (RAZE).—**rasure,** rā'zhūr, *n.* The act of scraping or erasing; an erasure.

rash, rash, *a.* [Same as L.G., Dan., and Sw. *rask*, Icel. *röskr*, D. and G. *rasch*, rash; perhaps from same root as G. *rad*, a wheel. Skr. *ratha*, a chariot.] Hasty in counsel or action; precipitate; resolving or entering on a project without due deliberation and caution; uttered, formed, or undertaken with too little reflection. ∴ A *rash* man is one who undergoes risk from natural impulsiveness; a *foolhardy* man foolishly incurs danger in defiance of and not believing in evil consequences; a *reckless* man sees but disregards consequences.—**rashly,** rash'li, *adv.* In a rash manner; precipitately; inconsiderately.—**rashness,** rash'nes, *n.* Precipitation; inconsiderate readiness to decide or act; a rash act.

rash, rash, *n.* [O.Fr. *rasche*, rash, scurf, itch; same origin as *rascal.*] An eruption on the skin, usually in the form of red spots or patches.

rasher, rash'ėr, *n.* [Probably a piece hastily cooked, from *rash, a.*] *Cookery*, a slice of bacon for frying or broiling.

Rasores, ra•sō'rēz, *n. pl.* [Lit. scrapers or scratchers, from L. *rado, rasum*, to scrape. RASE.] Gallinaceous birds or scratchers, an order of birds of which the common domestic fowl may be regarded as the type.—**rasorial,** ra•sō'ri•al, *a.* Pertaining to the Rasores; scratching the ground for food.

rasp, rasp, *v.t.* [O.Fr. *rasper*, Fr. *râper*, to scrape or rasp, from O.H.G. *raspôn*, to scrape together (D. *raspen*, Dan. *raspe*, Sw. *raspa*); akin to G. *raffen*, to sweep, E. *raff, raffle, rapier.*] To rub against with some rough implement; to file with a rasp; to grate; hence, *fig.* to grate harshly upon.—*v.i.* To rub or grate.—*n.* A coarse species of file with numerous separate projections or teeth; a raspberry.—**rasper,** ras'pėr, *n.* One who or that which rasps; a scraper.—**rasping,** ras'ping, *a.* Characterized by grating or scraping.—**raspy,** ras'pi, *a.* Grating; harsh; rough.

raspberry, raz'be•ri, *n.* [*Rasp* and *berry*; so named from the roughness of the fruit. Comp. G. *kratzbeere*—*kratzen*, to scratch, and *beere*, berry.] The well-known fruit of a plant extensively used by both the cook and the confectioner, and also in the preparation of cordials; also the plant itself; a derisive sound made by vibrating the tongue and lips (*slang*).

rasure. See RASE.

rat, rat, *n.* [A.Sax. *ræt*, a rat=D. *rat*, G. *ratte* (whence Fr. *rat*), L.G. and Dan. *rotte*, Gael. *radan*, Armor. *raz*, rat; root probably in L. *rodo*, to gnaw.] Any of various long-tailed rodents resembling, and allied to, the mouse, but considerably larger, brown or gray in color, and infesting houses, barns, stables, and ships; a sneaky person; one who betrays or deserts his associates; in underworld jargon, a criminal who discloses the identity of his accomplices to the police; a section of false hair (*colloq.*).—*To smell a rat*, to be suspicious that all is not right.—*v.i.* —*ratted, ratting.* To catch or kill rats; to forsake one's associates.—**ratsbane,** rats'bān, *n.* [*Rat* and *bane.*] Poison for rats; arsenious acid.—**ratter,** rat'ėr, *n.* One who rats; one whose business it is to catch rats; a terrier which kills rats.—**rattrap,** *n.* A trap for catching rats.

ratafia, rat•a•fē′a, *n.* [Sp., from Malay *arak*, arrack, and *tafia*, a spirit distilled from molasses.] A spirituous liquor flavored with the kernels of cherries, apricots, peaches, etc.; a kind of liqueur.

ratch, rach, *n.* [A softened form of *rack*.] *Mach.* a bar having angular teeth into which a pawl drops, to prevent machines from being reversed in motion; a rack or rack-bar. —**ratchet,** rach′et, *n.* [Dim. of *ratch*.] A piece, one extremity of which abuts against the teeth of a ratchet wheel; a click, pawl, or detent.—**ratchet wheel,** *n.* A wheel with pointed and angular teeth against which a ratchet abuts, used either for converting a reciprocating into a rotatory motion or for admitting of its motion in one direction only.

rate, rāt, *n.* [O.Fr. *rate*, from L. *rata* (*pars*, part, understood), from *ratus*, reckoned, ppr. of *reor*, to reckon, to calculate; akin *ratio*, *reason*, *ratify*.] The proportion or standard by which quantity or value is adjusted; price or amount fixed on anything with relation to a standard; a settled proportion; comparative value or estimate; degree as regards speed; a tax or sum assessed on property for public use according to its income or value; *navy*, the order or class of a ship according to its magnitude or force; the daily gain or loss of a chronometer or other timepiece.—*v.t.—rated, rating.* To settle or fix the value, rank, or degree of; to value or estimate; to fix the relative scale, rank, or position of (to *rate* a ship).—*v.i.* To be set or considered in a class.—**rateable,** rā′ta•bl, *a.* Ratable.—**ratable,** rā′ta•bl, *a.* Capable of being rated; reckoned according to a certain rate; liable by law to taxation.—**ratability,** rā•ta•bil′ī•ti, *n.* Quality of being ratable.—**ratably,** rā′ta•bli, *adv.* By rate or proportion.—*Rate of exchange*, the price per unit of money at which the currency of one country may be exchanged for the currency of another.—**rater,** rā′tėr, *n.* One who rates.—**rating,** rā′ting, *n.* The act of estimating; a fixing in rank or place; rank, as the *rating* of men and the *rating* of ships in the navy.

rate, rāt, *v.t.—rated, rating.* [Same word as Sw. *rata*, to blame; N. *rata*, to reject.] To chide with vehemence; to reprove; to scold; to censure violently.

ratel, rät′el, *n.* [D. *raat*, honeycomb.] The honey-eating badger, a native of India and the Cape of Good Hope.

rather, ra′THėr, *adv.* [Compar. of *rath*, quickly, from A. Sax. *hrathor*.] Preferably; more readily or willingly; with preference or choice; with better reason; more properly; more correctly speaking; to the contrary of what has been just stated (no better but *rather* worse); somewhat (*rather* pretty).

rathskeller, rats′kel•ėr, *n.* [G. *rat*, council, and *keller*, council.] A restaurant or bar, serving wine, beer, and light food, usually located below street level.

ratify, rat′i•fī, *v.t.—ratified, ratifying.* [Fr. *ratifier—ratus*, fixed by calculation, valid, firm (RATE), and *facio*, I make.] To confirm; to settle authoritatively; to approve and sanction; to make valid, as something done by a representative, agent, or servant.—**ratifier,** rat′i•fī•ėr, *n.* One who ratifies.—**ratification,** rat′i•fi•kā″shon, *n.* The act of ratifying or confirming; confirmation; authorization.

rating, *n.* See RATE.

ratio, rā′shi•ō, *n.* [L. *ratio*, *rationis*, reckoning, calculation, from *reor*, *ratus*, to think or suppose. (RATE.) *Reason*, *ration* are from same word.] Relation or proportion which one thing has to another in respect of magnitude or quantity; in a narrower sense, the numerical measure which one quantity bears to another of the same kind, expressed by the number found by dividing the one by the other; thus the ratio of 3 to 4 is the same as of 6 to 8, each being equivalent to ¾; sometimes called *geometrical ratio*, in opposition to *arithmetical ratio* or the difference between two quantities.

ratiocinate, rash•i•os′i•nāt, *v.i.—ratiocinated, ratiocinating.* [L. *ratiocinor*, *ratiocinatus*, from *ratio*, reason. RATIO.] To reason; to argue.—**ratiocination,** rash•i•os′i•nā″shon, *n.* [L. *ratiocinatio*.] The act or process of reasoning, especially of reasoning deductively.—**ratiocinative,** rash•i•os′i•nā•tiv, *a.* Characterized by ratiocination; argumentative.

ration, rā′shon, ra′shon, *n.* [Fr., from L. *ratio*, *rationis*, proportion. RATIO.] A daily allowance of provisions to soldiers and sailors; any fixed amount or quantity dealt out; allowance.—*v.t.* To supply with rations.

rational, rash′on•al, *a.* [Fr. *rationnel*, L. *rationalis*, from *ratio*, *rationis*, proportion. RATIO, REASON.] Having reason or the faculty of reasoning; endowed with reason: opposed to *irrational*; agreeable to reason; not absurd, foolish, preposterous, or the like; acting in conformity to reason; judicious; *arith.* and *alg.* a term applied to an expression in finite terms, the opposite of a *surd* or *irrational* quantity.—**rationale,** rash•o•näl′, *n.* [From L. *rationalis*, from *ratio*, *rationis*, in sense of reason, account, plan.] A statement of reasons; an account or exposition of the principles of some process, phenomenon, etc.—**rationalism,** rash′on•al•izm, *n. Theol.* a system of opinions deduced from reason as distinct from inspiration or revelation, or opposed to it; the interpretation of Scripture statements upon the principles of human reason to the disregard of revelation or anything supernatural.—**rationalist,** rash′on•al•ist, *n.* An adherent of rationalism; one who rejects the supernatural element in dealing with the Old and New Testaments, and disbelieves in revelation.—**rationalistic,** rash′on•al•is″tik, *a.* Relating to or accordant with rationalism.—**rationalistically,** rash′on•al•is″ti•kal•li, *adv.* In a rationalistic manner. —**rationality,** rash•o•nal′i•ti, *n.* The quality of being rational; power of reasoning; possession of reason; reasonableness. —**rationalize,** rash′on•al•īz, *v.t.* To explain or justify: *psych.* to devise logical or creditable motives for actions performed because of irrational, censorable, or unrecognized motives.—**rationalization,** *n.*—**rationally,** rash′on•al•li, *adv.* In a rational manner; reasonably; sensibly.

ratite, rat′īt, *a.* [From L. *ratis*, a raft.] Any of the division Ratitae with no ridge or keel on the sternum; birds such as the ostrich.

ratline, ratlin, rat′lin, *n.* [Probably from *raddling*, an E. dial. weaving term.] *Naut.* one of a series of small ropes or lines which traverse the shrouds horizontally, forming ladders for going aloft; also called *Ratling*.

ratoon, ra•tön′, *n.* [Sp. *retono*, a sprout or shoot.] A sprout from the root of the sugarcane which has been cut.

ratsbane. See RAT.

rattan, rat′an or rat•tan′, *n.* [Malay *rotan*.] The commercial name for the long trailing stems of certain species of palm from India and the Eastern Archipelago, employed for walking sticks, etc.; a cane or walking stick made of rattan.

ratteen, ra•tēn′, *n.* [Fr. *ratine*, ratteen.] A thick woolen stuff quilled or twilled.

ratten, rat′n, *v.t.* [Lit. to play a rat's trick upon, from prov. *ratten*, a rat.] To destroy or take away the tools or machinery of, a mischievous trick perpetrated upon those who work in defiance of trade unions.

ratter. See RAT.

rattle, rat′l, *v.i.—rattled, rattling.* [From an A.Sax. verb seen in *hraetele*, rattlewort = L.G. *ratteln*, D. *ratelen*, G. *rasseln*, Dan. *rasle*, to rattle; all from a root probably onomatopoetic.] To make a quick sharp noise rapidly repeated, as by the collision of bodies not very sonorous; to clatter; to speak eagerly and noisily; to chatter fluently.—*v.t.* To cause to make a rapid succession of sharp sounds.—*n.* A rapid succession of sharp clattering sounds; loud rapid talk; an instrument with which a clattering sound is made, formerly used by watchmen; also a child's toy constructed to produce a rattling sound; one who talks rapidly and without constraint; a jabberer; the horny organ at the extremity of the tail of the rattlesnake; the peculiar sound heard in the throat which immediately precedes and prognosticates death; the death rattle.—**rattler,** rat′lėr, *n.* One who rattles or talks away without thought; a giddy noisy person.—**rattling,** rat′ling, *p.* and *a.* Making a quick succession of sharp sounds; lively.—**rattlebrained,** *a.* Giddy; wild; rattleheaded.—

rattlehead, *n.* A giddy person.—**rattleheaded, rattlepated,** *a.* Noisy; giddy; unsteady.—**rattlesnake,** rat′-l•snāk, *n.* A venomous American snake having the tail terminating in a series of articulated horny pieces, which the animal moves in such a manner as to make a rattling sound.—**rattlesnake root, rattlesnake weed,** *n.* Plants so named from being used as a cure for the bite of the rattlesnake.—**rattletrap,** *n.* A shaky rickety object. (*Colloq.*)

raucous, ra̤′kus, *a.* [L. *raucus*, hoarse.] Hoarse; harsh, as the voice.—**raucity,** ra̤′si•ti, *n.* Harshness of sound; rough utterance; hoarseness.

ravage, rav′ij, *n.* [Fr. *ravage*, from *ravir*, to carry off, to ravish (which see).] Desolation or destruction by violence, either by men, beasts, or physical causes; devastation; ruin.—*v.t.*—*ravaged, ravaging.* [Fr. *ravager.*] To lay waste by force; to devastate; to pillage.—**ravager,** rav′i•jėr, *n.* One who ravages; a plunderer; a spoiler.

rave, rāv, *v.i.*—*raved, raving.* [O.Fr. *raver*, to be delirious, from L. *rabies*, madness. RABID.] To wander in mind or intellect; to be delirious, wild, furious, or raging, as a madman; to talk with false enthusiasm; to speak enthusiastically.—*v.t.* To utter wildly and excitedly.—**raving,** rā′ving, *p.* and *a.* Furious with delirium; mad.—*n.* Furious exclamation; irrational, incoherent talk.

ravel, rav′el, *v.t.*—*ravelled, ravelling.* [Same as O.D. *ravelen*, D. *rafelen*, to disentangle; connections uncertain.] To untwist; to unweave; to disentangle; to entangle; to make intricate; to involve.—*v.i.* To become entangled; to fall into perplexity and confusion.—**raveling,** rav′el•ing, *n.* Anything, as a thread, detached in the process of untwisting.

ravelin, rav′lin, *n.* [Fr. *ravelin*, from It. *ravellino, revellino*; probably from L. *re*, back, and *vallum*, a rampart.] A detached triangular work in fortification, with two embankments which form a projecting angle.

raven, rā′vn, *n.* [A.Sax. *hraefn*=Icel. *hrafn*, D. *raaf*, Dan. *ravn*, O.H.G. *hraban*, G. *rabe*. Like *crow*, ultimately from its cry.] A large bird of a black color, of the crow family, noted for its hoarse cry and plundering habits; found in every part of the globe.—*a.* Resembling a raven, especially in color; black (*raven* locks).

ravin, raven, rav′in, rav′en, *n.* [O.Fr. *ravine*, from L. *rapina*, rapine. RAVINE.] Prey; plunder.—*v.i.* To prey with rapacity; to show rapacity.—*v.t.* To devour; to eat with voracity. (O.T.)—**ravenous,** rav′en•us, *a.* Furiously voracious; hungry even to rage; eager for gratification (a *ravenous* appetite).—**ravenously,** rav′en•-us•li, *adv.* In a ravenous manner.—**ravenousness,** rav′en•us•nes, *n.*

ravine, ra•vēn′, *n.* [Fr. *ravine*, a ravine, from L. *rapina*, rapine, violence, from *rapio*, to seize, or carry away. RAPID.] A long deep hollow worn by a stream or torrent of water; any deep narrow gorge in a mountain, etc.; a gully.

ravioli, ra•vē•ō′li, *n.* [It. pl. of *raviolo.*] Small squares of dough enclosing ground meat, etc., which are cooked and served in a sauce.

ravish, rav′ish, *v.t.* [Fr. *ravir, ravissant*, from L. *rapio, rapere*, to seize, to snatch. RAPID.] To seize and carry away by violence; to have carnal knowledge of a woman by force and against her consent; to commit a rape upon; to deflower or violate; to transport with joy or delight; to enrapture; to enchant.—**ravisher,** rav′ish•ėr, *n.* One that ravishes.—**ravishing,** rav′ish•ing, *p.* and *a.* Such as to ravish; delighting to rapture; transporting.—**ravishingly,** rav′ish•ing•li, *adv.* In a ravishing manner.—**ravishment,** rav′ish•-ment, *n.* Ecstasy.

raw, ra̤, *a.* [A.Sax. *hreáw, hraew*=D. *raauw*, Dan. *raa*, Icel. *hrár*, O.H.G. *râo*, G. *roh*, raw; same root as L. *crudus*, raw, *cruor*, blood: Gr. *kreas*, flesh.] Not altered from its natural state by cooking; not roasted, boiled, or the like; not subjected to some industrial or manufacturing process; not manufactured (*raw* silk, *raw* hides); not mixed or diluted (*raw* spirits); not covered with the natural covering; having the flesh exposed; sore, as if galled; sensitive; immature; inexperienced; unripe in skill (*raw* soldiers); bleak; chilly; cold and damp (a *raw* day).—*n.* A raw, galled, or sore place, as on a horse.—**rawboned,** *a.* Having little flesh on the bones; gaunt; lean and large-boned.—**rawly,** ra̤′li, *adv.* In a raw manner; especially, in an ignorant or inexperienced manner.—**rawness,** ra̤′nes, *n.* The state or quality of being raw; want of cooking; state of being inexperienced; chilliness with dampness; bleakness.

ray, rā, *n.* [O.Fr. *ray*, a sunbeam, from L. *radius*, a ray.] A line of light, one of the lines that make up a beam; *fig.* a beam of intellectual light; a gleam; one of a number of diverging radii; *bot.* the radiating part of a flower; the outer part or circumference of a compound radiate flower; *ich.* one of the radiating bony spines in the fins of fishes.—*Becquerel rays*, rays emitted by radioactive elements.—*Roentgen rays*, rent′gen, or *X-rays*, rays of intense penetrating power, enabling an operator to detect a body within an organism, much used for surgical, and to some extent for industrial, purposes.—*Ultraviolet rays*, invisible rays having a wave length between the violet end of the visible spectrum and X-rays, used in physical therapy as a source of *Vitamin D.*—*Violet ray*, shortest of visible wave lengths of the spectrum.—*v.t.* To radiate; to shoot forth or emit rays; to cause to shine forth.—*v.i.* To shine forth or out, as in rays.

ray, rā, *n.* [Fr. *raie*, from L. *raia*, a ray.] One of a genus of cartilaginous fishes, of which the skate is a well-known example, having a flattened body, with the pectoral fins extremely broad and fleshy.

rayah, raia, rä′yä, *n.* In Turkey, a person not a Mohammedan who pays the capitation tax.

rayon, rā′on, *n.* [Arbitrarily formed from E. *ray*, beam.] A synthetic material formed by forcing viscose through tiny holes and drying the filaments.

raze, rāz, *v.t.*—*razed, razing.* [Same word as *rase*, Fr. *raser*, to raze, to shave, to demolish, from L. *rado, rasum*, to scrape. RASE.] To graze; to subvert from the foundation; to overthrow; to demolish; to erase; to efface; to extirpate; to destroy.

razor, rā′zor, *n.* [Fr. *rasoir*, from *raser*, to shave.] A keen-edged steel device used for shaving.—*Razorback*, *n.* A species of hog having long legs and a thin body; the rorqual whale. See RORQUAL.

re, rē. Shortened form of Latin legal expression *in re*, adopted in business correspondence: with reference to, in the matter of, a former communication or subject.

re, rā, *n.* *Music*, the name given to the second of the syllables used in solmization.

reabsorb, rē•ab•sorb′, *v.t.* To absorb or imbibe again.—**reabsorption,** rē•-ab•sorp′shon, *n.* The act of reabsorbing.

reach, rēch, *v.t.* [A.Sax. *raecan*, O.Fris. *réka*, G. *reichen*, to reach, to extend, to hold out; from same root as *rich, right, rack, rake*, etc.; L. *rego*, to govern, *rex*, a king, E. *regal.*] To extend or stretch out; to hold or put forth; to spread abroad: often followed by *out* and *forth*; to touch by extending the arm or something in the hand; to extend to; to stretch out as far, or as high as; to give with the hand (*reach* me a chair); to arrive at; to come to; to get as far as (the ship *reached* her port); to attain to by effort, labor, or study; to gain or obtain; to extend in action or influence to.—*v.i.* To extend in space (to *reach* to heaven); to extend in scope or power; to stretch out the hand in order to touch; to make efforts at attainment.—*To reach after*, to make efforts to attain to or obtain.—*n.* The act or power of reaching; distance to which one can reach; the sphere to which an agency or a power is limited; often the extent or limit of human faculties or attainments; scope; a stretch of water; a straight portion of a river between any two bendings.—**reacher,** rēch′ėr, *n.* One who reaches.

react, ri•akt′, *v.t.* To act or perform anew.—*v.i.* To return an impulse or impression; to resist the action of another body by an opposite force; to act in opposition; to act mutually or reciprocally upon each other, as two or more chemical agents.—**reactance,** ri•ak′tans. [*Re*, back, and *act.*] In an electric circuit carrying alternating current, that part of the impedance which is due to induction and capacity.—**reaction,** ri•ak′shon, *n.* The reciprocal action which two bodies or two minds exert on each other; action or tendency to revert from a present to a previous condition; in *politics*, a tendency to revert from a more to a less advanced policy; *physics*, the resistance made by a body to anything tending to change its state; *chem.* the mutual or reciprocal action of chemical agents upon each other; *pathol.* a vital phenomenon arising from the application of an external influence; depression or exhaustion consequent on excessive excitement or stimulation, or increase of activity succeeding depression.—*Reaction wheel*, a turbine wheel.—**reactionary,** ri•ak′shon•a•ri, *a.* Pertaining to, proceeding from, or favoring reaction.—**reactionary, reactionist,** ri•ak′shon•ist, *n.* A favorer of reaction; one who attempts to check or reverse political progress.—**reactive,** ri•ak′tiv, *a.* Having power to react; tending to reaction.

reactor, ri•ak′ter, *n. Phys.* a device for the production and control of atomic energy.

read, rēd, *v.t.* pret. & pp. *read* (red). [A.Sax. *raedan*, to discern, to advise, to read; Icel. *rátha*, to advise, to read; D. *raden*, to advise, to interpret; G. *rathen*, O.H.G. *ratan*, to advise; same root as L. *reor*, *raius*, to suppose (RATE). Akin *riddle*. It would have been better to have retained the old spelling *red* for the pret. & pp.; comp. *lead* and *led*.] To peruse; to go over and gather the meaning of (to *read* a book, an author); to utter aloud, following something written or printed; to reproduce in sound; to see through; to understand from superficial indications (to *read* one's face); to discover by marks; to study by reading (to *read* law); to explain; to interpret (to *read* a riddle).—*To read up*, to make a special study of.—*v.i.* To perform the act of perusing; to read many books; to study for a specific object; to stand written or printed (the passage *reads* thus); to have a certain effect when read; to be coherent; to make sense: said of a sentence.—*To read between the lines*, to perceive and appreciate the real motive or meaning of a writing or work, as distinguished from what is openly professed or patent.—*n.* A reading over; perusal.—*a.* (red). Instructed or knowing by reading: hardly used except with the adverb *well* (*well read* in history).—**readable,** rē′da•bl, *a.* Capable of being read; legible; worth reading.—**readability, readableness,** rē•da•bil′i•ti, rē′da•bl•nes, *n.* The state of being readable.—**readably,** rē′da•bli, *adv.* In a readable manner.—**reader,** rē′dėr, *n.* One who reads or peruses; one who studies; one whose office it is to read prayers, lessons, lectures, and the like to others; a reading book; one who corrects the errors in proof sheets; a corrector of the press.—**readership,** rē′dėr•ship, *n.* The office of a reader.—**reading,** rē′ding, *n.* The act of one who reads; perusal; study of books (a man of extensive *reading*); a public recital or delivery of something written; a particular version of a passage; a lection; view or interpretation of an author's meaning or intention; reproduction in accordance with such interpretation; rendering; *legislation*, the formal recital of a bill by the proper officer before the house which is to consider it (the bill passed the second *reading*).—*Thought reading*. See THOUGHT.—*a.* Addicted to the reading or study of books.—**reading desk,** *n.* A desk at which reading is performed.

readily, readiness. See READY.

readjust, rē•ad•just′, *v.t.* To adjust or settle again; to put in order again.—**readjustment,** rē•ad•just′ment, *n.* The act of readjusting.

readmission, readmittance, rē•ad•mish′on, rē•ad•mit′ans, *n.* The act of admitting again.—**readmit,** rē•ad•mit′, *v.t.* To admit again.

ready, red′i, *a.* [O.E. *redi*, *readi*, A.Sax. *raede*, ready=Dan. *rede*, Sw. *reda*, Icel. *reithr*, G. (*be*)*reit*, ready; perhaps from root of *ride*, *Array* is from this stem through the French.] Prepared at the moment; fit for immediate use; causing no delay from want of preparation; not slow, backward, dull, or hesitating (a *ready* apprehension); prompt; dexterous; not backward or reluctant; willing; inclined; offering itself at once; at hand; opportune, near, easy, convenient; on the point, eve, or brink: with *to*.—*Ready money*, means of immediate payment; cash.—*To make ready*, to make preparation; to get things in readiness.—**readily,** red′i•li, *adv.* In a ready manner; quickly; promptly; cheerfully.—**readiness,** red′i•nes, *n.* The state or quality of being ready; due preparation; aptitude; quickness; cheerfulness; alacrity.—**readymade,** *a.* Made or prepared beforehand, kept in stock ready for use or sale (*ready-made* clothes).—**ready-to-wear,** *n.* Ready-made clothes; clothes made beforehand in large quantities.—**ready-witted,** *a.* Having quick wit.

reaffirm, rē•af•fėrm′, *v.t.* To affirm again.—**reaffirmance,** rē•af•fėr′mans, *n.* A second affirmation or confirmation.

reagent, rē•ā′jent, *n.* [REACT.] *Chem.* a substance employed to detect another by a reaction.

real, rē′al, *a.* [O.Fr. *real*, (Fr. *réel*), L.L. *realis*, from L. *res*, a thing (whence *rebus*, *re-* of *republic*).] Actually being or existing; not fictitious or imaginary (*real* life); genuine; not artificial, counterfeit, or fictitious; not affected; not assumed (his *real* character); *law*, pertaining to things fixed, permanent, or immovable, as to lands and tenements (*real* estate); opposed to *personal* or *movable* (property).—*Real presence*, the alleged actual presence of the body and blood of Christ in the Eucharist, or the conversion of the substance of the bread and wine into the real body and blood of Christ.—**realism,** rē′al•izm, *n.* The doctrines or principles of a realist.—**realist,** rē′al•ist, *n. Metaph.* as opposed to *idealist*, one who holds the doctrine that there is an immediate or intuitive cognition of external objects, that external objects exist independently of our sensations or conceptions; *scholastic philos.* one who maintains that things, and not words, are the objects of dialectics: opposed to *nominalist*; *fine arts* and *literature*, one who endeavors to reproduce nature or describes real life just as it appears to him.—**realistic,** rē•al•is′tik, *a.* Pertaining to or characteristic of the realists; relating to realism.—**realistically,** rē•al•is′ti•kal•li, *adv.* In a realistic manner.—**reality,** ri•al′i•ti, *n.* [Fr. *réalité*.] The state or quality of being real; actual being or existence; actuality; truth; fact; that which is real as opposed to that which is imagination or pretense.—**realizable,** rē′al•ī•za•bl, *a.* Capable of being realized.—**realization,** rē′al•ī•zā″shon, *n.* The act of realizing.—**realize,** rē′al•īz, *v.t.*—*realized*, *realizing*. [Fr. *réaliser*.] To make real; to bring into being or act (to *realize* a scheme or project); to feel as vividly or strongly as if real; to bring home to one's own case or experience; to acquire as the result of labor or pains; to gain (to *realize* profit from trade); to sell for or convert into money (to *realize* one's stock in a railroad).—*v.i.* To turn any kind of property into money.—**realizer,** rē′al•ī•zėr, *n.* One who realizes.—**really,** rē′al•li, *adv.* In a real manner; in truth; actually; indeed; to tell the truth: often used familiarly as a slight corroboration of an opinion or declaration (well, *really*, I cannot say).—**realness,** rē′al•nes, *n.* The quality of being real; reality.—**realty,** rē′al•ti, *n.* [A contr. of *reality*.] *Law*, the fixed or permanent nature of that kind of property termed *real*; real property.

real, rē′al, *n.* [Sp. *real*, from royal.] A former Spanish coin.

realgar, rē•al′gar, *n.* [Fr. *réalgar*, from Sp. *rejalgar*, from Ar. *rahj*, powder, *al*, the, and *ghâr*, a mine.] A mineral consisting of sulfur and arsenic in equal equivalents; red sulfide of arsenic, a brilliant red pigment. See ORPIMENT.

realm, relm, *n.* [O.Fr. *realme* (Fr. *royaume*), from L. *regalis*, from *rex*, *regis*, a king. REGAL.] A kingdom; a king's dominions; hence, generally, region, sphere, domain.

ream, rēm, *n.* [O.Fr. *raime*, from Sp. *resma*, a ream, from Ar. *rizmah*, a bale, a packet, a ream.] A bundle or package of paper, consisting generally of 20 quires, or 500 sheets.

ream, rēm, *v.t.* [Increase, to enlarge, from *rúm*, space. ROOM.] To bevel out, as a hole in metal; to enlarge, as the bore of a cannon; *naut.* to widen the seams between a vessel's planks for the purpose of calking them.—**reamer,** rē′mėr, *n.* An instrument for enlarging a hole.

reanimate, rē•an′i•māt, *v.t.* To revive; to resuscitate; to restore to life or animation; to infuse new life or courage into.—**reanimation,** rē•an′i•mā″shon, *n.* The act of reanimating.

reap, rēp, *v.t.* [A.Sax. *rípan,* to reap; closely allied to Goth. *raupjan,* to pluck; D. *rapen,* to gather; L.G. *rapen,* to pluck. *Ripe* is from same stem.] To cut with a sickle, scythe, etc., as a grain crop; to cut down and gather; to gather when ripe or ready; to cut down the crop on; to clear of a grain crop (to *reap* a field); hence, to shave (*Shak.*); to receive as a reward, or as the fruit of labor or of works: in a good or bad sense.—*v.i.* To perform the act or operation of reaping; to receive the fruit of labor or works.—**reaper,** rē′pėr, *n.* One who reaps; a machine for cutting grain; a reaping machine.—**reaping machine,** *n.* A machine for cutting down standing corn, etc., and in many cases also for forming it into sheaves, moved by horses or tractors through the field.

reappear, rē•ap•pēr′, *v.i.* To appear again or anew.—**reappearance,** rē•-ap•pē′rans, *n.* A second or new appearance.

reappoint, rē•ap•point′, *v.t.* To appoint again.—**reappointment,** rē•-ap•point′ment, *n.* A renewed or second appointment.

rear, rēr, *n.* [O.F. *riere,* Pr. *reire,* from L. *retro,* behind—*re,* back, and suffix *tro,* denoting direction, from root corresponding to Skr. *tar,* to move. So *arrear,* from L. *ad,* to, and *retro.*] The part behind or at the back; the hind part; the background: generally with the definite article; specifically, the part of an army or a fleet which is behind the rest.—*a.* Pertaining to or in the rear; hindermost; last.—**rear admiral,** *n.* The third degree of the rank of admiral. ADMIRAL.—**rearmost,** rēr′mōst, *a.* Farthest in the rear; last of all.—**rearward,** rēr′ward, *n.* The rear guard; the latter part of anything.—*a.* At or toward the rear.

rear, rēr, *v.t.* [A.Sax. *raeran,* for *raeson,* to raise, caus. of *risan,* to rise. RAISE, RISE.] To lift or set up; to erect; to raise; to bring up, as young; to foster; to educate; to breed, as cattle; to build up; to construct (to *rear* an edifice).—*v.i.* To rise on the hind legs, as a horse; to assume an erect posture.

rearm, rē•ärm′, *v.t.* [Prefix, *re,* and *arm.*] To refurnish with arms.—**rearmament,** rē•är′ma•ment, *n.*

rearrange, rē′a•rānj, *v.t.* To arrange again; to put in proper order again.—**rearrangement,** rē•a•rānj′ment, *n.* A second or repeated arrangement.

reason, rē′zn, *n.* [Fr. *raison,* O.Fr. *reson,* from L. *ratio, rationis,* reason, plan, account, from *reor, ratus,* to think, to calculate. RATE, RATIFY, RATIO.] A motive, ground, or cause acting on the mind; the basis for any opinion, conclusion, or determination; a ground or a principle; what accounts for or explains a fact or phenomenon; final cause; explanation; a faculty of the mind by which it distinguishes truth from falsehood, and which enables the possessor to deduce inferences from facts or from propositions, and to combine means for the attainment of particular ends; the act of deducing consequences from premises; ratiocination; justice; equity; fairness; that which is dictated or supported by reason; moderate demands; claims which reason and justice admit or prescribe (to bring one to *reason*).—*In reason, in all reason,* in justice; with rational ground.—*v.i.* To exercise the faculty of reason; to deduce inferences justly from premises; to argue; to ratiocinate; to discuss, in order to make something understood.—*v.t.* To examine or discuss by arguments; to debate or discuss (to *reason* the point); to persuade by reasoning or argument.—**reasonable,** rē′zn•a•bl, *a.* Having the faculty of reason; rational; governed by reason; not given to extravagant notions or expectations conformable or agreeable to reason; not extravagant, excessive, or immoderate; fair; equitable (any *reasonable* demands); being in mediocrity; moderate; tolerable.—**reasonableness,** rē′zn•a•bl•nes, *n.* The quality of being reasonable.—**reasonably,** rē′-zn•a•bli, *adv.* In a reasonable manner; in consistency with reason; moderately; tolerably.—**reasoner,** rē′zn•ėr, *n.* One who reasons or argues.—**reasoning,** rē′zn•ing, *n.* The act or process of exercising the faculty of reason; ratiocination; the arguments employed; the proofs or reasons when arranged and developed.—**reasonless,** rē′zn•les, *a.* Destitute of reason; irrational; unreasonable.

reassemble, rē•as•sem′bl, *v.t.* To collect or assemble again.—*v.i.* To assemble or meet together again.

reassume, rē•as•sūm′, *v.t.* To resume; to take again.

reassure, rē•a•shör′, *v.t.* To assure anew; to restore courage to; to free from fear or terror; also, to reinsure.—**reassurance,** rē•a•shö′rans, *n.* Assurance or confirmation repeated; also reinsurance.

reaumur, rā′o•myu̇r, *n.* [Inventor's name.] A thermometric scale on which the fixed points are 0° and 80°, answering respectively to 32° and 212° F.; denoted by R. See *Fahrenheit.*

rebaptize, rē•bap•tīz′, *v.t.* To baptize a second time.—**rebaptism,** rē•-bap′tizm, *n.* A second baptism.

rebate, ri•bāt′, *v.t.*—*rebated, rebating.* [O.Fr. *rebatre*—*re,* back, and *batre,* L. *batuere,* to beat; akin *battle, batter, abate,* etc.] To blunt; to diminish, reduce, abate; to deduct or make a discount from.—*n.* (rē′bāt) Diminution; *com.* abatement in price; deduction.

rebate, rē•bāt′, *n.* See RABBET.

rebec, rebeck, rē′bek, *n.* [Fr. *rebec, rebebe,* from Ar. *rabâb,* a kind of musical instrument.] A stringed instrument introduced by the Moors into Spain, somewhat similar to the violin, and played with a bow.

rebel, reb′el, *n.* [Fr. *rebelle,* from L. *rebellis,* making war again—*re,* again, and *bellum,* war. DUEL.] One who revolts from the government to which he owes allegiance; one who defies and seeks to overthrow the authority to which he is rightfully subject. ∴ Syn. under INSURGENT.—*a.* Rebellious; acting in revolt.—*v.i.* (ri•bel′)—*rebelled, rebelling.* To revolt; to take up arms against the government of constituted authorities; to refuse to obey a superior; to shake off subjection; to turn with disgust or nausea; to conceive a loathing (his stomach *rebelled* at such food).—**rebellion,** ri•bel′yon, *n.* [L. *rebellio, rebellionis.*] The act of rebelling; an armed rising against a government; the taking of arms traitorously to resist the authority of lawful government; open resistence to, or refusal to obey, lawful authority. ∴ Syn. under INSURRECTION.—**rebellious,** ri•bel′-yus, *a.* Engaged in, or characterized by, rebellion; mutinous.—**rebelliously,** ri•bel′yus•li, *adv.* In a rebellious manner.—**rebelliousness,** ri•-bel′yus•nes, *n.*

rebirth, rē•bėrth′, *n.* [Prefix *re,* and *birth.*] A new, or second, birth; a renaissance.

rebound, ri•bound′, *v.i.* [Prefix *re,* and *bound;* Fr. *rebondir,* to rebound.] To spring or bound back; to fly back by elastic force after impact on another body.—*v.t.* To drive back; to cause to echo; to reverberate.—*n.* (*pron.* rē′bound). The act of flying back on collision with another body; resilience.

rebuff, ri•buf′, *n.* [Prefix *re,* back, and old *buff,* a blow, from O.Fr. *buffe, bufe,* a blow. BUFFET.] A beating, forcing, or driving back; sudden check; a repulse; refusal; rejection of solicitation.—*v.t.* To beat back; to offer sudden resistance to; to repel the advances of.

rebuild, rē•bild′, *v.t.* To build again; to build after having been demolished.

rebuke, ri•būk′, *v.t.*—*rebuked, rebuking.* [Anglo-F. *rebuker,* O.F. *rebuchier,* to beat or strike back.] To check with reproof; to reprehend sharply and summarily; to reprimand; to reprove.—*n.* A direct and severe reprimand; reproof; reprehension; a childing.—**rebuker,** ri•bū′kėr, *n.* One that rebukes.

rebus, rē′bus, *n.* [L., ablative plural of *res,* a thing—lit. by things, because the meaning is indicated by things.] A set of words written by figures or pictures of objects whose names resemble in sound those words or the syllables of which they are composed; thus, 'I can see you' might be expressed by figures of an eye, a can, the sea, and a ewe; hence, a kind of puzzle made up of such figures or pictures.

rebut, ri•but′, *v.t.*—*rebutted, rebutting.* [Fr. *rebuter, rebouter,* to put or thrust back—*re,* back, and *bouter,* to put, to thrust. BUTT.] To repel, as by counter evidence; to refute;

law, to oppose by argument, plea, or countervailing proof.—**rebuttal,** ri•but′al, *n.* The act of rebutting; refutation; confutation.—**rebutter,** ri•but′ėr, *n. Law*, the answer of a defendant to a plaintiff's surrejoinder.

recalcitrate, ri•kal′si•trāt, *v.i.*—*recalcitrated, recalcitrating.* [L. *recalcitro*, to kick back—*re*, back, and *calcitrare*, to kick, from *calx, calcis*, the heel.] To show repugnance or resistance to something; to be refractory.—**recalcitration,** ri•kal′si•trā″shon, *n.* Act of recalcitrating; opposition; repugnance.—**recalcitrant,** ri•kal′si•trant, *a.* Exhibiting repugnance or opposition; not submissive; refractory.

recall, ri•kạl′, *v.t.* To call or bring back; to take back; to revoke; to annul by a subsequent act; to revive in memory; to order to come back from a place or mission (to *recall* a minister from a foreign court).—*n.* A calling back; revocation; the power of calling back or revoking; the removal of an official from office by a popular vote.

recant, ri•kant′, *v.t.* and *i.* [L. *recantare*, to recant, to recall—*re*, back, and *canto*, freq. of *cano*, to sing. CHANT.] To retract; to unsay; to make formal contradiction of something which one had previously asserted.—**recantation,** rē•kan•tā′shon, *n.* The act of recanting; retraction; a declaration that contradicts a former one.—**recanter,** ri•kan′tėr, *n.* One who recants.

recapitulate, rē•ka•pit′ū•lāt, *v.t.*—*recapitulated, recapitulating.* [Fr. *recapituler*, L.L. *recapitulo, recapitulatum*—prefix *re*, and *capitulum*, a head or heading. CAPITULATE.] To repeat or summarize, as the principal things mentioned in a preceding discourse; to give a summary of the principal facts, points, or arguments of.—*v.i.* To repeat in brief what has been said before.—**recapitulation,** rē•ka•pit′ū•lā″shon, *n.* The act of recapitulating; a concise statement of the principal points in a preceding discourse, argument, or essay.—*Recapitulation theory*, the theory that ancestral stages are repeated in the life history.—**recapitulatory,** rē•ka•pit′ū•la•to•ri, *a.* Containing recapitulation.

recapture, rē•kap′chėr, *n.* The act of retaking; the retaking of goods from a captor; a prize retaken.—*v.t.* To capture back; to retake.

recast, rē•kast′, *v.t.* To cast or found again; to throw again; to mold anew; to throw into a new form.

recede, ri•sēd′, *v.i.*—*receded, receding.* [L. *recedo*—*re*, back, and *cedere*, to walk. CEDE.] To move back; to retreat; to withdraw; to withdraw from a claim or pretension; to relinquish what had been proposed or asserted (to *recede* from a demand, from propositions).—*v.t.* (rē′sēd). To cede back; to grant or yield to a former possessor.

receipt, ri•sēt′, *n.* [O.Fr. *recete, recepte* (Fr. *recette*), from L. *receptus*,-pp. of *recipere*, to receive. RECEIVE.] The act of receiving (the *receipt* of a letter); that which is received; *pl.* money drawn or received; drawings (his *receipts* were $20 a day); a recipe; a prescription of ingredients for any composition, as of medicines, etc.; hence, *fig.* plan or scheme by which anything may be effected; a written acknowledgment of something received, as money, goods, etc.—*v.t.* To give a receipt for; to discharge, as an account.—**receiptor,** ri•sēt′ėr, *n.* One who receipts; one who gives a receipt.

receive, ri•sēv′, *v.t.*—*received, receiving.* [O.Fr. *recever, receveir*, Fr. *recevoir*, from L. *recipio*—*re*, again, and *capio*, to take. CAPABLE.] To get or obtain; to take, as a thing given, paid, communicated, etc.; to accept; to take into the mind; to embrace; to allow or hold, as a belief, custom, tradition, etc.; to give acceptance to; to allow to enter; to welcome; to be the object of.—*v.i.* To entertain callers; to be a recipient; to convert electrical signals so as to make them perceptible to the senses, as in telephone, radio, or television.—**receivable,** ri•sēv′a•bl, *a.* Such as may be received (accounts *receivable*).—**receiver,** ri•sē′vėr, *n.* One who receives; a person appointed by a court to manage the affairs of an enterprise in reorganization or liquidation; a person appointed in some business for the purpose of winding up the concern; one who takes stolen goods from a thief, knowing them to be stolen; *chem.* a vessel for receiving and containing the product of distillation; a vessel to receive gases.—**receivership,** ri•sēv′ėr•ship, *n.* The legal status of an enterprise under jurisdiction of the court for the purpose of a trust, reorganization, or liquidation.—**receiving set,** *n.* A radio instrument, or set, used in the reception of radio programs or signals.

recense,† ri•sens′, *v.t.*—*recensed, recensing.* [L. *recensere*, to review or examine—*re*, again, and *censere*, to reckon. CENSOR.] To review; to revise.—**recension,** ri•sen′shon, *n.* An examination; enumeration; a revision of the text of an author by a critical editor; an edited version.

recent, rē′sent, *a.* [Fr. *récent*, from L. *recens, recentis*, recent; etym. unknown.] Of late origin, occurrence, or existence; new; not of remote date, antiquated style, and the like; modern; only made known or spoken of lately; fresh (*recent* intelligence); *geol.* applied to all accumulations and deposits whose remains belong exclusively to species still existing; occurring or formed since the glacial period.—**recently,** rē′sent•li, *adv.* Newly; lately; freshly; not long since.—**recentness,** rē′sent•nes, *n.*

receptacle, ri•sep′ta•kl or res′ep•ta•kl, *n.* [L. *receptaculum*, from *recipio, receptum*, to receive. RECEIVE.] That which receives, admits, or contains things; a place or vessel in which anything is received and contained; a repository; *bot.* a general term given to a part which receives or bears other parts; as, that part of a flower upon which the carpels are situated; that part of the axis of a plant which forms a sort of disk bearing the flowers.

reception, ri•sep′shon, *n.* [L. *receptio*, from *recipio*, to receive. RECEIVE.] A receiving or manner of receiving; receipt; treatment at first coming; welcome; entertaiment; a formal occasion or ceremony of receiving guests, official personages, etc.; admission or credence, as of an opinion or doctrine; acceptance or allowance; in *radio*, the act or process of receiving programs or signals.—**receptive,** ri•sep′tiv, *a.* Such as to receive readily (*receptive* of teaching); taking in; able to take in hold, or contain.—**receptivity, receptiveness,** rē′sep•tiv″i•ti, ri•sep′tiv•nes, *n.*—**receptor,** ri•sep′tėr, *n. Physiol.* a sense organ, especially a nerve ending, which receives stimuli.

recess, ri•ses′, *n.* [L. *recessus*, from *recedo, recessum.* RECEDE.] A withdrawing or retiring; a moving back (the *recess* of the tides); place of retirement or secrecy; private abode; the time or period during which public or other business is suspended (the Christmas *recess* of a school); a cavity, niche, or sunken space formed in a wall; an alcove or similar portion of a room.—*v.t.* To make a recess in; to put in a recess.—**recession,** ri•sesh′on, *n.* [L. *recessio, recessionis*, from *recedo*; in last sense directly from *re* and *cession.*] The act of receding; withdrawal; position relatively withdrawn; a cession or granting back; retrocession.—*Recession of the equinoxes*, the same as *Precession of the equinoxes.*—**recessional,** *n.* Glacial deposit remaining after the ice sheet receded; hymn or other verses sung after service, when the choir and clergy withdraw from their places.—**recessive,**† ri•ses′iv, *a.* Receding; going back.

recharter, rē•chär′tėr, *v.t.* To charter again; to grant another charter to.

recherché, rė•shâr•shā′, *a.* [Fr.] Much sought after; choice; rare; exquisite.

recidivist, ri•sid′i•vist, *n.* [Fr. *récidiviste*—L. *re*, back, *cado*, to fall.] A relapsed criminal or one who returns to crime.

recipe, res′i•pē, *n.* [L. *recipe*, take, receive, imper. of *recipio*, to take or receive. RECEIVE.] The first word of a physician's prescription; hence the prescription itself; now applied to a receipt for preparing, mixing, or cooking food to produce a particular dish.

recipient, ri•sip′i•ent, *n.* [L. *recipiens, recipientis*, ppr. of *recipio.* RECEIVE.] A person or thing that receives; one to whom anything is communicated.—*a.* Receiving.—**recipience, recipiency,** ri•sip′i•ens, ri•sip′i•en•si, *n.* A receiving; act or capacity of receiving; reception.

reciprocal, ri•sip′ro•kal, *a.* [L. *reci-*

procus, Fr. *réciproque*, alternating, reciprocal, probably connected with *re*, back, and *pro*, forward.] Acting with a backward and forward motion; moving backward and forward; reciprocating; done by each to the other; mutual; mutually interchangeable; *gram.* reflexive.—*Reciprocal* or *inverse proportion.* Under INVERSE.—*Reciprocal quantities, math.* quantities which, multiplied together, produce unity.—*Reciprocal ratio* is the ratio between the reciprocals of two quantities; thus the *reciprocal ratio* of 4 to 9 is that of 1-4th to 1-9th.—*n.* That which is reciprocal to another thing.—*Reciprocal of a quantity*, in *math.* the quotient resulting from the division of unity by the quantity; thus, the *reciprocal* of 4 is ¼, and conversely the *reciprocal* of ¼ is 4.—**reciprocally,** ri•sip′ro•kal•li, *adv.* In a reciprocal manner; mutually; interchangeably; inversely.—**reciprocality,** ri•sip′ro•kal″i•ti, *n.* The state or quality of being reciprocal.—**reciprocate,** ri•sip′ro•kāt, *v.i.—reciprocated, reciprocating.* To move backward and forward; to have an alternate movement; to alternate.—*v.t.* To interchange; to give and return mutually; to give in requital (to *reciprocate* favors).—**reciprocating,** ri•sip′ro•kāt•ing, *p.* and *a.* Alternating; moving backward and forward alternately.—*Reciprocating engine*, that form of engine in which the piston and piston rod move back and forth in a straight line, absolutely, or relatively to the cylinder.—**reciprocation,** ri•sip′ro•kā″shon, *n.* The act of reciprocating; interchange of acts; a mutual giving and returning; alternation.—**reciprocity,** res•i•pros′i•ti, *n.* The state or character of being reciprocal; reciprocal obligation or right; equal rights or benefits to be mutually yielded or enjoyed; especially equal commercial rights or privileges enjoyed mutually by two countries trading together.

recision, ri•sizh′on, *n.* [L. *recisio*—*re*, back, and *caedo*, to cut. EXCISION.] The act of cutting off.

recite, ri•sīt′, *v.t.—recited, reciting.* [Fr. *réciter*, from L. *recitare*—*re*, again, and *cito*, to cite. CITE.] To repeat, as something prepared, written down, or committed to memory beforehand; to rehearse, with appropriate gestures, before an audience; to tell over; to relate or narrate; to go over in particulars; to recapitulate.—*v.i.* To rehearse before an audience compositions committed to memory; to rehearse a lesson.—**reciter,** ri•sī′tėr, *n.* One that recites or rehearses; a narrator.—**recital,** ri•sī′tal, *n.* The act of reciting; the repetition of the words of another; narration; a telling of the particulars of an adventure or event; that which is recited; a story; a narrative; a musical entertainment given by a single performer (an organ *recital*).—**recitation,** res•i•tā′shon, *n.* The act of reciting; the delivery aloud, with appropriate gestures, before an audience, of a composition committed to memory, as an elocutionary exhibition; the rehearsal of a lesson by pupils before their instructor.—**recitative,** res′i•ta•tēv″, *n.* [It. *recitativo.*] *Music.* a species of vocal composition which differs from an air in having no definite rhythmical arrangement, and no strictly constructed melody; musical recitation or declamation; a piece of music to be sung recitatively.

reck, rek, *v.i.* [A.Sax. *reccan, récan*, to reck, regard; cog. O.Sax. *rókian*, Icel. *raekja*, O.H.G. *róhhian, geruochen*, to reck or care; perhaps same root as *reckon.*] *Obs.* To care; to mind; to heed; to regard; often followed by *of.*—*v.t.* To heed, regard, care for.—*It recks (impersonal)*, it concerns (*it recks* me not).—**reckless,** rek′les, *a.* Not recking; careless; heedless of consequences; mindless; with *of* before an object. ∴ Syn. under RASH.—**recklessly,** rek′les•li, *adv.* In a reckless manner.—**recklessness,** rek′les•nes, *n.* The state or quality of being reckless.

reckon, rek′n, *v.t.* [O.E. *reknen, rekenen*, A.Sax. *gerecnian, recenian* = D. *rekenen*, Dan. *regne*, Icel. *reikna*, Sw. *räkna*, G. *rechnen*, to reckon, number, esteem; perhaps from same root as *reck* or *right.*] To count; to number; to tell one by one; to calculate; to estimate by rank or quality; to esteem, account, repute, hold.—*v.i.* To make computation; to compute; to calculate; to make up or render an account; to adjust relations of desert and penalty; to think, suppose, imagine (in this sense American rather than English).—*To reckon on* or *upon*, to count or depend upon.—*To reckon with*, to call to account; to exact penalty of.—**reckoner,** rek′n•ėr, *n.* One who reckons; something that assists a person to reckon.—**reckoning,** rek′n•ing, *n.* The act of computing; calculation; a statement and comparison of accounts for adjustment; the charges made by a host in a hotel, tavern, etc. (to pay the *reckoning*); *naut.* the calculation of the position of a ship from the rate found by the log, and the course as determined by the compass.

reclaim, ri•klām′, *v.t.* [*Re* and *claim*; Fr. *réclamer*, to claim back, to reclaim a hawk, to protest; L. *reclamo*—*re*, back, and *clamo*, to call. CLAIM.] To claim back; to demand to have returned; to call back; to bring a hawk to the wrist by a certain call; to reduce from a wild to a tame or domestic state; to tame; to rescue from being wild, desert, or waste; to bring under cultivation; to bring back from error; to reform.—*v.i.* To cry out; to exclaim against anything; *Scots law*, to appeal to the inner house of the Court of Session.—*n.* The act of reclaiming; reformation.—**reclaimable,** ri•klā′ma•bl, *a.* Capable of being reclaimed.—**reclamation,** rek•la•mā′shon, *n.* The act of reclaiming; the act of bringing into cultivation; the bringing back of a person from evil courses; a demand; claim made; a remonstrance or representation.

recline, ri•klīn′, *v.t.—reclined, reclining.* [L. *reclino*, to bend back—*re*, back, and *clino*, to bend (whence also *incline, decline*); root same as that of E. to *lean.*] To lean to one side or sidewise; to lay down to rest (to *recline* the head).—*v.i.* To rest or repose; to take a recumbent position.—**recliner,** ri•klī′nėr, *n.* One who reclines.

recluse, ri•klös′, *a.* [Fr. *reclus*, fem. *recluse*, from L. *reclusus*, pp. of *recludo, reclusum*, to lay open, but in L.L. signifying to shut—*re*, again, back, and *claudere*, to shut. CLOSE.] Living shut up or apart from the world; retired; sequestered; solitary.—*n.* A person who lives in retirement or seclusion; a hermit; a religious devotee who lives in an isolated cell.—**reclusion,** ri•klö′zhon, *n.* A state of retirement from the world; seclusion.—**reclusive,** ri•klö′siv, *a.* Affording retirement from society; recluse.

recognize, rek′og•nīz, *v.t.—recognized, recognizing.* [From *recognisance* (which is older in English), O.Fr. *recognoissance*, from L. *recognosco*—*re* and *cognosco*. COGNITION, KNOW.] To recall or recover the knowledge of; to perceive the identity of, with a person or thing formerly known; to know again; to avow or admit a knowledge of; to acknowledge formally; to indicate one's notice by a bow or nod; *Parliamentary*, to give a speaker the floor in debate (by a presiding officer); to indicate appreciation of (to *recognize* services by a reward).—*v.i. Law*, to enter into recognizances.—**recognition,** rek•og•nish′on, *n.* [L. *recognitio.*] The act of recognizing or state of being recognized; a perceiving as being known; avowal; notice taken; acknowledgment.—*Recognition markings*, in birds and mammals, conspicuous markings supposed to aid mutual recognition by members of a species.—**recognitory,** ri•kog′ni•to•ri, *a.* Pertaining to recognition.—**recognizable,** rek′og•nī″za•bl, *a.* Capable of being recognized.—**recognizance,** ri•kog′ni•zans or ri•kon′i•zans, *n.* [Fr. *reconnaissance*, O.Fr. *recognoissance.*] Act of recognizing; recognition; mark or badge of recognition; token; *law*, an obligation which a man enters into before a proper tribunal, with condition to do some particular act, failure of which results in forfeiture.

recoil, ri•koil′, *v.i.* [Fr. *reculer*, from L. *re*, back, and *culus*, the posteriors; same root as in Gael. *cul*, W. *cil*, the back.] To rebound; to fall back; to take a sudden backward motion after an advance; to be forced to retreat; to return after a certain strain or impetus (the gun *recoils*); to start or draw back as from anything repulsive, alarming, or the like; to shrink.—*n.* (rē′koil). A starting or falling back; rebound; the rebound or resilience of a firearm when discharged; a shrinking back.

recoin, rē•koin′, *v.t.* To coin again.—**recoinage,** rē•koi′nij, *n.* The act of coining anew.

recollect, rek′ol•lekt, *v.t.* [Lit. to collect or gather again.] To recover or recall the knowledge of; to bring back to the mind or memory; to remember; *refl.* to recover resolution or composure of mind; to collect one's self. ∴ Syn. under REMEMBER.—**recollection,** rek•ol•lek′shon, *n.* The act of recollecting or recalling to the memory; a bringing back to mind; remembrance; the power of recalling ideas to the mind, or the period over which such power extends; that which is recollected; something recalled to mind. ∴ Syn. under MEMORY.—**recollective,** rek′-ol•lek′tiv, *a.* Having the power of recollecting.

re-collect, rē•kol•lekt′, *v.t.* To collect or gather again; to collect what has been scattered.

recombine, rē•kom•bīn′, *v.t.* To combine again.

recommence, rē•kom•mens′, *v.t.* and *i.* To commence again; to begin anew.—**recommencement,** rē•kom•mens ment, *n.* A commencement anew.

recommend, rek•om•mend′, *v.t.* [*Re* and *commend*; Fr. *recommander*, to recommend, to commend, to entrust.] To commend to another's notice; to put in a favorable light before another; to commend or give favorable representations of; to make acceptable; to attract favor to; hence, to *recommend itself*, to make itself approved; to advise, as to an action, practice, measure, remedy, etc.; to set forward as advisable.—**recommendation,** rek′om•men•dā″-shon, *n.* The act of recommending; a favorable representation; that which procures favor or a favorable reception.—**recommendatory,** rek•-om•men′da•to•ri, *a.* Serving to recommend.—**recommender,** rek•om•-men′dėr, *n.* One who recommends.

recommit, rē•kom•mit′, *v.t.* To commit again (as persons to prison); to refer again to a committee.—**recommitment, recommittal,** rē•-kom•mit′ment, rē•kom•mit′al, *n.* A second or renewed commitment; a renewed reference to a committee.

recompense, rek′om•pens, *v.t.*—*recompensed, recompensing.* [Fr. *récompenser*, L.L. *recompenso*—L. *re*, again, and *compenso, compensatum*, to compensate. COMPENSATE.] To give or render an equivalent to, as for services, loss, etc.; to reward; to requite; to compensate; to return an equivalent for; to make amends for by anything equivalent; to make compensation for.—*n.* An equivalent returned for anything given, done, or suffered, compensation, reward; amends.

reconcile, rek′on•sīl, *v.t.*—*reconciled, reconciling.* [Fr. *réconcilier*, from L. *reconcilio*—*re*, again, and *concilio*, to conciliate. CONCILIATE.] To conciliate anew, to restore to union and friendship after estrangement; to adjust or settle (differences, quarrels); to bring to acquiescence or quiet submission (to *reconcile* one's self to afflictions); to make consistent or congruous, followed by *with* or *to*; to remove apparent discrepancies from; to harmonize.—*v.i.* To become reconciled.—**reconcilement,** rek′on•sīl•ment, *n.* Reconciliation; renewal of friendship.—**reconciliation,** rek′on•sil•i•ā″shon, *n.* [L. *reconciliate.*] The act of reconciling parties at variance; renewal of friendship after disagreement or enmity; *Scrip.* atonement; expiation; the act of harmonizing or making consistent; agreement of things seemingly opposite or inconsistent.—**reconciliatory,** rek•-on•sil′i•a•to•ri, *a.* Able or tending to reconcile.—**reconcilable,** rek•on•-sī′la•bl, *a.* Capable of being again brought to friendly feelings; capable of being made to agree or be consistent; capable of being harmonized.

recondite, rek′on•dīt or re•kon′dīt, *a.* [L. *reconditus*, pp. or *recondo*—*re*, back, and *condo*, to conceal (as in *abscond*).] Hidden from the mental perception; abstruse; profound; dealing with things abstruse.

recondition, rē•kon•dish′un, *v.t.* To put something in good condition by repairing, adjusting, etc.

reconnaissance, re•kon′nā•sans, *n.* [Fr. RECONNOITER.] The act or operation of reconnoitering; preliminary examination or survey of a territory or of an enemy's position, for the purpose of directing military operations.—*Reconnaissance in force*, a demonstration by a considerable body of men for the purpose of discovering the position or strength of an enemy.

reconnoiter, reconnoitre, rek•on-noi′tėr, *v.t.*—*reconnoitered, reconnoitering.* [O.Fr. *reconnoitre*, Fr. *reconnaître*, from L. *recognosco*—*re*, again, and *cognosco.* The elements of the word are same as in *recognize* (which see).] To make a preliminary survey of; to examine or survey, as a tract or region, for military or engineering purposes.

reconquer, rē•kong′kėr, *v.t.* To conquer again; to recover by conquest; to recover; to regain.

reconsider, rē•kon•sid′ėr, *v.t.* To consider again; to turn over in the mind again; to take into consideration a second time, generally with the view of rescinding.—**reconsideration,** rē′kon•sid•ėr•ā″-shon, *n.* The act of reconsidering.

reconstruct, rē•kon•strukt′, *v.t.* To construct again; to rebuild.—**reconstruction,** rē•kon•struk′shon, *n.* Act of constructing again; something reconstructed; *U. S. History*, the governmental reorganization of the seceded states after the Civil War.

reconvene, rē•kon•vēn′, *v.t.* To convene or call together again.—*v.i.* To reassemble.

reconvert, rē•kon•vėrt′, *v.t.* To convert again.—**reconversion,** rē•kon•-vėr′zhon, *n.* A second or renewed conversion.

reconvey, rē•kon•vā′, *v.t.* To convey back or to its former place; to transfer back to a former owner.—**reconveyance,** rē•kon•vā′ans, *n.* The act of reconveying; the act of transferring back to a former proprietor.

record, ri•kord′, *v.t.* [Fr. *recorder*, to get by heart, formerly also to record, from L. *recordor*, to remember—*re*, again, and *cor, cordis*, the heart.] To preserve the memory of by written or other characters, to register; to note, to write down or enter in order to preserve evidence; to cause to be inscribed on a phonograph record, or on a wire or tape, as to *record* music; to imprint deeply on the mind or memory.—*n.* (rek′ord). Something set down in writing for the purpose of preserving the knowledge of it; a register; an authentic or official account of facts or proceedings, entered in a book for preservation; the book or document containing such; a public document; the known facts in a person's life, especially in that of a public figure; the best of recorded achievements in competitive sports as, the world's *record.*—*Court of record*, one of the higher courts in which the records of the suits are preserved.—*Phonograph record*, a cylinder or disc upon which a transcription of sound has been made.—**recorder,** ri•kor′dėr, *n.* One who records official transactions; in the United States, a judge with first jurisdiction in criminal cases, or a magistrate's jurisdiction; in England, the chief judicial officer of a borough or city; an old musical instrument, somewhat like a flageolet; a registering apparatus.

recount, ri•kount′, *v.t.* [Fr. *reconter*—*re*, and *conter*, to tell.] To relate in detail; to count again; to count ballots again when the result of the first count has been challenged by a defeated candidate.

recoup, ri•köp′, *n.* [From Fr. *recoupe*, cloth remaining after cutting out clothes, from *re*, back, and *couper*, to cut.] *Law*, a sum kept back; a deduction; discount.—*v.t. Law*, to keep back as a set-off or discount; hence, *refl.* to indemnify one's self for a loss or damage by a corresponding advantage.—**recoupment,** ri•köp′ment, *n.* The act of recouping.

recourse, ri•kōrs′, *n.* [Fr. *recours*, from L. *recursus*, a running back, a return, from *recurro*, to run back—*re*, back, and *curro*, to run. COURSE.] A going to, as for help or protection; a recurrence in difficulty, perplexity, need, or the like.

recover, ri•kuv′ėr, *v.t.* [O.Fr. *recovrer* (Fr. *recouvrer*), from L. *recuperare*, to recover; of doubtful origin.] To regain, to get or obtain after being lost; to get back; to restore from sickness, faintness, or the like; to revive; to cure; to heal; to retrieve; to make up for; to rescue; *law*, to gain as a compensation; to obtain in return for injury or debt; to obtain title to by judgment in a court of law.—*v.i.* To regain health after sickness; to grow well again; to regain a former state or condition, as after misfortune or disturbance of mind; to succeed in a lawsuit.—**recoverable**, ri•kuv′ėr•a•bl, *a.* Capable of being regained or recovered; obtainable from a debtor or possessor. —**recoverer**, ri•kuv′ėr•ėr, *n.* One who recovers.—**recovery**, ri•kuv′ėr•i, *n.* The act or power of regaining or getting again; restoration from sickness or faintness; restoration from low condition or misfortune; *law*, the obtaining of right to something by a verdict and judgment of court from an opposing party in a suit.

recreant, rek′ri•ant, *a.* [O.Fr. *recreant*, ppr. of *recroire*, L.L. *recredere*, to give in, to confess defeat—L. *re*, again, and *credo*, to believe. See MISCREANT.] Craven; yielding to an enemy; cowardly; mean-spirited; apostate; false.—*n.* One who basely yields; one who begs for mercy; a mean-spirited, cowardly wretch.—**recreantly**, rek′ri•ant•li, *adv.* In a recreant manner; basely; falsely.—**recreancy**, rek′ri•an•si, *n.* The quality of being recreant; cowardice.

recreate, rek′ri•āt, *v.t.*—*recreated, recreating.* [L. *recreo, recreatum*—*re*, again, and *creo*, to create. CREATE.] To revive or refresh after toil or exertion; to reanimate; as languid spirits or exhausted strength; to amuse; to divert; to gratify.—*v.i.* To take recreation.—*v.t.* (rē•kri•at′). [Directly from *re* and *create.*] To create or form anew.—**recreation**, rek•ri•ā′shon, *n.* The act of recreating or the state of being recreated; refreshment of the strength and spirits after toil; amusement; entertainment.—**recreative**, rek′ri•ā•tiv, *a.* Tending to recreate; refreshing; diverting.—**recreatively**, rek′ri•ā•tiv•li, *adv.* In a recreative manner.—**recreativeness**, rek′ri•ā•tiv•nes, *n.*

recrement, rek′ri•ment, *n.* [L. *recrementum*, from *recerno*—*re*, back, and *cerno*, to separate. SECRET.] Superfluous matter separated from that which is useful; dross; scoria; spume.—**recremental, recrementitious**, rek•ri•men′tal, rek′ri•men•tish″us, *a.* Drossy; consisting of superfluous matter separated from that which is valuable.

recriminate, ri•krim′i•nāt, *v.i.*—*recriminated, recriminating.* [L. *re*, again, and *criminor*, I accuse. CRIME.] To return one accusation with another; to charge an accuser with the like.—*v.t.* To accuse in return.—**recrimination**, ri•krim′i•nā″shon, *n.* The act of recriminating; the return of one accusation with another; *law*, an accusation brought by the accused against the accuser upon the same fact; a counter-accusation.—**recriminative, recriminatory**, ri•krim′i•ni•tiv, ri•krim′i•ni•to•ri, *a.* Recriminating or retorting accusation.

recross, rē•kros′, *v.t.* To cross again.

recrudescent, rē•krö•des′ent, *a.* [L. *recrudesco*—*re*, again, and *crudescere*, to become raw, from *crudus*, raw. CRUDE.] Recurring; renewing activity, as of an illness.—**recrudescence, recrudescency**, rē•krö•des′ens, rē•krö•des′en•si, *n.* The state of being recrudescent; *med.* increased severity of a disease after temporary remission.

recruit, ri•kröt′, *v.t.* [Fr. *recruter*, from *recrute*, a participial noun from O.Fr. *recroistre*, pp. *recrû*, from L. *recresco*—*re*, again, and *cresco*, to grow (seen in *crescent, increase*, etc.). CRESCENT.] To repair by fresh supplies; to restore the wasted vigor of; to renew the health, spirits, or strength of; to refresh; to supply with new men; to make up by enlistment (to *recruit* an army).—*v.i.* To gain new supplies of anything wasted; to gain flesh, health, spirits, etc.; to raise new soldiers.—*n.* A soldier newly enlisted.—**recruiter**, ri•kröt′ėr, *n.* One who recruits.—**recruitment**, ri•kröt′ment, *n.* The act of recruiting.

recrystallize, rē•kris′tal•īz, *v.t.* To crystallize a second time.—**recrystallization**, rē•kris′tal•i•zā″shon, *n.* The process of recrystallizing.

rectal. See RECTUM.

rectangle, rek′tang•gl, *n.* [L. *rectangulus*—*rectus*, right, and *angulus*, an angle.] A right-angled parallelogram; a quadrilateral figure having all its angles right angles.—**rectangular**, rek•tang′gū•lėr, *a.* Right angled; having an angle or angles of ninety degrees.—**rectangularly**, rek•tang′gū•lėr•li, *adv.* In a rectangular manner; with or at right angles.

rectify, rek′ti•fī, *v.t.*—*rectified, rectifying.* [Fr. *rectifier*, from L. *rectus*, right, and *facio*, to make.] To make or put right; to correct when wrong, erroneous, or false; to amend; to refine by repeated distillation or sublimation; to convert (alcohol) into gin, etc., by flavoring specially. —**rectifiable**, rek′ti•fī•a•bl, *a.* Capable of being rectified or set right.—**rectification**, rek′ti•fi•kā″shon, *n.* The act or operation of rectifying; the act of setting right that which is wrong; the process of refining or purifying by repeated distillation. —*Rectification of a globe*, the adjustment of it preparatory to the solution of a proposed problem.—**rectifier**, rek′ti•fī•ėr, *n.* One who or that which rectifies; one who refines by repeated distillations; a device for obtaining direct electric current from alternating current. See THERMIONIC VALVE.

rectilinear, rectilineal, rek•ti•lin′i•ėr, rek•ti•lin′i•al, *a.* [L. *rectus*, right, and *linea*, a line.] Bounded by straight lines; consisting of a straight line or of straight lines; straight.—**rectilinearly**, rek•ti•lin′i•ėr•li, *adv.* In a rectilinear manner; in a right line.

rectirostral, rek•ti•ros′tral, *a.* [L. *rectus*, straight, and *rostrum*, a beak.] Having a straight beak.

rectitude, rek′ti•tūd, *n.* [L. *rectitudo*, from *rectus*, pp. of *rego*, *rectum*, to keep or lead straight. REGENT.] Rightness of principle or practice; uprightness; integrity; honesty; probity; correctness.

recto, rek′tō, *n.* [L. *rectus*, right.] The right-hand page of an open book; the right-hand side of a sheet of paper, as opposed to *verso*, on the reverse.

rector, rek′tėr, *n.* [L. *rector*, a ruler, from *rego*, *rectum*, to rule, to keep right. RECTITUDE.] A clergyman of the Protestant Episcopal Church, elected by the vestrymen, who has charge of a parish, and to whom belong the parsonage and tithes; the chief elective officer of some universities, as in France and Scotland; in Scotland also the title of the headmaster of an academy or important public school.—**rectorial**, rek•tō′ri•al, *a.* Pertaining to a rector or to a rectory.—*Rectorial tithes*, great or praedial tithes.—**rectory**, rek′to•ri, *n.* A parish church or parish held by a rector; a rector's mansion or parsonage.

rectrix, rek′triks, *n.* pl. **rectrices**, rek•trī′sēz. [L. *rectrix*, a female governor. RECTOR.] One of the long quill feathers in the tail of a bird, which like a rudder direct its flight.

rectum, rek′tum, *n.* [L. *rectum*, straight, because once thought to be straight.] *Anat.* the third and last part of the large intestine opening at the anus.—**rectal**, rek′tal, *a.* Relating to the rectum.

recumbent, ri•kum′bent, *a.* [L. *recumbens, recumbentis*, ppr. of *recumbo* —*re*, back, and *cumbo*, to lie. INCUMBENT.] Leaning; reclining; lying down; reposing; inactive; *zool.* and *bot.* applied to a part that leans or reposes upon anything.—**recumbency**, ri•kum′ben•si, *n.* The state of being recumbent; the posture of reclining, or lying; rest; repose; idle state.—**recumbently**, ri•kum′bent•li, *adv.* In a recumbent posture.

recuperate, ri•kū′pėr•āt, *v.t.*—*recuperated, recuperating.* [L. *recupero, recuperatum.* RECOVER.] To recover; to regain.—*v.i.* To recover; to regain health.—**recuperation**, ri•kū′pėr•ā″shon, *n.* [L. *recuperatio.*] Recovery. —**recuperative, recuperatory**, ri•kū′pėr•a•tiv, ri•kū′pėr•a•to•ri, *a.* Tending to recovery; pertaining to recovery.

recur, ri•kėr′, *v.i.*—*recurred, recurring.* [L. *recurro*—*re*, and *curro*, to run. CURRENT.] To return; to return to the thought or mind; to have recourse; to turn for aid; to occur again or be repeated at a stated interval, or according to some regular rule.—**recurrence**, ri•kėr′ens, *n.* The act of recurring, or state of being recurrent; return; resort; recourse.—**recurrent**, ri•kėr′ent, *a.* Returning from time to time; turned back in its course.—**recurring**, ri•kėr′ing, *a.* Returning again.—*Recurring* or *circulating decimals.* See CIRCULATING.

recurvate, recurved, ri•kėr′vāt, ri•kėrvd′, *a.* [L. *re*, back, and *curvus*, bent.] *Bot.* bent, bowed, or curved backward or outward (a *recurvate* leaf, etc.).—**recurve**, ri•kėrv′, *v.t.*—*recurved, recurving.* To bend back.

recusant, rek′ū•zant, *a.* [Fr. *récu-*

sant, L. *recusans*, *recusantis*, ppr. of *recuso*, to refuse, to reject—*re*, back, and *causa*, cause.] Obstinate in refusal; refusing to acknowledge the supremacy of a sovereign, or to conform to the established rites of a church.—*n.* One obstinate in refusing; one who will not conform to general opinion or practice; specifically—*Eng. hist.* a nonconformist.—**recusancy,** rek′ū•zan-si, *n.* The state of being a recusant; the tenets of a recusant; nonconformity.

red, red, *a.* [A.Sax. *reád*, red; cog. Dan. and Sw. *röd*, Icel. *rauthr* (*raudr*), D. *rood*, G. *roth*, Goth. *rauds*; same root as in L. *rufus*, *ruber*, G. *erythros*, W. *rhudd*, Ir. and Gael. *ruadh*, red; Skr. *rudhira*, blood. Akin are *ruddy*, *russet*, *ruby*, *rubric*, etc.] Of a bright warm color resembling blood; a general term applied to many different shades or hues, as crimson, scarlet, vermillion, etc.; often used in forming compound words which are self-explanatory (*red-backed*, *red-breasted*, *red-cheeked*, etc.).—*Red admiral*, a beautiful species of butterfly.—*Red cedar*, a species of North American and West Indian juniper, of which the heartwood is in great demand for the manufacture of lead pencils.—*Red chalk.* REDDLE.—*Red deer*, the common stag, a native of the forests of Europe and Asia; still plentiful in the Highlands of Scotland.—*Red gum*, an eruptive skin disease to which infants are subject.—*Red herring*, the common herring highly salted, dried, and smoked, so as to keep for a long time; something cast in the path as a means of diverting the attention of persons, or the scent of hounds, from the real object; something to sidetrack an issue. (*Colloq.*)—*Red Indian* or *Red man*, one of the copper-colored aborigines of America.—*Red ochre*, a name common to a variety of pigments. — *Red orpiment.* REALGAR.—*Red pine*, a species of pine, the *Scotch* or *Norway Pine*.—*Red republican*, an extreme republican, so called because in the first French revolution the extreme republicans were in the habit of wearing a red cap; often contracted into *red* (he is one of the *reds*).—*n.* A red color; a color resembling that of arterial blood; one of the simple or primary colors; a red pigment; red hair; a red republican; one having radical political or social beliefs; a communist; an anarchist.—**redbreast,** red′brest, *n.* A singing bird so called from the color of its breast, also known as the *robin redbreast*, or simply as the *robin*.—**redcoat,** red′-kōt, *n.* A name formerly given to a British soldier because of his uniform.—**red cross.** A rectangular red cross on a white background, as a symbol of mercy.—**Red Cross,** an international society organized to serve humanity in first aid, medical care, and relief of human suffering in times of catastrophe.—**redden,** red′n, *v.t.* To make red.—*v.i.* To grow or become red.—**reddish,** red′-ish, *a.* Somewhat red; moderately red.—**redhand, redhanded,** *a.* With red or bloody hands; hence, in the very act, as if with red or bloody hands: said of a person caught in the perpetration of any crime.—**red-hot,** *a.* Red with heat; heated to redness.—**red lattice,** *n.* A lattice window painted red, formerly the customary badge of an inn or alehouse.—*Red-lattice phrases*, barroom talk.—**red lead,** *n.* An oxide of lead much used as a pigment, and commonly known by the name of *Minium*.—**red-letter,** *a.* Having red letters; marked by red letters.—*Red-letter day*, a fortunate or auspicious day; so called because the holidays or saints' days were marked in the old calendars with red letters.—**redness,** red′nes, *n.* The quality of being red; red color.—**redpoll,** red′pōl, *n.* [From the red color of the *poll* or head.] A name given to several species of finches.—**redskin,** *n.* A red Indian; a North American Indian.—**redstart,** red′-stärt, *n.* [*Start* is from A.Sax. *steort*, a tail.] A species of American warbler; a songbird nearly allied to the redbreast, widely diffused over Europe, Asia, and North Africa.—**red tape,** *n.* A sarcastic name for excessive regard to formality and routine without corresponding attention to essential duties: so named from the red tape used in tying up papers in government offices.—**redtapism,** *n.* Excessive official routine; strict and pedantic adherence to official formalities.—**redwing,** red′wing, *n.* An American blackbird with a red spot on the wing.—**redwood,** *n.* The name of various sorts of wood of a red color; an Indian dyewood; a coniferous tree of California, often growing 300 feet high, and its cedar-like wood.

redact, ri•dakt′, *v.t.* [L. *redigo*, *redactum*, to reduce to order—*re*, again, and *ago*, to bring.] To give a presentable literary form to; to act as redactor or editor of.—**redactor,** ri•dak′tėr, *n.* [Fr. *redacteur.*] One who redacts; an editor.—**redaction,** ri•dak′shon, *n.* [Fr.] Preparation for publication.

redan, ri•dan′, *n.* [Fr. *redan*, O.Fr. *redent*, from *re*, back, and *dent*, L. *dens*, *dentis*, a tooth; from its shape.] *Field fort*, the simplest kind of work employed, consisting of two parapets of earth raised so as to form a salient angle, with the apex toward the enemy.

reddle, red′l, *n.* [From *red*; comp. G. *röthel*, from *roth*, red.] Red chalk; a species of argillaceous ironstone ore used as a pigment and to mark sheep. Spelled also *Raddle*.

redeem, ri•dēm′, *v.t.* [Fr. *redimer*, L. *redimo*, to buy back, to ransom—*red*, *re*, back, and *emo*, to obtain or purchase. EXAMPLE, EXEMPT.] To buy back; to release from captivity or bondage, or from any obligation or liability to suffer or be forfeited, by paying an equivalent; to pay ransom or equivalent for; to ransom; to rescue; to perform, as a promise; to make good by performance; to make amends for; to atone for; to improve or employ to the best advantage (*redeeming* the time).—**redeemable,** ri•dē′ma•bl, *a.* Capable of being redeemed.—**redeemer,** ri•dē′mėr, *n.* One who redeems or ransoms; [*cap.*] the Saviour of the world, JESUS CHRIST.—**redemption,** ri•dem′shon, *n.* [L. *redemptio*: a doublet of *ransom*.] The act of redeeming; the state of being redeemed; ransom; *theol.* the deliverance of sinners from the penalty of God's violated law by the sufferings and death of Christ.—**redemptive,** ri•dem′tiv, *a.* Redeeming; serving to redeem.—**redemptory,** ri•dem′to•ri, *a.* Paid for ransom.

redeliver, rē•di•liv′ėr, *v.t.* To deliver back; to return to the sender; to liberate a second time.

redemand, rē•di•mand′, *v.t.* To demand back; to demand again.

redemption. See REDEEM.

redeposit, rē•di•poz′it, *v.t.* To deposit again or anew.

redintegrate, ri•din′ti•grāt, *v.t.*—*redintegrated*, *redintegrating*. [L. *re*, again, and *integer*, whole. ENTIRE.] To make whole again; to restore to a perfect state.—**redintegration,** ri•din′ti•grā″shon, *n.*

rediscover, rē•dis•kuv′ėr, *v.t.* [L. *re*, again, and *discover*.] To discover again or afresh.

redistrict, rē•dis′trikt, *v.t.* [L. *re*, again, and *district*.] To revise the districts of, usually for legislative purposes.

redolent, red′o•lent, *a.* [L. *redolens*, *redolentis*, ppr. of *redolere*, to emit a scent—*red*, back, and *olere*, to smell. ODOR.] Having or diffusing a sweet scent; giving out an odor; reminiscent: often with *of*.—**redolence,** red′o•lens, *n.*

redouble, rē•dub′l, *v.i.* [Prefix *re*, and *double*.] To multiply; to repeat often; to increase by repeated or continued additions.—*v.i.* To become twice as much; to become greatly or repeatedly increased.

redoubt, ri•dout′, *n.* [Fr. *redoute*, *reduit*, from L.L. *reductus*, a retired spot, from L. *reductus*, retired—*re*, back, and *duco*, to lead. DUKE.] *Fort.* a general name for nearly every class of works wholly enclosed and undefended by re-entering or flanking angles; a small enclosed temporary fieldwork.

redoubtable, ri•dout′a•bl, *a.* [O.Fr. *redoutable*, from *redoubter*, to fear—L. *re*, again, and *dubito*, to doubt. DOUBT.] Formidable; to be dreaded; terrible to foes; hence, valiant: often used in irony.—**redoubted,** ri•dout′ed, *p.* and *a.* Redoubtable; formidable; valiant.

redound, ri•dound′, *v.i.* [Fr. *redonder*, L. *redundo*, to overflow—*red*, back, and *undo*, to surge, from *unda*, a wave (seen also in *undulate*, *redundant*, *abound*).] To roll or flow back, as a wave; to conduce; to contribute; to result (this will *redound* to your benefit).—*n.* The coming back, as a consequence or effect; result.

redraft, rē•draft′, *v.t.* To draw or draft anew.—*n.* A second draft or copy; a second draft or order drawn for money.

redraw, rē•drą′, *v.t.* To draw again, as a second draft or copy.—*v.i.* *Com.* to draw a new bill of exchange.

redress, ri•dres′, *v.t.* [Fr. *redresser,* to straighten again, to put right. DRESS.] To remedy or put right, as a wrong; to repair, as an injury; to relieve of anything unjust or oppressive; to compensate; to make amends to.—*n.* Deliverance from wrong, injury, or oppression; undoing of wrong; reparation; indemnification.—**redresser.** ri•dres′ėr, *n.* One who gives redress.

reduce, ri•dūs′, *v.t.*—*reduced, reducing.* [L. *reduco*—*re,* back, and *duco,* to lead. DUKE.] To bring to any state or condition, good or bad; to bring (to power, to poverty, to order, etc.); to diminish in size, quantity, or value; to make less or lower; to bring to an inferior condition; to subdue; to bring into subjection; to bring under rules or within certain limits of description; to bring from a form less fit to one more fit for operation; *arith.* to change from one denomination into another without altering the value; *alg.* to bring to the simplest form with the unknown quantity by itself on one side, and all the known quantities on the other side; *metal.* to separate, as a pure metal from a metallic ore; *surg.* to restore to its proper place or state, as a dislocated or fractured bone.—*To reduce a design,* to make a copy of it smaller than the original.—*To reduce to the ranks,* to degrade for misconduct to the position of a private soldier.—**reducer,** ri•dū′sėr, *n.* One that reduces.—**reducible,** ri•dū′si•bl, *a.* Capable of being reduced; convertible.—**reducibly,** ri•dū′si•bli, *adv.* —**reduction,** ri•duk′shon, *n.* [L. *reductio.*] The act of reducing; conversion into another state or form; diminution; conquest; subjugation; *arith.* the bringing of numbers of one denomination into another; the arithmetical rule by which this is done; *alg.* the process of bringing equations to their simplest forms with the unknown quantity alone on one side, and the known ones on the other; the act of making a copy of a map, design, etc., on a smaller scale, preserving the proper proportions; *surg.* the operation of restoring a dislocated or fractured bone to its former place; *metal.* the operation of obtaining pure metals from metallic ores.—**reductive,** ri•duk′tiv, *a.* Having the power of reducing; tending to reduce.

redundant, ri•dun′dant, *a.* [L. *redundans, redundantis,* ppr. of *redundo.* REDOUND.] Superfluous; exceeding what is natural or necessary; superabundant; using more words than are necessary.—**redundance, redundancy,** ri•dun′dans, ri•dun′dan•si, *n.* The quality of being redundant; superfluity; superabundance; that which is redundant or superfluous.—**redundantly,** ri•dun′dant•li, *adv.* In a redundant manner.

reduplicate, ri•dū′pli•kāt, *v.t.*—*reduplicated, reduplicating.* [L. *reduplico, reduplicatum*—*er,* and *duplico,* to double. DUPLICATE.] To double again; to multiply; to repeat; *philol.* to repeat, as the initial syllable or the root of a word, for the purpose of marking past time.—*v.i. Philol.* to be doubled or repeated; to undergo reduplication.—*a.* Redoubled; repeated; *bot.* applied to a form of aestivation in which the edges of the sepals or petals are turned outward.—**reduplication,** ri•dū′pli•kā″shon, *n.* The act of doubling or reduplicating; *philol.* the repetition of a root or of the initial syllable (more or less modified), as in Gr. *pheugō,* to flee, perfect *pepheuga*; *did,* the reduplicated past of *do*; the new syllable formed by reduplication.

redware, red′wâr, *n.* [*red* + *ware,* seaweed.] An edible brownish seaweed found off the coast of New England.

redwing. See RED.

re-echo, rē•ek′ō, *v.t.* and *i.* To echo back; to reverberate again.—*n.* The echo of an echo; a second or repeated echo.

reed, rēd, *n.* [O.E. *rede,* A.Sax. *hreōd*=O.Sax. *ried,* D. *riet, ried,* O.H.G. *hriot,* Mod.G. *riet, ried*; also Ir. *readan,* Gael. *ribhid,* a reed.] A name applied to tall broad-leaved grasses growing in marshy places, or to their hollow stems; a musical instrument made from a reed; a rustic or pastoral pipe; a little tube through which a hautboy, bassoon, or clarinet is blown; one of the thin plates of metal whose vibrations produce the notes of an accordion, harmonium, etc.; *weaving,* a frame of parallel flat strips of wood or metal for separating the threads of the warp, and for beating the weft up to the web.—**reedbird.** RICEBIRD.—**reed grass,** *n.* A name given to various large grasses.—**reed pipe,** *n.* A musical pipe made of reed; a pipe in an organ sounding by means of a reed.—**reedy,** rēd′i, *a.* Abounding with reeds; resembling a reed; applied to a voice or musical instrument having a thin, harsh tone.

reef, rēf, *n.* [Same as D. *rif,* a roof; Icel. *rif,* Dan. *rev, riv,* Sw. *rev,* G. *riff,* reef; from root of *rive.*] A mass of rocks in the ocean lying at or near the surface of the water; among gold miners, a gold-bearing quartz vein.

reef, rēf, *n.* [From D. *reef,* a reef; L.G. *reff, riff,* Icel. *rif,* Dan. *rev, reb,* Sw. *ref,* reef; akin A.Sax. *reáf,* a garment. ROBE.] *Naut.* that part of a sail which can be drawn together by small cords, so as to contract the canvas in proportion to the increase of the wind.—*v.t. Naut.* to take a reef or reefs in; to reduce the extent of a sail by folding a certain portion of it and making it fast to the yard.—**reefer,** rēf′ėr, *n.* One who reefs; a close-fitting jacket of strong cloth.

reek, rēk, *n.* [A.Sax. *réc,* smoke, vapor; cog. O.Fris. *rék,* Icel. *reykr,* D. and L.G. *rook,* Dan. *rög,* Sw. *rök,* G. *rauch,* Lith. *rukis,* smoke.] Vapor; steam; exhalation; fume; smoke.—*v.i.* To smoke; to steam; to exhale; to emit vapor.—**reeky,** rēk′i, *a.* Giving out reek or fumes. (*Shak.*)

reel, rēl, *n.* [A.Sax. *hreól, reól,* a reel; Icel. *hraell,* a weaver's rod or sley.] A machine on which yarn is wound to form it into hanks, skeins, etc.; a revolving frame on which the logline is wound; a revolving appliance attached to the butt of a fishing rod, and around which the line is wound; the photographic film of a motion picture.—*v.t.* To wind upon a reel.

reel, rēl, *n.* [Gael. *righil,* a reel.] A lively dance peculiar to Scotland; the music for this dance, generally written in common time of four crotchets in a bar, but sometimes in jig time of six quavers; also, the Virginia Reel.

reel, rēl, *v.i.* [O.E. *reile, rele,* to roll, to reel; perhaps from *reel,* the implement.] To stagger or sway in walking; to whirl; to have a whirling or giddy sensation (my brain *reeled*). —*n.* A staggering motion, as that of a drunken man.

re-elect, rē•i•lekt′, *v.t.* To elect again.—**re-election,** rē•i•lek′shon, *n.* Election for a second term to an office, or a repeated election, as, for instance, the re-election of a president of the United States at the termination of his first four years in office.

re-emerge, rē•i•mėrj′, *v.i.* To emerge after being plunged, obscured, or overwhelmed.—**re-emergence,** rē•i•mėr′jens, *n.* The act of emerging again.

re-enact, rē•i•nakt′, *v.t.* To enact again.—**re-enactment,** rē•i•nakt′ment, *n.* The enacting or passing of a law a second time.

re-enforce, rē•in•fōrs′, *v.t.* To enforce anew; to reinforce.

re-engage, rē•in•gāj′, *v.t.* and *i.* To engage a second time.

re-enlist, rē•in•list′, *v.t.* and *i.* To enlist a second time.—**re-enlistment,** rē•in•list′ment, *n.* The act of re-enlisting.

re-enter, rē•en′tėr, *v.t.* To enter again or anew; *engr.* to cut deeper, as the incisions of a plate which are too faint.—**re-entrance,** rē•en′trans, *n.* The act of entering again.—**re-entry,** rē•en′tri, *n.* A new or second entry; the return, through the earth's atmosphere, of a space vehicle.

re-establish, rē•es•tab′lish, *v.t.* To establish anew.—**re-establishment,** rē•es•tab′lish•ment, *n.* The act of establishing again.

reeve, rēv, *n.* [A.Sax. *geréfa,* a steward, a person in authority; origin doubtful; *sheriff*=*shire-reeve.*] In England a bailiff; a steward; a peace officer: now used only in such words as *borough-reeve*, *port-reeve*, etc.

reeve, rēv, *n.* A bird, the female of the ruff.

reeve, rēv, *v.t.* and *i.*—*reeve* or *rove, reeving.* [From *reef*, the nautical term.] *Naut.* to pass the end of a rope through any hole in a block, thimble, ringbolt, etc.; to run or pass through such hole.

re-examine, rē•eg•zam′in, *v.t.* To examine anew.—**re-examination,** rē•eg•zam′i•nā″shon, *n.* A renewed or repeated examination.

re-export, rē•eks•pōrt′, *v.t.* To export again; to export after having been imported.—*n.* (rē•eks′pōrt). Any commodity re-exported.—**re-exportation,** rē•eks′pōr•tā″shon, *n.* The act of re-exporting.

refashion, rē•fash′on, *v.t.* To fashion or form into shape a second time.

refasten, rē•fas′n, *v.t.* To fasten again.

refection, ri•fek′shon, *n.* [L. *refectio, refectionis*, from *reficio*, to restore, to refresh—*re*, again, and *facio*, to make.] Refreshment after hunger or fatigue; a repast.—**refectory,** ri•fek′to•ri, *n.* An eating room; an apartment in convents where meals are taken.

refer, ri•fėr′, *v.t.*—*referred, referring.* [L. *refero, referre*, to bring back, to refer, etc.—*re*, back, and *fero*, to carry. FERTILE.] To trace back; to impute; to assign; to attribute to, as the cause, motive, or ground; to hand over, as to another person or tribunal for treatment, decision, etc. (to *refer* a matter to a third party); to appeal; to assign, as to an order, genus, or class; in all senses followed by *to.*—*v.i.* To respect; to have relation; to appeal; to have recourse; to apply; to consult (to *refer* to one's notes); to allude; to make allusion; to direct the attention. ∴ Syn. under ADVERT.—**referee,** ref•ė•rē′, *n.* One to whom a matter in dispute has been referred for settlement or decision; an arbitrator.—**reference,** ref′ėr•ens, *n.* The act of referring; the act of alluding; direct allusion; relation; respect, or regard (generally in the phrase *in* or *with reference to*); one of whom inquiries may be made in regard to a person's character, abilities, etc.; a passage or note in a work by which a person is referred to another passage.—*a.* Affording information when consulted.—*Reference Bible*, a Bible having brief explanations and references to parallel passages printed on the margin.—*Reference books*, books, such as dictionaries, etc., intended to be consulted as occasion requires. —*Reference library*, a library containing books which can be consulted on the spot.—**referendum,** ref•ėr•en′dum, *n.* [L., a thing to be referred.] The reference to public vote, for final approval or rejection, of measures proposed or passed by a representative assembly; a means of consulting public opinion by popular vote when a public body is unable to make decisions or take on itself the responsibility for a measure.

refill, rē•fil′, *v.t.* To fill again.—*n.* rē′fil, a product sold in a special container designed to be filled again when initial contents are consumed; the product made to fill again the container when original contents have been exhausted.

refine, ri•fīn′, *v.t.*—*refined, refining.* [Fr. *raffiner*, to refine—*re*, and *affiner* —*af* (for L. *ad*), to, and *fin*, fine. FINE.] To reduce to a pure state; to free from impurities; to purify; to reduce from the ore; to separate from other metals or from dross or alloy; to purify from what is coarse, inelegant, rude, and the like; to make elegant; to raise or educate, as the taste; to give culture to; to polish (to *refine* the manners, etc.).—*v.i.* To become pure or purer; to affect nicety or subtlety in thought or language.—**refined,** ri•fīnd′, *p.* and *a.* Polished or elegant in character; free from anything coarse or vulgar.—**refinement,** ri•fīn′ment, *n.* The act of refining or purifying, or state of being refined; the state of being free from what is coarse, rude, inelegant, or the like; elegance of manners, language, etc.; culture; a result of excessive elaboration, polish, or nicety; overnicety; an affected subtlety.—**refiner,** ri•fī′nėr, *n.* One that refines liquors, sugar, metals, or other things; an improver in purity and elegance; one who is overnice in discrimination, argument, reasoning, etc.—**refinery,** ri•fī′nėr•i, *n.* A place and apparatus for refining sugar, metals, or the like.

refit, rē•fit′, *v.t.*—*refitted, refitting.* To restore after damage or decay; to repair; to fit out anew.—*v.i.* To repair damages, especially to ships.—*n.* A repairing; the repair of a ship.

reflect, ri•flekt′, *v.t.* [L. *reflecto*—*re*, back, and *flecto*, *flexum*, to bend, seen in *flexure, deflect, inflect, inflection*, etc. FLEX.] To bend back; to turn, cast, or direct back; to throw off after striking or falling on any surface, and in accordance with certain physical laws (to *reflect* light, heat, or sound); to give back an image or likeness of; to mirror.—*v.i.* To throw back light, heat, sound, or the like; to return rays or beams; to throw or turn back the thoughts upon anything; to think or consider seriously; to revolve matters in the mind; to bring reproach; to cast censure or blame (do not *reflect* on his errors).—**reflection,** ri•flek′shon, *n.* The act of reflecting, or the state of being reflected; *physics*, the change of direction which light, heat, or sound experiences when it strikes upon a surface and is thrown back into the same medium from which it approached; that which is produced by being reflected; an image given back from a reflecting surface; attentive or continued consideration; meditation, contemplation, deliberation; a censorious remark or one attaching blame; reproach cast; *anat.* the folding of a membrane upon itself.—**reflective,** ri•flek′tiv, *a.* Throwing back rays; reflecting; exercising reflection; *gram.* reflexive.—**reflectively,** ri•flek′tiv•li, *adv.* In a reflective manner.—**reflectiveness,** ri•flek′tiv•nes, *n.*—**reflector,** ri•flek′tėr, *n.* One who reflects; that which reflects; a polished surface of metal or other suitable material for reflecting light, heat, or sound in any required direction; a reflecting telescope.

reflex, rē′fleks, *a.* [L. *reflexus*, ppr. of *reflecto.* REFLECT.] Turned backward; having a backward direction; reflective; introspective.—*Reflex actions*, those actions of the nervous system which are performed involuntarily, and often unconsciously, as the contraction of the pupil of the eye when exposed to strong light.—*n.* Reflection; image produced by reflection.—**reflexion,** ri•flek′shon. See REFLECTION.—**reflexive,** ri•flek′siv, *a,* Reflective; bending or turning backward; having respect to something past; *gram.* having for its direct object a pronoun which stands for the agent or subject, said of certain verbs (I *bethought myself*, the witness *forswore himself*); also applied to pronouns of this class.—**reflexively,** ri•flek′siv•li, *adv.*

refluent, ref′lu̦•ent, *a.* [L. *refluens, refluentis*—*re*, back, and *fluo*, to flow. FLUENT.] Flowing, surging, or rushing back; ebbing.—**refluence,** ref′lu̦•ens, *n.*

reflux, rē′fluks, *n.* [Prefix *re*, back, and *flux.*] A flowing back (the flux and *reflux* of the tides).

reforest, rē•for′est, *v.t.* and *i.* [L. *re*, again, and *forest.*] To replant an area with forest trees.

reform, ri•form′, *v.t.* [Fr. *réformer*, to reform or amend, from L. *reformare*—*re*, again, and *formo*, to form, from *forma*, form. FORM.] To change from worse to better; to introduce improvement in; to amend; to bring from a bad to a good state; to remove or abolish for something better.—*v.i.* To abandon evil and return to good; to amend one's behavior.—*n.* A rearrangement which either brings back a better order of things or reconstructs the present order in an entirely new form; reformation; amendment of what is defective, vicious, corrupt, or depraved.—**reformable,** ri•for′ma•bl, *a.* Capable of being reformed.—**reformation,** ref•or•mā′shon, *n.* The act of reforming or state of being reformed; correction or amendment of life, manners, or of anything objectionable or bad; the redress of grievances or abuses.—[*cap.*] The religious revolution of the sixteenth century which divided the Western Church into the two sections known as Protestant and Roman Catholic.—**reformatory,** ri•for′ma•to•ri, *a.* Tending to produce reformation.—*Reformatory*, a reform school.—*n.* An institution for the reception and reformation of juveniles who have already begun a career of criminality, and have been convicted.—**reformed,** ri•formd′, *p.* and *a.* Corrected; amended; restored to a good state; having turned from evil courses (a *reformed* profligate); [*cap.*] having accepted the principles of the Reformation and separated from the Church of Rome; especially those churches, such as the ones constituted in various parts of Europe by Zwingli, Calvin, and others, which also separated from Luther on various doctrines.—**reformer,** ri•for′mėr, *n.* One who effects a reformation or amendment; one who promotes or urges political or social reform.

re-form, ri•form′, *v.t.* [Directly from *re* and *form.*] To form again or anew; to give the same or another disposition or arrangement to (to *re-form* troops that have been scattered).—**re-formation,** rē•for•mā′shon, *n.* The act of forming anew; a second forming in order.

refract, ri•frakt′, *v.t.* [Fr. *refracter,* from L. *refringo, refractum,* to break up—*re,* and *frango, fractum,* to break. FRACTION.] To bend back sharply or abruptly; especially, *optics,* to deflect (a ray of light) at a certain angle on passing from one medium into another of a different density.—**refracting,** ri•frak′ting, *p.* and *a.* Serving or tending to refract; turning from a direct course.—*Refracting telescope,* a telescope in which the rays are refracted by an object glass, at the focus of which they are viewed by an eyepiece.—**refraction,** ri•frak′shon, *n.* The act of refracting or state of being refracted; a deflection or change of direction impressed upon rays of light or heat passing from one transparent medium into another of different density, as from air into water or vice versa—or upon rays traversing a medium the density of which is not uniform, as the atmosphere.—*Astronomical* or *atmospheric refraction,* the apparent angular elevation of the heavenly bodies above their true places, caused by the refraction of the rays of light in their passing through the earth's atmosphere.—*Double refraction,* the separation of a ray of light into two separate parts by passing through certain transparent mediums, as Iceland spar, causing objects to appear double.—**refractive,** ri•frak′tiv, *a.* Pertaining to refraction; serving or having power to refract.—**refractiveness,** ri•frak′tiv•nes, *n.*—**refractometer,** ri•frak•tom′et•ėr, *n.* An instrument for exhibiting and measuring the refraction of light.—**refractor,** ri•frak′tėr, *n.* A refracting telescope.

refractory, ri•frak′to•ri, *a.* [Fr. *réfractaire;* from L. *refractarius,* stubborn, from *refringo, refractum.* REFRACT.] Sullen or perverse in opposition or disobedience; obstinate in noncompliance; stubborn and unmanageable (a *refractory* child); resisting ordinary treatment, as metals that are difficult of fusion.—*n.* A refractory person.—**refractorily,** ri•frak′to•ri•li, *adv.* In a refractory manner; perversely; obstinately.—**refractoriness,** ri•frak′to•ri•nes, *n.* The quality of being refractory.

refragable, ref′ra•ga•bl, *a.* [L.L. *refragabilis,* from L. *refragor,* to oppose, to resist—*re,* back, and root of *frango,* to break. REFRACT.] Capable of being opposed or resisted; refutable.

refrain, ri•frān′, *n.* [Fr. *refrain,* from O.Fr. *refraindre,* L. *refringo*—*re,* again, and *frango,* to break. (REFRACT.) The *refrain,* therefore, is literally the break or interruption to the course of the piece.] The burden of a song; part of a poetic composition repeated at the end of every stanza; a kind of musical repetition.

refrain, ri•frān′, *v.t.* [Fr. *refréner,* to bridle in, to repress, from L. *refraeno*—*re,* back, and *fraenum,* a bit.] To hold back; to restrain; to curb; to keep from action: often *refl.*—*v.i.* To forbear; to abstain; to keep one's self from action or interference: followed by *from.*—**refrainer,** rē•frā′nėr, *n.* One who refrains.

refrangible, ri•fran′ji•bl, *a.* [L. *re,* and *frango,* to break. REFRACT.] Capable of being refracted; subject to refraction, as rays of light.—**refrangibility, refrangibleness,** ri•fran′ji•bil″i•ti, ri•fran′ji•bl•nes, *n.* The state or quality of being refrangible; susceptibility of refraction.

refresh, ri•fresh′, *v.t.* [O.Fr. *refreschir, refraischir* (Fr. *rafraîchir*), to refresh. FRESH.] To make fresh or vigorous again; to restore vigor or energy to; to give new strength to; to reinvigorate; to recreate or revive after fatigue, want, pain, or the like; to reanimate; to freshen.—**refresher,** ri•fresh′ėr, *n.* One who or that which refreshes; among lawyers, an additional fee paid to counsel when the case is adjourned from one term or sittings to another.—**refreshing,** ri•fresh′ing, *p.* and *a.* Acting or operating so as to refresh; invigorating; reviving; reanimating.—*n.* Refreshment.—**refreshingly,** ri•fresh′ing•li, *adv.* In a refreshing manner; so as to refresh.—**refreshment,** ri•fresh′ment, *n.* The act of refreshing; that which refreshes; that which gives fresh strength or vigor, as food, drink, or rest: in the plural almost exclusively applied to food and drink.

refrigerate, ri•frij′ėr•āt, *v.t.*—*refrigerated, refrigerating.* [L. *refrigero, refrigeratum,* to refrigerate—*re,* again, and *frigus, frigoris,* cold. FRIGID.] To cool; to allay heat; to keep cool; to chill or freeze foods, etc., in order to preserve them.—**refrigerant, refrigerative,** ri•frij′ėr•ant, ri•frij′ėr•a•tiv, *a.* Cooling; allaying heat.—*n.* A cooling agency; ice, or gases used in mechanical refrigerators; a medicine which abates fever (*med.*).—**refrigeration,** ri•frij′ėr•ā″shon, *n.* The abating of heat; the act or system of cooling or freezing foods, etc. in order to preserve them.—**refrigerator,** ri•frij′ėr•a•tėr, *n.* That which refrigerates, cools, or keeps cool; a box or room in which materials (usually foods) are kept cool, either by the action of ice or by evaporation of various liquid gases, as sulfur dioxide or ammonia; an apparatus that cools hot liquids or vapors rapidly.—**refrigeratory** ri•frij′ėr•a•to•ri, *a.* Cooling; mitigating heat.

refringent, ri•frin′jent, *a.* [L. *refringo*—*re,* back, and *frango,* to break. REFRACT.] Possessing the quality of refracting; refractive.

reft, reft, pret. & pp. of *reave.* Bereft.

refuge, ref′ūj, *n.* [Fr., from L. *refugium,* from *refugio*—*re,* again, and *fugio,* to flee (whence *fugitive*).] Shelter or protection from danger or distress; that which shelters or protects from danger, distress, or calamity; any place where one is out of the way of any evil or danger; an institution where the destitute or homeless find temporary shelter; a house of refuge; an expedient to secure protection or defense; a device, contrivance, shift.—*Cities of refuge,* among the Israelites, certain cities appointed to secure the safety of such persons as might unintentionally commit homicide.—*Harbors of refuge,* harbors which afford shelter to vessels in stress of weather.—*House of refuge,* an institution for the shelter of the homeless or destitute.—*v.t.*† To shelter; to protect.—*v.i.*† To take shelter.—**refugee,** ref•ū•jē′, *n.* [Fr. *réfugié.*] One who flees for refuge; one who in times of persecution or political commotion flees to a foreign country for safety.

refulgent, ri•ful′jent, *a.* [L. *refulgens, refulgentis,* ppr. of *refulgeo*—*re,* again, and *fulgeo,* to shine. FULGENT.] Casting a bright light; shining; splendid.—**refulgently,** ri•ful′jent•li, *adv.* In a refulgent manner.—**refulgence, refulgency,** ri•ful′jens, ri•ful′jen•si, *n.* The state or quality of being refulgent; splendor; brilliancy.

refund, ri•fund′, *v.t.* [L. *refundo,* to pour back, to restore—*re,* back, and *fundo,* to pour. FUSE.] To return in payment or compensation for what has been taken; to pay back; to restore; to reimburse.—**refunder,** ri•fun′dėr, *n.* One who refunds.

refurbish, rē•fėr′bish, *v.t.* To furbish a second time or anew.

refuse, ri•fūz′, *v.t.*—*refused, refusing.* [Fr. *réfuser,* to refuse; Pr. *refusar,* Sp. *rehusar;* supposed to owe its origin partly to L. *recusare,* to refuse; partly to *refutare,* to refute.] To deny, as a request, demand, invitation, or command; to decline to do or grant; often with an infinitive as object (he *refused* to give me the book); to decline to accept; to reject (to *refuse* an office); to deny the request of; to say no to (I could not *refuse* him).—*v.i.* To decline a request; not to comply.—*a.* (ref′ūs). Rejected; worthless; left as of no value.—*n.* That which is rejected as useless; waste matter.—**refusal,** ri•fū′zal, *n.* The act of refusing; denial of anything demanded, solicited, or offered for acceptance; option of taking or buying; preemption.—**refuser,** ri•fū′zėr, *n.* One who refuses.

refute, ri•fūt′, *v.t.*—*refuted, refuting.* [Fr. *réfuter,* L. *refutare*—*re,* back, and old *futo,* to pour, from root of *fundo,* to pour. CONFUTE, FUTILE, FUSE.] To disprove and overthrow by argument, evidence, or countervailing proof; to prove to be false or erroneous; to confute; to prove to be in error.—**refuter,** ri•fū′tėr, *n.* One who refutes.—**refutable,** ri•fū′ta•bl or ref′ū•ta•bl, *a.* Capable of being refuted.—**refutation,** ref•ū•tā′shon, *n.* The act of refuting or proving to be false or erroneous; overthrow by argument or countervailing proof.

regain, rē•gān′, *v.t.* To gain anew; to recover what has been lost; to reach again (they *regained* the shore).

regal, rē′gal, *a.* [L. *regalis,* from *rex, regis,* a king, from stem of *rego,* to rule, the same root being also seen in E. *right. Royal* is the same word; and *reign, regent,* etc., have the same origin, as also *-rect* in *correct, direct,* etc.] Pertaining to a king; kingly; royal. ∴ Syn. under ROYAL.—**regalia,** ri•gā′li•a, *n. pl.* [L. *regalia,* royal or regal things, nom. pl. neut. of *regalis,* regal.] The ensigns or symbols of royalty; the apparatus of a coronation, as the crown, scepter, etc.; the insignia or decorations of some society; showy clothes. —**regality,** ri•gal′i•ti, *n.* Royalty; sovereignty; kingship; sovereign right.—**regally,** rē′gal•li, *adv.* In a regal or royal manner; royally.

regale, ri•gāl′, *v.t.*—*regaled, regaling.* [Fr. *régaler,* to regale—*re,* and an old verb *galer,* to rejoice, probably from root of Goth. *gailjan,* to rejoice. GALA.] To entertain sumptuously or with something that gives great pleasure; to gratify, as the senses; to delight; to feast.—*v.i.* To feast; to fare sumptuously.—*n.* A splendid repast; a treat.—**regalement,** ri•gāl′ment, *n.* Entertainment; gratification.

regalia. See REGAL.

regard, ri•gärd′, *v.t.* [Fr. *regarder,* to regard, to observe—*re,* back, and *garder,* to guard. GUARD.] To look upon; to observe; to notice with some care; to pay attention to; to observe a certain respect toward; to respect, reverence, honor, esteem; to mind; to care for; to have or to show certain feelings toward; to view in the light of; to put on the same footing as.—*As regards* (impers.), with regard to; as respects; as concerns (as *regards* that matter I am of your opinion).—*n.* Look or gaze; aspect directed to another (*Shak.*); attention or care; heed; consideration; that feeling which springs from estimable qualities in the object; respect, esteem, reverence; relation; respect; reference; view: often in the phrases, *in regard to, with regard to*; *pl.* respects; good wishes; compliments (give my *regards* to the family).—**regardant,** ri•gär′dant, *a.* Regarding; watching; *her.* applied to an animal whose face is turned backward in an attitude of vigilance.—**regardful,** ri•gärd′fu̧l, *a.* Having or paying regard.—**regardfully,** ri•gärd′fu̧l•li, *adv.* In a regardful manner.—**regarding,** ri•gär′ding, *prep.* [Like *concerning, during,* a participle, now established as a preposition.] Respecting; concerning; in reference to (to be at a loss *regarding* something).—**regardless,** ri•gärd′les, *a.* Not having regard or heed; heedless; careless.—**regardlessly,** ri•gärd′les•li, *adv.* In a regardless manner; heedlessly; carelessly.—**regardlessness,** ri•gärd′les•nes, *n.* Heedlessness; negligence.

regatta, ri•gat′a, *n.* [It.] Originally a gondola race in Venice; now any sailing or rowing race in which a number of yachts or boats contend for prizes.

regelation, rē•je•lā′shon, *n.* [L. *re,* again, and *gelatio, gelationis,* a freezing. CONGEAL.] The phenomenon presented by pieces of moist ice which when placed in contact with one another freeze together even in a warm atmosphere.

regency. See REGENT.

regenerate, ri•jen′ėr•āt, *v.t.*—*regenerated, regenerating.* [L. *regenero, regeneratum*—*re,* again, and *genero,* to generate. GENERATE.] To generate or produce anew; to reproduce; *theol.* to cause to be born again; to change, as the heart and affections, from enmity or indifference to love of God. —*a.* Reproduced; *theol.* changed from a natural to a spiritual state.—**regeneracy,** ri•jen′ėr•a•si, *n.* The state of being regenerated.—**regeneration,** ri•jen′ėr•ā″shon, *n.* The act of regenerating or producing anew; *theol.* that change by which love of God and his law is implanted in the heart.—**regenerative,** ri•jen′ėr•ā•tiv, *a.* Producing regeneration; renewing. —**regeneratively,** ri•jen′ėr•ā•tiv•li, *adv.*

regent, rē′jent, *a.* [L. *regens, regentis,* ppr. of *rego,* to rule; cog. Skr. *râj,* to rule; from same root also E. *right.* REGAL.] Ruling; governing; exercising vicarious authority.—*n.* A governor; a ruler; one who governs a kingdom in the minority, absence, or disability of the sovereign; one of a certain standing who taught in universities: the word formerly in use for a *professor*; in the English universities, one who has certain peculiar duties of instruction or government. —**regentship,** rē′jent•ship, *n.* The office or dignity of a regent; regency. —**regency,** rē′jen•si, *n.* Rule; government; the office or jurisdiction of a regent; a body of men entrusted with the power of a regent.

regicide, rej′i•sīd, *n.* [Fr. *régicide,* from L. *rex, regis,* a king, and *caedo,* to slay.] A king-killer; one who murders a king; the killing or murder of a king.—**regicidal,** rej•i•sī′dal, *a.* Pertaining to regicide.

regime, re•zhēm′, *n.* [Fr. *régime,* from L. *regimen,* guidance, from *rego,* to govern.] Mode or system of management; government, especially as connected with certain social features; administration; rule.—*The ancient regime,* the political system which prevailed in France before the revolution of 1789.—**regimen,** rej′i•men, *n.* Orderly government; the regulation of diet, exercise, etc.; *gram.* government of words.

regiment, rej′i•ment, *n.* [Fr. *régiment,* from L.L. *regimentum,* from L. *regimen,* rule, from *rego,* to rule. REGIME, REGENT.] An organization of troops under the command of a colonel, consisting of several battalions, squadrons, or batteries in those branches of the army designated respectively as the infantry, cavalry, or artillery.—*v.t.* To form troops into regiments; to assign soldiers to a regiment; to organize civilians into groups to control their actions and indoctrinate their minds. —**regimentation,** rej•i•men•tā′shon, *n.* Strict control or uniformity imposed by external authority; the act of forming into groups.

region, rē′jun, *n.* [Fr. *région,* from L. *regio, regionis,* from *rego,* to rule. REGAL.] A large division of any space or surface considered as apart from others; especially, a tract of land, sea, etc., of considerable but indefinite extent; a country; a district; a part or division of the body (the *region* of the heart).—**regional,** rē′jun•al, *a.* Pertaining to a particular region; sectional.

register, rej′is•tėr, *n.* [Fr. *registre,* L.L. *registrum, regestrum,* a book of records—*re,* back, and *gero, gestum,* to carry. GESTATION.] An official written account or entry in a book regularly kept for preservation or for reference; a record; a list; the book in which records are kept; a document issued by the customs authorities as evidence of a ship's nationality; a contrivance for regulating the passage of heat or air in heating or ventilation; a device for automatically indicating the number of revolutions made or amount of work done by machinery, recording pressure, etc.; *printing,* the agreement of two printed forms to be applied to the same sheet, either on the same side, as in color printing, or on both sides as in a book or newspaper; *music,* the compass of a voice or instrument, or a portion of the compass; a stop or set of pipes in an organ.—*Lloyd's register.* See LLOYD'S.—*Lord register,* or *lord clerk register,* a Scottish officer of state who has the custody of the archives.—*v.t.* To record; to enter in a register.—*v.i. Printing,* to correspond exactly, as columns or lines of printed matter on opposite sheets.—**registered,** rej′is•tėrd, *p.* and *a.* Recorded in a register; enrolled.—*Registered company,* a joint-stock company entered in an official register, but not incorporated.—*Registered letter,* a letter the address of which is registered at a post office, for which a special fee is paid in order to secure its safe transmission. —**registrar,** rej′is•trär, *n.* [L.L. *registrarius.*] One whose business it is to write or keep a register; a keeper of records.—**registration,** rej•is•trā′shon, *n.* The act of inserting in a register.—**registry,** rej′is•tri, *n.* The act of entering in a register; the place where a register is kept; facts recorded; an entry.

reglet, reg′let, *n.* [Fr. *réglet,* from *règle,* rule, L. *regula.* REGULATE.] *Printing,* a strip of wood or metal used for separating pages in the chase, etc.; *arch.* a flat narrow molding between panels, etc.

regnal, reg´nal, *a.* [From L. *regnum*, a kingdom. REIGN.] Pertaining to the reign of a monarch.—*Regnal year*, the year of a sovereign's reign (as given in an act of the British Parliament).

regnant, reg´nant, *a.* [L. *regnans, regnantis*, ppr. of *regno*, to reign, from *regnum*, a kingdom.] Reigning as sovereign; predominant; prevalent.

regorge, rē•gorj´, *v.t.* [Prefix *re*, and *gorge*.] To vomit up; to disgorge.

regrant, rē•grant´, *v.t.* To grant back. —*n.* The act of granting back; a new or fresh grant.

regreet, rē•grēt´, *v.i.* To greet or salute again.

regress, rē´gres, *n.* [L. *regressus*, from *regredior*, to go back—*re*, back, and *gradior*, to go. GRADE.] Passage back; return; power or liberty of returning or passing back.—*v.i.* (ri•gres´). To go back; to return to a former place or state.—**regression,** ri•gresh´on, *n.* [L. *regressio*.] The act of passing back or returning; retrogression.—**filial regression.** [L. L. *filialis*, relating to offspring.] In heredity, a tendency to return to the average.—**regressive,** ri•gres´iv, *a.* Passing back; returning.

regret, ri•gret´, *n.* [Fr. *regret*, regret, *regretter*, O.Fr. *regreter*, to regret; from *re*, again, and the Teutonic verb seen in Icel. *gráta*, A.Sax. *graetan*, Sc. *greet*, to weep.] Grief or trouble caused by the want or loss of something formerly possessed; sorrowful longing; pain of mind at something done or left undone; remorse.—*v.t.—regretted, regretting*. To lament the loss of, or separation from; to look back at with sorrowful longing; to grieve at; to be sorry for. —**regretful,** ri•gret´fu̦l, *a.* Full of regret.—**regretfully,** ri•gret´fu̦l•li, *adv.* With regret.—**regrettable,** ri•gret´a•bl, *a.* Admitting of or calling for regret.

regular, reg´ū•lėr, *a.* [L. *regularis*, from *regula*, a rule, from *rego*, to rule. REGENT, REGAL.] Conformed to a rule; agreeable to a prescribed mode or customary form; normal; acting or going on by rule or rules; steady or uniform; orderly; methodical; unvarying; *geom.* applied to a figure or body whose sides and angles are equal, as a square, a cube, an equilateral triangle, an equilateral pentagon, etc.; *gram.* adhering to the common form in respect to inflectional terminations; *eccles.* belonging to a monastic order, and bound to certain rules; *bot.* symmetrical as regards figure and size and proportion of parts; colloquially, thorough, out-and-out, complete.—*Regular troops* or *regulars*; troops of a permanent army: opposed to *militia* or *volunteers*.—*Regular verb*, in English, one that forms the preterite and past participle in *d* or *ed*.—*n.* A monk who has taken the vows of some monastic order; a soldier belonging to a permanent army.—**regularity,** reg•ū•lar´i•ti, *n.* The state or quality of being regular; agreeableness to rule or established order; conformity to the customary type; steadiness or uniformity in a course. —**regularly,** reg´ū•lėr•li, *adv.* In a regular manner; in uniform order; at fixed intervals or periods; methodically; in due order.—**regulate,** reg´ū•lāt, *v.t.—regulated, regulating*. [L. *regulo, regulatum*, from *regula*, a rule.] To adjust by rule or established mode; to govern by or subject to certain rules or restrictions; to direct; to put or keep in good order; to control and cause to act properly.—**regulation,** reg•ū•lā´shon, *n.* The act of regulating; a rule prescribed by a superior as to the actions of those under his control; a governing direction; a precept.—**regulative,** reg•ū•lā´tiv, *a.* Regulating; tending to regulate.—**regulator,** reg´ū•lā•tėr, *n.* One who or that which regulates; a device or contrivance of which the object is to produce uniformity of motion or action; the governor of a steam engine.

regulus, reg´ū•lus, *n.* [L., a petty king or sovereign, a dim. of *rex, regis*, a king. REGAL.] A name originally applied by the alchemists to antimony, from the facility with which it alloyed with gold (the *king* of metals), now applied to metals which still retain to a greater or less extent the impurities they contained in the state of ore; [*cap.*] a star of the first magnitude in the constellation Leo.

regurgitate, rē•gėr´ji•tāt, *v.t.—regurgitated, regurgitating*. [L.L. *regurgito, regurgitatum*—L. *re, back*, and *gurges, gurgitis*, a whirlpool. GORGE] To pour or cause to rush or surge back; to pour or throw back in great quantity —*v.i.* To be poured back; to rush or surge back.—**regurgitation,** rē•gėr´ji•tā″shon, *n.* The act of regurgitating; *med.* the rising of some of the contents of the stomach into the mouth.

rehabilitate, rē•ha•bil´i•tāt, *v.t.—rehabilitated, rehabilitating*. [Fr. *réhabiliter*—*re*, and *habiliter*, to qualify, from *habile*, qualified, able. ABLE.] To restore to a former capacity or position; to reinstate; to re-establish in the esteem of others.—**rehabilitation,** rē•ha•bil´i•tā″shon, *n.* The act of rehabilitating.

rehash, rē•hash´, *v.t.* To hash anew; to work up old material in a new form.—*n.* Something made up of materials formerly used.

rehearse, ri•hėrs´, *v.t.—rehearsed, rehearsing*. [O.E. *reherce, reherse*, from O.Fr. *rehercer, reherser*, to repeat over again—*re*, again, and *hercer, herser*, to harrow, from *herce, herse*, a harrow. HEARSE.] To repeat, as what has already been said or written; to recite; to narrate, recount, relate; to recite or repeat in private for experiment and improvement, before giving a public representation (to *rehearse* a tragedy).—*v.i.* To go through some performance in private preparatory to public representation.—**rehearsal,** ri•hėr´sal, *n.* The act of rehearsing; narration; a telling or recounting; a trial performance (as of a play) made before exhibiting to the public.—**rehearser,** ri•hėr´sėr, *n.* One who rehearses.

Reichsbank, rīchs´bänk, *n.* [G.] The state bank of Germany.

reichsmark, rīchs´märk, *n.* [G.] The German monetary unit.

reign, rān, *v.i.* [O.Fr. *reigner*, Fr. *régner*, from L. *regnare*, to rule, from *regnum*, a kingdom, from *rego*, to rule. REGAL.] To possess or exercise sovereign power or authority; to hold the supreme power; to rule; to be predominant; to prevail; to have superior or uncontrolled dominion.—*n.* [O.Fr. *reigne*, Fr. *règne*, L. *regnum*, a kingdom.] Royal authority; sovereignty; the time during which a king, queen, or emperor reigns; empire; kingdom; power; sway.

reimburse, rē•im•bėrs´, *v.t.—reimbursed, reimbursing*. [Fr. *rembourser*—*re*, again, *en*, in, and *bourse*, a purse. PURSE.] To replace in a treasury; to pay back; to refund; to pay back to; to render an equivalent to for money or other expenditure.—**reimbursement,** rē•im•bėrs´ment, *n.* The act of reimbursing; repayment.

reimport, rē•im•pōrt´, *v.t.* To import again; to carry back to the country of exportation.—*n.* (rē•im´pōrt). Something reimported.—**reimportation,** rē•im´por•tā″shon, *n.* The act of reimporting; that which is reimported.

reimpose, rē•im•pōz´, *v.t.* To impose or levy anew.—**reimposition,** rē•im´pō•zish″on, *n.* Act of reimposing.

reimpression, rē•im•presh´on, *n.* A second impression; a reprint.

rein, rān, *n.* [Fr. *rêne*, O.Fr. *resne*, It. *redina*; from L. *retineo*, to retain. RETAIN.] The strap of a bridle, by which the rider or driver restrains and governs the horse, etc.; any thong or cord for the same purpose; *fig.* a means of curbing, restraining, or governing; restraint.—*To give the rein*, or *the reins*, to give license, to leave without restraint.—*To take the reins*, to take the guidance or government.—*v.t.* To govern, guide, or restrain by a bridle; to restrain.

reincarnation, rē•in•kär•na´shon, *n.* Belief that the soul returns after death to live in a new body.

reindeer, rān´dēr, *n.* [Icel. *hrein-dýri*, Sw. *rendjur*, Dan. *rensdyr*, a reindeer; said to be of Finnish or Lappish origin.] A deer of northern Europe and Asia, with broad branched antlers; used as a domestic animal among the Laplanders, to whom it furnishes food, clothing, and the means of conveyance.—**reindeer moss,** *n.* A lichen which constitutes almost the sole winter food for reindeer.

reinforce, rē•in•fōrs´, *v.t.* To strengthen; to strengthen with more troops, ships, etc.—*n.* An additional thickness given to any portion of an object in order to strengthen it; the part of a cannon nearest the breech. —*Reinforced concrete*, concrete in which steel bars are embedded, so as to increase the resistance of the structure to tension. — **reinforcement,** rē•in•fōrs´ment, *n.* The act of reinforcing; additional troops or forces to augment an army or fleet.

reinsert, rē•in•sėrt´, *v.t.* To insert a

second time.—**reinsertion,** rē•in•sėr′shon, *n.* The act of reinsertion, or what is reinserted.

reinstall, rē•in•stąl′, *v.t.* To install again.—**reinstallment,** rē•in•stąl′-ment, *n.* The act of reinstalling.

reinstate, rē•in•stāt′, *v.t.* To instate again; to place again in possession or in a former state.—**reinstatement,** rē•in•stāt′ment, *n.* The act of reinstating; reestablishment.

reinsurance, rē•in•shö′rans, *n.* A renewed or second insurance; a contract by which the first insurer relieves himself from the risks he has undertaken, and devolves them upon other insurers, called *reinsurers.* **reinsure,** rē•in•shör′, *v.t.* To insure again.—**reinsurer,** rē•in•shö′rėr, *n.* One who reinsures.

reinter, rē•in•tėr′, *v.t.* To inter again.

reintroduce, rē•in′tro•dūs″, *v.t.* To introduce again.—**reintroduction,** rē•in′tro•duk″shon, *n.* A second introduction.

reinvest, rē•in•vest′, *v.t.* To invest anew.

reinvigorate, rē•in•vig′o•rāt, *v.t.* To revive vigor in; to reanimate.

reis, rīs, *n.* [Ar.] A head; a chief; a captain.—*Reis effendi,* one of the chief Turkish officers of state.

reissue, rē•ish′ū, *v.i.* To issue or go forth again.—*v.t.* To issue, send out, or put forth a second time (to *reissue* bank-notes).—*n.* A second or renewed issue.

reiterate, rē•it′ėr•āt, *v.t.*—*reiterated, reiterating.* [L. *re,* again, and *itero, iteratum,* to repeat, from *iterum,* again. ITERATE.] To repeat again and again; to do or say (especially to say) repeatedly.—*a.* Reiterated.—**reiteration,** rē•it′ėr•ā″shon, *n.* The act of reiterating; repetition.—**reiterative,** rē•it′ėr•ā•tiv, *n.* A word or part of a word repeated so as to form a reduplicated word; *gram.* a word signifying repeated or intense action.

reject, ri•jekt′, *v.t.* [L. *rejicio, rejectum,* to reject—*re,* again, and *jacio,* to throw (whence also *eject, inject, project,* etc.) JET.] To throw away as useless or vile, to cast off; to discard; to refuse to receive; to decline haughtily or harshly; to refuse to grant.—*n.* rē′jekt, one who or that which is rejected.—**rejecter,** ri•jek′tėr, *n.* One who rejects or refuses.—**rejection,** ri•jek′shon, *n.* The act of rejecting; refusal to accept or grant.

rejoice, ri•jois′, *v.i.*—*rejoiced, rejoicing.* [O.E. *rejoisse, rejoyse,* from O.Fr. *rejoir, rejoissant,* Fr. *réjouir, réjouissant;* prefix *re,* and *éjouir,* older *esjoir*—L. *ex,* intens., and *gaudeo,* to rejoice. JOY.] To experience joy and gladness in a high degree; to be joyful; to exult; often with *at, in, on account of,* etc., or a subordinate clause.—*v.t.* To make joyful; to gladden.—**rejoicer,** ri•jois′ėr, *n.* One that rejoices; one that causes to rejoice.—**rejoicing,** ri•jois′ing, *n.* The act of expressing joy; procedure expressive of joy; festivity.

rejoin, rē•join′, *v.t.* To join again; to unite after separation; to join the company of again; to answer; to say in answer; to reply: with a clause as object.—*v.i.* To answer to a reply.—**rejoinder,** ri•join′dėr, *n.* [An infinitive form; Fr. *rejoindre,* to rejoin. *Attainder, remainder* are similar forms.] An answer to a reply; *law,* the fourth stage in the pleadings in an action, being the defendant's answer to the plaintiff's replication.

rejudge, rē•juj′, *v.t.* To judge again.

rejuvenate, rē•jū′ven•āt, *v.t.*—*rejuvenated, rejuvenating.* [L. *re,* again, and *juvenis,* young. JUVENILE.] To restore to youth; to make young again.—**rejuvenation,** rē•jū′ven•ā″-shon, *n.* The act of rejuvenating.

rejuvenescence, rē•jū′ven•es″ens, *n.* [L. *re,* and *juvenesco,* to grow young.] A renewing of youth; the state of being young again.—**rejuvenescent,** rē•jū′ven•es″ent, *a.* Becoming or become young again.—**rejuvenize,** rē•jū′ve•nīz, *v.t.* To render young again.

rekindle, rē•kin′dl, *v.t.* To kindle again, to inflame again; to rouse anew.

relapse, ri•laps′, *v.i.*—*relapsed, relapsing.* [L. *relabor, relapsus,* to slide back—*re,* back, and *labor, lapsus,* to slide. LAPSE.] To slip or slide back; to return to a former bad state or practice; to backslide; to fall back or return from recovery or a convalescent state.—*n.* A falling back into a former bad state, either of health or of morals.

relate, ri•lāt′, *v.t.*—*related, relating.* [Fr. *relater,* to state, to mention; L. *refero, relatum,* to refer, to bring back—*re,* back, and *latus,* brought (as in *elate, oblate, translate*).] To tell; to recite; to recount; to narrate the particulars of; to ally by connection or kindred.—*v.i.* To have reference or respect; to regard; to stand in some relation: with *to* following.—**related,** ri•lā′ted, *p.* and *a.* Allied; connected by blood or alliance, particularly by blood, standing in some relation or connection.—**relater,** ri•lā′tėr, *n.* One who relates.—**relation,** ri•lā′shon, *n.* [L. *relatio, relationis.*] The act of relating; that which is related or told; narrative; reference, respect, or regard; often in the phrase *in relation to;* connection perceived or imagined between things; a certain position of one thing with regard to another; the condition of being such or such in respect to something else; due conformity or harmony of parts; kinship; a kinsman or kinswoman; *math.* ratio; proportion; *logic,* one of the ten predicaments.—**relational,** ri•lā′shon•al, *a.* Indicating or specifying some relation: used in contradistinction to *notional* (a *relational* part of speech, as the pronoun, preposition, and conjunction).—**relationship,** ri•lā′shon•ship, *n.* The state of being related by kindred, affinity, or other alliance; kinship.—**relative,** rel′a•tiv, *a.* [L. *relativus.*] Having relation to or bearing on something; close in connection; pertinent; relevant; not absolute or existing by itself; depending on or incident to something else; *gram.* applied to a word which relates to another word, sentence, or part of a sentence called the antecedent, applied especially to certain pronouns, as *who, which,* and *that.*—*Relative motion,* the change of the place of a moving body with respect to some other body also in motion.—*Relative terms,* terms which imply some relation, as *guardian* and *ward, master* and *servant,* etc.—*n.* Something considered in its relation to something else; a person connected by blood or affinity, especially one allied by blood; a kinsman or kinswoman; *gram.* a word which relates to or represents another word, called its antecedent, or refers back to a statement; a relative pronoun.—**relatively,** rel′a•tiv•li, *adv.* In a relative manner; in relation to something else; not absolutely; comparatively; often followed by *to* (an expenditure large *relatively to.*—**relativism,** rel′a•tiv•izm, *n.* A theory that knowledge is relative to the limited nature of the mind.—**relativity,** rel•a•tiv′i•ti, *n.* The state of being relative; *phys.* a theory formulated by Albert Einstein that deals with the laws of mechanics and the velocity of light in a vacuum and considers mass and energy to be equivalent.—**relator,** ri•la′ter, *n. law,* an individual who furnishes information of an accusatory nature, or in whose behalf, or at whose instance, an information is filed, or a writ issued, as in the case of a quo warranto.

relax, ri•laks′, *v.t.* [L. *relaxo,* to relax—*re,* back, and *laxo,* to loosen, from *laxus,* loose. LAX.] To slacken; to make less tense or rigid; to make less severe or rigorous; to remit in strictness; to remit or abate in respect to attention, effort, or labor.—*v.i.* To become loose, feeble, or languid; to abate in severity; to become more mild or less rigorous; to remit in close attention; to unbend; to rest or seek recreation.—**relaxation,** ri•lak•sā′shon, *n.* [L. *relaxatio.*] The act of relaxing or state of being relaxed; a diminution of tension or firmness, remission of attention or application; recreation; an occupation giving mental or bodily relief after effort.

relay, rē•lā′, rē′lā, *n.* [Fr. *relais,* a relay of horses; originally, relief or release, from L. *re,* and *laxus,* loose.] A supply of anything stored up for affording relief from time to time, or at successive stages; a supply of horses placed on the road to be in readiness to relieve others; a squad of men to take a spell or turn of work at stated intervals; a telegraphic apparatus which, on receiving a feeble electric current, sends on a much stronger current.—*v.t.* To carry or pass on by stages.—**relay race,** a race between teams, in which each member of a team covers part of the total distance.

release, ri•lēs′, *v.t.*—*released, releasing.* [From O.Fr. *relesser, relaisser,* to release, to relinquish—prefix *re,* and *laisser*, to leave, from L. *laxare*, to loosen, from *laxus*, loose, lax. *Release*, *relax* are thus doublets. LAX.] To let loose again; to set free from restraint or confinement; to liberate; to free from pain, grief, or any other evil; to free from obligation or penalty; *law*, to give up or let go, as a claim.—*n.* Liberation from restraint of any kind, as from confinement or bondage; liberation from care, pain, or burden; discharge from obligation or responsibility.—**releaser,** ri•lēs′ėr, *n.* One who releases.

re-lease, rē•lēs′, *v.t.* [Prefix *re*, and *lease*.] To lease again or anew.

relegate, rel′e•gāt, *v.t.*—*relegated*, *relegating*. [L. *relego*, *relegatum*, to banish—*re*, back, and *lego*, to send. LEGATE.] To send away or out of the way; to consign to some obscure or remote destination; to banish.—**relegation,** rel•e•gā′shon, *n.* [L. *relegatio*.] The act of relegating; banishment; in ancient Roman law, banishment to a certain place for a certain time.

relent, ri•lent′, *v.i.* [Fr. *ralentir*, to slacken, to abate—prefix *re*, back, *a*, to, and *lent*, L. *lentus*, pliant, slow. LENIENT.] To become less harsh, cruel, or obdurate; to soften in temper; to become more mild; to yield, to comply.—**relentless,** ri•lent′les, *a.* Incapable of relenting; insensible to the distresses of others; merciless; implacable; pitiless.—**relentlessly,** ri•lent′les•li, *adv.* In a relentless manner; without pity.—**relentlessness,** ri•lent′les•nes, *n.* The quality of being relentless.

relevant, rel′e•vant, *a.* [Fr. *relevant*, ppr. of *relever*, to relieve, to help or aid. RELIEVE.] Lending aid or support‡; to the purpose; pertinent; applicable; bearing on the matter in hand (arguments not *relevant* to the case).—**relevantly,** rel′e•vant•li, *adv.* In a relevant manner.—**relevance, relevancy,** rel′e•vans, rel′e•van•si, *n.* The quality of being relevant; pertinence.

reliable, reliance, reliant, etc. See RELY.

relic, rel′ik, *n.* [Fr. *relique*, from L. *reliquiae*, remains—*re*, back, and *linquo*, to leave (as in *delinquent*, *relinquish*; same root as *license*, Gr. *leipō*, to leave.] That which is left after the loss or decay of the rest; a remaining fragment; the body of a deceased person; usually in *pl.*; something preserved in remembrance; a memento, souvenir, or keepsake; a bone or other part of saints or martyrs, or some part of their garments, etc., preserved, and regarded as of extraordinary sanctity and often as possessing miraculous powers.

relict, rel′ikt, *n.* [O.Fr. *relicte*, a widow, L. *relicta*, fem. of *relictus*, pp. of *relinquo*, to leave. RELIC.] A widow; a woman whose husband is dead.

relief, ri•lēf′, *n.* [Fr. *relief*, relief, a relieving, alleviation, also (like It. *rilievo*) artistic raised work, from *relever*. RELIEVE.] The removal of anything painful or burdensome by which some ease is obtained; ease from pain; alleviation; succor; what mitigates or removes pain, grief, or other evil; help given to the poor in the form of food, money, etc.; release from duty by a substitute or substitutes; *sculp.*, *arch.*, etc., the projection or prominence of a figure above or beyond the ground or plane on which it is formed, being of three kinds; high-relief (*alto-rilievo*), low-relief (*basso-rilievo*), and middle or half relief (*mezzo-rilievo*), according to the degree of projection, hence, a piece of artistic work in one or other of these styles; *painting*, the appearance of projection and solidity in represented objects, hence, prominence or distinctness given to anything by something presenting a contrast to it; *phys. geog.* the undulations or surface elevations of a country; *fort.* the height of a parapet from the bottom of the ditch; *feudal law*, a payment by the heir of a tenant made to his lord for the privilege of taking up the estate.—**relievable,** ri•lē′va•bl, *a.* Capable of being relieved; fitted to receive relief.—**relieve,** ri•lēv′, *v.t.*—*relieved*, *relieving*. [O.E. *releve*, from Fr. *relever*, to set up again, to release, to assist, from L. *relevare*, to lift up again—*re*, again, and *levare*, to raise, from *levis*, light. LEVITY.] To remove or lessen, as anything that pains or distresses; to mitigate; alleviate (pain, misery, wants); to free, wholly or partially, from pain, grief, anxiety, or anything considered to be an evil; to help, aid, or succor (the poor, the sick, etc.); to release from a post or duty by substituting another person or party (to *relieve* a sentinel); to obviate the monotony of by the introduction of some variety; to make conspicuous; to set off by contrast; to give the appearance of projection to.—**reliever,** ri•lē′vėr, *n.* One that relieves.

relievo, ri•lē′vō or rel•ē•ā′vō, *n.* A form of *Rilievo*.

relight, rē•līt′, *v.t.* To light anew; to rekindle.

religion, ri•lij′on, *n.* [Fr. *religion*, L. *religio*, *religionis*, perhaps from prefix *re*, and stem meaning to care for, to respect, allied to Gr. *elegō*, to heed.] The feeling of reverence which men entertain toward a Supreme Being; the recognition of God as an object of worship, love, and obedience; piety; any system of faith and worship (the *religion* of the Greeks, Jews, Hindus, Mohammedans, etc.)—*Established religion*, that form of religion in a country which is recognized and supported by the state.—*Natural religion*, the knowledge of God and of our duty which is derived from the light of nature.—*Revealed religion*, the knowledge of God and of our duty from positive revelation.—**religionism,** ri•lij′on•izm, *n.* The outward practice of religion; affected or false religion.—**religionist,** ri•lij′on•ist, *n.* A religious bigot; one who deals much in religious discourse; a partisan of a religion.—**religious,** ri•lij′us, *a.* [L. *religiosus*.] Pertaining or relating to religion; concerned with religion; set apart for purposes connected with religion; imbued with religion; pious; devout; devoted by vows to the practice of religion or to a monastic life (a *religious* order); bound by some solemn obligation; scrupulously faithful.—*n.* A religieux or religieuse.—**religiously,** ri•lij′us•li, *adv.* In a religious manner; piously; reverently; strictly; conscientiously.—**religiousness,** ri•lij′us•nes, *n.* The quality or state of being religious.

relinquish, ri•ling′kwish, *v.t.* [O.Fr. *relinquir*, *relinquissant*, from L. *relinquo*, to leave. RELIC.] To give up the possession or occupancy of; to withdraw from; to leave; to abandon; to give up the pursuit or practice of; to desist from; to renounce a claim to.—**relinquisher,** ri•ling′kwish•ėr, *n.* One who relinquishes.—**relinquishment,** ri•ling′kwish•ment, *n.* The act of relinquishing; the renouncing a claim to.

reliquary, rel′i•kwe•ri, *n.* [Fr. *reliquaire*, from L. *reliquiae*, relics. RELIC.] A depositary for relics; a casket in which relics are kept; a shrine.—**relique,** re•lēk′ or rel′ik, *n.* A relic.

reliquiae, ri•lik′wi•ė, *n. pl.* [L., remnants, remains. RELIC.] Relics; remains, fossil remains.

relish, rel′ish, *v.t.* [O.Fr. *relecher*, lit. to re-lick—*re*, again, and *léchér*, from O.H.G. *lecchon*, to lick. LICK.] To like the taste or flavor of; to be pleased with or gratified by; to have a liking for; to give an agreeable taste or flavor to; to savor or smack of.—*v.i.* To have a pleasing taste; to have a flavor.—*n.* The sensation produced by anything on the palate; savor; taste, commonly a pleasing taste; inclination; liking (a *relish for* something); delight given by anything; characteristic quality; savor or flavor; smack, a small quantity just perceptible; a pickled, spiced or glazed food served with the meat or fish course.—**relishable,** rel′ish•a•bl, *a.* Capable of being relished.

relive, rē•liv′, *v.i.* To live again; to revive.

reload, rē•lōd′, *v.t.* To load again.

relucent, ri•lū′sent, *a.* [L. *re*, back, and *luceo*, to shine. LUCID.] Throwing back light; luminous; shining; eminent.

reluctant, ri•luk′tant, *a.* [L. *reluctans*, *reluctantis*, ppr. of *reluctor*, to struggle—*re*, back, and *luctor*, to struggle, *lucta*, a struggle.] Striving against doing something; unwilling to do what one feels called on to do; acting with repugnance; averse; loth; granted with unwillingness (*reluctant* obedience).—**reluctantly,** ri•luk′tant•li, *adv.* In a reluctant manner; unwillingly.—**reluctance, reluctancy,** ri•luk′tans, ri•luk′tan•si, *n.* The state or quality of being reluctant; aversion; unwillingness; in magnetism, the resistance offered by a medium to the passage through it of lines of magnetic force; the reciprocal of permeability; also called magnetic resistance. Its unit is the OERSTED (which see).

relume, relumine, ri•lūm′, ri•lū′-min, *v.t.* [L. *re*, again, and *lumen*, light. LUMINARY.] To light anew; to illuminate again.

rely, ri•lī′, *v.t.*—*relied, relying.* [From Fr. *relier*, to bind, to attach—L. *re*, back, and *ligare*, to bind (hence *ligament*): formerly often used with reflexive pronouns (to *rely one's self upon*).] To rest with confidence, as when we are satisfied of the veracity, integrity, or ability of persons, or of the certainty of facts or of evidence; to have confidence; to trust: with *on* or *upon.*—**reliable,** ri•lī′a•bl, *a.* [This word (in use as early as 1569) was considered irregular by some 19th-century writers, but it is now considered perfectly acceptable.] Such as may be relied on; worthy of being relied on; to be depended on for support.—**reliableness, reliability,** ri•lī′a•bl•nes, ri•lī′a•bil″i•ti, *n.* The quality of being reliable.—**reliably,** ri•lī′a•bli, *adv.* In a reliable manner; so as to be relied on.—**reliance,** ri•lī′ans, *n.* The act of relying; dependence; confidence; trust; ground of trust.—**reliant,** ri•lī′ant, *a.* Having reliance; confident; self-reliant.—**relier,** ri•lī′ėr, *n.* One who relies.

remain, ri•mān′, *v.i.* [O.Fr. *remaindre*, to remain, from L. *remaneo* —*re*, back, and *maneo, mansi*, to stay. MANSION.] To continue in a place; to abide; to continue in an unchanged form or condition; to endure; to last; to stay behind after others have gone; to be left; to be left as not included or comprised; to be still to deal with.—*n.* That which is left; remainder; relic: chiefly used in the plural; specifically, *pl.*, that which is left of a human being after life is gone, that is the dead body; *pl.* the productions, especially the literary works, of one who is dead.—**remainder,** ri•mān′-dėr, *n.* [An infinitive form; comp. *rejoinder.*] That which remains; anything left after the removal of the rest; *arith.* etc., the sum or quantity that is left after subtraction or deduction; *law*, an estate limited so as to be enjoyed after the death of the present possessor or otherwise. —*a.* Remaining; left over.

remake, rē•māk′, *v.t.*—*remade, remaking.* To make anew; to make over again.

remand, ri•mand′, *v.t.* [Fr. *remander*, from L. *re*, and *mando*, to commit to one's charge. MANDATE.] To send, call, or order back; *law*, to send back to jail, as an accused party, in order to give time to collect more evidence.—*n.* The state of being remanded; the act of remanding.

remanent, rem′a•nent, *a.* [L. *remanens, remanentis*, ppr. of *remaneo.* REMAIN.] Remaining.

remark, ri•märk′, *n.* [Fr. *remarque*—*re*, and *marquo.* MARK.] The act of observing or taking notice; notice or observation; a brief statement taking notice of something; an observation; a comment.—*v.t.* To observe; to note in the mind; to express, as a thought that has occurred to the speaker; to utter by way of comment or observation.—**remarkable,** ri•-mär′ka•bl, *a.* Observable; worthy of notice; extraordinary; unusual; striking; noteworthy; conspicuous; distinguished.—**remarkableness,** ri•-mär′ka•bl•nes, *n.*—**remarkably,** ri•-mär′ka•bli, *adv.* In a remarkable manner; singularly; surprisingly.

remarry, rē•mar′i, *v.t.* To marry again or a second time.—*v.i.* To be married again or a second time.—**remarriage,** rē•mar′ij, *n.* Any marriage after the first; a repeated marriage.

remedy, rem′e•di, *n.* [L. *remedium*, from *re*, again, and *medeor*, to heal. MEDICAL.] That which cures a disease; any medicine or application which puts an end to disease and restores health (a *remedy for* the gout); that which corrects or counteracts an evil of any kind; relief; redress, legal means for recovery of a right.—*v.t.*—*remedied, remedying.* To cure; to heal; to repair or remove, as some evil; to redress; to counteract.—**remediable,** ri•mē′-di•a•bl, *a.* Capable of being remedied.—**remediably,** ri•mē′di•a•bli, *adv.*—**remedial,** ri•mē′di•al, *a.* [L. *remedialis.*] Affording a remedy; intended to remedy or cure something, or for the removal of an evil (*remedial* measures).—**remediless,** rem′e•di•les, *a.* Not admitting a remedy; incurable; irreparable.

remember, ri•mem′bėr, *v.t.* [O.Fr. *remembrer, se remembrer*, from L.L. *rememorare*—L. *re*, again, and *memorare*, to bring to mind, from *memor*, mindful. MEMOIR.] To have in the mind and capable of being brought back from the past; to bear or keep in mind; to be capable of recalling; not to forget; to put in mind; to remind; to think of; to keep in mind with gratitude, favor, affection, or other emotion.—*v.i.* To have something in remembrance; to recollect. ∴ *Remember* implies that a thing exists in the memory, but not that it is actually present in the thoughts at the moment. *Recollect* means that a fact, forgotten or partially lost to memory, is after some effort recalled. See MEMORY.—**rememberer,** ri•mem′bėr•ėr, *n.* One that remembers.—**remembrance,** ri•mem′brans, *n.* [O.Fr. *remembrance.*] The keeping of a thing in mind; power or faculty of remembering; limit of time over which the memory extends; what is remembered; a memorial; a keepsake; state of being mindful; regard. ∴ Syn. under MEMORY.—**remembrancer,** ri•-mem′bran•sėr, *n.* One who reminds; [*usually cap.*] an officer in the exchequer of England whose business is to record certain papers and proceedings, make out processes, etc.; a recorder; the name of an officer who collects debts due the sovereign.

remigrate, rē•mī′grāt, *v.i.* To migrate again; to return.—**remigration,** rē•mī•grā′shon, *n.* A migration to a former place.

remind, ri•mīnd′, *v.t.* To put in mind; to cause to recollect or remember (to *remind* a person of his promise).—**reminder,** ri•mīn′dėr, *n.* One who or that which reminds; a hint that serves to awaken remembrance.—**remindful,** ri•mīnd′fụl, *a.* Tending or adapted to remind.

reminiscence, rem•i•nis′ens, *n.* [Fr. *réminiscence*, L. *reminiscentia*, from *reminiscor*, to recall to mind—*re*, again, and *miniscor*, from root *men*, whence *mens*, the mind. MENTAL.] Recollection; that which is recollected or recalled to mind; a relation of what is recollected; a narration of past incidents within one's personal knowledge. ∴ Syn. under MEMORY.—**reminiscent,** rem•i•nis′-ent, *a.* Having remembrance; calling to mind.—*n.* One who calls to mind.

remise, ri•mīz′, *n.* [Fr., from *remettre*, L. *remitio.* REMISS.] *Law*, a granting back; a surrender; release, as of a claim.

remiss, ri•mis′, *a.* [L. *remissus*, relaxed, languid, not strict, pp. of *remitto*—*re*, back, and *mitto*, to send. MISSION.] Not energetic or diligent in performance; careless in performing duty or business; negligent; dilatory; slack; wanting earnestness or activity.—**remissibility,** ri•mis′-i•bil″i•ti, *n.* Capability of being remitted.—**remissible,** ri•mis′i•bl, *a.* Capable of being remitted or forgiven.—**remission,** ri•mish′on, *n.* The act of remitting; diminution or cessation of intensity; abatement; moderation; a giving up; the act of forgiving; forgiveness; pardon; a temporary subsidence of the force or violence of a disease or of pain.—**remissness,** ri•mis′nes, *n.* The state or quality of being remiss.—**remit,** ri•mit′, *v.t.*—*remitted, remitting.* [L. *remitto*, to send back, slacken, relax.] To relax in intensity; to make less intense or violent; to abate; to refrain from exacting; to give up in whole or in part (to *remit* punishment); to pardon; to forgive; to refrain from exacting punishment for (sins); to surrender; to resign; to send back; to put again into custody; *Scots law*, to transfer from one tribunal or judge to another; *com.* to transmit or send, as money, or other things in payment for goods received.—*v.i.* To slacken; to become less intense or rigorous; *med.* to abate in violence for a time (a fever *remits* at a certain hour every day); *com.* to transmit money, etc.—*n. Scots law*, the transferring of a cause from one tribunal or judge to another.—**remittal,** ri•mit′al, *n.* A remitting; a sending money to a distant place.—**remittance,** ri•mit′-ans, *n.* The act of transmitting money, bills, or the like, to a distant place, in return or payment for goods purchased; the sum remitted. —**remittent,** ri•mit′ent, *a.* [L. *remittens, remittentis*, ppr. of *remitto.*]

Temporarily ceasing; having remissions from time to time.—*Remittent fever*, any fever which suffers a decided remission of its violence during the twenty-four hours, but without entirely leaving the patient. —*n.* A remittent fever.—**remitter,** ri•mit′ėr, *n.* One who remits.

remnant, rem′nant, *n.* [Contr. from *remanent.* REMANENT.] What remains after the removal of the rest of a thing; the remaining piece of a web of cloth after the rest is sold; that which remains after a part is done or past; a scrap, fragment, little bit.—*a.* Remaining; yet left.

remodel, rē•mod′el, *v.t.*—*remodeled, remodeling.* To model or fashion anew.

remold, rē•mōld′, *v.t.* To mold again or anew.

remonetize, rē•mon′e•tīz, *v.t.*—*remonetized, remonetizing.* [L. *re*, again, and *moneta*, money. MONEY.] To restore to circulation in the shape of money; to make again the legal or standard money of account.—**remonetization,** rē•mon′et•i•zā″shon, *n.* The act of remonetizing.

remonstrate, ri•mon′strāt, *v.i.*—*remonstrated, remonstrating.* [O.Fr. *remonstrer* (Fr. *remontrer*); L.L. *remonstro*—L. *re*, again, and *monstro*, to show. MONSTER.] To exhibit or present strong reasons against an act, measure, or any course of proceedings; to expostulate.—**remonstrance,** ri•mon′strans, *n.* [O.Fr. *remonstrance.*] The act of remonstrating or expostulating; an expostulation; a strong statement of reasons against something; a paper containing such a statement.—**remonstrant, remonstrative,** ri•mon′strant, ri•mon′stra•tiv, *a.* Expostulatory; remonstrating.—**remonstrant, remonstrator,** ri•mon′strant, ri•mon′strā•tėr, *n.* One who remonstrates.

remora, rem′o•ra, *n.* [L., from *re*, back, and *mora*, delay.] The suckfish, a fish with flattened, adhesive disk on the top of the head, by which it attaches itself firmly to other fishes or to the bottoms of vessels; fabled by the ancients to have miraculous powers of delaying ships.

remorse, ri•mors′, *n.* [L.L. *remorsus*, a biting again, from L. *remordeo*, *remorsum*—*re*, again, and *mordeo*, to bite. MORSEL.] The keen pain or anguish excited by a sense of guilt; compunction of conscience for a crime committed; painful memory of wrongdoing.—**remorseful,** ri•mors′fu̧l, *a.* Full of remorse; impressed with a sense of guilt.—**remorsefully,** ri•mors′fu̧l•li, *adv.* In a remorseful manner.—**remorsefulness,** ri•mors′fu̧l•nes, *n.* The state of being remorseful.—**remorseless,** ri•mors′les, *a.* Without remorse; unpitying; cruel; insensible; pitiless.—**remorselessly,** ri•mors′les•li, *adv.* In a remorseless manner; pitilessly.—**remorselessness,** ri•mors′les•nes, *n.*

remote, ri•mōt′, *a.* [L. *remotus*, from *removeo*, to remove—*er*, and *moveo*, *motum*, to move. REMOVE.] Distant in place; far off; not near; distant in time, past or future; not directly producing an effect; not proximate (the *remote* causes of a disease); distant in consanguinity or affinity (a *remote* kinsman); slight; inconsiderable (remote resemblance). —*Remote control*, control from a point at some distance, as by a switchboard, by a movable actuating device electrically connected to a broadcasting station.—**remotely,** ri•mōt′li, *adv.* In a remote manner; at a distance; slightly; not closely.—**remoteness,** *n.*

remount, rē•mount′, *v.t.* and *i.* To mount again.—*n.* A fresh horse to mount.

remove, ri•möv′, *v.t.*—*removed, removing.* [O.Fr. *remouvoir*, from L. *removeo*, to remove—*re*, and *moveo*, to move. MOVE.] To shift from the position occupied; to put from its place in any manner; to displace from an office, post, or position; to take away by causing to cease; to cause to leave a person or thing; to put an end to; to banish (to *remove* a disease or grievance); to make away with; to cut off (to *remove* a person by poison).—*v.i.* To change place in any manner; to move from one place to another; to change the place of residence. ∴ *Move* is a generic term, including the sense of *remove*, but the latter is never applied to a mere change of posture without a change of place or position.—*n.* The act of removing; a removal; change of place; the distance or space through which anything is removed; an interval; stage; a step in any scale of gradation; a dish removed from the table to make room for something else.—**removability,** ri•mö′va•bil″i•ti, *n.* The capacity of being removable.—**removable,** ri•mö′va•bl, *a.* Capable of being removed.—**removal,** ri•mö′val, *n.* A moving from one place to another; change of place or site; the act of displacing from an office or post; the act of putting an end to (the *removal* of a grievance).—**removed,** ri•mövd′, *p.* and *a.* Changed in place; displaced from office; remote; separate from others. —**remover,** ri•mö′vėr, *n.* One who or that which removes, as paint *remover.*

remunerate, ri•mū′nėr•āt, *v.t.*—*remunerated, remunerating.* [L. *remunero*, *remuneratum*—*re*, back, and *munus*, *muneris*, a present, gift.] To reward; to recompense; to requite, in a good sense; to pay an equivalent to for any service, loss, or sacrifice.—**remuneration,** ri•mū′nėr•ā″shon, *n.* The act of remunerating; what is given to remunerate.—**remunerative,** ri•mū′nėr•ā•tiv, *a.* Affording remuneration; yielding a sufficient return.

renaissance, ren′e•säns″, *n.* [Fr. regeneration or new birth—*re*, again, and *naissance*, birth, L. *nascentia*, from *nascor*, *natus*, to be born. NATAL.] The revival of anything which has long been in decay or extinct; [*cap.*] the transitional movement in Europe from the Middle Ages to the modern world; specially applied to the time of the revival of letters and arts in the fifteenth century.—*Renaissance style*, the style of building and decoration which succeeded the Gothic, and sought to reproduce the forms of classical ornamentation.—**renascence,** ri•nās′ens, *n.* The state of being renascent; [*cap.*] also same as *Renaissance.*—**renascent,** ri•nās′ent, *a.* [L. *renascens.*] Rejuvenated.

renal, rē′nal, *a.* [L. *renalis*, from *ren*, pl. *renes*, the kidneys.] Pertaining to the kidneys.

rename, rē•nām′, *v.t.* To give a new name to.

Renard, ren′ärd, *n.* [Fr., from O.G. *Reinhard*, *Reginhart*, lit. strong in counsel, cunning—the name of a fox in a celebrated German epic poem.] A fox: a name used in fables, poetry, etc., also written *Reynard.*

rencounter, rencontre, ren•koun′tėr, ren•kon′tėr, *n.* [Fr. *rencontre* = *re-encounter.*] An abrupt or chance meeting of persons; a meeting in opposition or contest; a casual combat or action, as between individuals or small parties; a slight engagement between armies or fleets. —*v.t.*† To meet unexpectedly.—*v.i.* To meet an enemy unexpectedly; to come in collision; to fight hand to hand.

rend, rend, *v.t.*—pret. and pp. *rent.* [A.Sax. *rendan*, *hrendan*, to tear, to rend = O.Fris. *renda*, *randa*, N.Fris. *renne*, to cut, to rend; comp. W. *rhann*, Ir. *rann*, a part, Armor. *ranna*, to part, to separate.] To separate into parts with force or sudden violence; to tear asunder; to split; to take away with violence; to tear away.—*To rend the heart*, to affect with deep anguish or repentant sorrow.—*v.i.* To be or to become rent or torn; to split; to part asunder.—**render,** ren′dėr, *n.* One who rends or tears by violence.

render, ren′dėr, *v.t.* [Fr. *rendre*, from L. *reddo*, to restore, by the insertion of *n* before *d*—*re*, back, and *do*, to give.] To give in return; to give or pay back; to give, often officially, or in compliance with a request or duty; to furnish; to report (to *render* an account); to afford; to give for use or benefit (to *render* services); to make or cause to be or to convert; to invest with qualities (to *render* a fortress more secure); to translate from one language into another; to interpret or bring into full expression to others; to reproduce (to *render* a piece of music); to boil down and clarify (to *render* tallow).—*v.i. Naut.* to yield or give way to force applied; to pass freely through a block: said of a rope.—*n.* A return; a payment, especially a payment of rent.—**renderable,** ren′dėr•a•bl, *a.* Capable of being rendered.—**renderer,** ren′dėr•ėr, *n.* One who renders.

rendezvous, rän′de•vö, *n.* [Fr. *rendez-vous*, lit. render yourselves, repair to a place. RENDER.] A place appointed for the assembling of troops; the port or place where ships are ordered to join company;

an appointment; a place of meeting; a place at which persons commonly meet.—*v.i.*—*rendezvoused* (rän′de•vöd), *rendezvousing* (rän′de•vö•ing). To assemble at a particular place, as troops.

rendition, ren•dish′on, *n.* [L. *redditio.* RENDER.] A rendering or giving the meaning of a word or passage; translation; the act of reproducing or exhibiting artistically; the act of rendering up or yielding possession; surrender.

renegade, renegado, ren′e•gād, ren•ē•gā′dō, *n.* [Sp. *renegado,* Fr. *renégat,* L.L. *renegatus,* one who denies his religion—L. *re,* back, and *nego, negatum,* to deny. NEGATION, RUNAGATE.] An apostate from a religious faith; one who deserts to an enemy or who deserts one party and joins another: a deserter.

renege, ri•nig′, *v.t.* and *i.* [L.L. *renego.* RENEGADE.] To deny; to renounce; to play a card of another suit when able to follow suit; to go back on a promise.

renew, ri•nū′, *v.t.* To make new again; to restore to former freshness, completeness, or perfection; to restore to a former state, or to a good state, after decay or impairment; to make again (to *renew* a treaty); to begin again; to recommence (*renew* a fight); to grant or furnish again, as a new loan or a new note for the amount of a former one (to *renew* a bill).—*v.i.* To become new; to grow afresh; to begin again; not to desist.—**renewable,** ri•nū′a•bl, *a.* Capable of being renewed.—**renewal,** ri•nū′al, *n.* The act of renewing or of forming anew.

reniform, re′ni•form, *a.* [L. *ren,* a kidney.] Having the form or shape of the kidneys.

renitent, ri•nī′tent, *a.* [L. *renitens, renitentis,* ppr. of *renitor*—*re,* back, and *nitor,* to struggle.] Resisting pressure; acting against impulse; persistently opposed.—**renitency,** ri•nī′ten•si, *n.* The state of being renitent.

rennet, ren′et, *n.* [Also written *runnet,* and formed from the verb to *run,* O.E. *renne;* A.Sax. *rinnan,* to run, *gerinnan,* to curdle or coagulate; comp. G. *rennen,* to run, to curdle, *rennse,* rennet; D. *rinnen,* to curdle.] The prepared inner membrane of the calf's stomach, which has the property of coagulating milk.

rennet, ren′et, *n.* [Fr. *reinette,* dim. of *reine,* L. *regina,* a queen.] A kind of apple said to have been introduced in the reign of Henry VIII.

rennin, ren′nin, *n.* A milk-curdling ferment contained in gastric juice.

renounce, ri•nouns′, *v.t.*—*renounced, renouncing.* [Fr. *renoncer,* from L. *renuncio*—*re,* back, and *nuncio, nuntio,* to tell. NUNCIO.] To disown, disclaim, abjure, forswear; to refuse to own or acknowledge as belonging; to cast off or reject.—*v.i. Card playing,* not to follow suit when one has a card of the same sort; to revoke.—**renouncement,** ri•nouns′ment, *n.* The act of disclaiming or rejecting; renunciation.—**renunciation,** ri•nun′si•ā″shon, *n.* The act of renouncing; a disowning or disclaiming; rejecting.

renovate, ren′o•vāt, *v.t.*—*renovated, renovating.* [L. *renovo, renovatum*—*re,* again, and *novo,* to make new, from *novus,* new. NOVEL.] To renew; to repair and render as good as new; to restore to freshness or to a good condition.—**renovator,** ren′o•vā•tėr, *n.* One who or that which renovates.—**renovation,** ren•o•vā′shon, *n.* The act of renovating; renewal; repair; restoration.

renown, ri•noun′, *n.* [O.E. *renowne,* from Fr. *renom,* from L. *re,* and *nomen,* a name. NOUN.] The state of having a great or exalted name; exalted reputation derived from the widely spread praise of great achievements or accomplishments.—*v.t.* To make famous.—**renowned,** ri•nound′, *a.* Famous; celebrated for great and heroic achievements, for distinguished qualities, or for grandeur; eminent.

rensselaerite, rens′sel•âr•īt, *n.* [After Van *Rensselaer.*] A steatitic mineral with a fine compact texture, worked into inkstands and other articles.

rent, rent, pret. & pp. of *rend.*

rent, rent, *n.* [From pp. of *rend.*] An opening made by rending or tearing; a break or breach; a hole torn; schism.

rent, rent, *n.* [Fr. *rente,* It. *rendita,* that which is rendered or given up, from L.L. *rendo,* for L. *reddo,* to give up. RENDER.] A sum of money, or a certain amount of anything valuable, payable yearly for the use or occupation of lands or tenements; a compensation made to the owner by the user or occupier as a return for his occupancy.—*v.t.* To grant the possession and enjoyment of for a certain rent; to let on lease; to take and hold on the payment of rent.—*v.i.* To be leased or let for rent.—**rentable,** rent′a•bl, *a.* Capable of being rented.—**rental,** rent′al, *n.* A schedule or account of rents; the gross amount of rents drawn from an estate.—**renter,** rent′ėr, *n.* The lessee or tenant who pays rent.

renter, rent′ėr, *v.t.* [Fr. *rentraire*—*re,* back, *en,* in, and *traire,* from L. *trahere,* to draw. TRACT.] To fine-draw; to sew together, as the edges of two pieces of cloth.

renunciation. See RENOUNCE.

reoccupy, rē•ok′kū•pī, *v.t.* To occupy anew.

reopen, rē•ō′pen, *v.t.* To open again.—*v.i.* To be opened again; to open anew.

reorganize, rē•or′gan•īz, *v.t.* To organize anew; to reduce again to an organized condition.—**reorganization,** rē•or′gan•i•zā″shon, *a.* The act of organizing anew.

rep, repp, rep, *n.* [Perhaps from *rib.*] A dress fabric having a ribbed or corded appearance, the ribs being transverse.

repaint, rē•pānt′, *v.t.* To paint anew.

repair, ri•pâr′, *v.t.* [Fr. *réparer,* from L. *reparo*—*re,* again, and *paro,* to get or make ready. PARE.] To execute restoration or renovation on; to restore to a sound or good state after decay, injury, dilapidation, or partial destruction; to make amends for, as for an injury, by an equivalent; to give indemnity for.—*n.* Restoration to a sound or good state; supply of loss; reparation; state as regards repairing (a building in good or bad *repair*).—**repairable,** ri•pâ′ra•bl, *a.* Capable of being repaired; reparable.—**repairer,** ri•pâ′rėr, *n.* One who repairs.—**reparable,** rep′a•ra•bl, *a.* [L. *reparabilis.*] Capable of being repaired, restored to a sound state, or made good.—**reparably,** rep′a•ra•bli, *adv.* In a reparable manner.—**reparation,** rep•a•rā′shon, *n.* The act of repairing; repair; what is done to repair a wrong; indemnification for loss or damage, as demanded of Germany by the Allies after World War I for property damage done in France; satisfaction for injury; amends.—**reparative,** ri•par′a•tiv, *a.* Capable of effecting repair; tending to make good or amend defect.—*n.* That which restores to a good state; that which makes amends.

repair, ri•pâr′, *v.i.* [O.Fr. *repairer,* from L.L. *repatriare*—*re,* back, and *patria,* one's native country. PATRIOT.] To go to some place; to betake one's self; to resort.—*n.* The act of betaking one's self to any place; a resorting; haunt; resort.

repand, ri•pand′, *a.* [L. *repandus,* bent backward, turned up.] *Bot.* having an uneven, slightly sinuous margin, as a leaf.

repartee, rep•är•tē′, *n.* [Fr. *repartie*—*re,* back, and *partir,* from L. *partire,* to share, part, from *pars, partis,* a part. PART.] A smart, ready, and witty reply.

repartition, rē•pär•tish′on, *n.* A fresh partition or division.

repass, rē•pas′, *v.t.* To pass again; to pass or travel back over; to recross.—*v.i.* To pass or go back; to move back.

repast, ri•past′, *n.* [O.Fr. *repast,* Fr. *repas,* from L. *re,* again, and *pasco, pastum,* to feed. PASTOR.] The act of taking food; a meal; food; victuals (*Shak.*).—*v.t.* To feed; to feast.—*v.i.* To take food; to feast.

repatriate, rē•pā′tri•āt, *v.t.*—*repatriated, repatriating.* [L. *repatrio, repatriatum*—*re,* again, and *patria,* one's country. PATRIOT.] To restore to one's own country.—**repatriation,** rē•pā′tri•ā″shon, *n.* Return or restoration to one's own country.

repay, rē•pā′, *v.t.* To pay back; to refund; to make return or requital for.—*v.i.* To requite either good or evil.—**repayable,** rē•pā′a•bl, *a.* Capable of being repaid; liable to be repaid or refunded.—**repayment,** rē•pā′ment, *n.* The act of repaying or paying back; the money repaid.

repeal, ri•pēl′, *v.t.* [Fr. *rappeler*—*re,* back, and *appeler,* L. *appello,* to call upon, speak to. APPEAL.] To recall, as a law or statute; to revoke; to abrogate by an authoritative act, or by the same power that made or enacted.—*n.* The act of repealing; revocation; abrogation.—**repealable,** ri•pēl′a•bl, *a.* Capable of being repealed.

repeat, ri•pēt′, *v.t.* [Fr. *répéter,* from L. *repeto,* to seek again, to repeat—*re,* again, and *peto,* to seek. PETITION.] To do or perform again (to *repeat* an attempt); to go over, say, make, etc., again; to iterate; to recite; to rehearse; to say over (to *repeat* a lesson).—*n.* The act of repeating; repetition; *music,* a sign that a movement or part of a movement is to be twice performed.—*v.i.* To strike the hours (a *repeating* watch).—**repeatedly,** ri•pēt′ed•li, *adv.* With repetition; more than once; again and again.—**repeater,** ri•pēt′ėr, *n.* One that repeats, as illegally voting a second time in an election; a gun with extra shells in a chamber to facilitate rapid firing; one returned to prison for a further crime, having served one or more previous sentences; one that recites or rehearses; a watch that strikes the hours, etc., on the compression of a spring; *arith.* an interminate decimal in which the same figure continually recurs.—**repetend,** rep′e•tend, *n.* [L. *repetendum,* a thing to be repeated.] *Arith.* that part of a repeating decimal which recurs continually ad infinitum.—**repetition,** rep•e•tish′on, *n.* The act of doing or uttering a second time; the act of repeating or saying over; a reciting or rehearsing; what is repeated; something said or done a second time.—**repetitious,** rep•e•tish′us, *a.* Containing repetitions or statements repeated.—**repetitive,** ri•pet′i•tiv, *a.* Containing repetitions.

repel, ri•pel′, *v.t.—repelled, repelling.* [L. *repello—re,* back, and *pello,* to drive, as in *expel, compel, expulsion,* etc. PULSE.] To drive back; to force to return; to check the advance of; to repulse (to *repel* an enemy); to encounter with effectual resistance; to resist or oppose successfully (to *repel* an encroachment, an argument).—*v.i.* To cause repugnance; to shock; to act with force in opposition (electricity sometimes *repels*).—**repellent,** ri•pel′ent, *a.* Having the effect of repelling; able or tending to repel; repulsive; deterring.—*n.* That which repels.—**repeller,** ri•pel′ėr, *n.* One who or that which repels.

repent, ri′pent, *a.* [L. *repens, repentis,* ppr. of *repo,* to creep.] Creeping (a *repent* root, a *repent* animal).

repent, ri•pent′, *v.i.* [Fr. *repentir—se repentir,* to repent—L. *re,* and *pœnitere,* to repent, from *pœna,* pain. PENITENT, PAIN.] To feel pain, sorrow, or regret for something done or left undone by one's self; to experience such sorrow for sin as produces amendment of life; to be penitent.—*v.t.* To remember with compunction or self-reproach; to feel self-accusing pain or grief on account of (to *repent* rash words): formerly used in such phrases as I *repent me,* it *repented him* (impersonally).—**repentance,** ri•pen′tans, *n.* The act of repenting; the state of being penitent; contrition for sin; such sorrow for past conduct as produces a new life.—**repentant,** ri•pen′tant, *a.* Experiencing repentance; sorrowful for sin; expressing or showing sorrow for sin (*repentant* tears).—**repentantly,** ri•pen′tant•li, *adv.* In a repentant manner.—**repenter,** ri•pen′tėr, *n.* One that repents.

repeople, rē•pē′pl, *v.t.* To people anew; to furnish again with a stock of people.

repercuss, rē•pėr•kus′, *v.t.* [L. *repercutio, repercussum.* PERCUSS.] To beat or drive back (as sound or air); to make rebound.—**repercussive,** rē•pėr•kus′iv, *a.* Having the power of repercussion; causing to reverberate.

repercussion, rē•per•kush′in, *n.* [L. *repercussio,* from *repercussus,* pp. of *repercutere,* to drive back.] A driving back or being driven back; reverberation; a reciprocal action or effect (the *repercussions* of the plan).

repertoire, rep′ėr•twär, *n.* [Fr. *répertoire.* REPERTORY.] A list of dramas, operas, or the like, which can be performed by a dramatic or operatic company; those parts, songs, etc., that are usually performed by an actor, vocalist, etc.

repertory, rep′ėr•to•ri, *n.* [L. *repertorium,* from *reperio,* to find again—*re,* again, and *pario,* to produce. PARENT.] A storehouse or collection of things; a repertoire.

repetition, etc. See REPEAT.

repine, ri•pīn′, *v.i.—repined, repining* [O.E. *repoyne,* Fr. *repoindre,* to prick again—L. *re,* again, and *pungo,* to prick (PUNCTURE), influenced by verb to *pine.*] To fret one's self; to feel inward discontent which preys on the spirits; to indulge in complaint; to murmur: with *at* or *against.*

replace, ri•plās′, *v.t.* To put again in the former place; to repay; to refund; to fill the place of; to be a substitute for.—**replacement,** ri•plās′ment, *n.* The act of replacing; that which replaces, as *pl.* soldiers assigned to a decimated company.

replant, rē•plant′, *v.t.* To plant again; to reinstate.

repleader, rē•plē′dėr, *n. Law,* a second pleading or course of pleadings.

replenish, ri•plen′ish, *v.t.* [O.Fr. *replenir, replenissant,* from L. *re* again, and *plenus,* full, from *pleo,* to fill. PLENARY, COMPLETE.] To fill again after having been emptied or diminished; hence, to fill completely; to stock with numbers or abundance.—**replenisher,** ri•plen′ish•ėr, *n.* One who replenishes.—**replenishment,** ri•plen′ish•ment, *n.*

replete, ri•plēt′, *a.* [L. *repletus,* pp. of *repleo,* to fill again—*re,* again, and *pleo,* to fill. REPLENISH.] Completely filled; full; abounding; thoroughly imbued.—*v.t.* To fill to repletion or satiety.—**repletion,** ri•plē′shon, *n.* The state of being replete or completely filled; superabundant fullness; surfeit.

replevy, ri•plev′i, *v.t.—replevied, replevying.* [O.Fr. *replevir.*] *Law,* to recover possession of (as goods wrongfully seized) upon giving surety to try the right to them in court; to take back by writ of replevin.—**repleviable, replevisable,** ri•plev′i•a•bl, ri•plev′i•za•bl, *a. Law,* capable of being replevied.—**replevin, replevy,** ri•plev′in, *n. Law,* a personal action which lies to recover possession of goods or chattels wrongfully taken or detained.

replica, rep′li•ka, *n.* [It. *replica,* a reply, a repetition—L. *re,* back, and *plica,* a fold. REPLY.] A copy of a picture or piece of sculpture made by the hand that executed the original.

replicant, rep′li•kant, *n.* [L. *replicans, replicantis,* ppr. of *replico,* reply. REPLY.] *obs.* One who makes a reply.—**replication,** rep•li•kā′shon, *n.* An answer; a reply; a repetition; a copy; a replica.

replicate, rep′li•kāt, *a.* [L. *re,* back, and *plico,* to fold. REPLY.] *Bot.* folded or bent back.

reply, ri•plī′, *v.i.—replied, replying.* [O.Fr. *replier* (Mod.Fr. *répliquer*), to reply, from L. *replico,* to fold back, to reply—*re,* back, and *plico,* to fold. PLY, APPLY, EMPLOY.] To make answer in words or writing, as to something said or written by another; to answer; to respond; to do or give something in return for something else; to answer by deeds; to meet an attack by fitting action.—*v.t.* To return for an answer: often with a clause as object.—*n.* That which is said or written in answer to what is said or written by another; an answer; that which is done in consequence of something else; an answer by deeds; a counterattack.—**replier,** ri•plī′ėr, *n.* One who replies; an answerer, a respondent; a replicant.

report, ri•pōrt′, *v.t.* [Fr. *reporter,* to carry back; *rapporter,* to carry back, relate, report; the former from L. *reporto—re,* and *porto,* to carry, the latter from *re, ad,* and *porto.* PORT (carriage).] To bear or bring back, as an answer; to relate, as what has been discovered by a person sent to examine or investigate; to give an account of; to relate; to tell; to circulate publicly, as a story (as in the common phrase it is *reported,* that is, it is said in public); to give an official or formal account or statement of; to give an account of for public reading; to write out or take down from the lips of the speaker (the debate was fully *reported*); to lay a charge or make a disclosure against (I will *report* you).—*To be reported of,* to be well or ill spoken of.—*To report one's self,* to make known one's whereabouts or movements to the proper quarter.—*v.i.* To make a statement of facts; to take down in writing speeches from a speaker's lips; to discharge the office of a reporter.—*n.* An account brought back; a statement of facts given in reply to inquiry; a story circulated; hence, rumor; common fame; repute; public character (a man of good *report*); an account of a judicial decision, or of a case argued and determined in a court of law, etc.; an official statement of facts; an account of the proceedings, debates, etc., of a legislative assembly or other meeting, intended for publication; an epitome or fully written account of a speech; sound of an explosion; loud noise (the *report* of a gun).—**reportable,** ri•pōr′ta•bl, *a.* Fit to be reported.—**reporter,** ri•pōr′tėr, *n.* One who reports; a member of a newspaper staff whose duty it is to give an account of the proceedings of public meetings and entertainments, collect information respecting interesting or important events, and the like.—**reportorial,** ri•pōr′tō′ri•al, *a.* Relating to a reporter or reporters.

repose, ri•pōz′, *v.t.*—*reposed, reposing.* [Fr. *reposer,* to place again, to settle, to rest—*re,* again, and *poser.* POSE.] To lay at rest; to lay for the purpose of taking rest; to refresh by rest: frequently used reflexively; to lay, place, or rest in full reliance (to *repose* trust or confidence in a person).—*v.i.* To lie at rest; to sleep; to rest in confidence; to rely: followed by *on.*—*n.* [Fr. *repos.*] The act or state of reposing; a lying at rest; sleep; rest; quiet; rest of mind; tranquillity; settled composure; absence of all show of feeling; *painting,* an avoidance of obtrusive tints or of striking action in figures.—**reposal,** ri•pō′zal, *n.* The act of reposing or resting with reliance.—**reposeful,** ri•pōz′fųl, *a.* Full of repose; affording repose or rest; trustful.

reposit, ri•poz′it, *v.t.* [L. *repono, repositum*—*re,* back, and *pono,* to place. POSITION.] To lay up; to lodge, as for safety or preservation.—**reposition,** rē•po•zish′on, *n.* Act of repositing or laying up in safety.—**repository,** ri•poz′i•to•ri, *n.* [L. *repositorium.*] A place where things are or may be deposited for safety or preservation; a depository; a storehouse; a magazine; a warehouse; a shop.

repossess, rē•poz•zes′, *v.t.* To possess again.—**repossession,** rē•poz•zesh′on, *n.* The act or state of possessing again.

reprehend, rep•ri•hend′, *v.t.* [L. *reprehendo*—*re,* back, and *prehendo,* to lay hold of; seen also in *comprehend, apprehend, prehensile,* etc.] To charge with a fault; to chide sharply; to reprove; to take exception to; to speak of as a fault; to censure.—**reprehensible,** rep•ri•hen′si•bl, *a.* Deserving to be reprehended or censured; blameworthy; censurable; deserving reproof.—**reprehensibleness,** rep•ri•hen′si•bl•nes, *n.* The quality of being reprehensible.—**reprehensibly,** rep•ri•hen′si•bli, *adv.* In a reprehensible manner; culpably.—**reprehension,** rep•ri•hen′shon, *n.* [L. *reprehensio.*] The act of reprehending; reproof; censure; blame.—**reprehensive,** rep•ri•hen′siv, *a.* Containing reprehension or reproof.—**reprehensively,** rep•ri•hen′siv•li, *adv.* With reprehension.

represent, rep•ri•zent′, *v.t.* [Fr. *représenter,* from L. *repraesento,*—*re,* again, and *praesento,* to present. PRESENT.] To exhibit the image or counterpart of; to typify; to portray by pictorial or plastic art; to act the part of; to personate; to exhibit to the mind in language; to bring before the mind; to give an account of; to describe; to supply the place of; to speak and act with authority on behalf of; to be a substitute or agent for; to serve as a sign or symbol of (words *represent* ideas or things).—**representable,** rep•ri•zen′ta•bl, *a.* Capable of being represented.—**representation,** rep′ri•zen•tā″shon, *n.* The act of representing, describing, exhibiting, portraying, etc.; that which represents; an image or likeness; a picture or statue; exhibition of a play on the stage, or of a character in a play; a dramatic performance; a statement of arguments or facts, etc.; sometimes a written expostulation; a remonstrance; the representing of a constituency in a legislative assembly (the *representation* of a county in parliament); delegates or representatives collectively.—**representative,** rep•ri•zen′ta•tive, *a.* Fitted to represent, portray, or typify; acting as a substitute for another or others; performing the functions of others (a *representative* body); conducted by the agency of delegates chosen by the people (a *representative* government); *nat. hist.* presenting the full characteristics of the type of a group (a *representative* genius).—*n.* One who or that which represents; that by which anything is represented; something standing for something else; an agent, deputy, or substitute who supplies the place of another or others, being invested with his or their authority; *law,* one that stands in the place of another as heir.—*House of Representatives,* the lower house of the supreme legislative body (Congress) in the United States.—**representatively,** rep•ri•zen′ta•tiv•li, *adv.* In a representative manner.—**representativeness,** rep•ri•zen′ta•tiv•nes, *n.*

repress, ri•pres′, *v.t.* [Prefix *re,* and *press,* L. *reprimo, repressum.* PRESS.] To press back or down effectually; to crush, quell, put down, subdue (sedition, a rising); to check; to restrain.—**represser,** ri•pres′ėr, *n.* One who represses; one that crushes or subdues.—**repressible,** ri•pres′i•bl, *a.* Capable of being repressed.—**repression,** ri•presh′on, *n.* The act of repressing, restraining, or subduing; check; restraint.—**repressive,** ri•pres′iv, *a.* Having power to repress; tending to subdue or restrain.—**repressively,** ri•pres′iv•li, *adv.* In a repressive manner.

reprieve, ri•prēv′, *n.* [From O.Fr. *reprover, repruver,* to blame, condemn, from L. *reprobare,* to reject, condemn, meaning originally the rejection of a sentence already passed. REPROBATE.] The suspension of the execution of a criminal's sentence; respite; interval of ease or relief.—*v.t.*—*reprieved, reprieving.* To grant a reprieve or respite to; to suspend or delay the execution of for a time.

reprimand, rep′ri•mand, *n.* [Fr. *réprimande,* from L. *reprimenda,* a thing to be checked or repressed, from *reprimo, repressum,* to repress. REPRESS.] A severe reproof for a fault; a sharp rebuke; reprehension.—*v.t.* (rep•ri•mand′). To reprove severely; to reprehend; to reprove publicly and officially, in execution of a sentence.

reprint, rē•print′, *v.t.* To print again; to print a second or any new edition of; to renew the impression of.—*n.* (rē′print). A second or new impression of any printed work.

reprisal, ri•prī′zal, *n.* [Fr. *représaille,* from It. *rappresaglia,* from L.L. *reprisaliae,* from L. *reprehendo,* to take again; comp. *prize,* a capture, which is also from L. *prehendo.*] The seizure or taking of anything from an enemy by way of retaliation or indemnification; also, that which is so taken; any taking by way of retaliation; an act of severity done in retaliation.—*Letters of marque and reprisal.* See MARQUE.

reproach, ri•prōch′, *v.t.* [Fr. *reprocher,* O.Fr. *reprochier,* Pr. *repropchar,* to reproach, from L.L. *repropiare,* from L. *re,* back, and *prope,* near; lit. to bring near or set before. APPROACH, PROPINQUITY]. To charge with a fault in severe language; to censure with severity, opprobrium, or contempt, or as having suffered wrong personally; to upbraid.—*n.* A severe or cutting expression of censure or blame; blame for something considered outrageous or vile; contumely; source of blame; shame, infamy, or disgrace; object of contempt, scorn, or derision.—**reproachable,** ri•prō′cha•bl, *a.* Deserving reproach.—**reproachableness,** ri•prō′cha•bl•nes, *n.* The state of being reproachable.—**reproachably,** ri•prō′cha•bli, *adv.* In a reproachable manner.—**reproacher,** ri•prō′chėr, *n.* One who reproaches.—**reproachful,** ri•prōch′fųl, *a.* Containing or expressing reproach or censure; upbraiding; scurrilous; opprobrious; worthy of reproach; shameful; infamous.—**reproachfully,** ri•prōch′fųl•li, *adv.* In a reproachful manner.—**reproachfulness,** ri•prōch′fųl•nes, *n.* Quality of being reproachful.—**reproachless,** ri•prōch′les, *a.* Without reproach.

reprobate, rep′ro•bāt, *a.* [L. *reprobatus,* disapproved, rejected, pp. of *reprobo*—*re,* denoting reverse, and *probo,* to approve. PROBABLE, REPRIEVE, REPROVE.] Abandoned in sin; morally abandoned; depraved; profligate; lost to virtue or grace.—*n.* One who is very profligate or abandoned; a person abandoned to sin; one lost to virtue; a wicked, depraved wretch.—*v.t.*—*reprobated, reprobating.* [L. *reprobo, reprobatum.*] To disapprove with detestation or marks of extreme dislike; to contemn strongly; to condemn; to reject.—**reprobation,** rep•ro•bā′shon, *n.* The act of reprobating; condemnation; censure; rejection.—**reprobative,** rep′ro•bā•tiv, *a.* Conveying reprobation.

reproduce, rē•pro•dūs′, *v.t.*—*repro-*

duced, reproducing. To produce again or anew; to renew the production of; to generate, as offspring; to portray or represent; to bring to the memory or imagination.—**reproducer,** rē•pro•dū′sėr, *n.* One who or that which reproduces.—**reproduction,** rē•pro•duk′shon, *n.* The act or process of reproducing; the process whereby new individuals are generated and the perpetuation of the species ensured; that which is produced or presented anew.—**reproductive,** rē•pro•duk′tiv, *a.* Pertaining to reproduction; tending to reproduce.

reproof, ri•pröf′, *n.* [O.F. *reprueve,* reproof.] The expression of blame or censure addressed to a person; blame expressed to one's face; censure for a fault; reprehension; rebuke; reprimand.

reprove, ri•pröv′, *v.t.—reproved, reproving.* [Fr. *réprouver,* to blame, to censure; O.Fr. *reprover,* from L. *reprobare.* REPROBATE.] To chide; to reprehend; to express disapproval of (to *reprove* sins); to serve to admonish.—**reprovable,** ri•prö′va•bl, *a.* Worthy of being reproved; deserving reproof or censure.—**reproval,** ri•prö′val, *n.* Act of reproving; admonition; reproof.—**reprover,** ri•prö′vėr, *n.* One that reproves.—**reprovingly,** ri•prö′ving•li, *adv.* In a reproving manner.

reptile, rep′tīl, *a.* [Fr. *reptile,* from L. *reptilis,* creeping, from *repo, reptum,* to creep; akin to *serpo,* to creep. SERPENT.] Creeping; moving on the belly, or with small, short legs; groveling; low; mean; vile.—*n.* In a general sense, an animal that moves on its belly, or by means of small, short legs; a crawling creature; specifically, *zool.* an animal belonging to the class Reptilia; a groveling, abject, or mean person.—**reptilian,** rep•til′i•an, *a.* Belonging to the class of reptiles.—*n.* An animal of the class Reptilia; a reptile.

republic, ri•pub′lik, *n.* [Fr. *république,* L. *respublica—res,* an affair, interest, and *publica,* fem. of *publicus,* public. REAL, PUBLIC.] A commonwealth; a political community in which the supreme power in the state is vested either in certain privileged members of the community or in the whole community, and thus varying from the most exclusive oligarchy to a pure democracy.—*Federal republics,* of which the United States and Switzerland are examples, consist of a number of separate states bound together by treaty, so as to present the aspect of a single state with a central government, without wholly renouncing their individual powers of internal self-government.—**republican,** ri•pub′li•kan, *a.* Pertaining to or having the character of a republic; consonant to the principles of a republic. —*n.* One who favors or prefers a republican form of government; [*cap.*] a member of the Republican party in *U. S. politics.—Red Republican.* RED.—**republicanism,** ri•pub′li•kan•izm, *n.* Republican system of government; [*cap.*] principles and policies of the Republican party (*U.S.*); republican principles.

republication, rē•pub′li•kā″shon, *n.* The act of republishing; a new publication of something before published.

republish, rē•pub′lish, *v.t.* To publish anew; to publish again, as in a new edition.

repudiate, ri•pū′di•āt, *v.t.—repudiated, repudiating.* [L. *repudio, repudiatum,* to divorce, to cast off, from *repudium,* a casting off, a divorce.] To cast away; to reject; to discard; to disavow; to divorce; to refuse to acknowledge or to pay, as debt.—**repudiation,** ri•pū′di•ā″shon, *n.* [L. *repudiatio.*] The act of repudiating; rejection; disavowal; divorce; refusal on the part of a government to pay debts contracted by a former government.—**repudiator,** ri•pū′di•ā•tėr, *n.* One who repudiates.

repugnance, repugnancy, ri•pug′nans, ri•pug′nan•si, *n.* [Fr. *répugnance;* L. *repugnantia,* from *repugno,* to resist—*re,* against, and *pugno,* to fight. PUGNACIOUS.] The state of being opposed in mind; feeling of dislike for some action; reluctance; unwillingness; opposition in nature or qualities; contrariety.—**repugnant,** ri•pug′nant, *a.* [L. *repugnans, repugnantis,* ppr. of *repugno.*] Standing or being in opposition; contrary; at variance: usually followed by *to* (a statement *repugnant to* common sense); highly distasteful; offensive (a course *repugnant to* him).—**repugnantly,** ri•pug′nant•li, *adv.*

repulse, ri•puls′, *n.* [L. *repulsa,* from *repello, repulsum—re,* back, and *pello,* to drive. REPEL.] The condition of being repelled or driven back by force; the act of driving back; a check or defeat; refusal; denial.—*v.t.* —*repulsed, repulsing.* To repel; to drive back; to refuse; to reject.—**repulser,** ri•puls′ėr, *n.* One that repulses.—**repulsion,** ri•pul′shon, *n.* [L. *repulsio.*] The act of repelling; *physics,* a term often applied to the action which two bodies exert upon one another when they tend to increase their mutual distance.—**repulsive,** ri•pul′siv, *a.* Acting so as to repel; exercising repulsion; tending to deter or forbid approach or familiarity; repellent; forbidding. —**repulsively,** ri•pul′siv•li, *adv.* In a repulsive manner.—**repulsiveness,** ri•pul′siv•nes, *n.*

repurchase, rē•pėr′ches, *v.t.* To buy back; to regain by purchase.—*n.* The act of buying again; a new purchase.

repute, ri•pūt′, *v.t.—reputed, reputing.* [Fr. *réputer,* from L. *reputo,* to count over—*re,* and *puto,* to reckon, to estimate (as in *compute, impute,* etc.). PUTATIVE.] To hold in thought; to reckon, account, or consider as such or such; to deem.—*n.* Reputation; character, attributed by public report, especially good character; honorable name.—**reputed,** ri•pū′ted, *p.* and *a.* Generally considered; commonly believed, regarded, or accounted.—**reputedly,** ri•pū′ted•li, *adv.* In common opinion or estimation.—**reputable,** rep′ū•ta•bl, *a.* Being in good repute; held in esteem; not mean or disgraceful.—**reputably,** rep′ū•ta•bli, *adv.* In a reputable manner. — **reputation,** rep•ū•tā′shon, *n.* [L. *reputatio.*] Character by report; opinion of character generally entertained; character attributed; repute; in a good or bad sense; often favorable or honorable regard; good name.

request, ri•kwest′, *n.* [O.Fr. *requeste* (Fr. *requête*), from L. *requisita,* a thing required, a want, from *requiro, requisitum—re,* again, and *quaero, quaesitum,* to seek. QUEST.] The expression of desire to some person for something to be granted or done; an asking; a petition, prayer, entreaty; the thing asked for or requested; a state of being esteemed and sought after, or asked for (an article in much *request*). ∴ *Request* expresses less earnestness than *entreaty* and *supplication;* and supposes a right in the person requested to deny or refuse to grant, in this differing from *demand.—v.t.* To make a request for; to solicit or express desire for; to express a request to; to ask.

Requiem, rē′kwi•em, *n.* [Acc. case of L. *requies,* rest, respite, relaxation —*re,* again, and *quies,* rest, repose.] [*usually cap.*] A funeral dirge or service, containing the words '*Requiem* aeternam', etc., sung for the rest of a person's soul; a grand musical composition performed in honor of some deceased person.

require, ri•kwīr′, *v.t.—required, requiring.* [O.Fr. *requerre, requierre, requirre* (Fr. *requérir*), from L. *requiro, requirere,* to ask for. REQUEST.] To demand; to ask as of right and by authority; to insist on having; to ask as a favor; to call upon to act; to request; to have need or necessity for; to need or want (the matter *requires* great care, we *require* food); to find it necessary; to have to: with infinitives (you will *require* to go).—**requirement,** ri•kwīr′ment, *n.* The act of requiring; demand; that which requires the doing of something; an essential condition; something required or necessary.—**requisite,** rek′wi•zit, *a.* [L. *requisitus,* from *requiro.*] Required by the nature of things or by circumstances; necessary.—*n.* That which is necessary; something indispensable.—**requisitely,** rek′wi•zit•li, *adv.* In a requisite manner; necessarily.—**requisiteness,** rek′wi•zit•nes, *n.*—**requisition,** rek•wi•zish′on, *n.* [L. *requisitio.*] An application made as of a right; a demand; a demand for or a levying of necessaries by hostile troops from the people in whose country they are; a written call or invitation (a *requisition* for a public meeting); state of being required or much sought after; request.—*v.t.* To make a requisition or demand upon.

requite, ri•kwīt′, *v.t.—requited, requiting.* [From *re,* back, and *quit.* QUIT.] To repay either good or evil: in a good sense, to recompense or reward: in a bad sense, to retaliate on.—**requiter,** ri•kwī′tėr, *n.* One who requites.—**requital,** ri•kwī'tal, *n.* Return for any office, good or bad; recompense; reward.

reread, rē•rēd', *v.t.* To read again or anew.

reredos, rēr'dos, *n.* [Fr. *arrière dos—arrière,* behind, and *dos,* L. *dorsum,* the back. REAR, DORSAL.] The decorated portion of the wall behind and rising above the altar in a church.

reremouse, rēr'mous, *n.* [A.Sax. *hréremus,* from *hrénan,* to raise, to move, and *mús,* a mouse.] A bat. (*Shak.*)

rerun, re'run, *n.* An added running, as a later showing of a motion picture after its first run.—*v.t.* To run again.

resail, rē•sāl', *v.t.* or *i.* To sail back.

resale, rē'sāl, *n.* A sale at second hand; a second sale.

rescind, ri•sind', *v.t.* [Fr. *rescinder,* from L. *rescindo, rescissum—re,* again, and *scindo,* to cut (as in *concise, precise,* etc.).] To cut short‡; to abrogate; to revoke or annul by competent authority (to *rescind* a law, a judgment).—**rescission,** ri•sizh'on, *n.* [L. *rescissio, rescissionis.*] The act of rescinding; the act of abrogating or annulling.—**rescissory,** ri•sis'o•ri, *a.* [L. *rescissorius.*] Having power to rescind, abrogate, or annul.

rescript, rē'skript, *n.* [L. *rescriptum,* from *rescribo, rescriptum,* to write back—*re,* and *scribo,* to write. SCRIBE.] The answer or decision of a Roman emperor to some matter set before him; the decision by a pope of a question officially propounded; an edict or decree.

rescue, res'kū, *v.t.—rescued, rescuing.* [O.Fr. *rescoure, rescourre,* to rescue, from L. *re,* again, and *excutere,* to shake off.—*ex,* away, and *quiato, quassum,* to shake. QUASH.] To free from confinement, danger, or evil; to withdraw from a state of exposure to evil; *law,* to take by forcible or illegal means from lawful custody.—*n.* The act of rescuing; deliverance from restraint or danger; *law,* a forcible taking out of the custody of the law.—**rescuer,** res'kū•ėr, *n.* One that rescues.

research, ri•sėrch', *n.* [Prefix *re,* and *search;* Fr. *recherche.*] Diligent inquiry or examination in seeking facts or principles; laborious or continued search after truth; investigation.—*v.t.* To search again; to examine anew.—**researcher,** ri•sėr'chėr, *n.* One engaged in research.

reseat, rē•sēt', *v.t.* To seat or set again; to furnish with a new seat or seats.

resect, ri•sekt', *v.t.* [L. *reseco, resectum,* to cut off—*re,* back, and *seco,* to cut.] To cut or pare off.—**resection,** ri•sek'shon, *n.* [L. *resectio.*] *Surg.* the removal of the articular extremity of a bone, or of the ends of the bones in a false articulation.

resell, rē•sel', *v.t.* To sell again.

resemble, ri•zem'bl, *v.t.—resembled, resembling.* [Fr. *ressembler—re,* and *sembler,* to seem, from L. *similare,* from *similis,* like. SIMILAR.] To be like; to have similarity to in form, figure, or qualities; to liken; to compare.—**resemblance,** ri•zem'blans, *n.* The state or quality of resembling; likeness; similarity either of external form or of qualities; something similar; a similitude.—*Resemblance, general,* in animals, a harmonizing with surroundings producing inconspicuousness. May be protective, aggressive (deceiving prey), or both. May be capable of adjustment, i.e. *variable.—Resemblance, special,* in animals, resemblance to some specific object in surroundings, causing inconspicuousness. May be protective, etc.

resend, rē•send', *v.t.* To send again.

resent, ri•zent', *v.t.* [Fr. *ressentir,* from L. *re,* and *sentio,* to feel. SENSE.] To consider as an injury or affront; to be in some degree angry or provoked at; to take ill; to show such feeling by words or acts.—*v.i.* To be indignant; to feel resentment.—**resentful,** ri•zent'ful, *a.* Inclined or apt to resent; full of resentment.—**resentfully,** ri•zent'ful•li, *adv.* In a resentful manner.—**resentment,** ri•zent'ment, *n.* The act of resenting; the feeling with which one who resents is impressed; a deep sense of injury; anger arising from a sense of wrong; strong displeasure.

reserve, ri•zėrv', *v.t.—reserved, reserving.* [Fr. *réserver,* from L. *reservo—re,* back, and *servo,* to keep. SERVE.] To keep in store for future or other use; to withhold from present use for another purpose; to keep back for a time; to withdraw.—*n.* The act of reserving or keeping back; that which is reserved or retained from present use or disposal; something in the mind withheld from disclosure; a reservation; the habit of keeping back or restraining the feelings; a certain closeness or coldness toward others; caution in personal behavior; banking capital retained in order to meet average liabilities; a body of troops kept for an exigency.—*Federal Reserve Bank,* any of the 12 Federal banks which comprise the Federal Reserve System, and operate by the authority, and under the supervision, of the Federal Reserve Board.—**reservation,** rez•ėr•vā'shon, *n.* The act of reserving or keeping back; concealment or withholding from disclosure; something not expressed, disclosed, or brought forward; a keeping over of part of the consecrated elements for the communion of the sick; a tract of the public land reserved for some special use, as for schools, the use of Indians, etc.; a reserve; the act of having reserved for oneself, in advance, accommodations in a public place, as a reservation in a hotel, bus, theater, ship, etc.—*Mental reservation,* an intentional reserving or holding back of some word or clause, the speaker thus intending to set his conscience at rest while being guilty of deceit, or to keep his real sentiments secret.—**reserved,** ri•zėrvd', *p.* and *a.* Kept for another or future use; showing reserve in behavior; distant; cold.—**reservedly,** ri•zėr'ved•li, *adv.* In a reserved manner; with reserve.—**reservist,** ri•zėr'vist, *n.* A soldier of the reserve forces of an army, navy or militia organization.

reservoir, rez'ėr•vwar, *n.* [Fr. RESERVE.] A place where anything is kept in store; a place where water is collected and kept for use; an artificial lake or pond from which pipes convey water to a town.

reset, rē•set', *v.t.* To set again (to *reset* a diamond); *printing,* to set over again, as a page of matter.—*n.* The act of resetting; *printing,* matter set over again.

resettle, rē•set'l, *v.t.* and *i.* To settle again.—**resettlement,** rē•set'l•ment, *n.* The act of resettling.

reshape, rē•shāp', *v.t.* To shape again.

reship, rē•ship', *v.t.* To ship again; to ship again what has been imported.—**reshipment,** rē•ship'ment, *n.* The act of reshipping.

reside, ri•zīd', *v.i.—resided, residing.* [Fr. *résider,* from L. *resideo—re,* and *sedeo,* to sit, to settle down. SEDATE.] To dwell permanently or for a length of time; to have one's dwelling or home; to abide continuously; to abide or be inherent, as a quality; to inhere.—**residence,** rez'i•dens, *n.* The act of residing or abiding; period of abode; the place where a person resides; a dwelling; a habitation; a mansion or dwelling house.—**residency,** rez'i•den•si, *n.* The domicile of the chief executive's governmental representative to a possession or mandated territory; a territory in a protected state governed by a resident agent.—**resident,** rez'i•dent, *a.* [L. *residens, residentis.*] Dwelling or having an abode in a place for a continuance of time; residing.—*n.* One who resides or dwells in a place for some time; one residing; a public minister who resides at a foreign court; a kind of ambassador.—**residential,** rez•i•den'shal, *a.* Relating or pertaining to residence or to residents.—**residentiary,** rez•i•den'sher•i, *a.* Having residence.—*n.* One who is resident; an ecclesiastic who keeps a certain residence.

residue, rez'i•dū, *n.* [Fr. *résidu,* from L. *residuum,* what is left behind, from *residuus,* remaining, from *resideo.* RESIDE.] That which remains after a part is taken, separated, or dealt with in some way; that which is still over; remainder; the rest; *law,* the remainder of a testator's estate after payment of debts and legacies.—**residual,** ri•zid'ū•al, *a.* Having the character of a residue or residuum; remaining after a part is taken or dealt with.—*Residual air,* the air which remains in the chest and cannot be expelled, variously estimated at from 80 to 120 cubic inches.—**residuary,** ri•zid'ū•a•ri, *a.* Pertaining to a residue or part remaining; forming a residue or portion not dealt with.—*Residuary* *legatee*, the legatee to whom is bequeathed all that remains after deducting the debts and specific legacies.—**residuum,** re•zid′ū•um, *n.* [L.] That which is left after any process of separation or purification; a residue; the dregs or refuse; *law*, the part of an estate remaining after the payment of debts and legacies.

resign, ri•zīn′, *v.t.* [Fr. *résigner*, L. *resigno*, to resign—*re*, and *signo*, to mark, from *signum*, to sign. SIGN.] To assign or give back; to give up, as an office or post, to the person or authority that conferred it; hence, to surrender or relinquish; to give over; to withdraw, as a claim; to submit, particularly to Providence.—**resignation,** rez•ig•nā′shon, *n.* The act of resigning or giving up, as a claim, etc.; the state of being resigned or submissive; patience; quiet submission to the will of Providence; submission without discontent or repining.—**resigned,** ri•zīnd′, *p.* and *a.* Surrendered; given up; feeling resignation; submissive; patient.—**resignedly,** ri•zī′ned•li, *adv.* With resignation; submissively.

resile, ri•zil′, *v.i.*—*resiled, resiling.* [L. *resilio*, to leap or spring back—*re*, back, and *salio*, to leap. SALIENT.] To recede or withdraw from a purpose; to recoil; to return to original position.—**resilience, resiliency,** ri•zil′i•ens, ri•zil′i•en•si, *n.* The act of resiling; the act of rebounding; rebound from being elastic; the quantity of work given out by a body, such as a spring, that is compressed and then allowed to resume its former shape.—**resilient,** ri•zil′i•ent, *a.* Inclined to resile; rebounding.

resin, rez′in, *n.* [Fr. *résine*, from L. *resina*, resin. *Rosin* is the same word.] A flammable substance of sundry varieties found in most plants, and often obtained by spontaneous exudation, in some cases solid and brittle at ordinary temperatures, in others viscous or semifluid (in which case they are called *balsams*), valuable as ingredients in varnishes, and several of them used in medicine. *Rosin* is resin from coniferous trees.—*Fossil* or *mineral resins*, amber, petroleum, asphalt, bitumen, and other mineral hydrocarbons.—**resiniferous,** rez•i•nif′ėr•us, *a.* Yielding resin.—**resinous,** rez′i•nus, *a.* Pertaining to or obtained from resin; partaking of the qualities of resin; like resin.—*Resinous electricity*, negative electricity, that kind of electricity which is excited by rubbing resinous bodies with a woolen cloth, in distinction from that excited by rubbing glass, etc., which is termed *vitreous* or *positive electricity*.

resist, ri•zist′, *v.t.* [Fr. *résister*, from L. *resisto*, to withstand—*re*, and *sisto*, to place, to stand, from *sto*, to stand. STATE, STAND.] To withstand so as not to be impressed by; to form an impediment to; to oppose passively (certain bodies *resist* acids or a cutting tool); to act in opposition to; to strive or struggle against, actively.—*v.i.* To make opposition.—*n.* A sort of paste applied to calico goods to prevent color or mordant from fixing on those parts not intended to be colored.—**resistance,** ri•zis′tans, *n.* The act of resisting, whether actively or passively; a being or acting in opposition; the quality or property in matter of not yielding to force or external impression; a force acting in opposition to another force so as to destroy it, or diminish its effect; in *elect.* the property of a body that limits the strength of an electric current in it by causing part of the electrical energy to be dissipated in the form of heat, etc.: measured practically in *ohms.*—*Unit of resistance*, the standard of measurement of electric resistance; an ohm.—**resistant,** ri•zis′tant, *n.* One who or that which resists.—*a.* Making resistance; resisting.—**resister,** ri•zis′tėr, *n.* One who resists.—**resistible,** ri•zis′ti•bl, *a.* Capable of being resisted.—**resistibility,** ri•zis′ti•bil″i•ti, *n.* The quality of being resistible.—**resistless,** ri•zist′les, *a.* Incapable of being resisted or withstood; irresistible; powerless to resist (*Keats*).—**resistlessly,** ri•zist′les•li, *adv.* In a resistless manner; irresistibly.—**resistlessness,** ri•zist′les•nes, *n.*

resoluble, rez′o•lū•bl, *a.* [Fr. *résoluble.* RESOLVE.] Capable of being melted or dissolved.

resolute, rez′o•lūt, *a.* [Fr. *résolu*, pp. of *résoudre*, L. *resolvere*, to resolve. RESOLVE.] Having a fixed purpose; determined; steadfast; bold; firm.—**resolutely,** rez′o•lūt•li, *adv.* In a resolute manner; with fixed purpose; determinedly; boldly.—**resoluteness,** rez′o•lūt•nes, *n.* The quality of being resolute; unshaken firmness.—**resolution,** rez•o•lū′shon, *n.* [Fr. *résolution*, L. *resolutio.*] The character of being resolute; a resolve taken; a fixed purpose or determination of mind; the character of acting with fixed purpose; firmness; determination; a formal decision of a legislative or other body; the operation of resolving or separating the component parts of a body; the act of unraveling a perplexing question or problem; solution; *music*, the succession of a concord immediately after a discord; *med.* a removal or disappearance, as the disappearance of a tumor.—*Resolution of an equation*, in *alg.* the bringing of the unknown quantity by itself on one side, and all the known quantities on the other.—*Resolution of forces*, in *dyn.* the dividing of any single force into two or more others, which shall produce the same effect.—**resolutioner,** rez•o•lū′shon•ėr, *n.* One who joins in a resolution or declaration.

resolve, ri•zolv′, *v.t.*—*resolved, resolving.* [L. *resolvo*, to unloose, break up, dissolve, to determine, that is, to do away with (hence, to determine, that is, to do away with doubts or disputes)—*re*, back or again, and *solvo*, to loose. SOLVE.] To separate the component parts of; to reduce to constituent elements; to reduce to simple parts; to analyze; to disentangle of perplexities; to clear of difficulties (to *resolve* doubts); to explain; to fix in determination or purpose; to determine (usually in pp.); to melt; to dissolve; to form or constitute by resolution (the house *resolved* itself into a committee); to determine on; to express by resolution and vote; *med.* to disperse or remove, as an inflammation or a tumor; *math.* to solve.—*v.i.* To form an opinion or purpose; to determine; to determine by vote; to melt; to become fluid; to become separated into its component parts or into distinct principles.—*n.* That which has been resolved on; fixed purpose of mind; a settled determination; a resolution.—**resolved,** ri•zolvd′, *p.* and *a.* Having the mind made up; determined.—**resolvedly,** ri•zol′ved•li, *adv.* In a resolved manner; resolutely.—**resolvent,** ri•zol′vent, *a.* Having the power to resolve; causing solution.—*n.* That which has the power of causing solution; *med.* a discutient.—**resolver,** ri•zol′vėr, *n.* One who or that which resolves; one who determines.—**resolvability, resolvableness,** ri•zol′va•bil″i•ti, ri•zol′va•bl•nes, *n.* The property of being resolvable.—**resolvable,** ri•zol′va•bl, *a.* Capable of being resolved or separated into constituent parts; capable of being solved.

resonant, rez′o•nant, *a.* [L. *resonans, resonantis*, ppr. of *resono*—*re*, again, and *sono*, to sound. SOUND.] Capable of returning sound; resounding; full of sounds; echoing back.—**resonantly,** rez′o•nant•li, *adv.* In a resonant manner.—**resonance,** rez′o•nans, *n.* The state or quality of being resonant, the act of resounding.—**resonator,** rez′o•nā•tėr, *n.* An instrument for facilitating the analysis of compound sounds.

resort, ri•zort′, *v.i.* [O.Fr. *resortir*, Fr. *ressortir*, to go out again, to resort, from prefix *re*, and *sortir*, to go out, from L. *sortiri*, to obtain, to acquire by lot, from *sors, sortis*, lot. SORT.] To have recourse; to betake one's self (to *resort* to force); to go (to *resort* to a place); to repair frequently.—*n.* A betaking one's self; recourse; the act of visiting or frequenting; a place frequented; a haunt.

resound, ri•zound′, *v.t.* [O.E. *resoune*, from L. *resono*, to resound—*re*, again, and *sono*, to sound. SOUND.] To sound again; to echo; to extol.—*v.i.* To be filled with sound; to echo; to reverberate; to sound loudly; to be echoed; to be much mentioned.

resource, ri•sōrs′, *n.* [Fr. *ressource*, from O.Fr. *ressourdre*, to arise anew—*re*, again, and *sourdre*, L. *surgere*, to rise. SOURCE.] Any source of aid or support; an expedient; means yet untried; resort; *pl.* pecuniary means; funds; available means or capabilities of any kind.—**resourceful,** ri•sōrs′ful, *a.* Capable of utilizing resources.

respect, ri•spekt′, *v.t.* [Fr. *respecter*, from L. *respicio, respectum—re*, back, and obs. *specio*, to look. SPECIES.] To regard, heed, or consider; to have reference or regard to; to relate to; to view with some degree of reverence.—*To respect persons*, to show undue bias toward them; to be more favorable to one than to another.—*n.* [L. *respectus.*] A respecting or noticing with attention; regard; attention; a holding in high estimation or honor; the deportment which proceeds from esteem, regard, or reverence; partial or undue regard; bias (*respect* of persons); *pl.* an expression of regard, esteem, or deference (give him my *respects*); a point or particular (wrong in many *respects*); relation; reference: especially in the phrase *in* or *with respect to.*—**respectability,** ri•spek′ta•bil″i•ti, *n.* State or quality of being respectable.—**respectable,** ri•spek′ta•bl, *a.* Worthy of respect; having an honest or good reputation; belonging to a fairly good position in society; mediocre; not despicable (a *respectable* number of citizens).—**respectably,** ri•spek′ta•bli, *adv.* In a respectable manner; moderately; pretty well.—**respecter,** ri•spek′tėr, *n.* One that respects.—**respectful,** ri•spekt′fu̦l, *a.* Marked by respect; showing respect or outward regard; ceremonious.—**respectfully,** ri•spekt′fu̦l•li, *adv.* In a respectful manner; with respect.—**respectfulness,** ri•spekt′fu̦l•nes, *n.* The quality of being respectful.—**respecting,** ri•spek′ting, *ppr.* used as a *prep.* Regarding; in regard to; concerning.—**respective,** ri•spek′tiv, *a.* Relating or pertaining severally each to each; severally connected or belonging; several (our *respective* places of abode); relative; not absolute.—**respectively,** ri•spek′tiv•li, *adv.* In their respective relations; as each belongs to each.

respell, rē•spel′, *v.t.* To spell again; to spell in a new way; refers especially to spelling systems in which pronunciation is indicated.—**respelling,** rē•spel′ing, *n.* That which is respelled.

respire, ri•spīr′, *v.i.*—*respired, respiring.* [Fr. *respirer*, from L. *respiro—re*, and *spiro*, to breathe. SPIRIT.] To breathe; to inhale air into the lungs and exhale it, for the purpose of maintaining animal life; to re-recover breath; to rest, as after toil or suffering.—*v.t.* To breathe in and out, as air; to inhale and exhale; to breathe out; to send out in exhalations.—**respirable,** res′pi•ra•bl or ri•spī′ra•bl, *a.* Capable of or fit for being respired or breathed.—**respiration,** res•pi•rā′shon, *n.* [L. *respiratio.*] The act of respiring or breathing, in the higher animals performed by lungs and including inspiration or inhalation of air, and expiration or exhalation; in fishes performed by gills.—**respirator,** res′pi•rā•tėr, *n.* An appliance for breathing through, fitted to cover the mouth, or the nose and mouth, and used to exclude cold air, smoke, dust, etc.—**respiratory,** ri•spī′ra•to•ri, *a.* Pertaining to or serving for respiration.

respite, res′pit, *n.* [O.Fr. *respit*, from L. *respectus*, respect. RESPECT.] A temporary intermission of labor or suffering; prolongation of time for the payment of a debt; *law*, a reprieve; temporary suspension of the execution of an offender.—*v.t.*—*respited, respiting.* To give or grant a respite to, to reprieve.

resplendent, ri•splen′dent, *a.* [L. *resplendens, resplendentis*, ppr. of *resplendeo—re*, and *splendeo*, to shine. SPLENDID.] Very bright; shining with brilliant luster.—*Resplendent feldspar.* ADULARIA.—**resplendently,** ri•splen′dent•li, *adv.* In a resplendent manner.—**resplendence, resplendency,** ri•splen′dens,ri•splen′den•si,*n.* Brilliant luster; splendor.

respond, ri•spond′, *v.i.* [O.Fr. *respondre* (Fr. *répondre*), L. *respondeo—re*, back, and *spondeo*, to promise solemnly. SPONSOR, SPOUSE.] To make answer; to give a reply in words; to answer or reply in any way; to answer by action, to correspond; to suit.—*n.* In religious services, a short anthem or versicle chanted at intervals; a response.—**respondence, respondency,** ri•spon′dens, ri•spon′den•si, *n.* The state of being respondent; an answering.—**respondent,** ri•spon′dent, *a.* [L. *respondens, respondentis.*] Answering; conformable; corresponding.—*n.* One who responds; one who answers in a lawsuit; one who maintains a thesis in reply.—**response,** ri•spons, *n.* [L. *responsum.*] The act of responding or replying; reply; answer; an oracular answer; the answer of the congregation to the priest in the litany and other parts of divine service; a reply to an objection in formal disputation.—**responsibility,** ri•spon′si•bil″i•ti, *n.* The state of being responsible; that for which one is responsible; a trust, or the like, resting on a person; ability to answer in payment.—**responsible,** ri•spon′si•bl, *a.* Accountable; answerable; able to respond to any claim; involving responsibility.—**responsibly,** ri•spon′si•bli, *adv.* In a responsible manner.—**responsions,** ri•spon′shonz, *n.* [L. *responsio*, an answering.] The first examination which the students at Oxford are obliged to pass before they can take any degree, familiarly called *Smalls.*—**responsive,** ri•spon′siv, *a.* Answering; responding; correspondent; suited to something else.—**responsively,** ri•spon′siv•li, *adv.* In a responsive manner.—**responsiveness,** ri•spon′siv•nes, *n.*—**responsory,** ri•spon′so•ri, *a.* Containing answer.—*n.* A response; an antiphonary.

rest, rest, *n.* [A.Sax. *rest, raest*, rest, repose=Dan., Sw., and G. *rast*, D. *rust*, rest, Goth. *rasta*, a stage or place of rest on the road; root seen in Goth. *razn*, a house.] A state of quiet or repose; cessation of motion, labor, or action of any kind; freedom from everything that disquiets; peace; tranquillity; sleep; figuratively, the last sleep; death; a place of quiet; that on which anything leans for support; an article or appliance for support; *music*, an interval of silence between one sound and another, or the mark or character denoting the interval.—*v.i.* [A.Sax. *restan*, to rest.] To cease from action, motion, or work of any kind; to stop; to be free from whatever harasses or disturbs; to be quiet or still; to lie for repose; to sleep the final sleep; to die; to stand for support; to be supported; to be fixed in any state or opinion (to *rest* content); to rely (to *rest* on a man's promise); to be in a certain state or position, as an affair.—*To rest with*, to be in the power of; to depend upon (it *rests with* time to decide).—*v.t.* To lay at rest; to give rest or repose to; to quiet; to lay or place, as on a support.—*To rest one's self*, to take rest.—**restful,** rest′fu̦l, *a.* Full of rest; giving rest; quiet; being at rest.—**restfully,** rest′fu̦l•li, *adv.* In a state of rest or quiet.—**restfulness,** rest′fu̦l•nes, *n.* State of being restful.—**restless,** rest′les, *a.* Unresting; unquiet; continually moving; being without rest; unable to sleep; passed in unquietness; not satisfied to be at rest; unsettled; turbulent.—**restlessly,** rest′les•li, *adv.* In a restless manner; unquietly.—**restlessness,** rest′les•nes, *n.* Agitation; a state of disturbance or agitation of body or mind; inability to sleep or rest.

rest, rest, *n.* [Fr. *reste*, from *rester*, to rest, to remain, from L. *resto—re*, back, and *sto*, to stand. STATE.] That which is left after the separation of a part, either in fact or in contemplation: used with *the*; the remainder; the others; those not before included (in this sense plural); a surplus fund held in reserve by a bank, or other such company, to fall back upon in any great emergency.—*v.i.* [Fr. *rester.*] To be left; to remain; to continue to be.

restate, rē•stāt′, *v.t.* To state again.

restaurant, res′to•rant, *n.* [Fr.] A commercial establishment for the sale of refreshments; an eating-house.—**restaurateur,** res•tō′ra•tėr, *n.* [Fr.] The keeper of a restaurant.

restharrow, rest′har•ō, *n.* [For *arrestharrow.*] A European leguminous plant with pink flowers and long woody, tough roots, that arrest the harrow's prongs.

restiform, res′ti•form, *a.* [L. *restis*, a cord, and *forma*, form.] In the form of a cord.

restitution, res•ti•tū′shon, *n.* [L. *restitutio, restitutionis*, from *restituo*, to set up again—*re*, and *statuo*, to set. STATUTE.] The restoring of what is lost or taken away, especially taken away unjustly; amends; indemnification.

restive, res′tiv, *a.* [O.Fr. *restif*, drawing backward, refusing to go forward, from *rester*, L. *restare*, to stay back, to remain. REST (to remain).] Unwilling to go forward‡; refusing to rest or stand still; constantly fidgeting or moving about:

said of horses; hence, impatient under restraint or opposition: applied to persons.—**restively,** res′-tiv•li, *adv.* In a restive manner.—**restiveness,** res′tiv•nes, *n.*

restore, ri•stōr′, *v.t.*—*restored, restoring.* [O.Fr. *restorer* (Fr. *restaurer*), to restore, repair, reinstall, from L. *restauro,* to restore, to repair—*re,* again, and *stauro,* to make strong. STORE.] To bring back to a former and better state; to repair; to rebuild; to heal; to cure; to revive; to re-establish after interruption (to *restore* peace); to give back; to return after having been taken away; to bring or put back to a former position; to recover or renew, as passages of an author defective or corrupted; *fine arts,* to bring back from a state of injury or decay (to *restore* a painting); to complete by adding the defective parts.—**restoration,** res•to•rā′shon, *n.* The act of restoring; replacement; renewal; re-establishment; the repairing of injuries suffered by works of art, buildings, etc.; recovery of health.—*The Restoration,* the return of King Charles II in 1660, and the re-establishment of the English monarchy. In French history the terms *first* and *second Restoration* are respectively applied to the return of the Bourbons after Napoleon's abdication and after Waterloo.—**restorative,** ri•stō′ra•tiv, *a.* Capable of restoring strength, vigor, etc.—*n.* A medicine efficacious in restoring strength and vigor.—**restorer,** ri•stō′rėr, *n.* One who restores.

restrain, ri•strān′, *v.t.* [O.Fr. *restraindre* (Fr. *restreindre*), from L. *restringo*—*re,* back, and *stringo,* to draw tight. STRAIN.] To hold back; to hold in; to check; to hold from action; to repress; to restrict.—**restrainable,** ri•strā′na•bl, *a.* Capable of being restrained.—**restrainedly,** ri•strā′ned•li, *adv.* With restraint; with limitation.—**restrainer,** ri•strā′nėr, *n.* One who or that which restrains.—**restraint,** ri•strānt′, *n.* The act of restraining; a holding back or hindering from motion in any manner; hindrance of the will; a check to any tendency; abridgment of liberty; confinement; detention; that which restrains or hinders; a limitation.

restrict, ri•strikt′, *v.t.* [L. *restringo, restrictum*—*re,* back, and *stringo.* RESTRAIN.] To limit; to confine; to restrain within bounds.—**restriction,** ri•strik′shon, *n.* The act of restricting, or state of being restricted; that which restricts; a restraint; reservation.—**restrictive,** ri•strik′tiv, *a.* Having the quality of limiting or expressing limitation; imposing restraint.—**restrictively,** ri•strik′tiv•li, *adv.* In a restrictive manner; with limitation.

result, ri•zult′, *v.i.* [Fr. *résulter,* to result, originally to rebound, from L. *resulto,* to rebound, from *resilio*—*re,* back, and *salio,* to leap. RESILE.] To proceed, spring, or rise, as a consequence, from facts, arguments, premises, combination of circumstances, etc.; to ensue; to accrue; to have an issue; to terminate: followed by *in* (this measure will *result in* good or evil).—*Resulting force.* RESULTANT.—*n.* Consequence; conclusion; outcome; issue; effect; product; that which proceeds naturally or logically from facts, premises, or the state of things.—**resultant,** ri•zult′ant, *a.* Following as a result or consequence; resulting from the combination of two or more agents. —*n. Physics,* the force which results from the composition of two or more forces acting upon a body; the single force, velocity, acceleration, etc., to which several forces, velocities, accelerations, etc., are together equivalent.

résumé, rā′zū•mā, *n.* [Fr. RESUME.] A summing up; a recapitulation; a condensed statement; a summary.

resume, ri•zūm′, *v.t.*—*resumed, resuming.* [Fr. *résumer,* from L. *resumo*—*re,* and *sumo,* to take (as in *assume, consume,* etc.). SUMPTUOUS.] To take again; to take back; to take up again after interruption; to begin again.—**resumption,** ri•zum′shon, *n.* The act of resuming, taking back, or taking again.

resummon, rē•sum′on, *v.t.* To summon or call again; to recall; to recover.

resupinate, resupinated, ri•sū′pi•nāt, ri•sū′pi•nā•ted, *a.* [L. *resupinatus*—*re,* and *supinus,* lying on the back, supine.] Inverted; reversed; appearing as if turned upside down. —**resupination,** ri•sū′pi•nā″shon, *n.* The state of being resupinate or reversed.—**resupine,** rē•sū•pīn′, *a.* Lying on the back.

resurge,† ri•sėrj′, *v.i.* [L. *resurgo*—*re,* again, and *surgo,* to rise.] To rise again; to reappear, as from the dead. —**resurgence,** ri•sėr′jens, *n.* The act of rising again; resurrection.—**resurgent,** ri•sėr′jent, *a.* Rising again or from the dead.

resurrect, rez′ėr•rekt′, *v.t.* To raise from the dead; to restore to life or use.—**resurrection,** rez•ėr•rek′shon, *n.* [L. *resurrectio,* from *resurgo, resurrectum*—*re,* again, and *surgo,* to arise. SOURCE.] A rising again to life; [*cap.*] the rising of Christ after the Crucifixion.—**resurrectionist,** rez•ėr•rek′-shon•ist, *n.* One who steals bodies from the grave for dissection.

resurvey, rē•sėr•vā′, *v.t.* To survey again or anew; to review.—*n.* (rē•sėr′vā). A new survey.

resuscitate, ri•sus′i•tāt, *v.t.*—*resuscitated, resuscitating.* [L. *resuscito, resuscitatum*—*re,* again, and *suscito,* to rouse up—*sub,* and *cito,* to rouse, to summon, to cite. CITE.] To stir up anew; to revivify; to revive; particularly, to recover from apparent death.—*v.i.* To revive; to come to life again.—**resuscitable,** ri•sus′i•ta•bl, *a.* Capable of being resuscitated.—**resuscitation,** ri•sus′i•tā″-shon, *n.* The act of resuscitating; revivification; the restoring to animation of persons apparently dead.—**resuscitative,** ri•sus′i•tā•tiv, *a.* Tending to resuscitate.—**resuscitator,** ri•sus′i•tā•tėr, *n.* One who resuscitates.

ret, ret, *v.t.*—*retted, retting.* [D. *reten;* to ret flax; allied to *rot.*] To steep or macerate flax in water, in order to separate the fiber by incipient rotting.

retable, ri•tā′bl, *n.* [For *rear-table.*] *Arch.* a shelf or ledge behind an altar for holding candles or vases.

retail, rē′tāl, *v.t.* [Fr. *retail,* a piece cut off—*re,* again, and *tailler,* to cut, from L.L. *talea, talia,* a tally, L. *talea,* a stick (hence also *tailor, tally*). *Retail* is thus to sell by pieces cut off.] To sell in small quantities, or by the piece, in contradistinction to selling wholesale; to dispense in small quantities; to repeat a story to many persons.—*v.i.* To sell at retail, as, the coat *retails* for $50.—*n.* The sale of goods in small quantities.—*a.* Concerning the sale of anything in small quantities, as, a *retail* merchant, *retail* trade, etc.—**retailer,** ri•tāl′ėr, *n.* One who engages in retail trade.

retain, ri•tān′, *v.t.* [Fr. *retenir,* L. *retineo*—*re,* back, and *teneo,* to hold. TENANT.] To hold or keep in possession; to keep from departure or escape; to detain; to keep; not to lose or part with; to engage by the payment of a preliminary fee (to *retain* counsel).—**retainable,** ri•tā′na•bl, *a.* Capable of being retained.—**retainer,** ri•tā′nėr, *n.* One who or that which retains; one who is kept in service; a dependent; a servant, not a domestic; *law,* a preliminary fee given to counsel to secure their services or prevent their being secured by others; a retaining fee.—**retaining,** ri•tā′ning, *p.* and *a.* Keeping in possession; serving to retain.—*Retaining fee,* a retainer.—*Retaining wall,* a wall that is built to retain a bank of earth from slipping down; a revetment.—**retainment,** ri•tān′-ment, *n.* The act of retaining; retention.

retake, rē•tāk′, *v.t.* To take again; to recapture.

retaliate, ri•tal′i•āt, *v.t.*—*retaliated, retaliating.* [L. *retalio, retaliatum,* to retaliate—*re,* in return, and noun *talio,* like for like, retaliation, from *talis,* such.] To return the like for (to *retaliate* injuries or wrongs); to pay or requite by an act of the same kind as has been received, in a bad sense; that is, to return evil for evil. —*v.i.* To return like for like; to do injuries in return for injuries.—**retaliation,** ri•tal′i•ā″shon, *n.* The act of retaliating; the return of like for like; requital of evil by evil; reprisal; revenge.—**retaliative, retaliatory,** ri•tal′i•a•tiv, ri•tal′i•a•to•ri, *a.* Returning like for like; consisting in retaliation.

retard, ri•tärd′, *v.t.* [Fr. *retarder,* from L. *retardo*—*re,* and *tardo,* to delay, from *tardus,* slow. TARDY.] To obstruct in swiftness of course; to keep delaying; to impede; to clog; to hinder.—*n.* Retardation.—**retardation,** rē•tär•dā′shon, *n.* The act of retarding or delaying; *physics,* the act of hindering the free progress or velocity of a body; that which retards; an obstruction.—**retarder,** ri•tär′dėr, *n.* One that retards.—

retardment, ri•tärd′ment, *n.* The act of retarding.

retch, rech, *v.i.* [A.Sax. *hraecan,* to retch, to hawk; allied to *hraca,* the throat, a cough; Icel. *hraekja,* to spit, *hráki,* spittle.] To make an effort to vomit; to strain, as in vomiting.

retell, rē•tel′, *v.t.* To tell again.

retention, ri•ten′shon, *n.* [L. *retentio, retentionis,* from *retineo, retentum.* RETAIN.] The act of retaining or power of retaining; the faculty of remembering; power of memory; *med.* a morbid accumulation of matter in the body that should be evacuated.—**retentive,** ri•ten′tiv, *a.* Characterized by retention; having strong power of recollecting.—**retentiveness,** ri•ten′tiv•nes, *n.* The quality of being retentive.

retiary, rē′shi•e•ri, *a.* [From L. *rete,* a net.] Netlike; constructing or using a net or web to catch prey (*retiary* spiders).

reticence, reticency, ret′i•sens, ret′i•sen•si, *n.* [Fr. *réticence,* from L. *reticentia,* from *reticeo,* to be silent again—*re,* and *taceo,* to be silent. TACIT.] The quality of observing studied and continued silence; a refraining from talking; the keeping of one's counsel.—**reticent,** ret′i•sent, *a.* Having a disposition to be silent; reserved; not apt to speak about or reveal any matters.

reticular, ri•tik′ū•lėr, *a.* [L. *reticulum,* dim. of *rete,* a net.] Having the form of a net or of network; formed with interstices.—**reticulate,** re•tik′ū•lāt, *a.* [L. *reticulatus,* from *reticulum.*] Netted; resembling network; having distinct lines or veins crossing like network.—**reticulation,** ri•tik′ū•lā″shon, *n.* That which is reticulated; network; organization of substances resembling a net.—**reticule,** ret′i•kūl, *n.* [Fr. *réticule,* L. *reticulum,* dim. of *rete,* a net.] A kind of bag, formerly of network, but now of every description of materials, used by ladies for carrying in the hand; a micrometer attached to a telescope, having a network of fine fibers crossing at right angles.—**reticulum,** ri•tik′ū•lum, *n.* [L.] The honeycomb bag, or second cavity of the complex stomach of ruminants.

retiform, ret′i•form, *a.* [L. *retiformis*—*rete,* a net, and *forma,* form.] Having the form of a net in texture; composed of crossing lines and interstices.

retina, ret′i•na, *n.* [From L. *rete,* a net.] A membrane lining the interior of the eye behind, being a reticular expansion of the optic nerve, which receives the impressions from external objects.—**retinal,** ret′i•nal, *a.* Pertaining to the retina.—**retinitis,** ret•i•nī′tis, *n.* Inflammation of the retina.—**retinoscopy,** ret•i•nos′ko•pi, *n.* Examination of the retina.

retinite, ret′i•nīt, *n.* [Fr. *rétinite,* from Gr. *rētinē,* resin.] A translucent fossil resin; pitchstone.

retinue, ret′i•nū, *n.* [O.Fr. *retenue,* from *retenir,* to retain. RETAIN.] The attendants of a prince or other distinguished personage, chiefly on a journey or an excursion; a train of persons; a suite; a cortège.

retire, ri•tīr′, *v.i.*—*retired, retiring.* [Fr. *retirer*—*re,* back, and *tirer,* to draw, a word of Teutonic origin = Goth. *tairan,* E. to *tear.*] To withdraw; to go back; to draw back; to go from company or from a public place into privacy; to retreat from action or danger (to *retire* from battle); to withdraw from business or active life; to recede; to be bent or turned back (the shore *retires* to form a bay).—*v.t.* To designate as being no longer qualified for active service (to *retire* a military officer); to withdraw from circulation by taking up and paying (to *retire* a bill).—**retired,** ri•tīrd′, *p.* and *a.* Secluded from much society or from public notice; apart from public view (a *retired* life, a *retired* locality); private; secret; withdrawn from business or active life; having given up business (a *retired* merchant); given to seclusion; inclining to retirement.—*Retired list,* a list on which superannuated and deserving naval or military officers are placed.—**retirement,** ri•tīr′ment, *n.* The act of retiring; state of living a retired life; seclusion; privacy; retired or private abode.—**retiring,** ri•tī′ring, *p.* and *a.* Withdrawing; retreating; reserved; not forward or obtrusive; granted to or suitable for one who retires, as from public employment or service (a *retiring* allowance).

retort, ri•tort′, *v.t.* [L. *retorqueo, retortum,* to fling or cast back, to retort—*re,* back, and *torqueo, tortum,* to twist. TORTURE.] To return, as an argument, accusation, censure, or incivility (to *retort* the charge of vanity); to bend or curve back (a *retorted* line).—*v.i.* To return an argument or charge; to make a severe reply; to curl or curve back, as a line.—*n.* [The vessel is named from the neck being bent back or retorted.] A censure or incivility returned; a severe reply; a repartee; a flask-shaped vessel, to which a long neck is attached, employed for the purpose of distilling or effecting decomposition by the aid of heat; also applied to almost any apparatus in which solid substances, such as coal, wood, bones, etc., are submitted to destructive distillation (as *retorts* for producing coal gas).

retouch, rē•tuch′, *v.t.* To touch or touch up again; to improve by new touches; to revise.—*n.* A repeated touch; a revisal.

retrace, rē•trās′, *v.t.* [Prefix *re,* back, and *trace;* Fr. *retracer.*] To trace or track back; to go over again in the reverse direction.—**retraceable,** rē•trā′sa•bl, *a.* Capable of being retraced.

retract, ri•trakt′, *v.t.* [Fr. *rétracter,* from L. *retracto,* freq. of *retraho, retractum*—*re,* back, and *traho,* to draw. TRACT.] To draw back; to draw in (to *retract* the claws); to rescind; to withdraw, as a declaration, words, or saying; to disavow; to recant.—*v.i.* To take back statements; to unsay one's words.—**retractable,** ri•trak′ta•bl, *a.* Capable of being retracted.—**retraction,** ri•trak′shon, *n.* The act of retracting or drawing back; the act of recalling what has been said; recantation.—**retractile,** ri•trak′til, *a.* Capable of being drawn back.—**retractive,** ri•trak′tiv, *a.* Tending or serving to retract.—**retractor,** ri•trak′tėr, *n.* One who retracts; that which retracts or draws back; a muscle that draws back some part.

retreat, ri•trēt′, *n.* [Fr. *retraite,* from *retraire,* to withdraw, from L. *retrahere.* RETRACT.] The act of retiring; a withdrawing from any place; state of privacy or seclusion; place of retirement or privacy; a refuge; a place of safety or security; a military operation, either forced or strategical, by which troops retire before an enemy; a period of retirement with a view to self-examination, meditation, and special prayer.—*v.i.* To make a retreat; to retire from any position or place; to withdraw; to take shelter; to retire before an enemy.

retrench, ri•trensh′, *v.t.* [O.Fr. *retrencher* (Fr. *retrancher*)—*re,* and *trancher,* to cut. TRENCH.] To cut off, abridge, or curtail; to limit or restrict; *milit.* to furnish with a retrenchment.—*v.i.* To live at less expense; to practice economy.—**retrenchment,** ri•trensh′ment, *n.* The removing of what is superfluous; the act of curtailing or lessening; *milit.* an interior rampart cutting off a portion of a fortress from the rest, and to which a garrison may retreat.

retribute,† ret′ri•būt, *v.t.*—*retributed, retributing.* [L. *retribuo, retributum*—*re,* back, and *tribuo,* to assign, bestow. TRIBUTE.] To pay back; to requite; to compensate.—**retribution,** ret•ri•bū′shon, *n.* The act of requiting actions, whether good or bad; a reward, recompense, or requital; especially, a requital or punishment for wrong or evil done; evil justly befalling the perpetrator of evil; the distribution of rewards and punishments in a future life.—**retributive, retributory,** ri•trib′ū•tiv, ri•trib′ū•to•ri, *a.* Making retribution; rewarding for good deeds and punishing for offenses.

retrieve, ri•trēv′, *v.t.*—*retrieved, retrieving.* [Fr. *retrouver,* O.Fr. *retreuver,* to find again, to recover—*re,* again, and *trouver,* to find. TROVER.] To get again; to regain; to recover; to restore from loss or injury (to *retrieve* the credit of a nation); to make amends for; to repair.—**retrievable,** ri•trē′va•bl, *a.* Capable of being retrieved or recovered.—**retrieval,** ri•trē′val, *n.* Act of retrieving.—**retriever,** ri•trē′vėr, *n.* One who retrieves; a dog that goes in quest of game which a sportsman has shot.

retroact, rē•trō•akt′ or ret′rō•akt, *v.i.* To act backward; to act in opposition or in return.—**retroaction,** rē•trō•ak′shon or ret′, *n.* Action returned; reverse action; operation on something past or preceding.—**retroactive,** rē•trō•ak′tiv or ret′, *a.* Designed to retroact; affecting what is past; retrospective.—**retroactively,** rē•-trō•ak′tiv•li or ret′, *adv.*

retrocede, rē•tro•sēd′ or ret′ro•sēd, *v.i.* [L. *retro*, back, and *cedo*, to go. CEDE.] To go back; to give place; to retire.—*v.t.* To yield or cede back. —**retrocession,** rē•tro•sesh′on or ret′, *n.* The act of retroceding.

retrochoir, rē′tro•kwīr or ret′, *n.* [Prefix *retro*, and *choir*.] That part of a church situated behind the choir, or on the other side of it from the body of the building.

retrograde, rē′tro•grād or ret′, *n.* [L. *retro*, backward, and *gradior*, *gressus*, to go. GRADE.] Going or moving backward; specifically, *astron.* appearing to move from east to west in the sky: opposed to *direct*; declining from a better to a worse state.—*v.i.*—*retrograded*, *retrograding*. To go or move backward.—**retrogradation,** rē′tro•gra•dā″shon or ret′, *n.*

retrogress, ret•rō•gres′, *v.i.* [L. *retrogradus*, from *retrogressus*, pp. of *retrogradi*, to retrograde.] To move or step backward; to revert to a former state or condition.—**retrogression,** re•trō•gresh′on, *n.* The act of going backward.—**retrogressive,** re•trō•gres′iv, *a.*—**retrogressively,** re•trō•gres′iv•li, adv.

retrorocket, re″trō•rok′et, *n.* [Prefix *retro* and *rocket*.] A rocket used to retard the speed of a spacecraft with an impulse counter to the direction of flight.

retrorse, ri•trôrs′, *a.* [L. *retrorsus*, from *retro*, backward, and *versus*, turned.] *Bot.* turned backward.—**retrorsely,** ri•trôrs′li, *adv.* In a backward direction.

retrospect, ret′ro•spekt or rēt′, *n.* [L. *retro*, back, and *specio*, to look. SPECIES.] A looking back on things past; a review of past events.—**retrospection,** ret′ro•spek′shon or rēt′, *n.* The act or faculty of looking back on things past.—**retrospective,** ret′ro•spek′tiv or rēt′, *a.* Looking back on past events; having reference to what is past; affecting things past. —**retrospectively,** ret′ro•spek′tiv•li or rēt′, *adv.* In a retrospective manner.

retroversion, ret′ro•vėr′shon or rēt′, *n.* [L. *retro*, backward, and *verto*, *versum*, to turn.] A turning or falling backward.

return, ri•tėrn′, *v.i.* [Fr. *retourner*—*re*, back, and *tourner*, to turn. TURN.] To come back; to come or go back to the same place or state; to pass back; to come again; to reappear; to recur; to answer; to retort.—*v.t.* To bring, carry, or send back; to give back; to repay; to give in recompense or requital (to *return* good for evil); to give back in reply (to *return* an answer); to cast, throw, or hurl back; to render, as an account to a superior; to report officially; to transmit; to elect as a member of parliament.—*n.* The act of returning; the act of coming or going back (the *return* of a traveler, of the seasons); the act of giving or sending back; repayment; recompense; requital; restitution; that which is returned; the profit on labor, on an investment, undertaking, adventure, or the like; an account or official or formal report; *pl.* tabulated statistics for general information; also, a name for a light-colored mild-flavored kind of tobacco.—**returnable,** ri•tėr′na•-bl, *a.* Capable of being returned; *law*, legally required to be returned or delivered.—**return ticket,** *n.* A ticket issued by a common carrier for passage to a given point and return within a specified time; a round-trip ticket.

retuse, ri•tūs′, *a.* [L. *retusus*, pp. of *retundo*—*re*, back, and *tundo*, to hammer.] *Bot.* terminating in a rounded end, the center of which is somewhat depressed.

reunion, rē•ūn′yon, *n.* A second union; union after separation or discord; an assembly or festive gathering, as of friends, associates, etc.—**reunite,** rē•ū•nīt′, *v.t.* To unite again; to join after separation; to reconcile after variance.—*v.i.* To be united again; to join and cohere again.

revaluation, rē•val′ū•ā″shon, *n.* A second valuation.—**revalue,** rē•val′ū, *v.t.* To value again.

revamp, rē•vamp′, *v.t.* To vamp or patch up again; to rehabilitate.

reveal, ri•vēl′, *v.t.* [Fr. *révéler*, from L. *revelare*, to unveil—*re*, back, and *velo*, to veil. VEIL.] To make known, as something secret or concealed; to disclose; to divulge; to lay open; to betray; to make known by divine means; to communicate by supernatural revelation.—**revealable,** ri•-vē′la•bl, *a.* Capable of being revealed. —**revealer,** ri•vē′lėr, *n.* One who or that which reveals.—**revealment,**† ri•vēl′ment, *n.* The act of revealing. —**revelation,** rev•e•lā′shon, *n.* [L. *revelatio*.] The act of revealing; that which is revealed or made known; the Apocalypse; [*cap.*] the last book of the New Testament, containing the prophecies of St. John.—**revelator,**† rev′e•lā•tėr, *n.* One who makes a revelation; a revealer.

reveille, rev•e•lē′ or rev′e•li, *n.* [From Fr. *réveiller*, to awake—L. *re*, and *vigilo*, to watch. VIGIL.] *Milit.* beat of drum, bugle call, or other signal given about daybreak to awaken soldiers.

revel, rev′el, *n.* [O.Fr. *revel*, revelry, disorder, rebellion, from *reveler*, to rebel, from L. *rebellare*, to rebel. REBEL.] A feast with loose and noisy jollity; a festivity; a merrymaking.—*v.i.*—*reveled*, *reveling*. To feast with boisterous merriment; to carouse; to indulge one's inclination or caprice; to wanton; to take one's fill of pleasure.—**reveler,** rev′el•ėr, *n.* One who revels.—**revelry,** rev′el•ri, *n.* The act of engaging in a revel; noisy festivity; clamorous jollity.

revelation. See REVEAL.

revenge, ri•venj′, *v.t.*—*revenged*, *revenging*. [O.Fr. *revenger*, *revengier* (Fr. *revancher*)—*re*, in return, and *vengier*, *venger*, to avenge, from L. *vindicare*, to vindicate. VINDICATE.] To take vengeance for or on account of; to exact satisfaction for, under a sense of wrong or injury; to exact retribution for or for the sake of; to avenge; to inflict injury for or on account of, in a spiteful, wrong, or malignant spirit, and in order to gratify one's bitter feelings. [From the use of the verb with reflexive pronouns the expression *to be revenged* often has the sense of *to revenge one's self*, to take vengeance.] —*v.i.* To take vengeance.—*n.* The act of revenging; the executing of vengeance; retaliation; the deliberate infliction of pain or injury in return for an injury received; the desire of inflicting pain on one who has done an injury.—*To give one his revenge*, to offer one a return match after he has been defeated, as at chess or billiards. ∴ *Revenge* is the carrying into effect of a bitter desire to injure an enemy for a wrong done to one's self, or those closely connected with one's self, and is a purely personal feeling. *Vengeance* involves the idea of wrathful retribution, more or less just, and may arise from no personal feeling, but may be taken solely for another's wrong. —**revengeful,** ri•venj′fu̧l, *a.* Full of revenge; harboring revenge; vindictive. — **revengefully,** ri•venj′fu̧l•li, *adv.* In a revengeful manner; by way of revenge; vindictively.—**revengefulness,** ri•venj′fu̧l•nes, *n.*—**revenger,** ri•ven′jėr, *n.* One who revenges.

revenue, rev′e•nū, *n.* [Fr. *revenu*, lit. what comes back, from *revenir*, to return.] Income derived from an investment; receipts of a government from excise, taxes, imposts and duties, etc.—**revenue collector,** *n.* A governmental agent whose function it is to collect customs and excise.

reverberate, ri•vėr′bėr•āt, *v.t.*—*reverberated*, *reverberating*. [L.L. *reverbero*, *reverberatum*—L. *re*, back, and *verbero*, to beat, from *verber*, a lash, a whip.] To return, as sound; to send back; to echo; to reflect, as heat or light; to repel from side to side (flame *reverberated* in a furnace).—*v.i.* To rebound; to be reflected, as rays of light; to echo; to resound.—**reverberant,** ri•vėr′bėr•ant, *a.* Reverberating; returning sound; resounding.—**reverberation,** ri•vėr′-bėr•ā″shon, *n.* The act of reverberating; particularly, the act of reflecting or returning sound; a sound reverberated or echoed.—**reverberative,** ri•vėr′bėr•ā•tiv, *a.* Reverberant.—**reverberator,** ri•vėr′bėr•ā•tėr, *n.* That which reverberates.—**reverberatory,** ri•vėr′bėr•a•to•ri, *a.* Producing reverberation, acting by reverberation; reverberating.—*Reverberatory furnace*, a furnace with a low roof, so that the flame in passing to the chimney is reflected down on the hearth, where the material (ores, metal, etc.) to be operated on can be heated without coming in direct contact with the fuel.

revere, ri•vēr′, *v.t.*—*revered*, *revering*. [Fr. *révérer*, L. *revereor*—*re*, and *vereor*, to feel awe of, to fear; same root as in E. *wary*.] To regard with awe mingled with respect and affection; to venerate; to reverence.—

reverence, rev′ėr•ens, *n.* A feeling of deep respect and esteem mingled with affection; awe combined with respect; veneration; an obeisance; reverend character; a reverend personage; a common title of the clergy, used with the pronouns, *his, your,* etc.—*v.t.*—*reverenced, reverencing.* To regard with reverence.—**reverend,** rev′ėr•end, *a.* [L. *reverendus,* to be revered.] Worthy of reverence; a title of respect given to clergymen or ecclesiastics, and sometimes to Jewish rabbis.—**reverent,** rev′ėr•ent, *a.* Expressing reverence or veneration; humble; impressed with reverence.—**reverential,** rev•ėr•en′shal, *a.* Proceeding from reverence, or expressing it.—**reverentially,** rev•ėr•en′shal•li, *adv.* In a reverential manner.—**reverently,** rev′ėr•ent•li, *adv.* In a reverent manner.

reverie, rev′ėr•i, *n.* [Fr. *rêverie,* from *rêver,* to dream; akin to *rave.*] A waking dream; a brown study; a loose or irregular train of thoughts occurring in musing or meditation.

reverse, ri•vėrs′, *v.t.*—*reversed, reversing.* [L. *revertor, reversus*—*re,* back, and *verto,* to turn. VERSE.] To turn or put in an opposite or contrary direction or position; to turn upside down; to alter to the opposite; to make quite the contrary, or have contrary bearings or relations; to make void; to annul, repeal, revoke (to *reverse* a judgment or decree); *mach.* to cause to revolve in a contrary direction; to change the motion of.—*n.* The side presented when anything is turned in a direction opposite to its natural position; a complete change or turn of affairs: generally in a bad sense; a change for the worse; a misfortune; a cessation of success; a check; a defeat; a backhanded stroke in fencing (*Shak.*); that which is directly opposite or contrary; the contrary; the opposite (with *the*); the back or undersurface, as of a leaf or of a coin (OBVERSE).—*a.* Opposite; turned backward; having a contrary or opposite direction.—*Reverse curve,* a double curve formed of two curves in opposite directions, like the letter S.—**reversal,** ri•vėr′sal, *n.* The act of reversing.—**reversely,** ri•vėrs′li, *adv.* In a reverse manner; on the opposite.—**reverser,** ri•vėr′sėr, *n.* One who reverses.—**reversibility,** ri•vėr′si•bil″i•ti, *n.* The quality of being reversible; the capability of being reversed.—**reversible,** ri•vėr′si•bl, *n.* Capable of being reversed; capable of being turned outside in.—**reversibly,** ri•vėr′si•bli, *adv.* In a reversible manner.—**reversion,** ri•vėr′zhon, *n.* [L. *reversio.*] A reverting or returning; succession to a post or office after the present holder's term; *biol.* a return toward some ancestral type or character; atavism; *law,* the returning of an estate to the grantor or his heirs; a remainder.—**reversionary,** ri•vėr′zhon•e•ri, *a.* Involving or pertaining to a reversion.—**reversioner,** ri•vėr′zhon•ėr, *n.* One who has a reversion.—**revert,** ri•vėrt′, *v.t.* [L. *reverto*—*re,* back, and *verto,* to turn.] To turn or direct back; to reverse; to repel.—*v.i.* To return or come back to a former position; to turn back; to turn to something spoken of before; to go back to a former condition; *law,* to return to the possession of the donor, or of the former proprietor.—**revertible,** ri•vėr′ti•bl, *a.* Capable of being reverted or returned.

revest, rē•vest′, *v.t.* To reinvest; to vest again with possession or office.—*v.i.* To revert or return to a former owner.

revet, ri•vet′, *v.t.* revetted, *revetting.* [Fr. *revêtir,* to reclothe; L.L. *revestio*—L. *re,* again, and *vestio,* to clothe.] *Fort.* and *civil engin.* to face, as an embankment, with masonry or other material.—**revetment,** ri•vet′ment, *n. Fort.* a facing to a wall or bank, as of a scarp or parapet; *civil engin.* a retaining or breast wall.

revictual, rē•vit′l, *v.t.* To victual again; to furnish again with provisions.

review, ri•vū′, *v.t.* [Prefix *re,* again, and *view.*] To view or behold again; to revise; to notice critically; to write a critical notice of, after an examination in order to discover excellences or defects (to *review* a newly published book); to inspect; to make a formal or official examination of the state of, as of troops (to *review* a regiment); to look back on.—*n.* A second or repeated view; a reexamination; a critical examination of a new publication, with remarks; a criticism; a critique; the name given to certain periodical publications, consisting of essays, with critical examinations of new publications; an official inspection of military or naval forces, which may be accompanied by maneuvers and evolutions.—*v.i.* To make reviews; to be a reviewer (he *reviews* for the *Times*).—**reviewable,** ri•vū′a•bl, *a.* Capable of being reviewed.—**reviewer,** ri•vū′ėr, *n.* One that reviews; a writer in a review; one who critically examines a new publication.

revile, ri•vīl′, *v.t.*—*reviled, reviling.* [*Re* and *vile.*] To assail with opprobrious and contemptuous language; to vilify; to speak evil of.—**revilement,** ri•vīl′ment, *n.* The act of reviling.—**reviler,** ri•vī′lėr, *n.* One who reviles.

revise, ri•vīz′, *v.t.*—*revised, revising.* [Fr. *reviser;* L. *reviso*—*re,* again, and *viso,* to look at attentively, intens. of *video, visum,* to see. VISION.] To examine or reexamine and make corrections on; to review and amend.—*Revised Standard Version,* a mid-20th century translation of the Bible.—*n. Print.* a corrected proof.—**revision,** ri•vizh′on, *n.* What is revised.—**revisionism,** ri•vizh′on•ism, *n.* Among Marxists an asserted deviation from Marxism.—**revisory,** ri•vī′zo•ri, *a.*

revisit, rē•viz′it, *v.t.* To visit again; to come to see again.—**revisitation,** rē•viz′i•tā″shon, *n.* The act of revisiting.

revitalize, rē•vī′tal•īz, *v.t.* To restore vitality to; to bring back to life.

revive, ri•vīv′, *v.i.*—*revived, reviving.* [Fr. *revivre;* L. *re,* again, and *vivo,* to live. VITAL.] To return to life; to recover life; to recover new life or vigor; to be reanimated after depression; to recover from a state of neglect, oblivion, obscurity, or depression.—*v.t.* To bring again to life; to reanimate; to raise from depression or discouragement, to quicken; to refresh; to bring again into notice or vogue (to *revive* a scheme); to renew in the mind or memory.—**reviver,** ri•vī′vėr, *n.* One who or that which revives.—**revivification,** rē•viv′i•fi•kā″shon, *n.* The act of recalling to life.—**revivify,** rē•viv′i•fī, *v.t.*—*revivified, revivifying.* [Fr. *revivifier*—L. *re,* again, *vivus,* living, *facio,* to make.] To recall to life; to give new life or vigor to.—**reviviscence, reviviscency,** rev•i•vis′ens, rev•i•vis′en•si, *n.* The state of reviving; renewal of life.—**reviviscent,** rev•i•vis′ent, *a.* [L. *reviviscens,* ppr. of *revivisco,* to come to life again.] Reviving; regaining or restoring life or action.—**revival,** ri•vī′val, *n.* The act of reviving, or the state of being revived; recovery from apparent death; return to activity from a state of languor or depression; recovery from a state of neglect; a renewed and more active attention to religion; an awakening among large numbers of men to their spiritual concerns.—**revivalism,** ri•vī′val•izm, *n.* The spirit of religious revivals; excited feeling with respect to religion.—**revivalist,** ri•vī′val•ist, *n.* One who promotes revivals of religion.

revoke, ri•vōk′, *v.t.*—*revoked, revoking.* [Fr. *révoquer,* from L. *revocare*—*re,* back, and *voco,* to call. VOICE.] To call back‡; to annul by recalling or taking back; to make void; to cancel; to repeal; to reverse.—*v.i. Card playing,* to neglect to follow suit when the player can follow.—*n. Card playing,* the act of renouncing or failing to follow suit.—**revocable,** rev′e•ka•bl, *a.* [L. *revocabilis.*] Capable of being revoked.—**revocability,** rev′e•ka•bil″i•ti, *n.* The quality of being revocable.—**revocably,** rev′e•ka•bli, *adv.* In a revocable manner.—**revocation,** rev•e•kā′shon, *n.* [L. *revocatio.*] The act of recalling, revoking, or annulling; reversal; repeal.—**revocatory,** rev′e•ka•to•ri, *a.* Tending to revoke.

revolt, ri•vōlt′, *v.i.* [Fr. *révolter,* from It. *rivoltare, revoltare,* to revolt—*re,* and *volte, volta,* a volt, bounding, turn, from L. *volvo, volutum,* to roll. REVOLVE, VOLT.] To desert or go over to the opposite side; to renounce allegiance and subjection; to rise against a government in rebellion; to rebel; to be grossly offended or disgusted: with *at.*—*v.t.* To repel; to shock.—*n.* The act of revolting; change of sides; a renunciation of allegiance and subjection to one's government; rebellion. ∴ Syn. under INSURRECTION.—**revolter,** ri•vōl′tėr, *n.* One who revolts.—**revolting,** ri•-

vōl′ting, *a.* Causing abhorrence or extreme disgust.—**revoltingly,** ri•vōl′ting•li, *adv.* In a revolting manner.

revolute, rev′o•lūt, *a.* [L. *revolutus,* from *revolvo.* REVOLVE.] Rolled or curled backward or downward; *bot.* rolled spirally back or toward the lower surface.

revolution, rev•o•lū′shon, *n.* [L. *revolutio, revolutionis,* a revolving, from *revolvo, revolutum,* to revolve. REVOLVE.] The act of revolving or rotating; rotation; the circular motion of a body on its axis; the course or motion of a body round a center; one complete circuit made by a heavenly body round a center; a cycle of time; a radical change of circumstances or of system; a sudden and violent change of government, or in the political constitution of a country, mainly brought about by internal causes; in *Amer. hist.* the Revolutionary War or War of Independence (1775-83); in *Eng. hist.* applied distinctively to the convulsion by which James II was driven from the throne in 1688; *French Revolution,* a term usually applied to the violent reaction against absolutism, which began in 1789.—**revolutionary,** rev•o•lū′shon•e•ri, *a.* Pertaining to a revolution in government; tending to produce a revolution.—*n.* A person disposed toward a revolution.—**revolutionist,** rev•o•lū′shon•ist, *n.* The favorer of a revolution.—**revolutionize,** rev•o•lū′shon•īz, *v.t.* To bring about a revolution in; to effect a complete change in.

revolve, ri•volv′, *v.i.—revolved, revolving.* [L. *revolvo—re,* again, and *volvo,* to roll (as in *convolve, devolve, evolve,* etc.). WALLOW.] To turn or roll round an axis; to rotate; to move round a center; to circle; to move in an orbit; to pass away in cycles or periods (the years *revolve*). —*v.t.* To cause to turn round; to turn over and over in the mind; to meditate on.—**revolver,** ri•vol′vėr, *n.* One who or that which revolves; a firearm (generally a pistol) having a revolving barrel or breech cylinder so constructed as to discharge several shots in quick succession without being reloaded.—**revolving,** ri•vol′ving, *p.* and *a.* Turning; moving round.—*Revolving light,* in *lighthouses,* an arrangement such that there is exhibited once in one or two minutes a light gradually increasing to full strength, and then decreasing to total darkness; or a red and a white light may be exhibited alternately.—*Revolving storm,* a cyclone.

revue, re•vū′, *n.* [Fr.] A loosely constructed and spectacular theatrical exhibition of a topical character, depending on scenic and staging effects.

revulsion, ri•vul′shon, *n.* [L. *revulsio,* from *revello, revulsum—re,* again, and *vello,* to pull.] A violent separation; a sudden and violent change of feeling; *med.* the diverting of a disease from an organ in which it seems to have taken its seat.—**revulsive,** ri•vul′siv, *a.* Having the power of revulsion.—*n.* A medicine used for the power of revulsion.

reward, ri•wạrd′, *v.t.* [O.Fr. *rewarder,* from *re* and the Teutonic word *ward=guard,* so that *reward= regard.* WARD.] To give something to in return, either good or evil; to requite: commonly in a good sense; to bestow a recompense, remuneration, or token of favor upon: when evil is returned for injury *reward* signifies to punish.—*n.* That which is given in return for good or evil done or received, especially that which is in return for good; recompense; in a bad sense, punishment or requital of evil; the fruit of men's labor or works; a sum of money offered for taking or detecting a criminal, or for the recovery of anything lost.—**rewarder,** ri•wạr′dėr, *n.* One who rewards.

reword, rē•wėrd′, *v.t.* [Prefix *re* and *word.*] To repeat a statement, using different words; to rephrase a sentence, paragraph, etc.

rewrite, rē•rīt′, *v.t.* To write a second time; to write over again.

Reynard, rā′närd. See RENARD.

rhabdomancy, rab′do•man•si, *n.* [Gr. *rhabdos,* a rod, and *manteia,* divination.] Divination by a rod or wand; the discovery of things concealed in the earth, as ores of metals and springs of water by a divining rod.

Rhadamanthine, rad•a•man′thīn, rad•a•man′tīn, *a.* [From *Rhadamanthus,* one of the three judges of the lower world among the Greeks.] Severely or rigorously just.

Rhaetian, rē′shi•an, *a.* and *n.* Pertaining to the ancient Rhaeti, or their country Rhaetia (Tyrol, Grisons); a native or inhabitant of Rhaetia.—**Rhaetic,** rē′tik, *a.* Belonging to the Rhaetian Alps; the name of strata extensively developed in the Alps, and lying between the trias and lias.—**Rhaeto-Romanic,** *n.* A Romance tongue spoken in South Switzerland.

rhapsody, rap′so•di, *n.* [Gr. *rhapsōdia,—rhaptō, rhapsō,* to sew, and *odē,* a song. ODE.] Originally, a short epic poem, or portion of a longer epic such as would be recited by a rhapsodist at one time; a spoken or written work of an ecstatic sort, depending less on logical structure than emotional appeal; a musical composition of irregular form, resembling an improvisation, usually instrumental.—**rhapsodic, rhapsodical,** rap•sod′ik, rap•sod′i•kal, *a.* Pertaining to or consisting of rhapsody. —**rhapsodically,** rap•sod′i•kal•li, *adv.* In the manner of rhapsody.—**rhapsodist,** rap′so•dist, *n.* Among the ancient Greeks one who composed, recited, or sang poems; one whose profession was to recite or sing the verses of Homer and other poets; one who utters disconnected discourse.—**rhapsodize,** rap′so•dīz, *v.i.—rhapsodized, rhapsodizing.*

rhatany, rat′a•ni. See RATANY.

rhea, rē′a, *n.* [L.] The three-toed ostrich of South America.

Rhenish, ren′ish, *a.* Pertaining to the River Rhine (*Rhenish* wine).—*n.* Rhenish wine or Rhine wine.

rhenium, rē′ni•um, *n.* [From L. *Rhenus,* Rhine.] A rare metallic element with a high melting point. Symbol, Re; at. no., 75; at. wt., 186.2.

rheometer, rē•om′et•ėr, *n.* [Gr. *rheō,* to flow, and *metron,* measure.] Another name for the electrometer or galvanometer.—**rheoscope,** rē′o•skōp, *n.* [Gr. *rheō,* and *skopeō,* to view.] An instrument by which the existence of an electric current may be ascertained.—**rheostat,** rē′o•stat, *n.* [Gr. *rheō,* and *statos,* standing.] An instrument for regulating the strength of an electric current by means of adjustable resistances.—**rheotrope,** rē′o•trōp, *n.* [Gr. *rheō,* and *tropos,* a turn.] An instrument for reversing a current. [Of these terms in *rheo-,* only *rheostat* is now in use.]

rhesus, rē′sus, *n.* [Gr.] A small monkey common in China and India.

rhetoric, ret′o•rik, *n.* [Fr. *rhétorique,* L. *rhetorica,* from Gr. *hē rhētorikē* (*technē,* art, understood), from *rhētōr,* a public speaker, from *rheō,* to speak.] The art or branch of knowledge which treats of the rules or principles underlying all effective composition whether in prose or verse; the art which teaches oratory; the rules that govern the art of speaking with propriety, elegance, and force; rhetoric exhibited in language; eloquence, especially artificial eloquence; flashy oratory; declamation.—**rhetorical,** ri•tor′i•kal, *a.* Pertaining to, exhibiting, or involving rhetoric.—**rhetorically,** ri•tor′i•kal•li, *adv.* In a rhetorical manner; according to the rules of rhetoric.—**rhetorician,** ret•o•rish′an, *n.* One who teaches the art of rhetoric; one well versed in the rules and principles of rhetoric; a declaimer.

rheum, rūm, *n.* [Gr. *rheuma,* a flowing, rheum, from *rheō,* to flow.] A thin serous fluid secreted by the mucous glands, etc.; a cold.—**rheumy,** rū′mi, *a.*—**rheumatism,** rū′ma•tizm, *n.* A painful inflammation affecting muscles and joints of the human body, attended by swelling and stiffness.—**rheumatic,** rū•mat′ik, *a.*—**rheumatic fever,** *n.* An inflammatory disease of the pericardium and heart valves.

Rh factor, *n.* [From *rh*esus monkey, in which it was first noticed.] A substance present in the red blood cells of most human beings that can cause antigenic transfusion reactions in persons who lack the factor.

rhinal, rī′nal, *a.* [Gr. *rhis, rhinos,* the nose.] Pertaining to the nose.—**rhinencephalic,** rī′nen•se•fal″ik, *n.* [Gr. *rhis, rhinos,* and *enkephalos,* the brain.] Pertaining to the nose and brain or to the portion of the brain from which rise the olfactory nerves.

rhinestone, rīn′stōn, *n.* [From Fr. *caillou du Rhin,* stone of the Rhine]. A colorless glass or paste stone, frequently cut to imitate diamond.

rhinitis, ri•nī′tis, *n.* [N.L. from Gr.

rhin, rhis, nose, and *itis*, suffix used to denote any malady.] An inflammation of the nose and its mucous membrane.

rhino, rī´nō, *n.* [Slang.] Money, cash; a rhinoceros.

rhinoceros, rī•nos´e•ros, *n.* [L. *rhinoceros*; Gr. *rhinokerōs*, nose-horn—*rhis, rhinos*, the nose, and *keras*, a horn.] A large ungainly hoofed animal nearly allied to the hippopotamus, the tapir, etc., having a very thick skin which is usually thrown into deep folds, and deriving its name from the nasal bones usually supporting one or two horns, composed of matter somewhat analogous to that of hair.

rhinolith, rī´no•lith, *n.* [Gr. *rhis, rhinos*, nose, *lithos*, stone.] A concretion formed in the nose.—**rhinologist**, rī•nol´o•jist, *n.* One with a special knowledge of diseases of the nose.

rhinoplastic, rī•no•plas´tik, *a.* [Gr. *rhis, rhinos*, the nose, and *plassō*, to form.] Forming a nose.—*Rhinoplastic operation*, a surgical operation for forming an artificial nose, or restoring a nose partly lost.

rhinoscope, rī´no•skōp, *n.* [Gr. *rhis, rhinos*, the nose, and *skopeō*, to view.] A small mirror for inspecting the passages of the nose.—**rhinoscopy**, rī•nos´ko•pi, *n.* Use of the rhinoscope.

rhizocarpous, rī•zo•kär´pus, *a.* [Gr. *rhiza*, a root, and *karpos*, fruit.] *Bot.* having roots that endure many years, though the stems perish annually.

rhizoid, rīz´oid, *n.* [Gr. *rhiza*, a root, *eidos*, form.] In mosses, etc., one of the hair-like structures acting as roots.

rhizome, rī´zōm or riz´om, *n.* [Gr. *rhizōma*, a root from *rhiza*, a root.] *Bot.* a stem running along the surface of the ground, or partially subterranean, sending forth shoots at its upper end and decaying at the other, as in the ferns, iris, etc.

rhizomorphous, rī•zo•mor´fus, *a.* [Gr. *rhiza*, a root, *morphē*, shape.] Rootlike in form.

rho, rō, *n.* [Gr.] The seventeenth letter of the Greek alphabet, equivalent to the English *R*.

rhodium, rō´di•um, *n.* [From Gr. *rhodon*, a rose.] A silver-white metallic element found in platinum ores. Symbol, Rh; at. no., 45; at. wt., 102.905.

rhododendron, rō•do•den´dron, *n.* [Gr. *rhododendron*, lit. rose-tree—*rhodon*, a rose, and *dendron*, a tree.] An evergreen shrub of the genus *Rhododendron* having showy rose-purple or whitish flowers and found chiefly in the North Temperate Zone.

rhomb, rhombus, rom, rom´bus, *n.* [Fr. *rhombe*, L. *rhombus*, from Gr. *rhombos*.] A quadrilateral figure whose sides are equal and the opposite sides parallel, but the angles not right angles; a figure of a diamond or lozenge form; a solid bounded by six equal and similar rhombic planes; a rhombohedron.—**rhombic**, rom´bik, *a.* Having the figure of a rhomb; in crystallography, the system of crystals having three unequal axes mutually at right angles. TRIMETRIC.—**rhombohedral**, rom•bo•hē´dral, *a.* Relating to a rhombohedron.—**rhombohedron**, rom•bo•hē´dron, *n.* [Gr. *rhombos*, and *hedra*, a side.] A solid bounded by six rhombic planes.—**rhomboid**, rom´boid, *n.* A quadrilateral figure whose opposite sides and angles are equal, but which is neither equilateral nor equiangular; a solid having a rhomboidal form.—*a.* In the form of a rhomboid; rhomboidal; diamond shaped.—**rhomboidal**, rom•boi´dal, *a.* Having the shape of a rhomboid.

rhonchus, rong´kus, *n.* [L., from Gr. *rhonchos*, a snoring sound.] *Med.* the deep snoring which accompanies inspiration in some diseases, particularly in apoplexy; stertor.—**rhonchal**, rong´kal, *a.* Pertaining to rhonchus.

rhubarb, rö´bärb, *n.* [Fr. *rhubarbe*; L.L. *rheubarbarum*; Gr. *rhēon barbaron*, from *Rha*, the river Volga, and *barbaron*, barbarian.] The common name of a large herbaceous plant which yields leaf stalks used for making sauce, pies, etc.

rhumb, rum, *n.* [From *rhomb*.] *Navig.* a line which makes any given angle with the meridian; one of the thirty-two points of the compass; a rhumb line.—**rhumb line**, *n.* *Navig.* a line described by the course of a ship sailing steadily in any one direction except toward any of the cardinal points; a loxodromic curve.

rhyme, rīm, *n.* [O.E. *ryme, rime*, from A.Sax. *rīm*, number, rhyme = Icel. *rīm*, D. *rijm*, Dan. *riim*, G. *reim*, rhyme. The proper spelling is *rime*; the *h* has been inserted by influence of L. *rhythmus*. Gr. *rhythmos*, rhythm.] A correspondence of sound in the final portions of two or more syllables, more especially the correspondence in sound of the terminating word or syllable of one line of poetry with the terminating word or syllable of another; poetry; meter; a composition in verse; a poem, especially a short one; a verse, word, or termination rhyming with another.—*Male* or *masculine rhymes*, rhymes in which only the final syllables agree, as *strain, complain*.—*Female* or *feminine rhymes*, rhymes in which the two final syllables agree, the first being accented, as *motion, potion*.—*Rhyme royal*, a stanza of seven ten-syllable lines in the formation *a b a b b c c*, possibly from its use by James I of Scotland in *The King's Quair*.—The words *rhyme* and *reason* are often used in combination and negatively to imply lack of common sense or irrational conduct; as to act without *rhyme* or *reason*, to act recklessly, or without due thought and consideration.—*v.i.*—*rhymed, rhyming*. To accord in the terminational sounds; to form a rhyme; to make verses.—*v.t.* To put into rhyme.—**rhymer**, rī´mėr, *n.* One who makes rhymes; a poor poet.—**rhymester**, rīm´stėr, *n.* A rhymer; a poor or mean poet.

rhythm, riTHm, *n.* [L. *rhythmus*, from Gr. *rhythmos*, any regularly recurring vibratory motion, from root of *rheō*, to flow.] The measure of time or movement by regularly recurring impulses, sounds, etc., as in poetry, prose composition, and music, and by analogy, dancing; periodical emphasis; numerical proportion or harmony; rhyme; meter; verse; number. — **rhythmic, rhythmical**, riTH´mik, riTH´mi•kal, *a.* Pertaining to rhythm; having rhythm.—**rhythmically**, riTH´mi•kal•li, *adv.* In a rhythmical manner. — **rhythmics**, riTH´miks, *n.* That branch of music which treats of the length of sounds and of emphasis.

riant, rī´ant, *a.* [Fr. ppr. of *rire*, to laugh.] Laughing; gay; smiling.—**riancy**, rī´an•si, *n.* Character of being riant; cheerfulness; gaiety.

rib, rib, *n.* [A.Sax. *rib, ribb* = D. *rib, ribbe*, L.G. *ribbe*, Dan. *rib*, G. *rippe*, Icel. *rif*, a rib.] One of the curved bones springing from the vertebral column and enclosing a certain number of the important organs and viscera in man and other vertebrate animals; something resembling a rib in form, use, position, etc., as one of the bent timber or metallic bars which spring from the keel, and form or strengthen the side of a ship; a piece of timber or iron supporting an arched roof, as in domes, vaults, etc.; one of the principal veins or nerves in leaves of plants; one of the rods on which the cover of an umbrella is stretched; a prominent line or rising on cloth, as in corduroy. —*v.t.*—*ribbed, ribbing*. To furnish with ribs; to plow so as to leave riblike ridges somewhat apart.—**ribbing**, rib´ing, *n.* An assemblage or arrangement of ribs, as of a vaulted ceiling, on cloth, etc.; a kind of imperfect plowing, every alternate strip only being moved.

ribald, rib´ald, *n.* [O.Fr. *ribauld, ribault, ribaud*, lecherous; It. *ribaldo*, a ribald person, from O.H.G. *hribâ, hrîpa*, a prostitute.] A low, vulgar, brutal wretch; a lewd, coarse fellow; a foul-mouthed fellow.—*a.* Low; mean; vile; obscene.—**ribaldry**, rib´ald•ri, *n.* The talk of a ribald; obscene language; indecency.

ribbon, riband, rib´on, rib´and, *n.* [O.E. *ribane, riban, ribant*, etc., from O. and Prov.Fr. *riban*, Mod.Fr. *ruban*, perhaps from the Celtic; comp. Gael. *ribean*, a ribbon, a fillet for the hair; *rib, ribe*, a hair; Ir. *ribin*, a ribbon.] A fillet of silk, satin, etc.; a narrow web of silk, satin, or other material, generally used for an ornament, or for fastening some part of female dress; what resembles a ribbon in some respects; a narrow, thin strip of anything; a shred (sails torn to *ribbons*).—*Blue ribbon* and *red ribbon*, often used to designate the orders of the Garter and Bath respectively, the badge of the former being supported by a blue ribbon, and that of the latter by a red ribbon. BLUE RIBBON.—**ribbon**, rib´on, *v.t.* To adorn or furnish with ribbons; to make into shreds.—**ribbonfish**, *n.* A fish with a lengthened body much flattened on the sides.

rice, rīs, *n.* [O.Fr. *ris*, from L. *oryza*, from Gr. *oryza*, rice; of oriental origin.] A well-known cereal plant and its seed, probably a native of India, but now cultivated in all warm climates, the grain forming a large portion of the food of the inhabitants.—**ricebird,** *n.* A bird of the United States, allied to the buntings, so named from its feeding on rice. Called also *bobolink*, and *rice-bunting*.—**rice paper,** *n.* Paper made from rice straw, used in Japan and elsewhere; also, a substance prepared from the pith of a certain plant, brought from China, where it is used for painting upon and for the manufacture of fancy and ornamental articles.

rich, rich, *a.* [Partly from A.Sax. *rice*, rich, powerful, partly from Fr. *riche*, rich, the latter being from O.H.G. *riche*, rich, which again is cog. with A.Sax. *ríce*, Icel. *ríkr*, Goth. *reiks*, rich, the root being that of E. *right*.] Having abundant material possessions; wealthy: opposed to *poor*; hence, generally, well supplied; abounding; producing ample supplies; productive; fertile; composed of valuable or costly materials or ingredients; sumptuous; highly valued; costly; abounding in nutritive or agreeable qualities; especially, as applied to articles of food and drink, sweet, luscious, or highly flavored; largely gratifying the sense of sight; vivid; bright; agreeable to the sense of hearing; sweet; mellow; abounding in humor; highly provocative of amusement (a *rich* joke).—*The rich*, as a noun, rich men.—**riches,** rich′ez, *n.* [Formerly *richesse*, from Fr. *richesse* (singular noun), from *riche*, rich.] That which makes rich; abundant possessions; wealth; affluence. This word is really in the singular number, but is very rarely so used, the apparently plural termination having caused it to be regarded as a plural.—**richly,** rich′li, *adv.* In a rich manner; with riches; opulently; abundantly; splendidly; magnificently; highly.—**richness,** rich′nes, *n.* The state or quality of being rich; opulence; productiveness; fertility; magnificence; costliness; lusciousness; brilliancy; sweetness.

rick, rik, *n.* [A.Sax. *hreác*, a rick; cog. Icel. *hraukr*, a pile, W. *crug*, Ir. *cruach*, a heap, rick.] A stack or pile of corn or hay, the lower part generally of a cylindrical form, and the top part rounded or conical, and often thatched so as to protect the pile from rain.—*v.t.* To pile up in ricks.

rickets, rik′ets, *n.* [From old *wrick*, *wrikken*, to twist; allied to *wring*, *wriggle*.] A disease of children in which there is usually some distortion of the bones, due to faulty deposition of calcium, caused by vitamin deficiency and lack of sunlight.—**rickety,** rik′et•i, *a.* Affected with rickets; feeble or imperfect in general; shaky.

rickshaw, rik′sha̤, *n.* See *Jinrikisha*.

ricochet, rik′o•shā″, *n.* [Fr.; etym. unknown.] A rebounding from a flat surface, as of a stone from water or of a cannonball from the ground.—*Ricochet fire*, the firing of guns or mortars so as to cause balls or shells to roll or bound along.—*Ricochet battery*, a battery for firing in this manner.—*v.t.* (rik•o•shā′)—*ricochetted, ricochetting*. To operate upon by ricochet firing.—*v.i.* To skim, as a stone, along the surface of water; to strike and fly onward, as a cannonball.

rid, rid, *v.t.*—*rid* or *ridded* (pret. and pp.); *ridding*. [A.Sax. *hreddan*, to take or snatch; akin to Icel. *rydja* (*rythja*), Dan. *rydde*, to clear, to remove; D. *redden*, G. *retten*, to rescue.] To free; to deliver; to clear; to disencumber (to *rid* a person *of* pain, *of* a burden); to make away with‡; to remove by violence (*Shak.*)‡.—*pp.* or *a.* Free; clear (to be *rid* of trouble).—*To get rid of*, to free one's self from.—**riddance,** rid′ans, *n.* The act of ridding; a clearing away; a getting rid of something.—*A good riddance*, fortunate relief from something disagreeable.

ridden, rid′n, pp. of *ride*.

riddle, rid′l, *n.* [A.Sax. *hridder*, a fan for winnowing; cog. O.H.G. *hrîtarâ*, a sieve; from same root as L. *cerno*, Gr. *krinō*, to separate, judge. CRITIC.] A kind of large sieve with coarse meshes, employed for separating coarser materials from finer.—*v.t.*—*riddled, riddling*. To pass through or separate with a riddle; to perforate with balls, so as to make like a riddle (a house *riddled* with shot).

riddle, rid′l, *n.* [A.Sax. *raedels*, a riddle, from *raedan*, to read, discern, guess=D. *raadsel*, G. *räthsel*, a riddle. READ.] A proposition put in obscure or ambiguous terms to puzzle or exercise the ingenuity in discovering its meaning; something to be solved by conjecture; a puzzling question; an enigma; anything ambiguous or puzzling.—*v.t.*—*riddled, riddling*. To solve; to explain; to unriddle.—*v.i.* To speak ambiguously, obscurely, or enigmatically.

ride, rīd, *v.i.*—*rode*, pret. *ridden*, pp. *riding*, ppr. [A.Sax. *ridan*, to ride=L.G. *riden*, D. *rijden*, Icel. *rida*, Dan. *ride*, G. *reiten*, O.G. *rîtan*—to ride. *Raid* and *road*, as well as *ready*, are from this stem.] To travel or be carried on the back of an animal, as on a horse; to travel or be carried in a vehicle, as in a carriage or wagon; to be borne on or in a fluid (a ship *rides* at anchor); to have ability as an equestrian.—*To ride at anchor* (*naut.*), to lie at anchor; to be anchored.—*To ride to hounds*, to ride after hounds in fox hunting.—*v.t.* To sit or be supported on, so as to be carried (to *ride* a horse); to go over in riding (he *rode* three miles); to tyrannize or domineer over (as in debt-*ridden*).—*To ride down*, to trample on, or drive over in riding; to treat with extreme roughness or insolence.—*To ride out*, to continue afloat during, and withstand the fury of, as a vessel does a gale.—*n.* An excursion on horseback or in a vehicle; a road cut in a wood or through pleasure ground, for the amusement of riding.—**ridable,** rī′da•bl, *a.* Capable of being ridden; passable on horseback.—**rider,** rī′dėr, *n.* One who rides; one who breaks or manages a horse; formerly, a commercial traveler; any addition to a manuscript, or other document, inserted after its first completion; in legislative usage, a clause added to a bill, up for passage, often having nothing to do with the bill itself; certain mechanical parts, which overlie others or move along them.—**riderless,** rī′dėr•les, *a.* Having no rider.—**riding,** rī′ding, *p.* and *a.* Employed for riding on (a *riding* horse).

ridge, rij, *n.* [Softened form of older *rygge*, *rig*, from A.Sax. *hrycg*, *hrick*, a ridge, the back=Sc. *rig*, *rigg*, a ridge of land, Icel. *hryggr*, Dan. *ryg*, Sw. *rygg*, G. *rücken*, the back.] A long and narrow elevation on the earth's surface from which the ground slopes on either side; a long crest or summit (the *ridge* of a mountain, the *ridge* of a wave); a strip of ground thrown up by a plow or left between furrows; a strip of tilled land with a furrow on either side; the highest part of the roof of a building at the meeting of the upper end of the rafters.—*v.t.*—*ridged, ridging*. To form or make into a ridge; to furnish with a ridge or ridges.—*v.i.* To rise in ridges.—**ridgepiece, ridgeplate,** *n.* A piece of timber at the ridge of a roof against which the rafters abut.—**ridgy,** rij′i, *a.* Having a ridge or ridges; rising in a ridge.

ridicule, rid′i•kūl, *n.* [Fr. *ridicule*, from L. *ridiculus*, laughable, from *rideo*, *risum*, to laugh (seen also in *deride*, *risible*).] Expression or action intended to convey contempt and excite laughter; contemptuous mockery or jesting; wit of that species which provokes contemptuous laughter; that species of writing which excites contempt with laughter.—*v.t.*—*ridiculed, ridiculing*. To treat with ridicule; to mock; to make sport or game of; to deride.—**ridiculer,** rid′i•kū•lėr, *n.* One that ridicules.—**ridiculous,** ri•dik′ū•lus, *a.* [L. *ridiculus*, *ridiculosus*.] Worthy of or fitted to excite ridicule; laughable and contemptible.—**ridiculously,** ri•dik′ū•lus•li, *adv.* In a ridiculous manner.—**ridiculousness,** ri•dik′ū•lus•nes, *n.*

ridotto, ri•dot′tō, *n.* [It., from L. *reductus*, a retreat. REDOUBT.] In Italy, an entertainment consisting of singing and dancing.

rife, rīf, *a.* [A.Sax. *rýf*, rife, prevalent =Icel. *rífr* (allied to *reifa*, to enrich), O.D. *ryf*, *rijf*, plenteous.] Prevailing; prevalent; abundant; common; supplied or filled with in large numbers or great quantity; abounding in; replete.

riffraff, rif′raf, *n.* [A reduplication of *raff*, refuse.] Sweepings; refuse of anything; the rabble.

rifle, rī′fl, *v.t.*—*rifled, rifling*. [O.Fr. *rifler*, *riffler*, to sweep away, a word of Germanic origin, the same stem being seen in *raff, raffle.*] To seize and bear away by force; to snatch away; to strip; to rob; to pillage; to plunder.—*v.i.* To rob; to pillage. —**rifler,** rī′flėr, *n.* One that rifles; one that pillages; a robber.

rifle, rī′fl, *n.* [Lit. a grooved musket, being connected with Dan. *rifle,* a groove or fluting, *rifle,* to rifle a gun, *riffel,* a rifle; G. *riefeln,* to channel, *riefe,* a groove.] A gun the inside of whose barrel is grooved, or formed with spiral channels; *pl.* a body of troops armed with rifles.—*v.t.*—*rifled, rifling.* To groove; to channel. —*Rifled arms,* firearms in which spiral grooves, taking much less than one complete turn, are cut in the surface of the bore, thus giving the projectile greater accuracy and longer range.—**rifleman,** rī′fl•man, *n.* A soldier armed with a rifle; a sharpshooter.—**rifle pit,** *n.* A pit in front of an army, fort, etc., to afford cover to a single skirmisher.

rift, rift, *n.* [From *rive;* so Dan. *rift,* a rift, a rent] A cleft; a fissure; an opening made by riving or splitting. —*v.t.* To cleave; to rive; to split.—*v.i.* To burst open; to split.

rig, rig, *v.t.*—*rigged, rigging.* [Same as Dan. *rigge,* to rig; origin doubtful.] To dress; to clothe: generally with *out,* and used only colloquially; to furnish with apparatus or tackling; *naut.* to fit with shrouds, stays, etc.—*n.* Dress, usually gay or fanciful dress; *naut.* the peculiar style of the masts, sails, and rigging of any vessel. —**rigger,** rig′ėr, *n.* One who rigs; one whose occupation is to fit the rigging of a ship.—**rigging,** rig′ing, *n.* The ropes which support the masts, extend and contract the sails, etc., of a ship.

rigadoon, rig•a•dön′, *n.* [Fr. *rigadon, rigaudon,* from *Rigaud,* the inventor of the dance.] A gay brisk dance performed by one couple.

right, rīt, *a.* [A.Sax. *riht,* right, true, just, straight=D. *regt,* G. *recht,* O.G. *reht,* Goth. *raihts,* Icel. *rettr,* Dan. *ret;* participial forms cognate with L. *rectus,* straight, pp. of *rego, rectum,* to rule, direct (REGENT, REGAL.) *Reach* and *rich* are ultimately from same root.] In conformity with the rules which ought to regulate human action; in accordance with duty, truth, and justice, or the will of God; not wrong; just; equitable; fit; suitable; proper (the *right* man in the *right* place); real; true; not spurious (the *right* heir); not erroneous; according to fact or reality; not mistaken or wrong; not in error; not left, but its opposite; originally, no doubt, most useful or dexterous (the *right* hand); hence, being on the same side as the right hand (the *right* ear or eye); most favorable or convenient; opportune; properly done, made, placed, disposed, or adjusted; correct; to be placed or worn outward (the *right* side of cloth); straight; not crooked (a *right* line); hence, *math.* rising perpendicularly; having a perpendicular axis (a *right* cone); formed by one line or direction perpendicular to another (a *right* angle).—*At right angles,* so as to form a right angle or right angles; placed or standing perpendicularly. — *Right ascension.* Under ASCENSION.—*Right bank of a river,* the bank on the right hand of a person whose face is turned in the direction in which the water runs.—*adv.* [A.Sax. *rihte,* rightly.] In a right manner; justly; properly; correctly; in a great degree; very (*right* well; used especially in titles, as *right* honorable, *right* reverend; *right* noble); in a straight line; directly.—*Right and left,* to the right and to the left; in all directions.—*n.* What is right; the opposite of wrong; rectitude; a just claim (a *right* to fair play); legal or other claim or title; a prerogative; privilege belonging to one as member of a state, society, or community (natural, political, public *rights*); that which justly belongs to one; power of action; authority; legal power (a *right* to arrest malefactors); the side opposite to the left (on the *right*).—*Right of way,* the right of passing over land not one's own; the right of the public to a road or path over a certain piece of ground.—*Bill of Rights,* the declaration delivered by the two houses of parliament to the Prince of Orange, Feb. 13, 1688, in which the rights and privileges of the people were asserted; first ten amendments of U.S. Constitution.—*By right, by rights,* rightfully; in accordance with right; properly.—*To be in the right,* to be not wrong or in error; to have justice on one's side. —*To set to rights* or *to put to rights,* to put into good order.—*In one's own right,* by absolute right (peeresses *in their own right,* that is, as opposed to peeresses by marriage).—*v.t.* To put right; to restore to the natural or proper condition; to make correct from being wrong; to do justice to; to relieve from wrong.—*v.i.* To resume a vertical position, as a ship in the water after having been listed over.—**rightabout,** *adv.* In an opposite direction: used substantively in the phrase *to send to the rightabout,* to pack off; to dismiss; to cause to retreat.—**right-angled,** *a.* Containing a right angle or right angles.—**righter,** rīt′ėr, *n.* One who sets right; one who does justice or redresses wrong.—**rightful,** rīt′fụl, *a.* Having a right or just claim according to established laws (the *rightful* heir); being by right or by just claim (one's *rightful* property); just; consonant to justice (a *rightful* cause).—**rightfully,** rīt′fụl•li, *adv.* In a rightful manner.—**rightfulness,** rīt′fụl•nes, *n.* The state of being rightful.—**right hand,** *a.* Situated on the right hand, or in a direction from the right side; applied to one who is essential to another (our *right-hand* man).—**right-handed,** *a.* Using the right hand more easily and readily than the left.—**rightly,** rīt′li, *adv.* According to right or justice; properly; fitly; suitably; according to truth or fact; not erroneously; correctly.—**rightness,** rīt′nes, *n.* The state or quality of being right; correctness; rectitude.—**right whale,** *n.* [That is, the proper one to be caught.] The common or Greenland whale, from whose mouth whalebone is obtained.

righteous, rīt′yus, *a.* [A.Sax. *rihtwis,* righteous—*riht,* right, and *wis,* wise, prudent; similarly Icel. *rétt-viss,* righteous.] Upright; virtuous; acting in accordance with the dictates of religion or morality; free from guilt or sin; agreeing with right; just; equitable.—**righteously,** rīt′yus•li, *adv.* In a righteous manner; uprightly; justly.—**righteousness,** rīt′yus•nes, *n.* The quality of being righteous; *theol.* the state of being right with God; justification.

rigid, rij′id, *a.* [Fr. *rigide,* L. *rigidus,* from *rigeō,* to be stiff or numb; allied to Gr. *rhigeo,* to shiver, *rhigos,* cold; Skr. *rij,* to be stiff.] Stiff; stiffened; not pliant; not easily bent; *physics,* theoretically such as to resist change of form when acted on by any force; strict in opinion, practice, or discipline; severe in temper; opposed to *lax* or *indulgent;* inflexible; unmitigated; severely just (a *rigid* law or rule).—**rigidity, rigidness,** ri•jid′i•ti, rij′id•nes, *n.* The quality of being rigid.—**rigidly,** rij′id•li, *adv.* In a rigid manner; stiffly; inflexibly; severely; strictly.

rigmarole, rig′ma•rōl, *n.* [A corruption of *ragman-roll.*] A succession of confused or disjointed statements; an incoherent harangue; balderdash.

rigor, rig′or, *n.* [L. *rigor,* from *rigeo,* to be stiff. RIGID.] Rigidity; severity of life; austerity; strictness; exactness without allowance, latitude, or indulgence (to enforce moral duties with *rigor*); sternness; harshness; intensity of atmospheric cold (the *rigor* of winter). *Med.* a sudden coldness, attended by a shivering preceding certain fevers; a symptom which ushers in many diseases.—*Rigor mortis,* the stiffening of the body after death.—**rigorous,** rig′or•us, *a.* Characterized by rigor; severe; stringent; scrupulously accurate; very cold (*rigorous* weather).—**rigorously,** rig′or•us•li, *adv.* In a rigorous manner.—**rigorousness,** rig′or•us•nes, *n.* The state or quality of being rigorous.—**rigorism,** rig′or•izm, *n.* Rigidity in principles or practice.—**rigorist,** rig′or•ist, *n.* A person of severe or rigid principle or manners; a purist in style.

Rig-Veda, rig•vē′da, rig•vä′da, *n.* [Sanskrit.] The chief Veda (which see) of the Hindus.

rile, rīl, *v.t.* [A form of *roil.*] To stir to anger; to irritate. (*Colloq.*)

rill, ril, *n.* [Same as L.G. *rille,* a brook, a furrow.] A small brook; a rivulet; a streamlet.—*v.i.* To run in a small stream or in streamlets.—**rillet,** ril′et, *n.* [Dim. of *rill.*] A small stream; a rivulet.

rim, rim, *n.* [A.Sax. *rima,* rim, edge, lip; perhaps a Celtic word; comp. W. *rhim,* Armor. *rim,* a rim, a border.] The border, edge, or margin of a thing; a brim; the lower part of the belly or abdomen

(*Shak.*).—*v.t.*—*rimmed*, *rimming*. To be or to form a rim round.

rime, rīm, *n.* The more correct spelling of *Rhyme*.

rime, rīm, *n.* [A.Sax. *hrím*, rime = Icel. *hrím*, D. *rijm*, Dan. *riim*, Sw. *rim*—hoarfrost.] White or hoarfrost; congealed dew or vapor.—*v.i.*—*rimed*, *riming*. To freeze or congeal into hoarfrost.—**rimy,** rī'mi, *a.* Abounding with rime; frosty.

rimose, rimous, rī'mōs, rī'mus, *a.* [L. *rimosus*, from *rima*, a fissure or crack.] Full of chinks or fissures.

rind, rīnd, *n.* [A.Sax. *rind*, *hrind*, bark, crust = G. *rinde*, rind; same root as *rim*.] The outward coat or covering of trees, fruits, animals, etc.; bark; peel; husk; skin.—*v.t.* To take the rind from.

rinderpest, rin'dėr•pest, *n.* [Gr. *rinder*, pl. of *rind*, a horned beast, and *pest*, a plague.] A most virulent and eminently contagious disease or plague, affecting ruminant animals, especially cattle.

ring, ring, *n.* [A.Sax. *hring* = Icel. *hringr*, G., D., and Sw. *ring*, a ring. Akin are *range*, *rank*, *rink*, *harangue*, etc.] Anything in the form of a circular line or hoop; a circle of gold or other material worn on the fingers; a hoop of metal or other material used for a great variety of purposes; an area in which games or sports are performed; the arena of a hippodrome or circus; the enclosure in which pugilists fight; a space in which horses are exhibited or exercised; a circular group of persons; a combination of persons for a selfish end; as for controlling the market in stocks.—*The ring, the prize ring*, a term given to pugilism or those connected with pugilism.—*Fairy ring*. See FAIRY.—*Saturn's rings*, rings surrounding and nearly in the planet's equatorial plane, probably composed of swarms of meteorites or minute satellites.—*v.t.* To encircle; to surround with a ring or as with a ring; to make a cutting circularly round (a tree or branch).—**ringbolt,** *n.* An iron bolt with an eye, to which is fitted a ring of iron, used in ships.—**ringbone,** *n.* A callus growing on the pastern of a horse.—**ringdove,** *n.* A species of pigeon (the cushat or wood pigeon), so called from a circular marking on the neck.—**ringed,** ringd, *pp.* Surrounded with, or as with, a ring; having a ring or rings; encircled.—**ringleader,** ring'lē•dėr, *n.* One who leads a ring, as of dancers‡; the leader of any association of men engaged in violation of law, or an illegal enterprise.—**ringlet,** ring'let, *n.* [Dim. of *ring*.] A curl; particularly, a curl of hair.—**ringmaster,** *n.* One who has charge of the performances in a circus ring.—**ring ouzel,** *n.* A European bird of the thrush kind, resembling the blackbird, but having a white ring or bar on the breast.—**ringworm,** ring'wėrm, *n.* A contagious skin disease appearing in the form of rings or patches on different parts of the body, but most frequently on the scalp.

ring, ring, *v.t.*—pret. *rang* or *rung*, pp. *rang*. [A.Sax. *hringan*, to ring = Dan. *ringe*, Sw. *ringa*, Icel. *hringja*, O.D. *ringhen*, to ring.] To cause to sound, as a sonorous metallic body (to *ring* a bell); to repeat often, loudly, or earnestly; to sound (to *ring* one's praises); to attend on or celebrate by ringing.—*Ringing the changes*, a trick by which, in paying or receiving money, a rascal tries to confuse the person with whom he is dealing so that he may cheat him.—*v.i.* To sound, as a bell or other sonorous body; to resound; to have the sensation of sound continued; to tingle; to be filled with report or talk (the whole town *rings* with his fame).—*n.* The sound of a bell or other sonorous body; any loud sound continued, repeated, or reverberated; characteristic sound; a chime.—**ringer,** ring'ėr, *n.* One who rings; one who rings chimes on bells.

ringent, rin'jent, *a.* [L. *ringens*, *ringentis*, from *ringor*, to make wry facer, to gape.] *Bot.* labiated, with a space between the two lips like an open mouth.

rink, ringk, *n.* [A form of *ring*, an area, or of *rank*, a row.] That portion of a sheet of ice on which the game of curling is played, also used for ice skating; the players that make up a side at the games of curling and bowling; a smooth flooring, generally under cover, on which people skate with roller skates.

rinse, rins, *v.t.*—*rinsed*, *rinsing*. [O. Fr. *rinser*, *reinser*, Fr. *rincer*, to rinse, to wash, from Icel. *hreinsa* (Dan. *rense*), from Icel. *hreinn* (= Dan. *reen*, D. and G. *rein*, Goth. *hrains*), clean.] To wash lightly; to wash by laving water over; to cleanse the inner surface of by the introduction of water or other liquid.—**rinser,** rin'sėr, *n.* One who or that which rinses.

riot, rī'ot, *n.* [O.Fr. *riote*, disturbance, combat, Fr. *rioter*, to make a disturbance; origin doubtful.] An uproar; a tumult; excessive and expensive feasting; wild and loose festivity; revelry; *law*, a tumultuous disturbance of the peace.—*To run riot*, to act or move without control or restraint; to grow wildly or in rank abundance.—*Riot act*, an act of parliament for the prevention of tumultuous disturbances, after the reading of which by a magistrate to a mob, those who do not disperse may be treated as felons.—*v.i.* To revel; to act in an unrestrained or wanton manner; to raise a riot, uproar, or sedition.—*v.t.*† To pass or spend in riot. (*Tenn.*)—**rioter,** rī'ot•ėr, *n.* One who riots or engages in a riot.—**riotous,** rī'ot•us, *a.* Indulging in riot or revelry; tumultuous; guilty of riot.

rip, rip, *v.t.*—*ripped*, *ripping*. [Same as Dan. *rippe*, ro rip, to tear; allied probably to *rive*.] To separate or divide by cutting or tearing; to tear or cut open; to take out by cutting or tearing.—*n.* A rent.—**ripsaw,** *n.* A saw used for cutting wood along the grain.—**rip tide,** the clash of opposing tides or currents.

rip, rip, *n.* [Comp. D. *rap*, scab; Dan. *ripsraps*, riffraff.] A base or worthless person; a contemptible creature; a scamp.

riparian, ri•pâ'ri•an, *a.* [L. *ripa*, a bank.] Pertaining to the bank of a body of water.

ripe, rīp, *a.* [A.Sax. *ripe*, ripe = L.G. *ripe*, D. *rijp*, G. *reif*, ripe; allied to *reap*.] Ready for reaping; brought to perfection in growth or to the best state; mature; advanced to the state of being fit for use; fully developed; maturated; complete; finished; consummate (a *ripe* scholar); ready for action or effect (*ripe* for a war).—*v.t.* and *i.* To mature; to ripen.—**ripely,** rīp'li, *adv.* In a ripe manner; maturely; at the fit time.—**ripen,** rī'pn, *v.i.* To grow ripe; to be matured, as grain or fruit; to approach or come to perfection.—*v.t.* To mature; to make ripe.—**ripeness,** rīp'nes, *n.* The state of being ripe; maturity; perfection.

riposte, ri•pōst', *n.* [Fr., from It. *riposta*.] *Fencing*, the thrust or blow with which one follows up a successful parry; hence, a smart reply or repartee.

ripple, rip'l, *v.t.*—*rippled*, *rippling*. [A non-nasalized form corresponding to *rimple*, *rumple*.] To assume or wear a ruffled surface, as water when agitated or running over a rough bottom; to make a sound as of water running over a rough bottom.—*v.t.* To fret or dimple as the surface of water.—*n.* The fretting or ruffling of the surface of water; little curling waves.—**ripplingly,** rip'ling•li, *adv.* In a rippling manner.

ripple, rip'l, *v.t.* [Dim. from *rip*; like L.G. *repeln*, G. *riffeln*, to ripple.] To clean or remove the seeds or capsules from, especially from the stalks of flax.—*n.* A large comb or hatchel for separating the seeds or capsules from flax.

riprap, rip'rap, *n.* [Same as *riffraff*, Dan. *ripsraps*.] A foundation of stones thrown together without order, as in deep water or on a soft bottom.

Ripuarian, rip'ū•â"ri•an, *a.* Of or belonging to the division of Franks, opposed to the Salic, occupying the Rhine between the Moselle and the Meuse.

rise, rīz, *v.i.*—*rose*, pret., *risen*, pp., *rising*, ppr. [A.Sax. *rísan*, to rise, pret. *rás*, rose, pp. *risen* = Icel. *rísa*, Goth. *reisan* (in *urreisan*), to rise. This is the intransitive form of which *raise* is the causal or transitive, as also *rear*.] To move or pass from a lower position to a higher; to move upward; to ascend; to mount up; to change from a sitting, lying, or kneeling posture to a standing one; to become erect; to bring a sitting or a session to an end (the House *rose* at 11 p.m.); to get out of bed; to arise; to attain a height; to stand in height (a tree *rises* to 60 feet); to reach a higher level by increase of bulk or quantity (the tide *rises*); to swell or puff up in the process of fermentation, as dough and the like; to slope upward; to have an upward direction; to seem to mount up; frequently, to appear above the horizon, as the sun, moon, stars, etc.; to become apparent; to come forth; to appear (an eruption *rises* on the skin); to become audible (there *rose* a shout); to come into existence; to be produced; to spring; to increase in force, value, intensity, degree, etc. (the wind *rises*, a price *rises*); to take up arms; to go to war; to rebel or revolt; to attain a higher social position or rank; to increase in power or interest; said of style, thought, or discourse.—*n.* The act of rising; ascent; the distance through which anything rises (a *rise* of 6 feet); elevation, or degree of ascent (a gradual *rise* in the land); spring; source; origin; beginning; appearance above the horizon (the *rise* of the sun or a star); increase; advance (a *rise* in the price of wheat); advance in rank, honor, property, or fame.—*Rise of strata*, *geol.* opposite of *dip of strata.* DIP.—**riser,** rī'zėr, *n.* One that rises; the vertical face of a step of a stair.—**rising,** rī'zing, *p.* and *a.* Increasing in wealth, power, or distinction (a *rising* man); advancing to adult years (the *rising* generation).—*n.* The act of one who or that which rises; the appearance of the sun or a star above the horizon; the act of reviving from the dead; resurrection; an insurrection; a mutiny; an eminence or prominence.

risible, riz'i•bl, *a.* [Fr. *risible*, from L. *risibilis*, from *rideo, risum*, to laugh. RIDICULOUS.] Having the faculty or power of laughing; capable of exciting laughter; laughable; belonging to the phenomenon of laughter.—**risibility,** riz•i•bil'i•ti, *n.* The quality of being risible; proneness to laugh.

risk, risk, *n.* [Fr. *risque*, from Sp. *risco*, a steep rock, from L. *reseco*, to cut off—*re*, and *seco*, to cut. SECTION.] Hazard; danger; peril; exposure to harm; *com.* the hazard of loss, either of ship, goods, or other property; the amount which may be lost, as in insurance.—*To run a risk*, to incur hazard; to encounter danger.—*v.t.* To hazard; to expose to injury or loss; to venture; to dare to undertake.—**risky,** ris'ki, *a.* Dangerous; hazardous; full of risk.

risqué, ris•kā', *a.* [Fr. pp. of risquer.] Tending toward or verging on impropriety.

ritardando, rē•tär•dan'dō, *a.* [It.] *Music*, retarding; a direction to sing or play slower and slower.

rite, rīt, *n.* [Fr. *rite*, from L. *ritus*, a rite.] A formal act of religion or other solemn duty; a religious ceremony or usage; ceremonial.—**ritual,** rit'ū•al, *a.* [L. *ritualis.*] Pertaining to rites; consisting of rites; prescribing rites (the *ritual* law).—*n.* A book containing the rites or ordinances of a church or of any special service; the manner of performing divine service; ceremonial.—**ritualism,** rit'ū•al•izm, *n.* The system of rituals or prescribed forms of religious worship; observance of prescribed forms in religion; an excessive use of external forms in religion.—**ritualist,** rit'ū•al•ist, *n.* One skilled in ritual; one of the party in favor of an elaborate ritual in the Church of England.—**ritualistic,** rit'ū•al•is"tik, *a.* Pertaining to ritualism; characterized by the practices of the ritualists in the Church of England.—**ritually,** rit'ū•al•li *adv.* By ritual; by a particular rite.

rival, rī'val, *n.* [Fr. *rival*, from L. *rivalis*, pertaining to a brook, *rivales* those who use the same brook, hence competitors, rivals; from *rivus*, a brook, whence *rivulet.*] One who is in pursuit of the same object as another; one striving to reach or obtain something which another is attempting to obtain, and which one only can possess; a competitor; one who emulates or strives to equal or exceed another in excellence.—*a.* Having the same pretensions or claims standing in competition for superiority.—*v.t.*—*rivaled, rivaling.* To stand in competition with; to strive to equal or excel; to emulate.—**rivalry,** rī'val•ri, *n.* The act of rivaling; competition, a strife or effort to obtain an object which another is pursuing; emulation. ∴ Syn. under COMPETITION.

rive, rīv, *v.t.*—pret. *rived*; pp. *rived* or *riven*; ppr. *riving* [A Scandinavian word = Icel. *rifa*, Dan. *rive*, to rive, to tear; akin perhaps to *rip.*] To split; to cleave; to rend asunder by force.—*v.i.* To be split or rent asunder.

river, riv'ėr, *n.* [Fr. *rivière*, from L.L. *riparia*, a river, from L. *riparius*, pertaining to the banks of a river, from *ripa*, a bank.] A large stream of water flowing through a certain portion of the earth's surface and discharging itself into the sea, a lake, a marsh, or into another such stream.—**river horse,** *n.* The hippopotamus.—**riverine,** riv'ėr•īn, *a.* Belonging to a river; situated on a river.—**riverside,** *n.* The bank of a river.

rivet, riv'et, *n.* [Fr. *rivet*, a clinch, a a rivet; *river*, to rivet; origin doubtful, probably from the Teutonic; comp. Icel. *rifa*, to tack together, to sew together.] A short metallic pin or bolt passing through a hole and keeping two pieces of metal (or sometimes other substances) together; especially, a short bolt or pin of wrought iron formed with a head and inserted into a hole at the junction of two pieces of metal, the point after insertion being hammered broad so as to keep the pieces closely bound together.—*v.t.* To fasten with a rivet or with rivets; to clinch; *fig.* to fasten firmly; to make firm, strong, or immovable.—**riveter,** riv'et•ėr, *n.* One who rivets.

rivulet, riv'ū•let, *n.* [L. *rivulus*, dim. of *rivus*, a river (seen also in *derive, rival*).] A small stream or brook, a streamlet.

RNA, ribonucleic acid, a nucleic acid of the ribosomes and the cell nucleus. RNA is formed along a DNA template and in turn serves as template for the building of enzymes. RNA conveys genetic information from the chromosomes to the enzymes of the cell.

roach, rōch, *n.* [A.Sax. *reohhe*; akin to D. *roch*, a skate, G. *roche*, a roach or ray.] A European fish of the carp family; also see COCKROACH.

road, rōd, *n.* [A.Sax. *rad*, a riding, a journey on horseback, a road, from *ridan*, to ride. (RIDE.) *Raid* is a collateral form.] An open way or public passage; a piece of ground appropriated for travel, forming a line of communication between one city, town or place and another for foot passengers, cattle, or vehicles; generally applied to highways and as a generic term it includes high way, street, lane, etc.; a means or way of approach or access; a place where ships may ride at anchor at some distance from the shore.—*To take the road*, set out on a journey,—**roadbed,** rōd'bed, *n.* The foundation and surfacing of a road; in railroads cross ties and rails being included.—**roadhouse,** rōd'hous, *n.* An inn; usually beside a highway.—**road metal,** *n.* Broken stones used for macadamizing roads.—**roadstead,** rōd'sted, *n.* A place where ships may ride at anchor off the shore.—**roadster,** rōd'stėr, *n.* A horse well fitted for driving; an open-top automobile with one double seat.—**roadway,** rōd'wā, *n.* A highway; the part of a road used by horses, carriages, etc.

roam, rōm, *v.i.* [O.E. *rome*, also *rame*, to roam or rove; of doubtful connections; comp. O.H.G. *râmen*, to aim, to strive. *Ramble* is from this verb.] To wander; to ramble; to rove; to walk or move about from place to place without any certain purpose or direction.—*v.t.* To range; to wander over.—*n.* Act of wandering; a ramble.—**roamer,** rō'mėr, *n.* One who roams; a vagrant.

roan, rōn, *a.* [O.Fr. *roan*, Mod.Fr. *rouan*, It. *roano, rovano*, Sp. *ruano, roano*; origin. unknown.] Applied formerly to a horse of a bay, sorrel, or dark color, with numerous spots of gray or white; now generally applied to a color having a decided shade of red.—*n.* A leather used largely in bookbinding to imitate morocco, prepared from sheepskin; a horse of a roan color; a roan color.

roar, rōr, *v.i.* [A.Sax. *rárian*, L.G. *râren*, D. *reeren*, Prov. G. *reren, rören*, to roar; akin perhaps to Dan. *röst*, Icel. *raust*, the voice.] To cry with a full, loud, continued sound; to bellow, as a beast; to cry aloud, as in distress or anger; to make a loud, continued, confused sound, as winds, waves, a multitude of people shouting together, and the like; to laugh out loudly and continuously.—*v.t.* To cry out aloud; to shout.—*n.* A full loud sound of some continuance; the strong loud cry of a beast; the loud cry of a person in distress, pain, anger; a loud, continued, confused sound; outcry of joy or mirth.—**roarer,** rō′rėr, *n.* One who or that which roars; a broken-winded horse.—**roaring,** rō′ring, *n.* A loud cry, as of a beast; a continuous roar; loud continued sound, as of the billows of the sea; a disease of the bronchial tubes in horses.—*p.* and *a.* Characterized by roars or noise; disorderly; riotous.

roast, rōst, *v.t.* [O.Fr. *rostir* (Fr. *rôtir*), to roast, from O.H.G. *rostjan*, to roast (D. *roosten*, Sw. *rosta*, Dan. *riste*), or from the Celtic; Armor. *rosta*, W. *rhostiaw*, Gael. *roist*, to roast.] To cook or prepare for the table by exposure to the direct action of heat, on a spit, in an oven, or the like; to heat to excess; to dry and parch by exposure to heat; *metal.* to burn in a heap, as broken ore, in order to free it from foreign matters; colloquially, to banter severely.—*v.i.* To become roasted or fit for eating by exposure to fire.—*n.* That which is roasted, as a piece of beef; part of a slaughtered animal selected for roasting.—*a.* Roasted (*roast* beef).—**roaster,** rōs′tėr, *n.* One who or that which roasts; a machine or contrivance for roasting; an animal for roasting.

rob, rob, *v.t.*—*robbed, robbing.* [O. Fr. *rober*, to steal, from O.H.G. *roubôn*, Goth. *raubon*, to rob, a verb akin to A.Sax. *reáfian*, E. to *reave*, D. *rooven*, G. *rauben*—to seize; the origin being O.G. *raub* (A.Sax. *reáf*), a garment, clothing, spoil. ROBE.] To plunder or strip by force or violence; to deprive of something by stealing; to deprive unlawfully; to deprive (to *rob* a person *of* his peace of mind).—**robber,** rob′ėr, *n.* One who robs; one who commits a robbery.—**robbery,** rob′ėr•i, *n.* The act or practice of robbing; a taking away by violence or wrong; the forcible and felonious taking of something from the person of another.

roband, rob′and, *n. Naut.* a robbin or rope-band. ROBBIN.

robbin, rob′in, *n.* [From *rope* and *band.*] *Naut.* a short flat plaited piece of rope, with an eye in one end, used in pairs to tie square sails to their yards.

robe, rōb, *n.* [Fr. *robe*, from L.L. *rauba*, spoil, the taking of a man's garments, from O.G. *raub*, a garment, spoil (which in primitive times consisted chiefly of articles of dress). ROB.] A kind of gown or long loose garment worn over other dress; a gown or dress of a rich, flowing, or elegant style or make; a dressed buffalo (or bison) skin with the hair on.—*The robe*, or *the long robe*, the legal profession (gentlemen of *the long robe*).—*Master of the robes*, an officer in the royal household in England, whose duty consists in ordering the sovereign's robes; under a queen this office is performed by a lady, designated *Mistress of the robes.*—*v.t.*—*robed, robing.* To clothe in a robe; to attire; to invest.

robin, rob′in, *n.* [A familiar form of *Robert*; comp. the personal names of *Mag* and *Jack* in *magpie, jackdaw.*] The well-known European bird called also *Redbreast* and *robin redbreast*; in America a species of thrush with a red breast.

roborant, rob′o•rant, *a.* [L. *roborans roborantis*, ppr. of *roboro*, to make strong, from *robur*, strength.] Strengthening.—*n.* A medicine that strengthens; a tonic.

robot, rō′bot, *n.* [Czech *robotiti*, to work.] A mechanical device almost human in its functioning; an automaton; an unthinking but efficient person.

roburite, rō′bėr•īt, *n.* [L. *robur*, strength.] An explosive substance having as its basis ammonium nitrate.

robust, rō•bust′, *a.* [L. *robustus*, from *robus*, *robur*, strength. LABOR.] Possessed of or indicating great strength; strong; lusty; sinewy; muscular; vigorous.—**robustly,** rō•bust′li, *adv.* In a robust manner; vigorously.—**robustness,** rō•bust′nes, *n.* The quality of being robust; strength; vigor.—**robustious,** rō•bust′yus, *a.* Robust; sturdy; rough; boisterous.

roc, rok, *n.* [Ar. *rukh.*] The well-known monstrous bird of Arabian mythology.

rocambole, rok′am•bōl, *n.* [Fr., from G. *rockenbollen*—*rocken*, rye, and *bollen*, a bulb, because it grows among rye.] A kind of cultivated garlic.

Rochelle-salt, rō•shel′, *n.* [From being first prepared at *Rochelle* in France.] The double tartrate of soda and potash, used as a mild cathartic.

rochet, roch′et, *n.* [Fr. *rochet*, a blouse, a little jacket, from G. *rock*, O.H.G. *roch*, O.E. *rock*, a coat.] A sort of short surplice, with tight sleeves, and open at the sides, worn by bishops.

rock, rok, *n.* [Same as Icel. *rükkr*, Dan. *rok*, Sw. *rock*, a distaff; akin to D. *rokken*, G. *rocken.*] A distaff used in spinning.

rock, rok, *v.t.* [Same as Dan. *rokke*, to move, to shake; comp. G. *rucken*, to move.] To move backward and forward as a body resting on a support beneath; to cause to reel or totter; to make to sway; to move backward and forward in a cradle, chair, etc.; to lull; to quiet, as if by rocking in a cradle.—*v.i.* To be moved backward and forward; to reel.—**rocker,** rok′ėr, *n.* One who rocks anything, as a cradle; the curving piece of wood on which a cradle or rocking chair rocks; a rocking horse; a cradle or trough for washing ore by agitation.—**rocking chair,** *n.* An armchair mounted on rockers.—**rocking horse,** *n.* A wooden horse mounted on rockers; a hobby horse.—**rockshaft,** *n. Steam engines*, a shaft that oscillates or *rocks* on its journals instead of revolving.

rock, rok, *n.* [Fr. *roc*, either from a form *rupicus*, from L. *rupes*, a rock; or of Celtic origin.] A large mass of stony matter; a large fixed stone or crag; the stony matter constituting the earth's crust, as distinguished from soil, mud, sand, gravel, clay, peat; *geol.* any natural deposit or portion of the earth's crust, whatever be its hardness or softness; *fig.* defense, means of safety; asylum; a cause or source of peril or disaster; a name for a kind of hard stick candy.—**rocky,** rok′i, *a.* Full of rocks; hard; stony; obdurate.—**rockbound,** *a.* Surrounded or hemmed in by rocks.—**rock crystal,** *n.* Crystallized quartz, found both colorless, and of various gradations of color, as yellowish white, amber, purple, etc.—**rock oil,** *n.* Petroleum,—**rock rabbit,** *n.* The hyrax or 'coney' of Scripture.—**rockrose,** *n.* The plant *Cistus.*—**rock salt,** *n.* Mineral salt; common salt found in masses or beds.

rocket, rok′et, *n.* [It. *rocchetta*, from *rocca*, a distaff, a rock; from the German.] A cylindrical tube containing combustibles that upon ignition release gases, which upon expulsion thrust the tube through the air; used in pyrotechnics, signaling, and to carry explosives; hence a type of aircraft, such as a plane or missile, using this principle.

rocket, rok′et, *n.* [Fr. *roquette*, It. *ruchetta*, from It. *ruca*, L. *eruca*, rocket.] A name applied to various plants, one of which is the common garden rocket.

rococo, ro•kō′kō, *n.* [Fr., from *roc*, rock, from rockwork being a character of the style.] A debased variety of ornament of the time of Louis XIV and XV, characterized by meaningless scrolls and conventional shellwork; sometimes applied in contempt to anything bad or tasteless in decorative art.

rod, rod, *n.* [A.Sax. *ród*, a rod or beam, a rood or cross = D. *roede*, L.G. *rood*, *rode*, G. *ruthe*, rod; allied to L. *rudis*, a wand, from same root as Skr. *ruh*, to grow. *Rood* is a form of this word.] A shoot or slender stem of any woody plant; a wand; a straight slender stick; hence, an instrument of punishment or correction; a means of chastisement; a kind of scepter or badge of office; a fishing rod; an instrument for measuring; an enchanter's wand; a measure of length containing 5½ yards, or 16½ feet, often termed a *pole* or *perch.*

rode, rōd, pret. of *ride.*

rodent, rō′dent, *a.* [L. *rodens*, *rodentis*, ppr. of *rodo*, to gnaw (seen also in *erode*, *corrode*). Same root as *rado*, to shave or scrape. RASE] Gnawing; belonging or pertaining to the order of gnawing animals (Rodentia).—*n.* An animal that gnaws, as the squirrel, rat, mouse, etc.; a mammal of this order.

rodeo, rō'de•ō, *n.* [Sp.] A cattle market place or roundup; an exhibition of lassoing, horse breaking, and steer riding.

rodomont, rod'o•mont, *n.* [Fr. *rodomont*, from It. *rodomonte*, a bully, from *Rodomonte*, the name of the brave but somewhat boastful leader of the Saracens against Charlemagne in Ariosto's *Orlando Furioso*.] A vain boaster; a bully.—**rodomontade,** rod'o•mon•täd", *n.* [Fr.] Vain boasting; empty bluster or vaunting; rant.

roe, rō, *n.* [A.Sax. *rá*, *ráh*=Icel. *rá*, Dan. *raa*, D. *ree*, G. *reh*, roe, roebuck.] A roebuck; the female of the hart.—**roebuck,** rō'buk, **roe deer,** *n.* A species of European deer with erect cylindrical branched horns, of elegant shape and remarkably nimble.

roe, rō, *n.* [Akin to Dan. *rogn*, Icel. *hrogn*, G. *rogen*, roe, spawn; Sc. *ran*, *rawn*, the female roe.] The sperm or spawn of fishes; the roe of the male being called *soft roe* or *milt*, that of the female *hard roe* or *spawn*.

rogation, rō•gā'shon, *n.* [L. *rogatio*, *rogationis*, an asking, from *rogo*, *rogatum*, to ask, seen also in *abrogate*, *derogate*, *interrogate*, *prerogative*, etc.] A supplication; a litany.—*Rogation days*, the Monday, Tuesday, and Wednesday before Ascension day, the week in which they occur being called *Rogation week*, and the Sunday preceding *Rogation Sunday*: so called from the use of special prayers for an abundant supply of the fruits of the earth; in *Roman law*, a bill before the people waiting its sanction for conversion into a law.

rogue, rōg, *n.* [Probably a Celtic word; comp. Ir. *roguire*, a rogue; Fr. *rogue*, arrogant, from Armor, *rog*, arrogant, proud.] A vagrant; a vagabond; a wandering knave; a dishonest person; a rascal: applied generally to males; a name of slight tenderness and endearment; a wag; a sly fellow.—*Rogues' gallery*, a collection of photographs, kept in police files, of known criminals.—*Rogue's march*, a tune played when a bad character is discharged with disgrace from a regiment or from a ship of war.—**roguery,** rō'gėr•i, *n.* Knavish tricks; dishonest practices; waggery; arch tricks; mischievousness.—**roguish,** rō'gish, *a.* Knavish; fraudulent; dishonest; waggish; wanton; slightly mischievous.—**roguishly,** rō'gish•li, *adv.*—**roguishness,** rō'gish•nes, *n.*

roil, roil, *v.t.* [From O.Fr. *roille* (Fr. *rouille*), rust, mildew, from L. *robigo*, rust. *Rile* is a slightly different form.] To render turbid by stirring; to annoy or anger.

roister, rois'tėr, *v.i.* [From Fr. *rustre*, a boor, from L. *rusticus*, rustic; or connected with Sc. *roust*, to roar, Icel. *rosta*, a bawl, a riot.] To bluster; to swagger; to be noisy, vaunting, or turbulent.—**roisterer,** rois'tėr•ėr, *n.* One who roisters; a blustering or turbulent fellow.

role, rōl, *n.* [Fr., a roll, scroll, character in a play, from L. *rotulus*, a wheel. ROLL.] A play or character represented by an actor; any conspicuous part or function performed by anyone, as a leading public character.

roll, rōl, *v.t.* [O.Fr. *roeler*, *roler* (Fr. *rouler*), to roll; Pr. *rolar*, *rotlar*; from L.L. *rotulare*, from L. *rotulus*, *rotula*, a little wheel, from *rota*, a wheel (whence also *rotary*, *rotate*).] To cause to revolve by turning over and over; to drive onward by turning on itself; to move in a circular direction; to whirl or wheel (to *roll* the eyes); to turn about, as in one's mind; to revolve; to wrap round on itself by turning; to bind or involve in a bandage or the like; to enwrap; to press or level with a roller.—*To roll a drum*, to beat it with rapid continuous strokes.—*v.i.* To move along a surface by revolving; to turn over and over; to rotate; to run on wheels; to move circularly; to be tossed about; to move, as waves or billows, with alternate swells and depressions; to tumble or fall over and over; to wallow; to sound with a deep prolonged sound.—*n.* The act of rolling; something made or formed by rolling; that which is rolled up; a scroll; an official document; a list of the names of persons, as of students or soldiers; a register; a catalogue; a quantity of cloth or paper wound up in a cylindrical form; a small piece of dough rolled up into a cake before baking; the beating of a drum with strokes so rapid as to produce a continued sound; a prolonged deep sound.—*Rolls of court, of parliament*, etc., the parchments on which were engrossed its acts and proceedings and which constitute its records.—*Master of the rolls*. MASTER.—**roll call,** *n.* The act of calling over a list of names, as of men who compose a military body.—**roller,** rōl'ėr, *n.* One who or that which rolls; a cylinder which turns on its axis, used for various purposes, as smoothing, crushing, spreading out, and the like, in agriculture, gardening, roadmaking, etc.; that upon which something may be rolled up; that upon which a body can be rolled or moved along; a bandage; a long broad bandage used in surgery; a long, heavy, swelling wave, such as is seen setting in upon a coast after the subsiding of a storm.—**roller skate,** *n.* A skate mounted on small wheels or rollers, and used for skating upon asphalt or other smooth flooring.—**rolling,** rōl'ing, *p.* and *a.* Revolving; making a continuous noise; undulating; rising and falling in gentle slopes (the *rolling* land of the prairies).—**rolling mill,** *n.* A combination of machinery consisting of one or more sets of rollers, between which heated metal is passed and thereby subjected to a strong pressure, to be reduced to plates, bolts, bars, etc.—**rolling pin,** *n.* A cylindrical piece of wood with a handle on each end, for rolling dough or paste to a desired thickness.—**rolling stock,** *n.* The freight cars, coaches, locomotives, etc., of a railroad.

rollick, rol'ik, *v.i.* [A sort of dim. from *roll*.] To move in a careless, swaggering manner; to be jovial in behavior; to frolic.

roly-poly, rō'li•pō•li, *n.* [A jingling name derived from *roll*.] A sheet of pastry spread with jam and rolled into a pudding; a short, plump child or person; a well-rounded thing.

Romaic, ro•mā'ik, *n.* [Mod. Gr. *Romaike*, from L. *Roma*, Rome.] The vernacular language of modern Greece; the language of the uneducated or peasantry, a corrupted form of ancient Greek.—*a.* Relating to the modern Greek vernacular.

Roman, rō'man, *a.* [L. *Romanus*, from *Roma*, Rome, the principal city of the Romans in Italy.] Pertaining to or resembling Rome or the Roman people; pertaining to or professing the Roman Catholic religion; [*now usually not cap.*] applied to the common upright letter in printing, as distinguished from *italic*, and to numerals expressed by letters, and not in the Arabic characters.—*Roman candle*, a kind of firework, consisting of a tube which discharges upward a stream of white or colored stars.—*Roman Catholic*, of or pertaining to that branch of the Christian Church of which the pope or bishop of Rome is the head; hence, a *Roman Catholic* is a member of this church; and *Roman Catholicism* is a collective term for the principles, doctrines, rules, etc., of the Roman Catholic Church.—*Roman cement*, a dark-colored hydraulic cement, which hardens very quickly, and is very durable.—*Roman law*, the civil law; the system of jurisprudence finally elaborated in the ancient Roman Empire.—*Roman order of architecture*. Same as *Composite Order*.—*n.* A native or citizen of Rome; one enjoying the privileges of a Roman citizen.—**Romanism,** rō'man•izm, *n.* The tenets of the Church of Rome.—**Romanist,** rō'man•ist, *n.* A Roman Catholic.—**Romanize,** rō'man•īz, *v.t.*—*romanized*, *romanizing*. To latinize; to convert to the Roman Catholic religion.—*v.i.* To use Latin words or idioms; to conform to Roman Catholic opinions, customs, or modes of speech.

romance, ro•mans', *n.* [Fr. *romance*, from L.L. *Romanice* (*adv.*), 'in the Roman tongue', (that is in the provincial as opposed to the classical Latin), the adverb becoming a noun signifying a composition in this tongue.] Originally, a tale in verse, written in one of the Romance dialects; hence, any popular epic or any fictitious and wonderful tale in prose or verse; a kind of novel dealing with extraordinary and often extravagant adventures, or picturing an almost purely imaginary state or society; tendency of mind toward the wonderful and mysterious; romantic notions; something belonging rather to fiction than to everyday life; a fiction; ∴ Syn. under NOVEL.—[*cap.*] *a.* A term applied to the languages which arose in the south and west of Europe, based on the Latin as spoken in the provinces, and including Italian, French, Provençal, Spanish, Portuguese, and Romanian (which are therefore known as the *Romance* languages).—*v.i. romanced, romancing.* To devise and tell fictitious stories; to deal in extravagant stories.—**romancer,** ro•man′sėr, *n.* One who romances; a writer of romance.

Romanesque, rō•man•esk′, *n.* [Fr., from L. *Romanus,* Roman.] The style of architecture between the Roman and Gothic periods, characterized by round arches and vaults and by extensive ornament.—**Romanic,** ro•man′ik, *a.* Pertaining to the Romance languages or to the races speaking any of them.

Romanism, etc. See ROMAN.

Romansh, ro•mansh′, *n.* [Lit. *Romanish,* or derived from *Rome.*] A dialect based on the Latin, spoken in the Grisons of Switzerland.

romantic, ro•man′tik, *a.* [Fr. *romantique.* ROMANCE.] Pertaining to romance or romances; partaking of romance or the marvelous; fanciful, imaginative, or ideal; extravagant; chimerical; not belonging to real life; wildly picturesque; having striking natural features; full of wild or fantastic scenery. ∴ *Romantic* is used in relation to the imagination mainly, *sentimental* to the feelings. A *sentimental* person is given to displays of exaggerated feeling; a *romantic* person indulges his imagination in the creation and contemplation of scenes of an ideal life very different from the actual.—*Romantic school,* a term applied in literature and art to writers and critics who brought about a reaction from false classicalism, and strove to represent life in its actuality.—**romantically,** ro•man′ti•kal•li, *adv.* In a romantic manner.—**romanticism,** ro•man′ti•sizm, *n.* The state or quality of being romantic; a reaction in literature or art from classical to medieval or modern forms; romantic feeling.—**romanticist,** ro•man′ti•sist, *n.* One imbued with romanticism.

Romany, Rommany, rom′a•ni, *n.* A gypsy; the language spoken by the gypsies, a dialect brought from Hindustan and allied to the Hindustani.

romaunt, ro•mạnt′, *n.* [O.Fr.] A romantic ballad; a romance. (*Archaic.*)

Romish, rōm′ish, *a.* [From *Rome.*] Belonging to the Roman Catholic Church: used with a slightly contemptuous feeling, hence not by Catholics themselves.

romp, romp, *n.* [A slightly different form of *ramp.* RAMP.] A girl who indulges in boisterous play; energetic play or frolic.—*v.i.* To play boisterously; to leap and frisk about in play.—**romper,** *n.* One who romps; a type of dress or suit worn by an infant.—**rompish,** romp′ish, *a.* Given to romp.

rondeau, ron′dō, *n.* [Fr. *rondeau,* from *rond,* round.] A poem, commonly consisting of thirteen lines, of which eight have one rhyme and five another, and divided into three strophes, at the end of the second and third the beginning of the rondeau being repeated; a piece of music of three strains. Called also *Rondo.*

rondo, ron′dō. See RONDEAU.

ronion, ronyon, run′yun or ron′yon, *n.* [From Fr. *rogne,* itch, mange, from L. *robigo, robiginis,* rust.] A mangy, scabby animal; a scurvy person; a drab.

röntgen, roentgen, rent′gen, *a.* Pertaining to Konrad Röntgen or X-rays, which he discovered.—*Röntgen rays, n.* X-rays, which photograph through substances with varying degrees of clarity.

rood, röd, *n.* [The same word as *rod,* A.Sax. *ród,* a cross, a rod or pole; comp. D. *roede,* G. *ruthe,* a rod or switch and a measure of length.] A square measure, the fourth part of a statute acre, equal to 1210 square yards; a measure of 5½ yards in length; a rod, pole, or perch; also, a square pole, or 272½ square feet, used in estimating masonry work; a cross or crucifix; a large crucifix placed at the entrance to the chancel, often supported on the rood beam or rood screen.—**rood beam,** *n.* A beam across the entrance to the chancel of a church for supporting the rood.—**rood screen,** *n.* A screen or ornamental partition separating the choir of a church from the nave.

roof, röf, *n.* [A.Sax. *hróf,* a roof; cog. Icel. *hróf,* a shed under which ships are built; *ráf,* a roof; D. *roef,* a cover, a cabin.] The cover of any house or building irrespective of the materials of which it is composed; that which corresponds with or resembles the covering of a house, as the arch or top of a vault, a furnace, the top of a carriage, etc.; a canopy; the palate; a house.—*v.t.* To cover with a roof; to enclose in a house; to shelter.—**roofer,** röf′ėr, *n.* One who roofs.—**roofing,** röf′ing, *n.* The act of covering with a roof; the materials of which a roof is composed; the roof itself.—**roofless,** röf′les, *a.* Having no roof; having no house or home; unsheltered.—**rooftree,** *n.* A main beam in a roof.

rook, rụk, *n.* [A.Sax. *hróc,* D. *roek,* L.G. *rôk,* Icel. *hrókr,* Sw. *roka,* O.H.G. *hruoh,* probably from the cry which the bird utters; comp. Gael. *roc,* to croak, L. *raucus,* hoarse.] A bird resembling the crow, but differing from it in not feeding on carrion but on insects and grain, also in having the root of the bill bare of feathers; a cheat; a trickish rapacious fellow.—*v.i.* and *t.* To cheat; to defraud.—**rookery,** rụk′ėr•i, *n.* A wood used for nesting places by rooks; a neighborhood of poor mean dwellings; a squalid community; a resort of thieves; sharpers, etc. (*Brit.*).—**rookie,** *n.* A raw army recruit.—**rooky,** rụk′i, *a.* Inhabited by rooks.

rook, rụk, *n.* [Fr. *roc,* It. *rocco,* Sp. *roque,* from Per. and Ar. *rokh,* the rook or castle at chess.] *Chess,* one of the four pieces placed on the corner squares of the board; also called a *Castle.*

room, röm, *n.* [A.Sax. *rúm*=Icel. *rúm,* D. *ruim,* O.Sax., O.Fris., L.G., Sw., and Dan. *rum,* G. *raum,* room, space; Goth. *rums,* place, space; same root as L. *rus,* country. *Rummage* is a derivative.] Space; compass; extent of place, great or small; space or place unoccupied or unobstructed; fit occasion; opportunity; place or station once occupied by another; stead; an apartment in a house; any division separated from the rest by a partition; particular place or station (N.T.).—*To make room,* to open a way or passage; to remove obstructions.—**roomer,** *n.* One who rents a room without board.—**roomful,** röm′fụl, *n.* As much or as many as a room will hold.—**roommate,** *n.* One who shares a room.—**roomy,** röm′i, *a.* Having ample room; spacious.

roorback, rör′bak, *n.* A false and malicious report circulated by a political candidate at the last moment.

roost, röst, *n.* [A.Sax. *hróst,* D. *roost,* a roost; connections doubtful.] The pole or support on which fowls rest at night.—*At roost,* in a state of rest and sleep.—*v.i.* To occupy a roost; to lodge; to settle.—**rooster,** rös′tėr, *n.* The male of the domestic fowl; a cock.

root, röt, *n.* [From Icel. *rót,* Sw. *rot,* Dan. *rod;* connected with L. *radix* (whence *radical*), Gr. *rhiza,* root, E. *wort.*] That part of a plant which fixes itself in the earth, and by means of its radicles imbibes nutriment; a bulb, tuber, or similar part of a plant; that which resembles a root in position or function; the part of anything that resembles the root of a plant (the *root* of a tooth); foundation or base; the origin or cause of anything; that part of a word which conveys its essential meaning, as distinguished from the formative parts by which this meaning is modified; an ultimate form or element from which words are derived or regarded as having arisen; *math.* (of a quantity) any quantity that, when multiplied by itself a specified number of times, will exactly produce a stated quantity.—*To take root,* or *to strike root,* to become planted or fixed, or to be established.—*v.i.* To fix the root; to be firmly fixed; to be established.—*v.t.* To fix by the root; to plant and fix deep in the earth; to plant deeply to impress deeply and durably (principles *rooted* in the mind).—**root beer,** *n.* A nonalcoholic beverage made from various roots.—**rootless,** röt′les, *a.* Having no root.—**rootlet,** röt′let, *n.* A radicle; a little root.—**rootstock,** *n. Bot.* a prostrate rooting stem; a rhizome.—**rooty,** röt′i, *a.* Full of roots.

root, röt, *v.t.* [Formerly *wrote,* from A.Sax. *wrótan,* to root up, from *wrót*, Fris. *wrote*, a snout; D. *wroeten*, Icel. *róta*, Dan. *rode*, to root up as with the snout; akin G. *rûssel*, a snout.] To dig or burrow in with the snout; to turn up with the snout, as a swine; to tear up or out as if by rooting; to remove or destroy utterly; to exterminate: generally with *up*, *out*, *away*, etc.—*v.i.* To turn up the earth with the snout, as swine.

rope, rōp, *n.* [A.Sax. *ráp*, a rope= Icel. *reip*, D. *reep*, *roop*, G. *reif*, Goth. *raips*.] A cord of some thickness; a general name applied to cordage of greater circumference than string; a row or string of things tied together (a rope of onions).—*Rope's end*, a short piece of rope, or a hangman's noose; *fig.*, the end of one's opportunity.—*Rope of sand*, proverbially, a feeble union or tie; a band easily broken.—*To give a person rope*, to let him go on without check.—*v.i.*—*roped*, *roping*. To be formed into filaments from any glutinous or adhesive quality.—*v.t.* To fasten or tie with a rope or ropes; to pull by a rope.—**ropedancer,** *n.* One who dances or performs acrobatic feats on a rope extended at a greater or less height above the ground.—**roper,** rō′pėr, *n.* A ropemaker; one who ropes goods.—**ropery,** rō′pėr•i, *n.* A place where ropes are made; a ropewalk.—**ropewalk,** *n.* A long covered walk or a long building where ropes are manufactured.—**ropy,** rō′pi, *a.* [Lit. like a rope, forming ropes.] Having such consistence that it may be drawn into viscous filaments; stringy; glutinous.—*Ropy wine*, wine showing a flaky sediment and oily appearance.—**ropily,** rō′pi•li, *adv.* In a ropy or viscous manner.—**ropiness,** rō′pi•nes, *n.* The state of being ropy.

roquelaure, ro′ke•lōr, *n.* [From the Duke de *Roquelaure*.] A kind of short cloak used in the eighteenth century.

rorqual, ror′kwal, *n.* A large whale of several species, not an object of capture, as it yields little oil or whalebone.

rosaceous, rosary. See ROSE.

rose, rōz, *n.* [A.Sax. *rose*, Fr. *rose*, from L. *rosa*, a rose; allied to Gr. *rhodon*, a rose; probably from an Eastern source.] A well-known and universally cultivated plant and flower of many species and varieties, found in almost every country of the northern hemisphere, both in the Old and the New World; a knot of ribbon in the form of a rose, used as an ornament; a perforated nozzle of a pipe, spout, etc., to distribute water in fine shower-like jets; a popular name of the disease erysipelas; from its color; a circular card or disk; or diagram with radiating lines, as the compass card.—*Wars of the Roses*, the civil contest between the houses of York and Lancaster, the badge of the former house being a white, of the latter a red rose.—*Under the rose*, in secret; privately; in a manner that forbids disclosure.—*v.t.* To render rose-colored; to cause to flush or blush (*Poet.*)—**rosaceous,** ro•zā′shus, *a.* [L. *rosaceus*.] Roselike; composed of petals in a circular form (a *rosaceous* corolla); pertaining to the rose family of plants.—**rosaniline,** rō•zan′i•lin, *n.* [That is, *rose aniline*.] A substance obtained from aniline yielding a beautiful red dye.—**rosary,** rō′za•ri, *n.* [Lit. a chaplet or garland of roses.] A chaplet; a garland; formerly often adopted as a title of books, consisting of pieces culled from various authors; a string of beads used by Roman Catholics, on which they count their prayers, there being so many small beads each for an Ave Maria, and so many large ones each for a Paternoster.—**roseate,** rō′zi•āt, *a.* [L. *roseus*, rosy.] Full of roses; of a rose color; blooming.—**rosebud,** rōz′bud, *n.* The bud of a rose; the flower of the rose just appearing.—**rose color,** *n.* The color of the rose; *fig.* beauty; often fancied beauty or attractiveness. — **rose-colored,** *a.* Having the color of a rose; highly alluring.—**rose mallow,** *n.* Same as *Hollyhock*.—**rosette,** ro•zet′, *n.* [Fr., a dim. of *rose*.] An imitation of a rose, as by ribbon, used as an ornament or badge; *arch.* a flower ornament of frequent use in decorations and in all styles.—**rose water,** *n.* Water tinctured with roses by distillation.—**rose window,** *n.* *Arch.* a circular window divided into compartments by mullions or tracery radiating or branching from a center; called also *Catherine wheel* and *Marigold window*.—**rosewood,** *n.* The wood of South American trees, so named because when freshly cut it has a faint agreeable odor of roses; in the highest esteem for cabinetwork.

rosemary, rōz′ma•ri, *n.* [O.E. *rosmarine*, from L. *rosmarinus*, rosemary—*ros*, dew, and *marinus*, marine, from *mare*, the sea.] An evergreen shrub having a fragrant odor and a warm, pungent, bitterish taste.

roseola, rō•zē′o•la, *n.* [From L. *rosa*, a rose.] *Med.* a kind of rash or rose-colored efflorescence, occurring in connection with different febrile complaints.

Rosetta stone, ro•zet′a, *n.* A black basalt stele, with an inscription in hieroglyphics, demotic, and Greek, found in 1799 by Boussard, and important for having given Champollion a key for deciphering Egyptian hieroglyphics; it was acquired by the British in 1801, and is now in the British Museum.

Rosicrucian, rōz•i•krö′shi•an, *n.* [L. *rosa*, a rose, and *crux*, *crucis*, a cross, the name originating from that of the alleged founder *Rosenkreuz* (rosy cross).] One of a secret sect or society said to have originated in the fourteenth century, but brought into notice much more recently, whose members made great pretensions to a knowledge of the secrets of nature, and especially as to the transmutation of metals, the prolongation of life, etc., and were often known as Brothers of the Rosy Cross.—*a.* Pertaining to the Rosicrucians or their arts.—**rosicrucianism,** rōz•i•krö′shi•an•ism, *n.* The arts, practices, or doctrines of the Rosicrucians.

rosin, roz′in, *n.* [Corruption of *resin*.] The name given to resin when it is employed in a solid state for ordinary purposes; obtained from turpentine by distillation, the volatile oil coming over and the rosin remaining behind.—*v.t.* To rub or cover over with rosin.

rosolio, ro•zōl′i•ō, *n.* [It. *rosolio*.] A red wine of Malta; a species of liqueur.

rostel, ros′tel, *n.* [L. *rostellum*, dim. of *rostrum*, a beak. ROSTRUM.] *Bot.* any small beak-shaped process, as in the stigma of many violets.—**rostellate,** ros′tel•āt, *a.* Having a rostel.

roster, ros′tėr, *n.* [D. *rooster*, a thing for *roasting*, a gridiron, a table or list, a roster—the last meaning probably from perpendicular and horizontal lines of tabular statements giving a grated appearance. ROAST.] A list showing the rotation of those who relieve or succeed each other; a military list showing the rotation in which individuals, companies, regiments, etc., are called on to serve.

rostrum, ros′trum, *n.* [L., the beak of a bird or other animal, the beak of a ship, from *rodo*, to gnaw. RODENT.] The beak or bill of a bird or other animal; the beak of a ship, especially of an ancient war galley; an elevated place in the forum at Rome where orations, funeral harangues, etc., were delivered (so called because adorned with the *rostra* of captured ships); hence, a platform from which any speaker addresses his audience.—**rostral,** ros′tral, *a.* Pertaining to a rostrum; pertaining to the beak of a bird or other animal.—**rostrate,** ros′trāt, *a.* Furnished or adorned with beaks; beak-shaped; having a process resembling the beak of a bird.

rot, rot, *v.i.*—*rotted*, *rotting*. [A.Sax. *rotian*, to rot; D. *rotten*, Icel. *rotna*, to rot, *rotinn*, rotten (whence E. *rotten*, which is not used as the pp. of *rot*).] To decompose; to become putrid; to go to decay.—*v.t.* To make putrid; to cause to decompose; to bring to corruption; to expose to a process of partial rotting, as flax; to ret; used in the imperative as a sort of imprecation (*rot* it).—*n.* Putrefaction; a fatal distemper incident to sheep, caused by the liver fluke; a disease very injurious to the potato; the potato disease.

rota, rō′ta, *n.* [L. *rota*, a wheel.] An ecclesiastical court of Rome, composed of twelve prelates; a school roll or list; a roster.

Rotarian, rō•tâ′ri•an, *n.* One who belongs to a worldwide organization, originating in America, having for its object the promotion of international fellowship and high ethical standards between business and professional men and members of various industries.

rotary, rō′ta•ri, *a.* [From L. *rota*, a wheel; allied to G. *rad*, a wheel; W. *rhod*, a wheel, *rhedu*, to turn; Skr.

rathas, a chariot. Ultimately from L. *rota* are E. *round*, *roll*, *rowel*, etc.] Turning, as a wheel on its axis; pertaining to rotation; rotatory.—*Rotary converter*, a machine for converting alternating electric current into direct current.—*Rotary engine*. ROTATORY.—**rotate,** rō′tāt, *v.i.*—*rotated, rotating*. [L. *roto*, *rotatum*, to turn round, from *rota*, a wheel.] To revolve or move round a center; to turn round as a wheel; to act in turn or rotation.—*v.t.* To cause to turn round like a wheel.—*a. Bot.* wheel-shaped; monopetalous, spreading nearly flat without any tube.—**rotation,** rō•tā′shon, *n.* [L. *rotatio*, *rotationis*.] The act of rotating or turning; the motion of a solid body, as a wheel or sphere, about an axis; a return or succession in a series; established succession; the course in which persons leave their places or duties at certain times, and are succeeded by others; a recurring series of different crops grown on the same ground; the order of recurrence in cropping.—**rotational,** rō•tā′shon•al, *a.* Pertaining to rotation.—**rotator,** rō•tā′tėr, *n.* That which rotates or causes rotation; a muscle producing a rolling motion, as at the upper part of the thigh bone.—**rotatory,** rō′ta•to•ri, *a.* Pertaining to or consisting in rotation; exhibiting rotation; rotary.—*Rotatory* or *rotary steam engine*, an engine in which a rotatory motion is produced by the direct action of the steam without the intervention of reciprocating parts.—*Rotatory muscle*, a rotator.—**rotor,** rō′tor, *n.* [L. *rota*, a wheel.] The revolving part of an electric generator or motor.

rotche, roch, *n.* [D. *rotje*, a petrel; comp. Prov.G. *rätsche*, a duck.] A bird of the auk family; the little auk.

rote, rōt, *n.* [O.Fr. *rote*, a way, a *route*. ROUTE.] Repetition of words or sounds without attending to the signification; mere effort of memory: in the phrase *by rote*, by memory merely without intelligence.

rotifers, rō′ti•fėrz, *n. pl.* [L. *rota*, a wheel, and *fero*, to carry.] A class of animalcules, which, through the microscope, appear like revolving wheels, whence they have been called *wheel animalcules*.

rotogravure, rō•tō•gra•vūr′, *n.* [L. *rota* and *gravure*.] A printing process that utilizes engraved cylinders for plates; a newspaper section of rotogravure pictures.

rotor. See ROTARY.

rotten, rot′n, *a.* [A Scandinavian word=Icel. *rotinn*, Sw. *rutten*, rotten, a participle of an old verb akin to *rot*.] Putrid; decaying; decomposed by the natural process of decay; unsound; defective in principle; corrupt; fetid; ill-smelling.—*Rotten borough*, a name given to certain boroughs in England before the reform of 1832, which had fallen into decay and had a mere handful of voters, but which still retained the privilege of sending members to parliament.—**rottenly,** rot′n•li, *adv.* In a rotten manner; putridly; unsoundly.—**rottenness,** rot′n•nes, *n.* State of being rotten; putrefaction; unsoundness.—**rottenstone,** *n.* A soft stone much used for polishing household articles of brass or other metal, derived from the decomposition of siliceous limestones.

rotund, ro•tund′, *a.* [L. *rotundus*, formed from *rota*, a wheel. *Round* is a form of the same word. ROTARY, ROUND.] Round; spherical; globular; *bot.* circumscribed by one unbroken curve, or without angles.—**rotunda,** ro•tun′da, *n.* [It. *rotonda*. See above.] A round building; any building that is round both on the outside and inside.—**rotundity, rotundness,** ro•tun′di•ti, ro•tund′nes, *n.* Sphericity; circularity.

roué, rö′ā, *n.* [Fr. ppr. of *rouer*, to break on the wheel, from *roue*, L. *rota*, a wheel; lit. one worthy of suffering on the wheel. ROTARY.] A person devoted to a life of pleasure and sensuality; a rake.

rouge, rözh, *n.* [Fr. *rouge*, from L. *rubeus*, red.] A cosmetic prepared from a base, such as French chalk, sometimes an oil, and coloring matter, and used to add color to the cheeks or lips; a reddish powder, usually hydrated ferric oxide, used for polishing metals, etc.—*v.t.* and *i.* —*rouged, rouging*. To apply or use rouge. To paint or tinge with rouge.—**rouge et noir,** rözh•ā•nwär′, *n.* [Fr., red and black.] A game at cards played between a 'banker' and an unlimited number of persons, at a table marked with four spots of a diamond shape, two colored black and two red.

rough, ruf, *a.* [A.Sax. *rúh*, rough, shaggy; cog. D. *ruig*, *ruw*, L.G. *rug*, Dan. *ru*, G. *rauh*, *rauch*, rough; Lith. *raukas*, wrinkle.] Having prominences or inequalities; not smooth; having many irregularities of surface; harsh to the feel; unfinished; unpolished; shaggy; ragged; coarse; swelling into billows or breakers; stormy, as the sea or weather; not mild or gentle in character; boisterous; untamed; not mild or courteous; rude and brusque; harsh; severe; cruel; not refined or delicate; astringent; sour; harsh to the ear; grating; unharmonious; vague; crude (a *rough* guess).—*Rough diamond*, a diamond uncut; hence, *fig.* a person of genuine worth but rude and unpolished manners.—*Rough and ready*, of a hasty and unfinished sort; unpolished; unceremonious in manner, but reliable and always prepared for emergencies.—*v.t.* To give a rough appearance to; to make rough; to break in, as a horse; to shape out roughly, as a stone; to rough-hew.—*To rough it*, to submit to hardships; to put up for a time with rough accommodation. —*n.* The state of being coarse or in the original material; with *the* (materials or work in the *rough*); a rowdy; a rude coarse fellow; a bully. —**roughcast,** *v.t.* To form in its first rudiments; to mold without nicety or elegance; to cover with a coarse sort of plaster composed of lime and gravel (to *roughcast* a building).—*n.* The form of a thing in its first rudiments; a coarse kind of plastering for an external wall.—**roughen,** ruf′n, *v.t.* To make rough.—*v.i.* To grow or become rough.—**roughhew,** *v.t.* To hew coarsely without smoothing; to give the first form or shape to.—**roughly,** ruf′li, *adv.* In a rough manner; with uneven surface; harshly; severely; uncivilly; rudely; violently; not gently; boisterously; tempestuously.—**roughness,** ruf′nes, *n.* The state or quality of being rough; harshness to the taste or ear; unevenness of surface; asperity of temper; coarseness of behavior or address.—**roughrider,** *n.* One who breaks horses; [*cap.*] in the Spanish-American War, a soldier of the 1st U. S. Volunteer Cavalry organized and later led by Theodore Roosevelt. —**roughshod,** *a.* Shod with shoes armed with points.—*To ride roughshod, fig.* to pursue a violent or selfish course, regardless of others.

roulade, rö•läd′, *n.* [Fr., from *rouler*, to roll.] *Music*, a rapid run of notes, generally introduced as an embellishment.

rouleau, rö•lō′, *n.* pl. English **rouleaus,** rö•lōz, French **rouleaux,** rö•lō. [Fr., lit. a roll. ROLL.] A little roll; a roll of coin made up in paper.

roulette, rö•let′, *n.* [Fr., properly a little wheel, a castor, from *rouler*, to roll. ROLL.] A game of chance played with a ball at a table, in the center of which is a cavity surmounted by a revolving disk having its circumference divided into compartments colored black and red alternately, into any one of which the ball may drop; a tool furnished with a little toothed wheel.

round, round, *a.* [O.Fr. *roond*, round, Mod.Fr. *rond*, round, from L. *rotundus*, round, rotund, from *rota*, a wheel. ROTARY. *Rotund* is a doublet of this.] Having every part of the surface at an equal distance from the center; spherical; globular; circular; cylindrical; having a curved form; swelling; plump; not given as extremely accurate (in *round* numbers); large; considerable (a good *round* sum); full in utterance; candid. *Round dance*, a dance, as a polka, waltz, etc., in which the couples wheel round the room.—*Round game*, a game, as at cards, in which an indefinite number of players can take part, each on his own account.—*Round Table*, the table around which sat King Arthur and his knights.—*Round number*, a number that ends with a cipher, and may be divided by 10 without a remainder; a number not exact, but near enough the truth to serve the purpose.—*n.* That which is round, as a circle; a sphere, a globe; a series coming back to where it began (a *round* of toasts); a series of events or duties which come back to the point of commencement; the step of a ladder; a walk or circuit performed by a guard or an officer among sentinels; a short musical composition in which three or more voices, starting at the beginning of stated successive phrases, sing the same music (in unison or octave) the combination of all the parts producing correct harmony; a dance in a ring; a general discharge of firearms by a body of troops, in which each soldier fires once; ammunition for firing once.—*A round of beef*, a cut of the thigh through and across the bone.—*adv*. On all sides; circularly; not in a direct line; through a circle, as of friends or houses.—*All round*, over the whole place; in every direction.—*To bring one round*, to restore one to health, composure, or the like; to cause one to alter his opinions.—*To come round*, to change one's opinions; to be restored to health, or the like.—*To turn round*, to turn one's self about; to change one's side; to desert one's party.—*prep*. On every side of; around; about, in a circular course.—*To come or get round one*, to gain advantage over one by flattery or deception.—*v.t.* To make round; to make full or complete; to make full, smooth, and flowing.—*v.i.* To grow or become round; to become complete or full; to develop into the full type.—*To round to* (*naut.*), to turn the head of the ship toward the wind.—**roundabout,** round'a•bout, *a*. Indirect; going round; not straightforward.—*n*. A large horizontal wheel on which children ride; a merry-go-round; an armchair with a rounded back; a short close-fitting jacket; a circular dance.—**round-shouldered,** *a*. Having a round or slightly raised back or shoulders.—**rounder,** roun'dėr, *n*. One who makes the rounds of disreputable resorts; a dissolute spendthrift; [*pl.*] a game played chiefly in England, somewhat resembling baseball.—**round hand.** A style of penmanship in which the letters are round and full.—**Roundhead,** round'hed, *n*. A name given by the Cavaliers or adherents of Charles I to members of the Puritan or parliamentary party, from the latter having their hair closely cut, while the Cavaliers wore theirs long.—**roundhouse,** *n*. A circular building in which locomotives are repaired; a lockup‡; a cabin on the afterpart of the quarterdeck of a ship, having the poop for its roof.—**roundish,** round'ish, *a*. Somewhat round.—**roundly,** round'li, *adv*. In a round form; openly; plainly; without reserve; briskly; with speed; to the purpose; vigorously.—**roundness,** round'nes, *n*. The quality of being round; circularity; sphericity; cylindrical form; fullness; smoothness of flow; plainness of speech; positiveness.—**round robin.** A written petition, memorial, or remonstrance signed by names in a ring or circle that it may be impossible to ascertain who headed the list; a sport tournament arranged so that each contestant plays the same number of matches, resulting in the eventual elimination of the losers, an arrangement common in tennis.

roundel, roun'del, *n*. [Fr. *rondelle*, from *rond*, round. ROUND.] Anything having a round form; a round figure; a circle; a roundelay (which see).

roundelay, roun'de•lā, *n*. [O.Fr. *rondelet*, from Fr. *rond*, round. (ROUND.) The spelling has been influenced by *lay*, a song.] A sort of ancient poem, consisting of thirteen verses, of which eight are in one kind of rhyme and five in another; a song or tune in which the first strain is repeated; a dance in a circle.

roup, röp, *n*. A disease of poultry.

rouse, rouz, *v.t.*—*roused, rousing*. [Connected with O.H.G. *ruozjan*, to rouse.] To wake from sleep; to excite to thought or action from a state of idleness, languor, or inattention; to put into commotion; to agitate; to startle; to surprise; to drive from a lurking place or cover: a hunting term.—*v.i.* To awake from sleep or repose; to be excited to thought or action.—*n*. [Comp. D. *roes*, a bumper; G. *rausch*, drunkenness.] A carousal; a drinking frolic or festival. (*Tenn.*)—**rousing,** rou'zing, *p*. and *a*. Having power to awaken or excite; stirring.

rout, rout, *n*. [O.Fr. *route*, a company, a band, a division; lit. a portion broken off or separated; from L.L. *rupta*, from L. *ruptus*, broken, pp. of *rumpo*, to break. RUPTURE.] A company of persons; a rabble or multitude; a fashionable assembly or large evening party; an uproar; a brawl; the breaking or defeat of troops; the disorder and confusion of troops thus defeated.—*v.t.* To break the ranks of and put to flight in disorder; to defeat and throw into confusion; to drive or chase away; to dispel.

rout, röt, *v.t.* [Form of to *root*.] To turn up with the snout (as hogs); to root.

route, röt, *n*. [Fr. *route*, O.Fr. *rote*, a rut, way, path, from L.L. *rupta*, a path, properly *rupta via*, a path broken through forests, etc., from L. *ruptus*, broken, pp. of *rumpo*, to break. ROUT, a company. RUPTURE.] The course or way which is traveled or passed, or to be passed; a passing; a course; a march.—*To get the route* (*milit.*), to receive orders to quit one station for another; *route march*, a march performed for exercise and training, by a body of troops in full equipment.

routine, rö•tēn', *n*. [Fr., from *route*, a way: properly the way which one invariably takes through custom. ROUTE.] A round of business, amusements, or pleasure, daily or frequently pursued; a course of business or duties regularly returning; habit or practice adhered to by force of habit.—**routinist,** rö•tēn'ist, *n*. One addicted to routine.

rove, rōv, *v.i.*—*roved, roving*. [Originally to wander for plunder, a collateral form of *reave*, directly from the L.G. or D.; L.G. *roven*, D. *rooven*, Dan. *röve*, Sw. *röfva*, to rob; Icel. *ráfa*, *rápa*, to wander.] To wander; to ramble; to range; to go, move, or pass without certain direction in any manner.—*v.t.* To wander over.—**rover,** rō'vėr, *n*. One who roves; one who rambles about; a fickle or inconstant person; a pirate; *in archery*, a mark chosen at will or at random, chiefly in the phrase, *to shoot at rovers*, equivalent to *to shoot at random*.—**roving,** rō'ving, *n*. The act of rambling or wandering.

rove, rōv, *v.t.*—*roved, roving*. [Akin to *reeve* or to *ravel*.] To draw through an eye or aperture; to bring (wool or cotton) into that form which it receives before being spun into thread; to card into flakes, as wool, etc.—*n*. A roll of wool, cotton, etc., drawn out and slightly twisted.

row, rō, *n*. [A.Sax. *ráw*, a row; perhaps from same root as *room*, and meaning originally the space or interval between rows.] A series of persons or things arranged in a continued line; a line; a rank; a file.

row, rō, *v.t.* [A.Sax. *rówan*, to row= Icel. *róa*, Dan. *roe*, Sw. *ro*, D. *roeijen*, to row. *Rudder* is from same stem.] To impel along the surface of water by oars; to transport by rowing.—*v.i.* To labor with the oar; to be moved by means of oars.—*n*. An excursion taken in a boat with oars.—**rower,** rō'ėr, *n*. One that rows or manages an oar in rowing.

row, rou, *n*. [Perhaps short for *rowdydow*, a word used as imitative of noise or disturbance; or from *rouse*, *n*.] A riotous noise; a turbulent, noisy disturbance; a riot. (*Colloq.*)—*v.t.* To scold. (*Colloq.*)

rowan, rou'an, *n*. [Same as Dan. *rön*, *rönne-trae*, Sw. *rönn*, the rowan; akin perhaps to old *roun*, *round*, to whisper, *rune*, A.Sax. *run*, mystery, there being sundry superstitions connected with it.] See MOUNTAIN ASH.

rowdy, rou'di, *n*. [From *rowdydow*. See ROW, a disturbance.] A riotous turbulent fellow; a rough. (*Colloq.*)—*a*. Disreputable; blackguard. (*Colloq.*)—**rowdyish,** rou'di•ish, *a*. Belonging to a rowdy.—**rowdyism,** rou'di•izm, *n*. The conduct of a rowdy; turbulent blackguardism.

rowel, rou'el, *n*. [O.Fr. *rouelle*, dim. of *roue*, L. *rota*, a wheel. ROTARY.] The little wheel of a spur with sharp points for pricking the horse; a little flat ring or wheel on horses' bits; a roll of hair or silk passed through the flesh of horses, answering to a seton in surgery.

rowen, rou'en, *n*. [From O.F. *rewain*, *regain*. Second crop.] The aftermath.

royal, roi'al, *a*. [Fr. *royal*, from L. *regalis*, from *rex*, *regis*, a king. REGAL.] Pertaining or belonging to a king; pertaining to the crown; regal; becoming a king; kingly; princely; noble; generous; founded or originated by, in the service of, under the patronage of, or receiving support from royalty (*royal* navy); a term for a large size of paper.—*Royal Academy*, an incorporated society in London established for the promotion of the fine arts and having forty-two members.—*Royal assent*. See ASSENT.—*Royal grant*, a grant by letters patent from the crown.—*Royal Highness*, a title used in speaking to or of a prince or princess; also, the prince or princess thus referred to or addressed.—*Royal Standard*, a rectangular banner containing the Royal Arms. It is solely the prerogative of the sovereign, and may not be flown over any building in which the reigning monarch is not present.—*Royal Society*, a society authorized by Charles II in 1660 for the study of physical science, and which still flourishes in London. ∴ *Royal* denotes what pertains to the king as an individual, or is associated with his person (the *royal* family). *Regal* is applied primarily to what pertains to a king in virtue of his office; hence, to what becomes a king, and is nearly synonymous with princely, magnificent (*regal* state). *Kingly* signifies literally, like a king, hence, proper to or becoming a king, and it has often, like *royal*, reference to personal qualities.—*n. Naut.* a square sail spread immediately above the topgallant sail; a gold coin formerly current in England.—**royalism,** roi′al•izm, *n.* Attachment to a royal government.—**royalist,** roi′al•ist, *n.* An adherent of a king, or one attached to a kingly government; [*cap.*] *Eng. hist.* an adherent of Charles I and Charles II, opposed to *Roundhead* (which see).—**royalty,** roi′al•ti, *n.* The state or quality of being royal; condition or status of a person of royal rank; the person of a king; majesty (to stand in the presence of *royalty*); a right or prerogative of a king; a tax paid to the crown or to a superior on the produce of a mine, or to an inventor for the use of his patent.

rub, rub, *v.t.*—*rubbed, rubbing.* [Same word as Dan. *rubbe*, to rub, to scrub; akin also to W. *rhwb*, a rub, *rhwbiad*, a rubbing; Gael. *rub*, *rubadh*, Ir. *rubha*, a hurt, *rubadh*, attrition. *Rubbish, rubble* are derivatives.] To move along the surface of, or backward and forward upon, with friction; to apply friction to; to wipe; to clean; to scour; to smear all over; to gall or chafe; to gibe.—*To rub down*, to reduce to smaller dimensions by friction; to clean by rubbing, as a horse.—*To rub off*, to separate by friction.—*To rub out*, to erase; to obliterate.—*To rub up*, to burnish; to polish; to rouse to action.—*v.i.* To move along the surface of a body with pressure; to grate; to fret; to chafe; to get on or along with difficulty: usually with *on*, *along*, or *through* (to *rub through* the world).—An act of rubbing; something that renders motion or progress difficult; a difficulty or obstruction; a sarcasm; a gibe; something grating to the feelings.

rubasse, rụ•bas′, *n.* [Fr., from L. *rubeus*, red; akin *ruby*.] A lapidaries' name for a beautiful variety of rock crystal, speckled in the interior with minute spangles of specular iron, which reflect a color resembling that of the ruby.

rubber, rub′ėr, *n.* An elastic, resilient coherent solid made from the juice of certain trees and plants found chiefly in the tropics, and manufactured into tires, hose, water bottles, waterproofed fabrics, etc.; something made of this material, as an eraser, overshoe, etc.; a person who rubs, as a massager; a coarse file; a whetstone; *cards*, two games out of three, or a contest consisting of three games.—**rubberize,** *v.t.*—*rubberized, rubberizing.* To coat or impregnate with rubber so as to make waterproof or airtight.—**rubber-stamp,** *v.t.* To approve or endorse by printing with a stamping device; hence, to approve quickly without examination.

rubbish, rub′ish, *n.* [Influenced by *rub*, but from O.E. *robows*, *robeux*, *robrish*, a word of doubtful origin.] Refuse fragments of building materials; debris; waste or rejected matter; trash.—**rubbishy,** rub′ish•i, *a.* Characterized by rubbish; trashy; worthless. (*Colloq.*)

rubble, rub′l, *n.* [Akin to *rubbish*.] The upper fragmentary and decomposed portion of a mass of stone; stones of irregular shapes and dimensions, broken bricks, etc., used in coarse masonry, or to fill up between the facing courses of walls.—**rubblework,** *n.* Walls or masonry built of rubblestones.—**rubbly,** rub′l•i, *a.* Abounding in rubble.

rubefacient, rö•bi•fā′shi•ent, *a.* [L. *rubefaciens*, *rubefacientis*—*rubeo*, to be red, and *facio*, to make.] Making red; producing redness on the skin.—*n. Med.* a substance for external application which produces redness of the skin, not followed by a blister.

rubella, rö•bel′a, *n.* [L. *rubellus*, reddish, from *ruber*, red.] A disease resembling measles, accompanied by a reddish rash and other symptoms, but less serious than measles; called often *German Measles*.

rubellite, rö′bel•īt, *n.* [L. *rubellus*, dim. of *ruber*, red.] Red tourmaline, a siliceous mineral of a red color.

rubeola, rö•bē′o•la, *n.* [From L. *ruber*, red.] A name of measles.—**rubeoloid,** rö•bē′o•loid, *a.* Pertaining to or resembling rubeola.

rubescent, rö•bes′ent, *a.* [L. *rubescens*, *rubescentis*, ppr. of *rubesco*, from *rubeo*, to be red, from *ruber*, red.] Growing or becoming red; tending to a red color.

rubicelle, rö′bi•sel, *n.* [L. *rubeo*, to be red.] A variety of ruby of a reddish color, from Brazil.

Rubicon, röb′i•kon, *n.* The river forming the southern boundary of Caesar's province of Cisalpine Gaul, crossing which meant declaration of war. *Metaphorically*, to face any difficulty or crisis in a resolute manner.

rubicund, rö′bi•kund, *a.* [L. *rubicundus*, from *rubeo*, to be red.] Inclining to redness; ruddy; blood-red: said especially of the face.—**rubicundity,** rö•bi•kun′di•ti, *n.* The state of being rubicund; redness.

rubidium, rö•bid′i•um, *n.* [From L. *rubidus*, red—from the nature of its spectrum.] A silver-white metallic element, resembling, but more active than, potassium. Symbol, Rb; at. no., 37; at. wt., 85.47.

rubigo, rö•bī′gō, *n.* [L. *rubigo*, rust, *rubeus*, red. RUBY, RUST.] A kind of rust on plants, consisting of a parasitic fungus; mildew.—**rubiginous,** rö•bij′i•nus, *a.* Exhibiting or affected by rubigo; mildewed.

ruble, rö′bl, *n.* [Rus.] The unit of the Soviet money system divided into 100 kopecks.

rubric, rö′brik, *n.* [Fr. *rubrique*, from L. *rubrica* (*terra*), red earth, the title of a law in red, a law, from *ruber*, red. RUBY.] Some part of a manuscript or printed matter that is, or in former times usually was, colored red, to distinguish it from other portions; in law books, the title of a statute, formerly written in red letters; in prayer books, the directions and rules for the conduct of service, often printed in red; hence an ecclesiastical or episcopal rule or injunction; any formulated, fixed, or authoritative injunction of duty.—**rubric, rubrical,** rö′bri•kal, *a.* Pertaining to a rubric.—**rubricate,** rö′bri•kāt, *a.* Marked with red.—**rubrician,** rö•brish′an, *n.* One versed in rubrics; an adherent or advocate for the rubric.

ruby, rö′bi, *n.* [Fr. *rubis*, Sp. *rubi*, *rubin*, from L.L. *rubinus*, a carbuncle, from L. *rubeus*, red, reddish, *ruber*, red (akin *rubric*, *rust*).] A gem next to the diamond in hardness and value, of various shades of red, the most highly prized varieties being the crimson and carmine red; redness; red color; something resembling a ruby; a blotch on the face; a carbuncle; *printing*, a type smaller than nonpareil and larger than pearl.—*Rock ruby*, the most valued species of garnet.—*v.t.*—*rubied, rubying.* To make red.—*a.* Of the color, of the ruby; red.

ruche, ruching, rösh, rösh′ing, *n.* [Fr. *ruche*, a beehive. The stuff has its name from the quillings resembling honeycomb cells.] Quilled or goffered net, lace, silk, and the like, used as trimming for ladies' dress and bonnets. Spelled also *Rouche*.

ruck, ruk, *v.t.* [Icel. *hrukka*, a wrinkle, a fold, *rykkja*, to draw into folds; comp. Gael. *roc*, a wrinkle, to become wrinkled.] To wrinkle; to crease.—*n.* A wrinkle; a crease.

ruck, ruk, *n.* [Akin to *rick*, O.Sw. *ruka*, a heap.] An undistinguished crowd.

rudd, rud, *n.* [From the *ruddy* coloring.] A European fresh-water fish, with sides and belly yellow, marked with red; ventral and anal fins and tail deep red.

rudder, rud′ėr, *n.* [A.Sax. *róthor*, lit. rowing implement (the rudder being originally a kind of oar), from *rówan*, to row; D. *roeder*, Sw. *roder*, G. *ruder*, rudder. ROW, *v.t.*] The instrument by which a ship is steered; that part of the helm which consists of a piece of timber, broad at the bottom and attached to the sternpost by hinges, on which it turns; *fig.* that which guides or governs a course; in *aviation*, the subsidiary airfoil (in an airplane more or less perpendicular to the main supporting surfaces) by means of which an aircraft is turned to left or right.

ruddle, rud'l, *n.* [Akin to *ruddy, red.*] A species of red earth colored by iron, used for marking sheep.—*v.t.* To mark with ruddle.

ruddock, rud'ok, *n.* [A.Sax. *rudduc*, a dim. akin to *ruddy.*] A bird, the European robin redbreast.

ruddy, rud'i, *a.* [From A.Sax. *rud*, red, *rudu*, redness. RED.] Of a red color, or of a color approaching redness; of a lively flesh color, or the color of the Caucasian skin in high health; of a reddish shining color (*ruddy* gold).—*v.t.*—*ruddied, ruddying.* To make red or ruddy.

rude, röd, *a.* [Fr. *rude*, from L. *rudis*, in a natural state, rough, wild.] Unformed by art, taste, or skill; rough; rugged; coarse; of coarse manners; ignorant; untaught; clownish; uncivil; uncourteous; violent; boisterous.—**rudely,** röd'li, *adv.* In a rude manner; roughly; unskillfully; coarsely; uncivilly; violently; boisterously.—**rudeness,** röd'nes, *n.* The state or quality of being rude.

rudiment, rö'di•ment, *n.* [L. *rudimentum*, from *rudis*, rude. RUDE.] That which is in an undeveloped state; an unformed or unfinished beginning; an element or first principle of any art or science; especially in plural, the introduction to any branch of knowledge; the elements or elementary notions.—**rudimentary, rudimental,** rö•di•men'ta•ri, rö•di•men'tal, *a.* Pertaining to rudiments; elementary; initial; in an undeveloped state; imperfectly developed; in the first stage of existence; embryonic.—*Rudimentary organ.* See VESTIGE.

rue, rö, *v.t.*—*rued, ruing.* [A.Sax. *hreówan*, to rue=D. *rouwen*, G. *reuen*, to repent; same root as *crude*, L. *crudus*, raw, *cruel*, L. *crudelis*. Hence *ruth.*] To regret; to grieve for; to repent; to repent of and withdraw, or try to withdraw, from (to *rue* a bargain).—*v.i.* To have compassion; to become sorrowful, grieved, or repentant.—**rueful,** rö'fu̧l, *a.* Causing to rue or lament; mournful; sorrowful; expressing sorrow; suggesting sorrow or melancholy; pitiful.—**ruefully,** rö'fu̧l•li, *adv.* In a rueful manner.—**ruefulness,** rö'fu̧l•nes, *n.* The state of being rueful.

rue, rö, *n.* [Fr. *rue*, from L. *ruta*, from Gr. *rutē*, rue.] A plant with evergreen leaves and greenish-yellow flowers, used as a sudorific and a vermifuge.

rufescent, rö•fes'ent, *n.* [L. *rufescens*, from *rufus*, red.] Reddish; tinged with red.

ruff, ruf, *n.* [Connected with Prov. Fr. *rufo*, a crease or wrinkle, Armor. *roufen*, a wrinkle, a fold; Sp. *rufo*, frizzled, curled; comp. also D. *ruif*, a fold.] A large muslin or linen collar plaited, crimped, or fluted, formerly an important ornament of dress among both sexes; a species of pigeon having feathers disposed round its neck in the form of a ruff; a male bird of the sandpiper family, having the feathers of the neck standing out like a ruff, the female being called *reeve*; a low vibrating beat of a drum; a ruffle.

ruff, ruf, *n.* [Pg. *rufa*, a game with dice.] An old game at cards, the predecessor of whist; the act of trumping when you have no cards of the suit led.—*v.t. Card playing,* to trump instead of following suit.

ruff, ruf, *n.* [Origin unknown.] A small European fish of the perch family.

ruffian, ruf'i•an, *n.* [O.Fr. *rufien, ruffien*, a ruffian; Sp. *rufian*, a ruffian, a pimp; It. *ruffiano*, a pimp; probably of German origin.] A boisterous brutal fellow; a fellow ready for any desperate crime.—*a.* Like or belonging to a ruffian; brutal.—**ruffianism,** ruf'i•an•izm, *n.* The character or manners of ruffians.—**ruffianly,** ruf'i•an•li, *a.* Like a ruffian; bold in crimes; violent.

ruffle, ruf'l, *v.t.*—*ruffled, ruffling.* [A freq. of *ruff*=D. *ruyffeln*, to wrinkle.] To disorder; to rumple; to derange; to disarrange; to disturb the surface of; to cause to ripple or rise in waves; to agitate; to disturb (to *ruffle* the mind); to furnish or adorn with ruffles; to contract into plaits or folds.—*To ruffle one's feathers,* to irritate one; to make one angry.—*v.i.* To grow rough or turbulent; to put on airs; to swagger; often with an indefinite *it.*—*n.* A strip of plaited cambric or other fine cloth attached to some border of a garment, as to the wristband or bosom; a frill; a state of being disturbed or agitated; a low vibrating beat of the drum.—**ruffler,** ruf'l•ėr, *n.* A bully; a swaggerer.

rufous, rö'fus, *a.* [L. *rufus*, red; allied to *ruber*, red (whence *rubric*).] Reddish; of a yellowish or brownish red.

rug, rug, *n.* [Akin to Icel. *röggr*, a tuft, shagginess; Sw. *rugg, ragg*, rough hair. *Rugged* and *rag* are allied.] A floor covering of thick, heavy fabric with a nap or pile, mostly of wool, generally woven in one piece of a definite shape and design in distinction from a carpet; also a lap robe.

rugate, rö'gāt, *a.* [L. *ruga*, a wrinkle.] Wrinkled; rugose.

rugby, rug'bi, *n.* [From *Rugby* school.] A variety of football, played by fifteen men to a side, with an oval ball, handling being permitted.

rugged, rug'ed, *a.* [Closely akin to *rug.*] Full of rough projections on the surface; broken into irregular points or prominences (a *rugged* mountain, a *rugged* road); rough; shaggy; rough in temper; hard; crabbed; austere; rough to the ear; harsh; grating (*rugged* prose).—**ruggedly,** rug'ed•li, *adv.* In a rugged manner.—**ruggedness,** rug'ed•nes, *n.* The quality or state of being rugged.

rugose, rugous, rö'gōs, rö'gus, *a.* [L. *rugosus*, from *ruga*, a wrinkle.] Wrinkled; full of wrinkles.—**rugosity,** rö•gos'i•ti, *n.* A state of being rugose; a wrinkle; a pucker; a slight ridge.

ruin, rö'in, *n.* [Fr. *ruine*, from L. *ruina*, a falling down, downfall, ruin, from *ruo, rutum*, to fall, to rush down.] That change of anything which destroys it or entirely unfits it for use; destruction; overthrow; downfall; what promotes injury, decay, or destruction; bane; perdition; a building or anything in a state of decay or dilapidation; *pl.* the remains of a decayed or demolished city, house, fortress, etc.; the state of being destroyed or rendered worthless (to go to *ruin*).—*v.t.* To bring to ruin or destruction; to damage essentially; to destroy, defeat, demolish.—*v.i.* To fall into ruins; to run to ruin.—**ruinable,** rö'in•a•bl, *a.* Capable of being ruined.—**ruinate,** rö'i•nāt, *v.t.*—*ruinated, ruinating.* To ruin.—*a.* Brought to ruin; ruined; in ruins.—**ruination,** rö•i•nā'shon, *n.* The act of ruinating; subversion; overthrow; demolition.—**ruiner,** rö'in•ėr, *n.* One that ruins.—**ruinous,** rö'i•nus, *a.* [L. *ruinosus.*] Fallen to ruin; dilapidated; composed of ruins; bringing or tending to bring ruin.—**ruinously,** rö'i•nus•li, *adv.* In a ruinous manner; destructively.—**ruinousness,** rö'i•nus•nes, *n.*

rule, röl, *n.* [O.E. *reule, rewle*, from O.Fr. *reule, riule* (Fr. *règle*), from L. *regula*, a straight piece of wood, a ruler, a rule or pattern (whence *regular*), from *rego*, to keep straight, to govern. REGAL, RIGHT.] Government; sway; control; supreme command or authority; an established principle, standard, or guide for action; something settled by authority or custom for guidance and direction; a maxim, canon, or precept to be observed; the body of laws or regulations observed by a religious society and its members (the *rule* of St. Benedict); a point of law settled by authority; an instrument by which straight lines are drawn; an instrument for measuring short lengths, and performing various operations in mensuration; *arith.* a determinate mode prescribed for performing any operation and producing a certain result; *gram.* an established form of construction in a particular class of words, or the expression of that form in words.—*Rule of the road,* the regulation as to the side which drivers and equestrians are to keep in crossing or overtaking each other.—*Rule of thumb,* a rule suggested by a practical rather than a scientific knowledge.—*v.t.*—*ruled, ruling.* To govern; to exercise authority or dominion over; to control, conduct, guide; to mark with lines by a ruler; *law,* to establish by rule; to determine; to decide.—*v.i.* To have power or command; to exercise supreme authority: often followed by *over*; *com.* to stand or maintain a level (prices *rule* lower than formerly).—**ruler,** röl′ėr, *n.* One that rules or governs; one that assists in carrying on a government; an instrument made of wood, brass, ivory, etc., with straight edges or sides, by which straight lines may be drawn on paper or other substance, by guiding a pen or pencil along the edge.—**ruling,** röl′ing, *p.* and *a.* Governing; reigning; chief; prevalent; predominant.—*n.* A rule or point settled by a judge or court of law.

rum, rum, *n.* [Perhaps of West Indian origin; or from an old cant word *rumbooze*, good drink.] An alcoholic beverage distilled from a sugarcane product such as molasses.

rum, rum, *a.* [From an old cant word *rum, rome*, great, good, used in a contemptuous sense, from *Rom*, applied by themselves to the gypsies.] Old-fashioned; odd; queer. (*Slang.*)

rumble, rum′bl, *v.i.*—*rumbled, rumbling.* [Same as D. *rommelen*, Dan. *rumle*, G. *rummelen, rumpeln*, probably imitative of sound.] To make a low, heavy, continuous sound.—*n.* Such a sound; a rumbling; a seat for servants behind a carriage; an open rear seat in an automobile.—**rumbler,** rum′blėr, *n.* The person or thing that rumbles.—**rumblingly,** rum′bling•li, *adv.* In a rumbling manner.

rumen, rö′men, *n.* [L.] The upper or first stomach of animals which chew the cud.

ruminate, rö′mi•nāt, *v.i.*—*ruminated, ruminating.* [L. *rumino, ruminatum*, from *rumen*, the throat, the gullet.] To chew the cud; to chew again what has been slightly chewed and swallowed; to muse; to meditate; to think again and again; to ponder.—*v.t.* To chew over again; to muse or meditate on.—**ruminant,** rö′mi•nant, *a.* [L. *ruminans, ruminantis*, ppr. of *rumino.*] Chewing the cud; characterized by chewing again what has been swallowed (*ruminant* animals).—*n.* A member of an order of herbivorous hoofed mammals that chew the cud, as the camel, deer, goat, ox, etc.—**rumination,** rö•mi•nā′shon, *n.* The act of ruminating; the act of meditating; a musing or continued thinking.—**ruminator,** rö′mi•nā•tėr, *n.* One that ruminates.

rummage, rum′ij, *v.t.*—*rummaged, rummaging.* [Same as if *roomage*; originally a sea term signifying to stow goods in a ship's hold, or to remove them from the hold, from *rome*, an old form of *room*, or from D. *ruim*, the hold of a ship, a form of the same word. ROOM.] To search narrowly every place or part of, by looking into every corner and turning over goods or other things; to explore; to ransack.—*v.i.* To search a place narrowly by looking among things.—*n.* A searching carefully by looking into every corner and by tumbling over things.—**rummager,** rum′ij•ėr, *n.* One who rummages.

rummer, rum′ėr, *n.* [D. *roomer*, Sw. *remmer*, G. *rómer*, a large drinking glass; perhaps lit. a *Roman* glass.] A glass or drinking cup.

rummy. See RUM.

rumor, rumour, rö′mėr, *n.* [Fr. *rumeur*, from L. *rumor*, common talk. RUMBLE.] Flying or popular report; the common voice; a current story passing from one person to another, without any known authority for the truth of it; a mere report.—*v.t.* To tell or circulate by report; to spread abroad; to report.

rump, rump, *n.* [A Scandinavian word=Icel. *rumpr*, Sw. *rumpa*, D. *rompe*, G. *rumpf*, the trunk.] The end of the backbone of an animal, with the parts adjacent; the buttocks; *fig.* the fag end of something which lasts longer than the original body; *Eng. hist.* the fag end of the Long Parliament, after the expulsion of the majority of its members by Cromwell in 1648.

rumple, rum′pl, *v.t.*—*rumpled, rumpling.* [Same as D. *rompelen*, to rumple; akin to O.L.G. *rumpele*, a wrinkle; G. *rumpfen*, D. *rompelen*, to crimp, to wrinkle. *Rimple* is another form; comp. also *ripple.*] To wrinkle; to make uneven; to ruffle; to dishevel.—*n.* A fold or plait.

rumpus, rum′pus, *n.* [Perhaps imitative of a noise, like *rumble*; or allied to *romp.*] A riot; a great noise; disturbance. (*Colloq.*)

run, run, *v.i.* pret. *ran* (*run* is now incorrect); pp. *run*; ppr. *running.* [A.Sax. *rinnan* (pret. *ran*, pl. *runnon*, pp. *runnen*); O.Sax., Goth., and O.H.G. *rinnan*, D. *rennen, rinnen*, Icel. *renna*, G. *rennen*, to run; same root as in Skr. *ri*, to go.] To pass over the ground by using the legs more quickly than in walking; to contend in a race; hence, to enter into a contest; to flee for escape; to retreat hurriedly; to steal away; to extend quickly; to spread (the fire *runs* over a field); to rush or be carried along with violence (a ship *runs* against a rock); to move on wheels or runners, as a locomotive or sledge; to sail, as a ship; to pass or go back and forth from place to place; to ply (ships, railway trains, stagecoaches, etc., between different places); to move or pass, as a fluid, the sand in an hourglass, or the like; to be wet with a flowing liquid; to become fluid; to fuse; to melt; to spread on a surface; to spread and blend (colors *run* in washing; ink *runs* on damp paper); to discharge pus or other matter (an ulcer *runs*); to revolve on an axis or pivot; to turn, as a wheel; to continue going or in operation (an engine *runs*, the mills are *running*); to pass or proceed in thought or speech (to *run* from one topic to another); to pass from one state or condition to another (to *run* into error or into debt); to proceed or pass, as time; to have a certain course, track, or direction; to extend, stretch, lie (the street *runs* east and west); to have a certain written form; to read so or so to the ear (the lines *run* smoothly); to have a continued tenor or purport (the conversation *ran* as follows); to be popularly spread or received; to continue or be repeated for a certain time (the play *ran* for a hundred nights); to be carried to a pitch; to rise (debates *run* high); to grow exuberantly; to proceed or tend in growing; to continue in time before it becomes due and payable (a bill has ninety days to *run*).—*To run after*, to pursue or follow; to endeavor to obtain.—*To run against*, to come into collision with.—*To run at*, to attack with sudden violence; to rush upon.—*To run away*, to flee; to escape; to elope.—*To run away with*, to convey away in a hurried or clandestine manner; to join in eloping with; to bolt with; to start off with at a great pace (the horse *ran away with* the carriage).—*To run foul of*, to come into collision with.—*To run in* or *into*, to enter by running; to step in; to come or get into (to *run into* danger).—*To run on*, to be continued; to talk incessantly; to continue a course; *printing*, to be continued without a break or new paragraph.—*To run on all fours*, to run on hands and feet; to be coincident or concurrent; to be exactly analogous or similar to something else; to agree.—*To run out*, to stop after running to the end of its time, as a watch or sandglass; to come to an end; to expire (a lease *runs out* on October 1).—*To run over*, to overflow; to go over, examine, or recount cursorily (to *run over* all the particulars); to ride or drive over (to *run over* a child).—*To run through*, to spend quickly; to dissipate (he *ran through* his fortune).—*To run to seed*, said of herbaceous plants, which, instead of developing the produce for which they are valued, in a juicy state, shoot up, and yield, instead, flowers, and ultimately seed; hence, to become useless; to go to waste.—*To run up*, to rise; to grow; to increase (accounts *run up* very fast); to pass rapidly from bottom to top of (to *run up* a column of figures).—*v.t.* To cause to run or go quickly; to cause to be carried in a certain course (to *run* a ship aground); to cause to ply; to maintain in running (to *run* a stagecoach); to accomplish by running; to pursue, as a course; to incur; to encounter (to *run* the risk of being killed); to break through or evade (to *run* a blockade); hence, to smuggle; to import or export without paying duties; to push; to thrust; to pierce; to stab (to *run a* person through with a rapier); to pour forth in a stream; to melt; to melt and clarify; to form in a mold by melting; to carry on or conduct, as a hotel or other enterprise; to sew by passing the needle through and through in a continuous line.—*To run down*, to chase to weariness (to *run down* a stag); to run against and sink, as a vessel; to pursue with scandal or opposition.—*To run hard*, to press hard in a race or other competition;

to come very near beating; to press with jokes, sarcasm, or ridicule.—*To run in*, to take into custody, as by a policeman; to lock up. (*Slang*.)—*To run on* or *in*, *Print*. to carry on or continue, as a line, without break or a new paragraph.—*To run riot*. See RIOT.—*To run up*, to increase; to enlarge by additions (to *run up* a large account); to thrust up, as anything long and slender; to erect; especially, to erect hastily (to *run up* a block of buildings).—*To run the gantlet*. See GANTLET.—*n*. The act of running; a course run (a long *run*, a quick *run*); a trip; a pleasure trip or excursion (*colloq*.); particular or distinctive course, progress, tenor, etc.; continued course (a *run* of ill luck); a general or uncommon pressure or demand, as on a bank or treasury for payment of its notes; the distance sailed by a ship; a voyage; a passage from one place to another; a pair of millstones; a place where animals run or may run; especially, a large extent of grazing ground, called variously a *Cattle run*, a *Sheep run*, etc., according to the animals pastured; *music*, a succession of notes, either ascending or descending, played or sung rapidly.—*The common run* (or simply *the run*), that which passes under observation as usual or most general; the generality.—*By the run*, suddenly; quickly; at once; said of a fall or sudden descent.—*In the long run*, in the final result; in the conclusion or end.—*a*. Liquefied; melted; clarrified (*run* butter); run or conveyed ashore secretly; contraband (*run* brandy).—**runaway,** run′a•wā, *n*. One that flies from danger or restraint; one that deserts lawful service; a fugitive.—*a*. Acting the part of a runaway; escaping or breaking from restraint; accomplished or effected by running away or eloping (a *runaway* match).—**runnel,** run′l, *n*. A rivulet or small brook.—**runner,** run′ėr, *n*. One who runs; a racer; a messenger; an old name for a criminal detective; a slender prostrate stem sending out leaves and roots, as in the strawberry; any bird of the order Cursores; that on which a thing runs or slides (the *runner* or keel of a sleigh or skate).—*Runner-up*, a term applied, chiefly in golfing, but occasionally in other sports, to the player who is next to the winner in a competition.—**running,** run′ing, *p*. and *a*. Kept for racing (a *running* horse); in succession; without any intervening day, year, etc.; a semiadverbial usage (to visit two days *running*, to sow land two years *running*); discharging pus or matter.—*Running fight*, a fight kept up by the party pursuing and the party pursued.—*Running fire*, a constant fire of musketry or artillery.—*Out of the running*, out of the race.—*Running hand*, the style of handwriting in which the letters are formed without the pen being lifted from the paper.—*Running rigging*, the ropes used for hoisting a ship's sails, moving the yards, and the like: in distinction from *standing rigging*.—*n*. The act of one who runs; a quantity run (the first *running* of a still).

runagate, run′a•gāt, *n*. [Corruption of Fr. *renegat*. RENEGADE.] A fugitive; a vagabond; an apostate; a renegade.

runcinate, run′si•nāt, *a*. [L. *runcina*, a plane.] In *bot*. having curved indentations and lateral lobes turned backward, as in the dandelion leaf.

rundle, run′dl, *n*. [For *roundel*, from *round*.] A round; a step of a ladder.

rune, rön, *n*. [A.Sax. *run*, a rune, a mysterious or magical character, a mystery, a whisper; from root meaning to whisper, as in L. *rumor*, a rumor.] One of a particular set of alphabetic characters peculiar to the ancient northern nations of Europe, all the runes being formed almost entirely of straight lines, either single or in composition.—**runic,** rön′ik, *a*. Pertaining to runes.—*Runic wand*, *runic staff*, a willow wand inscribed with runes, used for purposes of divination.—*Runic rhyme*, rhyme where the melody or rhyme follows readily, or in ranks, as in the runes. (*Poe*.)

rung, rung, pp. of *ring*.

rung, rung, *n*. [A.Sax. *hrung*, a pole, a beam; Icel. *röng*, a rib in a ship; O.D. *ronghe*, a prop; G. *runge*, a short piece.] A heavy staff; the round or step of a ladder.

runlet, rundlet, run′let, rund′let, *n*. [For *roundlet*, from *round*.] A small barrel of no certain dimensions.

runnel. See RUN.

runt, runt, *n*. [Origin doubtful.] Any animal below the usual size of the breed; a variety of pigeon; a root of kale, colewort, or cabbage; a cudgel.

rupee, rö•pē′, *n*. [Hind. *rūpiyu*, a rupee, from Skr. *rūpya*, silver.] A silver coin, the unit of value in India.

rupture, rup′chėr *n*. [Fr. *rupture*, from L.L. *ruptura*, a breaking, from L. *rumpo*, *ruptum*, to break (seen also in *abrupt*, *corrupt*, *eruption*, *interrupt*, etc., and giving origin also to *route*, *rout*, etc.).] The act of breaking or bursting; the state of being broken or violently parted; *med*. same as hernia, especially hernia of the abdomen; a breach of concord either between individuals or nations; open hostility or war; a quarrel.—*v.t.*—*ruptured*, *rupturing*. To make a rupture in; to burst; to part by violence; to affect with or cause to suffer from rupture.—*v.i.* To suffer a breach or disruption.

rural, rö′ral, *a*. [L. *ruralis*, from *rus*, *ruris*, the country (whence also *rustic*); same root as *room*.] Pertaining to the country, as distinguished from a city or town; suiting the country or resembling it; pertaining to agriculture or farming.—*Rural dean*, in the Church of England, an ecclesiastic under the bishop and the archdeacon, in charge of the clergy of a district. **ruralist,** rö′ral•ist, *n*. One that leads a rural life.—**ruralize,** rö′ral•īz, *v.i.*—*ruralized*, *ruralizing*. To go into the country; to go to dwell in the country; to rusticate.—*v.t*. To render rural; to give a rural character to.—**rurally,** rö′ral•li, *adv*. In a rural manner.—**rurality,** rö•ral′i•ti, *n*. The quality of being rural.

ruse, röz, *n*. [Fr. *ruse*, from *ruser*, to dodge; O.Fr. *reuser*, to get out of the way, from L. *recusare*, to refuse. RECUSANT.] An artifice, trick, or stratagem; a wile.

rush, rush, *n*. [O.E. *rishe*, *rusche*, from A.Sax. *risce*, *ricse*, a rush; D. *rusch*, G. *rausch*; probably from L. *ruscum*, butcher's-broom.] The common name of herbaceous plants, usually growing in damp meadows and swamps, having round erect stems which are sometimes used for plaiting into mats, chair bottoms, etc., and which contain a large pith; used typically of anything weak or of trivial value; the merest trifle; a straw.—**rush candle,** *n*. A small taper made by the pith of a rush in tallow.—**rush light,** *n*. A rush candle or its light; hence, any weak flickering light.

rush, rush, *v.i.* [Akin to Dan. *ruske*, Sw. *ruska*, to shake; D. *ruischen*, G. *rauschen*, to rustle; O.G. *rûschen*, to rush, to roar; comp. also A.Sax. *hreósan*, to fall, to rush.] To move or drive forward with impetuosity, violence, and tumultuous rapidity; to enter with undue eagerness, or without due deliberation (to *rush* into a scheme).—*n*. A driving forward with eagerness and haste; a violent motion or course; an eager demand; a run.—**rusher,** rush′ėr, *n*. One who rushes.

rusk, rusk, *n*. [Perhaps akin to L.G. *rusken*, to crackle, as we have *cracknel*, a biscuit, from *crack*.] A slice of sweet light bread that is rebaked; zweiback.

Russ, rus, *a*. Pertaining to the Russians.—*n*. The language of the Russians; *sing*. and *pl*. a native or the natives of Russia.—**Russia leather,** rush′a, *n*. A strong, pliant, and waterproof leather, having a peculiar penetrating odor, due to the oil of birch used in its preparation, specially useful in binding books, the oil repelling insects.—**Russian,** rush′an, *a*. Pertaining to Russia.—*n*. A native of Russia; the language of Russia; Russ.—**Russophile,** rus′o•fīl, *n*. [*Russ*, and Gr. *philos*, a friend.] One whose sympathies lie toward Russia or her policy.—**Russophobia,** rus•o•fō′bi•a, *n*. [*Russ*, and Gr. *phobos*, fear.] A fear of Russia or the Russians.

russet, rus′et, *a*. [O.Fr. *rousset*, from L. *russus*, red, akin to *ruber*, red.] Of a reddish-brown color; coarse; homespun; rustic; from the general color of homespun cloth.—*n*. A kind of apple of a russet color and rough skin; a pigment of a rich transparent brown color obtained from madder.—*v.t*. To give a russet hue to; to change into russet.

rust, rust, *n*. [A.Sax. *rust*, rust—D. *roest*, Dan. *rust*, Sw. and G. *rost*, rust; so called from its *red* color, the root being that of *red*, *ruddy*, L. *ruber*, red (RUBRIC); *russus*, reddish (RUSSET).] The red or orange-yellow coating (an oxide of iron) which is formed on the surface of iron when exposed to air and moisture; a composition of iron filings and sal-ammoniac, with sometimes a little sulfur, moistened with water and used for filling fast joints; a parasitic fungus which attacks the leaves, glumes, stalks, etc., of cereals and grasses; any foul extraneous matter; corrosive or injurious accretion or influence.—*v.i.* To contract or gather rust; to be oxidized; to assume an appearance as if coated with rust; to degenerate in idleness or inaction. —*v.t.* To cause to contract rust; to impair by time and inactivity.—**rustily,** rus′ti•li, *adv.* In a rusty state; in a manner to suggest rustiness.—**rustiness,** rus′ti•nes, *n.* The state of being rusty.—**rusty,** rus′ti, *a.* Covered or affected with rust; having the color of rust; appearing as if covered with rust; impaired by inaction or neglect of use.

rustic, rus′tik, *a.* [L. *rusticus*, from *rus*, the country. RURAL.] Pertaining to the country; living in or found in the country; rural; plain; simple; not elegant, refined, or costly.—*Rustic work*, masonry worked with grooves between the courses, to look like open joints; summerhouses, garden seats, etc., made from rough limbs or branches of trees.—*n.* An inhabitant of the country; a clown; a swain.—**rustically,** rus′ti•kal•li, *adv.* In a rustic manner.—**rusticate,** rus′ti•kāt, *v.i.*—*rusticated, rusticating.* [L. *rusticor*, *rusticatus*.] To dwell or reside in the country.—*v.t.* To suspend from studies at a college or university and send away for a time by way of punishment.—**rustication,** rus•ti•kā′shon, *n.* The act of rusticating or state of being rusticated.—**rusticity,** rus•tis′i•ti, *n.* The state or quality of being rustic.

rustily, rustiness, rusty. See RUST.

rustle, rus′l, *v.i.*—*rustled, rustling.* [A.Sax. *hristlan*, to rustle, a dim. and freq. form corresponding to Icel. *hrista*, Dan. *ryste*, Sw. *rysta*, to shake, to tremble.] To make a quick succession of small sounds like the rubbing of silk cloth or dry leaves; to give out a slightly sibilant sound when shaken.—*v.t.* To cause to rustle; to steal (cattle); to do or get quickly and energetically.—*n.* A slight crackling sound as of dry leaves or silk.—**rustler,** rus′l•ėr, *n.* One who steals cattle; one who rustles.

rut, rut, *n.* [Fr. *rut*, O.Fr. *ruit*, the noise which deer make when they desire to come together, from L. to bellow.] The time during which deer and some other animals are under the sexual excitement.—*v.i. rutted, rutting.* To desire to come together for copulation: said of deer. —*v.t.* To cover in copulation.—**ruttish,** rut′ish, *a.* Lustful; libidinous.

rut, rut, *n.* [Same word as *route, rote.*] The track of a wheel, a line cut on the soil with a spade.—*v.t.*—*rutted, rutting.* To make ruts in or on with cart wheels; to cut a line on, as on the soil, with a spade.—**rutty,** rut′i, *a.* Full of ruts; cut by wheels, as a road.

rutabaga, rö•ta•bā′ga, *n.* [Origin doubtful.] The Swedish turnip.

ruth, röth, *n.* [From *rue*, comp. *truth*, from *true*.] Mercy; pity; tenderness; sorrow for the misery of another; sorrowful or tender regret. [*Mainly poet.*]—**ruthless,** röth′les, *a.* Having no ruth or pity; cruel; pitiless; barbarous.—**ruthlessly,** röth′les•li, *adv.* In a ruthless manner.—**ruthlessness,** röth′les•nes, *n.* Pitilessness.

ruthenium, rö•thē′ni•um, *n.* [From *Ruthenia*, a Latin name for Russia, having been first obtained in ore from the Ural.] A rare steel-gray metallic element of the platinum group. Symbol, Ru; at. no., 44; at. wt., 101.07.

rutile, rö′tīl, *n.* [L. *rutilus*, red, inclining to yellow.] Native titanic oxide, an ore of titanium of a reddish-brown color.

rye, rī, *n.* [A.Sax. *ryge*, Icel. *rúgr*, Dan. *rug*, Sw. *rog*, D. *rogge*, G. *roggen, rocken*, cog. Gr. *oryza*, rice.] A cereal plant which bears naked seeds furnished with awns like barley, much cultivated for food and as a spring forage crop for livestock; the seeds of this plant; whiskey distilled from these seeds.

S

S, s, es, the nineteenth letter of the English alphabet, a consonant representing a hissing sound.

sabadilla, sab•a•dil′a, *n.* The Spanish-American name for the seeds of a bulbous plant used in medicine.

Sabaism, sa•bā′izm, *n.* [Comp. Heb. *tsebâôth*, the heavenly host. SABAOTH.] The worship of the heavenly bodies, anciently practiced in western Asia.

Sabaoth, sa•bā′oth, *n.* [Heb. *tsebâôth*, armies, from *tsâbâ*, to assemble, to fight.] *Scrip.* armies; hosts.

Sabbath, sab′bath, *n.* [Heb. *shabbath*, rest, the day of rest.] The day which God appointed to be observed as a day of rest; originally the seventh day of the week, but in the Christian church the first day of the week is held sacred, in commemoration of the resurrection of Christ on that day; the Lord's day; Sunday; intermission of pain or sorrow; time of rest; the sabbatical year among the Israelites (O.T.). —*Sabbath-day's journey*, the distance which the Jews were permitted to travel on the Sabbath day, probably about an English mile. ∴ *Sabbath* is not strictly synonymous with *Sunday. Sunday* is the mere name of the day, *Sabbath* is the name of the institution. *Sunday* is the *Sabbath* of Christians, *Saturday* is the *Sabbath* of the Jews. But in the mouths of many it is equivalent to *Sunday*.—**Sabbatarian,** sab•ba•tâ′ri•an, *n.* One who observes the Sabbath with extraordinary or unreasonable rigor; one careful to abstain from work or relaxation on Sunday. Used also *adjectively*.—**Sabbatarianism,** sab•ba•tâ′ri•an•izm, *n.* The tenets of Sabbatarians.—**Sabbatic, Sabbatical,** sab•bat′ik, sab•bat′i•kal, *a.* [L. *sabbaticus*.] Pertaining to the Sabbath.—*Sabbatical year*, every seventh year, in which the Israelites were to allow their fields and vineyards to rest or lie without tillage; a period of absence, as granted a professor every seventh year.

Sabellian, sa•bel′i•an, *n.* A follower of *Sabellius*, a philosopher of Egypt in the third century A.D., who taught that there is one person only in the Godhead.—*a.* Of or belonging to the group of early inhabitants in Italy, including Sabines, Samnites, Campanians, Lucanians, and others.

saber, sabre, sā′bėr, *n.* [Fr. *sabre*, from D., Dan., and Sw. *sabel*, G. *säbel*, a saber; ultimate origin unknown.] A sword with a broad and heavy blade, thick at the back and a little curved toward the point, specially adapted for cutting; a cavalry sword.—*v.t. sabered, sabering*, or *sabred, sabring.* To strike, cut, or kill with a saber.

Sabines, sa′bīnz, *n.* The tribe north of Rome, and one of the Sabellian family.—**sabine,** *a.* Of or belonging to the Sabines, Horace's *Sabine* farm.

sable, sā′bl, *n.* [O.Fr. *sable*, from Pol. *sabol*, Russ. *sobol*, a Slavonic word.] A digitigrade carnivorous animal nearly allied to the marten, found chiefly in the northern regions of Asia, and hunted for its black, lustrous fur; the fur of the sable; a black or mourning suit or garment; the heraldic name for black.—*a.* Of the color of the sable; black; dark.—*v.t.*—*sabled, sabling.* To make sable or dark in color.

sabot, sa•bō′, *n.* [Fr. Origin unknown.] A wooden shoe worn by the peasantry in France, Belgium, etc.

sabotage, sa′bo•täzh, *n.* [Fr. from *saboter*, to work badly.] Malicious harm done to tools, machinery, production, etc., as by an employee during a labor dispute or by an enemy agent.—*v.t.* and *i.*—*sabotaged, sabotaging.* To harm by sabotage.—**saboteur,** sa•bo•tėr′, *n.* One who engages in sabotage.

sabulous, sab′ū•lus, *a.* [L. *sabulosus*, from *sabulum*, sand.] Sandy; gritty.—**sabulosity,** sab•ū•los′i•ti, *n.*

Sac, sak or säk, *n.* A member of the tribe of Algonquian Indians that once lived along the upper Mississippi River.

sac, sak, *n.* [L. *saccus*, a bag. SACK.] A bag or cyst of an animal or plant; a pouch; a receptacle for a liquid (the lachrymal *sac*).—**saccate,** sak′kāt, *a. Bot.* furnished with or having the form of a sac or pouch.—**sacculated,** sak′kū•lā•ted, *a.* Furnished with little sacs.—**saccule,** sak′kūl, *n.* [L. *sacculus*.] A little sac; a cyst; a cell.

saccate. See SAC.

saccharic, sak•kar′ik, *a.* [L. *saccharum*, sugar, from Gr. *sakchar*, *sakcharon*, sugar, a word of oriental origin. SUGAR.] Pertaining to or obtained from sugar or allied substances.—**saccharify,** sak•kar′i•fī, *v.t.* —*saccharified*, *saccharifying*. [Fr. *saccharifier*.] To convert into sugar.—**saccharin, saccharine,** sak′ka•rin, *n.* A substance, 300 to 500 times sweeter than cane sugar, derived from coal tar.—*a.* Pertaining to, or like sugar; sickeningly sweet.—**saccharoid, saccharoidal,** sak′ka•roid, sak′ka•roi•dal, *a.* Having a texture resembling that of loaf sugar. —**saccharometer, saccharimeter,** sak•ka•rom′et•ėr, sak•ka•rim′et•ėr, *n.* An instrument for determining the quantity of saccharine matter in any solution.

saccule. See SAC.

sacerdotal, sas•ėr•dō′tal, *a.* [L. *sacerdotalis*, from *sacerdos*, a priest. SACRED.] Pertaining to priests or the priesthood; priestly.—**sacerdotally,** sas•ėr•dō′tal•li, *adv.* In a sacerdotal manner.—**sacerdotalism,** sas•ėr•dō′tal•izm, *n.* Sacerdotal system or spirit; a tendency to attribute a lofty and sacred character to the priesthood; priestcraft.

sachem, sā′chem, *n.* A chief among some of the early American Indian tribes.

sachet, sa•shā′, *n.* [Fr.] A small bag for containing odorous substances.

sack, sak, *n.* [A.Sax. *sacc*, Dan. *säk*, D. *zak*, G. *sack*, Goth *sakkus*, from L *saccus*, Gr. *sakkos*, probably of Eastern origin, similar forms being also found in Hebrew and Coptic.] A bag, usually a large cloth bag, used for holding and conveying corn, wool, cotton, hops, and the like; a measure or weight which varies according to the article and country; a kind of loose gown or mantle formerly worn; a sacque.—*v.t.* To put in a sack or in bags.—**sackcloth,** sak′kloth, *n.* Cloth of which sacks are made; coarse cloth worn in mourning, distress, or penance.—**sackful,** sak′ful, *n.* As much as a sack will hold.—**sacking,** sak′ing, *n.* A coarse fabric of which sacks are made.

sack, sak, *v.t.* [Fr. *sac*, Sp. and Pg. *saco*, It. *sacco*, plunder; pillage; from the use of a *sack* in removing plunder. SACK, a bag.] To storm; to pillage; to devastate: usually said of a town; to dismiss an employee. (*Colloq.*).—*n.* The act of one who sacks; the storm and plunder of a town or city; also booty; spoil.—**sacker,** sak′ėr, *n.* One who sacks.

sack, sak, *n.* [Fr. *sec*, dry, from L. *siccus*, dry.] Formerly, a general name for different sorts of dry wines, more especially the Spanish, which were first extensively used in England in the sixteenth century.

sackbut, sak′but, *n.* [Fr. *saquebute*, from Sp. *sacabuche*, a kind of trumpet, from *sacar*, to draw, and *buche*, the stomach.] A musical instrument of the trumpet kind, so contrived that it can be lengthened or shortened according to the tone required, like the trombone; *Scrip.* a musical stringed instrument mentioned in Dan. iii., perhaps a kind of guitar.

sacque, sak, *n.* [A form of *sack*, Fr. *sac*, a bag. SACK.] A kind of loose gown or upper robe worn by ladies in the seventeenth and eighteenth centuries.

sacral. See SACRUM.

sacrament, sak′ra•ment, *n.* [L. *sacramentum*, a military oath of allegiance, an oath, from *sacer*, sacred (seen in *sacrifice*, etc.). SACRED.] *Theol.* an outward and visible sign of inward and spiritual grace; a solemn religious ceremony enjoined by Christ, to be observed by his followers, by which their special relation to him is created, or their obligations to him renewed and ratified. In the *R. Cath. Ch.* and the *Greek Ch.* there are seven sacraments, viz. baptism, confirmation, the Eucharist, penance, extreme unction, holy orders, and matrimony; but Protestants in general acknowledge but two sacraments, baptism and the Lord's supper. When used without any qualifying word by *sacrament* is meant the Eucharist or Lord's supper.—**sacramental,** sak•ra•men′tal, *a.* Constituting a sacrament or pertaining to it; having the character of a sacrament. — **Sacramentarian,** sak′ra•men•tâ″ri•an, *n.* A person holding some special view in regard to the sacraments.

sacrarium, sa•krâ′ri•um, *n.* [L., from *sacer*, sacred.] A chapel in the house of ancient Romans devoted to some particular divinity; the adytum of a temple; that part of a church where the altar is situated.

sacre, sā′kėr. See SAKER.

sacred, sā′kred, *a.* [Pp. of old *sacre*, to set apart, to consecrate; Fr. *sacrer*, from L. *sacrare*, from *sacer*, sacred (seen also in *sacrilege*, *sacrifice*, *consecrate*, *desecrate*, etc.); same root as in *sanction*, *sanctify*.] Set apart by solemn religious ceremony; dedicated to religious use; holy; not profane or common; relating to religion or the services of religion; not secular; consecrated; dedicated; devoted: with *to* (*sacred to* one's memory); entitled to the highest respect or reverence; venerable; not to be profaned or violated; inviolable; inviolate (a secret kept *sacred*). —*Sacred College*, the college of cardinals at Rome.—*Sacred Majesty*, a title once applied to the kings of England.—**sacredly,** sā′kred•li, *adv.* In a sacred manner; religiously; inviolably; strictly.—**sacredness,** sā′kred•nes, *n.* The state of being sacred; holiness; sanctity; inviolableness.

sacrifice, sak′ri•fīs, *n.* [Fr. *sacrifice*, from L. *sacrificium*, from *sacer*, sacred, and *facio*, to make. SACRED.] The offering of anything to God, or to a god; a consecratory rite; anything consecrated and offered to God or to a divinity; an immolated victim on an altar; surrender or loss made for gaining something else; a giving up of some desirable object in behalf of a higher object; the thing so devoted or given up; the selling of goods under cost price.—*v.t.*—*sacrificed*, *sacrificing*. To make an offering or sacrifice of; to consecrate or present to some divinity; to immolate on the altar of God either as an atonement for sin or to express gratitude; to destroy, surrender, or suffer to be lost for the sake of obtaining something else; to devote or give up with loss or suffering; to destroy; to kill.—*v.i.*—To offer up a sacrifice; to make offerings to God or to a deity by the slaughter and burning of victims, or some part of them, on an altar.—**sacrificer,** sak′ri•fīs•ėr, *n.* One that sacrifices.—**sacrificial,** sak•ri•fish′al, *a.* Pertaining to sacrifice; performing sacrifices; consisting in sacrifice.

sacrilege, sak′ri•lej, *n.* [Fr. *sacrilège*, from L. *sacrilegium*—*sacer*, sacred, and *lego*, to gather, to pick up.] The violation or profaning of sacred things; the alienating to common purposes what has been appropriated to religious uses; the stealing of goods out of any church or chapel.—**sacrilegious,** sak•ri•lē′jus, *a.* Guilty of or involving sacrilege; violating sacred things; profane; impious.—**sacrilegiously,** sak•ri•lē′jus•li, *adv.* In a sacrilegious manner.—**sacrilegiousness,** sak•ri•lē′jus•nes, *n.* The quality of being sacrilegious.

sacring, sā′kring, *n.* [Fr. *sacrer*, to make sacred.] Consecration. (*Tenn.*) —**sacring bell, Sanctus bell,** *n. R. Cath. Ch.* the small bell rung at the *sanctus* and at the elevation of the host in High Mass.

sacristan, sak′ris•tan, *n.* [L.L. *sacristanus*. *Sexton* is a contr. of this word.] An officer of the church who has charge of the sacristy and its contents.—**sacristy,** sak′ris•ti, *n.* [Fr. *sacristie*.] A room in a church where sacred utensils and clerical vestments are deposited; the vestry.

sacroiliac, sā•krō•il′i•ak, *a. Anat.* pertaining to both the sacrum and the ilium (*sacroiliac* ligaments).

sacrosanct, sak′rō•sangkt, *a.* [L. *sacrosanctus*—*sacer*, sacred, *sanctus*, holy.] Sacred and inviolable; holy and venerable.

sacrosciatic, sā′krō•sī•at″ik, *a.* [From *sacrum* and *sciatic*.] *Anat.* pertaining jointly to the sacrum and ischium.

sacrum, sā′krum, *n.* [L. *os sacrum*, the sacred bone.] *Anat.* the bone which forms the basis or inferior extremity of the vertebral column, said to derive its name from its having been offered in sacrifice, and hence considered sacred.—**sacral,** sā′kral, *a.* Pertaining to the sacrum.

sad, sad, *a.* [A.Sax. *saed*, satisfied, sated, weary, sick; Icel. *saddr*, sated, full; Goth. *saths*, satiated, full; cog. with L. *satur*, full, *satis*, enough. SATE, SATISTY.] Serious‡; sedate or grave‡; sorrowful; melancholy; mournful; affected with grief; downcast; gloomy; having the external appearance of sorrow; afflictive; calamitous; causing sorrow; bad; naughty; wicked.—**sadden,** sad′n, *v.t.* To make sad or sorrowful; to render melancholy or gloomy.—*v.i.* To become sad or sorrowful.—**sadly,** sad′li, *adv.* In a sad manner; sorrowfully; grievously; calamitously.—**sadness,** sad′nes, *n.* The state or quality of being sad; sorrowfulness; dejection.

saddle, sad′l, *n.* [A.Sax. *sadel, sadol*= Dan. *saddel,* Icel. *sothull,* G. *sattel,* a saddle; perhaps from L. *sedile,* a seat, from *sedeo,* to sit. Same root as *seat, set, sit.*] A seat to be placed on an animal's back for the rider to sit on; a padded piece of harness on an animal's back supporting the shafts of a vehicle.—*v.t.*—*saddled, saddling.* To put a saddle on; to load; to burden (to *saddle* a person with expense).—**saddlebag,** *n.* One of a pair of bags united by straps for carriage on horseback, one bag on each side.—**saddlebow,** *n.* The upper front part of a saddle, formed of two curved pieces united in an arch; a pommel.—**saddlecloth,** *n.* A cloth attached to a saddle, and extending over the loins of the horse; a housing. —**saddle horse,** *n.* A horse used for riding with a saddle.—**saddler,** sad′lėr, *n.* One whose occupation is to make saddles or harness generally.—**saddlery,** sad′lėr•i, *n.* The manufactures of a saddler; trade of a saddler.—**saddletree,** *n.* The wooden frame of a saddle.

Sadducee, sad′dū•sē, *n.* [Gr. *saddoukaios,* Heb. *tsadûkîm,* 'The righteous ones', 'The just.'] One of a sect or party among the ancient Jews, who denied the existence of any spiritual beings except God, believed that the soul died with the body, and therefore that there was no resurrection, and adhered to the written law alone. —**Sadduceeism,** sad′dū•sē•izm, *n.* The tenets of the Sadducees.—**Sadducean,** sad•dū•sē′an, *a.* Pertaining to or characteristic of the Sadducees.

sadism, sa′dizm, sā′dizm, *n.* [Fr. *sadisme,* after the Marquis de *Sade.*] Sexual gratification through inflicting pain on the love object; any morbid pleasure in inflicting pain.

safari, sa•fär′i, *n.* [Ar.] An expedition, especially for hunting; the members of such an expedition.

safe, sāf, *a.* [O.E. *sauf,* from Fr. *sauf,* safe, from L. *salvus,* safe (whence also *salvation*).] Free from or not liable to danger of any kind; free from or having escaped hurt, injury, or damage; not exposing to danger; securing from harm; no longer dangerous; placed beyond the power of doing harm; sound; whole (a *safe* conscience).—*n.* A box or chamber of great strength for preserving money, jewels, account books, and other valuable articles from thieves or against the action of fire; a ventilated or refrigerated receptacle in which meat is kept.—**safe conduct,** *n.* A convoy or guard for a person traveling in a foreign or hostile country; a writing serving as a pass or warrant of security to a traveler.—**safeguard,** sāf′gärd, *n.* One who or that which defends or protects; a defense; protection; a convoy or guard to protect a traveler; a passport; a warrant of protection to a traveler.—*v.t.* To guard; to protect.—**safekeeping,** *n.* The act of keeping in safety from injury or from escape; secure guardianship.—**safely,** sāf′li, *adv.* In a safe manner; without incurring danger; without hurt or injury; in safety; securely; carefully.—**safeness,** sāf′nes, *n.* The condition or quality of being safe; freedom from danger.—**safety,** sāf′ti, *n.* The state or quality of being safe; exemption from injury or loss; the state of not being liable to danger or injury; freedom from danger; preservation; the state or quality of not causing danger; close custody.—**safety belt,** *n.* A lifebelt; a strap for fastening a person to a seat or other object for his own protection.—**safety lamp,** *n.* A lamp for lighting coal mines without exposing workmen to the explosion of firedamp, the flame being enveloped in a cylinder of wire gauze, and thus prevented from igniting the inflammable gas.—**safety match,** *n.* A match which will light only on being rubbed on a specially prepared friction substance.—**safety pin,** *n.* A pin for articles of dress having its point fitting into a kind of sheath, so that it may not be readily withdrawn or prick the wearer or others.—**safety valve,** *n.* A contrivance for obviating or diminishing the risk of explosions in steam boilers, the principle of which consists in opposing the pressure within the boiler by such a force as will yield before it reaches the point of danger, and permit the steam to escape.

safflower, saf′flou•ėr, *n.* [From *saffron* and *flower.*] Bastard saffron, a plant cultivated in the south of Europe, Egypt, etc., on account of its flowers, which in their dried state form the safflower of commerce, and afford two coloring matters (also called safflower), a yellow and a red.

saffron, saf′ron, *n.* [Fr. *safran,* from Sp., Ar., and Per. *zaferân,* saffron.] A plant of the crocus genus with flowers of a purple color, the dried stigmata of which form the saffron of the shops, a substance of a rich orange color, used as a coloring and flavoring ingredient in culinary preparations, liqueurs, etc., and yielding an orange-red extract used in dyeing and painting.—*a.* Having the color of saffron flowers; yellow.—*v.t.* To tinge with saffron; to make yellow; to gild.

sag, sag, *v.i.*—*sagged, sagging.* [Allied to L.G. *sacken,* D. *zakken,* to sink; also perhaps to *sink.*] To incline or hang away owing to insufficiently supported weight; to sink in the middle; to hang off the perpendicular; to yield under the pressure of care, difficulties, or the like; to waver; *naut.* to incline to the leeward; to make leeway.—*v.t.* To cause to bend or give way.—*n.* The state or act of sagging.

saga, sä′ga, *n.* [Icel. *saga,* a tale, a history; from *segja,* E. to *say.* SAY.] An ancient Scandinavian legend or tradition of considerable length relating either mythical or historical events; a tale.

sagacious, sa•gā′shus, *a.* [L. *sagax, sagacis,* from *sagio,* to perceive keenly, from a root signifying to be sharp, seen in Gr. *sagaris,* a battleax, Skr. *saghnomi,* to kill.] Intellectually keen or quick; acute in discernment; discerning and judicious; shrewd; full of wisdom; sage; showing intelligence resembling that of man: said of the lower animals; quick of scent (*Milton*).—**sagaciously,** sa•gā′shus•li, *adv.* In a sagacious manner.—**sagaciousness,** sa•gā′shus•nes, *n.* The quality of being sagacious.—**sagacity,** sa•gas′i•ti, *n.* [L. *sagacitas.*] The quality of being sagacious; quickness of discernment; readiness of apprehension with soundness of judgment; shrewdness and common sense; intelligence resembling that of mankind (the *sagacity* of a dog).

sagamore, sag′a•mōr, *n.* Among some tribes of American Indians, a king or chief; a sachem.

sage, sāj, *n.* [Fr. *sauge,* from L. *salvia,* sage, from *salvus,* safe, sound; on account of the reputed virtues of the plant. SAFE.] A garden plant much used in cookery, and formerly also in great repute for its medicinal qualities.—*Sage apple,* an excrescence upon a species of sage caused by the puncture of an insect.—*Sagebrush,* an American shrub of the wormwood family.—*Sage cheese,* a kind of cheese flavored and colored green with the juice of sage.—*Sage cock,* a species of grouse of the Rocky Mountain region, which feeds on the leaves of the sagebrush.

sage, sāj, *a.* [Fr. *sage,* from L. *sapius,* wise, from *sapio,* to be wise (whence *sapient*).] Wise; sagacious; proceeding from wisdom; well-judged; grave; serious.—*n.* A wise man; a man venerable for years, and of sound judgment and prudence; a grave philosopher.—**sagely,** sāj′li, *adv.* In a sage manner; wisely.—**sageness,** sāj′nes, *n.* Wisdom; sagacity.

sagger, sag′ėr, *n.* [Prov.E. *saggard, saggar,* contr, for *safeguard.*] The case of fire clay in which fine stoneware is enclosed while being baked in the kiln.

sagittal, saj′i•tal, *a.* [L. *sagittalis,* from *sagitta,* an arrow.] Pertaining to an arrow; resembling an arrow; *anat.* applied to the suture which unites the parietal bones of the skull. —**Sagittarius,** saj•i•tâ′ri•us, *n.* [L., an archer.] One of the zodiacal constellations, which the sun enters Nov. 22; represented by the figure of a centaur in the act of shooting an arrow from his bow.—**sagittate,** saj′i•tāt, *a.* Shaped like the head of an arrow: used especially in *bot.*

sago, sā′gō, *n.* [Malay and Javanese *sagu,* sago, from Papuan *sagu,* bread.] A kind of starch produced from the stem of several palms of the East Indies, forming light, wholesome, nutritious food.

Sahib, sä′ib, *n.* [Hind., from Ar.

sahib, lord, master.] A term of respect used by the natives of India or Persia in addressing or speaking of Europeans.

said, sed, pret. and pp. of *say*; so written for *sayed*. Declared; uttered; aforesaid; before mentioned.

sail, sāl, *n.* [A.Sax. *segel*, *segl*, a sail = Icel. *segl*, G. and Sw. *segel*, Dan. *seil*, D. *zeil*; probably from an Indo-European root (*sagh*) meaning to check, to resist (the wind).] A piece of cloth, etc., spread to the wind to cause a vessel to move through the water, usually made of canvas; that portion of the arm of a windmill which catches the wind; a ship or other vessel: used as a plural with the singular form (a fleet of twenty *sail*); an excursion upon water; a passage in a vessel.—*Full sail*, with all sails set.—*To loose sails*, to unfurl them.—*To make sail*, to extend an additional quantity of sail.—*To set sail*, to expand or spread the sails; and hence, to begin a voyage.—*To shorten sail*, to reduce the extent of sail or take in a part.—*To strike sail*, to lower the sails suddenly, as in saluting or in sudden gusts of wind.—*Under sail*, having the sails spread.—*v.i.* To be impelled by the action of wind upon sails, as a ship, or by steam, cars, etc.; to be conveyed in a vessel on water; to pass by water; to set sail; to begin a voyage; to glide through the air; to pass smoothly along; to glide; to float (the clouds *sail*).—*v.t.* To pass over by means of sails; to move upon or pass over, as in a ship (to *sail* the seas); to fly or glide through; to navigate; to direct or manage the motion of.—**sailboat,** *n.* A boat propelled by or fitted for a sail or sails.—**sailcloth,** *n.* Canvas or duck used in making sails for ships, etc.—**sailer,** sā′lėr, *n.* A ship or other vessel with reference to her manner of sailing (a fast *sailer*).—**sailing,** sā′ling, *n.* The act of one who or that which sails; the art of navigation.—**sailor,** sā′lėr, *n.* A mariner; a seaman.

sainfoin, saintfoin, sān′foin, sānt′-foin, *n.* [Fr. *sainfoin*, from *sain*, wholesome, and *foin*, hay, or from *saint*, holy, and *foin*.] A leguminous plant cultivated for supplying fodder for cattle either in the green state or when converted into hay.

saint, sānt, *n.* [O.Fr., from L. *sanctus*, sacred, holy, pp. of *sancio*, to render sacred. SACRED.] A person sanctified; one eminent for piety and virtue; particularly applied to the apostles and other holy persons of early Christian times; one of the blessed in heaven; an angel (O. and N.T.); a person canonized by the Church of Rome: often contracted *St.* when coming before a personal name.—*St. Andrew's cross*, a cross shaped like the letter X.—*St. Anthony's fire*, erysipelas.—*St. Cuthbert's beads*, the detached and perforated joints of the fossil stems of encrinites.—*St. Elmo's fire*, a popular name for a meteoric appearance seen playing about the masts of a ship.—*St. George's ensign*, the distinguishing badge of ships of the British navy, consisting of a red cross on a white field, with the union flag in the upper quarter next the mast.—*St. Ignatius' bean*, the seed of a large climbing shrub nearly allied to that which produces nux vomica.—*St. John's bread*, the carob tree or its fruit.—*St. Vitus' dance*. See CHOREA.—*Saint's bell*. See SACRING BELL.—*v.t.*† To enroll among the saints; to canonize.—*v.i.* To act piously or with a show of piety. (*Shak.*)—**sainted,** sān′ted, *p.* and *a.* Canonized; holy; pious; entered into bliss; gone to heaven: often used as a euphemism for *dead*.—**sainthood,** sānt′hŏd, *n.* The character, rank, or position of a saint.—**saintly,** sānt′li, *a.* Resembling a saint; becoming a saint.—**saintliness,** sānt′li•nes, *n.* The quality or state of being saintly.—**saintship,** sānt′ship, *n.* The character or qualities of a saint.

Saint Patrick's Day, *n.* March 17, observed in honor of Ireland's patron saint, St. Patrick.

Saint Valentine's Day, *n.* February 14, feast day of a Christian martyr; a day when tokens of affection, valentines, are given.

sake, sāk, *n.* [A.Sax. *sacu*, contention; akin to A.Sax. *sacan*, Icel. *saka*, to contend, accuse, etc.] Final cause; purpose; account; regard to any person or thing: always with *for*.

sake, sä′kē, *n.* [Jap.] A Japanese wine made from rice.

saker, sā′kėr, *n.* [Fr. *sacre*, a falcon, then a piece of ordnance; Sp. and Pg. *sacre*, from Ar. *saqr*, a sparrow hawk.] A hawk; a species of falcon; formerly also a small piece of artillery.

sal, sal, *n.* [L. SALT.] Salt: a word much used by the older chemists and in pharmacy.—*Sal aeratus*. SALERATUS.—*Sal ammoniac* (am•mō′ni•ak), ammonium chloride, NH_4Cl, a salt much used in the arts and in pharmacy; a name derived from the temple of Jupiter *Ammon*, in Egypt, where it was originally made by burning camels' dung.—*Sal prunella*, nitrate of potash fused into cakes or balls and used for chemical purposes.—*Sal volatile*, (vo•lat′i•le), carbonate of ammonia; a spirituous solution of carbonate of ammonia flavored with aromatics.

salaam, sa•läm′, *n.* [Per. and Ar. *salâm*, Heb. *shalom*, peace.] A ceremonious salutation or obeisance among orientals.—*v.t.* and *i.* To perform the salaam; to salute with a salaam.

salable, sā′la•bl, *a.* See SALE.

salacious, sa•lā′shus, *a.* [L. *salax*, *salacis*, salacious, from *salio*, to leap.] Lustful; lecherous.—**salaciously,** sa•lā′shus•li, *adv.* Lustfully.—**salaciousness,** sa•lā′shus•nes, *n.* The quality of being salacious; lecherousness.

salad, sal′ad, *n.* [Fr. *salade*, It. *salata*, a salted dish, from *salare*, to salt, from L. *sal*, salt.] A general name for certain vegetables prepared and served so as to be eaten raw; chiefly lettuce, endive, radishes, green mustard, cresses, celery, and young onions.—*Salad days*, green, unripe age; days of youthful inexperience.—*Salad oil*, olive oil used in dressing salads.

salamander, sal•a•man′dėr, *n.* [L. and Gr. *salamandra*.] The name of harmless amphibian reptiles closely allied to the newts, formerly believed to be capable of living in fire; a kind of fire spirit or being supposed to live in fire; a large iron poker.—*Salamander's wool* or *hair*, fibrous asbestos. —**salamandrine,** sal•a•man′drin, *a.*

salami, sa•lä′mi, *n.* [It.] A kind of spiced sausage, usually flavored with garlic.

salary, sal′a•ri, *n.* [L. *salarium*, from *sal*, salt, originally salt money, money given to buy salt; hence, stipend, pay. SALT.] The recompense or consideration stipulated to be paid to a person periodically for services.

sale, sāl, *n.* [Icel. *sala*. SELL.] The act of selling; the exchange or transfer of a commodity for an agreed on price in money; opportunity of selling; demand; market; public transfer to the highest bidder; exposure of goods in a market or shop; auction.—*On sale, for sale*, to be bought or sold; offered to purchasers.—**salable,** sā′la•bl, *a.* Capable of being sold; finding a ready market; in demand.—**salability,** sā•la•bil′i•ti, *n.* The state of being salable.—**salably,** sā′la•bli, *adv.* In a salable manner.—**salesman,** sālz′man, *n.* One whose occupation is to sell goods or merchandise; a wholesale dealer, as a cattle, butter, hay, fish, or other *salesman*.

salep, sal′ep, *n.* [Ar. *sahleb*, salep.] The dried tuberous roots of different species of orchis, much valued in the East for its supposed stimulant properties and esteemed as a nutritious food.

saleratus, sal•e•rā′tus, *n.* [For *sal aeratus*, lit. aerated salt.] The prepared carbonate of soda and salt used for mixing with the flour in baking.

Salic, sal′ik, *a.* [Fr. *salique*, from the *Salian* Franks, or Franks settled on the river *Sala*.] A term applied to a law by which in France females were excluded from the throne.

salicaceous, sal•i•kā′shus, *a.* [L. *salix*, a willow.] Of or relating to the willow family of plants.—**salicin, salicine,** sal′i•sin, *n.* A bitter crystallizable substance extracted from willow bark and from that of the poplar, a valuable tonic.—**salicylic,** sal•i•sil′ik, *a.* [L. *salix*, and Gr. *hylē*, matter.] A term for an acid used as an antiseptic and for other purposes.

salient, sā′li•ent, *a.* [L. *saliens*, *salientis*, ppr. of *salio*, to leap (seen also in *sally*, *assail*, *assault*, *insult*, *result*, etc.).] Springing; shooting up or out; projecting outwardly (a *salient* angle); forcing itself on the notice or attention; conspicuous; prominent; forming a projecting angle or corner in a line of defense, for a jumping-off place; *her.* animals jumping, with both hind feet on the ground, and fore paws in the air.—**saliently,** sā′li•ent•li, *adv.* In a salient manner.—**salience,** sā′li•ens, *n.* The quality of being salient; projection; protrusion.

saliferous, sa•lif′ėr•us, *a.* [L. *sal,* salt, and *fero,* to produce.] Producing or bearing salt.

salify, sal′i•fī, *v.t.*—*salified, salifying.* [L. *sal,* salt, and *facio,* to make.] To form into a salt by combining an acid with a base.

salimeter, sa•lim′et•ėr, *n.* [L. *sal, salis,* salt, and Gr. *metron,* a measure.] An instrument for measuring the amount of salt present in any given solution.

salina, sa•lī′na, *n.* [Sp., from L. *sal,* salt. SALT.] A salt marsh; a saltpond enclosed from the sea; a place where salt is made from salt water; a saltworks.—**saline,** sa•līn′, *a.* [Fr. *salin,* from L. *sal,* salt.] Consisting of salt; partaking of the qualities of salt; salt.—*n.* [Fr. *saline.*] A salt spring, or a place where salt water is collected in the earth.—**salinity,** sa•lin′i•ti, *n.* The state of being salt; salineness. —**salinometer,** sal•i•nom′et•ėr, *n.* An apparatus for indicating the density of brine in the boilers of marine steam engines, and thus showing when they should be cleansed.

saliva, sa•lī′va, *n.* [L., akin to Gr. *sialon,* saliva; and to Gael. and Ir. *seile,* saliva, E. *slime.*] The fluid secreted by the salivary glands that begins the digestion of foods.—**salivary,** sal′i•va•ri, *a.* Pertaining to the saliva; secreting or conveying saliva (the *salivary* glands or ducts).—**salivate,** sal′i•vāt, *v.t.*—*salivated, salivating.* To cause to have an unusual secretion and discharge of saliva.

Salk vaccine, *n.* [After Jonas *Salk,* American physician.] A poliomyelitis vaccine, consisting of three strains of the virus grown on the kidney tissue of monkeys and treated with formaldehyde.

sallow, sal′ō, *n.* [A.Sax. *sealh*=Sc. *saugh,* Icel. *selja,* Dan. *saelje,* G. *sahl;* allied to L. *salix,* Gael. *seileach,* Ir. *sail,* a willow.] A shrub of the willow kind.

sallow, sal′ō, *a.* [A.Sax. *salu, sealwe,* sallow, dark=Icel. *sólr,* D. *saluwe,* O.H.G. *salo,* pale.] Of a pale, sickly color, tinged with a dark yellow; said especially of the skin or complexion.—*v.t.* To tinge with a sallow color.—**sallowness,** sal′ō•nes, *n.* The quality of being sallow.

sally, sal′i, *n.* [Fr. *saillie,* from *saillir,* to leap, from L. *salire,* to leap. SALIENT.] A leaping forth; a rush of troops from a besieged place to attack the besiegers; a spring or flight of intellect, fancy or imagination (a *sally* of wit); an act of levity or extravagance; a piece of wild gaiety; a frolic.—*v.i.*—*sallied, sallying.* To make a sally; to leap or rush out; to issue suddenly from a fortified place, to attack besiegers.—**sally port,** *n. Fort.* a postern or passage to afford egress to troops in making a sally.

salmagundi, sal•ma•gun′di, *n.* [Fr. *salmigondis.*] A dish of chopped meat, eggs, anchovies, red pickled cabbage, etc.; a mixture of various ingredients; a miscellany.

salmi, salmis, sal′mē, *n.* [Fr.] A ragout of woodcocks, larks, thrushes, etc.

salmon, sam′un, *n. sing.* and *pl.* [L. *salmo, salmonis,* from *salio,* to leap.] A large marine food and game fish that breeds in fresh water. The adult is steel blue in color and has fat, pinkish-orange flesh when cooked. The Pacific salmon, now more important than the Atlantic salmon, is caught in enormous numbers from Oregon to Alaska, the two chief species being the Chinook King, or Columbia River salmon, and the Blueback.—**salmonoid,** sam′un•oid, *a.* Belonging to the group of fishes of which the salmon is the type.—**salmon trout.** The European sea trout.

salon, sä•lon′, *n.* [Fr. *salon,* from It. *salone,* augmentative of *sala,* hall.] A drawing room or reception room in a large house; an assembly of guests; [cap.] an art exhibition.

saloon, sa•lön′, *n.* [Fr. *salon,* It. *salone,* from O.H.G. *sal,* a house=A.Sax. *sael,* a hall.] Any spacious apartment for the reception of company or for works of art; a large public room; an apartment for specific public use (the *saloon* of a steamer); in the United States, a shop where alcoholic beverages are sold and drunk.

saloop, sa•löp′, *n.* [See SALEP.] The plant sassafras; a drink made from powdered salep, or from sassafras.

salsify, sal′si•fī, *n.* [Fr. *salsifis,* goat's-beard.] A plant, called also purple goatsbeard. See GOATSBEARD.

salt, solt, *n.* [A.Sax. *sealt* (properly an adj.)=Fris., Dan., Sw., Icel., and Goth. *salt,* D. *zout,* G. *salz;* cog. W. *halen,* Gael. and Ir. *salann,* L. *sal* (Fr. *sel*), Gr. *hals* (=*sals*), salt.] A well-known substance in common use for seasoning and preserving food from the earliest ages, its chemical name being chloride of sodium, obtained from salt mines in the form of rock salt, or from seawater by simple evaporation; *chem.* a compound produced by the combination of a base (commonly a metallic oxide) with an acid; taste; smack; savor; wit; piquancy; pungency; sarcasm (Attic *salt*); a saltcellar; an old sailor (*colloq.*).—*Salt of lemons,* a substance prepared from oxalic acid and potassium carbonate, used to remove inkstains, etc.; also oxalic acid.—*Salt of Saturn,* acetate of lead; sugar of lead.—*Salt of soda,* carbonate of soda.—*Salt of sorrel,* oxalic acid; salt of lemons.—*Salt of tartar,* carbonate of potash.—*Salt of tin,* protochloride of tin, extensively used as a mordant in dyeing.—*Salt of vitriol,* sulfate of zinc.—*Spirit of salt,* muriatic or hydrochloric acid.—*To be worth one's salt,* to be worthy of one's hire.—*a.* Impregnated with salt; abounding in or containing salt; prepared with or tasting of salt; sharp; pungent.—*v.t.* To sprinkle, impregnate, or season with salt.—*To salt a mine,* to sprinkle it with a little of the precious metal in order to obtain a high price for the claim from an inexperienced person. —*To salt out,* to precipitate a substance from solution by the addition of ordinary, or other, salt.—**saltcellar,** *n.* [A tautological term, lit. a salt-dish, *cellar* being=Fr. *salière,* a saltcellar, from L. *sal,* salt.] A small vessel used for holding salt on the table.—**salter,** sol′tėr, *n.* One who salts; one that sells salt; a drysalter.—**saltern,** sol′tėrn, *n.* A saltworks; a building in which salt is made by boiling or evaporation.—**saltiness,** sol′ti•nes, *n.* The quality of being salty.—**saltish,** sol′tish, *a.* Somewhat salt.—**salt lick.** A place where salt lies exposed and where animals come to lick it; a salt spring —**salt marsh.** Land under pasture grasses subject to be overflowed by sea water.—**saltness,** solt′nes, *n.* The quality or state of being salt or impregnated with salt.—**saltpeter,** solt′pē•tėr, [*Salt* and L. *petra,* a stone.] A salt, called also *Niter* (which see).—**salts,** solts, *n. pl.* Epsom salt or other salt used as medicine.—**saltworks,** *n.* A place where salt is made.—**saltwort,** solt′-wėrt. A name applied to several plants yielding kelp.

saltant, sal′tant, *a.* [L. *saltans, saltantis,* ppr. of *salto,* to leap, from *salio.* SALIENT.] Leaping; jumping; dancing.—**saltation,** sal•tā′shon, *n.* [L. *saltatio.*] A leaping or jumping; beating or palpitation.—**saltatory,** sal′ta•to•ri, *a.* Leaping or dancing; adapted for leaping.

saltarello, sal•ta•rel′lo, *n.* [It.] A brisk Neapolitan dance.

saltigrade, sal′ti•grād, *a.* [L. *saltus,* a leap, *gradior,* to go.] Leaping; formed for leaping.

salubrious, sa•lū′bri•us, *a.* [L. *salubris,* from *salus, salutis,* health, safety; akin to *salvus,* safe. SAFE, SALUTARY.] Favorable to health; healthful; conducive to health, as *salubrious* water or food.—**salubriously,** sa•lū′bri•us•li, *adv.*—**salubriousness, salubrity,** sa•lū′bri•us•nes, sa•lū′bri•ti, *n.* The state or quality of being salubrious; healthfulness.

saluki, sa•lū′ki, *n.* A swift, sharp-eyed, graceful hunting dog bred in the Near East and Egypt. It has a long, narrow head, long silky ears, widely set legs, and a long hairy tail. Height about two feet.

salutary, sal′ū•te•ri, *a.* [Fr. *salutaire,* L. *salutaris,* from *salus, salutis,* health. SALUBRIOUS.] Wholesome; healthful; promoting health; contributing to some beneficial purpose; advantageous; profitable.—**salutarily,** sal′ū•te•ri•li, *adv.* In a salutary manner.—**salutariness,** sal′ū•te•ri•nes, *n.* The quality of being salutary.

salute, sa•lūt′, *v.t.*—*saluted, saluting.* [L. *saluto,* from L. *salus, salutis,* health. SALUBRIOUS, SAFE.] To address with expressions of kind wishes, or in order to show homage or courtesy; to greet; to hail; to greet by some act, as by uncovering the head, a bow, etc.; in the *army* or *navy*, to honor by a salute (see the noun).—*v.i.* To perform a salutation; to greet each other.—*n.* A salutation; a greeting; a kiss; a bow, or the like; in an *army* or *navy*, a compliment paid to a royal or other distinguished personage when squadrons or other bodies meet, and on various ceremonial occasions, by firing cannons or small arms, dipping colors or topsails, presenting arms, manning the yards, etc.—**saluter**, sa·lū′tėr, *n.* One who salutes.—**salutation**, sal·ū·tā′shon, *n.* [L. *salutatio*.] The act of saluting; that which is done or uttered in saluting; a greeting or salute.—**salutatory**, sa·lū″ta·tō′ri, *a.*—**salutatorian**, sa·lū′ta·to″ri·an, *n.* The graduating student who gives the salutatory address.

salvage, sal′vij, *v.t.* [Fr. from L.L. *salvare*, to save.] To retrieve a ship or its cargo, as from a wreck, etc.; to save from fire, etc.—*n.* Objects thus saved.

salvation, sal·vā′shon, *n.* [O.Fr. *salvation*, from L. *salvo*, *salvatum*, to save, from *salvus*, safe, same root as *salus*, *salutis*, safety (whence *salute*). SAFE, SALUBRIOUS.] The act of saving; preservation from destruction, danger, or great calamity; the redemption of man from the bondage of sin and liability to eternal death and the conferring on him of everlasting happiness; that which saves; the cause of saving.—*Salvation Army*, a society organized for the religious revival of the masses, having its proceedings conducted by generals, majors, captains, etc., of either sex, and by military forms.—**Salvationist**, sal·vā′shon·ist, *n.*

salve, salv, *v.t.* [From L. *salvo*, *salvatum*, to salve, from *salvus*, safe. SALVATION.] To save a ship or goods from destruction, as by shipwreck or fire.—**salvable**, sal′va·bl, *a.* Capable of being salved; admitting of salvation.—**salvage**, sal′vij, *n.* [L.L. *salvagium*, from L. *salvus*.] The act of saving a ship or goods from extraordinary danger, as from the sea, fire, an enemy, or the like; an allowance to which persons are entitled by whose voluntary exertions ships or goods have been saved; property thus saved.—**salvor**, sal′vor, *n.* One who saves a ship or goods from wreck or destruction.

salve, sav or salv, *n.* [A.Sax. *sealf*, a salve, an ointment=D. *zalve*, Dan. *salve*, G. *salbe*, O.H.G. *salba*, salve, allied to Skr. *sarpis*, ghee or clarified butter.] An adhesive substance to be applied to wounds or sores; a healing ointment; help; remedy.—*v.t.*—*salved*, *salving*. To apply salve to; to remedy.

salver, sal′vėr, *n.* [Sp. *salva*, a salver, also the previous tasting of a great man's food by a servant to see that it is wholesome, from L. *salvus*, safe. SALVATION.] A kind of tray or waiter for table service, or on which anything is presented to a person.

salvo, sal′vō, *n.* [From L. *salvo jure*, 'the right being intact', an expression used in reserving rights. SALVATION.] An exception or reservation; an excuse.

salvo, sal′vō, *n.* [Fr. *salve*, It. and Sp. *salva*, a salvo, a salute, from L. *salve*, hail, from *salvus*, safe. SALVATION.] A general discharge of guns intended for a salute or for some special purpose; a shouting or cheering.

salvor, sal′vor, *n.* See SALVE, to save.

samara, sam′a·ra, *n.* [L. *samara*, the seed of the elm.] *Bot.* a fruit with wing-like expansions, as in the fruit or *key* of the ash tree, elm, maple.

Samaritan, sa·mar′i·tan, *a.* Pertaining to *Samaria*, the principal city of the ten tribes of Israel; pertaining to the characters of a kind of ancient Hebrew writing probably in use before, and partly after, the Babylonish exile.—*n.* A native or inhabitant of Samaria; the language of Samaria; a Chaldean dialect; a charitable or benevolent person: in allusion to the 'good Samaritan' in the parable.

samarium, sa·mâr′i·um, *n.* [From Col. Samarski.] A metallic element of the rare-earth series, discovered in samarskite. Symbol, Sm; at. no., 62; at. wt., 150.35.

sambo, sam′bō, *n.* The offspring of a black person and a mulatto.

Sam Browne belt, sam·broun, *n.* A belt with a shoulder strap worn by military officers.

sambur, sambar, sam′bėr, *n.* A kind of large deer of northern India.

same, sām, *a.* [A.Sax. *same*, Icel. *samr*, Dan. and Sw. *samme*, O.Sax. and Goth. *sama*; allied to L. *similis* (whence *similar*, *simulate*), like *simul*, together; Gr. *hama*, together, *homos*, same; Skr. *sama*, like.] Identical; not different or other (the *same* man); of the identical kind, species, or degree; exactly similar, though not the specific thing (the *same* error); just mentioned or denoted: always preceded by *the* or *this*, *that*, etc.—*All the same*, nevertheless; notwithstanding.—**sameness**, sām′nes, *n.* The state of being the same; identity; similarity; want of variety.

samite, sa′mīt, *n.* [O.Fr. *samit*, from L.L. *samitum*, from Fr. *hexamiton*—*hex*, six, and *mitos*, a thread.] An old rich silk stuff interwoven with gold or embroidered.

samlet, sam′let, *n.* [Dim. of *salmon*.] A name for the parr.

samovar, sam′o·vär, *n.* [Russian.] A tea urn used in Russia in which the water is heated by an interior heating tube containing live coals.

Samoyeds, sam′o·yeds, *n.* The Mongolian race in Siberia; a breed of dog.

samp, samp, *n.* In the United States, food composed of corn, broken or bruised, boiled, and mixed with milk.

sampan, sam′pan, *n.* [Malay and Javanese.] A name applied to boats of various builds on the Chinese rivers, at Singapore, etc.

samphire, sam′fīr, *n.* [Corruption of Fr. (*herbe de*) *Saint Pierre* (St. Peter's herb).] Sea-fennel, a genus of plants whose leaves are used in pickles and salads.

sample, sam′pl, *n.* [O.Fr. *essample*, *example*, an example. EXAMPLE.] A pattern‡; an example‡; a small part or quantity of anything intended to be shown as evidence of the quality of the whole. ∴ Syn. under SPECIMEN.—*v.t.*—*sampled*, *sampling*. To take a sample of; to take a quantity from to serve as a sample (to *sample* sugar, etc.).—**sampler**, sam′plėr, *n.* One who samples.

sampler, sam′plėr, *n.* [From L. *exemplar*, a pattern, from *exemplum*, an example. SAMPLE, EXAMPLE.] A piece of fancy sewed or embroidered work done by girls for practice.

sanatorium, san·a·tō′ri·um, *n.* [Neut. of L.L. *sanatorius*.] A hospital for chronic diseases, such as tuberculosis.

sanbenito, san·be·nē′tō, *n.* [It. *sanbenito*, Sp. *sambenito*.] An upper garment painted with flames, figures of devils, etc., worn by persons going to the stake on the occasion of an auto-da-fé.

sanctify, sangk′ti·fī, *v.t.*—*sanctified*, *sanctifying*. [Fr. *sanctifier*, L. *sanctifico*, from *sanctus*, holy (whence *saint*), and *facio*, to make.] To make holy or sacred; to set apart to a holy or religious use; to hallow; to purify from sin or sinful affections; to make the means of holiness; to celebrate or confess as holy.—**sanctification**, sangk′ti·fi·kā″shon, *n.* The act of sanctifying or state of being sanctified; the act of God's grace by which the affections of men are purified from sin; conformity to the will of God; consecration.—**sanctifier**, sangk′ti·fī·ėr, *n.* One who sanctifies.

sanctimony, sangk′ti·mo·ni, *n.* [L. *sanctimonia*, from *sanctus*, holy. SAINT.] Piety‡, sanctity‡; the external appearance of devoutness; affected or hypocritical devoutness.—**sanctimonious**, sangk·ti·mō′ni·us, *a.* Making a show of sanctity; affecting the appearance of sanctity.—**sanctimoniously**, sangk·ti·mō′ni·us·li, *adv.* In a sanctimonious manner.—**sanctimoniousness**, sangk·ti·mō′ni·us·nes, *n.*

sanction, sangk′shon, *n.* [L. *sanctio*, from *sancio*, *sancire*, to render sacred or inviolable, whence *sanctus*, holy. SAINT.] An official act of a superior by which he ratifies and gives validity to the act of some other person or body; ratification or confirmation; authority; penalty incurred by the infringement of a command.—*Pragmatic sanction*. PRAGMATIC.—*v.t.* To give sanction to; to ratify; to give countenance to.

sanctity, sangk′ti·ti, *n.* [L. *sanctitas*, from *sanctus*, holy. SANCTION, SAINT.] The state or quality of being sacred or holy; holiness; saintliness; sacredness; inviolability.

sanctuary, sangk′chụ·a·ri, *n.* [L. *sanctuarium*, from *sanctus*, sacred.

SANCTITY.] A sacred or consecrated place; the temple at Jerusalem, particularly the most retired part of it, called the *Holy of Holies*; a house consecrated to the worship of God; a church; in the *R. Cath. Ch.* that part of a church where the altar is placed; the cella of an Egyptian, Greek, or Roman temple; a place of protection; a sacred asylum; right of affording such protection, a privilege attached to certain places in virtue of which criminals are protected from the law; refuge in a sacred place; shelter. —**sanctum,** sangk'tum, *n.* A sacred place; a private retreat or room (an editor's *sanctum*).—*Sanctum sanctorum*, 'the holy of holies'; the innermost or holiest place of the Jewish temple.—**Sanctus,** sangk'tus, *n.* An anthem beginning with the Latin word *sanctus*, holy.—**Sanctus bell,** *n.* Same as *Sacring bell*.

sand, sand, *n.* [A.Sax. *sand*=Dan., Sw., and G. *sand*, Icel. *sandr*, D. *zand*; probably from same root as L. *sabulum*, gravel.] Fine particles of stone, particularly of siliceous stone in a loose state, but not reduced to powder or dust, generally arising from disintegrated rock; *pl.* a tract of land consisting of sandy soil, like the deserts of Arabia; tracts of sand exposed by the ebb of the tide.—*v.t.* To sprinkle with sand; to drive upon a sandbank.—**sandbag,** *n.* A bag filled with sand or earth, and used in a fortification or for other purposes.—**sandblast,** *n.* A method used to engrave, clean, or abrade glass, rock, etc., by means of a stream of sand forced by compressed air or steam.—**sand-blind,** *a.* [Corrupted from *samblind*, from A.Sax. *sâm* (akin to L. *semi*), half.] Having imperfect sight. —**sandbur, sandburr,** *n.* A name for various weeds bearing prickly seed pods, growing in sandy places. —**sand crack,** *n.* A crack in the hoof of a horse.—**sand dollar,** *n.* A round, flat sea urchin found on sandy bottoms.—**sand eel,** *n.* A name of certain small fishes that bury themselves in the sand, and are also known by the name of launce.—**sanderling,** san'dėr•ling, *n.* [So called because it feeds among the moist sands of the shore.] A small wading bird which frequents the shores and feeds on small marine insects.—**sand flea,** *n.* The beach flea, the chigoe, or other flea which lives in sandy places.—**sand fly,** *n.* A minute dipterous insect whose bite is painful.—**sandglass,** *n.* A glass that measures time by the running of sand from one division of it to the other.—**sand grouse,** *n.* A genus of birds closely allied to the grouse, inhabiting arid sandy plains. —**sandiness,** san'di•nes, *n.* The state of being sandy.—**sand launce,** *n.* The sand eel.—**sand lily,** *n.* A stemless plant of western U. S., bearing stalks of lily-shaped flowers.—**sandman,** *n.* An imaginary person who puts sand into children's eyes to make them sleepy.—**sand martin,** *n.* The bank swallow.—**sandpaper,** *n.* Paper covered on one side with a fine gritty substance for polishing.—**sandpiper,** sand'pī•pėr, *n.* A name of several grallatorial birds allied to the snipe, plover, etc.—**sandstone,** sand'stōn, *n.* Stone composed of agglutinated grains of sand, which may be calcareous, siliceous, or of any other mineral nature, often known by the name of *freestone*.—**sandstorm,** *n.* A windstorm which blows along great clouds of sand.—**sand verbena** A plant, similar to the verbena, that grows in the dry, sandy soil of the western U. S.—**sandwort,** sand'wėrt, *n.* A name of several plants growing in sandy places.—**sandy,** san'di, *a.* Consisting of or abounding with sand; resembling sand; of the color of sand; of a yellowish-red color.

sandal, san'dal, *n.* [Fr. *sandale*, L. *sandalium*, from Gr. *sandalion*.] A kind of shoe, consisting of a sole fastened to the foot, generally by means of straps crossed over and worn round the ankle; a tie or strap for a shoe resembling that of a sandal.—**sandaled,** san'dald, *p.* and *a.* Wearing sandals; shaped like a sandal.

sandalwood, *n.* [Ar. *sandal*, sandalwood.] The wood of several trees of the East Indies and islands of the Pacific, with a strong scent which is very fatal to insects, and hence it is used for making cabinets, boxes, etc.—*Red sandalwood*, the wood of a tree of India, used as a dyewood.

sandarac, san'da•rak, *n.* [L. *sandaracha*, from Gr. *sandarachē*, a word of Oriental origin.] A resin which exudes from the bark of a valuable timber tree of Morocco, used as incense and for making varnish.

sandwich, sand'wich, *n.* [After an Earl of *Sandwich*, who brought it into fashion.] Two thin slices of bread with meat, fish, or the like, between.—**sandwich man,** *n.* A man carrying two advertising boards, one before and one behind.

sane, sān, *a.* [L. *sanus*, sound, whole, healthy (whence *sanatory*, *sanitary*); same root as Gr. *sōs*, safe.] Mentally sound; not deranged; having the regular exercise of reason and the other mental faculties.—**saneness, sanity,** sān'nes, san'i•ti, *n.* The state of being sane or of sound mind.

sang, sang, pret. of *sing*.

sangaree, sang'ga•rē, *n.* Wine and water sweetened and spiced, and sometimes iced; used as a refreshing drink.

sanguiferous, sang•gwif'ėr•us, *a.* [L. *sanguis*, blood, and *fero*, to carry.] Conveying blood, as the arteries and veins.

sanguinary, sang'gwi•ne•ri, *a.* [L. *sanguinarius*, from *sanguis*, blood; same root as *sucus* or *succus*, juice, *sugo*, to suck.] Consisting of blood; bloody; attended with much bloodshed; murderous; bloodthirsty.—**sanguinarily,** sang'gwi•ne•ri•li, *adv.* In a sanguinary manner.—**sanguinariness,** sang'gwi•ne•ri•nes, *n.*

sanguine, sang'gwin, *a.* [Fr. *sanguin*, from L. *sanguineus*, from *sanguis*, blood. SANGUINARY.] Having the color of blood; red; characterized by fullness of habit, vigor, activity of circulation, etc.; cheerful in temper; anticipating the best; not desponding; confident.—*n.* Blood color; bloodstone.—**sanguinely,** sang'gwin•li, *adv.* In a sanguine manner.—**sanguineness,** sang'gwin•nes, *n.* The state or quality of being sanguine.—**sanguineous,** sang•gwin'i•us, *a.* [L. *sanguineus*.] Appertaining to the blood; of the color of blood; sanguine; confident.—**sanguivorous,** sang•gwiv'o•rus, *a.* [L. *sanguis*, and *voro*, to eat.] Eating or subsisting on blood.—**sanguinolent,** sang•gwin'o•lent, *a.* [L. *sanguinolentus*.] Tinged or mingled with blood; bloody.

Sanhedrin, san'he•drin, *n.* [Heb. *sanhedrin*, from Gr. *sunedrion*—*sun* (or *syn*), with, together, and *hedra*, seat.] The great council among the Jews of Maccabean and later times, consisting of a president (generally the high priest) and seventy other members.

sanicle, san'i•kl, *n.* [Fr. *sanicle*, from L. *sano*, to heal—from its supposed healing virtues.] An umbelliferous plant of several species, also called *Selfheal*.

sanies, sā'ni•ēz, *n.* [L., bloody matter.] A thin reddish discharge from wounds or sores.—**sanious,** sā'ni•us, *a.* [L. *saniosus*.] Pertaining to sanies, or partaking of its nature and appearance.

sanitary, san'i•te•ri, *a.* [Fr. *sanitaire*, from L. *sanitas*, health, from *sanus*, sound. SANE.] Pertaining to or designed to secure health; relating to the preservation of health; hygienic. ∴ *Sanitary* and *sanatory* are not unfrequently confounded. *Sanitary* (from L. *sanitas*, health) has the general meaning of pertaining to health, hygienic; *sanatory* (directly from L. *sano*, *sanatum*, to make healthy) means pertaining to healing or curing; tending to cure.—**sanitarian,** san•i•tâ'ri•an, *n.* A promoter of, or one versed in, sanitary measures.—**sanitarium,** san•i•tâ'ri•um, *n.* A health retreat; a sanatorium.—**sanitation,** san•i•tā'shon, *n.* The adoption of sanitary measures for the health of a community; hygiene.

sanity, san'i•ti, *n.* See SANE.

sanjak, san'jak, *n.* [Turk., a standard.] A minor province of Turkey.

sank, sangk, pret. of *sink*.

sans, sanz, *prep.* [Fr., from L. *sine*, without.] Without; deprived of.—**sans-culotte,** sänz•kų•lot', *n.* [Fr., without breeches.] A fellow without knee breeches, a name originally given in derision to the popular party by the aristocrats in the beginning of the French Revolution of 1789; hence, a fierce republican of any country.—**sans-culottic,** sänz•kų•lot'ik, *a.* Revolutionary; republican. —**sans-culottism,** sänz•kų•lot'izm, *n.* Extreme republicanism.

Sanskrit, Sanscrit, san'skrit, *n.* [Skr. *sanskrita*, perfectly formed—*sam* (=Gr. *syn*), with, and *krita*, made, perfected, from *kri*, to make.]

The ancient language of the Hindus, being that in which most of their vast literature is written, one of the Aryan or Indo-European family of tongues. Also used as an adjective.—**sanskritist,** san'skrit•ist, *n.* A Sanskrit scholar.

Santa Claus, *n.* [Corruption of D. *Sint Klaas,* St. Nicholas.] The patron saint of children; the dispenser of gifts on Christmas Eve.

santonin, santonine, san'to•nin, *n.* [Gr. *santonion,* a kind of wormwood.] A substance obtained from the seeds of southernwood, a most efficacious vermifuge.

santorin, san'to•rin, *n.* An argillaceous mineral occurring on the island of *Santorin,* yielding an excellent cement.

sap, sap, *n.* [A.Sax. *saep*=D. *sap.* L.G. *sapp.* juice; akin Dan. and G. *saft,* juice, sap.] The juice or fluid which circulates in all plants, being as indispensable to vegetable life as the blood to animal life; vital juice; blood; sapwood; a stupid person.—*v.i.* To study. (*Colloq.*)—**sapless,** sap'les, *a.* Destitute of sap; dry; withered.—**sapling,** sap'ling, *n.* A young tree full of sap.—**sappy,** sap'i, *a.* Abounding with sap; juicy; succulent; young; stupid.—**sapsucker,** *n.* The name of several small woodpeckers.—**sapwood,** *n.* See ALBURNUM.

sap, sap, *v.t.*—*sapped, sapping.* [Fr. *saper,* from *sape,* L.L. *sapa,* a mattock.] To cause to fall, or to render unstable, by digging or wearing away the foundation; to undermine; to subvert; to destroy, as if by some secret, hidden, or invisible process.—*v.i.* To proceed by secretly undermining.—*n. Milit.* a ditch or trench by which approach is made to a fortress or besieged place within range of fire.—**sapper,** sap'ėr, *n.* One who saps; a soldier of an engineer corps, or who is trained in fortification or siege works.

sapanwood, sa•pan'wụd, *n.* A dyewood produced by a tree of southern Asia, which yields a red color.

sapid, sap'id, *a.* [L. *sapidus,* from *sapio,* to taste. SAPIENT.] Possessing savor or relish; savory.—**sapidity,** sa•pid'i•ti, *n.* The quality of being sapid; savor; relish.

sapient, sā'pi•ent, *a.* [L. *sapiens, sapientis,* wise, discreet, pp. of *sapio,* to taste, to know, to be wise; *sapid, insipid, savor, sage,* are of similar origin.] Wise; sage; knowing; discerning; proceeding from a wiseacre. (Now generally ironical, or used of affected wisdom.)—**sapience,** sā'pi•ens, *n.* [L. *sapientia,* wisdom.] The quality of being sapient; wisdom; sageness.—**sapiently,** sā'pi•ent•li, *adv.* In a sapient manner; sagely.

sapless, sapling. See SAP.

sapodilla, sap•o•dil'a, *n.* [Sp. *sapotilla,* from Mexican *zapotl.*] A large tree of the West Indies, yielding a fine fruit.

saponaceous, sap•o•nā'shus, *a.* [From L. *sapo, saponis,* soap.] Soapy; resembling soap; having the qualities of soap.—**saponify,** sa•pon'i•fī, *v.t.*—*saponified, saponifying.* [L. *sapo, saponis,* and *facio,* to make.] To convert into soap by combination with an alkali.—**saponifiable,** sa•pon'i•fī•a•bl, *a.* Capable of being saponified.—**saponification,** sa•pon'i•fi•kā"shon, *n.* Conversion into soap; the process in which fatty substances, through combination with an alkali, form soap.—**saponin,** sap'o•nin, *n.* A vegetable principle found in the root of soapwort and many other plants, causing water to froth like soap on being agitated.—**saponite,** sap'o•nīt, *n.* A silicate of magnesia and alumina, occurring in soft, soapy, amorphous masses.

sapor, sā'por, *n.* [L. SAPID.] Taste; savor.—**saporific,** sap•o•rif'ik, *a.* Producing taste or relish.—**saporous,** sap'or•us, *a.* Having flavor or taste.

sappadillo, sap•a•dil'ō. See SAPODILLA.

sapper. See SAP.

Sapphic, saf'ik, *a.* Pertaining to *Sappho,* a Grecian poetess; *pros.* applied to a kind of verse said to have been invented by Sappho.—*n.* A Sapphic verse.

sapphire, saf'īr, *n.* [L. *sapphirus,* Gr. *sappheiros,* of Eastern origin= Heb. *sappir,* Ar. *safir.*] A precious stone, next in hardness to the diamond, belonging to the corundum class, and of various shades of blue color; hence, a rich blue color; blue.—*Green sapphire,* the emerald.—*Red sapphire,* the oriental ruby.—*Violet sapphire,* the oriental amethyst.—*White* or *limpid sapphire,* a colorless or grayish transparent or translucent variety, sometimes sold as diamond.—*Yellow sapphire,* the oriental topaz.—*a.* Resembling sapphire; blue.—**sapphirine,** saf'fi•rin, *a.* Resembling sapphire; made of sapphire; of a rich blue.—*n.* A blue variety of spinel.

sappy. See SAP.

saprophagous, sa•prof'a•gus, *a.* [Gr. *sapros,* putrid, and *phagō,* to eat.] Feeding on substances in a state of decomposition.—**saprophyte,** sap'ro•fīt, *n.* [Gr. *sapros,* and *phyton,* a plant.] A plant that grows on decaying vegetable matter.—**saprophytic,** sap•ro•fit'ik, *a.* Pertaining to saprophytes.

sapsago, sap'sa•gō, *n.* [Corruption of G. *schabzieger.*] A kind of hard cheese made in Switzerland.

saraband, sarabande, sar'a•band, *n.* [Fr. *sarabande,* Sp. *zarabanda.*] A dance used in Spain, derived from the Saracens; a piece of music adapted to the dance.

Saracen, sar'a•sen, *n.* [L. *Saracenus,* from Gr. *Sarakēnos,* Ar. *Sharhiin,* Orientals, Easterns.] An Arabian or other Mussulman; any nation against which crusades were preached.—**Saracenic,** sar•a•sen'ik, *a.*

sarape, sä•räp'ā, *n.* [Mex.-Sp.] A shawl-like garment worn as a coat.

sarcasm, sär'kazm, *n.* [L. *sarcasmus,* from Gr. *sarkasmos,* a bitter laugh, from *sarkazō,* to tear flesh like dogs, to speak bitterly, from *sarx, sarkos,* flesh.] A bitter cutting expression; a satirical remark; a bitter gibe; a taunt.—**sarcastic,** sär•kas'tik, *a.* Characterized by sarcasm; bitterly cutting.—**sarcastically,** sär•kas'ti•kal•li, *adv.* In a sarcastic manner.

sarcenet, särs'net, *n.* [O.Fr. *sarcenet;* L.L. *saracenicum,* lit. cloth made by *Saracens.*] A species of fine thin woven silk used for linings, etc.

sarcocarp, sär'ko•kärp, *n.* [Gr. *sarx, sarkos,* flesh, and *karpos,* fruit.] *Bot.* the fleshy part of certain fruits, being the part which is usually eaten.

sarcoma, sär•kō'ma, *n.* [Gr. *sarkōma,* from *sarx, sarkos,* flesh.] A fleshy growth; *bot.* a fleshy disk.—**sarcomatous,** sär•kō'ma•tus, *a.* Relating to sarcoma.

sarcophagus, sär•kof'a•gus, *n.* pl. **sarcophagi,** sär•kof'a•jī, also **sarcophaguses** [Gr. *sarkophagos;* it was originally the name of a species of stone used for making coffins, and believed to have the property of consuming the dead bodies.] A coffin or tomb of stone; a kind of stone chest, generally more or less ornamented, for receiving a dead body.

sarcous, sär'kus, *a.* [Gr. *sarx, sarkos,* flesh.] Belonging to flesh or muscle.

sard, särd, *n.* [Fr. *sarde,* from *Sardes,* the ancient capital of Lydia.] A variety of carnelian of a deep blood red when held between the eye and the light.

sardine, sär•dēn', *n.* [Fr. *sardine,* from L. *sardina,* so called because caught near *Sardinia.*] A small fish allied to the herring and pilchard, large quantities of which are preserved, salted, and hermetically sealed in tin boxes with olive oil.

sardius, sär'di•us, *n.* A sort of precious stone, probably sard or carnelian. (O.T.)

sardonic, sär•don'ik, *a.* [Fr. *sardonique,* from L. *Sardonica herba,* the Sardinian herb, an herb said to cause a peculiar twitching of the face when eaten.] Not really proceeding from gaiety; forced; said of a laugh or smile; bitterly ironical; sarcastic; derisive and malignant: now the usual meaning.—**sardonically,** *adv.* In a sardonic manner; grimly; viciously.

sardonyx, sär'do•niks, *n.* [Gr. *sardonyx.* SARD, ONYX.] A precious stone, a beautiful variety of onyx, consisting of alternate layers of sard and white chalcedony.

sargasso, sargassum, sär•gas'ō, sär•gas'um, *n.* [Sp. *sargazo,* seaweed.] Gulfweed, floating on the surface of the sea, giving to part of the Atlantic the name *Sargasso Sea.*

sari, sä•ri', *n.* [Hind.] The chief garment of a Hindu woman, consisting of a long piece of cloth wound round the waist, with the one edge hanging down in front, the other taken up and thrown over the head.

Sarmatian, sär•mā'shi•an, *a.* Pertaining to *Sarmatia* and its inhabitants, supposed to be the ancestors of the Russians and Poles.

sarmentose, sarmentous, sär•men'tōz, sär•men'tus, *a. Bot.* having runners; having the character of a runner.

sarong, sa•rong′, *n.* [Malay.] A garment used in the Malay Archipelago, consisting of a cloth wrapped round the lower part of the body.

sarsaparilla, sär′sa•pa•ril″la, *n.* [Sp. *zarzaparrilla.*] The rhizome of several plants of tropical America and the East Indies, yielding a medicine valued on account of its mucilaginous and demulcent qualities.

sarsenet, särs′net, *n.* Same as *Sarcenet.*

sartorious, sär•tō′ri•us, *n.* [From L. *sartor,* a tailor.] A muscle of the thigh, so called because used in crossing the legs in sitting as tailors do.—**sartorial,** sär•tō′ri•al, *a.* Pertaining to a tailor.

Sarum use, sârum, *n.* Ecclesiastical phrase for the order of church service in the churches of Salisbury diocese before the Reformation.

sash, sash, *n.* [Per. *shash,* a sash, scarf, or shawl.] A band or scarf worn over the shoulder or round the waist for ornament, usually of silk, variously made and ornamented.—*v.t.* To dress with a sash.

sash, sash, *n.* [Fr. *châsse,* a frame, a sash, from L. *capsa,* a box, from *capio,* to take. CAPABLE.] The framed part of a window in which the glass is fixed; a similar part of a greenhouse, etc.; the frame in which a saw is fixed to prevent its bending when worked.—*v.t.* To furnish with sash windows.

sasin, sā′sin, *n.* An antelope, remarkable for its swiftness and beauty, abundant in the plains of India.

sassaby, sas′a•bi, *n.* A handsome South African antelope.

sassafras, sas′a•fras, *n.* [Fr. *sassafras,* from L. *saxifraga—saxum,* a stone, and *frango,* to break. SAXIFRAGE.] A kind of laurel, well known on account of the medicinal virtues of its root: so named because formerly used to *break* or dissolve *stone* in the bladder.

Sassenach, sas′en•*ach, n.* A name applied by the Celts of the British Isles to persons of Saxon race; a Saxon; an Englishman.

sassy, sas′i, *a.* A variation of *Saucy.* (U.S.).

Satan, sā′tan, *n.* [Heb., an adversary.] The devil or prince of darkness; the chief of the fallen angels; the archfiend.—**satanic, satanical,** sa•tan′ik, sa•tan′i•kal, *a.* Pertaining to Satan; resembling Satan; extremely malicious or wicked; devilish; infernal.—**satanically,** sa•tan′i•kal•li, *adv.* In a satanic manner; diabolically.—**Satanism,** sā′tan•izm, *n.* The evil and malicious disposition of Satan.

satchel, sach′el, *n.* [Also written *sachel,* a dim. of *sack,* the *k* sound having undergone the common softening to *ch.*] A little sack or bag; may be carried either by the hand or slung from the shoulder.

sate, sāt, *v.t.—sated, sating.* [Perhaps from A.Sax. *saed,* satisfied, satiated, the form having been influenced by *satisfy, satiate.* SATIATE, SAD.] To satisfy the appetite or desire of; to feed beyond natural desire; to glut; to satiate.

sateen, sa•tēn′, *n.* [From *satin.*] A kind of glossy fabric resembling satin, but having a woolen or cotton instead of a silken face.

satellite, sat′el•līt, *n.* [Fr. *satellite,* from L. *satelles, satellitis,* one who guards the person of a prince.] An obsequious dependent; a state dominated by another; a small planet revolving round a larger one; a man-made object orbiting a celestial body.

satiate, sā′shi•āt, *v.t.—satiated, satiating.* [L. *satio, satiatum,* to satisfy, to satiate, from *satis,* enough; akin to *satur,* full; akin *satisfy, saturate, satire.*] To satisfy the appetite or desire of; to feed or nourish to the full; to sate; to surfeit; to fill to repletion.—*a.* Filled to satiety; glutted; satiated†.—**satiation,** sā•shi•ā′shon, *n.* The state of being satiated or filled.—**satiable,** sā′shi•a•bl, *a.* Capable of being satiated or satisfied. —**satiability, satiableness,** sā′shi•a•bil″i•ti, sā′shi•a•bl•nes, *n.* The quality of being satiable or satisfied.—**satiety,** sa•tī′e•ti, *n.* [L. *satietas.*] The state of being satiated; an excess of gratification which excites wearisomeness or loathing; a being surfeited.

satin, sat′in, *n.* [Fr. *satin,* It. *setino.*] A species of glossy cloth (silk, rayon, nylon, etc.), of a thick, close texture with an overshot woof.—*a.* Belonging to or made of satin.—**satinet,** sat′i•net, *n.* [A dim. of *satin.*] A thin species of satin; a particular kind of twilled cloth, made of woolen weft and cotton warp, pressed and dressed to produce a glossy surface in imitation of satin.—**satinwood,** *n.* The wood of an Indian tree of a deep yellow color, heavy, and durable.—**satiny,** sat′i•ni, *a.* Resembling satin; having a surface or texture like satin.

satire, sat′īr or sat′ir, *n.* [L. *satira* (*i* short), or *satura,* a satire, a medley, an olio, lit. a full dish, from *satur,* full (whence *saturate*).] A poetical composition holding up vice or folly to reprobation; an invective poem; any literary production in which persons, manners, or actions are attacked with irony, sarcasm, or similar weapons; sarcastic ridicule; trenchant invective.—**satiric, satirical,** sa•tir′ik, sa•tir′i•kal, *a.* Belonging to satire; conveying or containing satire; given to satire; severe in language.—**satirically,** sa•tir′i•kal•li, *adv.* In a satirical manner.—**satiricalness,** sa•tir′i•kal•nes, *n.* Quality of being satirical.—**satirist,** sat′ir•ist, *n.* One who satirizes; one who writes satire.—**satirize,** sat′ir•īz, *v.t.—satirized, satirizing.* To assail with satire; to make the object of satire.

satisfy, sat′is•fī, *v.t.—satisfied, satisfying.* [Fr. *satisfaire,* O.Fr. *satisfier*—L. *satis,* enough, and *facio,* to make. SATIATE.] To grant fully the wants, wishes, or desires of; to supply to the full extent with what is wished for; to make content; to comply with the rightful demands of; to give what is due to; to pay, liquidate, requite; to fulfill the conditions of; to answer; to free from doubt, suspense, or uncertainty; to set at rest the mind.—*v.i.* To give satisfaction or content.—**satisfyingly,** sat′-is•fī•ing•li, *adv.* In a manner tending to satisfy.—**satisfier,** sat′is•fī•ėr, *n.* A person or thing that gives satisfaction.—**satisfaction,** sat•is•fak′-shon, *n.* [L. *satisfactio.*] The act of satisfying, or state of being satisfied; gratification of appetite or desire; contentment in possession and enjoyment; settlement of a claim due; payment; that which satisfies; compensation; atonement; the opportunity of satisfying one's honor by a duel. ∴ Syn. under CONTENTMENT. —**satisfactory,** sat•is•fak′to•ri, *a.* Giving or producing satisfaction; yielding content; relieving the mind from doubt or uncertainty; making amends or recompense; atoning.—**satisfactorily,** sat•is•fak′to•ri•li, *adv.* In a satisfactory manner; so as to give satisfaction.—**satisfactoriness,** sat•is•fak′to•ri•nes, *n.* The quality of being satisfactory.

satrap, sā′trap, *n.* [Gr. *satrapēs*; borrowed from the Persian.] A governor of a province under the ancient Persian monarchy; a prince; a petty despot.—**satrapy,** sā′trap•i, *n.* The government or jurisdiction of a satrap; a principality.

saturate, sach′ų•rāt, *v.t.—saturated, saturating.* [L. *saturo, saturatum,* from *satur,* filled (whence *satire*); from root of *satis,* enough. SATE, SATIATE.] To cause to become completely penetrated, impregnated, or soaked; to fill fully; to imbue thoroughly; to impregnate or unite with till no more can be received (air *saturated* with moisture).—*a.* Being full; saturated.—**saturable,** sach′ų•ra•bl, *a.* Admitting of being saturated.—**saturant,** sach′ų•rant, *a.* Saturating; impregnating to the full. —*n.* A substance which neutralizes acid in the stomach.—**saturation,** sach′ų•rā′shon, *n.* The act of saturation or state of being saturated; the combination of one body with another in such proportions as that they neutralize each other; solution continued till the solvent can contain no more.

Saturday, sat′ėr•dā, *n.* [A.Sax. *Saeterdaeg, Saeterndaeg,* lit. Saturn's day.] The seventh or last day of the week.

Saturn, sat′ėrn, *n.* [L. *Saturnus,* connected with *sero, satum,* to sow.] An ancient Italian deity, said to have instructed the people in agriculture, gardening, etc., and elevated them from barbarism to social order and civilization; one of the planets smaller than Jupiter, and more remote from the sun; *old chem.* an appellation given to lead.—**Saturnalia,** sat•ėr•nā′li•a, *n. pl.* [L.] In ancient Rome the festival of Saturn, celebrated as a period of unrestrained license and merriment; hence, any period of noisy license and revelry; unconstrained, licentious reveling.—**Saturnalian,** sat•ėr•nā′li•an, *a.* Pertaining to Saturnalia or revels; loose; dissolute.—**Saturnian,** sa•tėr′ni•an, *a.* Pertaining to Saturn, whose age or reign was called 'the golden age'; hence, happy; distinguished by happiness and simplicity.—*Saturnian verse*, an ancient and peculiar meter used by the Romans, in which the oldest Latin poems were written.—**saturnine,** sat′ėr•nīn, *a.* Supposed to be under the influence of the planet Saturn, which tended to make people morose; morose; of a gloomy temper; heavy; grave; phlegmatic.

satyr, sat′ėr, *n.* [L. *satyrus*, from Gr. *satyros*.] A sylvan deity or demigod of the Greeks and Romans, half man and half goat, the satyrs being common attendants on Bacchus, and distinguished for lasciviousness.—**satyriasis,** sat•i•rī′a•sis, *n.* A diseased venereal appetite in males.—**satyric,** sa•tir′ik, *a.* Pertaining to satyrs (a *satyric* drama).

sauce, sąs, *n.* [Fr. *sauce*, O.Fr. *saulse*, from L.L. *salsa*, sauce, from L. *salsus*, salted. SALT.] A condiment or composition (usually liquid) to be eaten with food for improving its relish, for whetting the appetite, or aiding digestion; pertness; insolence; saucy language.—*v.t.*—*sauced, saucing.* To add a sauce to; to season; to treat with pert language; to be saucy to; to make to pay or suffer (*Shak.*).—**saucebox,** *n.* A saucy, impudent fellow. (*Colloq.*)—**saucepan,** *n.* Originally, a pan for cooking sauces; now, a metallic vessel for boiling or stewing generally.

saucer, są′sėr, *n.* [Originally, a small pan or other vessel for sauce. SAUCE.] A piece of china or other ware in which a teacup or coffee cup is set; something resembling a saucer; a kind of flat caisson used in raising sunken vessels.

saucy, są′si, *a.* [From *sauce*, in the sense of pertness or impudence. SAUCE.] Showing impertinent boldness or impudent flippancy; treating superiors with impertinence; impudent; rude; pert; forward; expressive of impudence (a *saucy* eye).—**saucily,** są′si•li, *adv.* In a saucy manner; pertly; impudently.—**sauciness,** są′si•nes, *n.* The quality of being saucy.

sauerkraut, sour′krout, *n.* [G. *sauer*, sour, and *kraut*, herb, cabbage.] A German dish consisting of cabbage cut fine, pressed into a cask, with alternate layers of salt, and allowed to ferment.

saunter, sąn′tėr, *v.i.* [Origin obscure.] To wander idly; to walk leisurely along; to loiter; to linger; to dawdle.—*n.* A sauntering or place for sauntering.—**saunterer,** sąn′tėr•ėr, *n.* One that saunters.

Sauria, są′ri•a, *n. pl.* [From Gr. *sauros*, a lizard.] The term by which the great order of lizards is sometimes designated.—**saurian,** są′ri•an, *a.* Pertaining to the lizards; having lizard-like characters.—*n.* One of the order of scaly reptiles of which the lizard is a type.

saury, są′ri, *n.* A fish having a greatly elongated body covered with minute scales, while the jaws are prolonged into a long sharp beak.

sausage, są′sij, *n.* [O.Fr. *sausisse*, Fr. *saucisse*; from L.L. *salsa*, sauce (which see).] An article of food, consisting of chopped or minced meat, variously seasoned and stuffed into an animal intestine or other casing.

sauterne, sō•tėrn′, *n.* [Fr.] A white Bordeaux wine made near *Sauterne*, department of Gironde.

savable. See SAVE.

savage, sav′ij, *a.* [O.E. and O.Fr. *salvage* (Mod. Fr. *sauvage*), L.L. *salvaticus*, L. *silvaticus*, wild, from *silva*, a wood. SILVAN.] Pertaining to the forest or wilderness; wild; uncultivated; untamed; violent; brutal; uncivilized; untaught; rude; cruel; barbarous; inhuman.—*n.* A human being in his native state of rudeness; one who is untaught or uncivilized; a man of brutal cruelty; a barbarian.—**savagely,** sav′ij•li, *adv.* In a savage manner; cruelly; inhumanly.—**savageness,** sav′ij•nes, *n.* The quality of being savage; barbarism; cruelty; barbarousness.—**savagery,** sav′ij•ri, *n.* The state of being savage; a wild, uncultivated condition; cruelty; barbarity.—**savagism,** sav′ij•izm, *n.* The state of savages; savagery; barbarism.

savanna, savannah, sa•van′na, *n.* [Sp. *sabana*, properly a sheet for a bed, a plain, from L. *sabanum*, Gr. *sabanon*, a linen cloth.] An extensive open grassy plain or meadow in a tropical region: a word chiefly used in tropical America, though sometimes applied to any very large grassy plain or natural meadow.

savant, sä•vän′, *n.* [Fr., ppr. of *savoir*, L. *sapere*, to know.] A man of learning; a man of science; a man eminent for his acquirements.

save, sāv, *v.t.*—*saved, saving.* [Fr. *sauver*, from L. *salvare*, to save, from *salvus*, safe. SAFE, SALVATION.] To preserve from destruction or evil of any kind; to snatch, keep, or rescue from impending danger; to rescue from sin and eternal death; to deliver; to keep clear; to rescue from the power or influence of; to spare; to keep from doing or suffering: with a double object (to *save* a person trouble); to hinder from being spent or lost (to *save* time); to hinder from being used; to reserve or lay by; to lay up or hoard.—*To save appearances*, to preserve a good outside; to do something to avoid exposure or embarrassment.—*v.i.* To be economical; to hinder expense.—*prep.* [Originally an imperative.] Except; not including.—**savable,** sā′va•bl, *n.* Capable of being saved.—**save-all,** sāv′ąl, *n.* [*Save* and *all*.] A subordinate contrivance intended to save anything from being wasted.—**saver,** sā′vėr, *n.* One that saves.—**saving,** sā′ving, *p.* and *a.* Preserving from evil or destruction; frugal; not lavish; avoiding unnecessary expenses; incurring no loss, though not gainful (a *saving* voyage); reserving, as some title or right (a *saving* clause).—*n.* Something hoarded up; that which is saved: generally in plural.—*prep.* With exception; excepting.—**savingly,** sā′ving•li, *adv.* In a saving manner; with frugality or parsimony.—**savings account,** *n.* An account in a bank on which interest or interest dividends are usually paid and from which withdrawals may be made.—**savings bank,** *n.* A bank specially established for receiving and securely investing small savings, and for their accumulation at interest.

saveloy, sav′e•loi, *n.* [Fr. *cervelas*, from *cervelle*, the brains, from L. *cerebellum*. CEREBELLUM.] A highly seasoned dried sausage, originally made of brains, now made of young salted pork.

savin, savine, sav′in, *n.* [Fr. *savinier*, *sabine*, from L. *Sabina* (*herba*), the Sabine herb, savin.] A coniferous tree or shrub of the juniper kind.

savior, sāv′yėr, *n.* [O.Fr. *salveor* (Fr. *sauveur*), from L. *salvator*, from *salvare*, to save, *salvus*, safe. SAVE.] One who saves, preserves, or delivers from destruction or danger.—**Saviour,** *Jesus Christ*, the Redeemer, who is called *the Saviour* by way of distinction.

savor, sā′vėr, *n.* [O.Fr. *savor*, Mod. Fr. *saveur*, from L. *sapor*, from *sapio*, to taste. SAPIENT.] Flavor; taste; power or quality that affects the palate; odor (*Shak.*); characteristic property; distinctive quality.—*v.i.* To have a particular taste or flavor; to partake of the quality, nature, or appearance of something else; to smack; followed by *of* (his conduct *savors of* pride).—*v.t.* To like; to relish; to have the flavor or quality of.—**savoriness,** sā′vėr•i•nes, *n.* The condition or quality of being savory; pleasing taste or smell.—**savorless,** sā′vėr•les, *a.* Destitute of savor; insipid.—**savory,** sā′vėr•i, *a.* Having savor or relish; pleasing to taste; palatable; hence, agreeable in general.

savory, sā′vėr•i, *n.* [Fr. *savorée*, L. *satureia*, savory.] A European aromatic mint used as a culinary vegetable to flavor sauces and dishes.

savoy, sa•voi′, *n.* [Because brought from *Savoy*.] A variety of cabbage much cultivated for winter use.

Savoyard, sa•voi′ärd, *n.* A native or inhabitant of Savoy.

saw, są, pret. of *see*.

saw, są, *n.* [A.Sax. *saga*, *sage*, a saw = Dan. *sav*, Icel. *sōg*, D. *zaag*, O. *sąge*; same root as L. *seco*, to cut (SECTION).] A cutting instrument consisting of a blade, band, or disk of thin iron or steel, with a dentated or toothed edge.—*v.t.*—pret. *sawed*, pp. *sawed* or *sawn*. To cut with a saw; to form by cutting with a saw; to move through, as in the act of sawing (to *saw* the air).—*v.i.* To use a saw; to cut with a saw.—**sawdust,** *n.* The small fragments of wood or other material produced by the cutting of a saw.—**sawer,** są′ėr, *n.* One that saws; a sawyer.—**sawfish,** *n.* A fish allied to the sharks and rays: so called from the spines growing like teeth on both edges of its long bony snout.—**sawfly,** *n.* A hymenopterous insect, so called because the ovipositor of the females has serrated or toothed edges.—**sawmill,** *n.* A mill for sawing timber.—**sawpit,** *n.* A pit over which timber is sawed.—**saw-toothed,** *a.* Having teeth like a saw; serrated.—**sawyer,** sạ'yėr, *n.* [Formed like *lawyer, bowyer.*] One whose occupation is to saw timber into planks or boards, or to saw wood for fuel.

saw, sạ, *n.* [A.Sax. *sagu,* a saying, a saw, from stem of to *say.* SAY.] A saying; proverb; maxim.

saxatile, sak'sa•til, *a.* [L. *saxatilis,* from *saxum,* a rock.] Pertaining to rocks; living among rocks.

saxhorn, saks'horn, *n.* [After *A.J. Sax,* of Paris, the inventor.] A brass wind instrument with a wide mouthpiece, and three, four, or five cylinders, much employed in military bands. Called also *Sax-cornet.*

saxicolous, sak•sik'o•lus, *a.* [L. *saxum,* a rock, and *colo,* to inhabit.] *Bot.* growing on rocks.

saxifrage, sak'si•frij, *n.* [L. *saxifraga —saxum,* a stone, and *frango,* to break. The name was originally given to a plant supposed to be beneficial in removing stone in the bladder; but the saxifrages seem to have got the name rather from growing among rocks. SASSAFRAS.] A popular name of various plants, which mostly inhabit the colder and temperate parts of the northern zone, and are mostly rock plants.

Saxon, sak'son, *n.* [L. *Saxo,* pl. *Saxones,* A.Sax. *Seaxa,* pl. *Seaxe, Seaxan,* usually derived from *seax,* O.H.G. *sahs,* a short sword; G. *Sachse,* a Saxon.] One of the people who formerly dwelt in the northern part of Germany, and who invaded and conquered England in the fifth and sixth centuries; a Saxon of England as opposed to an Angle or Anglian; an Anglo-Saxon; one of the English race; the language of the Saxons; Anglo-Saxon; a native or inhabitant of modern Saxony.—*a.* Pertaining to the Saxons, their country, or their language; Anglo-Saxon; pertaining to modern Saxony.—**Saxonism,** sak'son•izm, *n.* An idiom of the Saxon or early English language.

saxophone, sak'so•fōn, *n.* A tubular brass or silver wind musical instrument, with a reed mouthpiece like that of the clarinet, having tonal finger keys.

say, sā, *v.t.* pret. & pp. *said,* ppr. *saying.* [A.Sax. *secgan,* to say=Icel. *segja,* D. *zeggen,* Dan. *sige,* G. *sagen,* to say.] To utter or express in words; to speak; to argue; to allege by way of argument; to give as an opinion; to repeat, rehearse, recite; to recite without singing; to answer; to utter by way of reply; to tell; to suppose; to assume; to take for granted: in this sense often elliptically (*say* 3000 men).—*It is said, they say,* it is commonly reported; people assert or maintain.—*To say nay,* to say no; to refuse.—*That is to say,* that is; in other words; otherwise. ∴ *Say* is especially common with a clause or words directly quoted after it, or with such objectives as *something, nothing, this, that,* etc.—*n.* What one has to say (he said his *say*); something said; a statement.—**sayer,** sā'ėr, *n.* One who says.—**saying,** sā'ing, *n.* That which is said; a sentence uttered; a proverbial expression; a maxim; an adage.

scab, skab, *n.* [A.Sax. *scaeb,* from L. *scabies,* scab, itch, from *scabo,* to scratch. Hence, *shabby.*] A sort of crust formed over a sore in healing; the mange in horses; a disease of sheep; blackleg; trade union term for nonunionist who takes the job of strikers.—**scabby,** skab'i, *a.* Abounding with scabs; diseased with scabs; mean; vile; worthless.—**scabbiness,** skab'i•nes, *n.* The state or quality of being scabbed or scabby.

scabbard, skab'erd, *n.* [Formerly *scaubert, scaberke, scaberge,* etc.; perhaps from A.Sax. *sceatha,* scathe, and *beorgan,* O.H.G. *bergan,* to protect (comp. *hauberk*), the scabbard being what prevents the weapon from doing harm when not in use.] The sheath of a sword or other similar weapon.—*v.t.* To put in a scabbard or sheath.

scabble, skab'l, *v.t.* In *masonry,* to dress with a rough slightly furrowed surface.

scabies, skā'bi•ēz, *n.* [L.] Scab; mange; itch.—**scabious,** skā'bi•us, *a.* [L. *scabiosus.*] Consisting of scabs; rough; itchy; leprous.—*n.* The plant devil's-bit and allied species, named from being formerly deemed of efficacy against scabby eruptions of the skin.

scabrous, skab'rus, *a.* [L. *scabrosus,* from *scaber,* rough, from *scabies,* scab.] Rough; having sharp points or little asperities.

scads, skads, *n.* Large amounts or quantity of, as *scads* of money. (*Slang.*)

scaffold, skaf'old, *n.* [O.Fr. *escafaut, eschafault* (Fr. *échafaud*); L.L. *scadafaltum,* from prep. *ex,* and *cadafaltum,* a scaffold, a catafalque. CATAFALQUE.] A temporary stage or platform; an elevated platform for the execution of a criminal; a temporary structure of timber for the workmen engaged in building or repairing houses, etc.—*v.t.* To furnish with a scaffold.—**scaffolding,** skaf'old•ing, *n.* A temporary combination of timberwork for supporting workmen engaged on some building.

scagliola, skal•yō'la, *n.* [It.] A composition of gypsum, splinters of marble, etc., imitative of marble, and used for enriching columns and internal walls of buildings.

scalar, skā'lar, *n.* A quantity that has no direction, as opposed to *vector* (which see). Scalar quantities are compounded by addition and subtraction.

scalariform, ska•la'ri•form, *a.* [L. *scalaria,* a ladder, and *forma,* form.] Shaped like a ladder; resembling a ladder.—*Scalariform vessels,* certain tubes met with in plants.

scalawag, skal'a•wag, *n.* [Origin unknown.] A worthless fellow; during the days of reconstruction after the Civil War, any white Southerner who espoused the radical Republican cause.

scald, skạld, *v.t.* [O.Fr. *eschalder* (Fr. *échauder*), It. *scaldare,* to scald, from L. *ex,* intens., and *caldus, calidus,* hot. CALDRON.] To burn and injure with or as with hot liquid; to expose to a strong heat over a fire or in water or other liquid (to *scald* milk). —*n.* A burn or injury from scalding. —**scalding,** skạl'ding, *a.* So hot as to scald.

scald, skạld, *a.* [That is *scalled,* or affected with *scall.* SCALL.] Covered with scurf or scab; scabby; scurvy; paltry; poor.

scald, skald, skạld, *n.* [Icel. *skáld,* Sw. *skald.*] An ancient Scandinavian poet, whose occupation was to compose poems in honor of distinguished men, and to recite and sing them on public occasions.

scale, skāl, *n.* [A.Sax. *scále, scálu,* the dish of a balance=Icel. *skál,* Dan. *skaal,* D. *schaal,* G. *schale,* a dish, a balance. *Scale,* a thin lamina, is allied. See next art.] The dish of a balance; also the balance itself, or whole instrument: in this sense generally in the plural.—*v.t.* To weigh, as in scales. [*Shak.*]

scale, skāl, *n.* [A.Sax. *scale,* a shell, a husk=Dan. *skael,* a scale; *skal,* rind, shell; Icel. *skel,* a shell; akin *shale, shell, skill, scull, skull,* and see above.] One of the overlapping plates on the exterior of certain animals; one of the thin, small plates which protect the skin of many fishes; one of the somewhat similar laminae of reptiles; anything resembling the scale of a fish or other animal; a thin flake or lamina (a *scale* of bone, iron, and the like); *bot.* a rudimentary leaf on the exterior of a leaf bud.—*v.t.*—*scaled, scaling.* To strip or clear of scales; to take off in thin laminae or scales; *gun.* to clean the inside of a cannon by exploding a little powder.—*v.i.* To come off in scales or thin layers.—**scale insect,** *n.* An insect, scale-like in form, injurious to plants.—**scale moss,** *n.* The popular name given to plants resembling moss, which grow on the trunks of trees, etc., and have small scale-like leaves.—**scaliness,** skā'li•nes, *n.* The state of being scaly.—**scaly,** skā'li, *a.* Covered or abounding with scales; having the form of scales or thin laminae.

scale, skāl, *n.* [L. *scala,* a ladder, from stem of *scando,* to mount; akin to Skr. *skand,* to ascend.] A ladder (*Milton*); anything graduated, especially when applied as a measure or rule; a mathematical instrument consisting of a slip of wood, ivory, etc., with spaces graduated and numbered on its surface, for measuring or laying off distances; any succession of ascending or descending steps or degrees; series of ranks; relative dimensions without difference in proportion of parts; a basis for a numerical system (the decimal *scale*); *music,* a succession of notes arranged in the order of pitch, and comprising the sounds that may occur in a piece of music written in a given key; the *diatonic scale*, having its eight notes ascending by five tones and two semitones; also the series of notes producible by voices or instruments (the *scale* of a violin).—*v.t.*—*scaled*, *scaling*. To climb, as by a ladder; to ascend by steps; to clamber up.—**scaler,** skā'lėr, *n.* One who scales.

scalene, ska•lēn', *a.* [Gr. *skalēnos*, limping, uneven.] A term applied to a triangle of which the three sides are unequal. *n.* A scalene triangle.

scall, skąl, *n.* [Same as Dan. *skal*, peel, husk, whence *skaldet*, bald; Icel. *skalli*, a bald head; akin to *scale*.] Scab; scurf; scabbiness. (O.T.)—*Dry scall*, psoriasis or itch.—*Moist scall*, eczema.—**scalled,** skąld, *a.* Scurfy; scabby; scald.

scallion, skal'yun, *n.* [O.Fr. *escalogne*, It. *scalogno*, from L. (*caepa*) *Ascalonia*, the onion of *Ascalon*.] A kind of onion; a shallot; a leek.

scallop, skal'op or skol'op, *n.* [O.Fr. *escalope*, from D. *schelp*, *schelpe*, shell, cockleshell; akin *scalp*, *scale*, etc.] A marine bivalve of the oyster family, used for food, one species of which occurs in abundance on the coast of Palestine, and was formerly worn by pilgrims as a mark that they had been to the Holy Land; a kind of dish for baking oysters in; a curving on the edge of anything, like the segment of a circle. Written also *Scollop*.—*v.t.* To cut the edge or border of into scallops or segments of circles.—**scalloped,** skal'opt or skol'opt, *p.* and *a.* Cut at the edge or border into scallops.—*Scalloped oysters*, oysters cooked (originally in shells) with bread crumbs, cream, etc.

scalp, skalp, *n.* [Akin to *scale*, *shell*, *skill*, *scallop*; comp. D. *schelp*, *schulp*, a shell; Icel. *skálpr*, a sheath.] The skull (*Shak.*); the outer covering of the skull; the skin of the head, or part of it, with the hair on it, torn off by the American Indians as a mark of victory over an enemy; a bed of mussels or oysters.—*v.t.* To deprive of the scalp.

scalpel, skal'pel, *n.* [L. *scalpellum*, dim. of *scalprum*, a knife, from *scalpo*, to cut, to scrape.] A knife used in anatomical dissections and surgical operations.

scammony, skam'o•ni, *n.* [L. *scammonia*, from Gr. *skammōnia*, from the Persian.] A gum resin of a bitter and acrid taste, obtained from a species of convolvulus, used in medicine as a drastic purge.

scamp, skamp, *n.* [Originally one who decamps or runs off without paying debts. See SCAMPER.] A worthless fellow; a knave; a swindler; a mean villain; a rogue.—*v.t.* To execute, as a piece of work, in a slim, dishonest, or perfunctory manner.—**scamper,** skam'pėr, *n.* One who scamps work.

scamper, skam'pėr, *v.i.* [From O.F. *escamper*, Pr. *escampar*, It. *scampare*, to save one's life, to escape; lit. to decamp, from L. *ex*, out of, and *campus*, a field. Hence *scamp*. CAMP.] To run with speed; to hasten away.—*n.* A hasty flight; a hurried run.

scan, skan, *v.t.*—*scanned*, *scanning*. [Formerly *scand*, from Fr. *scander*, to scan verse, from L. *scando*, to climb, to scan (seen in *ascend*, *descend*); Skr. *skand*, to climb.] To examine by counting the metrical feet or syllables; to read so as to indicate the metrical structure; to examine minutely or nicely; to scrutinize.—**scansion,** skan'shon, *n.* The act of scanning; the metrical structure of verse.

scandal, skan'dal, *n.* [Fr. *scandale*, from L. *scandalum*, Gr. *skandalon*, a snare, a scandal. *Slander* is a different form of this word.] Offense given by the faults or misdeeds of another; public reproach or reprobation; opprobrium; shame; something uttered which is false and injurious to reputation; defamatory talk; slander.—*v.t.* To throw scandal on; to slander.—**scandalize,** skan'dal•īz, *v.t.*—*scandalized*, *scandalizing*. To offend by some action considered very wrong or outrageous; to shock; to give offense to; to disgrace; to slander.—**scandalmonger,** *n.* One who deals in or retails scandal.—**scandalous,** skan'dal•us, *a.* Causing scandal or offense; shameful; disgraceful to reputation; libelous; slanderous.—**scandalously,** skan'dal•us•li, *adv.* In a scandalous manner; disgracefully; shamefully.

scandent, skan'dent, *a.* [L. *scandens*, *scandentis*, ppr. of *scando*, to climb.] *Bot.* climbing.

Scandinavian, skan•di•nā'vi•an, *a.* Relating to Scandinavia.—*Scandinavian tongues*, Icelandic, Norwegian, Danish, Swedish.

scandium, skan'di•um, *n.* [L. *Scandia*, Scandinavia.] A rare trivalent metallic element. Symbol, Sc; at. no., 21; at. wt., 44.956.

scansion. See SCAN.

Scansores, skan•sō'rēz, *n. pl.* [Lit. the climbers, from L. *scando*, to climb.] The order of climbing birds, such as the cuckoos, woodpeckers, parrots, etc., having feet with two toes turned backward and two forward.—**scansorial,** skan•sō'ri•al, *a.* Climbing or adapted to climbing; belonging to the Scansores.

scant, skant, *a.* [Same as Icel. *skamt*, short, brief; akin to Norse *skanta*, exactly measured; comp. Prov.E. and Sc. *skimp* or *skemp*, to give short measure.] Scarcely sufficient; rather less than is wanted for the purpose; not enough; having a limited supply; scarce; short (with *of*).—*v.t.* To limit; to stint; to keep on short allowance; to afford or give out sparingly; to be niggard of; to grudge.—*adv.* Scarcely; hardly; not quite.—**scantily, scantly,** skan'ti•li, skant'li, *adv.* In a scant or scanty manner.—**scantiness,** skan'ti•nes, *n.* The state or condition of being scant or scanty.—**scanty,** skan'ti, *a.* Wanting amplitude or extent; narrow; small; scant; not ample; hardly sufficient (a *scanty* supply).

scantling, skant'ling, *n.* [O.Fr. *eschantillon*, Fr. *échantillon*, a specimen, a pattern, from prefix *ex*, and *cantel*, a cantle.] A quantity cut for a particular purpose; a sample; a pattern; a small quantity; the dimensions of timber, stones, etc., in length, breadth, and thickness; timber less than five inches square; a kind of trestle for supporting a cask.

scape, skāp, *n.* [L. *scapus*, a stalk.] *Bot.* a radical stem bearing the fructification without leaves, as in the narcissus and hyacinth.—**scapiform,** skā'pi•form, *a. Bot.* In the form of a scape.

scape, skāp, *v.t.* and *i.* Short form of *escape*.—**scapegoat,** skāp'gōt, *n.* Among the ancient Jews, a goat which was sent into the wilderness bearing the iniquities of the people, which were laid on him by the hands of the high priest; hence, one made to bear the blame of others.—**scapegrace,** skāp'grās, *n.* A graceless fellow; a careless, idle, harebrained fellow.

scapolite, skap'o•līt, *n.* [Gr. *skapos*, a rod and *lithos*, a stone.] A mineral, a silicate, of alumina and lime, occurring often in long crystals.

scapula, skap'ū•la, *n.* [L.] The shoulderblade.—**scapular,** skap'ū•lėr, *a.* Pertaining to the scapula or the shoulder. — **scapular, scapulary,** skap'ū•lėr, skap'ū•le•ri, *n.* A kind of ecclesiastical garment consisting of two bands of woolen stuff going over the shoulders, one in front the other behind; a kind of badge, consisting of two small squares of brown stuff, of the same color as the Carmelite habit, connected by two lengths of tape, and worn in honor of the Virgin Mary; *surg.* a bandage for the shoulder blade; *ornithol.* a feather on the shoulder of a bird.

scar, skär, *n.* [Fr. *escarre*, *escharre*, L. *eschara*, from Gr. *eschara*, a scar or scab on a wound caused by burning.] The mark of a wound or an ulcer remaining after healing; a cicatrix; a hurt; a wound; *bot.* a mark left after the fall of a leaf, or on a seed after the separation of its stem.—*v.t.*—*scarred*, *scarring*. To mark with a scar or scars; to wound; to hurt.—*v.i.* To be covered with a scar; to form a scar.—**scarry,** skä'ri, *a.* Pertaining to scars; having scars or marks of old wounds.

scar, skär, *n.* [Same as Icel. *skor*, a rift in a precipice, *sker*, a rocky islet; Dan. *skjaer*, a cliff; root seen in *shear*, *short*.] A cliff; a naked detached rock; a bare and broken place on the side of a hill or mountain; a scaur.

scarab, skar'ab, *n.* [L. *scarabaeus*, a beetle.] One of a group of beetles of which the sacred beetle of the Egyptians, so frequently figured on their monuments, is the best known species; the figure of a beetle cut in hard stone, many of which are found in Egypt.

scaramouch, skar'a•möch, *n.* [Fr. *scaramouche*, It. *scaramuccia*, *scaramuccio*.] A buffoon in motley dress; [*cap.*] a personage, in Italian comedy, whose character was compounded of traits of vaunting and poltroonery; any poltroon or braggadocio.

scarce, skârs, *a.* [From O.Fr. *escars*, *eschars*, It. *scarso*, D. *schaars*, scarce, from L.L. *excarpsus*, *scarpsus*, for *excerptus*, pp. of L. *excerpo*, to pluck or cull out. EXCERPT.] Not plentiful or abundant; being in small quantity in proportion to the demand; deficient; seldom met with; rare; uncommon; unfrequent; scantily supplied; not having much: with *of*.—*To make one's self scarce*, to disappear voluntarily; to get out of the way.—**scarce, scarcely,** skârs′li, *adv.* Hardly; barely; but just; with difficulty. —**scarceness, scarcity,** skârs′nes, skâr′si•ti, *n.* The state or condition of being scarce; dearth; want; famine.

scare, skâr, *v.t.*—*scared, scaring.* [Akin to Icel. *skjarr*, apt to flee, shy, *skirra*, to drive away, G. *scheren*, to drive away; same root as *shear*.] To fright; to terrify suddenly; to strike with sudden terror.—*n.* A sudden fright or panic; a sudden terror inspired by a trifling cause; a causeless alarm.—**scarecrow,** skâr′krō, *n.* Anything set up to frighten crows or other birds from crops; anything terrifying without danger; a person so meanly clad as to resemble a scarecrow.

scarf, skärf, *n.* [Same as L.G. *scherf*, Dan. *skjaerf*, *skierf*, G. *scharpe*, O.H. G. *scherbe*, originally a pocket, hence the band suspending the pocket, a scarf.] A sort of light shawl; an article of dress of a light and decorative character worn round the neck or loosely round the shoulders, or otherwise.—**scarfskin,** *n.* [Perhaps for *scurfskin*.] The cuticle or epidermis; the outer thin integument of the body.

scarf, skärf, *n.* [Same as Sw. *skarf*, a joint; akin Dan. *skarre*, to scarf; Sc. *skare*, a scarf, to scarf.] *Carp.* the joint by which the ends of two pieces of timber are united so as to overlap and form a continuous piece. —*v.t.* To cut a scarf on; to unite by means of a scarf.—**scarf joint,** *n.* A joint formed by scarfing.

scarify, skar′i•fi, *v.t.*—*scarified, scarifying.* [Fr. *scarifier*, L. *scarifico*, from Gr. *skariphaomai*, to scratch open, from *skariphos*, a sharp-pointed instrument.] *Surg.* to make small cuts or incisions in the skin by means of a lancet or special instrument so as to draw blood without opening a large vein; to remove the flesh about a tooth in order to get a better hold of it; to stir the soil, as with a scarifier.—**scarification,** skar′i•fi•kā″shon, *n. Surg.* the act of scarifying.—**scarificator,** skar′i•fi•kā″tėr, *n.* An instrument used in scarification or cupping.—**scarifier,** skar′i•fī•ėr, *n.* One who or that which scarifies; *agri.* an implement with prongs employed for stirring the soil without reversing its surface or altering its form.

scarlatina, skär•la•tē′na, *n.* [From *scarlet*.] A serious contagious fever which especially attacks the young, accompanied by a scarlet eruption, sore throat, etc.; scarlet fever.

scarlet, skär′let, *n.* [O.Fr. *escarlate*, Mod. Fr. *écarlate*, It. *scarlatto*, a word of Persian origin.] A beautiful bright-red color, brighter than crimson; cloth of a scarlet color; scarlet robe or dress.—*a.* Of the color scarlet; of a bright-red color; dressed in scarlet (*Shak.*).—*Scarlet bean, Scarlet runner*, the kidney bean.—*Scarlet fever.* SCARLATINA.—**Scarlet Woman,** *n. Revelation* xvii. 4. A term applied by Protestants to Rome and Church of Rome.—**scarlet letter,** *n.* A scarlet "A" worn by women during Puritan times as a mark of adultery.

scarp, skärp, *n.* [From Fr. *escarpe*, from It. *scarpa*, a scarp, a slope, from O.H.G. *scarp*, Mod. G. *scharf*, E. *sharp*—the scarp being cut sharp or steep.] *Fort.* the interior slope of the ditch next the place, at the foot of the rampart.

scat, scatt, skat, *n.* [A.Sax. *sceat*, a tax, a coin; Icel. *skattr*, Dan. *skat*.] A tax.

scathe, skāᴛʜ, *n.* [A.Sax. *sceathan* = Icel. *skatha*, D. and G. *schaden*, to injure; Icel. *skathi*, Goth. *skathis*, D. and G. *schade*, injury.] Damage; injury; harm.—*v.t.*—*scathed, scathing.* To injure; to do damage to; to harm.—**scathing,** skā′ᴛʜing, *p.* and *a.* Injuring; damaging; harming; blasting.—**scatheless,** skāᴛʜ′les, *a.* Without scathe or harm; unharmed.

scatology, ska•tol′o•ji, *n.* [Gr. *skōr*, *skatos*, dung.] Knowledge of dung, or of savage practices in which dung or filth enters.

scatter, skat′ėr, *v.t.* [A.Sax. *scaterian*, to scatter; same word as *shatter*; Gr. *skedannymi*, to scatter, is of kindred origin.] To throw loosely about; to sprinkle; to strew; to besprinkle; to disperse; to dissipate; to separate or remove to a distance from each other; to disunite; to frustrate, disappoint, and overthrow (to *scatter* hopes, etc.). ∴ Syn. under DISPERSE.—*v.i.* To disperse; to separate from each other; to straggle apart.—**scatterbrain,** *n.* A thoughtless person; one incapable of concentration. (*Colloq.*)—**scatterbrained,** *a.* Giddy; heedless; thoughtless. (*Colloq.*)—**scatterer,** skat′ėr•ėr, *n.* One who scatters.

scaup, skạp, *n.* [A form of *scalp*.] A bed of shellfish (an *oyster-scaup*, a *musselscaup*); a species of duck which feeds on mollusks, etc.

scaur, skạr, *n.* [SCAR.] A scar or precipitous bank; a cliff.

scavenger, skav′en•jėr, *n.* [From *scavage*, L.L. *scavagium*, an old law term equivalent to *showage*, a duty on goods *shown*, from A.Sax. *sceawian*, to show. The scavenger was originally one who looked after the scavage. As to the insertion of *n* comp. *messenger*, *passenger*.] A person whose employment is to clean the streets of a city; a person similarly engaged.

scene, sēn, *n.* [Fr. *scène*; L. *scena*, from Gr. *skēnē*, a covered place, a tent, a stage, from root of Skr. *sku*, to cover. E. *shade*.] A stage; that part of a theater in which the acting is done; the imaginary place in which the action of a play is supposed to occur; the surroundings amid which anything is transacted; a whole series of actions and events connected and exhibited; an assemblage of objects displayed at one view; a place and objects seen together; a landscape; a view; one of the painted slides, hangings, or other devices used to give an appearance of reality to the action of a play; a part of a play, being a division of an act; an exhibition of strong feeling between two or more persons; a theatrical display of emotion; an artificial or affected action or course of action.—*Behind the scenes*, behind the scenery of a theater, at the back of the stage; hence, specially acquainted with the motives influencing the actions of a party or an individual.—**scenario,** si•nâ′ri•ō; It. pron. she•nä′rē•ō, *n.* [It.] An abstract of the chief incidents in any dramatic work arranged according to act and scene, giving a sort of skeleton of the piece.—**scenery,** sē′nėr•i, *n.* The paintings representing the scenes of a play; the general appearance or natural features of a place.—**scenic, scenical,** sē′nik or sen′ik, sē′ni•kal or sen′i•kal, *a.* Pertaining to the stage; dramatic; theatrical.—**scenographic,** sē•no•graf′ik, *a.* Pertaining to scenography; drawn in perspective.—**scenography,** si•nog′ra•fi, *n.* Representation or drawing according to the rules of perspective.

scent, sent, *n.* [For *sent*, from Fr. *sentir*, to perceive, to smell, from L. *sentire*, to perceive by the senses. SENSE.] That which, issuing from a body, affects the olfactory nerves of animals; odor; smell; the power of smelling; odor left on the ground enabling an animal's track to be followed; hence, course of pursuit; track.—*v.t.* To perceive by the olfactory organs; to smell; to perfume.—**scentless,** sent′les, *a.* Inodorous; destitute of smell.

scepter, sep′tėr, *n.* [Fr. *sceptre*, L. *sceptrum*, from Gr. *skēptron*, a staff, from *skēptō*, to prop or lean.] A staff or baton borne by a monarch or other ruler as a symbol of authority.—*The scepter*, royal power or authority.

schedule, sked′ūl (English shed′ūl), *n.* [O.Fr. *schedule*, from L. *schedula*, dim. of *scheda*, a scroll, from Gr. *schedē*, a leaf, from root of *schizō*, L. *scindo*, to split.] A sheet of paper or parchment containing a written or printed list; a list annexed to a larger document, as to a will, lease, etc.—*v.t.*—*scheduled, scheduling.* To make a tabular statement of times of projected operations, as of a train.

scheme, skēm, *n.* [Fr. *schème*, L. *schema*, from Gr. *schēma*, from *schein*, to hold, to keep.] A combination of things connected and adjusted by design; a system; a plan of something to be done; a project; the representation of any design or geometrical figure; a diagram.—*v.t.* —*schemed, scheming.* To plan, contrive, plot, project, design.—*v.i.* To form a plan; to contrive.—**schematic,** skē•mat′ik, *a.* Pertaining to a scheme.—**schematize,** skē′ma•-

tīz, *v.t.*—*schematized, schematizing.* To form into a scheme or schemes.—**schemer,** skē′mėr, *n.* One who schemes; a contriver; a plotter.—**scheming,** skē′ming, *p.* and *a.* Given to forming schemes; artful; intriguing.

scherif, she•rif′, *n.* See SHERIF.

scherzando, skert•sän′dō, *adv.* [It.] *Mus.* in a playful or sportive manner. —**scherzo,** skert′sō, *n.* [It.] A passage of a sportive character in musical pieces of some length, as in symphonies.

schism, sizm, *n.* [L. *schisma*; from Gr. *schisma*, from *schizō*, to divide; same root as L. *scindo*, to cut, A.Sax. *sceadan*, G. *scheiden*, to separate. SCHEDULE, SHED.] A split or division in a community; commonly, a division or separation in a church or denomination of Christians, occasioned by diversity of opinions; breach of unity among people of the same religious faith.—**schismatic, schismatical,** siz•mat′ik, siz•mat′i•kal, *a.* Pertaining to schism; partaking of the nature of schism; tending to schism.—**schismatic,** *n.* One who takes part in a schism.—**schismatically,** siz•mat′i•kal•li, *adv.* In a schismatical manner.

schist, shist, *n.* [Gr. *schistos*, divided, divisible, from *schizo*, to split. SCHISM.] A geological term applied to rocks which have a foliated structure and split in thin irregular plates; properly confined to metamorphic rocks (as gneiss) consisting of layers of different minerals.—**schistose, schistous,** shis′tōz, shis′-tus, *a.* Having the structure or character of schist.

schizocarp, shiz′o•kärp, or skiz′, *n.* [Gr. *schizō*, to split, *karpos*, fruit.] *Bot.* a dry fruit which splits at maturity into distinct one-seeded carpels.

schizoid, skiz′oid, *a.* [Gr. *schizein*, to split and suffix-*oid*, resembling.] Related to, or afflicted with, schizophrenia.

schizophrenia, skiz•o•frē′ni•a, *n.* [Gr. *schizo*, split and *phren*, mind and-*ia*, suffix.] A mental disorder in which there is a retreat from reality with personality disintegration.

schnapps, shnaps, *n.* [G. *schnapps*, D. *snaps*, a dram.] A dram of Hollands gin or other ardent spirits.

scholar, skol′ėr, *n.* [O.Fr. *escolier* (Fr. *écolier*), from L.L. *scholaris*, from L. *schola*, a school. SCHOOL.] One who attends a school; a learned person; a person of high attainments in learning; one that learns anything; a pedant†; an undergraduate in an English university who receives a portion of its revenues to furnish him with the means of prosecuting his studies.—**scholarly,** skol′ėr•li, *a.* Like a scholar; becoming a scholar or man of learning.—**scholarship,** skol′ėr•ship, *n.* The character of a scholar; attainments in science or literature; erudition; learning; an exhibition or regularly settled allowance of money for a scholar at some educational institution; a foundation for the support of a student.—**scholastic,** sko•las′tik, *a.* Pertaining to or suiting a scholar, school, or schools; characteristic of a scholar; pertaining to the Schoolmen of the middle ages, or those philosophers and divines who adopted the system of Aristotle, and spent much time on points of nice speculation. —*n.* One who adheres to the scholastic method; one of the schoolmen of the Middle Ages.

scholium, skō′li•um, *n.* pl. **scholiums** or **scholia** [Gr. *scholion*, from *scholē*, leisure, lucubration. SCHOOL.] A marginal note, annotation, or remark; an explanatory comment, such as those annexed to the Latin and Greek authors by the early grammarians.—**scholiast,** skō′li•ast, *n.* [Gr. *scholiastēs.*] One who makes scholiums; an ancient grammarian who annotated the classics.—**scholiastic,** skō•li•as′tik, *a.* Pertaining to a scholiast.

school, sköl, *n.* [A.Sax. *scól*, O.Fr. *escole*, from L. *schola*, from Gr. *scholē*, leisure, discussion, philosophy, a school.] A place in which persons are instructed in any species of learning; an educational establishment; a place in which instruction is imparted to the young; one of the seminaries of the scholastic philosophy of the middle ages; a body of pupils; the disciples or followers of a teacher; those who hold a common doctrine or accept the same teachings or principles (the Socratic *school*, painters of the Italian *school*); a system or state of matters prevalent at a certain time (the old *school*, the new *school*); any place of discipline or training,—*High school*, a school in which a superior education can be obtained; sometimes the chief public school in a town.—*Normal school.* NORMAL.—*a.* Relating to a school or to education; pertaining to the schoolmen; scholastic.—*v.t.* To instruct; to educate; to discipline; to chide and admonish; to reprove.—**school board,** an organized body of individuals appointed or elected to administer the affairs of the local public schools.—**schoolbook,** *n.* A book used in schools; a textbook.—**schoolboy,** *n.* A boy who attends school.—**schoolfellow, schoolmate,** *n.* An associate in school.—**schoolgirl,** *n.* A girl who attends school.—**schooling,** sköl′ing, *n.* Instruction in school.—**schoolman,** sköl′man, *n.* Teacher in medieval university; theologian using Aristotelian logic.—**schoolmaster,** sköl′mas•tėr, *n.* A man who presides over and teaches a school; a teacher, instructor, or preceptor of a school; one who or that which disciplines and instructs. —**schoolmistress,** sköl′mis•tres, *n.* The mistress of a school; a female who governs and teaches a school.—**schoolroom,** *n.* A room for teaching. —**schoolteacher,** *n.* One who gives regular instruction in a school.

school, sköl, *n.* [Same word as *shoal.*] A shoal or compact body (a *school* of fishes).

schooner, skön′ėr, *n.* [Properly *scooner*, from a New England word *scoon*, to skim or skip upon the water, to make ducks and drakes, the first vessel of the kind having been built at Gloucester, Mass., about 1713. *Scoon* is the A.Sax. *scunian*, E. to *shun.* SHUN.] A vessel with two masts, and her chief sails fore and aft sails, her mainsail and foresail being both extended by a gaff and a boom; a measure of beer about two-thirds of a pint.

schorl, shorl, *n.* [G. *schörl*, Sw. *skörl*, Dan. *skjörl*; comp. Dan. *skjör*, brittle.] A mineral of a pitchy luster and color, brittle texture, and capable of being rendered electric by heat or friction, usually occurring in granitic rocks, and often embedded in feldspar and quartz; tourmaline.—**schorlaceous,** shor•lā′shus, *a.* Pertaining to or containing schorl; resembling schorl.

schottische, shot′ish′, *n.* [G. *schottische*, Scottish, lit. a Scottish dance.] A dance performed by a lady and gentleman, resembling a polka; the music suited for such a dance is 2-4 time.

sciamachy, sī•am′a•ki, *n.* [Gr. *skia*, a shadow, and *machē*, a battle.] A fight with a shadow; an imaginary or futile combat.

sciatica, sī•at′i•ka, *n.* [L.L. *sciatica*, from Gr. *ischiadikos*, from *ischias*, a pain in the hip, from *ischion*, the hip.] Neuralgia of the sciatic nerve.—**sciatic,** sī•at′ik, *a.* Pertaining to the hip (the *sciatic* artery or nerve).

science, sī′ens, *n.* [Fr. *science*, from L. *scientia*, knowledge, from *scio*, to know (seen also in *conscious, conscience, nescience, sciolist*).] Knowledge; comprehension or understanding; knowledge coordinated, arranged, and systematized; hence, the knowledge regarding any one department of mind or matter coordinated, arranged, and systematized (the *science* of botany, of astronomy, etc.; mental *science*); art derived from precepts or built on principles; skill resulting from training; special skill.—*Applied science*, a science when its laws are employed and exemplified in dealing with concrete phenomena, as opposed to a *pure science*, as mathematics, when it treats of laws or general statements apart from particular instances.—*Natural science.* See NATURAL.—*Physical science.* PHYSICS.—*Moral science*, moral philosophy or ethics.—*The seven sciences* of antiquity, grammar, logic, rhetoric, arithmetic, geometry, music, and astronomy.—**sciential,** sī•en′shal, *a.* Pertaining to science.—**scientific,** sī•en•tif′ik, *a.* [L. *scientia*, knowledge, and *facio*, to make.] Pertaining to science; evincing or endowed with a knowledge of science; treating of science; well versed in science; according to the rules or principles of science.—**scientifically,** sī•en•tif′i•kal•li, *adv.* In a scientific manner; according to the rules or principles of science. —**scientist,** sī′ent•ist, *n.* A person versed in or devoted to science; a scientific man; a savant.

scilicet, si'li•set. [L.] To wit; videlicet; namely; abbreviated to *Scil.* or *Sc.*

scimitar, sim'i•tėr, *n.* [O.Fr. *cimeterre,* It. *scimitarra,* from Per. *shemshir, shimshir.*] An oriental sword, the blade of which is single-edged, short, curved, and broadest at the point end.

scincoid, sin'koid, *a.* Pertaining to the skink and allied animals.

scintilla, sin•til'la, *n.* [L.] A spark; a glimmer; the least particle; a trace.—**scintillant,** sin'til•lant, *a.* Sparkling.—**scintillate,** sin'til•lāt, *v.i.*—*scintillated, scintillating.* [L. *scintilla, scintillatum.*] To emit sparks; to sparkle or twinkle, as the stars.—**scintillation,** sin•til•lā'shon, *n.* The act of scintillating or sparkling; the twinkling of the stars.

sciolist, sī'ol•ist, *n.* [L. *sciolus,* a smatterer, dim. of *scius,* knowing, from *scio,* to know. SCIENCE.] One who knows things superficially; a smatterer.—**sciolistic,** sī•ol•is'tik, *a.* Pertaining to sciolism or a sciolist; superficial as to knowledge.

sciomancy, sī'o•man•si, *n.* [Gr. *skia,* a shadow, and *manteia,* divination.] Divination by shadows.

scion, sī'on, *n.* [Fr. *scion,* from L. *sectio, sectionis,* a cutting, from *seco,* to cut. SECTION.] A shoot or twig cut for the purpose of being grafted upon some other tree, or for planting; fig. a descendant; an heir.

scirrhus, skir'rus, *n.* [L. *scirrus,* from Gr. *skirrhos,* a hardened swelling or tumor.] *Med.* a hard tumor usually proceeding from the induration of a gland, and often terminating in a cancer.—**scirrhoid,** skir'roid, *a.* Resembling scirrhus.—**scirrhosity,** skir•ros'i•ti, *n.* The state of being scirrhous; also, a scirrhus or induration.—**scirrhous,** skir'rus, *a.* Proceeding from or of the nature of scirrhus; indurated; knotty.

scissel, sis'sel, *n.* [From L. *scindo, scissum,* to cut.] Clippings of various metals; the remainder of a plate of metal after the planchets or circular blanks have been cut out for the purpose of coinage.—**scissile,** sis'sil, *a.* Capable of being cut.—**scission,** sizh'on, *n.* [L. *scissio,* from *scindo,* to cut.] The act of cutting or dividing by an edged instrument; the state of being cut; division.

scissors, siz'ėrz, *n. pl.* [From O.Fr. *cisoires, ciseaux,* from L. *caedo,* to cut (CHISEL); but influenced by *scissor,* one who cuts, from *scindo, scissum,* to cut.] A cutting instrument consisting of two blades movable on a pin in the center, and which cut from opposite sides against an object placed between them; often spoken of as a *pair of scissors.*

sciurine, sī•ū'rīn, *a.* [L. *sciurus,* a squirrel. SQUIRREL.] Having the characters of the squirrel tribe.

scleretinite, skli•ret'i•nīt, *n.* [Gr. *sklēros,* hard, and *rētinē,* resin.] A black, hard, brittle mineral (or fossil) resin, nearly allied to amber.

scleroid, sklē'roid, *a. Bot.* having a hard texture.—**scleroma, sclerosis,** skli•rō'ma, skli•rō'sis, *n. Med.* induration of the cellular tissue.—**sclerosis,** skli•rō'sis. [Gr. *sklēros,* hard.] Hardening resulting from disease, especially of the nervous system and of arteries.—**sclerotic,** skli•rot'ik, *a.* [Gr. *sklerotes,* hardness.] Hard; firm (the *sclerotic* coat of the eye).—*n.* The firm white membrane which covers the posterior part of the eye, the front being covered by the transparent *cornea.*—**sclerotitis,** skle•rō•tī'tis, *n.* Inflammation of the sclerotic.—**sclerotium,** skle•rō'shum. [Gr. *sklerotēs,* hardness.] In fungi, a hard compact mass which germinates after a dormant period. See ERGOT.

scoff, skof, *n.* [Same as O.Fris. *schof,* sport; Icel. *skop, skaup,* mockery, ridicule; O.H.G. *scoph,* sport.] An expression of derision, mockery, scorn, or contempt; a gibe; a flout; an object of derision.—*v.i.* To show insolent ridicule or mockery; to utter contemptuous language; to mock; with *at* before the object.—*v.t.* To mock at; to ridicule.—**scoffer,** skof'ėr, *n.* One who scoffs; a mocker or scorner.—**scoffingly,** skof'ing•li, *adv.* In a scoffing manner; by way of derision.

scold, skōld, *v.i.* [Akin to Sc. *scald,* L.G. and D. *schelden,* Dan. *skielde,* G. *schelten,* to scold; Icel. *skjalla,* to clash; *skellr,* a crash; G. *schelle,* a bell.] To find fault in rude language; to utter harsh or rude rebuke; to make use of abuse or vituperation.—*v.t.* To chide with rudeness and ill-temper; to vituperate.—*n.* One who scolds; a noisy, foul-mouthed woman; a railing virago; a scolding; a brawl.—**scolder,** skōl'dėr, *n.* One that scolds.—**scolding,** skōl'ding, *n.* The act of one who scolds; a vituperative harangue; a rating.

Scolecida, sko•lē'si•da, *n. pl.* [From Gr. *skolēx,* an earthworm, a tapeworm.] The tapeworms and allied animals.—**scolex,** skō'leks, *n.* pl. **scolices,** skō'li•sēz. The larva of a tapeworm; a tapeworm embryo.

scoliosis, skō•li•ō'sis, *n.* [Gr. *skolios,* crooked.] A distortion or curvature of the spine to one side.

scollop, skol'op, *n.* [SCALLOP.] A kind of shellfish; a scallop; a curving indentation.—*v.t.* To form or cut with scollops.

sconce, skons, *n.* [O.Fr. *esconce,* shelter, a sconce; from L.L. *absconsa* (for *absconsa candela,* a hidden candle), a sconce, from L. *abscondo, absconsum,* to hide. ABSCOND.] A cover or screen; a cover or protection for a light; a case for a candle; the tube in a candlestick in which the candle is inserted; a fixed candlestick on a wall; a work for defense; bulwark; a fort, as at a pass or river; a covering for the head; a helmet; a head-piece; the head itself; the skull; table fine for breach of etiquette, etc.—*v.t.* To shelter; to ensconce.

scoop, sköp, *n.* [Same as D. *schop, schup,* spade, shovel; Sw. *skopa,* a scoop; akin to Dan. *skuffe,* a shovel.] A thin metallic shovel with capacious sides for lifting grain; a similar but smaller utensil for lifting sugar, flour, etc.; a large ladle with a long handle for dipping in fluids; a spoon-shaped surgical instrument; a sort of pan for holding coals; the publication of news before a competitor; news so published.—*v.t.* To take out with a scoop or as with a scoop; to lade out; to empty as with a scoop; to hollow out; to excavate; to publish news before (a competitor).—**scooper,** *n.*

scooter, scöt'ėr, *n.* A child's vehicle with a board set between tandem wheels, the child standing with one foot on the board and pushing with the other; a flat-bottomed sailboat with a raised prow and steel runners, to sail on ice or water.

scope, skōp, *n.* [It. *scopo,* mark, view, aim, L. *scopus,* Gr. *skopos,* a mark, aim, from Gr. *skeptomai,* to view.] A mark shot at‡; an aim or end kept in view; ultimate design or purpose; intention; free or wide outlook or aim; amplitude of intellectual range; space; liberty; sweep.

scorbutic, scorbutical, skor•bū'tik, skor•bū'ti•kal, *a.* [Fr. *scorbutique,* from *scorbut,* the scurvy, from D. *scheurbuik,* G. *scharbock,* scurvy.] Pertaining to or affected with scurvy.

scorch, skorch, *v.t.* [O.Fr. *escorcher, escorcer* (Fr. *écorcher*), to strip off the skin; from L. *excorticare*—*ex,* and *cortex, corticis,* bark (whence *cork*).] To burn superficially; to subject to a degree of heat that injures the surface; to parch.—**scorcher,** skorch'ėr, *n.* That which scorches; a hot day; a sharp rebuke; a person who drives at an excessive speed.—*v.i.* To be burned on the surface; to be parched.—**scorching,** skorch'ing, *a.* Such as to scorch.

score, skōr, *n.* [A.Sax. *scor,* a score, a notch, from *sceran,* to shear (see SHEAR); Icel. *skor,* an incision, a tally, the number twenty; *skora,* to number by notches; akin *scar* or *scaur, share, sheer, shire, shore, short.*] A notch; a cut made on a tally for the purpose of keeping account of something; the number twenty, as being marked off by a special or larger score; among archers, twenty yards; an account or reckoning kept by notches, marks, or otherwise; an account of dues; hence, what is due; a debt; the number of points made by players in certain games; account, reason, ground (he declined on the *score* of illness); a line drawn; a long superficial scratch; *music,* the original draft, or its transcript, of a musical composition with the parts for all the different voices or instruments.—*To go off at score,* to start, as a pedestrian, from the score or scratch; hence, to start off, generally.—*To quit scores,* to pay fully; to make even by giving an equivalent.—*v.t.*—*scored, scoring.* To make scores or scratches on; to furrow; to set down, as in account; to record; to mark; to note; to enter or register; to make a score of; to get for one's self, as points, hits, runs, etc., in certain games; *music,* to write out, as the different parts of a composition, in proper order and arrangement.—*v.i.* To make or keep a score; to make a point or hit, or a clever retort.—**scorer,** skō′rėr, *n.* One who scores; one who keeps the score or tally at games, matches, etc.; an instrument used in marking numbers, etc., on timber.

scoria, skō′ri•a, *n.* pl. **scoriae,** skō′ri•ē. [L. *scoria,* from Gr. *skōria,* from *skōr,* ordure.] The recrement of metals in fusion; the slag rejected after the reduction of metallic ores; dross; *pl.* the cinders of volcanic eruptions.—**scoriaceous,** skō•ri•ā′shus, *a.* Pertaining to scoria; partaking of the nature of scoria.—**scorification,** skō′ri•fi•kā″shon, *n.* The act or operation of scorifying.—**scorify,** skō′ri•fī, *v.t.* To reduce to scoria or drossy matter; to separate the dross from the valuable metal.

scorn, skorn, *n.* [O.Fr. *escorne,* affront, disgrace; *escorner,* It. *scornare,* to break off the horns, to affront, from L. *ex,* and *cornu,* a horn.] Extreme and passionate contempt; disdain springing from a person's opinion of the meanness and unworthiness of an object; the expression of this feeling; a scoff; a subject of extreme contempt or disdain.—*To think scorn,* to disdain; to despise.—*To laugh to scorn,* to deride; to make a mock of.—*v.t.* To hold in scorn; to despise; to disdain; to treat with scorn; to make a mock of.—*v.i.* To feel scorn or disdain; to show scorn.—**scorner,** skor′nėr, *n.* One that scorns; a despiser; a scoffer; a derider; one who scoffs at religion.—**scornful,** skorn′fu̧l, *a.* Full of scorn; contemptuous; disdainful.—**scornfully,** skorn′fu̧l•li, *adv.* In a scornful manner; contemptuously. —**scornfulness,** skorn′fu̧l•nes, *n.* The quality of being scornful.

Scorpio, skor′pi•ō, *n.* [L.] A constellation of the zodiac; the Scorpion.

scorpion, skor′pi•on, *n.* [L. *scorpio, scorpionis,* from Gr. *skorpiōn,* a scorpion.] An animal belonging to the Arachnida (spiders, etc.) having a pair of large nipping claws and a long jointed tail terminating with a venomous sting; a kind of painful scourge or whip (O.T.); [*cap.*] the eighth sign of the zodiac, which the sun enters about Oct. 23; an ancient military engine.—**scorpioid,** skor′pi•oid, *a.* Scorpion-like; *bot.* said of a peculiar twisted inflorescence, curved or circinate at the end.

scot, skot, *n.* [A.Sax. *scot,* Icel. *skot,* D. and L.G. *schot,* H. *schoss.*] Formerly a payment of money; a tax or contribution.—**scot-free,** *a.* Free from payment or scot; untaxed; unhurt.

Scot, skot, *n.* [A.Sax. *Scotta,* a Scot, *Scottas,* the Scots, originally the inhabitants of Ireland; origin quite unknown.] A native of Scotland or North Britain.—**scotch,** skoch, *a.* Pertaining to Scotland or its inhabitants; Scottish.—*Scotch fir,* the typical pine of Europe, especially of the northern and central parts, furnishing excellent timber, and turpentine, tar, resin, etc.—*Scotch mist,* a colloquial term for a wetting mist, like fine rain; or for a fine rain.—*Scotch pebble,* a name for varieties of agate, carnelian, etc.—*Scotch thistle,* a kind of thistle, so called because regarded as the national emblem of Scotland.—*n.* The dialect or dialects of English spoken in Scotland; collectively, the people of Scotland.—**Scotchman,** skoch′man, *n.* A native of Scotland; a Scot.—**Scots,** skots, *a.* Scotch (*Scots* law).—**Scotsman,** skots′man, *n.* SCOTCHMAN.—**Scotticism,** skot′i•sizm, *n.* An idiom or peculiar expression of the natives of Scotland.—**Scottish,** skot′ish, *a.* Pertaining to Scotland, its language, or its natives; Scotch.

scotch, skoch, *v.t.* [Perhaps Celtic; comp. Gael. *sgoch,* a cut; or Fr. *coche,* a notch, might have given a verb *escocher,* whence this word.] To cut with shallow incisions; to notch; to chop.—*n.* A slight cut or shallow incision; a line drawn on the ground, as in hopscotch.

scoter, skō′tėr, *n.* [Comp. Icel. *skoti,* a shooter; the name may mean diver or darter.] A diving duck found along the northern coasts of Europe and America.

scotia, skō′sha, *n.* [Gr. *skotia,* lit. darkness.] A hollow molding in the base of a column, so named from its surface being in shadow.

scotodinia, skot•ō•dī′ni•a, *n.* [Gr. *skotos,* darkness, and *dinos,* giddiness.] *Med.* giddiness, with imperfect vision.—**scotoma,** sko•tō′ma, *n.* [Gr. *skotoma,* from *skotos,* darkness.] Dizziness with dimness of sight.

Scotticism, Scottish. See SCOT.

scoundrel, skoun′drel, *n.* [Probably for *scounerel* or *scunerel,* one to be shunned or avoided, from A.Sax. *scunian,* to shun, an intermediate step being seen in Sc. *scunner, sconner,* to loathe, or as a noun, loathing; with *d* inserted as in *thunder, tender.*] A base, mean, worthless fellow; a rascal; a man without honor or virtue.—*a.* Belonging to a scoundrel; base; unprincipled.—**scoundrelly,** skoun′drel•li, *a.* Characteristic of a scoundrel; base; villainous.

scour, skour, *v.t.* [Same as Dan. *skure,* Sw. *skura,* G. *scheuern,* to scour; perhaps from O.Fr. *escurer,* from L. *excurare—ex,* intens., and *curare,* to clean, to care for. CURE.] To rub hard with something for the purpose of cleaning; to make clean or bright on the surface; to take grease or dirt out of the fabric of, by washing or chemical appliances; to cleanse away; to efface; to pass swiftly over; to brush along; to pass swiftly over in search of something or to drive away something; to overrun; to sweep clear.—*v.i* To clean by rubbing; to take dirt or grease out of cloth; to rove or range; to run with celerity; to scamper.—*n.* A kind of diarrhea or dysentery among cattle.—**scourer,** skour′ėr, *n.* One who or that which scours.

scourge, skėrj, *n.* [Fr. *escourgée,* a scourge; L.L. *excorrigiata,* from L. *ex,* intens., and *corrigia,* a rein, a shoe tie.] An instrument of the whip kind for the infliction of pain or punishment; a lash; a whip; hence a punishment; a vindictive affliction; one who greatly afflicts, harasses, or destroys; a whip for a top.—*v.t.—scourged, scourging.* To whip with a scourge; to whip severely; to lash; to chastise for correction; to afflict greatly; to harass.—**scourger,** skėr′jėr, *n.* One who scourges.

scout, skout, *n.* [O.Fr. *escoute,* a scout, from *escouter, escolter, esculter,* to hear, from L. *ausculto,* to listen. AUSCULTATION.] One sent out to gain and bring in information, especially to observe the motions and obtain intelligence regarding an enemy.—*v.i.* To act as a scout.—*v.t.* To watch closely; to observe the actions of.

scout, skout, *v.t.* [Icel. *skúta,* a taunt; perhaps from root of *shoot.*] To treat with disdain and contempt; to reject with scorn.

scow, skou, *n.* [D. *schouw,* a ferryboat.] A kind of large flat-bottomed boat used chiefly as a lighter or a ferryboat.

scowl, skoul, *v.i.* [Same as Dan. *skule,* to scowl; comp. Icel. *skaela,* to make a wry face.] To wrinkle the brows, as in frowning or displeasure; to let the brows droop; to look sullen or angry; to look gloomy, dark, or tempestuous.—*n.* A deep angry frown by depressing the brows; dark or tempestuous aspect, as of the heavens; gloom.

scrabble, skrab′l, *v.i.—scrabbled, scrabbling.* [A dim. of *scrape;* allied to *scribble* and *scramble.*] To make irregular, crooked marks; to scrawl; to scribble.—*v.t.* To mark with irregular lines or letters.—*n.* A scribble; a scrawl; a spelling game.

scrag, skrag, *n.* [Comp. Gael. *screag,* parched, shriveled; Icel. *skröggsligr,* scraggy, gaunt; Sc. *scrog,* a stunted bush.] Something thin or lean, with roughness.—*Scrag of mutton,* the bony part of the neck of a sheep's carcass.—**scragginess,** skrag′i•nes, *n.* The state or quality of being scraggy; leanness; roughness.—**scraggy,** skrag′i, *a.* Having an irregular broken surface; scragged; lean; bony.

scramble, skram′bl, *v.i.—scrambled, scrambling.* [Akin to D. *scrammen,* to scratch; Dan. *skramle,* to ramble; Sw. *skramla,* to clatter; also to *scrabble, scrape.*] To move or climb by the aid of the hands; to move on all fours; to snatch eagerly at anything; to struggle to get before others.—*n.* The act of scrambling; an eager contest for something, in which one endeavors to get the thing before another.—**scrambler,** skram′blėr, *n.* One who scrambles.

scrap, skrap, *n.* [Lit. what is *scraped;* same as Icel. *skrap,* scraps, trifles. SCRAPE.] A small piece; a detached, incomplete portion; a fragment; a fragment of something written or printed; a short or unconnected extract; a little picture suited to go along with others for ornamenting screens, boxes, etc.—*v.t.* To throw upon the *scrapheap*: used of outworn or antiquated machinery plant rendered useless; to supersede.—**scrapbook,** *n.* A book for the preservation of prints, engravings, etc., or of short pieces of poetry or other extracts from books; an album.—**scrappy,** skrap′i, *a.* Consisting of scraps; disconnected.

scrape, skrāp, *v.t.*—*scraped, scraping.* [Same as Icel. *skrapa*, to scrape, to scratch; L.G. and D. *schrapen*, Dan. *skrabe*, to scrape; akin *scrap*, *scramble*, perhaps *sharp*.] To rub the surface of with a sharp or rough instrument, or with something hard; to deprive of the surface coating by a sharp instrument; to grate harshly over; to clean with something sharp; to erase; to collect by laborious effort; to acquire, save, or gather penuriously: usually with *together.*—*To scrape acquaintance* with a person, to make one's self acquainted, lit. by bowing or scraping; to insinuate one's self into a person's acquaintance.—*v.i.* To roughen or remove a surface by rubbing; to make a harsh noise by rubbing; to play awkwardly on a violin or such like instrument; to rub the feet on the ground; to make an awkward bow, with a drawing back of the foot.—*n.* A rubbing with something hard on a surface; an awkward bow accompanied with a scraping of the foot; a disagreeable predicament; a difficulty; perplexity; distress.—**scraper,** skrā′pėr, *n.* One who or that which scrapes; an instrument with which anything is scraped; a metal instrument placed at or near the door of a house, upon which to scrape or clean the shoes.—**scraping,** skrā′ping, *n.* What is scraped from a substance, or is collected by scraping.

scratch, skrach, *v.t.* [O.E. *cratch*, to scratch; same as O.D. *kratsen*, Sw. *kratsa*, Dan. *kradse*, G. *kratzen*, to scratch, the *s* having been prefixed through the influence of *scrape*, etc.] To rub, tear, or mark the surface of with something sharp; to wound slightly by a point or points; to scrape with the nails so as not to wound; to write or draw awkwardly; to dig or excavate with the claws; to erase or blot out; to expunge; *horseracing*, to erase from the list of horses that are to compete in the race.—*To scratch out*, to erase; to obliterate.—*v.i.* To use the nails, claws, or the like, in tearing a surface, or in digging.—*n.* A break in a surface made by scratching; a slight furrow; a score; a light wound; a superficial laceration; a line up to which boxers are brought when they join fight; hence the vulgar phrase, to come up to the *scratch*, meaning to stand to the consequences, or appear when expected.—*a.* Taken at random or haphazard; heterogeneous; hastily collected (a *scratch* company of actors or of cricketers).—*Old Scratch*, the Devil; the *Skratti* of North European mythology. Akin to Bohemian *screti*, demon.—**scratcher,** skrach′ėr, *n.* One who or that which scratches; a bird which scratches for food, as the common fowl.

scrawl, skra̤l, *v.t.* [A contracted form of *scrabble*; comp. D. *schravelen*, to scratch.] To draw or mark awkwardly and irregularly; to write awkwardly or imperfectly; to scribble; to make irregular lines or bad writing on.—*v.i.* To write unskillfully and inelegantly.—*n.* A piece of unskillful, hasty, or bad writing.—**scrawl,** skra̤l, *n.* [Perhaps from *scrawl*, form of *crawl*.] A young crab. (*Tenn.*)—**scrawler,** skra̤′lėr, *n.* One who scrawls.

scrawny, skra̤′ni, *a.* Thin; rawboned.

screak, skrēk, *v.i.* [A form of *screech*, *shriek*=Sw. *shrika*, Icel. *skraekja*, to screak.] To scream or screech; to creak.

scream, skrēm, *v.i.* [Comp. Icel. *skramsa*, to scream; probably imitative, like *screech*, *shriek*, etc.] To cry out with a shrill voice; to utter a sudden, sharp outcry, as in a fright or in extreme pain; to shriek; to give out a shrill sound.—*n.* A shriek, or sharp shrill cry; a sharp, harsh sound.—**screamer,** skrē′mėr, *n.* One that screams; a South American grallatorial bird, remarkable for its harsh discordant voice.—**screaming,** skrē′ming, *p.* and *a.* Crying or sounding shrilly; causing screams of laughter (a *screaming* farce).

screech, skrēch, *v.i.* [A softened form of *screak*, Icel. *skraekja*, Sw. *skrika*, Dan. *skrige*, to screech; an imitative word.] To cry out with a sharp, shrill voice; to shriek.—*n.* A sharp, shrill cry; a harsh scream; a sharp, shrill noise.

screed, skrēd, *n.* [SHRED.] A shred or strip; a statement; a harangue or tirade.

screen, skrēn, *n.* [O.Fr. *escren*, *escrein*, *escran*, Fr. *écran*, a screen, perhaps from O.H.G. *skranna*, a table.] A framework or curtain used to shut out the sun, rain, cold, or to conceal something from sight; that which shelters, protects, or conceals; a wire sieve for sifting sand, lime, etc.; a surface on which a stereopticon picture or motion picture is projected; hence, collectively, motion pictures; *arch.* an ornamental partition of wood, stone, or metal in a church.—*v.t.* To shelter or protect from inconvenience, injury, or danger; to cover; to conceal; to sift by passing through a screen.—**screenings,** skrēn′ingz, *n. pl.* The refuse matter left after sifting coal, grain, etc.

screw, skrö, *n.* [Same as Dan. *skrue*, Sw. *skruf*, Icel. *skrúfa*, D. *schroef*, O.D. *schroeve*, L.G. *schruwe*, G. *shraube*, a screw.] A cylinder of wood or metal having a spiral ridge (the thread) winding round it in a uniform manner, so that the successive turns are all exactly the same distance from each other, and a corresponding spiral groove is produced: it forms one of the six mechanical powers, and is simply a modification of the inclined plane, the energy being transmitted by means of a hollow cylinder (the *female* screw) or equal diameter with the solid one (*male* screw), having a spiral channel cut on its inner surface so as to correspond exactly to the spiral ridge raised upon the solid cylinder; also, a screw propeller or a screw steamer; one who makes a sharp bargain; a skinflint; a small quantity of tobacco twisted up in a piece of paper.—*Archimedean, screw.* See ARCHIMEDEAN.—*Endless screw.* ENDLESS.—*Right and left screw*, a screw of which the threads upon the opposite ends run in different directions.—*Screw propeller*, an apparatus which, being fitted to ships and driven by steam, propels them through the water, and which, in all its various forms, is a modification of the common screw.—*A screw loose*, something defective or wrong with a scheme or individual.—*To put on the screw*, to bring pressure to bear on a person, often for the purpose of getting money.—*To put under the screw*, to influence by strong pressure; to coerce.—*v.t.* To apply a screw to; to press, fasten, or make firm by a screw; to force as by a screw; to wrench; to twist; to rack; to oppress by exactions; to distort.—*To screw down*, to fasten down by means of screws.—*To screw in*, to force in by screwing or twisting round.—*To screw out*, to force out by turning; *fig.* to extort.—*To screw up*, to fix up by screws; *fig.* to raise extortionately.—**screwdriver,** *n.* An instrument resembling a blunt chisel for driving in or drawing out screw nails.—**screwer,** skrö′ėr, *n.* One who or that which screws.—**screw jack,** *n.* A portable machine for raising great weights by the agency of a screw. JACK.—**screw pine,** *n.* The common name for useful trees which are natives of the East Indies, New Guinea, etc., and are remarkable for being supported above the ground by their aerial or adventitious roots.—**screw propeller,** *n.* A ship's screw.

scribble, skrib′l, *v.t.*—*scribbled scribling.* [Based partly on *scrabble*, partly on L. *scribo*, to write; comp. O.H.G. *skribeln*, to scribble.] To write with haste, or without care; to fill with careless or worthless writing.—*v.i.* To scrawl; to write without care or beauty.—*n.* Hasty or careless writing; a scrawl.—**scribbler,** skrib′lėr, *n.* One who scribbles or writes carelessly or badly; a petty author; a writer of no reputation.

scribble, skrib′l, *v.t.* [Sw. *skrubbla*, G. *schrubbeln*, to card, to scribble.] To card or tease coarsely; to submit, as cotton or wool, to a first rough teasing or carding.—**scribbler,** skrib′lėr, *n.* The machine which scribbles or teases cotton or wool.

scribe, skrīb, *n.* [Fr. *scribe*, from L. *scriba*, a clerk, a secretary, from *scribo*, *scriptum*, to write; seen also in *ascribe, describe, inscribe, subscribe, scripture, postscript,* etc.] One who writes; a penman; one skilled in penmanship; a secretary; an amanuensis; a notary; a copyist; a writer and doctor of the law among the ancient Jews; one who read and explained the law to the people. —*v.t.*—*scribed, scribing. Carp.* to mark by a rule or compasses; to mark for fitting accurately.—**scriber,** skrīb′ėr, *n.* A tool used by joiners for making lines on wood.

scrimmage, skrim′ij, *n.* [Corruption of *skirmish.*] A skirmish; a confused contest; a tussle; in *football,* a confused, close struggle round the ball.

scrimp, skrimp, *v.t.* [Dan. *skrumpe,* Sw. *skrumpna,* L.G. *schrumpen,* to shrink, to shrivel; akin to A.Sax. *scrimman,* to wither or shrivel.] To make too small or short; to scant; to limit or straiten.—*a.* Scanty; deficient; contracted.

scrip, skrip, *n.* [For *script,* L. *scriptum,* something written, from *scribo,* to write. SCRIBE.] A small writing; a certificate or schedule; *com.* a certificate of stock subscribed to a bank or other company; an interim writing entitling a party to a share or shares in any company, exchanged after registration for a formal certificate; a certificate of indebtedness, in lieu of currency, at times issued by government or a business concern.

script, skript, *n.* [L. *scriptum,* something written. SCRIP.] A typewritten or handwritten copy of a play showing the plot development usually by scenes and giving the directions for acting; a kind of handwriting that resembles printed characters; *printing,* type resembling or in imitation of handwriting; *law,* the original or principal document.

Scripture, skrip′chėr, *n.* [L. *scriptura,* a writing, from *scribo, scriptum,* to write. SCRIBE.] The books of the Old and New Testaments; the Bible: used by way of eminence and distinction, and often in the plural preceded by the definite article (*the Scriptures*); what is contained in the Scriptures; a passage or quotation from the Scriptures; a Bible text.—*a.* Relating to the Bible or the Scriptures; scriptural. (*Scripture* history).—**scriptural,** skrip′-chėr•al, *a.* Contained in or according to the Scriptures; biblical.—**scripturally,** skrip′chėr•al•li, *adv.* In a scriptural manner.

scrivener, skriv′nėr, *n.* [O.Fr. *escrivain* (with E. term. *-er* added); It. *scrivano,* from L.L *scribanus,* from L. *scribo,* to write. SCRIBE.] Formerly, a notary; a moneybroker; a financial agent.

scrofula, skrof′ū•la, *n.* [L *scrofulae,* swellings of the glands of the neck, scrofula.] A disease characterized by tubercle formation in the glandular and bony tissues, and generally showing itself by hard indolent tumors of the glands, particularly in the neck, which after a time suppurate and degenerate into ulcers. —**scrofulous,** skrof′ū•lus, *a.* Pertaining to scrofula; diseased or affected with scrofula.

scroll, skrōl, *n.* [O.Fr. *eskrol, escrou* (Fr. *écrou*), a scroll, a register; probably from the Teutonic; comp. Icel. *skrá,* a scroll, Sw. *skra,* a short writing.] A roll of paper or parchment; a writing formed into a roll; a list or schedule; an ornament of a somewhat spiral form; the volute of the Ionic and Corinthian capitals; the curved head of instruments of the violin family; a kind of volute at a ship's bow; a flourish added to a person's name in signing.—**scrollhead,** *n.* An ornament at the bow of a ship.—**scroll saw,** *n.* A saw with a long, ribbon-like blade used to saw out curved shapes.

scrotum, skrō′tum, *n.* [L.] The bag which contains the testicles.—**scrotal,** skrō′tal, *a.* Pertaining to the scrotum.

scrub, skrub, *v.t.*—*scrubbed, scrubbing.* [Same as Sw. *skrubba,* Dan. *skrubbe,* D. *schrobben,* L.G. *schrubben,* to scrub; allied to *scrape, scrabble,* or from *rub,* with initial *sc, sk,* intens.] To rub hard, as with a brush or with something rough, for the purpose of cleaning, scouring, or making bright; to scour by rubbing.—*v.i.* To be diligent and penurious.—*n.* A worn-out brush; a mean fellow; one that labors hard and lives meanly; something small and mean.—*a.* Mean; scrubby.—**scrubbed,** skrubd, *a.* See SCRUBBY. —**scrubber,** skrub′ėr, *n.* One who or that which scrubs; a hard broom or brush.—**scrubby,** skrub′i, *a.* Small and mean; insignificant; stunted in growth.

scrub, skrub, *n.* [Same word as *shrub,* A.Sax. *scrob,* Dan. dial. *skrub,* a shrub.] Close, low, or stunted trees or brushwood; low underwood.

scruff, skruf, *n.* The back of the neck; only in phrase, to take by the *scruff* of the neck.

scrunch, skrunsh, *v.t.* [From *crunch,* with *s* intens.] To crunch; to grind down.

scruple, skrö′pl, *n.* [Fr. *scrupule,* a scruple, from L. *scrupulus,* lit. a little sharp stone (dim. of *scrupus,* a sharp stone), the twenty-fourth part of anything, a trifling matter causing doubt or anxiety, doubt, uneasiness.] A weight of 20 grains; the third part of a dram, or the twenty-fourth part of an ounce in the old apothecaries' measure; any small quantity (*Shak.*); hesitation as to action from perplexity; doubt; hesitation, or perplexity arising from motives of conscience; a point causing hesitation; dubiety.—*v.i. scrupled, scrupling.* To have scruples; to hesitate; to doubt: often followed by an infinitive.—**scrupulosity,** skrö•pū•los′i•ti, *n.* [L. *scrupulositas.*] Scrupulousness; nice regard to exactness and propriety; hesitation from fear of acting wrongly.—**scrupulous,** skrö′pū•lus, *a.* [L. *scrupulosus.*] Full of scruples; hesitating to determine or to act; cautious in decision; careful; exact in regarding facts; precise; punctilious.—**scrupulously,** skrö′pū•lus•li, *adv.* In a scrupulous manner; carefully; precisely.—**scrupulousness,** skrö′pū•lus•nes, *n.* The state or quality of being scrupulous; scrupulosity; exactness; preciseness.

scrutiny, skrö′ti•ni, *n.* [L. *scrutinium,* from *scrutor,* to search carefully, to rummage, from *scruta,* trash, frippery.] Close investigation or examination; a minute inquiry; a critical examination; an examination by a competent authority of the votes given at an election, for the purpose of correcting the poll.—**scrutineer,** skrö•ti•nēr′, *n.* One who scrutinizes; one who acts as an examiner of votes, as at an election, etc.—**scrutinize,** skrö′ti•nīz, *v.t.*—*scrutinized, scrutinizing.* To subject to scrutiny; to investigate closely; to examine or inquire into critically. —*v.i.* To make scrutiny.—**scrutinizer,** skrö′ti•nī•zėr, *n.* One who scrutinizes.

scuba, skö′ba, *n.* [**S**elf **c**ontained **u**nderwater **b**reathing **a**pparatus.] Apparatus, including air tanks, that allows a swimmer to breathe underwater.

scud, skud, *v.i.*—*scudded, scudding.* [Comp. Sw. *skútta,* to run quickly; akin perhaps to *shoot.*] To run quickly or with precipitation; to fly with haste; *naut.* to run before a tempest with little or no sail spread. —*n.* The act of scudding; loose vapory clouds driven swiftly by the wind.

scudo, skö′dō, *n.* pl. **scudi,** skö′dē. [It., lit. a coin marked with a shield, a crownpiece, from L. *scutum,* a shield.] An Italian silver coin of different value in the different states in which it was issued.

scuffle, skuf′l, *v.i.*—*scuffled, scuffling.* [Freq. akin to A.Sax. *scufan,* Sw. *skuffa,* to shove; same word as *shuffle.* SHOVE.] To struggle or contend with close grapple; to fight tumultuously or confusedly.—*n.* A struggle in which the combatants grapple closely; any confused quarrel or contest; a tumultuous fight.

sculk, skulk, *v.i.* Same as *Skulk.*

scull, skul, *n.* [Origin uncertain; perhaps akin to *shell.*] An oar so short that one man can manage two, one on each side; an oar when used to propel a boat by being placed over the stern and worked from side to side.—*v.t.* To propel by sculls, or by moving and turning an oar over the stern.—**sculler,** skul′ėr, *n.* One who sculls; a boat rowed by sculls.

scullery, skul′ėr•i, *n.* [Perhaps from O.Fr. *escuelle, escuele,* a bowl, from L. *scutella,* dim. of *scutera,* a dish.] A place where culinary utensils are cleaned and kept; a back kitchen.

sculpin, skul′pin, *n.* A kind of small seafish.

sculpture, skulp′chėr, *n.* [Fr. *sculpture,* from L. *sculptura,* from *sculpo, sculptum* (also *scalpo*), to grave or carve.] The art of carving, cutting, or hewing stone or other materials into images of men, beasts, etc.;

the art of imitating natural objects in solid substances; statuary; carved work; a figure cut in stone or other solid substance, representing some real or imaginary object.—*v.t.*—*sculptured, sculpturing.* To represent in sculpture; to carve.—**sculptor,** skulp′tor, *n.* One who sculptures; one who carves or hews figures.—**sculptural,** skulp′chėr•al, *a.* Pertaining to sculpture.—**sculpturesque,** skulp′chėr•esk″, *a.* Possessing the character of sculpture; after the manner of sculpture.

scum, skum, *n.* [Same as Sw. and Dan. *skum,* G. *schaum,* D. *schuim,* O.H.G. *scûm,* scum, from a root meaning to cover (seen in *sky,* etc.). *Skim* is a derivative verb.] The extraneous matter which rises to the surface of liquors in boiling or fermentation; the scoria of molten metals; refuse; recrement.—*v.t.*—*scummed, scumming.* To take the scum from; to clear off the impure matter from the surface.—*v.i.* To throw up scum; to be covered with scum.—**scummy,** skum′i, *a.* Covered with scum; like scum.

scumble, skum′bl, *v.t.*—*scumbled, scumbling.* [Freq. of *scum.*] *Painting,* to cover thinly with semiopaque colors to modify the effect.—**scumbling,** skum′bling, *n.* The toning down of a picture by semitransparent colors.

scupper, skup′ėr, *n.* [Connected with *scoop,* or from O.Fr. and Sp. *escupir,* to spit; Armor. *skopa,* to spit.] A channel cut through the side of a ship for carrying off the water from the deck.

scurf, skėrf, *n.* [A.Sax. *scurf,* scurf; Icel. *skurfur* (pl.), Dan. *skurv,* Sw. *skorf,* G. *schorf,* scurf; allied to *scrape.*] Matter composed of minute portions of the dry external scales of the cuticle, which is continually being detached from the surface of the body; a layer of matter adhering to a surface; *bot.* the loose scaly matter that is found on some leaves, etc.—**scurfy,** skėr′fi, *a.* Covered with scurf; resembling scurf.

scurrile, skur′ril, *a.* [L. *scurrilis,* from *scurra,* a buffoon, a jester.] Such as befits a buffoon or vulgar jester; low; scurrilous.—**scurrility,** skur•ril′i•ti, *n.* The quality of being scurrilous; that which is scurrilous; low, vulgar, abusive language; grossness of abuse or invective; obscene jests, etc.—**scurrilous,** skur′ri•lus, *a.* Using low and indecent language; containing low abuse; foul; vile; obscenely jocular; opprobrious; abusive.—**scurrilously,** scur′ri•lus•li, *adv.*

scurry, skur′ri, *v.i.*—*scurried, scurrying.* [From HURRY.] To run rapidly; to hurry.—*n.* Hurry; haste.

scurvy, skėr′vi, *n.* [From O.E. *sceorf,* scurf.] A disease characterized by livid spots and general exhaustion, affecting persons who are deprived of vitamin C, and which is successfully treated, both as a preventive and as a curative agent, by lime or lemon juice.—*a.* Vile; mean; low; mischievous; malicious.—**scurvily,** skėr′vi•li, *adv.* Basely; meanly; with coarse and vulgar incivility.—**scurviness,** skėr′vi•nes, *n.* Meanness; vileness.—**scurvy grass,** *n.* [A corruption of *scurvy cress,* being used as a cure for *scurvy.*] The common name of several arctic species of cruciferous plants, with leaves that are eaten as a salad.

scut, skut, *n.* [Comp. W. *cwt,* a tail.] A short tail such as that of a hare or deer.

scutage, skū′tij, *n.* [L.L. *scutagium,* from L. *scutum,* a shield.] A tax on feudal tenants holding lands by knight's service; escuage.—**scutate,** skū′tāt, *a. Bot.* formed like an ancient round buckler; *zool.* protected or covered by large scales.

scutch, skuch, *v.t.* [Perhaps same as *scotch,* to cut, to strike.] To dress by beating; to separate the woody parts of the stalks of flax by beating.—**scutch, scutcher,** skuch, skuch′ėr, *n.* An implement or machine for scutching.

scutcheon, skuch′on, *n.* [A contr. of *escutcheon.*] A shield for armorial bearings; an escutcheon; the ornamental cover or frame to a keyhole.

scute, skūt, *n.* [L. *scutum,* a buckler.] A scale, as of a reptile, especially a large scale.—**scutellate,** skū′tel•lāt, *a.* Formed like a plate; covered with scutellae.—**scutellum,** skū•tel′lum, *n.* pl. **scutella,** skū•tel′la. [L. dim. of *scutum,* a shield.] *Bot.* the smaller cotyledon of wheat; the little cup or disk in lichens, containing tubes filled with sporules; *entom.* a part of the thorax of insects.—**scutiform,** skū′ti•form, *a.* Having the form of a buckler or shield.

scuttle, skut′l, *n.* [A.Sax. *scutel,* from L. *scutella,* dim. of *scutra,* a dish or platter.] A broad shallow basket; a wide-mouthed metal pan or pail for holding coals.

scuttle, skut′l, *n.* A square hole in the wall or roof of a house, with a lid; the lid itself; *naut.* a small hatchway with a lid for covering it; a hole in the side of a ship.—*v.t.*—*scuttled, scuttling. Naut.* to sink by making holes through the bottom.—**scuttle butt, scuttle cask,** *n.* A cask with a hole in it, covered by a lid, for holding fresh water for daily use in a ship.—**scuttlebutt,** *n.* A slang term for rumor, gossip.

scuttle, skut′l, *v.i.*—*scuttled, scuttling.* [For *scuddle,* a freq. of *scud.*] To run with affected precipitation; to hurry.—*n.* A quick pace; a short run.

scutum, skū′tum, *n.* pl. **scuta,** [L., a shield.] A shield-shaped plate; a scute.

scyphus, skī′fus, *n.* [Gr. *skyphos,* a cup or goblet.] *Bot.* the coronet or cup of such plants as narcissus.

scythe, sīTH, *n.* [Better written *sithe*; A.Sax. *sithe* for *sigthe,* the older form=Icel. *sigth*; from root of *sickle.*] A instrument used in mowing or reaping, consisting of a long curving blade fixed to a handle, which is swung by both arms.—*v.t.*—*scythed, scything.* To mow; to cut with a scythe.

scythian, sith′i•an, *a.* Pertaining to *Scythia,* the ancient name given to a vast territory north and east of the Black Sea, the Caspian, and the Sea of Aral.—*n.* A native of Scythia.

sea, sē, *n.* [A.Sax. *sae,* sea or lake= D. *see, zee,* Dan. *sö,* Icel. *saer,* G. *see,* Goth. *saivs.*] The continuous mass of salt water which covers great parts of the earth; the ocean; some special portion of this (the Polar *Sea,* the Black *Sea*); a name of certain lakes, especially when large (the *Caspian Sea,* the *Sea of Galilee*); a large wave; a surge (the vessel shipped a *sea*); the swell of the ocean; set of the waves; any large quantity (a *sea* of difficulties); a flood.—*At sea,* on the open sea; out of sight of land; in a vague uncertain condition; wide of the mark.—*At full sea,* at high water; hence, at the height.—*Beyond the sea* or *seas,* out of the realm or country.—*Cross sea, chopping sea,* waves moving in different directions.—*To go to sea, to follow the sea,* to follow the occupation of a sailor.—*Half seas over,* half drunk.—*The high seas* or *main sea,* the open ocean.—**sea anemone,** *n.* The popular name given to the actiniae.—**seaboard,** *n.* [*Sea,* and *board,* Fr. *bord,* side.] The seacoast; the country bordering on the sea.—*a.* Bordering on the sea.—**sea kale,** *n.* A kind of cabbage found on sandy shores of the sea.—**sea calf,** *n.* The common seal.—**seacoast,** *n.* The land immediately adjacent to the sea; the coast.—**sea cow,** *n.* A name given to the dugong and the manatee.—**sea cucumber,** *n.* A name given to several of the holothurians; the trepang or *bêche-de-mer.*—**sea devil,** *n.* The fishing-frog or toadfish.—**seadog,** *n.* The dogfish; the common seal; a sailor who has been long afloat (*colloq.*).—**sea duck,** *n.* One of the ducks that frequent the sea.—**sea eagle,** *n.* The white-tailed eagle of Europe; the bald eagle of America, found generally on the seacoast, as it is a fish-loving bird; the eagle ray, a fish of the Mediterranean and warmer seas.—**sea-ear,** *n.* The ear shell.—**seafarer,** sē′fâr•ėr, *n.* A traveler by sea; a mariner.—**seafaring,** sē′fâr•ing, *a.* Following the business of a seaman.—**sea fight,** *n.* An engagement between ships at sea.—**seafowl,** *n.* Any bird that lives by the sea and procures its food from it.—**seagirt,** *a.* Surrounded by the sea; forming an island.—**seagoing,** *a.* Applied to a vessel which makes foreign voyages, as opposed to a coasting or river vessel.—**sea green,** *a.* Having the green color of sea water; being of a faint green color.—**sea gull,** *n.* A gull or bird of the gull kind.—**sea hog,** *n.* The porpoise.—**sea holly,** *n.* The plant eryngo.—**sea horse,** *n.* The walrus; a small lophobranch fish, related to the pipefish, with head and neck likened to a horse; a fabled animal, half horse and half fish.—**sea-island,** *a.* Applied to a fine long-stapled variety of cotton grown on the islands off the coasts of South Carolina and Georgia.—**sea king,** *n.* A king of the sea; one of the piratical Northmen who infested the coasts of Western Europe in the eighth, ninth, and tenth centuries; a viking.—**sea legs,** *n. pl.* The ability to walk on a ship's deck when pitching or rolling.—**sea level,** *n.* The level of the surface of the sea, usually taken as the point from which to measure heights or depressions of the land.—**sea lion,** *n.* A name of several large seals, the best known of which has a mane on the neck, is 10 to 15 feet long, and is found in the Pacific.—**seaman,** sē′man, *n.* A man whose occupation is to assist in the navigation of ships; a mariner; a sailor.—*Able seaman,* a sailor who is well skilled in seamanship, and classed in the ship's books as such.—*Ordinary seaman,* one less skilled than an able seaman.—**seamanship,** sē′man•ship, *n.* The skill of a good seaman.—**seamark,** *n.* Any elevated object on land which serves for a direction to mariners; a beacon.—**sea mew,** *n.* A gull; a seagull.—**sea mile,** *n.* A nautical mile, the sixtieth part of a degree of latitude. See MILE.—**sea mouse,** *n.* A marine dorsibranchiate annelid found on the seacoast, splendidly colored.—**sea onion,** *n.* A plant. See SQUILL.—**sea otter,** *n.* A marine mammal closely allied to the common otter, and yielding a valuable fur.—**seaplane,** See HYDROPLANE.—**seaport,** sē′pōrt, *n.* A port, or a town with a port, on or near the sea.—**sea room,** *n.* Sufficient room at sea for a vessel to make any required movement.—**seascape,** sē′skāp, *n.* [Formed on the model of *landscape.*] A picture representing a scene at sea; a seapiece.—**sea serpent,** *n.* A name common to a family of snakes which frequent the seas of warm latitudes; an enormous animal of serpentine form said to have been repeatedly seen at sea, but as to the real existence of which naturalists are generally skeptical.—**seashore,** *n.* The shore of the sea; *law,* the ground between the ordinary high-water mark and low-water mark.—**seasick,** *a.* Affected with sickness or nausea from the pitching or rolling of a vessel.—**seasickness,** *n.* A nervous affection attended with nausea and vomiting, produced by the rolling or pitching of a vessel at sea.—**sea snake,** *n.* A serpent that inhabits the sea.—**sea squirt,** *n.* An ascidian.—**sea tangle,** *n.* The name of several species of seaweeds.—**sea urchin,** *n.* A roundish spiny echinoderm; an echinus.—**sea wall,** *n.* A strong wall on the shore to prevent encroachments of the sea.—**seaward,** sē′wėrd, *a.* Directed toward the sea.—*adv.* Toward the sea.—**seaware,** *n.* The algae thrown up by the sea, and made use of as manure, etc.—**seaway,** *n.* The sea as a route for travel; an ocean traffic lane; an inland waterway deep enough to admit ocean shipping; *naut.* progress made by a vessel through the waves.—**seaweed,** *n.* A name given generally to any plant growing in the sea, but more particularly to members of the nat. order Algae.—**seaworthiness,** *n.* The state of being seaworthy.—**seaworthy,** *a.* Applied to a ship in good condition and fit for a voyage.

seal, sēl, *n.* [A.Sax. *seol, seolh,* Sc. *selch, silch,* Icel. *selr,* Dan. *sael;* O.H.G. *selach;* origin doubtful.] A marine carnivorous mammal of numerous species, having both fore and hind feet forming a sort of swimming organs, largely hunted for their fur and blubber; the fur, which forms the valued sealskin of commerce, being obtained from some of the 'eared' species, or those that have external ears.—**sealer,** sēl′ėr, *n.* A seaman or a ship engaged in the seal fishery.—**sealskin,** *n.* The skin of the fur seal, which, with the fur on, is made into articles of clothing.

seal, sēl, *n.* [O.Fr. *seel,* from L. *sigillum,* a seal, dim. of *signum,* a sign. SIGN.] A piece of stone, metal, or other hard substance on which is engraved some figure or inscription, used for making an impression on some soft substance, as on the wax that makes fast a letter, or is affixed to documents in token of authenticity; the wax or other substance so impressed; the wax, wafer, or similar fastening of a letter or other paper; that which authenticates, confirms, or ratifies; assurance; pledge; that which effectually shuts or secures; that which makes fast.—*Great seal,* a nation's official seal used to authenticate public documents and papers.—*Privy-seal, lord privy-seal.* See under PRIVY.—*To set one's seal to,* to give one's authority to; to give one's assurance of.—*v.t.* To affix a seal to, as a mark of authenticity; hence, to confirm or ratify; to establish; to settle; to fasten and mark with a seal; to fasten securely, as with a wafer or with wax; to close hermetically; to shut or keep close (to *seal* one's lips); to confine securely.—**sealing wax,** *n.* A composition of resinous materials used for fastening folded papers and envelopes, and capable of receiving impressions of seals.

seam, sēm, *n.* [A.Sax. *seam,* a seam; Icel. *saumr,* Dan. and Sw. *söm,* D. *zoom,* G. *saum,* all from verb to *sew.* SEW.] A joining line formed by the sewing of two different pieces of cloth, etc., together; a suture; a scar or cicatrix; the line or space between planks joined together; *geol.* the line of separation between two strata; a thin layer or stratum, as of ore, coal, and the like, between two thicker strata.—*v.t.* To form a seam on; to unite with a seam; to mark with a cicatrix; to scar.—**seamer,** sēm′ėr, *n.* One who or that which seams.—**seamless,** sēm′les, *a.* Having no seam.—**seamstress,** sēm′stres, *n.* [A.Sax. *seámestre,* with term. *-ess* added.] A woman whose occupation is sewing; a sempstress.—**seamy,** sēm′i, *a.* Having a seam; containing seams or showing them, as the underside of a garment.—*Seamy side,* the darker side or hues of life, showing the evil side.

séance, sā′a̧ns, *n.* [Fr. *séance,* from *séant,* sitting, L. *sedens, sedentis,* ppr. of *sedeo,* to sit. SEDATE.] A session, as of some public body; among spiritualists, a sitting with the view of evoking spiritual manifestations or holding intercourse with spirits.

sear, sēr, *v.t.* [A.Sax. *seárian,* to parch, from *seár,* dry; akin to L.G. *soor,* O.D. *sore, soore,* D. *zoor,* dry.] To wither; to dry; to burn to dryness and hardness the surface of; to cauterize; to burn; to scorch; to make callous or insensible (a *seared* conscience); to brand.—*a.* [A.Sax. *sear.*] Dry; withered; no longer green and fresh (a *sear* leaf). Spelled also *Sere.*

sear, sēr, *n.* [Fr. *serre,* a lock, a bar, from L. *sera,* a bolt or bar.] The pivoted piece in a gunlock which enters the notches of the tumbler and holds the hammer at full or half cock.

search, sėrch, *v.t.* [O.E. *serche, cerche,* O.Fr. *cercher, cerchier* (Fr. *chercher*), to search, from L.L. *cercare, circare,* to search, to run about, from L. *circus,* a circle. CIRCLE.] To look over or through, for the purpose of finding something; to examine; to explore; to probe (to *search* a wound); to put to the test.—*v.i.* To make search; to make inquiry; to inquire.—*n.* The act of seeking or looking for something; inquiry; quest.—*Right of search,* the right of a belligerent to enter merchant vessels of neutral nations on the high seas, to search for an enemy's property, articles contraband of war, etc.—**searchable,** sėrch•a•bl, *a.* Capable of being searched.—**searcher,** sėrch′ėr, *n.* One who searches; an examiner or investigator; a prison warden who searches new prisoners.—**searching,** sėrch′ing, *p.* and *a.* Exploring; examining; investigating; penetrating; close; keen.—**searchlight,** *n.* An apparatus pivoted so as to project a strong beam of light in any desired direction; also, the beam of light.—**search warrant,** *n.* A warrant granted by a judge or magistrate to the police to enter premises in search of stolen goods or articles kept contrary to law.

season, sē′zn, *n.* [O.E. *seson, sesoun,* O.Fr. *seson, seison,* Mod.Fr. *saison,* lit. time of sowing, from L. *satio, sationis,* a sowing, from *sero, satum,* to sow.] One of the periods into which the year is naturally divided, as marked by its temperature, moisture, etc. (as spring, summer, autumn, and winter; the wet and the dry *season* of tropical countries); a convenient or suitable time; a proper conjuncture; the right time; a period of time not very long; a while; a time; that time of the year when a particular locality is most frequented by visitors (the London *season*); that part of the year when a particular trade, profession, or business is in its greatest activity (the theatrical *season*); that which gives a relish to food‡; seasoning‡.—*v.t.* To render suitable; to fit; to fit for any use by time or habit; to accustom; to inure; to acclimatize; to bring to the best state for use by any process (to *season* timber by drying or hardening); to render palatable; to flavor; to give a relish or zest to; to temper; to qualify by admixture.—*v.i.* To become suitable by time; to grow fit for use.—**seasonable,** sē'zn•a•bl, *a.* Suitable as to time or season; opportune; happening or being done in due season.—**seasonableness,** sē'zn•a•bl•nes, *n.* The state or quality of being seasonable.—**seasonably,** sē'zn•a•bli, *adv.* In due time; sufficiently early.—**seasonal,** sē'zn•al, *a.* Pertaining to the seasons.—**seasoner,** sē'zn•ėr, *n.* One who or that which seasons.—**seasoning,** sē'zn•ing, *n.* That which is added to any species of food to give it a higher relish; something added to enhance enjoyment.—**season ticket,** *n.* A ticket which entitles its holder to certain privileges during a specified period of time, as a pass for traveling by railroad, etc., issued at a cheap rate.

seat, sēt, *n.* [Same as Icel. *saeti, set,* Sw. *sate,* a seat, from root of *sit;* so L.G. *sitt,* G. *sitz.* SIT.] The place or thing on which one sits; something made to be sat in or on, as a chair, throne, bench, stool, or the like; a regular place of sitting; hence, a right to sit; a sitting (a *seat* in a church); place of abode; residence; a mansion in the country; the place where anything is situated, fixed, settled, or established; station; abode (a *seat* of learning, the *seat* of war).—*v.t.* To place on a seat; to cause to sit down; to place in a post of authority or a place of distinction; to settle; to fix in a particular place or country; to situate; to locate; to fix; to set firm; to assign seats to; to accommodate with room to sit; to fit up with seats.

sebaceous, si•bā'shus, *a.* [L.L. *sebaceus,* from L. *sebum,* tallow.] Pertaining to tallow or fat; made of, containing, or secreting fatty matter; fatty; *bot.* having the appearance of grease or wax.—**sebacic,** si•bas'ik, *a. Chem.* pertaining to fat; obtained from fat (*sebacic* acid).—**sebiferous,** si'bif'ėr•us, *a.* [L. *sebum,* and *fero,* to produce.] Producing fat or fatty matter.

seborrhea, seb'o•rē'a, *n.* [L. *sebum,* tallow, Gr. *rheō,* to flow.] Excess of the fatty secretion of the skin.

secant, sē'kant, *a.* [L. *secans, secantis,* ppr. of *seco,* to cut. SECTION.] Cutting; dividing into two parts.—*Secant plane,* a plane cutting a surface or solid.—*n. Geom.* a line that cuts another or divides it into parts; more especially, a straight line cutting a curve in two or more points; a straight line from the center of a circle cutting the circumference and proceeding till it meets a tangent to the same circle.

secede, si•sēd', *v.i.*—*seceded, seceding.* [L. *secedo*—*se,* apart, and *cedo,* to go. CEDE.] To withdraw from fellowship or association; to separate one's self; especially, to withdraw from a political or religious organization.—**seceder,** si•sē'dėr, *n.* One who secedes; [*cap.*] one of those Presbyterians who seceded from the Established Church of Scotland in 1733; any Scotch Presbyterian outside the Scottish Church.—**secession,** si•sesh'on, *n.* [L. *secessio.*] The act of seceding; the act of withdrawing from a political or religious organization.—**secessionism,** si•sesh'on•izm, *n.* The principles of secessionists.—**secessionist,** si•sesh'on•ist, *n.* One who advocates or engages in a secession; [*often cap.*] one who supported the secession of the Southern States of America in their struggle to break away from the Northern States.

secern, si•sėrn', *v.t.* [L. *secerno, secretum* (whence *secret*)—*se,* apart, and *cerno,* to separate.] To separate; to distinguish; to secrete.—**secernent,** si•sėr'nent, *n.* That which promotes secretion; *anat.* a secreting vessel.—*a.* Having the power of secreting; secretory.—**secernment,** si•sėrn'ment, *n.* The process of secreting.

secession. See SECEDE.

seclude, si•klöd', *v.t.*—*secluded, secluding.* [L. *secludo*—*se,* apart, and *claudo,* to shut. CLAUSE, CLOSE.] To shut up apart from company or society, and usually to keep apart for some time; *refl.* to withdraw into solitude.—**secludedly,** si•klö'ded•li, *adv.* In a secluded manner.—**seclusion,** si•klö'zhon, *n.* The act of secluding; the state of being secluded; retirement; privacy; solitude.—**seclusive,** si•klö'siv, *a.* Tending to seclude.

second, sek'und, *a.* [Fr. *second,* from L. *secundus,* second, from *sequor, secutus,* to follow. SEQUENCE.] Immediately following the first; next the first in order of place or time; repeated again; other; next to the first in value, power, excellence, or rank; inferior; secondary.—*n.* One next to the first; one who assists and supports another; one who attends another (his *principal*) in a duel and sees that his friend gets fair play; the sixtieth part of a minute of time or of that of a degree, that is, the second division next to the hour or degree; *music,* the difference between any sound and the next nearest sound above or below it, also a lower part added to a melody when arranged for two voices or instruments; *pl.* a coarse kind of flour.—*v.t.* To follow in the next place to; to follow up and support; to lend aid to; to assist; to promote; to encourage; to back; to support by one's voice or vote, as a motion or proposal brought forward in an assembly; to unite with in proposing some measure or motion.—**secondarily,** sek'un•de•ri•li, *adv.* In a secondary manner; secondly; in the second place.—**secondariness,** sek'un•de•ri•nes, *n.* The state of being secondary.—**secondary,** sek'un•de•ri, *a.* [L. *secondarius.*] Of second place, origin, rank, or importance; not primary; subordinate.—*Secondary circle,* in *geom.* and *astron.* a great circle passing through the poles of another great circle perpendicular to its plane.—*Secondary colors,* colors produced by the mixture of any two primary colors in equal proportions.—*Secondary fever,* a fever which arises after the crisis of some disease.—*Secondary planet,* a moon or satellite.—*Secondary strata, Secondary rocks, Secondary formation, geol.* the Mesozoic strata.—*Secondary tints, painting,* those of a subdued kind, such as grays, etc.—*n.* One who acts in subordination to another; a term for the feathers growing on the second bone of a bird's wing; a secondary circle; a secondary planet.—**secondhand,** *n.* Possession received from the first possessor or by transfer from a previous owner.—*At secondhand,* not from the first source or owner; by transmission (a report received *at secondhand*).—*a.* Not original or primary; received from another; not new; having been used or worn; dealing in secondhand goods (a *secondhand* bookseller).—**second rate,** *n.* The second order in size, quality, dignity, or value.—*a.* Of the second size, rank, quality, or value.—**second hand,** *n.* The hand of a watch that indicates seconds.—**second sight,** *n.* The power of seeing things future or distant; prophetic vision.

secrecy. See SECRET.

secret, sē'kret, *a.* [Fr. *secret,* from L. *secretus,* pp. of *secerno, secretum,* to set apart—*se,* apart, and *cerno,* to sift, distinguish. CONCERN, DISCERN.] Apart from the knowledge of others; private; known only to one or to few; kept from general knowledge; not made public; affording privacy; retired; secluded (a *secret* spot); secretive; not inclined to betray confidence; occult; mysterious; not apparent; privy; not proper to be seen.—*n.* Something studiously concealed; a thing kept from general knowledge; what is not or should not be revealed; a thing not discovered or explained; a mystery.—*In secret,* in privacy or secrecy; privately.—**secrecy,** sē'kre•si, *n.* A state of being secret or hidden; concealment from the observation of others; secret mode of proceeding; retirement; privacy; the quality of being secret; fidelity to a secret; the act or habit of keeping secrets.—**secretary,** sek're•te•ri, *n.* [L.L. *secretarius,* from L. *secretus,* secret; originally a confidant, one entrusted with secrets.] A person employed to write letters, draw up reports, records, and the like; one who carries on another's business correspondence or other matters requiring writing; a piece of furniture with conveniences for writing and for the arrangement of papers; an escritoire; an officer whose business is to superintend and manage the affairs of a particular department of government; a secretary of state.—**secretary bird,** *n.* An African bird of prey which renders valuable services by killing and eating serpents and other reptiles, so called from its long occipital plumes suggesting a secretary's quill behind his ear.—**secretarial,** sek•re•tâ′ri•al, *a.* Pertaining to a secretary.—**secretariat,** sek•re•tâ′ri•ăt, *n.* The office of a secretary; the place where a secretary transacts business.—**secretaryship,** sek′re•ta•ri•ship, *n.* The office or post of a secretary.—**secrete,** si•krēt′, *v.t.*—*secreted, secreting.* [L. *secerno, secretum,* to set apart.] To hide; to deposit in some secret place; *physiol.* to separate from the circulating fluid, as from the blood, sap, etc., and elaborate into a new product.—**secretin,** si•krēt′in, *n.* [From *secretion.*] A HORMONE (which see) secreted by the lining of the small intestine which stimulates the activity of the pancreas.—**secretion,** si•krē′shon, *n.* The act or process of secreting; the physiological process by which there are separated from the blood substances differing from the blood itself or from any of its constituents, as bile, saliva, mucus, urine, etc.; the process by which substances are separated from the sap of vegetables; the matter so secreted.—**secretive,** si•krē′tiv, *a.* Causing or promoting secretion; given to secrecy or to keep secrets.—**secretiveness,** si•krē′tiv•nes, *n.*—**secret service,** *n.* In the U. S., a division in the Treasury Department, for the purpose of detecting persons engaged in violating the laws of the U. S. relating to the Treasury Department, especially counterfeiting; and for protecting the person of the president of the U. S.

sect, sekt, *n.* [Fr. *secte,* from L. *secta,* from *seco, sectum,* to cut; or from *sequor, secutus,* to follow.] A body or number of persons who follow some teacher or leader, or are united in some settled tenets, chiefly in philosophy or religion; a school; a denomination.—**sectarian,** sek•tâ′ri•an, *a.* Pertaining to a sect or sects; strongly or bigotedly attached to a sect or religious denomination.—*n.* One of a sect; a strict member or adherent of a special denomination or party.—**sectarianism,** sek•tâ′ri•an•izm, *n.* The principles of sectarians; a narrow-minded devotion to the interests of a party.—**sectarianize,** sek•tâ′ri•an•īz, *v.t.* To imbue with sectarian principles or feelings.—**sectary,** sek′ta•ri, *n.* One that belongs to a sect; a schismatic; a sectarian.

sectile, sek′til, *a.* [L. *sectilis,* from *seco, sectum,* to cut (seen in *bisect, dissect, intersect,* etc.); same root as *scythe, saw.*] Capable of being cut, as with a knife.—**section,** sek′shon, *n.* [L. *sectio,* from *seco, sectum,* to cut.] The act of cutting; separation by cutting; a part cut or separated from the rest; a division; a portion; a distinct part or portion of a book or writing; the subdivision of a chapter, hence, the character §, often used to denote such a division; a paragraph; a distinct part of a country or people, community, class, etc.; a representation of a building or other object as it would appear if cut through by any intersecting plane, showing the internal structure; a small division of some military body, more especially the fourth part of a platoon, consisting of about ten men, commanded by a noncommissioned officer, and forming the normal fire unit; there are sixteen sections in a company. A *cavalry section* consists of from four to eight men. An *artillery section* comprises two guns, with the necessary men, horses, ammunition wagons.—*Conic sections.* See CONE.—**sectional,** sek′shon•al, *a.* Pertaining to a section; composed of or made up in several independent sections.—**sectionally,** sek′shon•al•li, *adv.* In a sectional manner.—**sector,** sek′tor, *n.* [L., a cutter.] *Geom.* a nearly triangular figure formed by two radii and the arc of a circle; a mathematical instrument so marked with lines of sines, tangents, chords, etc., as to fit all radii and scales, and useful in making diagrams, laying down plans, etc.; *milit.* an area of varying extent in war, over which operations are conducted.—*Dip sector,* an instrument used for measuring the dip of the horizon.—*Zenith sector.* See ZENITH.—**sectorial,** sek•tō′ri•al, *a.* Adapted or intended for cutting, as the cutting teeth of certain animals.

secular, sek′ū•lėr, *a.* [L. *saecularis,* from *saeculum,* an age or generation, a century, the times, the world.] Coming or observed at long intervals; extending over, taking place in, or accomplished during a very long period of time (the *secular* refrigeration of the earth); pertaining to this present world or to things not spiritual or sacred; disassociated with religious teaching or principles; not devoted to sacred or religious use; temporal; profane; worldly (*secular* education, *secular* music); not bound by monastic vows or rules (a *secular* priest as opposed to a *regular*).—*n.* An ecclesiastic not bound by monastic rules; a secular priest.—**secularism,** sek′ū•lėr•izm, *n.* Supreme or exclusive attention to the affairs of this life; the opinions or doctrines of the secularists.—**secularist,** sek′ū•lėr•ist, *n.* One who theoretically rejects every form of religious faith and every kind of religious worship; also, one who believes that education and other matters should be conducted without the introduction of a religious element.—**secularization,** sek′ū•lėr•ī•zā″shon, *n.* The act of secularizing or the state of being secularized.—**secularize,** sek′ū•lėr•īz, *v.t.*—*secularized, secularizing.* To make secular; to convert from religious or ecclesiastical to secular or common use.—**secularly,** sek′ū•lėr•li, *adv.* In a secular or worldly manner.—**secularity,** sek•ū•lar′i•ti, *n.* The state or quality of being secular.

secund, sē′kund, *a.* [L. *secundus,* second. SECOND.] *Bot.* applied to leaves or flowers which grow on one side of the stem; unilateral.—**secundine,** sē′kun•dīn, *n. Bot.* the outermost but one of the enclosing sacs of the ovulum; *zool.* all that remains in the womb after the birth of the offspring; the afterbirth: generally in the plural.

secure, si•kūr′, *a.* [L. *securus,* without care, unconcerned, free from danger, safe—*se,* apart, and *cura,* care, cure. *Sure* is this word in a more modified form.] Free from fear or apprehension; confident of safety; careless; unsuspecting; free from or not exposed to danger; in a state of safety; safe: often followed by *against* or *from;* such as to be depended on; capable of resisting assault or attack; stable; certain, sure, or confident: with *of;* in safe custody.—*v.t.*—*secured, securing.* To make secure; to guard effectually from danger; to protect; to make certain; to put beyond hazard; to assure; to enclose or confine effectually; to guard effectually from escape; to seize and confine (to *secure* a prisoner); to make certain of payment; to warrant against loss; to make fast or firm (to *secure* a door); to get possession of; to make one's self master of (to *secure* an estate).—**securely,** si•kūr′li, *adv.* In a secure manner; in security; safely.—**secureness,** si•kūr′nes, *n.* The feeling of security; the state of being secure; safety; security.—**securer,** si•kū′rėr, *n.* One who or that which secures.—**security,** si•kū′ri•ti, *n.* [Fr. *sécurité,* L. *securitas.*] The state of being secure; freedom from apprehension; confidence of safety; sometimes, over-confidence; freedom from danger or risk; safety; that which secures or makes safe; something that secures against pecuniary loss; surety; a person who engages himself for the performance of another's obligations; an evidence of property, as a bond, a certificate of stock, or the like (government *securities*).

sedan, si•dan′, *n.* Formerly, a covered chair or ornamental box for carrying one person, borne on poles by two men; a sedan chair; now, a type of automobile that holds from five to seven persons.

sedate, si•dāt′, *a.* [L. *sedatus,* from *sedo,* to calm or appease, to cause to subside, caus. of *sedeo,* to sit (seen also in *sedentary, sediment, session, preside, reside, supersede, assiduous,* etc.); same root as *sit.* SIT.] Calm or tranquil in feelings and manner; serene; unruffled by passion; staid; unmoved.—**sedately,** si•dāt′li, *adv.* In a sedate manner; calmly.—**sedateness,** si•dāt′nes, *n.* The state or quality of being sedate; composure of mind or manner; serenity; tranquillity.—**sedative,** sed′a•tiv, *a.* Tending to calm or tranquillize; *med.* allaying irritability and irritation; assuaging pain.—*n.* A medicine which allays irritability and irritation, and which assuages pain.

sedentary, sed′en•te•ri, *a.* [L. *sedentarius,* from *sedens, sedentis,* ppr. of *sedeo*, to sit. SEDATE.] Accustomed to sit much; requiring much sitting (a *sedentary* occupation); passed for the most part in sitting.—**sedentarily,** sed′en•te•ri•li, *adv.* In a sedentary manner.

sedge, sej, *n.* [A.Sax. *secg*=Sc. *segg*, L.G. *segge*, a reed, sedge; same root as in L. *seco*, to cut, being a plant with sword-like leaves.] The popular name of an extensive genus of grass-like plants growing mostly in marshes and swamps, and on the banks of rivers, distinguished from the grasses by having the stem destitute of joints.

sedilia, si•dil′i•a, *n. pl.* [L. *sedile*, a seat.] *Arch.* stone seats in the south wall of the chancel of many churches and cathedrals.

sediment, sed′i•ment, *n.* [L. *sedimentum*, from *sedeo*, to settle. SEDATE.] The matter which subsides to the bottom of water or any other liquid; settlings; lees; dregs.—**sedimentary,** sed•i•men′te•ri, *a.* Consisting of sediment; formed by sediment or matter that has subsided. —*Sedimentary rocks*, rocks which have been formed by materials deposited by water, and as a rule are stratified.—**sedimentation,** sed′i•men•tā″shon, *n.* The disposition or accumulation of sediment.

sedition, si•dish′on, *n.* [L. *seditio*, *seditionis*, discord, sedition—*sed*, apart, and *itio*, *itionis*, a going, from *eo*, *itum*, to go. ITINERANT.] A factious commotion in a state, not amounting to an insurrection; the stirring up of such a commotion; such offenses against the state as have the like tendency with, but do not amount to treason.—**seditionary,** si•dish′on•e•ri, *n.* An inciter or promoter of sedition.—**seditious,** si•dish′us, *a.* [L. *seditiosus*.] Pertaining to sedition; exciting or aiding in sedition; guilty of sedition.—**seditiously,** si•dish′us•li, *adv.* In a seditious manner.—**seditiousness,** si•dish′us•nes, *n.* The state or quality of being seditious.

seduce, si•dūs′, *v.t.*—*seduced*, *seducing*. [L. *seduco*—*se*, apart, and *duco*, to lead. DUKE.] To draw aside or entice from the path of rectitude and duty; to lead astray; to corrupt; specifically, to entice to a surrender of chastity.—**seducement,** si•dūs′ment, *n.* The act of seducing; seduction; the means employed to seduce. —**seducer,** si•dū′sėr, *n.* One that seduces; one who by deception or the like persuades a female to surrender her chastity.—**seducible,** si•dū′si•bl, *a.* Capable of being seduced. —**seduction,** si•duk′shon, *n.* [L. *seductio*, *seductionis*.] The act of seducing; the act or crime of persuading a female, by flattery or deception, to surrender her chastity. —**seductive,**† si•duk′tiv, *a.* Tending to seduce; apt to mislead by flattering appearances; alluring; enticing.—**seductively,** si•duk′tiv•li, *adv.* In a seductive manner.

sedulous, sed′ū•lus, *a.* [L. *sedulus*, from *sedeo*, to sit; as *assiduous*, from *assideo*. SEDATE.] Assiduous; diligent in application; steady and persevering in endeavors to effect an object; steadily industrious.—**sedulously,** sed′ū•lus•li, *adv.* In a sedulous manner; assiduously.—**sedulousness, sedulity,** sed′ū•lus•nes, se•dū′li•ti, *n.* The state or quality of being sedulous; assiduity.

see, sē, *v.t.*—pret. *saw*, pp. *seen*, ppr. *seeing*. [A.Sax. *seón*, to see=Icel. *sáj*, Dan. *see*, D. *zien*, Goth. *saihwan*, G. *sehen*—to see; same root as L. *sequor*, to follow.] To perceive by the eye; to behold; to perceive mentally; to form a conception or idea of; to understand; to comprehend; to give attention to; to examine; to attend or escort (to *see* a lady home); to have communication with; to meet or associate with; to visit (to go to *see* a friend); to experience; to know by personal experience (to *see* death). ∴ Simply to *see* is often an involuntary, and always a mechanical act; to *perceive* implies generally or always the intelligence of a prepared mind; to *observe* implies to look for the purpose of noticing.—*v.i.* To have the power or sense of sight; to perceive mentally; to discern; to understand: often with *through* or *into*; to examine or inquire; to consider; to be attentive; to take heed; to take care.—*To see to*, to be attentive to; to look after; to take care of.—*To see about a thing*, to pay some attention to it; to consider it.—*See to it*, look well to it; attend; consider; take care.—*Let me see*, *let us see*, phrases used to introduce the particular consideration of a subject.—*interj.* Lo! look! observe! behold!—**seeing,** sē′ing, *conj.* Because; inasmuch as; since; considering; taking into account that. —**seer,** sē′ėr or sēr, *n.* One who sees; one who foresees future events; a prophet.

see, sē, *n.* [From O.Fr. *se*, *sed*, from L. *sedes*, a seat, from stem of *sedeo*, to sit. SEDATE.] The seat of the power of a bishop; the diocese or jurisdiction of a bishop, archbishop, or, in Rome, of the pope.

seed, sēd, *n.* [A.Sax. *saed*, from *sáwan*, to sow; Icel. *saethi*, Dan. *saed*, D. *zaat*, G. *saat*. SOW.] The impregnated and matured ovule of a plant, containing an embryo, which may be developed, and converted into an individual similar to that from which it derives its origin; one of the grains or fruits of wheat and many other plants, though sometimes the seed is contained in the fruit; the fecundating fluid of male animals; the semen; that from which anything springs; first principle; progeny; offspring; children; descendants.—*To run to seed*. See RUN. —*v.i.* To produce seed; to shed the seed.—*v.t.* To sow; to supply with seed; to ornament with seed-like decorations.—**seedcake,** *n.* A sweet cake containing aromatic seeds.—**seediness,** sē′di•nes, *n.* State of being seedy; shabbiness.—**seed leaf,** *n.* *Bot.* the primary leaf developed from a cotyledon.—**seedling,** sēd′ling, *n.* A plant reared from the seed, and not from a layer, bud, etc.—*a.* Produced from the seed (a *seedling* pansy).—**seed pearl,** *n.* A small pearl resembling a grain or seed in size or form.—**seedsman,** sēdz′man, *n.* A person who deals in seeds; one who scatters seed (*Shak.*).—**seedtime,** *n.* The season proper for sowing.—**seed vessel,** *n.* *Bot.* the pericarp which contains the seeds.—**seedy,** sē′di, *a.* Abounding with seeds; running to seed; wornout; shabby; poor and miserable looking; feeling or appearing wretched, as after a debauch (*colloq.*).

seeing, *conj.* See SEE.

seek, sēk, *v.t.*—pret. and pp. *sought* (O.E. *sehe*, A.Sax. *sécan*, to seek, pret. *sóhte*, pp. *sóht*; Icel. *saekja*, Dan. *sõge*, Sw. *söka*, D. *zoeken*, G. *suchen*, Goth. *sokjan*; akin to *sake*. *Beseech* is from *seek*, with prefix *be-*.] To go in search or quest of; to look for; to search for; to take pains to find: often followed by *out*; to ask for; to solicit; to try to gain; to go to; to resort to; to have recourse to; to aim at; to attempt; to strive after (to *seek* a person's life or his ruin); to search.—*v.i.* To make search or inquiry; to endeavor; to make an effort or attempt; to try; to use solicitation.—*To seek after*, to make pursuit of; to attempt to find or take. —*To seek for*, to endeavor to find.—*To be to seek*, to require to be sought for; to be wanting or desiderated (the work is still *to seek*).—**seeker,** sēk′ėr, *n.* One that seeks; an inquirer.

seel, sēl, *v.t.* [Fr. *ciller*, *siller*, from *cil*, L. *cilium*, an eyelash.] To close the eyes of a hawk with a thread: a term of falconry; to blind; to hoodwink (*Shak.*).

seem, sēm, *v.i.* [A.Sax. *séman*, to conciliate, to adjust, to seem, from root of *same*.] To appear; to present the appearance of being; to be only in appearance and not really; to show one's self or itself; hence, to assume an air; to pretend; to appear to one's opinion or judgment; to be thought; to appear to one's self; to imagine; to feel as if (I still *seem* to hear his voice).—*It seems*, it would appear; it appears.—*It seems to me*= I think; I am inclined to believe. ∴ Formerly *seem* was often used impersonally in such phrases as *me seems*, *him seemed*; hence *meseems* as a single word.—**seemer,** sēm′ėr, *n.* One who seems; one who carries an appearance or semblance.—**seeming,** sēm′ing, *p.* and *a.* Appearing; having the appearance or semblance, whether real or not; specious or plausible in appearance.—*n.* Appearance; show; semblance, especially a false appearance.—**seemingly,** sēm′ing•li, *adv.* As it would seem; apparently; ostensibly; in appearance.—**seemliness,** sēm′li•nes, *n.* The state or quality of being seemly. —**seemly,** sēm′li, *a.* [Same as Icel. *saemiligr*, from *saemr*, fit, seemly.] Becoming; fitting.—*adv.* Becomingly.

seen, sēn, pp. of *see*.

seep, sēp, *v.i.* [A.Sax. *sīpian*, to absorb; akin *sip*.] To percolate; to ooze.—**seepage,** *n.* The act of seeping; also, the fluid that has seeped through.

seer. See SEE.

seesaw, sē′sa̤, *n.* [A reduplicated form of *saw*, the motion resembling the act of sawing.] A game in which two children, one on each end of a long piece of timber balanced on a support, move alternately up and down; a motion or action resembling that in seesaw.—*a.* Moving up and down or to and fro.—*v.i.* and *t.* To move up and down, or back and forth.

seethe, sēTH, *v.t.*—pret. *seethed*, pp. *seethed* or *sodden*, ppr. *seething*. [A. Sax. *seóthan*, to seethe; Icel. *sjótha*, G. *sieden*, to boil.] To boil; to prepare for food in boiling liquor; to soak; to steep and soften in liquor.—*v.i.* To be in a state of ebullition; to boil; to be hot.

seggar, seg′ėr, *n.* [Prov.E. *saggard*, *saggar*, contr, for *safeguard*.] The case of fire clay in which fine stoneware is enclosed while being baked in the kiln. Also SAGGER.

segment, seg′ment, *n.* [L. *segmentum*, from *seco*, to cut. SECTILE.] A part cut off or marked as separate from others; one of the parts into which a body naturally divides itself; a section; *geom.* a part cut off from any figure by a line or plane; the *segment of a circle*, being the part contained by an arc and its chord.—*v.i.* (seg•ment′). To divide or become divided up into segments.—**segmental,** seg•men′tal, *a.* Pertaining to, consisting of, or like a segment.—**segmentation,** seg•men•tā′shon, *n.* A division into segments; in animals (1), the division of the adult body into successive segments (rings, somites, and metameres), e.g. in Crustacea. (2) See CLEAVAGE.

segregate, seg′re•gāt, *v.t.*—*segregated, segregating*. [L. *segrego*, *segregatum*—*se*, apart, and *grex*, *gregis*, a flock. GREGARIOUS.] To separate from others; to set apart.—*v.i.* To separate or go apart.—*a.* Separate; select.—**segregation,** seg•re•gā′shon, *n.* The act of segregating; separation from others; dispersion.

seidlitz powder, sĭd′lits, *n.* An aperient medicine composed of Rochelle salt, bicarbonate of soda, and tartaric acid, taken while effervescing in water.

seignior, seigneur, sān′yėr, *n.* [Fr. *seigneur*, It. *signore*, Sp. *señor*, Pg. *senhor*, titles or words of respectful address, equivalent to Sir, Mr., gentleman; from L. *senior*, elder.] *Feudal law*, the lord of a fee or manor.—*Grand Seignior*, a title sometimes given to the Sultan of Turkey.—**seigniorage,** sān′yėr•ij, *n.* Something claimed by the sovereign or by a superior as a prerogative; the profit derived from issuing coins at a rate above their intrinsic value, or by giving back rather less in coin than is received in bullion; a royalty or share of profit; the money received by an author from his publisher for copyright of his works.—**seigniory,** sān′yėr•i, *n.* A lordship; power or authority as sovereign lord.

seine, sān, *n.* [Fr. *seine*, from L. *sagena*, Gr. *sagēnē*, a seine.] A large net for catching fish.

seise, sēz, *v.t. Law*, see SEIZE.—**seisin,** sē′zin, *n.* See SEIZIN.

seismic, seismal, sīz′mik, sīz′mal, *a.* [Gr. *seismos*, an earthquake, from *seiō*, to shake.] Pertaining to earthquakes.—**seismograph,** sīz′mo•graf, *n.* An electromagnetic instrument for registering the shocks and concussions of earthquakes.—**seismographic,** sīz•mo•graf′ik, *a.* Pertaining to seismography or the seismograph.—**seismography,** sīz•mog′ra•fi, *n.* A description or account of earthquakes.—**seismologic,** sīz•mo•loj′ik, *a.* Pertaining to seismology.—**seismologist,** sīz•mol′o•jist, *n.* A student of, or one versed in, seismology.—**seismology,** sīz•mol′o•ji, *n.* The science of earthquakes; that department of science which treats of volcanoes and earthquakes.—**seismometer, seismoscope,** sīz•mom′et•ėr, sīz′mo•skōp, *n.* An instrument for measuring the direction and force of earthquakes and similar concussions.

seize, sēz, *v.t.*—*seized, seizing*. [Fr, *saisir*, to seize, from O.H.G. *sezzan*. *sazjan*, Goth. *satjan*, to set. SET.] To suddenly lay hold of; to grip or grasp suddenly; to take possession by force, or by virtue of legal authority; to have a sudden and powerful effect on; to attack (a fever *seizes* a patient); to lay hold of by the mind; to comprehend; *naut.* to fasten two ropes, or different parts of one rope, together with a cord; *law*, to make possessed; to put in possession of: with *of* before the thing possessed.—*v.i.* With *on* or *upon*, to fall on and grasp; to take hold of; to take possession of.—**seizable,** sē′za•bl, *a.* Capable of being seized; liable to be taken.—**seizer,** sē′zėr, *n.* One who or that which seizes.—**seizin,** sē′zin, *n.* [Fr. *saisine*, seizin, from *saisir*, to seize.] *Law*, possession; the act of taking possession; the thing possessed.—**seizing,** sē′zing, *n. Naut.* the cord or cords used for fastening ropes together.—**seizor,** sē′zor, *n. Law*, one who seizes or takes possession.—**seizure,** sē′zhėr, *n.* The act of seizing or taking sudden hold; a taking into possession; the thing seized or taken possession of; a sudden attack of some disease.

sejant, sejeant, sē′jant, *a.* [O.Fr., from L. *sedere*, to sit.] Sitting, a heraldic term applied to an animal in the position of a sitting cat. When the fore paws are raised off the ground, the term is *sejant erect*.

selachian, si•lā′ki•an, *n.* [Gr. *selachos*, a shark.] Any fish of the shark or dogfish family.

selah, sā′lä, *n.* A Hebrew word in the Psalms, thought to have a meaning either devotional or musical.

seldom, sel′dom, *adv.* [A.Sax. *seldan*, *seldum*=Icel. *sjaldan*, Dan. *sielden*, D. *zelden*, G. *selten*; from A.Sax. *seld*, Goth. *sild*, rare.] Rarely; not often; not frequently.

select, si•lekt′, *v.t.* [L. *seligo*, *selectum*—*se*, from, and *lego*, to pick, cull, or gather. LEGEND.] To choose and take from a number; to take by preference from among others; to pick out; to cull.—*a.* Taken from a number by preference; picked out by reason of excellence; choice; picked.—**selection,** si•lek′shon, *n.* [L. *selectio*, *selectionis*.] The act of selecting; a taking by preference from a number; a thing or things selected from others.—*Natural selection*, that process in nature by which plants and animals best fitted for the conditions in which they are placed survive, propagate, and spread, while the less fitted die out and disappear; survival of the fittest.—**selective,** si•lek′tiv, *a.* Selecting; tending to select.—**selectness,** si•lekt′nes, *n.* The state or quality of being select.—**selector,** si•lek′tėr, *n.* One that selects.

selenium, si•lē′ni•um, *n.* [From Gr. *sēlēne*, the moon.] A nonmetallic element chemically resembling sulfur and tellurium and having an electrical resistance that changes under the action of light. Symbol, Se; at. no., 34, at. wt., 78.90.

selenography, sel•e•nog′ra•fi, *n.* [Gr. *selēnē*, the moon, and *graphō*, to describe.] A description of the moon and its phenomena; the art of picturing the face of the moon.—**selenographer, selenographist,** sel•e•nog′ra•fėr, sel•e•nog′ra•fist, *n.* One versed in selenography.—**selenographic,** si•lē′no•graf″ik, *a.* Belonging to selenography.—**selenology,** sel•e•nol′o•ji, *n.* [Gr. *selēnē*, and *logos*, description.] That branch of astronomical science which treats of the moon.

self, self; pl. **selves,** selvz. [A.Sax. *self*, *selfa*=D. *zelf*, Dan. *selv*, Icel. *sjálfr*, G. *selb*, Goth. *silba*.] A word affixed to certain personal pronouns to express emphasis or distinction; also when the pronoun is used reflexively. Thus for emphasis, I *myself* will write; I will examine for *myself*; thou *thyself* shalt go; thou shalt see for *thyself*. Reflexively, I abhor *myself*; he loves *himself*; we value *ourselves*. Sometimes *self* is separated from *my*, *thy*, etc., as *my* wretched *self*; and this leads to the similar use of *self* as a noun.—*n.* The individual as an object to his own reflective consciousness; one's individual person; personal interest; one's own private interest (he is always for *self*); a flower or blossom of a uniform color (with pl. **selfs**).—*Self* is the first element in innumerable compounds, generally of obvious meaning.—*a.*‡ Same; very same; still used in this sense in the compound *self-same*.—**self-abasement,** *n.* Degradation of one's self by one's own act.—**self-acting,** *a.* Acting of itself; applied to automatic contrivances for the manipulation of machines.—**self-assertive,** *a.* Forward in asserting one's self, or one's rights and claims.—**self-assertion,** *n.* The act of asserting one's self or one's own rights or claims; a putting one's self forward in an assuming manner.—**self-assured,** *a.* Self-confident; feeling secure in one's self.—**self-centered,** *a.* Devoted to self; egocentric; self-adoring.—**self-colored,** *a.* All of one color, as a blossom or piece of cloth.—**self-command,** *n.* Command of feelings; presence of mind; coolness.—**self-complacency,** *n.* Satisfaction with one's self or one's own doings.—**self-complacent,** *a.* Pleased with one's self or one's own doings; self-satisfied.—**self-conceit,** *n.* A high opinion of one's self; vanity. ∴ Syn. under EGOTISM.—**self-confidence,** *n.* The state or quality of being self-confident.—**self-confident,** *a.* Confident of one's own strength or powers; relying on the correctness of one's own judgment, or the competence of one's own powers, without other aid.—**self-conscious,** *a.* Conscious of one's states or acts as belonging to one's self; conscious of one's self as an object of observation to others; apt to think of how one's self appears.—**self-consciousness,** *n.* State of being self-conscious.—**self-contained,** *a.* Wrapped up in one's self; reserved; not communicative; relying on no outside aid or relations; sufficient within itself, as of a large estate, or as of a political state, sometimes called autarchy.—**self-contradictory,** *a.* Contradicting itself.—**self-control,** *n.* Control exercised over one's self; self-restraint; self-command.—**self-deceit, self-deception,** *n.* Deception concerning one's self, proceeding from one's own mistake.—**self-defense,** *n.* Defense of one's own person, property, or reputation.—**self-delusion,** *n.* The delusion of one's self; a delusion respecting one's self.—**self-denial,** *n.* The act of being self-denying.—**self-denying,** *a.* Denying one's self; forbearing to indulge one's own appetites or desires.—**self-destruction,** *n.* The destruction of one's self.—**self-devotion,** *n.* Sacrifice of one's own interests or happiness for the sake of others; self-sacrifice.—**self-distrust,** *n.* Distrust of one's self or one's own powers.—**self-educated,** *a.* Educated by one's own efforts or without the aid of teachers.—**self-esteem,** *n.* The esteem or good opinion of one's self.—**self-evident,** *a.* Evident without proof or reasoning; producing certainty or clear conviction upon a bare presentation to the mind.—**self-existence,** *n.* The quality of being self-existent.—**self-existent,** *a.* Existing by one's or its own nature or essence, independent of any other cause.—**self-explanatory,** *a.* Capable of explaining itself; bearing its meaning on its own face; obvious.—**self-governed,** *a.* Governed by one's self or itself.—**self-government,** *n.* The government of one's self; self-control; a system of government by which the mass of a nation or people appoint the rulers.—**self-help,** *n.* Assistance of or by one's self; the use of one's own powers to attain one's ends.—**self-importance,** *n.* High opinion of one's self; pride.—**self-important,** *a.* Important in one's own esteem; pompous.—**self-induction,** The production in a circuit of an induced current by the variation (especially starting or stopping) of the current in the same circuit; the unit is the *henry*.—**self-indulgence,** *n.* Free indulgence of one's passions or appetites.—**self-indulgent,** *a.* Indulging one's self; gratifying one's own passions, desires, or the like.—**self-interest,** *n.* Interest or concern for one's self; one's own advantage.—**selfish,** self′ish, *a.* Caring only or chiefly for self; regarding one's own interest chiefly or solely; proceeding from love of self; influenced solely by private advantage.—**selfishly,** self′ish•li, *adv.* In a selfish manner.—**selfishness,** self′ish•nes, *n.* The quality of being selfish; devotion to one's own interests with carelessness of others.—**self-knowledge,** *n.* The knowledge of one's own real character, abilities, worth, or demerit.—**self-love,** *n.* The love of one's own person or happiness; the natural feeling which impels every rational creature to preserve his life and promote his own happiness.—**self-made,** *a.* Made by one's self; having risen in the world by one's own exertions (a *self-made* man).—**self-opinion,** *n.* Exalted opinion of one's self; self-conceit.—**self-opinioned,** *a.* Valuing one's own opinion highly.—**self-pollination,** self•-pol′lin•a″shon. [From *pollen.*] Pollination of a flower by its own pollen.—**self-possessed,** *a.* Composed; not excited or flustered; cool; not disturbed.—**self-possession,** *n.* The possession of one's powers; presence of mind; calmness; self-command.—**self-preservation,** *n.* The preservation of one's self from destruction or injury.—**self-registering,** *a.* Registering automatically; an epithet applied to any instrument so contrived as to record its own indications of phenomena (a *self-registering* barometer, thermometer, or the like.)—**self-reliance,** *n.* Reliance on one's own powers.—**self-reliant,** *a.* Relying on one's self; trusting to one's own powers.—**self-renunciation,** *n.* The act of renouncing one's own rights or claims; self-abnegation.—**self-reproach,** *n.* The reproach or censure of one's own conscience.—**self-respect,** *n.* Respect for one's self or one's own character.—**self-restrained,** *a.* Restrained by itself or by one's own power of will.—**self-restraint,** *n.* Restraint or control imposed on one's self; self-command; self-control.—**self-righteous,** *a.* Righteous in one's own esteem; deeming one's self righteous above others.—**self-sacrifice,** *n.* Sacrifice of one's self or of self-interest.—**self-sacrificing,** *a.* Yielding up one's own interest, feelings, etc.; sacrificing one's self.—**selfsame,** *a.* The very same; identical.—**self-satisfied,** *a.* Satisfied with one's self.—**self-seeker,** *n.* One who seeks only his own interest.—**self-seeking,** *a.* Seeking one's own interest or happiness; selfish.—**self-styled,** *a.* Called or styled by one's self; called by a title assumed without warrant.—**self-sufficiency,** *n.* The state or quality of being self-sufficient.—**self-sufficient,** *a.* Independent of the aid of others; having undue confidence in one's own strength, ability, or endowments; conceited; overbearing.—**self-taught,** *a.* Taught by one's self; educated without a teacher (a *self-taught* genius).—**self-will,** *n.* Determination to have one's own way; willfulness; obstinacy.—**self-willed,** *a.* Governed by one's own will; willful; not accommodating or compliant; obstinate.

sell, sel, *v.t.*—pret. and pp. *sold.* [A.Sax. *sellan, syllan,* to give, to deliver up; L.G. *sellen,* Icel. *selja,* to sell, to deliver; Goth. *saljan,* to offer; akin *sale.*] To transfer to another for an equivalent; to give up for a consideration; to dispose of for something else, especially for money; correlative to *buy*; to make a matter of bargain and sale of; to take a bribe for; to betray.—*To sell one's life dearly,* to cause great loss to those who take one's life.—*To sell a person up,* to sell his goods to pay his creditors.—*v.i.* To practice selling; to be sold; to fetch a price.—*To sell out,* to dispose of one's property completely; *v.t.*—to fool a person, as by a trick or hoax. (*Slang.*)—*n.* A deception, a hoax. (*Colloq.*)—**seller,** sel′ėr, *n.* One who sells; a vender.

Seltzer water, selt′sėr, *n.* Originally, a mineral water imported from Germany; a manufactured effervescent water.

selvage, sel′vij, *n.* [From *self* and *edge*; lit. an edge formed of the stuff itself; comp. D. *zelfkant, zelfegge,* G. *selbende,* lit. self-edge, self-end.] A woven border, or border of close work, on a fabric made of the threads of the fabric; a list.

semantics, si•man′tiks, *n.* pl. [G. *semantikos,* significant, from *sēma,* sign.] The study of meaning; the study of historical change in meaning.—**semantic,** si•man′tik, *a.*

semaphore, sem′a•fōr, *n.* [G. *sēma,* sign, and *pherō,* to bear.] A system of visual signaling, which utilizes two flags held one in each hand.

semblance, sem′blans, *n.* [Fr. *semblance,* from *sembler,* to seem, to appear, from L. *similare, simulare,* to make like, from *similis,* like. SIMILAR.] Similarity; resemblance; external figure or appearance; form; a form or figure representing something; likeness; image.

semé, se•mā′, *a.* The heraldic term for powdered or sown, when used in connection with fleurs-de-lis.

semeiography, se•mī•og′ra•fi, *n.* [Gr. *sēmeion,* a sign, and *graphō,* to write.] The doctrine of signs; *pathol.* a description of the marks or symptoms of diseases.—**semeiology,** se•-mī•ol′o•ji, *n.* [Gr. *sēmeion,* and *logos,* discourse.] The doctrine of signs.

semen, sē′men, *n.* [L., from root of

sero, to sow.] The seed or fecundating fluid of male animals; sperm.

semester, si•mes′tėr, *n.* [L. *semestris*, half-yearly—*sex*, six, and *mensis*, month.] A period or term of six months.

semi, sem′i. [L. *semi*, Gr. *hēmi.*] A prefix signifying half; half of; in part; partially. The compounds are generally of very obvious meaning if the latter parts be known, and we give only a certain number of them below.

semiattached, sem′i•at•tacht″, *a.* Partially attached or united.—*Semiattached house*, one of two houses joined together, but both standing apart from others.

semibreve, sem′i•brēv, *n.* [From *semi* and *breve.*] *Music*, a note of half the duration or time of the breve, equivalent to two minims, four crotchets, or eight quavers.

semicircle, sem′i•sėr•kl, *n.* [L. *semicirculus.*] The half of a circle; the part of a circle comprehended between its diameter and half of its circumference; any body in the form of a half circle.—**semicircular,** sem•i•sėr′kū•lėr, *a.* Having the form of a half circle.

semicircumference, sem′i•sėr•kum″fėr•ens, *n.* Half the circumference.

semicolon, sem′i•kō•lon, *n.* [*Semi* and *colon.*] The punctuation mark or point (;), marking a pause of less duration than the colon, and more than the comma; used to distinguish the conjunct members of a sentence.

semiconscious, sem•i•kon′shus, *a.* Imperfectly conscious.

semicylinder, sem•i•sil′in•dėr, *n.* Half of a cylinder that is cut longitudinally by a plane.—**semicylindrical,** sem′i•si•lin″dri•kal, *a.* In the form of a semicylinder.

semidiameter, sem′i•dī•am″et•ėr, *n.* Half a diameter; a radius.

semidiurnal, sem′i•dī•ėr″nal, *a.* Pertaining to or accomplished in half a day; continuing half a day.

semifinal, sem′i•fī•nal, *a. Sports*, a match before the final or decisive one.—*n.* A semifinal match.

semifluid, sem•i•flū′id, *a.* Imperfectly fluid.—*n.* Semifluid matter.

semilunar, sem•i•lū′nėr, *a.* [L. *semi*, half, and *luna*, the moon.] Resembling in form a half moon.—*Semilunar valves, anat.* three valves at the beginning of the pulmonary artery and aorta.

semimute, sem′i•mūt, *a.* Applied to a person who, owing to losing the sense of hearing, has lost also to a great extent the faculty of speech.

seminal, sem′i•nal, *a.* [L. *seminalis*, from *semen*, seed, from stem of *sero*, to sow. SOW.] Pertaining to seed or semen, or to the elements of reproduction; contained in seed; germinal; rudimentary.

seminar, sem′i•när, *n.* [G. from L. *seminarium*, from *seminarius*, pertaining to seed.] A group of students studying under a professor, doing original research and study and then discussing the results.

seminary, sem′i•ne•ri, *n.* [L. *seminarium*, from *semen*, *seminis*, seed.] A place of education; any secondary school; college in which persons are instructed in theology.

semiography, se•mī•og′ra•fi, *n.* See SEMEIOGRAPHY.—**semiology,** se•mī•ol′o•ji, *n.* See SEMEIOLOGY.

semipalmate, semipalmated, sem•i•pal′māt, sem•i•pal′mā•ted, *a. Zool.* having the feet webbed only partly down the toes.

semiprecious, sem•i•presh′us, *a.* Lower in value than precious gems.

semiquaver, sem′i•kwā•vėr, *n. Music*, a note of half the duration of the quaver; the sixteenth of the semibreve.

semisolid, sem•i•sol′id, *a.* Partially solid.—*n.* A highly viscous substance.

Semite, sem′īt, *n.* [From *Sem* or *Shem*, eldest son of Noah.] A descendant of Shem; one of the Semitic races; a Shemite.—*a.* Belonging to Shem or his descendants.—**Semitic,** se•mit′ik, *a.* Relating to Shem or his descendants; pertaining to the Hebrew race or any of those kindred to it.—*Semitic* or *Shemitic languages*, an important group or family of languages, comprising the Hebrew, Phoenician, Arabic, Abyssinian, Chaldean, Assyrian, Babylonian.—**Semitism,** sem′it•izm, *n.*

semitone, sem′i•tōn, *n. Music*, half a tone; an interval of sound, as between *mi* and *fa* in the diatonic scale, which is only half the distance of the interval between *ut* (*do*) and *re*, or *sol* and *la*.—**semitonic,** sem•i•ton′ik, *a.* Pertaining to a semitone.

semitrailer, sem′i•trāl•ėr, *n.* A highway freight trailer, drawn by a motor truck (tractor).

semitransparent, sem′i•trans•pâ″rent, *a.* Half or imperfectly transparent.

semitropical, sem′i•trop″i•kal, *a.* Subtropical.

semivowel, sem′i•vou•el, *n.* A half vowel; a sound partaking of the nature of both a vowel and a consonant, as *l*, *m*, *r*.

semolina, sem•o•lē′na, *n.* [It. *semolino.*] The large hard grains retained in the bolting machine after the fine flour has been passed through it, or made separately, used for puddings.

sempiternal, sem•pi•tėr′nal, *a.* [Fr. *sempiternel*, L. *sempiternus*—*semper*, always, and *eternus*, eternal.] Eternal in futurity; everlasting; having beginning, but no end; also, without beginning or end.—**sempiternity,** sem•pi•tėr′ni•ti, *n.* Future duration without end; eternity.

sempstress, semp′stres, *n.* See SEAM.

senary, sēn′a•ri, *a.* [L. *senarius*, from *seni*, six each, from *sex*, six.] Of six; belonging to six; containing six.

senate, sen′it, *n.* [Fr. *sénat*, from L. *senatus*, from *senex*, old, aged; cog. with Goth. *sineigs*, Gr. *henos*, Skr. *sanas*, old. SENIOR, SIR.] Originally, in ancient Rome, a body of elderly citizens elected from among the nobles, and having supreme legislative power; hence, the upper branch of a legislature in various countries, as in France, the United States, etc.; in general, a legislative body; the legislative department of a government; the governing body of a university.—**senator,** sen′a•tor, *n.* A member of a senate.—**senatorial,** sen•a•tō′ri•al, *a.* Pertaining to a senator or senators; belonging to senators; in the United States, entitled to elect a senator.—**senatorship,** sen′a•tor•ship, *n.* The office or dignity of a senator.

send, send, *v.t.*—pret. and pp. *sent.* [A.Sax. *sendan*=Icel. *senda*, Dan. *sende*, D. *zenden*, G. *senden*, Goth. *sandjan*, to send; caus. of an old verb meaning to go.] To cause to go or pass from one place to another; to dispatch; to cause to be conveyed or transmitted; to impel; to propel; to throw; to cast; to commission, authorize, or direct to go and act; to cause to befall; to inflict (to *send* destruction); before certain verbs of motion, to cause to do the act indicated by the respective verb (to *send* the enemy *flying* in all directions).—*To send forth* or *out*, to put or bring forth; to emit.—*v.i.* To dispatch a message or a messenger for some purpose.—*To send for*, to request by message to come or be brought (to *send for* a physician).—**sender,** sen′dėr, *n.* One that sends.

sendal, sen′dal, *n.* [O.Fr. *cendal*, sendal; L.L. *cendalum*, from Gr. *sindon*, a fine Indian cloth, from *Sindhu*, the river Indus.] A light thin stuff of silk or thread.

Seneca, sen′e•ka, *n.* An Iroquois Indian tribe, formerly of western New York; the most warlike of the Five Nations.

senega, sen′e•ga, *n.* A drug consisting of the root of a plant of the United States, used in cough mixtures; the plant itself.

senescence, se•nes′ens, *n.* [L. *senesco*, from *senex*, old. SENATE.] The state of growing old.—**senescent,** se•nes′ent, *a.* Beginning to grow old.

seneschal, sen′es•shal, *n.* [O.Fr. *seneschal*, L.L. *senescallus*, *senescalcus*, from O.G. *senescalh*—*sene*, old, cognate with L. *senex* (seen in *senate*), and *scale*, *scalh*, a servant (seen also in *marshal*).] An officer in the houses of princes and dignitaries, who has the superintendence of feasts and domestic ceremonies; a steward.

senile, sē′nīl, *a.* [L. *senilis*, from *senex*, old. SENATE.] Pertaining to old age; proceeding from age; characterized by the weakness of old age.—**senility,** se•nil′i•ti, *n.* The state of being senile; old age; dotage.

senior, sēn′yėr, *a.* [L. *senior*, compar. of *senex*, old (SENATE). *Sir* is from *senior.*] More advanced in age; older; elder; being the elder of two persons of the same name (John Smith, *senior*); higher or more advanced in rank, office, or the like.—*n.* A person who is older than another (my *senior* by ten years); one that is older in office than another; one prior or superior in rank or office; an aged person; a student in the U. S. who is in his final year in college, a university, or high school.

—**seniority,** sēn•yor′i•ti, *n.* State of being senior; superior age; priority of birth; priority or superiority in rank or office, which presumes superior right to promotion.

senna, sen′na, *n.* [Ar. *senā*, senna.] The leaves of various species of *Cassia*, used as a laxative medicine in constipation, dyspepsia, etc.

sennit, sen′it, *n.* [From *seven* and *knit.*] *Naut.* a sort of flat braided cordage formed by plaiting rope yarns or spun yarn together.

sensation, sen•sā′shon, *n.* [Fr. *sensation*, L.L. *sensatio*, from L. *sentio*, *sensum*, to feel, to perceive. SENSE.] An impression made upon the mind through the medium of one of the organs of sense; feeling produced by external objects, or by some change in the internal state of the body; a feeling; the power of feeling or receiving impressions; feeling occasioned by causes that do not act on the senses; a purely spiritual or psychical affection (a *sensation* of awe, novelty, etc.); a state of some excitement (to create a *sensation*); what produces excited interest or feeling; often used as an adjective in the sense of causing excited interest or feeling (*sensation* novels, etc.).—*Sensation novels*, novels that produce their effect mainly by exciting and often improbable situations, as scenes of extreme peril, high-wrought passion, etc., depending but little on the delineation of character.—**sensational,** sen•sā′shon•al, *a.* Relating to or implying sensation or perception by the senses; producing sensation or excited interest or emotion (a *sensational* novel, a writer of the *sensational* school); pertaining to sensationalism.—**sensationalism,** sen•sā′shon•al•izm, *n. Metaph.* the theory or doctrine that all our ideas are solely derived through our senses; sensualism.—**sensationalist,** sen•sā′shon•al•ist, *n. Metaph.* a believer in or upholder of the doctrine of sensationalism.

sense, sens, *n.* [L. *sensus*, sensation, a sense, from *sentio*, *sensum*, to perceive by the senses (seen in *scent*, *sensual*, *consent*, *dissent*, *assent*, *resent*, *sentence*, *sentiment*, etc.).] One of the faculties by which man and the higher animals perceive external objects by means of impressions made on certain organs of the body, the senses being usually spoken of as five, namely, sight, hearing, taste, smell, and touch; perception by the senses; sensation; feeling; apprehension through the intellect; discernment; appreciation (no *sense* of beauty); moral perception; consciousness (a *sense* of shame); faculty of thinking and feeling; sound perception and reasoning; good judgment; understanding (a man of *sense*); rationality; view or opinion held in common (to speak the *sense* of a public meeting); meaning; import; signification of language.—*Common sense.* COMMON.—*To be in our senses*, to be in a sound state of mind; to have possession of our mental faculties; the contrary being to be *out of our senses*.—**senseless,** sens′les, *a.* Destitute of sense; having no power of sensation or perception; insensible; wanting feeling or sympathy; without sensibility; contrary to reason or sound judgment; unwise; foolish; nonsensical; wanting understanding; acting without judgment; stupid.—**senselessly,** sens′les•li, *adv.* In a senseless manner; foolishly; stupidly.—**senselessness,** sens′les•nes, *n.* The state or quality of being senseless; want of good sense; folly; stupidity.—**sensibility,** sen•si•bil′i•ti, *n.* The state or quality of being sensible; capability of sensation; capacity to experience emotion or feeling; the capacity of being impressed with such sentiments as those of sublimity, awe, wonder, etc.; delicacy or keenness of feeling; quick emotion or sympathy; that quality of an instrument which makes it indicate very slight changes of condition; sensitiveness (the *sensibility* of a thermometer).—**sensible,** sen′si•bl, *a.* [Fr. *sensible*, L. *sensibilis*, from *sensus.*] Capable of being perceived by the senses; capable of exciting sensation; perceptible; felt; capable of sensation or impression (the eye is *sensible* to light); capable of emotional influences; liable to impression or emotion; easily affected; perceiving or having perception either by the senses or the intellect; cognizant; persuaded; capable of indicating slight changes of condition; sensitive (a *sensible* thermometer); possessing or containing sense, judgment, or reason (a *sensible* remark); having good or sound sense; intelligent; reasonable; judicious.—**sensibleness,** sen′si•bl•nes, *n.* The state or quality of being sensible; sensibility.—**sensibly,** sen′si•bli, *adv.* In a sensible manner; perceptibly to the senses; with intelligence or good sense; judiciously.—**sensitive,** sen′si•tiv, *a.* [Fr. *sensitif*, L.L. *sensitivus.*] Having the capacity of receiving impressions from external objects; having feelings easily excited; readily and acutely affected; of keen sensibility; *physics*, easily affected, moved, or exhibiting change from some influence (a *sensitive* balance); *chem.* readily affected by the action of appropriate agents.—**sensitively,** sen′si•tiv•li, *adv.* In a sensitive manner.—**sensitiveness,** sen′si•tiv•nes, *n.* The state of being sensitive.—**sensitive plant,** *n.* A name given to several plants which display movements of their leaves in a remarkable degree under the influence of light and darkness, as also under mechanical and other stimuli.—**sensitivity,** sen•si•tiv′i•ti, *n.* The state of being sensitive or readily affected by the action of appropriate chemical or other agents; readiness of muscle or nerves to respond to stimuli.—**sensitize,** sen′si•tīz, *v.t.*—*sensitized*, *sensitizing*. To render capable of being acted on by the actinic rays of the sun or other means; a term in photography, etc.

sensorium, sen•sō′ri•um, *n.* [From L. *sensus*, sense.] The brain or any part of it considered as the general receptacle of impressions derived from the external world; the central seat of consciousness; a nerve center. —**sensorial,** sen•sō′ri•al, *a.* Sensory. —**sensory,** sen′so•ri, *a.* Relating to the sensorium; conveying sensation (*sensory* nerves).

sensual, sen′shū•al, *a.* [L. *sensualis*, from *sensus*, sense. SENSE.] Pertaining to the body, in distinction from the spirit; carnal; fleshly; pertaining to the gratification of the appetites; grossly luxurious; indulging in lust; voluptuous; pertaining to sensualism as a philosophical doctrine.—**sensualism,** sen′shū•al•izm, *n. Metaph.* that theory which bases all our mental acts and intellectual powers upon sensation; sensationalism, opposed to *intellectualism*; a state of subjection to the appetites; sensuality.—**sensualist,** sen′shū•al•ist, *n.* A person given to the indulgence of his appetites; a sensationalist in philosophy.—**sensualistic,** sen′shū•a•lis″tik, *a.* Upholding the doctrine of sensualism.—**sensuality,** sen•shū•al′i•ti, *n.* The quality of being sensual; devotedness to the gratification of the bodily appetites; indulgence in lust; carnality; fleshliness.—**sensualize,** sen′shū•al•īz, *v.t.*—*sensualized*, *sensualizing*. To make sensual; to debase by carnal gratifications.—**sensually,** sen′shū•al•li, *adv.* In a sensual manner.—**sensuous,** sen′shū•us, *a.* Pertaining to the senses; appealing to the senses; readily affected through the senses; alive to the pleasure to be received through the senses.—**sensuously,** sen′shū•us•li, *adv.* In a sensuous manner.—**sensuousness,** sen′shū•us•nes, *n.*

sent, sent, pret. and pp. of *send*.

sentence, sen′tens, *n.* [L. *sententia*, an opinion, a judgment, a maxim, a sentence, from *sentio*, to perceive. SENSE.] A judgment; a decision; a judgment pronounced by a court or judge upon a criminal; a maxim (*Shak.*); *gram.* a number of words containing complete sense or a complete thought and followed by a period, question mark, or exclamation point.—*v.t.*—*sentenced*, *sentencing*. To pronounce sentence or judgment on; to condemn; to doom to punishment.—**sentencer,** sen′ten•sėr, *n.* One who pronounces a sentence.—**sententious,** sen•ten′shus, *a.* [L. *sententiosus*, Fr. *sentencieux.*] Abounding in axioms or maxims; rich in judicious observations; having brevity and weight of meaning; pithy; terse.—**sententiously,** sen•ten′shus•li, *adv.*—In a sententious manner.—**sententiousness,** sen•ten′shus•nes, *n.* The quality of being sententious; brevity of expression combined with strength.

sentient, sen′shi•ent, *a.* [L. *sentiens*, *sentientis*, ppr. of *sentio*, to perceive. SENSE.] Capable of perceiving or feeling; having the faculty of perception; *physiol.* a term applied to those parts which are more susceptible of feeling than others.—**sen-**

tiently, sen′shi•ent•li, *adv.* In a sentient or perceptive manner.—**sentience, sentiency,** sen′shi•ens, sen′shi•en•si, *n.* The state of being sentient; feeling.

sentiment, sen′ti•ment, *n.* [Fr. *sentiment,* L.L. *sentimentum,* from L. *sentio,* to perceive. SENSE.] A thought prompted by feeling; a feeling respecting some person or thing; a particular disposition of mind in view of some subject; tendency to be swayed by feeling; emotion; sensibility; a thought or opinion; the thought or opinion contained in words, but considered as distinct from them; a thought expressed in striking words.—**sentimental,** sen•ti•men′tal, *a.* Having sentiment; apt to be swayed by sentiment; manifesting an excess of sentiment; artificially or mawkishly tender; appealing to sentiment rather than to reason. ∴ Syn. under ROMANTIC.—**sentimentalism,** sen•ti•men′tal•izm, *n.* Sentimentality.—**sentimentalist,** sen•ti•men′tal•ist, *n.* One who affects sentiment; the character of being sentimental or swayed by sentiment.—**sentimentality,** sen′ti•men•tal″i•ti, *n.* Affectation of fine feeling or exquisite sensibility; proneness to sentiment.—**sentimentalize,** sen•ti•men′tal•iz, *v.i.* To affect exquisite sensibility.—**sentimentally,** sen•ti•men′tal•li, *adv.* In a sentimental manner.

sentinel, sen′ti•nel, *n.* [Fr. *sentinelle;* It. *sentinella;* origin doubtful.] One who watches or keeps guard to prevent surprise; especially, a soldier set to guard any place from surprise; a sentry.—*v.t.*—*sentineled, sentineling.* To watch over as a sentinel; to furnish with a sentinel or sentinels.—**sentry,** sen′tri, *n.* [Corruption of *sentinel.*] A soldier placed on guard; a sentinel; guard; watch; duty of a sentinel.—**sentry box,** *n.* A small shed to cover and shelter a sentinel at his post.

sepal, sē′pal, *n.* [Fr. *sépale,* an invented term to correspond to *pétale,* a petal.] *Bot.* one of the separate divisions of a calyx when that organ is made up of various leaves.

separate, sep′a•rāt, *v.t.*—*separated, separating.* [L. *separo, separatum*—*se,* apart, and *paro,* to put or place. PARE.] To disunite; to divide; to part, in almost any manner, either things naturally or casually joined; to set apart from a number; to make a space between; to sever, as by an intervening space; to lie between.—*v.i.* To go apart; to withdraw from each other; to cleave or split; to come apart.—*a.* [L. *separatus,* pp. of *separo.*] Divided from the rest; parted from another or others; disjoined; unconnected; not united; distinct; withdrawn; alone; without company.—**separability, separableness,** sep′a•ra•bil″i•ti, sep′a•ra•bl•nes, *n.* The quality of being separable; divisibility.—**separable,** sep′a•ra•bl, *a.* [L. *separabilis.*] Capable of being separated or disjoined; divisible.—**separably,** sep′a•ra•bli, *adv.* In a separable manner.—**separately,** sep′a•rit•li, *adv.* In a separate or unconnected state; apart; distinctly; singly.—**separateness,** sep′a•rit•nes, *n.* The state of being separate.—**separation,** sep•a•rā′shon, *n.* [L. *separatio.*] The act of separating; the state of being separate; disjunction; disunion; disconnection; disunion of married persons; a cessation of conjugal cohabitation of man and wife.—*Judicial separation,* the separation of a husband and wife by decree of a court.—**separatism,** sep′a•rat•izm, *n.* The state of being a separatist; dissent.—**separatist,** sep′a•rat•ist, *n.* One who advocates separation; one who withdraws or separates himself from an established church; a dissenter.—**separator,** sep′a•rā•tėr, *n.* One who or that which separates; a name of several mechanical contrivances.—**separative,** sep′a•rā•tiv, *a.* Causing or used in separation.

sepia, sē′pi•a, *n.* [Gr. *sēpia,* the cuttle-fish or squid.] The cuttlefish; a species of brown pigment prepared from a black juice secreted by certain glands of the cuttlefish, and used in drawing.

sepoy, sē′poi, *n.* [Per. *sipahi,* a soldier.] A name given in Hindustan to the native soldiers in the British service.

sepsis, sep′sis, *n.* [Gr. *sēpsis,* putrefaction, from *sēpō,* to rot.] A poisoned state of the system, due to putrefaction; poisoning resulting from infection.—*Intestinal sepsis,* food poisoning caused by the eating of spoiled foods.—*Puerperal sepsis,* poisoning due to infection after childbirth.

septa, sep′ta, pl. of *septum.*

septal. See SEPTUM.

septarium, sep•tâ′ri•um, *n.* pl. **septaria,** sep•tâ′ri•a. [From L. *septum,* an enclosure, a wall, a partition.] A name given to spheroidal masses of calcareous marl, ironstone, or other matter, whose interior presents numerous fissures of some crystallized substance which divide the mass.

septate. See SEPTUM.

September, sep•tem′bėr, *n.* [L., from *septem,* seven.] The ninth month of the year, so called from being originally the seventh month from March, which was formerly the first month of the year.—**Septembrist,** *n.* One sharing as actor in the September massacres at Paris, in 1792, during the French Revolution.

septenary, sep′ten•a•ri, *a.* [L. *septenarius,* from *septeni,* seven each, from *septem,* seven.] Consisting of or relating to seven; lasting seven years; occurring once in seven years.

septennial, sep•ten′ni•al, *a.* [L. *septennis*—*septem,* seven, and *annus,* a year.] Lasting or continuing seven years; happening once in every seven years.—**septennially,** sep•ten′ni•al•li, *adv.* Once in seven years.

Septentrion, sep•ten′tri•on, *n.* [L. *septentrio, septentrionis,* from *septentriones,* the seven stars of the Great Bear—*septem,* seven, and *triones,* plowing oxen.] The north or northern regions.—**septentrional,** sep•ten′tri•on•al, *a.* Northern.

septet, septette, sep•tet′, *n.* [L. *septem,* seven.] *Music,* a composition for seven voices or instruments.

septic, sep′tik, *a.* [Gr. *sēptikos,* from *sēpō,* to putrefy.] Having power to promote putrefaction; causing putrefaction.—*n.* A substance causing putrefaction.

septicemia, sep•ti•sē′mi•a, *n.* [Gr. *sēptikos, sēptos,* putrefying, from *sēpō,* to putrefy, and *haima,* blood.] Blood poisoning by absorption into the circulation of poisonous or putrid matter.

septicidal, sep•ti•sī′dal, *a.* [L. *septum,* a partition, and *caedo,* to cut or divide. SEPTUM.] *Bot.* dividing or dehiscing at the septa or partitions.—**septifragal,** sep•tif′ra•gal, *a.* [L. *septum,* a partition, and *frango,* to break.] *Bot.* literally breaking from the partitions; applied to a mode of dehiscing in which the backs of the carpels separate from the dissepiments.

septillion, sep•til′yon, *n.* [From L. *septem,* seven, with termination of E. *million.*] In America and France a number consisting of a unit followed by 24 zeros (in Gt. Britain and Germany, by 42 zeros).

septuagenarian, sep′tū•a•je•nâ″ri•an, *n.* [L. *septuagenarius,* consisting of seventy, *septuageni,* seventy each, from *septem,* seven.] A person seventy years of age.—**septuagenary,** sep•tū•aj′e•ne•ri, *a.* Consisting of seventy or of seventy years; pertaining to a person seventy years old.—*n.* A septuagenarian.

Septuagesima, sep′tū•a•jes″i•ma, *n.* [L. *septuagesimus,* seventieth.] The third Sunday before Lent, so called because it is about seventy days before Easter.

Septuagint, sep′tū•a•jint, *n.* [L. *septuaginta,* seventy, from *septem,* seven.] A Greek version of the Old Testament (usually denoted by the symbol LXX) executed for the Jews of Alexandria and said to have been the work of seventy translators who were employed by Ptolemy Philadelphus, king of Egypt, about 280 B.C.

septum, sep′tum, *n.* pl. **septa,** sep′ta, [L. a partition, from *sepio,* to hedge in, to fence.] A partition; a wall separating cavities in animals or plants, as the cartilage between the nostrils; one of the partitions of an ovary or fruit.—**septal,** sep′tal, *a.* Belonging to or forming a septum.—**septate,** sep′tāt, *a.* Partitioned off into compartments by septa.

septuple, sep′tū•pl, *a.* [L. *septuplus,* from *septem,* seven.] Sevenfold.—*v.t.* To make sevenfold.

sepulcher, sep′ul•kėr, *n.* [L. *sepulchrum,* from *sepelio, sepultum,* to bury.] A tomb; a building, cave, etc., for interment; a burial vault; *eccles. arch.* a recess for the reception of the holy elements consecrated on Maunday Thursday till High Mass on Easter.—*v.t.*—*sepulchered, sepulchring.* To bury; to inter; to entomb.—**sepulchral,** se•pul′kral, *a.* [L. *sepulchralis.*] Pertaining to burial, to the grave, or to tombs; suggestive of a sepulcher; hence, deep, hollow in tone (a *sepulchral* tone of voice).—**sepulture,** sep′ul•chėr, *n.* [L. *sepultura,* from *sepelio, sepultum,* to bury.] Burial; act of interment; a sepulcher.

sequacious, si•kwā′shus, *a.* [L. *sequax, sequacis,* from *sequor,* to follow. SEQUENCE.] Following; disposed to follow a leader; logically consistent; consecutive in development or transition of thought.—**sequacity,** si•kwas′i•ti, *n.* State of being sequacious.

sequel, sē′kwel, *n.* [L. *sequela,* sequel, result, consequence, from *sequor,* to follow. SEQUENCE.] That which follows and forms a continuation; a succeeding part; consequence; result; event.—**sequela,** si•kwē′la, *n.* pl. **sequelae,** si•kwē′lē. [L., from *sequor.*] An adherent or band of adherents; a body of followers; *pathol.* the consequent of a disease; a morbid affection which follows another.

sequence, sē′kwens, *n.* [Fr. *séquence,* L.L. *sequentia,* from L. *sequens, sequentis,* ppr. of *sequor, secutus,* to follow (seen also in *sequel, second, prosecute, execute, consequent, ensue,* etc.).] A following or coming after; succession; a particular order or arrangement of succession; invariable order of succession; an observed instance of uniformity in following; a series of things following in a certain order; a set of playing cards immediately following each other, as king, queen, knave, etc.; *music,* the recurrence of a melodic figure in a different key to that in which it was first given; *R. Cath. Ch.* a hymn introduced into the mass on certain festival days, and coming immediately before the gospel.—**sequent, sequential,** sē′kwent, si•kwen′shal, *a.* [L. *sequens, sequentis.*] Following; succeeding; following by logical consequence.—**sequentially,** si•kwen′shal•li, *adv.* By sequence or succession.

sequester, si•kwes′tėr, *v.t.* [L. *sequestro,* to put into the hands of an indifferent person, from *sequester,* a depositary or trustee.] To set apart or separate from other things; *refl.* to retire or withdraw into obscurity; to seclude one's self; *law,* to separate from the owner for a time; to set apart, as the property of a debtor, until the claims of creditors be satisfied.—**sequestered,** si•kwes′tėrd, *p.* and *a.* Secluded; private; retired; separated from others; *law,* seized and detained for a time to satisfy a demand.—**sequestrable,** si•kwes′tra•bl, *a.* Liable to sequestration.—**sequestrate,** si•kwes′trāt, *v.t.*—*sequestrated, sequestrating. Law,* to sequester; to take possession of on behoof of creditors, as of the estate of a bankrupt, with the view of realizing it and distributing it equitably.—**sequestration,** sē′kwes•tra″shon, *n.* Retirement; seclusion from society; *law,* the separation of a thing in controversy from the possession of those who contend for it; the act of taking property from the owner for a time till the profits from it satisfy a demand; *Scots law,* the seizing of a bankrupt's estate, by decree of a competent court, for behoof of the creditors.—**sequestrator,** sē′kwes•trā•tėr, *n.* One who sequesters or sequestrates.

sequestrum, si•kwes′trum, *n.* [From L. *sequestro,* to sever.] *Pathol.* the portion of bone which is detached in necrosis.

sequin, sē′kwin, *n.* [Fr. *sequin,* from It. *zecchino,* from *zecca,* the mint, from Ar. *sikkah, sekkah,* a stamp.] A thin disk of metal, plastic, or other material, used to decorate clothing; a spangle.

sequoia, si•kwoi′a, *n.* [From *Sequoya,* the inventor of the Cherokee alphabet.] *Bot.* either of two species of coniferous California trees, genus *Sequoiadendron gigantum,* the big tree, and genus *Sequoia sempervirens,* the redwood, both of which can reach heights of more than 300 feet.

seraglio, se•räl′yō, *n.* [It. *serraglio,* partly from Turk. *serai,* Per. *sarai,* a palace, partly from It. *serrare,* to shut up, from L. *sera,* a bar.] The palace of a sultan; a harem.

serai, se•rī′, *n.* [Per. *serai,* a palace.] In Eastern countries, a place for the accommodation of travelers; a caravansary.

serape, se•rä′pā, *n.* [A Mexican word.] A blanket or shawl worn as an outer garment by the Mexicans, etc. See SARAPE.

seraph, ser′af, *n.* pl. **seraphs,** or **seraphim,** ser′a•fim. [From Heb. *seraph,* to burn, to be eminent or noble.] An angel of the highest order.—**seraphic, seraphical,** se•raf′ik, se•raf′i•kal, *a.* Pertaining to a seraph; angelic; inflamed with holy love or zeal.—**seraphically,** se•raf′i•kal•li, *adv.* In the manner of a seraph; angelically.

Serapis, si•rā′pis, *n.* The Greek name of an Egyptian deity considered as a combination of Osiris and Apis.

Serb, sėrb, *n.* [Native form.] A native or inhabitant of Serbia.

Serbonian, sėr•bō′ni•an, *a.* An epithet applied to a celebrated morass of ancient Egypt, fabled to have swallowed up whole armies; hence, *Serbonian bog* proverbially signifies a difficult or complicated state of matters; an inextricable mess.

sere, sēr, *a.* Same as *Sear.*

serenade, ser•e•nād′, *n.* [Fr. *sérénade,* from It. *serenata,* a serenade, clear fine weather at night, from L. *serenus,* serene.] An entertainment of music given at night by a lover to his mistress under her window, or performed as a mark of esteem and good will toward distinguished persons; also a piece of music characterized by soft repose in harmony with the stillness of night.—*v.t.*—*serenaded, serenading.* To entertain with a serenade.—*v.i.* To perform serenades or nocturnal music.—**serenader,** ser•e•nā′dėr, *n.* One who serenades.

serene, se•rēn′, *a.* [L. *serenus,* serene; allied to L. *sol,* the sun, Gr. *seirinos,* hot, scorching, *Seirios,* Sirius, Skr. *surya,* the sun.] Clear or fair, and calm; placid; quiet; unruffled; undisturbed; a form of address restricted to former sovereign princes of Germany, and the members of their families.—*v.t.*—*serened, serening.* To make serene.—**serenely,** se•rēn′li, *adv.* Calmly; quietly; with unruffled temper; deliberately.—**serenity,** se•ren′i•ti, *n.* [L. *serenitas.*] The quality or condition of being serene; clearness; calmness; quietness; stillness; peace.

serf, sėrf, *n.* [Fr. *serf,* from L. *servus,* a slave. SERVE.] A villein; one of those who in the middle ages were attached to the land and transferred with it, and liable to the lowest services; a forced laborer attached to an estate, as formerly in Russia; a slave.—**serfage, serfdom, serfhood,** sėrf′ij, sėrf′dom, sėrf′hud, *n.* The state or condition of a serf.

serge, sėrj, *n.* [Fr. *serge;* origin doubtful, perhaps L. *serica,* a silken fabric. SILK.] A kind of twilled worsted cloth of inferior quality.

sergeant, sär•jent, *n.* [Also written *serjeant;* from Fr. *sergent,* O.Fr. *serjent,* originally a servant, from L. *serviens, servientis,* ppr. of *servio,* to serve. SERVE.] A noncommissioned officer in the army of the grade next above corporal; a police officer in rank next below a captain or lieutenant; formerly in England, a lawyer of the highest rank; one of the servants of the British royal household. (In the last two meanings *serjeant* is the more usual spelling.)—**sergeancy,** sär′jen•si, *n.* The office of a sergeant.—**sergeant at arms.** An officer of a court, legislature, or other formal body, whose duty is to preserve order.—**sergeant major,** in the U. S. Army, the highest noncommissioned officer who assists the commanding officers of a battalion or regiment in the clerical work and supervises personnel.—**sergeantship,** *n.* The office of a sergeant.

sericeous, si•rish′us, *a.* [L. *sericeus,* from *sericum,* silk. SILK.] Pertaining to silk; consisting of silk; silky; *bot.* covered with very soft hairs pressed close to the surface.—**sericulture,** se′ri•kul•tūr, *n.* [L. *sericum,* silk, and *cultura,* cultivation.] The breeding and treatment of silkworms.—**sericulturist,** se•ri•kul′tū•rist, *n.* A cultivator of silkworms.

series, sē′rēz, *n. sing.* and *pl.* [L. *series,* same root as *sero,* to join, to weave together (seen also in *assert, insert, exert, desert*); Gr. *seira,* a cord; Skr. *sarat,* a thread.] A continued succession of similar things, or of things bearing a similar relation to each other; an extended rank, line, or course; a sequence; a succession; *geol.* a set of strata possessing some common mineral or fossil characteristic; *chem.* a group of compounds, each containing the same radical; *arith.* and *alg.* a number of terms or quantities in succession, each of which is related to the one before it according to a certain law.—**serial,** sē′ri•al, *a.* Pertaining to a series; consisting of or constituted by a series.—*n.* A tale or other composition running through successive numbers of a periodical work; a publication issued in successive numbers; a periodical.—**serially,** sēr′i•al•li, *adv.* In a series or in regular order.—**seriate,** sē′ri•at, *a.* Arranged in a series; pertaining to a series.—**seriately,** sē′ri•at•li, *adv.* In a regular series.—**seriatim,** sē•ri•ā′tim, *adv.* [L.] In regular order; one after the other.

serious, sē′ri•us, *a.* [Fr. *sérieux*, from L. *serius*, serious, earnest.] Grave in manner or disposition; solemn; not light, gay, or volatile; really intending what is said; being in earnest; not jesting; important; weighty; not trifling; attended with danger; giving rise to apprehension; deeply impressed with the importance of religion.—**seriously,** sē′ri•us•li, *adv.* In a serious manner; earnestly; gravely; solemnly.—**seriousness,** sē′ri•us•nes, *n.* The condition or quality of being serious; gravity; solemnity; earnest attention to religious concerns.—**seriocomic, seriocomical,** sē′ri•ō•kom″ik, sē′ri•ō•kom″i•kal, *a.* Having a mixture of seriousness and comicality.

sermon, sėr′mon, *n.* [L. *sermo, sermonis*, a speech or connected discourse, from *sero*, to join together. SERIES.] A discourse delivered in public, especially by a clergyman or preacher, for the purpose of religious instruction or the inculcation of morality, and grounded on some text or passage of Scripture; a similar discourse written or printed, whether delivered or not; a homily.—*v.t.* To tutor; to lesson; to lecture.—**sermonize,** sėr′mon•īz, *v.i.*—*sermonized, sermonizing*. To preach; to discourse.—*v.t.* To preach a sermon to.—**sermonizer,** sėr′mon•ī•zėr, *n.* One who sermonizes; a preacher.

serology, se•rol′o•jē, *n.* [Prefix *sero*, from L. *serum*, and combining form *logy*, science, theory.] The science that deals with the properties and effects of serums.

serosity. See SERUM.

serotinous, si•rot′i•nus, *a.* [L. *serotinus*, from *serus*, late.] *Bot.* appearing late in a season.

serous. See SERUM.

serpent, sėr′pent, *n.* [L. *serpens, serpentis*, from *serpo*, to creep; cog. Gr. *herpō*, to creep; Skr. *sarpa*, a serpent, from *srip*, to creep.] A reptile of an extremely elongated form, without feet, and moving by muscular contractions of the body; a snake; a powerful bass musical instrument, consisting of a conical tube of wood bent in a serpentine form; *fig.* a subtle or malicious person.—*Serpent stones* or *snake stones*, popular names sometimes applied to the ammonites.—**serpentine,** sėr′pen•tīn, *a.* [L. *serpentinus*.] Pertaining to or resembling a serpent; having the qualities of a serpent; subtle; winding or turning one way and the other like a moving serpent; spiral; crooked.—*Serpentine verse*, a verse which begins and ends with the same word.—*n.* A rock, usually a dark-colored green, red, brown, or gray, with shades and spots resembling a serpent's skin; much used for the manufacture of various ornamental articles.—*v.i.*—*serpentined, serpentining*. To wind like a serpent; to meander.

serpigo, sėr•pī′go, *n.* [L.L., from L. *serpo*, to creep.] A name for ringworm or similar skin disease.—**serpiginous,** sėr•pij′i•nus, *a. Med.* applied to certain diseases that creep from one part to another.

serrate, serrated, ser′rāt, ser′rā•ted, *a.* [L. *serratus*, from *serra*, a saw.] Notched on the edge like a saw; toothed.—**serration,** ser•rā′shon, *n.* Formation in the shape of a saw.—**serrature,** ser′ra•chėr *n.* A notching in the edge of anything, like a saw.

serrulate, serrulated, se′rū•lāt, se′rū•lā•ted, *a.* [L. *serrula*, dim. of *serra*, a saw.] Finely serrate; having very minute notches.—**serrulation,** se•rū•lā′shon, *n.* A small notching; an indentation.

serry,‡ ser′i, *v.t.* [Fr. *serrer*, to press, from L. *sero*, to lock, *sera*, a bolt or bar.] To crowd; to press together.—**serried,** ser′id, *p.* and *a.* Crowded; compacted; in close order (*serried* ranks of soldiers).

Sertularia, sėr•tū•lâ′ri•a, *n.* [L. *sertum*, a garland.] The genus of *Hydrozoa* commonly called *sea firs*.—**sertularian,** sėr•tū•lâ′ri•an, *n.* A member of the sea fir order.

serum, sē′rum, *n.* [L. *serum*, whey; Gr. *oros*, whey, serum; Skr. *sâra*, water.] The fluid part of the blood, a thin, pale, transparent liquid, obtained after coagulation; the clear, watery exudate of serous membranes; serum containing antitoxin and used to prevent and treat specific infections.—*Serum treatment*, treatment by the injection of ANTIBODIES (which see); the thin part of milk separated from the curd; whey.—**serous,** sē′rus, *a.* Pertaining to serum; having the character of serum.—**serosity,** si•ros′i•ti, *n.* The state of being serous.

serval, sėr′val, *n.* An African carnivorous animal.

serve, sėrv, *v.t.*—*served, serving*. [Fr. *servir*, from L. *servio, servire*, to serve, from *servus*, a servant, a slave; closely akin to *servo*, to preserve (as in *conserve, preserve, reserve*, etc.).] To perform regular or continuous duties in behalf of; to be in the employment of, as a domestic, slave, hired assistant, etc.; to work for; to render spiritual obedience and worship to; to minister to; to wait on at table or at meals; to set or arrange on a table for a meal: generally with *up*; to conduce to; to be sufficient for; to promote; to be of use to (to *serve* one's ends); to help by good offices; to administer to the wants of; to be in the place or instead of anything to; to be in lieu of (a sofa *served* him for a bed); to regulate one's conduct in accordance with the fashion, spirit, or demands of (to *serve* the time or the hour); to treat; to requite (he *served* me ill); to satisfy; to content (nothing would *serve* them but war); to handle, manage, or work (the guns were well *served*); *naut.* to protect from friction by winding something round; *law*, to deliver or transmit to; to present in due form.—*To serve out*, to deal out or distribute in portions.—*To serve one out*, to treat one according to his deserts; to take revenge on.—*To serve one right*, to treat one as he deserves.—*To serve the turn*, to meet the emergency; to answer the purpose.—*To serve a warrant*, to read it, and to seize the person against whom it is issued.—*To serve a writ*, to read it to the defendant, or to leave an attested copy at his usual place of abode.—*To serve an office*, to discharge the duties incident to it.—*v.i.* To be or act as a servant; to perform domestic offices; to discharge the requirements of an office; to act as a soldier, seaman, etc.; to answer a purpose; to be sufficient; to be of use; to suit (when occasion *serves*); to be convenient.—**server,** sėr′vėr, *n.* One who serves; a salver or small tray.—**servant,** sėr′vant, *n.* [Fr. *servant*, from *servir*, L. *servire*, to serve; *servant* is a doublet of *sergeant*.] One who serves or does services; a person who is employed by another for menial offices or other labor, and is subject to his command; a subordinate assistant or helper: often applied distinctively to domestics or domestic servants, those who for the time being form part of a household (Mrs. Smith has four *servants*).—*Servants' hall*, the room in a house set apart for the use of the servants in common, in which they take their meals, etc.—*Your humble servant, your obedient servant*, phrases of politeness formerly used, as in closing a letter.—*Servant of servants*, one debased to the lowest condition of servitude; a title (*servus servorum*) assumed by the popes.—**service,** sėr′vis, *n.* [Fr. *service*, from L. *servitium*.] The act of serving; the performance of labor or offices for another; menial duties; employment as a servant; menial employ or capacity (to be taken into a person's *service*); assistance or kindness rendered to another; kind office (has done me many *services*); duty performed; official function; especially military or naval duty; performance of the duties of a soldier or sailor (to see much *service* abroad); usefulness; benefit caused; profession of respect uttered or sent (my *service* to you); public religious worship or ceremony; religious rites appropriate to any event or ceremony (a marriage *service*); a set of dishes or vessels for the table (a tea *service*, a *service* of plate); the duty which a tenant owes to a lord for his fee.—*Service of a writ, process*, etc., the reading of it or due delivery of it to the person to whom notice is intended to be given.—**serviceable,** sėr′vis•a•bl, *a.* Capable of rendering useful service; fit for using; useful; doing service; active; diligent.—**serviceableness,**

sėr′vis•a•bl•nes, *n.* The state of being serviceable.—**servile,** sėr′vīl, *a.* [L. *servilis.*] Pertaining to or befitting a servant or slave; slavish (*servile* fear); held in subjection; dependent; cringing; fawning; meanly submissive.—**servilely,** sėr′vīl•li, *adv.* In a servile manner; slavishly.—**servileness, servility,** sėr′vīl•nes, sėr•vil′i•ti, *n.* The state or quality of being servile; mean submission; slavishness; slavish deference.—**servitor,** sėr′vi•tėr, *n.* [L.L., from L. *servio,* to serve.] A male servant; an attendant; a retainer; formerly, in Oxford University, a student aided by college funds and doing menial duties.—**servitude,** sėr′vi•tūd, *n.* [L. *servitudo.*] The condition of a menial, underling, or slave; involuntary subjection to a master; bondage; compulsory labor, such as a criminal has to undergo as a punishment (penal *servitude*); a state of slavish dependence. ∴ *Servitude* implies either the state of a voluntary servant or that of a slave; *slavery* is a stronger term, implying involuntary and compulsory servitude.—*a.* In *Scots law,* a right of way or otherwise over another's ground or property. See EASEMENT.

service tree, sėr′vis, *n.* [A corruption of L. *sorbus,* the sorb or service tree.] A British and European tree of the pear family, yielding a hard-grained timber and a small fruit, which is only pleasant in an over-ripe condition.

serviette, sėr•vi•et′, *n.* [Fr.] A table napkin.

servile, servitude, etc. See SERVE.

servomechanism, ser″vō•mek′an•izm, *n.* [Fr. *servo,* from *servo-moteur,* from L. *servus,* slave, servant, and Fr. *moteur,* motor.] An automatic device which controls great amounts of power through a small input of power, maintaining constant performance of a mechanism, as an automatic pilot.

sesame, ses′a•mi, *n.* [Gr. *sēsamē, sēsamon,* L. *sesamum.*] An annual herbaceous plant, the seeds of which yield a bland oil of a fine quality, which will keep many years without becoming rancid.—*Open Sesame,* the charm by which the door of the robbers' dungeon, in the tale of *Ali Baba and the Forty Thieves,* flew open; hence, a specific for gaining entrance into any place, or means of exit from it.—**sesamoid,** sēs′a•moid, *a.* Resembling the seeds of sesame in form.—*Sesamoid bones,* certain small bones formed at the articulations of the great toes, and occasionally the joints of the thumbs and in other parts.

sesquialteral, ses•kwi•al′tėr•al, *a.* [L. prefix *sesqui,* one and a half, and *alter,* other.] *Math.* a term applied to a ratio where one quantity or number contains another once and a half as much more; thus the ratio 9 to 6 is *sesquialteral.*—**sesquioxide,** ses•kwi•ok′sīd, *n.* A compound of oxygen and another element in the proportion of three equivalents of oxygen to two of the other.—**sesquipedalian, sesquipedal,** ses′-kwi•pe•dā″li•an, ses•kwip′i•dal, *a.* [L. *sesquipedalis—sesqui,* and *pes, pedis,* a foot.] Containing or measuring a foot and a half: often humorously applied to long words, as translation of Horace's '*sesquipedalia verba*'.

sessile, ses′īl, *a.* [L. *sessilis,* from *sedeo, sessum,* to sit. SEDATE.] *Zool.* and *bot.* attached without any sensible projecting support, a *sessile leaf* being one without a petiole or footstalk; a *sessile flower,* one having no peduncle; a *sessile gland,* one not elevated on a stalk.

session, sesh′on, *n.* [Fr. *session,* from L. *sessio, sessionis,* from *sedeo, sessum,* to sit. SEDATE.] A sitting; the sitting of a court, academic body, council, legislature, etc., for the transaction of business; the time or term during which such body transacts business regularly without breaking up; in Scotland, the kirk session, the lowest ecclesiastical court of the Presbyterian Church; *law,* generally in *pl.,* a sitting of a justice's court, as for granting local licenses, trying minor offenses, etc.—*Sessions of the peace,* in England, the sittings of the justice of the peace or magistrate.—*Petty sessions,* in England, the meeting of two or more justices for trying minor offenses without a jury.—*Court of Session,* the supreme civil court of Scotland.—**sessional,** sesh′on•al, *a.* Relating or belonging to a session or sessions.

sesterce, ses′tėrs, *n.* [Fr. *sesterce,* L. *sestertius,* lit. what contains two and a half—*semis,* a half, and *tertius,* a third.] A Roman coin or denomination of money, originally containing two asses and a half.

sestet, ses•tet′, *n.* [It. *sestetto,* from L. *sextus,* sixth, from *sex,* six.] *Music,* a composition for six voices or six instruments; the two concluding stanzas of a sonnet, consisting of three verses each; the last six lines of a sonnet.

set, set, *v.t.*—pret. and pp. *set,* ppr. *setting.* [Causative or factitive of *sit;* A.Sax. *settan,* to set, place, appoint, etc.; Icel. *setja,* Dan. *sette,* Goth. *satjan,* G. *setzen,* to set.] To make or cause to sit; to place in a sitting, standing, or any natural posture; to place upright (to *set* a box on its end or a table on its feet); to put, place, or fix; to put in a certain place, position, or station; to make or cause to be, do, or act; to put from one state into another (to *set* a person right, to *set* things in order); to fix as regards amount or value (to *set* a price on a house); to fix or settle authoritatively or by arrangement; to appoint; to assign (to *set* an hour for a journey); to estimate or rate (to *set* advice at naught); to regulate or adjust (to *set* a timepiece); to fit to music; to plant, as distinguished from *sowing;* to fix for ornament, as in metal (a diamond *set* in a ring); to adorn, as with precious stones; to intersperse; to stud; to reduce from a dislocated or fractured state (to *set* a joint); to fix mentally; to fix with settled purpose (to *set* the heart or affections); to stake at play (*Shak.*); to embarrass; to perplex; to pose (to be hard *set*); to put in trim for use (to *set* a razor or a saw); to apply or use in action; to employ: with *to* (to *set* spurs *to* one's horse); to incite; to instigate; to spur: often with *on;* to let to a tenant; *printing,* to place in proper order, as types; to compose; to put into type (to *set* a MS.: often with *up*); to make stiff or solid; to convert into curd (to *set* milk for cheese).—*To set against,* to oppose; to set in comparison.—*To set aside,* to omit for the present; to lay out of the question; to disregard; to abrogate (to *set aside* a verdict).—*To set at defiance,* to defy; to dare to combat.—*To set at ease,* to quiet; to tranquillize.—*To set at naught,* to regard as of no value or consideration; to despise.—*To set a trap* or *snare,* to prepare and place it so as to catch prey; to lay a plan to inveigle a person.—*To set at work,* to cause to enter on work or action.—*To set down,* to place upon the ground or floor; to enter in writing; to register.—*To set eyes on,* to fix the eyes in looking on; to behold.—*To set fire to,* to apply fire to; to set on fire.—*To set forth,* to present to view or consideration; to make known fully; to show; to promulgate; to publish.—*To set in order,* to adjust or arrange; to reduce to method.—*To set much* (*little,* etc.) *by,* to regard much; to esteem greatly.—*To set off,* to adorn; to decorate; to embellish; to show to the best advantage.—*To set* a person *on,* to instigate him; to prompt him to action.—*To set one's cap at.* Under CAP.—*To set one's self against,* to resist or oppose stubbornly; to be resolute against.—*To set one's teeth,* to press them close together.—*To set on fire,* to kindle; to inflame.—*To set on foot,* to start; to set agoing.—*To set over,* to appoint or constitute as supervisor, inspector, governor, or director.—*To set right,* to correct; to put in order.—*To set sail.* See SAIL.—*To set the teeth on edge.* See EDGE.—*To set the fashion,* to establish the mode; to determine what shall be the fashion.—*To set up,* to erect; to institute; to establish; to enable to commence a new business; to utter loudly (to *set up* a loud cry); to propose (to *set up* a doctrine); to raise from depression or to a sufficient fortune.—*v.i.* To pass below the horizon; to sink; to decline; to congeal or concrete; to solidify; to have a certain direction in motion; to flow; to tend (the current *sets* westward); to point out game, as a sportsman's dog; to undertake earnestly; to apply one's self; to face one's partner in dancing.—*To set about,* to begin; to take the first steps in.—*To set forth* or *forward,* to move or march; to begin to march; to advance.—*To set in,* to begin (winter *sets in* about December); to flow toward the shore (the tide *sets in*).—*To set off,* to start; to enter on a journey.—*Offset printing,* to employ the *offset* process, using intermediary smooth, rubber-faced cylinders that receive the impression from the plate and transfer the image to the paper instead of printing from the plate, thus permitting use of a variety of paper; the transfer from one sheet to another of printing ink before it has dried.—*Set up*, *p.* and *a.* Placed, put, fixed, etc.; regular; in due form; well arranged or put together (a *set* speech or phrase); fixed in opinion; determined; firm; obstinate; established; settled; appointed (*set* forms of prayer); predetermined; fixed beforehand (a *set* purpose); fixed; immovable.—*Set scene*, in theaters, a scene where there is a good deal of arrangement for the pose.—*n.* The act of setting; a group of similar things; a group of persons associated by common interests; a setting, as in a play; *math.* elements that are identified by some common characteristic; an electronic apparatus that functions as a unit (a radio *set*); permanent change of figure caused by pressure or being retained long in one position; a turn or bent; a direction or course (the *set* of a current).—*To make a dead set*, to make a determined onset, or an importunate application.—**setoff,** *n.* That which is used to set off the appearance of anything; an ornament; a counter claim or demand; a cross debt; an equivalent; *printing*, an offset, the impression from a printed page, the ink on which is not dry, to an opposite page.—**setscrew,** *n.* A screw screwed through one part tightly upon another to bring pieces into close contact.—**setter,** set′ėr, *n.* One who or that which sets; a kind of sportsman's dog, named from its habit of *setting* or crouching when it perceives the scent of game, and which is also trained to mark game by standing.—**setting,** set′ing, *n.* The act of one who or that which sets; a sinking below the horizon; that in which something, as a jewel, is set (a diamond in a gold *setting*).—**set-to,** *n.* A sharp contest; a fight at fisticuffs; a boxing match.

seta, sē′ta, *n.* pl. **setae,** sē′tē. [L., a bristle.] A bristle or sharp hair; especially a bristle or stiff hair-like appendage of plants and animals; the stalk that supports the theca, capsule, or sporangium of mosses.—**setaceous,** si•tā′shus, *a.* Bristly; set with bristles; having the character of setae.—**setiferous,** si•tif′ėr•us, *a.* Producing or having bristles.—**setiform,** sē′ti•form, *a.* Having the form of a bristle.—**setigerous,** si•tij′ėr•us, *a.* Covered with bristles; setiferous.

seton, sē′ton, *n.* [Fr. *séton*, from L. *seta*, a bristle—hair or bristles having been originally used for the purpose.] *Surg.* a skein of silk or cotton, or similar material, passed under the skin in order to maintain an artificial tissue.

setose, sē′tōs, *a.* [L. *setosus*, from *seta*, a bristle.] *Bot.* bristly; having the surface set with bristles.

settee, set•ē′, *n.* [From *set.*] A long seat with a back to it; a large sofa-shaped seat for several persons to sit in at one time.

settee, set•ē′, *n.* [Fr. *scétie*, *sétie.*] A vessel with a long sharp prow, carrying two or three masts with lateen sails; used in the Mediterranean.

setter, etc. See SET.

settle, set′l, *n.* [A.Sax. *setl*, a seat, a stool, a settle; from *set*. Comp. L. *sella*, a seat, for *sedla*, from *sedeo*, to sit. SET, SIT.] A bench to sit on; a stool—*v.t.*—*settled*, *settling*. [From *set*; a freq. in form = A.Sax. *setlan*, to seat, to place.] To place in a fixed or permanent position; to establish or fix in any line of life, in an office, business, situation, etc.; to change from a disturbed or troubled condition to one of tranquillity; to quiet, still, calm, compose (to *settle* the mind when agitated); to clear of dregs or sediment by causing them to sink; to cause to sink to the bottom; to determine, as something which is exposed to doubt or question; to free from uncertainty or wavering; to confirm; to adjust, as something in controversy; to bring to a conclusion; to finish (to *settle* a dispute); to make secure formally or legally (to *settle* an annuity on a person); to liquidate; to pay; to square or adjust (to *settle* an account, claim); to plant with inhabitants; to people; to colonize.—*v.i.* To become fixed or permanent; to assume a lasting form or condition; to establish a residence; to take up a permanent abode; to quit an irregular and desultory for a methodical life; to enter the married state; to change from a disturbed or turbid state to the opposite; to become free from dregs by their sinking to the bottom; to sink or fall gradually; to subside, as dregs from a liquid; to become lowered, as a building, by the sinking of its foundation; to become calm; to cease from agitation; to adjust differences; to come to an agreement. —**settled,** set′ld, *p.* and *a.* Established; stable; deep-rooted; unchanging (*settled* gloom, a *settled* conviction); orderly; methodical (a *settled* life).—**settlement,** set′l•ment, *n.* The act of settling or state of being settled; establishment in life; the act of colonizing or peopling; colonization; a tract of country colonized; a colony in its earlier condition; the liquidation of a claim or account; adjustment; arrangement; a legal deed by which property is settled; right from a certain connection with a particular parish, town, or locality to maintenance there if a pauper.—**settler,** set′lėr, *n.* One who settles; one who fixes his residence in a new colony; a colonist; that which settles or decides anything definitely (*colloq.*).—**settling,** set′ling, *n.* The act of one who settles; *pl.* dregs; sediment.

seven, sev′n, *a.* [A.Sax. *seofon* = D. *zeven*, Goth. and O.H.G. *sibun*, G. *sieben*, Icel. *sjau*, Dan. *syv*, W. *saith*, Ir. *seacht*, Rus. *semj*, L. *septem*, Gr. *hepta* (for *septa*), Per. *haft*, Skr. *saptan.*] One more than six or less than eight.—*n.* This number; a group of things amounting to this number; the symbol representing this number, as 7 or vii.—**sevenfold,** sev′n•fōld, *a.* Repeated or multiplied seven times.—*adv.* Seven times as much; in the proportion of seven to one.—**seventeen,** sev′n•tēn, *a.* and *n.* Seven and ten added.—**seventeenth,** sev′n•tēnth, *a.* Next in order after the sixteenth.—*n.* The next in order after the sixteenth; one of seventeen equal parts of a whole.—**seventh,** sev′nth, *a.* Next after the sixth; being one of seven equal parts of a whole.—*n.* One next in order after the sixth; one of seven equal parts of a whole; *music*, the interval of five tones and a semitone, embracing seven degrees of the diatonic scale, as from C to B; the seventh note of the diatonic scale reckoning upward; the B of the natural scale.—**seventhly,** sev′nth•li, *adv.* In the seventh place.—**seventy,** sev′n•ti, *a.* and *n.* [A.Sax. *seofontig*—*seofon*, seven, and *tig*, ten.] Seven times ten; the number made up of seven times ten.

sever, sev′ėr, *v.t.* [O.Fr. *sevrer*, *severer*, from L. *separare*, to separate. SEPARATE.] To part or divide by violence; to separate by cutting or rending; to part from the rest by violence; to disjoin, referring to things that are distinct but united by some tie (friends *severed* by death); to disunite.—*v.i.* To suffer disjunction; to be parted or rent asunder.—**severable,** sev′ėr•a•bl, *a.* Capable of being severed.—**severance,** sev′ėr•ans, *n.* The act of severing or state of being severed; separation; partition.

several, sev′ėr•al, *a.* [O.Fr. *several*, from *severer*. SEVER.] Separate; distinct; not common to two or more: in this sense chiefly a law term; single; individual (each *several* thing); more than two, but not very many; divers: used with plural nouns.—*n.* A few separately or individually; a small number singly taken: with a plural verb.—**severally,** sev′ėr•al•li, *adv.* Separately; distinctly; each by himself.—**severalty,** sev′ėr•al•ti, *n.* A state of separation from the rest, or from all others.

severe, si•vēr′, *a.* [Fr. *sévère*, from L. *severus*, serious, severe; seen also in *persevere*, *asseverate.*] Serious or earnest in feeling or manner; sedate; grave; austere; very strict in discipline or government; not indulgent; judging or criticizing harshly; strictly regulated by rule; rigidly methodical; not allowing unnecessary or florid ornament or the like (the *severest* style of Greek architecture); afflictive; distressing; violent; extreme; intense (*severe* pain or cold); difficult to be undergone; rigorous (a *severe* test or examination).—**severely,** si•vēr′li, *adv.* In a severe manner; rigidly; strictly; rigorously; painfully.—**severeness,** si•vēr′nes, *n.* Severity.—**severity,** si•ver′i•ti, *n.* [L. *severitas.*] The quality or state of being severe; extreme strictness;

rigor; harshness; intensity; extremity; keenness; extreme coldness or inclemency; cruel treatment; sharpness of punishment; strictness.

Sèvres, Sèvres ware, se′vr, *n.* A kind of beautiful porcelain ware, manufactured at *Sèvres,* in France.

sew, sō, *v.t.* [A.Sax. *siwian, seowian,* to sew=O.H.G. *siuwan,* Goth. *siujan,* Dan. *sye,* Icel. *sýja*; cog. L. *suo,* Skr. *siv,* to sew. *Seam* is from this stem.] To unite or fasten together with a needle and thread: to make or work by needle and thread.—*To sew up,* to close or unite by sewing.—*v.i.* To practice sewing; to join things with stitches.—**sewer,** sō′ėr, *n.* One who sews.—**sewing,** sō′ing, *n.* The act of sewing; dress goods that have been sewed.—**sewing machine,** *n.* A machine for sewing.

sewage, sū′ij, *n.* [From old verb *sew,* to drain, from O.F. *essuier,* to drain, from L. *ex,* out, and *aqua,* water.] The filthy matter which passes through drains, conduits, or sewers, leading away from human habitations.—**sewer,** sū′ėr, *n.* [O.Fr. *essuier, essuyer,* a drain, a conduit.] A subterranean channel or canal formed in towns and other places to carry off superfluous water, as well as excrementitious and other matters.—**sewerage,** sū′ėr•ij, *n.* The system of sewers; also, sewage.—*Sewerage* is generally applied to the system of sewers, and *sewage* to the matter carried off.

sewer, sū′ėr, *n.* [From O.Fr. *assegier,* to seat guests.] In medieval Europe, an officer who served up a feast and placed the guests.

sex, seks, *n.* [Fr. *sexe,* from L. *sexus,* a sex, from *seco,* to cut. SECTION.] The distinction between male and female, or that property or character by which an animal is male or female; the structure of plants which corresponds to sex in animals; one or other of the divisions of males and females; by way of emphasis, womankind; the female sex: generally with *the.*—**sexless,** seks′les, *a.* Having no sex.—**sexual,** sek′shụ•al, *a.* [L. *sexualis.*] Pertaining to sex or the sexes.—*Sexual system,* a system of classification founded on the distinction of sexes in plants.—**sexually,** sek′shụ•al•li, *adv.* In a sexual manner.—**sexuality,** sek•shụ•al′i•ti, *n.* The state or quality of being distinguished by sex.

sexagenary, sek•saj′e•na•ri, *a.* [L. *sexagenarius,* from *sexaginta,* sixty, from *sex,* six.] Pertaining to the number sixty; composed of or proceeding by sixties.—*n.* A sexagenarian.—**sexagenarian,** sek′sa•je•nâ″ri•an, *n.* A person aged sixty or between sixty and seventy.—*a.* Sixty years old; sexagenary.

Sexagesima, sek•sa•jes′i•ma, *n.* [L. *sexagesimus,* sixtieth.] The second Sunday before Lent, so called as being about the sixtieth day before Easter.—**sexagesimal,** sek•sa•jes′i•mal, *a.* Sixtieth; pertaining to the number sixty.—*Sexagesimal* or *sexagenary arithmetic,* a method of computation by sixties.—*Sexagesimal fractions,* or *sexagesimals,* fractions whose denominators are sixty or its multiple.

sexennial, sek•sen′ni•al, *a.* [L. *sex,* six, and *annus,* year.] Lasting six years, or happening once in six years.—**sexennially,** sek•sen′ni•al•li, *adv.* Once in six years.

sext, sekst, *n.* [Fr. *sexte,* L. *sixtus.*] [*often cap.*] The office in the Roman Catholic Church recited at the sixth hour or noon.

sextant, seks′tant, *n.* [L. *sextans, sextantis,* a sixth part, from *sex,* six.] The sixth part of a circle contained by two radii and an arc; an improved form of quadrant, capable of measuring angles of 120° and having an arc embracing 60° of a circle; chiefly employed as a nautical instrument for measuring the altitudes of celestial objects and their angular distances.

sextet, seks•tet′, *n.* A musical piece for six voices; the second part of the sonnet formation, opposed to the octave.

sextile, seks′til, *n.* The aspect of two planets when distant from each other sixty degrees or two signs, marked *.

sextillion, seks•til′yon, *n.* [From L. *sextus,* sixth, *sex,* six, and E. *million.*] In the American and French system, a number consisting of a unit followed by 21 zeros (in Gt. Britain and Germany, by 36 zeros).

sextodecimo, seks•tō•des′i•mō, *n.* [L. *sextus decimus,* sixteenth—*sextus,* sixth, and *decimus,* tenth.] A book folded so that each sheet makes sixteen leaves; the size of the book thus folded. Usually indicated thus, 16mo (pron. as sixteen-mo).

sexton, seks′ton, *n.* [Contr. from *sacristan* (which see).] An under officer of the church who takes care of the vessels, vestments, etc., and of the church generally, to which is added the duty of digging graves.

sextuple, seks′tū•pl, *a.* [L.L. *sextuplus,* from L. *sextus,* sixth, *sex,* six, with term. *-ple.*] Sixfold; six times as much.

sexual, sexually, etc. See SEX.

shabby, shab′i, *a.* [A softened form of *scabby*; Prov. E. *shabby,* itchy, mangy, from *shab,* itch. SCAR.] Threadbare or much worn; worn till no longer respectable; wearing much-worn clothes; mean; despicable.—**shabbily,** shab′i•li, *adv.* In a shabby manner.—**shabbiness,** shab′i•nes, *n.* The quality of being shabby.—**shabby-genteel,** *a.* Retaining in present shabbiness traces of former gentility.

shackle, shak′l, *n.* [A.Sax. *scacul, sceacul,* a shackle, probably originally a loose, dangling fastening, from *scacan, sceacan,* to shake.] A fetter, handcuff, or the like that confines the limbs so as to restrain the use of them; *fig.* that which obstructs or embarrasses free action; generally in pl.—*v.t.*—*shackled, shackling.* To fetter; to tie or confine the limbs of, so as to prevent free motion; *fig.* to bind or confine so as to embarrass action.

shad, shad, *n. sing.* and *pl.* [A.Sax. *sceadd,* G. *schade,* a shad.] A fish of the herring family which inhabits the Atlantic Ocean near the mouths of rivers, and ascends them to spawn.

shaddock, shad′ok, *n.* [After Captain *Shaddock,* who first brought it to the West Indies early in the eighteenth century.] A tree and its fruit, which is a large species of orange; a native of China. A small variety is called *grapefruit.*

shade, shād, *n.* [A.Sax. *scadu, sceadu,* shade. SHADOW.] A comparative obscurity, dimness, or gloom, caused by the interception of the rays of light; something that intercepts light, heat, dust, etc.; a cover for the flame of a lamp; a cover that confines the light of a lamp within a given area; a cover for the eyes; the dark or darker part of a picture; degree or gradation of light or brightness of color; a small or scarcely perceptible degree or amount (a price a *shade* higher); a shadow (*poet.*); the soul after its separation from the body; a spirit; a ghost; hence, *the shades,* the abode of spirits; Hades. ∴ *Shade* differs from *shadow,* as it implies no particular form or definite limit; whereas a *shadow* represents in form the object which intercepts the light.—*v.t.*—*shaded, shading.* To shelter or screen from light by intercepting its rays; to shelter from the light and heat of the sun; to cover with a shade or screen that intercepts light, heat, dust, etc.; to overspread with darkness or obscurity; to obscure; to shelter; to protect; *drawing* and *painting,* to put in darker colors to show where the light is less intense; to mark with gradations of color.—**shadeless,** shād′les, *a.* Without shade.—**shady,** shā′di, *a.* Abounding with shade or shades; casting or causing shade; sheltered from the glare of light or sultry heat; dark; tricky; ignoble.—**shadily,** shā′di•li, *adv.* In a shady manner; umbrageously.—**shadiness,** shā′di•nes, *n.* The state of being shady; umbrageousness.—**shading,** shā′ding, *n.* The effect of light and shade represented in a picture.

shadoof, sha•döf′, *n.* A contrivance employed in Egypt for raising water from the Nile, consisting of a long pole supported on an upright post and weighted at one end to serve as a counterpoise, the other end having a bucket or jar attached.

shadow, shad′ō, *n.* [A.Sax. *sceadu,* a shadow, *scadu,* a shade; O.Sax. *scado,* Goth. *skadus,* D. *schaduw,* G. *schatten*; from a root *skad,* Skr. *chhad,* to cover; comp. Gr. *skotos,* darkness.] The figure of a body projected on the ground or other surface by the interception of the light; a portion of space from which light is intercepted by an opaque body (to be in *shadow*); darkness or obscurity from intercepted light; *fig.* the shelter, protection, or security afforded by someone; a dark part of a picture; anything unsubstantial or unreal, though having the appearance of reality; a spirit; a ghost; a shade; an imperfect and faint representation; adumbration; a dim bodying forth; an inseparable companion or one that follows like a shadow; a type or mystical representation; slight or faint appearance.—*The shadow of death*, the approach of death or dire calamity.—*v.t.* To overspread with obscurity or shade; to intercept light or heat from; to shade; to cloud; to darken; to throw a gloom over; to protect; to screen from danger; to mark with slight gradations of color or light; to paint in obscure colors; to represent faintly or imperfectly; to represent typically: often followed by *forth*; to follow closely; to attend on like a shadow.—**shadowless,** shad′ō•les, *a.* Having no shadow.—**shadowy,** shad′ō•i, *a.* Full of shade or shadow; causing shade; gloomy; faintly representative; unsubstantial; unreal; dimly seen; obscure; dim; indulging in fancies or dreamy imaginations.

shady. See SHADE.

shaft, shaft, *n.* [From G. *schacht*, the shaft of a mine.] A narrow deep pit made into the earth as the entrance to a coal or other mine or for its ventilation.

shaft, shaft, *n.* [A.Sax. *sceaft*, a dart, arrow, spear, pole = Icel. *skaft*, *skapt*, Dan. *skaft*, D. and G. *schaft*; lit. the thing shaped or smoothed by shaving, from A.Sax. *scafan*, to shave; comp. L. *scapus*, a shaft; Gr. *skaptron*, *skēptron*, a staff.] An arrow; a spear or dart; the columnar part of anything; the body of a column between the base and the capital; the spire of a steeple; the handle of certain tools or instruments (the *shaft* of a hammer, ax, whip, etc.); a kind of large axle, as of a flywheel or the screw or paddles of a steamer; one of the bars between a pair of which a horse is harnessed to a vehicle; a thill; the pole of a carriage.—**shafting,** shaf′ting, *n.* A system of shafts through which motion is communicated in machinery.

shag, shag, *n.* [A.Sax. *sceacga*, coarse hair; akin to Icel. *skegg*, a beard, *skaga*, to stand out, *skagi*, a promontory.] Coarse hair or nap; rough woolly hair; a kind of cloth having a long coarse nap; a kind of tobacco cut into fine shreds; the crested or green cormorant.—*a.* Hairy; shaggy. (*Shak.*)—**shaggy, shagged,** shag′i, shag′ed, *a.* Rough with long hair or wool; rough; rugged.—**shagginess,** shag′i•nes, *n.* The state of being shaggy.

shagreen, sha•grēn′, *n.* [Fr. *chagrin*, Venetian, *sagrin*, from Turk. *sagri*, Per. *saghri*, shagreen. *Chagrin* is the same word.] A species of granulated leather prepared without tanning, from horse, ass, and camel skin, or made of the skins of the shark, sea otter, seal, etc.

shah, shä, *n.* [Per., a king, a prince (hence *chess*, *check*).] A title given by European writers to the monarch of Persia, who in his own country is designated by the compound appellation of *Padishah*; a chieftain or prince.

shake, shāk, *v.t.*—pret. *shook*; pp. *shaken*; ppr. *shaking*. [A.Sax. *scacan*, *sceacan*, pret. *scóc*, pp. *scacen*; Icel. and Sw. *skaka*, to shake; allied to D. *schokken*, to shake; G. *schaukeln*, to swing. SHOCK.] To cause to move with quick vibrations; to make to tremble, quiver, or shiver; to agitate; to remove by agitating or by a jolting, jerking motion; generally with *away*, *off*, *out*, etc.; to move from firmness; to threaten to overthrow; to cause to waver or doubt; to impair the resolution of; to depress the courage of; to give a tremulous sound to; to trill (a note in music).—*To shake hands*, to clasp right hands together mutually, as by two persons at meeting and parting, or to ratify or confirm an agreement.—*To shake hands with*, sometimes to take leave of; to give up; to take leave; to part.—*To shake off the dust from the feet*, a symbolic method of renouncing solemnly all intercourse or connection.—*To shake the head*, to express disapprobation, refusal, reproach, and the like.—*v.i.* To be agitated with a waving or vibratory motion; to tremble; to shiver; to totter.—*n.* A wavering rapid motion one way and the other; a shock or concussion; tremor; *mus.* a rapid reiteration of two notes; a trill; marked by the sign (*tr.*, abbreviation of *trill*) placed over the note; a crack or fissure in timber; *pl.* a trembling fit; specifically, ague; intermittent fever.—*Shake of the hand*, a friendly clasp of another's hand.—*No great shakes*, lit. no great windfall; hence, nothing extraordinary; of little value.—**shakedown,** *n.* A temporary bed; money obtained by extortion (*Slang*).—**Shaker,** shā′kėr, *n.* Member of a celibate religious sect founded in England in the eighteenth century, so called from a style of dancing which formed part of their ceremonial. Shakerism was practiced for some time in the U.S.A., but by mid-twentieth century was virtually extinct.—**shakiness,** shā′ki•nes, *n.* State or quality of being shaky.—**shaky,** shā′ki, *a.* Loosely put together; ready to come to pieces; unsubstantial; tottering; cracked or split, as timber.

Shakespearean, Shaksperian, shak′spē′ri•an, *a.* Relating to Shakespeare.—*n.* A scholar making Shakespeare's works his special field of study.

shako, shak′ō, *n.* [Fr. *schako*, from Hung, *csákó*, a shako.] A kind of military cap somewhat resembling a truncated cone, with a peak in front.

shale, shāl, *n.* [A form of *scale*, directly from G. *schale*, a shell, a thin layer. SHELL.] A shell or husk (*Shak.*); *geol.* a species of schist or schistous clay; a clayey rock having a slaty fracture, often found in strata in coal mines; an important variety being impregnated with bitumen and yielding paraffin, while another yields alum.—*v.t.* and *i.* To peel.

shall, shal, *auxiliary*. Pres. I *shall*, thou *shalt*, he *shall*, pl. 1, 2, and 3 *shall*; imperf. *should*, *shouldest* or *shouldst*, *should*, pl. *should*. [A.Sax. *sceal*, I shall, I have to, I ought; pl. *sculon*, pret. *sceolde*, *scolde*, inf. *sculon*; Icel. and Dan. *skal*, D. *zal*, G. *soll*, literal meaning seen in Goth. *skulan*, to owe, to have to pay.] In the first persons singular and plural it forms part of the future tense and future perfect, and simply foretells or declares what is to take place = am to, are to (I *shall* go, we *shall* go); in the second and third persons it implies control or authority on the part of the speaker, and is used to express a promise, command, or determination (you *shall* go, he *shall* go). Interrogatively, *shall* I go? *shall* we go? *shall* he go? *shall* they go? ask for direction or refer the matter to the determination of the person asked; *shall* you go? asks for information merely as to the future.—After *if*, etc., *shall*, in all persons, expresses simple futurity.—*Should*, though in form the past of *shall*, is not used to express simple past futurity unless in the indirect speech (I said I *should* go); it is very commonly used to express present as well as past duty or obligation (you *should* go, have gone).—It is also used to express a merely hypothetical case or a contingent future event, standing in the same relation to *would* that *shall* does to *will* (I *should* be glad if you *would* come).—Also often used in a modest way to soften a statement (I *should* think so).—*Shall* and *will* are often confounded by inaccurate speakers or writers. See WILL.

shalloon, sha•lön′, *n.* [Fr. *chalon*, a woolen stuff, said to be from *Châlons*, in France.] A slight woolen stuff.

shallop, shal′op, *n.* [Fr. *chaloupe*, a form of D. *sloep*, E. *sloop*.] A large boat with two masts, rigged like a schooner; a small light vessel with a small mainmast and foremast, with lugsails.

shallot, sha•lot′, *n.* [O.Fr. *eschalote*, from *Ascalon*.] A plant of the onion family having mild-flavored, clustered bulbs, and used in cooking and pickling; scallion.

shallow, shal′ō, *a.* [Same word as Icel. *skjálgr*, wry, oblique, the water being shallow where the beach sinks obliquely downward; comp. also *shoal*, *shelf*.] Not deep; having the bottom at no great distance from the surface (*shallow* water); having sides not raised much above the bottom (a *shallow* trough); not intellectually deep; not profound; superficial; silly.—*n.* A place where the water is not deep; a shoal.—*v.t.* To make shallow.—**shallowly,** shal′ō•li, *adv.* In a shallow manner; superficially.—**shallowness,** shal′ō•nes, *n.* The state or quality of being shallow; superficialness of intellect.

shalt, shalt, second person singular of *shall*: now only in poetic or solemn use.

sham, sham, *n.* [A form of *shame*; comp. Prov.E. *sham*, shame; *sham*, to blush for shame.] One who or that which deceives expectation; a trick or fraud; something counterfeit; an imposture.—*a.* False; counterfeit; pretended.—*v.t. shammed, shamming.* To make a pretense of in order to deceive; to feign (to *sham* illness).—*v.i.* To pretend; to make false pretenses.—**shammer,** sham′ėr, *n.* One that shams; an impostor.

shamanism, shā′man•izm, *n.* [Hind. and Per. *shaman*, an idolater.] An idolatrous religion of northern Asia and elsewhere, consisting mainly in a belief in sorcery, and in demons who require to be propitiated by sacrifices and rites; a sort of fetishism.—**shamanist,** shā′man•ist, *n.* A believer in shamanism.—**shaman,** shā′man, *n.* A priest or conjurer among those who profess shamanism.

shamble, sham′bl, *v.i.—shambled, shambling.* [A form of *scamble* (which see).] To walk awkwardly and unsteadily, as if the knees were weak.

shambles, sham′bls, *n.* pl. [A.Sax. *scamel*, *sceamol*, a bench, from L. *scammellum.*] A slaughterhouse; a place of great distruction or disorder.

shame, shām, *n.* [A.Sax. *sceamu*, *scamu*=Icel. *skamm*, *skömm*, Dan. and Sw. *skam*, G. *scham*, O.H.G. *scama*, shame; probably from root meaning to cover. Hence *sham.*] A painful sensation excited by the exposure of that which nature or modesty prompts us to conceal, or by a consciousness of guilt, or of having done something which injures reputation; the cause or reason of shame; reproach; disgrace; contempt.—*For shame!* an interjectional phrase signifying you should be ashamed; shame on you!—*To put to shame*, to cause to feel shame; to inflict shame or dishonor on.—*v.t. shamed, shaming.* To make ashamed; to cause to feel shame; to cover with reproach or ignominy.—*v.i.* To be ashamed.—**shamefaced,** shām′fāst, *a.* [Corrupted from *shamefast*, like *steadfast.*] Easily confused or put out of countenance; bashful; modest.—**shamefacedly,** shām′fāst•li, *adv.* Bashfully; with excessive modesty.—**shamefacedness,** shām′fāst•nes, *n.*—**shameful,** shām′ful, *a.* Bringing shame or disgrace; scandalous; disgraceful; raising shame in others; indecent.—**shamefully,** shām′ful•li, *adv.* In a shameful manner; disgracefully.—**shamefulness,** shām′ful•nes, *n.* The state or quality of being shameful; disgrace.—**shameless,** shām′les, *a.* Wanting modesty; brazen.—**shamelessly,** shām′les•li, *adv.*—**shamelessness,** shām′les•nes, *n.*

shammy, sham′i, *n.* [A corruption of *chamois*, the animal and its prepared skin.] The chamois; a kind of soft leather originally prepared from the skin of this animal, but now commonly made of the skin of the goat and sheep.

shampoo, sham•pö′, *v.t.* [Hind. *chāmpnā.*] To rub and squeeze the whole surface of the body of, stretching the limbs and joints, in connection with the hot bath, a practice introduced from the East; to rub the head vigorously with soap and water or some special cleansing preparation.—*n.* The act or operation of shampooing.

shamrock, sham′rok, *n.* [Ir. *seamrog*, Gael. *seamrag*, trefoil, white clover.] A plant regarded as the national emblem of Ireland; generally supposed to be white clover or else wood sorrel.

shandrydan, shan′dri•dan, *n.* A one-horse Irish conveyance.

shandygaff, shan′di•gaf, *n.* A mixture of beer and ginger beer or lemonade.

shank, shangk, *n.* [A.Sax. *scanca*, *sceanca*, the bone of the leg, the leg, *earm-scanca*, the armbone; Dan. and Sw. *skank*; G. and D. *schenkel*, the shank; akin perhaps *shin.*] The whole leg, or the part from the knee to the ankle; the tibia or shinbone; the part of the foreleg of a horse between the knee and the fetlock; that part of a tool or other thing which connects the acting part with a handle; the stem of an anchor connecting the arms and the stock.—*v.i.* In *bot.* to be affected with disease of the footstalk; to fall by decay of the footstalk: often with *off.*

shanny, shan′i, *n.* [Origin unknown.] A small fish allied to the blenny.

shan't, shänt. A colloquial contraction of *shall not.*

shanty, shan′ti, *n.* [Ir. *sean*, old, and *tig*, a house.] A hut or mean dwelling; a slight temporary building.

shape, shāp, *v.t.*—pret. *shaped*; pp. *shaped* or *shapen*; ppr. *shaping.* [A.Sax. *sceapan*, *scapan*=Goth. *skapjan*, Icel. *skapa*, Dan. *skabe*, O.H.G. *scafan*, G. *schaffen*, to shape, form, create; akin perhaps *shave.*] To form or create; to make; to mold or make into a particular form; to give form or figure to; to adapt to a purpose; to suit; to conceive or conjure up.—*v.i.* To square; to suit; to be adjusted.—*n.* External appearance of a body as determined by outlines or contours; make; figure; form; that which has form or figure; an appearance; a being; a pattern to be followed; a model; a mold; external manifestation of thought in words or action; *cookery*, a dish made of blanc-mange, rice, cornstarch, etc., which receives a particular form.—**shapeless,** shāp′les, *a.* Destitute of regular form; wanting symmetry of dimensions.—**shapelessness,** shāp′les•nes, *n.* The state of being shapeless.—**shapeliness,** shāp′li•nes, *n.* The state of being shapely.—**shapely,** shāp′li, *a.* Well formed; symmetrical.

shard, shärd, *n.* [A.Sax. *sceard*, from *sceran*, to shear. SHARE, SHEAR.] A broken piece of an earthen vessel; a potsherd; a fragment in general; the wingcase of a beetle; the leaves of the artichoke and some other vegetables whitened or blanched.

share, shâr, *n.* [A.Sax. *scearu*, a portion, lit. a *shearing*; *scear*, *scaer*, that which shears or divides, the share of a plow, both from *sceran*, to cut. Akin *sheer*, *shire*, *shore*, *short*, *skirt.* SHEAR.] A certain allotted quantity; a part bestowed; a portion; a part or portion of a thing owned by a number in common (*shares* in a bank); the iron blade of a plow which cuts the bottom of the furrow slice; a plowshare.—*v.t.—shared, sharing.* To divide in portions; to part among two or more; to partake or enjoy with others; to seize and possess jointly or in common.—*v.i.* To have part; to get one's portion; to be a sharer.—**sharecropper,** *n.* A tenant farmer who shares his crops with the owner of the land.—**sharer,** shâ′rėr, *n.* One who shares; one who participates in anything with another.

shark, shärk, *n.* [Origin uncertain; comp. D. *schrok*, a glutton, a greedy fellow.] A voracious carnivorous marine fish of which there are many species; a greedy, artful fellow; a sharper; a cheat.—*v.i.* To play the petty thief; to swindle.—*v.t.* To pick up hastily, slyly, or thievishly; with *up.*

sharp, shärp, *a.* [A.Sax. *scearp*, from the root of *scrape*, and perhaps of *shear*; L.G. *scharp*, D. *scherp*, Icel. *skarpr.* G. *scharf*, sharp.] Having a very thin edge or fine point; not blunt; having a keen cutting edge; pointed; peaked; bent at or forming an acute angle; acute of mind; quick to discern or distinguish; ingenious; shrewd; subtle; keen as regards the organs of sense; quick of sight; vigilant; attentive; affecting the organs of taste like fine points; sour; acid; acrid; piercing to the ear; penetrating; shrill; acrimonious; severe; sarcastic; cutting (a *sharp* rebuke); severely rigid; severe; eager for food; feeling the calls of hunger; fierce; fiery; violent (a *sharp* contest); afflicting, distressing, or painful; biting; piercing (*sharp* frost); gritty (*sharp* sand) emaciated (a *sharp* visage); keenly alive to one's own interest; barely honest; *phonetics*, applied to a sound pronounced or uttered with breath and not with voice; surd; not sonant (the *sharp* mutes in *p*, *t*, *k*); *mus.* raised a semitone; too high; so high as to be out of tune or above true pitch.—*n. Mus.* a note artificially raised a semitone, marked by the sign (♯); the sign itself; *pl.* the hard parts of wheat which require grinding a second time.—*v.t.* To make sharp; to sharpen.—*adv.* Sharply; exactly; to the moment; not a minute behind.—**sharpen,** shär′pn, *v.t.* To make sharp or sharper; to whet; to make more eager, active, intense, ingenious, etc.; to make more eager for any gratification; *mus.* to raise a semitone, or a little above the true pitch.—*v.i.* To grow or become sharp.—**sharper,** shär′pėr, *n.* A tricky fellow; a cheat; one who lives by cheating.—**sharply,** shärp′li, *adv.* In a sharp or keen manner; severely; rigorously; acrimoniously; keenly; violently; vehemently; with keen perception; wittily; abruptly; steeply.—**sharpness,** shärp′nes, *n.* The state or quality of being sharp; keenness of edge or point; pungency; acidity; keenness of appetite; severity of pain or affliction; severity of language; acuteness of intellect; quickness of sense or perception; keenness; severity (the *sharpness* of the air); keenness in transacting business; equivocal honesty.—**sharp-set,** *a.* Eager in appetite; affected by keen hunger.—**sharp-shooter,** *n.* A soldier or other person skilled in shooting with exactness.—**sharp-sighted,** *a.* Having quick sight; having acute discernment.—**sharp-witted,** *a.* Having the mental faculties acute.

Shasta daisy, shas•ta dā′zi, *n. Chrysanthemum maximum,* a large-flowered species of the common or oxeye daisy.

shatter, shat′ėr, *v.t.* [A softened form of *scatter;* to *shatter* is to smash into small pieces that scatter or fly apart.] To break at once into many pieces; to dash into splinters; to break up violently; to overthrow (a government, a person's intellect). —*v.i.* To be broken into fragments. —*n.* A fragment of many into which anything is broken.

shave, shāv, *v.t.*—pret. *shaved;* pp. *shaved* or *shaven;* ppr. *shaving.* [A.Sax. *sceafan,* to shave, scrape, smooth= Icel. *skafa,* Dan. *skave,* D. *schaaven,* Goth. *skaban,* G. *schaben;* same root as Gr. *skaptō,* to dig; L. *scabo,* to scrape.] To pare off from the surface of a body by a razor or other edged instrument; to pare close; to remove the hair from by a razor or other sharp instrument; to skim along or near the surface of; to sweep along; to oppress by extortion; to fleece.—*v.i.* To use the razor.—*n.* A cutting off of the beard; a thin slice or shaving; the act of passing so closely as almost to graze; an exceedingly narrow miss or escape (*colloq.*).—**shaver,** shā′vėr, *n.* One who shaves; one who is exacting and close in bargains or a sharp dealer; one who fleeces; a pillager; a youngster; a boy (*colloq.*).—**shavetail,** *n.* A newly commissioned second lieutenant.—**shaving,** shā′ving, *n.* The act of one who shaves; a thin slice pared off with a plane or other cutting instrument.

shawl, shạl, *n.* [Fr. *châle,* from Ar. and Per. *shâl,* a shawl.] An article of dress of various textures, usually of a square or oblong shape, worn by persons of both sexes in the East, but in the West chiefly by females as a loose body or shoulder covering. —*v.t.* To cover with a shawl.

shawm, shạm, *n.* [O.Fr. *chalemel,* Fr. *chalumeau,* a dim. of L. *calamus,* a reed, a reed pipe.] An old wind instrument similar in form to the clarinet.

she, shē, *pron.*—possessive and dative *her,* objective *her;* pl. *they, their, them.* [A.Sax. *seo,* the, that, the nom. fem. of the def. art.=G. *sie,* D. *zij,* Icel. *sjá.*] The nominative feminine of the pronoun of the third person; occasionally used as a noun; used also as a prefix denoting of the female sex (*she*-bear, *she*-cat).

sheaf, shēf, *n.* pl. **sheaves,** shēvz. [A.Sax. *scēaf,* a sheaf=L.G. *skof, schof,* D. *schoof,* Icel. *skauf,* G. *schaub;* from stem of *shove.*] A quantity of the stalks of wheat, rye, oats, or other plants, bound together; anything comparable to a sheaf of grain; a bundle of things tied together; a quiver full of arrows; a *sheaf catalogue,* a looseleaf catalogue.—*v.t.* To collect and bind; to make sheaves of.

shear, shēr, *v.t.*—pret. *sheared* or *shorn;* pp. *sheared* or shorn; pp. *shearing.* [A.Sax. *sceran,* to shear, to divide=D. *scheeren,* Icel. *skera,* Dan. *skjaere,* G. *scheren,* to shear; from a root which appears without the initial *s* in Gr. *keirō,* Skr. *kar,* to cut. Akin *share, sheer, shire, shore, short.*] To cut or clip the wool from; to cut the nap from (to *shear* cloth); to separate by shears; to cut or clip from a surface; *fig.* to strip of property; to fleece; to cut with a sickle (*Scotch*).—*v.i.* To cut; to penetrate by cutting.—**shearer,** shēr′ėr, *n.* One that shears.—**shearing stress,** *n.* That form of stress which tends to make one part of a body slide over the adjacent part.—**shears,** shērz, *n. pl.* An instrument consisting of two movable blades with bevel edges, used for cutting cloth and other substances by interception between the two blades; something in the form of the blades of shears, as an apparatus for raising heavy weights. SHEER.—**shearwater,** *n.* The name of several marine birds belonging to the petrel family, which skim over the waves.

sheatfish, shēt′fish, *n.* Same as *Silurus.*

sheath, shēth, *n.* [A.Sax. *scaeth*=D. and L.G. *schede,* Dan. *skede,* Icel. *skeithir* (pl.), G. *scheide,* a sheath; akin to *shed,* A.Sax. *sceádan,* to divide.] A case for the reception of a sword or other long and slender instrument; a scabbard; any somewhat similar covering; a petiole or leaf that embraces the branch from which it springs; the wing case of an insect.—**sheathe,** shēTH, *v.t.*—*sheathed, sheathing.* To put into a sheath or scabbard; to cover with a sheath or case; to protect by a casing or covering, as of copper (to *sheathe* a ship).—*To sheathe the sword* (*fig.*), to put an end to war or enmity; to make peace.—**sheather,** shē′THėr, *n.* One who sheathes.—**sheathing,** shē′THing, *n.* The act of one who sheathes; that which sheathes; the covering of copper, or an alloy containing copper, to protect a wooden ship's bottom.

sheave, shēv, *n.* [Same as O.D. *schijve,* D. *schijf,* Icel. *skifa,* Dan. *skive,* G. *scheibe,* a slice, a disc; akin to *schift.*] A grooved wheel in a block, mast, yard, etc., on which a rope works; the wheel of a pulley; a sliding scutcheon for covering a keyhole.

shebeen, shi•bēn′, *n.* [Irish.] An Irish smuggler's hut; a low public house; an unlicensed house where excisable liquors are sold.

shed, shed, *v.t.*—pret. and pp. *shed;* ppr. *shedding.* [A.Sax. *sceádan,* to separate, to disperse; G. *scheiden,* Goth. *skaidan,* to part, to separate; allied to L. *scindo,* to cut.] To let flow out; to let fall in drops (to *shed* tears, to *shed* blood); to cast or throw off, as a natural covering (to *shed* the leaves); to emit or give out (flowers *shed* fragrance); to cause to flow off without penetrating (a sloping roof *sheds* the rain); to divide; to cast off or part with, as the hair.—*v.i.* To let fall seed, a covering or envelope, etc.—*n.* A parting of the streams of a district; a watershed; *weaving,* the interstice between the different parts of the warp of a loom through which the shuttle passes.—**shedder,** shed′ėr, *n.* One who sheds.—**shedding,** shed′ing, *n.* The act of one that sheds; that which is shed or cast off; a parting or branching off.

shed, shed, *n.* [Perhaps originally a sloping roof or penthouse to *shed* off the rain.] A penthouse or covering of boards, etc., for shelter; a poor house or hovel; a hut; a large open structure for the temporary storage of goods, etc.

sheen, shēn, *a.* [A.Sax. *scíne, scóne,* bright, beautiful, akin to G. *schōn,* beautiful.] Bright; shining; glittering; showy. (*Poet.*)—*n.* Brightness; splendor.—**sheeny,** shē′ni, *a.* Bright; shining; fair.

sheep, shēp, *n. sing.* and *pl.* [A.Sax. *sceáp, scép,* sing. and pl.; L.G. and D. *schaap,* G. *schaf,* a sheep.] A ruminant animal nearly allied to the goat, and of great use to man both for its wool and its flesh; a silly fellow, the sheep being regarded as a stupid animal; leather prepared from sheepskin.—**sheepcot, sheepcote,** shēp′kot, shēp′kōt, *n.* A small enclosure for sheep; the cottage of a shepherd (*Shak.*).—**sheep-dip,** *n.* A sheep wash.—**sheep dog,** *n.* A dog for tending sheep; a collie.—**sheepfold,** shēp′fōld, *n.* A fold or pen for sheep.—**sheepish,** shēp′ish, *a.* Like a sheep; foolishly bashful; overmodest; diffident.—**sheepishly,** shēp′ish•li, *adv.* In a sheepish manner.—**sheepishness,** shēp′ish•nes, *n.* The quality of being sheepish.—**sheep's eye,** *n.* A modest, diffident look; a wishful glance; a leer.—*To cast a sheep's eye,* to direct a wishful or leering glance.—**sheepshearer,** *n.* One that shears the wool from sheep. —**sheepshearing,** *n.* The act or the occasion of shearing sheep.—**sheepskin,** *n.* The skin of a sheep, or leather prepared from it.—**sheep tick,** *n.* A dipterous insect parasitic on sheep, the blood of which it sucks.—**sheepwalk,** *n.* A tract of some extent where sheep feed.

sheer, shēr, *a.* [A.Sax. *scir,* pure, clear, bright; Icel. *skirr, skaer,* bright, clear; Goth. *skeirs,* clear, evident; G. *schier,* free from knots; probably from root of *shine.*] Pure or clear (*Shak.*)‡; simple; mere;

downright (*sheer* falsehood or ignorance); straight up and down; perpendicular; precipitous.

sheer, shēr, *v.i.* [A form of *shear*; so D. and G. *scheren*, to shear and to sheer.] To deviate from the line of the proper course; to slip or move aside: said especially of a ship.—*To sheer alongside*, to come gently alongside.—*To sheer off*, to move off or away.—*n.* The curve which the line of ports or of the deck presents to the eye when viewing the side of a ship; the sheer-strake of a vessel.

sheet, shēt, *n.* [A.Sax. *scéte*, a sheet, a flap, also *sceát*, a nook, a projecting corner, part, region, from *sceótan*, to shoot, the root-meaning being something shot out or extended. SHOOT.] A broad, large, thin piece of anything as paper, linen, iron, lead, glass, etc.; a large piece of linen or cotton cloth forming part of a set of bedclothes; a broad piece of paper, either unfolded as it comes from the manufacturer, or folded into pages; a piece of writing paper folded in two leaves; anything expanded; a broad expanse or surface (a *sheet* of water or of ice); *naut.* a rope fastened to the lower corner of a sail to extend and retain it in a particular situation.—*Three sheets in the wind*, tipsy; intoxicated.—*Sheet* is often used in composition to denote that the substance to the name of which it is prefixed is in the form of sheets or thin plates; as *sheet*-lead, *sheet*-glass, etc.—*v.t.* To furnish with sheets; to fold in a sheet; to cover as with a sheet.—**sheet anchor,** *n.* [That is, the anchor *shot*, or thrown out for preservation.] The largest anchor of a ship, which is shot out in extreme danger; *fig.* the chief support; the last refuge for safety.—**sheet glass,** *n.* A kind of crown glass blown at first in the form of a cylinder, which is afterward opened out to form a sheet.—**sheeting,** shēt'ing, *n.* Cloth for sheets.—**sheet lightning,** *n.* Lightning appearing in wide expanded flashes.

sheik, shēk or shāk, *n.* [Ar., an old man, an elder.] A title of dignity properly belonging to the chiefs of the Arabic tribes or clans, but now widely used among Moslems as a title of respect or reverence.

shekel, shek'el, *n.* [Heb., from *shakal*, to weigh.] An ancient weight and coin among the Jews: the weight probably equaled 250 grains Troy.

Shekinah, she•kī'na, *n.* [Heb. *shekinah*, from *shakan*, to rest.] The Jewish name for the symbol of the divine presence, which rested in the shape of a cloud or visible light over the mercy seat.

sheldrake, shel'drāk, *n.* [From *shield*, O.E. *sheld*, and *drake*, there being a somewhat shield-shaped chestnut patch on the breast.] A name of two species of European ducks, handsome birds that make their nests in rabbit burrows.

shelf, shelf, *n.* pl. **shelves,** shelvz. [A.Sax. *scelfe*, *scylfe*, a shelf; Icel. *skjálf*, a bench; comp. Sc. *skelb*, *skelve*, a splinter, a thin slice; akin to *shell*, *shale*, *scale*.] A board or platform of boards fixed horizontally to a wall for holding vessels, books, etc.; a ledge; a projecting ledge of rocks; a ledge of rocks in the sea; a shoal.—*To put* or *lay on the shelf*, to put aside or out of use; to lay aside, as from duty or active service.—*v.t.* To place on a shelf; to shelve.—**shelve,** shelv, *v.t.*—*shelved*, *shelving*. To place on a shelf; hence, to put aside out of active employment, or out of use; to dismiss; to furnish with shelves.—*v.i.* To slope, like a shelf or sandbank; to incline; to be sloping.—**shelving,** shel'ving, *p.* and *a.* Inclining; sloping; having declivity. —*n.* The shelves of a room, shop, etc., collectively.

shell, shel, *n.* [A.Sax. *scel*, *scell*=Icel. *skel*, D. *schel*, G. *schale*, husk, shell, peel; same root as *shale*, *scale*.] A hard outside covering, particularly that serving as a natural protection in certain plants and animals; the hard outside part of a nut; the hard covering or external skeleton of many invertebrate animals, as the crab, the oyster, etc.; the hard covering of some vertebrates, as the armadillo, tortoise, etc.; a carapace; the outside and calcareous layer of an egg; any outside framework; any slight hollow structure; a thin interior casket enclosed by a more substantial one which is called a vault; the outside plates of a boiler; a hollow projectile containing a bursting charge, which is exploded by a time or percussion fuse; a bomb. *Common* shells contain a charge of powder only. *High-explosive* shells are charged with *lyddite* or some similar substance, and act with tremendous power. *Armor-piercing* shells are used against armored ships. See also *Shrapnel*; in *magnetism*, a thin lamina, either plane or curved, magnetized in directions everywhere normal to its surface.—*v.t.* To strip or break off the shell of; to take out of the shell; to throw bombshells into, upon, or among; to bombard (to *shell* a fort, a town, etc.).—*v.i.* To fall off, as a shell, crust, or exterior coat; to cast the shell.—**shellfish,** *n. sing.* and *pl.* A mollusk or a crustacean, whose external covering consists of a shell, as oysters, crabs, etc.—**shell jacket,** *n.* An undress military jacket reaching only to the waist.—**shellac, shell-lac,** shel•lak', *n.* Seed lac melted and formed into thin cakes; a varnish made from this material. See LAC.—**shellproof,** *a.* Proof against shells; impenetrable by shells; bombproof. —**shell shock,** *n.* Neurosis caused by shellfire.—**shelly,** shel'i, *a.* Abounding with shells; covered with shells; consisting of a shell or shells.

shellac, she•lak', *n.* [*Shell* and *lac*, a resin.] A clear or yellowish wood finish prepared from lac dissolved in alcohol.—*v.t.*—*shellacked*,*shellacking*. To treat or cover with shellac.

shelter, shel'tėr, *n.* [Related to A.Sax. *scild*, a shield.] That which covers or defends from injury or annoyance; a protection; a refuge; a position affording cover or protection; a safe place; security.—*v.t.* To provide shelter for; to cover from violence, injury, annoyance, or attack; to protect; to place under cover; *refl.* to betake one's self to cover or a safe place.—*v.i.* To take shelter.—**shelterless,** shel'tėr•les, *a.* Destitute of shelter.

shelty, sheltie, shel'ti, *n.* A small strong horse from *Shetland*.

shelve. See SHELF.

Shemite, shem'īt, *n.* [SEMITE.] A descendant of Shem.—**Shemitic,** shem•it'ik, *a.* Pertaining to Shem; Semitic.

Sheol, shē'ol, *n.* A Hebrew word in the Old Testament, rendered by the King James Version, grave, hell, or pit.

shepherd, shep'ėrd, *n.* [A.Sax. *sceáp-hyrde*=*sheep-herd*.] A man employed in tending sheep in the pasture; one who exercises spiritual care over a community; a pastor.—*Shepherd kings*, the chiefs of a nomadic race from the East who conquered and ruled in Egypt in early times.—*Shepherd's crook*, a long staff having its upper end curved so as to form a hook, used by shepherds.—*Shepherd's dog*, a variety of dog employed by shepherds to assist them in looking after their flocks; a collie.—*Shepherd's* (or *shepherd*) *tartan*, a small black-and white-check pattern in cloth; cloth woven in this pattern. —**shepherdess,** shep'ėr•des, *n.* A woman that tends sheep.—**shepherd's-purse,** *n.* A common weed of worldwide distribution, having small white flowers, and small somewhat heart-shaped pods.

sherardizing, sher″ard•īz'ing, *n.* [After *Sherard* Cowper-Coles, the inventor.] A process of galvanizing articles by heating them in closed retorts with zinc dust.

sherbet, shėr'bet, *n.* [Ar. *sharbat*, from *sharaba*, to drink; akin *sirup*.] A favorite drink in the East, made of fruit juices, sweetened, and now usually frozen.

sherif, shereef, she•rēf', *n.* [Ar.] A descendant of Mohammed through his daughter Fatima and Hassan Ibn Ali; a prince; the chief magistrate of Mecca.

sheriff, sher'if, *n.* [A.Sax. *scire-geréfa*, a shire-reeve. SHIRE, REEVE.] The chief law enforcement officer of a county, usually elected for a term of years, who, with his appointed staff of deputy *sheriffs*, maintains law and order, executes mandates of the county court, maintains the jail and has custody of prisoners therein, and summons jurors to court sessions. In England, the chief officer of the crown in every county, whose duties are mainly honorary; in Scotland, the chief judge of a county, having under him one or more sheriffs-substitute.

sherry, sher'i, *n.* A species of wine, so called from *Xeres* in Spain, where it is made.—**sherry cobbler,** *n.* Sherry and fruit juices with iced water.

Shetland pony, shet'land pō'ni, *n.* A very small, hardy breed of pony originally bred in the Shetland Islands.

shew, shō. See SHOW.

shewbread, showbread, shō'bred, *n.* Unleavened bread which the Jewish priest placed before the Lord. (*Bible.*)

shiah, *n.* See SHIITE.

shibboleth, shib'o•leth, *n.* [Heb.] A word made the test to distinguish the Ephraimites from the Gileadites (Judg. xii); hence, the watchword of any party; a pet phrase of a party; a party cry.

shield, shēld, *n.* [A.Sax. *scild, scyld,* a shield, protection; Goth. *skildus,* Icel. *skjöldr,* G. *schild;* akin *shelter.*] A broad piece of defensive armor carried on the arm; a buckler, used in war for the protection of the body; anything that protects or defends; defense; protection; the person that defends or protects; *her.* the escutcheon or field on which are placed the bearings in coats of arms; *bot.* an apothecium.—*v.t.* To cover, as with a shield; to cover or protect from danger or anything hurtful or disagreeable, as a rubberized apron worn to *shield* the clothing; to defend; to protect.

shieling, shēl'ing, *n.* [From Icel. *skjól,* a shelter.] A hut for shepherds or for fishermen, etc.; a shed for sheltering sheep during the night.

shift, shift, *v.t.* [A.Sax. *scyftan,* to divide, to drive away=Dan. *skifte,* Icel. *skipta,* to divide, change, shift; akin to *shive, sheave,* or perhaps to *shove.*] To transfer from one place or position to another; to remove; to change; to substitute other clothes for; to dress in fresh clothes.—*v.i.* To change; to pass into a different form, state, or the like; to change place, position, or direction; to change dress, particularly the under garments; to resort to expedients; to adopt some course in a case of difficulty; to contrive.—*To shift about,* to turn quite round to a contrary side or opposite point; to vacillate.—*n.* A change, a substitution of one thing for another; an expedient tried in difficulty; a contrivance; a resource; one thing tried when another fails; a mean or base refuge or resort; an artifice; a woman's under garment; a chemise; a squad of men to take a spell or turn of work at stated intervals; the working time of a squad or relay of men; the spell of work; *mus.* a complete change of four notes by changing the position of the left hand in violin playing.—*To make shift,* or *to make a shift,* to contrive; to find ways and means.—**shifter,** shif'tėr, *n.* One who shifts (a scene-*shifter*); one who practices artifice.—**shiftiness,** shif'ti•nes, *n.* The quality of being shifty.—**shiftless,** shift'les, *a.* Destitute of expedients; not resorting to successful expedients.—**shiftlessness,** shift'les•nes, *n.* A state of being shiftless.—**shifty,** shif'ti, *a.* Full of shifts; fertile in expedients; especially fertile in evasions; given to tricks and artifices.

Shiite, Shiah, shē'īt, shē'a, *n.* [Ar. *shiah,* a multitude following one another.] A member of one of the two great sects into which Mohammedans are divided, the other sect being the Sunnites or Sunnis. They consider Ali as being the only rightful successor of Mohammed.

shillelagh, shillalah, shi•lā'le, shi•lā'la, *n.* [From *Shillelagh,* a barony in Wicklow famous for its oaks.] An Irish name for an oaken sapling or other stick used as a cudgel.

shilling, shil'ing, *n.* [A.Sax. *scylling*=O.Fris., O.Sax., Dan., and Sw. *skilling,* Goth. *skilliggs,* G. *schilling.*] A British coin equal to twelve pennies, or to one-twentieth of a pound sterling.

shilly-shally, shil'i•shal•i, *v.i.* [A reduplication of *shall I?* and equal to shall I or shall I not?] To act in an irresolute or undecided manner; to hesitate.—*n.* Foolish trifling; irresolution.

shimmer, shim'ėr, *v.i.* [A.Sax. *scimrian;* freq. of *scimian,* to gleam; Dan. *skimre,* G. *schimmern,* to gleam.] To emit a tremulous light; to gleam; to glisten.—*n.* A tremulous gleam or glistening.

shimmy, shimmey, shim'i, *n.* A dance in which the muscles are made to quiver; short for chemise.—*v.i.* To shake and quiver, as in the dance, or in vibration of the front wheels of an auto.

shin, shin, *n.* [A.Sax. *scin, scina,* the shin; D. *scheen,* the shin; Dan. *skinne,* the shin, a splint; G. *schiene,* a splint of wood, *schienbein,* the shinbone.] The forepart of the leg between the ankle and the knee, particularly of the human leg.—*v.i.* and *t.*—*shinned, shinning.* To climb a tree by means of the hands and legs alone.—**shinbone,** *n.* The bone of the shin; the tibia.

shindig, shin'dig, *n.* A merry, festive occasion, usually with dancing, sometimes tending to be riotous. (*Slang.*)

shindy, shin'di, *n.* A row; a quarrel. (*Slang.*)

shine, shīn, *v.i.*—*shone, shining.* [A. Sax. *scinan*=D. *schijnen,* Icel. *skina,* Dan. *skinne,* Goth. *skeinan,* G. *scheinen,* to shine; same root as in *shimmer, sheer.*] To emit rays of light; to give light; to beam with steady radiance; to exhibit brightness or splendor; to glitter or be brilliant; to be splendid or beautiful (to *shine* in society); to be noticeably visible.—*v.t.* To cause or make to shine.—*n.* Fair weather (*shine* and storm); sunshine; brilliancy; brightness.—**shiner,** shī'nėr, *n.* One who or that which shines; a black eye (*colloq.*); certain small fresh-water fish.—**shiny,** shī'ni, *a.* Characterized by sunshine; bright; luminous; glossy; brilliant.

shingle, shing'gl, *n.* [Corrupted from *shindle,* which, like G. *schindel,* was borrowed from L. *scindula,* a shingle, from L. *scindo,* to split.] A thin piece of wood, usually having parallel sides and thicker at one end than the other, used as a roof covering; a short haircut; a small signboard, as of a doctor or lawyer (*colloq.*)—*v.t.*—*shingled, shingling.* To cover with shingles; to perform the process of shingling on (to *shingle* iron).

shingles, shing'glz, *n.* pl. [From L. *cingulum,* a belt, from *cingo,* to gird.] A painful viral skin disease.

shinny, shinney, shin'i, *n.* Schoolboys' hockey; the curved stick used in playing the game.—*v.i.* and *t.* To climb, as a pole, with shins and arms (*colloq.*).

Shinto, Shintoism, shin'tō, shin'-tō•izm, *n.* [Chinese *shin,* god or spirit, and *to,* way or law.] The ancient religion of Japan—originally a form of nature worship, it is now much changed by Confucianism and Buddhism from China and Korea. Among certain sects the religious element is strong, while with others it is essentially nationalism incorporating polytheism, the divine emperor being descended from the sun goddess. Reverence of ancestors and worship of the spirits of departed heroes are dominant elements, with intense loyalty to the god-emperor.—**Shintoist,** shin'tō•ist. *n.* A believer in the Shinto religion.

ship, ship, *n.* [A.Sax. *scip,* a ship=L.G. *schipp,* D. *schip,* Icel. and Goth. *skip,* Dan. *skib,* O.H.G. *scif,* G. *schiff,* a ship. *Skiff* is the same word.] A vessel of some size adapted to navigation: a general term for vessels of whatever kind, excepting boats: sometimes restricted to a three-masted, square-rigged vessel.—*Ship's papers,* certain papers or documents required to be carried by ships, as a certificate of registry, bills of lading, etc.—*Ship of the line,* a man-of-war large enough and of sufficient force to take its place in a line of battle.—*Ship of the desert,* a sort of poetical name for the camel.—*v.t.*—*shipped, shipping.* To put on board of a ship or vessel of any kind; to transport in a ship; to take for service on board ship; *naut.* to fix in its proper place (to *ship* the tiller, the rudder).—*To ship off,* to send away by sea.—*To ship a sea,* to have a wave come aboard; to have the deck washed by a wave.—*v.i.* To go on board a vessel to make a voyage with it; to embark; to engage for service on board a ship.—**ship biscuit,** *n.* Hard coarse biscuit prepared for long keeping, and for use on board a ship.—**shipboard,** ship'-bōrd, *n.* The deck or the interior part of a ship: used only in the phrase *on shipboard.*—**shipbuilder,** *n.* One whose occupation is to construct ships; a naval architect; a shipwright.—**shipbuilding,** *n.* The art of constructing vessels for navigation.—**ship canal,** *n.* A canal through which vessels of large size can pass; a canal for seagoing vessels.—**ship chandler,** *n.* One who deals in cordage, canvas, and other furniture of ships.—**ship chandlery,** *n.* The business and commodities of a shipchandler.—**shipmate,** ship'māt, *n.* One who serves in the same ship with another;

a fellow sailor.—**shipment,** ship′-ment, *n.* The act of putting anything on board of a ship; the goods shipped or put on board.—**shipowner,** *n.* A person who owns a ship or ships, or any share therein.—**shipper,** ship′ėr, *n.* One who places goods on board a vessel for transportation.—**shipping,** ship′ing, *n.* Ships in general; the collective body of ships belonging to a country, port, etc.—*Shipping articles,* articles of agreement between the captain of a vessel and the seamen.—*a.* Relating to ships.—**ship-rigged,** *a.* Rigged like a ship, that is with square sails on all the masts.—**shipshape,** *a.* Having a seamanlike trim; hence, neat and trim; well arranged.—**shipworm,** *n.* The teredo, a mollusk very destructive to ships and submarine woodwork.—**shipwreck,** ship′rek, *n.* The wreck of a ship; the destruction or loss at sea of a ship; destruction; miscarriage; ruin.—*v.t.* To make to suffer shipwreck; to wreck; to cast away.—**shipwright,** ship′rīt, *n.* A workman who builds ships; a ship-carpenter.—**shipyard,** ship′yärd, *n.* A place near water in which ships are constructed.

shire, shīr, *n.* [A.Sax. *scire,* a division, from *sciran, sceran,* to *shear,* to divide. SHARE, SHEAR.] A name for the larger divisions into which Great Britain is divided, and practically corresponding to the term *county.*—*The shires,* those English counties the names of which terminate in 'shire', applied in a general way to the midland counties.

shirk, shėrk, *v.t.* and *i.* [Possibly a form of *shark.*] To avoid or get off unfairly or meanly; to seek to avoid the performance of duty.—*n.* One who seeks to avoid duty; the act of shirking.—**shirker,** shėr′kėr, *n.* One who shirks duty or danger.

shirred, shėrd, *a.* [Etymol. unknown.] Having cords or elastic threads inserted between two pieces of cloth or in the body of a fabric.

shirt, shėrt, *n.* [From Icel. *skyrta,* Dan. *skiorte,* a shirt; lit. a garment shortened. SHORT—*Skirt* is the same word.] A loose garment of linen, cotton, or other material, worn by men and boys under the outer clothes.—*v.t.* To put a shirt on; to clothe with a shirt.—**shirting,** shėr′-ting, *n.* Cloth suitable for shirts.—**shirtless,** shėrt′les, *a.* Wanting a shirt.

shittah tree, shit′ta, *n.* [Heb. *shittâh,* pl. *shittîm.*] A species of acacia which grows abundantly in the mountains of Sinai, and in some other Bible lands, and yields gum arabic, and also a hard close-grained timber.—**shittim wood,** shit′tim, *n.* The wood of the shittah tree.

shiver, shiv′ėr, *v.t.* [Icel. *skifa,* Dan. *schijf,* G. *scheibe,* all meaning slice, or small fragment; comp. G. *schiefern,* to splinter; O.D. *scheveren,* to break in pieces.] To break into many small pieces or splinters; to shatter.—*v.i.* To fall at once into many small pieces or parts.—*n.* [Comp. G. *schiefer,* a splinter, slate.] A small fragment into which a thing breaks by sudden violence.

shiver, shiv′ėr, *v.i.* [O.E. *chiver, chever;* comp. Prov.G. *schubbern,* to shiver; O.D. *schoeveren,* to shake; akin perhaps to *shift.*] To tremble, as from cold; to shake, as with ague, fear, horror, or excitement; to shudder; to quiver.—*n.* A shaking fit; a tremulous motion.—**shivery,** shiv′-ėr•i, *a.* Pertaining to shivering; characterized by shivering.

shoal, shōl, *n.* [A.Sax. *scolu, scalu,* a crowd, a shoal; perhaps same as *school.*] A great multitude assembled; a crowd; a throng.—*v.t.* To drive in shoals.

shoal, shōl, *n.* [Allied to *shallow.* SHALLOW.] A place where the water of a river, lake, or sea is shallow or of little depth; a sandbank or bar; a shallow.—*v.i.* To become more shallow (the water *shoals*).—*a.* Shallow; of little depth (*shoal* water).

shock, shok, *n.* [Same as D. *schok,* a bounce, a jolt (but perhaps directly from the derived Fr. *choc*); O. and Prov.G. *schock,* a shock; allied to *shake.*] A violent collision of bodies; a concussion; a violent striking or dashing against; violent onset; hostile encounter; a strong and sudden agitation; any violent or sudden impression or sensation; a blow to the feelings; *elect.* the effect on the animal system of a discharge of electricity from a charged body; *med.* a violent and sudden disorganization of the system, with perturbation of body and mind.—*v.t.* [Fr. *choquer,* from D. *schokken,* to jog, to jolt.] To shake by sudden collision; to strike against suddenly; to strike, as with horror, fear, or disgust; to offend extremely; to disgust; to scandalize.—*v.i.* To come together with a shock; to meet in sudden encounter.—**shocking,** shok′ing, *a.* Causing a shock of horror, disgust, or pain; causing to recoil with horror or disgust; extremely offensive or disgusting; very obnoxious or repugnant.—**shockingly,** shok′-ing•li, *adv.* In a shocking manner; disgustingly; offensively.

shock, shok, *n.* [O.Sax. *scoc,* threescore, D. *schok,* G. *schock,* Dan. *skok,* a heap, threescore.] A group or pile of stalks, usually of grain, placed upright in a field to dry before removal.—*v.t.* To arrange or stack in shocks, as *to shock corn.*

shock, shok, *n.* [Modified from *shag.*] A mass of close matted hair.—*a.* Shaggy; having shaggy hair.—**shockheaded,** *a.* Having a thick and bushy head of hair.

shod, shod, pret. and pp. of *shoe.*

shoddy, shod′i, *n.* [From *shod,* a provincial pp. of *shed*—the original meaning being fluff thrown off, or *shed,* from cloth in weaving.] The fiber from old woolen or worsted fabrics torn up or deviled by machinery, and mixed with fresh but inferior wool, to be respun and made into cheap cloth, etc.; the coarse or inferior cloth made from this.—*a.* Made of shoddy; *fig.* of a trashy or inferior character (*shoddy* literature).

shoe, shö, *n.* pl. **shoes,** shöz. [A.Sax. *sceō, sceōh*=Dan. and Sw. *sko,* Icel. *skór,* Goth. *skohs,* G. *schuh,* a shoe; probably from root seen in Skr. *sku,* to cover, L. *scutum,* a shield, etc.] A covering for the foot, usually of leather, composed of a thick kind for the sole, and a thinner kind for the upper; a plate or rim of iron nailed under the hoof of an animal, as a horse, to defend it from injury; anything resembling a shoe in form or use.—*v.t.*—pret. and pp. *shod,* ppr. *shoeing.* To furnish with shoes; to put shoes on; to cover at the lower end.—**shoeblack,** shö′blak, *n.* A person that cleans shoes.—**shoehorn,** *n.* A curved piece of polished horn (now also of sheet metal) used to aid in putting on shoes.—**shoelace,** *n.* A shoestring.—**shoemaker,** shö′-mā′kėr, *n.* One who makes or repairs shoes.—**shoemaking,** shö′mā•king, *n.* The trade of making or repairing shoes.—**shoer,** shö′ėr, *n.* One who puts shoes on horses.—**shoestring,** *n.* A shoelace.

shone, shōn, pret. and pp. of *shine.*

shook, shu̥k, pret. of *shake.*

shook, shu̥k, *n.* [A form of *shock,* a pile of sheaves.] The staves and headings sufficient for making one barrel, prepared for use and bound together.

shoot, shöt, *v.t.*—pret. and pp. *shot.* [A.Sax. *sceótan,* to shoot, to dart; Icel. *skjóta,* Dan. *skyde,* D. *schieten,* G. *schiessen,* to shoot, dart, etc.; closely akin are *shut, sheet, shuttle, skittle, scuttle,* etc.] To let fly with force; to propel, as from a bow or firearm (to *shoot* an *arrow,* a *ball*); to discharge; to let off; to fire off (to *shoot off* a gun); to hit, wound or kill with a missile discharged from a weapon; to discharge or propel with force; to empty out with rapidity or violence (to *shoot* rubbish into a hole); to push or thrust forward; to dart forth; to protrude; to put forth by way of vegetable growth; to pass rapidly through, under, or over (to *shoot* a rapids or a bridge).—*To shoot craps* or *dice,* to participate in a game of craps; to throw or roll out the dice in order to make a point.—*v.t.* To perform the act of discharging a bullet, an arrow, or other missile from an engine or mark); to be emitted; to dart forth; to rush or move along rapidly; to dart along (*shooting* stars); to be felt as if darting through one (*shooting* pains); to sprout; to put forth buds or shoots; to increase in growth; to grow taller or larger; to push or be pushed out; to project; to jut.—*To shoot ahead,* to move swiftly away in front; to outstrip competitors in rapidity.—*n.* A young branch which shoots out from the main stock; an annual growth; a kind of sloping trough for conveying coal, grain, etc., into a particular receptacle; a place for shooting rubbish; a weft thread in a woven fabric.—**shooter,** shöt′ėr, *n.* One that shoots; an implement for shooting; a ball shooting on the wickets at cricket.—**shooting,** shöt′-ing, *p.* and *a.* Pertaining to one who or that which shoots.—*n.* The act of one who shoots; sensation of a quick darting pain.—**shooting box,** *n.* A private lodge for the accommodation of a sportsman during the shooting season.—**shooting gallery,** *n.* A place, usually covered, for the practice of shooting at a mark, a covered shooting range.—**shooting star,** *n.* A meteor, a small celestial body passing with great velocity through the earth's atmosphere and becoming incandescent through friction with the resisting air.

shoot, shöt, *n.* [Fr. *chute,* modified by the verb *to shoot.*] Same as *Chute.*

shop, shop, *n.* [A.Sax. *sceoppa,* a booth, a storehouse; akin to O.D. *schop,* L.G. *schupp,* G. *schoppen, schuppen* a shed, booth, etc.] A building or apartment in which goods are sold at retail, generally with a frontage to a street or road, a building in which workmen carry on their occupation (a joiner's *shop,* a machine *shop*).—*To talk shop;* to speak of one's calling or profession only.—*v.i.—shopped, shopping.* To visit shops for purchasing goods; used chiefly in ppr.—**shopkeeper,** shop'kēp·ėr, *n.* A trader who sells goods in a shop or at retail, a tradesman.—**shopkeeping,** shop'kēp•ing, *n.* The business of keeping a shop.—**shoplifter,** shop'lift•ėr, *n.* One who steals from stores.—**shop steward,** *n.* The union member who is elected to represent the union in dealings with the management.—**shopworn,** shop'worn, *a.* Soiled or faded from being on display too long in a store.

shore, shōr, *n.* [A.Sax. *score,* the shore, from *sceran, sciran,* to shear; to divide; O.D. *schoore, schoor.* SHEAR.] The land immediately adjacent to a great body of water, as an ocean or sea, or to a large lake or river; the land along the edge of the water.—**shoreless,** shōr'les, *a.* Having no shore or coast; of indefinite or unlimited extent.

shore, shōr, *n.* [Lit. a piece *shorn* or cut to a certain length; same as D. and L.G. *schore, schoor,* Icel. *skortha,* a prop, a shore. SHEAR.] A prop; a piece of timber or iron for the temporary support of something, often resting obliquely against it.—*v.t.—shored, shoring.* To support by a shore or shores; to prop: usually with *up* (to *shore up* a building).—**shoring,** shōr'ing, *n.* A supporting with shores.

shorn, shorn, pp. of *shear.* Cut off; having the hair or wool cut off; deprived (a prince *shorn* of his honors).

short, short, *a.* [A.Sax. *sceort, scort.* short, from stem of *shear;* O.H.G, *scure,* short, cut off; Icel. *skort,* scantily supplied. SHEAR.] Not long; not having great length or linear extension; not extended in time; not of long duration; not reaching a certain point; limited in quantity; insufficient; inadequate; scanty; deficient (a *short* supply, *short* weight); scantily supplied or furnished; not possessed of a reasonable or usual quantity or amount (to be *short of* money or means); not tenacious or retentive (a *short* memory); not containing many words; curt; brief; abrupt; sharp; severe; uncivil (a *short* answer); breaking or crumbling readily in the mouth; crisp; brittle; friable; not prolonged in sound (a *short* vowel or syllable); followed by *of,* less than; below; inferior to (his escape was nothing *short of* a miracle). [*Short* is used in the formation of numerous self-explaining compounds, as *short-armed, short-eared, short-legged, short-tailed,* etc.]—*adv.* In a short manner; abruptly; suddenly.—*To come short,* to be unable to reach a certain necessary point or standard; to fall below expectations; to fail: generally followed by *of.*—*To fall short,* to become inadequate or insufficient (provisions *fall short*); to fail to reach a certain standard.—*To stop short,* to stop suddenly or abruptly; to arrest the steps at once; not to go so far as intended; not to reach the point indicated.—*To turn short,* to turn abruptly on the spot occupied.—*n.* A summary account (the *short* of the matter).—*In short,* in few words; briefly; to sum up in few words.—*The long and the short,* a brief summing up in decisive, precise, or explicit terms.—**shortage,** shor'tij, *n.* Amount short or deficient; an amount by which a sum of money is deficient.—**shortbread, shortcake,** *n.* A sweet and very brittle cake, in which butter or lard has been mixed with the flour.—**shortcoming,** short'kum•ing, *n.* A failing of the usual quantity or amount.—**short circuit,** *n.* A conductor of low resistance that is accidentally or otherwise connected between two points in a circuit.—**shorten,** shor'tn, *v.t.* To make short or shorter; to abridge; to curtail; to lessen; to diminish in extent or amount.—*To shorten sail,* to reef some of the sails set.—*v.i.* To become short or shorter; to contract.—**shortener,** shor'tn•ėr, *n.* One who or that which shortens.—**shorthand,** short'hand, *n.* A general term for any system of contracted writing; stenography.—**shorthanded,** *a.* Not having the necessary or regular number of hands or assistants.—**Shorthorn,** *n.* One of a valuable breed of cattle, having the horns shorter than in almost any other variety, and yielding flesh of excellent quality.—**short-lived,** short'-līvd, *a.* Not living or lasting long; being of short continuance.—**shortly,** short'li, *adv.* In a short or brief time or manner; soon; in few words.—**shortness,** short'nes, *n.* The quality of being short; briefness; brevity; conciseness; deficiency.—**shorts,** shorts, *n. pl.* The bran and coarse part of meal in mixture; smallclothes; breeches; abbreviated trousers for sports.—**shortsighted,** *a.* Not able to see far; myopic; nearsighted; not able to look far into futurity; not having foresight; characterized by a want of foresight (a *shortsighted* policy).—**shortsightedness,** *n.*—**shortstop,** short'stop, *n. Baseball,* the position between second and third bases.—**short wave,** *n. Radio,* electromagnetic waves 60 meters or less in length.—**short-winded,** *a.* Affected with shortness of breath.

shot, shot, *n.* pl. **shot** or **shots.** [From *shoot* (which see); A.Sax. *gescot,* an arrow.] The act of shooting; a discharge of a firearm or other missile weapon; one who shoots; a marksman; a missile, particularly a ball or bullet for firing from ordnance; cannon balls collectively (comprising *round shot, case shot, grapeshot,* etc.); small globular masses of lead for use with fowling pieces, etc.: in collective sense, often called distinctively *small shot;* the flight of a missile, or the range or distance through which it passes; range; reach; the whole sweep of a fisherman's nets thrown out at one time, also the number of fish caught in one haul of the nets; *weaving,* a single thread of weft carried through the warp at one run of the shuttle; *blasting,* a charge of powder or other explosive in a blasthole; an injection, as of serum (colloq.); a photograph.

shot, shot, *a.* [From pp. of *shoot.*] That which has been discharged; having a changeable color; spent physically or emotionally.—**shotgun,** *n.* A light, smoothbored gun for firing shot at short range; a fowling piece.—**shot put,** *n.* A field event in which contestants throw a metal ball (the shot) for maximum distance.

shot, shot, *n.* [A corruption of *scot* (which see).] A reckoning, or a person's share of a reckoning; share of expenses, as of a tavern bill.

shotten,‡ shot'n, *a.* [An old pp. of *shoot.*] Having ejected the spawn (a *shotten* herring). (*Shak.*)

should, shụd. The pret. of *shall.*

shoulder, shōl'dėr, *n.* [O.E. *shulder,* Sc. *shouther,* A.Sax. *sculdor*=Dan. *skulder,* Sw. *skuldra,* D. *schouder,* G. *schulter,* the shoulder, the shoulder blade.] The joint by which the arm of a human being or the foreleg of a quadruped is connected with the body; the bones and muscles of this part together; the upper joint of the foreleg of an animal cut for the market; that which resembles a human shoulder; a prominent or projecting part (the *shoulder* of a hill); a projection on various implements and articles.—*Shoulder-of-mutton sail,* a triangular sail set on a boat's mast.—*The cold shoulder,* a cold or cool reception of a person (to give a person *the cold shoulder*).—*To put one's shoulder to the wheel,* to assist in overcoming a difficulty; to give effective help.—*Shoulder to shoulder,* a phrase expressive of united action and mutual cooperation and support.—*v.t.* To push or thrust with the shoulder; to push with violence; to take upon the shoulder or shoulders; *milit.* to carry vertically at the side of the body and resting against the hollow of the shoulder (to *shoulder* arms).—*v.i.* To push forward; to force one's way, as through a crowd.—**shoulder blade,** *n.* The bone of the shoulder, or blade bone, covering the hind part of the ribs; the scapula.—**shoulder knot,** *n.* An ornamental knot of ribbon or lace worn on the shoulder. —**shoulder strap,** *n.* A strap worn on or over the shoulder, either to support the dress or as a badge of distinction.

shout, shout, *v.i.* [Perhaps a softened form of *scout*, or onomatopoetic.] To utter a sudden and loud cry, as in joy or exultation, or to call a person's attention.—*n.* A loud cry; a vehement and sudden outcry, particularly of a multitude of men, expressing joy, triumph, exultation, etc.—*v.t.* To utter with a shout.—**shouter,** shout'ėr, *n.* One that shouts.

shove, shuv, *v.t.*—*shoved, shoving.* [A.Sax. *scúfan*=O.Fris. *skuva*, Icel. *skýfa*, D. *schuiven*, Goth. *skiuban*, G. *schieben*, to shove; akin *shovel, scuffle.*] To force or push along, usually without a sudden impulse; to cause to slide by pushing; to press against; to jostle.—*To shove off*, to thrust or push away; to cause to move from shore by pushing with poles or oars.—*v.i.* To push or drive forward; to urge a course.—*To shove off*, to push a boat from shore.—*n.* An act of shoving; a push.

shovel, shuv'el, *n.* [A.Sax. *scofl* (from *scûfan*, to shove)=D. *schoffel*, Dan. *skovl*, G. *schaufel*, a shovel. SHOVE.] An implement consisting of a broad and slightly hollow blade, or a shallow scoop, with a long handle, used for removing coal, sand, earth, or other loose matter.—*v.t.*—*shoveled, shovelled, shoveling, shovelling.* To take up and throw with a shovel.—**shovelbill,** *n.* A variety of duck; a shoveler.—**shovelboard,** *n.* SHUFFLEBOARD.—A kind of game played by pushing coins or the like along a board toward certain marks; a game played on board ships by shoving wooden disks with a cue so that they shall rest in one of nine squares chalked on the deck.—**shoveler,** shuv'el•ėr, *n.* One who shovels; a species of duck.—**shovel hat,** *n.* A hat with a broad brim turned up at the sides, and projecting in front, worn by clergymen of the Church of England.—**shovelhead,** *n.* A species of shark; also a subspecies of sturgeon.

show, shō, *v.t.*—pret. *showed*; pp. *shown* or *showed*; also written *Shew, Shewed, Shewn.* [A.Sax. *sceáwian*, to behold, to show; D. *schouwen*, Dan. *skue*, G. *schauen*, Goth. *scavjan.*] To exhibit or present to the view; to place in sight; to display; to let be seen; to communicate; to reveal; to make known; to make apparent or clear by evidence, reasoning, etc.; to teach; to direct; to guide or usher; to conduct; to bestow, confer, afford (mercy, etc); to explain or to expound; to indicate; to point out.—*To show forth*, to manifest; to publish.—*To show off*, to exhibit in an ostentatious manner.—*To show up*, to usher or conduct up a stair; to hold up to ridicule or to contempt.—*v.i.* To appear; to become visible; to look; to be in appearance.—*To show off*, to make a show; to display one's self.—*n.* The act of showing; exposure to view or notice; appearance, whether true or false; semblance; outward aspect assumed; pretext; ostentatious display; parade; pomp; an object attracting notice; a sight or spectacle; an exhibition; a motion picture or a stage performance; a collection of curiosities exhibited for money (a flower *show*). —*A show of hands*, a raising of hands, as a means of voting.—**showboat,** *n.* A river steamboat with stage and a troupe of actors, used as a floating theater.—**showbread,** *n.* SHEWBREAD.—**showcase,** *n.* A case with glass on the top or front, within which articles are placed for sale or exhibition.—**showdown,** *n.* A concluding disclosure of facts and conditions concerning a matter.—**showily,** shō'i•li, *adv.* In a showy manner; with parade.—**showiness,** shō'i•nes, *n.* State of being showy; great parade.—**showing,** shō'ing, *n.* Exhibition.—**showman,** shō'man, *n.* One who exhibits a show.—**show-off,** *n.* Pretentious display; a person who shows off.—**showroom,** *n.* A room in which a show is exhibited; an apartment where goods are displayed.—**showy,** shō'i, *a.* Making a great show; gorgeous; gaudy.

shower, shou'ėr, *n.* [A.Sax. *scúr*=Icel. *skúr*, D. *schoer*, Sw. *skur*, O.H.G. *scûr*, G. *schauer*, a shower.] A fall of rain of short duration; a fall of things in thick and fast succession (a *shower* of stones); a surprise party given to a person at which those attending bring gifts for the guest of honor.—*v.t.* To pour down copiously and rapidly; to bestow liberally.—*v.i.* To rain in showers; to fall as a shower.—**shower bath,** *n.* A bath in which water is showered upon the person from above; plumbing and equipment installed for such a bath.—**showery,** shou'ėr•i, *a.* Raining in showers; abounding with falls of rain.

shrapnel, shrap'nel, *n.* [After General *Shrapnel*, the inventor.] A shell filled with bullets and a small bursting charge just sufficient to split the shell open and release the bullets at any given point.

shred, shred, *v.t.*—pret. and pp. *shred*; ppr. *shredding.* [A.Sax. *screádian*, to shred, from *screáde*, Sc. *screed*, a piece torn off; O.Fris. *skreda*, D. *schrooden*, O.H.G. *scrótan*, to tear. *Shroud* is akin.] To tear or cut into small pieces, particularly narrow and long pieces, as cloth or leather.—*n.* A piece torn or cut off; any torn fragment; a tatter; a fragment.

shrew, shrö, *n.* [O.E. *shrewe*, wicked, a wicked person; hence, obsol. *shrewe*, to curse, to (*be*)*shrew*, whence *shrewd*; A.Sax. *screawa*, the shrewmouse, lit. the evil or venomous mouse.] An ill-tempered woman; a nagging, scolding woman; a virago; a termagant; a shrewmouse.—**shrewish,** shrö'ish, *a.* Having the qualities of a shrew; vixenish.—**shrewishly,** shrö'ish•li, *adv.* In a shrewish manner.—**shrewishness,** shrö'ish•nes, *n.*—**shrewmouse,** *n.* [So called because its bite was once thought venomous.] A small harmless mammal, of the genus *Sorex*, with a long pointed snout, small eyes, short tail and brownish velvety fur, somewhat resembling a mouse, but belonging to the insectivorous animals, while the mouse is a rodent.

shrewd, shröd, *a.* [From old *shrewe*, to curse, *shrewe*, evil. SHREW.] Malicious or mischievous (*Shak.*)‡; astute; sagacious; discerning.—**shrewdly,** shröd'li, *adv.* In a shrewd manner; astutely; sagaciously; of *wind*, 'biting *shrewdly*' (*Hamlet*), in original sense.—**shrewdness,** shröd'nes, *n.* The quality of being shrewd; sagacity; acuteness of mind.

shriek, shrēk, *v.i.* [A form of *screak* and *screech.*] To utter a sharp shrill cry; to scream, as in a sudden fright, horror, or anguish.—*n.* A sharp shrill cry or scream; a shrill noise.—*v.t.* To utter with a shriek. —**shrieker,** shrē'kėr, *n.* One who shrieks.

shrievalty, shrē'val•ti, *n.* [From obsol. *shrieve*, a sheriff.] The office or jurisdiction of a sheriff.

shrike, shrīk, *n.* [From its *shrieking* cry.] The name of certain dentirostral insessorial birds which feed on mice, insects, small birds, etc., and often impale their prey on thorns; called also butcherbirds.

shrill, shril, *a.* [An imitative word akin to Sc. *skirl*, a screech, L.G. *skrell*, G. *schrill*, shrill.] Sharp or acute in tone; having a piercing sound; uttering an acute sound.—*v.i.* To utter an acute piercing sound.—*v.t.* To utter in a shrill tone.—**shrillness,** shril'nes, *n.* The quality of being shrill; acuteness of sound.—**shrilly,** shril'li, *adv.* In a shrill manner; with a sharp sound or voice.—*a.* (shril'i). Somewhat shrill.

shrimp, shrimp, *n.* [Akin to Sc. *scrimp*, to deal out sparingly; A.Sax. *scrymman*, to wither, G. *schrumpfen*, to shrivel.] A small crustacean allied to the lobster and crayfish, which burrows in sand, and is esteemed as food; a dwarfish creature; a manikin.

shrine, shrīn, *n.* [A.Sax. *scrin*, from L. *scrinium*, a box.] A box for holding the bones or other remains of departed saints; a reliquary; a tomb of shrine-like form; the mausoleum of a saint in a church; an altar; a place hallowed from its history or associations (a *shrine* of art).—*v.t.*—*shrined, shrining.* To place in a shrine; to enshrine.

shrink, shringk, *v.i.*—pret. *shrank* and *shrunk*; pp. *shrunk, shrunken* (the latter now always an adjective). [A.Sax. *scrincan*, O.D. *schrincken*, to shrink; from root of *shrimp, shrug.*] To contract spontaneously, as woolen cloth in water; to draw or be drawn into less compass by an inherent quality; to shrivel; to become wrinkled; to draw back, as from danger; to decline action from fear; to recoil; to draw the body together as in fear or horror.—*v.t.* To cause to contract by immersing in water.—*n.* The act of shrinking.—**shrinkage,** shringk'ij, *n.* The contraction of a material into less compass, as by soaking or by drying; hence, amount of depreciation in value, as of business assets; loss of weight, as of cotton in storage, etc.—**shrunken,** shrungk'n, *p.* and *a.* Having shrunk; shriveled up; contracted.

shrivel, shriv'el, *v.i.*—*shriveled, shriveling.* [Probably based partly on *rivel,* to shrivel, partly on *shrink.*] To contract or shrink; to draw or be drawn into wrinkles.—*v.t.* To contract into wrinkles.

shroud, shroud, *n.* [A.Sax. *scrúd,* a garment, a shroud; Icel. *skrúd,* shrouds, tackle; Dan. *skrud,* dress; from root of *shred.*] That which clothes, covers, or conceals; a garment; a covering; the dress of the dead; a winding sheet; *naut.* one of those large ropes that extend from the head of a mast to the right and left sides of the ship, to support the mast.—*v.t.* To envelop with some covering; to cover; to hide; to veil; to put a shroud or winding sheet on.—*v.i.* To take shelter.—**shroudless,** shroud'les, *a.* Without a shroud.

Shrovetide, *n.* [*Shrove,* pret. of *shrive,* and *tide,* time, season.] The time when the people were shriven preparatory to the Lenten season; the few days before Ash Wednesday.—**Shrove Tuesday,** *n.* Confession Tuesday; the Tuesday preceding the first day of Lent, or Ash Wednesday.

shrub, shrub, *n.* [A.Sax. *scrob,* a bush; perhaps from same root as *shrivel, shrimp. Scrub,* low shrubby trees, is the same word.] A low dwarf tree; a woody plant of a size less than a tree; or more strictly, a plant with several permanent woody stems dividing from the bottom.—**shrubbery,** shrub'ėr•i, *n.* An ornamental plantation of shrubs; growing shrubs.—**shrubby,** shrub'i, *a.* Full of shrubs; being or resembling a shrub; consisting of shrubs or brush.—**shrubbiness,** shrub'i•nes, *n.* The quality of being shrubby.

shrub, shrub, *n.* [Ar. *shurb,* a drink; allied to *syrup, sherbet.*] A liquor composed of lime or lemon juice and sugar, with spirit (chiefly rum).

shrug, shrug, *v.t.* and *i.*—*shrugged, shrugging.* [From root of *shrink;* allied to D. *schrikken,* G. *schrecken* to tremble.] To raise or draw up the shoulders, as in expressing dissatisfaction, aversion, etc.—*n.* A drawing up of the shoulders, a motion usually expressing dislike.

shuck, shuk, *n.* [Comp. *chuck,* to throw, husks being thrown away.] A shell or husk, as of an ear of corn or of a nut.—*v.t.* To tear off the husk.

shudder, shud'ėr, *v.i.* [Same as L.G. *schuddern,* O.D. *schudderen,* G. *schüttern,* to shake, to shiver, freq. forms from L.G. and D. *schudden,* G. *schütten,* O.H.G. *scuitan,* to shake; allied to E. *shed,* to cast.] To be strongly agitated or shaken, as by a qualm; to tremble; to quake violently, as with great horror.—*To shudder at,* to feel violent aversion to; to be filled with disgust at, as to *shudder* at the thought of, to *shudder* to think of.—*n.* An agitation or shaking of the body, resembling shivering or trembling, caused by a strong feeling of horror or disgust.

shuffle, shuf'l, *v.t.*—*shuffled, shuffling.* [A dim. from *shove,* like L.G. *schuffeln,* to shuffle. *Scuffle* is another form.] To shove rapidly one way and the other; to mix together by pushing or shoving; to put into a fresh order at random, as playing-cards.—*To shuffle off,* to push off; to rid one's self of.—*To shuffle up,* to throw together in haste.—*v.i.* To change the position; to shift ground; to prevaricate; to shift; to move with an irregular dragging gait; to shove the feet noisily to and fro on the floor or ground, to scrape the floor in dancing.—*To shuffle off,* to take leave or to start off (*colloq.*).—*n.* The act of one who shuffles; an evasion; a trick; an artifice; *dancing,* a rapid scraping movement with the feet, also the *double shuffle.*—**shuffleboard, shovelboard,** *n.* A game played by pushing disks toward certain marks; a game played on board ship by shoving disks with a cue, so that they will rest in one of nine squares on the deck.—**shuffler,** shuf'lėr, *n.* One who shuffles; one who plays mean tricks.

shun, shun, *v.t.*—*shunned, shunning.* [A.Sax. *scunian,* to shun; allied to D. *schuin,* oblique, *schuinen,* to slope. *Shunt* is from *shun,* as also *scoundrel.*] To keep clear of; to get out of the way of; to avoid; to eschew.

shunt, shunt, *v.i.* [From *shun.*] *Railroads,* to switch from one line of rails to another.—*v.t.* To cause to turn from one line of rails to another; to turn into a siding; hence (*colloq.*), to shove off; to free one's self of.—**shunter,** shunt'ėr, *n.* One who shunts.

shut, shut, *v.t.*—pret. and pp. *shut,* ppr. *shutting.* [O.E. *shuite, shitte,* A.Sax. *scyttan,* to bolt, to lock, to shoot the bolt, from *sceótan,* to shoot. (SHOOT.) A *shuttle* is what is *shot* or cast.] To close so as to prevent ingress or egress; to close up by bringing the parts together (a book, etc.); to forbid entrance into (to *shut* a port); to bar; to preclude; to exclude.—*To shut in,* to enclose; to confine; to cover or intercept the view of.—*To shut off,* to exclude; to intercept; to prevent the passage of.—*To shut out,* to preclude from entering; to exclude.—*To shut up,* to make fast the openings or entrances into; to enclose; to imprison; to lock or fasten in; to terminate or conclude; to cause to say nothing more (*colloq.*).—*v.i.* To close itself; to become closed.—*a.* Not resonant or sonorous; having the sound suddenly stopped by a succeeding consonant (as *o* in *got*).—*n.* The act of closing; close; a shutter.—**shutter,** shut'ėr, *n.* One who or that which shuts; a movable covering for a window.

shuttle, shut'l, *n.* [A.Sax. *scytel,* a shuttle, from *sceótan,* to shoot, because shot to and fro in weaving. SHOOT, SHUT.] An instrument used by weavers for passing the thread of the weft from one side of the web to the other between the threads of the warp; *sewing machines,* the sliding thread holder which carries the lower thread between the needle and the upper thread to make a lockstitch.—*v.i.* To scuttle; to hurry. (*Carl.*)—**shuttlecock,** *n.* [Cock = the bird.] A cork stuck with feathers made to be struck by a battledore in play; also the play.—*v.t.* To throw or bandy backward and forward like a shuttlecock.

shy, shī, *a.* [Same as Dan. *sky,* shy, skittish, G. *scheu,* shy, timid; akin to O.E. *schiech,* A.Sax. *sceóh,* Sc. *skiech,* Sw. *skygg,* shy. *Eschew* is akin to *shy.*] Keeping at a distance through caution or timidity; readily frightened; timid; sensitively timid; not inclined to be familiar; retiring; coy; reserved; cautious; wary; careful to avoid committing one's self: followed by *of.*—*v.i.*—*shied, shying.* To start away from an object that causes fear: said of a horse.—*v.t.* To throw (to *shy* a stone). (*Colloq.*)—**shyly,** shī'li, *adv.* In a shy or timid manner; coyly; diffidently.—**shyness,** shī'nes, *n.* The quality or state of being shy; reserve; coyness.

shyster, shī'ster, *n.* A tricky person; one without professional honor, especially an unethical lawyer.

si, sē. *Mus.* a name given in some systems to the seventh note of the natural or normal scale.

sialagogue, sialogogue, sī•al'a•gog, sī•al'o•gog, *n.* [Gr. *sialon,* saliva, and *agōgos,* leading.] A medicine that promotes the salivary discharge.

siamang, sī'a•mang, *n.* A quadrumanous animal, a kind of gibbon.

Siamese, sī•a•mēz', *n. sing.* and *pl.* A native or natives of Siam; the language of Siam.—**Siamese twins,** Eng and Chang, 1811-74, Chinese brothers, united from birth by a cartilaginous band; term used for any twins so united.

sib, sib, *a.* Related by blood; akin to.

Siberian, sī•bē'ri•an, *a.* Pertaining to Siberia.—*Siberian crab,* a Siberian tree of the apple genus.—*Siberian dog,* a variety of the dog, in northern regions employed in drawing sledges over the frozen snow.

sibilant, sib'i•lant, *a.* [L. *sibilans, sibilantis,* ppr. of *sibilo,* to hiss.] Hissing; making a hissing sound.—*n.* A letter that is uttered with a hissing of the voice, as *s* and *z.*—**sibilance, sibilancy,** sib'i•lans, sib'i•lan•si, *n.* The quality of being sibilant; a hissing sound as of *s.*—**sibilate,** sib'i•lāt, *v.t.*—*sibilated, sibilating.*

sibling, sib'ling, *n.* [From A.Sax. *sibb, gesib,* related, and suffix *ling.*] A brother or sister, without respect to sex.

sibyl, sib'il, *n.* [Gr. *sibylla.*] A name common to certain women mentioned by Greek and Roman writers, and said to have been endowed with a prophetic spirit; hence, a prophetess; a sorceress; a fortuneteller; a witch.—**sibylline,** sib'il•lēn, *a.* Pertaining to the sibyls; like the productions of sibyls; prophetical.—*Sibylline books*, certain books, containing directions as to the worship of the gods, the policy that should be observed by the Romans, etc., purchased by Tarquin the Proud from the Cumaean Sibyl.

Sicanian, si•kā'ni•an, *a.* Of or relating to the Sicani, the indigenous inhabitants of Sicily.

siccate, sik'āt, *v.t.*—*siccated, siccating.* [L. *sicco, siccatum,* to dry, from *siccus,* dry.] To dry very slowly for the purpose of preservation (*rare*).—**siccation,** sik•kā'shon, *n.* The act or process of drying.—**siccative,** sik'a•tiv, *a.* Drying; causing to dry by the slow elimination of moisture.—*n.* That which promotes the process of drying.

Sicilian, si•sil'i•an, *a.* Pertaining to Sicily.—*Sicilian Vespers,* the great massacre of the French in Sicily in 1282, on the evening of Easter Monday, the signal being the first stroke of the vesper bell.—*n.* A native or inhabitant of Sicily.

sick, sik, *a.* [A.Sax. *seóc*=Goth. *siuks,* L.G. *seek, siek,* D. *ziek,* Icel. *sjúkr,* G. *siech,* sick.] Affected with nausea; inclined to vomit; disgusted; feeling tedium; wearied (to be *sick of* flattery); affected with disease of any kind; not in health; ill; languishing; used by or set apart for sick persons (a *sick*-bed).—*The sick,* persons affected with disease.—**sick bay,** *n. Naut.* a portion of the main deck partitioned off for invalids.—**sickbed,** *n.* A bed on which one is confined by sickness.—**sicken,** sik'n, *v.t.* To make sick; to disease; to make squeamish or qualmish; to disgust.—*v.i.* To become sick; to fall ill; to feel sick; to become distempered; to languish.—**sickening,** sik'n•ing, *a.* Making sick; disgusting.—**sickish,** sik'ish, *a.* Indisposed; nauseating.—**sickishly,** sik'ish•li, *adv.* In a sickish manner.—**sickishness,** sik'ish•nes, *n.*—**sickliness,** sik'li•nes, *n.* The state of being sickly; insalubrity; the disposition to generate disease (the *sickliness* of a climate).—**sickly,** sik'li, *a.* Somewhat sick or ill; not healthy; attended with sickness; producing or tending to produce disease; faint; languid; appearing as if sick.—*adv.* In a sick manner or condition.—**sickness,** sik'nes, *n.* The state of being sick; disease; ill health; a disease; a malady; a particular state of the stomach which occurs under the forms of nausea, retching, and vomiting; any disordered state.

sickle, sik'l, *n.* [A.Sax. *sicel, sicol*=D. *sikkel,* G. *sichel,* Dan. *segel,* a sickle; a dim. form from root of *scythe.*] A reaping hook; a curved blade or hook of steel with a handle, for use with one hand in cutting grain, grass, etc.

side, sīd, *n.* [A.Sax. *síde*=Dan. *side,* Icel. *síða,* G. *seite,* a side; akin to A.Sax. *síd,* Icel. *síðr,* long.] The broad or long surface of a solid body, as distinguished from the *end,* which is of less extent; the exterior line of anything considered in length; the margin, edge, border; the part of an animal between the hip and shoulder (the right or left *side*); the part of persons on the right hand or the left; the part between the top and bottom; the slope of a hill or mountain (the *side* of Mount Etna); one of two principal surfaces opposed to each other; part whichever way directed; quarter in any direction; any party or interest opposed to another (on the same *side* in politics); line of descent traced through one parent (by the father's *side*); *geom.* any line which forms one of the boundaries of a straight-lined figure; also, any of the bounding surfaces of a solid; swagger; pomposity. (*Colloq.*)—*By the side of,* near to; closely adjoining.—*Side by side,* close together and abreast.—*To choose sides,* to divide a group for competition in exercises of any kind.—*To take a side,* to embrace the opinions of a party in opposition to another.—*a.* Lateral; being on the side; being from the side or toward the side; oblique; indirect (a *side* view).—*v.i.*—*Sided, siding.* To embrace the opinions of one party when opposed to another party; to engage in a faction; often followed by *with.*—**side arms,** *n. pl.* Arms carried at the side, as a revolver, sword, bayonet, etc.—**sideboard,** sīd'bōrd, *n.* A piece of dining room furniture, consisting of a kind of table with drawers or compartments used to hold dining utensils, etc.—**sidecar,** *n.* A single-seated car attached to the side of a motorcycle with one wheel supporting the off side; an intoxicating drink (*colloq.*).—**sided,** sī'ded, *a.* Having a side: used in composition (many-*sided*).—**side light,** *n.* Light admitted laterally; indirect information, upon a subject.—**sideling,** sīd'ling, *adv.* SIDELONG. (*Swift.*)—**sidelong,** sīd'long, *adv.* [*Side,* and term. *-long, -ling,* as in head*long,* dark*ling.*] Laterally; obliquely; in the direction of the side.—*a.* Lateral; oblique; not directly in front.—**sidesaddle,** *n.* A saddle for a woman, in which the feet are both on one side.—**sideslip,** *n.* A movement sideways of an airplane that may occur when the forward speed of the machine is unduly diminished.—**side view,** *n.* An oblique view; a side look.—**sidewalk,** *n.* A raised walk for foot passengers by the side of a street or road; a footway.—**sideways,** sīd'wāz, *adv.* SIDEWISE.—**sidewise,** sīd'wīz, *adv.* Toward one side; laterally; on one side.—**siding,** sī'ding, *n.* A short additional line of rails laid at the side of a main line for the purpose of switching.

sidereal, si•dē'rē•al, *a.* [L. *sideralis, sidereus,* from *sidus, sideris,* a star (seen also in *consider*).] Pertaining to the stars; starry; measured or marked by the apparent motions of the stars (*sidereal* time).—*Sidereal clock,* a clock adapted to measure sidereal time.—*Sidereal day,* the time in which the earth makes a complete revolution on its axis in respect of the fixed stars, being 23 hours, 56 minutes, 4.092 seconds.—*Sidereal system,* the general system of stars of which the solar system is a member.—*Sidereal year,* the period in which the fixed stars apparently complete a revolution in the heavens, being the exact period of the revolution of the earth round the sun, and containing 365.25 sidereal days.

siderite, sid'ėr•īt, *n.* [Gr. *sidērītēs,* from *sidēros,* iron.] Magnetic iron ore or loadstone; also native spathic iron ore, and a blue variety of quartz.—**siderolite,** sid'ėr•o•līt, *n.* [Gr. *sideros,* and *lithos,* a stone.] A meteoric stone chiefly consisting of iron.

siderostat, sid'ėr•o•stat, *n.* [L. *sidus, sideris,* a star, and Gr. *statos,* placed, standing, from *histēmi,* to stand.] An apparatus consisting of a mirror moved by clockwork and a fixed object-glass, for observing the light of the stars.

sidle, sī'dl, *v.i.*—*sidled, sidling.* [From *side.*] To go or move side foremost; to move to one side.

siege, sēj, *n.* [Fr. *siège,* from hypothetical L.L. *sedium, sidium,* from L. *sedeo,* to sit. SEDATE.] The investment of a fortified place by an army, and attack of it by passages and advance works that protect the besiegers; any continued endeavor to gain possession.

sienna, si•en'na, *n.* A ferruginous earth of a fine yellow color, from *Sienna* in Italy, used as a pigment.

sierra, si•er'ra, *n.* [Sp. from L. *serra,* a saw.] A chain of hills or mountains with jagged or sawlike ridges.

siesta, si•es'ta, *n.* [Sp.] A sleep or rest in the hottest part of the day indulged in by the Spaniards and others.

sieve, siv, *n.* [A.Sax. *sife,* a sieve; L.G. *seve,* D. *zeef,* G. *sieb;* perhaps made originally of rushes; comp. Prov.E. *seave,* Dan. *siv,* a rush.] An instrument for separating the smaller particles of substances from the grosser, usually in the form of a shallow circular vessel having its bottom made of basketwork, interwoven wires, hair, canvas, network, etc., according to circumstances.

sift, sift, *v.t.* [A.Sax. *siftan,* from *sife,* a sieve; L.G. *siften,* D. *ziften,* to sift. SIEVE.] To operate on by a sieve; to separate by a sieve, as the fine part of a substance from the coarse; to part, as by a sieve; to examine minutely or critically; to scrutinize.—**sifter,** sif'tėr, *n.* One who sifts; that which sifts; a sieve.

sigh, sī, *v.i.* [O.E. *syke,* A.Sax. *sican,* Sc. *sic, sich,* Dan. *sukke,* to sigh; D. *zugt,* a sigh; probably imitative of sound; comp. *sough,* noise of the wind.] To make a deep single respiration, as the involuntary expression of sorrow or melancholy; to grieve; to give out a similar sound (the wind *sighs*).—*To sigh for,* to long or wish ardently for.—*v.t.* To emit in sighs; to mourn; to express by sighs.—*n.* A single deep involuntary respiration; a simple respiration giving involuntary expression of some depressing emotion, as sorrow, melancholy, anxiety, or the like.—**sigher,** sī′ėr, *n.* One who sighs.

sight, sīt, *n.* [A.Sax. *gesiht*=G. *sicht*, Dan. and Sw. *sigte*; from stem of *see*; comp. *flight* and *flee*.] The act or power of seeing; perception of objects by the eye (to gain *sight* of land); the faculty of vision; range of unobstructed vision; open view (in *sight* of land); visibility; judgment or opinion from seeing; estimation (to find favor in one's *sight*); that which is beheld; a spectacle; particularly, something novel and remarkable; something worth seeing (the *sights* of a town); a great many individuals (*colloq.*); an appliance for guiding the eye in an optical instrument; a small elevated piece near the muzzle, or another near the breech, of a firearm, to aid the eye in taking aim.—*At sight, after sight*, terms applied to bills or notes payable on or after presentation.—*To take sight*, to take aim.—*v.t.* To get or catch sight of; to come in sight of; to see (to *sight* the land); to give the proper elevation and direction to by means of a sight (to *sight* a rifle or cannon).—**sighted,** sī′ted, *a.* Seeing in a particular manner (short-*sighted*, quick-*sighted*); having a sight or sights (a rifle *sighted* for 1000 yards).—**sighthole,** *n.* A hole to see through.—**sightless,** sīt′les, *a.* Wanting the power of seeing; blind.—**sightliness,** sīt′li•nes, *n.* The state of being sightly.—**sightly,** sīt′li, *a* Pleasing to the eye; striking to the view.—**sightseeing,** *n.* The act of seeing sights or visiting scenes of interest.—**sightseer,** *n.* One who goes to see sights or curiosities.

sigmoid, sigmoidal, sig′moid, sig•moi′dal, *a.* [From Gr. *sigma*, the letter Σ or C=S.] Curved like the letter sigma in its form C: applied in *anat.* to several parts, as the semilunar valves of the heart and the cartilages of the trachea.

sign, sīn, *n.* [Fr. *signe*, from L. *signum*, a mark, a sign, whence *signal*, *signet*, *assign*, *consign*, *design*, *resign*, etc., also *seal* from the dim. *sigillum*.] That by which anything is made known or represented; anything visible that indicates the existence or approach of something else; a token; a mark; an indication; a motion or gesture by which a thought is expressed or intelligence communicated; a prodigy; an omen; a miracle; a wonder; any symbol or emblem; that which, being external, represents or signifies something internal or spiritual; something conspicuously placed on or near a house, indicating the occupation of the tenant or giving notice of what is sold or made within; a signboard; *astron.* one of the twelve divisions of the ecliptic or zodiac, each containing 30 degrees, and named in succession Aries, Taurus, Gemini, Cancer, Leo, Virgo, Libra, Scorpio, Sagittarius, Capricornus, Aquarius, Pisces; *arith.* and *math.* a character indicating the relation of quantities, or an operation performed on them, as + (plus), — (minus), etc.; *mus.* any character, as a flat, sharp, dot, etc.—*v.t.* To express by a sign; to make known by gesture; to signify; to mark with a sign or symbol; to affix a signature to; to subscribe in one's own handwriting.—*v.i.* To make a sign or signal.—**signboard,** *n.* A board carrying notice of one's occupation, business or goods for sale.—**signer,** sī′nėr, *n.* One who signs or subscribes his name.—**sign manual,** *n.* A signature; the subscription of one's own name to a document; a royal signature.—**signpost,** *n.* A post on which a sign hangs.

signal, sig′nal, *n.* [Fr. *signal*, L.L. *signale*, from L. *signum*. SIGN.] A sign that is intended to communicate information, orders, or the like to persons at a distance, as by a motion of the hand, the raising of a flag, the showing of lights of various colors, etc.—*a.* Distinguished from what is ordinary; remarkable; notable; conspicuous: said of things.—*v.t.*—*signaled*, *signaling*. To communicate or make known by a signal or signals; to make signals to (the vessel *signaled* the forts).—*v.i.* To give a signal or signals.—**signalize,** sig′nal•īz, *v.t.*—*signalized*, *signalizing*. To make remarkable; to render distinguished; to distinguish by some fact or exploit: often used reflexively.—**signally,** sig′nal•li, *adv.* In a signal manner; eminently; remarkably; memorably.—**signalman,** *n.* One who signals; specifically, an official on a railway who works the signals.

signatory, sig′na•to•ri, *a.* [L. *signatorius*, pertaining to signing, from *signator*, a signer, from *signum*, a mark. SIGN.] Relating to the signing of documents; setting a signature to a document; signing a public document, as a treaty.—*n.* One who signs; the representative of a state who signs a public document.

signature, sig′na•chėr, *n.* [L.L. *signatura*, from L. *signo*, to sign. SIGN.] A stamp or mark impressed; the name of any person written with his own hand on a document; a sign manual; *printing*, a letter or figure at the bottom of the first page of each sheet or half sheet of a book to indicate their order; *mus.* the sign placed at the commencement of a piece of music to indicate the time and key.

signet, sig′net, *n.* [O.Fr. *signet*, dim. of *signe*, a sign. SIGN.] A seal; particularly, a seal for the authentication of royal grants or warrants.—*Writers to the signet*, a class of legal practitioners in Edinburgh who act generally as agents or attorneys in conducting causes before the Court of Session; originally they are said to have prepared writs for passing the royal signet.—**signeted,** sig′net•ed, *a.* Stamped or marked with a signet.—**signet ring,** *n.* A ring containing a signet or private seal.

signify, sig′ni•fī, *v.t.*—*signified*, *signifying*. [Fr. *signifier*, from L. *significo*—*signum*, a sign, and *facio*, to make. SIGN.] To make known by signs or words; to express or communicate to another by words, gestures, etc.; to give notice; to announce, declare, proclaim; to convey as its meaning; to mean; to import; to indicate; to matter or be of consequence: in particular phrases (it *signifies* much or little, it *signifies* nothing, what does it *signify?*).—**significance, significancy,** sig•nif′i•kans, sig•nif′i•kan•si, *n.* Meaning; import; that which is intended to be expressed; expressiveness; impressiveness; force; importance; moment.—**significant,** sig•nif′i•kant, *a.* [L. *significans*, *significantis*, ppr. of *significo*.] Bearing a meaning; expressive in an eminent degree; expressive or suggestive of something more than what appears (a *significant* look); standing as a sign of something; important; momentous.—**significantly,** sig•nif′i•kant•li, *adv.* In a significant manner; meaningly; expressively.—**signification,** sig′ni•fi•kā″shon, *n.* [L. *significatio*.] The act of signifying; that which is signified or expressed by signs or words; meaning; import; sense; notion conveyed.—**significative,** sig•nif′i•ka•tiv, *a.* [Fr. *significatif*.] Signifying; serving to signify; having meaning; expressive of a meaning.

signior, sēn′yor, *n.* An English form of the Italian *Signor*, Spanish *Señor*, a title of respect equivalent to the English *Sir* or *Mr.*, the French *Monsieur*, and the German *Herr*.—**signory,** sēn′yo•ri, *n.* A principality; a province (*Shak.*); an estate; a manor; dominion; power; a governing body.

Sikh, sēk, *n.* One of an Indian community, half religious, half military, which founded a state in the Punjab.

silence, sī′lens, *n.* [Fr. *silence*, from L. *silentium*, silence, from *sileo*, to be silent.] The condition prevailing when there is no noise; absence of sound; stillness; forbearance of speech; a holding of one's peace; taciturnity; a refraining from making known something; secrecy; absence of mention; oblivion —*v.t.*—*silenced*, *silencing*. To put to silence; to oblige to hold the peace; to cause to cease speaking; to restrain in reference to liberty of speech; to cause to cease sounding; to stop the noise of; to still, quiet, or appease (to *silence* scruples); to make to cease firing, especially by a vigorous cannonade (to *silence* guns or a battery).—*interj.* Used elliptically for let there be silence, or keep silence.—**silent,** sī′lent, *a.* [L. *silens*, *silentis*, ppr. of *sileo*.] Not speaking; mute; dumb; speechless; habitually taciturn; speaking little; not loquacious; not mentioning or proclaiming; making no noise or rumor; free from sound or noise; having or making no noise; having no sound in pronunciation (*e* is *silent* in *fable*).—**silently,** sī′-

lent•li, *adv.* In a silent manner.—**silentness,** sī′lent•nes, *n.* State of being silent; silence.

silhouette, sil′ö•et″, *n.* [Fr., from Etienne de *Silhouette,* French minister of finance in 1759, in derision of his excessive economy in regard to the finances.] A profile or shadow outline portrait filled in with a black color, the inner parts being sometimes indicated by lines of a lighter color.

silica, silex, sil′i•ka, sī′leks, *n.* [L. *silex, silicis,* a flint.] Oxide of silicon, an important substance constituting the characteristic ingredient of a great variety of minerals, among which rock crystal, quartz, chalcedony, and flint are nearly pure silica.—**silicate,** sil′i•kāt, *n.* A compound of silica with certain bases, as alumina, lime, magnesia, potash, soda, etc.—*Silicate paint,* natural silica, when dried and forming an almost impalpable powder, mixed with colors and oil.—**siliceous,** si•lish′us, *a.* Pertaining to silica, containing it, or partaking of its nature. —**silicic,** si•lis′ik, *a.* Pertaining to silica (*silicic* ether, *silicic* acid).—**silicide,** sil′i•sīd, *n.* [L. *silex, silicis,* a flint.] A compound of silicon with a metal.—**siliciferous,** sil•i•sif′ėr•us, *a.* [L. *silex,* and *fero,* to produce.] Producing silica; containing silica.—**silicification,** si•lis′i•fi•kā″shon, *n.* Petrifaction; conversion into stone by siliceous matter.—**silicify,** si•lis′i•fī, *v.t.*—*silicified, silicifying.* [L. *silex, silicis,* and *facio,* to make.] To convert into or petrify by silica.—*v.i.* To become impregnated with silica.

silicle, sil′i•kl, *n.* [L. *silicula,* dim. of *siliqua,* a pod.] *Bot.* a kind of seed vessel differing from a silique in being as broad as it is long, or broader.—**siliculose, siliculous,** si•lik′ū•lōs, si•lik′ū•lus, *a.* Having silicles or pertaining to them.—**silique,** si•lēk, *n.* [L. *siliqua,* a pod, also a very small weight.] *Bot.* the long pod or seed vessel of crucifers (as wallflower), dehiscing by two valves which separate from a central portion called the *replum.*—**siliquose, siliquous,** sil′i•kwōs, sil′i•kwus, *a. Bot.* bearing siliques.

silicon, sil′i•kon, *n.* [From L. *silex, silicis,* a flint.] A nonmetallic element constituting in combination more than one-fourth of the earth's crust, used in steelmaking. Symbol, Si; at. no., 14; at. wt., 28.086.

silicone, sil′i•kōn, *n. Chem.* a compound made by substituting silicon for carbon in substances such as oils, greases, synthetic rubber, and resins, to provide greater stability and resistance to temperature extremes.

silk, silk, *n.* [A.Sax. *seoloc,* silk, for *seric,* from L. *sericum,* Gr. *serikon,* silk, lit. Seric stuff, from *Seres,* the Greek name of the Chinese.] The fine, soft thread forming the cocoon of the larvae of various species of moths, the most important of which is the common silkworm moth, a native of the northern provinces of China; cloth made of silk; a garment made of this cloth.—*a.* Made of silk; silken.—*Silk gown,* the official robe of a queen's (or king's) counsel in England.—*To take silk,* to attain the rank of queen's counsel.—**silk cotton,** *n.* A silky fiber surrounding the seeds of several species of tropical American and Indian trees, used for stuffing mattresses, for covering hat bodies, etc.—**silken,** sil′kn, *a.* Made of silk; like silk; silky.—**silkiness,** sil′ki•nes, *n.* The state or quality of being silky.—**silkworm,** *n.* A worm which produces silk; the larva of various moths which spins a silken cocoon or case about the size of a pigeon's egg for the enclosure of the chrysalis.—**silky,** sil′ki, *a.* Made of silk; like silk; soft and smooth to the touch; delicate; tender.

sill, sil, *n.* [A.Sax. *syl, syll,* base, sill; Icel. *syll, svill,* Sw. *syll, swill,* G. *schwelle,* Goth. *sulja,* sill; perhaps from same root as L. *solum,* the ground, a base.] A stone or a piece of timber on which a structure rests; the horizontal piece of timber or stone at the bottom of a door, window, or similar opening; *mining,* the floor of a gallery or passage in a mine.

sillabub, sil′a•bub, *n.* [Origin doubtful.] A dish of wine or cider with cream or milk forming a soft curd.

silly, sil′i, *a.* [O.E. *seely,* A.Sax. *saelig,* prosperous; blessed; Icel. *saelligr,* G. *selig,* happy; from A.Sax. *sael,* Icel. *saell,* Goth. *sels,* good, happy.] Happy‡; guileless or inoffensive; helpless‡; foolish; weak in intellect; witless; simple; characterized by weakness or folly; showing folly; unwise; stupid.—**sillily,** sil′i•li, *adv.* In a silly manner; foolishly.—**silliness,** sil′i•nes, *n.* The quality of being silly.

silo, sī′lō, *n.* The pit in which green fodder is preserved in the method of ensilage. ENSILAGE.—*v.t.* To put into a silo.

silt, silt, *n.* [From Prov.E. *sile,* Sw. *sila,* to strain or filter.] A deposit of mud or fine soil from running or standing water; fine earthy sediment. —*v.t.* To choke or fill with silt or mud: often with *up.*—*v.i.* To percolate through crevices; to ooze.—**silty,** silt′i, *a.* Consisting of or resembling silt; full of silt.

Silurian, sī•lū′ri•an, *a.* Belonging to the *Silures,* an ancient people of South Wales.—*Silurian rocks, strata, system, geol.* the name given to a great succession of Paleozoic strata intervening between the Cambrian formation and the base of the old red sandstone; so called from the district where the strata were first investigated.

silva, sil′va, *a.* See SYLVA.

silvan, sil′van, *a.* See SYLVAN.

silver, sil′vėr, *n.* [A.Sax. *seolfer*= Icel. *silfr,* D. *zilver,* Dan, *sölv,* G. *silber,* Goth. *silubr.*] A white metallic element, ductile, malleable, and having the highest electrical and thermal conductivity of any substance—symbol, Ag (Latin, *argentum*); at. no., 47; at. wt., 107.870; money; coin made of silver; plate made of silver. GERMAN SILVER, NICKEL SILVER.—*Silver* is used in the formation of many self-explanatory compounds, as *silver*-bright, *silver*-clear, *silver*-white, etc.—*a.* Made of silver; resembling silver; silvery.—*Silver age,* the second mythological period in the history of the world, following the golden age. The term is also applied to the period of Roman literature subsequent to the most brilliant period, from about A.D. 14 to A.D. 180.—*v.t.* To cover superficially with a coat of silver; to cover with tinfoil amalgamated with quicksilver (to *silver* glass); to give a silvery sheen or silver-like luster to; to make hoary; to tinge with gray.—**silver certificate,** *n.* A certificate issued by a government against silver on deposit, used as legal tender.—**silverfish,** *n.* A fish of a white color with silvery lines, a variety of goldfish; a wingless insect. —**silver fox,** *n.* A fox of the northern parts of Asia, Europe, and America, with a valuable fur of a shining black color, intermingled with white. —**silvering,** sil′vėr•ing, *n.* The art of covering the surface of anything with silver, or with an amalgam of tin and mercury; the silver or amalgam laid on.—**silverly,** sil′vėr•li, *adv.* With a bright appearance, like silver. —**silver nitrate,** *n.* A salt of silver dissolved in nitric acid, used in photography and as an antiseptic.—**silversmith,** sil′vėr•smith, *n.* One whose occupation is to work in silver.—**silver-tongued,** *a.* Having a smooth tongue or speech.—**silverware,** *n.* A collective name for tableware, dishes, and ornaments made of silver.—**silvery,** sil′vėr•i, *a.* Like silver; containing silver; with luster.

simian, simious, sim′i•an, sim′i•us, *a.* [L. *simia,* an ape, from *simus,* flat-nosed.] Pertaining to apes or monkeys; apelike.—*n.* An ape or monkey, especially an anthropoid ape, as the gorilla and chimpanzee.

similar, sim′i•lėr, *a.* [Fr. *similaire,* from a hypothetical *similaris,* from L. *similis,* like; akin to *simul,* together, from root of E. *same. Dissemble, resemble, simulate,* etc., are akin.] Like; resembling; having a like form or appearance; like in quality; *geom.* having like parts and relations but not of the same magnitude.—*n.* That which is similar; something that resembles something else.—**similarity,** sim•i•lar′i•ti, *n.* The state of being similar; close likeness; perfect or partial resemblance.—**similarly,** sim′i•lėr•li, *adv.* In a similar or like manner; with resemblance in essential points.

simile, sim′i•lē, *n.* [L., a like thing, from *similis,* like. SIMILAR.] *Rhet.* the likening together of two things which, however different in other respects, have some strong point or points of resemblance; a poetic or imaginative comparison. METAPHOR. —**similitude,** si•mil′i•tūd, *n.* [L. *similitudo.*] Likeness; resemblance, in nature, qualities, or appearance; a comparison; a simile; a representation; a facsimile; similarity; guise.

simious. See SIMIAN.

simmer, sim′ėr, *v.i.* [Probably imitative of the gentle murmuring sound made by liquids beginning to boil or boiling very slowly.] To boil or bubble gently, or with a gentle hissing.

simony, sim′o•ni, *n.* [Fr. *simonie,* L.L. *simonia,* from *Simon* Magus, who wished to purchase the power of conferring the Holy Spirit. Acts, viii.] The buying or selling of ecclesiastical preferment; the presentation of anyone to an ecclesiastical benefice for money or reward.—**simoniac,** si•mō′ni•ak, *n.* [Fr. *simoniaque.*] One who practices simony. —**simoniacal,** sim•ō•nī′a•kal, *a.* Pertaining to, involving, or consisting of simony; guilty of simony.—**simoniacally,** si•mō•nī′a•kal•li, *adv.* In a simoniacal manner.

simoom, si•möm′, *n.* [Ar. *samûm,* from *samma,* to poison.] An intensely hot suffocating wind, laden with dust and sand, that blows occasionally in Africa and Arabia, generated by the extreme heat of the parched deserts. Also SIMOON.

simper, sim′pėr, *v.i.* [Akin to Prov.G. *simpern,* to be affectedly coy; Dan. *semper, simper,* coy.] To smile in a silly, affected manner.—*n.* A smile with an air of silliness; an affected smile or smirk.—**simperer,** sim′pėr•ėr, *n.* One who simpers.—**simperingly,** sim′pėr•ing•li, *adv.* In a simpering manner.

simple, sim′pl, *a.* [Fr. *simple,* from L. *simplex,* simple, from a root meaning one or unity (also in E. *same*), and that of *plica,* a fold (E. *ply*).] Not complex or compound; consisting of one thing or substance only; not complex or complicated; easily intelligible; clear; not given to deceit or duplicity; artless in manner; unaffected; inartificial; unadorned; plain; mere; being no more and no less (a *simple* knight); common; humble; weak in intellect; not wise or sagacious; silly; *bot.* consisting of one; not exhibiting divisions; *chem.* that has not been decomposed or separated into two or more elements; elementary.—*Simple interest.* Under INTEREST.—*n.* Something not mixed or compounded; a medicinal herb or a medicine obtained from an herb: so called because each vegetable was supposed to have one particular virtue.—**simple-minded,** *a.* Artless; undesigning; unsuspecting. — **simple-mindedness,** *n.* The character of being simple-minded.—**simpleness,** sim′pl•nes, *n.* The state or quality of being simple; simplicity.—**simpleton,** sim′pl•ton, *n.* [From *simple,* with French term. *-ton.*] One who is very simple; a silly or foolish person; a person of weak intellect.—**simplicity,** sim•plis′i•ti, *n.* [Fr. *simplicité,* L. *simplicitas.*] The state or quality of being simple, unmixed, uncompounded, or not complex; artlessness of mind; freedom from slyness or cunning; sincerity; freedom from artificial ornament; plainness; weakness of intellect; silliness. —**simplification,** sim′pli•fi•kā″shon, *n.* The act of simplifying.—**simplify,** sim′pli•fī, *v.t.*—*simplified, simplifying.* [Fr. *simplifier,* L.L. *simplificare,* L. *simplex,* and *facio,* to make.] To make simple; to bring to greater simplicity; to show an easier or shorter process for doing or making; to make plain or easy.—**simply,** sim′pli, *adv.* In a simple manner; without art or subtlety; plainly; merely; solely; weakly; foolishly.

simulacrum, sim•ū•lā′krum, *n.* pl. **simulacra,** sim•ū•lā′kra. [L.] An unreal or mock image or likeness; a phantom; a hollow, pretentious person.

simulate, sim′ū•lāt, *v.t.*—*simulated, simulating.* [L. *simulo, simulatum,* from *similis,* like. SIMILAR.] To assume the mere appearance or character of, without the reality; to counterfeit; to feign.—**simulation,** sim•ū•lā′shon, *n.* The act of simulating or of feigning to be that which one is not. ∴ *Simulation* denotes the assuming of a false character; *dissimulation,* the concealment of the true character.—**simulator,** sim′ū•lā•tėr, *n.* One who simulates.

simultaneous, sī′mul•tā″ni•us, *a.* [L. L. *simultaneus,* from L. *simul,* at the same time, akin to *similis,* like, E. *same.*] Taking place or happening at the same time; done at the same time; coincident in time.—**simultaneously,** sī′mul•tā″ni•us•li, *adv.* At the same time; together; in conjunction.—**simultaneousness, simultaneity,** sī′mul•tā″ni•us•nes, sī′mul•ta•nē″i•ti, *n.* The state or quality of being simultaneous; coincidence; concomitance.

sin, sin, *n.* [A.Sax. *synn, sinn,* sin; Icel. and Dan. *synd,* O.D. *sunde,* G. *sunde,* sin; connected with L. *sons, sontis,* guilty.] The voluntary departure of a moral agent from a custom prescribed by society or by divine law or divine command; moral depravity; wickedness; iniquity; an offense in general; a transgression.—*v.i.*—*sinned, sinning.* To commit a sin, to violate any known rule of duty; to offend in general; to transgress; to trespass: with *against* (to *sin against* good taste).—*To sin one's mercies,* to be unmindful of the gifts of Providence.—**sinful,** sin′fu̇l, *a.* Tainted with, or full of sin, wicked; containing sin or consisting of sin.—**sinfully,** sin′fu̇l•li, *adv.* In a sinful manner; wickedly.—**sinfulness,** sin′fu̇l•nes, *n.* The quality of being sinful.—**sinless,** sin′les, *a.* Free from sin; innocent.—**sinlessly,** sin′les•li, *adv.* In a sinless manner.—**sinlessness,** sin′les•nes, *n.* The state of being sinless.—**sinner,** sin′ėr, *n.* One who sins; one who fails in any duty or transgresses any law; an offender.

sinapism, sin′a•pizm, *n.* [Fr. *sinapisme,* L. *sinapismus,* from *sinapis,* Gr. *sinapi,* mustard.] A mustard poultice.

since, sins, *adv.* [O.E. *sins, sinnes, sithens, sithence,* all genitive forms from A.Sax. *siththan,* lit. after that. Comp. the genitives *hence, whence.*] From that time; after that time; from then till now; in the interval; before this or now; ago.—*prep.* Ever from the time of; subsequently to; after.—*conj.* From the time when (*since* I saw you last); because that; seeing that; inasmuch as.

sincere, sin•sēr′, *a.* [L. *sincerus,* sincere, pure, unmixed.] Pure; unmixed; being in reality what it appears to be; not feigned or simulated; not assumed; real; genuine; undissembling; guileless; frank; true. —**sincerely,** sin•sēr′li, *adv.* In a sincere manner.—**sincereness, sincerity,** sin•sēr′nes, sin•ser′i•ti, *n.* The quality of being sincere; freedom from hypocrisy; truthfulness; genuineness; earnestness.

sinciput, sin′si•put, *n.* [L.] The fore part of the head, in contradistinction to the *occiput* or back part.—**sincipital,** sin•sip′i•tal, *a.* Pertaining to the sinciput.

sine, sīn, *n.* [L. *sinus,* a bending, a curve, a bosom.] *Trigon.* the straight line drawn from one extremity of an arc perpendicular to the diameter passing through the other extremity. —*Versed sine* of an arc or angle, the segment of the diameter intercepted between the sine and the extremity of the arc.

sinecure, sī′ni•kūr, *n.* [L. *sine,* without, and *cura,* cure, care.] An ecclesiastical benefice without cure of souls; any office which has revenue without employment.—*v.t.* To place in a sinecure.—**sinecurist,** sī′ni•kūr•ist, *n.* One who holds a sinecure.

sinew, sin′ū, *n.* [A.Sax. *sinewe, sinu;* D. *zenuw;* G. *sehne,* Icel. *sin,* Dan. *sene,* a sinew.] The tough fibrous tissue which unites a muscle to a bone; a tendon; *fig.* that which gives strength or vigor; that in which strength consists.—*Sinews of war,* money as a means of carrying it on.—*v.t.* To knit or strengthen, as by sinews.—**sinewless,** sin′ū•les, *a.* Having no vigor.—**sinewy,** sin′ū•i, *a.* Consisting of or resembling a sinew or sinews; well braced with sinews; strong; vigorous; firm.

sinful, sinfulness, etc. See SIN.

sing, sing, *v.i.*—pret. *sang* or *sung;* pp. *sung.* [A.Sax. *singan,* pret. *sang,* pp. *sungen;* = Icel. *singja,* Dan. *synge,* D. *zingen,* G. *singen;* comp. Gael. *seinn,* to ring as a bell, to sing.] To utter words or sounds with musical inflections or melodious modulations of voice; to utter sweet sounds, as birds; to give out a small shrill or humming sound (the kettle *sings*); to tell or relate something in poetry or verse.—*v.t.* To utter with musical modulations of voice; to celebrate in song; to give praises to in verse; to relate or rehearse in poetry; to act or produce an effect on by singing (to *sing* one to sleep).—**singer,** sing′ėr, *n.* One who sings or whose occupation is to sing; a skilled or professional vocalist.—**singsong,** *n.* A drawling or monotonous tone, or wearying succession of tones; repetition of similar words or tones.—*a.* Drawling; monotonous.

singe, sinj, *v t.*—*singed, singeing.* [A. Sax. *sengan,* to singe, lit. to cause to sing, a caus. of *singan*, to sing; so also G. *sengen*, to singe.] To burn slightly or superficially; to burn the surface, ends, or outside of; to scorch; to remove the nap from, as cloth, by passing it over a red-hot roller, through a gas flame, or the like.—*n.* A burning of the surface; a slight burn.—**singer,** sin′jėr, *n.* One who or that which singes.

Singhalese, sing•ga•lēz′, *n. sing.* and *pl.* A native or natives of Ceylon; Cingalese.

single, sing′gl, *a.* [L. *singulus*, single, from root seen in *simple.*] Consisting of one alone; not double or more (a *single* star, a *single* act); often emphatic, even one (I shall not give you a *single* farthing); individual; considered as apart; alone; having no companion or assistant; unmarried (a *single* man, a *single* life); performed by one person, or by one person only opposed to another (*single* combat); honest; unbiased; sincere.—*Single blessedness*, the unmarried state; celibacy.—*Single entry*, a system of bookkeeping in which each entry appears only once on one side or other of an account.—*v.t.*—*singled*, *singling*. To select individually from among a number; to choose out separately from others: with *out* or similar words.—**single-breasted,** *a.* Applied to a coat or waistcoat which buttons only to one side.—**singlehanded,** *a.* Unassisted; by one's self; alone.—**singleness,** sing′gl•nes, *n.* The state or quality of being single; oneness; sincerity; freedom from duplicity.—**single-phase,** *a. Elect*. Having an alternating current of one phase.—**single tax,** a theory of tax on land values only for all revenue.—**singleton,** *n. Cards*, an only card of a suit in a hand.—**singletree,** *n.* A cross bar, pivoted at the center, to which one horse is hitched.—**singly,** sing′gli, *adv.* Individually; separately; each alone; without partners; honestly; sincerely.

singular, sing′gū•lėr, *a.* [L. *singularis*, from *singulus*, single. SINGLE.] Belonging to one; *gram.* denoting one person or thing (a *singular* noun); marked as apart from others; out of the usual course; odd (*singular* in his behavior); *gram.* the singular number; a word in this number.—**singularity,** sing•gū•lar′i•ti, *n.*—**singularly,** sing′gū•lėr•li, *adv.* In a singular manner; peculiarly; remarkably.

sinister, sin′is•tėr, *a.* [L., left, unlucky, bad; origin doubtful.] On the left hand or left side; left; *her.* the term which denotes the left side of the escutcheon, that is, the *right* side of a drawing of it; evil; bad; ill-intentioned; baneful; malign; unlucky; inauspicious.—**sinisterly,** sin′-is•tėr•li, *adv.* In a sinister manner.—**sinistral,** sin′is•tral, *a.* Belonging to the left hand; inclining to the left.—**sinistrorse,** sin′is•trors, *a.* [L. *sinistrorsus*, from *sinister*, left, and *vorsus*, *versus*, turned.] Directed to the left; turning or twining to the left: usually said of the stems of plants.—**sinistrous,** sin′is•trus, *a.* Sinister; on the left side; inclined to the left.

sink, singk, *v.i.*—pret. *sunk* or *sank*; pp. *sunk* (*sunken* being used as a participial adj). [A.Sax. *sincan* = Dan. *synke*, D. *zinken*, G. *sinken*, Goth, *sigkvan*, to sink.] To fall by the force of gravity; to descend through a medium of little resisting power, as water; to go to the bottom; to fall as from want of bodily strength; to take a lower position to the eye; to decline below the horizon; to be overwhelmed or depressed; to enter the mind and be impressed; to decline in worth, strength, estimation, etc.; to fall off in value; to decay; to decrease and become less deep; to subside.—*v.t.* To cause to descend below the surface; to immerse in a fluid; to cause to fall or drop; to make by digging or delving (to *sink* a well); to depress; to degrade; to bring low; to ruin; to crush; to invest (money) more or less permanently in any undertaking or scheme.—*n.* A basin to receive dirty water and liquid waste, ordinarily with a drainpipe connected and usually with a fresh-water supply, as in a kitchen; a sewer; *fig.* a place where vice and filth abound.—**sinker,** singk′ėr, *n.* One who or that which sinks; a weight, as on a fish line or net, to sink it; a doughnut (*slang*).—**sinkhole,** *n.* A place where drainage collects; a cesspool.—**sinking,** singk′ing, *p.* and *a.* Falling; subsiding; declining.—*Sinking fund*. See FUND.

sinless, sinner, etc. See SIN.

Sinn Fein, shin fān, *n.* [Irish, we ourselves.] An Irish Republican party, aiming at complete independence and separation, with the restoration of the old Irish tongue.

Sinologue, sin′o•log, *n.* [Fr. *sinologue*, from Gr. *Sina*, China, *Sinai*, the Chinese, and *logos*, discourse.] A student of the Chinese language, literature, history, etc.; one versed in Chinese.—**Sinology,** si•nol′o•ji, *n.* The knowledge of the Chinese language, etc.—**Sinological,** sin•o•loj′-i•kal, *a.* Pertaining to Sinology.—**Sinologist,** si•nol′o•jist, *n.* A Sinologue.

sinter, sin′tėr, *n.* A German name for a rock precipitated in a crystalline form from mineral waters.

sinuate, sin′ū•āt, *v.t.* [L. *sinuo*, to curve or bend, from *sinus*, a curve or bend.] To bend or curve in and out; to wind; to turn.—**sinuate, sinuated,** sin′ū•ā•ted, *a.* Winding; sinuous; *bot.* having large curved breaks in the margin, as in the oak leaf, having a wavy margin.—**sinuation,** sin•ū•ā′shon, *n.* A winding or bending in and out.—**sinuosity,** sin•ū•os′i•ti, *n.* The quality of being sinuous; a bending in and out; a bend in such a series; a wave line.—**sinuous,** sin′ū•us, *a.* [L. *sinuosus*.] Bending or curving in and out; of an undulating form; winding; crooked.—**sinuously,** sin′ū•us•li, *adv.* In a sinuous manner.

sinus, sī′nus, *n.* [L., a bend, curve, bay, etc.] Any cavity or channel in the body, as an air cavity in a bone, or a channel for venous blood; one of the cranial hollows that connects with the nasal cavities.—**sinusitis,** sī′nus•ī″tis, *n.* Inflammation of the sinuses.

sinusoidal, sī•nus•oi′dl, *a.* Following a periodic course, like the curve of sines.

Sioux, sö, *n. sing.* and *pl.* A classification of Indians in North America.

sip, sip, *v.t.*—*sipped*, *sipping*. [A lighter form of *sup* = D. and L.G. *sippen*, to sip.] To imbibe or take into the mouth in small quantities by the lips; to drink in or absorb in small quantities; to draw into the mouth; to suck up.—*v.i.* To drink a small quantity; to take a fluid in small quantities with the lips.—*n.* A small draught, taken with the lips.

siphon, sī′fon, *n.* [Gr. *siphōn*, a hollow tube, a reed.] A bent tube whose legs are of unequal length, used for drawing liquid out of a vessel, the shorter leg being inserted in the liquid and the longer hanging down outside: when the air is sucked from the tube the pressure of the atmosphere causes the liquid to rise in it and flow over; *zool.* a tube in certain mollusks conveying water to or from the gills.—**siphon bottle,** *n.* A bottle for aerated waters, which are discharged through a bent tube by the pressure of the gas.

sippet, sip′et, *n.* [Dim. of *sip* or *sop.*] A small sip; a little bit of something eatable; a small piece of bread served along with soup, broth, etc.

sir, sėr, *n.* [Fr. *sire*, from L. *senior*, an elder or elderly person. SENIOR.] A common mode of address now used without consideration of rank or status; a general title by which a speaker addresses the person he is speaking to; [*cap.*] the title distinctive of knights and baronets.

sirdar, sėr′där, *n.* [Hind. *sar-dār.*] A chieftain, captain, or hereditary noble in India; the head of the Egyptian army.

sire, sīr, *n.* [A form of *sir.*] A respectful title used in addressing a king or other sovereign prince; a father; a progenitor (used poetically); the male parent of a beast; particularly used of horses.—*v.t.*—*sired*, *siring*. To beget; to procreate: used especially of stallions.

siren, sī′ren, *n.* [Gr. *seirēn*, a siren.] *Greek myth.* a name of several sea nymphs, who by their singing fascinated those that sailed by their island, and then destroyed them; in works of art often represented as having partly the form of birds, sometimes only the feet of a bird; a charming, alluring, or enticing woman; a woman dangerous from her enticing arts; a genus of amphibians peculiar to the southern parts of the United States: called also *mud eels*; an instrument for measuring the number of sound waves or vibrations; an instrument producing a loud piercing sound and used as a fog or fire signal.—*a.* bewitching; fascinating (a *siren* song).—**sirenian,**

sī•rē′ni•an, *a.* and *n.* Belonging to, or one of, the Sirenia.

Sirius, sir′i•us, *n.* [Gr. *Seirios,* from *seirios,* hot, scorching.] A large and bright star called also the Dog star (which see).

sirloin, sėr′loin, *n.* [Formerly *surloin,* from Fr. *surlonge, surlogne,* a sirloin—*sur,* over, upon, and *longe, logne,* a loin. LOIN.] The loin, or upper part of the loin, of beef, or the part covering either kidney.

sirocco, si•rok′kō, *n.* [It., from Ar. *shoruk,* from *shark,* the east.] An oppressive relaxing wind coming from Northern Africa to Italy, Sicily, etc.; a variety of the Simoom.

sirup, syrup, sir′up, *n.* [Fr. *sirop,* It. *siroppo,* L.L. *syrupus,* from Ar. *sharāb,* beverage, syrup, whence also *sherbet* and *shrub.*] A saturated or nearly saturated solution of sugar in water; any sweet and somewhat viscous fluid; the uncrystallizable fluid finally separated from crystallized sugar in the refining process.—**sirupy, syrupy,** sir′up•i, *a.* Like syrup.

sisal, sisal hemp, sī′sal, *n.* The prepared fiber of the American aloe, used for cordage: from *Sisal,* in Yucatan.

siskin, sis′kin, *n.* [Dan. *sisgen,* Sw. *siska,* G. *zeisig.*] A well-known European songbird of the finch family, of color in general greenish.

sister, sis′tėr, *n.* [From Icel. *systir,* Sw. *syster,* a sister = D. *zuster,* A.Sax. *sweoster,* Goth. *swistar,* G. *schwester,* sister; cog. Rus. *sestra,* L. *soror,* Skr. *swasri.*] A female born of the same parents as another person; correlative to *brother*; a female fellow Christian; a female belonging to the same community (as the nuns in a convent).—*Sisters of Mercy.* See MERCY.—**sisterhood,** sis′tėr•hụd, *n.* The state of being a sister; a society of females united in one faith or one community.—**sister-in-law,** *n.* A husband's or wife's sister; also a brother's wife.—**sisterly,** sis′tėr•li, *a.* Like a sister; becoming a sister.

sistrum, sis′trum, *n.* [L., from Gr. *seistron,* from *seiō,* to shake.] A jingling instrument used by the ancient Egyptians in their religious ceremonies, consisting of a small metal frame with metal rods loosely inserted in it.

Sisyphean, sis•i•fē′an, *a.* [From *Sisyphus,* of *Greek myth.*; punished in the infernal world by having to roll to the top of a hill a huge stone which constantly rolled down again.] Entailing incessantly recurring toil; recurring unceasingly (a *Sisyphean* task).

sit, sit, *v.i.*—pret. and pp. *sat,* ppr. *sitting,* [A.Sax. *sittan* = Icel. *sitja,* D. *zitten,* G. *sitzen,* Goth. *sitan,* to sit; from root seen also in L. *sedeo,* to sit, *sedes,* a seat (whence *sedentary, siege,* etc.); Skr. *sad,* to sit. *Set* is the causative of this verb; *seat* is also akin.] To rest upon the haunches; to repose on a seat; to remain, rest, abide; to lie, bear, or weigh (grief *sits* heavy on his heart); to have a seat or position; to be placed; to incubate; to cover and warm eggs for hatching; to be suited to one's person; to fit or suit when put on; to assume a position in order to have one's portrait taken or a bust modeled; to have a seat in Congress (he *sat* for Ohio); to be convened, as an assembly; to hold a session; to be officially engaged in public business.—*To sit down,* to place one's self on a seat; to begin a siege (the enemy *sat down* before the town).—*To sit out,* to sit till all is done.—*To sit under,* to attend church for the purpose of hearing; to be a member of the congregation of.—*To sit up,* to rise from a recumbent posture; to refrain from lying down; not to go to bed.—*v.t.* To keep the seat upon (he *sits* a horse well); to place on a seat: used with *one's self, me, thee,* etc.—**sitter,** sit′ėr, *n.* One who sits; one who sits for his portrait.—**sitting,** sit′ing, *p.* and *a.* Holding the position of one who sits; incubating; occupying a place in an official capacity; holding a court.—*n.* The act of one who sits; the occasion on which one sits for a portrait or a bust; a session, a business meeting; the time during which one sits, as at books, at cards or dice; the space occupied by one person in a church pew.—**sitting room,** *n.* Sufficient space for sitting in; an apartment for sitting in; a parlor.

site, sīt, *n.* [L. *situs,* site, situation.] Situation, especially as regards relation to surroundings; local position; a plot of ground set apart for building.

sitology, sī•tol′o•ji, *n.* [Gr. *sitos, sition,* food, and *logos,* discourse.] That department of medicine which relates to the regulation of diet; dietetics.—**sitophobia, sitomania,** sī•to•fō′bi•a, si•to•mā′ni•a, *n.* [Gr. *phobos,* fear, *mania,* madness.] Morbid repugnance to or refusal of food.

situate, sit′ū•āt, *v.t.* [Fr. *situé,* situated, from L. *situs,* a site.] To place with respect to any other object; to fix permanently.—**situated,** sit′ū•ā•ted, *a.* [A later form of *situate,* but now more common.] Having a site; placed or permanently fixed with respect to any other object; being in any state or condition with regard to men or things: circumstanced.—**situation,** sit•ū•ā′shon, *n.* [Fr. *situation.*] Position or location in respect to physical surroundings; state, condition, or position with respect to society or circumstances; temporary state or position; place, post, or permanent employment.

sitz bath, sits, *n.* [G. *sitz-bad—sitz,* a seat, and *bad,* a bath.] A form of bath in which one can bathe sitting; a bath taken in a sitting posture.

Siva, sē′va, *n.* The name of the third god of the Hindu triad, in which he represents the principle of destruction.

Sivan, sē•vän′, *n.* The third month of the Jewish year, answering to part of May and part of June.

six, siks, *a.* [A.Sax. *six* = Icel., Dan., and Sw. *sex,* D. *zes,* G. *sechs,* Goth. *saihs,* L. *sex,* Gr. *hex,* Per. *shesh,* Skr. *shash,* six.] Twice three; one more than five.—*n.* The number of six or twice three; a symbol representing this number, as 6.—*At sixes and sevens,* in disorder and confusion.—**sixfold,** siks′fōld, *a.* and *adv.* Six times repeated.—**sixpence,** siks′pens, *n.* An English silver coin.—**sixpenny,** siks′pen•i, *a.* Worth sixpence; costing six pence.—**six-shooter,** *n.* A six-chambered revolver pistol.—**sixteen,** siks′tēn, *a.* and *n.* [A.Sax. *sixtýne.*] Six and ten; consisting of six and ten.—**sixteenmo,** siks′tēn•mō, *n.* See SEXTO-DECIMO.—**sixteenth,** siks′-tēnth, *a.* Next in order after the fifteenth.—*n.* One of sixteen equal parts into which a thing is divided.—**sixth,** siksth, *a.* The first after the fifth.—*n.* A sixth part; *mus.* an interval of two kinds, the *minor sixth,* consisting of three tones and two semitones, and the *major sixth,* composed of four tones and a semitone.—**sixthly,** siksth′li, *adv.* In the sixth place.—**sixtieth,** siks′ti•eth, *a.* Next in order after the fifty-ninth.—*n.* One of sixty equal parts of a thing.—**sixty,** siks′ti, *a.* and *n.* [A.Sax. *sixtig.*] Ten times six; the sum of six times ten.

sizar. See SIZE.

size, sīz, *n.* [Contr. for *assize,* and meaning originally quantity or dimensions *assessed* or settled. ASSESS, ASSIZE.] Extent of volume or surface; dimensions great or small; comparative magnitude; bulk; a conventional relative measure of dimension, as of shoes, gloves, etc.—*v.t.*—*sized, sizing.* To adjust or arrange according to size; to fix the standard of.—*Size up,* to estimate, to value, take correct estimate of person or thing.—**sizable,** sī′za•bl, *a.* Of considerable size; of suitable size; sometimes written *Sizeable.*—**sized,** sīzd, *p.* and *a.* Having a particular magnitude; commonly used in compounds.—**sizer,** sī′zėr, *n.* One who or that which sizes; a kind of gauge.—**sizar,** sī′zär, *n.* [From *size,* the term at Cambridge for an allowance of food from the buttery.] One of a class of students in Cambridge University who get their commons or food free and receive certain emoluments, ranking below the ordinary students.

size, sīz, *n.* [It. *sisa, assisa,* a kind of glue, size, akin to *size* above, meaning a settling substance.] A kind of weak glue used by painters (to mix with colors), paper manufacturers, etc.; a tenacious varnish used by gilders; matter resembling size.—*v.t.*—*sized, sizing.* To cover with size; to prepare with size.—**sizing,** sī′zing, *n.* The act of covering with size; the coating of size.

skate, skāt, *n.* [From D. *schaats,* or Dan. *skœite,* a skate.] A contrivance consisting of a steel runner or ridge fixed to a wooden sole, or to a light iron framework, fastened under the foot, and used to enable a person to glide rapidly over ice.—*v.i.*—*skated, skating.* To slide or move on skates.—**skater,** skā′tėr, *n.* One who skates.

skate, skāt, *n.* [Icel. *skata,* a skate; comp. L. *squatina,* the angel-fish.]

A name for several species of the ray family of fishes, having the body flat, and more or less approaching to a rhomboidal form.

skean, skēn, *n.* [Gael. *sgian,* Ir. *scian,* W. *ysgien,* a large knife.] A large knife used by the Irish and Highlanders of Scotland.

skeet, skēt, *n.* Trapshooting, as of clay pigeons hurled into the air.

skeg, skeg, *n.* [Icel. *skegg,* a beard, the cutwater of a ship.] The afterpart of a ship's keel.—*pl.* A kind of oats.

skein, skān, *n.* [Fr. *escaigne*; of Celtic origin.] A small hank of thread; a certain quantity of yarn put up together.

skeleton, skel′e•ton, *n.* [Gr. *skeleton,* a dried body, a mummy, *skeletos,* dried up, from *skellō,* to dry.] The hard firm pieces constituting the framework which sustains the softer parts of any animal, in vertebrates consisting of bony pieces; the bones of an animal body separated from the flesh and retained in their natural position; the supporting framework of anything; an outline or rough draft; the heads and outline of a literary performance; a very thin or lean person.—*A skeleton in every house,* something to annoy and to be concealed in every family.—*a.* Containing mere outlines or heads (a *skeleton* sermon).—*Skeleton proof,* an early proof of an engraving with the inscription outlined in hair strokes only.—**skeletonize,** skel′e•ton•īz, *v.t.* To form into a skeleton; to make a skeleton of.—**skeletal,** skel′e•tal, *a.* Pertaining to a skeleton.—**skeleton key,** *n.* A thin light key with nearly the whole substance of the bits filed away.

skep, skep, *n.* [A.Sax. *scep,* a basket, chest, box.] A sort of basket, narrow at the bottom and wide at the top; in Scotland, a beehive.

skeptic, skep′tik, *n.* [Fr. *sceptique,* from Gr. *skeptikos,* thoughtful, skeptic, from *skepsis,* speculation, doubt, from *skeptomai,* to examine critically.] One who doubts the truth of any principle or system of principles or doctrines; one who disbelieves or hesitates to believe; a disbeliever; a person who doubts the existence of God or the truth of revelation; one who disbelieves in the divine origin of Christianity.—**skeptical,** skep′ti•kal, *a.* Belonging to or characteristic of a skeptic or skepticism; holding the opinions of a skeptic.—**skeptic,** skep′tik, *a.* Skeptical.—**skeptically,** skep′ti•kal•li, *adv.* In a skeptical manner. —**skepticalness,** skep′ti•kal•nes, *n.* The state or quality of being skeptical.—**skepticism,** skep′ti•sizm, *n.* The doctrines or opinions of a skeptic; disbelief or inability to believe; doubt; incredulity; a doubting of the truth of revelation, or of the Christian religion.

sketch, skech, *n.* [O.Fr. *esquiche,* Mod.Fr. *esquisse,* from It. *schizzo,* a sketch, from L. *schedius,* Gr. *schedios,* offhand, sudden.] An outline or general delineation of anything; a first rough or incomplete draft; a picture rapidly executed and intended to give the general features or characteristic aspect; the first embodiment of an artist's idea in clay, on canvas, or on paper.—*v.t.* To draw a sketch of; to make a rough draft of; to give the principal points or ideas of; to delineate.—*v.i.* To practice sketching.—**sketcher,** skech′ėr, *n.* One who sketches.—**sketchily,** skech′i•li, *adv.* In a sketchy manner.—**sketchiness,** skech′i•nes, *n.* State of being sketchy.—**sketchy,** skech′i, *a.* Possessing the character of a sketch; not executed with finish or carefulness of detail; unfinished.

skew, skū, *a.* [Closely akin to Dan. *skiev,* Icel. *skeifr,* L.G. *schewe,* oblique, askew; allied to *shy.*] Having an oblique position; turned or twisted to one side.—*adv.* Awry; obliquely.—*v.t.* To put askew; to shape or form in an oblique way.—**skew arch,** *n.* An arch which is not at right angles to its abutments.

skewer, skū′ėr, *n.* [Prov.E. *skiver,* a skewer=*shiver,* a splinter.] A pin of wood or iron for fastening meat to a spit or for keeping it in form while roasting.—*v.t.* To fasten with skewers; to pierce or transfix.

ski, skē, *n.* [O.N. *skidh,* snowshoe.] A long, narrow snowshoe for running or traveling over snow.—**skijoring,** skē′jō•ring, *v.i.* Being drawn by a horse over snow or ice, wearing skis.—**ski jump,** skē jump, *n.* A jump by a performer on skis from a takeoff on a hillside.

skiagraphy, skī•ag′ra•fi, *n.* [Gr. *skiagraphia*—*skia,* a shadow, and *grapho,* to describe.] The act or art of correctly delineating shadows; the art of sketching objects with correct shading.—**skiagraph,** skī′a•graf, *n.* The section of a building to show its inside; an object shown by shadow, as by X-rays.—**skiagraphic, skiagraphical,** *a.*

skid, skid, *n.* [Dan. and Sw. *skid,* Icel. *skith,* a billet of wood.] A fender for a ship's side; a log or something else forming an inclined plane in loading or unloading heavy articles from trucks, etc.; uncontrolled sliding, as by an automobile on a slippery pavement; a platform upon which paper is piled and shipped from the mill to facilitate handling.—*Aviation, Tailskid,* part of the landing gear of an aircraft, arranged to slide along the ground.—*v.t.*—*skidded, skidding.* To check with a skid.—*v.i.* To slip, as a wheel, on a slippery surface without taking hold.—*Aviation,* sliding sideways in flight away from the center of the turn.

skiff, skif, *n.* [Fr. *esquif,* from O.G. *scif,* Mod.G. *schiff,* a ship. SHIP.] A popular name for any small boat.

skill, skil, *n.* [From Icel. *skil,* Dan. *skiel,* discrimination, discernment, from stem of Icel. *skilja,* A.Sax. *scylan,* to divide, to separate, to distinguish. *Scale, shell, scalp, scull, shale,* are akin.] Discernment; understanding; knowledge; wit; familiar knowledge of any art or science, united with readiness and dexterity in execution or performance; nice art in the application of knowledge of any kind; power to discern and execute; dexterity; aptitude.—**skillful,** skil′fụl, *a.* Having skill; skilled; well versed in any art; dexterous; expert; displaying or done with skill; clever.—**skillfully,** skil′fụl•li, *adv.* In a skillful manner; dexterously; expertly.—**skillfulness,** skil′fụl•nes, *n.* The quality of being skillful.—**skilled,** skild, *a.* Having skill or familiar knowledge, united with readiness and dexterity; expert; skillful.—**skilless,** skil′les, *a.* Wanting skill.

skillet, skil′et, *n.* [O.Fr. *escuellette,* dim. of *escuelle,* from L. *scutella,* a dish. SCUTTLE.] A kitchen pan with a long handle, used for frying and commonly called a frying pan.

skim, skim, *v.t.*—*skimmed, skimming,* [From *scum,* like *fill* from *full.*] To lift the scum from; to clear from any substance floating on the top; to take off from a surface; to pass near the surface of; to pass over lightly; to glance over in a superficial manner (to *skim* a newspaper article).—*v.i.* To pass lightly; to glide along.—**skimmer,** skim′ėr, *n.* One who or that which skims; a flat dish or ladle for skimming liquors; an aquatic swimming bird, called also *scissor-bill,* from its peculiar bill.—**skim milk,** *n.* Milk from which the cream has been taken.

skimble-skamble, *a.* Rambling, worthless stuff. (*Shak.*)

skimp, skimp, *v.t.* and *i.* [Origin not known.] To be sparing of.—*adj.* Meager.—**skimpy,** skim′pē, *adj.* Scanty; lacking in size; stingy.

skin, skin, *n.* [Same as Icel. and Sw. *skinn,* Dan. *skind,* skin.] The external layer or tissue of most animals; a pelt; the skin of an animal used as a vessel (wine-*skin*); any external covering resembling skin in appearance or use.—*v.t.*—*skinned, skinning.* To strip the skin or hide from; to flay; to peel.—*v.i.* To become covered with skin (a wound *skins* over). —**skindive,** skin′dīv, *v.i.* To swim with mask, fins, and breathing apparatus below the surface of the water. —**skinflint,** skin′flint, *n.* A niggardly person.—**skinner,** skin′ėr, *n.* One who skins; one who deals in skins, pelts, or hides.—**skinny,** skin′i, *a.* Consisting of skin, or of little more than skin; wanting flesh.

skink, skingk, *n.* [Gr. *skingkos,* a kind of lizard.] A small lizard of Egypt, etc.

Skinnerian, *a.* [From B. F. Skinner, a psychologist.] Pertaining to a type of functional analysis of behavior: involving the role of response and of its reinforcement from the environment in shaping learning behavior, which led to the development of the teaching machine.

skip, skip, *v.i.*—*skipped, skipping.* [Akin to Sw. *skimpa,* to run, *skumpa, skompa,* to skip.] To fetch quick leaps or bounds; to spring; to jump lightly; to pass without notice in reading; to make omissions in writing; often followed by *over.*—

v.t. To pass with a bound; to pass over intentionally in reading.—*n.* A leap; a bound; a spring.—**skipjack,** *n.* An upstart; a name given to certain beetles, from their being able to spring into the air, and thus regain their feet when laid on their backs.—**skipper,** skip′ėr, *n.* One who skips; the cheese maggot.—**skipping,** skip′ing, *p.* and *a.* Given to skips; moving with leaps.

skip, skip, *n.* [Icel. *skipa,* to place in order, to arrange.] In the games of bowls and curling, an experienced player chosen by each of the rival sides as their director or captain.

skipper, skip′ėr, *n.* [D. *schipper,* lit. a shipper, from *schip,* a ship. SHIP.] The master of a small trading or merchant vessel; a sea captain.

skirmish, skėr′mish, *n.* [O.Fr. *eskermir,* to fence; It. *schermire;* from O.H.G. *skirman,* to fight, to defend one's self, from *skirm,* a shield.] A slight fight in war, especially between small parties; a short, desultory kind of engagement; a short contest of any kind; a contention.—*v.i.* To fight slightly or in small parties.—**skirmisher,** skėr′mish•ėr, *n.* One that skirmishes.

skirt, skėrt, *n.* [The older form of *shirt.*] The lower and loose part of a coat or other garment; the edge of any part of dress; border; margin; extreme part; a woman's garment like a petticoat; the diaphragm or midriff in animals.—*v.t.* To border; to form the border or edge of; to run along the edge of.—*v.i.* To be on the border.

skit, skit, *n.* [From A.Sax. *scyte,* lit. a shooting, from *sceōtan,* to shoot. SHOOT.] A satirical or sarcastic attack; a pasquinade; a squib.—**skittish,** skit′ish, *a.* [Comp. Prov.E. *skit,* hasty.] Easily frightened; shy; wanton; volatile; changeable; fickle.—**skittishly,** skit′ish•li, *adv.* In a skittish manner.—**skittishness,** skit′ish•nes, *n.* The quality of being skittish; shyness; fickleness; wantonness.

skittles, skit′lz, *n. pl.* [From stem of A.Sax. *sceōtan,* to shoot, because shot at. (SKIT, SHOOT.) *Shuttle* is the same word.] A game played with nine pins set upright at one end of a skittle alley, the object of the player being to knock them over with as few throws as possible of a ball.—**skittle alley,** *n.* An oblong court in which the game of skittles is played.

skiver, skī′vėr, *n.* [Akin to *shive.*] An inferior leather made of split sheepskin.

skua, skua gull, skū′a, *n.* [N. *skua,* Icel. *skúfr,* the skua.] A powerful predatory bird of the gull family with strong hooked beak and claws.

skulk, skulk, *v.i.* [Dan. *skulke,* to sneak, allied to *skiule,* Icel. *skjól,* a cover, a hiding place.] To lurk; to keep in a place of concealment; to get out of the way in a sneaking manner; to shun doing one's duty.—**skulker,** skul′kėr, *n.* A person who skulks or avoids performing duties.

skull, skul, *n.* [Same as Sw. *skull, skoll,* a bowl or drinking cup; Dan. *skal,* a shell, *hjerneskal,* the skull (lit. brain-shell); the skull being so called from forming a kind of vessel. Allied to *scale* (of a balance) and to *shell.*] The cranium or bony case that forms the framework of the head and encloses the brain; the brain as the seat of intelligence.—**skullcap,** *n.* A cap fitting closely to the head or skull.

skunk, skungk, *n.* [Contr. from native American *seganku.*] An American carnivorous quadruped of the weasel family, provided with glands from which the animal can emit at pleasure an extremely fetid fluid; *metaphor.* a worthless, low fellow.

sky, skī, *n.* [Same as Icel. *ský,* Dan. and Sw. *sky,* a cloud; allied to A.Sax. *scúa,* a shade; also to E. *shade.* SHADE.] The apparent arch or vault of heaven; the firmament; that portion of the ethereal region in which meteorological phenomena take place; the region of clouds; the plural *skies* is often used in the same sense; weather, climate.—*Open sky,* open air; sky with no intervening cover or shelter.—*v.t. To sky a picture,* to give it a high position.—**sky-blue,** *a.* Of the blue color of the sky.—**skyey,** skī′i, *a.* Pertaining to the sky; ethereal.—**skylark,** *n.* A lark that mounts and sings as it flies, the common lark of Europe.—**skylight,** *n.* A window placed in the roof of a house, and having the same slope; a glazed aperture, in a ship's deck.—**skyline,** *n.* The horizon; a silhouette of trees or buildings against the sky.—**sky pilot,** *n.* Minister, preacher. (*Colloq.*)—**skyrocket,** *n. Fireworks,* a rocket that ascends high and burns as it flies; a species of firework.—**skysail,** *n.* A sail in a square-rigged vessel, next above the royal; sometimes called a *Sky-scraper* when it is triangular.—**skyscraper,** *n.* A high office building, characteristically American, which owes its origin to the lack of available land for building purposes.—**skyward,** skī′wėrd, *a.* and *adv.* Toward the sky.—**skywriting,** *n.* The writing in the air for advertising purposes done by means of oil vapors discharged from airplanes.

slab, slab, *n.* [Perhaps for *sklab,* and allied to Sc. *skelb,* a thin slice, E. *shelf.*] A thin flat regularly shaped piece of anything, as of marble or other stone; an outside piece taken from round timber in sawing it into boards, planks, etc.

slabber, slab′ėr, *v.i.* [Same as D. and L.G. *slabberen,* G. *schlabbern,* to slabber, freqs. of *slabben, schlabben,* to lap; *slaver* is akin.] To let the saliva fall from the mouth carelessly; to drivel; to slaver.—*v.t.* To sup up hastily, as liquid food; to beslobber; to besmear.

slack, slak, *a.* [A.Sax. *sleac,* slack, slow = O.D. and L.G. *slakk,* Icel. *slakr,* Sw. *slak;* same root (with *s* prefixed) as L. *languidus,* languid, *laxus,* lax. LANGUISH.] Not tense or tightly drawn; loose; relaxed; backward; not using due diligence; not earnest or eager; not in a press of business; not busy; dull as regards trade; *pl.* loose trousers.—*Slack water,* the time when the tide runs slowly, between ebb and flow.—*adv.* In a slack manner.—*n.* The part of a rope that hangs loose; small coal screened from household or furnace coal of good quality.—**slack, slacken,** slak′n, *v.i.* To become less tense or tight; to become remiss or backward; to become less violent; to abate; to languish; to flag.—*v.t.* To lessen the tension of; to loosen; to relax; to remit for want of eagerness; to abate; to retard; to repress; to check.—**slacker,** slak′ėr, *n.* One who performs his work or duties remissly; one who seeks to avoid duty, civil or military.—**slackly,** slak′li, *adv.*—**slackness,** slak′nes, *n.*

slack, slak, *v.t.* and *i.* Same as *Slake.*

slag, slag, *n.* [Same as Sw. *slagg,* G. *schlacke,* slag; comp. Icel. *slagna,* to flow over; *slag, slagi,* dampness.] The scoria from a smelting furnace or from a volcano; vitrified mineral matter removed in the reduction of metals; the fused dross of metal in a smelting furnace.

slain, slān, pp. of *slay.*

slake, slāk, *v.t.*—*slaked, slaking.* [Icel. *slôkva,* to slake; Sw. *släcka,* to quench thirst; akin to *slack.*] To quench (thirst, fire, rage); to extinguish; to abate; to reduce (quicklime) to the state of powder by mixing with water.—*v.i.* To be quenched; to become extinct; to slacken; to abate; to decrease.

slalom, sla′lom, *n.* [Nor.] A downhill skiing race, against time, over a zigzag course.

slam, slam, *v.t.*—*slammed, slamming.* [Same as Icel. *slaema, slamra,* to swing, to slam; comp. Sw. *slamra,* to jingle.] To close (a door, a lid) with force and noise; to shut with violence; to bang.—*v.i.* To shut or be closed violently or noisily, as a door.—*n.* A violent shutting of a door; at bridge, thirteen tricks is called a *grand slam,* and twelve, a *little slam.*

slander, slan′dėr, *n.* [O.E. *sclaunder, esclaundre,* from Fr. *esclandre,* from L. *scandalum,* Gr. *skandalon;* so that this word is simply *scandal* in another form.] A false tale or report maliciously uttered, and tending to injure the reputation of another; the uttering of such reports; aspersion; defamation; detraction.—*v.t.* To defame by slander; to injure by maliciously uttering a false report respecting; to calumniate.—**slanderer,** slan′dėr′ėr, *n.* One who slanders; a calumniator; a defamer.—**slanderous,** slan′dėr•us, *a.* Given to slander; uttering slander; containing slander or defamation; calumnious.—**slanderously,** slan′dėr•us•li, *adv.* In a slanderous manner; calumniously.—**slanderousness,** slan′dėr•us•nes, *n.*

slang, slang, *n.* [Connected with *sling,* being originally abusive language hurled at a person.] Colloquial language current among a certain class or classes, educated or uneducated, but having hardly the stamp of general approval, and often to be regarded as inelegant, incorrect, or even vulgar; often used adjectively (a *slang* word or expression).—*v.i.* To use slang; to engage in vulgar, abusive language.—*v.t.* To address with slang or ribaldry; to abuse with vulgar language.—**slangy,** slang'i, *a.* Of the nature of slang; addicted to the use of slang.

slant, slant, *a.* [Akin to Prov.E. *slent,* to slope; Sw. *slinta,* to slide or glide down; perhaps also to *slide.*] Sloping; oblique; inclined from a direct line, whether horizontal or perpendicular,—*v.t.* To give a slant or sloping direction to.—*v.i.* To slope; to lie obliquely.—*n.* An oblique direction or plane; a slope.—**slantingly,** slan'ting•li, *adv.* In a slanting manner.—**slantly, slantwise,** slant'li, slant'wīz, *adv.* Obliquely; in an inclined direction.

slap, slap, *n.* [Same as L.G. *slappe,* G. *schlappe,* a slap, *slappen, schlappen,* to slap; probably from the sound.] A blow given with the open hand, or with something broad.—*v.t.*—*slapped, slapping.* To strike with the open hand, or with something broad.—*adv.* With a sudden and violent blow; plump.—**slapdash,** *adv.* All at once; in a careless manner; at random. (*Colloq.*)

slash, slash, *v.t.* [O.Fr. *esclescher, esclischer,* from O.H.G. *slizan,* to split=E. to *slit.* SLIT.] To cut by striking at random; to cut with long incisions; to slit (to *slash* a garment).—*v.i.* To strike at random with an edged instrument.—*n.* A long cut; a cut made at random; a large slit in the thighs and arms of old dresses, to show a rich colored lining through the openings.—**slashing,** slash'ing, *p.* and *a.* Cutting up, sarcastic, or severe (*slashing* criticism).

slat, slat, *n.* [Perhaps akin to *slate* or, *slit.*] A long narrow slip of wood as in a venetian blind.—*v.i.* To strike against the mast with a flapping sound of the sails.

slate, slāt, *n.* [O.E. and Sc. *sclate,* O.Fr. *esclat* (Fr. *éclat*), a splinter, from *esclater,* to fly in splinters, from O.H.G. *slizan,* to split (E. to *slit*).] A name common to such rocks as are capable of being split readily into thin laminae in accordance with the planes of cleavage; a slab or thin piece of smooth argillaceous stone, used for covering buildings; a tablet for writing upon, formed of slate, or of an imitation of slate; a group of candidates selected to run for political office.—*v.t.*—*slated, slating.* To cover with slates; to select a prospective candidate for an office or position.—**slater,** slā'tėr, *n.* One whose occupation is to slate buildings; a popular name given to small crustaceous animals belonging to the isopods.—**slaty,** slā'ti, *a.* Resembling slate, having the nature or properties of slate.—*Slaty cleavage,* cleavage of rocks into thin plates or laminae in planes oblique to the stratification.

slattern, slat'ėrn, *n.* [From Prov.E. *slatter,* to spill carelessly, to waste; akin to Icel. *sletta,* to squirt; or akin to G. *schlotterig,* negligent; D. *slodderen,* to hang and flap.] A woman who suffers her clothes and house to be in disorder; one who is not tidy; a slut.—*a.* Resembling a slattern; slovenly; slatternly.—**slatternly,** slat'ėrn•li, *a.* Pertaining to a slattern; sluttish.

slaughter, sla̤'tėr, *n.* [From the stem of *slay*; same as Icel. *sláir,* raw flesh, *slátra,* to slaughter. SLAY.] The act of slaying or killing; great destruction of life by violent means; carnage; butchery; a killing of beasts for market.—*v.t.* To slay; to massacre; to butcher; to kill for the market.—**slaughterer,** sla̤'tėr•ėr, *n.* One who slaughters; a person employed in slaughtering; a butcher.—**slaughterhouse,** *n.* A house where beasts are killed for the market; an abattoir.—**slaughterous,** sla̤'tėr•us, *a.* Bent on killing; murderous.

Slav, slav, *n.* One of a race of Eastern Europe, comprising the Russians, Bulgarians, Serbians, Poles, Bohemians, etc.—**Slavic, Slavonic, Slavonian,** slav'ik, sla•von'ik, sla•vō'ni•an, *a.* Pertaining to the Slavs or Slavonians, or to their language.—*n.* The language of the Slavs, belonging to the family of Aryan tongues.

slave, slāv, *n.* [Fr. *esclave,* from G. *sklave,* originally a Slavonian, a captive Slavonian.] A bond servant; a person who is wholly subject to the will of another; a human being who is the property of another; one wholly under the dominion of any power (a *slave* to passion, to fear); an abject wretch; a drudge. (*Slave* is used in the formation of various self-explanatory compounds, as *slave-breeder, slave-catcher, slave-dealer, slave-market, slave-merchant, slave-owner,* etc.)—*v.i.*—*slaved, slaving.* To drudge; to toil; to labor as a slave.—**slavedriver,** *n.* An overseer of slaves at their work; hence, a severe or cruel master.—**slaveholder,** *n.* One who owns slaves.—**slaver,** slā'vėr, *n.* A person engaged in the slave trade; a slave trader; a vessel engaged in the slave trade.—**slavery,** slā'vėr•i, *n.* The state or condition of a slave; bondage; complete subjection; the system of keeping or holding slaves; exhausting and mean labor; drudgery. ∴ Syn. under SERVITUDE.—**slavish,** slā'vish, *a.* Pertaining to slaves; such as becomes a slave; servile; consisting in drudgery.—**slavishly,** slā'vish•li, *adv.* In a slavish manner.—**slavishness,** slā'vish•nes, *n.* The state or quality of being slavish.

slaver, slav'ėr, *v.i.* [Icel. *slafr,* slaver, *slafra,* to slaver; akin to *slabber, slobber.*] To suffer the spittle to issue from the mouth, to be besmeared with saliva.—*v.t.* To smear with saliva.—*n.* Saliva driveling from the mouth; drivel.

Slavonic. See SLAV.

slay, slā, *v.t.*—pret. *slew*; pp. *slain.* [A.Sax. *slahan,* or contr. *sleán,* to beat, to slay; D. *slaan,* Icel. *sla,* Goth. *slahan,* G. *schlagen*; akin *slaughter, sledge* (-hammer).] To put to death in any violent or sudden manner; to kill; to destroy; to ruin.—**slayer,** slā'ėr, *n.* One that slays; a killer; a murderer.

slay, slā, *n.* A weaver's reed; a sley. See SLEY.

sleave, slēv, *n.* [Probably akin to *slip*; comp. G. *schleife,* a loop, a knot.] Soft floss or unspun silk used for weaving. (*Shak.*)

sleazy, slē'zi, *a.* [Comp. G. *schleiszig,* worn out, threadbare, from *schleiszen,* to split, to wear out. SLIT.] Thin; flimsy; wanting firmness of texture (*sleazy* silk or muslin).

sled, sled, *n.* [D. *slede, sleede,* a sled; Dan. *slaede,* Icel. *sledi*; from stem of *slide.*] A vehicle on runners for use on snow or ice.—*v.t.*—*sledded, sledding.* To transport on a sled.

sledge, sledge hammer, slej, *n.* [A. Sax. *slecge,* a hammer, from *slahan, slagan,* to strike, to slay; so Icel. *sleggia,* a sledge hammer. SLAY.] A large heavy hammer used chiefly by smiths.

sledge, slej, *n.* [Formed from *sled,* or perhaps directly from D. *sleedie,* dim. of *sleede,* a sled.] A vehicle mounted on runners for the conveyance of loads over snow or ice, or the bare ground; a sled; a traveling carriage mounted on runners; a sleigh; the hurdle on which traitors were formerly drawn to execution.—*v.t.* and *i.*—*sledged, sledging.* To convey or travel in a sledge or sledges.—**sledge-chair,** *n.* A chair mounted on runners and propelled on the ice.

sleek, slēk, *a.* [Icel. *slikr,* smooth, sleek; connected with Icel. *sleikja,* Dan. *slikke,* to lick.] Having an even, smooth surface; having the hair smooth; glossy (*sleek* hair).—*v.t.* To make sleek; to render smooth, soft, and glossy; *fig.* to soothe; to calm.—**sleekly,** slēk'li, *adv.* In a sleek manner; glossily.—**sleekness,** slēk'nes, *n.* The quality of being sleek.

sleep, slēp, *v.i.*—pret. and pp. *slept.* [A.Sax. *slaepan, slépan*; D. and L.G. *slapen,* Goth. *slepan,* G. *schlafen,* to sleep; akin to *slip,* G. *schlaff,* loose, relaxed.] To be in that well-known state in which there is a suspension of the voluntary exercise of the powers of the body and mind, and which is periodically necessary to bodily health; to be dead; to lie in the grave; to be at rest; to be dormant or inactive (the question *sleeps* for the present); to assume a state as regards vegetable functions analogous to the sleeping of animals.—*v.t.* To pass in sleeping; with *away* (to *sleep away* the time); to get rid of, overcome, or recover from by sleeping: usually with *off* (to *sleep off* a fit of sickness).—*n.* A.Sax. *slaep,* D. *slaap,* Goth. *sleps,* G. *schlaf.*] That state in which the senses are more or less unaffected by external objects and the fancy or imagination only is active, and which is necessary to recruit both body and mind; slumber; death.—**sleeper,** slēp'ėr, *n.* A person or an animal that sleeps; an animal that lies dormant; a piece of timber on which are laid the ground joists of a floor; a beam on or near the ground for the support of some superstructure.—**sleepiness,** slēp'i•nes, *n.* The state or quality of being sleepy.—**sleeping,** slēp'ing, *p.* and *a.* Reposing in sleep; pertaining to sleep.—**sleeping car,** *n.* A railroad car fitted up with berths for passengers during night travel.—**sleeping sickness,** *n.* A disease prevalent in the African Congo and transmitted by the bite of the tsetse fly. Its victim becomes lethargic, soon sleeps all the time, becoming emaciated, and usually dies. Epidemic encephalitis; sleeping sickness of unknown etiology, believed to be caused by a virus infection; also called lethargic encephalitis. —**sleepless,** slēp'les, *a.* Without sleep; wakeful; having no rest; never resting.—**sleeplessly,** slēp'les•li, *adv.*—**sleeplessness,** slēp'les•nes, *n.*—**sleepwalker,** *n.* A somnambulist.—**sleepwalking,** *n.*—**sleepy,** slēp'i, *a.* Drowsy; inclined to or overcome by sleep; tending to induce sleep; heavy; inactive; sluggish.

sleet, slēt, *n.* [Akin to N. *sletta*; Icel. *slydda*, Dan. *slud*, G. *schlosse*, sleet.] Rain mingled with hail or snow.—*v.i.* To snow or hail with a mixture of rain.—**sleety,** slēt'i, *a.* Consisting of sleet; characterized by sleet.

sleeve, slēv, *n.* [A.Sax. *sléfe*, a sleeve; O.H.G. *slauf*, clothing; from root of *slip.*] The part of a garment that is fitted to cover the arm.—*To laugh in our sleeve*, to laugh privately or unperceived.—*v.t.*—*sleeved, sleeving.* To furnish with sleeves; to put in sleeves.—**sleeveless,** slēv'les, *a.* Having no sleeves; wanting a cover, pretext, or palliation; resultless; bootless (a *sleeveless* errand).

sleigh, slā, *n.* [D. *sleê*, a contr. form of *sleede*, a sled. SLED.] A vehicle mounted on runners for transporting persons on the snow or ice, of a more elegant form than a sledge.

sleight, slīt, *n.* [From O.E. *sleigh*, *sligh*, sly, like *height* from *high*; so Icel. *slaegth*, slyness, from *slaegr*, sly. SLY.] An artful trick; a trick or feat so dexterously performed that the manner of performance escapes observation; dexterous practice; dexterity.—*Sleight of hand*, legerdemain; prestidigitation.

slender, slen'dėr, *a.* [Same as O.D. *slinder*, thin, slender; comp. D. *slinderen*, *slidderen*, to wriggle, L.G. *slindern*, to glide; akin *slide.*] Small in diameter or thickness compared with the length; not thick; slim; thin; weak; slight (*slender* hope); inconsiderable; insufficient; inadequate; meager (*slender* means).—**slenderly,** slen'dėr•li, *adv.* Slightly; feebly; inadequately; meagerly.—**slenderness,** slen'dėr•nes, *n.* The state or quality of being slender; slimness; slightness; smallness.

slept, slept, pret. and pp. of *sleep.*

sleuth, slöth, *n.* A detective. (*colloq.*) See SLOT.

sleuthhound, slöth'hound, *n.* [Icel. *slóth*, the slot or track of an animal. SLOT.] A bloodhound.

slew, slū, pret. of *slay.*

slew, slū, *v.t.* To slue.

slice, slīs, *v.t.*—*sliced, slicing.* [O.Fr. *esclice*, a slice, a splinter, from O.H.G. *skleizan*, *slizan*, G. *schleiszen*, to break, to split. Akin *slate, slit.*] To cut into thin pieces, or to cut off a thin broad piece from; to cut into parts; to cut off in a broad piece. —*n.* A thin broad piece cut off; that which is thin and broad like a slice; a broad thin knife for serving fish at table.—**slicer,** slī'sėr, *n.* One who or that which slices.

slick, slik, *a.* [L.G. *slick*, G. *schlich.*] Dexterous, bland, glib, smooth, smart; having a smooth, glassy surface, as ice.

slide, slīd, *v.i.*—pret. *slid*, sometimes *slided*, pp. *slid, slidden*, ppr. *sliding.* [A.Sax. *slidan*, to slide; O.G. *sliten*, to slide; G. *schlitten*, a sledge; Lith. *slidus*, slippery. *Sledge* (the vehicle) and *sled* are allied.] To move along a surface by slipping; to slip; to glide; to amuse one's self with gliding over a surface of ice; to pass along smoothly; to pass silently and gradually from one state to another, generally from a better to a worse.—*v.t.* To thrust smoothly along; to thrust or push forward by slipping; to pass or put imperceptibly; to slip.—*n.* A smooth and easy passage; a prepared smooth surface of ice for sliding on; an inclined plane for facilitating the descent of heavy bodies; that part of an instrument or apparatus which slides or is slipped into or out of place.—**slider,** slī'dėr, *n.* One who or that which slides; the part of an instrument that slides.—**slidevalve,** *n.* A kind of valve regulating the admission or escape of steam or water in machinery.—**sliding,** slī'ding, *a.* Made so as to slide freely; fitted for sliding.—*n.* The act of one who slides; lapse; backsliding; the slipping of a body along a surface.—**slide rule,** *n.* A mathematical instrument, consisting of two parts, one of which slides along the other, and each having certain numbers engraved on it, such that when a given number on the one scale is brought to coincide with a given number on the other, the product of some other function of the two numbers is obtained by inspection.—**sliding scale,** *n.* A sliding rule; a scale or rate of payment which varies under certain varying conditions; a scale to settle wages by the rise and fall of the market price of the product of labor.

slight, slīt, *a.* [Same as O.L.G. *slight*, D. *slecht*, plain, common, mean; Icel. *sléttr*, smooth, common; G. *schlecht*, smooth; plain, bad; lit. perhaps 'beaten out smooth', the root being that of *slay.*] Not decidedly marked; small; trifling; insignificant (a *slight* difference); not strong or forcible (a *slight* impulse or effort); not severe or serious (a *slight* pain); not thorough or exhaustive (a *slight* examination); not firm or of strong construction; slim; slender; paltry; contemptible. —*n.* A moderate show of disrespect; contempt shown by neglect or inattention; intentional disregard.—*v.t.* To treat as unworthy of notice; to disregard intentionally; to treat with intentional neglect or superciliousness.—**slightingly,** slī'ting•li, *adv.* In a slighting manner; with disrespect.—**slightly,** slīt'li, *adv.* In a slight manner or measure; in a small degree; but little; somewhat.—**slightness,** slīt'nes, *n.* The quality of being slight; smallness; weakness; want of strength; triviality.

slily, slī'li, *adv.* See SLYLY, under SLY.

slim, slim, *a.* [Same as D. *slim*, L.G. *slimm*, Dan. and Sw. *slem*, Icel. *slaemr*, G. *schlimm*, all with the stronger sense of bad.] Slender; of small diameter or thickness in proportion to height; slight; unsubstantial; not executed with due thoroughness; cunning (S. Africa). —**slimness,** slim'nes, *n.* State or quality of being slim.

slime, slīm, *n.* [A.Sax. *slím*, Icel. *slím*, D. *slijm*, G. *schleim*, slime, slimy matter, mucilage, etc.; allied to G. *schlamm*, mud, perhaps to *lime*, *loam.*] A soft ropy, or glutinous substance; soft moist earth having an adhesive quality; viscous mud; asphalt or bitumen (O.T.); a mucous or viscous substance exuded from the bodies of certain animals; *fig.* anything of a clinging and offensive nature.—*v.t.*—*slimed, sliming.* To cover with slime; to make slimy.—**sliminess,** slī'mi•nes, *n.* The quality of being slimy; viscosity.—**slimy,** slī'mi, *a.* Abounding with slime; consisting of slime; overspread with slime.

sling, sling, *n.* [A.Sax. *slinge*, Sc. *slung*, Sw. *slunga*, Icel. *slanga*, O.G. *slinga*, a sling; G. *schlinge*, a noose or snare. See the verb.] An instrument for throwing stones or bullets, consisting of a strap or piece of leather to hold the missile and two strings attached to it; a sweep or swing; a sweeping stroke; a hanging bandage in which a wounded limb is sustained; a rope or chain specially arranged for raising or lowering heavy articles, as casks, bales, etc.; the strap to carry a rifle.—*Slings of a yard* (*naut.*), ropes or chains which suspend it by the middle.—*v.t.*—pret. and pp. *slung.* [A.Sax. *slingan*, to sling, to swing; Dan. *slynge*, Sw. *slinga*, Icel. *slyngva*, G. *schlingen*, to twist; same root as Icel. *slangi*, G. *schlange*, a serpent. *Slink* is akin.] To throw with a sling; to fling or hurl; to hang so as to swing; to place in slings in order to hoist or lower.—*v.i.* To move with long, swinging, elastic steps.—**slinger,** sling'ėr, *n.* One who slings or uses a sling.

sling, sling, *n.* [Comp. L.G. *slingen*, G. *schlingen*, to swallow.] A drink made of liquor or water, and served either hot (*hot toddy*) or with ice.

slink, slingk, *v.i.*—pret. and pp. *slunk* (pret. sometimes *slank*). [A. Sax. *slincan*, to slink, Sw. *slinka*; [perhaps from root of *sling*.] To sneak; to creep away meanly; to steal away.—*v.t.* To cast prematurely: said of the female of a beast.—*a.* Born or cast prematurely, as a calf.—*n.* A sneaking fellow; a calf brought away prematurely.

slip, slip, *v.i.*—*slipped* or *slipt*, *slipping*. [A.Sax. *slipan*, to slip, to guide; D. *slippen*, Dan. *slippe*, Icel. *sleppa*, G. *schleifen*, to slip.] To move smoothly along a surface; to slide; to glide; to have the feet slide; to fall by a false step; to depart or withdraw secretly; to sneak or slink: with *away*; to fall into error or fault; to err; to pass unexpectedly or imperceptibly; to glide; to enter by oversight: with *in* or *into* (some errors have *slipped in*); to escape insensibly, especially from the memory.—*To let slip*, to set free from the leash or noose, as a hound straining after a hare.—*v.t.* To put secretly or unobserved (*slipped* it into his pocket); to let loose (to *slip* the hounds); to disengage one's self from; to cast or suffer abortion of; to make a slip or slips of for planting.—*To slip off*, to take off noiselessly or hastily (to *slip off* one's shoes).—*To slip on*, to put on in haste or loosely.—*To slip a cable*, to let the end of it run out of the ship and sail without weighing anchor.—*n.* The act of slipping; an unintentional error or fault; a mistake inadvertently made (a *slip* of the pen); a departure from rectitude; a venial transgression; an indiscretion; a backsliding; a twig separated from the stock for planting or grafting; a scion (perhaps lit. a twig that can be *slipped* in); a leash or string by which a dog is held; a long narrow piece; a strip (a *slip* of paper); a child's pinafore; a loose covering or case (pillow-*slip*); a woman's fitted, dress-length undergarment with shoulder straps; an inclined plane upon which a vessel is supported while building or upon which she is hauled up for repair; also, a contrivance for hauling vessels out of the water for repairs, etc.; *pottery*, ground flint or clay mixed in water till of the consistence of cream for making porcelain; *geol.* a fault or dislocation of strata; *cricket*, one of the fielders who stands behind the wicket on the off side, and whose duty it is to back up the wicket-keeper; *pl.* that part of a theater at the sides of the stage where the flat scenes are slipped on and off.—*To give a person the slip*, to escape or desert from him.—**slipknot,** *n.* A knot which will not bear a strain, but slips.—**slipper,** slip′ėr, *n.* One who or that which slips or lets slip; loose, light footgear for household wear; a light shoe for formal evening wear.—**slippered,** slip′ėrd, *a.* Wearing slippers.—**slipperiness,** slip′ėr•i•nes, *n.* The state or quality of being slippery.—**slippery,** slip′ėr•i, *a.* [A. Sax. *sliper*, slippery.] Allowing or causing anything to slip or slide readily; so smooth as to cause slipping; not affording sure footing; not to be trusted to; ready to use evasions or the like; unstable; changeable; uncertain.—**slipshod,** slip′shod, *a.* Wearing slippers; wearing shoes down at heel; slovenly, especially with regard to literary qualities.—**slip-on,** *n.* An overcoat or other loose garment that can be easily slipped on or off.

slipslop, slip′slop, *n.* [A reduplication of *slop*.] Bad liquor; feeble composition.—*a.* Feeble; poor.

slit, slit, *v.t.*—pret. and pp. *slit* or *slitted*, ppr. *slitting*. [A.Sax. *slítan*, to tear; akin *slate*, *slice*, *slash*.] To cut lengthwise; to cut into long pieces or strips; to cut a long fissure in (to *slit* the ear or tongue); to cut in general.—*n.* A long cut; a long narrow opening; a slash.

slither, sliTH′ėr, *v.i.* [E. dial. *slidder*, A.Sax. *sliderian*.] To slide along, as on loose stones; to crawl or slide like a snake.—*v.t.* To send sliding.—**slithery,** sliTH′ėr•i, *a.*

sliver, sliv′ėr or slī′vėr, *v.t.* [A.Sax. *slifan*, to cleave, to split.] To cut into long thin pieces; to cut or rend lengthwise.—*n.* A long piece cut or rent off; a splinter; a small branch; *spinning*, a continuous strand of wool, cotton, or other fiber, in a loose untwisted condition.

slob, slob, *n.* Mud; slime; a person who is fat, untidy, and stupid.

slobber, slob′ėr, *v.i.* [A form of *slabber*.] To drivel; to slaver; to slabber.—*v.t.* To beslaver.—*n.* Slaver; liquor spilled; slabber.—**slobberer,** slob′ėr•ėr, *n.* One who slobbers.

sloe, slō, *n.* [A.Sax. *slâ*, Sc. *slaé*, D. and L.G. *slee*, G. *schlehe*, from L.G. *slee*, D. *sleeuw*, G. *schleh*, sour, astringent.] An American wild plum shrub called also *Blackthorn*; also its fruit, which is black and very austere.—**sloe gin,** *n.* An alcoholic beverage flavored with sloe plums.

slogan, slō′gan, *n.* [From Gael. *sluaghghairm*, lit. an army cry.] The war cry or gathering word or phrase of a Highland clan; hence, the watchword used by soldiers in the field; a catchword or phrase, as of a political party, or as in advertising.

sloop, slöp, *n.* [From D. *sloep*, L.G. *sluup*, *slupe*, a sloop; akin *shallop* (through the French).] A vessel with one mast, and often with nothing but fore-and-aft sails, the mainsail being extended by a gaff and a boom, and attached to the mast on its foremost edge.—*Sloop-of-war*, in the British navy, a vessel, of whatever rig, between a corvette and a gunboat.

slop, slop, *v.t.*—*slopped*, *slopping*. [Comp. Icel. *slöp*, offal of fish; Prov. G. *schloppen*, to swallow; E. *slobber*, *slabber*, also to *slip*.] To spill liquid upon; to soil by letting a liquid fall upon something.—*v.i.* To be spilled; to overflow, as some water has *slopped* on the floor.—*n.* A pool of spilled liquid, as produced by upsetting a cup or container of any kind; a quantity of water carelessly thrown about, as on a floor; *pl.* water that has been used for washing; liquid from utensils removed from bedrooms; swill or liquid garbage fed to swine; the clothes and bedding of a sailor.—**sloppily,** *adv.* In a sloppy manner; carelessly.—**sloppiness,** *n.* The state or condition of being sloppy (said of persons as well as things).—**sloppy,** *a.* Of a thin, liquid, or watery consistency; soaked; covered with a liquid; muddy; apt to splash, as *sloppy* roads, *sloppy* food, etc.; carelessly put together or performed; lacking sound construction, as *sloppy* work, a *sloppy* style, etc.; lacking restraint or sincerity, as *sloppy* sentiment.

slope, slōp, *n.* [From A.Sax. *slopen*, pp. of *slúpan*, to slip, akin to *slípan*, and D. *sluipen*, to slip. SLIP.] An oblique direction; a direction inclining obliquely downward; a declivity or acclivity; any ground whose surface forms an angle with the plane of the horizon.—*v.t.*—*sloped*, *sloping*. To form with a slope; to cause to slope; to direct obliquely; to incline.—*v.i.* To take an oblique direction; to descend in a slanting direction.—*To slope arms*, to place the rifle flat on the left shoulder, magazine outward.—**sloping,** slō′ping, *p.* and *a.* Oblique; inclining or inclined from a horizontal or other right line.—**slopingly,** slō′ping•li, *adv.* In a sloping manner; obliquely.

slot, slot, *n.* [Same as D. and L.G. *slot*, a lock, akin to D. *sluiten*, Dan. *slutte*, G. *schliessen*, to lock.] A bolt or bar; an oblong hole in a piece of metal, etc., as for the reception of a bolt; a trapdoor in the stage of a theater.—**slot machine,** an automatic mechanism, the operation of which is started by the insertion of coins; frequently used for gambling purposes.

slot, slot, *n.* [Same as Icel. *slóth*, a track or trail, *sleuth* in *sleuth*-hound.] The track of a deer, as followed by the scent or by the mark of the foot.

sloth, slōth or sloth, *n.* [From *slow*, and equivalent to *slowth* (like *growth* from *grow*); A.Sax. *slaewth*, slowness, from *sláw*, slow. SLOW.] Slowness‡; disinclination to action; sluggishness; indolence; laziness; idleness; the name of two South American mammals, adapted for living in trees but moving with great slowness on the ground.—*Australian sloth*, the koala.—**slothful,** slōth′fu̦l or sloth′fu̦l, *a.* Sluggish; lazy; indolent.—**slothfully,** slōth′ful•li or sloth′fu̦l•li, *adv.* In a slothful manner; sluggishly.—**slothfulness,** slōth′fu̦l•nes or sloth′fu̦l•nes, *n.* The state or quality of being slothful; the habit of idleness.

slouch, slouch, *n.* [Same as Icel. *slókr*, a dull inactive person; akin Sw. *sloka*, to droop, E. *slack*, *slug*, *sluggard*.] A stoop in walking; an ungainly clownish gait; an awkward clownish fellow; a depression or hanging down, as of the brim of a hat.—*v.i.* To have a downcast clownish gait or manner.—*v.t.* To depress; to cause to hang down.—**slouch hat,** *n.* A hat with a hanging brim.

slough, slou, *n.* [A.Sax. *slóh,* a slough; allied to G. *schlauch,* an abyss, the gullet, *schlucken,* to swallow.] A place of deep mud or mire; a hole full of mire.

slough, sluf, *n.* [Sc. *sloch,* a husk; G. *schlauch,* the skin of an animal stripped off.] The cast skin of a serpent or other animal; *surg.* the dead part which separates from the living in mortification, or the part that separates from a foul sore.—*v.i.* To come off, as the matter formed over a sore; a term in surgery.

Slovak, slō′vak, *a.* Of or belonging to the Slav race to the north of Hungary.

sloven, sluv′n, *n.* [Akin to L.G. *sluf,* D. *slof,* careless; D. *sloffen,* to trail one's feet; *slip* is perhaps allied.] A man careless of his dress or habitually negligent of neatness and order; a lazy fellow. *Slut* is the corresponding feminine term.—**slovenly,** sluv′n•li, *a.* Having the habits of a sloven; negligent of personal neatness; wanting neatness or tidiness; loose and careless (*slovenly* dress).—*adv.* In a slovenly manner.—**slovenliness,** sluv′n•li•nes, *n.* The state or quality of being slovenly.

Slovene, slō•vēn′, *a.* Of or belonging to the Slav race in Styria, Carinthia, etc.

slow, slō, *a.* [A.Sax. *slaw,* slow; Dan. *slöv,* Sw. *slö,* Icel. *sljór,* blunt, dull, slow. Hence *sloth.*] Moving a small distance in a long time; not swift; not quick in motion; extending over a long time; gradual; not ready; not prompt; inactive; tardy; dilatory; not hasty; acting with deliberation; indicating a time earlier than the true time (the clock is *slow*); dull; heavy; not lively; stupid.—*Slow coach,* a colloquial term for one who is slow in movement or deficient in quickness.—*Slow match.* See MATCH.—*adv.* Slowly.—*v.t.* To delay; to retard; to slacken in speed.—*v.i.* To slacken in speed.—**slowly,** slō′li, *adv.* In a slow manner; not rapidly; gradually; tardily; not hastily.—**slowness,** slō′nes, *n.* Want of speed or velocity; tardiness; want of readiness or promptness; dullness; dilatoriness; sluggishness.

slowworm, slō′wėrm, *n.* [Not from *slow,* but from A.Sax. *slá-wyrm,* lit. slayworm (from *slahan,* to slay), because it feeds on worms.] A name given to the blindworm. BLINDWORM.

sloyd, sloid, *n.* [Sw. *slöjd,* akin to E. *sleight.*] A system of manual training for pupils in schools, originating in Sweden.

slub, slub, *n.* [Perhaps akin to *slab, n.*] A roll of wool drawn out and slightly twisted by spinning machinery; a rove.—*v.t.—slubbed, slubbing.* To form into slubs.—**slubber,** slub′ėr, *n.* One who slubs; a slubbing machine.

sludge, sluj, *n.* [Also *slutch, slush, slich,* forms corresponding to L.G. *slick,* D. *slik*; *slijk,* dirt, mire, allied to E. *sleek.*] Mud; mire; soft mud.

slue, slū, *v.t.—slued, sluing.* [Perhaps from Icel. *snúa,* to turn, to twist, with change of *n* to *l.*] To turn or swing round (as the yard of a ship).

slug, slug, *n.* [Same as O.E. *slugge,* slow, sluggish. Akin to *slack* or *slouch.*] A sluggard; any of many usually terrestrial pulmonate gastropods, related to the land snail.

slug, slug, *n.* [Origin unknown.] A musket ball or bullet; a metal disk used in coin machines, especially one that is used illegally in place of money; *print.* a line of type cast as one piece; a single drink of liquor.—*v.t.—slugged, slugging.* To strike heavily, as with a fist.

slug, slug, *n.* [Akin to *slay*; comp. Prov. E. *slog,* to strike heavily.] A cylindrical, cubical, or irregularly shaped piece of metal used for the charge of a gun.

sluggard, slug′ėrd, *n.* [M.E. *sluggart.*] An habitually lazy fellow.—**sluggish,** slug′ish, *a.* Inactive; reacting slowly.—**sluggishness,** slug′ish•nes, *n.*

sluice, slös, *n.* [Same as D. *sluys, sluis,* Dan. *sluse,* G. *schleuse,* O.Fr. *escluse,* Fr. *écluse,* from L.L. *exclusa,* from L. *excludo, exclusum,* to shut out, to exclude. EXCLUDE.] A contrivance for excluding or admitting the inflow of a body of water; a waterway provided with a gate by which the flow of water is controlled; a floodgate; any vent for water; that through which anything flows.—*v.t.—sluiced, sluicing.* To let in a copious flow of water on; to wet or lave abundantly; to scour out or cleanse by means of sluices.—**sluice gate,** *n.* The gate of a sluice.

slum, slum, *n.* [Comp. Dan. *slam,* mire, mud.] A neighborhood with dilapidated houses and tenement buildings.

slumber, slum′bėr, *v.i.* [A.Sax. *slumerian,* from *sluma,* slumber; Dan. *slumre,* D. *sluimeren,* G. *schlummern,* to slumber. As to insertion of *b,* comp. *number, humble.*] To sleep lightly; to doze; to sleep; to be inert, or in a state of supineness or inactivity.—*n.* Light sleep; sleep not deep or sound; sleep; repose.—**slumberer,** slum′bėr•ėr, *n.* One that slumbers.—**slumberous, slumbrous,** slum′bėr•us, slum′brus, *a.* Inviting or causing sleep; soporific.

slump, slump, *v.i.* [Comp. Dan. *slumpe,* to stumble or light upon, from *slump,* chance, hazard.] To sink in walking, as in snow; to walk with sinking feet.—*n.* A sudden fall in prices or values.

slung, slung, pret. and pp. of *sling.*

slunk, slungk, pret. and pp. of *slink.*

slur, slėr, *v.t.—slurred, slurring.* [From Prov.E. *slur,* thin mud; comp. Icel. *slor,* filth; L.G. *slurren,* to trail the feet, D. *sloren,* to drag.] To soil or sully; to disparage by insinuation or innuendo; to speak slightingly of; to traduce; to pass lightly over; to say little of; to pronounce in an indistinct or sliding manner; *mus.* to sing or perform in a smooth, gliding style; to run (notes) into each other.—*n.* A slight reproach or disgrace; a stigma; *mus.* the blending of two or more notes; a curved mark indicating this.

slush, slush, *n.* [A form of *sludge.*] Sludge or watery mire; soft mud; wet, half-melted snow; a mixture of grease and other materials for lubrication; refuse fat or grease in ships; a mixture of white lead and lime with which the bright parts of machinery are covered to prevent them from rusting.—*v.t.* To cover or grease with slush.—**slushy,** slush′i, *a.* Consisting of soft mud, or of snow and water; resembling slush.

slut, slut, *n.* [Same as Dan. *slutte, slatte,* D. *slodde,* Prov. G. *schlutte,* a slut; comp. Dan. *slat,* loose, flabby.] A woman who is negligent of cleanliness and tidiness in her person, clothes, furniture, etc.; the correlative of *sloven*; a name of marked contempt for a woman.—**sluttish,** slut′ish, *a.* Like a slut or what is characteristic of a slut; devoid of tidiness or neatness.—**sluttishly** slut′ish•li, *adv.* In a sluttish manner.—**sluttishness,** slut′ish•nes, *n.* The qualities or practice of a slut; untidiness.

sly, slī, *a.* [O.E. *slie, slee,* from Icel. *slaegr,* sly; akin L.G. *slou,* Dan. *slu,* G. *schlau,* sly. Hence *sleight.*] Meanly artful; crafty; cunning; proceeding by underhand ways; wily; cautious; shrewd; arch; knowing (a *sly* remark).—*On the sly,* in a sly or secret manner; secretly.—**slyly,** slī′li, *adv.* In a sly manner; cunningly.—**slyness,** slī′nes, *n.* The quality of being sly; cunning; craftiness; archness.

smack, smak, *v.i.* [A.Sax. *smaeccan,* to taste, from *smaec,* smack, taste = D. *smaak,* Dan. *smag,* G. *geschmack,* taste; D. *smaken,* Dan. *smage,* G. *schmecken,* to taste.] To have a taste or flavor; to taste (it *smacks* of onions); to have a certain quality infused; to partake in character; to savor (it *smacks* of vanity).—*n.* A slight taste or flavor; savor; tincture; a slight or superficial knowledge; a smattering.

smack, smak, *v.i.* [Same as Sw. *smacka,* to smack; D. *smakken,* to smack the lips: imitative of the sound made.] To make a sharp noise with the lips; to kiss so as to make a sound with the lips.—*v.t.* To kiss with a sharp noise; to make a sharp noise by opening the mouth; to make a sharp noise by striking; to crack; to give a sharp stroke to, as with the palm.—*n.* A loud kiss; a quick sharp noise, as of a whip; a quick smart blow, as with the flat of the hand; a slap.—*adv.* In a sudden and direct manner, as if with a smack or slap.—**smacking,** smak′ing, *a.* Making a sharp brisk sound; brisk.

smack, smak, *n.* [Same as D. and L.G. *smak,* Dan. *smakke,* G. *schmake,* a smack.] A large sloop with a gaff-topsail and a running bowsprit; a small sloop used in the fishing trade.

small, smal, *a.* [A.Sax. *smael* = L.G. and D. *smal,* G. *schmal,* Goth. *smals,*

Sc. *sma'*, Dan. and Sw. *smaa*, Icel. *smá(r)*.] Little in size; not great or large; of minute dimensions; little in degree, quantity, amount, duration, or number; of little moment; trivial; petty; trifling; of little genius or ability; insignificant; of little strength or force; weak; gentle; soft; not loud; characterized by littleness of mind or character; narrow-minded; ungenerous; mean.—*Small fruits*, fruits raised in market gardens, such as strawberries, raspberries, and the like.—*The small hours*, the early hours of morning.—*n.* The small or slender part of a thing; *pl.* small-clothes; breeches.—**small arms,** *n. pl.* A general name for rifles, carbines, pistols, etc., as distinguished from cannon.—**small beer,** *n.* A species of weak beer.—**smallclothes,** *n. pl.* Breeches or trousers; smalls.—**small fry,** *n. pl.* Small creatures collectively; young children; persons of no importance.—**smallish,** smạl'-ish, *a.* Somewhat small.—**smallness,** smạl'nes, *n.* The state or quality of being small; littleness of size, quantity, degree, or value.—**smallpox,** *n.* A disease characterized by fever and a cutaneous eruption, propagated by contagion, and very dangerous, especially in persons that have not been vaccinated.—**small stuff** *n.* A nautical term referring to spun yarn, marline, and other small rope of various threads.—**small talk,** *n.* Light conversation; gossip.

smalt, smạlt, *n.* [It. *smalto*, from O.H.G. *smalzjan*, G. *schmelzen*, to melt, to *smelt*.] Glass tinged of a fine deep blue by the protoxide of cobalt, reduced to an impalpable powder, and employed as a pigment and coloring matter.—**smaltine** smạl'-tin, *n.* Gray or tin-white cobalt, consisting of arsenic and cobalt.

smaragd, smar'agd, *n.* [Gr. *smaragdos*, an emerald, a bright green stone.] An old name given to the emerald and other bright-green transparent stones.—**smaragdine,** sma•rag'din, *a.* Pertaining to emerald; of an emerald green.—**smaragdite** sma•-rag'dit, *n.* A mineral, called also *Green Diallage.*

smart, smärt, *n.* [A.Sax. *smeortan*, to smart, to feel pain; D. *smart*, *smert*, Dan. *smerte*, G. *schmerz*, pain, ache; allied to Rus. *smert*, Lith. *smertis*, death, being from a root seen in L. *mors*, death (whence *mortal*).] A sharp quick pain; a pricking local pain; severe pungent pain of mind; *v.i.* To feel a lively pungent pain; to be acutely painful; to feel sharp pain of mind; to suffer acute mental pain. —*a.* Causing a keen local pain; keen; severe; poignant; producing any effect with force and vigor; vigorous (a *smart* blow); sharp; severe (a *smart* skirmish); brisk; fresh (a *smart* breeze); acute and pertinent; witty; vivacious; lively; shrewd; fine in dress; spruce.—**smarten** smär'tn, *v.t.* To make smart; to render brisk, bright, or lively.—**smartly,** smärt'li, *adv.* In a smart manner; keenly; painfully; briskly; sharply; wittily; sprucely.—**smartness,** smärt'nes, *n.* The quality of being smart; pungency; keenness; quickness; liveliness; briskness; vivacity; spruceness.

smash, smash, *v.t.* [Perhaps formed from *mash* through the influence of *smite*; comp. G. *schmiss*, Sw. *smisk*, a dash, a blow.] To break in pieces by violence; to dash to pieces; to crush by a sudden blow.—*v.i.* To go to pieces; to go to utter wreck.—*n.* A breaking to pieces; ruin; bankruptcy.—**smasher,** smash'ėr, *n.* One who or that which smashes.

smatter, smat'ėr, *v.i.* To have a slight superficial knowledge; to talk superficially.—*n.* Slight superficial knowledge.—**smatterer,** smat'ėr•ėr, *n.* One who has only a smattering or slight superficial knowledge.—**smattering,** smat'ėr•ing, *n.* A slight superficial knowledge; an insignificant degree of acquirement (a *smattering* of law).

smear, smēr, *v.t.* [A.Sax. *smerian*, from *smeru*, grease; Icel. *smyrjan*, G. *schmieren*, to smear; D. *smeer*, Icel. *smjör*, Dan. *smör*, G. *schmeer*, grease.] To overspread with anything unctuous, viscous, or adhesive; to besmear; to daub; to soil.—*n.* A spot made as if by some unctuous substance; a stain; a blot or blotch.

smell, smel, *v.t.*—pret. and pp. *smelled* or *smelt.* [Allied to L.G. *smellen*, *smelen*, to smoulder, to smoke; D. *smeulen*, to smoulder; Dan. *smul*, dust, powder. Akin *smoulder*.] To perceive by the nose; to perceive the scent of; to perceive as if by the smell; to detect by sagacity.—*To smell out*, to find out by sagacity.—*To smell a rat.* See RAT.—*v.i.* To exercise the sense of smell; to give out odor or perfume; to affect the sense of smell; to have an odor or scent; to have a smack of any quality.—*n.* The sense or faculty of which the nose is the special organ; the faculty of perceiving by the nose; that which affects the olfactory organs; odor; scent.—**smelling salts,** *n. pl.* Ammonium carbonate, used for resuscitation and stimulation.

smelt, smelt, *n.* [A.Sax. and Dan. *smelt*.] A small edible fish allied to the salmon, inhabiting the salt water about the mouths of rivers and found in some lakes.

smelt, smelt, *v.t.* [Same as D. *smelten*, Dan. *smelte*, Icel. *smelta*, G. *schmelzen*, to melt, to liquefy; akin G. *schmelz*, fat. MELT.] To melt or fuse, as ore, for the purpose of separating the metal from extraneous substances.—**smelter,** smel'tėr, *n.* One who smelts ore.—**smeltery,** smel'-tėr•i, *n.* A house or place for smelting ores.—**smelting,** smel'ting, *n.* The process of obtaining metals from their ores by the action of heat, air, and fluxes.

smew, smū, *n.* [Perhaps for *ice-mew*; comp. the German names *ice-diver* and *mew-diver*.] A swimming bird of the merganser family, frequenting the seashore, lakes, and ponds; also called *White Nun.*

smile, smīl, *v.i.*—*smiled*, *smiling.* [Same as Dan. *smile*, Sw. *smila*, O.G. *smielen*, to smile; same root as Skr. *smi*, to smile.] To express pleasure or slight amusement by a special change of the features, especially the mouth: the contrary of to *frown*; to express slight contempt, sarcasm, or pity by a look; to sneer; to look gay and joyous (the desert *smiled*); to appear propitious or favorable.—*v.t.* To express by a smile (to *smile* content); to put an end to or dispel by smiling: with *away*.—*n.* A peculiar contraction of the features expressing pleasure, approbation, or kindness: opposed to *frown*; gay or joyous appearance; favor; countenance.—**smiler,** smī'lėr, *n.* One who smiles.—**smilingly,** smī'ling•li, *adv.*

smirch, smėrch, *v.t.* [From stem of *smear*.] To stain; to smear; to smudge.

smirk, smėrk, *v.i.* [A.Sax. *smercian*, *smearcian*, to smirk or smile; from stem of *smile*; comp. O.G. *smieren*, to smile.] To smile affectedly or wantonly; to look affectedly soft or kind.—*n.* An affected smile; a soft look.

smite, smīt, *v.t.*—pret. *smote*; pp. *smitten* or *smit*; ppr. *smiting*. [A.Sax. *smitan*, to smite=D. *smijten*, Dan. *smide*, G. *schmeissen*, to strike, to cast or fling; originally to smear or defile; comp. Sc. *smit*, to communicate a disease to; akin are *smudge*, *smut*.] To strike; to give a blow with the hand, something in the hand, or something thrown; to slay; to kill; to assail or visit with something evil; to blast; to afflict, chasten, punish; to strike or affect with love or other feeling.—*v.i.* To strike; to knock.—**smiter,** smī'tėr, *n.* One who smites.—**smitten,** smit'n, pp. of *smite*. Struck; affected with some passion; excited by beauty or something impressive.

smith, smith, *n.* [A.Sax. *smith*, a craftsman, a smith; Icel. *smithr*, Goth. *smitha*, D. *smid*, G. *schmidt*, a smith; not akin to *smooth*.] One who forges with the hammer; one who works in metals: often distinctively applied to a blacksmith.—*v.t.* To hammer into shape; to forge.—**smithery,** smith'ėr•i, *n.* A smithy; work done by a smith; the act or art of forging.—**smithy,** smith'i, *n.* [A.Sax. *smiththe*, a smithy.] The workshop of a smith.

smithereens, SMITH'er•ēnz", *n. pl.* [Perhaps from Ir. *smidirīn*, dim. of *smiodar*, fragment.] Small pieces; atoms; fragments, as *to blow*, *to smash*, *to smithereens.*

smock, smok, *n.* [A.Sax. *smocc*=Icel. *smokkr*, a smock; Sw. *smog*, a garment; lit. a garment one creeps into; comp. A.Sax. *smúgan*, Icel. *smjúga*, to creep. SMUGGLE.] A loose outer garment, usually of knee length, worn to protect other garments, and to keep them from being soiled.—*v.t.* To gather by stitching through material, following a desired pattern; to dress in a smock.

smog, smog, *n.* [Blend of *smoke* and *fog*.] Fog made thicker by the addition of smoke.

smoke, smōk, *n.* [A.Sax. *smoca*,

smoke=D. and L.G. *smook*, Dan. *smōg*, G. *schmauch*, smoke; comp. Gr. *smychō*, to burn slowly.] The exhalation or vaporous matter that escapes from a burning substance; especially the volatile particles expelled from burning vegetable matter; what resembles smoke; vapor; *fig.* idle talk; vanity; nothingness (it all ended in *smoke*); a continuous drawing in and puffing out of the fumes of burning tobacco.—*v.i.*—*smoked, smoking*. To emit smoke or vaporous matter; to give out visible vapor when heated; to inhale and exhale the fumes of burning tobacco; *fig.* to burn or rage (O.T.).—*v.t.* To apply smoke to; to foul by smoke; to hang in smoke; to fumigate; to drive out by smoke; to draw smoke from into the mouth and puff it out; to inhale the smoke of; to discover or find out; to make fun of (a person). —**smokehouse,** *n.* A building employed for the purpose of curing flesh or fish by smoking.—**smokejack** *n.* A machine for turning a roasting spit by means of a flywheel or wheels set in motion by the current of ascending air in a chimney.—**smokeless,** smōk′les, *a.* Having no smoke.—**smoker,** smō′kėr, *n.* One who smokes, especially tobacco; a place for smoking; a smoking concert.—**smokestack,** *n.* In steam vessels a name common to the funnel and the several escape pipes for steam beside it.—**smokily,** smō′ki•li, *adv.* In a smoky manner.—**smokiness,** smō′ki•nes, *n.* The state of being smoky.—**smoky,** smō′ki, *a.* Emitting smoke, especially much smoke; resembling smoke; filled with smoke; tarnished with smoke.—*Smoky quartz*, a variety of quartz of a smoky brown color, much the same as cairngorm.

smolder, smōl′dėr, *v.i.* [Perhaps from old *smorther*, and therefore the same word as *smother*; comp. also Dan. *smuldre, smulre*, to crumble, to molder, from *smul*, dust.] To burn in a stifled manner; to burn and smoke without flame; *fig.* to burn inwardly, as a thought, passion, and the like; to exist in a suppressed state.

smolt, smōlt, *n.* [Comp. Gael. *smal*, a spot.] A salmon when a year or two old, and when it has acquired its silvery scales.

smooth, smöTH, *a.* [A.Sax. *smoethe, smóthe*, also *smethe*, smooth; root doubtful.] Having a very even surface; free from asperities; not rough; evenly spread; glossy; gently flowing; not ruffled or undulating; falling pleasantly on the ear; not harsh or rugged; using language not harsh or rugged; bland; soothing; insinuating; without jolt or shock; equable as to motion.—*Smooth* is often used in the formation of self-explaining compounds, as *smooth*-haired, *smooth*-leaved, *smooth*-shaven, *smooth*-swarded, etc.—*n.* The act of making smooth; the smooth part of anything.—*v.t.* To make smooth; to make even on the surface by any means; to free from obstruction; to make easy; to palliate; to soften; to calm; to mollify; to allay.—**smoothbore,** *n.* A firearm with a smoothbored barrel and not rifled.—**smoothen,** smö′THn, *v.t.* To make smooth; to smooth.—**smoother,** smö′THėr, *n.* One who or that which smooths.—**smoothly,** smöTH′li, *adv.* In a smooth manner; evenly; not roughly or harshly; with bland, insinuating language.—**smoothness,** smöTH′nes, *n.* The state or quality of being smooth; evenness of surface; easy flow of words; blandness of address.

smote, smōt, pret. of *smite*.

smother, smuTH′ėr, *n.* [For older *smorther, smurther*, from A.Sax. *smorian*, to suffocate.] Stifling smoke; a suffocating dust.—*v.t.* To suffocate or stifle; to suffocate by closely covering, and by the exclusion of air; to cover close up, as with ashes, earth, etc.; *fig.* to suppress; to hide from public view.—*v.i.* To be suffocated; to smolder.—**smothery,** smuTH′ėr•i, *a.* Tending to smother; stifling; full of smother or dust.

smudge, smuj, *v.t.*—*smudged, smudging*. [A form of *smutch* (which see).] To smear or stain with dirt or filth; to blacken with smoke.—*n.* A foul spot; a stain; a smear; a smoldering fire used in an orchard to warm the air and protect the fruit from being destroyed by frost.

smug, smug, *a.* [Same as L.G. *smuck*, Dan. *smuk*, G. *schmuck*, handsome, fine, neat; akin to *smock*.] Neat; trim; spruce; fine; affectedly nice in dress; self-satisfied.—*v.t.*—*smugged, smugging*. To make smug or spruce.—**smugly,** smug′li, *adv.* In a smug manner; neatly; sprucely.—**smugness,** smug′nes, *n.* The state or quality of being smug; neatness; spruceness.

smuggle, smug′l, *v.t.*—*smuggled, smuggling*. [Same as L.G. *smuggeln*, Dan. *smugle*, G. *schmuggeln*, to smuggle, from stem of A.Sax. *smúgan*, Icel. *smjúga*, to creep. *Smock* is akin.] To import or export secretly and contrary to law; to manage, convey, or introduce clandestinely.—*v.i.*—To practice smuggling.—**smuggler,** smug′lėr, *n.* One who smuggles; a vessel employed in smuggling goods.—**smuggling,** smug′ling, *n.* The offense of importing or exporting prohibited goods or other goods without paying the legal duties.

smut, smut, *n.* [Akin to *smudge, smutch*; being from stem of *smite*; comp. D. *smet*, a blot, a stain.] A spot made with soot or coal; or the foul matter itself; obscene and filthy language; a disease of cereals, the farina of the seed being converted into a black soot-like powder.—*v.t.*—*smutted, smutting*. To stain or mark with smut or other dirty substance; to affect with the disease called smut. —*v.i.* To gather smut; to give off smut.—**smutty,** smut′i, *a.* Soiled with smut; affected with smut; obscene; not modest or pure.—**smuttily,** smut′i•li, *adv.* In a smutty manner.—**smuttiness,** smut′i•nes, *n.* The state or quality of being smutty.

smutch, smuch, *v.t.* [Closely allied to *smut*; same as Sw. *smuds*, Dan. *smuts*, G. *schmutz*, filth, dirt. *Smudge* is another form. SMUT.] To blacken with smoke, soot, or coal; to smudge. —*n.* A foul spot; a smudge; a black stain.

snack, snak, *n.* [Lit. a 'snatch' or morsel hastily taken. SNATCH.] A portion of food that can be eaten hastily; a slight, hasty repast; a share, as in the phrase, *to go snacks*, that is, to have a share.

snaffle, snaf′l, *n.* [Comp. D. *snavel*, a snout or animal's muzzle.] A bridle, consisting of a slender bit with a single rein and without a curb; a snaffle bit.—**snaffle bit,** *n.* A plain, slender bit having a joint in the middle.

snag, snag, *n.* [Comp. Icel. *snagi*, a small stake or peg.] A small projecting stump of a branch; a branch broken from a tree; the trunk of a large tree stuck by chance in a river with one end projecting so that steamboats, etc., are liable to strike on it.—*v.t.*—*snagged, snagging*. To trim by lopping branches, to injure by a snag.—**snaggy,** snag′i, *a.* Full of snags; having short stumps.

snail, snāl, *n.* [A.Sax. *snael*, contr. from *snaegel, snaegl*=Icel. *snigill*, Dan. *snegl*; dim. forms from root of *snake, sneak*, the name signifying creeping animal.] A slimy, slow-creeping, air-breathing mollusk differing from the slugs chiefly in having a spiral shell, but the latter are also sometimes popularly called *snails*; a slow-moving person; a sluggard; a drone; a piece of spiral machinery; a piece of metal forming part of the striking work of a clock.—**snail-paced,** *a.* Moving very slowly.

snake, snāk, *n.* [A.Sax. *snaca*; Icel. *snákr, snókr*, Sw. *snok*, Dan. *snog*. Akin *sneak, snail*.] A limbless reptile having an elongated body, some species having poison glands and certain upper teeth modified as fangs; a treacherous person, as *a snake in the grass*.—**snakeroot,** *n.* The popular name of various American plants reputed to be remedies for snake bites.—**snakeweed,** *n.* The plant bistort.—**snaky,** snā′ki, *a.* Pertaining to a snake or to snakes; resembling a snake; serpentine; winding; cunning; insinuating.

snap, snap, *v.t.*—*snapped, snapping*. [Same as L.G. and D. *snappen*, Dan. *snappe*, G. *schnappen*, to snap. *Snip* is a lighter form, and *snipe* is connected, probably also *neb*.] To bite suddenly; to seize suddenly with the teeth; to snatch suddenly or unexpectedly; to break upon suddenly with sharp, angry words: often with *up*; to crack; to make a sharp sound with (to *snap* the fingers); to shut with a sharp sound; to break with a sharp sound; to break short.—*To snap off*, to break or bite off suddenly.—*v.i.* To make a sudden effort to bite; to aim to seize with the teeth (to *snap at* a person's hand); to accept promptly (to *snap at* a proposal); to break short; to part asunder suddenly; to give a sharp cracking sound, such as that of the hammer of a firearm when it descends without exploding the charge; to utter sharp, angry words.—*n.* A sudden, eager bite; a sudden breaking or rupture of any substance; a sharp cracking sound: the spring catch of a purse, bracelet, and the like; a crisp kind of gingerbread nut or small cake.—*A cold snap*, a sudden severe time of cold weather.—**snapdragon,** *n.* An antirrhinum; a play in which raisins are snatched from burning brandy and put into the mouth.—**snapper,** snap′ėr, *n.* One that snaps.—**snapping turtle,** *n.* A large freshwater tortoise of the United States, which readily snaps at things.—**snappish,** snap′ish, *a.* Apt to snap or bite; apt to use sharp words; sharp in reply; tart; crabbed.—**snappishly,** snap′ish•li, *adv.* In a snappish manner; angrily; tartly.—**snappishness,** snap′ish•nes, *n.* The quality of being snappish.—**snapshot,** *n.* A photograph taken instantaneously.

snare, snâr, *n.* [A.Sax. *snear*, a snare, a noose; Icel. *snara*, Dan. *snare*, a snare, D. *snaar*, a string; from a root meaning to twist, seen also in L. *nervus*. NERVE.] A noose or set of nooses by which a bird or other living animal may be entangled; a gin; *fig.* something that serves to entangle or entrap a person.—*v.t.*—*snared, snaring.* To catch with a snare; to catch or take by guile.—**snarer,** snâ′rėr, *n.* One who lays snares or entangles.

snarl, snärl, *v.i.* [A freq. corresponding to old *snar*=L.G. and O.D. *snarren*, G. *schnarren*, to snarl; akin to *snore, snort.*] To growl, as an angry or surly dog; to talk in rude, murmuring terms.—**snarler,** snär′lėr, *n.* One who snarls.

snarl, snärl, *v.t.* [A freq. from *snare.*] To entangle; to involve in knots.—*n.* A knot; a complication; embarrassing difficulty.

snatch, snach, *v.t.* [Softened form of O. and Prov.E. *snack*, to snatch; D. and L.G. *snakken, snacken*, to snatch: probably a parallel form of *snap.*] To seize hastily or abruptly; to seize without permission or ceremony; to seize and transport away.—*v.i.* To attempt to seize suddenly; to snap or catch (to *snatch* at a thing).—*n.* A hasty catch or seizing; a catching at or attempt to seize suddenly; a small piece or fragment (a *snatch* of a song).—**snatch block,** *n.* A block used in ships, having an opening in one side to receive the bight of a rope.—**snatcher,** snach′ėr, *n.* One that snatches or takes abruptly.

sneak, snēk, *v.i.* [A.Sax. *snícan*, to creep, to sneak; Dan. *snige*, to creep. SNAKE.] To creep or steal privately; to go furtively, as if afraid or ashamed to be seen; to slink; to behave with meanness; to truckle.—*n.* A mean fellow; a cowardly, mean, underhand fellow.—**sneaker,** snē′kėr, *n.* One who sneaks; a kind of shoe; a kind of punchbowl.—**sneaking, sneaky,** snē′king, snē′ki, *a.* Pertaining to a sneak; acting like a sneak; mean; underhand.—**sneakingly,** snē′king•li, *adv.* In a sneaking manner.—**sneakiness,** snē′ki•nes, *a.* The quality of being sneaking.

sneer, snēr, *v.i.* [Same as Dan. *snaerre*, to snarl; allied to *snarl.*] To show contempt by turning up the nose, or by a particular cast of countenance; to insinuate contempt in words; to speak derisively.—*v.t.* To treat with sneers; to utter with a sneer.—*n.* A look of contempt or disdain; an expression of contemptuous scorn; indirect expression of contempt.—**sneerer,** snē′rėr, *n.* One that sneers.—**sneeringly,** snē′ring•li, *adv.* In a sneering manner.

sneeze, snēz, *v.i.*—*sneezed, sneezing.* [Same as *neese* with *s* prefixed; or modified from A.Sax. *sneósan*, D. *sniezen*, to sneeze.] To emit air through the nose audibly and violently by a kind of involuntary convulsive force, occasioned by irritation of the inner membrane of the nose.—*To sneeze at*, to show contempt for; to scorn.—*n.* The act of one who sneezes.—**sneezewort,** snēz′wėrt, *n.* A perennial herb, so called because the dried flowers and roots, when powdered, cause sneezing.

snick, snik, *n.* [Icel. *snikka*, to cut or work with a knife; D. *snik* a chisel.] A small cut or mark.—*v.t.* To cut; to clip.—**snickersnee,** snik′ėr•snē, *n.* [Comp. D. *snee*, a cut.] A large clasp knife.

snicker, snik′ėr, *v.i.* [Imitative of the sound.] To giggle; to snigger.

snide, snīd, *a.* [Origin unknown.] Derogatory in an insinuating way; dishonest or crooked; mean; low.

sniff, snif, *v.i.* [A lighter form of *snuff.*] To draw air audibly up the nose, sometimes as an expression of scorn; to snuff.—*v.t.* To draw in with the breath through the nose; to snuff; to smell.—*n.* The act of sniffing; the sound so produced; that which is taken by sniffing (a *sniff* of fresh air).

snigger, snig′ėr, *v.i.* [SNICKER.] To snicker; to giggle.—*n.* A suppressed laugh; a giggle.

snip, snip, *v.t.*—*snipped, snipping.* [Closely allied to *snap*, and same as D. and L.G. *snippen*, G. *schnippen, schnipfen*, to snip.] To cut off at once with shears or scissors; to clip; to shred.—*n.* A cut with shears or scissors; a bit cut off; a small shred.

snipe, snīp, *n.* [Same as Icel. *snípa*, a snipe; D. *snip*, L.G. *snippe*, Dan. *sneppe*, G. *schnepfe*, a snipe; akin *to snap, neb*, or *nib.*] A grallatorial bird frequenting marshy grounds, with a long straight bill, allied to the woodcock; a fool; a blockhead; a simpleton.—*v.t.* or *i.* To pick or snip off men with the rifle in war.—*Sea snipe*, the dunlin.—*Summer snipe*, the sandpiper.—**sniper,** *n.* A soldier who, from some unsuspected place of concealment, picks off those of the enemy that expose themselves to his fire.

snippet, snip′et, *n.* [Dim. of *snip*, a part.] A small part or share.—**snippety,** snip′et•i, *a.* Insignificant.

snivel, sniv′el, *v.i.*—*snivelled, snivelling.* [Akin to *sniff, snuff.*] To run at the nose; to cry or fret, as children, with snuffing or sniveling; to whimper.—**sniveler,** sniv′el•ėr, *n.* One who snivels or whines; one who weeps for slight causes.—**sniveling,** sniv′el•ing, *n.* The act or the noise of one who snivels.

snob, snob, *n.* [Origin unknown.] One who snubs people; one who deliberately ignores those whom he considers his social or intellectual inferiors; a smug, self-complacent individual; a person who apes gentility.—**snobbery, snobbishness,** snob′ėr•i, snob′ish•nes, *n.* The quality of being snobbish.—**snobbish,** snob′ish, *a.* Belonging to or resembling a snob; vulgarly ostentatious.—**snobbishly,** snob′ish•li, *adv.* In the manner of a snob.

snood, snöd, *a.* [A.Sax. *snod*, a snood; comp. Icel. *snúa*, to twist.] A fillet or ribbon for the hair.

snooze, snöz, *n.* [Imitative of the sound made in drawing the breath while asleep, and allied to *snore.*] A nap or short sleep.—*v.i.*—*snoozed, snoozing.* To slumber; to take a short nap. (*Colloq.*)

snore, snōr, *v.i.*—*snored, snoring.* [A.Sax. *snora*, a snoring; L.G. *snoren*, D. *snorken.*] To breathe with a rough hoarse noise in sleep.—*n.* A breathing with a harsh noise through the nose and mouth in sleep.—**snorer,** snō′rėr, *n.*

snorkel, snōr′kel, *n.* [G. *schnorchel.*] A tubular device for the intake and exhaust of air, permitting a submarine to cruise at periscope depth for long periods; other devices that resemble a snorkel in function.

snort, snort, *v.i.* [Akin to *snore*, D. *snorken.*] To force the air with violence through the nose, so as to make an abrupt noise.—*n.* A loud short sound produced by forcing the air through the nostrils.—**snorter,** snor′tėr, *n.* One who snorts.

snout, snout, *n.* [Same as L.G. *snute*, Sw. *snut*, Dan. *snude*, D. *snuit*, G. *schnautze*, a snout. *Snite* and *snot* are closely akin.] The long projecting nose of a beast, as that of swine; the nozzle or end of a pipe.

snow, snō, *n.* [A.Sax. *snáw*, snow= D. *sneeuw*, L.G. and Dan. *snee*, Sw. *snö*, Icel. *snjór* (also *snaer*), G. *schnee*, Goth. *snaivs*; cog. L. *nix*, Gr. *niphas* (without initial *s*).] Watery particles congealed into white crystals in the air, and falling to the earth in flakes.—*Red snow.* PROTOCOCCUS.—*v.i.* To fall in snow; used chiefly impersonally (it *snows*, it *snowed*).—*v.t.* To scatter or cause to fall like snow.—**snowball,** *n.* A ball of snow; a round mass of snow pressed or rolled together.—*v.t.* To pelt with snowballs.—*v.i.* To throw snowballs.—**snowberry,** *n.* A name of certain shrubs bearing fruits consisting of snow-white berries.—**snowbird,** *n.* The snow bunting.—**snowblind,** *a.* Affected with snow blindness.—**snow blindness,** *n.* An affection of the eyes caused by the reflection of light from the snow.—**snow-broth,** *n.* Snow and water mixed.—**snow bunting,** *n.* A bird belonging to the bunting family.—**snowdrift,** *n.* A driving snow; a bank of snow driven together by the wind.—**snowdrop,** snō′-drop, *n.* A garden plant, bearing solitary, drooping, and elegant white flowers, which appear very early in the year.—**snowflake,** *n.* A flake of falling snow.—**snow line,** *n.* The line above which mountains are covered with perpetual snow, varying according to latitude and local circumstances, being highest near the equator and lowest near the poles.—**snow plant,** *n.* Red snow; protococcus.—**snowplow,** *n.* An implement for clearing away the snow from roads, railroads, etc.—**snowshoe,** *n.* A kind of flat framework worn on the feet, made of wood alone, or consisting of a light frame crossed and recrossed by thongs, the broad surface thus presented keeping the wearer from sinking in the snow.—**snow-white,** *a.* White as snow; very white.—**snowy,** snō′i, *a.* White like snow; abounding with snow; covered with snow; white; pure; spotless; unblemished.

snub, snub, *v.t.*—*snubbed, snubbing.* [Same as older English *snib*; Icel. *snubba,* to snub, to chide, Dan. *snubbe,* to snap or snip off; akin to *snap, snip.*] To nip or check in growth‡; to check, stop, or rebuke with a tart sarcastic reply or remark; to slight designedly; to treat with contempt or neglect, as a forward or pretentious person.—*n.* A check; a rebuke.—**snub-nosed,** *a.* Having a short, flat nose.

snuff, snuf, *v.t.* [Same as D. *snuffen,* to snuff; *snuf,* a sniffing; akin Dan, *snöfte,* G. *schnupfen,* to snuff; akin *sniff, snivel, snuffle.*] To draw in with the breath; to inhale; to scent; to smell; to crop the snuff of, as of a candle.—*To snuff out,* to extinguish by snuffing.—*v.i.* To inhale air with noise, as dogs and horses; to snort or sniff; to sniff contemptuously.—*n.* An inhalation by the nose; a sniff; resentment; huff, expressed by a snuffing of the nose; a powdered preparation of tobacco inhaled through the nose; that part of a candle wick which has been charred by the flame.—**snuffbox,** *n.* A box for carrying snuff about the person.—**snuffer,** snuf′ėr, *n.* One that snuffs; *pl.* an instrument for removing the snuff of a candle.—**snuffy,** snuf′i, *a.* Resembling snuff in color; soiled with snuff, or smelling of it.

snuffle, snuf′l, *v.i.*—*snuffled, snuffling.* [Freq. of *snuff,* and = L.G. *snuffeln,* D. *snuffelen,* Sw. *snufla,* to snuffle. SNUFF.] To speak through the nose or with a nasal twang; to breathe hard through the nose.—*n.* A sound made by the passage of air through the nostrils; a speaking through the nose; an affected nasal twang.—**snuffler,** snuf′l·ėr, *n.* One who snuffles.

snug, snug, *a.* [Same as Icel. *snöggr,* short-haired, smooth; O.Dan. *snog,* Sw. *snygg,* neat, elegant; akin perhaps to *snag.*] Lying close and comfortable; neat, trim, and convenient.—*v.i.*—*snugged, snugging.* To lie close; to snuggle.—*v.t.* To put in a snug position; to place snugly.—**snuggery,** snug′ėri, *n.* A snug, warm habitation or comfortable place. (*Colloq.*)—**snuggle,** snug′l, *v.i.*—*snuggled, snuggling.* [A freq. and dim. from *snug.*] To lie close for convenience or warmth; to nestle.—**snugly,** snug′li, *adv.* In a snug manner; closely; comfortably.—**snugness,** snug′nes, *n.* The state or quality of being snug.

so, sō, *adv.* [A.Sax. *swá,* so, as; Icel. *svá, svo, so,* Goth. *sva, sve,* L.G. and G. *so,* D. *zoo.* It appears in *as, also, whosoever,* etc.] In this or that manner; to that degree (*so* long); thus (he does it *so*); in like manner or degree; after *as* (*as* thou art *so* were they); in such a manner; to such a degree: with *as* or *that* following (*so* fortunate *as* to escape); colloquially, extremely, very (it is *so* beautiful); as has been said or stated (it is *so,* do *so*); the case being such; accordingly; well (*so* you are here again, are you?); somewhere about this or that; thereby (a year or *so*); in wishes and asseverations (*so* help me Heaven! that is, may Heaven so help me as I speak truth).—*So forth, so on,* more of the same or a similar kind; et cetera.—*So so,* indifferent; middling; mediocre (a very *so so* affair).—*So, so,* an exclamation implying discovery or observation of some effect; ay, ay; well, well.—*So that,* to the end that; in order that; with the purpose or intention that; with the effect or result that.—*So then,* thus then it is that; the consequence is; therefore.—*conj.* Provided that; on condition that; in case that.—*interj.* Enough! that will do!—**so-and-so,** sō′and·sō, A certain person not mentioned by name; an indefinite person or thing. (*Colloq.*)

soak, sōk, *v.t.* [Probably akin to *suck.*] To let lie in a fluid in order to imbibe what it can contain; to macerate in water or other fluid; to steep; to drench; to wet thoroughly; to draw in by pores; to penetrate or permeate by pores.—*v.i.* To lie steeped in water or other fluid; to steep; to enter into pores or interstices; to drink intemperately; to tipple constantly.—**soakage,** sō′kij, *n.* Act of soaking; fluid imbibed.—**soaker,** sō′kėr, *n.* One who soaks; a constant drinker.

soap, sōp, *n.* [A.Sax. *sápe* = Sw. *sopa,* L.G. *sepe,* O.H.G. *seifa,* from same root as L. *sebum,* tallow.] A chemical compound of potash and soda with fat, soluble in water, and used for detergent or cleansing purposes; flattery (*slang*).—*v.t.* To rub or wash over with soap; to flatter (*slang*).—**soapstone,** *n.* A species of steatite.—**soapsuds,** *n.pl.* Suds; water well impregnated with soap.—**soapwort,** sōp′wėrt, *n.* A perennial plant common in gardens, the stems of which, upon being put in water, form a lather like soap.—**soapy,** sō′pi, *a.* Resembling soap; having the qualities of soap; smeared with soap; *fig.* flattering; unctuous; oily: said of persons, language, etc. (*colloq.*).

soar, sōr, *v.i.* [Fr. *essorer,* from L.L. *exaurare,* to take to the air—L. *ex,* out, and *aura,* the air.] To fly aloft, as a bird; to mount upward on wings or as on wings; to mount intellectually; to rise above what is prosaic or commonplace, etc.; to be transported with a lofty imagination, desires, etc.—*n.* A towering flight; ascent.

sob, sob, *v.i.*—*sobbed, sobbing.* [Akin to A.Sax. *seófian,* to sigh; G. *seufzen,* to sigh; E. *sough.*] To weep with convulsive catching of the breath.—*n.* A convulsive catching of the breath excited by mental emotion of a painful nature; a short convulsive sigh.

sober, sō′bėr, *a.* [Fr. *sobre,* from L. *sobrius,* sober, from *se,* apart, and *ebrius,* drunken.] Temperate in the use of intoxicating liquors; abstemious; not intoxicated; not drunk; not wild, visionary, or heated with passion; having the regular exercise of cool, dispassionate reason; dispassionate; calm; serious; grave; not bright, gay, or brilliant in appearance; dull-looking.—*v.t.* To make sober; to cure of intoxication, to make temperate, calm, or solemn.—*v.i.* To become sober, staid, or sedate; often with *down.*—**soberly,** sō′bėr·li, *adv.* In a sober manner; temperately; moderately; calmly; seriously; gravely.—**sober-minded,** *a.* Having a calm and temperate disposition.—**soberness,** sō′bėr·nes, *n.* The state or quality of being sober; sobriety; temperance; calmness.—**sobriety,** sō·brī′e·ti, *n.* [L. *sobrietas.*] Temperance in the use of intoxicating liquors; abstemiousness; moderation; freedom from the influence of strong drink; calmness; coolness; seriousness; gravity.

Sobranje, sō·brän′ye, *n.* The former Bulgarian Parliament.

sobriquet, so·bri·kā′, *n.* [Fr.] A nickname; a fanciful appellation.

socage, sok′ij, *n.* [L.L. *socagium,* socage; lit. the tenure of one over whom his lord had a certain jurisdiction, from A.Sax. *soc,* the privilege of holding a court in a district.] A tenure of land in medieval England by the performance of certain and determinate service.

soccer, sok′ėr, *n.* [Alteration of *association.*] A football game played with teams of 11, in which a round ball is advanced by kicking or by using any part of the body except the hands.

sociable, sō′shi·a·bl, *a.* [Fr. *sociable,* L. *sociabilis,* from *socio,* to associate or unite, from *socius,* a companion.] Inclined to associate or join in friendly intercourse; fond of companions; companionable; conversible; social.—*n.* An open carriage with seats facing each other.—**sociability, sociableness,** sō′shi·a·bil″i·ti, sō′shi·a·bl·nes, *n.* The quality of being sociable.—**sociably,** sō′shi•a•bli, *adv.* In a sociable manner; conversibly; familiarly.—**social,** sō′shal, *a.* [Fr. *social*, from L. *socialis*, from *socius*.] Pertaining to society; relating to man living in society, or to the public as an aggregate body; ready to mix in friendly converse; sociable; consisting in union or mutual converse; *bot.* growing naturally in large groups or masses; *zool.* living in communities, as wolves, deer, wild cattle, etc.; or as ants, bees, etc., which form co-operative communities.—*Social science*, the science dealing with all that relates to the social condition, or the relations and institutions which are involved in man's existence and his well-being as a member of an organized community; sociology.—*The social evil*, a term frequently applied to prostitution.—**socialism,** sō′shal•izm, *n.* The name applied to theories of social organization having for their aim the abolition of that individual action on which modern societies depend, and the substitution of a regulated system of cooperative action; especially, a system in which the government owns and controls the means of production and distribution.—**socialist,** sō′shal•ist, *n.* One who advocates socialism.—**socialite,** so′shal•it, *n.* A man or woman well known in social circles. (*Colloq.*)—**sociality,** sō•shi•al′i•ti, *n.* —**socialize,** sō′shal•iz, *v.t.*—*socialized, socializing.* To render social; to regulate according to socialism.—*v.i.* To participate in social activities.—**social security,** *n.* [often cap.] A U.S. government program that provides for old age and survivors insurance, contributions to state unemployment insurance, and old age assistance.—**social service,** *n.* Any work intended to promote the welfare of the sick, homeless, or destitute.—**social work,** *n.* Organized professional activities concerned with the study, treatment, and material aid to the socially maladjusted.

society, sō•sī′e•ti, *n.* [Fr. *société*, L. *societas*.] The relationship of men to one another when associated; companionship; fellowship; company; a body of persons united for the promotion of some object; the persons collectively who live in any region or at any period; the more cultivated portion of any community in its social relations and influences; those who give and receive formal entertainments mutually; used without the article.—*Society journal* or *newspaper*, a journal whose main object is to chronicle the sayings and doings of fashionable society.—*Society verses*, verses for the amusement of polite society; poetry of a light, entertaining, polished character.

Socinian, sō•sin′i•an, *a.* [From Laelius and Faustus *Socinus*, uncle and nephew, natives of Sienna, in Tuscany, the founders of the sect of Socinians in the sixteenth century.] Pertaining to Laelius or Faustus Socinus or their religious creed.—*n.* A follower of Socinus.—**Socinianism,** sō•sin′i•an•izm, *n.* The tenets of the Socinians; a belief akin to Unitarianism, rejecting the doctrine of the Trinity, the deity of Christ, the personality of the devil, and eternity of future punishment.

sociology, sō•shi•ol′o•ji, *n.* [L. *socius*, a companion, and Gr. *logos*, discourse. SOCIABLE.] The science which investigates the laws that regulate human society in all its grades; the science which treats of the general structure of society, the laws of its development, and the progress of civilization.—**sociologic, sociological,** sō′shi•o•loj″ik, sō′shi•o•loj″i•kal, *a.* Pertaining to sociology.—**sociologist,** sō•shi•ol′o•jist, *n.* One who treats of or devotes himself to the study of sociology.

sock, sok, *n.* [A.Sax. *socc*, from L. *soccus*, a kind of low-heeled shoe, especially worn by comic actors.] A knitted or woven covering for the foot, shorter than a stocking; the shoe worn by the ancient actors of comedy; hence, *the sock*, comedy in distinction from tragedy, which is symbolized by the buskin.—*v.i.* To strike violently, usually as with the fist, or with a bat in a game of baseball, as to *sock* the ball for a home run.

socket, sok′et, *n.* [O. Fr. *soquet*, a shoe.] An opening or cavity into which anything is fitted endwise; a hollow which receives and holds something else (the *sockets* of the teeth or of the eyes).

socle, sō′kl, *n.* [Fr. *socle*, *L. socculus*, dim. of *soccus*. SOCK.] *Arch.* a plain, low pedestal; also, a plain face or plinth at the lower part of a wall.

Socratic, sō•krat′ik, *a.* Pertaining to *Socrates* the Grecian sage, or to his language or manner of teaching and philosophizing; reaching conclusions by means of question and answer.—**Socratically,** sō•krat′i•kal•li, *adv.* In the Socratic manner.

sod, sod, *n.* [Same as L.G. and O.D. *sode*, D. *zode*.] The surface layer of the ground with the grass growing on it; a piece lifted from that surface; turf; sward.

soda, sō′da, *n.* [Sp. Pg. and It. *soda*, glasswort, barilla.] A name for various compounds of sodium, as sodium carbonate, bicarbonate of soda, and sodium hydroxide.—**soda cracker,** *n.* A crisp, white cracker made of yeast dough that has been neutralized with soda.—**soda water,** *n.* A sodium bicarbonate solution into which an acid, usually carbonic, has been added to cause effervescence.

sodality, sō•dal′i•ti, *n.* [L. *sodalitas*, from *sodalis*, a companion.] A fellowship or fraternity.

sodden, sod′n, pp. of *seethe*. Boiled; seethed; soaked and softened, as in water; thoroughly saturated; not well baked; doughy.

sodium, sō′di•um, *n.* [Named from its oxide *soda*.] A silver-white metallic element abundant in nature but always in a combined state and chemically very active. Symbol, Na (Latin, *natrium*); at. no., 11; at. wt., 22.9898.—**sodium carbonate,** *n.* Salt of soda.

Sodomite, sod′om•it, *n.* An inhabitant of Sodom; [*not cap.*] one guilty of sodomy.—**sodomitical,** sod•om•it′i•kal, *a.* Relating to sodomy.—**sodomy,** sod′omi, *n.* The sin attributed to the inhabitants of Sodom; a carnal copulation against nature.

soever, sō•ev′ėr. A word compounded of *so* and *ever*; generally used in composition to extend or render emphatic the sense of such words as *who*, *what*, etc., in *whosoever*, *whatsoever*, etc., from which it is sometimes separated.

sofa, sō′fa, *n.* [Fr. and Sp. *sofa*, a sofa, from Ar. *soffah*, a bench before a house.] A piece of upholstered furniture generally accommodating three or more people.—*Convertible sofa*, a sofa which may be converted into a bed.

soffit, sof′it, *n.* [Fr. *soffite*, It. *soffitta*, from L. *sub*, under, and *figo*, to fasten.] *Arch.* the lower surface of an arch or of an architrave; the under part of an overhanging cornice, of a projecting balcony, etc.

soft, soft, *a.* [A.Sax. *sófte*, softly; O.Sax, *saft*, O.D. *saeft*, *saft*; G. *sanft*, soft.] Easily yielding to pressure; easily impressible; yielding; the contrary of *hard*; not rough, rude, or violent; affecting the senses in a pleasant manner; delicate or pleasing to the touch; gentle or melodious to the ear; not glaring; not repelling or striking to the sight; easily yielding to persuasion or motives; facile, weak; not harsh, severe, or unfeeling; gentle; easily moved by pity; susceptible of tender affections; effeminate; not manly or courageous; foolish; simple; silly; quiet and refreshing (*soft* slumbers); readily forming a lather and washing well with soap (*soft* water); pronounced with more or less of a sibilant sound, as *c* in *cinder*, as opposed to *c* in *candle*; and *g* in *gin*, as opposed to *g* in *gift*.—*Soft goods*, textile goods; the wares of a draper or haberdasher.—*Soft palate*, that part of the palate which lies in the posterior part of the mouth.—*The softer sex*, the female sex.—*Soft soap*, a coarse kind of soap in a viscid form; as a *slang term*, flattery, blarney.—*adv.* Softly; gently; quietly.—*interj.* Be soft; hold; stop; not so fast.—**soften,** sof′n, *v.t.* To make soft or more soft; to make less hard; to mollify; to make less implacable or angry; to make less severe, harsh, or strong in language; to alleviate; to tone down.—*v.i.* To become soft or less hard; to become less harsh or cruel; to become milder.—**softener,** sof′n•ėr, *n.* One who or that which softens.—*Softening of the brain*, an affection of the brain, in which it becomes pulpy or pasty, often causing death.—**softhearted,** *a.* Having tenderness of heart.—**softly,** soft′li, *adv.* In a soft manner; not with force or violence; gently; not loudly; mildly; tenderly.—**softness,** soft′nes, *n.* The quality of being soft; the opposite of *hardness*; penetrability; susceptibility of tender feeling; weakness of mind or will; mildness; gentleness.—**soft-spoken,** *a.* Speaking softly; having a mild or gentle voice; mild; affable.

soil, soil, *v.t.* [O.Fr. *soillier* (Fr. *souiller*), to soil, lit. to act the pig, from L. *suillus*, pertaining to a swine, from *sus*, a swine. Sow, *n.*] To make dirty on the surface; to dirty; to defile; to tarnish; to sully; to dung; to manure.—*v.i.* To take on dirt; to take a soil or stain; to tarnish.—*n.* Foul matter upon another surface; stain; tarnish; defilement or taint.—**soil pipe,** *n.* A pipe for conveying from a house the foul or waste water, night soil, etc.

soil, soil, *n.* [O.Fr. *soil, soile* (Fr. *sol*), from L. *solum*, the soil. SOLID.] The upper stratum of the earth's crust; the mold, or that compound substance which furnishes nutriment to plants; earth; ground; land; country.

soil, soil, *v.t.* [O.Fr. *saouler*, to satiate, from *saoul*, L. *satullus*, sated, dim. of *satur*, sated, full. SATURATE.] To feed (cattle or horses) with fresh grass or green fodder instead of putting out to pasture.

soiree, swä•rā', *n.* [Fr. *soirée*, evening, an evening party, from *soir*, evening, from L. *serus*, late.] Originally, an evening party; now usually a reunion or social meeting of some society or body, at which tea and other refreshments are introduced during the intervals of music, speechmaking, etc.

sojourn, so•jėrn', *v.i.* [O.Fr. *sojorner*, from L. *sub*, under, and *diurnus*, diurnal. DIURNAL, DIARY.] To dwell for a time; to dwell as a temporary resident, or as a stranger, not considering the place a permanent habitation.—sō'jėrn, *n.* A temporary residence, as that of a traveler in a foreign land.—**sojourner,** so•jėrn'ėr, *n.*

sol, sōl, *n. Music*, the fifth tone of the diatonic scale.

sol, sol, *n.* [From *sol*ution.] A colloidal solution, composed of a liquid solvent and a liquid or very finely divided solid therein.

Sol, sol, *n.* [L.] The sun.

sol, sōl, *n.* A French coin no longer in use.

sol, sōl, *n.* A Peruvian coin.

solace, sol'is, *v.t.*—*solaced, solacing.* [O.Fr. *solace, solaz*, from L. *solatium*, from *solor, solatus*, to solace (seen in *console, disconsolate*).] To cheer in grief or under calamity; to relieve in affliction; to console; to comfort; to allay or assuage.—*n.* Comfort in grief; alleviation of grief or anxiety; what relieves in distress; recreation.—**solacement,** sol'is•ment, *a.* Act of solacing.

solanaceous, so•la•nā'shus, *a.* [L. *solanum*, nightshade.] Pertaining to plants of the nightshade family, which includes also the potato and tobacco.

solan goose, sō'lan, *n.* [Icel. *súlan*, the gannet.] The gannet.

solar, sō'lėr, *a.* [L. *solaris*, from *sol*, the sun; cog. Icel. *sál*, Goth. *sauil*, Ir. *sul*, the sun.] Pertaining to the sun; proceeding from, or produced by the sun; measured by the progress of the sun, or by its apparent revolution.—**solar battery,** a device using photovoltaic cells for storing the sun's energy as electricity.—*Solar cycle*, a period of twenty-eight years. CYCLE.—*Solar day.* DAY.—*Solar flowers*, those which open and shut daily at certain determinate hours.—**solar furnace,** a device for using sunlight as a direct source of heat. *Solar microscope*, a microscope in which the object is illuminated by the light of the sun concentrated upon it.—*Solar month*, the space of time in which the sun passes through one sign, or a twelfth part of the zodiac: 30 days, 10 hours, 29 minutes, 5 seconds.—*Solar spectrum*, the spectrum of sunlight.—*Solar spots*, dark spots that appear on the sun's disk sometimes so large as to be seen by the naked eye, very changeable in their number, figure, and dimensions.—*Solar system*, the system of which the sun is the center, and to which belong the planets, planetoids, satellites, comets, and meteorites, all directly or indirectly revolving round the central sun.—*Solar telegraph*, a telegraph in which the rays of the sun are projected from and upon mirrors.—*Solar time*, time as shown by a sundial, that is by the apparent motion of the sun.—*Solar year*, the time which the earth takes to go round the sun, 365 days, 5 hours, 48 minutes, 46 seconds.—*Arch.* a loft or upper room.

solarium, sō•lâr'i•um, *n.* [L.] A room for the treatment of patients by exposure to the sun.

solatium, sō•lā'shi•um, *n.* [L., consolation, solace. SOLACE.] Anything that alleviates or compensates for suffering or loss; a compensation in money.

sold, sōld, pret. and pp. of *sell.*

soldan,‡ sol'dan, *n.* A sultan.

solder, sod'ėr, *v.t.* [O.Fr. *solder*, *solider* (Fr. *souder*); lit. to make solid, from L. *solidus*, solid. SOLID.] To unite by a metallic substance in a state of fusion, which hardens in cooling, and renders the joint solid; *fig.* to unite or combine in general; to patch up.—*n.* A metal or metallic composition used in uniting other metallic substances by being fused between them. *Hard solders* are such as require a red heat to fuse them. *Soft solders* melt at a comparatively low temperature.—**solderer,** sod'ėr•ėr, *n.* One who solders.

soldier, sōl'jėr, *n.* [O.Fr. *soldier*, from L.L. *soldarius, solidarius*, from L. *soldus, solidus*, military pay; lit. a solid piece of money. SOLID.] A man who serves in an army; a common soldier or private; a man of military experience and skill, or a man of distinguished valor.—**soldierly,** sōl'jėr•li, *a.* Like or becoming a soldier; brave; martial; honorable.—**soldiership,** sol'jėr•ship, *n.* Military qualities or character; martial skill.—**soldiery,** sōl'jėr•i, *n.* Soldiers collectively; a body of military men.

sole, sōl, *n.* [Fr. *sole*, the sole of the foot, of a shoe, etc., the fish, from L. *solea*, a sandal, a sole, the fish, a sill, same origin as *solidus*, solid. SOLID, SOIL. *n.*] The under side of the foot; the bottom surface of a shoe or boot, or the piece of leather which constitutes the bottom; the part of anything that forms the bottom, and on which it stands; a marine fish belonging to the family of flat fishes, of an oblong form, probably so called from its shape.—*v.t.*—*soled, soling.* To furnish with a sole (to *sole* a shoe).

sole, sōl, *a.* [From L. *solus*, alone; which is of same origin as L. *salvus*, safe (whence *safe, salvation*), Gr. *holos*, entire, Skr. *sarva*, the whole. Akin *solitary, solitude, solemn, solid.*] Single; being or acting without another; alone in its kind; individual; *law*, single; unmarried (a femme *sole*).—**solely,** sōl'li, *adv.* Singly; alone; only; without another.

solecism, sol'e•sizm, *n.* [Gr. *soloikismos* from *Soloi*, in Cilicia, the Athenian colonists of which lost the purity of their language.] An impropriety in the use of language, arising from ignorance; a gross deviation from the idiom of a language, or a gross deviation from the rules of syntax; a violation of the rules of society.—**solecistic,** sol•e•sis'tik, *a.* Pertaining to or involving a solecism.

solemn, sol'em, *a.* [L. *sollemnis, sollennis*, that occurs every year, festal, solemn,—*sollus* all, every, and *annus*, a year SOLID.] Marked by religious rites or ceremonious observances; fitted to excite reverent or serious reflections; awe-inspiring; grave; impressive (a *solemn* silence) accompanied by seriousness or impressiveness in language or demeanor; earnest (a *solemn* promise); affectedly grave.—**solemnness,** sol'em•nes, *n.* The state or quality of being solemn; solemnity.—**solemnity,** so•lem'ni•ti, *n.* The state or quality of being solemn; gravity; impressiveness; mock gravity; a solemn or reverent rite or ceremony; a proceeding adapted to impress awe or reverence.—**solemnization,** sol'em•ni•zā"shon, *n.* The act of solemnizing, celebration.—**solemnize,** sol'em•nīz, *v.t.*—*solemnized, solemnizing.* [O.Fr. *solemniser.*] To dignify or honor by ceremonies; to celebrate; to perform with ritual ceremonies or according to legal forms: used especially of marriage; to make grave, serious, and reverential.—**solemnizer,** sol'em•nī•zėr, *n.* One who solemnizes.—**solemnly,** sol'em•li, *adv.* In a solemn manner; with religious ceremonies; with impressive seriousness; with all due form.

solenoid, sōl'en•oid, *n.* [Gr. *sōlen*, channel.] A coil of wire wound in the form of a helix, which, when traversed by an electric current, acts like a magnet.

sol-fa, sōl′fä, *v.i.* In *music*, to sing the notes of the scale in their proper pitch, using the syllables *do* (or *ut*), *re, mi, fa, sol, la, si.*—*v.t.* To sing to the syllables, *do, re, mi, fa, sol, la, si,* instead of to words.

solfeggio, sol•fej′i•ō, *n.* [It.] In *music*, a system of arranging the scale by the names *do* (or *ut*), *re, mi, fa, sol, la, si*; an exercise in scale singing; solmization.

solicit, so•lis′it, *v.t.* [Fr. *solliciter*, L. *solicitare*, from *sollicitus*, solicitous, from *sollus*, whole, and *cito, citum*, to agitate. SOLID, CITE.] To ask from with some degree of earnestness; to make petition to; to ask for with some degree of earnestness; to seek by petition; to awake or excite to action; to invite; to disturb or disquiet; to make anxious; *law*, to incite to commit a felony; to endeavor to influence by a bribe.—*v.i.* To make solicitation for some one or for a thing.—**solicitation,** so•lis′i•tā″shon, *n.* The act of soliciting; an earnest request; endeavor to influence to grant something by bribery; the offense of inciting a person to commit a felony.—**solicitor,** so•lis′i•tėr, *n.* One who solicits; an attorney; a law agent; one who represents another in court.—**solicitor general,** *n.* A law officer in the U. S. government, next in rank to the attorney-general, with whom he is associated in the management of the legal business of the nation.—**solicitous,** so•lis′i•tus, *a.* [L. *sollicitus*, anxious, uneasy.] Anxious; concerned; apprehensive; disturbed; restless.—**solicitously,** so•lis′i•tus•li, *adv.* Anxiously; with care and concern.—**solicitousness,** so•lis′i•tus•nes, *n.*—**solicitude,** so•lis′i•tūd, *n.* The state of being solicitous; uneasiness of mind occasioned by fear of evil or desire for good; concern; anxiety. ∴ Syn. under CARE.

solid, sol′id, *a.* [Fr. *solide*, from L. *solidus*, solid, firm, compact, from same root as *solum*, the soil (E. *soil*), *sollus*, whole (whence the *sol-* in *solicit, solemn*), *salvus*, safe (E. *safe*).] Possessing the property of excluding all other bodies from the space occupied by itself; impenetrable; firm; compact; opposed to *liquid* and *gaseous*; not hollow; full of matter; having all the geometrical dimensions—length, breadth, and thickness; cubic (a *solid* foot); strong; sound; substantial, as opposed to frivolous, fallacious, or the like; real; valid; financially sound or safe.—*Solid angle*, an angle formed by several planes or other surfaces meeting at one point; measured by the area intercepted on a sphere of unit radius with the point as center.—*Solid square*, a square body of troops; a body in which the ranks and files are equal.—*n.* A firm compact body with the particles firmly cohering, and thus distinguished from a *liquid* or a *gas*, whose particles yield to the slightest impression; *geom.* a body or magnitude which has three dimensions—length, breadth, and thickness.—*Regular solids*, those which are bounded by equal and regular planes.—**solidification,** so•lid′i•fi•kā″shon, *n.* The act or process of making solid; the passage of bodies from the liquid or gaseous to the solid state.—**solidify,** so•lid′i•fī, *v.t.*—*solidified, solidifying*. [L. *solidus*, solid, and *facio*, to make.] To make solid or compact, to cause to change from a liquid or a gas to a solid.—*v.i.* To become solid or compact.—**solidity,** so•lid′i•ti, *n.* [Fr. *solidité*, L. *soliditas*.] The state or quality of being solid; firmness; density; compactness: opposed to *fluidity*; strength or stability; massiveness; soundness; strength or validity as opposed to *weakness* or *fallaciousness*; the quantity of space occupied by a solid body; cubic content.—**solidly,** sol′id•li, *adv.* In a solid manner; firmly; compactly; on firm grounds.—**solidness,** sol′id•nes, *n.* Solidity.

solidarity, sol•i•dar′i•ti, *n.* [Fr. *solidarité*, from *solide*, solid.] Unity or communion of interests and responsibilities among nations or mankind in general.

solidungulate, sol•id•ung′gū•lāt, *a.* [L. *solidus*, solid, and *ungula*, a hoof.] Having hoofs that are whole or not cloven, as the horse, ass, zebra.—**solidus,** an oblique stroke /, an abbreviation for *shilling*, also used in fractions, as 2/3 for ⅔.

solifidian, sol•i•fid′i•an, *n.* [L. *solus*, alone, and *fides*, faith.] One who maintains that faith alone, without works, is necessary to justification.

soliloquy, so•lil′o•kwi, *n.* [L. *soliloquium*—*solus*, alone, and *loquor*, to speak. SOLE, LOQUACIOUS.] A talking to one's self; a monologue; a discourse not addressed to any person.—**soliloquize,** so•lil′o•kwīz, *v.i.*—*soliloquized, soliloquizing*. To utter a soliloquy; to talk to one's self.

solitaire, sol′i•târ, *n.* [Fr. *solitaire*, from L. *solitarius*. SOLITARY.] An article of jewelry in which a single gem is set; a game for a single person played on a board indented with thirty-three or thirty-seven hemispherical hollows and an equal number of balls; a card game which one can play alone.

solitary, sol′i•te•ri, *a.* [Fr. *solitaire*; L. *solitarius*, from *solus*, alone (whence *sole*). SOLE, *a.*] Being or living alone; being by one's self; not much visited or frequented; retired; lonely (a *solitary* residence); passed without company; shared by no companions (a *solitary* life); single; individual (a *solitary* example).—*n.* One that lives alone or in solitude; a hermit; a recluse.—**solitarily,** sol′i•te•ri•li, *adv.* In a solitary manner; alone.—**solitariness,** sol′i•te•ri•nes, *n.* The state of being solitary or apart from others; the state of not being frequented; loneliness.

solitude, sol′i•tūd, *n.* [Fr. *solitude*, from L. *solitudo*, from *solus*, alone. SOLITARY.] A state of being alone; loneliness; remoteness from society; destitution of inhabitants; a lonely place; a desert.

solmization, sol•mī•zā′shon, *n.* [From the syllables *sol, mi.*] *Mus.* the act or art of giving to each of the seven notes of the scale its proper sound or relative pitch; solfeggió.

solo, sō′lō, *n.* It. pl. **soli,** sō′lē, Eng. pl. **solos,** sō′lōz. [It., from L. *solus*, alone.] A tune, air, or strain to be played by a single instrument or sung by a single voice without or with an accompaniment.

solstice, sol′stis, *n.* [From L. *solstitium*—*sol*, the sun, *sto*, to stand. SOLAR, STATE.] The time of the year at which, owing to the annual revolution of the earth, the sun is at its greatest distance north or south from the equator, and begins to turn back, which happens at midsummer and midwinter, or June 21 and December 22; either of the two points in the ecliptic at which the sun appears to be at these dates.—**solstitial,** sol•stish′al, *a.* Pertaining to solstice; happening at a solstice.—*Solstitial points*, the two points in the ecliptic at which the sun arrives at the time of the solstices.—*Solstitial colure*, a great circle supposed to pass through the solstitial points.

soluble, sol′ū•bl, *a.* [L. *solubilis*, from *solvo*, to melt. SOLVE.] Susceptible of being dissolved in a fluid; capable of solution; *fig.* capable of being solved or resolved, as a mathematical problem; capable of being cleared up or settled by explanation, as a doubt, question, etc.—**solubility,** sol•ū•bil′i•ti, *n.* The quality of being soluble; susceptibility of being dissolved in a fluid; capability of being solved or cleared up.—**solubleness,** sol′ū•bl•nes, *n.* The state or character of being soluble; solubility.

solute, sol′ūt, *n.* [L. *solutio*, from *solvo*, to melt, dissolve. SOLVE.] A dissolved substance.—**solution,** so•lū′shon, *n.* The act of dissolving or state of being dissolved; the conversion of solid matter into liquid by means of a liquid (called the solvent); the combination of a liquid with a liquid or a gas to form a homogeneous liquid; the liquid thus produced; the preparation made by dissolving a solid in a liquid; the act of solving, clearing up, or explaining, explanation; *math.* the method of resolving a problem; *med.* the termination or the crisis of a disease.—*Chemical solution*, a perfect chemical union of a solid with a liquid.—*Mechanical solution*, the mere union of a solid with a liquid, without any alteration of the chemical properties of either.—*Solution of continuity*, a breach of continuity; a breach or rupture in a material substance.

Solvay process, sol′vā. [From *E. Solvay*, Belgian chemist.] A process for the manufacture of sodium carbonate, by the interaction of common salt, ammonia, and carbon dioxide.

solve, solv, *v.t.*—*solved, solving*. [L. *solvo, solutum*, to loosen, release, solve, for *se-luo*, from *se*, apart, and *luo*, to loosen; *solvo* is seen also in *absolve, dissolve, resolve, soluble, dissolute, resolute*, etc.] To explain or clear up the difficulties in; to make clear; to remove perplexity regarding; to operate upon by calculation or mathematical processes so as to bring out the required result (to *solve* a problem).—**solvency,** sol′ven•si, *n.* The state of being solvent; ability to pay all debts or just claims.—**solvent,** sol′vent, *a.* [L. *solvens, solventis*, ppr. of *solvo*.] Having the power of dissolving; able to pay all just debts.—*n.* Any fluid or substance that dissolves or renders liquid other bodies; a menstruum.—**solver,** sol′vėr, *n.* One who or that which solves.—**solvable,** sol′va•bl, *a.* Capable of being solved.—**solvability,** sol•va•bil′i•ti, *n.* Capability of being solved.

soma, sō′ma, *n.* [Gr. for *body*.] The body of a plant or animal exclusive of the germ cells.—**somatic,** sō•mat′ik, *a.* [Gr. *sōmatikos*, from *sōma, sōmatos*, the body.] Corporeal; pertaining to a body.—**somatics,** sō•mat′iks, *n.* Same as *Somatology*.—**somatology,** sō•ma•tol′o•ji, *n.* The doctrine of bodies or material substances; that branch of physics which treats of matter and its properties.

somber, som′bėr, *a.* [Fr. *sombre*, somber; Sp. and Pg. *sombra*, a shade; from L. *sub*, under, and *umbra*, a shade. UMBRAGE.] Dark in hue or aspect; dusky; gloomy; dismal; melancholy.—*v.t.* To make somber, dark, or gloomy; to shade.—**somberly,** som′bėr•li, *adv.* In a somber manner; darkly; gloomily.—**somberness,** som′bėr•nes, *n.* State or quality of being somber; gloominess.—**sombrous,** som′brus, *a.* Somber.

sombrero, som•brâr′ō, *n.* [Sp. from *sombra*, a shade. SOMBER.] A broad-brimmed hat.

some, sum, *a.* [A.Sax. *sum*, some, one, a certain; Goth. *sums*, Icel. *sumr*, Dan. *somme* (pl.), some; perhaps akin to *same*.] Expressing a certain indeterminate quantity or number, sometimes expressive of a considerable quantity (situated at *some* distance); indicating a person or thing not definitely known, or not specific: often followed by *or other* (*some* person *or other*); used before a word or number, with the sense of *about* or *near* (a village of *some* eighty houses); applied to those of one party; certain, in distinction from others (*some* men believe one thing, *others* another). It is often used without a noun and often followed by *of* (*some of* us, *some of* our provisions).—**somebody,** sum′bod•i, *n.* A person unknown or uncertain; a person indeterminate; a person of consideration.—**somehow,** sum′hou, *adv.* One way or other; in some way not yet known.—**someone,** sum′wun, *pron.* Somebody; some person.—*n.* A somebody.—**something,** sum′-thing, *n.* An indeterminate or unknown event or thing; an indefinite quantity or degree; a little; a person or thing of importance.—*adv.* In some degree or measure; somewhat; rather.—**sometime,** sum′tīm, *adv.* Once; formerly; at one time or other.—*a.* Having been formerly; former; late; whilom.—**sometimes,** sum′-tīmz *adv.* At times; at intervals; not always; now and then; once; formerly (*Shak.*).—**somewhat,** sum′-hwot, *n.* Something, though uncertain what; more or less; a certain quantity or degree, indeterminate.—*adv.* In some degree or measure; rather; a little.—**somewhere,** sum′-hwâr, *adv.* In or to some place or other unknown or not specified; in one place or another.—**somewhither,** sum′hwiTH•ėr, *adv.* To some indeterminate place.

somersault, somerset, sum′ėr•sạlt, sum′ėr•set, *n.* [Corrupted from O.Fr. *soubresault*, It. *soprassalto*, lit. an overleap; from L. *supra*, over, and *salio*, to leap.] A leap by which a person turns with the heels thrown over his head, completing a circuit, and again alights on his feet.

somite, sō′mīt, *n.* [Gr. *sōma*, body.] One of the successive rings or segments making up the bodies of certain animals.

somnambulate, som•nam′bū•lāt, *v.i.* [L. *somnus*, sleep, and *ambulo, ambulatum*, to walk.] To walk in sleep.—**somnambulation,** som•nam′bū•lā″-shon, *n.* The act of walking in sleep; somnambulism. — **somnambulator,** som•nam′bū•lā•tėr, *n.* A somnambulist; a sleepwalker.—**somnambulism,** som•nam′bū•lizm, *n.* The act or practice of walking in sleep, resulting from a peculiar perversion of the mental functions during sleep.—**somnambulist,** som•nam′bū•list, *n.* A person who walks in his sleep; a sleepwalker.— **somnambulistic,** som•nam′bū•lis″tik, *a.* Pertaining to or affected by somnambulism.

somniferous, som•nif′ėr•us, *a.* [L. *somnifer*—*somnus*, sleep, and *fero*, to bring.] Causing or inducing sleep; soporific.—**somnific,** som•nif′ik, *a.* [L. *somnus*, and *facio*, to make.] Causing sleep.

somnolence, somnolency, som′no•lens, som′no•len•si, *n.* [L. *somnolentia*, from *somnolentus*, sleepy, from *somnus*, sleep.] Sleepiness; drowsiness; inclination to sleep; *pathol.* a state intermediate between sleeping and waking.—**somnolent,** som′no•lent, *a.* Sleepy; drowsy; inclined to sleep.—**somnolently,** som′no•lent•li, *adv.* Drowsily.

son, sun, *n.* [A.Sax. *sunu*=Icel. *sonr, sunr*, Sw. *son*, Dan. *sōn*, Goth. *sunus*, G. *sohn*, Skr. *sûnu*, son; root seen in Skr. *su*, to beget.] A male child; the male issue of a parent, father, or mother: also used of animals; a male descendant; a term of affectionate address by an old man to a young one, a confessor to his penitent, a teacher to his disciple, etc.; a native of a country; a person strongly imbued by some quality (*sons* of light).—*The Son*, the second person of the Godhead; Christ: called also *Son of God* and *Son of Man*.—**son-in-law,** *n.* A man married to one's daughter.—**sonship,** sun′ship, *n.* The state of being a son.

sonant, sō′nant, *a.* [L. *sonans*, ppr. of *sono*, to sound. SOUND.] Pertaining to sound; sounding; uttered with voice and not breath merely; voiced, as the letters, *b, d* compared with *p, t*.—*n.* A sonant letter.

sonar, sō′när, *n.* [From *so*und *na*vigation *r*anging.] An apparatus that detects the presence of objects underwater by means of waves reflected from the objects.

sonata, so•nä′ta, *n.* [It., from L. *sonare*, to sound.] A musical composition for solo instruments, consisting of several movements, the allegro, adagio, rondo, and minuetto or scherzo.

song, song, *n.* [A.Sax. *sang, song*, from *singan*, to sing. SING.] That which is sung, whether by the human voice or a bird; a little poem to be sung; a vocal melody; an air for a single voice or several; a lay; a strain; poesy; verse.—*A mere song, an old song*, a trifle; an insignificant sum.

sonnet, son′et, *n.* [Fr. *sonnet*, from It. *sonetto*, a dim. from L. *sonus*, a sound. SOUND.] A short poem of fourteen lines, forming two stanzas of four verses each and two of three each, the rhymes being adjusted by a particular rule; a short poem, a song.—**sonneteer,** son•et•ēr′, *n.* [Fr. *sonnetier*.] A composer of sonnets; a small poet: usually in contempt.

sonometer, sō•nom′et•ėr, *n.* [L. *sonus*, sound, and Gr. *metron*, a measure.] An apparatus for illustrating the phenomena and laws of the vibrations of tense strings or wires; an apparatus for testing the acuteness of a person's hearing.

sonorous, so•nō′rus, *a.* [L. *sonorous*, from *sonus*, sound. SOUND.] Giving sound, as when struck; resonant; sounding; giving a clear, loud, or full-volumed sound; high sounding.—**sonorously,** so•nō′rus•li, *adv.* In a sonorous manner.—**sonorousness,** so•nō′rus•nes, *n.* The state or quality of being sonorous.

soon, sön, *adv.* [A.Sax. *sóna*, soon; O.Fris. *son, san*, Goth. *suns*, soon.] In a short time; shortly after any time specified or supposed; early; before any time supposed; quickly; speedily; readily; willingly; gladly (I would as *soon* do it).—*As soon as, so soon as*, immediately at or after another event.—*Sooner or later*, at some future time, near or remote.

soot, söt, *n.* [A.Sax. *sót*, soot=Icel. *sót*, Dan. *sod*, L.G. *sott*, soot.] A black substance formed from fuel in combustion, rising in fine particles and adhering to the sides of the chimney or pipe conveying the smoke.—*v.t.* To cover or foul with soot.—**sootiness,** söt′i•nes, *n.* The quality of being sooty.—**sooty,** söt′i, *a.* Pertaining to, producing, covered with, or resembling soot; fuliginous; dusky; dark.

soothe, SÖTH, *v.t.*—*soothed, soothing.* [Formerly to assent in a servile manner, to say yes to, from A.Sax. *gesóthian*, to confirm or show to be true, *sóth*, truth. SOOTH.] To please with blandishments or soft words;

to cajole; to make less angry or violent; to pacify; to assuage; to mitigate, ease, or allay.—**soother,** sö′THėr, *n.* One who or that which soothes.—**soothing,** sö′THing, *p.* and *a.* Such as to soothe; assuaging.—**soothingly,** sö′THing•li, *adv.* In a soothing manner.

soothsay, söth′sā, *v.i.* [From *sooth* and *say.*] To foretell; to predict. (N.T.)—**soothsayer,** söth′sā•ėr, *n.* One who foretells or predicts; a prophet.—**soothsaying,** söth′sā•ing, *n.* A foretelling; a prediction.

sop, sop, *n.* [Same as Icel. *soppa,* a sop, a sup; Sw. *soppa,* broth, soup; D. *sop*; L.G. *soppe,* a sop. Closely connected with *sup, soup.*] Something dipped in broth or liquid food, and intended to be eaten; something given to pacify: so called from the sop given to Cerberus to pacify him, in the ancient story.—*v.t.*—*sopped, sopping.* To steep or dip in liquor.—**soppy,** sop′i, *a.* Sopped or soaked in liquid; like a sop.

soph, sof, *n.* An abbreviation of *Sophister* and *Sophomore.*

sophism, sof′izm, *n.* [Fr. *sophisme,* from Gr. *sophisma,* a trick, a quibble, a sophism, from *sophos,* clever, wise.] A specious proposition; a specious but fallacious argument; a fallacy designed to deceive.—**Sophist,** sof′-ist, *n.* [Gr. *sophistēs,* a sophist.] One of a class of leading public teachers in ancient Greece during the fifth and fourth centuries B.C., many of whom were men who spent their time in verbal quibbles and philosophical enigmas, thus causing the term to take on a bad sense; [*not cap.*] a captious or fallacious reasoner; a quibbler.—**sophister,** sof′-is•tėr, *n.* A sophist; a quibbling disputant; a plausible fallacious reasoner; in the University of Cambridge, England, a student advanced beyond the first year of his residence; a soph.—**sophistic, sophistical,** so•-fis′tik, so•fis′ti•kal, *n.* Fallaciously subtle; containing sophistry; quibbling. ∴ Syn. under FALLACIOUS.—**sophistically,** so•fis′ti•kal•li, *adv.* In a sophistical manner; fallaciously.—**sophisticalness,** so•fis′ti•kal•nes, *n.*—**sophisticate,** so•fis′ti•kāt, *v.t.*—*sophisticated, sophisticating.* To pervert; to wrest from the truth; to adulterate; to render spurious by admixture.—**sophistication,** so•fis′-ti•kā″shon, *n.* The act of adulterating; adulteration; the act or art of quibbling; a quibble; artificial, narrow, complicated; of a person, worldly-wise; the process of disillusioning one.—**sophistry,** sof′ist•ri, *n.* Fallacious reasoning; reasoning sound in appearance only and intended to mislead.

sophomore, sof′o•mōr, *n.* [From Gr. *sophos,* wise, and *mōros,* foolish.] In American colleges, a student belonging to the second of the four classes; one next above a freshman.

soporiferous, sō•po•rif′ėr•us, *a.* [L. *soporifer*—*sopor, soporis,* sleep (cog. with Skr. *svap,* to sleep, Gr. *hypnos,* sleep), and *fero,* to bring.] Causing or tending to cause sleep; soporific.—**soporific,** sō•po•rif′ik, *a.* [L. *sopor,* and *facio,* to make.] Causing sleep; tending to cause sleep.—*n.* A drug or other thing that has the quality of inducing sleep.

soprano, so•prä′nō, *n.* It. pl. **soprani,** sō•prä′nē, E. pl. **sopranos,** so•prä′-nōz. [It., from *sopra,* L. *supra,* above.] The highest quality of female voice, whose ordinary easy range is from C below the treble staff to G or A above it; equivalent to *Treble,* a term which is falling out of use.

sorb, sorb, *n.* [Fr. *sorbe,* L. *sorbus,* the sorb.] The service tree or its fruit.—**sorb apple,** *n.* The fruit of the service tree.

Sorbonist, sor′bon•ist, *n.* A doctor of the *Sorbonne,* a celebrated institution founded in connection with the University of Paris in 1252 by Robert de *Sorbon,* chaplain and confessor of Louis IX.

sorcerer, sor′sėr•er, *n.* [Fr. *sorcier,* a sorcerer, from L.L. *sortiarius,* a caster of lots, from L. *sors, sortis,* a lot (whence also *sort*). As to the form of the word comp. *fruiterer,* Fr. *fruitier.*] A conjuror; an enchanter; a magician.—**sorceress,** sor′sėr•es, *n.* A female sorcerer.—**sorcery,** sor′sėr•i, *n.* [O.Fr. *sorcerie.*] Divination by the assistance or supposed assistance of evil spirits; magic; enchantment; witchcraft.

sordid, sor′did, *a.* [Fr. *sordide,* L. *sordidus,* form *sordes,* filth.] Filthy‡; base; mean; meanly avaricious; covetous; niggardly.—**sordidly,** sor′-did•li, *adv.* In a sordid manner; meanly; basely; covetously.—**sordidness,** sor′did•nes, *n.* The state or quality of being sordid; niggardliness.

sore, sōr, *a.* [A.Sax. *sár,* sore, a sore; Icel. *sárr,* sore, *sár,* a sore; Dan. *saar,* Goth. *sair,* a wound; G. *sehr,* very.] Painful; being the seat of pain; violent with pain; severe; distressing; tender, as the mind; easily annoyed or vexed; feeling aggrieved; galled.—*n.* A place in an animal body where the skin and flesh are ruptured or bruised, so as to be painful; a boil, ulcer, wound, etc.—*adv.* With painful violence; severely; sorely.—**sorely,** sōr′li, *adv.* In a sore manner; grievously; greatly; severely.—**soreness,** sōr′nes, *n.* The state of being sore.

sorghum, sor′gum, *n.* [From *sorgo,* its Italian name.] A cereal plant, one species of which is cultivated for fodder, grain, and juice; a sirup or molasses, boiled down from the plant juice.

sorites, sō•rī′tēz, *n.* [Gr. *sōreitēs,* from *sōros,* a heap.] *Logic,* a series of propositions so linked together that the predicate of each that precedes forms the subject of each that follows ($a=b$, $b=c$, $c=d$, therefore $a=d$); a logical sophism depending on numerical indetermination, the point at which a heap or other quantity precisely ceases to be such.

sororal, so•rō′ral, *a.* [L. *soror, sororis,* sister.] Pertaining to a sister or sisters; sisterly.—**sororicide,** so•rō′-ri•sīd, *n.* [L. *soror,* and *caedo,* to kill.] The murder of a sister; the murderer of a sister.

sorority, so•ror′i•ti, *n.* A fraternal organization of women, usually of a social nature, to promote their mutual welfare.

sorosis, so•rō′sis, *n.* pl. **soroses,** so•-rō′sēz. [From Gr. *sōros,* a heap.] *Bot.* a fleshy fruit composed of many flowers, seed vessels, and receptacles consolidated, as the pineapple or mulberry. (*cap.,* U.S.) A women′s club.

sorrel, sor′el, *a.* [A dim. from O.Fr. *sor, sore,* sorrel, from O.D. *sore,* akin to *sere.*] Of a reddish or yellowish brown color.—*n.* A reddish or yellow-brown color.

sorrel, sor′el, *n.* [Fr. *surelle,* sorrel, from O.H.G. *sûr,* sour. SOUR.] The popular name of certain perennial plants, a common species being a succulent acid herb used as a salad and potherb.

sorrel, so′rel, *n.* A buck of the third year.

sorrow, sor′ō, *n.* [O.E. *sorwe,* A.Sax. *sorg, sorh,* care, sorrow; Icel., Dan., and Sw. *sorg,* G. *sorge,* Goth. *saurga*—sorrow.] Pain of mind from loss of or disappointment in the expectation of good; grief; regret; sadness; mourning. ∴ Syn. under AFFLICTION.—*v.i.* To be affected with sorrow; to feel sorry; to grieve; to be sad.—**sorrowful,** sor′ō•fụl, *a.* Full of sorrow; exhibiting or producing sorrow; sad; mournful; dejected.—**sorrowfully,** sor′ō•fụl•li, *adv.* In a sorrowful manner.—**sorrowfulness,** sor′ō•fụl•nes, *n.*

sorry, sor′i, *a.* [Equivalent to *sore,* with term. *-y*; from A.Sax. *sárig,* from *sár,* sore: influenced in spelling by *sorrow.* SORE.] Grieved for the loss of some good; pained at some evil experienced or committed; often slight or transient regret (I am *sorry* you cannot come); mean; vile; worthless; pitiful (a *sorry* excuse).—**sorrily,** sor′i•li, *adv.* In a sorry or wretched manner.—**sorriness,** sor′-i•nes, *n.* Pitifulness; meanness; despicableness.

sort, sort, *n.* [Fr. *sorte,* sort, kind, from L. *sors, sortis,* a lot, a condition (seen also in *assort, consort, resort*).] A kind, species, class, or order (a *sort* of men); manner; form of being or acting; degree (in some *sort*); a set; a suit.—*Out of sorts,* out of order; not in one's usual state of health; unwell.—*v.t.* To separate and arrange in distinct classes or divisions; to assort; to arrange; to reduce to order.—*v.i.* To consort; to associate; to suit; to agree.—**sortable,** sor′ta•bl, *a.* Capable of being sorted.—**sorter,** sor′tėr, *n.* One who sorts (a letter-*sorter*; a wool-*sorter*).

sortie, sor′ti, *n.* [Fr., from *sortir,* to issue.] The issuing of troops from a besieged place to attack the besiegers; a sally.

sortilege, sor′ti•lej, *n.* [L. *sortilegium*—*sors,* lot, and *lego,* to select.] The act or practice of drawing lots; divination by lots.

sorus, sō′rus, *n.* pl. **sori,** sō′rī. [Gr.

sōros, a heap.] *Bot.* a cluster of spore cases on the back of the fronds of ferns.

SOS. An international radio distress signal sent out by a ship at sea which has encountered serious trouble.

sostenuto, sos•te•nö′to. [It., sustained.] *Mus.* a term implying that the note over which it is placed is to be held out its full length in an equal and steady manner.

sot, sot, *n.* [Fr. *sot*, a fool, probably from the Celtic; comp. Ir. *suthan*, a blockhead, *sotaire*, a fop.] A stupid person; a dolt; a person stupefied by excessive drinking; a habitual drunkard.—*v.t.*†—*sotted, sotting.* To stupefy; to besot.—*v.i.* To tipple to stupidity.—**sottish,** sot′ish, *a.* Pertaining to a sot; having the character of a sot.—**sottishly,** sot′ish•li, *adv.* In a sottish manner.—**sottishness,** sot′-ish•nes, *n.* The quality of being sottish; drunkenness.

soteriology, so•ti′ri•ol″o•ji, *n.* [Gr. *sōterios*, saving, salutary, and *logos*, discourse.] The science of health; the doctrine of salvation by Jesus Christ.

Sothic, soth′ik, *a.* [From *Sothis*, the Dog Star, at whose heliacal rising the year was supposed to commence.] Pertaining to the Dog Star. —*Sothic year*, the ancient Egyptian year of 365 ¼ days.

sottish, sottishness. See SOT.

sou, sö, *n.* [Fr., from L. *solidus*, a coin, a solid piece.] An old French copper coin, of varying value; a five-centime piece.

soubrette, sö•bret′, *n.* [Fr.] A waiting maid; the part of an intriguing servant girl in a comedy.

Souchong, sö•shong′, *n.* [Chinese, little sprouts.] A kind of black tea.

sough, suf, *v.i.* [O.E. *swough*, from A.Sax. *swōgan*, to sound.] To emit a rushing, moaning, or whistling sound, like that of the wind; to sound like the roar of the sea.—*n.* A sound of this kind; a rushing sound like that of the wind; a deep sigh.

sought, sat, pret. and pp. of *seek*.

soul, sōl, *n.* [O.E. and Sc. *saul*, A.Sax. *sáwel, sawl*; Icel. *sála*, Dan. *sjael*, D. *ziel*, Goth. *saivala*, G. *seele*, the soul.] The spiritual and immortal part in man; the immaterial spirit which inhabits the body; the moral and emotional part of man's nature; the seat of the sentiments or feelings; the animating or essential part; the vital principle; the essence (he is the very *soul* of honor); an inspirer or leader (the *soul* of an enterprise); courage or spirit; a spiritual being; a disembodied spirit; a human being; a person (not a *soul* present); a familiar term for a person (poor *soul*, he was a good *soul*).—*Cure of souls*, in the Church of England, an ecclesiastical charge.—*Soul* is used in many self-explanatory compounds; as *soul*-destroying, *soul*-entrancing, *soul*-felt, *soul*-stirring, *soul*-subduing, etc.—**soulless,** sōl′les, *a.* Without a soul; lifeless; spiritless; base; lacking nobility of nature.

sound, sound, *a.* [A.Sax. *sund*, sound, healthy; L.G., Dan., and Sw. *sund*, G. (*ge*)*sund*, D. *zond*; from root of L. *sanus*, sound. SANE.] Healthy; not diseased; not being in a morbid state (a *sound* mind, a *sound* body); uninjured; unhurt (a *sound* limb); free from imperfection or defect (*sound* timber, *sound* fruit); founded in truth; valid; that cannot be refuted (*sound* reasoning); correct; free from error; orthodox; founded in right and law; just (a *sound* claim); profound, unbroken, undisturbed (a *sound* sleep); heavy; laid on with force (a *sound* beating).—**soundly,** sound′li, *adv.* In a sound manner; healthily; validly; thoroughly; smartly (beat him *soundly*).—**soundness,** sound′nes, *n.* The state of being sound.

sound, sound, *n.* [A.Sax. *sund*, a strait, a sound; Icel., Dan., Sw., and G. *sund*, a sound; from root of *sunder*, or akin to *swim.*] A narrow passage or channel of water, as between the mainland and an isle, or connecting two seas; a strait.

sound, sound, *n.* [A.Sax. *sund*, a swimming, from *swimman*, to swim; it is also called the *swim.*] The air bladder of a fish.

sound, sound, *v.t.* [Fr. *sonder*, to sound; probably from the Teutonic *sund*, a strait. SOUND, a channel.] To measure the depth of; to fathom by sinking a plummet or lead attached to a line; *surg.* to examine by means of a probe; *fig.* to try or search out the intention, opinion, will, or desires of.—*v.i.* To use the line and lead in searching the depth of water.—*n. Surg.* any elongated instrument by which cavities of the body are sounded or explored.—**soundings,** sound′ingz, *n. pl.* The depths of water in rivers, harbors, along shores, and even in the open sea, which are ascertained by means of a sounding line.—**sounding lead,** *n.* The weight used at the end of a sounding line.—**sounding line,** *n.* A line for ascertaining the depth of water.—**soundless,** sound′les, *a.* Unfathomable.

sound, sound, *n.* [O.E. *soun, sowne*, from Fr. *son*, L. *sonus*, a sound (also in *consonant, dissonant, resonant, sonorous*, etc.), cog. Skr. *svan*, to sound. The *d* has been added, as in *round* (to whisper), *lend, hind* (a laborer).] That which is heard; the effect which is produced by the vibrations of a body affecting the ear; a noise; noise without signification; empty noise.—*v.i.* To make a noise; to give out a sound; to seem or appear when uttered; to appear on narration (this story *sounds* like a fiction); to be conveyed in sound; to be spread or published.—*v.t.* To cause to give out a sound; to play on; to utter audibly; to give a signal for by a certain sound (to *sound* a retreat); to publish or proclaim (to *sound* the praises of a great man).—**sound bow,** *n.* The part of a bell on which the clapper strikes.—**sounding,** soun′ding, *p.* and *a.* Causing sound; sonorous; having a lofty sound; bombastic (mere *sounding* phrases).—**sounding board, soundboard,** *n.* A canopy over a pulpit, etc., to direct the sound of a speaker's voice toward the audience; a thin board over which the strings of a pianoforte, violin, guitar, etc., are stretched.—**soundless,** sound′les, *a.* Having no sound; noiseless; silent; dumb.

soup, söp, *n.* [Fr. *soupe*, from G. *suppe*, D. *soep*, Dan. *suppe*, Icel. *súpa*—soup, broth, etc.: akin *sup, sip, sop.*] A kind of broth; a sort of food made generally by boiling meat, fish, etc., in water with various other ingredients.

soupçon, söp•son, *n.* [Fr., from O.Fr. *souspecon*, a suspicion. SUSPICION.] A very small quantity; a taste.

sour, sour, *a.* [A.Sax. *súr*, sour = Icel. *súrr*, Dan. *suur*, D. *zuur*, G. *sauer*; also found in Celtic: W. and Armor. *zur*—sour. SORREL.] Sharp to the taste; tart; acid; harsh of temper; crabbed; austere; morose; expressing discontent, displeasure, or peevishness (a *sour* word or look); become tart or acid by keeping, as milk.—*Sour grapes.* See GRAPE. *v.t.* To make acid or sour; to make cross, crabbed, or discontented (to *sour* the temper); to embitter.—*v.i.* To become acid; to acquire tartness; to become peevish, crabbed, or harsh in temper.—**sourish,** sour′ish, *a.* Somewhat sour; moderately acid.—**sourly,** sour′li, *adv.* In a sour manner; acidly; morosely; peevishly, discontentedly.—**sourness,** sour′nes, *n.* The state or quality of being sour; acidity; sharpness to the taste; asperity; harshness of temper.—**soursop,** *n.* A large succulent fruit closely allied to the custard apple.

source, sōrs, *n.* [Fr. *source*, O.Fr. *sorce*, from L. *surgo*, to rise, contr. for *surrigo*, for *sub-rego*—*sub*, under, and *rego*, to direct. SURGE, REGENT.] The spring or fountainhead from which a stream of water proceeds; one who or that which originates or gives rise to anything; first cause; origin.

souse, sous, *n.* [A form of *sauce.*] Pickle made with salt; sauce; pickled meat; the ears, feet, etc., of swine pickled; a guzzler (*slang*).—*v.t.*—*soused, sousing.* To steep in pickle; to plunge into water.

souse, sous, *v.i.* and *t.* [Comp. G. *sausen*, to rush.] To fall suddenly on; to guzzle, as liquor (*slang*).—*n.* A violent attack; a blow.—*adv.* With sudden violence.

soutane, sö•tän′, *n.* [Fr., from L.L. *subtana*, from L. *subtus*, beneath.] A cassock, usually black, worn by Roman Catholic clergy.

south, south, *n.* [A.Sax. *súth*; Icel. *suthr, sunnr*, Dan. *syd, sönden*, O.H. G. *sund*, Mod. G. *süd*, south; allied to *sun*, being the region of the sun.] One of the four cardinal points of the compass, directly opposite to the north; the region or locality lying opposite to the north; the wind that blows from the south; [*cap.*] the section of the U. S. below the Mason-Dixon line; the states of the cotton belt; Del., Md., Va., W. Va.,

N. C., S. C., Ky., Tenn., Fla., Ga., Ala., Miss., La., Tex., Okla., Ark., Mo.—*a.* Situated in the south, or in a southern direction; pertaining to the south; proceeding from the south.—*adv.* Toward the south; from the south.—**southeast,** *n.* The point of the compass equally distant from the south and east.—*a.* Pertaining to the southeast.—**southeaster,** *n.* A wind from the southeast.—**southeasterly, southeastern,** *a.* Southeast.—**southerliness,** suTH'ėr•li•nes, *n.* State of being southerly.—**southerly,** suTH'ėr•li, *a.* Lying in the south; coming from the south.—**southern,** suTH'ėrn, *a.* [A.Sax. *súthern*, from *súther*, *súth*, south.] Belonging to the south; lying on the south side of the equator; coming from the south.—*Southern Cross*, *n.* A bright constellation in the southern hemisphere, the principal stars of which form a cross.—**southerner,** suTHėr•nėr, *n.* An inhabitant or native of the south.—**southernly,** suTH'ėrn•li, *adv.* Toward the south.—**southernmost,** suTH'ėrn•mōst, *a.* Furthest toward the south.—**southernwood,** suTH'ėrn•wụd, *n.* A composite plant nearly allied to wormwood, formerly employed in medicine as a stomachic and stimulant.—**southing,** south'ing, *n.* Motion to the south; the time at which the moon or other heavenly body passes the meridian of a place; *navig.* and *survey.* the difference of latitude southward from the last point of reckoning. NORTHING.—**south pole,** *n.* The southern end of the earth's axis.—**southron, southern,** suTH'ron, suTH'ėrn, *n.* A native or inhabitant of a southern country or region.—**southward,** south'wėrd, *adv.* Toward the south.—*a.* Lying or situated toward the south; directed toward the south.—**southwest,** *n.* The point of the compass equally distant from the south and west.—*a.* Lying in the direction of the southwest; coming from the southwest.—**southwester,** *n.* A strong southwest wind; a waterproof hat with a flap hanging over the neck, worn in bad weather: frequently contracted into *Sou'wester*.—**southwesterly,** *a.* In the direction of southwest; coming from the southwest.—**southwestern,** *a.* Pertaining to the southwest.—**southwestward,** *a.* and *adv.* Toward the southwest.

souvenir, sö•ve•nēr', *n.* [Fr., from L. *subvenire*, to occur to mind.] That which reminds or revives the memory of anything; a keepsake.

sovereign, sov'rin, *a.* [O.Fr. *soverain*, Mod.Fr. *souverain*; from L.L. *superanus*, from L. *super*, above, over. The *g* has been erroneously inserted.] Supreme in power; possessing supreme dominion; royal; princely; paramount; efficacious in the highest degree (a *sovereign* medicine).—*n.* A supreme ruler; the person having the highest power or authority in a state, as a king, queen, emperor, etc.; a monarch.—**sovereignty,** sov'ėr•in•ti, *n.* The state of being a sovereign; the supreme power in a state; monarchical sway; supremacy; supreme excellence.

soviet, sov'i•et, *n.* [Rus.] The provincial, national, and federal councils or assemblies composed of representatives of workers, peasants, and soldiers, and culminating in the *Union of Soviet Socialist Republics*.

sow, sou, *n.* [A.Sax. *sugu*, *sú*, a sow=L.G. *suge*, O.D. *sowe*, G. *sau*, Dan. and Sw. *so*, sow; cog. L. *sus*, Gr. *hus*, sow; perhaps from root *su*, to bring forth (whence *son*).] The female of the swine; *founding*, the main channel into which metal is run from a smelting furnace. See under PIG.—*To have* or *get the right* (or *wrong*) *sow by the ear*, to pitch upon the right (or wrong) person or thing; to come to the right (or wrong) conclusion.

sow, sou, *n.* A medieval engine of attack, full of soldiers, covered at the tip, and propelled against the walls of a town or fortress; when crushed from the side of the besieged it was said 'to farrow'.—**sow thistle,** sou•this'l, *n.* A genus of composite plants in Britain, somewhat resembling thistles, and greedily eaten by various animals.

sow, sō, *v.t.*—pret. *sowed*, pp. *sówed* or *sown*, [A.Sax. *sáwan* (pret. *seow*; pp. *sáwen*), to sow=Icel. *sá*, Dan. *saae*, G. *säen*, Goth. *saian*; same root as L. *sero*, *satum*, to sow (whence *season*). *Seed* is from this stem.] To scatter, as seed upon the earth, for the purpose of growth; to plant by strewing; to stock with seed; to spread abroad; to disseminate; to propagate (to *sow* discord).—*v.i.* To scatter seed for growth and the production of a crop.—**sower,** sō'ėr, *n.* One who sows; a disseminator.

soy, soi, *n.* A sauce prepared in China and Japan from a bean for fish, meat, etc.—**soybean,** soi'bēn, *n.* A leguminous plant and its seed high in protein value, rich in vegetable oil, useful for both human food and forage, and from which are made, by chemical processing, paints and plastics. The plant is cultivated in China, Japan, Manchuria, and the United States.

spa, spä, *n.* A mineral spring; a place to which people resort for its mineral waters; from *Spa*, a celebrated watering place in Belgium.

space, spās, *n.* [Fr. *espace*, from L. *spatium*, space, from root *spa*, to stretch, seen in *span*.] Extension, considered independently of anything which it may contain; extension in all directions; any portion of extension; the interval between any two or more points or objects; quantity of time; the interval between two points of time; *printing*, the interval between words in printed matter; also a kind of blank type for separating words.—*mus.* one of the four intervals between the five lines of a staff.—*v.t.*—*spaced*, *spacing*. To arrange at proper intervals; to arrange the spaces in.—**space probe,** *n.* A craft launched into space to collect information by means of instruments it carries.—**spaceship,** spās'ship, *n.* A craft able to operate in the space beyond the earth's atmosphere.—**space time,** *n.* The four-dimensional world of events, separable (according to the theory of Minkowski and Einstein) into three dimensions of length and one of time.—**spacial,** spā'shi•al, *a.* Pertaining to space.—**spacious,** spā'shus, *a.* Enclosing an extended space; large in extent; wide; roomy.—**spaciously,** spā'shus•li, *adv.*—**spaciousness,** spā'shus•nes, *n.*

spade, spād, *n.* [A.Sax. *spada*=D., Dan., and Sw. *spade*, Icel. *spathi*, G. *spaten*; cog. Gr. *spathē*, any broad blade.] An instrument for digging, having a broad blade of iron and a stout handle, adapted to be used with both hands and one foot; *pl.* one of the four suits of playing cards.—*To call a spade a spade*, to call things by their proper names; to speak plainly and without mincing matters.—*v.t.* To dig with a spade; to pare the sward from with a spade.—**spadeful,** spād'fụl, *n.* As much as a spade will hold.

spadix, spā'diks, *n.* [L., a palm branch with its fruit; as an *adj.* date-brown.] *Bot.* a form of inflorescence, in which the flowers are closely arranged round a fleshy radius, and the whole surrounded by a large leaf called a spathe, as in palms.—**spadiceous,** spā•dish'us, *a.* *Bot.* growing within a spathe or spadix; forming a spadix.

spake, spāk. One of the forms of the preterite of *speak*, the more commonly used form being *spoke*.

span, span, *n.* [A.Sax. *span*, a span (the measure), *spannan*, to bind; Icel. *sponn*, Dan. *spand*, D. *span*, G. *spanne*, a span; same root as L. *spatium*, space; Gr. *spaō*, to draw (whence *spasm*).] The space from the point of the thumb to that of the little finger when extended; nine inches; the eighth of a fathom; a short space of time; the spread or extent of an arch between its abutments; a pair of horses; a yoke of animals; a team.—*v.t.*—*spanned*, *spanning*. To measure by the hand with the fingers extended, or with the fingers encompassing the object; to measure or reach from one side of to the other.—**spanner,** span'ėr, *n.* One that spans; a screw key.

span, span, pret. of *spin*.

spandrel, span'drel, *n.* [From O.Fr. *esplanader*, to level or make even. ESPLANADE.] *Arch.* the irregular triangular space comprehended between the outer curve or extrados of an arch and a straight-sided figure surrounding it.

spanemia, spa•nē'mi•a, *n.* [Gr. *spanis*, scarcity, and *haima*, blood.] Poverty or thinness of blood.

spangle, spang'gl, *n.* [Dim. of O.E. *spang*, A.Sax. *spange*, a buckle, a clasp, etc.; D. *spang*, Icel. *spöng*, a spangle, a stud.] A small circular ornament of metal stitched on an article of dress; any little thing sparkling and brilliant; a small sparkling object.—*v.t.*—*spangled*, *spangling*. To set, sprinkle, or adorn with spangles.—*v.i.*† To glitter; to glisten.

Spaniard, span′yėrd, *n.* A native of Spain.—**Spanish,** span′ish, *a.* Pertaining to Spain.—*n.* The language of Spain.—**Spanish fly,** *n.* See CANTHARIDES.

spaniel, span′yel, *n.* [O.Fr. *espagneul,* Mod.Fr. *épagneul,* lit. a little Spanish dog, from Sp. *espana,* L. *Hispania,* Spain.] A name given to several kinds of dogs all more or less elegant, some of them used for sporting purposes, others kept merely as pets; also, a cringing fawning person.

spank, spangk, *v.i.* [Same as Dan. *spanke,* to strut, to stalk; comp. Sc. *spang,* to leap.] To move with a quick lively step; to move or run along quickly.—*v.t.* To slap or smack, as with the open hand.—**spanker,** spang′kėr, *n.* One that spanks; a fast-going or fleet horse (*colloq.*); *naut.* a large fore-and-aft sail set upon the mizzenmast of a ship.—**spanking,** spangk′ing, *p.* and *a.* Moving with a quick lively pace; dashing; free-going. (*Colloq.*)

spanner, span′ėr, *n.* A tool with jaws or sockets at the end or ends of a lever; used for tightening nuts.

span-new, span′nū, *a.* [Icel. *spán-nýr,* span-new, lit. chip-new, splinter-new, from *spánn,* G. *span,* a chip; in allusion to work fresh from the hands of the workman.] Quite new.

spar, spär, *n.* [A.Sax. *spaer, spaerstán,* a kind of stone.] A mineralogical term for various crystallized, earthy, and some metallic substances, which easily break into rhomboidal, cubical, or laminated fragments with polished surfaces, as calcareous spar, fluorspar, etc.

spar, spär, *n.* [Same as Icel. *sparri, sperra,* Dan. *sparre,* D. *spar,* G. *sparren,* a beam, a bar.] A long piece of timber of no great thickness; a piece of sawed timber; a pole; *naut.* a long beam; a general term for masts, yards, booms, and gaffs.

spar, spär, *v.i.*—*sparred, sparring.* [O.Fr. *esparer* (It. *sparare*), to fling out the hindlegs, to kick, from L. *ex,* out, and Fr. *parer,* to parry. PARRY.] To rise and strike with the feet or spurs; said of cocks; to move the arms in a way suitable for immediate attack or defense; to fight with boxing gloves; to box.—*n.* A preliminary flourish of the fists; a boxing match; a contest with boxing gloves.

sparable, spar′a•bl, *n.* [Corruption of *sparrow bill,* from the shape.] A kind of nail driven into the soles of shoes and boots.

spare, spâr, *v.t.*—*spared, sparing.* [A.Sax. *sparian* = Icel. and Sw. *spara,* Dan. *spare,* G. and D. *sparen,* to spare; same root as L. *parco* (for *sparco*), to spare.] To use frugally; not to be profuse of; to part with; to do without; to dispense with; to omit; to forbear (in this sense often with an infinitive as object); to treat with pity, mercy, or forbearance; to forbear to afflict or punish; to forbear to inflict upon; to withhold from; to save, withhold, or gain, as from some engrossing occupation.—*v.i.* To be parsimonious or frugal; not to be liberal or profuse; to use mercy or forbearance.—*a.* [A.Sax. *spaer,* moderate, spare.] Scanty; not plentiful or abundant; such as may be spared; over and above what is necessary; superfluous; held in reserve; not required for present use (a *spare* anchor, a *spare* bed); lean; wanting flesh; meager; thin.—**sparely,** spâr′li, *adv.* In a spare manner; sparingly.—**spareness,** spâr′nes, *n.* State of being lean or thin; leanness.—**sparer,** spâ′rėr, *n.* One that spares.—**sparerib,** spâr′rib, *n.* [*Spare,* lean, and *rib.*] The piece of a hog taken from the side, consisting of the ribs with little flesh on them.—**sparing,** spâ′ring, *a.* Saving; parsimonious; chary (*sparing* of words).—**sparingly,** spâ′ring•li, *adv.* In a sparing manner; not abundantly; frugally; parsimoniously; not lavishly; seldom; not frequently.

sparge, spärj, *v.t.* [L. *spargo,* to sprinkle. ASPERSE.] To dash or sprinkle; to throw water upon malt in a shower of small drops.—**sparger,** spär′jėr, *n.* A sprinkler.

spark, spärk, *n.* [A.Sax. *spearca* = L.G. *sparke,* D. *spark, sperk,* also *sprank,* a spark; same root as *spring, sprinkle.*] A small particle of fire emitted from bodies in combustion; a small shining body or transient light; the light accompanying electric discharge; a particle (a *spark* of life; of courage).—*v.i.* To emit particles of fire; to sparkle.—**sparkle,** spär′kl, *v.i.*—*sparkled, sparkling.* [Freq. from *spark.*] To emit sparks; to shine as if giving out sparks; to glitter; to flash; to twinkle.—*v.t.* To emit with coruscations; to shine with.—*n.* A spärk; a luminous particle; a scintillation; luminosity; luster.—**sparkler,** spark′lėr, *n.* One who or that which sparkles.—**sparkling,** spärk′ling, *p.* and *a.* Emitting sparks. —**spark plug,** *n.* A part that fits into the cylinder of an internal-combustion engine, having two electrodes and providing the electric spark for combustion.

spark, spärk, *n.* [Same as Prov. E. *sprack,* lively, Icel. *sparkr,* sprightly; akin *spry.*] A brisk, showy, gay man; a lover; a gallant; a beau.—**sparkish,** spär′kish, *a.* Having the style or character of a spark.

sparrow, spar′ō, *n.* [A.Sax. *spearwa,* Goth. *sparwa,* Dan. *spurv,* Ital. *spörr,* G. *spar, sperling,* sparrow.] A well-known bird of the finch family, constantly seen in the vicinity of human dwellings, even in the midst of large cities.—**sparrow hawk,** *n.* A small European hawk, *Accipiter nisus,* very destructive to pigeons and small birds.

sparrowgrass, *n.* A corruption of *Asparagus.*

sparse, spärs, *a.* [L. *sparsus,* pp. of *spargo,* to strew, to sprinkle (as in *asperse, disperse, intersperse*); akin to Gr. *speirō,* to sow.] Thinly scattered; set or planted here and there; not dense; *bot.* not in any apparent regular order.—**sparsely,** spärs′li, *adv.* In a scattered or sparse manner; thinly.—**sparseness,** spärs′nes, *n.* The state of being sparse; scattered state.

Spartacist, spar′ta•sist, *n.* A member of the extreme Anarchist party in the German revolution of 1918.

Spartan, spär′tan, *a.* Pertaining to ancient *Sparta*; hence, hardy; undaunted.

spasm, spazm, *n.* [Fr. *spasme,* L. *spasmus,* from Gr. *spasmos,* from *spaō,* to draw, to wrench. SPAN.] *Med.* an abnormal, sudden, and more or less violent contraction of one or more muscles or muscular fibers, generally attended with pain.—**spasmodic, spasmodical,** spaz•mod′ik, spaz•mod′i•kal, *a.* [Gr. *spasmos,* and *eidos,* likeness.] Relating to spasm; consisting in spasm; convulsive; marked by strong effort, but of brief duration; violent and short-lived.—*Spasmodic school,* a name given in ridicule to certain modern authors whose writings were considered to be distinguished by an overstrained and unnatural style, e.g. Bailey, Dobell (*Aytoun*).—**spasmodic,** *a.* Of the nature of a spasm; convulsive; taking place by fits and starts; intermittent, as *spasmodic* attempts.—**spasmodically,** spaz•mod′i•kal•li, *adv.* In a spasmodic manner.—**spastic,** spas′tik, *a.* [Gr. *spastikos.*] Relating to spasm; spasmodic.

spat, spat, pret. of *spit.*

spat, spat, *n.* [Akin to verb to *spit.*] The spawn of shellfish; the developing spawn of the oyster.

spat, spat, *n.* [Abbrev. of *spatterdashes*?] Footwear round the ankles to keep the feet warm.

spathe, spāTH, *n.* [L. *spatha,* from Gr. *spathē,* a broad blade, a spathe.] *Bot.* a large membranaceous bract situated at the base of a spadix, which it encloses as a sheath.—**spathaceous, spathal,** spa•thā′shus, spā′thal, *a.* *Bot.* furnished with or formed like a spathe (*spathal* flowers).—**spathose,** spath′ōs, *a.* *Bot.* spathaceous.

spathic, spath′ik, *a.* [Fr. *spathique,* from *spath,* G. *spath,* spar.] Applied to minerals having an even lamellar or flatly foliated structure; sparry.—*Spathic iron,* carbonate of iron; an ore of iron of a foliated structure.—**spathose,** spath′ōs, *a.* Sparry; foliated in texture.

spatial. See SPACIAL.

spatter, spat′ėr, *v.t.* [Akin to *spit, spot.*] To scatter a liquid substance on; to sprinkle with anything liquid or semiliquid that befouls; to bespatter; to throw out in drops; *fig.* to asperse; to defame.—**spatterdash,** spat′ėr•dash, *n.* [*Spatter* and *dash.*] A covering of cloth or leather for the leg; a gaiter; a legging.

spatula, spat′ū•la, *n.* [L., dim. of *spatha,* Gr. *spathē,* a broad flat instrument. SPADE.] A sort of knife with a thin flexible blade, used by druggists, painters, etc., for spreading plasters, working pigments, etc.; an instrument used in the kitchen for turning pancakes, spreading icing on a cake, etc.; *surg.* a flat instrument for depressing the tongue in operations about the throat.

spavin, spav′in, *n.* [O.Fr. *espavent*; origin doubtful.] A disease of horses affecting the hock joint, or joint of the hind leg between the knee and the fetlock by which lameness is produced.—**spavined,** spav′ind, *a.* Affected with spavin.

spawn, spa̤n, *n.* [O.Fr. *espaundre*, to spawn, lit. to *expand*. EXPAND.] The eggs or ova of fishes, frogs, etc., when shed; the white fibrous matter from which fungi are produced; the mycelium of fungi; contemptuously, any offspring or product.—*v.t.* To deposit in the form of spawn; contemptuously, to bring forth or generate.—*v.i.* To deposit eggs, as fish, frogs, etc.—**spawner,** spa̤′nėr, *n.* A female fish.

spay, spā, *v.t.* [A Celtic word; Manx *spoiy*, Gael. *spoth*, to castrate.] To remove or destroy the ovaries of: a process applied to female animals, to incapacitate them for producing young.

speak, spēk, *v.i.*—pret. *spoke* (*spake* archaic or poetical); pp. *spoken.* [O.E. *speken*, A.Sax. *specan*, *sprecan*; same as D. and L.G. *spreken*, G. *sprechen*, to speak.] To utter words; to express thoughts by words; to utter a speech, discourse, or harangue; to talk; to discourse; to make mention; to tell by writing; to communicate ideas in any manner; to be expressive.—*To speak for*, to argue in favor of; to plead the cause of; to urge the claims of; to be the representative or spokesman of; to ask in marriage. (*Scrip.*)—*To speak out*, to speak loud or louder; to speak boldly or unreservedly.—*To speak up*, to speak in a loud or louder tone; to express one's thoughts freely.—*To speak well for*, to be a favorable indication of.—*To speak with*, to converse with. ∴ A man may *speak* by uttering a single word, whereas to *talk* is to utter sentiments consecutively; so, a man may be able to *speak* though he is not able to *talk*. *Speak* is also more formal in meaning; as, to *speak* before a brilliant audience; while *talk* implies a conversational manner of speaking.—*v.t.* To utter with the mouth; to utter articulately; to say; to declare (to *speak* the truth); to proclaim; to talk or converse in (to *speak* French); to address; to accost; to express in any way (her eyes *spoke* love).—*To speak a ship*, to hail and speak to her captain or commander.—**speaker,** spē′kėr, *n.* One who speaks; one that utters a speech in public, or one that practices public speaking; a person who is the mouthpiece or spokesman of another; a person who presides over a deliberative assembly, as of the House of Representatives.—**speaking,** spē′king, *a.* Used for the purpose of conveying speech (a *speaking* trumpet); forcibly expressive (a *speaking* likeness); extending to mere phrases of civility (a *speaking* acquaintance).—**speaking trumpet,** *n.* A trumpet-shaped instrument which enables the sound of the voice to be heard at a distance.—**speaking tube,** *n.* A tube for communicating orally from one room to another.

spear, spēr, *n.* [A.Sax. *spere*=D. and G. *speer*, Dan. *spaer*, Icel. *spjör*; comp. L. *sparus*, a hunting spear; probably akin to *spar.*] A long pointed weapon used in war and hunting, by thrusting or throwing; a lance; a pointed instrument with barbs, for stabbing fish, etc.—*v.t.* To pierce with, or as with, a spear; to kill with a spear.—**spearer,** spēr′ėr, *n.* One who spears.—**spearhead,** *n.* The metal point of a spear.—**spearman,** spēr′man, *n.* One who is armed with a spear.—**spearmint,** spēr′mint, *n.* An aromatic plant having spearshaped leaves.

special, spesh′al, *a.* [Fr. *spécial*, from L. *specialis*, from *species*, kind (which see).] Pertaining to something distinct or having a distinctive character; distinctive; particular; peculiar; differing from others; designed for a particular purpose or occasion; having a distinct field or scope.—*Special correspondent*, a person specially appointed to give an account of some important event or series of events for a newspaper.—*Special creation*, the obsolete theory that all species of plants and animals were created independently.—*Special pleading*, the business of a special pleader; the specious but unsound or unfair argumentation of one whose aim is victory rather than truth.—*n.* Any person or thing appointed for a special purpose or occasion, as a constable, a railroad train, etc.—**specialism,** spesh′al•izm, *n.* A particular branch or department of knowledge, devotion to some one subject.—**specialist,** spesh′al•ist, *n.* A person who devotes himself to a particular branch of a profession, art, or science; one who has a special knowledge of some particular subject.—**speciality,** spesh•i•al′i•ti, *n.* That property by which a person or thing is specially characterized; that in which one is specially versed; a quality or attribute peculiar to a species.—**specialization,** spesh′al•i•zā″shon, *n.* The act of specializing or devoting to a particular use or function; special determination.—**specialize,** spesh′al•īz, *v.t.*—*specialized*, *specializing.* To assign a specific use or purpose to; to devote or apply to a specific use or function.—**specially,** spesh′al•li, *adv.* In a special manner; particularly; especially; for a particular purpose.—**specialty,** spesh′al•ti, *n.* A particular point; that in which one is specially versed; a speciality; *law*, a special contract; an obligation or bond.

specie, spē′shi, *n.* [The ablative of L. *species*, used as an English word from its occurrence in the phrase 'paid in *specie*', that is, in visible coin.] Gold or silver coined, and used as a circulating medium; coin; in contradistinction to paper money.

species, spē′shēz, *n. sing.* and *pl.* [L. *species*, appearance, shape, sort, kind, from *specio*, to behold; akin to Gr. *skeptomai*, Skr. *pash*, to see. English words in which L. *specio* appears are very numerous, as *specious*, *specimen*, *specify*, *spite*, *spice*, *despise*, *aspect*, *prospect*, *respect*, *spectacle*, etc.] A kind, sort, or variety; a class, collection, or assemblage of things or beings classified according to attributes which are determined by scientific observation; a group of animals or plants which bear a close resemblance to each other in the more essential features of their organization, and produce similar progeny, several species uniting to form a *genus*; *logic*, a group of individuals agreeing in common attributes and designated by a common name.

specify, spes′i•fī, *v.t.*—*specified*, *specifying.* [Fr. *spécifier*, as if from a L. *specifico*—*species*, and *facio*, to make.] To mention or name distinctively; to designate in words, so as to clearly distinguish or limit.—**specific,** spe•sif′ik, *a.* [Fr. *spécifique.*] Pertaining to, characterizing, or constituting a species; marking something as a distinct species; tending to specify or particularize; definite; precise; *med.* possessed of peculiar efficacy in the cure of a particular disease.—*Specific center*, the locality where any species of animals or plants first appeared and from which it became diffused.—*Specific character*, that which distinguishes one species from every other species of the same genus; the essential character of a species.—*Specific gravity*, abbreviated *Sp. Gr.* or *S.G.*, the ratio of the weight of the given bulk of any substance to that of the same bulk of some standard substance, usually water for solids and liquids, air or hydrogen for gases; related to *relative density* as weight to mass, but represented by the same number in any case.—*Specific heat*, (S.H.), the ratio of the quantity of heat required to raise the temperature of a given mass of any substance through one degree to the quantity required to raise the same mass of a standard substance (water for solids and liquids, water or air for gases) through one degree. See ATOMIC HEAT.—*Specific inductive capacity*, for any substance, the ratio of the capacity of a condenser having that substance as a dielectric to the capacity of a similar condenser with air as the dielectric.—*Specific name*, the name which, appended to the name of the genus, constitutes the distinctive name of the species.—*Specific resistance*, for any substance, the resistance of a conductor of the substance of unit length and unit cross section.—*n.* A remedy which exerts a special action in the prevention or cure of a disease; an infallible or supposed infallible remedy; something certain to effect the purpose for which it is used; an unfailing agent.—**specifically,** spe•sif′i•kal•li, *adv.* In a specific manner; so far as concerns the species; definitely; particularly.—**specification,** spes′i•fi•kā″shon, *n.* The act of specifying; designation of particulars; particular mention; a statement describing the dimensions, details, etc., of any work about to be undertaken, as in building, engineering, etc.; an article, item, or particular specified.

specimen, spes′i•men, *n.* [L. *specimen,* an example or specimen, from *specio,* to behold. SPECIES.] One of a number of similar things intended to show the character of the whole, or of others not exhibited; a portion exhibited; a sample. ∴ A *specimen* exhibits the nature or character of a whole without reference to the relative quality of individual portions; a *sample* is a portion taken out of a quantity, and implies that the quality of the whole is to be judged by it; in many cases, however, the words are used indifferently.

specious, spē′shus, *a.* [Fr. *spécieux,* from L. *speciosus,* showy, beautiful, plausible, from *species,* show, appearance. SPECIES.] Pleasing to the eye‡; superficially fair, just, or correct; plausible; appearing well at first view (a *specious* argument, a *specious* objection). ∴ Syn. under COLORABLE.—**speciously,** spē′shus•li, *adv.* In a specious manner; with show of right or reason.—**speciousness,** spē′shus•nes, *n.* The quality of being specious; plausibility.—**speciosity,** spē•shi•os′i•ti, *n.* The state of being specious; a specious show.

speck, spek, *n.* [A.Sax. *specca,* a speck; akin L.G. *spaak,* a speck; *speckle* is a derivative.] A spot; a small discolored place in anything; a stain; a blemish; a small particle or patch.—*v.t.* To spot; to mark with specks or spots.

speckle, spek′l, *n.* [Dim. of *speck.*] A little spot in anything, of a different color from that of the thing itself; a speck.—*v.t.*—*speckled, speckling.* To mark with small specks or spots.

spectacle, spek′ta•kl, *n.* [Fr. *spectacle,* from L. *spectaculum,* from *specio,* to behold, freq. of *specio,* to see. SPECIES.] A show; a gazing stock; something exhibited as worthy of being seen; a gorgeous or splendid show; anything seen; a sight; *pl.* an optical instrument used to assist or correct some defect in the organs of vision, consisting of two lenses mounted in a light frame, so constructed as to adhere to the nose and temples, and keep the lenses before the eyes.—**spectacled,** spek′ta•kld, *a.* Furnished with or wearing spectacles.—**spectacular,** spek•tak′ū•lėr, *a.* Pertaining to or of the nature of a show or spectacle; pertaining to spectacles.

spectator, spek•tā′tor, *n.* [L., from *specto,* freq. of *specio,* to behold. SPECIES.] One who looks on; a beholder; one who is present at a play or spectacle.—**spectatorial,** spek•ta•tō′ri•al, *a.* Pertaining to a spectator.—**spectatress, spectatrix,** spek•tā′tres, spek•tā′triks, *n.* A female beholder or looker on.

specter, spek′tėr, *n.* [Fr. *spectre,* from L. *spectrum,* an appearance, an apparition, from *specto,* to behold. SPECIES.] An apparition; the disembodied spirit of a person who is dead; a ghost; a phantom.—**spectral,** spek′tral, *a.* Pertaining to a specter; ghostlike; pertaining to spectra; pertaining to the solar or other spectrum.—**spectrally,** spek′tral•li, *adv.* In a spectral manner; like a ghost or specter.—**spectroheliograph,** spek′tro•hēl″yo•graf, *n.* [L. *spectrum,* and Gr. *hēlios,* sun, and *graphō,* to write.] An instrument for photographing the sun by monochromatic light.—**spectrology,** spek•trol′o•ji, *n.* [*Spectrum,* and Gr. *logos,* discourse.] That branch of science which treats of the characteristic spectra of bodies.—**spectrometer,** spek•trom′et•ėr, *n.* [*Spectrum,* and Gr. *metron,* a measure.] An apparatus attached to a spectroscope for purposes of measurement.—**spectroscope,** spek′tro•skōp, *n.* [*Spectrum,* and Gr. *skopeō,* to look at.] The instrument employed in spectrum analysis, which by means of a prism or train of prisms produces a magnified image of any spectrum.—**spectroscopic, spectroscopical,** spek•tro•skop′ik, spek•tro•skop′i•kal, *a.* Pertaining to the spectroscope or spectroscopy.—**spectroscopically,** spek•tro•skop′i•kal•li, *adv.* By the use of the spectroscope.—**spectroscopist,** spek•tro′skop•ist, *n.* One who uses the spectroscope; one skilled in spectroscopy.—**spectroscopy,** spek″tro•skō′pi, *n.* That branch of science which is concerned with the use of the spectroscope and with spectrum analysis.—**spectrum,** spek′trum, *n.* pl. **spectra,** spek′tra, A specter‡; an image of something seen, continuing after the eyes are closed, covered, or turned away; the oblong figure or stripe, exhibiting the prismatic or rainbow colors or some of them, formed on a wall or screen by a beam of light, as of the sun, received through a small slit and refracted by being passed through a prism or series of prisms. The *solar spectrum* or spectrum of sunlight is colored transversely throughout its length, the colors shading insensibly into one another from red at the one end, through orange, yellow, green, blue, indigo, to violet at the other, and it is also crossed by a number of black lines having definite positions. The moon and planets have spectra like that of the sun, while each fixed star has a spectrum peculiar to itself, and the incandescent vapor of each elementary substance has its characteristic spectrum.—*Spectrum analysis,* the art or operation of examining spectra, whether of the heavenly bodies or of substances heated to incandescence, by means of the spectroscope, a means of detecting the presence of substances otherwise undetected.

specular. See SPECULUM.

speculate, spek′ū•lāt, *v.i.*—*speculated, speculating.* [L. *speculor, speculatus,* from *specula,* a look-out, from *specio,* to see. SPECIES.] To meditate; to consider a subject in its different aspects and relations; to theorize; to purchase goods, stock, or other things with the expectation of an advance in price and of selling the articles with a profit by means of such advance; to engage in speculation.—**speculation,** spek•ū•lā′shon, *n.* Mental view of anything in its various aspects and relations; contemplation; a theory or theoretical view; the laying out of money or incurring of extensive risks with a view to more than the usual success in trade; a hazardous commercial or other business transaction entered into in the hope of large profits.—**speculative,** spek′ū•lā•tiv, *a.* Given to speculation; contemplative; pertaining to, involving, or formed by speculation; theoretical; not verified by fact, experiment, or practice; pertaining to, or given to speculation in trade.—**speculatively,** spek′ū•lā•tiv•li, *adv.* In a speculative manner.—**speculativeness,** spek′ū•lā•tiv•nes, *n.* The state of being speculative.—**speculator,** spek′ū•lā•tėr, *n.* One who speculates or forms theories; a theorizer; one who speculates in trade; one who incurs great risks in the hope of great gain.—**speculatory,** spek′ū•la•to•ri, *a.* Speculative.

speculum, spek′ū•lum, *n.* [L., a mirror, from *specio,* to look, to behold. SPECIES.] A mirror or looking glass; *optics,* a reflecting surface, such as is used in reflecting telescopes, made of an alloy of copper and tin or of glass; *surg.* an instrument with a reflecting mirror attached for examining certain openings of the body.—*Speculum metal,* metal used for making the specula of reflecting telescopes—an alloy of two parts copper and one of tin.—**specular,** spek′ū•lėr, *a.* [L. *specularis.*] Having the qualities of a mirror or looking glass; having a smooth reflecting surface.—*Specular iron ore,* a hard, crystallized variety of hematite.

speech, spēch, *n.* [A.Sax. *spaec, spraec,* speech, from *specan, sprecan,* to speak. SPEAK.] The faculty of expressing thoughts by words or articulate sounds; the power of speaking; language; a particular language; the act of speaking with another; conversation; anything spoken; a discourse, oration, or harangue.—**speechify,** spēch′i•fī, *v.i.* —*speechified, speechifying.* To make a speech; to harangue. (*Humorous or contemptuous.*)—**speechless,** spēch′les, *a.* Destitute or deprived of the faculty of speech; dumb; mute; not speaking for a time; silent.—**speechlessness,** spēch′les•nes, *n.* The state of being speechless; muteness.

speed, spēd, *v.i.*—pret. and pp. *sped* or *speeded.* [A.Sax. *spēdan.* to hasten, to prosper, from *spēd,* haste, prosperity, from *spówan,* to thrive, same as

O.H.G. *spuön*, to succeed.] To make haste; to move with celerity; to have success; to prosper; to succeed; to have any fortune good or ill; to fare. —*v.t.* To dispatch or send away in haste; to hasten; to accelerate; to expedite; to help forward; to make prosperous; to cause to succeed; to dismiss with good wishes or friendly services; to kill or destroy: especially in pp. *sped* (*Shak.*).—*n.* Success; fortune; prosperity in an undertaking; swiftness; celerity; haste; impetuosity.—**Godspeed.** See GOD.—**speeder,** spē'dėr, *n.* One who speeds; a kind of machine for forwarding things in manufacture.—**speedy,** spē'di, *a.* Quick; nimble; rapid in motion; not dilatory or slow.—**speedily,** spē'di•li, *adv.* In a speedy manner; quickly; in a short time.—**speediness,** spē'di•nes, *n.* The quality of being speedy; quickness; dispatch.—**speedometer,** spēd•om'et•ėr, *n.* An instrument for indicating speed.—**speedwell,** spēd'wel, *n.* [From growing on roadsides, and, as it were, cheering travelers on their way.] The common name of plants of the genus *Veronica*, a favorite species being the germander speedwell.

speleology, spē•le•ol'o•ji, *n.* [Gr. *spēlaion*, cave, and suffix *logy*.] Exploration and study of caves.

spell, spel, *n.* [A.Sax. *spell*, a saying, tale, charm.] A charm consisting of some words of occult power; an incantation; any charm.

spell, spel, *v.t.* [M.E. *spellen* from O.Fr. *espeller*, of Germanic origin.] To repeat or write the letters of a word in order; to form by letters; to read; to read with labor or difficulty: often with *out*; to mean.—*v.i.* To form words with the proper letters.—**spellbind,** *v.t.*—*spellbound, spellbinding*. To hold the attention of as if by hypnotism; to fascinate.—**spellbound,** spel'bound, *a.* Bound as by a spell or charm.—**speller,** spel'ėr, *n.* One that spells; a spelling book.—**spelling,** spel'ing, *n.* The act of one who spells; orthography.—**spelling bee,** *n.* A spelling competition in which contestants are eliminated for misspelling a word.

spell, spel, *n.* [A.Sax. *spelian*, to supply the room of another; comp. D. and Sw. *spel*, G. *spiel*, play, game.] A piece of work done by one person in relief of another; a turn of work; a single period of labor; a period; a while or season.

spelt, spelt, *n.* [A.Sax. *spelt*, L.G. and D. *spelt*, G. *spelz*, from root of *split*.] An inferior kind of wheat. Called also *German wheat*.

spelt, spelt. A pret. and pp. of *spell*.

spelter, spel'tėr, *n.* [L.G. *spialter*, G. and D. *spiauter*, spelter, zinc; akin *pewter*.] A name often applied in commerce to zinc.

spencer, spen'sėr, *n.* An outer coat or jacket without skirts, named from an Earl *Spencer*, who first wore it.

spencer, spen'sėr, *n.* [Perhaps akin to *spanker*.] *Naut.* a fore-and-aft sail with a gaff and boom set abaft the fore and main masts.

spend, spend, *v.t.*—pret. and pp. *spent*. [A.Sax. *spendan*, borrowed from L. *expendo* or *dispendo*, to expend, to dispense. EXPEND, PENDANT.] To lay out (money); to part with in purchasing; to exhaust (to *spend* one's energies); to waste; to pass, as time; to suffer to pass away; to exhaust of force or strength; to waste (to *spend* efforts).—*v.i.* To make expense; to spend money.—**spender,** spen'dėr, *n.* One that spends; a prodigal; a lavisher.—**spendthrift,** spend'thrift, *n.* One who spends his means lavishly or improvidently; a prodigal: often used as an adjective (*spendthrift* ways).—**spent,** spent, pret. and pp. of *spend*. Worn out; wearied; exhausted; having deposited the spawn: said of a herring.—*Spent ball*, a cannon or rifle ball which reaches an object without sufficient force to pass through it, or to wound otherwise than by a contusion.

Spenserian, spen•sē'ri•an, *a.* Pertaining to the poet *Spenser*; applied to the style of versification adopted by Spenser in his *Faëry Queen*.

sperm, spėrm, *n.* [L. and Gr. *sperma*, *spermatos*, seed, from *speirō*, to sow.] The seminal fluid of animals; semen; spawn of fishes or frogs; a microscopic male cell, usually motile.—**spermaceti,** spėr•ma•se'ti, *n.* [Lit. sperm of whale; L. *sperma*, and *cetus*, a whale.] A fatty material obtained from a species of whale common in the Pacific.—**spermary,** spėr'ma•ri, *n.* The organ in male animals in which spermatozoa are produced.—**spermatic,** spėr•mat'ik, *a.* Seminal; pertaining to the semen, or conveying it.—**spermatium, -ia,** spėr•mā'shum, *n.* [Gr. *sperma*, *spermatos*, seed.] In fungi, a free nonmotile male cell.—**spermatogenous,** spėr•ma•toj'en•us, *a.* [Gr. *sperma*, and root *gen*, to produce.] Sperm-producing.—**spermatoid,** spėr'ma•toid, *a.* [Gr. *sperma*, and *eidos*, form.] Sperm-like; resembling sperm or semen.—**spermatophyte,** spėr'ma•to•fīt, *n.* [Gr. *sperma*, and *phyton*, plant.] The highest phylum of plants, the seed plants or flowering plants.—**spermatorrhea,** spėr'ma•to•rē"a, *n.* [Gr. *sperma*, and *rheō*, to flow.] Emission of the semen without copulation.—**spermatozoon,** spėr'ma•to•zō"on, *n.* pl. **spermatozoa,** spėr'ma•to•zō"a. [Gr. *sperma*, and *zōon*, a living being.] One of the microscopic animalcule-like bodies developed in the semen of animals and essential to impregnation.—**spermic,** spėr'mik, *a.* Pertaining to sperm or seed.—**sperm oil,** *n.* The oil of the spermaceti whale.—**sperm whale,** *n.* The spermaceti whale or cachalot.

spew, spū, *v.t.* [A.Sax. *spiwan*, to spew; D. *spouwen*, *spuwen*, G. *speien*, Icel. *spýja*, Goth. *speiwan*, to vomit; cog. L. *spuo*, to vomit. *Spit* is from same root.] To vomit; to eject from the stomach; to eject or to cast forth.—*v.i.* To vomit.—**spewer,** spū'ėr, *n.* One who spews.

sphacelate, sfas'e•lāt, *v.i.* [Gr. *sphakelos*, from *sphazō*, to kill.] To mortify; to become gangrenous, as flesh; to become carious, as a bone.—*v.t.* To affect with gangrene.—**sphacelation,** sfas•e•lā'shon, *n.* The process of becoming or making gangrenous; mortification.

sphagnum, sfag'num, *n.* [Gr. *sphagnos*, a kind of moss.] An important genus of mosses; peat moss, valuable for packing plants for transmission; much used in hospitals for dressing wounds.

sphene, sfēn, *n.* [From Gr. *sphēn*, a wedge, from the shape of its crystals.] A mineral composed of silicic acid, titanic acid, and lime.

sphenoid, sphenoidal, sfē'noid, sfē•noi'dal, *a.* [Gr. *sphēn*, a wedge, and *eidos*, form.] Resembling a wedge.—*Sphenoid bone*, a bone in the base of the skull, so named because it is wedged in amidst the other bones.—*n.* A wedge-shaped body; the sphenoid bone.—**spheno-.** As a prefix in anatomical terms means pertaining to the sphenoid.

sphere, sfēr, *n.* [L. *sphaera*, from Gr. *sphaira*, a ball, a globe.] A globular body; an orb or globe; a planet, star, or sun; a solid body the surface of which in every part is equally distant from a point within it called its center; the concave expanse of the heavens; circuit or range of action, knowledge, or influence; compass; province; rank or order of society.—*v.t.*—*sphered, sphering*. To place in a sphere or among the spheres; to form into a sphere.—**spheral,** sfē'ral, *a.* Pertaining to the spheres or heavenly bodies; rounded like a sphere.—**spherical, spheric,** sfer'i•kal, sfer'ik, *a.* [Fr. *sphérique*; L. *sphaericus*.] Having the form of a sphere; globular; pertaining or belonging to a sphere; relating to the orbs of the planets; planetary.—*Spherical angle*, an angle formed on the surface of a sphere by the intersection of two great circles.—*Spherical geometry*, that branch of geometry which treats of spherical magnitudes.—*Spherical triangle*, a triangle formed on the surface of a sphere by the mutual intersection of three great circles.—*Spherical trigonometry*, that branch of trigonometry which deals with spherical triangles.—**spherically,** sfer'i•kal•li, *adv.* In the form of a sphere.—**sphericity,** sfe•ris'i•ti, *n.* The state or quality of being spherical; globularity; roundness.—**spherics,** sfer'iks, *n.* *Geom.* the doctrine of the properties of the sphere.—**spheroid,** sfē'roid, *n.* A body not perfectly spherical; *geom.* a solid generated by the revolution of an ellipse about one of its axes, being either *oblate* or *prolate*.—**spheroidal,** sfi•roi'dal, *a.* Having the form of a spheroid; *crystal.* bounded by several convex faces.—*Spheroidal state*, the name given to the condition of a liquid when, on being placed on a red-hot plate, it assumes a spheroidal form and passes into the state of gas without boiling.—**spheroidicity,** sfi•roi•dis'i•ti, *n.* The quality of being spheroidal.—**spherometer,** sfi•rom′et•ėr, *n.* An instrument for measuring the thickness of small bodies when great accuracy is required, as the curvature of optical glasses, etc.—**spherule,** sfer′ūl, *n.* A little sphere or spherical body.—**spherulite,** sfer′ū•līt, *n.* [Gr. *sphaira,* and *lithos,* a stone.] A variety of obsidian found in rounded grains.—**sphery,** sfē′ri, *a.* Belonging to the spheres; resembling a sphere or orb.

sphincter, sfingk′tėr, *n.* [Gr. *sphingktēr,* from *sphingō,* to draw close.] *Anat.* a name applied to circular muscles or muscles in rings, which serve to close the external orifices of organs, as the sphincter of the mouth, of the anus, etc.

sphinx, sfingks, *n.* pl **sphinxes,** sfingk′sez. [L. *sphinx,* Gr. *sphingx.*] *Greek myth.* a she-monster often represented with the winged body of a lion and the breasts and head of a woman, said to have proposed a riddle to the Thebans and to have killed all who were not able to guess it, till Oedipus did so, whereupon the sphinx slew herself; hence, a person who puts puzzling questions; *Egyptian antiq.* a figure having the body of a lion and the head of a man, a ram, or a hawk.

sphragistics, sfra•jis′tiks, *n.* [Gr. *sphragis,* a seal.] The science of engraved seals, their history, peculiarities, and distinctions.

sphygmic, sfig′mik, *a.* [Gr. *sphygmos,* the pulse.] Of or pertaining to the pulse.—**sphygmograph,** sfig′mo•graf, *n.* An instrument which, when applied over an artery, indicates the character of the pulse.—**sphygmographic,** sfig•mo•graf′ik, *a.* Of or pertaining to the sphygmograph.—**sphygmometer,** sfig•mom′et•ėr, *n.* An instrument for counting the arterial pulsations; a sphygmograph.

spicate, spī′kāt, *a.* [L. *spicatus,* from *spica,* a spike.] *Bot.* having a spike or ear; eared like corn.

spice, spīs, *n.* [O.Fr. *espice* (Fr. *épice*), from L. *species,* species, kind, in late Latin, wares, spices, drugs, etc. SPECIES.] A vegetable production, fragrant, or aromatic to the smell and pungent to the taste, such as pepper, nutmeg, ginger, cinnamon, and cloves, used in sauces and in cookery; *fig.* a small admixture; a flavoring; a smack.—*v.t.*—*spiced, spicing.* To season with spice; to season, literally or figuratively.—**spicery,** spī′sėr•i, *n.* Spices collectively; a repository of spices.—**spicily,** spī′si•li, *adv.* In a spicy manner; pungently; with flavor.—**spiciness,** spī′si•nes, *n.* Quality of being spicy.—**spicy,** spī′si, *a.* Producing spice; abounding with spices; having the quality of spice; flavored with spice; aromatic; *fig.* pungent; piquant; keen.

spick-and-span, spik′and•span, *a.* or *adv.* [*Spick,* a spike, and span, a chip, a splinter. SPAN-NEW.] In full use adverbially with *new* = quite new; also used adjectively (a *spick-and-span* suit of clothes).

spicula, spik′ū•la, *n.* pl. **spiculae,** spik′ū•lē. [L. *spicula,* dim. of *spica,* a sharp point, a spike.] *Bot.* a small spike or spikelet; a pointed, fleshy, superficial appendage.—**spicular,** spik′ū•lėr, *a.* Resembling a dart; having sharp points.—**spiculate,** spik′ū•lāt, *a.* Covered with or divided into fine points.—**spicule,** spik′ūl, *n.* [L. *spicula.*] A little spike; a little sharp needle-shaped body.

spicy. See SPICE.

spider, spī′dėr, *n.* [For *spinder,* for *spinner,* one that spins; comp. G. *spinne,* a spider, from *spinnen,* to spin.] The common name of well-known animals of the class Arachnida, many of them remarkable for spinning webs for taking their prey and forming a convenient habitation; something supposed to resemble a spider, as a kind of gridiron, or a trivet to support vessels over a fire.—**spider monkey,** *n.* A name given to many species of New World monkeys.

spiegeleisen, spē′gel•ī•zn, *n.* [G.—*spiegel,* a mirror, and *eisen,* iron; from its fracture showing large smooth shining surfaces.] A kind of cast iron made from specular iron ore or hematite, containing much carbon and manganese, largely used in the Bessemer process of steelmaking.

spigot, spig′ot, *n.* [O.E. *spigotte, speget, spykette,* dim. forms from *spick* = *spike.*] A pin or peg used to stop a faucet, or a small hole in a cask of liquor; a faucet.

spike, spīk, *n.* [Same word as *pike* with initial *s*; Icel. *spík,* Sw. *spik,* a spike; cog. L. *spica,* a sharp point, an ear of corn; W. *yspig,* a spike.] A large nail or pin; a piece of pointed iron like a long nail, as on the top of walls, gates, etc.; a nail or instrument with which the vents of cannon are filled up; an ear of corn or other grain; *bot.* a species of inflorescence in which the flowers are sessile along a common axis.—*v.t.*—*spiked, spiking.* To fasten with spikes or long nails; to set with spikes; to fix upon a spike.—*To spike a gun* or *cannon,* to fill up the touchhole by driving a nail or steel pin with side springs forcibly into it, in order to render it unserviceable.—**spikelet,** spīk′let, *n. Bot.* a small spike making a part of a large one.—**spikenard,** spīk′närd, *n.* [The plant bears flowers in *spikes.* See NARD.] An aromatic herbaceous plant of the East Indies, the root of which is highly prized for its aromatic properties; a name given to several other plants, and to various fragrant essential oils.—**spiky,** spī′ki, *a.* In the shape of a spike; set with spikes.

spile, spīl, *n.* [Same as D. *spijl,* L.G. *spile,* a bar, a stake; G. *speil,* a skewer. SPILL, *n.*] A small peg or wooden pin used to stop a hole in a cask or barrel; a spigot.—*v.t.*—*spiled, spiling.* To supply with a spigot.

spill, spil, *n.* [Same as D. *spil,* G. *spille,* a spindle, a peg; allied to *spile, spell,* Sc. *spale,* a chip.] A spigot; a spile; a small slip of wood or strip of paper rolled up, used to light a lamp, etc.

spill, spil, *v.t.*—pret. and pp. *spilled* or *spilt.* [A.Sax. *spillan,* to spill; to ruin; L.G. and D. *spillen,* Icel. *spilla,* Dan. *spilde,* to spill, to waste; akin to *spill* above.] To suffer to fall or run out of a vessel; applied to fluids and to substances whose particles are small and loose; to suffer or cause to flow out; to shed (a man *spills* another's blood) to; throw from a horse or carriage (*colloq.*).—*v.i.* To be shed; to be suffered to fall, to be lost, or wasted.—**spillway,** *n.* In hydraulic engineering, a diversion for excess water from a river or reservoir; a gatelike mechanism of a dam to allow for the escape of superfluous water.

spin, spin, *v.t.*—pret. *spun* or *span*; pp. *spun*; ppr. *spinning.* [A.Sax. *spinnan* = D. and G. *spinnen,* Goth. *spinnan,* Dan. *spinde,* Icel. and Sw. *spinna*—to spin; same root as *span* and Gr. *spaō,* to draw. Hence *spindle, spinster, spider.*] To draw out and twist into threads, either by the hand or machinery (to *spin* wool, cotton, or flax); to draw out tediously (to *spin* out a tale); to extend to a great length; to whirl rapidly; to cause to turn with great speed (to *spin* a top); to form by the extrusion of a viscid fluid from their body, as spiders, silkworms, etc.—*To spin a yarn,* to tell a long story; originally a seaman's phrase.—*v.i.* To perform the act of making threads; to work at drawing and twisting threads; to move round rapidly; to whirl, as a top or a spindle; to run or drive with great rapidity; to go quickly (*colloq.*).—*n.* The act of spinning; a rapid run; a race; the rotation of an elongated projectile (a shell) about its long axis imparted to it by the rifling of the gun. See TWIST.—**spinner,** spin′ėr, *n.* One who or that which spins; a spider; a spinneret.—**spinneret,** spin′ėr•et, *n.* One of the nipple-like organs with which spiders form their webs.—**spinning jenny,** *n.* The first spinning machine by which a number of threads could be spun at once; invented about 1767 by James Hargreaves.—**spinning wheel,** *n.* A machine for spinning wool, cotton, or flax into threads by the hand.—**spinster,** spin′stėr, *n.* [*Spin,* and double fem. ter. *-ster, -ess.*] A woman who spins; an unmarried woman; formerly, in England, an unmarried woman of the nobility from a viscount's daughter downward.

spinach, spin′ich, *n.* [O.Fr. *espinoche,* It. *spinace,* Sp. *espinaca,* from L. *spina,* a spine—being named from the prickles on its fruit.] An annual plant (*Spinacia oleracea*), with hollow stems and edible, fleshy leaves, used as a vegetable.

spinal. See SPINE.

spindle, spin′dl, *n.* [A.Sax. *spindel,* lit. the instrument for spinning, from *spinnan,* to spin; so also, G., Sw., and Dan. *spindel.*] A slender rod by which the thread is twisted and wound in spinning; any slender pointed rod or pin which turns round or on which anything turns; an axis or arbor; a measure of yarn; in cotton, 15,120 yards; in linen, 14,400 yards.—*v.i.*—*spindled, spindling*. To shoot or grow in a long, slender stalk or body.—**spindlelegs, spindleshanks,** *n.* Long slender legs, or a person having such.—**spindle tree,** *n.* A small tree (genus *Euonymus*).

spindrift, spin′drift, *n.* [A form of *spoondrift*.] *Naut.* the blinding drift of salt water blown from the surface of the sea in hurricanes.

spine, spīn, *n.* [L. *spina*, a thorn, the spine, from a root seen also in *spike*. From the Latin come also *spinach, spinet, spinney*.] The backbone of a vertebrated animal, so called from the thorn-like processes of the vertebrae; a thorn; a sharp process from the woody part of a plant; a stout, rigid, and pointed process of the integument of an animal; a ridge of mountains, especially a central ridge.—**spinal,** spī′nal, *a.* Pertaining to the spine or backbone of an animal.—*Spinal column*, the backbone.—*Spinal cord, Spinal marrow*, the elongated mass of nervous matter contained in the osseous canal of the spine.—**spinescent,** spī•nes′ent, *a.* [L. *spinesco*, to grow thorny.] *Bot.* terminating in a spine; somewhat spinose.—**spiniferous,** spī•nif′ėr•us, *a.* Producing spines; bearing thorns; thorny.—**spinigerous,** spī•nij′ėr•us, *a.* Bearing a spine or spines.—**spininess,** spī′ni•nes, *n.* The quality of being spiny.—**spinosity,** spī•nos′i•ti, *n.* The state of being spinous or spinose.—**spinous, spinose,** spī′nus, spī′nōs, *a.* [L. *spinosus*.] Full of spines; armed with thorns; thorny.—**spinule,** spī′nūl, *n.* [L. *spinula*, dim. of *spina*.] A minute spine.—**spinulose,** spī′nū•lōs, *a. Bot.* covered with small spines.—**spiny,** spī′ni, *a.* Full of spines; thorny; like a spine; slender; perplexed; troublesome.

spinel, spinelle, spi•nel′, *n.* [Fr. *spinelle*, It. *spinella*, originally perhaps a mineral with spine-shaped crystals, from L. *spina*, a spine.] A species of corundum, which occurs in regular crystals and sometimes in rounded grains.

spinet, spin′et, *n.* [O.Fr. *espinette*, from L. *spina*, a spine, because its strings were twitched by spine-like pieces of quill. SPINE.] A stringed musical instrument, which differed from the virginal only in being of a triangular form; a small piano.

spiniferous. See SPINE.

spinifex, spin′i•feks, *n.* An excessively spiny grass, growing in tussocks, and covering large areas in Australia, where it forms a great impediment to travelers.

spinnaker, spin′a•kėr, *n.* [From *spin*, in sense of to go rapidly.] A triangular racing sail carried by yachts when running before the wind, on the opposite side to the mainsail.

spinner, spinneret, etc. See SPIN.

spinney, spinny, spin′i, *n.* [O.Fr. *espinaye*, from *espine*, a brier, from L. *spina*, a thorn.] A small wood with undergrowth; a clump of trees; a small grove.

spinose. See SPINE.

Spinozism, spi•nō′zizm, *n.* A system of pantheistic philosophy propounded by Baruch *Spinoza*, who was born in Amsterdam in 1632 of a Jewish family, and died at the Hague in 1677.—**Spinozist,** spi•nō′zist, *n.* A believer in the doctrines of Spinoza.

spinster. See SPIN.

spinthariscope, spin•thar′is•kōp, *n.* [Gr. *spinthēr*, a spark, *skopeō*, to view.] An instrument for demonstrating the physical properties of radium.

spinule, spiny. See SPINE.

spiracle, spī′ra•kl, *n.* [L. *spiraculum*, from *spirare*, to breathe. SPIRIT.] A breathing hole; an aperture for exhalation or inhalation; one of the breathing pores or apertures of the breathing tubes of insects.

spiraea, spī•rē′a, *n.* [Gr. *speiraia*.] A genus of plants, order Rosaceae, some of the species of which (as meadowsweet) are esteemed for their flowers.

spirant, spī′rant, *n.* [L. *spirans, spirantis*, ppr. of *spirare*, to breathe.] *Phonetics*, certain consonants that, when uttered, produce friction between the breath stream and parts of the oral passage (as between the upper and lower teeth in *see* or between the tongue and upper teeth in *thing*); a fricative.

spire, spīr, *n.* [L. *spira*, from Gr. *speira*, a spiral line, something twisted.] A winding line like the threads of a screw; a spiral; anything wreathed or contorted; a wreath; the convolutions of the spiral shell of a mollusk above the lowest or body whorl.—**spiral,** spī′ral, *a.* Winding round a fixed point or center like a watch spring; winding round a cylinder, and at the same time rising or advancing forward, like a corkscrew; pointed or shaped like a spire.—*Spiral nebula*, a nebula in the form of a double spiral, shining with white light, and supposed to be extremely remote.—*Spiral pump*, a form of the Archimedean screw.—*Spiral spring*, a coil whose rounds have the same diameter, and which is generally utilized by compression or extension in the line of its axis.—*n.* A curve which continually recedes from a center or fixed point while continuing to revolve about it; a helix or curve which winds round a cylinder like a screw.—*v.i. spiraled, spiralled, spiraling, spiralling*. To form, or move in, a spiral.—*v.t.* To arrange as, or form into, a spiral; to make, or cause, to spiral.—**spirally,** spī′ral•li, *adv.*—**spiry,** spī′ri, *a.* Of a spiral form.

spire, spīr, *n.* [A.Sax. *spir*, a spike or stalk; D. *spier*, a spire of grass; Dan. *spire*, a sprout, *spiir*, a spire; akin to *spear* and *spar*.] A body that shoots up to a point; the tapering portion of a steeple rising above the tower; a steeple; a stalk or blade of grass or other plant.—*v.i.*—*spired, spiring*. To shoot up pyramidically; to taper up.—**spired,** spīrd, *a.* Having a spire.

spirillum, spī•ril′um, *n.*; pl. **spirilla,** spī•ril′a. [From its *spiral* growth.] A microscopic germ of the bacteria class.

spirit, spir′it, *n.* [L. *spiritus*, breath, courage, the soul, life, from *spirare*, to breathe, seen also in *aspire, conspire, expire, inspire, respire*, etc. *Sprite* is the same word.] The intelligent, immaterial, and immortal part of man; the soul, as distinguished from the body which it occupies; a person considered with respect to his mental or moral characteristics; the human soul after it has quitted the body; an apparition; a specter; a ghost; a supernatural being; an angel, fairy, elf, sprite, demon, or the like; vivacity, animation, ardor, enthusiasm, courage, or the like; emotional state; mood; humor; often in the plural (to be in high or low *spirits*); the vital or essential part of anything; inspiring or actuating principle; essence; real meaning; intent, as opposed to the letter or formal statement; a liquid obtained by distillation, especially alcohol; *pl.* brandy, gin, rum, whisky, or other distilled liquor containing much alcohol (a glass of *spirits*).—*Animal spirits*, liveliness of disposition; constitutional briskness and gaiety.—*Holy Spirit*, or *the Spirit*, the Spirit of God, or the third person of the Trinity.—*v.t.* To animate with vigor; to encourage; to convey away secretly, as if by the agency of a spirit; to kidnap.—**spirited,** spir′it•ed, *a.* Animated; full of life; lively; full of spirit or fire (a *spirited* address); having a spirit of a certain character; used in composition (high-*spirited*, low-*spirited*).—**spiritedly,** spir′it•ed•li, *adv.* In a spirited manner; with spirit; with courage.—**spiritedness,** spir′it•ed-nes, *n.* The state.—**spiriting,** spir′it•ing, *n.* The work of a spirit; work done as if by a spirit.—**spiritless,** spir′it•les, *a.* Destitute of spirits; destitute of courage or fire; depressed; pusillanimous.—**spirit level,** *n.* A glass tube nearly filled with alcohol, for determining a line or plane parallel to the horizon, by the central position of an air bubble on its upper side.—**spirit rapping,** *n.* The name given to certain so-called spiritualistic manifestations, as audible raps or knocks on tables, table turning, etc.—**spiritual,** spir′i•chū•al, *a.* [L. *spiritualis*.] Pertaining to or consisting of spirit; not material; incorporeal; pertaining to the mind or intellect; mental; intellectual; pertaining to the soul or its affections as influenced by the Divine Spirit; proceeding from or controlled and inspired by the Holy Spirit; holy; sacred; divine; relating to sacred things; not lay or temporal; ecclesiastical.—**spiritualism,** spir′i•chū•al•izm, *n.* The state of being spiritual; spiritual character; the doctrine of the existence of spirit as distinct from matter; that system of philosophy according to which all that is real is spirit, soul, or mind, matter or the external world being either a succession of notions impressed on the mind by the Deity, or else a mere educt of the mind itself; the belief that communication can be held with departed spirits by means of phenomena manifested through a person of special susceptibility, called a *medium*.—**spiritualist,** spir′i•chū•al•ist, *n.* One whose state is spiritual; an adherent of spiritualism; one who believes that intercourse may be held with departed spirits through the agency of a *medium*; one who pretends to hold such intercourse.—**spiritualistic,** spir′i•chū•a•lis″tik, *a.* Relating to spiritualism.—**spirituality,** spir′i•chū•al″i•ti, *n.* The state or quality of being spiritual; spiritual character; immateriality; what belongs to the church or to religion, as distinct from *temporalities*; generally in plural. —**spiritualization,** spir′i•chū•al•i•zā″shon, *n.* The act of spiritualizing. —**spiritualize,** spir′i•chū•al•īz, *v.t.*—*spiritualized, spiritualizing.* To make spiritual or more spiritual; to infuse spirituality or life into; to inform with life; to convert into spirit, or to impart the properties of spirit to.—**spiritualness,** spir′i•chū•al•nes, *n.* The state or quality of being spiritual; spirituality.—**spirituous,** spir′i•chū•us, *a.* [Fr. *spiritueux.*] Containing alcohol as the characteristic ingredient; alcoholic.

spirochete, spī′ro•kēt, *n.* [Gr. *speira*, a coil, *chaitē*, a bristle.] Bacteria shaped like spiral threads.

spirt, spėrt, *v.t.* [Same as Icel. *spretta*, Sw. *spritta*, G. *spritzen*, to squirt, to spirt; A.Sax. *sprytan*, to sprout. *Spurt* is another form. SPROUT.] To throw or force out in a jet or stream (to *spirt* water from the mouth).—*v.i.* To gush or issue out in a small stream or jet.—*n.* A jet of water or other fluid.

spiry. See SPIRE.

spit, spit, *n.* [A.Sax. *spitu*, a spit = D. *spit*, *spet*, Dan. *spid*, Icel. *spýta*, G. *spiess*, a spit, a pike; akin G. *spitz*, pointed; from a root seen also in *spike*.] A long pointed spike or prong of metal, on which meat is roasted; a small point of land running into the sea; a long narrow shoal extending from the shore.—*v.t.*—*spitted, spitting.* To thrust a spit through; to put upon a spit; to thrust through; to pierce.

spit, spit, *v.t.*—pret. and pp. *spat* or *spit*, ppr. *spitting.* [A.Sax. *spittan* = Dan. *spytte*, Icel. *spýta*, to spit out; akin *spot*, *spatter*; same root as *spew*.] To eject from the mouth.—*v.i.* To throw out saliva from the mouth; to make a spitting or hissing noise as that of an angry cat.—*n.* What is ejected from the mouth; saliva.—**spitfire,** spit′fīr, *n.* A violent or passionate person; one who is irascible or fiery.—**spitter,** spit′ėr, *n.* One who spits.—**spittle,** spit′l, *n.* The moist matter which is secreted by the salivary glands; saliva ejected from the mouth.—**spittoon,** spit•tön′, *n.* A vessel to receive discharges of spittle.

spitchcock, spich′kok, *v.t.* [From *spit* and *stuck*, or *spit* and *cook*.] To split an eel lengthwise and broil it.—*n.* An eel split and broiled.

spite, spīt, *n.* [An abbreviated form of *despite* (which see).] A disposition to thwart and disappoint the wishes of another; a feeling of ill-will or malevolence; a manifestation of malevolence or malignity; chagrin; vexation.—*In spite of*, in defiance or contempt of; in opposition to all efforts of; notwithstanding.—*v.t.*—*spited, spiting.* To mortify; to thwart malignantly; to fill with spite or vexation.—**spiteful,** spīt′fu̧l, *a.* Filled with spite; having a malicious disposition; malignant; malicious.—**spitefully,** spīt′fu̧l•li, *adv.* In a spiteful manner.—**spitefulness,** spīt′fu̧l•nes, *n.* The state or quality of being spiteful.

spitfire, spittle, spittoon. See SPIT.

spitz dog, spits, *n.* [G. *spitz*, lit. pointed, from its pointed muzzle and ears.] A small variety of the Pomeranian dog, which has become a favorite lap-dog.

splanchnic, splangk′nik, *a.* [Gr. *splanchna*, the bowels.] Belonging to the entrails.—**splanchnology,** splangk•nol′o•ji, *n.* The doctrine of the viscera, or of diseases of the internal parts of the body.—**splanchnotomy,** splangk•not′o•mi, *n.* [Gr. *splanchna*, and *tomē*, a cutting.] *Anat.* the dissection of the viscera.

splash, splash, *v.t.* [A form of *plash*, with intens. *s* prefixed.] To spatter with water, or water and mud; to dash a liquid upon or over; to spatter; to cast or dash in drops.—*v.i.* To strike and dash about water, or something liquid.—*n.* A small quantity of water, or water and dirt, thrown upon anything; a stroke or fall of something in water; a noise from water dashed about; a spot of dirt or other discoloring matter; a blot; a daub.—**splashboard,** *n.* A broad piece in front of a wheeled vehicle, to ward off mud thrown up from the horses' heels.—**splasher,** splash′ėr, *n.* One who or that which splashes; a screen or guard placed over locomotive wheels.

splatter, splat′ėr, *v.i.* [Probably formed from *spatter*, like *splutter* from *sputter*.] To make a noise, as in water.

splay, splā, *v.t.* [Abbrev. from *display*.] To dislocate or break a horse's shoulder bone; *arch.* to slope or form with an angle, as the jambs or sides of a window.—*n. Arch.* a sloped surface, as when the opening through a wall for a door, window, etc., widens inward.—*a.* Spreading out; turned outward (a *splay*-foot).—**splayfooted,** *a.* Having feet with the toes turned outward; having flat feet.—**splayfoot,** *n.* A foot turning outward and with a flat under surface; a flat foot.

spleen, splēn, *n.* [L. *splen*, Gr. *splēn*, the spleen.] A spongy glandular organ situated in the upper part of the abdomen, forming one of the ductless glands concerned in the elaboration of the blood; the milt; anciently, supposed to be the seat of melancholy, anger, or vexation; hence, anger; latent spite; ill-humor; malice (to vent one's *spleen*); melancholy; low spirits; vapors.—**spleenful,** splēn′fu̧l, *a.* Full of or displaying spleen; splenetic; fretful; melancholy.—**spleenfully,** splēn′fu̧l•li, *adv.* In a spleenful manner.—**spleenwort,** splēn′wėrt, *n.* Any one of many tropical ferns, with long or linear sori on the upper side of a vein.

splendent, splen′dent, *a.* [L. *splendens, splendentis*, ppr. of *splendeo*, to shine.] Shining; resplendent; beaming with light; very conspicuous; illustrious.

splendid, splen′did, *a.* [Fr. *splendide*, L. *splendidus*, from *splendeo*, to shine.] Magnificent; gorgeous; dazzling; sumptuous; illustrious; grand; heroic; brilliant; noble; glorious.—**splendidly,** splen′did•li, *adv.* In a splendid manner; brilliantly; gorgeously; magnificently.—**splendidness,** splen′did•nes, *n.* The quality of being splendid.—**splendor, splendour,** splen′dėr, *n.* [L. *splendor.*] Great brightness; brilliant luster; magnificence; pomp; parade; brilliance; glory; grandeur; eminence; *her. in splendor*, the sun when thus depicted is completely surrounded with rays alternately waved and straight—to represent light and heat —and shows a human face on the disk.

splenetic, sple•net′ik or splen′e•tik, *a.* [L. *spleneticus*, from *splen*, the *splen*, the spleen. SPLEEN.] Affected with spleen; peevish; fretful.—*n.* A person affected with spleen.—**splenetical,** sple•net′i•kal, *a.* Splenetic.—**splenetically,** sple•net′i•kal•li, *adv.* In a splenetic manner.—**splenic,** splen′ik, *a.* [L. *splenicus.*] *Anat.* belonging to the spleen.—**splenitis,** sple•nī′tis, *n.* [Term. *-itis*, signifying inflammation.] Inflammation of the spleen.

splice, splīs, *v.t.*—*spliced, splicing.* [Same as Dan. *splisse, splidse*, D. *splitsen*, Sw. *splissa*, G. *splissen*, to splice. Closely akin to *split*, the ends of the rope being *split* in splicing.] To unite, as two ends of rope, by interweaving the strands of the ends; to unite by overlapping, as two pieces of timber; to unite in marriage (*slang*).—*n.* The joining of two ends of rope by interweaving the untwisted strands; the junction of two pieces of wood or metal by overlapping and fastening the ends.

splint, splint, *n.* [A nasalized form of *split* = Dan. Sw., and G. *splint*, a splinter. *Splinter* is a derivative.] A splinter; *surg.* a thin piece of wood or other substance, used to confine a broken bone when set, or to maintain any part of the body in a fixed position; *farriery*, the splint bone of a horse; a disease affecting the splint bone.—*v.t.* To confine or support by means of splints.—**splint bone,** *n.* One of the two small bones extending from the knee to the fetlock of a horse, behind the shank bone.

splinter, splin′ter, *n.* [Same as D. and G. *splinter*, a splinter; G. also *splitter*. SPLINT.] A fragment of anything split or shivered off; a thin piece of wood or other solid substance rent from the main body; a splint.—*v.t.* To split or rend into splinters or long thin pieces; to shiver; to support by a splint.—*v.i.* To be split or rent into long pieces; to shiver.—**splinter bar,** *n.* A crossbar in front of a wagon or other vehicle which supports the springs; a whippletree.

split, split, *v.t.*—pret. and pp. *split* (sometimes *splitted*); ppr. *splitting*. [Same as L.G. *splitten*, O.D. *splitten*, Dan. *splitte*, G. *spleiszen*; allied to *splice*; *splint*, *splinter*, are nasalized derivative forms.] To divide longitudinally or lengthwise; to separate or part in two from end to end by force; to rive; to cleave; to tear asunder by violence; to burst; to rend; to divide or break into parts as by discord; to separate into parts or parties.—*To split hairs*, to make too nice distinctions.—*To split the sides*, to burst with laughter.—*v.i.* To part asunder, especially lengthwise; to suffer disruption; to burst; to burst with laughter; to be dashed to pieces; to differ in opinion; to break up into parties; to inform upon one's accomplices or divulge a secret (*low*).—*n.* A crack, rent, or straight fissure; a division or breach as in a party; a flat strip of steel, cane, etc.; a cleft twig of willow, etc., used in basket weaving.—*p.* and *a.* Divided; cleft; rent in two.—*Split infinitive*, one with a word or words between 'to' and the verb.

splotch, splotch, *n.* [From *spot*, with inserted *l* (as in *spatter*, *splatter*, *sputter*, *splutter*), and term. borrowed from *blotch*.] A spot or stain; a daub; a smear.

splurge, splėrj, *n.* [Probably a coined word, suggested by *splash*, *surge*, or the like.] A showing off; great display or ostentation. (*Colloq.*)

splutter, splut′ėr, *n.* [From *sputter*, with inserted *l*. SPLOTCH.] A bustle; a stir.—*v.i.* To speak hastily and confusedly; to sputter.—**splutterer,** splut′ėr•ėr, *n.* One who splutters.

spodumene, spod′ū•mēn, *n.* [Gr. *spodoumenos*, converted into *spodos* or ashes.] A mineral, a silicate of aluminum and lithium, an emerald-green variety of which is used as a gem.

spoil, spoil, *v.t.* [Fr. *spolier*, from L. *spoliare*, to plunder, from *spolium*, plunder.] To plunder; to strip by violence; to rob; to seize by violence; to corrupt or vitiate; to render useless; to injure fatally; to ruin; to destroy.—*v.i.* To practice plunder; to lose the valuable qualities; to be corrupted; *colloq.* to long for, as 'he is spoiling for a fight'.—*n.* That which is taken from others by violence; plunder; booty; the slough or cast skin of a serpent or other animal.—**spoiler,** spoi′lėr, *n.* One that spoils.—**spoilfive,** *n.* A game of cards played with the whole pack, each player getting five cards; when no one takes three tricks the game is said to be spoiled.—**spoils system,** *n.* The practice of removing political incumbents from office to make room for the supporters of the incoming administration; during Jackson's administration, the doctrine was expressed by the comment: "To the victor belong the spoils."

spoke, spōk, pret. of *speak*.—**spoken,** spō′kn, pp. of *speak*. Used adjectivally for oral, as opposed to *written*; also used as equivalent to *speaking* in such compounds as civil-*spoken*.—**spokesman,** spōks′man, *n.* One who speaks for another or others.

spoke, spōk, *n.* [A.Sax. *spáca*=Icel. *spóki*, D. *speek*, L.G. *speke*, G. *speiche*; same root as *spike*, *spigot*, *pike*.] The radius of a wheel; one of the bars which are inserted in the hub or nave, and which serve to support the rim; the round of a ladder; one of the handles jutting from the circumference of the steering wheel of a vessel; a contrivance for fastening the wheel of a vehicle in order to prevent its turning when going down a hill.

spoliate, spō′li•āt, *v.t.*—*spoliated*, *spoliating*. [L. *spolio*, *spoliatum*, to plunder. SPOIL.] To plunder; to pillage; to despoil.—*v.i.* To practice plunder; to commit robbery.—**spoliation,** spō•li•ā′shon, *n.* The act of plundering; robbery; plunder.—**spoliator,** spō′li•ā•tėr, *n.* One who commits spoliation.

spondee, spon′dē, *n.* [L. *spondeus*, Gr. *spondeios*, from Gr. *spondē*, a solemn libation, such libations being accompanied by a slow and solemn melody.] A poetic foot of two long syllables, used in Greek and Latin poetry.—**spondaic,** spon•dā′ik, *a.* Pertaining to a spondee; composed of spondees.

sponge, spunj, *n.* [O.Fr. *esponge* (Fr. *éponge*), from L. *spongia*, Gr. *spongia*, a sponge.] A name given to Metazoa belonging to the phylum Porifera, consisting of jellylike, multicellular animals, whose skeletons are also known as sponges; a sponge skeleton composed of soft, light, spongin fibers, easily compressible, readily imbibing fluids, and as readily giving them out again upon compression; in common domestic use; one who meanly lives upon others; a sycophantic or cringing dependent; a parasite; a kind of mop for cleaning cannon after a discharge; the extremity or point of a horseshoe answering to the heel; *baking*, dough before it is kneaded and formed, when full of globules of carbonic acid, generated by the yeast; *metal.* iron in a soft or pasty condition, as delivered from the puddling furnace.—*To throw up the sponge*, to acknowledge that one is conquered or beaten; to submit; a phrase borrowed from the prize ring.—*v.t.*—*sponged*, *sponging*. To cleanse or wipe with a sponge; to efface; to destroy all traces of; to gain by sycophantic or mean arts.—*v.i.* To imbibe, as a sponge; to live by parasitic arts.—**spongecake,** *n.* A sweet cake; so called from its light make.—**sponger,** spun′jėr, *n.* One who sponges.—**sponginess,** spun′ji•nes, *n.* The quality or state of being spongy.—**sponging house,** *n.* In England, a house where persons arrested for debt were kept for twenty-four hours, in order that their friends might have an opportunity of settling the debt; so called from the extortionate charges made.—**spongy,** spun′ji, *a.* Resembling a sponge; soft and full of cavities; of an open, loose, easily compressible texture.

sponsal, spon′sal, *a.* [L. *sponsalis*, from *sponsus*, a spouse, from *spondeo*, *sponsum*, to promise. SPOUSE.] Relating to marriage or to a spouse.—**sponsion,** spon′shon, *n.* [L. *sponsio*, *sponsionis*, a solemn promise.] The act of becoming surety for another; an engagement made on behalf of a state by an agent not specially authorized.—**sponsor,** spon′sor, *n.* [L. *sponsor*, a surety.] A surety; one who binds himself to answer for another, and is responsible for his default; one who is surety for an infant at baptism; a godfather or godmother.—**sponsorial,** spon•sō′ri•al, *a.* Pertaining to a sponsor.

spontaneous, spon•tā′nē•us, *a.* [L. *spontaneus*, from *sponte*, of free-will.] Proceeding from natural inclination and without constraint or external force; voluntary; acting by its own impulse, energy, or natural law; self-originated.—*Spontaneous combustion.* See COMBUSTION.—*Spontaneous generation.* See GENERATION.—**spontaneously,** spon•tā′nē•us•li, *adv.* In a spontaneous manner.—**spontaneity,** spon•ta•nē′i•ti, *n.* The quality of being spontaneous.

spontoon, spon•tön′, *n.* [Fr. *sponton*, It. *spontone*, spontoon.] A kind of half pike, formerly borne by officers of infantry, and used for signaling orders.

spook, spök, *n.* [D. and L.G. *spook.*] A ghost or apparition.—**spooky,** **spookish,** spök′i, spök′ish, *a.* Pertaining to spooks; ghostly; haunted; unearthly.

spool, spöl, *n.* [Same as D. *spoel*, Dan. and Sw. *spole*, G. *spule*, spool.] A piece of cane or reed, or a hollow cylinder of wood, etc., used to wind thread or yarn on.

spoon, spön, *n.* [A.Sax. *spón*, Icel. *spónn*, *spánn*, Dan. and D. *spaan*, G. *span*, a chip, a splinter, originally a chip of wood for supping up liquids, same as *span*, in *span-new*.] A small domestic utensil, with a bowl or concave part and a handle, used at table for taking up and conveying to the mouth liquids and soft food; a foolish fellow; a simpleton.—*v.t.* To take up or out with a spoon or ladle; *cricket*, to hit a ball softly with the bat, affording an easy catch.—*v.i.* To act like a young lover—**spoonbill,** *n.* A grallatorial bird of the heron family, so called from the shape of the bill, which is somewhat like a spoon at the end.—**spoonful,** spön′fụl, *n.* As much as a spoon contains.

spoor, spör, *n.* [Borrowed from D. *spoor*, a track; the same word as A.Sax. and Icel. *spor*, G. *spur*, a track.] The track or trail of a wild animal or animals; used originally by travelers in South Africa.

sporadic, spo•rad′ik, *a.* [Gr. *sporadikos*, from *sporas*, dispersed, from *speirō*, to sow, to scatter. SPORE.] Separate; single; scattered; occurring here and there in a scattered manner.—*Sporadic disease*, a disease which occurs in single and scattered cases, in distinction from *epidemic* and *endemic.*—**sporadically,** spo•rad′i•kal•li, *adv.* In a sporadic manner.

spore, spōr, *n.* [Gr. *sporos*, a seed, from *speiro*, to sow.] The reproductive cell of cryptogamous plants, such as ferns, mosses, and mushrooms; *zool.* the minute reproductive cell of certain protozoa.—**sporangium,** spo•ran′ji•um, *n.* pl. **sporangia,** spo•ran′ji•a. *Bot.* the case in which the spores of cryptogams are formed. —**spore case,** *n. Bot.* the sporangium or covering of the spores of cryptogamic plants.—**sporiferous,** spo•rif′ėr•us, *a. Bot.* bearing spores.—**sporocarp,** spor′o•karp, *n.* [Gr. *sporos*, and *karpos*, a fruit.] A spore-producing body in red seaweeds, certain fungi, and some lower fern-like plants.—**sporocyst,** spo′rō•sist, *n. Bot.* the spore case of algals.—**sporogonium,** spor′o•gō″ni•um, *n.* [Gr. *sporos*, and *gonos*, offspring.] In mosses, the spore-producing 'fruit'. —**sporophyte,** spor′o•fīt, *n.* [Gr. *sporos*, and *phyton*, a plant.] *Bot.* the asexual stage in the life history.—**sporule,** spor′ūl, *n. Bot.* a little spore; a distinct granule within a spore.

sporran, spor′an, *n.* [Gael. *sporan.*] The pouch worn by Highlanders in full dress in front of the kilt, usually made of the skin of some animal with the hair on.

sport, spōrt, *n.* [An abbrev. of *disport.* DISPORT.] A pastime or amusement in which a person engages; a game; a diversion; a merry-making; an out-of-door recreation such as grown men indulge in, more especially hunting or fishing, also horseracing, etc.; such amusements collectively; amusement, fun, or enjoyment experienced; jest, as opposed to *earnest*; mockery; derision; object of mockery; any plant or animal deviating from the normal or natural condition or type; a monstrosity; a sportsman.—*In sport*, in jest; for play or diversion.—*v.t.* To divert; to make merry; used *refl.* (O.T.); to exhibit or wear in public (*colloq.*)—*v.i.* To play; to frolic; to make merry; to trifle.—**sportful,** spōrt′fụl, *a.* Full of sport; frolicsome; indulging in mirth or play; sportive.—**sportfully,** spōrt′fụl•li, *adv.* In a sportful manner.—**sportfulness,** spōrt′fụl•nes, *n.* The state of being sportful.—**sporting,** spōr′ting, *p.* and *a.* Belonging to or practicing sport or sports.—*Sporting man*, one who practices field sports; also, a horse-racer; one who patronizes pugilism, etc.—*Sporting chance*, or *offer*, an off chance, or offer made in a sporting spirit.—**sportive,** spōr′tiv, *a.* Engaging in sport; gay; frolic some; playful; amorous; wanton.—**sportively,** spōr′tiv•li, *adv.* In a sportive manner.—**sportiveness,** spōr′tiv•nes, *n.* The state of being sportive; playfulness; frolicsomeness.—**sports,** *n.* Athletic games.—**sportsman,** spōrts′man, *n.* One who pursues the sports of the field; one skilled in hunting, shooting, fishing, etc.—**sportsmanship,** spōrts′man•ship, *n.* The practice of sportsmen; skill in field sports.

sporule. See SPORE.

spot, spot, *n.* [Same as D. *spat*, Dan. *spætte*, a spot; Icel. *spotti*, *spottr*, a bit, a small piece; same root as *spit*, *spatter.*] A mark on a substance made by foreign matter; a speck; a place discolored; a stain on character or reputation; disgrace; reproach; blemish; a locality; any particular place; a small part of definite shape and different color from the ground on which it is.—*Upon the spot*, immediately; before moving.—*v.t.*—*spotted*, *spotting.* To make a spot, speck, or fleck upon; to stain; to tarnish; to mark with spots of color different from the ground; to note something as peculiar to, in order to identify; to catch with the eye; to recognize (*colloq.*).—**spotless,** spot′les, *a.* Free from spots; free from stain or impurity; pure; unspotted; immaculate.—**spotlessly,** spot′les•li, *adv.* In a spotless manner.—**spotlessness,** spot′les•nes, *n.* The state or quality of being spotless; freedom from spot or stain.—**spotted,** spot′ed, *p.* and *a.* Marked with spots.—*Spotted fever*, a species of typhus fever accompanied by an eruption of red spots.—**spotter,** *n.* One who, by watching the fall of shells, helps to ascertain the range for which the guns shall be set.—**spottiness,** spot′i•nes, *n.* The state or quality of being spotty.—**spotty,** spot′i, *a.* Full of spots; marked with discolored places; spotted.

spouse, spouz, *n.* [O.Fr. *espouse*, from L. *sponsus*, betrothed, pp. of *spondeo*, to promise solemnly, to engage one's self. ESPOUSE.] One engaged or joined in wedlock; a married person, husband, or wife.

spout, spout, *n.* [From stem of *spit*, *spew*, perhaps directly from D. *spuit*, a spout, *spuiten*, to spout.] A nozzle or projecting mouth of a vessel, used in directing the stream of a liquid poured out; an ajutage; a pipe or conduit; a pipe for conducting water as from a roof; a waterspout.—*v.t.* To pour out in a jet and with some force; to throw out through a spout or pipe; to utter in the manner of a mouthing actor or orator; to mouth. —*v.i.* To issue in a strong jet; to run as from a spout; to spurt; to make a speech, especially in a pompous manner.—**spouter,** spou′tėr, *n.* One who spouts; one who makes speeches in a pompous or affected manner.

sprag, sprag, *n.* [Allied to *sprig.*] A billet of wood; a prop for preventing the roof of a mine from sinking.—*v.t. spragged*, *spragging.* To prop by a sprag; to stop by putting a sprag in the spokes of a wheel.

sprain, sprān, *v.t.* [O.Fr. *espreindre*, to force out, to strain, from L. *exprimere*, *expressum*, to press out. EXPRESS.] To overstrain, as the muscles or ligaments of a joint so as to injure them, but without dislocation.—*n.* A violent straining or twisting of the soft parts surrounding a joint, without dislocation.

sprang, sprang, pret. of *spring.*

sprat, sprat, *n.* [Formerly also *sprot*, from D. and L.G. *sprot*, G. *sprotte*, sprat; allied to *sprout.*] A small fish of the herring family found in great abundance in European waters and excellent as food.

sprawl, sprạl, *v.i.* [A contr. word allied to Sc. *sprattle*, *sprachle*, to scramble, Dan. *spraelle*, to sprawl; Sw. *sprattla*, to palpitate.] To spread and stretch the body carelessly in a horizontal position; to lie or crawl with the limbs stretched out or struggling: to grow or spread irregularly or ungracefully.

spray, sprā, *n.* [Same as Dan. *sprag*, Sw. *spragg*, a spray; allied to *sprig* and *spring.*] A small shoot or branch (a *spray* of pearls, diamonds); the extremity of a branch; a twig; the small branches of a tree collectively.

spray, sprā, *n.* [A.Sax. *sprégan*, to pour; D. *spreijen*, to scatter; akin *spring*, *sprinkle.*] Water flying in small drops or particles, as by the force of wind, or the dashing of waves, or from a waterfall; the vapor from an atomizer.

spread, spred, *v.t.*—pret. and pp. *spread* (spred). [A.Sax. *spraedan*, to extend = L.G. *spreden*, D. *spreiden*, Dan. *sprede*, G. *spreiten*, to spread, to scatter.] To stretch or expand to a broader surface (a sheet, a carpet); to open out (the wings); to unfurl (a sail); to stretch; to cover by extending something; to overspread; to extend; to shoot to a greater distance in every direction (a tree *spreads* its branches); to put forth; to publish, as news or fame; to cause to be more extensively known; to propagate (a disease); to cause to affect greater numbers; to emit; to diffuse (perfume); to disperse; to scatter over a larger surface; to set and furnish with provisions.—*v.i.* To extend itself; to be extended or stretched; to be made known more extensively; to be propagated from one to another; to be diffused.—*n.* The act of spreading or state of being spread; extent; compass; a table, as spread or furnished with a meal; a feast (*colloq.*).—**spread eagle,** *n. Her.* an eagle having the wings and legs extended on each side of the body; also 'an eagle with two heads displayed'.—*a.* Pretentious; boastful; defiantly bombastic (a *spread-eagle* style).—**spreader,** spred'ėr, *n.* One who or that which spreads.

spree, sprē, *n.* [From Ir. *spre*, animation, spirit, vigor; comp. *spry*.] A merry frolic, a drinking frolic; a carousal.

sprig, sprig, *n.* [A.Sax. *sprec*, a branch; allied to *spray*, a twig.] A small shoot or twig of a tree or other plant; a spray; an offshoot, a slip; a youth; a lad: used as a term of slight disparagement (a *sprig* of nobility); an ornament resembling a sprig; a small square brad or nail without a head. In *her.* a *sprig* has five leaves attached to it, whereas a *slip* has only three.—**sprigged,** sprigd, *a.* Marked with ornaments resembling sprigs; fastened with sprigs.

spright, sprīt, *n.* [Contr. for *spirit*, and spelled erroneously, *sprite* being the better spelling.] A spirit or sprite; an elf. The spelling *spright* is now obsolete or obsolescent, but *sprightly* and not *spritely* is still the common spelling.—**sprightly,** sprīt'li, *a.* [Also written *spritely*.] Having the quality of a spirit or spright (*Shak.*); lively; spirited; brisk; airy; gay.—**sprightliness,** sprīt'li•nes, *n.* The quality of being sprightly; liveliness; briskness; vivacity.

spring, spring, *v.i.*—pret. *sprung* or *sprang* (sprung, sprang), pp. *sprung*. [A.Sax. *springan*, to spring, to leap = D. and G. *springen*, Sw. and Icel. *springa*, Dan. *springe*, from root seen also in *sprinkle*, *sprig*, *spray*.] To rise or come forth, as out of the ground; to shoot up, out, or forth; to begin to appear; to come to light; to issue into sight or knowledge; to take rise or origin; to issue or originate, as from ancestors, or from a country; to result, as from a cause, motive, principle, etc.; to leap; to jump; to fly back by elastic force; to start; to start or rise suddenly from a covert; to shoot; to issue with speed and violence; to warp or become warped; to become cracked (as a mast).—*To spring at*, to leap toward; to attempt to reach by a leap.—*To spring forth*, to leap out; to rush out. —*To spring in*, to rush in; to enter with a leap or in haste.—*To spring on* or *upon*, to leap on; to assault.—*v.t.* To start or rouse, as game; to cause to rise from a covert; to produce quickly or unexpectedly; to propose on a sudden; to crack; to weaken by a crack in the timber (to *spring* a mast); to pass by leaping; to jump over (to *spring* the fence).—*To spring a leak*, to have a leak open; to experience the opening of a leak.—*To spring a mine* (in the military sense), to cause it to explode; often used *fig.*—*n.* A leap; a bound; a flying back of a body by its elasticity; elastic power or force; an elastic body, made of various materials, as a strip or wire of steel coiled spirally, a steel rod or plate, etc., which, when bent or forced from its natural state, has the power of recovering it again in virtue of its elasticity; the springs of a railroad car or an automobile affording comfort in riding through their resiliency; springs are used to check recoil or diminish concussion; elliptic springs for railroad cars or for carriages, semi-elliptic or cantilever springs in automobile construction, and coil springs, spiral springs, and flat springs in many other mechanical devices; *fig.* that by which action is induced; mainspring; a natural fountain of water, owing its origin to the water which falls upon the earth; an issue of water from the earth, or the basin of water at the place of its issue; any source of supply; that from which supplies are drawn; one of the four seasons of the year (so called because plants *spring* or grow then); the vernal season; *fig.* the first and freshest part of any state or time; a crack in a mast or yard running obliquely or transversely; a rope passed out of a ship's stern, and attached to a cable proceeding from her bow, when she is at anchor; *arch.* the point of an arch that rests on its support.—**springboard,** *n.* An elastic board used in vaulting, etc.—**springbok,** *n.* [D., lit. the springing buck.] A species of antelope, nearly allied to the gazelle, very abundant in South Africa.—**springer,** spring'ėr, *n.* One who springs; *arch.* the lowest voussoir or bottom stone of an arch; the bottom stone of the coping of a gable; the rib of a groined roof or vault.—**spring tide,** *n.* The tide which happens at or soon after the new and full moon, and which rises higher than common tides; the time or season of spring; springtime.—**springtime,** *n.* The spring; the vernal season.—**springy,** spring'i, *a.* Having elasticity like that of a spring; elastic; light (a *springy* step); abounding with springs or fountains.

springe, sprinj, *n.* [From *spring*; comp. *swinge* from *swing*.] A noose attached to a spring or elastic body so as to catch a bird or other animal; a gin; a snare.

sprinkle, spring'kl, *v.t.*—*sprinkled*, *sprinkling*. [A dim. form from O.E. *sprinke*, A.Sax. *sprencan*, for *sprengan*, to sprinkle, caus. of *springan*, to spring; comp. D. *sprenkelen*, to sprinkle; G. *sprenkeln*, to speckle. SPRING.] To scatter in drops or particles; to cast or let fall in fine separate particles; to strew; to besprinkle; to bestrew; to bedrop.—*n.* A small quantity scattered; a sprinkling.—**sprinkler,** springk'lėr, *n.* One who sprinkles; a device for sprinkling; a fire extinguisher.—**sprinkling,** springk'ling, *n.* A small quantity falling in drops or particles; a small number or quantity scattered as if sprinkled.

sprint, sprint, *n.* [Akin to *spurt*.] A short race or run at high speed.

sprit, sprit, *n.* [A.Sax. *spreōt*, a sprout, a shoot; D. *spriet*, a sprit, *boeysprit*, the bowsprit.] A sprout‡; a small boom or spar which crosses the sail of a boat diagonally and thus extends and elevates it; also, the bowsprit of a vessel.—**spritsail,** *n.* A sail extended by a sprit; a sail, now disused, on a yard under a bowsprit.

sprite, sprīt, *n.* A spirit or spright; commonly, a kind of fairy, elf, or goblin.

sprocket wheel, sprok'et, *n.* A wheel with cogs or sprockets to engage with the links of a chain.

sprout, sprout, *v.i.* [Same as L.G. *spruten*, D. *spruiten*, to sprout; akin to A.Sax. *spreōtan*, to sprout, whence *spreōt*, a sprout. Akin *spirt*, *sprit*, *spurt*.] To shoot, as the seed of a plant; to germinate; to push out new shoots.—*n.* [D. *spruit*, a sprout.] The shoot or bud of a plant; a fresh outgrowth from a plant or tree; *pl.* young coleworts; Brussels sprouts.

spruce, sprös, *a.* [Lit. after the *Prussian* style, from *Spruce*, *Pruce*, formerly used for *Prussia*, *Prussian*.] Brisk‡; active (*Shak.*)‡: neat or smart in dress; trim; smug; dandified.—*v.t.*—*spruced*, *sprucing*. To trim or dress in a spruce manner.—*To spruce up*, to dress one's self sprucely or neatly.—**spruce,** *n.* [So-called because the tree was first known as a native of Prussia.] The name given to several species of trees of the pine family, yielding valuable timber; as the Norway spruce fir of Europe, and the white spruce, the black spruce, and the hemlock spruce of North America.—**spruce beer,** *n.* A fermented liquor made from sugar or molasses, and flavored with sprouts of the spruce fir.—**sprucely,** sprös'li, *adv.* In a spruce manner; trimly; nattily.—**spruceness,** sprös'nes, *n.* Trimness; nattiness.

sprung, sprung, pret. and pp. of *spring*.

spry, sprī, *a.* [Allied to *spree*; or to old *sprack*, N. *sprœk*, Sw. *spräk*, lively.] Nimble; active; vigorous; lively. (*Colloq.*)

spud, spud, *n.* [A form of *spade*; or akin to Dan. *spyd*, Icel. *spjot*, a spear, E. a *spit*.] A straight narrow spade with a long handle for digging up weeds, etc.; also, a small spade with a short handle; (*slang*) potato.

spume, spūm, *n.* [L. *spuma*, foam, from *spuo*, to spit out. SPEW.] Froth; foam; scum; frothy matter on liquors.—*v.i.* To froth; to foam; to spoom.—**spumescence,** spū•mes'ens, *n.* Frothiness.—**spumous, spumy,** spū'mus, spū'mi, *a.* [L. *spumosus*.] Consisting of froth or scum; foamy.

spun, spun, pret. and pp. of *spin*.—**spun yarn,** *n. Naut.* a cord formed of two, three, or more rope yarns twisted together.

spunk, spungk, *n.* [Ir. *sponc*, Gael. *spong*, tinder, touchwood, sponge; from L. *spongia*, a sponge.] Touchwood; tinder; tinder made from a species of fungus; amadou; a quick, ardent temper; mettle; pluck.

spur, spėr, *n.* [A.Sax. *spura*, *spora*, a spur; Icel. *spori*, Dan. *spore*, O.G. *spor*, Mod.G. *sporn*; from a root meaning to kick, seen also in *spurn*, *spurious*.] An instrument having a rowel or little wheel with sharp points, worn on horsemen's heels to prick the horses for hastening their pace; *fig.* an incitement or stimulus; a large or principal root of a tree; something that projects; a snag; the hard pointed projection on a cock's leg which serves as an instrument of offense and defense; *geog* a mountain, or mountain mass, that shoots from another mountain mass and extends for some distance; a small sidetrack of a railroad; *bot.* any projecting appendage of a flower resembling a spur.—*v.t.*—*spurred, spurring.* To prick with spurs; to urge or encourage to action; to incite; to instigate; to impel; to stimulate; to put spurs on; to furnish with spurs. —*v.i.* To spur one's horse to make it go fast; to ride fast; to press forward.—**spur gear, spur gearing,** *n.* Gearing in which spur wheels are employed.—**spurred,** spėrd, *a.* Wearing spurs; having prolongations or shoots like spurs.—**spurrier,** spėr′i•ėr, *n.* One whose occupation is to make spurs.—**spur wheel,** *n. Mach.* a wheel in which the teeth are perpendicular to the axis, and in the direction of radii.

spurge, spėrj, *n.* [O.Fr. *espurge,* spurge, from L. *expurgare,* to purge —*ex,* out of, and *purgo,* to purge. PURGE.] The common name of certain *Euphorbia,* plants with an acrid milky juice powerfully purgative.—**spurge laurel,** *n.* A Eurasian shrub with oblong evergreen leaves and yellow flowers.

spurious, spū′ri•us, *a.* [L. *spurius,* bastard, from same root as *sperno,* to despise. SPURN.] Not legitimate; bastard; not proceeding from the true source or from the source pretended; not genuine; counterfeit: adulterate.—*Spurious wing,* in *ornith.* the bastard wing.—**spuriously,** spū′ri•us•li, *adv.* In a spurious manner; falsely.—**spuriousness,** spū′ri•us•nes, *n.* The state or quality of being spurious.

spurn, spėrn, *v.t.* [A.Sax. *spurnan,* to spurn; Icel. *sporna, spyrna,* O.H.G. *spurnan, spornan,* to kick; same root as *spur,* and L. *sperno,* to despise, *spurius,* spurious.] To drive back or away, as with the foot; to kick; to reject with disdain; to treat with contempt.—*v.i.* To kick or toss up the heels; to dash the foot against something; to manifest disdain or contempt in rejecting anything.—*n.* A kick†; disdainful rejection; contemptuous treatment.—**spurner,** spėr′nėr, *n.* One who spurns.

spurry, spėr′i, *n.* [D. and O.Fr. *spurrie,* G. *spurrey, spurre.*] A small herb of the chickweed family, one species of which is cultivated as food for cattle.

spurt, spėrt, *v.t.* [A form of *spirt;* akin to *sprout;* comp. Icel. *sprettr,* a spurt.] To throw out in a stream or jet, as water; to spout; to squirt.—*v.i.* To gush out; to spirt.—*n.* A forcible gush of liquid; a jet; a sudden extraordinary effort for an emergency; a short sudden act.

sputnik, sput′nik, *n.* [Rus., traveling companion.] An artificial satellite.

sputter, sput′ėr, *v.i.* [Akin to *spout* or *spit;* same as L.G. *sputtern;* to sputter.] To emit saliva from the mouth in rapid speaking; to speak so rapidly as to emit saliva; to give out moisture (as green wood burning); to burn with some crackling or noise (as a candle).—*v.t.* To utter rapidly and with indistinctness; to jabber.—**sputterer,** sput′ėr•ėr, *n.* One that sputters.

sputum, spū′tum, *n.* pl. **sputa.** [L. *sputum,* spittle, *spuo,* to spit.] Spittle; matter expectorated.

spy, spī, *v.t.*—*spied, spying.* [O.Fr. *espier,* to spy, from O.H.G. *spehôn,* to search out or examine. Same root as in L. *specio,* to see, Skr. *spaç,* to look. SPECIES.] To gain sight of; to discover at a distance or in concealment; to espy; to gain a knowledge of by artifice; to explore; to view and examine secretly.—*v.i.* To search narrowly; to scrutinize; to pry.—*n.* A person who keeps a constant watch on the actions, motions, conduct, etc., of others; a secret emissary sent into the enemy's camp or territory to bring back intelligence.—**spyglass,** *n.* A telescope, especially a small telescope.

squab, skwob, *a.* [Akin Sw. *sqvabba,* a fat woman; Dan. *kvabbet,* fat, squab.] Fat; short and stout; bulky; unfledged; unfeathered.—*n.* A young unfledged pigeon; a short fat person; a kind of sofa or couch; a soft cushion.

squabble, skwob′l, *v.i.*—*squabbled, squabbling.* [Same as Sw. *sqvabbel,* a dispute; comp. L.G. *kabbeln,* to quarrel.] To engage in a noisy quarrel; to quarrel and fight noisily; to brawl; to wrangle; to debate peevishly; to dispute.—*v.t. Typog.* to put awry, as types that have been set up. —*n.* A scuffle; a wrangle; a petty quarrel.—**squabbler,** skwob′lėr, *n.* One who squabbles.

squad, skwod, *n.* [Abbrev. of *squadron.*] Any small party of men; *milit.* a small number of men assembled for drill or inspection.—*Awkward squad,* the recruits not yet fitted to take their place in the regimental line.

squadron, skwod′ron, *n.* [O.Fr. *esquadron* (Fr. *escadron*), from It. *squadrone,* a squadron, from *squadra,* a square—L. prefix *ex,* and *quadra,* a square. SQUARE.] In the United States Army formerly a unit composed of two or more troops of cavalry. This is the normal command of a major. In the United States Navy a squadron consists of one or more divisions of battleships, destroyers, or aircraft; any group organized for the performance of a specific service.

squalid, skwol′id, *a.* [L. *squalidus,* squalid, from *squaleo,* to be foul or filthy.] Foul; filthy; extremely dirty. —**squalidly,** skwol′id•li, *adv.* In a squalid, filthy manner.—**squalidness,** skwol′id•nes, *n.* The state of being squalid; filthiness.—**squalor,** skwol′ėr, *n.* Foulness; filthiness; coarseness.

squall, skwa̤l, *v.i.* [An imitative word; Icel. *skval,* a squall or scream, *skvala,* to scream; akin *squeal.*] To cry out; to scream or cry violently.—*n.* A loud scream: a harsh cry; a sudden and strong gust of wind; a sudden and vehement succession of gusts.—*A black squall,* one attended with dark clouds.—*A thick squall,* one accompanied with hail, sleet, etc.—*A white squall,* one which produces no diminution of light.—**squaller,** skwa̤l′ėr, *n.* One who squalls.—**squally,** skwa̤l•i, *a.* Abounding with sudden and violent gusts of wind; gusty.

squalor. See SQUALID.

squama, skwā′ma, *n.* pl. **squamae,** skwā′mē. [L., a scale.] A scale or scaly part of plants; a horny scale on animals.—**squamate,** skwā′māt, *a.* Squamose; covered with small scale-like bodies.—**squamous, squamose,** skwā′mus, skwā′mōs, *a.* [L. *squamosus.*] Covered with or consisting of scales; resembling scales; scaly.

squander, skwon′dėr, *v.t.* [Perhaps from A.Sax. *swindan, swand, swunden,* to waste away, vanish, with *q* inserted as in *squeamish* and vulgar *squim* for *swim,* etc.] To spend lavishly or profusely; to waste without economy or judgment.—**squanderer,** skwon′dėr•ėr, *n.* One who squanders; a spendthrift.

square, skwâr, *a.* [O.Fr. *esquarre,* a square; from L. prefix *ex,* and *quadra,* a square, from *quadrus,* square, from *quatuor,* four.] Having four equal sides and four right angles; forming a right angle; having rectilineal and angular rather than curved outlines; fair, just, or honest; adjusted so as to leave no balance (to make accounts *square*).—*Square measures,* the squares of lineal measures; superficial (a *square* inch, a *square* foot, a *square* yard, etc.).—*Square number,* the product of a number multiplied into itself.—*Square root, arith.* and *alg.* that root which being multiplied into itself produces the given number or quantity; thus, 8 is the square root of 64. —*All square,* all arranged; all right. (*Colloq.*)—*n.* A four-sided plane rectilineal figure, having all its sides equal and all its angles right angles; what nearly approaches this shape; a square surface; an area of four sides with houses on each side or on at least three; an instrument used by artificers, draftsmen and others, for testing or describing right angles; *arith.* and *alg.* the number or quantity produced by multiplying a number or quantity by itself; *milit.* a body of infantry formed into a rectangular figure with several ranks or rows of men facing on each side.—*On* or *upon the square,* all right; not objectionable; fair and strictly honest.—*v.t.*—*squared, squaring.* To make square; to reduce or bring accurately to right angles and straight lines; to reduce to any given standard; to compare with a standard; to adjust, regulate, accommodate, fit; to make even so as to leave no difference or balance; to settle (to *square* accounts); *math.* to multiply by itself; *naut.* to place at right angles with the mast or keel (to *square* the yards).—*To square the circle*, to determine the exact area of a circle in square measure.—*v.i.* To suit; to fit; to accord or agree (the facts do not *square with* the theory).—**squarely,** skwâr•li, *adv.* In a square form; fairly; honestly.—**squareness,** skwâr′nes, *n.* The state of being square; fairness in dealing. —**squarer,** skwâ′rėr, *n.* One who squares.—**square-rigged,** *a. Naut.* a term applied to a vessel most of whose sails are of a square shape and extended by yards suspended by the middle.—**square sail,** *n. Naut.* a sail extended on a yard suspended by the middle.—**square-toed,** *a.* Having the toes square.—**square-toes,** *n.* A precise, formal, old-fashioned personage. (*Colloq.*)

squarrose, squarrous, skwor′rōs, skwor′rus, *a.* [L. *squarrosus*, rough.] *Bot.* covered with processes or projecting points spreading at right angles or in a greater degree.

squash, skwosh, *v.t.* [O.Fr. *esquacher*, to crush, from L. *ex*, intens., and *coactare*, to constrain, from *cogo, coactum*, to force (whence *cogent*). *Squat* is akin.] To crush; to beat or press into pulp or a flat mass.—*n.* Something soft and easily crushed; something unripe and soft; an unripe pea pod; a sudden fall or shock of a heavy soft body.—**squasher,** skwosh′ėr, *n.* One who squashes.—**squashiness,** skwosh′i•nes, *n.* The state of being squashy.—**squashy,** skwosh′i, *a.* Soft or pulpy and green; soft and wet; miry; muddy.

squash, skwosh, *n.* [From American Indian name.] A plant, a kind of gourd, cultivated in America as an article of food; the flesh of this fruit boiled and mashed, served as a vegetable or used as a filling for pies; a drink, part of which is some fruit juice, e.g. *lemon squash.*

squat, skwot, *v.i.*—*squatted, squatting.* [From O.Fr. *quatir*, to squat, to bend, with *es*=L. *ex.* intens. prefixed; same origin as *squash, v.t.*] To sit down upon the hams or heels; to sit close to the ground; to cower, as an animal; to settle on land, especially public lands, without any title or right.—*v.t.* To put on the hams or heels; used reflexively.—*a.* Sitting close to the ground; cowering; short and thick, like the figure of an animal squatting.—*n.* The posture of one who squats.—**squatter,** skwot′ėr, *n.* One that squats; one that settles on unoccupied land, particularly public land, without a title.

squaw, skwa̤, *n.* [Amer. Indian.] Among American Indians, a female or wife.

squawk, skwa̤k, *v.i.* [Akin to *squeak.*] To cry with a loud harsh voice.

squeak, skwēk, *v.i.* [Imitative; comp. *squawk*, G. *quieken*, to squeak; Sw. *sqväka*, to cry like a frog.] To utter a sharp, shrill cry; to cry with an acute tone, as a pig, a mouse, or the like; or to make a sharp noise, as a wheel, a door, etc.; to break secrecy. —*n.* A sharp shrill cry or noise.—**squeaker,** skwē′kėr, *n.* One that squeaks.

squeal, skwēl, *v.i.* [A weaker form of *squall*, implying a shriller sound.] To cry with a sharp shrill voice, as certain animals do.—*n.* A shrill sharp cry; a squeak.

squeamish, skwē′mish, *a.* [Prov.E. *sweamish*, O. and Prov. *sweam*, an attack of sickness, from A.Sax. *swima*, a swimming or giddiness, or N. *sveim*, dizziness; akin to G. *schwindel*, dizziness. The *q* has been inserted partly through the influence of *qualmish.*] Having a stomach that is easily turned; excessively nice as to taste; fastidious; easily disgusted; scrupulous.—**squeamishly,** skwē′mish•li, *adv.* In a squeamish or fastidious manner.—**squeamishness,** skwē′mish•nes, *n.* The state or quality of being squeamish; fastidiousness.

squeeze, skwēz, *v.t.* — *squeezed, squeezing.* [Formerly *squise, squize*, from A.Sax. *cwisan*, to squeeze (with addition of initial *s*); L.G. *quese*, a bruise; Sw. *qväsa*, to crush; G. *quetschen*, to squash.] To press between two bodies; to press closely; to crush; to clasp closely; to press lovingly; to oppress so as to make to give money; to harass by extortion; to force by pressure.—*v.i.* To press; to press among a number of persons; to pass by pressing.—*n.* An application of pressure; a compression; a hug or embrace.—**squeezer,** skwē′zėr, *n.* One who or that which squeezes.

squelch, skwelch, *v.t.* [From Prov. E. *quelch*, a blow (with prefixed *s* through influence of *squash*, etc.); allied perhaps to *quell.*] To crush; to destroy.—*v.i.* To be crushed.—*n.* A flat heavy fall.

squib, skwib, *n.* [Origin uncertain.] A little pipe or hollow cylinder of paper filled with gunpowder, which on being ignited flies along, throwing out a train of sparks and bursting with a crack; a petty lampoon.

squid, skwid, *n.* [Probably from *squit*, English dialectical form of squirt.] Any of numerous 10-armed cephalopods, having a tapered body with caudal fins on each side.

squill, skwil, *n.* [L. *squilla, scilla*, Gr. *skilla*, a squill (both plant and animal).] A plant allied to the hyacinths, onions, etc., with a bulbous root used in medicine as a diuretic and expectorant; a crustaceous animal; a kind of shrimp.

squinch, skwinsh, *n. Arch.* a small arch (or several combined) formed across an angle, as in a square tower to support the side of a superimposed octagon.

squint, skwint, *a.* [Comp. Prov.E. *squinny, squiny*, to squint; D. *schuinte*, a slope, *schuin, schuinsch*, sloping, oblique.] Looking obliquely or askance; not having the optic axes coincident; said of the eyes; having distorted sight.—*v.i.* To look obliquely with the eyes; to have the axes of the eyes not coincident; to be affected with strabismus; to have an indirect reference.—*v.t.* To turn (the eye) to an oblique position; to cause to be squint.—*n.* An oblique look; an affection of the eyes in which the optic axes do not coincide; *arch.* an oblique opening through the walls of old churches, to enable a person in the transepts or aisles to see the high altar.—**squint-eyed,** *a.* Having eyes that squint; oblique; indirect.

squire, skwīr, *n.* [Contr. of *esquire.*] The title of a gentleman next in rank to a knight; in America, a title of office and courtesy, often given to justices of the peace.—*v.t.*—*squired, squiring.* To attend on as squire.

squirm, skwėrm, *v.t.* or *i.* [Origin obscure; perhaps suggested by *worm.*] To move like a worm or eel, with writhing or contortions.—*n.* A wriggling motion.

squirrel, skwir′el, *n.* [O.Fr. *esquirel, escurel* (Fr. *écureuil*), from L.L. *sciuriolus*, dim. of L. *sciurus*, Gr. *skiouros*, a squirrel—*skia*, shadow, and *oura*, tail.] A name common to various species of rodent mammals, mostly living in trees, and distinguished by their powers of leaping, and their usually long and bushy tails. Characteristic for the coniferous forests of North America are the red squirrels, while in the hardwood forests of the central and southern United States the gray and fox squirrels are at home. To the squirrel family belongs likewise the American ground squirrel or chipmunk, a burrowing rodent.—**squirrel corn,** *Dicentra canadensis*, one of the first spring flowers of the northern and eastern United States.

squirt, skwėrt, *v.t.* [Prov. E. *swirt*, L.G. *swirtjen*, to squirt, the *q* being inserted as in *squeamish.* Comp. Icel. *skvetta*, to squirt.] To eject from a narrow pipe or orifice in a stream. —*v.i.* To be ejected in a rapid stream; to spurt or spirt.—*n.* An instrument with which a liquid is ejected in a stream; a syringe; a small jet.—**squirter,** skwėr′tėr, *n.* One who squirts.

stab, stab, *v.t.*—*stabbed, stabbing.* [Allied to *staff*; comp. Gael. *stob*, Ir. *stobaim*, to stab; Gael. and Sc. *stob*, a stake, a prickle; also Goth. *stabs*, a rod; G. *stab*, a staff.] To pierce or wound with a pointed weapon; to kill by a pointed weapon; to drive in; to pierce in a figurative sense; to inflict keen or severe pain on.—*v.i.* To aim a blow with a pointed weapon; to be extremely cutting.—*n.* The thrust of a pointed weapon; a wound with a sharp-pointed weapon; keen, poignant pain. —**stabber,** stab′ėr, *n.* One who, or that which, stabs.

stable, stā′bl, *a.* [L. *stabilis*, from *sto*, to stand. STAND.] Firmly established; not to be easily moved, shaken, or overthrown; firmly fixed or settled; steady in purpose; firm in resolution; not fickle or wavering; abiding; durable.—**stability, stable-**

ness, sta•bil′i•ti, stā′bl•nes, *n.* The state or quality of being stable or firm; strength to stand without being moved or overthrown; steadiness.—**stabilizer,** stā″bi•līz′ėr, *n.* One who stabilizes; a substance added to another to prevent a change in physical state; a gyroscopic device that steadies a ship in rough seas; the horizontal part of the tail of an aircraft.

stable, stā′bl, *n.* [L. *stabulum,* a standing place, a stable, from *sto,* to stand. STABLE, *a.*] A building constructed for horses (rarely beasts generally) to lodge and feed in, and furnished with stalls and necessary equipments; the racing horses of certain stables; the persons connected with the ownership, management, and operations of the stables, as, the Whitney *stables.—v.t.—stabled, stabling.* To put or keep in a stable.—*v.i.* To dwell or lodge in a stable; to dwell, as beasts; to kennel.—**stableman,** *n.* A man who attends at a stable.—**stabling,** stā′bl•ing, *n.* A keeping in a stable; accommodation for keeping horses.

staccato, stak•kä′tō, *a.* [It., pp. of *staccare,* to separate.] *Mus.* a direction to perform the notes of a passage in a crisp, detached, distinct, or pointed manner.

stack, stak, *n.* [Same as Icel. *stakk*(*r*), Sw. *stack,* Dan. *stak,* a stack, a pile of hay; akin *stake, stick, stock.*] Corn in the sheaf, hay, peas, straw, etc., piled up in a regular form for keeping, and often thatched; a cord of wood containing 128 cubic feet in U. S.; a pile of indefinite quantity; a number of funnels or chimneys standing together; a single tall chimney; the funnel of a locomotive or steam vessel; a high rock detached; a columnar rock rising out of the sea.—*v.t.* To pile or build into the form of a stack; to make into a large pile.

stacte, stak′tē, *n.* [Gr. *staktē,* from *stazō,* to drop.] One of the sweet spices which composed the holy incense of the ancient Jews.

staddle, stad′l, *n.* [A.Sax. *stathol, stathel*; akin to *stead, steady, stand.*] A stack stand; a tree left uncut when others are cut down.

stadholder, stad′hōl•dėr, *n.* [D. *stadhouder—stad,* a city, and *houder,* holder.] Formerly, the chief magistrate of the United Provinces of Holland, also the governor or lieutenant-governor of a province.—**stadholdership,** stad′hōl•dėr•ship, *n.*

stadium, stā′di•um, *n.* pl. **stadia,** stā′di•a. [L., from Gr. *stadion.*] A Greek measure equal to 606 ft. 9 in.; the course for footraces in ancient Greece, flanked by terraced elevations with tiers of seats for spectators; (pl. **stadiums**) a similar modern structure used for athletic games.

staff, staf, *n.* pl. **staves, staffs,** stāvz, stafs (in last two senses always the latter). [A.Sax. *stæf,* a staff; D. and L.G. *staf,* Icel. *stafr,* Dan. *stav,* G. *stab,* a staff; same root as *stab, stem,* and Skr. *stabh, stambh,* to make firm.] A stick carried in the hand for support; a walking stick; *fig.* that which props or upholds; a support; a stick used as a weapon; a straight stick used as symbol of office; a baton; a rod with a curved head belonging to a bishop; the long handle of an instrument or weapon; *surv.* a graduated stick used in leveling; *naut.* a light pole on which to hoist and display the colors; *mus.* the five parallel lines, and the four spaces between them, on which notes and other musical characters are placed; *milit.* a body of officers whose duties refer to an army or regiment as a whole, and who are not attached to particular subdivisions; a number of persons, considered as one body, assisting in carrying on any undertaking (the editorial *staff* of a newspaper, a hospital *staff,* etc.).—**staff officer,** *n.* An officer upon the staff of an army or regiment.

stag, stag, *n.* [Same as O.E. *stag,* a young horse, a cock turkey; Sc. *staig,* a stallion; Icel. *steggr,* a male animal; from stem of A.Sax. *stīgan,* Icel. *stīga,* G. *steigen,* to mount; lit. the mounter. STAIR.] The male red deer, or a generic name of the red deer; the male of the hind; a hart; sometimes applied particularly to a hart in its fifth year; a man at a dance unaccompanied by a lady; a social gathering of men only.—**stag beetle,** *n.* One of the largest of American insects, distinguished by the enormous size of the horny and toothed mandibles in the males.

stage, stāj, *n.* [O.Fr. *estage* (Fr. *étage*), from hypothetical L. *staticum,* from *sto, statum,* to stand (whence *state, station,* etc.).] A floor or platform elevated above the ground or a common surface, as for an exhibition of something to public view; a scaffold; a staging; the raised platform or floor on which theatrical performances are exhibited; hence, *the stage,* the theater, the dramatic profession, the drama; the scene of any noted action or affair; a place of rest on a journey, as where a relay of horses is taken; a station; the distance between two places of rest on a road (a *stage* of 15 miles); a single step of a gradual process; degree of advance or progression, an increase or decrease, in rising or falling; a coach or other carriage running regularly from one place to another; a stagecoach; a wooden landing place at a quay or pier; a landing stage.—*v.t.* To put upon the theatrical stage.—**stagecoach,** *n.* A coach that runs by stages; a coach that runs regularly between two places for the conveyance of passengers.—**stage manager,** *n.* One who superintends the production and performance of a play, and who regulates all matters behind the scenes.—**stager,** stā′jėr, *n.* One that has long acted on the stage of life; a person of experience, or of skill derived from long experience.—**stage-struck,** *a.* Smitten with a love for the stage; seized by a passionate desire to become an actor.—**stage whisper,** *n.* A loud whisper; what is spoken on the stage in a subdued voice meant to indicate a whisper but loud enough to be heard by the audience; an aside.

stagger, stag′ėr, *v.i.* [From older *staker,* to stagger, Sc. *stacher, stacker,* Icel. *stakra,* to stagger.] To sway helplessly to one side and the other in standing or walking; to reel; to cease to stand firm; to hesitate; to become less confident or determined.—*v.t.* To cause to doubt and waver; to make to hesitate; to make less confident; to strike as incredible; to amaze.—*n.* A sudden swing or reel of the body, as if the person were about to fall; divergence from straightness, as when spokes or rivets are arranged on the two sides of a median line, or, in an airplane, when the leading edge of one plane falls behind that of the other; *pl.* a disease of horses and cattle attended with reeling or dizziness.—**staggeringly,** stag′ėr•ing•li, *adv.* In a staggering manner.

Stagirite, staj•i′rīt, *n.* Aristotle, from Stagira in Macedonia, his birthplace.

stagnate, stag′nāt, *v.i.—stagnated, stagnating.* [L. *stagno, stagnatum,* to stagnate (whence *stanch*), from *stagnum,* standing water, a pool (whence *stank, tank*).] To cease to run or flow; to have no current, as water; to become impure from want of current; to cease to be brisk or active; to become dull, quiet, or inactive (as trade).—**stagnancy,** stag′nan•si, *n.* The state of being stagnant.—**stagnant,** stag′nant, *a.* [L. *stagnans, stagnantis,* ppr. of *stagno.*] Not flowing; not running in a current or stream; standing, hence, impure from want of motion; inactive; dull; not brisk (trade is *stagnant*).—**stagnantly,** stag′nant•li, *adv.* In a stagnant manner.—**stagnation,** stag•nā′shon, *n.* The condition of being stagnant; the state of being without flow or circulation; the state of being very dull or inactive.

staid, stād, *a.* [From *stay,* to stop, to steady.] Sober; grave; steady; sedate; not volatile, flighty, or fanciful.—**staidly,** stād′li, *adv.* In a staid manner; sedately; soberly.—**staidness,** stād′nes, *n.* Gravity; sobriety; sedateness.

stain, stān, *v.t.* [An abbrev. of *distain* (which see); comp. *sport,* from *disport.* TINGE.] To discolor by the application of foreign matter; to make foul; to spot; to color, as wood, glass, etc., by a chemical or other process; to tinge with colors; to impress with figures or patterns in colors different from the ground (to *stain* paper for hangings); to soil or sully with guilt or infamy; to tarnish; to bring reproach on.—*v.i.* To take stains; to become stained or soiled; to grow dim.—*n.* A spot; discoloration from foreign matter; taint of guilt or evil; blot; blemish; disgrace; reproach; shame.—**stained,** stānd, *p.* and *a.*

Having a stain or stains; discolored; tarnished; produced by staining.—*Stained glass*, glass painted with metallic oxides or chlorides ground up with proper fluxes, and fused into its surface at a moderate heat.—**stainer,** stā′nėr, *n.* One who stains; a workman engaged in staining (paper-*stainer*).—**stainless,** stān′les, *a.* Free from stains or spots; free from the reproach of guilt; unblemished; immaculate.—**stainlessly,** stān′les•li, *adv.* In a stainless manner.

stair, stâr, *n.* [Lit. that by which a person mounts; A.Sax. *staeger*, from *stigan*, Icel. *stíga*, G. *steigen*, to mount, to climb, whence also *stag*, *stile* (on a fence), and the first part of *stirrup*.] A succession of steps rising one above the other arranged as a way between two points at different heights in a building, etc.; used often in plural in same sense, while the singular is also employed to mean a single step.—*Pair of stairs*, a set or flight of steps or stairs; more properly perhaps two flights.—*Flight of stairs*, a succession of steps in a continuous line or from one landing to another.—*Down stairs*, *below stairs*, in the basement or lower part of a house.—*Up stairs*, in the upper part of a house.—**staircase,** stâr′kās, *n.* The part of a building which contains the stairs.—**stairhead,** *n.* The top of a staircase.

stake, stāk, *n.* [A.Sax. *staca*, a stake = L.G. *stake*, D. *staak*, Dan. *stage*; from the root of *stick*, *stock*.] A piece of wood sharpened at one end and set in the ground, or prepared for setting, as a support to something, as part of a fence, etc.; the post to which one condemned to die by fire was fastened (to suffer at *the stake*); that which is pledged or wagered; that which is laid down to abide the issue of a contest, to be gained by victory or lost by defeat; something hazarded; the state of being pledged or put at hazard; preceded by *at* (his honor is *at stake*).—*v.t.*—*staked*, *staking*. To set and plant like a stake; to fasten; support, or defend with stakes; to mark the limits of by stakes; with *out* (to *stake out* land); to pledge; to lay down as stake; to hazard upon the issue of a competition, or upon a future contingency.—**stakeholder,** *n.* One who holds stakes, or with whom the stakes are deposited when a wager is laid.

stalactite, sta•lak′tīt, *n.* [From Gr. *stalaktos*, trickling or dropping, from *stalassō* or *stalazō*, to let fall drop by drop.] A mass of calcareous matter, usually in a conical or cylindrical form, pendent from the roofs of caverns, and produced by the filtration of water containing particles of carbonate of lime through fissures and pores of rocks.—**stalactitic, stalactitical,** sta•lak•tit′ik, sta•lak•tit′i•kal, *a.* Pertaining to or having the character of stalactite; resembling a stalactite; containing stalactites.—**stalagmite,** sta•lag′mīt, *n.* [Gr. *stalagmos*, a dropping, from *stalazo*, to drop.] A deposit of stalactitic matter on the floor of a cavern, sometimes rising into columns, which meet and blend with the stalactites above.—**stalagmitic, stalagmitical,** stal′ag•mit″ik, sta•lag•mit′i•kal, *a.* Relating to or having the form of stalagmite.

stale, stāl, *a.* [Akin to *stall*, the meaning being from standing long; comp. O.D. *stel*, that remains standing, quiet, ancient. STALL.] Vapid or tasteless from age; having lost its life, spirit, and flavor from being long kept; not new; not freshly made (*stale* bread); out of regard from use or long familiarity; trite; common; musty.—*v.t.*—*staled*, *staling*. To make vapid, useless, cheap, or worthless; to wear out.—**stalely,** stāl′li, *adv.* In a stale manner.—**stalemate,** *n. Chess-playing*, the position of the king when so situated that, though not in check, he cannot move without being placed in check, there being no other available move; in this case the game is drawn.—*v.t.* To subject to a stalemate in chess; hence, to perplex completely; to nonplus.—**staleness,** stāl′nes, *n.* The state of being stale.

stale, stāl, *v.i.* [Same as D. and G. *stallen*, Dan. *stalle*, Sw. *stalla*, to make water, from G. *stall*, A.Sax. *stael*, a stable. STALL.] To make water; to discharge urine, as horses and cattle.—*n.* Urine of horses and cattle.

stalk, sta̤k, *n.* [Same as Dan. *stilk*, Icel. *stilkr*, a stalk. STALL.] The stem or main axis of a plant; the pedicel of a flower, or the peduncle that supports the fructification of a plant; anything resembling a stalk.—**stalked,** sta̤kt, *a.* Having a stalk or stem.—**stalkless,** sta̤k′les, *a.* Having no stalk.

stalk, sta̤k, *v.i.* [A.Sax. *staelcan*, to go softly or warily; Dan. *stalke*, to stalk.] To walk softly or in a stealthy manner; to walk behind a stalking-horse; to pursue game by approaching softly and warily behind a cover; to walk in a lofty or dignified manner; to pace slowly.—*v.t. Sporting*, to pursue stealthily; to watch and follow warily for the purpose of killing.—*n.* A high, proud, stately step or walk.—**stalker,** sta̤′kėr, *n.* One who stalks; a kind of fishing net.—**stalking-horse,** *n.* A horse behind which a fowler conceals himself from the sight of the game; *fig.* anything thrust forward to conceal a more important object; a mask; a pretense.

stall, sta̤l, *n.* [A.Sax. *steall*, *stael*, place, stall, stable; Icel. *stallr*, D. *stal*, G. *stall*, Dan. *stald*, a stall, a stable, etc.; akin *stale*, *a.* and *v.*, *stalwart*, *stalk*, *n.*, etc.; same root as in *stand*.] The place where a horse or an ox is kept and fed; the division or compartment of a stable or cow house for one horse or ox; a bench or kind of table in the open air on which anything is exposed to sale; a small house or shed in which merchandise is exposed for sale or an occupation carried on (a butcher's *stall*); a fixed seat in the choir or chancel of a cathedral, church, etc., and mostly appropriated to some dignitary; *mining*, an opening made between pillars in the direction that the work is progressing or transversely.—*v.t.* To put into a stall or stable; to keep in a stall; to bring to a standstill unintentionally, e.g. a horse, automobile, electric motor, or airplane.—*v.i.* To live as in a stall; to dwell.—**stall-feed,** *v.t.* To fatten in a stall or stable (to *stall-feed* an ox).

stallion, stal′yun, *n.* [O.E. *stalon*, O.Fr. *estalon* (Fr. *étalon*), a stallion; from O.H.G. *stal*, E. *stall*; lit. the horse kept in the stall.] A horse not castrated; an entire horse.

stalwart, sta̤l′wėrt, *a.* [O.E. *stalword*, *stallworth*, from A.Sax. *staelweorth*, lit. worthy of place, from *stael*, stall, place. STALL.] Brave; bold; redoubted; daring; tall and strong; large and strong in frame.—**stalwartness,** sta̤l′wėrt•nes, *n.* The state or quality of being stalwart.

stamen, stā′men, *n.* pl. **stamens,** stā′menz, or **stamina,** stam′i•na, [L. *stamen*, pl. *stamina*, the warp of a web, a thread, the fiber of wood; from root *sta*, to stand.] *Bot.* the male organ of fructification in plants, situated immediately within the petals, and composed in most cases of three parts, the filament, the anther, and the pollen, of which the two latter are essential, the other not; pl. *stamina*, whatever constitutes the principal strength or support of anything; power of endurance; staying power; long lasting strength or vigor.—**staminal,** stam′i•nal, *a.* Pertaining to stamens or stamina; consisting in stamens or stamina.—**staminate,** stam′i•nāt, Furnished with stamens.—**stamineal,** sta•min′ē•al, *a.* [L. *stamineus*.] Consisting of stamens; possessing stamens; pertaining to the stamen.—**staminiferous,** sta•mi•nif′ėr•us, *a.* Bearing or having stamens.—**staminode,** stam′in•ōd, *n.* [From *stamen*.] A sterile stamen.

stammer, stam′ėr, *v.i.* [A freq. form from a root *stam*; A.Sax. *stamor*, *stamer*, Icel. *stamr*, *stammr*, stammering, speaking with difficulty; L.G. *stammern*, D. *stameren*, *stamelen*, G. *stammeln*, Icel. *stamma*, to stammer; allied to *stumble*.] To make involuntary breaks or pauses in speaking; to hesitate or falter in speaking; to speak with stops and difficulty; to stutter.—*v.t.* To utter with hesitation or imperfectly; frequently with *out*.—*n.* Defective utterance; a stutter.—**stammerer,** stam′ėr•ėr, *n.* One that stammers.—**stammeringly,** stam′ėr•ing•li, *adv.* With stammering.

stamp, stamp, *v.t.* [Same as Sw. *stampa*, Dan. *stampe*, D. *stampen*, G. *stampfen*, to stamp, nasalized forms corresponding to Icel. *stappa*, D. *stappen*, G. *stapfen*, to step; akin *step*.] To strike or press forcibly by thrusting the foot downward; to impress with some mark or figure;

to mark with an impression; to imprint; to fix deeply; to coin or mint; to affix a stamp (as a postage or receipt stamp) to; to cut out with a stamp; to crush by the downward action of a kind of pestle, as ore in a stamp mill.—*To stamp out*, to extinguish, as fire, by stamping on with the foot; hence, to extirpate; to eradicate; to suppress at once by strong measures.—*v.i.* To strike the foot forcibly downward.—*n.* The act of stamping; an instrument for making impressions on other bodies; a mark imprinted; an official mark set upon things chargeable with some duty or tax showing that the duty is paid; often used as a means of raising revenue; a small piece of stamped paper used by government; a postage stamp; an instrument for cutting materials (as paper, leather, etc.) into various forms by a downward pressure; general character fixed on anything (bears the *stamp* of genius); sort or character (a man of the same *stamp*); *metal.* a kind of hammer for crushing or beating ores to powder.—**Stamp Act,** *n.* An act passed by the British Parliament in 1765 imposing a duty on all paper, vellum, and parchment used in the American colonies. It was repealed in March, 1766, as a result of the colonists' opposition.—*Stamp booklet*, a small book containing a few leaves of postage stamps of low denomination, bound in thin cardboard and separated by oiled paper.—**stamping ground,** a person's most familiar surroundings or usual place of activity (his *old stamping ground*).—**stamp mill,** *n.* An engine by which ores are pounded by means of a stamp.

stampede, stam•pēd′, *n.* [Amer. Sp. *estampida*, a stampede; akin to *stamp*.] A sudden fright seizing upon large bodies of cattle or horses, on the prairies, and causing them to run for long distances.—*v.i.*—*stampeded*, *stampeding*. To take sudden flight, as if under the influence of panic terror.

stance, stans, *n.* [O.Fr. *estance*, a position, a standing.] Location, as for a building site; posture; manner of standing.

stanch, stänsh, *v.t.* [O.Fr. *estancher* (Fr. *étancher*), to stanch, from L.L. *stancare*, for L. *stagnare*, to make or be stagnant. STAGNATE.] To prevent the flow of, as of blood; to stop the flow of blood from; to dry up.—*v.i.* To stop, as blood; to cease to flow.—*a.* [Lit. made water-tight, and, as applied to a ship, not leaky.] Strong and tight; sound; firm in principle; steady; hearty; loyal (a *stanch* republican, a *stanch* friend).—**stancher,** stänsh′ėr, *n.* One who or that which stanches.—**stanchless,** stänsh′les, *a.* Incapable of being stanched; insatiable.—**stanchly,** stänsh′li, *adv.* In a stanch manner.—**stanchness,** stänsh′nes, *n.* The state or quality of being stanch; strongness and soundness; firmness in principle.

stanchion, stan′shon, *n.* [O.Fr. *estanson*, *estançon*, from *estance*, a support, from L.L. *stantia*, from L. *sto*, to stand. STAND.] A prop or support; a post or beam used for a support; an upright post or beam of different forms in ships.

stand, stand, *v.i.*—pret. and pp. *stood* (stöd). [A.Sax. *standan*, to stand, pret. *stód*, pp. *standen*=Icel. *standa*, O.H.G. *standan*, Goth. *standan*, D. *staan*, G. *stehen*; from root seen also in L. *sto*, Gr. (*hi*)*stanai*, Skr. *sthâ*; from same root are *stead*, *stall*, *still*, *stool*, etc., and through the French and Latin come *stage*, *state*, *station*, *stable*, etc.] To be stationary or at rest in an upright position; to be set upright; to be on end; to be as regards position or situation; to have its site or locality; to cease from progress; to come to a state of rest; to stop; to pause; to halt; to continue or remain without injury; to last; to endure; to maintain one's ground or position; to maintain a fixed or steady attitude; to persevere; to persist; to insist; to be placed as regards rank or order (*a stands* first); to be in a particular state or condition; to be (how *stands* the matter?); to be in the stead or place; to be equivalent (v *stands* for 5); to hold a certain course, as a ship; to be directed toward any local point; to measure from feet to head, or from bottom to top; to stagnate; to be valid; to have efficacy.—[*Note. Stand* with many adverbs receives the sense of motion as previous to coming to rest, and becomes equivalent to to step, go, come; as, to *stand* aloof, to *stand* apart, to *stand* aside, to *stand* back, to *stand* forth, etc.]—*To stand against*, to resist; to oppose.—*To stand by* (with *by* the adverb), to be present; to be near; to be placed or left aside; (with *by* the preposition) to support; to defend; to assist; not to desert.—*To stand fast*, to be fixed; to be unshaken.—*To stand for*, to espouse the cause of; to represent; to take the place of; to offer one's self as a candidate; *naut.* to direct the course toward.—Also, to endure, tolerate, or put up with, something undesired. *To stand from* (*naut.*), to direct the course from.—*To stand in*, or *stand in for* (*naut.*), to direct a course toward land or a harbor.—*To stand in* also means to take the place, temporarily, of another, as one actor for another at a rehearsal.—*To stand off*, to keep at a distance.—*To stand off and on* (*naut.*). to sail toward land and then from it.—*To stand* or *stand in* (with personal objects, the person being really in the dative), to cost (that coat *stood* him ten dollars or *in* ten dollars).—*To stand out*, to project; to be prominent; to persist in opposition or resistance.—*To stand to*, to apply one's self to; to remain fixed in (a purpose or opinion); to abide by; to adhere, as to a contract, etc.; to be consistent or tally with (it *stands to* reason).—*To stand up*, to rise to one's feet; to rise to make a claim or a declaration; to rise in opposition; to rise and stand on end (as one's hair).—*To stand up against*, to place one's self in opposition to; to resist.—*To stand up for*, to rise in defense of.—*To stand upon*, to set value on; to insist on; to attach a high value to; to be a stickler for (to *stand upon* ceremony).—*To stand with*, to be consistent.—*v.t.* To place on end; to endure; to sustain; to bear; to await; to undergo.—*To stand it*, to be able to endure or bear something.—*To stand one's ground*, to keep the ground, the station one has taken; to maintain one's position.—*To stand fire*, to remain while being shot at by an enemy without giving way.—*To stand trial*, to sustain the trial or examination of a cause.—*n.* A cessation of progress, motion, or activity; a stop; a halt; a point or condition beyond which no further progress is made; a state of hesitation or perplexity; a place or post where one stands; a station; a halt made for the purpose of resisting an attack; a small table or frame, on or in which articles may be put for support (an umbrella *stand*), or on which goods may be exposed for sale (a fruit *stand*); a place in a town where automobiles stand ready for hire, a cabstand; an erection or raised platform for spectators at open-air gatherings.—*Grand stand*, tiers of seats at a baseball, football, or other field.—*Stand of arms*, a musket or rifle with its usual appendages, as a bayonet, cartridge box, etc.—**standing,** stand′ing, *p.* and *a.* Permanent; not temporary; lasting; not transitory; stagnant; not flowing; fixed; not movable; remaining erect; not cut down; the relative position of a contestant in a tournament, or a team in a league, such as in baseball.—*Standing orders*, regulations made by a deliberative assembly respecting the manner in which business shall be conducted in it.—*Standing rigging*, the ropes which sustain the masts and remain fixed in their position, as the shrouds and stays.—*n.* The act of one who stands; duration of existence (a custom of long *standing*); station; place to stand in; power to stand; condition in society; relative position; rank; reputation.—**standpoint,** *n.* A fixed point or station; a basis or fundamental principle; a position or point of view from which a matter is considered.—**standstill,** *n.* A standing at rest; a stop.

standard, stand′ėrd, *n.* [From O.Fr. *estendart*, *estandart* (Fr. *étandard*), from the Teutonic verb to *stand* with suffix-*ard*.] A flag or ensign set up and round which men rally, or under which they unite for a common purpose; a flag or carved symbolical figure, etc., erected on a long pole or staff; a banner; the heraldic standard is a long, narrow pennant with a gold or parti-colored fringe; that which is established by competent authority as a rule or measure of quantity; a measure or weight by which others are to be regulated and adjusted; that which is established as a rule or model by public opinion, custom, or general consent; that which serves as a test or measure (a *standard* of morality, or of taste); *hort.* a tree or shrub which stands singly and not attached to any wall or support; *bot.* the upper petal or banner of a papilionaceous corolla; *carp.* any upright in a framing.—*a.* Serving as a standard; capable of satisfying certain conditions fixed by competent authority; fixed; settled; *hort.* not trained on a wall, etc.—**standard-bearer,** *n.* One who bears a standard.—**standardize,** stand′ärd•īz, *v.t.* To accept as a standard; to make in certain fixed or standard sizes, qualities, etc.

stanhope, stan′hōp, *n.* A light four-wheeled carriage without a top, with high seat and closed back; any high buggy of similar design.

stank, stangk, old pret. of *stink.*

stannic, stan′ik, *a.* [From L. *stannum,* tin.] Pertaining to tin; containing tin with valence four.—**stannous,** stan′us, *a.* Pertaining to, or containing tin; containing tin with valence two.

stanza, stan′za, *n.* [It. *stanza,* a stanza, abode, stop, etc., from L. *stans, stantis,* ppr. of *sto,* to stand. STATE.] A number of lines of poetry connected with each other, and properly ending in a full point or pause; a part of a poem containing every variation of measure in that poem, and successively repeated.—**stanzaic,** stan•zā′ik, *a.* Consisting of or relating to stanzas; arranged as a stanza.

stapelia, sta•pē′li•a, *n.* [After *Stapel,* a Dutch botanist.] A genus of fleshy African plants with beautiful flowers, many of which have the odor of rotten flesh.

stapes, stā′pēz, *n.* [L., a stirrup.] *Anat.* the innermost of the small bones of the ear, so called from its form.

staphylococcus, staf′il•o•kok″us, *n.* [Gr. *staphylē,* and *kokkos,* a berry.] In bacteria, a form consisting of a cluster of cocci.

staphyloraphy, staf•i•lor′a•fi, *n.* [Gr. *staphylē,* and *raphē,* a suture.] *Surg.* the operation of uniting a cleft palate.

staple, stā′pl, *n.* [Same as D. and G. *stapel,* a post, prop; so also Sw. *stapel,* Dan. *stabel*; same root as that of *stamp* and *step.*] According to old usage, a settled mart or market; an emporium; a town where certain commodities were chiefly taken for sale; hence, the principal commodity grown or manufactured in a country, district, or town; the principal element of or ingredient in anything; the chief constituent; the material or substance of anything; raw or unmanufactured material; the thread or pile of wool, cotton, or flax (wool of a long or coarse *staple*).—*a.* Pertaining to or being a mart or staple for commodities; mainly occupying commercial enterprise; established in commerce (a *staple* trade); chief; principal; regularly produced or made for market.—*v.t.*—*stapled, stapling.* To sort or adjust the different staples of, as wool.—**stapler,** stā′pler, *n.* A dealer in staple commodities; one employed in assorting wool according to its staple; a contrivance that drives thin wire staples through paper and clinches them to bind the paper.

staple, stā′pl, *n.* [A.Sax. *stapel,* a prop, trestle; really same as above word.] A loop of iron formed with two points to be driven into wood to hold a hook, pin, bolt, etc.

star, stär, *n.* [A.Sax. *steorra,* Sc. *starn,* Icel. *stjarna,* Goth. *stairno,* D. *ster,* O.D. *sterne,* G. *stern*; cog. L. *stella* (*or sterula*), also *astrum,* Gr. *astēr,* Armor. *stēren,* Skr. *târâ* (for *stârâ*), *stri,* to strew, from scattering light.] Any celestial body except the moon, the planets, comets, meteors, and nebulae; more strictly, any of the bodies that shine by their own light, as the sun, situated at immense distances from us, and doubtless, like our sun, the centers of systems similar to our own, distinctively called *fixed stars,* as they apparently do not change their relative positions as do the planets, the wanderers among the stars; that which resembles a star; a figure with points radiating like the spokes of a wheel; an ornamental figure rayed like a star worn upon the breast to indicate rank or honor; a radiated mark in writing or printing; an asterisk, thus, *: used as a reference to a note in the margin or to fill a blank in writing or printing where letters or words are omitted; a person of brilliant qualities; a brilliant theatrical or operatic performer; a movie star.—*v.t.*—*starred, starring.* To set or adorn with stars; to bespangle.—*v.i.* To shine as a star; to appear as an actor in a theater among inferior players.—**star apple,** *n.* A West Indian fruit somewhat resembling an apple.—**starfish,** *n.* A marine animal (one of the Echinodermata) which has the form of a star, with five or more rays radiating from a central disk.—**stargazer,** *n.* One who gazes at the stars; an astrologer.—**stargazing,** *n.* The act or practice of observing the stars with attention; astrology.—**starless,** stär′les, *a.* Having no stars visible or no starlight.—**starlight,** stär′līt, *n.* The light proceeding from the stars.—*a.* Lighted by the stars.—**starlike,** stär′līk, *a.* Resembling a star; bright; lustrous.—**starlit,** stär′-lit, *a.* Lighted by stars.—**starnose,** *n.* A North American mole with starlike rays at the extremity of its muzzle.—**starred,** stärd, *p.* and *a.* Studded or adorned with stars; influenced by the stars (ill-*starred*); marked with a star to indicate importance.—**stars and bars,** the first flag adopted by the Confederate States of America, having three bars of red, white and red, and a blue union with seven white stars.—**stars and stripes,** the flag of the United States, consisting of 13 horizontal stripes, alternately red and white, and a union having in a blue field 50 white stars to represent the states.—**Star-Spangled Banner,** a patriotic poem by Francis Scott Key, adopted as the national anthem of the United States by act of Congress in 1931.

starboard, stär′bōrd, *n.* [A.Sax. *steórbord,* that is, *steer-board,* from *steóran,* to steer, the old rudder being a kind of large oar used on the right side of the ship. STEER.] *Naut.* the right-hand side of a ship looking toward the stem or prow; opposed to *port* or old *larboard.*—*a.* Pertaining to the right-hand side of a ship; being or lying on the right side.

starch, stärch, *n.* [A softened form of *stark,* stiff, strong; lit. stuff that makes stiff. STARK.] A carbohydrate universally diffused in the vegetable world, and forming the greater part of all farinaceous substances; this substance as prepared for commerce, chiefly extracted from cereals or potatoes, and employed for stiffening cloth; *fig.* stiffness of a person's behavior or manner.—*v.t.* To stiffen with starch.—**starchiness,** stär′chi•nes, *n.*—**starchy,** stär′chi, *a.*

stare, stâr, *v.i.*—*stared, staring.* [A. Sax. *starian,* to stare, to gaze; D. and L.G. *staren,* G. *starren,* Icel. *stara;* lit. to look fixedly, the root being that of G. and Sw. *starr,* stiff, fixed, E. *stark,* stiff, strong.] To look with fixed eyes wide open; to gaze, as in admiration, surprise, horror, impudence, etc.—*v.t.* To affect or abash by gazing at; to look earnestly or fixedly at.—*To stare in the face,* (*fig.*) to be before the eyes, or undeniably evident.—*n.* The act of one who stares.—**starer,** stâ′rėr, *n.* One who stares or gazes.

stark, stärk, *a.* [A.Sax. *stearc,* stiff, hard; G. and Sw. *stark,* D. *sterk,* Icel. *sterkr*; akin G. *starr,* stiff; E. *stare. Starch* is a softened form.] Stiff; rigid, as in death; strong; rugged; powerful; mere; pure; downright (*stark* nonsense).—*adv.* Wholly; entirely (*stark* mad, *stark* naked).—**starkly,** stärk′li, *adv.* In a stark manner.

starling, stär′ling, *n.* [Dim. of *stare,* a starling. STARE.] The birds of the family Sturnidae, sometimes called American starlings; piles driven round piers of a bridge for its protection.

start, stärt, *v.i.* [O.E. *sterte, sturte, stirte,* not in A.Sax. or Icel.; allied to D. *storten,* Dan. *styrte,* G. *stürzen,* to rush, to spring.] To move suddenly and spasmodically; to make a sudden and involuntary motion of the body, caused by surprise, pain, or any sudden feeling; to shrink, to wince; to make a sudden or unexpected change of place; to spring up; to change condition at once; to set out; to commence a course, as a race, a journey, or the like; to shift or spring from a fixed position; to be dislocated.—*To start after*, to set out in pursuit of; to follow.—*To start against*, to become a candidate in opposition to; to oppose.—*To start up*, to rise suddenly, as from a seat; to come suddenly into notice.—*v.t.* To rouse suddenly from concealment; to cause to flee or fly (to *start* a hare); to begin; to set agoing; to originate (to *start* an enterprise, a newspaper); to cause to jump from its place; to make to lose its hold (to *start* a nail); to dislocate.—*n.* A sudden involuntary twitch, spring, or motion, caused by surprise, fear, pain, etc.; a sudden change of place; a quick movement; a bursting forth; a sally; a spasmodic effort; a beginning of action of motion; the setting of something agoing; first motion from a place, first motion in a race; the outset.—*To get* or *have the start*, to be beforehand with another; to get ahead; with *of*.—**starter,** stär′tėr, *n.* One who starts; one who sets out; one who sets persons or things in motion, as an official of a trolley line or a train dispatcher; *in automobile*, the electric motor that starts the gasoline engine; *at horse race*, one who starts as competitor in a race.—*Head start*, opposite of handicap, a favor, an advantage at a race for a supposedly inferior contestant.

startle, stär′tl, *v.i.*—*startled, startling*. [Dim. of *start*.] To move with a start or spasmodically; to start.—*v.t.* To excite by sudden alarm, surprise, or apprehension; to alarm.—*n.* A start of alarm.—**startling,** stärt′ling, *p.* and *a.* Such as to startle with fear or surprise; alarming; shocking. —**startlingly,** stärt′ling•li, *adv.* In a startling manner.

starve, stärv, *v.i.*—*starved, starving*. [A.Sax. *steorfan*, to perish of hunger or cold.—L.G. *starven*, D. *sterven*, G. *sterben*, to die.] To perish with or suffer extremely from hunger; to suffer from want; to be hard put to it through want of anything.—*v.i.* To kill or distress with hunger; to subdue by famine; to destroy by want; to deprive of force or vigor.—**starvation,** stär•vā′shon, *n.* [One of those words which have a Latin termination tacked on to an Anglo-Saxon base; comp. *flirtation, talkative, readable*, etc.] The state of starving or being starved; a suffering extremely from want of food.—**starveling,** stärv′ling, *a.* Hungry; lean; pining with want.—*n.* An animal or plant that is thin and weak through want of nutriment.

stasis, stā′sis, *n.* A stoppage of the normal flow of fluids in any organs of the body; a slackening of the blood current as in passive congestion.

state, stāt, *n.* [O.Fr. *estat*, state, condition, etc. (Fr. *état*); from L. *status*, state, position, from *sto*, to stand (seen also in *station, status, statue, stage, rest, arrest, constant, extant*, etc.). STAND.] Condition as determined by whatever circumstances; the condition or circumstances of a being or thing at any given time; situation; position; rank, condition, or quality; royal or gorgeous pomp; appearance of greatness, dignity; grandeur; a certain division of the community partaking in the government of their country; an estate (of the realm); a whole people united into one body politic; a commonwealth; the power wielded by the government of a country; the civil power (the union of church and *state*); one of the commonwealths or bodies politic which together make up a federal republic. —*v.t.*—*stated, stating*. To express the particulars of; to set down in detail; to explain particularly; to narrate; to recite.—**statecraft,** *n.* The art of conducting state affairs; statesmanship.—**stated,** stā′ted, *a.* Settled; established; fixed (stated hours or times).—**statedly,** stā′ted•li, *adv.* At stated or settled times; at regular intervals.—**statehouse,** *n.* The building in which the legislature of a state holds its sittings; the State Capitol. (*United States*).—**stateliness,** stāt′li•nes, *n.* The condition or quality of being stately; loftiness of mien; dignity.—**stately,** stāt′li, *a.* August; lofty; majestic; magnificent.—**statement,** stāt′ment, *n.* The act of stating; that which is stated; a narrative; a recital; the expression of a fact or of an opinion.—**stateroom,** *n.* A magnificent room in a palace or great house; a private room on a ship or train.—**States-General,** *n. pl.* The legislative assemblies of France before the revolution of 1789, and those of the Netherlands.—**statesman,** stāts′man, *n.* A man versed in the arts of government; a politician.—**statesmanlike,** stāts′man•līk, *a.* Having the manner or wisdom of statesmen; worthy of or becoming a statesman.—**statesmanship,** stāts′man•ship, *n.* The qualifications of a statesman; political skill.

statics, stat′iks, *n.* [Fr. *statique*, from Gr. *statikē*, statics, from *statikos*, causing to stop or stand; same root as *state, stand*.] That branch of dynamics which treats of the properties and relations of forces in equilibrium, the body upon which they act being in a state of rest. See DYNAMICS, MECHANICS.—**static,** stat′ik, *a.* Statical;—*n.* Disturbance of radio reception caused by outside electrical interference.—**statical,** stat′i•kal, *a.* Pertaining to bodies at rest or in equilibrium; acting by mere weight without producing motion (*statical* pressure).—*Statical electricity*, electricity produced by friction.

station, stā′shon, *n.* [Fr. *station*, L. *statio, stationis*, from *sto*, to stand. STATE.] The spot or place where anything stands, particularly where a person habitually stands or is appointed to remain for a time; post assigned; situation; position or locality; condition of life; social position; the place where the police force of any district is assembled when not on duty; a building or buildings on a railroad for the reception of passengers and goods intended to be conveyed, and where trains stop; *zool.* and *bot.* the peculiar locality where each species naturally occurs.—*Military station*, a place where troops are regularly kept in garrison.—*Naval station*, a harbor for war vessels, where there is a dockyard and every requisite for the repair of ships.—*v.t.* To assign a station or position to; to post; *refl.* to take up a post or position.—**stationary,** stā′shon•e•ri, *a.* [L. *stationarius*.] Remaining in the same station or place; not moving; fixed; remaining in the same condition.—*Stationary engine*, a steam engine in a fixed position; any steam engine other than a locomotive.—**stationer,** stā′shon•ėr, *n.* [From booksellers originally having a station or stall (L.L. *statio*) at fairs or in market places.] One who sells paper, pens, pencils, ink, and various other materials connected with writing.—*Stationers' hall*, the hall of the London Stationers' Company. The Guild of Stationers (i.e. booksellers and publishers) of London was founded in 1403.—**stationery,** stā′shon•er•i, *n.* The articles usually sold by stationers, as the various materials employed in connection with writing. —**station house,** *n.* A place of arrest or temporary confinement; a police station.—**stationmaster,** *n.* The official in charge of a railroad station.

statistics, sta•tis′tiks, *n.* [Fr. *statistique*, from Gr. *statos*, fixed, settled, from stem *sto*, to stand. STATE, STAND.] A collection of facts which admit of numerical statement and of arrangement in tables, especially facts illustrating the physical, social, moral, intellectual, political, industrial and economic condition of communities or classes of men; that department of political science which deals with such facts.—**statistical, statistic,** sta•tis′ti•kal, sta•tis′tik, *a.* Pertaining to statistics; containing statistics.—**statistically,** sta•tis′ti•kal•li, *adv.* In a statistical manner.—**statistician,** stat•is•tish′an, *n.* One versed in statistics.

stator, stā′tor, *n.* The stationary part of an electric generator or motor.

statoscope, stat′o•skōp, *n.* [Gr. *statos*, standing, and *skopein*, to view.] An instrument for registering the rise or fall of an aircraft.

statue, stat′ū, *n.* [Fr. *statue*, L. *statua*, from *statuo*, to set, to place, from stem of *sto*, to stand. STATE.] A lifelike representation of a human figure or animal in some solid substance, as marble, bronze, iron, wood; a sculptured cast or molded figure of some size and in the round.—*Equestrian statue*, a statue in which the figure is represented as seated on horseback.—**statuary,** stat′ū•e•ri, *n.* [L. *statuaria*, the art of statuary, *statuarius*, a statuary, from *statua*, a statue.] The art of carving or making statues, a branch of sculpture; statues regarded collectively; one that professes or practices the art of making statues.—**statuesque,** stat•ū•esk′, *a.* Partaking of or having the character of a statue.—**statuesquely,** stat•ū•esk′li, *adv.* In a statuesque manner.—**statuette,** stat•ū•et′, *n.* [Fr.] A small statue; a statue smaller than nature.

stature, stat′ūr, *n.* [L. *statura,* from *sto, statum,* to stand. STATE.] The natural height of an animal body; bodily tallness: generally used of the human body.

status, stā′tus, *n.* [L. *status,* state. STATE.] Standing or position as regards rank or condition; position of affairs.

statute, stat′ūt, *n.* [Fr. *statut,* L. *statutum,* from *statuo,* to set up, to fix, to determine, STATE.] A law proceeding from the government of a state; an enactment of the legislature of a state; especially one passed by a body of representatives; a written law; a permanent rule or law of a corporation.—*Statute law,* a statute; also, collectively, the enactments of a legislative assembly, in contradistinction to *common law.*—*v.i.* To ordain, of frequent occurrence in legal deeds. (*Scot.*)—**statutory,** stat′ū•to•ri, *a.* Enacted by statute; depending on statute for its authority.

stave, stāv, *n.* [From *staff,* through influence of the plural *staves.*] A pole or piece of wood of some length; one of the thin narrow pieces of timber of which casks, tubs, buckets, etc., are made; a stanza; a verse; *mus.* the *staff.*—*v.t.*—*staved, staving.* To break in a stave or staves of, or to break a hole in (in this sense pret. and pp. may be *stove*); to furnish with staves or rundles.—*To stave off,* lit. to push off with a staff; hence, to put off; to delay.—**staves,** stāvz, *n.* The plural of *staff* as well as of *stave.*

stavesacre, stāvz′ā•kėr, *n.* [A corruption of Gr. *staphisagria.*] Larkspur.

stay, stā, *v.i.*—pret. *staid, stayed;* ppr. *staying.* [O.Fr. *estayer,* to prop, support, keep steady, from O.D. or Fl. *staeye, staede,* a prop, *staeden,* to establish; akin to E. *stead, steady.*] To remain, continue, or be in a place; to abide; to dwell; to delay; to tarry; to be steady or firm; to continue in a state; to remain; to wait; to forbear to act; to stop; to come to a stand.—*v.t.* To prop or support (O.T.); to make to stop; to stop; to cause to cease (to *stay* operations); to delay; to keep back; to abide; to wait for; to await.—*To stay the stomach,* to satisfy hunger; to satisfy a strong desire.—*n.* A continuance in a place; abode for a time; continuance in a state or condition; stand; stop; obstacle; obstruction; a prop; a support; a piece in some structure performing the office of a brace or tie; *pl.* a kind of waistcoat, stiffened with whalebone or other material, worn by females, sometimes by men; a bodice; a corset: so called from the support it gives to the body.—**stayer,** stā′ėr, *n.* One who or that which stays; in sporting language, one who holds out long and steadily.

stay, stā, *n.* [A.Sax. *staeg*=Icel., Dan., Sw., D., and G. *stag,* a stay.] *Naut.* a strong rope used to support a mast, and leading from the head of one mast down to some other, or to some part of the vessel.—*In stays,* the situation of a vessel when she is going about from one tack to the other.—*To miss stays,* to fail in the attempt to tack about.—**staysail,** *n.* Any sail which hoists upon a stay.

stead, sted, *a.* [A.Sax. *stede*=D. and L.G. *stede,* Dan. *sted,* Icel. *stathr,* Goth. *staths,* G. *statt,* place, stead; from root of *stand;* hence, *steady, steadfast, bestead, bedstead, roadstead, homestead,* etc.] Place or room which another had or might have: preceded by *in,* as, David died, and Solomon reigned *in* his *stead;* hence *instead.*—*To stand a person in stead,* to be of use or advantage to him.—*v.t.* To be of use to; to benefit.

steadfast, sted′fast, *a.* [*Stead,* place, and *fast;* lit. firm in place.] Fast fixed; firm; constant or firm in resolution; resolute; not fickle or wavering. Written also *stedfast.*—**steadfastly,** sted′fast•li, *adv.* In a steadfast manner; with fixed eyes; firmly.—**steadfastness,** sted′fast•nes, *n.* The state of being steadfast; firmness of mind or purpose; constancy; resolution.

steady, sted′i, *a.* [A.Sax. *stedig,* from *stede,* place (STEAD); D. and Dan. *stadig,* G. *statig,* constant.] Firm in standing or position; firmly fixed; constant in mind or pursuit; not fickle; regular; constant; uniform.—*v.t.*—*steadied, steadying.* To make steady; to hold or keep from shaking, reeling, or falling; to support firmly.—*v.i.* To become steady; to regain or maintain an upright position.—**steadily,** sted′i•li, *adv.* In a steady manner; firmly; steadfastly; assiduously; unwaveringly.—**steadiness,** sted′i•nes, *n.* The state of being steady; firmness of mind or purpose; constancy; resolution.

steak, stāk, *n.* [A Scandinavian word; Icel. *steik,* Sw. *stek,* a steak; perhaps akin to *stick,* as being *stuck* on a spit to roast.] A slice of beef, pork, venison, etc., broiled or cut for broiling.

steal, stēl, *v.t.*—pret. *stole,* pp. *stolen* or *stole.* [A.Sax. *stelan,* to steal=D. *stelen,* Icel. *stela,* Goth. *stilan,* G. *stehlen,* to steal; same root as Gr. *stereo,* to deprive, Skr. *stenas,* a thief.] To take and carry away feloniously; to take clandestinely without right or leave; to gain or win by address or gradual and imperceptible means; to perform secretly; to try to accomplish clandestinely (to *steal* a look).—*To steal a march upon,* to gain an advantage over stealthily.—*v.i.* To practice or be guilty of theft; to withdraw or pass privily; to slip unperceived; to go or come furtively.—**stealer,** stē′lėr, *n.* One that steals; a thief.—**stealing,** stē′ling, *n.* The act of one who steals; theft.—**stealth,** stelth, *n.* [Comp. *heal, health; till, tilth.*] The act of stealing‡; a secret or clandestine method of procedure; a proceeding by secrecy.—**stealthily,** stel′thi•li, *adv.* In a stealthy manner; by stealth.—**stealthiness,** stel′thi•nes, *n.* The character of being stealthy.—**stealthy,** stel′thi, *a.* Done by stealth; accompanied by efforts at concealment; done furtively; furtive; sly.

steam, stēm, *n.* [A.Sax. *steam,* steam, smoke; D. *stoom,* Fris. *stoame,* steam; akin L.G. *stüm,* drift of snow or rain.] The vaporous or gaseous substance into which water is converted under certain circumstances of heat and pressure; the elastic aeriform fluid generated by heating water to the boiling point (212° F.); popularly, the visible moist vapor which rises from water, and from all moist and liquid bodies, when subjected to the action of heat.—*v.i.* To give out steam or vapor; to rise in a vaporous form; to pass off in visible vapor; to sail by the agency of steam.—*v.t.* To expose to steam; to apply steam to.—**steamboat,** *n.* A ship moved by the elastic power of steam acting upon machinery.—**steam boiler,** *n.* A strong metallic vessel of iron or steel plates riveted together, in which water is converted into steam for supplying steam engines, etc.—**steamcar,** *n.* A car drawn or driven by steam power.—**steam chest,** *n.* A box or chamber above a steam boiler to form a reservoir for the steam, and from whence it passes to the engine.—**steam engine,** *n.* An engine in which the elastic or expansive force of steam is made available as a source of motive power in the arts and manufactures, and in locomotion.—**steamer,** stē′mėr, *n.* A steamship; a road steamer; a fire engine the pumps of which are worked by steam; a vessel in which articles are subjected to the action of steam.—**steamship,** *n.* A ship propelled by steam.—**steamy,** stē′mi, *a.* Consisting of or abounding in steam; vaporous; misty.

steapsin, stē•ap′sin, *n.* [Gr. *stear,* fat, and *pepsin.*] A ferment in the gastric juice that acts on fats.

stearin, stearine, stē′a•rin, *n.* [Gr. *stear,* fat.] The chief ingredient of suet and tallow, or the harder ingredient of animal fats, oleine being the softer one.—**stearic,** stē•ar′ik, *a.* Pertaining to stearine.—*Stéaric acid,* a white, fatty acid.

steatite, stē′a•tīt, *n.* [Fr. *steatite,* from Gr. *stear, steatos,* fat, tallow.] A mineral consisting of magnesia and alumina, used in the manufacture of porcelain, in polishing marble, in the composition of crayons, etc.; soapstone.—**steatitic,** stē•a•tit′ik, *a.* Pertaining to steatite.

steatopygous, stē•a•top′i•gus, *a.* [Gr. *stear,* fat, and *pygē,* buttocks.] Having an accumulation of fat on the buttocks.

stedfast, sted′fast. See STEADFAST.

steed, stēd, *n.* [A.Sax. *stéd, stéda,* a steed; akin to *stud;* from stem of *stand.*] A horse; a horse for state or war; a word used chiefly in poetry and poetical or picturesque prose.

steel, stēl, *n.* [A.Sax. *stél, stýle,* steel=L.G.D. and Dan. *staal,* Icel. *stal,* G. *stahl,* O.G. *stahal;* root probably that of *stick, stake, steak,* etc.] Iron combined with a small portion of carbon, capable of showing great hardness and elasticity, and used in forming various kinds of instruments, edge tools, springs, etc., *fig.* a weapon, as a sword, spear, etc.; a kind of steel file for sharpening knives; a piece of steel for striking sparks from flint to ignite tinder or match; used to typify extreme hardness; sternness; rigor (a heart of *steel*).—*a.* Made of steel; resembling steel; unfeeling; rigorous.—*v.t.* To overlay, point, or edge with steel; to make hard or stubborn; to render insensible or obdurate (to *steel* one's heart against mercy).—**steel engraving,** *n.* The art of engraving upon steel plates; an impression or print from an engraved steel plate.—**steeliness,** stēl′i•nes, *n.* The state of being steely; great hardness.—**steely,** stēl′i, *a.* Made of or resembling steel; hard; stubborn.—**steelyard,** stēl′yard, *n.* [Apparently from *steel* and *yard*, but old forms of the name make this doubtful, though the real origin is not clear.] An instrument for weighing bodies, consisting essentially of a lever of unequal arms, the body to be weighed being applied at the shorter arm, while a weight is made to balance the body by being moved along the longer arm at a proper distance from the fulcrum.

steenbok, stēn′bok or stān′bok, *n.* [D. *steen*, stone, and *bok*, a buck.] A species of antelope of South Africa.

steep, stēp, *a.* [A.Sax. *steap*, high, steep; Icel. *steypthr*, high; probably allied to *stoop*, and signifying literally sinking down abruptly. *Steeple* is a derivative.] Ascending or descending with great inclination (as a roof, a slope); precipitous (hill, rock, etc.). —*n.* A precipitous place; a bold projecting rock; a precipice.—**steepen,**† stē′pn, *v.i.* To become steep.—**steeply,** stēp′li, *adv.* In a steep manner; with steepness; precipitously.—**steepness,** stēp′nes, *n.* The state of being steep; precipitousness.

steep, stēp, *v.t.* [Same as D. and G. *stippen*, Fris. *stiepen*, to dip, to steep; perhaps connected with *steep*, adjective.] To soak in a liquid; to macerate; to extract the essence of by soaking: often used figuratively (*steeped* to the lips in misery).—*n.* Something that is steeped or used in steeping; that in which things are steeped.—**steeper,** stē′pėr, *n.* One who steeps; a vessel in which things are steeped.

steeple, stē′pl, *n.* [A.Sax. *stépel*, *stýpel*, a steeple, a tower; L.G. *stipel*, a pillar; Icel. *stöpull*, a steeple; allied to *steep*.] A lofty erection attached to a church, public building, or other edifice, and generally intended to contain its bells; a tower surmounted by a spire.—**steeplechase,** *n.* A horse-race across country in which obstacles have to be jumped as they come in the way: so called because originally a church steeple or other conspicuous object served as a goal. —**steeplechaser,** *n.* One who rides, or the horse ridden, in steeplechases.—**steeple jack,** *n.* A man employed to repair steeples, tall chimneys, etc.

steer, stēr, *n.* [A.Sax. *steor*=D. and G. *stier*, Icel. *stjórr*, Goth. *stiur*, a steer, a bull; same root as Skr. *sthûra*, strong, and akin to L. *taurus*, Gr. *tauros* (for *stauros*), a bull.] A castrated male of the ox family; an ox.

steer, stēr, *v.t.* [A.Sax. *steóran*, *stýran*, to rule, steer; Dan. *styre*, Icel. *stýra*, G. *steuern*, to steer; Goth, *stiurjan*, to establish; same root as Gr. *stauros*, a stake.] To direct and govern the course of, by the movements of the helm; to control or govern; to direct; to guide.—*v.i.* To direct a vessel by the helm; to direct one's course at sea; to take a course at the direction of the helm; *fig.* to take or pursue a course in life.—**steerage,** stēr′ij, *n.* The steering of a ship; the hinder or stern part of a ship; that part of a ship allotted to the inferior class of passengers.—**steerageway,** *n. Naut.* that forward movement of a ship which enables the helm to act.—**steering wheel,** *n.* The wheel by which the rudder of a ship is governed.—**steersman,** stērz′man, *n.* One that steers; the helmsman of a ship.

steeve, stēv, *v.i.* [Akin to *stiff*; comp. D. *stevig*, stiff, firm.] *Naut.* to project from the bows at an angle instead of horizontally: said of a bowsprit.—*n. Naut.* the angle which the bowsprit makes with the horizon.

steinbok, stīn′bok, *n.* [That is, *stone buck*.] The German name of the ibex.

stele, stē′lē, *n.* pl. **stelae,** stē′lē. [Gr. *stélé*, a post, an upright stone, from stem *sta*, to stand.] A small column without base or capital, serving as a monument, a milestone, and the like; a sepulchral slab or column.

stellar, stel′lėr, *a.* [L. *stellaris*, from *stella*, a star. STAR.] Pertaining to stars; starry; full of stars; set with stars.—**stellate, stellated,** stel′lāt, stel′la•ted, *a.* [L. *stellatus*.] Resembling a star; radiated; *bot.* arranged in the form of a star.—**stelliferous,** stel•lif′ėr•us, *a.* Having or abounding with stars.—**stelliform,** stel′li•form, *a.* Like a star; radiated.—**stellular,** stel′ū•lėr, *a.* [L. *stellula*, dim. of *stella*, a star.] Having the appearance of little stars; *nat. hist.* having marks resembling stars.

stem, stem, *n.* [A.Sax. *stemn*, for *staefn*, *stefn*, a stem; Icel. *stofn*, *stomn*, Dan. *stamme*, D. *stam*, G. *stamm*: ultimately from root of *stand*. *Stem*, of a ship, is closely allied.] The principal body of a tree, shrub, or plant of any kind; the firm part which supports the branches; the ascending axis, as opposed to the root or descending axis; the stalk; also, a peduncle, pedicel, or petiole or leaf stem; the stock of a family; a race or generation of progenitors; anything resembling the stem of a plant; *mus.* the vertical line added to the head of a note.—**stemless,** stem′les, *a.* Having no stem; acaulous.

stem, stem, *n.* [Same as Icel. *stemni*, *stamn*, *stafn*, the stem of a ship; A.Sax. *stefn*, D. *steven*, a prow. See STEM above.] A curved piece of timber or combination of pieces to which the two sides of a ship are united at the fore end; the prow; the forward part of a vessel.—*From stem to stern*, from one end of the ship to the other.—*v.t.*—*stemmed*, *stemming*. To make way against by sailing or swimming; to press forward through; to dash against with the stem.

stem, stem, *v.t.* [Icel. *stemma*, Sw. *stamma*, G. *stemmen*, to dam, to bank up; perhaps allied to *stamp*.] To dam up; to stop; to check, as a stream or moving force.

stench, stensh, *n.* [A softened form of A.Sax. *stenc*, E. *stink*.] An ill smell; a stink.

stencil, sten′sil, *n.* [Perhaps from O.Fr. *estance*, a support, a stencil forming a guide or support in making letters, etc., from L. *sto*, to stand.] A thin plate of metal, leather, or other material, which has a pattern cut through it, and which is laid flat on a surface and brushed over with color so as to mark the surface below.—*v.t.*—*stenciled*, *stenciling*. To form by means of a stencil; to paint or color with stencils.—**stenciler,** sten′sil•ėr, *n.* One who works or paints in figures with a stencil.

stenograph, † sten′o•graf, *v.t.* [Gr. *stenos*, close, narrow, and *graphō*, to write.] To write or represent by shorthand.—*n.* A writing in shorthand.—**stenographer,** ste•nog′ra•fėr, *n.* One who is skilled in the art of shorthand writing.—**stenographic, stenographical,** sten•o•graf′ik, sten•o•graf′i•kal, *a.* Pertaining to stenography or shorthand; expressed in shorthand.—**stenography,** ste•nog′ra•fi, *n.* A generic term which embraces every system of shorthand.

stenosis, sten•ō′sis, *n.* [Gr. *stenos*, narrow.] *Med.* the narrowing of a channel or aperture.

stentorian, sten•tō′ri•an, *a.* [From *Stentor*, a Greek herald celebrated for his powerful voice.] Extremely loud or powerful (a *stentorian* voice); able to utter a very loud sound.

step, step, *v.i.*—*stepped*, *stepping*. [A.Sax. *steppan*, to step; O.Fris. *steppa*, O.Sax. *stapun*, D. and L.G. *stappen*, to step; A.Sax. *staepe*, D. *stap*, G. *stapfe*, a step. *Stamp* is allied, and *staple* is from same root.] To move the leg and foot in walking; to advance or recede by a movement of the foot or feet; to go; to walk; especially, to go a little distance and with a limited purpose (to *step* aside); to advance or come as it were by chance or suddenly (to *step* into an inheritance).—*To step aside*, to walk to a little distance; to deviate from the right path; to err.—*To step out*, to increase the length, but not the rapidity of the step.—*v.t.* To set (the foot)†; *naut.* to fix the foot of, as of a mast; to erect in readiness for setting sail.—*n.* A pace; an advance made by one removal of the foot in walking; one remove in ascending or descending a stair; the distance between the feet in walking or running; a small space or distance; a grade in progress or rank; a forward move; a higher grade of rank; print or impression of the foot; footprint; gait; manner of walking; sound of the feet; footfall; a proceeding; one of a series of proceedings; measure (to take *steps* in a matter); a foot piece for ascending or descending from a carriage; the round of a ladder; *pl.* a self-supporting ladder with flat steps; a stepladder; much used indoors; *naut.* a block or a solid piece supporting the heel of a mast.—*Step by step*, by a gradual and regular process; gradually; keeping pace.—**stepladder,** *n.* A portable ladder usually having flat steps, and its own means of support attached.—**stepper,** step′ėr, *n.* One who steps; one that has a gait good or bad: often applied to a horse.—**steppingstone,** *n.* A raised stone in a stream or in a swampy place to keep the feet dry in crossing; an aid by which an end may be accomplished or an object gained; an assistance to progress.

stepbrother, step′bruTH•ėr, *n.* [In this and following words *step-* is A.Sax. *steóp-*, Icel. *stjúp*, D. and G. *stief-*, a prefix of doubtful origin.] A brother by being a stepfather's or stepmother's son by a former wife or husband.—**stepchild,** step′chīld, *n.* The child of a husband or wife by a former wife or husband.—**stepdaughter,** step′da̤•tėr, *n.* The daughter of a husband or wife by a former wife or husband.—**stepfather,** step′fä•THėr, *n.* A mother's second or subsequent husband.—**stepmother,** step′muTH•ėr, *n.* A father's second or subsequent wife.—**stepparent,** *n.* A stepfather or stepmother.—**stepsister,** step′•sis•tėr, *n.* A stepfather's or stepmother's daughter by a former wife or husband.—**stepson,** step′sun, *n.* The son of a husband or wife by a former wife or husband.

steppe, step, *n.* [G. *steppe*, Rus. *stepy*′, a steppe.] A name applied to those extensive plains which stretch across the southeast of European Russia, round the shores of the Caspian and Aral Seas, and occupy the low lands of Siberia.

stercoraceous, stėr•ko•rā′shus, *a.* [L. *stercus, stercoris*, dung.] Pertaining to dung, or partaking of its nature.

stère, stēr, *n.* [Fr. *stère*, from Gr. *stereos*, solid.] The French unit for solid measure, equal to a cubic meter, or 35.3156 cubic feet.

stereo, ster′ē•ō, *n.* [Gr. *stereos*, solid.] A shortening of stereophonic and stereoscopy.—*a.* Stereophonic (a *stereo* record); stereoscopic.

stereobate, ster′ē•o•bāt, *n.* [Gr. *stereobates*—*stereos*, firm, *bainō*, to go.] *Arch.* a kind of continuous pedestal at the bottom of a wall.

stereochemistry, ster′i•o•kem″ist•ri, *n.* [Gr. *stereos*, solid.] A branch of chemistry which deals with the geometrical arrangement of the atoms of a molecule.—**stereochromy,** ster″i•o•krō′mi, *n.* [Gr. *stereos*, and *chrōma*, color.] A method of wall-painting by which the colors are covered with a varnish of water glass.—**stereochrome,** ster′i•o•krōm, *n.* A stereochromic picture.—**stereochromic,** ster′i•o•krōm″ik, *a.* Pertaining to stereochromy.—**stereogram, stereograph,** ster′i•o•gram, ster′i•o•graf, *n.* [Gr. *stereos*, and *graphō*, to write.] A diagram or picture which represents objects so as to give the impression of relief or solidity; a picture for a stereoscope.—**stereographic, stereographical,** ster′i•o•graf″ik, ster′i•o•graf″i•kal, *a.* Made according to the rules of stereography; delineated on a plane.—*Stereographic projection*, the projection or delineation of the sphere upon the plane of one of its great circles, the eye being at the pole of that circle.—**stereographically,** ster′i•o•graf″i•kal•li, *adv.* In a stereographic manner.—**stereography,** ster•i•og′ra•fi, *n.* The art of delineating solid bodies on a plane.—**stereoisomer,** ster′i•o•ī″so•mer, *n.* [Gr. *stereos*, solid, *isos*, equal, *meros*, a part.] A chemical compound having the same composition as some other compound but with its atoms differently arranged.—**stereometric, stereometrical,** ster′i•o•met″rik, ster′i•o•met″ri•kal, *a.* Pertaining to or performed by stereometry.—**stereometry,** ster•i•om′et•ri, *n.* The art of measuring solid bodies, etc.—**stereophonic,** ster′i•o•fon″ik, *a.* Applied to an acoustical system in which a number of acoustical elements are arranged so as to reproduce the spatial distribution of the original sound for the listener.—**stereopticon,** ster•i•op′ti•kon, *n.* [Gr. *stereos*, firm, *optikos*, optic.] An apparatus in which two magic lanterns are combined.—**stereoscope,** ster′i•o•skōp, *n.* [Gr. *stereos*, and *skopeo*, to view.] An optical instrument which enables us to look upon two pictures taken under a small difference of angular view, each eye looking upon one picture only, so that, as in ordinary vision, two images are conveyed to the brain as one, and the objects thus appear solid and real as in nature.—**stereoscopic, stereoscopical,** ster′i•o•skop″ik, stėr′i•o•skop″i•kal, *a.* Pertaining to the stereoscope; adapted to the stereoscope.—**stereoscopically,** ster′i•o•skop″i•kal•li, *adv.* In a stereoscopic manner; by means of the stereoscope.—**stereoscopist,** ster•i•os′ko•pist, *n.* One versed in the use of the stereoscope.—**stereoscopy,** ster•i•os′ko•pi, *n.* The art of using the stereoscope.—**stereotype,** ster′i•o•tīp, *n.* [Gr. *stereos*, and *typos*, type.] A metal plate, presenting on its upper surface a facsimile of a page of arranged types, being cast in a papier-maché, stucco, or other mold obtained from these types, and being used to print from in the same way, thus saving the types and allowing them to be used afresh at once.—*a.* Relating to the art of stereotyping or printing from stereotypes.—*v.t.*—*stereotyped, stereotyping*. To make a stereotype of; to prepare for printing by means of stereotype plates; *fig.* to fix firmly or unchangeably.—**stereotyped,** ster′i•o•tīpt, *p.* and *a.* Made or printed from stereotype plates; formed in a fixed, unchangeable manner (*stereotyped* opinions).—**stereotyper,** ster′i•o•tīp•ėr, *n.* One who stereotypes.—**stereotypic,** ster′i•o•tip″ik, *a.* Pertaining to stereotype plates.—**stereotypy,** ster′i•o•tī•pi, *n.* The art or business of making stereotype plates.

sterile, ster′il, *a.* [Fr. *stérile*, from L. *sterilis*, barren, unproductive; cog. Gr. *steiros*, barren, *stereos*, stiff; Skr. *stari*, a barren cow; G. *starr*, stiff, rigid; E. to *stare*.] Unfruitful; not fertile; barren; producing no young; not germinating; barren of ideas; destitute of sentiment; *bot.* bearing only stamens; staminate.—**sterility,** ste•ril′i•ti, *n.* [L. *sterilitas*.] The state of being sterile; unfruitfulness; barrenness.—**sterilize,** ster′il•īz, *v.t.*—*sterilized, sterilizing*. To make sterile or barren; to destroy the germs or microbes in.

sterlet, stėr′let, *n.* [Rus. *sterliad*.] A small species of sturgeon.

sterling, stėr′ling, *a.* [Probably from A.Sax. *steorra*, a star, because some early coins of exceptional purity were stamped with a star.] An epithet by which English money is distinguished, signifying that it is of the standard value (a pound *sterling*); hence, genuine; undoubted; of excellent quality (a work of *sterling* merit).

stern, stėrn, *a.* [A.Sax. *sterne, styrne*, stern; same root as to *stare*, and *stark*.] Severe, as regards facial expression; austere of aspect; gloomy; severe of manner; pitiless; harsh; rigidly steadfast; immovable.—**sternly,** stėrn′li, *adv.* In a stern manner; with an austere or stern countenance.—**sternness,** stėrn′nes, *n.* The state or quality of being stern; severity of look; severity or harshness of manner; rigor.

stern, stėrn, *n.* [A.Sax. *steorn*, a helm; akin to *steer*.] The hind part of a ship or boat.—*By the stern, naut.* more deeply laden abaft than forward.—**stern chase,** *n.* A chase in which one vessel follows in the wake of the other.—**stern chaser,** *n.* A cannon placed in a ship's stern, pointing backward.—**sternmost,** stėrn′mōst, *a.* Farthest in the rear; farthest astern.—**sternpost,** *n.* A principal piece of timber in a vessel's stern.—**sternway,** *n.* The movement of a ship stern foremost.—**stern-wheeler,** *n.* A vessel driven by a paddle wheel at the stern.

sternal, stėrn′al, *n.* [L. *sternum*, breastbone.] (1) In vertebrates, relating to the sternum. (2) In arthropods, the under side of the body. Cp. TERGAL. *a.* Pertaining to the sternum.—**sterno-** is used as a prefix to mean connected with the sternum.—**sternum,** stėr′num, *n.* The breastbone.

sternutation, stėr•nū•tā′shon, *n.* [L.

sternutatio, from *sternuto*, freq. of *sternuo*, to sneeze.] The act of sneezing.—**sternutative, sternutatory,** stėr•nū′ta•tiv, stėr•nū′ta•to•ri, *a.* Having the quality of exciting to sneeze. —*n.* A substance that provokes sneezing, as some kind of snuff.

stertorous, stėr′to•rus, *a.* [From L. *sterto*, to snore.] Characterized by a deep snoring, such as frequently accompanies apoplexy (a *stertorous* breathing).

stet, stet. [L., let it stand.] *Printing*, a word written upon proofs to signify that something which has been deleted is after all to remain.

stethometer, ste•thom′et•ėr, *n.* [Gr. *stēthos*, the breast, and *metron*, a measure.] An instrument for measuring the external movement in the chest during respiration.—**stethoscope,** steth′o•skōp, *n.* [Gr. *stethos*, and *skopeō*, to see.] An instrument used by medical men for listening to sounds within the thorax and other cavities of the body.—**stethoscopic, stethoscopical,** steth•o•skop′ik, steth•o•skop′i•kal, *a.* Pertaining to the stethoscope. —**stethoscopically,** steth•o•skop′i•kal•li, *adv.* By means of a stethoscope.—**stethoscopist,** steth′o•skop•ist, *n.* A person versed in the use of the stethoscope.—**stethoscopy,** ste•thos′ko•pi, *n.* The art of stethoscopic examination.

stevedore, stē′ve•dōr, *n.* [Sp. *estivador*, a packer of wool, etc., from *estivar*, to stow; from L. *stipare*, to cram, to stuff.] One whose occupation is to stow goods, packages, etc., in a ship's hold; one who loads or unloads vessels.

stew, stū, *v.t.* [From O.Fr. *estuver* (Fr. *étuver*), to stew, to bathe, from *estuve*, a stove; from O.H.G. *stupa*, a stove, a hot chamber. STOVE.] To boil slowly in a moderate manner or with a simmering heat.—*v.i.* To be boiled in a slow gentle manner, or in heat and moisture.—*n.* A house furnished with warm baths; a bagnio; a brothel; a dish cooked by stewing; a state of agitation or excitement.—**stewpan,** *n.* A pan in which meat and vegetables are stewed.

steward, stū′ėrd, *n.* [O.E. *styward*, A.Sax. *stiweard*—*stige*, a hall, and *weard*, a keeper.] A man employed to manage the affairs of a large estate or establishment; purveyor of provisions for institution, ship, etc.; waiter on ship, etc.; one who has affairs to superintend for another; in hotels and restaurants, one who selects, buys, and superintends the preparation of food or liquors; an officer of state (the lord high *steward* of England, one of the ancient great officers of state); an officer on a vessel who distributes provisions to the officers and crew; in passenger ships, a man who superintends the provisions and liquors, waits at table, etc. —**stewardess,** stū′ėrd•es, *n.* A female steward; a female who serves the passengers on an airplane, train, etc. —**stewardship,** stū′ėrd•ship, *n.* The office or functions of a steward.

sthenic, sthen′ik, *a.* [Gr. *sthenos*, strength.] *Med.* attended with morbid increase of vital energy and action in the heart and arteries.

stibial, stib′i•al, *a.* [L. *stibium*, antimony.] Pertaining to or having the qualities of antimony; antimonial.—**stibnite,** stib′nīt, *n.* An ore of antimony of a lead-gray color, yielding most of the antimony of commerce.

stich, stik, *n.* [Gr. *stichos*, a line, a verse.] A verse, of whatever measure or number of feet; a line of writing.—**stichic,** stik′ik, *a.* Consisting of lines or verses.—**stichometrical,** stik•o•met′ri•kal, *a.* Pertaining to stichometry.—**stichometry,** sti•kom′et•ri, *n.* [Gr. *stichos*, and *metron*, measure.] Measurement of books or writings by the number of lines which each contains.

stick, stik, *n.* [A.Sax. *sticca*, a stick, stake, spike; Icel. *stika*, a stick; closely akin to *stick* (verb), *stake*, *steak*, *stock*.] A piece of wood of indefinite size and shape; a branch of a tree or shrub cut or broken off; a rod or wand; anything shaped like a stick (a *stick* of sealing wax); *printing*, a composing stick.

stick, stik, *v.t.*—pret. and pp. *stuck*. [A.Sax. *stician*, to stab, pierce, adhere; Dan. *stikke*, D. *steken*, to pierce; G. *stecken*, to thrust, to stand fast; from a root *stig*, seen also in L. *stinguo*, to quench (as in *extinguish*), *stimulus* (for *stigmulus*), Gr. *stizō*, to prick, E. *sting*. *Stitch* is a softened form, and *stick*, *n.*, *steak*, *stake*, *stock*, *ticket*, *etiquette*, etc., are akin.] To pierce or stab (*Shak.*); to thrust so as to wound or penetrate; to fasten by piercing (to *stick* a pin); to thrust in; to attach by causing to adhere to the surface; to fix; to set; to fix in; to set with something inserted; to fix on a pointed instrument.—*To stick out*, to project; to thrust out; to be prominent; to refuse to treat or surrender; to hold out (to *stick out* for more favorable terms).—*To stick one's self up*, to put on grand airs.—*v.i.* To cleave to the surface, as by tenacity or attraction; to adhere; to be fixed by being thrust in; to remain where placed; to cling; to be hindered from making progress; to be brought to a stop by some impediment; to scruple; to hesitate; often with *at*.—*To stick by*, to adhere closely to; to be constant to.—*To stick to*, to be persevering in holding to; to abide firmly and faithfully by.—*To stick up*, to have an upright position; to stand on end. —*To stick up for*, to espouse the cause of; to defend.—**sticker,** stik′ėr, *n.* One who sticks (a bill-*sticker*).—**stickiness,** stik′i•nes, *n.* The quality of being sticky; viscousness; glutinousness.—**sticking plaster,** *n.* An adhesive plaster for closing wounds; court plaster.—**sticky,** stik′i, *a.* Having the quality of adhering to a surface; gluey; viscous.

stickle, stik′l, *v.i.*—*stickled*, *stickling*. [Modified by influence of *stick*, from O.E. *stihtle*, *stightle*, to rule, direct, from A.Sax. *stihtan*, to dispose, to govern.] To interpose between combatants and separate them‡; to arbitrate‡; to pertinaciously stick up for something, especially some trifle; to play fast and loose.—*v.t.* To arbitrate between or in‡.—**stickler,** stik′lėr, *n.* One who stickles or pertinaciously insists; an obstinate contender about things of little consequence.

stickleback, stik′l•bak, *n.* [O.E. *stickle*, a prickle, and *back*; from the spines on its back.] The popular name for certain very small fishes found in ponds and streams, and having spines on their backs, remarkable for building nests.

sticky. See STICK, *v.*

stiff, stif, *a.* [A.Sax. *stif*=O.Fris, *stef*, D. *stijf*, L.G. *stief*, G. *steif*; root in *stand*, Skr. *stha*, to stand. STAND.] Not easily bent; not flexible; rigid; not liquid or fluid; thick and tenacious; inspissated; drawn very tight; tense; not supple; not working smoothly or easily (*stiff* joints); not natural and easy; cramped; constrained (a *stiff* style of writing); haughty and unbending; formal in manner; blowing strongly; violent; not easily subdued; obstinate; stubborn; containing a good deal of spirits (a *stiff* glass of grog); *naut.* bearing a press of canvas without careening much.—**stiffen,** stif′n, *v.t.* To make stiff; to make less pliant or flexible.—*v.i.* To become stiff or stiffer; to become more rigid or less flexible; to become less susceptible of impression; to grow more obstinate.—**stiffener,** stif′n•ėr, *n.* One who or that which stiffens; a piece of stiff material inside a neckcloth.—**stiffly,** stif′li, *adv.* In a stiff manner; rigidly; unbendingly; obstinately; unyieldingly; in a constrained manner; formally.—**stiff-necked,** *a.* Stubborn; inflexibly obstinate.—**stiffness,** stif′nes, *n.* The state or quality of being stiff; want of pliableness, suppleness, or flexibility; rigidity; tension; viscidness; spissitude; stubbornness; formality or constraint of manner, expression, or writing.

stifle, stī′fl, *v.t.*—*stifled*, *stifling*. [Icel. *stifla*, to dam up (akin to *stiff*), the sense being influenced by old *stive*, to stuff up, from Fr. *estiver*, L. *stipare*, to cram close.] To kill by impeding respiration; to suffocate or greatly oppress by foul or close air; to smother; to deaden (flame, sound); to suppress or conceal; to repress; to keep from being known. —*v.i.* To suffocate; to perish by suffocation.

stifle, stī′fl, *n.* [Perhaps connected with *stiff*.] The joint of a horse next to the buttock, and corresponding to the knee in man.

stigma, stig′ma, *n.* pl. **stigmas** or **stigmata,** stig′ma•ta. [Gr. *stigma*, a prick with a pointed instrument, from *stizō*, to prick. STING.] A brand impressed with a red-hot iron on slaves and others; any mark of infamy; a brand of disgrace which attaches to a person; a natural mark on the skin; *bot.* the upper extremity of the style, and the part which in impregnation receives the pollen; *entomol.* one of the apertures in the bodies of insects communicating with the air vessels; *pl. stigmata,* marks said to have been supernaturally impressed upon the bodies of certain persons in imitation of the wounds on the crucified body of Christ (the *stigmata* of St. Francis).—**stigmatic, stigmatical,** stig•mat′ik, stig•mat′i•kal, *a.* Marked with a stigma, having the character of a stigma; *bot.* belonging to the stigma.—**stigmatic,** *n.* A person branded or marked with a natural stigma. (*Shak.*).—**stigmatization,** stig′ma•ti•zā″shon, *n.* The impression on the bodies of certain individuals of the marks of Christ's wounds.—**stigmatize,** stig′ma•tīz, *v.t.*—*stigmatized, stigmatizing.* [Fr. *stigmatiser,* Gr. *stigmatizō,* to brand.] To mark with a stigma or brand; to set a mark of disgrace on; to call or characterize by some opprobrious epithet.

stilbite, stil′bīt, *n.* [Gr. *stilbō,* to shine.] A mineral of a shining pearly luster; a kind of zeolite.

stile, stīl, *n.* [See STYLE.] The gnomon on the face of a dial to form the shadow.

stile, stīl, *n.* [A.Sax. *stigel,* a step, a ladder, from *stigan,* to mount, which appears also in *stair, stirrup,* being same as Icel. *stiga,* G. *steigen,* Goth. *steigan,* Skr. *stigh,* to ascend.] A step or series of steps, or a frame of bars and steps, for ascending and descending in getting over a fence.

stiletto, sti•let′tō, *n.* [It., dim. of *stilo,* a dagger, from L. *stilus,* a stile. STYLE.] A small dagger with a round pointed blade about 6 inches long; a pointed instrument for making eyelet holes in cloth, etc.—*v.t.* To stab or pierce with a stiletto.

still, stil, *a.* [A.Sax. *stille,* still, quiet, firm, fixed=D. *stil,* Dan. *stille,* G. *still;* from root of *stand,* seen also in *stall,* G. *stellen,* to place, etc. STAND.] Silent; noiseless; not loud; soft; low (a *still* small voice); quiet or calm; without agitation; motionless; not sparkling or effervescing.—*v.t.* [A.Sax. *stillan.*] To bring to silence; to make quiet; to check or restrain; to appease or allay.—*adv.* To this time; now no less than before; in future no less than formerly; always; time after time; continually; nevertheless; in spite of what has occurred; yet; in an increasing degree; even yet; very common with comparatives (*still* more). —*Still and anon,* at intervals and repeatedly.—**stillbirth,** *n.* State of being stillborn.—**stillborn,** *a.* Dead at the birth; abortive; produced unsuccessfully.—**still life,** *n.* Inanimate objects, such as dead animals, furniture, fruits, etc., represented by the painter's art.—**stillness,** stil′nes, *n.* The state or quality of being still; freedom from noise or motion; calmness; quiet; silence.—**stilly,** stil′i, *a.* Still; quiet.—*adv.* (stil′li). Silently; without noise; calmly; quietly.

still, stil, *n.* [Abbrev. from *distill.*] An apparatus for distilling or separating, by means of heat, volatile matters from substances containing them, and recondensing them into the liquid form; a distillery.—*v.t.* To distill.

stilt, stilt, *n.* [Same as Dan. *stylte,* Sw. *stylta,* L.G. and D. *stelt,* G. *stelze,* a stilt; root probably that of *stand.*] A long piece of wood with a rest for the foot, used in pairs for walking with the feet raised above the ground.—**stilted,** stilt′ed, *p.* and *a.* Elevated as if on stilts; hence, pompous; inflated; stiff and bombastic: said of language.

Stilton, stil′ton, *a.* Applied to a well-known and highly esteemed solid, rich, white cheese, originally made at *Stilton,* Huntingdonshire, England, but now chiefly made in Leicestershire.—*n.* Stilton cheese.

stimulate, stim′ū•lāt, *v.t.*—*stimulated, stimulating.* [L. *stimulo, stimulatum,* to prick, to urge on, from *stimulus,* a goad; root *stig,* as in Gr. *stizō,* to prick; allied to *stick, sting.*] To excite or animate to action by some pungent motive or by persuasion; to spur on; to incite, instigate, rouse; to excite greater vitality or keenness in; *med.* to produce a quickly diffused and transient increase of vital energy and strength of action in.—*v.i.* To act as a stimulus. —**stimulation,** stim•u•lā′shon, *n.* The act of stimulating; the effect produced; *med.* a quickly diffused and transient increase of vital energy. —**stimulative,** stim′ū•lā•tiv, *a.* Having the quality of stimulating.—*n.* That which stimulates.—**stimulant,** stim′ū•lant, *a.* [L. *stimulans, stimulantis,* ppr. of *stimulo.*] Serving to stimulate.—*n.* That which stimulates; a stimulus; *med.* an agent which produces a quickly diffused and transient increase of vital energy in the organism or some part of it; often applied distinctively to some kind of alcoholic liquors.—**stimulator,** stim′ū•lā•tėr, *n.* One that stimulates.—**stimulus,** stim′ū•lus, *n.* pl. **stimuli,** stim′u•lī. [L.] Something that incites to action or exertion; an incitement; a stimulant; *bot.* a sting, as in the nettle.

sting, sting, *v.t.*—pret. and pp. *stung.* [A.Sax. *stingan,* to pierce, to sting= Icel. and Sw. *stinga,* Dan. *stinge,* Goth. *stiggan* (i.e. *stingan*); nasalized forms corresponding to *stick;* akin also to *stink;* same root as in *stimulate.*] To pierce with the sharp-pointed organ with which certain animals and plants are furnished; to poison or goad with a sting; to give acute mental pain (*stung* with remorse or taunts).—*v.i.* To use a sting, as a bee.—*n.* [A.Sax. *sting,* Icel. *stingr.*] A sharp-pointed weapon which certain insects possess, and which they can thrust out from the hinder part of the body; a somewhat similar appendage of other animals, as scorpions; the thrust of a sting into the flesh; anything that gives acute pain; the biting, sarcastic, or cutting effect of words; the point, as in an epigram; that which gives acute mental pain; an impulse; a stimulus; *bot.* a hair which secretes a poisonous fluid, which, when introduced under the skin of animals, produces pain.—**stinger,** sting′ėr, *n.* One who or that which stings.—**stingingly,** sting′ing•li, *adv.* With stinging.—**sting ray,** *n.* A fish allied to the rays having a sharp bony spine on its tail.—**stingy,** sting′i, *a.* Having power to sting; stinging.

stingo, sting′gō, *n.* [Probably from *sting,* alluding to the sharpness of the taste.] Pungent or strong ale; rare good liquor. (*Colloq.*)

stingy, stin′ji, *a.* [Probably from *sting;* comp. *spring, springe; swing, swinge.*] Extremely close-fisted and covetous; meanly avaricious; niggardly; scanty.—**stingily,** stin′ji•li, *adv.* In a stingy or niggardly manner; meanly; shabbily.—**stinginess,** stin′ji•nes, *n.* The quality of being stingy; mean; covetousness; niggardliness.

stink, stingk, *v.i.*—pret. and pp. *stank, stunk.* [A.Sax. *stincan*=D. and G. *stinken,* Dan. *stinke,* to stink; closely allied to *sting, stick. Stench* is a derivative form.] To emit a strong offensive smell; hence, *fig.* to be in bad odor; to have a bad reputation.—*v.t.* To annoy with an offensive smell. —*n.* A strong offensive smell; a stench.—**stinkard,** stingk′ärd, *n.* A mean, paltry fellow.—**stinkpot,** *n.* An earthen pot filled with a stinking combustible mixture, formerly used in attacking an enemy's vessel at sea.

stint, stint, *v.t.* [A.Sax. *styntan,* to blunt or dull, from *stunt,* dull, stupid; akin Sw. *stunta,* Icel. *stytta,* to shorten. STUNT.] To restrict to a scanty allowance; to limit or make scanty.—*v.i.* To cease; to stop; to desist.—*n.* Limit or restraint set or observed; restriction as to quantity (to give money without *stint*).—**stinter,** stin′tėr, *n.* One who stints.

stipe, stipes, stīp, stī′pēz, *n.* [L. *stipes,* a stock, a trunk.] *Bot.* the petiole of the fronds of ferns; the stem of tree ferns; the stem of certain fungi.—**stipel,** stī′pel, *n. Bot.* a secondary stipule at the base of leaflets.—**stipiform,** stī′pi•form, *n. Bot.* having the appearance of an endogenous trunk.—**stipitate,** stī′pi•tāt, *a. Bot.* elevated on a stipe.

stipend, stī′pend, *n.* [L. *stipendium*—*stips,* a donation, and *pendo,* to weigh out.] Any periodical payment or compensation for services rendered; salary.—**stipendiary,** stī•pen′di•e•ri, *a.* [L. *stipendiarius.*] Receiving wages or salary; performing services for a stated compensation.—*n.* One who performs services for a settled salary or stipend.

stipes, stipitate. See STIPE.

stipple, stip′l, *v.t.*—*stippled, stippling.* [From D. *stippelen,* dim. of *stippen,* to make dots or points, from *stip,* a dot, a point; akin *stab.*] To engrave by means of dots, in distinction from engraving in lines.—*n.* Engraving by means of dots.

stipulate, stip′ū•lāt, *v.i.*—*stipulated, stipulating.* [L. *stipulor, stipulatus,* to stipulate, from *stipulus,* firm; akin *stipes,* a tree trunk; same root as *step, stand.*] To make an agreement or covenant to do or forbear anything; to contract; to settle terms; to bargain.—**stipulated,** stip′ū•lā•ted, *p.*

and *a.* Agreed on; covenanted.—**stipulation,** stip•ū•lā′shon, *n.* [L. *stipulatio, stipulationis.*] The act of stipulating; a contracting or bargaining; a point or matter settled by agreement; a particular article or item in a contract.—**stipulator,** stip′-ū•lā•tėr, *n.* One who stipulates.

stipule, stip′ūl, *n.* [L. *stipula*, a stalk, a straw, dim. of *stipes*, a trunk. STIPULATE.] *Bot.* a small leaf-like appendage to a leaf commonly situated at the base of the petiole in pairs, either adhering to it or standing separate.—**stipular,** stip′ū•lėr, *a. Bot.* belonging to, or standing in the place of stipules.—**stipulate,** stip′ū•lāt, *a. Bot.* having stipules.

stir, stėr, *v.t.*—*stirred, stirring.* [A. Sax. *styrian, stirian*, to stir, to move; allied to D. *storen*, Sw. *stora.* G. *stören*, to disturb; same root as *start, storm.*] To move or make to change place in any manner; to agitate the particles of; to bring into debate; to moot; to incite to action; to instigate; to excite; to awaken; to rouse, as from sleep.—*To stir up*, to incite; to instigate by inflaming passions; to excite; to give origin to (a mutiny, strife).—*v.i.* To move one's self; to change place; to be in motion; not to be still; to be on foot; to be already out of bed.—*n.* Agitation; tumult; bustle; public disturbance or commotion; excitement.—**stirrer,** stėr•ėr, *n.* One who stirs or is in motion; one who or that which puts in motion; an inciter or exciter; an instigator.—*Stirrer up*, an exciter; an instigator.—**stirring,** stėr′ing, *p.* and *a.* Active in business; bustling; animating; rousing; exciting.

stirk, stėrk, *n.* [A.Sax. *styrc, styric*, a dim. from *steor*, a steer.] A bullock or heifer between one and two years old.

stirrup, stir′up, *n.* [A.Sax. *stigráp, stiráp*, a stirrup, from *stigan*, to mount (O.E. *steye, stye*), and *ráp*, a rope; Icel. *stigreip.* STAIR, ROPE.] A strap hanging from a saddle, and having at its lower end a suitable appliance for receiving the foot of the rider, used to assist persons in mounting a horse; hence, anything resembling in shape and functions the stirrup of a saddle.—**stirrup cup,** *n.* A cup of liquor presented to a rider on having mounted his horse at parting.—**stirrup leather,** *n.* The leather portion of a stirrup.—**stirrup strap,** *n.* A stirrup leather.

stitch, stich, *v.t.* [Softened form of *stick*, Sc. *steke*, A.Sax. *stician*, to pierce; comp. G. *sticken*, to embroider, to stitch.] To sew; to sew by passing the needle through and through in a continuous line; to unite together by sewing.—*To stitch up*, to sew or unite with a needle and thread.—*v.i.* To practice stitching; to practice needlework.—*n.* A single pass of a needle in sewing; a single turn of the thread round a needle in knitting; *agri.* a furrow or ridge; a sharp pain in the side.—**stitcher,** stich′ėr, *n.* One that stitches.

stithy, stiTH′i, *n.* [Also *stiddy*, Sc. *studdy*, from Icel. *stethi*, an anvil; same root as *steady, stead.*] An anvil.

stiver, stī′vėr, *n.* [D. *stuiver*, Dan. *styver.*] An old Dutch coin and money of account, worth about two cents; used often as typical of insignificant value.

stoa, stō′a, *n.* [Gr., a porch.] *Greek arch.* a porch or portico.

stoat, stōt, *n.* [Armor. *stot, staot*, urine of animals, from the fetid fluid secreted by the anal glands.] The ermine.

stoccado, stoccata, stok•kä′dō, stok•-kä′ta, *n.* [Sp. *estocada*, It. *stoccata*, from Sp. *estoque*, It. *stocco*, a rapier, from G. *stock*, a stick. STOCK.] A stab; a thrust with a rapier.

stock, stok, *n.* [A.Sax. *stoc, stocc*, a stem, stick, block=D. and Dan. *stok*, Icel. *stokkr*, G. *stock*, stick, stock, block, etc., in the plural *stocks* (of a vessel); the root is that of *stick*, *v.* and *n.*, the primary notion being that which is stuck in and remains fast.] The stem or trunk of a tree or other plant; the stem in which a graft is inserted, or that furnishes grafts; a block; hence, what is lifeless and senseless (*stocks* and stones); a principal supporting or holding part in certain implements or tools; the wooden support to which the barrel, etc., of a rifle or like firearm is attached; the bar or crosspiece at the upper end of the shank of an anchor; the original race or line of a family; the progenitors and their direct descendants; lineage; family; the property which a merchant, tradesman, or company has invested in any business; capital invested in some commercial business or enterprise and contributed by individuals jointly; supply provided; store, provision, hoard; *agri.* the collective animals used or reared on a farm, or such animals collectively (prices of *stock* are low); a kind of stiff band or cravat worn round the neck; liquor in which meat, bones, vegetables, etc., have been boiled, used to form a foundation for soups and gravies; a cruciferous garden plant of various species, with a very sweet smell; *pl.* an instrument of punishment formerly used for petty offenders, consisting of a wooden frame in which their ankles or wrists were confined; *pl.* the frame of timbers on which a ship is supported while building.—*Stock in trade*, the goods kept for sale by a shopkeeper.—*To take stock*, to make an inventory of stock or goods on hand; hence, *to take stock of*, to make an estimate of or set a value on generally; to observe particularly for the purpose of forming an opinion.—*v.t.* To lay up in store; to put aside or accumulate for future use; to provide or furnish with stock; to supply with stock (to *stock* a farm, a warehouse).—*a.* Kept in stock; constantly ready for service; standing; permanent (a *stock* play, a *stock* jest).—**stockbroker,** stok′brō•kėr, *n.* A broker who purchases and sells stocks or shares for his customers.—**stock car,** *n.* A railroad car that carries livestock; a racing car that has an assembly-line chassis.—**stock company,** *n.* A corporation or company whose capital is represented in stock; a company of actors connected with a repertory theater.—**stock exchange,** *n.* The building, place, or mart where stocks or shares are bought and sold; an organized association of brokers or dealers in stocks.—**stock farmer,** *n.* A farmer who largely breeds livestock.—**stockholder,** stok′hōl•dėr, *n.* One who is the recorded owner of shares of stock in a corporation.—**stock market,** *n.* A market where stocks and bonds are bought and sold.—**stockpile,** stok′-pīl, *n.* A supply of material set aside for future use.—*v.t. stockpiled, stockpiling.* To store in a stockpile.—**stocky,** stok′i, *a.* Compact and sturdy in build.—**stockyard,** stok′yärd, *n.* A yard where livestock are kept for subsequent slaughter and shipping.

stockade, stok•ād′, *n.* [From *stock*, a stem or stake.] *Fort.* a fence or barrier constructed by planting upright in the ground trunks of trees or rough piles of timber; an enclosure made with posts.—*v.t.*—*stockaded, stockading.* To surround or fortify with sharpened posts fixed in the ground.

stocking, stok′ing, *n.* [Formerly called *stocks* or *nether stocks*, as distinguished from the *upper stocks* or knee breeches, *stock* here having the sense of stump or trunk, part of a body left when the limbs are cut off.] A close-fitting covering for the foot and leg, now usually knitted from woolen, cotton, nylon, or silk thread.

stodge, stoj, *v.t.* [Akin to *stock, stick, stoke.*] To stuff or cram.—**stodgy,** *a.* Crude; indigestible.

stoechiology, stē•ki•ol′o•ji, *n.* See STOICHIOLOGY.

Stoic, stō′ik, *n.* [Gr. *Stōikos*, from *Stōa, Stoa*, a porch in Athens where the philosopher Zeno taught.] A disciple of the philosopher Zeno, who founded a sect about 308 B.C., teaching that men should strive to be free from passion, unmoved by joy or grief, and submit without complaint to the unavoidable necessity by which all things are governed, regarding virtue as the highest good; hence, an apathetic person, or one who is indifferent to pleasure or pain.—*a.* Pertaining to the Stoics or their teaching.—**stoical,** stō′i•kal, *a.* Pertaining to the Stoics; able completely to repress feeling; manifesting or maintaining indifference to pleasure or pain.—**stoically,** stō′i•kal•li, *adv.* In the manner of a Stoic; without apparent feeling; with indifference to pain.—**stoicalness,** stō′-i•kal•nes, *n.*—**stoicism,** stō′i•sizm, *n.* The opinions and maxims of the Stoics; indifference to pleasure or pain; uncomplaining endurance; insensibility. [When referring to the philosophical sect these words should have a capital letter.]

stoichiology, stoi•ki•ol′o•ji, *n.* [Gr. *stoicheion*, an element or first principle, *logos*, discourse.] The science or doctrine of elements or first principles.—**stoichiometry,** stoi•ki•-om′et•ri, *n.* [Gr. *stoicheion*, an element.] A branch of chemistry which deals with atomic and molecular weights, or, more generally, with the relations of physical properties to composition.

stoke, stōk, *v.t.—stoked, stoking.* [Same as D. *stoken, stooken,* to poke or kindle a fire, from *stok,* a stick; akin to *stick, stock.*] To supply a fire with fuel, and attend to its combustion.—*v.i.* To act as a stoker.—**stokehole,** *n.* The mouth to the grate of a furnace.

stola, stō′la, *n.* pl. **stolae,** stō′lē. [L., from Gr. *stolē,* equipment, a stola, from *stellō,* to array.] A long garment worn by Roman matrons over the tunic, fastened round the body by a girdle.—**stole,** stōl, *n.* [O.Fr. *estole,* L. *stola.*] Originally, a garment resembling the stola; now a long narrow ornamental band or scarf with fringed ends, worn by ecclesiastics of the Roman and English churches, with the ends pendent in front to the knees.—*Groom of the stole,* the first lord of the bedchamber in the household of the English kings.

stole, stōl, pret. of *steal.*

stolen, stō′ln, pp. of *steal.*

stolid, stol′id, *a.* [L. *stolidus,* dull, doltish; akin to *stultus,* foolish; probably from root of L. *sto,* E. *stand.*] Slow in intellect; dull; heavy; stupid.—**stolidity, stolidness,** sto•lid′i•ti, stol′id•nes, *n.* The state or quality of being stolid; dullness; stupidity.

stolon, stō′lon, *n.* [L. *stolo, stolonis,* a sucker.] *Bot.* a sucker; a sucker taking root at intervals.—**stoloniferous,** stō•lon•if′ėr•us, *a.* Producing suckers.

stoma, stō′ma, *n.* pl. **stomata,** stō′ma•ta. [Gr. *stoma,* the mouth.] *Bot.* a minute orifice or pore in leaves, etc., through which exhalation takes place; *zool.* a breathing-pore of insects.—**stomatous,** stom′a•tus, *a.* Having stomata.

stomach, stum′ak, *n.* [L. *stomachus,* the gullet, the stomach, from Gr. *stomachos,* the gullet, from *stoma,* a mouth.] A membranous receptacle, the principal organ of digestion in man and some animals; in which food is prepared for yielding its nourishment to the body; a specialized cavity for the digestion of food in some of the simpler forms of animals; the desire of food caused by hunger; appetite; inclination; liking.—*v.t.* To bear without open resentment or without opposition; to brook (to *stomach* an affront).—**stomacher,** stum′ak•ėr, *n.* An ornamental covering for the breast, forming part of a lady's dress.—**stomachic,** sto•mak′ik, *a.* Pertaining to the stomach; strengthening the stomach; exciting the action of the stomach.—*n.* A medicine that strengthens the stomach and excites its action.

stomata. See STOMA.

stomatic, sto•mat′ik, *n.* [Gr. *stoma,* the mouth.] A medicine for diseases of the mouth.—*a.* Pertaining to a stoma or to stomata.—**stomatitis,** stom•a•tī′tis, *n. Pathol.* inflammation of the mouth.

stone, stōn, *n.* [A.Sax. *stán,* a stone, a rock = D. *steen,* Dan. and Sw. *sten,* Icel. *steinn,* G. *stein,* Goth. *stains,* stone; cog. Slav. *stjena,* Gr. *stia, stion,* a pebble. Probably from root *sta,* seen in *stand.*] A hard concretion of some species of earth or mineral matter, as lime, silex, clay, and the like—a *stone,* as distinguished from a *rock,* being usually a mass of no great size, and generally movable, whereas a *rock* is a solid and immovable portion of the earth's crust; the material obtained from stones or rocks; the kind of substance they produce (a house built of *stone*); *fig.* a type of hardness or insensibility (a heart of *stone*); a calculous concretion in the kidneys or bladder; the disease arising from such; a testicle; the nut of a drupe or stone fruit; a common measure of weight, the English standard stone being 14 lb. avoirdupois, though other values are in regular use; *printing,* the imposing stone.—*Meteoric stone.* See METEOR.—*Philosopher's stone.* See PHILOSOPHER.—*To leave no stone unturned,* to do everything that can be done; to spare no exertions.—*a.* Made of stone; like stone; pertaining to stone.—*v.t.—stoned, stoning.* To pelt with stones; to free from stones (to *stone* raisins).—**stoneblind,** *a.* Blind as a stone; perfectly blind.—**stonebroke,** *a. Colloq.* completely destitute of funds.—**stonechat,** *n.* An insessorial bird of the family of warblers, common in Europe, and often seen about heaps of stone in waste places.—**stonecrop,** *n.* [A.Sax. *stan-crop, crop* meaning cluster.] A name of a genus of plants that grow on rocks.—**stonecutter,** *n.* One whose occupation is to hew or cut stones for building, ornamental, or other purposes.—**stonecutting,** *n.* The business of a stonecutter.—**stone-deaf,** *a.* Deaf as a stone; totally deaf.—**stone fruit,** *n.* Fruit whose seeds are covered with a hard shell enveloped in the pulp, as peaches, cherries, plums, etc.; a drupe.—**stone lily,** *n.* A fossil encrinite.—**stonemason,** *n.* One who dresses stones for building, or builds with them.—**stoner,** stō′nėr, *n.* One who stones.—**stone wall,** *n.* A wall built of stones.—**stoneware,** *n.* A common species of glazed potter's ware made from a composition of clay and flint.—**stonework,** *n.* Work consisting of stone; mason's work of stone.—**stonily,** stō′ni•li, *adv.* In a stony manner.—**stoniness,** stō′ni•nes, *n.* The quality of being stony.—**stony,** stō′ni, *a.* Pertaining to, abounding in, or resembling stone; pitiless; obdurate; with rigid features.—**stonyhearted,** *a.* Hardhearted.

stood, stud, pret. and pp. of *stand.*

stook, stuk, *n.* [L.G. *stuke,* G. *stauch,* a heap of turf, flax, etc.] A shock of corn, consisting, when of full size, of twelve sheaves.—*v.t.* To set up in stooks.

stool, stöl, *n.* [A.Sax. *stól,* a seat = D. *stoel,* Sw. and Dan. *stol,* Icel. *stóll,* G. *stuhl,* Goth. *stolls*; cog. Slav. *stul,* *stol*; root in *stand, stall, still,* etc.] A seat without a back and with three or four legs, intended as a seat for one person; the seat used in evacuating the bowels; hence, an evacuation; a discharge from the bowels; the stump of a timber tree which throws up shoots; the cluster of shoots thus produced.—*Stool of repentance,* in Scotland, an elevated seat in the church on which persons in former times were made to sit during divine service as a punishment for fornication and adultery.

stoop, stöp, *v.t.* [A.Sax. *stúpian,* to stoop = O.D. *stoepen, stuipen,* Icel. *stúpa,* to stoop; Dan. *stupe,* to fall; Sw. *stupa,* to incline; akin *steep.*] To bend down the head and upper half of the body; to have the back bowed or bent and the head forward; to yield or submit; to condescend; to lower one's self; to dart down on prey, as a hawk; to pounce; to sink when on the wing.—*v.t.* To bend or bow downward and forward; to bow down; to bend forward (to *stoop* a cask of liquor).—*n.* The act of stooping; a habitual bend of the back or shoulders; a condescension; fall of a bird on his prey; swoop.—**stooper,** stöp′ėr, *n.* One who stoops.

stoop, stöp, *n.* [D. *stoep* (pron. *stoop*); the word was brought to America by the Dutch.] The steps at the entrance of a house; also, a porch with seats.

stop, stop, *v.t.—stopped, stopping.* [A.Sax. *stoppian,* to stop up; D. and L.G. *stoppen,* Dan. *stoppe,* Sw. and Icel. *stoppa,* to stop up; from L.L. *stuppo, stuppare,* to stop with tow, from L. *stuppa,* tow.] To close up by filling, stuffing, or otherwise; to fill up a cavity or cavities in (to *stop* a vent, the ears) to stanch or prevent from bleeding; to obstruct or render impassable (to *stop* a road or passage); to check, stay, arrest, impede, keep back, in a variety of usages; to regulate the sounds of with the fingers or otherwise (to *stop* a string); to retain or refuse to pay for some reason (to *stop* one's wages, an allowance of liquor).—*v.i.* To cease to go forward; to come to a standstill; to cease from any motion, habit, practice, or course of action; to check one's self; to stay; to reside temporarily.—*n.* A cessation of progressive motion; a hindrance of progress or action; interruption; pause; that which hinders or obstructs; obstacle, impediment, hindrance; one of the ventholes of a wind instrument; a collection or series of pipes in an organ giving sounds of a distinctive tone and quality; a point or mark in writing, intended to distinguish the sentences, part of a sentence, or clauses.—**stopcock,** *n.* A cock or faucet used to turn off or regulate the supply of water, gas, etc.—**stopgap,** *n.* That which fills up a gap; a temporary expedient.—**stoppage,** stop′ij, *n.* The act of stopping; arrest of progress or motion; a halt; a deduction made from pay or allowances.—**stopper,** stop′ėr, *n.* One who or that which stops; that which closes a vent or hole.—*v.t.* To close or secure with a stopper.—**stop watch,** *n.* A watch used in horseracing, etc., in which one of the hands can be stopped at once so as to mark with accuracy the time occupied.

stope, stōp, *n.* An excavation for the extraction of ore, the ore being cut so as to form a sort of staircase.

stopple, stop′l, *n.* [Dim. of *stop*: same as L.G. *stöppel*, G. *stöpfel*, *stöpsel*, a stopple.] That which stops or closes the mouth of a vessel; a stopper.—*v.t.*—*stoppled, stoppling*. To close with a stopple.

storax, stō′raks, *n.* [L. *storax*, *styrax*, from Gr. *styrax*, storax.] A resinous and odoriferous balsam formerly much employed in medicine, now used in perfumes.

store, stōr, *n.* [O.Fr. *estore*, store, provisions, from *estorer*, to erect, store, from the L. verb *stauro*, seen in *instauro*, to erect, *restauro*, to restore, from root of *sto*, *stare*, E. to *stand*.] A quantity collected, hoarded, or massed together; a supply; stock, hoard; specifically, *pl.* supplies, as of provisions, ammunition, arms, clothing, and the like, for an army, a ship, etc.; a great quantity or a large number; abundance; a storehouse or warehouse; a place where goods are kept for sale either by wholesale or retail, as a department *store*, a book *store*, etc., a shop.—*In store*, in stock; on hand; ready to be produced.—*To set store by*, to set a great value on; to appreciate highly.—*a.* Kept in store; containing stores; obtained at a store, as *store* clothes purchased readymade, as distinguished from clothes homemade or made to order.—*v.t.*—*stored, storing*. To collect or lay up in stock; to stock; to furnish or supply; to replenish (to *store* the mind with knowledge); to deposit in a warehouse.—**storage,** stō′rij, *n.* The act of storing; the act of depositing in a warehouse; a price for keeping goods in storage.—**storage battery,** *n.* A group of electric cells which can be charged again and again by sending currents through them.—**storehouse,** stōr′hous, *n.* A house in which things are stored; a magazine; a repository; a warehouse.—**storekeeper,** *n.* One who has the care of stores or of a store or warehouse.—**storer,** stō′rėr, *n.* One who lays up or forms a store.—**storeroom,** *n.* A room for the reception of stores.

stork, stork, *n.* [A.Sax. *storc*=D., Dan., and Sw. *stork*, Icel. *storkr*, G. *storch*, stork; root meaning doubtful.] A genus of tall wading birds resembling the herons, found in the vicinity of marshes and rivers, where they feed on frogs, lizards, fishes, etc.

storm, storm, *n.* [A.Sax. D., L.G., Dan., Sw., Icel. *storm*, G. *sturm*, storm, tempest, tumult; same root as in *stir*, *strew*.] A violent commotion of the atmosphere, producing or accompanied by wind, rain, snow, hail, or thunder and lightning; a tempest; a heavy fall of rain or snow; a violent disturbance in human society; a civil, political, or domestic commotion; a tumult; *milit.* a violent assault on a fortified place or strong position.—*Magnetic storm*, a violent and unusual disturbance of the magnetism of the earth over a wide area.—*v.t. Milit.* to take by storm; to assault (to *storm* a fortified town).—*v.i.* To be a storm: used impersonally (it *storms*); to be in a violent agitation or passion; to fume.—**storminess,** stor′mi•nes, *n.* The state of being stormy; tempestuousness.—**storm window,** *n.* An outer window to protect the inner from the weather.—**stormy,** stor′mi, *a.* Characterized by storm or tempest; tempestuous; boisterous; characterized by violence of feeling; passionate; angry.—*Stormy petrel.* See PETREL.

Storting, stor′ting, *n.* [Dan. *stor*, great, and *thing*, court.] The parliament or supreme legislative assembly of Norway.

story, stō′ri, *n.* [A short form of *history* (which see).] A narrative; an account of past events or transactions; history; an account of an incident or event; a short narrative about a matter or a person; a fictitious narrative less elaborate than a novel; a tale; a short romance; a lie; a falsehood (*euphemistic and colloq.*).—**storied,** stō′rid, *a.* Adorned with historical paintings or designs; referred to or celebrated in story or history; having stories, tales, or legends associated with it.—**storyteller,** *n.* One who tells stories, true or fictitious; a writer of stories; a euphemism for a liar.—**storytelling,** *n.* The act of relating stories; lying.

story, stō′ri, *n.* [From O.Fr. *estorer*, to build. STORE.] A stage or floor of a building; a set of rooms on the same floor or level.

stoup, stöp, *n.* [Same as Icel. *staup*, G. *stauf*, a pot, vessel, cup. See STOOP.] A basin for holy water placed in a niche at the entrance of Roman Catholic churches; a deep narrow vessel for holding liquids; a flagon.

stout, stout, *a.* [From O.Fr. *estout*, from D. *stout*, L.G. *stolt*, G. *stolz*, bold, haughty; perhaps from same root as *stilt*.] Strong; vigorous; robust; bold; intrepid; firmly or strongly built; having strength; rather corpulent; bulky or thickset in body (*colloq.*)—The strongest kind of porter.—**stouthearted,** *a.* Having a stout or brave heart.—**stoutly,** stout′li, *adv.* In a stout manner; boldly; strongly.—**stoutness,** stout′nes, *n.* The quality of being stout; sturdiness; corpulence; bodily bulk.

stove, stōv, *n.* [A.Sax. *stofe*, a stove; Icel. *stofa*, *stufa*, a bathing room with a stove; D. *stoof*, a stove; G. *stube*, a room; akin *stew*.] An apparatus to contain a fire for warming a room or house, or for cooking or other purposes, usually consisting of an enclosure of metal, brick, or earthenware; a house or room artificially heated to a high temperature, and used for drying and other purposes; *hort.* a hothouse in which artificial heat is maintained at a constantly high temperature.—*v.t.*—*stoved, stoving*. To heat, as in a stove.

stove, stōv, pret. of *stave*.

stow, stō, *v.t.* [Lit. to put into its place, from A.Sax. *stow*, a place; comp. D. *stouwen*, Dan. *stuve*, to stow, to pack.] To put away in a suitable place; to lay up; to pack; to compactly arrange anything in; to fill by packing closely.—**stowage,** stō′ij, *n.* The act of stowing; room for things to be stowed; money paid for stowing goods.—**stowaway,** stō′a•wā, *n.* One who attempts to obtain a free passage by concealing himself aboard a ship.

strabismus, stra•biz′mus, *n.* [Gr. *strabismos*, from *strabizō*, to squint, from *strabos*, squinting.] A defect in a person's eyes, rendering them incapable of looking exactly in the same direction, certain muscles not being of normal length; squinting.

strabotomy, stra•bot′o•mi, *n.* [Gr. *strabos*, squinting, *tome*, cutting.] A surgical operation to remedy squinting (*Strabismus*).

straddle, strad′l, *v.i.*—*straddle, straddling*. [For *stridle*, from *stride*.] To part the legs wide; to stand or walk with the legs far apart; to sit astride.—*v.t.* To stride over; to stand or sit astride of.—*n.* A standing or sitting with the legs far apart.

strafe, strāf, *v.t.* [From German slogan in World War I, *Gott strafe England*, God punish England.] To attack with a machine-gun from a low-flying aircraft.

straggle, strag′l, *v.i.*—*straggled, straggling*. [Freq. from O.E. *strake*, to wander, to stray, A.Sax. *strican*, to go. STRIKE.] To wander from the direct course or way; to scatter in marching; to rove; to shoot too far in growth; to grow with long irregular branches; to occur at intervals or apart from one another; to occur here and there.—**straggler,** strag′lėr, *n.* One who straggles, one who wanders from or is left behind by his fellows; something that stands apart from others.

straight, strāt, *a.* [The pp. of O.E. *strecche*, *streke*. A.Sax. *streccan*, to stretch (STRETCH); distinct from *strait*.] Passing from one point to another by the nearest course; not curved, bent, or crooked; direct (a *straight* line), according with justice and rectitude; not deviating from truth or fairness; upright.—*adv.* Immediately; directly; in the shortest time; in a straight line.—*n.* Straight part; straight direction.—**straight angle,** *n.* An angle of 180°.—**straightaway,** strāt′a•wā, *n.* A straight part of a course.—*adv.* Immediately.—**straightedge,** strāt′edj, *n.* A piece of material, as metal or wood, with straight edges for drawing straight lines or testing straight lines and surfaces.—**straighten,** strāt′en, *v.t.* and *i.* To make or become straight or straighter.—**straightener,** strā′tn•ėr, *n.*—**straightforward,** strāt′for•-

wėrd, *a.* Proceeding in a straight course; not deviating; upright; honest; open.—**straightforwardly,** strāt′-for•wėrd•li, *adv.*—**straightly,** strāt′li, *adv.*—**straightness,** strāt′nes, *n.*

strain, strān, *v.t.* [From O.Fr. *estrainare, estreindre, streindre,* to strain, wring, etc. (Fr. *étreindre*), from L. *stringo, stringere,* to strain, to draw tight, pp. *strictus, Strict, strait, stringent* are from same verb; so *constrain, restrain, restrict, constriction,* etc.] To stretch or draw tightly; to make tighter; to squeeze or clasp in an embrace; to injure or weaken by stretching or overtasking; to subject to too great stress or exertion; to harm by a twist or wrench; hence, to sprain; to exert to the utmost; to push to the utmost strength or exertion; *fig.* to push beyond the due limit; to carry too far; to do violence to (to *strain* the meaning of a text); to squeeze out; to purify by filtration; to filter.—*To strain a point,* to make a special and often inconvenient effort; to exceed one's duty; to overstep one's commission.—*v.i.* To exert one's self; to make violent efforts; to filter or be filtered; to percolate.—*n.* A violent effort; an excessive exertion of the limbs or muscles, or of the mind; an injurious stretching of the muscles or tendons; a continued course of action; general bearing; a poem; a song; a lay; a tune; a melody or part of a melody; especially, a section of a melody ending with a cadence; the subject or theme of a poem, discourse, etc.; tenor of discourse; *mech.* a definite alteration of form or dimensions experienced by a solid under the action of a stress; sometimes, in older usage, stress or force.—**strainer,** strā′nėr, *n.* One who strains; an instrument for filtration.

strain, strān, *n.* [O.E. *strene, streen, stren,* A.Sax. *strýnd,* stock, race, from *strýnan, streónan,* to produce.] Race; stock in a genealogical sense; family blood; quality or line in regard to breeding; natural disposition; turn; tendency.

strait, strāt, *a.* [From O.F. *estreit, estroit,* (Fr. *étroit*), narrow, from L. *strictus,* pp. of *stringo,* to draw tight. STRAIN, *v.t.*] Strict or rigorous‡; narrow; not wide.—*n.* A narrow pass or passage; a narrow passage of water between two seas or oceans (the plural is often used of one; the *Strait* or *Straits* of Gibraltar); distress; difficulty; distressing necessity.—**straiten,** strā′tn, *v.t.* To make strait; to contract, confine, hem in, narrow; to make tense or tight; to distress; to press with poverty or other necessity; to put in pecuniary difficulties: used especially in pp.—**straitlaced,** Having the stays or bodice tightly laced; constrained; strict in manners or morals; often excessively and puritanically strict.—**straitly,** strāt′li, *adv.* In a strait manner.—**straitness,** strāt′nes, *n.* The state or quality of being strait; narrowness; strictness.—**straitjacket,** *n.* A garment made of some strong material, with long sleeves, which are tied behind the body, used to restrain lunatics.

strake, strāk, *n.* [A form of *streak.*] A continuous line of planking or plates on a ship's side, reaching from stem to stern.

stramineous, stra•min′i•us, *a.* [L. *stramineus,* from *stramen,* straw.] Strawy; consisting of straw; like straw.

stramonium, stra•mō′ni•um, *n.* The thorn apple (*Datura Stramonium*), and a drug obtained from it similar to belladonna.

strand, strand, *n.* [A.Sax., D., Dan., Sw., and G. *strand,* Icel. *strōnd,* strand, shore, coast; root meaning is "edge".] A shore or beach of the sea or lake.—*v.i.* To drift or be driven on shore; to run aground; to have progress interrupted; to come to a standstill.—*v.t.* To drive or run aground on the seashore.

strand, strand, *n.* [Same as D. *streen,* G. *strähne,* a skein, a strand.] One of the twists or parts of which a rope is composed.

strange, strānj, *a.* [O.Fr. *estrange* (Fr. *étrange*), from L. *extraneus,* that is without, from *extra,* on the outside—*ex,* out, and affix *-tra* (as in *contra*). EXTERIOR.] Foreign; belonging to another country, not one's own; belonging to others; not before known, heard, or seen; new; wonderful; causing surprise; extraordinary; odd; unusual; not according to the common way; estranged; not familiar; unacquainted; not knowing.—*Strange sail* (*naut.*), an unknown vessel.—**strangely,** strānj′li, *adv.* In a strange manner; surprisingly; wonderfully; remarkably; in a distant and reserved manner.—**strangeness,** strānj′nes, *n.* The state or character of being strange.—**stranger,** strān′jėr, *n.* [O.F. *estranger.*] A foreigner; one of another place; one unknown or at least not familiar; one not knowing; one ignorant or unacquainted (a *stranger* to the affair); a guest; a visitor; one not admitted to fellowship.

strangle, strang′gl, *v.t.*—*strangled, strangling,* [O.Fr. *estrangler,* L. *strangulare,* to strangle, from Gr. *stranggalaō, stranggaloō,* to knot, *stranggō,* to tie tight; same root as E. *string.*] To destroy the life of by compressing the windpipe; to choke. *fig.* to suppress or stifle.—**strangler,** strang′glėr, *n.* One who or that which strangles.—**strangles,** strang′-glz, *n.pl.* A disorder which attacks horses, consisting of an abscess between the branches of the lower jaw.—**strangulation,** strang•gū•lā′-shon, *n.* [L. *strangulatio.*] The act of strangling; the state of being strangled; *med.* the state of a part too closely constricted, as the intestine in hernia.

strangury, strang′gū•ri, *n.* [L. *stranguria,* Gr. *strangouria*—*stranx, strangos,* a drop, and *ouron,* urine.] A disease in which there is pain in passing the urine, which is given out by drops.

strap, strap, *n.* [A collateral form of *strop,* from root of *stripe, strip*; or from L. *struppus,* a thong.] A long narrow slip of leather or other substance of various forms and for various uses, and often provided with a buckle; a plate, band, or strip of metal to connect or hold other parts together; a piece of leather for sharpening razors, etc.; in this sense often written *strop.*—*v.t.*—*strapped, strapping.* To chastise with a strap; to fasten or bind with a strap.—**strapper,** strap′ėr, *n.* One who uses a strap.—**strapping,** strap′ing, *a.* [Comp. *thumping, bouncing, thundering,* etc.] Tall and well made; handsome. (*Colloq.*)

strappado, strap′pā′dō, *n.* [O.Fr. *strapade,* It. *strappata,* from *strappare,* to pull.] An old punishment, consisting in having the hands of the offender tied behind his back, drawing him up by them by a rope, and then suddenly letting him drop.

strass, stras, *n.* [From the name of Strasser, its inventor.] A variety of flint glass used in the manufacture of artificial gems.

strata. See STRATUM.

stratagem, strat′a•jem, *n.* [Fr. *stratagème,* from L. *stratagema,* Gr. *stratēgēma,* from *stratēgos,* a general, from *stratos,* an army, *agō,* to lead.] An artifice in war; a plan or scheme for deceiving an enemy; a clever piece of generalship; any artifice; a trick to gain some advantage.—**strategic, strategical,** stra•tēj′ik, stra•tēj′i•kal, *a.* Pertaining to strategy; effected by strategy.—*Strategic point,* any point in the theater of warlike operations which affords to its possessor an advantage over his opponent.—**strategically,** stra•tēj′-i•kal•li, *adv.* In a strategic manner.—**strategist,** strat′e•jist, *n.* One skilled in strategy.—**strategy, strategics,** strat′e•ji, stra•tēj′iks, *n.* The science of forming and carrying out projects of military operations; generalship; the use of artifice or finesse in carrying out any project. ∴ *Strategy* refers to the operations or movements previous to a battle; *tactics* is the art of handling troops when in actual contact with the enemy.

strath, strath, *n.* [Gael. *srath.*] In Scotland, a valley of considerable size, often having a river running through it, giving it its distinctive name (*Strathspey, Strathdon,* etc.).—**strathspey,** strath′spā, *n.* In Scotland, a species of dance in duple time, resembling a reel, but slower; an air or piece of music for this dance.

stratify, etc. See STRATUM.

stratosphere, stra′to•sfēr, *n.* [L. *stratus,* spread, Gr. *sphaira,* a ball.] An upper part of the atmosphere, in which temperature does not vary with height.

stratum, strä′tum, *n.* pl. **strata,** strä′ta. [L., what is spread or stretched out, from *sterno, stratum,* to strew (whence also *street*); the root is that of E. *straw,* to strew.] A layer or bed of matter spread out; *geol.* a layer of any substance, as sand, clay, limestone, etc., which is deposited over a certain surface by the action of water, especially such a layer when forming one of a number superposed.—**stratify,** strat'i•fī, *v.t.* —*stratified, stratifying.* [Fr. *stratifier* —L. *stratum,* and *facio,* to make.] To form into strata or layers, as substances in the earth; to lay or arrange in strata.—**stratification,** strat'i•fi•kā"shon, *n.* The process by which are formed strata; an arrangement in strata or layers.—**stratified,** strat'i•fīd, *p.* and *a.* Arranged in layers or strata.—**stratiform,** strat'i•form, *a.* In the form of strata.—**stratigraphic, stratigraphical,** strat•i•graf'ik, strat•i•graf'i•kal, *a.* [L. *stratum,* and Gr. *graphō,* to describe.] Relating to strata or their arrangement.—**stratigraphically,** strat•i•graf'i•kal•li, *adv.* As regards stratigraphy or the disposition of strata.—**stratigraphy,** stra•tig'ra•fi, *n.* That department of geology which treats of the arrangement of strata, or the order in which they succeed each other.

stratus, strā'tus, *n.* [L. a strewing, a covering. STRATUM.] A low dense, horizontal cloud.

straw, strą, *n.* [A.Sax. *streáw,* straw= Icel. *strá,* Dan. *straa,* D. *stroo,* G. *stroh,* straw, akin to *strew;* cog. L. *stramen,* straw, from *sterno,* to strew. STRATUM, STREW.] The stalk or stem of certain species of grain, pulse, etc.; such stalks collectively when cut, and after being thrashed (no plural in this sense); used proverbially as typical of worthlessness (I don't care a *straw*).—*Man of straw,* the figure of a man formed of a suit of old clothes stuffed with straw; hence, the mere resemblance of a man; a person of little or no means or substance; an imaginary person.—**strawberry,** strą'be•ri, *n.* [A.Sax. *streáwberie, streów-berie,* from its habit of spreading or *strewing* itself along the ground.] A well-known fruit and plant, the fruit being succulent and bearing the seeds on its surface.—**strawboard,** *n.* Thick paper board made altogether or principally from straw.—**straw color,** *n.* The color of dry straw; a beautiful yellowish color.—**straw-colored,** *a.* Of a light yellow.

stray, strā, *v.i.* [O.Fr. *estrayer, extraier,* to wander, from O.Fr. *estrée,* It. *strada,* a road or street; from L.L. *strata,* a street, STREET.] To wander, as from a direct course; to go astray; *fig.* to wander from the path of duty or rectitude; to err; to roam or ramble; to run in a serpentine course; to wind.—*a.* Having gone astray; straggling.—*n.* Any domestic animal that wanders at large or is lost; an estray; *radio,* random electromagnetic waves, which interfere with radio reception. —**strayer,** strā'ėr, *n.* One who strays.

streak, strēk, *n.* [A.Sax. *strica,* a line, a stroke=Icel. *stryk.* Dan. *streg,* D. *streek,* a stroke, streak, line; akin *strike.*] A line or long mark of a different color from the ground; a layer in a mine; a stripe; *naut.* a strake; *mineral,* the color and appearance of a mineral when scratched.—*To strike a streak of bad luck,* to experience continuous misfortunes.—*v.t.* To form streaks on; to variegate with lines of color.—**streaky,** strē'ki, *a.* Having streaks; striped.

stream, strēm, *n.* [A.Sax. *streám,* a stream, a river=D. *stroom,* Icel. *straumr,* Dan. and Sw. *ström,* G. *strom;* from root seen in Skr. *sru,* to flow (with *t* inserted).] Any river, brook, or course of running water; a flow or gush of any fluid substance; a flow of air or gas or of light; a steady current; anything issuing as if in a flow.—*v.i.* To flow in a stream; to issue with continuance, not by fits; to issue or shoot in streaks; to float at full length in the air.—*v.t.* To send forth in a current or stream; to pour.—**streamer,** strē'mėr, *n.* A long narrow flag.—**streamline,** strēm'līn, *n.* A contour design which allows passage through air or water with a minimum of resistance, as the shape of an airplane or boat. —*v.t. streamlined, streamlining.*—To make streamlined; to alter or simplify for purposes of efficiency.—*a.* Designating a shape fashioned to offer the least resistance as it moves through air or water.—**streamlined,** *a.* Possessing fluid lines; stripped of nonessentials; brought up-to-date.—**stream of consciousness,** *n.* Thought considered as a series of processes moving forward constantly in time.

street, strēt, *n.* [A.Sax. *straet,* a street, from L. *strata (via),* a paved way, from *sterno, stratum,* to strew, to pave. STRATUM, STREW, STRAY.] A way or road in a city having houses on one or both sides, chiefly a main way, in distinction from a *lane* or *alley;* the houses as well as the open way.—**street Arab,** *n.* A neglected street boy.—**streetcar,** *n.* A passenger car which runs in a street, usually on rails.—**streetwalker,** *n.* A common prostitute.—**streetwalking,** *n.* The practice of a streetwalker.

strength, strength, *n.* [A.Sax. *strengthu,* strength, from *strang,* strong; comp. *length* and *long.* STRONG.] The muscular force or energy which an animal is capable of exerting; animal force; the quality of bodies by which they sustain the application of force without breaking or yielding; solidity or toughness (the *strength* of a bone); power or vigor of any kind; capacity for exertion (*strength* of mind, memory, evidence, argument, affection); power of resisting attacks; that on which confidence or reliance is placed; support; force or power in expressing meaning by words; vividness; intensity; intensity of some distinguishing or essential constituent; potency (*strength* of wine, poison, acid); legal or moral force or efficacy; force as measured or stated in figures; amount or numbers of an army, fleet, or the like; force proceeding from motion and proportioned to it; vehemence; impetuosity.—*On* or *upon the strength of,* in reliance upon the value of; on the faith of.—**strengthen,** streng'then, *v.t.* To make strong or stronger; to add strength to; to confirm; to establish; to encourage; to fix in resolution; to make greater; to add intensity to.—*v.i.* To grow strong or stronger. —**strengthener,** streng'then•ėr, *n.* One who or that which strengthens.

strenuous, stren'ū•us, *a.* [L. *strenuus,* vigorous, strenuous; allied to Gr. *strēnēs,* strong, hard.] Eager and constant in action; zealous; ardent: earnest.—**strenuously,** stren'ū•us•li, *adv.* Ardently; actively.—**strenuousness,** stren'ū•us•nes, *n.* Earnestness; active zeal.

streptococcus, strep'to•kok"us, *n.* [Gr. *streptos,* twisted, *kokkos,* a berry.] In bacteria, a form consisting of a chain of cocci.

streptomycin, strep'to•mī"sin, *n.* An antibiotic derived from a soil fungus; used against tuberculosis.

stress, stres, *n.* [O.Fr. *estrecer, estrecier* (Fr. *étrecir*), to straiten, to narrow, from L. *strictus,* pp. of *stringo, strictum,* to draw tight (whence *stringent, strain*). STRAIN.] Constraining, urging, or impelling force; pressure; urgency; violence (*stress* of weather); an effort or exertion; a strain; weight; any force tending to change the form or dimensions of a solid, that is, to produce a strain; also the reaction of the solid against the straining forces; importance or influence, imputed or ascribed (to lay *stress* on some point in argument); accent or emphasis; *mech.* force exerted in any direction or manner on bodies (*tensile* stress, etc.).

stretch, strech, *v.t.* [A softened form from A.Sax. *streccan,* to stretch=D. *strekken,* G. *strecken,* Dan. *sträkke,* to stretch. *Straight* is a derivative, and *strake, streak, strike, string, strong* are connected.] To draw out; to extend in length; to draw tight; to make tense; to extend, spread, expand in any direction; to reach out; to hold forth; to extend or distend forcibly; to strain; to exaggerate; to extend too far (to *stretch* a prerogative).—*To stretch a point.* Same as *To strain a point.*—*v.i.* To extend; to reach; to be continuous over a distance; to bear extension without breaking; to attain greater length.—*n.* A stretching or the state of being stretched; an effort; a strain; utmost extent or reach; an extended portion; an expanse.—*On* or *upon the stretch,* in a continuous effort or strain; straining one's powers.—*At* or *on a stretch,* at one effort; at one time.—**stretcher,** strech'ėr, *n.* One who or that which stretches; an instrument for widening gloves or for distending boots; a flat board on which corpses are laid out; a litter for carrying sick, wounded, or dead persons; *carp.* a tie timber in a frame; *naut.* a narrow piece of plank placed across a boat for the rowers to set their feet against.

strew, strö or strō, *v.t.*—pret. *strewed;*

pp. *strewed* or *strewn*. [A.Sax. *streowian*, to scatter=Goth. *straujan*, G. *streuen*, Icel. *strá*, Dan. and Sw. *strō*; same root as *straw*, *star* L. *sterno*, *stratum* (E. *stratum*), Skr. *stri*, to strew.] To scatter or sprinkle; always applied to dry substances separable into parts or particles; to cover by scattering or being scattered over; to throw loosely apart; to spread abroad; to disseminate. Also written *Strow* and formerly *Straw*.

stria, strī'a, *n.* pl. **striae,** strī'ē. [L.] A technical term for fine threadlike lines or streaks seen on the surface of shells, minerals, plants, etc.—**striate, striated,** strī'at, strī'a•ted, *a.* [L. *striatus*.] Marked with striae.—*Striated fiber*, the fiber of the voluntary muscles or those that the will can influence.—**striate,** *v.t.*—*striated, striating*. To mark with striae.—**striation,** strī•ā'shon, *n.* The state of being striated; striate markings; *geol.* the grooving of rock surfaces by masses of ice passing over them.

stricken, strik'n, pp. of *strike*. Struck; smitten; advanced (as in age—'well *stricken* in years').

strickle, strik'l, *n.* [From *strike*.] An instrument to strike grain to a level with the measure; an instrument for whetting scythes.

strict, strikt, *a.* [L. *strictus*, pp. of *stringo*, to draw tight; whence also *stringent*, *strain*. STRAIN.] Carefully adhering to or governed by some rule; carefully observed; rigorously nice (*strict* watch); rigorous as to rules or conduct (*strict* in religious observances); definite as to terms; stringent; rigidly interpreted; not loose or vague (the *strict* sense of a word).—**strictly,** strikt'li, *adv.* In a strict manner; with nice or rigorous accuracy; correctly; definitely; rigorously.—**strictness,** strikt'nes, *n.* The state or quality of being strict; exactness in the observance of rules; rigorous accuracy; precision; severity; stringency.

stricture, strik'chėr, *n.* [L. *strictura*, from *stringo*, *strictum*, to draw tight. STRICT.] A touch of sharp criticism; a censorious remark; censure; *med.* a morbid contraction of some mucous canal or duct of the body, especially the urethra.

stride, strīd, *v.i.*—pret. *strode*; pp. *stridden*; ppr. *striding*. [A.Sax. *stridan*, to stride, to walk, *bestridan*, to bestride; L.G. *striden*, to stride; comp. Dan. *stritte*, to straddle; also G. *streiten*, to contend, *streit*, Dan. *strid*, contest.] To walk with long steps; to stand with the feet far apart; to straddle.—*v.t.* To pass over at a step; to bestride.—*n.* A long step; a measured or pompous step; a lofty gait; the space measured by the legs far apart.

strident, strī'dent, *a.* [L. *stridens*, *stridentis*, ppr. of *strideo*, to creak.] Creaking; harsh; grating.—**stridulation,** strid•ū•lā'shon, *n.* A small, harsh, creaking noise, as made by some insects.—**stridulatory,** strid'ū•la•to•ri, *a.* Stridulous.—**stridulous,** strid'ū•lus, *a.* [L. *stridulus*.] Making a small creaking sound.

strife, strīf, *n.* [From Icel. *stríth*, war, strife; the *th* being changed to *f* by the influence of *strive*, O.Fr. *estriver*. STRIVE.] Exertion or contention for superiority; contest of emulation; emulation; contention in anger or enmity; discord; quarrel or war.

strigil, strij'il, *n.* [L. *strigilis*, from *stringo*, to graze, to scrape.] An instrument used by the ancients for scraping the skin at the bath.

strike, strīk, *v.i.*—pret. *struck*; pp. *struck*, *stricken*; ppr. *striking*. [A.Sax. *strícan*, to go rapidly in a straight course; *astrican*, to strike, to smite; D. *strijken*, to stroke; G. *streichen*, Icel. *strykja*, to stroke, to flog. *Stroke* is a derivative.] To pass or dart with rapidity (to *strike* into another path; the bullet *struck* through the door); to penetrate (the roots *strike* deep); to make a quick blow or thrust; to use one's weapons; to knock; to sound an hour (as a clock); to reach or act on an object (light *strikes* on the wall); to run or dash upon the shore, a rock, or bank; to be stranded; to lower a sail or a flag in token of respect, or to signify surrender (the ship *struck*); to yield; to quit work in order to compel an increase or prevent a reduction of wages, or for other reasons.—*To strike at*, to make or aim a blow at; to attack.—*To strike home*, to give an effective blow. —*To strike in*, to put in one's word suddenly; to interpose.—*To strike in with*, to conform to; to suit.—*To strike out*, to deliver a blow; to start to swim.—*To strike up*, to begin to play or sing.—*v.t.* To touch or hit with some force; to smite; to give a blow to; to give, deal, or inflict (with *blow* or similar word as object); to dash; to knock (with the instrument as object); to produce by a blow or blows (to *strike* fire); to stamp with a stroke; hence, to mint; to coin; to thrust in; to cause to enter or penetrate (a tree *strikes* its root deep); to cause to sound; to notify by sound; to impress (the mind) strongly; to affect sensibly with strong emotion (the scene *struck* him); to produce suddenly; to effect at once (to *strike* terror); to bring suddenly into some state or condition (to *strike* one dumb); to make and ratify (to *strike* a bargain); to lower, as the yards, flag, sails of a vessel.—*Well struck* or *stricken in years*, of an advanced age.—*To strike a balance*, in *bookkeeping*, to bring out the amount due on one or other of the sides of a debtor and creditor account; hence, in general, to ascertain on which side the preponderance is.—*To strike down*, to prostrate by a blow or illness; to fell. —*To strike off*, to separate by a blow; to erase from an account; to deduct; to impress; to print.—*To strike oil*, to find petroleum when boring for it; hence, to make a lucky hit (*colloq.*).—*To strike out*, to blot out; to efface; to erase; to plan or excogitate by a quick effort; to devise.—*To strike sail*, to lower or take in sail.—*To strike a tent*, to take it down.—*To strike up*, to drive up with a blow; to begin to play or sing.—*To strike work*, to cease work, especially till some dispute between employers and employed is settled.—*n.* An instrument for leveling a measure of grain, salt, etc.; a strickle; the act of a body of workmen discontinuing work with the object of compelling their employer to concede certain demands made by them; *geol.* the horizontal direction of the outcropping edges of tilted strata, running at right angles to the dip.—**striker,** strī'kėr, *n.* One who or that which strikes.—**striking,** strī'king, *a.* Such as to strike with surprise or other feeling; remarkable; forcible; impressive.—**strikingly,** strī'king•li, *adv.* In a striking manner; remarkably; strongly; impressively.

string, string, *n.* [A.Sax. *streng*=D. *streng*, Icel. *strengr*, Dan. and Sw. *sträng*, G. *strang*, string, cord; akin to *strong*, and to L. *stringo*, to draw tight (whence *strain*, *strict*), *strangulo*, to strangle.] A small rope, line, or cord used for fastening or tying things; a twine; a thread; a thread on which things are filed; and hence, a set of things on a line (a *string* of beads); the chord of a musical instrument which gives a sound by its vibrations; hence, *pl.* the stringed instruments of an orchestra; a line or chain of things following each other; a nerve or tendon of an animal body (the heart *strings*); a series of things connected or following in succession (a *string* of arguments).—*v.t.*—pret. and pp. *strung*. To furnish with strings; to put in tune the strings of; to put on a string (to *string* beads).—**stringcourse,** *n.* A narrow molding continued horizontally along the face of a building.—**stringed,** stringd, *a.* Having strings; produced by strings. — **stringer,** string'ėr, *n.* One who strings: an inside strake of plank or of plates in a ship; *carp.* a board that sustains some important part of a framework or structure. — **stringhalt,** *n.* A twitching of the hinder leg of a horse, constituting a defect, being a convulsive motion of the muscles of the hock.—**stringiness,** string'i•nes, *n.* The state of being stringy; fibrousness.—**stringy,** string'i, *a.* Consisting of strings or small threads; fibrous; filamentous; ropy; sinewy; wiry.

stringent, strin'jent, *a.* [L. *stringens*, *stringentis*, ppr. of *stringo*, to draw tight. STRICT, STRAIN.] Making strict claims or requirements; strict; rigid; making severe restrictions.—**stringently,** strin'jent•li, *adv.* In a stringent manner.—**stringency,** strin'jen•si, *n.* State or character of being stringent; strictness.

strip, strip, *v.t.*—*stripped*, *stripping*. [A.Sax. *strýpan*, to strip, to spoil; L.G. *strippen*, *stripen*, *strepen*, D. *stroopen*, G. *streifen*, to strip; closely akin to *stripe*.] To pull or tear off (a covering); to deprive of a covering; to remove the clothes from; to skin; to peel (to *strip* a tree *of* the bark); to deprive; to bereave; to despoil; to tear off the thread of a screw or bolt; to milk dry; to unrig (to *strip* a ship). —*v.i.* To take off the covering or clothes.—*n.* A narrow piece comparatively long; a stripe.—**stripper,** strip'ėr, *n.* One that strips.

stripe, strīp, *n.* [Closely akin to *strip* and=L.G. *stripe,* D. *streep,* Dan. *stripe,* G. *streif,* a stripe.] A long narrow division of anything of a different color from the rest; a streak; a strip or long narrow piece; a stroke made with a lash, rod, or scourge; a wale or weal.—*v.t.*—*striped, striping.* To make stripes upon; to form with lines of different colors.—**striped,** strīpt, *a.* Having stripes of different colors.

stripling, strip'ling, *n.* [From *strip, stripe,* with dim. term. *-ling;* primarily, a tall slender youth, one that shoots up suddenly; comp. *slip, scion.*] A youth in the state of adolescence, or just passing from boyhood to manhood; a lad.

strive, strīv, *v.i.*—pret. *strove,* pp. *striven,* ppr. *striving.* [O.Fr. *estriver,* to strive, from O.H.G. *streban,* G. *streben,* Dan. *straebe,* D. *streven,* to strive.] To make efforts; to endeavor with earnestness; to try; to contend; to struggle in opposition; to fight; to quarrel or contend with each other; to be in dispute or altercation; to vie. —**striver,** strī'vėr, *n.* One that strives.

strobilus, strobile, stro•bi'lus, stro'bil, *n.* [Gr. *strobīlus,* a pine cone.] *Bot.* a catkin the carpels of which are scalelike spread open, and bear naked seeds, as in the fruit of the pines; a pine cone.

stroboscope, stro'bo•skōp, *n.* [Gr. *strobos,* a whirling, and *skopein,* to view.] An instrument for observing the succession of phases in a periodic motion by intermittent illumination.

stroke, strōk, *n.* [From *strike.*] A blow; a knock; the striking of one body against another; a fatal assault or attack; a sudden attack of disease or affliction; a calamity; the striking of a clock; a dash in writing or printing; a line; the touch of a pen or pencil (a hair-*stroke*); a touch; a masterly effort (a *stroke* of genius); a successful attempt; the sweep of an oar; the stroke oar or strokesman; *steam-engine,* the entire movement of the piston from one end to the other of the cylinder.—**stroke oar,** *n.* The aftmost oar of a boat; also, the man that uses it.

stroke, strōk, *v.t.*—*stroked, stroking.* [A.Sax. *strácian,* to stroke=D. *strooken,* to stroke, to soothe; close akin to *strike.*] To rub gently with the hand in kindness or tenderness; to rub gently in one direction; to make smooth by gentle rubbing.—*n.* A caress; a gentle rubbing with the hand, expressive of kindness.

stroll, strōl, *v.i.* [Of doubtful origin: comp. Prov.G. *strolen, struolen,* to stroll.] To wander on foot slowly; to ramble idly or leisurely.—*Strolling player,* an inferior stage player who goes about from place to place and performs wherever an audience can be obtained.—*n.* A walking idly and leisurely; a ramble.—**stroller,** strōl'ėr, *n.* One who strolls; an itinerant player.

stroma, strō'ma, *n.* [Gr. *strōma,* a bed, from *strōnnymi,* to spread out.] *Anat.* the bed or foundation texture of an organ, or of any deposit; the framework of an organ; *bot.* the fleshy substance in some fungous plants; a thallus.

stromeyerite, strō•mī'ėr•īt, *n.* [After the chemist *Stromeyer.*] A steel-gray ore of silver, consisting of sulfur, silver, and copper.

strong, strong, *a.* [A.Sax. *strang, strong,* strong, robust=Icel. *strangr,* Dan. and D. *streng,* strong; G. *streng,* strict; same root as *string,* and L. *stringo,* to draw tight (whence *strict*). *Strength* is a derivative.] Having physical power; having the power of exerting great bodily force; robust; muscular; able or powerful mentally or morally; of great power or capacity (a *strong* mind, memory, imagination); naturally sound or healthy; hale; not easily broken; firm; solid; compact; well fortified; not easily subdued or taken (a *strong* fortress or position); having great military or naval power or force; having great wealth or resources; having force from moving with rapidity; violent; impetuous; adapted to make a deep impression on the mind or imagination; effectual; cogent; ardent or zealous (a *strong* supporter); having a particular quality or qualities in a great degree (a *strong* decoction, *strong* tea), containing much alcohol; intoxicating; affecting the senses forcibly (a *strong* light, scent, flavor); substantial; solid, but not of easy digestion; well established; firm; not easily overthrown or altered; vehement; earnest (a *strong* affection); having great resources; powerful; mighty; having great force or expressiveness; forcibly expressed; (preceded by numerals); amounting to; powerful to the extent of (an army 10,000 *strong*); *com.* tending upward in price; rising (a *strong* market); *gram.* applied to inflected words when inflection is effected by internal vowel change and not by adding syllables: *swim, swam, swum* is a *strong* verb (WEAK). *Strong* is used as an element in many self-explanatory compounds, as *strong*-backed, *strong*-bodied, *strong*-voiced, etc.—**stronghold,** strong'hōld, *n.* A fastness; a fortified place; a place of security.—**strongly,** strong'li, *adv.* In a strong manner; with strength, force, or power; firmly; forcibly; violently.—**strong-minded,** *a.* Having a strong or vigorous mind; having a masculine rather than a feminine turn of mind; unfeminine: applied ironically to women claiming equality with men.—**strong room,** *n.* A fireproof and burglarproof apartment in which valuables are kept.

strontia, stron'shi•a, *n.* An oxide of strontium occurring at *Strontian,* in Argyleshire, whence its name, a grayish-white powder, closely resembling baryta. The *nitrate of strontia* is sometimes used in making fireworks, as it communicates a magnificent red color to flame.—**strontian,** stron'shi•an, *n.* A name given to strontia.—*a.* Pertaining to strontia; containing strontia.—**strontianite,** stron'shi•an•īt, *n.* A mineral, native carbonate of strontia.

strontium, stran'she•um, *n.* [N.L. from *strontia.*] A soft, metallic metal of the alkaline-earth group, occurring only in a combined state: symbol, Sr; at. no., 38; at. wt., 87.62.—**strontium-90,** *n.* A heavy radioactive isotope of strontium that occurs in nuclear fallout and that is considered harmful.

strop, strop, *n.* [A.Sax. *stropp,* from L. *stroppus, struppus,* a thong.] A strip of leather, or a strip of wood covered with leather or other suitable material, used for sharpening razors; a razorstrop.—*v.t.*—*stropped, stropping.* To sharpen with a strop.

strophanthin, strō•fan'thin, *n.* [From *Strophanthus,* the plant—Gr. *strephō,* to turn, twist, *anthos,* flower.] A drug obtained from the seeds of an African plant; a muscle poison, but used in heart disease.

strophe, strō'fi, *n.* [Gr. *strophē,* from *strepho,* to turn.] The part of a Greek choral ode sung in turning from the right to the left of the orchestra, *antistrophe* being the reverse; hence, in lyric poetry, a term for the former of two corresponding stanzas, the latter being the *antistrophe.*—**strophic,** strō'fik, *a.* Relating to or consisting of strophes.

strove, strōv, pret. of *strive.*

strow, strō, *v.t.*—pret. *strowed;* pp. *strowed* or *strown.* Same as *Strew.*

struck, struk, pret. and pp. of *strike.*

structure, struk'chėr, *n.* [L. *structura,* from *struo, structum,* to build, seen in *construct, instruct, destruction, destroy, construe,* etc.] A building of any kind, but chiefly a building of some size or magnificence; an edifice; manner of building; make; construction; the arrangement of the parts in a whole (the *structure* of a sentence, rock of a columnar *structure*); manner of organization; mode in which different organs or parts are arranged.—**structural,** struk'chėr•al, *a.* Pertaining to structure.

struggle, strug'l, *v.i.* — *struggled, struggling.* [Formerly *stroggle, strogle;* of doubtful origin; comp. O.Sw. *strug,* a quarrel.] To make efforts with contortions of the body; to use great efforts; to labor hard; to strive. —*n.* A violent effort with contortions of the body; a contortion of distress; a forcible effort to attain an object; an effort to get on in the world; contest; strife.—**struggler,** strug'lėr, *n.* One who struggles.

strum, strum, *v.i.* [An imitative word.] To play unskillfully and coarsely on a stringed instrument. —*v.t.* To play on unskillfully or noisily; as, to *strum* a guitar.

struma, strö'ma, *n.* pl. **strumae,** strö'mē. [L., from *struo,* to build.] A scrofulous swelling or tumor; scrofula; sometimes goiter; *bot.* a swelling at the extremity of a petiole, next the lamina of a leaf.—**strumatic,**

strö•mat'ik, *a.* Strumose.—**strumose, strumous,** strö'mōs, strö'mus, *a.* Scrofulous; *bot.* having strumae.

strumpet, strum'pet, *n.* [Origin doubtful; perhaps from O.Fr. *strupre, stupre,* L. *stuprum,* fornication, debauchery.] A prostitute; a harlot. —*v.t.* To debauch.

strung, strung, pret. of *string.*

strut, strut, *v.i.—strutted, strutting.* [O.E. *strut, strout,* to swell or bulge, to strut; akin Dan. *strutte,* to strut, to stick out; L.G. *strutt,* sticking out; G. *strotzen,* to teem.] To walk with a lofty, proud gait and erect head; to walk with affected dignity or pompousness.—*n.* A lofty, proud step or walk with the head erect; affectation of dignity in walking; *carp.* a strengthening piece obliquely or diagonally placed; a brace; a stretching piece.—**strutter,** strut'ėr, *n.* One who struts.—**struttingly,** strut'ing•li, *adv.*

strychnine, strik'nin, *n.* [Gr. *strychnos,* nightshade.] An alkaloid obtained from nux vomica and used as a central nervous system stimulant.

stub, stub, *n.* [A.Sax. *styb,* a stub= Icel. *stubbi, stubbr, stobbi,* a stump, Dan. *stub,* stump, stubble; L.G. *stubbe,* D. *stobbe,* a stump: *stubble, stump, stubborn* are akin.] The stump of a tree or that part which remains in the earth when the tree is cut down; a stub nail.—*v.t.—stubbed, stubbing.* To grub up by the roots; to clear of roots.—**stubby,** stub'i, *a.* Abounding with stubs; short and thick.—**stub nail,** *n.* A nail broken off; a short thick nail.

stubble, stub'l, *n.* [A dim. form from *stub*; Dan. and Sw. *stub,* stubble.] The stumps of corn left in the ground; the part of the stalk left in the ground by the scythe or sickle.—**stubbled,** stub'ld, *a.* Covered with stubble.—**stubbly,** stub'li, *a.* Covered with stubble; resembling stubble; short and stiff (a *stubbly* beard).

stubborn, stub'orn, *a.* [From *stub,* A.Sax. *styb,* lit. like a *stub,* blockish, obstinate, with A.Sax. adj. term. *-or* and *-n* added.] Unreasonably or perversely obstinate; not to be moved or persuaded by reason; inflexible; refractory; not easily worked (as soil; metal); stiff; not flexible. ∴Syn. under OBSTINATE.—**stubbornly,** stub'orn•li, *adv.* In a stubborn manner; obstinately.—**stubbornness,** stub'orn•nes, *n.* Perverse obstinacy.

stucco, stuk'kō, *n.* [It., from O.H.G. *stucchi,* a crust.] A kind of fine plaster, used for cornices, moldings, etc., of rooms—a composition of fine sand, pulverized marble, and gypsum mixed with water; also, a popular name for plaster of Paris or gypsum. —*v.t.* To overlay with stucco.—**stuccoer,** stuk'kō•ėr, *n.* One who stuccoes.—**stuccowork,** *n.* Ornamental work of stucco, such as cornices, moldings, etc.

stuck, stuk, pret. and pp. of *stick.*—**stuckup,** *a.* Giving one's self airs of importance or superiority; aping the manners of one's superiors. (*Colloq.*)

stud, stud, *n.* [A.Sax. *studu,* a prop, a stud; Icel. *stoð,* Dan. *stōd,* D. *stut,* a prop, support; from stem of *steady.*] A nail with a large head, inserted chiefly for ornament; an ornamental knob; an ornamental button for a shirt front, transferable from one shirt to another; a supporting beam; a post or prop.—*v.t. studded, studding.* To adorn with studs or knobs; to set thickly, as with studs.

stud, stud, *n.* [A.Sax. *stód,* a stud (whence *stódhors,* a stallion); Icel. *stóð,* Dan. *stod,* a stud; akin *steed.*] A collection of breeding horses and mares; a person's horses collectively. —**studbook,** *n.* A book containing a genealogy or register of horses or cattle of particular breeds.—**studhorse,** *n.* A breeding horse.

studding sail, stud'ing, stunsl, *n.* [From *stud,* a support, or altered from *steadyingsail.*] *Naut.* a sail set on the outer edge of any of the principal sails during a light wind.

student, stū'dent, *n.* [L. *studens, studentis,* ppr. of *studeo,* to study.] A person engaged in learning something from books, or attending some educational institution, especially of the higher class; one studying anything; a scholar; a man devoted to books; a bookish man.—**studentship,** stū'dent•ship, *n.* The state of being a student.—**studied,** stud'id, *p.* and *a.* Made the subject of study; well considered; qualified by study; premeditated; deliberate (a *studied* insult).—**studiedly,** stud'id•li, *adv.* In a studied manner.—**studio,** stū'di•ō, *n.* [It., from L. *studium,* study.] The workroom of a painter, sculptor, or photographer; a place where an art is studied (a dance *studio*); a place where films are made; a place from which radio or television programs are transmitted.—**studious,** stu•di•us, *a.* [Fr. *studieux,* L. *studiosus.*] Given to study; devoted to the acquisition of knowledge from books; eager to discover something or to effect some object; earnest; eager (*studious* to please); attentive; careful: with *of*; deliberate; studied.—**studiously,** stū'di•us•li, *adv.* In a studious manner; with zeal and earnestness; diligently.—**studiousness,** stū'di•us•nes, *n.* The quality of being studious.—**study,** stud'i, *n.* [L. *studium,* zeal, study, from *studeo,* to study.] Application of mind to books, to arts or science, or to any subject for the purpose of learning what is not before known; earnest endeavor; diligence; a branch of learning studied; an object of study; a building or apartment devoted to study; a fit of thought; a reverie; *fine arts,* a work undertaken for improvement, or a preparatory sketch to be used in the composition of more finished works.—*v.i. studied, studying.* To apply the mind to books or learning; to dwell in thought; to ponder; to be zealous.—*v.t.* To apply the mind to for the purpose of learning; to consider attentively; to examine closely; to con over, or to commit to memory; to have careful regard to (one's interest, comfort, etc.); to be solicitous for the good of.

stuff, stuf, *n.* [O.Fr. *estoffe* (Fr. *étoffe*), stuff, material, from L. *stuppa,* tow. STOP.] Substance or matter indefinitely; the matter of which anything is formed; material; furniture; goods (O.T.); refuse or worthless matter; hence, foolish or irrational language; trash; *com.* a general name for fabrics of silk, wool, hair, cotton, etc.; particularly woolen, cloth of slight texture, for linings, etc.; a melted mass of turpentine, tallow, etc., with which ships are smeared for preservation.—*v.t.* [In this sense=G. *stopfen,* to stuff or cram; E. to *stop* up.] To fill by packing or crowding material into; to cram; to crowd in together; to fill or pack with material necessary to make complete (to *stuff* a cushion); to fill the skin of, as of a dead animal, for presenting and preserving its form; to fill mentally full; to put fraudulent ballots into; as, to *stuff* the ballot box; to crowd with facts or idle tales or fancies; *cookery,* to fill with seasoning (to *stuff* a leg of veal).—*v.i.* To feed gluttonously.—**stuffing,** stuf'ing, *n.* That which is used to fill something.—**stuffing box,** *n.* A box with packing that prevents leakage around a piston rod.

stuffy, stuf'i, *a.* [O.Fr. *estouffer,* to stifle, from *estoffe,* stuff. STUFF.] Difficult to breathe in; close; stifling; said of a room.—**stuffiness,** stuf'i•nes, *n.* The state of being stuffy; closeness; mustiness.

stultify, stul'ti•fī, *v.t.—stultified, stultifying.* [L. *stultus,* foolish; and *facio,* to make.] To make foolish; to make a fool of; to cause to appear as a fool. —**stultification,** stul'ti•fi•kā"shon, *n.* The act of stultifying.—**stultifier,** stul'ti•fī•ėr, *n.* One who stultifies.

stum, stum, *n.* [From D. *stom,* unfermented wine, must, from *stom,* G. *stumm,* Dan. and Sw. *stum,* dumb, mute.] Unfermented grape juice; must or new wine; wine made by must to ferment anew.—*v.t.—stummed, stumming.* To renew by mixing with must and fermenting anew.

stumble, stum'bl, *v.i.—stumbled, stumbling.* [O.E. *stomble, stomel*; allied to E. *stammer,* Prov. E. *stummer,* Icel. *stumra,* to stumble, N. *stumle,* to totter, L.G. *stumpeln,* to walk heavily.] To trip in walking; to make a false step; to stagger; to walk unsteadily; to fall into crime or error; to err; to strike upon without design; to light by chance; with *on* or *upon.*—*v.t.* To cause to stumble; to puzzle.—*n.* The act of stumbling; a trip in walking or running; a blunder.—**stumbler,** stum'blėr, *n.* One that stumbles.—**stumbling block,** *n.* Any cause of stumbling; that which forms a difficulty in one's way or which causes offense: used in figurative sense.—**stumblingly,** stum'bling•li, *adv.*

stump, stump, *n.* [A nasalized form of *stub,* and=Dan. *stump,* Icel. *stumpr,* D. *stomp,* G. *stumpf,* a stump. STUB.] The root part of a tree remaining in the earth after the tree is cut down; the part of a limb or other body remaining after the rest is cut off or destroyed (the *stump* of a tooth, of a lead pencil); one of the three posts constituting the wicket in a game of cricket.—*On the stump*, going through a district and making speeches. [Originally American; the stump of a tree being often used as a platform in lately cleared districts.] —*v.t.* To lop; to make a tour through delivering speeches for political or personal purposes (to *stump* the country); *cricket*, to put out of play by knocking down a stump or stumps while the batsman is out of the crease.—*v.i.* To walk stiffly, heavily, or noisily.—*To stump up*, to pay or hand over money. (*Colloq.*)—**stumpy,** stump'i, *a.* Full of stumps; short or stubby (*colloq.*).

stun, stun, *v.t.*—*stunned, stunning.* [A.Sax. *stunian*, to stun, from *stun*, noise; same root as Skr. *stan*, to thunder. ASTONISH.] To overpower the sense of hearing of; to confound by loud noise; to render insensible or dizzy by force or violence; to render senseless by a blow; to surprise completely; to overpower.—**stunner,** stun'ėr, *n.* Something first-rate; a person or thing of very showy appearance. (*Slang.*) —**stunning,** stun'ing, *a.* First-rate; excellent. (*Slang.*)

stung, stung, pret. and pp. of *sting.*

stunk, stungk, pret. of *stink.*

stunt, stunt, *v.t.* [From A.Sax. *stunt*, blunt, stupid; Sw. *stunt*, docked, short; akin Icel. *stuttr*, short, stunted; G. *stutzen*, to dock. STINT.] To hinder from free growth; to check in growth; to dwarf.—*n.* A check in growth.

stunt, stunt, *n.* A remarkable feat of skill; any enterprise, task, or undertaking.

stupa, stö'pa, *n.* [Skr. *stûpa.*] A Buddhist sacred monumental structure, commemorating some event or marking some spot.

stupe, stūp, *n.* [L. *stupa*, tow.] Flannel, flax, or similar substance wrung out of hot water, plain or medicated, applied to a wound or sore.

stupefy, stū'pe·fī, *v.t.*—*stupefied, stupefying.* [Fr. *stupéfier*, from L. *stupefacere*—*stupeo*, to be struck senseless, and *facio*, to make. STUPID.] To deprive of sensibility; to make dull or dead to external influences; to make torpid.—**stupefacient, stupefactive,** stū·pe·fā'shi·ent, stū·pe·fak'tiv, *a.* Having a stupefying power.—*n.* A medicine which produces stupor; a narcotic.—**stupefaction,** stū·pe·fak'shon, *n.* The state of being stupefied or stunned; a senseless state; insensibility; torpor.—**stupefier,** stū'pe·fī·ėr, *n.* One who or that which stupefies.

stupendous, stū·pen'dus, *a.* [L. *stupendus*, amazing, from *stupeo*, to be astonished. STUPID.] Striking dumb by magnitude; great and wonderful; of astonishing magnitude or elevation; grand.—**stupendously,** stū·pen'dus·li, *adv.* In a stupendous manner.—**stupendousness,** stū·pen'dus·nes, *n.*

stupid, stū'pid, *a.* [L. *stupidus*, from *stupeo*, to be astonished or struck senseless (seen also in *stupefy, stupendous*); perhaps same root as *stand.*] Bereft of consciousness, sense, or feeling; in a state of stupor; insensible; stupefied; devoid of understanding; possessed of dull gross folly; extremely dull of perception or understanding; nonsensical.—**stupidity, stupidness,** stū·pid'i·ti, stū'pid·nes, *n.* [L. *stupiditas.*] The state or quality of being stupid; stupor; astonishment; extreme dullness of understanding; dull foolishness.—**stupidly,** stū'pid·li, *adv.* In a stupid manner.—**stupor,** stū'por, *n.* [L. *stupor*, from *stupeo.*] Great diminution or total suspension of sensibility; a state in which the faculties are deadened or dazed; torpor.

sturdy, stėr'di, *a.* [O.Fr. *estourdi* (Fr. *étourdi*), stupid, inconsiderate, from L. *ex*, intens., and *torpidus*, torpid.] Stubborn‡; stiff-necked‡; exhibiting strength or force; forcible; vigorous; robust in body; strong; stout; vigorous and hardy.—**sturdily,** stėr'di·li, *adv.* In a sturdy manner; stoutly; lustily.—**sturdiness,** stėr'di·nes, *n.* The state or quality of being sturdy.

sturdy, stėr'di, *n.* [Gael. *stuird, stuirdean*, vertigo, sturdy.] A disease in sheep, marked by staggering, vertigo, stupor, etc.

sturgeon, stėr'jen, *n.* [Fr. *esturgeon*, from L.L. *sturio*, from O.H.G. *sturio*, A.Sax. *styria*, a sturgeon.] A genus of large fishes having a skin protected with rows of bony plates; flesh valuable as food; roes converted into caviar, and air bladder into isinglass.

stutter, stut'ėr, *v.i.* [Same as D. and L.G. *stotteren*, G. *stottern*, to stutter; freq. forms corresponding to Prov.E. *stut*, to stutter; Sc. *stot*, to rebound; Icel. *stauta*, to strike.] To stammer; to hesitate in uttering words.—*n.* A stammer; a hesitation in speaking.—**stutterer,** stut'ėr·ėr, *n.* One who stutters; a stammerer.—**stutteringly,** stut'ėr·ing·li, *adv.*

sty, stī, *n.* [A.Sax. *stige*, a sty or pen = Icel, *stía*, Dan. *sti*, Sw. *stia*, O.H.G. *stiga*, a sty. The first part of *steward* is this word.] A pen or enclosure for swine; any filthy hovel or place; a place of bestial debauchery.—*v.t.*—*stied, stying.* To shut up in a sty.

sty, stī, *n.* [A.Sax. *stigend*, a tumor on the eye, from *stigan*, to rise; akin *stair.*] A small inflammatory tumor on the edge of the eyelid, particularly near the inner angle of the eye.

Stygian, stij'i·an, *a.* [L. *Stygius*, from *Styx*, Gr. *Styx, Stygos*, the Styx, from *stygeō*, to hate.] Pertaining to Styx, fabled by the ancients to be a river of hell over which the shades of the dead passed; hence, hellish; infernal.

style, stīl, *n.* [Fr. *style*, from L. *stilus, stylus*, a stake, pointed instrument, style for writing, hence mode of expression; from root of *stimulus, stick, sting.* Spelling influenced by Gr. *stylos*, a pillar.] A pointed instrument used by the ancients for writing by scratching on wax tablets; anything of a similar kind; a pointed tool used in graving; a pointed surgical instrument; the pin or gnomon of a sundial; *bot.* the prolongation of the summit of the ovary which supports the stigma; manner of writing with regard to language; a distinctive manner of writing belonging to an author or body of authors: a characteristic mode of presentation in any of the fine arts; particular type of architecture pervading a building (the Gothic *style*); external manner, mode, or fashion; manner deemed elegant and appropriate; fashion (a person dressed in the *style*); a formal or official designation; title (a person's *style* and title); *chron.* a mode of reckoning time with regard to the Julian and Gregorian calendars. *Old Style* followed the Julian manner of computing the months and days, in which the year consists of 365 days and 6 hours, or something more than 11 minutes too much. The Gregorian or *New Style*, according to the calendar as reformed by Pope Gregory XIII in 1582, was adopted in England in 1752, and now almost everywhere prevails. ∴ Syn. under DICTION.—*v.t.*—*styled, styling.* To term; to name or call; to designate or denominate.—**stylet,** stī'let, *n.* *Surg.* a probe.—**stylar,** stī'lėr, *a.* Pertaining to a style.—**styliform,** stī'li·form, *a.* Having the shape of or resembling a style; styloid.—**stylish,** stīl'ish, *a.* Being in fashionable form or in high style; being quite in the mode or fashion; showy. —**stylishly,** stīl'ish·li, *adv* In a stylish manner; showily.—**stylishness,** stīl'ish·nes, *n.* The state or quality of being stylish; showiness.—**stylist,** stīl'ist, *n.* A writer or speaker who is careful of his style; a master of style.—**stylistic,** stī·lis'tik, *a.* Relating to style.—**stylography,** stī·log'ra·fi, *n.* A method of writing or engraving with a style.—**stylographic, stylographical,** stī·lo·graf'ik, stī·lo·graf'i·kal, *a.* Pertaining to stylography.—**styloid,** stī'loid, *a.* Having some resemblance to a style or pen.

stylite, stī'līt, *n.* [Gr. *stylītēs*, from *stylos*, a pillar.] A pillar saint, one of those ascetics who, by way of penance, passed the greater part of their lives on the top of high columns or pillars.

stylobate, stī'lō·bāt, *n.* [L. *stylobates, stylobata*, from Gr. *stylobatēs*—*stylos*, a pillar, and *bainō*, to go.] *Arch.* a continuous and unbroken pedestal or elevation upon which a range of columns stands.

stylography. See STYLE.

stylus, stī'lus, *n.* [L. *stilus*, a stake, a pointed instrument.] A sharp, pointed writing instrument, as that used on stencils; the tool used in cutting the grooves of an original phonograph record; the tool that rides in the grooves of a phonograph record and aids in sound reproduction.

stymie, stī'mi, *a.* The position in golf when the opponent's ball lies between the player's ball and the hole.

styptic, styptical, stip'tik, stip'ti·kal,

a. [L. *stypticus*, from Gr. *styptikos*, from *styphō*, to contract.] Astringent‡, having the quality of stopping the bleeding of a wound.—**styptic,** *n.* A substance that checks a flow of blood by application to the bleeding surface.—**stypticity,** stip•tis′i•ti, *n.* The quality of being styptic.

Styx, *n.* Chief river in Hades of the lower world which had to be crossed by the dead.

suasion, swā′zhon, *n.* [L. *suasio*, *suasionis*, from *suadeo*, *suasum*, to advise (as in *dissuade*, *persuade*).] The act of persuading.—**suasive,** swā′ziv, *a.* Having power to persuade.

suave, swäv, *a.* [Fr. *suave*, sweet, pleasant, from L. *suavis*, sweet; same root as *suadeo*, to persuade, and as E. *sweet*.] Gracious or agreeable in manner; blandly polite; pleasant.—**suavely,** swäv′li, *adv.* In a suave manner; blandly.

sub, sub, *n.* A colloquial contraction for submarine; also *pref.* under; inferior; somewhat.

subacid, sub•as′id, *a.* [L. *sub*, slightly.] Moderately acid or sour.—*n.* A substance moderately acid.

subacute, sub•a•kūt′, *a.* [L. *sub*, slightly.] Acute or pointed in a modified degree.

subah, sö′bä, *n.* [Per. and Hind., a province.] In India, a province or viceroyship.—**subahdar, subadar,** sö•bä•där′, *n.* A ruler of a province.

subalpine, sub•al′pīn, *a.* [L. *sub*, under.] Belonging to a region on lofty mountains immediately below the Alpine.

subaltern, sub′ąl•tėrn or sub•ąl′tėrn, *a.* [L. *subalternus*, subordinate—*sub*, under, *alter*, another.] Holding an inferior or subordinate position; in the army below the rank of a captain.—*n.* A commissioned military officer below the rank of captain.—**subalternate,** sub•ąl•tėr′nāt, *a.* Subordinate; successive.

subangular, sub•ang′gū•lėr, *a.* [L. *sub*, slightly.] Slightly angular.

subaquatic, subaqueous, sub•a•kwat′ik, sub•ak′wē•us, *a.* [L. *sub*, under, and *aqua*, water.] Being under water; *geol.* formed under water; deposited under water.

subarctic, sub•ark′tik, *a.* [L. *sub*, slightly.] Applied to a region or climate next to the arctic; approximately arctic.

subastringent, sub•as•trin′jent, *a.* [L. *sub*, slightly.] Astringent in a small degree.

subatomic, sub′a•tom″ik, *a.* [Prefix *sub*, under, and *atomic*.] Relating to particles smaller than atoms, as neutrons, electrons, protons, etc.

subaudition, sub•ą•dish′on, *n.* [L. *subauditio*, from *subaudio*, to understand or supply a word omitted—*sub*, under, and *audio*, to hear.] The act of understanding something not expressed.

subaxillary, sub•ak′sil•le•ri, *a.* [L. *sub*, under, and *axilla*, the arm-pit.] Under the armpit or the cavity of the wing; *bot.* placed under the axil.

subcartilaginous, sub•kär′ti•laj″i•nus, *a.* [L. *sub*, under or slightly.] Situated under or beneath cartilage; partially gristly.

subclass, sub′klas, *n.* [L. *sub*, under.] A subdivision of a class, consisting of allied orders, or superorders.

subclavian, sub•klā′vi•an, *a.* [L. *sub*, under, and *clavis*, a key, used in sense of Gr. *kleis*, the collarbone.] Situated under the clavicle or collarbone.

subcommittee, sub•kom•mit′ē, *n.* [L. *sub*, under.] An under committee; a part or division of a committee.

subconscious, sub•kon′shus, *a.* [Prefix *sub*, under, and *conscious*.] Operating below the level of consciousness but still existing in the mind.—*n.* Mental activities below the level of consciousness.

subcontract, sub•kon′trakt, *n.* [L. *sub*, under, and *contract*.] A contract under a previous contract.—**subcontractor,** sub•kon′trak•tėr, *n.*

subcutaneous, sub•kū•tā′nē•us, *a.* [L. *sub*, under, *cutis*, skin.] Situated immediately under the skin.—*Subcutaneous syringe*, a syringe for injecting substances beneath the skin.

subdeacon, sub′dē•kn, *n.* [L. *sub*, under.] In the *R. Cath. Ch.* an ecclesiastic subordinate to the deacon.

subdialect, sub′dī•a•lekt, *n.* [L. *sub*, under.] An inferior or less important dialect.

subdivide, sub•di•vīd′, *v.t.*—*subdivided, subdividing.* [L. *subdivido*—*sub*, under, and *divido*. DIVIDE.] To divide the parts of into more parts; to part into subdivisions.—*v.i.* To be subdivided.—**subdivision,** sub•di•vizh′on, *n.* The act of subdividing; one of the parts of a larger part.

subdominant, sub•dom′i•nant, *n.* [L. *sub*, under.] *Mus.* the fourth note of the diatonic scale lying a tone under the dominant or fifth of the scale.

subduct, sub•dukt′, *v.t.* [L. *subduco*, *subductum*—*sub*, under, and *duco*, to draw, to lead.] To withdraw; to take away; to subtract by arithmetical operation.—**subduction,** sub•duk′shon, *n.* The act of subducting; subtraction.

subdue, sub•dū′, *v.t.*—*subdued, subduing.* [O.Fr. *subduzer*, to subdue, from L. *sub*, under, and *duco*, to lead. DUKE.] To conquer and bring into subjection; to vanquish; to prevail over by some mild or softening influence; to gain complete sway over; to melt or soften (the heart, opposition); to tone down or make less glaring.

subeditor, sub•ed′i•tėr, *n.* [L. *sub*, under.] An assistant editor of a periodical or other publication.

subepidermal, sub•ep•i•dėr′mal, *a.* [L. *sub*, under.] Lying immediately under the epidermis.

suberose, suberous, sū′bėr•ōs, sū′bėr•us, *a.* [L. *suber*, cork.] Of the nature of cork.—**suberic,** sū•bėr′ik, *a.* Pertaining to cork.

subfamily, sub′fam•i•li, *n.* [L. *sub*, under.] *Nat. hist.* a subdivision of a family; a subordinate family.

subgenus, sub′jē•nus, *n.* [L. *sub*, under.] A subdivision of a genus comprising one or more species.—**subgeneric,** sub•je•ner′ik, *a.* Pertaining to a subgenus.

subgroup, sub′gröp, *n.* [L. *sub*, under.] In scientific classifications, the subdivision of a group.

subinfeudation, sub•in′fū•dā″shon, *n.* [L. *sub*, under.] The enfeoffment of a subordinate tenant by the holder of a fief.

subjacent, sub•jā′sent, *a.* [L. *subjacens*, *subjacentis*, from *subjaceo*, to lie under—*sub*, under, and *jaceo*, to lie (as in *adjacent*, *circumjacent*).] Lying under or below; *geol.* applied to rocks, beds, or strata which lie under or are covered by others.

subject, sub′jekt, *a.* [L. *subjectus*, pp. of *subjicio*, to place under—*sub*, under, and *jacio*, to throw (whence *object*, *eject*, *inject*, *jet*, etc.).] Placed under‡; being under the power and dominion of another; ruled by another state; liable, from extraneous or inherent causes; exposed (*subject to* headache). ∴ Syn. under LIABLE.—*n.* One who owes allegiance to a sovereign; one who lives under and owes allegiance to a government; a person as the recipient of certain treatment; that which is treated or operated on; a dead body for the purposes of dissection; that which is spoken of, thought of, treated of, or handled; matter dealt with; theme of discourse; *logic*, that term of a proposition of which the other is affirmed or denied; *gram.* that which is spoken of; the nominative of a verb; *philos.* the mind, soul, or personality of the thinker—the *Ego*; the thinking agent or principle, the *object*, which is its correlative, being anything or everything external to the mind; *mus.* the principal theme of a movement; *fine arts*, the incident chosen by an artist; the design of a composition or picture.—*v.t.* (sub•jekt′). To bring under; to subdue; to expose; to make liable; to cause to undergo; to expose, as in chemical or other operations; usually with *to* following in all senses (to *subject* a person *to* ridicule).—**subjection,** sub•jek′shon, *n.* The act of subjecting or subduing; the state of being under the control and government of another; subjugation; enthralment.—**subjective,** sub•jek′tiv, *a.* Relating to the subject, as opposed to the *object*; belonging to one's own mind and not to what is external; belonging to ourselves, the conscious *subject*; in *literature* and *art*, characterized by prominence of the personality of the author or artist (the writings of Shelley and Byron are *subjective*).—**subjectively,** sub•jek′tiv•li, *adv.* In a subjective manner; as existing in thought or mind.—**subjectiveness,** sub•jek′tiv•nes, *n.* Subjectivity.—**subjectivism,** sub•jek′tiv•izm, *n.* *Metaph.* the doctrine that all human knowledge is merely relative.—**subjectivity,** sub•jek•tiv′i•ti, *n.* The state of being subjective or in the mind alone; the character of exhibiting the individuality of an author or artist.—**subject matter,**

n. The theme or matter discussed or spoken of.

subjoin, sub•join′, *v.t.* [L. *sub*, under, near.] To add at the end; to add after something else has been said or written.

subjugate, sub′jū•gāt, *v.t.—subjugated, subjugating.* [L. *subjugo, subjugatum—sub*, under, and *jugum*, a yoke. JOIN, YOKE.] To subdue and bring under dominion; to conquer and compel to submit.—**subjugation,** sub•jū•gā′shon, *n.* The act of subjugating; subjection.—**subjugator,** sub′jū•gāt•ėr, *n.* One who subjugates.

subjunctive, sub•jungk′tiv, *a.* [L. *subjunctivus*, from *subjungo, subjunctum—sub*, under, near, and *jungo*, to join.] Subjoined‡; *gram.* designating a mood or form of verbs expressing condition, hypothesis, or contingency, generally subjoined or subordinate to another verb, and preceded by a conjunction.—*n. Gram.* the subjunctive mood.

subkingdom, sub′king•dum, *n.* [L. *sub*, under.] One of the great primary groups into which the animal kingdom is divided.

sublapsarian, sub•lap•sâ′ri•an, *n.* [L. *sub*, under, and *lapsus*, a sliding, a fall.] One who maintains the theological doctrine that God permitted the fall of man, and after it, elected certain persons to salvation passing over others.

sublease, sub′lēs, *n.* [L. *sub*, under.] *Law*, an under lease; a lease granted to a subtenant.—**sublessee,** sub•les•sē′, *n.* The receiver or holder of a sublease.

sublet, sub•let′, *v.t.* [L. *sub*, under.] To underlet; to let to another person, the party letting being himself lessee of the subject.

sublieutenant, sub′lū•ten•ant, *n.* An inferior or second lieutenant.

sublimate, sub′li•māt, *v.t.—sublimated, sublimating.* [L. *sublimo, sublimatum*, to raise, elevate. SUBLIME.] To bring by heat from the solid state into the state of vapor, which on cooling again becomes solid; *fig.* to refine and exalt; to elevate.—*n.* What is produced by sublimation.—*Corrosive sublimate.* See CORROSIVE.—*Blue sublimate*, a preparation of mercury with sulfur and sal ammoniac, used in painting.—**sublimation,** sub•li•mā′shon, *n.* The process of sublimating; a process by which solids are by heat converted into vapor that again becomes solid.

sublime, sub•līm′, *a.* [L. *sublimis*, elevated, exalted, lofty, sublime; perh. from *sub*, up to + *limes* limit.] High in place; elevated; high in excellence; elevated far above men in general by lofty or noble traits; said of persons; striking the mind with a sense of grandeur or power; calculated to awaken, or expressive of, awe, veneration, or lofty feeling; grand; noble: said of objects, of scenery, of an action or exploit, etc.—*The sublime*, what is sublime; sublimity; what is grand or lofty in style; the grand in the works of nature or art, as distinguished from the beautiful.—*v.t.—sublimed*, ppr. *subliming.* To exalt or render sublime; to dignify; to ennoble; to sublimate (which see). —*v.i.* To be susceptible of sublimation.—**sublimely,** sub•līm′li, *adv.* In a sublime manner; grandly; majestically; loftily.—**sublimeness,** sub•līm′nes, *n.* Sublimity.—**sublimity,** sub•lim′i•ti, *n.* [Fr. *sublimité*; L. *sublimitas.*] The state or quality of being sublime; grandeur; loftiness of nature or character; moral grandeur; loftiness of conception, sentiment, or style; elevation, whether exhibited in the works of nature or of art; the emotion produced by what is sublime.

subliminal, sub•lim′i•nal, *a.* [L.L. *sub*, under, *limen*, threshold.] Below consciousness; in the mind without our knowing it.

sublingual, sub•ling′gwal, *a.* [L. *sub*, under, *lingua*, the tongue.] Situated under the tongue.

sublunary, sub′lū•na•ri, *a.* [L. *sub*, under, *luna*, the moon.] *Lit.* situated under the moon; hence, pertaining to this world; mundane; earthly; worldly.—**sublunar,** sub•lū′nėr, *a.* Situated beneath the moon.

submarginal, sub•mär′ji•nal, *a.* [L. *sub*, near.] *Bot.* situated near the margin.

submarine, sub•ma•rēn′, *a.* [L. *sub*, under, and *mare*, the sea. MARINE.] Situated, existing, acting, or growing at some depth in the waters of the sea; remaining at the bottom or under the surface of the sea (*submarine* plants).—*n.* A vessel that can be submerged at will and sail under the water. Submarines are chiefly intended to attack other vessels by means of torpedoes.—*Submarine forest*, a collection of roots and stems of trees, etc., occupying the sites on which they grew, but now submerged by the sea.—*Submarine telegraph*, a telegraph cable laid along the bottom of the sea.

submaxillary, sub•mak•sil′la•ri, *a.* [L. *sub*, under, and *maxilla*, the jaw.] Situated under the jaw.

submediant, sub•mē′di•ant, *n.* [L. *sub*, under, *medius*, middle.] *Mus.* the sixth note of the diatonic scale, or middle note between the octave and subdominant.

submerge, sub•mėrj′, *v.t.—submerged, submerging.* [L. *submergo—sub*, under, and *mergo*, to plunge. MERGE.] To put under water; to plunge; to cover or overflow with water; to drown.—*v.i.* To plunge under water; to sink out of sight.—**submergence,** sub•mėr′jens, *n.* Act of submerging.—**submerse, submersed,** sub•mėrs′, sub•mėrst′, *a. Bot.* being or growing under water.—**submersible,** sub•mėr′si•bl, *n.* A submarine, especially one with projecting ballast tanks.—**submersion,** sub•mėr′shon, *n.* [L. *submersio, submersionis.*] The act of putting or state of being put under water or other fluid; a dipping or plunging; a state of being overflowed.

submit, sub•mit′, *v.t.—submitted, submitting.* [L. *submitto*, to put under, submit—*sub*, under, and *mitto*, to send. MISSION.] To yield to the power or will of another; used *refl.*; to place under the control of another; to surrender; to leave to the discretion or judgment of another; to refer.—*v.i.* To yield one's person to the power of another; to surrender; to yield one's opinion; to acquiesce; to be submissive; to yield without murmuring.—**submitter,** sub•mit′ėr, *n.* One who submits.—**submission,** sub•mish′on, *n.* [L. *submissio, submissionis.*] The act of submitting, yielding, or surrendering; the state of being submissive; humble or suppliant behavior; meekness; resignation; compliance with the commands of a superior; obedience.—**submissive,** sub•mis′iv, *a.* Disposed, or ready to submit; compliant; obedient; humble; meek. —**submissively,** sub•mis′iv•li, *adv.* In a submissive manner; meekly; humbly.—**submissiveness,** sub•mis′iv•nes, *n.* The character of being submissive; ready compliance; meekness.

submultiple, sub•mul′ti•pl, *n.* [L. *sub*, under.] A number or quantity which is contained in another a certain number of times.

subnormal, sub•nor′mal, *n.* [L. *sub*, under.] The portion of a diameter intercepted between the ordinate and the normal to any curve. Below normal.

suboccipital, sub•ok•sip′i•tal, *a.* [L. *sub*, under.] Being under the occiput.

suborbital, sub•or′bi•tal, *a.* [L. *sub*, under, and *orbital.*] Beneath the orbital cavity; not in orbit.

suborder, sub•or′dėr, *n.* [L. *sub*, under.] A subdivision of an order in classifications; a group of animals or plants greater than a genus and less than an order.

subordinate, sub•or′di•nāt, *a.* [L. *sub*, under, and *ordinatus*, pp. of *ordino*, to set in order, from *ordo*, order. ORDER.] Placed in a low order, class, or rank; occupying a lower position in a scale; inferior in nature, power, importance, etc.—*v.t.—subordinated, subordinating.* To place below something else; to make or consider as of less value or importance; to make subject.—*n.* One inferior in power, rank, dignity, office, etc.; one below and under the orders of another.—**subordination,** sub•or′di•nā″shon, *n.* The act of subordinating; gradation of ranks one below another; the state of being under control or government; subjection.—**subordinative,** sub•or′di•nā•tiv, *a.* Tending to subordinate.

suborn, sub•orn′, *v.t.* [Fr. *suborner*, from L. *suborno*, to prepare secretly, to suborn—*sub*, under, and *orno*, to equip, adorn. ORNAMENT.] To bribe to commit perjury; to induce to give false testimony or do some other wickedness.—**subornation,** sub•or•nā′shon, *n.* The crime of suborning.—*Subornation of perjury*, the inducing of any person to commit perjury.—**suborner,** sub•or′nėr, *n.* One who suborns.

subpoena, sub•pē′na, *n.* [L. *sub*, and *pœna*, pain, penalty.] *Law*, a writ or process commanding the attendance in a court of justice of the witness on whom it is served under a penalty.—*v.t.*—*subpoenaed, subpoenaing.* To serve with a writ of subpoena.

subscapular, sub•skap′ū•lėr, *a.* [L. *sub,* under.] Beneath the scapula or shoulder blade.

subscribe, sub•skrīb′, *v.t.*—*subscribed, subscribing.* [L. *subscribo*—*sub,* under, and *scribo,* to write. SCRIBE.] To write one's signature beneath; to sign one's own hand; to consent or bind one's self to by writing one's name beneath; to attest by writing one's name; to promise to give by writing one's name (to *subscribe* money).—*v.i.* To promise along with others a certain sum by setting one's name to a paper; to give consent; to assent; to enter one's name for a newspaper, a book, etc.—**subscriber,** sub•skri′bėr, *n.* One who subscribes; one who admits, confirms, or binds himself to a promise or obligation by signing his name; one who contributes to an undertaking by paying or promising; one who enters his name for a newspaper, periodical, book, or the like.—**subscript,** sub′skript, *a.* Underwritten; written below something.—**subscription,** sub•skrip′shon, *n.* [L. *subscriptio.*] The act of subscribing or signing; the signature attached to a paper; a sum subscribed or promised by signature; a sum contributed along with other subscribers; the amount subscribed.

subsequent, sub′si•kwent, *a.* [L. *subsequens, subsequentis,* ppr. of *subsequor,* to follow close after—*sub,* under, near, and *sequor,* to follow. SEQUENCE.] Following in time; coming or being after something else at any time, indefinitely; following in the order of place or succession; succeeding,—**subsequently,** sub′si•kwent•li, *adv.* In a subsequent manner, time, or position; afterward; later on.—**subsequence, subsequency,** sub′si•kwens, sub′si•kwen•si, *n.* The state of being subsequent.

subserve, sub•sėrv′, *v.t.*—*subserved, subserving.* [L. *subservio*—*sub,* under, and *servio,* to serve. SERVE.] To serve or be of advantage to; to be of service to; to assist or promote.—*v.i.* To serve in an inferior capacity; to be subservient.—**subservience, subserviency,** sub•sėr′vi•ens, sub•sėr′vi•en•si, *n.* The state of being subservient.—**subservient,** sub•sėr′vi•ent, *a.* [L. *subserviens,* ppr. of *subservio.*] Useful as an instrument to promote a purpose; serving to promote some end; acting as a subordinate instrument.—**subserviently,** sub•sėr′vi•ent•li, *adv.* In a subservient manner.

subside, sub•sīd′, *v.i.*—*subsided, subsiding.* [L. *subsido*—*sub,* under, and *sido,* to settle, akin to *sedeo,* to sit. SEDATE.] To sink or fall to the bottom; to settle, as lees; to sink or settle to a lower level, as a building; to fall into a state of quiet; to become tranquil; to abate.—**subsidence,** sub•sī′dens, *n.* The act or progress of subsiding; a gradually settling lower; a sinking into the ground (the *subsidence* of ground).

subsidiary, sub•sid′i•er•i, *a.* [L. *subsidiarius.* SUBSIDY.] Lending some aid or assistance; furnishing help; aiding or assisting; subordinate; contributory; pertaining to a subsidy.—*Subsidiary troops,* troops of one nation hired by another for military service.—*n.* One who or that which is subsidiary; an auxiliary; an assistant; a company controlled by another company by virtue of ownership of the controlling stock.

subsidy, sub′si•di, *n.* [L. *subsidium,* from *sub,* under, *sedeo,* to sit; lit. that which is placed beneath as a support. SUBSIDE.] A sum of money granted for a purpose; an aid or tax formerly granted by parliament to the crown for urgent occasions of the realm; a sum paid by one government to another to meet the expenses of carrying on a war.—**subsidize,** sub′si•dīz, *v.t.*—*subsidized, subsidizing.* To furnish with a subsidy; to purchase the assistance of by a subsidy.

subsist, sub•sist′, *v.i.* [Fr. *subsister,* from L. *subsistere*—*sub,* under, and *sisto, sistere,* to stand, to be fixed, from *sto,* to stand. STATE.] To exist; to have continued existence; to continue to retain the present state; to be maintained with food and clothing; to be supported; to live; to inhere in something else.—*v.t.* To support with provisions.—**subsistence,** sub•sis′tens, *n.* [Fr. *subsistance.*] Actual existence; that which furnishes support to animal life; means of support; support; livelihood; inherence in something else.—**subsistent,** sub•sis′tent, *a.* [L. *subsistens, subsistentis.*] Having existence; inherent.

subsoil, sub′soil, *n.* [L. *sub,* under.] The under-soil; the bed or stratum of earth or earthy matter which lies immediately under the surface soil.

subspecies, sub′spē•shiz, *n.* [L. *sub,* under.] A subordinate species; a division of a species.

substance, sub′stans, *n.* [Fr. *substance,* from L. *substantia,* substance, essence; from *substans, substantis,* ppr. of *substo*—*sub,* under, and *sto,* to stand. STATE.] That of which a thing consists or is made up; matter; material; a distinct portion of matter; a body; that which is real; that which constitutes a thing really a thing; the characteristic constituents collectively; the essential or material part; the purport; solidity; firmness; substantiality; material means and resources; goods; estate; *philos.* that which underlies all phenomena; that which exists independently and unchangeably, in contradistinction to *accident* or quality; *theol.* that in which the divine attributes inhere.—**substantial,** sub•stan′shal, *a.* Actually existing; real; not seeming or imaginary; corporeal; material; firm in substance or material; strong; solid; possessed of considerable substance, goods, or estate; moderately wealthy.—**substantiality,** sub•stan″shi•al″i•ti, *n.* The state of being substantial.—**substantially,** sub•stan′shal•li, *adv.* With reality of existence; strongly; solidly; in substance; in the main; essentially.—**substantialness,** sub•stan′shal•nes, *n.*—**substantiate,** sub•stan′shi•āt, *v.t.*—*substantiated, substantiating.* To make real or actual; to establish by proof or competent evidence; to verify; to make good; to prove.—**substantiation,** sub•stan′shi•ā″shon, *n.* The act of substantiating or proving; evidence; proof.—**substantival,** sub′stan•tī•val, *a.* Relating to or like a substantive.—**substantive,** sub′stan•tiv, *a.* [L. *substantivus,* self-existent; *substantivum verbum,* the substantive verb.] Betokening or expressing existence; depending on itself; independent.—*Substantive verb,* the verb *to be.*—*n. Gram.* a noun.—**substantively,** sub′stan•tiv•li, *adv.* In a substantive manner; in substance; essentially; *gram.* as a substantive or noun (an adjective used *substantively*).

substandard, sub•stan′dėrd, *a.* [L. *sub,* under, and *standard.*] Below standard; *insurance,* constituting a greater than normal risk; a pattern of linguistic usage that is below that of the prestige group of a particular speech community.

substitute, sub′sti•tūt, *v.t.*—*substituted, substituting* [L. *substituo, substitutum*—*sub,* under, and *statuo,* to place, to set (whence *statute,* etc.). STATE.] To put in the place of another; to put in exchange.—*n.* A person acting for or put in the room of another; a person who for a consideration serves in an army in the place of a conscript; one thing put in the place of another or serving the purpose of another.—**substitution,** sub•sti′tū′shon, *n.* The act of substituting or putting in place of another.

substratum, sub•strā′tum, *n.* [L. *sub,* under, and *stratum,* something spread. STRATUM.] That which is laid or spread under something; a stratum lying under another; subsoil; *metaph.* matter or substance in which qualities inhere.

substruction, sub•struk′shon, *n.* [L. *sub,* under, and *struo,* to build. STRUCTURE.] A mass of building below another; a foundation.—**substructure,** sub•struk′chėr, *n.* An under structure; a foundation.

subsultive, subsultory, sub•sul′tiv, sub•sul′to•ri, *n.* [From L. *subsilio, subsultum,* to leap up—*sub,* under, and *salio,* to leap.] Moving by sudden leaps or starts; having a spasmodic character.

subsume, sub•sūm′, *v.t.* [L. *sub,* under, and *sumo,* to take.] *Logic,* to include under a more general class or category.

subtangent, sub′tan•jent, *n.* [L. *sub,* under.] *Math.* the part of a produced diameter or produced axis, intercepted between an ordinate and a tangent, both drawn from the same point in a curve.

subtenant, sub•ten′ant, *n.* [L. *sub,*

under.] The tenant under a tenant; one who rents land or houses from a tenant.

subtend, sub•tend′, *v.t.* [L. *subtendo* —*sub*, under, and *tendo*, to stretch.] To extend under or be opposite to: a geometrical term said of the side of a triangle opposite an angle.

subterfuge, sub′tėr•fūj, *n.* [Fr. *subterfuge*, L.L. *subterfugium*, from L. *subter*, under, and *fugio*, to flee (whence *fugitive*, etc.).] A dishonest shift or expedient; a quirk, prevarication, or other artifice to escape censure or the force of an argument, or to justify opinions or conduct; a false excuse.

subterranean, subterraneous, sub•ter•rā′ni•an, sub•ter•rā′ni•us, *a.* [L. *subterraneus*—*sub*, under, and *terra*, the earth (whence *terrace*, *terrestrial*, *terrier*, etc.).] Being or lying at some depth in the earth; situated within the earth; underground.

subtle, sut′l, *a.* [O.E. *sotel*, *sotil*, *subtil*, O.Fr. *sutil*, *soutil*, *subtil* (Fr. *subtil*), from L. *subtilis*, slender, delicate, subtle, from *sub*, under, and *tela*, for *textela*, a web, from *texo*, to weave (whence *texture*).] Thin or tenuous in substance; not gross or dense; rare; delicate in texture or workmanship; acute or penetrating in intellect; capable of drawing nice distinctions; sly in design; cunning; artful; insinuating; cunningly devised.—**subtleness,** sut′l•nes, *n.* The quality of being subtle.—**subtlety,** sut′l•ti, *n.* The quality of being subtle; cunning; craftiness; wiliness; acuteness of intellect; nicety of distinction or discrimination.—**subtly,** sut′li, *adv.* In a subtle manner; artfully; cunningly; nicely; delicately; deceitfully; delusively.—**subtile,** sub′til or sut′l, *a.* A spelling of *subtle* as are also **subtilely, subtileness, subtilty, subtilization,** sub′til•i•zā″shon, *n.* The act of subtilizing; refinement in drawing distinctions, etc.—**subtilize,** sub′til•īz, *v.t.*—*subtilized*, *subtilizing*. To make subtle; to refine; to spin into niceties.—*v.i.* To refine in argument; to make nice distinctions.

subtonic, sub•ton′ik, *n.* [L. *sub*, under.] *Mus.* the semitone or note next below the tonic; the leading note of the scale.

subtorrid, sub•tor′id, *a.* [L. *sub*, slightly.] Approximately torrid; bordering on the torrid zone.

subtract, sub•trakt′, *v.t.* [L. *subtraho*, *subtractum*—*sub*, under, and *traho*, to draw. TRACT.] To withdraw or take from a number or quantity; to deduct.—**subtracter,** sub•trak′tėr, *n.* One who subtracts.—**subtraction,** sub•trak′shon, *n.* The act or operation of subtracting; the taking of a lesser number from a greater.—**subtractive,** sub•trak′tiv, *a.* Tending or having power to subtract.—**subtrahend,** sub′tra•hend, *n.* [L. *subtrahendus*, that must be subtracted.] The sum or number to be subtracted from another, which is called the minuend.

subtropical, sub•trop′i•kal, *a.* [L. *sub*, near, slightly.] Adjoining the tropics; indigenous to or characteristic of the regions lying near the tropics.

subulate, sū′bū•lāt, *a.* [From L. *subula*, an awl, from *suo*, to sew. SEW.] Shaped like an awl; slender and gradually tapering toward the end or point.

suburb, sub′ėrb, *n.* [L. *suburbium*—*sub*, under, near, and *urbs*, a city. URBAN.] An outlying part of a city or town; a part without the boundaries but in the vicinity of the town.—**suburban,** sub•ėr′ban, *a.*—**suburbanite,** sub•ėr″ban•īt′, *n.* One who dwells in a suburb.—**suburbia,** sub•ėr′bi•a, *n.* The suburbs of a city; suburbanites collectively.

subvene, sub•vēn′, *v.i.*—*subvened*, *subvening*. [From L. *subvenio*, *subventum*, to come to one's assistance—*sub*, under, and *venio*, *ventum*, to come (as in *advent*, *prevent*, etc.).] To arrive or happen so as to obviate something or afford relief.—**subvention,** sub•ven′shon, *n.* The act of coming to relieve or aid; a government grant or aid; pecuniary aid granted.

subvert, sub•vėrt′, *v.t.* [L. *subverto*, to overthrow—*sub*, under, and *verto*, to turn. VERSE.] To overthrow from the foundation; to ruin utterly; to destroy; to corrupt or pervert, as the mind.—**subverter,** sub•vėr′tėr, *n.* One who subverts.—**subversion,** sub•vėr′zhon, *n.* [L. *subversio*.] The act of subverting or overthrowing; overthrow; utter ruin; destruction.—**subversive,** sub•vėr′siv, *a.* Tending to subvert, overthrow, or ruin.

subway, sub′wā, *n.* [L. *sub*, under, and *way*.] An underground way; a passage under a street, usually with an electric railway.

succedaneous, suk•si•dā′ni•us, *a.* [L. *succedaneus*—*sub*, under, and *cedo*, to go. CEDE.] Supplying the place of something else; forming a substitute.—**succedaneum,** suk•si•dā′ni•um, *n.* pl. **succedanea,** suk•si•dā′ni•a. What supplies the place of or is used for something else; a substitute.

succeed, suk•sēd′, *v.t.* [Fr. *succéder*, from L. *succedo*, *successum*—*sub*, under, in place of, and *cedo*, to go. CEDE.] To take the place of in some post or position; to be heir or successor to; to come after; to be subsequent or consequent to. ∴ Syn. under FOLLOW.—*v.i.* To follow; to come next; to become heir; to ascend a throne after the removal or death of the occupant; to come down by order of succession; to devolve; to be fortunate or prosperous in any endeavor; to obtain the object desired; to turn out as wished; to have the desired result.—**succeeder,** suk•sē′dėr, *n.* One who succeeds; a successor.—**success,** suk•ses′, *n.* [L. *successus*, from *succedo*, *successum*.] The termination or result of any affair, whether happy or unhappy; the issue; more especially, a favorable or prosperous termination of anything attempted; good hap or fortune.—**successful,** suk•ses′fụl, *a.* Having or resulting in success; prosperous; fortunate. ∴ Syn. under FORTUNATE.—**successfully,** suk•ses′fụl•li, *adv.* In a successful manner; prosperously; favorably.—**succession,** suk•sesh′on, *n.* [L. *successio*, *successionis*, from *succedo*, *successum*.] A following of things in order, either in time or place; a series following one after the other; a series or line of descendants; successors collectively; a succession or coming to an inheritance; the act or right of entering upon an office, rank, etc., held by a predecessor.—*Law of succession*, or *law of descent*, the law according to which the inheritance of property is regulated, applied generally where the deceased party has died intestate, or in cases where the power of bequeathing property by will is limited by legislation.—*Apostolical succession*, the alleged transmission, through the episcopate, of the power and authority committed by Christ to his apostles for the guidance and government of the church.—**successional,** suk•sesh′on•al, *a.* Relating to succession; consecutive.—**successive,** suk•ses′iv, *a.* [L. *successivus*.] Following in an uninterrupted course or series, as persons or things, and either in time or place; coming one after another; consecutive.—**successively,** suk•ses′iv•li, *adv.* In a successive manner; in a series one after another.—**successiveness,** suk•ses′iv•nes, *n.*—**successor,** suk•ses′or, *n.* [L.] One that succeeds or follows; one that takes the place which another has left: correlative to *predecessor*.

succinct, suk•singkt′, *a.* [L. *succinctus*, tucked or girded up, succinct—*sub*, up, and *cingo*, *cinctum*, to gird. CINCTURE.] Compressed into few words; characterized by verbal brevity; brief; concise. ∴ Syn. under CONCISE.—**succinctly,** suk•singkt′li, *adv.* In a succinct manner; concisely.—**succinctness,** suk•singkt′nes, *n.* The quality of being succinct; conciseness.

succinic, suk•sin′ik, *a.* [L. *succinum*, amber.] Pertaining to amber; obtained from amber.

succor, suk′ėr, *v.t.* [O.Fr. *sucurre*, *soucourre* (Fr. *secourir*), from L. *succurro*, to run up to the aid of—*sub*, under, and *curro*, to run. CURRENT.] To help when in difficulty or distress; to assist and deliver from suffering; to aid or relieve.—*n.* Aid; help; assistance; particularly, assistance in difficulty or distress; the person or thing that brings relief.—**succorer,** suk′ėr•ėr, *n.* One who succors.

succory, suk′ko•ri, *n.* [A corruption of *chicory*.] Chicory.

succotash, suk′ko•tash, *n.* [From American Indian name.] Green maize and beans boiled together.

succulent, suk′kū•lent, *a.* [L. *succulentus*, from *succus*, juice.] Full of juice; juicy.—*Succulent plants*, plants remarkable for the thick and fleshy nature of their stems and leaves.—**succulently,** suk′ku•lent•li, *adv.* In a succulent manner; juicily.—**succulence, succulency,** suk′kū•lens, suk′-

kū•len•si, *n.* The quality of being succulent; juiciness.
succumb, suk•kum′, *v.i.* [L. *succumbo—sub*, under, and *cumbo*, to lie down (seen also in *incumbent, concubine*).] To sink or give way without resistance; to yield; to submit.
succursal, suk•kėr′sal, *a.* [Fr. *succursale*, from L.L. *succursus*, succor. SUCCOR.] Serving as a chapel of ease: said of a church attached to a parish church.—*n.* A chapel of ease; also a branch establishment.
succussion, suk′kush′on, *n.* [L. *succussio, succussionis*, a shaking—*sub*, under, and *quatio*, to shake.] The act of shaking; a shock; an aguish shaking.—**succussive,** suk•kus′iv, *a.* Characterized by shaking.
such, such, *a.* [Lit. so-like, from A. Sax. *swilc, swylc*, from *swa*=*so*, and *lic*=like; Icel. *slíkr*, G. *solch*, Goth. *swaleiks*. So *which*=who-like or why-like.] Of that or the like kind or degree; similar; like; the same as mentioned; so great (*such* baseness). *Such* is followed by *as* before the thing which is the subject of comparison; the article *a* or *an* is placed between it and the noun to which it refers (*such* a man), but *such* comes directly before nouns without the article (*such* weather).—*Such and such*, or *such or such*, used to represent an object generally or indefinitely, or to save particularizing.—*pron.* Such a person or thing; this or that, which was previously stated or is being stated, often in an inverted position (*such* is life).
suck, suk, *v.t.* [A.Sax. *súcan*, to suck, also *súgan*, like G. *saugen*, Icel. *sjúga, súga*, Dan. *suge*; cog. L. *sugo*, Gael. *sugaidh*, Ir. *suigim*, to suck.] To draw into the mouth by the action of the lips and tongue; to draw something from with the mouth; specifically, to draw milk from; to draw in or imbibe; to inhale; to absorb; to draw in as a whirlpool; to swallow up; to engulf.—*v.i.* To draw fluid into the mouth; to draw milk from the breast.—*n.* The act of drawing with the mouth; milk drawn from the breast by the mouth.—**sucker,** suk′ėr, *n.* One who or that which sucks; an organ in animals for sucking; the piston of a suction pump; a shoot or branch which proceeds from the roots or lower part of a stem; the sucking-fish; the lump-fish or lump-sucker; a toy consisting of a small piece of leather having a string attached to the center of it, soaked in water and pressed firmly down on a substance, when the atmospheric pressure causes it to adhere through the vacuum made when the string is pulled.—**suckfish,** *n.* The remora.—**suckle,** suk′l, *v.t.—suckled, suckling*. [Freq. from *suck*.] To give suck to; to nurse at the breast.—**suckling,** suk′ling, *n.* [From *suck* and term. *-ling*.] A young child at the breast.
sucrose, sū′krōs, *n.* [Fr. *sucre*, sugar.] A general name for the sugars identical with cane sugar.
suction, suk′shon, *n.* [O.Fr. *suction*, from L. *sugo, suctum*, to suck. SUCK.] The act of sucking; the sucking up of any fluid by the pressure of the external air when a vacuum is made.—**suction pump,** *n.* The common house or sucking pump as distinguished from the lifting or the force pump.—**suctorial,** suk•tō′ri•al, *a.* Adapted for sucking; living by sucking; capable of adhering by sucking.
sudation, sū•dā′shon, *n.* [L. *sudatio, sudationis*, from *sudo*, to sweat. SWEAT.] A sweating.—**sudatorium,** sū•da•tō′ri•um, *n.* [L.] A hot-air bath for producing perspiration.—**sudatory,** sū′da•to•ri, *n.* A sudatorium.—*a.* Sweating; perspiring.
sudd, sud, *n.* [Ar.] Floating vegetation obstructing boats in the Nile or other rivers.
sudden, sud′en, *a.* [O.Fr. *sodain, sudain, soubdain* (Fr. *soudain*), from L.L. *subitanus*, from L. *subitus*, sudden, from *subeo, subitum*, to steal upon—*sub*, under, and *eo*, to go. ITINERANT.] Happening without or with scarcely a moment's notice; coming unexpectedly; hastily put in use, employed, or prepared; quick; rapid; hasty; violent; passionate.—*On a sudden, of a sudden*, all at once; hastily; unexpectedly. *On the sudden*, is also used.—**suddenly,** sud′en•li, *adv.* In a sudden manner; unexpectedly; all at once.—**suddenness,** sud′en•nes, *n.* State of being sudden.
sudoriferous, sū•do•rif′ėr•us, *a.* [L. *sudor*, sweat (akin to E. *sweat*), and *fero*, to bear.] Producing sweat; secreting perspiration.—**sudorific,** sū•do•rif′ik, *a.* [L. *sudor*, and *facio*, to make.] Causing sweat.—*n.* A medicine that produces sweat; a diaphoretic.
Sudra, sö′dra, *n.* [Hind.] A member of the lowest of the four great castes among the Hindus.
suds, sudz, *n.* pl. [From stem of *seethe*; comp. G. *sud*, a seething, from *sieden*, to seethe.] Water impregnated with soap; a frothy mass.
sue, sū, *v.t.—sued, suing*. [O.Fr. *suir, sewir, sivir* (Fr. *suivre*), from a form *sequere*, for L. *sequi*, to follow (whence *pursue, ensue, suit, suite*). SEQUENCE.] To ply with love; to seek in marriage; to seek justice or right from by legal process; to institute a process in law against.—*To sue out*, to petition for and take out (to *sue out* a pardon).—*v.i.* To play the lover; to woo or be a wooer; to prosecute; to make legal claim; to seek by request; to petition; to plead.—**suability,** sū•a•bil′i•ti, *n.* Capability of being sued.—**suable,** sū′a•bl, *a.* Such as may be sued.—**suer,** sū′ėr, *n.* One who sues; a suitor.
suede, suède, swād, *n.* [Fr. *suède*, Sweden.] Tanned leather, such as kid, having a surface of soft, brushed nap.
suet, sū′et, *n.* [O.Fr. *seu, sieu* (Fr. *suif*), from L. *sebum*, tallow, grease.] The fatty tissue situated about the loins and kidneys of the ox, sheep, deer, etc., and which is harder than the fat from other parts.—**suety,** sū′et•i, *a.* Consisting of suet or resembling it.
suffer, suf′ėr, *v.t.* [O.Fr. *suffrir, sofferre* (Fr. *souffrir*), from L. *sufferre*, inf. of *suffero*, to suffer—*sub*, under and *fero*, to bear. BEAR, FERTILE.] To feel or bear with painful, disagreeable, or distressing effects; to undergo (to *suffer* pain); to be affected by (to *suffer* change, a loss); not to forbid or hinder; to allow.—*v.i.* To feel or undergo pain of body or mind; to undergo punishment; to be capitally executed; to be injured; to sustain loss or damage.—**sufferable,** suf′ėr•a•bl, *a.* Capable of being permitted or endured.—**sufferableness,** suf′ėr•a•bl•nes, *n.* The character of being sufferable.—**sufferably,** suf′ėr•a•bli, *adv.* In a sufferable manner.—**sufferance,** suf′ėr•ans, *n.* The state of suffering; endurance; patient endurance; passive consent by not forbidding or hindering; toleration; permission.—*On sufferance*, by passive permission or consent; without being positively forbidden; tolerated.—**sufferer,** suf′ėr•ėr, *n.* One who suffers; one who undergoes pain; one who sustains inconvenience or loss; one that permits or allows.—**suffering,** suf′ėr•ing, *n.* The bearing of pain, inconvenience, or loss; pain endured; distress.
suffice, suf•fīs′, *v.i.—sufficed, sufficing*. [O.E. *suffise*, from Fr. *suffire, suffisant*, L. *sufficio*, to be sufficient—*sub*, under, and *facio*, to make. FACT.] To be enough or sufficient; to be equal to the end proposed.—*v.t.* To satisfy; to equal to the wants or demands of.—**sufficient,** suf•fi′shent, *a.* [L. *sufficiens, sufficientis*, ppr. of *sufficio*.] Equal to the end proposed; adequate to wants; enough; of competent power or ability; qualified; capable.—**sufficiently,** suf•fi′shent•li, *adv.* To a sufficient degree; well enough; adequately; to a considerable degree.—**sufficiency,** suf•fish′en•si, *n.* The state of being sufficient or adequate; adequacy; capacity; adequate substance or means; a competence; a comfortable fortune; a supply equal to wants; self-conceit; self-confidence.
suffix, suf′fiks, *n.* [L. *suffixus*, pp. of *suffigo, suffixum*, to affix—*sub*, under, near, and *figo, fixum*, to fix. FIX.] A letter or syllable added or annexed to the end of a word; an affix; a postfix.—*v.t.* To add or annex (a letter or syllable) to a word.—**suffixion,** suf•fik′shon, *n.* The act of suffixing.
suffocate, suf′fo•kāt, *v.t.—suffocated, suffocating*. [L. *suffoco, suffocatum—sub*, under, and *faux, faucis*, the throat.] To choke or kill by stopping respiration; to stifle, as by depriving of air; to smother.—*v.i.* To become choked, stifled, or smothered.—**suffocatingly,** suf′fo•kāt′ing•li, *adv.* So as to suffocate.—**suffocation,** suf•fo•kā′shon, *n.* The act of suffocating; the condition of being suffocated, choked, or stifled.—**suffocative,** suf′fo•kā•tiv, *a.* Tending or able to choke or stifle.

Suffolk, suf′fok, *n.* A variety of English horse, strongly built, of a stout round shape.

suffragan, suf′fra•gan, *a.* [Fr. *suffragant*, L. *suffragans*, *suffragantis*, ppr. of *suffragor*, to vote for, from *suffragium*, a vote.] Assisting in ecclesiastical duties: said of bishops.—*n.* A bishop consecrated to assist another bishop in a portion of his diocese; any bishop in relation to his archbishop.

suffrage, suf′frij, *n.* [Fr. *suffrage*, L. *suffragium*, a vote.] A vote given in deciding a question, or in choice of a person; an opinion expressed; one's voice given; right to vote; the parliamentary franchise.—**suffragette,** suf•ra•jet′, *n.* A female advocate of female suffrage.—**suffragist,** suf′ra•jist, *n.* A supporter of some form of suffrage; a suffragette.

suffrutescent, suf•frö•tes′ent, *a.* [L. *sub*, slightly, and *frutex*, a shrub.] Moderately shrubby.—**suffruticose,** suf•frö′ti•kōs, *a.* In part shrubby; woody at the base.

suffumigate, suf•fū′mi•gāt, *v.t.* [L. *suffumigo*, *suffumigare*—*sub*, under, *fumus*, smoke.] To apply fumes or smoke to, as in medical treatment.—**suffumigation,** suf•fū′mi•gā″shon, *n.* The operation of suffumigating; fumigation.

suffuse, suf•fūz′, *v.t.*—*suffused*, *suffusing*. [L. *suffundo*, *suffusum*—*sub*, and *fundo*, to pour, to pour out. FUSE.] To overspread, as with a fluid or tincture; to fill or cover, as with something fluid (eyes *suffused* with tears, *suffused* with blushes).—**suffusion,** suf•fū′zhon, *n.* The act of suffusing or state of being suffused; a spreading over.

Sufism, sö′fizm, *n.* [Ar. *sufiy*, intelligent.] The doctrine of the Sufis, or Mohammedan mystics, of a pantheistic nature.

sugar, shụ′gėr, *n.* [Fr. *sucre*, from Ar. *sukkar*, sugar, from Per. *shakhara*, Prakrit *sakkara*, Skr. *çarkarâ*, grains of sand, sugar.] A well-known sweet granular substance, prepared chiefly from the expressed juice of the sugar cane, but obtained also from many other plants, as maple, beet, birch, parsnip, etc.; something resembling sugar in any of its properties; *fig.* honeyed or soothing words.—*Sugar of lead*, the acetate of lead, the crystals of which have a slight sweetness.—*Sugar of milk*, lactose.—*a.* Made of sugar.—*v.t.* To impregnate, season, sprinkle, or mix with sugar; *fig.* to sweeten, honey, or render acceptable.—*v.i.* To form sugar.—**sugarcane,** shụ″gėr•kān′, *n.* A tall, heavy grass, *Saccharum officinarum*, growing in warm regions, and the chief source of sugar.—**sugar beet,** *n.* A species of beet from whose juice sugar is obtained. —**sugar maple,** *n.* A species of maple tree, *Acer saccharum*, the main source of maple sugar, manufactured from the sap of which sugar is manufactured in considerable quantities in the United States and Canada.—**sugarplum,** *n.* A comfit or small sweetmeat made of boiled sugar, with flavoring and coloring ingredients.—**sugary,** shụ′gėr•i, *a.* Resembling, containing, or composed of sugar; sweet; *fig.* honeyed.

suggest, su•jest′ or sug•jest′, *v.t.* [L. *suggero*, *suggestum*, to put under, to suggest—*sub*, under, and *gero*, to bring. GESTURE.] To introduce indirectly to the mind or thoughts; to call up to the mind; to cause to be thought of; to recall; to propose with diffidence or modesty; to hint. ∴Syn. under HINT.—*v.i.* To make suggestions of evil.—**suggester,** su•jes′tėr or sug•jes′tėr, *n.* One that suggests.—**suggestion,** su•jes′chon or sug•jes′chon, *n.* The act of suggesting, or that which is suggested; a hint; a prompting, especially a prompting to do evil; temptation; *philos.* same as *Association*.—*Principle of suggestion*, association of ideas.—**suggestive,** su•jes′tiv or sug•jes′tiv, *a.* Calculated to suggest thoughts or ideas; suggesting what does not appear on the surface. —**suggestively,** su•jes′tiv•li or sug•jes′tiv•li, *adv.* By way of suggestion. —**suggestiveness,** su•jes′tiv•nes or sug•jes′tiv•nes, *n.* The state or quality of being suggestive.

suicide, sū′i•sīd, *n.* [From L. *sui*, of himself, and *caedo*, to kill (as in *homicide*, *parricide*).] Self-murder; the act of designedly destroying one's own life; one guilty of self-murder; a person who intentionally kills himself.—**suicidal,** sū•i•sī′dal, *a.* Pertaining to or of the nature of suicide. —**suicidally,** sū•i•sī′dal•li, *adv.* In a suicidal manner.

suit, sūt, *n.* [Fr. *suite*, succession, train, attendants, set, etc., from *suivre*, to follow. SUE.] A following‡; pursuit‡; the act of suing; a seeking for something by petition or entreaty; a request; a prayer; an attempt to win a woman in marriage; courtship; a set or number of things used together (a *suit* of curtains, a *suit* of clothes); a set of things of the same kind or stamp (a *suit* (or *suite*) of rooms); any of the four classes into which playing cards are divided; a retinue or train of attendants or followers (in this sense usually written *suite*); *law*, an action or process for the recovery of a right or claim.—*To follow suit*, to play a card of the same suit; hence, to do as another does.—*v.t.* To adapt; to make suitable; to become or be adapted to; to be suitable to; to fit; to be agreeable to; to fall in with the wishes or convenience of.—*v.i.* To agree; to correspond.—**suitable,** sū′ta•bl, *a.* Suiting or being in accordance; fitting; accordant; proper; becoming.—**suitableness, suitability,** sū′ta•bl•nes, sū•ta•bil′i•ti, *n.* The state or quality of being suitable, fitted, or adapted; fitness.—**suitably,** sū′ta•bli, *adv.* In a suitable manner; fitly.—**suite,** swēt, *n.* [Fr.] A company or number of attendants or followers; a retinue; a train; a connected series forming one whole (a *suite* of rooms). —**suitor,** sū′tor, *n.* A petitioner; an applicant; one who sues or entreats; one who solicits a woman in marriage; a wooer; a lover; *law*, a party to a lawsuit.

sulcate, sulcated, sul′kāt, sul′kā•ted, *a.* [L. *sulcatus*, from *sulcus*, a furrow.] Furrowed; grooved: applied especially to stems, leaves, etc., of plants; the surfaces of molluscous shells, etc. —**sulcation,** sul•kā′shon, *n.*

sulfa drug, *n.* Any of various sulfonamide drugs, a group of chemotherapeutic agents effective against bacterial infections.

sulfanilamide, sul•fa•nil′a•mīd, *n.* A synthetic drug used for its therapeutic action in numerous bacterial infections, as in pneumonia, gonorrhea, etc.

sulfate, sul′fāt, *n.* [From *sulfur*.] A salt of sulfuric acid or a compound of sulfuric acid and a base; as *sulfate* of copper, or blue vitriol; *sulfate* of iron, or green vitriol; *sulfate* of magnesium, or Epsom salts, etc.—**sulfatic,** sul•fat′ik, *a.* Relating to, containing, or resembling a sulfate.—**sulfide,** sul′fīd, *n.* A combination of sulfur with a metal or other element; a sulfuret.—**sulfite,** sul′fīt, *n.* A salt composed of sulfurous acid with a base.

sulfur, sulphur, sul′fėr, *n.* [L. *sulphur*, *sulfur*.] A nonmetallic element occurring free or combined in nature aud burning with a blue flame and a suffocating odor. Symbol, S; at. no., 16; at. wt., 32.064.—**sulfurate,** sul′fū•rit, *v.t.* To impregnate or combine with sulfur; to subject to the action of sulfur.—**sulfuration,** sul•fū•rā′shon, *n.* The subjection of a substance, such as straw plait, silks, woolens, etc., to the action of sulfur for the purpose of bleaching.—**sulfurator,** sul′fū•rā•tėr, *n.* An apparatus for fumigating or bleaching by the fumes of burning sulfur.—**sulfureous,** sul•fū′ri•us, *a.* Consisting of or having the qualities of sulfur; sulfurous.—**sulfureously,** sul•fū′ri•us•li, *adv.* In a sulfureous manner.—**sulfureousness,** sul•fū′ri•us•nes, *n.*—**sulfuret,** sul′fū•ret, *n.* A sulfide.—**sulfureted,** sul′fū•ret•ed, *a.* Having sulfur in combination.—*sulfureted hydrogen*, a compound of hydrogen and sulfur, a transparent colorless gas, recognized by its peculiar fetid odor, resembling that of putrid eggs, and very deleterious to animal life.—**sulfuric,** sul•fū′rik, *a.* Pertaining to sulfur.—*sulfuric acid*, oil of vitriol as it is called, from being first prepared from green vitriol (sulfate of iron), a compound of sulfur, oxygen, and hydrogen, colorless, oily, and strongly corrosive, used in the arts for innumerable purposes.—*sulfuric ether*, an incorrect name for ordinary ether (which contains no sulfur).—**sulfuring,** sul′fėr•ing, *n.* Sulfuration.—**sulfur-ore,** *n.* Iron pyrites yielding sulfur and sulfuric acid.—**sulfurous,** sul′fėr•us, *a.* Impregnated with sulfur; like sulfur; containing sulfur.—*Sulfurous oxide*, a gas formed by the combustion of sulfur in air or dry oxygen; also called *sulfur dioxide*; when led into water it forms *sulfurous acid*.—**sulfury,** sul′fėr•i, *a.* Partaking of

sulfur; having the qualities of sulfur.
sulky, sul'ki, *a.* [A.Sax. *solcen*, sluggish, sulky, pp. of *seolcan*, to languish.] Sullen; morose; doggedly keeping up ill-feeling and repelling advances.—*n.* A light two-wheeled carriage for a single person.—**sulkily,** sul'ki•li, *adv.* In a sulky manner; sullenly.—**sulkiness,** sul'ki•nes, *n.* Sullenness; moroseness.—**sulk,** sulk, *v.i.* To indulge in a sullen fit or mood.
sullen, sul'en, *a.* [O.E. *solein, solain*, O.Fr. *solain*, from L.L. *solanus*, from L. *solus*, alone, sole. SOLE.] Gloomily angry and silent; morose; sour; sulky; dismal; of a threatening aspect; somber.—**sullenly,** sul'en•li, *adv.* In a sullen manner; sulkily; with gloomy moroseness.—**sullenness,** sul'en•nes, *n.* The state or quality of being sullen; ill nature with silence.
sully, sul'i, *v.t.*—*sullied, sullying*. [Fr. *souiller* or A.Sax. *solian*, both meaning to soil.] To soil; to spot; to tarnish; to dim; *fig.* to stain, tarnish, or pollute (character *sullied* by infamous vices).—*v.i.* To be soiled or tarnished.
sulphur, sul'fer, *n.* See SULFUR.
sultan, sul'tan, *n.* [Ar. *sultân*.] The ordinary title of Mohammedan sovereigns, especially the ruler of Turkey, who assumed the title of sultan of sultans.—**sultana,** sul•tä'na, *n.* The consort of a sultan; the empress of the Turks; a sultaness; a kind of large raisin.—**sultanate,** sul'tan•āt, *n.* The rule or dominion of a sultan; sultanship.—**sultaness,** sul'tan•es, *n.* A sultana.—**sultanship,** sul'tan•ship, *n.* The office of a sultan.
sultry, sul'tri, *a.* [A form of *sweltry*, O.E. *sueltrie*, sultry, from *swelter*. SWELTER.] Very hot, burning, and oppressive; very hot and moist, or hot, close, and heavy (a *sultry* atmosphere).—**sultriness,** sul'tri•nes, *n.* The state of being sultry.
sum, sum, *n.* [O.Fr. *sume, some* (Fr. *somme*), from L. *summa*, a sum, fem. of *summus*, highest, superl. of *superus*, that is above, from *super*, above. SUPER.] The aggregate of two or more numbers, magnitudes, quantities, or particulars; the amount or total of any number of things added together; the whole or totality; a quantity of money; any amount indefinitely; the principal points viewed or aggregated together; the essence; the substance; an arithmetical problem to be solved.—*v.t.*—*summed, summing*. To add into one whole; to cast up; to bring or collect into a small compass; to comprise in a few words (to *sum up* arguments).—*To sum up evidence*, to recapitulate to the jury the different facts and circumstances which have been adduced in the evidence: said of the presiding judge in a jury court.—**summary,** sum'e•ri, *a.* Reduced into a narrow compass or into few words; succinct; concise; compendious; quickly executed; effected by a short way or method; *law*, said of proceedings carried on by methods intended to facilitate the dispatch of business.—*n.* [L. *summarium*, a summary.] An abridged or condensed statement or account; an abridgment or compendium containing the sum or substance of a fuller statement.—**summarily,** sum'e•ri•li, *adv.* In a summary manner; briefly; concisely; in a short way or method; without delay.—**summarize,** sum'e•rīz, *v.t.*—*summarized, summarizing*. To make a summary or abstract of; to represent briefly.—**summation,** sum•ā'shon, *n.* The act of forming a sum or total amount; an aggregate.
sumac, sumach, sū'mak, *n.* [Fr. *sumac*, Sp. *zumaque*, from Ar. *summâk*, sumach.] A genus of shrubs the leaves of which are much used for tanning; the leaves, shoots, etc., as forming an article of commerce.
summary, summation, etc. See SUM.
summer, sum'ėr, *n.* [A.Sax. *sumor, sumer*=O.H.G. and Icel. *sumar*, G. and Dan. *sommer*, Sw. *sommar*, D. *somer, zomer*; root doubtful.] That season of the year when the sun shines most directly upon any region; the warmest season of the year, which, north of the equator, may be roughly said to include June, July, and August.—*Indian summer*, a period of the autumn season characterized by dry, hazy, windless days.—*a.* Relating to summer (*summer heat*).—*v.i.* To pass the summer or warm season.—**summerhouse,** *n.* A small house or pavilion in a garden to be used in summer.—**summertime,** *n.* The summer season.
summer, sum'ėr, *n.* [Fr. *sommier*, a packhorse, a rafter, from L. *sagmarius*, from Gr. *sagma*, a pack-saddle.] *Building*, a lintel; a girder; a supporting beam.
summersault, sum'ėr•sạlt, *n.* See SOMERSAULT.
summerset, sum'ėr•set, *n.* See SOMERSAULT.
summit, sum'it, *n.* [Fr. *sommet*, dim. of O.Fr. *som*, a summit, from L. *summum*, highest part. SUM.] The top; the highest point; utmost elevation, as of rank; prosperity, etc.
summon, sum'on, *v.t.* [O.E. *somone*, O.Fr. *somoner*, F. *semondre*), from L. *summonere, submonere*—*sub*, under, privately, and *moneo*, to remind (whence *monition, monitor*, etc.).] To call or cite by authority to appear at a place specified; especially, to command to appear in a court of justice; to send for; to ask the attendance of; to call on; especially, to call upon to surrender; to call up; to excite into action or exertion: with *up* (*summon up* your courage).—**summoner,** sum'on•ėr, *n.* One who summons; also, a former name for an apparitor.—**summons,** sum'onz, *n.* [O.E. *somons, somounce*, O.Fr. *semonce, semonse*, a summons, fem. forms of *semons*, pp. of *semondre*.] A call by authority to appear at a place named, or to attend to some public duty; an invitation or asking to go to, or appear at, some place; *law*, a call by authority to appear in a court; also, the written or printed document by which such call is given; *milit.* a call to surrender.
sump, sump, *n.* [L.G., Sw., and Dan. *sump*, D. *somp*, G. *sumpf*, a swamp, pool.] A pond of water for use in saltworks; a pit for receiving metal on its first fusion; a reservoir at the lowest point of a mine, from which is pumped the water that accumulates there.
sumpter, sump'tėr, *n.* [O.Fr. *sommetier*, a packhorse driver; same origin as *summer*, a beam.] A horse that carries necessaries for a journey; a baggage horse; a packhorse.—*a.* Applied to a horse or mule that carries necessaries.
sumptuary, sump'chū•e•ri, *a.* [L. *sumptuarius*, from *sumptus*, expense, from *sumo, sumptum*, to use, spend—*sub*, under, and *emo*, to buy, to take (seen also in *exempt, prompt*, etc.).] Relating to expense; regulating expense or expenditure.—*Sumptuary laws*, laws made to restrain excess in apparel, food, or any luxuries.—**sumptuous,** sump'chū•us, *a.* [L. *sumptuosus*, from *sumptus*, cost, expense.] Costly; expensive; hence, splendid; magnificent.—**sumptuously,** sump'chū•us•li, *adv.* In a sumptuous manner; expensively; splendidly.—**sumptuousness,** sump'chū•us•nes, *n.* Costliness; magnificence.
sun, sun, *n.* [A.Sax. *sunne* (fem.)= Icel., O.H.G., and Goth. *sunna* (Goth. also *sunno*), G. *sonne*, L.G. *sunne*, D. *zon*; akin to Icel. *sól*, A.Sax. *sól*, L. *sol* (SOLAR); from a root meaning to shine.] The self-luminous orb which, being in or near the center of our system of worlds, gives light and heat to the earth and other planets; the sunshine or sunlight (to lie in the *sun*); anything eminently splendid or luminous; that which is the chief source of light, honor, glory, or prosperity; the luminary which constitutes the center of any system of worlds; a revolution of the earth round the sun; a year.—*Under the sun*, in the world; on earth; a proverbial expression.—*Sun of righteousness*, in *Scrip*. Christ.—*Sun and planet wheels*, a contrivance adopted by Watt in the steam engine, equivalent to a crank, the planet wheel being a toothed wheel fixed to the end of the connecting rod, and driving the fly-wheel by circling round a toothed wheel at the end of the fly-wheel shaft.—*v.t.*—*sunned, sunning*. To expose to the sun's rays; to dry in the sun.—**sunbeam,** sun'bēm, *n.* A ray of the sun.—**sunbird,** *n.* A name of small tropical insessorial birds, with plumage approaching in splendor that of the hummingbirds.—**sunbonnet,** *n.* A lady's bonnet having a shade as a protection from the sun.—**sunbow,** *n.* An iris formed by the refraction of light on the spray of cataracts, or on any rising vapor.—**sunburn,** *v.t.* To discolor or scorch by the sun; to tan.—**sunburst,** *n.* A sudden flash of sunlight.—**sundew,** *n.* A genus of plants which by a viscid substance entangle insects, and thus derive a certain amount of nutriment.—**sundial,** *n.* An instrument to show the time of day by

means of a shadow cast by the sun.—**sundog,** *n.* A luminous spot of the nature of a halo.—**sundown,** sun′-doun, *n.* Sunset; sunsetting.—**sun-dried,** *a.* Dried in the rays of the sun.—**sun-fish,** *n.* A genus of large fishes, so called on account of the almost circular form and shining surface of the typical species.—**sunflower,** sun′flou•ėr, *n.* A genus of plants, so named from the form and color of the flower, or from its habit of turning to the sun.—**sunless,** sun′les, *a.* Destitute of the sun or its rays; shaded.—**sunlight,** sun′līt, *n.* The light of the sun; sunshine.—**sunlit,** sun′lit, *a.* Lit or lighted by the sun.—**sunny,** sun′i, *a.* Like the sun; shining or dazzling with light or splendor; bright; exposed to the rays of the sun; lighted up or warmed by the direct rays of the sun.—**sunniness,** sun′i•nes, *n.* State of being sunny.—**sunrise,** sun′-rīz, *n.* The rising or appearance of the sun above the horizon; morning; the region where the sun rises; the east.—**sunset,** sun′set, *n.* The descent of the sun below the horizon; the time when the sun sets; evening; *fig.* close or decline; the region where the sun sets; the west.—**sunshine,** sun′shīn, *n.* The light of the sun; sunlight; *fig.* an influence acting like the rays of the sun; warmth; pleasantness; brightness; cheerfulness.—*a.* Sunshiny.—**sunshiny,** sun′shī•ni, *a.* Bright with the rays of the sun.—**sunstroke,** sun′-strōk, *n.* A kind of heat stroke with prostration caused by overexposure to the sun.

Sunday, sun′dā, *n.* [A.Sax. *sunnandaeg*, that is, day of the sun; G. *sonntag*, Dan. *söndag*, D. *zondag*; so called because this day was anciently dedicated to the *sun* or its worship.] The first day of the week; the Christian Sabbath; the Lord's day. SABBATH.—*a.* Belonging to the Lord's day or Christian Sabbath.—**Sunday school,** *n.* A school for religious instruction held on the Lord's day.

sunder, sun′dėr, *v.t.* [A.Sax. *sundrian*, *syndrian*, from *sundor*, *sunder*, asunder, apart; similarly Icel. *sundra*, Dan. *söndre*, D. *zonderen*, G. *sondern*, to separate. Hence *sundry*, *asunder*. *Sound*, a channel, is closely allied.] To part; to divide; to disunite in almost any manner, as by rending, cutting, or breaking.—*v.i.* To part; to be separated.—*n.* A separation or division into parts: used chiefly, if not exclusively, in the phrase *in sunder*, in two.

sundry, sun′dri, *a.* [A.Sax. *sundrig*, *syndrig*, from *sundor*, separate. SUNDER.] Several; more than one or two. —*All and sundry*, all both collectively and individually.—**sundries,** sun′driz, *n. pl.* Various small things, too minute or numerous to be individually specified.

sung, sung, pret. and pp. of *sing*.

sunk, sungk, pret. and pp. of *sink*.—**sunken,** sung′kn, *a.* Lying on the bottom of the sea or other water; low.—**sunk fence,** *n.* A ditch with a retaining wall on one side.

sunn, sunn hemp, sun, *n.* An East Indian material similar to hemp, used for cordage, canvas, etc.

Sunnites, sụn′īts, *n. pl.* The orthodox Mohammedans who receive the *Sunna* or traditionary law as of equal importance with the Koran.

sup, sup, *v.t.*—*supped, supping.* [A. Sax. *súpan*, to sup = Icel. *súpa*, L.G. *supen*, D. *zuipen*, O.G. *sufan*, G. *saufen*, to sip or sup. *Sip* is a lighter form of this, and *soup*, *sop*, are akin.] To take into the mouth with the lips, as a liquid; to imbibe; to sip; to have as one's lot; to be afflicted with (to *sup* sorrow).—*v.i.* To eat the evening meal.—*n.* A little taken with the lips; a sip.—**supper,** sup′ėr, *n.* [O.E. *soper*, O.Fr. *soper*, *super*, Mod.Fr. *souper*, to sup, supper (the inf. used as a noun), from the Teutonic.] The evening meal; the last repast of the day.—*Lord's supper*, the eucharist. LORD.—*v.i.* To take supper; to sup.—*v.t.* To give supper to.—**supperless,** sup′ėr•les, *a.* Wanting supper; being without supper.

super, sū′pėr, *n.* [L. *super*, above, beyond, besides (allied to E. *over*), whence *superus*, upper, comparative *superior*, superlative *supremus* or *summus* (whence *supreme, sum, summit*).] A contraction used colloquially for certain words of which it is the prefix; a supernumerary; specifically, a theatrical supernumerary.

superable, sū′pėr•a•bl, *a.* [L. *superabilis*, from *supero*, to overcome.] Capable of being overcome or conquered.

superabound, sū′pėr•a•bound″, *v.i.* [Prefix *super*, and *abound.*] To abound above or beyond measure.—**superabundance,** sū′pėr•a•bun″dens, *n.* More than enough; excessive abundance.—**superabundant,** sū′-pėr•a•bun″dent, *a.* Abounding to excess; being more than is sufficient. —**superabundantly,** sū′pėr•a•bun″-dent•li, *adv.* In a superabundant manner.

superadd, sū•pėr•ad′, *v.t.* [Prefix *super*, and *add.*] To add over and above; to add or join in addition.—**superaddition,** sū′pėr•ad•di″shon, *n.* The act of superadding; that which is superadded.

superannuate, sū•pėr•an′nū•āt, *v.t.*—*superannuated, superannuating.* [Prefix *super*, above, beyond, and L. *annus*, a year.] To allow to retire from service on a pension, on account of old age or infirmity; to give a retiring pension to.—*v.i.* To retire on a pension when disabled by length of years.—**superannuation,** sū•pėr•-an′nū•ā″shon, *n.* The state of being too old for office or business; retirement or removal from office with a pension, on account of long service or infirmity.

superb, sū•perb′, *a.* [Fr. *superbe*; L. *superbus*, proud, from *super*, above. SUPER.] Grand; august; stately; splendid; rich; sumptuous; showy; very fine; first-rate.—**superbly,** sū•-pėrb′li, *adv.* In a superb or splendid manner.—**superbness,** sū•pėrb′nes, *n.*

supercargo, sū•pėr•kär′gō, *n.* [Prefix *super*, and *cargo.*] *Lit.* a person over the cargo; a person in a merchant ship whose business is to manage the sales and superintend all the commercial concerns of the voyage.

superciliary, sū•pėr•sil′i•er•i, *a.* [L. *supercilium*, the eyebrow, also haughtiness or pride (as expressed by raising the brows)—*super*, above, and *cilium*, an eyelid.] Pertaining to the eyebrow; situated or being above the eyelid.—**supercilious,** sū•pėr•sil′i•us, *a.* [L. *superciliosus.*] Having a haughty air or manner; acting as if others were inferiors; haughty; overbearing; arrogant.—**superciliously,** sū•-pėr•sil′i•us•li, *adv.* In a supercilious manner; with an air of contempt.—**superciliousness,** sū•pėr•sil′i•us•nes, *n.* The state or quality of being supercilious; haughtiness.

superdominant, sū•pėr•dom′i•nant, *n.* [Prefix *super*, and *dominant.*] *Mus.* the note above the dominant; the sixth note of the diatonic scale.

superego, sū′pėr•ē″gō, *n.* [Prefix *super*, and *ego* (N.L. from L.), I.] A division of the psyche that is partly conscious, corresponding to conscience.

supereminent, sū•pėr•em′i•nent, *a.* [Prefix *super*, and *eminent.*] Eminent in a superior degree; surpassing others in excellence, power, authority, etc.—**supereminence,** sū•pėr•-em′i•nens, *n.* Eminence superior to what is common; distinguished eminence.—**supereminently,** sū•-pėr•em′i•nent•li, *adv.* In a supereminent manner.

supererogation, sū•pėr•er′o•gā•shon, *n.* [L. *supererogo*, *supererogatum*, to pay over and above—*super*, above, and *erogo*, to pay—*e*, *ex*, out, and *rogo*, to ask. ROGATION.] Performance of more than duty requires.—*Works of supererogation*, in the *R. Cath. Ch.* good works which are considered as not absolutely required of each individual for his salvation, and which it is believed God may accept in atonement for the defective service of another.—**supererogatory,** sū′pėr•e•rog″a•to•ri, *a.* Partaking of supererogation.

superfecundation, sū′pėr•fē•kun•-dā″shon, *n.* [L. *super*, over, and *fecundus*, fruitful.] Superfetation.

superfetate, sū•pėr•fē′tāt, *v.i.* [L. *superfeto*—*super*, over, after, and *feto*, to breed. FETUS.] To conceive after a prior conception.—**superfetation,** sū′pėr•fē•tā″shon, *n.* A second conception after a prior one, and by which two fetuses exist at once in the same womb.

superficies, sū•pėr•fish′ēz, *n.* [L., from *super*, upon, and *facies*, face. (FACE.) *Surface* is another form of the same word.] The surface; the exterior part or face of a thing, consisting of length and breadth without thickness, and therefore forming no part of the substance or solid content of a body.—**superficial,** sū•pėr•fish -al, *a.* [L. *superficialis.*] Lying on or pertaining to the surface; not penetrating the substance of a thing; not sinking deep; not deep or profound as regards knowledge; not learned or thorough; not going to the heart of things.—**superficiality,** sū•pėr•-

fish′i•al″i•ti, *n.* The quality of being superficial; want of depth or thoroughness; shallowness; a superficial person or thing.—**superficially,** sū•pėr•fish′al•li, *adv.* In a superficial manner; on the surface only; without going deep; slightly; not thoroughly. —**superficialness,** sū•pėr•fish′al•nes, *n.* Superficiality; shallowness.

superfine, sū•pėr•fīn′, *a.* [Prefix *super*, and *fine.*] Very fine; surpassing others in fineness; excessively or faultily subtle.

superfluity, sū•pėr•flū′i•ti, *n.* [Fr. *superfluité*, L. *superfluitas*, from *superfluus*, overflowing—*super*, above, and *fluo*, to flow. FLUENT.] A quantity that is over and above what is necessary; a greater quantity than is wanted; redundancy; something for show or luxury rather than use.—**superfluous,** sū•pėr′flu̦•us, *a.* [L. *superfluus.*] Being more than is wanted or sufficient; unnecessary from being in excess; redundant.—**superfluously,** sū•pėr′flu̦•us•li, *adv.* In a superfluous manner.—**superfluousness,** sū•pėr′flu̦•us•nes, *n.*

superheat, sū′pėr•hēt, *v.t.* [Prefix *super*, and *heat.*] To heat to an extreme degree; specifically, to heat steam, apart from contact with water, until it resembles a perfect gas.

superhuman, sū•pėr•hū′man, *a.* [Prefix *super*, and *human.*] Above or beyond what is human; hence, sometimes, divine.

superimpose, sū′pėr•im•pōz″, *v.t.* [Prefix *super*, and *impose.*] To lay or impose on something else.—**superimposition,** sū•pėr•im′po•zish″on, *n.* The act of superimposing or the state of being superimposed.

superincumbent, sū′pėr•in•kum″bent, *a.* [Prefix *super*, and *incumbent.*] Lying or resting on something else. —**superincumbence, superincumbency,** sū′pėr•in•kum″bens, sū′pėr•in•kum″ben•si, *n.* State of lying upon something.

superinduce, sū′pėr•in•dūs″, *v.t.* [Prefix *super*, and *induce.*] To bring in or on as an addition to something. —**superinduction,** sū′pėr•in•duk″shon, *n.* The act of superinducing.

superintend, sū′pėr•in•tend″, *v.t.* [L. *superintendo*, to have the oversight of—*super* and *intendo.* INTEND.] To have the charge and oversight of; to oversee with the power of direction; to take care of with authority.—**superintendence, superintendency,** sū′pėr•in•ten″dens, sū′pėr•in•ten″den•si, *n.* The act of superintending; care and oversight for the purpose of direction, and with authority to direct.—**superintendent,** sū′pėr•in•ten″dent, *n.* One who superintends or has the oversight and charge of something.—*a.* Overlooking others with authority.

superior, sū•pē′ri•ėr, *a.* [L., compar. of *superus*, upper, high, from *super*, above. SUPER.] More elevated in place; higher; higher in rank, office, or dignity; higher or greater in excellence; being beyond some power or influence; too great or firm to be affected by (*superior* to revenge); *bot.* growing above or upon anything (as the ovary when growing above the origin of the calyx); next the axis.—*Superior courts*, the highest courts in a state.—*Superior planets*, those that are more distant from the sun than the earth, as Mars, Jupiter, Saturn, Uranus, and Neptune.—*n.* One who is superior to or above another; one who is higher or greater than another in social station, rank, power, excellence, or qualities of any kind; the chief of a monastery, convent, or abbey; *Scots law*, one who has certain rights of feu over a property. —**superiority,** sū•pē′ri•or″i•ti, *n.* The state or quality of being superior; preeminence; higher rank or excellency.—**superiorly,** sū•pē′ri•ėr•li, *adv.* In a superior manner or position.

superjacent, sū•pėr•jā′sent, *a.* [L. *super*, above, and *jacens, jacentis*, ppr. of *jaceo*, to lie.] Lying above or upon.

superlative, sū•pėr′la•tiv, *a.* [L. *superlativus*, from *superlatus*—*super*, over, and *latus*, carried.] Of the highest pitch or degree; most eminent; surpassing all other (*superlative* wisdom or beauty); *gram.* applied to that form of an adjective or adverb which expresses the highest or utmost degree of the quality or manner. —*n.* That which is superlative; *gram.* the superlative degree of adjectives or adverbs; a word in the superlative degree.—**superlatively,** sū•pėr′la•tiv•li, *adv.* In a superlative manner; in the highest or utmost degree.—**superlativeness,** sū•pėr′la•tiv•nes, *n.* The state of being superlative.

superlunar, superlunary, sū•pėr•lū′nėr, sū•pėr•lū′na•ri, *a.* [L. *super*, above, *luna*, the moon.] Being above the moon; not sublunary or of this world.

superman, sū′pėr•man, *n.* The ideal superior man of the future in the philosophy of Nietzsche; also called *overman.*

supermarket, a large market store operating on a self-service, cash-and-carry basis.

supernal, sū•pėr′nal, *a.* [L. *supernus*, from *super*, above. SUPER.] Being or situated above us; relating to things above; celestial; heavenly.

supernatant, sū•pėr•nā′tant, *a.* [L. *super*, above, over, and *nato*, to swim.] Swimming above; floating on the surface.

supernatural, sū•pėr•nach′ė•ral, *a.* [Prefix *super*, and *natural.*] Being beyond or exceeding the powers or laws of nature; a term stronger than *preternatural*, and often equivalent to *miraculous.*—*The supernatural*, supernatural agencies, influence, phenomena, and so forth.—**supernaturalism,** sū•pėr•nat′ū•ral•izm, *n.* The state of being supernatural; *theol.* the doctrine that religion and the knowledge of God require a revelation from God.—**supernaturalist,** sū•pėr•nach′ė•ral•ist, *n.* One who upholds the principles of supernaturalism.—**supernaturally,** sū•pėr•nach′ė•ral•li, *adv.* In a supernatural manner.—**supernaturalness,** sū•pėr•nach′ė•ral•nes, *n.* The state or quality of being supernatural.

supernumerary, sū•pėr•nū′me•ra•ri, *a.* [L. *super*, above, beyond, and *numerus*, a number.] Exceeding a number stated or prescribed; exceeding a necessary or usual number. —*n.* A person or thing beyond a certain number, or beyond what is necessary or usual; especially a person not formally a member of an ordinary or regular body or staff of officials or employees; *milit.* in drill, the N.C.O.'s, etc., forming the third rank.

superphosphate, sū•pėr•fos′fāt, *n.* [Prefix *super*, and *phosphate.*] A specially soluble phosphate of calcium, used as a fertilizer.

superpose, sū•pėr•pōz′, *v.t.*—*superposed, superposing.* [Fr. *superposer*, from prefix *super*, and *poser*, to lay. POSE.] To lay upon, as one kind of rock on another.—**superposition,** sū′pėr•pō•zish″on, *n.* The act of superposing; a lying or being situated above or upon something; *geol.* the order in which mineral masses are placed upon or above each other, as more recent strata upon those that are older; *geom.* the process by which one magnitude may be conceived to be placed upon another.

supersaturate, sū•pėr•sach′u̦•rāt, *v.t.* [Prefix *super*, and *saturate.*] To saturate to excess.—**supersaturation,** sū′pėr•sach′u̦•rā″shon, *n.* Saturation to excess.

superscribe, sū•pėr•skrīb′, *v.t.*—*superscribed, superscribing.* [L. *superscribo*—*super*, over or above, and *scribo*, to write. SCRIBE.] To write on the top, outside, or surface; to put an inscription on; to write the name or address of one on the outside or cover of.—**superscription,** sū•pėr•skrip′shon, *n.* The act of superscribing; what is written or engraved on the outside or above something else; especially, an address on a letter.

supersede, sū•pėr•sēd′, *v.t.*—*superseded, superseding.* [O.Fr. *superseder*, L. *supersedere*, to sit over, to refrain, omit—*super*, above, and *sedeo*, to sit. SEDATE.] To make void, inefficacious, or useless by superior power, or by coming in the place of; to set aside; to suspend; to come or be placed in the room of; to displace; to replace (one person *supersedes* another).—**supersedure, supersession,** sū•pėr•sē′dūr, sū•pėr•sesh′on, *n.* The act of superseding.

supersensible, sū•pėr•sen′si•bl, *a.* [Prefix *super*, and *sensible, sensitive*, etc.] Beyond the reach of the senses. —**supersensual,** sū•pėr•sen′shö•al, *a.* Above or beyond the reach of the senses.

supersonic, sū′pėr•son″ik, *a.* [Prefix *super*, and *sonic* (L. *sonus*, sound).] Of a frequency higher than the human ear's audibility (approximately 20,000 cycles per second); of speeds that are faster than sound. —*n.* pl. The science of supersonic phenomena.

superstition, sū•pėr•stish′on, *n.* [L. *superstitio, superstitionis*, originally a standing still at, a standing in fear or amazement, hence superstition, from *supersto*, to stand over—*super*, over, and *sto*, to stand. STATE.] Belief in and reverence of things which are no proper objects of worship; a faith or article of faith based on ignorance of or on unworthy ideas regarding the Deity; a practice or observance founded on such a belief; credulity regarding the supernatural; belief in the direct agency of superior powers in certain affairs, as a belief in witchcraft or magic, or in supernatural phenomena, as apparitions, omens, etc.—**superstitious,** sū•pėr•stish′us, *a.* Pertaining or addicted to superstition; credulous in regard to the supernatural; proceeding from superstition.—**superstitiously,** sū•pėr•stish′us•li, *adv.* In a superstitious manner. —**superstitiousness,** sū•pėr•stish′us•nes, *n.*

superstratum, sū•pėr•strā′tum, *n.* [Prefix *super*, and *stratum*.] A stratum or layer above another, or resting on something else.

superstructure, sū•pėr•struk′chėr, *n.* [Prefix *super*, and *structure*.] Any structure built on something else; anything erected on a foundation or basis.

supersubtle, sū•pėr•sut′l, *a.* [Prefix *super*, and *subtle*.] Oversubtle; crafty in an excessive degree.

supertax, sūp′ėr•taks, *n.* [Prefix *super*, and *tax*.] An extra tax, usually graded, on incomes above some fixed amount.

supertonic, sū•pėr•ton′ik, *n.* [Prefix *super*, and *tonic*.] *Mus.* the note next above the tonic or key note; the second note of the diatonic scale.

supervene, sū•pėr•vēn′, *v.i.*—*supervened, supervening*. [L. *supervenio*—*super*, above, over, and *venio*, to come.] To come upon as something extraneous; to be added or joined; to take place; to happen.—**supervenient,** sū•pėr•vē′ni•ent, *a.* Coming upon as something additional; added; arising or coming afterward.—**supervention,** sū•pėr•ven′shon, *n.* The act of supervening.

supervise, sū•pėr•vīz , *v.t.*—*supervised, supervising*. [L. *super*, over, and *viso*, to look at, from *video, visum*, to see. VISION.] To oversee for direction; to superintend; to inspect.—**supervision,** sū•pėr•vizh′on, *n.* The act of supervising; superintendence; direction.—**supervisor,** sū•pėr•vī′zėr, *n.* One who supervises; an overseer; an inspector; a superintendent.—**supervisory,** sū•pėr•vī′zo•ri, *a.* Pertaining to or having supervision.

supine, sū•pīn′, *a.* [L. *supinus*, lying on the back, negligent, connected with *sub*, and Gr. *hypo*, under.] Lying on the back or with the face upward; opposed to *prone*; sloping backward; negligent; listless; indolent; inattentive.—*n.* (sū′pīn). [L. *supinum*; reason of the name not obvious.] A part of the Latin verb, really a verbal noun with two cases, an accusative in *-um*, and an ablative in *-u*.—**supinely,** sū•pīn′li, *adv.* In a supine manner; carelessly; indolently; listlessly.—**supineness,** sū•pīn′nes, *n.* Indolence; listlessness.—**supination,** sū•pī•nā′shon, *n.* The position of the hand extended outward with the palm upwards.—**supinator,** sū•pī•nā′tėr, *n.* A muscle which aids in turning the hand upward.

supper. See SUP.

supplant, sup•plant′, *v.t.* [Fr. *supplanter*, from L. *supplantare*, to trip up one's heels—*sub*, under, and *planta*, the sole of the foot. PLANT.] To trip up (*Mil.*)‡; to remove or displace by stratagem; to displace and take the place of.—**supplantation,** sup•plan•tā′shon, *n.* The act of supplanting.—**supplanter,** sup•plan′tėr, *n.* One who supplants.

supple, sup′l, *a.* [Fr. *souple*, from L. *suplex*, suppliant, bending—*sub*, under, and *plico*, to fold. SUPPLICATE.] Pliant; flexible; easily bent; yielding; not obstinate; capable of molding one's self to suit a purpose; flattering; fawning.—*v.t.*—*suppled, suppling*. To make supple or pliant; to make compliant, submissive, or yielding.—*v.i.* To become soft and pliant.—**supplejack,** *n.* A popular name given to various strong twining and climbing shrubs, the branches of which are imported into Europe from the West Indies for walking sticks.—**supplely,** sup′l•li, *adv.* In a supple manner.—**suppleness,** sup′l•nes, *n.* The quality of being supple or easily bent; pliancy; readiness of compliance; facility.

supplement, sup′le•ment, *n.* [L. *supplementum*, from *suppleo*, to fill up, to make full—*sub*, and *pleo*, to fill. SUPPLY.] An addition to anything, by which it is made more full and complete, especially an addition to a book, to a periodical publication, etc.; *trigon.* the quantity by which an arc or an angle falls short of 180 degrees or a semicircle. —*v.t.* To increase or complete by a supplement.—**supplemental, supplementary,** sup•le•men′tal, sup•le•men′te•ri, *a.* Of the nature of a supplement; serving to supplement; additional.

suppleness. See SUPPLE.

suppliant, sup′li•ant, *a.* [Fr. *suppliant*, ppr. of *supplier*, to entreat, from L. *supplico*, to *supplicate* (which see).] Entreating or begging earnestly; asking earnestly and submissively; supplicating; expressive of supplication.—*n.* A humble petitioner; one who entreats submissively.—**suppliantly,** sup′li•ant•li, *adv.* In a suppliant manner.

supplicate, sup′li•kāt, *v.t.*—*supplicated, supplicating*. [L. *supplico, supplicatum*, from *supplex, supplicis*, suppliant, lit. bending under (whence *supple*)—*sub*, under, and *plico*, to fold. PLY, *v.t.*] To entreat or beg humbly for; to seek by earnest prayer (to *supplicate* blessings); to address in prayer; to petition humbly (to *supplicate* God).—*v.i.* To petition with earnestness and submission; to implore; to beseech.—**supplication,** sup•li•kā′shon, *n.* [L. *supplicatio*.] The act of supplicating; humble and earnest prayer in worship; a petition; an earnest request.—**supplicatory,** sup′li•kā•to•ri, *a.* Containing supplication.—**supplicant,** sup′li•kant, *n.* One who supplicates or humbly entreats; a humble petitioner; a suppliant.—*a.* Earnestly entreating; suppliant.

supply, sup•plī, *v.t.*—*supplied, supplying*. [Fr. *suppléer*, to supply, from L. *supplere*, to fill up—*sub*, under, and *pleo*, to fill (seen also in *supplement, accomplish, complete, deplete, expletive, replete*, etc.). PLENTY.] To furnish with what is wanted (to *supply* a person *with* a thing); to afford or furnish a sufficiency for (to *supply* wants); to provide or furnish (to *supply* provisions); to serve instead of; to take the place of. —*n.* The act of supplying; a quantity supplied; a stock; a store; *pl.* the stores or articles necessary for an army or other great body of people; a grant of money provided by a national assembly to meet the expenses of government; the extent to which goods are produced to meet the demand.—**supplier,** sup•plī′ėr, *n.* One who supplies.

support, sup•pōrt′, *v.t.* [Fr. *supporter*, to support, bear, endure, etc., from L. *supporto*, to convey—*sub*, under, and *porto*, to carry (as in *export, import, report*, etc.). PORT, to carry.] To bear, uphold, prop up; to keep from falling or sinking; to endure without being overcome; to bear; to undergo; to uphold by aid or encouragement; to further, second, aid, assist; to keep from sinking, failing, or declining (to *support* the courage); to represent in acting on the stage; to act (to *support* a part); to be able to supply funds for or the means of continuing; to be able to carry on or continue; to maintain with the means of living; to provide for; to keep up by nutriment; to sustain (to *support* life, to *support* combustion); to make good or substantiate (a statement, an accusation); to second, as a proposal or motion at a public meeting.—*n.* The act of supporting; that which upholds or keeps from falling; a base, prop, foundation of any kind; sustenance or what maintains life; maintenance; livelihood; one who furnishes another's livelihood; the act of assisting, maintaining, vindicating, etc.; aid; help; succor; assistance.—**supportable,** sup•pōr′ta•bl, *a.* Capable of being supported; that may be tolerated; bearable; endurable.—**supportableness,** sup•pōr′ta•bl•nes, *n.* The state of being supportable.—**supportably,** sup•pōr′ta•bli, *adv.* In a supportable manner.—**supporter,** sup•pōr′tėr, *n.* One who supports or maintains; a defender; advocate, vindicator, adherent; one who accompanies and aids another; that which supports or keeps up; a prop, a pillar, etc.; *her.* a figure on each side of a shield appearing to support it; a band or truss for the support of any part.

suppose, sup•pōz′, *v.t.*—*supposed, supposing*. [Fr. *supposer*—*sup* for *sub*, under, and *poser*, to place.

POSE.] To lay down or regard as matter of fact for the sake of argument or illustration; to assume hypothetically; to take for granted; to imagine; to think to be the case; to require to exist or be true; to imply (creation *supposes* a creator).—*v.i.* To make or form a supposition; to think; to imagine.—**supposable,** sup•pō′za•bl, *a.* Capable of being supposed or imagined.—**supposal,** sup•pō′zal, *n.* A supposition.—**supposition,** sup•po•zish′on, *n.* The act of supposing; hypothesis; what is assumed hypothetically; an assumption; a conjecture.—**suppositional,** sup•po•zish′on•al, *a.* Based on supposition; hypothetical.—**suppositive,** sup•poz′i•tiv, *a.* Including or implying supposition.—*n.* A word implying supposition, as *if.*—**suppositively,** sup•poz′i•tiv•li, *adv.* With, by, or upon supposition.

supposititious, sup•poz′i•tish″us, *a.* [L. *supposititius*, from *suppono*, *suppositum*—*sub*, under, and *pono*, to place. POSITION.] Put by trick in the place belonging to another; substituted falsely; not genuine; counterfeit; spurious.—**supposititiously,** sup•poz′i•tish″us•li, *adv.* In a supposititious manner; spuriously.—**supposititiousness,** sup•poz′i•tish″us•nes, *n.*

suppress, sup•pres′, *v.t.* [L. *supprimo*, *suppressum*—*sub*, under, and *premo*, *pressum*, to press. PRESS.] To overpower and crush; to put down; to quell; to destroy (a revolt, mutiny, or riot); to restrain from utterance or vent; to check or keep in (to *suppress* the breath); to conceal; not to tell or reveal; to retain without making public.—**suppressible,** sup•pres′i•bl, *a.* Capable of being suppressed.—**suppression,** sup•presh′on, *n.* The act of suppressing, crushing, or putting down; the act of retaining from utterance, vent, or disclosure; concealment; the retaining of anything from public notice; *gram.* omission or ellipsis.—**suppressive,** sup•pres′iv, *a.* Tending to suppress.—**suppressor,** sup•pres′ėr, *n.* One who suppresses.

suppurate, sup′pū•rāt, *v.i.*—*suppurated, suppurating.* [L. *suppuro*, *suppuratum*—*sub*, and *pus*, *puris*, matter. PUS.] To generate pus or matter; to have a gathering of pus; to fester.—**suppuration,** sup•pū•rā′shon, *n.* The process of forming pus, as in a wound or abscess.—**suppurative,** sup′pū•rā•tiv, *a.* Tending to suppurate.—*n.* Something that promotes suppuration.

supralapsarian, sū′pra•lap•sâ″ri•an, *n.* [L. *supra*, above, and *lapsus*, a fall.] One who maintains that God decreed or preordained the fall of man and all its consequences, determining to save some and condemn others.—**supralapsarianism,** sū′pra•lap•sâ″ri•an•izm, *n.* The doctrine of the supralapsarians.

supraorbital, sū•pra•or′bi•tal, *a.* [Prefix *supra*, above, and *orbit.*] *Anat.* being above the orbit of the eye.

suprarenal, sū•pra•rē′nal, *a.* [L. *supra*, above, and *renes*, the kidneys.] *Anat.* situated above the kidneys.—*Suprarenal body.* See ADRENAL.

supreme, sū•prēm′, *a.* [L. *supremus*, from *superus*, upper, higher, from *super*, above. SUPER.] Highest in authority; holding the highest place in government or power; highest as to degree; greatest possible; utmost; *bot.* situated at the highest part or point.—*The Supreme*, the most exalted of beings; the sovereign of the universe; God.—**supremely,** sū•prēm′li, *adv.* With the highest authority; in the highest degree; to the utmost extent.—**supremacy,** sū•prem′a•si, *n.* The state or character of being supreme; highest authority or power.—*Papal supremacy*, the supreme authority which the pope formerly exercised over the churches of England, Scotland, and Ireland, and which still continues to be more or less recognized in some countries.—*Regal supremacy*, the authority which the sovereign of England exercises over the Church of England, as being its supreme head on earth.—*Oath of supremacy*, in Great Britain, an oath denying the supremacy of the pope in ecclesiastical or temporal affairs in that realm.

sura, sö′ra, *n.* [Ar.] A chapter of the Koran.

sural, sū′ral, *n.* [L. *sura*, the calf of the leg.] Pertaining to the calf of the leg.

surbase, sėr′bās, *n.* [Prefix *sur* (L. *super*), upon, and *base.*] *Arch.* the crowning molding or cornice of a pedestal; a border or molding above the base.—**surbased,** sėr′bāst, *a.* *Arch.* having a surbase.

surcharge, sėr•chärj′, *v.t.* [Prefix *sur* (L. *super*), over, and *charge.*] To overload; to overburden; to overcharge; to put an extra charge on.—*n.* An excessive or extra charge or burden; an overcharge.

surcingle, sėr′sing•gl, *n.* [O.Fr. *sursangle*, from *sur*, L. *super*, upon, and *cingulum*, a belt.] A belt or girth fastening a saddle or anything else on a horse's back; the girdle round a clergyman's cassock.

surcoat, sėr′kōt, *n.* [Prefix *sur* (L. *super*), over, and *coat.*] An outer garment formerly worn in a variety of forms; a loose sleeveless wrapper embroidered with the arms of a knight and girded round the waist with a sword belt, formerly worn by him over a coat of mail to protect it from wet.

surd, sėrd, *a.* [L. *surdus*, deaf, not sounding, stupid (seen also in *absurd*).] *Phonetics*, uttered with breath and not with voice; not sonant, as *t* compared with *d*, *p* with *b*, *f* with *v*; *math.* not capable of being expressed in rational numbers.—*n.* *Phonetics*, a nonsonant consonant; *math.* an irrational quantity; a quantity that cannot be expressed in finite terms, as the square root of 2.

sure, shör, *a.* [Fr. *sûr*, O.Fr. *seur*, *seür*, Pr. *segur*, from L. *securus*, unconcerned, secure—*se*, apart, and *cura*, care. The same word as *secure.* CURE.] Perfectly confident; certainly knowing and believing; certain; fully persuaded; certain to find or retain (*sure* of success); to be depended on; unfailing; firm; stable; secure; infallible (a *sure* remedy).—*To make sure*, to make certain; to secure so that there can be no failure of the purpose or object.—*adv.* Certainly; without doubt. (*Colloq.*)—**surefooted,** *a.* Not liable to stumble, slip, or fall.—**surely,** shör′li, *adv.* Certainly; undoubtedly; firmly; securely; verily.—**sureness,** shör′nes, *n.* The state of being sure or certain; certainty.—**surety,** shör′ti, *n.* Certainty; security; ground of security; security against loss or damage or for payment; *law*, one bound with and for another who is primarily liable, and who is called the principal; one who binds himself to stand good for another; a bail.—**suretyship,** shör′ti•ship, *n.* The state of being a surety; the obligation of a person to stand good for another. Written also *Suretiship.*

surf, sėrf, *n.* [For old *suffe*, the same as *sough*; or from a forgotten word of Indian origin.] The swell of the sea which breaks upon the shore, or upon sandbanks or rocks.—**surfboat,** *n.* A strong and buoyant boat capable of passing with safety through surf.—**surfboard,** *n.* A board used in the sport of riding toward shore on the surf.—**surfduck,** *n.* A species of duck frequent on the coasts of North America. Called also *surf scoter.*

surface, sėr′fis, *n.* [Fr. *surface*, from *sur*, upon, and *face*, face; L. *super*, and *facies.*] The exterior part of anything that has length and breadth; one of the limits that terminates a solid; the superficies; outside; *fig.* outward or external appearance; what appears on a slight or casual view; *geom.* a superficies; that which has length and breadth only.—*A plane surface* is that in which any two points being taken the straight line between them lies wholly in that surface.—*a.* Pertaining to the surface; external; superficial.—*v.t.*—*surfaced, surfacing.* To give a particular surface to; to work over the surface of.—**surface tension,** *n.* Of a liquid, the condition of the surface layer, which behaves like a stretched film.

surfeit, sėr′fit, *n.* [O.Fr. *surfait*, excess—*sur* (L. *super*), over, and *fait*, pp. of *faire*, L. *facere*, to do. FACT.] An overloading of the stomach by excess in eating and drinking; a gluttonous meal that deranges the stomach and system; disgust caused by excess; satiety.—*v.t.* To derange the stomach by excess in eating; to overload the stomach of; to fill to satiety and disgust; to cloy.—*v.i.* To suffer from a surfeit.—**surfeiter,** sėr′fit•ėr, *n.* One who surfeits; a glutton.

surge, sėrj, *n.* [O.Fr. *surgeon*, *sourgeon*, a spring, a spouting up, from L. *surgere*, to rise, from *sub*, under, and *rego*, to direct. SOURCE.] A large wave or billow; a great rolling swell of water; a heaving or swelling up; an undulation.—*v.i.*—*surged*, *surging*. To swell; to rise high and roll, as waves.

surgeon, sėr′jun, *n.* [O.E. *chirurgeon*, O.Fr. *surgien*, contr. for *chirurgien*, from L. *chirurgus*, Gr. *cheirourgos*, a surgeon—*cheir*, the hand, and *ergon*, work.] A medical man whose profession is to cure diseases or injuries of the body by manual operation or by medical appliances employed externally or internally, as distinguished from a physician.—**surgeoncy,** sėr′jun•si, *n.* The office of surgeon as in the army or navy.—**surgery,** ser′jėr•i, *n.* [For *surgeonry*.] The operative branch of medicine; that branch of medical science and practice which involves the performance of operations on the human subject; a room where surgical operations are performed.—**surgical,** sėr′ji•kal, *a.* Pertaining to surgery; done by means of surgery.

suricate, sū′ri•kāt, *n.* [South African name.] A carnivorous animal of South Africa, resembling the polecat or ferret, kept in houses like a cat.

surly, sėr′li, *a.* [Old form *sirly* or *syrly*; probably for *sir-like*, that is, magisterial, arrogant.] Arrogant‡; gloomily morose; sternly sour; cross and rude; churlish; rough or tempestuous.—**surlily,** sėr′li•li, *adv.* In a surly manner.—**surliness,** sėr′li•nes, *n.* The quality of being surly; gloomy moroseness; sour ill-nature.

surmise, sėr′mīz, *n.* [O.Fr. *surmise*, accusation, from *surmettre*, pp. *surmis*, *surmise*, to accuse, from prefix *sur*, L. *super*, upon, above, and *mettre*, L. *mittere*, to send. MISSION.] A thought or supposition with little or no ground to go upon; a guess or conjecture.—*v.t. surmise*, *surmising*, sėr•mīz′, sėr•mīz′ing. To guess; to conjecture.

surmount, sėr•mount′, *v.t.* [Fr. *surmonter*—*sur*, above, and *monter*, to mount. MOUNT.] To mount or rise above; to conquer; to overcome; to surpass.—**surmountable,** sėr•moun′ta•bl, *a.* Capable of being surmounted.

surmullet, sėr′mul•et, *n.* [Fr. *surmulet*, for *sormulet*, from O.Fr. *sor*, reddish-brown, sorrel, and *mulet*, a mullet. SORREL, MULLET.] A name for a variety of fishes allied to the perch family, of which the red surmullet inhabits the Mediterranean, and was prized by the Romans.

surname, sėr′nām, *n.* [Prefix *sur* (L. *super*), over and above, and *name*.] An additional name or appellation; a name or appellation added to the baptismal or Christian name, and which becomes a family name.—*v.t.* To give a surname to.

surpass, sėr•pas′, *v.t.* [Fr. *surpasser*—*sur*, over, and *passer*, to pass.] To exceed; to excel; to go beyond in anything good or bad.—**surpassable,** sėr•pas′a•bl, *a.* Capable of being surpassed.—**surpassing,** sėr•pas′ing, *p.* and *a.* Excellent in an eminent degree; exceeding others.—**surpassingly,** sėr•pas′ing•li, *adv.* In a degree surpassing others.

surplice, sėr′plis, *n.* [Fr. *surplis*, L.L. *superpellicium*, from L. *super*, over, and *pellicium*, a coat or tunic, lit. a skin coat, from *pellis*, a skin. PELL.] A white garment worn by priests, deacons, and choristers in the Anglican and Roman Catholic Churches over their other dress at religious services.

surplus, sėr′plus, *n.* [Fr. *surplus*, from *sur*, L. *super*, over and above, and *plus*, more.] That which remains when use or need is satisfied; more than suffices; overplus: often used adjectively (*surplus* population).—**surplusage,** sėr′plus•ij, *n.* Surplus; something not necessary or relevant to any matter.

surprise, sėr•prīz′, *n.* [Fr. *surprise*, from *surpris*, pp. of *surprendre*, to surprise—prefix *sur* (L. *super*), over, and *prendre*, L. *prendere*, *prehendere*, to seize. PRIZE.] The act of coming upon unawares, or of taking suddenly and without preparation; an emotion excited by something happening suddenly and unexpectedly; wonder; astonishment.—*v.t.*—*surprised*, *surprising*. To fall upon suddenly and unexpectedly; to attack or take unawares; to confuse or perplex; to strike with wonder or astonishment; to astonish; to lead, bring, or betray unawares.—**surprisal,** sėr•prī′zal, *n.* The act of surprising or taking unawares; a surprise.—**surpriser,** sėr•prī′zėr, *n.* One who surprises.—**surprising,** sėr•prī′zing, *p.* and *a.* Exciting surprise; wonderful; extraordinary.—**surprisingly,** sėr•prī′zing•li, *adv.* In a surprizing manner; astonishingly.

surrebutter, sėr•ri•but′ėr, *n.* [Prefix *sur*, over.] *Law*, the plaintiff's reply in pleading to a defendant's rebutter.—**surrejoinder,** sėr•ri•join′dėr, *n.* *Law*, the answer of a plaintiff to a defendant's rejoinder.

surrender, sėr•ren′dėr, *v.t.* [Fr. *surrendre*—*sur*, over, and *rendre*, to render. RENDER.] To yield to the power of another; to give or deliver up upon compulsion or demand; to resign in favor of another; to cease to claim or use; to relinquish; *refl.* to yield to any influence, passion, or power (to *surrender one's self* to grief).—*v.i.* To yield; to give up one's self into the power of another.—*n.* The act of surrendering; a yielding or giving up; the abandonment of an insurance policy by the party insured on receiving a portion of the premiums paid.

surreptitious, sėr•rep•tish′us, *a.* [L. *surreptitius*, from L. *surrepo*, to creep stealthily—*sub*, under, secretly, and *repo*, to creep. REPTILE.] Done by stealth or without proper authority; made or produced fraudulently.—**surreptitiously,** sėr•rep•tish′us•li, *adv.* In an underhand way; fraudulently.

surrogate, sur′ro•gāt, *n.* [L. *surrogatus*, substituted, pp. of *surrogo*, *surrogatum*, to put in another's place—*sub*, under, and *rogo*, to ask. ROGATION.] A deputy; the deputy of an ecclesiastical judge, most commonly of a bishop or his chancellor; in some states, a judicial officer corresponding to an ordinary judge.

surround, sėr•round′, *v.t.* [O.Fr. *suronder*, to overflow, from prefix *sur*, over, and L. *unda*, a wave (as in *abound*).] To encompass, environ, or enclose on all sides; to invest, as a city; to lie or be on all sides of; to form an enclosure round.—**surrounding,** sėr•roun′ding, *n.* An encompassing; one of those things that surround or environ; an environment: generally in plural (a dwelling and its *surroundings*).

surtax, sėr′taks, *n.* [Prefix *sur*, above, and *tax*.] A tax heightened for a particular purpose; an extra tax.

surtout, sėr•tö′, *n.* [Fr. *sur-tout*, over all—*sur*=L. *super*, over, and *tout*=L. *totus*, whole.] Originally, a man's coat to be worn over his other garments; in modern usage, an upper coat with long wide skirts; a frock coat.

surveillance, sėr•vāl′ans, *n.* [Fr., from *surveiller*, to watch over, from *sur*, L. *super*, over, and *veiller*, L. *vigilare*, to watch. VIGILANT.] Watch kept over some person or thing; oversight; superintendence.—*Police surveillance*, for a fixed time during which prisoners, after their release, have to report themselves periodically, is sometimes added to sentences.

survey, sėr•vā′, *v.t.* [O.Fr. *surveer*, *surveoir*—*sur* (L. *super*), over, and *veer*, *veoir* (Fr. *voir*), L. *videre*, to see. VISION.] To inspect or take a view of; to view as from a high place; to view with scrutinizing eye; to examine; to examine with reference to condition, situation, or value; to inspect for a purpose; to determine the boundaries, extent, position, natural features, etc., of, as of any portion of the earth's surface by means of measurements, and the application of geometry and trigonometry.—*n.* (sėr′vā or sėr•vā′). A general view; a look at or over; a close examination or inspection to ascertain condition, quantity, quality, etc.; the determination of dimensions and other topographical particulars of any part of the earth's surface; the plan or account drawn up of such particulars.—*Ordnance Survey*. See ORDNANCE.—*Trigonometrical survey*. TRIGONOMETRICAL.—**surveying,** sėr•vā′ing, *n.* The act of one who surveys; the operation or art of making a survey of a portion of the earth's surface by means of measurements and calculations.—*Land surveying*, the determination of the area, shape, etc., of a tract of land, usually of no very great extent.—*Marine surveying* consists in determining the forms of coasts, the positions and distances of islands, rocks, shoals, the depth of water, nature of the bottom, etc.—**surveyor,** sėr•vā′ėr, *n.* One who surveys; an overseer; one that views and examines for the purpose of ascertaining the condition or state of anything; one who practices the art of surveying.—**surveyorship,** sėr•vā′ėr•ship, *n.* The office of a surveyor.

survive, sėr•vīv′, *v.t.—survived, surviving.* [Fr. *survivre*, from L. *supervivo—super*, over, beyond, and *vivere* to live. VITAL, VIVACIOUS.] To outlive; to live beyond the life of; to live longer than; to live beyond (to *survive* one's usefulness).—*v.i.* To remain alive; to live after the death of another or after anything else.—**survival,** sėr•vī′val, *n.* The act of surviving; a living beyond the life of another person, or beyond any event; any habit, usage, or belief remaining from ancient times and existing merely from custom.—*Survival of the fittest*, the principle in natural selection that the animals and plants best suited to their surroundings survive, while the others die out. SELECTION.—*Survival value*, of a biological character, value as being helpful in the struggle for existence.—**surviving,** sėr•vī′ving, *p.* and *a.* Remaining alive; yet living.—**survivor,** sėr•vī′vėr, *n.* One who lives after the death of another, or after some event or time; *law*, the longer lived of two persons who have a joint interest in anything.—**survivorship,** sėr•vī′vėr•ship, *n.* The state of being a survivor.

susceptible, sus•sep′ti•bl, *a.* [Fr. *susceptible*, from L. *suscipio, susceptum—sus* for *sub*, under, and *capio*, to take. CAPABLE.] Capable of being acted on or affected in any way; admitting any change (*susceptible* of pain, of alteration); capable of emotional impression; readily impressed; impressible; sensitive.—**susceptibly,** sus•sep′ti•bli, *adv.* In a susceptible manner.—**susceptibility, susceptibleness,** sus•sep′ti•bil″i•ti, sus•sep′ti•bl•nes, *n.* The state or quality of being susceptible; sensitiveness; capacity for feeling or emotional excitement; sensibility; *magnetism*, the ratio between the intensity of magnetization in a magnetic substance and the magnetizing force producing it.—**susceptive,** sus•sep′tiv, *a.* Readily admitting or being affected by influence; susceptible.—**susceptivity,** sus•sep•tiv′i•ti, *n.* Susceptibility.

suslik, sus′lik, *n.* [Rus.] A pretty little animal of the marmot kind found in eastern Europe and western Asia.

suspect, sus•pekt′, *v.t.* [L. *suspicio, suspectum—sus* for *sub*, under, and *specio*, to look. SPECIES.] To have a vague belief or fear of the existence of; to imagine as probably existing (to *suspect* danger); to mistrust; to imagine to be guilty, but upon slight evidence or without proof; to hold to be uncertain; to doubt.—*n.* (sus′pekt) A suspected person; one suspected of a crime, or the like.—**suspicion,** sus•pish′on, *n.* [L. *suspicio, suspicionis.*] The act of suspecting; the feeling of one who suspects; the thought that there is probably something wrong; a notion that something is so or so.—**suspicious,** sus•pish′us, *a.* [L. *suspiciosus.*] Inclined to suspect; ready to entertain or entertaining suspicion; distrustful (*suspicious* of a person or his motives); indicating or exhibiting suspicion; adapted to raise suspicion (*suspicious* circumstances).—**suspiciously,** sus•pish′us•li, *adv.* In a suspicious manner; so as to excite suspicion.—**suspiciousness,** sus•pish′us•nes, *n.* The state or quality of being suspicious.

suspend, sus•pend′, *v.t.* [L. *suspendo —sus* for *sub*, under, and *pendo*, to hang. PENDANT.] To cause to hang; to hang up; to cause to cease for a time; to interrupt temporarily; to stay; to hold in a state undetermined (to *suspend* one's choice); to debar for a time from any privilege; to remove temporarily from an office; to cause to cease for a time from operation or effect.—*To suspend payment*, to formally stop paying debts from being insolvent.—*Suspended animation*, a temporary cessation of animation, especially from asphyxia.—*v.i.* To cease from operation; to stop payment or be unable to meet one's engagements.—**suspender,** sus•pen′dėr, *n.* One that suspends; one of a pair of braces for the trousers.—**suspense,** sus•pens′, *n.* [L. *suspensus*, suspended.] The state of having the mind or thoughts uncertain; uncertainty, with more or less apprehension or anxiety; indetermination; indecision; *law*, a temporary cessation.—**suspension,** sus•pen′shon, *n.* [L. *suspensio, suspensionis.*] The act of suspending or hanging up; the act of delaying, interrupting, or stopping for a time; a cessation of operation; a stoppage; temporary abeyance; the state of being in the form of particles floating undissolved in a fluid.—*Suspension of arms*, a short truce or cessation of operations during a war.—**suspensive,** sus•pen′siv, *a.* In a suspense; uncertain; doubtful.—**suspensor,** sus•pen′sor, *n.* Something which suspends; *bot.* the cord by which the embryo of some plants is suspended from the opening of the seed.—**suspensory,** sus•pen′so•ri, *a.* Serving to suspend; suspending.

suspicion, suspicious, etc. See SUSPECT.

suspire, sus•pīr′, *v.i.* [L. *suspiro*, to sigh—*sus* for *sub*, and *spiro*, to breathe. SPIRIT.] To fetch a long, deep breath; to sigh. (*Shak.*)—**suspiration,** sus•pi•rā′shon, *n.* A sigh.

sustain, sus•tān′, *v.t.* [O.Fr. *sustenir, sostenir* (Fr. *soutenir*), from L. *sustinere—sus* for *sub*, under, and *teneo*, to hold (as in *contain*, *retain*, etc.). TENANT.] To rest under and bear up; to support; to hold suspended; to keep from sinking in despondence; to keep alive; to furnish sustenance for; to nourish; to aid effectually; to keep from ruin; to endure without failing or yielding; to bear up against; to suffer; to undergo; to allow (an action) to proceed before a court; to hold valid in law; to establish by evidence; to confirm or corroborate.—**sustainable,** sus•tā′na•bl, *a.* Capable of being sustained.—**sustainer,** sus•tā′nėr, *n.* One who or that which sustains.—**sustenance,** sus′ten•ans, *n.* [O.Fr. *sustenance.*] The act of sustaining; maintenance; subsistence; that which supports life; food; provisions.—**sustentation,** sus•ten•tā′shon, *n.* [L. *sustentatio*, from *sustento*, intens. of *sustineo.*] Support; sustenance; support of life; the phenomenon of sustaining or supporting a heavier-than-air machine by the reaction of a deflected air stream; the flotation of a lighter-than-air machine by the displacement of an equal mass of air.

susurrus, sū•sur′rus, *n.* [L.] A soft, humming, murmuring sound; a whisper.—**susurrant,** sū•sur′ent, *a.* [L. *susurro*, to hum.] Whispering; susurrous.

sutler, sut′lėr, *n.* [O.D. *soeteler*, D. *zoetelaar*, a sutler, from *soetelen*, to perform menial offices or dirty work.] A person who follows an army and sells to the troops provisions, liquors, or the like.

sutra, sö′tra, *n.* [Skr., string.] A collection or string of aphorisms in the Sanskrit literature.

suttee, sut•tē′, *n.* [Skr. *sati*, from *sat*, good, pure; properly, a chaste and virtuous wife.] A Hindu widow who immolates herself on the funeral pile of her husband; the voluntary self-immolation by fire of a Hindu widow.—**sutteeism,** sut•tē′izm, *n.* The practice of self-immolation among Hindu widows.

suture, sū′chėr, *n.* [L. *sutura*, from *suo*, to sew.] The act of sewing; a seam; the line along which two things or parts are joined; *surg.* the uniting of the lips or edges of a wound by stitching; *anat.* one of the seams uniting the bones of the skull; *bot.* the seam of a dehiscent pericarp where the valves unite.—**sutural,** sū′chė•ral, *a.* Relating to a suture; *bot.* taking place at a suture.

suzerain, sö′ze•rān, *n.* [Fr. *suzerain*, from prefix *sus*, L. *sursum*, above, over, on type of *souverain*, from L. *super*, above.] A feudal lord or baron; a lord paramount.—**suzerainty,** sö′ze•rān•ti, *n.* The office or dignity of a suzerain; paramount authority or command.

swab, swob, *n.* [Same as Sw. *swab*, a mop; akin to D. *zwabber*, G. *schwabber*, Dan. *svabre*, a mop; comp. Prov. E. *swab*, G. *schwabbeln*, to splash; allied to *sweep*.] A mop for cleaning floors, ships' decks, and the like; a cleaner or sponge for the bore of a cannon; a term applied by sailors to an awkward, clumsy fellow.—*v.t.—swabbed, swabbing.* To clean with a swab or mop.—**swabber,** swob′ėr, *n.* An inferior officer in a warship whose business is to see that the ship is kept clean.

swaddle, swod′l, *v.t.—swaddled, swaddling.* [From A.Sax. *swaethil, swethel*, a swaddling-band; same origin as *swathe*. SWATHE.] To bind as with a bandage; to swathe; used generally of infants.—*n.* A cloth band round the body of an infant.—**swaddling, swaddling cloth,** *n.* A band or cloth wrapped round an infant.

Swadeshi, swa•dāsh′i, *n.* [Bengal,

'own country'. See SINN FEIN.] An Indian movement for boycotting foreign goods in order to secure political pressure and action.

swag, swag, *v.i.* [A form of *sway*; hence *swagger*.] To move, as something heavy and pendent; to sway.—*n.* Plunder, booty (*colloq.*).

swage, swāj, *n.* [O.Fr. *souage*, form, fashion.] A tool used by blacksmiths, etc., for stamping or molding heated metal into a required form.—*v.t.* To shape by means of a swage.

swagger, swag′ėr, *v.t.* [A freq. from *swag*; comp. Swiss *schwaggeln*, to stroll about.] To boast noisily; to bluster; to hector; to strut with a defiant or insolent air.—*v.t.* To influence by blustering or threats; to bully.—*n.* A piece of bluster; bravado or insolence in manner; an insolent strut.—**swaggerer,** swag′-ėr•ėr, *n.* One who swaggers; a blusterer; a bully.

swain, swān, *n.* [Same as Icel. *sveinn*, a youth, a servant; O.Sax. *swén*, Sw. *sven*, Dan. *svend*, A.Sax. *swán*.] A young man dwelling in the country; a peasant or rustic; a country gallant; a lover.

swallow, swol′ō, *n.* [A.Sax. *swalewe*, *swealwe*=D. *zwaluw*, Icel. and Sw. *svala*, Dan. *svale*, G. *schwalbe*, a swallow.] A name of certain insessorial birds remarkable for their extreme length of wing and velocity of flight, living on insects which they catch in the air, and in temperate climates coming in spring and departing when summer is over.—**swallowtail,** *n.* A plant, a species of willow; a swallow-tailed coat.—**swallow-tailed,** *a.* Of the form of a swallow's tail; having tapering or pointed skirts (a *swallow-tailed* coat).—**swallowwort,** *n.* The common celandine.

swallow, swol′ō, *v.t.* [A.Sax. *swelgan*, to swallow (pret. *swealg*, pp. *swolgen*)=L.G. *swalgen*, D. *zwelgen*, Dan. *svälge*, Icel. *svelgja*, G. *schwelgen*, to swallow.] To receive through the gullet into the stomach; to draw into an abyss or gulf; to engulf; to absorb; to take into the mind readily; to receive or embrace, as opinions; to drink in; to occupy or take up (to *swallow* time); to exhaust or consume; to put up with; to bear or take patiently (to *swallow* an affront).—*n.* Capacity for swallowing; voracity.—**swallower,** swol′ō•-ėr, *n.* One who swallows.

swam, swam, pret. of *swim*.

swamp, swomp, *n.* [Closely akin to *sump*, a pond, and to A.Sax. *swamm*, Dan. and Sw. *svamp*, Icel. *svöppr*, G. *schwamm*, a sponge; from root of *swim*.] A piece of spongy land, or low ground saturated with water; a bog, fen, marsh, or morass.—*v.t.* To plunge or sink in a swamp, or as in a swamp; to plunge into inextricable difficulties; *naut.* to overset, sink, or cause to become filled, as a boat in water; to whelm.—**swampy,** swom′pi, *a.* Consisting of swamp; low, wet, and spongy.

swan, swon, *n.* [A.Sax. *swan*=D. *zwaan*, Icel. *svanr*, Sw. *svan*, Dan. *svane*, G. *schwan*; probably from same root as Skr. *svan*, L. *sono*, to sound.] A long-necked web-footed bird of several species, frequenting rivers and ponds of fresh water, of great size, very graceful in the water, and generally having plumage of snowy whiteness, though a black species exists in Australia.—**swanherd,** swon′hėrd, *n.* One who tends swans.—**swannery,** swon′ėr•i, *n.* A place where swans are bred and reared.—**swansdown,** swonz′doun, *n.* The down of the swan; a fine, soft, thick woolen cloth; also, a thick cotton cloth with a soft nap on one side.—**swanskin,** swon′skin, *n.* The skin of a swan; a kind of fine twilled flannel.—**swan song,** swon′song, *n.* The last dying song or notes of a writer, from the fable of the dying swan.

swank, swank, *n.* [Akin to *swagger*.] Conceit.—*v.i.* To act so.

swap, swop, *v.t.*—*swapped*, *swapping*. [Allied to *sweep* and *swoop*; comp. G. *schwappen*, to strike, to swap; comp. *to strike a bargain*.] To strike with a sweeping stroke‡; to knock down; to swop; to barter; to exchange.—*n.* A blow; an exchange or barter.

sward, swạrd, *n.* [A.Sax. *sweard*, D. *zwoord*, Dan. *svaer*, Icel. *svördr*, G. *schwarte*, all signifying the skin or rind of bacon, hence sward.] The grassy surface of land; turf; greensward.—*v.t.* To cover with sward.

swarm, swạrm, *n.* [A.Sax. *swearm*, swarm=Icel. *svarmr*, Dan. *svaerm*, G. *schwarm*; from a root meaning to hum or buzz, seen in L. *susurrus*, a whisper; Skr. *svar*, to sound. SWEAR.] A large number or body of insects; the cluster of honey-bees which emigrate from a hive at once and seek new lodgings; any great number or multitude; a multitude of people in motion.—*v.i.* To depart from a hive in a swarm; to give out a swarm of bees; to throng in multitudes; to crowd; to be crowded or thronged with a multitude; to abound.

swarm, swạrm, *v.i.* [Perhaps akin to *swerve* or to *squirm*.] To climb a tree, pole, or the like by embracing it with the arms and legs, and scrambling; to shin.

swart, swarth, swạrt, swạrth, *a.* [A.Sax. *sweart*=Goth. *svarts*, L.G. *swartr*, Icel. *svartr*, G. *schwarz*, D. *zwart*, black, dark; same root as L. *sordidus*, sordid, filthy.] Being of a dark hue; moderately black; swarthy: said especially of the skin.—*v.t.* To make tawny.—**swarthy,** swạr′THi, *a.* Being of a dark hue or dusky complexion; tawny or black.—**swarthily,** swạr′THi•li, *adv.* With a swarthy hue.—**swarthiness,** swạr′THi•nes, *n.* The state of being swarthy; a dusky or dark complexion.—**swartness,** swạrt′-nes, *n.* The state of being swart or swarthy.

swash, swosh, *n.* [Probably from sound of splashing water; comp. Sw. *swassa*, to bluster, to swagger; akin *swish*.] A dashing or splash of water; liquid refuse or filth.—*v.i.* To splash water; to bluster; to make a show of valor; to dash or strike.—**swashbuckler,** *n.* A swaggering fellow; a bravo; a bully.—**swasher,** swosh′ėr, *n.* A braggart; a bully.—**swashing,** swosh′ing, *p.* and *a.* Like a swasher; swaggering; striking with great force; crushing.

swastika, swäs′ti•ka, swäs•tē′ka, *n.* [Skr. *svastika*, from *svasti*, well being.] An ancient symbol shaped like a Greek cross with an extension at right angles at the end of each of the four arms; emblem of Nazi party.

swath, swoth, *n.* [A.Sax. *swathu*, *swaethe*, a track, path, swath; D. *zwaad*, *zwade*, G. *schwaden*, a swath; akin to *swaddle*.] A band or bandage‡; a line of grass or corn cut and lying: the reach or sweep of a scythe.—**swathe,** swāTH, *v.t.*—*swathed*, *swathing*. [Icel. *svatha*, to swathe; A.Sax. *swethian*, to bind.] To bind with a band or bandage; to tie up in bundles or sheaves; to bind or wind about; to wrap.—*n.* A bandage.

sway, swā, *v.i.* [Same as Icel. *sveggja*, to make to sway, *sveigja*, to swerve; Dan. *svaie*, D. *swaaijen*, to swing; akin *swing*, *swag*.] To swing backward and forward; to be drawn to one side by weight; to incline or hang; to move or advance to one side; to have the judgment or feelings inclining one way; to have weight or influence; to bear rule; to govern.—*v.t.* To move backward and forward; to cause to incline to one side; to influence, govern, or direct.—*n.* A swing or sweep; power exerted in governing; rule; influence.

swear, swâr, *v.i.*—*swore*, *sworn*. [A.Sax. *swerian*, to swear; G. *schwören*, Goth. *svaran*, Icel. *sverja*, Sw. *svärja*, to swear.] To utter a solemn declaration, with an appeal to God for the truth of what is affirmed; to declare or affirm in a solemn manner; to promise upon oath; to give evidence on oath; to use profane language; to utter profane oaths.—*To swear by*, to treat as an infallible authority.—*v.t.* To affirm with an appeal to God; to utter on oath; to promise solemnly; to vow; to put to an oath; to bind by an oath; to utter in a profane manner.—**swearer,** swâ′rėr, *n.* One who swears.—**sworn,** swōrn, *pp.* Bound by oath.—*Sworn brothers*, companions in arms bound together by an oath; very close intimates.—*Sworn enemies*, enemies who have taken an oath or vow of mutual hatred; hence, determined or irreconcilable enemies.—*Sworn friends*, friends bound to be true to each other by oath; hence, close or firm friends.

sweat, swet, *n.* [A.Sax. *swaetan*, to sweat, from *swát*, sweat=Icel. *sveiti*, Sw. *svett*, Dan. *sved*, L.G. *sweet*, D. *zweet*, G. *schweiss*, sweat; from same root as L. *sudor*, sweat; Skr. *svedas*, sweat.] The moisture which comes out upon the skin of an animal; perspiration; the state of one who sweats; moisture exuded from any substance.—*v.i.* pret. and pp. *sweat* or *sweated*. To have sweat exuding from the skin; to perspire; to toil; to drudge; to emit moisture, as green plants in a heap.—*v.t.* To cause to give out sweat; to emit from the pores; to exude.—*To sweat coins,* more especially gold coins, to shake a number of them together in a bag, so that a portion of the metal is worn off, being then fraudulently appropriated.—**sweater,** swet′ėr, *n.* One who sweats; a grinding employer; a knitted or crocheted blouse.—**sweatily,** swet′i•li, *adv.* In a sweaty manner.—**sweatiness,** swet′i•nes, *n.* The state of being sweaty.—**sweating sickness,** *n.* An epidemic which made its appearance in England and on the Continent in the fifteenth and sixteenth centuries, characterized by profuse sweating, and frequently fatal in a few hours.—**sweating system,** *n.* The practice of employing poor people to make up clothes in their own houses at very low wages.—**sweaty,** swet′i, *a.* Moist with sweat; having the character of sweat; consisting of sweat.

Swede, swēd, *n.* A native of Sweden; a Swedish turnip.—**Swedish,** swē′dish, *a.* Pertaining to Sweden or its inhabitants.—*n.* The language of the Swedes.

Swedenborgian, swē•den•bor′ji•an, *a.* Relating to Emanuel *Swedenborg,* or to the doctrines taught by him.—*n.* One who holds the religious doctrines taught by Emanuel *Swedenborg,* a Swedish nobleman, born at Stockholm in 1688, who believed himself to have a divine revelation to found the New Jerusalem Church spoken of in the Apocalypse.—**Swedenborgianism,** swē•den•bor′ji•an•izm, *n.* The doctrines of the Swedenborgians.

sweep, swēp, *v.t.*—pret. and pp. *swept.* [From A.Sax. *swápan,* to sweep (pret. *sweóp,* pp. *swápen*= Icel. *sópa,* also *sveipa,* Goth. *sveipan,* G. *schweifen.* SWOOP.] To rub over with a broom or besom, for removing loose dirt; to clean by brushing; to remove or strike by a brushing stroke; to carry along or off (the wind *sweeps* the snow, a river *sweeps* away a dam); to destroy or carry off at a blow; to rub or trail over (to *sweep* the ground); to pass over so as to clear (to *sweep* the seas of ships); to move swiftly over or along; to carry the eye over; to draw or drag something over.—*v.i.* To pass or flow with swiftness and violence; to pass or brush along with celerity; to pass with pomp; to take in a view with progressive rapidity; to range.—*n.* The act of sweeping; the reach or range of a continued motion or stroke; the compass or reach of anything flowing or brushing along; the direction or turn of a curve, as of a road; compass or extent of excursion; range; a rapid survey with the eye; *naut.* a large oar used in small vessels to aid their progress; one who sweeps chimneys; the depth of strata of air disturbed by an airplane in motion.—**sweeper,** swē′pėr, *n.* One who sweeps.—**sweeping,** swē′ping, *p.* and *a.* Including many individuals or particulars in a single act or assertion; wide and comprehensive (a *sweeping* charge).—*n. pl.* Things collected by sweeping; rubbish.—**sweepingly,** swē′ping•li, *adv.* In a sweeping manner.—**sweepingness,** swē′ping•nes, *n.*—**sweepstake,** swēp′stāk, *n.* A gaming transaction in which a number of persons join in contributing a certain stake, which becomes the property of one or of several of the contributors under certain conditions; a prize made up of several stakes. Also called a *sweepstakes.*—**sweepy,** swē′pi, *a.* Moving in sweeps; sweeping.

sweet, swēt, *a.* [A.Sax. *swéte*=D. *zoet,* G. *süss,* Icel. *sœtr, sōtr,* Goth. *sutis;* same root as L. *suavis* (for *suadvis*), whence *suave;* Skr. *svâdus,* sweet, *svad,* to taste.] Having a pleasant taste or flavor like that of sugar or honey: opposed to *bitter;* pleasing to the smell; fragrant; pleasing to the ear; soft; melodious; pleasing to the eye; beautiful; pleasing or grateful to the mind; mild; gentle; kind; obliging; bland; not salt or salted; not stale; not sour; not putrescent. *Sweet herbs,* fragrant herbs cultivated for culinary purposes.—*A sweet tooth,* a great liking for sweet things or sweetmeats.—*n. pl.* Sweet things; sweetmeats; things that please (the *sweets* of domestic life).—**sweet bay,** *n.* A fragrant species of laurel.—**sweetbread,** *n.* The pancreas of an animal used as food.—**sweetbrier, sweetbriar,** *n.* A species of wild rose remarkable for the sweet smell of its leaves.—**sweeten,** swē′tn, *v.t.* To make sweet to the taste; to make pleasing or grateful to the mind; to make mild or kind; to increase the agreeable qualities of; to make pure and wholesome; to make mellow and fertile; to restore to purity.—*v.i.* To become sweet.—**sweetener,** swē′tn•ėr, *n.* One who or that which sweetens.—**sweetening,** swē′tn•ing, *n.* The act of one who sweetens; that which sweetens.—**sweet flag,** *n.* A plant of the arum family growing in wet places, the perennial rhizome of which is known as calamus, and is used in medicine, by confectioners, perfumers, etc.—**sweetheart,** swēt′härt, *n.* [From *sweet* and *heart.*] A lover, male or female.—*v.t.* To act the part of a male lover to; to pay court to.—**sweeting,** swē′ting, *n.* A sweet apple; a term of endearment.—**sweetish,** swē′tish, *a.* Somewhat sweet.—**sweetly,** swēt′li, *adv.* In a sweet manner; agreeably; harmoniously.—**sweet marjoram,** *n.* MARJORAM.—**sweetmeat,** swēt′mēt, *n.* An article of confectionery made wholly or principally of sugar; fruit preserved with sugar.—**sweetness,** swēt′nes, *n.* The quality of being sweet; fragrance; agreeableness to the ear; melody; gentleness; mildness; obliging civility.—**sweet oil,** *n.* Olive oil.—**sweet pea,** *n.* An annual much cultivated in gardens for its showy sweet-scented flowers.—**sweet potato,** *n.* A tropical plant of the convolvulaceous family largely cultivated for its edible roots.—**sweet-scented,** *a.* Having a sweet smell; fragrant.—**sweetsop,** *n.* A fruit and tree allied to the custard apple.—**sweet William,** *n.* A species of pink of many varieties, cultivated in gardens.

swell, swel, *v.i.*—pret. *swelled;* pp. *swelled* or *swollen* (the latter more frequently an adjective). [A.Sax. *swellan,* to swell=Icel. *svella,* D. *zwellen,* G. *schwellen,* to swell.] To grow bulkier; to dilate; to increase in size or extent; to rise or be driven into billows; to protuberate; to bulge out; to rise in altitude; to be puffed up with some feeling; hence, to strut; to look big; to grow and increase in the mind; to become larger in amount; to increase in intensity or volume, as sound.—*v.t.* To increase the size of; to cause to dilate or increase; to aggravate; to heighten; to inflate; to puff up.—*n.* The act of swelling; gradual increase; an elevation of land; an undulation; a succession of long unbroken waves setting in one direction, as after a storm; a billow; a surge; a gradual increase and decrease in the volume of musical sound; an arrangement in an organ whereby the player can increase or diminish the intensity of the sound; a familiar word for a person of rank or high standing, or for a showy, fashionable person; a dandy, a fop, or the like.—**swelling,** swel′ing, *n.* A tumor; a protuberance.—*p.* and *a.* Turgid; bombastic; grand; pompous.

swelter, swel′tėr, *v.i.* [From A.Sax. *sweltan,* to die, Goth. *swiltan,* Icel. *svelta,* Sw. *svälta,* Dan. *sulte,* to die. Hence *sultry,* for *sweltery.*] To be overcome and faint with heat.—*v.t.* To oppress with heat.

swept, swept, pret. and pp. of *sweep.*

swerve, swėrv, *v.i.*—*swerved, swerving.* [A.Sax. *sweorfan*=Icel. *svarfa,* D. *zwerven,* L.G. *swarven,* O.H.G. *suerban,* Goth. *svairban*—used of movements of various kinds.] To wander from any line prescribed or from a rule of duty; to deviate; to turn to one side; to incline; to waver.

swift, swift, *a.* [A.Sax. *swift,* from *swifan,* to move quickly, to revolve; Icel. *svífa,* to glide, G. *schweifen,* to sweep; same root as E. *sweep* and *swoop.*] Moving with great speed or rapidity; fleet; rapid; ready; prompt; coming suddenly or without delay; of short continuance; rapidly passing.—*adv.* In a swift or rapid manner; swiftly.—*n.* The name of birds of the family Apodidae, which have an outward resemblance to the swallows, the common swift having great powers of flight; the common European newt.—**swiftly,** swift′li, *adv.* In a swift or rapid manner; fleetly.—**swiftness,** swift′nes, *n.* The state or quality of being swift; rapid motion; celerity; rapidity.

swifter, swif′tėr, *n.* [Icel. *sviptingr,* a reefing rope.] *Naut.* a rope encircling a boat longitudinally to strengthen and defend her sides; one of a pair of shrouds above the others to strengthen the lower masts.

swig, swig, *v.t.*—*swigged, swigging.* [Perhaps from A.Sax. *swilgan,* to swallow; comp. *bag*=*balg*. SWALLOW.] To drink by large draughts; to drink off rapidly and greedily.—*v.i.* To take deep draughts.—*n.* A large draught.

swill, swil, *v.t.* [A.Sax. *swilian*, Sc. *sweel*, to wash; influenced by A.Sax. *swilgan*, to swallow. SWALLOW.] To wash (*Shak.*)‡; to drink grossly or greedily; to inebriate.—*v.i.* To drink greedily or to excess.—*n.* Drink taken in excessive quantities; the wash or mixture of liquid substances given to swine. Called also *Swillings*.

swim, swim, *v.i.*—pret. *swam* or *swum*; pp. *swum*; ppr. *swimming*. [A.Sax. *swimman*, to swim=L.G. *swimmen*, Icel. *svimma*, G. *schwimmen*—to swim; connected with *swamp*.] To be supported on water or other fluid; to float; to move through water by the motion of the hands and feet, or of fins; to glide with a smooth motion; to be flooded; to be drenched; to overflow.—*v.t.* To pass or cross by swimming; to cause to swim or float.—*n.* The act of swimming; period or extent of swimming; a smooth, gliding motion; the air bladder or sound of fishes.—**swimmer,** swim′ėr, *n.* One who swims; a bird that swims, as the duck and goose.—**swimming,** swim′-ing, *n.* The act or art of sustaining and propelling the body in water.—**swimmingly,** swim′ing•li, *adv.* In an easy gliding manner, as if swimming; smoothly; successfully.

swim, swim, *v.i.*—pret. *swam* or *swum*; pp. *swum*, ppr. *swimming*. [Same as Icel. *svima*, to be dizzy, *svimi*, dizziness; A.Sax. *swíma*, Dan. *svime*, a swoon; G. *schweimen*, to be dizzy. SQUEAMISH.] To be dizzy or giddy (the head *swims*).—**swimming,** swim′ing, *n.* A dizziness or giddiness.

swindle, swin′dl, *v.t.*—*swindled, swindling*. [Borrowed from G. *schwindeln*, to cheat, *schwindler*, a swindler, from *schwindel*, dizziness, infatuation.] To cheat and defraud grossly, or with deliberate artifice.—*n.* A fraudulent scheme intended to dupe people out of money; an act of cheatery; an imposition.—**swindler,** swin′dlėr, *n.* One who swindles; a cheat.

swine, swīn, *n. sing.* and *pl.* [A.Sax. *swín*,=D. *zwijn*, G. *schwein*, Dan. *sviin*, Icel. *svín*, Goth. *svein*, Pol. *swinia*, Bohem. *swine*; same root as *sow*, L. *sus*. SOW.] The domestic hog; members of the family Suidae, and whose flesh is much eaten under the name of *pork*; a pig or hog.—**swineherd,** swīn′hėrd, *n.* A herd or keeper of swine.—**swinish,** swīn′ish, *a.* Befitting swine; like the swine in filthiness; hoggish.—**swinishly,** swīn′ish•li, *adv.* In a swinish manner.—**swinishness,** swīn′ish•nes, *n.* Quality of being swinish.

swing, swing, *v.i.*—pret. and pp. *swung*. [A.Sax. *swingan*, to dash, to scourge=L.G. *swingen*, Dan. *svinge*, Sw. *swinga*, G. *schwingen*. *Swinge*, *swingle* are derivatives, and *swink*, *sway* connected forms.] To move to and fro, as a body suspended in the air; to oscillate; to sway; to be carried to and fro while hanging on something.—*v.t.* To make to sway or oscillate loosely; to whirl in the air; to wave; to brandish.—*To swing a ship*, to bring her head to each point of the compass in succession, in order to correct the compass by ascertaining the amount of local deviation.—*n.* The act of swinging; an oscillation; the sweep of a moving body; an apparatus suspended for persons to swing in; free course of conduct; unrestrained liberty or license: a "hot" variation of folk music, deviating from main theme with counter rhythm, characterized by improvisation and marked, syncopated rhythms.—**swingtree,** *n.* A crossbar by which a horse is yoked to a carriage, plow, etc., and to which the traces are fastened. Called also *singletree*.

swinge, swinj, *v.t.*—*swinged, swingeing*. [From *swing*; comp. *springe* from *spring*, *singe* from *sing*.] To beat soundly; to whip; to chastise.—**swingeing,** swin′jing, *a.* Great; large; huge. (*Colloq.*).—**swinger,** swin′jėr, *n.* One who swinges.

swingle, swing′gl, *v.t.*—*swingled, swingling*. [A freq. of *swing*.] To scutch flax by beating it.—*n.* A swingle staff. — **swingletree,** *n.* SWINGTREE under SWING.

swinish, swinishly. See SWINE.

swipe, swīp, *v.t.* and *i.*—*swiped, swiping*. [Akin to *sweep*, *swoop*.] To strike with a sweeping blow; to strike or drive with great force.—*vulg.* to steal.

swipe, swīp, *v.t.*—To strike with a sweeping motion; to wipe carelessly or quickly; to steal or snatch [*Slang.*]

swiple, swip′l, *n.* [From *swipe*, to strike.] The effective endpiece of a flail.

swirl, swėrl, *v.i.* [Akin to Dan. *svirre*, to whirl; same root as *swerve*.] To form eddies; to whirl in eddies.—*n.* A whirling motion; an eddy, as of water; a twist or curl in the grain of wood.

Swiss, swis, *n. sing.* and *pl.* A native or inhabitant (natives or inhabitants) of Switzerland.—*a.* Belonging to the Swiss or to Switzerland.—*Swiss muslin*, a fine open transparent cotton fabric.

switch, swich, *n.* [Same as O.D. *swick*, a switch; akin Icel. *svigi*, *sveigr*, a switch—from root of *swing* or *sway*.] A small flexible twig or rod; a movable piece of rail for turning a railroad train from one line to another; a device for making or breaking an electric circuit or changing direction of current.—*v.t.* To strike with a switch; to change or trade (to *switch* allegiance); to transfer from one line of rails to another.—*v.i.* To make a change. —**switchboard,** swich′bōrd, *n.* An apparatus consisting of a frame or panel on which are mounted switches for making electric-circuit connections, as for a series of lights in a building or theater; telephone wires in an exchange, etc.

Switzer, swit′zėr, *n.* A Swiss.

swivel, swiv′el, *n.* [From A.Sax. *swifan*, to move quickly, to revolve; akin *swift*.] A fastening that allows the thing fastened to turn freely round its axis.—*v.t.* *swiveled, swiveling*.—To turn around freely, as on an axis or swivel.—*v.i.* To turn or swing, as on a swivel.

swob, swob, *n.* A mop. See SWAB.—**swobber,** swob′ėr, *n.* A swabber.

swollen, swōl′en, *p.* and *a.* Swelled. See SWELL.

swoon, swön, *v.i.* [From A.Sax. *swógan*, to sigh, M.E. *swowen*, to swoon.] To faint; to sink into a fainting fit.—*n.* The state of one who swoons; a fainting fit.

swoop, swöp, *v.t.* [From A.Sax. *swápan*, to sweep, to swoop. SWEEP.] To dash upon while on the wing; to take with a sweep.—*v.i.* To descend upon prey suddenly from a height, as a hawk; to stoop.—*n.* The sudden pouncing of a rapacious bird on its prey; a falling on and seizing, as of a bird on its prey.

swop, swop, *v.t.* [SWAP.] To exchange; to swap.—*n.* An exchange; a barter.

sword, sōrd, *n.* [A.Sax. *sweord*=D. *zwaard*, L.G. *sweerd*, Dan. *zwærd*, Icel. *sverth*, G. *schwert*, a sword; allied to Skr. *çaru*, a dart or spear.] An offensive weapon having a long metal blade (usually steel), either straight and with a sharp point for thrusting, as the rapier; with a sharp point and one or two cutting edges for thrusting and striking, as the broadsword; or curved and with a sharp convex edge for striking, as the scimitar.—*The sword*, the emblem or symbol of justice, power, or authority, or of war, or used as equivalent to the military profession. —*Sword of state*, a sword borne before a king or other person of rank. —**sword bayonet,** *n.* A short sword which can be attached to a rifle like a bayonet.—**sword cane,** *n.* A cane or walking-stick containing a blade, as in a scabbard.—**sword dance,** *n.* A dance by one performer over crossed swords among the Scotch Highlanders.—**swordfish,** *n.* A fish allied to the mackerel tribe, remarkable for its elongated upper jaw, which forms a swordlike weapon.—**sword knot,** *n.* A ribbon or tassel tied to the hilt of a sword.—**swordplay,** *n.* A combat or fencing match with swords; a sword fight.—**swordplayer,** *n.* One who exhibits his skill in the use of the sword; a gladiator.—**swordsman,** sōrdz′man, *n.* A man who carries a sword; one skilled in the use of the sword.

swore, swōr, pret. **sworn,** swōrn, pp. of *swear*.

swung, swung, pret. and pp. of *swing*.

Sybarite, sib′a•rīt, *n.* [Fr. *Sybarite*, from L. *Sybarita*, Gr. *Sybaritēs*, an inhabitant of *Sybaris*, an ancient Greek city of southern Italy proverbial for the effeminacy and voluptuousness of its inhabitants.] A person devoted to luxury and pleasure; an effeminate person.—**Sybaritic, Sybaritical,** sib•a•rit′ik, sib•a•rit′i•kal, *a.* Luxurious; voluptuous; devoted to luxury or pleasure.

sycamine, sik'a•mīn, *n.* [Gr. *sykaminos.*] The mulberry. (N.T.)

sycamore, sik'a•mōr, *n.* [Fr. *sycomore,* L. *sycomorus,* from Gr. *sykomoros,* the fig-mulberry—*sykon,* fig, *moron,* mulberry.] A fruit tree of the fig family, common in Palestine, Arabia, etc.; a kind of maple, a well-known timber tree; a name frequently given in America to the plane tree, buttonwood, or cottonwood.

sycee, sī•sē', *n.* The fine silver of China cast into ingots weighing commonly rather more than a pound troy.

sycophant, sik'o•fant, *n.* [Gr. *sykophantēs,* a false accuser, slanderer—*sykon,* a fig, and *phainō,* to show; lit. a fig-shower; the reason for the name is unknown.] A parasite; a flatterer of princes and great men; a mean flatterer.—**sycophancy,** sik'o•fan•si, *n.* Obsequious flattery; servility.—**sycophantic, sycophantical,** sik•o•fan'tik, sik•o•fan'ti•kal, *a.* Belonging to or resembling a sycophant; obsequiously flattering.

sycosis, si•kō'sis, *n.* [Gr. *sykōsis,* from *sykon,* a fig.] A disease which consists of an eruption of tubercles on the bearded portion of the face and on the scalp.

syenite, sī'en•īt, *n.* A granitic rock of a grayish color, composed of quartz, hornblende, and feldspar; so called because abundant near *Syene* (sī•ē'nē) in Upper Egypt.—**syenitic,** sī•e•nit'ik, *a.* Containing or resembling syenite.—*Syenitic granite,* granite which contains hornblende.—*Syenitic porphyry,* fine-grained syenite containing large crystals of feldspar.

syllable, sil'a•bl, *n.* [Fr. *syllable,* L. *syllaba,* from Gr. *syllabē—syl* for *syn,* together, and root *lab,* to take; as to the termination comp. *participle, principle.*] A sound or combination of sounds uttered together, or at a single impulse of the voice, and constituting a word or part of a word; the least expression of language or thought; a particle.—*v.t.—syllabled, syllabling.* To utter; to articulate.—**syllabary,** sil'a•be•ri, *n.* A catalogue of the primitive syllables of a language.—**syllabic,** si•lab'ik, *a.* Pertaining to a syllable or syllables; consisting of a syllable or syllables.—**syllabically,** si•lab'i•kal•li, *adv.* In a syllabic manner.—**syllabicate,** si•lab'i•kāt, *v.t.* To form into syllables.—**syllabication,** si•lab'i•kā"shon, *n.* The act or method of dividing words into syllables.—**syllabify,** si•lab'i•fī, *v.t.* To form into syllables.

syllabub, sil'a•bub, *n.* See SILLABUB.

syllabus, sil'a•bus, *n.* [L., from the same source as *syllable.*] A brief statement of the heads of a discourse, of a course of lectures, etc.; an abstract; *R. Cath. Ch.* a summary enumeration of points decided by ecclesiastical authority; a document issued by Pope Pius IX in 1864, condemning various doctrines, institutions, etc.

syllepsis, sil•lep'sis, *n.* [Gr. *syllēpsis,* from *syl* for *syn,* with, and *lepsis,* taking.] A figure of speech by which one word is referred to another in the sentence to which it does not grammatically belong.

syllogism, sil'o•jizm, *n.* [L. *syllogismus,* from Gr. *syllogismos,* a syllogism, from *syl* for *syn,* with, and *logizomai,* to reckon, from *logos,* word, reason, etc.] *Logic,* a form of reasoning or argument, consisting of three propositions, of which the two first are called the *premises* (*major* and *minor*), and the last the *conclusion,* the conclusion necessarily following from the premises; thus: a plant has not the power of locomotion; an oak is a plant; therefore an oak has not the power of locomotion.—**syllogistic, syllogistical,** sil•o•jis'tik, sil•o•jis'ti•kal, *a.* Pertaining to a syllogism or to reasoning by syllogisms.—**syllogistically,** sil•o•jis'ti•kal•li, *adv.* In a syllogistic manner; by means of syllogisms.—**syllogize,** sil'o•jīz, *v.i.—syllogized, syllogizing.* To reason by syllogisms.—*v.t.* To put into the form of a syllogism.—**syllogizer,** sil'o•jī•zėr, *n.* One who syllogizes.

sylph, silf, *n.* [Fr. *sylphe,* a sylph; a word coined by Paracelsus. GNOME.] An elemental spirit of the air, according to the system of Paracelsus, generally used as feminine, and often applied figuratively to a woman of graceful and slender proportions.—**sylphid,** sil'fid, *n.* A diminutive of *sylph.*

sylva, sil'va, *n.* [L. *sylva, silva,* a wood or forest.] The forest trees of any region or country collectively. Written also *Silva.*—**sylvan,** sil'van, *a.* Pertaining to a wood or forest; abounding with trees; rural.—**sylviculture,** sil•vi•kul'chėr, *n.* The culture of forest trees; arboriculture.

symbiosis, sim•bi•ō'sis, *n.* [Gr. *syn,* together, *bios,* life.] A sort of parasitism in which two kinds of animals or plants, or a plant and animal, live in close relationship, the one being of service to the other for protection or food.

symbol, sim'bol, *n.* [L. *symbolum,* from Gr. *symbolon,* a symbol, from *symballō,* to infer, conclude—*sym* for *syn,* with, and *ballō,* to throw or put.] An object animate or inanimate standing for or calling up something moral or intellectual; an emblem; a type (the olive branch is the *symbol* of peace); a letter or character which is significant; a sign (as in chemistry, astronomy, etc.); a distinctive mark or attribute of office or duty; *theol.* a creed or confession of faith.—*v.t.* To symbolize.—**symbolic, symbolical,** sim•bol'ik, sim•bol'i•kal, *a.* Pertaining to a symbol or symbols; of the nature of a symbol; representative; *gram.* said of a class of words, such as pronouns, prepositions, etc. PRESENTIVE.—**symbolically,** sim•bol'i•kal•li, *adv.* In a symbolical manner; by symbols; typically.—**symbolism,** sim'bol•izm, *n.* The investing of objects or animals with a symbolic meaning; meaning expressed by symbols; symbols collectively.—**symbolist,** sim'bol•ist, *n.* One who symbolizes.—**symbolistic,** sim•bol•is'tik, *a.* Characterized by the use of symbols.—**symbolize,** sim'bol•īze, *v.t.—symbolized, symbolizing.* To represent by a symbol or by symbols; to serve as the symbol of; to regard or treat as symbolic.—*v.i.* To express or represent in symbols.—**symbology,** sim•bol'o•ji, *n.* [Gr. *symbolon,* and *logos,* discourse.] The art of expressing by symbols; symbols collectively and their meaning and use.

symmetry, sim'e•tri, *n.* [Gr. *symmetria,—sym* for *syn,* with, and *metron,* measure.] A due proportion in size and form of the parts of a body or structure to each other; such harmony of parts as produces a pleasing whole; the character of being well proportioned; *bot.* and *zool.* correspondence or similar distribution of parts in plants or animals; symmetrical disposition of organs.—**symmetric,** sim•met'rik, *a.* Symmetrical; used chiefly in mathematics.—**symmetrical,** sim•met'ri•kal, *a.* Possessing symmetry; well proportioned in all parts; handsome; finely made; *bot.* having the number of parts of one series corresponding with that of the other series (as, having five sepals, five petals, and five, or ten, or fifteen stamens); *math.* having corresponding parts or relations.—**symmetrically,** sim•met'ri•kal•li, *adv.* In a symmetrical manner.—**symmetricalness,** sim•met'ri•kal•nes, *n.*—**symmetrize,** sim'e•trīz, *v.t.* To make symmetrical.

sympathy, sim'pa•thi, *n.* [Fr. *sympathie,* L. *sympathia,* from Gr. *sympatheia—syn,* with, and *pathos,* suffering. PATHOS.] Feeling corresponding to that which another feels; a feeling that enables a person to enter into and in part share another's feelings; fellow-feeling; compassion; commiseration; *physiol.* and *pathol.* that relation of the organs and parts of a living body to each other whereby a disordered condition of one part induces more or less disorder in another part.—**sympathetic,** sim•pa•thet'ik, *a.* Expressive of, produced by, or exhibiting sympathy; having sympathy or common feeling with another; feeling-hearted; *physiol,* produced by sympathy.—*Sympathetic ink,* ink which does not appear on the paper until exposed to heat or chemicals.—*Sympathetic nervous system,* a set of nerves or nervous masses in vertebrate animals, arranged along the spine.—*Sympathetic sounds,* sounds produced from bodies by the vibrations of some other sounding body.—**sympathetically,** sim•pa•thet'i•kal•li, *adv.* In a sympathetic manner; with sympathy or fellow-feeling.—**sympathize,** sim'pa•thīz, *v.i.—sympathized, sympathizing.* To have a common feeling, as of bodily pleasure or pain; to feel in consequence of what another feels; to have fellow-feeling; to be sorry for another's suffering; to condole; to agree; to feel compassion.—**sympathizer,** sim'pa•thī•zėr, *n.* One who sympathizes.

symphony, sim′fo•ni, *n.* [L. *symphonia,* from Gr. *symphōnia—syn,* with, and *phōnē,* voice.] A consonance or harmony of sounds agreeable to the ear; harmony; *mus.* an elaborate composition for a full orchestra, consisting usually, like the sonata, of three or four contrasted but intimately related movements.—**symphonic,** sim•fon′ik, *a.* Pertaining to a symphony.—**symphonious,** sim•fō′ni•us, *a.* Agreeing in sound; harmonious.

symphysis, sim′fi•sis, *n.* [Gr. *symphysis,* from *sym* for *syn,* together, and *phyo,* to grow.] *Anat.* a growing together; the union of bones by cartilage; the point of union between two parts; a commissure.

symposium, sim•pō′zi•um, *n.* pl. **symposia,** sim•pō′zi•a. [Gr. *symposion,* from *syn,* with, *posis,* a drinking.] A feast where there is drinking; a convivial meeting; a discussion by writers in a periodical.—**symposiarch,** sim•pō′zi•ärk, *n.* [Gr. *symposiarchēs — symposion,* and *archē,* rule.] The president or manager of a feast.

symptom, sim′tom, *n.* [Gr. *symptōma —syn,* together, with *piptō,* to fall.] Any sign or token; what serves as evidence of something not seen; *med.* an affection which accompanies a disease, and from which the existence and nature of a disease may be inferred.—**symptomatic, symptomatical,** sim•to•mat′ik, sim•to•mat′i•kal, *a.* Being or serving as a symptom; indicating the existence of something else.—*Symptomatic disease,* a disease which proceeds from some prior disorder, and opposed to *idiopathic disease.*—**symptomatically,** sim•to•mat′i•kal•li, *adv.* By means of symptoms.—**symptomatology,** sim′to•ma•tol″o•ji, *n.* That part of medicine which treats of the symptoms of diseases.

synaeresis, si•ne′re•sis, *n.* [Gr. *synairesis—syn,* together, and *hairō,* to take.] *Gram.* the contraction of two syllables into one.

synagogue, sin′a•gog, *n.* [Fr. *synagogue,* Gr. *synagōgē—syn,* together, and *agō,* to bring.] A congregation of Jews met for the purpose of worship: a Jewish place of worship.—**synagogical,** sin•a•goj′i•kal, *a.* Pertaining or relating to a synagogue.

synaloepha, sin•a•lē′fa, *n.* [Gr. *synaloiphē, synaleiphō,* to melt together—*syn,* together, and *aleiphō,* to smear.] A suppression of some vowel or diphthong at the end of a word before another vowel or diphthong.

synapsis, sin•ap′sis. [Gr. *synapsis,* union.] A stage in the development of a germ cell, at which the chromatins become reduced in number.

synarthrosis, sin•är•thrō′sis, *n.* [Gr. *synarthrōsis—syn,* with, and *arthron,* a joint.] *Anat.* union of bones without motion.

synchronous, synchronal, sin′kro•nus, sin′kro•nal, *a.* [Gr. *syn,* with, and *chronos,* time (whence also *chronic, chronicle,* etc.).] Happening at the same time; contemporaneous; simultaneous.—**synchronism,** sin′kron•izm, *n.* Concurrence of two or more events or facts in time; simultaneousness; arrangement of contemporaneous events in tabular form.—**synchronistic,** sin•kron•is′tik, *a.* Pertaining to synchronism.—**synchronization,** sin′kron•i•zā″shon, *n.* The act of synchronizing.—**synchronize,** sin′kron•īz, *v.t.—synchronized, synchronizing.* To concur or agree in time.—*v.t.* To make to agree in time; to cause to indicate the same time, as one timepiece with another.—**synchronizer,** sin′kron•ī•zėr, *n.* One who or that which synchronizes.—**synchronously,** sin′kron•us•li, *adv.* Contemporaneously; at the same time.

synclastic, sin•klas′tik, *a.* Of surfaces, bending away from a tangent plane toward the same side all round, like a ball. See ANTICLASTIC.

synclinal, sin•klī′nal, *a.* [Gr. *syn,* together, and *klinō,* to incline or slope.] *Geol.* sloping downward in opposite directions so as to meet in a common point or line; dipping toward a common line or plane (*synclinal* strata); formed by or pertaining to strata dipping in such a manner (*synclinal* axis); opposed to *anticlinal.*—*n.* A synclinal line or axis.

syncope, sin′ko•pi, *n.* [Gr. *synkopē, syn,* together, and *koptō,* to strike, to cut off.] A contraction of a word by elision in the middle, as in *ne'er* for *never*; a suspension or sudden pause; *med.* a fainting or swooning; *mus.* syncopation.—**syncopate,** sin′ko•pāt, *v.t.—syncopated, syncopating.* To contract by syncope; *mus.* to treat with syncopation.—**syncopation,** sin•ko•pā′shon, *n.* The contraction of a word by elision; *mus.* the alteration of rhythm by driving the accent to that part of a bar not usually accented, the accented part of a bar being usually the first note.

syncretism, sing′kret•izm, *n.* [Gr. *synkrētismos.*] The attempted blending of irreconcilable principles or parties, as in philosophy or religion; opposed to *eclecticism.*—**syncretistic,** sing•kre•tis′tik, *a.* Pertaining to syncretism.—**syncretic,** sing•kret′ik, *a.* Pertaining to syncretism.

syndactyl, sin•dak′til, *a.* [Gr. *syn,* together, *daktylos,* a finger or toe.] *Ornithol.* having the external toe nearly as long as the middle, and partly united to it, as in the bee eater, kingfisher, etc.; or with some of the digits closely bound together.

syndesmology, sin•des•mol′o•ji, *n.* [Gr. *syndesmos,* a ligament, from *syn,* together, *desmos,* a band.] The department of anatomy that deals with the ligaments.—**syndesmosis,** sin•des•mō′sis, *n.* A connection of bones by a ligament.

syndic, sin′dik, *n.* [Gr. *syndikos,* helping in a court of justice, an advocate—*syn,* with, and *dikē,* justice.] An officer of government, invested with different powers in different countries; a person chosen to transact business for others.

syndicalism, sin′dik•al•izm, *n.* [Fr. *syndical,* of a trade union.] A system through which, by strikes, general or sympathetic, and otherwise, workmen aim at the domination of industry and capital.

syndicate, sin′di•kit, *n.* [F. *syndicat* from Gr. *syndic,* advocate.] A group of persons or organizations combined to carry out some project; a group of persons authorized to carry out transactions; a business concern that sells material for publication in various newspapers.—*v.t.*—sin″di•kāt′, *syndicated, syndicating.* To sell to a syndicate for publication; to operate as a syndicate.—*v.i.* To form a syndicate.

syndrome, sin′drōm, sin′dro•mā, *n.* [Gr. *syn,* with, and *dramein,* to run.] In medicine, concurrence of a group of symptoms.

synecdoche, si•nek′do•ki, *n.* [Gr., from *syn,* with, *ek,* out, *dechomai,* to receive.] A figure of speech by which the whole of a thing is put for a part, or a part for the whole (as *hands* for *workmen*).—**synecdochical,** sin•ek•dok′i•kal, *a.* Expressed by or implying synecdoche.

syneresis, si•ne′re•sis. See SYNAERESIS.

synergist, si•nėr′jist, *n.* [Gr. *syn,* with, and *ergon,* work.] One who maintains the co-operation of man with God in the conversion of sinners.

synizesis, sin•i•zē′sis, *n.* [Gr., from *syn,* with, and *hizō,* to sit.] *Med.* an obliteration of the pupil of the eye.

synod, sin′od, *n.* [Fr. *synode,* L. *synodus,* from Gr. *synodus—syn,* and *hodos,* a way, a journeying.] A council or meeting of ecclesiastics, especially bishops and clergy, to consult on matters of religion; among Presbyterians, a church court consisting of the members of several adjoining presbyteries; also, a meeting, convention, or council in general.—**synodic, synodical,** si•nod′ik, si•nod′i•kal, *a.* Pertaining to a synod; transacted in a synod; *astron.* pertaining to a conjunction or two successive conjunctions of the heavenly bodies.—*Synodical month,* the period from one conjunction of the moon with the sun to another: called also a *Lunation.*

synoecious, si•nē′shus, *a.* [Gr. *syn,* together, *oikos,* a house.] *Bot.* having male and female organs on the same head.

synonym, synonyme, sin′o•nim, *n.* [Fr. *synonyme,* from Gr. *synōnymos,* having the same signification—*syn,* with, and *onoma,* a name.] A word having the same, or nearly the same, signification as another in the same language; one of two or more words in the same language which have the same meaning.—**synonymic, synonymical,** sin•o•nim′ik, sin•o•nim′i•kal, *a.* Synonymous.—**synonymize,** si•non′im•īz, *v.t.—synonymized, synonymizing.* To express by words of the same meaning.—**synonymous,** si•non′i•mus, *a.* Having the character of a synonym; expressing the same thing.—**synonymously,** si•non′i•mus•li, *adv.* In a synonymous manner.—**synonymy,** si•non′i•mi, *n.* The quality of being synonymous.

synopsis, si•nop′sis, *n.* pl. **synopses,** si•nop′sēz. [Gr., from *syn,* with, and *opsis,* a sight, view.] A summary or brief statement giving a general view of some subject, as by means of short paragraphs; a conspectus.—**synoptic, synoptical,** si•nop′tik, si•nop′ti•kal, *a.* Affording a synopsis or general view.—*Synoptic gospels,* a term for the gospels of Matthew, Mark, and Luke, which present a synopsis of the same series of events, whereas in John's gospel the narrative and discourses are different.—**synoptic,** *n.* One of the synoptic gospels. —**synoptically,** si•nop′ti•kal•li, *adv.* In a synoptical manner.

synovia, si•nō′vi•a, *n.* [Gr. *syn,* with, and L. *ovum,* an egg.] A thick, viscid, yellowish-white fluid, somewhat resembling white of egg in appearance, secreted at the joints for the purpose of lubricating their surfaces.—**synovial,** si•nō′vi•al, *a.* Pertaining to or consisting of synovia.—**synovitis,** sin•o•vī′tis, *n.* [The term. *-itis* denotes inflammation.] Inflammation of the synovial membrane.

syntax, sin′taks, *n.* [Gr. *syntaxis,* arrangement, disposition, from *syn,* with, and *taxis,* order, from *tassō,* to put in order. TACTICS.] *Gram.* the construction of sentences; the due arrangement of words or members of sentences in their mutual relations according to established usage.—**syntactic, syntactical,** sin•tak′tik, sin•tak′ti•kal, *a.* Pertaining or according to the rules of syntax.—**syntactically,** sin•tak′ti•kal•li, *adv.* As regards syntax; in conformity to syntax.

synthesis, sin′the•sis, *n.* pl. **syntheses,** sin′the•sēz. [Gr. *synthesis,* a putting together, from *syn,* with, and *tithēmi,* to place.] The putting of two or more things together to form a whole: opposed to *analysis*; *logic,* the combination of separate elements of thought into a whole; *surg.* the operation by which divided parts are united; *chem.* the uniting of elements into a compound; composition or combination.—**synthetic, synthetical,** sin•thet′ik, sin•thet′i•kal, *a.* Pertaining to synthesis; consisting in synthesis; made by mixing certain ingredients.—*Synthetic processes,* in chemistry, processes by which naturally occurring compounds are built up artificially from their elements, or from simpler constituents. —**synthetically,** sin•thet′i•kal•li, *adv.* By synthesis or composition.

syphilis, sif′i•lis, *n.* [From *Syphilus,* hero of a 16th-century poem by Girolamo Fracastoro.] A contagious, usually venereal and sometimes congenital, disease, caused by the *Treponema pallidum* organism.—**syphilitic,** sif•ė•li′tik, *a.* Infected with syphilis.—**syphiloid,** sif′i•loid, *a.* Resembling or having the character of syphilis.

syphon, *n.* See SIPHON.

Syriac, sir′i•ak, *a.* [L. *Syriacus.*] Pertaining to Syria or its language.—*n.* The ancient language of Syria, a Semitic language differing little from Chaldee.

syringa, sī•ring′ga, *n.* [Gr. *syrinx, syringos,* a pipe—pipes having been made from the plants.] A genus of plants of which the lilac is the type; also a name of the mock orange.

syringe, si•rinj′, *n.* [From Gr. *syrinx, syringos,* a pipe, a tube.] An instrument used to inject or withdraw fluids from the body or from cavities of the body, consisting of a cylindrical tube with an airtight piston fitted with a handle. *v.t.*—*syringed, syringing.* To wash and cleanse or water by means of a syringe.

syrinx, si′ringks, *n.* [Gr. *syrinx,* a pipe.] The Pandean or Pan's pipes.

syrt, syrtis, sėrt, sėr′tis, *n.* [Fr. *syrte,* L. *syrtis,* Gr. *syrtis,* a sandbank.] A quicksand or sandbank.

syrup, sir′up, *n.* [O.E. *sirup,* from O.Fr. from L. from Ar. *sharab,* beverage.] A thick, sticky, flavored mixture of sugar and water.—**syrupy,** sir′up•i, *a.*

systaltic, sis•tal′tik, *a.* [Gr. *systaltikos*—*syn,* with, and *stellō,* to put.] *Med.* having alternate contraction and dilatation, as the heart.

system, sis′tem, *n.* [L. *systema,* Gr. *systēma,* from *syn,* together, and *histemi,* to set.] Any assemblage of things forming a regular and connected whole; things connected according to a scheme; a number of heavenly bodies acting on each other according to certain laws (the solar *system*); an assemblage or connected series of parts or organs in an animal body (the nervous *system*); also, the body itself as a functional unity or whole (to take poison into the *system*); a plan or scheme according to which things are connected into a whole (a *system* of philosophy); regular method or order (to have no *system* in working).—**systematic, systematical,** sis•te•mat′ik, sis•te•mat′i•kal, *a.* Pertaining to or consisting in system; methodical; proceeding according to system.—**systematically,** sis•te•mat′i•kal•li, *adv.* In a systematic manner; regularly; methodically.—**systematism,** sis′tem•at•izm, *n.* Reduction of facts to a system.—**systematist,** sis′tem•at•ist, *n.* One who forms or who adheres to a system.—**systematization,** sis′tem•at•ī•zā″shon, *n.* The act or process of reducing to system.—**systematize,** sis′tem•a•tīz, *v.t.*—*systematized, systematizing.* To reduce to system or regular method.—**systematizer,** sis′tem•a•tī•zėr, *n.* One who reduces things to system.—**systematology,** sis′tem•a•tol″o•ji, *n.* Knowledge or information regarding systems.—**systemic,** sis•tem′ik, *a.* Pertaining to a system; *physiol.* pertaining to the body as a whole (the *systemic* circulation of the blood); of hearts, containing pure blood only.—**systemize,** sis′tem•īz, *v.t.* See SYSTEMATIZE.

systole, sis′to•lē, *n.* [Gr. *systolé,* from *syn,* together, and *stello,* to put.] The contraction of the heart and arteries for forcing the blood through the system and carrying on the circulation: opposite to *diastole*; *gram.* the shortening of a long syllable.—**systolic,** sis•tol′ik, *a.* Relating to systole.

syzygy, siz′i•ji, *n.* [Gr. *syzygia*—*syn,* together, and *zygon,* a yoke. YOKE.] *Astron.* the conjunction or opposition of a planet with the sun, or of any two of the heavenly bodies.

T

T, t, tē, the twentieth letter of the English alphabet, closely allied to *d,* both being dentals.—*To a T,* exactly; with the utmost exactness (to suit *to a T*), the allusion being to a mechanic's T-square.

Taal, täl, *n.* [D. language.] Language of the Cape Dutch.

tab, tab, *n.* [Origin unknown.] A short projection, as a loop; a label; a tag; a close observation.—*v.t. tabbed, tabbing.*—To supply with tabs; to single out or designate.

tabard, tab′ėrd, *n.* [Fr. *tabard,* Sp. and Pg. *tabardo,* It. *tabarro,* L.L. *tabarrus, tabardus,* a cloak; origin doubtful.] A garment open at the sides, with wide sleeves or flaps reaching to the elbows; now only worn by the Officers of Arms. The tabard of a King of Arms is of velvet, that of a Herald of figured silk, and that of a Pursuivant of damask.

tabaret, tab′a•ret, *n.* [Probably connected with *tabby* or *tabard.*] A stout satin-striped silk used for furniture.

tabby, tab′i, *n.* [Fr. *tabis,* Sp., Pg., and It., *tabi,* L.L. *attabi,* from Ar. *attābi,* watered silk, from the quarter of Baghdad where this stuff was manufactured, named after a prince *Attab.*] A kind of rich silk or other stuff watered or figured; a cat of a mixed or brindled color; any cat; an ancient spinster.—*v.t.*—*tabbied, tabbying.* To water or cause to look wavy by the process of calendering (to *tabby* silk).—**tabbying,** tab′i•ing, *n.* The watering of stuffs between engraved rollers.

tabernacle, tab′ėr•nak•l, *n.* [L. *tabernaculum,* a tent, a dim. from *taberna,* a hut, a tavern. TAVERN.] A slightly constructed temporary habitation; the human frame as the temporary abode of the soul; [*cap.*] the movable building, so contrived as to be taken to pieces with ease, carried by the Jews during their wanderings in the wilderness; a temple; a place of worship; a small cell or repository for holy things; an ornamental chest on Roman Catholic altars for the consecrated vessels; *Goth. arch.* a canopied stall or niche; an arched canopy over a tomb; a tomb.—*Feast of tabernacles,* a festival of the Israelites to commemorate their dwelling in tents during their journeys in the wilderness, lasting eight days, during which the people dwelt in booths made of the branches of certain trees.—*v.i.* To sojourn.—**tabernacular,** tab•ėr•nak′ū•lėr, *a.* Pertaining to a tabernacle; sculptured with delicate tracery work.

tabes, tā′bēz, *n.* [L., from *tabeo,* to

waste away.] A disease consisting in a gradual wasting away of the whole body, accompanied with languor and depressed spirits.—**tabetic,** ta•bet'ik, *a.* Pertaining to tabes; consumptive. —**tabid,** tab'id, *a.* [L. *tabidus.*] Relating to tabes; wasted by disease.

table, tā'bl, *n.* [Fr. *table,* from L. *tabula,* a board, a painting, a tablet, etc., from root *ta,* to extend, and suffix *-bula* (as in *fabula,* a fable). Of allied origin are *tavern, tabernacle.*] An article of furniture consisting of a horizontal frame with a flat upper surface supported by legs; any detached flat surface, especially when horizontal; the fare or viands served on a table; the persons sitting at table; a thin piece of something for writing on; a tablet; a series of many items or particulars presented in one connected group, especially when the items are in lists or columns; a syllabus or index; a series of numbers which proceed according to some given law (*tables* of logarithms); *jewelry,* the upper and flat surface of a diamond or other precious stone; *pl.* an old name for the game of draughts or a similar game.—*The Lord's table,* the altar in a church; the sacrament of the Lord's supper. —*Round table.* ROUND.—*Twelve tables,* the tables containing a celebrated body of ancient Roman laws, which formed the basis of Roman jurisprudence.—*To lay on the table,* in parliamentary practice and in the usage of corporate and other bodies, to receive any document, as a report, motion, etc., but to agree to postpone its consideration indefinitely.—*To turn the tables,* to change the condition or fortune of contending parties, alluding to the vicissitudes of fortune in gaming.—*v.t.*—*tabled, tabling.* To form into a table or catalogue; to tabulate; to lay or place upon a table; to lay on the table in business meetings, whether public or private; to enter upon the record.—*a.* Appertaining to or provided for a table. —**tablecloth,** *n.* A cloth, usually of linen, for covering a table before the dishes are set for meals.—**table-d'hote,** tä'bl•dōt, *n.* [Fr. *table d'hôte,* lit. table of the host or landlord.] A common table for guests at a hotel; an ordinary.—**tableland,** *n.* A stretch of elevated flat land; a plateau.—**table linen,** *n.* The linen used for and at the table; napery.—**tablespoon,** *n.* The ordinary large spoon used at table as distinguished from a teaspoon.—**tablespoonful,** *n.* As much as a tablespoon will hold.

tableau, tab'lō, *n.* pl. **tableaux,** tab'lōz. [Fr. *tableau,* from *table,* a table.] A picture; a striking representation; performers grouped in a dramatic scene, or any persons regarded as forming a dramatic group. —*Tableau vivant* (vē•vän), a group of persons so dressed and placed as to represent some historical or fictitious scene; *lit.* a living picture.

tablet, tab'let, *n.* [Fr. *tablette,* dim. of *table.*] A small flat surface; a slab of wood or stone, or a metal plate bearing some device or inscription; a pad of paper; a small flattish cake, as of medicine.

taboo, ta•bö', *n.* [Of Polynesian origin.] The setting of something apart and away from human contact, either as consecrated or accursed, practiced among certain savage races; the state of being so set apart; prohibition of contact or intercourse.—*v.t.* To put under taboo; to interdict approach to or contact or intercourse with (a *tabooed* subject of conversation).

tabor, tabour, tā'bėr, *n.* [O.Fr. *tabour,* Fr. *tambour,* Sp. and Pg. *tambor,* probably from Per. *tabîr,* a tabor.] A small drum beaten with one stick, used as an accompaniment to a pipe or fife.—*v.i.* To play the tabor.—**taborer,** tā'bėr•ėr, *n.* One who beats the tabor.—**taboret, tabouret,** ta'bėr•et, *n.* A small tabor; a frame for embroidery, named from its shape.—**taborin,** ta'be•rēn, *n.* [Fr. *tabourin.*] A tabor; a tambourine.—**tabret,** ta'bret, *n.* [A dim. form.] A tabor.

tabu, ta•bö', *n.* See TABOO.

tabula, tab'ū•la, *n.* pl. **tabulae,** tab'ū•lē. [L. TABLE.] A table; a tablet; a flat portion of something; a horizontal plate across the cavity in certain corals.—**tabular,** tab'ū•lėr, *a.* [L. *tabularis,* from *tabula,* a table.] In the form of a table; having a flat surface; having the form of laminae or plates; set down in or forming a table or statement of items in columns; computed by the use of tables.—*Tabular spar,* silicate of lime, a mineral of a grayish-white color, occurring either massive or crystallized, in rectangular tabular crystals. —**tabularize,** tab'ū•lėr•īz, *v.t.* To make tables of; to tabulate.—**tabulate,** tab'ū•lāt, *v.t.*—*tabulated, tabulating.* To reduce to tables or synopses; to set down in a table of items.—*a.* Table-shaped; tabular.—**tabulation,** tab•ū•lā'shon, *n.* The throwing of data into a tabular form.

tacamahac, tak'a•ma•hak, *n.* A name of the balsam poplar of North America; a resin produced from a tree of Mexico and the West Indies.

tachometer, tak•om'et•ėr, *n.* [Gr. *tachus,* swift, *metron,* measure.] An instrument used in rapid surveying. An instrument for measuring velocity as of running water; a contrivance for indicating small variations in the velocity of machines.—**tachometry,** tak•om'et•ri, *n.* A system of rapid surveying, in which distances and bearings are determined by a modified form of theodolite, called a tachometer or tachymeter.

tachygraphy, ta•kig'ra•fi, *n.* [Gr. *tachys,* quick, and *graphō,* to write.] The art or practice of quick writing; shorthand; stenography. — **tachygraphic, tachygraphical,** tak•i•graf'ik, tak•i•graf'i•kal, *a.* Pertaining to tachygraphy or shorthand.

tachylyte, tak'i•līt, *n.* [Gr. *tachys,* swift, *lūō,* to loose.] Vitreous basalt, quickly fused under blowpipe.

tacit, tas'it, *a.* [L. *tacitus,* silent, from *taceo,* to be silent; cog. with Goth. *thahan,* to be silent.] Implied but not expressed in words; silent (*tacit* consent, a *tacit* agreement).—**tacitly,** tas'it•li, *adv.* Silently; by implication; without words.—**taciturn,** tas'i•tėrn, *a.* [L. *taciturnus,* from *tacitus,* silent.] Habitually silent; not apt to talk or speak.—**taciturnity,** tas•i•tėr'ni•ti, *n.* [L. *taciturnitas.*] The state or quality of being taciturn; habitual silence or reserve in speaking.—**taciturnly,** tas'i•tėrn•li, *adv.* In a taciturn manner; silently.

tack, tak, *n.* [Of Celtic origin; Ir. *taca,* Armor. *tach,* a nail; seen also in *attach, attack, detach.*] A small, short nail, usually having a broad head; a slight fastening or connection, as by a few stitches; *naut.* a rope for pulling the foremost lower corners of certain sails; the part of the sail to which the tack is fastened; the course of a ship as regards having the wind impelling her on the starboard or the port side; *Scots law,* a lease.—*v.t.* To fasten; to attach; to unite in a slight or hasty manner; to add on as a supplement or addition; to append.—*v.i.* To change the course of a ship so as to have the wind act from the starboard instead of the port side, or vice versa.—**tacket,** tak'et, *n.* A clout nail or hobnail. (*Scotch.*)

tackle, tak'l, *n.* [From the stem of *take*; L.G. and D. *takel,* Dan. *takkel,* Sw. *tackel,* tackle.] Apparatus, appliances, or equipment for various kinds of work; gear; one or more pulleys with a single rope, used for raising and lowering weights; the ropes and rigging, etc., of a ship. *v.t.*—*tackled, tackling.* To supply tackle; to apply tackle to; to set to work on vigorously; to seize and throw to the ground, as a football opponent.—**tackling,** tak'l•ing, *n.* Tackle; gear, rigging, etc.; instruments of action; harness, or the like.

tact, takt, *n.* [Fr. *tact,* touch, feeling, tact, from L. *tactus,* touch, from *tango, tactum,* to touch, from which also *tactile, tangent, tangible,* etc. TANGENT.] Touch†; peculiar skill or faculty; skill or adroitness in doing or saying exactly what is required by circumstances; the stroke in beating time in music.

tactics, tak'tiks, *n.* [Fr. *tactique,* Gr. *taktikē* (*technē,* art), the art of drawing up soldiers, from *tassō, taxō,* to arrange (seen also in *syntax, taxidermy*).] The science and art of disposing military or naval forces in order for battle, of maneuvering them in presence of the enemy or within the range of his fire, and performing military and naval evolutions. STRATEGY.—**tactic,** tak'tik, *n.* System of tactics.—**tactic, tactical,** tak'tik, tak'ti•kal, *a.* Pertaining to tactics.—**tactically,** tak'ti•kal•li, *adv.* According to tactics.—**tactician,** tak•tish'an, *n.* One versed in tactics.

tactile, tak'tīl, *a.* [Fr. *tactile,* from L. *tactilis,* from *tango,* to touch. TACT.] Capable of being touched or felt; tangible; pertaining to the sense of touch.—**taction,**† tak'shon, *n.* [L. *tactio.*] The act of touching; touch.—

tactual, tak'chū•al, *a.* Pertaining to the sense of touch; consisting in or derived from touch.

tadpole, tad'pōl, *n.* [Equivalent to *toadpoll*, that is toad with a big poll or head.] The young of the frog or allied animal in its first state from the spawn.

tael, tāl, *n.* In China, a denomination of silver money; also, a weight of 1½ oz.

ta'en, tān. Poetical contraction of *Taken.*

taenia, tē'ni•a, *n.* [L. *taenia*, from Gr. *tainia*, a fillet or ribbon.] The tapeworm; *arch.* the fillet or band which separates the Doric frieze from the architrave; *surg.* a ligature.

tafferel, *n.* See TAFFRAIL.

taffeta, taf'e•ta, *n.* [Fr. *taffetas*, It. *taffetà*, from Per. *tâftah*, pp. of verb *tâftan*, to weave.] A lustrous, silk-like fabric of plain weave, used especially in women's clothes.

taffrail, tafferel, taf'rāl, taf'e•rel, *n.* [D. *tafereel*, a panel, a picture, dim. of *tafel*, a table, a picture, from L. *tabula*, a table. TABLE.] *Naut.* the rail over the heads of the stern timbers; originally the upper flat part of a ship's stern.

taffy, taf'i, *n.* [Origin uncertain.] A light-colored, porous, viscous candy usually made with molasses.

tafia, ta'fi•a, *n.* [Fr. from Malay.] A variety of rum distilled from molasses.

tag, tag, *n.* [Same as Sw. *tagg*, a point; akin *tack*, *take.*] A metallic point on the end of a string; anything hanging loosely attached or affixed to another; the end or catchword of an actor's speech; something mean and paltry, as the rabble (*Shak.*); a young sheep of the first year.—*v.t.*—*tagged, tagging.* To fit with a tag or point; to fit one thing to another; to tack or join.—**tagger,** tag'ėr, *n.* One who tags.

tail, tāl, *n.* [A.Sax. *taegel*, *taegl*, a tail = Icel. *tagl*, L.G. and Sw. *tagel*, O.H.G. *zagal*, originally hair, as seen from Goth. *tagl*, hair.] That part of an animal which consists of the projecting termination of the spinal column, and terminates its body behind; the hinder or inferior part of a thing, as opposed to the head; any long terminal appendage or anything resembling or suggesting the tail of an animal; the other side of a coin from that which bears the head; the reverse; *aviation*, the after part of an aircraft, usually carrying controlling organs, e.g. rudders, elevators, fins.—*To turn tail*, to run away; to shirk an encounter.—*v.t.* To follow, droop, or hang like a tail. —**tailboard,** *n.* The movable board at the hinder end of a cart or wagon. —**tailpiece,** *n.* A piece forming a tail; an end piece; an appendage; a small picture or ornamental design at the end of a chapter or section in a book; the piece at the lower end of instruments of the violin kind to which the strings are fastened.—**tailrace,** *n.* The water which runs from the mill after it has produced the motion of the wheel.—**tailspin,** *n.* Spinning fall of an airplane out of control.

tail, tāl, *n.* [Fr. *taille*, a cutting, from *tailler*, to cut. TAILOR.] *Law*, limitation; abridgment.—*Estate tail*, or *estate in tail*, an entailed estate or estate limited to certain heirs.

tailor, tā'lėr, *n.* [Fr. *tailleur*, from *tailler*, to cut, from L.L. *taliare*, *taleare*, to cut, from L. *talea*, a rod, slip, cutting.] One whose occupation is to cut out and make clothing.—*v.t.* To fit with clothes; to style, especially clothing.—*v.i.* To do the work of a tailor.—**tailorbird,** *n.* An East Indian bird of the warbler family, so called because it constructs its nest by sewing leaves together, using the bill as a needle and a fiber as thread.—**tailormade,** ta'lėr•mād", *a.* Made and fitted by a tailor, as opposed to ready-made clothing.

taint, tānt, *v.t.* [O.Fr. *taindre*, pp. *taint*; (Mod. Fr. *teindre*, *teint*), from L. *tingere*, to wet or moisten; whence also *tinge*, *tincture*, *tint.*] To imbue or impregnate with something noxious or poisonous; to infect; to corrupt, as by incipient putrefaction; to sully or pollute.—*v.i.* To become infected or corrupted; to be affected with incipient putrefaction.—*n.* Something that infects or contaminates; infection; corruption; a stain; a blemish on reputation.—**taintless,** tānt'les, *a.* Free from taint or infection; pure.

Taiping, tī•ping, *n.* [Chinese, *t'ai p'ing*, great peace.] One who took part in the Chinese Rebellion of 1850-64. A dynasty name.

take, tāk, *v.t.*—pret. *took*; ppr. *taking*; pp. *taken.* [From Icel. and O.Sw. *taka*, Sw. *taga*, Dan. *tage*, to take, to seize, etc.; same root as L. *tango*, *tactum*, to touch (whence *tangible*, *tact*, etc.) *Tackle* is akin.] To receive or accept; correlative to *give*, and opposed to *refuse* or *reject*; to lay hold of; to seize; to grasp (*took* him by the throat); to lay hold of and remove; to carry off; to abstract (to *take* one's goods); to catch suddenly; to entrap; to circumvent; to surprise; to make prisoner of; to capture; to obtain possession of by arms (to *take* a town); to captivate, attract, allure; to understand or comprehend; to receive with good or ill will; to feel concerning (*take* an act amiss); to look upon as; to suppose, regard, consider (I *take* this to be right); to avail one's self of; to employ; to use (precaution, advice, etc.); to require or render necessary (the journey *takes* a week); not to let slip; to choose and make one's own; to select; to have recourse to; to betake one's self to (to *take* a course, shelter); to form or adopt (a resolution, a plan); to put on; to assume (to *take* shape); to receive and swallow (food, medicine); to copy; to draw (a portrait, a sketch); to put into writing; to note down; to fasten on, attack, or assail, as by a blast, a disease or the like; to be infected or seized with (to *take* a cold); to experience, indulge, feel (comfort, pride); to bear or submit to; to put up with; to enter into possession of by renting or leasing; to conduct, guide, convey, carry (to *take* one home); to leap over; to clear; to place one's self in; to occupy (to *take* a seat).—*To take aback*, to surprise or astonish; to confound.—*To take advantage of*, to use any advantage or benefit offered by; to catch or seize by surprise or cunning —*To take aim*, to aim.—*To take air*, to be divulged or disclosed.—*To take the air*, to *take an airing*, to walk or drive in the open air for refreshment.—*To take arms*, or *take up arms*, to commence war or hostilities.—*To take breath*, to stop in order to breathe or rest after exertion.—*To take care*, to be watchful, vigilant, or careful.—*To take care of*, to have the charge of; to keep watch over.—*To take down*, to remove to a lower position; hence, to humble; to abase; to pull to pieces; to put in writing; to write down.—*To take effect*, to produce the intended effect; to begin to act or come into operation.—*To take the field*, to commence the operations of a campaign.—*To take fire*, to become ignited or inflamed; *fig.* to become excited, as with anger or love.—*To take heart*, to become courageous or confident.—*To take to heart*, to be keenly or deeply affected by; to feel sensibly.—*To take heed*, to be careful or cautious.—*To take heed to*, to attend to with care.—*To take hold of*, to seize; to grasp; to lay hands on.—*To take horse*, to mount and ride.—*To take in*, to admit or bring into one's house; to encompass or embrace; to include; to comprehend; to draw into a less compass; to contract; to furl, as a sail; to receive into the mind; to admit the truth of; to circumvent; to cheat.—*To take in hand*, to undertake; to attempt to execute.—*To take in vain*, to use or utter unnecessarily, carelessly, or profanely.—*To take leave*, to bid farewell; to depart; to permit one's self; to use a certain license or liberty.—*To take notice of*, to regard or observe with attention; to pay some attention to; to make remarks on; to mention.—*To take oath*, to swear judicially or with solemnity.—*To take off*, to remove or lift from the surface, outside, or top; to divest one's self of; to remove to a different place; to kill; to make away with; to deduct; to withdraw; to call or draw away; to drink out; to mimic; to imitate, as in ridicule.—*To take on*, or *upon*, to undertake; to assume.—*To take out*, to remove from, within or from a number; to remove by cleansing or the like (to *take out* a stain).—*To take pains*, to use all one's skill, care, and the like.—*To take part in*, to share; to partake of.—*To take part with*, to join or unite with.—*To take one's part*, to espouse one's cause; to defend one.—*To take place*, to happen.—*To take root*, to strike a root; to put forth roots and grow;

to become firmly fixed or established.—*To take time,* to act without haste or hurry; to be in no haste or excitement; to require or necessitate a portion or period of time.—*To take thought,* to be solicitous or anxious.—*To take up,* to lift; to raise; to obtain on credit; to begin where another left off (to *take up* a narrative); to occupy, engross, or engage; to arrest or apprehend; to charge one's self with (a friend's cause, a quarrel); to enter upon; to adopt (a trade or occupation); to pay and receive (a bill at a bank)—*v.i.* To direct one's course; to betake one's self; to turn in some direction; to suit the public taste; to please; to have the intended effect; to catch hold; to admit of being made a portrait of.—*To take after,* to learn to follow; to imitate; to resemble.—*To take from,* to derogate or detract from.—*To take on,* to be violently affected; to grieve; to fret. (*Colloq.*)—*To take to,* to become fond of; to resort to.—*To take up with,* to dwell with; to associate with.—*n.* The quantity of anything taken; the quantity of fish taken at one haul or upon one cruise.—**taker,** tā′kėr, *n.* One that takes; one who catches; a captor.—**taking,** tā′king, *p.* and *a.* Alluring; engaging.—*n.* A seizing; agitation or distress of mind.

talapoin, tal′a•poin, *n.* A Buddhist monk of Burma or Siam.

talc, talk, *n.* [Fr. *talc,* Sp. and Pg. *talco,* from Ar. *talq,* talc.] A magnesian laminated mineral, unctuous to the touch, of a shining luster, translucent, and usually white, apple-green, or yellow, differing from mica in being flexible but not elastic. FRENCH CHALK.—**talcose, talcous,** tal′kōs, tal′kus, *a.* Like talc; consisting of talc; containing talc.

tale, tāl, *n.* [A.Sax. *talu,* speech, number; Icel. *tal, tala,* a speech, a number; Dan. *tal,* number, *tale,* talk, to talk; D. *tal,* number, *taal,* speech; G. *zahl,* number; akin tell.] An oral relation; a piece of information; a narrative of events that have really happened or are imagined to have happened; a short story, true or fictitious; a number or quantity reckoned, estimated, or set down; especially a reckoning by counting or numbering.—**talebearer,** *n.* A person who tells tales likely to breed mischief; one who carries stories and makes mischief by his officiousness.—**talebearing,** *n.* The act of spreading stories officiously; communication of secrets maliciously.—**taleteller,** *n.* One who tells tales or stories; a talebearer.

talent, tal′ent, *n.* [Fr. *talent,* L. *talentum,* from Gr. *talanton,* a thing weighed, a talent, from root *tal,* akin to Skr. *tul,* to lift up, L. *tollo,* to lift, O.E. and Sc. *thole,* to suffer.] An ancient weight and denomination of money; the Attic talent as a weight being about 56 lb.; the Hebrew talent as a weight equal to 93¾ lb.; a gift, endowment, or faculty (a *talent* for mimicry); mental endowments or capacities of a superior kind; general mental power. [In the latter senses probably borrowed from the Scriptural parable of the talents, Mat. xxv.] ∴ Syn. under GENIUS.

tales, tā′lēz, *n. pl.* [L. *talis,* such, of like sort, pl. *tales.*] *Law,* suitable persons who happen to be in a court, and from whom certain may be selected to supply any deficiency in the required number of jurors.—*To pray a tales,* to pray that the number of jurymen may be thus completed.

talipes, tal′i•pes, *n.* [L. *talus,* ankle, *pes,* foot.] The deformity called clubfoot.

talipot, tal′i•pot, *n.* [Singhalese name.] A palm of India, Ceylon, etc., the leaves of which are used for covering houses, making umbrellas, fans, as a substitute for writing paper, etc.

talisman, tal′is•man, *n.* [Fr. and Sp. *talisman,* from Ar. *telsamân,* pl. of *telsam,* a magical figure, from Byzantine Gr. *telesma,* incantation, from Gr. *teleō,* to accomplish, from *telos,* an end.] A charm consisting of a magical figure cut or engraved on stone or metal, and supposed to preserve the bearer from injury, disease, or sudden death; hence, something that produces extraordinary effects; an amulet; a charm.—**talismanic, talismanical,** tal•is•man′ik, tal•is•man′i•kal, *a.* Having the properties of a talisman; preservative against evils; magical.

talk, tạk, *v.i.* [A word related to *tale, tell,* in much the same way as *hark* to *hear, smirk* to *smile,* and *walk* to *well, wallow.*] To utter words; to speak; to converse familiarly; to hold converse; to prate; to confer; to reason.—*To talk to,* to remonstrate with; to reprove gently. ∴ Syn. under SPEAK.—*v.t.* To use as a means of conversation or communication (to *talk* French or German); to speak; to utter (to *talk* nonsense); to have a certain effect on by talking; *to talk one down*=to silence one with incessant talk; *to talk one out of*=to dissuade one from, as a plan, project, etc.; *to talk one over*=to gain one over by persuasion.—*To talk over,* to talk about; to discuss.—*n.* Familiar conversation; discourse; report; rumor; subject of discourse; a discussion.—**talkative,** tạ′ka•tiv, *a.* Apt to engage in conversation; freely communicative; chatty. [A hybrid word, E. with Latin termination, like *starvation.*]—**talkatively,** tạ′ka•tiv•li, *adv.* In a talkative manner.—**talkativeness,** tạ′ka•tiv•nes, *n.*—**talker,** tạ′kėr, *n.* One who talks; a loquacious person; a prattler.—**talking,** tạ′king, *a.* Given to talk; having the power of speech.

tall, tạl, *a.* [From W. *tàl,* tall, towering.] High in stature; long and comparatively slender: said of upright things; having height, great or small (how *tall* is he?); great; excellent; remarkable; extravagant; bombastic, as *tall* story, *tall* talk. [*Colloq.*]—**tallness,** tạl′nes, *n.* The state or quality of being tall.

tallage, tal′ij, *n.* [From Fr. *tailler,* to cut. TAILOR.] A term formerly applied to subsidies or taxes of various kinds.

tallow, tal′ō, *n.* [Same as Dan., Sw., and G. *talg,* Icel. *tólg,* D. *talk,* tallow; comp. Goth. *tulgus,* firm.] The harder and less fusible fat of animals melted and separated from the fibrous or membranous matter; also a fat obtained from some plants.—*v.t.* To grease or smear with tallow.—**tallowy,** tal′ō•i, *a.* Greasy; having the qualities of tallow.

tally, tal′i, *n.* [Fr. *taille,* a tally, a cutting, from *tailler,* to cut. TAILOR.] A piece of wood on which notches or scores are cut in order to keep an account; various bookkeeping forms; an accounting; a score, as in a game; correspondence or agreement with.—*v.t.*—*tallied, tallying.* To mark off by items; to make to correspond.—*v.i.* To make a tally; to agree exactly (your information *tallies* with mine).—**tallier,** tal′i•er, *n.* One who keeps a tally.

tallyho, tal′i•hō″, *interj.* and *n.* The huntsman's cry to urge on his hounds.

Talmud, täl′mụd *n.* [Chal. *talmûd,* instruction.] The body of the Hebrew civil and canonical laws, traditions, and explanations, or the book that contains them.—**Talmudic, Talmudical,** täl•mụd′ik, täl•mụd′i•kal, *a.* Pertaining to the Talmud; contained in the Talmud.—**Talmudist,** täl′mụd•ist, *n.* One versed in the Talmud.

talon, tal′on, *n.* [Fr. *talon,* the heel, from L. *talus,* the heel.] The claw of a bird of prey.

talus, tā′lus, *n.* [L. *talus,* the ankle.] *Anat.* the ankle bone or joint; *arch.* the slope or inclination of any work; *geol.* a sloping heap of broken rocks and stones at the foot of any cliff or rocky declivity.

tamandua, ta•man′dwa, *n.* A species of anteater.

tamarack, tam′a•rak, *n.* The black or American larch; hackmatack.

tamarin, tam′a•rin, *n.* [Native name in Cayenne.] A species of very small South American monkeys.

tamarind, tam′a•rind, *n.* [It. and Sp. *tamarindo,* Fr. *tamarin,* from Ar. *tamrhindī,* from *tamr,* fruit, date, and *hindī,* Indian.] A tropical leguminous tree, and also its seedpods, the preserved pulp of which is imported into European countries, and frequently employed in medicine, in fevers, etc.

tamarisk, tam′a•risk, *n.* [L. *tamariscus.*] A genus of shrubs or small trees belonging to southern Europe and Asia, some of them yielding manna.

tambour, tam′bör, *n.* [Fr. *tambour,* a drum, a tabor. TABOR.] A drum; *arch.* the naked part of Corinthian and Composite capitals, bearing some resemblance to a drum; the circular vertical part both below and above a cupola; a cylindrical stone as in the shaft of a column; a circular frame on which silk or other stuff is stretched to be embroidered.—*v.t.* and *i.* To embroider with a tambour; to work on a tambour frame.—**tambourine,** tam•-bu̧•rēn′, *n.* [Fr. *tambourin,* from *tambour.*] A musical instrument formed of a hoop, over which parchment is stretched like one end of a drum, and having small pieces of metal called jingles inserted in the hoop.

tame, tām, *a.* [A.Sax. *tam,* tame=D., Dan., Sw., and Goth. *tam,* Icel. *tamr,* G. *zahm,* tame; same root as in L. *domo,* to subdue, *dominus,* a lord; Skr. *dam,* to subdue. DAME.] Having lost its native wildness and shyness; accustomed to man; domesticated (a *tame* deer); wanting in spirit; submissive; spiritless; unanimated; without liveliness or interest; insipid; dull; flat (a *tame* poem, *tame* scenery).—*v.t. tamed, taming.* To make tame; to reduce from a wild to a domestic state; to subdue. —*v.i.* To become tame.—**tamable, tameable,** tā′ma•bl, *a.* Capable of being subdued; capable of being reclaimed from a wild or savage state. —**tameless,** tām′les, *a.* Incapable of being tamed; untamable.—**tamely,** tām′li, *adv.* In a tame manner; submissively; meanly; servilely; insipidly.—**tameness,** tām′nes, *n.* The quality of being tame; domestication; want of spirit or liveliness; dullness; flatness.—**tamer,** tā′mėr, *n.* One who tames.

Tamil, tam′il, *n.* One of a race of men inhabiting southern India, and belonging to the Dravidian stock; a Dravidian language spoken in India.

Tammany, tam′a•ni, *n.* [From a popular Indian chief of pre-Revolutionary times.]—*Tammany Hall,* the headquarters and organization of a Democratic political faction in New York City.

Tam o' Shanter, tam•o•shant′ėr, [*Burns* character.] A loosely woven round woolen cap worn by both sexes.

tamp, tamp, *v.t.* [From Fr. *tamponner;* akin to *tampion.*] To ram tight with tough clay or other substance, as a hole bored for blasting, after the charge is lodged.—**tamper,** tam′-pėr, *n.* One who tamps; an instrument used in tamping.

tamper, tam′pėr, *v.i.* [A form of *temper.*] To meddle or interfere; to try little experiments; to meddle so as to alter by corruption or adulteration; to influence toward a certain course by secret and unfair means; generally followed by *with* (to *tamper with* a document, a witness, etc.).—**tamperer,** tam′pėr•-ėr, *n.* One who tampers.

tampion, tam′pi•on, *n.* [From Fr. *tampon,* a nasalized form from *tapon,* a bung, from D. *tap*=E. *tap,* a plug. TAP.] The stopper of a cannon or other piece of ordnance; a tompion; a plug.

tam-tam, tam′tam, *n.* [Hind., from sound of drum.] A kind of native drum used in the East Indies; a Chinese gong; a tomtom.

tan, tan, *v.t.*—*tanned, tanning.* [Fr. *tanner,* to tan, from *tan,* oak bark, from Armor. *tann,* oak; akin *tawny.*] To convert into leather, as animal skins, by steeping them in an infusion of oak or some other bark, by which they are rendered firm, durable, and in some degree impervious to water; to make brown by exposure to the rays of the sun; to make sunburned; to beat, flog, or thrash (*colloq.*).—*v.i.* To become tanned (leather *tans* easily); to become tan-colored or sunburned.—*n.* The bark of the oak, willow, or other trees, as broken by a mill, and used for tanning; a yellowish-brown color like that of tan.—*a.* Of the color of tan; resembling tan; tawny.—**tannage,** tan′ij, *n.* The operation of tanning.—**tanner,** tan′-ėr, *n.* One whose occupation is to tan hides.—**tannery,** tan′ėr•i, *n.* A place where the operations of tanning are carried on; the art or process of tanning.—**tannate,** tan′āt, *n.* A salt of tannic acid.—**tannic,** tan′ik, *a.* Applied to an acid existing in oak, gallnuts, etc., and forming the efficient substance in tanning leather.—**tannin,** tan′in, *n.* Tannic acid.—**tanning,** tan′ing, *n.* The operation and art of converting raw hides and skins of animals into leather; a brown color produced on the skin by the sun.

tanager, tan′a•jėr, *n.* [Altered from Brazilian *tanagra.*] A genus of tropical American birds of the finch family, remarkable for their bright colors.

tandem, tan′dem, *adv.* [L., at length, that is, after some *time;* the English sense is by a pun or joke.] One before the other (to drive *tandem*).—*n.* A vehicle drawn by two horses harnessed one before the other; a cycle for two persons, one before the other.

tang, tang, *n.* [Imitative of a sound, like *twang,* metaphorically transferred to a strong taste.] A twang or sharp sound (*Shak.*); a taste or flavor; characteristic flavor, quality, or property; a smack or taste.—*v.i.* To ring; to twang.

tang, tang, *n.* [A modification of *tongue,* or allied to *tongs.*] A projecting part of an object which is inserted into and so secured to another; the part of a table knife or tool which fits into the handle; the tongue of a buckle.

tangent, tan′jent, *n.* [L. *tangens, tangentis,* ppr. of L. *tango, tactum,* to touch (whence also *contact, tact, tangible, taint, tax, task,* etc.; stem also in *contagion*).] *Geom.* a straight line which touches a circle or curve, and which being produced does not cut it; *trigon.* in a right-angled triangle, the tangent of an acute angle=opposite side ÷ adjacent side.—*To go* or *fly off at a tangent, fig.* to break off suddenly from one line of action, train of thought, or the like, and go on to something else.—*a.* Touching; forming a tangent.—**tangency,** tan′jen•si, *n.* State of being tangent; a contact or touching.—**tangential,** tan•jen′shal, *a.* Pertaining to a tangent; in the direction of a tangent.—*Tangential force,* force acting on a body at its surface, in a line which touches or lies in the surface.—**tangentially,** tan•jen′shal•li, *adv.* In the direction of a tangent.

tangerine, tan′jer•ēn, *n.* [*Tangier.*] A small orange; a reddish-orange color.

tangible, tan′ji•bl, *a.* [Fr. *tangible,* L. *tangibilis,* from *tango,* to touch. TANGENT.] Capable of being touched or grasped; perceptible by the touch; capable of being possessed or realized; real; actual; evident (*tangible* proofs).—**tangibility, tangibleness,** tan•ji•bil′i•ti, tan′ji•bl•nes, *n.* The quality of being tangible, or perceptible to the touch.—**tangibly,** tan′ji•bli, *adv.* So as to be perceptible to the touch.

tangle, tang′gl, *v.t.*—*tangled, tangling.* [Allied to Icel. *thöngull, thang,* Dan. and G. *tang,* tangle, seaweed; hence *entangle.*] To knit together confusedly; to interweave or interlace so as to be difficult to unravel; to entangle or entrap; to involve; to complicate.—*n.* A knot of threads or other things confusedly interwoven; a perplexity or embarrassment; a name given to some species of seaweed.

tanist, tan′ist, *n.* [Ir. and Gael. *tanaiste,* from *tan,* a region.] An elective prince or sovereign among the ancient Irish.—**tanistry,** tan′-ist•ri, *n.* An Irish custom of descent, according to which the tanist or prince was fixed by election, the right or succession not lying in the individual, but in the family to which he belonged.

tank, tangk, *n.* [For *stank,* from O.Fr. *estanc* (Fr. *étang*), Sp. *estanque,* from L. *stagnum,* a pond or pool. STAGNANT.] A cistern or vessel of large size to contain liquids; a reservoir; a pond for storing water in India; *milit.* an armored car with caterpillar wheels, protected by guns fired from inside, used for clearing trenches, destruction of iron barbed wire, etc.

tankard, tang′kerd, *n.* [O.Fr. *tanquart, tanquard,* O.D. *tanckaerd,* a tankard.] A rather large drinking vessel, with a cover, usually made of metal; a pitcher.

tanner, tannery, tannic, tannin, etc. See TAN.

tansy, tan′zi, *n.* [Fr. *tanaisie,* O.Fr. *tanasie,* tansy, from Gr. *athanasia,* immortality—because the dried flowers retain their natural appearance.] The popular name of a strongly scented perennial herb with much divided leaves and yellow flowers, formerly in repute as a tonic and anthelmintic; a dish made of eggs, cream, sugar, the juice of herbs, etc.

tantalite. See TANTALUM.

tantalize, tan′ta•līz, *v.t.*—*tantalized, tantalizing.* [From *Tantalus,* a mythical king of Lydia or Phrygia, who for divulging the secrets of his father Zeus was condemned to stand in water, which receded from him whenever he stooped to drink, while branches loaded with fruit, which always eluded his grasp, hung over his head.] To tease or torment by presenting something desirable to the view, but continually frustrating the expectations by keeping it out of reach; to excite by expectations or fears which will not be realized.—**tantalization,** tan′ta•li•zā″shon, *n.* The act of tantalizing; the torment of expectations frustrated.—**tantalizer,** tan′ta•lī•zėr, *n.* One that tantalizes.—**tantalizingly,** tan′ta•li•zing•li, *adv.* In a tantalizing manner.

tantalum, tan′ta•lum, *n.* [Named from the *tantalizing* difficulties in analyzing the ore.] A gray-white metallic element of the vanadium series, hard and ductile and resistant to single acids. Symbol, Ta; at. no., 73; at. wt., 180.948.—**tantalite,** tan′-ta•līt, *n.* An ore of tantalum.

Tantalus, tan′ta•lus, *n.* A stand for spirit bottles which is provided with a lock, and so constructed that, while the bottles are plainly visible, their contents cannot be got at without unlocking the stand.

tantamount, tan′ta•mount, *a.* [Fr. *tant*, L. *tantus*, so much, and E. *amount*.] Equivalent, as in value, force, effect, or signification.

tantivy, tan•tiv′i, *n.* [From the sound of galloping horses, or the note of a hunting horn.] A rapid, violent gallop, especially in hunting.

tantrum, tan′trum, *n.* [Origin obscure.] A burst of ill-humor; a display of temper; an illnatured caprice; used chiefly in plural.

Taoism, tou′izm, *n.* [Chinese *tao*, way or path.] A Chinese religion, non-theistic, teaching a pure morality, but associated with belief in magic, etc.

tap, tap, *v.t.—tapped, tapping.* [From Fr. *taper*, to tap, *tape*, a tap; from Prov. G. *tapp*, a blow, G. *tappen* to grope; Icel. *tapsa*, to tap; imitative of sound, like *pat*.] To strike with something small, or to strike with a very gentle blow; to pat gently.—*v.i.* To strike a gentle blow.—*n.* A gentle blow; a slight blow with a small thing.

tap, tap, *n.* [A.Sax. *taeppa*=L.G. *tappe*, D. and Dan. *tap*, Icel. *tappi*, G. *zapfen*, a tap, a faucet; akin *tip*, *top*, *tipple*, *tampion*, etc.] A pipe or hole through which liquor is drawn from a cask; a plug to stop a hole in a cask; a spigot; the liquor itself (*colloq.*): a taphouse or taproom; *engin.* a small tool for forming threads in drilled holes.—*v.t.* [Same as L.G. and D. *tappen*, Icel. and Sw. *tappa*, G. *zapfen*.] To pierce so as to let out a fluid (to *tap* a cask); to treat in any analogous way for the purpose of drawing something from (to *tap* telegraph wires).—**tapping,** tap′ing, *n.* The surgical operation of letting out a fluid by perforation, as in dropsy.—**taproom,** *n.* A room where beer is served from the tap; a common room for drinking in a tavern.—**taproot,** *n.* The main root of a plant, long and tapering, and penetrating the earth downward.—**tapster,** tap′stėr, *n.* A person employed in a tavern, etc., to tap or draw ale or other liquor.

tape, tāp, *n.* [A.Sax. *taeppe*, a fillet; akin to *tapestry*, *tippet*.] A narrow fillet or band; a narrow woven band of cotton or linen, used for strings and the like.—**tapeline, tape measure,** *n.* A tape painted to give it firmness and marked with inches, used in measuring.—**tape-record,** tāp′rē•kōrd, *v.t.* To record sounds on magnetic tape.—*v.i.* To make a tape recording.—**taperecorder,** tāp′-rē•kōrd•ėr, *n.*—**tapeworm,** *n.* Internal parasites composed of a number of flattened joints or segments, found in the intestines of warm-blooded vertebrates.

taper, tā′pėr, *n.* [A.Sax. *tapor*, *taper*, a taper, from Ir. *tapar*, W. *tampr*, a taper; comp. Skr. *tap*, to burn.] A small candle; a long wick coated with wax or other suitable material; a small light; tapering form; gradual diminution of thickness in an elongated object.—*a.* Long and regularly becoming slenderer toward the point; becoming small toward one end (*taper* fingers).—*v.i.* To become gradually slenderer or less in diameter; to diminish; to grow gradually less.—*v.t.* To cause to taper.—**taperingly,** tā′pėr•ing•li, *adv.*

tapestry, tap′es•tri, *n.* [Fr. *tapisserie*, tapestry, from *tapis*, tapestry, a carpet, from L. *tapes*, *tapete*, from Gr. *tapēs*, *tapētos*, a carpet, a rug.] A kind of woven hangings of wool and silk, often enriched with gold and silver, ornamented with figures of men, animals, landscapes, etc., and formerly much used for covering the walls and furniture of apartments, churches, etc.—*v.t.—tapestried*, *tapestrying*. To adorn with tapestry or as if with tapestry.

tapioca, tap•i•ō′ka, *n.* [Native American name.] A farinaceous substance prepared from cassava meal, which, while moist or damp, has been heated for the purpose of drying it on hot plates.

tapir, tā′pėr, *n.* [From the native Brazilian name.] A South American hoofed animal allied both to the hog and to the rhinoceros, with a nose resembling a small proboscis.

tapis, tap•ē′, *n.* [Fr., tapestry.] Carpeting or tapestry, formerly used to cover the table in a council chamber; hence, *to be on* or *upon the tapis*, to be under consideration, or on the table.

tappet, tap′et, *n.* [A dim. from *tap*, to strike gently.] A small lever connected with the valve of the cylinder of a steam engine; a small cam.

tapster, See TAP.

tar, tär, *n.* [A.Sax. *taro*, *tero*, tar=D. *teer*, Icel. *tjaro*, G. *theer*, tar; allied to *tree*.] A thick, dark-colored viscid product obtained by the destructive distillation of organic substances and bituminous minerals, as pine or fir, coal, shale, etc., used for coating and preserving timber and iron, for impregnating ships' ropes and cordage, etc.; a sailor, contraction of *tarpaulin* (which see) (*Macaulay*, *H.*, chap. ii).—*v.t.—tarred*, *tarring*. To smear with tar.—*To tar and feather* a person, to pour heated tar over him and then cover with feathers, as is sometimes done by mobs to obnoxious persons.—**tarry,** tär′i, *a.* Consisting of tar, or like tar; partaking of the character of tar; smeared with tar.

tarantass, tar•an•tas′, *n.* A covered Russian carriage without springs.

tarantula, tä•ran′tū•la, *n.* [It. *tarantola*, from L. *Tarentum*, now *Taranto*, in the south of Italy.] Any of various large, hairy spiders of the family Theraphosidae, whose bite may be painful but is not poisonous to man. —**tarantella,** tar•an•tel′la, *n.* [It.] A swift, whirling Italian dance in six-eight measure; the music for the dance.—**tarantism,** ta•ran′tizm, *n.* [It. *tarantismo*.] A fabulous dancing disease, said to be caused by the tarantula; a disease resembling St. Vitus's dance.

taraxacum, ta•rak′sa•kum, *n.* [From Ar. or Per. *tarashaqūn*, taraxacum.] Dandelion or its roots as used medicinally.

tarboosh, tär′bösh, *n.* [Ar. name.] A red woolen skullcap formerly worn by Turkish men; a fez.

tardigrade, tär′di•grād, *a.* [L. *tardus*, slow, *gradus*, step.] Slow-paced; moving or stepping slowly; pertaining to the tardigrades.—*n.* One of a family of edentate mammals comprising the sloths.

tardy, tär′di, *a.* [Fr. *tardif*, tardy, as if from a form *tardivus*, from L. *tardus*, slow (seen in *retard*).] Moving with a slow pace or motion; slow; late; dilatory; not up to time; reluctant.—**tardily,** tär′di•li, *adv.* In a tardy manner; with slow pace; slowly.—**tardiness,** tär′di•nes, *n.* The state or quality of being tardy; slowness; dilatoriness; unwillingness; reluctance.

tare, târ, *n.* [Origin obscure.] A name of different species of leguminous plants, called also vetch.

tare, târ, *n.* [Fr. *tare*, from Sp. *tara*, from Ar. *tarha*, deduction.] *Com.* a deduction from the gross weight of goods as equivalent to the weight of the package containing them.

target, tär′get, *n.* [A dim. from O.Fr. *targue*, *targe*, from O.H.G. *zarga*, G. *zarge*, a frame, border, etc.] A shield or buckler of a small kind, circular in form; the mark set up to be aimed at in archery, musketry, or artillery practice and the like.—**targeteer,** tär•get•ēr′, *n.* One armed with a target.

Targum, tär′gum, *n.* [Chal. *targûm*, interpretation, from *targem*, to interpret; akin *dragoman*.] A translation or paraphrase of the Hebrew Scriptures in the Aramaic or Chaldee language, made after the Babylonish captivity, when Hebrew began to die out as the popular language.

tariff, tar′if, *n.* [Fr. *tarif*, Sp. *tarifa*, from the Ar. *tarif*, explanation, information, a list of fees to be paid, from *'arafa*, to inform.] A list of goods with the duties or customs to be paid for the same, either on importation or exportation; a table or scale of charges generally (a hotel *tariff*).

tarlatan, tär′la•tan, *n.* [Bengali *tarnatan*, a fine muslin.] A thin cotton stuff resembling gauze, used in costuming, etc.

tarn, tärn, *n.* [Icel. *tjörn*, Sw. *tärn*, a tarn.] A small mountain lake or pool, especially one which has no visible feeders.

tarnish, tär′nish, *v.t.* [Fr. *ternir*, ppr. *ternissant*, from O.H.G. *tarnjan*, to conceal; akin to A.Sax. *dernan*, Sc. *dern*, to hide.] To diminish or destroy the luster of; to soil or sully; to cast a stain or disgrace upon.—*v.i.* To lose luster; to become dull.—*n.* A spot; a blot; soiled state.

taro, tä′rō, *n.* [Native name.] A plant of the arum family, cultivated in the Pacific Islands for the sake of its esculent root.

tarpaulin, tär•pa̤′lin, *n.* [*Tar*, and old *pauling*, a covering for a cart or wagon, equivalent to *palling*, from *pall*, a cover.] Tarred canvas used to cover the hatchways, etc., on shipboard, and to protect agricultural produce, goods, etc., from the weather; a sailor's hat covered with painted or tarred cloth.

Tarpeian, tar•pē′an, *a.* [L. *Tarpeius.*] Of the hillside or rock from which in early Rome criminals were cast down.

tarpon, tär′pon, *n.* [Origin unknown.] A fine large sea fish of the Southern United States and West Indies, belonging to the herring family, and giving excellent sport to the angler.

tarragon, tar′a•gon, *n.* [Sp. *taragona*, It. *targone*, from L. *draco*, a dragon.] A plant used for perfuming vinegar.

tarry, tar′i, *v.i.—tarried, tarrying.* [From A.Sax. *tergan*, *tyrgan*, to torment, to tease, hence to tire, to delay=D. *tergen*, G. *zergen*, to provoke; akin *tire.*] To stay; to abide; to remain behind; to wait; to put off going or coming; to delay; to linger.—*v.t.* To wait for.

tarry, tär′i, *a.* See TAR.

tarsier, tär′si•ėr, *n.* [Fr. *tarsier*, from the length of its *tarsus.*] A nocturnal animal of the lemur family inhabiting the East Indies.

tarsometatarsus, tär′sō•met•a•tär″-sus, *n. Ornith.* same as *Tarsus.*

tarsus, tär′sus, *n.* pl. **tarsi,** tär′sī. [Gr. *tarsos*, the flat part of the foot.] *Anat.* that part of the lower limb which in man is known as the ankle; also the thin cartilage at the edges of the eyelids; *entom.* the last segment of the legs; *ornith.* that part of the leg (or properly the foot) of birds which extends from the toes to the first joint above; the shank.—**tarsal,** tär′sal, *a.* Pertaining to the tarsus.

tart, tärt, *a.* [A.Sax. *teart*, acid, sharp, from stem of *teran*, to tear.] Sharp tasting; severe; female of questionable morals.—**tartly,** tärt′li, *adv.* In a tart manner; sharply.—**tartness,** tärt′nes, *n.* Acidity; sharpness, asperity.

tart, tärt, *n.* [Fr. *tarte*, *tourte*, Sp. *torta*, *tarta*, It. *torta*, a tart, from L. *tortus*, ppr. of *torqueo*, to twist, lit. a piece of pastry in a twisted form; comp. a *roll*, from being rolled. TORTURE.] A piece of pastry, consisting of fruit baked and enclosed in paste; a prostitute.

tartan, tär′tan, *n.* [Fr. *tartane*, It., Sp., and Pg. *tartana*; of Eastern origin.] A vessel used in the Mediterranean, with a single mast bearing a large lateen sail, and with a bowsprit and foresail.

tartan, tär′tan, *n.* [Fr. *tiretaine*, *tirtaine*, linsey-woolsey; of unknown origin.] A species of woolen cloth, checkered or cross-barred in various colors; traditionally worn by Scottish Highlanders, each clan having its own pattern. Also, the pattern itself, as *Stuart* tartan, *MacQueen* tartan, etc.—*a.* Consisting of or resembling tartan.

tartar, tär′tėr, *n.* [Fr. *tartre*, It. and Sp. *tartaro*, L.L. *tartarum*, the hard deposit in wine casks; perhaps from Ar. *durd*, sediment, dregs.] A hard pink or red crust deposited from wines not completely fermented, a compound of tartaric acid and potassium, also called *argol*; also, a concretion which sometimes forms on the teeth.—*Cream of tartar*, purified tartar.—*Salt of tartar*, carbonate of potassium obtained by calcining cream of tartar.—*Tartar emetic*, a compound of tartaric acid, potassium, and antimony, used as an emetic, purgative, diaphoretic, sedative, etc.—**tartaric,** tär•tar′ik, *a.* Pertaining to, or obtained from tartar.—*Tartaric acid*, the acid of tartar existing in grapes and other fruits, but principally in cream of tartar, used in calico printing and in medicine, etc.—**tartarous,** tär′-tar•us, *a.* Consisting of tartar, or partaking of its qualities.—**tartrate,** tär′trāt, *n.* A salt of tartaric acid.

Tartar, tär′tar, *n.* [A corruption of the native name *Tatar.*] A native of Tartary; a very irascible or rigorous person; [*often not cap.*]—*To catch a tartar*, to assail a person who proves too strong for the assailant.—*a.* Pertaining to the Tartars.

Tartarean. See TARTARUS.

Tartarus, tär′ta•rus, *n.* [Gr. *Tartaros.*] Among the Greeks and Romans a name for the lower world or infernal regions; hell.—**Tartarean,** tär•tâ′rē•an, *a.* Pertaining to Tartarus; infernal.

tartlet. See TART, *n.*

tartly, tartness. See TART, *a.*

Tartufe, tär•töf′, *n.* [Fr.] Religious hypocrite or impostor, from the character in Molière's play of the name.

tasimeter, ta•sim′et•ėr, *n.* [Gr. *tasis*, a stretching, from *teinō*, to stretch, and *metron*, a measure.] An instrument invented by Edison for measuring extremely slight variations of pressure, temperature, moisture, etc., by variations produced in the force of an electric current.—**tasimetric,** tas•i•met′rik, *a.* Pertaining to the tasimeter.

task, task, *n.* [O.Fr. *tasque*, *tasche*, (Fr. *tâche*), a task, from L.L. *tasca*, by metathesis from *taxa* (=*tacsa*), from L. *taxo*, to tax. TAX.] A labor or work imposed by another; a piece of work to be done; what duty or necessity imposes; a lesson to be learned; a portion of study imposed by a teacher; an undertaking; burdensome employment; toil.—*To take to task*, to reprove; to reprimand.—*v.t.* To impose a task upon; to oppress with labor.—**task force,** *n.* A temporary grouping, especially of military units, under one leader in order to undertake a specific project.

Tasmanian, taz•mā′ni•an, *a.* Pertaining to Tasmania.—*Tasmanian devil*, the dasyure.—*Tasmanian wolf*, a carnivorous marsupial of Tasmania of nocturnal habits and very destructive to sheep.—*n.* A native or inhabitant of Tasmania.

tassel, tas′el, *n.* [O.Fr. *tassel*, a knob or knot, a button, from L. *taxillus*, a small cube or die, dim. of *talus*, a die, a small bone.] A pendent ornament, consisting generally of a roundish mold covered with twisted threads of silk, wool, etc., and having threads hanging down in a fringe; anything resembling a tassel.—*v.i. tasseled, tasseling.* To put forth a tassel or flower, as Indian corn.—*v.t.* To adorn with tassels.—**tasseled,** tas′eld, *a.* Furnished or adorned with tassels.

taste, tāst, *v.t.—tasted, tasting.* [O.Fr. *taster* (Fr. *tâter*), to handle, feel, taste, from hypothetical *taxitare*, freq. of L. *taxare*, to touch repeatedly, from *tango*, *tactum*, to touch (whence *tact*, etc.). TANGENT.] To try by the touch of the tongue; to perceive the relish or flavor of; to try by eating; to eat; to become acquainted with by trial; to experience (to *taste* death); to partake of (to *taste* happiness).—*v.i.* To eat or drink a little by way of trial; to have a smack or flavor; to have a particular relish or savor; to smack or savor (it *tastes* of garlic); to have experience or enjoyment.—*n.* The act of tasting; a particular sensation excited by certain bodies when applied to the tongue, palate, etc., and moistened with saliva; the sense by which we perceive this by means of special organs in the mouth; intellectual relish or discernment; appreciation and liking; nice perception; the faculty of discerning beauty, proportion, symmetry, congruity, or whatever constitutes excellence, particularly in the fine arts and literature; discernment of what is fit or becoming; manner or style as tested by this faculty; manner, with respect to what is pleasing (a work in good *taste*, a remark in bad *taste*); a small portion tasted; a small bit.—**tasteful,** tāst′fu̇l, *a.* Having much flavor; savory; possessing good taste; showing or produced in good taste.—**tastefully,** tāst′fu̇l•li, *adv.* In a tasteful manner; with good taste.—**tastefulness,** tāst′fu̇l•nes, *n.* The state or quality of being tasteful.—**tasteless,** tāst′les, *a.* Having no taste;

insipid; having no power of giving pleasure; stale; flat; void of good taste; showing or executed with bad taste.—**tastelessly,** tāst′les•li, *adv.* In a tasteless manner.—**tastelessness,** tāst′les•nes, *n.*—**taster,** tās′tėr, *n.* One who tastes; one who tests food, provisions, or liquors by tasting samples; an instrument by which something is tasted in order to judge of its quality.—**tastily,** tās′ti•li, *adv.* In a tasty manner.—**tasty,** tās′ti, *a.* Palatable; good to the taste; tasteful; showing good taste.

tat, tat, *v.t.* and *i.*—*tatted, tatting.* To make a type of lace by hand.—**tatting,** tat′ing, *n.* A kind of lace woven or knitted from sewing thread, with a somewhat shuttle-shaped implement; the act of making such lace.

tatter, tat′ėr, *n.* [Icel. *töturr, tötturr,* tatters, rags; akin to *totter.*] A rag or a part torn and hanging to the thing.—**tatterdemalion,** tat′ėr•di•mā″li•on, *n.* [E. *tatter,* Fr. *de,* from, and O.Fr. *maillon,* long clothes.] A ragged fellow.—**tattered,** tat′ėrd, *p.* and *a.* Rent in tatters; hanging in rags; ragged.

tattle, tat′l, *v.i.*—*tattled, tattling.* [Like *titter,* an imitative word; comp. L.G. *tateln,* to gabble; G. *tattern,* to prattle.] To prate; to talk idly; to use many words with little meaning; to tell tales; to blab.—*v.t.* To utter in a prating way.—*n.* Idle talk or chat; trifling talk.—**tattler,** tat′lėr, *n.* One who tattles.—**tattling,** tat′ling, *a.* Given to idle talk; apt to tell tales. —**tattlingly,** tat′ling•li, *adv.* In a tattling manner.

tattoo, tat•tö′, *n.* [Formerly *taptoo,* from D. *taptoe,* the tattoo—*tap,* a tap or spigot, and *toe* (pron. as E. *to*), to, being primarily the signal for the closing of drinking houses.] A beat of drum and bugle call at night, giving notice to soldiers to repair to their quarters.—*Devil's tattoo,* an idle drumming with the fingers upon a table, etc.

tattoo, tat•tö′, *v.t.* and *i.* [A Polynesian word.] To prick the skin and stain the punctured spots with a coloring substance, forming lines and figures upon the body.—**tattooer,** tat•tö′ėr, *n.* One who tattoos.—**tattooing,** tat•tö′ing, *n.* The act of one who tattoos; the design produced by a tattooer.

tau, taŭ, *n.* [Gr.] The nineteenth letter of the Greek alphabet.

taught, tạt, pret. and pp. of *teach.*

taunt, tạnt, *v.t.* [O.Fr. *tanter, tenter,* to tempt, to provoke, from L. *tentare, temptare,* to try. TEMPT.] To reproach with severe or insulting words; to twit scornfully or insultingly; to upbraid.—*n.* A bitter or sarcastic reproach; insulting invective.—**taunter,** tạn′tėr, *n.* One who taunts.—**tauntingly,** tạn′ting•li, *adv.* In a taunting manner; insultingly.

taunt, tạnt, *a.* [O.Fr. *tant,* L. *tantus,* so great.] *Naut.* high or tall: said of masts.

taupe, tōp, *n.* [Fr. mole.] A yellowish-gray color similar to that of the moleskin.

Taurus, tạ′rus, *n.* [L., a bull; allied to E. *steer* (an ox). STEER.] The Bull, one of the twelve signs of the zodiac, which the sun enters about the 20th of April.—**taurine,** tạ′rīn, *a.*

taut, tạt, *a.* [A form of *tight* or closely allied to it.] Tight; not slack; applied to a rope or sail.

tautog, tạ•tog′, *n.* [The plural of *taut,* the Indian name.] A fish of the wrasse family caught on the New England coasts.

tautology, tạ•tol o•ji, *n.* [Gr. *tautologia—tautos,* the same, and *logos,* word.] A useless repetition of the same idea or meaning in different words; needless repetition.—**tautological,** tạ•to•loj′i•kal, *a.* Involving tautology; repeating the same thing. — **tautologically,** tạ•to•loj′i•kal•li, *adv.* In a tautological manner.—**tautologist,** tạ•tol′o•jist, *n.* One who uses tautology.—**tautologize,** tạ•tol′o•jīz, *v.i.*—*tautologized, tautologizing.* To repeat the same thing in different words.

tautomerism, tạ•tom′er•izm, *n.* [Gr. *tauto,* the same, *meros,* part.] *Org. chem.* property of a substance which in its reactions behaves sometimes like one of two isomeric forms, sometimes like the other.

tavern, tav′ėrn, *n.* [Fr. *taverne,* Pr., Sp., and It. *taverna,* from L. *taberna,* a shed, a tavern, from root of *tabula,* a board. TABLE.] A place where alcoholic drinks are sold and food may be served, the term displacing bar and saloon since repeal of the prohibition laws in the United States; a taproom; formerly an inn.

tawdry, tạ′dri, *a.* [From *St. Audrey,* otherwise called St. Etheldreda, at whose fair, held in the isle of Ely, laces and cheap gay ornaments are said to have been sold.] Fine and showy, without taste or elegance; tastelessly but showily ornamental.—**tawdrily,** tạ′dri•li, *adv.*—**tawdriness,** tạ′dri•nes, *n.*

tawny, tạ′ni, *a.* [O.Fr. *tané,* Fr. *tanné,* tanned, tawny, pp. of *tanner,* to tan. TAN.] Of a yellowish dark color, like things tanned, or persons who are sunburned.—*v.t.* To make tawny; to tan.

tax, taks, *n.* [Fr. *taxe,* from *taxer,* to tax, from L. *taxo, taxare,* to handle, to rate, to censure, from stem of *tango,* to touch (whence also *tangent, task, taste,* etc.).] A charge imposed by governmental authority upon property, individuals, or transactions to raise money for public purposes; a levy by civil authority on the property, real or personal, of an individual or corporation, or a levy on income, inheritance, or the purchase or holdings of commodities; *fig.* a strain, serious burden, or heavy demand, as *a tax on one's strength, one's endurance,* etc.—*v.t.*—To impose a rate or duty upon for governmental purposes; to subject to a strain, to make heavy demands upon, as *to tax one's patience*; to accuse of, charge with, or impute to, as *to tax a man with rudeness*; *law,* to fix judicially and allow or disallow the items of charge or cost in any judicial matter.—*Capital stock tax,* a tax imposed upon a corporation, for the privilege of doing business, based upon the value of its capital stock.—*Direct tax,* a tax paid directly by the consumer such as on gasoline, theater tickets, etc.—*Franchise tax,* a tax on rights and privileges granted by a franchise.—*Hidden tax,* a tax paid indirectly by the consumer, frequently without his being aware of it.—*Income tax,* a graduated tax on the product or income derived from a person's property or business. —*Inheritance tax,* a tax on transfer of inherited wealth.—*Nuisance tax,* a small amount levied on miscellaneous transactions, such as theater tickets, and paid by the purchaser.—*Poll tax,* a head tax, usually on all adult males, but also frequently on women and children as well; a tax on a person without reference to property owned or business followed. —*Personal-property tax,* a levy on such movable things as chattels, mortgages, bonds, stocks, etc., as distinguished from real estate.—*Real-estate tax,* a direct tax on real property.—*Sales tax,* a small percentage tax imposed either on the person making the sale or on the purchaser. —*Social-security tax,* a tax paid in equal amounts by employers and employees to provide funds for old-age pensions of employees.—*Surtax,* an additional tax; a tax in excess of a normal tax.—**taxability, taxableness,** tak•sa•bil′i•ti, tak′sa•bl•nes, *n.* The state of being taxable.—**taxable,** tak′sa•bl, *a.* Subject or liable to taxation. —**taxably,** tak′sa•bli, *adv.* In a taxable manner.—**taxation,** tak•sā′shun, *n.* [L. *taxatio, taxationis.*] The act of laying a tax or of imposing taxes by the proper authority; the raising of revenue required for public service by means of taxes; the aggregate of taxes.—**tax-exempt,** *a.* Exempt from taxation, as certain government bonds.—**taxpayer,** *n.* One who pays a tax; a small building or money-earning equipment on a valuable property to meet taxes on the land.

taxicab, tak″si•kab′, *n.* [From E. *taxi*meter and *cab.*] An automobile carrying passengers for a fare.—**taxi,** tak′si, *v.t.* To ride in a taxicab; *avi.* to operate an airplane under its own power at low speeds over the ground or water.—*v.i.* To transport by taxicab.—*n.* Short form of *taxicab.*

taxidermy, tak′si•dėr•mi, *n.* [Gr. *taxis,* an arranging, order, *derma,* skin.] The art of treating the skins of animals so that they retain their natural appearance, and also of stuffing and mounting them.

tea, tē, *n.* [From Chinese *t'e,* tea.] The dried leaves of a shrub extensively cultivated in China, India and Japan, etc.; the plant itself; a decoction or infusion of tea leaves in boiling water, used as a beverage; a social gathering at which tea is usually served.—**tea caddy,** *n.* A small box for holding the tea used in a household.—**teacake,** *n.* A light kind of cake eaten with tea.—**teacup,** *n.* A small cup for drinking tea.—**teakettle,** *n.* A portable kettle in which water is boiled for making tea.—**teapot,** *n.* A vessel with a spout in which tea is infused, and from which it is poured into teacups.—**teaspoon,** *n.* A small spoon used in drinking tea.—**teaspoonful,** *n.* As much as a teaspoon holds.

teach, tēch, *v.t.*—pret. and pp. *taught.* [From A.Sax. *taecan.* to teach, show, command; allied to *tihan,* to accuse; Goth. *teihan,* G. *zeigen,* to point out; cog. L. *dico,* to say (whence *diction,* etc.); Gr. *deiknymi,* Skr. *diç,* to point out. *Token* is akin.] To impart instruction to; to guide the studies of; to instruct; to impart the knowledge of; to instruct, train, or give skill in the use, management, or handling of; to let be known; to tell; to show how; to show.—*v.i.* To practice giving instruction; to perform the business of a preceptor.—**teachable,** tēch'a•bl, *a.* Capable of being taught; apt to learn; docile.—**teachableness,** tēch'a•bl•nes, *n.* The quality of being teachable; aptness to learn; docility.—**teacher,** tēch'ėr, *n.* One who teaches or instructs; a preceptor; a tutor; a preacher; a minister of the gospel.—**teaching,** tēch'ing, *n.* The act or business of instructing; instruction.

teaching machine, tēch'ing ma•shēn', *n.* A mechanical device by means of which the student answers a given set of questions and is immediately informed as to whether the answer was right, the device being usually set up in such a way that the student must repeatedly answer each question until he has supplied the right answer.

teak, tēk, *n.* [Tamil name.] A tree growing in different parts of the East Indies, and yielding a strong, durable, and most valuable timber.

teal, tēl, *n.* [Same as *tel* or *tal* in D. *teling, taling,* a teal; origin doubtful.] One of several short-necked freshwater ducks, especially the blue-winged *teal* and the green-winged *teal.*

team, tēm, *n.* [A.Sax. *teám,* offspring, a series, a row, whence *týman,* to teem; akin to O.Fris. *tam,* offspring; D. *toom,* a brood; from same stem as *tow, tug.*] A flock of young animals, especially young ducks; two or more horses, oxen, or other beasts harnessed together for drawing; the persons forming one of the parties or sides in a game, match, or the like.—**teamster,** tēm'stėr, *n.* One who drives a team or truck.

tear, tēr, *n.* [A.Sax. *teár,* a tear=Icel. *tár,* Dan. *taare,* G. *zähre,* Goth. *tager*; cognate Gr. *dakry,* O.L. *dacryma,* L. *lacryma,* Ir. *dear,* W. *daiger,* Gael. *deur*; from a root meaning to bite.] A drop of the limpid fluid secreted by a special gland, and appearing in the eyes or flowing from them, especially through excessive grief or joy; any transparent drop of fluid matter; also a solid, transparent drop, as of some resins.—**teardrop,** *n.* A tear.—**tearful,** tēr•fụl, *a.* Abounding with tears; shedding tears.—**tear gas,** *n.* A gas which causes temporary partial blindness, used by police and in war in tear shells, tear grenades, etc.

tear, târ, *v.t.*—pret. *tore* (formerly *tare*), pp. *torn.* [A.Sax. *teran,* to rend =Goth. (*ga*)*tairan,* to break; G. *zehren,* D. *teren,* Dan. *taere,* to consume; same root as Gr. *derō,* to flay; Skr. *dar,* to split. *Tire* is akin.] To separate the parts of by pulling; to pull apart by force; to form fissures or furrows in by violence; to lacerate; to wound; to divide by violent measures; to disturb, excite, or disorganize violently (*torn* by factions); to drag; to move or remove by pulling or violently; to cause or make by rending (to *tear* a hole).—*To tear up,* to remove from a fixed state by violence; to rend completely.—*To tear the hair,* to pull it in a violent or distracted manner: often as a sign of grief.—*v.i.* To be rent or torn; to rage; to act with turbulent violence.—*n.* A rent; a fissure.—*Tear and wear,* deterioration by long or frequent use.

tease, tēz, *v.t.*—*teased, teasing.* [A. Sax. *taesan,* to pluck, to tease=Dan. *taese, taesse,* to tease wool; D. *teezen,* to pick, to tease; akin G. *zausen,* to tug, tear. *Teasel* is from this, and *touse, tousy, tussle,* are allied.] To pull apart the adhering fibers of; to comb or card, as wool or flax; to vex with importunity; to annoy or irritate by petty requests or by raillery.

teasel, teazel, tē'zel, *n.* [A.Sax. *taesl,* teasel, from *taesan,* to tease. TEASE.] The fuller's thistle, cultivated for its heads or burrs, which have numerous hooked bracts, and are employed to raise the nap of woolen cloths; any contrivance similarly used in the dressing of woolen cloth.—*v.t.* To subject to the action of teasels.—**teaseler,** tē'zel•ėr, *n.* One who uses the teasel.

teat, tēt, *n.* [A.Sax. *tit, titt,* a teat= L.G. and O.D. *titte,* G. *zitze,* Ir. and Gael. *did,* a teat.] The projecting organ through which milk is drawn from the breast or udder of females; a nipple; a dug of a beast; a pap.

Tebeth, tē beth, *n.* [Heb.] The tenth month of the Jewish ecclesiastical year.

techily, techiness. See TECHY.

technetium, tek•nē'shi•um, *n.* A metallic element, identified spectroscopically in platinum and columbium compounds and produced artificially by bombardment of molybdenum. Symbol, Tc; at. no., 43.

technical, tek'ni•kal, *a.* [L. *technicus,* from Gr. *technikos,* from *technē,* art.] Pertaining to the mechanical arts; specially appertaining to an art, science, profession, handicraft, business, or the like.—**technic,** tek'nik, *n.* Method of manipulation in any art; artistic execution.—*a.* Technical.—**technicality,** tek•ni•kal'i•ti, *n.* The character of being technical; a technical feature or peculiarity; a technical expression.—**technically,** tek'-ni•kal•li, *adv.* In a technical manner.—**technician,** tek•nish'an, *n.* One skilled in any technical art.—**technique,** tek•nēk', *n.* Expert method of execution or manner of performance.—**technological,** tek•no•loj'i•kal, *a.* Pertaining to technology.—**technologist,** tek•nol'o•jist, *n.* One versed in technology.—**technology,** tek•-nol'o•ji, *n.* The application of science to industrial use.

techy, tetchy, tech'i, *a.* [From old *teche, tache,* a blemish, a vice, from Fr. *tache,* a spot.] Peevish; fretful; irritable; testy.—**techily,** tech'i•li, *adv.* In a techy manner; peevishly.—**techiness,** tech'i•nes, *n.* The state or quality of being techy.

tectonic, tek•ton'ik, *a.* [Gr. *tektonikos,* from *tektōn, tektonos,* a carpenter, a builder.] Pertaining to building or construction, or to the earth's structure.—**tectonics,** tek•-ton'iks, *n.* The art of constructing with utility as well as taste.

tectrices, tek'tri•sēz, *n. pl.* [From L. *tego, tectum,* to cover.] *Ornith.* the feathers which cover the quill feathers of the wing; the coverts.

ted, ted, *v.t.*—*tedded, tedding.* [From W. *teddu,* to spread out.] *Agri.* to spread to the air after being mown; to turn and scatter new-mowed grass or hay.—**tedder,** ted'ėr, *n.* One who teds; an implement that spreads newly mown grass.

tedium, tē'di•um, *n.* [L. *taedium,* from *taedet,* it wearies.] Irksomeness; wearisomeness.—**tedious,** tēd'yus, *a.* [O.Fr. *tedieux,* L. *taediosus.*] Involving or causing tedium; tiresome from continuance or slowness; wearisome; monotonous.—**tediously,** tēd'yus•li, *adv.* In a tedious manner; so as to weary.—**tediousness,** tēd'yus•nes, *n.* The quality of being tedious; wearisomeness.

tee, tē, *n.* [Icel. *tja,* to mark, to note.] A point of aim or starting-point in certain games, as quoits, curling, and golf; more particularly, the little pin or heap of sand on which golfers set the ball for the first stroke toward each hole.—*v.t.* To set the ball in this position.

teel, tēl, *n.* [Indian name.] Indian sesame.

teem, tēm, *v.i.*—[A.Sax. *teman, tyman,* to produce. TEAM.] To bring forth young; to be pregnant; to be stocked to overflowing; to be prolific or abundantly fertile.—*v.t.* To produce; to bring forth.—**teeming,** *a.* Overflowing; crowded, as a *teeming* city.

teens, tēnz, *n. pl.* The years of one's age having the termination *-teen,* beginning with thir*teen* and ending with nine*teen,* during which period a person is said to be in his or her *teens.*

teeth, tēth, pl. of *tooth.*—**teethe,** tēTH, *v.i.* See TOOTH.

teetotal, tē'tō•tal, *a.* [Formed by reduplication of initial letter of *total,* for the sake of emphasis; comp. *tee-totum.*] Pertaining to total abstinence; totally abstaining from intoxicants.—**teetotalism,** tē'tō•tal•izm, *n.* The principles or practice of teetotalers.—**teetotaler, teetotaller,** tē•-tō'tal•ėr, *n.* One who binds himself to entire abstinence from intoxicating liquors, unless medically prescribed; a total abstainer.

teetotum, tē•tō'tum, *n.* [That is

T-totum, totum represented by T, from the T marked upon it and standing for L. *totum*, the whole, the whole stakes being won when T turns up; comp. *teetotal*.] A small four-sided toy of the top kind, made to spin by the fingers, and used by children in a game of chance, the result depending on which side turns up.

tegmen, teg′men, *n.* pl. **tegmina,** teg′mi•na, [L., from *tego*, to cover.] A covering or tegument; *bot.* the inner skin which covers the seed.

tegular, teg′ū•lėr, *a.* [L. *tegula*, a tile, from *tego*, to cover.] Resembling a tile; consisting of tiles.

tegument, teg′ū•ment, *n.* [L. *tegumentum*, from *tego*, to cover.] A cover or covering; a natural covering, as of an animal; an integument.—**tegumentary,** teg•ū•men′te•ri, *a.* Pertaining to teguments.

teil, teil tree, tēl, *n.* [Fr. *teil*, from L. *tilia*, a lime-tree.] The lime tree.

telamon, tel′a•mon, *n.* pl. **telamones,** tel•e•mō′nēz. [Gr. *telamōn*, a bearer.] *Arch.* the figure of a man employed as a column or pilaster. See ATLANTES.

telautograph, te•lą′to•graf, *n.* [Gr. *tēle*, far, and E. *autograph*.] A telegraph that produces a facsimile of the person's handwriting who sends a message.

teledu, tel′e•dö, *n.* [Native name.] A Javanese carnivorous animal allied to the skunk, and, like it, able to give out an abominable stench.

telegony, te•leg′o•ni, *n.* [Gr. *tēle*, far, *gonos*, offspring.] The hypothetical influence of a sire on subsequent offspring by a different sire.

telegram, tel′e•gram, *n.* [Gr. *tēle*, far, and *gramma*, what is written, from *graphō*, to write.] A communication sent by telegraph; a telegraphic message or dispatch.—**telegraph,** tel′e•graf, *n.* A general name for any apparatus for conveying intelligence beyond the limits of distance at which the voice is audible; now usually restricted to the electric telegraph, which consists essentially of a battery or other source of electric power, of a wire or conductor for conveying the electric current from one station to another, of the apparatus for transmitting the current, and of the indicator or signaling instrument; a telegraphic communication; a telegram.—*Telegraph cable.* See CABLE.—*v.t.* To convey or announce by telegraph.—**telegraphic, telegraphical,** tel•e•graf′ik, tel•e•graf′i•kal, *a.* Pertaining to the telegraph; made by a telegraph; communicated by a telegraph.—**telegraphically,** tel•e•graf′i•kal•li, *adv.* By means of a telegraph.—**telegraphist,** tel•eg′raf•ist, *n.* One who works a telegraph.—**telegraphy,** te•leg′ra•fi, *n.* The art or practice of communicating by telegraph.

telemeter, te•lem′et•ėr, *n.* [Gr. *tēle*, far, and *metron*, a measure.] An instrument used among artillery for determining the distance from the gun of the object fired at; an apparatus by which the variations recorded by any physical or other instrument can be shown at a distance by means of electricity.—**telemetry,** te•lem′e•tri, *n.* Measurement or observation by means of a telemeter.

teleology, tel•i•ol′o•ji, *n.* [Gr. *telos*, *teleos*, an end, and *logos*, discourse.] The science or doctrine of final causes; the science treating of the end or design for which things were created.—**teleological,** tel′i•o•loj″i•kal, *a.* Pertaining to teleology.—**teleologically,** tel′i•o•loj″i•kal•li, *adv.* In a teleological manner.—**teleologist,** tel•i•ol′o•jist, *n.* One versed in teleology; one who investigates the final cause or purpose of phenomena, or the end for which each has been produced.

teleostean, tel•i•os′ti•an, *a.* [Gr. *teleos, teleios*, complete, and *osteon*, a bone.] A term applied to an order of fishes having a well-ossified skeleton, and including almost all familiar food fishes.—*n.* One of this division of fishes.

telepathy, te•lep′a•thi, *n.* [Gr. *tēle*, far, *pathos*, feeling.] The communication of feelings or impressions between persons at a distance from each other.—**telepathic,** tel•e•path′ik, *a.* Pertaining to telepathy.

telephone, tel′e•fōn, *n.* [Gr. *tēle*, at a distance, and *phōnē*, sound.] Any instrument which transmits sound beyond its natural limits of audibility; more especially, an instrument transmitting sound and words uttered by the human voice by means of electricity and conducting wires, the vibrations of a metal plate that receives the sounds at one end of the wire giving rise to corresponding vibrations at the other end which reproduce the sound.—**telephote,** tel′e•fōt, *n.* A telegraphic apparatus for reproducing pictures at a great distance.—**telephotograph,** tel′e•fōt″o•graf, *n.* A photograph reproduced by wire or wireless by means of a device using the scanning beam of a photoelectric cell on a sensitized medium.—**telephotography,** tel′e•fo•tog″ra•fi, *n.* Process of photographing by means of the telephoto lens; also process of transmitting the telephotograph.—**telephoto lens,** *n.* A compound telescopic lens for photographing objects at a distance.

telescope, tel′e•skōp, *n.* [Gr. *tēleskopos*, seeing afar, from *tēle*, at a distance, and *skopeō*, to view.] An optical instrument essentially consisting of a set of lenses fixed in a tube or a number of sliding tubes, by which distant objects are brought within the range of distinct, or more distinct vision.—*v.t.* To drive the parts of into each other, like the movable joints of a pocket telescope (the train was *telescoped* by the collision).—**telescopic, telescopical,** tel′e•skop•ik, tel′e•skop•i•kal, *a.* Pertaining to a telescope; performed by a telescope; seen only by a telescope; seeing at a great distance; having the power of extension by joints sliding one within another.—**telescopically,** tel•e•skop′i•kal•li, *adv.*

telespectroscope, tel•e•spek′tro•skōp, *n.* A telescope and spectroscope combined.

teletype, tel′e•tīp, *n.* A system of communication by which messages may be sent by wire through an electrical sending device with keys similar to a typewriter, and transmitted to a receiving station which reproduces the typed message.

television, tel″e•vizh′on, *n.* The transmission of scenes or moving pictures by conversion of light rays to electrical waves, which are reconverted to reproduce the original image.

telic, tel′ik, *a.* [Gr. *telos*, end.] *Gram.* denoting end or purpose.

tell, tel, *v.t.*—pret. and pp. *told*. [A.Sax. *tellan*, to tell, announce, count=O.Fris. *tella*, D. *tellen*, Dan. *taelle*, Icel. *telja*, to tell, number, etc.; G. *zählen*, to number. Closely akin to *tale*.] To express in words; to say; to relate, narrate, rehearse (to *tell* a story); to make known by words; to disclose; to confess; to acknowledge (to *tell* a secret); to discern so as to be able to say (to *tell* one from another); to distinguish; to decide upon; to enumerate; to count; to inform; to give an order or request to.—*To tell off*, to count off; especially, to count off, detach, or select for some special duty.—*v.i.* To give an account; to make report; to play the informer; to blab; to take effect; to produce a marked effect (every shot *tells*).—*To hear tell*, to hear mention made; to learn by hearsay.—**teller,** tel′ėr, *n.* One who tells; one who numbers; one appointed to count votes, as in a lodge or public election; a functionary in a banking establishment whose business is to receive and pay money over the counter.—**telling,** tel′ing, *p.* and *a.* Operating with great effect; highly effective; impressive (a *telling* speech).—*n.* The act of one that tells.—**telltale,** *a.* Telling tales; officiously revealing; blabbing.—*n.* One who improperly discloses private concerns; one who tells that which prudence should suppress; an instrument or device of various kinds, usually automatic, for counting or registering.

tellural, tel′ū•ral, *a.* [L. *tellus, telluris*, the earth.] Pertaining to the earth.—**tellurian,** tel•ū′ri•an, *a.* Pertaining to the earth or to an inhabitant of the earth.—*n.* An inhabitant of the earth.—**telluric,** tel•ū′rik, *a.* Pertaining to the earth or to tellurium.—*Telluric acid*, an oxyacid of tellurium.—**telluride,** tel′ū•rīd, *n.* A compound of tellurium with an electropositive element.—**tellurion,** tel•ū′ri•on, *n.* A kind of orrery showing the changes of the seasons, etc.—**tellurium,** tel•ū′ri•um, *n.* [From L. *tellus*, earth.] A nonmetallic element usually occurring in nature combined with metals. Symbol, Te; at. no., 52; at. wt., 127.61.—**tellurous,** tel•ū′rus, *a.* Pertaining to, or obtained from, tellurium.

telpherage, tel′fėr•ij, *n.* [Crude formation from *tele*, far, *phero*, to carry.]

A system of transporting goods in a light car suspended from a cable and electrically propelled.

telson, tel′son, *n.* [Gr., an extremity.] The last joint in the abdomen of Crustacea.

telstar, tel′star, *n.* [Gr. *tēle*, far, and *star*.] Any of a series of small, experimental U.S. communications satellites, designed to study broadbeam microwave communications, radiation, and tracking techniques.

temblor, tem•blōr′, *n.* [Sp.] An earthquake.

temerity, te•mer′i•ti, *n.* [L. *temeritas*, rashness, from *temere*, rashly.] Heedlessness of consequences; extreme venturesomeness; recklessness; rashness.—**temerarious,** tem•-e•râ′ri•us, *a.* [L. *temerarius*.] Rash; reckless: careless.

temper, tem′pėr, *v.t.* [Fr. *tempérer*, from L. *temperare*, to regulate, mix properly, temper, from *tempus*, *temporis*, time. TEMPORAL.] To qualify by intermixture (to *temper* justice with mercy); to moderate; to calm; to form to a proper degree of hardness (to *temper* iron or steel).—*n.* Disposition or constitution of the mind, with regard to the passions and affections; heat of mind; irritation; the state of a metal as to its hardness; middle character; mean or medium.—**temperable,** tem′pėr•a•bl, *a.* Capable of being tempered.—**temperament,** tem′pėr•a•ment, *n.* [L. *temperamentum*, admixture, moderation, etc., from *tempero*.] Due mixture of elements or qualities; adjustment of opposing influences; that individual peculiarity of physical organization by which the manner of acting, feeling, and thinking of each person is permanently affected (a person of a sanguine, or of a melancholy, *temperament*); *mus.* a certain adjustment of the tones or intervals of the scale of fixed-toned instruments, as the organ, piano, and the like, with the view of removing an apparent imperfection, and fitting the scale for use in all keys without offense to the ear.—**temperance,** tem′pėr•ans, *n.* [L. *temperantia*, moderation, sobriety, from *tempero*, to temper.] The observance of moderation; temperateness; moderation in regard to the indulgence of the natural appetites and passions; restrained or moderate indulgence; sobriety; sometimes loosely used to mean total abstinence from intoxicants.—**temperate,** tem′pėr•it, *a.* [L. *temperatus*.] Moderate; showing moderation; moderate as regards the indulgence of the appetites or desires; abstemious; sober; not violent or excessive as regards the use of language; reasonable; calm; measured; not going beyond due bounds; moderate as regards amount of heat; not liable to excessive heats (a *temperate* climate).—*Temperate zones*, the spaces on the earth between the tropics and the polar circles, where the heat is less than in the tropics, and the cold less than in the polar circles.—**temperately,** tem′pėr•it•li, *adv.* In a temperate manner or degree; moderately; soberly; calmly; sedately.—**temperateness,** tem′pėr•it•nes, *n.* The quality of being temperate; moderation; reasonableness.—**temperature,** tem′pėr•a•chėr, *n.* [L. *temperatura*, due measure, temperature.] Constitution or temperament; the state of a body or of a region of the earth with regard to heat, the degree or intensity of the heat effects of a body.—**tempered,** tem′-pėrd, *a.* Having a certain disposition or temper; disposed; often used in composition (a good-*tempered*, bad-*tempered* man).

tempera, tem′pe•ra, *n.* [It.] *Painting*, the same as *Distemper*.

tempest, tem′pest, *n.* [O.Fr. *tempeste*, from L. *tempestas*, time, season, a tempest, from *tempus*, time. TEMPORAL.] An extensive current of wind rushing with great velocity and violence; a storm of extreme violence; a hurricane; a violent tumult or commotion.—**tempestuous,** tem•-pes′chū•us, *a.* [L. *tempestuosus*.] Belonging to a tempest; very stormy; blowing with violence; subject to fits of stormy passion.—**tempestuously,** tem′pes′chū•us•li, *adv.* In a tempestuous manner.—**tempestuousness,** tem•pes′chū•us•nes, *n.*

Templar. See TEMPLE

template, *n.* See TEMPLET.

temple, tem′pl, *n.* [Fr. *temple*, from L. *templum*, a temple, originally a place marked or cut off, from root *tem* in Gr. *temnō*, to cut, whence Gr. *temenos*, a temple.] An edifice dedicated to the service of some deity or deities; originally, an edifice erected for some Roman deity; [*cap.*] one of the three successive edifices at Jerusalem dedicated to the worship of Jehovah; an edifice erected among Christians as a place of public worship; a church; [*cap.*] a semimonastic establishment in London inhabited by the knights Templars and receiving its name from them; the buildings erected on this site and occupied by lawyers or students of law.—**Templar,** tem′-plėr, *n.* One of a religious military order first established at Jerusalem about 1118 A.D. for the protection of pilgrims traveling to the Holy Land and of the Holy Sepulcher, and so named from their residence at Jerusalem being connected with the church and convent of the Temple; *Masonic order*, Knight Templar.

temple, tem′pl, *n.* [O.Fr. *temple* (Fr. *tempe*), the temple, from L. *tempus*, time, also a temple of the head. TEMPORAL.] The flat portion of either side of the head between the forehead and ear.

templet, template, tem′plet, tem′-plāt, *n.* [Comp. Fr. *temple*, *templet*, a mechanical appliance of several kinds.] A flat thin board or piece of sheet iron whose edge is shaped in some particular way, so that it may serve as a guide or test in making an article with a corresponding contour; a short piece of timber or a stone placed in a wall to support a girder, beam, etc.

tempo, tem′pō, *n.* [It. *tempo*, time.] *Mus.* a word used to express the degree of quickness with which a piece of music is to be executed; musical time.

temporal, tem′pe•rel, *a.* [L. *temporalis*, from *tempus*, *temporis*, time, season, etc. (seen in *tense*, *n.*, *contemporary*, *extempore*).] Pertaining to this life or this world; secular; opposed to *spiritual* and *ecclesiastical*; measured or limited by time, or by this life or state of things; having limited existence; opposed to *eternal*; *gram.* relating to a tense; pertaining to the temple or temples of the head.—*n.* Anything temporal or secular; a temporality.—**temporality,** tem•pe•ral′i•ti, *n.* The state or quality of being temporal; a secular possession; *pl.* revenues of an ecclesiastic from lands, tithes, etc.; opposed to *spiritualities*.—**temporally,** tem′pe•rel•li, *adv.* In a temporal manner; with respect to time or this life only.—**temporarily,** tem″pe•rer′i•li, *adv.* In a temporary manner; for a time; provisionally.—**temporary,** tem′pe•re•ri, *a.* [L. *temporarius*.] Lasting for a time only; existing or continuing for a limited time; transient; provisional.—**temporize,** tem′pe•rīz, *v.i.*—*temporized*, *temporizing*. [Fr. *temporiser*, from L. *tempus*, *temporis*, time.] To comply with or humor the time or occasion; to try to suit both sides or parties; to trim; to use politic devices.—**temporization,** tem′pe•ri•zā″shon, *n.* The act of temporizing.—**temporizer,** tem′pe•rī•zėr, *n.* One who temporizes.

tempt, temt, *v.t.* [O.Fr. *tempter* (Fr. *tenter*), from L. *temptare*, *tentare*, to try, prove, test, incite, intens. of *tendo*, *tentum*, to stretch; same root as Gr. *teinō*, Skr. *tan*, to stretch. (TEND, THIN.) *Taunt* is of same origin.] To incite or solicit to an evil act; to entice to something wrong by some specious argument or inducement; to seduce; to invite; to try; to induce; to try the patience of; to put to a test.—**temptable,** tem′ta•bl, *a.* Liable to be tempted.—**temptation,** tem•tā′shon, *n.* The act of tempting or state of being tempted; enticement to evil; that which is presented as an inducement to evil; an enticement; an allurement to anything indifferent or even good (*colloq.*).—**tempter,** tem′tėr, *n.* One who tempts; one who entices to evil.—**tempting,** tem′ting, *a.* Adapted to entice or allure; attractive; seductive.—**temptingly,** tem′ting•li, *adv.* In a tempting manner.—**temptingness,** tem•ting•nes, *n.*—**temptress,** temt′res, *n.* A female who tempts or entices.

ten, ten, *a.* [A.Sax. *ten*, *týn*=D. *tien*, Goth. *taihun*, G. *zehn*, Icel. *tíu*, Sw. *tio*, Dan. *ti*; cog. L. *decem*, Gr. *deka*, Skr. *deçan*; W. *deg*, Armor. *dek*, Ir. *deag*, Gael. *deich*.] Twice five; nine and one.—*n.* The number of twice five; a figure or symbol denoting ten units, as 10 or X; a playing card with ten spots.—**tenth,** tenth, *a.* First after the ninth.—*n.*

The tenth part; one of ten equal parts into which a whole is divided.—**tenthly,** tenth′li, *adv.* In the tenth place.—**tenfold,** ten′fōld, *a.* and *adv.* Ten times greater or more.

tenable, ten′a•bl, *a.* [Fr. *tenable,* from *tenir,* L. *tenere,* to hold (seen also in *tenant, tenacious, tenement, tenor, tenure, abstain, contain, obtain, retain,* etc.); same root as in *tendo,* to stretch, *tempto,* to tempt. TEND, TEMPT.] Capable of being held, maintained, or defended against an assailant, or against attempts to take it.—**tenability,** ten•a•bil′i•ti, *n.* The state of being tenable.

tenacious, te•nā′shus, *a.* [L. *tenax, tenacis,* from *teneo,* to hold. TENABLE.] Holding fast, or inclined to hold fast; inclined to retain; with *of* before the thing held; retentive; apt to retain long what is committed to it (a *tenacious* memory); apt to adhere to another substance; adhesive; tough; having great cohesive force among the constituent particles.—**tenaciously,** te•nā′shus•li, *adv.* In a tenacious manner.—**tenaciousness,** te•nā′shus•nes, *n.* The state or quality of being tenacious.—**tenacity,** te•nas′i•ti, *n.* [Fr. *tenacité,* L. *tenacitas.*] The quality of being tenacious; adhesiveness; that property of material bodies by which their parts resist an effort to force or pull them asunder, or the measure of the resistance of bodies to tearing or crushing.

tenaille, tenail, te•nāl′, *n.* [Fr. *tenaille,* from *tenir,* L. *tenere,* to hold. TENABLE.] *Fort.* an outwork or rampart in the main ditch immediately in front of the curtain, between two bastions.

tenant, ten′ent, *n.* [Fr. *tenant,* holding, ppr. of *tenir,* L. *tenere,* to hold. TENABLE.] A person who holds or possesses lands or tenements by any kind of title, either in fee, for life, for years, or at will; one who occupies lands or houses for which he pays rent; one who has possession of any place; a dweller; an occupant.—*v.t.* To hold or possess as a tenant.—*v.i.* To live as a tenant; to dwell.—**tenancy,** ten′en•si, *n.* A holding or possession as tenant; period of occupancy as tenant; tenure.—**tenantable,** ten′ent•a•bl, *a.* In a state of repair suitable for a tenant.—**tenantless,** ten′ent•les, *a.* Having no tenant; unoccupied.—**tenantry,** ten′ent•ri, *n.* The body of tenants.

tench, tensh, *n.* [O.Fr. *tenche* (Fr. *tanche*), from L. *tinca,* a tench.] A fish of the carp family inhabiting most of the lakes of Europe.

tend, tend, *v.i.* [L. *tendo,* to stretch out, to extend, to bend one's footsteps (seen also in *attend, extend, contend, intend, superintend, tent,* etc.); same root as L. *teneo,* to hold, Gr. *teinō,* Skr. *tan,* to stretch. THIN, TENDER, *a.* TENABLE.] To move in a certain direction; to be directed; to have influence toward producing a certain effect; to conduce or contribute.—**tendency,** ten′den•si, *n.* [Fr. *tendance.*] An inclining or contributing influence; aptness to take a certain course; inclination; effect of giving a certain bent or direction.

tend, tend, *v.t.* [Contr. from *attend.*] To accompany as an assistant or protector; to watch; to guard; to look after; to take care of; to attend to.—*v.i.* To attend; to wait, as attendants or servants; to attend as something inseparable; to be attentive (*Shak.*).—**tendance,** ten′dans, *n.* Act of tending or attending.—**tender,** ten′dėr, *n.* One that tends; *naut.* a small vessel attending a larger one with stores, or to convey intelligence; *rail.* a special car attached to a steam locomotive, for carrying the fuel, water, etc.

tender, ten′dėr, *v.t.* [Fr. *tendre,* to reach or stretch out, from L. *tendo, tendere,* to stretch out. TEND, to move, etc.] To present for acceptance; to offer in payment or satisfaction of a demand.—*n.* An offer of money or any other thing in satisfaction of a debt or liability; any offer for acceptance; an offer in writing to execute some specified work, or to supply certain specified articles, at a certain rate; the thing offered.

tender, ten′dėr, *a.* [Fr. *tendre,* from L. *tener,* tender, from same root as *tenuis,* thin, *tendo,* to stretch (whence *tend*), *teneo,* to hold (as in *tenable*), and E. *thin.* The *d* is inserted as in *gender, thunder.*] Easily injured; delicate; very sensible to pain; very susceptible of any sensation; not hardy; weak; easily affected by the distresses of another (a *tender* heart); sympathetic; affectionate; fond; pathetic; careful not to hurt or injure; gentle; unwilling to pain; apt to give pain or to annoy when spoken of (a *tender* subject).—*v.t.*‡ To hold dear; to esteem (*Shak.*).—**tenderfoot,** *n.* *Amer.* A newcomer, one who is unaccustomed to the ways of a place; a boy scout or girl scout beginner.—**tenderhearted,** *a.* Very susceptible of the softer passions of love, pity, or kindness.—**tenderloin,** *n.* The strip of meat along the backbone in beef, or pork; also, in cities, the section where vice abounds.—**tenderly,** ten′dėr•li, *adv.* In a tender manner; with tenderness; mildly; gently; kindly; fondly; affectionately.—**tenderness,** ten′dėr•nes, *n.* The state or character of being tender; delicacy; readiness to be hurt.

tendon, ten′don, *n.* [Fr. *tendon,* from L. *tendo,* to stretch. TEND.] *Anat.* a hard, insensible cord or bundle of fibers by which a muscle is attached to a bone or other part which it serves to move.—*Tendon of Achilles,* the large tendon connecting the calf of the leg with the heel.—**tendinous,** ten′di•nus, *a.* [Fr. *tendineux.*] Partaking of the nature of tendons; full of tendons; sinewy.

tendril, ten′dril, *n.* [O.Fr. *tendrillon,* a tendril, from *tendre,* tender. TENDER.] *Bot.* a slender spiral shoot of a plant that winds round another body for the purpose of support.

tenebrific, ten•e•brif′ik, *a.* [L. *tenebrae,* darkness, and *facio,* to make.] Producing darkness.—**tenebrous,** ten′e•brus, *a.* [L. *tenebrosus.*] Dark; gloomy.

tenement, ten′e•ment, *n.* [O.Fr. *tenement,* L.L. *tenementum,* from L. *teneo,* to hold. TENABLE.] An abode; a habitation; a dwelling; an apartment or apartments in a building used by one family; *law,* any species of permanent property that may be held.—**tenementary,** ten•e•men′te•ri, *a.* Capable of being leased; held by tenants.—**tenement house,** *n.* A house or block of building divided into dwellings for separate families.

tenesmus, ti•nes′mus, *n.* [L., from Gr. *teinesmos,* from *teinō,* to stretch to strain.] *Med.* a continual inclination to void the contents of the bowels, accompanied by straining, but without any discharge.

tenet, ten′et, *n.* [L. *tenet,* he holds. TENABLE.] Any opinion, principle, dogma, or doctrine which a person believes or maintains as true.

tenfold. See TEN.

tennis, ten′is, *n.* [Said to be from Fr. *tenez,* take it (from *tenir,* L. *tenere,* to hold), a word which the French use when the ball is struck.] An ancient game in which players alternately drive a ball against a wall with rackets; short for *lawn tennis,* a game in which the ball must pass back and forth over a net and land within a marked court; the player failing to return the ball losing the point.

tenon, ten′on, *n.* [Fr. *tenon,* from *tenir,* L. *tenere,* to hold. TENABLE.] A projecting piece on the end of a piece of wood fitted for insertion into a corresponding cavity or mortise in order to form a joint.—*v.t.* To fit with a tenon.

tenor, ten′ėr, *n.* [L. *tenor,* a holding on, course, tenor, from *teneo,* to hold. TENABLE.] Prevailing course or direction; general course or drift of thought; general spirit or meaning; purport; substance (the *tenor* of a discourse); *mus.* the highest of the adult male chest voices; so called because in former times the leading melody was given to this voice; the part above the bass in harmonized music; one who sings a tenor part.—*a.* *Mus.* adapted for singing or playing the tenor.—*Tenor clef,* the C clef, placed on the fourth line.

tenrec, ten′rek, *n.* [Native Madagascar name.] An animal allied to the hedgehog, inhabiting Madagascar.

tense, tens, *a.* [L. *tensus,* pp. of *tendo,* to stretch. TEND.] Stretched until tight; strained to stiffness; rigid; not lax.—**tensely,** tens′li, *adv.* In a tense manner; with tension.—**tenseness,** tens′nes, *n.* The state of being tense.—**tensile,** ten′sil, *a.* Pertaining to tension; capable of tension.—**tensility,** ten•sil′i•ti, *n.* The quality of being tensile.—**tension,** ten′shon, *n.* [L. *tensio, tensionis.*] The act of stretching or straining; the state of being stretched or strained to stiffness; tightness; mental strain; *mech.* the force by which a bar, rod, or string is pulled when forming part of any system; *elect.* intensity, or the degree to which a body is excited, as estimated by the electrometer; *physics,* elastic force.—*The tension of a gas,* the degree of pressure it exerts on the containing surface.—**tensity,** ten′si•ti, *n.* State of being tense; tenseness. —**tensor,** ten′sor, *n. Anat.* a muscle that extends or stretches the part to which it is fixed.

tense, tens, *n.* [O.Fr. *tens,* Mod.Fr. *temps,* time, from L. *tempus,* time. TEMPORAL.] *Gram.* one of the forms which a verb takes in order to express the time of action or of that which is affirmed.

tensile, tension, etc. See TENSE, *a.*

tent, tent, *n.* [Fr. *tente,* L.L. *tenta,* a tent, lit. something stretched out or extended, from L. *tendo, tentum,* to stretch. TEND.] A portable house consisting of some flexible covering, such as skins, matting, or canvas stretched and sustained by poles.—*v.i.* To lodge in a tent; to tabernacle. —**tented,** tent′ed, *a.* Covered or furnished with tents.

tent, tent, *v.t.* [Fr. *tenter,* from L. *tentare,* to feel, to try. TEMPT.] To probe; to keep open with a tent or pledget.—*n. Surg.* a roll of lint or linen, etc., used to dilate an opening in the flesh, or keep open a sore from which matter is discharged.

tentacle, ten′ta•kl, *n.* [L.L. *tentaculum,* from L. *tento,* to handle, to feel. TEMPT.] *Zool.* an elongated appendage on the head of many invertebrate animals, used as an instrument of prehension or as a feeler. —**tentacular,** ten•tak′ū•lėr, *a.* Of the nature of a tentacle.

tentative, ten′te•tiv, *a.* [Fr. *tentatif,* from L. *tento, tentatum,* to try, to test. TEMPT.] Based on or consisting in trial or experiment; experimental; empirical.—*n.* An essay; a trial.—**tentatively,** ten′ta•tiv•li, *adv.* By way of experiment or trial.

tenter, ten′tėr, *n.* [From provincial *tent,* to tend or attend.] A person in a manufactory who looks after machines, so that they may be in proper order.

tenter, ten′tėr, *n.* [From L. *tentus,* stretched, from *tendo, tentum,* to stretch. TEND.] A frame used in cloth manufacture to stretch the pieces of cloth, and make them set or dry even and square; a tenterhook.—*On the tenters,* on the stretch; on the rack; in suspense.—*v.t.* To stretch on tenters.—**tenterhook,** *n.* A hook for stretching cloth on a tenter; *fig.* anything that painfully strains, racks, or tortures, chiefly used in the expression *to be on tenterhooks.*

tenth, tenthly. See TEN.

tenuity, te•nū′i•ti, *n.* [L. *tenuitas,* from *tenuis,* thin, from root meaning to stretch, as in E. *thin.*] The state of being thin or fine; thinness; slenderness; rarity; thinness, as of a fluid.—**tenuous,** ten′ū•us, *a.* Thin; slender; rare; subtle; not dense.

tenure, ten′ūr, *n.* [Fr. *tenure,* L.L. *tenura,* from L. *teneo,* to hold. TENABLE.] The act, manner, or right of holding property, especially real estate; manner of holding or possessing in general; the terms or conditions upon which anything is held or possessed (life is held on a precarious *tenure*).

teocalli, tē•o•kal′li, *n.* [Lit. God's house.] A temple among the aboriginal Indians of Mexico and Central America.

tepee, tē′pē, tep′ē, *n.* [Amer. Ind.] The American Indian cone-shaped tent.

tepid, tep′id, *a.* [L. *tepidus,* warm, from *tepeo,* to be warm; same root as Skr. *tap,* to burn.] Moderately warm; lukewarm.—**tepidness, tepidity,** tep′id•nes, ti•pid′i•ti, *n.* Moderate warmth; lukewarmness.

teraph, ter′af, *n.* pl. **teraphim,** ter′af•im. [Heb.] A household deity or image reverenced by the ancient Hebrews.

teratology, ter•a•tol′o•ji, *n.* [Gr. *teras, teratos,* a prodigy, and *logos,* discourse.] That branch of biological science which treats of monsters or malformations in the vegetable and animal kingdoms.—**teratological,** ter′a•to•loj″i•kal, *a.* Pertaining to teratology.—**teratologist,** ter•a•tol′o•jist, *n.* One versed in the study of teratology.

terbium, tėr′bi•um, *n.* [From Ytterby, Swedish town.] A metallic element of the rare-earth series. Symbol, Tb; at. no., 65; at. wt., 158.924.

tercel, tėr′sel, *n.* [Fr. *tiercelet,* tiercelet, a dim. from *tierce,* L. *tertius,* third—because said to be a third less than the female.] A male hawk or falcon.

tercentenary, tėr•sen′ten•e•ri, *a.* [L. *ter,* thrice, and E. *centenary.*] Comprising three hundred years.—*n.* A festival in commemoration of some event that happened three hundred years before; the three-hundredth anniversary of any event.

tercet, tėr′set, *n.* [Fr.] *Mus.* a third; *poetry,* a group of three rhyming lines; a triplet.

terebinth, ter′e•binth, *n.* [L. *terebinthus,* from Gr. *terebinthos,* the turpentine tree.] The turpentine tree; a name for various resinous exudations, both of fluid and solid.—**terebinthine,** ter•e•bin′thin, *a.* Pertaining to turpentine.

teredo, te•rē′dō, *n.* pl. **teredos,** [L. from Gr. *terēdōn,* from *tereō,* to bore.] A wormlike molluscous animal, the shipworm, well known on account of the destruction it causes by perforating submerged wood in order to form a habitation.

terete, te•rēt′, *a.* [L. *teres, teretis,* rounded off—properly, rubbed off—from *tero,* to rub.] Cylindrical and smooth; long and round; columnar, as some stems of plants.

tergal. See TERGUM.

tergeminate, tėr•jem′i•nāt, *a.* [L. *tergeminus*—*ter,* thrice, and *geminus,* double.] Thrice double; three-paired; threefold; triple.

tergiversate, tėr′ji•vėr•sāt, *v.i.*—*tergiversated, tergiversating.* [L. *tergiversor, tergiversatus,* from *tergum,* the back, and *versor,* to turn, from *verto,* to turn. VERSE.] To practice evasion; to make use of shifts or subterfuges.—**tergiversation,** ter′ji•vėr•sā″shon, *n.* The act of tergiversating; subterfuge; evasion; the act of changing or of turning one's back upon one's opinions; a turning against a cause formerly advocated.—**tergiversator,** tėr′ji•vėr•sā•tėr, *n.* One who practices tergiversation.

tergum, tėr′gum, *n.* [L., the back.] The convex upper plate of each segment of a crustacean.—**tergal,** tėr′gal, *a. Anat.* pertaining to the back; dorsal.

term, tėrm, *n.* [Fr. *terme,* an end, end, word, speech, period, etc., from L. *terminus,* a boundary (whence *terminal, terminate, determine,* etc.); akin Gr. *terma,* limit; same root as L. *trans,* E. *through.*] A limit; a bound or boundary; the time for which anything lasts; a time or period fixed in some way; a period during which instruction is regularly given to students in certain universities and colleges; the time in which a superior law court is held or is open for the trial of causes (but the law terms of the superior courts in England are now called 'sittings'); a day on which rent or interest is regularly payable, such as Lady Day or Michaelmas Day; a word by which something fixed and definite is expressed; particularly, a word having a technical meaning; *pl.* in a general way, words or language (to speak in vague *terms*); *pl.* conditions or propositions stated and offered for acceptance (state your *terms*); *pl.* relative position or footing (on good *terms* with a person); *logic,* the expression in language of the notion obtained in an act of apprehension; the subject or the predicate of a proposition; *alg.* a member of a compound quantity connected with another or others by the signs of addition and subtraction.—*Terms of a fraction,* the numerator and denominator.—*To make terms,* to come to an agreement.—*To come to terms,* to agree.—*To bring to terms,* to reduce to submission or to conditions.—*v.t.* To name; to denominate.—**termless,** tėrm′les, *a.* Having no term; boundless; endless.

termagant, tėr′ma•gent, *n.* [O.Fr. *Tervagant,* It. *Tervagante, Trivagante;* probably a name of Eastern origin. Termagant was a fabled deity of the Mohammedans introduced into the old moralities or other shows, in which he figured as a most violent personage.] A brawling, turbulent woman; a virago.—*a.* Furious; scolding.

terminate, tėr′mi•nāt, *v.t.*—*terminated, terminating.* [L. *termino, terminatum,* to bound, to terminate. TERM.] To bound; to limit; to form the extreme point or side of; to put an end to; to complete; to put the finishing touch to.—*v.i.* To be limited in space; to stop short; to end; to come to a limit in time.—*a.* Capable of coming to an end (a *terminate* decimal).—**termination,**

tėr•mi•nā′shon, *n.* The act of terminating; an ending or concluding; the end of a thing or point where it ends; limit in space; end in time; *gram.* a part annexed to the root or stem of an inflected word; the syllable or letter that ends a word; conclusions; issue; result.—**terminational,** tėr•mi•nā′shon•al, *a.* Pertaining to or forming a termination. —**terminative,** tėr′mi•nā•tiv, *a.* Terminating; definitive.—**terminatively,** tėr′mi•nā•tiv•li, *adv.*—**terminator,** tėr′mi•nāt•ėr, *n.* One who or that which terminates.—**terminable,** tėr′mi•na•bl, *a.* Capable of being terminated; coming to an end after a certain term.—**terminableness,** tėr′mi•na•bl•nes, *n.* —**terminal,** tėr′mi•nal, *a.* Relating to or forming the end or extremity; placed at the end of something.—*n.* That which terminates; an extremity; the clamping screw at each end of a voltaic battery ; a passenger or freight station (an airline *terminal*).

terminology, tėr•mi•nol′o•ji, *n.* [From L. *terminus,* with meaning of term or appelation, and Gr. *logos,* discourse.] The science of technical terms; theory regarding the proper use of terms; collectively, the terms used in any art, science, and the like; nomenclature. ∴ Syn. under NOMENCLATURE.—**terminological,** tėr′min•o•loj″i•kal, *a.* Of or pertaining to terminology.—**terminologically,** tėr′min•o•loj″i•kal•li, *adv.* In a terminological manner; in the way of terminology.

terminus, tėr′mi•nus, *n.* pl. **termini,** tėr′mi•nī. [L. TERM.] A boundary; a limit; a landmark; the extreme station at either end of a railroad or important section of a railroad.

termite, tėr′mīt, *n.* [From L. *termes, termitis,* a woodworm.] An insect of the order Isoptera, commonly called white ants, which live in communities and destroy wood.

termless. See TERM.

tern, tėrn, *n.* [Dan. *terne,* Icel. *therna,* a tern.] A long-winged bird of the gull family, which, from its manner of flight, forked tail, and size, has received the name of *sea swallow.*

tern, tėrn, *a.* [L. *terni,* three each, from *ter,* thrice, *tres,* three.] Threefold; consisting of three.—**ternary,** tėr′na•ri, *a.* [L. *ternarius.*] Proceeding by threes; consisting of three; arranged in order by threes.—**ternate,** tėr′nāt, *a.* [L.L. *ternatus.*] Arranged in threes; *bot.* having three leaflets on a petiole.—**ternately,** tėr′nāt•li, *adv.* In a ternate manner.

Terpsichore, tėrp′sik′o•rē, *n.* [Greek name, from *terpō,* (fut. *terpsō*), to delight, and *choros,* dancing.] *Greek myth.* one of the Muses, the inventor and patroness of the art of dancing and lyrical poetry.—**Terpsichorean,** tėrp′si•kō•rē″an, *a.* Relating to Terpsichore.—*The Terpsichorean art,* dancing.

terra, ter′a, *n.* [L. *terra.* Hence *terrace, terrestrial, terrier, tureen, inter,* etc.] Earth; the earth.—*Terra firma,* firm or solid earth; dry land, in opposition to water.—*Terra incognita* (in-kog′ni•ta), an unknown or unexplored region.—*Terra japonica* (ja•pon′i•ka), catechu, formerly supposed to be a kind of earth from Japan, hence the name.—**terra cotta,** *n.* [It., lit. baked or cooked earth.] A mixture of fine clay and fine-grained white sand with crushed pottery, first slowly air dried, then baked in a kiln into the hardness of stone, much used for statues, figures, vases, etc.

terrace, ter′is, *n.* [Fr. *terrasse,* from L.L. *terracia,* from L. *terra,* earth. TERRA.] A raised level space or platform of earth, supported on one or more sides by masonry, a bank of turf, or the like; a level space on a sloping surface; a street or row of houses along the face or top of a slope; often applied arbitrarily.—*v.t.*—*terraced, terracing.* To form into a terrace; to cut into terraces.

terra cotta, ter′ä kot″ä, *n.* [It., lit., baked earth.] A fired clay used for statuettes, vases, architectural purposes, as roofing and ornamentation, etc.

terrain, te•rān′, *n.* [Fr. from L. *terrenus,* earth.] Any land area; a piece of earth or ground; the physical features of a piece of land.

terrapin, ter′a•pin, *n.* [Algonquin *torope,* turtle.] A name of several species of fresh-water tortoises, whose flesh is much esteemed.

terraqueous, ter•ak′wi•es, *a.* [From L. *terra,* land, and *aqua,* water. TERRA.] Consisting of land and water, as the globe or earth.

terrene, ter•ēn′, *a.* [L. *terrenus,* from *terra,* earth. TERRA.] Pertaining to the earth; earthy; terrestrial.

terreplein, ter′plān, *n.* [Fr.] *Fort.* that part of a rampart on which the guns are placed.

terrestrial, ter•es′tri•al, *a.* [L. *terrestris,* from *terra,* the earth. TERRA.] Pertaining to the earth; existing on this earth; earthly; as opposed to *celestial*; pertaining to the world; mundane; pertaining to land as opposed to water; confined to or living on land; opposed to *aquatic.*—*Terrestrial magnetism.* See MAGNETISM.—*n.* An inhabitant of the earth.

terrible, ter′ri•bl, *a.* [Fr. *terrible,* from L. *terribilis,* from *terreo,* to frighten.] Adapted to excite fear, awe, or dread; dreadful; formidable; excessive; extreme.—**terribleness,** ter′ri•bl•nes, *n.* The quality of being terrible.—**terribly,** ter′ri•bli, *adv.* In a terrible manner; dreadfully; excessively.

terricolous, ter•rik′o•lus, *a.* [L. *terra,* earth, *colo,* to inhabit.] Inhabiting the earth; living in the soil.

terrier, ter′i•ėr, *n.* [Fr. *terrier,* the hole of a rabbit, from *terre,* L. *terra,* the earth; equivalent therefore to burrow dog.] A small and courageous variety of dog that follows animals into their burrows or holes.

terrier, ter′i•ėr, *n.* [Fr. *terrier,* land-book.] A book in which landed property is registered and described.

terrify, ter′ri•fī, *v.t.*—*terrified, terrifying.* [L. *terreo,* to frighten, and *facio,* to make. TERRIBLE.] To frighten extremely; to alarm or shock with fear.—**terrific,** ter•rif′ik, *a.* [L. *terrificus.*] Dreadful; terrifying; causing terror.—**terrifically,** ter•rif′i•kal•li, *adv.* Terribly; frightfully.

terrigenous, ter•rij′en•us, *a.* [L. *terra,* the earth, and root *gen,* to bring forth.] Earth-born; produced by the earth.

territory, ter′ri•to•ri, *n.* [L. *territorium,* from *terra,* earth. TERRA.] Any separate tract of land as belonging to a state, city, or other body; a dominion; a region; a country; in the United States a region not yet admitted as a state into the Union, but with an organized government.—**territorial,** ter•ri•tō′ri•al *a.* Pertaining to a territory; limited to a certain district.—*n.* A member of the Territorial Army.—*Territorial Army* the force organized for home defense, levied in definite areas of territory.—**territorially,** ter•ri•tō′ri•al•li, *adv.* In regard to territory.

terror, ter′ror, *n.* [L. *terror,* from *terreo,* to frighten. TERRIBLE.] Fear that agitates the body and mind; dread; fright; the cause of extreme fear.—*King of terrors,* death.—*Reign of terror,* in the first French revolution, that period during which the rulers made the execution of all opponents the principle of their governments, extending from April, 1793, to July, 1794.—**terrorism,** ter′ror•izm, *n.* A system of government by terror; intimidation.—**terrorist,** ter′ror•ist, *n.* One who rules by intimidation.—**terrorize,** ter′ror•īz, *v.t.* To impress with terror; to repress or domineer over by means of terror.

terry, ter′i, *n.* [Fr. *tirer,* to draw.] A textile fabric with a long, smooth pile, such as plush or velvet.—**terry cloth,** a cloth or fabric with this type of pile.

terse, tėrs, *a.* [L. *tersus,* pp. of *tergo,* to rub or wipe.] Free from superfluity; neat and concise; pithy; said of style or language.—**tersely,** tėrs′li, *adv.* In a terse manner; concisely.—**terseness,** tėrs′nes, *n.* Neatness and conciseness of style.

tertial, tėr′shal, *a.* and *n.* [L. *tertius,* third.] A term applied to the feathers growing on the innermost joint of a bird's wing.

tertian, tėr′shan, *a.* [L. *tertianus,* from *tertius,* third.] *Med.* having its paroxysm every other day (a *tertian* fever).

tertiary, tėr′shi•e•ri, *a.* [L. *tertiarius,* from *tertius,* third, from *ter,* thrice, *tres,* three.] Of the third order, rank, or formation; third.—*Tertiary color,* a color produced by the mixture of two secondary colors.—*Tertiary formation, geol.* the third great division of stratified rocks, lying immediately above the Secondary and resting on the chalk, being followed by the post-Tertiary.—*n. Geol.* the Tertiary system of rocks; *ornith.* a tertial.

tessellated, tes′e•lā•ted, *a.* [L. *tessella,* a dim. of *tessera,* a square.] Formed by inlaying differently colored materials in little squares, triangles, or other geometrical figures, or by mosaic work.—**tessellation,** tes•e•lā′shon, *n.*

tessera, tes′e•ra, *n.* pl. **tesserae,** tes′e•rē. [L., a cube, a die.] A small cube of marble, precious stone, ivory, glass, wood, etc., used to form tessellated pavements and for like purposes; a small square of bone, wood, etc., used as a token or ticket in ancient Rome.

test, test, *n.* [O.Fr. *test* (Fr. *têt*), from L. *testum,* an earthen vessel, from *testa,* a shell. TESTY.] Any critical trial and examination; means of trial; a standard; a series of questions or exercises used as a means of measuring knowledge, reasoning capacity, skill, intelligence, etc., of an individual or group.—*v.t.* To bring to trial and examination; to prove by a fixed standard or by experiment. —**tester,** tes′tėr, *n.***test paper,** *n.* A paper impregnated with some chemical reagent, and serving to detect the presence of certain substances by change of color when they touch it.—**test tube,** *n.* A glass tube to contain substances to be chemically tested.

test, test, *n.* [L. *testa,* a shell, etc. See TEST above.] *Zool.* the outside hard covering of certain animals, as the shell of Mollusca or of the sea urchin; *bot.* the outer integument of a seed.—**testacean,** tes•tā′shen, *n.* A testaceous animal; a mollusk with a shell.—**testaceous,** tes•tā′shus, *a.* [L. *testaceus.*] Having a molluscous shell; having the character of a test or shell.

testacy. See TESTAMENT.

testament, tes′ta•ment, *n.* [L. *testamentum,* from *testor,* to be a witness, to make a will, from *testis,* a witness; similarly *testify, testimony, attest, contest,* etc.] *Law,* a duly executed document in writing, by which a person declares his will as to the disposal of his estate and effects after his death; a will; [*cap.*] the name of each general division of the canonical books of the sacred Scriptures (the Old *Testament,* the New *Testament*): when used alone the word is often limited to the New Testament.—**testamentary,** tes•te•men′te•ri, *a.* Pertaining to a will or to wills; bequeathed or arranged by will.—**testate,** tes′tāt, *a.* [L. *testatus.*] Having made and left a will.—**testacy,** tes′ta•si, *n.* The state of being testate.—**testator,** tes•tā′ter, *n.* A man who makes and leaves a will at death.—**testatrix,** tes•tā′triks, *n.* [L.] A woman who makes and leaves a will at death.

tester, tes′tėr, *n.* [O.Fr. *testiere,* a headpiece, from *teste* (Fr. *tête*) a head, from L. *testa,* an earthen pot, the skull, the head. TEST.] The square canopy over a four-post bedstead; a flat canopy, as over a pulpit, tomb, and the like; an old French silver coin, so named from the *teste* (head) upon it.

testes, tes′tēz, *n. pl.* [L.] *Anat.* the testicles.

testicle, tes′ti•kl, *n.* [L. *testiculus,* dim. of *testis,* a testicle.] One of the glands which secrete the seminal fluid in males.—**testicular, testiculate,** tes•tik′ū•lėr, tes•tik′ū•lit, *a. Bot.* shaped like a testicle.

testify, tes′ti•fī, *v.i.*—*testified, testifying.* [O.Fr. *testifier,* from L. *testificari*—*testis,* a witness, and *facio,* to make. TESTAMENT.] To make a solemn declaration, verbal or written to establish some fact; *law,* to give evidence under oath; to declare a charge.—*v.t.* To affirm or declare solemnly; *law,* to affirm under oath before a tribunal, for the purpose of proving some fact.—**testification,** tes′ti•fi•kā″shon, *n.* [L. *testificatio.*] The act of testifying or giving evidence.—**testifier,** tes′ti•fī•ėr, *n.* One who testifies.

testily, testiness. See TESTY.

testimony, tes′ti•mo•ni, *n.* [L. *testimonium,* from *testis,* a witness. TESTAMENT.] A solemn declaration or affirmation made for the purpose of establishing or proving some fact; evidence; declaration; attestation; witness; anything equivalent to a declaration or protest; divine revelation.—**testimonial,** tes•ti•mō′ni•al, *n.* A certificate in favor of someone's character; a certificate of qualifications; a gift or token of appreciation raised by subscription in acknowledgment of an individual's services, or to show respect for his worth.

testis, tes′tis, *n.* pl. **testes,** tes′tēz. [L., witness.] A testicle.

teston, testoon, tes′tön, *n.* [It. *testone.*] An early silver coin of several European countries.

testudo, tes•tū′dō, *n.* [L., from *testa,* a shell.] Among the ancient Romans a cover from missiles formed by soldiers holding their shields over their heads and standing close to each other; *zool.* the land tortoise.—**testudinal,** tes•tū′di•nal, *a.* Pertaining to the tortoise.—**testudinarious,** tes•tū′di•nâ″ri•us, *a.* Resembling a tortoiseshell in color.—**testudinate,** tes•tū′di•nit, *a.* Resembling the back of a tortoise; arched; vaulted.

testy, tes′ti, *a.* [O.Fr. *testu* (Fr. *têtu*), headstrong, willful, from *teste* (Fr. *tête*), the head, from L. *testa,* potsherd, shell. TEST, TESTER.] Fretful; peevish; easily irritated.—**testily,** tes′ti•li, *adv.* In a testy manner; fretfully.—**testiness,** tes′ti•nes, *n.* The state or quality of being testy.

tetanus, tet′a•nus, *n.* [Gr. *tetanos,* tetanus, from *teinō,* to stretch. THIN.] A disease caused by the tetanus bacillus and characterized by spasm of voluntary muscles, especially of the jaw.

tetchy, tech′i. See TECHY.

tête-à-tête, tāt•e•tāt, *adv.* [Fr., lit. head to head.] Face to face; in private; in close confabulation.—*n.* A private interview with no one present but the parties concerned.

tether, teTH′ėr, *n.* [Same as Icel. *tjóthr,* a tether, *tjóthra,* to tether; O.Fris. *tieder,* L.G. *tider,* O.Sw. *tiuther,* cord, tether; from same root as to *tie.*] A rope or chain by which a grazing animal is confined within certain limits; *fig.,* range of opportunity.—*v.t.* To confine with a tether.

tetrabranchiate, tet•ra•brang′ki•āt, *a.* [Gr. *tetra-,* four, and *branchia,* gills.] Having four gills: applied to an order of cephalopods.

tetrachord, tet′ra•kord, *n.* [Gr. *tetrachordon*—*tetra-,* four, and *chordē,* a chord.] A scale of four notes; half of the octave scale.

tetrad, tet′rad, *n.* [Gr. *tetras, tetrados,* the number four.] The number four; a collection of four things.

tetradynamous, tet•ra•din′a•mus, *a.* [Gr. *tetra-,* four, and *dynamis,* power.] *Bot.* having hermaphrodite flowers with six stamens, four longer than the other two.

tetragon, tet′ra•gon, *n.* [Gr. *tetragōnon*—*tetra-,* four, and *gōnia,* an angle.] *Geom.* a figure having four angles; a quadrangle, as a square, a rhombus, etc.—**tetragonal,** te•trag′on•al, *a.* Having four angles or sides; of a system of crystals having all three axes equal, and two of them at right angles to each other.

tetrahedron, tet•ra•hē′dron, *n.* [Gr. *tetra-,* four, and *hedra,* a base.] A triangular pyramid having four equal and equilateral faces; a solid bounded by four equal triangles.—**tetrahedral,** tet•ra•hē′dral, *a.* Having the form of a tetrahedron.—**tetrahedrite,** tet•ra•hē′drīt, *n.* Fahlerz.

tetralogy, te•tral′o•ji, *n.* [Gr. *tetralogia*—*tetra-,* four, and *logos,* discourse.] A collection of four dramatic compositions, three tragic and one satiric, which were exhibited together on the Athenian stage.

tetramerous, te•tram′ėr•us, *a.* [Gr. *tetra-,* four, and *meros,* a part.] Consisting of four parts; *bot.* having the parts in fours; *entom.* having four-jointed tarsi.

tetrameter, te•tram′et•ėr, *n.* [Gr. *tetra-,* four, and *metron,* measure.] *Pros.* a verse consisting of four measures.

tetrander, te•tran′dėr, *n.* [Gr. *tetra-,* four, and *anēr, andros,* a male.] *Bot.* a monoclinous or hermaphrodite plant having four stamens.—**tetrandrous,** te•tran′drus, *a. Bot.* monoclinous or hermaphrodite and having four stamens.

tetrapetalous, tet•ra•pet′al•us, *a.* [Gr. *tetra-,* four, and *petalon,* a leaf.] *Bot.* containing four distinct petals.

tetrapteran, te•trap′tėr•an, *n.* [Gr. *tetra-,* four, and *pteron,* a wing.] An insect which has four wings.—**tetrapterous,** te•trap′tėr•us, *a.* Having four wings.

tetrarch, tet′rärk, *n.* [Gr. *tetrarchēs*—*tetra-,* four, and *archē,* rule.] A Roman governor of the fourth part of a province; a petty king or sovereign.—**tetrarchate, tetrarchy,** tet′rär•kāt, tet′rär•ki, *n.* The office or jurisdiction of a tetrarch, or the district under his rule.

tetraspore, tet′ra•spōr, *n.* [Gr. *tetra-,* four, and E. *spore.*] *Bot.* among the algae a collection of spores, of which usually there are four.

tetrastich, te•tras′tik, *n.* [Gr. *tetra-,* four, and *stichos,* verse.] A stanza or poem in four verses (or lines).

tetrasyllable, tet′ra•sil•a•bl, *n.* [Gr. *tetra-*, four, and *syllabē*, syllable.] A word consisting of four syllables.—**tetrasyllabic, tetrasyllabical,** tet′-ra•si•lab″ik, tet′ra•si•lab″i•kal, *a.* Consisting of four syllables.

tetratomic, tet•ra•tom′ik, *a.* [Gr. *tetra-*, four, and E. *atomic.*] Such that one atom in composition is equivalent to four atoms of hydrogen.

tetravalent, tet•ra•vāl′ent, *a.* See QUADRIVALENT.

tetter, tet′ėr, *n.* [A.Sax. *tetr*, G. *zitter*, tetter; comp. Skr. *dadru*, tetter.] A vague name of several cutaneous diseases affecting man, as herpes, impetigo, etc.; a cutaneous disease of animals, which may be communicated to man.

Teutonic, tū•ton′ik, *a.* [L. *Teutones*, the Teutons; a Latinized form of their native name; akin *Dutch.*] Belonging to the Teutons or the peoples of Germanic origin in general; Germanic; pertaining to the languages spoken by these peoples, which include Gothic, Anglo-Saxon and English, Dutch, German, Icelandic, Norse, Danish, and Swedish.—*n.* The language or languages collectively of the Teutons.

text, tekst, *n.* [Fr. *texte*, from L. *textus*, a tissue, a text, from *texo*, *textum*, to weave.] The main part of a written work; the original words of a writer, as distinct from a translation, abridgment, etc.; a selection from Scripture, usually as a subject for a sermon, etc.; any theme; an authority for something; a textbook. —**textbook,** tekst′bu̥k, *n.* A book used by a student in some branch of study. —**texthand,** *n.* A large hand in writing.—**textual,** teks′chū-al, *a.* Pertaining to or contained in the text.—**textualist,** teks′chū•al•ist, *n.* One who can readily quote texts; one who adheres strictly to a text.—**textually,** teks′chū•al•li, *adv.* In accordance with the text; placed in the text of a work.—**textuary,** teks′chū•a•ri, *a.* Textual.

textile, teks′til, *a.* [L. *textilis*, from *texo*, to weave. TEXT.] Woven or capable of being woven; formed by weaving.—*n.* A fabric made by weaving.

textual, etc. See TEXT.

texture, teks′chėr, *n.* [L. *textura*, from *texo*, *textum*, to weave. TEXT.] A fabric formed by weaving; the disposition or connection of threads or filaments interwoven; the disposition of the elementary constituent parts of any solid body; the grain or peculiar character of a solid.

thalamus, thal′a•mus, *n.* pl. **thalami,** thal′a•mī. [Gr. *thalamos*, a bedroom.] A part in the brain at the origin of the optic nerve; *bot.* the receptacle of a flower or part on which the carpels are placed.

thaler, tä′lėr, *n.* [G. DOLLAR.] A former German coin, value 3 marks.

Thalia, thāl′ya, *n.* [Gr. *Thaleia.*] The Muse of comedy and the patroness of pastoral and comic poetry.

thallium, thal′i•um, *n.* [Gr. *thallos*, a young green shoot—from the green line it gives in the spectrum.] A rare metallic element, soft and malleable, resembling lead, and having poisonous compounds. Symbol, Tl; at. no., 81; at. wt., 204.37.—**thallic, thallious,** thal′ik, thal′i•us, *a. Chem.* pertaining to or containing thallium.

thallophyte, thal′o•fīt, *n.* [Gr. *thallos*, young shoot, *phyton*, plant.] Any one of the lowest phylum (Thallophyta) of plants, comprising the algae, bacteria, lichens, and fungi; with some minor groups.

Thammuz, tä′mu̥z, *n.* [Heb.] The tenth month of the Jewish civil year, answering to part of June and part of July; a Syrian deity for whom the Hebrew idolatresses held an annual feast or lamentation; supposed identical with Adonis.

than, THan, *conj.* [Originally same as *then*; 'this is better *than* that' is equivalent to 'this is better *then* that'.] A particle used after certain adjectives and adverbs which express comparison or diversity, such as *more, better, other, otherwise, rather, else*, etc., for the purpose of introducing the second member of the comparison: sometimes used to govern an objective like a preposition.

thanatoid, than′a•toid, *a.* [Gr. *thanatos*, death, and *eidos*, resemblance.] Resembling death; deathlike. —**thanatopsis,** than•a•top′sis, *n.* [Gr. *opsis*, a view.] A view or contemplation of death.

thane, thān, *n.* [A.Sax. *thegen, thegn, thén*, a thane=Icel. *thegen*, a warrior; O.H.G. *degan*, G. *degen*, a warrior; akin to O.E. *thee*, A.Sax. *theón*, to thrive.] A title of honor among the Anglo-Saxons; an Anglo-Saxon baron; a landed proprietor.

thanks, thangks, *n.* pl. [A.Sax. *thanc*, Goth. *thagks*, Icel. *thōkk*, D. and G. *dank*, thanks; from stem of *think.*] Expressions of gratitude; kind thoughts; a shortened form of *thank you.*—**thank,** thangk, *v.t.* To express one's gratitude to for a favor; to make acknowledgments to for kindness bestowed.—*I will thank you*, a phrase of civility introducing a request.—*Thank you*, a colloquial or informal contraction of the phrase *I thank you.*—**thankful,** thangk′fu̥l, *a.* Impressed with a sense of kindness received and ready to acknowledge it; grateful; expressive of thanks.—**thankfully,** thangk′fu̥l•li, *adv.* Gratefully.—**thankfulness,** thangk′fu̥l•nes, *n.* Gratefulness; gratitude.—**thankless,** thangk′les, *a.* Unthankful; ungrateful; not deserving or not likely to gain thanks (a *thankless* task).—**thanklessly,** thangk′les•li, *adv.* In a thankless manner.—**thanklessness,** thangk′les•nes, *n.* — **thanksgiving,** thangks′giv•ing, *n.* The act of rendering thanks; a public celebration of divine goodness; [*cap.*] a day set apart for such a celebration; a form of words expressive of thanks to God.—**thankworthy,** thangk′wėr•THi, *a.* Worthy of or deserving thanks; meritorious.

that, THat, *a.* and *pron.* pl. **those,** THōz. [A.Sax. *thaet*, neut. of the demonstrative and def. art. *the* or *se* and=Goth. *thata*, Icel. *that*, D. *dat*, G. *das*, Skr. *tat*; akin *the, these, this, there*, etc. THE.] A word used as pointing to a person or thing before mentioned or supposed to be understood (*that* man, *that* city); frequently used in opposition to *this* (I will take *this* book, you can take *that* one): often used without a noun as a demonstrative pronoun, and also as a relative pronoun, in many cases equivalent to *who* or *which*; *who* being generally used for persons, *which* for things, and *that* for either. When governed by a preposition the latter is put at the end of the clause (the book *that* I read *from*).—*conj.* Introducing a reason: because (not *that* I care); introducing an end or purpose (speak *that* I may hear); introducing a result or consequence (so weak *that* he cannot stand); introducing a clause as the subject or object of the principal verb (we know *that* he is dead).—*adv.* To such a degree or extent (it was *that* large).

thatch, thach, *n.* [A.Sax. *thaec*, thatch, *theccan*, to thatch; Icel. *thak*, a roof, thatch; D. *dak*, G. *dach*, a roof; Dan. *daekke*, D. *dekken*, G. *decken*, to cover; same root as L. *tego*, *tectum*, to cover, Gr. *tegos*, *stegos*, a roof, Skr. *sthag*, to cover. *Deck* is allied.] Straw, rushes, reeds, heath, etc., used to cover the roofs of buildings or stacks of hay or grain.—*v.t.* To cover with straw, reeds, or some similar substance.—**thatcher,** thach′ėr, *n.* One who thatches.

thaumatrope, tha̤′ma•trōp, *n.* [Gr. *thauma*, *thaumatos*, a wonder, and *trepō*, to turn.] An optical toy, which by revolving causes two pictures to seem connected.

thaumaturgy, tha̤′ma•tėr•ji, *n.* [Gr. *thaumatourgia*—*thauma*, *thaumatos*, a wonder, and *ergon*, work.] The act of performing something wonderful; wonder-working; magic; legerdemain.—**thaumaturge, thaumaturgist,** tha̤′ma•tėrj, tha̤′ma•tėr•jist, *n.* A dealer in miracles; a miracle worker.—**thaumaturgic, thaumaturgical,** tha̤•ma•tėr′jik, tha̤•ma•tėr′-ji•kal, *a.* Pertaining to thaumaturgy.

thaw, tha̤, *v.i.* [A.Sax. *tháwan*, to thaw, Icel. *thá*, a thaw, *theyja*, to thaw; D. *dooi*, thaw, *dooijen*, to thaw; G. *thauen*, to melt, to thaw; comp. Gr. *tēkō*, to melt.] To melt, as ice or snow; to become so warm as to melt ice and snow: said of the weather, and used impersonally; *fig.* to become less cold, formal, or reserved; to become genial.—*v.t.* To melt ice or snow; to make less cold or reserved.—*n.* The melting of ice or snow; warmth of weather, such as liquefies ice.

the, THē or THi, *def. art.* or *definitive a.* [A.Sax. *the*, masc. nom. corresponding to *that*=O.Sax. and O.Fris. *the*, D. and L.G. *de*, Sw. and Dan. *den*, G. *der*. The *the* before comparatives represents the A.Sax. instrumental case *thi, thý.*] Used before nouns with a specifying or limiting effect (*the* laws of our country); used before a noun in the singular number to denote a species by way of distinction or a single thing representing the whole (*the* elephant is sagacious); prefixed to adjectives to give them the force of abstract nouns (a passion for *the* sublime and beautiful); used before adjectives and adverbs in the comparative degree it means by that; by how much; by so much (*the longer* we continue in sin *the more difficult* it is to reform).

theanthropism, thē•an′thro•pizm, *n.* [Gr. *theos,* God, and *anthrōpos,* man.] A state of being God and man; a conception of God or of gods as possessing qualities essentially human.

thearchy, thē′är•ki, *n.* [Gr. *theos,* God, and *archē,* rule.] Government by God; theocracy; a body of deities or divine rulers.

theater, theatre, thē′e•tėr, *n.* [Fr. *théâtre,* from L. *theatrum,* from Gr. *theatron,* from *theaomai,* to see, *thea,* a view.] A building for the representation of dramatic spectacles; a playhouse; a room with seats rising stepwise for public lectures, anatomical demonstrations, etc.; the locality where events take place (the *theater* of war).—**theatric, theatrical,** thi•at′rik, thi•at′ri•kal, *a.* Pertaining to a theater or to scenic representations; calculated for display; meretricious; artificial; false.—**theatrically,** thi•at′ri•kal•li, *adv.* In a theatrical manner.—**theatricals,** thi•at′ri•kalz, *n. pl.* A dramatic performance, especially in a private house.—**theatrics,** thi•at′riks, *n. Plural in form but takes singular construction.* That skill which is involved in the writing, directing and staging of a dramatic presentation; stagecraft; dramaturgy.

theca, thē′ka, *n.* pl. **thecae,** thē′sē. [L., from Gr. *thēkē,* a case.] A sheath or hollow case; *bot.* the spore-case of ferns, mosses, and other cryptogams. —**thecal,** thē′kal, *a.* Pertaining to a theca.

thee, THē, *pron.* [A.Sax. *thé,* dat. and accus. of *thu,* thou.] The objective and dative case of *thou.*

theft, theft, *n.* [A.Sax. *theōfthe,* theft, from *theōf,* a thief. Final *th* became *t* as in *height.*] The wrongfully taking away the goods of another with intent to deprive him of them; the act of stealing.

theine, thein, thē′in, *n.* [From *Thea,* the generic name of the tea plant.] A bitter principle found in tea, coffee, and some other plants; caffeine.

their, THâr, *a.* [From Icel. *theirra,* their=A.Sax. *thaera,* of them: the genitive pl. of which *the, that,* are nominatives.] Pertaining or belonging to them.—**theirs,** THârz. A possessive or genitive, properly a double genitive of *they,* used without a noun following, either as a nominative, objective, or simple predicate.

theism, thē′izm, *n.* [Fr. *théisme,* from Gr. *theos,* God, seen also in *theocracy, theology, atheism,* etc.] The belief or acknowledgment of the existence of a God, as opposed to *atheism.*— **theist,** thē′ist, *n.* One who believes in the existence of a God. ∴ Syn. under DEIST.—**theistic, theistical,** thē•is′tik, thē•is′ti•kal, *a.* Pertaining to theism or to a theist.

them, THem, *pron.* [Originally a dative corresponding to *their*=Icel. *theim,* A.Sax. *thám.*] The dative and objective case of *they;* those persons or things; those.—**themselves,** THem•selvz′, *pron.* pl. of *himself, herself, itself.*

theme, thēm, *n.* [Gr. *thema,* a proposition, a theme, a root word, from Gr. *tithēmi,* to place.] A subject or topic on which a person writes or speaks; a subject of discourse or discussion; a short dissertation composed by a student on a given subject; *philol.* the part of a noun or a verb unchanged in declension or conjugation; *mus.* a series of notes selected as the text or subject of a new composition; the leading subject in a composition or movement.— **thematic,** thē•mat′ik, *a.* Relating to a theme or themes.

theme, thēm, *n.* [Gr. *thema.*] One of the provinces, twenty-nine in number, of the old Byzantine Empire.

then, THen, *adv.* [A.Sax. *thenne, thanne, thonne,* then, an acc. form belonging to the pronominal stem *the, thaet;* same word as *than.*] At that time, referring to a time specified, either past or future; soon afterward or immediately; at another time (now and *then*).—*By then,* by the time when or that.—*Till then,* until that time. Often used elliptically, like an adjective, for *then existing;* but this usage is discountenanced by careful writers.—*conj.* In that case; in consequence; therefore; for this reason.

thenar, thē′nar, *n.* [Gr. *thenar,* from *thenō,* to strike.] *Anat.* the palm of the hand or the sole of the foot.— **thenal,** thē′nal, *a.* Pertaining to the thenar.

thence, THens, *adv.* [O.E. *thens, thennes, thannes,* genitive forms from A.Sax. *thanan, thonon,* thence; comp. *hence, whence.*] From that place; from that time; for that reason; from this; out of this; not there; elsewhere; absent.—*From thence,* though pleonastic, is supported by custom and good usage.—**thenceforth,** THens′fōrth, *adv.* From that time forward. —**thenceforward,** THens′for•wėrd, *adv.* From that time or place onward.

theobromine, thē•ō•brō′min, *n.* [From *Theobroma,* the generic name of the cacao tree—Gr. *theos,* God, and *brōma,* food.] A crystalline compound found in the seeds of cacao, analogous to theine.

theocracy, thē•ok′ra•si, *n.* [Gr. *theokratia*—*theos,* God, and *kratos,* power.] Government of a state by the immediate direction of God; the state thus governed.—**theocrat,** thē′o•krat, *n.* One who lives under a theocracy.— **theocratic, theocratical,** thē•o•krat′ik, thē•o•krat′i•kal, *a.* Pertaining to a theocracy; administered by the immediate direction of God.

theocrasy, thē•ok′ra•si, *n.* [Gr. *theos,* God, and *krasis,* mixture.] An intimate union of the soul with God in contemplation; a mixture of the worship of different gods.

theodicy, thē•od′i•si, *n.* [Gr. *theos,* God, and *dikē,* justice.] A vindication of the ways of God with a theory as to the existence of evil; a doctrine as to the being, attributes, and government of God, and the immortality of the soul.

theodolite, thē•od′o•līt, *n.* [Origin doubtful; perhaps from Gr. *thea,* a seeing, *hodos,* way, and *litos,* smooth.] A surveying instrument for measuring horizontal and vertical angles by means of a telescope the movements of which can be accurately marked on two graduated circles.—**theodolitic,** thē•od′o•lit″ik, *a.* Pertaining to a theodolite; made by a theodolite.

theogony, thē•og′o•ni, *n.* [Gr. *theogonia*—*theos,* a god, and *gone,* generation.] A poem treating of the generation and descent of gods; doctrine as to the genealogy or origin of heathen deities.—**theogonic,** thē•o•gon′ik, *a.* Relating to theogony.

theology, thē•ol′o•ji, *n.* [Gr. *theologia* —*theos,* God, and *logos,* discourse.] The science of divine things or of the Christian religion; the science which treats of God and man in all their known relations to each other. —**theologian,** thē•o•lō′ji•an, *n.* A person well versed in theology; a divine. —**theologic, theological,** thē•o•loj′ik, thē•o•loj′i•kal, *a.* Pertaining to theology.—**theologically,** thē•o•loj′i•kal•li, *adv.* In a theological manner; according to theology.—**theologize,** thē•ol′o•jīz, *v.i.*—*theologized, theologizing.* To theorize or speculate upon theological subjects.—**theologizer,** thē•ol′o•jī•zėr, *n.* One who theologizes.

theomachy, thē•om′a•ki, *n.* [Gr. *theos,* a god, and *machē,* combat.] A fighting against the gods; a strife or battle among the gods.

theopathy, thē•op′a•thi, *n.* [Gr. *theos,* God, and *pathos,* passion.] Emotion excited by the contemplation of God; piety, or a sense of piety.—**theopathetic, theopathic,** thē′o•pa•thet″ik, thē•o•path′ik, *a.* Relating to theopathy.

theophany, thē•of′a•ni, *n.* [Gr. *theos,* God, and *phainomai,* to appear.] A manifestation of God to man by actual appearance in the form of man.

theorbo, thē•or′bō, *n.* [It. *tiorba,* Fr. *téorbe.*] A musical instrument somewhat like a large lute, with two necks, to one of which the bass strings were attached.

theorem, thē′o•rem, *n.* [Gr. *theōrēma,* from *theōreō,* to look, to view. THEORY.] A position laid down as an acknowledged truth or established principle; *math.* a proposition to be proved by a chain of reasoning; *alg.* and *analysis,* a rule expressed by symbols or formulae (the binomial *theorem*).—**theorematic,** the′o•re•mat″ik, *a.* Pertaining to a theorem; comprised in a theorem.

theory, thē′o•ri, *n.* [L. *theōria,* a theory, from Gr. *theoria,* a looking at, theory, from *theōreō,* to see, from *theōros,* an observer.] A supposition explaining something; a doctrine or scheme of things resting merely on speculation; hypothesis; plan or system suggested; an exposition of the general or abstract principles of any science (the *theory* of music or of medicine); the science or rules of an art, as distinguished from the practice; a philosophical explanation of phenomena; a connected arrangement of facts according to their bearing on some real or hypothetical law or laws.—**theoretic, theoretical,** thē•o•ret′ik, the•o•ret′i•kal, *a.* [Gr. *theorētikos.*] Pertaining to theory; depending on theory or speculation; speculative; not practical.—**theoretically,** thē•o•ret′i•kal•li, *adv.* In or by theory; in speculation; speculatively; not practically.—**theoretics,** thē•o•ret′iks, *n. pl.* The speculative parts of a science; speculation.—**theorist, theorizer,** thē′o•rist, thē′o•rī•zėr, *n.* One who forms theories.—**theorize,** thē′o•rīz, *v.i.*—*theorized, theorizing.* To form a theory; to form opinions solely by theory; to speculate.

theosophy, thē•os′o•fi, *n.* [Gr. *theosophia,* knowledge of divine things—*theos,* God, and *sophia,* wisdom, from *sophos,* wise.] Knowledge of divine things; a knowledge of the Divine Being obtained by spiritual ecstasy, direct intuition, or special individual relations.—**theosophic, theosophical,** thē•o•sof′ik, thē•o•sof′i•kal, *a.* Pertaining to theosophy.—**theosophically,** thē•o•sof′i•kal•li, *adv.* In a theosophical manner; with direct divine illumination.—**theosophism,** thē•os′of•izm, *n.* Pretension to divine illumination.—**theosophist,** thē•os′of•ist, *n.* One who pretends to divine illumination, or to derive his knowledge from divine revelation.

therapeutic, therapeutical, ther•a•pū′tik, ther•a•pū′ti•kal, *a.* [Gr. *therapeutikos,* from *therapeuō,* to nurse, serve, or cure.] Curative; pertaining to the healing art.—**therapeutics,** ther•a•pū′tiks, *n.* That part of medicine which relates to the composition, application, and operation of remedies.—**therapeutist,** ther•a•pū′tist, *n.* One versed in therapeutics.—**therapy,** ther′a•pi, *n.* Therapeutics, as in *electrotherapy.*

there, THâr, *adv.* [A.Sax. *ther, thaer,* there, a locative case of the pronominal stem *the, that, then,* etc. In *thereafter, thereby,* etc., the dative case fem. sing. of the definite article.] In that place; at that place: often opposed to *here, there* generally denoting the place most distant; in that object or matter; at that point; after going to such a length; into that place; to that place; thither; often used to begin sentences before a verb when there is an inversion of the subject (*there* came many strangers to the town).—*Here and there, neither here nor there.* See HERE.—**thereabout, thereabouts,** THâr′a•bout, THâr′a•bouts, *adv.* Near that place; near that number, degree, or quantity.—**thereafter,** THâr•af′tėr, *adv.* According to that; accordingly; after that; afterward.—**thereat,** THâr•at′, *adv.* At that place; at that place or event; on that account.—**thereby,** THâr•bī′, *adv.* By that; by that means; annexed or attached to that; by or near that place; near that number or quantity.—**therefor,** THâr•for′, *adv.* For that or this or it.—**therefore,** THâr′for, *conj.* or *adv.* [*There,* the dat. sing. fem. of the old def. art., and *for.*] For that or this reason, referring to something previously stated; consequently; in return or recompense for this or that.—**therefrom,** THâr•from′, *adv.* From this or that.

therein, THâr•in′, *adv.* In that or this place, time, or thing; in that or this particular point or respect.—**thereinto,** THâr•in•tö′, *adv.* Into that or that place.—**thereof,** THâr•ov′, *adv.* Of that or this.—**thereon,** THâr•on′, *adv.* On that or this; thereupon.—**thereto, thereunto,** THâr•tö′, THâr•un•tö′, *adv.* To that or this.—**theretofore,**† THâr•tu̧•fōr′, *adv.* Before that time; the counterpart of *heretofore.*—**thereunder,** THâr•un′dėr, *adv.* Under that or this.—**thereupon,** THâr•up•on′, *adv.* Upon that or this; in consequence of that; at once; without delay.—**therewith,** THâr•with′, *adv.* With that or this.—**therewithal,** THâr•with•a̧l′, *adv.* With that or this; therewith.

theriac, thi′ri•ak, *n.* [L.*theriac a,* Gr. *thēriakē,* from *thērion,* a wild beast.] A name given anciently to various substances esteemed efficacious against the effects of animal or other poison.—**theriacal,** thi•rī′a•kal, *a.* Medicinal; serving as an antidote.

theriomorphic, thē•ri•o•mor′fik, *a.* [Gr. *thērion,* animal, *morphē,* shape.] Having the form of an animal.

therm, therm, *n.* [Gr. *thermos,* hot.] A unit of heat, equal to 100,000 British thermal units.—**thermal, thermic,** thėr′mal, thėr′mik, *a.* Pertaining to heat; warm.—*Thermal springs, thermal waters,* hot springs.—*Thermal capacity.* See CAPACITY.

thermionic, thėr′mi•on″ik, *a.* [Gr. *therm* and *ion.*] Pertaining to electrons emitted by heating an electrode to incandescence.—*Thermionic valve,* an exhausted glass bulb with two or more, usually three, electrodes, viz. the metal plate, or anode, the grid, and filament. The filament when heated gives off electrons, which have a negative charge, so that a positive current of electricity can flow from plate to filament, but not in the reverse direction. The valve is important in wireless telegraphy and telephony.—**thermally,** thėr′mal•li, *adv.* In a thermal manner; with reference to heat.—**thermochemistry,** *n.* That branch of chemistry in which heat is of importance.

thermodynamics, thėr′mō•di•nam″iks, *n.* pl. [Gr. *thermo* and *dynamic.*] The branch of physics concerned with heat and its relation to mechanical energy and with the conversion of one to the other.—**thermodynamic,** thėr′mō•di•na″mik, *a.*

thermoelectricity, thėr′mō•e•lek•tri″si•ti, *n.* [Gr. *thermo* and *electricity.*] Electricity produced from the direct action of heat.—**thermoelectric,** thėr′mō•ē•lek″trik, *a.*—**thermoelectric couple,** *n.* The connection of two dissimilar conductors for the production of thermoelectricity, when there is a temperature difference between the two conductors.—**thermocouple,** thėr″mō•cup′l, *n.* A thermoelectric couple. —**thermograph,** thėr′mo•graf, *n.* An instrument for automatically recording variations of temperature.—**thermometer,** thėr•mom′et•ėr, *n.* [Gr. *thermos,* warm, and *metron,* measure.] An instrument by which the temperatures of bodies are ascertained, usually a closed glass tube containing mercury or alcohol, which expands or contracts in accordance with the variations of temperature.—**thermometric, thermometrical,** thėr•mo•met′rik, thėr•mo•met′ri•kal, *a.* Pertaining to a thermometer; made by a thermometer.—**thermometry,** thėr•mom′ė•tri, *n.* The measurement of temperature.

thermonuclear, thėr′mō•nū″kli•ėr, *a.* [Gr. *thermo* and *nuclear.*] Concerning changes in the nucleus of atoms that require extremely high temperatures for their inception; pertaining to a thermonuclear bomb.

thermopile, thėr′mo•pīl, *n.* An instrument that measures minute degrees of temperature.

thermoplastic, thėr′mo•plas″tik, *a.* [Gr. *thermo* and *plastic.*] Becoming plastic when heated and hardening again when cooled.

Thermos, thėr′mos, *n.* [A trademark.] A vacuum bottle which maintains the temperature of liquids.

thermoscope, thėr′mo•skōp, *n.* An instrument that indicates temperature changes and measures heat effects.

thermostat, thėr′mō•stat, *n.* [Gr. *thermo* and *stat,* from N.L. *stata* from Gr. *statēs,* one that stops.] An automatic device used to maintain a steady temperature, as in a room or in an automobile engine, usually by turning a heating or cooling system off and on.

thesaurus, thi•sa̧′rus, *n.* [L. *thesaurus,* from Gr. *thesauros,* from (*ti*)*thēmi,* to place.] A treasury; a lexicon or treasury of words.

these, THēz, *pron.* and *a.,* pl. of *this.*

thesis, thē′sis, *n.* pl. **theses,** thē′sēz. [L. *thesis,* Gr. *thesis,* a position, from (*ti*)*thēmi,* to set.] A position or proposition which a person advances and maintains; a subject propounded for a school or college exercise; the exercise itself; an essay or dissertation; *pros.* the part of a foot on which the depression of the voice falls: opposed to *arsis.*

Thespian, thes′pi•an, *a.* [From *Thespis,* who played an important part in the early history of the drama in Greece about B.C. 535.] Relating to Thespis, or [*sometimes not cap.*] to dramatic acting in general; hence, the *Thespian art* is equivalent to *the drama.*

theta, thā′ta, thē′ta, *n.* [Gr. *thēta,* of Semitic origin.] The eighth letter of the Greek alphabet.

theurgy, thē′ėr•ji, *n.* [Gr. *theourgia,* from *theos,* a god, and *ergon,* work.] The working of some divine or supernatural agency in human affairs; a working or producing effects by spiritual means; magic.—**theurgic, theurgical,** thē•ėr'jik, thē•ėr'ji•kal, *a.* Pertaining to theurgy.—**theurgist,** thē'ėr•jist, *n.* One who pretends to theurgy.

thews, thūz, *n. pl.* [Perhaps same as A.Sax. *theáwas,* manners, habits.] Muscles, sinews, strength.—**thewy,** thū'i, *a.* Brawny; muscular.

they, THā, *pron.*; poss. case *their,* obj. case *them.* [Partly from A.Sax. *thá,* nom. pl. of the def. art., partly from Icel. *their,* they, nom. pl. of the pers. pron.] The pl. form for *he, she,* or *it,* thus denoting more than one person or thing.

thiamine, thī'a•min, *n.* [Gr. *thi,* combining form, and *amine* (*ammonia* and suffix *ine*).] A B-complex vitamin necessary for the metabolism and for nerve function; vitamin B.

thick, thik, *a.* [A.Sax. *thicce*=O.Fris. *thikke,* Icel. *thykkr,* Dan. *tyk,* D. *dik,* G. *dick,* thick.] Having more or less extent measured through and through or otherwise than in length or breadth: said of solid bodies; relatively of great dimensions when thus measured: opposed to *thin, slender, slim*; dense; having great consistence (*thick* fog or smoke); foggy or misty; close set or planted; closely crowded together; close; following each other closely (blows *thick* as hail); without due flexibility of articulation (*thick* utterance); stupid; gross; very friendly or familiar (*colloq.*).—*n.* The thickest part, or the time when anything is thickest.—*Thick and thin,* whatever is in the way; all obstacles or hindrances.—*adv.* In close succession one upon another; fast or close together.—**thicken,** thik'n, *v.t.* To make thick or thicker.—*v.i.* To become thick or thicker.—**thickening,** thik'n•ing, *n.* Something put into a liquid or mass to make it more thick.—**thicket,** thik'et, *n.* [Comp. G. *dickicht,* from *dick,* thick.] A wood or collection of trees or shrubs closely set.—**thickhead,** *n.* A stupid fellow; a blockhead; a numskull.—**thickish,** thick'ish, *a.* Somewhat dull.—**thickly,** thik'li, *adv.* In a thick manner or condition; to considerable depth on a surface; closely.—**thickness,** thik'nes, *n.* The state of being thick in any sense of the word; measure through from surface to surface; density; consistence; closeness or crowded state; clumsy indistinctness of speech.—**thickset,** thik'-set, *a.* Close set or planted; having a short thick body; thick; stout:

thief, thēf, *n.* pl. **thieves,** thēvz. [A.Sax. *theóf*=Icel. *thjófr,* Sw. *tjuf,* D. *dief,* G. *dieb,* Goth. *thjubs,* thief; root doubtful.] A person who steals or is guilty of theft; one who deprives another of property secretly or without open force: as opposed to a *robber,* who openly uses violence.—*Thieves' Latin,* a jargon used by thieves.—**thieve,** thēv, *v.i.*—*thieved, thieving.* To steal; to practice theft.—*v.t.* To take by theft; to steal.—**thievery,** thē'vėr•i, *n.* The practice of stealing; theft.—**thievish,** thē'vish, *a.* Given to stealing; of the nature of theft.—**thievishly,** thē'vish•li, *adv.* In a thievish manner.—**thievishness,** thē'vish•nes, *n.*

thigh, thī, *n.* [A.Sax. *theóh,* the thigh=Icel. *thjó,* O.H.G. *dioh,* D. *dij,* O.D. *dygh,* thigh.] The thick fleshy portion of the leg between the knee and the trunk.—**thighbone,** *n.* The bone of the thigh; the femur.

thill, thil, *n.* [A.Sax. *thill, thille,* a stake, board; Icel. *thili, thil,* a deal, a plank; G. *diele,* a board; same root as Skr. *tala,* surface.] The shaft of a cart, gig, or other carriage.

thimble, thim'bl, *n.* [A.Sax. *thýmel,* a thimble, from *thúma,* thumb; having no doubt been first worn on the thumb, as the sailor's thimble still is. THUMB.] A metal cap or cover for the finger, used in sewing for driving the needle through; *naut.* an iron ring with a rope spliced round it.—**thimbleful,** thim'bl•fu̧l, *n.* As much as a thimble would hold; hence; a very small quantity.—**thimblerig,** thim'bl•rig, *n.* [From *rig,* a trick.] A sleight-of-hand trick, played with three thimbles and a small ball or pea.—**thimblerigger,** thim'bl•-rig•ėr, *n.* One who practices the trick of thimblerig.

thin, thin, *a.* [A.Sax. *thynne,* thin=Icel. *thunnr,* D. *dun,* Sw. *tunn,* G. *dünn,* cog. L. *tenuis,* Skr. *tanus,* thin; W. *tenau, teneu,* thin, rare; Ir. *tana,* thin, slender; all from root, *tan,* to stretch; seen also in L. *tendo,* to stretch, E. *tend*; Gr. *tonos*; G. *tonus,* E. *tone*; L. *tener,* E. *tender,* etc.] Not thick; having little extent from one surface to the opposite (a *thin* plate, a *thin* board); slight; flimsy (a *thin* veil); rare; not dense; said of aeriform fluids; deficient in body or substance; said of liquids or semiliquids; not close or crowded; sparse; not abundant (*thin* grass); not numerously filled; slim; slender; lean; faint; feeble; destitute of fullness or volume, as sound; often used adverbially in composition as the first element in compounds (*thin*-clad).—*v.t.*—*thinned, thinning.* To make thin in all its senses,—*v.i.* To diminish in thickness; to grow or become thin; with *out, away,* etc.—**thinly,** thin'li, *adv.* In a thin, loose, scattered manner.—**thinner,** thin'ėr, *n.* One who thins or makes thin.—**thinness,** thin'nes, *n.* The state of being thin.—**thin-skinned,** *a.* Having a thin skin; hence, unduly sensitive; easily offended; irritable.

thine, THīn, *pronominal adj.* [A.Sax. *thin,* thine, genit. of *thú,* thou. The loss of the *n* produced *thy.* THOU.] Thy; belonging to thee; used with or without a noun, and either for a nominative or objective or a predicate. ∴ *Thine,* like *thou,* is now used only in poetry or the solemn style, *your* and *yours* otherwise taking its place.

thing, thing, *n.* [A.Sax. *thing,* a meeting, cause, affair, etc.; L.G. and G. *ding,* thing, matter, Dan. and Sw. *ting,* Icel. *thing,* a court, an assembly; root doubtful.] Whatever exists, or is conceived to exist, as a separate entity; whatever may be spoken or thought of; an inanimate object; a creature; applied to man and animals in pity, contempt, tenderness, or admiration; a transaction, matter, circumstance, event; *pl.* clothes, personal belongings, luggage.—*The thing,* as it ought to be: a colloquial phrase applied to an ideal or typical condition.

think, thingk, *v.i.*—pret. and pp. *thought.* [A.Sax. *thincan, thencan,* to think=Goth. *thagkjan,* G. and D. *denken,* Icel. *thekkja,* Dan. *taenke*; allied to *thank,* and to A.Sax. *thyncan,* to seem, whence *methinks.*] To have the mind occupied on some subject; to revolve ideas in the mind; to perform any mental operation; to cogitate; to muse; to meditate; to consider; to deliberate; to judge, conclude, be of opinion (I *think* it will rain); to purpose, design, intend; to imagine, suppose, fancy.—*To think of,* to estimate; to esteem (to *think* little *of* a book).—*To think on* or *upon,* to meditate or muse on; to light on or discover by meditation (to *think on* an expedient).—*v.t.* To form in the mind; to imagine; to hold in opinion; to regard, consider, esteem; to form a conception of.—*To think scorn,* to disdain; to scorn.—*To think shame,* to feel shame; to be ashamed.—**thinkable,** thingk'a•bl, *a.* Capable of being thought; conceivable; cogitable.—**thinker,** thingk'ėr, *n.* One who thinks; one who reasons or meditates (a deep *thinker*); one who writes on speculative subjects.—**thinking,** thingk'ing, *a.* Able to think; having the faculty of thought.—*n.* The act or state of one who thinks; thought; cogitation.—**thinkingly,** thingk'ing•li, *adv.* By thought.

thinly, thinness, etc. See THIN.

thio, thī'ō, *n.* [Gr. *theion* sulfur.] An adjective or combining form, indicating the presence of sulfur in a compound.

thiosulfate, thī•ō•sul'fāt, *n.* Any salt of thiosulfuric acid, $H_2S_2O_3$, analogous to sulfuric acid, H_2SO_4.

third, thėrd, *a.* [A.Sax. *thridda*; cog. Goth. *thridja,* Icel. *thrithi,* Sw. *tredje,* Dan. *tredie,* D. *derde,* G. *dritte,* Gr. *tritos,* L. *tertius,* Skr. *tritiya,* W. *trydy,* Gael. *treas*—all from words signifying *three.* THREE.] Next after the second; being one of three equal parts into which anything is divided.—*Third estate,* the commons, as distinguished from clergy and nobility. See ESTATE.—*Third person, gram.* the person spoken of; *the third person* in the Trinity, the Holy Spirit.—*n.* The third part of anything; the sixtieth part of a second of time; *mus.* an interval consisting of three conjunct degrees of the scale; the upper of the two notes including this interval.—**thirdly,** thėrd'li, *adv.* In the third place.—**third-rate,** *a.* Next below second-rate; quite inferior; in the *navy,* applied to a certain class of men-of-war.

thirst, thėrst, *n.* [A.Sax. *thyrst, thurst,* thirst=Sw. and Dan. *törst,*

Icel. *thorsti*, D. *dorst*, G. *durst*, Goth. *thaurstei*, thirst; allied to Icel. *thurr*, G. *dürr*, dry, the root being that of L. *torridus*, torrid, *terra*, the earth, the dry land; Gr. *tersomai*, to be dry; Skr. *tarsh*, to thirst.] The desire, uneasiness, or suffering occasioned by want of drink; vehement desire for drink; a want and eager desire after anything (a *thirst* for knowledge).—*v.i.* [A.Sax. *thyrstan*, Icel. *thyrsta*.] To experience thirst; to have desire to drink; to have a vehement desire for anything. —**thirster,** thėrs'tėr, *n.* One who thirsts.—**thirsty,** thėrs'ti, *a.* [A.Sax. *thyrstig*.] Feeling a painful sensation for want of drink; having thirst; very dry; parched; having a vehement desire of anything.—**thirstily,** thėrs'ti•li, *adv.* In a thirsty manner. —**thirstiness,** thėrs'ti•nes, *n.* The state of being thirsty.

thirteen, thėr'tēn, *a.* [A.Sax. *threótyne*, lit. three-ten.] Ten and three.—*n.* The number which consists of ten and three.—**thirteenth,** thėr'tēnth, *a.* The third after the tenth; being one of thirteen equal parts of a thing. —*n.* One of thirteen equal parts of anything.

thirty, thėr'ti, *a.* [A.Sax. *thrittig*, *thritig*, from *threó*, *thré*, three, and *-tig*, ten=L. *decem*, Gr. *deka*, ten.] Thrice ten; ten three times repeated. —*n.* The number which consists of three times ten.—**thirtieth,** thėr'ti•eth, *a.* The next in order after the twenty-ninth; being one of thirty equal parts of a thing.—*n.* One of thirty equal parts of anything.

this, THis, *a.* and *pron.* pl. **these,** THēz, [A.Sax. masc. *thes*, fem. *theos*, neut. *this*, from the pronominal stem seen in *the*, *that*, *thither*, etc., and A.Sax. *se*, *sa*, he (=Skr. *sa*, he).] A demonstrative used with or without a noun to denote something that is present or near in place or time, or something just mentioned: often opposed to *that* (the latter referring to something more remote); applied to time, *this* may refer to the present time; now; to time next to come, or to time immediately ended; frequently used to signify present state, condition, etc.

thistle, this'l, *n.* [A.Sax. *thistel*, a thistle=Icel. *thistill*, G. and D. *distel*, Sw. *tistel*, Sc. *thrissle*, thistle; origin doubtful.] The common name of a tribe of prickly plants of numerous species, most of them inhabitants of Europe; regarded as the national emblem of Scotland.

thither, THiTH'ėr, *adv.* [A.Sax. *thider*, Icel. *thathra*, thither, there; from demonstrative stem seen in *the*, *that*, and suffix *ther*=*tra* in Skr. *tatra*, there, from root *tar*, to go.] To that place: opposed to *hither*; to that end or result.—*Hither and thither*, to this place and that; one way and another.—**thitherward,** THiTH'ėr•wėrd, *adv.* Toward that place.

tho, THō. A contraction of *though*.

thole, tholepin, thōl, *n.* [A.Sax. *thol*, a thole-pin=Icel. *thollr*, a thole-pin, a wooden peg; L.G. *dolle*, D. *dol*, a thole.] A pin inserted into the gunwale of a boat to serve as a fulcrum for the oar in rowing; often in pairs, the oar resting between; also written *Thowl*.

Thomist, tō'mist, *n.* A follower of the scholastic philosophy of *Thomas* Aquinas, in opposition to *Scotist*.

thong, thong, *n.* [A.Sax. *thwang*, *thwong*, a thong; Icel. *thvengr*, a strap, a latchet.] A strap of leather used for fastening anything; a long narrow strip of leather or similar material.

Thor, thor, *n.* [Icel. *Thórr*, from older *Thonor*, equivalent to A.Sax. *thunor*, E. *thunder*. THUNDER.] The second principal god of the ancient Scandinavians, the god of thunder; son of Odin. *Thursday* is called after him.

thorax, thō'raks, *n.* [Gr. *thōrax*, the chest, a breastplate.] The cavity of the body formed by the spine, ribs, and breastbone, and containing the lungs, heart, etc.; the chest; the corresponding portion of animals; the portion of an insect between the head and abdomen.—**thoracic,** thō•ras'ik, *a.* Pertaining to or contained in the thorax or chest.—*Thoracic duct*, *anat.* the vessel which receives the chyle conveyed by the lacteals, and carries it along the spine to the left subclavian vein, where it enters the blood.

thorium, thō'ri•um, *n.* [From *Thor*, the Scandinavian deity.] A radioactive metallic element isolated from thorite and other minerals as a heavy gray metal, used as an oxide in gas mantles. Symbol, Th; at. no., 90; at. wt., 232.038.—**thoria,** thō'ri•a, *n.* An oxide of thorium.—**thorite,** thō'rīt, *n.* A mineral found in Norway containing thorium.

thorn, thorn, *n.* [A.Sax. *thorn*=Icel. *thorn*, Goth. *thaurnus*, Dan. *torn*, D. *doorn*, G. *dorn*; same word as Pol. *tarn*, Bohem. *trn*. Probably from a root meaning to pierce, seen also in *through*, *thrill*, etc.] A common name of trees and shrubs armed with spines or prickles, as the blackthorn, buckthorn, and especially the common hawthorn; any sharp-pointed spiny or prickly process growing on a plant; *fig.* anything that annoys or torments sharply; a care or trouble.—**thorn apple,** *n.* An annual plant of the potato family with narcotic properties, used medicinally.—**thornback,** *n.* A species of skate with spines on its back and tail.—**thorny,** thor'ni, *a.* Full of thorns, spines, or prickles; prickly; vexatious; harassing.

thorough, thur'ō, *a.* [Same word as *through*.] Going completely to the end; extending to all particulars; complete; perfect.—*Thorough bass*, the mode of expressing chords by means of figures placed over or under a given bass, such figures indicating the harmony *through* all the other parts; also sometimes used as equivalent to *harmony*.—**thoroughbred,** *a.* Of pure or unmixed breed, bred from a sire and dam of purest blood; hence, high spirited; mettlesome.—*n.* An animal, especially a horse, of pure blood.—**thoroughfare,** thur'ō•fâr, *n.* [A.Sax. *thurhfaru*.] An unobstructed way; especially an unobstructed road or street for public traffic.—**thoroughgoing,** *a.* Going or ready to go all lengths; extreme.—**thoroughly,** thur'ō•li, *adv.* In a thorough manner; fully; completely.—**thoroughness,** thur'o•nes, *n.*—**thoroughpaced,** *a.* *Lit.* trained to go through all the paces of a well-trained horse; hence, going all lengths; downright; consummate.

thorp, thorpe, thorp, *n.* [A.Sax. *thorp*=Icel. *thorp*, Sw. and Dan. *torp*, D. *dorp*, G. *dorf*, a village, a hamlet.] A group of houses standing together in the country; a hamlet; a village.

those, THōz, *a.* and *pron.* Historically the plural of *this*, being another form of *these*, but used as plural of *that*.

Thoth, thoth, *n.* An Egyptian divinity whom the Greeks considered to be identical with Hermes (Mercury).

thou, THou, *pron.*; obj. and dat. *thee*, pl. *ye* or *you*. [A.Sax. *thú*, genit. *thín*, dat. and acc. *thé*, nom. pl. *gé*, genit. *eówer*, dat. and acc. *eów*; Icel. *thú*, Goth. *thu*, D., Dan., and G. *du*; L. *tu*, Gr. *su*, *tu*, Skr. *tvam*, Slav. *ti*, W. *ti*, Gael. *tu*, thou.] The second personal pronoun in the singular number, used to indicate the person spoken to; but in ordinary language the plural form *you* is now universally substituted, *thou* being used in the poetical or solemn style, as also among the Friends, or Quakers.

though, THō, *conj.* [A.Sax. *theáh*, though=Icel. *thó*, Dan. *dog*, D. and G. *doch*, Goth. *thauh*, though; from stem of *that*, *the*.] Granting or allowing it to be the fact that; notwithstanding that.—*As though*, as if.—*What though*, elliptically for what though the fact or case is so. ∴ Syn. under WHILE, ALTHOUGH.—*adv.* However; for all that.

thought, tha̤t, pret. and pp. of *think*.

thought, tha̤t, *n.* [A.Sax. *thoht*, *gethoht*, from *thencan*, to think, pret. *thohte*, pp. *gethoht*; Icel. *thótti*, G. *gedacht*. THINK.] The act or power of thinking; cogitation; meditation; that which is thought; an idea; a conception; a judgment; a fancy; a conceit; deliberation; reflection; solicitude.—*A thought*, a small degree or quantity. (*Colloq.*)—*Second thoughts*, maturer reflection; after-consideration.—**thoughtful,** tha̤t'fu̧l, *a.* Full of thought; contemplative; meditative; attentive; careful; mindful; full of anxiety; solicitous.—**thoughtfully,** tha̤t'fu̧l•li, *adv.* In a thoughtful manner.—**thoughtfulness,** tha̤t'fu̧l•nes, *n.* Serious attention; solicitude.—**thoughtless,** tha̤t'les, *a.* Free from thought or care; heedless; negligent; lightminded.—**thoughtlessly,** tha̤t'les•li, *adv.* Without thought; carelessly.—**thoughtlessness,** tha̤t'les•nes, *n.* The quality of being thoughtless, inconsiderate or careless; heedlessness; inattention.

thousand, thou′zand, *n.* [A.Sax. *thúsend*=Icel. *thús-hund, thús-hundrath*, Dan. *tusind*, D. *duizend*, Goth. *thúsundi*, G. *tausend*.] The number of ten hundred; proverbially, a great number.—*a.* Denoting the number of ten hundred, or proverbially, a great number indefinitely.—**thousandfold,** thou′zand•fōld, *a.* Multiplied by a thousand.—**thousandth,** thou′-zandth, *a.* Completing the number of a thousand; being one of a thousand equal parts of anything.—*n.* The thousandth part of anything.

thrall, thrạl, *n.* [A.Sax. *thrael*=Icel. *thraell*, Sw. *träl*, Dan. *trael*, a serf, a slave.] One in bondage.—**thralldom,** thrạl•dum, *n.* Slavery; bondage.

thrash, thresh, thrash, thresh, *v.t.* [A.Sax. *threscan, therscan*, to thrash (corn), to beat=Icel. *threskja*, Sw. *trōska*, Dan. *taerske*, D. *dorschen*, G. *dreschen*, Goth. *thriskan*; comp. Lith. *trasketi*, to rattle.] To beat out or separate the grain or seeds from by a flail or threshing machine, or by treading with oxen; to beat soundly with a stick or whip; to drub.—*v.i.* To drive out grain from straw.—**thrasher, thresher,** thrash′ėr, thresh′ėr, *n.* One who thrashes grain; a species of shark which uses its tail as a weapon.—**thrashing, threshing,** thrash′ing, thresh′ing, *n.* The operation by which grain is thrashed; a beating or drubbing.

thrasonical, thra•son′i•kal, *a.* [From *Thraso*, a boaster in old comedy.] Given to bragging; boastful.

thrave, thrāv, *n.* [Icel. *threfi*, a thrave; Dan. *trave*, a score of sheaves.] Two shocks of a grain crop of twelve sheaves each.

thread, thred, *n.* [A.Sax. *thraed*, lit. what is twisted, from *thráwan*, to twist, to throw; similarly Icel. *thrádr*, Dan. *traad*, D. *draad*, G. *draht*, thread. THROW.] A fine cord, especially such as is used for sewing; the filaments of fibrous substances, such as cotton, flax, silk, or wool, spun out into a slender line; anything resembling this; any slender filament; continued course or tenor (the *thread* of a discourse); the prominent spiral part of a screw.—*v.t.* To pass a thread through the eye or aperture of; to pass or go through, as through a narrow way or any intricate course.—**threadbare,** thred′bâr, *a.* Having the nap worn off so as to show the separate threads; hence, trite; hackneyed; used till it has lost novelty or interest.—**threader,** thred′-ėr, *n.* One who threads.—**thready,** thred′i, *a.* Like thread; filamentous; containing thread.

threat, thret, *n.* [A.Sax. *threat*, threat, punishment; from stem of A.Sax. *threotan*, to tire, harass; Goth. *thriutan*, G. (*ver*) *drieszen*, to annoy; allied to L. *trudo*, to thrust (in *intrude*).] A menace; a declaration of an intention to inflict punishment, loss, or pain on another.—**threaten,** thret′n, *v.t.* To use threats toward; to declare an intention of injuring; to menace; to menace by action; to act as if intending to injure; to exhibit the appearance of bringing something evil or unpleasant on (the clouds *threaten* us with rain); to show to be impending (the sky *threatens* a storm).—*v.i.* To use threats or menaces.—**threateningly,** thret′n•ing•li, *adv.*

three, thrē, *a.* [A.Sax. *thri, threo*= Goth. *threis*, Icel. *thrir*, Dan. *tre*, D. *drie*, G. *drei*; cog. W., Ir., and Gael. *tri*, Lith. *trys*, L. *tres*, Gr. *treis*, Skr. *tri*.] Two and one.—*Three-times-three*, three cheers thrice repeated.—*n.* The number which consists of two and one; a symbol representing this.—*Rule of three*, the arithmetical rule otherwise called *Proportion*.—**three-decker,** *n.* A vessel of war carrying guns on three decks.—**threefold,** thrē′fōld, *a.* Consisting of three in one; triple.—*adv.* In a threefold manner; trebly.—**threepence,** *n.* A silver coin of Great Britain.—**threepenny,** *a.* Worth three pence or six cents, hence, of little worth.—**three-phase,** *a. Elect.* a system of alternating current supply, in which there are three circuits differing in phase by 120° from each other.—**three-ply,** *a.* Threefold; consisting of three strands, or three thicknesses, etc.

threne, thrēn, *n.* [L. *threnus*, from Gr. *threnos*, lamentation.] [*obs.*] A complaint or lamentation.—**threnodial,** thri•nō′di•al, *a.* Pertaining to a threnody; elegiac.

thresh, thresh, *v.t.* [A.Sax. *thresean, threscan*, to thrash (corn), to beat.] To separate seed from (as grain) by mechanical means; to discuss repeatedly; to hit repeatedly.—*v.i.* To thresh, as grain; to strike repeatedly, as with a whip. See also THRASH.

threshold, thresh′ōld, *n.* [A.Sax. *therscwald, therscold, therxold*, from *therscan*, to thrash or thresh, and apparently *wald*, a wood, timber, because this bar was threshed or trod upon by the feet.] A doorsill; the stone or piece of timber which lies under a door; hence, entrance; beginning; outset (the *threshold* of an argument).—*Threshold of consciousness, psych.* the point at which a stimulus to the sensory organism is just sufficiently intense to be felt.

threw, thrö, pret. of *throw*.

thrice, thrīs, *adv.* [O.E. *thries, thryes*, from *thrie*, three, with genit. term., like *once, twice*.] Three times; also often used for emphasis or intensity (*thrice* blessed, etc.).

thrift, thrift, *n.* [From Icel. *thrift*, THRIVE.] A thriving state or condition (*Shak.*)‡; economical management in regard to property; economy; frugality; a plant which grows on mountains and along the seacoasts of the North Temperate Zone.—**thriftily,** thrif′ti•li, *adv.* In a thrifty manner; frugally.—**thriftiness,** thrif′ti•nes, *n.* The quality of being thrifty; economy; frugality.—**thriftless,** thrift′les, *a.* Having no thrift; profuse; extravagant.—**thrifty,** thrif′ti, *a.* Having thrift; careful in husbanding resources; frugal; economical.

thrill, thril, *v.t.* [A.Sax. *thyrlian, thyrelian* (from *thirl, thyrel*, a hole= *tril* of nos*tril*), to pierce=D. *drillen*, to bore, to drill troops (whence E. to *drill*); same root as *through*.] To pierce in a figurative sense; to effect with a keen emotion, as of delight or excitement.—*v.i.* To penetrate, to produce a tingling sensation; to act tremulously, to vibrate; to feel a shivering sensation running through the body; to shiver; to quiver or move with a tremulous movement.—*n.* A warbling; a trill; a thrilling sensation.

thrive, thrīv, *v.i.*—pret. *throve*; pp. *thriven* (thriv′n); ppr. *thriving*. [From Icel. *thrífask*, to thrive (a reflexive verb, *sk* meaning self, as in *bask*), whence also *thrift*, thrift; Dan. *trives*, to thrive.] To prosper or succeed; to be fortunate; to increase in goods and estate; to keep increasing one's acquisitions; to be marked by prosperity (a *thriving* business); to go on or turn out well; to have a good issue; to grow vigorously or luxuriantly; to flourish.—**thriver,** thrī′vėr, *n.* One who thrives.—**thriving,** thrī′ving, *a.* Being prosperous; advancing in wealth; flourishing.—**thrivingly,** thrī′ving•li, *adv.* In a thriving or prosperous way.

thro', thrö, *a.* Contraction of *Through*.

throat, thrōt, *n.* [A.Sax. *throte*; akin G. *drossel*, the throat, the throttle; comp. D. *strot*, throat; hence *throttle*.] The anterior part of the neck of an animal, in which are the gullet and windpipe; the fauces; the pharynx; an opening or entrance somewhat resembling the throat (the *throat* of a valley); *bot.* the mouth of a monopetalous corolla; *arch.* the part of a chimney between the gathering and the flue; *fort.* same as *Gorge*.—*To lie in one's throat*, to lie outrageously.—**throaty,** thrō′ti, *a.* Guttural; uttered back in the throat.

throb, throb, *v.i.*—*throbbed, throbbing*. [O.E. *throbbe*; origin doubtful.] To beat, as the heart or pulse, with more than usual force or rapidity; to palpitate; to quiver or vibrate.—*Throbbing pain*, a pain augmented by the pulsation of the arteries.—*n.* A beat or strong pulsation; palpitation.

throe, thrō, *n.* [A.Sax. *threá*, affliction, from *threówan*, to afflict; akin Icel. *thrá*, a throe, a hard struggle.] Extreme pain; agony; the anguish of travail in childbirth; a cleaving tool; a frow.

thrombus, throm′bus, *n.* [L., from Gr. *thrombos*, a clot.] A fibrinous clot of blood which forms in and obstructs a blood vessel.—**thrombosis,** throm′bō•sis, *n.* [Gr.] *Pathol.* the obstruction of a blood vessel by a thrombus.

throne, thrōn, *n.* [O.Fr. *throne*, L. *thronus*, from Gr. *thronos*, a seat, chair.] An elevated and ornamental chair of state used by a king, emperor, pope, bishop, etc.; the official chair of a presiding official of certain societies; sovereign power and dignity; also, the wielder of that power; usually with *the*.—*v.t.*—

throned, throning. To place on a royal seat; to enthrone; to exalt.

throng, throng, *n.* [A.Sax. *thrang, throng*, a crowd, from *thringan*, to crowd; Icel. *thrǒng*, G. *drang*, a crowd, distress; D. and G. *dringen*, to crowd.] A multitude of persons pressed into a close body; a crowd; a great number; a number of things crowded or close together (a *throng* of words).—*v.i.* To crowd together; to come in multitudes.—*v.t.* To crowd or press; to annoy with a crowd of living beings; to fill with a crowd.

throstle, thros'l, *n.* [A dim. corresponding to *thrush*; A.Sax. *throstle*, G. and Dan. *drossel*, a thrush. THRUSH.] The song thrush or mavis; a machine for spinning wool, cotton, etc., from the rove.

throttle, throt'l, *n.* [From *throat.*] The windpipe or trachea; the throat; the valve that controls the amount of fuel vapor that enters the cylinders of an internal-combustion engine; the lever controlling this valve.—*v.t.* —*throttled, throttling*. To choke or strangle; to suppress, as if by choking; to cut the flow of by means of a throttle.—**throttle valve,** *n.* *Steam engines*, a valve which regulates the supply of steam to the cylinder.

through, thru, thrö, *prep.* [O.E. *thurgh, thurch*, A.Sax. *thurh*, G. *durch*, D. *door*, Goth. *thaírh*; cog. W. *trw*, Armor, *tre*, through; L. *trans*, over, across; the root is Indo-European *tar*, Skr. *tri, tar*, to penetrate, seen also in E. *thrill, trite*, etc. *Thorough* is the same word.] From end to end or from side to side of; between the sides or walls of (to pass *through* a gate); by the agency of; by means of; on account of; over the whole surface or extent of; throughout; among or in the midst of, in the way of passage; among, in the way of experiencing; from beginning to end of.—*adv.* From one end or side to the other; from beginning to end; to the end; to completion.—*To carry through*, to complete; to accomplish.—*To fall through*, to come to an unsuccessful issue; to fail.—*To go through with* something, to prosecute it to the end.—*a.* Going with little or no interruption from one important place or center to another (a *through* passenger, a *through* journey).—**throughout,** thrö•out', *prep.* Quite through in every part of; from one extremity to the other of.—*adv.* Everywhere; in every part.

throve, thrōv, pret. of *thrive.*

throw, thrō, *v.t.*—*threw* (thrö), *thrown* (thrōn). [A.Sax. *thráwan*, to twist (as to *throw* silk), to throw; akin D. *draaijen*, G. *drehen* to twist, to turn; same root as L *torqueo*, to twist, to throw (whence *torture*). *Thread* is a derivative.] To fling or cast in any manner; to hurl, to dash: often *refl.* (*threw* himself on the enemy); to prostrate, as in wrestling; to overturn; to divest one's self of; to shed; to give violent utterance or expression to; to send (to *throw* defiance); to put on or over with haste or negligence; to wind or twist two or more filaments of, as of silk, so as to form one thread; *pottery*, to form or shape roughly on a wheel or throwing engine.—*To throw away*, to cast away; to part with or bestow without compensation; to spend recklessly; to squander; to waste; to reject; to refuse.—*To throw back*, to cast or hurl back; to reject; to retort.—*To throw by*, to cast or lay aside as useless.—*To throw down*, to cast on the ground; to overturn; to subvert; to destroy.—*To throw in*, to cast or fling in or into; to put in or deposit along with others; to interpolate; to give or add to the bargain.—*To throw off*, to cast off or aside; to discard; to reject; to print at one impression.—*To throw one's self on* or *upon*, to resign one's self to the favor, benevolence, protection, etc., of.—*To throw open*, to open suddenly or widely; to give free or unrestricted admission to.—*To throw out*, to cast out; to eject; to reject or discard; to expel; to construct so as to project; to emit; to insinuate (to *throw out* a hint).—*To throw over*, to discard; to abandon.—*To throw up*, to erect or build rapidly; to resign; to abandon; to eject from the stomach; to vomit. —*v.i.* To perform the act of casting or flinging; to cast dice.—*n.* The act of one who throws; a cast; a cast of dice; hence, risk; venture; decision of fortune; *geol.* and *mining*, a dislocation of strata up or down.—**thrower,** thrō'ėr, *n.* One who throws; a person who twists silk; a throwster.—**throwster,** thrō'stėr, *n.* One who throws or twists silk.

thrum, thrum, *n.* [Allied to D. *dreum*, thrum; Icel. *thrōmr*, margin, edge; same root as L. *terminus*, an end.] The end of a weaver's web; the fringe of threads by which it is fastened to the loom, and from which the cloth when woven has to be cut; coarse yarn.

thrum, thrum, *v.i.*—*thrummed, thrumming*. [Akin to *drum*; comp. *strum.*] To play coarsely or unskillfully on a stringed instrument; to make a drumming noise.—*v.t.* To play roughly on with the fingers; to drum; to tap.

thrush, thrush, *n.* [A.Sax. *thrisc*, a thrush; akin to Icel. *thröstr*, Sw. *trost*, Rus. *drozd*; same root as L. *turdus*, a thrush. *Throstle* is a dim. form.] A passerine bird of various species, including the song thrush or mavis, the missel thrush, etc., celebrated for their powers of song.

thrush, thrush, *n.* [From Icel. *thurr*, dry, and=Dan. *tröske*, Sw. *torsk*, the thrush; akin *thirst.*] *Pathol.* a disease characterized by vesicles of a pearl color, affecting the lips and mouth; aphthae; also an inflammatory and suppurating disease in the feet of the horse.

thrust, thrust, *v.t.*—pret. and pp. *thrust.* [O.E. *thriste, threste*, from Icel. *thrýsta*, to thrust, probably same root as L. *trudo*, to thrust.] To push or drive with force; to impel: usually followed by *away, from, in, off*, etc.—*To thrust on*, to impel; to urge.—*To thrust through*, to pierce; to stab.—*To thrust out*, to expel; to push out or protrude.—*To thrust one's self in* or *into*, to obtrude; to intrude.—*v.i.* To make a push; to make a lunge with a weapon.—*n.* A violent push or drive, as with the hand or foot or with a pointed weapon; a lunge. *arch.* the force exerted by any body against another body, such as the force exerted by rafters or beams against the walls supporting them; the pushing force of a rocket or a jet-engine.

thud, thud, *n.* [Imitative; comp. A.Sax. *thoden*, din.] The sound produced by a blow upon a comparatively soft substance; a blow causing a dull sound.

Thug, thug, *n.* [Hind.] A member of a peculiar association of robbers and assassins formerly prevalent in India, who strangled their victims partly from religious motives.—**thuggee,** thug•gē', *n.* The profession and practices of the Thugs.

Thule, thū'lē, *n.* The name given by the ancients to the most northern country which they knew of, supposed to have been Iceland, Norway, or the Shetland Islands; often spoken of by the Romans as *ultima Thule*, remotest Thule; hence, *fig.*, a farthest point or limit.

thulium, thū'li•um, *n.* [From *Thule*, a northernmost region.] A metallic element of the rare-earth series. Symbol, Tm; at. no., 69; at. wt., 168.934.

thumb, thum, *n.* [A.Sax. *thuma*, the thumb=Dan. *tomme*, D. *duim*, G. *daumen*, from root seen in L. *tumeo*, to swell, whence *tumid*. *Thimble* is a derivative.] The short, thick finger of the human hand, or the corresponding member of other animals.—*Under one's thumb*, under one's power or influence.—*Rule of thumb*. See RULE.—*v.t.* To soil or wear with the thumb or the fingers, or by frequent handling.—**thumbkin,** thum'kin, *n.* An instrument of torture for compressing the thumbs by means of screws. Called also *Thumbscrew.*—**thumbscrew,** *n.* A screw to be turned by the finger and thumb; the thumbkin.

Thummim, thum'im, *n. pl.* A Hebrew word denoting perfections. The *Urim* and *Thummim* were worn in the breastplate of the high priest, but what they were is not known.

thump, thump, *n.* [Allied to Dan. *dump*, a plunge, *dump*, dull, low; D. *dompen*, to plunge; perhaps of imitative origin; comp. *bump, plump.*] The sound made by the sudden fall of a heavy body; hence, a heavy blow given with anything that is thick.—*v.t.* To strike or beat with something thick or heavy.—*v.i.* To strike or fall with a heavy blow.

thunder, thun'dėr, *n.* [From A.Sax. *thunor*, thunder (with insertion of *d.* as in *gender, jaundice*); D. *donder*, G. *donner*; cog. L. *tonitru*, Per. *tundur*; same root as L. *tonare*, to sound, E. *stun*, G. *stöhnen*, to groan, Gr.

stonos, a groaning. THOR.] The sound which follows a flash of lightning; a report due to the sudden disturbance of the air produced by a violent discharge of atmospheric electricity or lightning; any loud noise (*thunders* of applause); an awful or startling denunciation or threat (the *thunders* of the Vatican). —*v.i.* To make thunder; often impersonal (it *thundered* yesterday); to make a loud noise, particularly a heavy sound of some continuance.—*v.t.* To emit as with the noise of thunder; to utter or issue by way of threat or denunciation.—**thunderbolt,** thun″dėr•bolt′, *n.* A flash of lightning with an accompanying clap of thunder; something that stuns abruptly or violently; *her.* a charge consisting of a double twisted column of flame, having two rays or darts of lightning in saltire and two wings joined on to the center; a dreadful threat, denunciation, or censure; a fulmination.—**thunderclap,** *n.* A clap or burst of thunder; a thunderpeal.—**thundercloud,** *n.* A cloud that produces lightning and thunder, of dark and dense appearance.—**thunderer,** thun′dėr•ėr, *n.* One who thunders; an epithet of Jupiter.—**thunderhead,** *n.* A kind of cumulus cloud.—**thundering,** thun′dėr•ing, *a.* Producing or characterized by a loud rumbling or rattling noise, as that of thunder or artillery; large or extraordinary (*colloq.*).—**thunderous,** thun′dėr•us, *a.* Producing thunder; making a noise like thunder; giving a loud and deep sound.—**thunderpeal,** *n.* A peal or clap of thunder.—**thundershower,** *n.* A shower that accompanies thunder.—**thunderstone,** *n.* A thunderbolt (*Shak.*); a variety of crystalline iron pyrites; a belemnite; a flint arrowhead.—**thunderstruck,** thun′dėr•struk, *p.* and *a.* Astonished; amazed; struck dumb by something surprising or terrible suddenly presented.

thuribler, thū′ri•bl, *n.* [L. *thuribulum*, from *thus*, *thuris*, frankincense.] A kind of censer in the shape of a covered vase, perforated to allow the fumes of incense to escape.—**thurifer,** thū′ri•fėr, *n. R. Cath. Ch.* the attendant who carries the thurible.

Thursday, thėrz′dā, *n.* [That is, *Thor's day*, the day consecrated to Thor, the old Scandinavian god of thunder.] The fifth day of the week.

thus, THus, *adv.* [A.Sax. *thus*, akin to *thes*, *theos*, *this*, this. THIS.] In this way, manner, or state; accordingly; things being so; to this degree or extent; so (*thus* wise). —*Thus far, thus much,* to this point; to this degree.

thwack, thwak, *v.t.* [Modified from A.Sax. *thaccian*, to stroke gently; Icel. *thjökka*, to thwack. *Whack* is another form.] To strike, bang, beat, or thrash.—*n.* A heavyblow with something flat or heavy; a bang.

thwart, thwa̤rt, *a.* [From Icel. *thvert*, transverse; Sw. *tvärt*, Dan. *tvert*, across; *tvär*, *tver*, cross; akin A.Sax. *thweorh*, across, perverse.] Transverse; being across something else.—*v.t.* To place or pass over‡; to cross, as a purpose; to frustrate or defeat (a design, a person).—*n.* Opposition†; the seat of a boat placed athwart it.—**thwarter,** thwa̤r′tėr, *n.* One who thwarts.

thy, THī, *pron.* [THINE.] Belonging or pertaining to thee; possessive pronoun of the second person singular.

thylacine, thī′la•sīn, *n.* [Gr. *thylakos*, a pouch.] The Tasmanian wolf.

thyme, tīm, *n.* [L. *thymum*, from Gr. *thymon*, thyme, from *thyō*, to smell.] A genus of small undershrubs, of which the common or garden thyme is a favorite on account of its aromatic odor.—**thymol,** tīm′ol, *n.* [From *thyme*, *oleum*, oil.] A crystalline substance obtained from oil of thyme; a strong antiseptic and disinfectant, used as a gargle, for inhalation, in skin diseases, etc.

thymus, thī′mus, *n.* [From Gr. *thymos*, thyme, being compared to the flower of this plant by Galen.] *Anat.* a glandular body situated behind the sternum or breastbone in children, often entirely disappearing in adults.

thyroid, thyreoid, thī′roid, thī′ri•oid, *a.* [Gr. *thyreos*, a shield, *eidos*, form.] Resembling a shield; applied to one of the cartilages of the larynx, to a gland situated near that cartilage, and to the arteries and veins of the gland.—**thyroid gland,** *n.* A ductless gland attached to the front of the larynx. It produces an internal secretion that helps to regulate the nutrition of the body.

thyrsus, thėr′sus, *n.* [L. *thyrsus*, from Gr. *thyrsos*, a thyrsus.] An attribute or emblem of Bacchus and his followers, consisting of a spear or staff wrapped round with ivy and vine branches, and often with a pine cone at the point; *bot.* a form of inflorescence resembling a panicle but denser and closer.—**thyrsoid, thyrsoidal,** thėr′soid, thėr′soi•dal, *a. Bot.* having somewhat the form of a thyrsus.

thyself, THī•self′, *pron.* A pronoun used after *thou*, to express distinction with emphasis; or used without *thou*, its usage being similar to that of *myself*, etc.

ti, tē, *n.* [Variation of *si.*] *Mus.* the seventh note of the diatonic scale.

ti, tē, *n.* A liliaceous plant of the Pacific islands, etc., with a highly nutritious root.

tiara, ti•ä′ra, *n.* [L. and Gr. *tiara*, from Per.] A woman's headband decorated, usually, with jewels or flowers.

tibia, tib′i•a, *n.* [L., a musical pipe, the large bone of the leg.] A kind of pipe, the commonest musical instrument of the Greeks and Romans; *anat.* the large bone of the lower leg; the shinbone; *entom.* the fourth joint of the leg.—**tibial,** tib′i•al, *a.* Pertaining to the tibia.

tic, tik, *n.* [Fr. *tic*, spasm.] A convulsive twitching of certain muscles of the face; also *tic-douloureux* of facial neuralgia.

tick, tik, *n.* [Contr. of *ticket.*] Credit; trust.—*To buy upon tick*=to buy on a *ticket* or note, or on credit.

tick, tik, *n.* [L.G. *teke*, D. *teek*, G. *zecke*, a tick.] The name common to certain small parasitical arachnidans or mites which infest sheep, oxen, dogs, goats, etc.

tick, tik, *n.* [Same as D. *tijk*, G. *zieche*, a cover, a tick, from L. *theca*, Gr. *thēkē*, a case, a cover.] The cover or case which contains the feathers, wool, or other materials of a bed; ticking.—**ticking,** tik′ing, *n.* A strong striped linen or cotton fabric used for the ticks of beds, mattresses, etc.

tick, tik, *v.i.* [From the sound; comp. D. *tikken*, to touch slightly and quickly, as with a pen, to dot.] To make a small noise by beating or otherwise, as a watch; to give out a succession of small sharp noises—*n.* A small distinct noise, as that of a watch or clock; a small dot.—*v.t.* To mark with a tick or dot; to check by writing down a small mark: generally with *off.*—**ticker,** tik′ėr, *n.* A device for facilitating detection of continuous waves; a telegraphic receiving instrument for the stock exchange that records quotations.

ticket, tik′et, *n.* [Fr. *étiquette*, O.Fr. *etiquet*, a bill, note, ticket, label, etc., from G. *stecken*, to stick, a ticket being something stuck on. STICK, ETIQUETTE.] A label stuck on the outside of anything to give notice of something concerning it; a small piece of paper, cardboard, or the like, with something written or printed on it, and serving as a notice, acknowledgment, etc.; a certificate or token of a share in a lottery or the like; a card or slip of paper given as a certificate of right of entry to a place of public amusement, or to travel on a railroad or by other public conveyance.—*The ticket*, the right or correct thing. (*Slang*).—*v.t.* To distinguish by a ticket; to put a ticket on.

ticking. See TICK.

tickle, tik′l, *v.t.*—*tickled, tickling.* [A freq. of *tick*, to touch lightly; or by metathesis from A.Sax. *citelian*=Sc. *kittle*, D. *kittelen*, G. *kitzeln*, to tickle.] To touch lightly and cause peculiar thrilling sensation, which commonly causes laughter; to titillate; to please by slight gratification; to stir up to pleasure; to flatter; to cajole; to puzzle.—**tickler,** tik′lėr, *n.* One who tickles or pleases; something that puzzles or perplexes (*colloq.*).—**tickling,** tik′ling, *n.* A sensation similar to that produced by being tickled.—**ticklish,** tik′lish, *a.* Easily tickled; in an unsteady or critical state; difficult; nice; critical. —**ticklishly,** tik′lish•li, *adv.* In a ticklish manner.—**ticklishness,** tik′lish•nes, *n.*

tidbit, tid′bit, *n.* [Origin uncertain.] A choice, delicate bit of food; a choice bit of anything, as news.

tide, tīd, *n.* [A.Sax. *tíd*, time, season, hour=Icel. *títh*, Sw. and Dan. *tid*, D. *tijd*, G. *zeit*, time; same root as *time*. The tides are times of rising and falling of the sea. Hence *tidy*, *tidings*, *betide*.] Time; season; the alternate rising and falling of the waters of the ocean, and of bays, rivers, etc., connected therewith, depending on the relative position of the moon, and in a less degree of the sun; the whole interval between high and low water; a state of being at the height or acme (*Shak.*); stream; flow; current (a *tide* of blood); course or tendency of influences or circumstances; current. See NEAP, SPRING, EBB, FLOOD.—*v.t.* or *i.*—*tided*, *tiding*. To drive with the tide or stream. *To tide over*, to surmount by favorable incidents, by prudence, and management, or by aid from another.—**tidal**, tī′dal, *a.* Pertaining to tides; showing tides.—*Tidal harbor*, a harbor in which the tide ebbs and flows, not having a dock with flood gates.—*Tidal river*, a river up which the tide flows to a certain point in its course.—*Tidal train*, a railroad train which runs in connection with a steamer, and whose running is therefore regulated by the state of the tide.—*Tidal wave*, tide wave.—**tidal wave,** *n.* Great sea waves following earthquakes, or floods caused by the piling up of water in hurricanes; the daily tides caused by the gravitational attraction of the moon upon the earth; the spring tides at new and full moon, when earth, sun and moon are in a direct line.

tidings, tī′dingz, *n. pl.* [Lit. events that happen or *betide*; Icel. *tithindi* (pl.), tidings, news; Dan. *tidende*, D. *tijding*, G. *zeitung*. TIDE.] News; information; intelligence; account of what has taken place and was not before known.

tidy, tī′di, *a.* [From *tide*, time, season; like D. *tijdig*, Dan. and Sw. *tidig*, G. *zeitig*, timely, seasonable. TIDE.] Seasonable‡; arranged in good order or with neatness; dressed or kept with neatness; neat; trim; practicing neatness; moderately large or great (*colloq.*).—*v.t.*—*tidied*, *tidying*. To make neat or tidy; to put in good order.—*n.* A piece of knitted or crotchet work for hanging over the back of a chair, the arms of a sofa, or the like.—**tidily,** tī′di•li, *adv.* In a tidy manner.—**tidiness,** tī′di•nes, *n.* The quality of being tidy.

tie, tī, *v.t.*—*tied*, *tying*. [A.Sax. *týge*, a rope, from *teón*, to pull; akin *tug*, *tow*.] To fasten with a band or cord and knot; to bind; to fasten; to knit; to unite so as not to be easily parted; to limit or bind by authority or moral influence; to restrain; to confine; to oblige.—*To tie down*, to fasten so as to prevent from rising; to restrain, restrict, or confine; to impose stipulations on.—*To tie up*, to fasten up; to confine or restrain; to annex such conditions so that it cannot be sold or alienated.—*n.* Something used to fasten or bind; a fastening; an ornamental knot; a necktie; a bond; an obligation, moral or legal (the *ties* of blood or of friendship); *building*, a beam or rod which secures parts together and is subjected to a tensile strain; *mus.* a curved line written over or under notes of the same pitch to indicate that the sound is to be unbrokenly continued to the time value of the combined notes; a state of equality among competing or opposed parties, as in certain games, competitions among marksmen, etc.; a contest in which two or more competitors are equally successful.—*To play* or *shoot off a tie*, to go through a second contest (the first being indecisive) to decide who is to be the winner.—**tie beam,** *n.* The beam which connects the bottom of a pair of principal rafters in a roof.

tier, tēr, *n.* [Fr. *tire*, from *tirer*, to draw.] A row; a rank, particularly when two or more rows are placed one above another.

tierce, tērs, *n.* [Fr., a third, third part, from L. *tertius*, third, from *tres*, three.] Formerly a liquid measure equal to one-third of a pipe, or 42 wine gallons, equal to 35 imperial gallons; a cask for salt provisions, etc.; *mus.* a major or minor third; *fencing*, a position in which the wrist and nails are turned downward, the weapon of the opponent being on the right of the fencer.

tiff, tif, *n.* [Originally a sniff; comp. N. *taev*, *taeft*, scent.] A small draft of liquor; a pet or fit of peevishness; a slight altercation or quarrel. —*v.i.* To be in a pet.—*v.t.* To sip; to drink.

tiffany, tif′a•ni, *n.* [O.Fr. *tiffer*, to adorn.] A species of gauze or very thin silk.

tiffin, tif′in, *n.* [From Prov.E. *tiffing*, eating or drinking out of due season. TIFF.] In India a lunch or slight repast between breakfast and dinner.

tiger, tī′gėr, *n.* [Fr. *tigre*, from L. and Gr. *tigris*, a tiger, from O.Per. *tigrâ*, an arrow.] A large and dreaded carnivorous mammal of the cat family found in Southern Asia, about the size of the lion, but more catlike and having a striped body; it is usually driven out of its haunts by natives and shot by sportsmen seated on elephants.—**tiger beetle,** *n.* A name given to certain beetles that feed upon other insects.—**tiger cat,** *n.* A domestic cat having the striped appearance of a tiger.—**tigerish, tigrish,** tī′gėr•ish, tī′grish, *a.* Resembling, pertaining to, or characteristic of a tiger.—**tiger lily,** *n.* A garden lily with orange-colored flowers spotted with black.—**tiger moth,** *n.* A name of various moths having wings richly streaked.—**tigress,** tī′gres, *n.* The female of the tiger.

tight, tīt, *a.* [O.E. *thite*, *thiht*, *thyht*= Icel. *théttr*, tight, Dan. *taet*, tight, close, D. *digt*, G. *dicht*, thick, solid, dense; perhaps allied to *thick*.] Having the parts or joints so close as to prevent the passage of fluids; impervious to air, gas, water, etc.; compactly or firmly built or made; sound and strong; as applied to persons, well-knit, sinewy, strong; firmly packed or inserted; not loose; fitting too close to the body; tensely stretched or strained; taut; not slack (a *tight* rope); not easy to be obtained; not to be had on ordinary terms; said of money when capitalists are disinclined to speculate (*commercial slang*).—**tighten,** tī′tn, *v.t.* To make tight; to draw tighter.—**tightener,** tī′tn•ėr, *n.* One who or that which tightens.—**tightly,** tīt′li, *adv.* In a tight manner; closely; compactly.—**tightrope,** *n.* A tightly stretched rope on which an acrobat performs feats.—**tights,** tīts, *n.pl.* Tight-fitting breeches; a covering worn on the legs by acrobats, actors, dancers, and the like.

tigress, etc. See TIGER.

tike, tīk, *n.* [Icel. *tik*, Sw. *tik*, a bitch, a cur.] A dog; a cur; a boor; a clown.

til, tēl, *n.* Indian sesame.

tilbury, til′be•ri, *n.* [From the name of the inventor, a London coach builder in the beginning of the nineteenth century.] A gig or two-wheeled carriage without a top or cover.

tilde, til′de, *n.* [Sp.] The mark over the Spanish *n* when pronounced with a slightly added *y* sound, as in señor, cañon, etc.

tile, tīl, *n.* [A.Sax. *tigel*, from L. *tegula*, a tile, from *tego*, to cover (seen also in *tegument*, *detect*, *protect*), from same root as E. *thatch*, *deck*.] A kind of thin slab of baked clay, used for covering the roofs of buildings, paving floors, lining furnaces and ovens, constructing drains, etc.; a tube or tunnel-shaped piece of baked clay for drains; a tall stiff hat (*slang*).—*Encaustic tiles*. See ENCAUSTIC.—*v.t.*—*tiled*, *tiling*. To cover with tiles; *Freemasonry*, to guard against the entrance of the uninitiated by placing the tiler at the closed door.—**tiler,** tī′lėr, *n.* A man who makes or who lays tiles; the doorkeeper of a Freemasons' lodge. —**tiling,** tī′ling, *n.* Covering a roof with tiles; tiles collectively.

till, til, *n.* [Formerly a drawer in general, from A.Sax. *tyllan*, to draw; comp. D. *tillen*, O.Fris. *tilla*, to lift, to raise.] A money box in a shop, warehouse, etc.; a cash drawer.

till, til, *n.* [Comp. W. *tel*, compact.] A kind of hard clayey earth; boulder clay; *geol.* unstratified boulder clay or any unstratified alluvial formation of considerable thickness.

till, til, *prep.* [Same as Icel. and Dan. *til*, Sw. *till*; perhaps allied to G. *ziel*, end, aim.] To the time of; until (wait *till* next week); often used before verbs and clauses (I will wait *till* you arrive); also to, as far as, or up to.—*Till now*, to the present time.—*Till then*, to that time.

till, til, *v.t.* [A.Sax. *tilian*, to labor, to till; lit to make fit or good, from *til* (A.Sax. and Goth.), fit, good; allied to D. *telen*, to cultivate, to breed; O.G. *zilôn*, to cultivate. *Toil* is a closely allied form.] To plow and prepare for seed, and to dress the crops of; to cultivate; to labor.—**tillable,** til′a•bl, *a.* Capable of being tilled; arable.—**tillage,** til′ij, *n.* The operation or art of tilling land; cultivation; culture; husbandry.—

tiller, til′ėr, *n.* One who tills.—*Naut.* the bar or lever fitted to the head of a rudder to turn the helm of a ship or boat in steering.

tiller, til′ėr, *n.* [Comp. A.Sax. *telgor*, a plant, a shoot; akin D. *telen*, to breed.] The shoot of a plant springing from the root; a sucker.—*v.i.* To put forth shoots from the root.

tilt, tilt, *n.* [A.Sax. *teld*, a tent=Dan. and L.G. *telt*, Icel. *tjald*, G. *zelt*, tent.] A tent‡; the cloth covering of a cart or wagon; a canopy or awning over the after part of a boat.—*v.t.* To cover with a tilt or awning.

tilt, tilt, *v.t.* [From A.Sax. *tealt*, unsteady or unstable; comp. O.Fris. *tilla*, D. and L.G. *tillen*, to raise, to heave up; Sw. *tulta*, to waddle; Icel. *tōlt*, an amble.] To raise one end of, as of a cask, for discharging liquor; to heave up at an angle; to hammer or forge with a tilthammer.—*To tilt up, geol.* to throw up abruptly at a high angle of inclination (the strata are *tilted up*).—*v.i.* To run or ride and thrust with a lance; to joust, as in a tournament; to fight similarly; to rush as in combat; to rise into a sloping position; to heel.—*n.* A thrust; a military exercise on horseback, in which the combatants attacked each other with lances; a tilthammer; inclination forward (the *tilt* of a cask); *geol.* the throwing up of strata at a high angle of inclination.—**tilter,** til′tėr, *n.* One who tilts; one who jousts.—**tilthammer,** *n.* A large hammer worked by steam or water power, lifted by a cam or projection on the axle of a wheel and again allowed to fall on the mass on the anvil.

tilth, tilth, *n.* [A.Sax. *tilth*, culture, from *tilian*, to till; comp. *spilth*, from *spill*.] The operation of tilling; tillage; husbandry; the state of being tilled; tilled ground.

timber, tim′bėr, *n.* [A.Sax. *timber*, timber, wood, structure=Icel. *timbr*, Dan. *tōmmer*, D. *timmer*, G. *zimmer*; lit. building materials, the root being that of Gr. *demō*, to build, L. *domus*, a house (whence *domestic*, *domicile*, etc.).] Trees cut down and suitable for building purposes; trees felled and partly prepared for use; growing trees yielding wood suitable for constructive purposes; one of the main beams of a fabric; *naut.* a curving piece of wood forming the rib of a ship (with a plural in this and preceding sense).—*v.t.* To furnish with timber.—**timbered,** tim′-bėrd, *p.* and *a.* Furnished with timbers; covered with growing timber.

timbre, tim′br, or tan•br, *n.* [Fr., from L. *tympanum*, a drum.] *Mus.* the quality which distinguishes any given tone or sound of one instrument or voice from the same tone or sound of another instrument or voice, and which depends on the harmonics co-existing with the fundamental tone and their relative intensities.

timbrel, tim′brel, *n.* [A dim. of Fr. *timbre*, a bell, originally a drum. See above.] A kind of drum or tabor; a tambourine.

time, tīm, *n.* [A.Sax. *tíma*, time, hour, season; Icel. *tími*, Sw. and Dan. *time*; akin to *tide*, being from the same root but with a different termination.] The measure of duration; a particular portion or part of duration, whether past, present, or future, and either a space or a point, a period or a moment; occasion; season; moment; a proper occasion; opportunity (to bide our *time*); period at which any definite event occurred or person lived; an age (the *time* of James I); an allotted period of life; the present life; existence in this world; prevailing state of circumstances: generally in plurəl (good *times*, bad *times*); leisure (I have not *time* to speak with you); hour of death or of travail (his *time* was come); a performance or repetition among others; *mus.* the style of movement marked by the regular grouping of a certain and equal number of notes, or of more or less notes equal in time value to that certain number through all the bars of a movement; rhythm; the absolute velocity or rate of movement at which a piece is executed.—*At times*, at distinct intervals of duration.—*The time*, the present age; the present period (men of the *time*); also, any period definitely referred to.—*Absolute time*, time considered without relation to bodies or their motions; duration flowing on uniformly.—*Relative time*, the sensible measure of any portion of duration.—*Apparent time*, time regulated by the apparent motion of the sun; time as shown by a properly adjusted sundial; solar time.—*Astronomical time*, mean solar time reckoned through the twenty-four hours.—*Civil time*, mean time adapted to civil uses, and distinguished into years, months, days, etc.—*Common time, mus.* See COMMON.—*Equation of time*. Under EQUATION.—*In time*, in good season; at the right moment; sufficiently early; before it is too late; in the course of things; by degrees; eventually.—*Mean time*, or *mean solar time*, time regulated by the average or mean. See MEAN.—*Nick of time*, the exact point of time required by necessity or convenience; the critical moment.—*Sidereal time*. See SIDEREAL.—*Solar time*. Same as *Apparent time*.—*Time enough*, in season; early enough.—*Time out of mind*, or *time immemorial*, time beyond the memory of man.—*To kill time*, to occupy one's self so as to make it pass without too much tediousness.—*To lose time*, to fail to take full advantage of time or opportunity; to go too slow (as a watch or clock).—*v.t.*—*timed, timing*. To adapt to the time or occasion; to regulate as to time; to mark or ascertain the time or rate of.—*v.i.* To keep time; to harmonize.—**time-honored,** *a.* Honored for a long time; venerable and worthy of honor by reason of antiquity and long continuance.—**timekeeper,** *a.* A clock, watch, or chronometer; a person who keeps or marks the time, as that during which a number of workmen work.—**timeless,** tīm′les, *a.* Unseasonable; without end.—**timeliness,** tīm′li•nes, *n.* The quality of being timely.—**timely,** tīm′li, *a.* Seasonable; being in good time; sufficiently early.—**timeous,** tī′mus, *a.* Timely; seasonable.—**timepiece,** *n.* A clock, watch, or other instrument to measure time, especially a small portable clock.—**timeserver,** *n.* One who meanly and for selfish ends adapts his opinions and manners to the times; one who obsequiously complies with the ruling power.—**timeserving,** *a.* Obsequiously complying with the humors of men in power.—*n.* The conduct of a timeserver.—**timetable,** *n.* A table or register of times, as of the hours to be observed in a school, of the departure and arrival of railroad trains, steamboats, etc.

timid, tim′id, *a.* [L. *timidus*, from *timeo*, to fear.] Fearful; wanting courage to meet danger; timorous; not bold.—**timidity, timidness,** ti•mid′i•ti, tim′id•nes, *n.* The state or quality of being timid.—**timidly,** tim′id•li, *adv.* In a timid manner; weakly; without courage.

timocracy, tī•mok′ra•si, *n.* [Gr. *timokratia*—*timē*, honor, worth, and *krateō*, to rule.] A form of government in which a certain amount of property is requisite as a qualification for office.—**timocratic,** tī•mō•krat′-ik, *a.* Pertaining to timocracy.

timorous, tim′or•us, *a.* [L.L. *timorosus*, from L. *timor*, fear, from *timeo*, to fear. TIMID.] Fearful of danger; timid; destitute of courage; indicating or marked by fear.—**timorously,** tim′or•us•li, *adv.* In a timorous manner.—**timorousness,** tim′or•us•nes, *n.* The state or quality of being timorous.

timothy grass, *n.* [First recommended by *Timothy* Hanson.] A kind of hard, coarse grass extensively cultivated for hay.

timous, timeous. See TIME.

tin, tin, *n.* [A.Sax., D., Dan., and Icel. *tin*, Sw. *ten*, G. *zinn*; not connected with L. *stannum*, tin.] A silver-white, malleable, ductile metallic element, used as a protective coating and in alloys. Symbol, Sn (Latin, *stannum*); at. no., 50; at. wt., 118.69.—*v.t.*—*tinned, tinning*. To cover with tin, or overlay with tin foil.—**tin foil,** *n.* Pure tin, or the metal alloyed with a little lead, beaten and rolled into thin sheets.—**tin hat,** *n.* A soldier's shrapnel helmet.—**tinman,** tin′man, *n.* A manufacturer of, or dealer in tinware.—**tinner,** tin′ėr, *n.* One who works in a tin mine; a tinman.—**tinny,** tin′i, *a.* Pertaining to, abounding with, or resembling tin.—**tin plate,** *n.* Thin sheet iron coated with tin, in order to protect it from oxidation or rust; white-iron.—**tinsmith,** *n.* One who makes articles of tin or tin plate.—**tinstone,** *n.* One of the principal ores of tin.—**tinware,** tin′wâr, *n.* Articles made of tinned iron.

tinamou, tin′a•mö, *n.* [The native name.] A gallinaceous bird of South

America, the species varying in size from a pheasant to a quail.

tincal, ting'kal, *n.* [Malay *tingkal,* Hind. and Per. *tinkâr.*] The commercial name of borax in its crude or unrefined state, employed in refining metals.

tinct, tingkt, *n.* A tint or tincture. (*Obsolete or poetical.*)

tinctorial, tingk•tō'ri•al, *a.* [From L. *tinctor,* a dyer. TINCTURE.] Pertaining to colors or dyes.

tincture, tingk'chėr, *n.* [L. *tinctura,* from *tingo, tinctum.* TINGE.] A tinge or shade of color; slight taste superadded to any substance; slight quality added to anything; *med.* an extract or solution of the active principles of some substance in a solvent, the latter being often proof spirit: so called from usually possessing color; *tinctures* is the heraldic name for what are commonly called 'colors'. The 'metals' (gold and silver) are included in the 'tinctures' together with the five 'colors': red, blue, green, black, and purple.—*v.t.*—*tinctured, tincturing.* To tinge or impart a slight foreign color to; to impregnate; to imbue.

tinder, tin'dėr, *n.* [A.Sax. *tynder, tender,* from *tyndan, tendan,* to kindle (Dan. *taende,* G. *zünden*)=Sw. and L.G. *tunder,* Icel. *tundr,* D. *tonder,* G. *zunder,* tinder.] An inflammable substance generally composed of partially burned linen, used for kindling fire from a spark struck with a steel and flint.—*German tinder.* AMADOU.—**tinderbox,** *n.* A box in which tinder is kept.—**tindery,** tin'-dėr•i, *a.* Like tinder; inflammable.

tine, tīn, *n.* [O.E. *tinde,* A.Sax. *tind*= Icel. *tindr,* Dan. *tind, tinde,* L.G. and Sw. *tinne,* same root as *tooth.*] The tooth or spike of a fork; a prong; the tooth of a harrow; a point or prong of a deer's horn.—**tined,** tīnd, *a.* Furnished with tines.

tinea, tin'ē•a, *n.* [L., a gnawing worm, a bookworm, a moth.] A term for ringworm or similar diseases of the skin.

ting, ting, *n.* [Imitative; comp. *tinkle, jingle*; L. *tinnio,* to tinkle.] A sharp sound, as of a bell; a tinkling.—*v.i.* To sound or ring.

tinge, tinj, *v.t.*—*tinged, tinging.* [L. *tingo, tinctum,* to moisten, stain, dye (seen also in *tincture, tint, taint, distain,* whence *stain*); cog. Gr. *tenggō,* to wet.] To mix or imbue with some foreign substance so as to slightly affect or modify the color, taste, or qualities of; to give a certain smack, flavor, or quality to; to color. —*n.* A slight degree of color, taste, flavor, or quality infused or added to something; tincture; tint; smack.

tingle, ting'gl, *v.i.*—*tingled, tingling.* [A dim. from *ting.*] To feel a kind of thrilling sensation, as in hearing a small sharp ringing sound; to feel a sharp, thrilling pain; to have a thrilling, sharp, or penetrating sensation.—*v.t.* To cause to give a sharp ringing sound; to ring.—**tingling,** ting'gl•ing, *n.* A thrilling, jarring, tremulous sensation.

tinker, ting'kėr, *n.* [From *tink, ting,* a sharp metallic sound.] A mender of kettles, pans, and the like; a repair; a cobbling or botching.—*v.t.* To mend like a tinker; to mend clumsily; to cobble; to botch.—*v.i.* To work at tinker's work; to cobble; to keep making petty repairs.

tinkle, ting'kl, *v.i.*—*tinkled, tinkling.* [A freq. from *tink, ting,* imitative of sound.] To make small, quick, sharp sounds, as by striking on metal; to clink; to jingle; to resound with a small sharp sound; to tingle.—*v.t.* To cause to make sharp, quick, ringing sounds; to ring.—*n.* A small, quick, sharp, ringing noise.—**tinkling,** tingk'ling, *n.* A small, quick, sharp sound.

tinner, etc. See TIN.

tinnitus, tin•nī'tus, *n.* [L., a ringing, a tingling, from *tinnio,* to ring.] *Med.* a ringing in the ears.

tinsel, tin'sel, *n.* [Fr. *étincelle,* O.Fr. *estincelle,* from L. *scintilla,* a spark (whence also *scintillate*).] Thin shining metallic plate or foil for ornamental purposes; cloth or tissue of silk and silver threads; cloth overlaid with foil; something superficially showy, and more gay than valuable. —*a.* Consisting of tinsel; showy to excess; specious; superficial.—*v.t.*—*tinseled, tinseling.* To adorn with tinsel or with something showy and without value.

tint, tint, *n.* [It. *tinta,* Fr. *teint,* from L. *tinctus,* pp. of *tingo.* TINGE.] A slight coloring or tincture distinct from the ground or principal color; a hue; a tinge; degree of intensity of a color.—*v.t.* To tinge; to give a slight coloring to.

tintinnabular, tintinnabulary, tin•tin•nab'ū•lėr, tin•tin•nab'ū•le•ri, *a.* [L. *tintinnabulum,* a bell, from *tintinno,* a freq. from *tinnio,* to ring.] Of or relating to bells or their sound. —**tintinnabulation,** tin'tin•nab•ū•lā"shon, *n.* A tinkling or ringing sound, as of bells.

tiny, tī'ni, *a.* [M.E. *tyne,* tiny.] Very small; little; puny.

tip, tip, *n.* [D. *tip,* L.G. and Sw. *tipp,* a tip; allied to *tap.*] A gentle stroke; a tap; gratuity; present in money; an item of private information, especially in regard to the chances of horses engaged for a race, for betting purposes (slang).—*v.t.*—*tipped, tipping.* To give as a money gift, usually for some service rendered; to tap.

tip, tip, *n.* [M.E.] A small, pointed end, as the tip of a pencil; an end piece, as a cap.—*v.t.*—*tipped, tipping.* To form the tip of; to cover or adorn the tip of.—*To tip off,* to drink off.—*To tip up,* to raise up one end of.—*To tip the wink,* to direct a wink to another as a sign of caution or the like (*slang*).—**tipcart,** *n.* A cart which can be canted up to empty its contents.—**tipcat,** *n.* A game in which a small pointed piece of wood called a cat is made to jump from the ground by being struck on the tip with a stick.—**tipstaff,** *n.* pl. **tipstaves,** A staff tipped with metal; an officer who bears such a staff; a constable; a sheriff's officer.—**tipster,** tip'stėr, *n.* One who for a fee sends tips for betting purposes.—**tiptoe,** tip'tō, *n.* The tip or end of the toe.—*To be* or *to stand on tiptoe, fig.* to be on the strain; to be interested or anxious.

tip, tip, *v.t.* and *i.*—*tipped, tipping.* [M.E. *type,* of uncertain origin.] To upset; to overthrow; to slant or incline.—*n.* A tilt; a tipped position.

tippet, tip'et, *n.* [A.Sax. *taeppet,* a tippet, from L. *tapete,* cloth. TAPESTRY.] A sort of cape covering the shoulders, and sometimes descending as far as the waist.

tipple, tip'l, *v.i.*—*tippled, tippling.* [Freq. and dim. from *tip,* to tilt or turn up; akin *tipsy.*] To drink spirituous or intoxicating liquors habitually; to drink frequently, but without getting drunk.—*v.t.* To drink, sip, or imbibe often.—*n.* Liquor taken in tippling; drink.—**tippler,** tip'lėr, *n.* One who tipples; a toper; a soaker.

tipsy, tip'si, *a.* [Connected with *tipple*; comp. Prov.G. *tips, tipps,* drunkenness.] Overpowered or muddled with strong drink; intoxicated, but not helplessly drunk; fuddled.—**tipsily,** tip'si•li, *adv.* In a tipsy manner.—**tipsiness,** tip'si•nes, *n.* The state of being tipsy.

tiptop, tip'top, *a.* [From *tip* and *top,* or a reduplication of *top* (like *dingdong, slipslop,* etc.).] First-rate; excellent or perfect in the highest degree. (*Colloq.*)

tirade, tī'rād, *n.* [Fr. *tirade,* from *tirer,* to draw, from the Germanic verb=E. to *tear.*] A long violent speech; a declamatory flight of censure or reproof; a series of invectives; a harangue.

tire, tīr, *n.* [For *tier* from *tie.*] A band or hoop, as of steel or rubber (solid or pneumatic) forming the tread of a vehicle wheel.

tire, tīr, *v.t.*—*tired, tiring.* [A.Sax. *teorian,* to tire; *tirian, tirigan,* to vex, annoy; D. *tergen,* to irritate.] To exhaust the strength of by toil or labor; to fatigue; to weary; to exhaust the attention or patience of, with dullness or tediousness.—*To tire out,* to weary or fatigue to excess; to exhaust.—*v.i.* To become weary; to have the patience exhausted.—**tiredness,** tīrd'nes, *n.* The state of being wearied; weariness.—**tiresome,** tīr'sum, *a.* Fitted or tending to tire; fatiguing; wearisome; tedious.—**tiresomely,** tīr'sum•li, *adv.* In a tiresome manner.—**tiresomeness,** tīr'sum•nes, *n.* Wearisomeness; tediousness.

'tis, tiz. A common contraction of *It is.*

Tishri, tish'ri, *n.* [Heb.] A Hebrew month answering to part of September and part of October.

tissue, tish'ū, *n.* [Fr. *tissu,* woven, pp. of *tisser,* to weave, from L. *texere,* to weave. TEXT.] A woven or textile fabric; cloth interwoven with gold or silver, or with colored figures; *fig.* a mass of connected particulars (a *tissue* of falsehood); *animal anat.* one of the primary layers composing any of the parts of animal bodies;

vegetable anat. the minute elementary structures of which the organs of plants are composed.—**tissue paper,** *n.* A very thin, gauze-like paper, used for protecting engravings in books, wrapping delicate articles, etc.

tit, tit, *n.* [Same as Icel. *tittr*, a small bird, a tit; Dan. *tite*, a sandpiper; N. *tite*, a titmouse; originally anything small.] A small bit; a morsel; a small horse; the titmouse; a contemptuous term for a woman.—*Tit for tat*, an equivalent in the way of revenge or repartee.

Titan, tī'tan, *n. Greek myth.* one of the twelve children of Heaven and Earth, said to have been of gigantic size and enormous strength, and to have been defeated by Zeus and thrown into Tartarus; poetical for the sun.—**Titaness,** tī•'tan•es, *n.* A female Titan; a female personage of surpassing power.—**Titania,** ti•tā'ni•a, *n.* [Among the Romans a name of Diana.] The queen of Fairyland and consort of Oberon.—**titanic,** tī•tan'ik, *a.* Pertaining to the Titans; enormous in size or strength; huge; vast.

titanium, tī•tā'ni•um, *n.* [So called in fanciful allusion to the *Titans*.] A white metallic element, occurring in practically all rocks; used in metallurgy and for light, strong alloys. Symbol, Ti; at. no., 22; at. wt., 47.90.—**titanate,** tī'tan•āt, *n.* A salt of titanic acid.—**titanic,** tī•tan'ik, *a.* Pertaining to titanium.—*Titanic acid*, dioxide of titanium, called also *Titanic oxide*.—**titaniferous,** tī•tan•if'ėr•us, *a.* Producing titanium.

titbit. Same as TIDBIT.

tithe, tīTH, *n.* [O.E. *tethe*, *tiethe*, *teothe*, from A.Sax. *teótha* (for *teóntha*), the tenth. TEN.] The tenth part of anything; the tenth part of the profits of land and stock and the personal industry of the inhabitants, allotted to the clergy for their support; hence, any small part or proportion.—*Commutation of tithes*, the conversion of tithes into a rent-charge payable in money, and chargeable on the land.—*v.t.*—*tithed, tithing.* To levy a tithe on; to tax to the amount of a tenth.—*v.i.* To pay tithes.—**tithable,** tī'THa•bl, *a.* Subject to the payment of tithes.—**tither,** tī'THėr, *n.* One who collects tithes.—**tithing,** tī'THing, *n.* The levying or taking of tithes; a tithe; formerly in England, a number or company of ten householders, who, dwelling near each other, were sureties or free pledges to the king for the good behavior of each other.

titian, tish'an, *n.* [After *Titian*, It. painter (1477-1576).] A brownish-orange color made famous by Titian.

titillate, tit'i•lāt, *v.i.*—*titillated, titillating.* [L. *titillo, titillatum*, to tickle.] To tickle; to give a slight relish or pleasure to.—**titillation,** tit•i•lā'shon, *n.* The act of tickling; any slight pleasure.—**titillative,** tit'i•lā•tiv, *a.* Tending to titillate or tickle.

titivate, tittivate, tit'i•vāt, *v.t.* [Perhaps from *tidy*.] To put in order; to make look smart or spruce; to adorn. (*Slang.*)

titlark, tit'lärk, *n.* [From *tit*, a small bird, and *lark*.] A common small bird somewhat resembling a lark; a pipit.

title, tī'tl, *n.* [O.Fr. *title* (Fr. *titre*), from L. *titulus*, a title.] An inscription or superscription on anything as a name by which it is known; a label; the inscription at the beginning of a book or other composition, containing the subject of the work or its particular designation; a particular section or division of a writing, especially a chapter or section of a law book; an appellation of dignity, distinction, or pre-eminence given to persons; the appellation or honor distinctive of a sovereign, prince, or nobleman; a name or appellation in general; a claim; a right; *law*, right of ownership, or the sources of such right; the instrument or document which is evidence of a right.—*v.t.*—*titled, titling.* To name; to call; to entitle.—**titled,** tī'tld, *a.* Having a title; especially, having a title of nobility.—**title deed,** *n.* A writing evidencing a man's right or title to property.—**title page,** *n.* The page of a book which contains the title.—**title role,** *n.* The part in a play which gives its name to it, as Hamlet in the play of the same name.

titmouse, tit'mous, *n.* pl. **titmice,** tit'mīs. [From *tit*, a small thing, a small bird, and *mouse*, by corruption from A.Sax. *máse* (D. *mees*, G. *meise*), a titmouse.] A name of several common insessorial birds, small and active, feeding on seeds, insects, etc., with shrill, wild notes.

titration, tī•trā'shun, *n.* [Fr. *titer*, titrate.] *Chem.* a method of determining the strength of a solution or the concentration of a substance in solution by finding the smallest amount of a liquid reagent of known strength necessary to change the solution or substance into another form.—**titrate,** tī'trāt, *v.t.* and *i.*—*titrated, titrating.* To subject to or perform titration.

titter, tit'ėr, *v.i.* [An imitative word, like *snigger*, *tattle*, etc.] To laugh with a stifled sound or with restraint.—*n.* A restrained laugh.

tittle, tit'l, *n.* [O.Fr. *title*, a title, a tittle. TITLE.] A small particle; a jot; an iota.

tittle-tattle, *n.* [A reduplication of *tattle*; an imitative word.] Idle trifling talk; empty prattle.—*v.i.* To talk idly; to prate.

titubate,† tit'ū•bāt, *v.t.* and *i.* [L. *titubo, titubatum*, to stumble.] To stumble; to rock or roll, as a curved body on a plane.—**titubation,** tit•ū•bā'shon, *n.* A stumbling; *med.* restlessness; fidgets.

titular, tit'ū•lėr, *a.* [Fr. *titulaire*; from L. *titulus*, a title. TITLE.] Being such or such by title or name only; having the title to an office without the duties of it.—*n.* One who has merely the title of an office; one who may lawfully enjoy an ecclesiastical benefice without performing its duties.—**titularly,** tit'ū•lėr•li, *adv.* In a titular manner; by title only.—**titulary,** tit'ū•le•ri, *a.* and *n.* Same as *Titular*.

tizzy, tiz'i, *n.* [Origin unknown.] A state of being highly excited and baffled over a trifle.

tmesis, tmē'sis, *n.* [Gr. *tmēsis*, from *temnō*, to cut.] *Gram.* the division of a compound word into two parts, with one or more words between (of whom *be* thou *ware*).

TNT. See TRINITROTOLUENE.

to, tu̧, or when emphasized tö, *prep.* [A.Sax. *tó*, to, toward, for, etc. = D. *toe*, L.G. *to*, G. *zu*, Goth. *du*; cog. Ir. and Gael. *do*, Slav. *do*.] Denoting motion toward a place or thing (going *to* church); toward (point *to* the sky); opposed to *from*; indicating a point or limit reached (count *to* ten); denoting destination, aim, or design (born *to* poverty); denoting an end or consequence (*to* our cost); denoting addition, junction, or union (tied *to* a tree); compared with; often used in expressing ratios or proportions (three is *to* twelve as four is *to* sixteen); denoting opposition or contrast (face *to* face); often used in betting phrases (my hat *to* a halfpenny); according to; in congruity or harmony with (suited *to* his taste); denoting correspondency or accompaniment (dance *to* an air); in the character or quality of (took her *to* wife); for; denoting the relation of the dative in other languages (given *to* me); marking an object (a dislike *to* spirituous liquors); the sign of the infinite mood of a verb, or governing the gerundial infinitive or gerund (slow *to* believe; we have *to* pay it).—*adv.* Forward; on; often denoting motion toward a junction, union, or closing (shut the door *to*).—*To and fro*, forward and backward; up and down.

toad, tōd, *n.* [A.Sax. *tádie*.] Any of numerous frog-like, tailless, leaping amphibians living on land but breeding in water.—**toadeater,** *n.* A fawning, obsequious parasite; a mean sycophant; a toady.—**toadfish,** *n.* A fish, the angler or fishing-frog.—**toadflax,** *n.* The name of several indigenous British plants allied to the antirrhinum.—**toadstone,** *n.* Bufonite.—**toadstool,** *n.* A fungus with a fleshy, umbrella-shaped cap; a poisonous mushroom.—**toady,** tō'di, *n.* A self-seeking flatterer. a toadeater. —*v.t.* —*toadied, toadying.* To fawn upon in a servile manner; to play the toady or sycophant to.—**toadyism,** tō'di•izm, *n.* Mean sycophancy; servile adulation; nauseous flattery.

toast, tōst, *v.t.* [O.Fr. *toster*, from L. *tostum*, pp. of *torreo*, to toast. TORRENT.] To dry and scorch (a piece of bread) by the heat of a fire; to warm thoroughly (to *toast* the feet); to drink to the success of or in honor of.—*n.* Bread scorched by the fire; a piece of such bread put in a beverage; a lady whose health is drunk in honor or respect; anyone or anything named in honor in drinking; a sentiment proposed for general acceptance in drinking.—**toaster,** tōs′tėr, *n.* One who toasts; an instrument for toasting bread, cheese, etc.—**toastmaster,** *n.* A person who announces the toasts; the person presiding at a dinner.

tobacco, to•bak′ō, *n.* A plant of the nightshade family, a native of the warmer parts of America, and now extensively cultivated in various regions; also the prepared leaves, used for smoking and chewing or in the form of snuff.—**tobacconist,** to•bak′o•nist, *n.* A dealer in tobacco; a manufacturer of tobacco.

toboggan, to•bog′an, *n.* [Corruption of Amer. Indian *odabagan,* a sled.] A kind of flat-bottomed sled turned up in front, used for sliding down snow-covered slopes.—*v.i.* To use such a sled; to fall rapidly, as stock prices (*Slang*).

tocher, to*ch*′ėr, *n.* [Gael. *tochradh,* Ir. *tochar,* a portion or dowry.] The dowry which a wife brings to her husband by marriage. (*Scotch.*)

tocsin, tok′sin, *n.* [Fr. *tocsin,* O.Fr. *toquesin;* from *toque,* a stroke, and *sin, sein,* a bell, from L. *signum,* a sign. TOUCH, SIGN.] An alarm bell; a bell rung as a signal or for the purpose of giving an alarm.

today, tu̧•dā′, *n.* [A.Sax. *to-daeg—tó,* to, and *daeg,* day.] The present day. —*adv.* On this day.

toddle, tod′l, *v.i.—toddled, toddling.* [A freq. akin to *totter;* comp. G. *zotteln,* to toddle.] To walk with short steps in a tottering way, as a child or an old man.—*n.* A little toddling walk.—**toddler,** tod′l•ėr, *n.* One who toddles; a young child.

toddy, tod′i, *n.* [Hind.] The sweet juice of certain palms; palm wine; also, a mixture of spirit and hot water sweetened.

to-do, tu̧•dö, *n.* Ado; bustle; hurry; commotion. (*Colloq.*)

tody, tō′di, *n.* [L. *todus,* a small bird.] A tropical passerine bird of gaudy plumage, allied to the kingfishers.

toe, tō, *n.* [A.Sax. *tá,* toe = Icel. *tá,* Sw. *to,* Dan. *taa,* G. *zehe,* the toe.] One of the small members which form the extremity of the foot; the fore part of a shoe, stocking, etc. —*v.t.—toed, toeing.* To touch or reach with the toes; to supply with a toe; to drive slantingly, as a nail. —*v.i.* To tiptoe.—*Toe the line,* to adhere tenaciously to some rule or standard.

toffee, toffy, tof′i, *n.* [Alteration of *taffy.*] A hard candy made by boiling sugar, or molasses.

toft, toft, *n.* [A Scandinavian word; Icel. and Dan. *toft,* an enclosed field near a house.] A messuage; a house and homestead.

toga, tō′ga, *n.* [L., from stem of *tego,* to cover.] The principal outer garment worn by males among the ancient Romans; a sort of loose robe.—**togated,** tō′gā•ted, *a.* [L. *togatus.*] Dressed in a toga or gown.

together, tu̧•geTH′ėr, *adv.* [A.Sax. *tōgaedere—to,* to, *gador, geador,* at once. GATHER.] In company; unitedly; in concert; in the same place; at the same time; so as to be contemporaneous; the one with the other; mutually; into junction or a state of union; without intermission; on end.

toggery, tog′ėr•i, *n.* [Perhaps humorously formed from L. *toga.*] Clothes; garments. (*Slang.*)

toggle, tog′l, *n.* [Connected with *tag* or *tug.*] *Naut.* a pin through the bight or eye of a rope, or in a similar position, to prevent slipping. —**toggle switch,** *n. Elect.* a switch with a projecting arm that moves through a small arc to open or close a circuit.

toil, toil, *v.i.* [Perhaps from O.D. *teulen, tuylen,* to labor, *tuyl,* tillage, toil; O.Fris. *teula,* to labor, *teule,* labor; akin to *till.*] To exert strength continuously with pain and fatigue of body or mind, particularly of the body; to labor; to work; to drudge.—*v.t.* To labor on; to exhaust or overlabor.—*n.* Labor with pain and fatigue; labor that oppresses the body or mind.—**toiler,** toi′lėr, *n.* One who toils.—**toilful,** toil′ful, *a.* Full of toil; laborious.—**toilsome,** toil′sum, *a.* Attended with toil; laborious; fatiguing.—**toilsomely,** toil′sum•li, *adv.* In a toilsome manner.—**toilsomeness,** toil′sum•nes, *n.* Laboriousness.—**toilworn,** *a.* Worn out or exhausted with toil.

toilet, toi′lit, *n.* [Fr. *toilette,* formerly a sort of cloth, from *toile,* cloth.] A bathroom; a lavatory; the act or process of dressing; attire; dress.—*To make one's toilet,* to dress.—**toiletry,** toi′let•ri, *n.* Articles or preparations used in making one's toilet.—**toilette,** toi•let′, *n.* A woman's toilet, consisting of bathing, dressing, application of cosmetics, and hair grooming.—**toilet water,** *n.* A mildly scented liquid used during or after bathing.

toils, toilz, *n.* pl. [L. *tela,* a web.] Anything suggestive of a net or a snare.

Tokay, tō•kā′, *n.* A highly prized wine produced at *Tokay* in Hungary, made of white grapes, and distinguished by its aromatic taste.

token, tō′kn, *n.* [A.Sax. *tácen, tácn,* a token = Icel. *tákn, teiken,* D. *teeken,* G. *zeichen,* Goth. *taikns.* TEACH.] A sign; a mark; indication; symptom; a memorial of friendship; a souvenir; a metal disk issued as a fare by a transportation company.—*a.* Given as a guarantee, in partial payment of a debt (a *token* payment).

told, tōld, pret. and pp. of *tell.*

Toledo, to•lē′dō, *n.* A sword blade of the finest temper, named from *Toledo* in Spain, formerly famous for its sword blades.

tolerate, tol′ėr•āt, *v.t.—tolerated, tolerating.* [L. *tolero, toleratum,* to bear or support, from root seen in *tollo,* to lift up, *tuli,* I have borne; Skr. *tul,* to bear; E. to *thole.*] To suffer to be or to be done without prohibition or hindrance; to allow or permit; to treat in a spirit of patience and forbearance; not to judge of or condemn with bigotry.—**toleration,** tol•ėr•ā′shon, *n.* [L. *toleratis.*] The act of tolerating; allowance given to that which is not wholly approved; the recognition by the state of the right of private judgment in matters of faith and worship; a disposition to tolerate or not to judge or deal harshly in cases of difference of opinion or conduct; tolerance.—**tolerator,** tol′ėr•ā•tėr, *n.* One who tolerates.—**tolerable,** tol′ėr•a•bl, *a.* [L. *tolerabilis.*] Capable of being borne or endured; supportable, either physically or mentally; sufferable; moderately good or agreeable; not contemptible; passable; middling.—**tolerably,** tol′ėr•a•bli, *adv.* In a tolerable manner; moderately well; passably.—**tolerance,** tol′ėr•ans, *n.* [L. *tolerantia.*] The quality of being tolerant; the capacity or the act of enduring; a disposition to be patient and indulgent toward those whose opinions or practices differ from one's own; *engin.* the permitted amount of deviation from exact dimensions as specified.—**tolerant,** tol′ėr•ant, *a.* [L. *tolerans, tolerantis,* ppr. of *tolero.*] Inclined or disposed to tolerate; favoring toleration; forbearing; able to endure or suffer.—**tolerantly,** tol′ėr•ant•li, *adv.* In a tolerant manner.

toll, tōl, *n.* [A.Sax. *toll,* tax or tribute = Icel. *tollr,* Sw. *tull,* Dan. *told,* D. *tol,* G. *zoll,* toll, duty, custom, from stem of *tell,* to count.] A tax or duty imposed for some liberty or privilege, as the sum charged for leave to offer goods in a market or fair; a fixed charge made by those entrusted with the maintenance of roads, streets, bridges, etc., for the passage of persons, goods, and cattle.—*v.i.*‡ To pay toll; to exact or levy toll.—**tollage,** tōl′ij, *n.* Toll; payment of toll.—**toll bar,** *n.* A bar or gate to prevent persons or traffic passing without payment of toll.—**tollgate,** *n.* A gate where toll is taken; a toll bar.—**tollgatherer,** *n.* The man who takes toll.—**tollhouse,** *n.* A house placed by a road near a tollgate, where the man who takes the toll is stationed.—**tollman,** *n.* A tollgatherer; the keeper of a toll bar.

toll, tōl, *v.i.* [M. E. *tollen,* to pull, entice.] To give out the slowly measured sounds of a bell when struck at uniform intervals, as at funerals.—*v.t.* To cause (a bell) to sound with strokes slowly and uniformly repeated; to indicate by tolling or striking; to draw attention to by slowly repeated sounds of a bell; to ring for or on account of.—*n.* The sounding of a bell with slow, measured strokes.

tolu, tō′lö, *n.* A fragrant resin or balsam produced by a tree of South America, first brought from Santiago de *Tolu,* in New Granada, and used in coughs, etc.

toluene, tol′ū•ēn, *n.* [From *tolu.*] A coal-tar product used in the preparation of trinitrotoluene, a high explosive.

tom, tom, *n.* A popular contraction of *Thomas,* used in slight contempt (a *tomfool*), or in the names of certain animals.—**tomboy,** tom′boi, *n.* A rude boisterous boy; a wild, romping girl; a hoyden.—**tomcat,** *n.* A male cat, especially a full-grown male cat. —**tomfool,** tom′föl, *n.* A great fool; a trifler.—**tomfoolery,** tom•föl′ėr•i, *n.* Foolish trifling; ridiculous behavior; silly trifles; absurd ornaments or knick-knacks.

tomahawk, tom′a•hąk, *n.* [From Virginian Indian *tamahaac, tamohake,* a hatchet.] An American Indian hatchet, used in the chase and in war, not only in close fighting, but by being thrown to a considerable distance.—*v.t.* To strike, cut, or kill with a tomahawk.

tomato, to•mā′tō or to•mä′tō, *n.* pl. **tomatoes.** [Sp. *tomate,* from Mexican *tomatl.*] A tropical American plant of the potato family and its nutritious fruit, which is pulpy, acid, and usually red.

tomb, töm, *n.* [Fr. *tombe,* It. *tomba,* L.L. *tumba,* from Gr. *tymba, tymbos,* a mound, from root of L. *tumeo,* to swell, *tumulus,* a mound.] A grave; a chamber or vault formed for the reception of the dead; a monument erected in memory of the dead; any sepulchral structure.—*v.t.* To bury; to entomb.—**tombstone,** töm′stōn, *n.* A stone erected over a grave; a sepulchral stone.

tombac, tombak, tom′bak, *n.* [Fr. *tombac,* from Malay *tambaga,* copper.] An alloy of copper and zinc, used as an imitation of gold for cheap jewelry. When arsenic is added it forms *white tombac.*

tomboy, tomcat. See TOM.

tome, tōm, *n.* [Fr. *tome,* from L. *tomus,* a portion of a book, a book, from Gr. *tomos,* a section, from *temnō,* to cut.] A volume, forming part of a larger work; a book, usually a ponderous one.

tomentose, tomentous, tō•men′tōs, tō•men′tus, *a.* [L. *tomentum,* down.] Covered with hairs so close as scarcely to be discernible, or with a whitish down like wool; downy; nappy: used chiefly in botany.—**tomentum,** tō•men′tum, *n.* Pubescence; downy matter.

tomfool. See TOM.

tommy, tom′i, *n.* [From the name *Thomas Atkins,* used casually in specimen forms given in Army Regulations.] A private soldier in the British army.

tommy, tom′i, *n.* (*Slang.*) A penny roll; bread; provisions; goods given to a workman in lieu of wages; the system of paying workmen in goods in place of money; the truck system.

tommyrot, tom″i•rot′, *n.* [E. dial. *tommy,* fool, and *rot.*] Nonsense; rank foolishness.

tomorrow, tų•mor′ō, *n.* [*To* and *morrow.* Comp. *today, tonight.*] The day after the present; or, adverbially, on the day after the present; also used adjectively.

tompion, tom′pi•on, *n.* [Fr. *tampon,* a stopple. TAMPION.] The tampion or stopper of a cannon; the plug in a flute.

tom-tom, tom′tom, *n.* [Imitative, from Hind. *tam-tam.*] A type of drum, usually beaten with the hands.

ton, tun, *n.* [A.Sax. *tunne,* a butt, a large vessel. TUN.] A weight equal to 2,000 pounds avoirdupois (in Gt. Britain 2,240 pounds); a unit of the inside capacity of a ship, equal to 100 cubic feet; a unit of volume of freight capacity, usually approximately 40 cubic feet.—**tonnage,** tun′ij, *n.* The cubical content or burden a ship can carry; the ships of a port or nation collectively estimated by their burden in tons.

tone, tōn, *n.* [Fr. *ton,* tone, accent, style, manner, etc., L. *tonus,* a sound, a tone, from Gr. *tonos,* a stretching, a tone, note, strength, etc., from *teinō,* to stretch, cog. with L. *tendo,* to stretch, and E. *thin. Tune* is the same word.] Any sound considered with relation to its pitch, its quality or timbre, or its strength or volume; a modulation of the voice, as expressing some feeling; accent; a sing-song manner of speaking; a drawl; a musical sound; also one of the larger intervals between certain contiguous notes of the diatonic scale (known as *major* or *minor*); the peculiar quality of sound of any voice or instrument; timbre; that state of a living body in which all the parts and organs have due tension or are well-strung; healthy activity of the organs; state or temper of mind; mood; the general or prevailing character, as of morals, manners, or sentiments; *painting,* a harmonious relation or the colors of a picture in light and shade; the characteristic expression of a picture as distinguished by its color.—*v.t.*—*toned, toning.* To give a certain tone to; to utter in an affected tone.—*To tone down,* to soften the coloring of; to give a lower tone to; to render less pronounced or decided (to *tone down* a statement); to soften.—**toneless,** tōn′les, *a.* Having no tone; unmusical.—**tonal,** tō′nal, *a.* Pertaining to tone.—**tonality,** tō•nal′i•ti, *n. Mus.* the peculiarity characteristic of modern compositions due to their being written in definite keys, thereby conforming to certain defined arrangements of tones and semitones; tonal quality.—**tonic,** ton′ik. *a.* Relating to tones; based on the first tone of a musical scale; a syllable bearing the primary accent; *med.* increasing the mental or physical tone of the system.—*n.* Something that invigorates, restore, stimulates, etc.; *mus.* the keynote, or first note, of a scale.—**tonic sol-fa.** A term applied to a system of writing and teaching music, the leading features of which are the substitution of letters denoting sounds, and of strokes, commas, and colons, denoting time for the notes, etc., of the ordinary notation.—**tone deaf,** *a.* Not sensitive to differences in musical pitch. —**tone language,** *n.* A language (such as Chinese) in which differences in tone result in differences in the meaning of a word.—**tone poem,** *n.* An instrumental composition intended to suggest poetic images.

tongs, tongz, *n. pl.* [A.Sax. *tange,* pl. *tangan,* tongs=D. and Dan. *tang,* Icel. *töng,* G. *zange,* tongs; same root as Gr. *daknō,* to bite.] An instrument of metal, a kind of large nippers, used for handling things, particularly fire or heated metals.

tongue, tung, *n.* [A.Sax. *tunge,* a tongue, speech=L.G. and Dan. *tunge,* Icel. and Sw. *tunga,* Goth. *tuggo,* G. *zunge;* cog. O.L. *dingua,* L. *lingua,* a tongue (whence *lingual, linguist*).] The fleshy movable organ within an animal's mouth, subserving the purposes of taste, prehension of food, swallowing, and in man of articulation or speech also; the instrument of speech (a bitter *tongue*); speech; the whole sum of words used by a particular nation; a language; a nation as distinguished by their language (O.T.); anything considered to resemble an animal's tongue; a point or strip of land running out into a sea or lake; a long low promontory; a tapering jet of flame; the pin of a buckle or brooch which pierces the strap, ribbon, or object to be fastened.—*To have on* (or *at*) *the tip* (or *end*) *of one's tongue,* to be on the point of uttering, telling, or speaking.—*To hold one's tongue,* to keep silence. —*v.t.*—*tongued, tonguing.* To scold; *mus.* to modify tone with the tongue in playing, as in the flute.—**tongue-and-groove joint,** *n.* A joint with a projecting strip on the edge of one board and a matching groove on another.—**tongue in cheek,** *a.* and *adv.* With irony, insincerity, parody, etc.—**tongue-tied,** *a.* Not able, as from shyness, to speak freely.—**tongue twister,** *n.* A word, phrase, sentence, etc., that is difficult to say because of a succession of similar sounds.

tonic, etc. See TONE.

tonight, tu•nīt′, *n.* [Comp. *today, tomorrow.*] The present night.—*adv.* In the present night, or the night after the present day.

tonite, tōn′īt, *n.* [L. *tono,* to thunder.] A very powerful explosive agent prepared from pulverized guncotton.

tonka bean, tong′ka bēn, *n.* [From *tonka,* the name of the bean in Guyana.] The fruit of a shrubby leguminous plant of Guyana, containing a single seed, the odor of which is extremely agreeable.

tonnage. See TON.

tonsil, ton′sil, *n.* [L. *tonsilla,* a tonsil, a mooring pole for a boat.] *Anat.* one of two oblong masses of lymphoid tissue, located on each side of the throat, or fauces.—**tonsillitis,** ton•sil•ī′tis, *n.* Inflammation of the tonsils.—**tonsillectomy,** ton′si•lek″-to•mē, *n.* A surgical operation for the removal of the tonsils.

tonsile, ton′sīl, *a.* [L. *tonsilis,* from *tondeo, tonsum,* to clip or shear.] *Obs.* Capable of or fit to be clipped.—**tonsorial,** ton•sō′ri•al, *a.* Pertaining to a barber or to shaving.—**tonsure,** ton′shėr, *n.* [L. *tonsura,* the act of shaving or clipping.] The act of clipping or shaving; the round bare place on the heads of the Roman Catholic priests and monks formed by shaving or cutting the hair.—**tonsured,** ton′shėrd, *a.* Having a tonsure; hence, clerical.

tontine, ton′tēn, *n.* [Fr. *tontine,* from its inventor *Tonti,* an Italian of the seventeenth century.] An annuity shared by subscribers to a loan, with the benefit of survivorship, the annuity being increased as the subscribers die, until at last the whole goes to the last survivor, or to the last two or three.

too, tö, *adv.* [A form of *to,* the preposition; A.Sax. *tó,* meaning both *to* and *too.* Comp. G. *zu,* to and too.] Over; more than enough; denoting excess (*too* long, *too* short); sometimes with merely an intensive force=very, exceedingly (I should only be *too* glad); likewise; also; in addition; besides; over and above (a painter and a poet *too*).—*Too, too,* repeated, denotes excess emphatically.

took, tụk, pret. of *take.*

tool, töl, *n.* [A.Sax. *tól,* a tool, probably from stem of *tawian,* to make, to prepare. TAW.] Any implement used by a craftsman or laborer at his work; an instrument employed in the manual arts for facilitating mechanical operations; a person used by another as an instrument to accomplish certain ends; a word of reproach.—*Machine tool.* See MACHINE. ∴ *A tool* differs from an *implement* in being more general or less specific, and from an *instrument* in being always used in reference to the manual arts; agricultural *implements*; gardeners' *tools*; joiners' *tools*; surgical *implements*; mathematical *instruments*; musical *instruments.* —*v.t.* To shape with a tool; to drive, as a vehicle (*slang*).

toon, *tön, n.* The wood of an East Indian tree, highly valued as a furniture wood.

toot, töt, *v.i.* [Same as D. *toeten,* G. *tuten,* Sw. *tuta,* to blow a horn, to toot; imitative of sound.] To make a noise like that of a pipe or horn.—*v.t.* To sound, as a horn.—*n.* A sound blown on a horn; a similar noise.—**tooter,** tö′tėr, *n.* One who toots.

tooth, töth, *n.* pl. **teeth,** tēth. [A.Sax. *tóth,* pl. *téth* (comp. *foot, feel*; *goose, geese*)=D., Sw., and Dan. *tand,* Icel. *tōnn* (for *tōnd*), G. *zahn,* Goth. *tunthus*; cog. W. *dant,* L. *dens, dentis,* Gr. *odous, odontos,* Skr. *danta*—tooth; from root meaning to divide, seen also in Gr. *daiō,* to divide.] One of the projecting bony growths in the jaws of vertebrate animals, serving as the instrument of mastication; taste; palate; any projection resembling the tooth of an animal in shape, position, or office; a small, narrow, projecting piece, usually one of a set (as of a comb, a saw, a rake, a wheel).—*Tooth and nail* (lit. by biting and scratching), with one's utmost power; by all possible means of attack and defense.—*To one's teeth,* in open opposition; directly to one's face.—*In the teeth of,* in direct opposition to.—*To cast* something *in one's teeth,* to taunt one with something; to retort reproachfully.—*In spite of one's teeth,* in open defiance of; in opposition to every effort.—*To show the teeth,* to threaten (like a snarling dog).—*To set the teeth on edge,* to cause a tingling or grating sensation in the teeth.—*v.t.* To furnish with teeth; to cut into teeth.—**teethe,** tēTH, *v.i.* —*teethed, teething.* To have the teeth grow.—**teething,** tē′THing, *n.* The growth of the teeth in the young; dentition.—**toothache,** töth′-āk, *n.* Pain in a tooth or in the teeth arising from decay.—**toothbrush,** *n.* A small brush for cleaning the teeth.—**toothed,** tötht, *p.* and *a.* Having teeth or cogs; having projecting points somewhat like teeth.—**toothless,** töth′les, *a.* Having no teeth; deprived of teeth.—**toothpick,** töth′pik, *n.* A small instrument for picking substances from the teeth.—**toothsome,** töth′sum, *a.* Palatable; grateful to the taste.—**toothsomeness,** töth′sum•nes, *n.* Pleasantness to the taste; palatableness.

top, top, *n.* [A.Sax. *top,* top=D. and Dan. *top,* summit; Icel. *toppr,* a tuft or lock of hair, top; G. *zopf,* a tuft, a crest. *Tip, tap* (of a cask); *tuft,* are allied.] The highest part of anything; the most elevated or uppermost point; the summit; upper surface; the highest place or rank; the most honorable position; the utmost degree; the height; the crown of the head (from *top* to toe); the head or upper part of a plant; *pl.* top boots; *woolen manuf.* the combed wool ready for the spinner; *naut.* a sort of platform surrounding the head of the lower masts, serving to extend the shrouds, and for the convenience of men aloft.—*The top of one's bent,* the utmost of one's inclination or liking (fooled to *the top of his bent*).—*a.* Being on the top or summit; highest (*top* speed).—*v.i.*—*topped, topping.* To rise aloft; to be eminent. —*v.t.* To cover on the top; to cap; to rise above; to surpass; to take off the top or upper part of; to rise to the top of.—*To top off,* to complete by putting on the top; hence, to finish; to complete.—**top boots,** *n. pl.* Boots having tops of light-colored leather, used chiefly for riding.—**topcoat,** *n.* An upper or over coat.—**topdress,** *v.t.* To spread manure on the surface of.—**topdressing,** *n.* A dressing of manure laid on the surface of land.—**topgallant,** top′gal•ant, *a. Naut.* being the third of the kind above the deck; above the topmast and below the royal mast (the *topgallant* mast, yards, etc.).—**top hamper,** *n. Naut.* any unnecessary weight either aloft or about the upper decks.—**topheavy,** *a.* Having the top or upper part too heavy for the lower. —**topknot,** *n.* An ornamental knot or bow worn on the top of the head, as by women; the crest of a bird.—**topmast,** top′mast, *n. Naut.* the second mast from the deck, or that which is next above the lower mast, main, fore, or mizzen.—**topmost,** top′mōst, *a.* Highest; uppermost.—**topper,** top′ėr, *n.* One who tops or excels; anything superior. (*Colloq.*).—**topping,** top′ing, *p.* and *a.* Rising aloft; preeminent; surpassing; fine; noble; gallant.—**topsail,** top′sāl, *n. Naut.* the second sail above the deck on any mast (main, fore, or mizzen).—**topsoil,** *n.* The upper part or surface of the soil.—**topside,** top′sīd, *n. Naut.* the outer part of a ship above the water line.—*adv.* On the deck of a ship; in a commanding position.

top, top, *n.* [D. *top,* G. *topf,* a top or point.] A child's toy, shaped like a pear, made to whirl on its point by means of a string.

topaz, tō′paz, *n.* [Fr. *topaze,* L. *topazus,* from Gr. *topazos,* the yellow or oriental topaz; comp. Skr. *tapus,* fire.] A gem harder than quartz, transparent or translucent, and having the color yellow, white, green, or blue.

tope, tōp, *n.* [Originally a Cornish word.] A fish of the shark kind, attaining a length of six feet.

tope, tōp, *n.* [Skr. *stûpa,* a tope.] A species of Buddhist monument occurring in India and Southeastern Asia, intended for the preservation of relics or the commemoration of some event (STUPA).

tope, tōp, *v.i.* [From Fr. *toper,* to cover a stake in gaming, to accept an offer (hence, it might mean to vie in drinking); of German origin and akin to *tap,* to strike] *Obs.* To drink hard; to drink strong or spirituous liquors to excess.—**toper,** tō′-pėr, *n.* One who drinks to excess; a drunkard; a sot.

Tophet, tō′fet, *n.* [Heb., lit. a place to be spit on.] A place near Jerusalem where the idolatrous Jews worshiped the fire gods and sacrificed their children; hence, the place of torment in a future life.

tophus, tō′fus, *n.* [L. *tophus,* tufa or tuff.] *Surg.* a soft tumor on a bone; also, a concretion in the joints.

topiary, tō′pi•e•ri, *a.* [L. *topiarius,* from *topia* (*opera*), ornamental gardening, from Gr. *topos,* a place.] Shaped by clipping, pruning, or training.—*Topiary work,* the trimming of thickets, trees, or hedges into fantastic shapes.

topic, top′ik, *n.* [Fr. *topiques,* subjects of conversation, from L. *topica,* Gr. *topika* (pl.), the name of a work by Aristotle on *topoi* or commonplaces, from *topos,* a place, a commonplace, a topic.] Originally a general maxim or dictum regarded as being of use in argument or oratory; a general truth; in common usage, the subject of any discourse; any subject that is discussed or spoken of for the time being; the matter treated of.—**topical,** top′-i•kal, *a.* Pertaining to a topic; pertaining to a place or locality; local; *med.* pertaining to a particular part of the body (a *topical* application).—**topically,** top′i•kal•li, *adv.* Locally; with limitation to a part or place.

topography, to•pog′ra•fi, *n.* [Gr. *topos*, place (hence *topic*), and *grapho*, to describe.] The description of a particular place, city, town, parish, or tract of land; the detailed description of any country or region; distinguished from geography in dealing with the minuter features.—**topographer,** to•pog′raf•ėr, *n.* One who deals with topography.—**topographic, topographical,** top•o•graf′ik, top•o•graf′i•kal, *a.* Pertaining to topography; descriptive of a place or country.—**topographically,** top•o•graf′i•kal•li, *adv.* In the manner of topography.

toponomy, to•pon′o•mi, *n.* [Gr. *topos*, a place, and *onoma*, a name.] The place names of a country or district.

topple, top′l, *v.i.*—*toppled, toppling.* [From *top.*] To fall forward, as something tall or high; to tumble down; to be on the point of falling.—*v.t.* To throw down.

topsy-turvy, top′si•tėr•vi, *a.* or *adv.* [A word of uncertain origin.] In an inverted posture; with the top or head downward and the bottom upward.

toque, tōk, *n.* [Fr., from Armor. *tôk*, W. *toc*, a hat or bonnet.] A woman's brimless hat of soft fabric.

tor, tor, *n.* [W. *tor*, a bulge, a hill; allied to L. *turris*, a tower.] A high pointed rock or hill.

Torah, tō′ra, *n.* [Heb.] Mosaic law, the Pentateuch.

torch, torch, *n.* [Fr. *torche*, It. *torcia*, from L.L. *tortia*, from L. *torqueo*, *tortus*, to twist.] A light to be carried in the hand; anything that inspires (the *torch* of truth); a portable device for producing a flame, as in welding.—**torchbearer,** *n.* One whose office is to carry a lighted torch.—**torchlight,** *n.* The light of a torch.

tore, tōr, pret. of *tear.*

toreador, tor″e•a•dor′, *n.* [Sp., from *toro*, a bull.] A general name for a bullfighter in Spain, especially one who fights on horseback.

toreutic, to•rū′tik, *a.* [Gr. *toreutikos*, from *toreutēs*, an embosser, from *toreuo*, to emboss, to work in relief.] Pertaining to carved or sculptured work, especially to work in relief.

torment, tor′ment, *n.* [O.Fr. *torment* (Fr. *tourment*), from L. *tormentum*, an engine for hurling missiles, a rack, torture, from *torqueo*, *tortum*, to twist. TORTURE.] Extreme pain; anguish of body or mind; torture; what causes such pain.—*v.t.* (tor•ment′). To put to extreme pain or anguish; to inflict excruciating pain on; to torture; to afflict; to tease, vex, or harass; to annoy.—**tormentor,** tor•men′tėr, *n.*

tormentil, tor′men•til, *n.* [Fr. *tormentille*, from L. *tormentum*, pain—because said to allay the pain of toothache.] Eurasian weed with small yellow flowers, and large woody roots sometimes used in tanning.

torn, tōrn, pp. of *tear.*

tornado, tor•nā′dō, *n.* pl. **tornadoes,** tor•nā′dōz. [Sp. *tornado*, a return, from *tornar*, to turn. TURN.] A violent whirling wind; a whirlwind or tempest, usually accompanied with severe thunder, lightning, and torrents of rain; a typhoon or hurricane.

torose, torous, tō′rōs, tō′rus, *a.* [L. *torosus*, from *torus*, a protuberance.] *Bot.* and *zool.* protuberant; swelling in knobs.

torpedo, tor•pē′do, *n.* pl. **torpedoes,** tor•pē′dōz. [L., from *torpeo*, to be stiff, numb, or torpid.] A fish allied to the rays, noted for its power of discharging electric shocks when irritated; a cigar-shaped submarine missile about 21 feet in length, 21 inches in diameter, and weighing about 1½ tons, filled with an explosive which is discharged on impact, propelled and steered by its own mechanism, capable of traveling accurately a distance of 10,000 yards, stabilized by a gyroscope, used in naval warfare for destroying or damaging enemy ships at sea.—*v.t.* To sink by a torpedo.—**torpedo boat,** *n.* A vessel specially intended to attack with torpedoes, and having one or more torpedo tubes.—**torpedo tube,** *n.* A tube for the discharge of torpedoes.

torpid, tor′pid, *a.* [L. *torpidus*, from *torpeo*, to be numb, motionless.] Having lost motion or the power of motion and feeling; numb; dull; sluggish; inactive.—**torpidity, torpidness,** tor•pid′i•ti, tor′pid•nes, *n.* The state of being torpid; numbness; insensibility; inactivity; sluggishness.—**torpidly,** tor′pid•li, *adv.* In a torpid manner; numbly; dully.—**torpescence,** tor•pes′ens, *n.* A becoming torpid or benumbed.—**torpor,** tor′pėr, *n.* [L.] Loss of motion or sensation; torpidity; numbness; sluggishness.—**torporific,** tor•pe•rif′ik, *a.* [L. *torpor*, and *facio*, to make.] Tending to produce torpor.

torque, tork, *n.* [From L. *torques*, a twisted neck chain, from *torqueo*, to twist.] *Archaeol.* a personal ornament, consisting of a stiff collar, formed of a number of gold wires twisted together, or of a thin twisted metal plate, worn round the neck as a symbol of rank by certain ancient nations, as by the ancient Britons, Gauls, and Germans—*Mech.* a system of forces equivalent to a couple, and therefore having a twisting or turning effect.

torrefy, tor′e•fī, *v.t.*—*torrefied, torrefying.* [Fr. *torréfier*, from L. *torreo*, to roast, and *facio*, to make. TORRENT.] To dry, roast, scorch, or parch by a fire; *metal.* to roast, as metallic ores.—**torrefaction,** tor•e•fak′shon, *n.* The operation of drying or parching by a fire.

torrent, tor′ent, *n.* [Fr. *torrent*, from L. *torrens*, *torrentis*, a torrent, from *torrens*, burning, roaring, ppr. of *torreo*, *tostum*, to burn; same root as E. *thirst. Torrid, toast*, are of same origin.] A violent stream, as of water, lava, or the like; *fig.* a violent or rapid flow; a flood (a *torrent* of words or eloquence.)—**torrential,** *a.* Pertaining to a torrent.

torrid, tor′id, *a.* [L. *torridus*, from *torreo*, to roast. TORRENT.] Dried with heat; parched; violently hot; burning or parching.—*Torrid zone, geog.* the broad belt round the middle of the earth which is included between the tropics, and divided into two parts by the equator, and where the heat is always great.—**torridity, torridness,** tor•id′i•ti, tor′id•nes, *n.* The state of being torrid.

torsion, tor′shon, *n.* [L.L. *torsio*, from L. *torqueo*, *torsi*, to twist. TORTURE.] The act of twisting; the twisting, wrenching, or straining of a body; *mech.* deformation produced by twisting; strain set up in a body by forces acting in opposite directions about the same axis of rotation; *surg.* twisting of the cut end of a small artery for the purpose of checking hemorrhage.—*Torsion balance*, an instrument for estimating the intensity of a small force (as of electricity) by the force with which a thread or wire resists twisting, as observed by the angle made by an arm horizontally suspended from the thread or wire.—**torsional,** tor′shon•al, *a.* Pertaining to torsion.

torsk, torsk, *n.* [Sw. and Dan. *torsk*, a codfish or torsk.] A fish of the cod tribe, caught in great quantities and salted and dried as food.

torso, tor′sō, *n.* [It., lit. a trunk or stump.] *Sculp.* the trunk of a statue lacking head and limbs; in anatomy, the human trunk minus head and limbs.

tort, tort, *n.* [Fr., from L. *tortus*, twisted, from *torqueo*, to twist. TORTURE.] A legal term for any wrong or injury to person or property.—**tortious,** tor′shus, *a.* Of the nature of or implying tort or injury.—**tortiously,** *adv.*

tortile, tor′til, *a.* [From L. *torqueo*, *tortum*, to twist. TORTURE.] Twisted; wreathed; coiled.

tortoise, tor′tis, *n.* [Lit. twisted or distorted animal (referring to its peculiar limbs), from O.Fr. *tortis*, fem. *tortisse*, twisted, from L. *torqueo*, *tortum*, to twist. TORTURE.] A name common to a family of land reptiles covered with a flattened shell, a kind of bony box, from which the head and legs protrude. TURTLE.—**tortoise shell,** *n.* The shell, or more strictly the scutes or scales, of the tortoise and other allied reptiles, used in the manufacture of combs, snuffboxes, etc., and in inlaying and other ornamental work.

tortuous, tor′chū•us, *a.* [L. *tortuosus*, from *tortus*, twisted, pp. of *torqueo*, to twist. TORTURE.] Twisted; wreathed; winding; *fig.* proceeding in a circuitous and underhand manner; taking an oblique and deceitful course; not open and straightforward.—**tortuously,** tor′chū•us•li, *adv.* In a tortuous or winding manner.—**tortuousness,** tor′chū•us•nes, *n.* The state of being tortuous.—**tortuosity,** tor•chū•os′i•ti, *n.* The state of being tortuous.

torture, tor′chėr, *n.* [Fr. *torture*, from L. *tortura*, a twisting, torture, from *torqueo, tortum*, to twist, torture (seen also in *torment, torsion, tortoise, torch*, also, *distort, extort*, etc.); same root as E. to *throw*, G. *drehen*, to turn.] Excruciating pain; extreme anguish of body or mind; agony; torment; severe pain inflicted judicially, either as a punishment for a crime or for the purpose of extorting a confession; the act of inflicting excruciating pain. —*v.t.—tortured, torturing*. To pain to extremity; to torment bodily or mentally; to punish with torture; to wrest greatly from the right meaning. —**torturer**, tor′chėr•ėr, *n*. One who tortures; a tormentor.

torus, tō′rus, *n*. [L., a swelling or protuberance.] *Arch*. a large molding used in the bases of columns, having a semicircular section; *bot*. the receptacle of a flower.

Tory, tō′ri, *n*. [From Irish *toruighe* or *toiridhe*, a pursuer, an Irish outlaw or plunderer.] A political party name first used in England about 1679, and applied originally in reproach to all supposed abettors of the imaginary Popish Plot; then to those who refused to concur in excluding a Roman Catholic prince (in the particular instance James II) from the throne; latterly it was generally applied to those adverse to changes in the constitution; in American history, a loyalist, one who during the War of Independence submitted to the claims of England against the colonies.—**Toryism**, tō′ri•izm, *n*. The principles or practices of the Tories.

toss, tos, *v.t.* [Probably Scand., as in Norw. *tossa*, sprinkle, spread out.] To throw with the hand; to pitch; to fling; to cast; to throw up with a sudden or violent motion; to jerk (to *toss* the head); to dash about (to be *tossed* on the waves); to agitate; to make restless.—*To toss off*, to swallow at one gulp; to drink hastily. —*v.i.* To roll and tumble; to be in violent commotion; to writhe; to be flung or dashed about.—*To toss, to toss up*, to throw up a coin, and decide something by the side turned up when it falls.—*To toss oars*, to raise them perpendicularly with blades uppermost as a salute.—*n*. A throwing with a jerk; the act of tossing; a throw or jerk of the head; the tossing up of a coin to decide something.—**tosser**, tos′ėr, *n*. One who tosses.—**tosspot**, *n*. A toper.—**tossup**, *n*. The throwing up of a coin to decide something; hence, an even chance or hazard.

tot, tot, *n*. [Dan. *tot*, Icel. *tottr, tuttr*, applied to dwarfish persons; perhaps allied to *tit*.] Anything small or insignificant; used as a term of endearment; a young child; a small quantity of liquor.

tot, tot, *v.t.—totted, totting*. [Abbrev. of *total*.] To sum; generally with *up*. (*Colloq*.)

total, tō′tal, *a*. [L. *totalis*, from *totus*, whole; akin to *tot*, so many, *tam*, so, *tantus*, so great.] Pertaining to the whole; comprehending the whole; entire (the *total* sum); complete in degree; absolute (a *total* wreck); thorough. ∴ Syn. under COMPLETE. —*n*. The whole; the whole sum or amount; an aggregate.—**totality**, tō•tal′i•ti, *n*. The whole or total sum; whole quantity or amount.—**totally**, tō′tal•li, *adv*. **totalitarian**, tō•tal′i•târ″i•an, *n*. Of or pertaining to a highly national socialistic state, or the philosophy of its government, headed by a political party whose control is omnipotent and absolute.—**totalitarianism**, to•tal′i•târ″i•an•izm, *n*. A national socialistic philosophy of government in which the state is omnipotent and absolute, superseding the welfare of its citizenry, the will of the state being expressed through a leader or a dictator.

tote, tōt, *v.t.—toted, toting*. [Origin unknown.] To carry, especially on one's person or in the arms.—*n*. The act of toting; a burden.

totem, tō′tem, *n*. [Algonquian (Chippewa) *ototeman*, his brother-sister kin.] An object, especially a plant or animal, serving as an emblem of a family or clan; a representation (carved or painted) of such an object; an object with which a family, clan, or other group feels a kinship, often a blood kinship.

tother, tuTH′ėr. A colloquialism for *the other*; the initial *t* being the final *t* of *that* (old neuter article).

totipalmate, tō•ti•pal′māt, *a*. and *n*. [L. *totus*, entire, and *palma*, a palm.] A term applied to swimming birds whose hind toe is united with the others in a continuous membrane (as the pelican).

totter, tot′ėr, *v.i.* [O.E. *toteren*; allied to *toddle*, and to G. *zotteln*, to trot; comp. also A.Sax. *tealtrian*, to totter, from *tealt*, unstable.] To appear as if about to fall when standing or walking; to walk unsteadily; to be on the point of falling; to threaten to topple down.—**tottery**, tot′ėr•i, *a*. Unsteady; shaking.

toucan, tö′kan, *n*. [Fr. *toucan*, Pg. and Braz. *tucano*: imitative of its cry.] The name of a family of scansorial birds of tropical America, distinguished by their enormous beak.

touch, tuch, *v.t.* [Fr. *toucher*, O.Fr. *tucher, tocher, toquer*=Sp. and Pg. *tocar*, It. *toccare*, to touch, from O.H.G. *zuchon*, to draw, to pull; G. *zucken*, to twitch; E. to *tuck*.] To perceive by the sense of feeling; to come in contact with in any manner, but particularly by means of the hand, finger, etc.; to hit or strike against; to harm; to meddle or interfere with; hence, to taste or eat; to come to; to reach or arrive at; to relate to or concern (a person or thing); to mark or delineate slightly; to add a slight stroke or strokes to, as with a pen, pencil, brush, etc.; to handle in a skillful or special manner (as a musical instrument); to discourse of; to write about; to make a mere reference to; to move or strike mentally; to excite with compassion or other tender emotion; to melt or soften the heart of; to make an impression on physically; to act on; *geom*. to meet without cutting; to be in contact with.—*To touch off*, to sketch hastily; to finish by touches. —*To touch up*, to repair or improve by slight touches or emendations.—*v.i.* To be in contact; to take effect; to say a few words in discourse.—*Touch and go*, a phrase used either substantively or adjectively and applied to something, such as an accident, which had almost happened; a close shave.—*To touch at*, to come or go to in a voyage without staying.—*To touch on*, to mention slightly; to say very little about.—*n*. The act of touching, or the state of being touched; contact; the sense of feeling which resides in the nervous papillae of the skin and forms one of the five senses; a state in which one or other of two parties has a knowledge of the other's position, opinions, etc.; a certain degree of some feeling, affection, or emotion (a *touch* of pity); a trait; a characteristic; a small quantity or degree; a smack; a little; a successful effort or attempt; a stroke (a *touch* of genius); a stroke of a pen, pencil, or the like; the act of the hand on a musical instrument; the peculiar handling usual to an artist, and by which his works may be known; the resistance of the keys of a musical instrument to the fingers.—**touchable**, tuch′a•bl, *a*. Capable of being touched.—**touchdown**, tuch′doun, *n*. *Football*, the act of scoring six points, by moving the ball over the opponent's goal line.—**touchhole**, *n*. The vent of a cannon or other species of firearms, by which fire is communicated to the charge.—**touching**, tuch′ing, *a*. Affecting; moving; pathetic.—*pp*. used as *prep*. Concerning; relating to; with respect to.—**touchingly**, tuch′ing•li, *adv*. In a manner to touch the passions; pathetically; feelingly.—**touch-me-not**, *n*. A plant the seed vessel of which, being touched and irritated when ripe, projects the seeds to some distance.—**touchstone**, tuch′stōn, *n*. A hard black siliceous stone used in ascertaining the purity of gold and silver, the streak made by rubbing the article on it being compared with that made by the touch needle, the quality of which is known; *fig*. any test or criterion by which the qualities of a thing are tried.—**touchwood**, tuch′wu̧d, *n*. The soft white substance into which wood is converted by the action of several fungi, serving the purpose of tinder.

touchy, tuch′i, *a*. [A form of *techy*, *tetchy*, brought into use by the influence of *touch*.] Apt to take offense; irritable; irascible; hence **touchily, touchiness.**

tough, tuf, *a*. [A.Sax. *tóh*, tough; akin to D. *taai*, G. *zähe*, Prov.G. *zach*, tough.] Having the quality of flexibility without brittleness; yielding to force without breaking; having tenacity; tenacious; strong; able to endure hardship; viscous; durable; stubborn; unmanageable.—**toughen**, tuf′n, *v.i.* To grow tough.—*v.t.* To make tough.—**toughly**, tuf′li, *adv*. In a tough manner.—**toughness**, tuf′-

nes, *n.* The quality of being tough; flexibility with firm adhesion of parts; viscosity; tenacity; strength of constitution or texture.

toupee, tö•pā′, *n.* [Fr. *toupet,* dim. from O.Fr. *toupe,* a tuft, from G. *zopf,* tuft. TOP.] A curl or artificial lock of hair; a small wig or upper part of a wig.

tour, tör, *n.* [Fr. *tour,* a turn, trip, tour, etc.; same origin as *turn.*] A round or circuit; a journey in a circuit; a roving journey; a lengthy jaunt or excursion; turn or succession (a *tour* of duty): a military use of the word.—*v.i.* To make a tour.—**tourist,** tör′ist, *n.* One who makes a tour; one who travels for pleasure.

touraco, tö•rak′ō, *n.* An African insessorial bird of the family of plantain eaters.

tourbillion, tör•bil′yon, *n.* [Fr. *tourbillon,* a whirlwind.] An ornamental whirling firework.

tour de force, tör′de fōrs″, *n.* [Fr.] A feat of skill or strength; a clever accomplishment.

tourmaline, tör′ma•lin, *n.* [Fr. from *toramalli,* a name given to it in Ceylon.] A mineral of various colors, frequently black or colorless, crystallized in three-sided or six-sided prisms, often found in granitic rocks and possessing strong electrical properties. Black tourmaline is schorl; red tourmaline, rubellite.

tournament, tör′na•ment, *n.* [O.Fr. *tourneiment, tournoyement,* from *tourneier, tournoyer,* to turn or twirl about. TURN.] A martial sport or species of combat performed in former times by knights on horseback for the purpose of exercising and exhibiting their courage, prowess, and skill in arms; a tilting match; hence, any contest of skill in which a number take part (a chess *tournament*).—**tourney,** tėr′ni, *n.* [O.Fr. *tournei.*] A tournament.—*v.i.* To tilt; to engage in a tournament.

tourniquet, tör′ni•ket, *n.* [Fr., from *tourner,* to turn.] A surgical bandage which is tightened by twisting with a stick or a pad tightened with a screw or elastic, to arrest hemorrhage.

touse, touz, *v.t.*—*toused, tousing.* [Same as L.G. *túsen,* G. *zausen,* to pull; akin to *tease.*] *Dial.* To pull or drag; to disorder the hair of; to tousle.—**tousle,** tou′zl, *v.t.* To put into disorder; to dishevel; to rumple. (*Colloq.*)

tout, tout, *v.i.* [Formerly *toot, tote,* to pry, peep, from A.Sax. *tótian,* to stick out or project.] To solicit for customers; to give a tip on a racehorse, especially with the expectation of some compensation.—*v.t.* To solicit for importunately; to spy on.

tow, tō, *v.t.* [From stem of A.Sax. *teóhan, teón,* to draw, to tug, whence *tohlíne,* a towing line; akin Icel. *toga,* G. *ziehen,* to draw; Scot. *tow,* Icel. *taug, tog,* D. *touw,* a rope or cord; cog. L. *duco,* to lead. Akin *tug, tie.*] To drag, as a boat or ship, through the water by means of a rope.—*n.* The state of being towed (to take a boat in *tow*).—**towage,** tō′ij, *n.* The act of towing.—**towboat,** *n.* A boat employed in towing.—**tow path,** *n.* A path along a canal, made by men or by animals towing boats.—**towline, towrope,** tō′līn, tō′rōp, *n.* A rope used for towing.

tow, tō, *n.* [A.Sax. *tow,* tow; akin Icel. *tó,* a tuft.] The coarse and broken part of flax or hemp separated from the finer part by the hatchel or swingle.—**towhead,** tō′hed, *n.* A person with flaxen or very pale blond hair; a head of such hair.

toward, towards, tu̩•wa̩rd′, tu̩•wa̩rdz′, *prep.* [A.Sax. *tóweard, tóweardes*—*tó,* to, and *-weard,* expressing direction. *Towards* is an adverbial genitive.] In the direction of; in regard or with respect to (well-disposed *toward* us); tending or contributing to; in aid of; for; nearly; about (*toward* three o'clock).—*Toward* was formerly sometimes divided by tmesis (*to* God*ward*).—*adv.* In a state of preparation; being carried on.—**toward,** tō′wėrd, *a.* [Lit. bending or turned to; comp. *froward,* in the opposite sense.] Pliable; docile; ready to do or learn; apt.—**towardliness,** tō′wėrd•li•nes, *n.* The quality of being toward; aptness; docility.—**towardly,** tō′wėrd•li, *a.* Docile; tractable.

towel, tou′el, *n.* [Fr. *touaille,* from O.H.G. *twahilla, dwahilla,* a towel, from *twahan,* A.Sax. *thweán* (for *thweahan*), Goth. *thvahan,* to wash.] A cloth or soft paper, for wiping the hands and face, especially after washing; a similar cloth for wiping in domestic use, as a *dish towel.*—**toweling,** tou′el•ing, *n.* Cloth or other material for towels, usually in narrow widths.

tower, tou′ėr, *n.* [O.E. *tour,* from Fr. *tour,* a tower, from L. *turris,* a tower; cog. Gr. *tyrris, tyrsis,* Ir. *túr,* W. *twr,* Gael. *torr,* a heap, a tower.] A lofty narrow building of a round, square, or polygonal form, either insulated or forming part of a church, castle, or other edifice; a tall, movable wooden structure anciently used in storming a fortified place; a citadel; a fortress.—*v.i.* To rise or fly high; to soar; to be lofty; to stand sublime.—**towered,** tou′ėrd, *a.* Having towers; adorned or defended by towers.—**towering,** tou′ėr•ing, *a.* Very high or lofty; extreme; violent; outrageous (a *towering* rage).

town, toun, *n.* [A.Sax. *tun,* inclosure, homestead, town = O.Sax. and Icel. *tún,* homestead, D. *tuin,* a fence; G. *zaun,* a hedge; allied to Celt. *dun,* fortress, town.] Originally a walled or fortified place; then houses enclosed with a wall; hence, any collection of houses larger than a village; a large assemblage of adjacent houses intersected by streets; often opposed to *country*; the metropolis, county town, or the particular city, etc., in or near which the speaker or writer is (to go to *town,* to be in *town*); the inhabitants of a town (all the *town* talks of it).—To *go to town,* to venture, especially when noted success is achieved (*slang*).—*a.* Pertaining to or characteristic of a town; urban.—**town clerk,** *n.* The clerk of a municipal corporation, who keeps the records of the town and town council.—**town crier,** *n.* A public official who issues proclamations in a town, formerly by loud verbal announcement.—**town hall,** *n.* A large hall or building belonging to a town or borough in which the town council holds its meetings, and offices are maintained for the town officials and courts.—**town house,** *n.* A house in a city, particularly one owned by one who also has a country residence; one of a number of individual housing units constructed with a common roof, front wall, and rear wall.—**town meeting,** *n.* A meeting held for townspeople to discuss town matters; such a meeting that constitutes the legal authority of a town.—**townsfolk,** touns′fōk, *n.* pl. The people of a town or city; townspeople.—**township,** toun′ship, *n.* An administrative division of a county.—**townsman,** tounz′man, *n.* An inhabitant of a town; one of the same town with another.—**townspeople,** tounz′pē•pl, *n. pl.* The inhabitants of a town, especially as distinguished from country folk.

towrope. See TOW, *v.t.*

toxemia, toks•ē′mi•a, *n.* [M.L. *toxicus,* from L. *toxicum,* poison.] Blood poisoning, especially that caused by bacterial toxins.

toxic, tok′sik, *a.* [Gr. *toxikon,* poison, originally for arrows, from *toxon,* a bow.] Pertaining to poisons; poisonous.—**toxicant,** tok′si•kant, *n.* A poison of a stimulating, narcotic, or anesthetic nature.—**toxicological,** tok′si•ko•loj″i•kal, *a.* Pertaining to toxicology.—**toxicologically,** tok′si•ko•loj″i•kal•li, *adv.* In a toxicological manner.—**toxicologist,** tok•si•kol′o•jist, *n.* One who treats of poisons.—**toxicology,** tok•si•kol′o•ji, *n.* [Gr. *toxikon,* poison, *logos,* discourse.] The doctrine of poisons; that branch of medicine which treats of poisons and their antidotes.

toxin, toks′in, *n.* [See TOXEMIA.] A poisonous substance, chemically allied to proteins, occurring in a plant or animal.

toxoid, tok′soid, *n.* [Combining form Gr. *tox,* bow, and suffix, *oid,* like.] A toxin, such as that of tetanus, treated chemically to eliminate its poisonous qualities, used as an agent (when injected) to induce the formation of antibodies.

toxophilite, tok•sof′i•līt, *n.* [Gr. *toxon,* a bow, and *philos,* loving.] A lover of archery.

toy, toi, *n.* [Same as Dan. *töi,* D. *tuig,* G. *zeug,* as in Dan. *lege-toi,* D. *speeltuig,* G. *spiel-zeug,* a plaything or toy; same root as *tug, tow.*] A plaything for children; a bauble; a thing for amusement and of no real value; a trifling object.—*v.i.* To dally amorously; to trifle; to play.—**toyer,** toi′ėr, *n.* One who toys.

trace, trās, *n.* [Fr. *trace,* trace, track, outline, etc., from *tracer,* to trace, from L.L. *tractiare,* from L. *tractus,* pp. of *traho, trahere,* to draw; whence also *tract, tractable, train, trait, treat, abstract, detract, extract,* etc. In last sense directly from O.Fr. *trais*, pl. of *trait*, the trace of a carriage, from *traire*, L. *trahere*, to draw.] A mark left by anything passing; a track; any mark, impression, or appearance left when the thing itself no longer exists; visible evidence of something having been; token; vestige; a minute quantity or insignificant particle; one of the straps, chains, or ropes by which a carriage, wagon, etc., is drawn.—*v.t.*—*traced, tracing.* To follow by traces left; to track out; to follow by vestiges or indications; to draw or delineate with marks; to draw in outline; to copy, as a drawing or engraving, by following the lines and marking them on a sheet superimposed, through which they appear. —*v.i.* To walk; to travel.—**traceable,** trās′a•bl, *a.* Capable of being traced. —**traceably,** trās′a•bli, *adv.* So as to be traced.—**tracer,** trās′ėr, *n.* One who or that which traces.—**tracery,** trās′ėr•i, *n. Arch.* ornamental openwork in stone in the head of a Gothic window, showing curves and flowing lines intersecting in various ways and enriched with foliations; any similar ornamental work.—**tracing,** trās′ing, *n.* The act of one who traces; a copy of an original design or drawing made by following its lines through a transparent medium.

trachea, tra′kē•a, *n.* pl. **tracheae,** tra′kē•ē. [L. *trachia*, Gr. *tracheia*, from *trachys*, rough, from the inequalities of its cartilages.] The windpipe, a cartilaginous and membranous pipe through which the air passes into and out of the lungs; *bot.* one of the spiral vessels of plants; *zool.* one of those vessels in insects, etc., which receive air and distribute it to every part of the interior of the body.—**tracheal,** tra′kē•al, *a.* Pertaining to the trachea.—**tracheitis,** tra•kē•ī′tis, *n.* Inflammation of the windpipe.—**tracheotomy,** tra•kē•ot′o•mi, *n.* [*Trachea*, and Gr. *tomē*, a cutting, from *temnō*, to cut.] *Surg.* the operation of cutting into the trachea, as in cases of suffocation; bronchotomy; laryngotomy.

trachyte, tra′kīt, *n.* [Gr. *trachys*, rough.] A feldspathic rock abundant among the products of volcanoes, and often containing crystals of glassy feldspar, with sometimes hornblende and mica.—**trachytic,** tra•kit′ik, *a.* Pertaining to trachyte or consisting of it.

track, trak, *n.* [O.Fr. *trac*, a track or course, from D. and L.G. *trek*, *treck*, a drawing, *trekken*, *trecken*, to draw.] A mark left by something that has passed along; a mark left by the foot of man or beast; a trace; a footprint; a road; a beaten path; course followed; path; the course of a railroad; the permanent way.—*v.t.* To follow the traces of, as in hunting an animal; to observe the path of, as an artificial satellite; to traverse; to carry on the feet (as mud) and deposit upon (as a floor).—*v.i.* To follow a track; to leave tracks, as on a floor.—**tracker,** trak′ėr, *n.*—**trackless,** trak′les, *a.*

tract, trakt, *n.* [L. *tractus*, a drawing, a district, from *traho*, *tractum*, to draw or drag.] Verses of scripture sung in place of the alleluia in a Mass on various occasions, especially from Septuagesima to the day before Easter; any area; an indefinite region of land or water; a system of organs or parts of the body having some purpose, as the digestive tract.

tract, trakt, *n.* [M.E. from L. *tractatus*, treatise.] A short treatise for distribution, usually in the form of a pamphlet, especially on a religious or political subject.—**Tractarian,** trak•tâ′ri•an, *n.* A term applied to the writers of the '*Tracts* for the Times', a series of papers published at Oxford between 1833 and 1841, written by Anglican scholars, and showing a considerable leaning toward Roman Catholicism; also a person who supports such opinions. —**Tractarianism,** trak•tâ′ri•an•izm, *n.* The doctrine or teaching of the Tractarians.—**tractate,** trak′tāt, *n.* A treatise, a tract.

tractable, trak′ta•bl, *a.* [L. *tractabilis*, from *tracto*, to handle, treat.] Capable of being easily trained or managed; very amenable to discipline; docile; governable.—**tractableness, tractability,** trak′ta•bl•nes, trak•ta•bil′i•ti, *n.* The state or quality of being tractable; docility.—**tractably,** trak′ta•bli, *adv.* In a tractable manner.

Tractarian. See TRACT.

tractile, trak′til, trak′tīl, *a.* [From *traction* and suffix, *ile*.] Ductile; capable of being drawn out.

traction, trak′shon, *n.* [Fr. *traction*, from L. *traho*, *tractum*, to draw. TRACT.] The act of drawing or pulling; the act of drawing a body along a plane, as when a vessel is towed in water or a carriage upon a road or railroad.—**traction engine,** *n.* A steam locomotive engine for dragging heavy loads on common roads. —**tractive,** trak′tiv, *a.* Serving to pull or draw; drawing along.—**tractor,** trak′ter, *n.* A vehicle driven by an internal-combustion engine, especially as used in agriculture.—*Tractor airplane*, an airplane in which the propeller is mounted in front of the main lifting surfaces. See PROPELLER.

trade, trād, *n.* [TREAD.] Regular employment or way of life; the business which a person carries on for procuring subsistence or for profit; occupation; particularly a mechanical or mercantile employment or a handicraft, as distinguished from an art or profession; the business of exchanging commodities for other commodities or for money; commerce; traffic; collectively; those who are engaged in any trade; a trade wind.—*Board of trade*, an organization for the advancement and protection of business interests; also the place where commercial exchange occurs. Commodities, bonds, or stocks are usually traded in a place of this kind.—*a.* Pertaining to trade or a particular trade.—*v.i. traded, trading.* To barter or to buy and sell; to traffic; to carry on commerce; to engage in affairs generally; to deal or have dealings.—*v.t.* To sell or exchange in commerce; to barter.—**trade acceptance,** a bill of exchange, a promissory note originating from a merchandise transaction.—**trademark,** *n.* A distinctive mark or device adopted by a manufacturer or producer, and impressed on his goods, labels, etc., to distinguish them from those of others.—**trade name,** the name given to an article by traders, in distinction from its composition, chemical or otherwise. —**trader,** trā′dėr, *n.* One engaged in trade or commerce; a vessel employed regularly in any particular trade.—**trade school,** *n.* A school teaching the theory and practice of a trade.—**tradesman,** trādz′man, *n.* A shopkeeper; a mechanic.—**trade union,** *n.* An organization of workers representing the members in dealings with the management on matters such as wages and working conditions; a labor union.—**trade wind,** *n.* A wind that blows almost always in the same direction, especially those blowing in the area of about 30° north latitude to 30° south latitude, from northeast to southwest in the Northern Hemisphere and from southwest to northeast in the Southern Hemisphere. —**trading post,** *n.* A station of a trading company carrying on trade in sparsely settled regions, where trade is carried on with the natives, as the fur-trading posts of the Hudson's Bay Company.—**trading stamp.** A printed stamp of a certain value, given by the dealer to the customer and redeemable by the dealer in the purchase of other merchandise.

tradition, tra•dish′on, *n.* [Fr. *tradition*, from L. *trado*, to hand over, deliver.] The handing down of opinions, doctrines, practices, rites, and customs from father to son, or from ancestors to posterity by oral communication; that which is handed down from age to age by oral communication; a doctrine or statement of facts so handed down.—**traditional,** tra•dish′on•al, *a.* Pertaining to or derived from tradition; communicated from ancestors to descendants by word only; transmitted from age to age without writing.—**traditionalism,** tra•dish′on•al•izm, *n.* Adherence to or importance placed on tradition.—**traditionalist,** tra•dish′on•al•ist, *n.* One who holds to tradition or traditionalism.—**traditionally,** tra•dish′on•al•li, *adv.* By tradition; by oral transmission.—**traditionary,** tra•dish′on•e•ri, *a.* Traditional.—**traditionist,** tra•dish′on•ist, *n.* One who adheres to tradition. —**traditive,**† trad′i•tiv, *a.* Pertaining to or based on tradition; traditional.

traduce, tra•dūs′, *v.t.*—*traduced, traducing.* [L. *traduco*, *traducere*, to lead along, exhibit, disgrace, defame—*trans*, over, and *duco*, to lead. DUKE.] To misrepresent willfully; to defame; to calumniate; to vilify.—**traducer,** tra•dū′sėr, *n.* One that traduces; a slanderer; a calumniator.

traffic, traf′ik, *n.* [Fr. *trafic*, It.

traffico, prob. from. L. *transfero*, to bear across, transport.] An interchange of goods or merchandise between countries, communities, or individuals; trade; commerce; goods or persons passing along a road, railroad, canal, steamboat route, etc., viewed collectively; dealings; intercourse.—*v.i.*—*trafficked, trafficking.* [Fr. *trafiquer*, Sp. *traficar* or *trafagar*.] To trade; to buy and sell wares; to carry on commerce; to have business or dealings; to deal; to trade meanly or mercenarily.

tragacanth, trag'a•kanth, *n.* [L. *tragacantha, tragacanthum*, from Gr. *tragakantha*—*tragos*, a goat, and *akantha*, a thorn.] Goat's-thorn, a leguminous plant yielding a gummy juice used in confectionery; a variety of gum familiarly termed gum dragon or gum tragacanth, used as a demulcent in coughs and for other purposes.

tragedy, traj'e•di, *n.* [L. *tragœdia*, from Gr. *tragó(i)dia*, tragedy—*tragos*, a he-goat, and *ódē, o(i)de*, a song, from *aeidó*, to sing.] That kind of drama in which some fatal or mournful event is the main theme; a fatal and mournful event; any event in which human lives are sacrificed; a murderous deed.—**tragedian,** tra•jē'di•an, *n.* [L. *tragœdus*.] A writer of tragedy; an actor of tragedy.—**tragedienne,** tra•jē'di•en" *n.* [Fr. *tragédienne*.] A female actor of tragedy; a tragic actress.—**tragic, tragical,** traj'ik, traj'i•kal, *a.* [L. *tragicus*.] Pertaining to tragedy; of the nature or character of tragedy (in this sense *Tragic* is now the more common form); connected with or characterized by bloodshed or loss of life; murderous; dreadful; calamitous.—**tragically,** traj'i•kal•li, *adv.* In a tragic or tragical manner.—**tragicalness,** traj'i•kal•nes, *n.*—**tragicomedy,** *n.* A kind of dramatic piece in which serious and comic scenes are blended, and of which the event is not unhappy.—**tragicomic, tragicomical,** *a.* Pertaining to tragicomedy.

tragus, trāg'us, *n.* [From Gr. *tragos*, a goat, being sometimes furnished with a tuft of hair suggesting the beard of a goat.] *Anat.* a small cartilaginous eminence at the entrance of the external ear.

trail, trāl, *v.t.* [From old *traile*, a sledge, from L. *tragula*, a sledge, a dragnet, from *traho*, to draw. TRACE.] To draw behind or along the ground; to drag.—*v.i.* To sweep over a surface by being pulled or dragged; to grow with long slender and creeping shoots or stems, as a plant; to follow as a detective.—*To trail arms*, to carry the rifle obliquely, muzzle forward, butt near ground.—*n.* A track followed by a hunter; anything drawn to length (a *trail* of smoke); the end of the stock of a gun carriage which rests upon the ground when a gun is in position for firing.—**trailer,** trāl'ėr, *n.* One who trails; a plant which cannot grow upward without support; a car pulled by a motor vehicle; a house on wheels, attachable to an automobile and fitted with camping conveniences.—**trailing edge,** *n.* In an airplane, the rear edge of the wing.

train, trān, *v.t.* [Fr. *traîner*, O.Fr. *traïner, trahiner*, to draw, from L.L. *trahinare*, from L. *trahere*, to draw. TRACE.] To draw along‡; to trail‡; to draw by artifice; to entice; to educate; to rear and instruct: often followed by *up*; to form to any practice by exercise; to drill; to discipline; to break; to tame and reduce to docility; to teach to perform certain actions (to *train* dogs); to subject to proper regimen and exercise for the performance of some special exertion or feat (to *train* horses for the Derby); *gardening*, to form to a desired shape by growth and pruning, etc.—*v.i.* To undergo some special drill or discipline; to subject one's self to a special course of exercise and regimen for an athletic or other feat.—*n.* That which is drawn along behind; that part of a gown or robe which trails behind the wearer; the tail of a comet, meteor, etc.; the tail of a bird; the after part of a gun carriage; a succession of connected things; a series; way or course of procedure; regular method; course; a number or body of followers or attendants; a retinue; a procession; a connected line of cars on a railroad together with the locomotive; a line of combustible material to lead fire to a charge or mine; a set of wheels, or wheels and pinions, as in a watch.—*Train of artillery*, a certain number of pieces, with attendants, carriages, etc., organized for a given duty.—**trainable,** trān'a•bl, *a.* Capable of being trained.—**trainer,** trā'nėr, *n.* One who trains; one who prepares men, horses, etc., for the performance of certain feats, as a boxer for a prizefight, or a horse for racing.—**training,** trān'ing, *p.* and *a.* Teaching and forming by practice.—*Training college*, a normal school.—*n.* The act of one who trains; the process of educating; education; drill; course of exercise and regimen. —**training ship,** *n.* A ship equipped with instructors, officers, etc., to train lads for the sea.

train oil, trān, *n.* [D. and L.G. *traan*, Dan. and Sw. *tran*, G. *thran*, train oil; comp. D. *traan*, G. *thräne*, a tear, a drop.] The oil procured from the blubber or fat of whales.

traipse, trāps, *v.i.* [Perhaps from O.Fr. *trespasser*, to pass across.] To walk sloppily or carelessly; *also* trapes.

trait, trāt or trā, *n.* [Fr., a trait, a stroke, from L. *tractus*, a drawing. TRACT.] A stroke; a touch; a distinguishing or peculiar feature; a peculiarity.

traitor, trā'tėr, *n.* [O.Fr. *traïtor* (Fr. *traître*), from L. *traditor*, from *trado*, to deliver up (whence *tradition*)—*trans*, over, and *do, datum*, to give.] One who violates his allegiance and betrays his country; one guilty of treason; one who, in breach of trust, plays into the hands of an enemy; one guilty of perfidy or treachery.—*a.* Traitorous.—**traitorous,** trā'tėr•us, *a.* Acting the traitor; treacherous; perfidious; consisting in or partaking of treason.

traject, tra•jekt', *v.t.* [L. *trajicio, trajectum*—*trans*, across, over, and *jacio*, to throw. JET.] To throw, cast, or make to pass through.—**trajection,** tra•jek'shon, *n.* The act of trajecting.

trajectory, tra•jek'tė•ri, *n.* [L. *trans*, across, and *jacere*, to throw.] The path described by a body, such as a missile, comet, satellite, bullet, etc., in space.

tram, tram, *n.* [It. *trama*, from L. *trama*, weft.] A kind of doubled silk thread, in which two or more strands are twisted together.

tram, tram, *n.* [E. dial, a coal wagon.] A mining car, running on a track; any of various other vehicles on rails.

trammel, tram'el, *n.* [Fr. *tramail, trémail*, a net, from L.L. *tramaculum, tremaculum*, a kind of fishing net, from L. *tres*, three, and *macula*, a mesh.] A kind of net for catching birds or fish; a kind of shackles for regulating the motions of a horse and making him amble; whatever hinders activity, freedom, or progress; an instrument for drawing ovals, used by joiners and mechanics; a beam-compass.—*v.t.*—*trammeled, trammeling.* To confine; to hamper; to shackle.—**trammeler, trammeller,** tram'el•ėr, *n.* One who or that which trammels.

tramontane, tra•mon'tān, *a.* [It. *tramontano*, from L. *transmontanus*—*trans*, beyond, and *mons*, mountain.] Lying or being beyond the mountains, originally applied by the Italians to those on the other side of the Alps; hence, foreign; barbarous.—*n.* A dweller in a tramontane region, especially the country north of the Alps mountains; so, a barbarian, a stranger.

tramp, tramp, *v.t.* [Same as L.G. *trampen*, Dan. *trampe*, Sw. *trampa*, to tramp; nasalized forms corresponding to D. and G. *trappen*, to tread; akin *trap, trip*.] To tread under foot; to trample; to travel over on foot (to *tramp* a country).—*v.i.* To travel on foot; to hike.—*n.* A homeless vagrant who wanders along the roads from place to place, sleeps in the open, and lives by begging and by working occasionally for short periods; sound of a heavy tread, as of a regiment marching past; a cargo steamer making journeys to any port as the occasion arises, without having any regular ports of call, and without making any scheduled voyages; a flat plate of iron on a shoe or upper edge of a spade to protect the shoe when pressing the spade into the ground.—*To look like a tramp*, to present a dirty, disreputable, shabby appearance.—**tramper,** tram'pėr, *n.* One who tramps.—**trample,** tram'pl, *v.t.* —*trampled, trampling.* [A freq. from *tramp*; like D. *trampelen*, G. *trampeln*, to trample.] To tread under foot; to tread down; to prostrate by treading; to crush with the feet; to treat with pride, contempt, and insult.—*v.i.* To tread in contempt;

to tread with force; to stamp.—**trampler,** tram'pl•ėr, *n.* One who tramples.

trampoline, tramp'e•lin, *n.* [G. *trampolin,* a springboard.] A framed resilient strip of canvas or other material for feats of bouncing, jumping, tumbling, etc.

trance, trans, *n.* [Fr. *transe,* from L. *transitus,* a passage, from *trans,* across, beyond, and *eo, itum,* to go; so that *trance* and *transit* are doublets.] An ecstasy; a state in which the soul seems to have passed out of the body, or to be rapt into visions; a state of insensibility to the things of this world; a state of perplexity or bewilderment; *med.* same as *Catalepsy.*—*v.t.*—*tranced, trancing.* To entrance; to place in or as in a trance; to charm; to enchant.

tranquil, tran'kwil, *a.* [Fr. *tranquille,* from L. *tranquillus,* quiet, calm.] Quiet; calm; undisturbed; peaceful; not agitated.—**tranquillity,** tran•kwil'i•ti, *n.* [L. *tranquillitas.*] The state of being tranquil; quietness; calmness.—**tranquilize,** tran'kwil•īz, *v.t.* and *i.*—*tranquilized, tranquilizing.* To make or become tranquil or calm.—**tranquilizer,** tran'kwil•ī•zėr, *n.* A drug that calms but does not affect one's mental alertness.—**tranquilly,** tran'kwil•li, *adv.* In a tranquil manner; quietly; peacefully.

transact, tran•zakt', *v.t.* [L. *transigo, transactum*—*trans,* across, through, and *ago,* to lead, act.] To carry through, perform, or conduct (business affairs, etc.); to do; to perform; to manage; to complete; to carry through.—**transaction,** tran•zak'shon, *n.* The doing or performing of any business; some piece of business; a proceeding; an affair; *pl.* reports containing papers or abstracts of papers, speeches, discussions, etc., read or delivered at the meetings of certain learned societies.—**transactor,** tran•zak'tėr, *n.* One who transacts.

transalpine, tran•zal'pīn, *a.* [L. *transalpinus,* from *trans,* beyond, and *Alpinus,* pertaining to the *Alps.*] Lying or being beyond the Alps; generally used in regard to Rome; opposed to *Cisalpine.*

transatlantic, tranz•at•lan'tik, *a.* [L. *trans,* beyond, and *Atlantic.*] Lying or being beyond the Atlantic; crossing the Atlantic (a *transatlantic* line of steamers).

transcend, tran•send', *v.t.* [L. *transcendo*—*trans,* beyond, and *scando,* to climb (as in *ascend, descend,* etc.) SCAN.] To rise above or beyond; to be or go beyond the grasp or comprehension of; to surpass, outgo, excel, exceed.—**transcendence, transcendency,** tran•sen'dens, tran•sen'den•si, *n.*—**transcendent,** tran•sen'dent, *a.* Superior or supreme in excellence; surpassing others; going beyond or transcending human experience.—**transcendental,** tran•sen•den'tal, *a.* Transcendent; beyond the reach of ordinary, everyday, or common thought and experience.—**transcendentalism,** tran•sen•den'tal•izm, *n.* A system of philosophy which contends that there are realities that may be perceived by thought over and above the realities of worldly experience, usually associated with Emerson.—**transcendentalist,** tran•sen•den'tal•ist, *n.*

transcontinental, trans'kon•ti•nen"tal, *a.* [L. *trans,* across, and *continental.*] Extending across a continent; located on the farther side of a continent.

transcribe, tran•skrīb', *v.t.*—*transcribed, transcribing.* [L. *transcribo*—*trans,* over, and *scribo,* to write. SCRIBE.] To write over again or in the same words; to make a written copy; to copy oral material on paper; to copy speech by means of a phonetic system; to record, as on magnetic tape.—**transcript,** tran'skript, *n.* A written copy (as a student's record) made from an original record; an imitation.—**transcription,** tran•skrip'shon, *n.* The act of transcribing or copying; a copy; a transcript; *mus.* the arrangement of a composition for some instrument or voice other than that for which it was originally composed.

transept, tran'sept, *n.* [L. *trans,* across, and *septum,* an inclosure.] *Arch.* that portion of a church built in the form of a cross, which is between the nave and choir and projects externally on each side so as to form the short arms of the cross.

transfer, trans•fėr', *v.t.*—*transferred, transferring.* [L. *transfero*—*trans,* and *fero,* to carry (as in *defer, confer,* etc.). FERTILE.] To convey from one place or person to another; to transmit (ownership or control) to another; to change; to produce a copy on one surface from another.—*v.i.* To go from one place, situation, etc., to another; to leave one school and enroll at another.—*n.* trans'fėr. The act of transferring; that which is transferred.—**transferable,** trans•fėr'a•bl, *a.* Capable of being transferred; capable of being legitimately passed into the possession of another.—**transferee,** trans•fėr'ē', *n.* The person to whom a transfer is made.—**transference,** trans'fėr•ens, *n.* The act of transferring; the act of conveying from one place, person, or thing to another; the passage of anything from one place to another.—**transferrer,** trans•fėr'ėr, *n.* One who transfers.

transfigure, trans•fig'ūr, *v.t.*—*transfigured, transfiguring.* [Fr. *transfigurer,* from L. *transfiguro*—*trans,* over, and *figura,* figure. FIGURE.] To change the outward form or appearance of; to transform in appearance; to give an elevated or glorified appearance to; to elevate and glorify; to idealize.—**transfiguration,** trans•fig'ū•rā"shon, *n.* A change of form or figure; [*cap.*] the supernatural change in the personal appearance of the Saviour on the mount; an ecclesiastical feast held on August 6 in commemoration of this.

transfix, trans•fiks', *v.t.* [L. *transfigo, transfixum*—*trans,* through, and *figo,* to fix. FIX.] To pierce through as with a pointed weapon.—**transfixion,** trans•fik'shon, *n.* The act of transfixing.

transform, trans•form', *v.t.* [Fr. *transformer,* from L. *transformare*—*trans,* across, and *forma,* form.] To change the form of; to give a new form to; to metamorphose; to change into another substance; to transmute; to change the character or disposition of.—*v.i.*† To be changed in form; to be metamorphosed.—**transformation,** trans•for•mā'shon, *n.* The act or operation of transforming; the state of being transformed; an entire change in form, appearance, nature, disposition, etc.; a metamorphosis; false hair worn by women on the top and front of the head.—*Transformation scene,* a gorgeous scene at the end of the burlesque of a pantomime, in which the chief characters are supposed to be transformed into those that take part in the immediately following harlequinade.—**transformative,** trans•for'ma•tiv, *a.* Having power or tendency to transform.—**transformer,** trans•for'mėr, *n. Elect.* an appliance for altering pressure in alternating current circuits.

transfuse, trans•fūz', *v.t.*—*transfused, transfusing.* [Fr. *transfuser,* from L. *transfundo, transfusum*—*trans,* over, and *fundo, fusum,* to pour. FUSE.] To transfer by pouring; to cause to be instilled or imbibed; to instill; *surg.* to transfer (blood) from the veins or arteries of one animal to those of another.—**transfusible,** trans•fū'zi•bl, *a.* Capable of being transfused.—**transfusion,** trans•fū'zhon, *n.*—**transfusive,** trans•fū'ziv, *a.* Tending or having power to transfuse.

transgress, trans•gres', *v.t.* [Fr. *transgresser,* from L. *transgredior, transgressus*—*trans,* across, and *gradior,* to pass. GRADE.] To overpass, as some law or rule prescribed; to break or violate; to infringe,—*v.i.* To offend by violating a law; to sin.—**transgression,** trans•gresh'on, *n.* The act of transgressing; the breaking or violation of any law; a trespass; an offense.—**transgressor,** trans•gres'ėr, *n.* One who transgresses; an offender; an evildoer.

tranship, tran•ship', *v.t.*—*transhipped, transhipping.* To convey or transfer from one ship to another.—**transhipment,** tran•ship'ment, *n.* The act of transhipping.

transient, tran'shent, *a.* [L. *transiens,* ppr. of *transeo,* to pass away—*trans,* across, and *eo,* to go. Akin *transition, transit, trance.* ITINERANT.] Passing quickly away; of short duration; not permanent, lasting, or durable; momentary; passing. ∴ *Transient* implies shortness of duration; *transitory,* uncertainty of duration; while *fleeting* refers to something in the act of passing away.—**transiently,** tran'shent•li, *adv.* In a transient manner.—**transience, transiency, transientness,** tran'shens, tran'shen•si, tran'shent•nes, *n.* The state or quality of being transient; evanescence; fugitiveness.

transistor, tran•zis'ter, *n.* An electronic device using a semiconductor, such as germanium or silicon, and performing many of the functions of an electron tube.

transit, tran′sit, *n.* [L. *transitus,* a passing across, from *transeo, transitum,* to go over. *Trance* is a doublet of this word. TRANSIENT.] The act of passing; a passing over or through; the process of conveying; passage; conveyance (the *transit* of goods through a country); *astron.* the passage of a heavenly body across the meridian of any place; the passage of one heavenly body over the disk of a larger one, as of the planets Mercury and Venus over the sun's disk; the transits of the latter being of great importance as affording the best known means of determining the sun's parallax, and consequently the dimensions of the planetary system.—**transit instrument,** *n.* An important astronomical instrument, which consists essentially of a telescope so fixed as to move in the plane of the meridian, the principal use of it being to determine the exact moment when a celestial body passes the meridian of the place of observation.—**transition,** tran•sizh′on or tran•zish′on, *n.* [L. *transitio.*] Passage from one place or state to another; change or process of change; *mus.* a change in the course of a composition from one key to another, or the passage from one major scale to another more or less related.—*Transition rocks, geol.* a name formerly given to the lowest uncrystalline stratified rocks, as marking the transition from the non-fossiliferous to the fossiliferous periods.—**transitional,** tran•sizh′on•al, *a.* Containing or involving transition.—**transitive,** tran′si•tiv, *a.* Having the power of passing or making transition; *gram.* taking an object after it; denoting action passing to an object that is expressed (a *transitive* verb).—*n.* A transitive verb.—**transitively,** tran′si•tiv•li, *adv.* In a transitive manner.—**transitiveness,** tran′si•tiv•nes, *n.* State of being transitive.—**transitorily,** tran′si•to•ri•li, *adv.* In a transitory manner; with short continuance.—**transitoriness,** tran′si•to•ri•nes, *n.* The state of being transitory.—**transitory,** tran′si•to•ri, *a.* [L. *transitorius,* from *transeo.*] Passing away without continuance; unstable and fleeting; short and uncertain. ∴ Syn. under TRANSIENT.

translate, trans•lāt, *v.t.—translated, translating.* [O.Fr. *translater,* from L. *translatus—trans,* across, and *latus,* borne or carried.] To remove from one place to another†; to take up to heaven without dying (N.T.); to transfer from one office or charge to another; to remove a bishop from one see to another; in the Scotch Church, to transfer a minister from one parish to another; to transform (*Shak.*)‡; to render into another language; to interpret; to explain by using other words; to express in other terms.—*v.i.* To be engaged in or practice translation.—**translatable,** trans•lā′ta•bl, *a.* Capable of being translated.—**translation,** trans•lā′shon, *n.* The act of translating; a removal or motion from one place to another; the removal of a person from one office to another; especially the removal of a bishop from one see to another; also applied to the removal of the relics of a saint from one place to another; the removal of a person to heaven without subjecting him to death; the act of turning into another language; that which is produced by turning into another language; a version.—**translation,** trans•lā′shon, *n.* [L. *translatus,* carried across.] That form of motion in which all the particles of a body move parallel to a fixed line with the same velocity. Comp. ROTATION and REVOLUTION.—**translator,** trans•lā′tėr, *n.* One who translates.

transliterate, trans•lit′ėr•āt, *v.t.—transliterated, transliterating.* [L. *trans,* across, over, and *litera,* a letter. LETTER.] To express or write in the alphabetic characters of another language; to spell in different characters intended to express the same sound.—**transliteration,** trans•lit′ėr•ā″shon, *n.* The act of transliterating; a rendering in equivalent alphabetic characters.

translucent, trans•lū′sent, *a.* [L. *translucens, translucentis—trans,* through, and *luceo,* to shine. LUCID.] Transmitting rays of light, but not so as to render the form or color of objects beyond distinctly visible; transparent.—**translucence, translucency,** trans•lū′sens, trans•lū′sen•si, *n.* The state of being translucent; transparency.—**translucently,** trans•lū′sent•li, *adv.* In a translucent manner.—**translucid,** trans•lū′sid, *a.* [L. *translucidus.*] Transparent; clear; translucent.

transmarine, trans•ma•rēn′, *a.* [L. *transmarinus—trans,* across, and *mare,* the sea. MARINE.] Lying or being beyond the sea.

transmigrate, tranz•mī′grāt, *v.i.—transmigrated, transmigrating.* [L. *transmigro, transmigratum—trans,* across, and *migro,* to migrate.] To migrate; to pass from one country or region to another; to pass from one animal body into another.—**transmigration,** tranz•mī•grā′shon, *n.* The act of transmigrating; the passing of a soul into another body after death; metempsychosis.—**transmigrator,** tranz′mī•grā•tėr, *n.* One who transmigrates.—**transmigratory,** tranz•mī′gra•to•ri, *a.* Passing from one place, body, or state to another.

transmit, tranz•mit′, *v.t.—transmitted, transmitting.* [L. *transmitto, transmissum—trans,* across, through, and *mitto,* to send. MISSION.] To cause to pass or be conveyed from one point to another; to communicate by sending; to send from one person or place to another; to hand down.—*v.i.* To send, as a radio signal.—**transmitter,** trans•mit′ėr, *n.* One who or that which transmits; the sending instrument in telegraphy, radio, etc.—**transmissible, transmittible,** trans•mis′i•bl, trans•mit′i•bl, *a.* —**transmission,** trans•mish′on, *n.* The act of transmitting, or the state of being transmitted; transference; a passing through, as of light through glass; *mach.* the gear that transmits power from the engine to the drive wheels of an automobile; *radio,* the passage of radio waves from the sending to the receiving site.

transmogrify, trans•mog′ri•fī, *v.t.—transmogrified, transmogrifying.* [A fanciful formation from *trans.*] To transform into some other person or thing; to change entirely the appearance of. (*Humorous.*)—**transmogrification,** trans•mog′ri•fi•kā″shon, *n.* A transformation. (*Humorous.*)

transmute, trans•mūt′, *v.t.—transmuted, transmuting.* [L. *transmuto—trans,* across, through, and *muto,* to change, from same root as *moveo,* to move. MOVE.] To change from one nature, form, or substance into another; to change into another thing or body; to metamorphose; to transform.—**transmutability, transmutableness,** trans•mū′ta•bil″i•ti, trans•mū′ta•bl•nes, *n.* The quality of being transmutable.—**transmutable,** trans•mū′ta•bl, *a.* Capable of being transmuted.—**transmutation,** trans•mū•tā′shon, *n.* [L. *transmutatio.*] The act of transmuting, or state of being transmuted; change into another substance, form, or nature; *alchemy,* the changing of base metals into gold or silver.—*Transmutation of energy,* in *physics,* the theory that any one of the various forms of energy may be converted into one or more of the other forms (as electricity into heat).—**transmuter,** trans•mū′tėr, *n.* One that transmutes.

transoceanic, trans′ō•shi•an″ik, *a.* [L. *trans,* across, and *oceanic.*] Crossing the ocean; beyond the ocean.

transom, tran′sum, *n.* [Short for *transommer, transummer,* from *trans,* across, and *summer,* a beam; or from L. *transtrum,* a transom.] A strengthening beam across the stern of a ship; a horizontal bar of stone or timber across a mullioned window; the crossbar separating a door from the fanlight above it; the piece of wood or iron joining the cheeks of gun carriages.

transpadane, trans′pa•dān, *a.* [L. *transpadanus—trans,* across, and *Padus,* the Po.] Being beyond the river Po.

transparent, trans•pâ′rent, *a.* [Fr. *transparent,* from L. *trans,* across, through, and *parens, parentis,* ppr. of *pareo,* to appear (seen also in *apparent, appear*).] Having the property of transmitting rays of light so that bodies can be distinctly seen through; pervious to light; diaphanous; pellucid; *fig.* such as to be easily seen through; not sufficient to hide underlying feelings.—**transparently,** trans•pâ′rent•li, *adv.* In a transparent manner; clearly.—**transparency,** trans•pâ′ren•si, *n.* The quality or condition of being transparent; perviousness to light; something transparent; a picture painted on transparent or semitransparent materials, to be viewed by light shining through it.

transpicuous, trans•pik′ū•us, *a.* [L. *trans*, through, and *specio*, to see.] Transparent; pervious to the sight.

transpierce, trans•pērs′, *v.t.* [Prefix *trans*, and *pierce*.] To pierce through.

transpire, trans•pīr′, *v.t.—transpired, transpiring.* [Fr. *transpirer*, from L. *trans*, across, and *spiro*, to breathe. SPIRIT.] To excrete through the pores of the skin; to send off in vapor; to perspire; to exhale.—*v.i.* To be emitted through the pores of the skin; to exhale; to pass off in insensible perspiration; to become public gradually; to come to light; to ooze out; to leak out; to take place; to happen.—**transpiration,** trans•pi•rā′shon, *n.* The act or process of transpiring; exhalation of moisture through the skin; exhalation of watery vapor from the leaves of plants.—**transpiratory,** trans•pī′ra•to•ri, *a.* Pertaining to transpiration; transpiring; exhaling.

transplant, trans•plant′, *v.t.* [Prefix *trans*, and *plant*; Fr. *transplanter*.] To remove and plant in another place; to remove from one place to another; to remove and settle or establish for residence in another place.—**transplantation,** trans•plan•tā′shon, *n.* The act of transplanting; the shifting of a plant from one spot to another; *surg.* the removal of a part of the human body to supply a part that has been lost.—**transplanter,** trans•plan′tėr, *n.* One who or that which transplants.

transpontine, trans•pon′tīn, *a.* [L. *trans*, beyond, and *pons*, *pontis*, bridge.] Situated beyond the bridge; across the bridge; sensational, melodramatic, of the type of plays in London on the Surrey side of the Thames and London Bridge.

transport, trans•pōrt′, *v.t.* [Fr. *transporter*, from L. *transportare—trans*, across, and *porto*, to carry. PORT (to carry).] To carry or convey from one place to another; to hurry or carry away by violence of passion; to carry away or ravish with pleasure; to absorb.—*n.* (trans′pōrt). Transportation; conveyance; a vessel engaged in transporting goods and passengers; a ship employed for carrying soldiers, war equipment, etc.; a vehement emotion; passion; rapture; ecstasy.—**transportability,** trans•pōr′ta•bil″i•ti, *n.* The capacity of being transported.—**transportable,** trans•pōr′ta•bl, *a.* Capable of being transported.—**transportation,** trans•pōr•tā′shon, *n.* The act of transporting; a conveyance from one place to another; a ticket purchased to travel on some public carrier such as a bus, train, etc.

transpose, trans•pōz′, *v.t.—transposed, transposing.* [Fr. *transposer*, prefix *trans*, and *poser*, to place. POSE, COMPOSE.] To change the place or order of by putting each in the place of the other; to cause to change places; *alg.* to bring, as any term of an equation, over from one side to the other side; *gram.* to change the natural order of words; *mus.* to change the key of.—**transposer,** trans•pō′zėr, *n.* One who transposes.—**transposal,** trans•pō′zal, *n.* The act of transposing; transposition.—**transposition,** trans•po•zish′on, *n.* The act of transposing or state of being transposed; *alg.* the bringing over of any term of an equation from one side to the other side; *rhet.* a change of the natural order of words for effect; *mus.* the change of a composition to a key either higher or lower than the original.—**transpositional,** trans•po•zish′on•al, *a.* Pertaining to transposition.

transship. See TRANSHIP.

transubstantiate, tran•sub•stan′shi•āt, *v.t.* [L. *trans*, over, and *substantia*, substance.] To change to another substance.—*v.i.* To undergo transubstantiation.—**transubstantiation,** tran•sub•stan′shi•ā″shon, *n.* Change of substance; *theol.* the conversion of the *substance* of the bread and wine in the eucharist into the *substance* of the body and blood of Christ, while the *accidents* remain unchanged, a belief held by Roman Catholics and others.

transude, tran•sūd′, *v.i.—transuded, transuding.* [L. *trans*, across, through, and *sudo*, to sweat; allied to E. *sweat*.] To pass or ooze through the pores of a substance.—**transudation,** tran•sū•dā′shon, *n.* The act or process of transuding; osmose.

transuranic, trans•ū•ran′ik, *a.* [L. *trans*, across, and *uranic*, from Gr. *ouranos*, heaven.] Having a higher atomic number than uranium.

transverse, trans•vėrs′ or trans′vėrs, *a.* [L. *transversus—trans*, across, and *versus*, turned. VERSE.] Lying or being across or in a cross direction; lying in a direction across other parts.—*Transverse axis* or *diameter*, in *conic sections*, the diameter which passes through the foci.—*Transverse stress*, that form of stress which bends a structure and tends to break it in pieces.—*Transverse vibrations*, vibrations executed in a direction perpendicular to that in which the undulation advances, e.g. those of light.—**transversely,** trans•vėrs′li, *adv.* In a transverse manner; in a cross direction.—**transversal,** trans•vėr′sal, *a.* Transverse; lying crosswise.—**transversally,** trans•vėr′sal•li, *adv.* In a direction crosswise.

trap, trap, *n.* [A.Sax. *traeppe*, *treppe*, a trap=O.D. *trappe*, O.H.G. *trapo*.] A contrivance that shuts suddenly, used for taking game and other animals; any device or contrivance to betray or catch unawares; an ambush; a drain trap; a familiar name for a carriage, on springs, of any kind.—*v.t.—trapped, trapping.* To catch in a trap; to ensnare; to take by stratagem.—*v.i.* To set traps for game.—**trapper,** trap′ėr, *n.*—**trapshooting,** trap′shōt•ing, *n.* Shooting at clay pigeons that are thrown into the air by traps.

trap, trap, *n.* [Dan. *trap*, Sw. *trapp*, G. *trapp*, the rock, from Dan. *trappe*, Sw. *trappa*, G. *treppe*, a stair, stairs; akin to *trap* above. The rock was named from the terraced or step-like arrangement seen in many of these rocks.] A kind of movable ladder or steps; a kind of ladder leading up to a loft; *geol.* a name applied to the multifarious igneous rocks of the Paleozoic and Secondary epochs that cannot be classed as either granitic or volcanic, comprising basalt, clinkstone, greenstone, felstone, etc.—**trappean,** trap•ē′an, *a.* Pertaining to the rock known as trap; resembling trap.—**trap door,** *n.* A door in a floor or roof, with which when shut it is flush or nearly so.

trap, trap, *v.t.—trapped, trapping.* [O.E. *trappe*, a horse-cloth; same word as Sp. *trapo*, L.L. *trapus*, cloth, Fr. *drap*, cloth; akin *drape*.] To adorn; to dress with ornaments.—**trappings,** trap′ingz, *n. pl.* Ornamental accessories, as the ornaments put on horses; ornaments generally; dress; finery.—**traps,** traps, *n. pl.* Small or portable articles for dress, furniture, etc.; goods; furniture; luggage.

trapan, tra•pan′, *v.t.* Same as *Trepan* (to ensnare).

trapezium, tra•pē′zi•um, *n.* [L., from Gr. *trapezion*, a little table, dim. of *trapeza*, a table, for *tetrapeza*, lit. four-footed thing.] *Geom.* a plane figure contained by four straight lines, none of them parallel; *anat.* a bone of the wrist, so named from its shape.—**trapeze,** tra•pēz′, *n.* A trapezium; *gymnastics*, a sort of swing, consisting of one or more crossbars suspended by two cords at some distance from the ground, on which various feats are performed.—**trapeziform,** tra•pē′zi•form, *a.* Having the form of a trapezium.—**trapezohedron,** tra•pē′zo•hē″dron, *n.* A solid bounded by twenty-four equal and similar trapezoidal planes.—**trapezoid,** trap′e•zoid, *n. Geom.* a plane four-sided figure having two of its opposite sides parallel.—**trapezoidal,** trap•e•zoi′dal, *a.* Having the form of a trapezoid.

trapping. See TRAP.

trappings, trap′ingz, *n.* pl. [M.E. *trappen*, from *trappe*, cloth.] Ornamental accessories or dress.

Trappist, trap′ist, *n.* [From the abbey of La *Trappe*, in Normandy, the headquarters of the order.] A member of a religious order of the Roman Catholic Church, founded in 1664, and remarkable for the austere life led by the monks.

trash, trash, *n.* [Comp. Icel. *tros*, rubbish, leaves and twigs picked up for fuel.] Loppings of trees; sugarcanes from which the juice has been expressed; waste or worthless matter; rubbish; refuse; dross; dregs; a worthless person.—*v.t.* To free from superfluous twigs or branches; to lop.—**trashily,** trash′i•li, *adv.* In a trashy manner.—**trashiness,** trash′i•nes, *n.* The state or quality of being trashy.—**trashy,** trash′i, *a.* Composed of or resembling trash, rubbish, or dross; waste; rejected; worthless; useless.

trass, tras, *n.* [Prov. G. *trass, tarrass,* trass, from Fr. *terrasse,* earthwork, from L. *terra,* earth. TERRACE.] A volcanic production consisting of ashes and scoriae, found near Coblentz, and used as a cement.

trauma, tra̤′ma. [Gr. *trauma,* a wound.] A wound; mental instability due to shock.—**traumatic,** tra̤•mat′-ik, *a.* Pertaining to or applied to wounds; adapted to the cure of wounds.—*n.* A medicine useful in the cure of wounds.—**traumatism,** tra̤′mat•izm, *n. Pathol.* the condition of the system occasioned by a grave wound.

travail, trav′āl, *v.i.* [From Fr. *travailler,* to labor, *travail,* labor, toil; originally an apparatus of bars to restrain a vicious horse, from L. *trabs,* a beam. (TRAVE.) *Travel* is the same word.] To toil‡; to suffer the pangs of childbirth.—*n.* Severe toil‡; parturition; childbirth.

trave, trāv, *n.* [O.Fr. *traf, tref,* It. *trave,* a beam, from L. *trabs, trabis,* a beam. TRAVAIL.] A cross beam‡; a wooden frame to confine an unruly horse while shoeing.

travel, trav′el, *v.i.*—*traveled, traveling.* [A different orthography and application of *travail.*] To pass or make a journey from place to place on foot, on horseback, or in any conveyance; to visit distant or foreign places; to journey; to go from place to place for the purpose of obtaining orders for goods, collecting accounts, etc., for a commercial house; to proceed or advance in any way; to pass.—*v.t.* To journey over; to pass.—*n.* The act of traveling or journeying; journeying to a distant country or countries; *pl.* an account of occurrences and observations made during a journey.—**traveled,** trav′eld, *p.* and *a.* Having made many journeys; hence, experienced.—**traveler,** trav′el•ėr, One who travels.—**traveler's check,** *n.* A draft issued by a bank or an express company, payable to the buyer upon endorsement in the presence of a payer.—**travelogue, travelog,** trav′e•la̤g, *n.* A lecture on travel, often illustrated with slides or a film; a film, describing a place or places.

traverse, trav′ėrs, *a.* [O.Fr. *travers, transvers,* from L. *transversus.* TRANSVERSE.] Transverse; being in a direction across something else.—*Traverse sailing,* where a ship makes several courses in succession, the track being zigzag, and the directions of its several parts lying more or less athwart each other.—*n.* A transverse piece; an untoward accident; *fort.* a portion of parapet thrown across the covered way at certain points; *naut.* the zigzag track described by a ship when compelled to sail on different courses; *arch.* a gallery or loft of communication in a church or other large building; *law,* a denial of what the opposite party has advanced in any stage of the pleadings; *surv.* a number of measured lengths and bearings forming a connected series.—*v.t.*—*traversed, traversing.* To cross; to lay in a cross direction; to thwart; to bring to nought; to wander over; to cross in traveling; *gun.* to turn and point in any direction; *carp.* to plane in a direction across the grain of the wood; *law,* to deny what the opposite party has alleged.—*v.i.* To use the motions of opposition in fencing (*Shak.*); to turn, as on a pivot; to swivel.—*adv.* Athwart; crosswise.—**traversable,** trav′ėr•sa•bl, *a.* Capable of being traversed.—**traverser,** trav′-ėr•sėr, *n.* One who traverses; *rail.* a traverse table.

travertine, travertin, trav′ėr•tin, *n* [It. *travertino, tibertino, tiburtino,* L. *lapis Tiburtinus,* from being formed by the waters of the Anio at *Tibur,* now Tivoli.] A white concretionary limestone deposited from the waters of springs holding carbonate of lime in solution.

travesty, trav′es•ti, *v.t.*—*travestied, travestying.* [Fr. *travestir,* to disguise, to travesty, from L. *trans,* over, and *vestio,* to clothe. VEST.] To give such a literary setting to as to render ludicrous after having been previously handled seriously; to burlesque.—*n.* A burlesque treatment or setting of a subject which had been originally handled in a serious or lofty manner.

trawl, tra̤l, *n.* [From Fr. *trôler,* to lead, to drag. TROLL.] A long line from which short lines with baited hooks are suspended, used in sea fishing, a trawl net.—*v.i.* To fish with a trawl net.—**trawler,** tra̤′lėr, *n.* One who trawls; a fishing vessel which uses a trawl net.

tray, trā, *n.* [A.Sax. *treg,* a tray; connected with *trough.*] A small shallow wooden vessel used for various domestic purposes, as kneading, mincing, etc.; a sort of salver or waiter on which dishes and the like are presented.

treacherous, trech′ėr•us, *a.* [O.Fr. *tricheor* (Fr. *tricheur*), a trickster, from O.Fr. *tricher, trecher,* to cheat, to trick; of Germanic origin, and akin to *trick.*] Characterized by treason or violation of allegiance or faith pledged; faithless; traitorous; deceptive; illusory.—**treacherously,** trech′ėr•us•li, *adv.* In a treacherous manner; traitorously; faithlessly; perfidiously.—**treacherousness,** trech′ėr•us•nes, *n.* The quality of being treacherous.—**treachery,** trech′ėr•i, *n.* [Fr. *tricherie,* trickery.] Violation of allegiance or of faith and confidence; treason; perfidy.

treacle, trē′kl, *n.* [O.Fr. *triacle,* corrupted from L. *theriaca,* from Gr. *thēriaka* (*pharmaka,* drugs, understood), antidotes against the bites of venomous animals, from *thērion,* a wild beast, dim. of *thēr,* an animal.] A medicine formerly believed to be capable of curing or preventing the effects of poison; molasses.

treacle, trē′kl, *n.* [Origin same as preceding.] Molasses; a sirup by-product in the refining of sugar.

tread, tred, *v.i.*—pret. *trod;* pp. *trod, trodden.* [A.Sax. *tredan,* pret. *traed,* to tread = O.Fris. *treda,* D. and L.G. *treden,* Dan. *traede,* Icel. *trotha,* G. *treten,* Goth. *trudan,* to tread; root same as *tramp. Trade* is from this verb.] To set the foot down or on the ground; to press with the foot; to step; to walk with a more or less measured or cautious step; to copulate, as fowls.—*To tread on* or *upon,* to trample; to set the foot on in contempt.—*To tread upon the heels of,* to follow close upon.—*v.t.* To step or walk on; to beat or press with the feet; to perform by motions of the feet; to dance, to crush under the foot; to trample in contempt or hatred; to copulate with, as a male bird.—*To tread down,* to crush or destroy, as by tramping under foot.—*To tread out,* to press out with the feet; to destroy or extinguish, as by treading or trampling.—*To tread the stage* or *the boards,* to perform a part in a drama.—*n.* A step or stepping; way of walking; gait; the flat horizontal part of the step of a stair.—**treader,** tred′ėr, *n.* One who treads.—**treadle,** tred′l, *n.* The part of a loom or other machine which is moved by the foot; a treddle; the albuminous cords which unite the yoke of the egg to the white.—**treadmill,** *n.* A machine employed in prison discipline, the usual form of which is a wheel caused to revolve by the weight of the prisoners treading on steps on its periphery.

treason, trē′zon, *n.* [O.Fr. *traison* (Fr. *trahison*), from L. *traditio,* a delivering up, from *trado,* to deliver up—*trans,* over and *do,* to give. *Treason* and *tradition* are doublets. TRADITION.] A betrayal of trust, treachery; perfidy; disloyalty or treachery to one's country; any attempt to overthrow the government of a state to which one owes allegiance; the crime of giving aid and comfort to the enemies of one's country.—**treasonable,** trē′zon•a•bl, *a.* Pertaining to or consisting of treason; disloyal; treacherous.—**treasonably,** trē′zon•a•bli, *adv.* In a treasonable manner.

treasure, trezh′ėr, *n.* [O.E. *tresoure,* Fr. *trésor,* L. *thesaurus,* from Gr. *thēsauros,* a store, treasure, from root of *tithēmi,* to put or place (whence also *thesis, theme,* etc.).] Wealth accumulated; particularly, a stock or store of money in reserve; a great quantity of anything collected for future use; something very much valued.—*v.t.*—*treasured, treasuring.* To hoard up; to collect for future use; to accumulate; to store; to retain carefully in the mind; to regard as precious; to prize.—**treasurer,** trezh′ėr•ėr, *n.* One who has the care of a treasure or treasury; one who has the charge of collected funds, such as those belonging to incorporated companies or private societies; a public officer who receives and disburses the money collected from taxes, duties, imposts, etc.—**treasurership,** trezh'-ėr•ėr•ship, *n.* The office of treasurer. —**treasure trove,** trōv, *n.* [O.Fr. *trové,* Mod. Fr. *trouvé,* found. TROUBADOUR.] *Law.* money, gold, silver plate, or bullion found hidden in the earth or in any private place the owner of which is not known.—**treasury,** trezh'ėr•i, *n.* A place or building where public revenues are deposited, and public debts discharged; [*often cap.*] that department of a government which has charge of the finances; the officials constituting such a department; [*cap.*] one of the ten major departments of the executive branch of the U. S. federal government, the head of which is a member of the Cabinet; *fig.* a collection of valuable information or facts.—*Secretary of the Treasury,* a member of the Cabinet who is responsible to the President and who supervises the collection of all Federal taxes, safeguards and expends public funds, and is in charge of such divisions as the Bureau of Customs, Bureau of Engraving and Printing, Internal Revenue Service, Bureau of the Mint, Bureau of Narcotics, United States Secret Service, and the United States Coast Guard.—**treasury note,** trezh'-ėr•i•nōt, *n.* A demand note issued by the United States Treasury, and by law made a legal tender at its face value for all debts, public and private.

treat, trēt, *v.t.* [Fr. *traiter,* O.Fr. *traicter,* to handle, to treat, from L. *tractare,* a freq. of *traho, tractum,* to draw (whence also *tract, trace, trait, train,* etc.). TRACE.] To behave to or toward; to act well or ill toward; to use in any manner; to handle in a particular manner, in writing or speaking, or by any of the processes of art; to entertain without expense to the guest; to give food or drink to; to manage in the application of remedies (to *treat* a patient); *chem.* to subject to the action of some other substance.—*v.i.* To discourse; to handle in writing or speaking; followed usually by *of;* to negotiate; to propose terms of accommodation.—*n.* An entertainment given as a compliment or expression of regard; anything which affords much pleasure; some unusual gratification.—*To stand treat,* to pay the expenses of an entertainment for another or others.—**treater,** trē'tėr, *n.* One who treats.—**treatise,** trē'tiz, *n.* [O.Fr. *tretis, traitis.*] A written composition on some subject, in which the principles of it are discussed or explained; usually of considerable length.—**treatment,** trēt'ment, *n.* The act or the manner of treating; management; manipulation; manner of dealing with substances; usage; good or bad behavior toward a person; manner of applying remedies to cure.—**treaty,** trē'ti, *n.* [Fr. *traité.*] The act of treating or negotiating for the adjustment of differences, or for forming an agreement; negotiation; an agreement, league, or contract between two or more nations or sovereigns.

treble, treb'l, *a.* [O.Fr. *treble,* from L. *triplus,* triple. TRIPLE.] Threefold; triple; *mus.* pertaining to the highest or most acute sounds; playing or singing the highest part or most acute sounds.—*n.* The highest vocal or instrumental part in a concerted piece of music; a soprano voice; a soprano singer.—*v.t.*—*trebled, trebling.* To make thrice as much.—**treble clef,** *n. Mus.* a clef on which G is above middle C and on the second line of the staff (also called G clef).

tree, trē, *n.* [A.Sax. *treów, treó,* a tree=Icel. *tré,* Dan. *trae,* Sw. *trä,* O.D. *tree,* Goth. *triu,* tree, wood; cog. W. *derw,* an oak; Gr. *drus,* an oak, *doru,* a spear; Skr. *dru,* a tree. *Tar* is allied.] A perennial plant having a woody trunk of considerable size, from which spring branches, or, in the palms, fronds; something resembling a tree, consisting of a stem or stalk and branches; as, a genealogical *tree;* a generic name for many wooden pieces in machines or structures; as, axle-*tree,* saddle-*tree,* etc.—*Tree of life,* the tree which grew in the midst of the garden of Eden; also, arborvitae.—*v.t.*—*treed, treeing.* To drive to a tree; to cause to take refuge in a tree (a dog *trees* a squirrel).—*v.i.* To take refuge in a tree, as a wild animal.—**tree fern,** *n.* The names given to ferns found in tropical countries which attain the size of trees.—**tree frog,** *n.* A variety of frog which climbs trees, and remains there all summer living upon insects.—**treeless,** trē'-les, *a.* Destitute of trees.—**treenail,** trē'nāl, *n.* A cylindrical pin of hardwood used for securing the planking of wooden ships to the frames, or parts to each other.

trefoil, trē'foil, *n.* [O.Fr. *trefoil,* trefoil, from L. *tres,* three, and *folium,* a leaf.] A three-leaved plant, as the white and red clover, etc., so well known as fodder plants; an ornament used in Gothic architecture representing the form of a three-lobed leaf.

trek, trek, *n.* [Afrikaans from Middle D. *trekken,* to haul.] A journey by ox wagon, especially a migration by a large group.—*v.i.*—*trekked, trekking.* To journey or migrate by ox wagon. —*v.t.* To pull: said of a draft animal.

trellis, trel'is, *n.* [Fr. *treillis,* latticework, from *treille,* an arbor, from L. *trichila,* a bower or arbor.] A structure or frame of crossbarred work or latticework, used for supporting plants; a kind of espalier for climbing plants or for training fruit trees; a reticulated framing or latticework of wood or metal, for screens, doors, or windows.—**trelliswork,** *n.* Latticework.

trematode, trem'a•tōd, *a.* [Gr. *trēma, trēmatos,* a hole, a pore.] A term applied to certain annuloid parasitic worms living in the intestines of animals, some of them being called flukeworms.

tremble, trem'bl, *v.i.*—*trembled, trembling.* [Fr. *trembler,* from L. *tremulus,* trembling, from *tremo,* to tremble=Gr. *tremō,* to tremble. The *b* is inserted as in *number. Tremor, tremulous, tremendous* have same origin.] To shake involuntarily, as with fear, cold, weakness, etc.; to shudder: said of persons; to be moved with a quivering motion; to shake; to totter: said of things; to quaver, as sound.—*n.* The act or state of trembling; an involuntary shaking or shivering through cold or fear.—**trembler,** trem'blėr, *n.* One who trembles.—**trembling,** trem'bling, *p.* and *a.* Shaking, as with fear, cold, or weakness; quaking; shivering.—*Trembling poplar,* the aspen.—*n.* The act or state of shaking involuntarily; a tremor or quaking of the earth.—**tremblingly,** trem'bling•li, *adv.* In a trembling manner.

tremendous, tri•men'dus, *a.* [L. *tremendus,* lit. to be trembled at, from *tremo,* to tremble. TREMBLE.] Sufficient to excite fear or terror; terrible; awful; dreadful; hence, such as may astonish by magnitude, force, or violence.—**tremendously,** tri•men'dus•li, *adv.* In a tremendous manner; dreadfully; terrifically.

tremolite, trem'o•līt, *n.* [From Val *Tremola,* a valley in the Alps where it was discovered.] A mineral regarded as a variety of hornblende, found in dolomite, crystalline limestone, etc.

tremolo, trem'o•lō, *n.* [It., from L. *tremulus,* tremulous.] *Mus.* a rapid quavering effect in playing or singing; a vibration of the voice in singing, suitable for the production of certain effects.

tremor, trem'ėr, *n.* [L., from *tremo,* to tremble. TREMBLE.] An involuntary trembling; a shivering or shaking; a quivering or vibratory motion.—**tremulous,** trem'ū•lus, *a.* [L. *tremulus,* from *tremo.*] Trembling; affected with fear or timidity; shaking; shivering.—**tremulously,** trem'ū•lus•li, *adv.* In a tremulous manner; tremblingly.—**tremulousness,** trem'ū•lus•nes, *n.* Shakiness.

trenail, trē'nāl. Same as *Treenail.*

trench, trensh, *v.t.* [O.Fr. *trencher,* to cut off (Fr. *trancher*), perhaps from L. *truncare,* to lop, from *truncus,* a log, a trunk.] To cut or dig, as a ditch; to furrow deeply with the spade or plow; to break up and prepare for crops by deep digging; to fortify by a ditch and rampart of earth; to intrench. INTRENCH.—*v.i.* To encroach; with *on* or *upon.*—*n.* A long narrow cut in the earth; a ditch; *milit.* a deep ditch, with a parapet or breastwork, cut for defense (as in a siege or a position taken up) or to interrupt the approach of an enemy.—*To open the trenches,* to begin to dig or to form the lines of approach.—**trenchant,** tren'shant, *a.* [O.Fr. *trenchant.*] Cutting; sharp; keen; unsparing; severe.—**trencher,** tren'-

shėr, *n.* [In second sense, lit. that on which food is *trenched* or cut.] One who trenches or cuts; a wooden plate on which meat may be cut or carved, or on which it is eaten.—**trencherman,** *n.* A hearty feeder; a table companion.—**trench foot,** *n.* A condition of the feet resembling frostbite, frequently terminating in gangrene, and caused by exposure to wet and cold.—**trench fever,** *n.* An infectious disease with feverish symptoms, transmitted by vermin.

trend, trend, *v.i.* [Lit. to bend circularly, from stem of A.Sax. *trendel, tryndel,* a circle; Fris. *trind, trund,* Dan. and Sw. *trind,* round; closely akin to *trundle.*] To extend or lie along in a particular direction; to stretch (the coast *trends* to the south).—*n.* Inclination of a coast or other line in a particular direction.

trepan, tri•pan′, *n.* [Fr. *trépan,* It. *trapano,* from Gr. *trypanon,* an auger, a surgical instrument, from *trypē,* a hole.] *Surg.* an instrument in the form of a crown saw for removing portions of the bones of the skull, and thus relieving the brain from pressure.—*v.t.*—*trepanned, trepanning.* To operate on by the trepan.—**trepanning,** tri•pan′ing, *n.* The operation of using the trepan.

trepan, tri•pan′, *v.t.*—*trepanned, trepanning.* [Formerly *trapan,* from O.Fr. *trappan,* from *trappe,* a trap. TRAP.] To ensnare or entrap; to inveigle in some deceitful manner.—*n.* A snare; a cheat; a deceiver.—**trepanner,** tri•pan′ėr, *n.* One who trepans; a cheat.

trepang, tri•pang′, *n.* [Malay name.] The sea slug, sea cucumber, or *bêche-de-mer,* found in the eastern seas, and used as food in China.

trephine, tri•fīn′ or tri•fēn′, *n.* [Fr. *tréphine,* modified form of *trépan.*] An improved form of the trepan.

trepidation, trep•i•dā′shon, *n.* [L. *trepidatio,* from *trepido,* to tremble, from *trepidus,* trembling, from obsolete *trepo,* to turn=Gr. *trepō,* to turn.] An involuntary trembling; a state of terror; a trembling of the limbs, as in paralytic affections; the oscillation of the ecliptic formerly assumed to account for the phenomenon of the precession of the equinoxes. (*Mil.,* P.L., iii, 483).

trespass, tres′pas, *v.i.* [O.Fr. *trespasser,* from *tres*=L. *trans,* beyond, and *passer,* to pass. PASS.] To pass over a boundary line and enter unlawfully upon the land of another; to intrude; to encroach; to commit any offense; to transgress; to violate any divine law or any known rule of duty.—*n.* The act of one who trespasses; a violation of some law or rule laid down; any voluntary transgression of the moral law; sin; *law,* any transgression of the law not amounting to felony; especially wrong done by entering on the grounds of another.—**trespasser,** tres′pas•ėr, *n.* One who commits a trespass.

tress, tres, *n.* [Fr. *tresse,* It. *treccia,* a tress, plait of hair, from Gr. *tricha,* in three parts, from the usual mode of plaiting the hair; allied to *three.*] A lock or curl of hair; a ringlet.

trestle, tres′l, *n.* [O.Fr. *trestel* (Fr. *tréteau*), a trestle; from Armor. *treustel,* from *treust, trest,* W. *trawst,* a beam.] A sort of frame with three or four legs attached to a horizontal piece; a braced framework of steel, timber, or piles, serving as a support for a road or railroad running over a gully, ravine, etc.

tret, tret, *n.* [Fr. *trait,* from O.Fr. *traire,* to draw, from L. *trahere,* to draw. TRACE.] An allowance to purchasers of certain goods for waste or refuse matter.

trews, tröz, *n. pl.* The tartan trousers of Highlanders or soldiers in Highland regiments.

trey,‡ trā, *n.* [O.Fr. *trei,* Fr. *trois,* L. *tres,* three.] A three at cards or dice. (*Shak.*)

triable. See TRY.

triad, trī′ad, *n.* [Gr. *trias, triados,* from *treis, tria,* three.] A unity of three; three united; a trinity; *mus.* the common chord formed of three radical sounds, a fundamental note, its third, and its fifth; *chem.* an elementary substance, each atom of which will combine with three atoms of a monad.

trial. See TRY.

triangle, trī′ang•gl, *n.* [Fr. *triangle,* from L. *triangulum*—*tres, tria,* three, and *angulus,* an angle.] *Geom.* a figure bounded by three lines and containing three angles, the lines or sides being straight in a plane triangle, and parts of circles in spherical triangles; a musical instrument of percussion, made of a rod of steel bent into this shape, open at one of the angles; a three-cornered straightedge, used by draftsmen, etc.; a kind of gin for raising heavy weights; *milit.* three halberts stuck in the ground and united at the top, to which soldiers were bound when flogged.—**triangular,** trī•ang′gū•lėr, *a.* Having three angles; having the form of a triangle; three-cornered.—*Triangular compass,* a compass having three legs by means of which any triangle or any three points may be taken off at once.—*Triangular pyramid,* a pyramid whose base is a triangle.—**triangularity,** trī•ang′gū•lar″i•ti, *n.* Quality of being triangular.—**triangularly,** trī•ang′gū•lėr•li, *adv.* After the form of a triangle.—**triangulate,** trī•ang′gū•lāt, *v.t.*—*triangulated, triangulating.* To make triangular; *surv.* to divide into triangles, or survey by dividing into triangles.—**triangulation,** trī•ang′gū•lā″shon, *n.* The reduction of the surface of an area to triangles for the purpose of a trigonometrical survey.

triarchy, trī′är•ki, *n.* [Gr. *treis,* three, and *archē,* rule.] Government by three persons.

Trias, trī′as, *n.* [Gr. *trias,* the number three.] *Geol.* a name given to the upper new red sandstone, from its being composed in Germany of three well-marked groups, only the highest and lowest of which are known in England.—**Triassic,** trī•as′ik, *a.* Pertaining to or composed of Trias.

triatomic, trī•a•tom′ik, *a.* [Gr. *treis,* three, and *atomos,* an atom.] *Chem.* consisting of three atoms; having three atoms in the molecule.

tribasic, trī•bā′sik, *a.* [Gr. *treis,* three, and *basis,* base.] *Chem.* applied to acids which combine with three equivalents of a base.

tribe, trīb, *n.* [L. *tribus,* one of the three bodies into which the Romans were originally divided, from *tres,* three. THREE.] A division, class, or distinct portion of a people or nation; a family or race descending from the same progenitor, and kept distinct, as the twelve tribes of Israel; a nation or family of savages, forming a subdivision of a race; a number of persons of any character or profession; in contempt; a term used by some naturalists to denote a number of things having certain characters or resemblances in common (a *tribe* of plants); a division of animals or plants intermediate between order and genus.—**tribal,** trī′bal, *a.* Belonging to a tribe; characteristic of a tribe.

tribrach, trī′brak, *n.* [Gt. *tribrachys*—*treis,* three, and *brachys,* short.] *Pros.* a poetic foot of three short syllables; a word of three short syllables.

tribulation, trib•ū•lā′shon, *n.* [Eccles. L. *tribulatio,* distress, from L. *tribulo, tribulatum,* to thrash, from *tribulum,* a threshing sledge for dragging over corn; akin *tero, tritum,* to rub (whence *trite, contrite* heart).] That which occasions affliction or distress; severe affliction; distress; trouble; trial.

tribune, trī′būn or trib′ūn, *n.* [L. *tribunus,* a tribune, magistrate, or officer, from *tribus,* tribe; in latter senses short for *tribunal.*] An officer in ancient Rome who represented a tribe for certain purposes; an officer or magistrate chosen by the common people of Rome to protect them from the oppression of the patricians; also a military officer commanding a division or legion; a raised seat or stand; the throne of a bishop; a sort of pulpit or rostrum where a speaker stands to address an assembly.—**tribunal,** trī•bū′nal, *n.* [L. *tribunal,* from *tribunus,* a tribune.] The seat of a judge; a bench for judges; a court of justice.—**tribunate,** trī′bū•nāt, *n.* Tribuneship.—**tribuneship,** trī′būn•ship or trib′ūn•ship, *n.* The office of a tribune.—**tribunitial,** trib•ū•nish′al, *a.* Pertaining to tribunes.

tribute, trib′ūt, *n.* [Fr. *tribut,* L. *tributum,* from *tribuo,* to give, to bestow, perhaps from *tribus,* a tribe. TRIBE.] An annual or stated sum paid by one prince or nation to another, either as an acknowledgment of submission or by virtue of some treaty; the obligation of contributing; a personal contribution; anything done or given, as that which is due or observed (a *tribute* of respect).—**tributary,** trib′-

ū•te•ri, *a.* [L. *tributarius.*] Paying tribute to another; subject; subordinate; inferior; yielding supplies of anything; contributing.—*n.* An individual, government, or state that pays tribute; *geog.* an affluent; a stream which contributes water to another stream.—**tributarily,** trib′ū•te•ri•li, *adv.* In a tributary manner.

trice, trīs, *v.t.*—*triced, tricing.* [Same as M.E. *trisen,* Dan. *tridse,* to hoist, *tridse,* a pulley; Sw. *trissa,* a pulley.] *Naut.* to haul or tie up by means of a small rope; to hoist.

trice, trīs, *n.* [From M.E. *trisen,* to pull, hoist.] A very short time; a moment, now used only in the phrase *in a trice* (literally *in a single pull*), in an instant or moment.

triceps, trī′seps, *n.* pl. **tricepses,** tri′seps•iz. [L. from *tres,* three, and *caput,* head.] A muscle having three heads, especially the extensor running along the back of the upper arm.

trichina, tri•kī′na, *n.* pl. **trichinae,** tri•kī′nē. [From Gr. *thrix, trichos,* a hair.] A minute nematode worm, whose larvae cause trichinosis.—**trichinosis,** trik′i•nō″sis, *n.* A disease of the intestines and muscle tissue, caused by the presence of trichinae.

trichocyst, trik′o•sist, *n.* [Gr. *thrix, trichos,* a hair, and *kystis,* a bag.] A cell capable of emitting thread-like filaments, found in Infusoria.—**trichogyne,** trīk′o•jin, *n.* [Gr. *thrix,* and *gynē,* a woman.] In red seaweeds a receptive thread-like projection from the female organ.—**trichome,** trī′kōm, *n.* A hair or other outgrowth from the epidermis.

trichotomy, trī•kot′o•mi, *n.* [Gr. *tricha,* thrice, and *tomē,* a cutting.] Division into three parts.—**trichotomous,** trī•kot′o•mus, *a.* Divided or branching by threes; trifurcate.

trichromatic, trī•krōm•at′ik, *a.* [Prefix *tri-,* and Gr. *chroma,* color.] Pertaining to three colors, especially to red, green, and violet, which, according to the trichromatic theory, are fundamental in color sensation; or to red, yellow, and blue, which are primary colors so far as regards mixtures of pigments.

trick, trick *n.* [O.F. *tricher,* to deceive, from L. *tricor,* to play tricks.] An artifice; a stratagem; a fraudulent contrivance for an evil purpose; a cheat; a knack or art; a sleight-of-hand performance; the legerdemain of a juggler; a particular practice or habit; an action peculiar to a person (a *trick* of frowning); anything mischievously and roguishly done; a prank; a frolic; *card-playing,* all the cards played in one round; *naut.* a spell; a turn; the time allotted to a man to stand at the helm.—*v.t.* To deceive; to impose on; to defraud; to cheat; to draw in outline, as with a pen; to delineate without color, as heraldic devices [In last sense directly from D. *trekken,* to draw, to delineate.]—*v.i.* To live by deception and fraud.—**tricker,** trik′ėr, *n.* One who tricks; a deceiver; a cheat; a trickster.—**trickery,** trik′er•i, *n.* The practice of tricks; imposture; cheating; artifice.—**trickish,** trik′ish, *a.* Given to tricks; artful; knavish.—**trickishly,** trik′ish•li, *adv.* In a trickish manner.—**trickishness,** trik′ish•nes, *n.*—**tricksiness,** trik′si•nes, *n.* The quality of being tricksy; playfulness.—**trickster,** trik′stėr, *n.* One who practices tricks; a deceiver; a cheat.—**tricksy,** trik′si, *a.* Full of tricks and devices; artful; given to pranks. **tricky,** trik′i, *a.* Trickish; mischievous.

trick, trik, *v.t.* [From above word, or from W *treciaw,* to trick out, from *trec,* harness, gear.] To dress; to decorate; to set off; to adorn fantastically; often followed by *out.*—**tricking,** trik′ing, *n.* Dress; ornament.

trickle, trik′l, *v.i.*—*trickled, trickling.* [Probably for *strickle,* from A.Sax. *strícan,* to go. STRIKE.] To flow in a small gentle stream; to run down in drops.

tricktrack, trik•trak, *n.* A kind of backgammon.

triclinic, trī•klin′ik, *a.* [Gr. *treis,* three, *klinō,* to incline.] *Crystal.* having three unequal axes intersecting obliquely.—**triclinium,** trī•klin′i•um, *n.* [L., from Gr. *triklinion.*] Among the Romans, a couch running round three sides of a table, for reclining on at meals; the dining room in which such a couch was laid.

tricolor, trī′kul•ėr, *n.* [Fr. *tricolore,* of three colors—L. *tres,* three, and *color,* color.] A flag having three colors; a flag having three colors arranged in equal stripes, adopted in France as the national ensign during the first revolution, the colors being blue, white, and red, divided vertically.

tricorn, trī′korn, *a.* [Fr. *tricorne,* from L. *tricornis.*] Having three corners or horns.

tricostate, trī•kos′tāt, *a.* [L. *tri*=*tres,* three, and *costa,* a rib.] *Bot.* having three ribs or ridges; three-ribbed.

tricot, trē′ko, *n.* [Fr. from *tricoter,* to knit.] A knitted fabric of nylon, wool, cotton, silk, or rayon, usually used as underwear.

tricuspid, tricuspidate, trī•kus′pid, trī•kus′pi•dāt, *a.* [L. *tri*=*tres,* three, and *cuspis, cuspidis,* a point.] Having three cusps or points; *bot.* three-pointed; ending in three points.

tricycle, trī′si•kl, *n.* [Gr. *tri*=*treis,* three, and *kyklos,* a circle, a wheel.] A form of velocipede with three wheels, generally two wheels parallel to each other, and a steering wheel either in front or in the rear.

trident, trī′dent, *n.* [L. *tridens, tridentis*—*tri*=*tres,* three, and *dens, dentis,* a tooth.] Any instrument of the form of a fork with three prongs; the scepter or spear with three barbed prongs with which Poseidon (Neptune), the sea god, is represented.—**tridentate, tridentated,** trī•den′tāt, trī•den′tā•ted, *a.* Having three teeth.

Tridentine, trī•den′tīn, *a.* [L. *Tridentum,* Trent.] Pertaining to Trent, or to the celebrated ecumenical council which met in that city in 1545.

tridimensional, trī•di•men′shon•al, *a.* [Prefix *tri,* three, and *dimension.*] Having three dimensions.

triennial, trī•en′ni•al, *a.* [L. *triennium,* the space of three years—*tri*=*tres,* three; and *annus,* a year.] Continuing three years; happening every three years.—**triennially,** trī•en′ni•al•li, *adv.* Once in three years.

trier, trī′er, *n.* One who tries or attempts; one who tests or experiments; one who tests judicially; a judge.

trierarch, trī′ėr•ärk, *n.* [Gr. *triērēs,* a trireme, and *archē,* rule.] The commander of a Greek trireme; also, one who was obliged to build ships and furnish them at his own expense.—**trierarchy,** trī″ėr•är′ki, *n.* The office or function of a trierarch.

trifid, trī′fid, *a.* [L. *trifidus*—*tri*=*tres,* three, and *findo, fidi,* to divide.] *Bot.* split into three lobes or parts by clefts; tridentate.

trifle, trī′fl, *n.* [O.E. *trifle, trofle, trufle,* a trifle, from O.Fr. *trufle, truffe,* mock, gibe; perhaps of Teutonic origin; comp. Icel. *truff,* trumpery.] A thing of very little value or importance; a paltry toy, bauble, or luxury; a silly or unimportant action, remark, or the like; a kind of light dish or fancy confection.—*v.i.*—*trifled, trifling.* To act or talk without seriousness or with levity; to indulge in light amusements.—*To trifle with,* to treat as a trifle; to make a toy or a fool of; to mock.—*v.t.* To waste to no good purpose; to spend; usually followed by *away.*—**trifler,** trī′fl•ėr, *n.* One who trifles.—**trifling,** trī′fl•ing, *p.* and *a.* Acting with levity; frivolous; being of small value or importance; trivial.—**triflingly,** trī′fl•ing•li, *adv.*

trifocal, trī•fō′kal, *a.* [Fr. *tri,* from L. *tri, tres,* three, and *focal.*] Having three focal lengths, as an eyeglass lens.—*n.* pl. Eyeglasses with three focal lengths.

trifoliate, trifoliated, trī•fō′li•āt, trī•fō′li•ā•ted, *a.* [L. *tri*=*tres,* three, and *folium,* a leaf.] Having three leaves.—**trifoliolate,** trī•fō′li•o•lāt, *a.* Having three leaflets.

triforium, trī•fō′ri•um, *n.* [L. *tri*=*tres,* three, and *foris,* pl. *fores,* a door.] *Gothic arch.* a gallery above the arches of the nave of a church, generally in the form of an arcade.

triform, trī′form, *a.* [L. *triformis*—*tri*=*tres,* three, and *forma,* shape.] Having a triple form or shape.

trifurcate, trifurcated, trī•fėr′kāt, trī•fėr′kā•ted, *a.* [L. *tri*=*tres,* three, and *furca,* a fork.] Having three branches or forks; trichotomous.

trig, trig, *v.t.*—*trigged, trigging.* [Comp. W. *trigaw,* to stay, to tarry; Pr. *trigar,* to stop.] To stop, as the wheel of a vehicle, by putting something down to check it.—*n.* A stone, wedge, etc., used for this purpose.

trig, trig, *a.* [Sw. *trygg,* Dan. *tryg,* secure, safe.] Trim; spruce; neat.

trigger, trig'ėr, *n.* [D. *trekker,* trigger, from *trekken,* to draw; allied to *trick, track.*] The lever which, on being pulled back, liberates the hammer of the lock of a gun or pistol; any similar device; an initiating stimulus (the icy water was the *trigger* that caused the illness).—*v.t.* To fire; to cause the explosion of something; to initiate.—*v.i.* To release a trigger.

triglyph, trī'glif, *n.* [Gr. *tri=treis,* three, and *glyphē,* sculpture.] *Arch.* an ornamental block in Doric friezes, repeated at equal intervals, having on its face two small perpendicular channels and a half channel on either side.—**triglyphic, triglyphical,** trī•glif'ik, trī•glif'i•kal, *a.* Pertaining to triglyphs.

trigon, trī'gon, *n.* [Fr. *trigone,* L. *trigonum,* from Gr. *trigōnon—tri= treis,* three, and *gōnia,* an angle.] A triangle; *astrol.* the junction of three signs of the zodiac; an ancient triangular lyre.—**trigonal, trigonous,** trī'gon•al, trī'gon•us, *a.* Triangular; *bot.* having three prominent longitudinal angles, as a style or ovary.

trigonometry, trig•o•nom'et•ri, *n.* [From Gr. *trigōnon,* a triangle (*treis,* three, and *gōnia,* an angle), and *metron,* a measure.] The measuring of triangles, or the science of determining the sides and angles of triangles by means of certain parts which are given, of high importance in astronomy, navigation, and surveying. It is of two kinds, *plane trigonometry,* treating of triangles described on a plane, and *spherical trigonometry,* of those described on the surface of a sphere.—**trigonometric, trigonometrical,** trig'o•no•met"rik, trig'o•no•met"ri•kal, *a.* Pertaining to trigonometry; performed by or according to the rules of trigonometry.—*Trigonometrical survey,* the survey of a country carried on from a single base, which must be measured with the most extreme accuracy, by the computation of observed angular distances and careful geodetical operations.—**trigonometrically,** trig'o•no•met"ri•kal•li, *adv.* In a trigonometrical manner; by trigonometry.

trigraph, trī'graf, *n.* [Gr. *tri=treis,* three, *gramma,* a letter, *graphē,* a writing.] A name given to three letters having one sound; a triphthong, as *eau* in *beau.*

trihedron, trī•hē'dron, *n.* [Gr. *tri= treis,* three, and *hedra,* side.] A figure having three equal sides.—**trihedral,** trī•hē•dral, *a.* Having three equal sides.

trijugate, trijugous, trī'jū•gāt, trī'jū•gus, *a.* [L. *tri=tres,* three, *jugum,* yoke.] *Bot.* in three pairs, as a pinnate leaf with three pairs of leaflets.

trilateral, trī•lat'er•al, *a.* [L. *tri= tres,* three, *latus, lateris,* a side.] Having three sides, as a triangle.—**trilaterally,** trī•lat'er•al•li, *adv.* With three sides.

trilinear, trī•lin'i•ėr, *a.* [L. *tri=tres,* three, and *linea,* a line.] Composed or consisting of three lines.

trilingual, trī•ling'gwal, *a.* [L. *tri= tres,* three, and *lingua,* a tongue.] Consisting of three languages.

triliteral, trī•lit'er•al, *a.* [L. *tri= tres,* three, and *litera,* a letter.] Consisting of three letters; combining three letters, as the roots in the Semitic family of tongues.—*n.* A word consisting of three letters.

trill, tril, *n.* [Perhaps imitative of sound=D. *trillen,* Dan. *trille,* to trill.] *Mus.* a rapid alteration of two tones a degree apart; a similar sound, as of a bird warbling; the vibration of an articulatory speech organ against another, as with the tongue against the alveolar ridge (back of the upper teeth) in pronouncing *r.* —*v.t.* To utter with, or as if with, a trill.—*v.i.* To sing or play an instrument with a trill.

trillion, tril'yon, *n.* [Formed from *tri-,* three, and *million.*] In the U. S. and France, a million, times a million, or a thousand billions; a digit followed by twelve zeros (1,000,000,000,000). In Gt. Britain and Germany, a million billions (1,000,000,000,000,000,000).

trilobate, trilobed, trī•lō'bāt, trī'lōbed, *a.* [Gr. *tri=treis,* three, and *lobos,* a lobe.] Having three lobes.

trilobite, trī'lo•bīt, *n.* [Gr. *tri=treis,* three, and *lobos,* a lobe.] One of an extinct and widely distributed family of Paleozoic Crustacea abundant in the Silurian strata, having the body divided into three lobes, which run parallel to its axis.—**trilobitic,** trī•lo•bit'ik, *a.* Pertaining to or resembling a trilobite.

trilocular, trī•lok•ū•lėr, *a.* [L. *tri= tres,* three, and *loculus,* a cell, dim. of *locus,* a place.] *Bot.* three-celled; having three cells for seeds.

trilogy, tril'o•ji, *n.* [Gr. *trilogia,* from *treis, tria,* three, and *logos,* speech, discourse.] A series of three works each in a certain sense complete in itself, yet together forming one connected whole.

trim, trim, *v.t.—trimmed, trimming.* [A.Sax. *trymian,* to prepare, to set in order, from *trum,* firm, strong; O.Sax. *trimm,* firm, L.G. *betrimmen,* to make firm.] To put in due order for any purpose; to adjust; to invest, embellish, or decorate, as with ribbons, braid, lace, etc. (to *trim* a gown); to bring to a neat or orderly condition by removing superfluous appendages or matter; to clip, pare, shave, prune, lop, or the like (to *trim* the hair, a hedge, or a tree); *carp.* to dress, as timber, *naut.* to adjust the weights in a ship or boat, so that it shall sit well on the water and sail well.—*v.i.* To hold a middle course or position between parties, so as to appear to favor each.—*a.* Being neat and in good order; properly adjusted; having everything appropriate and in its right place; tight; snug; neat; tidy; smart.—*n.* Dress; garb; state of preparation; order; condition; mood; disposition; the state of a ship by which she is well prepared for sailing.—**trimly,** trim'li, *adv.* In a trim manner or condition. —**trimmer,** trim'ėr, *n.* One who trims; a laborer who arranges the cargo of coal on board a ship; one who fluctuates between parties, especially political parties, or tries to keep on good terms with each.—**trimming,** trim'ing, *n.* The act of one who trims; the act of one who fluctuates between parties; ornamental appendages to a garment; *pl.* the accessories to any dish or article of food (*colloq.*).—**trimness,** trim'nes, *n.* The state or quality of being trim.

trimerous, trī'mėr•us, *a.* [Gr. *tri= treis,* three, and *meros,* a part.] *Bot.* consisting of three parts; *entom.* applied to beetles (Trimera) having three-jointed tarsi.

trimester, trī•mes'tėr, *n.* [Fr. *trimestre,* from L. *trimestris*—prefix *tri,* three, and *mensis,* a month.] A term or period of three months.—**trimestral, trimestrial,** trī•mes'tral, trī•mes'tri•al, *a.* Pertaining to a trimester; occurring every three months; quarterly.

trimeter, trim'et•ėr, *n.* [Gr. *tri= treis,* three, and *metron,* a measure.] A line or verse of poetry consisting of three measures (often of two iambic feet each).

trimorphism, trī•mor'fizm, *n.* [Gr. *tri=treis,* three, and *morphē,* form.] The state or property of having three distinct forms; *crystal.* the property of crystallizing in three fundamentally different forms.—**trimorphic, trimorphous,** trī•mor'fik, trī•mor'fus, *a.* Characterized by trimorphism; having three distinct forms.

Trimurti, tri•mör'ti, *n.* [Skr., from *tri,* three, and *mûrti,* body.] The Hindu trinity, Brahma the creator, Vishnu the preserver, and Siva the destroyer, conceived as an inseparable unity.

trinal, trine, trī'nal, trīn, *a.* [L. *trinus,* threefold, from *tres,* three.] Threefold; triple.—**trine,** *n.* The aspect of planets distant from each other 120 degrees; a triad.

trinitrotoluene, trī•nī'trō•tol"ū•ēn, *n.* [From *tri-, nitric,* and *toluene.*] A high explosive, made by treating toluene with nitric acid; also called T.N.T.

trinity, trin'i•ti, *n.* [Fr. *trinité,* from L. *trinitas,* from *trinus,* threefold, from *tres,* three. THREE.] A union of three in one; the state of being three; [*cap.*] *theol.* the union of three persons in one Godhead; [*cap.*] the Father, the Son, and the Holy Spirit; a symbolical representation of the mystery of the Trinity frequent in Christian art.—*Trinity Sunday,* the Sunday next after Whitsunday, observed in honor of the Trinity.—*Trinity House,* an incorporation having its headquarters in London, entrusted with the regulation and management of the lighthouses and buoys of the shores and rivers of England, with supervision of those of Scotland and Ireland.—**Trinitarian,** trin•i•tâ'ri•an, *a.* Pertaining to the Trinity, or to the doctrine of the Trinity.—*n.* One who believes the doctrine of the Trinity.—

Trinitarianism, trin•i•tâ'ri•an•izm, *n.* The doctrine of Trinitarians.

trinket, tring'ket, *n.* [Probably a nasalized form of *tricket,* from *trick,* to dress out.] A small ornament, as a jewel, a ring, and the like; a thing of no great value; a trifle.—*v.i.* To hold secret communication; to intrigue; to traffic.

trinomial, trī•nō'mi•al, *a.* [Gr. *tri*=*treis,* three, and *nome,* a division.] *Alg.* consisting of three terms connected by the signs + or −.—*n. Alg.* a quantity of three terms.

trio, trē'ō, *n.* [It., from L. *tres,* three.] Three united; *mus.* a composition for three voices or three instruments; the performers of a trio.

triode, trī•ōd', *n.* [Prefix *tri,* and Gr. *hodos,* way.] An electron tube with three electrodes.

triolet, trē'o•let, *n.* [Dim. of *trio.*] A stanza of eight lines in which the first line is repeated after the third, and the first and second lines after the sixth.

trioxide, tri•äk'sīd, *n.* [L. *tri,* three, and *oxide.*] An oxide having three atoms of oxygen per molecule.

trip, trip, *v.i.*—*tripped, tripping.* [A lighter and non-nasalized form akin to *tramp* and = Dan. *trippe,* Sw. *trippa,* D. *trippen,* G. *trippen, trippeln,* to trip. TRAMP, TRAP.] To run or step lightly; to move the feet nimbly, as in running, walking, dancing; to stumble and come near to fall; to make a false step; to lose the footing; to offend against morality, propriety, or rule; to err; to go wrong.—*v.t.* To cause to fall by striking the feet suddenly from under the person; to cause to stumble or make a false step; often followed by *up*; to catch in a fault or mistake (*Shak.*); *naut.* to loose (an anchor) from the bottom by its cable.—*n.* A light short step; a lively movement of the feet; a short journey or voyage; an excursion or jaunt; a causing to stumble or fall; a stumble; a false step; an error; a mistake.—**trip hammer,** *n.* A large hammer used in forges; a tilthammer.—**tripper,** trip'ėr, *n.* One who trips or trips up; one who walks nimbly.—**tripping,** trip'ing, *a.* Stepping quickly or lightly; quick; nimble.

tripartite, trī'pär•tīt, *a.* [L. *tripartitus*—*tri*=*tres,* three, and *partitus,* pp. of *partior,* to part. PART.] Divided into three parts; having three corresponding parts; made between three parties (a *tripartite* treaty); *bot.* divided into three parts down to the base, but not wholly separate.—**tripartitely,** trī'pär•tīt•li, *adv.* In a tripartite manner.—**tripartition,** trī•pär•tish'on, *n.* A division into three parts; a division by three.

tripe, trīp, *n.* [Fr. *tripe,* Sp. and Pg. *tripa,* It. *trippa,* tripe; of Celtic origin; W. *tripa,* Ir. *triopas,* Armor. *stripen,* tripe.] The stomach of ruminating animals when prepared for food.

tripedal, trip'e•dal, *a.* [L. *tripedalis*—*tri*=*tres,* three, and *pes, pedis,* a foot.] Having three feet.

tripersonal, trī•pėr'son•al, *a.* [Prefix *tri,* three, and *personal.*] Consisting of three persons.

tripetaloid, trī•pet'al•oid, *a.* [Gr. *tri treis,* three, *petalon,* a leaf.] *Bot.* appearing as if furnished with three petals.—**tripetalous,** trī•pet'al•us, *a.* Having three petals.

triphthong, trif'thong or trip'thong, *n.* [Gr. *tri*=*treis,* three, and *phthongē,* sound.] A combination of three vowels in a single syllable; three vowel characters representing a single sound (*eau* in *beau*); a trigraph.

tripinnate, trī•pin'āt, *a.* [Prefix *tri,* three, and *pinnate, pinnatifid, pinnatisect.*] *Bot.* trebly pinnate: said when the leaflets of a bipinnate leaf are themselves pinnate.

triple, trip'l, *a.* [Fr. *triple,* from L. *triplus,* threefold, triple, from *tres, tria,* three, and term. *-plus,* as in *double* (which see). *Treble* is a doublet of this.] Consisting of three united; threefold; three times repeated; treble.—*Triple crown,* the crown worn by the popes, consisting of three crowns placed one above another, surrounding a high cap or tiara.—*Triple time, mus.* time or rhythm of three beats, or of three times three beats, in a bar.—*v.t.*—*tripled, tripling.* To make threefold or thrice as much or as many; to treble.—**triplet,** trip'let, *n.* [Dim. from *triple.*] A collection or combination of three of a kind, or three united; three verses or lines of poetry rhyming together; *mus.* a group of three notes of equal time value, to be performed in the time of two, indicated by a slur and the figure 3; a combination of three lenses; one of three children at a birth.—**triply,** trip'li, *adv.* In a triple or threefold manner; trebly.

triplicate, trip'li•kit, *a.* [L. *triplicatus,* pp. of *triplico,* to triple—*tres,* three, and *plico,* to fold. PLY.] Made thrice as much; threefold.—*Triplicate ratio,* in *math.* the ratio which the cubes of two quantities bear to one another, compared with the ratio which the quantities themselves bear to each other.—*n.* A third thing corresponding to two others.—**triplication,** trip•li•kā'shon, *n.* The act of trebling or making threefold.—**triplicity,** tri•plis'i•ti, *n.* [From L. *triplex, triplicis,* triple.] The state of being triple or threefold.

triply. See TRIPLE.

tripod, trī'pod, *n.* [Gr. *tripous, tripodos*—*tri*=*treis,* three, *pous, podos,* a foot.] A name for various ancient utensils or articles of furniture resting on three feet; the seat from which the priestesses at Delphi gave oracular responses; a three-legged frame or stand for supporting a theodolite, compass, etc.

tripoli, trip'o•li, *n.* A kind of siliceous rottenstone, soft, and of a yellowish gray or white color, composed of the shields of microscopic Infusoria and Diatomaceae, originally brought from *Tripoli,* used in polishing metals, marbles, glass, etc.

tripper, tripping. See TRIP.

tripterous, trip'ter•us, *a.* [Gr. *tri*=*treis,* three, and *pteron,* a wing.] Three-winged: said of a leaf.

triptych, trip'tik, *n.* [Gr. *tri*=*treis,* three, and *ptychē,* a fold or folding.] A picture, carving, or other representation in three compartments side by side; most frequently such as is used for an altarpiece; a writing tablet in three parts, two of which might be folded over the middle part; hence, sometimes, a book or treatise in three parts or sections.

triquetrous, trī•kwē'trus, *a.* [L. *triquetrus,* triangular, from *tres, tria,* three.] Three-sided; triangular; *bot.* having three acute angles with concave faces, as the stems of many plants; three-edged: three-cornered.

triradiate, trī•rā'di•āt, *a.* [L. *tri*=*tres,* three, and *radius,* a ray.] Having three rays.

trireme, trī'rēm, *n.* [L. *triremis*—*tri*=*tres,* three, and *remus,* an oar.] A galley or vessel with three benches or ranks of oars on a side, a common class of warship among the ancient Greeks, Romans, Carthaginians, etc.

trisect, trī•sekt', *v.t.* [L. *tri*=*tres,* three, and *seco, sectum,* to cut. SECTION.] To cut or divide into three equal parts.—**trisection,** trī•sek'shon, *n.* The division of a thing into three parts; particularly, in geometry, the division of an angle into three equal parts.

trisepalous, trī•sep'al•us, *a.* [Prefix *tri,* and *sepal.*] *Bot.* having three sepals.

triserial, trī•sē'ri•al, *a.* [Prefix *tri,* three, and *series.*] *Bot.* arranged in three rows, one beneath another.

trismus, tris'mus, *n.* [Gr. *trismos,* gnashing of the teeth, from *trizō,* to gnash.] A species of tetanus affecting the under jaw with spastic rigidity; lockjaw.

trisoctahedron, tris•ok'ta•hē"dron, *n.* [Gr. *tris,* three times, *oktō,* eight, and *hedra,* face.] A solid bounded by twenty-four equal faces, three corresponding to each face of an octahedron.

trispermous, trī•spėr'mus, *a.* [Gr. *tri*=*treis,* three, and *sperma,* seed.] *Bot.* three-seeded; containing three seeds.

tristichous, trī'stik•us, *a.* [Gr. *tri*=*treis,* three, and *stichos,* a row.] *Bot.* arranged in three rows.

trisyllable, tris'sil•a•bl, *n.* [L. *tri*=*tres,* three, and *syllaba,* syllable.] A word consisting of three syllables.—**trisyllabic, trisyllabical,** tris•si•lab'ik, tris•si•lab'i•kal, *a.* Pertaining to a trisyllable; consisting of three syllables.

trite, trīt, *a.* [L. *tritus,* pp. of *tero, tritum,* to rub, to wear (seen also in *triturate, contrite, detritus,* etc.); root *tar, tra,* to pierce, etc., as in prep. *trans.* TRY.] Used till so common as to have lost its novelty and interest; commonplace; hackneyed; stale.—**tritely,** trīt'li, *adv.* In a trite or commonplace manner; stalely.—**triteness,** trīt'nes, *n.* The quality of being trite; commonness; staleness.

tritheism, trī'thē•izm, *n.* [Gr. *tri*=*treis,* three, and *Theos,* God.] The opinion that the Father, Son, and

Holy Spirit are three beings or Gods.—**tritheist,** trī'thē•ist, *n.* One who believes that there are three distinct Gods in the Godhead, that is, three distinct substances, essences, or hypostases.—**tritheistic, tritheistical,** trī•thē•is'tik, trī•thē•is'ti•kal, *a.* Pertaining to tritheism.

Triton, trī'ton, *n.* [From *Triton*, the Greek sea deity, a son of Poseidon and Amphitrite.] One of certain subordinate sea deities among the Greeks and Romans, having their lower extremities fish-like; a genus of gasteropodous mollusks with trumpet-like shells; a genus of batrachian reptiles comprehending the newts.

tritone, trī'tōn, *n.* [Gr. *tri=treis*, three, and *tonos*, a tone.] *Mus.* a dissonant interval consisting of three tones or of two major and one minor tone, or of two tones and two semitones.

triturate, trich'e•rāt, *v.t.*—*triturated, triturating.* [L.L. *trituro, trituratum*, to grind, from L. *tritus*, pp. of *tero*, to wear. TRITE.] To rub or grind to a very fine powder.—**triturable,** trich'e•ra•bl, *a.* Capable of being triturated.—**trituration,** trich'e•rā'shon, *n.* The act of triturating; levigation.

triumph, trī'umf, *n.* [L. *triumphus*, a triumph; allied to Gr. *thriambos*, a festal song, a procession in honor of Bacchus.] *Rom. antiq.* a magnificent procession in honor of a victorious general, in which he entered the city riding in a chariot and followed by his army—the highest military honor which a general could obtain; hence, the state of being victorious; victory; conquest; joy or exultation for success; great gladness; rejoicing.—*v.i.* To enjoy a triumph; to celebrate victory with pomp; hence, to rejoice for victory; to obtain victory; to meet with success; to prevail; to exult upon an advantage gained; especially, to exult or boast insolently.—**triumphal,** trī•um'fal, *a.* [L. *triumphalis.*] Pertaining to triumph; commemorating or used in celebrating a triumph or victory.—*Triumphal arch*, originally a temporary arch erected in connection with the triumph of a Roman general, and through which he and his army passed; afterward a massive and ornamental permanent structure; a decorated temporary arch in public rejoicings.—**triumphant,** trī•um'fant, *a.* [L. *triumphans, triumphantis*, ppr. of *triumpho*, to triumph.] Rejoicing for victory or as for victory; triumphing; exulting; victorious; graced with conquest.—**triumphantly,** trī•um'fant•li, *adv.* In a triumphant manner; in the manner of a conqueror; with joy and exultation.

triumvir, trī•um'vėr, *n.* [L. *tres*, genit. *trium*, three, and *vir*, man.] One of three men united in office.—**triumvirate,** trī•um'vi•rāt, *n.* A coalition of three men in office or authority; in Roman history the coalition in 59 B.C. between Caesar, Pompeius, and Crassus, and that in 43 B.C. between Antonius, Octavianus, and Lepidus; government by three men in coalition; a party of three men; three men in company or forming one company.

triune, trī'ūn, *n.* [L. *tri=tres*, three, and *unus*, one.] Three in one: [*cap.*] applied to express the unity of the Godhead in a trinity of persons.—**triunity,** trī•ū'ni•ti, *n.* The state of being triune; trinity.

trivalent, trī•vāl'ent or triv'a•lent, *a.* [Prefix *tri*, three, and L. *valeo*, to be worth.] Having a valency of three.

trivalve, trī'valv, *n.* [Prefix *tri*, three, and *valve.*] Anything having three valves, especially a shell with three valves.

trivet, triv'et, *n.* [Corruption of *three-feet* or *three-foot*, or of Fr. *trépied*, from L. *tripes, tripedis*, a three-footed stool—*tres*, three, and *pes, pedis*, a foot.] Anything supported by three feet; a kind of iron frame or stand whereon to place vessels for boiling, etc., or to receive something placed before the fire: frequently used as a proverbial comparison indicating stability, inasmuch as having three legs to stand on it is never unstable ('right as a *trivet*').

trivia, triv'ē•a, *n.* pl. [N.L. back-formation of L. *trivalis*, trivial.] Unessential items; trifles; unimportant matters.

trivial, triv'i•al, *a.* [Fr. *trivial*, from L. *trivialis*, belonging to the public streets, hence common, from *trivium*, a place where three roads meet, a crossroad—*tri=tres*, three, and *via*, a way, a road.] Commonplace; trifling; insignificant; of little worth or importance; inconsiderable; occupying one's self with trifles; trifling.—*Trivial name*, in *classification*, same as *specific name*; also used for the common English name.—**trivialism,** triv'i•al•izm, *n.* A trivial matter or mode of acting.—**triviality,** triv•i•al'i•ti, *n.* The state or quality of being trivial; a trivial thing; a trifle.—**trivially,** triv'i•al•li, *adv.* In a trivial or trifling manner; lightly; inconsiderably; insignificantly.—**trivium,** triv'i•um, *n.* A collective term given in the schools of the middle ages to the first three liberal arts—grammar, rhetoric, and logic. See QUADRIVIUM.

triweekly, trī'wēk•li, *a.* Occurring or appearing once every three weeks; also, happening or appearing thrice a week.

trocar, trō'kär, *n.* [Fr. *trocar*, from *trois*, three, and *carre*, a square, a face, the instrument having a triangular face.] A perforating surgical instrument used in cases of dropsy, etc., for drawing off the fluid.

trochanter, trō•kan'tėr, *n.* [Gr. *trochantēr*, from *trochazō*, to run along, from *trechō*, to run.] *Anat.* a process of the upper part of the thigh bone to which are attached the muscles which rotate the limb.

trochar, trō'kär, *n.* Same as *Trocar*.

troche, trō'ki, *n.* [Gr. *trochos*, something circular, a round ball or cake.] A small medicinal lozenge.

trochee, trō'kē, *n.* [L. *trochaeus*, Gr. *trochaios*, from *trechō*, to run.] *Pros.* a foot of two syllables, the first long and the second short.—**trochaic,** trō•kā'ik, *a.* [L. *trochaicus.*] Pertaining to or consisting of trochees.—*n.* A trochaic verse.

trochilus, trok'il•us, *n.* [L. *trochilus*, Gr. *trochilos.*] A small bird said in ancient legend to enter the crocodile's mouth and eat matters from among his teeth; also, *arch.* same as *Scotia*.

trochlea, trok'li•a, *n.* [L., a pulley, from Gr. *trochalia*, from *trochalos*, running, from *trechō*, to run.] A pulley-like cartilage connected with one of the superior muscles of the eye.—**trochlear,** trok'li•ėr, *a.* Pulley-shaped.

trochoid, trō'koid, *n.* [Gr. *trochos*, a wheel, and *eidos*, resemblance.] *Geom.* the curve otherwise called cycloid; *anat.* a trochoidal articulation.—**trochoidal,** trō•koi'dal, *a.* Pertaining to a trochoid; *anat.* said of a species of joint in which one bone rotates upon another (as in the elbow).

trod, trod, pret. of *tread*.

trodden, trod'n, pp. of *tread*.

troglodyte, trog'lo•dīt, *n.* [Gr. *trōglodytēs*, a troglodyte, from *trōglē*, a cavern, and *dyō*, to enter.] A cavedweller; a name given by the ancient Greeks to the cavedwellers on the coast of the Red Sea and on the Upper Nile; hence, one living in seclusion.—**troglodytic,** trog'lo•dit"ik, *a.* Pertaining to troglodytes.

trogon, trō'gon, *n.* [Gr. *trōgōn*, gnawing.] A name of certain tropical birds with long tail plumes and most gorgeous plumage.

Trojan, trō'jan, *a.* Pertaining to ancient Troy, a city in Asia Minor, the scene of a ten-year war, described in Homer's *Iliad*, which was caused by the kidnaping of Helen, wife of Menelaus, by Paris.—**Trojan,** *n.* A citizen of ancient Troy; a plucky, diligent person.

troll, trōl, *v.t.* [From the Celtic, partly through the French: W. *trōliaw*, to trundle, to roll; *trol*, a roller; Armor. *trôel*, a twining plant; Fr. *trôler*, to lead about, to drag. TRAWL.]

troll, trōl, *v.t.* [M.E. *trollen*, to roll.] **To cause to move in a circular motion; to sing parts in succession; to sing in a gay manner; to pull through the water in fishing** (to *troll* a lure); to fish in this way.—*v.i.* To fish by trolling a lure; to sing joyfully.—**troller,** trōl'ėr, *n.*

troll, trōl, *n.* [Icel. *troll*, Dan. and Sw. *trold*, L.G. *droll*; hence E. *droll.*] A name of certain supernatural beings in Scandinavian mythology and literature, dwelling in the interior of hills and mounds; described as in some respects obliging and neighborly but also given to thieving.

trolley, trolly, trol'i, *n.* [Akin to *troll*, to roll.] A device so constructed as to run on an overhead rail or cable; a grooved wheel or bow-shaped device, mounted on electric trains and streetcars, for conducting electrical energy from an overhead wire.

trollop, trol'op, *n.* [Comp. Sc. *trollop*,

trallop, a loose hanging rag; Armor. *trul*, a rag or tatter, *trulen*, a slatternly woman; Ir. *troll*, corruption; Gael. *truaill*, to pollute; also G. *trulle*, a trull. *Trull* is allied.] A woman loosely dressed; a slattern; a prostitute.

trombone, trom′bōn, *n.* [It., aug. of *tromba*, a trumpet. TRUMP.] A deep-toned, brass wind instrument of the trumpet family, having a cylindrical metal tube doubled back on itself and ending in a bell-shaped section, pitch being controlled by a movable section called the slide.

trompe, tromp, *n.* [Fr. *trompe*, a tube, a trumpet.] The blowing machine used in a certain process of smelting iron.

trona, trō′na, *n.* [Ar. *natrun*, niter.] Same as *Natron*.

troop, tröp, *n.* [Fr. *troupe*, It. *truppa*, Sp. *tropa*, from L.L. *troppus*, a troop.] A collection of people; a number; a multitude; a body of soldiers; pl. soldiers in general; an organized group of Boy or Girl Scouts.—**troopship,** tröp′ship, *n.* A ship for transporting members of the armed forces.—*v.i.* To collect in numbers; to gather in crowds; to march in a body or in company; to march in haste: often with *off*.—**trooper,** tröp′ėr, *n.* A private soldier in a body of cavalry; a horse-soldier.

Tropaeolum, trō•pē′o•lum, *n.* [Gr. *tropaion*, a trophy, the leaves being shield-shaped, the flowers helmet-shaped.] A genus of South American trailing or climbing plants of the geranium family, some of them well known as Indian cress and nasturtium.

trope, trōp, *n.* [Fr. *trope*, from L. *tropus*, from Gr. *tropos*, a trope or figure, a turn, from *trepō*, to turn. TROPHY, TROPIC.] *Rhet.* a figurative use of a word; a word or expression used in a different sense from that which it properly possesses; a figure of speech.—**tropical,** trop′i•kal, *a.* Figurative; rhetorically changed from its original sense.—**tropically,** trop′i•kal•li, *adv.* In a tropical manner.—**tropism,** trōp′ism, *n.* The natural tendency of an organism to respond to an external stimulus.—**tropology,** tro•pol′o•ji, *n.* [Gr. *tropos*, trope, *logos*, discourse.] A rhetorical mode of speech, including tropes.—**tropologic, tropological,** trop•o•loj′ik, trop•o•loj′i•kal, *a.* Varied or characterized by tropes; figurative.—**tropologically,** trop′o•loj′i•kal•li, *adv.* In a tropological manner.—**troposphere,** trop′o•sfēr, *n.* [Gr. *tropos*, and *sphere*.] A lower part of the atmosphere, in which temperature falls with increasing height. See STRATOSPHERE.

trophy, trō′fi, *n.* [Fr. *trophée*, the spoil of an enemy, from L. *tropaeum*, from Gr. *tropaion*, a trophy, from *tropē*, a putting to rout, lit. a turning, from *trepō*, to turn. TROPE.] Among the Greeks and Romans a monument or memorial in commemoration of some victory, consisting of arms and spoils of the vanquished enemy, hung on the trunk of a tree or on a pillar; hence, anything taken and preserved as a memorial of victory, as captured arms, standards, etc.; anything serving as an evidence of victory.—**trophied,** trō′fid, *a.* Adorned with trophies.

tropic, trop′ik, *n.* [Fr. *tropique*, L. *tropicus*, Gr. *tropikos*, turning, pertaining to a turn, from *tropē*, a turning.] The name of two circles of the celestial sphere, each 23½° distant from the Equator, the northern one being called the *tropic of Cancer*, and the southern the *tropic of Capricorn*; pl. the regions lying between the tropics.—*a.* Tropical; pertaining to the tropics.—**tropical,** trop′i•kal, *a.* Pertaining to the tropics; being within the tropics; incident to the tropics (*tropical* diseases). See also under TROPE.—**tropic bird,** *n.* A tropical web-footed bird of the pelican family, wonderfully powerful on the wing.

tropism, trōp′izm, *n.* [Gr. *trope*, a turning.] *Biol.* the natural tendency of an organism to respond to an external stimulus.

tropology, etc. See TROPE.

troposphere, trop′o•sfēr, *n.* [Fr. *troposphère*, from Gr. *tropos*, a turn, and *sphere*.] The layer of atmosphere just below the stratosphere, at an altitude of about seven to ten miles.

trot, trot, *v.i.*—*trotted, trotting.* [Fr. *trotter*, It. *trottare*, from L. *tolutare*, to trot, modified into *tlutare, tlotare, trotare.*] To move faster than in walking; to walk or move fast; to run.—*n.* The pace of a horse or other quadruped more rapid than a walk; an endearing term used to a child; a contemptuous term for an old man or woman.—*v.t.* To cause to trot; to ride at a trot.—**trotter,** trot′ėr, *n.* One who trots; a trotting horse; the foot of an animal, especially of a sheep.

troth, trōth, *n.* [A form of *truth*.] Truth; faith; fidelity; veracity.—*To plight one's troth*, to pledge one's faith; to betroth one's self.

troubadour, trö′ba•dör, *n.* [Fr. *troubadour*, from Pr. *trobador*, a troubadour (Sp. *trovador*, It. *trovatore*), from *trobar*, Fr. *trouver*, to find, originally to invent or compose new poems, from L.L. *tropare*, to sing, from L. *tropus*, a song, a trope. TROPE.] A name given to a class of early poets who first appeared in Provence, in France, and flourished from the eleventh to the latter part of the thirteenth century, their poetry being lyrical and amatory.

trouble, trub′l, *v.t.*—*troubled, troubling.* [Fr. *troubler*, by metathesis and alteration from L. *turbula*, dim. of *turba*, a crowd, confusion; akin *turbid, turbulent, disturb, perturb.*] To put into confused motion; to agitate; to disturb; to annoy, fret, or molest; to afflict; to distress; to put to some slight labor or pains: used in courteous phraseology.—*n.* Distress of mind or what causes such; grief, great perplexity; affliction; anxiety; annoyance; pains; labor; exertion; *mining*, a fault or interruption in a stratum, especially a stratum of coal.—*To take the trouble*, to be at the pains; to give one's self inconvenience.—**troubler,** trub′l•ėr, *n.* One who troubles or disturbs.—**troublesome,** trub′l•sum, *a.* Giving or causing trouble; harassing; annoying; vexatious; importunate.—**troubleshooter,** trub″l•shöt′ėr, *n.* A person who locates and corrects trouble sources, as in mechanical equipment; a person talented in settling disputes, as of a political, business, or diplomatic nature.

trough, traf, *n.* [A.Sax. *trog*, *troh*= Icel., D., and G. *trog*, Dan. *trug*, a trough; akin *tray*.] A vessel of wood, stone, or metal, generally rather long and not very deep, for holding water, foodstuff for animals, or the like; a channel or spout for conveying water; anything resembling a trough in shape, as a depression between two ridges or between two waves; a basin-shaped or oblong hollow.

trounce, trouns, *v.t.*—*trounced, trouncing.* [O.Fr. *troncer*, *troncir*, to cut or break off or into pieces, from L. *truncus*, a trunk. TRUNK.] To punish or to beat severely; to castigate.

troupe, tröp, *n.* [Fr., same as *troop*.] A troop; a company; particularly, a company of actors, dancers, acrobats, etc.—**trouper,** tröp′ėr, *n.* One who performs as a member of a troupe, as of actors.

trousers, trou′zėrz, *n.pl.* [For older *trouses, trowses*, a kind of drawers, from O.Fr. *trousses*, a kind of hose, from *trousse*, a truss, case, or cover. TRUSS.] A garment worn by men and boys, extending from the waist to the ankles, covering the lower part of the trunk, and each leg separately.

trousseau, trö•sō′, *n.* [Fr., from *trousse*, a bundle, a truss. TRUSS.] The clothes and general outfit of a bride.

trout, trout, *n.* [Fr. *truite*, from L.L. *trutta*, L. *tructa*, from Gr. *trōktēs*, a kind of fish, from *trōgō*, to gnaw.] The common name of fresh-water species of the salmon family, such as the rainbow trout, the brook trout, etc.

trouvère, trouveur, trö•vâr′ trö•vėr′, *n.* [Fr. *trouver*, to find. TROUBADOUR.] A name given to the ancient poets of Northern France, corresponding to the *Troubadours* of Provence; but their productions partake of a narrative or epic character.

trover, trō′vėr, *n.* [O.Fr. *trover*, Fr. *trouver*, to find. TROUBADOUR.] *Law*, the gaining possession of goods by finding or by other means than purchase; a form of action at law to recover goods or damages, now abolished.

trow, trō, *v.i.* [A.Sax. *treówian, treówan*, to believe, lit. to believe to be *true*. TRUE.] To believe; to trust; to think or suppose.

trowel, trou′el, *n.* [Fr. *truelle*, from L. *trulla*, a small ladle, dim. of *trua*, a stirring-spoon, a ladle.] A tool somewhat resembling a small spade, used for spreading and dressing mortar and plaster, etc.; a similar gardener's tool, used in taking up plants and for other purposes.—*To lay on* (flattery or the like) *with a trowel*, to lay it on thickly and coarsely.—*v.t.*—*troweled, troweling*. To dress or form with a trowel.

troy, troy weight, troi, *n.* [From *Troyes*, in France.] A weight chiefly used in weighing gold and silver, divided into 12 ounces, each of 20 pennyweights, each of 24 grains. The pound troy=5760 grains; the pound avoirdupois 7000.

truant, trö'ant, *n.* [O.Fr. *truant* (Fr. *truand*), a vagabond, from the Celtic; Armor. *truant*, vagabond, W. *truan*, wretched, Ir. and Gael. *truaghan*, poor.] One who shirks or neglects his duty; an idler; especially, a child who stays from school without leave. —*To play truant*, to stay from school without leave.—*a.* Shirking duty; willfully absent from an appointed place; idle.—**truancy,** trö'an•si, *n.*

truce, trös, *n.* [Properly a plural; O.E. *trews, trewse, trewis*, O.Fr. *trues* (pl.), a truce, from O.H.G. *triuwa, triwa*, G. *treue*, faith; akin *true, trust*.] *Milit.* a suspension of arms by agreement of the commanders of the opposing armies; an armistice; any temporary intermission or cessation; short quiet.—*Flag of truce*. See FLAG.

truck, truk, *v.i.* [Fr. *troquer*, to truck, to barter, from Sp. *trocar*, to exchange.] To exchange commodities; to barter.—*v.t.* To exchange; to give in exchange; to barter; to put in a truck; to convey by truck.—*n.* Exchange of commodities; barter; payment of wages in goods; commodities appropriate for barter or for small trade.—*Truck system*, the practice of paying the wages of workmen in goods instead of money, which was prevalent previously in the mining and manufacturing districts of Britain.—**truck farm,** *n.* A farm on which vegetables are raised for market.

truck, truk, *n.* [From L. *trochus*, a hoop, from Gr. *trochos*, a wheel.] A small carriage or barrow with two low wheels, for heavy packages; a heavy motor vehicle used for transport; *gun.* a circular piece of wood like a wheel fixed on an axletree, for moving ordnance; *naut.* the small circular wooden cap at the extremity of a flagstaff or of a topmast.—*v.t.* To convey or transport by truck. —*v.i.* To truck goods.—**truckage,** truk'ij, *n.* Money paid for conveyance of goods on a truck; freight.—**trucker,** truk'ėr, *n.* One who drives a truck; a company engaged in transporting goods by truck.—**truckle,** truk'l, *n.* A small wheel or caster. —*v.t.* To move on rollers; to trundle. —**truckle bed,** *n.* A bed that runs on wheels and can be stored under another bed.

truckle, truk'l, *v.i.*—*truckled, truckling*. [Dim. of *truck*, to barter; or from *truckle* bed, because inferiors slept in them.] To yield or bend obsequiously to the will of another; to cringe; usually with *to*.—**truckler,** truk'lėr, *n.* One who truckles.

truculent, truk'ū•lent, *a.* [L. *truculentus*, from *trux, trucis*, fierce, savage.] Fierce; savage; barbarous; inspiring terror; ferocious.—**truculently,** truk'ū•lent•li, *adv.* In a truculent manner.—**truculence, truculency,** truk'ū•lens, truk'ū•len•si, *n.* [L. *truculentia*.] The quality of being truculent; savageness; fierceness.

trudge, truj, *v.i.*—*trudged, trudging*. [Probably a modification of *tread*, through the influence of *drudge*.] To travel on foot with fatigue or more or less painful exertion; to travel or march with labor or effort.

true, trö, *a.* [A.Sax. *treówe* (whence *treowian*, to *trow*)=Icel. *trúr*, Dan. *tro*, D. *trouw*, G. *treu*, faithful, true; cog. Skr. *dhru*, to be fixed. Akin *truce, trust, troth*.] Conformable to fact; not false or erroneous; free from falsehood; truthful; genuine; not counterfeit, false, or pretended; firm or steady in adhering to promises, to friends, or the like; faithful; loyal; honest; exact; correct; right; conformable to law and justice; legitimate; rightful.—*True bill, law*, a bill of indictment endorsed by the grand jury after evidence as containing a well-founded accusation.—*v.t.* To give a right form to; to make exactly straight, square, level, or the like: a workman's term.—**true blue,** *a.* An epithet applied to a person of inflexible honesty and fidelity; stanch; inflexible.—*n.* A person of inflexible honesty or stanchness.—**truelove,** *n.* One truly loved or loving; one whose love is pledged to another; a sweetheart.—**truelove knot, truelover's knot,** *n.* A kind of double knot, made with two bows on each side interlacing each other and with two ends—the emblem of affection.—**trueness,** trö'nes, *n.* The quality of being true; sincerity; genuineness; accuracy.—**truepenny,** trö'pen•i, *n.* A familiar phrase for an honest fellow.—**truism,** trö'izm, *n.* An undoubted or self-evident truth.—**truly,** trö'li, *adv.* In a true manner; exactly; faithfully; honestly; legitimately; in reality; in fact.—**truth,** tröth, *n.* [A.Sax. *treówthe*, from *treówe*, true. Formed similarly to *sloth, filth*, etc.] The state or quality of being true; conformity to fact or reality; veracity; purity from falsehood; fidelity; constancy; genuineness; that which is true; a true statement; fact; reality; verity; a verified fact.—*In truth*, in reality; in sincerity.—*Of a truth*, truly; certainly.—**truthful,** tröth'fu̦l, *a.* Full of truth; loving and speaking the truth.—**truthfully,** tröth'fu̦l•li, *adv.* In a truthful manner.—**truthfulness,** tröth'fu̦l•nes, *n.* The state or character of being truthful.

truffle, truf'l, *n.* [O.Fr. *trufle*, Fr. *truffe*; origin uncertain.] An edible and much-esteemed fungus growing a few inches beneath the surface of the ground, of a dark color, of a roundish form, and without visible root.

truism. See TRUE.

trull, trul, *n.* [Of similar origin with *trollop*.] A low vagrant strumpet; a drab.

truly. See TRUE.

trump, trump, *n.* [Contr. from *triumph*, which formerly had sense of *trump*. See TRIUMPH.] A winning card; one of the suit of cards which takes any of the other suits; a good fellow; a person upon whom one can depend (*colloq.*).—*To put to one's trumps*, to reduce to the last expedient.—*v.t.* To take with a trump card; to put a trump card upon in order to win.

trump, trump, *n.* [Fr. *trompe*, a trumpet or horn; Sp. and Pg. *trompa*, It. *tromba*, a trumpet; comp. O.H.G. *trumba, trumpa*, a drum; Lith. *truba*, a herdsman's horn. Akin *trombone*. Hence *trumpet*.] A wind instrument of music; a trumpet.

trump, trump, *v.t.* [Fr. *tromper*, to deceive, to dupe, probably from *trompe*, a trumpet, alluding to mountebanks or charlatans who summoned people by a trumpet.] To obtrude or impose unfairly.—*To trump up*, to devise; to forge (to *trump up* a story).—**trumpery,** trum'pėr•i, *n.* [Fr. *tromperie*, fraud; trumpery is what deceives by false show.] Worthless finery; things worn out and of no value; rubbish.—*a.* Trifling; worthless.

trumpet, trum'pet, *n.* [Fr. *trompette*, a dim. of *trompe*, a trumpet. TRUMP, a trumpet.] A wind instrument of music made of brass or silver, having a clear ringing tone; one who praises or propagates praise. EAR TRUMPET, SPEAKING TRUMPET.—*Feast of trumpets*, a feast among the Jews, so called from the blowing of trumpets in the temple with more than usual solemnity.—*v.t.* To publish by sound of trumpet; hence, to blaze or noise abroad; to proclaim.—**trumpeter,** trum'pet•ėr, *n.* One who sounds a trumpet; one who proclaims, publishes, or denounces; a variety of the domestic pigeon; a grallatorial bird of South America, called also *Agami*. —**trumpet flower,** *n.* A name applied to various large tubular flowers.

truncate, trung'kāt, *v.t.* [L. *trunco, truncatum*, to cut short, from *truncus*, mutilated, and as substantive, the trunk of a tree.] To shorten by cutting abruptly; to lop; to cut short.—*a.* Truncated; *bot.* appearing as if cut short at the tip (a *truncate* leaf).—**truncation,** trung•kā'shon, *n.* The act of truncating or state of being truncated; cutting off.

truncheon, trun'shon, *n.* [O.Fr. *tronchon*, Fr. *tronçon*, from *tronche, tronce*, a trunk, staff, etc., L. *truncus*. TRUNK.] A short staff; a cudgel; a tree the branches of which have been lopped off to produce rapid growth.—*v.t.* To beat with a truncheon; to cudgel.—**truncheoned,** trun'shond, *a.* Furnished with a truncheon.

trundle, trun'dl, *v.i.*—*trundled, trundling*. [A.Sax. *tryndel, trendel*, a circle, a wheel; akin Sw. and Dan. *trind*, round. TREND.] To roll, as on little wheels; to roll; to bowl along.—*v.t.* To wheel or move on wheels; to cause to roll (to *trundle* a hoop).—*n.* A little wheel; a castor; a small carriage with low wheels; a truck.—**trundle bed,** *n.* A truckle bed.

trunk, trungk, *n.* [Fr. *tronc,* trunk or stem, main body, broken shaft of a column, a charity box; from L. *truncus,* mutilated, and as noun, trunk or stem, body, piece cut off, etc. (whence also *truncheon, truncate*).] The elephant's *trunk* should have been *trump,* being from Fr. *trompe,* a trumpet, a proboscis, but the word was confused with this. TRUMP.] The woody stem of trees; that part which supports the branches; the body of an animal without the limbs, or considered as apart from the limbs; the main body of anything relatively to its branches or ramifications; a box or chest, often one covered with leather for containing clothes, etc.; the long snout or proboscis of an elephant; also, a similar organ of other animals, as the proboscis of an insect; a tube, usually wooden, to convey air, dust, broken matter, grain, etc.; a trough to convey water from a race to a water wheel, etc.; a flume; a boxed passage for air to or from a blast apparatus or blowing engine; *pl.* trunk hose.—**trunk hose,** *n. pl.* [Named probably from being *truncated* or cut short.] A kind of short wide breeches gathered in above the knees, or immediately under them, and worn during the reign of Henry VIII, Elizabeth, and James I.—**trunk line,** *n.* The main line of a railroad, canal, etc.

trunnion, trun'yon, *n.* [Fr. *trognon,* a stump, from *tronc,* L. *truncus,* trunk of a tree. TRUNK.] A knob projecting on each side of a gun, mortar, etc., serving to support it on the carriage; *steam engines,* a hollow gudgeon on each side of an oscillating cylinder to support it, and through which steam enters.

truss, trus, *n.* [Fr. *trousse,* a bundle, in pl. trunk hose, breeches (whence E. *trousers*), from *trousser,* O.Fr. *trosser, trusser,* to tuck up, to pack; L.L. *tortiare,* to twist, from L. *torqueo, tortum,* to twist. TORTURE.] A bundle, especially a small hand-packed bundle of dry goods; a quantity, as of hay or straw tied together; *surg.* a bandage used in cases of rupture to keep up the parts or for other purposes; a tuft of flowers at the top of the main stalk of certain plants; an umbel; *building,* a combination of timbers, of iron, or of timbers and iron work, so arranged as to constitute an unyielding frame; *arch.* a large corbel or modillion supporting some object projecting from the face of a wall.—*v.t.* To put in a bundle; to pack up: often with *up*; to seize and carry off: said of birds of prey; to draw tight and tie the laces of, as of garments; to make fast, as the wings of a fowl to the body in cooking it; to skewer; to pull up by a rope or ropes; to hang.—**trussing,** trus'ing, *n.* The timbers, etc., which form a truss.—*a. Her.* applied to a bird of the eagle or falcon type preying upon anything.

trust, trust, *n.* [From stem of *true, trow*=Icel. *traust,* trust, confidence; Dan. and Sw. *trost,* G. *trost,* consolation, hope. TRUE.] A reliance or resting of the mind on the integrity, veracity, justice, friendship, etc., of another person; a firm reliance on promises or on laws or principles; confidence; confident expectation; assured anticipation; belief; hope; reliance or belief without examination (to take opinions on *trust*); the transfer of goods, property, etc., in confidence of future payment; credit; a person confided in and relied on; that which is committed or entrusted to one; something committed to one's care for use or for safekeeping; the state of being confided to another's care and guard; safekeeping; care; management; *law,* the conveying of property to one party (the *trustee*) in confidence that he will apply it for the benefit of a third party or to some specified purpose.—*v.t.* To place confidence in; to rely on; to depend upon; to believe; to receive as true; to rely on with regard to the care of; to entrust (to *trust* him *with* money); to commit, as to one's care; to leave to one's self or to itself without fear of consequences; to sell to upon credit or in confidence of future payment; to be confident; to hope confidently; followed by a clause.—*v.i.* To have trust or reliance; to confide readily; to practice giving credit; to sell in reliance upon future payment.—*To trust in,* to confide in; to rely on.—*To trust to,* to depend on; to have confidence in.—*a.* Held in trust (*trust* property).—**trustee,** trus•tē', *n.* A person appointed to hold property, to take care of and apply the same for the benefit of those entitled to it.—**trusteeship,** trus•tē'ship, *n.* The office of a trustee.—**truster,** trus'tėr, *n.*—**trustful,** trust'fụl, *a.* Full of trust; trusting; worthy of trust; trusty.—**trustfully,** trust'fụl•li, *adv.* In a trustful manner.—**trust fund,** *n.* Money, stocks, bonds, etc., held in trust.—**trustily,** trust'i•li, *adv.*—**trustiness,** trust'i•nes, *n.*—**trust territory,** *n.* A territory, which is not self-governing, that is placed under the administration of the United Nations.—**trustworthiness,** trust'wėr•THi•nes, *n.*—**trustworthy,** trust'wėr•THi, *a.* Worthy of trust or confidence.—**trusty,** trus'ti, *a.* Admitting of being safely trusted.

truth, truthful, etc. See TRUE.

try, trī, *v.t.*—*tried, trying.* [Fr. *trier,* to pick, cull, select; same as It. *triare, tritare,* to grind, bruise, examine; L.L. *tritare,* to thrash (corn), from L. *tritum,* pp. of *tero,* to rub, to cleanse corn by threshing. TRITE.] To sift or pick out‡; to purify, assay, or refine, as metals; to test or prove by experiment; to make experience of; to subject to some severe test or experience; to cause suffering or trouble to; to examine or inquire into, especially, to examine judicially; to subject to the examination and decision or sentence of a tribunal; to attempt; to undertake; to make experiment with; to see what will result from using or employing.—*To try on,* to put on, as a garment, to see if it fits.—*v.i.* To exert strength; to endeavor; to prove by a test.—*To try back,* to go back, as in search of a road that one has missed.—*n.* The act of trying; a trial, experiment.—**triable,** trī'a•bl, *a.* Capable of being tried; fit to be tried or stand trial.—**trial,** trī'al, *n.* The act of trying or testing in any manner; an attempt; a test; experiment; a becoming acquainted by experience; that which tries or afflicts; that which tries the character or principle; affliction; temptation; the state of being tried; a process for testing qualification; an examination; *law,* the examination of a cause in controversy between parties before a proper court.—**trial and error,** *n.* A process in which a result is reached through a series of tests in which invalid solutions are eliminated.—**trial balloon,** *n.* A balloon sent aloft to test wind velocity, etc.; any statement of intention that is meant to test public opinion of that intention.—**trying,** trī'ing, *a.* Severely testing one's powers.—**tryout,** trī'-out, *n.* A test to determine a person's qualifications for something; an audition.

trypanosome, trip'an•o•sōm, *n.* A parasitic protozoan, infesting the blood of animals, including man, being usually introduced by the bite of an insect. It is the cause of various diseases, e.g. sleeping sickness.

tryptophane, trip'to•fān, *n.* [Gr. *truein,* to rub down, *phainein,* to show.] An amino acid, or an iodine derivative, supposed to be the active substance in the secretion of the thyroid gland.

tryst, trist, *n.* [Closely akin to *trust*; Icel. *treysta,* to trust.] An appointment to meet; a rendezvous; a market (Falkirk *Tryst*).—*v.i.* To agree to meet at any particular time or place.—**trysting place,** *n.* An arranged meeting place.

tsar, tsär, *n.* CZAR.—**tsarina, tsaritsa,** tsä•rē'na, tsä•rit'sa, *n.* CZARINA.

tsetse, tset'si, *n.* [Native name.] A South African two-winged fly that can transmit the parasite that causes African sleeping sickness.

T square, tē'skwâr, *n.* A T-shaped ruler for making parallel lines.

tub, tub, *n.* [Same as L.G. *tubbe,* D. *tobbe,* a tub.] An open wooden vessel formed with staves, bottom, and hoops; a half barrel open above; a small cask or barrel for liquor; any wooden structure resembling a tub; *mining,* a corve or bucket for raising coal or ore from the mine.—*A tale of a tub,* an idle or silly fiction; a cock-and-bull story.—*v.t.*—*tubbed, tubbing.* To plant or set in a tub (to *tub* plants).—*v.i.* To wash; to make use of a bathing tub.—**tubbing,** tub'-ing, *n.* Material for tubs; the lining of the shaft of a mine, of an artesian well, etc., to prevent falling in of the sides.

tuba, tū'ba, *n.* [L. a trumpet.] A large musical instrument of brass, low in pitch, and resembling the bombardon.

tube, tūb, *n.* [Fr. *tube*, from L. *tubus*, a tube, *tuba*, a trumpet.] A pipe; a hollow cylinder of wood, metal, glass, india rubber, etc., used for the conveyance of fluids and for various other purposes; any similar object; a vessel of animal bodies or plants which conveys a fluid or other substance; an electron tube.—*v.t.*—*tubed, tubing.* To furnish with a tube. —**tubiform,** tū'bi•form, *a.* Having the form of a tube; tubular.—**tubing,** tūb'ing, *n.* The act of making or providing with tubes; a series of tubes; material for tubes.—**tubular,** tū'byu̦•lėr, *a.* [From L. *tubulus*, dim. of *tubus*, a tube.] Having the form of a tube or pipe; consisting of a pipe; fistular.—*Tubular boiler*, a form of boiler in which the connection between the fire and the chimney is made by a large number of tubes surrounded by the water, which is heated by the gases, etc., passing through the tubes.—*Tubular bridge*, a bridge formed of a great rectangular iron or steel tube, through which the roadway or railway passes.—**tubulate,** tū'byu̦•lit, *a.* Made in the form of a small tube; furnished with a small tube.—**tubulation,** tū•byu̦•lā'shon, *n.* The act of making tubular.—**tubulous,** tū'byu̦•lus, *a.* Tubular.

tuber, tū'bėr, *n.* [L., a swelling, tumor, protuberance; same root as *tumid, tumor*.] An underground fleshy stem or modification of the root of plants (as in the potato), roundish in shape, of annual duration, and with buds from which new plants are produced; *surg.* a knot or swelling in any part.—**tubercle,** tū'bėr•kl, *n.* [L. *tuberculum*, dim. from *tuber*.] A small tuber; a little projecting knob; *anat.* a natural small rounded body or mass; *pathol.* one of certain small masses of morbid matter which may be developed in different parts of the body, but are most frequently observed in the lungs (in the disease consumption).—**tubercular,** tū•bėr'kyu̦•lėr, *a.* Of the character of a tubercle, affected with tuberculosis. —**tuberculous,** tū•bėr'kyu̦•lus, *a.*—**tuberculin,** tū•bėr'kyu̦•lin, *n.* An extract used as a test for the presence of tuberculosis.—**tuberculosis,** tū•bėr'kyu̦•lō"sis, *n.* A disease due to infection with the tubercle bacillus, the commonest sites of infection being the lungs and joints.—**tuberous, tuberose,** tū'ber•us, tū'ber•ōs, *a.* Covered with knobby or wartlike prominences; knobbed; *bot.* having tubers; resembling a tuber.

tuberose, tūb'rōz or tū'be•rōz, *n.* [From the Latin specific name *tuberosa*, which means simply 'tuberous'; so Fr. *tubéreuse*, Sp. *tuberosa*.] An odoriferous plant with a tuberous root, a favorite flower and much cultivated.

tubing, tubular, etc. See TUBE.

tuck,‡ tuk, *n.* [From Fr. *estoc*, It. *stocco*, a rapier, from G. *stock*, a stick.] A rapier. (*Shak.*)

tuck, tuk, *v.t.* [Same as L.G. *tucken*, G. *zucken*, Sw. *tocha*, to draw together, to contract; akin *tug, tow, touch*.] To put into smaller compass by folding; to fold in or under; to gather up; to gather the bedclothes close around (to *tuck* a child into a bed).—*v.i.* To contract; to draw together.—*Tuck in*, to partake freely of food or dainties (*colloq.*).—*n.* A fold sewed in some part of a dress to shorten it, especially a horizontal fold made on a skirt.—*Tuck-shop*, a schoolboy name for the shop where pastry, confectionery, and the like are sold.—**tucker,** tuk'ėr, *n.* One who or that which tucks; an ornamental frilling of lace or muslin round the top of a woman's dress.

tuckahoe, tuk'a•hō, *n.* [Algonquian Indian word meaning globular.] Various bulbous roots used by Indians as bread.

tucket, tuk'et, *n.* [From It. *toccata*, a prelude, from *toccare*, to touch. TOUCH.] A flourish on a trumpet; a fanfare. (*Shak.*)—**tuck,** tuk, *n.* [From *tucket*.] The sound produced by beating a drum; beat.

Tudor, tū'dor, *a.* The dynasty and the style of architecture during the reigns of Henry VII, Henry VIII, Edward VI, Mary, Elizabeth, deriving from Owen Tudor, grandfather of Henry VII.—*Tudor rose, her.* a double rose, having a white center with red petals, or vice versa, and intended to conjoin the emblems of the Houses of York and of Lancaster.

Tuesday, tūz'di, *n.* [A.Sax. *Tiwesdaeg*, that is, Tiw's day, the day of *Tiw*, the Northern Mars, or god of war; so Icel. *týsdagr, tyrsdagr*, Sw. *tisdag*, Dan. *tirsdag*, G. *dienstag*. Comp. *Thursday* = *Thor's* day.] The third day of the week.

tufa, tuff, tū'fa, tuf, *n.* [It. *tufa*, Fr. *tuf*, a kind of porous stone, from L. *tophus*, tuff, tufa.] *Geol.* a term originally applied to a light porous rock composed of cemented scoriae and ashes, but now to any porous vesicular compound. —**tufaceous,** tū•fā'shus, *a.* Pertaining to or resembling it.

tuft, tuft, *n.* [From Fr. *touffe*, a tuft, a thicket, with addition of *t* (comp. *graft* and *graff*); from G. *zopf*, Icel. *toppr*, a tuft = E. *top*. TOP.] A collection of small flexible or soft things in a knot or bunch (a *tuft* of flowers, a *tuft* of feathers); a cluster; a clump (a *tuft* of trees); in English universities, a slang term for a young nobleman student: so called from the gold *tuft* on the cap formerly worn by him.—*v.t.* To adorn with or as with tufts or a tuft.—**tufted,** tuf'ted, *p.* and *a.* Adorned with a tuft or tufts; growing in tufts or clusters.—**tufthunter,** *n.* A hanger-on or toady in the society of titled persons.—**tufthunting,** *n.* The practice of a tufthunter.—**tufty,** tuf'ti, *a.* Abounding with tufts; growing in tufts.

tug, tug, *v.t.*—*tugged, tugging.* [A.Sax. *teóhan, teón*, to tug or pull; pret. pl. *tugon*, pp. *togen*; Icel. *toga, tjúga*, to draw; G. *zug*, a pull; akin *tow*, to pull, *tuck, tie*.] To pull with effort; to haul; to strain at; to drag by means of a steam tug.—*v.i.* To pull with great effort; to labor; to strive; to struggle.—*n.* A pull with the utmost effort; a supreme effort; the severest strain or struggle (the *tug* of war); a tugboat.—*Tug-of-war*, a trial of strength between two parties at opposite ends of a rope, each striving to pull the other over a certain mark.—**tugboat,** *n.* A strongly built steamboat used for towing sailing and other vessels.—**tugger,** tug'ėr, *n.* One who tugs.

tuition, tū•ish'on, *n.* [L. *tuitio, tuitionis*, guardianship, from *tueor, tuisus*, to see, to look to.] Guardianship or superintendence‡; instruction; tutorship; teaching; payment for instruction.—**tuitionary,** tū•ish'on•e•ri, *a.* Pertaining to tuition.

tulip, tū'lip, *n.* [Fr. *tulipe*, from Sp. *tulipa, tulipan*, It. *tulipano*, a tulip, from Turk. *tulipant*, a turban, the name being given to the flower from its similarity. TURBAN.] A plant of the lily family of many species, much cultivated for the beauty of the flowers.—**tulipomania,** tū'lip•o•ma"ni•a, *n.* [*Tulip*, and L. *mania*, madness.] A violent passion for the cultivation or acquisition of tulips.—**tulip tree,** *n.* An American tree bearing flowers resembling the tulip, one of the most magnificent forest trees of temperate North America.—**tulipwood,** *n.* A beautiful striped, rose-colored wood, the produce of a Brazilian tree, much used for inlaying.

tulle, tūl, *n.* A kind of thin, open net, silk fabric, originally manufactured at *Tulle* in France, much used in female headdresses, collars, etc.

tumble, tum'bl, *v.i.*—*tumbled, tumbling.* [From Dan. *tumle*, Sw. *tumla*, to tumble, allied to A.Sax. *tumbian*, to dance, D. *tuimelen*, to tumble, G. *taumeln*, to reel, to stagger.] To roll about by turning one way and the other; to toss the body about; to roll; to lose footing and fall; to be precipitated; to play acrobats' tricks.—*v.t.* To turn or throw about for examination or search; to toss over carelessly; to disorder; to rumple; to throw down; to precipitate.—*n.* A fall; a rolling over.—**tumbler,** tum'blėr, *n.* One who tumbles; one who plays the tricks of an acrobat turning summersaults, etc.; a large drinking glass, originally one that had not a base that it could stand on; a variety of the domestic pigeon, so called from its practice of turning over in flight; a sort of spring latch in a lock which detains the bolt until a key lifts it.

tumbrel, tumbril, tum'brel, tum'bril, *n.* [O.Fr. *tumberel*, from *tomber*, to fall, because tilted up to be emptied; of Germanic origin and akin to *tumble*. TUMBLE.] A dungcart; a low vehicle with two wheels used by farmers; a covered cart or carriage with two wheels, which accompanies troops for conveying the tools of pioneers, ammunition,etc.

tumefy, tū'mi•fī, *v.t.—tumefied, tumefying.* [Fr. *tuméfier*, from L. *tumeo*, to swell, and *facio*, to make. TUMID.] To swell or cause to swell or be tumid.—*v.i.* To swell; to rise in a tumor.—**tumefaction,** tū•mi•fak'shon, *n.* A swelling up; a tumor.—**tumescence,** tū•mes'ens, *n.* The state of growing tumid; tumefaction.

tumid, tū'mid, *a.* [L. *tumidus*, from *tumeo*, to swell, from root *tu*, producing also *tumulus, tumultus, tumor, tuber*, etc. (whence *tumult, tumor*, etc.). Akin *tomb.*] Being swelled, enlarged, or distended; swollen; protuberant; swelling in sound or sense; pompous; bombastic. —**tumidity, tumidness,** tū•mid'i•ti, tū'mid•nes, *n.* The state or quality of being tumid.—**tumidly,** tū'mid•li, *adv.* In a tumid manner or form.—**tumor, tumour,** tū'mėr, *n.* [L. *tumor, tumoris*, from *tumeo*, to swell.] *Surg.* a morbid enlargement or swelling; more strictly, a permanent swelling occasioned by a new growth, and not a mere enlargement of a natural part.

tumult, tū'mult, *n.* [L. *tumultus*, from *tumeo*, to swell. TUMID.] The commotion, disturbance, or agitation of a multitude; an uproar; violent commotion or agitation, with confusion of sounds; irregular or confused motion.—**tumultuary,** tu•mul'tū•e•ri, *a.* [L. *tumultuarius.*] Disorderly; promiscuous; confused; restless; agitated; unquiet.—**tumultuous,** tu•mul'chu̦•us, *a.* [L. *tumultuosus.*] Full of tumult, disorder, or confusion; conducted with tumult; disorderly; agitated; disturbed, as by passion or the like; turbulent; violent.—**tumultuously,** tu•mul'chu̦•us•li, *adv.* In a tumultuous manner; with turbulence.—**tumultuousness,** tu•mul'chu̦•us•nes, *n.*

tun, tun, *n.* [A.Sax. *tunne*, a butt= Icel., Sw., and O.H.G. *tunna*, L.G. *tunne*, D. *ton*, G. *tonne*, cask, tun; perhaps a Celtic word=Ir. and Gael. *tunna, tonna*; comp. W. *tynell. Ton* is the same word; *tunnel* is a derivative.] Originally any large cask or vessel for containing liquids; hence, a certain measure or quantity which contained 4 hogsheads or 252 gallons. —*v.t.—tunned, tunning.* To put into casks.

tuna, tö'na, *n.* A prickly pear, genus *Opuntia*, native to Central America.

tuna, tö'na, *n.* A large fish of the mackerel family, found in the warm-water regions of the Atlantic and Pacific oceans; a tunny.

tundra, tun'dra, *n.* A term applied to the immense stretches of flat boggy country in the northern part of Siberia.

tune, tūn, *n.* [A form of *tone.* TONE.] A rhythmical, melodious series of musical tones produced by one voice or instrument, or by several voices or instruments in unison; an air; a melody; correct intonation in singing or playing; adjustment of a musical instrument so as to produce its tones in correct key relationship, or in harmony with other instruments; frame of mind; mood; temper for the time being.—*To the tune of*, to the sum or amount of. (*Colloq.*)—*v.t.—tuned, tuning.* To put into or cause to be in tune; to sing with melody or harmony; to attune; to put into the proper state; to adapt.—**tunable,** tūn'a•bl, *a.* Capable of being put in tune or made harmonious; musical; tuneful.—**tunableness,** tūn'a•bl•nes, *n.* The state or quality of being tunable.—**tunably,** tūn'a•bli, *adv.* In a tunable manner; musically.—**tunefully,** tūn'fu̦l•li, *adv.* In a tuneful manner; harmoniously; musically.—**tuneless,** tūn'les, *a.* Unmusical; unharmonious; not expressed musically; without voice or utterance.—**tuner,** tūn'ėr, *n.* One who tunes; one whose occupation is to tune musical instruments.—**tuning fork,** *n.* A steel instrument with two prongs, designed when set in vibration to give a musical sound of a certain fixed pitch.—**tune-up,** tūn'-up, *n.* A routine adjustment to bring to the highest efficiency, especially an automobile.

tungsten, tung'sten, *n.* [Sw. and Dan., from *tung*, heavy, and *sten*, stone.] A gray-white metallic element, occurring in wolframite and other minerals, and used in alloys and for electric-light filaments. Symbol, W (*wolframium*); at. no., 74; at. wt., 183.85. Called also *wolfram.*—**tungstenic, tungstic,** tung•sten'ik, tung'stik, *a.* Pertaining to or obtained from tungsten (*tungstic* acid).

Tungusic, tu̦n•gu̦s'ik, *a.* A term applied to a group of Turanian tongues spoken by tribes in the northeast of Asia.

tunic, tū'nik, *n.* [L. *tunica*, a tunic.] A very ancient form of under garment worn by both sexes, and fastened by a girdle or belt about the waist; at the present day a loose garment worn by women and boys drawn in at the waist and reaching not far below it; a military surcoat; the garment worn by a knight over his armor; the full-dress, short uniform coat worn by soldiers; *anat.* a membrane that covers or composes some part or organ (the *tunics* or coats of the eye, the *tunics* of the stomach, etc.); a natural covering; an integument; *bot.* any loose membranous skin not formed from epidermis; the skin of a seed.—**tunicate, tunicated,** tū'ni•kāt, tū'ni•kā•ted, *a. Bot.* covered with a tunic or membranes; coated; *zool.* enveloped in a tunic or mantle.

tunnel, tun'el, *n.* [From Fr. *tonnelle*, an arbor, a tunnel, from *tonne*, L.L. *tunna*, a cask. TUN.] A subterranean passage cut through a hill, a rock, or any eminence, or under a river, a town, etc.—*v.t.* and *i.—tunneled, tunneling.* To cut a tunnel through or under.

tunny, tun'i, *n.* [It. *tonno*, Fr. *thon*, from L. *thynnus*, from Gr. *thynnos*, a tunny, from *thynō*, to dart.] A food fish of the mackerel family, attaining a length of from four to even twenty feet, and found in immense quantities in the Mediterranean, there being also an American species taken chiefly for the oil it yields. A tuna.

tup, tup, *n.* [Comp. L.G. *tuppen, toppen*, to push, to butt.] A ram.

Turanian, tū•rā'ni•an, *a.* [Persian *Turan*, a name for the Turks and kindred races.] A term applied to the Altaic family of languages, which includes the Ugrian or Finnish, Turkish, Mongolian, etc.

turban, tėr'ban, *n.* [O.E. *turband, turbant, tulibant*, etc., from Turk. *tulbend, dulbend*, Per. *dulband*, turban.] A headdress consisting of a cap around which a long scarf is wound, worn by men in certain Asiatic countries, especially by Moslems.

turbary, tėr'be•ri, *n.* [L.L. *turbaria*, from O.H.G. *turba*, E. *turf.*] A place where turf is cut; the right of cutting turf.

Turbellaria, tėr•bel•lâ'ri•a, *n. pl.* [From L. *turba*, a crowd, a stir, from the currents caused by their moving cilia.] An order of annuloid animals nearly all aquatic and non-parasitic, including the nemertids and others.

turbid, tėr'bid, *a.* [L. *turbidus*, from *turba*, a crowd, or *turbare*, to trouble (as in *disturb, perturb, turbulent*). TROUBLE.] Having the lees or sediment disturbed; muddy; foul with extraneous matter; not clear; said of liquids of any kind.—**turbidity, turbidness,** tėr•bid'i•ti, tėr'bid•nes, *n.* The state of being turbid.

turbinate, turbinated, tėr'bi•nāt, tėr'bi•nā•ted, *a.* [From *turbo, turbinis*, a top.] Shaped like a whipping-top; *conch.* spiral or wreathed conically from a larger base to the apex like a top; *bot.* shaped like a top or cone inverted.—**turbination,** tėr•bi•nā'shon, *n.* The act of spinning or whirling, as a top.

turbine, tėr'bīn, *n.* [L. *turbo, turbinis*, that which spins or whirls round, a top.] A kind of horizontal water wheel, made to revolve by the escape of water through orifices, under the influence of pressure derived from a fall; an engine in which rotary motion is produced by the direct impact of steam, gas or vapor upon a series of projections on the circumference of a cylinder free to revolve. —**turbojet,** tėr'bō•jet, *n.* A propulsion system in which turbine power drives a compressor supplying air to a burner that, in turn, burns gases, which then pass over the turbine and through a nozzle, producing a rearward thrust.—**turboprop,** tėr'bō•prop, *n.* A turbopropeller engine; an aircraft driven by such an engine.—**turbopropeller engine,** *n.* A jet engine powered by a propeller that is driven by turbine power.

turbit, tėr'bit, *n.* A variety of the domestic pigeon remarkable for its short beak.

turbot, tėr'bot, *n.* [Fr. *turbot*, O.D. *turbot*, perhaps from L. *turbo*, a whipping-top, like Gr. *rhombos*, which means both top and turbot, there being a supposed similarity in shape.] A well-known and highly esteemed species of flatfish native to the North Atlantic Ocean, often weighing from 70 to 90 lb.

turbulent, tėr'bū•lent, *a.* [L. *turbulentus,* from *turbare,* to disturb. TURBID.] Being in violent commotion; tumultuous; disposed to insubordination and disorder; riotous; disorderly.—**turbulence, turbulency,** tėr'bū•lens, tėr'bū•len•si, *n.* The state or quality of being turbulent; riotous disposition; unruliness. —**turbulently,** tėr'bū•lent•li, *adv.* In a turbulent manner.

Turco, tėr'ko, *n.* The name given by the French to Arab sharpshooters in their army.

Turcoman, tėr'ko•man, *n.* See TURKOMAN.

tureen, tū•rēn', *n.* [From Fr. *terrine,* a tureen, lit. an earthen vessel, from *terre*=L. *terra,* earth. TERRA.] A rather large deep vessel for holding soup or other liquid food at the table.

turf, tėrf, *n.* pl. **turfs,** tėrfs, now seldom **turves,** tėrvz. [A.Sax. *turf*= D. *turf,* Icel., Sw., and L.G. *torf,* Dan. *törv,* turf.] The surface or sward of grass lands; a piece of earth with the grass growing on it; a sod; a kind of peaty substance cut from the surface of the ground and used as fuel.—*The turf,* the racecourse; and hence, the occupation or profession of horseracing.—*v.t.* To cover with turf or sod.—**turfiness,** tėr'fi•nes, *n.* The state or quality of being turfy.—**turfy,** tėr'fi, *a.* Abounding or covered with turf; having the qualities or appearance of turf; connected with the turf or race-ground; characteristic of horseracing; sporting.

turgent, tėr'jent, *a.* [L. *turgens, turgentis,* ppr. of *turgeo,* to swell.] Swelling; tumid; turgid.—**turgescence, turgescency,** tėr•jes'ens, tėr•jes'en•si, *n.* The act of swelling or state of being swelled; inflation; bombast; *med.* superabundance of humors in any part of the body.—**turgescent,** tėr•jes'ent, *a.* [L. *turgescens.*] Growing turgid; in a swelling state.—**turgid,** tėr'jid, *a.* [L. *turgidus,* from *turgeo.*] Swelled; bloated; distended beyond its natural state; inflated; bombastic (a *turgid* style).—**turgidly,** tėr'jid•li, *adv.* In a turgid manner; pompously. —**turgidity, turgidness,** tėr•jid'i•ti, tėr'jid•nes, *n.* The state or quality of being turgid; distention beyond its natural state.

Turk, tėrk, *n.* A native of Turkey; a cruel person.

turkey, tėr'ki, *n.* [So called because it was erroneously believed to have come from *Turkey.*] A large gallinaceous bird native to America, including wild and domestic varieties; its flesh is a table delicacy.—**turkey buzzard,** *n.* A common species of the vulture family having a distinct resemblance to a turkey.—**turkey cock,** *n.* A male turkey.—**Turkey red,** *n.* [Because originally produced by madder from Turkey.] A brilliant and durable red color produced by madder.—**Turkish bath,** *n.* A bath in which profuse perspiration is produced in steam rooms, after which one has a massage and cold shower.

Turko, tėr'ko, *n.* Same as *Turco.*

Turkoman, tėr'ko•man, *n.* One of a nomadic Tartar people of Asia, occupying a territory east and southeast of the Caspian Sea.

turmeric, tėr'mer•ik, *n.* [Fr. *terre merite,* from L. terra merita, "a deserving earth" from the earthy appearance of the prized rhizomes.] A name of one or two East Indian plants of the ginger family, whose rhizomes are used as a condiment, a yellow dye, and as a chemical test for the presence of alkalies.

turmoil, tėr'moil, *n.* [Origin doubtful; comp. *tumult* and *moil.*] Harassing labor; molestation by tumult; commotion; disturbance.—*v.t.* To harass with commotion; to trouble; to molest.—*v.i.* To be in commotion.

turn, tėrn, *v.t.* [O.Fr. *turner, torner* (Fr. *tourner*), to turn, from L. *tornare,* to turn in a lathe, from *tornus,* a lathe, from Gr. *tornos,* a turner's chisel; same root as L. *tero, tritum* (E. *trite*), to grind, etc.; akin *tour, tournament, tornado, detour,* etc.] To cause to move round on a center or axis, or as on a center or axis; to put into circular motion; to rotate or revolve; to shape by means of a lathe; to direct or put into a different way, course, direction, or channel (to *turn* a person from a purpose, to *turn* the eyes toward); to apply or devote (to *turn* one's self to trade); to put to some use or purpose; to shift or change with respect to the top, bottom, front, back, sides, or the like; to reverse; to invert; to bring the inside of out; to change to another opinion or party; to convert; to translate; to alter into something else; to metamorphose; to transform, transmute, change; to revolve or ponder (*turn* the matter over); to consider and reconsider; to change from a fresh, sweet, or natural condition; to cause to ferment, become sour, or the like; to put, bring, or place in a certain state or condition (*turned* into ridicule).—*To turn adrift,* to expel from some place or office; to throw upon one's own resources.—*To turn against,* to direct toward or against; to use to one's disadvantage (his argument was *turned against* himself); to render unfavorable, hostile, or opposed to.—*To turn aside,* to ward off; to avert (a blow).—*To turn away,* to dismiss, discharge, or discard; also, to avert. —*To turn back,* to cause to return the same way; to drive back.—*To turn down,* to fold or double down; to reject (a proposal).—*To turn off,* to dismiss or put away; to discharge; to accomplish; to produce complete (the printer *turned off* 10,000 copies); to shut off, as a fluid, by means of a stopcock, valve, etc. (to *turn off* the gas).—*To turn on,* to admit, as a fluid, by means of a stopcock or valve (to *turn on* the gas).—*To turn out,* to drive out; to expel; to put out to pasture; to produce as the result of labor; to furnish in a complete state (to *turn out* 1000 pieces of cloth); to bring the inside of out; to bring out to view.—*To turn over,* to change the position of the top, bottom, or sides of; to overturn; to transfer; to put into different hands; to do business, sell goods, or draw money to the amount of (he *turns over* $500 a week); to open and turn the leaves of as of a book.—*To turn over a new leaf,* to take a different and better line of conduct.—*To turn up,* to bring from below to the top, to dig up (to *turn up* the soil); to bring a different surface or side uppermost; to place with the face upward (to *turn up* a card); to tilt up; to bring the end, tip, or point uppermost (to *turn up one's nose,* an expression of contempt); to refer to in a book.—*To turn upon* (or *on*), to cause to operate on or against.—*To turn the back,* to turn away; to go off; to flee.—*To turn the back on* or *upon,* to withdraw one's favor, friendship, or assistance from.—*To turn a corner,* to go or pass round a corner.—*To turn the edge of,* to blunt or render dull.—*To turn an enemy's flank, line, position,* etc., to maneuver so as to pass round his forces and attack him from behind or on the side.—*To turn one's hand,* to apply or adapt one's self.—*To turn one's head* or *brain,* to make one giddy or dizzy; to deprive of one's reason or judgment; to infatuate.—*To turn a penny,* or *the penny,* to keep one's money in brisk circulation; to increase one's capital by business.—*To turn the scale,* to make one side of the balance go down; *fig.* to decide in one way or another; to give superiority or success.—*To turn the stomach,* to cause nausea, disgust, or loathing.—*To turn the tables,* to overthrow a formerly victorious rival, antagonist, or the like. —*To turn tail,* to retreat with ignominy; to flee like a coward.—*v.i.* To have a circular or rotatory motion; to move round; to revolve or rotate; *fig.* to depend, as on the chief point for decision or the like; to hinge (the question *turns* upon this); to move the body, face, or head in another direction; to change the position or posture of the body, as in bed; to retrace one's steps; to go or come back; to return; to offer opposition; to show fight; to take an opposite or a new course; to be directed (the road *turns* to the right); to have recourse (knew not where to *turn*); to be transformed or transmuted; to be converted; in a general sense, to become; to grow (to *turn* pale); to change from a fresh or sweet condition; to become sour or spoiled, as milk, wine, cider; to become dizzy or giddy, as the head or brain; to reel; to become nauseated or qualmish, as the stomach; to become inclined in another direction; to change from ebb to flow or from flow to ebb, as the tide; to have a consequence; to result (to *turn* to account).—*To turn about,* to turn the face in another direction.—*To* *turn again*, to return.—*To turn against*, to become unfavorable, unfriendly, or hostile to.—*To turn aside*, to leave a straight course; to withdraw from the presence of others.—*To turn away*, to deviate; to move the face in another direction; to avert one's looks.—*To turn back*, to go or come back; to return.—*To turn in*, to bend or double or point inward; to enter; to go to bed (*colloq.*).—*To turn off*, to diverge; to deviate from a course (the road *turns off* to the right).—*To turn on* or *upon*, to show sudden anger or hostility to; to confront in a hostile or angry manner; to depend or hinge.—*To turn out*, to bend or point outward; to come abroad; to appear outside; to get out of bed; to prove in the result or issue; to terminate; to result (the affair *turned out* better).—*To turn over*, to move, shift, or change from side to side, or from top to bottom; to roll; to tumble.—*To turn to*, to apply or betake one's self to; to direct one's mind or attention to.—*To turn up*, to point upward; to come to light; to occur; to appear.—*n.* The act of turning; a revolution or rotation; one round of a rope or cord; the point or place of deviation from a straight line; a winding; a bend; a flexure; an angle; a short walk, promenade, or excursion; alteration of course; new direction or tendency; change or alteration generally; vicissitude; opportunity enjoyed in alternation with another or others, or in rotation; due chance, time, or opportunity; occasion; occasional act of kindness or malice (a good or ill *turn*); purpose; requirement; use; exigence (to serve our *turn*); form, shape, or mold; manner; fashion; character or temper; a short spell or a little job (*colloq.*); a nervous shock, such as is caused by alarm or sudden excitement (*colloq.*); *mus.* the sign ∾ indicating a certain way of playing a group of notes.—*By turns*, one after another; alternately; at intervals.—*In turn*, in due order of succession.—*To a turn*, to a nicety; exactly; perfectly.—*To take turns*, to take each other's place alternately.—*Turn of life*, the period of life in women between the ages of 45 and 50, when the menses cease naturally.—*Turn and turn about*, alternately; successively; by turns.—**turncoat,** *n.* One who forsakes his party or principles.—**turndown,** *a.* Folded or doubled down (a *turndown* collar).—**turner,** tėr′nėr, *n.* One who turns; one whose occupation is to form things with a lathe.—**turnery,** tėr′nėr•i, *n.* The act of turning articles by the lathe; articles made by or formed in the lathe; a place where articles are turned.—**turning,** tėr′ning, *n.* A bend or flexure; the art or operation of shaping articles in a lathe.—**turnkey,** tėrn′kē, *n.* [One who *turns* the *key* in locks.] A person who has charge of the keys of a prison for opening and fastening the doors.—**turnout,** *n.* A coming forth; a number of persons who have *come out* on some particular occasion (a great *turnout* of spectators); that which is brought prominently forward or exhibited; hence, an equipage; a horse or horses and carriage; the net quantity of produce yielded.—**turnover,** *n.* The act or result of turning over; the amount of money turned over or drawn in a business, as in a retail shop, in a given time.—**turnpike,** tėrn′pīk, *n.* [Originally a turning frame with *pikes* or *spikes* projecting.] A turnstile; a gate set across a road in order to stop traffic or travelers, till toll is paid; a tollbar or tollgate; a turnpike road.—**turnpike road,** *n.* A road on which there are turnpikes or tollgates.—**turnspit,** tėrn′spit, *n.* A person who turns a spit; a dog allied to the terrier, formerly employed to drive a wheel to turn the spit for roasting in kitchens.—**turnstile,** tėrn′stīl, *n.* A post surmounted by four horizontal arms which move round as a person pushes by them.—**turnstone,** tėrn′stōn, *n.* A bird of the plover family, so called from its practice of turning up small stones in search of worms, etc., on which it feeds.—**turntable,** *n.* A circular revolving platform used for shifting railroad cars from one line of rails to another, and for reversing engines on the same line of rails.

turner, tėr′nėr, *n.* [Fr. *tournois.*] Old Scottish coin, bearing thistle, from French standard, like plack (Fr. *plaque*), groat (Fr. *gros*), and bawbee (Fr. *bas billon*), the reckoning in Scotland up to about 1760.

turnip, tėr′nip, *n.* [The latter part is A.Sax. *naep*, Icel. *naepa*, Sc. *neip*, a turnip, from L. *napus*, a turnip; the first syllable is perhaps E. *turned* meaning rounded.] A cruciferous, biennial plant, allied to the cabbage, with a solid bulbous root, much cultivated as food for sheep and cattle, especially in winter, and as a flavoring for soups, etc.

turnsole, tėrn′sōl, *n.* [Fr. *tournesol*, from *tourner*, to turn, and L. *sol*, the sun.] A plant whose flower is said to turn toward the sun; a leguminous plant the juice of which is rendered blue by ammonia and air, and which serves as a test for acids; the purple dye obtained from this plant.

turpentine, tėr′pen•tīn, *n.* [D. *terpentijn*, O.Fr. *turbentine*, turpentine, from L. *terebinthus*, Gr. *terebinthos*, the turpentine tree.] An oleoresinous substance obtained from coniferous trees; an oil distilled from turpentine, used as a paint solvent and thinner.

turpeth, tėr′peth, *n.* [From Fr. *turbith*, *turbit*, Sp. *turbit*, from Per. *turbed*, *tirbid*, the plant, the name being given to the mineral on account of its medicinal properties and yellow color like the roots of the plant.] The root of a convolvulus of Ceylon, Malabar, and Australia, which has cathartic properties; also, turpeth mineral.—**turpeth mineral,** *n.* Yellow basic sulfate of mercury, formerly used as a drug.

turpitude, tėr′pi•tūd, *n.* [L. *turpitudo*, from *turpis*, foul, base.] Inherent baseness or vileness of principle, words, or actions; shameful wickedness; moral depravity.

turquoise, tėr′koiz, *n.* [Fr. *turquoise*, so called because brought originally from *Turkey*, Fr. *Turquie.*] A greenish-blue opaque precious stone, a favorite gem in rings and other articles of jewelry.

turret, tur′et, *n.* [O.Fr. *tourette*, dim. of *tour*, a tower, from L. *turris*, a tower. TOWER.] A little tower on a building; an armored shelter on a warship containing, and revolving with, a gun. Distinguished from BARBETTE.—**turreted,** tur′et•ed, *p.* and *a.* Formed like a turret; furnished with turrets.—**turrilite,** tur′i•līt, *n.* [L. *turris*, a tower, and Gr. *lithos*, a stone.] A fossil cephalopod, the shells of which, spiral, turreted, chambered, occur in the cretaceous formations.

turtle, tėr′tl, *n.* [Probably a corruption of *tortoise*, or Sp. *tortuga*, a tortoise.] The name given to the sea tortoise, found in warm climates, the most important species being the green turtle, the flesh of which is so much prized as a luxury at the tables of the rich.

turtledove, tėr′tl•duv, *n.* [A.Sax. *turtle*, a corruption of L. *turtur*, a turtledove, whence also D. *tortel*, G. *turtel*, Icel. *turtil.*] A bird of the pigeon family, smaller than the ordinary domestic pigeon, celebrated for the constancy of its affection, and therefore much sung by poets and appealed to by lovers.

Tuscan, tus′kan, *a.* Pertaining to *Tuscany*, in Italy.—*Tuscan order*, one of the five orders of architecture, devoid of ornaments, and having columns that are never fluted.—*n.* An inhabitant of Tuscany; *arch.* the Tuscan order.

tush, tush, *interj.* An exclamation indicating rebuke, impatience, or contempt, and equivalent to pshaw!

tush, tush, *n.* [A form of *tusk.*] A long pointed tooth; a tusk; applied especially to certain of the teeth of horses.—**tushed,** tusht, *a.* Tusked.

tusk, tusk, *n.* [A.Sax. *tusc*, *tux*, a tusk; probably for *twisc*, from *twá*, two.] The long, pointed, and often protruding tooth on each side of the jaw of certain animals, as in the elephant; the canine tooth of the boar, walrus, hippopotamus, etc.; the share of a plow, a harrow tooth, or the like.—**tusked,** tuskt, *a.* Furnished with tusks.—**tusker,** tus′kėr, *n.* An elephant that has its tusks developed.

tussah silk, tusseh silk, tus′sa, tus′se, *n.* A strong, coarse, brown silk obtained from the cocoons of a wild Bengal silkworm.

tussle, tus′l, *n.* [A form of *tousle*, to pull about roughly.] A struggle; a conflict; a scuffle.—*v.i.*—*tussled*, *tussling.* To struggle; to scuffle.

tussock, tus′ok, *n.* [Modified from older *tuske*, *tushe*, a tuft, a bush; Dan. *dusk*, a tuft, a tassel.] A clump, tuft, or small hillock of growing grass.—**tussock moth,** *n.* A light, brownish-gray moth, so called from the tufts of hair growing on the caterpillar.

tut, tut, *interj.* An exclamation used to check or rebuke, or to express impatience or contempt; synonymous with *tush.*

tutelage, tū′tel•ij, *n.* [From L. *tutela,* protection, from *tueor,* to defend (whence also *tutor, tuition*).] Guardianship; protection bestowed; the state of being under a guardian; protection enjoyed.—**tutelar, tutelary,** tū′tel•ėr, tū′tel•e•ri, *a.* [L. *tutelaris.*] Having the guardianship or charge of protecting a person or a thing; guardian; protecting.

tutenag, tū′te•nag, *n.* The Indian name of zinc or spelter; also an alloy of copper, nickel, and zinc, used for table ware, etc.

tutor, tū′tor, *n.* [L., a defender or guardian, from *tueor,* to defend. TUTELAGE.] One who has the care of the education of another; a private instructor; a teacher or instructor in anything; *law,* a guardian.—*v.t.* To instruct; to teach; to train or discipline.—**tutorage,** tū′tor•ij, *n.* The office of a tutor or guardian; guardianship.—**tutorial,** tū•tō′ri•al, *a.* Belonging to a tutor or instructor.—**tutorship,** tū′tor•ship, *n.* The office of a tutor; guardianship; tutelage.

tutti, töt′ti. [It., from L. *totus,* pl. *toti,* all.] *Mus.* all; a direction to every performer to take part in the execution of the passage or movement.

tutty, tut′i, *n.* [Fr. *tutie,* Pg. *tutia,* from Ar. *tútiya.*] An impure protoxide of zinc, collected from the chimneys of smelting furnaces, and used as a polishing powder.

tuxedo, tuk•sē′dō, *n.* [From *Tuxedo* Park, N. Y.] Men's semiformal evening dress usually consisting of a dark single or double breasted, tailless jacket, dark tie, and, often, a cummerbund.—**tux,** tuks, *n.* A short form of *tuxedo.*

tuyère, twi•yâr′ or tụ•yâr′, *n.* [Fr. *tuyère,* akin to *tuyau,* a pipe.] The nozzle of the pipe that introduces the blast of a blast furnace; the blast pipe itself, of which there are usually two.

twaddle, twod′l, *v.i.*—*twaddled, twaddling.* [Older form *twattle,* also *twittle, twittle-twattle*; an imitative word like *tattle, twitter,* etc.] To talk in a weak, silly, or tedious manner; to prate.—*n.* Empty, silly talk; a twaddler.—**twaddler,** twod′lėr, *n.* One who twaddles.—**twaddling,** twod′ling, *n.* The act of one who twaddles; silly talk.

twain, twān, *a.* [O.E. *tweyne, tweyen,* etc., A.Sax. *twegen,* from *twá,* two= O.Fris. *twêne,* Dan. *tvende,* G. *zween.* TWO.] Two. [Obsolete unless in poetry.]—*n.* A pair; a couple.

twang, twang, *n.* [Imitative of a resonant sound; akin to *tang.*] sharp quick sound; an affected modulation of the voice; a kind of nasal sound; aftertaste; tang.—*v.i.* To sound with a quick sharp noise; to make the sound of a string which is stretched and suddenly pulled; to utter with a sharp or nasal sound.—*v.t.* To make to sound, as by pulling and letting go suddenly; to utter with a short, sharp sound.—*interj.* Imitative of a sharp, quick sound, as that made by a bowstring.

Twankay, twang′ke, *n.* [Chinese.] A sort of green tea.

twattle, twot′l, *v.i.* and *n.* An older form of *Twaddle.*

tweak, twēk, *v.t.* [A.Sax. *twiccian,* to twitch=L.G. *twikken,* D. *zwikken,* G. *zwicken*; an older form of *twitch.*] To twitch; to pinch and pull with a sudden jerk.—*n.* A sharp pinch or jerk; a twitch.

tweed, twēd, *n.* [Originally called *tweels,* that is *twills,* but this name was misread into *tweeds,* when the goods were sent to London, the idea being that they were so called from the river *Tweed.*] A twilled woolen fabric, principally for men's wear, the manufacture of which is largely carried on in the south of Scotland.

tweedledum and **tweedledee,** *n.* The difference of nothing, between two trifles; adapted from lines by John Byrom (1692-1763) expressing the rivalry between the musical followers of Handel and Bononcini.

'tween, twēn, *prep.* A contraction of *Between.*

tweezers, twē′zėrz, *n. pl.* [Formerly *tweezes,* from *tweeze,* a surgeon's box of instruments, a case containing scissors, penknife, or similar articles, from Fr. *étuis,* pl. of *étui,* O.Fr. *estui,* a case or sheath (of Germanic origin).] Small pincers used to pluck out hairs, etc.; small forceps.

twelve, twelv, *a.* [A.Sax. *twelf*=O. Sax. *twelif,* O.Fris. *twelef,* D. *twaalf,* Icel. *tólf.* Goth. *tvalif,* O.H.G. *zwelif,* Mod. G. *zwölf.* Formed similarly to *eleven,* the elements being *two,* A.Sax. *twá,* and a suffix= *ten.* ELEVEN.] The sum of two and ten; twice six.—*n.* The number which consists of ten and two; a symbol representing twelve units, as 12 or xii.—**twelfth,** twelfth, *a.* The second after the tenth; the ordinal of twelve; being one of twelve equal parts of anything.—*n.* One of twelve equal parts of anything.—**Twelfth-night,** twelfth′nīt, *n.* The evening of the festival of the Epiphany.—**twelvemonth,** twelv′munth, *n.* One year.

twenty, twen′ti, *a.* [A.Sax. *twéntig,* from *twegen,* two, *twain,* and *-tig,* ten; *-tig* being cog. with L. *decem,* ten; so D. and L.G. *twintig,* G. *zwanzig,* Goth. *tvaitigjus.*] Twice ten; proverbially, an indefinite number.—*n.* The number of twice ten; a score; a symbol representing this, as 20 or xx.—**twentieth,** twen′ti•eth, *a.* The ordinal of twenty; being one of twenty equal parts of anything.—*n.* One of twenty equal parts.—**twentyfold,** *a.* Twenty times as many.

twibil, twī′bil, *n.* [A.Sax. *twibill,* from *twi*=*two,* and *bill, bil,* an axe, a bill.] A kind of double ax or mattock.

twice, twīs, *adv.* [O.E. *twies,* from A.Sax. *twi, twý,* two or double—*twice* like *thrice,* being an adverbial genitive.] Two times; doubly.

twiddle, twid′l, *v.t.*—*twiddled, twiddling.* [Perhaps based on *twirl* and *fiddle.*] To twirl, in a small way; to touch lightly, or play with.—*v.i.* To play with a tremulous quivering motion.

twig, twig, *n.* [A.Sax. *twig,* akin to *twá,* two, alluding to the bifurcation of the branch; L.G. *twieg,* D. *twijg,* G. *zweig,* a twig. TWO.] A small shoot or branch of a tree or other plant, of no definite length or size.

twig, twig, *v.t.*—*twigged, twigging.* [Ir. and Gael. *tuig,* to perceive, discern.] To take notice of; to observe keenly. (*Colloq.*)—*v.i.* To see; to apprehend or understand. (*Colloq.*)

twilight, twī′līt, *n.* [From *twi,* double (as in *twibill*). A.Sax. *twi, twý,* akin to *twá, two,* and *light.*] The faint light which is reflected upon the earth after sunset and before sunrise; crepuscular light; usually applied to evening twilight, morning twilight being called *dawn*; a faint light in general; hence, a dubious or uncertain medium through which anything is seen or examined (the *twilight* of early history).—*a.* Imperfectly illuminated; seen, done, or appearing by twilight.

twill, twil, *v.t.* [Same as L.G. *twillen,* to make double; akin G. *zwillich,* twill; akin to *twin, two,* and the prefix *twi* of *twilight, twibill.*] To weave in such a manner as to produce a kind of diagonal ribbed appearance upon the surface of the cloth.—*n.* A variety of textile fabric so woven as to have the appearance of parallel diagonal lines or ribs over the surface; the raised lines made by twilling.

twin, twin, *n.* [A.Sax. *twin,* double, *getwinne,* twins, from *twi,* two; so Icel. *tvennr, tvinnr,* a pair; G. *zwilling,* a twin; akin *twill, two, twain,* etc.] One of two young produced at a birth by an animal that ordinarily bears but one; one very much resembling another.—*The Twins,* a constellation and sign of the zodiac; Gemini.—*a.* Applied to one or two born at a birth; very much resembling something else.—**twinborn,** *a.* Born at the same birth with another.—**twinned,** twind, *a.* Produced at one birth, like twins.—**twin-screw,** *a.* and *n.* A steam vessel having two screw propellers on separate shafts and revolving in opposite directions so as to counteract the tendency to lateral vibration.

twine, twīn, *v.t.*—*twined, twining.* [A.Sax. *twinan,* from *twi,* two; so D. *twijnen,* Icel. *tvinna,* to double, to twine. TWIN.] To twist; to form by twisting two or more threads or fibers; to entwine; to encircle.—*v.t.* To wind circularly or spirally; to make flexures; to ascend or grow up in convolutions about a support (the plant *twines*).—*n.* A strong thread composed of two or three smaller threads or strands twisted together; a small cord or string.

twinge, twinj, *v.t.—twinged, twinging.* [Akin to Icel. *thvinga*, to weigh down, to oppress, Dan. *tvinge*, D. *zwingen*, to constrain.] To affect with a sharp, sudden pain; to torment with pinching or sharp pains; to pinch; to tweak.—*v.i.* To have a sudden, sharp, local pain.—*n.* A sudden, sharp pain; a darting, local pain of momentary continuance; a pinch; a tweak.

twinkle, twing'kl, *v.i.—twinkled, twinkling.* [A.Sax. *twinclian*, to twinkle, a dim. and freq. corresponding to O.E. *twinken*, G. *zwinken*, to wink with the eyes; nasalized forms corresponding to *twitch.*] To open and shut the eyes rapidly; to gleam; to sparkle; said of the eyes; to flash at intervals; to shine with a tremulous, intermitted light; to scintillate.—*n.* A wink or quick motion of the eye; a gleam or sparkle of the eye or of a star; a twinkling.—**twinkling,** twingk'ling, *n.* The act of that which twinkles; a quick movement of the eye; a wink; the time taken up in winking the eye; an instant.

twirl, twėrl, *v.t.* [Allied to Fris. *twierren*, to whirl, D. *dwarl*, a whirling, *dwarlen*, to whirl, O.G. *twirel*, what turns rapidly; Swiss *zwirlen*, to twirl.] To cause to turn round with rapidity; to cause to rotate rapidly, especially with the finger.—*v.i.* To revolve with velocity; to be whirled round.—*n.* A rapid circular motion; a twist; a convolution.

twist, twist, *v.t.* [A.Sax. *twist*, a cord, from stem of *twá*, two; hence allied to *twine, twill, twig*, etc.; similarly L.G. and D. *twist*, Dan. and Sw. *tvist*, G. *zwist*, discord, division in two parties.] To form by winding strands together; to twine; to form into a thread from many fine filaments; to contort; to crook spirally; to wreathe; to insinuate; to pervert; to turn from the true form or meaning.—*To twist round one's finger*, to completely control the opinions and actions of.—*v.i.* To be united by winding round each other; to be twisted.—*n.* The act of twisting; the result of the act; a convolution; a contortion; a flexure; what is formed by twisting, as a cord, thread, etc.; manufactured tobacco in the form of a thick cord; the spiral in the bore of a rifled gun.—**twister,** twis'tėr, *n.* One that twists.

twit, twit, *v.t.—twitted, twitting.* [O.E. *atwite, atwiten*, A.Sax. *aetwitan* to twit, reproach—*aet*, at, and *witan*, to blame; Sc. *wite*, blame; akin to Icel. *vita*, to fine.] To vex or annoy by bringing to remembrance a fault, imperfection, or the like; to taunt; to upbraid, as for some previous act.—**twitter,** twit'ėr, *n.* One who twits or reproaches.

twitch, twich, *v.t.* [A form of *tweak.*] To pull with a sudden jerk; to snatch.—*v.i.* To be suddenly contracted, as a muscle.—*n.* A pull with a jerk; a short quick pull; a short, spastic contraction of the muscles; a noose twisted around the upper lip of a horse to keep him quiet when shoeing.

twitch grass, twich'gras, *n.* See COUCH GRASS.

twitter, twit'ėr, *v.i.* [Imitative of sound, like G. *zwitschern*, D. *kwetteren*, to twitter.] To utter a succession of small, tremulous, intermitted notes, as certain birds do.—*n.* A small intermitted noise or series of chirpings, as the sound made by a swallow.

'twixt, twikst. A contraction of *Betwixt*; used in poetry and colloquially.

two, tö, *a.* [A.Sax. *twá*=Icel. *tveir, tvö*, Goth. *tvai*, D. *twee*, G. *zwei*, Rus. *dwa*, Lith. *du*, L. and Gr. *duo*, Ir. and Gael. *da, do*. Per. *do*, Hind. *do, doo*, Skr. *dvi, dvau. Twin, twine, twill, twain, twist*, etc., are connected.] One and one together: often used indefinitely for a small number (a word or *two, two* or three hours).—*In two*, into two parts; asunder.—*n.* The number which consists of one and one; the symbol representing it as 2 or ii.—**two-faced,** *a.* Having two visages, like the Roman deity Janus; given to equivocation or doubledealing; insincere.—**twofold,** tö'fōld, *a.* Double; multiplied by two; *bot.* two and two together growing from the same place (*twofold* leaves).—*adv.* In a double degree; doubly.—**two-handed,** *a.* Having two hands; requiring the two hands to grasp (a *two-handed* sword).—**twopence,** tup'ens, *n.* In Great Britain, a small silver coin.—**twopenny,** tup'en•i, *a.* Of the value of twopence; hence, of little worth.—**two-ply,** *a.* Having two strands, as cord, or two thicknesses, as cloth, carpets.

Tyburn, tī'bėrn, *n.* The old place of the gallows in London.

tycoon, tī•kön', *n.* [Chinese *Tai-koon*, great lord.] The generalissimo of the Japanese army, and formerly virtual emperor and real ruler of the country; wealthy businessman.

tyke, tīk, *n.* [TIKE.] A dog; a base fellow. (*Shak.*)

tymbal, tim'bal, *n.* [Fr. *timbale*, It. *timballo, taballo*, from Ar. *thabal*, a drum.] A kind of kettledrum.

tympan, tim'pan, *n.* [Fr. *tympan*, L. *tympanum*, from Gr. *tympanon, typanon*, a drum, from *typtō*, to beat.] A drum‡; *arch.* same as *tympanum*; *printing*, a frame attached to the handpress or platen machine, and covered with parchment or cloth, on which the blank sheets are put in order to be laid on the form to be impressed.—**tympanic,** tim•pan'ik, *a.* Like a tympanum or drum; *anat.* pertaining to the tympanum.—**tympanites,** tim•pa•nī'tēz, *n. Med.* a distention of the abdomen from a morbid collection of air in the intestines.—**tympanitic,** tim•pa•nit'ik, *a.* Relating to or affected with tympanites.—**tympanitis,** tim•pa•nī'tis, *n.* Inflammation of the lining membrane of the middle ear or tympanum.—**tympanum,** tim'pa•num, *n. Anat.* the drum of the ear, a cavity of an irregular shape, constituting the middle ear; *arch.* the triangular space in a pediment; *mach.* a drum-shaped wheel with spirally curved partitions, by which water is raised for the purposes of irrigation; *bot.* a membranous substance stretched across the theca of a moss.—**tympany,** tim'pan•i, *n.* Tympanites; inflation of language; bombast.

type, tīp, *n.* [Fr. *type*, from L. *typus*, from Gr. *typos*, a blow, an impression, a mark, a type, from root of *typtō*, to strike.] A distinguishing mark or stamp; an emblem; an allegorical or symbolic representation of some object, which is called the *antitype*; a symbol; what prefigures something else; an example of any class considered as eminently possessing the properties or characters of the class; the ideal representative of a group; distinctive plan of structure; the model or pattern which becomes the subject of a copy; *printing*, a rectangular piece of metal, wood, or other hard material having a raised letter, figure, or other character on the upper end, which, when inked, gives impressions on paper; such types collectively.—*In type*, set up, ready for printing.—*v.t.* To serve as type of; to typify; to typewrite.—**type founder,** *n.* A person who makes type by casting.—**typefounding,** *n.* The founding or casting of printing types.—**typefoundry,** *n.* A place where types are cast.—**type metal,** *n.* An alloy of lead, antimony, and tin.—**typescript,** *n.* Matter produced by a typewriter.—**typesetter,** *n.* One who sets up type; a compositor; a typesetting machine.—**typesetting,** *n.* The act or process by which type is set up to be printed from.—**typewrite,** *v.t.* To print by a typewriter.—**typewriter,** *n.* A keyboard machine for producing writing resembling type impressions; one who uses such machine.—**typist,** tīp'ist, *n.* One who uses a typewriter.—**typical, typic,** tip'i•kal, tip'ik, *a.* Pertaining to a type; serving as or having the character of a type; emblematic; figurative —**typically,** tip'i•kal•li, *adv.* In a typical manner. —**typicalness,** tip'i•kal•nes, *n.*—**typification,** tip'i•fi•kā"shon, *n.* The act of typifying.—**typifier,** tip'i•fī•ėr, *n.* One who typifies.—**typify,** tip'i•fī, *v.t.—typified, typifying.* To represent by an image or resemblance; to serve as the type of; to prefigure; to exemplify.—**typographer,** tī•pog'raf•ėr, *n.* A printer.—**typographic, typographical,** tīp•o•graf'ik, tīp•o•graf'i•kal, *a.* Pertaining to printing.—**typographically,** tīp•o•graf'i•kal•li, *adv.* By means of types; after the manner of printers.—**typography,** tī•pog'ra•fi, *n.* [Gr. *typos*, and *graphō*, to write.] The art of printing; matter printed; style in which anything is printed.

typhlitis, tif•lī'tis, *n.* [Gr. *typhlos*, blind (referring to caecum, from L.

caecus, blind), and term. *-itis*, denoting inflammation.] *Med.* inflammation of the caecum or blind gut.

typhoon, tī•fön′, *n.* [Chinese *tai-fong*, great wind, influenced by Gr. *typhōn*, a whirlwind.] A cyclone or hurricane that occurs in the western Pacific Ocean and the China Sea.

typhus, tī′fus, *n.* [Gr. *typhos*, stupor or coma.] A contagious disease caused by *Rickettsia* and spread by lice, symptoms being high fever, severe fatigue and depression, and an eruption that gives the skin a deep livid color, etc.—**typhoid,** tī′foid, *a.* Pertaining to or resembling typhus.—*Typhoid fever*, a continued fever, characterized by abdominal pains and diarrhea, and analogous in many respects to eruptive fevers. Known also as *Enteric* and *Gastric Fever*.—**typhous,** tī′fus, *a.* Relating to typhus.

typical, typography. etc. See TYPE.

tyrant, tī′rant, *n.* [O.Fr. *tiran, tirant*, from L. *tyrannus*, from Gr. *tyrannos*, a lord, a despotic ruler. The final *t* has been added, as in *pheasant, peasant*, etc.] Originally, in ancient Greece, one who had usurped the ruling power without the consent of the people or at the expense of the existing government; a usurper; hence, a monarch or other ruler or master who uses power to oppress those under him; a cruel sovereign or master; an oppressor.—**tyrannic,** ti•ran′ik, *a.* Tyrannical.—**tyrannical,** ti•ran′i•kal, *a.* [Fr. *tyrannique*, Gr. *tyrannikos.*] Pertaining to or acting as a tyrant; unjustly severe in government; oppressive to subordinates; despotic; cruel.—**tyrannically,** ti•ran′i•kal•li, *adv.* In a tyrannical manner; oppressively.—**tyrannicalness,** ti•ran′i•kal•nes, *n.*—**tyrannicide,** ti•ran′i•sīd, *n.* [L. *tyrannus*, and *caedo*, to kill.] The act of killing a tyrant; one who kills a tyrant.—**tyrannize,** tir′an•īz, *v.i.*—*tyrannized, tyrannizing.* [Fr. *tyranniser.*] To act the tyrant; to exercise arbitrary power; to rule with unjust and oppressive severity.—**tyrannous,** tir′an•us, *a.* Tyrannical; unjustly severe; oppressive.—**tyrannously,** tir′an•us•li, *adv.* In a tyrannous manner.—**tyranny,** tir′an•i, *n.* The rule of a tyrant; despotic exercise of power; cruel government; undue severity; oppression; a cruel or oppressive act.

tyrian, tir′i•an, *n.* A native of ancient Tyre, the famous Phoenician city.—*a.* Pertaining to Tyre; of a purple color.—*Tyrian purple*, a celebrated purple dye formerly prepared at Tyre from shell-fish.

tyro, tī′rō, *n.* [L. *tiro*, a raw recruit, a novice.] A novice or mere beginner; a beginner in learning.

Tyrolese, tī′rol•ēz or tir′ol•ēz, *a.* Belonging or relating to the Tyrol or Tirol.—*n. sing.* and *pl.* A native of the Tyrol; the people of the Tyrol.—**Tyrolienne,** tē•rōl•yen′, *n.* [Fr.] A Tyrolese popular melody, in which rapid alternation of the natural and falsetto voice is introduced.

tzar, tzarina, tsär, tsä•rē′na. Same as *Czar, Czarina.*

U

U, u, ū. The twenty-first letter and the fifth vowel in the English alphabet.

ubiety, ū•bī′e•ti, *n.* [From L. *ubi*, where.] The state of being somewhere.

ubiquitous, ū•bik′wi•tus, *a.* [From L. *ubique*, everywhere.] Existing or being everywhere; omnipresent.—**ubiquitously,** ū•bik′wi•tus•li, *adv.* In a ubiquitous manner.—**ubiquity,** ū•bik′wi•ti, *n.* The state of being ubiquitous; existing everywhere at the same time; omnipresence.

U-boat, ū′bōt, *n.* A German submarine (from German *unterseeboot*).

udder, ud′ėr, *n.* [A.Sax. *uder*=O. Fris. *uder*, O.H.G. *ûtar*, G. *euter*; cog. L. *uber*, Gr. *outhar*, Skr. *ûdhar*, an udder.] The glandular organ or bag of cows and other quadrupeds, in which the milk is secreted and retained for the nourishment of their young.

udometer, ū•dom′et•ėr, *n.* [L. *udus*, moist, wet, and Gr. *metron*, measure.] A pluviometer; a rain gauge.

UFO. See FLYING SAUCER.

ugh, ug, *interj.* **An expression of horror or recoil.**

ugly, ug′li, *a.* [O.E. *uggely, uglike*, from *uggr*, fear, and *-ligr*=E. *-like, -ly*; akin Icel. *ugga*, to fear, E. *awe.*] Possessing qualities opposite to beauty; offensive to the sight; deformed; morally repulsive; hateful.—*n.* A kind of sun-shade formerly worn by ladies in front of their bonnets.—**uglily,** ug′li•li, *adv.* In an ugly manner.—**ugliness,** ug′li•nes, *n.* The quality of being ugly; want of beauty; deformity of person; moral repulsiveness.

Ugrian, ö′gri•an, *a.* [From name of a Finnish tribe.] Applied to the Finnic group of Turanian tongues and peoples, comprising the Lapps, Finns, and Magyars. By some used as equivalent to Turanian.

uhlan, ö′lan, *n.* [G. *uhlan*, from Polish *ulan*, a lancer.] A name given to light cavalry soldiers in the Russian, Austro-Hungarian, and German armies. Written also *Ulan.*

ukase, ū•kās′, *n.* [Rus., from *kasati*, to show.] A Russian edict or order emanating from the government, and having the force of law.

ukulele, ū′ku•lā″lē, *n.* [Hawaiian, from *uku*, insect, and *lele*, to jump, from the motion of the fingers.] A small guitar-like instrument with four strings, originally from Portugal.

ulcer, ul′sėr, *n.* [Fr. *ulcère*, from L. *ulcus, ulceris*, an ulcer or sore, akin Gr. *helkos*, an ulcer or wound.] A sore in any of the soft parts of the body, and attended with a secretion of pus or some kind of discharge.—**ulcerate,** ul′sėr•āt, *v.i.*—*ulcerated, ulcerating.* To be formed into an ulcer.—*v.t.* To affect with an ulcer or with ulcers.—**ulceration,** ul•sėr•ā′shon, *n.* [L. *ulceratio.*] The process of becoming ulcerous; the state of being ulcerated; an ulcer.—**ulcerative,** ul′sėr•ā•tiv, *a.* Pertaining to ulcers.—**ulcerous,** ul′sėr•us, *a.* Having the nature or character of an ulcer; affected with an ulcer or with ulcers.—**ulcerously,** ul′sėr•us•li, *adv.*—**ulcerousness,** ul′sėr•us•nes, *n.*

ulema, ö•le•mä′, *n.* [Ar. *ulemâ*, wise or learned men.] The collective name of the hierarchical corporation of learned men in Turkey, who have charge of the department of government relating to sacred matters; composed of the Imams, the Muftis, and the Cadis.

ullage, ul′ij, *n.* [O.Fr. *eullage*, the filling up of leaky wine vessels, from *œil*, the eye, the bunghole, from L. *oculus*, the eye. OCULAR.] The quantity that a cask wants of being full.

ulna, ul′na, *n.* pl. **ulnae,** ul′nē. [L. *ulna*, elbow, arm, an ell. ELL.] The larger of the two bones of the forearm, reaching from the elbow to the wrist, its upper extremity forming the point of the elbow; *old law*, an ell.—**ulnar,** ul′nėr, *a.* Pertaining to the ulna.

ulotrichous, ū•lot′ri•kus, *a.* [Gr. *oulotrichos*, from *oulos*, crisp or curly, and *thrix, trichos*, hair.] Pertaining to the crisp- or woolly-haired races of man.

ulster, ul′stėr, *n.* A long loose overcoat for either a male or a female, originally made of frieze cloth in Ulster.

ulterior, ul•tē′ri•or, *a.* [L., compar. from *ulter*, beyond, further. ULTRA.] Being beyond or on the further side; not at present in view or consideration; more remote; distant (*ulterior* views or objects).—**ulteriorly,** ul•tē′ri•or•li, *adv.* More distantly; remotely.

ultima, ul′ti•ma, *n.* [L. *ultimus*, last, furthest, superl. of *ulter*, further. ULTERIOR.] *Gram.* the last syllable of a word.—**ultimate,** ul′ti•mit, *a.* Furthest; most remote in place; last or final; arrived at as a final result; such that we cannot go beyond; incapable of further resolution or analysis.—*Ultimate analysis, chem.* the resolution of a substance into its absolute elements opposed to *proximate analysis*, or the resolution of a substance into its constituent compounds.—**ultimately,** ul′ti•mit•li, *adv.* As an ultimate or final result; at last; finally.—**ultimatum,** ul•ti•mā′tum, *n.* pl.—**ultimatums,** ul•ti•mā′tumz. Any final proposal or statement of conditions in diplomatic negotiations, the final terms offered by a negotiator or party.—**ultimo,** ul′ti•mō, *a.* [L. *ultimo mense*, in the last month.] Last, as distinguished from the current month and all others; usually contracted to *ult.*—**ultimogeniture,** ul′ti•mo•jen″i•cher, *n.* The custom or practice by which the youngest child succeeds to an inheritance, as *borough-English* in England opposed to *primogeniture*.

ultra, ul'tra, *prefix*, *a.* and *n.* [L. *ultra*, beyond, from pronominal root seen in *ille*, that person, he, and *-tra*, as in *contra*, *intra*, etc. *Outrage* is from this word.] A Latin preposition used as a prefix, in sense of beyond; exceedingly; in a high degree (*ultra*-conservative, *ultra*-liberal); also as an independent adjective, to signify beyond due limit; extreme (*ultra* measures); and as a noun, to signify one who advocates extreme views or measures, an ultraist.—**ultraism,** ul'tra•izm, *n.* The principles of men who advocate extreme measures.—**ultraist,** ul'-tra•ist, *n.* One who pushes a principle or measure to extremes.

ultrahigh frequency, *n.* Electromagnetic radiation (radio waves) having a frequency of from 300 to 3,000 megacycles.

ultramarine, ul'tra•ma•rēn", *a.* [L. *ultra*, and *marinus*, marine.] Situated or being beyond the sea; deep blue. —*n.* A beautiful and durable sky-blue color, formed of the mineral called lapis-lazuli.

ultramicroscopic, ul'tra•mī'krō•-skop"ik, *a.* Being too small to be seen by an ordinary microscope.—**ultramontane,** ul•tra•mon'tān, *a.* [L. *ultra*, and *mons*. mountain.] Being or lying beyond the mountains; tramontane; belonging to the Italian or ultra-papal party in the Church of Rome; holding the doctrines of ultramontanism.—*n.* One who belongs to the Italian or ultra-papal party in the Church of Rome; one holding the doctrines of ultramontanism.—**ultramontanism,** ul•-tra•mon'ten•izm, *n.* The views of that party in the Church of Rome who place an absolute authority in matters of faith and discipline in the hands of the pope.

ultramundane, ul•tra•mun'dān, *a.* [L. *ultra*, and *mundus*, world.] Being beyond the world, or beyond the limits of our system.

ultrasonic, ul'tra•son"ik, *a.* [L. *ultra*, beyond, and *sonic*, sound.] Pertaining to sound of about 20,000 cycles per second: beyond the range of human audibility; supersonic.

ultraviolet, ul'tra•vi"o•let, *a.* Pertaining to radiation beyond the visible spectrum, at the violet end.

ululate, ul'ū•lāt, *v.i.* [L. *ululo*, *ululatum*, to howl.] To howl, as a dog or wolf.—**ululant,** ul'ū•lant, *a.* Ululating; howling.—**ululation,** ul•ū•-lā'shon, *n.* A howling, as of the wolf or dog; a wailing.

umbel, um'bel, *n.* [L. *umbella*, a little shade, dim. of *umbra*, a shade. UMBRAGE.] *Bot.* a particular mode of inflorescence, which consists of a number of flower stalks or pedicels, nearly equal in length, spreading from a common center, each bearing a single flower, as in the ivy, carrot, etc.—**umbellar,** um•bel'ėr, *a.* Pertaining to an umbel; having the form of an umbel.—**umbellate, umbellated,** um'bel•āt, um'bel•ā•-ted, *a.* Bearing umbels; umbel-like. —**umbelliferous,** um•bel•lif'ėr•us, *a.* Producing umbels; bearing umbels.—**umbellule,** um'bel•ūl, *n.* Dim. of *umbel. Bot.* a small or partial umbel.

umber, um'bėr, *n.* [L. *umbro*, a shade, or from *Umbria*, a district of Italy, where, according to some, it was first obtained.] A soft earthy combination forming a pigment of an olive-brown color in its raw state, but much redder when burnt. —*v.t.* To color with umber; to shade or darken.

umbilical, um•bil'i•kal or um•bi•-lī'kal, *a.* [L. *umbilicus*, the navel; akin to G. *omphalos*, the navel.] Pertaining to the navel; formed in the middle like a navel; navel-shaped; central.—*Umbilical cord*, *anat.* a cord-like structure which passes from the navel of the fetus or embryo of the higher mammalia to the placenta; the navel string.—**umbilicate, umbilicated,** um•bil'i•-kāt, um•bil'i•kā•ted, *a.* Navel-shaped; *bot.* fixed to a stalk by a point in the center.—**umbilicus,** um•bi•lī'kus, *n.* [L.] *Anat.* the navel; *bot.* the part of a seed by which it is attached to the placenta; the hilum; *conch.* a circular depression in the lower whorl of many spiral univalves.

umbles, um'blz, *n. pl.* The humbles or entrails of a deer.—**umblepie,** um'bl•pī, *n.* See HUMBLE PIE.

umbo, um'bō, *n.* [L. *umbo*, a boss on a shield, any boss or knob.] The boss or protuberant part of a shield; *bot.* the knob in the center of the pileus or hat of the fungus tribe; *conch.* the projection of a bivalve shell situated immediately above the hinge.—**umbonate,** um'-bo•nāt, *a.* Bossed; knobbed in the center; *bot.* round with a projecting point in the center.

umbra, um'bra, *n.* [L., a shadow.] *Astron.* the total shadow of the earth or moon in an eclipse, or the dark cone projected from a planet or satellite on the side opposite to the sun, as contrasted with the *penumbra*; the dark central portion of a sunspot surrounded by a brighter annular portion.

umbrage, um'brij, *n.* [O.Fr. *umbrage*, Fr. *ombrage*, from L. *umbra*, a shade (whence also *umbel*, *umbrella*, *adumbrate*).] A shade; shadow; shade caused by foliage; hence, the feeling of being overshadowed; jealousy of another, as standing in one's light or way; suspicion of injury; offense; resentment.—**umbrageous,** um•-brā'jus, *a.* [Fr. *ombrageux*.] Shading; forming a shade; shady; shaded (an *umbrageous* garden).—**umbrageously,** um•brā'jus•li, *adv.* In an umbrageous manner.—**umbrageousness,** um•brā'jus•nes, *n.*

umbrella, um•brel'la, *n.* [It. *ombrella*, an umbrella, dim. of *ombra*, a shade, from L. *umbra*, a shade. UMBRAGE.] A portable shade, screen, or canopy of silk, cotton, etc., extended on an expanding frame composed of bars of steel, cane, etc., inserted in, or fastened to a rod or stick, and carried in the hand for sheltering the person from the rays of the sun, or from rain or snow.—**umbrella tree,** *n.* The magnolia tree with umbrella-like leaves at end of branches.

Umbrian. The followers in painting of Raphael and Perugino.

umbriferous, um•brif'ėr•us, *a.* [L. *umbra*, a shade, and *fero*, to bear. UMBRAGE.] Casting or making a shade.

umiak, ö'mi•ak, *n.* [Eskimo.] A flat-bottomed skin boat usually rowed by women.

umlaut, ųm'lout, *n.* [Gr., from prefix *um*, indicating alteration, and *laut*, sound=change of sound.] *Philol.* the change of a vowel in one syllable through the influence of a vowel in the syllable immediately following—a common feature in several of the Teutonic tongues; mutation.

umpire, um'pīr, *n.* [From O.E. *noumpere*, *nowmpere*, *nompere*, and with loss of initial *n* (as in *apron*), *owmper*, etc., from O.Fr. *nonper*, not equal, odd—L. *non*, not, and *par*, equal, a pair. PAIR. Lit. an odd person, in addition to a pair.] A person to whose sole decision a controversy or question between parties is referred; one agreed upon as arbiter of decisions in baseball and other sports events.—**umpirage,** um'pīr•ij, *n.* The post of umpire; the act of one who arbitrates as umpire; arbitrament.

un-. A prefix derived from two sources and with two uses, viz. those of negation and those of reversal or undoing. As expressive of simple negation it is A.Sax. *un-* (Goth. *un-*, D. *on-*, L. *in-*, all signifying not); and in this sense it is used chiefly before adjectives, past participles passive, and present participles used adjectively, being also prefixed to some nouns as in *un*truth, *un*dress, *un*rest, *un*wisdom, etc. Before some words of Latin origin it may be used alternatively with *in* or *non*; thus *un*alterable, *in*alterable; *un*elastic, *in*elastic, and *non*-elastic. As expressing reversal it represents A.Sax. *on-*, *ond-*, *and-*, *an-* in *answer* (Icel. and Goth. *and-*, G. *ant-*, L. *ante*, before), and is generally prefixed to active transitive verbs, as, *un*do, *un*learn, *un*lock, *un*make, etc. As adjectives and participles with the prefix *un-*, simply in the sense of not, are almost unlimited in number, and their meaning generally quite obvious, many of them are omitted from this work. When such words, however, have a special signification or usage of their own, and are not simply to be explained as equivalent to 'not' and their latter element, they are here given (as, for instance, *unaccountable*, *unruly*, *unconscionable*, *unparalleled*, etc.). Verbs and nouns with the other *un* as a prefix are also carefully defined.

unabashed, un•a•basht', *a.* Not abashed or daunted; not put to shame or confusion.

unabated, un•a•bāt'ed, *a.* Not diminished in strength or violence.

unable, un•ā'bl, *a.* Not able; not having sufficient ability; not equal for some task. ∴ Syn. under INCAPABLE.

unabridged, un•a•brijd′, *a.* Not abridged; not shortened.

unaccented, un•ak•sent′ed, *a.* Not accented; having no accent.

unacceptable, un•ak•sep′ta•bl, *a.* Not acceptable or pleasing; not welcome; not such as will be received with pleasure.

unaccommodating, un•ak•kom′mo•dāt•ing, *a.* Not ready to accommodate or oblige.

unaccompanied, un•ak•kum′pa•nid, *a.* Having no attendants, companions, or followers; *mus.* performed or written without an accompaniment.

unaccomplished, un•ak•kom′plisht, *a.* Not accomplished; not performed completely; not having accomplishments.

unaccountable, un•ak•koun′ta•bl, *a.* Not to be accounted for; not explicable; such that no reason or explanation can be given.

unaccredited, un•ak•kred′it•ed, *a.* Not accredited; not authorized.

unaccustomed, un•ak•kus′tumd, *a.* Not accustomed; not habituated.

unacknowledged, un•ak•nol′ejd, *a.* Not acknowledged or recognized; not owned, confessed, or avowed.

unacquainted, un•ak•kwān′ted, *a.* Not having formed an acquaintance; not having knowledge; followed by *with.*

unadjusted, un•ad•just′ed, *a.* Not adjusted, settled, or regulated.

unadmonished, un•ad•mon′isht, *a.* Not cautioned, warned, or advised.

unadorned, un•a•dornd′, *a.* Not adorned; not decorated; not embellished.

unadulterated, un•a•dul′tėr•āt•ed, *a.* Not adulterated; genuine; pure.

unadvisable, un•ad•vī′za•bl, *a.* Not advisable; not to be recommended; not expedient; not prudent.—**unadvised,** un•ad•vīzd′, *a.* Done without due consideration; rash.—**unadvisedly,** un•ad•vī′zed•li, *adv.* Imprudently; indiscreetly.

unaffected, un•af•fek′ted, *a.* Not having the feelings moved; not showing affectation; natural; not artificial; simple; not hypocritical; sincere.—**unaffectedly,** un•af•fek′ted•li, *adv.* In an unaffected manner; naturally; simply; sincerely.

unaided, un•ād′ed, *a.* Not aided; not assisted.

unallied, un•al•līd′, *a.* Having no alliance or connection, either by nature, marriage, or treaty.

unalloyed, un•al•loid′, *a.* Not alloyed; having no admixture of alloy; without disturbing elements (*unalloyed* happiness or satisfaction).

unalterable, un•a̤l′tėr•a•bl, *a.* Not alterable; unchangeable; immutable.—**unaltered,** un•a̤l′tėrd, *a.* Not altered or changed.

unambiguous, un•am•big′ū•us, *a.* Not of doubtful meaning; plain; clear; certain.

unambitious, un•am•bi′shus, *a.* Free from ambition; not affecting show; not showy or prominent.

unamiable, un•ā′mi•a•bl, *a.* Not amiable or lovable not adapted to gain affection.

unaneled,‡ un•a•nēld′ *a.* or *pp.* [From *un,* not, old *an-* for *on,* and A.Sax. *elan,* to oil, from *ele,* oil.] Not having received extreme unction. (*Shak.*)

unanimous, ū•nan′i•mus, *a.* [L. *unanimus,* of one mind—*unus,* one, and *animus,* mind. ANIMAL.] Being of one mind; agreeing in opinion or determination; formed by unanimity (a *unanimous* vote).—**unanimously,** ū•nan′i•mus•li, *adv.* With entire agreement of minds.—**unanimity,** ū•na•nim′i•ti, *n.* The state of being unanimous.

unanswerable, un•an′sėr•a•bl, *a.* Not to be satisfactorily answered; not capable of refutation.

unappealable, un•ap•pēl′a•bl, *a.* That cannot be carried to a higher court by appeal; not to be appealed from.

unappeasable, un•ap•pēz′a•bl, *a.* Not to be appeased or pacified.

unapproachable, un•ap•prō′cha•bl, *a.* That cannot be approached; inaccessible; not to be equaled.

unappropriate, un•ap•prō′pri•āt, *a.* Not appropriate; inappropriate.—**unappropriated,** un•ap•prō′pri•ā•ted, *a.* Not appropriated; not applied to any specific object; not granted to any person, company, or corporation (*unappropriated* lands).

unapproved, un•ap•prövd′, *a.* Not having received approbation.

unapt, un•apt′, *a.* Not apt; dull; not ready to learn; unfit; unsuitable (*Shak.*).

unarmed, un•ärmd′, *a.* Not having on arms or armor; not equipped.

unasked, un•askt′, *a.* Not asked; not invited; unsolicited; not sought by entreaty or care.

unaspirated, un•as′pi•rā•ted, *a.* Having no aspirate; pronounced or written without an aspirate.

unassailable, un•as•sā′la•bl, *a.* Incapable of being assailed; not to be moved or shaken from a purpose.

unassuming, un•as•sūm′ing, *a.* Not assuming; not bold or forward; not arrogant; modest.

unattached, un•at•tacht′, *a.* Not attached; *law,* not taken on account of debt; *milit.* not belonging to any one company or regiment, or on half pay; said of officers.

unattainable, un•at•tā′na•bl, *a.* Not to be gained or obtained.

unattempted, un•at•temp′ted, *a.* Not attempted; not tried; not essayed.

unattended, un•at•tend′ed, *a.* Not accompanied; having no retinue or attendance.

unau, ö•nou′, *n.* [South American.] The two-toed sloth of Brazil.

unauthentic, un•a̤•then′tik, *a.* Not authentic; not genuine or true.—**unauthenticated,** un•a̤•then′ti•kā•ted, *a.* Not attested; not shown to be genuine.

unauthorized, un•a̤′thor•īzd, *a.* Not warranted by proper authority; not duly commissioned.

unavailing, un•a•vā′ling, *a.* Not having the effect desired; of no avail; ineffectual; useless; vain.

unavoidable, un•a•voi′da•bl, *a.* Not avoidable; not to be shunned; inevitable.

unaware, un•a•wâr′, *a.* Not aware; not knowing; not cognizant. Sometimes used adverbially for *unawares.*—**unawares,** un•a•wârz′, *adv.* [An adverbial genitive, like *betimes,* etc.] Unexpectedly; without previous preparation; inadvertently.—*At unawares,* unexpectedly.

unbalanced, un•bal′anst, *a.* Not balanced; not in equipoise; not brought to an equality of debit and credit.

unbar, un•bär′, *v.t.* To remove a bar or bars from; to unfasten; to unlock.

unbearable, un•bâr′a•bl, *a.* Not to be borne or endured; intolerable.

unbecoming, un•bi•kum′ing, *a.* Not becoming; improper; indecorous.—**unbecomingly,** un•bi•kum′ing•li, *adv.* Indecorously.

unbefitting, un•bi•fit′ing, *a.* Not fitting or suitable; unsuitable; unbecoming.

unbelief, un•bi•lēf′, *n.* Incredulity; the withholding of belief; infidelity; disbelief of divine revelation; disbelief of the truths of the gospel.—**unbelievable,** un•bi•lē′va•bl, *a.* Such as cannot be believed; impossible to believe.—**unbeliever,** un•bi•lē′vėr, *n.* One who does not believe; an infidel; one who discredits revelation, or the mission and doctrines of Christ.—**unbelieving,** un•bi•lē′ving, *a.* Incredulous; infidel; discrediting divine revelation.

unbend, un•bend′, *v.i.* To become relaxed or not bent; to rid one's self of constraint; to act with freedom; to give up stiffness or austerity of manner.—*v.t.* To free from bend or flexure; to relax; to set at ease for a time (to *unbend* the mind); *naut.* to unfasten from the yards and stays, as sails.—**unbending,** un•ben′ding, *p.* and *a.* Unyielding; resolute; inflexible.—**unbendingly,** un•ben′ding•li, *adv.* Obstinately.

unbeseeming, un•bi•sēm′ing, *a.* Unbecoming; not befitting.

unbias, un•bī′as, *v.t.* To free from bias, prejudice, or prepossession.—**unbiased,** un•bī′ast, *a.* Free from bias, undue partiality, or prejudice; impartial.

unbidden, un•bid′n, *a.* Not commanded; spontaneous; uninvited; not requested to attend.

unbind, un•bīnd′, *v.t.* To untie; to unfasten; to loose; to set free from shackles.

unbleached, un•blēcht′, *a.* Not bleached; not whitened by bleaching.

unblemished, un•blem′isht, *a.* Not blemished; free from turpitude or reproach; untarnished; pure; spotless (*unblemished* reputation).

unblest, un•blest′, *a.* Not blest; excluded from benediction; hence, cursed; wretched; unhappy.

unblushing, un•blush′ing, *a.* Not blushing; destitute of shame; impudent.—**unblushingly,** un•blush′ing•li, *adv.* In an unblushing or shameless manner.

unbolt, un•bōlt′, *v.t.* To remove a bolt from; to unfasten; to open.—**unbolted,** un•bōlt′ed, *p.* and *a.* Freed from fastening by bolts; (in this sense of different origin) not bolted or sifted (*unbolted* meal).

unborn, un•born′, *a.* Not yet born; future; to come; never born or brought into existence.

unbosom, un•bu̇′zum, *v.t.* To reveal in confidence; to disclose, as one's secret opinions or feelings: often used with reflexive pronouns (to *unbosom himself*).

unbought, un•bạt′, *a.* Not bought; obtained without money or purchase.

unbound, un•bound′, *a.* Not bound; loose; not tied; not bound by a bookbinder; not bound by obligation or covenant; also, pret. of *unbind*.

unbounded, un•boun′ded, *a.* Having no bound or limit; unlimited in extent; very great; excessive.

unbrace, un•brās′, *v.t.* To remove the braces from; to free from tension; to loosen; to relax.

unbridle, un•brī′dl, *v.t.* To free from the bridle; to let loose.—**unbridled,** un•brī′dld, *p.* and *a.* Loosed from the bridle; hence, unrestrained; unruly; violent; licentious.

unbroken, un•brō′kn, *a.* Not broken; not violated; not subdued; not tamed and rendered tractable; not interrupted.

unbuckle, un•buk′l, *v.t.* To loose from buckles; to unfasten the buckle or buckles of.

unburden, un•bėr′dn, *v.t.* To rid of a load or burden; to relieve the mind or heart of, as by disclosing what lies heavy on it: with reflexive pronouns (to *unburden oneself*).

unburied, un•ber′id, *a.* Not buried; not interred.

unburnt, un•bėrnt′, *a.* Not burned; not consumed or injured by fire; not hardened in fire, as brick.

unbutton, un•but′n, *v.t.* To loose the buttons of.

uncanny, un•kan′i, *a.* [Scotch and occasional in English.] Not canny; eerie; mysterious; not of this world; of evil and supernatural character.

unceasing, un•sēs′ing, *a.* Not ceasing; not intermitting; continual.

unceremonious, un•ser′e•mō″ni•us, *a.* Not using ceremony or form; not ceremonious; familiar.—**unceremoniously,** un•ser′e•mō″ni•us•li, *adv.* In an unceremonious manner; without ceremony; informally.

uncertain, un•sėr′tin, *a.* Not certain; doubtful; not certainly known; ambiguous; not having certain knowledge; not sure; unreliable; not to be depended on; undecided; not having the mind made up; not steady; fitful; fickle; inconstant; capricious.—**uncertainly,** un•sėr′tin•li, *adv.* In an uncertain manner.—**uncertainty,** un•sėr′tin•ti, *n.* The quality or state of being uncertain; want of certainty; doubtfulness; state of doubting; dubiety; hesitation; something not certainly and exactly known; a contingency.

unchain, un•chān′, *v.t.* To free from chains or slavery; to let loose.

unchallenged, un•chal′enjd, *a.* Not challenged or called to account; not objected to; not called in question.

unchangeable, un•chān′ja•bl, *a.* Not capable of change; immutable; not subject to variation.—**unchanging,** un•chān′jing, *a.* Suffering no alteration; unalterable.

uncharitable, un•char′i•ta•bl, *a.* Not charitable; ready to think evil or impute bad motives; harsh; censorious; severe in judging.—**uncharitableness,** un•char′i•ta•bl•nes, *n.* The quality of being uncharitable.—**uncharitably,** un•char′i•ta•bli, *adv.* In a manner contrary to charity.

unchaste, un•chāst′, *a.* Not chaste; not continent; libidinous; lewd.—**unchastity,** un•chas′ti•ti, *n.* The quality of being unchaste; incontinence; lewdness.

unchristian, un•kris′chen, *a.* Contrary to the laws or opposed to the spirit of Christianity.

uncial, un′shi•al, *a.* [From L. *uncia*, an inch, the letters being about an inch long. OUNCE.] A term applied to letters of a large size used in ancient Latin and Greek manuscripts.—*n.* An uncial letter.

unciform, un′si•form, *a.* [L. *uncus*, a hook, and *forma*, form.] Hook-like; having a curved or hooked form.—**uncinate,** un′si•nāt, *a.* [L. *uncinatus.*] *Bot.* hooked at the end, as an awn.

uncircumcised, un•sėr′kum•sīzd, *a.* Not circumcised.—**uncircumcision,** un•sėr′kum•si″zhon, *n.* Absence or want of circumcision.

uncivil, un•siv′il, *a.* Not courteous; ill-mannered; rude; coarse.—**uncivilized,** un•siv′il•īzd, *a.* Not civilized or reclaimed from savage life; rude; barbarous; savage.

unclaimed, un•klāmd′, *a.* Not claimed; not demanded; not called for.

unclasp, un•klasp′, *v.t.* To loose or undo the clasp of; to open what is clasped.

uncle, ung′kl, *n.* [O.Fr. *uncle* (Fr. *oncle*), from L. *avunculus*, an uncle, a dim. of *avus*. a grandfather.] The brother of one's father or mother; also applied to the husband of one's aunt; pawnbroker (*colloq.*).

unclean, un•klēn′, *a.* Not clean; foul, dirty; filthy; morally impure; foul with sin; wicked; evil; ceremonially impure according to the Jewish law.—**uncleanly,** un•klen′li, *a.* Foul; filthy; dirty; indecent; unchaste; obscene.

uncloak, un•klōk′, *v.t.* To deprive of the cloak; to tear the disguise from; to unmask.

unclose, un•klōz′, *v.t.* To open; to disclose; to lay open.

unclothe, un•klōTH′, *v.t.* To strip of clothes; to make naked; to divest of covering.—**unclothed,** un•klōTHd′, *p.* and *a.* Stripped of clothing; not clothed; wanting clothes.

unclouded, un•kloud′ed, *a.* Free from clouds; free from gloom; clear.

uncoil, un•koil′, *v.t.* and *i.* To unwind or open, as the turns of a rope or a spiral spring; to open out its coils, as a snake.

uncollected, un•kol•lek′ted, *a.* Not collected; not received; not having one's thoughts collected.

uncolored, un•kul′ėrd, *a.* Not colored; not heightened in description.

uncomely, un•kum′li, *a.* Not comely; wanting grace; unbecoming.

uncomfortable, un•kum′fėr•ta•bl, *a.* Affording no comfort; causing bodily discomfort; giving uneasiness; uneasy; ill at ease.

uncommitted, un•kom•mit′ed, *a.* Not committed or done; not referred to a committee; not pledged by anything said or done.

uncommon, un•kom′on, *a.* Not common; infrequent; rare; remarkable; extraordinary.—**uncommonly,** un•kom′on•li, *adv.* Rarely; not usually; remarkably.

uncommunicative, un•kom•mū′ni•kā•tiv, *a.* Not apt to communicate to others; reserved.

uncompanionable, un•kom•pan′yon•a•bl, *a.* Not companionable or sociable.

uncomplaining, un•kom•plā′ning, *a.* Not complaining; not disposed to murmur or complain.

uncompromising, un•kom′pro•mī•zing, *a.* Not accepting of any compromise; not agreeing to terms; inflexible.

unconcern, un•kon•sėrn′, *n.* Want of concern; freedom from solicitude; cool and undisturbed state of mind.—**unconcerned,** un•kon•sėrnd′, *a.* Feeling no concern or solicitude; easy in mind; having or taking no interest; not affected.—**unconcernedly,** un•kon•sėrnd′li, *adv.* In an unconcerned manner; without anxiety; coolly.—**unconcernedness,** un•kon•sėrnd′nes, *n.*

unconditional, un•kon•dish′on•al, *a.* Not limited by any conditions; absolute; unreserved.—**unconditionally,** un•kon•dish′on•al•li, *adv.* Without terms or conditions.—**unconditioned,** un•kon•dish′end, *a. Metaph.* a word employed to designate that which has neither conditions, relations, nor limitations either as regards space or time; used commonly in the noun phrase *the unconditioned*, that is, the absolute, the infinite.

unconfined, un•kon•fīnd′, *a.* Not confined; free from restraint or control; not having narrow limits; wide and comprehensive.

unconfirmed, un•kon•fėrmd′, *a.* Not firmly established; not strengthened or established by additional testimony; not confirmed according to the church ritual.

unconformable, un•kon•for′ma•bl, *a.* Not consistent; *geol.* applied to strata whose planes do not lie parallel with those of the strata above or below but have a different inclination.

unconnected, un•kon•nek′ted, *a.* Not connected; separate; not coherent; not joined by proper transitions or dependence of parts; loose; rambling.

unconquerable, un•kong′kėr•a•bl, *a.* Not conquerable; not to be overcome in contest; incapable of being subdued or brought under control; insuperable.

unconscionable, un•kon′shon•a•bl, *a.* Not conscionable; exceeding the limits of any reasonable claim or expectation; inordinate; unreasonable (an *unconscionable* demand or claim).—**unconscionably,** un•kon′-shon•a•bli, *adv.*

unconscious, un•kon′shus, *a.* Not conscious; devoid of consciousness; having no mental perception; not knowing; not perceiving.—*Unconscious mind,* that part of the mind whose states and activity remain permanently out of consciousness; distinguished from conscious mind and subconscious mind.—**unconsciously,** un•kon′shus•li, *adv.* In an unconscious manner; without perception.—**unconsciousness,** un•kon′-shus•nes, *n.* The state of being unconscious; want of perception.

unconstitutional, un•kon′sti•tū″-shon•al, *a.* Not agreeable to the constitution of a country; contrary to the principles of the constitution.—**unconstitutionally,** un•kon′sti•tū″-shon•al•li, *adv.*

unconstrained, un•kon•strānd′, *a.* Free from constraint; voluntary; having no feeling that checks one's words or actions.

uncontested, un•kon•test′ed, *a.* Not contested; not disputed.

uncontrollable, un•kon•trōl′a•bl, *a.* That cannot be controlled, ruled, or restrained; ungovernable.

unconverted, un•kon•vėr′ted, *a.* Not converted; not turned from one faith to another.

unconvinced, un•kon•vinst′, *a.* Not convinced; not persuaded.—**unconvincing,** un•kon•vin′sing, *a.* Not sufficient to convince.

uncork, un•kork′, *v.t.* To draw the cork from.

uncorrected, un•ko•rek′ted, *a.* Not corrected; not revised; not reformed or amended; not chastised.

uncorrupted, un•ko•rup′ted, *a.* Not corrupted; not depraved.

uncouple, un•ku′pl, *v.t.* To loose, as dogs coupled together; to disjoin.

uncourteous, un•kėr′tē•us, *a.* Not courteous; uncivil; unpolite.

uncouth, un•köth′, *a.* [A.Sax. *uncúth,* unknown—*un,* not, and *cúth,* pp. of *cunnan,* to know. CAN.] Strange; odd in appearance; awkward; ungainly.—**uncouthly,** un•köth′li, *adv.* Oddly; strangely; awkwardly.—**uncouthness,** un•köth′nes, *n.* Oddness; strangeness.

uncovenanted, un•kuv′e•nan•ted, *a.* Not promised by covenant; not proceeding from the covenant made between God and his people through Christ; a theological term, as in the phrase *uncovenanted mercies*; that is, such mercies as God may be pleased to show to those not sharing in the covenant.

uncover, un•kuv′ėr, *v.t.* To remove a cover or covering from; to divest of a cover or covering; hence, to lay bare; to disclose.—*v.i.* To bare the head; to take off one's hat.—**uncovered,** un•kuv′ėrd, *p.* and *a.* Deprived of a cover; not provided with a cover or covering; bare; naked.

uncreated, un•krē•ā′ted, *p.* and *a.* Not yet created; not produced by creation.

uncrippled, un•krip′ld, *a.* Not crippled or lamed; not having the powers of motion, activity, usefulness, etc., impaired.

uncritical, un•krit′i•kal, *a.* Not critical; wanting in critical powers; not according to the rules of criticism.

uncrown, un•kroun′, *v.t.* To deprive of a crown; to dethrone.

unction, ungk′shon, *n.* [L. *unctio, unctionis,* from *ungo, unctum,* to anoint (whence *unguent, ointment, anoint*); same root as Skr. *anj,* to anoint.] The act of anointing or rubbing with an unguent, ointment, or oil; an unguent; a salve; *fig.* something soothing or lenitive; that quality in language, mode of address, or manner, which excites devotion or sympathy; religious fervor; sham devotional fervor; oiliness.—*Extreme unction.* See EXTREME.—**unctuous,** ungk′chụ•us, *a.* Of an oily or greasy character; fat and clammy; soapy; greasy or soapy to the feel when rubbed or touched by the fingers, a characteristic of steatite and other minerals; nauseously bland, sympathetic, devotional, or the like; oily; fawning.—**unctuously,** ungk′chụ•us•li, *adv.* In an unctuous manner.—**unctuousness, unctuosity,** ungk′-chụ•us•nes, ungk•chụ•os′i•ti, *n.* The state or quality of being unctuous.

uncultivated, un•kul′ti•vā•ted, *a.* Not cultivated or tilled; rough or rude in manners; not improved by labor, study, care, or the like.

uncurl, un•kėrl′, *v.t.* To straighten out, as something curled.—*v.i.* To fall from a curled state, as ringlets; to become straight.

uncut, un•kut′, *a.* Not cut; not cut open at the edges, as the leaves of a book.

undamaged, un•dam′ijd, *a.* Not damaged; not made worse.

undated, un•dā′ted, *a.* Not dated; having no date.

undaunted, un•dạn′ted, *a.* Not daunted; not depressed by fear; fearless; intrepid.—**undauntedly,** un•dạn′-ted•li, *adv.* In an undaunted manner; boldly; intrepidly.—**undauntedness,** un•dạn′ted•nes, *n.* Boldness; intrepidity.

undé, undē, *a. Her.* wavy.

undecagon, un•dek′a•gon, *n.* [L. *undecim,* eleven, and Gr. *gōnia,* an angle.] A hendecagon.

undeceive, un•di•sēv′, *v.t.* To free from deception, misapprehension, or mistake, whether caused by others or by ourselves; to open one's eyes.

undecided, un•di•sī′ded, *a.* Not decided or determined; not settled; not having the mind made up; hesitating; irresolute.

undecked, un•dekt′, *a.* Not having a deck (an *undecked* vessel).

undeclinable, un•di•klī′na•bl, *a.* Not to be declined; *gram.* indeclinable.

undefended, un•di•fen′ded, *a.* Not defended; being without works of defense; *law,* not characterized by a defense being put forward.

undefinable, un•di•fī′na•bl, *a.* Not definable; indefinable.—**undefined,** un•di•fīnd′, *a.* Not defined; not having its limits distinctly marked or seen.

undemonstrative, un•di•mon′stra•tiv, *a.* Not demonstrative; not apt to let the feelings betray themselves; reserved; cold in manner.

undeniable, un•di•nī′a•bl, *a.* Incapable of being denied; indisputable; evidently true.—**undeniably,** un•di•nī′a•bli, *adv.* Indisputably.

under, un′dėr, *prep.* [A.Sax. *under,* under, among = Sw. and Dan. *under,* Icel. *undir,* D. *onder,* G. *unter,* Goth. *undar*; cog. L. *inter,* Skr. *antar,* in the midst, under. The term. *-ter, -dar, -tar* is the compar. suffix, and the root portion is akin to the prepositions *in, on.*] In a lower place or position than; so as to be overtopped, overhung, or covered by; beneath; denoting a state of being loaded, oppressed, or distressed by; subject to the government, direction, instruction, or influence of; in a state of liability or limitation with respect to; inferior to in rank, social position, etc.; inferior to or less than with respect to number, quantity, value, etc.; falling short of; included in; in the same category, division, class, etc., as; with the character, pretext, or cover of; being the subject of (*under* discussion).—*Under arms,* fully armed and equipped so as to be ready for action.—*Under fire,* exposed to the enemy's shot; taking part in a battle or engagement.—*Underground,* below the surface of the ground.—*Under one's hand, signature, seal,* or the like, attested or confirmed by writing one's name, or by affixing a seal.—*Under sail,* having the sails unfurled or spread out to catch the wind; hence, in motion.—*Under the breath,* with a low voice; in a whisper; very softly.—*Under the rose,* in secret.—*Underwater,* below the surface of the water.—*Under way, naut.* having just weighed anchor or left moorings and making progress through the water.—*adv.* In a lower or subordinate condition or degree (to keep a person *under*).—*To knock under.* KNOCK.—*Under,* with its adverbial force, is frequently used as the first element of a compound with verbs and adjectives, when it denotes not sufficiently or imperfectly (*under*bred, *under*done); or it may have reference to literal inferiority of place (to *under*mine, etc.).—*a.* Lower in position, rank, or degree; subject; subordinate (*under* sheriff). *Under,* in this sense, is often used with nouns as the first element of a compound.

underagent, un•dėr•ā′jent, *n.* A subordinate agent.

underbid, un•dėr•bid′, *v.t.* To bid less than, as in auctions; to offer to execute work or the like at a lower price than.

underbred, un′dėr•bred, *a.* Of inferior breeding or manners; vulgar.

underbrush, un′dėr•brush, *n.* Shrubs and small trees in a wood, growing under large trees; undergrowth.

underbuy, un•dėr•bī′, *v.t.* To buy at a lower price than.

undercharge, un•dėr•chärj′, *v.t.* To charge less than a fair price for; to take too low a price from.—*n.* (un′dėr•chärj). Too low a charge or price.

underclothes, underclothing, un′dėr•klōTHz, un′dėr•klōTH•ing, *n.* Clothes worn under others or next the skin.

undercroft, un′dėr•kroft, *n.* [*Under,* and *croft,* a corruption of *crypt.*] A vault under the chancel of a church.

undercurrent, un′dėr•kur•ent, *n.* A current below the surface of the water; *fig.* an influence at work out of sight or not readily apparent.

underdeveloped, un′dėr•dē•vel″upd, *a.* Not properly developed; not achieving potential industrial ability (an *underdeveloped* country).

underdo, un•dėr•dö′, *v.t.* To do less thoroughly than is requisite.

underdog, un′dėr•dog, *n.* One who loses, or is predicted to lose, a contest; one who is not favored to win; one who is persecuted.

underestimate, un•dėr•es′ti•māt, *v.t.* To estimate at too low a rate.—*n.* An estimate at too low a rate.

underexpose, un′dėr•eks•pōs″, *v.t.* To expose (photographic film) for an insufficient length of time.—**underexposure,** un′dėr•eks•pō″zhėr, *n.*

undergo, un•dėr•gō′, *v.t.* To be subjected to; to experience (to *undergo* changes).

undergraduate, un•dėr•grad′ū•āt, *n.* A student or member of a university or college who has not taken his first degree.

underground, un′dėr•ground, *a.* Being below the surface of the ground.—*adv.* Beneath the surface of the earth.—*n.* A secret conspiratorial group usually organized for revolutionary purposes; a group organized secretly in an occupied or totalitarian country, especially in wartime.

undergrowth, un′dėr•grōth, *n.* Shrubs or small trees growing among large ones.

underhand, un′dėr•hand, *adv.* By secret means; in a clandestine manner and often with a bad design.—*a.* Working by stealth; clandestine.—**underhanded,** un′dėr•han•ded, *a.*

underhung, un′dėr•hung, *a.* Projecting beyond the upper jaw; applied to the under jaw.

underlaid, un•dėr•lād′, *p.* and *a.* Having something lying or laid beneath (sand *underlaid* with clay).

underlay, un•dėr•lā′, *v.t.* To lay beneath; to put under; to support by laying something under.

underlet, un•dėr•let′, *v.t.* To let below the value; to sublet.

underlie, un•dėr•lī′, *v.t.*—pret. *underlay,* pp. *underlain,* ppr. *underlying.* To lie beneath; to be situated under; to be at the basis of; to form the foundation of; to be subject or liable to.—*v.i.* To lie beneath.—**underlying,** un•dėr•lī′ing, *a.* Lying beneath or under; *geol.* applied to rocks or strata lying below others.

underline, un′dėr•līn, *v.t.* To mark underneath or below with a line; to underscore.

underling, un′dėr•ling, *n.* [*Under,* and term. *-ling.*] An inferior person or agent; a mean sorry fellow.

undermine, un•dėr•mīn′, *v.t.* To form a mine under; to sap; to make an excavation beneath, especially for the purpose of causing to fall, or of blowing up; *fig.* to subvert clandestinely; to injure by secret or dishonorable means.—**underminer,** un•dėr•mī′nėr, *n.*

undermost, un′dėr•mōst, *a.* Lowest in place, rank, or condition.

underneath, un•dėr•nēth′, *adv.* [*Under,* and *-neath,* as in *beneath.* NETHER.] Beneath; in a lower place.—*prep.* Under; beneath.

underpay, un•dėr•pā′, *v.t.* To pay insufficiently.

underpin, un•dėr•pin′, *v.t.* To pin or support underneath; to place something under for support or foundation when a previous support is removed.—**underpinning,** un•dėr•pin′ing, *n.* The act of one who underpins; the solid building or other supports introduced beneath a wall, etc., already constructed.

underplot, un′dėr•plot, *n.* A plot subordinate to another plot, as in a play or a novel; an underhand clandestine scheme.

underprivileged, un′dėr•priv″e•lejd, *a.* Deprived of certain rights or opportunities to which one is entitled.

underprop, un•dėr•prop′, *v.t.* To prop from beneath; to uphold.

underrate, un•dėr•rāt′, *v.t.* To rate too low; to undervalue.

underscore, un•dėr•skōr′, *v.t.* To underline or draw a line or lines under.

undersecretary, *n.* A secretary subordinate to the principal secretary.

undersell, un•dėr•sel′, *v.t.* To sell cheaper than.

undershoot, un′dėr•shöt, *v.t.* To shoot short of; to fail to reach in aiming at.—**undershot,** un′dėr•shot, *a.* Moved by water passing under, or acting on the lowest part: said of a water wheel, and opposed to *overshot.*

undershrub, un′dėr•shrub, *n.* A plant of shrubby habit, but scarcely attaining the dimensions of a shrub.

underside, un′dėr•sīd, *n.* The lower side or side underneath.

undersign, un•dėr•sīn′, *v.t.* To write one's name at the foot or end of; to subscribe.—**undersigned,** un•dėr•sīnd′, *p.* and *a.* Subscribed at the bottom or end.—*The undersigned,* the person or persons signing any document; the subscriber or subscribers.

undersized, un′dėr•sīzd, *a.* Being of a size or stature less than common; dwarfish.

undersoil, un′dėr•soil, *n.* Soil beneath the surface; subsoil.

undersong, un′dėr•song, *n.* The burden or accompaniment of a song; a subordinate strain.

understand, un•dėr•stand′, *v.t.*—pret. and pp. *understood,* formerly sometimes incorrectly *understanded.* [A.Sax. *understandan,* to understand, lit. to stand under—*under,* and *standan,* to stand; so O.Fris. *understonda,* Icel. *undirstanda.*] To apprehend or comprehend fully; to know or apprehend the meaning of; to perceive or discern by the mind; to have just and adequate ideas of; to comprehend; to see through; to be informed; to learn: governing a clause; to suppose to mean; to interpret (how do you *understand* it?); to take as meant or implied; to infer; to assume; to supply or leave to be supplied mentally; to recognize as implied or meant although not expressed.—*To give to understand, to let understand, to make understand,* to tell; to inform; to let know.—*v.i.* To have the use of the intellectual faculties; to have understanding; to be informed by another; to learn.—**understanding,** un•dėr•stan′ding, *a.* Knowing; skillful; intelligent.—*n.* The act of one who understands or comprehends; comprehension; apprehension and appreciation; discernment; intelligence between two or more persons; anything mutually understood or agreed upon; that power by which we perceive, conceive, and apprehend.

understate, un•dėr•stāt′, *v.t.* To state or represent less strongly than the truth will bear; to state too low.—**understatement,** un•dėr•stāt′ment, *n.* The act of understating; a statement under the truth.

understock, un•dėr•stok′ *v.t.* To supply insufficiently with stock (a farm).

understrapper, un′dėr•strap•ėr, *n.* [Comp. *strapper,* in local sense of groom.] A petty fellow; an inferior agent.

understratum, un′dėr•strā•tum, *n.* A substratum; subsoil.

understudy, un′dėr•stu•di, *n.* A player who makes a study of a theatrical part so as to be able to take it in the absence of the regular performer.

undertake, un•dėr•tāk′, *v.t.*—pret. *undertook,* pp. *undertaken,* ppr. *undertaking.* To take on one's self; to lay one's self under obligations to perform or execute; to pledge one's self to do; often with infinitives; to engage in; to take in hand; to set about; to attempt; to warrant; to answer for; to guarantee: often governing a clause (*undertook* that he would go).—**undertaker,** un•dėr•tā′kėr, *n.* One who undertakes any business.—(un″dėr•tāk′ėr). One who directs and provides things necessary for a funeral; one who has an undertaking establishment; a mortician.—**undertaking,** un•dėr•tāk′ing, *n.* That which a person undertakes; an enterprise; a promise; an engagement.—(un″dėr•tāk′ing). The business of an undertaker.

undertenant, un′dėr•ten•ant, *n.* The tenant of a tenant; one who holds lands or tenements of a tenant.

undertone, un′dėr•tōn, *n.* A low or subdued tone; a tone lower than is usual, as in speaking.

undertow, un′dėr•tō, *n.* A current of water below the surface in a different direction from that at the surface; the backward flow of a wave breaking on a beach.

undervalue, un•dėr•val′ū, *v.t.* To

value or estimate below the real worth; to esteem lightly; to despise; to hold in mean estimation.—**undervaluation,** un•dėr•val′ū•ā″shon. *n.* The act of undervaluing.

underwear, un′dėr•wâr, *n.* A wearing under the outer clothing.

underwent, un•dėr•went′, pret. of *undergo.*

underwood, un′dėr•wu̧d, *n.* Small trees and bushes that grow among large trees; coppice; underbrush.

underworld, un′dėr•wėrld, *n.* The lower world; the place of departed souls; Hades; the criminal element.

underwrite, un•dėr•rīt′, *v.t.* To write below or under; to subscribe; to subscribe or set one's name to a policy of insurance along with others, for the purpose of becoming answerable for loss or damage to a certain amount; to issue insurance on life, fire, theft, etc.—**underwriter,** un′dėr•rīt•ėr, *n.* A marine insurer; a person who practices the business of insuring anything, so called because he writes his name at the foot of the policy of insurance; one who insures subscriptions to stocks, bonds, etc.—**underwriting,** un′dėr•rīt•ing, *n.*

undeserved, un•di•zėrvd′, *a.* Not deserved; not merited.—**undeserving,** un•di•zėr′ving, *a.* Not deserving; not having merit.

undesigned, un•di•zīnd′, *a.* Not intended; unintentional.—**undesigning,** un•di•zīn′ing, *a.* Not having any underhand design; not having any hidden motive.

undesirable, un•di•zī′ra•bl, *a.* Not desirable; not to be wished.

undetermined, un•di•tėr′mind, *a.* Not determined; not decided, fixed, or settled.

undeviating, un•dē′vi•ā•ting, *a.* Not departing from a rule, principle, or purpose; steady; regular.

undigested, un•di•jes′ted, *a.* Not digested; not acted on or prepared by the stomach; not properly prepared by the stomach; not properly prepared or arranged; crude.

undignified, un•dig′ni•fīd, *a.* Not dignified; not consistent with dignity.

undiluted, un•di•lū′ted, *a.* Not diluted or mixed with water; not tempered with any admixture.

undine, un•dēn′, *n.* [From L. *unda,* a wave.] A water-spirit of the female sex, resembling in character the sylphs or spirits of the air, and corresponding somewhat to the naiads of classical mythology.

undiscernible, un•diz•zėr′ni•bl, *a.* That cannot be discerned or discovered; invisible.—**undiscerning,** un•diz•zėr′ning, *a.* Not discerning; wanting judgment or discrimination.

undischarged, un•dis•chärjd′, *a.* Not discharged; not freed from obligation.

undisciplined, un•dis′si•plind, *a.* Not disciplined; not properly trained; raw.

undiscoverable, un•dis•kuv′ėr•a•bl, *a.* That cannot be discovered or found out.—**undiscovered,** un•dis•kuv′ėrd, *a.* Not discovered; not laid open to view; lying hid.

undiscriminating, un•dis•krim′i•nā•ting, *a.* Not discriminating or distinguishing; disregarding or not perceiving differences.

undisguised, un•dis•gīzd′, *a.* Not disguised; not covered with a mask; hence, open; candid; artless.

undismayed, un•dis•mād′, *a.* Not dismayed; not disheartened by fear; undaunted.

undisposed, un•dis•pōzd′, *a.* Not set apart; not allocated; not appropriated; with *of* (goods *undisposed of*).

undisputed, un•dis•pū′ted, *a.* Not disputed; not called in question.

undissolvable, un•diz•zol′va•bl, *a.* Incapable of being dissolved or melted; incapable of being loosened or broken.—**undissolved,** un•diz•zolvd′, *a.* Not dissolved; not melted; not loosened, broken, etc.

undistinguishable, un•dis•ting′gwish•a•bl, *a.* Incapable of being distinguished by the eye; not to be distinctly seen; not to be known or distinguished by the intellect by any peculiar property.—**undistinguished,** un•dis•ting′gwisht, *a.* Not having any distinguishing mark; not treated with any particular respect; not famous; not distinguished by any particular eminence.

undisturbed, un•dis•tėrbd′, *a.* Free from interruption; not molested or hindered; calm; tranquil; not agitated.

undiversified, un•di•vėr′si•fīd, *a.* Not diversified or varied; uniform.

undivided, un•di•vī′ded, *a.* Not divided; unbroken; whole (one's *undivided* attention).

undo, un•dö′, *v.t.*—pret. *undid;* pp. *undone.* [With *un-* in sense of reversal. UN.] To reverse, as something which has been done; to annul; to untie or unfasten; to unravel; to open out; to bring ruin or distress upon; to ruin the morals, reputation, or prospects of; to destroy; to impoverish.—**undoer,** un•dö′ėr, *n.* One who undoes; one who reverses what has been done; one who ruins.—**undoing,** un•dö′ing, *n.* The reversal of what has been done; ruin; destruction.—**undone,** un•dun′, *pp.* Untied or unfastened, reversed; ruined.

undo, un•dö′, *v.t.* [With *un-,* not.] To leave unperformed.—**undone,** un′dun, *pp.* Not done or performed.

undoubted, un•dou′ted, *a.* Not doubted; not called in question; indubitable; indisputable.—**undoubtedly,** un•dou′ted•li, *adv.* Without question; indubitably.—**undoubting,** un•dou′ting, *a.* Not doubting; not hesitating respecting facts; not fluctuating in uncertainty.

undraw, un•dra̧′, *v.t.* To draw aside or open.

undreamed, undreamt, un•drēmd′, un•dremt′, *a.* Not dreamed; not thought of; not imagined; often followed by *of.*

undress, un•dres′, *v.t.* To divest of clothes; to strip; to disrobe; to take the dressing or bandages from.—*v.i.* To take off one's dress or clothes.—*n.* (un′dres). A loose negligent dress; also, ordinary dress, as opposed to full dress or uniform.—**undressed,** un•drest′, *p.* and *a.* Divested of dress; not attired; not prepared; in a raw state.

undrinkable, un•dring′ka•bl, *a.* Not drinkable; not fit for drinking.

undue, un•dū′, *a.* Not due; not yet demandable by right (a debt, money); not right; not lawful; improper; unworthy; erring by excess; excessive; inordinate (an *undue* attachment to forms).—**unduly,** un•dū′li, *adv.* Improperly; unlawfully; unwarrantably; inordinately.

undulate, un′dū•lāt, *v.i.*—*undulated, undulating.* [L.L. *undulo, undulatum,* from L. *undula,* a little wave, dim. of *unda,* a wave (seen also in *inundate, abundant, abound, redundant,* etc.); from a root seen also in E. *water.*] To have a wavy motion; to rise and fall in waves; to move in curving or bending lines; to wave.—*v.t.* To cause to wave, or move with a wavy motion.—**undulate, undulated,** un′dū•lāt, un′dū•lā•ted, *a.* Wavy; having a waved surface.—**undulation,** un•dū•lā′shon, *n.* The act of undulating; a waving motion; a wavy form; *physics,* a vibratory motion transmitted through some fluid medium by impulses communicated to the medium; any one vibration of such fluid.—**undulatory,** un′dū•la•to•ri, *a.* Having an undulating character; moving in the manner of waves; pertaining to such a motion.—*Undulatory theory,* the theory which regards light as the effect on the eye of vibrations propagated from a luminous source by undulations in the subtle medium (ether) presumed to pervade all space.

unduly. See UNDUE.

undutiful, un•dū′ti•fu̧l, *a.* Not dutiful; not performing or not in accordance with duty; disobedient; rebellious; irreverent.

undying, un•dī′ing, *a.* Not dying; not subject to death; immortal.

unearned, un•ėrnd′, *a.* Not merited by labor or services.—*Unearned increment,* the increase in the value of land not due to any expenditure on the part of the owner, as when it arises from growth of population.

unearth, un•ėrth′, *v.t.* To drive or bring forth from an earth or burrow; to bring to light; to discover or find out.—**unearthly,** un•ėrth′li, *a.* Not earthly; not terrestrial; supernatural; weird.

uneasy, un•ē′zi, *a.* Feeling some degree of pain either mental or physical; unquiet; troubled; anxious; constrained; cramped; stiff; awkward; causing constraint, discomfort, or want of ease; irksome.—**uneasily,** un•ē′zi•li, *adv.* In an uneasy manner.—**uneasiness,** un•ē′zi•nes, *n.* The state of being uneasy; want of ease or comfort, physical or mental.

uneatable, un•ē′ta•bl, *a.* Not eatable; not fit to be eaten.

unedified, un•ed′i•fīd, *a.* Not edified.—**unedifying,** un•ed′i•fī•ing, *a.* Not edifying; not improving to the mind; not beneficial morally.

uneducated, un•ed′ū•kā•ted, *a.* Not educated; illiterate.
unembarrassed, un•em•bar′ast, *a.* Not embarrassed; not perplexed or put to some confusion of feeling; free from pecuniary difficulties.
unembellished, un•em•bel′isht, *a.* Not embellished.
unemotional, un•i•mō′shon•al, *a.* Not emotional; free from emotion or feeling; impassive.
unemphatic, un•em•fat′ik, *a.* Not emphatic; having no emphasis or stress of voice.
unemployed, un•em•ploid′, *n.* Not employed; having no work or occupation; at leisure; not being in use.—*The unemployed,* working people who are out of work.
unending, un•en′ding, *a.* Not ending; having no end; perpetual; eternal.
unendurable, un•en•dū′ra•bl, *a.* Not to be endured; intolerable.
unengaged, un•en•gājd′, *a.* Not engaged; free from obligation to any person; free from attachment that binds; disengaged; unoccupied; not busy.
unenlightened, un•en•lī′tend, *a.* Not enlightened; not mentally or morally illuminated.
unenterprising, un•en′tėr•prī•zing, *a.* Not enterprising; not adventurous.
unentertaining, un•en′tėr•tā•ning, *a.* Not entertaining or amusing.
unenviable, un•en′vi•a•bl, *a.* Not enviable; not to be envied or viewed with envy (an *unenviable* notoriety).—**unenvied,** un•en′vid, *a.* Not envied; exempt from envy.
unequal, un•ē′kwal, *a.* Not equal; not of the same size, length, breadth, quantity, quality, strength, talents, age, station; inadequate; insufficient; not equable or uniform.—**unequaled,** un•ē′kwald, *a.* Not to be equaled; unparalleled; unrivaled.—**unequally,** un•ē′kwal•li, *adv.* In an unequal manner or degree.
unequivocal, un•i•kwiv′o•kal, *a.* Not equivocal; not doubtful; clear; evident; not ambiguous.—**unequivocally,** un•i•kwiv′o•kal•li, *adv.* In an unequivocal manner.
unerring, un•ėr′ing, *a.* Committing no mistake; incapable of error; incapable of missing the mark; certain.—**unerringly,** un•ėr′ing•li, *adv.* In an unerring manner.
unessential, un•es•sen′shal, *a.* Not essential; not constituting the real essence; not absolutely necessary; not of prime importance.—*n.* Something not essential or of absolute necessity.
uneven, un•ē′vn, *a.* Not level, smooth, or plain; rough; not straight; crooked; not uniform or equable; changeable; not fair, just, or true; *arith.* odd; not divisible by 2 without a remainder.—**unevenly,** un•ē′vn•li, *adv.* In an uneven manner.—**unevenness,** un•ē′vn•nes, *n.* The state or quality of being uneven; inequality of surface; want of uniformity; variableness.
unexceptionable, un•ek•sep′shon•a•bl, *a.* Not liable to any exception or objection; unobjectionable; faultless; excellent; admirable.—**unexceptionably,** un•ek•sep′shon•a•bli, *adv.* In an unexceptionable manner; perfectly; admirably.
unexecuted, un•ek′si•kū•ted, *a.* Not executed; not performed; not having the proper attestations or forms that give validity.
unexhausted, un•egz•has′ted, *a.* Not exhausted; not spent or used up; not worn out with fatigue.
unexpected, un•eks•pek′ted, *a.* Not expected; not looked for; unforeseen; sudden.—**unexpectedly,** un•eks•pek′ted•li, *adv.* At a time or in a manner not expected or looked for; suddenly.
unexpired, un•eks•pīrd′, *a.* Not having come to an end or termination; not having reached the date at which it is due (an *unexpired* promissory note or bill).
unexplored, un•eks•plōrd′, *a.* Not explored; not examined by any traveler.
unfading, un•fā′ding, *a.* Not liable to fade; not losing strength or freshness of coloring; not liable to wither or to decay.
unfailing, un•fā′ling, *a.* Not liable to fail; ever fulfilling a hope, promise, or want; sure; certain.
unfair, un•fâr′, *a.* Not fair; not honest; not impartial; disingenuous; using trick or artifice; proceeding from trick or dishonesty.—**unfairly,** un•fâr′li, *adv.* In an unfair or unjust manner.—**unfairness,** un•fâr′nes, *n.* The character of being unfair; injustice; bias.
unfaithful, un•fāth′ful, *a.* Not observant of promises, vows, allegiance, or duty; faithless; violating trust or confidence; violating the wedding vow.—**unfaithfully,** un•fāth′ful•li, *adv.* In an unfaithful manner.—**unfaithfulness,** un•fāth′ful•nes, *n.* The quality of being unfaithful.
unfamiliar, un•fa•mil′yėr, *a.* Not familiar; not well known by frequent use; having an element of strangeness.—**unfamiliarity,** un•fa•mil′i•ar″i•ti, *n.* The state of being unfamiliar.
unfashionable, un•fash′on•a•bl, *a.* Not according to the prevailing fashion or mode; not complying in dress or manners with the reigning custom.
unfasten, un•fas′n, *v.t.* To loose; to unbind; to untie.
unfathered, un•fä′THėrd, *a.* Having no father; fatherless; having no acknowledged father.
unfathomable, un•faTH′um•a•bl, *a.* Incapable of being fathomed or sounded; too deep to be measured.
unfavorable, un•fā′vėr•a•bl, *a.* Not favorable; not propitious; discouraging; giving an adverse judgment or opinion; somewhat prejudicial.—**unfavorably,** un•fā′vėr•a•bli, *adv.* In an unfavorable manner; adversely; with some censure.
unfeeling, un•fē′ling, *a.* Devoid of feeling; insensible; without sensibility; devoid of sympathy with others; hard-hearted.—**unfeelingly,** un•fē′ling•li, *adv.* In an unfeeling or cruel manner.
unfeigned, un•fānd′, *a.* Not feigned; not counterfeit; not hypocritical; real; sincere.—**unfeignedly,** un•fā′ned•li, *adv.* In an unfeigned manner.
unfelt, un•felt′, *a.* Not felt; not perceived.
unfeminine, un•fem′in•in, *a.* Not feminine; not according to the female character or manners.
unfenced, un•fenst′, *a.* Having no fence.
unfermented, un•fėr•men′ted, *a.* Not fermented; not having undergone fermentation, as liquor; not leavened or made with yeast, as bread.
unfetter, un•fet′ėr, *v.t.* To loose from fetters; to unchain; to unshackle; to free from restraint; to set at liberty.—**unfettered,** un•fet′ėrd, *a.* Unshackled; free from restraint; unrestrained.
unfilial, un•fil′i•al, *a.* Unsuitable to a son or daughter; not becoming a child.
unfinished, un•fin′isht, *a.* Not finished; not complete; imperfect; wanting the last hand or touch.
unfit, un•fit′, *a.* Not fit; improper; unsuitable; unbecoming; said of things; wanting suitable qualifications, physical or moral; not suited or adapted; not competent; of persons.—*v.t.* To render unfit; to make unsuitable; to deprive of the strength, skill, or proper qualities for anything.—**unfitly,** un•fit′li, *adv.* In an unfit manner; not properly; unsuitably.—**unfitness,** un•fit′nes, *n.* The quality of being unfit.—**unfitting,** un•fit′ing, *a.* Improper; unbecoming.
unfix, un•fiks′, *v.t.* To make no longer fixed or firm; to loosen from any fastening; to detach; to unsettle.
unflagging, un•flag′ing, *a.* Not flagging; not drooping; maintaining strength or spirit.
unflattering, un•flat′ėr•ing, *a.* Not flattering; not coloring the truth to please; not affording a favorable prospect.
unfledged, un•flejd′, *a.* Not yet furnished with feathers; not having attained to full growth or experience.
unflinching, un•flinch′ing, *a.* Not flinching; not shrinking.
unfold, un•fōld′, *v.t.* To open the folds of; to expand; to spread out; to lay open to view or contemplation; to disclose; to reveal.—*v.i.* To become gradually expanded; to open out; to become disclosed or developed; to develop itself.
unforced, un•fōrst′, *a.* Not forced or compelled; not constrained; not feigned; not artificially assumed or heightened; not strained; easy; natural.
unforeseen, un•fōr•sēn′, *a.* Not foreseen; not foreknown.—*The unforeseen,* that which is not foreseen or expected.
unforgivable, un•for•giv′a•bl, *a.* Incapable of being forgiven; unpardonable.—**unforgiven,** un•for•giv′n, *a.* Not forgiven; not pardoned.—**unforgiving,** un•for•giv′ing, *a.* Not forgiving; not disposed to overlook or pardon offenses; implacable.

unforgotten, un•for•got′n, *a.* Not forgot; not lost to memory; not overlooked; not neglected.
unformed, un•formd′, *p.* and *a.* Not having been formed; not fashioned; not molded into regular shape.
unfortified, un•for′ti•fīd, *a.* Not fortified; not having fortifications; not strengthened by means of adventitious spirit, as wine.
unfortunate, un•for′che•nit, *a.* Not successful; not prosperous; unlucky; unhappy.—*n.* One who is unfortunate; a woman who has lapsed from virtue; a prostitute.—**unfortunately,** un•for′che•nit•li, *adv.* In an unfortunate manner; by ill fortune; unhappily.
unfounded, un•foun′ded, *a.* Having no real foundation; groundless; idle; baseless.
unfree, un•frē′, *a.* Not free; in bondage.
unfrequent, un•frē′kwent, *a.* Not frequent; infrequent.—**unfrequented,** un•fri•kwen′ted, *a.* Rarely visited; seldom resorted to by human beings; solitary.
unfriended, un•fren′ded, *a.* Wanting friends; not countenanced or supported.—**unfriendliness,** un•frend′li•nes, *n.* The quality of being unfriendly; want of kindness; disfavor.—**unfriendly,** un•frend′li, *a.* Not friendly; not kind or benevolent; not favorable.—*adv.* In an unkind manner; not as a friend.
unfrock, un•frok′, *v.t.* To deprive or divest of a frock; hence, to deprive of the character and privileges of a priest or clergyman.
unfruitful, un•fröt′fu̧l, *a.* Not producing fruit or offspring; barren; unproductive; not fertile (an *unfruitful* soil); not productive of good (an *unfruitful* life); fruitless; ineffectual.—**unfruitfulness,** un•fröt′fu̧l•nes, *n.* The quality of being unfruitful.
unfulfilled, un•fu̧l•fild′, *a.* Not fulfilled; not accomplished.
unfunded, un•fun′ded, *a.* Not funded; having no permanent fund established for the payment of its interest; said of government debt when it exists in the form of treasury notes or the like.
unfurl, un•fėrl′, *v.t.* To loose from a furled state; to expand to the wind.
unfurnish, un•fėr′nish, *v.t.* To strip of furniture; to strip in general.—**unfurnished,** un•fėr′nisht, *a.* Not furnished; not supplied with furniture; unsupplied; unprovided in general.
ungainly, un•gān′li, *a.* [From *un-*, not, and old *gainly*, *geinly*, from Icel. *gegn*, ready, serviceable; akin to *-gain* in *again*.] Clumsy; awkward; uncouth; ill-shaped in person.—**ungainliness,** un•gān′li•nes, *n.* The state or character of being ungainly; clumsiness; awkwardness.
ungallant, un•gal′ant, *a.* Not gallant; uncourtly to ladies.
ungathered, un•gaᴛʜ′ėrd, *a.* Not gathered; not culled; not picked.
ungenerous, un•jen′ėr•us, *a.* Not generous; not showing generosity or liberality of mind or sentiments; illiberal; mean.—**ungenerously,** un•jen′ėr•us•li, *adv.* In an ungenerous manner; illiberally.
ungentle, un•jen′tl, *a.* Not gentle; harsh; rude.
ungentlemanly, un•jen′tl•men•li, *a.* Not becoming a gentleman; such as no gentleman would do.
ungifted, un•gif′ted, *a.* Not gifted; not endowed with peculiar faculties.
ungird, un•gėrd′, *v t.* To loose or free from a girdle or band; to divest of a girdle or what is girt on; to unbind.
unglazed, un•glāzd′, *a.* Not furnished with glass (as windows); wanting glass windows; not covered with vitreous matter (*unglazed* pottery).
unglue, un•glö′, *v.t.* To separate, as anything that is glued or cemented.
ungodly, un•god′li, *a.* Not godly; careless of God; godless; wicked; impious; sinful.—**ungodliness,** un•god′li•nes, *n.* Impiety; wickedness.
ungovernable, un•guv′ėr•na•bl, *a.* Incapable of being governed, ruled, or restrained; refractory; unruly; wild; unbridled.—**ungoverned,** un•guv′ėrnd, *a.* Not governed; unbridled; licentious.
ungraceful, un•grās′fu̧l, *a.* Not graceful; wanting grace and elegance; inelegant; clumsy.—**ungracefully,** un•grās′fu̧l•li, *adv.* In an ungraceful manner; awkwardly; inelegantly.—**ungracefulness,** un•grās′fu̧l•nes, *n.* The quality of being ungraceful.
ungracious, un•grā′shus, *a.* Unmannerly; rude; not well received; not favored.—**ungraciously,** un•grā′shus•li, *adv.* In an ungracious manner.—**ungraciousness,** un•grā′shus•nes, *n.* State of being ungracious.
ungrammatical, un•gram•mat′i•kal, *a.* Not according to the rules of grammar.—**ungrammatically,** un•gram•mat′i•kal•li, *adv.* In a manner contrary to the rules of grammar.
ungrateful, un•grāt′fu̧l, *a.* Not grateful; not feeling thankful or showing gratitude; making ill returns for kindness; unpleasing; unacceptable; disagreeable; harsh.—**ungratefully,** un•grāt′fu̧l•li, *adv.* In an ungrateful manner.—**ungratefulness,** un•grāt′fu̧l•nes, *n.* The state or character of being ungrateful; ingratitude.
ungrounded, un•groun′ded, *a.* Having no foundation or support; groundless; baseless; unfounded.
ungrudging, un•gruj′ing, *a.* Not grudging; freely giving; liberal; hearty.
ungual, ung′gwal, *a.* [From L. *unguis*, a nail, claw, or hoof.] Pertaining to a nail, claw, or hoof; having a nail, claw, or hoof.—**unguiculate,** ung•gwik′ū•lāt. Clawed; having claws.
unguarded, un•gär′ded, *a.* Not guarded; having no guard or watch; not being on one's guard; not attentive to danger; not cautious; negligent; not done or spoken with caution.
unguent, ung′gwent, *n.* [L. *unguentum*, from *ungo*, to anoint. UNCTION.] Any soft composition used as an ointment, or for the lubrication of machinery.
unguided, un•gī′ded, *a.* Not guided, led, or conducted; not regulated; ungoverned.
unguis, ung′gwis, *n.* pl. **ungues,** ung′gwēz. [L., nail or claw.] A nail, claw, or hoof of an animal. *Bot.* a claw-like portion of a petal.
ungula, ung′gū•la, *n.* [L. *ungula*, a hoof, dim. of *unguis*, a nail or claw. UNGUAL.] A hoof, as of a horse; *geom.* a part cut from a cylinder, cone, etc., by a plane passing obliquely through the base and part of the curved surface; so named from its shape.—**Ungulata,** ung•gū•lā′ta, *n. pl.* The hoofed quadrupeds, a large and important order of the Mammalia, including the pig, horse, rhinoceros, etc., in one section; and the ox, sheep, deer, and all other ruminants in another. ARTIODACTYL, PERISSODACTYL.—**ungulate,** ung′gū•lāt, *n.* A hoofed quadruped; one of the order Ungulata or hoofed animals.—*a.* Hoof-shaped; having hoofs.
unhackneyed, un•hak′nid, *a.* Not hackneyed; not stale, flat, or commonplace from frequent use or repetition.
unhallowed, un•hal′ōd, *a.* Not hallowed, consecrated, or dedicated to sacred purposes; unholy; profane; impious.
unhampered, un•ham′pėrd, *a.* Not hampered, hindered, or restricted.
unhand, un•hand′, *v.t.* To take the hand or hands from; to release from a grasp; to let go.
unhandily. See UNHANDY.
unhandsome, un•hand′sum, *a.* Not handsome; not well formed; not beautiful; not generous or liberal; unfair; mean; unbecoming.
unhandy, un•han′di, *a.* Not handy; not dexterous; not skillful and ready in the use of the hands; not convenient; awkward.—**unhandily,** un•han′di•li, *adv.* In an unhandy manner.
unhanged, un•hangd′, *a.* Not hung or hanged; not punished by hanging.
unhappy, un•hap′i, *a.* Not happy; not cheerful or gay; in some degree miserable or wretched; marked by ill fortune or mishap; ill-omened; evil.—**unhappily,** un•hap′i•li, *adv.* In an unhappy manner; unfortunately; by ill fortune; as ill luck would have it.—**unhappiness,** un•hap′i•nes, *n.* The state of being unhappy; misfortune; ill luck.
unharmed, un•härmd′, *a.* Not harmed or injured.
unhealthy, un•hel′thi, *a.* Wanting health; not sound and vigorous of body; habitually weak or indisposed; wanting vigor of growth; unfavorable to the preservation of health (an *unhealthy* season or city); adapted to generate disease; unwholesome; insalubrious (an *unhealthy* climate); not indicating health; resulting from bad health; morbid.—**unhealthily,** un•hel′thi•li, *adv.* In an unwholesome or unsound manner.—**unhealthiness,** un•hel′thi•nes, *n.* The state or quality of being unhealthy.
unheard, un•hėrd′, *a.* Not heard; not perceived by the ear; not admitted

to audience.—*Unheard-of,* unprecedented; such as was never known before; not known to fame; not celebrated.

unheeded, un•hē'ded, *a.* Not heeded; disregarded; neglected; unnoticed. —**unheedful,** un•hēd'fu̦l, *a.* Not heedful; unheeding; not cautious; inattentive; careless; inconsiderate. —**unheeding,** un•hē'ding, *a.* Not heeding; careless; negligent.

unhesitating, un•hez'i•ta•ting, *a.* Not hesitating; not remaining in doubt; prompt; ready.

unhinge, un•hinj', *v.t.* To take from the hinges; to unsettle; to render unstable or wavering; to discompose or disorder (the mind, opinions); to put quite out of sorts; to incapacitate by disturbing the nerves.

unhitch, un•hich', *v.t.* To disengage from a fastening.

unholy, un•hō'li, *a.* Not holy; not sacred; not hallowed or consecrated; impious; wicked.—**unholily,** un•hō'li•li, *adv.* In an unholy manner.—**unholiness,** un•hō'li•nes, *n.* The quality or state of being unholy.

unhonored, un•on'ėrd, *a.* Not honored; not regarded with veneration; not celebrated.

unhook, un•hu̦k', *v.t.* To loose from a hook; to undo the hook or hooks of.

unhoped, un•hōpt', *a.* Not hoped for; not so probable as to excite hope.—*Unhoped for,* unhoped; not hoped for.

unhorse, un•hors', *v.t.* To throw or strike from a horse; to cause to fall from the saddle; to remove the horse or horses from.

unhouse, un•houz', *v.t.* To drive from the house or habitation; to deprive of shelter.—**unhoused,** un•houzd', *p.* and *a.* Having no house or home; deprived of a house, home, roof, or shelter.

unhouseled,‡ unhouselled,‡ un•hou'zeld, *a.* [HOUSEL.] Not having received the sacrament. (*Shak.*)

unhurt, un•hėrt', *a.* Not hurt; not harmed; free from wound or injury. —**unhurtful,** un•hėrt'fu̦l, *a.* Not hurtful.

Uniat, ū'ni•at, *n.* One of the Oriental Christian Churches, which, while having its own religious forms, recognizes unity under Papal supremacy.

uniaxial, ū•ni•ak'si•al, *a.* [L. *unus,* one, and *axis.*] Having but one axis.

unicameral, ū•ni•kam'ėr•al, *a.* [L. *unus,* one, *camera,* a chamber.] Consisting of a single chamber; said of a legislative body.

unicellular, ū•ni•sel'ū•lėr, *a.* [L. *unus,* one, and E. *cellular.*] Consisting of a single cell; exhibiting only a single cell.

unicorn, ū'ni•korn, *n.* [L. *unicornis,* onehorned—*unus,* one, and *cornu,* horn.] An animal with one horn; a fabulous animal having the head, neck, and body of a horse, the legs of a deer, the tail of a lion, and a long horn growing out of the forehead.—*Sea unicorn,* the narwal or narwhal.

unicostate, ū•ni•kos'tāt, *a.* [L. *unus,* one, and *costa,* a rib.] *Bot.* having one large vein running down the center called the *midrib.*

unific, ū•nif'ik, *a.* [L. *unus,* one, and *facio,* to make.] Making one; forming unity.—**unification,** ū'ni•fi•kā"shon, *n.* The act of uniting into one.

unifilar, ū•ni•fī'lėr, *a.* [L. *unus,* one, and *filum,* a thread.] Having only one thread: applied to a magnetometer consisting of a magnetic bar suspended by a single thread.

uniflorous, ū•ni•flō'rus, *a.* [L. *unus,* one, and *flos, floris,* flower.] *Bot.* bearing one flower only.

uniform, ū'ni•form, *a.* [Fr. *uniforme,* L. *uniformis—unus,* one, and *forma,* form.] Having always the same form; not changing in shape, appearance, character, etc.; not varying in degree or rate; equable; invariable; of the same kind or matter all through; homogeneous; consistent at all times; conforming to one rule or mode.—*n.* A dress of the same kind, fabrics, fashion, or general appearance as others worn by the members of the same body, whether military, naval, or any other, intended as a distinctive costume.—**uniformity,** ū•ni•for'mi•ti, *n.* The state or character of being uniform; a state of matters in which sameness is exhibited; freedom from variation or difference; conformity to one type.—*Act of uniformity,* in *Eng. hist.* an act of parliament passed in the reign of Charles II (1662) regulating the form of worship to be observed in all the churches.—**uniformly,** ū'ni•form•li, *adv.* In a uniform manner; invariably.—**uniformness,** ū'ni•form•nes, *n.* State of being uniform; uniformity.

unify, ū'ni•fī, *v.t.* [L. *unus,* one, and *facio,* to make.] To form into one; to reduce to unity; to view as one.—**unification,** ū'ni•fi•kā"shon, *n.* The act of unifying.

unilateral, ū•ni•lat'ėr•al, *a.* [L. *unus,* one, and *latus, lateris,* side.] One-sided; pertaining to one side; *bot.* growing chiefly to one side.

unilluminated, un•il•lū'mi•nā•ted, *a.* Not illuminated; not enlightened; dark; ignorant.

unilocular, ū•ni•lok'ū•lėr, *a.* [L. *unus,* one, and *loculus,* cell, dim. of *locus,* a place.] Having one cell or chamber only; not divided into cells (a *unilocular* pericarp).

unimaginable, un•im•aj'i•na•bl, *a.* Not capable of being imagined, conceived, or thought of; inconceivable.

unimpaired, un•im•pârd', *a.* Not impaired; not diminished; not enfeebled by time or injury.

unimpassioned, un•im•pash'end, *a.* Not impassioned; not moved or actuated by passion; calm; tranquil; not violent.

unimpeachable, un•im•pēch'a•bl, *a.* Not impeachable; not to be called in question; blameless; irreproachable.

unimportance, un•im•por'tans, *n.* Want of importance or consequence. —**unimportant,** un•im•por'tant, *a.* Not important; not of great moment.

unimposing, un•im•pō'zing, *a.* Not imposing; not commanding respect or awe.

unimpressible, un•im•pres'i•bl, *a.* Not impressible; not sensitive; apathetic.

unimproved, un•im•prövd', *a.* Not made better or wiser; not used for a valuable purpose; not tilled; not cultivated.

unincorporated, un•in•kor'po•rā•ted, *a.* Not incorporated; not mixed or united in one body; not associated or united in one body politic.

uninhabitable, un•in•hab'i•ta•bl, *a.* Not inhabitable; unfit to be the residence of men.—**uninhabited,** un•in•hab'i•ted, *a.* Not inhabited; having no inhabitants.

uninjured, un•in'ju̦rd, *a.* Not injured; not hurt; suffering no harm.

uninspired, un•in•spīrd', *a.* Not having received any supernatural instruction or illumination; not produced under the direction or influence of inspiration.

uninstructed, un•in•struk'ted, *a.* Not instructed or taught; not educated; not furnished with instructions.—**uninstructive,** un•in•struk'tiv, *a.* Not serving to instruct or improve the mind.

unintelligent, un•in•tel'i•jent, *a.* Not having reason or understanding; not having the mental faculties acute; not showing intelligence; dull. —**unintelligibility,** un•in•tel'i•ji•bil•i•ti, *n.* The quality of being not intelligible.—**unintelligible,** un•in•tel'i•ji•bl, *a.* Not intelligible; not capable of being understood; meaningless.—**unintelligibly,** un•in•tel'i•ji•bli, *adv.* In an unintelligible manner.

unintentional, un•in•ten'shon•al, *a.* Not intentional; done or happening without design.—**unintentionally,** un•in•ten'shon•al•li, *adv.* Without design or purpose.

uninterested, un•in'tėr•es•ted, *a.* Not interested; not personally concerned; not having the mind or feelings engaged.—**uninteresting,** un•in'tėr•es•ting, *a.* Not capable of exciting an interest, or of engaging the mind or passions.

unintermitted, un•in'tėr•mit"ed, *a.* Not intermitted; not suspended for a time; continuous.—**unintermitting,** un•in'tėr•mit"ing, *a.* Not intermitting; not ceasing for a time; incessant.

uninterrupted, un•in'tėr•rup"ted, *a.* Not interrupted; unintermitted; incessant.

uninvited, un•in•vī'ted, *a.* Not having received an invitation; unbidden.

union, ūn'yon, *n.* [Fr. *union,* from L. *unio, unionis,* oneness, unity, later a union, from *unus,* one (seen also in *unit, unity, unique, universal,* etc.); allied to E. *one.* ONE.] The act of joining two or more things into one, and thus forming a compound body; the state of being united; junction; coalition; concord; agreement and conjunction of mind, will, affections, or interest; that which is formed by a combination of individual things or persons; a combination; a confederation; a confederacy; two or more parishes united into one whole for better administration, as Union Methodist Church; a permanent combination among workmen engaged in the same occupation or trade; a trade union; a joint, screw, etc., uniting parts of machinery, or the like; a kind of coupling; a mixed fabric of cotton, flax, jute, silk, wool, etc.—**unionism,** ūn′yon•izm, *n.* The principle of union, attachment to the federal union of the United States.—*Trade unionism,* designed to unite all workers into organizations for improving working conditions.—**unionize,** to form into a union, as the employees of a factory.—**union jack,** U. S. Navy, a pilot flag.

uniparous, ū•nip′a•rus, *a.* [L. *unus,* one, *pario,* to bear.] Producing one at a birth; *bot.* having but one peduncle.

unipolar, ū•ni•pō′lėr, *a.* [L. *unus,* one, *polus,* a pole.] Having but one pole; capable of receiving only one kind of electricity.

unique, ū•nēk′, *a.* [Fr. *unique,* from L. *unicus,* from *unus,* one. UNION.] Without a like or equal; unmatched; unequaled; single in its kind of excellence.—**uniquely,** ū•nēk′li, *adv.* So as to be unique.—**uniqueness,** ū•nēk′nes, *n.*

unisexual, ū•ni•sek′shū•al, *a.* [L. *unus,* one, *sexus,* a sex.] Having one sex only; *bot.* applied to plants having separate male and female flowers.

unison, ū′ni•son, *n.* [L. *unus,* one, and *sonus,* sound. UNION, SOUND.] *Mus.* the state of sounding at the same pitch; the combination of two or more sounds equal in pitch, or at one or more octaves apart; hence, accordance; harmony.—**unisonant, unisonous,** ū•nis′o•nant, ū•nis′o•nus, *a.* Being in unison; concordant.

unit, ū′nit, *n.* [E. *unitas,* unity, from *unus,* one. UNION.] A single thing or person regarded as having oneness for the main attribute; a single one of a number; an individual; *arith.* one, the least whole number; *math.* and *physics,* any known determinate quantity by the constant repetition of which any other quantity of the same kind is measured (as a foot-pound, a gram, a dyne); *war,* any self-contained portion of a military force, comprising men, vehicles, etc., ready to act or to be employed together. There may be fighting, medical, transport, etc., units.

Unitarian, ū•ni•tâ′ri•an, *n.* [From L. *unitas,* unity, from *unus,* one. UNION.] One who ascribes divinity to God the Father only; one of a religious sect distinguished by the denial of the received doctrine of the Trinity; also, a monotheist.—*a.* Pertaining to Unitarians or their doctrines.—**Unitarianism,** ū•ni•tâ′ri•an•izm, *n.* The doctrines of Unitarians.

unite, ū•nīt′, *v.t.*—*united, uniting.* [L. *unio, unitum,* from *unus,* one. UNION.] To combine or conjoin, so as to form one; to incorporate in one; to associate by some bond, legal or other; to join in interest, affection, or the like; to ally; to couple; to cause to adhere; to attach.—*v.i.* To become one; to become incorporated; to coalesce; to commingle; to join in an act; to concur.—**united,** ū•nī′ted, *p.* and *a.* Joined or combined; made one.—*United Brethren,* a religious community commonly called Moravians. MORAVIAN.—*United Presbyterians,* the Presbyterian church formed in Scotland by the union in 1847 of certain bodies who had seceded from the Established Church.—**unitedly,** ū•nī′ted•li, *adv.* In a united manner; jointly; amicably.—**unitive,** ū′ni•tiv, *a.* Having the power of uniting.

unity, ū′ni•ti, *n.* [L. *unitas,* from *unus,* one. UNION.] The property of being one; oneness; concord; agreement; oneness of sentiment, affection, and the like; the principle by which a uniform tenor of story and propriety of representation are preserved in literary compositions; *math.* any definite quantity taken as one, or for which 1 is made to stand in calculation.—*The unities* (of *time, place,* and *action*), formerly deemed essential to a classical drama, demanded that there should be no shifting of the scene from place to place, that the whole series of events should be such as might occur within the space of a single day, and that nothing should be admitted irrelevant to the development of the single plot.

univalent, ū•ni•vāl′ent, *a.* [L. *unus,* one, *valere,* to be strong.] Having a valency of one, like a hydrogen atom.

univalve, ū′ni•valv, *a.* [L. *unus,* one, and E. *valve.*] Having one valve only, as a shell or pericarp.—*n.* A shell having one valve only; a mollusk with a shell composed of a single piece, usually of a conical and spiral form.—**univalved, univalvular,** ū′ni•valvd, ū•ni•val′vū•lėr, *a.* Having one valve only; univalve.

universal, ū•ni•vėr′sal, *a.* [L. *universalis,* from *universus,* universal, lit. turned into one—*unus,* one, and *versus,* turned. UNION, VERSE.] Extending to or comprehending the whole number, quantity, or space; pervading all or the whole; all-embracing; all-reaching; total; whole; comprising all the particulars.—*Universal church,* the church of God throughout the universe.—*Universal joint,* a form of joint or coupling allowing free swiveling in any direction.—*Universal proposition, logic,* one in which the subject is taken in its widest extent and the predicate applies to everything which the subject can denote.—*n.* A general notion or idea; a predicable; a universal proposition.—**Universalism,** ū•ni•vėr′sal•izm, *n. Theol.* the doctrine of the Universalists.—**Universalist,** ū•ni•vėr′sal•ist, *n.* One who holds the doctrine that all men will finally be saved, in opposition to the doctrine of eternal punishment.—**universality,** ū′ni•vėr•sal″i•ti, *n.* The state of being universal.—**universally,** ū•ni•vėr′sal•li, *adv.* In a universal manner; with extension to the whole; without exception.—**universe,** ū′ni•vėrs, *n.* [L. *universum,* the universe, neut. of the adj. *universus.*] The general system of things; all created things viewed as constituting one system or whole; the world. ∴ *World* properly signifies this globe and everything inhabiting it. *Universe* designates the entire mass of worlds, with everything associated with them.—**university,** ū•ni•vėr′si•ti, *n.* [L. *universitas,* the whole of anything; the universe; later, an association, corporation, company, etc.] An establishment or corporation for the purposes of instruction in all or some of the most important branches of science and literature, and having the power of conferring certain honorary dignities, termed *degrees,* in several faculties, as arts, medicine, law, and theology.

unjust, un•just′, *a.* Not just; not acting according to law and justice; contrary to justice and right.—**unjustly,** un•just′li, *adv.* In an unjust manner; wrongfully.

unjustifiable, un•jus′ti•fī″a•bl, *a.* Not justifiable; not to be vindicated or defended.

unkempt, un•kemt′, *a.* Uncombed; hence, rough; slovenly dressed; untidy; unpolished; unrefined.

unkennel, un•ken′el, *v.t.* To drive or force from a kennel; to rouse from secrecy or a close retreat.

unkind, un•kīnd′, *a.* Wanting in kindness, affection, or the like; harsh; cruel.—**unkindliness,** un•kīnd′li•nes, *n.* Unkindly conduct.—**unkindly,** un•kīnd′li, *a.* Unkind; ungracious.—*adv.* In an unkind manner; without kindness or affection; harshly.—**unkindness,** un•kind′nes, *n.* The quality of being unkind; want of kindness or affection; unkind conduct; an unkind act.

unknit, un•nit′, *v.t.* To separate so as to be no longer knit; to smooth out (the brow).

unknowable, un•nō′a•bl, *a.* Incapable of being known or discovered.—**unknowing,** un•nō′ing, *a.* Not knowing; ignorant.—**unknown,** un•nōn′, *a.* Not known; not discovered or found out; not ascertained: often used adverbially in the phrase *unknown to*=without the knowledge of (he did it *unknown to* me).

unlace, un•lās′, *v.t.* To loose the lacing or fastening of; to unfasten by untying the lace of.

unlade, un•lād′, *v.t.* To take out the cargo of; to remove, as a load; to discharge.

unlamented, un•la•men′ted, *a.* Not lamented; whose loss is not deplored.

unlatch, un•lach′, *v.i.* To open by lifting the latch.

unlawful, un•la̧′fu̧l, *a.* Contrary to law; illegal; begotten out of wedlock; illegitimate.—**unlawfully,** un•la̧′fu̧l•li, *adv.* In an unlawful manner; illegally; illegitimately.—**unlawfulness,** un•la̧′fu̧l•nes, *n.* The quality of being unlawful; illegality.

unlearn, un•lėrn′, *v.t.* To divest one's self of the acquired knowledge of; to forget the knowledge of.—**un-**

learned, un•lėr'ned, *a.* Not learned or erudite; ignorant; illiterate; inexperienced.—*a.* (un•lėrnd'). Not made known by study; not known.

unleash, un•lēsh', *v.t.* To free from a leash; to let go.

unleavened, un•lev'nd, *a.* Not leavened; not raised by leaven or yeast.

unless, un•les', *conj.* [For *on less* (than), the older forms being *onles, onlesse*=on lower terms, on any lower condition.] If it be not that; if ... not; supposing that ... not; except; excepting. By omission of a verb *unless* may have the force of a preposition=except, but for.

unlettered, un•let'ėrd, *a.* Unlearned; untaught; ignorant.

unlicensed, un•lī'senst, *a.* Not having a license or legal permission; done or undertaken without due license.

unlike, un•līk', *a.* Not like; having no resemblance.—*Unlike quantities, math.* quantities expressed by different letters or by the same letters with different powers.—*Unlike signs,* the signs *plus* (+) and *minus* (—).—**unlikelihood, unlikeliness,** un•līk'li•hụd, un•līk'li•nes, *n.* The state of being unlikely; improbability.—**unlikely,** un•līk'li, *a.* Such as cannot be reasonably expected; improbable; not holding out a prospect of success; likely to fail; unpromising.—**unlikeness,** un•līk'nes, *n.* Want of resemblance; dissimilarity.

unlimber, un•lim'bėr, *v.t.* To take off the limbers; to prepare for action.

unlimited, un•lim'i•ted, *a.* Not limited; boundless; indefinite; unconfined; not restrained.

unlink, un•lingk', *v.t.* To separate the links of; to loose, as something fastened by a link.

unload, un•lōd', *v.t.* To take the load from; to discharge or disburden; to remove from a vessel or vehicle; *fig.* to relieve from anything onerous or troublesome; to withdraw the charge from (to *unload* a gun).

unlock, un•lok', *v.t.* To unfasten something which has been locked; to open, in general; to lay open.

unlooked-for, un•lökt'for, *a.* Not looked for; not expected; not foreseen.

unloose, un•lös', *v.t.* To loose; to untie; to undo; to set free from hold or fastening; to set at liberty.

unlovely, un•luv'li, *a.* Not lovely; tending rather to repel; not beautiful or attractive.

unlucky, un•luk'i, *a.* Not lucky or fortunate; not successful in one's undertakings; resulting in failure, disaster, or misfortune; ill-omened; inauspicious.—**unluckily,** un•luk'i•li, *adv.* In an unlucky manner; unfortunately; by ill luck.—**unluckiness,** un•luk'i•nes, *n.* The state of being unlucky; ill fortune.

unmake, un•māk', *v.t.* To destroy the essential form and qualities of; to cause to cease to exist.—**unmade,** un•mād', *p.* and *a.*

unman, un•man', *v.t.* To deprive of the character or qualities of a man; to deprive of manly courage and fortitude; to dishearten; to overpower with womanish weakness; to emasculate.—**unmanly,** un•man'li, *a.* Not manly, or the reverse of manly; effeminate; womanish; childish; unbecoming in a man; cowardly.—**unmanliness,** un•man'li•nes, *n.* State of being unmanly; effeminacy.—**unmanned,** un•mand', *p.* and *a.* Deprived of the qualities of a man; rendered effeminate or weak.

unmanageable, un•man'ij•a•bl, *a.* Not manageable; not easily restrained or directed; not controllable; beyond control.

unmannerly, un•man'ėr•li, *a.* Not mannerly; not having good manners; rude; ill-bred.—**unmannerliness,** un•man'ėr•li•nes, *n.* Want of good manners; rudeness of behavior.

unmanufactured, un•man'ū•fak"-chėrd, *a.* Not manufactured; not wrought into the proper form for use.

unmarketable, un•mär'ket•a•bl, *a.* Not fit for the market; not saleable.

unmask, un•mask', *v.t.* To strip of a mask or of any disguise; to lay open to view.—*v.i.* To put off a mask.

unmatched, un•macht', *a.* Matchless; having no equal.

unmeaning, un•mēn'ing, *a.* Having no meaning or signification; mindless; senseless.

unmeasured, un•mezh'ėrd, *a.* Not measured; plentiful; beyond measure; immense; infinite; excessive; immoderate.

unmeet, un•mēt', *a.* Not meet or fit; not worthy or suitable.

unmelodious, un•me•lō'di•us, *a.* Not melodious; wanting melody; harsh.

unmentionable, un•men'shon•a•bl, *a.* Incapable of being mentioned; unfit for being mentioned or noticed.—*n.pl.* Articles of dress not to be mentioned in polite circles. (*Colloq. and humorous.*)

unmerciful, un•mėr'si•ful, *a.* Not merciful; cruel; inhuman; merciless; unconscionable.—**unmercifully,** un•mėr'si•fụl•li, *adv.* In an unmerciful manner; cruelly.

unmerited, un•mer'i•ted, *a.* Not merited or deserved; obtained without service or equivalent; not deserved through wrongdoing.

unmindful, un•mīnd'ful, *a.* Not mindful; not heedful; regardless.

unmistakable, un•mis•tāk'a•bl, *a.* Not capable of being mistaken or misunderstood; clear; evident.

unmitigable, un•mit'i•ga•bl, *a.* Not capable of being mitigated, softened, or lessened.—**unmitigated,** un•mit'-i•gā•ted, *a.* Not mitigated; not softened or toned down; perfect in badness; having no redeeming feature (an *unmitigated* scoundrel).

unmixed, unmixt, un•mikst', *a.* Not mixed; pure; unadulterated; unalloyed.

unmolested, un•mō•les'ted, *a.* Not molested or disturbed; free from disturbance.

unmoor, un•mör', *v.t. Naut.* to loose from anchorage or moorings.

unmoved, un•mövd', *a.* Not moved; not changed in place; not changed in purpose or resolution; unshaken; firm; not touched by passion or emotion; calm; cool.

unmuffle, un•muf'l, *v.t.* To uncover by removing what muffles or conceals.

unmusical, un•mū'zi•kal, *a.* Not musical; not melodious.

unmuzzle, un•muz'l, *v.t.* To remove a muzzle from; to free from restraint.

unnamable, un•nām'a•bl, *a.*—Incapable of being named; indescribable.—**unnamed,** un•nāmd', *a.* Not having received a name; not mentioned.

unnatural, un•nat'ū•ral, *a.* Not natural; contrary to the laws of nature; contrary to the natural feelings; acting without the affections of our common nature; not representing nature; forced; affected; artificial.—**unnaturally,** un•nat'ū•ral•li, *adv.* In an unnatural manner; in opposition to natural feelings and sentiments.—**unnaturalness,** un•nat'ū•ral•nes, *n.*

unnavigable, un•nav'i•ga•bl, *a.* Incapable of being navigated.

unnecessary, un•nes"e•ser'i, *a.* Not necessary; needless; not required by the circumstances of the case.—**unnecessarily,** un•nes"e•ser'i•li, *adv.* In an unnecessary manner; needlessly.

unneighborly, un•nā'bėr•li, *a.* Not neighborly; not suitable to the duties of a neighbor; not kind and friendly.

unnerve, un•nėrv', *v.t.* To deprive of nerve, force, or strength; to enfeeble; to deprive of coolness or composure of mind.

unnoticed, un•nō'tist, *a.* Not observed; not regarded; not treated with the usual marks of respect.

unnumbered, un•num'bėrd, *a.* Not numbered; innumerable; indefinitely numerous.

unobjectionable, un•ob•jek'shon•a•bl, *a.* Not liable to objection; incapable of being condemned as faulty, false, or improper; unexceptionable.

unobscured, un•ob•skūrd', *a.* Not obscured; not darkened or overcast.

unobservable, un•ob•zėr'va•bl, *a.* Not observable; not discoverable.—**unobservant, unobserving,** un•ob•zėr'vant, un•ob•zėr'ving, *a.* Not observant; not attentive; heedless.—**unobserved,** un•ob•zėrvd', *a.* Not observed, noticed, or regarded; not heeded.

unobstructed, un•ob•struk'ted, *a.* Not obstructed; not filled with impediments; not hindered.

unobtrusive, un•ob•trö'siv, *a.* Not obtrusive; not forward; modest.

unoccupied, un•ok'kū•pīd, *a.* Not occupied; not possessed; not employed or taken up in business or otherwise.

unofficial, un•of•fish'al, *a.* Not official; inofficial.

unopposed, un•op•pōzd', *a.* Not opposed; not resisted; not meeting with any obstruction or opposition.

unorganized, un•or'gan•īzd, *a.* Not organized; *bot.* inorganic.

unorthodox, un•or'tho•doks, *a.* Heterodox; heretical.

unostentatious, un•os'ten•tā"shus, *a.* Not ostentatious; not making show and parade; modest; not glaring or showy; not pretentious; inconspicuous.

unowned, un•ōnd', *a.* Having no

known owner; not acknowledged or admitted

unpack, un•pak′, *v.t.* To take from a package; to remove a wrapper from; to unload.

unpaid, un•pād′, *a.* Not paid; not discharged, as a debt; not having received what is due; not receiving a salary or wages.—*Unpaid for,* not paid for; taken on credit.

unpalatable, un•pal′a•ta•bl, *a.* Not palatable; disgusting to the taste; not such as to be relished; disagreeable to the feelings.

unparalleled, un•par′a•leld, *a.* Having no parallel or equal; unequaled; matchless; such that nothing similar was ever seen.

unpardonable, un•pär′dn•a•bl, *a.* Not to be forgiven; incapable of being pardoned.

unparliamentary, un•pär′le•men″te•ri, *a.* Contrary to the usages or rules of proceeding of parliamentary bodies; not such as can be used or uttered in a parliamentary assembly; unseemly, as language.

unpatriotic, un•pā′tri•ot″ik, *a.* Not patriotic.

unpaved, un•pāvd′, *a.* Not paved; having no pavement.

unpeople, un•pē′pl, *v.t.* To deprive of inhabitants; to depopulate; to dispeople.

unperceivable, un•pėr•sē′va•bl, *a.* Incapable of being perceived; not perceptible.

unphilosophic, unphilosophical, un•fil′e•sof″ik, un•fil′e•sof″i•kal, *a.* Not philosophic; the reverse of philosophic; not according to the principles of sound philosophy.

unpin, un•pin , *v.t.* To loose from pins; to unfasten or undo what is held together by a pin or pins.

unpitied, un•pit′id, *a.* Not pitied; not regarded with sympathetic sorrow.—**unpitying,** un•pit′i•ing, *a.* Having no pity; showing no compassion.

unplagued, un•plāgd′, *a.* Not plagued, harassed, or tormented.

unpleasant, un•plez′ant, *a.* Not pleasant; not affording pleasure; disagreeable. — **unpleasantly,** un•plez′ant•li, *adv.* In a manner not pleasing.—**unpleasantness,** un•plez′ant•nes, *n.* Disagreeableness.—**unpleasing,** un•plē′zing, *a.* Unpleasant; offensive; disagreeable.

unplumbed, un•plumd′, *a.* Not plumbed or measured by a plumb line; unfathomed.

unpoetic, unpoetical, un•pō•et′ik, un•pō•et′i•kal, *a.* Not poetical; not having poetical qualities; not proper to or becoming a poet.

unpolluted, un•pol•lū′ted, *a.* Not polluted or defiled; pure.

unpopular, un•pop′ū•lėr, *a.* Not popular; not having the public favor.—**unpopularity,** un•pop′ū•lar″i•ti, *n.* The state of being unpopular.—**unpopularly,** un•pop′ū•lėr•li, *adv.* Not popularly.

unpractical, un•prak′ti•kal, *a.* Not practical; impractical.

unpracticed, un•prak′tist, *a.* Not having been taught by practice; raw; unskillful.

unprecedented, un•pres′e•den•ted, *a.* Having no precedent; not matched by any other instance; unexampled.—**unprecedentedly,** un•pres′e•den•ted•li, *adv.* Without precedent; exceptionally.

unprejudiced, un•prej′ū•dist, *a.* Not prejudiced; free from undue bias or prepossession; unbiased; impartial.

unpremeditated, un•prē•med′i•tā•ted, *a.* Not previously meditated or prepared in the mind; not previously purposed or intended; not done by design.

unprepared, un•pri•pârd′, *a.* Not prepared; not fitted or made suitable or ready; not brought into a right or suitable condition in view of a future event, contingency, danger, or the like.—**unpreparedness,** un•pri•pâ′red•nes, *n.*

unprepossessing, un•prē′poz•zes″ing, *a.* Not having a prepossessing or winning appearance; not attractive or engaging.

unpresentable, un•pri•zen′ta•bl, *a.* Not fit for being presented to company or society.

unpretending, un•pri•ten′ding, *a.* Not pretending to any distinction; making no pretensions to superiority; unassuming.

unprincipled, un•prin′si•pld, *a.* Not having settled principles; destitute of virtue; profligate; immoral; iniquitous; wicked.

unprivileged, un•priv′i•lejd, *a.* Not enjoying a particular privilege or immunity.

unproductive, un•pre•duk′tiv, *a.* Not productive; not producing large crops; not making profitable returns for labor; not producing profit or interest; not producing articles for consumption or distribution; not producing any effect.

unprofessional, un•pre•fesh′on•al, *a.* Not pertaining to one's profession; contrary to the rules or usages of a profession; not belonging to a profession.

unprofitable, un•prof′i•ta•bl, *a.* Not profitable; bringing no profit; serving no useful end; useless; profitless.—**unprofitableness,** un•prof′i•ta•bl•nes, *n.* Uselessness.

unprohibited, un•prō•hib′i•ted, *a.* Not forbidden; lawful.

unpromising, un•prom′is•ing, *a.* Not affording a favorable prospect of success, of excellence, of profit, etc.

unpronounceable, un•pre•noun′sa•bl, *a.* Incapable of being pronounced; unfit for being named; unmentionable.

unpropitious, un•pre•pish′us, *a.* Not propitious or favorable; inauspicious.

unprosperous, un•pros′pėr•us, *a.* Not attended with success; unfortunate.—**unprosperously,** un•pros′pėr•us•li, *adv.* Unsuccessfully; unfortunately.

unprotected, un•pre•tek′ted, *a.* Not protected or defended; without protector or guardian.

unproved, un•prövd′, *a.* Not tested or known by trial; not established as true by proof.

unprovided, un•pre•vī′did, *a.* Not provided; not supplied.

unprovoked, un•pre•vōkt′, *a.* Not provoked; not proceeding from provocation or just cause.

unpublished, un•pub′lisht, *a.* Not made public; not published or issued from the press to the public, as a manuscript or book.

unpunctual, un•pungk′chū•al, *a.* Not punctual; not exact as to time.

unpunished, un•pun′isht, *a.* Suffered to pass with impunity.

unqualified, un•kwol′i•fīd, *a.* Not having the requisite qualifications; without sufficient talents, abilities, or accomplishments; not legally competent to act; not having passed the necessary examinations and received a diploma or license; not modified by conditions or exceptions (*unqualified* praise).

unquenchable, un•kwensh′a•bl, *a.* Incapable of being quenched, extinguished, or the like.

unquestionable, un•kwes′chen•a•bl, *a.* Not to be doubted or called in question; indubitable; certain.—**unquestionably,** un•kwes′chen•a•bli, *adv.* Without doubt; indubitably.—**unquestioned,** un•kwes′chend, *a.* Not called in question; not doubted; not interrogated.

unquiet, un•kwī′et, *a.* Not calm or tranquil; restless; agitated; disturbed.

unravel, un•rav′el, *v.t.* To disentangle; to disengage or separate; to clear from complication or difficulty; to unriddle; to unfold or bring to a denouement, as the plot or intrigue of a play.—*v.i.* To be unfolded; to be disentangled.

unread, un•red′, *a.* Not perused; not instructed by books.—**unreadable,** un•rē′da•bl, *a.* Incapable of being read or deciphered; illegible; not worth reading; so dull or ill-written as to repel readers.

unready, un•red′i, *a.* Not prepared; not fit; not prompt.

unreal, un•rē′al, *n.* Not real; not substantial; having appearance only.—**unreality,** un•ri•al′i•ti, *n.* Want of real existence; that which has no reality.

unreason, un•rē′zn, *n.* Want of reason; folly; absurdity.—**unreasonable,** un•rē′zn•a•bl, *a.* Not agreeable to reason; not guided by reason; exceeding the bounds of reason; exorbitant; immoderate; unconscionable.—**unreasonableness,** un•rē′zn•a•bl•nes, *n.* The state or quality of being unreasonable.—**unreasonably,** un•rē′zn•a•bli, *adv.* In an unreasonable manner; excessively; immoderately.—**unreasoning,** un•rē′zn•ing, *a.* Not having reasoning faculties; characterized by want of reason; not taking a reasonable view.

unreclaimed, un•ri•klāmd′, *a.* Not brought to a domestic state; not tamed; not brought into tillage; not reformed; not called back from vice to virtue.

unrecognizable, un•rek′og•nī″za•bl, *a.* Incapable of being recognized; irrecognizable.

unrecompensed, un•rek′om•penst, *a.* Not rewarded or requited.

unreconciled, un•rek′on•sīld, *a.* Not

reconciled; not made consistent; not restored to friendship or favor; still at enmity.

unrecorded, un•ri•kor′ded, *a.* Not recorded or registered; not kept in remembrance by public monuments.

unredeemed, un•ri•dēmd′, *a.* Not redeemed; not ransomed; not recalled into the treasury or bank by payment of the value in money (*unredeemed* bills); not having any countervailing quality; unmitigated.

unrefined, un•ri•fīnd′, *a.* Not purified; not polished in manners, taste, or the like.

unreformed, un•ri•formd′, *a.* Not reclaimed from vice; not corrected or amended.

unregarded, un•ri•gär′ded, *a.* Not heeded; neglected; slighted.

unregeneracy, un•ri•jen′ėr•a•si, *n.* State of being unregenerate.—**unregenerate, unregenerated,** un•ri•jen′ėr•āt, un•ri•jen′ėr•ā•ted, *a.* Not regenerated or renewed in heart; remaining at enmity with God.

unregistered, un•rej′is•tėrd, *a.* Not entered in a register.

unrelated, un•ri•lā′ted, *a.* Not connected by blood or affinity; having no connection of any kind.

unrelenting, un•ri•len′ting, *a.* Not becoming lenient, gentle, or merciful; relentless; hard; pitiless.

unreliable, un•ri•lī′a•bl, *a.* Not reliable; not to be relied or depended on.

unrelieved, un•ri•lēvd′, *a.* Not eased or delivered from pain; not succored; not delivered from distress; not released from duty.

unremembered, un•ri•mem′bėrd, *a.* Forgotten.

unremitted, un•ri•mit′ed, *a.* Not remitted; not forgiven; not having a temporary relaxation.—**unremitting,** un•ri•mit′ing, *a.* Not abating; not relaxing for a time; incessant; continued.

unremovable, un•ri•mö′va•bl, *a.* Fixed; irremovable; immovable.

unrepaid, un•ri•pād′, *a.* Not compensated; not requited.

unrepealed, un•ri•pēld′, *a.* Not repealed, revoked, or abrogated; remaining in force.

unrepentant, un•ri•pen′tant, *a.* Not penitent; not contrite for sin.

unrepresented, un•rep′ri•zen″ted, *a.* Not represented; not having a representative or person to act in one's stead; not yet put on the stage.

unrequited, un•ri•kwī′ted, *a.* Not requited; not recompensed; not reciprocated.

unreserved, un•ri•zėrvd′, *a.* Not reserved or restricted; not withheld in part; full; entire; open; frank; concealing nothing.—**unreservedly,** un•ri•zėr′ved•li, *adv.* Without limitation or reservation; frankly; without concealment.—**unreservedness,** un•ri•zėr′ved•nes, *n.*

unresisted, un•ri•zis′ted, *a.* Not resisted or opposed.—**unresisting,** un•ri•zis′ting, *a.* Not making resistance; submissive.

unrest, un•rest′, *n.* Disquiet; want of tranquillity; uneasiness; unhappiness.—**unresting,** un•res′ting, *a.* Never resting or ceasing; continually in motion.

unrestrained, un•ri•strānd′, *a.* Not restrained or controlled; not limited; uncontrolled; licentious; loose.—**unrestraint,** un•ri•strānt′, *n.* Freedom from restraint.

unrestricted, un•ri•strik′ted, *a.* Without restriction; not limited or confined.

unrevenged, un•ri•venjd′, *a.* Not having obtained revenge; not having taken vengeance; remaining without vengeance taken.

unrewarded, un•ri•wa̤r′ded, *a.* Not having received a reward; not compensated by reward bestowed; unrequited.

unriddle, un•rid′l, *v.t.* To solve or explain; to interpret.

unrighteous, un•rī′chus, *a.* Not righteous; not just; wicked; not honest and upright; of persons or things.—**unrighteously,** un•rī′chus•li, *adv.* Unjustly; wickedly.—**unrighteousness,** un•rī′chus•nes, *n.* Injustice; a violation of the principles of justice and equity; wickedness.

unripe, un•rīp′, *a.* Not ripe; not mature; not fully prepared; not completed.—**unripeness,** un•rīp′nes, *n.* Want of ripeness; immaturity.

unrivaled, un•rī′vald, *a.* Having no rival or equal; peerless; incomparable.

unrobe, un•rōb′, *v.t.* To take off a robe; to undress; to disrobe.

unroll, un•rōl′, *v.t.* To open out, as something rolled or convolved; to lay open or display.—*v.i.* To unfold; to uncoil.

unromantic, un•ro•man′tik, *a.* Not romantic; not given to romantic fancies; having nothing of romance connected with it.

unroof, un•röf′, *v.t.* To strip off the roof or roofs of.

unroot, un•röt′, *v.t.* To tear up by the roots; to extirpate; to eradicate.

unruffled, un•ruf′ld, *a.* Calm; tranquil; not agitated; not disturbed.

unruly, un•rö′li, *a.* Disregarding restraint; disposed to violate laws; turbulent; ungovernable; disorderly.—**unruliness,** un•rö′li•nes, *n.* Disregard of restraint; turbulence.

unsaddle, un•sad′l, *v.t.* To take the saddle from.

unsafe, un•sāf′, *a.* Not affording or accompanied by complete safety; not free from danger; perilous; hazardous.—**unsafely,** un•sāf′li, *adv.* Not without danger.

unsaid, un•sed′, *a.* Not spoken; not uttered.

unsaintly, un•sānt′li, *a.* Not like a saint; unholy.

unsalable, un•sā′la•bl, *a.* Not salable; not meeting a ready sale; that cannot find a purchaser.

unsanctified, un•sangk′ti•fīd, *a.* Unholy; profane; wicked; not consecrated.

unsatisfactory, un•sat′is•fak″te•ri, *a.* Not satisfactory; not satisfying; not giving satisfaction. — **unsatisfied,** un•sat′is•fīd, *a.* Not having enough; not gratified to the full; not content; not pleased; not convinced or fully persuaded; unpaid.—**unsatisfying,** un•sat′is•fī•ing, *a.* Not affording full gratification; not convincing the mind.

unsavory, un•sā′vėr•i, *a.* Not savory; tasteless; insipid; disagreeable to the taste or smell; unpleasing; offensive.

unsay, un•sā′, *v.t.* To recant or recall after having been said; to retract; to take back.

unscathed, un•skāTHd′, *a.* Not scathed or injured; without scathe; uninjured.

unschooled, un•sköld′, *a.* Not schooled; not taught; illiterate.

unscrew, un•skrö′, *v.t.* To draw the screws from; to unfasten by screwing back.

unscriptural, un•skrip′cher•el, *a.* Not agreeable to the Scriptures; not warranted by the authority of the Word of God.

unscrupulous, un•skrö′pyu̥•lus, *a.* Having no scruples; regardless of principle. —**unscrupulously,** un•skrö′pyu̥•lus•li, *adv.* In an unscrupulous manner.—**unscrupulousness,** un•skrö′pyu̥•lus•nes, *n.* Want of scrupulousness.

unseal, un•sēl′, *v.t.* To open after having been sealed.

unsearchable, un•sėr′cha•bl, *a.* Incapable of being discovered by search; inscrutable; mysterious.

unseasonable, un•sē′zn•a•bl, *a.* Not seasonable; not agreeable to the time of the year; ill-timed; untimely; not suited to the time or occasion.—**unseasonableness,** un•sē′zn•a•bl•nes, *n.* The quality of being unseasonable. —**unseasonably,** un•sē′zn•a•bli, *adv.* Not seasonably; not at the most suitable time.—**unseasoned,** un•sē′znd, *a.* Not seasoned; not kept and made fit for use; not inured; not flavored with seasoning.

unseat, un•sēt′, *v.t.* To remove from a seat; to throw from one's seat on horseback; to depose from a seat in the House of Representatives or the Senate.

unseaworthy, un•sē′wėr•THi, *a.* Not fit for a voyage; said of ships not in a fit state to encounter the ordinary perils of a sea voyage.

unseconded, un•sek′un•ded, *a.* Not supported; not assisted; without anyone to second.

unsectarian, un•sek•tâ′ri•an, *a.* Not sectarian; not characterized by any of the peculiarities of a sect; not belonging to any one sect.

unseeing, un•sē′ing, *a.* Wanting the power of vision; blind.

unseemly, un•sēm′li, *a.* Not seemly; not becoming; indecorous; indecent. —*adv.* Indecently; unbecomingly.—**unseemliness,** un•sēm′li•nes, *n.* Uncomeliness; indecency; indecorum.

unseen, un•sēn′, *a.* Not seen; invisible.—*The unseen,* that which is unseen; especially, the world of spirits; the hereafter.

unselfish, un•sel′fish, *a.* Not selfish or unduly attached to one's own interest.

unsentimental, un•sen′ti•men″tal, *a.* Not apt to be swayed by sentiment; matter-of-fact.

unserviceable, un•sėr′vis•a•bl, *a.* Not

bringing advantage, use, profit, or convenience; useless.

unsettle, un•set'l, *v.t.* To change from a settled state; to unhinge; to make uncertain or fluctuating; to disorder the mind of; to derange.—**unsettled,** un•set'ld, *p.* and *a.* Not fixed in resolution; unsteady or wavering; disturbed or troubled; not calm or composed; having no fixed place of abode; apt to change one's abode or occupation; displaced from a fixed or permanent position; not adjusted; unpaid; not occupied by permanent inhabitants.

unsex, un•seks', *v.t.* To deprive of the qualities of sex; to transform in respect to sex; usually, to deprive of the qualities of a woman.

unshackle, un•shak'l, *v.t.* To unfetter; to set free from restraint.

unshaken, un•shā'kn, *a.* Not shaken; not agitated; not moved in resolution; firm; steady.

unshaped, unshapen, un•shāpt' un•shā'pn, *a.* Shapeless; misshapen; deformed.—**unshapely,** un•shāp'li, *a.* Ill formed.

unsheathe, un•shēTH', *v.t.* To draw from the sheath or scabbard.—*To unsheathe the sword,* often equivalent to to make war.

unshed, un•shed', *a.* Not shed; not spilt.

unship, un•ship', *v.t.* To take out of a ship or other water craft; *naut.* to remove from the place where it is fixed or fitted.

unshod, un•shod', *a.* Having no shoes.

unshorn, un•shorn', *a.* Not sheared; not clipped.

unshrinking, un•shringk'ing, *a.* Not withdrawing from danger or toil; not recoiling.

unsifted, un•sif'ted, *a.* Not separated by a sieve; not critically examined.

unsightly, un•sīt'li, *a.* Disagreeable to the eye; repulsive; ugly; deformed.

unsisterly, un•sis'tėr•li, *a.* Not like or becoming a sister.

unsized, un•sīzd', *a.* Not sized or stiffened; not made with size (*unsized* paper).

unskillful, unskilful, un•skil'fụl, *a.* Not skillful; having no or little skill; wanting knowledge and dexterity.—**unskillfully, unskilfully,** un•skil'fụl•li, *adv.* Without skill or dexterity; clumsily.—**unskillfulness,** un•skil'fụl•nes, *n.* The quality of being unskillful; want of skill.—**unskilled,** un•skild', *a.* Destitute of skill or practical knowledge.—*Unskilled labor,* labor not requiring special skill or training; simple manual labor.

unslaked, un•slākt', *a.* Not slaked or quenched; not mixed with water and so reduced to powder (*unslaked* lime).

unsling, un•sling', *v.t. Naut.* to release from slings.

unsociable, un•sō'she•bl, *a.* Not sociable; not suitable for society; not inclined for society; not free in conversation; not companionable.—**unsociableness, unsociability,** un•sō'she•bl•nes, un•sō'she•bil''i•ti, *n.* The state or quality of being unsociable.—**unsociably,** un•sō'she•bli, *adv.*—**unsocial,** un•sō'shal, *a.* Not social; not adapted to society; not caring to mix with one's fellows.

unsoiled, un•soild', *a.* Not soiled; unpolluted; pure.

unsold, un•sōld', *a.* Not sold; not transferred for a consideration.

unsolicited, un•se•lis'i•ted, *a.* Not solicited; not applied to or petitioned; not asked for; not eagerly requested.

unsophisticated, un•se•fis'ti•kā•ted, *a.* Not sophisticated; not adulterated; unmixed; pure; in the natural and simple state; natural; void of the conventionalities or artificialities of polite society.

unsought, un•sạt', *a.* Not searched for; unasked for; unsolicited.

unsound, un•sound', *a.* Not sound or healthy; corrupt; decayed; not solid, firm, or the like; not founded on truth or correct principles; not valid; erroneous; not orthodox.—**unsoundly,** un•sound'li, *adv.* In an unsound manner.—**unsoundness,** un•sound'nes, *n.* Want of soundness; want of strength or solidity; weakness; erroneousness; defectiveness.

unsowed, unsown, un•sōd', un•sōn', *a.* Not sowed; not planted with seed; not scattered on land for growth; not propagated by seed scattered.

unsparing, un•spâ'ring, *a.* Not parsimonious; profuse; not merciful or forgiving; severe; rigorous in treatment.

unspeakable, un•spē'ka•bl, *a.* Incapable of being spoken or uttered; unutterable; ineffable.—**unspeakably,** un•spē'ka•bli, *adv.* Unutterably.

unspecified, un•spes'i•fīd, *a.* Not specified or particularly mentioned.

unspent, un•spent', *a.* Not spent; not used or wasted; not exhausted.

unspiritual, un•spir'i•chö•al, *a.* Carnal; worldly.

unspoken, un•spō'kn, *a.* Not spoken or uttered.

unspotted, un•spot'ed, *a.* Free from spots; free from moral stain; untainted with guilt; unblemished; faultless; pure.

unstable, un•stā'bl, *a.* Not stable; inconstant; irresolute; wavering.—**unstableness,** un•stā'bl•nes, *n.* Instability.

unstained, un•stānd', *a.* Not stained; not polluted, tarnished, or dishonored.

unstamped, un•stampt', *a.* Not having a stamp impressed or affixed (an *unstamped* receipt or letter).

unsteady, un•sted'i, *a.* Not steady; shaking; staggering; reeling; wavering; fluctuating; not constant in mind; fickle; unsettled; not regular, equable, or uniform; varying.—**unsteadily,** un•sted'i•li, *adv.* In an unsteady manner; without steadiness; waveringly; totteringly; restlessly; inconsistently.—**unsteadiness,** un•sted'i•nes, *n.* Want of firmness, fixedness, or stability; restlessness; inconstancy.

unstinted, un•stin'ted, *a.* Not stinted; bestowed abundantly; rather profuse or lavish.

unstop, un•stop', *v.t.* To free from a stopper, as a bottle or cask; to free from obstruction.

unstrained, un•strānd', *a.* Not purified by straining; not forced; easy or natural.

unstratified, un•strat'i•fīd, *a.* Not consisting of a series of strata or layers (as is the case with rocks deposited by water), but forming amorphous masses.

unstring, un•string', *v.t.* To deprive of strings; to relax or untune the strings of; to take from a string; to relax the tension of; to loosen or relax (the nerves).—**unstrung,** un•strung', *pp.* Deprived of strings; having the nerves shaken.

unstudied, un•stud'id, *a.* Not studied; not premeditated; not labored; easy; natural; ignorant; unskilled.

unsubdued, un•sub•dūd', *a.* Not brought into subjection; not conquered.

unsubstantial, un•sub•stan'shal, *a.* Not substantial or solid; not real; not having substance.—**unsubstantiality,** un•sub•stan'shi•al''i•ti, *n.* The state or quality of being unsubstantial; want of substance or reality.

unsuccessful, un•suk•ses'ful, *a.* Not successful; having met with no success; not fortunate in the result or issue.

unsuitable, un•sū'ta•bl, *a.* Not suitable, fit, or adapted; unfit; improper.—**unsuitableness,** un•sū'ta•bl•nes, *n.* Unfitness.—**unsuitably,** un•sū'ta•bli, *adv.* Unfitly; inadequately.—**unsuited,** un•sū'ted, *a.* Not suited or adapted; unfit.

unsullied, un•sul'id, *a.* Not sullied; not stained or tarnished; free from imputation of evil; pure; stainless.

unsung, un•sung', *a.* Not sung; not celebrated in song.

unsupported, un•sup•pōr'ted, *a.* Not supported; not upheld; not sustained; not countenanced; not aided.

unsuppressed, un•se•prest', *a.* Not suppressed; not subdued or put down.

unsurpassed, un•sėr•past', *a.* Not excelled, exceeded, or outdone.

unsusceptible, un•sus•sep'ti•bl, *a.* Not susceptible; insusceptible.

unsuspected, un•sus•pek'ted, *a.* Not suspected; not an object of suspicion.—**unsuspecting,** un•sus•pek'ting, *a.* Not imagining that any ill is designed; free from suspicion.—**unsuspicious,** un•sus•pish'us, *a.* Not inclined to suspect or to imagine evil; unsuspecting.

unswathe, un•swāTH', *v.t.* To take a swathe from; to relieve from a bandage or bandages.

unswept, un•swept', *a.* Not swept; not cleaned by sweeping; not passed over by a sweeping motion.

unswerving, un•swėr'ving, *a.* Not deviating from any rule or standard; unwavering; firm.

unsymmetrical, un•sim•met'ri•kal, *a.* Wanting symmetry or due proportion of parts.

unsystematic, un'sis•te•mat''ik, *a.* Not systematic; wanting a proper system.

untainted, un•tān'ted, *a.* Not tainted; not impregnated with foul matter;

not putrescent; not sullied; unblemished.

untamable, untameable, un•tā′-ma•bl, *a.* Not capable of being tamed.—**untamed,** un•tāmd′, *a.* Not reclaimed from wildness; not domesticated; not subdued or brought under control.

untarnished, un•tär′nisht, *a.* Not soiled or tarnished; unstained; unblemished.

untaught, un•tạt′, *a.* Not instructed or educated; unlettered; unskilled; unschooled; not made the subject of teaching.

untaxed, un•takst′, *a.* Not charged with or liable to pay taxes; not charged with any fault.

unteach, un•tēch′, *v.t.* To cause to forget, disbelieve, or give up what has been taught.—**unteachable,** un•tē′cha•bl, *a.* That cannot be taught; indocile.

untempered, un•tem′pėrd, *a.* Not tempered; not duly mixed; not regulated, moderated, or controlled.

untenable, un•ten′a•bl, *a.* Not tenable; that cannot be held in possession; that cannot be maintained by argument; not defensible.

untenanted, un•ten′an•ted, *a.* Not occupied by a tenant; not inhabited.

unthanked, un•thangkt′, *a.* Not having received thanks; not repaid with acknowledgments.—**unthankful,** un•thangk′fụl, *a.* Ungrateful; not making acknowledgments for good received.

unthinkable, un•thingk′a•bl, *a.* That cannot be made an object of thought; incogitable.—**unthinking,** un•thingk′ing, *a.* Not heedful; inconsiderate; not indicating thought or reflection.—**unthinkingly,** un•thingk′ing•li, *adv.* Without reflection; thoughtlessly.

unthread, un•thred′, *v.t.* To draw or take out a thread from.

unthrifty, un•thrif′ti, *a.* Prodigal; profuse; lavish; wasteful.

untie, un•tī′, *v.t.* To loosen, as a knot; to undo; to unfasten; to unbind; to set loose.

until, un•til′, *prep.* [O.E. *un,* unto, akin to A.Sax. *oth,* to, and *ende,* end, plus *til* or *till,* till.] Up to some time (he remained *until* dinner); before some time (the seeds cannot grow *until* it rains); before (he cannot leave *until* tomorrow).—*conj.* Up to some time that; before some time that; to a point that.

untillable, un•til′a•bl, *a.* Incapable of being tilled; barren.—**untilled,** un•tild′, *a.* Not cultivated.

untimely, un•tīm′li, *a.* Not timely; not done or happening in the right season; inopportune; premature.—*adv.* Before the natural time; unseasonably.

untiring, un•tī′ring, *a.* Not becoming tired or exhausted; unwearied.

untitled, un•tī′tld, *a.* Having no title of rank; not belonging to the nobility.

unto, un′tö, *prep.* [Prefix *und* and *to.* UNTIL.] To.

untold, un•tōld′, *a.* Not told; not related; too great to be counted.

untouchable, un•tuch′a•bl, *a.* Exempt from control or criticism; that which may not be touched; beyond reach.—*n.* One of a hereditary lower caste in India whose touch was thought to defile a person of a higher caste.

untouched, un•tucht′, *a.* Not hit; not meddled with; uninjured; not mentioned; not affected; not affected emotionally.

untoward, un•tō′ėrd *a.* Froward; perverse; not easily guided or taught; awkward; inconvenient; vexatious.

untraceable, un•trās′a•bl, *a.* Incapable of being traced or followed.

untracked, un•trakt′, *a.* Not tracked; not marked by footsteps.

untractable, un•trak′ta•bl, *a.* Not tractable; intractable; refractory.

untrained, un•trānd′, *a.* Not trained; not disciplined, not instructed.

untrammeled, un•tram′eld, *a.* Not trammeled or fettered; free to act.

untransferable, un•trans•fėr′a•bl, *a.* Incapable of being transferred or passed from one to another.

untranslatable, un•trans•lā′ta•bl, *a.* Not capable of being translated or rendered into another language.

untraveled, un•trav′eld, *a.* Not traversed by passengers; not having gained experience by travel.

untried, un•trīd′, *a.* Not tried; not attempted; not showing capabilities by trial or proof given; not having passed trial; not heard and determined in a court of law.

untrod, untrodden, un•trod′, un•trod′n, *a.* Not having been trod; not marked by the feet; unfrequented.

untroubled, un•trub′ld, *a.* Free from trouble; not disturbed by care, sorrow, or business; not agitated or ruffled; not raised into waves.

untrue, un•trö′, *a.* Not true; false; contrary to the fact; not faithful to another; not to be trusted; inconstant in love.—**untruly,** un•trö′li, *adv.* Falsely; not according to reality.

untrustworthy, un•trust′wėr•THi, *a.* Not worthy of being trusted; not deserving of confidence.

untruth, un•tröth′, *n.* The quality of being untrue; contrariety to truth; want of veracity; want of fidelity; a false assertion; a lie.—**untruthful,** un•tröth′fụl, *a.* Wanting in truth or veracity.

untunable, un•tū′na•bl, *a.* Not capable of being tuned; discordant; not musical.—**untune,** un•tūn′, *v.t.* To put out of tune; to disorder; to confuse.

untutored, un•tū′tord, *a.* Untaught; uninstructed; rude.

untwine, un•twīn′, *v.t.* To untwist; to open or separate after having been twisted; to cause to cease winding round and clinging.—*v.i.* To become untwined.

untwist, un•twist′, *v.t.* To separate and open, as threads twisted; to turn back from being twisted.—*v.i.* To become untwisted.

unused, un•ūzd′, *a.* Not employed; disused; that has never been used; not accustomed.

unusual, un•ū′zhö•al, *a.* Not usual; not common; rare.—**unusually,** un•ū′zhö•al•i, *adv.* In an unusual manner; not commonly.

unutterable, un•ut′ėr•a•bl, *a.* Incapable of being uttered or expressed; ineffable; inexpressible.—**unutterably,** un•ut′ėr•a•bli, *adv.* Inexpressibly.—**unuttered,** un•ut′ėrd, *a.* Not uttered or spoken.

unvalued, un•val′ūd, *a.* Not valued or prized; neglected.

unvaried, un•vâ′rid, *a.* Not varied; not altered; not diversified; always the same.—**unvarying,** un•vâ′ri•ing, *a.* Not altering; uniform.

unvarnished, un•vär′nisht, *a.* Not overlaid with varnish; *fig.* not artfully embellished; plain.

unveil, un•vāl′, *v.t.* To remove a veil from; to disclose to view.—*v.i.* To remove one's veil.

unventilated, un•ven′ti•lā•ted, *a.* Not ventilated; not purified by a free current of air.

unveracious, un•ve•rā′shus, *a.* Not veracious; untruthful.

unversed, un•vėrst′, *a.* Not versed or skilled; unacquainted.

unvoiced, un•voist′, *a.* Not spoken; unuttered; *phonetics,* not uttered with voice as distinct from breath.

unwarlike, un•war′līk, *a.* Not warlike; not used to or fond of war; not military.

unwarrantable, un•wor′an•ta•bl, *a.* Not defensible; not justifiable; improper.—**unwarrantably,** un•wor′an•ta•bli, *adv.* In a manner that cannot be justified; unjustifiably.—**unwarranted,** un•wor′an•ted, *a.* Not authorized; not assured or certain; not guaranteed.

unwary, un•wâ′ri, *a.* Not wary or vigilant against danger; not cautious; unguarded.—**unwarily,** un•wâ′ri•li, *adv.* Without vigilance and caution; heedlessly.

unwashed, un•wosht′, *a.* Not washed; not cleansed by water; filthy.—*The great unwashed,* a phrase first applied by Burke to the artisan class, now used to designate the lower classes generally; the mob; the rabble.

unwavering, un•wā′vėr′ing, *a.* Not wavering; not unstable; fixed; steadfast.

unwearied, un•wē′rid, *a.* Not tired; not fatigued; indefatigable; assiduous.

unweave, un•wēv′, *v.t.* To undo what has been woven; to disentangle.

unwed, un•wed′, *a.* Unmarried.

unweeded, un•wē′ded, *a.* Not cleared of weeds.

unwelcome, un•wel′kum, *a.* Not welcome; not pleasing or grateful; not well received.

unwell, un•wel′, *a.* Indisposed; not in good health; ailing.

unwept, un•wept′, *a.* Not wept for; not lamented; not mourned.

unwholesome, un•hōl′sum, *a.* Not wholesome; unfavorable or prejudicial to health; insalubrious; causing sickness; not sound; diseased.

unwieldy, un•wēl′di, *a.* [From *un,* not, and old *weldy, wieldy,* active. WIELD.] Movable with difficulty; too bulky and clumsy to move or be moved easily; unmanageable from weight; ponderous.—**unwieldiness,** un•wēl′di•nes, *n.* Heaviness; difficulty of being moved or managed.

unwilling, un•wil′ing, *a.* Not willing; loath; disinclined; reluctant.—**unwillingly,** un•wil′ing•li, *adv.* Against one's will; reluctantly.—**unwillingness,** un•wil′ing•nes, *n.* Loathness; disinclination; reluctance.

unwind, un•wīnd′, *v.t.* To wind off; to disentangle.—*v.i.* To admit of being unwound.

unwinking, un•wingk′ing, *a.* Not winking; not shutting the eyes; not ceasing to wake or watch.

unwisdom, un•wiz′dom, *n.* Want of wisdom; foolishness; unwise conduct or speech.—**unwise,** un•wīz′, *a.* Not wise; defective in wisdom; foolish; injudicious.—**unwisely,** un•wīz′li, *adv.* Foolishly; injudiciously; indiscreetly.

unwitnessed, un•wit′nest, *a.* Not witnessed; not attested by witnesses.

unwitting, un•wit′ing, *a.* Not knowing; unconscious; unaware.—**unwittingly,** un•wit′ing•li, *adv.* Without knowledge or consciousness; inadvertently.

unwomanly, un•wu̇′man•li, *a.* Unbecoming a woman.

unwonted, un•wun′ted, *a.* Not wonted; not common; unusual; infrequent; unaccustomed.—**unwontedly,** un•wun′ted•li, *adv.* In an unaccustomed manner.—**unwontedness,** un•wun′ted•nes, *n.* Uncommonness; rareness.

unworldly, un•wėrld′li, *a.* Not influenced by worldly or sordid motives.—**unworldliness,** un•wėrld′li•nes, *n.* State of being unworldly.

unworthy, un•wėr′THi, *a.* Not deserving; not worthy (*unworthy of* confidence); worthless; vile; base; beneath the character (work *unworthy of* the man).—**unworthily,** un•wėr′THi•li, *adv.* Not according to desert.—**unworthiness,** un•wėr′THi•nes, *n.* Want of worth or merit.

unwounded, un•wön′ded, *a.* Not hurt; not injured in body.

unwrap, un•rap′, *v.t.* To open or undo, as what is wrapped up; to take off a wrapper from.

unwreathe, un•rēTH′, *v.t.* To untwist or untwine.

unwritten, un•rit′n, *a.* Not reduced to writing; oral; not written upon; blank.—*Unwritten law,* a law not formulated in any written document.

unwrought, un•ra̤t′, *a.* Not manufactured; not worked up.

unyielding, un•yēl′ding, *a.* Unbending; unpliant; stiff; firm; obstinate.

unyoke, un•yōk′, *v.t.* To loose from a yoke.

up, up, *adv.* [A.Sax. *up, upp,* up = D. and Dan. *op,* Icel. *upp,* Sw. *up, upp,* Goth. *iup,* G. *auf;* akin to *over.*] The opposite of *down;* to a higher place or position; from a lower to a higher place; on high; aloft; raised; upright; erect; no longer in bed; in a state of action; in commotion, excitement, insurrection, or the like; higher or advanced in price, rank, social standing, etc.; to a more complete or mature condition; reaching a certain point; as far as: with *to* (*up to* the roof); not below or inferior: with *to* (*up to* one's expectations); denoting approach or arrival (to bring *up* troops); quite; thoroughly: often used to intensify a verb (to eat *up* all the food); in a place where it is kept when not used; in a state of being brought together or into close compass; often used elliptically for rise up, go up, etc.; followed by *with* in this elliptical use it signifies set up, erect, raise (*up with* the flag, he *up with* his hand).—*All up,* all over; completely done or ruined; come to an end (it is *all up* with him).—*To come up with,* to overtake.—*The time is up,* the allotted time is past.—*To have one up* or *pull one up,* to bring one before a magistrate or court of justice.—*Up and down,* here and there; hither and thither; from one place to another.—*prep.* From a lower to a higher place or point on; at or in a high or higher position on; toward the interior (generally the more elevated part) of a country; in a direction from the coast, or toward the head or source of a stream.—*n.* Used in the phrase *ups and downs,* rises and falls; alternate states of prosperity and the contrary; vicissitudes.—It is also used adjectively in such expressions as the *up* line of a railroad. See compounds below.—**uppish,** up′ish, *a.* Proud; arrogant; putting on airs.—**uppishness,** up′ish•nes, *n.* The quality of being uppish.

upas, ū′pas, *n.* [Malay, poison.] The poisonous sap of a large moraceous tree (*Antiaris toxicaria*) of Asia, used as arrow poison.

upbear, up•bâr′, *v.t.* To bear or raise aloft; to elevate; to sustain aloft; to support.

upbeat, up′bēt, *n. Mus.* an unaccented beat in a measure.

upbraid, up•brād′, *v.t.* [O.E. *upbreyden* from A.Sax. *ūpbregdan.*] To criticize, reproach, or scold severely for some fault.—*v.i.* To utter criticisms.

upbringing, up′bring•ing, *n.* The process of rearing, said especially of children.

upcoming, up′kum′ing, *a.* That which is approaching; nearing.

upcountry, up′kun•tri, *a.* Pertaining to the interior of a country.—*adv.* up•kun′tri.—*n.* up′kun•tri.

update, up•dāt′, *v.t.* To bring something, as a design, etc., up to date.

upend, up•end′, *v.t.* To place on end.—*v.i.* To rise on end.

upgrade, up′grād, *n.* An upward slope.—*v.t.* up•grād′. To improve; to raise the standards of.

upheaval, up′he″val, *n.* A violent disruption or change.

uphill, up′hil, *n.* An upward slope; ascent.—*a.* Ascending; with difficulty; situated on high ground.—*adv.* up•hil′. Upward on a hill; against adversity or difficulty.

uphold, up•hōld′, *v.t.*—pret. *upheld,* pp. *upholding.* To give support, as against opposition.

upholsterer, up•hōl′stėr•ėr, *n.* [Lengthened from older *upholster* to resemble *fruiterer, poulterer;* lit. an *upholder.* Comp. *undertaker* as to similar specialized meaning.] One who furnishes houses with curtains, carpets, cushions for chairs and sofas, etc.—**upholster,** up•hōl′stėr, *v.t.* To furnish with upholstery.—**upholstery,** up•hōl′stėr•i, *n.* The business or goods of an upholsterer.

upkeep, up′kēp, *n.* The state of being maintained; maintenance; the cost of maintenance.

upland, up′land, up•land′, *n.* Elevated land, as a plateau, especially land not near the sea.

uplift, up′lift, *n.* An improvement of conditions, especially emotionally; influences meant to uplift.—*v.t.* up•lift′. To elevate; to improve conditions.—*v.i.* To rise.

upon, up•on′, *prep.* [A.Sax. *uppon,* upon—*upp,* up, and *on,* on. UP, ON.] On; especially, resting on; at or in contact with the upper or outer part of a thing; resting, lying, or placed in contact with: all but synonymous with *on,* though sometimes rather more emphatic.

upper, up′ėr, *a.* Higher in position, rank, etc.; referring to the (usually) smaller branch of a bicameral legislature; constituting a level near the surface of the earth.

uppercase, u′pėr•kās″, *n.* Capital letters.

upper-class, u′pėr•klas″, *a.* Pertaining to a social class that is usually thought of as superior; the junior and senior classes of a college or high school.

uppercut, up′ėr•kut, *n.* A blow executed with the arm curved and in an upward direction.

uppermost, up″ėr•most′, *a.* In the highest position; of first consideration.

uppish, up′ish, *a.* Uppity.

uppity, up′i•ti, *a.* [Origin uncertain.] Arrogant; presumptuous.

upraise, up•rāz′, *v.t.* To raise or lift up.

uprear, up•rēr′, *v.t.* To rear up; to raise.

upright, up′rīt, *a.* [That is *right,* or directly, *up.*] Erect; perpendicular; erect on one's feet; pricked up; shooting directly from the body; adhering to rectitude; of inflexible honesty; conformable to rectitude.—*n.* Something standing erect; a vertical piece in some structure.—**uprightly,** up′rīt•li, *adv.* In an upright manner; perpendicularly; honestly; justly.—**uprightness,** up′rīt′nes, *n.* The quality or condition of being upright; honesty; integrity; probity.

uprise, up•rīz′, *v.i.*—pret. *uprose* (sometimes in poetry *uprist*), pp. *uprisen.* To rise up, as from bed or from a seat; to ascend above the horizon; to slope upward.—**uprising,** up•rī′zing, *n.* The act of rising up; rise; an ascent or declivity; a riot; a rebellion.

uproar, up′rōr, *n.* [From D. *oproer,* uproar, tumult = Dan. *uprōr,* Sw. *upror,* G. *aufruhr,* from *op, up, auf,* up, and D. *roeren,* Dan. *rōre,* Sw. *rōra,* G. *ruhren,* to stir; the spelling being affected by *roar.*] A violent disturbance and noise; bustle and clamor; a noisy tumult.—**uproarious,** up•rō′ri•us, *a.* Making an uproar or tumult; tumultuous.—**uproari-**

ously, up•rō'ri•us•li, *adv.* With great noise and tumult.

uproot, up•röt', *v.t.* To tear up by the roots, or as if by the roots; to eradicate.

upset, up•set', *v.t.*—pret. *upset*, pp. *upsetting*. To overturn; to disturb emotionally; to shorten and thicken, usually by hammering on the ends of something; to win a contest unexpectedly.—*n.* up'set. The act of overturning; an unexpected victory; the act of putting into disorder.

upshot, up'shät, *n.* The conclusion or result of something; the gist.

upside down, *adv.* [From M.E. *up so down.*] In a position in which the upper part is underneath; in great confusion.

upsilon, ūp'si•lon, *n.* [Gr.] The twentieth letter of the Greek alphabet, corresponding to the English *u*.

upstairs, up•stârz', *adv.* To a higher floor; up the stairs.—*a.* up'stârz. On an upper floor; pertaining to the upper floors.

upstanding, up'stand"ing, up'stand•ing, *a.* Erect; upright; having integrity.

upstart, up'stärt, *n.* One who has risen quickly from a low position to one of power and wealth.

upstream, up'strēm', *adv.* Toward the source of river or stream.

upward, upwards, up'wėrd, up'wėrdz, *adv.* [A.Sax. *upweard.*] Toward a higher from a lower position; toward a better level; more or higher; toward later years.

Ural-Altaic, ū'ral•al•tā"ik, *n.* A hypothesized language family consisting of the Finno-Ugric group (notably Finnish, Estonian, and Hungarian) and the Altaic group (notably Turkish and Mongolian, with numerous other languages spoken in the Caucasus, cental Asia, and to the east of Mongolia).

Urania, ū•rā'ni•a, *n.* [L. *Urania*, Gr. *Ourania*, lit. 'the Heavenly', from *ouranos*, heaven.] The muse of astronomy, generally represented holding in her left hand a celestial globe.—**uranic,** ū•ran'ik, *a.* Pertaining to the heavens; celestial; pertaining to uranium.—**uraninite,** ū•ran'in•īt, *n.* [From *uranium.*] A mineral closely allied to *pitchblende*, which is considered to be a massive and altered form. These minerals consist largely of uranium, and also contain cerium and thorium, but are chiefly important as sources of radium.—**uranite** ū'ran•īt, *n.* An ore of uranium, of a green or yellow color.—**uranium,** ū•rā'ni•um, *n.* A radioactive metallic element, occurring in pitchblende and carnotite; isotope U^{235} is used in atomic fission. Symbol, U; at. no., 92; at. wt., 238.03. —**uranography,** ū•ra•nog'ra•fi, *n.* [Gr. *ouranos*, heaven, and *graphō*, to describe.] The determination of the positions of the heavenly bodies, the construction of celestial maps and globes, etc.—**uranous,** ū'ra•nus, *a.* Pertaining to the metal uranium.—**Uranus,** ū'ra•nus, *n.* [The Greek name of heaven.] A deity of Greek mythology, father of Kronos or Saturn; *astron.* one of the primary planets, the most distant of all except Neptune, possessing several satellites.

urban, ėr'ban, *a.* [L. *urbanus*, from *urbs*, a city (seen also in *suburb*).] Belonging to or included in a town or city (*urban* population).—**urbane,** ėr•bān', *a.* Courteous; polite; suave; elegant or refined.—**urbanity,** ėr•ban'i•ti, *n.*—**urbanize,** ėr"ban•iz', *v.t.* To cause to take on the qualities of a city; to impart ways of a city to.

urceolate, ėr'si•o•lāt, *a.* [From L. *urceolus*, dim. of *urceus*, a pitcher.] *Bot.* shaped like a pitcher; swelling or bulging out like a pitcher.

urchin, ėr'chin, *n.* [Prov. Fr. *hurchon*, *hirchon*, Fr. *hérisson*, O.Fr. *ericon*, from L.L. *ericio*, *ericionis*, from L. *ericius*, a hedgehog, from *er*=Gr. *chēr*, hedgehog.] A hedgehog; a familiar, half-chiding name sometimes given in sport to a child; a sea urchin.

Urdu, ụr'dö, *n.* [Hind. camp.] The Hindustani language springing from the union of the Mohammedan invaders with their various camp followers.

urea, ū'rē•a, *n.* [From the *ur* of *urine.*] A crystalline compound which exists in healthy urine, and may also be prepared artificially.—**ureter,** ū•rē'tėr, *n.* The duct or tube that conveys the urine from the kidney to the bladder.—**urethra,** ū•rē'thra, *n.* The canal by which the urine is conducted from the bladder and discharged.

Uredo, ū•rē'dō, *n.* [L. blight of plants, from *uro*, to burn.] A genus of parasitic fungi, causing such diseases in plants as smut, rust, etc.

uremia, ū•rē'mi•a, *n.* [Gr. *ouron*, urine, and *haima*, blood.] A condition in which materials normally eliminated by urination are retained in the blood stream.

urge, ėrj, *v.t.*—*urged*, *urging*. [L. *urgeo*, *urgere*, to press, push, urge; same root as A.Sax. *wrecan*, to wreak.] To press, impel, or force onward; to press the mind or will of; to serve as a motive or impelling cause; to stimulate; to press or ply hard with arguments, entreaties, or the like; to importune; to solicit earnestly; to press upon attention; to insist on (to *urge* an argument).—*v.i.* To press forward.—**urgency,** ėr'jen•si, *n.* The state or character of being urgent; importunity; earnest solicitation; pressure of necessity.—**urgent,** ėr'jent, *a.* [L. *urgens*, *urgentis.*] Pressing; necessitating or calling for immediate action; eagerly soliciting; pressing with importunity.—**urgently,** ėr'jent•li, *adv.*

uric, ū'rik, *a.* [From *ur* in *urine.*] Pertaining to or obtained from urine.—**uric acid,** *n.* An odorless, tasteless, white acid, $C_5H_4N_4O_3$, present in urine.

Urim, ū'rim, *n.* [Heb. *urîm*, lights or flames, pl. of *ûr*, flame.] A kind of ornament or appendage belonging to the habit of the Jewish high priest in ancient times, along with the Thummim, in virtue of which he gave oracular answers to the people.

urine, ū'rīn, *n.* [Fr. *urine*, from L. *urina*, allied to Gr. *ouron*, urine; Skr. *vâri*, water; A.Sax. *ûrig*, humid; Icel. *úr*, drizzling rain.] An animal fluid secreted by the kidneys, whence it is conveyed into the bladder by the ureters, and through the urethra discharged.—**urinal,** ū'ri•nal, *n.* [L. *urinal.*] A vessel for receiving urine in cases of incontinence; a convenience, public or private, for the accommodation of persons requiring to pass urine.—**urinalysis,** ū•ri•nal'i•sis, *n.* The act of analyzing the chemical elements of urine.—**urinary,** ū'ri•na•ri, *a.* Pertaining to urine or to the organs connected with its secretion and discharge.—*Urinary organs*, the kidneys, the ureters, the bladder, and the urethra.—*n.* A reservoir for the reception of urine, etc., for manure.—**urinate,** ū'ri•nāt, *v.i.* To discharge urine.—**urinogenital,** ū'ri•no•jen"i•tal, *a.* Pertaining to the urinary and genital organs.

urn, ėrn, *n.* [L. *urna*, from *uro*, to burn, as being made of burned clay.] A kind of vase—a term somewhat loosely applied; a rather large vessel with a foot or pedestal, and a stopcock, employed to keep hot water at the tea table; a tea urn; a vessel in which the ashes of the dead are kept; a cinerary urn; *bot.* the spore case of mosses.

urogenital, ū•ro•jen'i•tal, *a.* Urinogenital.

uropod, ū'ro•pod, *n.* [Gr. *oura*, tail, *pous*, *podos*, foot.] A name of certain posterior appendages of the abdomen in crustaceans, serving as feet.

uropygium, ū•ro•pij'i•um, *n.* [Gr. *ouropygion.*] *Ornith.* the rump of birds.—**uropygial,** ū•ro•pij'i•al, *a.* Pertaining to the uropygium.

uroscopy, ū•ros'ko•pi, *n.* [Gr. *ouron*, urine, and *skopeō*, to view.] The judgment of diseases by inspection of the urine.

Ursa, ėr'sa, *n.* [L., a she-bear, a constellation.] A name of two constellations: *Ursa Major*, the Great Bear, one of the most conspicuous of the northern constellations, situated near the pole, and popularly called *Charles's Wain* or the *Plow*; and *Ursa Minor*, the Little Bear, the constellation which contains the polestar.—**ursine,** ėr'sīn, *a.* [L. *ursinus.*] Pertaining to or resembling a bear.

Ursuline, ėr'sū•lin, *a.* Applied to an order of nuns who took their name from St. *Ursula*, and who devote themselves to the succor of poverty and sickness, and the education of female children.

urticaceous, ėr•ti•kā'shus, *a.* [L. *urtica*, a nettle, from *uro*, to burn.] *Bot.* pertaining to plants of the nettle family.—**urticaria,** ėr•ti•kā'ri•a, *n.*

urticaria, ėr•ti•ka'ri•a, *n.* [N.L. from L. *urtica*, nettle.] An allergic reaction characterized by eruptions on the skin or mucous membrane, caused by internal or external contact with the causative irritant; nettle rash; hives.

urus, ū'rus, *n.* [L.] The mountain bull or *Bos urus*, described by Caesar, which ran wild in Gaul in the period of the Roman invasion, probably now extinct though relationship is claimed for an English species.

us, us, *pron.* [A.Sax. *ús*, acc. and dat.; Goth. *unsis, uns*, G. *uns*, us.] The objective or accusative case of *we*; the dative of *we*, used after certain verbs, such as verbs of *giving*.

usage, usance. See USE.

use, ūs, *n.* [O.Fr. *us*, use, from L. *usus*, use, a using, service, need, from *utor, usus*, to use (whence also *utility, utensil, usury, abuse*, etc.).] The act of employing anything, or the state of being employed; employment; conversion to a purpose (*to make use of*, that is, to use or employ); the quality that makes a thing proper for a purpose; utility; service; convenience; need for employing; exigency (I have no *use* for it); continued or repeated practice; wont; usage; a liturgical form of service for use in a diocese (the *Sarum use*). —*Use and wont*, the common or customary practice.—*v.t.* (ūz)—*used, using*. [Fr. *user*, from L.L. *usare*, to use, from *usus*, pp. of L. *utar*, to use.] To employ or make use of; to act with or by means of; to do work with; to consume or exhaust by employment (to *use* flour for food); to practice or employ (to *use* treachery); to make a practice of; to act or behave toward; to treat (to *use* one ill); to accustom; to render familiar by practice.—*To use up*, to consume entirely by using; to exhaust or wear out the strength of.—*v.i.* To be accustomed; to be in the habit; to be wont.—**usable,** ū′za•bl, *a.* Capable of being used.—**usage,** ū′zij, *n.* [Fr. *usage*, from *user*, to use.] Treatment; behavior of one person toward another; long-continued practice; customary way of acting; custom; practice; established mode of employing some particular word.—**usance,** ū′zans, *n.* [Fr. *usance*, from *user*, to use.] Usury; interest paid for the loan of money; the time which in certain countries is allowed by custom or usage for the payment of bills of exchange drawn on those countries.—**useful,** ūs′fu̧l, *a.* Valuable for use; suited or adapted to the purpose; beneficial; profitable.—**usefully,** ūs′fu̧l•li, *adv.* In a useful manner; profitably; beneficially.—**usefulness,** ūs′fu̧l•nes, *n.* The state or quality of being useful; profitableness.—**useless,** ūs′les, *a.* Having no use; unserviceable; producing no good end; not advancing the end proposed.—**uselessly,** ūs′les•li, *adv.* Without profit or advantage.—**uselessness,** ūs′les•nes, *n.* Unfitness for any valuable purpose or for the purpose intended.—**user,** ū′zėr, *n.* One who uses.—**usual,** ū′zhū•al, *a.* [L. *usualis*, Fr. *usuel*.] In common use; customary; ordinary; frequent. —**usually,** ū′zhū•al•li, *adv.* Customarily; ordinarily.—**usualness,** ū′zhū•al•nes, *n.* Commonness; frequency.

Ushas, u̧′shas, *n.* [From Skr. *ush*, to shine.] The Hindu goddess of dawn.

usher, ush′ėr, *n.* [O.Fr. *ussier, uissier, hussier*, Fr. *huissier*, a door-keeper, from O.Fr. *uis, huis*, from L. *ostium*, a door.] An officer or servant who had care of the door of a court, hall, chamber, etc.; hence, an officer whose business is to introduce strangers or to walk before a person of rank; an under-teacher or assistant to a schoolmaster or principal teacher.—*v.t.* To act as an usher toward; to introduce, as forerunner or harbinger; generally followed by *in, forth*, etc.

usquebaugh, us′kwi•ba̧, *n.* [Ir. and Gael. *uisge-beatha*, whisky, lit. water of life. WHISKY.] Whisky.

ustulate, us′tū•lāt, *a.* [L. *ustulatus*, pp. of *ustulo*, dim. of *uro, ustum*, to burn.] *Bot.* blackened as if burned.—**ustulation,** us•tū•lā′shon, *n.* The act of burning or searing; the operation of expelling a substance by heat, as sulfur from ores.

usual, usually, etc. See USE.

usufruct, ū′zū•frukt, *n.* [L. *usufructus—usus*, use, and *fructus*, fruit.] *Law*, the use and enjoyment of lands or tenements without the right to alienate such.

usurp, ū•zėrp′, *v.t.* [Fr. *usurper*, from L. *usurpare*, from *usus*, use, and *rapio*, to seize. USE, RAPID.] To seize and hold possession of by force or without right; to appropriate or assume illegally or wrongfully (a throne, power, or rank).—*v.i.* To be or act as a usurper; to encroach.—**usurpation,** ū•zėr•pā′shon, *n.* The act of usurping; the seizing or occupying the place or power of another without right; especially, the unlawful occupation of a throne; an encroaching.—**usurper,** ū•zėr′pėr, *n.* One who usurps; one who seizes power or position without right.

usury, ū′zhu̧•ri, *n.* [O.E. *usure*, later, *usurie*, from Fr. *usure*, L. *usura*, interest for money lent, lit. a using, from *utor* to use. USE.] Interest for money‡; an excessive or inordinate premium for the use of money borrowed; extortionate interest; the practice of taking exorbitant or excessive interest.—**usurer,** ū•zhu̧r•ėr, *n.* Formerly, any person who lent money on interest; now, one who lends money at an exorbitant rate of interest.—**usurious,** ū•zhū′ri•us, *a.* Pertaining to or practicing usury; taking exorbitant interest for the use of money.—**usuriously,** ū•zhū′ri•us•li, *adv.* In a usurious manner.—**usuriousness,** ū•zhū′ri•us•nes, *n.* The state or quality of being usurious.

ut, u̧t, *n.* The first or key note in the musical scale of Guido d'Arezzo (being the initial word in a Latin hymn, from the first syllable of each of the succeeding lines of which the names of the other notes were also taken), now superseded by *do*.

Ute, ūt, *n.* [Ute, *Yuta*.] A group of Shoshonean American Indians at one time living in Colorado, Utah, and New Mexico.

utensil, ū•ten′sil or ū′ten•sil, *n.* [Fr. *utensile*, from L. *utensilis*, fit for use, from *utor*, to use. USE.] An implement; an instrument; particularly, an instrument or vessel used in domestic business.

uterine, ū′tėr•in, *a.* [L. *uterinus*, from *uterus*, the womb.] Pertaining to the womb; born of the same mother but by a different father.

uterus, ū′tėr•us, *n.* [L. womb, abdomen.] The organ in female mammals in which young are contained and usually fed during development before birth; the womb.

utility, ū•til′i•ti, *n.* [L. *utilitas*, from *utilis*, useful, from *utor*, to use. USE.] The state or quality of being useful; usefulness.—**utilitarian,** ū•til′i•tâ″ri•an, *a.* [From *utility*.] Consisting in or pertaining to utility; holding forth utility as a standard in ethics or politics.—*n.* One who holds the doctrine of utilitarianism.—**utilitarianism,** ū•til•i•tâ″ri•an•izm, *n.* The doctrine that the greatest happiness of the greatest number should be the end and aim of all social and political institutions; or the doctrine that utility is the standard of morality, that actions are right in proportion as they tend to promote happiness, wrong as they tend to produce the reverse of happiness.—**utilization,** ū′til•i•zā″shon, *n.* The act of utilizing or turning to account.—**utilize,** ū′til•īz, *v.t.*—*utilized, utilizing*. [Fr. *utiliser*, from *utile*, L. *utilis*, useful.] To turn to profitable account or use; to make useful; to adapt to some useful purpose.

utmost, ut′mōst, *a.* [A.Sax. *útemest*, uttermost, outmost, a double superlative, being from *utema*, which itself is a superlative, and *mest*, also a superlative termination; similarly *aftermost*. *Outmost* is another form; *utter* is the comparative.] Being at the farthest point or extremity; farthest out; most distant; extreme; being in the greatest or highest degree; often used substantively, signifying the most that can be; greatest power, degree, or effort (strained to *the utmost*, try *your utmost*).

Uto-Aztecan, ū′tō•az′tek•an, *n.* [*Ute* and *o* and *Aztec*.] A language phylum consisting of Nahuatlan, Taracahitian, Piman, and Shoshonean families.

Utopia, ū•tō′pi•a, *n.* [Lit. the land of Noplace, from Gr. *ou*, not, and *topos*, a place.] A name invented by Sir Thomas More, and applied by him to an imaginary island which he represents as enjoying the utmost perfection in laws, politics, etc., as contrasted with the defects of those which then existed; [*not cap.*] hence. [*not cap.*] a place or state of ideal perfection.—**Utopian,** ū•tō′pi•an, *a.* Pertaining to Utopia; [*not cap.*] founded upon or involving imaginary or ideal perfection.—*n.* An inhabitant of Utopia; [*not cap.*] an ardent but unpractical reformer.

utricle, ū′tri•kl, *n.* [L. *utriculus*, dim. of *uter, utris*, a bottle of hide or skin.] A little bag or reservoir; a microscopic cell in an animal or vegetable structure; any thin bottle-like or bladder-like body in plants.—**utricular, utriculate,** ū•trik′ū•lėr, ū•tirk′ū•lāt, *a.* Having utricles; resembling a utricle or bag.

utter, ut′ėr, *a.* [A.Sax. *utor, uttor,* compar. of *ut,* out.] Complete; total; entire; perfect.—**utterly,** ut′-ėr•li, *adv.* Completely.

utter, ut′ėr, *v.t.* [O.E. *uttren* from *utter,* outside, from A.Sax. *ut,* out.] To articulate as a sound; to pronounce; to express in words; to put forth.—**utterer,** ut′ėr•ėr, *n.*

utterance, ut′ėr•ans, *n.* [UTTER.] Something spoken, especially a public expression; speech; style of speaking.

uttermost, ut′ėr•mōst, *a.* Extreme; being in the furthest, greatest, or highest degree; utmost; used also substantively, like *utmost.*

uvea, ū′vi•a, *n.* [From L. *uva,* a grape—from resembling a grape skin.] *Anat.* the black layer on the back part of the iris.—**uveous,** ū′vi•us, *a.* Resembling a grape or a bunch of grapes.

uvula, ū′vū•la, *n.* [L., dim. of *uva,* a grape, the uvula.] The small conical fleshy substance which hangs from the soft palate over the root of the tongue.—**uvular,** ū′vū•lėr, *a.* Pertaining to the uvula.

uxorious, uk•sō′ri•us, *a.* [L. *uxorius,* from *uxor, uxoris,* a wife.] Excessively or foolishly fond of one's wife; doting on one's wife.—**uxoriously,** uk•sō′ri•us•li, *adv.* In an uxorious manner.—**uxoriousness,** uk•sō′ri•us•nes, *n.* The state or quality of being uxorious.—**uxorial**†, uk•sō′ri•al, *a.* Pertaining to a wife or married woman.—**uxoricide,** uk•sor′i•sīd, *n.* [L. *uxor,* and *caedo,* to kill.] The murder of a wife by her husband; a husband who murders his wife.

V

V, v, vē, the twenty-second letter of the English alphabet, formerly, as a character, used indiscriminately with *u.*

vacant, vā′kant, *a.* [L. *vacans, vacantis,* ppr. of *vaco,* to be empty, to have leisure (from same stem, *vacuity, vacuum*).] Having no contents; empty; unfilled; void; not occupied or filled by an incumbent, possessor, or official; unoccupied; unemployed; not required to be spent in work; leisure; free (*vacant* hours); free from thought; not given to thinking, study, reflection, or the like; wanting intelligent facial expression; inane.—**vacancy,** vā′-kan•si, *n.* The quality or state of being vacant; empty space; vacuity; a space between objects; an unoccupied space; an unoccupied interval of time; an unoccupied post, position, or office; a situation or office destitute of a person to fill it; vacuity or inanity.—**vacate,** va•kāt′, *v.t.—vacated, vacating.* To make vacant; to quit the occupancy or possession of; to leave empty or unoccupied; to make void or of no validity.—**vacation,** va•kā′shon, *n.* [Fr. *vacation,* L. *vacatio.*] The act of vacating; the act of leaving without an occupant; a stated interval in a round of duties, holidays; the time when a post has no occupant.

vaccinate, vak′si•nāt, *v.t.—vaccinated, vaccinating.* [L. *vaccinus,* pertaining to a cow, from *vacca,* a cow.] To inoculate with the cowpox virus in order to procure immunity from smallpox; to inoculate.—*v.i.* To perform a vaccination.—**vaccination,** vak•si•nā′shon, *n.* The act of vaccinating; inoculation with vaccine; the scar remaining after vaccination.—**vaccine,** vak′sēn, *a.* [L. *vaccinus.*] Pertaining to cows or to cowpox.—*n.* A preparation having the virus of cowpox, used in vaccination; a preparation of organisms administered to produce immunity to a particular disease.

vacillate, vas′i•lāt, *v.i.—vacillated, vacillating.* [L. *vacillo, vacillatum,* to sway to and fro, perhaps allied to E. *wag.*] To waver; to move one way and the other; to fluctuate in mind or opinion; to be unsteady or inconstant.—**vacillating,** vas′i•lā•ting, *p.* and *a.* Moving so as to vacillate; unsteady in opinion or resolution; wavering.—**vacillatingly,** vas′i•lā•ting•li, *adv.* In a vacillating manner.—**vacillation,** vas•i•lā′shon, *n.* [L. *vacillatio.*] The act of vacillating; a wavering; vacillating conduct; fluctuation of mind; unsteadiness; change from one object to another; inconstancy.

vacuity, vacuousness, va•kū′i•ti, vak′ū•us•nes, *n.* [L. *vacuitas,* from *vacuus,* empty. VACANT.] The state of being empty or unfilled; emptiness; a space unfilled or unoccupied, or occupied with an invisible fluid only; a vacuum; freedom from mental exertion; absence of thought; absence of intelligence in look; vacant expression.—**vacuole,** vak′-ū•ōl, *n.* [A dim. from *vacuum.*] A minute cell or cavity in the tissue of organisms, as in the Protozoa.—**vacuous,** vak′ū•us, *a.* [L. *vacuus.*] Empty; unfilled; void; vacant.

vacuum, vak′ū•um, *n.* [L., an empty space, neut. sing. of *vacuus,* empty.] Space empty, or space devoid of all matter or body; an enclosed space from which air is completely removed.—*a.* Pertaining to a vacuum device (a *vacuum* cleaner).—**vacuum bottle,** *n.* A container having a vacuum between an inner and outer wall, used to keep liquids hot or cold for long periods.—**vacuum cleaner,** *n.* An electrical appliance that utilizes suction to pick up dirt.—**vacuum-packed,** vak′ūm•pakt″, *a.* Having a partial vacuum created before being hermetically sealed.—**vacuum tube,** *n.* An electron tube.

vade mecum, vā•di mē′kum, *n.* [L. *vade mecum,* go with me.] A book or other thing that a person constantly carries with him; a manual.

vagabond, vag′a•bond, *a.* [Fr. *vagabond,* from L. *vagabundus,* wandering, from *vagor,* to wander; from *vagus,* wandering, whence E. *vague.*] Wandering; going from place to place without settled habitation; pertaining to a vagrant or idle stroller.—*n.* An idle worthless stroller from place to place without fixed habitation or visible means of earning an honest livelihood; an idle, worthless fellow; a scamp; a rascal.—**vagabondage,** vag′a•bon•-dij, *n.* The state or condition of a vagabond.

vagary, va•gâ′ri, *n.* [From It. *vagare,* to wander, or directly from L. *vagari,* to wander (whence *vagabond,* etc.).] A wandering of the thoughts; a wild freak; a whim; a whimsical purpose.

vagina, va•jī′na, *n.* [L., a sheath.] *Bot.* and *anat.* a name for any part having the character of a sheath; the canal in females leading from the exterior to the womb.—**vaginal,** va•jī′nal or vaj′i•nal, *a.* Pertaining to or resembling a sheath; pertaining to the vagina.—**vaginate,** vaj′i•nat, *a.* *Bot.* sheathed; invested by the tubular base of the leaf.

vagrant, vā′grant, *a.* [Formerly *vagarant,* same origin as *vagary.*] Wandering without any settled habitation; pertaining to one who wanders; unsettled; moving without any certain direction.—*n.* A wanderer; one without a settled home or habitation; an idle wanderer or stroller; a vagabond; a tramp; *law,* a term for various minor offenders, such as beggars, prostitutes, fortune-tellers, and other impostors.—**vagrancy,** vā′gran•si, *n.* A state of wandering without settled home; the condition of being a vagrant.

vague, vāg, *a.* [Fr. *vague,* from L. *vagus,* wandering. VAGABOND.] Wandering‡; vagabond‡; unsettled as regards meaning, scope, or the like; indefinite; hazy; uncertain; doubtful; proceeding from no known authority; of uncertain origin or foundation (a *vague* report).—**vaguely,** vāg′li, *adv.* In a vague, uncertain, unsettled manner.—**vagueness,** vāg′nes, *n.* The character of being vague; want of clearness; haziness.

vagus or **vagus nerve,** vā′gus, *n.* Same as PNEUMOGASTRIC NERVE.

vain, vān, *a.* [Fr. *vain,* vain, empty, vainglorious, etc., from L. *vanus,* empty, void (whence also *vanish, evanescent*); same root as to *wane, want.*] Having no real value or importance; unsubstantial; empty; idle; worthless; unsatisfying; producing no good result; fruitless; ineffectual; light-minded; foolish; silly; proud of petty things or of trifling attainments; having a foolish craving for the admiration or applause of others; puffed up; inflated; conceited.—*In vain,* to no purpose; without effect; ineffectually.—*To take the name of God in vain,* to use the name of God with levity or profaneness.—**vainglorious,** vān•-glō′ri•us, *a.* Feeling or proceeding from vainglory; vain to excess of one's own achievements; boastful.—**vaingloriously,** vān•glō′ri•us•li, *adv.* With vainglory or empty pride.—**vainglory,** vān•glō′ri, *n.* Glory, pride, or boastfulness that is vain or empty; tendency to unduly exalt one's self or one's own performances; vain pomp or show.—**vainly,** vān′li, *adv.* In a vain manner; without effect; to no purpose; in vain; in a conceited manner; foolishly.—**vainness,** vān′nes, *n.* The state of being vain; empty pride; vanity.—**vanity,** van′i•ti, *n.* [Fr. *vanité* L. *vanitas.*] The quality or state of being vain; worthlessness; falsity; unrealness; want of substance to satisfy desire; the desire of indiscriminate admiration; empty pride, inspired by an overweening conceit of one's personal attainments or decorations; ambitious display; anything empty, visionary, or unsubstantial. ∴ Syn. under EGOTISM.—*Vanity Fair,* the vain show of this world, sketched in Bunyan's *Pilgrim's Progress,* and in Thackeray's novel of the name.

vair, vâr, *n.* [O.Fr. *vair,* from L. *varius,* various, variegated.] An old name for a kind of fur, said to have been the skin of a species of squirrel with a gray back and white belly; *her.* one of the furs represented by little pieces like shields alternately silver and blue.

Vaisya, vīs′ya, *n.* A member of the third caste among the Hindus, comprehending merchants, traders, and cultivators.

valance, valence, val′ans, val′ens, *n.* [From Norm. *valaunt,* O.Fr. *avalant,* descending, hanging down, from *avaler,* to let down. VAIL (to let down).] The drapery hanging round a bed, from the head of window curtains, from a couch, etc.

vale, vāl, *n.* [Fr. *val,* from L. *vallis,* a valley. VALLEY.] A tract of low ground between hills; a valley; more poetical and less general than *valley*.

valediction, va•le•dik′shon, *n.* [L. *valedico, valedictum—vale,* and *dico,* to say.] A farewell; a bidding farewell.—**valedictory,** va•le•dik′to•ri, *a.* Bidding farewell; pertaining to a leave-taking.—*n.* A farewell; a farewell utterance.—**valedictorian,** va′le•dik•tō″ri•an, *n.* The member of a graduating class who gives the valedictory address at a commencement, usually the person with the highest academic rank.

valence, valency, vā′lens, vā′len•si, *n.* [L.L. *valentia,* strength, *valeo,* to be strong. VALID.] *Chem.* the combining strength or capacity of atoms, referred to hydrogen as a standard; the force which determines with how many atoms of an element an atom of another element will combine.

Valenciennes, va•len′si•enz″, *n.* A rich variety of lace made at *Valenciennes* in France.

valentine, val′en•tīn, *n.* A sweetheart selected or got by lot on St. *Valentine's* Day, February 14th; a letter or missive of an amatory or satirical kind, sent by one person to another on St. Valentine's Day.

valerian, va•lē′ri•an, *n.* [Supposed to be from the Emperor *Valerianus,* who had benefited from it.] The common name of a genus of perennial herbs, having small red or white flowers, which are collected for their medicinal properties.—*Valerian oil,* an aromatic essential oil obtained from the root of the great wild valerian.

valet, val′et, *n.* [Fr. *valet,* O.Fr. *varlet, vaslet,* a lad, a servant; dim. of *vassal.* VASSAL. *Varlet* is the same word.] A manservant who attends on a gentleman's person.

valetudinarian, val•e•tū′di•nâ″ri•an, *a.* [L. *valetudinarius,* from *valetudo,* good or ill health, from *valeo,* to be well. VALID.] Sickly; in a poor state of health; infirm; seeking to recover health.—*n.* A person of an infirm or sickly constitution; one who is seeking to recover health.—**valetudinarianism,** val•e•tū′di•nâ″ri•an•izm, *a.* A state of feeble health; infirmity.—**valetudinary,** val•e•tū′di•ne•ri, *n.* and *a.* Same as *Valetudinarian.*

Valhalla, val•hal′la, *n.* [Icel. *valhöll,* the hall of the slain—*valr,* slaughter, and *höll,* a hall.] In the Scandinavian mythology the palace of immortality, inhabited by the souls of heroes slain in battle; *fig.* any edifice which is the final resting place of many of the heroes or great men of a nation.

valiant, val′yant, *a.* [Fr. *vaillant,* from *valoir,* L. *valere,* to be strong. VALID.] Brave; courageous; intrepid in danger; puissant; performed with valor; heroic.—**valiantly,** val′yant•li, *adv.* In a valiant manner.—**valiantness,** val′yant•nes, *n.* The quality of being valiant; valor.

valid, val′id, *a.* [Fr. *valide,* L. *validus,* strong, powerful, from *valeo,* to be strong, to be well (seen also in *value, valiant, valour, valetudinary, avail, prevail,* etc.).] Sufficiently supported by actual fact; well grounded; sound; just; good; not weak or defective; having sufficient legal strength or force; good or sufficient in point of law.—**validate,** val′i•dāt, *v.t.* To make valid; to confirm.—**validity, validness,** va•lid′i•ti, val′id•nes, *n.* The state or quality of being valid; strength or cogency from being supported by fact; justness; soundness; legal strength or force; sufficiency in point of law.—**validly,** val′id•li, *adv.* In a valid manner; so as to be valid.

valise, va•lēs′, *n.* [Fr.] A small leather bag or case for holding a traveler's equipment; a portmanteau.

Valkyrie, val•kē′ri, *n.* [Icel. *valkyrja—valr,* the slain, and *kjósa,* to select.] One of the maidens of Odin, who led to Valhalla the souls of those who fell in battle, where they ministered at their feasts.—**Valkyrian,** val•kē′ri•an, *a.* Of or relating to the Valkyries.

valley, val′i, *n.* [Fr. *vallée,* O.Fr. *valee,* from *val,* a *vale,* from L. *vallis,* a valley.] Any hollow or surface depression of some width bounded by hills or mountains, and usually traversed by a stream or river; a vale; the internal angle formed by the meeting of the two inclined sides of a roof.

valonia, va•lō′ni•a, *n.* [It. *vallonia,* from Mod. Gr. *balania,* the holm-oak, from Gr. *balanos,* an acorn, an oak.] The acorn cups of a species of oak exported from the Levant for the use of tanners and dyers.

valor, val′or, *n.* [O.Fr. *valor,* Mod. Fr. *valeur,* L.L. *valor,* worth, from L. *valeo,* to be strong. VALID.] That quality which enables a man to encounter danger with firmness; personal bravery, especially as regards fighting; intrepidity; prowess.—**valorous,** val′or•us, *a.* Brave; courageous; valiant; intrepid.—**valorously,** val′or•us•li, *adv.* In a valorous manner; valiantly.

value, val′ū, *n.* [O.Fr. *value,* the fem. of *valu,* pp. of *valoir,* from L. *valere,* to be strong, to be worth. VALID.] Worth; that property or those properties of a thing which render it useful or estimable; the degree of such property or properties; utility; importance; what makes a person of some account, estimation, or worth; estimate of worth; price equal to the worth; market price; the money for which a thing is sold or will sell; equivalent in the market; import; precise signification (the *value* of a word or phrase); *mus.* the relative length or duration of a tone or note.—*v.t.—valued, valuing.* To estimate the worth of; to rate at a certain price; to appraise; to consider with respect to importance; to rate, whether high or low; to have in high esteem; to prize; to regard; to hold in respect and estimation.—**valued,** val′ūd, *p.* and *a.* Regarded as of high value; highly esteemed.—**valueless,** val′ū•les, *a.* Being of no value; having no worth; worthless.—**valuable,** val′ū•a•bl, *a.* Having value or worth; having a high value; having qualities which are useful and esteemed; precious.—*n.* A thing, especially a small thing, of value; a choice article of personal property; usually in the plural.—**valuableness,** val′ū•a•bl•nes, *n.* The quality of being valuable; preciousness.—**valuation,** val•ū•ā′shon, *n.* The act of valuing; the act of setting a price; appraisement; estimation; value set upon a thing; estimated worth.—**valuator,** val′ū•ā•tėr, *n.* One who sets a value; an appraiser.

valve, valv, *n.* [Fr. *valve,* from L. *valvae,* folding doors.] A leaf of a folding door; a movable lid or partition adapted to a tube or orifice, and so formed as to open communication in one direction and to close it in the other, used to regulate the admission or escape of water, gas, or steam; *anat.* a partition within the cavity of a vessel, opening to allow the passage of a fluid in one direction, and shutting to prevent its return (the *valves* of the heart); *bot.* one of the divisions of any dehiscent body; *conch.* one of the separable portions of the shell of a mollusk.—**valvular,** val′vū•lėr, *a.* Containing valves; having the character of, or acting as, a valve.

vamoose, va•mös′, *v.t.* or *i.* (*Slang.*) [Sp. *vamos,* let us go.] To quit, to depart.

vamp, vamp, *n.* [Formerly *vampey,* from Fr. *avant-pied*—*avant,* before, and *pied,* the foot. VAN (front).] The upper leather of a boot or shoe; any piece or patch intended to give an old thing a new appearance; a piece added for appearance sake; *mus.* an improvised accompaniment.—*v.i.* To put a new vamp or upper leather on; to furnish up; to give a new appearance to; to patch.

vamp, vamp, *n.* (*Slang.*) Short for VAMPIRE.—*v.t.* and *t.* To beguile men; to act the part of a vampire.

vampire, vam′pīr, *n.* [Fr. from G. *vampyr,* from Serb. *vampir, vampira,* a vampire.] A kind of spectral being or ghost still possessing a human body, believed to leave the grave during the night and suck the blood of living men and women while they are asleep; an adventuress; a woman who uses her physical charms in such a manner as to allure or debase a man; a siren; an extortioner.—**vampire bat,** *n.* A bloodsucking bat of South America of several species, with long sharp teeth.

van, van, *n.* [Abbrev. from *vanguard,* from Fr. *avant-garde*—*avant,* before, and *garde,* guard. AVAUNT, GUARD.] The front of an army, or the front line or foremost division of a fleet.

van,‡ van, *n.* [Fr. *van,* from L. *vannus,* a van or fan for winnowing. FAN.] A fan or any contrivance for winnowing grain; a wing.

van, van, *n.* [Abbrev. from *caravan.*] A caravan; a covered vehicle used by tradesmen and others for carrying goods.

vanadium, va•nā′di•um, *n.* [From *Vanadis,* a surname of the Scandinavian goddess of love, Freya.] A silver-white hard metallic element, occurring in certain minerals and used in alloy steels to impart hardness and strength. Symbol, V; at. no., 23; at. wt., 50.942.—**vanadic, vanadous,** va•nad′ik, van′a•dus, *a.* Pertaining to vanadium.

Vandal, van′dal, *n.* [L. *Vandali, Vinduli, Vindili,* the Vandals.] One of a Teutonic race who pillaged Rome in the fifth century, and unsparingly destroyed the monuments of art and the productions of literature; [*not cap.*] hence, one who willfully or ignorantly destroys any work of art, literature, or the like.—**Vandal, Vandalic,** van•dal′ik, *a.* Pertaining to or resembling the Vandals.—**vandalism,** van′dal•izm, *n.* Willful or ignorant destruction of works of art or literature; hostility to art or literature.

Vandyke, van•dīk′, *n.* A pointed collar of lace or sewed work worn by both sexes during the reign of Charles I, and to be seen in portraits painted by Vandyke; a pointed beard.—*Vandyke brown,* a pigment obtained from a kind of peat or bog-earth, of a fine, deep, semi-transparent brown color.

vane, vān, *n.* [O.E. *fane,* a banner, a weathercock, from A.Sax. *fana*= O.H.G. *fano,* G. *fahne,* D. *vaan,* a flag; Goth. *fana,* cloth; cog. L. *pannus,* cloth.] A weathercock, arrow, or thin slip of metal, wood, etc., placed on a spindle at the top of a spire, tower, etc., for the purpose of showing by its turning and direction which way the wind blows; any somewhat similar device or contrivance; the broad part of a feather on either side of the shaft; one of the plates or blades of a windmill, a screw propeller, etc.

vang, vang, *n.* [D. *vangen,* G. *fangen,* to catch.] *Naut.* a steadying-rope from a gaff to the ship's side.

vanguard, van″gärd′, *n.* [For *vantguard, avantguard,* from O.Fr. *avantgarde* from *avant,* before, and *garde,* guard.] *Milit.* the troops in the front ranks of an army; the forefront, or those who are in the forefront, of a movement or action.

vanilla, va•nil′a, *n.* [From Sp. *vainilla,* dim. of *vaina,* a scabbard, from L. *vagina,* a scabbard; the pod resembles a scabbard.] A genus of orchidaceous plants, natives of tropical America, the fleshy podlike fruit of several species of which is remarkable for its fragrant odor and is used in medicine, confectionery, and perfumery.

vanish, van′ish, *v.i.* [From L. *vanesco, evanesco,* to vanish, to pass away (through the old French), from *vanus,* vain. VAIN.] To disappear; to pass from a visible to an invisible state; to pass beyond the limit of vision; to be annihilated or lost; to be no more; *math.* to become less and less till the value is nothing, or is denoted by 0.—*Vanishing point,* the point in a view or picture at which all parallel lines in the same plane tend to meet when correctly represented in a picture.

vanity. See VAIN.

vanquish, vang′kwish, *v.t.* [From Fr. *vaincre,* pret. *vainquis,* subj. *vainquisse,* O.Fr. *veinquir,* from L. *vincere,* to conquer. VICTOR.] To conquer, overcome, or subdue in battle; to defeat in any contest; to get the better of; to confute; to overpower; to prostrate; to be too much for. ∴ Syn. under CONQUER.—**vanquishable,** vang′kwish•a•bl, *a.* Capable of being vanquished; conquerable.—**vanquisher,** vang′kwish•ėr, *n.* A conqueror; a victor.

vantage, van′tij, *n.* [Fr. *avantage,* ADVANTAGE.] Advantage; vantage ground.—**vantage ground,** *n.* Superiority of position or place; the place or condition which gives one an advantage over another; favorable position.

vapid, vap′id, *a.* [L. *vapidus,* vapid, having lost spirit, same root as *vapor.*] Having lost its life and spirit; insipid; dead; flat; dull; unanimated; spiritless.—**vapidly,** vap′id•li, *adv.* In a vapid manner.—**vapidity, vapidness,** va•pid′i•ti, vap′id•nes, *n.* The state or quality of being vapid; deadness; flatness; dullness; want of life or spirit.

vapor, vapour, vā′pėr, *n.* [L. *vapor,* steam; vapor; akin to *vapidus,* vapid, having lost flavor, *vappa,* vapid wine.] An exhalation or fume; a gaseous substance; visible steam; the gaseous form which any solid or liquid substance assumes when heated; also specifically used of a gas below its critical temperature; any visible diffused substance floating in the atmosphere, as fog or mist; hazy matter; something unsubstantial, fleeting, or transitory; a mental fume; a vain imagination; an unreal fancy; *pl.* an old name for a nervous hypochondriacal or hysterical affection; the blues.—*Vapor density,* the density of a substance in the state of vapor, referred to air or hydrogen as the standard; of importance in chemistry in determining the molecular weight.—*v.i.* To boast or vaunt with ostentatious display; to bully; to hector; to brag; to bounce.—**vaporer,** vā′pėr•ėr, *n.* One who vapors, brags, or bullies; a braggart, bully, or boaster.—**vaporing,** vā′pėr•ing, *p.* and *a.* Boasting; given to boast or brag.—*n.* Boastful or windy talk.—**vaporish,** vā′pėr•ish, *a.* Affected by vapors; hypochondriac; whimsical; fanciful.—**vapory,** vā′pėr•i, *a.* Vaporous; full of vapors.—**vaporiferous,** vā•pėr•if′ėr•us, *a.* [L. *vapor,* and *fero,* to bear.] Conveying or producing vapor.—**vaporific,** vā•pėr•if′ik, *a.* [L. *vapor,* and *facio,* to make.] Forming vapor; converting into steam, or into a volatile form.—**vaporizable,** vā′pėr•ī•za•bl, *a.* Capable of being vaporized.—**vaporization,** vā′pėr•i•zā″shon, *n.* The act of vaporizing; conversion into vapor.—**vaporize,** vā′pėr•īz, *v.t.*—*vaporized, vaporizing.* To convert into vapor by the application of heat or artificial means; to cause to evaporate; to sublimate.—*v.i.* To pass off in vapor.—**vaporizer,** vā′pėr•īz′ėr, *n.* In oil engines, a contrivance for converting the oil fuel into fine spray.—**vaporose,** vā′pėr•ōs, *a.* Vaporous.—**vaporous,** vā′pėr•us, *a.* Being in the form of, or having the character of vapor; full of vapors or exhalations; promoting exhalation or effluvia; unsubstantial; vainly imaginative or soaring; whimsical.

vaquero, vä•kâr′ō, *n.* [Sp., a cowherd, from *vaca,* L. *vacca,* a cow.] In Mexico and the western United States, a herdsman, a cowboy.

Varangian, va•ran′ji•an, *n.* [Icel. *Vaeringjar,* lit. confederates or sworn men, from *várar,* an oath.] One of those Scandinavians, Anglo-Saxons, etc., who entered the service of the Byzantine emperors and became the Imperial Guard.

variable, variance, etc. See VARY.

varicella, var•i•sel′la, *n.* [Dim. of

variola, the smallpox.] The chickenpox.

varicocele, var″i•kō•sēl′, *n.* [L. *varix*, a dilated vein, and Gr. *kēlē*, a tumor.] A varicose enlargement of the spermatic veins, or the veins of the scrotum.

varicose, var′i•kōs, *a.* [L. *varicosus*, from *varix*, a varicose vein.] Exhibiting a morbid enlargement or dilation, knotty and irregular in shape, as often seen in the veins of the lower extremities, which sometimes burst with considerable hemorrhage.—**varicosity,** var•i•kos′-i•ti, *n.* The state of being varicose.

variegate, vâ′ri•e•gāt, *v.t.*—*variegated, variegating.* [L. *variego, variegatum*, to variegate, from *varius*, various, and term. from *ago*, to do. VARY.] To diversify by means of different tints or hues.—**variegated,** vâ′ri•e•gā•ted, *p.* and *a.* Diversified with tints or hues; *bot.* irregularly marked with spots of a light color; said of leaves.—**variegation,** vâ′ri•e•gā″shon, *n.* The state of being variegated; diversity of colors, especially on the leaves or petals of plants.

variety. See VARY.

variola, va•rī′o•la, *n.* [Fr. *variole*, Mod. L. *variola*, smallpox, from L. *varius*, spotted,] The smallpox.—**variolar, variolous,** va•rī′o•lėr, va•rī′o•lus, *a.* Pertaining to or designating the smallpox.—**variolite,** va•rī′o•līt, *n.* [Gr. *lithos*, stone.] A porphyritic rock in which the embedded substances are imperfectly crystallized, or are rounded, giving a spotted appearance.—**variolitic,** va•rī′o•lit″ik, *a.* Pertaining to variola; thickly marked with small round specks or dots; spotted.—**varioloid,** va•rī′o•loid, *a.* Resembling variola; spotted.

variorum, vâ•ri•ō′rum, *a.* [From L. *editio cum notis variorum*, an edition with the notes of various persons.] A term applied to an edition of some work in which the notes of different commentators are inserted (a *variorum* edition of Shakespeare).

various. See VARY.

varix, vâ′riks, *n.* pl. **varices,** vâr′i•sēz. [L.] A varicose vein. VARICOSE.

varlet, vär′let, *n.* [O.Fr. *varlet, vaslet*, VALET.] Anciently, a page or knight's follower; an attendant on a gentleman; hence, a term of contempt for one in a subordinate or menial position; a low fellow; a rascal.—**varletry,** vär′let•ri, *n.* The rabble; the crowd.

varnish, vär′nish, *n.* [From Fr. *vernis*, varnish, *vernisser, vernir*, to varnish, from L. *vitrinus*, glassy, from *vitrum*, glass—varnish giving a glassy surface. VITREOUS.] A solution of resinous matter, forming a clear limpid fluid, used by painters, cabinetmakers, etc., for coating the surface of their work in order to give it a shining, transparent, and hard surface, capable of resisting the influences of air and moisture; what resembles varnish either naturally or artificially; a glossy or lustrous appearance; outside show; gloss.—*v.t.* To lay varnish on; to give an improved appearance to; to give a fair coloring to; to gloss over.—**varnisher,** vär′nish•ėr, *n.* One who varnishes; one who gives a fair external appearance.—**varnish tree,** *n.* The name of certain trees found chiefly in India, Burma, and China, which exude resinous juices employed as varnishes.

varus, vâ′rus, *a.* [L. *varus.*] Knock-kneed, in-kneed.

vary, vâ′ri, *v.t.*—*varied, varying.* [Fr. *varier*, from L. *variare*, to vary, from *varius*, variegated, diverse, various.] To alter in form, appearance, substance, or position; to make different by a partial change; to change; to diversify; *mus.* to embellish, as a melody or theme with passing notes, arpeggios, etc.—*v.i.* To alter or be altered in any manner; to suffer change; to appear in different forms; to differ or be different; to be unlike or diverse; to change, as in purpose, opinion, or the like; to deviate; to swerve; to alternate; to disagree; to be at variance; *math.* to be subject to continual increase or decrease.—**variable,** vâ′ri•a•bl, *a.* Capable of varying, changing, or altering; liable to change; often changing; changeable (*variable* winds); fickle; unsteady; inconstant; capable of being varied or changed.—*Variable quantities, math.* quantities subject to continual increase or diminution.—*Variable stars*, stars which undergo a periodical increase and diminution of their luster.—*n.* That which is variable; a variable quantity; a shifting wind as opposed to a trade wind; hence *the variables*, the region between the northeast and the southeast trade winds.—**variableness, variability,** vâ′ri•a•bl•nes, vâ′ri•a•bil″i•ti, *n.* The state or quality of being variable.—**variably,** vâ′ri•a•bli, *adv.* In a variable manner; changeably; mutably; inconstantly.—**variance,** vâ′ri•ans, *n.* Difference that produces dispute or controversy; disagreement; dissension; discord.—*At variance*, in disagreement; in a state of dissension; in enmity.—**variant,** vâ′ri•ant, *a.* Different; diverse; variable; varying.—*n.* Something that is really the same, though with a different form; a different reading or version.—**variation,** vâ•ri•ā′shon, *n.* [L. *variatio.*] The act or process of varying; partial change in the form, position, state, or qualities of the same thing; alteration; mutation; change; modification; the extent to which a thing varies; the amount or rate of change; the act of deviating; deviation; *gram.* change of termination of words; inflection; *astron.* any deviation from the mean orbit or mean motion of a heavenly body occasioned by another disturbing body; *physics* and *navig.* same as *declination*; *mus.* one of a series of ornamental changes or embellishments in the treatment of a tune, movement, or theme during several successive repetitions.—*Calculus of variations*, a branch of analysis, the chief object of which is to find what function of a variable will be a maximum or minimum on certain prescribed conditions.—**varied,** vâ′rid, *p.* and *a.* Altered; changed; characterized by variety; diversified; consisting of various kinds or sorts differing from each other; diverse; various.—**varier,** vâ′ri•ėr, *n.* One who varies. (*Tenn.*)—**varietal,** va•rī′e•tal, *a.* Pertaining to a variety, as distinguished from an individual or a species.—**variety,** va•rī′e•ti, *a.* [L. *varietas*, from *varius.*] The state or quality of being varied or various; intermixture or succession of different things, or of things different in form; diversity; multifariousness; manysidedness; a collection or number of different things; a varied assortment; something different from others of the same general kind; a sort; a kind; in scientific classifications, a subdivision of a species of animals or plants; according to the evolution theory, a species in process of formation.—**variform,** vâ′ri•form, *a.* Having different shapes or forms.—**variometer,** vâ•ri•om′etėr, *n.* [From *vary*, and Gr. *metron*, a measure.] *Wireless tel.* an inductance coil whose inductance can be varied by moving a part of the coil with reference to the remainder.—**various,** vâ′ri•us, *a.* [L. *varius.*] Differing from each other; different; diverse; manifold; divers; several; exhibiting different characters; multiform.—**variously,** vâ′ri•us•li, *adv.* In various or different ways; with diversity; diversely; multifariously.

vascular, vas′kū•lėr, *a.* [L. *vasculum*, a vessel, dim. of *vas*, a vessel.] Pertaining to the vessels or tubes connected with the vital functions of animals or plants, and especially making up the circulatory system; consisting of, containing, or operating by means of animal or vegetable vessels.—*Vascular plants*, flowering plants and ferns, as contrasted with *cellular* plants.—*Vascular tissue*, tissue composed of small vessels like the woody tissue or substance of flowering plants: used in contradistinction to *cellular*.—*Vascular system, anat.* the system formed by all the blood vessels, lacteals, etc.—**vascularity,** vas•kū•lar′i•ti, *n.* The state or quality of being vascular.—**vasculose,** vas′kū•lōs, *a. Bot.* same as *Vascular*.—*n.* The substance constituting the principal part of the vessels of plants.—**vasculum,** vas′-kū•lum, *n.* A botanist's case for carrying specimens as he collects them; *bot.* a pitcher-shaped leaf.

vase, vāz or väz, *n.* [Fr. *vase*, from L. *vasum* (rarely used for *vas*), a vessel; akin *vessel, vascular.*] A vessel of some size of various materials, forms, and purposes, often merely serving for ornament, *arch.* a sculptured ornament representing the vessels of the ancients, as incense pots, flowerpots, etc.; the body of a Corinthian or Composite capital.—**vasomotor,** vas•ō•mō′tėr, *a.* [L. *vas*, a vessel, and *motor*, a mover.] Applied to the system of nerves distributed over the muscular coats of the blood vessels.

vassal, vas'al, *n.* [Fr. *vassal*, L.L. *vassallus*, a vassal, dim. of *vassus*, a domestic, from Armor. *gwaz*, W. *gwas*, a youth, a servant. Of same origin are *valet*, *varlet*.] A feudal tenant holding lands under a lord, and bound by his tenure to feudal services; a subject; a dependent; a retainer; a servant; a bondman; a slave.—*a.* Servile; subservient.—**vassalage,** vas'al•ij, *n.* The state of being a vassal; servitude; dependence; slavery.

vast, vast, *a.* [Fr. *vaste*, from L. *vastus*, waste, desert, vast, huge (hence, *vasto*, to lay waste, to *devastate*); allied to G. *wüste*, a desert. WASTE.] Waste or desert‡; lonely‡; of great extent; boundless; huge in bulk and extent; immense; very great in numbers or amount; very great as to degree or intensity.—*n.* A boundless waste or space; immensity. (*Poetical.*)—**vastly,** vast'li, *adv.* Very greatly; to a vast extent or degree.—**vastness,** vast'nes, *n.* The quality of being vast; great extent; immensity; greatness in general.—**vasty,**‡ vas'ti, *a.* Vast; boundless; very spacious. (*Shak.*)

vat, vat, *n.* [Also *fat*, a vat, from A.Sax. *faet*, a vat=D. *vat*, Icel. and Sw. *fat*, a vat, G. *fass*, a cask.] A large vessel for holding liquors; a large vessel of the tub kind; a tun; a wooden tank or cistern.—*v.t.*—*vatted*, *vatting*. To put in a vat.

vatic,† vat'ik, *a.* [L. *vates*, a prophet.] Pertaining to a prophet; oracular; inspired.

Vatican, vat'i•kan, *n.* A most extensive palace at Rome upon the Vatican hill, the residence of the pope; hence, the *Vatican* is equivalent to the papal power or government.—*Vatican Council*, the Ecumenical Council which met in the Vatican in 1870, and declared the infallibility of the pope to be a dogma of the church.—**Vaticanism,** vat'i•kan•izm, *n.* The doctrines and tenets promulgated by the Vatican; ultramontanism.

vaticinate, va•tis'i•nāt, *v.i.*—*vaticinated*, *vaticinating*. [L. *vaticinor*, *vaticinatus*, to prophesy, from *vates*, a prophet.] To prophesy; to practice prediction.—*v.t.* To prophesy; to foretell.—**vaticination,** va•tis'i•nā″shon, *n.* A prediction; a prophecy.—**vaticinator,** va•tis'i•nā•tėr, *n.* One who vaticinates or predicts.

vaudeville, vōd'vēl, *n.* [Fr. *vaudeville*, from O.Fr. *Vau de Vire*, *Val de Vire*, the valley of the Vire, in Normandy —originally applied to songs of Oliver Basselin, who lived there.] A French name for a light, gay song, consisting of several couplets and refrain or burden, sung to a familiar air; in the U.S. various types of entertainment, as song and dance acts, humorous skits, comic dialogues, and juggling acts.

Vaudois, vōd•wä, *n.* [*Vaud* in Switzerland.] An inhabitant of the Pays de Vaud, a Waldense.

vault, vạlt, *n.* [O.Fr. *vaulte*, *voulte* (Fr. *voûte*) from L.L. *volta*, *voluta*, a vault, from L. *volvo*, *volutum*, to turn round, to roll. VOLUBLE.] An arched roof; a concave roof or rooflike covering (the *vault* of heaven); *arch.* a continued arch; an arched apartment, a compartment built of steel or fireproof brick for the storing of valuables; a safe.—*v.t.* To form with a vault or arched roof; to arch.—**vaulted,** vạl'ted, *p.* and *a.* Arched; concave; covered with an arch or vault.—**vaulting,** vạl'ting, *n.* Vaulted work; vaults collectively.

vault, vạlt, *n.* [Fr. *volte*, from It. *volta*, a turn, a leap or vault, from *volvo*, *volutum*, to roll, to turn. Hence this word is a doublet of *Vault* above.] A leap or spring, a bound; a leap by means of a pole, or assisted by resting the hand or hands on something.—*v.i.* To leap; to bound, to spring; to exhibit equestrian or other feats of tumbling or leaping.—**vaulter,** vạl'tėr, *n.* One that vaults; a leaper; a tumbler.—**vaulting,** vạl'ting, *n.* The art or practice of a vaulter.

vaunt, vạnt, *v.i.* [From Fr. *vanter*, to vaunt, from L.L. *vanitare*, to boast, from L. *vanus*, vain. VAIN.] To boast; to talk with ostentation; to brag; to glory; to exult.—*v.t.* To boast of; to magnify or glorify with vanity; to display or put forward boastfully.—*n.* A boast; a brag.—**vaunter,** vạn'tėr, *n.* A boaster; a man given to vain ostentation.—**vauntingly,** vạn'ting•li, *adv.* Boastfully; with vain ostentation.

vavasor, vav'a•sor, *n.* [O.Fr. *vavassor*, L.L. *vavassor*, *vasvassor*, probably a contr. of *vassus vassorum*, the vassal of vassals. VASSAL.] A principal vassal not holding immediately of the sovereign but of a great lord, and having himself vassals.

veal, vēl, *n.* [O.Fr. *veel* and *vedel*, from L. *vitellus*, dim. of *vitulus*, a calf; from root of L. *vetus*, *veteris*, old (whence *veteran*, Gr. (*v*)*etos*, a year).] The flesh of a calf killed for the table.

vector, vek'tor, *n.* [L. a bearer or carrier, from *veho*, to carry.] A quantity, such as a velocity or a force, which has direction as well as magnitude, and is compounded by the parallelogram law; also a radius vector. See RADIUS.

Veda, vä'dä or vē'da, *n.* [Skr., from *vid*, to know; cog. L. *video*, E. *wit*, to know. WIT.] The general name for the body of ancient Sanskrit hymns, with accompanying comments, believed by the Hindus to have been revealed by Brahma, and on which the Brahmanical system is based.—**Vedanta,** ve•dän'ta, *n.* A system of philosophy among the Hindus founded on the Vedas.—**Vedic,** vē'dik, *a.* Relating to a Veda or the Vedas.

vedette, vi•det', *n.* [Fr. *vedette*, from It. *vedetta*, a vedette, from *vedere*, L. *videre*, to see. VISIBLE.] A sentinel on horseback stationed on an outpost or elevated point to watch an enemy and give notice of danger; a picket or outpost.

veer, vēr, *v.i.* [Fr. *virer*, to turn, veer, tack, etc.; from L.L. *virare*, to turn, from L. *viria*, a ring, a bracelet; akin *environ*.] To shift or change direction, as the wind; to go round; to change the direction of its course by turning (as a ship); to turn round, vary, be otherwise minded: said in regard to persons, feelings, intentions.—*v.t.* *Naut.* to direct into a different course; to wear or cause to change a course by turning the stern to windward, in opposition to *tacking*.

vegetable, vej'e•ta•bl, *a.* [Fr. *végétable*, from L. *vegetabilis*, enlivening, from *vegeto*, to enliven, from *vegetus*, lively, from *vegeo*, to rouse, excite; from root seen also in *vigor*, *vigilant*.] Belonging, pertaining, or peculiar to plants; having the characteristics of a plant or plants.—*Vegetable ivory*. IVORY NUT.—*Vegetable mold*, mold consisting wholly or chiefly of humus.—*n.* A plant; often distinctively, a plant used for culinary purposes, or used for feeding cattle and sheep or other animals.—**vegetal,** vej'e•tal, *a.* Having the characteristics or nature of a plant; pertaining to that class of vital phenomena common to plants and animals.—*n.* A plant; a vegetable. (*Johnson.*)—**vegetarian,** vej•e•tâ'ri•an, *n.* One who abstains from animal food, and maintains that vegetable food is the only kind proper for man.—*a.* Belonging to the diet or system of the vegetarians.—**vegetarianism,** vej•e•tâ'ri•an•izm, *n.* The theory and practice of living solely on vegetable food.—**vegetate,** vej'e•tāt, *v.i.*—*vegetated*, *vegetating*. [In form from L. *vegeto*, *vegetatum*, to enliven, but in meaning from *vegetable*.] To grow in the manner of plants; hence, to live a monotonous, useless life; to have a mere existence.—**vegetation,** vej•e•tā'shon, *n.* The process of growing exhibited by plants; vegetable growth; vegetables or plants in general or collectively.—**vegetative,** vej'e•tā•tiv, *a.* Growing as plants; having the power to produce or support growth in plants.—**vegetativeness,** vej'e•tā•tiv•nes, *n.* The quality of being vegetative.

vehement, vē'e•ment, *a.* [Fr. *véhément*, from L. *vehemens*, *vehementis*, eager, vehement, lit. carried out of one's mind, from *veho*, to carry, and *mens*, *mentis*, the mind. VEHICLE, MENTAL.] Proceeding from or characterized by strength or impetuosity of feeling; very eager or urgent; fervent; passionate; acting with great force or energy (*vehement* wind, fire); energetic; violent; very forcible.—**vehemently,** vē'e•ment•li, *adv.* With great force and violence; urgently; passionately.—**vehemence,** vē'e•mens, *n.* [Fr. *véhémence*, L. *vehementia*.] The character or quality of being vehement; violent ardor; fervor; impetuosity; fire; impetuous force; boisterousness; violence.—**vehemency,** vē'e•men•si, *n.* Vehemence.

vehicle, vē'i•kl, *n.* [L. *vehiculum*, a vehicle, a carriage, from *veho*, to carry (seen also in *inveigh*, *vehement*), from a root seen also in E. *wagon*, *way*.] Any kind of carriage moving on land; a conveyance; that which is used as the instrument of conveyance, transmission, or communication (language is the *vehicle* for conveying ideas), a substance in which medicine is taken; a menstruum or medium in which paints, gums, varnishes, etc., are dissolved and prepared for use.—**vehicular,** vē•hik′ū•lėr, *a.* Pertaining to a vehicle; of the nature of a vehicle.

veil, vāl, *n.* [O.Fr. *veile, vaile* (Fr. *voile*), from L. *velum*, a sail, a veil, from root seen also in *veho*, to carry, and in E. *way, wagon.*] Something hung up or spread out to intercept the view; a screen; a curtain; especially, a more or less transparent piece of dress worn to conceal, shade, or protect the face; *fig.* anything that prevents observation; a covering, mask, disguise, or the like; *anat.* the soft palate.—*To take the veil*, to assume the veil on becoming a nun; to retire to a nunnery. —*v.t.* To cover or conceal with a veil; to enshroud; to envelop; to keep from being seen; to conceal from view; to conceal, figuratively; to mask; to disguise.

vein, vān, *n.* [Fr. *veine*, from L. *vena*, a vein, also natural bent, genius, same root as *veho*, to carry. VEHICLE, VEIL.] One of a system of membranous canals or tubes distributed throughout the bodies of animals for the purpose of returning the impure blood from the extremities, surfaces, and viscera to the heart and lungs; a tube or an assemblage of tubes through which the sap of plants is transmitted along the leaves; a crack or fissure in a rock, filled up by substances different from the rock, and which may either be metallic or nonmetallic; a streak or wave of different color appearing in wood, in marble, etc.; disposition or cast of mind; particular mood, humor, or disposition for the time being.—*v.t.* To fill or furnish with veins; to streak or variegate with veins.—**veined,** vānd, *a.* Full of veins; streaked; variegated; *bot.* having vessels branching over the surface, as a leaf.—**veinlet,** vān′let, *n.* A vein branching off from a larger vein.—**veiny,** vā′ni, *a.* Full of veins.

velar, vē′lėr, *a.* [L. *velum*, a veil. VEIL.] Pertaining or relating to a veil; pertaining to the veil of the palate.—**velarium,** vē•lâ′ri•um, *n.* An awning stretched over an ancient Roman theater or amphitheater, these buildings being open to the sky.—**velate,** vē′lāt, *a. Bot.* having a veil; veiled.

veld, veld, felt, *n.* [D. *veld*, a field=E. *field.*] A term in S. Africa for open unenclosed country.

velitation, vel′i•tā″shon, *n.* [L. *velites*, light-armed soldiers.] A preliminary skirmish, a slight controversy.

velleity, vel•lē′i•ti, *n.* [Fr. *velléité*, from L. *velle*, to will.] *Philos.* volition in the weakest form; an indolent or inactive wish or inclination toward a thing.

vellicate, vel′i•kāt, *v.t.* [L. *vellico*, *vellicatum*, from *vello*, to pull.] To twitch.—**vellication,** vel•i•kā′shon, *n.* A twitching; a convulsive twitching of muscles.

vellum, vel′um, *n.* [Fr. *vélin*, from L. *vitulinus*, pertaining to a calf, from *vitulus*, a calf. VEAL.] A fine kind of parchment made of calf's skin, and rendered clear, smooth, and white for writing on.—**vellumy,** vel′um•i, *a.* Resembling vellum.

velocipede, ve•los′i•pēd, *n.* [From L. *velox*, and *pes, pedis*, a foot.] A light vehicle or conveyance consisting mainly of wheels and driven or impelled by the feet of the rider or pair of riders; a bicycle or tricycle.

velocity, ve•los′i•ti, *n.* [Fr. *vélocité*, from L. *velocitas, velocitatis*, from *velox, velocis*, swift, rapid.] Quickness or speed in motion or movement; swiftness; rapidity; not applied to the movements of animals, or but rarely; *physics*, rate of motion, differing from speed in involving direction as well as magnitude.—*Velocity potential*, in the theory of fluid motion, a quantity varying from point to point of space, and having the property that its rate of change per unit length in any direction gives the component velocity in that direction.—*Virtual velocity*, an infinitesimal displacement of the point of application of a force measured in the direction of the force.

velours, vel′ör, *n.* [Fr. *velours*, L. *villosus.*] A substance of felt or other velvety combinations, much used in the construction of silk hats, women's hats, etc.

velum, vē′lum, *n.* [L., a veil.] *Bot.* the horizontal membrane connecting the margin of the pileus of a fungus with the stipes; *anat.* the veil of the palate.

velutinous, ve•lū′ti•nus, *a.* [From It. *veluto*, velvet. VELVET.] Resembling velvet; velvety.

velvet, vel′vet, *n.* [O.E. *velouette, velwet, vellute*; L.L. *velluetum, vellutum*; It. *veluto*, from L. *villus*, shaggy hair.] A rich silk stuff, covered on the outside with a close, short, fine, soft shag or nap; a cotton stuff manufactured in the same way, distinctively called *velveteen* or *cotton velvet*; a delicate hairy integument covering a deer's antlers in the first stages of growth.—*a.* Made of velvet; soft and delicate like velvet.—**velveteen,** vel•ve•tēn′, *n.* A cloth made of cotton in imitation of velvet; cotton velvet.—**velvety,** vel′ve•ti, *a.* Made of or resembling velvet; smooth, soft, or delicate in surface.

venal, vē′nal, *a.* [L. *venalis*, venal, for sale, from *venum*, sale; akin *vend.*] Ready to sell one's self for money or other consideration and entirely from sordid motives; ready to accept a bribe; mercenary.—**venality,** vē•nal′i•ti, *n.* Prostitution of talents, offices, or services for money or reward; mercenariness.

venation, vē•nā′shon, *n.* [From L. *vena*, a vein.] *Bot.* the manner in which the veins of leaves are arranged.

vend, vend, *v.t.* [From L. *vendo*, to sell, from *venum*, sale, and *do*, to give. VENAL.] To sell.—**vendee,** ven•dē′, *n.* The person to whom a thing is sold: opposed to *vendor.*—**vender,** ven′dėr, *n.* One who vends or sells.—**vendible,** ven′di•bl, *a.* Capable of being sold; saleable; marketable.—**vendibility,** ven•di•bil′i•ti, *n.* The state of being saleable. —**vendibly,** ven′di•bli, *adv.* In a saleable manner.—**vendor,** ven′dor, *n.* A seller.

vendace, ven′dās, *n.* [O.Fr. *vendese*, Fr. *vandoise*, the dace; origin unknown.] A white fish found in a few British lakes, and in some of the rivers and lakes of Sweden; very delicate eating.

vendetta, ven•det′tä, *n.* [It., from L. *vindicta*, revenge. VINDICTIVE.] A blood feud; the practice of the nearest of kin executing vengeance on the murderer of a relative, as among the Corsicans, Arabs, etc.

vendue,‡ ven′dū, *n.* [O.Fr. *vendue*, from *vendre*, to sell. VEND.] A sale by auction.

veneer, ve•nēr′, *n.* [From G. *furnier*, a veneer, *furnieren*, to veneer, from Fr. *fournir*, to furnish (which see).] A thin piece of wood (sometimes ivory or other substance) laid upon another of a less valuable sort, so that the whole article appears to be of the more valuable sort.—*v.t.* To overlay or face over with veneer; *fig.* to put a fine superficial show on; to gild.—**veneering,** ve•nēr′ing, *n.* The act of one who veneers; the material laid on; *fig.* superficial show.

venerate, ven′ėr•āt, *v.t.*—*venerated, venerating.* [L. *veneror, veneratus*, to venerate, from the stem of *Venus, Veneris*, Venus, love; allied to Skr. *van*, to worship, to love. VENUS.] To regard with respect and reverence; to reverence; to revere; to regard as hallowed. — **veneration,** ven•ėr•ā′shon, *n.* [L. *veneratio.*] The highest degree of respect and reverence; a feeling or sentiment excited by the dignity, wisdom, and goodness of a person, or by the sacredness of his character, and with regard to place, by whatever makes us regard it as hallowed.—**venerator,** ven′ėr•ā•tėr, *n.* One who venerates.—**venerable,** ven′ėr•a•bl, *a.* [L. *venerabilis.*] Worthy of veneration; deserving of honor and respect; to be regarded with awe and reverence; hallowed by associations.—**venerableness,** ven′ėr•a•bl•nes, *n.* The state or quality of being venerable.—**venerably,** ven′ėr•a•bli, *adv.* So as to excite veneration or reverence.

venereal, ve•nē′ri•al, *a.* [L. *venereus*, from *Venus, Veneris.*] Pertaining to sexual love or its indulgence; relating to or arising from sexual intercourse. —**venery,** ven′ėr•i, *n.* Sexual intercourse.

venery, ven′ėr•i, *n.* [Fr. *vénerie*, from O.Fr. *vener*, L. *venari*, to hunt, whence also *venison.*] The act or exercise of hunting; the sports of the chase.

venesection, ven•e•sek′shon, *n.* [L. *véna*, vein, and *sectio*, a cutting.] The operation of opening a vein for letting blood; bloodletting; phlebotomy.

Venetian, ve•nē′shi•an, *a.* Pertaining to Venice in Northern Italy.—*Venetian blind,* a blind made of thin narrow transverse slips of wood, so connected as to overlap each other when closed, and to show a series of open spaces for the admission of light and air when in the other position. [In this usage the capital letter need not be employed.]—*Venetian chalk, Venetian talc.* Same as *French Chalk.*—*Venetian door,* a door with long narrow side lights.—*Venetian red,* a burnt ocher which owes its color to the presence of an oxide of iron.—*Venetian white,* a carefully prepared carbonate of lead.—*n.* A native of Venice; a venetian blind.

vengeance, ven′jans, *n.* [Fr. *vengeance,* from *venger,* to revenge, from L. *vindicare,* to avenge. VINDICATE.] Punishment inflicted in return for an injury or an offense, generally implying indignation on the part of the punisher and more or less justice in the nature of the punishment. ∴ Syn. under REVENGE. The word is often used in curses or imprecations (a *vengeance* on you!); the phrase *with a vengeance!* is expressive of excess in degree, vehemence, violence, and the like (a forced march, *with a vengeance!*).—**vengeful,** venj′fụl, *a.* Vindictive; retributive; revengeful.—**vengefully,** venj′fụl•li, *adv.* In a vengeful manner; vindictively.

venial, vē′ni•al, *a.* [L. *venialis,* from L. *venia,* pardon; akin to *Venus* (which see).] That may be forgiven; pardonable; not deeply sinful; excusable; that may pass without censure.—**venialness, veniality,** vē′ni•al•nes, vē•ni•al′i•ti, *n.* Quality of being venial.—**venially,** vē′ni•al•li, *adv.* In a venial manner; pardonably.

venison, ven′zn or ven′i•zn, *n.* [O.Fr. *venison* (Fr. *venaison*), from L. *venatio,* a hunting, from *venari,* to hunt (whence *venery,* hunting).] The flesh of such wild animals as are taken in the chase and used as human food; in modern usage restricted to the flesh of animals of the deer kind.

venom, ven′om, *n.* [O.E. *venim, venime,* O.Fr. *venim, venin,* Mod.Fr. *venin,* from L. *venenum,* poison.] The poisonous fluid secreted by certain animals and introduced into the bodies of other animals by biting, as in the case of serpents, and stinging, as in the case of scorpions, bees, etc.; hence, spite; malice; malignity; virulency.—**venomous,** ven′om•us, *a.* Full of venom; noxious to animal life from venom; poisonous; malignant; spiteful; malicious.—**venomously,** ven′om•us•li, *adv.* In a venomous manner; malignantly; spitefully.—**venomousness,** ven′om•us•nes, *n.*

venous, vē′nus, *a.* [L. *venosus,* from *vena,* a vein. VEIN.] Pertaining to a vein or to veins; contained in veins (*venous* blood, distinguishable from arterial blood by its darker color); consisting of veins; *bot.* veined or venose.—**venose,** vē′nōs, *a. Bot.* having numerous branched veins, as leaves.—**venosity,** vi•nos′i•ti, *n.* The state or quality of being venous or venose.

vent, vent, *n.* [From Fr. *vent,* wind, air, from L. *ventus,* wind (in *ventilate*), so that the original meaning would be airhole; or same as *fent.*] A small aperture or opening; the priming and firing aperture of a gun; the touchhole; the anus; the opening at which the excrements of birds and fishes are discharged; the flue or funnel of a chimney; an outlet; means of outward manifestation or expression (a *vent* for one's feelings); utterance; expression.—*To give vent to,* to suffer to escape; to keep no longer pent up (anger or the like).—*v.t.* To let out; to give passage to; to emit; to keep no longer pent up in one's mind; to pour forth; to utter; to publish.

vent, vent, *n.* [Fr. *vente,* sale, a market from L. *vendo, venditum,* to sell. VEND.] A selling; sale; market.

ventage, ven′tij, *n.* [From Fr. *vent,* L. *ventus,* wind. VENTILATE.] A small hole, as of a flute.—**ventail,** ven′tāl, *n.* [Fr. *ventail,* L.L. *ventaculum,* from L. *ventus.*] The movable front of a helmet.

venter, ven′tėr, *n.* [L., the belly.] *Anat.* the abdomen or lower belly; the belly of a muscle; *law,* the womb.

ventilate, ven′ti•lāt, *v.t.*—*ventilated, ventilating.* [L. *ventilo, ventilatum,* to winnow, to ventilate, from *ventus,* wind; same root as Skr. *vâ,* to blow, E. *wind.*] To expose to the free passage of air or wind; to supply with fresh and remove vitiated air; to expose to common talk or consideration; to let be freely discussed.—**ventilation,** ven•ti•lā′shon, *n.* [L. *ventilatio.*] The act of ventilating; the replacement of vitiated air by pure fresh air; the art or operation of supplying buildings, mines, and other confined places with a necessary quantity of fresh air; public examination or discussion of questions or topics.—**ventilative,** ven′ti•lā•tiv, *a.* Belonging to ventilation.—**ventilator,** ven′ti•lā•tėr, *n.* One who ventilates; a contrivance for keeping the air fresh in any close space.

ventrad, vent′rad, *a.* [From L. *venter, ventris,* the belly, and *ad,* toward.] Toward the ventral surface.—**ventral,** ven′tral, *a.* Belonging or pertaining to the belly, or to the surface of the body opposite to the dorsal side or back.—**ventricle,** ven′tri•kl, *n.* [L. *ventriculus,* dim. of *venter,* belly.] A small cavity in an animal body serving some function.—*Ventricles of the heart,* two cavities of the heart (distinguished as *right* and *left*), which propel the blood into the arteries.—**ventricose,** ven′tri•kōs, *a.* [L. *ventricosus.*] Swelled out; *bot.* swelling out in the middle.—**ventricular,** ven•trik′ū•lėr, *a.* Pertaining to a ventricle; distended in the middle.—**ventriloquism,** ven•tril′o•kwizm, *n.* [L. *ventriloquus,* a ventriloquist—*venter,* and *loquor,* to speak, the notion being that the voice proceeded from the belly.] The act, art, or practice of speaking or uttering sounds by employing the vocal organs in such a manner that the voice appears to come, not from the person, but from some distance, as from the opposite side of the room, from the cellar, etc.—**ventriloquist,** ven•tril′o•kwist, *n.* One who practices or is skilled in ventriloquism.—**ventriloquize,** ven•tril′o•kwīz, *v.i.* To practice ventriloquism.—**ventriloquial,** ven•tri•lō′kwi•al, *a.* Pertaining to ventriloquism.

venture, ven′chėr *n.* [Abbrev. of *aventure,* old form of *adventure,* from Fr. *aventure,* L. *ad,* to, and *venturus,* about to come, from *venio,* to come (seen also in *advene, advent, convene, convent, covenant, event, invent, prevent, revenue,* etc.). COME.] An undertaking of chance or danger; the risking or staking of something; a hazard; a scheme for making gain by way of trade; a commercial speculation; the thing put to hazard; something sent to sea in trade; chance; luck; contingency.—*At a venture,* at hazard; without seeing the end or mark, or without foreseeing the issue.—*v.i.*—*ventured, venturing.* To dare; to have courage or presumption to do, undertake, or say something; to run a hazard or risk; to risk one's self.—*v.t.* To expose to hazard; to risk; to expose one's self to.—**venturer,** ven′chėr•ėr, *n.* One who ventures.—**venturesome,** ven′chėr•sum, *a.* Inclined to venture; venturous.—**venturesomely,** ven′chėr•sum•li, *adv.* In a venturesome manner.—**venturesomeness,** ven′chėr•sum•nes, *n.*—**venturous,** ven′chėr•us, *a.* Daring; bold; intrepid; adventurous.—**venturously,** ven′chėr•us•li, *adv.* Daringly; fearlessly; boldly.—**venturousness,** ven′chėr•us•nes, *n.*

venue, ven′ū, *n.* [Fr. *venue,* a coming, from *venir,* L. *venire,* to come. VENTURE.] *Fencing,* a coming on; an onset; a bout; a turn; a thrust; *law,* a locality; the place where an action is laid, or the trial of a cause takes place.

venule, ven′ūl, *n.* [L. *venula,* a small vein. VEIN.] A small vein.

Venus, vē′nus, *n.* [L. *Venus, Veneris* (hence *venereal*), cog. with A.Sax. *wine,* Icel. *vinr,* O.G. *wini,* a friend, Skr. *van,* to love, to worship. VENERATE, VENIAL.] The goddess of beauty and love among the Romans, often identified with the Greek *Aphrodite*; a planet having its orbit between Mercury and the earth, the most brilliant of all the planetary bodies, sometimes the morning, sometimes the evening star.

veracious, ve•rā′shus, *a.* [L. *verax, veracis,* from *verus,* true. VERY.] Observant of truth; habitually disposed to speak truth; characterized by truth; true.—**veraciously,** ve•rā′shus•li, *adv.* In a veracious manner; truthfully.—**veracity,** ve•ras′i•ti, *n.* The state or quality of being veracious or true; regard to or observance of truth; truthfulness; truth; agreement with actual fact.

veranda, ve•ran′da, *n.* [Pg. *varanda*, from Skr. *varanda*, a veranda, from *vri*, to cover.] A kind of open portico, or a sort of light external gallery attached to the front of a building, with a sloping roof supported on slender pillars.

veratrin, veratrine, ve′ra•trin, *n.* [L. *veratrum*, hellebore.] A vegetable alkaloid found in plants of the hellebore genus, used as external application in neuralgia and rheumatism.

verb, vėrb, *n.* [Fr. *verbe*, from L. *verbum*, a word, a verb; same root as E. *word*.] *Gram.* that part of speech whose essential function is to predicate or assert something in regard to something else (the subject or thing spoken of), divided into *active* and *neuter*, *transitive* and *intransitive*, etc.—**verbal,** vėr′-bl, *a.* [L. *verbalis*.] Spoken; expressed to the ear in words; oral; respecting words only and not things; literal; having word answering to word (a *verbal* translation); *gram.* derived from a verb (a *verbal* noun).—*n. Gram.* a noun derived from a verb.—**verbalism,** vėr′bl•izm, *n.* Something expressed orally.—**verbalist,** vėr′bl•ist, *n.* One who deals in words merely; a literal adherent to, or a minute critic of words.—**verbalization,** vėr′-bl•i•zā″shon, *n.* The act of verbalizing.—**verbalize, verbify,** vėr′bl•īz, vėr′bi•fī, *v.t.* To convert into a verb; to use as a verb,—*v.i.* To use many words; to be verbose or diffuse.—**verbally,** vėr′bl•li, *adv.* In a verbal manner; by words uttered; orally; word for word.—**verbatim,** vėr•bā′-tim, *adv.* [L.] Word for word; in the same words (to tell a story *verbatim*). —*Verbatim et literatim* (lit•ėr•ā′tim), word for word, and letter for letter.—**verbiage,** vėr′bi•ij, *n.* [Fr.] Verbosity; use of many words without necessity; wordiness.—**verbose,** vėr•-bōs′, *a.* [L. *verbosus*.] Abounding in words; using or containing more words than are necessary; wordy; prolix.—**verbosely,** vėr•bōs′li, *adv.* In a verbose manner; wordily.—**verboseness, verbosity,** vėr•bōs′nes, vėr•bos′i•ti, *n.* The state or quality of being verbose; wordiness; prolixity.

verbena, vėr•bē′na, *n.* [L. *verbena*, any green bough used in sacred rites.] A genus of plants, mostly American, one species of which, common vervain, was formerly supposed to possess remarkable virtues, others are cultivated for the great beauty of their flowers.

verbiage, verbose, etc. See VERB.

verdant, vėr′dant, *a.* [From Fr. *verdir*, to grow green, O.Fr. *verd*, green, from L. *viridis*, green.] Green with herbage or foliage covered with growing plants or grass; green in knowledge; simple by reason of inexperience (*colloq.*).—**verdancy,** vėr′dan•si, *n.* Greenness; rawness; inexperience.—**verdantly,** vėr′dant•-li, *adv.* In a verdant manner.—**verd antique,** vėrd•an•tēk′, *n.* [Fr., from *verd*, green, *antique*, ancient.] The green incrustation seen on ancient coins, brass or copper; *mineral.* an aggregate of serpentine and white crystallized marble, having a greenish color; also, a green porphyry used as marble.—**verderer, verderor,** vėr′dėr•ėr, vėr′dėr•or, *n.* [Fr. *verdier*, L.L. *viridarius*.] An official having charge of the trees, etc., in a royal forest.

verdict, vėr′dikt, *n.* [L.L. *verdictum*, *veredictum*, from L. *vere*, truly, and *dictum*, something declared, from *dico*, *dictum*, to say. VERY, DICTION.] The answer of a jury given to the court concerning any matter of fact in any cause committed to their trial and examination; hence, a decision, judgment, or opinion pronounced in general.

verdigris, vėr′di•grēs, *n.* [O.Fr. *verd-de-gris*, verdigris, apparently from *verd*, green, *de*, of, *gris*, gray; but rather from *verd de Grèce*, lit. green of Greece. VERDANT.] A substance obtained by exposing copper to the air in contact with acetic acid, used as a pigment, as a mordant, and otherwise.

verditer, vėr′di•tėr, *n.* [Fr. *verd-de-terre*, green of earth. VERDANT.] A blue or bluish-green pigment, generally prepared by decomposing nitrate of copper with chalk.

verdure, vėr′dūr, *n.* [Fr. *verdure*, greenness, green vegetation, from *verd*, *vert*, green, from L. *viridis*, green. VERDANT.] Greenness or freshness of vegetation; green plants or foliage.—**verdurous,** vėr′dūr•us, *a.* Covered with verdure; verdant.

verge, vėrj, *n.* [Fr. *verge*, a rod, mace, ring, or hoop, from L. *virga*, a rod.] A rod or staff of office; a mace; a ring or circle (*Shak.*)‡; compass; space; room; scope; the extreme side or edge of anything; the brink, border, margin, limit.—**verger,** vėr′-jėr, *n.* One who carries a verge; an officer who bears the verge or staff of office before a bishop, dean, or other dignitary; the official who takes care of the interior of the fabric of a church.

verge, vėrj, *v.i.*—*verged*, *verging*. [L. *vergo*, to turn, to incline.] To tend downward; to bend; to slope; to tend; to incline; to approach; to border.

veridical,† ve•rid′i•kal, *a.* [L. *veridicus*—*verum*, truth, and *dico*, to say. VERDICT.] Truth-telling; veracious.

verify, ver′i•fī, *v.t.*—*verified*, *verifying*. [Fr. *vérifier*, from L. *verus*, true, and *facio*, to make. VERY.] To prove to be true; to confirm; to establish the truth, correctness, or authenticity of.—**verifiable,** ver′i•fī•-a•bl, *a.* Capable of being verified.—**verification,** ver′i•fi•kā″shon, *n.* The act of verifying; authentication; confirmation.—**verificative,** ver′i•-fi•kā″tiv, *a.* Serving to verify.—**verifier,** ver′i•fī•ėr, *n.* One who or that which verifies.

verily, ver′i•li, *adv.* [From *very*.] In truth; in very truth or deed; in fact; certainly; really; in sincere earnestness.

verisimilar, ver•i•sim′i•lėr, *a.* [L. *verisimilis*—*verus*, true, and *similis*, like. VERY, SIMILAR.] Having the appearance of truth; probable; likely. —**verisimilitude,** ver′i•si•mil″i•tūd, *n.* [L. *verisimilitudo*.] The appearance of truth; probability; likelihood.

verity, ver′i•ti, *n.* [Fr. *vérité*, from L. *veritas*, from *verus*, true. VERY.] The quality of being true or real; true or real nature; reality; truth; fact; a true assertion or tenet; a truth.—*Of a verity*, in very truth or deed; of a truth; certainly,—**veritable,** ver′i•ta•bl, *a.* [Fr. *véritable*.] True; agreeable to truth or fact; real; actual.—**veritably,** ver′i•ta•bli, *adv.* In a veritable or true manner; truly.

verjuice, vėr′jūs, *n.* [Fr. *verjus*, from *verd*, *vert*, L. *viridis*, green, and *jus*, juice. VERDANT, JUICE.] An acid liquor expressed from crab apples, unripe grapes, etc., used for culinary and other purposes; *fig.* sourness or acidity of temper, manner, or expression.

vermeil, vėr′mil, *n.* [Fr. *vermeil*. VERMILLION.] Vermilion; a bright, beautiful red, the color of vermilion (*poet.*); silver or bronze gilt; a liquid applied to a gilded surface to give luster to the gold.

vermicelli, vėr•mi•chel′li, *n.* [It., lit. little worms, pl. of *vermicello*, from L. *vermiculus*, dim. of *vermis*, a worm. VERMIN.] An Italian food preparation of flour, yolks of eggs, sugar, and saffron, in the form of long, slender tubes or threads.

vermicide, vėr′mi•sīd, *n.* [L. *vermis*, a worm, and *caedo*, to kill. VERMIN.] A substance which destroys intestinal worms; a worm killer.

vermicular, vėr•mik′ū•lėr, *a.* [From L. *vermiculis*, a little worm, dim. of *vermis*, a worm. VERMIN.] Pertaining to worms; resembling a worm; particularly resembling the motion of a worm; peristaltic.—*Vermicular* or *vermiculated work*, mosaic work showing knots or windings resembling the tracks of worms; a species of rusticated masonry appearing as if eaten into or formed by the tracks of worms. —**vermiculate,** vėr•mik′ū•lāt, *a.* Wormlike in shape or appearance; crawling or creeping like a worm. —**vermiculation,** vėr•mik′ū•lā″shon, *n.* Motion in the manner of a worm; a wormlike ornament or body of any kind; the state of being worm-eaten.—**vermicule,** vėr′mi•kūl, *n.* A little worm.—**vermiculite,** vėr•-mik′ū•līt, *n.* [L. *vermiculus*, and Gr. *lithos*, a stone.] *Geol.* a short worm track seen on the surface of many flagstones.—**vermiform,** vėr′mi•-form, *a.* [L. *vermis*, and *forma*, form.] Having the form or shape of a worm or of its motions.—**vermifuge,** vėr′mi•fūj, *n.* A medicine or substance that destroys or expels intestinal worms; an anthelmintic.

vermilion, vėr•mil′yon, *n.* [Fr. *vermillon*, from *vermeil*, vermilion, red, from L. *vermiculus* (dim. of *vermis*, a worm), a little worm, the kermes insect, hence a scarlet color such as that obtained from the kermes insect. This color was formerly called *worm dye*. VERMIN.] The red sulfide of mercury or cinnabar; a bright red pigment formed of this, or artificially prepared from a preparation of sulfur and mercury; a color such as that of the above pigment; a beautiful red color.—*v.t.* To color with vermilion; to cover with a delicate red.

vermin, vėr′min, *n. sing.* and *pl.*: used chiefly in plural. [Fr. *vermine*, vermin, parasitic insects, from L. *vermis*, a worm (seen also in *vermicular*, *vermilion*, *vermicelli*, etc.) cog. E. *worm*. WORM.] A name given to the smaller mammalia or certain birds which damage man's crops or other belongings, and to noxious or destructive insects or the like; also used of noxious human beings.—**vermination,** vėr•mi•nā′shon, *n.* The breeding of parasitic vermin; a gripping of the bowels.—**verminous,** vėr′mi•nus, *a.* Caused by or arising from the presence of vermin on the body.

vermouth, vėr′möth, *n.* [Fr. *vermout*, *vermouth*, from G. *wermuth*, absinthe. WORMWOOD.] A liquor compounded of white wine and flavored with aromatics.

vernacular, vėr•nak′ū•lėr, *a.* [L. *vernaculus*, domestic, indigenous, from *verna*, a slave born in his master's house, a native.] Belonging to the country of or place of one's birth; belonging to the speech that we all naturally acquire, or more particularly to the everyday idiom of a place.—*n.* One's mother tongue; the native idiom of a place.—**vernacularism,** vėr•nak′ū•lėr•izm, *n.* A vernacular idiom.—**vernacularly,** vėr•nak′ū•lėr•li, *adv.* In agreement with the vernacular manner.

vernal, vėr′nal, *a.* [L. *vernalis*, from *ver*, spring; cog. Icel. *vár*, Dan. *vaar*, the spring; from root signifying to be bright, to burn, seen in *Vesta*, *Vesuvius*, etc.] Belonging to the spring; appearing in spring; belonging to youth; the spring of life.—*Vernal equinox*. See EQUINOX.—**vernation,** vėr•nā′shon, *n.* [L. *verno*, *vernatum*, to be spring-like.] *Bot.* the disposition of the nascent leaves within the bud.

vernier, vėr′ni•ėr, *n.* [From the inventor, Peter *Vernier*, of Brussels, who died 1637.] A small sliding scale parallel with the fixed scale of a barometer, theodolite, or other instrument, used for measuring fractional parts of the divisions on the fixed graduated scale.

Veronal, ver′o•nal, *n.* A white, crystalline substance used as a hypnotic.

veronica, ve•ron′i•ka, *n.* [From a supposed female saint of the name of *Veronica*.] A genus of plants including the various species of speedwell.

verrucose, ver′ū•kōs, *a.* [L. *verrucosus*, warty, from *verruca*, a wart.] Warty; having little knobs or warts on the surface.

versant, vėr′sant, *n.* [Fr. *versant*, a mountain slope, from *verser*, to shed, to pour, from L. *versare*, to turn, freq. of *verto*. VERSE.] All that part of a country which slopes or inclines in one direction; general slope of surface; aspect.

versatile, vėr′sa•til, *a.* [L. *versatilis*, from *verso*, to turn, freq. of *verto*, *versus*, to turn. VERSE.] Capable of being moved or turned round; turning with ease from one thing to another; readily applying one's self to a new task or to various subjects; many-sided; *bot.* turning like the needle of a compass; fixed but freely movable.—**versatilely,** vėr′sa•til•li, *adv.* In a versatile manner.—**versatility, versatileness,** vėr•sa•til′i•ti, vėr′sa•til•nes, *n.* The state or quality of being versatile; the faculty of easily turning one's mind to new tasks or subjects; facility in taking up various intellectual pursuits.

verse, vėrs, *n.* [L. *versus*, a row, a line in writing, a verse, from *verto*, *versum*, to turn; seen also in *advert*, *convert*, *revert*, *adverse*, *converse*, *inverse*, *version*, *vertex*, etc.; same root as E. *worth* (verb).] A line of poetry consisting of a certain number of metrical feet; poetry; metrical language; poetical composition; versification; a short division of the chapters in the Scriptures; a short division of a poetical composition; a stanza.—**versicle,** vėr′si•kl, *n.* [L. *versiculus*, dim. of *versus*.] A little verse; a short verse in a church service spoken or chanted by the priest or minister alternately with a response by the people.—**versicular,** vėr•sik′ū•lėr, *a.* Pertaining to verse or verses.—**versification,** vėr′si•fi•kā″shon, *n.* The act or practice of composing poetic verse; a turning into verse; the construction of poetry; metrical composition.—**versifier,** vėr′si•fī•ėr, *n.* One who versifies; one who makes verses; one who converts into verse.—**versify,** vėr′si•fī, *v.i.*—*versified*, *versifying*. [Fr. *versifier*, L. *versificare*—*versus*, a verse, and *facio*, to make.] To make verses.—*v.t.* To relate in verse; to treat as the subject of verse; to turn into verse.

versed, vėrst, *a.* [Fr. *versé*, from L. *versatus*, pp. of *versor*, to turn about frequently, to be engaged, from *verto*. VERSE.] Thoroughly acquainted; practiced; skilled.

version, vėr′zhon, *n.* [From L. *verto*, *versum*, to turn, change, translate.] A translation; that which is rendered from another language (the revised *version* of the Scriptures); a statement or account of incidents or proceedings from some particular point of view; *med.* uterine displacement; change of fetal position.

verso, vėrs′ō, *n.* pl. **versos,** vėrs′ōz. [L. *verso* (*folio*), on the turned leaf.] *Print.* the left-hand page of a book or manuscript; the back of an object, as of a coin.

verst, vėrst, *n.* A Russian measure of length, containing 1166²/₃ yards, or two-thirds of a mile.

versus, vėr′sus, *prep.* [L., against, turned in the direction of. VERSE.] Against; used chiefly in legal phraseology (Doe *versus* Roe) and in sports (Yale *vs.* Brown).

vert, vėrt, *n.* [Fr. *vert*, green, from Latin *viridis*, green. VERDANT.] *Forest law*, everything within a forest that grows and bears a green leaf; *her.* a green color, expressed in engraving by diagonal lines drawn downward from left to right.

vertebra, vėr′te•bra, *n.* pl. **vertebrae,** vėr′te•brē. [L. *vertebra*, a joint, a joint or vertebra of the spine, from *verto*, to turn. VERSE.] One of the bones of which the spine or backbone of an animal consists; *pl.* the spine.—**vertebral,** vėr′te•bral, *a.* Pertaining to the vertebrae (the *vertebral* column, that is, the spine); vertebrate.—*n.* A vertebrate animal.—**Vertebrata,** vėr•te•brā′ta, *n. pl.* A division of the animal kingdom, consisting of those animals which possess a backbone, including the fishes, amphibians, birds, reptiles, quadrupeds, and man.—**vertebrate,** vėr′te•brāt, *n. Zool.* a member of the Vertebrata.—*a.* Having a spine or vertebral column.

vertex, vėr′teks, *n.* pl. **vertexes,** vėr′tek•sez, or **vertices,** vėr′ti•sēz, [L. *vertex*, an eddy, top, summit, lit. a turning point, from *verto*, to turn. VERSE.] The highest or principal point; apex; top; crown; summit; *math.* the point in any figure opposite to and most distant from the base; the point of a conic section where the axis meets the curve.—**vertical,** vėr′ti•kal, *a.* Relating to the vertex; situated at the vertex; directly overhead; in a position perpendicular to the plane of the horizon; upright; plumb.—*Vertical angles*, the opposite angles made by two straight lines which intersect each other.—*Vertical circle*, *astron.* a great circle passing through the zenith and the nadir.—*Vertical plane*, a plane perpendicular to the plane of the horizon.—*Vertical steam-engine*, an engine in which the piston moves vertically, or straight up and down.—*n.* A vertical circle, plane, or line.—*Prime vertical*, *astron.* that vertical circle which passes through the zenith and the east and west points of the horizon.—**vertically,** vėr′ti•kal•li, *adv.* In a vertical manner, position, or direction.—**verticalness, verticality,** vėr′ti•kal•nes, vėr•ti•kal′i•ti, *n.* The state of being vertical.

verticil, vėr′ti•sil, *n.* [L. *verticillus*, dim. of *vertex*, a whirl. VERTEX.] *Bot.* a mode of inflorescence in which the flowers surround the stem in a kind of ring; a whorl.—**verticillate, verticillated,** vėr•tis′i•lāt, vėr•tis′i•lā•ted, *a. Bot.* growing in a whorl, or on the same plane round the axis.

vertigo, vėr′ti•gō, *n.* [L. *vertigo*, from *verto*, to turn. VERSE.] Dizziness or swimming of the head; giddiness arising from some disorder of the system.—**vertiginous,** vėr•tij′i•nus, *a.* [L. *vertiginosus*.] Affected with vertigo; giddy; apt to make one giddy.

vertu, vėr′tö, It. pron. ver•tö′, *n.* [It. *vertū*, *virtū*, virtue, goodness, excellence, etc.] Excellence in objects of art or curiosity; objects of art, antiquity, or curiosity taken collectively.

Vertumnus, vėr•tum′nus, *n.* [L. *vertumnus*, from *verto*, to turn.] The Latin god of the changing seasons of the year, husband of Pomona.

vervain, vėr′van, *n.* [Fr. *verveine*, from L. *verbena*. VERBENA.] The popular name of some plants of the genus *Verbena*, formerly believed to have medicinal properties.

verve, verv, *n.* [Fr.] Poetical or artistic rapture or enthusiasm; great spirit; energy; rapture; enthusiasm.

very, ver′i, *adv.* [O.E. *verri*, *veray*, *verray*, *verrei*, from O.Fr. *verai*, Fr. *vrai*, true, from a L.L. form *veracus*, from L. *verax*, veracious, from *verus*, true (seen also in *verify*, *verity*, *aver*, *verdict*, etc.); cog. D. *waar*, G. *wahr*, true.] In a high degree; to a great extent; extremely; exceedingly.—*a.* Veritable; real; true; actual; often placed before substantives to indicate that they must be understood in their full, unrestricted sense (my *very* heartstrings); to denote exact conformity with what is expressed by the word, or to express identity (the *very* words); to give emphasis or force generally (even your *very* eyes). [*Very* is sometimes met with in the comparative and superlative.]

Very light, ve•ri′līt, *n.* [After Lieut. *Very*, the inventor.] The commonest make of British star shell, used for purposes of observation and signaling.

vesical, ves′i•kal, *a.* [L. *vesica*, a bladder.] Pertaining to the bladder. —**vesicate,** ves′i•kāt, *v.t.*—*vesicated*, *vesicating*. To raise vesicles or blisters on; to blister.—**vesication,** ves•i•kā′shon, *n.* The process of blistering.—**vesicant,** ves′i•kant, *n.* A blistering application or agent.—**vesicatory,** ves′i•ka•to•ri, *a.* Having the property, when applied to the skin, of raising a blister; blistering.—*n.* A blistering agent.—**vesicle,** ves′i•kl, *n.* [Fr. *vésicule*, L. *vesicula*, a little bladder, dim. of *vesica*.] Any small bladder-like structure, cavity, cell, or the like in a body; a little sac or cyst; a small blister or pustule on the skin.—**vesicular,** ve•sik′ū•lėr, *a.* Pertaining to or consisting of vesicles; bladdery; cellulose; full of interstices.—**vesiculate,** ve•sik′ū•lāt, *a.* Full of vesicles; vesicular.

vesper, ves′pėr, *n.* [L., akin to Gr. *Hesperos*, the evening, the evening star; same root as *west*.] The evening star; hence, the evening; *pl.* the time of evening service in some churches; *pl.* evening worship or service.—*Sicilian vespers.* See SICILIAN.—*a.* Relating to the evening or to vespers.—**vespertine,** ves′pėr•tin, *a.* [L. *vespertinus*.] Pertaining to the evening, of flowers opening in evening, of stars sinking to horizon at evening, of birds that fly in the evening.

vespiary, ves′pi•a•ri, *n.* [From L. *vespa*, a wasp. WASP.] A nest or colony of wasps, hornets, etc.

vessel, ves′el, *n.* [O.Fr. *vessel*, *veissel* (Fr. *vaisseau*), from L. *vascellum*, a dim. of *vas*, a vessel. VASE.] A utensil proper for holding liquors and other things, as a barrel, kettle, cup, dish, etc.; a ship; a craft of any kind, but usually one larger than a mere boat; *anat.* any tube or canal in which the blood or other humors are contained, secreted, or circulated; *bot.* a canal or tube in which the sap is contained and conveyed; *fig.* in scriptural phraseology, a person into whom anything is conceived as poured or infused (a chosen *vessel*, *vessels* of wrath).—*The weaker vessel*, applied in a jocular way to a woman, a usage borrowed from 1 Pet. iii. 7.

vest, vest, *n.* [Fr. *veste*, from L. *vestis*, a garment, a vest (whence also *vesture*, *vestry*, *vestment*, *invest*, *divest*); cog. Gr. (*v*)*esthēs*, dress; Skr. *vas*, to put on; Goth. *vasjan*, to clothe.] A garment or dress; a short sleeveless garment worn by men under the coat, covering the upper part of the body; a waistcoat.—*v.t.* To clothe; to invest or clothe, as with authority; to endow; to confer upon (*vested with* power); to confer possession or enjoyment of (to *vest* dominion *in* a person).—*v.i.* To devolve; to take effect, as a title or right (the estate *vests in* the heir).—**vested,** ves′ted, *p.* and *a.* Clothed; habited; *law*, not in a state of contingency or suspension; fixed (*vested* rights or interests in property).—**vesting,** ves′ting, *n.* Cloth for vests.

Vesta, ves′ta, *n.* [L.] One of the great divinities of the ancient Romans, the virgin goddess of the hearth, in honor of whom a sacred fire was kept constantly burning under the charge of six stainless virgins; *astron.* one of the asteroids; a wax match which ignites by friction.—**vestal,** ves′tal, *a.* [L. *vestalis*.] Pertaining to Vesta; pure; chaste.—*n.* Among the ancient Romans, a virgin consecrated to Vesta; hence, a virgin or woman of spotless chastity; a nun.

vestibule, ves′ti•būl, *n.* [Fr. *vestibule*, from L. *vestibulum*, a vestibule, from same root as Skr. *vas*, to dwell; E. *was*.] A passage, hall, or antechamber next the outer door of a house; a lobby; a hall; *anat.* a cavity belonging to the labyrinth of the ear.—**vestibular,** ves•tib′ū•lėr, *a.* Pertaining to or resembling a vestibule.

vestige, ves′tij, *n.* [L. *vestigium*, a footprint (seen also in *investigate*).] A footprint‡; a trace, mark, or appearance of something which is no longer present or in existence; remains of something long passed away; in plants and animals, structures which have been reduced as a result of adaptation.

vestment, vest′ment, *n.* [O.Fr. *vestement*, [L. *vestimentum*, from *vestio*, to clothe. VEST.] A covering or garment; some part of clothing or dress; especially, some part of outer clothing.—*Ecclesiastical* or *sacerdotal vestments*, articles of dress or ornament worn by clergymen in the celebration of divine service.

vestry, ves′tri, *n.* [Fr. *vestiaire*, L. *vestiarium*, a wardrobe, from *vestis*, a garment. VEST.] A place or room appendant to a church, where the ecclesiastical vestments are kept, and where the clergy robe themselves; in *England*, a parochial assembly, so called from its meetings being held in the vestry; a select number of ratepayers elected to carry on the local government of a parish.—**vestryman,** *n.* One of a vestry board.

vesture, ves′chėr, *n.* [O.Fr. *vesture*. VEST.] A garment or garments generally; clothing; apparel; dress; that which invests or covers; envelope; integument.—**vestured,** ves′chėrd, *a.* Clothed; enveloped.

vesuvian, ve•sū′vi•an, *n.* The mineral idocrase; a kind of match for lighting cigars, etc.

vetch, vech, *n.* [O.Fr. *veche*, *vesse*, Mod. Fr. *vesce*, It. *veccia*, from L. *vicia*, a vetch, cog. Gr. *bikas*, a vetch. *Fitch* is another form.] The popular name of plants allied to the bean, some of them, as the common tare, cultivated for fodder to cattle.—**vetchling,** vech′ling, *n.* [Dim. of *vetch*.] A name for various vetchlike plants.

veteran, vet′e•ran, *a.* [L. *veteranus*, from *vetus*, *veteris*, old; same root as Gr. (*v*)*etos*, a year, seen also in L. *vitulus*, a calf. VEAL.] Having been long exercised in anything; long praticed or experienced in war and the duties of a soldier.

veterinary, vet′e•ri•ne•ri, *a.* [L.L. *veterinarius*, pertaining to beasts of burden, from L. *veterinae*, beasts of burden.] Pertaining to the art or science of treating the diseases of domestic animals (a *veterinary* surgeon, a *veterinary* college or school). —**veterinarian,** vet′e•ri•nâr″i•an, *n.* One who is authorized to practice veterinary medicine.

veto, vē′tō, *n.* [L. *veto*, I forbid.] The power which one branch of a legislature has to negative the resolutions of another branch; the power of governors and of the president of the U. S. to interdict a measure passed by the legislature.—*v.t.*—*vetoed*, *vetoing*. To put a veto on; to forbid; to interdict.

vex, veks, *v.t.* [Fr. *vexer*, to vex, from L. *vexare*, to vex, a freq. or intens. of *veho*, *vectum*, to carry. VEHICLE.] To excite slight anger or displeasure in; to trouble by petty or light annoyances; to irritate, fret, plague, annoy; to make sorrowful; to grieve or distress.—**vexation,** vek•sā′shon, *n.* The act of vexing or state of being vexed; irritation; annoyance; cause of irritation; affliction.—**vexatious,** vek•sā′shus, *a.* Causing vexation; annoying; mortifying.—**vexatiously,** vek•sā′shus•li, *adv.* In a vexatious manner.—**vexatiousness,** vek•sā′shus•nes, *n.*—**vexed,** vekst, *p.* and *a.* Annoyed; troubled; much disputed or contested; causing contention (a *vexed* question).

vexillum, vek'sil•um, *n.* [L., a dim. of *vellum*, a veil. VEIL.] The standard of the cavalry of ancient Rome; *bot.* the standard or fifth petal placed at the back of a papilionaceous corolla.—**vexillary,** vek'si•le•ri, *a.* Pertaining to an ensign or standard; *bot.* pertaining to or having a vexillum.—**vexillary,** *n.* A standard bearer.

via, vī'a, *prep.* [L., a way or road. WAY.] By way of (to send or travel *via* airplane).

viable, vī'a•bl, *a.* [Fr., likely to live, from *vie*, L. *vita*, life. VITAL.] Capable of sustaining independent life, said of a newborn child.—**viability,** vī•a•bil'i•ti, *n.* The state of being viable.

viaduct, vī'a•dukt, *n.* [L. *via*, way, and *ductus*, a leading, a duct. WAY, DUKE.] A long bridge or series of arches conducting a railroad or road over a valley or district of low level.

vial, vī'al, *n.* [A modification of *phial.*] A small glass vessel or bottle; a phial.

viand, vī'and, *n.* [Fr. *viande*, viands, food, from L.L. *vivanda*, provisions, from L. *vivo*, to live. VITAL.] Meat dressed; food; victuals; used chiefly in the plural.

viaticum, vī•at'i•kum, *n.* [L. *viaticus*, pertaining to a way or road, from *via*, way. VOYAGE.] Provisions for a journey; *R. Cath. Ch.* the communion or eucharist given to a dying person.

vibrate, vī'brāt, *v.i.*—*vibrated, vibrating.* [L. *vibro, vibratum*, to vibrate, brandish, shake.] To swing; to oscillate; to move one way and the other; to play to and fro; to produce a vibratory or resonant effect; to quiver.—*v.t.* To move or wave to and fro; to oscillate; to cause to quiver; to measure by vibrating or oscillating (a pendulum which *vibrates* seconds).—**vibraculum,** vī•brak'ū•lum, *n.* pl. **vibracula,** vī•brak'ū•la. A long filamentous appendage in polyzoa.—**vibrant,** vī'brant, *a.* L. *vibrans, vibrantis*, ppr. of *vibro.*] Vibrating; tremulous; resonant.—**vibratile,** vī'bra•tīl, *a.* Adapted to or used for vibratory motion; vibratory.—**vibratility,** vī•bra•til'i•ti, *n.* The quality of being vibratile.—**vibration,** vī•brā'shon, *n.* [L. *vibratio, vibrationis.*] The act of vibrating; an oscillation or swing of a pendulum or similar body; one of a series of rapid tremulous motions produced in a body or substance; the tremulous motion of a sonorous body.—**vibratory,** vī'bra•to•ri, *a.* Consisting in or belonging to vibration; causing to vibrate; vibrating.

Vibrio, vī'bri•ō, *n.* [From *vibrate.*] A genus of bacteria, having the form of curved filaments, with a wavy motion.

vibrissae, vī•bris'sē, *n. pl.* [L. *vibrissae*, the hairs in the nostrils.] The stiff, long bristles on the head in many mammals; the hairs about the mouth of certain birds, as the flycatchers.

vicar, vik'ėr, *n.* [Fr. *vicaire*, from L. *vicarius*, forming a substitute, from *vicis*, change (whence prefix *vice* in *viceroy*, etc., *vicissitude*).] A substitute in office; a representative; the priest of a parish in England who receives only the smaller tithes or a salary.—**vicarage,** vik'ėr•ij, *n.* The benefice of a vicar; the house or residence of a vicar.—**vicar apostolic,** *n. R. Cath. Ch.* a bishop who possesses no diocese, but who exercises jurisdiction over a certain district by direct authority of the pope.—**vicar-general,** *n.* The official assistant of a bishop or archbishop.—**vicarial, vicariate,** vī•kâ'ri•al, vī•kâ'ri•āt, *a.* Pertaining to a vicar; vicarious; delegated.—**vicarious,** vī•kâ'ri•us, *a.* [L. *vicarius.*] Belonging to a deputy or substitute; delegated; filling the place of another; performed or suffered for, or instead of, another.—**vicariously,** vī•kâ'ri•us•li, *adv.* In the place of another; substitution.—**vicarship,** vik'ėr•ship, *n.* The office of a vicar.

vice, vīs, *n.* [Fr. *vice*, from L. *vitium*, vice, blemish, fault, error, crime, from root *vi*, to twist.] A defect, fault, or blemish; a fault or bad trick in a horse; any immoral or evil habit or practice; a moral failing; a particular form of wickedness or depravity; the indulgence of impure or degrading appetites or passions; depravity or corruption of manners (an age of *vice*); the character in the old Morality Plays, dressed in the habit of a fool, furnished with a dagger of lath, whose chief employment was to belabor the devil.—**vicious,** vish'us, *a.* [Fr. *vicieux*, L. *vitiosus*, from *vitium*, vice.] Characterized by vice; faulty; defective; imperfect; addicted to vice; depraved; wicked; contrary to morality; evil; bad (*vicious* examples); not genuine or pure; faulty; incorrect (a *vicious* style in language); addicted to bad tricks (a *vicious* horse).—**viciously,** vish'us•li, *adv.* In a vicious manner.—**viciousness,** vish'us•nes, *n.* The quality or state of being vicious.

vice, vī'si, *prep.* [L. *vice*, in the room of, ablative of *vicis*, change, turn, etc., the stem being seen also in *vicar, vicissitude.*] In place of; in room of (A.B. appointed to be captain *vice* C.D. promoted).—**vice versa,** *adv.* [L.] Contrariwise; the reverse; the terms or the case being reversed.

vice, vīs. [Fr. *vice-*, from L. *vice*. See above.] A prefix denoting position second in rank; sometimes used by itself as a noun, the context making the intended meaning clear.—**vice-admiral,** *n.* An officer next in rank and command to the admiral.—**vice-admiralty,** *n.* The office of a vice-admiral.—**vice-chancellor,** *n.* An officer next to a chancellor; a judge in the chancery division of the High Court of Justice in England; an officer of a university who discharges certain duties of the chancellor.—**vice-consul,** *n.* One who acts in the place of a consul; a consul of subordinate rank.—**vicegerency,** vīs•jē'ren•si, *n.* The office of a vicegerent.—**vicegerent,** vīs•jē'rent, *n.* [Fr. *vicegerent*—*vice*, and L. *gerens, gerentis*, ppr. of *gero*, to act. GESTURE.] An officer who is deputed to exercise the powers of another; a substitute; one having a delegated power.—**vice-presidency,** *n.* The office of vice-president.—**vice-president,** *n.* An office bearer next in rank below a president.—**viceregal,** *a.* Pertaining to a viceroy.—**viceroy,** vīs'roi, *n.* [Fr. *viceroi; vice*, in the place of, and *roi*, L. *rex*, a king. REGENT.] One who rules in the name of the king (or queen) with regal authority.—**viceroyalty, viceroyship,** vīs•roi'al•ti, vīs'roi•ship, *n.* The dignity or jurisdiction of a viceroy.

vicenary, vis'e•ne•ri, *a.* [L. *vicenarius*, from *viceni*, twenty.] Belonging to or consisting of twenty.

vicennial, vi•sen'ni•al, *a.* [L. *viceni*, twenty, and *annus*, a year.] Lasting or continuing twenty years.

viceregal, viceroy, etc. See VICE- (prefix).

vicinage, vis'in•ij, *n.* [O.Fr. *veisinage* (Fr. *voisinage*), neighborhood, from L. *vicinus*, neighboring, from *vicus*, a village, akin to Gr. (*v*)*oikos*, Skr. *veca*, a house.] Neighborhood; the place or places adjoining or near; the vicinity.—**vicinity,** vi•sin'i•ti, *n.* [L. *vicinitas*, from *vicinus*, neighboring.] The quality of being near; propinquity; proximity; nearness in place; neighborhood; the adjoining district, space, or country.

vicious, etc. See VICE.

vicissitude, vi•sis'i•tūd, *n.* [L. *vicissitudo*, from *vicis*, a change. VICAR.] A passing from one state or condition to another; change, especially in regard to the affairs of life or the world; mutation.—**vicissitudinary,** vi•sis'i•tū"di•ne•ri, *a.* Subject to vicissitudes.—**vicissitudinous,** vi•sis'i•tū"di•nus, *a.* Full of vicissitude; characterized by changes.

victim, vik'tim, *n.* [Fr. *victime*, from L. *victima*, a victim, lit. a well-grown beast; same root as *vigour*, *wax* (to grow).] A living being sacrificed to some deity, or in the performance of a religious rite; a person or thing destroyed; a person sacrified in the pursuit of an object; a person who suffers severe injury from another; one who is cheated or duped; a gull.—**victimize,** vik'tim•īz, *v.t.*—*victimized, victimizing.* To make a victim of; to make the victim of a swindling transaction.

victor, vik'tėr, *n.* [L. from *vinco*, *victum* to conquer (seen also in *convince, evince, invincible, vanquish*).] One who wins or gains the advantage in a contest; especially, one who conquers in war.—*a.* Victorious.—**victoria,** vik•tō'ri•a, *n.* [L. *victoria*, victory, hence the name of the British queen.] A kind of four-wheeled carriage, with a calash top, seated for two persons, and with an elevated driver's seat in front.—

Victoria cross, a British naval and military decoration granted for bravery.

Victorian, vik•tō′ri•an, *a.* [From Queen *Victoria* (Eng.).] Pertaining to the reign of Queen Victoria, especially to the values of that society; characteristic of the Victorian age: typically thought of as being a time of inflexible, narrow moral standards and of hypocrisy.—*n.* One living during the Victorian age.

victorious, vik•tō′ri•us, *a.* [Fr. *victorieux,* from L. *victoriosus.*] Having conquered in battle or contest; being victor; conquering; associated with victory; indicating victory.—**victoriously,** vik•tō′ri•us•li, *adv.*—**victory,** vik′to•ri, *n.* The defeat of an enemy in battle or of an antagonist in a contest; the superiority gained in any contest.

victual, vit′l, *n.* [O.Fr. *vitaille,* Mod. Fr. *victuaille,* from L.L. *victualia,* provisions, *victualis,* pertaining to food, from L. *victus,* food, from *vivo, victum,* to live. VITAL.] Provision of food; provisions: now generally in plural and signifying food for human beings, prepared for eating.—*v.t. victualed, victualing.* To supply with food.—*v.i.* To eat.

vicuna, vi•kön′ya, *n.* [Sp. *vicuna,* from native name.] A South American animal of the camel family, closely allied to the llama, yielding short, soft, silken fur used for making delicate fabrics.

video, vid′ē•ō, *a.* [From L. *videre,* to see, and *o.*] Pertaining to the transmission or reception of television images; the visible, as opposed to the audible, portion of a television transmission.—*n.* Television.—**video tape,** *n.* A magnetic tape on which visual images can be recorded for repeat broadcasts.

vidette, vi•det′, *n.* See VEDETTE.

vie, vī, *v.i.* [Contr. from old *envie, envye* (accent on last), from Fr. *envier,* to invite, to vie in games, from L. *invitare.* INVITE.] To strive for superiority; to contend.

Viennese, vē•en•ēz′, *n. sing.* and *pl.* A native of *Vienna*; natives of Vienna.

view, vū, *n.* [O.Fr. *veue* (Fr. *vue*), from *veü, veu,* L.L. participle *vidutus,* from L. *video, videre,* to see. VISION.] The act of looking, seeing, or beholding; survey; look; sight; a mental survey; consideration; range of vision; power of seeing or perception, either physical or mental; that which is viewed, seen, or beheld; a sight or spectacle presented; scene; prospect; a scene portrayed; a representation of a landscape or the like; manner or mode of looking at things; judgment; opinion; way of thinking; something looked toward or forming the subject of consideration; intention; purpose (to act with a *view* to happiness).—*Field of view,* the whole region or space within the range of vision.—*Point of view,* the direction from which a thing is seen; hence, *fig.* the particular mode or manner in which a subject is considered; standpoint.—*On view,* open or submitted to public inspection; exhibited to the public.—*v.t.* To see; to look on; to examine with the eye; to inspect; to survey; to survey intellectually; to consider.—*v.i.* To look; to take a view.—*In view of,* considering the consequences of.—*With a view to,* for the purpose of.—**viewless,** vū′les, *a.* Not capable of being viewed or seen; invisible.

vigesimal, vī•jes′i•mal, *a.* [L. *vigesimus,* twentieth, from *viginti,* twenty.] Twentieth.

vigil, vij′il, *n.* [Fr. *vigile,* vigil, from L. *vigilia,* a watch, from *vigil,* watchful, from *vigeo,* to be vigorous, from root seen in E. *wake.* VIGOR, WAKE.] The act of keeping awake; forbearance from sleep; a period of sleeplessness; a watch or watching; a devotional watching; devotions performed during the customary hours of sleep; *eccles.* the eve or evening or whole day preceding a festival, as Christmas, Easter, or some principal saint's day.—**vigilance,** vij′i•lans, *n.* The state or quality of being vigilant; watchfulness; circumspection; *her.* a crane *in its vigilance* is depicted standing on one leg and clasping a stone in the talons of the other foot.—**vigilant,** vij′i•lant, *a.* [L. *vigilans, vigilantis,* ppr. of *vigilo,* to watch.] Watchful; ever awake and on the alert; circumspect.—**vigilantly,** vij′i•lant•li, *adv.* Watchfully; circumspectly.

vignette, vin•yet′ or vi•net′, *n.* [Fr., dim. of *vigne,* L. *vinea,* a vine.] An ornament representing vine leaves, tendrils, and grapes, such as those with which capital letters in ancient manuscripts were often surrounded; hence, flowers, head and tail pieces, etc., in printed books; any woodcut or engraving not enclosed within a definite border; a small photographic portrait.

vigor, vig′or, *n.* [L. *vigor,* vigor, from *vigeo,* to be strong; from root also seen in *vigil, vegetable, victim.*] Active strength or force of body in animals; physical strength; strength of mind; intellectual force; energy; strength in animal or vegetable nature or action.—**vigorous,** vig′or•us, *a.* Possessing vigor or physical strength; strong; lusty; exhibiting or resulting from vigor, energy, or strength of either body or mind; powerful; energetic.—**vigorously,** vig′or•us•li, *adv.* In a vigorous manner; forcibly; with active exertions.—**vigorousness,** vig′or•us•nes, *n.* Strength; force; energy.

viking, vīk′ing, *n.* [Icel. *vikingr,* lit. one who frequents bays and fiords—*vik,* a bay, and term. *-ing,* one who belongs to or is descended from (*r* being the masc. art.).] A rover or sea robber belonging to the predatory bands of Northmen who infested the European seas during the eighth, ninth, and tenth centuries.

vilayet, vē•lä•yet′, *n.* [Turk.] Any province of the Turkish Empire.

vile, vīl, *a.* [Fr. *vil, vile,* from L. *vilis,* worthless, vile.] Worthless; despicable; morally base; depraved; bad; wicked; villainous.—**vilely,** vīl′li, *adv.* Basely; shamefully; odiously; worthlessly.—**vileness,** vīl′nes, *n.* The state or quality of being vile; moral or intellectual baseness; degradation; sinfulness; extreme badness.—**vilify,** vil′i•fī, *v.t.*—*vilified, vilifying.* [L. *vilifico*—*vilis,* vile, and *facio,* to make.] To attempt to degrade by slander; to defame; to traduce.—**vilifier,** vil′i•fī•ėr, *n.* One who defames or traduces.—**vilification,** vil′i•fi•kā″shon, *n.* The act of vilifying or defaming.

vilipend, vil′i•pend, *v.t.* [L. *vilipendo,* to hold in slight esteem—*vilis,* worthless, vile, and *pendo,* to weigh, to value. VILE, PENDANT.] To express a disparaging or mean opinion of; to slander.

villa, vil′a, *n.* [L. *villa,* a country house, farm, villa, a contr. of *vicula,* from *vicus,* a village. VICINAGE, VILLAIN.] A country residence, usually of some size and pretension; a rural or suburban mansion.—**village,** vil′ij, *n.* [Fr. *village,* from L. *villa.*] An assemblage of houses smaller than a town or city and larger than a hamlet.—*a.* Pertaining to a village; hence, rustic.—**villager,** vil′i•jėr, *n.* An inhabitant of a village.

villain, vil′in, *n.* [O.Fr. *villain, villein, vilein* (Fr. *vilain*), from L.L. *villanus,* a farm servant, from *villa,* a country house. VILLA.] A feudal serf; a man of the lowest grade in feudal times; hence, a boor, peasant, or clown; latterly; a man extremely depraved, and capable or guilty of great crimes; a vile, wicked person.—**villainous,** vil′in•us, *a.* Pertaining to a villain; very wicked or depraved; vile; proceeding from depravity; sorry; mean.—**villainously,** vil′in•us•li, *adv.* In a villainous manner.—**villainy,** vil′in•i, *n.* The quality of being villainous; extreme depravity; great wickedness; a villainous act; a crime; an action of deep depravity.

villanelle, vil′e•nel, *n.* [Fr.] A French two-rhyme measure of nineteen lines.

villein, vil′en, *n.* [O.Fr. *villein.* VILLAIN.] A feudal tenant of the lowest class.—**villenage, villeinage,** vil′en•ij, *n.* A feudal tenure of lands and tenements by base services, and at the will of a lord.

villi, vil′lī, *n.pl.* [Pl. of L. *villus,* hair.] *Anat.* fine small fibers like the pile of velvet, as on the internal coat of the intestinal canal; *bot.* long, straight, and soft hairs covering fruit, flowers, etc.—**villiform,** vil′i•form, *a.* Having the form or character of villi.—**villosity,** vil•los′i•ti, *n.* The state of being villous.—**villous,** vil′lus, *a.* [L. *villosus,* from *villus,* hair.] Abounding with villi; having the surface covered with fine hairs or woolly substance.

vim, vim, *n.* [L. acc. of *vis,* strength.] Vigor, energy. (*Colloq.*)

vimen, vī′men, *n.* [L. *vimen, viminis,* from *vieo,* to weave.] *Bot.* a long and flexible shoot of a plant.

vinaceous, vī•nā′shus, *a.* [L. *vinaceus,* from *vinum,* wine.] Belonging to wine or grapes; of the color of wine.

vinaigrette, vin•i•gret′, *n.* [Fr., from *vinaigre,* vinegar.] A small box of gold, silver, etc., with perforations, for holding aromatic vinegar (in a sponge) or smelling salts; used like a smelling bottle.

vincible, vin'si•bl, *a.* [From L. *vinco,* to conquer. VICTOR.] Capable of being conquered or subdued.

vinculum, ving'kū•lum, *n.* [L., from *vincio,* to bind.] A bond of union; a bond or tie; *alg.* a line over a quantity of several terms in order to connect them together as one quantity.

vindicate, vin'di•kāt, *v.t.*—*vindicated, vindicating.* [L. *vindico, vindicatum,* to lay claim to, to avenge or revenge, from *vindex, vindicis,* one who lays claim, perhaps from root meaning desire, love (in *Venus*), and *dico,* to declare. Of same origin are *vengeance, avenge, revenge.*] To assert a right or claim to†; to prove (a claim) to be just or valid; to maintain the cause or rights of; to deliver from wrong, oppression, or the like; to support or maintain against denial, censure, or objections; to defend (to *vindicate* a theory); to justify.—**vindicable,** vin'di•ka•bl, *a.* That may be vindicated.—**vindication,** vin•di•kā'shon, *n.* [L. *vindicatio, vindicationis.*] The act of vindicating; justification against censure, objections, or accusations; the proving of anything to be just; defense from wrong or oppression, by force or otherwise.—**vindicator,** vin'di•kā•tėr, *n.* One who vindicates.—**vindicatory,** vin'di•ka•to•ri, *a.* Tending to vindicate; justificatory.—**vindictive,** vin•dik'tiv, *a.* [L. *vindicta,* revenge.] Revengeful; given to revenge.—**vindictively,** vin•dik'tiv•li, *adv.* By way of revenge; revengefully.—**vindictiveness,** vin•dik'tiv•nes, *n.* Revengeful spirit; revengefulness.

vine, vīn, *n.* [O.Fr. *vine* (Fr. *vigne*), a vine; from L. *vinea,* a vine, from *vineus,* adj. from *vinum,* wine. WINE.] A well-known climbing plant with a woody stem, producing the grapes of commerce; the trailing or climbing stem of a plant.—**vinedresser,** *n.* One who trims or prunes vines.—**vinery,** vī'nėr•i, *n.* A kind of greenhouse where vines are cultivated by artificial heat.—**vineyard,** vin'yėrd, *n.* A plantation of vines producing grapes.—**vinosity,** vī•nos'i•ti, *n.* State or quality of being vinous.—**vinous,** vī'nus, *a.* [L. *vinosus,* from *vinum,* wine.] Having the qualities of wine.—*Vinous fermentation,* the fermentation that produces wine from grape juice.

vinegar, vin'e•gėr, *n.* [Fr. *vinaigre,* from *vin,* L. *vinum,* wine, and *aigre,* L. *acer,* sharp, sour. WINE, EAGER.] Dilute and impure acetic acid, usually obtained by the souring or acetification of fermented fruit juices, or an infusion of malt; anything really or metaphorically sour; sourness of temper.—*Aromatic vinegar,* a vinegar holding camphor and essential oils in solution.—*Wood vinegar.* PYROLIGNEOUS ACID.—**vinegarette,** vin'e•gėr•et, *n.* A vinaigrette.

vinery, vineyard. See VINE.

vinous. See VINE.

vintage, vin'tij, *n.* [Partly from *vintner,* partly from Fr. *vendange,* vintage, from L. *vindemia,* the vintage—*vinum,* wine, and *demo,* to take away. VINE.] The gathering of a crop of grapes; the crop produced; the wine from the crop of grapes in one season.—**vintager,** vin'ta•jėr, *n.* One engaged in the vintage.

vintner, vint'nėr, *n.* [O.E. *viniter,* O.Fr. *vinetier,* from L.L. *vinitarius,* from L. *vinum,* wine. VINTAGE.] One who deals in wine; a wineseller; a licensed victualler; a taverner.

viol, vī'ol, *n.* [Fr. *viole,* It. *viola,* Pr. *viola, viula,* L.L. *vidula,* a viol, from L. *vitulari,* to celebrate a festival (perhaps by killing a calf—*vitulus,* a calf).] An ancient stringed musical instrument of much the same form as the violin.—**viola,** vi•ō'la, *n.* [It.] A large kind of violin, to which the part between the second violin and the bass is generally assigned.—**violist,** vi•ōl'ist, *n.* A player on the viol or viola.

Viola, vī'o•la, *n.* [L.] The violet, an extensive genus of plants.—**violaceous,** vī•o•lā'shus, *a.* [L. *violaceus.*] Pertaining to the violet family; resembling the violet in color.

violable. See VIOLATE.

violate, vī'o•lāt, *v.t.*—*violated, violating.* [L. *violo, violatum,* to violate; akin to *vis,* force.] To treat roughly and injuriously; to do injury to; to outrage; to break in upon; to disturb; to desecrate; to treat with irreverence; to profane or profanely meddle with; to infringe; to sin against; to transgress; to ravish; to commit rape on.—**violable,** vī'o•la•bl, *a.* Capable of being violated.—**violation,** vī•o•lā'shon, *n.* The act of violating; desecration; profanation; infringement; transgression.—**violator,** vī'o•lā•tėr, *n.* One who violates; one who infringes or transgresses; one who profanes or desecrates.—**violence,** vī'o•lens, *n.* [L. *violentia,* from *violentus,* violent.] The quality of being violent; vehemence; intensity of action or motion; highly excited feeling; impetuosity; injury done to anything which is entitled to respect or reverence; profanation; violation; unjust force; outrage; attack; assault.—**violent,** vī'o•lent, *a.* [L. *violentus,* violent; akin *violate.*] Characterized by the exertion of force accompanied by rapidity; impetuous; furious; effected by violence; not coming by natural means (a *violent* death); acting or produced by unlawful, unjust, or improper force; unreasonably vehement; passionate; severe; extreme; sharp or acute (*violent* pains).—**violently,** vī'o•lent•li, *adv.* In a violent manner; by violence; forcibly; vehemently.

violet, vī'o•let, *n.* [Fr. *violet, violette,* from *viole,* L. *viola,* a violet; allied to Gr. (*v*)*ion,* a violet.] The common name of a genus of plants that includes the pansy and other well-known species.

violin, vī'o•lin, *n.* [It. *violino,* a dim. of *viola.* VIOL.] A well-known musical instrument of wood, having four catgut strings stretched by means of a bridge over a hollow body, and played with a bow; a fiddle.—**violinist,** vī'o•lin•ist, *n.* A person skilled in playing on a violin.

violoncello, vē'o•lon•chel"ō, vī'ō•lon•sel"ō, *n.* [It., a dim. of *violone,* which is an augmentative of *viola,* a viol. VIOL.] A powerful and expressive bow instrument of the violin kind, held by the performer between the knees, and filling a place between the violin and double bass.—**violoncellist,** vē'o•lon•chel"ist, vī'o•lon•sel"st, *n.* A performer on the violoncello.

viper, vī'pėr, *n.* [Fr. *vipère,* from L. *vipera,* from *vivus,* alive, and *pario,* to bring forth, as bringing forth its young alive.] A name of certain poisonous serpents, including the common viper or adder; a mischievous or malignant person.—**viperine,** vī'pėr•īn, *a.* [L. *viperinus.*] Pertaining to a viper or to vipers.—**viperous,** vī'pėr•us, *a.* Having the qualities of a viper; malignant; venomous.

virago, vi•rā'gō, *n.* [L., a heroic maiden, a heroine, a female warrior, from *vir,* a man. VIRILE.] A manlike woman; a bold, impudent, turbulent woman; a termagant.

virescent, vī•res'sent, *a.* [L. *virescens, virescentis,* ppr. of *viresco,* to grow green, incept. verb from *vireo,* to be green.] Slightly green; beginning to be green.

virgate, vėr'gāt, *a.* [From L. *virga,* a rod.] Having the shape of a rod or wand.—*n.* [L. *virga,* a rod, in L.L. a measure of land, like *rod, pole,* or *perch.*] A yard-land.

virgin, vėr'jin, *n.* [O.Fr. *virgine,* L. *virgo, virginis,* a virgin, root as *virga,* a twig.] A woman who has had no carnal knowledge of man; a maiden of inviolate chastity; a man who has preserved his chastity; the sign or the constellation Virgo.—*a.* Pertaining to a virgin; maidenly; modest; chaste; untouched; fresh; unsullied.—**virginal,** vėr'jin•al, *n.* [Fr. *virginal,* from being commonly played by young ladies or virgins.] An obsolete keyed musical instrument resembling the spinet.—**virginity,** vėr•jin'i•ti, *n.* [L. *virginitas.*] The state of being a virgin; perfect chastity.—**virgin's-bower,** *n.* A plant of the Clematis genus.—**Virgo,** vėr'gō, *n.* One of the twelve signs of the zodiac, which the sun enters about August 22.

viridity, vi•rid'i•ti, *n.* [L. *viriditas,* from *viridis,* green. VERDANT.] Greenness; verdure.

virile, vir'īl or vir'il, *a.* [Fr. *viril,* from L. *virilis,* from *vir,* a man; cog. A.Sax. *wer,* Icel. *verr,* a man; Gr. *hērōs,* a hero; Skr. *vira,* a hero. From L. *vir* comes also *virtus,* E. *virtue.*] Pertaining to a man as opposed to a woman; masculine; not puerile or feminine.—**virility,** vi•ril'i•ti, *n.* [Fr. *virilité,* L. *virilitas.*] Manhood; the power of procreation; masculine conduct, character, vigor, or spirit.

virtu, vėr'tö, *n.* [It. *virtù.*] Same as *Vertu.*

virtue, vėr'chö, *n.* [Fr. *vertu,* virtue,

goodness, power, efficacy, from L. *virtus, virtutis*, properly manliness, bravery, hence worth, excellence, virtue, from *vir*, a man. VIRILE.] Moral goodness; uprightness; morality: the opposite of *vice*; a particular moral excellence (the *virtue* of temperance); specifically, female purity; chastity; any good quality, merit, or accomplishment; an inherent power or property (the medicinal *virtues* of plants); efficacy; active, efficacious power.—*By virtue of, in virtue of*, by or through the efficacy or authority of.—*Cardinal virtues*. CARDINAL. —*Theological virtues*, the three virtues, Faith, Hope, and Charity.—**virtual,** vėr′chṳ•al, *a.* [Fr. *virtuel.*] Being in essence or effect, not in fact; not actual but equivalent, so far as result is concerned (a *virtual* denial of a statement).—**virtually,** vėr′chṳ•al•li, *adv.* In a virtual manner; in efficacy or effect if not in actuality. —**virtuous,** vėr′chṳ•us, *a.* Imbued with or proceeding from virtue; morally good; practicing the moral duties and abstaining from vice; often specifically, chaste; pure: applied to women.—**virtuously,** vėr′chṳ•us•li, *adv* In a virtuous manner.

virtuoso, vėr•chṳ•ō′sō, *n* pl. **virtuosi,** vėr•chṳ•ō′sē. [It. VERTU.] One skilled in or having a taste for artistic excellence; one skilled in antiquities, curiosities, and the like.

virulent, vi′rū•lent, *a.* [Fr. *virulent*, from L. *virulentus*, poisonous, from *virus*, poison. VIRUS.] Extremely poisonous or venomous; very actively injurious to life; very noxious or baneful; very bitter in enmity; malignant.—**virulently,** vi′rū•lent•li, *adv.* With malignant activity; with bitter spite.—**virulence,** vi′rū•lens, *n.* [Fr. *virulence*, L. *virulentia.*] The quality of being virulent; intensity of destructive quality.

virus, vī′rus, *n.* [L., poison; allied to Gr. *ios* (for *vios, visos*), Skr. *visha*, Ir. *fi*, poison.] A group of submicroscopic infective agents, thought to be either living organisms, or complex proteins capable of multiplying in living cells. Viruses cause diseases as rabies, smallpox, and mumps; a harmful influence.

visa, vē′za, *n.* [Fr. *visé*, pp. of *viser*, to put a visé to, from L. *visus*, seen, *video, visum*, to see. VISION.] An endorsement made upon a passport, denoting that it has been examined and found correct.

visage, viz′ij, *n.* [Fr. *visage*, from L. *visus*, a look.] The face, countenance, or look of a person.

vis-à-vis, vē•za•vē′, *adv.* [Fr., lit. face to face, from O.Fr. *vis*, a visage, L. *visus*, a look. VISAGE.] In a position facing each other; standing or sitting face to face.

viscera, vis′e•ra, *n.pl.* [L. *viscera*, pl. of *viscus, visceris*; akin to *viscid.*] The entrails; the bowels.—**visceral,** vis′e•ral, *a.* Pertaining to the viscera.—*Visceral arches and clefts*, in vertebrates, thickenings and slits on the side of the neck. The latter place the cavity of the throat in communication with the exterior.

viscid, vis′sid, *a.* [L.L. *viscidus*, clammy, from L. *viscum*, the mistletoe, birdlime.] Sticking or adhering, and having a ropy or glutinous consistency; semi-fluid and sticky.—**viscidity,** vis•sid′i•ti, *n.* The state or quality of being viscid; glutinousness: stickiness.

viscose, vis′kōs, *n.* [L. L. *viscosus.*] A viscous solution prepared by treating cellulose with caustic alkali and carbon disulfide, used in making cellophane, rayon, etc.—**viscosity,** vis•kos′i•ti, *n.* The quality of being viscous; stickiness; glutinousness.—**viscous,** vis′kus, *a.* Glutinous; sticky; adhesive; tenacious.

viscount, vī′kount, *n.* [Lit. a vice-count; O.E. *viconte*, O.Fr. *viceconte, viscomte*, Fr. *vicomte*. VICE, COUNT.] A degree or title of nobility next in rank to an earl, and above that of baron.—**viscountess,** vī′kount•es, *n.* The wife of a viscount, or a lady having equal rank.—**viscounty,** vī′koun•ti, *n.* The quality or rank of a viscount.

viscous. See VISCID.

viscus, vis′kus, *n.* [L. See VISCERA.] One of the viscera; one of the organs (as the heart, liver, etc.) contained in the larger cavities of the body.

vise, vīs, *n.* [O.Fr. *vis, viz*, a screw, a winding stair, from L. *vitis*, a vine.] A device having two jaws operated by a lever, cam, etc., used for holding an object being worked on.

Vishnu, vish′nö, *n.* [Skr. *Vishnu*, from *vish*, to pervade.] The Hindu deity, called 'the Preserver', who, with Brahma and Siva, forms the *trimurti*, or trinity.

visible, viz′i•bl, *a.* [L. *visibilis*, from *video, visum*, to see. VISION.] Perceivable by the eye; capable of being seen; in view; apparent.—*Visible church*, the whole body of professed believers in Christ on earth.—*Visible speech*, a system of alphabetical characters designed to represent every possible articulate utterance of the organs of speech, each organ and every mode of action having its appropriate and suggestive symbol. —**visibility, visibleness,** viz•i•bil′i•ti, viz′i•bl•nes, *n.* The state or quality of being visible; condition of the atmosphere with reference to the ease with which objects can be seen through it: chiefly used in aviation, and with such adjectives as good, low, poor, moderate.—**visibly,** viz′i•bli, *adv.* Perceptibly to the eye; manifestly; obviously.

Visigoth, viz′i•goth, *n.* One of the Western Goths, as distinguished from the *Ostrogoths*, or Eastern Goths. GOTH, OSTROGOTH.—**Visigothic,** viz•i•goth′ik, *a.* Pertaining to the Visigoths.

vision, vizh′on, *n.* [Fr. *vision*, from L. *visio, visionis*, from *video, visum*, to see, from root seen also in Gr. (*v*)*idein*, to see, (*v*)*oida*, I know; Skr. *vid*, to know; E. *wit, wot*. The Latin verb is seen also in *visual, visible, visit, visage, vista, advise, evident, provide*, Fr. *vue*, E. *view*, etc.] The act or faculty of seeing; the power or faculty by which we perceive the forms and colors of objects; sight; that which is seen; an object of sight; something supposed to be seen otherwise than by the ordinary organs of sight; something seen in a dream, trance, or the like; an apparition; a phantom; a mere creation of fancy; fanciful view.—**visional,** vizh′on•al, *a.* Pertaining to a vision.—**visionary,** vizh′on•e•ri, *a.* [Fr. *visionnaire.*] Apt to behold visions of the imagination; given to indulging in daydreams, fanciful theories, or the like; not real; having no solid foundation; imaginary.—*n.* One who sees visions or unreal sights; one who forms impracticable schemes.

visit, viz′it, *v.t.* [Fr. *visiter*, from L. *visitare*, a freq. from *viso*, to go to see, from *video, visum*, to see. VISION.] To go or come to see (a person or thing); to make a call upon; to proceed to in order to view; to come or go to generally; to afflict; to overtake or come upon; said especially of diseases or calamities; to send a judgment upon; to inflict punishment for.—*v.i.* To practice going to see others; to make calls.—*n.* The act of visiting; a going to see a person, place, or thing; a short stay of friendship, ceremony, business, curiosity, etc.; a call.—**visitant,** viz′i•tant, *n.* One who visits; a visitor.—**visitation,** viz•i•tā′shon, *n.* [L. *visitatio.*] A visit‡: a formal or judicial visit by a superior, superintending officer, etc.; a special dispensation or judgment from heaven; communication of divine favor or goodness, more usually of divine indignation and retribution.—**visitatorial,** viz′i•ta•tō″ri•al, *a.* Pertaining to a judicial visitor or visitation.—**visitor,** viz′i•tor, *n.* One who visits; a caller; a guest.

visor, vizor, vīz′ėr, *n.* [Fr. *visière*, a visor, from O.Fr. *vis*, the face or visage. VISAGE.] A mask used to conceal the face or disguise the wearer; the movable face guard of a helmet; a shield worn above the eyes to protect them from glare.

vista, vis′ta, *n.* [It., sight, view, from L. *video, visum*, to see. VISION.] A view or prospect through an avenue, as between rows of trees; the trees that form the avenue.

visual, vizh′ū•al, *a.* [Fr. *visuel*, L.L. *visualis*, from L. *visus*, sight. VISION.] Pertaining to sight; used in sight; serving as the instrument of seeing. —*Visual angle*, the angle formed at the eye by the rays of light from the extremities of the object.—*Visual education*, a modern method of teaching by presenting objects or pictures to supplement that which is being taught.—*Visual purple*, a rose-colored substance, sensitive to light, found in the retina of the eye. Its decomposition by light is supposed to be an essential step in the process which leads to the sensation of vision.—**visualize,** vizh′ū•al•īz, *v.t.*—*visualized, visualizing*. To form a mental picture of anything.

vital, vī′t'l, *a.* [Fr. *vital*, from L.

vitalis, vital, pertaining to life, from *vita* (for *vivita*), life, from stem of *vivus*, living, *vivo*, *victum*, to live (whence also *vivid*, *vivacity*, *victual*, *viand*, etc.); from a root seen also in E. *quick*.] Pertaining to life, either animal or vegetable; contributing to life; necessary to life; being the seat of life; being that on which life depends (a *vital* part); hence, absolutely necessary; essential; indispensable.—*Vital functions*, those functions on which life immediately depends, as the circulation of the blood, respiration, digestion, etc.—**vitality,** vi•tal′i•ti, *n.* The state of showing vital powers; the principle of life; animation; manifestation of life or of a capacity for lasting.—**vitalization,** vī•t′l•i•zā′shon, *n.* The act of vitalizing.—**vitalize,** vī′t′l•īz, *v.t.*—*vitalized*, *vitalizing*. To give life to; to furnish with the vital principle.—**vitally,** vī′t′l•li, *adv.* In a vital manner; essentially (*vitally* important).—**vitals,** vī′t′lz, *n. pl.* Internal parts or organs of animal bodies essential to life; the part of a complex whole essential to life.

vital statistics, *n.* Statistics of births, marriages, deaths, health, and disease.

vitamin, vī′ta•min, *n.* [L. *vita*, life, and *amine*.] One of several substances necessary for animal nutrition, and occurring in minute quantities in natural foods.

vitellus, vi•tel′us, *n.* [L., the yoke of an egg.] The yoke of an egg; a membrane enclosing the embryo in some plants.—**vitelline,** vi•tel′lin, *n.* A substance consisting of casein and albumen in the yolk of birds' eggs.

vitiate, vish′i•āt, *v.t.*—*vitiated*, *vitiating*. [L. *vitio*, *vitiatum*, from *vitium*, a fault, vice. VICE.] To render faulty or imperfect; to injure the quality or substance of; to impair; to spoil; to render invalid or of no effect; to invalidate.—**vitiation,** vish•i•ā′shon, *n.* The act of vitiating.

viticulture, vit′i•kul•chėr, *n.* [L. *vitis*, a vine, and *cultura*, culture.] The culture or cultivation of the vine.

vitreous, vit′ri•us, *a.* [L. *vitreus*, from *vitrum*, glass; same root as *video*, to see. VISION.] Pertaining to or obtained from glass; consisting of glass; resembling glass (the *vitreous* humor of the eye, a transparent gelatinous fluid occupying the posterior of the globe).—*Vitreous electricity*, that produced by rubbing glass, as distinguished from *resinous electricity*.—**vitreousness,** vit′ri•us•nes, *n.* The quality of being vitreous.—**vitrescence,** vi•tres′sens, *n.* The quality of being vitrescent.—**vitrescent,** vi•tres′sent, *a.* Turning into glass; tending to become glass.—**vitrescible,** vi•tres′si•bl, *a.* Capable of being vitrified.—**vitric,** vit′rik, *a.* Of a glassy nature.—**vitrifaction, vitrification,** vit•ri•fak′shon, vit′ri•fi•kā″shon, *n.*—**vitrifiable,** vit′ri•fī•a•bl, *a.* Capable of being vitrified.—**vitriform,** vit′ri•form, *a.* Having the form or resemblance of glass.—**vitrify,** vit′ri•fī, *v.t.*—*vitrified*, *vitrifying*. [L. *vitrum*, and *facio*, to make.] To convert into glass by fusion or the action of heat.—*v.i.* To become glass; to be converted into glass.

vitriol, vit′ri•ol, *n.* [Fr. *vitriol*, L.L. *vitriolum*, vitriol, from L. *vitrum*, glass. VITREOUS.] The common name of sulfuric acid and of many of its compounds, which, in certain states, have a glassy appearance.—*Blue vitriol* or *copper vitriol*, sulfate of copper.—*Green vitriol*, copperas.—*Lead vitriol*, sulfate of lead.—*Oil of vitriol*, concentrated sulfuric acid.—*Red vitriol*, a sulfate of cobalt; also, red sulfate of iron.—*White vitriol*, sulfate of zinc.—**vitriolize,** vit′ri•ol•īz, *v.t.* To convert into a vitriol.—**vitriolization,** vit′ri•ol•i•zā″shon, *n.* The act of conversion into a vitriol.—**vitriolic,** vit•ri•ol′ik, *a.* Pertaining to vitriol; having the qualities of vitriol.

vitta, vit′a, *n.* pl. **vittae,** vit′ē. [L.] A headband, fillet, or garland; *bot.* a name given to the receptacles of oil in the fruits of umbelliferous plants, as anise, fennel, caraway, etc.—**vittate,** vit′āt, *a.* Filleted; *bot.* striped lengthwise.

vituline, vit′ū•līn, *a.* [L. *vitulinus*, from *vitulus*, a calf. VEAL.] Belonging to a calf or to veal.

vituperate, vī•tū′pe•rāt, *v.t.*—*vituperated*, *vituperating*. [Fr. *vituperer*, from L. *vitupero*, *vituperatum*—*vitium*, a vice, a fault, and *paro*, to prepare. VICE, PARE.] To blame with abusive language; to abuse; to rate; to objurgate.—**vituperation,** vī•tū′pe•rā″shon, *n.* [L. *vituperatio*.] The act of vituperating; abuse; railing.—**vituperative,** vī•tū′pe•rā•tiv, *a.* Containing or expressing abusive censure; abusive.—**vituperatively,** vī•tū′pe•rā•tiv•li, *adv.* With vituperation; abusively.—**vituperator,** vī•tū′pe•rāt•ėr, *n.* One who vituperates.

vivacious, vi•vā′shus, *a.* [L. *vivax*, *vivacis*, from *vivus*, alive. VITAL.] Lively; active; sprightly in temper or conduct; proceeding from or characterized by sprightliness.—**vivaciously,** vi•vā′shus•li, *adv.* With vivacity, life, or spirit.—**vivaciousness,** vi•vā′shus•nes, *n.* Vivacity; liveliness.—**vivacity,** vi•vas′i•ti, *n.* [L. *vivacitas*.] Liveliness of manner or character; sprightliness of temper or behavior; animation; briskness; cheerfulness; spirit.

vivandière, vē•vänd•yâr′, *n.* [Fr. VIAND.] A female attached to French and other continental regiments, who sells provisions and liquor.

vivarium, vi•vâ′ri•um, *n.* pl. **vivaria,** vi•vâ′ri•a. [L., from *vivus*, alive. VITAL.] A place artificially prepared for keeping animals alive, in as nearly as possible their natural state.

viva voce, vī′va vō′si, *adv.* [L., by the living voice.] By word of mouth; orally; sometimes used adjectively (a *viva voce* examination).

vivid, viv′id, *a.* [L. *vividus*, from *vivus*, alive. VITAL.] Exhibiting the appearance of life or freshness; bright; clear; lively; fresh (*vivid* colors); forming brilliant images or painting in lively colors; realistic.—**vividly,** viv′id•li, *adv.* In a vivid or lively manner; with strength or intensity; in bright or glowing colors; with animated exhibition to the mind.—**vividness,** viv′id•nes, *n.* The quality of being vivid; liveliness; brightness.

vivify, viv′i•fī, *v.t.*—*vivified*, *vivifying*. [Fr. *vivifier*, L. *vivificare*—*vivus*, alive, and *facio*, to make.] To endue with life; to animate; to make to be living.—*v.i.* To impart life or animation.—**vivification,**† viv′i•fi•kā″shon, *n.* The act of vivifying.

viviparous, vi•vip′a•rus, *a.* [L. *vivus*, alive, and *pario*, to bear.] Producing young in a living state, as distinguished from *oviparous*, producing eggs.—**viviparously,** vi•vip′a•rus•li, *adv.* In a viviparous manner.—**viviparity, viviparousness,** viv•i•par′i•ti, vi•vip′a•rus•nes, *n.* State or character of being viviparous.

vivisection, viv•i•sek′shon, *n.* [From L. *vivus*, alive, and *sectio*, *sectionis*, a cutting.] The dissection of, or otherwise experimenting on, a living animal, for the purpose of ascertaining or demonstrating some fact in physiology or pathology.—**vivisector,** viv′i•sek•tėr, *n.* One who practices vivisection.

vixen, vik′sen, *n.* [A.Sax. *fixen*, *fyxen*, a she-fox, fem. of *fox* (with change of *f* to *v*); comp. G. *füchsin*, a she-fox, *fuchs*, a fox.] A she-fox; a froward, turbulent, quarrelsome woman; a scold; a termagant.—**vixenish,** vik′sen•ish, *a.* Pertaining to a vixen.—**vixenly,** vik′sen•li, *a.* Having the qualities of a vixen.

viz. A contraction of L. *videlicet*, meaning namely, to wit, and read as so.

vizier, viz′i•ėr or vi•zēr′, *n.* [Fr. *vizir*, from Ar. *wazir*, a vizier, lit. a bearer of burdens, a porter, from *wazara*, to bear a burden.] The title of high political officers in the Turkish Empire and other Mohammedan states; a minister of state.—*Grand vizier*, the president of the divan; the prime minister.—**vizierate,** viz′i•ėr•āt or vi•zēr′āt, *n.* The office, state, or authority of a vizier.—**vizierial,** vi•zē′ri•al, *a.* Pertaining to a vizier.

vizor, vīz′or, *n.* See VISOR.

vocable, vō′ka•bl, *n.* [L. *vocabulum*, from *voco*, to call. VOICE.] A word; a term; a word without regard to its meaning.—**vocabulary,** vō•kab′ū•le•ri, *n.* [Fr. *vocabulaire*, from L. *vocabulum*.] A list or collection of words arranged in alphabetical order and briefly explained; a wordbook; sum or stock of words employed; range of language (a limited *vocabulary*).

vocal, vō′kal, *a.* [L. *vocalis*, from *vox*, voice. VOICE.] Pertaining to the voice or speech; uttered or modulated by the voice; endowed or as if endowed with a voice; *phonetics*, voiced or sonant: said of certain sounds; having a vowel character.—*Vocal chords*, two elastic membranous folds so attached to the cartilages of the larynx and to muscles that they may be stretched or relaxed, so as to modify the sounds produced by their vibration.—**vocalist,** vō′kal•ist, *n.* A vocal musician; a singer.—**vocality,** vō•kal′i•ti, *n.* The quality of being vocal.—**vocalization,** vō′-kal•i•zā″shon, *n.* Act of vocalizing; the state of being vocalized.—**vocalize,** vō′kal•īz, *v.t.*—*vocalized, vocalizing.* To form into voice; to make vocal; to utter with voice and not merely breath; to make sonant.—**vocally,** vō′kal•li, *adv.* In a vocal manner; with voice; verbally.

vocation, vō•kā′shon, *n.* [Fr. *vocation,* from L. *vocatio,* from *voco, vocatum,* to call. VOICE.] A calling or designation to a particular state or profession; a summons; a call; employment; calling; occupation; trade.—**vocative,** vok′a•tiv, *a.* [L. *vocativus,* from *voco,* to call.] Relating to calling or addressing by name; applied to the grammatical case in which a person or thing is addressed.—*n.* The vocative case.

vociferate, vō•sif′ėr•āt, *v.i.*—*vociferated, vociferating.* [L. *vocifero, vociferatum*—*vox, vocis,* the voice, and *fero,* to bear. VOICE, FERTILE.] To cry out with vehemence; to exclaim.—*v.t.* To utter with a loud voice or clamorously; to shout.—**vociferation,** vō•sif′ėr•ā″shon. *n.* The act of vociferating; a violent outcry; clamor; exclamation.—**vociferous,** vō•sif′ėr•us, *a.* Making a loud outcry; clamorous; noisy.—**vociferously,** vō•sif′ėr•us•li, *adv.* In a vociferous manner.—**vociferousness,** vō•sif′ėr•us•nes, *n.*

vodka, vod′ka, *n.* An intoxicating spirit distilled from potatoes or various cereals, and much used in Russia.

vogue, vōg, *n.* [Fr. *vogue,* fashion, lit. rowing of a ship, from It. *voga,* a rowing, from G. *wogen,* to wave, akin E. *wag, wave.*] The prevalent mode or fashion; popular repute or estimation; now almost exclusively used in the phrase *in vogue,* that is, in fashion, held in esteem for the time being.

voice, vois, *n.* [O.E. *voys,* O.Fr. *vois,* Mod. Fr. *voix,* from L. *vox, vocis,* voice, a word, from stem of *vocare,* to call (seen also in *vocation, vocative, vocal, vowel, advocate, convoke, invoke,* etc.); allied to Skr. *vach,* to speak.] The sound uttered by the mouths of living creatures, whether men or animals; especially, human utterance in speaking, singing, or otherwise; the sound made when a person speaks or sings; the faculty of uttering audible sounds; the faculty of speaking; language; a sound produced by an inanimate object; sound emitted; the right of expressing an opinion; vote; suffrage (you have no *voice* in the matter); *phonetics,* sound uttered with resonance of the vocal chords, and not with breath merely; sonant utterance; *gram.* a form of verb inflection (active *voice,* middle *voice,* passive *voice*).—*v.t.*—*voiced, voicing.* To utter, declare, or proclaim.—**voiced,** voist, *a.* Furnished with a voice; *phonetics,* sonant.—**voiceful,** vois′fu̧l, *a.* Having a voice; vocal.—**voiceless,** vois′les, *a.* Having no voice, utterance, or vote.

void, void, *a.* [O.Fr. *voide, vuide* (Fr. *vide*), empty, void, from L. *viduus,* widowed, bereaved; allied to E. *widow.* Hence also *avoid, devoid.*] Empty or not containing matter; having no holder or possessor; vacant; unoccupied; devoid; destitute (*void of* learning); not producing any effect; ineffectual; in vain; having no legal or binding force; null (a deed not duly signed and sealed is *void*).—*n.* An empty space; a vacuum.—*v.t.* [O.Fr. *voidier,* to empty.] To make or leave vacant; to quit or vacate; to emit, throw, or send out; to evacuate from the bowels.—**voidable,** voi′da•bl, *a.* Capable of being voided.—**voidance,** voi′dans, *n.* The act of voiding; ejection from a benefice; vacancy, as of a benefice.—**voided,** *a. Her.* a charge is voided when the center is cut out and only a framework left round the edge.—**voider,** voi′dėr, *n.* One who voids.

volant, vō′lant, *a.* [Fr. *volant,* flying, from *voler,* L. *volare,* to fly.] Flying; nimble; rapid; *her.* represented as flying.—**volar,**† vō′lėr, *a.* Pertaining to flight; used in flying (the *volar* membranes of bats).—**volplane,** vol′-plān, *n.* and *v. Aviation,* to alight with a long glide downward.

Volapük, vō′la•pūk, *n.* [An invented name based on the words *world* and *speak;* world speech.] An artificial language intended for universal use, its vocables being based on English and other words, changed so as to be easily uttered, and its grammar or syntax of the simplest and most regular kind.

volar, vō′lėr, *a.* [L. *vola,* palm.] Relating to the palm or sole of foot.

volatile, vol′a•til, *a.* [Fr. *volatil,* from L. *volatilis,* from *volo, volatum,* to fly.] Having the quality of passing off by spontaneous evaporation; diffusing more or less freely in the atmosphere; passing off insensibly in vapor; of a lively, brisk, or gay temperament; fickle; apt to change.—**volatility,** vol•a•til′i•ti, *n.* The quality of being volatile; capability of evaporating or dissipating; flightiness; fickleness.—**volatilization,** vol′a•til•i•zā″shon, *n.* The act or process of volatilizing.—**volatilize,** vol′a•til•īz, *v.t.*—*volatilized, volatilizing.* [Fr. *volatiliser.*] To cause to exhale or evaporate; to cause to pass off in vapor or invisible effluvia.

volcano, vol•kā′nō, *n.* pl. **volcanoes,** vol•kā′nōz. [It. *volcano, vulcano,* Fr. *volcan,* from L. *Vulcanus,* the god of fire; cog. Skr. *ulkā,* fire.] A hill or mountain more or less perfectly cone shaped, with a circular cuplike opening or basin (called a *crater*) at its summit, from which are sent out clouds of vapor, gases, showers of ashes, hot fragments of rocks, and streams of lava.—**volcanic,** vol•-kan′ik, *a.* Pertaining to volcanoes; changed or affected by the heat of a volcano.—*Volcanic foci,* subterranean centers of igneous action, from which minor exhibitions diverge.—*Volcanic glass,* obsidian.—*Volcanic rocks,* rocks which have been formed by volcanic agency.—**volcanism,** vol′kan•izm, *n.* State of being volcanic; volcanic power.—**volcanist,** vol′kan•ist, *n.* One versed in volcanoes; a vulcanist.—**volcanization,** vol′kan•i•zā″shon, *n.* The process of volcanizing.—**volcanize,** vol′kan•īz, *v.t.*—*volcanized, volcanizing.* To subject to volcanic heat and modify by its action.

vole, vōl, *n.* [Fr., from *voler,* to fly.] A deal at cards that draws all the tricks.

vole, vōl, *n.* [Also called *vole-mouse,* perhaps for *wold-mouse.*] A name of several rodent animals, resembling, and in many cases popularly bearing, the names of rats and mice, as the short-tailed field mouse, the water rat, etc.

volition, vō•lish′on, *n.* [L. *volitio,* from *volo,* to will; same root as E. *will.* VOLUNTARY.] The act of willing; the exercise of the will; the power of willing; will.—**volitional,** vō•lish′on•al, *a.* Pertaining to volition.—**volitive,** vol′i•tiv, *a.* Having the power to will; originating in the will; *gram.* used in expressing a wish or permission (a *volitive* proposition).

volley, vol′i, *n.* [Fr. *volée,* a flight, from *voler,* L. *volare,* to fly. VOLATILE.] A flight of missiles, as of shot, arrows, etc.; a simultaneous discharge of a number of missile weapons, as small arms; in tennis, a return of the ball before it touches the ground.—*v.t.*—*volleyed, volleying.* To discharge with a volley, or as if with a volley.—*v.i.* To be discharged at once or with a volley.

volleyball, vol′i•ba̧l, *n.* [From *volley* and *ball.*] A game in which two teams volley a large, inflated ball over a net.

volplane, *n.* and *v.* See VOLANT.

volt, vōlt, *n.* [Fr. *volte,* from L. *volvo, volutum,* to turn. VAULT.] A bound or spring; *fencing,* a sudden movement or leap to avoid a thrust.

volt, vōlt, *n.* [From *Volta,* the discoverer of voltaism.] The practical unit of electromotive force, or potential difference.—**voltage,** vōl′tij, *n.* Electromotive force expressed in volts.—**voltaic,** vol•tā′ik, *a.* Pertaining to ordinary current electricity or galvanism.—*Voltaic battery,* an apparatus consisting of a combination of voltaic cells.—*Voltaic cell,* a contrivance for producing electric current, consisting in its simplest form of a jar containing an electrolyte, such as dilute sulfuric acid, and two metals, such as copper and zinc. When the metals are joined by a wire a current flows. See GALVANIC.—*Voltaic electricity,* current electricity, produced chemically,—**voltaism,** vol′ta•izm, *n.* Voltaic electricity; galvanism.—**voltameter,** vol•tam′et•ėr, *n.* [*Voltaic,* and Gr. *metron,* measure.] An electrolytic means for measuring the strength of a current.—**voltmeter,** volt′mē•-tėr, *n.* [After A. *Volta,* Gr. *metron,* a measure.] An instrument for measuring electrical pressure, or difference of potential, in volts.

voluble, vol'ū•bl, *a.* [Fr. *voluble,* L. *volubilis,* revolving, fluent, voluble, from *volvo, volutum,* to roll (whence also *vault, volume, revolve, involve, convolution,* etc.); cog. E. *wallow, walk.*] Having a great flow of words or glibness of utterance; speaking with over great fluency; over fluent; *bot.* twisting; applied to stems which twist or twine round other bodies.—**volubly,** vol'ū•bli, *adv.* In a voluble or fluent manner.—**volubility, volubleness,** vol•ū•bil'i•ti, vol'ū•bl•nes, *n.* [Fr. *volubilité,* L. *volubilitas.*] The quality of being voluble in speech; over great fluency or readiness of the tongue; unchecked flow of speech.

volume, vol'ūm, *n.* [Fr. *volume,* from L. *volumen,* a roll, a roll of manuscript, a book, from *volvo,* to roll. VOLUBLE.] A roll of manuscript, such as anciently formed a book; a book; a tome; a part or portion of an extended work that is bound up together in one cover; something of a convolved, rounded, or swelling form; a coil; a convolution; a wreath (*volumes* of smoke); the bulk or solid content of a body, measured e.g. in cubic feet or cubic centimeters; a quantity as having a certain bulk (a *volume* of a gas); *mus.* quantity, fulness, power, or strength of tone or sound.—**volumed,** vol'ūmd, *a.* Having the form of volumes or rounded masses; consisting of rolling masses.—**volumetric,** vol•ū•met'rik, *a. Chem.* pertaining to estimation by measured volumes of standard solutions of reagents.—*Volumetric analysis,* a method of chemical analysis in which the quantity of a substance present in a solution is estimated by the amount of a standard solution required to produce a certain reaction.—*Volumetric efficiency* (*aviation*), the ratio of the volume of charge or mixture induced into the cylinder of a gasoline engine to the volume which would completely fill the cylinder.—**volumetrically,** vol•ū•met'ri•kal•li, *adv.* By volumetric analysis.

voluminous, vo•lū'mi•nus, *a.* [Fr. *volumineux,* from L. *volumen, voluminis,* a volume. VOLUME.] Consisting of many coils or complications (*Mil.*); of great volume; bulky; having written much; producing books that are bulky or writing many of them (a *voluminous* writer).—**voluminously,** vo•lū'mi•nus•li, *adv.* In a voluminous manner.—**voluminousness,** vo•lū'mi•nus•nes, *n.*

voluntary, vol'un•te•ri, *a.* [L. *voluntarius,* from *voluntas,* will, choice, from *voluns,* for *volens,* part. pres. of *volo, velle,* to will (whence *volition,* (*bene*)*volence,* (*male*)*volence*); cog. E. *will.*] Proceeding from the will; done of one's own accord or free choice; spontaneous; not prompted or suggested by another; of one's or its own accord or choice; subject to or controlled by the will; regulated by the will; endowed with free will; pertaining to the doctrines of the voluntaries (a *voluntary* church).—*n.* A person who maintains that churches should be supported entirely by voluntary contributions, and should be quite free from connection with the state; *mus.* an organ solo performed at the beginning, during, or at the end of a church service.—**voluntarily,** vol'un•te•ri•li, *adv.* In a voluntary manner; spontaneously.—**voluntariness,** vol'un•te•ri•nes, *n.* The character of being voluntary; spontaneity.—**voluntaryism,** vol'un•te•ri•izm, *n.* The principle of supporting religion by voluntary effort and association.—**volunteer,** vol•un•tēr', *n.* [Fr. *volontaire.*] A person who enters into any service of his own free will; a person who of his own free will offers the state his services in a military capacity without the stipulation of a substantial reward; a person belonging to one of the corps of riflemen, artillery, engineers, etc., who voluntarily undergo a military training.—*v.t.* To offer or bestow voluntarily.—*v.i.* To enter into any service of one's free will.

voluptuary, vo•lup'chū•e•ri, *n.* [L. *voluptuarius,* from *voluptas,* pleasure, akin to *volo,* to wish. VOLUNTARY.] A man wholly given up to luxury or the gratification of the appetite and sensual pleasures; a sensualist.—**voluptuous,** vo•lup'chū•us, *a.* [L. *voluptuosus.*] Pertaining to sensual pleasure; gratifying the senses; exciting or tending to excite sensual desires; sensual.—**voluptuously,** vo•lup'chū•us•li, *adv.* In a voluptuous manner; luxuriously; sensually.—**voluptuousness,** vo•lup'chū•us•nes, *n.* The state or quality of being voluptuous.

volute, vo•lūt', *n.* [L. *voluta,* a volute, from *volutus,* pp. of *volvo, volutum,* to roll. VOLUBLE.] *Arch.* a kind of spiral scroll used in the Ionic, Corinthian, and Composite capitals, of which it is a principal ornament.—**volution,** vo•lū'shon, *n.* A spiral turn; a convolution.

volva, vol'va, *n.* [L., a wrapper.] *Bot.* a wrapper or bag that envelops certain fungi when young.

vomer, vō'mėr, *n.* [L., a plowshare.] *Anat.* the slender thin bone between the nostrils.—**vomerine,** vō'mėr•in, *a.* Pertaining to the vomer.

vomit, vom'it, *v.t.* [From L. *vomo, vomitum,* to vomit; allied to Gr. *emō* (for *vemō*), Skr. *vam,* to vomit.] To throw up or eject from the stomach; to belch forth; to emit.—*v.i.* To eject the contents of the stomach by the mouth; to spew.—*n.* The matter ejected from the stomach; an emetic.—*Black vomit,* dark-colored matter ejected from the stomach in the last stage of yellow fever; hence, yellow fever.—**vomitory,** vom'i•to•ri, *n.* [L. *vomitorius,* causing vomiting, *vomitoria,* passages for exit in a theater.] An emetic; *arch.* an opening or door in an ancient theater and amphitheater which gave ingress or egress to the people.

voodoo, vö'dö, *n.* [Perhaps of African origin.] Among the West Indies and some Southern States Negroes, a person who professes to be a sorcerer, or to possess mysterious powers; such mysterious and malign powers collectively; an evil spirit. Also used adjectively.—**voodooism,** vö'dö•izm, *n.* [*often cap.*] Voodoo beliefs or practices.

voracious, vō•rā'shus, *a.* [L. *vorax, voracis,* from *voro,* to devour; same root as Gr. *bora,* food; Skr. *gar,* to swallow.] Greedy for eating; eating food in large quantities; rapacious; ready to devour or swallow up.—**voraciously,** vō•rā'shus•li, *adv.* In a voracious manner; ravenously.—**voracity,** vō•ras'i•ti, *n.* The quality of being voracious.

vortex, vor'teks, *n.* pl. **vortices,** vor'ti•sēz, or **vortexes,** vor'tek•sez. [L., from *verto,* anciently *vorto,* to turn. VERSE.] A whirling or gyratory motion in any fluid, whether liquid or aeriform; a whirlpool or a whirlwind; an eddy.—*Vortex ring,* a ring of fluid matter, which may be regarded as composed of rotating circles placed side by side, like beads on a string, as the singular smoke rings which are sometimes produced in smoking tobacco.—**vortical, vorticose,** vor'ti•kal, vor'ti•kōs, *a.* Pertaining to a vortex; whirling; turning.—**vortically,** vor'ti•kal•li, *adv.* In a vortical manner; whirlingly.

votary, vō'ta•ri, *n.* [From L. *votum,* a vow. VOTE.] One devoted, consecrated, or engaged by a vow or promise; a person devoted, given, or addicted to some particular service, worship, study, or state of life.—**votarist,** vō'ta•rist, *n.* A votary.—**votaress,** vō'ta•res, *n.* A female devoted to any service, worship, or state of life.

vote, vōt, *n.* [Fr. *vote,* a vote, from L. *votum,* a vow, wish, will, from *voveo, votum,* to vow (seen also in *devote, devout*). VOW.] The expression of a desire, preference, or choice in regard to any measure proposed, in which the person voting has an interest in common with others; a suffrage; that by which will or preference is expressed in elections or in deciding proposals; a ballot, a ticket, etc.; a thing conferred by vote; a grant.—*v.i.*—*voted, voting.* To give a vote; to express or signify the mind, will, or preference in electing men to office or the like.—*v.t.* To elect by some expression of will; to enact, establish, or grant by vote.—**voter,** vō'tėr, *n.* One who votes or has a legal right to vote; an elector.—**votive,** vō'tiv, *a.* [L. *votivus,* from *votum,* a vow.] Given, paid, or consecrated, in consequence of some vow.—*A votive offering,* a tablet, picture, etc., dedicated in consequence of the vow of a worshiper.—**votively,** vō'tiv•li, *adv.* In a votive manner; by vow.

vouch, vouch, *v.t.* [O.Fr. *vocher,* from L. *vocare,* to call; hence *avouch.* VOICE.] To declare, assert, affirm, or attest; to maintain by affirmations; to warrant; to answer for.—*v.i.* To bear witness; to give testimony or attestation; to maintain; to assert; to aver.—**voucher,** vouch′ėr, *n.* One who vouches; a paper or document which serves to confirm and establish facts of any kind; the written evidence of the payment of a debt, as a discharged account or the like.

vouchsafe, vouch•sāf′, *v.t.—vouchsafed, vouchsafing.* [From *vouch* and *safe,* to vouch or attest as safe; formerly often as two words.] To condescend to grant; to concede (to *vouchsafe* an answer).—*v.i.* To condescend; to deign; to yield.—**vouchsafement,** vouch•sāf′ment, *n.* The act of vouchsafing.

voussoir, vös•wär′, *n.* [Fr., akin in origin to *vault.*] One of a series of stones, etc., shaped like truncated wedges, with which an arch is constructed, the uppermost or middle one of which is called the keystone.

vow, vou, *n.* [O.Fr. *vou,* Mod. Fr. *vœu,* a vow, from L. *votum,* a vow; hence really the same word as *vote. Avow* is a derivative.] A solemn promise; an engagement solemnly entered into; an oath made to God, or to some deity, to perform some act on the fulfillment of certain conditions; a promise to follow out some line of conduct, or to devote one's self to some act or service.—*v.t.* To promise solemnly; to give, consecrate, or dedicate by a solemn promise, as to a divine power; to threaten solemnly or upon oath (to *vow* vengeance).—**vower,** vou′ėr, *n.* One who makes a vow.

vowel, vou′el, *n.* [Fr. *voyelle,* from L. *vocalis,* vocal, lit. a vocal letter, from *vox, vocis,* the voice. VOICE.] A sound produced by the vibration of the vocal chords during which air passes directly over the tongue and escapes from the mouth without obstruction by, or friction with, any part of the mouth; the letter or character that represents such a sound.—*a.* Pertaining to a vowel; vocal.

voyage, voi′ij, *n.* [Fr. *voyage,* a journey; It. *viaggio,* Sp. *viage*; from L. *viaticum,* from *viaticus,* pertaining to a journey, from *via,* a way (seen also in *viaduct, deviate, obviate, obvious, previous, convey,* etc.); same root as E. *way.*] Formerly, a journey by sea or by land; now, a journey by sea from one place, port, or country to another, especially a journey by water to a distant place or country.—*v.i.—voyaged, voyaging.* To take a journey or voyage; to sail or pass by water.—*v.t.* To travel; to pass over.—**voyager,** voi′ij•ėr, *n.* One who makes a voyage.

Vulcan, vul′kan, *n.* [L. *Vulcanus* or *Volcanus* (hence *volcano*); akin Skr. *ulkā,* a fire.] The Roman deity who presided over fire and the working of metals; the name given in 1859 to a hypothetical intra-Mercurial planet, now considered to have no existence.—**Vulcanian,** vul•kā′ni•an, *a.* Pertaining to Vulcan, or to works in iron, etc.; [*not cap.*] volcanic; *geol.* pertaining to vulcanism.—*Vulcanian theory,* the Plutonic theory. See PLUTONIC.—**vulcanism,** vul′kan•izm, *n.* The phenomena due to the internal heat of the earth, as volcanoes, hot springs, etc.

vulcanite, vul′kan•īt, *n.* [From *Vulcan.*] A hard, vulcanized rubber.

vulcanization, vul′kan•i•zā″shon, *n.* [From *Vulcan.*] A process of treating rubber chemically in order to reduce plasticity and increase stability and elasticity.—**vulcanize,** vul′kan•īz, *v.t.—vulcanized, vulcanizing.* To subject to the process of vulcanization.—*v.i.* To undergo vulcanization.

vulgar, vul′gėr, *a.* [Fr. *vulgaire,* from L. *vulgaris,* from *vulgus,* the common people, the crowd.] Pertaining to the common people or the multitude; plebeian; common; ordinary; in general use; hence, national; vernacular (the *vulgar* tongue); pertaining to the lower or less refined class of people; hence, somewhat coarse; rude; boorish; low.—*Vulgar fractions.* See FRACTION.—*The vulgar,* the common people collectively; the uneducated, uncultured class of people.—**vulgarian,** vul•gâ′ri•an, *n.* A vulgar person.—**vulgarism,** vul′gėr•izm, *n.* Vulgarity; a vulgar phrase or expression.—**vulgarity,** vul•gar′i•ti, *n.* The quality of being vulgar; coarseness or clownishness of manners or language; an act of low manners.—**vulgarize,** vul′gėr•īz, *v.t.—vulgarized, vulgarizing.* To make vulgar or common.—**vulgarly,** vul′gėr•li, *adv.* In a vulgar manner; commonly; by popular usage; coarsely; clownishly.—**vulgarness,** vul′gėr•nes, *n.* Vulgarity.—*The Vulgate* (L. *vulgata editio,* the edition made public or given to all), the authorized Latin version of the Scriptures in the Roman Catholic Church.

vulnerable, vul′nėr•a•bl, *a.* [Fr. *vulnerable,* from L. *vulnero,* to wound, from *vulnus, vulneris,* a wound.] Capable of being wounded; liable to injury; subject to be affected injuriously.—**vulnerability, vulnerableness,** vul′nėr•a•bil″i•ti, vul′nėr•a•bl•nes, *n.* The quality of being vulnerable.—**vulnerary,** vul′nėr•e•ri, *a.* [L. *vulnerarius.*] Useful in healing wounds.—*n.* Any plant, drug, or composition useful in the cure of wounds.

vulpine, vul′pīn, *a.* [L. *vulpinus,* from *vulpes,* a fox.] Pertaining to the fox; resembling the fox; cunning.—**vulpicide,** vul′pi•sīd, *n.* [L. *vulpes,* and *caedo,* to kill.] The practice of killing foxes; a fox killer.

vulpinite, vul′pin•īt, *n.* [From *Vulpino,* in Italy, where it is found.] A variety of gypsum sometimes employed for small statues and other ornamental work.

vulture, vul′chėr, *n.* [O.Fr. *vultor,* L. *vultur,* same root as *vulnerable.*] The name of well-known raptorial birds which live chiefly on carrion.—**vulturine,** vul′chėr•in, *a.* [L. *vulturinus.*] Having the qualities of or resembling the vulture. Also **vulturous.**

vulva, vul′va, *n.* [L. *vulva, volva,* a wrapper, the womb, from *volvo,* to roll.] *Anat.* the opening of the external parts of generation in the female.—**vulvo-uterine,** *a.* Pertaining to the vulva and the uterus.

vying, vī′ing, *p.* and *a.* Competing; emulating. See VIE.

W

W, w, dub′l•yu̧, is the twenty-third letter of the English alphabet, taking its form and name from the union of two V's or U's.

wabble, wob′l, *v.i.—wabbled, wabbling.* [WOBBLE.] To vacillate; to wobble.—*n.* A rocking unequal motion, as of a top imperfectly balanced.—**wabbly,** wob′li, *a.* Inclined to wabble; unsteady.

Wac, wak, *n.* [From the initials.] A member of the Women's Army Corps.

wacke, wak′e, *n.* [G. *wacke, grauwacke,* wacke, graywacke.] A soft earthy variety of traprock, generally of a grayish-green color, and usually containing crystals.

wad, wod, *n.* [Same word as Sw. *vadd,* Dan. *vat,* G. *watte,* wad.] A soft mass of fibrous material, as raw cotton or the like, used for stuffing, stopping an aperture, etc.; a little mass of some soft or flexible material, used for stopping the charge of powder in a gun and pressing it close to the shot.—*v.t.—wadded, wadding.* To furnish with a wad; to stuff or line with wadding, as a garment.—**wadding,** wod′ing, *n.* A fabric of cotton fiber or the like, used for stuffing various parts of articles of dress; material for ramming down above the charge of firearms.

waddle, wod′l, *v.i.—waddled, waddling.* [A dim. and freq. formed from *wade.*] To sway or rock from side to side in walking; to walk in a tottering or vacillating manner; to toddle.—**waddler,** wod′lėr, *n.* One who waddles.

wade, wād, *v.i.—waded, wading.* [A.Sax. *wadan,* to go, to wade=L.G. *waden,* Icel. and Sw. *vada,* D. *waden,* G. *waten,* to wade; same root as L. *vado,* to go. INVADE.] To walk through any substances that impedes or hinders the free motion of the limbs (as long grass or snow); to move stepwise through a fluid; to move or pass with difficulty or labor.—*v.t.* To pass or cross by wading; to ford.—**wader,** wā′dėr, *n.* One who wades; specifically, the name applied to such birds as the heron, snipe, rail, etc. GRALLATORES.

wadi, wady, wäd′i, *n.* [Ar. *wādi.*] The channel of a watercourse which is dry, except in the rainy season; a watercourse; a term used chiefly in the topography of certain Eastern or North African countries.

wadmal, wadmoll, wod′mal, wod′mol, *n.* [Icel. *vad-mâl,* Sw. *vadmal,*

Dan. *vadmel.*] A coarse cloth formerly manufactured.

Waf, waf, *n.* [*W*omen in the *A*ir *F*orce.] A member of the women's component of the U.S. Air Force.

wafer, wā′fėr, *n.* [G. *waffel*, D. *wafel*, a thin cake, a wafer.] A small thin sweet cake; a thin circular portion of unleavened bread, used in the Roman Catholic celebration and administration of the Eucharist; a small thin disk of dried paste used for sealing letters, etc.; any similar disk.

waffle, wof′l, *n.* [D. *wafel*, G. *waffel*, WAFER.] An indented batter cake baked between the two metal plates of a waffle iron.—**waffle iron,** *n.* A utensil having two hinged plates that can be heated in order to cook waffle batter.

waft, wäft, *v.t.* [Closely akin to *wave*, and to Sw. *vefta*, to waft, Dan. *vifte*, to waft, to fan; *vift*, a puff.] To convey through water or air; to make to sail or float; to buoy up; to keep from sinking.—*v.i.* To sail or float.—*n.* The act of one who or that which wafts; a sweep; a breath or current, as of wind.—**waftage,** wäf′tij, *n.* The act of wafting or state of being wafted.—**wafter,** wäf′tėr, *n.* One who wafts.

wag, wag, *v.t.*—*wagged*, *wagging*. [A.Sax. *wagian*, to wag, to shake; Sw. *vagga*, to wag, Icel. *vaga*, to wag, to waddle, D. *waggeten*, to stagger, G. *wackeln*, to waggle; akin *wagon*, *wain*, *weigh*, *way*, *wave*.] To cause to move backward and forward, or from side to side alternately; to cause to oscillate or vibrate slightly; to wave.—*v.i.* To move backward and forward; to hang loosely and shake; to oscillate; to sway; to be in motion or action; to move off or away; to be gone.—*n.* [Most likely a shortening of the old term *waghalter*, one likely to *wag* in a *halter* or gallows. Comp. Sc. *hempte*, a gallows bird, a frolicsome fellow, lit. one fitted for the hempen rope.] A person who is fond of making jokes; one who is full of frolicsome tricks; a humorist; a wit; a joker.—**waggery,** wag′ėr•i, *n.* The manner, action, or pranks of a wag; jocular sayings; pleasantry.—**waggish,** wag′ish, *a.* Belonging to a wag; full of sportive or jocular tricks, actions, sayings, etc.; frolicsome.—**waggishly,** wag′ish•li, *adv.* In a waggish manner; in sport.—**waggishness,** wag′ish•nes, *n.*

wage, wāj, *v.t.*—*waged*, *waging*. [O. Fr. *wager*, to pledge, to promise (hence, to pledge one's self to combat), Fr. *gager*, to stake, to pledge, from L.L. *vadium*, *wadium*, Goth. *wadi*, a pledge, same word as A.Sax. *wed*, a pledge. WED. *Gage* is another form of this word.] To engage in (a contest); to carry on (war); to undertake.—*n.* A gage or pledge‡; hire; wages.—**wages,** wā′jez, *n. pl.* [O.Fr. *wage*, *gage*, a pledge; *wages* are what the person hiring another has pledged himself to give.] The payment given for services performed; the price paid for labor; hire; recompense. Though a plural, *wages* sometimes has a verb in the singular.

wager, wā′jėr, *n.* [O.Fr. *wageure*, *gageure*, from L.L. *vadiatura*, from *wadium*, a pledge. WAGE.] An occasion on which two parties bet; a bet; the stake laid; the subject of a bet.—*Wager of battle*, the legal trial of a cause by combat either between the parties themselves or their champions, formerly in practice in England.—*v.t.* To hazard on the issue of some question that is to be decided; to bet; to stake.—*v.i.* To make a bet; to bet.—**wagerer,** wā′jėr•ėr, *n.* One who wagers.

wages. See WAGE.

waggle, wag′l, *v.i.*—*waggled*, *waggling*. [A freq. and dim. from *wag*.] To move with a wagging motion; to sway or move from side to side.—*v.t.* To cause to wag frequently and with short motions.

wagon, wag′on, *n.* [From D. *wagen*, rather than from A.Sax. *waegen*, a wagon (whence *wain*); Icel. and Sw. *vagn*, Dan. *vogn*, G. *wagen*; lit. what carries, from stem of *weigh*; cog. Skr. *vah*, L. *veho*, to carry (whence *vehicle*); akin also *way*, *wag*, etc.] A four-wheeled vehicle for the transport of heavy loads.—*v.t.* To transport or carry in a wagon.—**wagonage,** wag′on•ij, *n.* Money paid for conveyance by wagon.—**wagoner,** wag′on•ėr, *n.* One who drives a wagon; the constellation Charles's Wain or Ursa Major.—**wagonette,** wag•on•et′, *n.* [Dim. of *wagon*.] An open four-wheeled pleasure vehicle of light construction, seated for six or eight persons.

wagtail, wag′tāl, *n.* A small bird of several species, distinguished by its brisk and lively motions, as well as by the length of its tail, which it jerks up and down incessantly, hence the name; a pert person.

Wahabee, Wahabi, wa•hä′bi, *n.* [From Abdel *Wahab*, a reformer of Mohammedanism about 1760.] A member of a very strict sect of Mohammedans in Arabia.

waif, wāf, *n.* [O.Fr. *waif*, *gaif*, a waif; of Scandinavian origin, like E. *waive*.] A stray or odd article; an article that no one claims; goods found of which the owner is not known; a wanderer; a neglected, homeless wretch.

wail, wāl, *v.t.* [From Icel. *vaela*, *vála*, to wail or lament; perhaps connected with *woe*.] To lament; to bewail.—*v.i.* To express sorrow audibly; to lament; to howl or moan.—*n.* Loud weeping; violent lamentation.

wain, wān, *n.* [A.Sax. *waen*, a contracted form of *waegen*, a wagon, from *wegan*, to carry. WAGON, WEIGH.] A four-wheeled vehicle for the transportation of goods; a wagon; [*cap.*] a constellation, Charles's Wain.

wainscot, wān′skot, *n.* [From D. *wagenschot*, wainscot, for *wageschot*, from *waeg*, a wall, and *schot*, boarding, a covering of boards.] A wooden lining or boarding of the walls of rooms, usually made in panels.—*v.t.* To line with wainscot.—**wainscoting,** *n.* Wainscot, or the material used for it.

waist, wāst, *n.* [A.Sax. *waestm*, growth, stature, form, from stem of *wax*, to grow.] That part of the human body which is immediately below the ribs or thorax, or between the thorax and hips; the middle part of a ship, or that part between the foremast and mainmast.—**waistband,** wāst′band, *n.* A band round the waist; the band at the top of a pair of trousers.—**waistcoat,** wāst′kōt, *n.* A garment worn, usually by men, under a doublet; *British*, a man's vest.—**waistline,** wāst′līn, *n.* The line with the smallest circumference around the part of the body between the chest and the hips; the place where the upper and lower parts of a dress meet.

wait, wāt, *v.i.* [O.Fr. *waiter* (Fr. *guetter*), to watch or lie in wait, from *waite*, a watchman or sentinel, from O.H.G. *wahta*, a watchman; akin E. *watch*, *wake*.] To stay or rest in expectation or patience; to perform the duties of a servant or attendant; to serve at table.—*To wait on* or *upon*, to attend upon; to perform menial services for; to visit on business or for ceremony; to attend or follow, as a consequence; to accompany.—*v.t.* To stay or wait for; to await.—*n.* The act of waiting; a waiting in concealment; ambush; a musician who with others promenades the streets in the night about Christmas time, performing music appropriate to the season.—*To lie in wait*, to lie in ambush; hence, *fig.* to lay snares or make insidious attempts.—**waiter,** wā′tėr, *n.* One who waits; a male attendant on the guests in a hotel, inn, or similar place; a salver or small tray.—**waiting,** wā′ting, *n.* The act of staying in expectation; attendance.—*In waiting*, in attendance (lords *in waiting*, certain officers of the royal household).—**waiting maid, waiting woman,** *n.* A female servant who attends a lady.—**waitress,** wāt′res, *n.* A female attendant in a restaurant, etc.

waive, wāv, *v.t.* [Icel. *veifa*, to swing loosely, to vibrate. WAIF.] To relinquish or give up; not to insist on or claim; to forego.—**waiver,** wāv′ėr, *n. Law*, to voluntarily relinquish a known right, claim, or privilege; the legal document or written statement giving notice of such an act.

wake, wāk, *v.i.* pret. and pp. *woke* or *waked*; ppr. *waking*. [A.Sax. *wacan*, also *wacian*, to arise, to wake, to be awake; Icel. *vaka*, D. and L.G. *waken*, Goth. *vakan*, G. *wachen*, to wake; cog. with L. *vigil*, watchful (whence *vigilant*). Hence *waken*, *watch*.] To be awake; to continue awake; not to sleep; to cease to sleep; to be aroused; to be excited from a torpid or inactive state; to be put in motion; to revel or carouse late at night.—*v.t.* To rouse from sleep; to excite or stir; to put in motion or action, often with *up*; to hold a wake for.—*n.* [A.Sax. *wacu*, a watching, a vigil.] Vigils;

the feast of the dedication of a parish church, formerly kept by watching all night; a merry-making; a festive gathering (*Shak.*); the watching of a dead body prior to burial by the friends and neighbors of the deceased.—**waking,** wā'-king, *p.* and *a.* Being awake; rousing from sleep; exciting.—*Waking hours,* the hours when one is awake.—**wakeful,** wāk'fųl, *a.* Keeping awake after going to bed; watchful; vigilant.—**wakefully,** wāk'fųl•li, *adv.* In a wakeful manner.—**wakefulness,** wāk'fųl•nes, *n.* The state of being wakeful; indisposition to sleep.—**waken,** wā'kn, *v.i.* [A.Sax. *waecnan,* to become awake, from *wacan,* to wake.] To wake; to cease to sleep.—*v.t.* To excite or rouse from sleep; to awaken; to excite to action; to rouse; to stir; to produce; to call forth (to *waken* love or fear).—**wakener,** wā'kn•ėr, *n.* One who or that which wakens.—**wakening,** wā'-kn•ing, *n.* The act of one who wakens; a ceasing from sleep.—**waker,** wā'kėr, *n.* One who wakes.

wake, wāk, *n.* [Same as Prov. E. *wake,* a row of grass; Icel. *vök,* a channel for a vessel in ice.] The track which is left by a ship in the water, and which may be seen to a considerable distance behind.

Waldenses, wol•den'sēz, *n.* [From Peter *Waldo* or *Waldus,* the founder of the sect in the twelfth century.] A sect of Christians in Northern Italy whose faith is substantially that of the Reformed churches, formerly much persecuted.

wale, wāl, *n.* [A.Sax. *walu,* a wale= O.Fris. *walu,* Icel. *völr,* Goth. *walus,* a rod, a staff. Hence *wale* in *gunwale.*] A streak or stripe produced by the stroke of a rod or whip on animal flesh; a weal; a plank from one end of a ship to another a little above the waterline.—*v.t.*—*waled, waling.* To mark with wales or stripes.

Walhalla, wąl•hal'la, *n.* See VALHALLA.

walk, wąk, *v.i.* [A.Sax. *wealcan,* to roll, to turn about, to rove (whence *wealcere,* a fuller, origin of the name *Walker*)=Icel. *válka,* Dan. *valke,* G. *walken,* to full; same root as *wallow, well,* L. *volvo,* to roll (whence *voluble,* etc.).] To step along; to advance by alternate steps, lifting one foot past the other without running; to go or travel on foot; to go or come, as used in the ceremonious language of invitation (*walk* in); to haunt or show itself in some place, as a specter; to conduct one's self; to pursue a particular course of life. —*v.t.* To pass over or through on foot; to cause to walk or step slowly. —*n.* The act of one who walks; the pace of one who walks; a short excursion on foot, for pleasure or exercise; manner of walking; gait; a place in which one is accustomed to walk; an avenue, promenade, or the like; sphere of action; a department, as of art, science, or literature; way of living; a tract or piece of ground in which animals graze; a sheepwalk; a district habitually served by an itinerant vendor of any commodity.—**walker,** wąk'ėr, *n.*—**walkie talkie,** *n.* A portable radio equipped with a transmitter and receiver, used for two-way communication.—**walking papers,** *n.* A dismissal, as from a job (colloq.).—**walking stick,** *n.* A stick used to aid in walking.—**walk-on,** wąk'on, *n.* A minor role in a play or film that does not, usually, entail speaking, but merely walking on to the stage. —**walk out,** *v.i.* To go on strike; to exit suddenly.—**walkout,** wąk'out, *n.*—**walk-up,** wąk'up, *a.* Pertaining to a building or apartment that does not have an elevator.

wall, wąl, *n.* [A.Sax. *weall,* a wall, a rampart=O.Sax., O.Fris., and D. *wal,* Dan. *val,* Sw. *vall,* G. *wall,* a rampart; from L. *vallum,* a fence of stakes, a rampart (seen also in *interval*), from *vallus,* a stake.] A structure of stone, brick, or other materials, of some height and breadth, serving to enclose a space, form a division, support superincumbent weights, etc.; the side of a building or room; a solid and permanent enclosing fence; a rampart; a fortified enceinte or barrier; in this sense often spoken of as plural; means of security or protection; *mining,* the rock enclosing a vein.—*To go to the wall,* to get the worst of a contest; to be overpowered.—*To push* or *thrust to the wall,* to crush by superior power.—*v.t.* To enclose with a wall; to defend by walls; to fill up with a wall.—**walled,** wąld, *p.* and *a.* Provided with a wall or walls; fortified.—**wallflower,** wąl'flou•ėr, *n.* The name of a cruciferous plant—a biennial or perennial herb or undershrub—which exhales a delicious odor, and is a great favorite in gardens; so called because in its wild state it grows on old walls and in stony places.—**wallpaper,** *n.* Paper for covering room walls; paper hangings.—**wall plate,** *n.* A piece of timber fixed horizontally in or on a wall, under the ends of girders, joists, and other timbers.

wallaby, wol'a•bi, *n.* [Native Australian.] The name of several varieties of the Australian kangaroo.

wallah, wol'la, *n.* [Anglo-Indian.] Person employed about or concerned with something.—*Competition-wallah,* Indian civil servant appointed by examination.

wallet, wol'et, *n.* [Probably a corruption of old *watel,* a bag. WATTLE.] A small folder used to carry money, cards, etc.; a billfold; a bag used to carry small articles while travelling.

walleye, *n.* [Icel. *vagl-eygr,* wall-eyed, from *vagl,* a beam or defect in the eye.] An eye in which the iris is of a very light gray or whitish color: said commonly of horses.—**walleyed,** *a.* Having such an eye: said of horses; glaring-eyed; fierce-eyed (*Shak.*).

Walloon, wal•lön', *n.* [From a Teutonic word meaning foreign, seen also in *walnut, Welsh.*] One of the descendants of the old Gallic Belgae who occupy part of Belgium and northeastern France, speaking a French dialect containing Gallic and Low German words; the language of the Walloons.

wallop, wol'op, *v.t.* To thrash; beat soundly. (*Colloq.*)

wallow, wol'ō, *v.i.* [A.Sax. *wealwian,* to roll; akin to E. to *well* up; same root as L. *volvo,* to roll. VOLUBLE.] To roll one's body on the earth, in mire, or in other substance; to tumble and roll in anything soft; to live in filth or gross vice.—**wallower,** wol'ō•ėr, *n.* One who wallows.

walnut, wąl'nut, *n.* [A.Sax. *wealh-hnut,* a walnut, lit. a foreign nut—*wealh,* foreign, and *hnut,* nut; so G. *wallnuss,* D. *walnoot.* WELSH.] A large handsome tree and its fruit, a native of Persia, yielding timber of great value as a cabinet and furniture wood.

walrus, wol'rus, *n.* [From D. *walrus,* a walrus, lit. a whale-horse—*wal,* a whale, and *ros,* a horse; so G. *wallross,* Dan. *valros,* Sw. *vallross,* A.Sax. *hors-hwael,* Icel. *hross-hvalr,* horse-whale.] A large marine carnivorous mammal of the Arctic regions allied to the seal; also known as the morse, sea horse, and sea cow; hunted for its oil and for the ivory of its tusk.

waltz, wolts, *n.* [Short for G. *walzer,* from *walzen,* to roll, to waltz; akin to *welter.*] A dance performed by two persons, who, almost embracing each other, swing round the room with a whirling motion; the music composed for the dance.—*v.i.* To dance a waltz.—**waltzer,** wolt'sėr, *n.* A person who waltzes.

wamble, wom'bl, *v.i.* [Same as Dan. *vamle,* to nauseate; akin Icel. *vaema,* to loathe, *vaema,* nausea.] To be disturbed with nausea: said of the stomach.

wampum, wom'pum, *n.* [American Indian; said to mean white.] Small beads made of shells, used by the American Indians as money, or wrought into belts, etc., as an ornament.

wan, won, *a.* [A.Sax. *wan, won, wann,* dark, dusky.] Having a pale or sickly hue; languid of look; pale; gloomy: often applied to water.—*v.i.* To grow or become wan. (*Poetical.*) —**wanly,** won'li, *adv.* In a wan manner; palely.—**wanness,** won'nes, *n.* Paleness; a sallow, dead color.

wand, wond, *n.* [Same as Dan. *vaand,* O.Sw. *wand,* Icel. *vondr,* Goth. *wandus,* a twig, a wand; probably akin to *wind* (*v.*), from its flexibility.] A long slender stick; a rod; a rod or similar article, having some special use or character; a staff of authority; a rod used by conjurors or diviners.

wander, won'dėr, *v.i.* [A.Sax. *wandrian,* to wander=O.D. *wanderen,* Dan. *vandre,* Sw. *vandra,* G. *wandern,* to wander; freq. forms akin to *wend.* WEND, WIND (verb).] To ramble here and there without any certain course or object in view; to roam; to stroll; to leave home; to go through the world; to deviate; to err; to be delirious; not to be under the guidance of reason.—*v.t.* To travel over without a certain course; to traverse.—**wanderer,** won′dėr•ėr, *n.* One who wanders.—**wandering,** won′dėr•ing, *p.* and *a.* Given to wander; roaming; unsettled.—*n.* A traveling without a settled course; peregrination; aberration; deviation; mental aberration.—**wanderingly,** won′dėr•ing•li, *adv.* In a wandering manner.

wanderoo, won•de•rö′, *n.* A monkey inhabiting the East Indies.

wane, wān, *v.i.*—*waned, waning.* [A. Sax. *wanian,* to diminish, become less, from *wan,* deficient; akin *want.*] To diminish; to decrease or grow less: particularly applied to the illuminated part of the moon, as opposed to *wax;* to decline; to approach its end (the autumn *wanes*). —*n.* Decrease of the illuminated part of the moon to the eye of the spectator; decline (his fortunes were on the *wane*).

wangle, wang′gl, *v.* To gain one's ends by devious or unscrupulous methods.

wanly, wanness, etc. See WAN.

want, wont, *n.* [From Icel. *vant,* neut. of *vanr,* lacking, wanting, *vanta,* to be lacking; akin *wane, wan-* in *wanton.*] The state of not having; absence or scarcity of what is needed or desired; lack; need; necessity (to supply one's *wants*); poverty; indigence; lack of the necessaries of life (to suffer from *want*).—*v.t.* To be without; not to have; to lack; to have occasion for; to require; to need; to feel a desire for; to long for.—*v.i.* To be deficient; to be lacking; to be absent or not present where required or expected; to be in want.

wanton, won′ton, *a.* [O.E. *wantowen, wantoun,* undisciplined, dissolute, from *wan,* prefix denoting want or deficiency (A.Sax. *wan,* lacking), and *towen,* A.Sax. *togen,* pp. of *teón,* to draw, to educate. WANT, TUG.] Indulging the natural impulses or appetites without restraint; licentious; lustful; unrestrained in various ways, as in gaiety or sport; playful; frolicsome; sportive; playing freely or without constraint (*wanton* ringlets); unrestrained in growth; growing too luxuriantly; arising from recklessness or disregard of right or consequences; unprovoked (*wanton* mischief).—*n.* A lascivious man or woman; a pampered, petted creature. —*v.i.* To revel; to frolic unrestrainedly; to sport or dally in lewdness.—**wantonly,** won′ton•li, *adv.* In a wanton manner; without cause or provocation.—**wantonness,** won′ton•nes, *n.* The state or quality of being wanton; lewdness; negligence of restraint; sportiveness.

wap, wop, *v.t.* To beat; to whop. (*Colloq.*)

wapentake, wo′pn•tāk, *n.* [Lit. a *weapontaking* or weapon-touching—from the men of a district touching the arms of a superior in token of fealty.] The name formerly given in some of the northern shires of England, and still given in Yorkshire, to a division of the county, corresponding to a *hundred.*

wapiti, wäp′i•ti, *n.* [Indian name.] The North American deer usually called elk, closely resembling the European red deer, though larger.

wappenschaw, wapinschaw, wä′pn•shạ, wa′pin•shạ, *n.* [Lit. a *weaponshow.*] In Scotland, a review of persons under arms, made formerly at certain times in every district; afterward applied in some quarters to the periodical gatherings of the volunteer corps of a district.

war, wạr, *n.* [A.Sax. *wár,* O.D. *werre,* O.H.G. *werra,* war (whence Fr. *guerre,* war); akin to G. *wirren,* to embroil, confuse; D. *war,* entanglement; perhaps allied to *worse.*] A contest between nations or states (*international war*), or between parties in the same state (*civil war*), carried on by force of arms; the profession of arms; art of war; a state of violent opposition or contest; hostility; enmity (feelings at *war* with each other).—*Articles of war.* See ARTICLE.—*Council of war.* See COUNCIL.—*v.i.*—*warred, warring.* To make or carry on war; to carry on hostilities; to contend; to strive; to be in a state of opposition.—**war cry,** *n.* A cry or phrase used in common by a body of troops or the like in charging an enemy.—**war dance,** *n.* A dance engaged in by savage tribes before a warlike excursion; a dance simulating a battle.—**warfare,** wạr′fâr, *n.* Military service; military life; hostilities; war.—*v.i.* To carry on warfare; to engage in war.—**war game,** *n.* A conference training exercise in which strategic and tactical concepts are tested in a simulated battle.—**war head,** *n.* The section of any missile that contains the explosive charge.—**warmonger,** wạr′mong•gėr, *n.* One who seeks to bring about war.—**war paint,** *n.* Paint put on the face and other parts of the body by savages before going to war.—**warpath,** wạr′path, *n.* The route or path taken on going to war: used chiefly in regard to the American Indians.—**warrior,** wạr′i•ėr, *n.* A soldier; a man engaged in military life; a brave soldier.—**warship,** wạr′ship, *n.* A ship constructed for engaging in naval warfare; a man-of-war.

warble, wạr′bl, *v.t.*—*warbled, warbling.* [O.Fr. *werbler,* from O.H.G. *hwerbalôn,* G. *wirbeln,* to whirl, to warble. WHIRL.] To sing in a trilling, quavering, or vibrating manner; to modulate with turns or variations; to sing or carol generally; to utter musically.—*v.i.* To have a trilling, quavering, or vibrating sound; to carol or sing with smoothly gliding tones; to trill.—*n.* A soft, sweet flow of melodious sounds, a trilling, flexible melody; a carol; a song.—**warbler,** wạr′blėr, *n.* One who warbles; a songbird; the popular name given to members of a dentirostral family of birds comprising most of the small woodland songsters of Europe and North America.

warble, wạr′bl, *n.* [Perhaps from O. Sw. *var,* pus and *bulde,* tumor.] A small tumor on the backs of cattle, containing the maggot or larva of a fly.

ward, wạrd, *v.t.* [A.Sax. *weardian* to guard, from *weard,* a guard, a watch; G. *wart,* Icel. *vörthr,* Goth. *vards,* guard. From the G. are Fr. *garder,* E. *guard, regard, reward.* Akin to *wary.*] To fend off; to keep from hitting; to turn aside, as anything mischievous that approaches: often followed by *off.*—*n.* [Partly from A.Sax. *weard,* a guard, partly from the verb.] The act of guarding; guard (to keep watch and *ward*); a defensive motion or position in fencing or the like; the state of being under a guard; confinement; custody; guardianship; one who is guarded; specifically, a minor who is under guardianship; a certain division or section of a town or city, such as is constituted for the convenient transaction of local public business; one of the apartments into which a hospital is divided; a curved ridge of metal inside a lock to oppose the passage of a key which has not a corresponding notch; the notch in the key.—**warden,** wạr′den, *n.* [O.Fr. *wardein, gardein*—a Germanic word with a Latin termination=*anus.*] A guard or watchman; an officer of rank in charge of something; a keeper; the title given to the head of some colleges and to the superior of some conventual churches.—*Warden of a church.* CHURCHWARDEN. See CHURCH.—**wardenship, wardenry,** wạr′den•ship, wạr′den•ri, *n.* The office of a warden.—**wardrobe,** wạrd′rōb, *n.* A place in which clothes are kept, often a piece of furniture resembling a press or cupboard; wearing apparel in general.—**wardroom,** *n.* The messroom of the chief officers in a warship.—**wardship,** wạrd′ship, *n.* The office of a ward or guardian; guardianship; also pupilage.

ware, wâr, *n.* [A.Sax. *waru*=D. *waar,* Icel. *vara,* Dan. *vare,* G. *waare,* ware, merchandise; perhaps connected with *worth* (value), *wary.*] Articles of merchandise; goods; commodities; manufactures of a particular kind: properly a collective noun, as in the compounds china*ware,* hard*ware,* tin*ware,* etc., but generally used in the plural form when articles for sale of different kinds are meant. —**warehouse,** wâr′hous, *n.* A house in which wares or goods are kept; a building for storing imported goods on which customs dues have not been paid; a store for the sale of goods wholesale; also a building for storage purposes.—*v.t.* To deposit or secure in a warehouse.—**warehouseman,** wâr′hous•man, *n.* One who keeps a warehouse; one who is employed in a warehouse.

warfare. See WAR.

warily, wariness. See WARY.

warlike. See WAR.

warlock, wạr′lok, *n.* [Icel. *varthlokur, varthlokkur,* lit. weird songs or spells, the name being transferred from the things to the person who used them, or O.E. *waerloga*, deceiver.] A male witch; a wizard or sorcerer.

warm, wạrm, *a.* [A.Sax. *wearm*, warm = O.Sax., G., and D. *warm*, Icel. *varmr*, Dan. and Sw. *varm*, warm.] Having heat in a moderate degree; not cold; having the sensation of heat; feeling hot; flushed; subject ot heat; having prevalence of heat (a *warm* climate); full of zeal, ardor, or affection; zealous; ardent (a *warm* friend); somewhat ardent or excitable; irritable (a *warm* temper); somewhat excited; nettled; brisk; keen (a *warm* contest); wealthy; moderately rich; well-off (*colloq.*).—*Warm colors*, such as have yellow or yellow-red for their basis: opposed to *cold colors*, such as blue and its compounds.—*Warm tints*, *cold tints*, modifications of the preceding.—*v.t.* To make warm; to communicate a moderate degree of heat to; to interest; to excite ardor or zeal in; to animate; to inspirit; to give life to; to flush; to cause to glow.—*v.i.* To become moderately heated; to become ardent or animated.—*n.* A warming; a heating. (*Colloq.*)—**warm-blooded,** *a.* Having warm blood: *zool.* said of mammals and birds, in contradistinction to fishes, amphibians, and reptiles, or cold-blooded animals.—**warm-hearted,** *a.* Having warmth of heart; cordial; sincere; hearty. — **warm-heartedness,** *n.* Warmth or kindness of heart; cordiality.—**warming pan,** *n.* A covered pan with a long handle for warming a bed with ignited coals.—**warmly,** wạrm′li, *adv.* In a warm manner; with warmth or heat; with warmth of feeling; eagerly; ardently; hotly.—**warmth, warmness,** wạrmth, wạrm′nes, *n.* The quality or state of being warm; the sensation of heat; gentle heat; hearty kindness or good feeling; ardor; zeal; fervor; earnestness; slight anger or irritation; *painting*, that glowing effect which arises from the use of warm colors.

warn, wạrn, *v.t.* [A.Sax. *warnian*, *wearnian*, to warn, to take heed, from *wearn*, refusal, denial; Icel. and Sw. *varna*, G. *warnen*, to warn; of same origin as *ware*, *wary*.] To give notice of approaching or probable danger or evil, that it may be avoided; to caution against anything that may prove injurious; to advise; to expostulate with; to inform previously; to give notice to.—**warner,** wạr′nėr, *n.* One who warns.—**warning,** wạr′ning, *n.* Caution against danger, or against faults or evil practices which incur danger; previous notice; a notice given to terminate the relation of master and servant or landlord and tenant.—*Warning coloration*, in animals, conspicuous marks and colors that indicate the presence of obnoxious qualities.—**warningly,** wạr′ning•li, *adv.* In a warning manner.

warp, wạrp, *v.t.* [From A.Sax. *weorpan*, pret. *wearp*, to throw, to cast; Icel. *verpa*, to throw, and reflexively, to warp or shrink, also *varpa*, to throw; Dan. *varpe*, to warp a vessel; Goth. *vairpan*, G. *werfen*, to throw. Akin *wrap*. As to first meaning comp. *cast* in sense of twist.] To turn or twist out of shape, or out of a straight direction, by contraction (the heat of the sun *warps* boards); to turn aside from the true direction; to pervert (the mind or judgment); *naut.* to tow or move, as a ship into a required position, by means of a rope attached to something; *agri.* to fertilize by artificial inundation from rivers which hold large quantities of earthy matter in suspension.—*v.i.* To twist, or be twisted from straightness; to turn from a straight, true, or proper course; to deviate; to swerve; to wind yarn off bobbins to form the warp of a web; *naut.* to work forward by means of a rope.—*n.* [A.Sax. *wearp*, the warp of cloth, from *weorpan*, to cast; so D. *werp*, O.H.G. *warf*, warp.] *Weaving*, the threads which are extended lengthwise in the loom and crossed by the woof; *naut.* a rope used in moving a ship by attachment to an anchor, post, etc.; a towing-line; *agri.* an alluvial deposit of water artificially introduced upon low lands; a tidal deposit of marine silt; the twist of wood in drying.—**warper,** wạr′pėr, *n.* One who warps; one who or that which prepares warp for weaving.

warrant, wor′ant, *v.t.* [O.Fr. *warantir*, *garantir* (Fr. *garantir*), to warrant, *warant*, *garant*, a warrant, from O.H.G. *warjan*, to give bail for, to defend; G. *gewähren*, to warrant; akin *wary*, *ward*.] To give an assurance or surety to; to guarantee; to give authority or power to do or forbear anything; to justify, sanction, support, allow; to give one's word for or concerning; to assert as undoubted; to furnish sufficient grounds or evidence to; to give a pledge or assurance to or in regard to (to *warrant* goods to be as said).—*n.* An authority granted by one person to another to do something which he has not otherwise a right to do; a document or anything that authorizes an act; security; guarantee; pledge; a voucher; an attestation; a document or negotiable writing authorizing a person to receive money or other thing; an instrument giving power to arrest or execute an offender; *army* and *navy*, a writ or authority inferior to a commission.—**warrantable,** wor′ant•a•bl, *a.* Justifiable; defensible; lawful.—**warrantably,** wor′ant•a•bli, *adv.* Justifiably; legally.—**warranter,** wor′ant•ėr, *n.* One who warrants.—**warrant officer,** *n.* An officer in the army or navy next below a commissioned officer, acting under a warrant from a department of state, and not under a commission.—**warranty,** wor′an•ti, *n.* A legal deed of security; any promise from a vendor to a purchaser, that the thing sold is such as represented; *insur.* an absolute condition, noncompliance with which voids the insurance.

warren, wor′en, *n.* [O.Fr. *warene*, *warenne*, of similar origin to *warrant*.] A piece of ground appropriated to the breeding and preservation of game or rabbits; a preserve for keeping fish in a river.—**warrener,** wor′en•ėr, *n.* The keeper of a warren.

warrior. See WAR.

wart, wạrt, *n.* [A.Sax. *wearte*, a wart = Icel. *varta*, Dan. *vorte*, D. *wrat*, G. *warze*; same root as L. *verruca*, a wart.] A small dry hard growth in the skin, most common on the hands; a spongy excrescence on the hinder pasterns of a horse; a roundish glandule on the surface of plants.—**wart hog,** *n.* A species of swine found in Africa notable for its large tusks and warty growths or excrescences on the cheeks.—**warty,** wạr′ti, *a.* Covered with warts; of the nature of warts.

wary, wâ′ri, *a.* [Formed from *ware*, wary, aware (the *-ware* of *a-ware*, *be-ware*), from A.Sax. *waer*, cautious = Icel. *varr*, Dan. and Sw. *var*, Goth. *vars*; from root of L. *vereor*, to regard, to dread. (REVERE.) Of kindred origin are *warn*, *warrant*, *ward*, *guard*, etc.] Carefully watching against deception, artifices, and dangers; ever on one's guard; cautious; circumspect; prudent; careful, as to doing or not doing something.—**warily,** wâ′ri•li, *adv.* In a wary manner; cautiously.—**wariness,** wâ′ri•nes, *n.* The quality or state of being wary.

was, woz. [A.Sax. *ic waes*, I was, *hé waes*, he was, *thú waere*, thou wert, pl. *waeron*, were; inf. *wesan*, to be; Icel. *vesa* or *vera*, to be; G. *wesen*, to be, *war*, I was; Dan. *vaere*, Sw. *vara*, to be; allied to Goth. *visan*, to dwell, to be; Skr. *vas*, to dwell. See also AM, BE.] The past tense of the verb to be; as, I *was*, thou *wast* or *wert*, he *was*; we, you, or they *were*. The subjunctive is seen in if I *were*, or *were* I to go; if thou *wert*; *wert* thou; *were* they, etc.

wash, wosh, *v.t.* [A.Sax. *wascan*, to wash = L.G. *wasken*, Dan. *vaske*, Sw. *vaska*, G. *waschen*; same root as *water*.] To apply water or other liquid to, for the purpose of cleansing; to scour, scrub, or the like, with water or other liquid; to cover with water or other liquid; to overflow or flow along; to wet copiously; to remove by ablution, literally or figuratively; with *away*, *off*, *out*, etc.; to sweep away by a rush of water (a man *washed* overboard); to cover with a watery or thin coat of color; to tint lightly or thinly; to overlay with a thin coat of metal; to separate from earthy and lighter matters by the action of water (to *wash* gold, to *wash* ores).—*v.i.* To perform the act of ablution on one's own person; to perform the business of cleansing clothes in water; to stand the operation of washing without being injured, spoiled, or destroyed; hence, to stand being put to the proof; to stand the test (*colloq.*).—*n.* The act of washing; the clothes washed on one occasion; the flow or sweep of water; a piece of ground sometimes overflowed; a shallow; waste liquor containing the refuse of food, such as is often given to pigs; swill or swillings; the fermented wort from which spirit is extracted; a liquid used for toilet purposes, such as a liquid dentifrice, a hair wash, etc.; a lotion; a thin coat of color spread over surfaces; a thin coat of metal.—**washable,** wosh′a•bl, *a.*—**wash and wear,** *a.* Pertaining to fabric that needs little or no ironing after washing.—**washboard,** wosh′bōrd, *n.* A board with a ribbed surface for washing clothes.—**washbowl,** wosh′-bōl, *n.* A bowl for water, used for washing the hands and face; a sink. —**washcloth,** wosh′clạth, *n.* A small cloth used for washing one's body; a washrag.—**washer,** wosh′ėr, *n.* One who or that which washes; an annular disk or flat ring of metal, leather, or other material, used to reduce friction, etc.—**washerwoman,** wosh′-ėr•wụm•an, *n.* A woman who washes clothes for hire.—**washing machine,** *n.* A machine for washing clothes.—**washout,** wosh′out, *n.* The washing out or away of earth by rain or a flood; a complete failure or defeat.—**washroom,** wosh′röm, *n.* A room that has washing and toilet accommodations.—**washy,** wosh′i, *a.* Watery; diluted; thin; feeble.

wasp, wosp, *n.* [A.Sax. *wæsp,* by metathesis for *wæps;* D. *wesp,* G. *wespe;* cog. L. *vespa* (for *vepsa*), a wasp, Lith. *wapsa,* a gad-fly.] The common name applied to various hymenopterous insects which live in societies, and consist of males, females, and neuters, the latter two classes being armed with powerful and in some cases highly venomous stings; *fig.* a person characterized by ill-nature, irritability, or petty malignity.—**waspish,** wos′pish, *a.* Resembling a wasp in form; having a wasplike waist; snappish; irritable; irascible.

wassail, wos′el, *n.* [A.Sax. *wes hael, wæs hael,* be hale, that is, health be to you, an old pledge or salutation in drinking—*wes,* imper. of *wesan,* to be. WAS, HALE.] A festive occasion where drinking and pledging of healths are indulged in; a drinking bout; a carouse; the liquor used on such occasions, especially about Christmas or the New Year.—*v.i.* To hold a merry drinking meeting.—**wassailer,** wos′el•ėr, *n.* One who takes part at a wassail or drinking feast; a reveler.

Wassermann test, wos′ėr•man, *n.* A serum reaction used for the detection of syphilis; named after August Wassermann, a German bacteriologist (1866-1925).

waste, wāst, *v.t.*—*wasted, wasting.* [O.Fr. *waster,* to waste, lay waste (later *gaster,* Mod.Fr. *gâter,* to spoil), from O.H.G. *wasten,* from L. *vastare,* to lay waste, *vastus,* vast, waste. VAST.] To bring to desolation; to devastate; to desolate; to ravage; to wear away gradually; to spend uselessly, vainly, or foolishly; to squander; *law,* to damage, injure, or impair, as an estate, voluntarily, or by allowing the buildings, fences, or the like, to go to decay.—*v.i.* To decrease gradually; to be consumed; to dwindle.—*a.* Resembling a desert or wilderness; desolate; not cultivated; producing no crops nor timber; rendered unfit for its intended use; spoiled in making or handling; refuse.—*To lay waste,* to render desolate; to devastate.—*n.* The act of wasting or process of being wasted; lavish expenditure; gradual decrease in quantity, strength, value, etc.; a desert region; a wilderness; a tract of land not in cultivation, and producing little or no herbage or wood.—*To run to waste,* to become useless, exhausted, or spoiled from want of proper attention, care, or skill.—**wastage,** wās′-tij, *n.* Loss by use, decay, leakage, and the like.—**wastebasket,** *n.* A basket used in offices, etc., to hold waste papers.—**wasteful,** wāst′fụl, *a.* Causing waste; grossly thriftless; ruinous; lavish; prodigal.—**wastefully,** wāst′fụl•li, *adv.* In a wasteful manner.—**wastefulness,** wāst′fụl•nes, *n.* Lavishness; prodigality.—**wasteness,** wāst′nes, *n.* The state of being waste; desolation.—**wastepaper,** *n.* Spoiled or used paper.—**waste pipe,** *n.* A pipe for waste water, etc.; an overflow pipe.—**waster,** wās′tėr, *n.* One who wastes; a squanderer; a prodigal; a growth in the snuff of a candle causing it to waste; an article spoiled in the making.—**wasting,** wās′ting, *p.* and *a.* Desolating; laying waste; sapping the bodily strength (a *wasting* disease).—**wastrel,** wās′-trel, *n.* An idle, worthless fellow; a waster.

watch, woch, *n.* [A.Sax. *waecce,* a watch, a watching, from stem of *wacan,* to wake. WAKE.] A keeping awake for the purpose of attending, guarding, preserving, or the like; a vigil; vigilant attention; vigilance; a guard or number of guards; a watchman or body of watchmen; the time during which a person or body of persons are on guard; a division of the night, when the precautionary setting of a watch is most generally necessary; *naut.* the period of time occupied by each part of a ship's crew alternately while on duty; a certain part of the officers and crew of a vessel who together attend to working her for an allotted time; a small timepiece, now universally circular in shape, to be carried in the pocket or about the person.—*v.i.* To be or continue without sleep; to keep vigil; to be attentive, circumspect, or vigilant; to be closely observant; to give heed; to act as a watchman, guard, sentinel, or the like; to look forward with expectation; to be expectant; to wait.—*To watch over,* to be cautiously observant of; to guard from error and danger.—*v.t.* To look with close attention at or on; to keep a sharp lookout on or for; to regard with vigilance and care; to have in keeping; to tend; to guard; to look for; to wait for.—**watchdog,** *n.* A dog kept to watch or guard premises and property.—**watcher,** woch′ėr, *n.* One who watches.—**watch fire,** *n.* A fire kept up in the night as a signal or for the use of a guard.—**watchful,** woch′fụl, *a.* Careful to observe; observant; giving wary attention; vigilant.—**watchfully,** woch′fụl•li, *adv.* Vigilantly; heedfully. —**watchfulness,** woch′fụl•nes, *n.* Vigilance; heedfulness; wary attention.—**watchmaker,** *n.* One whose occupation is to make and repair watches.—**watchmaking,** *n.* The art of making watches; the business of a watchmaker.—**watchman,** woch′man, *n.* A person set to pay heedful attention over something; one who holds a post of observation; a guard; a sort of night policeman; the caretaker of a building by night.—**watchtower,** *n.* A tower on which a sentinel is placed to watch for enemies.—**watchword,** woch′wėrd, *n.* The word given to sentinels and such as have occasion to visit guards, as a token by which a friend is known from an enemy; a countersign; a password, motto, or maxim.

water, wạ′tėr, *n.* [A.Sax. *waeter,* water=O.Sax. *watar,* D. and L.G. *water,* G. *wasser;* akin to Icel. *vatn,* Sw. *vatten;* Goth. *wato,* water; from root seen also in L. *udus,* wet, *unda,* a wave (whence *undulate*); Gr. *hydōr,* Skr. *udan,* water. Akin *wet, otter.*] A compound substance, consisting of hydrogen and oxygen in the proportion of 2 volumes of the former gas to 1 volume of the latter; a fluid covering about three-fifths of the entire surface of the earth, and forming an essential constituent of vegetable and animal organisms; this fluid as opposed to *land* (to travel by *water*); any natural collection of it; sometimes used of other fluids, humors, etc.; urine; the color or luster of a diamond or other precious stone (a diamond of the first *water,* that is, perfectly pure and transparent).—*Water of crystallization,* the water which unites chemically with many salts during the act of crystallizing.—*Water-vascular system,* in echinoderms, a set of tubes containing sea water; concerned with breathing and locomotion.—*To hold water,* to be able to retain water without leaking; hence, *fig.* to be correct, valid, or well grounded: said of arguments, theories, etc.—*v.t.* To irrigate; to overflow or wet with water; to supply with water or streams of water (a country well *watered*); to supply with water for drink (to *water* horses); to subject to a calendering process, as silk, etc., in order to make it exhibit a variety of undulated reflections and plays of light.—*v.i.* To shed water or liquid matter (his eyes *water*); to take in water (the ship put into port to *water*); to gather saliva as a symptom of appetite.—**water chestnut,** *n.* A water plant, *Trapa natans,* with a horned, edible nut, often used in Chinese-American food.—**water closet,** *n.* A room for defecation and excretion; a privy.—**water color,** *n.* A pigment for which water is used as a vehicle; a painting executed with such a pigment.—**water-cool,**

wa̤'tėr•köl, *v.t.* To cool by means of (usually) circulating water (as in an automobile engine).—**watercourse,** wa̤'tėr•kours, *n.* A stream of water; a channel.—**water cress,** *n.* An aquatic plant much used as a salad.—**water cure,** *n.* Hydropathy. —**waterfall,** wa̤'tėr•fa̤l, *n.* A fall or perpendicular descent of the water of a river or stream; a cascade; a cataract.—**waterfowl,** wa̤'tėr•foul, *n.* A bird that lives about rivers, lakes, or on or near the sea; an aquatic fowl.—**water gas,** *n.* An illuminating gas obtained by decomposing water. —**water gate,** *n.* A floodgate; a gate used to control the flow of water.—**water glass,** *n.* A soluble alkaline silicate made by boiling silica in an alkali, as soda or potash, used to give surfaces, as of walls, a durable covering resembling glass.—**water hammer,** *n.* The violent shaking of moving water against the sides of a pipe, especially a steam pipe.—**water hen,** *n.* The gallinule or moor hen.—**wateriness,** wa̤'tėr•i•nes, *n.* The state of being watery.—**watering,** wa̤'tėr•ing, *n.* The act of supplying with water; the process of giving a wavelike appearance or ornamentation whereby an article is made to exhibit a wavy luster and different plays of light; tabbying.—**watering place,** *n.* A place where water may be obtained, as for a ship, for cattle, etc.; a place to which people resort at certain seasons in order to drink mineral waters, or for bathing, etc., as at the seaside.—**watering pot,** *n.* A hand vessel for sprinkling water on plants.—**watering trough,** *n.* A trough in which cattle and horses drink.—**water jacket,** *n.* An outer casing containing cooling water, e.g., in an internal-combustion engine.—**waterless,** wa̤'tėr•les, *a.* Destitute of water.—**water level,** *n.* A leveling instrument in which water is employed, consisting of a bent glass tube open at both ends, and having the ends turned up. —**water lily,** *n.* The common name of several genera of aquatic plants distinguished for their beautiful flowers and large floating leaves.—**water line,** *n.* The line of flotation in a ship; one of those horizontal lines supposed to be described by the surface of the water on the bottom or side of a ship.—**waterlogged,** *a.* Lying like a log on the water: applied to a ship when by leaking and receiving a great quantity of water into her hold she has become so heavy as to be nearly or altogether unmanageable, though still afloat.—**water main,** *n.* A conduit through which water flows.—**waterman,** wa̤'tėr•man, *n.* A boatman; a ferryman; one who plies for hire on rivers, etc. —**watermark,** wa̤'tėr•märk, *n.* The mark indicating the rise and fall of water; any distinguishing device or devices indelibly stamped in the substance of a sheet of paper.—**watermelon,** wa̤'tėr•mel•on, *n.* A plant, *Citrullus vulgaris,* and its fruit, oblong in shape and having a pinkish watery pulp, extensively cultivated in dry hot parts of the world, the fruit abounding with a sweetish refreshing liquor, and the pulp remarkably delicious.—**water meter,** *n.* An instrument that measures the quantity of water that passes through it, as a gasmeter measures gas.—**water mill,** *n.* A mill whose machinery is moved by water.—**water ouzel,** *n.* The dipper, a European bird of the thrush family that can walk about under the surface of water.—**water parting,** *n.*—**water polo,** *n.* A game, played in water, in which two teams try to score by throwing an inflated ball into a goal.—**water power,** *n.* The power of water employed or capable of being employed as a prime mover in machinery.—**waterproof,** wa̤'ter•pröf, *a.* Impervious to water.—*v.t.* To render impervious to water, as cloth, leather, etc.—**water rat,** *n.* An aquatic rodent of the vole genus which lives in the banks of streams or lakes.—**water sapphire,** *n.* A transparent precious stone of an intense blue color found in Ceylon.—**watershed,** wa̤'tėr•shed, *n.* [*Shed* has sense of parting.] An imaginary line which runs along the ridge of separation between adjacent seas, lakes, or river basins, and represents the limit from which water naturally flows in opposite directions.—**waterside,** *n.* The bank or margin of a lake; the seashore.—**water ski,** wa̤'tėr skē, *n.* A ski used in gliding behind a power boat over the surface of water. —**water-ski,** wa̤'tėr•skē, *v.i.*—**water snake,** *n.* A snake or serpent that lives in water; a sea-snake.—**water spaniel,** *n.* The name of two varieties of the spaniel, excellent swimmers. —**waterspout,** wa̤'tėr•spout, *n.* A meteorological phenomenon consisting of a pillar of dark cloud caused to revolve by a whirlwind and forming a vast funnel, which descends to the sea.—**watertight,** wa'tėr•tīt, *a.* So tight as to retain or not to admit water; stanch.—**water tower,** *n.* A tower or vertical pipe having a supply of water, used to maintain a water level.—**waterway,** wa̤'tėr•wā, *n.* That part of a river, arm of the sea, etc., through which vessels enter or depart.—**water wheel,** *n.* A kind of wheel moved by water and employed to turn machinery.—**waterworks,** wa̤'tėr•wėrks, *n.* pl. The aggregate of constructions and appliances for the collection, storage, and distribution of water for the use of communities.—**water vapor,** *n.* Water in gaseous form especially when diffused in the air and below the boiling point (in contrast to steam).—**watery,** wa̤'tėr•i, *a.* Pertaining to water; resembling water; wet; moist; tasteless; insipid; vapid; spiritless; thin or transparent, as a liquid.

watt, wot, *n.* [After James *Watt.*] The practical unit of power, or rate of conveying energy, used in electricity; the power of a current of one ampere driven by an electrical pressure of one volt, viz. 10^7 ergs per second.—**wattage,** wot'ij, *n.* Power expressed in watts.—**watt-hour,** wot'our', *n.* A unit of work: the power of one watt operating for one hour.—**wattmeter,** wot"mē'tėr, *n.* An instrument that directly measures circuit power in watts.

wattle, wot'l, *n.* [A.Sax. *watel, watul,* a wattle, a hurdle, etc.] A hurdle made of interwoven rods or wands; the fleshy lobe that grows under the throat of the domestic fowl, or any appendage of the like kind.—*v.t.*—*wattled, wattling.* To twist, interweave, or interlace (twigs or branches); to plat (to *wattle* a hedge); to form by platting twigs.—**wattled,** wot'ld, *a.* Furnished with wattles, as a cock or turkey; in *her.* the term indicates that the wattles of a cock or cockatrice are of a different tincture from the rest of the body.

wattle, wot'l, *n.* A name in Australia for various species of acacia, some of them with beautiful flowers.

wattlebird, wot'l, *n.* A name of certain Australian birds of the honey-eater family, having wattles hanging below the ear.

wave, wāv, *v.i.*—*waved, waving.* [From A.Sax. *wafian,* to waver or hesitate through astonishment; Icel. *veifa,* to wave, to vibrate; O.G. *waben,* to fluctuate. *Waver, waft,* are derivative forms.] To move loosely backward and forward; to float or flutter; to undulate; to be moved as a signal; to beckon.—*v.t.* To move one way and the other; to brandish; to signal to by waving the hand or the like; to beckon.—*n.* [O.E. *wawe,* a wave of the sea, from A.Sax. *waeg,* a wave (akin to *wag*); modified by the verb above.] A swell or ridge on the surface of water or other liquid resulting from the oscillatory motion of its component particles, when disturbed from their position of rest by any force; especially, a swell or surge on the surface of the sea or other large body of water by the action of the wind; a billow; *physics,* a vibration propagated from one set of particles of an elastic medium to the adjoining set, and so on; anything resembling a wave; one of a series of undulating inequalities on a surface; an undulation; a swelling outline; that which advances and recedes, rises and falls, comes and goes, etc., like a wave; the undulating line or streak of luster on cloth watered and calendered; a signal made by waving the hand, a flag, or the like.—**wave length,** *n.* The distance between the crests of or hollows between two adjacent waves. —**wavelet,** wāv'let, *n.* A small wave; a ripple on water.—**waviness,** wā'vi•nes, *n.* The state or quality of being wavy.—**wavy,** wā'vi, *a.* Rising or swelling in waves; full of waves; *bot.* undulating on the border or on the surface.

Wave, wāv, *n.* [*W*omen *A*ccepted for *V*olunteer *E*mergency Service.] A woman serving in the women's component of the U.S. Navy.

waver, wā'vėr, *v.i.* [A freq. corresponding to the verb to *wave,* to fluctuate = Icel. *vafra*, to hover.] To play or move to and fro; to flutter; to be unsettled in opinion; to be undetermined; to fluctuate; to vacillate; to hesitate; to be in danger of falling or failing; to totter; to reel.—**waverer,** wā′vėr•ėr, *n.* One who wavers; one who is unsettled in doctrine, faith, or opinion.—**waveringly,** wā′vėr•ing•li, *adv.* In a wavering, doubtful, or fluctuating manner.

wax, waks, *n.* [A.Sax. *weax*, wax = G. *wachs*, Icel. and Sw. *vax*, Dan. *vox*, D. *vas*; cog. Pol. *vosk*, Rus. *voska*, Lith. *waszkas*, wax.] A thick, viscid, tenacious substance, excreted by bees from their bodies, and employed in the construction of their cells; any substance resembling this in appearance or properties; a vegetable product which may be regarded as a concrete fixed oil; vegetable wax; a tenacious substance excreted in the ear; earwax; a substance used in sealing letters; sealing-wax; a thick resinous substance used by shoemakers for rubbing their thread.—*v.t.* To smear or rub with wax.—**waxen,** wak′sn, *a.* Made of wax; resembling wax; covered with wax.—**wax myrtle,** *n.* The candleberry tree.—**wax palm,** *n.* A species of S. American palm, which exudes a thick secretion, consisting of resin and wax.—**waxwing,** *n.* The name of a dentirostral bird, so called because it has small, oval, horny appendages on the secondaries of the wings of the color of red sealing wax.—**waxwork,** *n.* Work in wax; figures formed of wax in imitation of real beings; a place where a collection of such figures is exhibited.—**waxy,** wak′si, *a.* Resembling wax; made of wax; abounding in wax.

wax, waks, *v.i.*—pret. *waxed*; pp. *waxed* or *waxen* (the latter now only poetical). [A.Sax. *weaxen*, to grow, to become = Icel. *vaxa*, Dan. *voxe*, Sw. *växa*, G. *wachsen*, D. *wassen*, to wax; allied to L. *augeo* (whence *augment*), Skr. *vakshâmi*, to increase, to wax; from a root seen also in L. *vigor*, E. *vigeur*, *vegetable*, etc.] To increase in size; to grow; to become larger or show a larger disk (as the moon); to become (to *wax* strong).

way, wā, *n.* [A.Sax. *weg*, a way, road, passage = Dan. *vei*, Sw. *väg*, Icel. *vegr*, D. and G. *weg*, Goth. *vigs*, way; from a root meaning to move, go, take, carry, seen also in E. *wagon*, *weigh*, *wain*, L. *via*, a way (in *viaduct*), *veho*, to carry (whence *vehicle*), *velum*, a sail (E. *veil*), *vehemens*, E. *vehement*, etc.] A track or path along or over which one passes or journeys; a path, route, or road of any kind; distance (a good *way* off); path or course in life; direction of motion; means by which anything is accomplished; scheme; device; plan; method or manner of proceeding; mode; style; usual or habitual mode of acting or behaving; plan or mode of action selected; course approved of as one's own; sphere of observation (to come in one's *way*); *naut.* progress or motion through the water; *pl.* the timbers on which a ship is launched.—*To give way*, to break or fall, as under pressure or a strain; to make room for another person passing; to yield; to submit.—*To go one's way* or *ways*, to take one's departure; to set out.—*To go the way of all the earth*, to die. (O.T.)—*To lead the way*, to go in front; to act the part of a leader, guide, etc.—*To make way*, to give room for passing; to stand aside; to give place.—*To make one's way*, to find and keep a successful career; to advance in life by one's own exertions.—*To take one's way*, to follow one's own settled opinion, inclination, or fancy.—*By the way*, in the course of the journey; in passing; without necessary connection with the main subject; parenthetically.—*By way of*, as being; to serve as or in lieu of.—*In the way*, in a position or of such a nature as to obstruct or impede.—*In the way of*, in a favorable position for doing or getting.—*On the way*, in going or traveling along; advancing toward completion.—*Out of the way*, not in the proper course or position; not where it can be found or met with; concealed or lost; out of the beaten track; hence, extraordinary; striking.—*Milky Way.* GALAXY.—*Right of way*, in *law*, a privilege which a person or persons have of going over another's ground.—*Ways and means*, methods; resources; facilities; means for raising money for governmental purposes; resources of revenue.—**waybill,** *n.* A list of passengers or goods carried by rail or other public conveyance.—**wayfarer,** wā′fâ•rėr, *n.* One who journeys or travels; a traveler; a passenger.—**wayfaring,** wā′fâ•ring, *a.* Being on a journey; traveling.—**waylay,** wā•lā′ or wā′lā, *v.t.*—pret. and pp. *waylaid*; ppr. *waylaying*. [*Way* and *lay*.] To watch insidiously in the way, with a view to seize, rob, or slay; to beset in ambush.—**waylayer,** wā•lā′ėr or wā′lā•ėr, *n.* One who waylays.—**wayside,** wā′sīd, *n.* The side, border, or edge of a road or highway.—*a.* Growing, situated, etc., by or near the side of the way (*wayside* flowers).—**wayworn,** *a.* Worn or tired by travel.

wayward, wā′wėrd, *a.* [For *awayward*; comp. *froward*, *toward*.] Full of peevish caprices or whims; froward; perverse.—**waywardly,** wā′wėrd•li, *adv.* Frowardly; perversely.—**waywardness,** wā′wėrd•nes, *n.* Frowardness; perverseness.

we, wē, *pron.*, pl. of *I*. [A.Sax. *wé*, O.Sax. *we*, *wi*, Icel. *vér*, *vaer*, Dan. and Sw. *vi*, D. *wij*, G. *wir*, Goth. *weis*; cog. Skr. *vayam*, we.] I and another or others; I and he or she, or I and they. *We* is frequently used by individuals, as editors, authors, and the like, when alluding to themselves, in order to avoid the appearance of egotism; and the plural style is also used by kings and otherwise heads of countries.

weak, wēk, *a.* [Same as Icel. *veikr*, *veykr*, Sw. *vek*, Dan. *veg*, L.G. and D. *week*, G. *weich*, pliant, soft, weak, the A.Sax. form being *wác*; allied to Gr. (*v*)*eikein*, to yield. *Wick*, *wicker*, are from same root.] Not strong; wanting physical strength; feeble; infirm; not able to sustain a great weight or strain; easily broken; brittle; frail; wanting in ability to perform functions or office (a *weak* stomach, *weak* eyes); deficient in force of utterance (a *weak* voice); unfit for effective attack or defense (a *weak* fortress or body of troops); deficient in essential or characteristic ingredients (*weak* tea, etc.); deficient in intellectual power or judgment; silly; not decided or confirmed (*weak* faith); vacillating; wanting resolution; easily moved or worked upon; facile; wanting moral courage; not supported by the force of reason or truth (*weak* arguments); ineffective; not founded in right or justice; deficient in force of expression; not affecting the mind or the senses strongly; slight; *gram.* a term applied when inflection is effected by adding a letter or syllable (*love*, *loved* as compared with *rise*, *rose*); distinguished from *strong*.—*Weak side*, that side of a person's character on which he is most easily influenced or affected.—**weaken,** wē′kn, *v.t.* To make weak or weaker; to enervate; to enfeeble.—*v.i.* To become weak or weaker.—**weakener,** wē′kn•ėr, *n.* One who or that which weakens.—**weakling,** wēk′ling, *n.* A feeble creature.—**weakly,** wēk′li, *adv.* In a weak manner; with little physical strength; faintly; not forcibly; with feebleness of mind or intellect; injudiciously.—*a.* Not strong of constitution; infirm.—**weakness,** wēk′nes, *n.* The state or quality of being weak; want of physical, mental, or moral strength; feebleness; want of strength of will or resolution; want of cogency; a defect; a failing.

weal, wēl, *n.* [A.Sax. *wela*, prosperity, lit. the state of being well, from *wel*, well; Dan. *vel*, Sw. *väl*. WELL.] A sound, healthy, prosperous state; welfare; prosperity; happiness.—The *public*, *general*, or *common weal*, the interest, well-being, prosperity of the community, state, or society.—**wealth,** welth, *n.* [From *well*, and suffix *th*; comp. *health*, *sloth*, etc.] Well-being or welfare‡; a collective term for riches; material possessions in all their variety; affluence; opulence; profusion; abundance; *pol. econ.* all and only such objects as have both utility and can be appropriated in exclusive possession, and therefore exchanged.—**wealthy,** wel′thi, *a.* Having wealth; having large possessions in lands; affluent; rich; opulent; large in point of value; ample.—**wealthily,** wel′thi•li, *adv.* In a wealthy manner; richly.—**wealthiness,** wel′thi•nes, *n.* State of being wealthy, affluent; richness.

weal, wēl, *n.* The mark of a stripe. WALE.

weald, wēld, *a.* [A.Sax. *weald*, a forest tract; akin G. *wald*, a wood or forest. It is a form of *wold.*] A piece of open forest land; a wold.

wealth, wealthy, etc. See WEAL.

wean, wēn, *v.t.* [A.Sax. *wenian*, to accustom, whence *áwenian*, to wean; Icel. *venja*, to accustom; Dan. *vaenne*, to accustom, *vaenne fra brystet*, to wean, lit. to accustom from the breast; from stem seen in *wont.* WONT.] To accustom to do without the mother's milk as food; to reconcile to the want of the breast; to detach or alienate, as the affections, from any object of desire; to reconcile to the want or loss of something; to disengage from any habit.—**weanling,** wēn′ling, *n.* A child or other animal newly weaned.

weapon, wep′on, *n.* [A.Sax. *waepen*, a weapon=Icel. *vápon*, Dan. *vaaben*, Sw. *vapen*, D. *wapen*, G. *waffe*, a weapon, Goth. *wepna* (pl.), arms.] Any instrument of offense or defense; an instrument for contest or for combating enemies; an instrument that may be classed among arms; *bot.* a thorn, prickle, sting, or the like, with which plants are furnished for defense.

wear, wâr, *v.t.*—pret. *wore*, pp. *worn.* [A.Sax. *werian*, to wear (on the body); O.H.G. *werian*, to put on; Icel. *verja*, Goth. *wasjan*, to clothe; same root as in L. *vestis*, a garment. VEST.] To carry covering or appendant to the body, as clothes, weapons, ornaments, etc.; to have on; to deteriorate or destroy (clothes, etc.) by frequent or habitual use; to waste or impair by rubbing or attrition; to destroy by degrees; to produce by constant rubbing or attrition (to *wear* a channel); to have or exhibit an appearance of; to exhibit; to show (to *wear* a glad face).—*To wear away*, to impair or destroy by gradual or imperceptible action.—*To wear off*, to remove or diminish by attrition.—*To wear out*, to wear till useless; to waste by degrees; to tire or harass completely; to waste the strength of.—*v.i.* To be undergoing gradual impairment or diminution; to waste gradually; to pass away, as time; to make gradual progress (winter *wore* over). —*To wear well* or *ill*, to be wasted away slowly or quickly; to be affected by time or use with difficulty or easily.—*To wear off*, to pass away by degrees.—*n.* The act of wearing; the state of being worn; diminution by friction, use, time, or the like; style of dress; fashion or vogue in costume.—*Wear and tear*, loss or deterioration by wearing or ordinary use; tear and wear.—**wearable,** wâr′a•bl, *a.* Capable of being worn.—**wearer,** wâr′ėr, *n.* One who wears.—**wearing,** wâr′ing, *a.* Applied to what is worn (*wearing* apparel).

wear, wâr, *v.t.* [A form of *veer.*] *Naut.* to bring on the other tack by turning the vessel round, stern toward the wind.

weary, wē′ri, *a.* [A.Sax. *wérig*, weary, perhaps from *wór*, a swampy place, the word originally having reference to the fatigue of walking on wet ground.] Having the strength much exhausted by toil or violent exertion; tired; fatigued; impatient of the continuance of something painful, irksome, or the like; sick; disgusted (*weary* of life); tiresome; irksome.—*v.t.—wearied, wearying.* To make weary; to tire; to fatigue; to exhaust the patience of; to harass by anything irksome.—*v.i.* To become weary; to tire.—**wearily,** wē′ri•li, *adv.* In a weary manner; like one fatigued.—**weariness,** wē′ri•nes, *n.* The state of being weary or tired; lassitude or exhaustion of strength induced by labor; fatigue; tedium; ennui; languor.—**wearisome,** wē′ri•sum, *a.* Causing weariness; tiresome; irksome; monotonous.—**wearisomely,** wē′ri•sum•li, *adv.* Tediously.—**wearisomeness,** wē′ri•sum•nes, *n.* Tiresomeness; tediousness.

weasand, wē′zand, *n.* [A.Sax. *wásend*, the windpipe; O.Fris. *wasende*, O.H.G. *weisunt.*] The windpipe. Written also *Wesand*, *Wezand*, and *Weazand.*

weasel, wē′zl, *n.* [A.Sax. *wesle*=D. *wezel*, Dan. *vaesel*, G. *wiesel*, weasel.] A small carnivorous animal distinguished by the length and slenderness of its body, feeding on mice, rats, moles, and small birds; a lean, mean, sneaking fellow.

weather, weTH′ėr, *n.* [A.Sax. *weder*= D. and L.G. *weder*, Icel. *vethr*, Sw. *väder*, G. *wetter*; supposed to be from same root as *wind. Wither* is a derivative.] The atmospheric conditions at any particular time; the state of the atmosphere with respect to its temperature, pressure, humidity, motions, or any other meteorological phenomena.—*v.t.* To bear up against and come through, though with difficulty (to *weather* a gale); hence, to bear up against and overcome, as danger or difficulty; *naut.* to sail to the windward of.—*v.i. Geol.* to suffer change, disintegration, or waste, by exposure to the weather, as a rock or cliff.—*a. Naut.* toward the wind; windward: opposite of *lee.*—**weatherbeaten,** *a.* Beaten or harassed by the weather; seasoned by exposure to every kind of weather.—**weatherboard,** *n.* That side of a ship which is toward the wind; the windward side; one of a set of overlapping boards on a roof.—**weatherboarding,** *n.* Overlapping boards nailed on roofs, etc.—**weatherbound,** *a.* Delayed by bad weather.—**weathercock,** weTH′ėr•kok, *n.* A vane or figure on the top of a spire, which turns with the wind and shows its direction; so called from the figure of a cock being a favorite form of vane; a fickle, inconstant person.—**weathered,** weTH′ėrd, *p.* and *a.* Wasted, worn, or discolored by exposure to atmospheric influences; said of stones or rock surfaces.—**weather gauge,** *n. Naut.* the situation of one ship to the windward of another.—**weatherglass,** *n.* An instrument to indicate the state of the atmosphere; a term popularly applied to the barometer.—**weatherman,** weTH′ėr•man, *n.* One who reports, forecasts, and predicts weather.—**weather map,** *n.* A chart showing weather conditions in an area at a particular time.—**weatherproof,** weTH′ėr•pröf, *a.* Able to withstand the effects of weather.—**weathervane,** weTH′ėr•vān, *n.* A weathercock.

weave, wev, *v.t.*—pret. *wove*, ppr. *weaving*, pp. *woven*; pret. and pp. formerly often *weaved.* [A.Sax. *wefan*, to weave=D. *weven*, Icel. *vefa*, Dan. *vaeve*, G. *weben*, to weave; cog. Skr. *vabh*, to weave. Akin *web*, *weft*, *woof.*] To form by interlacing anything flexible, such as thread, yarn, filaments, or strips of different materials; to form by a loom; to form a tissue with; to entwine into a fabric; to unite by intermixture or close connection; to work up into one whole (to *weave* incidents into a story); to contrive or construct with design (to *weave* a plot).—*v.i.* To work with a loom; to become woven.—**weaver,** wē′vėr, *n.* One who weaves or whose occupation is to weave; an aquatic insect, the whirlwig beetle; a weaver bird.—**weaverbird,** *n.* An insessorial tropical bird, so called from its nest being woven of various vegetable substances.—**weaving,** wē′ving, *n.* The act of one who weaves; the act or art of producing cloth or other textile fabrics.

web, web, *n.* [A.Sax. *web*, *webb*, from stem of *weave.* WEAVE.] That which is woven; the whole piece of cloth woven in a loom; something resembling this; a large roll of paper such as is used for newspapers and the like; the blade of a saw; a flat portion of various things; the membrane which unites the toes of many waterfowl; the threads or filaments which a spider spins; a cobweb; *fig.* anything carefully contrived and put together, as a plot or scheme. —**webbed,** webd, *a.* Having the toes united by a membrane or web.—**webbing,** web′ing, *n.* A strong fabric or hemp, 2 or 3 inches wide, for supporting the seats of stuffed chairs, sofas, etc.—**webfoot,** *n.* A foot whose toes are united by a web or membrane.

weber, vā′ber, *n.* [From Wilhelm Edouard *Weber*, a German physicist.] The unit of magnetic flux; practically obsolete, the name *Gauss* or *Maxwell* being used.

wed, wed, *v.t.*—*wedded, wedding*; *wed* as pret. and pp. also occurs. [A.Sax. *weddian*, to engage, to pledge, from *wed*, a pledge; similarly Goth. (*ga*)*wadjan*, to pledge, to betroth, from *wadi*, a pledge. Akin *gage*, *wage*, *wager.*] To marry; to take for husband or for wife; to join in marriage; to unite closely by passion or prejudice; to unite inseparably.—*v.i.* To marry; to contract matrimony.—**wedded,** wed′ed, *a.* Pertaining to matrimony (*wedded* life); intimately connected or joined together.—**wedding,** wed′ing, *n.* Marriage; nuptial ceremony; nuptial festivities.—*Silver wedding, golden wedding, diamond wedding,* the celebrations of the twenty-fifth, the fiftieth, and the seventy-fifth anniversaries of a wedding. ∴ Syn. under MARRIAGE.— *a.* Pertaining to a wedding.—**wedlock,** wed′lok, *n.* [A.Sax. *wedlāc,* a pledging, from *wed,* a pledge, and *lâc,* sport, a gift, latterly used as a mere termination of abstract nouns.] MARRIAGE.

wedding. See WED.

wedge, wej, *n.* [A.Sax. *wecg,* a wedge=Icel. *veggr,* Dan. *vaegge,* Sw. *vigg,* D. *wig,* G. *weck,* wedge; perhaps akin to *wag, way, weigh,* and signifying lit. the mover.] A piece of wood or metal, thick at one end and sloping to a thin edge at the other, used in splitting wood, rocks, etc.; one of the mechanical powers, a mass of metal, especially if resembling a wedge in form; anything in the form of a wedge.—*The thin* or *small end of the wedge,* is used figuratively of an initiatory move of small apparent importance, but calculated to produce ultimately an important effect.—*v.t.*—*wedged, wedging.* To split with a wedge or with wedges; to rive; to drive as a wedge is driven; to crowd or compress closely; to fasten with a wedge or with wedges; to fix in the manner of a wedge.

Wedgwood ware, wej′wụd, *n.* [After Josiah *Wedgwood* (1730-1795) of Etruria, Staffordshire, the inventor.] A superior kind of semivitrified pottery capable of taking on the most brilliant and delicate colors, and much used for ornamental ware, as vases, etc.

wedlock. See WED.

Wednesday, wenz′di, *n.* [A.Sax. *Wódnesdaeg,* that is Woden's day. Woden is the same as Odin. ODIN.] The fourth day of the week; the next day after Tuesday.

wee, wē, *a.* [A form of *way,* its present meaning being due to its frequent usage in the phrase 'a little *we*' (or *wea*)=a little way, a little bit.] Small; little (*Colloq.*)

weed, wēd, *n.* [A.Sax. *weód,* a weed. D. *wiede,* weeds; affinities doubtful.] The general name of any plant that is useless or troublesome; a plant such as grows where it is not wanted, and is either of no use to man or injurious to crops; a sorry, worthless animal; a leggy, loose-bodied horse; a cigar.—*v.t.* To free from weeds or noxious plants; to take away, as noxious plants; to extirpate; to free from anything hurtful or offensive.—**weeder,** wēd′-ėr, *n.* One that weeds; a weeding tool.—**weedgrown,** *a.* Overgrown with weeds.—**weedless,** wēd′les, *a.* Free from weeds.—**weedy,** wēd′i, *a.* Consisting of weeds; abounding with weeds; worthless for breeding or racing purposes (a *weedy* horse).

weed, wēd, *n.* [A.Sax. *waed, waede,* a garment; O.Fris. *wede,* D. (*ge*)*waad,* Icel. *váđ;* from same root as Goth. *ga-widan,* to bind, and as E. *withy.*] A garment‡; *pl.* mournings, especially the mourning dress of a widow.

week, wēk, *n.* [A.Sax. *wice,* a week=D. *week,* Icel. *vika,* a week; akin G. *woche,* a week; root doubtful.] The space of seven days; the space from one Sunday to another.—*This* (*that*) *day week,* the same day a week afterward; the corresponding day in the succeeding week.—**weekday,** *n.* Any day of the week except Sunday.—**weekly,** wēk′li, *a.* Pertaining to a week or weekdays; lasting for a week; happening or done once a week.—*adv.* Once a week.—*n.* A periodical, as a newspaper, appearing once a week.

weep, wēp, *v.i.*—pret. and pp. *wept.* [A.Sax. *wépan,* to weep, from *wóp,* clamor, outcry; O.Sax. *wopian,* Goth. *wopjan,* to cry; cog. Rus. *vopit,* Lith. *vapiti,* to weep; L. *vox,* voice; Skr. *vach,* to speak.] To manifest grief or other strong passion by shedding tears; to drop or flow like tears; to let fall drops; to rain; to give out moisture; to have the branches drooping or hanging downward; to droop.—*v.t.* To lament, bewail, or bemoan; to shed tears for; to shed or let fall drop by drop; to pour forth in drops, as if tears; to get rid of by weeping; followed by *away, out,* etc.—**weeper,** wē′pėr, *n.* One who weeps; a sort of white linen cuff or band on a dress, worn as a badge of mourning.

weever, wē′vėr, *n.* [O.Fr. *wivre, guivre,* from L. *vipera,* a viper; akin *wyvern.*] An edible fish of the North Atlantic Ocean which inflicts wounds with the spines of its first dorsal fin.

weevil, wē′vil, *n.* [A.Sax. *wifel,* L.G. and D. *wevel,* G. *wiebel;* cog. Lith. *wabalas,* a beetle.] The name applied to various insects of the beetle family, distinguished by the prolongation of the head, so as to form a sort of snout or proboscis; dangerous enemies to the agriculturist, from destroying grain, fruit, etc.—**weevily,** wē′vil•i, *a.* Infested by weevils.

weft, weft, *n.* [A.Sax. *weft,* the woof, from *wefan,* to weave; so Icel. *veftr.* WEAVE.] The woof of cloth; the threads that are carried in the shuttle and cross the warp.

weigh, wā, *v.t.* [A.Sax. *wegan,* to lift, to weigh, to move; *waeg,* a balance, a pair of scales; D. *wegen,* to weigh; Icel. *vega,* to bear, lift, move; G. *wiegen,* to rock; same root as *way, wain, wag,* etc.] To raise or bear up; to lift so that it hangs in the air (to *weigh* anchor); to examine by the balance so as to ascertain how heavy a thing is; to pay, allot, or take by weight; to consider for the purpose of forming an opinion or coming to a conclusion; to estimate; to balance; to compare.—*To weigh down,* to preponderate over; to oppress with weight or heaviness; to overburden.—*v.i.* To have weight; to be equal in weight to (to *weigh* a pound); to be considered as important; to have weight in the intellectual balance; to bear heavily; to press hard.—*n.* A wey; *naut.* a corruption of *way,* used only in the phrase *under weigh.*—**weigher,** wā′-ėr, *n.* One who or that which weighs.—**weight,** wāt, *n.* [O.E. *weght, wight,* A.Sax. *wiht.*] That property of bodies by which they tend toward the center of the earth; the measure of the force of gravity as determined for any particular body; the amount which anything weighs; a certain mass of brass, iron, or other substance to be used for determining the weight of other bodies (a pound *weight*); a heavy mass; something heavy; in clocks, one of the two masses of metal that by their weight actuate the machinery; pressure; burden (the *weight* of grief); importance; influence; efficacy; consequence; moment; impressiveness; *med.* a sensation of oppression or heaviness.—*Dead weight,* a heavy and oppressive burden.—*v.t.* To add or attach a weight or weights to; to add to the heaviness of.—**weightily,** wā′ti•li, *adv.* In a weighty manner; heavily; ponderously.—**weightiness,** wā′ti•nes, *n.*—**weightlessness,** wāt′les•nes, *n.* The condition of free fall in which an object moves solely according to its own inertia and any gravitational forces acting upon it.—**weighty,** wā′ti, *a.* Having great weight; heavy; ponderous; important; momentous; grave.

weir, wēr, *n.* [A.Sax. *waer, wer,* a fence, an inclosure for fish; G. *wehr,* weir, dam; lit. a fence or defense being akin to *ward, ware, wary, warren.*] A dam across a stream to stop and raise the water, for the purpose of conveying water to a mill for irrigation, etc.; a fence of twigs or stakes set in a stream for catching fish.

weird, wērd, *n.* [A.Sax. *wyrd, wird,* fate, destiny, from stem of *weorthan,* G. *werden,* Goth. *wairthan,* to become, to be. WORTH, *v.*] Destiny; a person's allotted fate.—*a.* Connected with fate or destiny; able to influence fate; partaking of the supernatural; unearthly; suggestive of unearthliness.—**weirdness,** wērd′nes, *n.*

Weismannism, vīs′män•iz′m, *n.* A theory of heredity propounded by the German biologist August Weismann (1834-1914), which regards the germ plasm as the basis of heredity and denies the possibility of the transmission of acquired characteristics.

welcome, wel′kum, *a.* [Equivalent to *well come.*] Received with gladness; admitted willingly to one's house and company; producing gladness on its reception; grateful; pleasing; free to have or enjoy; in phrases of courtesy.—*n.* Salutation of a newcomer.—*To bid welcome,* to receive with professions of friendship, kindness, or gladness.—*v.t.*—*welcomed, welcoming.* To salute a newcomer with kindness; to receive hospitably and cheerfully; to accept or meet with gladness (to *welcome* death).—**welcomer,** wel′kum•ėr, *n.*

weld, wold, weld, wōld, *n.* [O.E.

welde, wolde, Sc. *wald*; origin unknown.] An annual herb (*Reseda luteola*) from which a yellow dye is obtained.

weld, weld, *v.t.* [O.E. *welle,* Sc. *waul* (the final *d* has been added) = G. and D. *wellen,* to boil, to weld; Sw. *walla,* to weld; same word as *well,* to boil, to bubble up.] To unite or join together into firm union, as two pieces of metal, by heating until brought to a semiliquid or liquid state and then allowing them to run together; *fig.* to unite very closely (*welded* by affection).—*n.* A junction of two pieces of metal by welding.—**welder,** wel′dėr, *n.*

welfare, wel′fâr, *n.* [Lit. a state of *faring well.* WELL, FARE.] A state of exemption from misfortune, calamity, or evil; the enjoyment of health; well-being; prosperity.—**welfare state,** *n.* A political system in which the state assumes the function of providing for the welfare of the people.—**welfare work,** *n.* Organized work designed to improve the living conditions, etc., of a group in a society.

welkin, wel′kin, *n.* [O.E. *welkne, wolkne,* A.Sax. *wolcen, wolcn,* a cloud, pl. the sky; G. *wolke,* O.H.G. *wolchan,* a cloud.] The sky; the vault of heaven. (*Poetical.*)

well, wel, *n.* [A.Sax. *well, wella,* a well, fountain, *weallan,* to well up, to boil; Icel. *vell,* a boiling, D. *wel,* a spring, Dan. *vael,* a spring, G. *welle,* a wave, *wallen,* to boil; from root of *walk, wallow,* L. *volvo,* to roll (whence *volume,* etc.).] A spring; a fountain; an artificial structure from which water is obtained, often a round pit sunk perpendicularly into the earth to reach a supply of water; a compartment at the bottom of certain things; a compartment in a fishing vessel having holes to let in water so that fish may be kept alive; *arch.* the space in a building in which winding stairs are placed; *fig.* a spring, source, or origin.—*v.i.* To spring or issue forth, as water from the earth; to flow; to bubble up.—**wellspring,** *n.* A fountain; a source of continual supply.

well, wel, *a.* [A.Sax. *wel,* well, enough, much = D. *wel,* Icel. and Dan. *vel,* Sw. *väl,* Goth. *waila,* G. *wohl,* well; of same origin as *will,* and meaning originally according to one's *will.* Akin *weal, wealth.*] Not ill; in accordance with wish or desire (the business turned out *well*); satisfactory; often in impersonal usages (it is *well*); being in health; not ailing or sick; having recovered; comfortable; being in favor; favored (to be *well* with the king); just; right; proper (was it *well* to do this?). —*adv.* In a proper manner; justly; rightly; not ill or wickedly; in a satisfactory manner; skillfully; with due art (the work is *well* done); sufficiently; very much (I like it *well*); to a degree that gives pleasure; with praise; commendably (to speak *well* of one); conveniently; suitably (I cannot *well* go); easily; fully; adequately; thoroughly; considerably; not a little (*well* advanced in life). This word is often merely expletive or used to avoid abruptness (*well,* the work is done; *well,* let us go; *well, well,* be it so).—*As well,* rather right, convenient, or proper than otherwise (it may be *as well* to inform you before you go).—*As well as,* together with; and also; not less than; one as much as the other (a sickness long *as well as* severe).—*Well enough,* in a moderate degree; so as to give satisfaction, or so as to require no alteration.—*Well nigh,* nearly; almost.—*To be well off,* to be in a good condition, especially as to property.—**well-behaved,** *a.* Of good conduct or behavior.—**well-being,** wel′bē″ing, *n.* Welfare; happiness; prosperity.—**wellborn,** *a.* Born of a noble or respectable family; not of mean birth. —**well-bred,** *a.* Of good breeding; polite; cultivated; refined; of good breed, stock, or race.—**welldoing,** *n.* Performance of duties; upright conduct.—**well-favored,** *a.* Handsome; well-formed; pleasing to the eye.—**well-founded,** *a.* Founded on good and valid reasons.—**well-informed,** *a.* Well furnished with information; intelligent.—**well-known,** *a.* Fully known; generally known or acknowledged.—**well-meaning,** *a.* Having a good intention. —**well off,** *a.* In comfortable circumstances; having a good store of wealth; fortunate.—**well-read,** *a.* Having read a great deal; conversant with books.—**well-spoken,** *a.* Spoken well or with propriety; speaking well; fair-spoken; civil; courteous.—**well-timed,** *a.* Done at a proper time; opportune.—**well-to-do,** *a.* Being in easy circumstances; well off; prosperous.—**well-wisher,** *n.* One who wishes the good of another.

Welsbach burner, wels′bak, *n.*[After A. von *Welsbach,* the inventor.] A gas burner in which air is admitted into the stream of gas, and combustion of the mixture raises an incandescent mantle to white heat.

Welsh, welsh, *a.* [A.Sax. *welisc, waelisc,* lit. foreign, from *waelh,* a foreigner; similarly G. *wälsch, welsch,* is foreign, especially French or Italian, and *Wälschland* is Italy. So *wal*nut is the welsh or foreign nut. Akin *Walloon,* Corn*wall.*] Pertaining to Wales or to its people; Cymric.—*Welsh rabbit.* See RABBIT. —*n.* The language of Wales, a member of the Celtic family, forming with the Breton and now extinct Cornish the Cymric group; the inhabitants of Wales.—**Welshman,** welsh′man, *n.* A native of the principality of Wales.

welsher, welsh′ėr, *n.* [Yorkshire *welch,* a failure, a form of *welk,* to fail, to fade = D. and G. *welken,* to fade.] One who makes a bet and does not pay if he loses (*slang*).

welt, welt, *n.* [Probably from W. *gwald,* a hem, a welt.] A border; a kind of hem or edging; a strip of leather sewed round the edge of the upper of a boot or shoe and the inner sole, and to which the outer sole is afterward fashioned; an inflamed stripe raised on the skin by a blow; a wale.—*v.t.* To furnish with a welt; to raise welts on the skin by striking or thrashing.

welter, wel′tėr, *v.i.* [From A.Sax. *wealtan,* to roll; L.G. *weltern,* Sw. *vältra,* G. *wälzen,* to roll, to wallow, to welter; same root as *walk, wallow.* Akin *waltz.*] To wallow; to tumble about; to roll or wallow in some foul manner; to rise and fall, as waves.

wen, wen, *n.* [A.Sax. *wenn,* D. *wen,* L.G. *ween,* Prov.G. *wenne,* a swelling, a wart.] A tumor without inflammation or change of color of the skin.—**wennish, wenny,** wen′ish, wen′i, *a.* Having the nature of a wen.

wench, wensh, *n.* [O.E. *wenche,* from *wenchel,* a child, A.Sax. *wencel,* weak; allied to G. *wanken,* to totter. WINK.] A familiar expression applied to a woman, especially a young woman, in any variation of tone between tenderness and contempt; in a bad sense, a young woman of loose character.—*v.i.* To frequent the company of women of ill fame.—**wencher,** wensh′ėr, *n.* One who wenches; a lewd man.

wend, wend, *v.i.*—pret. and pp. *wended. Went,* which is really the pret. of this verb, is now detached from it and used as pret. of *go.* [A.Sax. *wendan,* to turn, to go = Icel. *venda,* Dan. *vende,* D. and G. *wenden,* to change, to turn: a caus. of the verb to *wind,* to turn, to twist. WIND.] To go; to pass to or from a place; to travel.—*v.t.* To go; to direct: in the phrase *to wend one's way*; also used reflexively (*wend thee* homeward).

went, went, old pret. and pp. of *wend*: now used as the pret. of *go,* or vulgarily as its pp.

wept, wept, pret. and pp. of *weep.*

were, wėr. [See WAS.] The indicative past tense plural of the verb to *be,* and the past or imperfect subjunctive —*wert* being used as second person singular.

werewolf, wēr′wu̧lf, *n.* [A.Sax. *werewulf,* lit. man-wolf, from *wer* (Icel. *verr,* Goth. *wair*), a man, and *wulf,* wolf; *wer* is cog. with L. *vir,* a man. VIRILE.] A man transformed for a time or periodically into a wolf; a man by day and a wolf by night; a lycanthrope.

wergild, weregild, wėr′gild, wēr′-gild, *n.* [A.Sax. *wergild*—*wer,* man, and *gild, geld,* a payment.] Formerly a fine of varying amount for manslaughter and other crimes against the person, by paying which the offender got rid of every further obligation or punishment.

wert, wėrt. See WERE.

Wesleyan, wes′li•an, *a.* Pertaining to John *Wesley,* or the religious sect (the Methodists) established by him about 1739.—*n.* One who adopts the principles and doctrines of Wesleyanism.—**Wesleyanism,** wes′li•an•-izm, *n.* The system of doctrines and church polity of the Wesleyan Methodists.

west, west, *n.* [A.Sax. *west,* west, westward=D. *west*, Icel. *vestr*, Dan. and Sw. *vest*, G. *west* (whence Fr. *ouest*); probably related to Gr. *hesperos*, L. *vesper*, referring to the evening.] That point of the horizon where the sun sets at the equinox, and midway between the north and south points; the region of the heavens near this point; the region or tract lying opposite the east, or nearer the west point than another point of reckoning.—[*cap.*] In the U. S. the whole region west of the Mississippi River, the land of unlimited possibilities.—*a.* Being in the west or lying toward the west; western; coming or moving from the west or western region.—*adv.* To the western region; at the westward; more westward.—*v.i.*—To pass to the west; to assume a westerly direction.—**westering,** wes'-tėr•ing, *p.* and *a.* Passing to the west. (*Poet.*)—**westerly,** wes'tėr•li, *a.* Being toward the west; situated in the western region; coming from the westward.—*adv.* Tending, going, or moving toward the west.—**western,** wes'tėrn, *a.* Being in the west, or in the direction of west; moving or directed to the west; proceeding from the west (a *western* breeze).—**westerner,** wes'tėr•nėr, *n.* A native or inhabitant of the west.—**westernmost,** wes'tėrn•mōst, *a.* Farthest to the west; most western.—**westing,** wes'ting, *n.* Space or distance westward; space reckoned from one point to another westward from it.—**westward, westwards,** west'wėrd, west'wėrdz, *adv.* [A.Sax. *west*, and *-weard*, denoting direction. *Westwards* is an adverbial genitive.] Toward the west; in the direction of the west.

wet, wet, *a.* [O.E. and Sc. *weet*, A.Sax. *waet*, Icel. *vátr*, Dan. *vaad*, wet; akin to *water*.] Containing water; soaked with water; having water or other liquid upon the surface; rainy; drizzly; very damp (*wet* weather).—*n.* Water or wetness; moisture or humidity in considerable degree; rainy weather; rain.—*v.t.*—pret. and pp. *wet* or *wetted* (the latter regularly in the passive to avoid confusion with the adjective *wet*), ppr. *wetting*. To make wet; to moisten, drench, or soak with water or other liquid; to dip or soak in liquor.—**wetness,** wet'-nes, *n.* The state of being wet; a watery or moist state of the atmosphere; moisture.—**wet nurse,** *n.* A woman who suckles and nurses a child not her own: opposed to *dry nurse*.

wether, weTH'ėr, *n.* [A.Sax. *wether*, a ram; a word common to the Teutonic tongues, and allied to L. *vitulus*, a calf, lit. a yearling. VEAL.] A castrated ram.

whack, hwak, *v.t.* [THWACK.] To thwack; to give a hearty or resounding blow to. (*Colloq.*)—*v.i.* To strike or continue striking anything with smart blows. (*Colloq*).

whale, hwāl, *n.* [A.Sax. *hwael*, a whale; Icel. *hvalr*, Sw. and Dan. *hval*, *hvalfish* (whalefish), D. *walvisch*, G. *wallfisch*.] The common name given to the larger mammals of the order Cetacea, the two types being the toothed whales and the whalebone whales, which are valuable on account of the oil and the whalebone that they furnish.—**whaleboat,** hwāl'-bōt, *n.* A strong boat, double bowed, that is used in the hunting of whales.—**whalebone,** hwāl'bōn, *n.* A well-known elastic horny substance which adheres in thin parallel plates to the upper jaw of certain species of whales; baleen.—**whaler,** hwā'lėr, *n.* A person or ship employed in the whale fishery.

whap, hwop, *v.t.* Same as WHOP.

wharf, hwąrf, *n.* pl. **wharfs,** hwąrfs, or **wharves,** hwąrvz. [A.Sax. *hwerf*, *hwearf*, a turning, a bank, a wharf; O.Sw. *hwarf*, a turning, a wharf; Icel. *hvarf*, a turning, a shelter; D. *werf*, a wharf, a yard, a turn. Perhaps originally an embankment or dam that turns the course of a stream; from A.Sax. *hweorfan*, Icel. *hverfa*, to turn.] A quay of wood or stone on a roadstead, harbor, or river, alongside of which ships are brought to load or unload.—*v.t.* To place or lodge on a wharf.—**wharfage,** hwąr'-fij, *n.* Money paid for using a wharf; a wharf or wharfs collectively.—**wharfinger,** hwąr'fin•jėr, *n.* [For *wharfager*, the *n* being inserted as in *messenger*, *passenger*.] A person who owns or who has the charge of a wharf.

what, hwot, *pron.* [A.Sax. *hwaet*, what, also, why, lo, etc., neut. of *hwá*, who. WHO.] An interrogative pronoun used in asking questions as to things, and corresponding in many respects to *who*, but used adjectively as well as substantively (*what's* the matter? I do not know *what* the matter is; *what* stuff is this?). Used alone in introducing a question it has an emphatic force, or is almost an interjection, equivalent to is it possible that? really? (*what*, do you believe that?); hence, such expressions as, *what if*=what would be the consequence if? what will it matter if? *what of*=what follows from? why need you speak of? *what though*=what does it matter though? granting or admitting that. Used to introduce an intensive or emphatic phrase or exclamation, and when employed adjectively it is equivalent to how great . . .! how remarkable . . .! how extraordinary . . .! (*what* a season it has been!). It often has the force of a compound relative pronoun: when used substantively=the thing (or things) which; that which (I know *what* you mean): when used adjectively=the . . . which; the sort or kind of . . . which; such . . . as (*what* money I have is my own). It also stands for whatever or whoever; whatsoever or whosoever (come *what* will). In such phrases as, *I tell you what*, *I'll tell you what*, etc., *what* is used to lay some stress on what is about to be stated.—*What's his (its) name? what do you call it?* etc., colloquial phrases generally signifying that the speaker cannot supply a definite name or word.—*What not*, is used in concluding an enumeration of several articles or particulars, and is equivalent to something more which I need not mention; et cetera.—*To know what's what*, to know the nature of things; to be knowing.—*What ho!* an exclamation of calling.—*What with* (repeated), partly by or in consequence of (*what with* one thing *what with* another the scheme miscarried).—**whatever,** hwot•ev'ėr, *pron.* Anything soever that; be it what it may that; all that: used substantively; of any kind soever; be what may the: used adjectively.—**whatnot,** *n.* A stand or piece of household furniture having shelves for papers, books, etc.—**whatsoever,** hwot•sō•ev'ėr, *pron.* No matter what thing or things: more emphatic that *whatever*.

wheal, hwēl, *n.* [In first meaning from A.Sax. *hwele* (?), putrefaction.] A pimple or pustule; a wale or weal.

wheat, hwēt, *n.* [A.Sax. *hwaete*=Sc. *white*, Icel. *hveiti*, Sw. *hvete*, Dan. *hvede*, D. *weit*, Goth. *hwaiteis*, G. *weizen*. Lit. the *white* grain. WHITE.] A plant belonging to the grass family, of several varieties; the seeds collectively of the plant.—**wheat cake,** *n.* A griddle cake, or pancake, made with wheat flour.—**wheat germ,** *n.* The embryo of a kernel of wheat, used as a source of vitamins.

wheatear, hwēt'ēr, *n.* [A.Sax. *hwít*, white, *aers*, posteriors.] A bird akin to the stonechat, having a conspicuous white patch at the base of the tail.

Wheatstone's bridge, hwēt'stōnz, *n.* [After Sir Charles *Wheatstone*, inventor.] *Elec.* an instrument for measuring the resistance of an electrical conductor.

wheedle, hwē'dl, *v.t.*—*wheedled*, *wheedling*. [Probably from G. *wedeln*, to fan, to wag the tail; hence to flatter.] To entice by soft words; to gain over by coaxing and flattery; to cajole; to procure by coaxing.—*v.i.* To flatter; to coax.—**wheedler,** hwēd'ler, *n.* One who wheedles.—**wheedling,** hwēd'ling, *a.* Coaxing; flattering.

wheel, hwēl, *n.* [A.Sax. *hweól*, contr. from *hweowol*; akin D. *wiel*, Dan. *hjul*, Icel. *hjol*, *hvél*; connections doubtful.] A circular frame or solid disk turning on an axis; as applied to carriages, a wheel usually consists of a nave, into which are inserted radiating spokes connecting it with the periphery or circular ring; any apparatus or machine the essential feature of which is a wheel (a spinning-*wheel*, a potter' s *wheel*); a circular frame with projecting handles and an axle on which are wound the ropes or chains connecting it with the rudder for steering a ship; an instrument of torture formerly used, the victim being fastened on it and his limbs broken by successive blows; a whirling round; a revolution or rotation; circumgyration. — *Wheel and axle*, one of the mechanical powers, an application of the general principle of the lever, consisting of a cylindrical axle on which a wheel is firmly fastened, power being applied to the wheel and a weight raised by a rope coiled round the axle.—*Wheels within wheels*, a complication of circumstances, motives, influences, or the like.—*To put one's shoulder to the wheel*. See SHOULDER. —*v.t.* To cause to turn round or revolve; to give a circular motion to; to rotate; to whirl; to convey in a wheeled vehicle; to give a circular direction or form to.—*v.i.* To turn on an axis or as on an axis; to revolve; to rotate; to turn round; to make a circular flight; to roll forward or along; to march, as a body of troops, round a point that serves as a pivot.—**wheel animal, wheel animalcule,** *n.* A rotifer.—**wheelbarrow,** *n.* A frame or box with a wheel in front and two handles behind, rolled by a single individual. —**wheel bug,** *n.* An insect of North America which feeds upon the blood of other insects.—**wheelchair,** *n.* A chair mounted on wheels and used by invalids.—**wheeled,** hwēld, *a.* Having wheels: often in composition (a two-*wheeled* carriage).—**wheeler,** hwē'lėr, *n.* One who wheels; a maker of wheels; a wheel horse, or one next the wheels of the carriage.—**wheel horse,** *n.* WHEELER.—**wheelhouse,** *n. Naut.* a kind of house built over the steering wheel in large ships. —**wheel lock,** *n.* A kind of old musket lock with a wheel which revolved against a flint, for producing sparks.—**wheelman,** hwēl'man, *n.* One who uses a bicycle or tricycle or similar conveyance.—**wheelwork,** *n.* The combination of wheels which communicate motion to one another in machinery.—**wheelwright,** *n.* A man whose occupation is to make wheels.

wheeze, hwēz, *v.i.*—*wheezed, wheezing.* [A.Sax. *hwésan, hwaesan,* to wheeze; Dan. *hvaese,* Icel. *hvaesa,* to hiss: an imitative word, akin to *whisper, whistle.*] To breathe hard and with an audible sound, as persons affected with asthma.—**wheezy,** hwē'zi, *a.* Affected with or characterized by wheezing.

whelk, hwelk, *n.* [A.Sax. *weolc, weluc,* allied to *wealcan,* to turn: lit. a twisted shell. WALK.] An edible mollusk with a spiral shell, used for food in Europe.

whelk, hwelk, *n.* [Dim. from *wheal,* a pustule.] A pustule or pimple. (*Shak.*)

whelm, hwelm, *v.t.* [Apparently modified from old *whelve, whelfe,* to overturn, to cover over, from A.Sax. *hwylfan,* to vault over, from *hwealf,* a vault or arch = Icel. *hválf,* Sw. *hvalf,* a vault.] To throw over so as to cover‡; to engulf; to swallow up; to ruin or destroy by overpowering disaster.

whelp, hwelp, *n.* [A.Sax. *hwelp* = D. *welp,* G. *welf,* Dan. *hvalp,* Icel. *hvelpr,* a whelp.] The young of the canine species, and of several other beasts of prey; a puppy; a cub; a son; a young man: in contempt or sportiveness.—*v.i.* To bring forth whelps.—*v.t.* To bring forth, as a bitch does; hence to give birth to or originate: in contempt.

when, hwen, *adv.* [A.Sax. *hwaenne, hwonne,* O.Fris. *hwenne,* G. *wann, wenn,* Goth. *hwan,* when; akin to *who.* Comp. L. *quum, quando,* when, *qui,* who.] At what or which time: used interrogatively (*when* did he come?); at the time that; at or just after the moment that: used relatively (he came *when* I went); at which time; at the same time that; while; whereas (you were absent *when* you should have been present); which time; then; preceded by *since* or *till.*—**whenever,** hwen•ev'ėr, *adv.* At whatever time.—**whensoever,** hwen•sō•ev'ėr, *adv.* At whatever time.

whence, hwens, *adv.* [O.E. *whennes,* from *when* by affixing a genitive termination, as in *hence, thence, twice,* etc.] From what place; from what or which source, origin, premises, antecedents, principles, facts, and the like; how: used interrogatively (*whence* and what art thou?); from which: referring to place, source, origin, facts, arguments, etc., and used relatively (the place *whence* he came).—*From whence,* although a pleonastic mode of expression, is used by good writers.—**whencesoever,** hwens•sō•ev'ėr, *adv.* From whatsoever place or cause or source.

where, hwâr, *adv.* [A.Sax. *hwaer,* akin to *who, what,* like *there* and *that.*] At or in what place; in what position, situation, or circumstances: used interrogatively; at or in the place in which; in which case, position, circumstances, etc.: used relatively; to which place; whither: used both interrogatively and relatively.—**whereabout,** hwâr•a•bout', *adv.* Near what or which place; the place near which; concerning or about which: also frequently used as a noun (a notice of your *whereabout*).—**whereabouts,** hwâr•a•bouts', *adv.* Near what or which place; whereabout: often used substantively (I do not know his *whereabouts*).—**whereas,** hwâr•az', *conj.* The fact or case really being that; when in fact; the thing being so that; considering that things are such that.—**whereat,** hwâr•at', *adv.* At which: used relatively; at what: used interrogatively.—**whereby,** hwâr•bī', *adv.* By which: used relatively; by what: used interrogatively.—**wherefore,** hwâr'for, *adv.* and *conj.* For which reason: used relatively; why; for what reason: relatively; why; for what reason: used interrogatively.—**wherein,** hwâr•in', *adv.* In which; in which thing, time, respect, etc.: used relatively; in what thing, time, etc.: used interrogatively.—**whereinto,** hwâr•in'tö, *adv.* Into which: used relatively; into what: used interrogatively.—**whereof,** hwâr•ov', *adv.* Of which: used relatively; of what: used interrogatively.—**whereon,** hwâr•on', *adv.* On which: used relatively; on what: used interrogatively.—**wheresoever,** hwâr•sō•ev'ėr, *adv.* In what place soever; in whatever place.—**wherethrough,** hwâr'thrö, *adv.* Through which; by reason of which.—**whereto,** hwâr•tö', *adv.* To which: used relatively; to what; to what end: used interrogatively.—**whereupon,** hwâr•up•on', *adv.* Upon which; upon what; immediately after and in consequence of which.—**wherever,** hwâr•ev'ėr, *adv.* At whatever place. —**wherewith, wherewithal,** hwâr•with', hwâr•with•ạl', *adv.* With which: used relatively; with what: used interrogatively.—*The wherewith, the wherewithal,* a sufficiency of resources or money.

wherry, hwer'i, *n.* [Perhaps akin to Icel. *hverfr,* crank, said of vessels, and to A.Sax. *hweorfan,* to turn. WHARF.] In England, a light shallow boat, seated for passengers, and plying on rivers.

whet, hwet, *v.t.*—pret. and pp. *whetted* or *whet,* ppr. *whetting.* [A.Sax. *hwettan,* to whet, from *hwaet,* sharp, keen, bold; so Icel. *hvetja,* from *hvatr,* bold; D. *wetten,* G. *wetzen,* to whet.] To sharpen by rubbing on or with a stone; to sharpen in general; to make keen, or eager; to excite; to stimulate (to *whet* the appetite); to provoke.—*n.* The act of sharpening; something that provokes or stimulates the appetite.—**whetstone,** *n.* A stone for sharpening cutlery or tools by friction.

whether, hweTH'ėr, *pron.* [A.Sax. *hwaether,* which of two, also conj.; O.H.G. *hwedar,* Goth. *hwathar*; from the interrogative *who,* and comparative suffix *-ther,* as in *hither, other,* etc.] Which of two; which one of the two: used interrogatively and relatively.—*conj.* Which of two or more alternatives; used to introduce the first of a series of alternative clauses, the succeeding clause or clauses being connected by *or* or by *or whether.*—*Whether or no,* in either alternative; in any case.

whew, hwū, *v.i.* [Imitative.] To whistle with a shrill pipe, as plovers. —*interj.* A sound expressing astonishment, aversion, or contempt.

whey, hwā, *n.* [A.Sax. *hwaeg* = D. *wei, hui,* L.G. *wey,* whey.] The watery part of milk separated from the more coagulable part, particularly in the process of making cheese.—**wheyey,** hwā'i, *a.* Partaking of or resembling whey.—**wheyface,** *n.* A face white or pale, as from fear.—**wheyfaced,** *a.* Having a white or pale face; palefaced.—**wheyish,** hwā'ish, *a.* Wheyey; thin; watery.

which, hwich, *pron.* [A.Sax. *hwilc, hwylc,* contr. from *hwilic,* lit. *whylike,* from *hwi,* instrumental case of *whá,* who, *whaet,* what, and *líc,* like; so Icel. *hvílíkr,* Dan. *hvilken,* Goth. *hveleiks,* D. *welk,* G. *welch.* Comp. *such* = *so-like.* Like *who, which* was originally an interrogative; as such it is of any gender, but as a relative it is now only neuter. It is both singular and plural.] An interrogative pronoun, by which one or more among a number of persons or things (frequently one of two) is inquired for; used adjectively or substantively (*which* man is it? *which* are the articles you mean?); a relative pronoun, serving as the neuter of *who*: often used adjectively, the relative coming before the noun by a kind of inversion (within *which* city he resides); used as an indefinite pronoun, standing for any one which (take *which* you will).—**whichever, whichsoever,** hwich•ev′ėr, hwich•sō•ev′ėr, *pron.* No matter which; anyone: used both as an adjective and as a noun.

whiff, hwif, *n.* [Imitative of the sound of blowing; comp. *puff*, W. *chwif*, a whiff, a puff, *chwaf*, a quick gust.] A sudden expulsion of air, smoke, or the like from the mouth; a puff; a gust of air conveying some smell.—*v.t.* To puff; to throw out in whiffs; to smoke.—*v.i.* To emit puffs, as of smoke; to puff; to smoke.—**whiffle,** hwif′l, *v.i.* [Probably from *whiff*; but comp. D. *weifelen*, to waver; Icel. *veifla*, to shake often.] To veer about, as the wind; to change from one opinion or course to another; to use evasions; to prevaricate.—**whiffler,** hwif′lėr, *n.* One who whiffles; a piper or fifer; hence, a harbinger (*Shak.*).

Whig, hwig, *n.* [From the name *whiggamores* applied to a body of Covenanters who marched from the southwest of Scotland to Edinburgh in 1648, said to be from *whiggam*, a word used in Southwestern Scotland in driving horses; akin to Sc. *whig*, to jog along briskly, the connections of this being doubtful.] A name once given to the members of a political party in Britain: opposed to *Tory*; later applied to the more conservative section of the Liberal party, and opposed to *Radical*; one who sympathized with the American Revolution in contradistinction to the *Royalists* and *Tories* who favored allegiance to the King; a political party in the United States (1834-1854) that favored a protective tariff, and was succeeded by the present Republican party.

while, hwīl, *n.* [A.Sax. *hwil*, a time, a space of time; D. *wijl*, *wijle*, Goth. *hweila*, G. *weile*, a time; Icel. *hvíla*, a place of rest; Dan. *hvile*, rest; allied to L. *quies*, rest. QUIET.] A time; a space of time; especially, a short space of time during which something happens or is to happen or be done.—*The while*, in the meantime. —*Worthwhile*, worth the time which it requires; worth the time and pains, or the trouble and expense.—*conj.* During the time that; as long as; at the same time that. ∴ *While* implies less of contrast in the parallel than *though*, sometimes, indeed, implying no contrast at all (*while* I admire his bravery, I esteem his moderation; but *though* I admire his courage, I detest his cruelty).—*v.t.*—*whiled, whiling.* To cause to pass pleasantly and without irksomeness, languor, or weariness; usually with *away* (to *while away* time).

whilom,‡ hwī′lom, *adv.* or *adj.* [A. Sax. *hwilum*, dat. pl. of *hwil*, a time. WHILE.] Formerly; once; quondam.

whim, hwim, *n.* [Probably akin to Icel. *hvima*, to wander with the eyes; Sw. *hvimsa*, to be unsteady; Dan. *vimse*, to skip about. Comp. also W. *chwim*, motion.] A sudden turn of the mind; a freak; a capricious notion; a kind of large capstan worked by horse power or steam for raising ore, water, etc., from the bottom of a mine.—**whimsey,** hwim′zi, *n.* A whim; a freak; a capricious notion.—**whimsical,** hwim′zi•kal, *a.* [From *whimsey.*] Full of whims; freakish; capricious; odd in appearance; fantastic.—**whimsicality, whimsicalness,** hwim•zi•kal′i•ti, hwim′zi•kal•nes, *n.* The state or quality of being whimsical; an oddity; a whim.—**whimsically,** hwim′zi•kal•li, *adv.* Freakishly.

whimbrel, hwim′brel, *n.* [Perhaps from its cry resembling a *whimpering.*] A European bird closely allied to the curlew, but considerably smaller.

whimper, hwim′pėr, *v.i.* [Akin to G. *wimmern*, to whimper, and to *whine*, both being imitative words.] To cry with a low, whining, broken voice.—*v.t.* To utter in a low, whining, or crying tone.—*n.* A low, peevish, broken cry.—**whimperer,** hwim′pėr•ėr, *n.* One who whimpers.

whimsey. See WHIM.

whin, hwin, *n.* [W. *chwyn*, weeds.] Gorse; furze. FURZE.—**whinchat,** *n.* A passerine European bird commonly found among broom and furze.—**whinny,** hwin′i, *a.* Abounding in whins.—**whinstone,** hwin′stōn, *n.* [Probably first given to the blocks of whinstone often found lying in waste places.] A name for greenstone, and also applied to any dark-colored and hard unstratified rock.

whine, hwīn, *v.i.*—*whined, whining.* [A.Sax. *hwinan*, to whiz; Icel. *hvína*, Dan. *hvine*, to whiz; imitative words like *whiz*, *whir*, etc.] To express distress or complaint by a plaintive drawling cry; to complain in a mean or unmanly way; to make a similar noise, as dogs or other animals.—*n.* A drawling plaintive tone; a mean or affected complaint.—**whiner,** hwī′nėr, *n.* One who whines.—**whiningly,** hwī′ning•li, *adv.* In a whining manner.

whinny, hwin′i, *v.i.*—*whinnied, whinnying.* [Imitative and akin to *whine*; comp. L. *hinnio*, to whinny.] To neigh.—*n.* The neigh of a horse; a low neigh.

whip, hwip, *v.t.*—*whipped, whipping.* [Allied to D. *wippen*, to skip, to toss; *wip*, a swing, a swipe; O.D. *wippe*, a whip; L.G. *wippen*, Dan. *vippe*, to see-saw; G. *wippen*, to rock, to see-saw, etc.; comp. also W. *chwip*, a quick turn; *chwipiaw*, to move briskly.] To take or seize with a sudden motion; to carry or convey suddenly and rapidly: with *away*, *out*, *up*, and the like; to sew slightly; to form into gathers; to overlay, as a rope or cord, with a cord, twine, or thread going round and round; to strike with a lash or with anything tough and flexible; to lash; to flog; to drive with lashes; to make to spin round with lashes (to *whip* a top); to lash in a figurative sense; to treat with cutting severity; to fish in with rod and line; to beat into a froth, as eggs, cream, etc.—*To whip in*, to keep from scattering, as hounds in a hunt; hence, to bring or keep the members of a party together.—*v.i.* To start suddenly and run; to turn and run, with *away*, *round*, etc.—*n.* An instrument for driving horses, cattle, etc., or for correction, consisting commonly of a handle, to which is attached a thong of plaited leather; a lash; a coachman or driver of a carriage (a good *whip*); a member of parliament or other legislative body who secures the attendance of as many members as possible at important divisions; a call made upon members to be in their places at a certain time.—**whipcord,** *n.* A hard-twisted cord of which lashes for whips are made.—**whip hand,** *n.* The hand that holds the whip in riding or driving.—*To have the whip hand of*, to have an advantage over.—**whiplash,** *n.* The lash or striking end of a whip.—**whipper,** hwip′ėr, *n.* One who whips.—**whipper-in,** *n.* One who keeps hounds from wandering, and *whips* them *in*, if necessary.—**whippersnapper,** *n.* A diminutive, insignificant person; a whipster.—**whipping,** hwip′ing, *n.* Punishment with a whip; flagellation.—**whipping boy,** *n.* A boy educated with a prince and punished in his stead.—**whipping post,** *n.* A post to which offenders were tied when whipped.—**whippoorwill,** *n.* The popular name of an American bird, allied to the European goatsucker or nightjar, so called from its cry.—**whipsaw,** *n.* A thin, narrow saw set in a frame.

whippet, hwip′et, *n.* A breed of dog resembling the greyhound but smaller, used chiefly for coursing and racing; *milit.* a light tank which can move quickly.

whir, hwėr, *v.i.* [From the sound, partly influenced in meaning by *whirl*; comp. *whiz.*] To whiz; to fly, dart, revolve, or otherwise move quickly with a whizzing or buzzing sound.—*n.* The buzzing or whirring sound made by a quickly revolving wheel, a partridge's wings, and the like.—**whirring,** hwėr′ing, *n.* The sound of something that whirs; the sound of a partridge's or pheasant's wings.

whirl, hwėrl, *v.t.* [A freq. corresponding to A.Sax. *hweorfan*, to turn (whence *wharf*); equivalent to Icel. and Sw. *hvirfla*, Dan. *hvirvle*, O.D. *wervelen*, G. *wirbeln*, similar frequentatives.] To turn round or cause to revolve rapidly; to turn with velocity; to carry away by means of something that turns round.—*v.i.* To turn round rapidly; to revolve or rotate swiftly; to move along swiftly as in a wheeled vehicle.—*n.* A turning with velocity; rapid rotation; something that moves with a whirling motion; a hook used in twisting, as in a rope machine; *bot.* and *conch.* same as *Whorl.*—**whirlabout,** *n.* Something that whirls with velocity; a whirligig.—**whirler,**

hwėr′lėr, *n.* One who or that which whirls.—**whirligig,** hwėr′li•gig, *n.* [*Whirl* and *gig.*] A toy which children spin or whirl round.—**whirlpool,** hwėrl′pöl, *n.* A circular eddy or current in a river or the sea produced by the configuration of the channel, by meeting currents, by winds meeting tides, etc.—**whirlwind,** hwėrl′-wind, *n.* A whirling wind; a violent wind moving in a circle, or rather in a spiral form, as if moving round an axis, this axis having at the same time a progressive motion.

whisk, hwisk, *v.t.* [Same as Dan. *viske*, to wipe, from *visk*, a wisp, a bunch; Icel. *visk*, a wisp; Sw. *viska*, to wipe; akin to *wash.*] To sweep, brush, or agitate with a light, rapid motion, to move with a quick, sweeping motion.—*v.i.* To move nimbly and with velocity.—*n.* A rapid, sweeping motion, as of something light; a sudden puff or gale; a wisp or small bunch; a brush or small besom; *cookery*, an instrument for rapidly agitating certain articles, as cream, eggs, etc.—**whisker,** hwis′-kėr, *n.* One who or that which whisks; the hair growing on the cheeks of a man, formerly also the hair on the upper lip, the mustache; the bristly hairs growing on the upper lip of a cat or other animal at each side.—**whiskered,** hwis′kėrd, *a.* Having whiskers; formed into whiskers.

whisky, whiskey, hwis′ki, *n.* [Ir. and Gael. *uisge-beatha*, whisky, usquebaugh, lit. water of life—*uisge*, water, *beatha*, life.] An alcoholic liquor distilled generally from barley, but sometimes from corn, rye, sugar, etc.

whisper, hwis′pėr, *v.i.* [A.Sax. *hwisprian*, to whisper, an imitative word, like G. *wispern*, O.D. *whisperen*, and Icel. *hviskra*, to whisper. Comp. *whistle*, *whist*, *whizz*, etc.] To speak with a low, hissing, or sibilant voice; to speak softly or without sonant breath; to make a low, sibilant sound, as the wind.—*v.t.* To say in a whisper or under the breath.—*n.* A low, soft, sibilant voice; the utterance of words with the breath merely; what is uttered by whispering; a low, sibilant sound, as of the wind.—**whisperer,** hwis′pėr•ėr, *n.* One who whispers; one who tells secrets.—**whispering,** hwis′pėr•ing, *p.* and *a.* Speaking in a whisper; making secret insinuations of evil; backbiting; making a low, sibilant sound.—*Whispering gallery* or *dome*, a gallery or dome in which the sound of words uttered in a low voice or whisper is communicated to a greater distance than under ordinary circumstances.—**whisperingly,** hwis′pėr•ing•ly, *adv.* In or with a whisper.

whist, hwist, *interj.* [Akin to *hush*, *hist.*] Silence! hush! be still!—*a.* Silent; still.—*n.* A game of cards usually played by four persons with a standard 52-card pack in which a point is scored for each trick in excess of six that is taken.

whistle, hwis′l, *v.i.*—*whistled*, *whistling*. [A.Sax. *hwistlian*, to whistle, to pipe; Dan. *hvisle*, Sw. *hvissla*, to whistle; Icel. *hvisla*, to whisper; all imitative words like *whisper*, *wheeze*, *whizz*, etc.] To utter a kind of musical sound by pressing the breath through a small orifice formed by contracting the lips; to utter a sharp or piercing tone, or series of tones, as birds; to pipe; to produce a shrill sound; to sound with a loud shrill wind instrument; to sound shrill or like a pipe.—*v.t.* To utter or modulate by whistling; to call, direct, or signal by a whistle.—*To whistle off*, to send off by a whistle; to send from the fist in pursuit of prey: a term in falconry.—*n.* The sound produced by one who whistles; any similar sound; the shrill note of a bird; a sound of this kind from an instrument; an instrument or apparatus for producing such a sound; the instrument sounded by escaping steam used on railroad engines, steamships, etc.; the mouth or throat (in the colloquial phrase *to wet one's whistle*=to take a drink or dram).—*To pay for one's whistle*, or *to pay dear for one's whistle*, to pay a high price for something one fancies; to pay dearly for indulging one's taste or wish.—**whistler,** hwis′lėr, *n.* One who whistles.

whit, hwit, *n.* [By metathesis from A.Sax. *wiht*, a creature, a wight, a whit. WIGHT.] The smallest part or particle imaginable; an iota; a title: used generally with a negative (not a *whit* better).

white, hwīt, *a.* [A.Sax. *hwít*, white= D. *wit*, Icel. *hvítr*, Dan. *hvid*, Sw. *hvit*, G. *weiss*, Goth. *hveits*; cog. Skr. *çveta*, white, *çvit*, to shine. Hence *wheat*, the *white* grain.] Being of the color of pure snow; not tinged or tinted with any of the proper colors or their compounds; snowy; the opposite of black or dark; pale; pallid; bloodless, as from fear or cowardice; pure and unsullied; gray, grayish-white or hoary, as from age, grief, fear, etc. (*white* hair); lucky; favorable (a *white* day).—*n.* The color of snow; the lightest coloring matter or pigment or the hue produced by such; a part of something having the color of snow; the central part of the butt in archery; the albumen of an egg; that part of the ball of the eye surrounding the iris or colored part; a member of the white race of mankind.—*v.t.* To make white; to whiten.—**white ant,** *n.* A termite.—**whitebait,** hwīt′bāt, *n.* A very small fish of the herring kind, much prized for eating.—**whitebeard,** hwīt′bērd, *n.* An old man.—**white blood cell,** *n.* A leukocyte; a blood cell not having hemoglobin.—**whitecollar,** hwīt′kol′-ėr, *a.* Pertaining to salaried workers whose jobs require a well-groomed appearance.—**white corpuscle,** *n.* A white blood cell.—**white elephant,** *n.* A pale-colored Indian elephant, sometimes venerated in India, Ceylon, Burma and Thailand; a useless object.—**white feather,** *n.* A symbol of cowardice, a term introduced from cockfighting, a gamecock having no white feathers; generally used in such phrases as *to show the white feather*=to show cowardice.—**whitefish,** hwīt′fish, *n.* One of many freshwater food fish that are related to the salmon and the tuna.—**white flag,** *n.* A flag used to signal a truce or surrender.—**white friar,** *n.* A friar of the Carmelite order, whose habit is white.—**white gold,** *n.* An alloy of gold, usually containing nickel, that resembles platinum.—**Whitehall,** hwit′hạl, *n.* The British government, so-called because many of the governmental buildings are on the street *Whitehall.*—**white heat,** *n.* The temperature, usually between 1,500° and 1,600° centigrade, at which an object becomes incandescent.—**White House,** *n.* The mansion in which the U.S. president lives; the executive branch of the U.S. government.—**white lead,** *n.* A carbonate of lead much used in painting; ceruse. See LEAD.—**white leather,** *n.* Leather prepared with alum and salt, and therefore of a white color.—**white lie,** *n.* A lie for which some kind of excuse can be offered; a harmless or non-malicious falsehood.—**white-livered,** hwīt′liv′-ėrd, *a.* Cowardly; dastardly.—**whiten,** hwī′tn, *v.t.* To make white; to bleach; to blanch.—*v.i.* To grow white; to turn or become white.—**whitener,** hwī′tn•ėr, *n.*—**whiteness,** hwīt′nes, *n.*—**white pine,** *n.* A valuable pine of Canada and the northern United States.—**white poplar,** *n.* A poplar that has the under side of the leaves white.—**white supremacy,** *n.* The notion that the Caucasian race is inherently superior to the Negro race and that the Negro should thus be subordinate to the Caucasian in all relationships.—**whitewash,** hwīt′-wosh, *n.* A wash or liquid for whitening something; a composition of lime and water, or of whiting, size, and water, for whitening walls, ceilings, etc.—*v.t.* To cover with whitewash; hence, *fig.* to clear from imputations; to restore the reputation of; colloquially, to clear from the effects of bankruptcy by passing through a judicial process.—**whitewasher,** hwīt′wosh•ėr, *n.* One who whitewashes.—**whitewood,** *n.* A name applied to a number of trees.—**whitish,** hwī′tish, *a.* Somewhat white.

whither, hwiTH′ėr, *adv.* [A.Sax. *hwider*, whither, from stem of *who*, *what*, and suffix *-ther*; closely akin to *whether.*] To what place; used interrogatively; to which place; used relatively. *Where* has now to a considerable extent taken the place of *whither.*—**whithersoever,** hwiTH′-ėr•sō•ev•ėr, *adv.* To whatever place.

whiting, hwī′ting, *n.* [From *white*; in first meaning with dim. term. *-ing*; in second with term. of verbal noun.] A small fish of the cod tribe which abounds on all the British coasts, and forms a delicate article of food; chalk pulverized and freed from impurities, used in whitewashing, for cleaning plate, etc.

whitlow, hwit′lō, *n.* [A corruption of

whickflaw for *quick-flaw*, lit. *flaw* or sore of the *quick*.] An inflammation affecting one or more of the joints of the fingers, generally terminating in an abscess; an inflammatory disease of the feet in sheep.

Whitsunday, hwit′sun•di, *n.* [Lit. white Sunday. The name was given because Pentecost was formerly a great season for christenings, in which white robes are a prominent feature.] The seventh Sunday after Easter; a festival of the church in commemoration of the descent of the Holy Spirit on the day of Pentecost; in Scotland, a term-day (May 15, or May 26 Old Style).—**Whitmonday,** *n.* The Monday following Whitsunday; in England generally observed as a holiday.—**Whitsun,** hwit′sun, *a.* Pertaining to Whitsuntide.—*Whitsun Monday, Tuesday,* etc., the Monday, Tuesday, etc., following Whitsunday.—**Whitsuntide,** hwit′sun•tīd, *n.* [*Whitsun,* and *tide,* time, season.] The season of Pentecost.

whittle, hwit′l, *n.* [O.E. *thwitel,* dim. from A.Sax. *thwitan,* to cut; O.E. and Sc. *white,* to cut with a knife.] A knife; rarely now used except in provincial English or Scotch.—*v.t.*—*whittled, whittling.* To cut or dress with a knife.

whiz, hwiz, *v.i.*—*whizzed, whizzing.* [An imitative word; comp. *wheeze, whistle, whir,* etc.] To make a humming or hissing sound, like an arrow or ball flying through the air.—*n.* A sound between hissing and humming.

whiz-bang, hwiz-bang, *n.* A small high-velocity shell which burst before the report of the gun was heard.

who, hö, *pron. relative*; possessive **whose,** höz; objective **whom,** höm. [A.Sax. *hwá,* who, masc. and fem., *whaet,* what, neut.; always an interrogative; Icel. *hver, hvat,* Dan. *hvo, hvad,* D. *wie, wat,* G. *wer, was,* Goth. *hvas, hvo, hvata*; cog. L. *qui,* W. *pwy,* Gael. and Ir. *co,* Per. *ki,* Skr. *kas,* who. Akin are *when, where, whither, which,* etc. WHY, HOW.] A relative and interrogative pronoun always used substantively (that is, not joined with a noun), and with relation to a person or persons; used interrogatively who = what or which person or persons? of what personality (*who* is he? I do not know *who* he is); used relatively = that; which person; sometimes used elliptically for *he, they,* or *those, who* or *whom.*—*As who should say,* as one who should say; as if he should say. ∴ *Who, Which, That.* These agree in being relatives, *who* being used for persons, *which* for things, and *that* for either; but *that* has often more preciseness, and in some cases it cannot be used for *who* ('James *who*', not 'James *that*').—**whoever,** hö•ev′ėr, *prin.* Any person whatever; no matter who.—**whoso,** hö′sō, *pron.* Whosoever; whoever.—**whosoever,** hö•sō•ev′ėr, *pron.* Whoever; whatever person.—**whosesoever,** höz•sō•ev′ėr, *pron.* Of whatever person; the possessive or genitive case of *whosoever.*

whoa, hwō′a, *exclam.* Stop! stand still!

whole, hōl, *a.* [O.E. *hole, hool* (the *w* being erroneous, as in *whore*), from A.Sax. *hál,* whole, sound, safe; D. *heel,* Icel. *heill,* G. *heil,* Goth. *hails,* healthy, sound, whole. HALE, HEAL, HOLY.] In a healthy state; sound; well; restored to a sound state; healed, unimpaired; uninjured; not broken or fractured; not defective or imperfect; entire; complete; comprising all parts, units, etc., that make up an aggregate; all the; total (the *whole* city).—*Whole number,* an integer, as opposed to a fraction. ∴ Syn. under COMPLETE.—*n.* An entire thing; a thing complete in itself; the entire or total assemblage of parts; a complete system; a regular combination of parts.—*Upon the whole,* all circumstances being considered; upon a review of the entire matter.—**wholeness,** hōl′nes, *n.* The state of being whole, entire, or sound; entireness; totality.—**wholesale,** hōl′sāl, *n.* Sale of goods by the entire piece or large quantity, as distinguished from *retail.*—*a.* Pertaining to the trade by wholesale; dealing by wholesale; *fig.* in great quantities; extensive and indiscriminate.—**wholesome,** hōl′sum, *a.* [*Whole,* and affix-*some.*] Tending to promote health; good for the bodily system; nourishing; healthful; favorable to morals, religion, or prosperity; salutary.—**wholesomely,** hōl′sum•li, *adv.* In a wholesome manner.—**wholesomeness,** hōl′sum•nes, *n.* The quality of being wholesome; salutariness.—**wholly,** hōl′li, *adv.* [For *whole-ly.*] Entirely; completely; perfectly; totally; exclusively.

whoop, hoop, *v.i.* [Perhaps from Fr. *houper,* to whoop, an imitative word; comp. *hoot.* Hence *whooping cough.*] To shout with a loud, clear voice.—*n.* A shout; a loud clear call.—**whooping cough,** *n.* A disease, *esp.* of children, characterized by paroxysms of coughing ending in prolonged crowing or respiratory whoop.

whop, hwop, *v.t.*—*whopped, whopping.* [W. *chwapiaw,* to strike, from *chwap,* a stroke.] To strike; to beat. (*Colloq.*)—**whopper,** hwop′ėr, *n.* [The idea of greatness or bulk is often associated with that of a blow; thus a *striking* likeness is an impressive likeness.] Anything uncommonly large; a manifest lie. (*Colloq.*)

whore, hōr, *n.* [A.Sax. *hóre,* Icel. *hóra,* Dan. *hore,* D. *hoer,* G. *hure,* a whore; same root as L. *carus,* dear; Skr. *kâma,* love. The *w* has intruded as in *whole.*] A woman who prostitutes her body for hire; a harlot; a prostitute; a lewd woman.—*v.i.*—*whored, whoring.* To have to do with prostitutes.—*v.t.* To corrupt by lewd intercourse.—**whoredom,** hōr′dum, *n.* Fornication; idolatry (O.T.).—**whoremonger,** hōr′mung•gėr, *n.* One who has to do with whores; a fornicator; a lecher.—**whorish,** hō′rish, *a.* Incontinent; unchaste.—**whorishly,** hō′rish•li, *adv.* In a whorish manner.—**whorishness,** hō′rish•nes, *n.*

whorl, hworl, *n.* [A form of *whirl,* which is also used in same sense.] A ring of leaves or other organs of a plant all on the same plane; a verticil; a turn of the spire of a univalve cell; the fly of a spindle, generally made of wood, sometimes of hard stone.—**whorled,** hworld, *a.* Furnished with whorls; verticillate.

whortleberry, hwor′tl•be•ri, *n.* [From A.Sax. *wyrtil,* a small shrub, dim. of *wort,* a wort. WORT.] The bilberry and its fruit.—**whort,** hwort, *n.* The fruit of the whortleberry or the shrub itself.

whose, whoso, etc. See WHO.

why, hwī, *adv.* [A.Sax. *hwí, hwý,* the instrumental case of *hwá,* who, *hwaet,* what. *How* is a form of the same word. WHO.] For what cause, reason, or purpose; wherefore; interrogatively (direct or indirect); for what reason or cause; for what; wherefore; used relatively.—*Why so,* for what reason; wherefore. *Why* is sometimes used substantively (the how and the *why*).—*interj.* Used emphatically or to enliven the speech or to draw attention.

wick, wik, *n.* [A.Sax. *weoca, wecca,* a wick; D. *wiek,* a wick, a plug for a wound; Sw. *veke,* Dan. *vaege,* a wick; allied to *weak* (being pliant) and to *wicker.*] A sort of loose spongy string or band which draws up the oil in lamps or the melted tallow or wax in candles to be burned.

wicked, wik′ed, *a.* [From old *wicke, wikke,* wicked (comp. *wretched*), apparently from A.Sax. *wicca,* a wizard, *wicce,* a witch. WITCH.] Evil in principle or practice; doing evil; sinful; bad; wrong; iniquitous; mischievous; prone or disposed to mischief, often good-natured mischief; roguish.—**wickedly,** wik′ed•li, *adv.* In a wicked manner; viciously; corruptly; immorally.—**wickedness,** wik′ed•nes, *n.* The state or quality of being wicked; depravity; sinfulness; vice; crime; sin; a wicked act.

wicker, wik′ėr, *a.* [O.E. *wikir, wiker,* a withy, from stem of *weak*; comp. Sw. *wika,* to plait, to bend; Dan. *vegre,* a withy, G. *wickel,* a roll. WEAK, WICK.] Made of plaited twigs or osiers; covered with such plaited work.—*n.* A small pliant twig; a withe; a basket.—**wickerwork,** *n.* A texture of twigs; basketwork.

wicket, wik′et, *n.* [O.Fr. *wiket* (Fr. *guichet*), from Icel. *víkja,* to turn, to bend, same word as A.Sax. *wícan,* to yield. WEAK.] A small gate or doorway, especially a small door forming part of a larger one; a hole in a door; *cricket,* the object at which the bowler aims, consisting of three upright rods, having two small pieces lying in grooves along their tops; the ground on which the wickets are set.

wide, wīd, *a.* [A.Sax. *wíd,* wide, broad, extensive = D. *wijd,* Icel. *vidr,* Sw. and Dan. *vid,* G. *weit,* wide; connections doubtful.] Having a great or considerable distance or extent between the sides; broad; opposed to *narrow*; having a great extent every way; vast; extensive; *fig.* not narrow or limited; enlarged; liberal; broad to a certain degree (three feet *wide*); failing to hit a mark; hence, remote or distant from anything, as truth, propriety, or the like.—*adv.* To a distance; to a considerable extent or space; far; far from the mark or from the purpose; astray.—**wide-awake,** *a.* On the alert; ready prepared; knowing. (*Colloq.*)—*n.* [So called because worn greatly by smart sporting men.] A species of soft felt hat with a broad brim turned up all round.—**widely,** wīd′li, *adv.* In a wide manner or degree; with great extent each way; very much; greatly; far.—**widen,** wī′dn, *v.t.* To make wide or wider; to extend the breadth of.—*v.i.* To grow wide or wider; to extend itself.—**wideness,** wīd′nes, *n.* The state or quality of being wide; breadth; large extent in all directions.—**widespread,** *a.* Spread to a great distance; extending far and wide.—**width,** width, *n.* [Comp. *breadth, length.*] Breadth; wideness.

widgeon, wij′on, *n.* [Fr. *vigeon, vingeon*, names of ducks; comp. L. *vipio, vipionis*, a small crane.] A migratory bird allied to the duck family, which breeds in high northern latitudes.

widow, wid′ō, *n.* [A.Sax. *widuwe, wuduwe*, a widow = D. *weduwe*, L.G. *wedewe*, G. *wittwe*, Goth. *widuwo*; cog. Rus. *vdovā*, L. *vidua*, from *viduus*, deprived (VOID); Skr. *vidhavâ*, a widow.] A woman who has lost her husband by death, and who remains still unmarried; also used adjectively (a *widow* lady).—*v.t.* To reduce to the condition of a widow; to bereave of a husband or mate; to strip of anything good.—**widower,** wid′ō•ėr, *n.* A man who has lost his wife by death.—**widowhood,** wid′ō•hu̦d, *n.* The state of a man or woman whose husband or wife is dead, and who has not married again; the state of being a widow.

width. See WIDE.

wield, wēld, *v.t.* [O.E. *welden*. A.Sax. (*ge*)*weldan*, (*ge*)*wyldan*, from *wealdan*, to rule; Icel. *valda*, G. *walten*, to rule; Goth. *valdan*, to govern; same root as L. *valeo*, to be strong. VALID.] To use in the hand or hands with full command or power; to hold aloft or swing freely with the arm; to use or employ with the hand; to manage, employ, or have full control over.—*To wield the scepter*, to govern with supreme command.—**wieldable,** wēl′da•bl, *a.* Capable of being wielded.—**wielder,** wēl′dėr, *n.* One who wields.—**wieldy,** wēl′di, *a.* Capable of being wielded; wieldable.

wife, wīf, *n.* pl. **wives,** wīvz. [A.Sax. *wīf*, a woman, a wife = D. *wijf*, Icel. *vīf*, Dan. *viv*, G. *weib*, a woman; root doubtful. This word gives the first syllable of *woman*.] Originally, any woman of mature age; still so used in compounds (ale-*wife*, fish-*wife*); a woman or female of any age who is united to a man in wedlock; the correlative of *husband*.—**wifehood,** wīf′hu̦d, *n.* State and character of a wife.—**wifeless,** wīf′les, *a.* Without a wife; unmarried.—**wifely,** wīf′li, *a.* Like a wife; becoming a wife.

wig, wig, *n.* [The final syllable of *periwig*.] An artificial covering of hair for the head.—**wigged,** wigd, *a.*

wigan, wig′an, *n.* [From *Wigan* in Lancashire.] A stiff, open canvas-like fabric, used for stiffening and protecting the lower inside surface of skirts, etc.

wight, wīt, *n.* [A.Sax. *wiht, wuht*, a creature, a thing; D. *wicht*, a baby; G. *wicht*, creature, fellow; Goth. *waihts, waiht*, a thing. Perhaps originally 'moving creature', allied to *wag, weigh*. *Whit* is the same word, and it is also contained in *aught, naught* or *nought*.] A being; a human being; a person either male or female.

wight, wīt, *a.* [Icel. *vigr*, neut. *vigt*, warlike, fit for war, from *vig* (A.Sax. *wig*), war; akin Sw. *vig*, agile, nimble.] Having warlike prowess; strong and active; agile. (*Poet.*)

wigwam, wig′wom, *n.* [A native Indian term.] A hut of the American Indians of the Great Lakes region.

wild, wīld, *a.* [A.Sax. *wild*, wild, not tame; savage = Sc. *will*, Icel. *villr*, wild, astray, bewildered; Dan. and Sw. *vild*, D. *wild*, G. *wild*, Goth. *wiltheis*, wild; akin to *will*, an animal that is wild, also wandering at its will. WILL.] Living in a state of nature; roving at will; not tame; not domestic; savage; uncivilized; ferocious; sanguinary; growing or produced without culture; not cultivated; desert; uncultivated; as left by nature (a *wild* scene); turbulent; tempestuous; stormy; furious; in both a physical and moral sense; violent; unregulated; passionate (a *wild* outbreak of rage); disorderly in conduct; frolicsome; wayward; reckless; rash; not based on reason or prudence; wanting order or regularity; extravagant; fantastic; indicating strong emotion or excitement; excited; bewildered; distracted (a *wild* look); excessively eager; ardent to pursue, perform, or obtain.—*To run wild*, to take to a wild life, or to a loose way of living; to escape from cultivation and grow in a wild state.—*n.* A desert; an uninhabited and uncultivated tract or region.—**wild boar,** *n.* An animal of the hog kind, the ancestor of the domesticated swine.—**wildcat,** *n.* A ferocious animal closely akin to the domestic cat, but larger and has a shorter, bushier tail.—**wildfire,** wīld′fīr, *n.* A composition of inflammable materials readily catching fire and hard to be extinguished; a kind of lightning unaccompanied by thunder; a name for erysipelas; also a name for an eruptive disease, a species of lichen.—**wildfowl,** *n.* A name given to various birds pursued as game, but ordinarily restricted to waterfowl.—**wild goose,** *n.* A migratory North American game bird that breeds in the cold regions, and is usually gray and brown in color.—*Wild-goose chase*, the pursuit of anything in ignorance of the direction it will take; a foolish pursuit or enterprise.—**wilding,** wīl′ding, *n.* A plant that grows wild or without cultivation.—**wildly,** wīld′li, *adv.* In a wild state or manner; savagely; with disorder, perturbation, or distraction; extravagantly; irregularly.—**wildness,** wīld′nes, *n.* The state of being wild; desert or uncultivated state; savageness; fierceness; distraction; great perturbation of look.—**wild oats,** *n.* Weeds and grass of the genus *Avena*; youthful excesses or indiscretions.—*To sow one's wild oats*, to indulge in youthful excesses, dissipations, or follies; *to have sown one's wild oats*, to have given up youthful dissipation; to have settled down.—**wildwood,** *n.* Belonging to wild or unfrequented woods.

wildebeest, wil′da•bēst, *n.* [Afrikaans *wildebees*, from *wilde*, wild and *bees*, ox.] A gnu.

wilder, wil′dėr, *v.t.* [From the *wilder-* of *wilderness*; hence *bewilder*.] To cause to lose the way or track; to puzzle with mazes or difficulties; to bewilder.—**wilderment,** wil′dėr•ment, *n.* Bewilderment.

wilderness, wil′dėr•nes, *n.* [Formed with suffix *-ness* from older *wilderne*, a wilderness, from A.Sax. *wilder*, a wild animal, from *wild*, wild, *deór*, an animal; comp. D. *wildernis*, G. *wildniss*, wilderness.] A desert; a tract of land or region uncultivated and uninhabited by human beings, whether a forest or a wide barren plain; a portion of a garden set apart for things to grow in unchecked luxuriance.

wile, wīl, *n.* [A.Sax. *wíle, wil*, wile; Icel. *vél, vael*, artifice, craft, trick; connections doubtful. *Guile* is the same word, but has come to us directly from the French. GUILE.] A trick or stratagem practiced for ensnaring or deception; a sly, insidious artifice.—*v.t.*—*wiled, wiling*. To draw or turn away, as by diverting the mind; to cajole or to wheedle (Sc.).—**wilily,** wī′li•li, *adv.* In a wily manner; insidiously; craftily; cunningly.—**wiliness,** wī′li•nes, *n.* The character of being wily; cunning; guile.—**wily,** wī′li, *a.* Capable of using wiles; full of wiles; subtle; cunning; crafty.

will, wil, *n.* [A.Sax. *willa*, will, from *willan*, to desire, and = D. *wil*, Icel. *vili*, Dan. *villie*, Sw. *vilja*, G. *wille*, will. See the verb.] That faculty or power of the mind by which we determine either to do or not to do something; the power of control which the mind possesses over its own operations; volition; power of resisting impulse; determination; the determination or choice of one possessing authority; wish or pleasure of a superior; strong wish or inclination (it is against my *will*); *law*, the legal declaration of a man's intentions as to what he wishes to be performed after his death in relation to his property; a testament; the written paper containing such a disposition of property. GOOD WILL, ILL WILL.—*At will*, at pleasure; as one wishes.—*With a will*, with willingness and pleasure; heartily.—*v. aux.*, pres. I *will*, thou *wilt*, he *will*; past *would*; no past participle. [A.Sax. *willan*, pret. *wolde*; D. *willen*, Icel. *vilja*, Dan. *ville*, to will; G. *will*, I will infin. *wollen*, to be willing; cog. L. *volo*, I will, *velle*, to will (VOLITION); Gr. *boulomai*, I will. Akin *well*, *weal*, *wild*.] A word denoting either simple futurity or futurity combined with volition according to the subject of the verb. In the first person it expresses willingness, consent, intention, or promise; and when emphasized, determination or fixed purpose (I *will* go); simple futurity with the first person being expressed by *shall* (SHALL). In the second and third persons *will* expresses only a simple future or certainty, the idea of volition, purpose, or wish being then lost.—**would**, wụd, past tense of *will*, stands in the same relation to *will* that *should* does to *shall*, being seldom or never a preterite indicative pure and simple, but mainly employed in subjunctive, conditional, or optative senses, in the latter case having often the force of an independent verb.—*v.t.* [From the noun rather than from the auxiliary verb. In this use the conjugation is regular, pres. ind. I *will*, thou *willest*, he *wills*, etc., pret. and pp. *willed*.] To determine by an act of choice (a man may move if he *wills* it); to ordain; to decree; to desire or wish; to intend; to dispose of by testament; to give as a legacy; to bequeath.—*v.i.* [From the noun.] To form a volition; to exercise an act of the will; to desire; to wish; to determine; to decree.—**willing**, wil′ing, *a.* Ready to do or grant; having the mind inclined; not averse; desirous; ready; borne or accepted voluntarily; voluntary.—**willingly**, wil′ing•li, *adv.* In a willing manner; with one's free choice or consent; without reluctance; voluntarily; readily; gladly.—**willingness**, wil′ing•nes, *n.*—**willful**, wil′fụl, *a.* Governed by one's own will without yielding to reason; not to be moved from one's notions or inclinations; obstinate; refractory; wayward; done by design; intentional (*willful* murder).—**willfully**, wil′fụl•li, *adv.* In a willful manner; waywardly; obstinately; by design; intentionally.—**willfulness**, wil′fụl•nes, *n.* Obstinacy; stubbornness; perverseness; intention; character of being done by design.

will-o'-the-wisp, *n.* See IGNIS FATUUS.

willow, wil′ō, *n.* [A.Sax. *welig*, *wilig*, D. *wilg*, L.G. *wilge*, a willow.] A name for numerous well-known species of plants of a treelike or shrubby habit, valuable for a variety of purposes, including basketmaking; an instrument for opening and disentangling locks of wool previous to manufacture.—**willow pattern**, *n.* A well-known design on stoneware and porcelain dishes, in imitation of a Chinese design; so called from a willow tree (or what may pass for one) which is a prominent object in it.—**willow herb**, *n.* A herb with pinkish-purple flowers and long leaves like those of the willow.—**willowy**, wil′ō•i, *a.* Abounding with willows; resembling a willow; slender and graceful.

wilt, wilt, *v.i.* [Akin to *welk*, to fade.] To fade; to loose freshness; to droop; to grow weak.—*v.t.* To cause to wilt. —*n.* The act of wilting; a virus disease of caterpillars; a disease of plants.

Wilton carpet, *n.* [Made originally at *Wilton*.] A variety of Brussels carpet in which the loops are cut open into an elastic velvet pile.

wily. See WILE.

wimble, wim′bl, *n.* [Same (with inserted *b*) as Sc. *wimmle* or *wummle*, Dan. *vimmel*, an auger; akin D. *wemelen*, to bore, *weme*, an auger; Sw. *wimla*, G. *wimmeln*, to be in tremulous movement. *Gimlet* is a dim. form. GIMLET.] An instrument of the gimlet, auger, or brace kind used for boring holes.

wimple, wim′pl, *n.* [A.Sax. *winpel*, a wimple=D. *wimpel*, Icel. *vimpill*, Dan. *vimpel*, G. *wimpel*, a pennon; perhaps akin to *whip*, *gimp*.] A former female headdress laid in plaits over the head and round the chin, sides of the face, and neck, still worn by nuns.—*v.t.*—*wimpled*, *wimpling*. To cover, as with a wimple or veil; hence, to hoodwink. —*v.i.* To resemble or suggest wimples; to undulate; to ripple (a brook that *wimples* onward).

win, win, *v.t.*—pret. and pp. *won* (wun), ppr. *winning*. [A.Sax. *winnan*, to strive, labor, fight, struggle=D. *winnen*, Icel. *vinna*, Dan. *vinde*, G. (*ge*)*winnen*, to fight, strive, win, etc., Goth. *winnan*, to endure; from root meaning to desire eagerly, seen also in the name of the goddess *Venus*; akin *wean*, *wont*.] To gain by proving one's self superior in a contest; to be victorious in; to gain as victor; to gain possession of by fighting; to get into one's possession by conquest (to *win* a fortress); to gain, procure, or obtain in a general sense, but especially implying labor, effort, or struggle; to allure to kindness or compliance; to gain or obtain, as by solicitation or courtship; to gain to one's side or party, as by solicitation or other influence.—*v.i.* To be superior in a contest or competition; to be victorious; to gain the victory.—**winner**, win′ėr, *n.* One who wins.—**winning**, win′ing, *a.* Attracting; adapted to gain favor; charming (a *winning* manner).—*n.* The sum won or gained by success in competition or contest; usually in the pl.—**winningly**, win′ing•li, *adv.* In a winning manner; charmingly.—**winning post**, *n.* A post or goal in a racecourse, the order of passing which determines the issue of the race.

wince, wins, *v.i.*—*winced*, *wincing*. [Formerly also *winch*, from O.Fr. *guinchir*, *guenchir*, *winchir* (?), from O.G. *wenken*, to start aside. Akin to *wink*.] To twist or turn, as in pain or uneasiness; to shrink; to start back.—*n.* The act of one who winces; a start, as from pain.

winch, winsh, *n.* [A.Sax. *wince*, a winch, a reel for thread; akin *wince*, *wink*, *winkle*.] The crank for turning an axle; a hoisting machine in which an axis is turned by a crank-handle, and a rope or chain wound round it so as to raise a weight.

wind, wind, in poetry often wīnd, *n.* [A.Sax. *wind*=D. and G. *wind*, Dan. and Sw. *vind*, Icel. *vindr*, Goth. *winds*; cog. L. *ventus*, W. *gwynt*, wind. The root is in Goth. *waian*, Skr. *vâ*, to blow. *Weather* is from same root.] Air naturally in motion with any degree of velocity; a current of air; a current in the atmosphere, as coming from a particular point; a point of the compass, especially one of the cardinal points (O.T.); air artificially put in motion (the *wind* of a cannonball); breath modulated by the respiratory organs or by an instrument; power of respiration; lung power; breath; empty or unmeaning words; idle or vain threats; gas generated in the stomach and bowels; flatulence.—*Between wind and water*, in that part of a ship's side which is frequently brought above the water by the rolling of the vessel.—*How the wind blows* or *lies*, the direction of the wind; *fig.* position or state of affairs; how matters stand.—*In the wind's eye*, *in the teeth of the wind*, directly toward the point from which the wind blows; right against the wind.—*Something in the wind*, something within the region of suspicion or surmise, without being acknowledged or announced (colloq.).—**windage**, win′dij, *n. Gun.* the difference between the diameter of the bore of a firearm and that of the ball or shell; the influence of the wind in deflecting a missile; the extent of such deflection.—**windbag**, wind′bag, *n.* A bag filled with wind; a man of mere words; a noisy pretender.—**Windbreaker**, wind′brāk•ėr, *n.* [Trademark.] An outer jacket made of a wind-resistant material.—**windfall**, wind′fal, *n.* Fruit blown from a tree; timber blown down; an unexpected legacy; any unexpected piece of good fortune.—**windiness**, win′di•nes, *n.*—**wind instrument**, *n.* An instrument of music, played by breath or wind, as the flute, horn, organ, harmonium, etc.—**windjammer**, wind′jam•ėr, *n.* A merchant sailing ship or one of its crew.—**windmill**, wind′mil, *n.* A mill driven by the force of the wind, and used for grinding corn, pumping water, etc.—**windpipe**, wind′pīp, *n.* The passage for the breath to and from the lungs; the trachea.—**windrow**, win′drō, *n.* A row or line of hay raked together for the purpose of being rolled into cocks or heaps.—

windshield, wind'shēld, *n.* A protective, transparent shield in front of the passengers in a vehicle.—**wind tunnel,** *n.* A passage through which wind of known velocity, etc., can be blown in order to test, and experiment with, objects, as aircraft or missile parts.—**windward,** wind'wėrd, *n.* The point from which the wind blows.—*a.* On the side toward which the wind blows.—*adv.* Toward the wind.—**windy,** win'di, *a.* Consisting of wind; formed by gales; tempestuous; boisterous; exposed to the wind; resembling the wind; as empty as the wind; flatulent.

wind, wind, *v.t.* [WIND.] To perceive or follow by scent; to expose to the wind; to render short of breath; to rest in order to restore breath; to regulate the wind of an organ pipe. —*v.i.* To scent game; to stop for breath.

wind, wīnd, *v.t.* [WIND.] To cause to sound by blowing; to sound on a horn. —*v.i.* To produce a sound on a horn.

wind, wīnd, *v.t.*—pret. and pp. *wound* (occasionally *winded*). [A.Sax. *windan*, to wind, twist, twine=D. and G. *winden*, Icel. and Sw. *vinda*, Goth. *windan*; akin *wand, wend, wander*.] To coil round something; to form into a ball or coil by turning; to turn by shifts and expedients; *refl.* to insinuate; to bend or turn to one's pleasure; to enfold or encircle.—*To wind off*, to unwind; to uncoil.—*To wind up*, to coil up into a small compass; to bring to a conclusion, as a speech or operation; to make a final settlement of; to coil anew the spring or draw up the weights of (a watch or clock).—*v.i.* To turn around something; to have a spiral direction; to have a course marked by bendings; to meander; to make one's way by bendings.—*To wind up*, to come to a conclusion; to conclude; to finish.—**winder,** wīn'dėr, *n.* One who or that which winds yarn or the like; an instrument or machine for winding.—**winding,** wīn'ding, *a.* Bending; having curves or bends; spiral.—*n.* A turn or turning; a bend.—**windingly,** wīn'ding•li, *adv.* In a winding form.—**winding sheet,** *n.* A sheet in which a corpse is wrapped; a piece of tallow or wax hanging down from a burning candle; regarded as an omen of death.—**windup,** *n.* The conclusion or final settlement of any matter; the closing act; the close.

windlass, wind'las, *n.* [Partly from D. *windas*, or Icel. *vindass*, lit. winding-beam; partly from old *windle*, a wheel or reel, a dim. from the verb to *wind*.] A modification of the wheel and axle, consisting of a horizontal barrel turned by a winch or by levers, for raising a weight that hangs at the end of a rope or chain wound on to a barrel.

windlestraw, win'dl•strạ, *n.* [A.Sax. *windelstreow*, properly straw for plaiting, from *windel*, a basket, from *windan*, to wind. WIND.] A name given to various species of grasses; a stalk of grass.

window, win'dō, *n.* [O.E. *windoge, windohe*, from Icel. *vindauga*, a window, lit. a wind-eye—*vindr*, wind, and *auga*, an eye. WIND, EYE.] An opening in the wall of a building for the admission of light or of light and air when necessary; an opening resembling or suggestive of a window; the sash or other thing that covers the aperture.—**window dressing,** *n.* Merchandise attractively displayed in a shop window; an exaggerated statement made with the intention of giving unfavorable facts an attractive appearance.

Windsor chair, *n.* A kind of strong, plain, polished chair, made entirely of wood, seat as well as back.

wine, wīn, *n.* [A.Sax. *win*, borrowed (like D. *wijn*, Icel. *vín*, G. *wein*) from L. *vinum*, wine, akin to *vitis*, the vine, the twining plant (cog. with E. *withy*), the root being seen also in E. to *wind, wire*, etc.] An alcoholic liquor obtained by the fermentation of the juice of the grape or fruit of the vine; also, the juice of certain fruits prepared in imitation of this (currant *wine*, gooseberry *wine*).—*Quinine wine*, sherry with sulfate of quinine in solution.—*Spirit of wine*, alcohol.—**winebibber,** *n.* One who drinks much wine.—**wine cellar,** *n.* An apartment or cellar for stowing wine. —**wineglass,** *n.* A small glass in which wine is drunk.—**winegrower,** *n.* One who cultivates a vineyard and makes wine.—**wine palm,** *n.* A palm from which palm wine is obtained.—**wine press,** *n.* An apparatus in which the juice is pressed out of grapes.—**winy,** wī'ni, *a.* Having the taste or qualities of wine.

wing, wing, *n.* [Same as Sw. and Dan. *vinge*, Icel. *vaengr*, a wing; probably akin to *wag*.] One of the anterior limbs in birds, specially modified and provided with feathers, in most cases serving as organs of flight; an organ used for flying by some other animals, as insects and bats; act of flying; flight (to take *wing*); that which moves or acts like a wing, as the sail of a windmill, of a ship, etc.; a projection of a building on one side of the central or main portion; a lateral extension of anything; a leaf of a gate or double door; one of the sides of the stage of a theater; also, one of the long narrow scenes which fill up the picture on the side of the stage; the half of a regiment or larger body, termed 'right' and 'left' when in line 'leading' and 'rear' when in column. —*On the wing*, flying (to shoot wild fowl *on the wing*); speeding to its object; on the road.—*v.t.* To furnish with wings; to enable to fly; to transport by flight (to *wing* me home); to move in flight through; to traverse by flying (to *wing* the air); to wound in the wing; to disable a wing or limb of.—*To wing a flight* or *way*, to proceed by flying; to fly.—**wing case,** *n.* The hard case which covers the wings of beetles, etc.; the elytron.—**winged,** wingd, *a.* Having wings; swift; rapid; passing quickly; *bot.* and *conch.* same as *Alate*.—**wingless,** wing'les, *a.* Having no wings.—**winglet,** wing'let, *n.*—**wingspan,** wing'span, *n.* The length of an aircraft's wing from tip to tip.—**wingspread,** wing'spred, *n.* The distance between the tips of spread wings (as of a bird).

wink, wingk, *v.i.* [A.Sax. *wincian*, to wink; akin to *wancol*, unsteady; D. *winken, wenken*, Icel. *vanka*, to wink; Dan. *vinke*, Sw. *vinka*, to wink or nod; G. *winken*, to beckon; root perhaps same as in *weak*, G. *weichen*, to yield or turn aside. Akin *wince, winch*.] To close and open the eyelids quickly and involuntarily; to blink; to nictitate; to give a significant hint by motion of the eyelids; to twinkle; to connive; to seem not to see; to shut the eyes willfully: with *at* (to *wink at* faults). —*n.* The act of closing the eyelids quickly; no more time than is necessary to shut the eyes; a hint given by shutting the eye with a significant cast.—**winker,** wing'kėr, *n.* One who winks; one of the blinds of a horse; a blinker.

winkle, wing'kl, *n.* A common abbreviation of *Periwinkle*.

winner, winning, etc. See WIN.

winnow, win'ō, *v.t.* [A.Sax. *windwian*, to winnow, from *wind*, the wind. (WIND.) Comp. L. *ventilare*, to winnow, from *ventus*, the wind.] To drive the chaff from by means of wind; to fan; *fig.* to examine, sift, or try, as for the purpose of separating falsehood from truth.—*v.i.* To separate chaff from corn.—**winnower,** win'ō•ėr, *n.* One who or that which winnows.

winsome, win'sum, *a.* [A.Sax. *wynsum*, pleasant, delightful, from *wynn*, delight, joy (akin to *win*), and term. *sum*, later *-some*.] Attractive; agreeable; engaging.

winter, win'tėr, *n.* [A.Sax. *winter*, winter=D. and G. *winter*, Sw. and Dan. *winter*, Icel. *vetr, vitr* (for *vintr*), Goth. *vintrus*; allied to *wind* or to *wet*.] The cold season of the year, which in northern latitudes may be roughly said to comprise December, January, and February; a year; the part being used for the whole; also often used as an emblem of any cheerless situation.—*a.* Belonging to winter.—*v.i.* To pass the winter; to hibernate.—*v.t.* To keep, feed, or manage during the winter (to *winter* cattle).—**winter cress,** *n.* A name of two cruciferous plants, one of them bitter and sharp to the taste, and sometimes used as a salad. —**wintergreen,** *n.* The common name of certain perennial plants allied to the heaths, some of which are medicinal, while an American species yields an oil, used in confectionery and to disguise the taste of disagreeable medicines.—**winterly,** win'tėr•li, *a.* Wintery; cheerless.—**wintertide,** *n.* The winter season.—**winter wheat,** *n.* Wheat sown in autumn.—**wintry, wintery,** win'tri, win'tėr•i, *a.* Suitable to winter; brumal; cold; bleak and cheerless.

winy. See WINE.

winze, winz, *n.* [Icel. *vinza*, to winnow, from *vindr*, wind.] A small shaft in a mine sunk from one level to another, for ventilation or communication.

wipe, wīp, *v.t.—wiped, wiping.* [A.Sax. *wipian*, to wipe; akin to L.G. *wiep*, G. *wif*, a wisp of straw, and to *whip* and *wisp.*] To rub with something soft for cleaning; to clean by gentle rubbing; to strike or brush gently; often with *off*, *up*, *away*, etc.—*To wipe away*, to remove by gentle rubbing; *fig.* to remove or take away in general (to *wipe away* a reproach).—*To wipe out*, to efface; to obliterate.—*n.* The act of one who wipes; a rub for the purpose of cleaning; a gibe; a jeer.—**wiper,** wī′pėr, *n.*

wire, wīr, *n.* [A.Sax. *wír*=L.G. *wire*, Icel. *virr*, Dan. *vire*, wire, allied to L. *viriae*, bracelets; of same root as *wind*, to twist, *withe.*] A thread of metal; a fine or slender metal rod of uniform diameter; such metallic threads collectively; a telegraph wire, hence, the telegraph.—*v.t.—wired, wiring.* To bind with wire; to apply wire to; to snare by means of a wire; to send by telegraph.—*v.i.* To communicate by means of the telegraph.—**wire cloth,** *n.* A texture of wire intermediate between wire gauze and wire netting.—**wiredraw,** wīr′dra̤, *v.t.* To form into wire by forcibly pulling through a series of holes; to draw or spin out to great length and tenuity.—**wire-drawer,** wīr′dra̤•ėr, *n.* One who draws metal into wire.—**wire drawing,** wīr′dra̤•ing, *n.* The act or art of extending ductile metals into wire; the drawing out of an argument or discussion to prolixity by useless distinctions, disquisitions, etc.— **wire gauze,** *n.* A kind of stiff close fabric made of fine wire.—**wireless,** wīr′les, *a.* Having no wires; operating with radio waves, not connected by wires; a shortening of wireless telegraphy or wireless telephone; *British*, radio.—**wire netting,** *n.* A texture of wire used for light fencing, etc.—**wirephoto,** *n.* wīr″fō′tō. A photograph transmitted over telephone wires by electronic impulses and subsequently reproduced at the receiving end.—**wirepuller,** wīr′pul•lėr, *n.* One who pulls the wires of puppets, hence, one who instigates the actions of others without his influence appearing; an intriguer.—**wiretap,** wīr′tap, *v.i.—wiretapped, wiretapping.* To tap, as a telephone, in order to monitor transmissions.—*n.* An act of wiretapping; the connection made during wiretapping.—**wiretapper,** wīr″tap′ėr, *n.*—**wire-work,** wīr′wėrk, *n.* Some kind of fabric made of wire.—**wireworker,** wīr″wėrk′ėr, *n.* One who manufactures articles from wire.—**wireworm,** *n.* A name for several kinds of larvae or grubs very destructive to crops, the name being given from the cylindrical form and hardness of these grubs.—**wire-wove,** *n.* Applied to a paper of fine quality and glazed.—**wiry,** wī′ri, *a.* Made of wire; like wire; tough; lean and sinewy.—**wiriness,** wī′ri•nes, *n.* The state or quality of being wiry.

wise, wīz, *a.* [A.Sax. *wís*, wise, prudent=D. *wijs*, Icel. *víss*, Dan. *viis*, G. *weise*, wise; from same root as *wit*, *wot*, L. *video*, to see (VISION). The wise man is therefore the man that sees and knows. WIT.] Having the power of discerning and judging correctly; possessed of discernment, judgment, and discretion; prudent; sensible; sage; judicious; experienced; skilled; *Scrip.* godly; pious.—*Wise man*, a man skilled in hidden arts; a sorcerer.—*Wise woman*, a witch; a fortuneteller.—**wisdom,** wiz′dom, *n.* [A.Sax. *wisdóm*, from *wis*, and term. *-dóm*=Icel. *vísdómr*, Sw. *visdom*, Dan. *viisdom.*] The quality of being wise; the power or faculty of forming the fittest and best judgment in any matter presented for consideration; sound judgment and sagacity; prudence; discretion; sound common sense; often opposed to *folly*; *Scrip.* right judgment concerning religious and moral truth; godliness.—**wisdom tooth,** *n.* A large back double tooth, so named because not appearing till a person is grown up.—**wisely,** wīz′li, *adv.* In a wise manner; judiciously; discreetly.

wise, wīz, *n.* [A.Sax. *wíse*, manner=D. *wijs*, Icel. *vís*, *visa*, Dan. *viis*, G. *weise*; originally, knowledge or known way; akin to the adjective *wise*. *Guise* is the same word.] Manner; mode; now used only in such phrases as *in any wise*, *in no wise*, etc., or in composition, as in like*wise*, length*wise*, etc., having then much the same force as *-ways* in length*ways*, etc.

wiseacre, wīz′ā•kėr, *n.* [Corrupted from G. *weissager*, a soothsayer, from O.H.G. *vizzago*, *vizago*, a seer =A.Sax. *witega*, a seer, lit. one who is wise or knowing; akin to *wit* and *wise.*] One who makes pretensions to great wisdom; a would-be wise person.

wish, wish, *v.i.* [O.E. *wische*, *wusche*, A.Sax. *wýscan*, to wish, from *wúsc*, a wish; D. and G. *wunsch*, a wish; allied to Skr. *van*, to love, *vanchh*, to desire, L. *Venus*, the goddess, *veneror*, to venerate. WIN, VENERATE.] To have a desire; to long; with *for* before the object.—*v.t.* To desire; to long for; often governing an infinitive or a clause; to frame or express desires concerning; to desire to be (with words completing the sense; to *wish* one well, to *wish* himself rich); to imprecate; to invoke (to *wish* one evil).—*n.* A desire; a longing; an expression of desire; a request; a petition; the thing desired.—**wishbone,** *n.* A fowl's merrythought.—**wisher,** wish′ėr, *n.* One who wishes or expresses a wish.—**wishful,** wish′fu̦l, *a.* Having a desire; desirous; with *of* before an object; showing desire; longing.—**wishfully,** wish′fu̦l•li, *adv.* Longingly; wistfully.—**wishfulness,** wish′fu̦l•nes, *n.*

wish-wash, wish′wosh, *n.* [A reduplication of *wash*, thin or waste liquor.] Any sort of weak, thin drink.—**wishy-washy,** wish′i•wosh′i, *a.* Very thin and weak; diluted; hence, feeble; wanting in substantial qualities.

wisp, wisp, *n.* [O.E. *wispe*, *wesp*, *wips*; akin to L.G. *wiep*, *vippa*, a wisp, also to *whip.*] A bundle of straw or other like substance; a bunch of fibrous matter; a whisk or small broom; an ignis fatuus or will-o'-the-wisp.

wist, wist, pret. of *wit*.

wistful, wist′fu̦l, *a.* [Modified from old *wistly*, observantly, from *wist*, known, pp. of *wit*, to know.] Anxiously observant; pensive from the absence or want of something; earnest from a feeling of desire; longing.—**wistfully,** wist′fu̦l•li, *adv.* In a wistful manner; pensively; longingly.—**wistfulness,** wist′fu̦l•nes, *n.*

wit, wit, *v.t.* and *i.*; present tense, I. *wot*, thou *wottest* or *wotst*, he *wots* or *wot*; pl. *wot*; pret. *wist* in all persons; ppr. *witting*, also *wotting*. [A.Sax. *witan* to know; pres. *ic wát*, I wot; pl. *witon*, pret. sing. *wiste*, pl. *wiston*, pp. *wist*; D. *weten*, pret. *wist*; Icel. *vita*, pret. *vissa*; Dan. *vide*, pret. *vidste*; Goth. *witan*, pret. *wissa*; G. *wissen*, pret. *wusste*; cog. L. *video*, *visum*, to see (VISION), Gr. (*v*)*idein*, to see, (*v*)*eidenai*, to know, Skr. *vid*, to know, to perceive. Hence *wit*, the noun, *witness*. Akin are *wise*, *wizard.*] To know; to be or become aware; to learn. *To wit* is now used parenthetically to call attention to something particular, or as introductory to a detailed statement of what has been just before mentioned generally, and is equivalent to namely, that is to say.—**wittingly,** wit′ing•li, *adv.* Knowingly; not inadvertently or ignorantly.

wit, wit, *n.* [A.Sax. *wit*, *gewit*, knowledge, mind, understanding; Icel. *vit*, Dan. *vid*, G. *witz*, understanding, wit. See WIT, *v.*] Intellect, understanding or mental powers collectively; a faculty or power of the mind (he has all his *wits* about him); wisdom; sagacity; the faculty of associating ideas in a new and ingenious, and at the same time natural and pleasing way exhibited in apt language; a quality or faculty akin to humor, but depending more on point or brilliancy of language; facetiousness; a person possessing this faculty; one distinguished for bright or amusing sayings; a humorist.—*The five wits*, the five senses.—*At one's wits' end*, at a loss what further steps or measures to adopt; unable to think further.—*To live by one's wits*, to live by shifts or expedients, as one without a regular means of living.—**witless,** wit′les, *a.* Destitute of sense or understanding; silly; senseless; foolish.—**witlessly,** wit′les•li, *adv.* Sillily; foolishly.—**witlessness,** wit′les•nes, *n.*—**witling,** wit′ling, *n.* [Dim. from *wit.*] A person who has little wit; a pretender to wit.—**witted,** wit′ed, *a.* Having wit or understanding; used chiefly in composition (a quick-*witted* boy).—**witticism,** wit′i•sizm, *n.* [From *witty*; comp. such words as *Atticism, Gallicism.*] A witty sentence, phrase, or remark; an observation characterized by wit.—**witty,** wit′i. *a.* [A.Sax. *witig.*] Possessed of wit, smartly or cleverly facetious; bright and amusing.—**wittily,** wit′i•li, *adv.* In a witty manner; with wit.—**wittiness,** wit′i•nes, *n.* The quality of being witty.

witch, wich, *n.* [A.Sax. *wicce,* a witch, *wicca,* a wizard; origin doubtful, perhaps akin to *wit.* Hence *wicked.*] A person of either sex given to the black art; a woman supposed to have formed a compact with the devil or with evil spirits, and by their means to operate supernaturally; one who practices sorcery or enchantment; a bewitching or charming young woman.—**witchcraft,** wich′kraft, *n.* The practices of witches; sorcery; power more than natural; enchantment; fascination.—**witch doctor,** *n.* One in primitive tribes who practices magic: similar to a medicine man and shamen.—**witch-hunt,** wich′hunt, *n.* A searching and punishing of one accused of practicing witchcraft; an unwarranted, and often unfair, investigation of a dissenter.—**witch hazel,** *n.* An American shrub with yellow flowers; a preparation from this shrub, used on bruises and sprains.—**witching,** wich′ing, *a.* Bewitching; suited to enchantment or witchcraft.—*n.* The practice of witchcraft or sorcery.

witenagemot, wit″en•a•ge•mōt′, *n.* [A.Sax. *witena,* gen. pl. of *wita,* a wise man. *(ge)mót,* a meeting, a moot. WIT, MEET.] Among the Anglo-Saxons, the great national council or parliament, consisting of athelings or princes, nobles or ealdormen, the large landholders, principal ecclesiastics, etc.

with, WITH, *prep.* [A.Sax. *with,* nearby, against, toward; Icel. *vith,* against, toward, along with; Dan. *ved,* near, with, against. The A.Sax. *wither,* opposite, against (seen in *withers*), is a comparative from this; like Icel. *vithr,* D. *weder,* G. *wieder,* Hence *withal, within, without, withdraw, withhold,* etc.] Against; competing against (to fight, contend, or vie *with*); not apart from; in the company of; on the side of or in favor of; in the estimation, consideration, or judgment of (*with* you art is useless); having as a concomitant, consequence, or appendage (*with* a blush); so as to contract or correspond; immediately after (*with* that he left); correspondence; through or by, as means, cause, or consequence (pale *with* fear).—*With child,* pregnant; in the family way.

withal, WITH•ạl′, *adv.* [*With* and *all.*] With the rest; together with that; likewise.—*prep.* With; used after relatives or equivalent words, and transposed to the end of a sentence or clause.

withdraw, WITH•drạ′, *v.t.*—pret. *withdrew*; pp. *withdrawn.* [Prefix *with,* against, opposite to, and *draw.*] To draw back or in a contrary direction; to lead, bring, or take back; to recall; to retract.—*v.i.* To retire from or quit a company or place; to go away; to retreat.—**withdrawal,** WITH•drạ′al, *n.* Act of withdrawing or taking back; a recalling.—**withdrawn,** WITH•drạn′, *a.* Retiring; shy; introspective.

withe, withy, with or WITH, WITH′i, *n.* [A.Sax. *withig,* willow, withe; Icel. *vithja, vith,* a withy, a withe; Dan. *vidie,* Sw. *vide, vidja,* G. *weidė,* a willow; allied to Gr. *ítea* (for *vitea*), a willow; from a root meaning to twist or bend, seen also in L. *vimen,* a withe, *vitis,* a vine. WINE.] A willow or osier; a willów or osier twig; a flexible twig used to bind something; a fastening of plaited or twisted twigs.

wither, WITH′ėr, *v.i.* [Lit. to *weather,* to suffer from or expose to the weather. WEATHER.] To dry and shrivel up, as a plant; to lose freshness and bloom; to fade; to become dry and wrinkled, as from the loss of animal moisture; to lose pristine freshness, bloom, or vigor; to decline; to pass away.—*v.t.* To cause to fade; to make sapless and shrunken; to cause to lose bloom; to shrivel; to blight, injure, or destroy, as by some malign or baleful influence.

withers, WITH′ėrz, *n. pl.* [Lit. the parts that act against or resist, from A.Sax. *wither,* against, from prep. *with,* against.] The junction of the shoulder bones of a horse, forming an elevation at the springing of the neck.

withhold, WITH′hōld′, *v.t.*—pret. and pp. *withheld.* [*With,* in sense of against, and *hold.*] To hold back; to restrain; to keep from action; to retain; to keep back; not to grant.—**withholder,** WITH•hōl′dėr, *n.* —**withholding tax,** *n.* An income tax that is deducted at the source of payment.

within, WITH•in′, *prep.* [A.Sax. *withinnan*—*with,* against, towards, and *innan,* within, inwardly, from *in,* in.] In the inner or interior part or parts of; inside of; opposed to *without*; in the limits, range, reach, or compass of; not beyond; inside or comprehended by the scope, limits, reach, or influence of; not exceeding, not overstepping, etc.—*adv.* In the interior or center; inwardly; internally; in the mind, heart, or soul; in the house or dwelling; indoors; at home.—*From within,* from the inside; from within doors, etc.

without, WITH•out′, *prep.* [A.Sax. *withútan,* without—*with,* toward, against, and *út,* out.] On or at the outside or exterior of; out of; opposed to *within*; out of the limits, compass, range, or reach of; beyond; not having or not being with; in absence or destitution of; deprived of; not having.—*conj.* Unless; except; now rarely used by correct speakers and writers.—*adv.* On the outside; outwardly; externally; out of doors.—*From without,* from the outside; opposite to *from within.*

withstand, WITH•stand′, *v.t.*—pret. and pp. *withstood.* [*With,* in sense of against, and *stand.*] To resist, either with physical or moral force; to oppose.—*v.i.* To resist; to make a stand.—**withstander,** WITH•stan′dėr, *n.* One that withstands; an opponent.

withy. See WHITE.

witless, witling, etc. See WIT, *n.*

witness, wit′nes, *n.* [A.Sax. *witnes,* testimony, lit. what one knows, from *witan,* to know. WIT.] Attestation of a fact or event; testimony; that which furnishes evidence or proof; a person who knows or sees anything; one personally present; *law,* one who sees the execution of an instrument, and subscribes it for confirmation of its authenticity; a person who gives testimony or evidence in a judicial proceeding. —*With a witness,*‡ effectually; with a vengeance; so as to leave some mark as a testimony behind.—*v.t.* To attest; to testify; to see or know by personal presence; to be a witness of; to give or serve as evidence or token of; to subscribe as witness.—*v.i.* To bear testimony; to give evidence.—**witnesser,** wit′nes•ėr, *n.* —**witness stand,** *n.* The area from which a witness in a court gives evidence; witness box.

witticism, wittily, etc. See WIT, *n.*

wittingly. See WIT, *v.*

witty. See WIT, *n.*

wive,‡ wīv, *v.i.* and *t.* [From *wife.*] To marry; to provide with a wife; to take for a wife.—**wives,** wīvz, pl. of *wife.*

wizard, wiz′ėrd, *n.* [From *wise,* and term. *-ard.*] Originally, a wise man; a sage; latterly, an adept in the black art; a sorcerer; an enchanter; a magician; a conjurer.

wizen, wiz′n, *a.* [A.Sax. *wisnian,* to become dry, akin to Icel. *visna,* to wither, from *visinn,* withered, palsied.] Hard, dry, and shriveled; withered.—**wizened,** wīz′end, *a.* Shriveled; dried up.

woad, wōd, *n.* [A.Sax. *wád,* D. *weede,* Dan. *vaid, veid,* G. *waid, weid,* woad; connected with L. *vitrum,* woad.] A cruciferous plant, the pulped and fermented leaves of which yield an excellent blue dye.—**woaded,** wōd′ed, *a.* Dyed or colored blue with woad.

wobble, wob′l, *v.i.*—*wobbled, wobbling.* [Also *wabble*; akin to L.G. *wabbeln,* G. *wabern, weibeln, weiben,* to move to and fro.] To move unsteadily in rotating or spinning; to rock; to vacillate.

Woden, wō′den, *n.* [Akin to A.Sax. *wód,* mad; G. *wuth,* rage; or to *wind.*] The Anglo-Saxon form of the name of the deity called by the Norse Odin. *Wednesday* derives its name from him.

woe, wō, *n.* [A.Sax. *wá*; often as an interjection, as in *wá lá wá*, woe lo woe! wellaway! D. *wee*, Icel. *vei*, Dan. *vee*, G. *weh*, Goth. *vai*; a natural sound of grief, like L. *vae*! Gr. *ouai*! alas.] Grief; sorrow; misery; heavy calamity. *Woe* is frequently used in denunciations either with a verb or alone; it is also used in exclamations of sorrow, a pronoun following being then in the dative (*woe is me*). The phrase '*Woe worth* the day', means *woe be to* the day. WORTH, *v.i.*—**woebegone,** wō'bi·gon, *a.* [That is, surrounded or overwhelmed with woe, *begone* being from A.Sax. *began*, to surround—*be*, by, and *gán*, to go.] Overwhelmed with woe; immersed in grief and sorrow.—**woeful, woful,** wō'fụl, *a.* Full of woe; afflicted; sorrowful; expressing woe; doleful; distressful; piteous; wretched.—**woefully, wofully,** wō'-fụl·li, *adv.* Sorrowfully; lamentably; wretchedly; miserably; extremely.—**woefulness, wofulness,** wō'fụl·-nes, *n.*

wold, wōld, *n.* [A.Sax. *wald*, *woald*, a wood; O.Sax., O.Fris., and G. *wald*, a wood or forest. *Weald* is the same word.] A wood; a forest; a weald or open country; a low hill; a down; in the plural, a hilly district or a range of hills.

wold, wōld, *n.* A plant. See WELD.

wolf, wụlf, *n.* pl. **wolves,** wụlvz. [A. Sax. *wulf*=D. and G. *wolf*, Icel. *úlfr*, Dan. *ulv*, Sw. *ulf*, Goth. *wulfs*; cog. L. *lupus*, Gr. *lukos*, Skr. *vrika*, a wolf; traced to a root meaning to tear.] A carnivorous quadruped belonging to the dog family, and closely related to the dog, swift of foot, crafty, and rapacious, but, in general, cowardly and stealthy; hence, a term for a person considered ravenous, cruel, cunning, or the like; *mus.* a jarring discordant sound produced by instruments tuned to unequal temperament.—*To cry wolf*, to raise a false alarm; in allusion to the shepherd boy in the fable.—*To keep the wolf from the door*, to keep away hunger or want.—**wolf dog,** *n.* A large kind of dog kept to keep off or destroy wolves.—**wolf fish,** *n.* An edible fish 6 or 7 feet long, so called from its ferocious aspect and habits. Called also *Sea-cat, Sea-wolf*.—**wolfish,** wụlf'ish, *a.* Like a wolf; savage.—**wolfishly,** wụlf'ish·li, *adv.* In a wolfish manner.—**wolfsbane,** *n.* A poisonous plant of the aconite kind, yielding the virulent poison aconitin; monkshood or aconite.

wolfram, wụl'fram, *n.* [G. *wolfram*—*wolf*, wolf, *ram*, *rahm*, froth, cream, soot.] See TUNGSTEN.

wollastonite, wol'as·ton·it, *n.* Same as *Tabular spar*.

wolverine, wụl'vėr·ēn, *n.* [Origin uncertain.] A carnivorous North American mammal, *Gulo luscus*.

woman, wụm'an, *n.* pl. **women,** wim'en. [A.Sax. *wifman*, later *wimman*, from *wif*, wife, and *man*, in its primitive sense of human being, person. WIFE, MAN.] The female of the human race; an adult or grownup female, as distinguished from a girl; a female attendant on a person of rank.—**womanhood,** wụm'-an·hụd, *n.* The state, character, or collective qualities of a woman.—**womanish,** wụm'an·ish, *a.* Suitable to a woman; feminine; effeminate; often in a contemptuous sense.—**womanishly,** wụm'an·ish·li, *adv.* Effeminately.—**womanishness,** wụm'-an·ish·nes, *n.* State or quality of being womanish.—**womankind,** wụm'an·kīnd, *n.* Women in general; the female sex.—**womanliness,** wụm'an·li·nes, *n.* Quality of being womanly.—**womanly,** wụm'an·li, *a.* Becoming or suiting a woman; feminine, in the praiseworthy sense; not masculine.

womb, wöm, *n.* [A.Sax. *wamb*, *womb*, the belly=D. *wam*, Icel. *vómb*, Dan. *vom*, G. *wamme*, *wampe*, Goth. *wamba*, the belly.] The belly or stomach‡; the uterus of a female; something likened to this; any large or deep cavity that receives or contains anything.

wombat, wom'bat, *n.* [Corruption of the native name *womback* or *wombach*.] A marsupial mammal of Australia and Tasmania, about the size of a badger; it inhabits a burrow and feeds on roots.

women, pl. of *woman*.

won, wun, pret. and pp. of *win*.

wonder, wun'dėr, *n.* [A.Sax. *wundor* =D. *wonder*, G. *wunder*, Icel. *úndr*, Sw. and Dan. *under*; perhaps akin to *wind* (*v.*), *wend*, a prodigy being such as to turn a person away through awe.] That emotion which is excited by something new, strange, and extraordinary, or that arrests the attention by its novelty, grandeur, or inexplicableness; a feeling less than *astonishment*, and much less than *amazement*; a cause of such feeling; a strange or extraordinary thing; a prodigy.—*A nine days' wonder*, something that causes a sensation or astonishment for a short time.—*v.i.* To be struck with wonder; to marvel; to be amazed; to look with or feel admiration; to entertain some doubt and curiosity; to be in a state of expectation, mingled with doubt and slight anxiety; followed by a clause.—**wonderer,** wun'dėr·er, *n.* One who wonders.—**wonderful,** wun'dėr·fụl, *a.* Adapted to excite wonder; strange; astonishing; marvelous.—**wonderfully,** wun'dėr·fụl·li, *adv.* In a wonderful manner; surprising; strangely; colloquially often equivalent to very.—**wonderfulness,** wun'dėr·fụl·nes, *n.* The state or quality of being wonderful.—**wonderingly,** wun'dėr·ing·li, *adv.* With wonder.—**wonderland,** *n.* A land of wonders or marvels.—**wonderment,** wun'dėr·ment, *n.* Wonder; surprise; astonishment.—**wonder-struck,** wun'dėr·struk, *a.* Struck with wonder or surprise.—**wonder-work,** *n.* A prodigy; a miracle.—**wonder-worker,** *n.* One who performs wonders.—**wondrous,** wun'-drus, *a.* Such as to excite wonder; wonderful; marvelous; strange.—*adv.* In a wonderful degree; remarkably; exceedingly (*wondrous* wise).—**wondrously,** wun'drus·li, *adv.* In a strange or wonderful manner or degree.

won't, wōnt. A contraction for *will not*.

wont, wunt, *a.* [For older *woned*, a participle or participial adjective, from A.Sax. *wuna*, *gewuna*, custom, habit, or from the kindred *wunian*, to dwell; akin Icel. *vani*, custom, *vanr*, accustomed. WEAN, WIN.] Accustomed; having a certain habit or custom; using or doing customarily.—*n.* [From A.S. *wuna*, habit, custom, and M.E. *wone*.] Custom; habit; use.—*v.i.* pret. *wont*; pp. *wont*, *wonted*. [For old *wone*, to be accustomed, to dwell. The pret. and pp. *wont* are thus put for *woned*, and *wonted* is a doubled form.] To be accustomed or habituated; to use; to be used.—**wonted,** wun'ted, *p.* and *a.* Customary or familiar from use or habit; usual; accustomed; made or having become familiar by using, frequenting, etc.

woo, wö, *v.t.*—*wooed*, *wooing*. [A. Sax. *wógian*, to woo, from *wóh*, genit. *wóges*, bent, bending; the meaning is therefore to bend or incline another toward one's self.] To court; to solicit in love; to invite; to seek to gain or bring about; to court (to *woo* destruction).—*v.i.* To make love.—**wooing,** wö'ing, *n.* Courtship; time of courtship.

wood, wụd, *n.* [A.Sax. *wudu*, a wood, timber; akin O.D. *wede*, Icel. *vithr*, Dan. and Sw. *ved*, wood, a tree; comp. W. *gwydd*, trees, shrubs.] A large collection of growing trees; a forest; the substance of trees or their trunks; timber; *pl.* wind instruments in an orchestra, such as the flute, clarinet, oboe, etc.—*v.i.* To take in or get supplies of wood.—*v.t.* To supply with wood, or get supplies of wood for.—**woodbine, woodbind,** wụd'bīn, wụd'bīnd, *n.* [BINE.] The wild honeysuckle; formerly the bindweed.—**woodchat,** *n.* A species of butcherbird or shrike.—**woodchuck,** *n.* A species of marmot common in the United States and Canada; the ground hog.—**wood coal,** *n.* Charcoal; also lignite or brown coal.—**woodcock,** wụd'kok, *n.* A bird allied to the snipe but with a more robust bill and shorter legs.—**woodcraft,** wụd'-kraft, *n.* Skill in anything which pertains to woods or forests; skill in hunting deer, etc.—**woodcut,** *n.* An engraving on wood, or a print from such engraving.—**woodcutter,** *n.* A person who cuts wood; an engraver on wood.—**woodcutting,** *n.* The act or employment of cutting wood; wood engraving.—**wooded,** wụd'ed, *a.* Supplied or covered with wood (land well *wooded*).—**wooden,** wụd'n, *a.* Made of wood; consisting of wood; ungainly; awkward; without spirit or expression.—**wood engraver,** *n.* An artist who engraves on wood.—**wood engrav-**

ing, *n.* The art of engraving on wood, or of producing by special cutting tools a design or picture in relief on the surface of a block of wood (generally box), from which impressions can be taken by means of an ink or pigment.—**woodenly,** wụd′n•li, *adv.*—**wodiness,** wụd′i•nes, *n.*—**woodland,** wụd′land, *n.* Land covered with wood.—*a.* Relating to woods; sylvan.—**woodman,** wụd′man, *n.* A forester; one who fells timber.—**wood nymph,** *n.* A goddess of the woods; a dryad.—**woodpecker,** wụd′pek•ėr, *n.* The name for certain climbing birds that feed on insects and their larvae which they find on trees.—**woodpile,** wụd′pīl, *n.* A stack of piled-up wood for fuel.—**wood pulp,** *n.* Pulp from wood, widely used in making paper.—**woodruff,** wụd′ruf, *n.* A well-known plant cultivated in gardens for the beauty of its whorled leaves and simple white blossoms, but chiefly for the fragrance of its leaves.—**wood sorrel,** *n.* A small species of sorrel, supposed by some to be the Irish shamrock.—**wood spirit,** *n.* A crude spirit obtained by distilling wood in closed vessels.—**wood vinegar,** *n.* A sort of vinegar obtained by the distillation of wood.—**woodwind,** wụd′wind, *n.* Wind instruments, including the flute, the oboe, clarinet, bassoon, and sometimes the saxophone.—**woodwork,** *n.* Work formed of wood; the part of any structure that is made of wood.—**woody,** wụd′i, *a.* Abounding with wood; consisting of wood; ligneous; pertaining to woods.

wooer. See WOO.

woof, wöf, *n.* [O.E. *oof, owef,* from A.Sax. *ówef,* from prefix *ó,* for *on,* and *wefan,* to weave. WEAVE.] The threads that cross the warp in weaving; the weft; texture.

wool, wụl, *n.* [A.Sax. *wull, wul,* = D. *wol,* G. *wolle,* Goth. *wulla,* Icel. and Sw. *ull,* Dan. *uld;* allied to L. *villus,* shaggy hair, *vellus,* a fleece; from a root signifying to cover, seen also in L. *vallis,* a valley, and in *valeo,* to be strong. VALID.] That soft species of hair which grows on sheep and some other animals; the fleecy coat of the sheep; also applied to other kinds of hair, especially short, crisped, and curled hair like that of a Negro; any fibrous or fleecy substance resembling wool.—**woolen,** wụl′en, *a.* Made of wool; consisting of wool; pertaining to wool.—*n.* Cloth made of wool, such as blanketings, serges, flannels, tweeds, broadcloth, and the like.—**woolgathering,** *n.* The act of gathering wool; usually applied figuratively to the indulgence of idle fancies; a fruitless pursuit.—**woolgrower,** *n.* A person who raises sheep for the production of wool.—**woolliness,** wụl′i•nes, *n.* The state of being woolly.—**woolly,** wụl′i, *a.* Consisting of wool; resembling wool; clothed or covered with wool; *bot.* covered with a pubescence resembling wool.—**woolpack,** wụl′pak, *n.* A bag of wool.—**woolsack,** wụl′sak, *n.* A sack or bag of wool; the seat of the lord-chancellor in the House of Lords, a large square bag of wool, without back or arms, covered with red cloth.—**wool stapler,** *n.* A dealer in wool; a sorter of wool.

word, wėrd, *n.* [A.Sax. *word,* a word = D. *woord,* G. *wort,* Icel., Sw., and Dan. *ord,* Goth. *waurd;* cog. Lith. *vardas,* name; L. *verbum,* a word (whence *verb*); from a root meaning to speak, seen in Gr. (*v*)*eirō,* to speak.] A single articulate sound, or a combination of articulate sounds or syllables, uttered by the human voice, and by custom expressing an idea or ideas; a vocable; a term; speech exchanged; conversation; talk; in this sense plural; information; tidings; in this sense without an article and only as a singular (to send *word* of one's safe arrival); a watchword; a password; a motto; a term or phrase of command; an injunction; an order; an assertion or promise; an affirmation on honor; a declaration; with possessives (to take him at his *word*); terms or phrases interchanged in contention, anger, or reproach; in plural, and often qualified by *high, hot, harsh, sharp,* etc.—*The Word,* the Scriptures, or any part of them; the second person of the Trinity; the Logos.—*Word for word,* in the exact words or terms; verbatim; exactly.—*By word of mouth,* by actual speaking; orally.—*Good word,* expressed good opinion; a recommendation (to speak a *good word* for a person).—*In word,* in mere phraseology.—*In a word,* in *one word,* briefly; to sum up; in short.—*To eat one's words,* to retract what one has said.—*A word and a blow,* a threat and its immediate execution.—*v.t.* To express in words; to phrase.—**wordbook,** *n.* A vocabulary; a dictionary; a lexicon.—**wordily,** wėr′di•li, *adv.* In a wordy manner.—**wordiness,** wėr′di•nes, *n.* The quality of being wordy; verbosity.—**wording,** wėr′ding, *n.* Expression in words; form of expression.—**wordless,** werd′les, *a.* Not speaking; silent.—**wordy,** wėr′di, *a.* Using many more words than are necessary; verbose; consisting of words; verbal.

wore, wōr, pret. of *wear.*

work, wėrk, *n.* [A.Sax. *worc, weorc* = D. *werk,* Icel. and Sw. *verk,* Dan. *vaerk,* G. *werk,* work; from same root as Gr. (*v*)*ergon,* work.] Exertion of energy, physical or mental; effort directed to some purpose or end; toil; labor; employment; the matter upon which one is employed, engaged, or laboring; that which engages one's time or attention; an undertaking; an enterprise; a task; that which is done; performance; deed; feat; achievement; goings-on; that which is made or produced; a product of nature or art; a literary or artistic performance; a composition; some extensive structure, as a dock, bridge, fortification, etc.; any establishment where labor is carried on extensively (an iron *work*), the plural being often applied to one such establishment; *mech.* the overcoming of resistance; the act of producing a change of configuration in a system in opposition to a force which resists that change.—*Unit of work,* a foot-pound. See FOOT.—*v.i.*—pret. and pp. *wrought* or *worked.* [From the noun; A.Sax. *wircan, wyrcan;* pret. *worhte,* pp. *geworht.*] To make exertion for some end or purpose; to be engaged or employed on some task, labor, duty, or the like; to labor; to toil; to be engaged in an employment or occupation; to perform the duties of a laborer, workman, man of business, etc.; to be in motion, operation, or activity (the machine *works* well); to act; to operate; to have or take effect; to exercise influence; to tend or conduce (things *work* to some end); to be tossed or agitated, as the sea; to be in agitation; to boil (passion *works* in him); to make way laboriously and slowly; to act as a purgative or cathartic; to ferment, as liquors.—*To work against,* to act in opposition to; to oppose actively.—*To work on* or *upon,* to act on; to influence.—*v.t.* To bestow manual labor upon; to carry on the operations of (to *work* a mine or quarry); to bring about; to effect, perform, do (to *work* mischief); to keep at work; to keep busy or employed (he *works* his horses, his servants; to bring by action to any state (to *work* one's self out); to make or get by labor or exertion (to *work* one's way); to make into shape; to fashion; to mold; to embroider; to operate on, as a purgative; to purge; to cause to ferment, as liquor.—*To work a passage,* to give one's work or services as an equivalent for passage money.—*To work in* or *into,* to intermix gradually, as in the process of manufacture; to cause to enter or penetrate by repeated efforts; to introduce artfully; to insinuate (he *works* himself *into* favor).—*To work off,* to get rid of by some gradual process; to produce, as separate articles of the same kind from a machine or the like.—*To work out,* to effect by continued labor or exertion; to solve, as a problem; to exhaust by drawing all the useful material (to *work out* a mine).—*To work up,* to stir up; to excite; to agitate; to use up in the process of manufacture or the like; to elaborate (to *work up* a story or article).—**workable,** wėr′ka•bl, *a.* That can be worked or that is worth working.—**workaday,** wėr′ka•dā, *a.* Working day; everyday; toiling.—**workbag,** *n.* A small bag used by ladies for containing needlework, etc., a reticule.—**workbox,** *n.* A small box for holding needlework, etc.—**worker,** wėr′kėr, *n.* One who works; a laborer; a toiler; a performer; a working bee; sterile or neuter bees, ants, and other insects that work.—**workhouse,** wėrk′hous, *n.* A house of correction where petty offenders are incarcerated and put to work.—**working,** wėr′king, *p.* and *a.* Engaged in bodily toil; laborious; industrious; taking an active part in a business (a *working* partner).—*n.* The act of laboring; fermentation; movement; operation. —**working day,** *n.* Any day on which work is ordinarily performed, as distinguished from Sundays and holidays; such part of the day as is devoted or allotted to work.—*a.* Relating to days on which work is done; plodding; laborious.—**workman,** wėrk′man, *n.* Any man employed in work, especially manual labor; a laborer; a toiler; a worker; a skillful artificer or operator.—**workmanlike,** wėrk′man•līk, *a.* Skillful; well performed.—**workmanly,** wėrk′man•li, *a.* Skillful; workmanlike.—**workmanship,** wėrk′man•ship, *n.* The art or skill of a workman; the style or character of work performed on anything; operative skill; the result or objects produced by a workman, artificer, or operator.—**workpeople,** *n.* People engaged in labor, particularly manual labor.—**workshop,** wėrk′shop, *n.* A shop or building where any work or handicraft is carried on.—**workwoman,** wėrk′wụm•an, *n.* A woman who performs any work.

world, wėrld, *n.* [A.Sax. *world, worold* =O.Sax. *werold,* D. *wereld,* Icel. *veröld,* Sw. *verld,* O.H.G. *weralt,* G. *welt*; lit. man-age, age of man, age, hence, course of time, world; from A.Sax. *wer,* a man (cog. with L. *vir,* whence *virile, virtue*), and *eld, yld,* age, akin to *old.*] The earth and all created things thereon; the terraqueous globe; the universe; any celestial orb or planetary body; a large portion or division of our globe (the Old *World,* or eastern hemisphere; the New *World,* or western hemisphere; the Roman *world*); the earth as the scene of human existence and action; any state or sphere of existence (a future *world*); a domain, region, or realm (the *world* of dreams, of art); the human race; the aggregate of humanity; the public; the people among whom one lives; the life of humanity at large; the people united by a common faith, aim, pursuit, etc. (the religious *world* the heathen *world*); the people exclusively interested in secular affairs; the unregenerate or ungodly part of humanity. It is sometimes used to signify a great multitude or quantity; a great degree or measure (a *world* too large); it is also used in emphatic phrases expressing perplexity or surprise (what in the *world* am I to do?). —*World without end,* to all eternity; eternally; unceasingly.—*For all the world,* exactly; precisely; entirely.—*The world's end,* the remotest part of the earth.—**worldliness,** wėrld′li•nes, *n.* The state of being worldly.—**worldling,** wėrld′ling, *n.* One who is devoted exclusively to the affairs and interests of this life.—**worldly,** wėrld′li, *a.* Belonging to the world or present state of man's existence; temporal; secular; desirous of temporal benefit or enjoyment. **world power,** *n.* A country that is powerful enough to affect the whole (political) world by its actions.—**world series,** *n.* A seven-game series played between the champion of the American and National leagues at the end of the regulation baseball season.

worm, wėrm, *n.* [A.Sax. *wyrm,* a worm, a serpent = D. *worm,* G. *wurm,* Goth. *waurms,* Icel. *ormr,* Dan. and Sw. *orm*; cog. L. *vermis,* a worm (whence *vermicular* and *vermin*).] A term loosely applied to many small creeping animals, entirely wanting feet or having but very short ones; any somewhat similar creature; an intestinal parasite of lengthened form; *pl.* the disease due to the presence of such parasites; a maggot; a canker; an epithet of scorn, disgust, or contempt; anything vermicular or spiral; the thread of a screw; the spiral pipe of a still placed in a vessel of cold water, and through which the vapor of the substance distilled is conducted to cool and condense it; a small vermicular ligament under the tongue of a dog, often cut out to prevent the young dog from gnawing things.—*v.i.* To advance by wriggling; *refl.* to insinuate one's self; to work gradually and secretly. —*v.t.* To effect by slow and stealthy means; to extract or get at slyly or cunningly (to *worm* a secret out of a person); to cut the worm from a dog. —**worm-eaten,** *a.* Gnawed by worms; having a number of internal cavities made by worms.—**wormseed,** *n.* The seed of a species of wormwood brought from the Levant, and used as an anthelmintic.—**worm wheel,** *n.* A wheel which gears with an endless screw.—**wormy,** wėr′mi, *n.* Containing a worm or worms; earthy; grovelling.

wormwood, wėrm′wụd, *n.* [A corruption of a name having no connection with *worm* or *wood*; A.Sax. *wermód,* D. *wermoet,* G. *wermuth*; lit. *ware-mood,* mind-preserver (from some old notion as to its virtues), the *wer* being akin to *ware* (in *beware*), *wary.* (WARY, MOOD.) The plant was used as a remedy for worms, hence the corruption.] A well-known plant, celebrated for its intensely bitter, tonic, and stimulating qualities; bitter feeling, mortification (*gall and wormwood*).

worn, worn, pp. of *wear.*—**wornout,** *a.* Destroyed or much injured by wear; wearied; exhausted with toil.

worry, wur′i, *v.t.*—pret. and pp. *worried.* [O.E. *wirie, wurie, worowe,* etc.; from A.Sax. *wyrgan,* seen in *á-wyrgan,* to strangle, to injure; D. *worgen, wurgen,* G. *würgen,* to strangle; akin to *wring, wrong,* nasalized forms.] To seize by the throat with the teeth; to tear with the teeth, as dogs when fighting; to harass with importunity or with care and anxiety; to plague, tease, bother, vex, persecute.—*v.i.* To be unduly careful and anxious; to be in solicitude or trouble; to fret.—*n.* The act of worrying or mangling with the teeth; perplexity; trouble; anxiety; harassing turmoil.—**worrying,** wur′i•ing, *p.* and *a.* Troubling; harassing; fatiguing.—**worrier,** wur′i•ėr, *n.* One that worries.—**worriment,** wur′i•ment, *n.* Worry; anxiety.—**worrisome,** wur′i•sum, *a.* Causing worry.

worse, wėrs, *a.* [A.Sax. *wyrsa,* adj., *wyrs,* adv.; Icel. *verr, verri,* Dan. *vaerre,* Goth. *wairs,* adv., *wairsiza,* adj.; same root as G. *wirren,* to entangle, E. *war. Worse* and *worst* are used as comparative and superlative to *ill* and *bad.*] Bad or ill in a greater degree; less good or perfect; of less value; inferior; more unwell; more sick; in poorer health; in a less favorable situation; more ill off; also used substantively, often with *the*; loss; defeat; disadvantage; something less good or desirable (*worse* remains behind).—*adv.* In a manner more evil or bad; in a smaller or lower degree; less (it pleases him *worse*); in a greater manner or degree: with a notion of evil (he hates him *worse*).—**worsen,** wėr′sn, *v.i.* To grow worse; to deteriorate.—**worser,** wėr′sėr, *a.* and *adv.* A redundant comparative of *worse,* sometimes used by good writers.—**worst,** wėrst, *a.* Bad in the highest degree, whether in a moral or physical sense.—*n.* The most evil, aggravated, or calamitous state or condition: usually with *the.*—*adv.* Most ill or extreme; most intensely (he hates us *worst*).—*v.t.* To get the advantage over in conquest; to defeat; to overthrow.

worship, wėr′ship, *n.* [From *worth,* and term. *-ship*; A.Sax. *weorthscipe,* honor.] A title used in addressing certain magistrates and others of rank or station; the performance of devotional acts in honor of a deity; the act of paying divine honors to a Supreme Being; religious exercises; reverence; submissive respect; loving or admiring devotion.—*v.t.*—*worshiped* or *worshipped, worshiping* or *worshipping.* To pay divine honors to; to reverence with respect; to perform religious service to; to adore; to idolize.—*v.i.* To perform acts of adoration; to perform religious service.—**worshipful,** wėr′ship•fụl, *a.* Worthy of honor; honorable; a term of respect especially applied to magistrates and corporate bodies. — **worshipfully,** wėr′ship•fụl•li, *adv.* Respectfully; honorably. —**worshipfulness,** wėr′ship•fụl•nes, *n.*—**worshiper, worshipper,** wėr′ship•ėr, *n.* One who worships; one who pays divine honors to any being; one who adores.

worst. See WORSE.

worsted, wụs′ted, *n.* [From *Worsted,* in Norfolk, where it was first manufactured.] A variety of woolen yarn or thread, spun from long-staple wool, used in knitting stockings, etc.

wort, wėrt, *n.* [A.Sax. *wyrt,* a plant = G. *wurz,* Goth. *wurts,* Icel. and Dan. *urt.* This word is contained in *orchard,* and is of same root as *root, radical* (which see).] A plant; an herb: now used chiefly in compounds (liver*wort,* fig*wort,* spleen*wort*).

wort, wėrt, *n.* [A.Sax. *wyrte,* wort, must; Icel. *virtr,* O.D. *wort,* G. *würze,* wort; probably akin to above word.] New beer unfermented or in the act of fermentation; the sweet infusion of malt.

worth, wėrth, *v.i.* [A.Sax. *weorthan,* to be or to become=Icel. *vertha,* Dan. *vorde,* D. *worden,* G. *werden,* Goth. *wairthan;* same root as in L. *verto,* to turn, whence E. *verse* (which see).] To be; to become; to betide: now used only in the phrases woe *worth* the day, woe *worth* the man, etc., equivalent to woe *be to* the day, etc.

worth, wėrth, *n.* [A.Sax. *weorth, wurth,* price, value, honor, or as an adj. valuable, honorable, with similar forms in the other Teutonic languages; perhaps from root meaning to guard, as in *wary, beware.*] That quality of a thing which renders it valuable; value; money value; price; rate; value in respect of mental or moral qualities; desert; merit; excellence.—*a.* Equal in value or price to; deserving of (a cause *worth* defending); having estate to the value of; having a fixed or specified value.—*Worthwhile.* See WHILE.—**worthily,** wėr′THi•li, *adv.* In a worthy manner; suitably; excellently; deservedly; justly; according to merit.—**worthiness,** wėr′THi•nes, *n.* The state or quality of being worthy or well-deserved; excellence; dignity; virtue.—**worthless,** wėrth′les, *a.* Having no value; having no dignity or excellence; mean; contemptible; unworthy; not deserving.—**worthlessly,** wėrth′les•li, *adv.* In a worthless manner.—**worthlessness,** wėrth′les•nes, *n.* The state of being worthless.—**worthy,** wėr′THi, *a.* Having worth; excellent; deserving praise; valuable; estimable; applied to persons and things; such as merits; deserving (*worthy* of love or hatred); suitable; proper; fitting.—*n.* A person of worth or distinguished for estimable qualities; a local celebrity; a character (a village *worthy*).

would, wụd, pret. of *will.* See WILL.—**would-be,** *a.* Wishing to be; vainly pretending to be (a *would-be* philosopher).—*n.* A vain pretender.

wound, wönd, *n.* [A.Sax. *wund,* a wound; also, as an adjective, wounded, from *winnan,* to fight; D. *wonde,* Icel. *und,* Dan. *vunde,* G. *wunde,* a wound. WIN.] A cut, breach, or rupture in the skin and flesh of an animal caused by violence; an injury in a soft part of the body from external violence; a similar injury to a plant; any injury, hurt, or pain, as to the feelings.—*v.t.* To inflict a wound on; to cut, slash, or lacerate; to hurt the feelings of; to pain.—*v.i.* To inflict hurt or injury.—**woundless,** wönd′les, *n.* Unwounded; unharmed; invulnerable.

wound, wound, pret. and pp. of *wind.*

wove, wōv, pret. and sometimes pp. of *weave.*—*Wove* or *woven paper,* writing paper made with a surface of uniform appearance, without watermark or lines.—**woven,** wō′vn, pp. of *weave.*

wrack, rak, *n.* [A form of *wreck;* the seaweed is so called as being cast up by the waves. Comp. Dan. *vrag,* wreck, *vrage,* to reject, Sw. *vrak,* wreck, refuse, *vraka,* to reject. WRECK.] A popular name for seaweeds generally, but more especially when thrown ashore by the waves; also, a wreck‡; ruin‡.—*v.t.*‡ To wreck; to destroy.

wrack, rak, *n.* [RACK.] A thin, flying cloud; a rack.

wraith, rāth, *n.* [Gael. and Ir. *arrach,* a specter or apparition.] An apparition in the exact likeness of a person, supposed to be seen before or soon after the person's death; an apparition.

wrangle, rang′gl, *v.i.*—*wrangled, wrangling.* [A freq. from *wring,* A. Sax. *wringan,* pret. *wrang,* to press.] To dispute angrily; to brawl; to altercate; to engage in discussion and disputation; to argue; to debate.—*n.* An angry dispute; a noisy quarrel.—**wrangler,** rang′glėr, *n.* One who wrangles; an angry or noisy disputant; a cowboy or herdsman [in this sense, from Sp. *caballerango.*] **wrangling,** rang′gling, *n.* Angry disputation or altercation.

wrap, rap, *v.t.*—*wrapped, wrapping.* [O.E. *wrappe,* formed by metathesis from *warp,* in old sense of to throw, hence to throw clothes or the like round. WARP, LAP (to fold), ENVELOP.] To fold together; to arrange so as to cover something; to envelop or muffle; to cover up or involve generally.—*To be wrapped up in,* to be bound up with or in; to be involved in; to be engrossed in or entirely devoted to (*wrapped up* in his studies).—*n.* An outer article of dress for warmth; a wrapper.—**wrapper,** rap′ėr, *n.* One who wraps; that in which anything is wrapped; an outer covering; a loose upper garment; a lady's dressing gown or the like.—**wrapping,** rap′ing, *a.* Used for wrapping (*wrapping* paper).—*n.* That in which anything is wrapped; a wrapper.

wrasse, ras, *n.* [W. *wrach.*] A genus of prickly-spined, edible fish (family Labridae), with oblong scaly bodies and a single dorsal fin, related to the parrot fish, and inhabiting temperate waters.

wrath, räth, *n.* [A.Sax. *wraeththo,* wrath, from *wráth,* wrathful, wroth; Icel. *reithi,* wrath, from *reithr,* wroth, from *rítha,* for *vritha,* to writhe or twist; Sw. and Dan. *vrede,* wrath; akin to *writhe, wreathe, wrest.*] Violent anger; vehement exasperation; indignation; rage. ∴ Syn. under ANGER.—**wrathful,** räth′fụl, *a.* Full of wrath; wroth; greatly incensed; raging; furious; impetuous.—**wrathfully,** räth′fụl•li, *adv.* In a wrathful manner.—**wrathfulness,** räth′fụl•nes, *n.* Vehement anger.

wreak, rēk, *v.t.* [A.Sax. *wrecan,* to punish, to revenge, originally to banish or drive away=D. *wreken,* to avenge or revenge; Icel. *reka,* to repel; G. *rächen,* to revenge; Goth. *wrikan,* to persecute; same root as L. *urgeo,* E. to *urge. Wretch, wreck,* are closely akin.] To revenge or avenge; to inflict or cause to take effect (to *wreak* vengeance, rage, resentment, etc.).

wreath, rēth, *n.* [A.Sax. *wraeth,* from *wrīthan,* to twist. WRITHE.] Something twisted or curled; a twist or curl; a garland; a chaplet; an ornamental twisted bandage to be worn on the head.—**wreathe,** rēTH, *v.t.*—*wreathed, wreathing.* To form into a wreath; to make or fashion by twining or twisting the parts together; to entwine; to intertwine; to surround with a wreath; to twine round; to encircle.—*v.i.* To twine circularly; to be interwoven or entwined.—**wreathen,** rē′THn, an old *pp.* Wreathed; twisted.

wreck, rek, *n.* [Same as A.Sax. *wraec,* exile, punishment (from *wrecan,* to *wreak,* originally to drive), the special meaning of shipwreck being seen in D. *wrak,* a wreck; Dan. *vrag,* O.Dan. *vrak,* a wreck, Icel. *rek* for *vrek,* Sw. *wrak,* what is drifted ashore. *Wrack,* seaweed cast up, is the same word. WRACK, WREAK.] The destruction of a vessel by being driven ashore, dashed against rocks, or the like; shipwreck; the ruins of a ship stranded or floating about; goods which, after a shipwreck, have been thrown ashore by the sea; destruction or ruin generally; a person whose constitution is quite ruined; the remains of anything destroyed, ruined, or fatally injured.—*v.t.* To cause to become a wreck; to cast away, as a vessel, by violence, collision, or otherwise; to cause to suffer shipwreck; to ruin or destroy generally, physically or morally.—**wreckage,** rek′ij, *n.* The act of wrecking; the remains of a ship or cargo that has been wrecked; material or parts recovered from any demolished building or structure.—**wrecker,** rek′ėr, *n.* One who plunders the wrecks of ships; one whose occupation is to recover cargo or goods from wrecked vessels; one engaged in the business of tearing down buildings and removing the debris: a demolisher.

wren, ren, *n.* [A.Sax. *wrenna,* a wren; allied perhaps to *wraene,* lascivious.] A name of various small birds; more especially a well-known insessorial little bird, of brisk and lively habits, with a comparatively strong and agreeable song.

wrench, rensh, *n.* [Same as A.Sax. *wrence, wrence,* deceit, fraud (a figurative meaning); allied to G. *renken,* to sprain, to wrench; O.D. *wronck,* contortion; akin *wring, wrong, wrinkle.*] A violent twist, or a pull with twisting; a sprain; an injury by twisting, as in a joint; an instrument consisting essentially of a bar of metal having jaws adapted to catch upon the head of a bolt or a nut to turn it; a screw-key; the combination of a single force and a couple in a plane at right angles to its line of action. Any system of forces whatever can be reduced to a wrench.—*v.t.* To pull with a sudden, sharp, violent jerk (*to wrench a plant out of the ground; to wrench a box open*); to twist, jerk, or tear from the normal position, as a tendon, ligament, etc.

of the body; to distort the meaning of what is said.

wrest, rest, *v.t.* [A.Sax. *wraestan,* to writhe, to twist; Icel. *reista* (for *vreista*), Dan. *vriste,* to wrest, to twist; akin to *writhe, wreathe, wrist; wrestle* is a derivative.] To twist; to wrench; to apply a violent twisting force to; to extort or bring out, as by a twisting, painful force; to force, as by torture; to turn from truth or twist from the natural meaning by violence; to pervert.—*n.* A wrench or twist; an instrument of the wrench or screw-key kind; a key to tune stringed musical instruments with.—**wrester,** res′tėr, *n.* One who wrests.

wrestle, res′l, *v.i.*—*wrestled, wrestling.* [A freq. of *wrest*; A.Sax. *wraestlian,* D. *wrastelen, worstelen,* to wrestle.] To contend by grappling, and trying to throw down; to struggle, strive, or contend.—*v.t.* To contend with in wrestling.—*n.* A bout at wrestling; a wrestling match.—**wrestler,** res′lėr, *n.*—**wrestling,** res′-ling, *n.* The sport of unarmed, hand-to-hand grappling, in which two contestants seek to throw each other.

wretch, rech, *n.* [A.Sax. *wraecca,* an outcast, an exile, from *wrecan,* to banish, to wreak. WREAK, WRECK.] A miserable person; one sunk in the deepest distress; one who is supremely unhappy; a worthless mortal; a mean, base, or vile person; often used by way of slight or ironical pity or contempt, like *thing* or *creature*.—**wretched,** rech′ed, *a.* [From *wretch*; similar in formation to *wicked*.] Miserable or unhappy; sunk into deep affliction or distress; calamitous; very afflicting; worthless; paltry; very poor or mean; despicable.—**wretchedly,** rech′ed•li, *adv.* In a wretched manner; miserably; meanly; contemptibly.—**wretchedness,** rech′ed•nes, *n.* The state or quality of being wretched.

wriggle, rig′l, *v.i.*—*wriggled, wriggling.* [Freq. from older *wrig, wrigge,* to wriggle; so D. *wriggelen,* to wriggle, a freq. from *wrikken,* Dan. *vrikke,* to wriggle; akin *wry, wrench, wring, wrong.*] To move the body to and fro with short motions like a worm or an eel; to move with writhing or twisting of the body; hence, to proceed in a mean, groveling manner; to work by paltry shifts or schemes (to *wriggle* into one's confidence).—*n.* The motion of one who wriggles; a quick twisting motion like that of a worm or an eel.—**wriggler,** rig′lėr, *n.* One who wriggles.

wright, rīt, *n.* [A.Sax. *wyrhta,* a worker, a maker, from *wyrht,* a work, from *wyrcan,* to work. WORK.] An artisan or artificer; a worker in wood; a carpenter: now chiefly used in compounds, as in ship*wright,* wheel*wright,* also play*wright.*

wring, ring, *v.t.*—pret. and pp. *wrung.* [A.Sax. *wringan,* to wring, strain, press = L.G. and D. *wringen,* Dan. *vraenge,* Sw. *vränga,* G. *ringer,* to wring, twist, etc., all nasalized forms of stem seen in *wriggle,* and in A.Sax. *wrigian,* to bend (whence *wry*), and akin to *wrong.*] To twist and squeeze or compress; to pain, as by twisting, squeezing, or racking; to torture; to distress (to *wring* one's heart); to squeeze or press out; hence, to extort or force (to *wring* a confession or money from a person).—*To wring off,* to force off by wringing or twisting.—*To wring out,* to squeeze out by twisting; to free from a liquid by wringing.—*v.i.* To writhe; to twist, as with anguish.—**wringer,** ring′ėr, *n.* One who wrings; an apparatus for forcing water from clothes, after they have been washed, by compression between rollers.

wrinkle, ring′kl, *n.* [A.Sax. *wrincle* a wrinkle = O.D. *wrinckle,* a wrinkle; a dim. form corresponding to Dan. *rynke,* Sw. *rynka,* a wrinkle; akin to *wring, wrench,* etc.] A small ridge or a furrow, formed by the shrinking or contraction of any smooth substance; a crease; a fold.—*v.t.*—*wrinkled, wrinkling.* To contract into wrinkles or furrows; to furrow; to crease.—*v.i.* To become contracted into wrinkles.—**wrinkly,** ring′kli, *a.* Somewhat wrinkled; puckered; creasy.

wrinkle, ring′kl, *n.* [Dim. from A. Sax. *wrenc, wrence,* a trick. WRENCH.] A valuable hint; a new or good idea; a notion; a device. (*Colloq.*)

wrist, rist, *n.* [A.Sax. *wrist, handwrist,* the wrist; lit. the turning joint, from *writhan,* to twist; Dan. and Sw. *vrist,* Icel. *rist* (for *vrist*), the instep; G. *rist,* the wrist, the instep. WRITHE, WREST.] The joint by which the hand is united to the arm, and by means of which the hand moves on the forearm; the carpus.—**wristband,** rist′band, *n.* The band or part of a sleeve, especially of a shirt sleeve, which covers the wrist.—**wristlock,** rist′lok, *n.* A hold upon a wrestler's wrist which makes use of his arms and hands impossible.

writ, rit, *n.* [A.Sax. *writ, gewrit,* a writing, a writ; from *wrītan,* to write.] That which is written, particularly applied to the Scriptures (holy *writ,* sacred *writ*); a formal document or instrument in writing; *law,* a precept issued by competent authority commanding a person to do a certain act therein specified.

write, rīt, *v.t.*—pret. *wrote* (formerly also *writ*); pp. *written*; ppr. *writing.* [A.Sax. *wrītan,* pret. *wrát,* pp. *writen,* to write = Icel. *ríta,* to scratch, write; Sw. *rita,* to draw, to trace; D. *rijten,* G. *reissen,* to tear. Originally it meant to scratch marks with something sharp.] To form or trace by a pen, pencil, graver, or other instrument; to produce by tracing legible characters expressive of ideas; to set down in letters or words; to inscribe; to cover with characters or letters; to make known or express by means of characters formed by the pen, etc.; to compose and produce as author; to style in writing; to entitle; *fig.* to impress deeply or durably.—*v.i.* To trace or form characters with a pen, pencil, or the like, upon paper or other material; to be engaged in literary work; to be an author; to conduct epistolary correspondence; to convey information by letter or the like.—**writer,** rī′tėr, *n.* One who writes; a member of the literary profession.—**writing,** rī′ting, *n.* The act or art of setting down words or characters on paper or other material, for the purpose of recording ideas; anything written; a literary or other composition; a manuscript; a book; an inscription.—**written,** rit′n, *a.*—**writeup,** *n.* A story, especially one written for a newspaper; copy (slang).

writhe, rīTH, *v.t.*—*writhed, writhing.* [A.Sax. *writhan,* to writhe, wreath, twist = Icel. *rítha* (for *vritha*), Dan. *vride,* Sw. *vrida,* to writhe; from same root as *worth* (verb), L. *verto,* to turn (VERSE).] To twist with violence (to *writhe* the body); to distort; to wrest.—*v.i.* To twist the body about, as in pain.

wrong, rong, *a.* [A participial form from *wring*; Dan. *vrang,* Icel. *rangr, vrangr,* wrong; D. *wrang,* sour, harsh (lit. twisting the mouth). WRING.] Not right; not fit or suitable; not according to rule, wish, design, or the like; not what ought to be.—*n.* What is not right, especially morally; a wrong or unjust act.—*adv.* In a wrong manner; erroneously; incorrectly.—*v.t.* To treat with injustice; to deal harshly or unfairly with; to do injustice to by imputation; to think ill of unfairly.—**wrongdoer,** rong•dö′ėr, *n.*—**wrongdoing,** rong•-dö′ing, *n.*—**wrongfulness,** rong′fụl•-nes, *n.*—**wrongheaded,** rong′hed•ed, *a.* Wrong; stubborn adherence to an opinion.—**wrongheadedly,** rong′-hed•ed•li, *adv.*—**wrongheadedness,** rong′hed•ed•nes, *n.*—**wrongly,** rong′-li, *adv.*—**wrongness,** rong′nes, *n.*

wroth, rạth, *a.* [A.Sax. *wráth,* angry, enraged (whence *wrath*), lit. twisted, from *writhan,* to twist or writhe. WRATH, WRITHE.] Very angry; much exasperated; wrathful.

wrought, rạt, *a.* [O.E. from pp. *worken,* to work.] Formed or fashioned, especially when beaten to a shape with a tool; hammered; highly excited (he was *wrought* up).

wrung, rung, pret. and pp. of *wring.*

wry, rī, *a.* [A.Sax. *wrigian,* to bend, to turn, to incline; akin to *wriggle* (which see).] Abnormally bent or turned to one side; twisted; distorted; crooked.—**wryly,** rī′li, *adv.* In a wry, crooked, or distorted manner.—**wryneck,** rī′nek, *n.* A twisted or distorted neck; a small bird allied to the woodpeckers: so called from the singular manner in which it twists its neck.

Wyandot, wī′an•dot, *n.* A member tribe of the Iroquois Indians.

Wyandotte, wī′an•dot, *n.* A breed of domestic fowls.

wych-elm, wich, *n.* [O.E. *wiche, wyche,* A.Sax. *wice,* a name applied to various trees; allied to *wicker.*] A variety of elm with large leaves and sometimes pendulous branches, forming a 'weeping' tree.

wye, wī, *n.* The letter Y.

wyvern, wī′vėrn, *n.* [O.Fr. *wivre, vivre* (with *n* added as in *bittern*), a viper, a dragon, from L. *vīpera,* a viper. VIPER, WEEVER.] A heraldic monster, a sort of dragon, with two wings, two legs, and a tapering body.

X

X, x, eks, the twenty-fourth letter of the English alphabet, representing the sounds *ks, gz, z, ksh, gzh.*

xanthic, zan′thik, *a.* [Gr. *xanthos*, yellow.] Tending toward a yellow color; yellowish.—*Xanthic flowers*, flowers which have yellow for their type, and which are capable of passing into red or white, but never into blue.

xanthin, zan′thin, *n.* [Gr. *zanthos*, yellow.] A yellow pigment; yellow coloring.

Xanthippe, zan•tip′ē, *n.* [Wife of Socrates.] A shrew.

xanthophyll, zan′tho•fil, *n.* [Gr. *xanthos*, yellow, *phyllon*, a leaf.] The yellow coloring matter of withering leaves.

xanthous, zan′thus, *a.* [Gr. *xanthos*, yellow.] Of the fair-haired type; having brown, auburn, yellow, flaxen, or red hair.

X chromosome, *n.* The sex chromosome carrying the factors of sex determination and usually occurring paired (*XX*) in a female and singly (*X*Y) in a male. See also Y CHROMOSOME.

xebec, zē′bek, *n.* [Sp. *xabeque*, from Turk. *sumbeki*, a xebec; Ar. *sumbûk*, a small vessel.] A small three-masted vessel having both square and lateen sails, and sometimes used in the Mediterranean.

xenogenesis, zen•o•jen′e•sis, *n.* [Gr. *xenos*, strange, and *genesis*, birth.] Heterogenesis, the production of offspring entirely unlike their parents.—**xenogenetic,** zen″o•je•net′ik, *a.* Pertaining to xenogenesis.

xenon, zen′on, *n.* [Gr. *xenos*, stranger.] A colorless, odorless, gaseous element, very rare and chemically inactive. Symbol, Xe; at. no., 54; at. wt., 131.3.

xerasia, zē•rā′zi•a, *n.* [From Gr. *xēros*, dry.] A disease of the hair, which becomes dry and ceases to grow.—**xeroderma,** zē•ro•dėr′ma, *n.* [Gr. *derma*, skin.] A morbid dryness of the skin, in its severest form constituting fish-skin disease.—**xerophthalmia,** zē•rof•thal′mi•a, *n.* [Gr. *ophthalmos*, the eye.] A dry, red soreness or itching of the eyes.

xerophyte, ze′ro•fīt, *n.* [Gr. *xēros*, dry, *phyton*, a plant.] A plant adapted to live in surroundings where water is scarce (deserts) or difficult to absorb (moors).

xiphoid, zif′oid, *a.* [Gr. *xiphos*, a sword, and *eidos*, likeness.] Shaped like or resembling a sword.

Xmas, *n.* (*X*, symbol for Christ; *mas*, contraction of Mass.) Christmas (*Colloq.*).

X-ray, eks′rā, *n.* [Called *X*, unknown, because of its nature previously being unknown.] Electromagnetic radiation of very short wavelength, produced (usually) by bombarding a metal target with electrons in a vacuum, used to penetrate solids, as in medical treatment, taking photographs of the inside of the body, etc.—*v.t.* To examine or treat by X-ray.—**X-ray photograph,** *n.* A radiograph made by utilizing X-ray.—**X-ray therapy,** *n.* Medical treatment, as for cancer, involving the use of X-ray.—**X-ray tube,** *n.* A vacuum tube in which X-rays are produced.

xylem, zī′lem, *n.* Woody tissue, in botany opposed to *phloem.*

xylene (xylol), zī′lēn (zī′lol), *n.* [Gr. *xylon*, wood.] A transparent liquid distilled from coal tar, and used in microscopic work as a solvent.

xylite, zī′līt, *n.* [Gr. *xylon*, wood.] Ligniform asbestos, mountain wood, or rock wood.—**xylograph,** zī′lo•graf, *n.* [Gr. *xylon*, and *graphō*, to write or engrave.] A wood engraving.—**xylographer,** zī•log′ra•fėr, *n.* One who engraves on wood.—**xylographic, xylographical,** zī•lo•graf′ik, zī•lo•graf′i•kal, *a.* Relating to xylography.—**xylography,** zī•log′ra•fi, *n.* Wood engraving; a process of decorative painting on wood.—**xyloid,** zī′loid, *a.* [Gr. *xylon*, and *eidos*, form.] Having the nature of wood; resembling wood.—**xylophagous,** zī•lof′a•gus, *a.* [Gr. *phagō*, to eat.] Eating or feeding on wood.—**xylophone,** zī′lo•fōn, zil′o•fōn, *n.* [Gr. *xylon*, wood, *phōnē*, sound.] A musical instrument using wooden bars graduated to produce the notes of the scale when struck with a small wooden hammer.—**xyloretine,** zī′lō•rē•tin, *n.* [Gr. *rhetine*, resin.] A resinous substance found in connection with the pine trunks of certain peat mosses.

Y

Y, y, wī, the twenty-fifth letter of the alphabet, sometimes a vowel, sometimes a consonant.

yacht, yot, *n.* [From O.D. *jacht*, Mod.D. *jagt*, a yacht, a chase, from *jagen*, G. *jagen*, Dan, *jage*, to hunt.] A light and elegantly fitted up vessel, used for either pleasure trips or racing, or as an offshore residence, now usually motor-powered.—*v.i.* To sail or cruise in a yacht.—**yachting** yot′ing, *a.* Belonging to a yacht or yachts.—**yachtsman,** yots′man, *n.* One who keeps or sails a yacht.

yager, yā′gėr, *n.* [G. *jager*, lit. a huntsman, from *jägen*, to hunt. YACHT.] A soldier in certain regiments of light infantry in the armies of various German states.

Yahoo, yä′hö, *n.* [Coined by Swift.] A name given by Swift, in *Gulliver's Travels*, to a race of brutes having the form of man and all his degrading passions; [*not cap.*] hence, a rude, boorish, uncultivated character.

Yahweh, yä′wā, *n.* [Heb.] Jehovah.

yak, yak, *n.* [Thibetan.] A kind of ox with long silky hair, a bushy mane, and horse-like tail, inhabiting Tibet and the Himalayas.

yam, yam, *n.* [Pg. *inhame*, a yam; Senegal *nyami.*] A large esculent tuber or root produced by a genus of tropical plants, forming a wholesome and nutritious food.

yammer, yam′ėr, *n.* [O.E. *yomeren*, to murmur, to be sad, from A.Sax. *gēomrian*, to be sad.] To talk constantly; to chatter; to whimper; to whine.—*v.t.* To say in complaint.

yang, yäng, *n.* [Chinese (Mandarin).] The active, or male, principle, which in Chinese thought is said to produce (with the female counterpart, *yin*) all that exists.

yank, yangk, *n.* [Origin unknown.] A sudden pull; a jerk.—*v.t.* To pull away from with a sudden, strong movement.—*v.i.* To pull with a sudden movement.

Yank, yangk, *n.* [A shortening of *Yank*ee.] Yankee.

Yankee, yang′kē, *n.* [Probably a corrupt pronunciation of some Dutch personal name starting with *Jan*; dates from before 1683.] A cant name for a citizen of New England; often applied more widely to natives of the United States.

yap, yap, *v.i.* [Imitative of sound.] To yelp; to bark.—*n.* The cry of a dog; a bark; a yelp.

yapok, yap′ok, *n.* An opossum of Brazil and Guiana, aquatic in its habits and resembling a small otter.

yard, yärd, *n.* [A.Sax. *gyrd, gird*, a rod, a yard measure=D. *garde*, G. *gerte*, a rod, a twig; Goth. *gazds*, a goad; cog. with L. *hasta*, a spear.] The British and American standard measure of length, equal to 3 feet or 36 inches, the foot being practically the unit; also 9 square feet and 27 cubic feet (the square and cubic yard); a long cylindrical piece of timber in a ship, slung crosswise to a mast, and supporting and extending a sail.—**yardarm,** *n.* The end of a ship's yard.—*Yardarm and yardarm*, the situation of two ships lying along-side of each other so near that their yardarms cross or touch.—**yardmaster,** yärd″mas′tėr, *n.* One in charge of a lumber yard or a railroad yard.—**yardstick,** *n.* A stick, 3 feet in length, used as a measure of cloth, etc.

yard, yärd, *n.* [A.Sax. *geard*, a yard, a court, etc.; Icel. *garthr*, an enclosure (E. *garth*); Dan. and D. *gaard*, a garden; G. *garten*, a garden; same root as L. *hortus*, a garden. Akin *garden, gird*, to surround. *Orchard* contains this word.] A small piece of enclosed ground adjoining a house; an enclosure within which any work or industry is carried on (a brick-*yard*, a dock*yard*, etc.).—*v.t.* To enclose (as cattle) in a yard.

yare, yâr, *a.* [A.Sax. *gearu*, prepared ready, yare; akin *garb, gear.*] Ready; quick; dexterous.

yarn, yärn, *n.* [A.Sax. *gearn* yarn= D. *garen*, Icel. Sw. Dan. and G. *garn* yarn; comp. Icel. *garnir*, intestines; Gr. *chordē*, a chord, an intestine.] Any kind of thread prepared for weaving into cloth; one of the threads of which a rope is composed; *fig.* a long story or tale (colloq.).

yarrow, yar′ō, *n.* [A.Sax. *gearwe*, D. *gerw*, G. *garbe*, O.G. *garwe*, yarrow.] An odorous herb, also called *Milfoil.*

yataghan, yat′a•gan, *n.* [Turk.] A dagger-like saber about 2 feet long, the handle without a cross guard, worn in Mohammedan countries.

yaw, ya̤, *v.i.* [Comp. prov. G. *gagen*, to rock, to move unsteadily.] To steer wild; to deviate from the line of her course in steering: said of a ship.—*n.* A temporary deviation of a ship or vessel from the line of her course.

yawl, ya̤l, *n.* [From D. *jol*, a yawl, a skiff; Sw. *julle*, Dan. *jolle*, a jolly boat, a yawl. *Jolly* in *jolly boat* is this word.] A small ship's boat, usually rowed by four or six oars; a jolly boat; the smallest boat used by fishermen.

yawl, ya̤l, *v.i.* [Akin to *yowl, yell.*] To cry out; to howl; to yell.

yawn, ya̤n, *v.i.* [A.Sax. *gánian*, to yawn, to gape; akin Sc. *gant*, to yawn; Gr. *gāhnen*, to yawn; from root seen in Gr. *chainō*, L. *hio*, to gape; also in G. *gans*, E. *gander*, *goose*. From same root are *chasm*, *chaos*.] To have the mouth open involuntarily through drowsiness or dullness; to gape; to open wide; to stand open, as a chasm or gulf, or the like.—*n.* An involuntary opening of the mouth from drowsiness; a gaping or opening wide.

yaws, ya̤z, *n.* [African *yaw*, a raspberry.] A contagious disease of the African races characterized by cutaneous tumors, growing to the size of a raspberry.

Y chromosome, *n.* A sex chromosome that occurs in male cells and was once thought to carry the factors determining maleness; in species of animals having a differentiation between sex chromosomes, the mate of the X chromosome. See also X CHROMOSOME.

ye, yē, *pron.* [A.Sax. *gé*, ye, you, nom. pl. corresponding to *thú*, thou; D. *gij* Dan. and Sw. *i* Goth. *jus.* YOU.] Properly the nominative plural of the second personal pronoun but in later times also used as an objective; now used only in the sacred and solemn style, in common discourse and writing *you* being exclusively used.

yea, yā *adv.* [A.Sax. *geá*, yea, indeed =Icel. *já*, D. Dan. Sw. and G. *ja*, Goth. *ja, jai*, yea, yes; allied to Goth. *jah*, and; L. *jam*, now. YES.] Yes: the opposite of *nay*; also used like nay=not this alone, not only so but also.

yean, yēn, *v.t.* and *i.* [A.Sax. *eánian*, *eacnian*, from *eácen*, gravid, lit. increased, being pp. of *eacan*, to increase, to *eke.* EKE.] To bring forth young, as a goat or sheep; to lamb.—**yeanling,** yēn′ling, *n.* A lamb; an eanling.

year, yēr, *n.* [A.Sax. *geár*, *gér*=D. *jaar*, L.G. *jôr*, G. *jahr*, Goth. *jêr*, Icel. ár, Dan. *aar*; cog. Slav. *jaro*, spring; Zend *yâre*, a year. Perhaps from root *i*, to go, seen in L. *eo*, *ire*, to go.] The period of time during which the earth makes one complete revolution in its orbit, comprehending what are called the twelve calendar months, or 365 days from January 1 to December 31.—*Civil year*, the tropical or solar year. —*Common year*, a year of 365 days, as distinguished from *leap year*.—*Ecclesiastical year*, from Advent to Advent.—*Leap year.* LEAP.—*Lunar year*, a period of 12 lunar months, or 354 days.—*Tropical* or *solar year*, the period from the time the sun is on one of the tropics till its return again to it, being 365 days, 5 hours, 48 minutes, 46 seconds.—*Year of grace*, any year of the Christian era. —**yearbook,** yēr′bu̇k, *n.* A book published every year, each issue supplying fresh information on matters in regard to which changes are continually taking place.—**yearling,** yēr′ling, *n.* An animal one year old or in the second year of his age.—*a.* Being a year old.—**yearly,** yēr•li, *a.* Annual; happening every year.—*adv.* Annually; once a year.

yearn, yėrn, *v.i.* [A.Sax. *geornian*, *gyrnan*, to yearn, from *georn*, desirous; Icel. *gjarn*, eager, whence *girna*, to desire; Goth. *gairns*, desirous, *gairnjan*, to long for; Dan. *gierne*, D. *gaarne*, G. *gern*, willingly.] To feel mental uneasiness from longing desire; to be filled with eager longing; to have a wistful feeling.—**yearning,** yėr′ning, *a.* Longing; having longing desire.—*n.* The feeling of one who yearns; a strong feeling of tenderness, pity, or longing desire.—**yearningly,** yėr′-ning•li, *adv.*

yeast, yēst, *n.* [O.E. *yest*, from A.Sax. *gist*, akin to M.H.G. *jest*, foam, and to Gr. *zein*, to boil.] Barm; ferment; cells of a culture of a species of *Saccharomyces*, such as *Saccharomyces cerevisiae*, or brewers yeast, a byproduct from brewing.—*German yeast*, common yeast collected, drained, and pressed till nearly dry.—*Patent yeast*, yeast collected from a wort of malt and hop, and treated similarly to German yeast.—*Artificial yeast*, a dough of flour and a small quantity of common yeast made into small cakes and dried, which, if kept free from moisture, long retains its fermentative property.—**yeasty,** yēs′-ti, *a.*

yelk, yelk, *n.* The yolk of an egg.

yell, yel, *v.i.* [A.Sax. *gellan*, *gyllan*, to yell=Icel. *gella*, *gjalla*, D. *gillen*, to yell; G. *gellen*, to resound; allied to A.Sax. *galan*, to sing, whence *-gale* in *nightingale.*] To cry out with a sharp, disagreeable noise; to shriek hideously; to cry or scream as with agony or horror.—*n.* A sharp, loud, harsh outcry; a scream or cry of horror, distress, or agony.

yellow, yel′ō, *a.* [A.Sax. *geolo*, *geolu*, yellow; akin D. *geel*, G. *gelb*, Icel. *gulr*, Dan. and Sw. *guul*, yellow; from same root as *gold.* Gr. *chloē*, green herb, *cholē*, bile (cog. with E. *hall*).] Being of a pure bright golden color, or of a kindred hue; traitorous, cowardly (*slang*).—*Yellow berries*, called also *French berries*, the fruit of a species of buckthorn, used by dyers and painters for staining yellow.—*Yellow journalism*, a type of writing and press reporting which stresses sensational and unpleasant or horrifying aspects and details.—*Yellow ocher*, an earthy pigment colored by the oxide of iron.—*Yellow soap*, a common soap composed of tallow, resin, and soda, to which some palm oil is occasionally added.—*n.* One of the prismatic colors; a bright golden color.—*v.t.* To render yellow. —*v.i.* To grow yellow.—**yellow fever,** *n.* An infectious febrile disease common in the West Indies and neighboring regions, attended with yellowness of the skin, caused by a filterable virus and transmitted by the bite of the *Aedes* (*Stegomyia*) mosquito.—**yellowhammer,** yel″ō-ham′ėr, *n.* A passerine songbird of Europe, called also *Yellow Bunting*, from its predominantly yellow plumage.—**yellow jacket,** *n.* A wasp common to America, having bright yellow stripes.—**yellow metal,** *n.* A sheathing alloy of copper and zinc; Muntz's metal.—**yellow pine,** *n.* A North American tree, the wood of which is largely employed and is extensively exported.—**yellowthroat,** yell″ō•thrōt′, *n.* A small North American songbird of the warbler species.

yelp, yelp, *v.i.* [O.E. *yelpen*, *gelpen*, A.Sax. *gilpan*, to boast; Icel. *gjálpa*, to yelp; allied to *yell.*] To utter a sharp or shrill bark; to give a sharp, quick cry, as a dog, either in eagerness or in pain or fear.—*n.* A sharp bark or cry caused by fear or pain.

yen, yen, *n.* [Japanese.] A monetary unit of Japan, equal to 100 sen.

yen, yen, *n.* [Chinese (Cantonese) *yan*, craving.] A craving; a desire.—*v.i.*—*yenned*, *yenning.* To desire (he *yenned* for some candy).

yeoman, yō′man, *n.* pl. **yeomen,** yō′-men. [O.E. *yeman*, *yoman*; supposed to be equivalent to Fris. *gaman*, *gamon*, a villager, a man of a *ga* or village, from *ga*=G. *gau*, Goth. *gawi*, a district.] In England a man of small estate in land, not ranking as one of the gentry; one who farms his own land; a farmer; a member of the yeomanry cavalry.—*Yeoman of the guard*, in England, a bodyguard of the sovereign, habited in the costume of Henry VIII's time, and commanded by a captain and other officers.—**yeomanry,** yō′-man•ri, *n.* Yeomen collectively.

yes, yes, *adv.* [A.Sax. *gese*, *gise*, from *geá*, yea, and *sí*, *sý*, be it so, let it be, 3d sing. pres. subj. of the substantive verb in A.Sax.=G. *sei*, let it be; akin to L. *sim*, may it be; from root *as.* YEA, AM, ARE.] A word which expresses affirmation or consent: opposed to *no.*

yest, yest, *n.* Same as *Yeast.*

yester, yes′tėr, *a.* [A.Sax. *geostra*, *giestra*, *gystra*, yesterday's, *geostran daeg*, yesterday; *gystran niht*, yesternight; D. *gisteren*, G. *gestern*, yesterday; Goth. *gistra*, *gistra dagis*, tomorrow. These are comparative forms, applied to L. *hesternus*, of yesterday, and to Gr. *chthes*, Skr. *hyas*, yesterday.] Belonging to the day preceding the present; next before the present; mostly in composition.—**yesterday,** yes′tėr•di, *n.* The day next before the present; often used for time not long gone by. *Yesterday, yesternight,* etc., are used without the preposition *on* or *during.*—**yestereve,** yes′tėr•ēv, *n.* The evening last past.—**yestermorn, yestermorning,** yes′tėr•morn, yes•tėr•mor′ning, *n.* The morn or morning last past.—**yesternight,** yes′tėr•nīt, *n.* The night last past.

yet, yet, *adv.* [A.Sax. *get, git,* yet, still; equivalent etymologically to *yea to* or *yea too.*] In addition; over and above; further; still; used especially with comparatives (*yet* more surprising); at this or at that time, as formerly; now or then, as at a previous period (while *yet* young); at or before some future time; before all is done (he'll suffer *yet*); thus far; hitherto (a letter not *yet* sent off); often accompanied by *as* in this sense (I have not met him *as yet*); though the case be such; nevertheless.—*conj.* Nevertheless; notwithstanding; however.

yew, yū, *n.* [A.Sax. *iw,* the yew; O.H.G. *iwa,* G. *eibe,* D. *iif,* Icel. *ýr*; cog. W. *yw, ywen,* Armor. *ivin,* Corn. *hivin,* the yew.] An evergreen tree allied to the conifers, yielding a hard and durable timber used for cabinet work and formerly for making bows; frequently planted in churchyards, and thus associated with death, perhaps from its poisonous leaves.

Yiddish, yid′ish, *n.* [Yiddish, *yidish,* shortening of *yidish daytsch,* Jewish German.] A German language spoken by Jews, primarily in eastern Europe and in places to which Jews from eastern Europe have migrated, usually written in Hebrew characters. —**Yiddish,** yid′ish, *a.*

yield, yēld, *v.t.* [A.Sax. *gildan, gieldar,* to yield, pay, render=Icel. *gjalda,* Dan. *gjelde,* to yield, Sw. *gälla,* to be of consequence; D. *gelden,* G. *gelten,* to be worth, to avail, etc.; akin *guild.*] To give in return or by way of recompense; to produce as return for labor or capital; to produce generally; to bring forth, give out, or furnish (trees *yield* fruit); to afford; to grant or give (to *yield* consent); to give up, as to superior power; to relinquish; to surrender: in this sense often followed by *up.*—*To yield up the ghost* or *life,* to die.—*v.i.* To give way, as to superior force; to submit; to surrender; to give way, as to entreaty, argument, etc.; to comply; to consent; to give place, as inferior in rank or excellence.—*n.* Amount yielded; product; return; particularly product resulting from growth or cultivation.—**yielder,** yēl′dėr, *n.*—**yielding,** yēl′ding, *a.* Ready to submit, comply, or yield; compliant; unresisting.—**yieldingly,** yēl′ding•li, *adv.*

yodel, yodle, yō′dl, *v.t.* and *i.* [German Swiss.] To sing by continuously and suddenly changing from a chest voice to a falsetto voice.

yoga, yō′ga, *n.* [*Skr.,* lit., union.] [Cap.] a Hindu philosophy that teaches the suppression of all activity of the body so that the self may achieve distinction, and thus liberation, from the body; a system of exercises aimed at attaining control over body and mind.

yogurt, yoghurt, yō′gėrt, *n.* [Turk.]A thick, acidic milk food made from fermented milk, often flavored.

yoicks, yoiks, *interj.* An old foxhunting cry.

yoke, yōk, *n.* [A.Sax. *geoc, ioc,* a yoke=D. *juk, jok,* G. *joch,* Goth. *juk,* Icel. and Sw. *ok,* Dan. *aag*; cog. L. *jugum,* Gr. *zygon,* Skr. *yuga,* a yoke, from a root meaning to join, seen in Skr. *yuj,* to join; L. *jungo,* to join. JOIN.] A part of the gear or tackle of draft animals, particularly oxen, passing across their necks and so that two are connected for drawing; a pair of draft animals, especially oxen, yoked together; something resembling a yoke in form or use; a frame to fit the shoulders and neck of a person for carrying pails or the like; *fig.* servitude, slavery, or burden imposed; something which couples or binds together; a bond of connection; a tie.—*v.t.*—*yoked, yoking.* To put a yoke on; to join in a yoke; to couple; to join with another.—*v.i.* To be joined together.—**yokefellow,** *n.* One associated with another in labor; one connected with another by marriage; a partner; a mate.

yokel, yō′kl, *n.* [Perhaps from *yoke*= one who drives yoked animals, or akin to *gawk.*] A rustic or countryman; a bumpkin.

yolk, yōk, *n.* [A.Sax. *geoleca,* lit. the yellow of the egg, from *geolu,* yellow. YELLOW.] The yellow part of an egg; the vitellus; the yelk; the unctuous secretion from the skin of sheep which renders the pile soft and pliable.

Yom Kippur, yäm′kip″ėr, *n.* [Heb. *yōm,* day, and *kippūr,* atonement.] A Jewish holiday observed by fasting on the 10th day of the Jewish month, Tishri.

yon, yon, *a.* [A.Sax. *geon,* yon, that; Goth. *jains,* G. *jener,* that; of pronominal origin, and akin to Skr. *yas,* who.] That; those; referring to an object at a distance; yonder: now chiefly used in the poetic style.—**yonder,** yon′dėr, *a.* Being at a distance within view; that or those, referring to persons or things at a distance.—*adv.* At or in that place there.

Yorkshire pudding, *n.* [From *Yorkshire,* England.] A pudding made with a batter of eggs, flour, and milk, which is baked in meat drippings.

Yorkshire terrier, *n.* [From *Yorkshire,* England.] A dog having short legs, a long body, and long hair that is bluish silver except on the head and chest, which are tan.

you, yö, *pron.* [A.Sax. *eów,* dat. and acc. pl. of the pronoun of the second person, *ye* being properly the nom. pl.; O.Sax. *iu,* D. *u,* you, *gij,* ye; O.H.G. *iu,* you, *iuwar,* your; cog. Skr. *yuyam,* you. YE.] The person or persons being addressed; pronoun of the second person.

young, yung, *a.* [A.Sax. *geong, giung, iung*=D. *jong,* G. *jung,* Goth. *juggs,* Icel. *ungr, jungr,* Dan. and Sw. *ung*; cog. L. *juvenis* (whence *juvenile*), Skr. *juvan,* young.] Being in the first or early stage of life or growth; not yet arrived at maturity; not old; being in the early part of existence; not yet far advanced; having the appearance of early life; fresh or vigorous; having little experience; raw; green; pertaining to one's early life.—*n.* pl. The offspring of an animal collectively.—*With young,* pregnant; gravid.—**young-eyed,** yung′īd, *a.* Having the fresh bright eyes or look of youth.—**youngish,** yung′ish, *a.* Somewhat young.—**youngling,** yung′ling, *n.* An animal in the first part of life; also, a young person. —**youngster,** yung′stėr, *n.* A young person; a lad.—**younker,** yung′kėr, *n.* A young fellow; a lad; a youngster.

your, yu̧r, *a.* [A.Sax. *eówer*=D. *uwer,* G. *euer*; the possessive corresponding to *ye, you,* and therefore properly plural (*thy* being the singular), but now like *you* used as singular or plural.] Pertaining or belonging to you.—**yours,** yu̧rz, *poss. pron.* A double possessive of *you*; that or those which belong to you; belonging to you; used with or without direct reference to a preceding noun; your property; your friends or relations.—**yourself,** yu̧r•self′, *pron.* pl. **yourselves,** yu̧r•selvz′. You, not another or others; you, in your own person or individually: used distinctively or reflexively.

youth, yūth, *n.* [A. Sax. *geóguth,* for *geonguth* (=*youngth, young* and *-th*), from *geong,* young. YOUNG.] The state or quality of being young; youthfulness; the part of life between childhood and manhood; a young man; a stripling or lad; young persons collectively.—**youthful,** yūth′fu̧l, *a.* Being in the early stage of life; young; pertaining to the early part of life; suitable to the first part of life; fresh or vigorous, as in youth.—**youthfully,** yūth′fu̧l•li, *adv.* In a youthful manner.—**youthfulness,** yūth′fu̧l•nes, *n.* The state or quality of being youthful.

yowl, youl, *v.i.* [Akin to *yell.*] To give a long distressful or mournful cry, as a dog.—*n.* A long distressful or mournful cry, as that of a dog.

yperite, ēp′ėr•īt, *n.* [After the Belgian town of *Ypres.*] Mustard gas.

ytterbium, i•tėr′bi•um, *n.* A rare metallic element, one of the rare-earth metals. Symbol, Yb; at, no., 70; at. wt., 173.04.

yttria, it′ri•a, *n.* A metallic oxide or earth, having the appearance of a white powder; the protoxide of yttrium, discovered in 1794 in a mineral found at *Ytterby* in Sweden, whence the name.

yttrium, i′trē•um, *n.* [N.L. from *yttria,* yttrium oxide.] A metallic element of the rare-earth group, occurring in minerals. Symbol, Y; at. no., 39; at. wt., 88.905.

yucca, yuk'ka, *n.* [From some American tongue.] A genus of American plants of the lily family, of considerable size, with white flowers in large panicles, and long rigid, pointed leaves.

yule, yöl, *n.* [A.Sax. *geól, giúl, iúl, geóhol,* Christmas; Icel. *jól,* Dan. *juul,* Sw. *jul;* originally a pagan festival; etymol. doubtful. *Jolly* is from this through the French.] The Old English and still the Scotch and Northern English name for Christmas.—**yule log, yule block,** *n.* A large log of wood forming the basis of a Christmas fire in the olden time.—**yuletide,** *n.* The time or season of Yule or Christmas.

Z

Z, z, zē, the last letter of the English alphabet, equivalent to the s in *wise, ease,* etc.

zaffer, zaf'ėr, *n.* [Fr. *zafre, safre, saffre,* Sp. *zafre;* probably of Arabic origin.] Impure oxide of cobalt; the residuum of cobalt after the sulfur, arsenic, and other volatile matters have been expelled by calcination, much used by enamelers and porcelain manufacturers as a blue color.

zamia, zā'mi•a, *n.* [L. *zamia,* a fir cone.] A genus of plants of the cycad order, the stem of some of which yields a starchy pith used for food.

zamindar, ze•mēn•där', *n.* Same as *Zemindar.*

zany, zā'ni, *n.* [Fr. *zani,* from It. *zanni, zane,* a zany or clown; originally simply a familiar and abbreviated pronunciation of *Giovanni,* John.] A buffoon or merry-andrew.—**zanyism,** zā'ni•izm, *n.* The character or practice of a zany; buffoonery.

zareba, za•rē'ba, *n.* A temporary camping place surrounded by a fence of bushes, stones, etc., used in the Sudan.

zax, zaks, *n.* [A.Sax. *seax,* Icel. *sax,* a knife of short sword.] An instrument used by slaters for cutting and dressing slates.

zeal, zēl, *n.* [Fr. *zèle,* from L. *zelus,* Gr. *zēlos,* zeal; from stem of *zeō,* to boil, which is akin to E. *yeast,* JEALOUS.] Passionate ardor in the pursuit of anything; eagerness in any cause or behalf, good or bad; earnestness; fervency; enthusiasm. —**zealot,** zel'ot, *n.* One who is zealous or full of zeal; one carried away by excess of zeal; a fanatical partisan.—**zealotry,** zel'ot•ri, *n.* Behavior of a zealot; excessive zeal; fanaticism.—**zealous,** zel'us, *a.* Inspired with zeal; warmly engaged or ardent in the pursuit of an object; fervent; eager; earnest.—**zealously,** zel'us•li, *adv.* —**zealousness,** zel'us•nes, *n.*

zebec, zebeck, zē'bek, *n.* Same as *Xebec.*

zebra, zē'bra, *n.* [A native African word.] A quadruped of southern Africa allied to the horse and ass, nearly as large as a horse, white, striped with numerous brownish-black bands.—**zebrawood,** *n.* A South American wood somewhat resembling the skin of a zebra in color, used by cabinetmakers.

zebu, zē'bū, *n.* [The Indian name.] A species of ox found extensively in India, and regarded with veneration by the Hindus, having one, or more rarely two, humps of fat on the shoulders.

zechin, zek'in, *n.* [It. *zecchino,* Fr. *sequin.* SEQUIN.] A sequin.

zedoary, zed'ō•e•ri, *n.* [Sp. and Pg. *zedoaria,* from Ar. and Pers. *zedwâr,* zedoary.] An Asiatic root used for similar purposes as ginger.

zemindar, ze•mēn•där', *n.* [Per. *zemindâr,* a landholder—*zemin,* land, and *dār,* holding, a holder.] In India, a landholder or landed proprietor, subject to the payment of the land tax or government land revenue.

Zen, zen, *n.* [Japanese.] A movement within Buddhism that emphasizes the direct attainment of enlightenment.

zenana, ze•nä'na, *n.* [Hind. *zananah,* from Per. *zan,* a woman.] The portion of a house exclusively for the females in a family of good caste in India.

Zend-Avesta, zend•a•ves'ta, *n.* [Fr. from M.Per. *Avastāk va Zand,* Avesta and Commentary.] The collective name for the sacred writings of the Parsees, ascribed to Zoroaster.

zenith, zē'nith, *n.* [Fr. *zenith,* from Sp. *zenit, zenith,* a corruption of Ar. *samt, sent,* abbreviated for *samt-ur-ras, samt-er-ras,* way of the head, zenith, *samt* being a way (*ras,* head). Akin *azimuth.*] The vertical point of the heavens at any place, or point right above a spectator's head; the upper pole of the celestial horizon; *fig.* the highest point of a person's fortune; culminating point. —*Zenith distance,* the arc intercepted between a heavenly body and the zenith.—**zenithal,** zē'nith•al, *a.*

zeolite, zē'o•līt, *n.* [Gr. *zeō,* to boil, *lithos,* stone; so named from boiling and swelling when heated by the blowpipe.] A generic name of hydrated double silicates in which the principal bases are aluminum and calcium.

zephyr, zephyrus, zef'ėr, zef'i•rus, *n.* [L. *zephyrus,* from Gr. *zephyros,* allied to *zophos,* darkness, gloom, the west.] The west wind; also poetically, any gentle breeze.

zeppelin, zep'lin, *n.* [From Count Ferdinand von *Zeppelin,* German manufacturer.] A cylindrical dirigible balloon having a rigid frame structure and internal gas cells.

zero, zē'rō, *n.* [Fr. *zéro,* It. and Sp. *zero,* by contraction from Ar. *sifr,* a cipher; the same word as *cipher.*] No number or quantity; number or quantity diminished to nothing; a cipher; nothing; *phys.* the point of a graduated instrument at which its scale commences; the starting point on a graduated scale, generally represented by the symbol 0.—*a.* Pertaining to zero; lacking.—*Ceiling zero,* having vision limited to 50 feet or less.—*Zero visibility,* having visibility limited to 165 feet or less. —*v.t.* To adjust the zero setting of (*zero-in* a rifle); to concentrate fire power in a specific area.—*v.i.* To adjust fire to a single target; to focus attention.

zest, zest, *n.* [Fr. *zeste,* the peel of an orange or lemon; from L. *schistus,* Gr. *schistos,* split, divided, from *schizō,* to split (whence also *schism, schist*).] Originally, a piece of orange or lemon peel, used to give flavor to liquor, hence, that which serves to enhance enjoyment; a relish; keen enjoyment; gusto.

zeta, zā'ta, zē'ta, *n.* [Gr. *zēta.*] The sixth letter of the Greek alphabet.

zeugma, zūg'ma, *n.* [Gr. *zeugma,* from *zeugnymi,* to join, same root as E. *yoke.*] A figure in grammar in which two nouns are joined to a verb suitable to only one of them, but suggesting another verb suitable to the other noun; or in which an adjective is similarly used with two nouns.

Zeus, zūs, *n.* The supreme divinity among the Greeks; generally treated as the equivalent of the Roman Jupiter.

zibet, zib'et, *n.* [CIVET.] An animal closely akin to the civet.

zigzag, zig'zag, *n.* [Fr. *zig-zag,* from G. *zick-zack,* reduplicated from *zacke,* a tooth or sharp point.] Something that consists of straight lines or pieces with short sharp turns or angles; a zigzag molding; a chevron.—*a.* Having sharp and quick turns or flexures.—*v.i.*—*zigzagged, zigzagging.* To move or advance in a zigzag fashion; to form zigzags.

zinc, zingk, *n.* [Fr. *zinc,* G., Sw., and Dan. *zink;* allied to G. *zinn,* tin.] A bluish-white metallic element occurring in combination, used as protective coating, in alloys, as reducing agent, in zinc compounds, etc.—symbol, Zn; at. no., 30; at. wt., 65.37.—*v.t.*—*zinked, zinking.* To coat or cover with zinc.—**zinc blende,** *n.* Native sulfide of zinc, a brittle transparent or translucent mineral.—**zincite,** zingk'īt, *n.* Native oxide of zinc.—**zincographer,** zing•kog'ra•fėr, *n.* One who practices zincography.—**zincographic, zincographical,** zing•ko•graf'ik, zing•ko•graf'i•kal, *a.* Relating to zincography. —**zincography,** zing•kog'ra•fi, *n.* An art similar to lithography, the stone printing surface of the latter being replaced by that of a plate of polished zinc.—**zincous,** zingk'us, *a.* Pertaining to zinc, or to the positive pole of a voltaic battery.—**zinc white,** *n.* Oxide of zinc, a pigment now largely substituted for white lead as being more permanent and not poisonous.

zingiberaceous, zinziberaceous, zin'ji•bėr•ā"shus, zin'zi•bėr•ā"shus, *a.* [L. *zingiber, zinziber,* ginger.] Pertaining to ginger, or to the order of plants of which ginger is the type.

Zionism, zī'on•ism, *n.* [From *Mount*

Zion, in Jerusalem.] A Jewish national movement for the re-establishment of the Jews in Israel.

zipper, zip′ėr, *n.* [From the trademark.] A fastener consisting of two fabric strips set with metal, plastic, nylon, etc., teeth that pass through a center piece and that interlock and close when the center piece is slid up between them.

zircon, zėr′kon, *n.* [Pers. *zargun*, Ar. *zarqun*, gold-colored.] A mineral ($ZrSiO_4$) of a zirconium silicate occurring in lustrous brown or gray prisms, often used as a gem.

zirconium, zėr•kō′ni•um, *n.* [N.L. from *zircon*.] A white, soft, ductile, metallic element obtained from the zircon and other minerals, used in steel production and as structural material for nuclear reactors. Symbol, Zr; at. no., 40; at. wt., 91.22.

zither, zithern, zith′ėr, zith′ėrn, *n.* [G., from L. *cithara*. CITHARA.] A flat, stringed musical instrument consisting of a sounding box with thirty-one strings, played with the right hand, the strings being stopped with the left.

zodiac, zō′di•ak, *n.* [Fr. *zodiaque*, L. *zodiacus*, the zodiac, from Gr. *zōdiakos* (*kyklos*, circle, understood), from *zōdion*, dim. of *zōon*, an animal.] An imaginary belt or zone in the heavens, extending about 8° on each side of the ecliptic, within which the motions of the sun, moon, and principal planets are confined.—**zodiacal,** zō•dī′a•kal, *a.* Pertaining to the zodiac.—*Zodiacal light*, a luminous tract lying nearly in the ecliptic, its base being on the horizon, seen at certain seasons either in the west after sunset or in the east before sunrise.

zombi, zombie, zom′bi, *n.* [West African.] A voodoo snake god; the power that, according to voodoo belief, can enter and reanimate a dead body; any of various mixed drinks, usually containing rum, fruit juice, and brandy.

zone, zōn, *n.* [L. *zona*, a belt or girdle, a zone of the earth, from Gr. *zōnē*, a girdle, from *zōnnymi*, to gird.] A girdle or belt; any well-marked band or stripe running round an object; *geog.* one of the five great divisions of the earth, bounded by circles parallel to the Equator, named according to the temperature prevailing in each, the *torrid zone*, two *temperate zones*, and two *frigid zones*; *nat. hist.* any well-defined belt within which certain forms of plant or animal life are confined.—**zoned,** zōnd, *a.* Wearing a zone; having zones or bands resembling zones.—**zonule,** zō′nūl, *n.* A little zone, band, or belt.—**zonal,** zō′nal, *a.*—**zonate,** zō′nāt, *a. Bot.* marked with zones or concentric bands of color.

zoo, zö, *n.* [Shortening of *zoological garden*.] A park or zoological garden in which animals are kept for public exhibition.

zooglea, zō′o•glē″a, *n.* [Gr. *zōon*, an animal, *gloia*, glue.] An aggregation of bacteria in a slimy colony.

zoography, zō•og′ra•fi, *n.* [Gr. *zōon*, an animal, and *graphō*, to describe.] A description of animals, their forms and habits.—**zoographer,** zō•og′ra•fėr, *n.* One who describes animals.—**zoographic, zoographical,** zō•o•graf′ik, zō•o•graf′i•kal. *a.* Pertaining to zoography.

zooid, zō′oid, *a.* [Gr. *zōon*, an animal, and *eidos*, likeness.] Resembling or pertaining to an animal.—*n.* An organic body, as a cell or a spermatozoön, in some respects resembling a distinct animal; one of the more or less completely independent organisms produced by gemmation or fission, as in polyzoa, tapeworms, etc.

zoolatry, zō•ol′a•tri, *n.* [Gr. *zōon*, an animal, and *latreia*, worship.] The worship of animals.

zoology, zō•ol′o•ji, *n.* [Gr. *zōon*, an animal, and *logos*, discourse.] That science which treats of the natural history of animals, or their structure, physiology, classification, habits, and distribution.—**zoological,** zō•o•loj′i•kal, *a.* Pertaining to zoology.—*Zoological garden*, a garden in which a collection of living animals is kept.—**zoologically,** zō•o•loj′i•kal•li, *adv.* In a zoological manner.—**zoologist,** zō•ol′o•jist, *n.* One who studies or is well versed in zoology.

zoom, zöm, *v.i.* [Imitative.] To make a continuous hum or buzz; to pilot an aircraft suddenly upward at high speed; to move quickly toward or away from with a motion picture or television camera in order to make the image on the screen approach or retreat from the viewer.—*v.t.* To cause to zoom.—*n.* The act of zooming; a zooming sound.

zoomorphic, zō•o•mor′fik, *a.* [Gr. *zōon*, an animal, *morphē*, shape.] Pertaining to animal forms; exhibiting animal forms.—**zoomorphism,** zō•o•mor′fizm, *n.* The state of being zoomorphic.

zoophile, zō′o•fīl, *n.* [Gr. *zōon*, an animal, *philos*, love.] A lover of animals.

zoophyte, zō′o•fīt, *n.* [Gr. *zōon*, an animal, *phyton*, a plant.] A name loosely applied to many plant-like animals, as sponges, corals, sea anemones, sea mats, and the like.—**zoophytic,** zō•o•fit′ik, *a.*

zoosperm, zō′o•sperm, *n.* [Gr. *zōon*, an animal, and *sperma*, seed.] One of the spermatozoa of animals.

zoospore, zō′o•spōr, *n.* [Gr. *zōon*, an animal, *spora*, a sowing, seed.] A spore of algae, fungi, etc., which can move spontaneously to some extent by its cilia or long filiform processes.—**zoosporic,** zō•o•spor′ik, *a.* Pertaining to zoospores.

zootomy, zō•ot′o•mi, *n.* [Gr. *zōon*, an animal, and *tomē*, a cutting, from *temnō*, to cut.] The anatomy of the lower animals; that branch of anatomical science which relates to the structure of the lower animals.—**zootomical,** zō•o•tom′i•kal, *a.* Pertaining to zootomy.—**zootomist,** zō•ot′o•mist, *n.* One who dissects animals.

Zoroastrian, zor•o•as′tri•an, *a.* Pertaining to *Zoroaster*, whose system of religion was the national faith of ancient Persia, and is embodied in the Zend-Avesta.—*n.* A believer in this religion.—**Zoroastrianism,** zor•o•as′tri•an•izm, *n.* The religion founded by Zoroaster, one feature of which was a belief in a good and an evil power or deity perpetually striving against each other.

Zouave, zö•äv′, *n.* [Fr., from the name of a tribe inhabiting Algeria.] A soldier belonging to certain light-infantry corps in the French army, originally organized in Algeria, and having a dress of a somewhat Turkish fashion.

Zulu, zö′lö or zū•lū′, *n.* A member of the Bantu nation of Natal; the Bantu language of the Zulu people.

Zuñi, zö′nye, *n.* [Sp. from Keresan *sīni*, middle.] A tribe of North American Indians living in a pueblo in western New Mexico; a member of the Zuñi tribe; the language of the Zuñi.

zygapophysis, zig•a•pof′i•sis, *n.* [Gr. *zygon*, a yoke, and *apophysis*.] *Anat.* one of the processes by which the vertebrae articulate with each other.

zygoma, zī•gō′ma, *n.* [Gr. *zygōma*, from *zygon*, a yoke.] *Anat.* the prominence of the cheekbone, or the part that joins it with the cranium.—**zygomatic,** zī•go•mat′ik, *a.* Pertaining to the cheek bone.

zygomorphic, zī′go•mor″fik, *n.* [Gr. *zeugos*, a pair, *morphē*, form.] Of flowers, with bilateral symmetry (irregular).

zygospore, zī′go•spōr, *n.* [Gr. *zeugos*, a pair, *sporos*, fruit.] *Bot.* a spore formed by union of two gametes, or reproductive cells.

zygote, zī′gōt, *n.* [Gr. *zeugos*, a pair.] *Biol.* the product of fusion of two gametes.

zymic, zim′ik, *a.* [Gr. *zymē*, leaven.] Pertaining to a ferment or to fermentation; causing fermentation.—**zymologic,** zī•mo•loj′ik, *a.* Pertaining to zymology.—**zymologist,** zī•mol′o•jist, *n.* One skilled in zymology.—**zymology,** zī•mol′o•ji, *n.* The doctrine of ferments and fermentation.—**zymometer,** zī•mom′e•tėr, *n.* An instrument for ascertaining the degree of fermentation of a fermenting liquor.—**zymosis,** zī•mō′sis, *n.* Fermentation; a zymotic disease; the origin or production of such diseases.—**zymotic,** zī•mot′ik, *a.* Pertaining to, or produced by, fermentation.—*Zymotic diseases*, epidemic, endemic, contagious, or sporadic diseases, supposed to be produced by some morbific principle acting on the system like a ferment.

zymurgy, zī′mėr•ji, *n.* [Gr. *zymē*, and *ergon*, work.] That part of chemistry which treats of the scientific principles of the fermentation process, as in winemaking, brewing, distilling, and the preparation of yeast and vinegar.

ENCYCLOPEDIC SUPPLEMENTS

DICTIONARY OF

SYNONYMS AND ANTONYMS

A Treasury of Words of Similar and Contrasted Meaning

THOUGHTS are as many-colored and swift-changing as the sunset. They soar up into new realms. They are as endless and various as life itself. Words, by contrast, are pedestrian and limited in number; they plod along in pursuit. Yet if ideas are to be expressed and communicated to others, the right words must be found, the words whose meanings are most suitable. As an aid in this search a dictionary of synonyms and antonyms is of great value. The meanings of synonyms are similar but not identical. Consider the nice shades of meaning presented by the synonyms of DELIGHT*—enjoyment, pleasure, happiness, transport, ecstasy, gladness, rapture, bliss;* ECSTASY *carries an overtone of excitement;* BLISS *suggests tranquil, perfect contentment;* RAPTURE *lies somewhere between;* TRANSPORT *suggests a joy so great as to lift a person out of himself;* GLADNESS *sounds a more social, hearty, human note;* PLEASURE *describes the qualities of a simple sensation; and so so. No two words are identical in thought-content; if they were there would be no need for two. The writer cannot pull one out of a sentence and push in another, like a mason laying bricks of like size, weight, and color. The writer instead must select with care. Usually this selection comes naturally, but when it does not, the writer must search for the correct word—the right word used in the right place and at the right moment to render a new thought imperishable. This dictionary is a simple, effective means for locating these elusive words.*

Abaft, aft, sternward, behind.
Ant.—Forward, ahead, afore, before.

Abandon, forsake, leave, desert, renounce, relinquish, resign, quit, forego, let go, waive, abjure, abdicate.
Ant.—Retain, hold, maintain, support, uphold, defend, keep, cherish, undertake, assert.

Abandoned, dissolute, wicked, reprobate, profligate, flagitious, corrupt, depraved, vicious, bad, sinful, unchaste.
Ant.—Worthy, virtuous, upright, good, chaste.

Abandonment, leaving, desertion, dereliction, renunciation, defection.
Ant.—Protection, maintenance, support.

Abase, lower, humble, humiliate, degrade, depress, disgrace, dishonor, bring down.
Ant.—Exalt, elevate, honor, raise, promote.

Abasement, degradation, fall, degeneracy, humiliation, abjection, debasement, servility.
Ant.—Exaltation, promotion, elevation, dignity, honor.

Abash, bewilder, disconcert, discompose, confound, confuse, shame.
Ant.—Encourage, cheer, animate, embolden, incite.

Abate, lessen, diminish, bate, reduce, decrease, remove, suppress, lower, moderate.
Ant.—Increase, extend, amplify, continue, enlarge.

Abbreviate, abridge, shorten, condense, contract, curtail, reduce, epitomize.
Ant.—Lengthen, extend, prolong, produce, expand, enlarge, amplify.

Abbreviation, abridgment, contraction, condensation, compression.
Ant.—Extension, expansion, enlargement, amplification.

Abdicate, give up, forsake, relinquish, quit, forego, surrender, vacate, resign, renounce.
Ant.—Occupy, retain, maintain.

Abet, help, encourage, instigate, incite, stimulate, aid, assist.
Ant.—Resist, oppose, hinder.

Abettor, accessory, accomplice, assistant, promoter, instigator, coadjutor, associate, companion, confederate.
Ant.—Foe, antagonist, opponent, counteractor, baffler, adversary.

Abhor, dislike intensely, view with horror, hate, detest, abominate, loathe, nauseate.
Ant.—Love, like, adore.

Abide, stay, dwell, live with, tarry, remain, await, wait, sojourn, tolerate.
Ant.—Depart, migrate, move, proceed, avoid, shun.

Abiding. (See Lasting.)

Ability, capacity, capability, talent, faculty, qualification, aptitude, skill, efficiency, power, dexterity, aptness.
Ant.—Inability, incapacity, incapability, imbecility, unreadiness, stupidity, incompetency, inefficiency.

Abject, degraded, groveling, low, mean, base, ignoble, despicable, vile, servile, contemptible, wretched.
Ant.—Dignified, worthy, noble, independent, honorable, haughty, arrogant.

Abjure, recant, recall, revoke, retract, forswear, disclaim, renounce, repudiate.

Ant.—Claim, assert, profess, vindicate, retain, maintain, hold.

Able, strong, powerful, vigorous, robust, brawny, skillful, competent, efficient, capable, telling.

Ant.—Inefficient, incapable, unable, weak, ineffective.

Abnegation, denial, abstinence, stint.

Ant.—Indulgence, assertion, license.

Abnormal, unnatural, anomalous, irregular, eccentric, unusual.

Ant.—Normal, natural, ordinary, customary, usual, regular.

Abode, residence, habitation, dwelling, domicile, home, quarters, house, lodging, (with the idea of permanence).

Ant.—(With the idea of transience)—Halt, perch, tent, vestry, place.

Abolish, revoke, abrogate, annul, cancel, annihilate, extinguish, vitiate, invalidate, nullify, destroy.

Ant.—Establish, enforce, institute, restore, repair, erect, continue, sustain, support.

Abominable, hateful, detestable, odious, vile, execrable, foul.

Ant.—Delectable, desirable, admirable, enjoyable, pure, lovable, amiable, gracious, delightful, pleasing.

Abominate. (See Hate.)

Abortive, fruitless, ineffectual, idle, inoperative, vain, futile.

Ant.—Successful, fruitful, complete, perfect.

About, nearly, approximately, generally, concerning, regarding, relative to, with regard to, as to, respecting, with respect to, referring to, around.

Ant.—Precisely, exactly, away, away from, irrelevant.

Abridge. (See Abbreviate.)

Abridgment, epitome, summary, synopsis, compendium, abstract.

Ant.—Amplification, expansion, expatiation, dilation.

Abroad, away, apart, adrift.

Ant.—At home, near, close by.

Abrupt, sudden, unexpected, sharp, harsh, rough, rugged, steep, craggy, precipitous, hasty.

Ant.—Expected, slow, smooth, easy, undulating, courteous, polished.

Abscond, decamp, bolt, run off, steal away.

Ant.—Appear, emerge, show, stay, remain.

Absent, *a.* departed, inattentive, abstracted, not attending to listless, dreamy.

Ant.—Present, attentive, evident, imminent, existent.

Absolute, unconditional, unqualified, entire, complete, unrestricted, despotic, arbitrary, tyrannous, imperative, authoritative, imperious.

Ant.—Conditioned, conditional, incomplete, imperfect, relative, dependent, accountable, contingent.

Absolve. (See acquit.)

Absorb, swallow up, engulf, imbibe, consume, engross, merge, monopolize.

Ant.—Exude, emit, eject, dispense, dissipate.

Abstain. (See Refrain.)

Abstemious. (See Temperate.)

Abstract. (See Abridgment.)

Abstract, *v.* draw from, steal, purloin, remove, part, separate.

Ant.—Add, unite, return, adduce, restore.

Abstruse, recondite, profound, hidden, occult.

Ant.—Easy, clear, plain, obvious, patent, trite.

Absurd, preposterous, ridiculous, irrational, silly, foolish, unreasonable, nonsensical, inconsistent.

Ant.—Sagacious, sensible, rational, reasonable, wise, consistent, sound.

Abundance, plenty, competency, sufficiency, more than enough, fullness.

Ant.—Scarcity, paucity, scantiness, deficiency, dearth, less than enough.

Abundant, plentiful, plenteous, teeming, copious, ample.

Ant.—Deficient, scarce, insufficient, scant, exhausted.

Abuse, *v.* asperse, revile, vilify, calumniate, defame, scandalize, malign, traduce, disparage, ill-use.

Ant.—Praise, laud, extol, protect, respect, cherish.

Abuse, *n.* invective, scurrility, ribaldry, contumely, obloquy, opprobrium, vituperation.

Ant.—Praise, commendation, eulogy, applause.

Accede, consent, assent to, acquiesce, comply with, concur, coincide, submit.

Ant.—Dissent, refuse, decline, withdraw, demur, protest, oppose.

Accelerate, quicken, hasten, hurry, expedite, forward, dispatch.

Ant.—Retard, hinder, delay, obstruct, clog, drag, block.

Accept, take, receive, admit, acknowledge.

Ant.—Refuse, decline, reject, disown.

Acceptable, agreeable, pleasing, pleasurable, gratifying, grateful, welcome, desirable.

Ant.—Unpleasant, disagreeable, unwelcome, objectionable.

Access, admission, approach, avenue, admittance.

Ant.—Exclusion, repulse, rejection, departure.

Accession, increase, augmentation, enlargement, addition, reinforcement.

Ant.—Decrease, loss, subtraction, weakening.

Accident, contingency, chance, fortuity, casualty, mishap, disorder.

Ant.—Law, purpose, ordainment, provision, preparation.

Acclamation, applause, plaudit, exultation, shouting, cheering, jubilation, outcry.

Ant.—Obloquy, execration, silence, censure.

Acclivity, ascent, rise, incline.

Ant.—Declivity, descent.

Accommodate, adapt, adjust, fit, suit, serve, supply, furnish.

Ant.—Inconvenience, put out, disoblige, incommode.

Accompany, attend, go with, escort, convey.

Ant.—Leave, avoid, desert, abandon, quit.

Accomplice. Confederate, accessory, abettor, coadjutor, assistant, ally, associate.

Ant.—Adversary, opponent, enemy.

Accomplish, do, effect, finish, execute, achieve, complete, perfect, consummate, perform, attain.

Ant.—Fail, defeat, frustrate, disconcert, baffle, mar, ruin, spoil.

Accomplishment, attainment, qualification, acquirement.

Ant.—Defect, disability.

Accord, agree, consent, grant, allow, admit, concede.

Ant.—Differ, disagree, withhold, refuse, deny.

Accordant, compatible, harmonious, consonant, consistent, consenting, acquiescent.

Ant.—Different, incompatible, inharmonious, inconsistent.

Accost, address, speak to, stop, salute, greet, hail.

Ant.—Shun, pass, elude, ignore, avoid.

Account, narrative, description, narration, relation, de-

tail, recital—money, reckoning, bill, charge.
Ant.—Misrepresentation, confusion, distortion, caricature.

Accountable, punishable, answerable, amenable, responsible, liable.
Ant.—Absolute, supreme, irresponsible, independent.

Accredited, authorized, commissioned, empowered, entrusted.
Ant.—Unauthorized, uncommissioned.

Accumulate, collect, bring together, amass, gather, heap, increase.
Ant.—Dissipate, disperse, diminish, scatter, waste.

Accumulation, concentration, store, mass, collection.
Ant.—Dissipation, dispersion, diminution.

Accurate, correct, exact, precise, nice, truthful.
Ant. Inaccurate, inexact, incorrect, faulty, defective.

Accuse, arraign, charge, incriminate, tax with.
Ant.—Acquit, absolve, exonerate, release, vindicate, discharge.

Accustom, use, inure, habituate, familiarize.
Ant.—Disaccustom, dishabituate, wean, estrange.

Acerbity, asperity, sharpness, acrimony, roughness, acidity.
Ant.—Sweetness, gentleness, softness, mildness.

Achieve, do, accomplish, effect, fulfil, execute, gain, win.
Ant.—Fail, lose, miss.

Achievement, feat, exploit, accomplishment, attainment, performance, acquirement, gain.
Ant.—Failure, loss, abortion.

Acknowledge, admit, confess, own, avow, grant, recognize, allow, concede, indorse.
Ant.—Repudiate, disown, disclaim, disavow, deny.

Acme, summit, apex, climax, end, culmination.
Ant.—Base, depth, foot, nadir.

Acquaint, inform, tell, enlighten, apprise, make aware, make known, notify, communicate.
Ant.—Ignore, deceive, misguide, mislead, hoodwink.

Acquaintance, knowledge, familiarity, intimacy, cognizance, fellowship, companionship.
Ant.—Ignorance, unfamiliarity, inexperience.

Acquiesce, assent, agree, accede, consent, coincide with, concur.
Ant.—Dissent, demur, object, protest, resist, oppose.

Acquire, get, obtain, attain, gain, procure, win, earn, reap, secure.
Ant.—Lose, forfeit, forego, miss, surrender.

Acquit, absolve, pardon, forgive, discharge, set free, clear.
Ant.—Condemn, constrain, charge, accuse, compel.

Acrimonious, sharp, acrid, stinging, harsh, pungent, piquant, poignant, sour, acid.
Ant.—Amiable, smooth, bland, mild, friendly, pleasant.

Act, do, operate, make, perform, play, enact.

Action, deed, achievement, feat, exploit, accomplishment, battle, engagement, agency, instrumentality, movement.
Ant.—Inaction, rest, repose, quiet, cessation, quiescence.

Active, lively, sprightly, alert, agile, nimble, brisk, quick, supple, prompt, vigilant, laborious, industrious.
Ant.—Lazy, passive, indolent, inactive, slow, heavy, clumsy.

Actual, real, positive, genuine, certain.
Ant.—Fictitious, imaginary.

Actuate, instigate, move, impel, induce, prompt, persuade.
Ant.—Dissuade, prevent, deter, hinder, discourage.

Acute, sharp, shrewd, keen, intelligent, penetrating, piercing, severe.
Ant.—Dull, obtuse, stupid, blunt, heavy, chronic.

Adage, maxim, aphorism, proverb, apothegm, byword, saw.
Ant.—Discourse, harangue, yarn, inquisition.

Adapt, accommodate, suit, fit, conform, adjust.
Ant.—Misfit, misconform, misapply.

Addicted, devoted, wedded, attached, given up to, dedicated, prone, inclined, disposed.
Ant.—Unaddicted, unaccustomed, indisposed, disinclined, free from, detached, untrammeled.

Addition, increase, accession, augmentation, reinforcement.
Ant.—Subtraction, abstraction, decrease, decline, separation.

Address, *n.* tact, skill, ability, dexterity, deportment, demeanor.
Ant.—Awkwardness, unmannerliness, clumsiness.

Address, *v.* accost, greet, speak to, approach.
Ant.—(See Accost.)

Adherent, follower, partisan, pupil, disciple.
Ant.—Opponent, enemy, antagonist, adversary.

Adhesion, adherence, attachment, fidelity, devotion.
Ant.—Desertion, opposition, treason, unfaithfulness, aversion, antipathy, alienation, aloofness.

Adieu, good-by, *au revoir*, farewell, leave-taking, valediction.
Ant.—Welcome, greeting, recognition, salutation.

Adjacent, near to, adjoining, contiguous, conterminous, bordering, neighboring.
Ant.—Remote, distant.

Adjourn, postpone, defer, prorogue, delay.
Ant.—Conclude, consummate, complete, dispatch, terminate, continue.

Adjunct, appendage, appurtenance, dependency, help, auxiliary.
Ant.—Essence, body, clog, impediment, drawback, hindrance, autonomy.

Adjust, right, fit, accommodate, adapt, arrange, settle, regulate, organize, reconcile.
Ant.—Dislocate, disarrange, derange, disturb, disorder, confuse, disorganize.

Administer, award, accord, give, serve, supply, afford, contribute, dispense, execute, perform.
Ant.—Withhold, retain, refuse, withdraw, divert, mismanage.

Admirable, striking, surprising, wonderful, astonishing.
Ant.—Detestable, abominable, horrible, hideous.

Admire, wonder, approve, appreciate, affect.
Ant.—Abhor, abominate, dislike, despise, disapprove.

Admit, receive, allow, grant, permit, acknowledge, tolerate.
Ant.—Exclude, debar, reject, repudiate, disavow, deny, prohibit.

Admonition, warning, notice, caution, censure, advice, rebuke, dissuasion.
Ant.—Encouragement, countenance, applause, aid, instigation.

Adopt, take, select, assume, appropriate, choose.
Ant.—Reject, discard, renounce, repudiate, abandon.

Adorn, beautify, decorate, embellish, ornament, gild.
Ant.—Mar, spoil, deform, deface, despoil.

Adroit, skillful, clever, dexterous, expert, apt.
Ant.—Awkward, clumsy, unskillful, inexpert, lubberly.

Adulation. (See Flattery.)

Advance, adduce, assign, allege, bring forward, promote, progress, further.
Ant.—Hinder, retard, withhold, degrade, oppose, decrease.

Advancement, preferment, promotion, progress.
Ant.—Degradation, hindrance, opposition, retrogression.

Advantage, benefit, good, profit, utility, service.
Ant.—Disadvantage, unprofitableness, uselessness, harmfulness.

Advantageous, beneficial, profitable, salutary.
Ant.—Disadvantageous, unprofitable, useless, harmful, hurtful, noxious.

Adventure, incident, occurrence, casualty, contingency, accident, event.
Ant.—Matter of fact, matter of course, routine, rut.

Adventurous, bold, daring, enterprising, chivalrous, rash, precipitate, foolhardy.
Ant.—Unadventurous, timid, cautious, hesitating.

Adversary, opponent, antagonist, enemy, foe, rival, opposer.
Ant.—Friend, ally, assistant, accomplice, abettor, accessory.

Adverse, opposed, contrary, opposite, counteractive, hostile, repugnant, antagonistic.
Ant.—Favorable, propitious, fortunate, amicable, lucky.

Adversity, misfortune, sorrow, affliction, calamity, disaster.
Ant.—Prosperity, happiness, success.

Advertise, publish, announce, proclaim, promulgate.
Ant.—Conceal, suppress, hush, hoodwink.

Advice, warning, counsel, instruction, information, deliberation, consultation, reflection, consideration.
Ant.—Remonstrance, prohibition, dissuasion, expostulation.

Advise, acquaint, inform, communicate, notify, tell, persuade, prompt, incite.
Ant.—Misinform, deceive, delude, dissuade, deter, prohibit, remonstrate.

Advocate, counsel, defender, upholder.
Ant.—Accuser, impugner, adversary.

Aerial, airy, light, volatile, ethereal, empyreal.

Affability, courteousness, courtesy, urbanity, politeness, suavity.
Ant.—Haughtiness, contemptuousness, gruffness, discourtesy, superciliousness.

Affair, business, matter, question, subject, concern.

Affect, influence, act upon, feign, pretend, assume.
Ant.—Eschew, shun, dislike, repudiate.

Affecting. (See Pathetic.)

Affection, fondness, attachment, kindness, love, tenderness, endearment, condition, state, inclination.
Ant.—Insensibility, indifference, repugnance, repulsion, aversion, distaste, hatred.

Affectionate, fond, kind.
Ant.—Harsh, cold, unfeeling.

Affinity, relationship, alliance, union, kin, kindred, relation, analogy, sympathy.
Ant.—Antipathy, dissimilarity, disconnection, unlikeness, antagonism.

Affirm, assert, asseverate, declare, aver, swear, protest, state, maintain.
Ant.—Deny, contradict, dispute, demur, doubt, oppose.

Affix. (See Attach.)

Afflict, grieve, give pain, distress, trouble, torment, agonize.
Ant.—Console, relieve, assuage.

Affluence. (See Wealth.)

Afford, produce, bestow, grant, give, impart, communicate, confer, spare.
Ant.—Withhold, stint, withdraw, retain, grudge.

Affray, brawl, fray, quarrel, contention, altercation, wrangle, broil, strife, fracas.
Ant.—Order, tranquillity, pacification.

Affright. (See Frighten.)

Affront, injury, wrong, insult, offense, outrage.
Ant.—Amends, homage, apology, salutation.

Afraid, fearful, timid, timorous, faint-hearted.
Ant.—Bold, courageous, heroic, fearless, audacious, venturesome.

Afterward, hereafter, subsequently, ultimately.
Ant.—Previously, hitherto, heretofore.

Age, period, time, date, generation, era, epoch, antiquity, senility.
Ant.—Moment, instant, infancy, youth, childhood.

Aged, old, elderly, senile, anile, ancient, antiquated.
Ant.—Young, youthful, recent, fresh, juvenile.

Agency, instrumentality, influence, operation, management.
Ant.—Counteraction, opposition, neutralization, interference.

Aggrandize, exalt, promote, prefer, advance, elevate.
Ant.—Debase, degrade, disgrace, dishonor, depress.

Aggravate, tantalize, irritate, inflame, provoke, chafe, nettle, embitter, exasperate, increase, enhance, heighten, make worse, magnify.
Ant.—Soothe, soften, palliate, attenuate, alleviate, mitigate, diminish.

Aggregate, *n.* total, entire, complete, the whole.
Ant.—Unit, part, element, ingredient.

Aggregate, *v.* heap up, amass, accumulate, get together.
Ant.—Separate, dissipate, disperse, divide, segregate.

Aggression, encroachment, assault, attack, offense, invasion.
Ant.—Resistance, repulsion, retreat, withdrawal.

Agile, lively, sprightly, nimble, brisk, quick, supple, alert, wide-awake.
Ant.—Slow, heavy, awkward, ponderous, inert.

Agitate, convulse, disturb, stir, move, shake, oscillate, upheave.
Ant.—Calm, soothe, allay, compose, smooth, pacify.

Agonize, distress, rack, torture, writhe, excruciate, pain.
Ant.—Soothe, relieve, ease, compose, comfort.

Agony, anguish, pain, distress, suffering, woe, torture.
Ant.—Peace, enjoyment, comfort, composure, relief.

Agree, consent, assent, accede, acquiesce, comply, coincide, tally, concur.
Ant.—Disagree, differ, dissent, demur, decline.

Agreeable, gratifying, pleasant, pleasing, amiable, pleasurable, welcome, acceptable, suitable, jocular, smiling, charming.
Ant.—Disagreeable, offensive, unpleasant, obnoxious, unwelcome, rude, curt, gruff.

Agreement, concurrence, coincidence, concord, compact, contract, bargain, covenant, stipulation, accordance, harmony, unison.

Ant.—Disagreement, discord, promise, parole.

Aid, help, assist, coöperate, relieve, succor, further, forward, contribute, conduce, tend, facilitate, abet.

Ant.—Oppose, retard, resist, deter, baffle, withstand.

Ailing, unwell, sickly, diseased, ill.

Ant.—Well, healthy, sound, strong.

Aim. (See Purpose.)

Alacrity, readiness, willingness, agility, quickness, activity, promptitude.

Ant.—Slowness, repugnance, reluctance, unwillingness.

Alarm, terror, fright, affright, dismay, consternation, disquietude.

Ant.—Security, quiet, confidence, peace.

Alert. (See Agile.)

Alienate, estrange, withdraw from, transfer, assign, convey.

Ant.—Conciliate, retain, endear, secure.

Allay. (See Soothe.)

Allege, affirm, declare, maintain, adduce, advance, assign.

Ant.—Contradict, deny, disprove, refute, gainsay.

Allegory, parable, metaphor, fable.

Ant.—Fact, history.

Alleviate, assuage, mitigate, soothe, solace, relieve, abate, diminish, extenuate, soften.

Ant.—Aggravate, increase, augment, embitter.

Alliance, affinity, union, connection, relation, confederacy, combination, coalition, league, confederation.

Ant.—Antagonism, enmity, divorce, discord, hostility, separation, disruption.

Allot, apportion, appropriate, appoint, distribute, assign.

Ant.—Withhold, retain, misappropriate, refuse.

Allow, let, permit, admit, concede, yield, grant, give, tolerate, suffer, sanction, authorize.

Ant.—Disallow, refuse, resist, object, deny, withhold, protest.

Allude, refer, hint, insinuate, imply, intimate, suggest.

Ant.—State, demonstrate, declare, mention, specify.

Allure, entice, attract, decoy, tempt, seduce.

Ant.—Warn, scare, alarm, deter.

Alteration, change, variation, transition, changeableness, mutability.

Ant.—Fixity, permanence, stability, conservation, changelessness, identity.

Altercation. (See Quarrel.)

Alternating, intermittent, interrupted.

Ant.—Continual, constant.

Altitude, height, elevation, tallness, loftiness.

Ant.—Depth, lowness, depression, shortness, declination.

Altogether, wholly, totally, entirely, perfectly, completely, utterly.

Ant.—Partly, partially, separately, individually, imperfectly.

Always. (See Ever.)

Amalgamate, join, compound, mix, fuse, unite, consolidate.

Ant.—Separate, decompose, disintegrate, disunite.

Amass. (See Accumulate.)

Amazing, astonishing, wondrous, surprising, marvelous, stupendous, astounding.

Ant.—Commonplace, trivial, usual, ordinary, familiar, customary.

Ambassador, envoy, plenipotentiary, minister.

Ambiguous, equivocal, uncertain, vague, dubious, enigmatical.

Ant.—Plain, clear, obvious, unmistakable, indisputable, unequivocal, unambiguous.

Ameliorate, improve, amend, better.

Ant.—Injure, spoil, mar, debase, deteriorate.

Amenable, responsible, accountable, answerable for, liable, subject, tractable.

Ant.—Unamenable, independent, irresponsible, autocratic.

Amend, improve, correct, better, mend. (See Ameliorate.)

Ant.—Impair, injure.

Amends, compensation, recompense, restoration, reparation, atonement, restitution.

Ant.—Offense, injury, fault, insult.

Amiable, loving, pleasing, engaging, good, kind.

Ant.—Hateful, abominable, churlish, disagreeable, illnatured.

Amicable. (See Friendly.)

Ample, complete, full, wide, spacious, capacious, extensive, liberal, expansive, diffusive.

Ant.—Scanty, narrow, stingy, mean, insufficient.

Amplification, enlargement, exegesis, expansion, development.

Ant.—Abbreviation, curtailment, epitome, retrenchment.

Amusement. (See Recreation.)

Analogy, similarity, affinity, purity, resemblance.

Ant.—Dissimilarity, inaffinity, inequality, incongruity, disproportion.

Ancient. (See Aged.)

Anger, *v.* vex, exasperate, enrage, inflame, irritate, kindle, provoke, imbitter, incense.

Ant.—Please, amuse, gratify, soothe, pacify.

Anger, *n.* wrath, passion, rage, fury, indignation, ire, choler, bile, exasperation, irritation, resentment, pique.

Ant.—Peace, peacefulness, peaceableness, appeasement, good nature, poise, self-control, forbearance, good will, conciliatoriness, good temper.

Angry, passionate, irascible, choleric, hasty, sullen, moody, incensed, irritated, enraged, provoked, nettled, piqued, exasperated, wrathful.

Ant.—Peaceful, calm, good-tempered, forgiving, forbearing.

Anguish. (See Agony.)

Animate, cheer, enliven, inspire, encourage, embolden, inspirit, instigate, urge.

Ant.—Dishearten, deter, depress, discourage.

Animation, life, vivacity, spirit, buoyancy, elasticity, activity, alacrity.

Ant.—Deadness, dullness, inertness, spiritlessness.

Animosity, enmity, malignity, hostility, antagonism, hatred, antipathy, aversion.

Ant.—Concord, companionship, friendship, alliance, unanimity, harmony, regard.

Annals, chronicles, records, registers, historical accounts.

Ant.—Traditions, legends, romance.

Annex. (See Attach.)

Annihilate, destroy, annul, extinguish, nullify, obliterate, efface.

Ant.—Perpetuate, keep, preserve, conserve, foster, protect.

Announce, declare, make known, publish, advertise, proclaim, report, notify, give out.

Ant.—Conceal, hush, suppress, withhold, stifle, bury.

Annoy, vex, tease, chafe, molest, incommode, inconvenience.

Ant.—Accommodate, please, quiet, gratify, regard.

Annul, revoke, abolish, abrogate, repeal, cancel, destroy, extinguish, quash, nullify.

Ant.—Exact, establish, institute, confirm, maintain.

Anomalous, irregular, abnormal, eccentric.
Ant.—Regular, ordinary, normal.

Antagonism. (See Animosity.)

Antagonist. (See Adversary.)

Antagonistic. (See Adverse.)

Anterior, prior, preceding, antecedent, previous, foregoing, former.
Ant.—Posterior, later, subsequent, succeeding.

Anticipate, forestall, foretaste, prejudge, prearrange, obviate.
Ant.—Misapprehend, recall, undo.

Antipathy, dislike, aversion, repugnance, contrariety, opposition, hatred, antagonism, hostility, feeling against.
Ant.—Affinity, amity, sympathy, attraction, fellow-feeling, harmony.

Antithesis, contrast, opposition.
Ant.—Equivalent, alike, counterpart, equal.

Anxiety, care, solicitude, attention, eagerness, trouble.
Ant.—Contentment, confidence, peace, apathy, nonchalance, contentedness.

Apathy. (See Indifference.)

Aphorism, adage, maxim, saying.
Ant.—Lecture, exhortation, speech, disquisition.

Apocryphal, uncertain, unauthentic, legendary, doubtful, spurious.
Ant.—Authentic, genuine, verified, attested, undisputed.

Appal. (See Dismay.)

Apparent, easily seen, visible, palpable, clear, plain, transparent, evident, unmistakable, unambiguous, manifest, obvious, self-evident.
Ant.—Unapparent, uncertain, dubious, unobservable, unseen, indistinguishable, mistakable, ambiguous, apocryphal, indistinct.

Appeal, refer, invoke, invocate, call upon.
Ant.—Deprecate, protest, disavow, disclaim.

Appearance, air, look, aspect, manner, mien—advent, apparition.
Ant.—Disappearance, non-appearance, concealment.

Appease. (See Soothe.)

Appellation, name, denomination, cognomen, title, designation.
Ant.—Anonymousness, namelessness.

Applaud, praise, extol, commend, approve.
Ant.—Disapprove, denounce, decry, execrate.

Applause. (See Acclamation.)

Appoint, assign, allot, ordain, depute, order, prescribe, constitute, settle, determine.
Ant.—Recall, cancel, suspend, withdraw, withhold.

Apportion. (See Allot.)

Appreciate, value, prize, esteem.
Ant.—Undervalue, misjudge, ignore, depreciate.

Apprehend, think, feel, conceive, imagine, take, arrest, seize, fancy, anticipate, fear, dread, understand.
Ant.—Misapprehend, misconceive, lose, miss, ignore.

Approbation, approval, concurrence, assent, consent.
Ant.—Disapprobation, disapproval, censure, dissatisfaction, refusal, denial, disclaimer.

Appropriate, *v.* (See Assume.) Ascribe, arrogate, usurp.
Ant.—Yield, render, surrender.

Appropriate, *a.* peculiar, particular, exclusive, apt.
Ant.—Inappropriate, unsuitable.

Approval. (See Approbation.)

Arbitrary, despotic, imperious, domineering, tyrannous.
Ant.—Limited, considerate, lenient, modest, mild.

Arbitrator, arbiter, judge, umpire, referee.
Ant.—Appellant, claimant, litigant, disputant.

Ardent, eager, fervid, hot, fiery, glowing, passionate.
Ant.—Cool, cold, indifferent, apathetic, passionless, phlegmatic.

Argue, discuss, dispute, debate, reason upon.
Ant.—Dictate, assent, command, propound.

Arise, flow, emanate, spring, proceed, rise, issue.
Ant.—Sink, fall.

Arouse, stir up, awaken, vivify, excite, stimulate.
Ant.—Allay, compose, quiet, assuage, pacify, deaden.

Arrange, put in order, place, assort, classify, regulate, dispose, adjust.
Ant.—Derange, disarrange, confuse, disturb, jumble, disorder.

Arrant, notorious, flagrant, heinous, flagitious, atrocious, monstrous.
Ant.—Slight, moderate, small, inconspicuous.

Array, *n.* rank, order, disposal, disposition, arrangement.
Ant.—Confusion, disorder, rout.

Array, *v.* range, place, draw up, marshal, dress, deck out.
Ant.—Disarray, derange, displace.

Arrest, stop, apprehend, withhold, keep back, restrain, seize.
Ant.—Liberate, free, discharge, dismiss.

Arrogance, assumption, haughtiness, pride, loftiness.
Ant.—Humility, modesty, servility, bashfulness, diffidence, politeness.

Art, skill, tact, aptitude, adroitness, expertness, cunning, subtlety.
Ant.—Inexpertness, unskillfulness.

Artful, disingenuous, sly, tricky, insincere.
Ant.—Candid, frank, straightforward, sincere.

Artifice, trick, stratagem, machination, deception, cheat, imposture, delusion, finesse.
Ant.—Openness, simplicity, fairness, candor, honesty.

Ascend, climb, mount, rise, soar, tower, scale.
Ant.—Descend, fall, sink.

Ascendency, superiority, influence, authority, sway, mastery.
Ant.—Subjection, inferiority, disadvantage, subordination.

Ascent. (See Acclivity.)

Ask, request, entreat, solicit, beg, claim, demand, invite, question.
Ant.—Command, order, insist, dictate, exact.

Aspect, light, view, appearance, complexion, feature, air, look, mien, countenance.

Asperity, acrimony, acerbity, harshness, smartness, pungency, poignancy, tartness, roughness.
Ant.—Mildness, gentleness, sweetness, softness, pleasantness.

Asperse, accuse falsely, malign, slander, traduce, defame, scandalize, disparage, depreciate, vilify.
Ant.—Eulogize, laud, extol, praise, defend, uphold.

Assault, *v.* assail, attack, invade, encounter, storm.
Ant.—Defend, protect, repulse, retaliate.

Assemble, congregate, collect, gather, muster, bring together.
Ant.—Disperse, disrupt, adjourn, depart.

Assembly, assemblage, collection, group, company, muster, congregation, convention, congress, diet, council, convocation, conclave, synod, meeting, audience.
Ant.—Dispersion, disunion, adjournment, individual.

Assent, *v.* consent, accede, acquiesce, comply, concur.
Ant.—Dissent, disagree, differ, disclaim, protest.

Assert. (See Affirm.)

Assign, adduce, allege, advance, bring forward, appoint, allot, appropriate, apportion.
Ant.—Refuse, withhold, withdraw, retain.

Assist. (See Aid.)

Assistant, auxiliary, helper, supporter, sustainer, aide, adjutant.
Ant.—Opponent, enemy, foe, antagonist, rival, obstructionist, hinderer.

Associate, colleague, ally, partner, coadjutor, comrade, companion, consort.
Ant.—Rival, foe, alien.

Association, company, society, confederacy, union, partnership, fellowship, companionship, connection, alliance, combination.
Ant.—Disunion, separation, independence, solitude, individuality.

Assuage, compose, calm, pacify, allay, soothe, conciliate, appease, tranquilize, mitigate, alleviate, palliate, mollify.
Ant.—Excite, aggravate, increase, provoke, inflame, incite, stimulate.

Assume, pretend to, arrogate, usurp, appropriate, affect, wear, suppose.
Ant.—Abandon, concede, render, surrender, grant, allow, doff, prove, demonstrate.

Assurance, confidence, certainty, consciousness, conviction, effrontery, impudence.
Ant.—Bashfulness, reserve, unobtrusiveness, decency.

Astonishing. (See Amazing.)

Athletic, stalwart, powerful, brawny, muscular, robust, able-bodied.
Ant.—Weak, sickly, puny, slight, unmuscular.

Atrocious, flagitious, heinous, enormous, flagrant, villainous, monstrous, inhuman, nefarious.
Ant.—Laudable, honorable, noble, admirable.

Attach, affix, append, annex, adjoin, connect, stick, conciliate, attract, win.
Ant.—Detach, disengage, unfasten, untie, disconnect, alienate, repel, estrange.

Attack, *v.* assail, assault, impugn, encounter.
Ant.—Defend, resist, repulse, aid, repel, shield, shelter, support, protect.

Attempt, effort, exertion, endeavor, essay, trial, experiment.
Ant.—Neglect, laziness, inaction, abandonment.

Attend, go with, accompany, escort, wait on, listen, hearken, heed.
Ant.—Leave, forsake, abandon, wander, disregard.

Attentive, careful, intent, wistful, vigilant, studious, considerate.
Ant.—Inattentive, indifferent, careless, abstracted, absent, distracted, remiss.

Attest, testify, witness, prove, vouch, confirm, establish, evidence.
Ant.—Contradict, refute, disprove, oppugn, deny.

Attire, *n.* dress, apparel, garments, clothes, habiliments, robes, vestment, costume.
Ant.—Nudity, bareness, dishabille, disarray, exposure.

Attitude, posture, position, pose.
Ant.—Movement, gesture, gesticulation, exercise, deportment, bearing, action.

Attract, draw to, allure, entice, charm, wheedle.
Ant.—Repel, repulse, deter, estrange, alienate.

Attractive, winning, charming, captivating, fascinating, bewitching, enchanting, agreeable.
Ant.—Unattractive, uninteresting, repulsive, unpleasant, disagreeable, forbidding.

Attribute, quality, property, mark, characteristic, accomplishment, attainment.
Ant.—Essence, nature, substance.

Audacious. (See Bold.)

Audacity, boldness, effrontery, hardihood.
Ant.—Meekness, humility.

Augment, increase, enlarge, extend, stretch out, spread out.
Ant.—Reduce, diminish, deduct, reserve, impoverish.

August, majestic, noble, dignified, stately, gorgeous, exalted.
Ant.—Mean, common, vulgar, despicable, paltry, undignified.

Auspicious, fortunate, favorable, propitious, prosperous, lucky, happy.
Ant.—Inconspicuous, unpropitious, unlucky, unhappy, discouraging, hopeless.

Austere, rigid, severe, rigorous, stern, harsh, hard, strict.
Ant.—Indulgent, genial, easy, luxurious, mild, tender, kindly, dissolute, dissipated.

Authoritative, powerful, conclusive, potent, commanding, swaying, imperative, imperious.
Ant.—Weak, inconclusive, vague, indeterminate, indefinite.

Authority, weight, force, power, domination, supremacy, ground, justification.
Ant.—Spuriousness, weakness, usurpation, wrong, groundlessness.

Authorized, accredited, empowered, commissioned.
Ant.—Unauthorized, uncommissioned, unempowered, self-appointed, self-assumed.

Auxiliary, assistant, helping, conducive, furthering, instrumental.
Ant.—Hindrance, opposing, retarding, obstructive, cumbersome.

Avail, advantage, profit, use, benefit, service, utility.
Ant.—Disadvantage, loss, injury.

Available, profitable, advantageous, useful, beneficial.
Ant.—Unavailable, useless, inoperative, unprocurable, nonconducive, irrelevant.

Avarice, covetousness, cupidity, greed, rapacity.
Ant.—Generosity, liberality, profuseness, extravagance, unselfishness, waste.

Avaricious, niggardly, miserly, parsimonious.
Ant.—Generous, free-handed.

Aversion. (See Antipathy.) Dislike, hatred, repugnance.
Ant.—Affection.

Avocation, business, occupation, employment, calling, office, engagement, function, profession, trade.
Ant.—Idleness, leisure, holiday.

Awaken, arouse, excite, stir up, vivify.
Ant.—Stupefy, soothe, quiet, pacify, compose.

Award, adjudge, adjudicate, judge, determine, allot.
Ant. Retain, withhold, refuse, misapportion.

Aware, sensible, conscious, cognizant.

Ant.—Unaware, ignorant, uninformed, unconscious.

Awe, dread, fear, reverence.
Ant.—Familiarity.

Awkward, clumsy, unpolished, rough, untoward.
Ant.—Graceful, elegant, neat, polished, dexterous, skillful, adroit, handy.

Awry, crooked, wry, bent, curved, oblique.
Ant.—Straight, right, true, direct.

Axiom, adage, aphorism, apothegm, byword, maxim, proverb, saying, saw.
Ant.—Fallacy, babble, chatter, prattle, prate.

B

Bad, evil, wicked, unsound, unwholesome, baneful, deleterious, pernicious, noisome, noxious, sinful.
Ant.—Good, fit, wholesome, sound, virtuous, suitable, reputable, honorable, excellent.

Baffle, defeat, discomfort, bewilder, frustrate, foil, balk, confound, disconcert.
Ant.—Aid, help, assist, encourage, promote, abet.

Balance, weigh, poise, neutralize, counteract, equalize, adjust.
Ant.—Overbalance, upset, tilt.

Balk. (See Baffle.)

Balmy, fragrant, sweet-scented, odoriferous, odorous, perfumed.
Ant.—Harsh, rough, malodorous, nasty, unpleasant, sour.

Baneful. (See Bad.)

Banquet, feast, fete, entertainment, festival.
Ant.—Fast, abstinence, starvation.

Banter, mockery, derision, raillery, irony, teasing.
Ant.—Argument, discussion.

Barbarous, savage, brutal, cruel, inhuman, ruthless, merciless, remorseless, unrelenting, uncivilized, rude.
Ant.—Polite, civilized, refined, humane.

Bargain, agreement, convention, compact, stipulation, covenant, contract, transaction.
Ant.—Loss, failure, cheat.

Base, bad, low, mean, sordid, groveling, ignoble, ignominious, dishonorable, vile, counterfeit, deep.
Ant.—Lofty, exalted, refined, pure, noble, esteemed, honored, shrill, worthy.

Battle, combat, engagement, action, conflict, contest, fight.
Ant.—Peace, truce, council, armistice, mediation, arbitrament.

Bear, hold, sustain, support, endure, carry, maintain, convey, transport, waft, suffer, tolerate, undergo, put up with.
Ant.—Drop, eject, reject, decline, resign, refuse.

Bearing, manner, deportment, demeanor, behavior, conduct.

Beastly, brutal, brutish, sensual.
Ant.—Human, refined, gentle, lofty, pure, kindly.

Beat, strike, knock, hit, belabor, thump, dash, vanquish, overpower, conquer, defeat, overthrow, rout.
Ant.—Caress, pat, stroke, defend, shield, fail, surrender.

Beautiful, elegant, beauteous, handsome, fair, pretty, fine.
Ant.—Ugly, homely, foul, hideous, disagreeable, deformed, unattractive, unsightly.

Beautify. (See Adorn.)

Becoming, befitting, comely, decent, fit, proper, suitable, seemly.
Ant.—Unbecoming, unseemly, indecent, ungrateful, incongruous, improper.

Beg, ask, beseech, implore, entreat, crave, solicit, supplicate.
Ant.—Demand, extort, exact, require, give, confer, donate.

Beginning, commencement, outset, opening, inception, start, origin.
Ant.—End, close, termination, conclusion, completion, consummation.

Behavior, carriage, conduct, deportment, demeanor.

Behold, see, look, discern, view, descry, observe.
Ant.—Ignore, disregard, overlook, miss.

Belief, faith, credence, credit, trust, confidence, reliance, conviction, persuasion.
Ant.—Unbelief, disbelief, distrust, denial, heresy, doubt.

Below, beneath, under, underneath, lower, inferior, subordinate.
Ant.—Above, over, aloft, top, overhead, superior.

Bend, lean, incline, distort, stoop, descend, condescend, yield, submit.
Ant.—Stiffen, break, advance, resist.

Benediction, blessing, commendation, approval.
Ant.—Malediction, curse, disapproval, censure, execration.

Benefaction, gift, donation, alms, charity.
Ant.—Confiscation, deprivation, reservation.

Beneficent, benevolent, bountiful, bounteous, munificent, liberal, generous.
Ant.—Cruel, hard, oppressive, griping, stern, grinding, covetous, miserly.

Benefit, advantage, good, profit, service, ability, avail, use, favor, kindness, civility.
Ant.—Injury, loss, evil, disadvantage, detriment, harm.

Benevolence, beneficence, benignity, kindness, generosity, humanity, tenderness.
Ant.—Maleficence, unkindness, cruelty, harshness, churlishness, malevolence, malignity, brutality, inhumanity.

Bent, tendency, bias, inclination, disposition, prepossession, propensity, predilection, proneness.
Ant.—Disinclination, indisposition, aversion.

Bereave, deprive, strip, dispossess, disarm, divest.
Ant.—Replenish, benefit, enrich, give, compensate, satisfy.

Beseech. (See Supplicate.)

Beset, surround, encompass, embarrass, hem, beleaguer.
Ant.—Liberate, abandon, free.

Betimes, early, soon, shortly, ere long.
Ant.—Late, slowly, sluggishly, behindhand.

Betoken, forebode, bode, portend, augur, presage, prognosticate, signify, foreshadow.
Ant.—Belie, hide, mask, mislead, misindicate.

Better. (See Amend.)

Bewail. (See Lament.)

Bewilder. (See Perplex.)

Bewitch. (See Captivate.)

Bias. (See Bent.)

Bicker, wrangle, dispute, dissent, argue, contend, jar.
Ant.—Agree, converse, chat.

Bid, offer, proffer, tender, propose, call, invite, summon.
Ant.—Forbid, deter, prohibit, restrain.

Bide, wait, stay, remain, tarry, endure, await.
Ant.—Quit, depart, move, migrate, resist, adjourn.

Bigoted, illiberal, prejudiced, narrow, limited, intolerant.
Ant.—Liberal, tolerant, unprejudiced, broad.

Bind, tie, restrain, restrict, connect, link, engage, oblige.
Ant.—Unbind, untie, loose, loosen, unfasten, liberate, free, acquit.

Binding, astringent, costive, valid, obligatory, stringent, constraining.
Ant.—Loosening, purgative, freeing.

Bitter, harsh, pungent, poignant, stinging, sharp, tart, intense.
Ant.—Sweet, mellow, pleasant, affable, kindly.

Black, dark, murky, pitchy, inky, Cimmerian.
Ant.—White, light, radiant, shining, glorious.

Blacken, defame, calumniate, slander, scandalize, asperse.
Ant.—Whiten, eulogize, vindicate, clear.

Blame, reprove, reprehend, censure, condemn, reprobate, reproach, chide, upbraid.
Ant.—Praise, approve, exonerate, exculpate, laud, eulogize.

Blameless, inculpable, guiltless, sinless, innocent, immaculate, unsullied, unblemished, spotless, pure.
Ant.—Guilty, blameworthy, faulty, answerable, criminal, culpable.

Bland, soft, gentle, mild, kind, gracious, benign, benignant.
Ant.—Harsh, abrupt, rough, disagreeable, unpleasant.

Blank, confused, confounded, dumfounded, abashed, nonplussed, disconcerted, empty, unfilled.
Ant.—Filled, modified, qualified, mitigated.

Blast, blight, wither, shrivel, destroy.
Ant.—Nurture, cherish, save, shield, protect.

Blatant, noisy, clamorous, braying, bellowing, vociferous.
Ant.—Soft, noiseless, quiet, reserved, refined.

Blemish, *v.* stain, blur, sully, spot, obscure, dim, ruin, spoil, mar.
Ant.—Improve, clarify, cleanse, renovate, renew, purify, ornament.

Blemish, *n.* flaw, speck, defect, imperfection, fault.
Ant.—Adornment, embellishment, purity, unsulliedness.

Blend, mix, amalgamate, mingle, commingle, compound, fuse.
Ant.—Divide, dissociate, separate, disintegrate.

Blessedness, bliss, happiness, felicity, beatitude.
Ant.—Wretchedness, unhappiness, sorrowfulness.

Blind, sightless, eyeless, unseeing, ignorant, prejudiced, heedless.
Ant.—Clear-sighted, keen, far-sighted, aware, conscious, prudent.

Bliss, ecstasy, felicity, blessedness, blissfulness.
Ant.—Woe, misery, suffering, wretchedness.

Blithe, gay, blithesome, cheerful, merry, sprightly, vivacious.
Ant.—Heavy, dull, dejected, sullen, cheerless, gloomy, sorrowful.

Blockhead, dunce, dolt, dullard, numskull, jolthead, loggerhead, ignoramus.
Ant.—Sage, adept, savant, philosopher, master.

Bloodshed, carnage, slaughter, butchery, massacre.
Ant.—Peace, amity, festival.

Bloom, blossom, bud, sprout, germinate, shoot forth.
Ant.—Decay, blight, blast, wither.

Blot, speck, flaw, stain, blur, blemish, defect.
Ant.—Perfection, blamelessness, clearness.

Bluff, blustering, burly, swaggering, hectoring, bullying.
Ant.—Courteous, polished, graceful, reserved, elegant.

Blunder, mistake, error, delusion, hallucination, fault, oversight.
Ant.—Correctness, accuracy, exactness, truthfulness, foresight, correction.

Blunt, pointless, obtuse, edgeless, impolite, rough, rude.
Ant.—Sharp, keen, pointed, acute, polished, courteous, refined.

Boast, glory, triumph, vaunt, brag.
Ant.—Deprecate, cringe, whine, whimper, to be modest.

Bodily, corporal, corporeal, material, physical, wholly, collectively, unitedly.
Ant.—Spiritually, ghostly, partially, piecemeal, fragmentarily.

Boisterous, violent, furious, impassioned, impetuous, vehement, stormy, turbulent.
Ant.—Peaceful, calm, serene, self-possessed.

Bold, fearless, undaunted, dauntless, brave, daring, adventurous, intrepid, audacious, impudent, contumacious.
Ant.—Timid, fearful, shy, inadventurous, bashful, retiring.

Bondage, slavery, thralldom, vassalage, servitude, serfdom, captivity, imprisonment, confinement.
Ant.—Freedom, liberty, independence, liberation, manumission.

Booty, plunder, loot, pillage.
Ant.—Restitution, confiscation, forfeiture, penalty.

Border, edge, brim, rim, verge, brink, margin, confine, boundary, frontier.
Ant.—Center, interior, space, substance.

Bound, *v.* limit, circumscribe, confine, restrict, restrain, terminate.
Ant.—Open, free, release, liberate.

Boundless, unbounded, infinite, unlimited, interminable.
Ant.—Bounded, limited, finite.

Bounty, munificence, liberality, generosity, benevolence, beneficence, charity, benignity, humanity.
Ant.—Illiberality, closeness, miserliness, stinginess, churlishness.

Brag. (See Boast.)

Brand, mark, stigmatize, denounce.
Ant.—Honor, decorate, eulogize.

Brave, courageous, gallant, chivalrous, daring, audacious, adventurous, valorous, heroic, valiant, bold, dauntless, intrepid, magnanimous, fearless.
Ant.—Cowardly, fearful, timorous, weak-kneed, traitorous, ungallant, timid, weak, craven, cringing, cowering.

Bravery, courage, valor.
Ant.—Cowardice.

Brawny. (See Athletic.)

Break, fracture, shatter, burst, rend, rack, violate, infringe, transgress, demolish, destroy, crush, pound, squeeze.
Ant.—Join, conjoin, heal, repair, readjust, renovate, restore, mend.

Breed, beget, engender, generate, hatch, brood, incubate, produce.
Ant.—Extirpate, destroy, eradicate, stifle.

Breeze, blast, gale, gust, hurricane, storm, tempest.

Brevity, shortness, conciseness, succinctness.
Ant.—Prolixity, diffusiveness, protraction, length, elongation.

Brief, short, concise, compendious, succinct, summary.
Ant.—Long, prolix, interminable, protracted.

Bright, clear, lucid, transparent, limpid, lustrous, translucent, shining, brilliant, luminous, radiant, gleaming, clever, witty.

Ant.—Dull, dim, cheerless, dead, murky, muddy, opaque, sullen, dejected, imbecile, foolish, stupid, muggy.

Brisk, active, agile, nimble, lively, quick, sprightly, prompt, alert, assiduous, vigorous, vigilant.

Ant.—Slow, sluggish, indolent, dully, heavy, inactive, stagnant.

Brittle, fragile, frangible, frail, breakable.

Ant.—Elastic, tough, strong, solid.

Broad, wide, large, ample, expanded, extensive, liberal, indelicate, coarse, generic.

Ant.—Narrow, restricted, limited, confined, illiberal, bigoted, refined, delicate, specific, pointed.

Broil. (See Affray.)

Brook, suffer, bear, endure, submit to.

Ant.—Resist, resent, reject, combat.

Bruise, break, crush, squeeze, pulverize, triturate.

Ant.—Heal, soothe, comfort, repair, renovate, strengthen.

Brutal, cruel, inhuman, merciless, ferocious, remorseless, ruthless, barbarous, savage, irrational, sensual.

Ant.—Humane, civilized, tender, kind, gentle, polished, generous.

Bud, sprout, germinate, blossom, shoot forth.

Ant.—Seed, flower, wither, die.

Build, erect, raise, construct, found.

Ant.—Overthrow, undermine, lower, tear down, raze, destroy.

Bulk, size, dimension, magnitude, greatness, bulkiness, bigness, largeness, massiveness.

Ant.—Portion, particle, atom, smallness, diminution.

Buoyancy, floatableness, lightness, elasticity, animation, spirit, vivacity.

Ant.—Heaviness, sinkableness, depression, dejection, moodiness.

Burden, *v.* load, encumber, embarrass, oppress, afflict.

Ant.—Unburden, ease, alleviate, assuage, lighten, liberate, console, mitigate.

Burial, interment, sepulture.

Ant.—Resurrection.

Burning, glowing, ardent, fervid, impassioned, fervent, fiery, hot, blazing.

Ant.—Cool, extinguishing, smoldering, latent, sluggish.

Burst, break, crack, split, rend.

Ant.—Cohere, hold, stand, join, repair.

Bury, inter, inhume, entomb, immure.

Ant.—Disinter, exhume, excavate, expose, aggravate.

Business, vocation, employment, engagement, occupation, art, profession, trade.

Ant.—Avocation.

Bustle, stir, tumult, fuss.

Ant.—Quiet, repose.

Buy, purchase, gain, get, obtain, bribe.

Ant.—Sell, vend, hawk, dispose of.

By and By, anon, shortly, ere long, soon.

Ant.—Now, immediately, at once.

C

Cabal, combination, intrigue, faction, conspiracy, plot.

Ant.—Legislation, council, parliament, government.

Cajole, coax, wheedle, flatter, fawn, lure.

Ant.—Scold, warn, chide, blame, antagonize, displease.

Calamitous, disastrous, unfortunate, unlucky, hapless, fatal, luckless, ill-fated, ill-starred.

Ant.—Felicitous, fortunate, auspicious, propitious, advantageous.

Calamity, disaster, misfortune, mischance, mishap.

Ant.—Good fortune, windfall, luck.

Calculate, compute, estimate, count, consider, reckon, suppose.

Ant.—Miscalculate, conjecture, risk, chance, guess.

Called, termed, designated, denominated, named.

Ant.—Miscalled, misnamed.

Calling. (See Employment.)

Callous, hard, obdurate, impenitent, unfeeling, insensible, insensitive, unsusceptible.

Ant.—Sensitive, susceptible, soft, tender.

Calm, *v.* (See Soothe.)

Calm, *a.* quiet, undisturbed, serene, placid, composed, collected, imperturbable, tranquil, pacific, unruffled, still.

Ant.—Disturbed, noisy, riotous, frantic, excited, stormy, unsettled.

Calumniate, vilify, revile, accuse falsely, asperse, malign, traduce, slander, defame, scandalize, disparage.

Ant.—Eulogize, vindicate, clear.

Calumny, slander, false accusation, aspersion, defamation.

Ant.—Eulogy, panegyric, vindication, clearance.

Cancel, blot out, obliterate, expunge, efface, wipe out, rub out, erase, quash, abolish, annul, repeal, abrogate, revoke, destroy, invalidate, nullify.

Ant.—Enact, enforce, reënact, perpetuate, confirm.

Candid, fair, honest, open, artless, ingenuous, frank, sincere, plain.

Ant.—Unfair, unjust, disingenuous, insincere.

Canvass, discuss, contest, controvert, sift, examine, dispute, solicit, apply for.

Ant.—Ignore, disregard, admit, pass.

Capable, able, qualified, competent, efficient, fitted, susceptible, clever, skillful.

Ant.—Incapable, dull, unqualified, inefficient, unfitted, stupid, awkward, shiftless, incompetent, inadequate.

Capacious, roomy, ample, spacious, extensive.

Ant.—Limited, shallow, restricted, narrow, petty.

Capacity, capability, skill, ability, faculty, power, talent, efficiency, caliber, size.

Ant.—Incapacity, inability, stupidity, insufficiency, narrowness, contractedness.

Caprice, freak, whim, humor, crotchet, fancy.

Ant.—Plan, reason, determination, decision, deliberation.

Captious, touchy, testy, cross, petulant, peevish, fretful, carping, censorious.

Ant.—Approving, appreciative, encouraging, commendatory, equable, well-balanced.

Captivate, charm, enchant, fascinate, enrapture, bewitch, enchain, enamor, confine, imprison.

Ant.—Liberate, free, release, disenchant.

Captivity, imprisonment, confinement, bondage, slavery, thralldom, servitude, serfdom.

Ant.—Freedom, emancipation, liberty.

Capture, catch, seize, grasp, arrest, apprehend.

Ant.—Release, let go, miss, free, liberate, acquit.

Care, anxiety, solicitude, concern, attention, regard, circumspection, caution, foresight, prudence, heed, attention.

Ant.—Carelessness, disregard, neglect, indifference, temerity, improvidence, heedlessness, negligence.

Career, history, course, race, passage, life.
Ant.—Incident, fact.

Caress, fondle, hug, embrace, kiss.
Ant.—Persecute, annoy, tease, vex, spurn, buffet, rebuff.

Carnage, slaughter, butchery, massacre.

Carnal, fleshly, sensual, voluptuous, luxurious, secular, worldly.
Ant.—Spiritual, ethereal, exalted, refined, pure, temperate.

Carnival, revel, rout, masquerade, festivity.
Ant.—Fast, mortification, Lent.

Carriage, walk, bearing, deportment, gait, manner, behavior, demeanor, vehicle, conveyance.
Ant.—Miscarriage, misconduct, mismanagement.

Carry, bear, sustain, convey, transport.
Ant.—Set down, drop, abandon, surrender.

Case, condition, state, circumstance, plight, predicament, suit, process, cause.
Ant.—Theory, supposition, conjecture, fancy, hypothesis.

Cast down, downcast, dejected, depressed, discouraged, melancholy.
Ant.—Raised, elevated, encouraged, excited, animated, impressed.

Casualty, accident, contingency, incident, occurrence, event, adventure.
Ant.—Appointment, enactment, assignment, provision.

Catalogue, list, roll, record, inventory, index.
Ant.—Individual, unit, fact.

Catch, overtake, lay hold of, grasp, seize, capture, grip, clutch, snatch, arrest, apprehend.
Ant.—Lose, miss, escape, release, liberate, misapprehend.

Catching. (See Contagious.)

Cause, *n.* source, origin, agent, producer, creator, motive, reason, incentive, inducement, incitement, impulse, effort, work, operation.
Ant.—Effect, result, end, issue, production, accomplishment, consequence.

Cause, *v.* occasion, make, induce, originate, give rise to, evoke, provoke, incite.
Ant.—Effect, prosecute, conduct, apply.

Caution, care, vigilance, circumspection, admonition, warning, notice.
Ant.—Heedlessness, recklessness, temerity, indifference, carelessness.

Cavity, gap, hollow, aperture, chasm, opening.
Ant.—Surface, level, projection, plain, abrasion.

Cease, leave off, desist, discontinue, pause, end.
Ant.—Continue, begin, start, prosecute.

Cede, give up, surrender, relinquish, quit, forego.
Ant.—Claim, adhere to, hold, take, accept.

Celebrate, commend, applaud, laud, extol, magnify, glorify.
Ant.—Decry, disgrace, hiss, shame, blame, condemn.

Celebrated, famous, renowned, far-famed, illustrious, glorious.
Ant.—Unknown, obscure, undistinguished, mean, disgraced.

Celerity, rapidity, velocity, swiftness, quickness, speed, fleetness.
Ant.—Slowness, sluggishness, inertness, tardiness.

Celestial, heavenly, divine, godlike, seraphic, angelic, radiant.
Ant.—Terrestrial, earthly, mortal, human, infernal.

Censure, *v.* blame, reprove, reprehend, reprobate, condemn, upbraid, animadvert, criticize.
Ant.—Praise, approve, encourage, commend, eulogize.

Ceremonial, official, imposing, ritual.
Ant.—Ordinary, private, unostentatious.

Certain, sure, indubitable, unquestionable, unfailing, secure, real, actual, positive, assured, true.
Ant.—Uncertain, dubious, exceptional, doubtful, undecided, irregular, occasional, casual, hesitating.

Certify, testify, vouch, declare, avow, prove, evidence.
Ant.—Disprove, disavow, misinform.

Cessation, intermission, rest, pause, discontinuance, abeyance, suppression, stop.
Ant.—Continuance, continuity, incessancy.

Chafe, fret, irritate, gall, vex, chagrin, worry, annoy.
Ant.—Soothe, smooth, calm, console.

Champion, leader, chieftain, head, hero.
Ant.—Private, renegade, traitor, miscreant, poltroon, coward.

Chance, accident, fortune, casualty, hazard, luck, fate.
Ant.—Law, rule, sequence, causation, purpose, design, plan.

Change, *v.* alter, vary, transform, exchange, barter, modify, qualify, shift, veer, substitute.
Ant.—Retain, conserve, stabilize, hold, fix, clinch.

Change, *n.* variety, alteration, alternation, vicissitude.
Ant.—Stability, fixity, unchangeableness, monotony, uniformity.

Changeable, variable, undecided, hesitating, unsteady, vacillating, fluctuating, wavering, inconstant, unsteadfast, unstable, versatile, restless, fickle, fitful, capricious, mutable.
Ant.—Regular, settled, steady, stationary, consistent, uniform, immutable, unchangeable, unmovable, steadfast, dependable.

Character, cast, turn, tone, description, nature, disposition, reputation, class, order, sort, kind, mature, repute, standing.
Ant.—Vagueness, anonymousness.

Characteristic, peculiar to, sign of, distinctive, specific.
Ant.—Common, general, ordinary, generic, indistinctive.

Characterize, name, designate, denominate, describe, particularize, style.
Ant.—Suggest, hint, insinuate.

Charge, *v.* accuse, impeach, arraign, inculpate, attack, assault, carry.
Ant.—Acquit, discharge, clear, free, liberate, defend.

Charge, *n.* care, custody, ward, trust, management, cost, price, expense, account, fee, bill, assault, shock, onset, attack, accusation, impeachment, imputation.

Charity, kindness, benignity, beneficence, benevolence, tenderness.
Ant.—Uncharitableness, harshness, cruelty, inhumanity.

Charm, enchant, enrapture, fascinate.
Ant.—Repel, disgust.

Chary, wary, cautious, prudent, careful, sparing, reluctant.
Ant.—Liberal, lavish, profuse, eager.

Chastise, correct, castigate, punish.
Ant.—Indulge, pamper, spoil, demoralize, degrade.

Chastity, purity, continence, virtue.
Ant.—Lewdness, immorality.
Cheap, inexpensive, inferior, common.
Ant.—Dear, expensive, costly.
Cheat, *v.* defraud, trick, beguile, deceive, gull, dupe, delude, hoodwink.
Ant.—Deal fairly with, guide, undeceive, compensate, remunerate.
Cheat, *n.* deception, imposture, fraud, delusion, artifice, deceit, trick, imposition, impostor, rogue, trickster.
Ant.—Honesty, openness, exposure, artlessness, genuineness, dupe, gull, victim.
Check, curb, restrain, repress, control, counteract, chide, reprimand, reprove, rebuke.
Ant.—Loose, liberate, instigate, accelerate, indulge, abet.
Cheer, *v.* exhilarate, animate, inspirit, inspire, enliven, gladden, comfort, solace.
Ant.—Depress, sadden, dispirit, dishearten.
Cheerful, gay, merry, sprightly.
Ant.—Mournful, sad, doleful.
Cheerfulness, gaiety, sprightliness, merriment, mirth, liveliness, vivacity, joviality.
Ant.—Depression, sorrow, tearfulness.
Cheerless, disconsolate, brokenhearted, comfortless, inconsolable, desolate, forlorn.
Ant.—Cheerful, lively, gay, happy, bonny, blithe, pleasant.
Cherish, nourish, nurture, nurse, foster, sustain, value.
Ant.—Dislike, hate, despise, stifle, abandon, discard.
Chief, principal, main, supreme, paramount, leader, head, chieftain, champion, cardinal.
Ant.—Inferior, subordinate, minor, unimportant, lower, defective, mean.
Choice, option, preference, election, selection, rare, select, precious, valuable.
Ant.—Necessity, rejection, compulsion, refusal, common, ordinary, inferior, cheap, valueless.
Choose, prefer, select, elect, call, pick.
Ant.—Refuse, leave, dismiss, reject, decline, ignore.
Circuitous, roundabout, tortuous, flexuous, tiresome.
Ant.—Straight, direct, linear.
Circulate, spread, diffuse, disseminate, propagate.
Ant.—Suppress, hush, avert, cease, stagnate.
Circumlocution, verbosity, ambiguousness.
Ant.—Terseness, conciseness, directness, coherence, simplicity.
Circumspection, watchfulness, vigilance, caution, deliberation, thoughtfulness, wariness.
Ant.—Heedlessness, recklessness, thoughtlessness, carelessness.
Circumstance, situation, condition, position, fact, incident, happening.
Cite, quote, adduce, summon, call.
Ant.—Discredit, dispute, contradict, dishonor.
Civil, polite, complaisant, affable, courteous, obliging, urbane, well-bred.
Ant.—Disobliging, boorish, clownish, churlish, uncivil.
Civilize, polish, humanize, cultivate, refine.
Ant.—Demoralize, debase, vitiate, spoil, depress, injure.
Claim, *v.* ask, demand, challenge, call for, plead, insist.
Ant.—Disclaim, waive, forego, abandon, concede, surrender, repudiate.
Clamor, outcry, fuss, noise, hubbub, uproar.
Ant.—Silence, acquiescence, quiet, reticence.
Clandestine, hidden, secret, private, furtive, surreptitious.
Ant.—Open, public, advertised, announced, unconcealed.
Class, order, rank, degree, grade, category, caste, tribe.
Ant.—Individuality, singularity, specialty, isolation, alienation, division.
Clause, stipulation, proviso, term, article, portion, section.
Ant.—Document, instrument, paper.
Clean, cleanse, clarify, purify.
Ant.—Dirty, vitiate, befoul, deteriorate, stain.
Clear, *v.* absolve, acquit, liberate, deliver, release, set free, unbind, clarify, disentangle, extricate.
Ant.—Involve, implicate, contaminate, befoul, pollute, encumber, embarrass.
Clear, *a.* apparent, palpable, visible, obvious, plain, evident, manifest, unmistakable, distinct, intelligible, transparent, limpid, bright, lucid, vivid.
Ant.—Indistinct, thick, muddy, opaque, turbid, foul, unintelligible, dubious, entangled, confused.
Clemency. (See Mercy.)
Clever, skillful, expert, dexterous, adroit.
Ant.—Dull, stupid, slow, awkward, bungling, clumsy, unskilled, botched.
Climax, summit, height, consummation, acme, culmination.
Ant.—Anti-climax, base, floor, depth.
Climb, get up, scale, mount, soar, tower, ascend.
Ant.—Descend, drop, fall, slip, tumble.
Cling, hold, stick, adhere, attach, cleave, hang, embrace.
Ant.—Relax, forego, drop, abandon, let go.
Cloak, mask, veil, cover, blind, disguise, screen.
Ant.—Revelation, exposition, showing, exposure.
Clog, encumber, burden, hinder, impede, obstruct, embarrass, trammel, fetter.
Ant.—Aid, assist, help, release, encourage, instigate.
Close, *v.* conclude, shut, end, terminate, finish, stop.
Ant.—Open, initiate, protract, conduct.
Close, *a.* compact, solid, firm, dense, shut, fast.
Ant.—Wide, open, spacious, ample, airy, unconfined, public, liberal, frank.
Clothed, clad, dressed.
Ant.—Naked, disrobed, undressed.
Clothes, garments, vestments, dress, habiliments, apparel, attire, array, raiment, vesture, drapery.
Ant.—Nudity, nakedness, nature, disarray.
Cloudy, dim, obscure, dark, dusky, murky, indistinct, shadowy, mysterious.
Ant.—Clear, bright, distinct, palpable, open, limpid.
Clumsy, awkward, unpolished, uncourtly, ponderous.
Ant.—Adroit, clever, skillful, dexterous, adept, handy.
Clutch, grasp, lay hold of, catch, seize, grip.
Ant.—Liberate, let go, release, emancipate.
Coagulate, thicken, curdle, mix, blend.
Ant.—Rarefy, expand, dissipate.
Coalition, alliance, union, confederacy, league, combination.
Ant.—Dissociation, disruption, disagreement.
Coarse, rough, rude, rugged, gruff, harsh, vulgar, immodest, unpolished.

Ant.—Fine, delicate, choice, refined, polished, well-bred, high-minded.

Coax, cajole, wheedle, flatter, fawn.

Ant.—Coerce, intimidate, impel, instigate, drive.

Cogent, forcible, strong, valid, irresistible, resistless.

Ant.—Weak, feeble, powerless, ineffectual.

Coincidence, concurrence, correspondence, agreement.

Ant.—Design, purpose, adaptation, variation, difference.

Cold, frigid, wintry, unfeeling, stoical.

Ant.—Hot, fiery, impetuous, impulsive.

Colleague, fellow, compeer, companion, partner, assistant.

Ant.—Competitor, opponent, rival, antagonist.

Collect, gather, assemble, muster, congregate, accumulate, hoard.

Ant.—Distribute, dispense, divide, sort, dispose, deal.

Collected, composed, placid, calm, serene, cool, attentive.

Ant.—Distracted, excited, bewildered, dazed, scared.

Collision, clash, clashing, striking together, encounter, conflict.

Ant.—Divergence, shave, opposition, escape.

Color, hue, tint, tinge, complexion, dye, stain.

Ant.—Achromatism, paleness, nakedness, transparency.

Colorable, ostensible, plausible, specious.

Colossal. (See Enormous.)

Combat, *n.* engagement, conflict, contest, fight, action, battle.

Ant.—Peace, surrender, submission, truce, arbitration, mediation, reconciliation.

Combat, *v.* oppose, resist, withstand, thwart.

Ant.—Help, aid, assist, reconcile.

Combination, alliance, union, league, confederacy, coalition, conspiracy, synthesis, cabal, plot.

Ant.—Disunion, dissolution, division, opposition, analysis.

Comely, becoming, decent, seemly, agreeable, graceful, shapely.

Ant.—Unseemly, ungraceful, unshapely, homely.

Comfort, solace, console, encourage, revive.

Ant.—Discomfort, trouble, annoy, grieve, wound.

Comfortless, cheerless, forlorn, disconsolate, inconsolable, desolate, wretched.

Ant.—Comfortable, cheerful, happy, bright, gay, easy, pleasant.

Comic, funny, laughable, ludicrous, droll.

Ant.—Pathetic, tearful, sad, melancholy, doleful.

Command, order, decree, injunction, mandate, precept, behest.

Ant.—Entreaty, supplication, petition, prayer, wish, intimation.

Commence, begin, enter upon, initiate, inaugurate.

Ant.—Terminate, end, finish, complete, conclude.

Commend, praise, applaud, extol, eulogize, recommend.

Ant.—Blame, censure, condemn, denounce, disapprove.

Comment, note, observe, criticize, expatiate, explain, illustrate.

Ant.—Confuse, obscure, misinterpret, mystify, misconceive.

Commerce, dealing, trade, traffic, intercourse, interchange, reciprocity, business, barter.

Ant.—Stagnation, dullness, inactivity, interdict, embargo.

Commit, perpetrate, do, intrust, confide, consign.

Ant.—Omit, miscommit, misconsign, misentrust, fail.

Commodity, goods, merchandise, wares.

Common, vulgar, low, mean, frequent, ordinary, usual, general, universal.

Ant.—Refined, excellent, unusual, rare, scarce, uncommon, exceptional, extraordinary.

Communicate, make known, divulge, disclose, reveal, impart, tell, adjoin, attach.

Ant.—Secrete, suppress, conceal, reserve, withhold, disjoin.

Communion, fellowship, converse, share, association, participation, Lord's Supper, Eucharist, sacrament.

Ant.—Exclusion, deprivation, non-participation, alienation.

Community, society, commonwealth, social state, aggregation, association, order, nationality, fraternity.

Ant.—Segregation, secession, independence, individuality, rivalry, hostility, animosity.

Commute, substitute, change, alter, exchange, barter.

Ant.—Perpetuate, disallow, misappropriate.

Companion, comrade, coadjutor, partner, ally, associate, confederate, fellow, colleague.

Ant.—Rival, foe, antagonist, adversary.

Company, association, society, assembly, assemblage, audience, corporation, troop, horde, crew.

Ant.—Individual, separation, rivalry, opposition, antagonism.

Comparison, simile, similitude, illustration.

Ant.—Contrast, opposition, dissociation.

Compass, encircle, environ, encompass, invest, enclose, surround, beset, bring about, realize.

Ant.—Expand, unfold, amplify, display, fail, bungle, botch.

Compassion, pity, commiseration, sympathy, condolence, clemency.

Ant.—Cruelty, hard-heartedness, unforgiveness, vindictiveness, severity.

Compassionate, kind, merciful, clement, benign, gracious, benignant.

Ant.—Uncompassionate, unkind, hard, cruel, severe, vindictive, relentless.

Compatible, consistent, consonant, accordant, harmonious.

Ant.—Incompatible, inconsistent, discordant, hostile, antagonistic, incongruous.

Compel, force, constrain, coerce, enforce, oblige, necessitate.

Ant.—Persuade, convince, coax, allure, induce, tempt, seduce, lead.

Compendious, brief, short, succinct, concise, condensed.

Ant.—Diffuse, vague, prolix, cumbrous.

Compendium, compend, abridgment, abstract.

Ant.—Enlargement.

Compensate, recompense, make amends, remunerate, requite.

Ant.—Injure, damage, cheat, dissatisfy, defraud.

Compensation, amends, recompense, remuneration, requital, reward.

Ant.—Injury, loss.

Competent, able, capable, efficient, qualified, fitted, clever, skillful, sufficient, adequate.

Ant.—Incompetent, weak, inadequate, unqualified, unfit.

Competitor, candidate, rival, aspirant, antagonist.

Ant.—Colleague, assistant, partner, auxiliary.

Complain, murmur, lament, regret, repine.
Ant.—Rejoice, approve, applaud, exult.

Complaint, malady, disease, distemper, disorder.
Ant.—Health, sanity, soundness.

Complete, accomplish, fulfill, realize, execute, effect, achieve, conclude, finish, end, fill up, terminate.
Ant.—Begin, commence, inaugurate.

Complex, compound, complicated, involved, intricate.
Ant.—Simple, obvious, plain, direct.

Complicated. (See Complex.)

Compliment, praise, flatter, adulate, applaud.
Ant.—Insult, wound, condemn, blame.

Comply. (See Accede.) Conform, submit, yield.
Ant.—Refuse, reject, oppose.

Compose, construct, form, compound, put together, constitute, soothe, calm, quiet, lull, hush, frame, indite.
Ant.—Dissect, analyze, pull apart, destroy, imitate, excite, annoy.

Composed, serene, placid, calm, collected.
Ant.—Decomposed, excited, bewildered, irritated, vexed, angry.

Compound. (See Complex.)
Ant.—Simple, unmixed.

Comprehend, comprise, take in, embrace, contain, embody, include, conceive, imagine, apprehend, grasp, perceive, understand.
Ant.—Exclude, except, misunderstand, mistake.

Comprehension, capacity, capability, knowledge, intelligence, understanding.
Ant.—Misunderstanding, misconception.

Comprehensive, extensive, broad, wide, inclusive.
Ant.—Exclusive, narrow, restricted, shallow.

Compress, condense, press, squeeze, abridge.
Ant.—Expand, dilate, diffuse.

Comprise, embrace, contain, include, comprehend, embody.
Ant.—Exclude, except, omit, reject.

Compromise, arbitrate, adjust, concede, implicate, involve, entangle, embarrass, discredit.
Ant.—Aggravate, perpetuate, extricate, exonerate, disentangle.

Compulsion, constraint, force, coercion.
Ant.—Persuasion, coaxing, inducement, temptation, seduction.

Compute. (See Calculate.)

Comrade. (See Companion.)

Conceal, hide, secrete, disguise, dissemble, suppress.
Ant.—Reveal, exhibit, expose, publish, divulge, confess, avow, uncover.

Concede. (See Allow.)

Conceited, proud, vain, egotistical, affected.
Ant.—Humble, natural, simple, unaffected, honest.

Conceive, think of, imagine, suppose, comprehend, understand, design, believe.
Ant.—Misconceive, execute, express, produce.

Concern. (See Affair.)

Concerning, respecting, with regard to, regarding, with reference to, with respect to, relative to, in relation to, about.
Ant.—Omitting, disregarding.

Concert, contrive, devise, design, manage.
Ant.—Oppose, disregard, mismanage.

Concise. (See Brief.)

Conclude. (See Close.)

Conclusion, inference, deduction.

Concord, concert, chorus, harmony, unity.
Ant.—Discord, disagreement, variance, animosity.

Concourse, crowd, confluence, conflux, assembly, mob.
Ant.—Solitude, dispersion, conclave, desertion, cabal.

Concur. (See Agree.)

Condemn, blame, reprobate, reprove, reproach, upbraid, censure, reprehend, doom, sentence, disapprove.
Ant.—Acquit, absolve, exonerate, pardon, approve, justify.

Condense. (See Compress.)

Condition, state, plight, case, predicament, category, stipulation, covenant, article, term.
Ant.—Relation, dependence, situation, circumstance, concession, fulfillment, adaptation.

Condolence, sympathy, commiseration, compassion.
Ant.—Congratulation, exultation, indifference.

Conduce, contribute, subserve, lead, tend, incline, avail, aid, converge.
Ant.—Indispose, counteract, deject, neutralize.

Conduct, guide, lead, direct, manage, bring, control, govern, regulate.
Ant.—Misconduct, mislead, miscarry, mismanage.

Confederate. (See Abettor.)

Confer, bestow, give, discourse, converse, consult.
Ant.—Withdraw, withhold, contrast, conjecture, dissociate.

Confide, trust, repose, depend, rely, believe.
Ant.—Doubt, distrust, disbelieve.

Confidence, assurance, trust, faith, reliance, hope.
Ant.—Doubt, distrust, disbelief, misgiving.

Confident, dogmatic, positive, absolute, bold, presumptuous, sanguine.
Ant.—Doubtful, fearful, weak, cowardly.

Confine, limit, bound, circumscribe, restrict, restrain, shut up.
Ant.—Expand, extend, widen, loosen, liberate.

Confirm, ratify, establish, substantiate, corroborate, settle, strengthen, approve, attest.
Ant.—Cancel, annul, repeal, abrogate, refute, weaken, upset, contradict, combat.

Conflict, combat, contest, contention, struggle.
Ant.—Peace, quiet.

Conflicting, jarring, discordant, irreconcilable.
Ant.—Congruous, harmonious, consistent.

Conform, agree with, comply with, act according to, harmonize, adapt, suit.
Ant.—Deviate, dissent, disagree, secede, vary.

Confound, confuse, disconcert, bewilder, stun, astound, absorb.
Ant.—Elucidate, unravel, arrange, classify, enlighten.

Confused, muddled, mixed, promiscuous, indistinct, deranged, disordered, disorganized, bewildered.
Ant.—Clear, simple, plain, obvious, transparent, elucidated.

Confusion, disorder, derangement, disorganization, chaos, anarchy, misrule.
Ant.—Order, simplicity, clarity, arrangement.

Confute, disprove, refute, impeach.
Ant.—Approve, second.

Congregate, assemble, collect, gather, muster, convene, convoke, bring together.
Ant.—Separate, disperse, depart, go away.

Conjecture, guess, surmise, supposition, hypothesis.
Ant.—Inference, deduction, proof, fact, calculation.
Conjure, adjure, beseech, entreat, implore.
Ant.—Deprecate, protest, remonstrate, expostulate.
Connect, join, link, bind.
Ant.—Disconnect, separate, unbind, break apart, dissociate.
Connected, joined, related, akin, kindred, relative, cognate, congenial.
Ant.—Unconnected, foreign, unrelated, opposed.
Connection. (See Alliance.)
Conquer, vanquish, subdue, overcome, subjugate, surmount, defeat, master.
Ant.—Succumb, surrender, resign, lose, fail, fall, cede, fly, retire, yield.
Conscious, cognizant, aware, sensible.
Ant.—Unconscious, unaware, unsensible.
Consecrate, sanctify, hallow, devote, dedicate.
Ant.—Desecrate, secularize, profane, pollute.
Consent. (See Assent.)
Consequence, effect, result, event, issue, sequence.
Ant.—Cause, antecedence, origin, causation.
Consider, reflect, regard, weigh, ponder, deliberate, think, observe, investigate.
Ant.—Guess, hazard, conjecture, disregard, ignore, forget.
Considerate, thoughtful, reflective, deliberate, prudent, provident, careful, judicious, cautious.
Ant.—Inconsiderate, thoughtless, careless, rude, selfish.
Consistent, accordant, constant, compatible.
Ant.—Inconsistent, shifting, self-contradictory.
Console, soothe, comfort, solace.
Ant.—Harrow, worry, harass.
Consort. (See Associate.)
Conspicuous, distinguished, noted, marked, prominent, eminent, preeminent, illustrious, famed.
Ant.—Inconspicuous, unknown, unimportant, unnoticeable.
Conspiracy, plot, treachery, intrigue.
Ant.—Legislation, congress, parliament, revolution.
Constancy, stability, firmness, steadiness.
Ant.—Fickleness, flightiness.
Constantly, ever, always, continually, perpetually, incessantly, everlastingly.
Ant.—Never, seldom, irregularly, occasionally, accidentally.
Constitute, make, form, compose, mold.
Ant.—Decompose, dissolve, destroy, abrogate, disorganize, annul.
Constitutional, legal, regulated, organized, radical, rooted, fundamental.
Ant.—Unconstitutional, tyrannous, revolutionary, accidental.
Constrain. (See Compel.)
Construct, build, make, erect, compile, constitute.
Ant.—Destroy, demolish, derange, overthrow.
Construction, interpretation, version, explanation, view, reading, meaning.
Ant.—Misconstruction, misinterpretation, misunderstanding.
Consult, advise with, take counsel, deliberate, debate.
Ant.—Dictate, explain, expound, direct, order, command.
Consume, burn, absorb, spend, swallow, imbibe, engulf, devour, use, appropriate, utilize, employ.
Ant.—Construct, discard, disuse, reject.
Contagious, infectious, pestilential, miasmatic, catching.
Ant.—Noncommunicable.
Contain, comprise, comprehend, include, embrace, hold, incorporate, embody.
Ant.—Drop, exclude, emit, discharge, afford, yield.
Contaminate, corrupt, defile, pollute, taint.
Ant.—Purify, ennoble.
Contemn, despise, disdain, scorn, scout.
Ant.—Respect, revere, venerate, regard, esteem, honor.
Contemplate, meditate, muse, think, observe, behold, ponder.
Ant.—Ignore, overlook, waive, abandon.
Contemporary, contemporaneous, coeval, simultaneous.
Ant.—Antecedent, prior, past, future, asynchronous.
Contemptible, despicable, paltry, pitiful, vile, mean.
Ant.—Noble, worthy.
Contemptuous, disdainful, scornful, supercilious, insolent.
Ant—Humble, affable, courteous, respectable, modest, bashful.
Contend, contest, debate, argue, dispute, cope, strive, vie, wrangle, struggle, combat.
Ant.—Relinquish, surrender, concede, allow, waive, resign, succumb.
Contest. (See Contend.)
Contiguous. (See Adjacent.)
Contingency, casualty, accident, incident, occurrence, adventure, event.
Ant.—Purpose, design, order, cause.
Continual, unceasing, incessant, continuous, perpetual, uninterrupted, unremitting, endless, everlasting, constant.
Ant.—Occasional, rare, fitful, casual, interrupted, intermittent.
Continually, always, ever, constantly, incessantly, unceasingly, uninterruptedly, perpetually.
Ant.—Sometimes, occasionally, rarely, fitfully, interruptedly.
Continuance. (See Continuation.)
Continuation, continuance, endurance, duration, sequence, prolongation.
Ant.—Interruption, cessation, break, gap, discontinuance, pause.
Continue, persist, persevere, pursue, prosecute.
Ant.—Cease, stop, halt.
Contortion, distortion, twisting, writhing, wrestling, wrenching.
Ant.—Symmetry, uniformity, contour, configuration.
Contract, *v.* abbreviate, curtail, shorten, condense, abridge, retrench, reduce, agree.
Ant.—Expand, dilate, amplify, elongate, concede.
Contract, *n.* agreement, compact, bargain, stipulation, covenant.
Ant.—Release, dissolution.
Contradict, deny, gainsay, oppose.
Ant.—Confirm, strengthen.
Contrary. (See Adverse.)
Contribute, give to, coöperate, conspire, supply.
Ant.—Refuse, withhold, misapply.
Contrition, repentance, penitence, remorse.
Ant.—Impenitence, callousness, obduracy, reprobation.
Contrivance, plan, device, scheme, design, invention.
Ant.—Chance, venture, hazard.
Controversy, debate, contest, discussion, disquisition, dispute.

Ant.—Agreement, unanimity, coincidence.

Convene, call together, bring together, convoke, assemble, congregate, muster.

Ant.—Disperse, dismiss, disband.

Convenient, commodious, suitable, adapted, handy, timely.

Ant.—Inconvenient, awkward, useless, unseasonable, untimely.

Convention. (See Assembly.)

Conventional, usual, ordinary, fashionable.

Ant.—Natural, unusual, immutable, invariable, compulsory, unfashionable.

Conversation, dialogue, conference, talk, parley, colloquy, chat.

Ant.—Speech, oration, harangue, soliloquy, monologue, silence.

Convert, change, turn, transform, apply.

Ant.—Divert, conserve, perpetuate, clinch, alienate.

Convey. (See Carry.)

Convivial, joyous, festal, social, sociable, hospitable.

Ant.—Churlish, unsociable, ascetic, inhospitable, austere.

Convocation. (See Assembly.)

Convulse, upheave, upturn, shake, agitate.

Ant.—Soothe, compose, assuage.

Cool, cold, frigid, dispassionate, unimpassioned, calm, undisturbed, composed, collected, tranquil.

Ant.—Warm, disturbed, heated, irritated, excited, inflamed.

Coöperate, assist, abet, conspire, conduce, contribute.

Ant.—Oppose, thwart, rival, counteract, antagonize.

Copious. (See Abundant.)

Copy, model, pattern, imitation, exemplar, transcript, facsimile, illustration, duplicate.

Ant.—Original, prototype, example.

Corporal. (See Bodily.)

Corpulent. (See Stout.)

Correct, *v.* right, mend, amend, rectify, better, reform, improve, chasten.

Ant.—Corrupt, falsify, spare.

Correct, *a.* accurate, exact, precise, proper, faultless, strict, impeccable.

Ant.—Incorrect, false, untrue, faulty, wrong, muddled.

Correspond, fit, tally, answer, suit, agree, match.

Ant.—Differ, disagree, jar, clash, vary.

Correspondence, letters, intercourse, communication, commerce, coincidence, concurrence.

Ant.—Conversation, colloquy, difference, reservation, withdrawal.

Corrupt, *v.* contaminate, defile, taint, pollute, infect, adulterate, demoralize, deprave, spoil.

Ant.—Purify, cleanse, ameliorate, better, mend, repair, renovate.

Corrupt, *a.* depraved, debased, vitiated, demoralized, profligate.

Ant.—Incorrupt, pure, undefiled, good, honest.

Corruption, defilement, contamination, pollution, infection, adulteration, vice, depravity, corruptness.

Ant.—Purity, honesty, goodness, amelioration.

Cost, price, charge, expense, outlay.

Ant.—Receipt, profit, revenue, income, emolument.

Council. (See Assembly.)

Counsel. (See Advice.)

Count, calculate, compute, reckon, number, sum, estimate, rate.

Ant.—Underestimate, guess, hazard, conjecture.

Countenance, encourage, patronize, support, confirm, sanction.

Ant.—Discountenance, discourage, oppose, confront.

Counterfeit, spurious, forged, imitated, supposititious, false.

Ant.—True, real, genuine, authentic, veritable.

Countless, innumerable, numberless, incalculable, unnumbered.

Ant.—Few, scant, sparse, numbered, limited.

Courage, resolution, fearlessness, prowess, bravery, fortitude, chivalry, intrepidity, boldness, firmness.

Ant.—Timidity, cowardice, pusillanimity, poltroonery.

Course, way, road, route, passage, race, career, series, process, succession.

Ant.—Disorder, deviation, error, caprice.

Courteous, affable, conciliating, kind, urbane.

Ant.—Rude, churlish, arrogant, uncivil, ungracious.

Courteousness. (See Affability.)

Covenant. (See Contract.)

Cover, shelter, screen, hide, overspread, overshadow, cloak, conceal, secrete.

Ant.—Expose, reveal, betray, exhibit, produce.

Covert, secret, clandestine, hidden, latent, concealed, cabalistic, mysterious.

Ant.—Open, exposed, exhibited, revealed.

Covet, desire, wish for, long for, aspire to.

Ant.—Dislike, despise, undervalue.

Covetousness, avarice, cupidity.

Ant.—Beneficence, abnegation, renunciation.

Cowardice, fear, timidity, pusillanimity.

Ant.—Courage, intrepidity.

Cozen, cheat, gull, dupe, defraud, impose upon, deceive, wheedle.

Ant.—Undeceive, disabuse, enlighten.

Crafty, cunning, artful, sly, subtle, wily, tricky.

Ant.—Honest, open, frank, candid, straightforward, artless, sincere.

Crave, beg, entreat, solicit, beseech, implore, supplicate.

Ant.—Demand, insist, require, seize.

Crazy, imbecile, foolish, crack-brained, brainless, idiotic.

Ant.—Sound, robust, clever, vigorous, talented, learned.

Create, make, form, cause, produce, generate, engender, invent.

Ant.—Destroy, annihilate, demolish.

Credence, belief, faith, confidence.

Ant.—Disbelief, distrust, denial.

Credential, missive, diploma, title, testament, seal, warrant, letter, introduction.

Ant.—Autocracy, self-appointment, self-constitution.

Credit, belief, trustworthiness, reputation, security, honor.

Ant.—Disbelief, distrust, censure, disgrace, shame.

Credulity, gullibility, simplicity.

Ant.—Incredulity, scepticism, suspiciousness, shrewdness.

Crest, top, summit, apex, head, crown.

Ant.—Base, foot, bottom, sole.

Crime, offense, misdeed, misdemeanor, felony, sin, vice.

Ant.—Good deed, well-doing, duty, obligation, exploit, virtue, rectitude.

Criminal, illegal, felonious, vicious, iniquitous, sinful, guilty, nefarious, immoral.

Ant.—Lawful, right, just, virtuous, moral, meritorious.

Cripple, weaken, impair, curtail, cramp.
Ant.—Strengthen, renovate, augment, ease.

Criterion, test, touchstone, proof, standard.
Ant.—Glance, conjecture, haphazard.

Critical, nice, exact, fastidious, precarious, ticklish, crucial, important, hazardous.
Ant.—Uncritical, loose, easy, indiscriminate, inexact, safe, decided, settled.

Criticize, examine, scan, analyze, discuss, anatomize.
Ant.—Overlook, survey, slur, skim.

Crooked, bent, oblique, devious, corrupt.
Ant.—Straight, direct, upright.

Cross, ill-tempered, fretful, ill-humored, crusty, peevish, fractious.
Ant.—Amiable, genial, good-humored, good-tempered.

Crude, raw, undigested, unconsidered, half-studied, harsh, unshaped, unfinished, unrefined, ill-prepared.
Ant.—Refined, finished, ripe, well-prepared, well-digested, well-considered, elaborate.

Cruel, savage, barbarous, inhuman, malignant, brutal.
Ant.—Humane, forbearing, merciful, benevolent, generous, kind, gentle.

Cultivate, promote, foster, improve, cherish.
Ant.—Neglect, discourage, blight, blast, uproot, eradicate.

Cultivation, culture, refinement.
Ant.—Barbarism, boorishness.

Cupidity. (See avarice.)

Curb, restrain, hold, check, moderate.
Ant.—Loosen, release, liberate, instigate, incite, impel.

Curiosity, inquisitiveness, interest, rarity, celebrity, oddity.
Ant.—Abstraction, indifference, heedlessness, disregard, bagatelle, song, cipher.

Curious, inquiring, inquisitive, searching, interrogative, prying, peeping, peering, rare, odd.
Ant.—Indifferent, incurious, uninterested, trite, common.

Curse, malediction, anathema, bane, blight.
Ant.—Blessing, benediction, joy, crown, glory.

Cursory, summary, rapid, superficial, desultory, hasty, slight.
Ant.—Minute, elaborate, profound, thorough, painstaking.

Custody, keeping, guardianship, conservation, care.
Ant.—Neglect, exposure, abandonment, liberation, discharge.

Custom, manner, habit, use, prescription, fashion, practice.
Ant.—Law, regulation, command, rule, disuse, unconventionality.

Cut, sever, slice, sunder, avoid.
Ant.—Unite, splice, accost, approach, address, salute.

Cutting, sharp, biting, trenchant, piercing, bitter, sarcastic.
Ant.—Mild, soothing, conciliatory, indulgent, consoling.

Cynical, sarcastic, snarling, sneering, cross-grained.
Ant.—Lenient, tolerant, genial, complaisant, urbane.

D

Dainty, choice, luxurious, rare, refined, tasteful, exquisite, epicurean, fastidious.
Ant.—Coarse, common, dirty, nasty, gluttonous.

Damage, injure, hurt, loss, impair.
Ant.—Benefit, repair, bless, compensate, enhance, improve.

Danger, peril, hazard, risk, jeopardy.
Ant.—Security, safety, precaution, custody, defense.

Dare, venture, face, brave, hazard, risk, defy.
Ant.—Shun, dread, fear, shrink, cower.

Dark, black, dusky, sable, swarthy, opaque, obscure, abstruse, unintelligible, blind, ignorant, dim, shadowy, somber, joyless, mournful, sorrowful, dismal.
Ant.—Light, fair, white, bright, radiant, transparent, lucid, intelligible, plain, festive, luminous, clear.

Dash, hurl, cast, throw, drive, rush, fly, speed.
Ant.—Creep, crawl.

Data, facts, grounds, postulates.
Ant.—Assumption, conjectures, inferences.

Dauntless, valiant, gallant, fearless, intrepid.
Ant.—Timid, cautious, cowardly.

Dawn, gleam, begin, rise, open, break.
Ant.—Wane, set, sink, close, depart, end.

Dead, defunct, deceased, departed, gone, inanimate, lifeless, insensible, heavy, unconscious, dull, spiritless.
Ant.—Living, alive, animate, vivacious, stirring, bustling.

Deadly, fatal, destructive, mortal.
Ant.—Life-giving, immortal.

Deaf, insensible, disinclined, averse, inexorable.
Ant.—Attentive, alive, acute, interested, sensible, willing.

Dear, beloved, precious, costly, expensive.
Ant.—Despised, cheap.

Death, departure, demise, decease, dissolution, mortality, expiration.
Ant.—Birth, growth, rise, life, spirit, vigor, activity, action, vitality, inauguration.

Debase, degrade, lower, depress, deprave, deteriorate, corrupt, alloy.
Ant.—Enhance, exact, raise, purify, improve, promote.

Debatable, dubious, doubtful, uncertain, problematical, unsettled.
Ant.—Indisputable, incontestable, certain, sure.

Debate. (See Argue.)

Debility, weakness, feebleness, lassitude, languor.
Ant.—Strength, energy, vigor, nerve, robustness.

Debt, obligation, liability, default.
Ant.—Credit, assets, gift, gratuity, trust, favor.

Decay, decline, wane, dwindle, waste, ebb, decrease, disintegrate.
Ant.—Flourish, luxuriate, grow, increase, rise.

Decayed, rotten, corrupt, unsound, decomposed, faded, unprosperous, impoverished.
Ant.—Sound, thriving, flourishing, wholesome, fresh, healthful.

Deceit, cheat, imposition, trick, delusion, guile, beguilement, treachery, sham.
Ant.—Truthfulness, sincerity, candor.

Deceive, cheat, delude, impose upon, over-reach, gull, dupe.
Ant.—Enlighten, inform.

Decide, determine, settle, adjudicate, terminate, resolve.
Ant.—Waver, suspend, moot, brood over, cogitate, doubt, misjudge, vacillate.

Decipher, interpret, read, spell, solve.
Ant.—Vacillate.

Decision, determination, conclusion, resolution, firmness.
Ant.—Indecision, uncertainty, irresolution, weakness.

Declaim, speak, debate, harangue, recite.
Ant.—Read, study, write, compose.

Declamation, oratory, elocution, harangue, effusion, debate.

Declaration, avowal, statement, manifestation, profession.
Ant.—Denial, concealment, suppression.

Declivity, descent, fall, slope, incline.
Ant.—Ascent, rise, mountain, verticality.

Decorum, seemliness, propriety, dignity, order.
Ant.—Disorder, impropriety, disturbance,

Decrease, diminish, lessen, wane, decline, retrench, curtail, reduce.
Ant.—Increase, amplify, expand, extend, grow, augment, wax.

Decree, decision, determination, law, edict, order, manifesto, rule, verdict.
Ant.—Request, hint, intimation, suggestion.

Decrepit. (See Infirm.)

Dedicate, devote, consecrate, offer, set, apportion, assign.
Ant.—Misuse, alienate, misapply, misappropriate.

Deed, act, action, achievement, commission, instrument, document.
Ant.—Nonperformance, omission, failure, invalidation, reversion.

Deem, judge, estimate, consider, think, suppose, conceive.

Deep, profound, subterranean, submerged, designing, abstruse, learned.
Ant.—Shallow, superficial, familiar, artless, undesigning, easy, plain.

Deface, injure, mar, spoil, disfigure.
Ant.—Beautify, improve.

Default, lapse, forfeit, omission, absence, want, failure, neglect.
Ant.—Maintenance, appearance, presence, place, satisfaction, attention, effort, assiduity, diligence.

Defeat, conquer, overcome, worst, rout, frustrate, baffle.
Ant.—Succumb to, surrender, aid, advance, establish.

Defect, imperfection, flaw, fault, blemish.
Ant.—Supply, sufficiency, compensation, ornament, beauty, perfection.

Defend, guard, protect, justify.
Ant.—Abandon, betray, defeat, accuse, charge, retreat.

Defense, excuse, plea, vindication, bulwark, rampart.
Ant.—Desertion, abandonment, surrender, exposure, accusation, charge.

Defer, delay, postpone, put off, prorogue, adjourn.
Ant.—Hasten, press, urge, hurry, expedite.

Deference. (See Honor.)

Deficient, short, wanting, inadequate, scanty, incomplete.
Ant.—Complete, sufficient, full, correct, satisfactory, adequate.

Defile, pollute, corrupt, sully, contaminate, spoil, stain, desecrate.
Ant.—Cleanse, purify, ameliorate, better, hallow, sanctify.

Define, fix, settle, determine, limit, circumscribe.
Ant.—Confuse, obscure, mystify, misstate, confound, dilate, distend.

Definite, precise, exact, correct, fixed, determined.
Ant.—Indefinite, vague, obscure, undefined, confused.

Deformity, ugliness, disfigurement, hideousness, monstrosity.
Ant.—Regularity, grace, beauty, ornament.

Defray, meet, liquidate, pay, discharge, quit.
Ant.—Repudiate, dishonor, dissatisfy, misappropriate.

Degenerate, debased, fallen, impaired.
Ant.—Regenerated, advanced, improved.

Degree, grade, extent, measure, mark, range, quantity, amount, limit.
Ant.—Space, mass, magnitude, size.

Dejected. (See Melancholy.)

Deliberate, *v.* consider, meditate, consult, ponder, debate.
Ant.—Hazard, risk, chance.

Deliberate, *a.* purposed, intentional, designed, determined.
Ant.—Irresolute, playful, hasty, quick, dictated, suggested, rash, ill-considered.

Delicacy, nicety, daintiness, refinement, tact, softness, modesty.
Ant.—Coarseness, indelicacy, roughness, rudeness, vigor, robustness, boorishness, indecency.

Delicate, tender, fragile, dainty, refined.
Ant.—Coarse, rough, clownish.

Delicious, sweet, palatable.
Ant.—Nauseous.

Delight, enjoyment, pleasure, happiness, transport, ecstasy, gladness, rapture, bliss.
Ant.—Pain, suffering, sorrow, trouble, misery, discomfort, dejection, disappointment, depression, distress, melancholy, annoyance.

Deliver, liberate. free, rescue, pronounce, hand to, give.
Ant.—Confine, hold, take, capture, retain, appropriate.

Demand, claim, insist.
Ant.—Disclaim, waive, petition, request, supplicate.

Demonstrate. (See Prove.) Show, exhibit, illustrate.
Ant.—Hide, conceal, obscure.

Denominate, name, call, designate, denote.
Ant.—Misname, miscall, describe, suggest.

Denude, strip, divest, lay bare.
Ant.—Invest, clothe, drape, ornament, enrich.

Deny. (See Refuse.)

Depart. (See Leave.) Quit, decamp, retire, withdraw, vanish.
Ant.—Remain, abide, stay.

Department, section, division, office, branch, province.
Ant.—Institution, establishment, state, whole, body.

Deprive, strip, bereave, despoil, rob, divest.
Ant.—Supply, invest, endow, compensate, present, donate, bestow.

Depute, appoint, commission, charge, entrust, delegate, authorize, accredit.
Ant.—Recall, dismiss, discharge, supersede.

Deputy, vicegerent, lieutenant, representative, agent, commissioner, delegate, proxy, substitute.
Ant.—Principal, master, chief, head, ruler, sovereign.

Derision, scorn, contempt, contumely, disrespect.
Ant.—Respect, regard, admiration, deference.

Derivation, origin, source, beginning, cause, etymology, root, spring, analysis.
Ant.—Result, issue, application, use.

Describe, draw, delineate, portray, explain, illustrate, define, picture.
Ant.—Confuse, caricature, distrust, suggest.

Desecrate. (See Defile.) Profane, secularize, misuse, abuse, pollute.
Ant.—Sanctify, consecrate, dedicate, employ, devote, purify, solemnize.

Desert, wild, waste, wilderness, solitude, void.

Ant.—Garden, oasis, pasture, field.

Deserve, merit, earn, justify, win.
Ant.—Forfeit, lose.

Design, delineation, sketch, drawing, cunning, contrivance, artfulness.
Ant.—Structure, execution, performance, result, issue, candor, fairness, sincerity, chance, accident.

Desirable, expedient, advisable, valuable, acceptable, proper, judicious, beneficial, profitable, good.
Ant.—Undesirable, unadvisable, unprofitable, evil, detestable, obnoxious.

Desire, longing, affection, craving.
Ant.—Loathing, aversion, hate, repugnance, abomination.

Desist, cease, stop, discontinue, drop, abstain, forbear.
Ant.—Persist, continue, proceed, persevere.

Desolate, bereaved, forlorn, forsaken, deserted, wild, waste, bare, bleak, lonely.
Ant.—Cheerful, attended, consoled, cultivated, sheltered, fertile, frequented, gay, contented, happy.

Despair, hopelessness, despondency, desperation.
Ant.—Hope, confidence, elation, sanguineness, anticipation.

Desperate, wild, daring, audacious, determined, reckless.
Ant.—Hopeful, remediable, cautious, timid, propitious, calm, unmoved.

Despised, degraded, worthless.
Ant.—Admired.

Destination, purpose, intention, design, consignment, object, end, fate, doom, use, scope, goal, aim.

Destine, purpose, intend, design, devote.
Ant.—Divert, alienate, misapply.

Destiny, fate, decree, doom, end.
Ant.—Will, freedom, volition, choice.

Destitute. (See Devoid.)

Destroy. (See Annihilate.)

Destructive. (See Hurtful.) Detrimental, noxious, injurious, deleterious, baleful, baneful, subversive.
Ant.—Creative.

Desuetude, disuse, discontinuance.
Ant.—Continuance.

Desultory, rambling, discursive, loose, unmethodical, superficial, unsettled, erratic, fitful, spasmodic.
Ant.—Consecutive, continuous, methodical, systematic, periodical, diligent, serious, thorough, painstaking.

Detail, *n.* particular, specification, minutiae.
Ant.—Generalities.

Detail, *v.* particularize, enumerate, specify.
Ant.—Generalize, abstract, condense, sketch, amalgamate.

Detect. (See Discover.)

Deter, warn, stop, dissuade, dispirit, discourage, dishearten, terrify, scare.
Ant.—Prompt, tempt, encourage, incite, persuade.

Detest. (See Hate.)

Detract, lessen, deteriorate, depreciate, diminish.
Ant.—Enhance, raise, increase, augment.

Detriment. (See Harm.) Loss, injury, deterioration.
Ant.—Benefit, help.

Detrimental. (See Hurtful.)

Develop, amplify, expand, enlarge, enunciate, unfold.
Ant.—Envelop, compress, restrict, contract, involve, stunt, dwarf, stultify.

Device, artifice, expedient, contrivance.
Ant.—Openness, fortune, luck, hazard.

Devious, tortuous, circuitous, round-about, distorted.
Ant.—Direct, plain, straightforward, frequented.

Devoid, void, wanting, destitute, unendowed, unprovided.
Ant.—Provided, supplied, furnished, replete, full, complete.

Devolve, impose, place, charge, commission, befall, fall on.
Ant.—Deprive, withhold, cancel, alienate, lapse.

Devoted. (See Fond.) Attached, absorbed, dedicated.
Ant.—Indifferent.

Devotion, piety, devoutness, religiousness, dedication, love, attachment.
Ant.—Aversion, indifference, antipathy, alienation, apathy.

Devour, eat, consume, gorge, swallow, bolt.
Ant.—Disgorge, vomit, emit.

Dictate, prompt, suggest, enjoin, order, command.
Ant.—Follow, obey, echo, answer, repeat.

Dictatorial, imperative, imperious, domineering, arbitrary, tyrannical, overbearing, commanding.
Ant.—Persuasive, humble, subservient, submissive, meek.

Die, expire, depart, perish, decline, languish, wane, sink, fade, decay.
Ant.—Live, begin, originate, grow strong, flourish, luxuriate.

Diet, food, nourishment, nutriment, sustenance, victuals, fare, cheer, regimen.
Ant.—Abstinence, starvation, fasting, gluttony.

Difference, separation, discord, dissent, disagreement, estrangement, variety.
Ant.—Similarity, sympathy, agreement, likeness, uniformity, identity, consonance, harmony.

Different, various, manifold, diverse, unlike, separate, distinct.
Ant.—Similar, like, congruous.

Difficult, hard, intricate, involved, perplexing, obscure, unmanageable.
Ant.—Easy, plain, simple, lucid, tractable, favorable, clear.

Diffuse, discursive, prolix, diluted, copious.
Ant.—Terse, laconic, epigrammatic, condensed, concise.

Dignify, aggrandize, elevate, invest, exalt, advance, promote, honor.
Ant.—Degrade, disgrace, humiliate, dishonor.

Dilapidation, ruin, decay, disintegration, crumbling, demolition.
Ant.—Solidity, freshness, integrity, roundness, reparation, structure.

Dilate, stretch, widen, expand, swell, distend, enlarge, descant, expatiate.
Ant.—Contract, narrow, restrict, constrict, concentrate, epitomize, condense, shrink.

Dilatory, tardy, procrastinating, behind-hand, lagging, dawdling, lingering, slack.
Ant.—Prompt, alert, eager, beforehand, vigilant, nimble, quick, precipitate, swift, headlong.

Diligence, care, assiduity, attention, heed, industry.
Ant.—Indifference, carelessness, heedlessness, idleness, negligence.

Dimension, measurement, size, configuration, delineation.
Ant.—Segment, part, sector, fragment, mismeasurement.

Diminish, decrease, lessen, reduce, contract, curtail, retrench.
Ant.—Increase.

Dingy, dim, dull, dusky, rusty, colorless, obscure, dead, somber.

Ant.—Bright, radiant, lustrous, shiny, glossy, gleaming.

Diplomatic, judicious, knowing, wise, prudent, sagacious.
Ant.—Undiplomatic, injudicious, awkward, bungling, ill-managed.

Disability, unfitness, incapacity.
Ant.—Ability, fitness, qualification, merit, power.

Discern, descry, observe, recognize, see, discriminate, separate, perceive.
Ant.—Overlook, confound, omit, confuse, blend, mingle, involve.

Discernible, visible, conspicuous, manifest, palpable.
Ant.—Indiscernible, invisible, impalpable, obscure, minute.

Discernment, discrimination, far-sightedness, clearsightedness, penetration, observation, sagacity.
Ant.—Dullness, heedlessness, blindness, stupidity.

Discipline, order, strictness, training, coercion, punishment, organization.
Ant.—Disorder, confusion, rebellion, disorganization, encouragement, demoralization.

Disclose. (See Reveal.)

Discomfort, disquiet, vexation, annoyance, trouble.
Ant.—Comfort, ease, pleasure, agreeableness.

Disconcert, abash, confuse, confound, upset, baffle, derange, discompose, frustrate, discomfit.
Ant.—Rally, aid, untangle, encourage, arrange, order.

Disconsolate, sad, forlorn, melancholy, unhappy, desolate, woeful.
Ant.—Cheerful, joyous, blithe, merry, happy.

Discover, make known, find, invent, contrive, expose, reveal, detect.
Ant.—Conceal, suppress, mask, screen, cover, lose, secrete, miss.

Discredit, *v.* disbelieve, distrust, disgrace, dishonor.
Ant.—Credit, believe, trust.

Discredit, *n.* disgrace, disrepute, dishonor.
Ant.—Credit, honor, trust, faith, belief.

Discreditable, shameful, disgraceful, scandalous, disreputable.
Ant.—Honorable, favorable, worthy, confident, trusty, creditable.

Discreet, cautious, prudent, wary, judicious, considerate, politic, provident.
Ant.—Indiscreet, foolish, impudent, thoughtless, unwary, reckless, silly.

Discrepancy, difference, disagreement, variance.
Ant.—Agreement, consonance, similarity.

Discrimination, discernment, acuteness, judgment, caution.
Ant.—Obtuseness, gullibility.

Discuss. (See Argue.)

Disdain. (See Scorn.)

Disease, complaint, malady, disorder, ailment, sickness.
Ant.—Health, wholesomeness.

Disgrace, *n.* disrepute, reproach, dishonor, shame, odium.
Ant.—Honor, favor, confidence, trust.

Disgrace, *v.* (See Dishonor.) Debase, degrade, defame, discredit.
Ant.—Exalt.

Disgust, dislike, distaste, loathing, abomination, abhorrence.
Ant.—Fondness, partiality, liking, desire, avidity, relish, admiration.

Dishonest, unjust, fraudulent, unfair, deceitful, cheating, deceptive, wrongful.
Ant.—Honest, just, honorable, equitable, right, upright.

Dishonor, disgrace, shame, degrade, ravish, pollute.
Ant.—Honor, justify, improve, enhance, raise, better.

Dislike. (See Antipathy.)

Dismal, dreary, gloomy, lonesome, dull, melancholy, sad, pitiable, cheerless.
Ant.—Cheerful, gay, propitious, joyous, lively.

Dismay, *v.* terrify, frighten, scare, daunt, appal, dishearten.
Ant.—Inspirit, encourage, allure.

Dismay, *n.* terror, dread, fear, fright.
Ant.—Assurance, confidence.

Dismiss, send off, discharge, discard, banish.
Ant.—Recall, retain, detain, keep.

Disorder, disease, malady, complaint, confusion, derangement.
Ant.—Order, health, sanity, arrangement, method, system.

Disorderly, irregular, confused, lawless, unruly.
Ant.—Orderly, regular, systematized, lawful, governable, amenable, pure.

Disown. (See Renounce.)

Dispel. (See Scatter.) Drive away, disperse, dissipate.
Ant.—Collect, gather.

Disperse. (See Dispel.)

Display, show, spread out, exhibit, expose.
Ant.—Hide, conceal.

Displease, offend, vex, anger, provoke, irritate.
Ant.—Please, amuse, gratify.

Dispose, arrange, array, place, order.
Ant.—Confuse, disarrange.

Dispute, *v.* argue, contest, contend, question, impugn.
Ant.—Waive, concede, allow, forego, assent.

Dispute, *n.* argument, debate, controversy, quarrel, disagreement.
Ant.—Agreement, decision, council, harmony.

Disregard, slight, neglect, despise, disparage.
Ant.—Regard, honor, exalt, listen, attend, hear.

Dissent, disagree, differ, vary.
Ant.—Assent.

Dissolve. (See Melt.)

Distance, interval, remoteness, space.
Ant.—Nearness, proximity, adjacency, contact, presence.

Distinct, clear, plain, obvious, different, separate.
Ant.—Dim, obscure.

Distinguish, perceive, discern, mark out, divide, discriminate.
Ant.—Miss, overlook, confound, confuse.

Distinguished, famous, glorious, far-famed, noted, illustrious, eminent, celebrated.
Ant.—Undistinguished, dishonored, disgraced, unknown, obscure, ordinary.

Distract, disturb, perplex, bewilder.
Ant.—Calm, soothe, reassure.

Distress, trouble, pain, afflict, grieve, take, seize, distrain.
Ant.—Soothe, compose, console, comfort, please, gratify.

Distribute, allot, share, dispense, apportion, deal.
Ant.—Receive, retain, withhold, restrict, keep, collect.

Disturb, derange, discompose, agitate, rouse, interrupt, confuse, annoy, trouble, vex, worry, perplex.
Ant.—Soothe, pacify, compose, quiet, order, arrange.

Disuse, discontinuance, abolition, desuetude.
Ant.—Use.

Divert, please, gratify, amuse, entertain, alter, change, deflect.
Ant.—Annoy, disturb, distress, prolong, continue, confine.

Divide, part, separate, sever, deal out, distribute, sunder.
Ant.—Unite, join, gather, convene, classify, combine, associate.

Divine, Godlike, holy, heavenly, sacred; *n.* a parson, clergyman, minister.
Ant.—Profane, unholy, devilish, satanic, ungodly, fiendish, diabolical.

Do, effect, make, perform, accomplish, finish, transact.
Ant.—Undo, omit, neglect.

Docile, tractable, teachable, compliant, tame.
Ant.—Stubborn, obstinate, intractable, mulish, unruly, pig-headed.

Doctrine, tenet, articles of belief, creed, dogma, teaching.
Ant.—Practice, conduct, action, duty, deed, performance.

Doleful, dolorous, woebegone, rueful, dismal, piteous.
Ant.—Joyous, happy, cheerful, merry.

Domicile. (See Abode.)

Doom, sentence, verdict, judgment, fate, lot, destiny.
Ant.—Pardon, liberation, respite, acquittal, salvation.

Doubt, uncertainty, suspense, hesitation, scruple, ambiguity.
Ant.—Certainty, precision, decision, conviction, determination, clearness, satisfaction, belief, faith.

Draw, pull, haul, attract, inhale, sketch, drag.
Ant.—Push, carry, propel, repel, impel, throw, thrust, describe, exhale.

Dread, fear, horror, terror, alarm, dismay, awe.
Ant.—Courage, confidence, assurance, boldness.

Dreadful, fearful, frightful, shocking, awful, horrible, horrid, terrific.
Ant.—Hopeful, inspiriting, encouraging, promising, attractive, pleasing, desirable.

Dress, clothing, attire, apparel, garments, costume, garb, livery.
Ant.—Nudity, nakedness, undress, disarrangement.

Drift, purpose, meaning, scope, aim, tendency, direction.
Ant.—Aimlessness, vagueness, indefiniteness, pointlessness.

Drill, train, teach, discipline, perforate, bore.
Ant.—Disorder, confuse, disarrange.

Drive, force, urge, press, compel, guide, direct.
Ant.—Draw, pull, hinder, obstruct, discourage.

Droll, funny, laughable, comic, whimsical, queer, amusing, absurd.
Ant.—Sad, lugubrious, funereal, tragic, solemn, grave, mirthless.

Drown, inundate, swamp, submerge, overwhelm, engulf.
Ant.—Dry, drain, expose, air, ventilate, resuscitate, emerge.

Drowsy, sleepy, heavy, dozy.
Ant.—Awake, alive, alert, vigilant.

Dry, arid, parched, lifeless, dull, tedious, uninteresting, meager, tiresome.
Ant.—Wet, moist, juicy, fresh, lively, entertaining, damp.

Due, owing to, attributable to, just, fair, proper, right.
Ant.—Undue, irrelative, independent, unfair, improper, deficient, exorbitant, unjust.

Dull, stupid, blunt, gloomy, sad, dismal, commonplace, opaque, cloudy.
Ant.—Sharp, clever, lively, animated, bright, brilliant, clear, interesting, entertaining.

Dunce, simpleton, fool, ninny, idiot.
Ant.—Sage, philosopher.

Dupe. (See Cheat.)

Durable, lasting permanent, abiding, continuing.
Ant.—Perishable, unstable, transient, evanescent, ephemeral, fleeting.

Dutiful. (See Obedient.)

Dwell, stay, stop, abide, sojourn, linger, tarry.
Ant.—Move, travel, wander, roam, migrate, flit, stray.

Dwindle, pine, waste, diminish, decrease, fall off.
Ant.—Enlarge, increase, flourish, develop, augment, grow.

E

Eager, hot, ardent, impassioned, forward, impatient.
Ant.—Listless, cool, indifferent, sluggish, diffident, detached.

Early, soon, by and by, shortly, ere long, anon, betimes.
Ant.—Late, backward, tardy, belated.

Earn, acquire, obtain, win, gain, achieve.
Ant.—Steal, lose, spend, waste, forfeit, forego.

Earnest, *a.* ardent, serious, grave, solemn, warm.
Ant.—Playful, flippant, idle, irresolute, indifferent, trifling, frivolous.

Earnest, *n.* pledge, pawn.

Ease, *n.* comfort, rest.
Ant.—Worry, discomfort, unrest.

Ease, *v.* calm, alleviate, allay, mitigate, appease, assuage, pacify, disburden, rid.
Ant.—Trouble, annoy, vex, incommode, excite, worry, disturb.

Easy, light, comfortable, unconstrained.
Ant.—Difficult, hard.

Eccentric, irregular, anomalous, singular, odd, abnormal, wayward, particular, strange, fussy, meticulous.
Ant.—Regular, ordinary, customary, normal, usual.

Eclipse, shade, overcast, cloud, overshadow.
Ant.—Brighten, reveal, enhance, heighten.

Economical, sparing, saving, provident, thrifty, frugal, careful, niggardly.
Ant.—Extravagant, wasteful, improvident, generous, loose, open-handed, prodigal, lavish.

Edge, border, brink, rim, brim, margin, verge.
Ant.—Middle, center.

Efface, blot out, expunge, obliterate, wipe out, cancel, erase.
Ant.—Restore, revive, portray, delineate, preserve, insert.

Effect, *n.* consequence, result, issue, event, execution, operation.
Ant.—Cause, origin, source, antecedent, purpose, reason, motive.

Effect, *v.* accomplish, fulfil, realize, achieve, execute, operate, complete.
Ant.—Prevent, obviate, mar, frustrate, fail, fall short, yield.

Effective, efficient, operative, serviceable.
Ant.—Weak, ineffective, futile, inoperative, vain, ineffectual, footless.

Effects. (See Property.)

Efficacy, efficiency, energy, agency, instrumentality.
Ant.—Inefficiency, uselessness, futility.

Efficient, effectual, effective, competent, capable, able, fitted.
Ant.—Inefficient, useless, unable, unfitted, incompetent, futile, feckless.

Eject, thrust out, cast out, expel, oust, dislodge, throw out, dispossess.
Ant.—Receive, retain, accept, accommodate, lodge, welcome, admit, inject, introduce.

Elaborate, labored, studied.

Ant.—Simple, plain, unstudied.

Elapse, lapse, guide, pass.
Ant.—Wait, abide, hold, continue.

Elastic, ductile, flexible.
Ant.—Inelastic, rigid, inflexible, tough.

Elementary, primary, rudimentary, physical, material, natural, component, constituent, ultimate.
Ant.—Enveloped, organized, immaterial, incorporeal.

Eligible, fit, desirable.
Ant.—Ineligible, unfit, unworthy, worthless.

Eliminate, drive out, expel, thrust out, eject, cast out, dislodge, banish, proscribe, oust.
Ant.—Add, import, foist, involve, invite, welcome.

Eloquence, oratory, rhetoric, declamation.

Elucidate, make plain, explain, clear up, illustrate.
Ant.—Mystify, obscure, confuse, muddle, perplex.

Elude, evade, escape, avoid, shun.
Ant.—Meet, confront, encounter, defy.

Embarrass, perplex, entangle, abash, distress, trouble.
Ant.—Assist, help.

Embellish, adorn, decorate, bedeck, beautify, deck.
Ant.—Disfigure, deface, mar.

Embolden, encourage, inspirit, animate, cheer, urge, impel, stimulate.
Ant.—Discourage, dishearten, deter.

Embrace, clasp, hug, comprise, comprehend, contain, include, embody, incorporate.
Ant.—Exclude, reject, except.

Eminent, illustrious, distinguished, signal, conspicuous, noted, prominent, elevated, renowned, famous, glorious.
Ant.—Low, obscure, unknown, unimportant.

Emit, discharge, give out, throw out, exhale, vent.
Ant.—Admit, inhale.

Emotion, perturbation, agitation, trepidation, tremor, mental conflict.
Ant.—Insensibility, indifference, impassiveness, stoicism, poise, repose, calm.

Employ, occupy, busy, take up with, engross, use, apply.
Ant.—Dismiss, discard, misuse, discharge.

Employment, business, avocation, engagement, office, function, trade, profession, occupation, calling, vocation.
Ant.—Idleness, slothfulness, leisure.

Empty, *v.* evacuate, exhaust, drain, draw out.
Ant.—Fill, supply, replenish, glut, swell, increase.

Empty, *a.* void, devoid, hollow, unfilled, unoccupied, unfurnished.
Ant.—Full, supplied, occupied, inhabited.

Enchanted, charmed, captivated, fascinated, spellbound, transported, enchained, entranced, electrified, wrapt.
Ant.—Disenchanted, disgusted, repelled, horrified.

Encircle. (See Encompass.)

Enclose, fence in, confine, circumscribe.
Ant.—Expose, open, disclose, develop.

Encompass, encircle, surround, environ, beset, begird, invest.
Ant.—Open, expose, expand, avoid, withdraw.

Encounter, attack, conflict, combat, assault, onset, engagement, battle, action.
Ant.—Escape, retreat, surrender, defeat, plight.

Encourage, countenance, support, foster, cherish, sanction, inspirit, embolden, animate, cheer, incite, urge, impel, stimulate.
Ant.—Discourage, dissuade, deter, dispirit, daunt, deject, depress.

End, *n.* aim, terminal, object, purpose, result, conclusion, upshot, close, expiration, termination, extremity.
Ant.—Beginning, commencement, introduction, incipiency.

Endanger. (See Imperil.)

Endeavor, try, attempt, essay, strive, aim.
Ant.—Relax, shirk.

Endless, everlasting, perpetual, deathless, undying, imperishable, infinite, interminable.
Ant.—Terminable, limited, transient, brief, periodic, finite.

Endorse. (See Ratify.)

Endue, invest, endow, enrich, store.
Ant.—Denude, strip, deprive, divest, spoil.

Endurance, fortitude, patience, resignation.
Ant.—Weakness, cowardice.

Endure, last, continue, support, bear, sustain, suffer, brook, submit to, undergo.
Ant.—Perish, succumb, stop, give way, fail, wane.

Enemy, adversary, foe, antagonist, opponent.
Ant.—Friend, comrade.

Energetic, effectual, efficacious, powerful, binding, stringent, forcible, nervous, active, industrious.
Ant.—Lazy, slothful, ineffectual, weak, slow, idle, indolent, passive, sluggish.

Energy, force, vigor, efficacy, potency, strength.
Ant.—Laziness, weakness, slowness.

Engage, employ, busy, occupy, attract, invite, allure, entertain, engross, take up, enlist.
Ant.—Refuse, dismiss, discard, disengage, withdraw.

Engagement, word, promise, battle, action, combat, conflict.
Ant.—Declination, refusal, dismissal, retreat.

Engross, absorb, engulf, take up, occupy, engage, monopolize.

Engulf, swallow, absorb, imbibe, drown, submerge, bury, entomb, overwhelm.
Ant.—Cast out, disgorge, disperse, dissipate, eject, emit, exude.

Enjoin, order, ordain, appoint, prescribe.
Ant.—Release, recall, dispense, dissuade, accept, follow, obey, yield, submit.

Enjoyment, pleasure, gratification.
Ant.—Pain, sorrow, sadness.

Enlarge, increase, extend, augment, broaden, swell.
Ant.—Diminish, contract.

Enlighten, illumine, illuminate, instruct, inform.
Ant.—Obscure, perplex, confuse.

Enliven, animate, cheer, vivify, stir up, inspire, exhilarate.
Ant.—Deaden, benumb, dispirit.

Enmity, invidiousness, animosity, hatred, hostility, ill-will, malignity, maliciousness.
Ant.—Love, affection, esteem, cordiality, friendliness, good will.

Enormous, gigantic, colossal, huge, vast, immense, prodigious.
Ant.—Diminutive, insignificant, trivial, ordinary, venial, little, small, petty.

Enough, sufficient, plenty, abundance.
Ant.—Bare, scant, inadequate, insufficient, want, lack, paucity, poverty.

Enraged, infuriated, raging, wrathful, maddened.

Ant.—Soothed, quieted, tamed, pacified, pacific, mollified.

Enrapture, captivate, enchant, fascinate, charm, bewitch.
Ant.—Repel, revolt.

Enroll, enlist, list, register, re cord.
Ant.—Disrate, disqualify.

Entangle, embarrass, inveigle, implicate, involve, compromise, ensnare, entrap.
Ant.—Disentangle, unravel, extricate.

Enterprise, adventure, undertaking, effort, endeavor, attempt.
Ant.—Matter of fact, indifference.

Entertainment. (See Recreation.)

Enthusiasm, zeal, ardor, fervor, warmth, fervency, earnestness, devotion, intensity, vehemence.
Ant.—Indifference, coldness, callousness, repugnance, contempt, ennui, caution, wariness.

Enthusiast, fanatic, visionary.
Ant.—Indifferentist.

Entice. (See Allure.)

Entire, whole, complete, perfect, total.
Ant.—Partial, broken, incomplete, impaired.

Entitled, named, designated, denominated, styled, characterized, qualified, fit.
Ant.—Unentitled, unfit, disqualified, disabled.

Entrance, entry, inlet, ingress, porch, portal.
Ant.—Exit, egress, departure.

Entreat, beg, crave, solicit, beseech, implore, supplicate.
Ant.—Command, insist, order, bid, enjoin.

Enumerate, tell, relate, narrate, recount, specify, detail, reckon.
Ant.—Lump, mass, miscount, confound.

Envy, invidiousness, jealousy, suspicion, grudging.
Ant.—Satisfaction, generosity, gratification.

Epitome, abridgment, compendium, abstract, summary, digest.
Ant.—Amplification, expansion, enlargement, whole.

Equal, *n.* fellow, colleague, companion, peer, compeer.
Ant.—Inferior, superior, enemy, opponent.

Equal, *a.* equable, even, uniform, alike, adequate, sufficient, compensating, equivalent, impartial, same, like.
Ant.—Unequal, uneven, unlike, inadequate, insufficient, disparate, dissimilar, different.

Equitable. (See Just.)

Era. (See Age.)

Eradicate, root out, extirpate, exterminate, annihilate.
Ant.—Implant, inculcate, instill.

Erase, scratch out, blot out, expunge, efface, cancel.
Ant.—Insert, mark, add, write, delineate.

Erect, set up, raise, elevate, construct, establish, institute, found.
Ant.—Lower, depress, overthrow, demolish, remove, destroy.

Erroneous, incorrect, inaccurate, faulty, inexact.
Ant.—Exact, correct.

Error, mistake, fallacy, blunder, fault.
Ant.—Correct, true, proper, accuracy, precision.

Escape, elude, evade.
Ant.—Confront, encounter, meet, incur.

Escort. (See Accompany.)

Especially, particularly, specially, mainly, principally, chiefly.
Ant.—Generally, universally, commonly.

Essay, attempt, dissertation, tract, treatise.

Essential, necessary, indispensable, requisite, vital.
Ant.—Accidental, unnecessary, superfluous, redundant.

Establish, institute, found, organize, confirm, settle, fix, build up, strengthen.
Ant.—Overthrow, demolish, destroy, disestablish, unsettle, upset, refute, suppose, guess.

Estate, domain, demesne, lands, property, possessions.

Esteem, prize, value, appreciate, respect, regard, reverence, venerate, revere, defer to.
Ant.—Dislike, decry, undervalue, depreciate, contemn, scorn.

Estimate, calculate, appraise, compute, rate.

Estrangement, abstraction, alienation.
Ant.—Reconciliation.

Eternal, everlasting, endless, infinite, perpetual, deathless, immortal, undying, imperishable.
Ant.—Temporal, finite, transient, ephemeral, limited.

Evade, elude, equivocate, prevaricate, baffle.
Ant.—Confront, meet, encounter.

Evasion, shift, subterfuge, prevarication, quibble, equivocation.
Ant.—Honesty, uprightness, frankness, straightforwardness.

Even, equal, equable, smooth, plain, level, uniform.
Ant.—Uneven, unequal, variable, inclined, abrupt, rough, jagged.

Event, incident, occurrence, accident, adventure, issue, result, consequence.
Ant.—Cause, antecedent, operation, inducement, tendency.

Ever, always, eternally, everlastingly, evermore, aye, perpetually, continually, incessantly, endless, infinite.
Ant.—Never, momentarily, transiently.

Evidence, *n.* testimony, deposition, declaration.
Ant.—Surmise, conjecture, concealment, refutation.

Evidence, *v.* manifest, evince, demonstrate, exemplify.
Ant.—Conceal, surmise, hide, conjecture.

Evident. (See Apparent.)

Evil, ill, wicked, bad, unfair, mischievous, harmful, misfortune.
Ant.—Good, wholesome, beneficial, felicitous.

Evince, show, argue, prove, evidence, manifest, demonstrate.
Ant.—Conceal, suppress, negative.

Evoke, call out, invite, summon, challenge, provoke, elicit, produce.
Ant.—Silence, seal, prevent, stop, allay, stifle.

Exact, accurate, nice, particular, punctual.
Ant.—Careless, slip-shod.

Exaggerate, overstate, heighten, amplify, enlarge.
Ant.—Understate, mitigate, modify, qualify, palliate.

Exalt, raise, elevate, erect, lift up, dignify, ennoble.
Ant.—Debase, lower, depress, dishonor, defame, humble, degrade.

Examination, search, inquiry, research, scrutiny, investigation.
Ant.—Conjecture, hazard, guess.

Example, pattern, sample, model, specimen, copy, instance.
Ant.—Principle, law, rule, system, material, substance.

Exasperate. (See Irritate.)

Exceed, surpass, excel, outdo, transcend.
Ant.—Fall short.

Except, unless, save, saving, but.
Ant.—Counting, including, reckoning, admitting.
Exceptional, uncommon, rare, extraordinary.
Ant.—Usual, commonplace.
Excess, superfluity, redundance, redundancy.
Ant.—Deficiency, shortcoming, failure, temperance.
Excessive, exorbitant, extortionate, unreasonable, immoderate, inordinate, extravagant.
Ant.—Insufficient, scant, inadequate.
Exchange. (See Change.)
Excitable, irritable, susceptible.
Ant.—Insensible, composed, quiet, cool, self-possessed.
Excite, incite, arouse, awaken, stir up, disquiet, disturb, agitate, provoke, irritate, rouse.
Ant.—Allay, calm, quiet, pacify, quell, lull, soothe.
Exclaim, call out, shout, cry, ejaculate.
Ant.—Write, whisper, sign, intimate.
Exclude, shut out, debar, preclude, seclude.
Ant.—Admit, include, open, retain, conserve.
Exclusive, sole, only, alone.
Ant.—Comprehensive, inclusive.
Excursion, trip, ramble, tour, jaunt.
Ant.—Rest, peace, quiet, home.
Excusable, pardonable, venial.
Ant.—Inexcusable, unpardonable.
Excuse, palliate, mitigate, acquit, justify, absolve, dispense, exempt.
Ant.—Exact, charge, compel, condemn, accuse.
Execrable, abominable, detestable, hateful, accursed, cursed.
Ant.—Laudable, desirable, eligible, respectable.
Execute, accomplish, effect, fulfill, release, achieve, complete, finish, perform.
Ant.—Neglect, omit, drop, nullify, mar, frustrate, defeat.
Exempt, free, cleared.
Ant.—Subject, inculpated, incriminated.
Exemption, freedom, immunity, privilege.
Ant.—Liability, responsibility, amenableness.
Exercise, exert, practice, pursue, carry on.
Ant.—Rest, ease, relax, respite.
Exhale, emit, give out, smoke, steam.
Ant.—Absorb, inhale.
Exhaust, spend, drain, empty, deliberate.
Ant.—Fill, replenish, augment, invigorate, refresh.
Exhaustive, thorough, complete.
Ant.—Cursory, superficial.
Exhibition, show, sight, spectacle, pageant, representation.
Ant.—Concealment, mark, suppression, secretion.
Exigency, emergency.
Exile, banishment, deportation, expatriation, expulsion, proscription.
Ant.—Reinstate, recall, welcome, domesticate.
Exonerate, clear, acquit, absolve, discharge, justify.
Ant.—Charge, accuse, condemn.
Exorbitant. (See Excessive.)
Expand, spread, diffuse, dilate, extend, enlarge, amplify, unfold, develop.
Ant.—Contract, curtail, restrict, condense.
Expectation, expectancy, waiting for, hope, anticipation, confidence, trust.
Ant.—Realization, verification, exhibition.
Expedient, fit, necessary, essential, requisite.
Ant.—Inexpedient, disadvantageous, unfit.
Expedite, accelerate, quicken, hasten, facilitate, forward, advance.
Ant.—Hinder, retard, delay, obstruct, restrain.
Expel. (See Eject.)
Expend. (See Spend.)
Expensive, costly, dear, valuable, sumptuous.
Ant.—Cheap, poor, worthless, economical.
Experience, experiment, trial, proof, test.
Ant.—Conjecture, theory, hazard, hypothesis, intuition.
Experiment, proof, trial, test.
Expert. (See Adroit.)
Expire. (See Die.)
Explain, expound, interpret, elucidate, clear up, illustrate.
Ant.—Mystify, obscure, confound, confuse, muddle, perplex, misinterpret.
Explicit, express, plain, definitive, positive, determinate.
Ant.—Implicit, implied, suggested, limited, obscure.
Exploit. (See Achievement.)
Expound. (See Explain.)
Express, *a.* explicit, plain, positive, definitive, determinate, categorical.
Ant.—General, vague, undefined, loose.
Express, *v.* declare, enunciate pronounce, articulate, denote utter, signify, testify, intimate, tell.
Ant.—Hint, conceal, mystify, obscure, retain.
Expressive. (See Significant.)
Expunge. (See Erase.)
Exquisite, preëminent, superlative, consummate.
Ant.—Common, coarse, ordinary.
Extend, increase, stretch, elongate.
Ant.—Abridge, abbreviate, shorten.
Extensive, comprehensive, wide, large, expansive, diffusive.
Ant.—Contracted, limited, restricted, narrow.
Exterior, outward, outer, external.
Ant.—Internal, inner, inward.
Exterminate, eradicate, root out, annihilate, extinguish.
Ant.—Propagate, populate, increase, augment.
Extinguish, abolish, destroy, extirpate, eradicate, kill.
Ant.—Establish, propagate, promote, fan, encourage, aid, replenish.
Extort, exact, wrest, wring, draw from.
Ant.—Coax, wheedle, cajole, cheat.
Extract, draw out, elicit, pump.
Ant.—Restore, resist, replace, incorporate.
Extraordinary, remarkable, signal, eminent, uncommon, peculiar, marvelous.
Ant.—Ordinary, usual, common, frequent.
Extravagant, prodigal, lavish, profuse, excessive, wild, absurd.
Ant.—Frugal, parsimonious, sound, economical, niggardly.
Extreme, utmost, farthest, most distant, last, extravagant.
Ant.—Initial, primal, beginning, moderate, judicious.
Extricate, free, disengage, disentangle, disembarrass, liberate.
Ant.—Involve, enmesh, encompass, encircle.
Exuberant, plenteous, plentiful, luxuriant, abundant, rich.
Ant.—Scant, deficient, sparse, mean.
Exultation, transport, joy, triumph, elation.
Ant.—Depression, sorrow, grief, mournfulness.

F

Fable, apologue, novel, romance, tale.

Fabricate, invent, frame, feign, forge, coin, make, construct.
Ant.—Narrate, copy, represent, portray, repeat, demolish, spoil.

Face, *n.* visage, countenance.

Face, *v.* front, confront, encounter.
Ant.—Avoid, escape, shun, elude.

Facetious, jocose, jocular, pleasant, witty.
Ant.—Grave, serious, dull, lugubrious.

Facile, easy, pliable, flexible, docile, manageable.
Ant.—Obstinate, determined, inflexible, self-willed.

Fact, reality, incident, circumstance, truth, deed.
Ant.—Fiction, falsehood, lie, delusion, invention, romance, supposition, theory.

Factor, agent.

Fail, to fall short, be deficient, decline, become bankrupt, waste away.
Ant.—Succeed, accomplish.

Failing, imperfection, weakness, frailty, foible, miscarriage, mishap.
Ant.—Virtue, power, vigor, strength.

Failure, omission, neglect, default.
Ant.—Success, achievement.

Faint, languid, weak, low, timid, dim, pale, feeble.
Ant.—Strong, vigorous, fresh, prominent, conspicuous, glaring, forcible.

Fair, clear, bright, just, honest, equitable, impartial, reasonable.
Ant.—Lowering, dull, cloudy, gloomy, foul, ugly, unfair, fraudulent, dishonorable, dishonest.

Faith, belief, creed, orthodoxy.
Ant.—Disbelief, infidelity, heterodoxy.

Faithful, true, loyal, constant.
Ant.—Faithless, treacherous, perfidious.

Faithless, unfaithful, false-hearted, treacherous.
Ant.—Faithful, true, firm, loyal.

Fall, drop, sink, droop, decline, tumble.
Ant.—Rise, ascend, mount, climb, soar.

False, untrue, mendacious.
Ant.—True, correct, real, genuine, sound, authentic.

Falsehood, untruth, story, lie, fabrication, fib, falsity.
Ant.—Truth, fact, verity, reality, honesty.

Falter, halt, stammer, stutter, hesitate.
Ant.—Persevere, speed, proceed.

Fame, reputation, glory, renown, celebrity, honor, credit.
Ant.—Silence, disgrace, dishonor, hush, ignominy.

Familiar, free, frank, affable, conversant, intimate.
Ant.—Unfamiliar, new, unacquainted, rare, strange, uncommon.

Family, household, house, lineage, ancestry, race.
Ant.—Strangers, foreigners.

Famous, famed, celebrated, renowned, illustrious.
Ant.—Obscure, unknown, inconspicuous.

Fanciful, imaginative, ideal, fantastical, whimsical, capricious, grotesque, erratic.
Ant.—Natural, regular, sober, orderly, truthful, literal, practical, unimaginative.

Fancy, imagination, notion, conceit, vagary, frolic, inclination, liking, humor, thought.
Ant.—Reality, fact, law, truth, verity, aversion, common sense.

Farewell, good-bye, adieu, leave-taking.
Ant.—Welcome, hail.

Farthest, most distant, extreme, remotest, utmost, uttermost.
Ant.—Nearest, adjacent, next, adjoining, neighboring.

Fascinate. (See Captivate.)

Fashion, custom, manner, mode, practice, form, usage, style, conformity.
Ant.—Eccentricity, strangeness, shapelessness.

Fast, firm, solid, constant, steadfast, stanch, stable, steady, unyielding, inflexible, unswerving, wild, dissipated, gay, rapid, quick, fleet, expeditious.
Ant.—Loose, insecure, slow, tardy, virtuous, respectable, sluggish.

Fasten, fix, tie, link, stick, hold, affix, attach, annex.
Ant.—Unfasten, loose, undo, relax, detach, remove.

Fat, obese, corpulent, pursy, unctuous, rich.
Ant.—Lean, slender, barren, poor, scant.

Fatal, deadly, mortal, lethal, inevitable.
Ant.—Beneficial, wholesome, nutritious, salubrious, harmless.

Fatigue, weariness, lassitude, languor, enervation, exhaustion.
Ant.—Freshness, vigor, activity, vivacity.

Fault, blemish, imperfection, vice, failure, defect, omission.
Ant.—Perfection, correctness, completeness.

Favor, benefit, kindness, civility, grace, gift, boon.
Ant.—Disfavor, disapproval, refusal, denial, prohibition.

Fear, fright, terror, dismay, alarm, dread, trepidation, timidity, timorousness, consternation, apprehension.
Ant.—Boldness, confidence, courage, trust, assurance, bravery.

Fearful, afraid, timid, nervous, timorous, dreadful, awful, frightful, horrible, distressing, shocking.
Ant.—Fearless, bold, audacious, confident, hopeful, alluring, attractive.

Fearless. (See Brave.)

Fee, charge, bill, account, reckoning.
Ant.—Favor, gift.

Feeble, weak, infirm, nerveless, forceless, failing, frail, enfeebled, debilitated, enervated, impotent, paralyzed, palsied.
Ant.—Strong, robust, active, effective, successful.

Feeling, emotion, sentiment, impression, sensation, consciousness, sensibility, susceptibility.
Ant.—Insensibility, coldness, callousness, imperturbability.

Feign. (See Pretend.)

Felicity, happiness, bliss, blessedness, beatitude, blissfulness.
Ant.—Unhappiness, sadness, gloominess, wretchedness.

Fell, cruel, inhuman, barbarous, merciless, ruthless, pitiless, remorseless, relentless, savage, ferocious, brutal.
Ant.—Generous, chivalrous, humane, lenient, propitious.

Fellow, comrade, equal, companion, colleague, mate.
Ant.—Foe, stranger, opponent, opposite, antagonist.

Fellowship, brotherhood, society, companionship, acquaintance, familiarity, intimacy.
Ant.—Severance, enmity, vendetta, disconnection.

Ferocious, fierce, savage, ravenous, voracious, cruel, inhuman, fell, barbarous, furious, wild.
Ant.—Gentle, docile, tame, harmless, calm, mild.

Fertile, fruitful, prolific, teeming, pregnant, productive, rich, luxuriant, plenteous.

Ant.—Sterile, barren, unfruitful, unproductive, unimaginative.

Fervid, glowing, ardent, impassioned, fervent, warm.
Ant.—Passionless, cool, apathetic, indifferent, phlegmatic.

Festal, festive, convivial, joyous, gay.
Ant.—Gloomy, deserted, solitary, sad, ascetic.

Feud, fray, affray, broil, quarrel, dispute, enmity, strife.
Ant.—Friendliness, clanship, sympathy, reconciliation.

Fickle, unstable, inconstant, restless, fitful, variable, changeable.
Ant.—Reliable, stable, unchangeable, steady, trustworthy, uniform.

Fiction, romance, invention, falsehood, fabrication.
Ant.—Fact, truth, verity, reality.

Fidelity, faithfulness, honesty, integrity, exaction.
Ant.—Treachery, disloyalty, untruthfulness, infidelity, inaccuracy.

Fiendish, diabolic, demoniacal, devilish.
Ant.—Angelic, divine, celestial.

Fierce. (See Furious.)

Fiery, hot, glowing, ardent, fervid, impassioned, passionate, high-spirited, fervent, vehement.
Ant.—Cold, icy, tame, passionless, mild, quenched.

Fight, battle, action, engagement, combat, conflict, contest, encounter, contention, struggle.
Ant.—Pacification, reconciliation, truce, retreat.

Figure, image, allegory, emblem, type, symbol, form, shape, metaphor, picture.
Ant.—Misrepresentation, disfigurement, deformity.

Fill, satisfy, content, store, replenish, glut, gorge, stuff.
Ant.—Empty, drain, exhaust, diminish, subside, ebb.

Filthy, dirty, dingy, unclean, gross.
Ant.—Pure, sweet, clean.

Final, ending, ultimate, last, latest, conclusive, decisive.
Ant.—Inaugural, incipient, rudimentary, progressive, current.

Find, descry, discover, espy.
Ant.—Lose, overlook.

Fine, refined, delicate, pure, nice, handsome, pretty, beautiful, elegant, showy, subtle, minute.
Ant.—Coarse, large, rough, blunt, rude, illiberal, paltry.

Fine, forfeit, forfeiture, mulct, penalty.
Ant.—Gift, donation.

Finite, limited, bounded, terminable.
Ant.—Infinite, unlimited, eternal, boundless.

Fire, glow, heat, warmth.
Ant.—Cold.

Firm, strong, robust, sturdy, fast, steadfast, stable, solid, constant, fixed.
Ant.—Loose, insecure, weak, irresolute, indulgent, wavering, unreliable, yielding.

First, primary, primitive, pristine, primeval, original, foremost, chief, earliest, paramount.
Ant.—Last, subordinate, subsequent, hindmost.

Fit, *v.* suit, adapt, adjust, equip, prepare, qualify, accommodate.
Ant.—Misfit, unsuit, misadjust, disqualify.

Fit, *a.* apt, suitable, meet, befitting, becoming, decent, decorous, expedient.
Ant.—Unfit, unsuitable, inadequate, inappropriate, inexpedient, unbecoming.

Fitful, fickle, unstable, unsteadfast, inconstant, mutable, versatile, restless.
Ant.—Regular, systematic, orderly, sober, equable.

Fix, *v.* fasten, tie, link, enlink, attach, stick, settle, establish, determine, define, limit.
Ant.—Unfix, displace, unfasten, untie, unsettle, disarrange, remove, disturb, change, transfer.

Flagitious, disgraceful, scandalous, heinous, monstrous, wicked.
Ant.—Honorable, creditable, meritorious, pardonable, excusable.

Flame, blaze, flare, flash, glare.

Flashy, showy, ostentatious, gaudy, pompous, tawdry.
Ant.—Subdued, dull, colorless, dim.

Flat, level, horizontal, even, insipid, mawkish, dull, spiritless, tasteless, lifeless.
Ant.—Hilly, rolling, uneven, mountainous, exciting, thrilling, rugged.

Flattery, adulation, servility, cajolery.
Ant.—Insult, rebuke, reprimand, satire, censure.

Flavor, taste, relish, savor.
Ant.—Tastelessness, insipidity.

Flaw. (See Defect.)

Fleeting, temporary, transient, transitory, short-lived, ephemeral.
Ant.—Lasting, permanent, long-lived, eternal.

Fleetness, quickness, celerity, swiftness, speed, rapidity, velocity.
Ant.—Slowness, tardiness, inertness, sluggishness, laziness.

Flexible, pliant, lithe, supple, ductile, pliable.
Ant.—Rigid, inflexible, hard, tough, inelastic, stiff, unbending.

Flicker, flutter, quiver, waver, glimmer.
Ant.—Blaze, gleam, shine, stream.

Flightiness, levity, lightness, giddiness.
Ant.—Gravity, heaviness, sobriety.

Flimsy, light, weak, superficial, shallow.
Ant.—Solid, sound, substantial, cogent, strong.

Fling, cast, throw, hurl, toss.
Ant.—Hold, keep, retain, grasp, snatch, arrest.

Flippancy, pertness, sauciness, lightness.
Ant.—Respect, gravity, sobriety, flattery, obsequiousness.

Flock, throng, crowd, swarm, shoal, congregate, assemble.
Ant.—Separate, disperse, scatter.

Flood, deluge, inundation, overflow, submersion, drowning.
Ant.—Drought, scarcity, drain, ebb, subsidence.

Flourish, thrive, prosper, wave, brandish.
Ant.—Decay, decline, fade, arrest, sheathe, ground, degenerate.

Flowery, florid, ornate, embellished.
Ant.—Bare, nude, sober, chaste.

Fluctuate, waver, hesitate, oscillate, scruple, change.
Ant.—Persist, abide, stay, stick, adhere.

Fluctuating, wavering, hesitating, oscillating, vacillating, changing.
Ant.—Firm, steadfast, decided, resolute, stable.

Fluent, flowing, glib, voluble, unembarrassed, ready.
Ant.—Labored, strained, dribbling, difficult, unready, hesitating, halting.

Fly, soar, mount, tower.
Ant.—Crawl, sink, decline, descend.

Foe. (See Adversary.)

Foil, balk, defeat, frustrate, baffle.
Ant.—Aid, abet, assist, promote, advance, encourage.

Fold, wrap, envelop.
Ant.—Unfold, disengage, expose.

Folks, persons, people, individuals.

Follow, succeed, ensue, imitate, copy, pursue.
Ant.—Lead, precede, disobey, avoid, elude, cause, originate, create.

Follower, partisan, disciple, retainer, pursuer, successor, adherent.
Ant.—Leader, teacher, rival, antagonist, predecessor, superior.

Folly, silliness, foolishness, imbecility, weakness.
Ant.—Wisdom, prudence, sense, judgment, sanity, reasonableness.

Fond, enamored, attached, affectionate, loving, tender, devoted.
Ant.—Distant, irresponsive, unloving, averse, austere, insensible.

Fondness, affection, attachment, kindness, love.
Ant.—Aversion, dislike, hate.

Food, meal, repast, victuals, meat, viands, diet.
Ant.—Drink, want, starvation, hunger.

Fool, idiot, buffoon, zany, clown.
Ant.—Philosopher, student, scholar.

Foolhardy, venturesome, incautious, hasty, adventurous, rash.
Ant.—Cautious, careful, provident.

Foolish, simple, silly, irrational, brainless, imbecile, crazy, absurd, preposterous, ridiculous, nonsensical.
Ant.—Sensible, wise, sane, sagacious, prudent, judicious, advisable, discreet.

Fop, dandy, dude, beau, coxcomb, puppy, jackanapes.
Ant.—Gentleman.

Foppish, dandified, dressy.
Ant.—Modest, dowdy, slovenly, unaffected.

Forage, spoil, pillage, depredate, plunder.
Ant.—Purchase, buy, protect, shield.

Forbear, abstain, refrain, withhold.
Ant.—Indulge, seek.

Force, *v.* compel, coerce, oblige, necessitate.
Ant.—Persuade, ask, coax.

Force, *n.* strength, vigor, dint, might, energy, power, violence, army, host.
Ant.—Weakness, feebleness, inefficiency, debility.

Forcible, strong, vigorous, energetic, effective, operative, powerful, cogent, irresistible.
Ant.—Weak, feeble, inefficient, disabled, ineffective, tame.

Forebode, presage, portend, augur.

Forecast, forethought, foresight, premeditation, prognostication.
Ant.—Result, effect, end, record, afterthought.

Forego, abandon, quit, relinquish, let go, waive.
Ant.—Insist.

Foregoing, antecedent, anterior, preceding, previous, prior, former.
Ant.—Subsequent, succeeding, latter, following.

Forerunner, herald, harbinger, precursor, omen.
Ant.—Successor, follower, issue, result.

Foresight, forethought, forecast, premeditation.
Ant.—Result, record, guess, hazard, issue.

Foretell. (See Predict.)

Forge, coin, invent, frame, feign, fabricate, counterfeit, falsify.
Ant.—Detect, expose, shatter, batter, shiver, blast, verify.

Forget, lose, overlook.
Ant.—Remember, recollect, retain, treasure, learn.

Forgive, pardon, condone, remit, absolve, acquit, excuse, except.
Ant.—Condemn, accuse, punish.

Forlorn, forsaken, abandoned, deserted, desolate, lone, lonesome.
Ant.—Cherished, beloved.

Form, *n.* ceremony, solemnity, observance, rite, figure, shape, conformation, fashion, appearance, representation, semblance.
Ant.—Informality, illegality, mockery, distortion, vagueness.

Form, *v.* make, create, produce, constitute, arrange, fashion, mold, shape, frame.
Ant.—Deform, derange, dislocate, distort, dissipate, analyze, destroy, demolish.

Formal, ceremonious, precise, exact, stiff, methodical, affected, regular, correct.
Ant.—Informal, easy, unceremonious, incomplete, incorrect, natural, unconventional, careless.

Former, antecedent, anterior, previous, prior, preceding, foregoing.
Ant.—Latter, succeeding, subsequent, posterior, future.

Formidable, terrible, dreadful, fearful, shocking, horrible.
Ant.—Contemptible, despicable, weak, trivial.

Forsake. (See Abandon.)

Forsaken, abandoned, forlorn, deserted, desolate, lone, lonesome.
Ant.—Cherished, protected, defended, pursued, supported, upheld.

Forthwith, immediately, directly, instantly, instantaneously.
Ant.—Soon, presently, by and by, hereafter, anon.

Fortify, strengthen, garrison, reinforce, intrench.
Ant.—Weaken, invalidate, dismantle.

Fortitude, endurance, resolution, fearlessness, dauntlessness, strength, courage.
Ant.—Timidity, faintness, delicacy, effeminacy, weakness.

Fortunate, lucky, happy, auspicious, prosperous, successful.
Ant.—Unfortunate, unlucky, unhappy, luckless.

Fortune, chance, fate, luck, doom, destiny, property, possession, riches.
Ant.—Misfortune, poverty.

Forward, *a.* onward, progressive, confident, presumptuous, bold, imprudent.
Ant.—Backward, slow, tardy, indifferent, retiring, modest.

Forward, *v.* further, advance, promote, prefer.
Ant.—Deter, retard, retain, hinder, obstruct.

Foster, cherish, nurse, tend, harbor, nurture.
Ant.—Neglect, disregard.

Foul, dirty, impure, nasty, filthy, unclean, defiled.
Ant.—Pure, clean.

Found, ground, base, rest, build, institute, establish, set up.
Ant.—Uproot, disestablish, subvert, overthrow, demolish.

Foundation, ground, basis, groundwork, establishment.
Ant.—Superstructure, building, disestablishment.

Fractious, cross, petulant, touchy, captious, testy, peevish, fretful, splenetic.
Ant.—Good-humored, agreeable, genial, blithesome, tractable, submissive, pliant.

Fragile, brittle, frail, delicate, feeble.
Ant.—Tough, hardy, stout, strong, sturdy, solid.

Fragment, piece, scrap, chip, remains, remnant, leaving.
Ant.—Bulk, body, mass, whole, solid, entity.

Fragrant, spicy, sweet-scented, balmy, perfumed.
Ant.—Malodorous, stinking, fetid, scentless.

Frailty, weakness, failing, foible, imperfection, fault, blemish.
Ant.—Strength, perfection.

Frame, form, construct, invent, coin, fabricate, forge, mold, feign, make, compose.
Ant.—Sunder, destroy, dissolve, rend.

Franchise, right, exemption, immunity, privilege, suffrage, freedom.
Ant.—Obligation, disqualification, disability, jurisdiction.

Frank, artless, candid, sincere, free, easy, familiar, open, ingenuous, plain.
Ant.—Disingenuous, close, reserved, taciturn, tricky, insincere, wily, shifty.

Frantic, distracted, mad, furious, raving, frenzied.
Ant.—Sane, sober, calm, collected, composed, unruffled, quiet, subdued, peaceful, normal.

Fraternize, coöperate, consort, associate with.
Ant.—Oppose, renounce, abjure, foreswear.

Fraud, deception, deceit, duplicity, guile, cheat, imposition.
Ant.—Honesty, straightforwardness, fairness.

Fray. (See Affray.)

Freak, fancy, humor, vagary, whim, caprice, crotchet.
Ant.—Purpose, resolution, consistency.

Free, *a.* liberal, generous, bountiful, bounteous, munificent, frank, artless, candid, familiar, open, unconfirmed, unreserved, unrestricted, exempt, clear, loose, easy, careless, independent, unconfined.
Ant.—Illiberal, biased, bound, shackled, restricted, clogged, impeded, subject, amenable, qualified, slavish, stingy, artful.

Free, *v.* release, set free, deliver, rescue, liberate, enfranchise, emancipate, exempt, affranchise.
Ant.—Bind, shackle, restrict, clog, hinder, enslave, disenfranchise, confine, imprison.

Freedom, liberty, independence, unrestraint, familiarity, license, franchise, exemption, privilege.
Ant.—Slavery, bondage, serfdom.

Frequent, often, common, usual, general.
Ant.—Rare, few, solitary, scanty, casual, infrequent, unique, exceptional.

Fresh, new, novel, recent, modern, blooming, ruddy.
Ant.—Stale, old, weary, stagnant, faded, decayed, pallid, sickly, musty, putrid, former.

Fret, gall, chafe, agitate, irritate, vex.
Ant.—Soothe, console, please, appease.

Fretful. (See Fractious.)

Friendly, amicable, social, sociable, kindly.
Ant.—Hostile, inimical, adverse, antagonistic, distant, reserved, cool.

Fright. (See Alarm.)

Frighten, scare, affright, dismay, appal, terrify, daunt.
Ant.—Compose, reassure, allay, soothe, rally, embolden.

Frightful, fearful, dreadful, dire, direful, terrific, awful, horrible, horrid.
Ant.—Pleasing, attractive, fair, beautiful, lovely, gentle.

Frivolous, trifling, trivial, petty, silly.
Ant.—Serious, earnest, grave, important.

Frolic, gambol, play, game, sport, prank, spree, lark.
Ant.—Occupation, work, business, study, purpose.

Front. (See Face.)

Frugal, provident, economical, saving, temperate.
Ant.—Intemperate, profuse, extravagant, self-indulgent, wasteful, prodigal.

Fruitful, fertile, prolific, productive, abundant, plentiful, plenteous.
Ant.—Unfruitful, barren, sterile, useless, fruitless.

Fruitless, vain, useless, idle, abortive, bootless, unavailing, without avail.
Ant.—Fruitful, profitable, valuable, successful.

Frustrate, defeat, foil, disappoint, balk.
Ant.—Aid, abet, forward, push, incite, instigate, encourage, assist, help, satisfy.

Fulfill, accomplish, complete, effect.
Ant.—Neglect, ignore, disappoint, falsify, bungle, fail.

Fullness. (See Abundance.)

Fully, completely, abundantly, perfectly.
Ant.—Partially, partly.

Fulsome, coarse, gross, sickening, offensive, rank.
Ant.—Chaste, sober, nice, delicate, moderate.

Fun. (See Humor.)

Funereal, dismal, dark, mournful.
Ant.—Festive, joyous, lively.

Furious, violent, boisterous, vehement, dashing, sweeping, rolling, impetuous, frantic, distracted, stormy, angry, raging, fierce.
Ant.—Calm, sober, quiet, composed, sane, dull, unruffled, unrestrained, placid.

Further. (See Advance.)

Fury. (See Anger.)

Futile, trifling, trivial, frivolous, useless.
Ant.—Effective, powerful, cogent, useful, solid, capable.

G

Gaiety, merriment, jollity, mirth, hilarity.
Ant.—Sadness, sorrow, melancholy, gravity.

Gain, *n.* profit, emolument, advantage, benefit, winnings, earnings.
Ant.—Loss, forfeiture, disadvantage, failure.

Gain, *v.* get, acquire, obtain, attain, procure, earn, win, achieve, reap, reach, realize.
Ant.—Lose, forfeit, suffer, fail.

Gainsay, contradict, deny, dispute.
Ant.—Affirm, verify, confirm, attest, witness.

Gallant, brave, bold, courageous, gay, fine, showy, intrepid, fearless, heroic.
Ant.—Cowardly, churlish, discourteous, rude, coarse, timid. shrinking, fearful, timorous.

Gallantry, prowess, courage, bravery, valor, heroism, boldness, fearlessness, politeness.
Ant.—Cowardice, timidity, rudeness, barbarity.

Galling, irritating, chafing, vexing.
Ant.—Soothing.

Gambol, frisk, prank, play, spree, caper.
Ant.—Droop, flag, tire, work, study.

Game, play, pastime, diversion, sport, amusement.
Ant.—Toil, work, business, duty, study, labor, drudgery.

Gang, company, band, horde, mob, troop, crew.
Ant.—Individual.

Gap, breach, chasm, hollow, cavity, cleft, crevice, rift, chink.

Garble, mutilate, misquote, distort, pervert, falsify.
Ant.—Quote, cite, extract, recite.

Garnish, embellish, adorn, beautify, deck, decorate.
Ant.—Denude, strip, dismantle, spoil, mark, pollute, deface, defile.

Gather, collect, pick, cull, assemble, muster, infer.
Ant.—Scatter, disperse.

Gaudy, showy, tawdry, gay, glittering, bespangled, flashy.
Ant.—Rich, simple, handsome, chaste, somber, dark, plain.

Gaunt, emaciated, scraggy, meager, lank, attenuated, spare, lean, thin, skinny.
Ant.—Sleek, fat, well-fed, unctuous, plump, stout.

Gay, cheerful, merry, lively, jolly, sprightly, blithe.
Ant.—Sad, melancholy, grave, heavy, somber, dull, solemn, funereal, doleful, dismal.

Generate, make, form, beget, produce.

Generation, formation, race, breed, stock, kind, age, era.
Ant.—Eternity, immortality, perpetuity.

Generous, beneficent, noble, honorable, bountiful, liberal, free.
Ant.—Stingy, mean, selfish, illiberal, ignoble, niggardly, close, parsimonious, miserly.

Genial, cordial, hearty, festive, joyous, warm.
Ant.—Ungenial, cold, distant, harsh, deadly.

Genius, talent, taste, nature, character, cleverness, intellect, invention, adept.
Ant.—Stupidity, imbecility, stolidity, inanity, dullness.

Genteel, refined, polished, fashionable, polite, well-bred.
Ant.—Boorish, clownish, rude, uncultivated.

Gentle, placid, mild, meek, tame, bland, docile.
Ant.—Rough, rude, harsh, coarse, fierce, savage, uncouth, boisterous, obstreperous.

Genuine, real, true, unaffected, sincere, authentic, veritable.
Ant.—Spurious, synthetic, fictitious, adulterated, false, deceptive.

Germane, relative, allied, related, pertinent.
Ant.—Foreign, alien, irrelevant, unconnected.

Gesture, attitude, action, posture.

Get, obtain, earn, gain, attain, procure, achieve.
Ant.—Lose, forfeit, surrender, forego, fail.

Ghastly, pallid, wan, hideous, grim, shocking.
Ant.—Ruddy, blooming, fresh, comely, buxom, florid, high-colored, hectic, radiant.

Ghost, specter, sprite, apparition, shade, phantom.
Ant.—Substance, body, animal, organism.

Gibe, scoff, sneer, flout, jeer, mock, taunt, deride.
Ant.—Salute, compliment, hail, welcome, greet, cheer, encourage, applaud, approve.

Giddy, unsteady, flighty, thoughtless, lofty.
Ant.—Steady, stationary, wary, composed, slow, ponderous, thankful, low, reliable, poised, well-balanced, dependable.

Gift, donation, benefaction, grant, alms, gratuity, boon, present, faculty, talent.
Ant.—Earnings, purchase, compensation, remuneration, forfeit, surrender, stupidity, inanity.

Gigantic, enormous, colossal, huge, vast, prodigious, immense.
Ant.—Diminutive, little, tiny, small, wee.

Gild. (See Adorn.)

Gird, belt, encircle, enclose, engird.
Ant.—Open, expand, ungird, disclose.

Give, grant, bestow, confer, yield, impart.
Ant.—Withhold, retain, refuse, deny, withdraw, take, absorb.

Glad, pleased, cheerful, joyful, gladsome, gratified, cheering.
Ant.—Sorry, unhappy, dismal, despondent, sad, melancholy, depressed.

Glare, flare, glisten, glitter, dazzle, gleam.
Ant.—Flicker, glimmer, sparkle, scintillate.

Gleam, glare, glimmer, glance, glitter, shine, flash.

Glee, gaiety, merriment, mirth, joviality, joy, hilarity.
Ant.—Sorrow, despondency, sadness.

Glib, voluble, fluent, flowing, ready, flippant.
Ant.—Stammering, slow, hesitating, abrupt, rough.

Glide, slip, slide, run, roll on.
Ant.—Jump, skip, hop, tumble, stumble, fall.

Glimmer, flicker, gleam, glitter.

Glimpse, glance, look, glint.
Ant.—Scrutiny, analysis, investigation, inspection, exposure.

Glitter, flicker, gleam, shine, glisten, radiate.

Gloom, cloud, darkness, dimness, blackness, dullness, sadness.
Ant.—Light, brightness, radiance, clearness, joy.

Gloomy, lowering, lurid, dim, dusky, sad, glum.
Ant.—Bright, clear, gay, merry.

Glorify, magnify, celebrate, adore, exalt, elevate, honor.
Ant. Debase, degrade, decry, defame, censure, abuse, overthrow, ruin, dishonor, disgrace.

Glorious, famous, renowned, celebrated, illustrious, distinguished, conspicuous, noble, exalted, grand.
Ant.—Degraded, infamous, unknown, debased, dishonored.

Glory, honor, fame, renown, splendor, grandeur.
Ant.—Ignominy, dishonor, degradation, obscurity, infamy, shame, disgrace.

Glowing. (See Hot.)

Glut, gorge, stuff, cram, cloy, satiate, block up, fill to repletion, inundate.
Ant.—Empty, drain, draw off, starve.

Go, depart, proceed, move, budge, stir.
Ant.—Come, stand, stay, abide, remain, persist, endure.

God, Creator, Lord, Almighty, Jehovah, Omnipotence, Providence.
Ant.—Beelzebub, Lucifer, Satan, the devil.

Godly, righteous, devout, holy, pious, religious.
Ant.—Wicked, godless, impious.

Good, *n.* benefit, weal, advantage, profit, boon.
Ant.—Hurt, evil, injury, detriment, disadvantage, calamity, affliction, mischief, harm, loss.

Good, *a.* virtuous, righteous, upright, just, true, pious, efficient, reputable.
Ant.—Bad, evil, wrong, mean, disgraceful, imperfect, vicious, invalid, fictitious, wicked.

Goodly, comely, pleasant. graceful, desirable, considerable.
Ant.—Unpleasant, undesirable, inconsiderable, small.

Gorge, glut, fill, cram, stuff, satiate.
Ant.—Empty, starve.

Gorgeous, superb, grand, magnificent, splendid.
Ant.—Dowdy, dingy, bare, cheap, poor, mean, squalid.

Govern, rule, manage, command, direct, mold, sway.

Ant.—Misgovern, misrule, misdirect, tyrannize, comply, obey, submit, yield.

Government, rule, administration, cabinet, constitution, state, control, sway.

Ant.—Anarchy, revolution, rebellion.

Graceful, becoming, elegant, beautiful, comely.

Ant.—Ungraceful, awkward, deformed, gawky, ungainly, clumsy.

Gracious, merciful, beneficent, courteous, civil, kindly.

Ant.—Haughty, ungracious, churlish, disdainful, curt.

Gradual, slow, progressive.

Ant.—Sudden, instantaneous, intermittent, broken, periodic.

Grand, majestic, stately, dignified, lofty, elevated, exalted, splendid, gorgeous, superb, magnificent, sublime, pompous.

Ant.—Small, little, inferior, common, paltry, insignificant, undignified, petty, unimposing, shabby, poor, mean.

Grant, *v.* bestow, impart, give, yield, cede, allow, confer, invest.

Ant.—Withhold, deny, withdraw, reserve, absorb, take, assume, engross.

Grant, *n.* gift, boon, donation.

Graphic, forcible, pictorial, telling, picturesque, vivid.

Ant.—Weak, unpicturesque, undescriptive, vague, maundering, illusive.

Grasp, catch, seize, grip, clasp, grapple.

Ant.—Loose, lose, abandon, relinquish, release, surrender, let go.

Grasping, greedy, avaricious, covetous, miserly.

Ant.—Generous, benevolent, philanthropic.

Grateful, agreeable, pleasing, welcome, thankful.

Ant.—Ungrateful, unacceptable, disagreeable, unpleasant, harsh, thankless.

Gratification, enjoyment, pleasure, delight, reward.

Ant.—Abstinence, abnegation, stinting, pain, dislike, disappointment.

Grave, *a.* serious, sedate, thoughtful, solemn, sober, important, weighty, pressing, heavy.

Ant.—Joyous, merry, frivolous, facetious, light, trivial, giddy, flighty.

Grave, *n.* tomb, sepulcher, vault.

Gravity, weight, heaviness, importance, moment, seriousness.

Ant.—Lightness, buoyancy, smallness, frivolity, triviality.

Great, big, huge, large, majestic, vast, grand, noble, august.

Ant.—Little, narrow, puny, few, scanty, short, mean, ignoble, weak, small, petty, unimportant.

Greediness, avidity, eagerness, voracity.

Ant.—Abstinence, temperance, indifference, content, generosity.

Grief, sorrow, affliction, trial, woe, tribulation.

Ant.—Joy, gladness, mirth, pleasure.

Grieve, mourn, lament, sorrow, pain, hurt, wound, bewail.

Ant.—Exult, rejoice, ease, console, soothe.

Grievous, painful, afflicting, heavy, baneful, unhappy, disastrous, calamitous, baleful.

Ant.—Joyous, pleasant, glad, acceptable, light, delightful, enjoyable.

Grind, crush, oppress, grate, harass, afflict.

Ant.—Bless, help.

Grisly, ghastly, terrible, hideous, grim, dreadful.

Ant.—Pleasing, beautiful.

Gross, coarse, outrageous, unseemly, shameful, indelicate, entire, whole.

Ant.—Pure, refined, partial, net, delicate, fine.

Groundless, unfounded, baseless, ungrounded, gratuitous.

Ant.—Well-founded, authoritative, authentic, substantial.

Group, assembly, cluster, collection, clump, order, class.

Grovel, crawl, cringe, fawn, sneak.

Ant.—Soar, aspire, mount, rise.

Grow, increase, expand, advance.

Ant.—Diminish, contract, die, wane, fail, decay, decrease, shrink.

Growl, grumble, snarl, murmur, complain, croak, find fault, repine.

Ant.—Chuckle, cackle, grin, acquiesce, purr, approve, applaud, rejoice.

Grudge, malice, rancor, spite, pique, hatred, aversion.

Ant.—Welcome, liking, affection, attachment.

Gruff, rough, rugged, blunt, rude, harsh, surly, bearish.

Ant.—Affable, mild, pleasant, smooth, courteous, agreeable, amiable, polite.

Grumble. (See Growl.)

Guard *v.* (See Defend.)

Guard *n.* (See Protection.)

Guess. (See Surmise.)

Guide, lead, conduct, direct, regulate, manage, superintend.

Ant.—Mislead, misconduct, betray, deceive.

Guile, deceit, fraud, artifice, trickery.

Ant.—Honesty, candor, sincerity, frankness.

Guilt, crime, offense, sin.

Ant.—Honesty, truth, frankness, straightforwardness, virtue.

Guiltless, harmless, innocent.

Ant.—Guilty, harmful, sinful, criminal, noxious.

Guise, manner, aspect, mien, habit, dress.

Ant.—Individual, life, mind, soul, self.

Gull. (See Cheat.)

Gush, stream, flow, rush, spout.

Ant.—Drip, drop, dribble, trickle, ooze, filter.

Gust, breeze, blast, gale, squall.

Ant.—Calm, quiet.

H

Habit, custom, practice.

Habitation. (See Abode.)

Habitual, usual, customary, accustomed, wonted, regular, ordinary.

Ant.—Unusual, rare, exceptional, occasional, extraordinary.

Hail, greet, salute, welcome, accost, call, address.

Ant.—Ignore, pass, cut, avoid.

Hale. (See Healthy.)

Hallow, consecrate, sanctify, venerate, dedicate, enshrine.

Ant.—Desecrate, abominate, profane, execrate.

Halt, rest, pause, falter, limp, hop, hobble.

Ant.—Advance, speed, proceed, progress.

Handle, manage, use, wield, feel.

Ant.—Drop, mismanage, bungle, abstain.

Handsome, pretty, elegant, graceful, ample, beautiful, fine.

Ant.—Uncomely, ugly, ill-looking, coarse.

Handy, near, convenient, ready, dexterous.

Ant.—Remote, inconvenient, unhandy, awkward, unwieldy.

Happen, betide, befall, occur.

Ant.—Ordain, ordered, caused.

Happiness, felicity, bliss, prosperity, well-being, welfare, beatitude, blessedness.

Ant.—Unhappiness, sorrow,

grief, despair, misery, sadness.

Happy, prosperous, successful, lucky, fortunate, glad.
Ant.—Unhappy, sorrowful, miserable, dull, sorry, disconsolate.

Harass. (See Perplex.)

Harbor, *n.* port, haven, asylum, refuge.
Ant.—Exposure, peril, voyage, toil.

Harbor, *v.* shelter, indulge, foster, cherish, entertain.
Ant.—Exclude, eject, expel, banish, dismiss.

Hard, firm, solid, flinty, unfeeling, harsh, cruel, difficult, arduous.
Ant.—Soft, fluid, liquid, elastic, brittle, easy, mild, lenient, tender, simple, yielding.

Hardihood. (See Audacity.)

Hardy, manly, masculine, vigorous, courageous, brave, heroic, intrepid, stout, strong, firm.
Ant.—Weak, fragile, delicate, effeminate, enervated.

Harm, evil, ill, misfortune, mischief, mishap, injury, hurt, detriment, wrong, infliction.
Ant.—Benefit, boon, improvement, compensation, reparation, favor, kindness.

Harmless, safe, innocuous, innocent.
Ant.—Hurtful, noxious, poisonous.

Harmonious, symphonious, accordant, amicable.
Ant.—Discordant, incongruous, harsh, grating, riotous.

Harsh, rough, severe, rigorous, gruff, rugged, blunt, grating, jarring, sour, morose.
Ant.—Smooth, soft, melodious, suave, kindly, gentle, mild.

Hasten, push on, press on, accelerate, quicken, expedite, hurry, dispatch, speed.
Ant.—Retard, impede, obstruct, hesitate, halt, delay, hinder.

Hasty, quick, precipitate, rash, excitable, hot, fiery, passionate, angry, cursory, slight, hurried, ill-advised.
Ant.—Slow, careful, calm, reflective, thoughtful, deliberate.

Hate, detest, abominate, abhor, loathe, dislike.
Ant.—Love, cherish, like, approve.

Hateful, odious, detestable, execrable, abominable, loathsome, repulsive.
Ant.—Lovable, desirable, delightful, attractive, pleasant.

Hatred, enmity, ill-will, rancor.
Ant.—Friendship, love.

Haughtiness, arrogance, pride.
Ant.—Modesty, meekness, humility.

Haughty, arrogant, disdainful, supercilious, proud.
Ant.—Meek, humble.

Havoc, destruction, desolation, devastation.
Ant.—Prosperity, conservation, augmentation, enrichment.

Hazard, peril, imperil, jeopardize, risk, dare, conjecture, venture, chance.
Ant.—Insure, protect, guard, think, know, determine.

Haze, fog, mist, rime.
Ant.—Clearness, transparency, brightness.

Head. (See Chief.)

Heal, cure, remedy, reconcile.
Ant.—Hurt, wound, harm, pierce.

Healthy, hearty, hale, sound, strong, wholesome, salubrious, salutary.
Ant.—Unhealthy, unsound, delicate, sick, weak, noxious, injurious.

Heap, accumulate, amass, pile up.
Ant.—Disperse, scatter.

Hear, hearken, overhear, listen.
Ant.—Ignore, disregard, refuse.

Hearty, healthy, cordial, sincere, warm.
Ant.—Insincere, cool.

Heavenly, celestial, divine, seraphic, angelic.
Ant.—Hellish, diabolical, devilish.

Heaviness, dullness, gloom, lethargy, torpor.
Ant.—Lightness, buoyancy, joyousness, animation.

Heavy, weighty, massive, dull, drowsy, insipid, oppressive, inert, slow, burdensome, ponderous.
Ant.—Light, agile, active, quick, brisk, animated, joyous.

Heed, mind, attend to, regard, notice, care, give attention.
Ant.—Disregard, slight, ignore, pay no heed, overlook.

Height, top, crisis, acme, apex, climax, zenith.
Ant.—Depth, base, lowness, depression, abasement.

Heighten, amplify, exaggerate, raise, enhance, increase, exalt, elevate.
Ant.—Lower, depress, debase, diminish, tone, modify.

Heinous, atrocious, flagitious, flagrant.
Ant.—Venial, trifling.

Help, aid, assist, relieve, succor.
Ant.—Hinder, block, check, counteract, embarrass, impede, retard.

Heretic, sectary, sectarian, schismatic, dissenter, nonconformist.

Heroic, courageous, brave, bold, intrepid, fearless, gallant.
Ant.—Cowardly, craven, dastardly, timid.

Hesitate, falter, pause, demur, scruple, stammer, stutter.
Ant.—Resolve, decide, determine, proceed.

Hew, cut, fell, hack, chop.
Ant.—Mold, model, form.

Hidden, secret, occult, mysterious.
Ant.—Open, exposed, revealed, understood, apparent, evident.

Hide, *v.* conceal, disguise, secrete, cover, screen.
Ant.—Expose, exhibit, discover, betray, show.

Hideous, ghastly, grim, grisly, frightful, horrible, ugly.
Ant.—Attractive, beautiful, graceful, lovely, entrancing, pretty.

High, tall, lofty, elevated, proud, conceited.
Ant.—Low, depressed, stunted, mean, base, deep.

Hilarity, mirth, glee, jollity, merriment, joviality.
Ant.—Despair, grief, sorrow, mournfulness, depression.

Hinder, thwart, retard, stop, prevent, impede, obstruct.
Ant.—Expedite, promote, facilitate, accelerate, assist, relieve, succor.

Hint, suggest, allude, refer, intimate, insinuate.

Hire, pay, allowance, salary, wages, stipend.
Ant.—Gratuity, present.

Hit, strike, dash, beat, thump.
Ant.—Miss, mischance, fail, err.

Hoard, heap up, treasure, lay up, store.
Ant.—Waste, squander, dissipate.

Hoax. (See Trick.)

Hoist. (See Lift.)

Hold, have, possess, keep, detain, retain.
Ant.—Drop, abandon, release, forego, vacate, surrender, fail, let go.

Holiness, sanctity, piety, sacredness.
Ant.—Wickedness, impiety.

Hollow, vacant, empty, void.
Ant.—Solid, full, strong, firm, genuine, sound.

Holy, sacred, pious, devout, religious, divine, saintly, blessed.
Ant.—Unholy, profane, evil, impure, cursed, polluted, abominable, worldly.
Homage, respect, deference, honor, veneration.
Ant.—Defiance, treason, rebellion, disaffection.
Home. (See Abode.)
Homely, plain, ugly, coarse.
Ant.—Beautiful.
Honest, upright, honorable, conscientious, virtuous.
Ant.—Dishonest, tricky, deceitful, fraudulent, guileful.
Honesty, integrity, purity, probity, sincerity, veracity, virtue, justice, uprightness.
Ant.—Dishonesty, fraud, deceit, deception, guile.
Honor, *n.* homage, dignity, grandeur, deference, respect, regard, reverence, esteem.
Ant.—Disrespect, irreverence, abasement, dishonor, ignominy.
Honor, *v.* reverence, revere, venerate, respect, dignify, exalt.
Ant.—Disrespect, despise, obscure, dishonor.
Hope, expectation, expectancy, trust, confidence, anticipation.
Ant.—Despair, despondency, disbelief.
Hopeless, desperate, pessimistic.
Ant.—Buoyant, hopeful, optimistic.
Horrible, fearful, dreadful, dire, direful, frightful, terrible, terrific, horrid.
Ant.—Lovely, desirable, enjoyable, beautiful, fair, amiable.
Hostile. (See Adverse.)
Hostility. (See Enmity.)
Hot, ardent, fervent, fiery, burning, glowing, intense, passionate.
Ant.—Cold, cool, indifferent, passionless.
House. (See Abode.)
However, nevertheless, notwithstanding, yet.
Huge. (See Enormous.)
Humanity, kindness, benevolence, philanthropy, tenderness, sensibility.
Ant.—Inhumanity, bestiality, unkindness, cruelty.
Humble, *v.* lower, debase, degrade, disgrace, humiliate, mortify, abase.
Ant.—Raise, enhance, honor, elevate, exalt, promote.
Humble, *a.* lowly, modest, submissive, unpretending, unassuming, plain, unostentatious, simple.
Ant.—Eminent, proud, boastful, arrogant, pretentious, haughty, overbearing, supercilious.
Humor, satire, wit, jocularity, temper, mood, frame, fun.
Ant.—Seriousness, gravity, sorrow, grief, nature.
Hunt, seek, chase.
Hurl. (See Fling.)
Hurry, *v.* hasten, speed, expedite, precipitate.
Ant.—Hinder, retard, restrain, obstruct, dally, tarry.
Hurt, annoy, grieve, vex, wound.
Ant.—Heal, soothe, repair, console, benefit, compensate.
Hurtful, pernicious, baneful, deleterious, noxious, detrimental, prejudicial, destructive.
Ant.—Advantageous, useful, beneficial, healthy, wholesome.
Husbandry, cultivation, tillage.
Hush, lull, calm, still, quiet, silence.
Ant.—Noise, riot, gale, disturbance, boisterousness.
Hypocrisy, deceit, pretense, cant.
Ant.—Honesty, candor, openness, virtue, fanaticism.
Hypocrite, dissembler, imposter.
Hypothesis, theory, supposition.

I

Idea, imagination, conception, notion, thought, sentiment, impression.
Ant.—Object, form, subject, thing, reality.
Ideal, imaginary, imaginative, fancied.
Ant.—Physical, material, real, actual, palpable, visible, tangible.
Identical, same, self-same, particular.
Ant.—Different, distinct, contrary, opposed, separate.
Idiot. (See Fool.)
Idle, lazy, indolent, inactive, unemployed.
Ant.—Busy, employed, occupied, industrious, filled, populated.
Ignominious, shameful, scandalous, infamous.
Ant.—Creditable, reputable, honorable, noble.
Ignominy, shame, disgrace, obloquy, infamy, reproach.
Ant.—(See Honor.)
Ignorant, unlearned, illiterate, unlettered, uninformed, uneducated.
Ant.—Learned, wise, informed, educated, cultured, cultivated, erudite.
Ill, *n.* evil, wickedness, misfortune, mischief, harm.
Ant.—Good, blessing.
Ill, *a.* sick, indisposed, unwell, diseased.
Ant.—Well, healthy, sound, hearty.
Illegal, unlawful, illicit, contraband, illegitimate.
Ant.—Lawful, legal, legitimate, honest.
Illimitable, infinite, boundless, immeasurable, unlimited.
Ant.—Limited, finite.
Illiterate, ignorant, unlettered, unlearned, untaught, uninstructed.
Ant.—Learned, educated.
Illness, sickness, indisposition, disease, disorder, malady, ailment.
Ant.—Health, vigor, soundness, activity.
Ill-tempered, crabbed, sour, surly, acrimonious.
Ant.—Good-natured, amiable.
Illusion, deception, phantasm, fallacy.
Ant.—Reality, body, substance.
Illusory, imaginary, chimerical, visionary.
Ant.—Real, actual, tenable.
Illustrate, explain, elucidate, clear.
Ant.—Obscure, confuse, mystify, darken.
Illustrious, celebrated, glorious, noble, eminent, distinguished, famous, renowned.
Ant.—Infamous, disreputable, ignominious, disgraceful, obscure, unknown.
Ill-will, enmity, hatred, antipathy.
Ant.—Good-will, benevolence.
Image, likeness, picture, representation, effigy.
Ant.—Original, substance, subject, reality, truth, verity.
Imaginary, ideal, fanciful, illusory.
Ant.—Real, true, substantial, satisfactory, solid, actual, tangible.
Imagine, conceive, fancy, apprehend, think, presume.
Ant.—Prove, demonstrate, depict, exhibit, substantiate.
Imbecility, silliness, senility, dotage.
Ant.—Wisdom, shrewdness, sagacity, cleverness.
Imbibe. (See Absorb.)
Imitate, copy, ape, mimic, mock, counterfeit.

Ant.—Alter, distort, caricature, modify, misrepresent, vary, originate, invent.

Immaculate, unspotted, spotless, unsullied, stainless.

Ant.—Defiled, impure, corrupt, sinful, contaminated, polluted, soiled, spotted, bedraggled.

Immediate, pressing, instant, next, at once, proximate, contiguous.

Ant.—Distant, far, future, remote.

Immediately, instantly, forthwith, directly, instanter, presently, straightway.

Ant.—By and by, distantly, remotely.

Immense, enormous, vast, huge, prodigious, monstrous.

Ant.—Tiny, diminutive.

Immerse, dip, plunge, douse, souse.

Ant.—Dry, drain, air, ventilate, hoist out.

Immigration, colonization, settlement.

Ant.—Emigration, exodus.

Immunity, privilege, prerogative, exemption.

Ant.—Liability, obligation, impost, jurisdiction, responsibility.

Immure, confine, shut up, imprison.

Ant.—Release, dismiss, acquit, escape.

Impair, injure, diminish, decrease.

Ant.—Enhance, improve, augment, repair, increase, build up, perfect.

Impart, give, reveal, divulge, disclose, discover, bestow, afford.

Impartial, just, equitable, unbiased.

Ant.—Partial, prejudiced, interested.

Impassioned, passionate, glowing, burning, fiery, vehement, intense, impetuous.

Ant.—Cool, impassive, indifferent, unresponsive.

Impeach, accuse, charge, arraign, censure.

Ant.—Acquit, absolve, vindicate, condone, discharge, excuse, forgive, overlook, pardon, release.

Impede, obstruct, hinder, retard, prevent.

Ant.—Help, aid, assist.

Impediment, obstacle, obstruction, hindrance, barrier.

Ant.—Aid, assistance.

Impel, encourage, animate, induce, incite, instigate, embolden.

***Ant.*—Retard, check.**

Impending, imminent, threatening.

Ant.—Distant, remote.

Imperative, commanding, dictatorial, authoritative, despotic, peremptory, dogmatic, domineering, overbearing.

Ant.—Indulgent, lenient, supplicatory, optional, discretional, complaisant, compliant, docile, mild, submissive, yielding.

Imperfection, blemish, fault, defect, vice.

Ant.—Beauty, perfection.

Imperil, peril, endanger, hazard, jeopardize.

Ant.—Defend, secure, protect, shield, rescue, save, deliver.

Imperious, dictatorial, commanding, authoritative, imperative, lordly, domineering, overbearing.

Ant.—(See Imperative.)

Impertinent, intrusive, meddling, officious, rude, saucy, impudent, insolent.

Ant.—Pertinent, related, appropriate, fit, proper, applicable, courteous, suave, polite.

Impervious, impassable, inaccessible, impenetrable.

Ant.—Penetrable, explorable, traversable.

Impetuous, violent, boisterous, furious, vehement, rapid, impulsive, hasty.

Ant.—Slow, thoughtful, deliberate, leisurely, calm.

Impious, profane, irreligious, godless.

Ant.—Pious, sacred, godly, religious, reverent.

Implicate, involve, entangle, embarrass, compromise.

Ant.—Extricate, acquit, disconnect, exonerate, clear, exculpate.

Implore. (See Entreat.)

Imply, involve, comprise, infold, import, denote, signify.

Ant.—Express, state, declare, pronounce.

Importance, signification, significance, avail, consequence, weight, gravity, moment.

Ant.—Unimportance, irrelevance, triviality, meanness, insignificance, pettiness.

Important, pressing, momentous, material, weighty, grave.

Ant.—Unimportant, insignificant, trivial, irrelevant, petty, mean.

Impose, put, place, set, fix, lay.

Ant.—Remove, unburden.

Imposing, impressive, striking, majestic, august, noble, grand.

Ant.—Ineffective, undignified, petty, insignificant, trivial.

Imposition. (See Cheat.)

Impost, tax, duty, custom, excise, tribute, toll.

Ant.—Exemption, immunity, proceeds, revenue.

Impostor. (See Cheat.)

Impotence, weakness, incapacity, infirmity, frailty, feebleness.

Ant.—Power, strength, vigor.

Impotent, weak, feeble, helpless, enfeebled, nerveless, infirm.

Ant.—Strong, capable, effectual.

Impregnate. (See Saturate.)

Impression, feeling, sentiment, sensation, stamp, edition, susceptibility.

Ant.—Apathy, insensibility.

Impressive, stirring, forcible, exciting, affecting, moving.

Ant. Unimpressive, ordinary, common, laughable, ludicrous, ineffective, undignified, petty, insignificant.

Imprison, confine, incarcerate, shut up, immure.

Ant.—Liberate, set free.

Imprisonment, incarceration, captivity, durance, confinement.

Ant.—Freedom, release, acquittal, liberty.

Improve, amend, better, mend, reform, rectify, ameliorate.

Ant.—Debase, lower, disgrace, abase, drag down, make worse, deteriorate, aggravate, corrupt, impair, injure, mar.

Improvement, progress, proficiency, amendment, correction, advancement.

Ant.—Debasement, retrogression, blemish, fault.

Improvident, prodigal, careless, incautious, imprudent, wasteful, reckless, rash.

Ant.—Thrifty, careful, prudent, provident.

Impudence, assurance, impertinence, confidence, insolence, rudeness.

Ant.—Courtesy, courteousness, attention, flattery, compliment, good breeding, politeness, affability.

Impudent, impudence, saucy, brazen, bold, impertinent, forward, rude, insolent, immodest, shameless, aggressive.

Ant.—Gentle, polite, decorous.

Impugn, gainsay, oppose, attack, assail.

Ant.—Confirm, prove, establish, evidence.

Impulse, motive, incentive, incitement, instigation.

Impulsive, rash, hasty, forcible, violent.
Ant.—Deliberate, thoughtful, cool, quiet, self-restrained.

Impure, mixed, adulterated, tainted, foul.
Ant.—Pure, good, unadulterated, honest.

Imputation, blame, censure, reproach, charge, accusation.
Ant.—Withdrawal, retraction, acquittal.

Inability, weakness, impotence, incapacity, incapability.
Ant.—Ability, power, strength, capacity, capability.

Inactive, inert, lazy, slothful, sluggish, idle, indolent.
Ant.—Active, smart, energetic, alert.

Inadvertency, error, oversight, blunder, inattention, carelessness, negligence.

Inanimate, lifeless, dead, defunct, inert, extinct.
Ant.—Animate, alive, sensible, active, lively.

Incapable, unable, inadequate, incompetent, insufficient, unfit.
Ant.—Able, competent, fitted.

Incentive, motive, inducement, impulse.
Ant.—Deterrent.

Incessantly, always, unceasingly, continually, perpetually.
Ant.—Occasionally, periodically, intermittently, never.

Incident. (See Circumstance.)

Incidental, accidental, casual, contingent, occasional.
Ant.—Essential, invariable, regular, irrelative, uniform, inherent.

Incite, urge, instigate, excite, provoke, stimulate, encourage, impel.
Ant.—Deter, dishearten, discourage.

Inclemency, harshness, rigor, intensity, severity.
Ant.—Clemency, mercifulness, mildness, geniality.

Inclination, incline, leaning, slope, disposition, tendency, bent, bias, affection, attachment, wish, liking, desire.
Ant.—Aversion, distaste, dislike, repugnance.

Incline, slope, lean, slant, tend, bend, turn, bias, dispose.
Ant.—Indispose, disincline, deter.

Inclose, surround, shut in, fence in, cover, wrap.
Ant.—Exclude, debar, eject.

Include, comprehend, comprise, contain, embrace, take in, hold.
Ant.—Exclude, except, shut out, enclose.

Incoherent, loose, unconnected, incongruous, inconsistent, incompatible.
Ant.—Coherent, clear, continuous, intelligible.

Incommode, annoy, plague, molest, disturb, inconvenience, trouble.
Ant.—Accommodate, oblige, supply, reconcile, fit.

Incompetent, incapable, unable, inadequate, insufficient.
Ant.—Competent, capable, effective.

Incomplete, imperfect, defective, unexecuted.
Ant.—Complete, perfect, finished.

Inconstant, changeable, unsteadfast, unstable, fickle, restless, fitful, variable.
Ant.—Constant, stable, firm, changeless, faithful, steady.

Inconvenience. (See Incommode.)

Increase, *v.* extend, enlarge, augment, dilate, expand, amplify, raise, enhance, aggravate, magnify, grow.
Ant.—Decrease, diminish, modify, contract, narrow, lessen, dwindle, shrink.

Increase, *n.* augmentation, accession, addition, enlargement, extension.
Ant.—Decrease, diminution, shrinkage.

Inculcate, impress, infuse, instil, implant.
Ant.—Insinuate, suggest, disavow, abjure, denounce.

Incumbent, obligatory.

Incursion, inroad, invasion, irruption, aggression.
Ant.—Retreat, retirement, withdrawal, settlement.

Indefinite, vague, uncertain, unsettled, loose, lax.
Ant.—Definite, exact, bounded, settled, fixed, unalterable, precise.

Indicate, point out, show, mark, declare.
Ant.—Conceal, contradict, falsify, misindicate.

Indication, mark, sign, note, symptom, token.
Ant.—Silence, misdirection, surmise, guess.

Indifference, apathy, carelessness, listlessness, insensibility.
Ant.—Interest, eagerness, gravity, ardor, affection, importance, significance, application, assiduity.

Indigence, want, penury, poverty, destitution, privation, neediness.
Ant.—Abundance, wealth, richness, affluence, plenty.

Indignation, anger, wrath, ire, resentment.

Indignity, insult, affront, outrage, obloquy, opprobrium, reproach, ignominy.
Ant.—Deference, compliment, homage, respect, honor.

Indiscriminate, promiscuous, chance, indistinct, confused.
Ant.—Careful, select, discerning, sorted, chosen, picked.

Indispensable, essential, necessary, requisite, expedient.
Ant.—Dispensable, unnecessary, useless, inexpedient, supernumerary.

Indisputable, undeniable, undoubted, incontestable, indubitable, unquestionable, sure, infallible.
Ant.—Disputable, debatable, doubtful, contestable, fallible, uncertain, questionable, erroneous, mistaken.

Indistinct, uncertain, indiscriminate, confused, ambiguous, disputable, questionable, doubtful.
Ant.—Distinct, certain, exact, clear, plain, intelligible, indisputable, sure.

Indite, compose, couch, frame.

Indolent. (See Lazy.)

Indorse, ratify, confirm, superscribe.
Ant.—Repudiate, abandon, abjure.

Induce. (See Instigate.)

Inducement. (See Motive.)

Indulge, cherish, foster, fondle.
Ant.—Deny, refuse.

Ineffectual, useless, vain, unavailing, fruitless, abortive, inoperative.
Ant.—Effective.

Inequality, disparity, disproportion, unevenness, dissimilarity.
Ant.—Equality, justice, fairness, evenness, purity, similarity.

Inestimable, invaluable, priceless.
Ant.—Estimable, worthless, cheap, mean, poor.

Inevitable, unavoidable, not to be avoided, certain.
Ant.—Avoidable, uncertain, indeterminate, doubtful, unlikely.

Infamous, scandalous, shameful, ignominious, opprobrious, disgraceful.
Ant.—Famous, honorable, reputable, celebrated, renowned noble.

Infect, pollute, contaminate, taint, defile, corrupt.
Ant.—Purify, disinfect.

Infectious. (See Contagious.)
Inference, deduction, corollary, conclusion, consequence.
Ant.—Premise, statement, argument, guess, assumption.
Inferior, secondary, subaltern, subordinate.
Ant.—Superior, better, greater, higher.
Infernal, diabolical, fiendish, devilish, hellish.
Ant.—Celestial, godly, heavenly, saintly.
Infest, annoy, plague, harass, disturb, haunt, beset.
Ant.—Regale, refresh, gratify, comfort.
Infidelity, unbelief, distrust, incredulity, disbelief, unfaithfulness.
Ant.—Faith, belief, trust, orthodoxy.
Infinite, boundless, unbounded, illimitable, unlimited.
Ant.—Limited, bounded, narrow, confined.
Infirm, weak, feeble, enfeebled, decrepit.
Ant.—Firm, strong, sound, forcible, active, cogent, robust, sturdy, vigorous.
Inflame, anger, irritate, enrage, incense, nettle, aggravate, embitter, exasperate, chafe.
Ant.—Cool, quench, extinguish, allay, pacify, quiet, soothe.
Inflict, lay on, impose.
Ant.—Remove, alleviate, suspend, spare.
Influence, *v.* bias, sway, prejudice, prepossess.
Influence, *n.* credit, favor, reputation, character, weight, authority, sway, ascendency.
Ant.—Neutrality, inefficacy, weakness, powerlessness.
Inform, communicate, tell, report, acquaint, apprise, notify, disclose, reveal, divulge.
Ant.—Be silent, conceal, retain, mislead, deceive.
Infraction, infringement, encroachment, invasion, intrusion.
Ant.—Observance, integrity, maintenance, respect.
Infringe, invade, intrude, contravene, break, transgress, violate.
Infuse, instil, ingraft, implant, inspire, breathe into, impart.
Ant.—Dry, drain, retract, divert, suck, withdraw.
Ingenuous, artless, candid, generous, open, frank, plain, sincere,
Ant.—Disingenuous, sly, reserved, mean, insincere, crafty, cunning.
Ingratitude, unthankfulness, thanklessness.
Ant.—Gratitude, thankfulness.
Ingress, entry, entrance, inlet.
Ant.—Egress, exit, outlet.
Inhabit, dwell in, reside in, occupy.
Ant.—Abandon, forsake, migrate.
Inherit, enjoy, possess, obtain.
Ant.—Earn, bequeath, devise.
Inhuman, cruel, brutal, savage, barbarous, ruthless, merciless, ferocious.
Ant.—Human, merciful, civilized, kind, gentle.
Iniquity, injustice, grievance, wrong.
Ant.—Justice, integrity, virtue, holiness.
Injunction. (See Order.)
Injure, damage, hurt, deteriorate, wrong, aggrieve, harm, spoil, mar, sully.
Ant.—Benefit, profit, repair, ameliorate, enhance, help.
Injurious, hurtful, baneful, pernicious, deleterious, noxious, prejudicial, wrongful, damaging.
Ant.—Beneficial, helpful.
Injustice, wrong, iniquity, grievance.
Ant.—Justice, right, law, probity, righteousness.
Inlet. (See Ingress.)
Innocent, guiltless, sinless, harmless, inoffensive, innoxious.
Ant.—Guilty, responsible, sinful, corrupt, bad, impure.
Innocuous, harmless, safe, innocent.
Ant.—Hurtful, injurious.
Innovation, alteration, novelty.
Ant.—Conservation, maintenance, archaism.
Inoffensive, harmless, innocent, innoxious, unoffending.
Ant.—Offensive, obnoxious, pernicious, harmful.
Inordinate, intemperate, irregular, disorderly, excessive, immoderate.
Ant.—Moderate, just, regular, temperate, orderly.
Inquiry, investigation, examination, research, scrutiny, disquisition, question, query, interrogation.
Ant.—Conjecture, guess, assumption, supposition, hypothesis.
Inquisitive, prying, peeping, curious, peering.
Ant.—Indifferent, careless, incurious, dull, blind.
Insane, mad, deranged, delirious, demented.
Ant.—Sane, healthy, sound, normal, rational.
Insanity, lunacy, madness, mental aberration, delirium.
Ant.—Sanity.
Inscribe, dedicate, devote, impress, engrave.
Ant.—Erase, expunge, obliterate, efface, deface.
Inside, interior, within, inland.
Ant.—Without, outside, extraneously, externally.
Insidious, sly, treacherous, crafty, artful, wily.
Ant.—Sincere, straightforward, undesigning.
Insinuate, hint, intimate, suggest, infuse, ingratiate, introduce.
Ant.—State, affirm, propound, announce, withdraw, retract, extract.
Insipid, dull, flat, mawkish, tasteless, vapid, inanimate, lifeless.
Ant.—Racy, intense, strong, full-flavored, bright, sparkling.
Insist, persist, persevere, urge.
Ant.—Waive, yield, concede, surrender, forego.
Insolent, rude, saucy, pert, impertinent, abusive, scurrilous, opprobrious, insulting, offensive, outrageous.
Ant.—Deferential, polite, modest, respectful, considerate, courteous.
Inspect, examine, investigate, overhaul, supervise.
Ant.—Glance, overlook.
Inspire, animate, exhilarate, enliven, cheer, breathe, inhale.
Ant.—Depress, discourage, dispirit, deter.
Instability, mutability, fickleness, mutableness, wavering.
Ant.—Stability, durability, firmness, strength.
Install, induct, inaugurate, invest.
Ant.—Eject, degrade, dismiss, deprive.
Instance. (See Example.)
Instantaneous, direct, immediate, momentary, quick.
Ant.—Enduring, continuing, periodic, long, eternal.
Instantly, immediately, forthwith, straightway, directly, instanter.
Ant.—Soon, by and by, sometime.
Instigate, stir up, persuade, animate, incite, urge, stimulate, encourage, induce.
Ant.—Discourage, deter, dispirit, hinder, obstruct, abstain, depress, dishearten.
Instil, implant, inculcate, infuse, insinuate.

Ant.—Drain, extract, remove, eliminate, strain, deter, uproot, deaden, dull.

Institute, establish, found, erect, begin, form, organize, prescribe.

Ant.—Disestablish, overthrow, bankrupt, complete, finish, subvert.

Instruct, inform, teach, educate, enlighten.

Ant.—Misinform, misinstruct, misguide, mislead, deceive, barbarize, brutalize.

Instrument, tool, implement, utensil, medium, channel, agent.

Ant.—Bar, preventive, obstruction, hindrance, counteragent, opponent.

Instrumental, conducive, assistant, helping, ministerial.

Ant.—Non-instrumental, foreign, opposed, hindrance, hindering, impedimental.

Insufficiency, inadequacy, incompetency, incapability, deficiency, lack.

Ant.—Sufficiency, abundance, plenty, enough, richness, amplitude.

Insult, affront, outrage, indignity, blasphemy.

Ant.—Respect, honor, praise, flattery, compliment, esteem.

Insulting, insolent, rude, saucy, impertinent, abusive.

Ant.—Polite, well-mannered, gentle.

Insurrection, rebellion, mutiny, revolt, sedition.

Ant.—Law, peace, order, government, submission, subjection, obedience, bondage, servitude, pacification.

Integrity, uprightness, honesty, probity, entirety, entireness, completeness, rectitude, purity.

Ant.—Dishonesty, roguery, rascality, fraud, duplicity, meanness, chicanery.

Intellect, understanding, sense, brains, mind, intelligence, ability, talent, genius.

Ant.—Matter, force, passion, body, mechanism, organism, brute force, sense.

Intellectual, mental, ideal, metaphysical, learned.

Ant.—Unintellectual, bodily, physical, ignorant, stupid, real, actual.

Intelligence, advice, information, instruction, notice, intellect, spirit, report, news.

Ant.—Stupidity, dullness, ignorance, misunderstanding, concealment, silence, misguidance.

Intelligent, understanding, enlightened, instructed, knowing.

Ant.—Unintelligent, ignorant, foolish, stupid.

Intelligible, clear, obvious, plain, distinct.

Ant.—Unintelligible, obscure, dull, indistinct, incoherent, abstruse.

Intemperate, immoderate, excessive, drunken, inordinate.

Ant.—Temperate, moderate, self-restrained, ascetic, austere, severe.

Intend. (See Propose.)

Intense, ardent, earnest, glowing, fervid, burning, vehement, strained, forced, excessive, extreme.

Ant.—Indifferent, apathetic, cool, dispassionate, phlegmatic, cold, inert, uninterested.

Intent, purpose, design, intention, drift, view, aim, purport, meaning.

Intentional, designed, intended, contemplated, premeditated, studied.

Ant.—Unintentional, fortuitous, accidental, casual.

Inter, bury, entomb, inhume.

Ant.—Disinter, exhume, resurrect.

Intercede, interpose, interfere, mediate, advocate.

Intercourse, commerce, connection, intimacy, acquaintance.

Ant.—Reticence, cessation, suspension, opposition, isolation, separation, aloofness, detachment.

Interdict, forbid, prohibit, inhibit, proscribe, debar, restrain from.

Ant.—Grant, allow, indulge, concede, permit.

Interfere, interpose, meddle, intermeddle.

Ant.—Avoid, retire, stand off, withdraw.

Interior, inward, inner, inside, internal, intrinsic, inherent, innate.

Ant.—Exterior, outside, adjacent, external.

Intermediate, intervening, interjacent, between.

Ant.—Surrounding, outside, extreme, enclosing.

Interminable, endless, infinite, unlimited, illimitable, boundless, limitless, unending, inexhaustible.

Ant.—Terminable, brief, moderate, curt, short, concise, limited.

Intermission, cessation, pause, rest, stop, stoppage, interruption.

Ant.—Continuity, perpetuity, permanence, uninterruptedness.

Internal. (See Interior.)

Interpose, intercede, arbitrate, mediate, interfere, meddle.

Ant.—Retire, recede, remove, hold aloof, withdraw, retract.

Interpret, elucidate, explain, expound, unfold, decipher, translate, declare.

Ant.—Misinterpret, falsify, distort, mistake, misrepresent.

Interpretation, version, rendering, sense, construction, explanation.

Ant.—Misinterpretation, distortion, mistake, error, falsification.

Interrupt, disturb, hinder, break, divide.

Ant.—Continue, prosecute, expedite.

Interval, intermission, space, period, gap.

Ant.—Continuity, simultaneousness.

Intervention, agency, interposition, mediation.

Ant.—Non-intervention, continuity, opposition, encouragement, instigation.

Intimate, hint, suggest, insinuate, express, signify, impart, tell.

Ant.—Conceal, retain, withhold, reserve.

Intimidate, frighten, dishearten, alarm, affright, scare, appal, daunt, cow, quail, browbeat.

Ant.—Encourage, inspirit, animate, reassure, cheer, countenance, embolden, inspire, promote.

Intolerable, insufferable, insupportable, unendurable, unbearable.

Ant.—Tolerable, allowable, endurable, supportable, bearable.

Intoxicated, drunk, tipsy, inebriated, fuddled, muddled.

Ant.—Sober, sane, depressed, melancholy, clearheaded.

Intrepid, bold, brave, daring, fearless, dauntless, undaunted, courageous, valorous, valiant, heroic, gallant, chivalrous, doughty.

Ant.—Cowardly, faint-hearted, fearful.

Intricacy, difficulty, complexity, complication, involution, perplexity.

Ant.—Simplicity, directness, obviousness, clearness.

Intrigue, plot, conspiracy, combination, artifice, ruse, cabal, amour.

Ant.—Rebellion, insurrection,

candor, openness, honesty, probity.

Intrinsic, genuine, sterling, native, real, true, natural.

Ant.—Extrinsic, acquired, borrowed, added, assumed, pretended.

Introduce, present, bring in, usher, begin.

Ant.—Estrange, eject, conclude, terminate, end.

Introduction, preface, prelude, exordium, prologue, preamble.

Ant.—Conclusion, completion, end.

Intrude, force in, obtrude, trench, infringe, invade, interfere.

Ant.—Withdraw, hold back, retire, restrain, withhold.

Intrust. (See Commit.)

Inundate, drown, overflow, deluge, flood, submerge, overwhelm.

Ant.—Drain, dry, parch, burn.

Inure. (See Accustom.)

Invade, attack, assail, infringe, encroach, trench, intrude, violate.

Ant.—Vacate, abandon, evacuate, relinquish.

Invalidate, quash, cancel, overthrow, vacate, nullify, annul.

Ant.—Confirm, strengthen, sustain.

Invasion, trespass, incursion, irruption, inroad, aggression, raid, foray.

Invective, abuse, reproach, railing, censure, sarcasm, satire.

Ant.—Commendation, eulogy, panegyric, laudation, praise, encouragement.

Invent, devise, contrive, frame, fabricate, discover, design, find out.

Ant.—Imitate, copy, reproduce.

Invert, upset, overturn, overthrow, subvert, reverse.

Ant.—Erect, fix, conserve, establish, ground.

Invest, surround, besiege, endue, clothe.

Investigation, examination, search, inquiry, research, scrutiny.

Inveterate, confirmed, chronic, malignant.

Ant.—Incipient, unformed, undeveloped, inchoate.

Invidious, unfair, partial, envious, hateful, odious, malignant.

Ant.—Fair, impartial, considerate, due, just, benevolent, charitable, generous, kindly, humane.

Invigorate, brace, harden, nerve, strengthen, fortify.

Ant.—Enervate, depress, sadden, frighten, weaken, enfeeble.

Invincible, unconquerable, impregnable, insuperable, insurmountable.

Ant.—Weak, powerless, spiritless, puny, vulnerable.

Invisible, unseen, imperceptible, impalpable, unperceivable.

Ant.—Visible, seen, perceptible, palpable, tangible, evident, actual.

Invite, summon, challenge, ask, call, bid, request, allure, attract, solicit.

Ant.—Forbid, exclude, expel, discard, repel, cut, ignore.

Invoke, invocate, call upon, appeal, refer, implore, beseech.

Ant.—Ignore, defy, warn, inhibit, deprecate, avoid, dodge, elude, shun.

Involuntary, compulsory, exacted, coercive.

Ant.—Voluntary, spontaneous, free, deliberate, optional.

Involve, implicate, entangle, compromise, envelop.

Ant.—Separate, extricate, disconnect, disentangle, remove.

Inward, interior, internal, inner.

Ant.—Outward, exterior, external.

Ire. (See Anger.)

Irksome, tedious, wearisome, tiresome, annoying.

Ant.—Pleasant, delightful.

Irony, sarcasm, satire, ridicule, raillery.

Ant.—Compliment, seriousness, honesty.

Irrational, foolish, silly, imbecile, brutish, unreasonable, absurd, preposterous, ridiculous.

Ant.—Rational, right, correct, learned, cultivated, reasonable, logical, sensible, sane, sound.

Irregular, eccentric, anomalous, inordinate, intemperate.

Ant.—Regular, ordinary, common, temperate, established, fixed, formal, methodical.

Irreligious, profane, godless, impious, sacrilegious, desecrating.

Ant.—Religious, pious, orthodox, sacred, holy, saintly, godly.

Irreproachable, blameless, spotless, irreprovable, unblemished.

Ant.—Reproachable, blamable, censurable, reprovable, blame-worthy, faulty, culpable.

Irresistible, resistless, unopposed, irrepressible.

Ant.—Resistible, defensible, repressible.

Irresolute, wavering, undetermined, undecided, vacillating.

Ant.—Resolute, determined, bold, decided, firm, persistent.

Irritable, excitable, irascible, susceptible, sensitive, hasty.

Ant.—Calm, good-tempered, cool, quiet, composed, placid.

Irritate, aggravate, worry, provoke, embitter, madden, exasperate, displease.

Ant.—Soothe, mollify, pacify, caress, comfort.

Issue, *v.* emerge, rise, proceed, flow, spring, emanate.

Ant.—Cause, originate, commence, order.

Issue, *n.* end, upshot, effect, result, offspring, progeny.

J

Jade, harass, weary, tire, worry.

Ant.—Refresh, recruit, invigorate, inspirit, cheer, relieve, soothe, help.

Jangle, wrangle, conflict, disagree.

Ant.—Agree, debate, discourse, quiet, assuage.

Jarring, discordant, conflicting, inconsonant, inconsistent.

Ant.—Harmonious, consistent.

Jaunt, ramble, excursion, trip.

Jealousy, suspicion, envy, invidiousness, covetousness.

Ant.—Liberality, indulgence, toleration, indifference, confidence, trust.

Jeer, sneer, scoff, mock, deride, banter.

Ant.—Flatter, fawn, compliment, eulogize.

Jeopardize, hazard, peril, endanger.

Ant.—Safeguard, protect.

Jeopardy, risk, peril, hazard, danger, chance, venture.

Ant.—Safety, security, provision, insurance.

Jest, joke, sport, diversion.

Ant.—Gravity, seriousness, sobriety.

Jocose, jocular, jolly, facetious, witty, pleasant.

Ant.—Serious, earnest, melancholy, grave, lugubrious.

Jocund, light-hearted, lively, sprightly, vivacious, sportive, merry, mirthful, blithesome.

Ant.—Melancholy, dull, grave, mournful, cheerless, sorrowful.

Join, accompany, go with, add, unite, append, adjoin, combine, confederate, league.
Ant.—Separate, leave, subtract, disconnect, oppose.
Jolly, merry, gay, mirthful, genial, joyous.
Ant.—Sad, mournful, cheerless, morose, gloomy.
Journey, tour, travel, passage.
Joviality. (See Merriment.)
Joy, delight, gladness, charm, pleasure, ecstasy, rapture, transport, mirth.
Ant.—Sorrow, pain, trouble, misery, melancholy, grief, affliction, despondency, sadness.
Joyful, glad, rejoicing, exultant.
Ant.—Mournful, sorrowful, despondent.
Judge, justice, referee, arbitrator.
Judgment, discernment, discrimination, sagacity, intelligence, sentence, decision, order, award, understanding.
Ant.—Insagacity, inquiry, argument, speculation, proposition, investigation.
Judicious, wise, sage, thoughtful, discerning, just.
Ant.—Unwise, foolish, imprudent, injudicious, indiscreet, rash, blind, impolitic, unjust.
Juicy, succulent, bibulous, spongy.
Ant.—Dry, parched, wizened.
Jump, leap, bound, spring.
Ant.—Fall, crawl, glide, walk, run.
Junction, union, alliance, connection, confederacy, combination.
Ant.—Separation, disunion, dispersion, division, segregation, divergence.
Juncture, contact, touch, conjuncture, crisis.
Ant.—Course, arrangement, provision, preparation.
Just, right, proper, fair, equitable, impartial, honest, sound, reasonable, lawful.
Ant.—Unjust, unfair, partial, inexact, dishonorable, unsound.
Justice, right, equity, law.
Ant.—Injustice, wrong, partiality, unfairness, illegality.
Justify, excuse, clear, exonerate, defend, absolve.
Ant.—Condemn, censure, convict, protest, accuse, inculpate.
Justness, accuracy, correctness.
Ant.—Error, fallacy.
Juvenile, young, youthful, boyish, infantile, childish.
Ant.—Mature, aged, manly, womanly, adult, elderly.

K

Keen, sharp, acute, penetrating, cutting, biting, stinging, sarcastic, satirical.
Ant.—Blunt, dull, blind, indifferent, languid.
Keep, retain, hold, detain, preserve, maintain, sustain, obey, continue, celebrate, save.
Ant.—Release, liberate, send, dismiss, betray, neglect, divulge, abandon, discard, disobey, forsake, desert, disregard.
Key. (See Solution.)
Kill, murder, assassinate, slay, massacre, butcher.
Ant.—Vivify, resuscitate, animate, save, protect.
Kind, *a.* thoughtful, affable, gentle, meek, tender, good, gracious, compassionate, indulgent, forbearing.
Ant.—Unkind, harsh, severe, cruel, hard.
Kind, *n.* species, sort, class, genus, nature, character.
Ant.—Opposite, contrary.
Kindle, ignite, enkindle, awaken, arouse, stir up, excite.
Ant.—Extinguish, quench, suppress, allay.
Kindred, affinity, relatives, kinsfolk.
Ant.—Strangers, foreigners, disconnection.
Kinsfolk. (See Kindred.)
Knave, rogue, scoundrel, rascal.
Ant.—Gentleman, dupe, simpleton, innocent.
Knavish, roguish, dishonest, fraudulent.
Ant.—Honest, square, fair.
Knowledge, learning, scholarship, acquirements, attainments, information, understanding, erudition, science.
Ant.—Ignorance, inexperience, illiteracy, incomprehensibility, stupidity, folly.

L

Labor, work, task, toil, exertion, effort, drudgery.
Ant.—Indolence, ease, inactivity, rest, recreation, facility, skill, idleness, leisure.
Laborious, hard-working, industrious, diligent, assiduous, active, toilsome, wearisome.
Ant.—Idle, lazy, indolent, easy, light, simple.
Lack, want, need, require, deficiency, scarcity, insufficiency.
Ant.—Supply, satisfy, plenty, abundance.
Laconic, short, brief, concise, curt.
Ant.—Prolix, garrulous, loquacious, prosy, long.
Lag, tarry, linger, loiter, saunter.
Ant.—Hasten, hurry, rush, press, speed.
Lame, limp, halt, hobble, weak, hesitating.
Ant.—Agile, robust, efficient, telling, effective.
Lament, grieve, mourn, regret, bewail, deplore, bemoan, weep.
Ant.—Welcome, hail, rejoice, exult, triumph.
Language, speech, tongue, dialect, phraseology, idiom.
Ant.—Muteness, jargon, gibberish, cry, whine, howl.
Languid, weak, faint, drooping.
Ant.—Strong, healthy, robust, active.
Lank, lean, thin, skinny, meager, scraggy.
Ant.—Plump, rounded, short, full.
Lapse, elapse, glide, pass.
Ant.—Fix, stay, stand, arrest, stop, retain.
Large, big, great, huge, vast, extensive, wide, liberal.
Ant.—Small, mean, narrow, contracted, scanty, petty, illiberal, bigoted.
Lascivious, loose, unchaste, lustful, lewd, lecherous.
Ant.—Chaste, modest.
Lash, scourge, whip, flog, beat, fasten.
Ant.—Anoint, smooth, rub, unfasten.
Lassitude, weariness, fatigue, languor.
Ant.—Health, strength, activity, freshness.
Last, latest, hindmost, utmost, extreme, final, ultimate.
Ant.—First, initiatory, opening, foremost, highest, next, nearest.
Lasting, durable, abiding, permanent, perpetual, continuing.
Ant.—Ending, transient, ephemeral.
Latent, hidden, secret, occult, inscrutable.
Ant.—Visible, apparent, manifest, conspicuous, explicit.
Laud. (See Praise.)
Laudable, commendable, praiseworthy.
Ant.—Blamable.
Laughable, ridiculous, comical, droll, ludicrous.
Ant.—Serious, grave.
Lavish, profuse, extravagant, prodigal,

Ant.—Chary, sparing, close, niggardly, mean, economical.

Lawful, legal, legitimate, rightful, constitutional, licit.

Ant.—Unlawful, illegal, wrong, lawless, unfair, ungovernable, inequitable.

Lax, loose, vague, dissolute, licentious, remiss.

Ant.—Concise, coherent, compact, strict, rigid, severe, conscientious.

Lazy, idle, indolent, slothful, sluggish, inactive.

Ant.—Industrious, energetic, laborious, active, alert.

Lead, conduct, guide, direct, induce, persuade, influence.

Ant.—Mislead, dissuade, follow, abandon, leave, misguide.

Leader. (See Chief.)

Leading, principal, chief, governing, ruling, important.

Ant.—Unimportant, subordinate, inferior, lower, succeeding, following.

League, alliance, confederacy, combination, coalition, union.

Ant.—Dissolution, neutrality, secession, disunion, alienation.

Lean, *a.* thin, scraggy, lank, skinny, meager.

Ant.—Fat, stout, brawny, plump.

Lean, *v.* incline, tend, bend, slope, rest, repose, confide.

Ant.—Erect, straighten, rise, raise, stabilize.

Leap. (See Jump.)

Learned, erudite, scholarly.

Ant.—Ignorant.

Learning, knowledge, scholarship, erudition, lore.

Ant.—Ignorance, illiteracy, intuition, revelation, inspiration.

Leave, *n.* liberty, license, permission.

Ant.—Prohibition, prevention, refusal, restriction.

Leave, *v.* quit, relinquish, renounce, give up, retire, depart, go, withdraw, abandon.

Ant.—Pursue, prosecute, seek, court, hold, keep, support, occupy, cherish, shelter, nurture, harbor, foster, entertain.

Legal. (See Lawful.)

Legend, fable, myth, memoir, chronicle.

Ant.—Fact, history, transaction, substantiation.

Legitimate, legal, lawful, genuine, fair.

Ant.—Illegitimate, illicit, unallowable, unfair, bastard.

Leisure, vacation, recess, freedom, convenience, ease.

Ant.—Toil, labor, business, employment, occupation, engagement.

Lengthen, extend, elongate, protract, prolong.

Ant.—Condense, abbreviate, shorten, contract.

Lessen, abate, diminish, decrease, lower, subside.

Ant.—Lengthen, increase, extend, elongate.

Let. (See Allow.)

Letter, epistle, note, communication.

Ant.—Word, speech, conversation.

Level, even, plain, smooth, flat.

Ant.—Uneven, unequal, rough, rolling, inclined.

Levity, giddiness, lightness, flightiness.

Ant.—Gravity, earnestness, seriousness.

Liable, exposed to, subject to, amenable.

Ant.—Independent, autocratic.

Libel, lampoon, pasquinade, defamation, calumny.

Ant.—Eulogy, panegyric, puff, encomium, apology, vindication.

Liberal, generous, bountiful, bounteous, munificent, plentiful.

Ant.—Illiberal, mean, ungenerous, bigoted, prejudiced.

Liberate, set free, free, deliver, discharge, release, let go.

Ant.—Confine, immure, imprison, restrict, bind, enslave.

Liberty, leave, permission, freedom, independence.

Ant.—Slavery, servitude, dependence, submission, constraint.

Licentious, loose, lax, dissolute, rakish, unbridled, debauched.

Ant.—Temperate, strict, sober, ascetic, rigid.

Lie, untruth, falsehood, falsity, fabrication, fiction, invention, story.

Ant.—Truth, fact, verity.

Life, animation, vivacity, buoyancy, spirit, history, career, existence.

Ant.—Death, decease, lethargy, torpor, dullness.

Lifeless, dead, inanimate, inert, sluggish.

Ant.—Vigorous, lively, animated.

Lift, raise, elevate, erect, exalt, hoist.

Ant.—Sink, depress, degrade, lower, cast, hurl.

Light, illuminate, illumine, enlighten, lighten.

Ant.—Darken, obscure, dim, shade, mystify, misinterpret.

Lightness, levity, flightiness, volatility, giddiness, inconstancy, frivolity.

Ant.—Darkness, gravity, seriousness.

Likelihood. (See Probability.)

Likeness, picture, image, effigy, resemblance, similarity, representation, similitude.

Ant.—Original, unlikeness, dissimilarity, inequality, disparity, difference, variation.

Likewise, also, too, as well.

Ant.—Nor, otherwise.

Limit, *n.* extent, boundary, bound, border.

Ant.—Extension, infinity.

Limit, *v.* bound, circumscribe, restrict, confine.

Ant.—Extend, prolong, release, loosen.

Limpid. (See Clear.)

Lineage, descent, family, house, generation.

Linger, tarry, loiter, wait, lag, saunter.

Ant.—Hasten, speed, press, push, expedite, urge, quicken.

Link, tie, bind, join, chain.

Ant.—Disjoin, break, untie, unbind.

Liquid, fluid, juicy, watery, fluent, limpid.

Ant.—Solid, hard, congealed, dry, harsh, discordant.

List. (See Catalogue.)

Listen, list, hearken, heed, attend to.

Ant.—Ignore, disregard, refuse, repudiate.

Listless, indifferent, indolent, careless, languid.

Ant.—Eager, attentive, active, earnest, awake, interested.

Literal, actual, real, positive, true.

Ant.—General, metaphorical, figurative, free.

Little, small, diminutive, dwarf, tiny, short, scanty, brief, slight, weak, petty, paltry.

Ant.—Big, bulky, large, enormous, huge, long, full, much, important, liberal, generous, noble, great.

Live, exist, subsist, dwell, act.

Ant.—Die, perish, wither, vanish, fade, fail, depart.

Livelihood, living, support, sustenance, subsistence, maintenance.

Ant.—Want, starvation, beggary.

Lively, active, brisk, quick, sprightly, prompt, buoyant, racy, vivacious, jocund, merry, sportive, sprightly.

Ant.—Lifeless, listless, dull, indifferent, torpid, insensible, slow, languid, sluggish.

Loath, *a.* reluctant, backward, unwilling.

Ant.—Eager, willing, alert, anxious.

Loathe. (See Abhor.)

Lofty, high, tall, elevated, exalted.

Ant.—Low, depressed, stunted, undignified.

Logical, sound, argumentative, conclusive.

Ant.—Illogical, inconclusive, fallacious.

Loiter, wait, linger, tarry, saunter, lag.

Ant.—Hasten, hurry, speed, rush.

Long, extended, extensive.

Ant.—Short, brief, concise.

Look, see, witness, view, eye, inspect, appear, seem, behold, scan, survey, watch, regard.

Ant.—Overlook, hide, avert, miss, lurk.

Loose, vague, indefinite, lax, slack, dissolute, licentious, rakish, wanton.

Ant.—Tied, fast, bound, tight, compact, accurate, exact, logical, conscientious.

Lose, miss, forfeit.

Ant.—Gain, obtain, secure, achieve.

Loss, damage, detriment, waste, deprivation.

Ant.—Gain, advantage, satisfaction, recovery, economy, profit.

Lot, destiny, future, doom.

Loud, noisy, clamorous, vociferous, blustering, riotous, turbulent, tumultuous.

Ant.—Soft, quiet, gentle, subdued, dulcet, inaudible, low.

Love, endearment, affection, attachment, fondness.

Ant.—Hatred, dislike, coldness, indifference, repugnance, malice.

Lovely, charming, amiable, delightful.

Ant.—Homely, unlovely, unattractive, hideous, plain.

Lover, suitor, sweetheart, wooer.

Ant.—Rival, foe, opponent.

Low, humble, lowly, base, mean, filthy, foul, gentle, abject.

Ant.—High, tall, elevated, raised, loud, eminent, lofty, noble.

Lower, reduce, humble, humiliate, degrade, debase.

Ant.—Hoist, raise, heighten, increase, elevate.

Luck. (See Chance.)

Lucre, gain, profit, emolument, money.

Ant.—Loss, poverty, dross, failure, privation.

Ludicrous. (See Ridiculous.)

Lull, quiet, hush, still, calm.

Ant.—Storm, tempest, tumult, excitement.

Lunacy, derangement, madness, insanity, aberration, mania.

Ant.—Sanity, reason, intelligence, lucidity.

Lurid, gloomy, murky, lowering.

Ant.—Bright, luminous.

Luscious, honeyed, sweet, mellifluous.

Ant.—Sour, sharp, tart, bitter.

Luster, splendor, brightness, brilliancy, effulgence, refulgence.

Ant.—Dimness, dullness, darkness, cloudiness, gloom.

Lusty, stout, strong, able-bodied, stalwart, robust, muscular.

Ant.—Infirm, weak, disabled, effete, listless.

Luxuriant, overflowing, exuberant, redundant, abundant.

Ant.—Poor, mean, small, sparse, meager.

Luxury, plenty, profuseness, voluptuousness.

Ant.—Asceticism, self-denial, hardship, poverty.

M

Machination, stratagem, imposture, fraud, cheat, trick, plot, intrigue, cabal, conspiracy.

Ant.—Artlessness, directness, candor.

Mad, wild, frantic, distracted, furious, rabid, insane, crazy, delirious, violent.

Ant.—Sane, sensible, composed, sober, rational, quiet.

Madden, irritate, enrage, exasperate.

Ant.—Calm, soothe, pacify, assuage.

Madness, mental aberration, insanity, lunacy, mania, frenzy, rage, fury.

Ant.—Sanity, sense, composure, sobriety, rationality.

Magisterial, august, dignified, majestic, pompous, stately.

Ant.—Pitiful, wretched.

Magnanimous, generous, august, dignified, noble, exalted, lofty.

Ant.—Mean, petty, paltry, spiteful.

Magnificence, splendor, grandeur, gorgeousness, pomp.

Ant.—Tameness, tawdriness, pettiness, smallness.

Magnify, enlarge, extol, applaud, laud, amplify.

Ant.—Diminish, contract, curtail, extenuate, decry.

Magnitude. (See Size.)

Maim, mutilate, mangle, cripple, lame.

Ant.—Mend, strengthen, restore.

Main, chief, principal, leading, first.

Ant.—Portion, inferior, subordinate.

Maintain. (See Support.)

Majestic, dignified, noble, stately, pompous, grand.

Ant.—Mean, small, undignified, petty.

Majesty, grandeur, dignity.

Ant.—Meanness, debasement, degradation.

Make, create, form, produce, mold, shape, construct, gain, fashion, cause, constitute, establish, execute, frame.

Ant.—Destroy, demolish, annihilate, dismember, undo, defeat, miss, lose, mar, break, unmake.

Malady, ailment, disease, distemper, disorder, sickness, illness.

Ant.—Health, vigor, soundness.

Malediction, curse, imprecation, denunciation, anathema, execration.

Ant.—Benediction, eulogy, compliment, blessing.

Malevolent, malicious, virulent, malignant.

Ant.—Benevolent, kindly.

Malice, spite, rancor, ill-feeling, grudge, pique, animosity, ill-will.

Ant.—Charity, toleration, love, kindness, affection, benignity, good-will.

Malicious, virulent, malignant, wicked, malevolent.

Ant.—Kind, lovable, affectionate, charitable, good.

Manacle, chain, shackle, fetter.

Ant.—Free, liberate.

Manage, contrive, concert, direct, handle, control, regulate.

Ant.—Mismanage, misconduct, upset, derange.

Management, direction, superintendence, care, economy,

Ant.—Maltreatment, mismanagement, misconduct, neglect, remissness.

Mangle, maim, tear, lacerate, mutilate, cripple, rend.

Ant.—Heal, mend, secure, unite, weld.

Mania, madness, insanity, lunacy.

Ant.—Sanity.

Manifest, exhibit, clear, plain, evident, open, apparent, visible.

Ant.—Hidden, occult.

Manifold, several, sundry, various, divers, complex, many, numerous.
Ant.—Limited, few, scant, rare, homogeneous, plain, simple, uncombined, uniform.

Manly, masculine, hardy, vigorous, courageous, brave, heroic.
Ant.—Effeminate, childish, unmanly, dastardly, weak, boyish, timid, feminine.

Manner, habit, custom, way, air, look, appearance, mode, style, fashion.

Manners, morals, habits, behavior, carriage.
Ant.—Misbehavior, awkwardness, misdemeanor.

Many, numerous, several, sundry, divers, various, manifold.
Ant.—Few, scarce, rare, infrequent.

Mar, injure, spoil, ruin, disfigure.
Ant.—Ameliorate, improve.

March, tramp, tread, walk, step, pace.
Ant.—Halt, stop, stand, rest, crawl, creep, jump, skip, run.

Margin, edge, rim, border, brink, verge.
Ant.—Center, middle.

Marine, maritime, nautical, naval.
Ant.—Territorial, land, earthly.

Mark, *n.* sign, note, symptom, token, indication, trace, vestige, track, badge, brand.
Ant.—Erasure, effacement, obliteration, plainness, avoidance, neglect.

Mark, *v.* impress, print, stamp, engrave, note, notice, remark, show, indicate, designate.
Ant.—Ignore, overlook, omit, misindicate.

Marriage, wedding, nuptials, matrimony, wedlock.
Ant.—Celibacy, virginity, divorce.

Marsh. (See Swamp.)

Martial, military, warlike, soldierlike.
Ant.—Peaceful, civil.

Marvel, wonder, miracle, prodigy.

Marvelous, wonderful, wondrous, amazing, miraculous.
Ant.—Commonplace, usual.

Masculine. (See Manly.)

Mask, visor, cloak, veil, blind.
Ant.—Truth, exposure, detection, openness, candor.

Massacre, carnage, slaughter, butchery.
Ant.—Deliverance, quarter, ransom.

Massive, bulky, heavy, weighty, ponderous, solid, substantial.
Ant.—Slight, frail, light, slender, flimsy.

Master, possessor, proprietor, head, owner.
Ant.—Servant, slave, subject, property, pupil.

Masterly, skillful, clever, expert, dexterous, adroit.
Ant.—Clumsy, rude, unskilled.

Mastery, dominion, rule, sway, ascendancy, supremacy, authority, victory.
Ant.—Submission, tutelage, guidance, obedience, failure, defeat, surrender.

Matchless, unrivaled, unequaled, unparalleled, peerless, incomparable, inimitable, surpassing, unique.
Ant.—Common, ordinary, commonplace, usual.

Material, corporeal, bodily, physical, temporal, momentous, essential, important.
Ant.—Immaterial, spiritual, metaphysical, ideal, nonessential, ethereal.

Matrimony. (See Marriage.)

Mature. (See Ripe.)

Mawkish, insipid, flat, spiritless, vapid.
Ant.—Savory, sound, pungent, palatable.

Maxim, adage, apothegm, proverb, saying, byword, saw, truism, dictum.
Ant.—Enigma, sophism, quibble, absurdity, paradox, demonstration.

Meager, poor, lank, emaciated, barren, dry, uninteresting.
Ant.—Stout, fat, brawny, fertile, copious, rich, abundant, fruitful.

Mean, *a.* stingy, niggardly, low, abject, vile, ignoble, degraded, contemptible, vulgar, despicable.
Ant.—Generous, openhanded, extravagant, noble, lofty, dignified, exalted, extreme, excessive.

Mean, *v.* design, purpose, intend, contemplate, signify, denote, indicate.

Meaning, signification, import, acceptation, sense, purport, drift.

Means, way, manner, method, mode, resources, instrument.
Ant.—End, purpose, object.

Mechanic. (See Workman.)

Meddlesome, officious, intermeddling, interfering.
Ant.—Helpful, unofficious, unobtrusive.

Mediate, intercede, interpose, interfere, arbitrate.
Ant.—Combat, excite, irritate.

Mediocrity, commonplace, mean, average.
Ant.—Superiority, excellence, distinction.

Meditate, think, reflect, muse, plan.
Ant.—Execute, enact, complete, consummate.

Medium, means, organ, channel, instrument.

Medley, mixture, variety, diversity, miscellany, confusion, hodge-podge.
Ant.—Classification, order, arrangement, assortment, grouping.

Meek, unassuming, mild, gentle, yielding.
Ant.—Bold, arrogant, proud, high-spirited, haughty.

Meet, apt, fit, suitable, expedient, proper.
Ant.—Unsuitable, unfit, unmeet.

Meeting. (See Assembly.)

Melancholy, low-spirited, dispirited, dreamy, sad, dejected.
Ant.—Merry, lively, sprightly, blithesome, cheerful, happy, jolly, buoyant.

Mellow, ripe, mature, soft.
Ant.—Unripe, sour, harsh, crabbed, dry, immature.

Melodious, musical, tuneful, silver, dulcet, sweet.
Ant.—Discordant, grating, harsh.

Melt, liquefy, fuse, dissolve, moisten.
Ant.—Consolidate, freeze, congeal, crystallize.

Memoir, narrative, chronicle, legend, life, history.
Ant.—Myth, tradition, romance.

Memorable, signal, distinguished, marked, famous, remarkable, extraordinary.
Ant.—Ordinary, insignificant, petty, trivial, unimportant.

Memorial, monument, memento, commemoration, annals, archives.
Ant.—Obliteration, erasure, effacement.

Memory, remembrance, recollection, fame.
Ant.—Forgetfulness, oblivion.

Menace, threat.

Mend, amend, correct, better, ameliorate, improve, rectify, repair.
Ant.—Impair, damage, mar, corrupt, spoil, prevent.

Menial, servant, domestic, drudge.
Ant.—Master, lord, sovereign, autocrat.

Mention, tell, name, communicate, impart, divulge, reveal, disclose, inform, acquaint.
Ant.—Conceal, retain, withhold, suppress, omit, forget.

Mercenary, sordid, selfish, avaricious.
Ant.—Generous, prodigal, liberal, unselfish.

Merchant, trader, tradesman, dealer.
Ant.—Salesman, peddler, jobber, employee.

Merciful, compassionate, lenient, clement, tender, gracious, kind.
Ant.—Merciless, cruel, unmerciful, pitiless, remorseless, brutal, unfeeling.

Merciless, hard-hearted, cruel, unmerciful, pitiless, remorseless, unrelenting.
Ant.—(See Merciful.)

Mercy, leniency, mildness, clemency, compassion, pity.
Ant.—Vengeance, cruelty, harshness, execution.

Merit, worth, desert, excellence.
Ant.—Badness, demerit, imperfection, defect, fault, failing.

Merited, deserved, condign, suitable, adequate, proper.
Ant.—Unmerited, undeserved, improper.

Merriment, mirth, joviality, jollity, hilarity.
Ant.—Soberness, sobriety, gravity, moroseness, lugubriousness, sorrow, sadness, melancholy.

Merry, cheerful, mirthful, joyous, gay, lively, sprightly, blithe, blithesome, jovial, sportive, jolly, hilarious.
Ant.—Melancholy, dispirited, sad, gloomy, sober, grave, mournful, morose.

Metaphorical, figurative, allegorical, symbolical.
Ant.—Literal, exact, actual.

Method, way, manner, mode, process, order, rule, system, regularity.
Ant.—Disorder, assumption, hazard, guess-work, conjecture, chaos, confusion, irregularity.

Mien, air, behavior, look, manner, aspect, appearance.

Mighty, powerful, potent.
Ant.—Weak, impotent, feeble, infirm.

Migratory, roving, strolling, wandering, vagrant.
Ant.—Settled, sedate, permanent, fixed, stationary.

Mild, soft, meek, gentle, kind, calm, moderate.
Ant.—Violent, wild, fierce, savage, strong, severe, harsh, bitter.

Military, soldierlike, martial, warlike.
Ant.—Unmilitary, peaceful, civil, civilian, nonmartial.

Mimic, imitate, ape, mock.
Ant.—Change, distort, transform, vary.

Mind, *v.* heed, advert to, regard.
Ant.—Disregard, ignore, overlook, miss.

Mind, *n.* sentiment, opinion, idea, notion, intellect, understanding.
Ant.—Body, limbs, action, conduct, object, aversion.

Mindful, observant, attentive, heedful, thoughtful, careful.
Ant.—Regardless, inattentive, mindless, oblivious, heedless, careless.

Mingle, mix, blend, compound, amalgamate.
Ant.—Separate, sift, sort, analyze, eliminate, unravel.

Minister, *n.* official, divine, clergyman, ecclesiastic, parson, curate, incumbent.
Ant.—Citizen, layman.

Minister, *v.* administer, contribute, supply.
Ant.—Rule, command, exact.

Minute, particular, specific, circumstantial, microscopic.
Ant.—Big, huge, enormous, superficial, general, comprehensive.

Mirth, joy, merriment, gladness, festivity, joviality, hilarity, cheerfulness, vivacity, gaiety, fun, jollity.
Ant.—Sadness, sorrow, trouble, gravity, sobriety, melancholy.

Miscellaneous, promiscuous, indiscriminate, mixed.
Ant.—Selected, classified, orderly, systematized, homogeneous.

Miscellany, medley, diversity, variety, mixture.
Ant.—System, order, group, collection, classification.

Mischance, calamity, disaster, misfortune, mishap, misadventure.
Ant.—Chance, design, purpose, predestination, law.

Mischief, injury, harm, damage, hurt, evil, ill.
Ant.—Compensation, benefit, favor, good, advantage, blessing, boon, remedy, service.

Misconception, misapprehension, misunderstanding, mistake.
Ant.—Conception, understanding, truth, verity.

Miscreant, rogue, caitiff, villain, ruffian.
Ant.—Benefactor, philanthropist.

Miserable, unhappy, wretched, distressed, afflicted.
Ant.—Happy, contented, comfortable, respectable, worthy, gay.

Miserly, stingy, niggardly, avaricious, griping.
Ant.—Prodigal, extravagant, generous, liberal, open-handed.

Misery, wretchedness, woe destitution, penury, priva tion, beggary.
Ant.—Happiness, comfort, content, respect, worth, luxury, ease, good fortune.

Misfortune, disaster, calamity, mishap, catastrophe.
Ant.—Good luck, windfall.

Misguide, mislead, dazzle, beguile, deceive.
Ant.—Guide, lead, show, conduct, aid, help, encourage.

Mislead. (See Misguide.)

Misrule, anarchy, confusion.
Ant.—Rule, order, stability, government, peace.

Miss, omit, lose, fail, miscarry.
Ant.—Meet, accost, address, conduct, grasp, accomplish, understand.

Mission, commission, legation, embassy, errand.
Ant.—Assumption, usurpation, self-appointment, relaxation, pleasure.

Mistake, *n.* (See Error.)

Mistake, *v.* err, fail, misconceive, misapprehend.
Ant.—Apprehend, recognize, know, affirm.

Misty, murky, dark, dim, obscure, cloudy, shadowy, dusky.
Ant.—Bright, clear, lucid.

Mitigate, alleviate, relieve, abate, diminish.
Ant.—Aggravate, enhance, enlarge, increase, extend.

Mix. (See Mingle.)

Mixture. (See Variety.)

Mob, crowd, concourse, multitude, throng, bevy.
Ant.—Individual, meeting, congregation.

Mock, mimic, imitate, ape, deride, ridicule.
Ant.—Salute, respect, admire, compliment, copy.

Mode. (See Method.)

Model, copy, pattern, specimen, example, standard, type.
Ant.—Imitation, copy, execution, production, work.

Moderate, temperate, abstemious, sober, abstinent.
Ant.—Excessive, extravagant, intemperate, violent, immoderate, reckless.

Moderation, temperance, sobriety, abstemiousness.
Ant.—Excess, intemperance, extravagance.

Modern, novel, new, recent, present.
Ant.—Bygone, ancient, past, olden, antiquated.

Modest, chaste, virtuous, bashful, reserved, meek.
Ant.—Immodest, bold, vulgar, coarse, forward, pushing, assertive, impudent.

Moist, wet, damp, dank, humid, fertile, marshy, swampy.
Ant.—Arid, dry, parched.

Molest, annoy, incommode, discommode, incommodate, vex, tease, disturb.
Ant.—Soothe, caress, pacify, mollify.

Moment, consequence, weight, importance, instant, trice.
Ant.—Triviality, unimportance, insignificance, age, period.

Monotonous, unvaried, dull, tiresome, undiversified.
Ant.—Varied, diversified, different, relieved, diverse.

Monster, ruffian, villain, brute, prodigy.
Ant.—Beauty, gem, jewel, angel.

Monstrous, shocking, dreadful, horrible, prodigious, portentous, marvelous, abnormal, flagrant, huge, immense.
Ant.—Fair, comely, shapely, beautiful, ordinary, familiar, reasonable, just, excellent, superior, transcendent.

Monument, memorial, record, remembrancer, cenotaph.

Mood, humor, vein, temper, disposition, nature, character.

Moral, regular, strict, virtuous, ethical.
Ant.—Immoral, vicious, bad, physical, material.

Morass. (See Swamp.)

Morbid, sick, ailing, sickly, diseased, corrupted.
Ant.—Healthy, sound, wholesome, normal.

Morning, daybreak, morn, dawn, sunrise, forenoon, a.m.
Ant.—Evening, afternoon, night, sunset, p.m.

Morose, gloomy, sullen, surly, fretful, crabbed, crusty.
Ant.—Genial, kindly, gentle, indulgent, joyous, merry, gay.

Mortal, human, deadly, fatal, destructive.
Ant.—Divine, immortal, celestial, life-giving, eternal, everlasting.

Mortify, vex, chagrin, grieve, hurt, afflict, annoy, rot, putrefy.
Ant.—Please, gratify, delight, indulge, pamper, heal, recover.

Motion, proposition, proposal, movement, change, action.
Ant.—Rest, equilibrium, stability, fixity, inaction, quiescence, quiet, repose, stillness.

Motionless, still, stationary, torpid, stagnant.
Ant.—Active, unstable, nervous, moving.

Motive, cause, reason, principle, inducement, incentive, impulse, spur, stimulus.
Ant.—Result, end, action, effort, deed, attempt.

Motley, heterogeneous, diversified, mixed.
Ant.—Uniform, homogeneous, alike.

Mottled, dappled, dotted, spotted, flecked, speckled.
Ant.—Uniform, unspotted, clear.

Mount, ascend, arise, rise, soar, tower, climb, scale.
Ant.—Descend, fall.

Mournful, sad, sorrowful, lugubrious, grievous, doleful, heavy.
Ant.—Happy, joyous, hilarious.

Move, actuate, impel, induce, prompt, instigate, persuade, stir, agitate, propel, push.
Ant.—Stand, stop, rest, stay, allay, deter, prevent, arrest, halt.

Moving, affecting, touching, pathetic, melting.
Ant.—Laughing, ridiculous, absurd, ineffective.

Much, ample, plenteous, copious.
Ant.—Little, scant, short, near.

Muffle, deaden, disguise, conceal, cover, shroud.
Ant.—Unfold, exhibit, reveal.

Multitude, crowd, throng, host, mob, swarm.
Ant.—Paucity, scarcity, sprinkling, few, handful.

Munificent, bounteous, bountiful, generous, liberal.
Ant.—Niggardly, mean, beggarly, miserly.

Murder, kill, assassinate, slay, massacre, dispatch.
Ant.—Resuscitate, revivify, protect, shield, guard.

Murky, dark, dusky, dim, cloudy, misty, shadowy.
Ant.—Clear, light, pleasant, bright.

Muse, meditate, contemplate, think, reflect, cogitate, ponder.
Ant.—Stir, act, move, perform.

Music, harmony, melody, symphony.
Ant.—Discord, babel, harshness, noise.

Musical, tuneful, melodious, harmonious, dulcet, sweet.
Ant.—Discordant, harsh, inharmonious, unmelodious, noisy.

Muster, collect, rally, assemble, congregate.
Ant.—Dismiss, disperse, disband, relegate.

Musty, stale, sour, fetid.
Ant.—Fresh, odorous, aromatic, fragrant, sweet.

Mutable, inconstant, unsteadfast, unstable, fickle, alterable, restless, fitful, variable, changeable, unsteady.
Ant.—Immutable, permanent, changeless, eternal.

Mute, dumb, silent, speechless, quiet.
Ant.—Voluble, garrulous, loquacious, talkative.

Mutilate, maim, cripple, disable, disfigure.

Mutinous, insurgent, seditious, tumultuous, turbulent, riotous.
Ant.—Orderly, obedient, quiet, pacific.

Mutual, reciprocal, interchangeable, correlative.
Ant.—Disconnected, separate, unrequited, unshared.

Mysterious, dark, obscure, hidden, secret, dim, mystic, enigmatical, unaccountable.
Ant.—Clear, plain, obvious, simple, explained, understood, open.

Mystify, confuse, perplex, puzzle.
Ant.—Enlighten, inform, guide, elucidate, clear, explain.

Myth, fable, legend, fiction, parable.
Ant.—Fact, history, narration, truth.

N

Naked, nude, bare, uncovered, unclothed, rough, rude, simple.
Ant.—Dressed, robed, clothed, protected, veiled, shrouded, covered, clad.

Name, *v.* denominate, style, designate, term, call, christen, specify, entitle.
Ant.—Misname, miscall, hint, suggest.

Name, *n.* appellation, designation, denomination, title, cognomen, reputation, character, fame, credit, repute.
Ant.—Misnomer, anonymity, pseudonym.

Narrate, tell, relate, detail, recount, describe, enumerate, rehearse, recite.

Ant.—Suppress, conceal, hide, retain, withhold, misrepresent, deny, hush up.

Narrow, bigoted, illiberal, contracted, confined, circumscribed, straightened, limited.
Ant.—Liberal, tolerant, generous, wide, broad, ample, easy.

Nasty, filthy, foul, dirty, unclean, impure, indecent, gross, vile.
Ant.—Nice, pure, agreeable, pleasant, good, proper.

Nation, people, community, realm, state.
Ant.—Individuals, subjects, dependents, colonists.

Native, real, genuine, indigenous, vernacular, mother, inborn.
Ant.—Foreign, alien, imported, acquired, artificial, assumed, affected.

Natural, original, regular, normal, spontaneous.
Ant.—Unnatural, abnormal, adventitious, fictitious, affected, forced.

Nausea, qualm, seasickness, disgust, loathing, aversion.
Ant.—Relish, enjoyment, taste, health.

Nautical. (See Marine.)

Near, nigh, neighboring, close, adjacent, contiguous, intimate.
Ant.—Far, distant, remote, off, foreign, removed.

Neat, nice, spruce, trim, precise, pure.
Ant.—Slovenly, careless, dirty, unclean, nasty.

Necessary, needful, expedient, essential, requisite, indispensable.
Ant.—Unnecessary, contingent, unessential, accidental, casual, optional, discretional, abortive, bootless, futile, ineffectual, nugatory, vain, valueless, worthless.

Necessitate, compel, force, oblige.
Ant.—Ask, suggest, hint, supplicate, beg, dissuade, hinder, impede, inhibit, prevent, restrain.

Necessity, need, occasion, exigency, emergency, urgency, want, poverty, requisite.
Ant.—Uncertainty, uselessness. superfluity, competence, casualty, contingency, freedom, choice, fortuity, option, possibility, uncertainty.

Need, *n.* necessity, distress, poverty, indigence, want, penury.

Need, *v.* require, want, lack.

Needful. (See Necessary.)

Neglect, *v.* disregard, slight, omit, overlook.
Ant.—Respect, consider, notice, observe, attend, regard, foster, cherish, nourish.

Neglect, *n.* omission, failure, default, negligence, remissness, carelessness, slight.
Ant.—Care, watchfulness.

Neighborhood, vicinity, nearness, adjacency, proximity, environs.
Ant.—Remoteness, distance.

Nerve, fiber, sinew, tendon, force, pluck, courage.
Ant.—Timidity, cowardice, hesitation.

Nerveless, feeble, impuissant, weak, forceless, enfeebled, debilitated, enervated, impotent, paralyzed, palsied.
Ant.—Strong, healthy, sound, active, bold, fearless.

Nervous, timid, timorous, shaky.
Ant.—Cool, collected, calm, confident, brave.

Nettle. (See Aggravate.)

Neutralize, counterbalance, counteract.
Ant.—Enhance, intensify.

New, fresh, recent, novel, modern.
Ant.—Old, ancient, antique, antiquated, obsolete, trite, worn-out.

News, tidings, intelligence, information.
Ant.—Antiquity, oldness, staleness.

Nice, good, fine, delicate, exact, accurate, particular, precise, fastidious.
Ant.—Coarse, rude, rough, nasty, unscrupulous, inexact, inaccurate, careless, unpleasant.

Niggardly. (See Miserly.)

Nigh. (See Near.)

Nimble, active, brisk, lively, alert, quick, agile, prompt.
Ant.—Clumsy, dilatory, heavy, inert, sluggish, unready.

Nobility, aristocracy, greatness, grandeur, peerage.
Ant.—Obscurity, plebeian, meanness, commonalty, smallness.

Noble, exalted, elevated, dignified, illustrious, great, grand, stately, lofty.
Ant.—Ignoble, mean, plebeian, paltry, small, low, vile.

Nocturnal, nightly, gloomy, dark.
Ant.—Diurnal, light, daily, brilliant, solar.

Noise, cry, outcry, clamor, row, din, uproar, tumult.
Ant.—Stillness, hush, silence, music, note, melody, quiet.

Nominate, name, entitle, appoint, invest, present.
Ant.—Suggest, indicate, recall, deprive, cancel, withdraw.

Nonsensical, silly, irrational, absurd, foolish.
Ant.—Sensible, rational, sane.

Notable, remarkable, plain, evident, signal, striking, rare.
Ant.—Obscure, insignificant.

Note, mark, token, symbol, sign, indication, remark, comment.

Noted, remarkable, distinguished, renowned, eminent.
Ant.—Obscure, unknown.

Notice, *n.* advice, notification, intelligence, information, warning.
Ant.—Neglect, oversight, disregard, slight, omission.

Notice, *v.* mark, note, observe, attend to, regard, heed.
Ant.—ignore, overlook.

Noticeable. (See Remarkable.)

Notification. (See Notice.)

Notify, publish, acquaint, communicate, inform, declare, apprise.
Ant.—Suppress, withhold, conceal, bury, hide.

Notion, conception, idea, belief, opinion, sentiment, impression.
Ant.—Misconception, misapprehension, falsification.

Notorious, noted, well-known, renowned, infamous, open, obvious, ill-famed.
Ant.—Suspected, reported, famous, mysterious, secret, unknown.

Nourish, nurture, cherish, foster, supply.
Ant.—Starve, blight, destroy, wither, kill, famish.

Nourishment, diet, food, sustenance, nutrition.

Novel, new, modern, fresh, recent, unused, strange, rare.
Ant.—Old, ancient, old-fashioned.

Noxious, hurtful, deadly, poisonous, deleterious, baneful.
Ant.—Wholesome, healthy, useful, beneficial, helpful, advantageous.

Nugatory, ineffectual, futile, useless, null, void.
Ant.—Potent, serious, important, efficacious, successful.

Nullify, annul, vacate, invalidate, repeal, quash, cancel.
Ant.—Confirm, establish.

Number. (See Count.)

Numerous, many, sundry, various, several.
Ant.—Few, sparse, scant.

Nuptials. (See Marriage.)

Nurture. (See Nourish.)

Nutrition, food, diet, nutriment, nourishment.
Ant.—Exhaustion, starvation, inanition.

O

Obdurate, hard, callous, hardened, unbending, graceless, unfeeling, insensible, unsusceptible.
Ant.—Tender, softened, flexible, yielding, amenable, docile, tractable.

Obedient, compliant, submissive, dutiful, respectful.
Ant.—Disobedient, rebellious, mutinous, antagonistic, obstinate, stubborn.

Obese, fat, corpulent, fleshy.
Ant.—Attenuated, thin, slender.

Obey, conform, comply, submit, yield.
Ant.—Resist, rebel, violate, transgress, disobey.

Object, *n.* aim, end, purpose, design, mark, butt.

Object, *v.* oppose, except, contravene, impeach, deprecate.
Ant.—Agree, comply, aid, help, abet, encourage, assent, uphold.

Obligation, duty, favor, engagement, contract, bond.
Ant.—Choice, freedom, exemption.

Oblige, compel, bind, engage, coerce, constrain, force, impel, accommodate, gratify.
Ant.—Release, acquit, induce, persuade, annoy, disobey.

Obliging, accommodating, civil, courteous, considerate.
Ant.—Discourteous, rude, perverse, disobliging.

Obliterate, erase, blot out, expunge, efface.
Ant.—Insert, mark, note, introduce.

Obloquy, odium, reproach, censure, abuse, scurrility, opprobrium, shame.
Ant.—Praise, encomium, encouragement, congratulation.

Obnoxious, hateful, offensive, unpopular, objectionable.
Ant.—Pleasant, wholesome, salutary, beneficial, popular, agreeable.

Obscene, lewd, foul, filthy, indecent, indelicate, shameless.
Ant.—Pure, modest, virtuous, decent.

Obscure, *a.* dim, misty, cloudy, shadowy, dusky, dark, gloomy, indistinct, unknown, humble, unintelligible, undistinguished.
Ant.—Plain, distinct, lucid, bright, luminous, prominent, eminent, distinguished.

Obscure, *v.* shade, dim, cloud, darken.
Ant.—Lighten, brighten, unveil, expose.

Observance, form, etiquette, ceremony, solemnity, rite, celebration, usage, custom.
Ant.—Disuse, omission, informality, disrespect, neglect, unconventionality.

Observant, watchful, mindful, attentive, heedful.
Ant.—Unobservant, heedless, careless, neglectful, unmindful.

Observation, remark, comment, notice.
Ant.—Inattention, oversight, inadvertence, disregard.

Observe, keep, fulfill, heed, obey, perform, notice, remark, watch.
Ant.—Omit, miss, ignore, fail, disregard.

Obsolete, disused, antiquated, old-fashioned, ancient, old.
Ant.—Current, extant, modern, fashionable.

Obstacle, difficulty, impediment, stumbling-block, barrier, hindrance, obstruction.
Ant.—Aid, incentive, encouragement, help.

Obstinate, firm, dogged, pertinacious, perverse, intractable, stubborn, headstrong, contumacious, obdurate.
Ant.—Docile, complaisant, amenable, yielding, irresolute.

Obstruct, hinder, prevent, impede, bar, clog, barricade, choke, interrupt.
Ant.—Clear, open, facilitate, expedite, aid, help, advance, promote.

Obtain. (See Acquire.)

Obtuse, stolid, heavy-headed, dull, stupid, unintelligent.
Ant.—Acute, sharp, clever, intelligent.

Obviate, prevent, preclude, hinder, provide, against.
Ant.—Necessitate, compel, order.

Obvious. (See Apparent.)

Occasion, *n.* necessity, need, event, opening, ground, reason, opportunity.
Ant.—Untimeliness, unseasonableness.

Occasion, *v.* cause, make, create, induce, generate.
Ant.—Frustrate, hinder, mar.

Occasional, accidental, casual, incidental.
Ant.—Frequent, often, always, permanent, continual.

Occult, secret, hidden, unknown, invisible, dark, mysterious.
Ant.—Plain, clear, open, familiar, exposed.

Occupation, occupancy, profession, holding, tenure, business, trade, avocation, calling, engagement, office, pursuit.
Ant.—Idleness, indolence, rest, enjoyment, leisure, resignation, abandonment.

Occur, happen, take place, appear, offer, present itself.
Ant.—Pass, threaten, impend.

Odd, singular, eccentric, strange, extraordinary, whimsical, comical, droll, uneven.
Ant.—Usual, regular, normal, common, balanced, aggregate, matched, even.

Odious, hateful, loathsome, execrable, detestable, abominable, disgusting, repulsive.
Ant.—Pleasant, pleasing, acceptable, delectable.

Odor. (See Smell.)

Offend, displease, vex, nettle, irritate, shock, transgress, err.
Ant.—Conciliate, gratify, indulge, please.

Offense, affront, insult, outrage, indignity, misdeed, trespass, transgression, wrong, misdemeanor, injustice.
Ant.—Defense, innocence, gentleness, favor, right.

Offensive, insulting, rude, saucy, impertinent, distasteful, obnoxious, opprobrious, insolent, abusive.
Ant.—Defensive, grateful, pleasant, agreeable, savory, admirable, beautiful, sweet, charming, worthy.

Offer, present, bid, tender, proffer, extend, propose, volunteer.
Ant.—Withdraw, retract, retain, withhold, divert.

Office, business, post, situation, duty, charge, benefit, service, counting-house, function, place.
Ant.—Leisure, vacancy, sinecure, home.

Officer, functionary, official, commandant.
Ant.—Private, civilian, member, servant, subordinate.

Officious, busy, obtrusive, interfering, meddling.
Ant.—Modest, retiring, unofficious, negligent.

Offspring, issue, progeny, descendants, children.
Ant.—Ancestry, paternity.

Often, frequently, recurrently, repeatedly, many times.
Ant.—Seldom, infrequently, never.

Old, aged, superannuated, ancient, antique, antiquated, obsolete, old-fashioned.
Ant.—Young, new, modern.

Omen, presage, prognosis.

Omission, oversight, failure, neglect, default.
Ant.—Attention, insertion, notice, performance.

Omit, leave out, miss, overlook.
Ant.—Insert, notice, perform, do.

One, common, united, single, individual, undivided.
Ant.—Plurality, multitude, variety, diversity.

Onerous, burdensome, heavy, laborious, responsible, oppressive, toilsome.
Ant.—Light, easy, trivial, slight.

Onward, forward, ahead, progressive.
Ant.—Backward, back, retrograde.

Ooze, exude, drop, percolate, filter.
Ant.—Pour, rush, flow, stream.

Opaque, dull, dark, cloudy.
Ant.—Transparent, translucent, clear, bright.

Open, *a.* candid, frank, unreserved, free, ingenuous, sincere, clear, fair, unaffected, genuine, undisguised, unfolded.
Ant.—Close, shut, reserved, unavailable, settled, hidden, dark.

Open, *v.* unclose, unlock, unseal, exhibit, dissolve, spread, expand, begin.
Ant.—Close, shut, cover, conceal, inclose, mystify.

Opening, breach, aperture, gap, rent, hollow, chasm, cleft, crevice, cranny, fissure, chink, chance.
Ant.—Obstruction, enclosure, close, end, conclusion.

Operate, act, do, make, work, labor.
Ant.—Cease, rest, fail, stop.

Operation, action, agency, instrumentality, force, effort, enterprise.
Ant.—Cessation, inaction, rest, inefficacy.

Operative, stringent, effective, serviceable, binding.
Ant.—Inoperative, ineffectual.

Opinion, view, idea, sentiment, feeling, notion, impression, conviction, theory, judgment, belief.
Ant.—Knowledge, verity, fact.

Opinionated, conceited, egotistical.
Ant.—Decorous, modest, unassuming, unpretentious.

Opponent. (See Adversary.)

Opportune, seasonable, timely, fit, well-timed, proper.
Ant.—Inopportune, untimely, unseasonable, infelicitous.

Opportunity, occasion, chance, opening.
Ant.—Unseasonableness, lapse, omission.

Oppose, combat, bar, hinder, resist, withstand, contradict, thwart.
Ant.—Aid, abet, help, support, expedite, sustain, give way, yield, succumb.

Opposing, conflicting, jarring, neutralizing.
Ant.—Agreeing, supporting, aiding, helping.

Opposite, adverse, diverse, contrary, hostile, antagonistic, repugnant, incompatible, paradoxical, facing.
Ant.—Agreeing, coincident, neighboring.

Oppress, overburden, overbear, overtask, persecute, abuse.
Ant.—Encourage, support, assist, befriend.

Opprobrious, abusive, scurrilous, insulting, offensive, outrageous, shameful.
Ant.—Eulogistic, panegyrical, flattering, pleasing, honorable.

Opprobrium, disgrace, odium, infamy, ignominy, obloquy.
Ant.—Honor, respect, glory, praise.

Option, choice, preference, election, discretion.
Ant.—Obligation, necessity, compulsion.

Opulent. (See Rich.)

Oral, verbal, spoken, parole.
Ant.—Written, documentary.

Oration, address, speech, harangue, discourse.
Ant.—Essay, letter.

Ordain, order, consecrate, prescribe, enjoin, institute.
Ant.—Revoke, cancel, annul, subvert, disestablish.

Order, *n.* succession, series, method, rule, class, rank, decree, law, injunction, precept, command, system, regularity.
Ant.—Disorder, confusion, inversion, execution, disarrangement, misrule, anarchy.

Order, *v.* appoint, prescribe, enjoin, command, direct, arrange, range, dispose, regulate, organize, adjust, classify.
Ant.—Disorder, revoke, cancel, confuse, invert, execute.

Orderly, regular, systematic, methodical, quiet, peaceable.
Ant.—Disorderly, irregular, riotous.

Ordinance, decree, law, statute, edict, regulation.
Ant.—Custom, usage, prescription.

Ordinary, common, vulgar, plain, customary, settled, wonted, conventional, habitual, usual.
Ant.—Extraordinary, uncommon, strange, marvelous, remarkable, unconventional, unusual.

Organic, fundamental, rooted, elemental.
Ant.—Accidental, unimportant, inorganic, vegetal.

Organization, structure, form, instrumentality, construction.
Ant.—Disruption, disorganization, dismemberment, adjournment.

Organize, dispose, arrange, regulate, adjust.
Ant.—Disband, break up, disorganize, dismember, distort, adjourn.

Orifice, aperture, opening.
Ant.—Stopper, plug, obstruction.

Origin, commencement, original, beginning, rise, source, spring, cause, occasion.
Ant.—Termination, conclusion, extinction, end.

Original, first, primary, pristine, primeval, peculiar, odd.
Ant.—Derived, subsequent, terminal, later, modern, plagiarized.

Originate, create, form, spring, ooze, issue, proceed, begin.
Ant.—Prosecute, conduct, apply.

Ornament, adorn, beautify, deck, embellish, emblazon.
Ant.—Disfigure, disgrace, brand, spoil, mar.

Ostensible, manifest, visible, outward, colorable, professed.
Ant.—Real, genuine, concealed, actual, veritable.

Ostentation, display, pomp, show, parade, vaunting, boasting.
Ant.—Reserve, modesty, diffidence, unobtrusiveness.

Oust, remove, eject, expel, dislodge, evict.
Ant.—Install, restore, reinstate.

Outcry, cry, clamor, noise, scream, yell.
Ant.—Quiet, silence, acclamation, plaudit.

Outer. (See Exterior.)

Outlandish, strange, foreign, alien, barbarous, clownish.
Ant.—Regular, modish, fashionable, native.

Outline, sketch, plan, draft, contour.

Ant.—Form, substance, figure, ground, space.

Outlive, survive.

Outrage, affront, abuse, injury, insult, offense, indignity.

Ant.—Favor, moderation, self-control, coolness, calmness.

Outrageous, monstrous, flagrant, violent, furious, wild.

Ant.—Moderate, reasonable, justifiable.

Outset, commencement, start, beginning, opening.

Ant.—Close, termination, end, conclusion.

Outskirts, suburbs, environs, precincts.

Ant.—Interior, center, heart.

Outward, outer, external, exterior, extrinsic, extraneous, outside.

Ant.—Inward, internal, intrinsic, toward, homeward, inner, interior.

Over, above.

Ant.—Under, beneath.

Overbalance, outweigh, preponderate.

Overbear, bear down, overwhelm, overpower, subdue.

Overbearing, haughty, proud, arrogant.

Ant.—Gentle.

Overcome. (See Defeat.)

Overflow, inundate, submerge, deluge, flood.

Ant.—Subside, drain, exhaust.

Overlook, inspect, survey, excuse, forgive, pardon, neglect, miss.

Ant.—Visit, scrutinize, investigate, mark.

Overrule, supersede, suppress.

Oversight, inadvertence, inattention, neglect, mistake, error, omission, inspection, superintendence.

Ant.—Scrutiny, correction, emendation, attention, mark, notice, overspread, overrun.

Overt, open, public, notorious, manifest, patent.

Ant.—Covert, secret, clandestine.

Overthrow, prostrate, demolish, overturn, destroy, ruin, upset, beat, defeat, discomfit, rout.

Ant.—Restore, reinstate, regenerate, revive, construct, build.

Overture, proposal, offer, invitation, resolution.

Ant.—Inaction, quiescence.

Overturn, overthrow, invert, reverse, subvert.

Ant.—Establish, fortify.

Overwhelm, drown, overbear, oppress, overpower, subdue, crush, defeat, vanquish.

Ant.—Raise, reëstablish, rescue, extricate, maintain, restore, support, uphold.

Owe, indebted, beholden.

Ant.—Repay, liquidate, defray.

Own, acknowledge, admit, confess, recognize, hold, have, possess.

Ant.—Disown, abjure, disavow, forfeit, lose, alienate.

Owner, proprietor, possessor, master, holder.

Ant.—Servant, subordinate, lessee.

P

Pacific, peaceful, peaceable, mild, gentle, calm, quiet.

Ant.—Warlike, tumultuous, harsh, quarrelsome, exasperating.

Pacify, appease, calm, quiet, still, soothe.

Ant.—Excite, exasperate, irritate, provoke, rouse.

Pagan, Gentile, heathen, idolator.

Ant.—Believer, Christian.

Pageantry, pomp, splendor, show, magnificence.

Pain, *n.* anguish, agony, distress, suffering, pang, grief, qualm.

Ant.—Pleasure, joy, felicity, enjoyment, delight, ease, amusement, comfort, happiness.

Pain, *v.* agonize, rack, torment, torture, trouble, annoy.

Ant.—Relieve, ease, refresh, please, gratify.

Paint, color, represent, portray, delineate, depict.

Ant.—Daub, caricature, misrepresent, misdepict, describe.

Palatable, tasteful, savory, appetizing.

Ant.—Unpalatable, disagreeable, sour, unsavory.

Pale, pallid, wan, whitish, sallow, faint.

Ant.—Ruddy, deep, high-colored, conspicuous.

Palliate, extenuate, allay, soothe, soften.

Ant.—Expose, denounce, exaggerate, aggravate.

Pallid, pale, wan.

Ant.—Florid, rubicund, flushed.

Palpable. (See Apparent.)

Palpitate, flutter, pant, throb, pulsate.

Ant.—Pause, stop, cease.

Paltry, contemptible, pitiful, mean, sorry, despicable, shabby, beggarly.

Ant.—Admirable, magnificent, candid, straightforward, estimable.

Panegyric, eulogy, encomium, eulogium, praise.

Ant.—Satire, sarcasm, invective, tirade.

Pang, throe, twinge, agony, anguish, pain, distress.

Ant.—Delight, glow, enjoyment, pleasure, gratification.

Pant. (See Palpitate.)

Parable, fable, allegory, simile, similitude.

Ant.—History, fact, narrative.

Parade, show, ostentation, vainglory, procession, spectacle.

Ant.—Concealment, modesty, humility, plainness, retirement.

Parallel, equal, parity, analogous, like, similar.

Ant.—Divergent, different, opposed, incongruous.

Paramount, supreme, principal, chief.

Ant.—Minor, inferior, subordinate.

Parasite, flatterer, sycophant, toady.

Ant.—Friend, antagonist, traducer, calumniator.

Pardon, forgive, absolve, overlook, excuse, remit, acquit, discharge, set free, clear, liberate.

Ant.—Condemn, punish, accuse.

Parent, author, origin, source, cause.

Ant.—Offspring, child, issue, effect, progeny.

Parson, clergyman, incumbent, curate, minister.

Ant.—Layman, member, sinner.

Part, separate, divide, sever, dissever, disunite, break, division, portion, share, fraction.

Ant.—Join, annex, compound, add, unite, aggregate, amount, entirety, mass, sum, total, whole.

Partake, participate, share.

Ant.—Forfeit, relinquish.

Partial, biased, prejudiced, limited, incomplete.

Ant.—Impartial, just, fair, equitable, total, universal, whole.

Participate. (See Partake.)

Particular, singular, exact, nice, punctual, minute, careful, distinct, odd, strange.

Ant.—General, universal, comprehensive, rough, coarse.

Particularly, primarily, especially, chiefly.

Ant.—On the whole, generally.

Partisan. (See Adherent.)

Partition, part, divide, apportion, distribute.

Ant.—Unite, coalesce, include, collect, incorporate.

Partner, colleague, coadjutor, associate, sharer, confederate, spouse.

Ant.—Rival, opponent, competitor, antagonist.

Partnership, union, connection, firm, house, association. company, companionship, society.

Ant.—Dissolution, separation, disunion.

Party, faction, confederacy, combination, detachment, clique, league.

Ant.—Individual, nation, state.

Pass, elapse, glide, slip, slide.

Ant.—Stay, remain, stand, wait.

Passage, journey, course, road, route, avenue, channel, clause, sentence.

Ant.—Halt, rest, stop, discourse, essay.

Passion, anger, rage, fury, vehemence, impetuosity, love, affection.

Ant.—Apathy, indifference, coolness, frigidity.

Passionate, angry, excitable, fiery, vehement, impetuous, glowing, burning, ardent, hot, hasty, irritable.

Ant.—Impassionate, cool, deliberate, apathetic, quiet.

Passive, unresisting, unopposing, submissive, enduring, patient.

Ant.—Active, alert, positive, vehement.

Pastime, sport, play, recreation, amusement, diversion.

Ant.—Business, study, labor, task, work.

Path. (See Road.)

Pathetic, moving, touching, affecting, melting, tender.

Ant.—Ludicrous, funny, unaffecting, farcical.

Patience, resignation, endurance, fortitude.

Ant.—Resistance, impatience, rebellion, inconstancy.

Patient, passive, submissive meek.

Ant.—Hasty, irascible.

Patronize, befriend, favor, countenance, support.

Ant.—Discountenance, oppose, oppress, disfavor.

Pattern. (See Model.)

Pause, demur, hesitate, deliberate, intermit, suspend.

Ant.—Continue, proceed, advance, persist, persevere.

Pay, *n.* wages, salary, hire, stipend, recompense.

Ant.—Present, gratuity, gift.

Pay, *v.* liquidate, lessen, discharge, extinguish, reward.

Ant.—Defraud, repudiate, hoard, retain, deprive.

Peace, quiet, calm, tranquillity, repose, amity.

Ant.—War, noise, tumult, disorder, strife, discord, riot, trouble, turbulence.

Peaceable, pacific, peaceful, quiet.

Ant.—Troublesome, riotous.

Peaceful, tranquil, quiet, still, pacific, undisturbed, calm placid, serene, mild, gentle.

Ant.—Warlike, pugnacious, savage, hostile, fierce, violent.

Peasant, countryman, rustic, bumpkin, clodpole, swain.

Ant.—Citizen, townsman, autocrat, lord.

Peculiar, particular, exclusive, remarkable, signal, special, singular, uncommon.

Ant.—General, universal, ordinary, common, public.

Pedantic, priggish, pedagogical, learned.

Ant.—Modest, unaffected.

Peel, skin, rind, husk.

Ant.—Heart, core.

Peerless, unequaled, unmatched, matchless, unique.

Ant.—Ordinary, commonplace, mediocre.

Peevish, ill-natured, touchy, testy, captious, fractious, cross, fretful, petulant, cynical, irascible.

Ant.—Genial, good-natured, good-tempered, complaisant.

Penal, punitive, retributive, corrective.

Ant.—Honorary, remunerative, reparatory.

Penalty, fine, amercement, mulct, forfeiture.

Ant.—Reward, wages, premium, prize, compensation, remuneration.

Penetrate, pierce, perforate, bore, fathom, reach, enter, stab, transfix.

Ant.—Withdraw, fail, depart, leave, issue, vacate.

Penetration, insight, sharpness, acuteness, sagacity, discernment, discrimination.

Ant.—Dullness, shallowness, obtuseness, ignorance, stupidity.

Penitence, contrition, repentance, remorse.

Ant.—Obduracy, congratulation, approval, hard-heartedness.

Pensive, thoughtful, meditative, dreamy, melancholy, dejected, depressed, cheerless, drooping.

Ant.—Vacant, careless, thoughtless, joyous, unreflective.

Penury, poverty, indigence, beggary, destitution, want, need, privation.

Ant.—Competence, wealth, affluence.

People, commonalty, populace, mob, nation, tribe, race, clan, citizenry.

Ant.—Ruler, government, nobility, aristocracy.

Perceive, see, discern, distinguish, observe, understand, know, comprehend, note.

Ant.—Overlook, miss, misconceive, misobserve, ignore, lose, misapprehend.

Perception, seeing, sense, perceptibility, sensibility, susceptibility, sensation, apprehension, conviction, conception, notion, idea.

Ant.—Insensibility, ignorance, misapprehension.

Peremptory, absolute, positive, arbitrary, despotic, decisive, imperative.

Ant.—Suggestive, entreating, mild, gentle.

Perennial, imperishable, undying, immortal, deathless, enduring, perpetual.

Ant.—Occasional, periodical, uncertain, deficient.

Perfect, complete, whole, entire, finished, unbroken, thorough, mature, ripe, absolute.

Ant.—Imperfect, faulty, deficient, objective, scant, fallible, blemished, spoiled.

Perfidious, faithless, treacherous, insidious, unfaithful.

Ant.—True, staunch, faithful, honorable.

Perforate. (See Penetrate.)

Perform. (See Accomplish.)

Performer, actor, player, comedian, tragedian.

Ant.—Spectator, looker-on, audience.

Perfume, odor, scent, fragrance, aroma, smell, incense.

Ant.—Stench, stink, fetor, reek.

Perhaps, perchance, possibly, peradventure.

Ant.—Certainly, inevitably, without doubt.

Peril, danger, hazard, jeopardy, risk, venture, insecurity, pitfall, snare.

Ant.—Security, safety, certainty.

Period. (See Age.)

Periodically, statedly, spasmodically, fitfully.

Ant.—Continually.

Perish. (See Die.)

Permanent, durable, abiding, enduring, lasting, fixed, stable.

Ant.—Transient, ephemeral, fleeting, frail, transitory.

Permission, permit, leave, liberty, license.
Ant.—Prohibition, denial, refusal, prevention, hindrance.
Permit, allow, tolerate.
Ant.—Forbid, interdict.
Pernicious. (See Hurtful.)
Perpetual, constant, continual, continuous, endless, eternal, lasting, incessant, ceaseless, unceasing, uninterrupted.
Ant.—Occasional, transient, periodic, momentary, accidental, casual.
Perplex, embarrass, harass, confuse, bewilder, entangle, involve, puzzle.
Ant.—Clear, enlighten, elucidate, simplify, explicate.
Persecute, oppress, harrow, afflict, worry, annoy.
Ant.—Encourage, inspirit, abet, support.
Persevere, continue, persist, pursue, proceed.
Ant.—Lag, fail, rest, withdraw, refrain, abstain.
Persons, men, people, folks, individuals.
Ant.—Collection, assembly, nation, state.
Perspicuous, clear, plain, distinct, unequivocal, unmistakable, intelligible.
Ant.—Obscure, confused, unintelligible.
Persuade, exhort, urge, allure, incite, influence, entice, prevail upon.
Ant.—Deter, disincline, dissuade, coerce, compel, order, discourage, restrain.
Pert, forward, flippant, saucy, impertinent, impudent.
Ant.—Modest, bashful, demure, staid.
Pertinacious, obstinate, inflexible, stubborn, determined.
Ant.—Inconstant, irresolute, volatile, unreliable.
Pertinent, fit, relevant, proper, appropriate, applicable, related.
Ant.—Alien, discordant, unrelated, unconnected, repugnant.
Pervade, diffuse, spread, permeate, overspread, fill.
Perverse, awkward, cross, untoward, petulant, peevish, crooked, froward, wayward, stubborn.
Ant.—Docile, complaisant, obliging, amenable, gentle.
Pest, bane, plague, ruin, pestilence, taint.
Ant.—Benefit, blessing, good.
Pestilential, contagious, infectious, epidemical, mischievous, pernicious, noxious, baneful, destructive.
Ant.—Innocuous, pure, genial, wholesome, salubrious, salutary, nutritive, healthy.
Petition, prayer, supplication, entreaty, request, suit, appeal.
Ant.—Protest, command, injunction, demand, exaction, requirement.
Petty, trifling, trivial, frivolous, insignificant, small, little.
Ant.—Large, liberal, broad, noble, generous.
Petulant. (See Peevish.)
Phantom. (See Ghost.)
Philanthropic, charitable, kind, benevolent, gracious.
Ant.—Selfish, egotistical, misanthropic, morose.
Philosophy, science, knowledge.
Ant.—Ignorance, stupidity.
Phlegmatic, frigid, cold, heavy, unfeeling, apathetic.
Ant.—Passionate, active, energetic, interested, alert.
Physical, material, corporeal, tangible, natural, bodily.
Ant.—Spiritual, mental, immaterial, moral, intangible.
Pick, pluck, choose, cull, select, gather.
Ant.—Reject, discard, repudiate, relegate, bunch.
Picture, likeness, painting, image, resemblance, drawing, representation, effigy, engraving, print, illustration.
Ant.—Original, landscape, scene, body, nature.
Picturesque, graphic, imaginative.
Ant.—Unpicturesque, tame, desolate, cheerless, homely.
Pierce, penetrate, perforate, bore, broach, tap.
Ant.—Blunt, soothe, allay, lull, compose.
Piety, religion, sanctity, holiness, devotion, grace, godliness.
Ant.—Impiety, ungodliness, profanity, hypocrisy.
Pile, *v.* heap, accumulate, hoard, amass, collect.
Ant.—Demolish, scatter, upset, overthrow, disperse, separate.
Pile, *n.* building, edifice, structure, thread, fiber.
Pilfer, filch, steal, purloin.
Ant.—Restore, refrain.
Pillage. (See Plunder.)
Pillar, column, shaft, post, support.
Ant.—Base, capitol, arch, wall.
Pilot, guide, steer, direct, conduct.
Ant.—Mislead, betray, lose, misdirect.
Pious, holy, godly, saintly, devout, religious.
Ant.—Impious, ungodly, sinful, hypocritical, bad.
Piquant, pungent, acrid, smart, keen, biting, harsh, stinging, cutting, racy.
Ant.—Tame, dull, flat, insipid.
Pique. (See Spite.)
Pitch, fling, cast, launch, throw.
Ant.—Draw, pull, hold, restrain, push.
Piteous, doleful, pitiable, mournful, sad, deplorable, woeful, rueful.
Ant.—Joyous, pleasant, comfortable, desirable, delectable, cheerful, gay, genial, happy, merry, mirthful.
Pith, gist, kernel, cream, strength, marrow.
Ant.—Dressing, surroundings, verbiage.
Pithy, terse, concise, forcible, strong.
Ant.—Fruitless, vapid, weak, diluted, insipid.
Pitiless. (See Merciless.)
Pity, *n.* compassion, sympathy, condolence, mercy.
Ant.—Cruelty, pitilessness, hard-heartedness, relentlessness, brutality.
Place, *n.* position, spot, site, post, situation, station.
Place, *v.* put, set, lay, dispose, order, organize, array, marshal, arrange.
Ant.—Disturb, remove, disarrange, misplace, uproot, transport, confuse, derange, mislay, perturb, unsettle.
Placid, serene, calm, peaceful, tranquil, unruffled, mild.
Ant.—Ruffled, troubled, stormy, excited, agitated, disturbed.
Plague, annoy, molest, vex, tease, trouble, harass, torment.
Ant.—Please, gratify, amuse, soothe, comfort, allay.
Plain, even, level, flat, smooth, apparent, visible, clear, obvious, intelligible, certain, evident, manifest, distinct, palpable, open, candid, frank, sincere, free, ingenuous, overt.
Ant.—Uneven, undulatory, rough, broken, abrupt, confused, obstructed, uncertain, dubious, ambiguous, enigmatical, fair, beautiful, artful, secret, hidden.
Plaintive, doleful, sad, mournful, melancholy.
Ant.—Joyous, exultant, glad, cheerful, cheering.
Plastic, pliant, ductile, tractile.
Ant.—Stubborn, unyielding, unmalleable, inflexible.
Plaudit. (See Acclamation.)
Plausible, specious, ostensible, feasible.

Ant.—Unmistakable, genuine, sterling, true.

Play, game, sport, pastime, amusement, gambol, drama.
Ant.—Occupation, labor, business, work, idleness, toil, drudgery.

Playful, sportive, lively, jocund, merry, gay, sprightly, vivacious, racy, buoyant.
Ant.—Inert, slow, sluggish, sad, melancholy.

Plea, excuse, apology, defense, vindication, entreaty.
Ant.—Charge, accusation, impeachment, action.

Plead, defend, vindicate, exonerate, justify, exculpate, excuse.
Ant.—Charge, accuse, impeach, condemn.

Pleasant. (See Agreeable.)

Please, gratify, satisfy, content, delight, fascinate, indulge, pacify.
Ant.—Displease, dissatisfy, annoy, trouble, vex, irritate.

Pleasure, comfort, enjoyment, gratification, joy, delight, rapture, charm.
Ant.—Pain, suffering, affliction, trouble, asceticism.

Plebeian, ignoble, vulgar, lowborn.
Ant.—Patrician, noble, aristocratic, high-born, high-bred.

Pledge, pawn, earnest, security, surety, guaranty.

Plentiful, abundant, ample, copious, plenteous.
Ant.—Rare, scanty, scarce.

Plenty, enough, sufficiency, abundance, fullness.
Ant.—Scantiness, insufficiency.

Pliable, pliant, flexible, lithe, supple, yielding, docile.
Ant.—Stiff, brittle, stubborn, unbending, unmanageable.

Plot, *n.* stratagem, conspiracy, combination, confederacy, scheme, plan.
Ant.—Action, execution, deed, resolution, law.

Plot, *v.* concoct, hatch, frame, contrive, conspire.
Ant.—Resolve, consult, debate, discover, defeat.

Pluck, courage, mettle, spirit, nerve.
Ant.—Timidity, cowardice.

Plump, fleshy, round, fat, full, chubby.
Ant.—Lean, thin, wizened, shriveled, emaciated, lank, weak.

Plunder, pillage, booty, loot, spoil, robbery, depredation.

Plunge, dive, dip, douse, sink.
Ant.—Emerge, issue, rise, extricate.

Poetical, metrical, versified, imaginative, dreamy, fictitious.
Ant.—Prosaic, unmetrical, commonplace, historical, mathematical, logical, sober.

Poignant, sharp, keen, biting, severe, deep, intense, stinging.
Ant.—Blunt, dull, gentle, shallow.

Point, peaked, sharp, marked, keen, severe.
Ant.—Pointless, aimless, feeble, inexpressive.

Poise, balance, equilibrium, equipoise.
Ant.—Instability.

Poison, bane, pest, venom, virus, infection.
Ant.—Purification, disinfectant, antidote.

Policy, plan, device, stratagem, management.
Ant.—Conjecture, hazard, mismanagement.

Polish, brighten, burnish, glaze, civilize, cultivate, refine.
Ant.—Dull, scratch, mar, spoil, dim, barbarize.

Polite, refined, genteel, civil, accomplished, well-bred.
Ant.—Awkward, rude, uncouth, ill-bred, discourteous, boorish.

Politeness. (See Affability.)

Politic, wise, political, civil, judicious, prudential.
Ant.—Imprudent, unwise, improvident, impolitic.

Pollute, contaminate, soil, defile, taint, infect, corrupt, deprave, demoralize.
Ant.—Purify, clarify, disinfect, filter.

Pomp, parade, display, gorgeousness, splendor, grandeur, pageantry, show.
Ant.—Quiet, simplicity, privacy, plainness, unceremoniousness.

Pompous, majestic, stately, grand, august, dignified, lofty, inflated, bombastic.
Ant.—Unassuming, modest, unobtrusive.

Ponder. (See Reflect.)

Ponderous, heavy, weighty, massive, bulky.
Ant.—Light, trifling, airy, volatile, subtle.

Poor, indigent, needy, penniless, necessitous, deficient, scanty.
Ant.—Rich, wealthy, affluent, abundant, liberal, ample, moneyed, sufficient.

Populace, people, commonalty, multitude, mob.
Ant.—Nobility, aristocracy, government, individual.

Popular, common, general, prevailing, favorite.
Ant.—Exclusive, restricted, scientific, unpopular, odious.

Port, harbor, haven, entrance, portal.
Ant.—Sea, ocean, coast.

Portend, foreshow, augur, presage, forebode, betoken, threaten.
Ant.—Avert, contradict, nullify, negative, preclude.

Portion, part, division, share, piece, bit, section, fragment, parcel.
Ant.—Whole, substance, bulk, mass.

Portly, majestic, stately, grand, dignified, burly, stout.
Ant.—Thin, undignified, unimposing, mean.

Portray, draw, sketch, paint, depict, delineate, represent, describe.
Ant.—Caricature, misrepresent, misportray, suggest.

Position, place, locality, situation, spot, site, action, gesture, posture, attitude.
Ant.—Displacement, absence.

Positive, actual, true, real, certain, sure, definitive, fixed, confident, dogmatic, absolute, peremptory, decided, certain.
Ant.—Negative, fictitious, imaginary, contingent, dependent, conditional, implied, dubious, uncertain, doubtful.

Possess, have, own, hold, occupy.
Ant.—Abandon, renounce, surrender, lose, forfeit, resign.

Possessor, owner, proprietor.

Possible, practicable, likely, feasible, practical.
Ant.—Impossible, impracticable, visionary.

Possibly, perhaps, peradventure, perchance, haply.
Ant.—Certain, without doubt, positively, never.

Poverty, penury, indigence, need, want.
Ant.—Wealth, plenty, abundance, riches, affluence.

Power, authority, force, strength, dominion.
Ant.—Weakness, futility.

Powerful, mighty, potent.
Ant.—Futile, trivial, useless, weak.

Practical, serviceable, useful, experienced, skillful.
Ant.—Impracticable, theoretical, unserviceable, awkward.

Practice, custom, habit, manner, use, usage, exercise.
Ant.—Theory, speculation, disuse, inexperience, idleness.

Praise, *n.* approval, eulogy, commendation, applause, exaltation, honor.

Ant.—Blame, censure, disapproval.

Praise, *v.* commend, extol, eulogize, panegyrize, laud, applaud, glorify.

Ant.—Condemn, reprove, disapprove, censure, blame.

Praiseworthy, laudable, honorable, commendable, meritorious, worthy.

Ant.—Blamable, censurable, reprehensible.

Prate, tattle, babble, chat, chatter, prattle, gossip.

Ant.—Orate, speak, debate, discuss.

Pray. (See Supplicate.)

Prayer, petition, entreaty, request, suit.

Preamble, preface, introduction.

Ant.—Peroration, finale, conclusion, essay, body.

Precarious, doubtful, dubious, uncertain, insecure, unsettled.

Ant.—Safe, certain, assured, systematic, immutable.

Precaution, care, forethought.

Ant.—Improvidence, carelessness, thoughtlessness.

Precede, lead, go before, herald.

Ant.—Succeed, follow.

Precedence, priority, preeminence, preference, antecedence.

Ant.—Inferiority, sequence, posteriority.

Precept, command, injunction, mandate, direction, order, rule, law, maxim, doctrine, principle.

Ant.—Suggestion, hint, prompting, impulse.

Preceptor, teacher, tutor, instructor, schoolmaster.

Ant.—Pupil, scholar, student.

Precincts, borders, limits, bounds, confines, districts.

Ant.—Heart, center, nucleus.

Precious, valuable, costly, dear, estimable.

Ant.—Worthless, valueless, unvalued.

Precipitate, *v.* hurry, hasten, cast down, expedite.

Ant.—Hinder, restrain, retard, deter, obstruct.

Precipitate, *a.* hasty, hurried, rash, premature.

Ant.—Deliberate, slow, shallow, inclined, undulating, level.

Precise, accurate, correct, particular, exact, nice, punctilious.

Ant.—Indefinite, vague, inexact, rough, loose, inaccurate, unceremonious.

Preclude, prevent, obviate, hinder, debar.

Ant.—Admit, promote, further, advance.

Precursory, preceding, anterior, prefatory.

Ant.—Subsequent, consequent, eventual, posterior.

Predecessor, ancestor, forefather, progenitor, forerunner.

Ant.—Successor, junior, posterity.

Predict, foretell, prognosticate, prophesy, foreshadow.

Ant.—Tell, narrate, recount, recall, report.

Predilection, preference, partiality, bias, prejudice.

Ant.—Aversion, antipathy, disinclination, apathy.

Predominant, prevailing, prevalent, ascendant, overruling.

Ant.—Subordinate, inferior.

Preëminence, priority, precedence, antecedence, superiority.

Ant.—Inferiority, equality.

Preface. (See Preamble.)

Prefer, choose, fancy, select, raise, exalt, promote, further.

Ant.—Reject, postpone, defer, withhold, degrade, debase.

Pregnant, prolific, teeming, replete, enceinte.

Ant.—Sterile, barren, void, meaningless.

Prejudice, prepossession, bias, partiality, detriment, harm.

Ant.—Impartiality, fairness, judgment, advantage.

Preliminary, prefatory, introductory, previous, antecedent.

Ant.—Subsequent, following, succeeding.

Prelude, introduction, preface, prologue.

Ant.—Sequel, conclusion.

Premature, precipitate, rash, hasty, untimely, early.

Ant.—Timely, seasonable, opportune.

Premeditation, forethought, forecast.

Ant.—Hazard, impromptu, extemporization.

Premium, recompense, reward, bonus, bribe.

Ant.—Penalty, fine, forfeit, depreciation.

Prepare, fit, equip, qualify, make ready, furnish, adapt, adjust, arrange.

Ant.—Derange, demolish, subvert, misfit.

Preponderate, predominate, prevail, overbalance, outweigh, outbalance.

Ant.—Fail, sink, succumb.

Prepossessing, charming, engaging, taking, attractive, winning.

Ant.—Repulsive, unprepossessing, disagreeable.

Preposterous, irrational, foolish, absurd, ridiculous.

Ant.—Reasonable, fair, just, moderate, sound, right.

Prerogative, privilege, immunity, right, exemption.

Ant.—Disqualification, disfranchisement.

Presage, foresee, predict, portend, augur, forebode, prognosticate, betoken, threaten.

Ant.—Fulfill, occur, recall, report, announce.

Prescribe, appoint, ordain, dictate, decree, enjoin, impose, order.

Ant.—Prohibit, discountenance, suggest.

Present, *a.* existing, subsistent, nigh, immediate, instant, current.

Ant.—Absent, distant, remote, separate.

Present. (See Gift.)

Present, *v.* offer, exhibit, give, introduce.

Ant.—Accept, take, receive, retain, withhold.

Presentiment, foreboding, foretaste, anticipation, forethought.

Ant.—Surprise, miscalculation, accident, foreknowledge.

Preserve, keep, save, secure, defend, uphold, embalm, protect, guard, spare.

Ant.—Damage, impair, abandon, injure.

Press, compress, crush, squeeze, oppress, gall, urge, enforce, impress, crowd, harass.

Ant.—Relax, ease, free, relieve, liberate, entice, allure.

Pressure, urgency, exigency, hurry, crushing, squeezing.

Ant.—Relief, ease, liberty.

Presume, suppose, think, infer, believe, conjecture, apprehend.

Ant.—Deduce, prove, argue, hesitate, distrust.

Presumptuous, presuming, overconfident, forward, arrogant, bold, rash, foolhardy.

Ant.—Modest, diffident, bashful, hesitating.

Pretend, feign, affect, simulate, profess.

Ant.—Substantiate, test, verify, detect, refute.

Pretense, cloak, mask, garb, pretext, excuse, plea, subterfuge.

Ant.—Reality, truth, candor, fact, actuality, openness.

Pretext. (See Pretense.)

Pretty. (See Beautiful.)

Prevail, predominate, obtain, succeed.

Ant.—Fail, sink, succumb, abolish, disappear.

Prevailing, proper, prevalent, ruling, ascendant, predominant, general.

Ant.—Mitigated, diminishing, subordinate, powerless, isolated, sporadic.

Prevalence, influence, custom, power, operation, preponderance.

Ant.—Disuse, decay, obsoleteness, disappearance, abolition.

Prevaricate, quibble, cavil, equivocate.

Ant.—Affirm, maintain, prove, substantiate.

Prevent, impede, thwart, obviate, hinder, obstruct, bar, neutralize, preclude.

Ant.—Promote, aid, expedite, encourage, advance, cause.

Previous, preceding, foregoing, antecedent, anterior, prior, introductory, preparatory, preliminary.

Ant.—Subsequent, succeeding, following, later.

Prey, food, victim, sacrifice, spoil, booty, ravage.

Ant.—Rights, earnings, wages, due.

Price, cost, charge, expense, figure, value, worth.

Ant.—Discount, allowance, donation, gift.

Priceless, invaluable, inestimable.

Ant.—Cheap, valueless.

Pride, arrogance, haughtiness, vanity, self-esteem, lordliness, conceit, loftiness, vainglory.

Ant.—Meekness, modesty, humility, lowliness.

Priggish, dandified, foppish, affected, coxcombical.

Ant.—Sensible, unaffected, plain, honest.

Prim, precise, demure, formal, starched, stiff, priggish.

Ant.—Informal, easy, genial, natural.

Primary, first, earliest, primitive, pristine, original, primeval.

Ant.—Secondary, subordinate, inferior, subsequent, later.

Prime, primal, first, capital, first-rate, perfect, excellent.

Ant.—Inferior, impaired, deteriorated, defective.

Primitive, old-fashioned, first, pristine, ancient, antiquated, primeval.

Ant.—Modern, modish, civilized, sophisticated.

Princely, royal, regal, stately, august, noble, munificent.

Ant.—Lowly, beggarly, mean.

Principal, chief, leading, first, highest, supreme, main, essential.

Ant.—Subordinate, secondary, subject, auxiliary, minor.

Principally, chiefly, essentially, mainly.

Ant.—Secondarily, subsequently.

Principle, ground, reason, motive, impulse, maxim, rule, rectitude, integrity.

Ant.—Action, issue, exercise, application.

Print, mark, impress, stamp, imprint.

Ant.—Write, speak, engrave.

Prior. (See Previous.)

Pristine. (See Primary.)

Privacy, solitude, retirement, seclusion, retreat, secrecy, concealment.

Ant.—Publicity, exposure, notoriety.

Privation, loss, bereavement, destitution, poverty, want.

Ant.—Supply, benefaction, compensation, recovery, restitution.

Privilege, immunity, advantage, favor, prerogative, exemption, right, claim.

Ant.—Prohibition, inhibition, exclusion, disqualification, damage, detriment, drawback, loss, obstacle, obstruction.

Prize, *n.* seizure, capture, booty, spoil, loot, plunder, trophy, palm.

Ant.—Loss, forfeiture, penalty, sacrifice, failure, infamy.

Prize, *v.* esteem, rate, appraise, assess, value.

Ant.—Dislike, abhor, condemn, despise.

Probability, chance, likelihood, appearance, presumption.

Ant.—Improbability, unlikelihood.

Probity, honesty, integrity, uprightness, sincerity, soundness, rectitude.

Ant.—Dishonesty, rascality, vice, fraud, deceit.

Problematical, uncertain, doubtful, dubious, questionable, disputable, suspicious.

Ant.—Certain, sure, undoubted, proved.

Procedure. (See Proceeding.)

Proceed, move, pass, advance, arise, issue, emanate.

Ant.—Recede, retreat, stand, stop, stay, discontinue.

Proceeding, transaction, measure, step, procedure, process, course, form, progress, progression, suit, trial, case.

Ant.—Inaction, abandonment, desistence, deviation.

Procession, train, march, caravan, retinue, cavalcade, cortege.

Ant.—Rabble, mob, confusion, rout.

Proclaim, advertise, announce, publish, declare, promulgate, report.

Ant.—Conceal, suppress, secrete, contain.

Proclivity, propensity, tendency, bias, bent, proneness, aptitude.

Ant.—Aversion, indisposition, disinclination.

Procrastinate, delay, defer, adjourn, postpone, put off, dally.

Ant.—Hurry, complete, finish.

Procure, obtain, acquire, gain, get, reap, win, earn.

Ant.—Miss, lose, forfeit.

Prodigal, extravagant, improvident, lavish, profuse, wasteful.

Ant.—Frugal, economical, close, saving, miserly.

Prodigious, enormous, huge, vast, amazing, astonishing, remarkable, astounding, surprising, wonderful.

Ant.—Insignificant, small.

Prodigy, wonder, miracle, marvel, monster.

Ant.—Imposture, individual, nature.

Produce, yield, give, generate, occasion, realize, show, lengthen.

Ant.—Retain, withhold, destroy, contract, reduce.

Profane, impious, irreligious, unhallowed, secular, unholy, ungodly, godless.

Ant.—Pious, sacred, holy, devout, reverend.

Profess, affect, pretend, feign, own.

Ant.—Renounce, repudiate, abjure.

Profession, occupation, business, trade, vocation, office, employment, engagement, avowal.

Proffer, volunteer, offer, propose, tender.

Ant.—Withhold, detain, refrain.

Proficiency, advancement, progress, improvement, skill, dexterity.

Ant.—Failure, backwardness, awkwardness.

Proficient, adept, master, expert.

Ant.—Tyro, amateur, novice, dunce.

Profit, gain, emolument, advantage, benefit, service, avail, use.

Ant.—Loss, detriment, damage, waste.

Profligate, abandoned, dissolute, depraved, vicious, degenerate, corrupt, demoralized.
Ant.—Virtuous, honest, principled, conscientious, good, upright, honorable.
Profound, deep, penetrating, solemn, abstruse, recondite, fathomless.
Ant.—Shallow, superficial, slight.
Profuse, extravagant, prodigal, lavish, improvident, excessive, copious, plentiful.
Ant.—Scanty, sparing, parsimonious, poor, miserly, niggardly, economical.
Progeny, children, descendants, race, offspring, issue.
Ant.—Stock, parentage, ancestry.
Prognosticate. (See Predict.)
Progress, advancement, progression, growth, improvement, movement, march.
Ant.—Delay, stoppage, retrogression, failure, relapse.
Prohibit, hinder, debar, prevent, forbid, interdict, inhibit.
Ant.—Permit, grant, allow, sanction.
Project, *n.* design, plan, scheme, contrivance, device.
Ant.—Hazard, chance, venture.
Project, *v.* shoot, discharge, throw, hurl, jut, protrude, bulge.
Ant.—Withdraw, draw, pull, attract, recoil, retain.
Prolific, fertile, productive, generative, fruitful, teeming.
Ant.—Barren, sterile.
Prolix, diffuse, long, prolonged, tedious, tiresome, wordy, verbose, prosaic.
Ant.—Concise, brief, succinct.
Prolong. (See Lengthen.)
Prominent, eminent, conspicuous, jutting, important, leading, marked.
Ant.—Inconspicuous, minor, unimportant, receding, indented, engraved, obscure.
Promiscuous, mixed, miscellaneous, mingled, indiscriminate, heterogeneous.
Ant.—Sorted, select, arranged, reserved, exclusive, nice, choice.
Promote, encourage, aid, further, advance, forward.
Ant.—Repress, hinder, discourage, check, allay, dishonor, abase.
Prompt, *v.* incite, animate, urge, impel.
Prompt, *a.* expeditious, quick, alert, agile, active, brisk, ready.
Ant.—Tardy, late, sluggish, behind-hand.
Promptitude, readiness, promptness, quickness, alacrity, activity, briskness.
Ant.—Unreadiness, tardiness, hesitation, inaction.
Promulgate, publish, announce, advertise, proclaim, declare, spread.
Ant.—Suppress, conceal, stifle, hush, discountenance.
Prone, inclining, prostrate, flat, tending, apt.
Ant.—Averse, disinclined, indisposed.
Pronounce, articulate, speak, utter, deliver, express, enunciate, declare, affirm.
Ant.—Mispronounce, suppress, stifle, silence, mumble.
Proof, demonstration, evidence, testimony, experience, trial, experiment, test, assay.
Ant.—Disproof, failure, fallacy, invalidity.
Prop, bolster, brace, buttress, maintain, sustain, support, stay.
Propagate, spread, circulate, diffuse, disseminate, extend, breed, increase, generate.
Ant.—Extinguish, contract, suppress, reduce, diminish, fail, die, decrease.
Propensity, inclination, disposition, bias, proneness, tendency, bent, predilection, proclivity.
Ant.—Aversion, disinclination, indisposition.
Proper, legitimate, right, just, fair, equitable, honest, suitable, fit, befitting, decent, pertinent, appropriate, meet, becoming, benefiting, adapted.
Ant.—Improper, wrong, unsuitable, common, indecent, unbecoming, unseemly.
Property, goods, possessions, wealth, estate, peculiarity, quality, attribute, effects.
Ant.—Poverty, want, failure, penury, aspect, essence.
Prophesy, foretell, predict, prognosticate.
Ant.—Recount, tell, relate.
Propitiate, conciliate, reconcile.
Ant.—Alienate, estrange, exasperate.
Propitious, fortunate, promising, favorable, auspicious, timely.
Ant.—Unpropitious, hostile, untimely, unfavorable.
Proportion, rate, ratio, degree.
Ant.—Disproportion, asymmetry.
Proposal, offer, tender, overture, proposition.
Ant.—Withdrawal, order, command, warning, prohibition.
Propose, purpose, intend, mean, move, propound, design, offer, proffer, bid, tender.
Ant.—Chance, risk, venture, revoke.
Proprietor, possessor, owner, master.
Ant.—Lessee, servant, subordinate.
Propriety, expediency, fitness, justness, decorum, correctness.
Ant.—Impropriety, indecorum, unconventionality.
Prorogue, adjourn, postpone, delay, defer.
Ant.—Convene, call, assemble, prolong.
Prosecute, continue, pursue, persevere, persist, arraign.
Ant.—Discontinue, abandon, exonerate, acquit.
Prospect, view, survey, landscape, perspective, vista, scene, promise, hope.
Ant.—Obscurity, darkness, cloud, hopelessness, improbability.
Prosper, succeed, flourish, grow rich, thrive, advance.
Ant.—Fail, lose.
Prosperity, welfare, well-being, weal, happiness, good luck.
Ant.—Poverty, failure.
Prostrate, oppressed, trampled on, abject, paralyzed.
Ant.—Erect, upright, restored, vertical, revived.
Protect. (See Defend.)
Protection, shield, defense, preservation, guard, shelter.
Ant.—Betrayal, abandonment, exposure.
Protest, denounce.
Ant.—Sanction, endorse, acquiesce, agree.
Protract. (See Lengthen.)
Protrude, jut, project, bulge, shoot out, suspend.
Ant.—Recede, indent, incline.
Proud, stately, vain, lofty, arrogant, conceited, boastful, grand, assuming, haughty, vainglorious.
Ant.—Humble, meek, lowly, affable, deferential.
Prove, examine, assay, evince, demonstrate, establish, confirm, manifest, argue, attest, verify.
Ant.—Disprove, refute, contradict.
Proverb, adage, maxim, aphorism, saying, byword, saw.
Ant.—Essay, dissertation, oration, yarn.
Provide, procure, prepare, furnish, supply, arrange, get

Ant.—Neglect, overlook, withhold, retain, refuse, appropriate.

Provident, careful, cautious, thrifty, prudent, economical.
Ant.—Improvident, reckless, careless.

Provision, food, supplies, clause, duty, function.
Ant.—Neglect, oversight, want, destitution, pittance.

Provoke. (See Irritate.)

Proximity, nearness, vicinity, neighborhood.
Ant.—Distance, remoteness, separation.

Proxy, deputy, agent, representative, substitute, delegate.

Prudence, carefulness, judgment, discretion, wisdom.
Ant.—Imprudence, rashness, indiscretion, silliness, recklessness, heedlessness.

Prurient, itching, craving, hankering, longing.
Ant.—Pure-minded.

Pry, scrutinize, peep, peer, look into, search.
Ant.—Disregard, overlook, connive.

Public, common, general, open, notorious.
Ant.—Private, personal, secret, secluded.

Publish, proclaim, advertise, announce, declare, divulge, disclose, reveal, issue, bring out, print.
Ant.—Suppress, reserve, conceal, whisper, deny.

Puerile, youthful, juvenile, boyish, childish, infantile, trifling, weak, silly.
Ant.—Manly, vigorous, powerful, cogent, strong, mature.

Pull, draw, haul, gather, drag, tug.
Ant.—Push, eject, propel.

Punctilious, nice, particular, formal, precise.
Ant.—Unceremonious, unconventional, unscrupulous, negligent, careless.

Punctual, exact, precise, nice, particular, prompt, timely.
Ant.—Late, tardy, dilatory, unpunctual.

Pungent, acrid, acrimonious, piquant, smart, keen, stinging.
Ant.—Soothing, mellow, luscious, unctuous.

Punish, chastise, castigate, correct, chasten, scourge, whip.
Ant.—Reward, remunerate, approve, indemnify.

Pupil, scholar, disciple, learner, student, ward, tyro.
Ant.—Teacher, master, adept, guardian.

Purchase. (See Buy.)

Pure, unmixed, unspotted, unsullied, real, unadulterated, genuine, unblemished, spotless, immaculate, absolute.
Ant.—Impure, foul, corrupt, stained, defiled, sullied, tarnished, guilty.

Purify, clarify, clear, cleanse.
Ant.—Blacken, befoul, corrupt, stain, defile, sully.

Purloin. (See Steal.)

Purport, tenor, sense, meaning, import, drift, spirit, intent, signification.
Ant.—Statement, assertion, declaration, proposition.

Purpose, *n.* object, design, intention, view, aim, drift, end.
Ant.—Chance, fate, hazard, lot, accident.

Purpose, *v.* (See Propose.)

Pursue, chase, hunt, track, follow, prosecute.
Ant.—Catch, hold, stop, withdraw, retire, abandon.

Push, thrust, impel, urge, press, drive.
Ant.—Pull, draw, drag.

Putative, supposed, reputed, credited, deemed, reported.
Ant.—Real, veritable, authenticated, actual.

Putrefy, rot, decompose, corrupt, decay.
Ant.—Purify, preserve, freshen, disinfect, embalm.

Puzzle, perplex, confound, embarrass, bewilder, confuse, pose, mystify.
Ant.—Enlighten, instruct, illumine, clear, solve, explain, clarify.

Q

Quack, impostor, pretender, charlatan, empiric, mountebank, faker.
Ant.—Dupe, gull, victim, authority, adept, expert, master, savant.

Quail, cow, daunt, dismay, intimidate, flinch, quake, tremble.
Ant.—Stand, defy, face, endure.

Quaint, artful, curious, farfetched, fanciful, odd, singular.
Ant.—Commonplace, ordinary, common, modern, dowdy, conventional, customary.

Quake, quail, shake, tremble, shudder, quiver.
Ant.—Stand, rest, calm.

Qualification, capacity, fitness, capability.
Ant.—Disqualification, incapacity, unfitness.

Qualified, competent, fitted, adapted.
Ant.—Incompetent, ineligible.

Qualify, fit, adapt, suit, abate, modify, soften.
Ant.—Disqualify, unfit, absolve, incapacitate.

Quality, property, attribute, peculiarity, rank, fashion, distinction, character, station.
Ant.—Nondescript, incapacity, indistinctiveness, negation, being, essence, nature, substance.

Quantity, amount, sum, deal, portion, part, division, share.
Ant.—Deficiency, insufficiency, loss, diminution.

Quarrel, altercation, brawl, broil, tumult, feud, affray, disagreement, wrangle.
Ant.—Peace, agreement, harmony, friendliness, amity, reconciliation.

Quarrelsome, irritable, hot, fiery, irascible.
Ant.—Peaceable, mild, meek, conciliatory, genial.

Quash. (See Annul.)

Queer, quaint, whimsical, odd, strange, eccentric, singular.
Ant.—Ordinary, familiar, common, usual.

Quell. (See Subdue.)

Querulous, complaining, repining, doubting, fretting.
Ant.—Contented, satisfied, genial, cheerful, long-suffering, patient, resigned.

Query. (See Question.)

Question, ask, interrogate, subject, point, doubt, dispute, query, inquire.
Ant.—Answer, state, assert, dictate, concede, endorse, allow, reply.

Questionable, doubtful, uncertain, disputable, suspicious.
Ant.—Certain, evident, obvious, indisputable.

Quibble, cavil, evade, equivocate, prevaricate.

Quick, lively, ready, prompt, alert, nimble, agile, active, brisk, expeditious, adroit, fleet, rapid, swift, impetuous, sweeping, dashing, clever, sharp.
Ant.—Slow, tardy, sluggish, inert, inactive, dull, deliberate.

Quicken, accelerate, hasten, expedite, dispatch, animate, revive, vivify.
Ant.—Retard, delay, clog, detain, discourage.

Quickness, speed, velocity, celerity, swiftness, fleetness.

Quiescence, quiet, quietude, rest, repose, tranquillity, dormancy, abeyance, stillness, silence.
Ant.—Agitation, unrest, mo-

ion, noise, disturbance, excitement, tumult.

Quiet, *v.* calm, still, hush, lull, pacify, soothe.
Ant.—Rouse, excite, disturb, urge, agitate.

Quiet, *n.* (See Quiescence.)

Quit, relinquish, abandon, leave, forego, give up, resign, cede, surrender.
Ant.—Hold, seek, occupy, bind, enforce, enter.

Quite, altogether, completely, wholly, entirely, totally.
Ant.—Barely, hardly, partially, imperfectly.

Quiver. (See Quake.)

Quixotic, romantic, wild, freakish.
Ant.—Rational, reasonable, humdrum.

Quote, note, repeat, cite, adduce.
Ant.—Misquote, contradict, disprove, retort, refute.

R

Rabid, mad, furious, raging, frantic.
Ant.—Rational, sane, sober, reasonable.

Race, ancestry, course, match, pursuit, career, family, clan, house, lineage, pedigree.

Rack, torture, agonize, wring, excruciate, distress, harass.
Ant.—Soothe, comfort, console.

Racy, spicy, pungent, smart, spirited, lively, vivacious.
Ant.—Dull, insipid.

Radiance, splendor, brightness, brilliance, luster, glare, brilliancy.
Ant.—Dullness, darkness, gloom, obscurity.

Radiate, shine, gleam, glitter, glisten, sparkle, coruscate.
Ant.—Darken, dull, converge.

Radical, organic, innate, fundamental, original, constitutional, inherent, complete, entire, uncompromising.
Ant.—Adventitious, superficial, partial, derived, extraneous, unimportant, conservative, moderate.

Rage, *n.* anger, indignation, choler, fury, passion, frenzy.
Ant.—Reason, moderation, temperance, calm, mildness, softness.

Rage, *v.* storm, rave, fret, chafe, fume.
Ant.—Calm, assuage, cool.

Rail, censure, bluster, scold.
Ant.—Flatter, compliment, approve.

Raiment, clothes, vestments, garments, attire, garb, dress, apparel.
Ant.—Nudity, nakedness, nature.

Raise, hoist, lift, exalt, heave, heighten, aggregate, elevate, erect, levy.
Ant.—Lay, cast, depress, lower, depreciate, lull, quiet, calm, compose, destroy.

Rally, assemble, congregate, recall, inspirit, animate.
Ant.—Demoralize, disperse, disband.

Ramble, *n.* excursion, tour, jaunt.
Ant.—Rest, quiet.

Ramble, *v.* wander, stroll, roam, rove, range, expatiate, stray.
Ant.—Hasten, speed, drive, run.

Rampant, prevalent, overruling, imperious, domineering, luxuriant, frisky, headstrong.
Ant.—Curbed, controlled, disciplined, demure.

Rampart, bulwark, defense, fence, security, guard, fortification, fort.
Ant.—Exposure, vulnerability.

Rancid, fetid, rank, stinking, sour, tainted.
Ant.—Sweet, pure, fresh, fragrant.

Rancor, malignity, hatred, hostility, antipathy, animosity, enmity, ill-will, spite.
Ant.—Forgiveness, gentleness, mildness, clemency.

Rank, order, degree, dignity, consideration, distinction, nobility.
Ant.—Disorder, confusion, commonalty.

Ransack, rummage, pillage, overhaul, explore, plunder.
Ant.—Skim, survey, overlook, leave, omit.

Ransom, emancipate, free, unfetter.
Ant.—Prosecute, hold, detain, indict, fine, forfeit, imprison, chain, fetter.

Rant, bombast, cant.
Ant.—Eloquence, rhetoric, reason, argument, sincerity, truth.

Rapacious, ravenous, voracious, greedy, grasping.
Ant.—Frugal, contented, liberal, bountiful, generous.

Rapidity, quickness, swiftness, speed, velocity, celerity, fleetness, activity, expedition, dispatch.
Ant.—Slowness, delay, tardiness.

Rapt, ecstatic, transported, ravished, entranced, spellbound, charmed, enchanted, delighted.
Ant.—Agonized, tortured, pained, indifferent, distracted.

Rapture, ecstasy, transport, delight, bliss.
Ant.—Agony, torture, pain, ennui, dejection, despair.

Rare, scarce, singular, uncommon, incomparable, unusual, unique.
Ant.—Common, commonplace, frequent, abundant, numerous, usual, mean, dense, cheap, worthless, ordinary.

Rascal, rogue, scoundrel, knave, vagabond, scamp.

Rash, hasty, precipitate, foolhardy, venturesome, adventurous, thoughtless, heedless, reckless, careless.
Ant.—Wary, cautious, timid, discreet, deliberate, reluctant, reasoned.

Rate, value, compute, appraise, estimate.

Ratify, confirm, establish, substantiate, sanction, endorse.
Ant.—Reject, repudiate, abrogate, annul, nullify, protest, oppose.

Rational, reasonable, sagacious, judicious, wise, intellectual, sensible, sane, sound.
Ant.—Irrational, insane, weak, silly, absurd, injudicious, unreasonable, mad.

Ravage, overrun, overspread, desolate, devastate, despoil, destroy, swoop.
Ant.—Spare, preserve, protect, shield, indemnify, beautify, improve, build up.

Ravenous. (See Rapacious.)

Raving, distracted, frantic, mad, furious, angry, violent.
Ant.—Quiet, calm, reasonable, sane.

Ravish, entrance, enrapture, transport, enchant, charm, delight, violate, abuse, captivate.
Ant.—Disgust, displease, annoy, shield, protect, honor, disenchant, nauseate, repel.

Raze, demolish, destroy, overthrow, ruin, dismantle.
Ant.—Raise, erect, build, restore, strengthen.

Reach, touch, stretch, attain, gain, arrive at.
Ant.—Fail, miss, cease, stop, fall short.

Ready, prepared, ripe, apt, prompt, adroit, dexterous, handy.
Ant.—Slow, tardy, late, reluctant, awkward, clumsy, unprepared, unwilling, constrained, dilatory.

Real, actual, literal, positive, certain, genuine, true, veritable, practical.

Ant.—Fictitious, unreal, imaginary, false, untrue, spurious, artificial, assumed, pretended, mythical.

Realize, accomplish, achieve, effect, gain, get, acquire, comprehend.

Ant.—Fail, lose, miss, dissipate, falsify, misrepresent.

Reap, gain, get, acquire, obtain.

Ant.—Sow, plant, waste, lose, squander, scatter.

Rear, lift, elevate, erect, breed, raise, train.

Ant.—Kill, destroy, demolish, stifle.

Reason, *n.* motive, design, end, argument, proof, cause, purpose, ground.

Ant.—Pretext, fallacy, folly, aimlessness.

Reason, *v.* deduce, draw from, trace, infer, conclude.

Reasonable, rational, wise, honest, fair, right, just.

Ant.—Unreasonable, foolish, perverse.

Rebellion, conspiracy, insurrection, revolt, anarchy.

Ant.—Support, adherence, law, order, authority, control, domination, government, organization, rule, sovereignty.

Rebuff, repel, repulse, rebuke, reprimand, reprove, check.

Ant.—Welcome, hail, encourage.

Recall, revoke, reclaim, call back, annul, cancel.

Ant.- Send, appoint, delegate, forget.

Recant, abjure, retract, revoke, recall.

Ant.—Propound, assert, maintain, declare, hold.

Recapitulate, repeat, recite, rehearse, enumerate.

Ant.—State, say, deliver, pronounce.

Recede, retire, retreat, withdraw, ebb.

Ant.—Advance, proceed, approach, flow, uphold.

Receive, accept, take, admit, entertain.

Ant.—Give, impart, reject, discharge, emit, bestow.

Recent, fresh, late, new, novel, modern.

Ant.—Ancient, antiquated, archaic.

Reception, levee, receipt, admission, receiving.

Ant.—Dismissal, denial, protest, rejection, repudiation, egress, exclusion, exit, repulse.

Recess, retreat, depth, niche, vacation, alcove, intermission.

Ant.—Projection, promontory, protrusion, work.

Reciprocal, mutual, alternate, interchangeable.

Ant.—Partial, nonreciprocal.

Recite, relate, tell, repeat, rehearse, recapitulate.

Ant.—Write, read, hear, misquote, misrepresent.

Reckless, heedless, regardless, careless, indifferent, unmindful, headstrong, imprudent, wild.

Ant.—Careful, heedful, cautious, timid, considerate, wary.

Reckon. (See Calculate.)

Reclaim, recall, reform, regain, recover.

Ant.—Vitiate, corrupt, debase.

Recline, lean, rest, repose, lie.

Ant.—Erect, raise, rise, stand.

Recognize, acknowledge, own, confess, avow, concede, remember.

Ant.—Ignore, overlook, cut, disown, repudiate, forget.

Recollect, bear in mind, remember, think of, recall.

Ant.—Forget, lose, disown.

Recompense, *v.* indemnify, compensate, repay, redeem, remunerate, reimburse, requite.

Ant.—Ignore, hurt, dissatisfy.

Reconcilable, placable, forgiving, consistent.

Ant.—Irreconcilable, inconsistent, incompatible.

Reconcile, conciliate, pacify, propitiate, harmonize.

Ant.—Estrange, alienate, separate, sever.

Record, *v.* enroll, note, register, chronicle.

Ant.—Suppress, obliterate, erase, withhold.

Record, *n.* chronicle, register, note, trace, minute, memorandum.

Ant.—Oblivion, obliteration.

Recount, relate, rehearse, narrate, detail, describe, enumerate, state.

Ant.—Falsify, hear, listen.

Recover, regain, repossess, retrieve, repair, restore, rally.

Ant.—Lose, forget, miss, impair, decay, decline, relapse.

Recreant, cowardly, base, dastardly, craven, fearful, timid.

Ant.—Faithful, true, loyal.

Recreation, sport, pastime, play, amusement, game, fun, entertainment.

Ant.—Weariness, toil, work, labor, fatigue, vocation.

Recruit, repair, replenish, renew, refresh, restore, replace, invigorate.

Ant.—Waste, lose, impair, relapse, decay.

Rectify. (See Correct.)

Rectitude. (See Integrity.)

Recumbent, leaning, lying, resting, reposing.

Ant.—Erect, vertical, standing.

Redeem, ransom, get back, recover, atone for, recompense, make amends, rescue, deliver, save, free.

Ant.—Profit, lose, abandon, betray, surrender, condemn.

Redolent, odorous, aromatic, fragrant, odoriferous.

Redound, tend, conduce, contribute, add.

Ant.—Fail, miss, defeat, frustrate.

Redress, remedy, repair, abate, relieve, mitigate, cure.

Ant.—Wrong, impair, aggravate, intensify, confirm, perpetuate, oppress, injure.

Reduce, abate, lessen, decrease, diminish, lower, abridge, shorten, conquer, curtail.

Ant.—Enlarge, increase, augment, extend, broaden, expand, invigorate, restore, liberate, transform, amplify, lengthen.

Redundant, superfluous, unnecessary, excessive, luxuriant.

Ant.—Defective, requisite, necessary.

Reel, stagger, totter, falter, roll.

Ant.—Walk, stand, run.

Refer, appeal, allude, revert, relate, belong.

Ant.—Disconnect, separate, alienate, misapply.

Referee, umpire, judge, arbitrator, arbiter.

Ant.—Litigant, opponent, adversary.

Refined, polite, courtly, polished, genteel, purified, cultured.

Ant.—Coarse, vulgar, gross, rude, blunt, unsophisticated, uncultivated, boorish, ill-bred, bourgeois.

Reflect, consider, think, ponder, muse, censure, reprove, cogitate.

Ant.—Disregard, overlook.

Reform, amend, correct, mend, better, restore, ameliorate, improve, reclaim.

Ant.—Corrupt, deform, impair, vitiate, debase.

Reformation, reform, improvement, amendment.

Ant.—Corruption, ruin.

Refrain, abstain, keep from, restrain, govern, forbear, desist from, refuse.

Ant.—Persist, continue, indulge, venture.

Refresh, revive, enliven, cheer, renew, vivify, regale, feast.

Ant.—Oppress, weary, tire, fatigue, exhaust, enervate.

Refuge, asylum, protection, sanctuary, shelter, retreat, harbor.

Ant.—Exposure, peril, snare.

Refund, reimburse, pay back, repay, return, restore.

Ant.—Expend, embezzle, appropriate, steal, divert, withhold.

Refuse, *v.* deny, reject, repudiate, decline, withhold.

Ant.—Grant, concede, afford, yield, comply, accept, avow, acknowledge.

Refuse, *n.* dregs, dross, scum, rubbish, leavings, remains.

Ant.—Cream, flower, prime.

Refute, disprove, falsify, negative.

Ant.—Prove, confirm, establish, affirm, accept.

Regain. (See Recover.)

Regale, feast, entertain, delight, refresh, gratify.

Ant.—Starve, stint, refuse, tantalize.

Regard, attend to, advert, mind, heed, notice, behold, view, consider, respect, reverence, revere.

Ant.—Disregard, miss, overlook, despise, hate, misjudge, slight.

Regardless, indifferent, careless, heedless, unmindful, reckless, inconsiderate, disregarding.

Ant.—Careful, attentive, prudent, cautious, scrupulous, mindful.

Register. (See Record.)

Regret, grief, sorrow, lamentation, repentance, remorse.

Ant.—Indifference, exultation, callousness, satisfaction, complacency, delight.

Regular, orderly, methodic, systematical, uniform, unvaried, customary, ordinary, stated, periodical.

Ant.—Irregular, exceptional, abnormal, erratic, uncertain, rare, disorderly, confused.

Regulate, arrange, adjust, organize, govern, rule, methodize.

Ant.—Disorder, confuse, misrule.

Rehearse, narrate, repeat, recite, recount, tell, relate.

Ant.—Exhibit, perform, misrepresent.

Reimburse, refund, repay, satisfy, indemnify.

Ant.—Embezzle, defraud, retain, appropriate.

Rein, restrain, moderate, govern, control, check.

Ant.—Indulge, loose, vent.

Reiterate, repeat, reproduce, renew.

Ant.—Retract, reverse, contradict, cancel.

Reject, repel, renounce, decline, refuse, repudiate.

Ant.—Hail, welcome, accept, choose, select, admit.

Rejoice, delight, joy, gladden, exult, revel.

Ant.—Mourn, grieve, lament, weep.

Rejoinder, retort, parry, reply, answer, replication.

Related, cognate, connected, kindred, akin.

Ant.—Separated, disconnected, opposed, different.

Relation, narration, narrative, account, recital, detail, affinity, kinsman.

Ant.—Disunion, disconnection, dissociation, irrelevancy.

Relax, abate, slacken, loosen, soften, relent.

Ant.—Tighten, stretch, bend, intensify, brace, grow.

Release, free, extricate, disengage, liberate, loosen.

Ant.—Bind, constrain, confine, fetter, imprison.

Relent. (See Relax.)

Relevant, fit, proper, suitable, appropriate, pertinent, apt.

Ant.—Irrelevant, impertinent, inappropriate.

Reliance, trust, hope, dependence, confidence.

Ant.—Distrust, misgiving, suspicion, diffidence, doubt.

Relief, succor, aid, help, redress, alleviation.

Ant.—Oppression, trouble, exhaustion, weariness, injury, hurt, harm.

Religious, pious, godly, holy, devout, sacred.

Ant.—Irreligious, profane, ungodly, skeptic, impious.

Relinquish, forsake, give up, resign, surrender, quit, leave, forego.

Ant.—Retain.

Relish, taste, flavor, piquancy, gusto.

Ant.—Insipidity, disrelish.

Reluctant, unwilling, averse, loath, disinclined.

Ant.—Eager, active, ready, forward, willing, prompt.

Remain, stop, tarry, halt, abide, stay, continue, sojourn, wait.

Ant.—Fly, vanish, go, disappear, hasten, depart.

Remark, note, heed, comment, observe.

Ant.—Disregard, overlook, miss.

Remarkable, unusual, rare, noteworthy, noticeable, extraordinary, observable, striking.

Ant.—Ordinary, common, everyday, commonplace.

Remedial, healing, curative, mitigating.

Ant.—Noxious, hurtful, deleterious, unhealthy, unwholesome.

Remedy, help, relief, redress, cure, specific, reparation.

Ant.—Evil, ill, disease, hurt, plague, provocation, embarrassment, hindrance, interference, obstruction, opposition.

Remember, recall, recollect, mind.

Ant.—Forget, overlook, disregard.

Remonstrate, object, protest, expostulate.

Ant.—Acquiesce, submit, coincide.

Remorse, self-condemnation, anguish, penitence.

Ant.—Indifference, complacency, self-approval.

Remorseless, pitiless, relentless, cruel, ruthless, merciless, barbarous.

Ant.—Compassionate, humane, gentle, lenient, merciful.

Remote, distant, far, secluded, indirect.

Ant.—Near, close, immediate, proximate, present, urgent, adjacent, approximate.

Remove, displace, dislodge, withdraw, suppress, eject, oust.

Rend, tear, disunite, split, lacerate.

Ant.—Repair, unite, piece, patch, perpetuate.

Render, present, restore, return, requite, give.

Ant.—Keep, retain, withhold, appropriate.

Renew. (See Refresh.)

Renounce, reject, abjure, quit, forego, abandon, forsake, resign, relinquish, disown.

Ant.—Acknowledge, recognize, maintain, assert, own, avow, profess, defend.

Renown, distinction, reputation, fame, glory, celebrity.

Ant.—Infamy, disgrace, dishonor, disrepute, ignominy, oblivion.

Repair, mend, retrieve, recover, restore.

Ant.—Impair, injure, waste, deteriorate.

Repay, reimburse, reward, refund, return, requite.

Ant.—Defraud, cheat, extort, embezzle, confiscate.

Repeat, recite, relate, reproduce, recapitulate, rehearse.

Ant.—Discontinue, drop, stop, ignore, suppress, conceal, misquote.

Repeatedly, again and again, frequently, often.
Ant.—Occasionally, seldom, infrequently.

Repel, reject, refuse, deter, repulse, beat back.
Ant.—Propel, advance, encourage, promote, attack, charge.

Repentance, self-reproach, penitence, contrition, remorse.
Ant.—Impenitence, obduracy, self-approval.

Replace, reinstate, refund, restore.
Ant.—Move, remove, derange, deprive.

Report, announce, notify, tell, communicate, relate.
Ant.—Silence, hush, suppress, conceal.

Repose, *n.* quiet, quietude, peace, ease, rest, sleep.
Ant.—Unrest, agitation, disturbance, commotion, tumult.

Repose, *v.* rest, recline, lie, settle, confide.
Ant.—Rise, move, labor, remove.

Reprehend. (See Censure.)

Represent. (See Portray.)

Repress, quell, crush, subdue, check, curb, restrain.
Ant.—Raise, rouse, excite, agitate, encourage, incite, stimulate, fan.

Reprieve, pardon, acquittal, respite.
Ant.—Conviction, condemnation.

Reprimand. (See Reprove.)

Reprobate, villain, ruffian, miscreant, castaway.
Ant.—Example, paragon, model, pattern.

Reproduce, propagate, imitate, represent, copy.
Ant.—Stifle, extinguish, exterminate, misrepresent.

Reprove, chide, rebuke, reprimand, scold.
Ant.—Praise, approve, commend, extol.

Repudiate, disavow, disown, discard, denounce, disclaim.
Ant.—Acknowledge, avow, admit.

Repugnant, antagonistic, averse, adverse, hostile, unwilling, distasteful.
Ant.—Friendly, harmonious, agreeable, consistent, congruous, acceptable.

Repulsive, odious, forbidding, ugly, disagreeable, revolting,
Ant.—Attractive, charming, agreeable.

Request, desire, beg, ask, beseech, entreat.
Ant.—Command, order, insist, dictate, enjoin, exact.

Requite. (See Repay.)

Rescue, save, preserve, recover, recapture, retake.
Ant.—Endanger, expose, imperil, abandon, surrender.

Research, inquiry, examination, lore, learning, investigation.
Ant.—Oversight, ignorance, superficiality.

Resemblance, similarity, semblance, likeness, image.
Ant.—Unlikeness, difference, dissimilarity.

Resent, resist, oppose, repel, rebel.
Ant.—Overlook, submit, pardon.

Resentment, ire, indignation, anger, umbrage, animosity.
Ant.—Forgiveness, mildness, calmness.

Reserve, shyness, modesty, coyness, reservation.
Ant.—Frankness, candor, openness, forwardness, pertness.

Resign, relinquish, leave, abandon, abdicate, forego.
Ant.—Retain, grasp, claim, appropriate, hold.

Resist, withstand, oppose, check, thwart, hinder.
Ant.—Encourage, promote, aid, help, submit, suffer, tolerate, permit.

Resolute, determined, steadfast, decided, steady, constant, persevering, dogged, unshaken, unflinching.
Ant.—Irresolute, weak, undecided, inconstant, vacillating.

Resolution, determination, resolve, decision, motion, courage, fortitude, firmness, conversion.
Ant.—Indecision, inconstancy, composition, union, synthesis.

Resort, fly to, retreat, repair, retire, go.
Ant.—Shun, ignore, avoid, discard.

Resound, echo, reëcho, ring, respond, reverberate.
Ant.—Whisper, murmur, mutter, die.

Resources, means, materials, devices, expedients, wealth, riches.
Ant.—Destitution, poverty, want, exhaustion.

Respect, regard, prefer, venerate, defer.
Ant.—Despise, condemn, disregard, dishonor.

Respectable, good, worthy, laudable, esteemed, reputable, decent, fair.
Ant.—Disreputable, bad, unworthy, mean.

Respite, reprieve, interval, stop.
Ant.—Completion, consummation, execution, performance.

Respond, reply, answer, rejoin, correspond, tally, accord.
Ant.—Ignore, overlook, disregard, disagree, differ.

Rest, repose, slumber, quiet, cessation, peace, tranquillity, interval, remainder, residue.
Ant.—Motion, commotion, tumult, noise.

Restive, obstinate, stubborn, impatient, uneasy.
Ant.—Docile, tractable, manageable

Restoration, renewal, renovation, return, recovery, revival, reparation.
Ant.—Loss, lapse, forfeiture, abandonment, waste, seizure.

Restore, replace, refund, repair, refresh, heal, cure.
Ant.—Remove, displace, appropriate, deprive, demolish, injure.

Restrain, repress, check, stop, limit, hinder, withhold.
Ant.—Promote, advance, urge, incite, aid, loosen, amplify, enlarge, extend.

Result, end, termination, conclusion, effect, issue, consequence.
Ant.—Beginning, cause, origin, antecedent.

Resume, recommence, begin again, renew.
Ant.—Drop, interrupt, discontinue.

Retain, keep, hold, restrain, retard, detain, engage, hire.
Ant.—Abandon, forfeit, surrender, give up.

Retaliate, repay, revenge, requite, retort.
Ant.—Pardon, condone, forgive.

Retard. (See Impede.)

Retire. (See Depart.)

Retreat, departure, retirement, withdrawal, asylum, shelter, refuge.
Ant.—Advance, approach, publicity, exposure, prominence.

Retrench, reduce, abbreviate, diminish, curtail, contract, lessen, economize.
Ant.—Increase, extend, enlarge, augment, amplify.

Retribution, penalty, punishment, requital.
Ant.—Pardon, reprieve, escape.

Retrieve, recover, rescue, regain, restore, repair.
Ant.—Lose, forfeit, impair, surrender.

Retrospect, review, reminiscence, survey.

Return, reappear, recur, revert, repay, requite, yield.

Ant.—Depart, leave, go, vanish, disappear, appropriate, withhold.

Reveal, disclose, show, divulge, expose, publish.

Ant.—Hide, obscure, conceal, cover, cloak.

Revel, feast, carouse, luxuriate, banquet, wallow.

Ant.—Fast, abstain.

Revenge, vengeance, retaliation, requital, retribution.

Ant.—Pardon, remission, forgiveness.

Revengeful, unforgiving, spiteful, resentful, vindictive.

Ant.—Forgiving, generous, compassionate.

Revenue, produce, income, fruits, proceeds, wealth, assets.

Ant.—Expenditure, expense, waste, liabilities, debts, outgo.

Reverence, honor, respect, awe, veneration, deference, worship, homage.

Ant.—Irreverence, dishonor, contempt, contumely, execration.

Reverse, repeal, revoke, invert, overturn, overthrow, subvert.

Ant.—Order, arrange, place, ordain, affirm.

Review, retrospect, retrospection, survey, revision, criticism.

Ant.—Glance, look, establishment.

Revile, vilify, calumniate, asperse, slander, reproach, abuse, scandalize.

Ant.—Flatter, compliment, eulogize.

Revise, review, reconsider.

Ant.—Overlook, skim, dismiss, reject, turn down.

Revive, refresh, renew, renovate, animate, resuscitate, vivify, cheer, comfort.

Ant.—Extinguish, kill, depress, exhaust, droop, wither, dishearten.

Revolt, rebel, resist, shock.

Ant.—Obey, submit, acquiesce.

Revolting, shocking, disgusting, frightful, horrible.

Ant.—Attractive, pleasing, charming, genial.

Revolve, turn, circulate, whirl, twirl, wheel, rotate.

Ant.—Stand, proceed, fly, walk.

Reward, recompense, compensation, remuneration, requital, bounty, premium.

Ant.—Punishment, earnings, wages.

Rich, wealthy, affluent, opulent, copious, ample, abundant, exuberant, plentiful, fertile, fruitful, gorgeous, superb.

Ant.—Poor, needy, indigent, barren, sterile, unfruitful, destitute.

Ridicule, laugh at, deride, mock, lampoon, rally, chaff.

Ant.—Venerate, respect, salute, honor.

Ridiculous, ludicrous, droll, absurd, preposterous, grotesque, comical, laughable.

Ant.—Serious, grave, sober, important, weighty, majestic.

Right, *a.* lawful, correct, true, straight, direct, just, proper, fit, suitable.

Ant.—Wrong, unjust, untrue, incorrect, crooked, dishonest, bad, vile.

Right, *n.* claim, privilege, equity, justice.

Ant.—Wrong, injustice, falsehood, emptiness, encroachment, violence.

Righteous, godly, upright, just, fair, honest, virtuous.

Rigid, rigorous, austere, unyielding, stern, harsh, severe, unmitigated, firm, stringent.

Ant.—Pliant, docile, flexible, yielding, mild.

Riot, commotion, tumult, uproar, row, disturbance, confusion.

Ant.—Peace, order, law.

Ripe, ready, mellow, complete, mature.

Ant.—Raw, green, crude, immature, imperfect, unfit.

Rise, *v.* (See Ascend.)

Rise, *n.* origin, source, spring, fountainhead, beginning, acclivity, ascent, increase.

Ant.—End, subsidence, sinking, termination, disappearance, conclusion.

Rival, competitor, antagonist, opponent.

Ant.—Accomplice, ally, friend, helper, supporter.

Road, way, highway, route, course, path, pathway, anchorage.

Roam, ramble, rove, wander, stray, stroll.

Ant.—Hurry, speed, fly, hasten, abide, remain.

Roar, thunder, peal, howl, yell, vociferate.

Ant.—Silence, hush, whisper, breathe.

Robbery, theft, plunder, pillage, larceny, depredation.

Ant.—Restoration, protection.

Robust, strong, lusty, vigorous, sinewy, stout, sturdy, stalwart, able-bodied.

Ant.—Weak, frail, delicate, fragile, sickly, puny.

Rogue, scamp, knave, rascal, villain, scoundrel, cheat, swindler, sharper, miscreant.

Ant.—Gentleman, citizen, victim.

Roll. (See Catalogue.)

Romantic, sentimental, poetic, sensitive, fictitious, ideal.

Ant.—Practical, prosaic, literal, unvarnished.

Room, hall, chamber, apartment, space.

Ant.—Infinity, meadow, field, atmosphere.

Rough, craggy, uneven, shaggy, rugged, blunt, rude, gruff, harsh.

Ant.—Smooth, even, level, sleek, calm, tranquil, refined, courteous, finished.

Round, circular, entire, spherical, complete, plump.

Ant.—Square, oblong, convex, lean.

Rout, defeat, discomfit, beat, overthrow, scatter.

Route, road, course, march, way, journey, path, direction.

Ant.—Ramble, wandering, hazard, chance.

Rove. (See Roam.)

Row, tumult, commotion, riot, disturbance, uproar, broil, affray.

Ant.—Peace, quiet, order.

Rubbish, fragments, debris, litter, wreck, dross, refuse, trash.

Ant.—Valuables, trinkets, property.

Rude, rugged, rough, uncouth, unpolished, harsh, gruff, impertinent, saucy, flippant, impudent, insolent, churlish.

Ant.—Refined, modest, bashful, civil, courteous, polished, elegant, gentle, calm, peaceful, serene, polite, well-bred.

Rugged. (See Rough.)

Ruin, destruction, wreck, havoc, desolation, ravage, defeat, overthrow.

Ant.—Success, rise, prosperity, completeness, integrity, regeneration, organization.

Rule, sway, method, system, law, maxim, precept, guide, formula, regulation, government, standard, test.

Ant.—Irregularity, chance, hazard, exception, deviation.

Ruling, prevalent, predominant, ascendant, dominant.

Ant.—Unimportant, unessential, minor, subordinate.

Rumor, hearsay, talk, fame, report, bruit.

Ant.—Verification, fact, proof, evidence.

Rumple, wrinkle, crumple, pucker, crease.

Ant.—Smooth, flatten, arrange.

Run, flee, scamper, fly, hasten, go, flow.

Ant.—Walk, saunter, lounge, stay, stop, halt, hold, fail, drop, hesitate.

Rupture, fracture, breach, burst, disruption, hostility.

Ant.—Union, coalition, fusion, junction.

Rush, stream, sweep, dash, press, roll.

Ant.—March, halt, lag, hesitate.

Rustic, rural, countrified, rude, coarse, simple.

Ant.—Urbane, elegant, refined, polished.

Ruthless, cruel, savage, barbarous, inhuman, merciless, remorseless, relentless, unrelenting.

Ant. -Forbearing, careful, tender, gentle, lenient, compassionate, considerate, kind.

S

Sacred, holy, hallowed, divine, consecrated, devoted, dedicated.

Ant. Profane, unholy, common, secular.

Sad, sorrowful, mournful, dull, dismal, downcast, lugubrious, dejected, gloomy, cheerless.

Ant.—Joyous, gay, cheerful, glad, happy, blithe.

Safe, sure, secure, certain, substantial, trustworthy, reliable, harmless.

Ant.—Unsafe, insecure, dangerous, hazardous, perilous.

Sagacious, shrewd, discerning, sage, wise, prudent, acute, discriminating, intelligent.

Ant.—Dull, obtuse, stolid, unintelligent.

Salary, wages, allowance, pay, stipend, hire, remuneration.

Ant.—Gift, gratuity, reward.

Salient, striking, remarkable, prominent, projecting, jutting.

Ant.—Minor, inconsiderable, retreating, retiring.

Salutation, greeting, address, welcome, congratulation.

Ant.—Disregard, scorn, affront, cut.

Sample, specimen, model, pattern, example, illustration.

Ant.—Exception, nondescript, variety, phenomenon.

Sanction, confirm, countenance, encourage, support, ratify, authorize.

Ant.—Discountenance, disallow, prohibit, nullify, disapprove, oppose.

Sane, sober, lucid, sound, rational.

Ant.—Crazy, mad, insane.

Sanguine, hopeful, confident.

Ant.—Desponding, distrustful, suspicious, misgiving.

Sarcasm, satire, irony, chaff, ridicule, mockery.

Ant.—Eulogy, compliment, panegyric.

Satiate, glut, gorge, satisfy, surfeit.

Ant.—Stint, starve.

Satire. (See Sarcasm.)

Satisfaction, gratification, compensation, amends, recompense, remuneration, contentment, complacency, payment.

Ant.—Discontent, dissatisfaction, grievance, vexation, annoyance, fraud, wrong, demand, claim, offense.

Satisfy, please, gratify, convince, satiate, glut, gorge.

Ant.—Dissatisfy, displease, annoy, stint, starve, puzzle, tantalize.

Saturate, steep, soak, imbue, impregnate.

Ant.—Drain, empty, dry.

Saucy, impertinent, rude, impudent, insolent, flippant.

Ant.—Civil, deferential, obsequious, servile, modest, respectful, polite.

Savage. (See Barbarous.)

Save, rescue, deliver, keep, hold, husband, redeem, spare, retrench, economize.

Ant.—Lose, betray, abandon, destroy, surrender, impose, promote, induce, cause, endanger, risk, lavish, waste.

Savory, tasty, piquant, tasteful, palatable.

Ant.—Dry, flavorless, distasteful, nauseous.

Scandalize, shock, disgust, offend, calumniate, vilify, revile, malign, traduce, defame, slander.

Ant.—Praise, respect, honor, please, commend oneself.

Scanty, bare, pinched, insufficient, slender, meager.

Ant.—Ample, full, liberal, bountiful, generous, sufficient, adequate.

Scarce, rare, singular, uncommon, unique, wanting, unusual.

Ant.—Common, frequent, abundant, plentiful.

Scarcity, dearth, famine, lack, want.

Ant.—Plenty, abundance, frequency.

Scare, *v.* (See Frighten.)

Scatter, strew, spread, fling around, disseminate, disperse, dissipate, dispel.

Ant.—Collect, gather, heap, save, accumulate, unite.

Scheme, design, plan, project, theory, intrigue, plot.

Ant.—Blunder, misconception, chance.

Scholar, disciple, pupil, student.

Ant.—Teacher, master, professor.

Science, knowledge, learning, scholarship.

Ant.—Ignorance, inexperience.

Scoff, jibe, jeer, sneer, deride, taunt, twit.

Ant.—Salute, respect, compliment, honor.

Scope, range, purpose, intention, drift, aim, tendency, design, view, tenor, purport.

Ant.—Aimlessness, accident, deviation.

Scorn, contempt, disdain, mockery, sneer.

Ant.—Esteem, regard, honor, respect.

Scraggy. (See Lean.)

Scrap. (See Fragment.)

Scruple, hesitate, doubt, waver.

Ant.—Proceed, decide, determine, act.

Scrupulous, strict, nice, conscientious, precise.

Ant.—Reckless, unscrupulous, confident, self-complacent.

Scrutinize, examine, sift, investigate, inquire into.

Ant.—Overlook, disregard, miss, glance.

Search, exploration, scrutiny, inquiry, investigation, examination, research, quest, pursuit.

Ant.—Abandonment, withdrawal, stoppage.

Season, time, period, occasion, term, spell.

Ant.—Untimeliness, unseasonableness.

Seasonable, timely, fit, opportune, convenient, suitable.

Ant.—Unseasonable, unsuitable, unexpected, inopportune.

Seclusion. (See Privacy.)

Secondary, second, inferior, under, subordinate, minor, unimportant.

Ant.—Primary, leading, prominent, important.

Secrecy. (See Privacy.)

Secret, concealed, hidden, clandestine, sly, underhand, private, latent.

Ant.—Public, open, exposed, known, notorious, disclosed.

Secular, worldly, temporal, civil, lay, profane.
Ant.—Religious, clerical, monastic, spiritual.

Secure. (See Safe.)

Sedate, settled, grave, composed, calm, quiet, serene, staid.
Ant.—Flighty, ruffled, frolicsome, indiscreet, playful.

Sedition, insurrection, rebellion, revolt, mutiny, tumult, riot.
Ant.—Union, allegiance, fealty, quiet, obedience, order.

Seditious, factious, tumultuous, turbulent, insurgent, mutinous, rebellious, incendiary.
Ant.—Obedient, orderly, quiet, calm, peaceful.

Seduce, allure, attract, decoy, entice, abduct, inveigle, deprave.
Ant.—Force, compel, command, overpower, save, convert.

Sedulous, assiduous, diligent, industrious, indefatigable, constant, persevering.
Ant.—Idle, inconstant, wandering, distracted.

See, behold, view, witness, eye, spy, descry, discern, perceive, understand, observe, note, mark, discover.
Ant.—Miss, overlook, disregard, misunderstand, ignore.

Seek, look for, search, explore, examine, find out, discover, detect, ask.
Ant.—Avoid, shun, elude, discard, abandon, ignore.

Seem, look, appear.
Ant.—Belie, misrepresent, differ.

Seemly, fit, suitable, becoming, decent, decorous, comely.
Ant.—Unseemly, unbecoming, unfit, unsuitable, improper, indecent, incongruous.

Seize, capture, catch, grasp, clutch, snatch, take, arrest, apprehend, bind, fasten.
Ant.—Loose, dismiss, liberate, abandon, drop, unfasten.

Seldom, rarely, unfrequently.
Ant.—Often, frequently, invariably.

Select, elect, prefer, choose, pick, cull.
Ant.—Lump, sweep.

Selfish, egotistical, self-seeking, earthly, sordid, mercenary, venal, greedy.
Ant.—Unselfish, disinterested, generous, liberal, magnanimous, considerate.

Sell, vend, dispose of, hawk, retail.
Ant.—Give, bestow, present.

Send, transmit, forward, dispatch.
Ant.—Detain, withhold, deny, recall.

Seniority, eldership, superiority, priority.
Ant.—Juniority, inferiority, subordination.

Sensation, perception, apprehension, feeling, impression.
Ant.—Apathy, insensibility.

Sense, discernment, appreciation, view, opinion, feeling, perception, sensibility, susceptibility, thought, judgment, signification, import, significance, meaning, purport, wisdom.
Ant.—Ignorance, folly, nonsense, insensibility, stolidity, misconception, misinterpretation, thoughtlessness.

Senseless, foolish, imbecile, brainless, absurd, nonsensical, unmeaning, silly.
Ant.—Sensible, wise, practical.

Sensible, wise, intelligent, reasonable, sober, sound, conscious, aware.
Ant.—Insensible, ignorant, intangible, invisible, impalpable, foolish, stupid, senseless.

Sensual, carnal, fleshly, voluptuous, animal.
Ant.—Spiritual, intellectual, abstemious, ascetic.

Sentiment, thought, feeling, notion, sensation, apprehension, opinion, impression, conviction.

Separate, distinct, different, unconnected, disconnected, detached, disjoined, severed.
Ant.—United, joined, tied, wedded, linked, consolidated, connected, fused, collected.

Sequel, end, close, termination, conclusion.
Ant.—Original, beginning, opening.

Serene. (See Calm.)

Series. (See Order.)

Serious. (See Grave.)

Service. (See Benefit.)

Servile, mean, low, abject, sneaking.
Ant.—Independent, refractory, stubborn, defiant, rebellious.

Set, put, place, lay, arrange, locate, settle.
Ant.—Remove, lift, raise, transfer, loosen, detach.

Settle, arrange, adjust, regulate, organize, conclude, determine, fix, ratify, confirm.
Ant.—Unsettle, remove, disturb, disorder, misplace, disarrange, upset.

Sever, break, disconnect, dissever, separate, detach.
Ant.—Unite, connect, include, join.

Several, sundry, divers, various, many.
Ant.—One, same, identical, united, total, analogous, homogeneous, similar.

Severe, harsh, stern, stringent, unmitigated, rough, unyielding.
Ant.—Gentle, considerate, lenient, kind, genial, indulgent, gay, cheerful, joyous, mild.

Shade, shadow, dim, obscure, cloud.
Ant.—Light, illuminate, shine, glare, expose.

Shake, tremble, shudder, shiver, quake, quiver.
Ant.—Secure, fix, fasten, strengthen, stand, calm, compose, pacify, quiet, soothe.

Shallow, superficial, flimsy, slight.
Ant.—Deep, thorough.

Shame, disgrace, dishonor, immodesty, indecency.
Ant.—Honor, glory, renown, credit.

Shameful, dishonorable, degrading, scandalous, disgraceful, outrageous.
Ant.—Honorable, noble, upright.

Shameless, arrant, immodest, impudent, indecent, indelicate, brazen.
Ant.—Becoming, seemly, fitting.

Shape, form, fashion, mold, model.
Ant.—Distort, derange, pervert, caricature.

Share, portion, lot, division, quantity, quota, contingent.
Ant.—Whole, mass, aggregate, entirety.

Sharp, pointed, biting, pungent, acute, keen, shrewd, clever, witty, penetrating, piercing, shrill.
Ant.—Blunt, dull, obtuse, rounded, hollow, light, trivial, mild, gentle, tender, indifferent, careless.

Shatter, shiver, derange, disorder.
Ant.—Construct, organize, compose.

Shed, pour, effuse, spread, spill, diffuse.
Ant.—Absorb, collect, assume, retain.

Shelter, *n.* asylum, refuge, retreat, cover, haven, security.
Ant.—Exposure, betrayal.

Shelter, *v.* cover, screen, lodge, protect.
Ant.—Expose, endanger, imperil, betray.

Shift, *v.* transpose, contrive, change, alter, veer.
Ant.—Locate, fasten, fix, plant.
Shift, *n.* evasion, expedient, resource, alternative.
Ant.—Location, permanence, fixity.
Shine, glow, gleam, glisten, glitter, radiate, sparkle, glare.
Ant.—Fade, wane.
Shiver, shatter, break, quake, shudder, quiver, tremble.
Ant.—Steady, stiffen, stand.
Shock, offend, disgust, appall, dismay, scare, stun, terrify.
Ant.—Gratify, please, delight, amuse.
Shocking, disgusting, revolting, dreadful, terrible.
Ant.—Pleasing, charming, delightful, creditable, attractive.
Short, brief, concise, curt, compendious, succinct, summary.
Ant.—Long, protracted, extended, unlimited, ample, abundant, complete, diffuse.
Shorten. (See Abbreviate.)
Show, exhibition, sight, representation, spectacle, scene, pageant, ostentation.
Ant.—Secrecy, disguise, concealment, suppression, disappearance.
Showy, pompous, gorgeous, fine, gay, grand.
Ant.—Quiet, subdued, unnoticeable.
Shrewd. (See Sagacious.)
Shudder. (See Tremble.)
Shut, close, preclude.
Ant.—Open, expand, unfasten, unclose.
Shy, timid, reserved, coy.
Ant.—Bold, impudent, forward, audacious.
Sick, ill, diseased, disordered, distempered, indisposed, unwell, ailing, sickly, unhealthy, morbid.
Ant.—Well, whole, healthy, strong, robust, normal, sound.
Sickness, illness, indisposition, disease, disorder.
Ant.—Health, soundness.
Side, edge, verge, margin, border, party, cause, interest, policy.
Ant.—Center, core, body, interior, neutrality, opposition.
Sight, seeing, perception, view, vision, spectacle, show.
Ant.—Blindness, invisibility, disappearance, oversight.
Sign, token, proof, indication, symbol, emblem, type, symptom, mark, omen, signal, badge.
Ant.—Misinformation, falsification, misrepresentation.
Signal, remarkable, noted, notable, extraordinary, eminent, conspicuous, memorable, important.
Ant.—Ordinary, common, unimportant, unnoticeable.
Significant, expressive, indicative, momentous, material, important.
Ant.—Insignificant, meaningless, unimportant, mute, slight, negligible.
Signification, import, sense, meaning.
Signify, express, declare, intimate, imply, denote, mean, betake.
Ant.—Conceal, suppress, nullify, refute, neutralize.
Silence, stillness, quiet, calm, secrecy, speechlessness, dumbness.
Ant.—Noise, clamor, din, tumult, roar, agitation, publicity, celebrity, loquacity, outcry.
Silent, dumb, mute, speechless.
Ant.—Talkative, noisy.
Silly, simple, imbecile, foolish, witless, unwise, indiscreet, nonsensical.
Ant.—Sagacious, intelligent, astute, wise, discreet, prudent, rational, sound.
Similar, resembling, alike, corresponding.
Ant.—Different, unlike, dissimilar, alien, incongruous.
Simile, comparison, similitude.
Simple, silly, imbecile, foolish, elementary, unmixed, mere, plain, frank, open, shallow, single, uncompounded, artless.
Ant.—Complex, double, mixed, various, compound, elaborate, complicated, sagacious, wise, abstruse.
Simulate, dissimulate, dissemble, pretend.
Ant.—Exhibit, expose, manifest, proclaim, show, vaunt.
Sin, wrong, wickedness, iniquity, crime, ungodliness, evil.
Ant.—Goodness, virtue, righteousness, purity, holiness.
Sincere, unvarnished, genuine, honest, unaffected, upright, true, plain, frank, candid, cordial, hearty, pure, real.
Ant.—Insincere, false, feigned, pretended, dishonest, affected.
Single, sole, unmarried, singular, particular, individual, only.
Ant.—Plural, many, collective, double, numerous, frequent, married.
Singular, particular, odd, curious, eccentric, queer, strange, rare, scarce.
Ant.—Common, frequent, ordinary, usual, customary, general.
Sinister, unfair, disingenuous, dishonest, bad, evil.
Ant.—Honest, right, fair, lucky, fortunate, attractive.
Sink, droop, descend, suppress, conceal, submerge.
Ant.—Rise, ascend, mount, soar, swell, increase.
Situation, condition, plight, predicament, state, position.
Size, greatness, bulk, magnitude, largeness, dimension, bigness, extent.
Ant.—Smallness, littleness, minuteness, pettiness.
Sketch. (See Portray.)
Skillful. (See Adroit.)
Skulk, sneak, hide, cover, sink, shroud, shelter, veil.
Ant.—Show, parade, issue.
Slack, loose, remiss, careless, negligent, backward, weak, slow.
Ant.—Tight, tense, diligent, alert, active, eager.
Slacken, loosen, unbind, relax, abate, flag, moderate.
Ant.—Tighten, increase, freshen.
Slander, *v.* defame, asperse, calumniate, traduce, detract, scandalize, revile, vilify, abuse, malign, vilipend.
Ant.—Vindicate, commend, praise, honor, extol, eulogize, flatter, glorify.
Slander, *n.* calumny, libel, vilification, defamation.
Ant.—Praise, commendation, applause.
Slaughter, bloodshed, carnage, butchery.
Ant.—Peace, order, arbitration.
Slavery, servitude, enthrallment, thralldom.
Ant.—Freedom, liberty.
Slay. (See Kill.)
Sleek, glossy, shiny, velvety, silken.
Ant.—Rough, bristly, hairy.
Sleep, doze, drowse, nap, slumber.
Ant.—Toil, wake, watch, work.
Sleepy, sluggish, lazy, somnolent, slumberous, drowsy, lethargic.
Ant.—Wakeful, vigilant, alert, awake, active.
Slender, slim, thin, small, trivial, slight, fragile.
Ant.—Stout, robust, thick, massive.
Slight. *a.* (See Slender.)
Slippery, smooth, glossy, unsafe, deceptive, evasive.
Ant.—Rough, firm, secure, safe, stable, trustworthy.
Slovenly, loose, negligent, disorderly.

Ant.—Trim, neat, tidy, orderly, careful.

Slow, dilatory, tardy, sluggish, tedious, dull, lazy.

Ant.—Quick, fast, rapid, alert, active, ready, prompt.

Sly, cunning, astute, crafty, artful, subtle, wily, underhand.

Ant.—Open, frank, artless, undesigning.

Small, little, diminutive, minute, slight, trivial.

Ant.—Great, large, big, bulky, ample, stout, spacious, strong, important, liberal.

Smart, quick, keen, brisk, sharp, caustic, severe, clever, witty, showy, spruce.

Ant.—Dull, heavy, slow, stupid, sluggish, dowdy, shabby, clownish.

Smear, daub, besmear, begrime, varnish, spatter.

Ant.—Polish, scour, scrape.

Smell, odor, scent.

Smite, beat, strike, slay, kill, afflict, chasten, punish.

Ant.—Soothe, caress, console.

Smoke, fumes, vapor, nothing, moonshine, triviality.

Ant.—Substance, importance, flame, reality.

Smooth, *a.* suave, bland, even, level, plain, polished, flat, mild.

Ant.—Rough, uneven, rugged, harsh, blunt.

Smooth, *v.* level, flatten, ease, calm, allay, mollify.

Ant.—Roughen, smear, dent, groove, excite, aggravate.

Smother, gag, strangle, allay, stifle, conceal, choke, suffocate.

Ant.—Fan, ventilate, resuscitate, foster, cherish, publish.

Snare. (See Trap.)

Snatch, pluck, pull, twitch, catch, clutch, grasp, grip.

Ant.—Restore, release, unhand.

Sneer, scoff, taunt, jibe, mock.

Ant.—Compliment, eulogy, deference.

Snug, close, compact, concealed, comfortable.

Ant.—Exposed, loose, uncomfortable, bare.

Soak, wet, moisten, steep, drench, saturate, macerate, imbrue.

Ant.—Dry, air, wring, bleach, desiccate, drain.

Soar, rise, mount, tower, ascend, aspire.

Ant. Drop, sink, descend, alight.

Sober, moderate, abstemious, abstinent, sedate, temperate, cool, calm, dispassionate, reasonable, self-possessed.

Ant.—Intemperate, drunk, intoxicated, excited, impassioned, agitated, furious, extravagant, eccentric.

Sociable, social, convivial, conversable, familiar, companionable, genial, friendly.

Ant.—Unsociable, ungenial, morose, retiring, bashful.

Social, civil, civic, sociable, convivial, friendly, hospitable, communicative.

Ant.—Individual, personal, solitary, physical, hostile, inimical, unkind, unsocial.

Society, association, company, corporation, companionship, community, fellowship, fraternity.

Ant.—Individuality, personality, separation, privacy.

Soft, supple, flexible, yielding, docile, tractable, manageable, mild, gentle, meek, tender, mellow.

Ant.—Hard, tough, rigid, unyielding, coarse, harsh, rough, unkind, stern, sharp, ascetic, resolute, cruel, exacting, flinty, hardened, obdurate.

Soften, civilize, mollify, mitigate.

Ant.—Harden, barbarize, excite, infuriate.

Soil, *v.* stain, sully, tarnish, begrime, defile, dirty.

Ant.—Cleanse, purify, bleach.

Sojourn, *v.* (See Dwell.)

Solace. (See Comfort.)

Sole, only, solitary, single, alone, individual, exclusive.

Ant.—Plural, numerous, collective.

Solemn. (See Grave.)

Solemnity, ceremony, rite, observance, form, celebration, sanctity, sacredness, impressiveness.

Ant.—Gaiety, profanity, triviality, desecration, vulgarity.

Solicit, ask, crave, beg, urge, pray, entreat, beseech, implore, supplicate, importune, invite.

Ant.—Demand, require, exact, claim.

Solicitude. (See Anxiety.)

Solid, hard, firm, stable, substantial, compact, dense, strong, valid.

Ant.—Hollow, soft, yielding, frail, brittle, elastic, weak, invalid, unsound.

Solitary, alone, sole, only, single.

Ant.—Manifold, multitudinous, many, numerous.

Solution, explanation, answer, key.

Ant.—Mystification, obscurity.

Somber, dull, grave, gloomy, cloudy, murky, dusky, sable, dark, mournful, funereal, lugubrious.

Ant.—Bright, gay, sunny, joyous.

Song, ballad, carol, ditty, lay, strain, poem, hymn, anthem.

Ant.—Speech, prose, sermon.

Soothe, soften, allay, appease, relieve, assuage, compose, calm, quiet, still, hush, lull, pacify, mitigate.

Ant.—Rouse, excite, ruffle, irritate, agitate, aggravate, annoy, infuriate.

Sordid, earthly, selfish, mean, covetous, niggardly, greedy, close, dirty, foul, gross, vile, base.

Ant.—Pure, generous, unselfish, honorable, profuse, lavish, prodigal, extravagant.

Sorrow, affliction, distress, grief, trouble, sadness, mourning.

Ant.—Joy, gladness, rejoicing.

Sorry, grieved, pained, hurt, afflicted, vexed, shabby, paltry, worthless, vile, sorrowful, sad, poor, insignificant.

Ant.—Glad, pleased, delighted, gratified, fine, respectable.

Sort, species, kind, quality, class, genus, nature, character.

Ant.—Unlikeness, eccentricity, phenomenon, uniqueness.

Soul, spirit, life, reason, intellect, vitality, energy, courage, feeling, person, animation, vivacity, mind.

Ant.—Materiality, body, organism, physiology.

Sound, *a.* healthy, orthodox, unbroken, unimpaired, firm, weighty, valid, sane.

Ant.—Unsound, imperfect, partial, broken, impaired, unhealthy, weak, frail, fragile, diseased, rotten.

Sound, *n.* tone, noise.

Ant.—Silence.

Sound, *v.* ring, peal, clash, clang, investigate, gauge.

Ant.—Silence, hush, overlook, disregard.

Sour, acid, sharp, tart, rancid, harsh, pungent, piquant, crabbed, morose, peevish.

Ant.—Sweet, wholesome, mellow, genial, kindly.

Source, origin, spring, fount, cause, rise, beginning, commencement.

Ant.—Mouth, end, exit, issue, result, effect.

Sovereign, regal, royal, imperial, principal, chief, predominant, paramount, effectual.

Ant.—Inferior, subject, subordinate, subservient, weak, inefficient.

Space, room, interval, extent, expanse, field, place, site, station.

Ant.—Limitation, restriction, confinement, proximity.

Spacious, ample, roomy, capacious, extensive, large, wide.

Ant.—Narrow, limited, cramped, confined.

Spare, *v.* afford, give, store, forbear.

Ant.—Spend, squander, lavish, scatter, indulge.

Spare, *a.* meager, scanty, frugal, stinted, lean, thin.

Ant.—Ample, plentiful, abundant, profuse, liberal, generous, bountiful, available.

Sparkle, shine, flash, gleam, twinkle, glitter, glisten, glare, bubble, effervesce.

Ant.—Smolder, stagnate, expire.

Sparse, scanty, thin.

Ant.—Luxuriant, abundant.

Speak, converse, say, tell, talk, discourse, utter, express, confer.

Ant.—Hush, sing, write, chant, conceal.

Special, exceptional, peculiar, particular, distinctive, specific.

Ant.—General, universal, common, generic.

Specify, particularize, state, designate, mention.

Ant.—Generalize, lump, combine, confound.

Specimen, model, sample, illustration, example, instance.

Ant.—Exception, anomaly, nondescript, freak.

Specious, colorable, plausible, showy.

Ant.—Absurd, ridiculous, inadmissible, unreasonable.

Spectacle, show, display, sight, scene, exhibition, representation, pageant.

Speculation, contemplation, consideration, view, theory, scheme, conjecture.

Ant.—Realization, proof, fact, verification, certainty.

Speedy, early, quick, fast, rapid, swift, fleet.

Ant.—Late, slow. tardy, loitering, lingering.

Spend, expend, disburse, exhaust, squander, lavish, waste, consume, dissipate.

Ant.—Retain, save, hoard, accumulate, economize.

Spirit, breath, life, essence, soul, specter, apparition, ghost, courage, zeal, mood, temper, principle.

Ant.—Body, substance, flesh, frame, embodiment, torpor, deadness, timidity, dejection.

Spiritual, divine, religious, incorporeal, immaterial, ecclesiastical, ghostly.

Ant.—Material, carnal, fleshly.

Spite, rancor, spleen, malice, malevolence, ill will, grudge, pique, vindictiveness.

Ant.—Good will, kindliness, benevolence.

Spleen. (See Spite.)

Splendid, magnificent, grand, brilliant, showy, superb, sumptuous, pompous, glorious, illustrious, signal.

Ant.—Tame, somber, dull, obscure, unimposing, mean, poor, ordinary, ineffective.

Split, cleave, break, burst, crack, divide, separate.

Ant.—Unite, cohere, coalesce, combine, agree, consolidate.

Spoil, destroy, mar, impair, injure, plunder.

Ant.—Preserve, improve, better, enrich, endow.

Spontaneous, voluntary, willing, gratuitous.

Ant.—Involuntary, compulsory, necessitated.

Sporadic, isolated, rare.

Ant.—General, prevalent.

Sport, amusement, diversion, recreation, pastime, game, play, frolic.

Ant.—Work, business, earnestness.

Spread, extend, disperse, expand, diffuse, distribute, circulate, propagate, disseminate, unfurl, scatter.

Ant.—Contract, gather, furl, fold, close, shut, secrete, suppress, restrict, hush, conceal, check, condense, confine, restrain.

Sprightly. (See Gay.)

Spring, rise, proceed, issue, flow, emerge, leap, bound, jump, fountain, source.

Ant.—Alight, land, drop, arrive, issue, end, terminate.

Sprout, bud, germinate, shoot forth, spring.

Ant.—Blight, wither, decay.

Spruce. (See Neat.)

Spur, goad, incite, urge, stimulate.

Ant.—Hold, discourage, rein, check, restrain, deter.

Spurious, counterfeit, fictitious, unauthentic, false, unsound.

Ant.—Genuine, true, veritable, legitimate, authentic.

Squalid, foul, filthy, dirty, unclean, poverty-stricken.

Ant.—Cleanly, wholesome, trim neat, tidy.

Squander, waste, consume, dissipate.

Ant.—Save, retain, hoard, hold, acquire, get.

Squeeze. (See Press.)

Stable, firm, established, solid, substantial, constant, staunch, steadfast, steady, fast, standing, permanent, perpetual.

Ant.—Unstable, weak, infirm, insecure, precarious, frail, transient, evanescent.

Staff, prop, support, stay.

Stagger, reel, totter.

Stagnant, motionless, lifeless, tideless, standing.

Ant.—Brisk, flowing, rapid, lively, seething, restless.

Staid, steady, sober, demure, grave, sedate.

Ant.—Unsteady, flighty, indiscreet, eccentric, agitated.

Stain, color, dye, blot, befoul, soil, tarnish, sully, pollute, mar, injure, spoil, discolor, spot.

Ant.—Purify, cleanse, wash, decorate, honor, blemish.

Stammer. (See Hesitate.)

Stamp, mark, impress, impression, print, genus, kind, description, make, mold, type.

Stand, stop, rest, stagnate, endure, halt.

Ant.—Move, proceed, advance, progress, yield, fall, fail, run, vanish, depart.

Standard, criterion, measure, gauge, test, rule.

Standing, status, ground, station, rank, position.

Ant.—Insecurity, precariousness.

Starved, famished, lean, ill-fed, emaciated.

Ant.—Fat, well-fed, plump.

State, *n.* condition, commonwealth, realm.

State, *v.* specify, particularize, say, declare, propound, avow, narrate, recite.

Ant.—Suppress, conceal, suppose, imply, deny, retract, contradict, hear.

Station, standing, position, post, office, situation, state, rank, location.

Stationary, immovable, fixed, motionless.

Ant.—Movable, changeable, migratory, alterable, unfixed, loose.

Stay, remain, abide, continue, await, wait for, dwell, support, sustain, hold, stop, restrain, arrest, hinder.

Ant.—Go, leave, depart, move, proceed, hasten, speed, send, expedite, free.

Steadfast, constant, staunch, firm, resolved.

Ant.—Wavering, capricious, uncertain, dubious, irresolute.

Steady, firm, fixed, constant, regular.

Ant.—Unsteady, changeable, variable, inconstant.

Steal, purloin, pilfer, filch, embezzle.

Ant.—Buy, restore, renew.

Steep, precipitous, abrupt, hilly, craggy.

Ant.—Easy, level, gradual, accessible.

Sterile, unfruitful, barren, waste, unproductive.

Ant.—Fertile, fruitful, productive, luxuriant, cultivated.

Sterling, genuine, pure, unalloyed, unadulterated, sound, substantial.

Ant.—False, fictitious, specious, pretentious, unreliable.

Stern, harsh, severe, austere, rigid, rigorous, strict.

Ant.—Lenient, kindly, easy, genial.

Stifle, extinguish, choke, suffocate, smother.

Stigma, mark, brand, infamy, disgrace, blot, stain.

Ant.—Decoration, laurels, credit, renown.

Still. (See Motionless.)

Stimulate. (See Encourage.)

Stingy, close, mean, niggardly, sparingly.

Ant.—Liberal, generous, lavish, bountiful.

Stint, limit, stop, restrict.

Ant.—Lavish, pour, heap, squander.

Stipulate, bargain, contract, agree on, engage, covenant.

Ant.—Retract, decline, refuse, withdraw, disagree, protest.

Stir, budge, move, agitate, disturb, excite, arouse.

Ant.—Still, quiet, pacify, soothe, repress.

Stock. (See Store.)

Stolid, obtuse, heavy-headed, doltish, dull, senseless.

Ant.—Acute, quick, clever, bright, sensitive.

Stoop, bend, yield, condescend.

Ant.—Rise, erect, stand.

Stop, close, plug, cork, seal, arrest, check, hinder, impede, bar, terminate.

Ant.—Open, clear, unseal, promote, speed, hasten, proceed.

Store, stock, fund, supply, hoard, provision, treasury.

Ant.—Emptiness, lack, want, consumption, exhaustion.

Stormy, tempestuous, boisterous, blustering, roaring, raving, rough.

Ant.—Calm, quiet, peaceful, tranquil.

Stout, robust, athletic, vigorous, stalwart, corpulent, strong, lusty.

Ant.—Lean, thin, slender, weak, frail, feeble, timid.

Straight, right, direct, undeviating.

Ant.—Crooked, circuitous, curved, winding.

Strain, stretch, tighten, exert, filter.

Ant.—Loosen, relax, slacken.

Strait, narrow, confined.

Ant.—Broad.

Strange, odd, surprising, singular, eccentric, rare, uncommon, unusual.

Ant.—Familiar, usual, ordinary, common, regular, general.

Stranger, foreigner, alien.

Ant.—Neighbor, friend, acquaintance, countryman, comrade, associate.

Stratagem, artifice, trick, deception, cheat, imposture, delusion, deceit, plot, plan, device.

Ant.—Openness, frankness, blunder, defect.

Stray, rove, ramble, err, digress, deviate, wander.

Ant.—Adhere, abide, stick, return.

Strength, power, might, authority, force, vigor.

Ant.—Weakness, feebleness, infirmity, frailty, softness, insecurity, invalidity.

Strengthen, fortify, reinforce, invigorate, consolidate, establish, substantiate, confirm.

Ant.—Weaken, loosen, shake, undermine, diminish, abrogate, annul, cancel, destroy.

Strenuous, vigorous, zealous, vehement, bold, ardent, strong, resolute.

Ant.—Weak, feeble, irresolute.

Stress, emphasis, force, accent, strain, weight, pressure.

Ant.—Lightness, touch, triviality, unimportance.

Stretch, spread, expand, extend, lengthen, elongate.

Ant.—Contract, abbreviate, shorten, shrink, curtail.

Strict, close, accurate, correct, exact, nice, stringent, rigorous, severe.

Ant.—Loose, lax, indulgent, lenient, inaccurate.

Strife, struggle, quarrel, contention, discord, disagreement, bickering, wrangle.

Ant.—Peace, amity, friendship, reconciliation, good will.

Strike, hit, beat, smite, touch.

Ant.—Avoid, graze, miss, escape, pass.

Strip, denude, divest, bare, despoil, rob, rifle.

Ant.—Clothe, invest, endow, enrich, compensate.

Strive, labor, struggle, aim, contend, vie, contest, endeavor.

Ant.—Submit, succumb, yield, withdraw.

Strong, forcible, cogent, powerful, fortified, potent, sturdy, stalwart, hale, robust, sinowy, athletic, hardy, firm.

Ant.—Weak, frail, powerless, defenseless, feeble, sickly, infirm, calm, gentle, delicate, impotent, moderate, brittle, tender.

Struggle. (See Strive.)

Stubborn. (See Obstinate.)

Study, thought, consideration, care, attention, application.

Ant.—Idleness, ease, carelessness, negligence.

Stupendous, astounding, amazing, marvelous, wondrous.

Ant.—Ordinary, unimposing, small.

Stupid, stolid, dull, obtuse, foolish, witless.

Ant.—Bright, quick, clever, sagacious, sensible, intelligent.

Sturdy. (See Strong.)

Suavity. (See Affability.)

Subdue, conquer, overpower, vanquish, subjugate, overcome, tame, quell.

Ant.—Exalt, fortify, liberate, strengthen, aggrandize.

Subject, *a.* exposed to, liable, obnoxious.

Ant.—Exempt, immune.

Subject, *n.* inferior, subordinate.

Ant.—Superior.

Sublime, grand, noble, raised, exalted, lofty, elevated, eminent, high.

Ant.—Low, mean, base, ignoble, inglorious, ordinary.

Submerge, inundate, drown, deluge, flood, sink.

Ant.—Raise, extricate, dry, save.

Submissive. (See Obedient.)

Submit, succumb, comply, yield, surrender.

Ant.—Resist, oppose, object, withdraw, resume, recover, retain, hold, keep.

Subsequent, later, posterior, following, succeeding.

Ant.—Prior, former, earlier, anterior, previous, preceding, antecedent.

Substantial, real, true, solid, substantive, tangible, responsible, durable.

Ant.—Unreal, imaginary, fictitious, visionary, immaterial, weak, frail, ghostly, unsubstantial, flimsy.

Substitute. (See Deputy.)
Subterfuge, evasion, shift, quirk, subtlety, artifice, dodge.
Ant.—Candor, openness, frankness, honesty, challenge, assertion, exhibition.
Subtle, cunning, crafty, astute, sly, wily, artful, shrewd.
Ant.—Simple, artless, open, frank, rough, undiscerning.
Subtract, deduct, subduct, withdraw, remove, take.
Ant.—Add, import, give, bring.
Succeed, flourish, thrive, prosper, follow.
Ant.—Fail, lose, miss, precede, anticipate.
Successful, fortunate, lucky, happy.
Ant.—Unsuccessful, unfortunate, unlucky.
Succession, order, series, rotation, lineage, race.
Ant.—Irregularity, disorder, failure, intermission, break, gap.
Succinct, brief, short, concise.
Ant.—Prolix, diffuse, discursive, long.
Succor. (See Aid.)
Succumb. (See Submit.)
Sudden, abrupt, quick, unexpected, unlooked for, unanticipated.
Ant.—Gradual, expected, anticipated, slow.
Suffer, bear, endure, tolerate, admit, allow, let, permit.
Ant.—Resist, repel, reject, forbid, ignore.
Suffocate. (See Smother.)
Suggest, hint, allude, refer, intimate, insinuate, propose.
Ant.—Declare, insist, demand, dictate, enunciate.
Suit, serve, adapt, agree, answer, fit, please, harmonize, accord.
Ant.—Differ, disagree, misfit, vary.
Suitable, seemly, fit, apt, becoming, expedient, convenient, eligible.
Ant.—Unsuitable, discordant, unbecoming, unfitting.
Sulky, sullen, gloomy, morose, fretful.
Ant.—Genial, kindly, obliging.
Sully, stain, tarnish, soil, spoil, blemish, mar, disgrace, dishonor.
Ant.—Purify, cleanse, glorify, ennoble, dignify.
Sum, amount, quantity, total, whole, problem, aggregate.
Ant.—Part, portion, item, imperfection.
Summary, *n.* abstract, epitome, digest, abridgment, compendium.
Ant.—Expansion, dilution, explanation.
Summary, *a.* short, brief, concise, compendious, succinct.
Ant.—Tedious, protracted, circuitous, formal, slow.
Summit, top, height, culmination, acme, apex, zenith.
Ant.—Bottom, depth, base, foot, nadir.
Summon, call, fetch, cite, bid, challenge, convoke.
Ant.—Send, discharge, remit, disband, dissolve, dismiss.
Sumptuous, costly, expensive, dear, valuable, princely, superb.
Ant.—Poor, mean, inexpensive, sordid, beggarly, frugal.
Superb, princely, grand, splendid, magnificent.
Ant.—Mean, commonplace, shabby.
Supercilious, haughty, arrogant, insolent.
Ant.—Affable, courteous, modest.
Superficial, shallow, flimsy, slight, imperfect, external, outer, untrustworthy.
Ant.—Deep, profound, abstruse, accurate, exact, thorough.
Superfluous, needless, excessive, useless, unnecessary.
Ant.—Essential, necessary, required, scant, deficient.
Superintend, supervise, overlook, control, direct, manage.
Superior, higher, upper, noble, head, better, excellent.
Ant.—Inferior, lower, worse, subordinate, ordinary.
Superlative, highest, greatest, extreme, supreme, exquisite.
Ant.—Lowest, common, ordinary.
Supernatural, miraculous, preternatural.
Ant.—Natural, physical, human.
Supersede, overrule, annul, set aside, suspend, supplant.
Ant.—Confirm, perpetuate, continue, supply.
Supine, indolent, sluggish, lazy, listless, dull, apathetic, torpid, inactive, careless.
Ant.—Active, energetic, diligent, indefatigable.
Supple, lithe, flexible, pliant, bending, yielding, compliant.
Ant.—Firm, stiff, stubborn, inflexible, unbending, independent.
Supplicate, pray, beg, solicit, beseech, importune, entreat, implore, crave.
Ant.—Order, command, insist, demand.
Supply, furnish, give, grant, afford, provide, minister, contribute, yield.
Ant.—Expand, use, consume, absorb, demand, withhold.
Support, sustain, prop, uphold, maintain, help, befriend, assist, countenance, patronize, favor, second, further, forward, promote, nurture, nourish, foster.
Ant.—Drop, abandon, betray, surrender, discontinue, oppose, discourage, weaken, exhaust, subvert, suppress.
Suppose, presume, conceive, apprehend, imagine, think, assume, believe, deem.
Ant.—Prove, demonstrate, deny, negative.
Supposition. (See Conjecture.)
Supposititious, spurious, false, theoretical, speculative.
Ant.—Genuine, true, real.
Suppress, repress, crush, quell, restrain, put down, stifle, overwhelm, smother, check, stop.
Ant.—Raise, support, fan, excite, incite, instigate, aggravate, publish, spread, disseminate.
Supreme, paramount, highest, greatest, principal.
Ant.—Inferior, subordinate, subject, lower.
Sure, infallible, certain, indisputable, unmistakable, doubtless, firm, safe, secure, confident, positive, assured.
Ant.—Uncertain, ignorant, dubious, doubtful, weak, precarious, insecure, transient, fallible.
Surfeit, glut, gorge, cloy, pall, satiate.
Ant.—Stint, deprive, starve.
Surly, gloomy, morose, sulky, sullen, splenetic, ill-natured, rough, gruff.
Ant.—Genial, kindly, pleasant, happy.
Surmise, presume, conjecture, guess, suppose, suspect.
Ant.—Prove, establish, verify, state.
Surmount, overcome, subdue, vanquish, conquer, surpass, exceed.
Ant.—Succumb, fail, miss, submit, lose.
Surpass, excel, exceed, outdo, outstrip, surmount.
Ant.—Fail, foil, miss, equal.
Surplus, remainder, overplus, residue, excess, balance.
Ant.—Deficiency, deficit.
Surprise, astonish, amaze, startle, alarm.
Ant.—Forewarn, prepare, premonish.

Surrender, cede, give up, deliver, yield, relinquish, resign, abandon.
Ant.—Resist, defeat, retain, vindicate, withhold.

Surreptitious, underhand, furtive, stealthy, clandestine.
Ant.—Open, frank, honest, ingenuous.

Surround, environ, encompass, encircle, invest, besiege, inclose, embrace.
Ant.—Open, expose, liberate, free, exclude, shut out.

Survey, examine, scrutinize, review, view, inspect, reconnoiter.
Ant.—Overlook, ignore, miss, disregard.

Susceptible, sensitive, excitable, tender, sensible.
Ant.—Insusceptible, insensitive, impassive, cold.

Suspect, fear, surmise, guess, conjecture.
Ant.—Trust, credit, confide.

Suspense, doubt, uncertainty, anxiety, solicitude, respite, rest, pause.
Ant.—Settlement, decision, determination.

Suspicion, misgiving, jealousy, distrust, mistrust.
Ant.—Belief, trust, confidence.

Suspicious, doubtful, questionable, mistrustful.
Ant.—Trusting, confident.

Sustain, support, maintain.

Sustenance, support, living, livelihood, subsistence, maintenance, sustentation.
Ant.—Starvation, exhaustion, inanition.

Swallow, absorb, imbibe, engulf, engross, consume, devour.
Ant.—Vomit, disgorge, discharge.

Swamp, bog, fen, morass, marsh, quagmire.
Ant.—Field, meadow, river, lake, pond, hill.

Sway, influence, government, authority, dominion, supremacy, ascendancy, rule.
Ant.—Meekness, obedience, subservience, subjection.

Swear, declare, depose, testify, curse, blaspheme.
Ant.—Guess, surmise, conjecture, hesitate.

Sweet, sugary, luscious, delicious, pleasing, mild, gentle, winning.
Ant.—Sour, bitter, offensive, nasty, discordant, repulsive, unwholesome, tainted.

Swell, heave, rise, enlarge, enhance, heighten, dilate, expand, augment.
Ant.—Contract, lessen, diminish, reduce, condense, narrow.

Swift, quick, fleet, speedy, rapid, prompt, ready, eager.
Ant.—Slow, tardy, lazy, loitering, sluggish.

Sycophant, flatterer, parasite, adulator, toady, hanger-on.
Ant.—Friend, rival, opponent.

Symmetry, proportion
Ant.—Deformity, disproportion, shapelessness.

Sympathy, commiseration, condolence, pity, compassion, agreement, fellow-feeling, union, concert.
Ant.—Antipathy, unkindness, harshness, maleficence, cruelty, churlishness, malignity, brutality, inhumanity, malevolence.

Symptom, token, sign, note, mark, suggestion.
Ant.—Misindication, mistake.

Synopsis, epitome, syllabus.
Ant.—Oration, essay, dilation, expansion.

System, method, arrangement, regularity, order, rule, plan, scheme.
Ant.—Disorder, confusion, chance, fortuity.

Systematic, orderly, regular, methodical.
Ant.—Chaotic, confused.

T

Tacit, silent, implied, understood, implicit.
Ant.—Open, avowed, declared, expressed.

Tact, adroitness, expertness, skill, nicety, discrimination, dexterity.
Ant.—Indiscretion, ignorance, awkwardness, mistake.

Tactics, strategy, policy, diplomacy.
Ant.—Blunder, mistake.

Taint, contaminate, defile, pollute, corrupt, infect, vitiate, disgrace.
Ant.—Purify, cleanse, disinfect, efface.

Take, accept, receive, catch, seize, remove, abstract.
Ant.—Drop, reject, abandon, lose, miss, repel, give.

Talent, ability, faculty, genius, cleverness, gift, endowment, capability.
Ant.—Imbecility, stupidity, incompetence.

Talk, conversation, chat, gossip, dialogue, discourse, report, rumor.
Ant.—Writing, correspondence, literature.

Talkative, garrulous, loquacious, prating, chattering, chatty, communicative.
Ant.—Taciturn, silent, reserved, close, mute, reticent.

Tall. (See High.)

Tally, match, suit, correspond, agree, accord, harmonize.
Ant.—Differ, disagree.

Tame, gentle, domesticated, mild, docile, tedious, dull.
Ant.—Wild, savage, undomesticated, fierce, spirited, animated, exciting, lively.

Tangible, palpable, solid, substantial, material, perceptible.
Ant.—Intangible, impalpable, spiritual, incomprehensible.

Tantalize, aggravate, provoke, irritate, tease, vex, frustrate.
Ant.—Gratify, soothe, satisfy.

Tantamount, equivalent, synonymous, equal to.

Tardy. (See Slow.)

Tarry, await, stay, remain, lag, loiter, abide, lodge, dwell.
Ant.—Press, push, speed, haste.

Tart, sour, sharp, keen, acrid, bitter, acrimonious.
Ant.—Mellow, sweet, mild, genial, kindly, oily, polite, courteous.

Task, business, work, labor, toil, lesson.
Ant.—Relaxation, amusement, leisure, hobby.

Taste, judgment, discernment, perception, sensibility, relish, gusto, zest, nicety, elegance, refinement, flavor, savor.
Ant.—Indiscrimination, indiscernment, indelicacy, insipidity, coarseness, tastelessness.

Tasteless, flat, insipid, mawkish, vapid, dead, stale.
Ant.—Savory, toothsome, palatable, elegant, refined.

Taunt, gibe, jeer, sneer, scoff, twit, deride, reproach.
Ant.—Compliment, eulogy, panegyric.

Tax, toll, duty, rate, assessment, impost, contribution, custom, excise.
Ant.—Gift, wages, reward, remuneration.

Teach, instruct, inform, educate, inculcate, train, direct, guide, counsel, advise.
Ant.—Mislead, misinform, misguide.

Teacher, schoolmaster, professor, preceptor, instructor, tutor.
Ant.—Pupil, student, scholar.

Tear, rend, break, lacerate, sever, sunder.
Ant.—Mend, unite.

Tease, vex, plague, torment, irritate, disturb, provoke, taunt, tantalize.
Ant.—Soothe, gratify, please, delight, fascinate, comfort.

Tedious, slow, dilatory, tardy, wearisome, irksome, dreary, tiresome, prosy, sluggish.
Ant.—Quick, exciting, interesting, amusing, delightful.

Teeming, prolific, fertile, pregnant, fruitful, full, fraught, replete, swarming.
Ant.—Barren, scant, sparse, few.

Tell, number, enumerate, count, state, mention, communicate, apprise, impart, reveal, inform, ascertain, signify, acquaint, notify, intimate, report.
Ant.—Hear, listen, repress, suppress, misreport, misquote, misjudge.

Temerity, foolhardiness, audacity, rashness, heedlessness.
Ant.—Timidity, caution, calculation.

Temperate, abstinent, moderate, sober, abstemious, calm, cool, sedate, frugal.
Ant.—Intemperate, immoderate, self-indulgent, torrid, frigid.

Temporal, worldly, terrestrial, mundane, secular, transient.
Ant.—Religious, spiritual, eternal, sacerdotal.

Temporary, present, immediate, transient, partial, fleeting, transitory.
Ant.—Perpetual, lasting, complete, perfect, permanent, final, stable.

Temporize, fence, maneuver, procrastinate.
Ant.—Act, decide, determine, confirm.

Tempt, allure, try, test, attract, decoy, entice, seduce.
Ant.—Dissuade, deter, warn, frighten, repel.

Tenable, defensible, sound, reasonable.
Ant.—Indefensible, weak, fallacious, irrational, absurd.

Tenacious, cohesive, pertinacious, retentive.

Tend, keep, watch, guard, manage, incline, nurture.
Ant.—Betray, desert, abandon.

Tendency, inclination, leaning, propensity, proclivity, proneness, predisposition, drift, aim, bias.
Ant.—Disinclination, aversion, deviation, tangency.

Tender, *v.* offer, proffer, produce, bid.
Ant.—Withhold, withdraw, retain.

Tender, *a.* mild, kind, bland, indulgent, compassionate, gentle.
Ant.—Strong, sturdy, hardy, tough, cruel, careless, rough, rude, unfeeling.

Tenet, opinion, position, view, conviction, belief.

Tenor, meaning, drift, intent, sense, purport.
Ant.—Incoherence, irrelevance, variance.

Tension, strain, force, stretch, tightness.
Ant.—Looseness, laxity, slackness.

Term, designation, boundary, limit, period, time.

Terminate, close, end, conclude, complete, finish, stop.
Ant.—Begin, commence, initiate, establish, progress.

Terrestrial, worldly, earthly, mundane, sublunary.
Ant.—Celestial, infernal.

Terrible, awful, terrific, tremendous, fearful, dreadful, shocking, frightful, horrible,
Ant.—Ordinary, commonplace, pleasant.

Terrify. (See Frighten.)

Territory, dominion, domain.

Terror. (See Alarm.)

Terse, neat, smooth, compact, concise, succinct, pithy, forcible, energetic.
Ant.—Coarse, rough, rude, dispersed, diffuse, prolix.

Test, criterion, standard, ordeal, experience, experiment, trial, proof.
Ant.—Error, blunder, oversight.

Testify, depose, declare, swear, attest, witness, prove, certify.
Ant.—Falsify, disprove, silence.

Testimony, witness, confirmation, attestation, proof, evidence.
Ant.—Refutation, contradiction, disproof, argument.

Thankful, grateful, obliged.

Thankless, ungracious, profitless, ungrateful, unthankful.
Ant.—Thankful, profitable, reciprocative.

Thaw, melt, dissolve, liquefy.
Ant.—Freeze, congeal.

Theatrical, dramatic, showy, ceremonious, meretricious.
Ant.—Simple, quiet, subdued, plain, unaffected.

Theft, robbery, depredation, spoliation.

Theme, subject, topic, text, essay.

Theory, speculation, scheme, plea, hypothesis, conjecture.
Ant.—Fact, proof, verity, practice.

Therefore, accordingly, consequently, hence.

Thick, dense, close, compact, solid, coagulated, muddy, turbid, misty, foggy, vaporous.
Ant.—Thin, rare, fine, sparse, strained, pure, limpid, slight, clear, distinct.

Thin, slim, slender, slight, flimsy, lean, attenuated, scraggy, emaciated, diluted, gaunt, meager.
Ant.—Thick, dense, solid, close, bulky, deep, fat, obese, rotund.

Think, cogitate, consider, reflect, ponder, contemplate, meditate, muse, conceive, fancy, imagine, apprehend, hold, esteem, reckon, consider, deem, believe, opine, regard.
Ant.—Guess, hazard, conjecture, doubt.

Thorough, accurate, correct, trustworthy, reliable, complete.
Ant.—Superficial, inaccurate.

Thought, idea, conception, imagination, fancy, conceit, notion, supposition, care, provision, consideration, opinion, view, sentiment, reflection, deliberation.

Thoughtful, considerate, careful, cautious, heedful, diligent, contemplative, reflective, provident, pensive, dreamy.
Ant.—Thoughtless, inconsiderate, rash, precipitate, heedless.

Thoughtless, inconsiderate, rash, improvident, precipitate, heedless.

Threat, menace, intimidation.
Ant.—Promise, encouragement allurement.

Threatening, imminent, impending, menacing, intimidating, foreboding.
Ant.—Encouraging, promising, reassuring, enticing.

Thrifty, sparing, careful, prudent, economical, frugal, saving, provident.
Ant.—Prodigal, wasteful, extravagant.

Thrive, flourish, prosper, increase, succeed, grow, fatten.
Ant.—Decay, fade, wither, waste, languish, droop.

Throw, propel, cast, hurl, fling.
Ant.—Retain, revoke, hold, restrain, draw, haul.

Thrust, push, drive, force, impel, urge.
Ant.—Draw, retract, snatch.

Tickle, amuse, titillate, gratify.
Ant.—Irritate, hurt, annoy, vex.

Tide, current, stream, course, influx.

Ant.—Stagnation, stoppage, cessation, subsidence.

Tidings. (See News.)

Tidy, orderly, neat, spruce, clean, cleanly.

Ant.—Untidy, dirty, unclean, slovenly.

Tie, *v.* bind, restrain, restrict, oblige, secure, unite, join.

Ant.—Untie, unbind, sever, separate, release, free, loose.

Tie, *n.* band, ligament, ligature.

Tight, tense, stretched, not slack, small.

Ant.—Loose, slack, open, lax, large.

Time, duration, season, period, era, age, date, span, spell.

Ant.—Eternity, indetermination, space.

Timely, seasonable, opportune, early, judicious.

Ant.—Untimely, late, inopportune, unseasonable.

Timid, timorous, fearful, afraid, pusillanimous, cowardly, dastardly, faint-hearted.

Ant.—Bold, daring, courageous, rash, venturesome, audacious.

Tinge, flavor, taste, color, dye.

Ant.—Disinfect, erase.

Tint, shade, tinge, hue, color, stain, dye, complexion.

Ant.—Pallor, bleaching, achromatism.

Tiny, small, little, diminutive, wee, lilliputian.

Ant.—Huge, large, gigantic, bulky.

Tipsy. (See Intoxicated.)

Tire, exhaust, fatigue, bore, weary, jade, harass, dispirit.

Ant.—Enliven, refresh, animate, amuse, excite.

Title, denomination, designation, name, appellation, style, dignity, epithet, right.

Toil, work, task, travail, pain, labor, drudgery.

Ant.—Ease, relaxation, rest, amusement, pleasure.

Token. (See Sign.)

Tolerable, passable, ordinary, middling.

Ant.—Intolerable, unbearable, insupportable, insufferable.

Tolerate, allow, admit, receive, suffer, permit, let, endure, abide.

Ant.—Repel, prohibit, reject, resist, disallow, forbid, refuse.

Tomb. (See Grave.)

Tone, style, manner, mode, sound, intonation, pitch.

Ant.—Laxity, silence, hush.

Top, summit, apex, head, crown, surface.

Ant.—Foot, bottom, base, foundation.

Torment, torture, tease, worry, persecute, pain, offend, tantalize, plague.

Ant.—Soothe, gratify, please, delight, amuse.

Torpid, benumbed, numb, dull, stupid, sluggish, inert.

Ant.—Lively, animated, gay, nimble, brisk, active.

Torrid, burning, hot, parching, scorching, sultry.

Ant.—Frigid, arctic, cold, cool, fresh, temperate, icy, freezing.

Tortuous, twisted, winding, crooked, indirect.

Ant.—Straight, direct.

Torture, torment, anguish, agony.

Ant.—Ecstasy, rapture, bliss, delight, relieve, ease, refresh, please, gratify.

Total, sum, gross, whole, aggregate, entire, complete.

Ant.—Part, item, portion.

Totally, entirely, quite, altogether, fully, wholly.

Ant.—Partly, partially, incompletely.

Totter, falter, reel, rock, tremble, shake, stagger.

Ant.—Steady, stand, stay.

Touching, tender, affecting, moving, pathetic.

Ant.—Amusing, ridiculous, indifferent, joyous, pleasant, comfortable, desirable, delectable, cheerful, gay, genial, happy, merry, mirthful.

Tough, strong, hard, firm, leathery, difficult.

Ant.—Soft, yielding, tender, fragile, brittle.

Tour. (See Excursion.)

Trace, derive, deduce, follow, pursue, track.

Ant.—Miss, lose, stop, retreat, fail.

Tractable, docile, manageable, amenable.

Ant.—Refractory, unmanageable, intractable, obstinate, stubborn.

Trade, traffic, commerce, dealing, occupation, employment, office.

Ant.—Profession, idleness, leisure, relaxation.

Traditional, oral, uncertain, transmitted, apocryphal, legendary, unverified.

Ant.—Written, documentary, certainty, fact, history, truth, verity.

Traduce. (See Calumniate.)

Traffic, trade, exchange, commerce, intercourse.

Tragedy, disaster, calamity, affliction, catastrophe.

Ant.—Joy, delight, boon, prosperity, comedy.

Tragic, mournful, calamitous, fatal, sorrowful.

Ant.—Comical, joyous, gay, light.

Train, educate, instruct, discipline, drill, inure.

Ant.—Force, break, disqualify, misdirect.

Trammel, fetter, shackle, clog, bond, chain, impediment, hindrance.

Ant.—Freedom, liberation, extrication.

Tranquil, peaceful, unruffled, still, quiet, hushed.

Ant.—Agitated, disturbed, anxious, excited, restless, uneasy, noisy, boisterous.

Transact, perform, conduct, manage, negotiate, treat.

Ant.—Mismanage, misconduct, fail.

Transaction, negotiation, occurrence, proceeding, affair.

Ant.—Nonperformance, mismanagement, suspension.

Transcend, surmount, overstep, exceed, surpass, excel, eclipse.

Ant.—Fail, fall, foil.

Transcendent, consummate, surpassing, unrivaled, unexampled, matchless, incomparable.

Ant.—Ordinary, attainable, common, average.

Transfer, make over, convey, remove, copy, transmit.

Ant.—Retain, keep, withhold, fix, appropriate, receive.

Transform, change, metamorphose, transfigure, transmute.

Ant.—Perpetuate, conserve, arrest.

Transgress, pass, exceed, violate, infringe, offend, trespass.

Ant.—Observe, keep, obey, fulfill, respect.

Transient, fleeting, passing, transitory, temporary, short-lived.

Ant.—Permanent, lasting, abiding, perpetual, enduring.

Transition, change, shifting, variation, transmutation.

Ant.—Stability, permanence, perpetuity.

Transmit, remit, dispatch, convey, send, forward.

Ant.—Retain, keep, withhold.

Transparent, clear, limpid, lucid, obvious.

Ant.—Opaque, thick, turbid, mysterious, questionable.

Transport, *n.* bliss, ecstasy, rapture, carriage, conveyance.

Ant.—Agony, distress, annoyance, vexation.

Transport, *v.* ravish, delight, enrapture, bear, carry, convey, remove, banish.
Ant.—Vex, displease, annoy, stop, hold, retain.
Transpose, change, reverse, shift.
Ant.—Retain, fix, keep.
Trap, snare, ambush, stratagem, pitfall.
Ant.—Warning, beacon, lighthouse, premonition.
Trappings, gear, ornaments, tackle, harness, paraphernalia.
Ant.—Nudity, nakedness, dismantlement.
Trash, nonsense, twaddle, trifles, dross.
Ant.—Sense, wisdom, usefulness, goods, property.
Travel, trip, ramble, excursion, journey, tour, voyage, peregrination.
Ant.—Rest, halt, stop, settlement.
Traverse, cross, pass, thwart, obstruct.
Ant.—Pass, omit, sanction, overlook, elude, avoid.
Treacherous, traitorous, disloyal, treasonable, faithless, false-hearted, perfidious, sly, false.
Ant.—True, faithful, open, honest, chivalric, trustworthy.
Treason, treachery, disloyalty, disaffection.
Ant.—Openness, fidelity, honor, chivalry.
Treasure, riches, wealth, stock, store, reserve.
Ant.—Trash, offal, refuse, dregs, scum.
Treat, negotiate, bargain, entertain, feast.
Ant.—Drop, abandon, decline, maltreat, mismanage, misarrange, trifle.
Treaty, convention, negotiation, agreement, contract.
Ant.—Neutrality, noninterference.
Tremble, quake, shake, quiver, shudder, totter.
Ant.—Steady, settle, still, calm.
Tremendous, awful, fearful, frightful, terrible.
Ant.—Unimposing, unappalling, inconsiderable.
Tremulous, trembling, jarring, quivering, vibrating, shaking.
Ant.—Motionless, smooth, equable.
Trenchant, cutting, sharp, severe, sarcastic.
Ant.—Weak, impotent, unavailing.
Trend, incline, diverge, bend, tend, stretch.
Ant. Continue, proceed, advance.
Trepidation. (See Fear.)
Trial, experiment, test, gauge, proof, ordeal, essay, trouble, temptation, affliction, cause, action, suit.
Ant.—Hazard, guess, theory, conjecture, relief, refreshment, oversight, disregard.
Tribulation, affliction, grief, distress, trouble, misery, woe.
Ant.—Joy, rejoicing, gladness, rest, delight.
Tribute, tax, impost, subsidy, duty, charge, custom, offering, contribution.
Ant.—Gift, wages, reward, remuneration.
Trick, fraud, cheat, artifice, stratagem, guile, deception, imposition, freak, antic, vagary, hoax.
Ant.—Exposure, artlessness, honesty, fairness, candor, openness.
Trifle, *n.* bauble, toy, gewgaw, bagatelle.
Ant.—Treasure, portent, phenomenon, crisis, importance, urgency, necessity.
Trifle, *v.* toy, play, dally.
Ant.—Treat, cope, tackle, grapple, deal.
Trifling, slight, silly, trivial, petty, unimportant, light.
Ant.—Important, grave, serious.
Trim, compact, snug, neat, nice, tidy, clean, spruce.
Ant.—Slovenly, untidy, loose, negligent.
Trip, mistake, error, blunder, excursion, tour, ramble, jaunt.
Ant.—Stand, speed, prosper, succeed.
Trite, stale, old, ordinary, commonplace, hackneyed.
Ant.—Original, novel, startling, unusual.
Triumph, achievement, ovation, victory, conquest, jubilation.
Ant.—Defeat, failure, discomfiture, disappointment.
Triumphant, elated, victorious, exultant.
Ant.—Unsuccessful, beaten, baffled, worsted, humiliated.
Trivial, trifling, petty, small, frivolous, unimportant, insignificant.
Ant.—Important, weighty.
Troop, assemblage, multitude, gang, band, horde, company.
Ant.—Scarcity, few, individual, bevy, squad.
Trouble, *v.* afflict, distress, agitate, annoy, tease, harass, perplex, disturb, grieve, oppress, aggrieve.
Ant.—Soothe, calm, allay, please, delight, gratify, refresh, entertain.
Trouble, *n.* affliction, distress, grief, tribulation, adversity, calamity, disaster, misfortune, anxiety, sorrow, misery, plague, torment.
Ant.—Happiness, pleasure, delight, joy, gladness, amusement.
Troublesome, tiresome, irksome, sore, grievous, arduous.
Ant.—Easy, pleasant, amusing, light.
Truant, idling, loitering, vagabond, shirking, vagrant.
Ant.—Diligent, industrious, loyal, faithful.
True, genuine, actual, sincere, honest, upright, veritable, real, veracious, authentic, exact, accurate, correct, truehearted, unaffected.
Ant.—False, untrue, fictitious, erroneous, spurious, counterfeit, faithless, fickle, unfounded, dubious.
Trumpery, trivial, worthless, tawdry.
Ant.—Valuable, costly, good.
Trunk, stem, stalk, body, proboscis, chest, box.
Trust, believe, credit, hope, expect.
Ant.—Distrust, suspect, discredit, doubt, disbelieve, resume, withdraw.
Try, attempt, endeavor, strive, struggle, test, examine, prove.
Ant.—Ignore, reject, abandon, decline, withdraw.
Tumble. (See Fall.)
Tumult, ferment, outbreak, brawl, fray, turbulence, uproar, commotion, hubbub, disturbance, riot.
Ant.—Peace, quiet, order, tranquillity, subsidence.
Tumultuous, turbulent, riotous, disorderly, disturbed, confused, unruly.
Ant.—Peaceful, orderly, quiet, tranquil, reposeful.
Tune, tone, air, melody, strain.
Turbid, foul, thick, muddy, impure, unsettled.
Ant.—Clear, crystal, crystalline, transparent, limpid, pure.
Turbulent. (See Tumultuous.)
Turn, *v.* revolve, circulate, whirl, twirl, wheel, incline, inflect, deviate.
Ant.—Fix, stand, stop, arrest, continue, proceed, perpetuate.
Turn, *n.* spiral, maze, labyrinth, cast, bent, tendency, character, tone, manner, round.

Ant.—Straightness, stability, fixity, immobility, uniformity.

Turpitude, depravity, vileness, baseness, wickedness, sin.

Ant.—Goodness, nobility, virtue, excellence.

Tutor. (See Teacher.)

Twine, twist, wind, embrace, entwine.

Ant.—Untwine, untwist, unwind, detach, disengage, separate, sever, disunite.

Twirl. (See Turn.)

Type, emblem, symbol, figure, sign, kind, sort, letter.

Ant.—Caricature, monstrosity, deviation, eccentricity.

Tyrannical, cruel, severe, absolute, arbitrary, despotic.

Ant.—Humane, kindly, liberal, generous, just.

Tyrant, oppressor, despot, autocrat, persecutor.

Ant.—Philanthropist, judge.

Tyro, novice, beginner, learner.

Ant.—Adept, expert, master, professor.

U

Ugly, unsightly, ill-favored, hideous, plain, homely.

Ant.—Attractive, fair, beautiful, handsome, seemly.

Ulterior, further, more distant, beyond, succeeding.

Ant.—Immediate, present, prior, hither.

Ultimate, furthest, last, latest, final, eventual.

Ant.—Proximate, preliminary, prior, intermediate.

Umbrage, offense, dissatisfaction, displeasure, resentment.

Ant.—Complacency, satisfaction, gratification.

Umpire, referee, arbitrator, judge, arbiter.

Ant.—Litigant, disputant.

Unaffected. (See Genuine.)

Unanimity, accord, agreement, unity, concord.

Ant.—Variance, discord, dissent, disagreement.

Unanimous, agreeing, like-minded.

Ant.—Dissentient,disagreeing.

Unanswerable, indisputable, unquestionable, undeniable.

Ant.—Questionable, doubtful, disputable.

Unbind, loosen, untie, unfasten, set free.

Ant.—Bind, tie, hold, fasten.

Unbounded, boundless, excessive, infinite, unsparing, unstinted, interminable.

Ant.—Finite, bounded, restricted, narrow.

Unbridled, wanton, licentious, dissolute, loose, lax.

Ant.—Austere, severe, ascetic, virtuous, self-controlled, restrained.

Uncertain, doubtful, dubious, questionable, fitful, equivocal, ambiguous, indistinct, variable, fluctuating.

Ant.—Certain, dependable.

Uncivil, rude, discourteous, disrespectful, disobliging

Ant.—Civil, well-mannered, well-behaved, courteous.

Unclean, dirty, foul, filthy, sullied.

Ant.—Clean, immaculate, spotless.

Uncommon, rare, strange, scarce, singular, unique, unusual, choice.

Ant.—Common, ordinary, average, usual.

Unconcerned, indifferent, careless, apathetic,

Ant.—Anxious.

Uncouth, strange, odd, clumsy, ungainly.

Ant.—Polite, neat, trim, courtly, graceful, polished, refined, well-bred.

Uncover, reveal, strip, expose, lay bare, divest.

Ant.—Cover, clothe, conceal, suppress, hide.

Under, below, underneath, beneath, subordinate, lower, inferior.

Ant.—Over, above, superior.

Understand, know, comprehend, apprehend.

Ant.—Misunderstand, ignore, declare, state, express.

Understanding, knowledge, intellect, intelligence, faculty, comprehension, mind, reason.

Ant.—Ignorance, misunderstanding, misapprehension, body, material, matter, substance.

Undertake, engage in, embark in, agree, promise.

Ant.—Abandon, drop, decline, discontinue, desist, dismiss, neglect, omit.

Undisturbed, quiet, still, tranquil, placid, peaceful.

Ant.—Disturbed, annoyed, irritated, troubled, vexed.

Undo, annul, frustrate, untie, unfasten, destroy.

Ant.—Unite, bind.

Uneasy, restless, disturbed, unquiet, stiff, awkward.

Ant.—Calm, easy, quiet, peaceful, composed, equable, unembarrassed.

Unequal, uneven, not alike, irregular, insufficient.

Ant.—Equal, alike, similar, even.

Unequaled, matchless, unique, novel, new, unheard of.

Ant.—Common, habitual, normal.

Unfair, wrongful, dishonest, unjust.

Ant.—Fair, just, equable, rational, honest, right, equitable.

Unfit, *a.* improper, unsuitable, untimely, incompetent, inconsistent.

Ant.—Fit, able, capable, ready, timely, qualified, competent, seemly, proper.

Unfit, *v.* disable, disqualify, incapacitate.

Ant.—Fit, enable, qualify.

Unfold, unravel, disclose, unbosom, divulge, display, reveal, declare, develop, explain.

Ant.—Fold, conceal, suppress, hide.

Unfortunate, calamitous, ill-fated, unlucky, wretched, unhappy, miserable.

Ant.—Fortunate, happy, lucky, cheerful, gay, joyous.

Unfriendly, inhospitable, ungenial, unkind, disobliging.

Ant.—Friendly, hospitable, amicable, kindly.

Ungainly, awkward, clumsy, lumbering, uncouth.

Ant.—Pretty, graceful.

Unhappiness, misery, wretchedness, distress, woe.

Ant.—Happiness, pleasure, delight, joy.

Unhappy, miserable, wretched, distressed, afflicted, painful, disastrous, dreary, dismal, drear.

Ant.—Happy, joyous, gay, merry, pleased, delighted, fortunate.

Uniform, regular, symmetrical, equal, even, alike, unvaried.

Ant.—Variable, varying, diverse, heterogeneous, irregular, bizarre, eccentric, varied, unlike.

Uninterrupted, incessant, continuous, perpetual, unceasing, endless.

Ant.—Intermittent, recurrent.

Union, junction, combination, alliance, confederacy, league, coalition, agreement, concert.

Ant.—Separation, disunion, divorce, secession, discord, disagreement, division.

Unique, unequaled, uncommon, rare, choice, matchless, unequal.

Ant.—Ordinary, commonplace, common.

Unison, harmony, concord, agreement, union.

Ant.—Discord, disunion, variance.

Unite, join, conjoin, combine, connect, add, attach, incorporate, embody, clench, merge, concert.
Ant.—Separate, sever, divide, part, sunder, disintegrate, disrupt.

Unity, oneness, concord, uniformity, agreement.
Ant.—Plurality, multitude, complexity, discord, variety, diversity.

Universal, general, all, entire, total, catholic.
Ant.—Special, particular, partial, local, exclusive, sectional, limited.

Unlimited, infinite, absolute, boundless, undefined.
Ant.—Limited, finite.

Unreasonable, foolish, silly, absurd, preposterous, ridiculous, immoderate.
Ant.—Reasonable, rational, sensible, certain, logical, sagacious, undeniable, wise.

Unrivaled, unequaled, unique unexampled, incomparable, matchless.
Ant.—Equaled, common, ordinary, average, mediocre.

Unroll, unfold, open, discover.
Ant.—Conceal, suppress, mask, screen, cover, lose, secrete, miss.

Unruly, ungovernable, unmanageable, refractory.
Ant.—Gentle, governable, manageable, tractable, docile.

Unseemly, unbecoming, indecorous, unsuitable, unfit, unbefitting.
Ant.—Decorous, polite, respectful, obedient, refined.

Unsteady, wavering, unstable, variable, fickle, restless, fitful.
Ant.—Steady, fixed, firm, stable.

Untruth. (See Lie.)

Unusual, rare, singular, uncommon, remarkable, strange, extraordinary, unwonted.
Ant.—Usual, common, average, ordinary.

Upbraid. (See Blame.)

Uphold, maintain, defend, sustain, support, vindicate.
Ant.—Drop, betray, abandon, oppose, attack, abjure, renounce, desert.

Upright, vertical, perpendicular, erect, just, equitable, fair, pure, honorable.
Ant.—Inclined, horizontal, inverted, dishonest, corrupt, prone, iniquitous.

Uprightness, honesty, integrity, fairness, goodness, probity, honor, virtue.
Ant.—Dishonesty, vice.

Uproar, tumult, row, riot, disturbance, brawl, noise, clamor.
Ant.—Peace, quiet, order, silence.

Uproot, eradicate, exterminate, weed out.
Ant.—Sow, implant, cultivate, nurture, foster.

Urbanity. (See Affability.)

Urge, incite, impel, push, drive, instigate, stimulate, press, induce, solicit.
Ant.—Hold, restrain, retain, prohibit, retard, hinder, obstruct, impede, hold back, discourage.

Urgent, pressing, important, imperative, immediate, serious, cogent, wanted.
Ant.—Unimportant, trivial, insignificant, feeble, inconclusive, powerless, weak.

Usage, custom, fashion, practice, prescription.
Ant.—Anomaly, exception.

Use, *n.* usage, practice, habit, custom, advantage, utility, benefit, application, avail.
Ant.—Disuse, obscurity, neglect, desuetude.

Use, *v.* employ, exercise, occupy, practice, accustom, inure.
Ant.—Discard, suspend, ignore, avoid, abuse.

Useful, advantageous, serviceable, available, helpful, beneficial, good.
Ant.—Useless, fruitless, ineffectual, unavailable, unprofitable, bootless, futile, null, unavailing, unserviceable, vain, worthless.

Useless, unserviceable, fruitless, idle, profitless, vain, ineffectual.
Ant.—Useful, advantageous, helpful, beneficial.

Usual, ordinary, common, accustomed, habitual, wonted, customary, general.
Ant.—Unusual, uncommon, rare, exceptional, extraordinary, abnormal, irregular.

Usurp, arrogate, seize, appropriate, assume.
Ant.—Receive, inherit, accept, yield, render, surrender.

Utility. (See Use.)

Utmost, farthest, remotest, uttermost, greatest.
Ant.—Nearest, next.

Utter, *a.* extreme, excessive, sheer, mere, pure.
Ant.—Moderate, palliative, partial, superficial.

Utter, *v.* speak, articulate, pronounce, express, issue.
Ant.—Suppress, repress, hush, stifle, retain, hear, conceal, hide.

Utterly, totally, completely, wholly, quite, entirely, altogether.
Ant.—Partly, partially, in a measure, incompletely.

V

Vacant, empty, unfilled, unoccupied, thoughtless, unthinking.
Ant.—Full, filled, employed, engaged, occupied, thoughtful, tenanted.

Vacation, holiday, recreation.
Ant.—Term, business.

Vagrant, wanderer, beggar, tramp, vagabond, rogue.
Ant.—Workman, gentleman, laborer.

Vague, unsettled, undetermined, uncertain, indefinite, pointless.
Ant.—Definite, specific, limited, determined, strict, precise.

Vain, useless, fruitless, empty, worthless, inflated, proud, unreal, unavailing, conceited, vapid.
Ant.—Solid, real, substantial, sound, efficient, effectual, potent, modest, humble.

Valiant, brave, bold, valorous, courageous, gallant.
Ant.—Timid, cowardly, craven, cringing, timorous.

Valid, weighty, strong, powerful, sound, binding, efficient.
Ant.—Invalid, weak, powerless, unsound, false, insufficient, void.

Valor, courage, gallantry, boldness, bravery, heroism.
Ant.—Cowardice.

Valuable, precious, costly, dear, expensive, inestimable.
Ant.—Valueless, cheap, poor, worthless, mean.

Value, appraise, assess, reckon, appreciate, estimate, price, esteem, treasure.
Ant.—Despise, underrate, undervalue, disregard, dislike, scorn, contemn.

Vanish, disappear, melt, fade, dissolve.
Ant.—Appear, approach, loom, emerge.

Vanity, emptiness, conceit, self-conceit, affectedness.
Ant.—Substance, reality, truth, simplicity, modesty, humility, fullness.

Vanquish. (See Conquer.)

Vapid, dull, flat, insipid, stale, tame.
Ant.—Spirited, animated, pungent, pithy, sparkling, brilliant.

Vapor, fume, smoke, mist, fog, steam.
Ant.—Water, substance, fluid.

Variable, changeable, unsteady, inconstant, shifting, wavering, fickle, restless.
Ant.—Invariable, firm, constant, true, unchangeable, staunch, inimitable, changeless, stable.

Variance, disagreement, dissension, jarring, quarrel.
Ant.—Unity, reconciliation, harmony, peace, consent.

Variation, change, diversity, deviation, discrepancy, difference.
Ant.—Continuance, fixity, law, rule, uniformity, harmony.

Variety, difference, diversity, change, diversification, mixture, medley, miscellany.
Ant.—Uniformity, species, type, specimen, sameness, monotony.

Vary, change, alter, modify, diversify, variegate, differ, disagree.
Ant.—Perpetuate, strengthen, conform, harmonize.

Vast, enormous, spacious, boundless, mighty, immense, colossal, gigantic, huge, prodigious.
Ant.—Confined, limited.

Vaunt, boast, puff, hawk, advertise, flourish, parade, brag, display, flaunt.
Ant.—Suppress, conceal, disparage, decry, detract, cover.

Vehement, furious, ardent, fervid, burning, raging, eager, impetuous, forcible, vigorous.
Ant.—Mild, feeble, subdued, cold, passionless, weak.

Veil, screen, hide, intercept, mask, conceal, cover, disguise.
Ant.—Unveil, expose, strip, denude, exaggerate.

Velocity, swiftness, quickness, fleetness, celerity, speed, rapidity.
Ant.—Slowness, languor, inactivity, sluggishness.

Vend. (See Sell.)

Venerable, grave, sage, wise, old, reverend.
Ant.—Contemptible, despicable, young, foolish, frivolous, flighty.

Venial, pardonable, excusable, justifiable.
Ant.—Unpardonable, mortal, inexcusable, grave, serious.

Venom, poison, virus, spite, malice, malignity.
Ant.—Antidote, cure, corrective, remedy.

Venture, *n.* speculation, chance, peril, stake.
Ant.—Caution, calculation, insurance, protection, safety, assurance, security.

Venture, *v.* dare, risk, jeopardize, adventure, hazard.
Ant.—Calculate, reserve, insure, protect, guard, think, know, determine.

Veracity, truth, truthfulness, credibility, accuracy.
Ant.—Falsehood, deceit, imagination, fiction, fraud, lie, untruth.

Verbal, oral, spoken, literal, unwritten.
Ant.—Written, documentary, recorded.

Verdict, judgment, finding, decision, answer.
Ant.—Indecision, indetermination.

Verge. (See Border.)

Versatile, unsteady, changeable, unfixed, wavering, vacillating, oscillating, fluctuating, inconstant, fickle, restless, manifold.
Ant.—Immovable, fixed, onesided, uniform, narrow, limited, stolid, immobile.

Versed, skilled, practiced, conversant, clever, proficient.
Ant.—Awkward, unskilled, ignorant, strange, unfamiliar.

Vexation, chagrin, mortification.
Ant.—Pleasure, gratification.

Vibrate, oscillate, swing, sway, wave, undulate, thrill.
Ant.—Stand, remain, proceed, advance.

Vice, corruption, depravity, pollution, immorality, wickedness, guilt, iniquity, crime, fault, defect, blemish, vileness.
Ant.—Virtue, purity, perfection, goodness, holiness, integrity, morality.

Vicious, corrupt, depraved, debased, bad, contrary, unruly, demoralized, profligate, faulty, malicious.
Ant.—Pure, sound, perfect, virtuous, good.

Victim, sacrifice, food, prey, sufferer, dupe, gull.
Ant.—Sacrificer, seducer, attacker, fraud, cheat.

Victuals, viands, bread, meat, repast, provisions, fare, food.

View, *n.* thought, notion, sentiment, opinion, perspective, landscape, purpose, intention, design, light, aspect, end.
Ant.—Darkness, blindness, deception, error, delusion, misconception.

View, *v.* look, see, behold, eye, observe, scan, regard, prospect, survey.
Ant.—Ignore, overlook, disregard, miss, misjudge, oversight.

Vigilant, watchful, wakeful, observant, cautious, careful.
Ant.—Careless, inattentive, indifferent.

Vigorous, healthy, strong, powerful, energetic, stalwart, robust, hardy, firm, spirited, determined.
Ant.—Weak, feeble, powerless, debilitated, inactive, indolent, irresolute.

Vile, ignoble, base, low, worthless, abject, sordid, mean, dishonorable, sinful, wicked, vicious.
Ant.—Good, noble, exalted, pure, honorable, costly, rare, precious.

Vilify, debase, degrade, slander, decry, defame, scandalize, upbraid, brand, stigmatize, denounce.
Ant.—Purify, refine, exalt, raise, improve, praise, laud.

Vindicate, justify, assert, uphold, support, defend.
Ant.—Fail, abandon, surrender, forego, nullify, destroy, subvert, vitiate, condemn.

Vindictive, spiteful, resentful, revengeful, unforgiving.
Ant.—Forgiving, generous, merciful, forbearing.

Violate, infringe, transgress, disobey, injure, hurt, ravish.
Ant.—Respect, foster, cherish, protect, regard, preserve, obey.

Violence, passion, rage, fury, vehemence, outrage, injustice.
Ant.—Mildness, self-restraint, gentleness, forbearance, self-control, obedience, protection.

Violent, forcible, raving, raging, passionate, furious, rapid, dashing, sweeping, rolling, boisterous, impetuous, vehement.
Ant.—Mild, feeble, calm, soft, gentle, quiet.

Virtuous, just, upright, moral, chaste, pure, honest.
Ant.—Vicious, bad, corrupt, debased, impure, immoral.

Visible. (See Apparent.)

Vision, apparition, dream, ghost, phantom, specter.
Ant.—Fact, reality, realization, verity.

Vital, living, necessary, essential, indispensable.
Ant.—Mortal, lifeless, unnecessary, unimportant, immaterial.

Vivacious, lively, brisk, gay, merry, racy, sprightly.
Ant.—Dead, lifeless, dull, stolid, moody, heavy, sullen, torpid, sluggish.

Vivid, lively, clear, lucid, bright, sunny, glowing, graphic.
Ant.—Dull, opaque, obscure, somber, dim, dusky, cloudy, pale, wan.
Vocation, profession, calling, trade, business, employment, office, mission.
Ant.—Leisure, incapacity.
Vogue, usage, way, custom, fashion, use, practice.
Ant.—Disuse, disrepute.
Void, null, invalid, unfilled, empty, hollow, useless, nugatory.
Ant.—Occupied, full, solid, valid, efficacious, sound.
Volume, book, scroll, bulk, size, capacity.
Ant.—Pamphlet, sheet, minuteness, smallness.
Voluntary, free, spontaneous, unconstrained, deliberate.
Ant.—Compulsory, involuntary, coercive.
Voluptuary, epicure, sensualist.
Ant.—Stoic, moralist.
Voracious, ravenous, rapacious, greedy.
Ant.—Generous.
Voracity, greediness.
Vote, suffrage, voice.
Vouch, certify, affirm, asseverate, aver, assure.
Ant.—Deny.
Vulgar, common, general, popular, ordinary, rude, coarse, low.
Ant.—Scientific, philosophic, restricted, technical, select, choice, refined, polite, well-bred.
Vulnerable, assailable, weak, exposed, tender.
Ant.—Invulnerable, impregnable, unassailable.

W

Waft, transport, bear, convey.
Ant.—Push, pull, drag, draw.
Wag, humorist, jester, joker, wit.
Ant.—Dullard, butt.
Wage, make, carry on, engage in, undertake.
Ant.—Desist, stop, abandon.
Wages, salary, hire, allowance, stipend, pay, remuneration, earnings, compensation.
Ant.—Gratuity, gift, premium, grace, bonus.
Wait, await, abide, bide, stay, remain, tarry, expect, look for.
Ant.—Speed, hasten, press, abandon, avoid, reject, shun.
Waive, forego, relinquish, let go.
Ant.—Press, urge, claim, arrest, enforce.
Wake, waken, awaken, arouse, stir up, excite, kindle, provoke.
Ant.—Soothe, allay, hush, quiet, tranquilize.
Wakeful, sleepless, vigilant, wary, watchful.
Ant.—Drowsy, dreamy, sleepy, somnolent.
Wander, stroll, ramble, gad, rove, roam, range, stray, err, deviate, swerve.
Ant.—Rest, stop, halt, lie, anchor, alight, moor, pause, repose.
Wandering, vagrant, roving, strolling, discursive.
Ant.—Stationary, fixed, immovable, permanent.
Want, *v.* need, lack, require, desire, wish, crave for.
Ant.—Supply, offer, demand, give, afford, furnish.
Want, *n.* poverty, penury, indigence, destitution, privation, necessity, need, lack, scarcity.
Ant.—Supply, sufficiency, provision, abundance, production, adequacy, plenty.
Wanton, licentious, libertine, unrestrained, unbridled, uncurbed, dissolute, loose, lax.
Ant.—Staid, sober, demure, austere, formal, deliberate.
Ward, avert, parry, fend, repel, turn aside, guard, defend.
Ant.—Attack, betray, surrender.
Warlike, bellicose, hostile, inimical, military.
Ant.—Friendly, peaceful.
Warm, fervid, affectionate, attached, devoted, ardent, fervent, glowing.
Ant.—Frigid, cold, tepid, indifferent, passionless.
Warmth, ardor, fervency, fervor, cordiality, vehemence, heat, fervidness, glow.
Ant.—Frigidity, frost, coldness, calmness, indifference, apathy, slowness.
Warning. (See Admonition.)
Warrant, guarantee, insure, assure, secure, justify.
Ant.—Endanger, nullify, invalidate, repudiate.
Wary, careful, cautious, circumspect, guarded, watchful, heedful, prudent, vigilant.
Ant.—Unwary, unsuspecting, heedless, unguarded, foolhardy, reckless, intrepid.
Wash, clean, rinse, wet, moisten.
Ant.—Soil, foul, contaminate, dirty, stain.
Waste, *v.* squander, dissipate, lavish, destroy, decay, dwindle, wither.
Ant.—Restore, repair, preserve, protect, husband, economize, hoard, accumulate, multiply, develop, save.
Waste, *a.* desolate, stripped, bare, dreary, unproductive, wild, uncultivated.
Ant.—Fertile, productive, cultivated.
Wasteful, extravagant, profligate.
Ant.—Economical, frugal.
Watchful, alert, vigilant, attentive, cautious, heedful, observant, circumspect, wakeful.
Ant.—Heedless, incautious, drowsy, careless, unwary, distracted.
Wave, breaker, billow, surge.
Waver, *v.* hesitate, scruple, fluctuate, vacillate, flicker, quiver, flutter.
Ant.—Determine, decide, settle, rest, repose, abide, hold fast, stay, stick.
Wavering, unsteady, unsettled, fluctuating, changeable, inconstant, variable.
Ant.—Steady, constant, fixed, immovable, changeless.
Way, method, plan, system, means, manner, mode, form, fashion, course, process, road, route, track,. path, habit, practice.
Ant.—Chance, hazard, conjecture, luck.
Wayward, obstinate, stubborn, unruly, perverse.
Ant.—Docile, manageable, amenable.
Weak, feeble, infirm, enfeebled, debilitated, powerless, helpless, emaciated, prostrate, thin, watery, diluted, flimsy, slight, poor, silly, defenseless.
Ant.—Strong, vigorous, robust, muscular, powerful, tough, stout, sturdy, hard, potent, efficient, spirited, animated, sound, judicious, determined, forcible, able.
Weaken, enfeeble, debilitate, unnerve, paralyze, emaciate, attentuate, dilute, enervate, invalidate.
Ant.—Strengthen, empower, invigorate, confirm.
Weakness, feebleness, infirmity, frailty, silliness, imbecility, prostration, defect, failing, foible.
Ant.—Strength, power, nerve, spirit, vigor, activity, efficiency.
Wealth, riches, opulence, affluence, plenty, mammon, abundance.
Ant.—Poverty, destitution, indigence, scarcity, impecuniosity.

Wear, bear, carry, last, consume.
Ant.—Doff, abandon.
Weariness, exhaustion, languor, lassitude, fatigue.
Ant.—Buoyancy, vigor.
Wearisome, tedious, tiresome.
Ant.—Interesting, entertaining.
Weary, tired, fatigued, exhausted, worn, faint, harass, jade, tire, fatigue.
Ant.—Fresh, vigorous, renovated, hearty, refresh, inspire.
Wedding, marriage, nuptials, espousal.
Ant.—Divorce, celibacy, singleness.
Weight, heaviness, pressure, oppression, burden, load, value, gravity.
Ant.—Lightness, weakness, levity, triviality, worthlessness.
Welcome, acceptable, agreeable, pleasing, grateful, pleasurable, gratifying, pleasant, satisfying.
Ant.—Unwelcome, ungrateful, distasteful, unpleasant, disagreeable, disappointing, distressing, hateful, melancholy, mournful, painful, woeful, wretched.
Welfare, good fortune, prosperity, happiness, success.
Ant.—Adversity, reverse, failure, ill luck, unhappiness, harm, hurt.
Well-being, happiness, prosperity, welfare.
Ant.—Adversity, poverty.
Wheedle. (See Coax.)
Whet, sharpen, incite, excite, provoke, stimulate.
Ant.—Blunt, pall, deaden, satiate, nauseate.
Whimsical, odd, singular, capricious, fanciful, fantastic, fantastical.
Ant.—Staid, serious, sober, sedate, orderly.
Whirl. (See Turn.)
White, snowy, pure, spotless, unspotted, unblemished, stainless, clean.
Ant.—Black, impure, stained, dirty, foul.
Whole, sound, healthy, well, total, all, entire, perfect, complete, integral, aggregate, undivided.
Ant.—Sick, unsound, impaired, partial, imperfect, incomplete, part.
Wholesome, nutritious, healthy salubrious, healing, salutary.
Ant.—Unwholesome, unhealthy, deleterious, detrimental.
Wholly, entirely, totally, altogether, quite, perfectly, completely, utterly.
Ant.—Partially, partly, in part, mostly.
Wicked, bad, ill, unjust, irreligious, ungodly, godless, profane, impious, unhallowed, black, dark, foul, atrocious, villainous, monstrous, outrageous, profligate, abandoned, iniquitous, nefarious.
Ant.—Good, virtuous, just, moral, upright, honest, pure, stainless, sinless, incorrupt, spotless, honorable, esteemed, immaculate.
Wickedness, evil, sin, crime, criminality, guilt, iniquity, offense, vileness, turpitude, corruption, vice, pollution.
Ant.—Goodness, virtue, order, law, honor, purity.
Wide, broad, ample, large, expanded, diffuse, extensive.
Ant.—Narrow, contracted, limited.
Wild, savage, uncivilized, loose, irregular, disorderly, untamed, undomesticated, unruly.
Ant.—Tame, civilized, cultivated, inhabited, regular, peaceful, domesticated, docile, gentle, mild, regulated, sane, coherent, sensible, calm.
Wilful, perverse, stubborn, self-willed, headstrong, obstinate.
Ant.—Thoughtful, considerate, amenable, docile, manageable, accidental, unintentional.
Will, determination, resolution, volition, wish, desire.
Willingly, voluntarily, spontaneously, gratuitously.
Ant.—Unwillingly, involuntarily, grudgingly.
Win, get, obtain, gain, procure, effect, accomplish, achieve, realize.
Ant.—Lose, fail, miss, forfeit, alienate.
Wind, coil, twine, wreathe, turn, bend, curve, twist.
Ant.—Unwind, untwist, uncoil, straighten.
Winning, attractive, charming, captivating, fascinating, bewitching, enchanting, dazzling, brilliant.
Ant.—Repulsive, unattractive, displeasing, disagreeable, hateful, unlovely.
Wisdom, sense, knowledge, learning, prudence, judgment, intelligence, sagacity, information, foresight, far-sightedness.
Ant.—Ignorance, imprudence, folly, foolishness, improvidence.
Wise, intelligent, learned, skilled, judicious, rational, discreet, prudent.
Ant.—Ignorant, foolish, stupid, imprudent, indiscreet.
Wit, mind, intellect, understanding, genius, imagination, humor, satire, irony, mirth, fun, raillery.
Ant.—Dullness, vapidity, stupidity, platitude, commonplace, solemnity, stolidity.
Withdraw, retreat, retire, go back, recede, recall, regress, retrograde, take back.
Ant.—Offer, proffer, produce, afford, confirm, reiterate, repeat.
Withhold, keep back, restrain, arrest, hinder, abstain, refrain, keep from, desist from, refuse, retain, reserve.
Ant.—Grant, furnish, afford, provide, allow, give, permit, encourage, incite, aid, help, abet.
Withstand, oppose, resist, thwart, confront.
Ant.—Yield, submit, surrender, support, encourage, aid.
Witness, attest, testify, evidence, prove, certify, vouch, see, behold, view, observe.
Ant.—Refute, invalidate.
Wizard, juggler, magician, conjurer, necromancer, sorcerer.
Ant.—Dupe, dolt, ignoramus.
Woe, distress, sorrow, affliction, disaster, trouble.
Ant.—Joy, gladness, comfort, happiness, prosperity, blessing.
Wonder, *n.* amazement, surprise, astonishment, admiration, miracle, marvel, prodigy, curiosity.
Ant.—Indifference, apathy, expectation, familiarity, triviality, anticipation, commonplace, truism.
Wonder, *v.* admire, amaze, astonish, surprise.
Wonderful, marvelous, wondrous, amazing, astonishing, striking, surprising, admirable.
Ant.—Common, regular, normal, usual, customary, expected, anticipated, calculated, natural.
Wondrous. (See Wonderful.)
Word, term, expression, accent, promise, engagement, account, tidings, message, order, command.
Ant.—Idea, conception.
Work, *n.* employment, business, occupation, performance, production, toil, task labor, achievement, action, drudgery

Ant.—Rest, nonperformance, leisure, holiday, ease, idleness, play, recreation, repose.

Work, *v.* labor, toil, drudge, strive, exert, ply.

Ant.—Rest, sleep, play, refresh, amuse, enjoy.

Workman, artisan, mechanic, craftsman, artificer, journeyman, operative.

Ant.—Idler, tramp, vagrant, vagabond.

Worldly, terrestrial, mundane, temporal, secular, carnal, earthly.

Ant.—Unworldly, spiritual, religious, moral.

Worry, plague, tease, torment, vex, annoy, irritate, fret.

Ant.—Soothe, calm, gratify, please, amuse, quiet.

Worship, adore, revere, venerate, reverence, deify, idolize, honor, respect.

Ant.—Despise, blaspheme, rail, jeer, loathe, abominate, curse, execrate.

Worth, price, value, desert, merit, virtue, excellence.

Ant.—Worthlessness, demerit, cheapness.

Worthless, useless, valueless, frivolous, corrupt, dissolute, abject, base, cheap, degraded, ignoble, low, mean, vile.

Ant.—Valuable, worthy, rich, rare, costly, estimable, excellent, noble, precious, admirable, virtuous, esteemed, exalted, honorable, honored, pure.

Worthy, excellent, deserving, eligible, preferable, meritorious, estimable, commendable, laudable, praiseworthy.

Ant.—Worthless, useless, valueless.

Wrap, muffle, envelop, fold, encase.

Ant.—Unwind, unfold, unwrap, develop, expose, show.

Wrath. (See Anger.)

Wrathful, angry, ireful, enraged, infuriated, exasperated.

Ant.—Calm, pleased, quiet.

Wreck, debris, ruins, havoc, rubbish.

Ant.—Perfection, completeness.

Wretched, deplorable, miserable, unhappy, distressed, afflicted, unfortunate, afflicting, disastrous, calamitous, dreary, dismal.

Ant.—Prosperous, happy, admirable, noble, worthy, elated.

Wretchedness, misery, woe, distress, misfortune, calamity, disaster, affliction, unhappiness.

Ant.—Happiness, prosperity, pleasure, joy.

Writer, scribe, penman, author, scribbler, amanuensis, clerk, secretary.

Ant.—Speaker, orator, reader.

Writhe, distort, contort, twist, wrest, wrench, wring.

Ant.—Quiet, soothe, calm, rest.

Written, penned, inscribed, transcribed.

Ant.—Traditional, verbal.

Wrong, bad, evil, incorrect, erroneous, unsuitable, improper, unjust, dishonesty, injustice, injury, partiality, unfairness, untruth.

Ant.—Right, fit, proper, suitable, correct, accurate, just, fair, moral, beneficial, equity, fairness, integrity, law, justice, rectitude, truth, virtue.

Wry, twisted, distorted, awry, crooked, askew.

Ant.—Straight, right, fit, just, proper, comely, true.

Y

Yawn, gape, open wide.

Ant.—Close, snap.

Yearly, annually, year by year, per annum.

Ant.—Momentarily, eternally, weekly, daily, monthly.

Yearn, hanker after, long for, desire, crave.

Ant.—Despise, loathe, recoil, dislike, avoid, turn from.

Yell, bellow, cry out, scream.

Yellow, golden, saffron-like.

Yelp, bark, sharp cry, howl.

Yeoman, farmer, freeholder, commoner.

Ant.—Esquire, gentleman.

Yet, besides, nevertheless, however, ultimately, notwithstanding, still, at last, so far, thus far.

Yield, bear, give, afford, impart, bestow, abdicate, resign, cede, surrender, relinquish, relax, forego, let go, waive, comply, accede, acquiesce, succumb, submit, quit, give up, assent.

Ant.—Withdraw, withhold, retain, deny, refuse, assert, claim, disallow, resist, dissent, protest, struggle, strive, decline, demur, object, oppose.

Yielding, supple, pliant, bending, compliant, submissive, unresisting.

Ant.—Unyielding, stubborn, dogged, persevering, obstinate, resolute.

Yoke, couple, link, connect, associate, join, unite.

Ant.—Unyoke, unhitch, sever, disconnect, separate, liberate, release, divorce, alienate, detach, disjoin, divide, part.

Yore, long ago, long since.

Ant.—Now.

Young, juvenile, inexperienced, youthful.

Ant.—Old, ancient, tried.

Youth, boy, lad, minority, adolescence, juvenility.

Ant.—Man, maid, woman, maturity, majority, senility, age.

Youthful, young, juvenile, boyish, girlish, puerile.

Ant.—Old, aged, senile, mature.

Z

Zeal, fervor, ardor, earnestness, enthusiasm, energy, eagerness.

Ant.—Apathy, indifference, torpor, coldness, detachment.

Zealot, bigot, partisan, fanatic.

Ant.—Renegade, traitor, deserter.

Zealous, warm, ardent, fervent, enthusiastic, anxious.

Ant.—Careless, indifferent, unconcerned.

Zenith, top, apex, summit, pinnacle, climax.

Ant.—Bottom, nadir.

Zest, relish, gusto, flavor.

Ant.—Distaste, disrelish, detriment, indifference, apathy, disgust, dislike.

CONCISE TREASURY OF
POPULAR QUOTATIONS

Selections from the writings of the foremost authors, poets, and philosophers of all time

Compiled by Gertrude Zimmerman

He ranged his tropes and preached up patience,
Backed his opinions with quotations.

MATTHEW PRIOR,
Paulo Purganti and His Wife

Ability

No one knows what it is that he can do till he tries.

PUBLILIUS SYRUS

Natural abilities are like natural plants; they need pruning by study.

FRANCIS BACON. *Essays*

Every person is responsible for only the good within his abilities, and for no more, and no one can tell whose sphere is the largest.

GAIL HAMILTON,
Country Living and Country Thinking

They can because they think they can.

VERGIL

And all may do what has by man been done.

EDWARD YOUNG, *Night Thoughts*

The winds and waves are always on the side of the ablest navigators.

EDWARD GIBBON,
Decline and Fall of the Roman Empire

Absence

Absence makes the heart grow fonder.

THOMAS HAYNES BAYLY, *Isle of Beauty*

It so falls out,
That what we have we prize not to the worth
Whiles we enjoy it; but being lacked and lost,
Why, then, we reck the value.

WILLIAM SHAKESPEARE,
Much Ado about Nothing

Say, is not absence death to those who love?

ALEXANDER POPE, *Autumn*

Abuse

Abuse, if you slight it, will gradually die away; but if you show yourself irritated you will be thought to have deserved it.

TACITUS

Accomplishment (*See also* Deeds)

Something attempted, something done,
Has earned a night's repose.

HENRY WADSWORTH LONGFELLOW,
The Village Blacksmith

Action (*See also* Deeds)

Let us do or die.

ROBERT BURNS, *Bannockburn*

Deeds let escape are never to be done.

ROBERT BROWNING, *Sordello*

Actions are our epochs.

LORD BYRON, *Manfred*

Action is transitory—a step, a blow—
The motion of a muscle—this way or that—
'Tis done; and in the after-vacancy
We wonder at ourselves like men betrayed.

WILLIAM WORDSWORTH,
The White Doe of Rylstone

The keen spirit
Seizes the prompt occasion, makes the thought
Start into instant action, and at once
Plans and performs, resolves and executes!

HANNAH MORE, *Daniel*

Be good, sweet maid, and let who will be clever;
Do noble things, not dream them, all day long.

CHARLES KINGSLEY, *A Farewell*

Count that day lost whose low descending sun
Views from thy hand no worthy action done.

AUTHOR UNKNOWN. FROM STANIFORD'S *Art of Reading*

Let us, then, be up and doing,
With a heart for any fate;
Still achieving, still pursuing,
Learn to labor and to wait.

HENRY WADSWORTH LONGFELLOW, *A Psalm of Life*

The all of things is an infinite conjugation of the verb *to do*.

THOMAS CARLYLE, *The French Revolution*

Better to reign in hell than serve in heaven.

JOHN MILTON, *Paradise Lost*

Only the actions of the just
Smell sweet and blossom in the dust.

JAMES SHIRLEY, *Contention of Ajax and Ulysses*

Actions of the last age are like almanacs of the last year.

SIR JOHN DENHAM, *The Sophy*

In every deed of mischief he had a heart to resolve, a head to contrive, and a hand to execute.

EDWARD GIBBON, *Decline and Fall of the Roman Empire*

Actions speak louder than words.

Proverb

Handsome is as handsome does.

OLIVER GOLDSMITH, *The Vicar of Wakefield*

Admiration

Fools admire, but men of sense approve.

ALEXANDER POPE, *Essay on Criticism*

A fool always finds a greater fool to admire him.

NICHOLAS BOILEAU

Advancement (*See also* Ambition)

Some rise by sin, and some by virtue fall.

WILLIAM SHAKESPEARE, *Measure for Measure*

Adversity

Great things thro' greatest
hazards are achiev'd,
And then they shine.

BEAUMONT AND FLETCHER, *Loyal Subject*

Of all the horrid, hideous notes of woe,
Sadder than low-songs on the midnight blast,
Is that portentous phrase, "*I told you so.*"

LORD BYRON, *Don Juan*

Who has not known ill fortune, never knew
Himself, or his own virtue.

MALLET AND THOMSON, *Alfred*

We bleed, we tremble, we forget, we smile;
The mind turns fool before the cheek is dry.

EDWARD YOUNG, *Night Thoughts*

Into each life some rain must fall,
Some days must be dark and dreary.

HENRY WADSWORTH LONGFELLOW, *The Rainy Day*

The greatest works of admiration,
And all the fair examples of renown,
Out of distress and misery are grown.

SAMUEL DANIEL, *Earl of Southampton*

Advice

One gives nothing so liberally as advice.

LA ROCHEFOUCAULD, *Maximes*

We ask advice, but we mean approbation.

CHARLES CALEB COLTON, *Lacon*

The worst men give oft the best advice.

PHILIP JAMES BAILEY, *Festus*

Let him be so,
For counsel still is folly's deadly foe.

WILLIAM SHAKESPEARE, *London Prodigal*

Write down the advice of him who loves you, though you like it not at present.

Proverb

I pray thee cease thy counsel,
Which falls into mine ears as profitless
As water in a sieve.

WILLIAM SHAKESPEARE, *Much Ado about Nothing*

Aging (*See also* Old Age; Middle Age; Youth)

Old man, forswear that dogged rumba
Go home and yield to Christian slumba.

MARGARET FISHBACK, *Time for a Quick One*[1]

Every man desires to live long, but no man would be old.

JONATHAN SWIFT, *Thoughts on Various Subjects*

In youth, what disappointments of our own making: in age, what disappointments from the nature of things.

EDWARD YOUNG, *True Estimate of Human Life*

Like our shadows,
Our wishes lengthen as our sun declines.

EDWARD YOUNG, *Night Thoughts*

---

[1]Copyright 1940, by Margaret Fishback. Reprinted by permission of Harcourt, Brace and Company, Inc.

Oh, sir! I must not tell my age.
They say women and music should never be dated.

OLIVER GOLDSMITH, *She Stoops to Conquer*

In youth we run into difficulties, in old age, difficulties run into us.

JOSH BILLINGS (HENRY WHEELER SHAW)

Our youth we can have but today,
We may always find time to grow old.

BISHOP BERKELEY, *Can Love Be Controlled by Advice?*

Youth is a blunder, manhood a struggle; old age a regret.

BENJAMIN DISRAELI, *Coningsby*

Young men soon give and soon forget affronts;
Old age is slow in both.

JOSEPH ADDISON, *Cato*

Agreeability

"My idea of an agreeable person," said Hugo Bohun, "is a person who agrees with me."

BENJAMIN DISRAELI, *Lothair*

Amazement

And still they gazed, and still the wonder grew,
That one small head could carry all he knew.

OLIVER GOLDSMITH, *The Deserted Village*

Ambition (*See also* Advancement; Aspiration)

'T is a common proof,
That lowliness is young ambition's ladder,
Whereto the climber-upward turns his face;
But when he once attains the utmost round,
He then unto the ladder turns his back,
Looks in the clouds, scorning the base degrees
By which he did ascend.

WILLIAM SHAKESPEARE, *Julius Caesar*

Ambition has but one reward for all:
A little power, a little transient fame,
A grave to rest in, and a fading name.

WILLIAM WINTER, *Queen's Domain*

Oh, sons of earth! Attempt ye still to rise
By mountains pil'd on mountains to the skies?
Heaven still with laughter the vain toil surveys,
And buries madmen in the heaps they raise.

ALEXANDER POPE, *Essay on Man*

And the final event to himself (Mr. Burke) has been, that, as he rose like a rocket, he fell like the stick.

THOMAS PAINE, *Letter to the Addressers*

I hate the man who builds his name
On ruins of another's fame.

JOHN GAY, *Fables*

Fain would I climb, but that I fear to fall.

SIR WALTER RALEIGH, *Historie of the World*

Men at some time are masters of their fates:
The fault, dear Brutus, is not in our stars,
But in ourselves that we are underlings.

WILLIAM SHAKESPEARE, *Julius Caesar*

He who surpasses or subdues mankind
Must look down on the hate of those below.

LORD BYRON, *Childe Harold's Pilgrimage*

Reign, and keep life in this our deep desire
Our only greatness is that we aspire.

JEAN INGELOW, *A Snow Mountain*

They that stand high have many blasts to shake them;
And if they fall they dash themselves to pieces.

WILLIAM SHAKESPEARE, *Richard III*

Ambition is an idol on whose wings
Great minds are carry'd only to extreme;
To be sublimely great, or to be nothing.

THOMAS SOUTHERNE, *The Loyal Brother*

Look not too high, lest a chip fall in your eye.

Proverb

The boast of heraldry, the pomp of pow'r,
And all that beauty, all that wealth e'er gave,
Await alike the inevitable hour:
The paths of glory lead but to the grave.

THOMAS GRAY, *Elegy in a Country Churchyard*

Americanism

To be prepared for war is one of the most effectual means of preserving peace.

GEORGE WASHINGTON, *Speech to both Houses of Congress*

We join ourselves to no party that does not carry the flag, and keep step to the music of the Union.

RUFUS CHOATE, *Letter to Whig Convention*

Liberty and union, now and forever, one and inseparable!

DANIEL WEBSTER, *Speech on Foote's Resolution*

The people's government, made for the people, made by the people, and answerable to the people.

DANIEL WEBSTER, *Second Speech on Foote's Resolution*

Let our object be our country, our whole country, and nothing but our country.

DANIEL WEBSTER, *Address on Laying of the Corner-stone of the Bunker Hill Monument*

Sink or swim, live or die, survive or perish, I give my hand and my heart to this vote.

DANIEL WEBSTER, *Eulogy on Adams and Jefferson*

I shall on all subjects have a policy to recommend, but none to enforce against the will of the people.

ULYSSES S. GRANT,
First Inaugural Address

Independence now and Independence forever.

DANIEL WEBSTER,
Eulogy on Adams and Jefferson

The world must be made safe for democracy.

WOODROW WILSON,
War Address to Congress

And ne'er shall the sons of Columbia be slaves,
While the earth bears a plant, or the sea rolls its waves.

ROBERT TREAT PAINE,
Adams and Liberty

Then join hand in hand, brave Americans all;
By uniting we stand, by dividing we fall.

JOHN DICKINSON,
The Liberty Song

Let independence be our boast,
Ever mindful what it cost;
Ever grateful for the prize,
Let its altar reach the skies!

JOSEPH HOPKINSON,
Hail, Columbia

Our country! in her intercourse with foreign nations may she always be in the right; but our country, right or wrong!

STEPHEN DECATUR, *Toast*

There is no right to strike against the public safety by anybody, anywhere, any time.

CALVIN COOLIDGE,
Letter to Samuel Gompers

In the field of world policy, I would dedicate this nation to the policy of the good neighbor.

FRANKLIN DELANO ROOSEVELT,
First Inaugural Address

This generation of Americans has a rendezvous with destiny.

FRANKLIN DELANO ROOSEVELT,
Speech Accepting Renomination

We aim at the assurance of a rounded and permanent national life. We do not distrust the future of essential democracy.

FRANKLIN DELANO ROOSEVELT,
First Inaugural Address

The test of our progress is not whether we add more to the abundance of those who have much; it is whether we provide enough for those who have too little.

FRANKLIN DELANO ROOSEVELT,
Second Inaugural Address

We must be the great arsenal of democracy.

FRANKLIN DELANO ROOSEVELT,
Fireside Chat, Dec. 29, 1940

We do not see faith, hope and charity as unattainable ideals, but we use them as stout supports of a nation fighting the fight for freedom in a modern civilization.

FRANKLIN DELANO ROOSEVELT,
Renomination Speech

This hand, to tyrants ever sworn the foe,
For Freedom only deals the deadly blow;
Then sheathes in calm repose the vengeful blade,
For gentle peace in Freedom's hallowed shade.

JOHN QUINCY ADAMS

I believe this government cannot endure permanently half slave and half free.

ABRAHAM LINCOLN,
Speech, Republican State Convention, 1858

Speak softly and carry a big stick: you will go far.

THEODORE ROOSEVELT, *Address*

Blandishments will not fascinate us, nor will threats of a "halter" intimidate. For, under God, we are determined that, wheresoever, whensoever, or howsoever we shall be called to make our exit, we will die free men.

JOSIAH QUINCY,
Observations on the Boston Port Bill

We have met the enemy, and they are ours.

OLIVER H. PERRY,
Dispatch to General Harrison

Freedom of religion; freedom of the press; freedom of person under the protection of the habeas corpus; and trial by juries impartially selected, —these principles form the bright constellation which has gone before us, and guided our steps through an age of revolution and reformation.

THOMAS JEFFERSON,
First Inaugural Address

It is not best to swap horses when crossing a stream.

ABRAHAM LINCOLN,
upon his renomination.

With malice toward none, with charity for all, with firmness in the right, as God gives us to see the right, let us strive on to finish the work we are in.

ABRAHAM LINCOLN,
Second Inaugural Address

That this nation, under God, shall have a new birth of freedom; and that government of the people, by the people, for the people, shall not perish from the earth.

ABRAHAM LINCOLN,
Speech at Gettysburg

To the memory of the Man, first in war, first in peace, and first in the hearts of his countrymen.

COL. HENRY LEE, *Eulogy on Washington*

We mutually pledge to each other our lives, our fortunes, and our sacred honour.

THOMAS JEFFERSON,
Declaration of Independence

The God who gave us life, gave us liberty at the same time.

THOMAS JEFFERSON,
Summary View of the Rights of British America

We hold these truths to be self-evident; that all men are created equal; that they are endowed by their Creator with certain unalienable Rights; that among these are Life, Liberty, and the pursuit of Happiness.

THOMAS JEFFERSON,
Declaration of Independence

Our federal Union, it must be preserved.

ANDREW JACKSON, *Toast*

Is life so dear, or peace so sweet, as to be purchased at the price of chains and slavery? Forbid it, Almighty God! I know not what course others may take; but, as for me, give me liberty, or give me death!

PATRICK HENRY, *Speech*

He serves his party best who serves the country best.

RUTHERFORD B. HAYES,
Inaugural Address

I only regret that I have but one life to lose for my country.

NATHAN HALE,
[Last words before being executed.]

God reigns, and the Government at Washington lives.

JAMES A. GARFIELD

They that can give up essential liberty to obtain a little temporary safety deserve neither liberty nor safety.

BENJAMIN FRANKLIN,
Historical Review of Pennsylvania

We must all hang together, else we shall all hang separately.

BENJAMIN FRANKLIN,
[Remark during signing of Declaration of Independence.]

Nothing is certain but death and taxes.

BENJAMIN FRANKLIN,
Letter to Leroy

The financial honor of this government is of too vast importance, is entirely too sacred to be the football of party politics.

WILLIAM MCKINLEY

I am for America because America is for the common people.

WILLIAM MCKINLEY

We go to war only to make peace. We never went to war with any other design. We carry the national conscience wherever we go.

WILLIAM MCKINLEY

God and man have linked the nations together.

WILLIAM MCKINLEY

No material greatness, no wealth, no accumulation of splendor, is to be compared with those humble and homely virtues which have generally characterized our American homes.

BENJAMIN HARRISON

We want no more land. We do want to improve what we have, and want to see our neighbors improve and grow so strong that the design of any other country could not endanger them.

ULYSSES S. GRANT

Performance should be made square with promise.

THEODORE ROOSEVELT

The country's honor must be upheld at home and abroad.

THEODORE ROOSEVELT

What is wanted is not more law, but a better public opinion.

JAMES G. BLAINE

He mocks the people who proposes that the government shall protect the rich that they in turn may care for the laboring poor.

GROVER CLEVELAND

An American citizen could not be a good citizen who did not have hope in his heart.

GROVER CLEVELAND

Public officers are the servants and agents of the people. Subordinates in public place should be selected and retained for their efficiency, and not because they may be used to accomplish partisan ends.

GROVER CLEVELAND

The declaration that our people are hostile to a government made by ourselves and for themselves, and conducted by themselves, is an insult.

JOHN ADAMS, *Address*

Ancestry

Our ancestors are very good kind of folks; but they are the last people I should choose to have a visiting acquaintance with.

RICHARD BRINSLEY SHERIDAN, *The Rivals*

Anger

Never forget what a man says to you when he is angry.

HENRY WARD BEECHER, *Life Thoughts*

Anger is like
A full-hot horse, who being allow'd his way,
Self-mettle tires him.

WILLIAM SHAKESPEARE, *Henry VIII*

Wise anger is like fire from a flint: there is great ado to get it out; and when it does come, it is out again immediately.

MATTHEW HENRY

When anger rushes, unrestrain'd to action,
Like a hot steed, it stumbles in its way:
The man of thought strikes deepest, and strikes safest.

RICHARD SAVAGE, *Sir Thomas Overbury*

A man's disposition is never well known till he be crossed.

FRANCIS BACON, *Advancement of Learning*

Well, no offense:
Thar ain't no sense
In gittin' riled.

FRANCIS BRET HART, *Jim*

Anger is short madness.

HORACE

He who conquers his wrath overcomes his greatest enemy.

PUBLILIUS SYRUS

Delay is the best remedy for anger.

SENECA, *De Ira*

Anger, when it is long in coming, is the stronger when it comes, and the longer felt.

FRANCIS QUARLES

The elephant is never won with Anger,
Nor must that man who would reclaim a lion
Take him by the teeth.

EARL OF ROCHESTER, *Valentinian*

Angling

The pleasant'st angling is to see the fish
Cut with her golden oars the silver stream,
And greedily devour the treacherous bait.

WILLIAM SHAKESPEARE,
Much Ado about Nothing

Angling is somewhat like Poetry, men are to be born so.

IZAAK WALTON, *The Compleat Angler*

Anticipation

All things that are,
Are with more spirit chased than enjoy'd.

WILLIAM SHAKESPEARE,
Merchant of Venice

Expectation in a weak mind makes an evil greater and a good, less: but in a resolved mind it digests an evil before it comes; and makes a future good, long before present. I will expect the worst, because it may come: the best, because I know it will come.

BISHOP JOSEPH HALL,
Meditations and Vows

Nothing is so good as it seems beforehand.

GEORGE ELIOT, *Silas Marner*

To swallow gudgeons ere they're catched,
And count their chickens ere they're hatched.

SAMUEL BUTLER, *Hudibras*

Antiquity

Nothing can be preserved that is not good.

RALPH WALDO EMERSON,
In Praise of Books

Apology

Apologies only account for that which they do not alter.

BENJAMIN DISRAELI,
Speech in the House of Commons

Appearance

You can't judge a horse by the harness.

Proverb

Great men are seldom over-scrupulous in the arrangement of their attire.

CHARLES DICKENS, *Pickwick Papers*

Costly thy habit as thy purse can buy,
But not expressed in fancy;
rich, not gaudy:
For the apparel oft proclaims the man.

WILLIAM SHAKESPEARE, *Hamlet*

All that glisters is not gold,
Gilded tombs do worms infold.

WILLIAM SHAKESPEARE,
Merchant of Venice

By outward show let's not be cheated;
An ass should like an ass be treated.

JOHN GAY, *Fables*

And many a withering thought lies hid, not lost,
In smiles that least befit who wears them most.

LORD BYRON, *Corsair*

Things are seldom what they seem;
Skim milk masquerades as cream.

SIR WILLIAM SCHWENCK GILBERT,
H. M. S. Pinafore

The Devil hath power
To assume a pleasing shape.

WILLIAM SHAKESPEARE, *Hamlet*

All is not gold that glitters.

Proverb

Fine feathers, they say, make fine birds.

ISAAC BICKERSTAFF, *The Padlock*

A goodly apple rotten at the heart;
O, what a goodly outside falsehood hath!

WILLIAM SHAKESPEARE,
Merchant of Venice

Argument

Be calm in arguing; for fierceness makes
Error a fault, and truth discourtesy.

SIR WILLIAM TEMPLE

When much dispute has past,
We find our tenets just the same as last.

ALEXANDER POPE, *Moral Essays*

Who, too deep for his hearers, still went on refining.
And thought of convincing while they thought of dining.

OLIVER GOLDSMITH, *Retaliation*

Art

To me more dear, congenial to my heart,
One native charm, than all the gloss of art.

OLIVER GOLDSMITH, *The Deserted Village*

Art is not imitation but illusion.

CHARLES READE, *Christie Johnstone*

Art is the child of Nature.

HENRY WADSWORTH LONGFELLOW, *Keramos*

Art may make a suit of clothes; but Nature must produce a man.

DAVID HUME, *Essays*

For Art may err, but Nature cannot miss.

JOHN DRYDEN, *The Cock and the Fox*

The course of Nature is the art of God.

EDWARD YOUNG, *Night Thoughts*

Aspiration (*See also* Ambition)

Alas! we make
A ladder of our thoughts, where angels step,
But sleep ourselves at the foot: our high resolves
Look down upon our slumbering acts.

LETITIA ELIZABETH LANDON, *A History of the Lyre*

Screw your courage to the sticking place,
And we'll not fail.

WILLIAM SHAKESPEARE, *Macbeth*

Too low they build who build beneath the stars.

EDWARD YOUNG, *Night Thoughts*

Hitch your wagon to a star.

RALPH WALDO EMERSON, *Society and Solitude*

To be, or not to be: that is the question.

WILLIAM SHAKESPEARE, *Hamlet*

Assurance (*See also* Confidence)

Assurance is two-thirds of success.

Proverb

Authors

Authors, like coins, grow dear as they grow old:
It is the rust we value, not the gold.

ALEXANDER POPE, *Imitation of Horace*

The author who speaks about his own books is almost as bad as a mother who talks about her own children.

BENJAMIN DISRAELI, *Speech at Glasgow*

Autumn

The melancholy days are come, the saddest of the year,
Of wailing winds, and naked woods, and meadows brown and sere.

WILLIAM CULLEN BRYANT, *Death of the Flowers*

And in his hand a sickle he did holde,
To reape the ripened fruit the which the earth had yold.

EDMUND SPENSER, *Faerie Queene*

The year growing ancient,
Not yet on summer's death, nor on the birth
Of trembling winter.

WILLIAM SHAKESPEARE, *Winter's Tale*

Wild is the music of autumnal winds
Amongst the faded woods.

WILLIAM WORDSWORTH

Thrice happy time,
Best portion of the various year, in which
Nature rejoiceth, smiling on her works,
Lovely, to full perception wrought.

JOHN PHILIPS, *Cyder*

Awareness

To know ourselves diseased is half our cure.

ALEXANDER POPE

Bad News

For evil news rides post, while good news baits.

JOHN MILTON, *Samson Agonistes*

Ill news comes apace.

Proverb

Beauty

The flowers anew returning seasons bring,
But beauty faded has no second spring.

AMBROSE PHILLIPS, *Pastoral*

Beauty from order springs.

WILLIAM KING, *The Art of Cookery*

Beauty's of a fading nature—
Has a season and is gone!

ROBERT BURNS, *Will Ye Go and Marry Katie?*

Beauty is but skin deep.

Proverb

The saying that beauty is but skin deep is but a skin-deep saying.

HERBERT SPENCER, *Essays*

A thing of beauty is a joy forever;
Its loveliness increases; it will never
Pass into nothingness.

JOHN KEATS, *Endymion*

Beauty is a very handy thing to have, especially for a woman who ain't handsome.

JOSH BILLINGS (HENRY WHEELER SHAW)

If eyes were made for seeing,
Then Beauty is its own excuse for being.

RALPH WALDO EMERSON, *The Rhodora*

In beauty faults conspicuous grow;
The smallest speck is seen on snow.

JOHN GAY, *Fables*

'Tis not a lip, or eye, we beauty call,
But the joint force and full result of all.

ALEXANDER POPE, *Essay on Criticism*

Beauty is but a flower
Which wrinkles will devour.

THOMAS NASH, *Summer's Last Will and Testament*

Believing

A man lives by believing something; not by debating and arguing about many things.

THOMAS CARLYLE

Man prefers to believe what he prefers to be true.

FRANCIS BACON, *Aphorisms*

What we ardently wish, we believe.

EDWARD YOUNG, *Night Thoughts*

Bitterness

But hushed be every thought that springs
From out the bitterness of things.

WILLIAM WORDSWORTH, *Elegiac Stanzas*

Blushing

The man that blushes is not quite a brute.

EDWARD YOUNG, *Night Thoughts*

Boasting

Would you know the qualities in which a man is wanting? Examine those of which he boasts.

SÉGUR, *Poems*

The honor is overpaid,
When he that did the act is commentator.

JAMES SHIRLEY

The empty vessel makes the greatest sound.

Proverb

Books

Who kills a man, kills a reasonable creature, God's image; but he who destroys a good book kills reason itself.

JOHN MILTON, *Areopagitica*

Books, like friends, should be few and well chosen.

SAMUEL PATERSON, *Joineriana*

God be thanked for books. They are the voices of the distant and the dead, and make us heirs of the spiritual life of past ages.

WILLIAM ELLERY CHANNING, *Self-Culture*

Books are the best things, well used; abused, among the worst.

RALPH WALDO EMERSON

Some books are to be tasted, others to be swallowed, and some few to be chewed and digested.

FRANCIS BACON, *Essay on Studies*

A good book is the precious lifeblood of a master-spirit embalmed and treasured up on purpose to a life beyond life.

JOHN MILTON, *Areopagitica*

Bores

Again I hear the creaking step!—
He's rapping at the door!—
Too well I know the boding sound
That ushers in a bore.

JOHN GODFREY SAXE, *My Familiar*

We always get bored with those whom we bore.

LA ROCHEFOUCAULD, *Maximes*

Borrowing

A man in debt is so far a slave.

RALPH WALDO EMERSON

The human species, according to the best theory I can form of it, is composed of two distinct races, *the men who borrow* and *the men who lend.*

CHARLES LAMB, *Two Races*

Let us all be happy and live within our means, even if we have to borrow the money to do it with.

ARTEMUS WARD, *Natural History*

Neither a borrower nor a lender be:
  For loan oft loses both itself and friend;
  And borrowing dulls the edge of husbandry.

WILLIAM SHAKESPEARE, *Hamlet*

Creditors have better memories than debtors.

Proverb

When debtors once have borrowed all we have to lend, they are very apt to grow shy of their creditors' company.

SIR JOHN VANBRUGH, *The Provoked Wife*

Bravado

His bark is worse than his bite.

GEORGE HERBERT, *Jacula Prudentum*

The robbed that smiles steals something from the thief.

WILLIAM SHAKESPEARE, *Othello*

The Schoolboy, with his satchel in his hand,
Whistling aloud to bear his courage up.

ROBERT BLAIR, *The Grave*

Bravery (*See also* Courage)

None but the brave deserves the fair.

JOHN DRYDEN, *Alexander's Feast*

Breeding

A man's own good breeding is his best security against other people's ill manners.

LORD CHESTERFIELD, *Letters to His Son*

Brevity

Brevity is the soul of wit.

WILLIAM SHAKESPEARE, *Hamlet*

Carelessness

Many little leaks may sink a ship.

THOMAS FULLER, *Holy and Profane States*

Cause and Effect

Shallow men believe in luck, believe in circumstances. Strong men believe in cause and effect.

RALPH WALDO EMERSON, *Conduct of Life*

Caution

Great estates may venture more,
But little boats should keep near shore.

BENJAMIN FRANKLIN, *Poor Richard's Almanac*

They that fear the adder's sting, will not come near his hissing.

GEORGE CHAPMAN, *Widow's Tears*

Slow and steady wins the race.

DAVID LLOYD, *Fables*

Caution is the parent of safety.

Proverb

Celebrity

Celebrity is the chastisement of merit and the punishment of talent.

SÉBASTIEN R. N. CHAMFORT

Celebrity is the advantage of being known to people whom we don't know, and who don't know us.

SÉBASTIEN R. N. CHAMFORT

Certainty

In this world, nothing is certain but death and taxes.

BENJAMIN FRANKLIN, *Letter*

There is nothing certain in man's life but that he must lose it.

OWEN MEREDITH, *Clytemnestra*

The only thing that is certain is that nothing is certain.

PLINY THE ELDER, *Historia Naturalis*

Chance

Chance is the providence of adventurers.

NAPOLEON BONAPARTE

A fool must now and then be right by chance.

WILLIAM COWPER, *Conversations*

Change

A rolling stone gathers no moss.

STEPHEN GOSSON, *Ephemerides of Phialo*

Life belongs to the living, and he who lives must be prepared for changes.

JOHANN WOLFGANG VON GOETHE

The stone that is rolling can gather no moss;
For master and servant oft changing is loss.

THOMAS TUSSER, *Five Hundred Points of Good Husbandry*

Character

Character is simply a habit long continued.

PLUTARCH

I leave my character behind me.

RICHARD BRINSLEY SHERIDAN, *School for Scandal*

Character is a reserve force which acts directly by presence and without means.

RALPH WALDO EMERSON

Character is the result of a system of stereotyped principles.

DAVID HUME

Charity

The best investment I know of is charity: you git your principal back immediately, and draw a dividend every time you think of it.

JOSH BILLINGS (HENRY WHEELER SHAW)

Charity begins at home, but should not end there.

Proverb

Alas for the rarity of Christian charity
Under the sun!

THOMAS HOOD, *Bridge of Sighs*

They serve God well
Who serve his creatures.

CAROLINE ELIZABETH NORTON, *Lady of La Garaye*

Children

The wise child handles father and mother
By playing one against the other.

OGDEN NASH, *The Face is Familiar*[1]

Children know,
Instinctive taught, the friend or foe.

SIR WALTER SCOTT, *Lady of the Lake*

Then spare the rod, and spoil the child.

SAMUEL BUTLER, *Hudibras*

How sharper than a serpent's tooth it is
To have a thankless child!

WILLIAM SHAKESPEARE, *King Lear*

Choice

A man is too apt to forget that in this world he cannot have everything. A choice is all that is left him.

H. MATHEWS, *Diary of an Invalid*

Descend a step in choosing a wife, ascend a step in choosing thy friend.

The Talmud

Christianity (*See also* Religion)

Christianity is an idea
and as such is immortal like every idea.

HEINRICH HEINE, *Religion and Philosophy*

Christianity is the root of all democracy, the highest fact in the rights of man.

NOVALIS

Christianity is a religion that can make men good, only if they are good already.

GEORG WILHELM FRIEDRICH HEGEL

Christmas

At Christmas play and make good cheer,
For Christmas comes but once a year.

THOMAS TUSSER, *Five Hundred Points of Good Husbandry*

Circumstances

Circumstances alter cases.

THOMAS CHANDLER HALIBURTON, *The Old Judge*

Everyone is as God has made him, and oftentimes a great deal worse.

MIGUEL DE CERVANTES, *Don Quixote*

Who does the best his circumstance allows,
Does well, acts nobly—angels could no more.

EDWARD YOUNG, *Night Thoughts*

Civilization

Civilization is the eternal sacrifice of one generation to the next.

BULWER-LYTTON, *Alice*

Cleanliness

Cleanliness is near of kin to godliness.

Proverb

Cleanliness is, indeed, next to godliness.

JOHN WESLEY, *Sermon on Dress*

Common Sense

Common sense is not so common.

VOLTAIRE

Comparison

None but himself can be his parallel.

LOUIS THEOBALD, *The Double Falsehood*

Leave her, and I will leave comparing thus;
She and comparisons are odious.

JOHN DONNE, *Elegie VIII*

Complaints

Constant complaints never get pity.

Proverb

They who complain most are most to be complained of.

MATTHEW HENRY

Compromise

All great alterations in human affairs are produced by compromise.

SYDNEY SMITH, *Catholic Question*

Throw no gift againe the giver's head;
For better is halfe a lofe than no bread.

JOHN HEYWOOD, *Proverbs*

Compulsion

Nothing is pleasant
Joined with a must.

ROBERT BRIDGES, *Nero*

Who overcomes
By force hath overcome but half his foe.

JOHN MILTON, *Paradise Lost*

Conceit

Every man thinks his own geese, swans.

Proverb

He's so full of himself that he is quite empty.

Proverb

Conceit may puff a man up, but never prop him up.

JOHN RUSKIN

Concentration

Concentration is the secret of strength in politics, in war, in trade, in short in all the management of human affairs.

RALPH WALDO EMERSON

Confession

An open confession is good for the soul.

Proverb

A fault confessed is half redressed.

Proverb

Confidence

Confidence is a thing that cannot be produced by compulsion.

DANIEL WEBSTER, *Speech*

Confidence is a plant of slow growth in an aged bosom.

WILLIAM PITT, *Speech*

For they can conquer who believe they can.

RALPH WALDO EMERSON
Society and Solitude

Conscience

A burthen'd conscience
Will never need a hangman.

BEAUMONT AND FLETCHER,
Laws of Comedy

Whatever creed be taught or land be trod,
Man's conscience is the oracle of God!

LORD BYRON, *The Island*

Let his tormentor, Conscience, find him out.

JOHN MILTON, *Paradise Regained*

Better be with the dead,
Than on the torture of the mind to lie
In restless ecstasy.

WILLIAM SHAKESPEARE, *Macbeth*

The fond fantastic thing call'd conscience,
Which serves for nothing but to make men cowards.

THOMAS SHADWELL, *The Libertine*

Conscience, good my lord,
Is but the pulse of reason.

SAMUEL TAYLOR COLERIDGE, *Zapolya*

Conscience, the bosom-hell of guilty man!

JAMES MONTGOMERY, *The Pelican Island*

Conscience, in most souls, is like an English sovereign—it reigns, but it does not govern.

WILLIAM HURRELL MALLOCK,
The New Republic

Here, here it lies; a lump of lead by day;
And in my short, distracted, nightly slumbers,
The hag that rides my dreams.

JOHN DRYDEN

There is no future pang
Can deal that justice on the self-condemn'd
He deals on his own soul.

LORD BYRON, *Manfred*

A guilty conscience needs no accuser.

Proverb

A quiet conscience makes one so serene.

LORD BYRON, *Don Juan*

Conscience is the chamber of justice.

ORIGEN

Constancy

When change itself can give no more,
It is easy to be true.

SIR CHARLES SEDLEY,
Reasons for Constancy

Contentment

Show me a thoroughly contented person, and I will show you a useless one.

JOSH BILLINGS (HENRY WHEELER SHAW)

Contentment consisteth not in adding more fuel, but in taking away some fire.

THOMAS FULLER

Controversy

He that wrestles with us strengthens our nerves and sharpens our skill. Our antagonist is our helper.

EDMUND BURKE,
Reflections on the Revolution in France

Conversation

Silence and modesty are very valuable qualities in conversation.

MICHEL DE MONTAIGNE

Conversation is an art in which a man has all mankind for competitors.

RALPH WALDO EMERSON

Coöperation

For when was honey ever made
With one bee in the hive.

THOMAS HOOD, *The Last Man*

Two heads are better than one.

JOHN HEYWOOD, *Proverbs*

Corporations

They (corporations) cannot commit trespass nor be outlawed, nor excommunicate, for they have no souls.

SIR EDWARD COKE,
Case of Sutton's Hospital

Correction (*See also* Criticism)

Correction is good administered in time.

Proverb

Corruption

Corruption is like a ball of snow, when once set a-rolling it must increase.

CHARLES CALEB COLTON

For sweetest things turn sourest by their deeds;
Lilies that fester smell far worse than weeds.

WILLIAM SHAKESPEARE, *Sonnets*

Courage (*See also* Daring)

They also serve who only stand and wait.

JOHN MILTON

'Tis more brave to live than to die.

OWEN MEREDITH, *Lucile*

True valor lies half way between cowardice and rashness.

MIGUEL DE CERVANTES, *Don Quixote*

He is not valiant that dares die,
But he that boldly bears calamity.

PHILIP MASSINGER, *The Maid of Honour*

A brave man struggling with adversity is a spectacle for the gods.

SENECA

Do have the courage not to adopt another's courage.

RALPH WALDO EMERSON, *Society and Solitude*

Courage consists not in blindly overlooking danger, but in meeting it with the eyes open.

JEAN PAUL RICHTER

Courtesy

Politeness costs nothing and gains everything.

LADY MARY WORTLEY MONTAGU, *Letters*

Life is not so short but that there is always room for courtesy.

RALPH WALDO EMERSON, *Social Aims*

Good manners never can intrude.

EDWARD MOORE, *Fable*

Cowardice

The coward threatens when he is safe.

JOHANN WOLFGANG VON GOETHE

Faint heart ne'er won fair lady.

MIGUEL DE CERVANTES, *Don Quixote*

Criticism

People in general will much better bear being told of their vices or crimes than of their little failings or weaknesses.

LORD CHESTERFIELD, *Letters to His Son*

Some of their capsules survive among the classic punchlines of all times, especially those typed in acid.

WALTER WINCHELL

Those best can bear reproof who merit praise.

ALEXANDER POPE, *Essay on Criticism*

It is much easier to be critical than correct.

BENJAMIN DISRAELI, *Speech*

Culture

Culture is not a substitute for life, but the key to it.

WILLIAM HURRELL MALLOCK, *The New Republic*

Curiosity

Curiosity is the kernel of the forbidden fruit.

THOMAS FULLER

Curiosity is lying in wait for every secret.

RALPH WALDO EMERSON

Curses

Curses, like young chickens, come home to roost.

ROBERT SOUTHEY, *The Curse of Kehama*

Custom

Custom then is the great guide of human life.

DAVID HUME, *Concerning Human Understanding*

To follow foolish precedents, and wink
With both our eyes, is easier than to think.

WILLIAM COWPER, *Tirocinium*

Danger

Everything is sweetened by risk.

ALEXANDER SMITH, *Dreamthorp*

Without danger we cannot get beyond danger.

GEORGE HERBERT, *Jacula Prudentum*

A danger will never be overcome without danger.

PUBLILIUS SYRUS

Danger for danger's sake is senseless.

VICTOR HUGO

When the house of your neighbor is on fire, your own is in danger.

Proverb

Daring (*See also* Courage)

Who bravely dares must sometimes risk a fall.

TOBIAS SMOLLET, *Advice*

I dare do all that may become a man;
Who dares do more is none.

WILLIAM SHAKESPEARE, *Macbeth*

Dare to do something worthy of transportation and imprisonment, if you wish to be somebody.

JUVENAL

Daybreak

The morning steals upon the night,
Melting the darkness.

WILLIAM SHAKESPEARE, *The Tempest*

Death

I have a rendezvous with Death,
At some disputed barricade,
When Spring comes back with rustling shade,
And apple-blossoms fill the air.

ALAN SEEGER,
I Have a Rendezvous With Death[1]

The dead they sleep, a long, long sleep;
The dead they rest, and their rest is deep;
The dead have peace, but the living weep.

SAMUEL HOFFENSTEIN, *Year In, You're Out*[2]

I am glad God saw Death and gave Death a
Job taking care of all who are tired of living.

CARL SANDBURG, *Junkman*[3]

If I fear at all, I fear dying—I do not fear death.

SAMUEL TAYLOR COLERIDGE, *Letters*

Death lays his icy hand on kings;
Scepter and crown
Must tumble down,
And in the dust be equal made
With the poor, crooked scythe and spade.

JAMES SHIRLEY,
Contention of Ajax and Ulysses

Death is, to a certain extent, an impossibility which suddenly becomes a reality.

JOHANN WOLFGANG VON GOETHE

Let no man fear to die; we love to sleep all,
And death is but the sounder sleep.

FRANCIS BEAUMONT,
Humorous Lieutenant

No life that breathes with human breath
Has ever truly longed for death.

ALFRED, LORD TENNYSON,
The Two Voices

Death, kind Nature's signal of retreat.

SAMUEL JOHNSON,
The Vanity of Human Wishes

Death joins us to the great majority.

EDWARD YOUNG, *The Revenge*

It seems to me most strange that men should fear;
Seeing that death, a necessary end,
Will come when it will come.

WILLIAM SHAKESPEARE,
Julius Caesar

All that lives must die,
Passing through nature to eternity.

WILLIAM SHAKESPEARE, *Hamlet*

[1]Reprinted by permission of Charles Scribner's Sons.

[2]Published by Liveright Publishing Corp., N.Y. Copyright by Samuel Hoffenstein, 1930.

[3]From Chicago Poems by Carl Sandburg. Copyright 1916 by Henry Holt and Company, Inc. Copyright 1944 by Carl Sandburg. Used by permission of the publishers.

He that begins to live, begins to die.

FRANCIS QUARLES, *Hieroglyph*

A man can die but once.

WILLIAM SHAKESPEARE,
King Henry IV

Deception

Oh, what a tangled web we weave,
When first we practice to deceive.

SIR WALTER SCOTT, *Marmion*

If a man deceive me once, shame on him; if twice, shame on me.

Proverb

It is a double pleasure to deceive the deceiver.

Proverb

Deeds (*See also* Action)

Deeds are the pulse of time.

GEORGE ELIOT, *Daniel Deronda*

We live in deeds, not years; in thoughts, not breaths;
In feelings, not in figures on a dial.

PHILIP JAMES BAILEY, *Festus*

The deed is everything; the fame is nothing.

JOHANN WOLFGANG VON GOETHE

Defense

Never make a defense or apology before you be accused.

CHARLES I, *Letter to Lord Wentworth*

Democracy (*See also* Americanism)

Democracy means simply the bludgeoning of the people, by the people, for the people.

OSCAR WILDE,
Soul of Man Under Socialism

A democracy is a state in which the government rests directly with the majority of the citizens.

JOHN RUSKIN

Democracy started from men's thinking that if they are equal on any count, they are equal absolutely.

ARISTOTLE, *Politics*

Dependency

Affairs that depend on many rarely succeed.

FRANCESCO GUICCIARDINI

Depression

All day the darkness and the cold
Upon my heart have lain,
Like shadows on the winter sky,
Like frost upon the pane.

JOHN GREENLEAF WHITTIER,
On Receiving an Eagle's Quill

Despair (*See also* Grief *and* Sorrow)

Despair is the conclusion of fools.

BENJAMIN DISRAELI, *Sibyl*

It is a miserable state of mind to have few things to desire, and many things to fear.

FRANCIS BACON, *Essays*

Destruction

A thousand years scarce serve to form a state;
An hour may lay it in the dust.

LORD BYRON, *Childe Harold's Pilgrimage*

Difficulties

All things are difficult before they are easy.

THOMAS FULLER, *Gnomologia*

Difficulties are meant to rouse, not discourage.

WILLIAM ELLERY CHANNING

Dignity

Where boasting ends there dignity begins.

EDWARD YOUNG, *Night Thoughts*

There is a certain dignity to be kept up in pleasures as well as in business.

LORD CHESTERFIELD, *Letters to His Son*

A life both dull and dignified.

SIR WALTER SCOTT, *Marmion*

Diplomacy

A drop of honey catches more flies than a hogshead of vinegar.

Proverb

Toward men, and toward God, she maintained a respectful attitude, lightened by the belief that in a crisis she could deal adequately with either of them.

ROBERT NATHAN, *The Road of Ages*[1]

Disappointment

Blessed is he who expects nothing, for he shall never be disappointed.

ALEXANDER POPE, *Letter to Gay*

Things sweet to taste
  Prove in digestion, sour.

WILLIAM SHAKESPEARE, *Richard II*

I never loved a tree or flower,
But 'twas the first to fade away.

THOMAS MOORE, *Lalla Rookh*

Discipline

He that has learned to obey will know how to command.

SOLON

[1]Reprinted by permission of Alfred A. Knopf, Inc.

Discontent

Who with a little can not be content,
Endures an everlasting punishment.

ROBERT HERRICK, *Hesperides*

What makes us discontented with our condition is the absurdly exaggerated idea we have of the happiness of others.

Proverb

Discontent is the first step in the progress of a man or a nation.

OSCAR WILDE, *A Woman of No Importance*

Discretion

Abhor a knave and pity a fool in your heart, but let neither of them unnecessarily see that you do so.

LORD CHESTERFIELD, *Letters to His Son*

Discussion

In political discussion heat is in inverse proportion to knowledge.

J. G. C. MINCHIN, *The Growth of Freedom in the Balkan Peninsula*

Disgrace

In shame there is no comfort, but to be beyond all bounds of shame.

SIR PHILIP SIDNEY, *Arcadia*

A man may survive distress, but not disgrace.

Proverb

Disgraces are much like cherries—one draws another.

GEORGE HERBERT, *Jacula Prudentum*

Disorder

Disorder makes nothing at all, but unmakes everything.

JOHN STUART BLACKIE

Doubts

If a man will begin with certainties, he shall end in doubts; but if he will be content to begin with doubts, he shall end in certainties.

FRANCIS BACON, *Advancement of Learning*

By doubting we come at the truth.

CICERO

Our doubts are traitors
And make us lose the good we oft might win
By fearing to attempt.

WILLIAM SHAKESPEARE, *Measure for Measure*

Dreams

We are such stuff
As dreams are made on; and our little life
Is rounded with a sleep.

WILLIAM SHAKESPEARE, *The Tempest*

Drink

Candy is dandy
But liquor is quicker.

OGDEN NASH, *The Face is Familiar*[1]

There is nothing which has yet been contrived by man by which so much happiness is produced as by a good tavern or inn.

SAMUEL JOHNSON,
in Boswell's *Life of Johnson*

Some men are like musical glasses—to produce their finest tones you must keep them wet.

SAMUEL TAYLOR COLERIDGE

Drink not the third glass, which thou canst not tame
When once it is within thee.

GEORGE HERBERT, *The Church Porch*

Drink! for you know not whence you came, nor why:
Drink! for you know not why you go, nor where.

OMAR KHAYYAM, *The Rubaiyat*

Great men should drink with harness on their throats.

WILLIAM SHAKESPEARE,
Timon of Athens

Sweet fellowship in shame;
One drunkard loves another of the name.

WILLIAM SHAKESPEARE,
Love's Labour's Lost

Best while you have it use your breath:
There is no drinking after death!

BEAUMONT AND FLETCHER, *Rollo*

Duty

He gives nothing but worthless gold
Who gives from a sense of duty.

JAMES RUSSELL LOWELL,
Vision of Sir Launfal

Do the duty that lies nearest thee; which thou knowest to be a duty.
The second duty will already become clearer.

THOMAS CARLYLE, *Sartor Resartus*

I slept, and dreamed that life was Beauty;
I woke, and found that life was Duty.

ELLEN HOOPER, *The Dial*

You would not think any duty small
If you yourself were great.

GEORGE MACDONALD, *Willie's Question*

[1]Copyright 1931, 1933, 1936, 1938 by Ogden Nash. Reprinted by permission of Little, Brown & Co.

New occasions teach new duties.

JAMES RUSSELL LOWELL,
The Present Crisis

Earnestness

Earnestness is enthusiasm tempered by reason.

BLAISE PASCAL

Eating

He hath eaten me out of house and home.

WILLIAM SHAKESPEARE, *Henry IV*

Unquiet meals make ill digestions.

WILLIAM SHAKESPEARE,
Comedy of Errors

Eavesdropping

Listen at the keyhole,
and you'll hear news of yourself.

Proverb

Education

Deep versed in books, and shallow in himself.

JOHN MILTON, *Paradise Regained*

The bookful blockhead, ignorantly read,
With loads of learned lumber in his head.

ALEXANDER POPE,
Essay on Criticism

A smattering of everything and a knowledge of nothing.

CHARLES DICKENS, *Sketches by Boz*

Better build schoolrooms for the boy,
Than cells and gibbets for the man.

ELIZA COOK,
A Song for the Ragged Schools

'Tis education forms the common mind;
Just as the twig is bent the tree's inclined.

ALEXANDER POPE, *Moral Essays*

Egoism

Every man is of importance to himself.

SAMUEL JOHNSON

Encouragement

Correction does much, but encouragement does more.

JOHANN WOLFGANG VON GOETHE

Enemies

Man is his own worst enemy.

CICERO

Enjoyment

Enjoy when you can, and endure when you must.

JOHANN WOLFGANG VON GOETHE

We're charmed with distant views of happiness,
But near approaches make the prospect less.

THOMAS YALDEN, *Against Enjoyment*

A man of pleasure is a man of pains.

EDWARD YOUNG, *Night Thoughts*

A day in such serene enjoyment spent
Were worth an age of splendid discontent!

JAMES MONTGOMERY, *Greenland*

Enthusiasm

Enthusiasm is the genius of sincerity, and truth accomplishes no victories without it.

BULWER-LYTTON, *The Last Days of Pompeii*

Nothing great was ever achieved without enthusiasm.

RALPH WALDO EMERSON, *Circles*

It is unfortunate, considering that enthusiasm moves the world, that so few enthusiasts can be trusted to speak the truth.

ARTHUR JAMES BALFOUR, *Letter to Mrs. Drew*

No wild enthusiast ever yet could rest,
Till half mankind were like himself possess'd.

WILLIAM COWPER, *Progress of Error*

Envy

People hate those that make them feel their own inferiority: therefore conceal all your learning carefully.

LORD CHESTERFIELD, *Letters to His Son*

How bitter a thing it is to look into happiness through another man's eyes!

WILLIAM SHAKESPEARE, *As You Like It*

Envy is but the smoke of low estate
Ascending still against the fortunate.

LORD BROOKE, *Alaham*

Envy is a necessary evil; it is a little goad which forces us to do yet better.

VOLTAIRE

Envy is better worth having than pity.

Proverb

For one man who sincerely pities our misfortunes, there are a thousand who sincerely hate our success.

CHARLES CALEB COLTON, *Lacon*

Fools may our scorn, not envy, raise,
For envy is a kind of praise.

JOHN GAY, *Fables*

Base envy withers at another's joy
And hates the excellence it cannot reach.

JAMES THOMSON, *The Seasons*

Equality

Equality is the sacred law of humanity.

FRIEDRICH SCHILLER

Sauce for the goose is sauce for the gander.

JONATHAN SWIFT, *Journal to Stella*

Oh, East is East, and West is West, and never the twain shall meet,
Till earth and sky stand presently at God's great judgment seat;
But there is neither East nor West, Border nor Breed nor Birth,
When two strong men stand face to face, though they come from the ends of the earth!

RUDYARD KIPLING, *The Ballad of East and West*

But our captain counts the image of God, nevertheless his image, cut in ebony as if done in ivory.

THOMAS FULLER, *The Good Sea-Captain*

Error

There is no anguish like an error of which we feel ashamed.

BULWER-LYTTON, *Ernest Maltravers*

Honest error is to be pitied, not ridiculed.

LORD CHESTERFIELD, *Letters to His Son*

For there is no error so crooked but it hath in it some lines of truth.

MARTIN FARQUHAR TUPPER, *Proverbial Philosophy of Truth in Things False*

Errors like straws upon the surface flow;
He who would search for pearls must dive below.

JOHN DRYDEN, *All for Love*

Evil

Evil is only good perverted.

HENRY WADSWORTH LONGFELLOW, *The Golden Legend*

But evil is wrought by want of thought,
As well as want of heart.

THOMAS HOOD, *The Lady's Dream*

A little evil is often necessary for obtaining a great good.

VOLTAIRE, *Baron d'Otranto*

Exaggeration

Exaggeration is to paint a snake and add legs.

Proverb

Example

Examples would indeed be excellent things were not people so modest that none will set them, and so vain that none will follow them.

JULIUS CHARLES HARE

How far that little candle throws his beams!
So shines a good deed in a naughty world.

WILLIAM SHAKESPEARE, *Merchant of Venice*

From another's evil qualities a wise man corrects his own.

PUBLILIUS SYRUS

Example is the school of mankind and they will learn at no other.

EDMUND BURKE, *Letter on a Regicide Peace*

Excess

A surfeit of the sweetest things,
The deepest loathing to the stomach brings.

WILLIAM SHAKESPEARE, *Midsummer Night's Dream*

Thus each extreme to equal danger tends:
Plenty, as well as want, can sep'rate friends.

ABRAHAM COWLEY, *Davideis*

Enough is as good as a feast: . . . too much of a good thing is good for nothing.

THEODORE HOOK, *Danvers*

Excuses

A bad excuse is better, they say, than none at all.

STEPHEN GOSSON, *The Schoole of Abuse*

An excuse uncalled for becomes an obvious accusation.

Law Maxim

Existence

I think, therefore I am.

RENÉ DESCARTES

Experience

Experience is the best of schoolmasters.

Proverb

Sad experience leaves no room for doubt.

ALEXANDER POPE, *January and May*

Experience makes us able pilots in the waves of fortune.

EDWARD YOUNG, *True Estimate of Human Life*

Experience is the best teacher, only the school-fees are heavy.

GEORG WILHELM FRIEDRICH HEGEL

A burnt child dreads the fire.

Proverb

I had rather have a fool to make me merry than experience to make me sad.

WILLIAM SHAKESPEARE, *As You Like It*

The best of prophets of the future is the past.

LORD BYRON, *Letter*

The years teach much which the days never know.

RALPH WALDO EMERSON, *Experience*

For Time will teach thee soon the truth,
There are no birds in last year's nest!

HENRY WADSWORTH LONGFELLOW, *It Is Not Always May*

He jests at scars that never felt a wound.

WILLIAM SHAKESPEARE, *Romeo and Juliet*

A sadder and a wiser man,
He rose the morrow morn.

SAMUEL TAYLOR COLERIDGE, *The Ancient Mariner*

By pain men come to greater pains,
And by indignities men come to dignities.

FRANCIS BACON, *Essays*

It is costly wisdom that is bought by experience.

ROGER ASCHAM, *The Schoolmaster*

Extravagance

Fond pride of dress is, sure, a very curse;
Ere fancy you consult, consult your purse.

BENJAMIN FRANKLIN, *Poor Richard's Almanac*

A fool and his money are soon parted.

Proverb

Extremity

Who love too much, hate in the like extreme.

ALEXANDER POPE, *The Odyssey of Homer*

Virtuous and vicious every man must be,
Few in the extreme, but all in the degree.

ALEXANDER POPE, *Essay on Man*

Eyes

Drink to me only with thine eyes,
And I will pledge with mine.

BEN JONSON, *To Celia*

From women's eyes this doctrine I derive:
They are the ground, the books, the academes,
From whence doth spring the true Promethean fire.

WILLIAM SHAKESPEARE, *Love's Labour's Lost*

Her glance, how wildly beautiful.

LORD BYRON

Those eyes
Soft and capacious as a cloudless sky.

WILLIAM WORDSWORTH

Her eyes are homes of silent prayer.

ALFRED, LORD TENNYSON, *In Memoriam*

Face

Was this the face that launch'd a thousand ships,
And burnt the topless towers of Ilium?

CHRISTOPHER MARLOWE, *Faustus*

Facts

A fact in our lives is valuable not so far as it is true, but as it is significant.

JOHANN WOLFGANG VON GOETHE

Facts are stubborn things.

JARED ELLIOT

Failure

I am not now in fortune's power:
He that is down can fall no lower.

SAMUEL BUTLER, *Hudibras*

A man of intellect without energy added to it is a failure.

SÉBASTIEN R. N. CHAMFORT

In the lexicon of youth, which fate reserves for a bright manhood, there is no such word as—*fail!*

BULWER-LYTTON, *Richelieu*

Fairness

Let the other side also have a hearing.

SENECA

Faith

Our faith comes in moments; our vice is habitual.

RALPH WALDO EMERSON, *The Over-Soul*

Faith builds a bridge from the old world to the next.

EDWARD YOUNG

Faith is a higher faculty than reasoning.

PHILIP JAMES BAILEY, *Festus*

Faith is the subtle chain
That binds us to the Infinite: the voice
Of a deep life within.

ELIZABETH OAKES SMITH, *Faith*

Pin not your faith on another's sleeve.

Proverb

The faith that stands on authority is not faith.

RALPH WALDO EMERSON, *The Over-Soul*

O welcome, pure-eyed Faith, white-handed Hope,
Thou hovering angel, girt with golden wings!

JOHN MILTON, *Comus*

Call no faith false which e'er has brought
Relief to any laden life,
Cessation from the pain of thought,
Refreshment 'mid the dust of strife.

LEWIS MORRIS, *Songs of Two Worlds*

Man then, has not invented God;
He has developed Faith,
To meet a God already there.

EDNA ST. VINCENT MILLAY, *Conversation at Midnight*[1]

Fame

Fame is a fickle food
Upon a shifting plate.

EMILY DICKINSON, *The Single Hound*[2]

One crowded hour of glorious life
Is worth an age without a name.

SIR WALTER SCOTT, *Old Mortality*

Unblemished let me live, or die unknown;
O grant an honest fame, or grant me none!

ALEXANDER POPE, *The Temple of Fame*

To live in hearts we leave behind,
Is not to die.

THOMAS CAMPBELL, *Hallowed Ground*

Here we may reign secure, and in my choice
To reign is worth ambition, though in hell.

JOHN MILTON, *Paradise Lost*

With fame in just proportion, envy grows;
The man that makes a character, makes foes.

EDWARD YOUNG, *Epistle to Pope*

The evil that men do lives after them;
The good is oft interred with their bones.

WILLIAM SHAKESPEARE, *Julius Caesar*

Men's evil manners live in brass; their virtues
We write in water.

WILLIAM SHAKESPEARE, *King Henry VIII*

Lives of great men all remind us
We can make our lives sublime,
And, departing, leave behind us
Footprints on the sands of time.

HENRY WADSWORTH LONGFELLOW, *A Psalm of Life*

Fame is a revenue payable only to our ghosts.

SIR GEORGE MACKENZIE

Glories, like glow-worms, afar off shine bright,
But looked to near have neither heat nor light.

JOHN WEBSTER, *The White Devil*

What's fame? A fancied life in others' breath,
A thing beyond us, even before our death.

ALEXANDER POPE, *Essay on Man*

For what is fame
But the benignant strength of one transformed
To joy of many?

GEORGE ELIOT, *Armgart*

---

[1]Published by Harper & Brothers. Copyright 1937 by Edna St. Vincent Millay.

[2]From *Poems by Emily Dickinson*, edited by Martha Dickinson Bianchi and Alfred Leete Hampson; published by Little, Brown & Co.

Passion for fame; a passion which
is the instinct of all great souls.

EDMUND BURKE, *Speech on American Taxation*

Happy is the man who hath never known what it is to taste of fame—to have it is a Purgatory, to want it is a Hell!

BULWER-LYTTON, *Last of the Barons*

A little rule, a little sway,
A sunbeam in a winter's day,
Is all the proud and mighty have
Between the cradle and the grave.

JOHN DYER, *Grongar Hill*

Familiarity

Familiarity breeds contempt.

Proverb

Familiarity begets boldness.

SHACKERLEY MARMION, *The Antiquary*

Fanaticism

Fanaticism soberly defined,
  Is the false fire of an o'erheated mind.

WILLIAM COWPER

Fashion

Darling, what is that?
Are you sure it is a hat?

OGDEN NASH, *The Face is Familiar*[1]

The girdle business goes to pot
In summer, when the weather's hot.

MARGARET FISHBACK, *Time For a Quick One*[2]

There is not so variable a thing in Nature as a lady's head-dress.

JOSEPH ADDISON, *The Spectator*

This is our chief bane, that we live not according to the light of reason, but after the fashion of others.

SENECA, *Octavia*

What used to be vices are become fashions.

SENECA

Fashion too often makes a monstrous noise,
  Bids us, a fickle jade, like fools adore
The poorest trash, the meanest toys.

PETER PINDAR, *Odes to the Royal Academicians*

Disguise it as you will,
  To right or wrong 'tis fashion guides us still.

JOSEPH WARTON, *Fashion*

[1]Copyright 1931, 1933, 1936, 1938 by Ogden Nash. Reprinted by permission of Little, Brown & Co.
[2]Copyright 1940 by Margaret Fishback. Reprinted by permission of Harcourt, Brace and Company, Inc.

Fate

For this is Wisdom; to love, to live
To take what fate, or the Gods, may give.
To ask no question, to make no prayer,
To kiss the lips and caress the hair,
Speed passion's ebb as you greet its flow
To have,—to hold—and,—in time,—let go!

LAURENCE HOPE, *The Complete Love Lyrics*[1]

And whether I came in love or hate,
That I came to you was written by fate.

LAURENCE HOPE, *The Complete Love Lyrics*

Human reason needs only to will more strongly than fate and she is fate.

THOMAS MANN, *The Magic Mountain*[2]

Thus, envious of another's state
Each blamed the partial hand of fate.

JOHN GAY, *Fables*

What fates impose, that men must needs abide;
It boots not to resist both wind and tide.

WILLIAM SHAKESPEARE, *Henry VI*

Things are where things are, and as fate has
  willed,
So shall they be fulfilled.

ROBERT BROWNING, *Agamemnon*

Heaven from all creatures hides the book of Fate.

ALEXANDER POPE, *Essay on Man*

Faults

The greatest fault, I should say, is to be conscious of none.

THOMAS CARLYLE, *Heroes and Hero Worship*

When you have done a fault, be always pert and insolent and behave yourself as if you were the injured person.

JONATHAN SWIFT, *Rules that Concern Servants*

We keep the faults of others before our eyes; our own behind our backs.

SENECA

He is all fault who hath no fault at all.

ALFRED, LORD TENNYSON, *Lancelot and Elaine*

And he that does one fault at first
And lies to hide it, makes it two.

ISAAC WATTS, *Songs for Children*

If we had no faults, we should not take so much pleasure in noticing them in others.

LA ROCHEFOUCAULD

[1]Reprinted by permission of Dodd, Mead & Company. Copyright by Malcolm J. J. S. Nicolson 1905–1933.
[2]Reprinted by permission of Alfred A. Knopf, Inc.

We never admit our faults, excepting through vanity.

LA ROCHEFOUCAULD

Whosoever does not know how to recognize the faults of great men is incapable of estimating their perfections.

VOLTAIRE

They say, best men are moulded out of faults.

WILLIAM SHAKESPEARE, *Measure for Measure*

Bad men excuse their faults, good men will leave them.
He acts the third crime that defends the first.

BEN JONSON, *Catiline*

Condemn the fault, and not the actor of it.

WILLIAM SHAKESPEARE, *Measure for Measure*

Fear

And feels a thousand deaths, in fearing one.

EDWARD YOUNG, *Night Thoughts*

Fear always springs from ignorance.

RALPH WALDO EMERSON

Nothing is terrible except fear itself.

FRANCIS BACON, *Fortitudo*

We have won against the most dangerous of our foes. We have conquered fear.

FRANKLIN DELANO ROOSEVELT, *Speech Accepting Renomination*

Feelings

Those who would make us feel—must feel themselves.

CHARLES CHURCHILL, *The Rosciad*

There are some feelings that time cannot benumb.

LORD BYRON, *Childe Harold's Pilgrimage*

Feelings are like chemicals, the more you analyze them, the worse they smell.

CHARLES KINGSLEY

Nothing is lost on him who sees
With an eye that feeling gave;
For him there's a story in every breeze,
And a picture in every wave.

THOMAS MOORE, *Boat Glee*

Fickleness

Man wants but little here below,
Nor wants that little long.

OLIVER GOLDSMITH, *The Hermit*

Man wants but little; nor that little long.

EDWARD YOUNG, *Night Thoughts*

Flattery

Strive not to hew your path through life—
it really doesn't pay;
Be sure the salve of flattery soaps all you
do and say.

EUGENE FIELD, *Uncle Eph*[1]

But when I tell him he hates flatterers,
He says he does, being then most flattered.

WILLIAM SHAKESPEARE, *Julius Caesar*

O flatt'ry!
How soon thy smooth insinuating oil
Supples the toughest food!

ELIJAH FENTON, *Mariamne*

When flattery does not succeed it is not the fault of flattery, but of the flatterer.

PIERRE GASTON, *Maxims*

Flatterers look like friends, as wolves like dogs.

GEORGE CHAPMAN, *Conspiracy of Charles, Duke of Byron*

If we did not flatter ourselves, the flattery of other people would not harm us.

LA ROCHEFOUCAULD

Foolishness

Since trifles make the sum of human things,
And half our misery from our foibles springs.

HANNAH MORE, *Sensibility*

For fools rush in where angels fear to tread.

ALEXANDER POPE, *Essay on Criticism*

Forgetfulness

And out of mind as soon as out of sight.

LORD BROOKE

Forgiveness

The offender never pardons.

GEORGE HERBERT, *Jacula Prudentum*

"I can forgive, but I cannot forget," is only another way of saying, "I cannot forgive."

HENRY WARD BEECHER, *Life Thoughts*

Forgive! How many will say "forgive," and find
A sort of absolution in the sound
To hate a little longer.

ALFRED, LORD TENNYSON, *Sea Dreams*

Fortune

O Fortune, unkind to men of talent, how unequally do you distribute your rewards!

SENECA, *Hercules Furens*

[1]From *The Poems of Eugene Field*. Reprinted by permission of Charles Scribner's Sons.

Extremes of fortune are true wisdom's test
And he's of men most wise who bears them best.

RICHARD CUMBERLAND, *Philemon*

A great fortune is a great bondage.

SENECA, *De Consolatione*

Too poor for a bribe, and too proud to importune,
He had not the method of making a fortune.

THOMAS GRAY

Fortune knows
We scorn her most, when most she offers blows.

WILLIAM SHAKESPEARE, *Antony and Cleopatra*

Freedom (*See also* Americanism)

No man loveth his fetters, be they made of gold.

JOHN HEYWOOD, *Proverbs*

When liberty is gone,
Life grows insipid and has lost its relish.

JOSEPH ADDISON

Liberty too must be limited in order to be possessed.

EDMUND BURKE, *Letter*

Liberty is not in any form of government. It is in the heart of free man; he carries it with him everywhere.

JEAN JACQUES ROUSSEAU *Emile, or Education*

Men rattle their chains to show that they are free.

Proverb

The love of liberty is the love of others; the love of power is the love of ourselves.

WILLIAM HAZLITT, *The Toad Eaters*

Pray you use your freedom and so far, if you please, allow me mine.

PHILIP MASSINGER, *Duke of Milan*

The cause of Freedom is the cause of God.

WILLIAM LISLE BOWLES, *To Edmund Burke*

He is a free man whom the truth makes free.

WILLIAM COWPER, *Winter Morning Walk*

The greatest glory of a freeborn people is to transmit that freedom to their children.

WILLIAM HARVARD, *Regulus*

A day, an hour, a virtuous liberty
Is worth a whole eternity in bondage.

JOSEPH ADDISON, *Cato*

O liberty! liberty! how many crimes are committed in thy name!

MADAME ROLAND

Freedom has a thousand charms to show,
That slaves, howe'er contented, never know.

WILLIAM COWPER, *Table Talk*

Error of opinion may be tolerated where reason is left free to combat it.

THOMAS JEFFERSON, *First Inaugural Address*

Free Speech (*See also* Americanism)

This is true liberty, when freeborn men,
having to advise the public, may speak free.

JOHN MILTON, *Translation of Euripides*

To speak his thought is ever freeman's right,
In peace and war, in council and in fight.

ALEXANDER POPE, *Iliad of Homer*

Friendship

Friendship! mysterious cement of the soul!
Sweetener of life! and solder of society!

ROBERT BLAIR, *The Grave*

Friends are as dangerous as enemies.

THOMAS DE QUINCEY, *Essay on Schlosser's Literary History*

After their friendship there is nothing so dangerous as to have them for enemies.

LORD CHESTERFIELD, *Letters to His Son*

Friendship is Love without his wings.

LORD BYRON, *L'Amitié est l'Amour sans Ailes*

Lay this unto your breast:
Old friends, like old swords, still are trusted best.

JOHN WEBSTER, *The Duchess of Malfi*

A stranger's kindness oft exceeds a friend's.

THOMAS MIDDLETON

Ships that pass in the night, and speak each other in passing,
Only a signal shown, and a distant voice in the darkness.
So on the ocean of life we pass and speak one another.
Only a look and a voice, then darkness again and a silence.

HENRY WADSWORTH LONGFELLOW, *Tales of a Wayside Inn*

An open foe may prove a curse,
But a pretended friend is worse.

JOHN GAY, *Fables*

A broken friendship may be soldered, but will never be sound.

Proverb

Tell me the company you keep, and I'll tell you who you are.

Proverb

A pleasant possession is useless without a comrade.

SENECA

A friend to everybody is a friend to nobody.

Proverb

It is prosperity that gives us friends, adversity that proves them.

Proverb

Women do not have friends—they only have rivals.

EDMOND GONDINET, *Jonathan*

The only way to have a friend is to be one.

RALPH WALDO EMERSON, *Friendship*

Friendship excels kinship.

CICERO

There is little friendship in the world, and least of all between equals.

FRANCIS BACON, *Of Followers*

Old friends are best. King James used to call for his old shoes; they were easiest for his feet.

JOHN SELDEN, *Friends*

The friends thou hast, and their adoption tried,
Grapple them to thy soul with hoops of steel.

WILLIAM SHAKESPEARE, *Hamlet*

Fulfillment

He gave to misery (all he had) a tear;
He gained from heaven ('twas all he wished) a friend.

THOMAS GRAY,
Elegy in a Country Churchyard

Futility

You cannot get blood out of a stone.

Proverb

'Tis no good planting boiled potatoes.

CHARLES HADDON SPURGEON,
John Ploughman

Gain

Gain cannot be made without some other person's loss.

PUBLILIUS SYRUS

Genius

Time, place, and action may with pains be wrought,
But Genius must be born; and never can be taught.

JOHN DRYDEN, *Epistle to Congreve*

Genius can only breathe freely in an atmosphere of freedom.

JOHN STUART MILL, *Liberty*

Since when was genius found respectable?

ELIZABETH BARRETT BROWNING,
Aurora Leigh

Adverse fortune reveals genius; prosperity hides it.

HORACE

No great genius is without an admixture of madness.

ARISTOTLE

God

God never made his work for man to mend.

JOHN DRYDEN, *Epistle to John Dryden*

God will estimate success one day.

ROBERT BROWNING,
Prince Hohenstiel-Schwangau

If God had not existed it would have been necessary to invent him.

VOLTAIRE,
To the author of The Three Impostors

If God is not in us, He never existed.

VOLTAIRE, *La Loi Naturelle*

God moves in a mysterious way
His wonders to perform;
He plants his footsteps in the sea
And rides upon the storm.

WILLIAM COWPER,
Light Shining out of Darkness

God sends us meat, the devil sends us cooks.

Proverb

God's mills grind slow, but sure.

GEORGE HERBERT,
Jacula Prudentum

Though the mills of God grind slowly,
yet they grind exceeding small;
Though with patience He stands waiting,
with exactness grinds He all.

HENRY WADSWORTH LONGFELLOW, *Retribution*

God tempers the wind to the shorn lamb.

LAURENCE STERNE,
A Sentimental Journey

God is more truly imagined than expressed, and He exists more truly than He is imagined.

ST. AUGUSTINE,
De Trinitate

He was a wise man who originated the idea of God.

PLATO, *Sisyphus*

God is the brave man's hope, and not the coward's excuse.

PLUTARCH, *Morals*

God made the country, and man made the town.

WILLIAM COWPER, *The Task*

God enters by a private door into every individual.

RALPH WALDO EMERSON, *Intellect*

God's in His Heaven—
All's right with the world.

ROBERT BROWNING, *Pippa Passes*

God, I can push the grass apart
And lay my fingers on Thy heart.

EDNA ST. VINCENT MILLAY, *Renascence*[1]

Goodness

Good, the more communicated, more abundant grows.

JOHN MILTON, *Paradise Lost*

There is some soul of goodness in things evil,
Would men, observingly, distil it out.

WILLIAM SHAKESPEARE, *Henry IV*

Gossip

A cruel story runs on wheels, and every hand oils the wheels as they run.

OUIDA, *Moths*

He's gone, and who knows how he may report
Thy words by adding fuel to the flame?

JOHN MILTON, *Samson Agonistes*

Who by aspersions throw a stone
At the head of others, hit their own.

GEORGE HERBERT, *Charms and Knots*

None are so fond of secrets as those who do not mean to keep them.

CHARLES CALEB COLTON, *Lacon*

There is no radical cure for the busybody, no more than there is for the fleas on a long-haired dog—if you get rid of the fleas you have got the dog left, and if you get rid of the dog you have got the fleas left, and so, where are you?

JOSH BILLINGS (HENRY WHEELER SHAW)

Take not informers' words on trust.

JOHN GAY, *Fables*

Who deals in slander lives in strife.

JOHN GAY, *Fables*

I remember that a wise friend of mine did usually say: That which is everybody's business is nobody's business.

IZAAK WALTON, *The Compleat Angler*

Government (*See also* Americanism)

Every nation has the government it deserves.

JOSEPH DE MAISTRE, *Letter*

Spare the spurs, boy, and hold the reins more firmly.

OVID, *Metamorphoses*

You can only govern men by serving them
The rule is without exception.

VICTOR COUSIN

[1]Published by Harper & Brothers. Copyright 1912, 1940 by Edna St. Vincent Millay.

A manly assertion by each of his individual rights and a manly concession of equal rights to every other man, is the law of good citizenship.

BENJAMIN HARRISON

Gratitude

No metaphysician ever felt the deficiency of language so much as the grateful.

CHARLES CALEB COLTON, *Lacon*

Wherever I find a great deal of gratitude in a poor man, I take it for granted there would be so much generosity if he were a rich man.

ALEXANDER POPE, *Thoughts on Various Subjects*

Only fools are unable to support that crushing load which we call gratitude.

EUGÈNE MARIN LABICHE, *M. Perrichon*

One good turn deserves another.

Proverb

Greatness

High stations tumult, but not bliss, create;
None think the great unhappy but the great.

EDWARD YOUNG, *Love of Fame*

Some are born great, some achieve greatness,
and some have greatness thrust upon 'em.

WILLIAM SHAKESPEARE, *Twelfth Night*

Little minds are tamed and subdued by misfortune,
But great minds rise above it.

WASHINGTON IRVING, *The Sketch Book*

Nothing is more simple than greatness; indeed, to be simple is to be great.

RALPH WALDO EMERSON, *Literary Ethics*

To be great is to be misunderstood.

RALPH WALDO EMERSON, *Self-Reliance*

It is always interesting, in the case of a great man, to know how he affected the women of his acquaintance.

LORD MORLEY, *Burke*

The world knows nothing of its greatest men.

SIR HENRY TAYLOR, *Philip van Artevelde*

Great wits and valors, like great estates,
Do sometimes sink with their own weights.

SAMUEL BUTLER, *Hudibras*

He is only a great man, who can neglect the applause of the multitude, and enjoy himself independent of its favor.

RICHARD STEELE, *Spectator*

Grief (*See also* Despair *and* Sorrow)

Grief best is pleased with grief's society.

WILLIAM SHAKESPEARE, *Rape of Lucrece*

No greater grief than to remember days
Of joy when misery is at hand.

DANTE ALIGHIERI, *Hell*

The private wound is deepest.

WILLIAM SHAKESPEARE, *Two Gentlemen of Verona*

When griefs have partners they are better borne.

THOMAS MIDDLETON, *Your Five Gallants*

Light burdens long borne grow heavy.

GEORGE HERBERT, *Jacula Prudentum*

None knows the weight of another's burden.

GEORGE HERBERT, *Jacula Prudentum*

Half of the ills we hoard within our hearts
Are ills because we hoard them.

BRYAN WALLER PROCTER, *Mirandola*

While grief is fresh, any attempt to divert it only irritates.

SAMUEL JOHNSON

Depend upon it, that, if a man talks of his misfortunes, there is something in them that is not disagreeable to him; for where there is nothing but pure misery, there never is any recourse to the mention of it.

SAMUEL JOHNSON

A great sorrow is a great repose, and you will come out from your grief stronger than when you entered it.

ALEXANDRE DUMAS, *Mme. de Chamblay*

Guilt

Guilt proves the hardest nearest home.

JAMES HOGG, *The Pedlar*

Habit

Habit, the instrument of nature, is a great leveler: the familiarity which it induces takes off the edge both of our pleasures and our sufferings.

WILLIAM PALEY, *Natural Theology*

Habit becomes a kind of second nature which acts as a motive for many of our actions.

CICERO

Happiness

The lesson we suffer the most in learning:
That a happy man is a man forgetful of all the
torturing ills around him.

EDWIN ARLINGTON ROBINSON, *The Night Before*[1]

All who joy would win
Must share it—happiness was born a twin.

LORD BYRON, *Don Juan*

No man is happy. Man strives all his life through for imaginary happiness, which he seldom attains, and if he does, it is only to be disillusioned.

ARTHUR SCHOPENHAUER, *Emptiness of Existence*

The little-known art of being happy.

VOLTAIRE, *Sur l'Usage de la Vie*

One is never so happy or so unhappy as one imagines.

LA ROCHEFOUCAULD, *Maximes*

A man must seek his happiness and inward peace from objects which cannot be taken away from him.

WILHELM VON HUMBOLDT

And there is ev'n a happiness
That makes the heart afraid.

THOMAS HOOD, *Ode to Melancholy*

Know then this truth (enough for man to know),
Virtue alone is happiness below.

ALEXANDER POPE, *Essay on Man*

When one is contented, there is no more to be desired; and when there is no more to be desired, there is an end of it.

MIGUEL DE CERVANTES, *Don Quixote*

Happy he who has succeeded in learning the causes of things.

VERGIL

Happy he who dares courageously to defend what he loves.

OVID

O happiness! our being's end and aim!
Good, pleasure, ease, content! whate'er thy name:
That something still which prompts the eternal sigh,
For which we bear to live, or dare to die.

ALEXANDER POPE, *Essay on Man*

Happiness depends, as Nature shows,
Less on exterior things than most suppose.

WILLIAM COWPER, *Table Talk*

Haste

The more haste the lesse speede.

JOHN HEYWOOD, *Proverbs*

Haste makes waste, and waste makes want, and want makes strife between the good man and his wife.

Proverb

[1]From *The Children of the Night,* published by Charles Scribner's Sons.

Hate

Now hatred is by far the longest pleasure!
Men love in haste, but they detest at leisure.

LORD BYRON, *Don Juan*

People hate the ones who make them feel their own inferiority.

LORD CHESTERFIELD, *Letters*

Love, friendship, respect, will never unite people as much as a common hatred for something.

ANTON PAVLOVICH CHEKHOV, *Note-Books*

They did not know how hate can burn
In hearts once changed from soft to stern.

LORD BYRON

In time we hate that which we often fear.

WILLIAM SHAKESPEARE, *Antony and Cleopatra*

Hatred is like fire—it makes even light rubbish deadly.

GEORGE ELIOT, *Janet's Repentance*

Hell

Hell is paved with good intentions.

JAMES BOSWELL, *Life of Samuel Johnson*

Heroes

In short, he was a perfect cavaliero,
And to his very valet seemed a hero.

LORD BYRON, *Beppo*

Every hero becomes a bore at last.

RALPH WALDO EMERSON, *Representative Men*

Whoe'er excels in what we prize
Appears a hero in our eyes.

JONATHAN SWIFT

History (*See also* Americanism)

History, a distillation of Rumour.

THOMAS CARLYLE, *The French Revolution*

History is full of the errors of states and princes.

BENJAMIN FRANKLIN, *Autobiography*

Home

'Mid pleasures and palaces though we may roam,
Be it ever so humble, there's no place like home.

JOHN HOWARD PAYNE, *Home, Sweet Home*

Our friends are as true, and our wives are as
comely,
And our home is still home, be it ever so homely.

CHARLES DIBDIN, *Songs*

Honesty

Honesty rare as a man without self-pity,
Kindness as large and plain as a prairie wind.

STEPHEN VINCENT BENÉT, *John Brown's Body*[1]

And looks the whole world in the face,
For he owes not any man.

HENRY WADSWORTH LONGFELLOW, *The Village Blacksmith*

Honesty is the best policy.

BENJAMIN FRANKLIN, *Poor Richard's Almanac*

Too much honesty never harmed a man.

JOHN CLARKE, *Paroemiologia*

It is my own opinion that every man cheats in his own way, and he is only honest who is not discovered.

SUSANNAH CENTLIVRE, *The Artifice*

An honest tale speeds best, being plainly told.

WILLIAM SHAKESPEARE, *King Richard III*

He that loseth his honestie hath nothing else to lose.

JOHN LYLY, *Euphues*

Hope

The worst is not
So long as we can say, "this is the worst."

WILLIAM SHAKESPEARE, *King Lear*

The miserable have no other medicine,
But only hope.

WILLIAM SHAKESPEARE, *Measure for Measure*

While there is life there's hope.

JOHN GAY, *The Sick Man and the Angel*

Hope springs eternal in the human breast.

ALEXANDER POPE, *Essay on Man*

The rose is fairest when it is budding new,
And hope is brightest when it dawns from fears.

SIR WALTER SCOTT, *Lady of the Lake*

Hope never leaves a wretched man that seeks her.

BEAUMONT AND FLETCHER, *The Captain*

It has been well said: "Man is based on Hope; he has properly no other possession but Hope; this habitation of his is named the Place of Hope."

THOMAS CARLYLE, *The French Revolution*

---

[1]From *Selected Works of Stephen Vincent Benét*, published by Rinehart & Company, Inc. Copyright 1927, 1928 by Stephen Vincent Benét.

But love can hope where reason would despair.
LORD LYTTELTON, *Epigram*

Above the cloud with its shadow is the star with its light.
VICTOR HUGO

A drowning man will catch at a straw.
Proverb

The wretch condemned with life to part,
Still, still on hope relies;
And every pang that rends the heart
Bids expectation rise.
OLIVER GOLDSMITH, *The Captivity*

Hope, like the gleaming taper's light,
Adorns and cheers our way;
And still, as darker grows the night
Emits a brighter ray.
OLIVER GOLDSMITH, *The Captivity*

Hope! thou nurse of young desire.
ISAAC BICKERSTAFF, *Love in a Village*

Hope, of all ills that men endure,
The only cheap and universal cure.
ABRAHAM COWLEY, *For Hope*

Hospitality

Profusion is the charm of hospitality.
Have plenty, if it be only beer.
WILLIAM MAKEPEACE THACKERAY, *Barmecide Banquets*

Human Being

On a human being: an ingenious assembly of portable plumbing.
CHRISTOPHER MORLEY, *Human Being*[1]

Humanity

All that is human must retrograde if it do not advance.
EDWARD GIBBON, *Decline and Fall of the Roman Empire*

Love, hope, fear, faith—these make humanity;
These are its sign, and note and character.
ROBERT BROWNING, *Paracelsus*

O wearisome condition of humanity!
LORD BROOKE, *Mustapha*

Human Nature

We have hearts within:
Warm, live, improvident, indecent hearts.
ELIZABETH BARRETT BROWNING, *Aurora Leigh*

You cannot slander human nature; it is worse than words can paint it.
CHARLES HADDON SPURGEON, *Salt-Cellars*

Our soul is full of a thousand internal contrarieties.
PLATO, *Republic*

Every heart, when sifted well,
Is a clot of warmer dust,
Mix'd with cunning sparks of hell.
ALFRED, LORD TENNYSON, *The Vision of Sin*

No one likes to be disturbed at meals or love.
LORD BYRON, *Don Juan*

Hobbes clearly proves that every creature
Lives in a state of war by nature.
JONATHAN SWIFT, *Poetry*

Man dreams of Fame, while woman wakes to Love.
ALFRED, LORD TENNYSON, *Merlin and Vivien*

Human nature will not flourish, any more than a potato, if it be planted and replanted for too long a series of generations, in the same worn-out soil.
NATHANIEL HAWTHORNE, *The Scarlet Letter*

Humility

Humility is a virtue all preach, none practice, and yet everybody is content to hear.
JOHN SELDEN, *Humility*

Hypocrisy

Hypocrisy is the homage vice pays to virtue.
LA ROCHEFOUCAULD, *Maximes*

Yet do I fear thy nature;
It is too full o' the milk of human kindness.
WILLIAM SHAKESPEARE, *Macbeth*

Who dares think one thing, and another tell,
My heart detests him as the gates of hell.
ALEXANDER POPE, *The Iliad*

When I see a merchant over-polite to his customers, begging them to take a little brandy, and throwing his goods on the counter, thinks I, that man has an ax to grind.
BENJAMIN FRANKLIN, *Poor Richard's Almanac*

He holds with the hare, and runs with the hound.
Proverb

An hypocrite is a gilded pill, composed of two natural ingredients, natural dishonesty, and artificial dissimulation.
SIR THOMAS OVERBURY, *Characters: An Hypocrite*

Idleness

An idle brain is the devil's workshop.
Proverb

[1]Reprinted by permission of J. B. Lippincott Company.

An idler is a watch that wants both hands:
As useless when it goes as when it stands.

WILLIAM COWPER, *Retirement*

Absence of occupation is not rest,
A mind quite vacant is a mind distressed.

WILLIAM COWPER, *Retirement*

Idleness is only the refuge of weak minds, and the holiday of fools.

LORD CHESTERFIELD, *Letters to His Son*

The doer is better than the critic, and the man who strives stands far above the man who stands aloof.

THEODORE ROOSEVELT

Ignorance

Where ignorance is bliss
'Tis folly to be wise.

THOMAS GRAY, *Ode on a Distant Prospect of Eton College*

Have the courage to be ignorant of a great number of things, in order to avoid the calamity of being ignorant of everything.

SYDNEY SMITH, *Lectures on Moral Philosophy*

From ignorance our comfort flows,
The only wretched are the wise.

MATTHEW PRIOR

A blind man should not judge of colors.

Proverb

Your ignorance is the mother of your devotion to me.

JOHN DRYDEN, *The Maiden Queen*

Imagination

To see a world in a grain of sand,
And a heaven in a wild flower.

WILLIAM BLAKE, *Auguries of Innocence*

Don't let us make imaginary evils, when you know we have so many real ones to encounter.

OLIVER GOLDSMITH, *The Good-Natured Man*

Imitation

Imitation is the sincerest of flattery.

CHARLES CALEB COLTON, *Lacon*

No man was ever great by imitation.

SAMUEL JOHNSON, *Rasselas*

Imperfection

Roses have thorns, and silver fountains mud;
Clouds and eclipses stain both moon and sun,
And loathsome canker lies in sweetest bud.

WILLIAM SHAKESPEARE, *Sonnet*

Every bean hath its black.

Proverb

Every white will have its black,
And every sweet its sour.

THOMAS PERCY, *Reliques*

Improvement

And make each day a critic on the last.

ALEXANDER POPE, *Essay on Criticism*

Wise men ne'er sit and wail their loss,
But cheerly seek how to redress their harms.

WILLIAM SHAKESPEARE, *Henry VI*

Inconsistency

The greatest men
May ask a foolish question now and then.

PETER PINDAR, *The Apple Dumpling and the King*

Do not grudge
  To pick out treasures from an earthen pot.
The worst speak something good.

GEORGE HERBERT, *The Church Porch*

Indication

A cold hand, a warm heart.

Proverb

Indispensability

Trust me, To-day's Most Indispensables,
Five hundred men can take your place or mine.

RUDYARD KIPLING, *Departmental Ditties*

Individuality

Literary history and all history is a record of the power of minorities, and of minorities of one.

RALPH WALDO EMERSON, *Progress of Culture*

Whatever crushes individuality is despotism, by whatever name it may be called.

JOHN STUART MILL, *Liberty*

Absolute individualism is an absurdity.

HENRI FRÉDÉRIC AMIEL

Inevitability

Come what come may;
Time and the hour run through the roughest day.

WILLIAM SHAKESPEARE, *Macbeth*

Innocence

An innocent heart is a brittle thing, and one false vow can break it.

BULWER-LYTTON, *Last of the Barons*

Insight

A moment's insight is sometimes worth a life's experience.

OLIVER WENDELL HOLMES, *The Professor at the Breakfast Table*

Instinct

And to all this fame he rose,
Only following his nose.

WILLIAM COWPER, *On a Pointer Dog*

Swift instinct leaps; slow reason feebly climbs.

EDWARD YOUNG, *Night Thoughts*

Institution

An institution is the lengthened shadow of one man.

RALPH WALDO EMERSON, *Self-Reliance*

Insult

A moral, sensible, and well-bred man
Will not affront me, and no other can.

WILLIAM COWPER, *Conversation*

There is nothing that people bear more impatiently, or forgive less, than contempt; and an injury is much sooner forgotten than an insult.

LORD CHESTERFIELD, *Letters to His Son*

Insults are like bad coins; we cannot help their being offered to us, but we need not take them.

CHARLES HADDON SPURGEON, *Salt-Cellars*

Intelligence

All men see the same objects, but all men do not equally understand them. Intelligence is the tongue that discerns and tastes them.

THOMAS TRAHERNE, *Centuries of Meditations*

Intentions

When any great design thou dost intend,
Think on the means, the manner and the end.

SIR JOHN DENHAM

Interference

Those who in quarrels interpose,
Must often wipe a bloody nose.

JOHN GAY, *Fables*

Irritation

Rub a galled horse, he will kick.

Proverb

Jealousy

Jealousy,
. . . the injur'd lover's hell.

JOHN MILTON, *Paradise Lost*

O! beware, my lord, of jealousy;
It is the green-eyed monster which doth mock
The meat it feeds on.

WILLIAM SHAKESPEARE, *Othello*

A jealous woman believes everything her passion suggests.

JOHN GAY, *The Beggar's Opera*

What frenzy dictates, jealousy believes.

JOHN GAY, *Dione*

Love is strong as death; jealousy is cruel as the grave.

The Song of Solomon

Judgment

Give every man thine ear but few thy voice:
Take each man's censure, but reserve thy judgment.

WILLIAM SHAKESPEARE, *Hamlet*

Remember, when the judgment's weak the prejudice is strong.

KANE O'HARA, *Midas*

Men see a little, presume a great deal, and so jump to the conclusion.

JOHN LOCKE

I am monarch of all I survey;
My right there is none to dispute.

WILLIAM COWPER, *Verses Supposed to be Written by Alexander Selkirk*

'Ere you remark another's sin,
Bid thy own conscience look within.

JOHN GAY, *Fables*

We are firm believers in the maxim that, for all right judgment of any man or thing, it is useful, nay, essential, to see his good qualities before pronouncing on his bad.

THOMAS CARLYLE, *Goethe*

And how his audit stands who knows, save heaven?

WILLIAM SHAKESPEARE, *Hamlet*

'Tis with our judgments as our watches, none
Go just alike, yet each believes his own.

ALEXANDER POPE, *Essay on Criticism*

Be to her virtues very kind;
Be to her faults a little blind.

MATTHEW PRIOR, *An English Padlock*

Justice

Give the devil his due.

Proverb

Every dog must have his day.

JOHN THOMAS RANDOLPH, *The Townsman's Petition*

Let Hercules himself do what he may,
The cat will mew, and dog will have his day.

WILLIAM SHAKESPEARE, *Hamlet*

Whoso diggeth a pit shall fall therein.

Proverbs

Kissing

Kissing an unwilling pair of lips is as mean a victory as robbing a bird's nest, and kissing too willing ones is about as unfragrant a recreation as making bouquets out of dandelions.

JOSH BILLINGS (HENRY WHEELER SHAW)

Knowledge (*See also* Learning)

What can we reason but from what we know?

ALEXANDER POPE, *Essay on Man*

Knowledge dwells
In heads replete with thoughts of other men:
Wisdom, in minds attentive to their own.

WILLIAM COWPER, *The Task*

Knowledge is a treasure but practice is the key to it.

Proverb

Half our knowledge we must snatch, not take.

ALEXANDER POPE, *Moral Essays*

Knowledge is not happiness, and science
But an exchange of ignorance for that
Which is another kind of ignorance.

LORD BYRON, *Manfred*

Knowledge is the antidote to fear.

RALPH WALDO EMERSON, *Courage*

A man without knowledge, and I have read,
May well be compared to one that is dead.

THOMAS INGELEND,
The Disobedient Child

Knowledge is power.

FRANCIS BACON, *Meditationes Sacrae*

A man is but what he knoweth.

FRANCIS BACON, *In Praise of Knowledge*

Knowledge comes, but wisdom lingers.

ALFRED, LORD TENNYSON,
Locksley Hall

Knowledge is of two kinds. We know a subject ourselves, or we know where we can find information upon it.

SAMUEL JOHNSON,
in Boswell's *Life of Johnson*

No man's knowledge, here, can go beyond his experience.

JOHN LOCKE,
Essay on the Human Understanding

He who knows not and knows not that he knows not is a fool—avoid him!
He who knows and knows not that he knows is asleep—waken him!
He who knows not and knows that he knows not wants beating—beat him!
But he who knows and knows that he knows is a wise man—know him.

Proverb

Laughter

There is one kind of a laugh that I always did recommend; it looks out of the eye first with a merry twinkle, then it creeps down on its hands and knees and plays around the mouth like a pretty moth around the blaze of a candle, then it steals over into the dimples of the cheeks and rides around in those little whirlpools for a while, then it lights up the whole face like the mellow bloom on a damask rose, then it swims up on the air, with a peal as clear and as happy as a dinner-bell, then it goes back again on gold tiptoes like an angel out for an airing, and lies down on its little bed of violets in the heart where it came from.

JOSH BILLINGS (HENRY WHEELER SHAW)

How much lies in laughter: the cipher-key, wherewith we decipher the whole man.

THOMAS CARLYLE, *Sartor Resartus*

Laughter is my object; 'tis a property
In man essential to his reason.

THOMAS RANDOLPH,
The Muses' Looking-Glass

And the loud laugh that spoke the vacant mind.

OLIVER GOLDSMITH, *The Deserted Village*

Laugh while you can. Everything has its time.

VOLTAIRE

Law

Laws are like cobwebs that entangle the weak, but are broken by the strong.

SOLON

Law is the protector of the weak.

FRIEDRICH SCHILLER

A good law is one that holds, whether you recognize it or not; a bad law is one that cannot, however much you ordain it.

JOHN RUSKIN

Learning (*See also* Knowledge)

A little learning is a dangerous thing;
Drink deep, or taste not the Pierian spring;
There shallow draughts intoxicate the brain,
And drinking largely sobers us again.

ALEXANDER POPE,
Essay on Criticism

Learn, but learn from the learned.

CATO

The mind is slow in unlearning what it has been long in learning.

SENECA, *Troades*

Knowledge is proud that he has learned so much.
Wisdom is humble, that he knows no more.

WILLIAM COWPER, *Winter Walk at Noon*

Learned fools are the greatest fools.

Proverb

Learning makes the wise wiser, but the fool more foolish.

Proverb

All men naturally desire to know.

ARISTOTLE

Happy is the man who sees his folly in his youth.

Proverb

Learning by study must be won;
'Twas ne'er entailed from son to son.

JOHN GAY, *Fables*

Liberalism

Liberalism is trust of the people, tempered by prudence; Conservatism, distrust of the people, tempered by fear.

WILLIAM EWART GLADSTONE

Lies

And, after all, what is a lie? It is but the truth in masquerade.

LORD BYRON, *Don Juan*

Liars should have good memories.

Proverb

A lie travels round the world while Truth is putting on her boots.

CHARLES HADDON SPURGEON, *Truth and Falsehood*

Life (or) Living

Gather ye rosebuds while ye may—
This is the sum of his earthy day.
And when the whole of it's done and said,
"Up, to the office . . . and so to bed."

FRANKLIN P. ADAMS, *So Much Velvet*[1]

Man to the last is but a forward child;
So eager for the future, come what may,
And to the present so insensible!

SAMUEL ROGERS, *Reflections*

Life is indestructible:
Its holy flame forever burneth:
From Heaven it came, to Heaven returneth.

ROBERT SOUTHEY, *The Curse of Kehama*

To live and move among men, the heart must break or harden.

SÉBASTIEN R. N. CHAMFORT

[1]Copyright 1924 by Doubleday & Company, Inc. Reprinted by permission.

Life is short and the art long.

HIPPOCRATES, *Aphorisms*

Life is a game, at which everybody loses.

SARKADI SCHULLER, *Within Four Walls*

Life is real! Life is earnest!
And the grave is not its goal.

HENRY WADSWORTH LONGFELLOW, *Psalm of Life*

Live every day as if thy last.

MARCUS AURELIUS

We are born crying, live complaining, and die disappointed.

Proverb

Life is a series of surprises.

RALPH WALDO EMERSON

The web of our life is of a mingled yarn, good and ill together.

WILLIAM SHAKESPEARE, *All's Well That Ends Well*

Live while you live, the epicure would say,
And seize the pleasures of the present day.

PHILIP DODDRIDGE, *Epigram on His Family Motto*

Life differs from the play only in this . . . it has no plot . . . all is vague, desultory, unconnected . . . till the curtain drops with the mystery unsolved.

BULWER-LYTTON, *Godolphin*

Life is a great bundle of little things.

OLIVER WENDELL HOLMES, *Professor at the Breakfast Table*

Let Nature and let Art do what they please,
When all is done, Life's an incurable disease.

ABRAHAM COWLEY, *Ode to Dr. Scarborough*

Limitation

There is no stretching of power. 'Tis a good rule: Eat within your stomach, act within your commission.

JOHN SELDEN

As we advance in life we learn the limits of our abilities.

JAMES ANTHONY FROUDE, *Short Studies on Great Subjects*

Logic

Take a straw and throw it up into the air, you may see by that which way the wind is.

JOHN SELDEN, *Libels*

Cause and effect are two sides of one fact.

RALPH WALDO EMERSON, *Circles*

Set a thief to catch a thief.

Proverb

Loneliness (*See also* Solitude)

So lonely 'twas, that God Himself
Scarce seemed there to be.

SAMUEL TAYLOR COLERIDGE, *The Ancient Mariner*

Love

Here's my strength and my weakness, gents—
I loved them until they loved me.

DOROTHY PARKER, *Not So Deep As a Well*[1]

Oh, gallant was the first love, and glittering and fine;
The second love was water, in a clear white cup;
The third love was his, and the fourth was mine;
And after that, I always get them all mixed up.

DOROTHY PARKER, *Not So Deep As a Well*[1]

Ah, when Love comes his wings are swift;
His ways are full of quick surprise;
'Tis well for those who have the gift
To seize him even as he flies.

LAURENCE HOPE, *The Complete Love Lyrics*[2]

Why is Love such a sorrowful thing,
This I never could understand:
Pain and passion are linked together,
Ever I find them hand in hand.

LAURENCE HOPE, *The Complete Love Lyrics*[2]

Love's a thing that's never out of season.

BARRY CORNWALL

A woman in love is a very poor judge of character.

J. G. HOLLAND

In dreams and in love there are no impossibilities.

JÁNOS ARANY

You should be more concerned with being lovely than being loved.

A. BERGGREN, *The Lionhearted*

Love looks not with the eyes, but with the mind;
And therefore is winged Cupid painted blind.

WILLIAM SHAKESPEARE, *A Midsummer Night's Dream*

For aught that I could ever read,
Could ever hear by tale or history,
The course of true love never did run smooth.

WILLIAM SHAKESPEARE, *A Midsummer Night's Dream*

And yet, to say the truth,
reason and love keep little company
together now-a-days.

WILLIAM SHAKESPEARE, *A Midsummer Night's Dream*

[1]From *The Portable Dorothy Parker.* Copyright 1926, 1944 by Dorothy Parker. Reprinted by permission of Viking Press, Inc.
[2]Copyright by Malcolm J. J. S. Nicolson 1905–1933. Reprinted by permission of Dodd, Mead & Company.

Of all the pain, the greatest pain,
It is to love, but love in vain.

ABRAHAM COWLEY, *Anacreontics*

We are all born for love. It is the principle of existence, and its only end.

BENJAMIN DISRAELI, *Sibyl*

God, from a beautiful necessity, is Love.

MARTIN FARQUHAR TUPPER, *Of Immortality*

In the spring a young man's fancy lightly turns to thoughts of love.

ALFRED, LORD TENNYSON, *Locksley Hall*

It's good to be off wi' the old love
Before ye be on wi' the new.

SIR WALTER SCOTT, *The Bride of Lammermoor*

Love and a red nose can't be hid.

THOMAS HOLCROFT, *Duplicity*

Heaven has no rage like love to hatred turned,
Nor hell a fury like a woman scorned.

WILLIAM CONGREVE, *The Mourning Bride*

They sin who tell us Love can die:
With Life all other passions fly,
All others are but vanity.

ROBERT SOUTHEY, *The Curse of Kehama*

Pains of love be sweeter far
Than all other pleasures are.

JOHN DRYDEN, *Tyrannic Love*

Love lives in cottages as well as in courts.

JOHN RAY, *English Proverbs*

Say thou dost love me, love me, love me—toll
The silver iterance!—only minding, Dear,
To love me also in silence with thy soul.

ELIZABETH BARRETT BROWNING, *Sonnets from the Portuguese*

Man's love is of man's life a thing apart;
It is woman's whole existence.

LORD BYRON, *Don Juan*

All mankind loves a lover.

RALPH WALDO EMERSON, *Love*

In their first passion women love their lover; and in all the others, they love love.

LA ROCHEFOUCAULD, *Maximes*

They do not love that do not show their love.

JOHN HEYWOOD, *Proverbs*

I feel it when I sorrow most:
It is better to have loved and lost
Than never to have loved at all.

ALFRED, LORD TENNYSON, *In Memoriam*

Love is a platform upon which all ranks meet.

SIR WILLIAM SCHWENCK GILBERT, *H. M. S. Pinafore*

Then, must you speak
Of one that loved not wisely but too well.

WILLIAM SHAKESPEARE, *Othello*

Such is the nature of women, . . . not to love when we love them, and to love when we love them not.

MIGUEL DE CERVANTES, *Don Quixote*

Let me not to the marriage of true minds
Admit impediments: love is not love
Which alters when it alteration finds.

WILLIAM SHAKESPEARE, *Sonnets*

Of all the paths lead to a woman's love,
Pity's the straightest.

BEAUMONT AND FLETCHER, *The Knight of Malta*

No sooner met but they looked, no sooner looked than they loved, no sooner loved than they sighed, no sooner sighed but they asked one another the reason, no sooner knew the reason but they sought the remedy.

WILLIAM SHAKESPEARE, *As You Like It*

Love sought is good, but given unsought is better.

WILLIAM SHAKESPEARE, *Twelfth Night*

But love is blind and lovers cannot see
The pretty follies that themselves commit.

WILLIAM SHAKESPEARE, *Merchant of Venice*

Men have died from time to time, and worms have eaten them, but not for love.

WILLIAM SHAKESPEARE, *As You Like It*

Friendship is constant in all other things
Save in the office and affairs of love:
Therefore all hearts in love use their own tongues;
Let every eye negotiate for itself
And trust no agent.

WILLIAM SHAKESPEARE, *Much Ado About Nothing*

Speak low if you speak love.

WILLIAM SHAKESPEARE, *Much Ado about Nothing*

That man that hath a tongue, I say, is no man,
If with his tongue he cannot win a woman.

WILLIAM SHAKESPEARE, *Two Gentlemen of Verona*

We learn only from those we love.

JOHANN WOLFGANG VON GOETHE, *Conversation with Eckermann*

All is fair in love and war.

FRANCIS EDWARD SMEDLEY, *Frank Fairleigh*

Two souls with but a single thought,
Two hearts that beat as one.

FRIEDRICH HALM, *Ingomar the Barbarian*

Change everything but your loves.

VOLTAIRE, *Sur l'Usage de la Vie*

Who ever loved
that loved not at first sight?

CHRISTOPHER MARLOWE, *Hero and Leander*

Those who are faithful know only the trivial side of love: it is the faithless who know love's tragedies.

OSCAR WILDE, *Picture of Dorian Gray*

When poverty comes in at the door, love creeps out at the window.

THOMAS FULLER, *Gnomologia*

It is an unhappy circumstance that the man so often should outlive the lover.

WILLIAM CONGREVE, *The Way of the World*

Love reckons hours for months, and days for years;
And every little absence is an age.

JOHN DRYDEN, *Amphitryon*

He that will win his dame, must do
As love does when he bends his bow;
With one hand thrust the lady from,
And with the other pull her home.

SAMUEL BUTLER, *Hudibras*

The heart once broken is a heart no more,
And is absolved from all a heart must be;
All that it signed or chartered heretofore
Is cancelled now, the bankrupt heart is free.

EDNA ST. VINCENT MILLAY, *Fatal Interview*[1]

I find some woman bearing as I bear
Love like a burning city in the breast.

EDNA ST. VINCENT MILLAY, *Fatal Interview*[1]

Man

Two and two are merely four
And often less and never more,
And I, for all the world's advance,
An upright mammal wearing pants.

SAMUEL HOFFENSTEIN, *Year In, You're Out*[2]

His words are bonds, his oaths are oracles;
His love sincere, his thoughts immaculate;
His tears, pure messengers sent from his heart;
His heart as far from fraud as heaven from earth.

WILLIAM SHAKESPEARE, *Two Gentlemen of Verona*

---

[1]Published by Harper & Brothers. Copyright 1930 by Edna St. Vincent Millay.

[2]Published by Liveright Publishing Corp., N.Y. Copyright by Samuel Hoffenstein, 1930.

Man!
Thou pendulum betwixt a smile and tear.

LORD BYRON, *Childe Harold's Pilgrimage*

Men are but children of a larger growth.

JOHN DRYDEN, *All for Love*

Men of few words are the best men.

WILLIAM SHAKESPEARE, *King Henry V*

Man has his will—but woman has her way.

OLIVER WENDELL HOLMES, *Prologue*

Man is the creature of circumstance.

ROBERT OWEN, *The Philanthropist*

Man's the creature of habit.

CHARLES DICKENS, *The Battle of Life*

Man is the hunter; woman is his game.

ALFRED, LORD TENNYSON, *The Princess*

Man is an embodied paradox, a bundle of contradictions.

CHARLES CALEB COLTON, *Lacon*

Man is Nature's sole mistake.

SIR WILLIAM SCHWENCK GILBERT, *Princess Ida*

Man punishes the action, but God the intention.

Proverb

Ah! how unjust to nature, and himself,
Is thoughtless, thankless, inconsistent man!

EDWARD YOUNG, *Night Thoughts*

Marriage

Marriage, at best, is but a vow,
Which all men either break or bow.

SAMUEL BUTLER, *The Lady's Answer to the Knight*

When I said I would die a bachelor,
I did not think I should live till I were married.

WILLIAM SHAKESPEARE, *Much Ado about Nothing*

Some marry in haste, and then set down and think it careful over.

JOSH BILLINGS (HENRY WHEELER SHAW)

Marriages are made in Heaven.

Proverb

Thus grief still treads upon the heels of pleasure;
Married in haste, we may repent at leisure.

WILLIAM CONGREVE, *The Old Bachelor*

Oh! how many torments lie in the small circle of a wedding-ring!

COLLEY CIBBER, *The Double Gallant*

Is not marriage an open question, when it is alleged, from the beginning of the world, that such as are in the institution wish to get out, and such as are out wish to get in?

RALPH WALDO EMERSON, *Representative Men: Montaigne*

Marry your son when you will; your daughter when you can.

GEORGE HERBERT, *Jacula Prudentum*

Needles and pins, needles and pins!
When a man marries his trouble begins.

Old Nursery Rhyme

Advice to person about to marry.—Don't.

HENRY MAYHEW, *Punch's Almanac*

One was never married, and that's his hell; another is and that's his plague.

ROBERT BURTON, *Anatomy of Melancholy*

Choose not alone a proper mate,
But a proper time to marry.

WILLIAM COWPER, *Pairing Time*

Remember, it's as easy to marry a rich woman as a poor woman.

WILLIAM MAKEPEACE THACKERAY, *Pendennis*

In married life three is company and two none.

OSCAR WILDE, *The Importance of Being Earnest*

Marriage has many pains, but celibacy has no pleasures.

SAMUEL JOHNSON, *Rasselas*

Melancholy

There is a mood
(I sing not to the vacant and the young),
There is a kindly mood of melancholy,
That wings the soul, and points her to the skies.

JOHN DYER, *The Ruins of Rome*

Melancholy is a fearful gift;
What is it but the telescope of truth?

LORD BYRON

Melancholy
Sits on me, as a cloud along the sky,
Which will not let the sunbeams through, nor yet
Descend in rain, and end.

LORD BYRON

Go,—you may call it madness, folly;
You shall not chase my gloom away!
There's such a charm in melancholy
I would not, if I could, be gay.

SAMUEL ROGERS, *To ———*

There's not a string attuned to mirth
But has its chord in melancholy.

THOMAS HOOD, *Ode to Melancholy*

Memory

How cruelly sweet are the echoes that start,
When memory plays an old tune on the heart!

ELIZA COOK, *Old Dobbin*

Of joys departed,
Not to return, how painful the remembrance!

ROBERT BLAIR, *The Grave*

I remember, I remember
How my childhood fleeted by—
The mirth of its December,
And the warmth of its July.

WINTHROP MACKWORTH PRAED, *I Remember, I Remember*

Mercy (*See also* Pity)

The quality of mercy is not strain'd;
It droppeth as the gentle rain from heaven
Upon the place beneath; it is twice bless'd:
It blesseth him that gives, and him that takes.

WILLIAM SHAKESPEARE, *Merchant of Venice*

Teach me to feel another's woe,
To hide the fault I see;
That mercy I to others show,
That mercy show to me.

ALEXANDER POPE, *The Universal Prayer*

They who forgive most shall be most forgiven.

PHILIP JAMES BAILEY, *Festus*

To err is human, to forgive divine.

ALEXANDER POPE, *Essay on Criticism*

Sweet Mercy is nobility's true badge.

WILLIAM SHAKESPEARE, *Titus Andronicus*

Middle Age (*See also* Aging)

Life declines from thirty-five.

SAMUEL JOHNSON, *To Mrs. Thrale, When Thirty-five*

And man not old, but mellow, like good wine.

STEPHEN PHILLIPS, *Ulysses*

Be wise with speed;
A fool at forty is a fool indeed.

EDWARD YOUNG, *Love of Fame*

At thirty, man suspects himself a fool;
Knows it at forty, and reforms his plan.

EDWARD YOUNG, *Night Thoughts*

A man of 40 today has nothing to worry him but falling hair, inability to button the top button, failing vision, shortness of breath, a tendency of the collar to shut off all breathing, trembling of the kidneys to whatever tune the orchestra is playing, and a general sense of giddiness when the matter of the rent is brought up. 40 is Life's Golden Age.

ROBERT BENCHLEY, *From Bed to Worse*[1]

Mind

The mind's the standard of the man.

ISAAC WATTS, *False Greatness*

My mind to me a kingdom is;
Such perfect joy therein I find
As far exceeds all earthly bliss
That God and nature hath assigned.

SIR EDWARD DYER, *Byrd's Psalmes*

A mind not to be changed by place or time.
The mind is its own place, and in itself
Can make a heaven of hell, a hell of heaven.

JOHN MILTON, *Paradise Lost*

Mischief

For Satan finds some mischief still,
For idle hands to do.

ISAAC WATTS, *Songs for Children*

Misery (*See also* Grief)

Misery acquaints a man with strange bedfellows.

WILLIAM SHAKESPEARE, *The Tempest*

Mockery

Mockery is the fume of little hearts.

ALFRED, LORD TENNYSON, *Guinevere*

Moderation

Out of moderation a pure happiness springs.

JOHANN WOLFGANG VON GOETHE, *Die Natürliche Tochter*

Moderation is the silken string running through the pearl-chain of all virtues.

THOMAS FULLER, *Of Moderation*

Modesty

Modesty is the only sure bait when you angle for praise.

LORD CHESTERFIELD, *Letters to His Son*

Money

Sing a song of sixpence,
And sing it till you die;
And this I'll bet, you'll never get
A pocketful of rye.

SAMUEL HOFFENSTEIN, *Year In, You're Out*[2]

Certainly, there are lots of things in life that
money won't buy, but it's very funny—
Have you ever tried to buy them without money?

OGDEN NASH, *The Face is Familiar*[3]

---

[1]Reprinted by permission of Harper & Brothers.

[2]Published by Liveright Publishing Corp., N.Y. Copyright by Samuel Hoffenstein, 1930.

[3]Copyright 1931, 1933, 1936, 1938 by Ogden Nash. Reprinted by permission of Little, Brown & Co.

But the jingling of the guinea helps the hurt that honor feels.

ALFRED, LORD TENNYSON, *Locksley Hall*

The almighty dollar—that great object of universal devotion throughout our land!

WASHINGTON IRVING, *The Creole Village*

If you would know the value of money, go and try to borrow some; for he that goes a-borrowing goes a-sorrowing.

BENJAMIN FRANKLIN, *Poor Richard's Almanac*

The lust of gold succeeds the rays of conquest;
The lust of gold, unfeeling and remorseless!
The last corruption of degenerate man.

SAMUEL JOHNSON, *Irene*

Gold—Gold! gold! gold! gold!
Bright and yellow, hard and cold.

THOMAS HOOD, *Miss Kilmansegg*

And his best riches, ignorance of wealth.

OLIVER GOLDSMITH, *The Deserted Village*

For what is worth in anything
But so much money as 'twill bring?

SAMUEL BUTLER, *Hudibras*

Make money! If you can, make money honestly; if not, by whatever means you can, make money.

HORACE

There are few ways in which a man can be more innocently employed than in getting money.

SAMUEL JOHNSON

Put not your trust in money; put your money in trust.

American saying

Money is like muck, not good except it be spread.

FRANCIS BACON, *Of Seditions*

Yes, ready money *is*
Aladdin's lamp.

LORD BYRON, *Don Juan*

Americans have little faith. They rely on the power of the dollar.

RALPH WALDO EMERSON, *Man the Reformer*

Moonlight

This night methinks is but the daylight sick.
It looks a little paler; 'tis a day,
Such as the day is when the sun is hid.

WILLIAM SHAKESPEARE, *Merchant of Venice*

How sweet the moonlight sleeps upon this bank!
Here will we sit, and let the sounds of music
Creep in our ears; soft stillness and the night
Become the touches of sweet harmony.

WILLIAM SHAKESPEARE, *Merchant of Venice*

The queen of night, whose large command
Rules all the sea, and half the land.

SAMUEL BUTLER, *Hudibras*

Morals

Morals are a personal affair; in the war of righteousness every man fights for his own hand.

ROBERT LOUIS STEVENSON, *Lay Morals*

Morning

The silent hours steal on,
And flaky darkness breaks within the east.

WILLIAM SHAKESPEARE, *Richard III*

Sweet is the breath of morn, her rising sweet,
With charm of earliest birds.

JOHN MILTON, *Paradise Lost*

At length the world, renew'd by calm repose,
Was strong for toil, the dappled morn arose.

THOMAS PARNELL, *The Hermit*

I now, an early riser, love to hail
The dreamy struggles of the stars with light,
And the recovering breath of earth, sleep-drowned
Awakening to the wisdom of the sun.

PHILIP JAMES BAILEY, *Festus*

Night wanes—the vapours round the mountains curl'd
Melt into morn, and light awakes the world.

LORD BYRON, *Laura*

Music

Music hath charms to soothe the savage breast,
To soften rocks, or bend a knotted oak.

WILLIAM CONGREVE, *The Mourning Bride*

The only universal tongue.

SAMUEL ROGERS, *Italy*

Of all noises, I think music the least disagreeable.

SAMUEL JOHNSON, in the *Morning Chronicle*

Music is the only sensual pleasure without vice.

SAMUEL JOHNSON, *Apothegms*

O Music! sphere-descended maid,
Friend of pleasure, wisdom's aid!

WILLIAM COLLINS, *The Passions*

Names

What's in a name? That which we call a rose
By any other name would smell as sweet.

WILLIAM SHAKESPEARE, *Romeo and Juliet*

Nature

Nature is content with little; grace with less; but lust with nothing.

MATTHEW HENRY, *Genesis*

Accuse not Nature; she hath done her part;
Do thou but thine.

JOHN MILTON, *Paradise Lost*

But who can paint
Like Nature? Can imagination boast,
Amid its gay creation, hues like hers?

JAMES THOMSON, *The Seasons*

Nature, exerting an unwearied power,
Forms, opens, and gives scent to every flower;
Spreads the fresh verdure of the field, and leads
The dancing Naiads through the dewy meads.

WILLIAM COWPER, *Table Talk*

Nothing is great but the inexhaustible wealth of nature.

RALPH WALDO EMERSON, *Resources*

Nature alone is antique and the oldest art a mushroom.

THOMAS CARLYLE, *Sartor Resartus*

Nature and Nature's laws lay hid in night:
God said, 'Let Newton be!' and all was light.

ALEXANDER POPE,
Epitaph Intended for Sir Isaac Newton

Nature is God's, Art is man's instrument.

SIR THOMAS OVERBURY, *A Wife*

Nature is a mutable cloud, which is always and never the same.

RALPH WALDO EMERSON, *History*

Nature, so far as in her lies,
Imitates God.

ALFRED, LORD TENNYSON,
On a Mourner

Nature is the art of God.

SIR THOMAS BROWNE,
Religio Medici

Nearness

A man's best things are nearest him,
Lie close about his feet.

LORD HOUGHTON, *The Men of Old*

Necessity

All things happen by necessity; in nature there is neither good nor bad.

BENEDICT SPINOZA

Need makes the old wife trot.

Proverb

Necessity is the mother of invention.

Proverb

Necessity does the work of courage.

GEORGE ELIOT, *Romola*

Night

Light thickens; and the crow
Makes wing to the rooky wood;
Good things of day begin to droop and drowse,
Whiles night's black agents to their prey do rouse.

WILLIAM SHAKESPEARE, *Macbeth*

'Tis now the very witching time of night,
When churchyards yawn, and hell itself breathes out.

WILLIAM SHAKESPEARE, *Hamlet*

This dead of night, this silent hour of darkness,
Nature for rest ordain'd, and soft repose.

NICHOLAS ROWE, *The Fair Penitent*

Now sunk the sun; the closing hour of day
Came onward, mantled o'er with sober grey;
Nature in silence bade the world repose.

THOMAS PARNELL

How like a widow in her weeds, the night,
Amid her glimmering tapers, silent sits!
How sorrowful, how desolate, she weeps
Perpetual dews, and saddens nature's scene.

EDWARD YOUNG, *Night Thoughts*

In sable pomp, with all her starry train,
The night resum'd her throne.

RICHARD GLOVER

How beautiful is night!
A dewy freshness fills the silent air;
No mist obscures, nor cloud, nor speck, nor stain
Breaks the serene of heaven.

ROBERT SOUTHEY, *Thalaba*

The night
Shows stars and women in a better light.

LORD BYRON, *Don Juan*

Night—the nurse of thoughts.

HENRY VAUGHAN, *Daphnis*

Nobility

Noble by birth, yet nobler by great deeds.

HENRY WADSWORTH LONGFELLOW,
Tales of a Wayside Inn

Do noble things, not dream them, all day long.

CHARLES KINGSLEY, *A Farewell*

Nonsense

A little nonsense, now and then,
Is relished by the wisest men.

Unknown—old nursery rhyme

A careless song, with a little nonsense in it now and then, does not misbecome a monarch.

HORACE WALPOLE,
Letter to Sir Horace Mann

Nose

Lightly was her slender nose
  Tip-tilted like the petal of a flower.

ALFRED, LORD TENNYSON, *Gareth and Lynette*

Oaths

I'll take thy word for faith, not ask thine oath;
Who shuns not to break one will sure crack both.

WILLIAM SHAKESPEARE, *Pericles*

Obscurity

Full many a flower is born to blush unseen,
And waste its sweetness on the desert air.

THOMAS GRAY, *Elegy in a Country Churchyard*

Observation

Let observation, with extensive view,
Survey mankind from China to Peru.

SAMUEL JOHNSON, *Vanity of Human Wishes*

Rightly viewed, no meanest object is insignificant; all objects are as windows, through which the philosophic eye looks into Infinitude itself.

THOMAS CARLYLE, *Sartor Resartus*

I pity the man who can travel from Dan to Beersheba, and cry, "'Tis all barren!"

LAURENCE STERNE, *In the Street*

Oh wad some power the giftie gie us
To see oursels as ithers see us!

ROBERT BURNS, *To a Louse*

Men are born with two eyes, but with one tongue in order that they should see twice as much as they say.

CHARLES CALEB COLTON, *Lacon*

The difference between landscape and landscape is small; but there is a great difference between the beholders.

RALPH WALDO EMERSON, *Nature*

You must look into people as well as at them.

LORD CHESTERFIELD, *Letters to his Son*

Obstacles

Every path hath a puddle.

GEORGE HERBERT, *Jacula Prudentum*

Obstinacy

An obstinate man does not hold opinions, but they hold him.

ALEXANDER POPE, *Moral Essays*

Ocean

Roll on, thou deep and dark blue Ocean,—roll!
Ten thousand fleets sweep over thee in vain:
Man marks the earth with ruin,—his control
Stops with the shore.

LORD BYRON, *Childe Harold's Pilgrimage*

Offense

Who fears t'offend takes the first step to please.

COLLEY CIBBER, *Love in a Riddle*

Old Age (*See also* Aging *and* Youth)

What is the worst of woes that wait on age?
What stamps the wrinkle deeper on the brow?
To view each loved one blotted from life's page,
And be alone on earth as I am now.

LORD BYRON, *Childe Harold's Pilgrimage*

When our vices leave us, we flatter ourselves with the idea that we are leaving them.

LA ROCHEFOUCAULD, *Maximes*

Men of age object too much, consult too long, adventure too little, repent too soon.

FRANCIS BACON, *Essays: Youth and Age*

Crabbed age and youth
Cannot live together.

WILLIAM SHAKESPEARE, *The Passionate Pilgrim*

Old age, a second-child, by Nature curst
  With more and greater evils than the first,
  Weak, sickly, full of pains, in every breath
  Railing at life, and yet afraid of death.

CHARLES CHURCHILL, *Gotham*

Last scene of all,
That ends this strange eventful history,
Is second childishness, and mere oblivion;
Sans teeth, sans eyes, sans taste, sans everything.

WILLIAM SHAKESPEARE, *As You Like It*

An old man's twice a child.

PHILIP MASSINGER, *The Bashful Lover*

Whatever poet, orator or sage
May say of it; old age is still old age.

HENRY WADSWORTH LONGFELLOW, *Morituri Salutamus*

Forty is the old age of youth, fifty is the youth of old age.

VICTOR HUGO

See how the world its veterans rewards!
A youth of frolics, an old age of cards.

ALEXANDER POPE, *Moral Essays*

Opinion

New opinions are always suspected, and usually opposed, without any other reason, but because they are not already common.

JOHN LOCKE, *An Essay concerning Human Understanding*

Remember that all things are only opinion and that it is in your power to think as you please.

MARCUS AURELIUS

The absurd man is he who never changes his opinions.

AUGUSTE BARTHÉLEMY

Human nature causes us to be dependent on other people's opinion in a way completely out of proportion to its value.

ARTHUR SCHOPENHAUER, *On Women*

I have bought
  Golden opinions from all sorts of people.

WILLIAM SHAKESPEARE, *Macbeth*

Men are never so good or so bad as their opinions.

SIR JAMES MACKINTOSH, *Ethical Philosophy*

The man who never alters his opinion is like standing water, and breeds reptiles of the mind.

WILLIAM BLAKE, *Proverbs of Hell*

Opportunity

There is an hour in each man's life appointed
To make his happiness if then he seize it.

FLETCHER AND MASSINGER, *The Custom of the Country*

Jupiter himself cannot bring back lost opportunity.

PHAEDRUS

There is a tide in the affairs of men,
Which, taken at the flood, leads on to fortune.

WILLIAM SHAKESPEARE, *Julius Caesar*

A wise man will make more opportunities than he finds.

FRANCIS BACON, *Essays: Of Ceremonies and Respects*

Gather ye rose-buds while ye may,
Old Time is still a-flying,
And this same flower, that smiles today,
Tomorrow will be dying.

ROBERT HERRICK, *To the Virgins, to Make Much of Time*

When the sunne shineth, make hay.

JOHN HEYWOOD, *Proverbs*

Age is opportunity no less
  Than youth itself, though in another dress.

HENRY WADSWORTH LONGFELLOW, *Morituri Salutamus*

A little fire is quickly trodden out;
Which, being suffered, rivers cannot quench.

WILLIAM SHAKESPEARE, *King Henry VI*

Strike whilst the iron is hot.

JOHN WEBSTER, *Westward Ho*

It is good to make hay while the sun shines.

Proverb

Every man has a goose that lays golden eggs, if he only knew it.

Proverb

Oppression

Press not a falling man too far!

WILLIAM SHAKESPEARE, *King Henry VIII*

Optimism

Men in general are fain to believe that which they wish to be true.

JULIUS CAESAR

Order

The heavens themselves, the planets and this
  centre,
Observe degree, priority, and place,
Insisture, course, proportion, season, form,
Office and custom, in all line of order.

WILLIAM SHAKESPEARE, *Troilus and Cressida*

Order is Heaven's first law.

ALEXANDER POPE, *Essay on Man*

Originality

There is nothing new under the sun.

THOMAS BABINGTON MACAULAY, *Essay on the Diary of Madame D'Arblay*

Oysters

Oysters are not good in a month that hath not an R in it.

Proverb

Pain

Pain pays the income of each precious thing.

WILLIAM SHAKESPEARE, *Rape of Lucrece*

A man deep-wounded may feel too much pain
To feel much anger.

GEORGE ELIOT, *Spanish Gypsy*

Pain is no longer pain when it is past.

MARGARET J. PRESTON, *Nature's Lesson*

Parenthood

Where yet was ever found a mother
  Who'd give her booby for another?

JOHN GAY, *The Mother, the Nurse and the Fairy*

A mother is a mother still,
The holiest thing alive.

SAMUEL TAYLOR COLERIDGE, *The Three Graves*

It is a wise father that knows his own child.

WILLIAM SHAKESPEARE, *Merchant of Venice*

Parting

Such partings break the heart they fondly hope to heal.

LORD BYRON, *Childe Harold's Pilgrimage*

So sweetly she bade me adieu,
I thought she bade me return.

WILLIAM SHENSTONE, *A Pastoral*

Good night, good night! parting is such sweet sorrow.

WILLIAM SHAKESPEARE, *Romeo and Juliet*

Farewell!
For in that word,—that fatal word,—howe'er
We promise—hope—believe,—there breathes despair.

LORD BYRON, *The Corsair*

Farewell—Farewell! a word that must be, and hath been:
A sound which makes us linger,—yet—farewell.

LORD BYRON, *Childe Harold's Pilgrimage*

Stand not upon the order of your going
But go at once.

WILLIAM SHAKESPEARE, *Macbeth*

They who go
Feel not the pain of parting; it is they
Who stay behind that suffer.

HENRY WADSWORTH LONGFELLOW, *Michael Angelo*

The joys of meeting pay the pangs of absence;
Else who could bear it?

NICHOLAS ROWE, *Tamerlane*

My greatest grief is that I leave
No thing that claims a tear.

LORD BYRON, *Childe Harold's Pilgrimage*

Past

Wondrous and awful are thy silent halls,
O kingdom of the past!
There lie the bygone ages in their palls,
Guarded by shadows vast.

JAMES RUSSELL LOWELL, *To the Past*

Patience

Patience, that blending of moral courage with physical timidity.

THOMAS HARDY, *Tess of the D'Urbervilles*

All things come to him who will but wait.

HENRY WADSWORTH LONGFELLOW, *Tales of a Wayside Inn*

Arm the obdured breast
With stubborn patience as with triple steel.

JOHN MILTON, *Paradise Lost*

Beware the fury of a patient man.

JOHN DRYDEN, *Absalom and Achitophel*

How poor are they, that have not patience!
What wound did ever heal, but by degrees?

WILLIAM SHAKESPEARE, *Othello*

Patriotism (*See also* Americanism)

The age of virtuous politics is past,
And we are deep in that of cold pretence.
Patriots are grown too shrewd to be sincere:
And we too wise to trust them.

WILLIAM COWPER, *The Task*

Breathes there a man with soul so dead,
Who never to himself hath said
This is my own, my native land?

SIR WALTER SCOTT, *The Lay of the Last Minstrel*

Peace

Two things I have found that are lovely,
Though most things are sullen and grey;
One: Peace—but what mortal has found him, and
Passion—but when would he stay?

LAURENCE HOPE, *The Complete Love Lyrics*[1]

But the real and lasting victories are those of peace, and not of war.

RALPH WALDO EMERSON, *Worship*

The arts of peace are great,
And no less glorious than those of war.

WILLIAM BLAKE, *King Edward III*

Peace hath her victories,
No less renowned than war.

JOHN MILTON, *Sonnet: To the Lord General Cromwell*

Persistence

Attempt the end, and never stand to doubt;
Nothing's so hard but search will find it out.

RICHARD LOVELACE, *Seek and Find*

Persuasion

Few are open to conviction, but the majority of men to persuasion.

JOHANN WOLFGANG VON GOETHE

Pity

Pity speaks to grief
More sweetly than a band of instruments.

BARRY CORNWALL, *The Florentine Party*

Plans

The best laid schemes of mice and men
Gang aft a-gley;
And leave us naught but grief and pain
For promised joy.

ROBERT BURNS, *To a Mouse*

Pleasure

Follow pleasure, and then will pleasure flee;
Flee pleasure, and pleasure will follow thee.

JOHN HEYWOOD, *Proverbs*

Pleasures are like poppies spread—
You seize the flower, its bloom is shed.

ROBERT BURNS, *Tam o' Shanter*

Pleasure that comes unlook'd for is thrice welcome.

SAMUEL ROGERS, *Italy, An Interview*

Rich the treasure,
Sweet the pleasure,
Sweet is pleasure after pain.

JOHN DRYDEN, *Alexander's Feast*

Let us have wine and women, mirth and laughter;
Sermons and soda-water the day after.

LORD BYRON, *Don Juan*

Pleasure is very seldom found where it is sought.

SAMUEL JOHNSON, in *The Rambler*

Rarity enhances pleasures.

JUVENAL

To really enjoy pleasures you must know how to leave them.

VOLTAIRE

Pleasure is more powerful than all fear of the penalty.

JOHANN WOLFGANG VON GOETHE

Plenty

Plenty corrupts the melody.

ALFRED, LORD TENNYSON, *The Blackbird*

Plenty is the child of peace.

WILLIAM PRYNNE, *Histriomastix*

Poetry

To get at the eternal strength of things,
And fearlessly to make strong songs of it,
Is, to my mind, the mission of that man
The World would call a poet.

EDWIN ARLINGTON ROBINSON, *Octaves*[1]

Poetry is the child of nature, which, regulated and made beautiful by art, presenteth the most harmonious of all other compositions.

JAMES SHIRLEY, *Preface to Beaumont and Fletcher*

[1]From *The Children of the Night*, published by Charles Scribner's Sons.

Poetry, the queen of arts.

THOMAS SPRAT, *Ode upon the Poems of Abraham Cowley*

There is a pleasure in poetic pains
Which only poets know.

WILLIAM COWPER, *The Task*

Possession

What we have, we have;
What we spent, we had;
What we left, we lost.

Epitaph of Edward Courtenay

One bird in the hand is worth two in the bush.

Proverb

The thing possessed is not the thing it seems.

SAMUEL DANIEL, *The History of the Civil Wars*

No man can lose what he never had.

IZAAK WALTON, *The Compleat Angler*

Better one byrde in hand than ten in the wood.

JOHN HEYWOOD, *Proverbs*

Them as ha' never had a cushion don't miss it.

GEORGE ELIOT, *Adam Bede*

Postponement

Be wise today; 'tis madness to defer.

EDWARD YOUNG, *Night Thoughts*

Defer not till tomorrow to be wise:
Tomorrow's sun to thee may never rise.

WILLIAM CONGREVE, *Letter to Cobham*

Never leave that till tomorrow which you can do today.

BENJAMIN FRANKLIN, *Poor Richard's Almanac*

Never do today what you can do as well tomorrow; because something may occur to make you regret your premature action.

AARON BURR, in a letter

By the street of By-and-By
One comes to the house of never.

Proverb

Poverty

Poverty is no disgrace to a man, but it is confoundedly inconvenient.

SYDNEY SMITH, *Lady Holland*

Poverty is a bully if you are afraid of her, or truckle to her. Poverty is good-natured if you meet her like a man.

WILLIAM MAKEPEACE THACKERAY, *Philip*

Poverty makes some humble, but more malignant.

BULWER-LYTTON, *Eugene Aram*

Poverty, the reward of honest fools.

COLLEY CIBBER, *Richard III*

Power

Power is the grim idol that the world adores.

WILLIAM HAZLITT, *Political Essays*

Practice

Practice what you preach.

EDWARD YOUNG, *Love of Fame*

An ounce of practice is worth a pound of preaching.

Proverb

Praise

The love of praise, howe'er concealed by art,
Reigns more or less, and glows in every heart.

EDWARD YOUNG, *Love of Fame*

Say not that she did well or ill,
Only, "She did her best."

DINAH MARIA CRAIK, *Poems*

As a rule we only praise in order to be praised.

LA ROCHEFOUCAULD, *Maximes*

Do you wish people to speak well of you?
Don't yourself.

BLAISE PASCAL, *Pensées*

The art of praising is the beginning of the art of pleasing.

VOLTAIRE, *La Pucelle*

And those that paint them truest praise them most.

JOSEPH ADDISON, *The Campaign*

Prayer

I was not born for courts or great affairs;
I pay my debts, believe, and say my prayers.

ALEXANDER POPE,
Epistle to Dr. Arbuthnot

Prayer is the spirit speaking truth to Truth.

PHILIP JAMES BAILEY, *Festus*

He prayeth best who loveth best
All things, both great and small.

SAMUEL TAYLOR COLERIDGE,
The Ancient Mariner

He prayeth well who loveth well
Both man and bird and beast.

SAMUEL TAYLOR COLERIDGE,
The Ancient Mariner

Precaution

A stitch in time saves nine.

Proverb

Look ere ye leape.

JOHN HEYWOOD, *Proverbs*

It is too late to shutte the stable door when the steede is stolne.

JOHN LYLY, *Euphues*

Look before you ere you leap;
For as you sow y'are like to reap.

SAMUEL BUTLER, *Hudibras*

Preference

What's one man's poison, signor,
Is another's meat or drink.

BEAUMONT AND FLETCHER,
Love's Cure

Every one to his taste.

Proverb

Prejudice

All seems infected that the infected spy,
As all looks yellow to the jaundiced eye.

ALEXANDER POPE,
Essay on Criticism

Preparedness

All things are ready, if our minds be so.

WILLIAM SHAKESPEARE, *Henry V*

A wise man in time of peace prepares for war.

HORACE, *Satires*

Present

The present is never a happy state to any human being.

SAMUEL JOHNSON,
in Boswell's *Life of Johnson*

One today is worth two tomorrows.

BENJAMIN FRANKLIN,
Poor Richard's Almanac

Pride

Pride goeth before destruction,
And an haughty spirit before a fall.

Proverbs

Pride,
Howe'er disguised in its own majesty,
Is littleness.

WILLIAM WORDSWORTH,
Poems Written in Youth

Pride that dines on vanity sups on contempt.

BENJAMIN FRANKLIN,
Poor Richard's Almanac

Procrastination

Procrastination is the thief of time.

EDWARD YOUNG, *Night Thoughts*

Profit

No one was ever ruined by taking a profit.
Stock Exchange Saying

Ill blows the wind that profits nobody.
WILLIAM SHAKESPEARE, *Henry VI*

Progress

Necessity invented stools,
Convenience next suggested elbow-chairs,
And luxury the accomplish'd sofa last.
WILLIAM COWPER, *The Task*

Progress is
The law of life; man is not man as yet.
ROBERT BROWNING, *Paracelsus*

Progress is the development of order.
AUGUSTE COMTE

All things, going upwards or downwards, are in a perpetual flux.
HERACLITUS

Promises

Men apt to promise are apt to forget.
Proverb

They promise mountains, but perform molehills.
CHARLES HADDON SPURGEON, *Ploughman's Pictures*

Quarreling

Quarrels would not last long if the fault was only on one side.
LA ROCHEFOUCAULD

When one will not, two cannot quarrel.
Proverb

Quiet

Quiet to quick bosoms is a hell.
LORD BYRON, *Childe Harold's Pilgrimage*

Quotations

He ranged his tropes and preached up patience,
Backed his opinions with Quotations.
MATTHEW PRIOR, *Paulo Purganti and His Wife*

The wisdom of the wise and the experience of ages may be preserved by quotations.
ISAAC D'ISRAELI, *Curiosities of Literature*

Rain

The clouds consign their treasures to the fields,
And softly shaking on the dimpled pool
Prelusive drops, let all their moisture flow,
In large effusion, o'er the freshen'd world.
JAMES THOMSON, *The Seasons*

Reality

Consult the dead upon the things that were,
But the living only on things that are.
HENRY WADSWORTH LONGFELLOW, *The Golden Legend*

Few men have imagination enough for the truth of reality.
JOHANN WOLFGANG VON GOETHE

Reason

A man's vanity tells him what is honour, a man's conscience what is justice.
WALTER SAVAGE LANDOR, *Imaginary Conversations*

Every why hath a wherefore.
WILLIAM SHAKESPEARE, *The Comedy of Errors*

Passion and prejudice govern the world; only under the name of reason.
JOHN WESLEY, *Letter to Joseph Benson*

The sublime and the ridiculous are often so nearly related, that it is difficult to class them separately. One step above the sublime makes the ridiculous, and one step above the ridiculous makes the sublime again.
THOMAS PAINE, *Age of Reason*

When a man has not a good reason for doing a thing, he has one good reason for letting it alone.
REV. THOMAS SCOTT, *Commentary on the Bible*

Reconcilement

Never can true reconcilement grow
Where wounds of deadly hate have pierc'd so deep.
JOHN MILTON, *Paradise Lost*

Reflection

The world is a looking-glass, and gives back to every man the reflection of his own face.
WILLIAM MAKEPEACE THACKERAY, *Vanity Fair*

Reform

A reform is a correction of abuses: a revolution is a transfer of power.
EDWARD BULWER-LYTTON, *Speech in the House of Commons*

Every reform, no matter how necessary, will by weak minds be carried to an excess, which will itself need reforming.
SAMUEL TAYLOR COLERIDGE, *Biographia Literaria*

Regret

Be early what, if you are not, you will, when it is too late, wish you had been.

LORD CHESTERFIELD, *Letters to His Son*

For of all sad words of tongue or pen,
The saddest are these: "It might have been!"

JOHN GREENLEAF WHITTIER, *Maud Muller*

Rejoicing

It's a poor heart that never rejoices.

Proverb—CHARLES DICKENS, *Barnaby Rudge*

Relationship

Almost all of our sorrows spring out of our relations with other people.

ARTHUR SCHOPENHAUER

Religion

The writers against religion, whilst they oppose every system, are wisely careful never to set up any of their own.

EDMUND BURKE, *A Vindication of Natural Society*

To be of no church is dangerous. Religion, of which the rewards are distant, and which is animated only by Faith and Hope, will glide by degrees out of the mind, unless it be invigorated and reimpressed by external ordinances, by stated calls to worship, and the salutary influence of example.

SAMUEL JOHNSON, *Life of Milton*

Atheism is rather in the lip than in the heart of man.

FRANCIS BACON, *Essays of Atheism*

There is no greater disagreement than one about Religion.

MONTANUS, in *Micah*

There is only one religion, though there are a hundred versions of it.

GEORGE BERNARD SHAW

By night an atheist half believes a God.

EDWARD YOUNG, *Night Thoughts*

Nobody can deny but that religion is a comfort to the distressed, a cordial to the sick, and sometimes a restraint on the wicked.

LADY MARY WORTLEY MONTAGU, *Letter to the Countess of Bute*

Forgetfulness of all religion leads to the forgetfulness of the duties of man.

JEAN JACQUES ROUSSEAU, *Emile*

Man is by his constitution a religious animal.

EDMUND BURKE, *Reflections on the Revolution in France*

Every man has his religion. We differ about trimming.

JOHN SELDEN

The practice of true Religion consists principally in two great branches, giving honor to God, and doing good to men.

SAMUEL CLARKE, *Sermons*

Remedy

Extreme remedies are very appropriate for extreme diseases.

HIPPOCRATES, *Aphorisms*

Feed a cold and starve a fever.

Proverb

The best physicians are, Dr. Diet, Dr. Quiet, and Dr. Merryman.

SYDNEY SMITH

Remembrance

How sharp the pang of this remembrance is!

WILLIAM SHAKESPEARE, *The Tempest*

Repentance

Repentance is the weight of indigest meals eat yesterday.

GEORGE ELIOT, *Spanish Gypsy*

Reputation

But he that filches from me my good name
Robs me of that which not enriches him
And makes me poor indeed.

WILLIAM SHAKESPEARE, *Othello*

At every word a reputation dies.

ALEXANDER POPE, *The Rape of the Lock*

It is not as thy mother says, but as thy neighbors say.

Proverb

He that hath an ill name is half hang'd, ye know.

JOHN HEYWOOD, *Proverbs*

A man's reputation is something like his coat, there is certain chemicals that will take the stains and greese spots out of it, but it always has a second-handed kind of a look, and generally smells strong of the chemicals.

JOSH BILLINGS (HENRY WHEELER SHAW)

'Tis thus that on the choice of friends
Our good or evil name depends.

JOHN GAY, *Fables*

Resignation

What's gone and what's past help
Should be past grief.

WILLIAM SHAKESPEARE, *A Winter's Tale*

Trust no Future, howe'er pleasant!
Let the dead Past bury its Dead!

HENRY WADSWORTH LONGFELLOW, *A Psalm of Life*

A great man commands the affections of the people. A prudent man does not complain when he has lost them.

JUNIUS, *Letters*

Things without all remedy
Should be without regard; what's done is done.

WILLIAM SHAKESPEARE, *Macbeth*

When remedies are past, the griefs are ended.

WILLIAM SHAKESPEARE, *Othello*

Resourcefulness

Fight fire with fire, and craft with craft.

HENRY WADSWORTH LONGFELLOW, *The Cobbler of Hagenau*

If the mountain will not come to Mohammed, Mohammed will go to the mountain.

MOHAMMED

The mouse that always trusts to one poor hole
Can never be a mouse of any soul.

ALEXANDER POPE, *The Wife of Bath*

Foul cankering rust the hidden treasure frets,
But gold that's put to use more gold begets.

WILLIAM SHAKESPEARE, *Venus and Adonis*

Revenge

Revenge is a kind of wild justice.

FRANCIS BACON, *Revenge*

Revenge is a confession of pain.

SENECA, *De Ira*

Revenge, at first though sweet,
Bitter ere long back on itself recoils.

JOHN MILTON, *Paradise Lost*

Revenge is profitable, gratitude is expensive.

EDWARD GIBBON, *Decline and Fall of the Roman Empire*

Sweet is revenge—especially to women.

LORD BYRON, *Don Juan*

Reward

The reward of a thing well done is to have done it.

RALPH WALDO EMERSON, *New England Reformers*

How blest is he who crowns, in shades like these,
A youth of labour with an age of ease.

OLIVER GOLDSMITH, *The Deserted Village*

As you brew, so shall you bake.

Proverb

Ridicule

I defy the wisest man in the world to turn a truly good action into ridicule.

HENRY FIELDING, *Joseph Andrews*

Of all the griefs that harass the distrest,
Sure the most bitter is a scornful jest.

SAMUEL JOHNSON, *London*

Ridicule is a weak weapon, when levelled at a strong mind;
But common men are cowards and dread an empty laugh.

MARTIN FARQUHAR TUPPER, *Proverbial Philosophy of Ridicule*

Right and Wrong

It is the greatest good to the greatest number which is the measure of right or wrong.

JEREMY BENTHAM, *Works*

He who discusses is in the right, he who disputes is in the wrong.

CLAUDE DE RULHIÈRE, *Disputes*

Routine

We all of us live too much in a circle.

BENJAMIN DISRAELI, *Sybil*

Rumor

That talkative maiden, Rumour.

GEORGE ELIOT, *Felix Holt*

Satire

Satire has always shone among the rest,
And is the boldest way, if not the best,
To tell men freely of their foulest faults,
To laugh at their vain deeds, and vainer thoughts.

DRYDEN AND MULGRAVE, *Essay on Satire*

Satire's power: 'tis her corrective part
To calm the wild disorders of the heart,
To point the arduous height where glory lies,
And teaches mad Ambition to be wise.

ALEXANDER POPE, *Essay on Satire*

Satire should, like a polished razor keen,
Wound with a touch that's scarcely felt or seen.

LADY MARY WORTLEY MONTAGU, *To the Imitator of the First Satire of Horace*

Scepticism

Scepticism is slow suicide.

RALPH WALDO EMERSON, *Self-Reliance*

A wise scepticism is the first attribute of a good critic.

JAMES RUSSELL LOWELL, *Among My Books*

Science

Science is organized knowledge.

HERBERT SPENCER, *Education*

Sea

The Sea, beloved by a thousand ships,
Is maiden ever, and fresh and free.
Ah, for the touch of her cool green lips,
Carry me out to Sea!

LAURENCE HOPE, *The Complete Love Lyrics*[1]

Self-Control

And mistress of herself,
though china fall.

ALEXANDER POPE, *Moral Essays*

If you cannot keep your own counsel, how can you expect another person to keep it.

Proverb

Self-Defense

The smallest worm will turn, being trodden on.

WILLIAM SHAKESPEARE, *King Henry VI*

Self-defense is nature's eldest law.

JOHN DRYDEN, *Absalom and Achitophel*

Self-Reliance

God helps them that help themselves.

Proverb

There is no dependence that can be sure but a dependence upon one's self.

JOHN GAY, *Letter to Swift*

And all your fortune lies beneath your hat.

JOHN OLDHAM, *To a Friend*

What weapons has the lion but himself?

JOHN KEATS, *King Stephen*

Self-Respect

It is necessary for the happiness of man that he be mentally faithful to himself.

THOMAS PAINE, *The Age of Reason*

Sense of Humor

The man who cannot laugh is not only fit for treasons, stratagems, and spoils; but his whole life is already a treason and a stratagem.

THOMAS CARLYLE, *Sartor Resartus*

A sense of humour sharp enough to show a man his own absurdities will keep him from the commission of all sins, or nearly all, except those that are worth committing.

SAMUEL BUTLER, *Life and Habit*

A mind is not completely well organized that is deficient in a sense of humour.

SAMUEL TAYLOR COLERIDGE, *Table Talk*

[1]Copyright 1905–1933 by Malcolm J. J. S. Nicolson. Reprinted by permission of Dodd, Mead & Company.

Senses

Sight has to do with the understanding; hearing with reason; smell with memory. Touch and taste are realistic and depend on contact; they have no ideal side.

ARTHUR SCHOPENHAUER, *Psychological Observations*

Sentimentalism

The heart has reasons of which reason has no knowledge.

BLAISE PASCAL, *Pensées*

Silence

And I oft have heard defended
Little said is soonest mended.

GEORGE WITHER, *The Shepherd's Hunting*

Wise men say nothing in dangerous times.

JOHN SELDEN, *Table Talk*

Be checked for silence
But never tax'd for speech.

WILLIAM SHAKESPEARE, *All's Well that Ends Well*

Silence in woman is like speech in man.

BEN JONSON, *Silent Woman*

Great joys, like griefs, are silent.

SHACKERLEY MARMION, *Holland's Leaguer*

Silence gives consent.

OLIVER GOLDSMITH, *The Good-Natured Man*

Silence is deep as Eternity; speech is shallow as Time.

THOMAS CARLYLE, *Sir Walter Scott*

Macaulay is like a book in breeches. . . . He has occasional flashes of silence, that make his conversation perfectly delightful.

SYDNEY SMITH, *Lady Holland's Memoir*

Be silent, or say something better than silence.

Proverb

A fool when he is silent is counted wise.

Proverb

Silence is a still noise.

JOSH BILLINGS (HENRY WHEELER SHAW)

Similarity

Birds of a feather will fly together.

Proverb

Like will to like.

JOHN HEYWOOD, *Proverbs*

Sin

Give me your love for a day, a night, an hour;
If the wages of sin are Death I am willing to pay.

LAURENCE HOPE, *The Complete Love Lyrics*[1]

Commit
The oldest sins the newest kind of ways.

WILLIAM SHAKESPEARE, *King Henry IV*

He that falls into sin is a man; that grieves at it is a saint; that boasteth of it is a devil.

THOMAS FULLER, *Holy and Profane States*

The way to Hell's a seeming Heav'n.

FRANCIS QUARLES, *Emblemes*

No vice is complete by itself (i.e., one vice leads to another).

SENECA

Sincerity

Every man alone is sincere; at the entrance of a second person hypocrisy begins.

RALPH WALDO EMERSON, *Friendship*

Sky

The silence that is in the starry sky.

WILLIAM WORDSWORTH, *Song at the Feast of Brougham Castle*

Sleep

Blessings on him who invented sleep, the mantle that covers all human thoughts, the food that appeases hunger, the drink that quenches thirst, the fire that warms cold, the cold that moderates heat, and lastly, the general coin that purchases all things, the balance and weight that equals the shepherd with the king, and the simple with the wise.

MIGUEL DE CERVANTES, *Don Quixote*

O sleep! it is a gentle thing,
Beloved from pole to pole.

SAMUEL TAYLOR COLERIDGE, *The Ancient Mariner*

O bed! bed! delicious bed!
That heaven upon earth to the weary head!

THOMAS HOOD, *Miss Kilmansegg: Her Dream*

Come, Sleep; O Sleep! the certain knot of peace,
The baiting-place of wit, the balm of woe,
The poor man's wealth, the prisoner's release,
Th' indifferent judge between the high and low.

SIR PHILIP SIDNEY, *Astrophel and Stella*

Thou has been called, O sleep! the friend of Woe;
But 'tis the happy that have called thee so.

ROBERT SOUTHEY, *The Curse of Kehama*

Society

Society is now one polished horde,
  Formed of two mighty tribes, the Bores and Bored.

LORD BYRON, *Don Juan*

Society is a masked ball, where every one hides his real character, and reveals it by hiding.

RALPH WALDO EMERSON, *Worship*

Solitude

In solitude where we are least alone.

LORD BYRON, *Childe Harold's Pilgrimage*

I was never less alone than when by myself.

EDWARD GIBBON, *Memoirs*

For solitude sometimes is best society.

JOHN MILTON, *Paradise Lost*

That inward eye
Which is the bliss of solitude.

WILLIAM WORDSWORTH, *I Wandered Lonely as a Cloud*

One can be instructed in society, one is inspired only in solitude.

JOHANN WOLFGANG VON GOETHE

Conversation enriches the understanding, but solitude is the school of genius.

EDWARD GIBBON

Sorrow (*See also* Grief *and* Despair)

Sorrow concealed, like an oven stopp'd,
Doth burn the heart to cinders.

WILLIAM SHAKESPEARE, *Titus Andronicus*

The busy have no time for tears.

LORD BYRON, *The Two Foscari*

Great Sorrows cannot speak.

JOHN DONNE, *Elegy on Death*

When sorrows come, they come not single spies,
But in battalions!

WILLIAM SHAKESPEARE, *Hamlet*

Speculation

All's to be fear'd where all is to be gain'd.

LORD BYRON, *Werner*

Speech

And men talk only to conceal the mind.

EDWARD YOUNG, *Love of Fame*

The true use of speech is not so much to express our wants as to conceal them.

OLIVER GOLDSMITH, *The Bee*

Discretion of speech is more than eloquence.

FRANCIS BACON, *Essays: Of Discourse*

Words are the only things that last forever.

WILLIAM HAZLITT,
Table-Talk: On Thought and Action

Words are like leaves; and where they most abound,
Much fruit of sense beneath is rarely found.

ALEXANDER POPE, *Essay on Criticism*

Blessed is the man who, having nothing to say, abstains from giving us wordy evidence of the fact.

GEORGE ELIOT, *Theophrastus Such*

What is not in a man cannot come out of him surely.

JOHANN WOLFGANG VON GOETHE

First among the evidences of an education I name correctness and precision in the use of the mother tongue.

NICHOLAS MURRAY BUTLER

Language most shows a man; speak, that I may see you.

BEN JONSON, *Explorata*

Talking is one of the fine arts . . . and its fluent harmonies may be spoiled by the intrusion of a single harsh note.

OLIVER WENDELL HOLMES

His words, like so many nimble and airy servitors, trip about him at command.

JOHN MILTON, *Apology for Smectymnuus*

Drawing is speaking to the eye; talking is painting to the ear.

JOSEPH JOUBERT

And it is so plain to me that eloquence, like swimming, is an art which all men might learn, though so few do.

RALPH WALDO EMERSON

Mend your speech a little, lest it may mar your fortunes.

WILLIAM SHAKESPEARE, *King Lear*

You may blot what is written, but the spoken word can never be recalled.

HORACE

God has given us tongues so that we may say something pleasant to our fellow men.

HEINRICH HEINE, *Confessions*

Accent is the soul of speech, it gives it feeling and truth.

JEAN JACQUES ROUSSEAU, *Emile*

Spelling

I spell by ear altogether, spelling a word the way it sounds, which frequently is much simpler than the way these academic sharps put it.

IRVIN S. COBB, *Exit Laughing*[1]

Spring

Come, gentle Spring! ethereal mildness, come!

JAMES THOMSON, *The Seasons*

First, lusty spring, all dight in leaves of flowers
That freshly budded, and new blossoms did wear
In which a thousand birds had built their bowers.

EDMUND SPENSER, *Faerie Queene*

Hail, bounteous May, that dost inspire
Mirth, youth, and warm desire:
Woods and groves are of thy dressing,
Hill and dale doth boast thy blessing.

JOHN MILTON, *On May Morning*

In these green days
Reviving sickness lifts her languid head;
Life flows afresh and young-ey'd health exalts
The whole creation round.

JAMES THOMSON, *The Seasons*

O Spring! of hope, and love, and youth, and gladness,
Wind-winged emblem! brightest, best, and fairest
Whence comest thou?

PERCY BYSSHE SHELLEY

Wide flush the fields: the softening air is balm;
Echo the mountains round; the forest smiles;
And every sense, and every heart, is joy.

JAMES THOMSON, *The Seasons*

Stars

There they stand,
Shining in order like a living hymn
Written in light.

NATHANIEL PARKER WILLIS, *Poems*

Ye stars, that are the poetry of heaven.

LORD BYRON,
Childe Harold's Pilgrimage

The Sky
Spreads like an ocean hung on hight
Bespangled with those isles of light
So wildly, spiritually bright.

LORD BYRON, *Siege of Corinth*

Stealth

Stolen waters are sweet,
And bread eaten in secret is pleasant.

Proverbs

Strangers

The largest part of mankind are nowhere greater strangers than at home.

SAMUEL TAYLOR COLERIDGE

Strength

O, it is excellent
To have a giant's strength; but it is tyrannous
To use it like a giant.

WILLIAM SHAKESPEARE,
Measure for Measure

Subtlety

A beauty masked, like the sun in eclipse,
Gathers together more gazers than if it shined out.

WILLIAM WYCHERLEY, *The Country Wife*

Success (*See also* Fame)

The secret of success is constancy to purpose.

BENJAMIN DISRAELI,
Speech at the Crystal Palace

They never fail who die
In a great cause.

LORD BYRON, *Marino Faliero*

Suicide

Self-destruction is the effect of cowardice, in the highest extreme.

DANIEL DEFOE, *An Essay Upon Projects*

Suitability

Suit the action to the word, the word to the action.

WILLIAM SHAKESPEARE, *Hamlet*

Summer

Now comes thy glory in the summer months,
With light and heat refulgent.

JAMES THOMSON

'Twas noon; and every orange-bud
Hung languid o'er the crystal flood,
Faint as the lids of maiden eyes
Beneath a lover's burning sighs!

CLEMENT CLARK MOORE

The Spring's gay promise melted into thee,
Fair Summer! and thy gentle reign is here;
Thy emerald robes are on each leafy tree;
In the blue sky thy voice is rich and clear.

WILLIS GAYLORD CLARK

Thus gazing on thy void and sapphire sky,
O, Summer! in my inmost soul arise
Uplifted thoughts to which the woods reply.

WILLIS GAYLORD CLARK

Sun

Pleasant the sun,
When first on this delightful land he spreads
His orient beams, on herb, tree, fruit, and flower,
Glistering with dew.

JOHN MILTON, *Paradise Lost*

For like a god thou art, and on thy way
Of glory sheddest, with benignant ray,
Beauty and life, and joyance from above.

ROBERT SOUTHEY

There was not, on that day, a speck to stain
The azure heaven; the blessed sun alone,
In unapproachable divinity,
Career'd, rejoicing in his field of light.

ROBERT SOUTHEY

I marvel not, O sun! that unto thee,
In adoration man should bow the knee,
And pour the prayer of mingled awe and love.

ROBERT SOUTHEY

Blest power of sunshine! genial Day,
What balm, what life is in thy ray!
To feel thee is such real bliss.

THOMAS MOORE, *Lalla Rookh*

Centre of light and energy! thy way
Is through the unknown void; thou hast thy throne,
Morning and evening, and the close of day,
Far in the blue, untended, and alone.

JAMES GATES PERCIVAL, *Poems*

And we watch it down the west,
As it early sings to rest;
Then, with sorrow at our hearts,
Sigh—"How soon the sun departs!"

CAROLINE MAY

Superiority

Among the blind the one-eyed is a king.

Proverb

Never seem wiser, nor more learned, then the people you are with.

LORD CHESTERFIELD, *Letters to His Son*

Be wiser than other people if you can; but do not tell them so.

LORD CHESTERFIELD, *Letters to His Son*

How much a dunce that has been sent to roam
Excels a dunce that has been kept at home.

WILLIAM COWPER, *The Progress of Error*

Superstition

Superstition is the religion of feeble minds.

EDMUND BURKE,
Reflections on the Revolution in France

Suspicion

Suspicion always haunts the guilty mind;
The thief doth fear each bush an officer.

WILLIAM SHAKESPEARE, *Henry VI*

He that hides treasure
Imagines every one thinks of that place.

THOMAS MIDDLETON, *The Old Law*

Every true man's apparel fits your thief.

WILLIAM SHAKESPEARE,
Measure for Measure

Sympathy

The drying up a single tear has more of honest fame, than shedding seas of gore.

LORD BYRON, *Don Juan*

Tact

Reprove thy friend privately,
Commend him publicly.

Proverb

Talent

Talent is that which is in a man's power; genius is that in whose power a man is.

JAMES RUSSELL LOWELL, *Among My Books*

A really great talent finds its happiness in execution.

JOHANN WOLFGANG VON GOETHE

Talking

A bird is known by its note, and a man by his talk.

Proverb

Temperament

We boil at different degrees.

RALPH WALDO EMERSON,
Society and Solitude: Eloquence

Temptation

The only way to get rid of temptation is to yield to it.

OSCAR WILDE, *Picture of Dorian Gray*

When a man is tempted to do a tempting thing, he can find a hundred ingenious reasons for gratifying his liking.

WILLIAM MAKEPEACE THACKERAY,
Pendennis

No man is matriculated to the art of life till he has been well tempted.

GEORGE ELIOT, *Romola*

Thinking

There is nothing either good or bad, but thinking makes it so.

WILLIAM SHAKESPEARE, *Hamlet*

A moment's thinking is an hour in words.

THOMAS HOOD, *Hero and Leander*

Thoroughness

Whatever is worth doing at all, is worth doing well.

LORD CHESTERFIELD,
Letter to His Godson

Carry on every enterprise as if all depended on the success of it.

RICHELIEU

Thought

Thought alone is eternal.

OWEN MEREDITH, *Lucile*

Thought is the property of him who can entertain it, and of him who can adequately place it.

RALPH WALDO EMERSON,
Representative Men: Shakespeare

They are never alone that are accompanied with noble thoughts.

SIR PHILIP SIDNEY, *Arcadia*

Thrift

A penny saved is a penny gained.

Proverb

For age and want, save while you may;
No morning sun lasts a whole day.

BENJAMIN FRANKLIN,
Poor Richard's Almanac

Thrift is too late at the bottom of the purse.

SENECA

Time

Time is a great legalizer, even in the field of morals.

HENRY L. MENCKEN, *A Book of Prefaces*[1]

It (the value of time) is in everybody's mouth, but in few people's practice.

LORD CHESTERFIELD, *Letters to His Son*

Our todays and yesterdays
Are the blocks with which we build.

HENRY WADSWORTH LONGFELLOW,
The Builders

Time *wasted* is existence; *used* is life.

EDWARD YOUNG, *Night Thoughts*

The inaudible and noiseless foot of Time.

WILLIAM SHAKESPEARE,
All's Well that Ends Well

Sweet childish days, that were as long
As twenty days are now.

WILLIAM WORDSWORTH,
To a Butterfly

I recommend you to take care of the minutes for the hours will take care of themselves.

LORD CHESTERFIELD, *Letters to His Son*

Catch, then, O catch the transient hour;
Improve each moment as it flies;
Life's a short Summer, man a flower;
He dies,—alas! how soon he dies!

SAMUEL JOHNSON, *Winter*

---

[1]Reprinted by permission of the publishers, Alfred A. Knopf, Inc.

Dost thou love life? Then do not squander time, for that is the stuff life is made of.

BENJAMIN FRANKLIN, *Poor Richard's Almanac*

Time, who in the twilight comes to mend
All the fantastic day's caprice.

ROBERT BROWNING, *Strafford*

Unhappy is he who trusts only to time for his happiness.

VOLTAIRE

Trifles

Think nought a trifle, though it small appear;
Small sands the mountain, moments make the year,
And trifles life.

EDWARD YOUNG, *Love of Fame*

Trivia

At every trifle scorn to take offence;
That always shows great pride or little sense.

ALEXANDER POPE, *Essay on Criticism*

Those who occupy their minds too much with small matters generally become incapable of great.

LA ROCHEFOUCAULD, *Maximes*

A man must be well off who is irritated by trifles, for in misfortune trifles are not felt.

ARTHUR SCHOPENHAUER

Troubles

I never knew any man in my life who could not bear another's misfortunes perfectly like a Christian.

ALEXANDER POPE, *Thoughts on Various Subjects*

Every one can master a grief but he that has it.

WILLIAM SHAKESPEARE, *Much Ado about Nothing*

For there was never yet philosopher
That could endure the toothache patiently.

WILLIAM SHAKESPEARE, *Much Ado about Nothing*

Truth

Truth is the highest thing that man may keep.

GEOFFREY CHAUCER, *The Frankeleyn's Tale*

Children and fools speak the truth.

Proverb

Truth from his lips prevailed with double sway,
And fools who came to scoff remained to pray.

OLIVER GOLDSMITH, *The Deserted Village*

Truth, crushed to earth, shall rise again:
The eternal years of God are hers;
But Error, wounded, writhes with pain,
And dies among his worshippers.

WILLIAM CULLEN BRYANT, *The Battle-Field*

Truth is as impossible to be soiled by any outward touch as the sunbeam

JOHN MILTON, *The Doctrine and Discipline of Divorce*

Truth is truth
To the end of reckoning.

WILLIAM SHAKESPEARE, *Measure for Measure*

Some falsehood mingles with all truth.

HENRY WADSWORTH LONGFELLOW, *The Golden Legend*

This above all: to thine own self be true,
And it must follow, as the night the day,
Thou canst not then be false to any man.

WILLIAM SHAKESPEARE, *Hamlet*

'Tis not enough your counsel still be true;
Blunt truths more mischief than nice falsehoods do.

ALEXANDER POPE, *Essay on Criticism*

Beauty is truth, truth beauty,—that is all
Ye know on earth, and all ye need to know.

JOHN KEATS, *Ode on a Grecian Urn*

Children and fooles speake true.

JOHN LYLY, *Endymion*

Errors, like straws, upon the surface flow;
He who would search for pearls, must dive below.

JOHN DRYDEN, *All For Love*

It is strange, but true; for truth is always strange;
Stranger than fiction.

LORD BYRON, *Don Juan*

All nature is but art, unknown to thee;
All chance, direction, which thou canst not see;
All discord, harmony, not understood;
All partial evil, Universal Good;
And, spite of pride, in erring reason's spite,
One truth is clear, Whatever is, is right.

ALEXANDER POPE, *Essay on Man*

No pleasure is comparable to the Standing upon the vantage-ground of truth.

FRANCIS BACON, *Essay on Truth*

It is the customary fate of new truths to begin as heresies and to end as superstitions.

THOMAS HENRY HUXLEY, *Science and Culture*

I do not know what I may appear to the world, but to myself I seem to have been only like a boy playing on the sea-shore, and diverting myself in now and then finding a smoother pebble, or a prettier shell than ordinary, whilst the great ocean of truth lay all undiscovered before me.

ISAAC NEWTON, in Brewster's *Memoirs of Newton*

It is more from carelessness about truth than from intentional lying, that there is so much falsehood in the world.

SAMUEL JOHNSON to JAMES BOSWELL

Without courage there cannot be truth, and without truth there can be no other virtue.

SIR WALTER SCOTT

It often requires more bravery to tell the simple truth than it does to win a battle.

JOSH BILLINGS (HENRY WHEELER SHAW)

Uncertainty

Many things fall out between the cup and the lip.

Proverb

Lest men suspect your tale untrue,
Keep probability in view.

JOHN GAY, *The Painter Who Pleased Nobody and Everybody*

Unchanging

The sun, which passeth through pollutions and itself remains as pure as before.

FRANCIS BACON, *Advancement of Learning*

Understanding

We do not comprehend ruins until we are ourselves in ruin.

HEINRICH HEINE

Everyone hears only what he understands.

JOHANN WOLFGANG VON GOETHE

Ungratefulness

Cast no dirt into the well that gives you water.

Proverb

Unsympathetic

Laugh, and the world laughs with you,
Weep, and you weep alone.

ELLA WHEELER WILCOX, *Way of the World*

Be always as merry as ever you can
For no one delights in a sorrowful man.

Proverb

Valuation

Forbidden wares sell twice as dear.

DENHAM, *Natura Naturalia*

Oh, God! that bread should be so dear,
And flesh and blood so cheap!

THOMAS HOOD, *The Song of the Shirt*

A thing you don't want is dear at any price.

Proverb

A crown, if it hurt us, is hardly worth wearing.

PHILIP JAMES BAILEY, *Festus*

Variety

A man who can do everything can do nothing.

Proverb

The great source of pleasure is variety.

SAMUEL JOHNSON, *Life of Butler*

Vary everything, except your loves.

VOLTAIRE

Versatility

Who can be wise, amazed, temperate and furious,
Loyal and neutral, in a moment.

WILLIAM SHAKESPEARE, *Macbeth*

Vice

I have found that one big vice in a man is apt to keep out a great many smaller ones.

FRANCIS BRET HARTE, *Two Men of Sandy Bar*

Virtue

And virtue, though in rags, will keep me warm.

HORACE, *Odes*, translated by Dryden

Why to true merit should they have regard?
They know that virtue is its own reward.

JOHN GAY, *Epistle to Methuen*

Wants

A man never feels the want of what it never occurs to him to ask for.

ARTHUR SCHOPENHAUER

War (*See also* Americanism)

The arms are fair,
When the intent of bearing them is just.

WILLIAM SHAKESPEARE, *Henry IV*

War's a brain-spattering, windpipe-slitting art,
Unless her cause by right be sanctified.

LORD BYRON, *Don Juan*

Wars are to be undertaken in order that it may be possible to live in peace without molestation.

CICERO, *De Officiis*

War is just to those to whom war is necessary.

TITUS LIVIUS, *History*

For what can war but endless war still breed?

JOHN MILTON, *Sonnets: To Lord Fairfax*

Worse than war is the fear of war.

SENECA, *Thyestes*

War should be long in preparing in order that you may conquer the more quickly.

PUBLILIUS SYRUS, *Sententiae*

Warning

Coming events cast their shadows before.

THOMAS CAMPBELL, *Lochiel's Warning*

The fox barks not when he would steal the lamb.

WILLIAM SHAKESPEARE, *Henry VI*

Waste

The world is too much with us; late and soon,
Getting and spending, we lay waste our powers:
Little we see in Nature that is ours.

WILLIAM WORDSWORTH, *Miscellaneous Sonnets*

Thoughts shut up want air,
And spoil, like bales unopened to the sun.

EDWARD YOUNG, *Night Thoughts*

Our wasted oil unprofitably burns,
Like hidden lamps in old sepulchral urns.

WILLIAM COWPER, *Conversation*

Water

Water, water, everywhere,
Nor any drop to drink.

SAMUEL TAYLOR COLERIDGE, *The Ancient Mariner*

Wickedness

There is a method in man's wickedness;
It grows up by degrees.

BEAUMONT AND FLETCHER, *King and No King*

Willingness

In idle wishes fools supinely stay;
Be there a will,—and wisdom finds a way.

GEORGE CRABBE, *The Birth of Flattery*

Nothing is impossible to a willing heart.

JOHN HEYWOOD, *Proverbs*

Wind

Thou wind!—
Which art the unseen similitude of God
The Spirit; His most meet and mightiest sign!

PHILIP JAMES BAILEY, *Festus*

Winter

See, winter comes to rule the varied year,
Sullen and sad, with all his rising train;
Vapours, and clouds and storms.

JAMES THOMSON, *The Seasons*

Let winter come! let polar spirits sweep
The darkening world and tempest-troubled deep
Though boundless snows the wither'd heath deform.

THOMAS CAMPBELL, *The Pleasures of Hope*

Lastly came winter, clothed all in frieze,
Chattering his teeth for cold that did him chill;
Whilst on his hoary beard his breath did freeze.

EDMUND SPENSER, *Faerie Queene*

And pale concluding winter comes at last,
And shuts the scene.

JAMES THOMSON, *The Seasons*

Wisdom

Some are wise, and some are otherwise.

Proverb

To know
That which before us lies in daily life,
Is the prime wisdom.

JOHN MILTON, *Paradise Lost*

What is it to be wise?
'Tis but to know how little can be known;
To see all other's faults, and feel our own.

ALEXANDER POPE, *Essay on Man*

And he is oft the wisest man,
Who is not wise at all.

WILLIAM WORDSWORTH, *The Oak and the Broom*

Have more than thou showest,
Speak less than thou knowest,
Lend less than thou owest,
Ride more than thou goest.

WILLIAM SHAKESPEARE, *King Lear*

Wishes (or) Wishing

Thy wish was father, Harry, to that thought.

WILLIAM SHAKESPEARE, *Henry IV*

Wishing, of all employments is the worst.
Philosophy's reverse; and health's decay!

EDWARD YOUNG, *Night Thoughts*

We look before and after, and pine for what is not.

PERCY BYSSHE SHELLEY, *Ode to a Skylark*

Wit

Don't put too fine a point on your wit for fear it should get blunted.

MIGUEL DE CERVANTES, *The Little Gypsy*

Women

A girl whose cheeks are covered with paint,
Has an advantage with me over one whose ain't.

OGDEN NASH, *The Face is Familiar*[1]

Women are wacky. Women are vain.
They'd rather be pretty than have a good brain.

MARGARET FISHBACK, *Time For a Quick One*[2]

Women are to be talked to as below men, and above children.

LORD CHESTERFIELD, *Letters to His Son*

No is not a negative in a woman's mouth.

SIR PHILIP SIDNEY, *Arcadia*

Have you not heard it said full oft,
A woman's nay doth stand for nought?

WILLIAM SHAKESPEARE, *The Passionate Pilgrim*

My only books
Were women's looks,
And folly's all they've taught me.

THOMAS MOORE, *Irish Melodies*

There are three classes into which all elderly women that I ever knew were to be divided: first, that dear old soul; second, that old woman; third, that old witch.

SAMUEL TAYLOR COLERIDGE, *Table Talk*

Her voice was ever soft,
Gentle, and low, an excellent thing in woman.

WILLIAM SHAKESPEARE, *King Lear*

Sir, a woman preaching is like a dog's walking on his hind legs. It is not done well; but you are surprised to find it done at all.

SAMUEL JOHNSON, in Boswell's *Life of Johnson*

Let men say whate'er they will,
Woman, woman, rules them still.

ISAAC BICKERSTAFF, *The Sultan*

She's beautiful, and therefore to be wooed:
She is a woman; therefore to be won.

WILLIAM SHAKESPEARE, *Henry VI*

The happiest women, like the happiest nations, have no history.

GEORGE ELIOT, *The Mill on the Floss*

A mill and a woman are always in want of something.

Proverb

A mill, a clock, and a woman, always want mending.

Proverb

If she be not so to me,
What care I how fair she be?

GEORGE WITHER, *The Shepherd's Resolution*

Such, Polly! are your sex—part truth, part fiction;
Some thought, much whim, and all a contradiction.

RICHARD SAVAGE, *Verses to a Young Lady*

She who ne'er answers till a husband cools,
Or, if she rules him, never shows she rules.

ALEXANDER POPE, *Moral Essays*

A beautiful woman is the "hell" of the soul, the "purgatory" of the purse, and the "paradise" of the eyes.

FONTENELLE

Work

By the work one knows the workman.

LA FONTAINE

Run if you like, but try to keep your breath;
Work like a man, but don't be worked to death.

OLIVER WENDELL HOLMES, *A Rhymed Lesson*

A woman's work, grave sirs, is never done.

From a poem read by LAURENCE EUSDEN at a Cambridge Commencement

Labor makes us insensible to sorrow.

CICERO

Life gives nothing to mortals except with great labor.

HORACE

Labor is often the father of pleasure.

VOLTAIRE, *Discours*

Labor has a bitter root but a sweet taste.

Proverb

World

All the world's a stage,
And all the men and women merely players.

WILLIAM SHAKESPEARE, *As You Like It*

The world is a comedy to those that think, a tragedy to those who feel.

HORACE WALPOLE, *Letter to Sir Horace Mann*

It is a very good world to live in,
To lend, or to spend, or to give in;
But to beg or to borrow, or to get a man's own,
It is the very worst world that ever was known.

Attributed to the EARL OF ROCHESTER

Why, then the world's mine oyster,
Which I with sword will open.

WILLIAM SHAKESPEARE, *The Merry Wives of Windsor*

The history of the world is the judgment of the world.

FRIEDRICH SCHILLER—*Resignation*

Worry

But what torments of pain you endured
From evils that never arrived!

RALPH WALDO EMERSON, *Conduct of Life*

The mind that is anxious about the future is miserable.

SENECA

Present fears
Are less than horrible imaginings.

WILLIAM SHAKESPEARE, *Macbeth*

Writers

But show me a writer who when not writing for pay deliberately writes for fun or for self-expression, and I'll show you one of the rarest cases of freakish misapplication in the entire dime museum of human nature.

IRVIN S. COBB, *Exit Laughing*[1]

No man but a blockhead ever wrote except for money.

SAMUEL JOHNSON,
in Boswell's *Life of Johnson*

Look, then, into thine heart, and write!

HENRY WADSWORTH LONGFELLOW,
Voices of the Night

Some write, confin'd by physic; some, by debt;
Some, for 'tis Sunday; some because 'tis wet;
Another writes because his father writ,
And proves himself a bastard by his wit.

EDWARD YOUNG, *Epistle to Mr. Pope*

'Tis pleasant, sure, to see one's name in print;
A book's a book although there's nothing in't.

LORD BYRON,
English Bards and Scotch Reviewers

Talent alone cannot make a writer. There must be a man behind the book.

RALPH WALDO EMERSON, *On Goethe*

Beneath the rule of men entirely great,
The pen is mightier than the sword.

BULWER-LYTTON, *Richelieu*

Most wretched men
Are cradled into poetry by wrong;
They learn in suffering what they teach in song.

PERCY BYSSHE SHELLEY,
Julian and Maddalo

[1]Copyright 1941. Used by special permission of the publishers, The Bobbs-Merrill Company, Inc.

Of all those arts in which the wise excel,
Nature's chief masterpiece is writing well.

JOHN SHEFFIELD, *Essay on Poetry*

If you would learn to write, 'tis in the street you must learn it.

RALPH WALDO EMERSON,
Society and Solitude

Wrongs

Wrongs do not leave off there where they begin,
But still beget new mischiefs in their course.

SAMUEL DANIEL,
The History of the Civil War

Youth

Youth is wholly experimental.

ROBERT LOUIS STEVENSON,
A Letter to a Young Gentleman

The whining school-boy with his satchel,
And shining morning face, creeping like snail
Unwillingly to school.

WILLIAM SHAKESPEARE, *As You Like It*

My salad days,
When I was green in judgement.

WILLIAM SHAKESPEARE,
Antony and Cleopatra

Zeal

Zeal without knowledge is a runaway horse.

Proverb

Zeal without knowledge is the sister of folly.

Proverb

Zeal is like fire, it needs both feeding and watching.

Proverb

DICTIONARY OF CLASSICAL MYTHOLOGY

A KNOWLEDGE OF THE CLASSICS *and an acquaintance with the imaginary characters, places, and incidents of ancient mythology which have been such an inspiring influence to writers of all ages add greatly to one's enjoyment of literature, art, and conversation. Few people outside literary and educational pursuits have sufficient opportunity or leisure to acquire or keep up a knowledge of this particular branch of learning. It is important, therefore, to present in dictionary form the stories of gods, goddesses, heroes, and heroines of the old Grecian and Roman literature. It will lead to a better understanding of the countless references which are made from time to time in the literature of the day to classic subjects. It is a great wonderland of poesy and romance, and forms a realm all its own, the realm of antiquity's gods and demons and of prehistoric heroes.*

Abderus, armor-bearer to Hercules. He was torn to pieces by the mares of Diomedes.

Absyrtus, a son of Aeetes, king of Colchis, who was murdered by his sister Medea when she fled with Jason.

Acamas, son of Theseus and Phaedra, who went with Diomedes to demand Helen from the Trojans and afterward took part in the Trojan War.

Acantha, a nymph, loved by Apollo and transformed into the acanthus.

Acarnas and **Amphoterus,** sons of Alcmaeon and Callirrhoe.

Acestes, king of Drepanum, who assisted Priam at Troy and after the war entertained Aeneas during his stay at Drepanum.

Achaei, the descendants of Achaeus, who constituted one of the chief divisions of the ancient Greeks.

Achaemenides, son of Adramastus, who was abandoned by Ulysses on the coast of Sicily and was later found by Aeneas.

Achates, a friend of Aeneas, known for his fidelity; whence the term *fidus Achates.*

Acheloides, the Sirens, daughters of Achelous.

Achelous, son of Oceanus and Tethys, god of the river Achelous in Epirus. Contending with Hercules for Dejanira, he changed himself into a serpent. Later, after Achelous had turned himself into an ox, Hercules broke one of his horns and defeated him.

Acheron, a son of Ceres, who was changed into a river in Tartarus for supplying the Titans with water in their battle with the gods. Over this river Charon ferried the souls of the dead.

Acherusia, a lake near Memphis, said to have been connected with the lower world. Across this lake the bodies of the dead were ferried by Charon.

Achilles, most famous of the Greek heroes that fought at Troy, son of Peleus and Thetis. When an infant, he was plunged by his mother into the Styx and made invulnerable except in the heel, by which she held him. During the Trojan War he quarreled with Agamemnon about Briseis and for a time refrained from fighting. But when his friend Patroclus was killed, he rejoined his comrades and slew Hector at the Scaean Gate. Ultimately Achilles himself was slain, wounded by an arrow in his vulnerable heel.

Achillides, Pyrrhus, son of Achilles.

Acis, a Sicilian shepherd, son of Faunus and Simaethis, who fell in love with the sea-nymph Galatea. Jealous of her love, the Cyclops Polyphemus crushed Acis to death with a rock. He was changed by Galatea into a stream on Mount Aetna.

Aconteus, a hunter, changed into stone at the sight of Medusa's head during the nuptials of Perseus and Andromeda.

Acrisius, son of Abas and Ocalea and father of Danae.

Actaeon, son of Aristaeus and Autonoe, who, because he watched Diana bathing, was changed into a stag and devoured by his own dogs.

Admeta, daughter of Eurystheus and priestess of Juno's temple at Argos. To obtain for Admeta the girdle of the queen of the Amazons was the ninth labor imposed upon Hercules by Eurystheus.

Admetus, king of Thessaly and husband of Alcestis. Apollo, who served him for a time as shepherd, urged the Fates to spare Admetus' life if some other person should be willing to die for him. Alcestis offered herself as substitute. Admetus was one of the Argonauts and was present at the hunt of the Calydonian boar.

Adonis, son of Cinyras and Myrrha and beloved by Venus. While hunting, he was killed by a wild boar and was transformed by Venus into the anemone. The gods of the underworld allowed him to spend six months of every year on earth with Venus.

Adrastus, king of Sicyon and leader of the Seven against Thebes, of whom he alone survived. Ten years later he led the Epigoni, sons of the Seven, to destroy Thebes.

Aeacus, son of Jupiter and Aegina. After the inhabitants of Aegina had been destroyed by pestilence, Jupiter transformed ants into human beings, whom Aeacus called *Myrmidons.* Aeacus with Minos and Rhadamanthus became a judge in the lower world.

Aeetes, king of Colchis and father of Medea, Absyrtus, and Chalciope. It was to his court that Phryxus fled on the back of a ram. After the ram had been sacrificed, its golden fleece was given to Aeetes.

Aegeus, king of Athens and father of Theseus. While at the court of Pittheus in Troezen, he married the king's daughter Aethra. Departing before the birth of his son, Aegeus told her to send Theseus to him as soon as he could lift the stone under which he had concealed his sword. Years later, when the young man arrived in Athens, his life was threatened by Medea, who meanwhile had married his father. Theseus soon sailed to Crete, where he destroyed the Minotaur. On his return voyage he forgot to hoist white sails—the pre-arranged signal of success—and Aegeus, concluding that his son was dead, threw himself from a high rock into the sea, which was named after him the Aegean.

Aegis, the shield of Jupiter, in the center of which was represented the Gorgon's head.

Aegisthus, king of Argos, son of Thyestes and Pelopea. He murdered Atreus to avenge the crime perpetrated against his father and ascended the throne of Mycenae, banishing Agamemnon and Menelaus. But Aegisthus at length became reconciled to the Atridae and during Agamemnon's absence at Troy was made guardian of his wife Clytemnestra. He fell in love with her, and the two murdered Agamemnon on his return from the Trojan War. Subsequently they themselves were killed by Orestes, son of Agamemnon.

Aeneades, descendants of Aeneas.

Aeneas, a Trojan prince, son of Venus and Anchises. At Troy he fought bravely against Diomedes and Achilles. After the storming of the city he rescued his father, his son, and the household gods and fled from the flaming ruins. With a number of companions he built twenty ships and set out for the Thracian Chersonesus; from there he sailed to Delos, the Strophades, Crete, and Epirus; thence to Drepanum, in Sicily, where he buried his father. On the voyage to Italy, the ships were driven upon the African coast near Carthage. In this city he was entertained by Queen Dido, whose unrequited love for him led her to commit suicide. Aeneas sailed back to Sicily, thence to Cumae, where the Sibyl conducted him to the lower world. After a voyage of seven years and the loss of thirteen ships, he reached the Tiber. Latinus, king of Latinum, promised him his daughter Lavinia, already betrothed to Turnus. War ensued, and in a combat with Aeneas Turnus was killed. Aeneas later married Lavinia, in whose honor he built the town of Lavinium, and succeeded Latinus as king of Latium. After a short reign he died, either killed in war with the Etruscans or drowned in the river Numicus. The Caesars traced their origin to him, and his wanderings form the subject of Vergil's *Aeneid*.

Aeolus, son of Hippotes and god of the winds, who lived in the island of Aeolia. He presented Ulysses, on his return to Ithaca, with all the adverse winds tied in bags; but his companions from curiosity opened them, and so Ulysses was driven out of his course.

Aerope, wife of Atreus and mother of Agamemnon, Menelaus, and Anaxibia.

Aesacus, son of Priam by Alexirrhoe or by Arisba. Falling passionately in love with Hesperia, he pursued her till she despaired of escape; she flung herself into the sea and was transformed into a bird. At the same time Aesacus was changed into a cormorant.

Aesculapius, the god of healing and son of Apollo. He was killed by Jove's thunderbolt for restoring men to life.

Aeson, father of Jason and brother of Pelias, who succeeded his father as king in Iolchus but was deposed by Pelias. In old age Aeson was restored to youth by Medea's magic powers.

Agamemnon, king of Mycenae and Argos, brother of Menelaus, and son of Atreus. On the death of Atreus, Thyestes seized Argos, and Agamemnon with Menelaus was forced to leave the city. The brothers fled to Tyndareus, king of Sparta, who gave them his daughters in marriage: Clytemnestra to Agamemnon, and Helen to Menelaus. Later Tyndareus helped them to recover their father's kingdom; Agamemnon established himself at Mycenae, and Menelaus succeeded Tyndareus at Sparta. When Paris ran off with Helen, Agamemnon assumed command of the forces against Troy and fought with great valor. After the war Cassandra foretold his murder by Clytemnestra, but he nevertheless returned to Argos, where, as he was leaving the bath, Clytemnestra and Aegisthus murdered him.

Agenor, king of Phoenicia, son of Neptune and Libya, father of Cadmus, Phoenix, Cilix, and Europa. He was an ancestor of Dido, queen of Carthage.

Aglaia, one of the Graces, daughter of Jupiter and Eurynome.

Ahenobarbus, an ancestor of Nero, so named because his beard was changed to bronze by Castor and Pollux for refusing to believe in the victory at Lake Regillus.

Ajax, son of Telamon and next to Achilles the most famous Greek warrior. He sought to gain possession of the arms of Achilles after the latter's death. Informed that they had been awarded to Ulysses, he lost his mind and slaughtered a flock of sheep which he mistook for the sons of Atreus; then he stabbed himself, and where the blood from his wound sank into the earth appeared the hyacinth. The lesser Ajax was the son of Oileus and was swiftest of the Greeks after Achilles. On his return from Troy he was shipwrecked by Athena. He was rescued, but later for boasting of his escape he was killed by lightning.

Albion, Neptune's son by Amphitrite, who introduced astronomy and shipbuilding.

Alcathous, son of Pelops and king of Megara. Accused of slaying his brother Chrysippus, he escaped to Megara, killed a lion that had destroyed the king's son, and succeeded to the throne.

Alcestis, daughter of Pelias and Anaxibia and wife of Admetus. She willingly sacrificed her life to save Admetus from death. Through Hercules' efforts, however, she was brought back from the lower world and returned to her husband.

Alcimede, mother of Jason by Aeson.

Alcinous, son of Nausithous and Periboea, king of Phaeacia. He married his niece, Arete, by whom he had a daughter, Nausicaa.

Alcithoe, daughter of Minyas, king of Thessaly. Her spindle was changed into a vine, her yarn into ivy, and she herself into a bat because she ridiculed Bacchus.

Alcmaeon, son of Amphiaraus and Eriphyle. He was driven to madness by the thought of having killed his mother. He fled from home and after a time married Arsinoe. But because he left her to marry Callirrhoe, her brothers killed him.

Alcmene, daughter of Electryon, who was promised in marriage to Amphitryon on condition that he avenge the death of her brothers. In Amphitryon's absence, however, Jupiter assumed his form and became the father of Alcmene's son Hercules.

Alectryon, a youth placed on guard in order to warn Mars of the approach of Phoebus while the god of war was visiting Venus. Alectryon was transformed into a cock for falling asleep.

Alpheus, the god of the river Alpheus in Arcadia. He fell in love with Arethusa, who was transformed by Diana into a fountain in the small island of Ortygia, near Syracuse. The Alpheus was said to flow under the sea and come to the surface in Ortygia.

Althaea, wife of Oeneus and mother of Meleager.

Amalthaea, daughter of King Melissus of Crete. She fed the infant Jupiter with goat's milk.

Amata, wife of King Latinus, who betrothed her daughter Lavinia to Turnus before Aeneas' arrival. When Amata learned that Aeneas had killed Turnus, she committed suicide.

Amazons, a race of warlike women dwelling in Asia Minor, who came to the help of Troy during the Trojan War.

Ambrosia, the food of the gods, which preserved for them their immortality.

Ammon, an ancient Egyptian divinity, identified with Jupiter and frequently referred to as Jupiter Ammon. The god was sometimes represented as a ram. One of his temples, renowned for its oracle, was in an oasis of the Libyan Desert, nine days' journey from Alexandria.

Amphiaraus, son of Oicles and Hypermnestra. He took part in the hunt of the Calydonian boar and in the Argonautic expedition. He was a great prophet; and though he foresaw the fatal end, he was persuaded by his wife Eriphyle to join the expedition of Adrastus against Thebes, where the earth swallowed him up before his enemies could kill him.

Amphion, a famous musician, the twin brother of Zethus, born to Jupiter by Antiope on Mount Cithaeron, where she had fled to avoid the wrath of Dirce. A shepherd succored the infants and when they had grown to manhood, they besieged Lycus, their granduncle, in Thebes, murdered him, and tied his wife Dirce to a wild bull, which dragged her to her death. Amphion became king of Thebes. While building the wall about the city, he played on his lyre, and the stones moved into position of their own accord. Niobe, daughter of Tantalus, was his wife.

Amphitrite, the daughter of Oceanus and Tethys and mother of Triton by Neptune.

Amphitryon, king of Thebes, who, because he avenged the deaths of the sons of Electryon, was appointed his successor and given his daughter Alcmene in marriage. While Amphitryon was absent, Jupiter appeared to Alcmene in the form of her husband and became the father of her child.

Amycus, son of Neptune, who became king of Melia. He was a skillful boxer but was killed by Pollux during a match.

Amyntor, king of Argos, who blinded his son Phoenix for insulting Clytia, his concubine.

Amyone, daughter of Danaus and Europa, who married Enceladus and killed him on the marriage night. Of the fifty Danaids she alone was absolved from the task of filling the leaky vessel in Hades because she had supplied Argos with water during a drought.

Anaxibia, sister of Agamemnon and wife of Nestor.

Ancaeus, an Argonaut killed at the Calydonian hunt.

Anchises, father of Aeneas and son of Capys and Themis. His surpassing beauty attracted Venus, herself the goddess of beauty, who fell in love with him and bore him Aeneas. After the fall of Troy Anchises was carried out of the city on the shoulders of his son. He accompanied Aeneas on his subsequent wanderings but died before reaching Italy.

Anchurus, the son of Midas, who sacrificed his life by leaping into a fissure in the earth. An oracle had declared that this chasm would not cease to swallow whatever appeared above it until Midas had thrown in what was most dear to him.

Androcles, a slave who was thrown to the wild animals in the Roman arena but was spared by a lion from whose foot he had once extracted a thorn in an African cave. Amazed at the lion's behavior, the Roman officials pardoned Androcles and presented him with the lion.

Androgynae, a race of hermaphrodites, who lived in the region of Africa beyond the Nasamones.

Andromache, wife of Hector and mother of Astyanax. The passage in Homer's *Iliad* describing her farewell to Hector as he is about to leave for battle, is one of the best-known passages in the poem. After her husband's death and the fall of Troy, Andromache became the prize of Pyrrhus. Pyrrhus died, and she married Helenus, a fellow-captive.

Andromeda, wife of Perseus and daughter of Cepheus, king of Aethiopia. Her mother was Cassiopeia, who boasted that she was more beautiful than the Nereids. Out of revenge for this insult to the sea nymphs, Neptune inundated the land and sent a sea monster to ravage the shore. To appease the god of the sea, Cepheus was commanded by the oracle of Ammon to chain his daughter to a rock out in the sea. Perseus came to the rescue, however, by turning the monster to stone with the magic head of Medusa. Andromeda was saved and became the wife of Perseus.

Antaeus, a Libyan giant and wrestler, son of Terra and Neptune, who was vanquished by Hercules. Realizing that Antaeus' strength depended upon contact with his mother Earth, Hercules lifted him from the ground and crushed the life out of him.

Antigone, daughter of Oedipus by Jocasta, who defied the order of Creon, king of Thebes, that the body of her brother Polynices remain unburied. Condemned to be buried alive, Antigone killed herself.

Antilochus, son of Nestor and Eurydice, killed at Troy by Memnon.

Antiope, daughter of Nycteus, king of Thebes, who was wooed by Jupiter. To escape her father's anger, she fled to Mount Cithaeron, where her twin sons Amphion and Zethus were born.

Antiphus, son of Priam, who was killed by Agamemnon.

Aon, son of Neptune and king of Boeotia, after whom the Boeotians were called Aones, and the country Aonia.

Aphrodite, the goddess of love and beauty, identified with Venus by the Romans.

Apollo, god of light and prophecy and patron of the arts. He was the son of Jupiter and Latona and was born on Delos, which before had been a floating island, but was now anchored with chains to the bottom of the sea. Apollo became a renowned physician and himself instructed his son Aesculapius in medicine. When the latter was killed by Jupiter's thunderbolt for having restored the dead to life, Apollo took vengeance on the Cyclopes, who had forged the bolt. For this rash act he was ordered to shepherd the flocks of Admetus. Thereafter he aided Neptune in building the walls of Troy; however, because the king, Laomedon, refused him the promised reward, he sent a pestilence upon the inhabitants. Apollo's oracles were at Delphi—famed throughout the ancient world—Delos, Claros, Tenedos, Cyrrha, and Patara. The epithets most frequently applied to him were *Pythius*, *Phoebus*, *Cynthius*, and *Lycius*.

Arachne, daughter of Idmon of Colophon, who was so expert in weaving that she challenged Minerva. She chose for designs scenes which depicted the foibles of the gods. Angered by such insults, Minerva tore up the web. Arachne hanged herself in despair and was transformed into a spider—which hangs by the thread it spins.

Arcas, son of Jupiter and Callisto, who ruled over Pelasgia, which was called Arcadia after him.

Ares, the Greek god of war, identified with Mars.

Arethusa, a nymph who was pursued by the river-god Alpheus and changed by Diana into a fountain.

Argia, daughter of Adrastus, who married Polynices and was put to death by Creon for burying her husband against Creon's orders.

Argiphontes, a name meaning "slayer of Argus," which was given to Mercury because he killed the hundred-eyed Argus.

Argo, the ship used by Jason and his companions in their search for the Golden Fleece.

Argonauts, the companions of Jason on the *Argo*, among whom were Hercules, Theseus, Aesculapius, Nestor, Orpheus, Castor and Pollux.

Argus, a giant possessed of a hundred eyes, of which only two were asleep at a time. He was ordered by Juno to keep watch on Io, but Jupiter sent Mercury to kill him; afterward his eyes were put on the tail of Juno's sacred peacock.

Ariadne, the daughter of Minos of Crete. Having fallen in love with Theseus, she gave him some thread by means of which he was able to find his way out of the labyrinth. After Theseus had killed the Minotaur, he married Ariadne but deserted her later at Naxos. Bacchus gave her a crown of seven stars, which was turned into a constellation.

Arion, a famous musician, who, when returning from Sicily to Corinth with rich prizes, was threatened with death by the sailors. He leapt into the sea, and a dolphin, charmed by his playing, carried him safely to land.

Aristaeus, a Libyan shepherd, son of Apollo and Cyrene, who was reared by the Seasons and nourished with nectar and ambrosia. He married Autonoe, by whom he had a son Actaeon. He was indirectly responsible for the death of Eurydice, for in fleeing from his advances, she stepped on a snake and died of its bite. He was the first to teach men the art of keeping bees.

Arne, daughter of Aeolus, wooed by Neptune in the form of a bull.

Artemis, a Greek goddess, the guardian of forests and wild animals, who was identified with Diana.

Aruntius, a Roman intoxicated by Bacchus for ridiculing his rites and killed by his daughter Medullina, whom he had insulted.

Ascalaphus, son of Acheron, who, having been appointed by Pluto to watch Proserpina in the Elysian Fields, testified that the goddess had eaten pomegranates. For his spying Proserpina changed him into an owl.

Ascanius, son of Aeneas and Creusa and founder of Alba Longa.

Astarte, a Syrian goddess, corresponding to the Greek Aphrodite.

Asteria, daughter of Coeus, the Titan, and mother of Hecate. Courted by Zeus in the form of an eagle, she threw herself into the sea, where she was changed into an island, which was later called Delos.

Astraea, daughter of Astraeus and goddess of justice during the Golden Age. Disgusted with the wickedness of mortals, she returned to heaven and was transformed into the constellation Virgo. She is represented as holding a pair of scales in one hand and a sword in the other.

Astyanax, son of Hector and Andromache, who was thrown from the walls of Troy by the victorious Greeks.

Atalanta, the name of two mythological characters. The daughter of Jasus, the Arcadian, was a huntress, who took part in the hunt for the Calydonian boar and shared with Meleager in the prize of victory. The daughter of Schoeneus, of Boeotia, was also a huntress, but she is known best for her ability in foot-racing. Refusing to marry anyone who could not outrun her, she insisted that all her suitors run a race with her in which the penalty of defeat was death. At last Hippomenes (or Milanion, according to others) defeated her. From Venus he had obtained three golden apples and, as he ran, he threw them down, one after another. Atalanta, fascinated by them, stopped to pick them up, and thus Hippomenes won the race and married Atalanta.

Ate, the goddess of infatuation, who led men into rash actions.

Athamas, king of Orchomenos and son of Aeolus. He married Nephele, who bore him Phryxus and Helle. Later he divorced her and married Ino, by whom he had Learchus and Melicertes. Ino was jealous of Nephele's children and persuaded an oracle to predict that a pestilence then raging could only by their sacrifice be arrested. On being led to the altar Phryxus and Helle fled to Colchis through the air on a golden ram, whose fleece was later sought by Jason. During the voyage Helle fell off into the sea, hence called the Hellespont. Juno dispatched the Fury Tisiphone to torture Athamas to madness. In this condition he killed Learchus, whereupon Ino threw herself into the sea and was changed into a sea-goddess.

Athena, a Greek goddess, corresponding to the Roman Minerva.

Atlantides, the seven daughters of Atlas: Maia, Electra, Taygeta, Sterope, Merope, Alcyone, and Celaeno.

Atlantis, an island said to have existed in the Atlantic, west of Gibraltar. It was once rich and powerful and blessed with every beauty but was later swallowed up by the ocean owing to the increasing wickedness of its inhabitants.

Atlas, son of Iapetus and Clymene and father of the Hesperides, Hyades, and Pleiades. He lived in northern Africa and carried the heavens on his shoulders. Perseus, after vanquishing the Gorgons, sought refuge with him. Because assistance was denied him, Perseus produced Medusa's head and changed Atlas into a mountain.

Atreus, son of Pelops by Hippodamia and king of Mycenae. Suspected of the murder of his half brother Chrysippus, he fled to Argos and succeeded Eurystheus as king, marrying his daughter Aerope, who bore him Agamemnon and Menelaus. Thyestes, the brother of Atreus, who had been banished for seducing Aerope, sent Plisthenes, Atreus' eldest son by a former wife, to murder his own father. But Plisthenes was killed by Atreus. On learning that he had slain his own son, Atreus murdered the two sons of Thyestes and served them up to their father at a banquet. For this crime Atreus and his house were cursed by the gods, and he himself was finally killed by Aegisthus.

Atrides, any one of the descendants of Atreus but especially Agamemnon or Menelaus.

Atropos, one of the Fates, the goddess that cut the thread of life.

Attis, or **Atys,** a Phrygian god of fertility, who died and came to life again. He was loved by Cybele and was represented as a beautiful youth.

Augeas, king of Elis, owner of 3,000 oxen, whose enormous stables had not been cleaned for thirty years. The job of cleaning out the stalls was one of the twelve labors imposed on Hercules; for this work Augeas promised him a tenth of his herd. When Hercules diverted the waters of the Alpheus to send them through the stables, Augeas regarded this as a trick and refused to give him the reward. Hercules, therefore, conquered Elis and killed Augeas.

Aurora, daughter of Hyperion and Thea and goddess of the dawn, who rose from the couch of her husband Tithonus before the break of day. She is depicted as a veiled figure riding in a rose-colored chariot drawn by white horses and opening the gates of day.

Auster, the south wind, that brought rain and fog in winter and hot, dry air in summer.

Autolycus, son of Mercury, an Argonaut, and a notorious cattle thief. He was able to deceive the owners by changing the marks on the cattle, but Sisyphus, son of Aeolus, got the better of him by putting his marks under the feet of his oxen.

Automedon, son of Dioreus, charioteer to Achilles and afterward to Pyrrhus.

Avernus, a lake between Cumae and Puteoli, the waters of which were so fatal that no birds could live near it. It was one of the entrances to Tartarus.

B

Bacchanalia, a Roman festival in honor of Bacchus, marked by wild revelry.

Bacchantes, devotees of Bacchus, who danced and threw themselves about in barbaric abandonment at the Bacchanalia.

Bacchus, the god of wine, son of Jupiter and Semele. He was saved by Jupiter from Juno's jealous wrath, which compassed his mother's death, and was intrusted to Ino. While living on Mount Nysa Bacchus discovered how to make wine from grapes and afterward traveled to many foreign lands to teach the art of cultivating the vine, tilling the soil, and collecting honey. He is generally represented as crowned with vine and ivy-leaves. He married Ariadne after she was deserted by Theseus at Naxos.

Baucis, the wife of Philemon, who lived with her husband in a small cottage in Phrygia, where they were visited by Jupiter and Mercury in disguise. As a reward for the hospitality extended to them, Jupiter transformed the cottage into a splendid temple. Baucis and Philemon lived to a ripe old age and at death were changed into trees before the temple's doors.

Bellerophon, the son of Glaucus, who was sent by Iobates, king of Lycia, to attack the Chimaera, a fire-breathing monster. This action had been urged upon the king by his son-in-law, Proetus, whose wife accused Bellerophon of seducing her. Aided by Minerva, Bellerophon succeeded in destroying the Chimaera. Thereafter he tried to fly to heaven on his winged horse Pegasus, but Jupiter sent a gadfly to sting the horse and Bellerophon was thrown to earth. He wandered about, lame and blind, for the rest of his life.

Bellona, the goddess of war, daughter of Phorcys and Ceto, and companion or sister of Mars. Her priests, called Bellonarii, inflicted wounds on themselves when offering sacrifices.

Bergion, a giant, son of Neptune, who was killed with stones thrown from heaven, when he opposed Hercules.

Beroe, the nurse of Semele, whose form Juno assumed when she appeared before Semele. Juno persuaded Semele to obtain proof as to whether it was actually Jupiter who was visiting her.

Bomonicae, the youths who were whipped at the altar of Diana Orthia during her festivals. The one who cried out the least was awarded the prize.

Bona Dea, Roman goddess of fecundity. At her festival, celebrated on the 1st of May, no male was permitted to be present.

Boreas, the north or northeast wind, who carried away Orithyia to Mount Haemus in Thrace. According to one version he was the son of Astraeus and Aurora. He possessed twelve mares of such fleetness that they could cross the sea without getting their feet wet.

Branchus, son of Smicrus of Miletus, to whom Apollo gave the power of prophecy.

Briareus, son of Coelus and Terra, a giant with a hundred arms and fifty heads, who helped the Olympians against the Titans.

Briseis, a beautiful woman who was part of the spoils appropriated by Achilles after the conquest of Lyrnessus. Later Agamemnon claimed her, causing Achilles to withdraw from the Trojan War. After the death of Patroclus she was given back to Achilles.

Bucephalus, favorite horse of Alexander the Great, which died in India.

Busiris, king of Egypt and son of Neptune and Libya. When Hercules was in Egypt, Busiris had him bound hand and foot and carried to the altar. Hercules freed himself, however, and slew both Busiris and his courtiers.

C

Cacus, a giant, son of Vulcan and Medusa, who lived in a cave on the Aventine Hill. He stole some of the cattle of Hercules and dragged them by the tails into his cave. Hercules heard them low, however, and strangled Cacus.

Cadmus, son of Agenor, who, unable to find his sister Europa and not wishing to return home without her, consulted the Delphic oracle as to where he should settle. The oracle told him to follow a certain cow and to found a city where the cow should lie down. He killed a dragon, which lived near the spot where the cow lay down, and sowed its teeth in the ground. The armed men who sprang from the dragon's teeth formed the original population of Thebes. Cadmus later married Harmonia, who was the daughter of Venus.

Caduceus, the magic wand of Mercury, with which he conducted the souls of mortals across the Styx and raised the dead to life.

Caeneus, a girl transformed by Neptune into a man, who took part in the Calydonian hunt. Later he was transformed into a bird, but in Elysium he became a girl again.

Calchas, the Greek soothsayer and high priest who was chosen to accompany the Greeks to Troy. He declared that the fleet could not sail until Iphigenia was sacrificed; that the plague could not be stopped till Chryseis was restored to her father; and that Troy could not be taken without Achilles' aid, nor without a ten years' siege.

Calliope, the Muse of epic poetry, daughter of Jupiter and Mnemosyne. She was the mother of Orpheus by Apollo.

Callirrhoe, daughter of Scamander, who married Tros and became the mother of Ganymede and Assaracus. Coresus fell in love with her, but she scorned him. This angered Bacchus, whose priest Coresus was, and the god sent a pestilence; whereupon the oracle demanded that Callirrhoe should be sacrificed. Coresus, compelled to lead the nymph to the altar, stabbed himself. Callirrhoe fled to Attica and there on the brink of a fountain killed herself.

Callisto, one of Diana's attendants and a daughter of King Lycaon, of Arcadia, who was changed into a bear and placed in the sky among the stars.

Calydon, a city of Aetolia, which was devastated by a boar sent by Diana in revenge for the neglect of her rites. This disaster gave rise to the famous hunt for the Calydonian boar, in which many heroes took part. Meleager succeeded in slaying the animal and presented its head to Atalanta.

Calypso, a sea nymph and queen of Ogygia. She offered Ulysses hospitality on his being shipwrecked, fell in love with him, and detained him seven years.

Camenae, fountain nymphs and goddesses of prophecy, who were identified with the Greek Muses.

Camilla, a warlike Volscian heroine, who was killed in the war between Aeneas and Turnus.

Capaneus, one of the Seven against Thebes, son of Hipponous and Astinome, and husband of Evadne. Having vowed to take Thebes in spite of Jupiter, he was killed with a stroke of lightning. On hearing the news Evadne committed suicide.

Cassandra, daughter of Priam and Hecuba, to whom Apollo granted the gift of prophecy. When she resisted him, however, he ordered that no one should believe her. After the fall of Troy, she became the captive of Agamemnon, who took her to Mycenae, where Clytemnestra put her to death.

Cassiopeia, mother of Andromeda and wife of Cepheus.

Castalia, a fountain on Mount Parnassus, sacred to Apollo and the Muses.

Castor, twin brother of Pollux and noted for his skill in taming horses. The two brothers joined in the Calydonian hunt and Argonautic expedition. In the struggle with Idas and Lynceus, Castor was slain and after the death of Pollux the brothers were placed among the stars as the Gemini.

Cecrops, founder and first king of Athens.

Celaeno, a daughter of Atlas; also one of the Harpies.

Centaurs, a race of creatures half horse, half human, who inhabited Mount Pelion. They engaged in the famous contest with the Lapithae. Later the greater number of them were killed by Hercules, and the rest driven to Mount Pindus.

Cerberus, the three-headed dog which kept watch over the gates of Hades. It was one of the labors of Hercules to bring Cerberus to the upper world.

Ceres, the Roman goddess of the earth's produce, especially of grain, who was identified with Demeter. When her daughter Proserpina was carried away by Pluto, Ceres in her anger caused the earth to withhold its fruits and was appeased only when Proserpina was brought back. But since she had eaten a pomegranate seed in Hades, Proserpina had to spend half of each year in the lower world.

Chaos, the unfathomable abyss from which the earth, its first occupants, and all else gradually proceeded.

Charon, son of Erebus, whose duty it was to ferry the souls of the dead over the waters of the

Styx and the Acheron to the infernal regions, receiving an obolus for each passenger; hence the ancient Roman custom of putting an obolus into the mouth of a corpse before interment.

Charybdis, a whirlpool in the Strait of Messina, exceedingly perilous to ships, which in avoiding Charybdis often ran aground on Scylla.

Chimaera, a monster shaped like a lion in front, a dragon behind, and a goat in the middle, which devastated Lycia until it was killed by Bellerophon.

Chiron, the most famous of the centaurs, killed by an arrow from the bow of Hercules.

Chryseis, a daughter of a priest of Apollo, taken prisoner by the Greeks and given to Agamemnon. Her father, Chryses, asked for her release, but Agamemnon refused; whereupon Apollo sent a plague upon the Greeks. To free them from this curse, Agamemnon had to surrender Chryseis.

Circe, daughter of Helios and Perseis and famous as a sorceress. After murdering her husband, she was banished to the island of Aeaea, to which Ulysses and his companions were later driven. Receiving them into her palace, she served them a magic concoction, touched them with her wand, and turned them into swine. Ulysses himself, who was saved by partaking of a herb that made the magic potion powerless, forced Circe to turn his companions back into men.

Clio, the Muse of history.

Clotho, one of the Fates, the goddess that spun the thread of life.

Clytemnestra, daughter of Tyndareus and Leda; sister of Castor, Pollux, and Helen; and wife of Agamemnon. While her husband was at Troy, she lived with Aegisthus in adultery. On Agamemnon's return she murdered him; later she herself was slain by her son Orestes.

Clytie, a water nymph, who fell in love with Apollo. She was transformed by him into a sunflower, so that she might always be turned toward him in his daily journey across the sky.

Comus, the god of revelry and feasting.

Coriolanus, a Roman patrician, exiled because of his haughty bearing toward the people. He joined the Volscians and led them against Rome but was finally persuaded by his mother and wife to retreat without attacking the city.

Cornucopia, the horn of plenty, presented by Jupiter to Amalthaea in return for her having fed him while young with goat's milk.

Creon, king of Thebes, whose decree condemning Antigone to be buried alive was the cause of her suicide, as well as that of her lover, Haemon, who was Creon's own son.

Cronus, one of the Titans, son of Uranus and Gaea, and father of Jupiter, Neptune, Pluto, Juno, Ceres, and Vesta. He was identified with Saturn by the Romans.

Cupid, son of Venus and god of love, who pierced the hearts of gods and men with arrows of desire. He was identified with Eros.

Cybele, a Phrygian goddess, worshiped as mother of the gods. She was identified with the Greek goddess Rhea and the Roman Magna Mater.

Cyclopes, a race of shepherds of gigantic stature with only one eye, which was in the middle of the forehead. They lived near Mount Aetna and assisted Vulcan at his forges.

D

Daedalus, a cunning craftsman, who flew from Crete to Italy with his son Icarus by means of wings fastened to their shoulders with wax. Daedalus arrived safely, but Icarus, flying too near the sun, which melted the wax, fell into the sea.

Danaë, daughter of Acrisius, king of Argos, and mother of Perseus. An oracle predicted that some day her son would kill his grandfather, Acrisius. To prevent such a calamity, the king had his daughter imprisoned in a dungeon so that no one might marry her. But she was visited by Jupiter, who distilled himself into a shower of gold. After the birth of Perseus, she and the child were put in a chest and thrown into the sea, but they drifted to the shore of Seriphus and were saved. The oracle's prediction came true, for Acrisius was accidentally killed by a quoit thrown by Perseus.

Danaus, son of Belus and twin brother of Aegyptus. Aegyptus had fifty sons, Danaus had fifty daughters. To escape his brother and his nephews, Danaus fled with his daughters to Argos and there became king. Hearing of their uncle's success, the sons of Aegyptus betook themselves to Argos and demanded his daughters for wives. On the wedding night each wife killed her husband with a dagger provided by Danaus. Only one escaped, Lynceus, who killed Danaus.

Daphne, a nymph who was loved by Apollo but did not return his love. She fled, pursued by the god, and when she could run no more, she was changed into a laurel. Thereafter the laurel was Apollo's favorite tree.

Daphnis, a Sicilian shepherd, famous as a flutist. He was struck with blindness for faithlessness to a naiad.

Dardanus, son of Jupiter and Electra, who was the founder of Troy and the ancestor of the Trojans.

Dejanira, wife of Hercules and sister of Meleager, for whose love Achelous fought a fierce battle with Hercules. Afterward, jealous of her husband's attentions toward Iole, Dejanira steeped one of his robes in the poisonous blood of Nessus. The poison entered his body, and as he tried to pull off the garment, which clung to his skin, he tore away huge layers of flesh.

Delphi, a city in central Greece, famous for the temple and oracle of Apollo.

Demeter, Mother Earth, identified with the Roman goddess, Ceres.

Deucalion, son of Prometheus and husband of Pyrrha. Deucalion and Pyrrha were the only persons that survived the deluge sent by Jupiter to destroy the inhabitants of the earth. In order to repeople the earth, they were ordered to throw behind them the bones of their mother; therefore, picking up some stones from Mother Earth, they flung these behind them. The stones cast by Deucalion were transformed into men, and those by Pyrrha into women.

Diana, goddess of hunting, daughter of Jupiter and Latona, and twin sister of Apollo. She was also goddess of the moon. Two of her famous temples were at Ephesus and Taurus.

Dido, queen of Carthage, who fled from Tyre with a large number of friends and followers and established a colony on the coast of Africa opposite Sicily. She assisted Aeneas after he had been shipwrecked and fell in love with him. When he left her to sail on to Italy, she killed herself.

Diomedes, son of Tydeus and king of Argos, who was a prominent Greek chieftain in the Trojan War. He fought with Mars in single combat, wounding him so severely that the god of war retired from the battle.

Dionysus, the god of wine and vegetation, who was identified with Bacchus.

Dioscuri, a name applied to Castor and Pollux, twin sons of Tyndareus and Leda. They rescued their sister Helen from Theseus, took part in the Argonautic expedition, and performed many other great deeds while on earth. Pollux was famed for his skill in boxing, Castor for his ability to manage horses. The Dioscuri were regarded as the patrons of seafarers. At the request of Pollux, Jupiter allowed them to share alternate days in the upper and the lower world.

Dirce, wife of Lycus, who herself suffered the torture which she planned to inflict upon Antiope: to be tied to the horns of a wild bull and dragged to her death.

Dryads, wood nymphs; the spirits or souls of trees. They were not immortal; each Dryad came to life and died with her tree.

E

Echo, a mountain nymph who diverted the attention of Juno while Jupiter made love to other nymphs. When Juno discovered the deception, she transformed her into an echo, depriving her of the power of speaking except when spoken to. Echo pined away with love for Narcissus, until only her voice remained.

Electra, daughter of Agamemnon, who sent her brother Orestes to King Strophius in Phocis in order to protect him from Clytemnestra, her mother. After Orestes had avenged his father's death by killing his mother, Electra married her brother's good friend Pylades.

Elysium, the abode of the spirits of the blessed.

Endymion, a shepherd on Mount Latmos, a beautiful youth loved by Selene, who chose perpetual sleep in preference to death. He sleeps in a cave in Caria, where Selene visits him by night.

Erato, the Muse of love poetry.

Erebus, son of Chaos, who is one of the deities of the lower world. He is a personification of that dread darkness through which departing souls pass to Hades.

Eros, the Greek god of love, identified with Cupid.

Eteocles, a son of Oedipus and Jocasta. After his father's death, he and his brother Polynices agreed to reign in alternate years, Eteocles taking the first turn. At the end of his year, however, he refused to relinquish the throne. Polynices, therefore, appealed to Adrastus, king of Argos, whose daughter he had married. Adrastus sent an army and seven of his bravest generals (the Seven against Thebes) to his son-in-law's aid, and a severe conflict ensued. In the end the two brothers agreed to settle their differences by single combat, and both were slain.

Eumenides, avenging spirits, known also as Furies.

Euphrosyne, one of the Graces, daughter of Jupiter and Eurynome.

Europa, daughter of Agenor, king of Phoenicia. She was loved by Jupiter, who assumed the form of a white bull and carried her off to Crete, where she became the mother of Minos, Sarpedon, and Rhadamanthus.

Eurydice, wife of Orpheus, who was granted permission to leave Hades and accompany her husband to the world above on condition that he should not turn around to look at her until they had reached the upper world. But Orpheus, unable to resist the temptation, turned around. Eurydice had disappeared.

Eurystheus, king of Mycenae, who imposed on Hercules the "twelve labors."

Euterpe, the Muse of lyric poetry.

Evander, son of Mercury, who was leader of a group of Arcadian colonists that settled in Italy. He joined Aeneas in the war against Turnus.

F

Fates, three daughters of Jupiter and Themis, who controlled the actions and destinies of man: Clotho, Lachesis, and Atropos.

Faunus, an old Italian divinity, protector of agriculture and shepherds. He was identified with the Greek Pan.

Flora, the goddess of flowers.

Furies, three hideous, winged females, sprung from the blood of the mutilated Uranus: Alecto, Tisiphone, and Megaera. They were avenging deities, who pursued and punished the guilty, especially murderers.

G

Galatea, the name of two mythological characters. The sea nymph of this name, who fell in love with Acis, was the daughter of Nereus and Doris. The other Galatea was the girl whom Aphrodite brought to life when she transformed Pygmalion's statue of a maiden into a living form.

Ganymede, cupbearer to the gods, a mortal youth of such grace and beauty that Jupiter had him carried off to Olympus on the back of an eagle.

Genius Loci, the special divinity assigned to a particular place or region.

Glaucus, the name of several mythological characters, of whom two deserve to be identified: Glaucus, the father of Bellerophon; and Glaucus, the Boeotian fisherman, who was changed by Oceanus into a divinity of the sea and granted the gift of prophecy by Apollo. His oracles are highly prized by fishermen.

Golden Fleece, the hide of the golden ram, intrusted by Phryxus to Aeetes and guarded by Argus, the hundred-eyed dragon. It was for the purpose of obtaining this fleece that Jason fitted out the Argonautic expedition.

Gorgons, three hideous wenches, whose heads were covered with snakes instead of hair. The one most frequently mentioned is Medusa. The others are Stheno and Euryale.

Graces, three daughters of Jupiter—Euphrosyne, Aglaia, and Thalia—who represented the perfection of grace in body and mind. They are known also as the Charites and are usually shown as attendants of Venus.

H

Hades, a name applied both to the ruler and to the regions of the underworld. The ruler, known also as Pluto, was the son of Saturn and the brother of Jupiter and Neptune. His wife was Proserpina. Hades is often represented as seated on a throne, with Cerberus lying at his feet.

Haemon, son of Creon and lover of Antigone. On hearing that his sweetheart had committed suicide, he too killed himself.

Hamadryads, tree nymphs, usually called Dryads.

Harpies, greedy monsters with female heads, long claws, and wings, sent by the gods to torment mortals.

Hebe cupbearer to the gods and daughter of Jupiter and Juno. She was represented as the goddess of youth and was called Juventas by the Romans.

Hecate, goddess of sorcery and witchcraft, often represented with three heads, who personified the darkness and terror of night. She was identified both with Diana and with Proserpina. Her domain extended over heaven, earth, and hell. She particularly haunted cross-roads and was associated with the howling of dogs.

Hector, son of Priam and Hecuba and husband of Andromache, who was the leader of the Trojan forces and the most valiant of them all. After killing Patroclus in battle, he was himself slain by Achilles, whom he had provoked to fight again. Hector's body was dragged in triumph three times around the walls of Troy. Jupiter then interposed and ordered the body to be given up to Priam for burial.

Hecuba, wife of Priam and queen of Troy, who saw her husband and her sons killed by the Greeks. After the capture of Troy, she fell to the lot of Ulysses and accompanied the conquerors on their voyage back to Greece. While in the Thracian Chersonesus, after trying to avenge the murder of her son Polydorus, she cast herself into the sea.

Helen, daughter of Jupiter and Leda, famed for her beauty. In her youth she was carried off to Attica by Theseus and Pirithous but was rescued by her brothers, Castor and Pollux. She became the wife of Menelaus, king of Sparta, but later Paris, son of Priam, persuaded her to forsake her husband and accompany him to Troy. To avenge this insult, Menelaus urged the Greek princes to attack Troy. When Paris was killed, in the ninth year of the war, Helen married Deiphobus. Shortly afterward she betrayed him in order to regain the favor of Menelaus. She went back to Menelaus and lived with him until his death.

Helenus, son of Priam and Hecuba, famous for his prophetic powers, who settled in Epirus after the Trojan War and was married to Andromache.

Helicon, a mountain in Boeotia, sacred to Apollo and the Muses.

Helios, or **Sol,** the god of the sun, who daily drove his four-horsed chariot across the sky.

Helle, daughter of Nephele and Athamas, who during her flight on the golden ram fell into the strait separating Europe from Asia, the strait later named the Hellespont in her honor.

Hephaestus, the Greek god of fire, identified with Vulcan.

Hera, wife of Zeus, identified with Juno.

Heracles or **Hercules,** son of Jupiter and Alcmene, renowned for his strength. While yet in his cradle he strangled two serpents which Juno had sent to destroy him. Before reaching manhood he killed the lion of Mount Cithaeron. Afterward, having been driven mad by Juno, he killed his own children and those of his brother. On recovering he was so stricken with grief that he exiled himself and went to consult the oracle of Apollo at Delphi. He was commanded to serve Eurystheus for twelve years, during which period he performed twelve labors. The gods assisted him in his tasks, and he carried them out successfully. His first labor was to kill the lion of Nemea, which he choked to death; the second, to destroy the nine-headed Lernaean hydra, which he killed with his club; the third was to capture the Arcadian stag, which he caught in a trap; the fourth, to kill the wild boar of Erymanthus; the fifth, to clean the Augean stables; the sixth, to kill the carnivorous birds of Stymphalis; the seventh, to capture the wild bull of Crete; the eighth, to capture the mares of Diomedes; the ninth, to obtain the girdle of the queen of the Amazons; the tenth, to capture the oxen of Geryon; the eleventh, to obtain the golden apples from the garden of the Hesperides; and the twelfth, to bring Cerberus, the three-headed dog of Hades, to the upper world. Hercules was now free from service to Eurystheus and returned to Thebes. He married Dejanira, daughter of Oeneus of Calydon. When Nessus, a centaur, tried to abduct her, Hercules shot him with a poisoned arrow. The dying Nessus told Dejanira to keep his blood, as it would always preserve her husband's love. Later, fearing that she was being supplanted by Iole, Dejanira sent Hercules a garment soaked in the blood of Nessus, which poisoned him. After his death he was taken to Olympus and endowed with immortality.

Hermes, messenger of the gods, identified with Mercury.

Hero, the sweetheart of Leander, who killed herself when she learned that her lover had been drowned.

Hesperides, the three daughters of Atlas and Hesperis, appointed to guard the golden apples which Earth gave Juno at her marriage to Jupiter. The dragon, Ladon, which was always on guard at the foot of the tree, was slain by Hercules when he seized the apples.

Hesperus, the evening star, king of the Western Lands.

Hippocrene, a fountain at the foot of Mount Helicon, dedicated to the Muses. It began to flow when the ground was struck by the hoofs of the winged horse, Pegasus.

Hippolytus, son of Theseus, who, having spurned the advances made by Phaedra, his stepmother, was accused of attempting to dishonor her.

Horatius Cocles, a Roman soldier, who with two comrades held off the Etruscan army from the bridge across the Tiber, while his fellow-soldiers were cutting down the bridge. When the bridge was destroyed, he leaped into the river and swam safely to the Roman shore.

Hyacinthus, a beautiful youth, accidentally killed by Apollo while playing quoits. From his blood sprang the hyacinth.

Hydra, a many-headed monster. The Lernaean hydra, which Hercules slew, was a water serpent with nine heads, one of which was immortal. For each head cut off, two would grow in its place unless the wound was cauterized. Hercules succeeded in burning away eight of its heads and buried the ninth under a rock.

Hygeia, goddess of health, daughter of Aesculapius.

Hylas, a beautiful youth loved by Hercules, who accompanied him on board the *Argo*. While Hylas was drawing water at a spring, a nymph drew him into the water and drowned him.

Hymen, or Hymenaeus, the god of marriage, represented as a youth bearing a bridal torch.

Hyperion, one of the Titans, son of Uranus and Gaea. He was the father by Thea of Helios, the sun-god; of Selene, the moon-goddess; and of Eos, goddess of the dawn.

I

Icarus, son of Daedalus, who fell into the sea, named after him the Icarian Sea.

Io, princess of Argos and daughter of Inachus. She was loved by Jupiter, who, to allay the suspicions of Juno, transformed her into a heifer. But Juno was aware of the change and put Argus to watch her. When Argus was killed by Mercury, Juno tormented Io with a gadfly, which drove her from place to place until she reached the Nile, where she recovered her form and bore a son to Jupiter.

Iphigenia, daughter of Agamemnon and Clytemnestra, who was offered as a sacrifice to Artemis. At the outbreak of the Trojan War a priest of Apollo declared that the wrath of the gods, which had been aroused by Agamemnon's killing of a sacred stag, could not be appeased except by the sacrifice of Iphigenia; and furthermore, that contrary winds would detain the fleet until this was done. As the priest, raising his kinfe, was about to perform the sacrifice, Artemis carried Iphigenia off to Tauris and substituted a hind. The Greeks proceeded against Troy. Afterward Iphigenia, who meanwhile had become a priestess, was instrumental in saving the life of her brother Orestes when he was about to be sacrificed.

Iris, goddess of the rainbow, who was often sent as a messenger by the gods.

Ixion, king of Thessaly, who had promised his father-in-law, Deioneus, a valuable gift but being unable to obtain it, put him to death in order to be released from his promise. After a long period of expiation, he was summoned by Jupiter to Mount Olympus and placed at the table of the gods. But Ixion, ill requiting the hospitality of his host, began to make love to Juno. As a punishment Ixion was sent to Hades and there tied to a fiery wheel, that never ceased to revolve.

J

Janus, an old Italian divinity, represented with two faces, turned in opposite directions. He was the god of beginnings and entrances; wherefore, the first month of the year was named after him, and gates and doorways were under his protection. His temple at Rome was open in time of war and closed in time of peace.

Jason, son of Aeson and leader of the Argonautic expedition. When his father was driven from the throne by Pelias, Jason was rescued and brought up by the centaur Chiron. Grown to manhood, he demanded the restitution of his father's kingdom, a request which Pelias promised to satisfy if Jason would bring him the Golden Fleece, kept by Aeetes in the custody of a dragon. Accordingly, Jason had a ship built, which was named the *Argo*. He assembled a crew and set out for Colchis. King Aeetes agreed to part with the fleece if Jason would perform several seemingly impossible deeds, such as yoking the fire-breathing oxen and sowing the dragon's teeth. He accomplished these tasks with the help of Medea, Aeetes' daughter, who had fallen in love with him. Shortly thereafter Jason returned home with the fleece, taking Medea with him. After several years he deserted her for another woman. Medea was driven mad with jealousy and in revenge killed her children by Jason. Years later Jason was killed by a beam that fell from his ship, the *Argo*.

Juno, daughter of Cronus and Rhea, sister and wife of Jupiter, and queen of heaven. She was an exacting and jealous wife, taking severe vengeance upon the numerous mortal maidens of whom Jupiter became enamored, as well as upon their offspring. She was the mother of Mars, Vulcan, and Hebe. In the Trojan War she was on the side of the Greeks.

Jupiter, son of Cronus and Rhea, father of gods and men, and lord of Olympus. He was brought up in a cave on Mount Ida so that he might be safe from his father, who had eaten all his other children. With the help of the Cyclopes he defeated Cronus and the other Titans and thus became master of the world. He gave the sea to Neptune, the infernal regions to Pluto, reserving heaven for himself. He is usually depicted as seated on a throne, with thunderbolts in one hand and a scepter of cypress in the other, wearing a wreath of olive or myrtle.

L

Lachesis, one of the Fates, the goddess that measured the thread of life.

Laertes, king of Ithaca, and father of Ulysses.

Laocoön, brother of Anchises, priest of Apollo and later of Neptune, who warned the Trojans against bringing the wooden horse into Troy. While the people hesitated whether to accept or reject his advice, two giant serpents emerged from the sea and attacked his sons. Rushing to their rescue, Laocoön himself was attacked, and all three persons were strangled.

Laodamia, wife of Protesilaus, in answer to whose prayers her husband was restored to life for three hours. When he died a second time, Laodamia died with him.

Laomedon, father of Priam and king of Troy, for whom Neptune built the walls of Troy. When Laomedon refused to give the promised reward, Neptune sent a monster to plague the city. The king was prepared to sacrifice his daughter to the beast, but Hercules appeared, rescued her, and slew the monster. Because Laomedon again broke his promise, Hercules attacked the city and killed him.

Lapithae, a people of Thessaly, who engaged in battle with the centaurs at the marriage feast of Hippodamia and Pirithous, their king.

Lares, ancient Roman divinities, the deified spirits of ancestors, who shielded their descendants against harm.

Latona, or **Leto,** daughter of Coeus and Phoebe and mother by Jupiter of Apollo and Diana. Persecuted by Juno, she wandered from place to place until Jupiter gave her a refuge on Delos, where she gave birth to her children.

Leander, a youth of Abydos, who swam nightly across the Hellespont to visit his sweetheart, Hero, living in Sestos. He was guided by a lamp which she hung out from a tower, but one stormy night the light was blown out, and Leander, losing his way, was drowned. On seeing his body washed up by the waves, Hero threw herself into the sea and was drowned.

Leda, wife of Tyndareus, king of Sparta, who was loved and approached by Jupiter in the form of a swan. She brought forth two eggs, from one of which sprang Helen and from the other Castor and Pollux.

M

Mars, the god of war, son of Jupiter and Juno, and lover of Venus.

Medea, a sorceress, wife of Jason, who murdered her own children to take vengeance upon her husband.

Medusa, one of the Gorgons, a terrible monster with hissing serpents for hair, whose face turned the beholder into stone. She was killed by Perseus, who, while observing her image in a mirror, cut off her head with his sword.

Meleager, son of Oeneus and Althaea, who took part in the Argonautic expedition and led the chase for the Calydonian boar. It had been decreed by the Fates that he should live only so long as a certain firebrand should remain unconsumed. Accordingly, his mother snatched the brand from the fire and jealously guarded it. When Althaea heard of Meleager's slaying of the boar, she went to the temple to return thanks. On the way, however, she came upon the bodies of her brothers, who had been slain by Meleager because they protested against the skin's being given to Atalanta. This so incensed Althaea that she cast the fatal brand into the fire, and when the brand was consumed, Meleager was dead.

Melpomene, the Muse of tragedy.

Menelaus, son of Atreus, brother of Agamemnon, and king of Sparta, who was one of the prominent Greek generals in the Trojan War. The abduction of his wife, Helen, was the cause of that war.

Mentor, friend of Ulysses and tutor of Telemachus, to whom was intrusted the care and education of the son of Ulysses during the latter's absence at Troy. The word "mentor" has become proverbial for a wise and faithful counselor.

Mercury, son of Jupiter and Maia, messenger of the gods, god of commerce, and patron of travelers, shepherds, traders, and robbers. Many of his exploits turn upon thievery or mischief. He wore a winged cap and had wings attached to his ankles that he might transport himself from place to place with the speed of the wind.

Midas, king of Phrygia, who, having done Bacchus a service, was permitted to choose his reward. Accordingly, he asked that whatever he touched be turned into gold. His prayer was granted. But when the food he touched, the clothes he wore, the water he washed in, turned into gold, he soon asked that the gift be revoked. On another occasion, because Midas ventured to remark that Pan made better music than Apollo, he was given ass's ears. At first, his barber was the only man to find out. Midas could not keep the secret to himself, however, and whispered it into a hole in the earth. Later, in this place, reeds grew up and as they were shaken by the wind they murmured and thus revealed the secret.

Minerva, goddess of wisdom, arts, and defensive warfare, who sprang full-grown from Jupiter's head. She was impervious to the passion of love and is depicted as wearing a helmet and carrying a shield. She was patron goddess of Athens, which was awarded to her as the result of a contest with Neptune, in which the city was to fall to the one who should present the more useful gift. Neptune produced the horse, and Minerva the olive.

Minos, the name of two kings of Crete. The one was a famous lawgiver, son of Jupiter and Europa, who became a judge in the lower world. The other was a grandson of the above-mentioned king, whose wife, Pasiphae, gave birth to a monster, the Minotaur. Minos had refused to sacrifice a white bull sent him by Neptune in answer to his prayer. As punishment for the king's perfidy Neptune drove his queen mad with love for the bull. To confine the offspring of this vile love affair, Minos commissioned Daedalus to construct a prison, known as the labyrinth.

Minotaur, the half-bull, half-human creature, offspring of Pasiphae and a bull, which was confined in the Cretan labyrinth by Minos. Every year the monster devoured seven youths and seven maidens sent as tribute by the Athenians. Finally, with Ariadne's help the Minotaur was slain by Theseus.

Morpheus, son of Somnus, who was the god of sleep and dreams. He is generally represented as a chubby, winged child, holding poppies in his hand.

Muses, daughters of Jupiter and Mnemosyne, nine divinities who presided over the arts. Their names and the arts assigned to them were: Clio, history; Euterpe, lyric poetry; Thalia, comedy; Melpomene, tragedy; Terpsichore, choral dance and song; Erato, erotic poetry; Polyhymnia, religious poetry and song; Urania, astronomy; Calliope, epic poetry.

N

Naiads, water nymphs, the daughters of Jupiter.

Narcissus, a beautiful youth, son of the river-god Cephissus, with whom the nymph Echo fell in love. But Narcissus did not return her love. To avenge what she regarded as a rebuke to herself, Venus, the goddess of love, caused him to become enamored of his own reflection in the waters of a stream. Unable to embrace or kiss the image, he pined away until he was changed into a flower, the narcissus.

Nemesis, goddess of vengeance and daughter of Night, who relentlessly meted out punishment to evildoers and lawbreakers.

Neoptolemus, or **Pyrrhus,** son of Achilles, who fought at Troy and later settled in Epirus, where he was killed by Orestes.

Nephele, wife of Athamas and mother of Phryxus and Helle.

Neptune, son of Saturn and Rhea and brother of Jupiter and Pluto, who was god of the sea. He made love to Amphitrite by assuming the form of a dolphin. His greatest gift to mankind was the horse. He is usually represented as seated in a chariot, drawn across the sea by brazen-hoofed horses, attended by Tritons and nymphs, and holding a trident in his hand.

Nereus, a sea divinity, son of Oceanus and Terra, and husband of Doris, by whom he had fifty daughters, called the Nereids. He was gifted with prophecy and lived in the Aegean Sea.

Nessus, a centaur slain by Hercules.

Nestor, king of Pylos, the oldest of the Greek commanders in the Trojan War, who was known for his wise counsel.

Niobe, daughter of Tantalus and wife of Amphion, whose intense pride in her children was the cause of their destruction. Because she had seven sons and seven daughters, she sneered at the goddess Latona, who had only two children, Apollo and Diana. Latona roused her children to take revenge for this insult. Apollo killed all Niobe's sons, while Diana killed all her daughters. Niobe herself was transformed by Jupiter into stone, from which streamed incessant tears.

Nisus, king of Megara, whose lock of purple hair (on which his life and fortune depended) was snipped off by his daughter Scylla and presented to King Minos, with whom she had fallen deeply in love. Nisus was transformed into a sea-eagle, and his daughter into a monster of barking dogs and hissing serpents.

Notus, the south wind, called also Auster.

Nymphs, female divinities that inhabited certain objects or places in nature. There were (1) Oceanids and Nereids, who were sea nymphs; (2) Naiads, fresh-water nymphs; (3) Dryads and Hamadryads, tree nymphs; and (4) Oreads, mountain nymphs.

O

Oceanus, son of Uranus and Gaea, brother of Cronus, and husband of Tethys, who was god of the sea and father of all river-gods and water nymphs.

Odysseus, the hero of the Odyssey, commonly called Ulysses.

Oedipus, king of Thebes, son of Laius and Jocasta, who unwittingly murdered his father and married his mother. An oracle had foretold that the son of Laius, if he should reach manhood, would be the slayer of his father. Therefore, as soon as the boy was born, he was ordered to be put to death, but Jocasta gave the child to a servant, who carried him to Mount Cithaeron. There he was discovered by a shepherd and brought up as his own child. After he had grown to manhood, he chanced to meet his father one day, who was driving along in his chariot. The road being narrow, the king ordered the stranger to make way for him. Oedipus refused, and in the encounter that ensued Laius was slain by his own son, as the oracle had predicted. Proceeding to Thebes, Oedipus found the population of the city threatened with destruction by the Sphinx, a monster sent by Juno, which proposed to all passers-by a riddle and destroyed those who failed to solve it. The kingdom and the hand of the queen were offered to whoever might find the solution and thereby free the people from the monster. Oedipus guessed the riddle. He became king and married his own mother, thus fulfilling the prophecy. Later, Thebes was visited by a plague, and an oracle declared that the epidemic would not cease until the murderer of Laius was discovered. Eventually, Oedipus became aware of his identity. Jocasta hanged herself, and Oedipus put out his eyes. Afterward he left Thebes, accompanied by his daughter Antigone, and died at Colonus, near Athens.

Oenomaus, a son of Mars by Sterope, the daughter of Atlas. He was king of Elis and father of Hippodamia.

Oenone, a nymph whom Paris married and later abandoned for Helen. On account of the indignities which she had suffered, she refused to heal the wound received by him in the battle before Troy. But when his injury proved fatal, she was overcome with remorse and hanged herself.

Olympus, a lofty mountain on the border between Macedonia and Thessaly, which was the abode of the gods.

Omphale, daughter of Jardanus and queen of Lydia, whom Hercules was forced to serve as slave for having murdered his friend Iphitus. She fell in love with him and freed him from slavery.

Oreads, the nymphs that inhabited mountains and caves.

Orestes, son of Agamemnon and Clytemnestra. who killed his mother and her paramour, Aegisthus, to avenge his father's death. Thereafter he was haunted by the Furies and fled from country to country. Afterward, by Apollo's command, he submitted to trial before the Areopagus at Athens and, being acquitted, returned to Argos and ascended the throne.

Orion, a famous giant and hunter, who asked for the hand of Merope, daughter of Oenopion, king of Chios. As the price of betrothal Oenopion set him the task of clearing the island of wild beasts. This deed Orion quickly accomplished. Instead of receiving his reward, however, he was made drunk and had his eyes put out by the king. Afterward, having recovered his eyesight by facing the rising sun, he took revenge on the king. Orion, after his death, was placed in the sky, where a constellation bears his name.

Orpheus, a famous lyrist, son of Apollo and Calliope, and husband of Eurydice, who received his lyre from Apollo and played upon it so exquisitely that all things, inanimate as well as animate, were charmed. He was one of the heroes of the Argonautic expedition and on his return married Eurydice. After Eurydice had died from the sting of a serpent, Orpheus followed her to Hades and begged Pluto to allow her to accompany him back to earth. His request would be granted, he was told, if he would not look at Eurydice until the borders of Hades had been passed. The temptation was too great however. He looked—and lost her forever. In grief for her he spurned the Thracian women, who became incensed and tore him to pieces during the celebration of the Bacchanalia.

Ossa, a mountain in Thessaly, on which the Giants piled Mount Pelion in order to climb to the heavens.

P

Palamedes, the ambassador sent by the Greek chieftains to urge Ulysses to join the expedition against Troy. Ulysses, pretending to be insane, yoked an ass and an ox to the plow and began to sow his land with salt. In order to test him, Palamedes placed Ulysses' son in the furrow before the plow. He was convinced that Ulysses was sane when he turned the plow aside to avoid striking his son.

Palladium, an image of Pallas Athene at Troy, on which the safety of the city depended; it was stolen by Ulysses and Diomedes.

Pallas, or **Pallas Athene,** the Greek goddess identified with Minerva.

Pan, the god of woods, fields, and shepherds, son of Mercury and a wood nymph. He is represented as having two small horns, a flat nose, and the lower limbs of a goat. He was very fond of music and enjoyed dancing with the nymphs. But he was also mischievous and frightened people who walked through the forests at night.

Pandora, the first woman ever to have been created, who was intended by Jupiter as a curse for mankind. (Till that time the human race, in some mysterious manner, had survived without the aid of woman.) Because Prometheus had stolen fire from heaven, Jupiter decided to punish man: He created woman. Since to this new work of creation all the gods and goddesses contributed something, it was called Pandora, "The gift of all the gods." Pandora married Epimetheus and presented him with a box given to her by the gods. Although she was forbidden to open it, she nevertheless lifted the cover, and there escaped every kind of human ill and plague, which quickly spread throughout the world. "Hope" alone remained in the box.

Parcae, the goddesses that shaped the destinies of gods and men. They are usually referred to as the Fates and are three in number: Clotho, Lachesis, and Atropos.

Paris, son of Priam, whose abduction of Helen, wife of Menelaus, was the cause of the Trojan War. He was brought up as a shepherd and married Oenone, a nymph of Mount Ida. At the marriage of Peleus and Thetis the goddess of discord, Eris, threw a golden apple, inscribed "For the fairest," among the assembled guests. Juno, Venus, and Minerva each claimed the apple, and so Jupiter thought it best to let Paris pass judgment. He decided in favor of Venus, who had promised him the most beautiful woman for a wife. The fairest of women proved to be Helen, the wife of Melenaus. Paris fell in love with her and took her with him to Troy. The Trojan War was the result. After Paris was wounded, he returned to Oenone. But she refused to heal the wound, and Paris died.

Parnassus, a mountain in Phocis, dedicated to the Muses and to Apollo and Bacchus.

Pasiphae, daughter of Helios, wife of Minos, and mother of Ariadne and the Minotaur.

Pasithea, or **Aglaia,** one of the Graces.

Patroclus, friend of Achilles, who was killed in battle by Hector. When Achilles refused to fight, Patroclus, wearing the armor of his friend, led the Greeks into battle. He fought bravely, but was slain. The desire to avenge his death brought Achilles back into the field.

Pax, the Roman goddess of peace.

Pegasus, the winged horse, which sprang from the blood of the slain Medusa. Mounted on this horse, Bellerophon soared through the air to conquer the Chimaera. Thereafter he wanted to scale the heavens on the back of Pegasus, but the horse threw him and flew up to Olympus alone.

Peleus, son of Aeacus and father of Achilles, who married the Nereid Thetis.

Pelias, father of Alcestis and uncle of Jason, who, having received the crown from his brother during the minority of Jason, refused later to surrender his authority. To prevent Jason from seizing the throne, he sent him in search of the Golden Fleece. When Pelias had grown old, his daughters requested Medea to rejuvenate their father. Medea consented, realizing that this would be the means of getting revenge. As a preliminary act in rejuvenation, she persuaded them, it was necessary for them to kill their father. But instead of restoring the old man to youth, she fled the country.

Pelion, a mountain of Thessaly. In their wars against the gods, the Giants placed Pelion on Mount Ossa to scale the heavens with greater ease.

Pelops, son of Tantalus, who was slaughtered by his father and served up to the gods. He was later restored to life, while Tantalus was sent to Tartarus. He won Hippodamia as his bride by defeating her father, Oenomaus, in a chariot race, in which death awaited the loser. The son of Pelops and Hippodamia was Atreus.

Penelope, wife of Ulysses, who was besieged by more than a hundred suitors during her husband's absence at Troy. She firmly believed that Ulysses would return and therefore delayed a decision as long as possible. Finally she promised to make a choice when she had completed a certain robe which she was then weaving. By undoing at night what she had woven during the day, she was able to put off the suitors until Ulysses returned.

Penthesilea, queen of the Amazons, killed at Troy by Achilles.

Pentheus, king of Thebes, who was killed by his mother, Agave, and her sisters during a celebration in honor of Bacchus.

Persephone, the Greek form of Proserpina.

Perseus, son of Jupiter and Danae and husband of Andromeda, who was sent by Polydectes to kill the monster Medusa. Obtaining winged shoes and Pluto's helmet, which rendered him invisible, he flew to the land of the Gorgons. He found them asleep, cut off Medusa's head, and flew away with it to Seriphus. There, by means of the magic Gorgon's head, he turned Polydectes and his court into stone.

Phaedra, daughter of Minos, who married Theseus after he had deserted her sister Ariadne. She fell in love with Hippolytus, the son of Theseus by Antiope, but was rejected by him.

Phaethon, son of Apollo, who was killed while driving his father's chariot across the sky.

Philemon, husband of Baucis, who was changed into a tree.

Phoebus, an epithet applied to Apollo.

Phryxus, son of Athamas and Nephele, who with his sister Helle rode through the air on the back of the golden ram.

Pleiades, daughters of Atlas, who, being pursued by Orion, appealed to the gods for help. Jupiter transformed them into doves and placed them among the stars.

Pluto, son of Cronus and Rhea and brother of Jupiter, to whom was assigned the kingdom of the lower world. His queen was Proserpina, the daughter of Ceres, whom he seized and carried off to the world below. Pluto is known also as Hades.

Pollux, son of Jupiter and Leda and twin brother of Castor, who was known for his skill in boxing.

Polyhymnia, the Muse of sacred poetry and song.

Polyphemus, son of Neptune and the most renowned of the Cyclopes, who was the rival of Acis for the affections of Galatea. When Ulysses with twelve of his companions entered his cave, Polyphemus devoured six of the men. Later, while Polyphemus was asleep, Ulysses put out his eye—the lone, huge eye in the middle of his forehead.

Poseidon, the Greek god of the sea, identified with Neptune.

Priam, king of Troy, husband of Hecuba, and father of Hector and Paris. In the fighting before Troy, he was killed by Neoptolemus.

Priapus, a Roman god of fertility.

Prometheus, a Titan, who stole fire from heaven for the benefit of mankind. For his crime he was chained by Jupiter to a rock on Mount Caucasus, where an eagle kept tearing at his liver until he was rescued by Hercules.

Proserpina, daughter of Ceres, wife of Pluto, and queen of the nether world. One day as she was playing with her companions, Pluto saw her and took her with him to the realm of the dead.

Proteus, a soothsayer who lived in a cave on the island of Pharos. He could be made to utter his prophecies only while asleep, since at other times he had the power of changing his shape so that he could not be recognized.

Psyche, a nymph whom Cupid married and visited nightly, concealing his features from her and leaving before dawn. She contrived to see him one night, however. Lighting her lamp, she was enraptured with his beauty. He was awakened by a drop of oil which fell on his face, and he fled immediately. Thereafter she wandered in search of him, incurring the hatred of Venus, who tried to thwart the lovers. Psyche ultimately joined Cupid in heaven and was endowed with immortality.

Pygmalion, a sculptor who carved an ivory statue of a woman and, falling in love with it, appealed to Venus to breathe life into it. The statue came to life and the woman, who was named Galatea, loved and married Pygmalion.

Pylades, friend of Orestes and husband of Electra.

Pyrrha, wife of Deucalion.

Pyrrhus, another name for Neoptolemus.

Python, the famous serpent of the caves of Mount Parnassus, which was slain by Apollo. It was born of the mud left by the Deluge.

R

Remus, twin brother of Romulus.

Rhadamanthus, son of Jupiter and Europa, who at his death was appointed one of the three judges in Hades, Minos and Aeacus being the other two.

Rhea, goddess of the earth, wife of Saturn, and mother of Jupiter.

Romulus, twin brother of Remus, son of the vestal virgin Sylvia. His mother was condemned to be buried alive. The children, set adrift on the Tiber, were rescued and suckled by a she-wolf. Afterward Romulus and Remus founded a city, named Rome in honor of Romulus.

S

Saturn, the god of agriculture, identified with the Greek Cronos, a son of Uranus and Terra, who usurped his father's kingdom, his brothers assenting on condition that he would not bring up any male children. Saturn, therefore, devoured his sons as soon as they were born, but his wife, Rhea, concealed from her husband her sons Jupiter, Neptune, and Pluto and gave him large stones to swallow instead of her male offspring. It was this that led to the Titans' making war upon Saturn and his ultimate overthrow by his son Jupiter.

Satyrs, rustic divinities addicted to sensual pleasure and associated with the worship of Bacchus.

Scylla, a rock near the Italian coast in the Strait of Messina, dangerous to mariners. In avoiding this peril, a boat was often drawn into Charybdis, a dangerous whirlpool near the opposite shore.

Selene, goddess of the moon.

Semele, daughter of Cadmus and mother of Bacchus. Hera, jealous of Jupiter's love, persuaded Semele to ask him to come to her in his true form. By the lightning, in which he came, Semele was killed, but she gave birth to Bacchus, whom Jupiter kept alive by enclosing him in his thigh till it was time for the child to be born.

Sibyls, women with the gift of prophecy, one of whom compiled the Sibylline Books, which were kept in Rome.

Silenus, a jovial old Satyr, companion of Bacchus.

Sirens, sea nymphs who by their song lured all who heard them to their death.

Sisyphus, son of Aeolus, who was punished in the underworld by having to roll uphill a huge rock, which, as soon as it reached the top, always rolled down again.

Sol, the sun-god.

Somnus, god of sleep and father of Morpheus.

Styx, the chief river of the underworld.

T

Tantalus, a son of Jupiter, who, for revealing his father's secrets, was punished in Tartarus with a raging thirst. Water and fruits that he saw close at hand always receded from his grasp.

Tartarus, the depths of Hades.

Telemachus, son of Ulysses and Penelope.

Tereus, a Thracian king, who married Procne, daughter of Pandion of Athens, and later abandoned her to marry her sister Philomela, whose tongue he cut out. But the sisters communicated with each other; and Procne killed her son Itys and served up his flesh to Tereus. The sisters fled, pursued by Tereus. They were changed by the gods into birds: Procne became a swallow, Philomela a nightingale, and Tereus a hawk.

Terpsichore, the Muse of choral song and dance.

Tethys, daughter of Uranus and wife of Oceanus.

Thalia, the Muse of Comedy; also one of the Graces.

Themis, one of the Titans, goddess of law and justice, who was mother by Jupiter of the Fates and the Hours.

Theseus, son of Aegeus, king of Athens, and legendary hero of Attica. His most famous exploit was the slaying of the Minotaur. He went to Crete as one of the youths whom the Athenians sent annually to Minos. Ariadne, daughter of Minos, fell in love with him, and with her help he slew the Minotaur and escaped from the labyrinth. He took Ariadne away with him but deserted her in the island of Naxos. Among his other adventures were the battle with the Amazons, whose queen he seized, and the carrying off of Helen from Sparta to Athens, whence she was rescued by Castor and Pollux. His friendship with Pirithous was proverbial.

Thetis. (See **Peleus.**)

Thisbe, the sweetheart of Pyramus, whose parents objected to her love affair. The lovers, consequently, arranged to meet secretly one day at the tomb of Ninus. As Thisbe reached the place, she saw a lion and fled, letting fall her cloak. When Pyramus arrived and found the torn garment, he thought she had been murdered; and therefore he killed himself. Thereafter Thisbe returned and, at the sight of her dead lover, put an end to her life also.

Tiresias, a Theban, whom the gods blinded and, in compensation for the loss of his sight, gave the power of prophecy.

Titans, a race of giants, who waged ten years' war with Jupiter and were ultimately conquered and imprisoned in a cavern near Tartarus.

Tithonus, son of Laomedon and brother of Priam, for whom his wife, Aurora, secured immortality, but not eternal youth. In consequence, he gradually shriveled up.

Triton, a divinity of the sea, son of Neptune, who calmed the waves by blowing his trumpet.

Turnus, an Italian prince, who opposed Aeneas' settlement in Italy and was killed by him in battle.

Tyndareus, husband of Leda.

U

Ulysses, son of Laertes, husband of Penelope, and king of Ithaca. The wiliest of the Greek leaders at Troy, he was the inventor of the wooden horse. His wanderings home from Troy, which form the subject of Homer's *Odyssey*, lasted twenty years. Finally he reached home and killed the suitors by whom Penelope had been surrounded during his absence.

Uranus, god of the heavens, husband of Earth, who was dethroned by his son Saturn.

V

Venus, goddess of love and daughter of Jupiter and Dione. According to later legend she was born of the foam of the sea. She received the beauty prize in the judgment of Paris. Cupid was her son.

Vesta, the goddess of the hearth.

Vulcan, god of fire and son of Jupiter and Juno, who made the armor of the gods and had his workshops in volcanic mountains.

Z

Zephyrus, the west wind.

Zeus, the Greek name for Jupiter.

FOREIGN WORDS AND PHRASES

ENGLISH is one of the richest languages in the world. Its ancestor, Anglo-Saxon, was augmented at the time of the Norman Conquest by a veritable wealth of Old French words, themselves derived from Latin, and during the Renaissance received a large influx of pure Greek and Latin words. Since that time many other foreign words have been adopted, being fitted more smoothly into the English language by changes in spelling and pronunciation. But there are other foreign words which, although used by writers of English, have retained their original form intact; the student or author should know them, since for one reason or another they have proved extremely useful. Some of these foreign phrases express a certain idea more concisely than could any combination of English words—"The Greeks had a word for it," as the saying goes. Others have a historical flavor and significance that would be lost if they were Anglicized. Phrases such as coup d'état, tour de force, bête noire, vox populi, status quo, *and* raison d'être *are in common use today. Latin and Greek phrases also appear frequently as mottoes and inscriptions, such as* semper fidelis, requiescat in pace, labor omnia vincit, mens sana in corpore sano, *and* nemo me impune lacessit. *The following dictionary of foreign words and phrases is intended to enrich the appreciation of the student and general reader, and to provide a ready answer for many oft-recurring questions.*

à bas. [Fr.] Down, down with.
Ab initio. [L.] From the beginning.
à bon chat, bon rat. [Fr.] Tit for tat.
à bon marché. [Fr.] Cheap; a good bargain.
Ab origine. [L.] From the origin.
Ab ovo. [L.] From the egg; from the beginning.
Absit invidia. [L.] Let there be no ill-will; envy apart.
Absit omen. [L.] May the omen be averted.
Ab uno disce omnes. [L.] From one specimen judge of all the rest.
Ab urbe condita. [L.] From the building of the city; *i.e.*, Rome.
à cheval. [Fr.] On horseback.
Ad captandum vulgus. [L.] To attract or please the rabble.
Ad finem. [L.] To the end.
Ad hoc. [L.] For this special object or duty.
Ad infinitum. [L.] To infinity.
à discrétion. [Fr.] At discretion; unrestricted.
Ad libitum. [L.] At pleasure.
Ad nauseam. [L.] To disgust or satiety.
Ad rem. [L.] To the purpose; to the point.
Adsum. [L.] I am present; here!
Ad unguem. [L.] To the nail; to a nicety; exactly; perfectly.
Ad utrumque paratus. [L.] Prepared for either case.
Ad valorem. [L.] According to the value.
Aere perennius. [L.] More lasting than brass.
Affaire d'amour. [Fr.] A love affair.
Affaire d'honneur. [Fr.] An affair of honor; a duel.
Affaire de cœur. [Fr.] An affair of the heart.
A fortiori. [L.] With stronger reason.
Age quod agis. [L.] Attend to what you are about.
à grands frais. [Fr.] At great expense.
à haute voix. [Fr.] Aloud.
à la belle étoile. [Fr.] Under the stars; in the open air.
à la bonne heure. [Fr.] In good time; very well.
à l'abri. [Fr.] Under shelter.
à la dérobée. [Fr.] By stealth.
à la française. [Fr.] After the French mode.
à la mode. [Fr.] According to the custom or fashion.
à l'envi. [Fr.] Emulously; so as to vie.
Al fresco. [It.] In the open air; cool.
Allez-vous-en. [Fr.] Away with you.
Allons. [Fr.] Let us go; come on; come.
Alter ego. [L.] Another self.
Amende honorable. [Fr.] Satisfactory apology; reparation.
A mensa et toro. [L.] From bed and board.
à merveille. [Fr.] To a wonder; marvellously.
Amor patriae. [L.] Love of country.
Amour propre. [Fr.] Self-love; vanity.
Ancien régime. [Fr.] The ancient or former order of things.
Anno aetatis suae. [L.] In the year of his or her age.
Anno Christi. [L.] In the year of Christ.
Anno Domini. [L.] In the year of our Lord.
Anno mundi. [L.] In the year of the world.
Anno urbis conditae. [L.] In the year from the time the city (Rome) was built.
Annus mirabilis. [L.] Year of wonder.
Ante meridiem. [L.] *Before noon.*
à outrance. [Fr.] To a finish.
Aperçu. [Fr.] A general sketch or survey.
à peu près. [Fr.] Nearly.
à pied. [Fr.] On foot.
A posteriori. [L.] From the effect to the cause.
Après nous le déluge. [Fr.] After us the deluge.
à propos de bottes. [Fr.] Apropos of boots; foreign to the subject or matter in hand.
à propos de rien. [Fr.] Apropos of nothing; without a motive.
Arbiter elegantiarum. [L.] A judge or supreme authority in matters of taste.
Arcades ambo. [L.] Arcadians both; fellows of the same stamp.
Argent comptant. [Fr.] Ready money.
Argumentum ad hominem. [L.] An argument to the individ-

ual man; *i.e.* to his interests and prejudices.

Arrière pensée. [Fr.] Mental reservation.

Ars est celare artem. [L.] It is true art to conceal art.

Ars longa, vita brevis. [L.] Art is long, life is short.

Artium magister. [L.] Master of Arts.

Au contraire. [Fr.] On the contrary.

Au courant. [Fr.] Fully acquainted with matters.

Au fait. [Fr.] Well acquainted with; expert.

Au fond. [Fr.] At bottom.

Auf Wiedersehen. [Ger.] Au revoir.

Au reste. [Fr.] As for the rest.

Au revoir. [Fr.] Adieu until we meet again.

Aut Caesar aut nullus. [L.] Either Caesar or nobody.

Aux armes! [Fr.] To arms!

Avant propos. [Fr.] Preliminary matter; preface.

à votre santé. [Fr.] To your health.

B

Bas bleu. [Fr.] A blue-stocking; a literary woman.

Beaux yeux [Fr.] Fine eyes; good looks.

Ben trovato. [It.] Well invented.

Bête noire. [Fr.] A black beast; a bugbear.

Bon ami. [Fr.] Good friend.

Bon gré, mal gré. [Fr.] With good or ill grace; willing or unwilling.

Bon jour. [Fr.] Good day; good morning.

Bonne et belle. [Fr.] Good and handsome.

Bonne foi. [Fr.] Good faith.

Bon soir. [Fr.] Good evening.

Breveté. [Fr.] Patented.

C

Cacoëthes scribendi. [L.] An itch for writing.

Caeteris paribus. [L.] Other things being equal.

Carpe diem. [L.] Enjoy the present day; improve the time.

Casus belli. [L.] That which causes or justifies war.

Causa sine qua non. [L.] An indispensable cause or condition.

Cause célèbre. [Fr.] A famous case.

Caveat emptor. [L.] Let the buyer beware.

Cela va sans dire. [Fr.] That goes without saying; that is a matter of course.

C'est-à-dire. [Fr.] That is to say.

C'est autre chose. [Fr.] That's quite another thing.

Chacun à son goût. [Fr.] Every one to his taste.

Châteaux en Espagne. [Fr.] Castles in the air.

Chemin de fer. [Fr.] Iron road; a railway.

Cherchez la femme. [Fr.] Look for the woman.

Chère amie. [Fr.] A dear (female) friend.

Ci gît. [Fr.] Here lies.

Civis Romanus sum. [L.] I am a Roman citizen.

Cogito, ergo sum. [L.] I think, therefore I exist.

Comme il faut. [Fr.] As it should be.

Communi consensu. [L.] By common consent.

Compagnon de voyage. [Fr.] A travelling companion.

Compos mentis. [L.] Sound of mind.

Compte rendu. [Fr.] An account rendered; a report.

Con amore. [It.] With love; very earnestly.

Conditio sine qua non. [L.] A necessary condition.

Conseil d'état. [Fr.] A council of state; a privy-council.

Contra bonos mores. [L.] Against good manners; in violation of good morals.

Coram nobis. [L.] Before us; in our presence.

Cordon sanitaire. [Fr.] A line of guards to prevent the spreading of contagion or pestilence.

Coup. [Fr.] A stroke.—*Coup d'essai*, a first attempt.—*Coup d'état*, a sudden decisive blow in politics; a stroke of policy. —*Coup de grâce*, a finishing stroke.—*Coup de main*, a sudden attack or enterprise.—*Coup de maître*, a master stroke.—*Coup d'œil*, a rapid glance of the eye.—*Coup de pied*, a kick.—*Coup de soleil*, sunstroke.—*Coup de théâtre*, a theatrical effect.

Credo quia absurdum. [L.] I believe because it is absurd.

Cui bono? [L.] For whose advantage? to what end?

Cum grano salis. [L.] With a grain of salt.

Cum privilegio. [L.] With privilege.

Currente calamo. [L.] With a running or rapid pen.

D

Dame d'honneur. [Fr.] Maid of honor.

De bonne grâce. [Fr.] With a good grace.

De facto. [L.] In fact; actually.

Dégagé. [Fr.] Free; easy; unconstrained.

De gustibus non est disputandum. [L.] There is no disputing about tastes.

De haut en bas. [Fr.] Contemptuously.

Dei gratia. [L.] By the grace of God.

De jure. [L.] From the law; by right.

Delenda est Carthago. [L.] Carthage must be destroyed.

De mortuis nil nisi bonum. [L.] Say nothing but good of the dead.

De novo. [L.] Anew.

Deo adjuvante. [L.] God assisting.

Deo favente. [L.] God favoring; with God's favor.

Deo gratias. [L.] Thanks to God.

Deo juvante. [L.] With God's help.

Deo volente. [L.] God willing; by God's will.

De profundis. [L.] Out of the depths.

Dernier cri. [Fr.] The latest fad of fashion.

Dernier ressort. [Fr.] A last resource.

Deus ex machina. [L.] A god from some mechanical device.

Dies Irae. [L.] Day of wrath.

Dieu et mon droit. [Fr.] God and my right.

Dieu vous garde. [Fr.] God protect you.

Dii penates. [L.] Household gods.

Dis aliter visum. [L.] It is otherwise decreed by the gods.

Disjecta membra. [L.] Scattered remains.

Divide et impera. [L.] Divide and rule.

Dolce far niente. [It.] Sweet idleness.

Dominus vobiscum. [L.] The Lord be with you.

Dramatis personae. [L.] The persons or characters in a drama.

Dum vivimus, vivamus. [L.] While we live, let us live.

Durante vita. [L.] During life.

E

Ecce homo. [L.] Behold the man!

Editio princeps. [L.] The first printed edition of a book.

Emeritus. [L.] Retired or superannuated after long service.

En ami. [Fr.] As a friend.

En arrière. [Fr.] In the rear; behind; back.

En attendant. [Fr.] In the meantime.

En avant. [Fr.] Forward.

En déshabillé. [Fr.] In undress.

En effet. [Fr.] In effect; substantially; really.
En famille. [Fr.] With one's family; in a domestic state.
Enfants perdus. [Fr.] Lost children; a group of men forming a forlorn hope.
Enfant terrible. [Fr.] A child who is always making inopportune and embarrassing remarks.
Enfant trouvé. [Fr.] A foundling.
Enfin. [Fr.] In short; at last; finally.
En rapport. [Fr.] In harmony; in agreement.
En revanche. [Fr.] In requital; in return.
En route. [Fr.] On the way.
En suite. [Fr.] In company; in a set.
Entente cordiale. [Fr.] Cordial understanding, especially between two states.
Entourage. [Fr.] Surroundings; adjuncts.
Entre nous. [Fr.] Between ourselves.
E pluribus unum. [L.] One out of many; one composed of many.
Eppur si muove. [It.] Yet it does move.
Esprit de corps. [Fr.] The animating spirit of a collective body, as a regiment.
Esse quam videri. [L.] To be rather than to seem.
Est modus in rebus. [L.] There is a medium in all things.
Et caetera (or *Et cetera*). [L.] And the rest.
Et hoc (or *Et id*) *genus omne.* [L.] And everything of the sort.
Et sequentes, Et sequentia, [L.] And those that follow.
Et sic de similibus. [L.] And so of the like.
Et tu, Brute! [L.] And thou also, Brutus!
Ex animo. [L.] Heartily; sincerely.
Ex cathedra. [L.] From the chair. (Since 1870 the Pope has claimed to be infallible when speaking *ex cathedra.*)
Exceptio probat regulam. [L.] The exception proves (or tests) the rule.
Exempli gratia. [L.] By way of example.
Ex necessitate rei. [L.] From the necessity of the case.
Ex nihilo nihil fit. [L.] Out of nothing, nothing comes.
Ex officio. [L.] By virtue of office.
Ex parte. [L.] From one side only.
Experto credite. [L.] Trust one who has had experience.
Ex post facto. [L.] After the deed is done; retrospective.
Extra muros. [L.] Beyond the walls.

F

Facile princeps. [L.] Easily preeminent; indisputably the first.
Facilis descensus Averni (or *Averno*). [L.] The descent to Avernus (or hell) is easy.
Faire suivre. [Fr.] Please forward.
Fait accompli. [Fr.] A thing already done.
Far niente. [It.] The doing of nothing.
Festina lente. [L.] Hasten slowly.
Fiat justitia, ruat caelum. [L.] Let justice be done though the heavens should fall.
Fiat lux. [L.] Let there be light.
Fidei Defensor. [L.] Defender of the faith.
Fide, non armis. [L.] By faith, not by arms.
Fides Punica. [L.] Punic or Carthaginian faith; treachery.
Fidus Achates. [L.] Faithful Achates; a true friend.
Fille de joie. [Fr.] A prostitute.
Finem respice. [L.] Look to the end.
Finis coronat opus. [L.] The end crowns the work.
Flagrante delicto. [L.] In the commission of the crime.
Fons et origo. [L.] The source and origin.
Fortiter in re. [L.] With firmness in acting.
Fronti nulla fides. [L.] There is no trusting to outward features.
Fuit Ilium. [L.] Troy has been, but is no more.
Functus officio. [L.] Having per formed one's office or duty; hence, out of office.
Furor loquendi. [L.] A rage for speaking.
Furor poeticus. [L.] Poetical fire.

G

Gallice. [L.] In French.
Garçon. [Fr.] A boy; a waiter.
Garde du corps. [Fr.] A bodyguard.
Garde mobile. [Fr.] A guard liable to general service.
Gardez la foi. [Fr.] Keep the faith.
Gaudeamus igitur. [L.] So let us be joyful.
Genius loci. [L.] The pervading spirit.
Gens d'armes. [Fr.] Men at arms.
Gens de guerre. [Fr.] Military men.
Gens de lettres. [Fr.] Literary men.
Gentilhomme. [Fr.] A gentleman.
Germanicè. [L.] In German.
Gloria in Excelsis. [L.] Glory (to God) in the highest.
Gloria Patri. [L.] Glory be to the Father.
Gnothi seauton. [Gr.] Know thyself.
Grace à Dieu. [Fr.] Thanks to God.
Guerre à outrance. [Fr.] War to the uttermost.

H

Habent sua fata libelli. [L.] Books have their own fates.
Hic et ubique. [L.] Here and everywhere.
Hic jacet. [L.] Here lies.
Hic labor, hoc opus est. [L.] This is labor, this is toil.
Hinc illae lacrimae. [L.] Hence these tears.
Hoi polloi. [Gr.] The many; the vulgar; the rabble.
Homme d'affaires. [Fr.] A man of business.
Homme d'esprit. [Fr.] A man of wit or genius.
Homo sum; humani nihil a me alienum puto. [L.] I am a man; I count nothing human indifferent to me.
Homo unius libri. [L.] A man of one book.
Honi soit qui mal y pense. [O.Fr.] Evil to him who evil thinks.
Horae subsecivae. [L.] Leisure hours.
Horresco referens. [L.] I shudder as I relate.
Hors de combat. [Fr.] Disabled; put out of the fight.
Hors de la loi. [Fr.] In the condition of an outlaw.
Hors de propos. [Fr.] Not to the point or purpose.
Hors-d'oeuvre. [Fr.] A dish served at the commencement of a meal; an appetizer. (Lit., Outside of work.)
Hos ego versiculos feci: tulit alter honores. [L.] I wrote these lines; another got the credit for them.
Humanum est errare. [L.] To err is human.

I

Ibidem. [L.] At the same place (in a book).
Ich dien. [Ger.] I serve: motto of the Prince of Wales.
Id est. [L.] That is: often contracted *i.e.*
Ignoratio elenchi. [L.] Ignorance of the point in question.

Ignotum per ignotius. [L.] The unknown (explained) by the still more unknown.

Il penseroso. [It.] The pensive man.

Imperium in imperio. [L.] A state within a state.

In aeternum. [L.] Forever.

In articulo mortis. [L.] At the point of death.

In curia. [L.] In court.

In dubio. [L.] In doubt.

In esse. [L.] In being; in actuality.

In extenso. [L.] At full length.

In extremis. [L.] At the point of death.

Infra dignitatem. [L.] Below one's dignity.

In futuro. [L.] In future; henceforth.

In hoc signo vinces. [L.] In this sign thou shalt conquer.

In limine. [L.] At the threshold.

In loco. [L.] In the place; in the natural or proper place.

In loco parentis. [L.] In the place of a parent.

In medias res. [L.] Into the midst of things.

In memoriam. [L.] To the memory of; in memory.

In nomine. [L.] In the name of.

In nuce. [L.] In a nut-shell.

In omnia paratus. [L.] Prepared for all things.

In partibus infidelium. [L.] In parts belonging to infidels, or countries not adhering to the Roman Catholic faith.

In perpetuum. [L.] Forever.

In petto. [It.] Within the breast; in reserve.

In posse. [L.] In possible existence; in possibility.

In praesenti. [L.] At the present moment.

In propria persona. [L.] In one's own person.

In re. [L.] In the matter of.

In saecula saeculorum. [L.] For ever and ever.

In situ. [L.] In its original situation.

In statu quo. [L.] In the former state.

Inter alia. [L.] Among other things.

Inter nos. [L.] Between ourselves.

Inter se. [L.] Among themselves.

In toto. [L.] In the whole; entirely.

Intra muros. [L.] Within the walls.

In transitu. [L.] On the passage.

In vacuo. [L.] In empty space; in a vacuum.

In vino veritas. [L.] There is truth in wine; truth is told under the influence of liquor.

Ipse dixit. [L.] He himself said it; a dogmatic saying or assertion.

Ipsissima verba. [L.] The very words.

Ipso facto. [L.] By the fact itself; in the nature of the case.

Italicè. [L.] In Italian.

J

Jacta est alea. [L.] The die is cast.

Je ne sais quoi. [Fr.] I know not what; a something or other.

Jeu de mots. [Fr.] A play on words; a pun.

Jeu d'esprit. [Fr.] A display of wit; a witticism.

Judicium Dei. [L.] The judgment of God.

Juris utriusque doctor. [L.] Doctor of both the civil and canon law.

Jus canonicum. [L.] The canon law.

Jus civile. [L.] The civil law.

Jus divinum. [L.] The divine law.

Jus gentium. [L.] The law of nations.

Jus gladii. [L.] The right of the sword.

Juste milieu. [Fr.] The golden mean.

L

Labor omnia vincit. [L.] Labor conquers everything.

Lapsus calami. [L.] A slip of the pen.

Lapsus linguae. [L.] A slip of the tongue.

Lapsus memoriae. [L.] A slip of the memory.

Lares et penates. [L.] Household gods.

Latinè dictum. [L.] Spoken in Latin.

Laus Deo. [L.] Praise to God.

L'avenir. [Fr.] The future.

Le beau monde. [Fr.] The fashionable world.

Legatus a latere. [L.] A papal ambassador.

Le grand monarque. [Fr.] The great monarch: Louis XIV of France.

Le pas. [Fr.] Precedence in place or rank.

Le roi est mort; vive le roi! [Fr.] The king is dead; long live the king!

Lèse-majesté. [Fr.] High-treason.

L'état, c'est moi. [Fr.] I am the state.

Le tout ensemble. [Fr.] The whole together.

Lettre de cachet. [Fr.] A sealed letter containing private orders; a royal warrant.

Lex loci. [L.] The law or custom of the place.

Lex non scripta. [L.] Unwritten law; common law.

Lex scripta. [L.] Statute law.

Lex talionis. [L.] The law of retaliation.

L'inconnu. [Fr.] The unknown.

Lite pendente. [L.] During the trial.

Litera scripta manet. [L.] The written letter remains.

Loco citato. [L.] In the place cited.

Locus sigilli. [L.] The place of the seal.

Lucus a non lucendo. [L.] Used as typical of an absurd derivation—*lucus*, a grove, having been derived by an old grammarian from *luceo*, to shine—'from not shining.'

Lusus naturae. [L.] A sport or freak of nature.

M

Ma chère. [Fr.] My dear (fem.).

Ma foi. [Fr.] Upon my faith.

Magna est veritas, et praevalebit. [L.] Truth is mighty, and will prevail.

Magni nominis umbra. [L.] The shadow of a great name.

Magnum opus. [L.] A great work.

Maison de santé. [Fr.] A private asylum or hospital.

Maître d'hôtel. [Fr.] A house-steward.

Maladie du pays. [Fr.] Home-sickness.

Mala fide. [L.] With bad faith; treacherously.

Mal de mer. [Fr.] Sea-sickness.

Malgré nous. [Fr.] In spite of us.

Mardi gras. [Fr.] Shrove Tuesday.

Mare clausum. [L.] A closed sea; a bay.

Mariage de convenance. [Fr.] Marriage from motives of interest rather than of love.

Mariage de la main gauche. [Fr.] Left-handed marriage; morganatic marriage.

Mauvaise honte. [Fr.] False modesty.

Mauvais goût. [Fr.] Bad taste.

Mauvais sujet. [Fr.] A bad subject; a worthless scamp.

Me judice. [L.] I being judge; in my opinion.

Memento mori. [L.] Remember death.

Mens sana in corpore sano. [L.] A sound mind in a sound body.

Meum et tuum. [L.] Mine and thine.

Mirabile dictu. [L.] Wonderful to relate.

Mirabile visu. [L.] Wonderful to see.

Mise en scène. [Fr.] The getting up for the stage, or the putting on the stage.

Modus operandi. [L.] Manner of working.

Mon ami. [Fr.] My friend (masc.).

Mon cher. [Fr.] My dear (masc.).

Monumentum aere perennius. [L.] A monument more lasting than brass.

Motu proprio. [L.] Of his own accord.

Multum in parvo. [L.] Much in little.

Mutatis mutandis. [L.] With the necessary changes.

N

Natura abhorret vacuum. [L.] Nature abhors a vacuum.

Necessitas non habet legem. [L.] Necessity has no law.

Nee. [Fr.] Born: used to indicate a married woman's maiden name.

Nemine contradicente. [L.] No one speaking in opposition; without opposition.

Nemo me impune lacessit. [L.] No one assails me with impunity.

Ne plus ultra. [L.] Nothing further; the uttermost point; perfection.

Nihil ad rem. [L.] Nothing to the point.

Nil admirari. [L.] To be astonished at nothing.

Nil desperandum. [L.] There is no reason for despair.

Ni l'un ni l'autre. [Fr.] Neither the one nor the other.

N'importe. [Fr.] It matters not.

Nisi Dominus frustra. [L.] Unless God be with us all is in vain.

Noblesse oblige. [Fr.] Rank imposes obligations.

Nolens volens. [L.] Willing or unwilling.

Noli me tangere. [L.] Touch me not.

Nolle prosequi. [L.] To be unwilling to prosecute.

Nom de guerre. [Fr.] A war name; a pseudonym; a pen name: often, incorrectly, *nom de plume.*

Non compos mentis. [L.] Not of sound mind.

Non libet. [L.] It does not please me.

Non liquet. [L.] The case is not clear; not proven.

Non possumus. [L.] We cannot (comply).

Non sequitur. [L.] It does not follow.

Nosce te ipsum. [L.] Know thyself.

Noscitur a sociis. [L.] He is known by his companions.

Nota bene. [L.] Mark well.

Nous avons changé tout cela. [Fr.] We have changed all that.

Nous verrons. [Fr.] We shall see.

Novus homo. [L.] A new man; one who has raised himself from obscurity.

Nulla dies sine lineâ. [L.] Not a day without a line; no day without something done.

Nulli secundus. [L.] Second to none.

Nunquam non paratus. [L.] Never unprepared; always ready.

O

Obiit. [L.] He, or she, died.

Obiter dictum. [L.] A thing said by the way.

Oderint dum metuant. [L.] Let them hate provided they fear.

Odi et amo. [L.] I hate and love.

Odi profanum vulgus. [L.] I loathe the profane rabble.

Odium theologicum. [L.] The hatred of theologians for one another; the bitterness of theological controversy.

Omne ignotum pro magnifico. [L.] Whatever is unknown is held to be magnificent.

Omne solum forti patria. [L.] Every soil is a brave man's country.

Omnia vincit amor. [L.] Love conquers all things.

Omnia vincit labor. [L.] Labor overcomes all things.

Operose nihil agunt. [L.] They laboriously do nothing.

Ora et labora. [L.] Pray and work.

Ora pro nobis. [L.] Pray for us.

Ore rotundo. [L.] With round full voice.

Origo mali. [L.] Origin of the evil.

O sancta simplicitas! [L.] O holy simplicity.

O tempora! O mores! [L.] O the times! O the manners!

Otium cum dignitate. [L.] Ease with dignity.

P

Pace. [L.] By leave of; not to give offence to.—*Pace tua,* with your consent.

Palmam qui meruit ferat. [L.] Let him who has won the palm wear it.

Par excellence. [Fr.] By way of eminence.

Pari passu. [L.] With equal pace; step for step.

Par nobile fratrum. [L.] A noble pair of brothers; two just alike.

Parole d'honneur. [Fr.] Word of honor.

Pars pro toto. [L.] Part for the whole.

Particeps criminis. [L.] An accomplice in crime.

Parturiunt montes; nascetur ridiculus mus. [L.] The mountains are in labor; an absurd mouse will be born.

Parvis componere magna. [L.] To compare great things with small.

Passim. [L.] Everywhere; all through.

Pater patriae. [L.] Father of his country.

Patres conscripti. [L.] Conscript fathers; Roman senators.

Pax vobiscum. [L.] Peace be with you.

Peccavi. [L.] I have sinned; I admit my mistake.

Peine forte et dure. [Fr.] Strong and severe punishment; a kind of judicial torture.

Pensée. [Fr.] A thought.

Per. [L.] For; through; by.—*Per annum.* By the year; annually.—*Per capita.* For each person.—*Per centum.* By the hundred.—*Per contra.* Contrariwise.—*Per diem.* By the day; daily.—*Per saltum.* By a leap or jump.—*Per se.* By or in itself.

Per ardua ad astra. [L.] Through difficulties to the stars; to achieve fame in spite of obstacles.

Pereant qui ante nos nostra dixerunt. [L.] May those perish who have said our good things before us.

Persona grata. [L.] A person who is held in special favor.

Petitio principii. [L.] A begging of the question.

Peu à peu. [Fr.] Little by little.

Pied-à-terre. [Fr.] A resting-place; a temporary lodging; an occasional abode.

Pis aller. [Fr.] The worst or last shift.

Place aux dames. [Fr.] Make way for the ladies.

Poco a poco. [It.] Little by little.

Poeta nascitur, non fit. [L.] The poet is born, not made.

Point d'appui. [Fr.] Point of support.

Pons asinorum. [L.] The ass' bridge; a name for the fifth proposition of the first book of Euclid.

Post hoc; ergo propter hoc. [L.] After this; therefore on account of this.

Pour prendre congé. [Fr.] To take leave.
Preux chevalier. [Fr.] A brave knight.
Primo. [L.] In the first place.
Primum mobile. [L.] The source of motion; the mainspring.
Principiis obsta. [L.] Resist the first beginnings.
Pro aris et focis. [L.] For our altars and our hearths.
Pro bono publico. [L.] For the good of the public.
Pro et contra. [L.] For and against.
Profanum vulgus. [L.] The profane vulgar.
Pro forma. [L.] For the sake of form.
Proh pudor. [L.] O, for shame!
Propaganda fide. [L.] For extending the faith.
Pro patria. [L.] For our country.
Pro rege, lege, et grege. [L.] For the king, the law, and the people.
Pro re nata. [L.] For some special circumstance which has arisen.
Prudens futuri. [L.] Thoughtful of the future.
Punica fides. [L.] Punic or Carthaginian faith; treachery.

Q

Quantum libet. [L.] As much as you please.
Quantum meruit. [L.] As much as he deserved.
Quantum mutatus ab illo. [L.] How changed from what he once was.
Quantum sufficit. [L.] As much as suffices.
Quelque chose. [Fr.] Something; a trifle.
Quem Deus vult perdere, prius dementat. [L.] Whom God wishes to destroy, he first makes mad.
Quid pro quo. [L.] Something in return; an equivalent.
Qui facit per alium facit per se. [L.] He who does a thing by another's agency does it himself.
Quis custodiet ipsos custodes? [L.] Who shall keep the keepers themselves?
Qui s'excuse s'accuse. [Fr.] He who excuses himself accuses himself.
Qui va là? [Fr.] Who goes there?
Quoad hoc. [L.] To this extent.
Quocunque modo. [L.] In whatever way.
Quod avertat Deus! [L.] Which may God avert!
Quod erat demonstrandum. [L.] Which was to be proved or demonstrated.
Quod erat faciendum. [L.] Which was to be done.
Quod vide. [L.] Which see.
Quot homines, tot sententiae. [L.] Many men, many minds.

R

Raison d'état. [Fr.] A reason of state.
Raison d'être. [Fr.] The reason for a thing's existence.
Rara avis in terris, nigroque simillima cygno. [L.] A rare bird on earth, and very like a black swan (formerly believed to be non-existent).
Reductio ad absurdum. [L.] The reducing of a position to an absurdity.
Requiescat in pace. [L.] May he (or she) rest in peace.
Res gestae. [L.] Things done; exploits.
Res judicata. [L.] A case or suit already settled.
Respice finem. [L.] Look to the end.
Resurgam. [L.] I shall rise again.
Revenons à nos moutons. [Fr.] Let us return to our sheep; let us return to our subject.
Ruat caelum. [L.] Let the heavens fall.
Rus in urbe. [L.] The country in town.

S

Sal Atticum. [L.] Attic salt; *i.e.* wit.
Salus populi suprema est lex. [L.] The safety of the people is the highest law.
Salvo jure. [L.] The right being safe.
Salvo pudore. [L.] Without offence to modesty.
Sans peur et sans reproche. [Fr.] Without fear and without reproach.
Sans souci. [Fr.] Without care.
Sapere aude. [L.] Dare to be wise.
Sartor resartus. [L.] The botcher repatched; the tailor patched or mended.
Satis quod sufficit. [L.] What suffices is enough.
Satis superque. [L.] Enough, and more than enough.
Satis verborum. [L.] Enough of words; no more need be said.
Sauve qui peut. [Fr.] Let him save himself who can.
Savoir-faire. [Fr.] The knowing how to act; tact.
Savoir-vivre. [Fr.] Good-breeding; refined manners.
Secundum artem. [L.] According to art or rule; scientifically.
Semper fidelis. [L.] Always faithful.
Semper idem. [L.] Always the same.
Semper paratus. [L.] Always ready.
Sic itur ad astra. [L.] Such is the way to the stars, or to immortality.
Sic passim. [L.] So here and there throughout; so everywhere.
Sic semper tyrannis. [L.] Ever so to tyrants.
Sic transit gloria mundi. [L.] Thus passes away the glory of this world.
Sicut ante. [L.] As before.
Sic vos non vobis mellificatis apes; nidificatis aves; vellera fertis oves. [L.] So not for yourselves do you bees make honey; birds build nests; sheep wear fleeces.
Similia similibus curantur. [L.] Like things are cured by like.
Si monumentum requiris, circumspice. [L.] If you seek his monument, look around you.
Simplex munditiis. [L.] Plain in her adornments.
Sine curâ. [L.] Without charge or care.
Sine die. [L.] Without a day being appointed.
Sine dubio. [L.] Without the slightest doubt.
Sine morâ. [L.] Without delay.
Sine qua non. [L.] Without which, not; something indispensable.
Si parva licet componere magnis. [L.] If small things may be compared with great.
Siste, viator. [L.] Stop, traveller.
Sit tibi terra levis. [L.] Light lie the earth upon thee.
Si vis me flere dolendum est primum ipse tibi. [L.] If you wish me to weep, you must first feel grief yourself.
Si vis pacem, para bellum. [L.] If you wish for peace, prepare for war.
Splendide mendax. [L.] Nobly untruthful; untrue for a good object.
Sponte sua. [L.] Of one's (or its) own accord.
Statu quo ante bellum. [L.] In the state in which things were before the war.
Status quo. [L.] The state in which.
Sua cuique voluptas. [L.] Every man has his own pleasures.
Suaviter in modo, fortiter in re. [L.] Gentle in manner, resolute in execution.
Sub judice. [L.] Under consideration.
Sub paena. [L.] Under a penalty.

Sub rosa. [L.] Under the rose; privately.
Sub silentio. [L.] In silence.
Sub voce. [L.] Under such or such a word.
Sui generis. [L.] Of its own peculiar kind.
Summum bonum. [L.] The chief good.
Suppressio veri. [L.] A suppression of the truth.
Supra vires. [L.] Beyond one's strength.
Sur le tapis. [Fr.] On the carpet; under discussion.
Suum cuique. [L.] Let every one have his own.
Suus cuique mos. [L.] Everyone has his particular habit.

T

Tabula rasa. [L.] A smooth or blank tablet.
Taedium vitae. [L.] Weariness of life.
Tant mieux. [Fr.] So much the better.
Tant pis. [Fr.] So much the worse.
Te judice. [L.] You being the judge.
Tempora mutantur, nos et mutamur in illis. [L.] The times are changing and we with them.
Tempus edax rerum. [L.] Time, the devourer of all things.
Tempus fugit. [L.] Time flies.
Tenax propositi. [L.] Tenacious of purpose.
Terminus ad quem. [L.] The term or limit to which.
Terminus a quo. [L.] The term or limit from which.
Terra incognita. [L.] An unknown land.
Tertium quid. [L.] A third something; a nondescript.
Toga virilis. [L.] The manly toga; the dress of manhood.
To kalon. [Gr.] The beautiful; the chief good.
Tot homines, quot sententiae. [L.] So many men, so many minds.
Totidem verbis. [L.] In just so many words.
Totis viribus. [L.] With all his might.
Toto caelo. [L.] By the whole heavens; diametrically opposite.
Toujours perdrix. [Fr.] Always partridge; always the same thing over again.
Toujours prêt. [Fr.] Always ready.
Tour de force. [Fr.] A feat of strength or skill.
Tout à fait. [Fr.] Wholly; entirely.
Tout à l'heure. [Fr.] Instantly.
Tout au contraire. [Fr.] On the contrary.
Tout à vous. [Fr.] Wholly yours.
Tout de suite. [Fr.] Immediately.
Tout ensemble. [Fr.] The whole taken together.
Tu quoque. [L.] Thou also.

U

Ubi bene, ibi patria. [L.] Where it is well there is one's country.
Ubi supra. [L.] Where above mentioned.
Ultra vires. [L.] Beyond one's power.
Una voce. [L.] With one voice; unanimously.
Uno animo. [L.] With one mind; unanimously.
Usque ad nauseam. [L.] To disgust.
Usus loquendi. [L.] Usage in speaking.
Utile dulci. [L.] The useful with the pleasant.
Ut infra. [L.] As below.
Uti possidetis. [L.] As you hold in possession.
Ut supra. [L.] As above.

V

Vae victis. [L.] Woe to the vanquished.
Variae lectiones. [L.] Various readings.
Varium et mutabile semper femina. [L.] Woman is ever changeful and capricious.
Veni, vidi, vici. [L.] I came, I saw, I conquered. [Caesar's message home when he conquered Pharnaces, king of Pontus].
Ventre à terre. [Fr.] At full gallop.
Verbatim et literatim. [L.] Word for word and letter for letter.
Verbum sat sapienti. [L.] A word is enough for a wise man.
Veritas vincit. [L.] Truth conquers.
Vestigia nulla retrorsum. [L.] No returning footsteps; no traces backward.
Via media. [L.] A middle course.
Vide et crede. [L.] See and believe.
Vide supra. [L.] See what is stated above.
Vi et armis. [L.] By force and arms; by main force.
Vincit omnia veritas. [L.] Truth conquers all things.
Virginibus puerisque canto. [L.] I sing to maids and to boys.
Virtute et fide. [L.] By or with virtue and faith.
Virtute et labore. [L.] By virtue and labor.
Virtute securus. [L.] Secure through virtue.
Vis comica. [L.] Comic power or talent.
Vis inertiae. [L.] The power of inertness.
Vis medicatrix naturae. [L.] The healing power of nature.
Vita brevis, ars longa. [L.] Life is short, art is long.
Vive la bagatelle. [Fr.] Long live trifling.
Voilà. [Fr.] Behold; there is; there are.
Voilà tout. [Fr.] That's all.
Voilà une autre chose. [Fr.] That's another thing; that is quite a different matter.
Volenti non fit injuria. [L.] No injustice is done to the consenting person.
Vox et praeterea nihil. [L.] A voice and nothing more; sound but no sense.
Vox populi, vox Dei. [L.] The voice of the people is the voice of God.
Vulgo. [L.] Commonly.

STUDENTS' AND AUTHORS'
MANUAL OF INFORMATION

MODERN ENGLISH USAGE - ABBREVIATIONS - BASIC REFERENCE WORKS
WRITING TO SELL - PROOFREADING AND PROOFREADERS' MARKS
MUSICAL SIGNS AND ABBREVIATIONS - EFFECTIVE PUBLIC SPEAKING

MODERN ENGLISH USAGE

This section is designed to point out some of the basic grammatical terms necessary for correct speech and writing. In addition, rules are given for the proper use of those forms of pronouns and verbs which are usually most troublesome.

The Parts of Speech

All words belong to one of eight categories, called the parts of speech. Every good dictionary indicates to which of these categories a word belongs. The parts of speech are the following:

NOUN. The name of a *person, place, thing,* or *idea.*

Nouns may be classified as follows:

a) Common: the name used to identify any object in general, such as *man, flower, dog, house,* etc.
b) Proper: the name of a specific person, place, or thing, such as *Washington, Walt Whitman, Statue of Liberty.*
c) Abstract: the name of that which is perceived through the intellect, such as *virtue, justice, morality.*
d) Concrete: the name of that which has a physical existence and is perceived through the senses, such as *man, desk, machine,* etc.
e) Collective: the name of a class composed of many individual parts, such as *government, company, crowd, congress, faculty, jury,* etc.

PRONOUN. A word that takes the place of a noun.

Pronouns may be classified as follows:

a) Personal: *I, thou, you, he, she, it, we, ye, you, they.*
b) Demonstrative: *this, that, these, those.*
c) Relative: *who, whose, whom, which, that.*
d) Indefinite: *anyone, each, both, someone, either,* etc.
e) Interrogative: *who, whose, whom, what, which.*
f) Reflexive: *myself, yourself, himself, herself, itself,* etc.
g) Intensive: *myself, yourself, himself, herself,* etc. The reflexive and intensive pronouns have the same forms; the distinction in function is determined by their position in the sentence. Thus, in the sentence "I wash *myself*," *myself* is a reflexive pronoun; whereas, in the sentence "I *myself* do the washing," *myself* is an intensive pronoun.
h) Reciprocal: *each other, one another.*

VERB. A word that indicates an action or state of being. Verbs permit of the following classification:

a) *Transitive verbs* have their meaning completed by a direct object. In the sentence, "He threw the ball," *threw* is a transitive verb, and *ball* the direct object.
b) *Intransitive verbs* cannot take a direct object. In the sentence, "The man walks slowly," *walks* is an intransitive verb and *slowly* is an adverb.
c) *Copulative verbs* (linking verbs) link a subject with a predicate noun or adjective, are usually restricted to a form of the verb *to be,* and are sometimes classified as intransitive verbs because they cannot take an object. In "Art *is* life," "Men *are* mortal," the copulas are *is* and *are* respectively, because they link *art* to *life,* and *men* to *mortal.*

Verbs show the following characteristics:

a) Mood indicates the manner in which the action takes place. Moods can be classified as:

1) Indicative: expresses a simple fact, declarative or interrogative.
   It is cold.
   Are you going?
2) Imperative: expresses a command or request.
   Sit down.
   Please don't go.
3) Subjunctive: expresses doubt, exhortation, wish, permission, sup-

position, expectation, possibility, condition contrary to fact, intention.

If I *were* you, I should do it.
Would that it *were* so.
He *may* go to the theatre tonight, but I doubt that he will.

4) Conditional: expresses contingency, the verbal phrases being formed with *should* and *would*. This mood is sometimes regarded as a function of the subjunctive.

b) Tense indicates the time of an action. The *simple* tenses, present, past, and future, merely indicate the time of an action; the *compound* tenses, present perfect, past perfect, and future perfect, indicate the extent to which an action was completed. The *emphatic* forms occur only in the simple present and past tenses, and are used to give emphasis to a statement. The *progressive* forms occur in all simple and compound tenses to show continuity of action at the time of reference.

c) Voice indicates the manner in which the action of the verb is related to the subject. When the subject is acting, the voice is *active;* when the subject is acted upon, the voice is *passive*.

d) Number indicates whether the subject of the verb refers to one person or thing, *singular*, or more than one, *plural*.

e) Person, *first, second, third*, is indicated by the inflectional ending of the verb; *I call, he calls.*

Verbals are verb forms which have the function of a noun or adjective. In the sentence, "*To walk* is pleasant," the infinitive *to walk* has the function of a noun, and is the subject of the verb *is*. In the sentence, "*Walking* is pleasant," the gerund *walking* has the function of a noun, and is the subject of the verb *is*. In the sentence, "*Seizing* the opportunity, he rode to popularity," the participle *seizing* has the function of an adjective, modifying *he*.

ADVERB. A word that modifies a verb, adjective, or another adverb. Adverbs may be classified as follows:

a) Time: answers the question *when?* In the sentence, "It rained *yesterday*," *yesterday* is an adverb of time.

b) Place: answers the question *where?* In the sentence, "The men marched *forwara*," *forward* is an adverb of place or direction.

c) Manner: answers the question *how?* In the sentence, "It rained *hard*," *hard* is an adverb of manner.

ADJECTIVE. A word that modifies a noun or pronoun. Adjectives may be classified as follows:

a) Limiting: the definite article *the*, and the indefinite articles *a, an*.

b) Descriptive: denotes condition or quality, as a *red* building, a *good* deed, an *upright* man, etc.

c) Pronominal: derived from pronouns.
1) Possessive: *my, his, her, its, our, your, their.*
2) Demonstrative: *this, that, these, those.*
3) Interrogative: *what, which, whose.*
4) Relative: *which, whose.*
5) Indefinite: *neither, some, every, each, other*, etc.

d) Numeral
1) Cardinal: *one, two, three*, etc.
2) Ordinal: *first, second, third*, etc.

PREPOSITION. A word that expresses the relation of a noun or pronoun to some other word in the sentence. The noun or pronoun governed by the preposition is always in the objective case. Hence, it is wrong to say "Between you and *I*," because *I* is a nominative form; the correct form is the objective *me*, because the pronoun is the object of the preposition *between*. The preposition and its object constitute a *prepositional phrase*. Prepositional phrases may be used as adjectives or adverbs. In the sentence, "He has a pot of *gold*," the prepositional phrase *of gold* is used as an adjective to modify the noun *pot*; in the sentence, "The book *lies on the table*," the prepositional phrase *on the table* is used as an adverb to modify the verb *lies*.

CONJUNCTION. A word that connects words, phrases, or clauses. Conjunctions may be classified as:

a) Coordinating: connects words, phrases, or independent clauses.
1) Pure conjunctions: *and, but, or, for.*
2) Correlatives: *either . . . or, neither . . . nor, not only . . . but also, both . . . and*, etc.
3) Conjunctive adverbs: *hence, consequently, besides, moreover, therefore, nevertheless*, etc.

b) Subordinating: introduces a subordinate clause, and connects it with the main clause.
1) Those that introduce adjectival clauses: *who, which, that.*
2) Those that introduce adverbial clauses: *although, because, since, though, if, as if*, etc.
3) Those that introduce noun clauses: *that.*

INTERJECTION. An exclamatory word that expresses strong or sudden feeling, having no grammatical function in the construction of a sentence: *ah, alas, oh, bah, pshaw,* etc.

Sentence Structure

A *simple sentence* is the expression of a single thought. It may also be defined as an independent clause. (A clause is a group of words containing a subject and a predicate.)

> The first reports came at eleven o'clock.

A *compound sentence* is formed by joining two or more simple sentences, or at least two independent clauses.

> We waited all evening, but the first reports did not come until eleven.

A *complex sentence* consists of one independent clause and one or more dependent clauses. (Dependent clauses do not make complete statements; they do the work of an adverb, adjective, or noun.)

> Although we waited all evening, we did not receive a report until eleven o'clock. (The clause introduced by *although* is adverbial.)

The *compound-complex sentence.*

> The men who were chosen were excellent players; they had had a great deal of experience, and they worked well together.

In the above sentence there are three independent clauses, and one dependent, *who were chosen,* which is an adjectival clause.

Writers without much experience often use a compound sentence when a complex would be more effective, that is, when one of the parts of the sentence is really subordinate to the other in thought. For example: "I was very tired, and so I went to bed early," might be written "Because I was very tired, I went to bed early." Good writers vary the sentence structure to gain emphasis and to avoid monotony.

SENTENCE ANALYSIS.—Every clause consists of a *subject* (the thing talked about), a *verb* or *predicate* (which makes a statement about the subject), and when the verb is not complete, an *object* (with a transitive verb) or a *predicate noun* or *adjective* (with a linking verb). The remaining words in the clause are modifiers of one of these elements.

> The old house which we purchased from Mr. Jones has been a constant source of expense.

This is a complex sentence. The independent or main clause is *The old house has been a constant expense.* The dependent clause is *which we purchased from Mr. Jones.*

In the independent clause *house* is the subject. It is modified by the adjectives *the* and *old* and by the adjectival clause *which we purchased from Mr. Jones. Has been* is the verb. *Source* is the predicate noun and it is modified by the adjectives *a* and *constant.*

In the adjectival clause, *we* is the subject; *purchased* is a transitive verb modified by the prepositional phrase (used like an adverb) *from Mr. Jones; which* is the direct object.

> They promised us that the boat would be ready, and having done business with them before, we accepted their promise.

This is a compound-complex sentence, consisting of two independent clauses connected by *and,* and one dependent clause, *that the boat would be ready.*

In the first independent clause, *they* is the subject; *promised* is the transitive verb; the noun clause *that the boat would be ready* is the direct object; *us* is the indirect object.

In the second independent clause, *we* is the subject, modified by the adjective-participial phrase *having done business with them before; accepted* is the verb; *promise* is the object, modified by the possessive adjective, *their.*

In the dependent noun clause, *boat* is the subject, modified by *the; would be* is the linking verb; *ready* is the predicate adjective; *that* is used only to introduce the clause.

In the participial phrase, the verbal *having done* has an object, *business,* and an adverbial modifier, the phrase *with them.*

It is possible, then, to account for the use of every word in any sentence.

DECLENSION OF THE NOUN

	Singular	Plural
NOMINATIVE	dog	dogs
POSSESSIVE	dog's	dogs'
OBJECTIVE	dog	dogs
NOMINATIVE	man	men
POSSESSIVE	man's	men's
OBJECTIVE	man	men

THE CORRECT USE OF PRONOUNS.—Because pronouns have different forms for each of the three cases in the English inflectional system, they offer more difficulty than perhaps any other part of speech. People are often puzzled about the use of *who* and *whom;* they are uncertain whether *everyone* is singular or plural. It is to meet these questions that the following rules are given.

CASES OF PRONOUNS

NOMINATIVE CASE	Used for the subject or predicate nominative.
POSSESSIVE CASE	Used to indicate ownership.
OBJECTIVE CASE	Used for the objects of verbs and prepositions.

Declension of the Pronoun

Personal

First Person, Masculine and Feminine

	Singular	Plural
NOMINATIVE	I	we
POSSESSIVE	*my, mine	*our, ours
OBJECTIVE	me	us

Second Person, Masculine and Feminine

	Singular	Plural
NOMINATIVE	you	you
POSSESSIVE	*your, yours	*your, yours
OBJECTIVE	you	you

Third Person, Masc., Fem., Neuter

	Singular			Plural
NOMINATIVE	he	she	it	they
POSSESSIVE	his	*her, hers	its	*their, theirs
OBJECTIVE	him	her	it	them

*These forms are pronominal adjectives.

Relative

	Singular	Plural
NOMINATIVE	who	who
POSSESSIVE	whose	whose
OBJECTIVE	whom	whom

Rules for Use of Pronouns

1. Use the Nominative Case as the subject of a finite verb.

"He is taller than *I*." *I* is the subject of *am* (understood).

"Explain the situation to *whoever* comes first." *Whoever* is the subject of *comes*, not the object of the preposition *to*.

"He is the man *who* we believe should be elected." *Who* is the subject of *should be elected*, not the object of *believe*.

2. Use the Nominative Case after the various forms of the linking verb *be* (*was, were, is, are, have been*, etc.)

"It was *he* who called."

"The leaders were Tom, Dick, Harry, John, and *I*."

"We are certain it is *they*."

3. Use the Possessive Case to modify a gerund.

"We objected to *his* leaving."

"*Dick's* losing the ball stopped the game."

"I am certain of *their* having been there."

4. Use the Objective Case for the object of a verb.

"I invited Mary and *him*."

"She likes John better than *me*." *Me* is the object of *she likes* (understood).

"*Whom* did you see?" *Whom* is the object of *did see*.

"Give the dictionary to *whomever* you see."

Whomever is the object of *see*.

5. Use the Objective Case for the object of a preposition.

"She gave the dictionary to Helen and *me*."

"They were all there except *him*."

"Three of *us* boys went camping in Wisconsin."

Pronouns—Number

Use a *singular* pronoun to refer to the indefinite words *anyone, either, everyone, each, every, nobody*.

"*Everyone* should have *his* own dictionary."

"*Each one* of the girls read *her* essay."

"If *anyone* wishes help, *he* must ask for it."

"*Neither* of the boys could express *his* ideas."

Agreement of Subject and Verb

1. Use a singular verb with a singular subject. "Mary *doesn't* like to work." *Don't* would be wrong in this sentence. Do not say *he don't, she don't, it don't*, because these are contractions of *he do not, she do not, it do not*.

"Each of the boys *is* capable in his own way." *Each* is singular.

"Neither Tom nor Peter is eligible." When the two parts of the subject are joined by *nor, or, but*, the verb agrees in number with the noun or pronoun nearest to it.

"Every member of the committee *agrees* to the proposal."

"John, together with his companion, *is* here." *John*, alone, is the subject of this sentence.

2. Use a plural verb with a plural subject. "There *are* several varieties of apples in the basket." *Varieties* is the subject of *are*. "Applause and flattery *are* the breath of his existence." A compound subject, i.e., two words joined by *and*, requires a plural verb unless the two words designate the same person or thing, as in the sentence: "His guide and protector *is* Mr. Collins."

3. Collective nouns (words like *group, crowd, committee, choir, faculty, congress*) may take either a singular or plural verb according to the meaning intended.

"The *company* has been ordered to the coast." *Company* is here thought of as a unit.

"The *company* are not all willing to take the risk." Here *company* is considered as plural because several individuals are meant.

CONJUGATION OF THE VERB "TO CALL":

ACTIVE VOICE

Indicative Mood

Singular	Plural
Present Tense	
Simple	
1. I call	we call
2. you call	you call
3. he calls	they call
Emphatic	
1. I do call	we do call
2. you do call	you do call
3. he does call	they do call
Progressive	
1. I am calling	we are calling
2. you are calling	you are calling
3. he is calling	they are calling
Past Tense	
Simple	
1. I called	we called
2. you called	you called
3. he called	they called
Emphatic	
1. I did call	we did call
2. you did call	you did call
3. he did call	they did call
Progressive	
1. I was calling	we were calling
2. you were calling	you were calling
3. he was calling	they were calling
Future Tense	
Simple	
1. I shall call	we shall call
2. you will call	you will call
3. he will call	they will call
Emphatic	
1. I will call	we will call
2. you shall call	you shall call
3. he shall call	they shall call
Progressive	
1. I shall be calling	we shall be calling
2. you will be calling	you will be calling
3. he will be calling	they will be calling
Present Perfect	
Simple	
1. I have called	we have called
2. you have called	you have called
3. he has called	they have called
Progressive	
1. I have been calling	we have been calling
2. you have been calling	you have been calling
3. he has been calling	they have been calling

Singular	Plural
Past Perfect	
Simple	
1. I had called	we had called
2. you had called	you had called
3. he had called	they had called
Progressive	
1. I had been calling	we had been calling
2. you had been calling	you had been calling
3. he had been calling	they had been calling
Future Perfect	
Simple	
1. I shall have called	we shall have called
2. you will have called	you will have called
3. he will have called	they will have called
Progressive	
1. I shall have been calling	we shall have been calling
2. you will have been calling	you will have been calling
3. he will have been calling	they will have been calling

Subjunctive Mood

Singular	Plural
Present Tense	
Simple	
1. if I call	if we call
2. if you call	if you call
3. if he call	if they call
Emphatic	
1. if I do call	if we do call
2. if you do call	if you do call
3. if he do call	if they do call
Progressive	
1. if I be calling	if we be calling
2. if you be calling	if you be calling
3. if he be calling	if they be calling
Past Tense	
Simple	
1. if I called	if we called
2. if you called	if you called
3. if he called	if they called
Emphatic	
1. if I did call	if we did call
2. if you did call	if you did call
3. if he did call	if they did call
Progressive	
1. if I were calling	if we were calling
2. if you were calling	if you were calling
3. if he were calling	if they were calling

Singular	Plural
Present Perfect	
Simple	
1. if I have called	if we have called
2. if you have called	if you have called
3. if he has called	if they have called
Progressive	
1. if I have been calling	if we have been calling
2. if you have been calling	if you have been calling
3. if he has been calling	if they have been calling
Past Perfect	
Simple	
1. if I had called	if we had called
2. if you had called	if you had called
3. if he had called	if they had called
Progressive	
1. if I had been calling	if we had been calling
2. if you had been calling	if you had been calling
3. if he had been calling	if they had been calling

Conditional Mood

Present Tense

Singular	Plural
Simple	
1. I should call	we should call
2. you would call	you would call
3. he would call	they would call
Emphatic	
1. I would call	we would call
2. you should call	you should call
3. he should call	they should call
Progressive	
1. I should be calling	we should be calling
2. you would be calling	you would be calling
3. he would be calling	they would be calling

Perfect

Singular	Plural
Simple	
1. I should have called	we should have called
2. you would have called	you would have called
3. he would have called	they would have called
Progressive	
1. I should have been calling	we should have been calling
2. you would have been calling	you would have been calling
3. he would have been calling	they would have been calling

Imperative Mood

SIMPLE: call
EMPHATIC: do call
PROGRESSIVE: be calling

Present Infinitive

SIMPLE: to call
PROGRESSIVE: to be calling
GERUND: calling

Perfect Infinitive

SIMPLE: to have called
PROGRESSIVE: to have been calling
GERUND: having called

Participles

PRESENT: calling
PAST: (lacking)
PERFECT SIMPLE: having called

PASSIVE VOICE

Indicative Mood

Singular	Plural
Present Tense	
1. I am called	we are called
2. you are called	you are called
3. he is called	they are called
Past Tense	
1. I was called	we were called
2. you were called	you were called
3. he was called	they were called
Future Tense	
1. I shall be called	we shall be called
2. you will be called	you will be called
3. he will be called	they will be called
Present Perfect	
1. I have been called	we have been called
2. you have been called	you have been called
3. he has been called	they have been called
Past Perfect	
1. I had been called	we had been called
2. you had been called	you had been called
3. he had been called	they had been called
Future Perfect	
1. I shall have been called	we shall have been called
2. you will have been called	you will have been called
3. he will have been called	they will have been called

Subjunctive Mood

Singular	Plural
Present Tense	
1. if I be called	if we be called
2. if you be called	if you be called
3. if he be called	if they be called

Singular	Plural
Past Tense	
1. if I were called	if we were called
2. if you were called	if you were called
3. if he were called	if they were called
Present Perfect	
1. if I have been called	if we have been called
2. if you have been called	if you have been called
3. if he has been called	if they have been called
Past Perfect	
1. if I had been called	if we had been called
2. if you had been called	if you had been called
3. if he had been called	if they had been called

Conditional Mood

Present	
1. I should be called	we should be called
2. you would be called	you would be called
3. he would be called	they would be called
Perfect	
1. I should have been called	we should have been called
2. you would have been called	you would have been called
3. he would have been called	they would have been called

Imperative Mood

SIMPLE: be called

Present Infinitive

SIMPLE: to be called
GERUND: being called

Perfect Infinitive

SIMPLE: to have been called
GERUND: having been called

Participles

PRESENT: being called
PAST: called
PERFECT: having been called

Capitalization

Capital letters are employed to give emphasis to particular words, namely proper nouns and proper adjectives. The difficulty in this principle lies in determining when a noun or adjective is proper, and when a noun or adjective is common. It would be difficult, if not impossible, to list here an exhaustive set of rules to cover every instance. The following rules, however, will be found helpful insofar as they do apply to problems in capitalization met daily.

1. Capitalize the first word (*a*) of a sentence, (*b*) of a direct quotation, (*c*) of a line of poetry, or (*d*) of a formally introduced series of items or phrases following a colon.

a) The room was uncomfortably warm.

b) Turning quickly she said, "Please go now."

c) Then I felt like some watcher of the skies,
When a new planet swims into his ken:
Or like stout Cortez when with eagle eyes
He stared at the Pacific—and all his men
Look'd at each other with wild surmise—
Silent, upon a peak in Darien.

d) The analysis revealed the following: Carbon, six parts; hydrogen, twelve parts; oxygen, six parts.

The first word of a fragmentary quotation is not capitalized.

He thought the play "was good, but amateurish."

The first word following a colon is not capitalized if that which follows merely expands, qualifies, or makes clearer the sense of that which precedes the colon.

Intelligence cannot be acquired or increased: it is native.

History shows that wars settle nothing: they merely unsettle things.

2. Capitalize the interjection *O*, but none of the other interjections.

O powerful western fallen star!
O shades of night—O moody, tearful night!
O great star disappear'd—O the black murk that hides the star!
O cruel hands that hold me powerless—O helpless soul of me!
O harsh surrounding cloud that will not free my soul.

3. Capitalize all proper nouns.

Bohemia	King Philip of Macedon
China	John Macadam
America	Adam
Louis Pasteur	

4. Words derived from proper nouns, and retaining a proper meaning are capitalized.

Bohemian (of Bohemia)
American (of America)
Venetian (of Venice)
Moroccan (of Morocco)
Parisian (of Paris)

a. Do not capitalize words derived from proper nouns for which a common or specialized meaning has been developed.

china	anglicize
morocco	pasteurize
venetian blinds	philippic
plaster of paris	macadam

5. Capitalize common nouns and adjectives which form an essential part of a proper name, as of streets, parks, specific buildings, geographical names, etc.

Chestnut Street	Delaware River
Franklin Parkway	Blair County
Michigan Avenue	Mount Everest
Cermak Road	Gulf of Mexico
Fairmount Park	Panama Canal
Elverson Building	Chesapeake Bay

a. Do not capitalize descriptive place references:

the valley of the Nile
the river Seine
the gorge of the Colorado

b. The following are never capitalized:

aqueduct	lock
breakwater	pier
buoy	slip
dike	spillway
ditch	tunnel
drydock	watershed
floodway	weir
levee	wharf

c. The following are always capitalized when they follow a proper name:

Archipelago	Harbor
Bay	Highway
Bayou	Hill
Borough	Hook
Canal (for ships)	Inlet
Canyon	Island
Cape	Isle
Channel	Lake
County	Mount
Creek	Mountain
Desert	Narrows
Falls	Peninsula
Forest	Plateau
Fork (stream)	River
Fort	Sea
Gap	Sound
Glacier	Spring
Gulch	Valley
Gulf	Woods

6. Capitalize the *d'*, *da*, *della*, *van*, and *von* when not preceded by a title or forename.

De Maupassant, but Guy de Maupassant
Van Gogh, but Vincent van Gogh
Von Tirpitz, but Alfred von Tirpitz
Della Robbia, but Luca della Robbia

a. In American and British names these particles are usually capitalized without regard to the above rule, but individual usage should be followed.

William De Morgan
Thomas De Quincey
Lucretia Van Zandt
Henry van Dyke (his usage)

7. Capitalize the names of organized bodies and their members to distinguish them from the common meaning.

Republican Party, a Republican; but, a republican (one who believes in a republican form of government).
Democratic Party, a Democrat; but, a democrat (one who believes in democracy).
an Elk; but, an elk (an animal.)

8. Capitalize *territory*, *state*, *nation*, *union*, *empire*, etc. only when these words refer to a particular political division.

the United States: the Republic, the Nation, the Union; but a republic, a nation, a union.
the British Empire: the Empire; but an empire.
Cook County: the County; but a county.

9. Capitalize descriptive terms used to designate a definite geographical region or feature.

the Middle Atlantic States
the Far East; the Near East
the Continental Divide
the North Pole; the South Pole
the Western Hemisphere

10. Capitalize names of months and days of the year.

January	Sunday
February	Monday
March, etc.	Tuesday, etc.

11. Capitalize names of historic events and eras, holidays, and ecclesiastical feast and fast days.

World War	Renaissance
Mexican War	Fourth of July
Middle Ages	Shrove Tuesday

12. Capitalize personification in figures of speech.

For Nature is neither kind nor cruel, merciless nor merciful; she follows inexorably her immutable laws.
The Chair introduced the guest speaker.

13. Capitalize all nouns and adjectives denoting the Deity, and all pronouns referring to the same.

the Holy Ghost	Jehovah
the Lord	Yahweh
the Almighty	Allah
Son of Man	the Virgin

14. Capitalize all names of creeds, religious bodies and their adherents.

Nicene Creed	Methodist Church
Augsburg Confession	Protestant
	Buddhist
Christian	Mohammedan

15. Capitalize all names for the Bible, books of the Bible, and all other sacred books.

Holy Writ	the Koran
Scriptures	the Vedas
Exodus	the Upanishads
Septuagint	the Talmud

a. Do not capitalize adjectives derived from such nouns.

apocryphal	scriptural
koranic	biblical

16. Capitalize all titles preceding a name.

Doctor Smith	King George
Professor Gibbs	General Butler
President Truman	Justice Roberts

a. Capitalize a title in the second or third person.

Your Honor	Mr. President
Your Grace	Mr. Chairman
His Holiness	His Excellency

17. Capitalize the first word and every important word in the English title of a book, poem, play, article, essay, work of art, piece of music, report, publication, legal case, and historic document.

The Dawn of Civilization (book)
Caliban in the Coal Mines (poem)
Pillars of Society (drama)
Old Lamps for New (essay)
Dinner for Threshers (painting)
Death and Transfiguration (music)

Punctuation

The purpose of punctuation is to aid the reader in assimilating the thought expressed through the written word.

Although very little conscious thought is given to punctuation in the actual reading of printed or written matter—the mind automatically stopping at periods, pausing for commas, and preparing for a change of thought at dashes—a thorough knowledge of the fundamental rules governing the correct use of punctuation marks is indispensable to the writer who wishes to express his thoughts, ideas, and feelings clearly, accurately, and logically.

The following rules will be found to embrace all cases arising in the course of ordinary formal and informal writing.

1. When reading, notice all punctuation closely and try to reason out why the marks encountered are used.

2. When writing, first organize in your mind what you want to say and then use only sufficient punctuation to insure the accurate conveyance of your thoughts.

3. Never use any mark of punctuation without a definite reason for so doing.

4. Give particular attention to the use of the comma, as ignorance of the rules governing this mark is the major cause of punctuation trouble.

The Comma.—The function of the comma is to break up the sentence into separate thoughts in the interest of clarity and ease of reading.

1. Use a comma between each element of pairs and series unless the pairs are connected by a coordinating conjunction.

The ride was long, exhausting.
The ride was long, hot, exhausting.
The ride was long and exhausting.

2. Use a comma before the *and* in a series having the form of *a*, *b*, and *c*.

We brought ham, pickles, and eggs.

3. Use a comma before any one of the conjunctions (*and*, *but*, *for*, *or*, *neither*, *nor*) when it joins a pair of main clauses.

He said he would be there, and I do not doubt his word.
Many are called, but few are chosen.
He read the book quickly, for he was late.
She will be there, or I am mistaken.

4. Use a comma to introduce a short, direct quotation in the form of a complete sentence and also at the end of a quotation if it is followed by explanatory, unquoted remarks. (Introducing a direct quotation with a colon is permissible if the quoted sentence is long.)

The cynic replied, "Diplomacy is the art of lying."
"Diplomacy is the art of lying," replied the cynic.
"Diplomacy," replied the cynic, "is the art of lying."

5. Use a comma before and after such elements as *for example*, *to be sure*, *in fact*, *however*, *nevertheless*, and *therefore*, when they are used parenthetically.

We do not, for example, favor a moratorium.
He was, in fact, unequal to the work.
She will go, therefore, at six o'clock.

6. Use commas to enclose a geographical name explaining a preceding geographical name.

They lived in Chicago, Illinois, for many years.

7. Use commas to enclose a date explaining a preceding date.

In April, 1918, his regiment moved to the front.
On April 24, 1918, his regiment moved to the front.
Early in the morning of Monday, April 24, his regiment moved to the front.

8. Use commas to enclose any element taken from its natural position and placed elsewhere.

Their new car, when running at top speed, will go faster than 90 miles an hour.

9. Use a comma between the parts of a name or phrase when they are written in reverse order.

Buchanan, James B.
Psychology, History of
Nouns, Use of
Chemistry, Organic

10. Enclose appositives with commas.

U. S. Grant, the great Civil War general, was short in stature.

11. Enclose absolute phrases with commas.

It is my belief, conditions being what they are, that war is inevitable.

12. Use a comma to separate two words or figures that might otherwise be confusing.

To Henry, Scott was a hero.
In 1939, 40 ships were lost.
January 24, 1939.
Instead of 10, 25 men answered the call for volunteers.

13. Use a comma to indicate the omission of a word.

He is tall; she, short.
The former illustrates the use of a semicolon; the latter, a comma.

14. Use a comma after a phrase or subordinate clause that precedes a main clause.

Caught on a reef, the vessel foundered and was lost.
Although a severe winter had been anticipated, we were pleasantly surprised by its mildness.

a. Do not use a comma after a main clause if the following adverbial clause is its logical completion.

This testimony is inadmissible because it is prejudicial.
The project can be completed only if all cooperate.

15. Use a comma between two of the same or similar words to avoid confusion.

That which is, is neither good nor bad.
That which was, is no more.
What will be, will be.

16. Use a comma before the abbreviations or degrees *Jr.*, *Sr.*, *M.A.*, *M.D.*, *Ph.D.*, etc.

Charles H. Leiter, Jr.
Anthony Ennis, M.D.
D.S. Platon, Ph.D.

17. Use a comma to separate thousands, millions, billions, etc. in numbers of four or more digits.

3,197	3,284,962
52,012	653,039,253

a. Do not use a comma in figures of four or more digits in telephone numbers, serial numbers, dates, and radio wave lengths.

Murray Hill 9912
A.D. 1925
No. F87831084 A
1170 kilocycles; 820 meters

18. Use a comma after a title or phrase in direct address.

Sir, the end is not yet.
Mr. President, the gentleman is out of order.
Gentlemen, we shall now proceed to the order of the day.

19. Use a comma between title and name of organization where *of* or *of the* has been omitted.

Commander, Fourth Army Corps
President, University of Chicago
Superintendent, Board of Health

THE DASH.—The dash may often be substituted for the comma, semicolon, colon, or parenthesis mark. It is used to enclose or introduce short elements and has great force. It should be used only in extreme cases, when other forms of punctuation are inadequate—and only then.

1. Substitute a dash for a semicolon when more effective grouping is desired.

The shouting ceased—all was quiet; evidently the mob had dispersed.

2. The dash may be used to call attention to a word or group of words following it.

He works hard—too hard, in fact.
The American character may be described in one word—courage.

3. The dash is useful at the end of a long series to introduce material concerning that series.

> With careful study, with diligent practice, with the desire for improvement—with all these, one should be able to succeed.

4. Use dashes to enclose parenthetical elements where commas would be weak or parentheses undesirable.

> Ruth—the best hitter in the league—has powerful shoulders.
>
> He thinks—and rightly—that the disease can be eradicated.

5. Use the dash to indicate an interruption or an unfinished sentence.

> He goes on to say that—. But never mind; it's of no importance.
>
> "This thing has be—."

6. Use a dash to link letters, figures, or letters and figures.

DO—X	1938—40
RZ—1	January—March
$5—$10	Monday—Thursday

7. Use a dash when there is repetition for additional or especial emphasis.

> We are now faced with a new problem—the problem of isolating the germ.

8. Use a dash for summarizing.

> Washington, Jefferson, Jackson—all had the same idea.

THE SEMICOLON.—This mark is used to coordinate main clauses.

1. Use the semicolon between pairs of main clauses not connected by a coordinating conjunction (*and, but, for, or, neither, nor*).

> You may help him; I will not.

2. Use the semicolon between pairs of main clauses not connected by a coordinating conjunction especially when a conjunctive adverb (*therefore, nevertheless, however, otherwise*, etc.) is present.

> You may help him; however, I will not.

3. Use the semicolon between pairs of main clauses where a coordinating conjunction is present if such clauses are long, contain commas, or if emphasis is desired.

> It is most unusual; and it should not be tolerated.
>
> It is not just to the people, the state, or the country; and although difficult, a proper decision must be made.

4. Use the semicolon to separate statements so closely related that a comma would be too weak and a period too strong.

> It was so in the past; it is so in the present; and if the past and the present may be taken as a valid indication of the future, it will always remain so.

THE COLON.—The colon is a mark of punctuation used to introduce a clause or phrase that amplifies or is in explanation of a preceding clause.

1. Use the colon to introduce a clause that supplements or explains the preceding clause in a sentence.

> Everett's speech was soon forgotten: he was too much occupied with form rather than substance.
>
> We live on a planet, not on a star: a star is a sun.

2. Use the colon to introduce formally a direct, lengthy quotation, or any other formal matter.

> These are his principal qualifications: attention to detail; many years of experience; and an instinctive ability to sell merchandise.
>
> He said: "I do not accept as valid the proposition that time goes. It would not be difficult to demonstrate that time is ageless; and it would also be easy to demonstrate that human beings are not ageless. No, it is we who go, not time."

3. Use the colon to express time.

> 8:30 A.M.
> 12:25 P.M.

4. Use the colon after the salutation of a letter.

Dear Sir:	Gentlemen:
My dear Sir:	Dear Madam:

5. Use the colon in biblical and other citations.

> Luke 4:7
> N. Y. Times, Nov. 20, 21:7

6. Use the colon in proportions.

> 1:3: :3:9
> The ratio was 16:1.

PARENTHESES

1. Use parentheses to enclose that part of a sentence intended to be read as a side remark provided the removal of such part would not destroy the sense of the context. Also, use parentheses to enclose complete sentences intended as side remarks.

Robert was playing great football (for the thrill of it; not merely to win) and several times staved off defeat.

We hurried home the next day. (It was only too true that the river had risen. We were ruined.) But with characteristic vigor we began building anew.

2. Use parentheses to enclose an independent clause inserted in a sentence.

The work (he was preeminently fitted for it) absorbed his attention for weeks.

3. Enclose with parentheses references to tables, diagrams, etc.

The cost of living (See Chart II) has risen slowly but surely.

4. Use parentheses to enclose figures or letters used in enumerations.

The immediate results were these: (1) a cornering of the market, (2) a decrease in available material, (3) an advance in prices.

BRACKETS.—Brackets are used to enclose an explanatory remark in a quoted passage. They are rarely, if ever, used in a business letter. For all practical purposes the secretary can attain the same ends with parentheses.

"The rise of absolutism [Fascism, Hitlerism, etc.] has its roots in postwar conditions," the speaker said.

QUOTATION MARKS

1. Use quotation marks to enclose all direct quotations.

Patrick Henry said, "Give me liberty, or give me death."

2. Use single quotation marks to mark a quotation within a quotation.

The coach said: "I heard one of our men say, 'It was the hardest game of the season.' "

3. When a quotation consists of more than one paragraph, use quotation marks before each paragraph, but at the end of only the last one.

"________________________________
____
__________.

"________________________________
____
__________________________."

4. When quoting poetry consisting of more than one stanza, use quotation marks before each stanza, but at the end of only the last stanza.

"Under the wide and starry sky,
Dig the grave and let me die.
Glad did I live and gladly die,
And I laid me down with a will.

"This be the verse you grave for me:
Here he lies where he longed to be;
Home is the sailor, home from sea,
And the hunter home from the hill."
—ROBERT LOUIS STEVENSON.

5. Enclose slang expressions, colloquialisms, technical words, or a word used in a humorous or ironical way, in quotation marks when such expressions are not in keeping with the style of writing in which they occur.

His wife is undoubtedly "Lord High Chancellor of the Exchequer" in their household.

He got himself "all balled up."

6. The comma and period are always placed inside the quotation marks.

"I shall come," she said, "if it does not rain."

The semicolon, exclamation mark, colon, question mark, and dash are all placed outside the quotation marks except when they form part of the quoted passage or when the quotation is not accompanied by such expressions as *he said, she replied*, etc.

Did she say, "I have lost my book"?
"May I come in now?" he asked.
"They're off!"
"Where?"
"At Latonia."

7. Dialogue should be written in separate paragraphs.

"Come in," she said, "and get warm."

"Thank you," he replied, "it is very cold tonight."

8. Enclose definitions requiring explanation with single quotation marks; for translations use double quotation marks.

Facetious means 'humorous' or 'jocular.'

Verboten means "forbidden."

9. Since there are no italics on a typewriter, quote the names of ships, of musical compositions, of art works, and the titles of books and pictures, or indicate italics by underlining.

The U. S. S. "Pennsylvania"
DaVinci's "The Last Supper"
Theodore Dreiser's <u>An American Tragedy.</u>
George Gershwin's <u>Rhapsody in Blue</u>

THE PERIOD

1. Use the period at the end of a declarative sentence.

The soft rays of the morning sun illuminated the gold in the ripening wheat.

As the sun began to slip away the mountain underwent a slow progression in color, from warmer to cooler, from green through blue to purple, until a mere outline was left against a dusky sky which finally melted into the darkness of night.

2. Use the period at the end of an imperative sentence.

Hang up your coat.
Come to the fair.
Be there on time.

3. Use the period at the end of an indirect question.

Tell me what he said.
I should like to know how you do it.
I asked him what time it was.

4. Use the period after an abbreviation.

viz.	D. C.
N. Y.	q.v.
etc.	SW.

a. Do not use a period after the symbols for chemical elements.

Ag (silver)	K (potassium)
Au (gold)	O (oxygen)
Fe (iron)	S (sulphur)

b. Do not mistake a contraction for an abbreviation: a contraction is not followed by a period.

ass'n	assn.	sup't	supt.
m'g'r	mgr.	Penn'a	Penn.

5. Do not use a period after Roman numerals except in enumeration used in an outline.

George VI
Haakon VII
Gustavus V
I. The Colonial Period
II. The Ante-Bellum Period
III. The Post-Bellum Period
IV. The Twentieth Century

6. Do not use a period after *per cent, MS, MSS.*

the Cotton MS (manuscript)
25 per cent

7. Always put the period within quotation marks.

I have read "Leaves of Grass."
He did not see the performance of "Mourning Becomes Electra."

THE EXCLAMATION POINT.—This mark is used at the end of a declarative sentence or after an exclamation within the sentence to convey the idea of strong feeling, surprise, or irony.

Here, get down from there!
What! the only one we have! and I'm not to use it!
Voting in a totalitarian state is an expression of popular sentiment? Popular sentiment, indeed!

THE QUESTION MARK

1. Use the question mark at the end of every sentence that asks a question.

How fast are we going?
"How fast are we going?" he asked.
Can there not be such a thing as an absolute event quite independent of cause?

2. Use the question mark within the sentence when it is desirable to emphasize each element separately.

Where now is his love of country? his political integrity? his unblemished record?

3. Use the question mark within parentheses to indicate doubt or uncertainty as to the correctness of the word or fact preceding it.

Charles I, born in 1660 (?), was king of Sicily.

THE APOSTROPHE.—The apostrophe is used to indicate the omission of one or more letters from a word or to form the possessive of certain nouns as indicated in the rules following.

1. Use the apostrophe to indicate the omission of one or more letters from a word, or figures from a number.

I can't do it now.
He wouldn't do it then.
The class of '98 met in Chicago.

2. Use the apostrophe and *s* to form the possessive of singular nouns of not more than one syllable including those which end in *s*.

Fred's, James's, Mr. Jones's.

Some writers still use only the apostrophe for the possessive of singular nouns ending in *s*; but the 's is preferable.

3. Use the apostrophe alone when forming the possessive of plural nouns ending in *s*, or nouns ending in *s* and consisting of more than one syllable; add *s* with the apostrophe in the case of plural nouns which do not end in *s*.

The Smiths' house.
Girls', soldiers', children's, men's.
The *New Testament* contains Jesus' parables.

4. Use the apostrophe and *s* to indicate joint possession.

George and Mary's book.
Chase and Sanborn's coffee.

5. Use the apostrophe and *s* to form the possessive of indefinite pronouns.

One's, other's, another's, either's.
Somebody else's coat.

The above rule does not apply to *its, hers, his, ours, yours, theirs, whose.*

6. Use the apostrophe and *s* to form the plural of a letter, a figure, or of a word used as a noun.

There are two *f's* in *affect*.
Your *8's* are not legible.
He uses too many *if's* and *but's.*

Faulty Expressions

The following glossary of faulty expressions, while by no means exhaustive, is representative of the most common forms of incorrect usage. The secretary should avoid, in business correspondence, obsolete and archaic words, slang and vulgarisms. Although provincialisms and colloquialisms are permissible in conversation, their usage in a business letter detracts from its dignity and effectiveness. Too, the type of English frequently used in newspapers, written in a loose, racy, smart, or sensational style, should not be employed in business correspondence. The English may not be incorrect, but it lacks the character and dignity in keeping with the tone of a business letter, and is, therefore, to be avoided. The expressions listed here are those which are avoided by persons of good training. The secretary will do well to study them carefully.

ACCEPT, EXCEPT. These words should not be confused. *Accept* means *to receive*, as *I accept your kind offer. Except* means *to exclude.*

The law excepts no one.

A.D. *In the year of our Lord.* The A.D. should precede the date and never be used with *in*, since that would be superfluous. Nor should the A.D. be used when speaking of a century.

Wrong: He died in 1865 A.D.
Right: He died A.D. 1865.
Wrong: We live in the 20th century A.D.
Right: We live in the 20th century of the Christian Era.

AD. Colloquialism for advertisement. Although acceptable in speech it should be avoided in formal writing.

Colloq.: Your ad was placed in the Sunday News.
Preferable: Your advertisement was inserted in the Sunday News.

ADAPT, ADEPT. These words are carelessly confused. *Adapt* is a verb and means *to adjust*, as *He adapted the idea to his own needs. Adept* is an adjective and means *skilled*, as *He is adept at figures.*

ADVISE. Means *to offer an opinion* but is frequently used in business correspondence to mean *inform* or *tell*. In this sense, *inform* or *tell is* preferable to *advise.*

Permissible: Please be advised that the merchandise has been shipped.
Preferable: We wish to inform you that the merchandise has been shipped.

AFFECT, EFFECT. *Affect* is always a verb and means *to influence*, as *A high tariff will affect our cotton exports. Effect*, as a verb, means *to cause*, as *I want to effect a settlement;* as a noun it means *result*, as *Some believe that for every effect there is a cause.*

AFTER. This should not be used with a past participle, but may be used with the present participle.

Wrong: After having read the poem, I could appreciate it.
Right: Having read the poem, I could appreciate it.
Or also: After reading the poem, I could appreciate it.

AGGRAVATE. This means *to make an already bad condition worse* and, though sanctioned by popular usage, should not be used in the sense of *irritate, annoy*, or *provoke.*

Popular: His petty behavior aggravated me.
Preferable: His petty behavior irritated me.

AGREE TO, AGREE WITH. These are idiomatic expressions with different meanings. *Agree to* means *to give assent to*, as *I did not agree to pay that sum of money. Agree with* means *to be in accord with*, as *I agree with him in principle, but differ as to method.*

AIN'T. This word has been the subject of much controversy, but most authorities agree that it should never be used except in written colloquial dialogue. In its place should be used *is it not?, am I not?* (but never the British-Hollywood vulgarism *aren't I*), *are we not?* etc.

ALL OF. The *of* is superfluous.

Bad: He gave all of his property to charity.
Better: He gave all his property to charity.

ALL THE FARTHER, HIGHER, FASTER. These are frequently used incorrectly for *as far as, as high as, as fast as. All the* is correct when used in the sense of *just so much.*

Right: Disregarding the warning, we climbed all the higher.
Right: That day we climbed as high as 5,000 feet.
Wrong: Is this all the farther we are going?

ALLOW. The word means *to permit, to approve.* The provincial meaning *to think* or *believe* should be avoided.

Provincial: I allow that's so.
Preferable: I think that is so.

ALLUDE, DELUDE, ELUDE. *Allude* means *to refer to indirectly,* as *He alluded to unethical practitioners in the profession. Delude* means *to deceive,* as *He was deluded by the man's apparent honesty. Elude* means *to escape,* as *The gist of the story eludes me.*

ALLUSION, ILLUSION. *Allusion* has the meaning of *a casual reference,* as *There were many humorous allusions to human foibles in the drama. Illusion* has the meaning of a *false* or *deceptive appearance,* as *He lulled himself into a feeling of false security by an illusion of wealth.*

ALREADY, ALL READY. Both of these are correct, but each one has a different meaning. *Already* has the meaning of *beforehand* or *by now,* as *The merchandise has already arrived. All ready* has the meaning of *everything* or *everybody ready,* as *They are all ready.*

ALRIGHT, ALL RIGHT. There is no such word as the former; the latter is the correct spelling and should not be overworked in the sense of *very well.*

ALTAR, ALTER. The former is a noun and means *a shrine,* the latter is a verb and means *to change.*

ALTOGETHER, ALL TOGETHER. Both expressions are correct but have different meanings. The former means *wholly, totally;* the latter, *everybody* or *everything together.*

ALUMNUS, ALUMNI; ALUMNA, ALUMNAE. The first two are the masculine singular and plural forms respectively; the last two are the feminine singular and plural forms respectively.

AMONG, BETWEEN. The former is used of more than two persons, things, or groups, as, *You are among friends.* The latter is used where there are only two, as *This is between you and me.*

AND ETC. The *and* is unnecessary since *etc.* is the abbreviation of *et cetera* which means *and the rest.*

ANXIOUS, EAGER. While both words imply *interest,* the former carries the added implication of *worry,* as *He is anxious about your health;* but *He is eager to learn new things.*

ANY. Do not use for *at all* as *He has not played any this game.* When comparing an object with another in the same class, use *any other:* "I like roast beef better than *any other* meat."

ANYHOW. Anyway is to be preferred as an adverb.

ANYPLACE, EVERY PLACE, NO PLACE, SOMEPLACE. These are colloquial expressions and should not be used for *anywhere, everywhere, nowhere,* and *somewhere.*

APT, LIABLE, LIKELY. Care should be exercised in the use of these words. *Apt* means *suitable; liable* implies *damage, danger, expense; likely* means *probable, suitable.*

Wrong: He is liable to go.
Right: He is likely to go.
Or: It is likely that he will go.

APPROPRIATE. *To appropriate* means *to set apart for a special purpose.* Do not use for *take.*

AROUND. Do not use for *about* in the sense of *nearly.*

AS . . . AS, SO . . . AS. Use the latter in negative comparisons: "Jane is not *so* tall *as* Mary."

ASCENT, ASSENT. The former means an *upward slope, a climb;* the latter, *consent.*

AT. Vulgar in *Where do you work at? Where* means *at what place.*

AUTO. A colloquialism for automobile and should not be used in formal writing.

AWFUL, AWFULLY. Used only to express profound fear or reverence. Never use in the sense of *very.*

B

BAD, BADLY. The former is an adjective and is properly used with verbs relating to the senses of seeing, feeling, smelling, etc.; the latter is an adverb. Thus, *I feel bad* means I feel ill; but as an adverb, *He limped badly.*

BALANCE. Do not use to indicate *remainder* except in a financial sense.

BEING AS, BEING THAT. Do not use for *since, because.*

BELONG TO BE. Do not use for *should be, ought to be.*

BESIDE, BESIDES. Modern usage confines the former to giving the idea of *by the side of* and the latter to *in addition to, moreover.*

BIANNUAL, BIENNIAL. The former means *twice a year;* the latter, *once in two years.*

BLAME IT ON. Do not use for *blame* (*some one*) *for.*

BOGUS. Slang. Say *counterfeit,* or *false.*

BOTH ALIKE. . Omit *both,* "They are *alike.*"

BRAINY. A colloquialism for *intelligent.*

BUNCH. Colloquial for *a group of people.*

BUSINESS. Do not use for *right,* as "He has no *right* (not *business*) to go there."

BUT THAT, BUT WHAT. *But that* means *except that:* "I have no doubt *that* I will go (not *but that*)." *But what* is a colloquialism for *that* or *but that.* Correctly used in a sentence such as "I will do nothing *but what* I want to do," since *but what* means *except what.*

C

CALCULATE. Use only in a mathematical sense and not in the sense of *think* or *suppose.*

CAN, MAY. The former carries the idea of *ability;* the latter of *permission.*

CANNOT HELP BUT. Two idioms are confused, *can but* and *cannot help. Help* should be followed by a gerund: "He cannot help *liking* them."

CAN'T HARDLY. Do not use for *can hardly.*

CAN'T SEEM TO. Do not use for *seem not to* or *seem unable to.*

CAPACITY. Do not use for *ability.*

CAPITAL, CAPITOL. The former refers to the city, the latter to the building.

CASE. Commonly used indiscriminately in place of *instance, condition, situation, contingency,* etc. Better usage often dictates the choice of the more specific word.

CENSER, CENSOR, CENSURE. The first refers to a *vessel for burning incense,* the second refers to a person who approves or withholds, and the third to *condemnation.*

CHARACTERISTIC. Frequently used vaguely. It means *that which pertains to or indicates the character,* as "Dignity is one of the *characteristics* of a well-bred person."

CLAIM. Should not be used in the sense of *say, assert, maintain.* Its specific meaning is *to demand as a right* (usually in a legal sense).

Loose: He claims he saw it happen.
Better: He says that he saw it happen.

CLEVER. Commonly used for *agreeable, good-natured, witty.* Use the more specific word.

COINCIDENCE. Means *the occurring of two or more events.* Do not use of a single event.

COMMON, MUTUAL. The former means *belonging to two or more persons;* the latter means *reciprocal* or *interchangeable.* Do not confuse.

COMPARE TO, WITH. Use the former to imply *rivaling,* the latter, and more formal expression, to liken two objects of real or supposed resemblance. Thus, one would say, "*Compared to* the sun the earth is small, but some of the other planets *compare* favorably in size *with* the sun."

COMPLEMENT, COMPLIMENT. The former means *that which completes a thing* or *that which is complete;* the latter, *an expression of praise or delicate flattery.* Do not confuse.

CONSCIOUS, CONSCIENCE. Sometimes confused. The former means *aware;* the latter refers to moral sensibility. Thus, one may be *conscious* of the distinction between good and evil, but it is one's *conscience* that decides whether he shall do good or evil.

CONSIDERABLE. Sometimes incorrectly used for *considerably,* for *much,* or for *a great deal of.*

CONTINUAL, CONTINUOUS. Frequently confused. The former means *in rapid succession;* the latter, *without cessation.*

CONTRARY. Should not be used for *perverse.*

CONTRAST FROM. Incorrectly used for *contrast to* or *contrast with.*

CORPORAL, CORPOREAL. The former means *relating to the body as opposed to the mind;* the latter, *pertaining to matter or a material body.*

CORRESPOND TO, WITH. The former means *to be in accord* or *harmony,* as "The part that I have *corresponds to* the part that you have." The latter means *to exchange* letters as "I *correspond* regularly *with* Mr. Jones."

COULD OF. A vulgar corruption that should never be used for *could have.* This applies also to *had of, may of, might of, should of,* etc.

COUNCIL, COUNSEL, CONSUL. The first, *a deliberative body,* the second, *advice,* or *to give advice,* the third, *a commercial representative of a foreign government.*

COUPLE. Use only to indicate two persons or objects connected or linked in some way.

CREDIBLE, CREDITABLE. The former means *believable;* the latter, *praiseworthy.*

CROWD. Sanctioned by colloquial usage in the sense of a *social group* or *clique,* but should be avoided in formal writing.

CUNNING. Means *crafty, sly, designing.* Do not use for *attractive, pleasing.*

CURRANT, CURRENT. The former, *a berry;* the latter, *that which is passing.*

CUSTOM, HABIT. Communities, social groups, and institutions have customs, but individuals have habits. Thus, "It is the *custom* of this academy to make an annual award for outstanding research in chemistry"; but "I am in the *habit* of brushing my teeth twice daily."

D

DATA. The plural of *datum.* Say "data are."

DATE. Colloquially acceptable for an *appointment* or *social engagement,* but should not be used to indicate the person dated.

DEAL. A colloquialism for *transaction, bargain.*

DEFINITELY, DEFINITIVELY. The former means *precisely, with assurance;* the latter, *finally, conclusively, with exactness.*

DELIVER. It is better to say "He *gave* a lecture," "He *made* an oration."

DEMISE. Do not use for *death.* The word means *the passing of some authority, distinction, or privilege to another, perhaps by death.*

DEPOT. Means *warehouse, storage place.* May be used to indicate a freight warehouse but not a building for railway passengers. Say *station.*

DEPRECATORY, DEPRECIATORY. The former

means *apologetic;* the latter, *tending to depreciate.* Do not confuse.

DETRACT, DISTRACT. The former means *to take away from;* the latter, *to bewilder, harass mentally.*

DIALECTAL, DIALECTICAL. The former means *characteristic of a dialect;* the latter, *pertaining to dialectics.*

DIE. Say *die of* not *die with.*

Wrong: He died with a heart attack.
Right: He died of a heart attack.

DIFFER FROM, WITH. Use the former to express *unlikeness,* as "These two objects *differ from* each other only in color." The latter indicates a *disagreement of opinion,* as "I *differ with* you on that point."

DISEASED, DECEASED. The former, *afflicted with a disease;* the latter, *dead.*

DISINTERESTED. Frequently misused for *uninterested. Disinterested* means *without self-interest; uninterested* means *lacking interest.*

DISTINCTLY, DISTINCTIVELY. The former means *plainly;* the latter, *in a way to distinguish one thing from another.*

DOESN'T, DON'T. The former is the contraction of *does not;* the latter is the contraction of *do not.* Say "*He doesn't*" not "*He don't*"; "*They don't,*" not "*They doesn't.*"

DONE. Never use for *did.* "He *did* the work," not "He *done* the work."

DOUBT. This word is always followed by *whether* when uncertainty of choice is to be indicated, as "I doubt *whether* he did that." It is followed by *that* when a strong negative probability is to be expressed, as "I doubt *that* he did it."

DOVE. *Dived,* not *dove,* should be used as the past tense of *dive.*

DUAL, DUEL. The former, *composed of two;* the latter, *a combat between two persons.*

DUE TO. This is an adjective phrase and should not be used to modify a verb, as in, "I was late *due to* the heavy snow." Say, "I was late *because of* the heavy snow."

E

EACH OTHER, ONE ANOTHER. Use the former when referring to two; the latter when referring to more than two.

ECONOMIC, ECONOMICAL. The former refers to *the science of economics;* the latter to *saving, frugality.*

EFFICACY, EFFICIENCY. The former means *power to produce effects;* the latter, *dispatch with which such effects are produced.* Thus, "Because of their belief in the *efficacy* of prayer Roman legions always sought the blessings of the gods before entering a battle, but it was upon the superior discipline and general *efficiency* of their troops that the Romans relied for victory."

EGOISM, EGOTISM. These terms are alike in implying self-interest, but the latter suggests offensive exaltation of self.

EITHER, BOTH, EACH. *Either* should be used only to indicate one or the other of two; *both* means *the one and the other, two together; each* refers to one of a number considered individually.

ELEGANT. Means notable for *neatness, propriety,* and *refinement.* It should not be used for *good, enjoyable, pleasant.*

ELEMENT, FACTOR, PHASE. Frequently used vaguely. *Element* means *a constituent principle, essential part; factor* means *an agency that contributes to a result; phase* means *one stage in the development of a thing.*

EMIGRATE, IMMIGRATE. The former means *to go out of a country or place;* the latter, *to go into a country or place.*

EMINENT, IMMANENT, IMMINENT. The first, *distinguished;* the second, *indwelling;* the third, *impending.*

ENTHUSE. A vulgarism for the phrases, *to become enthusiastic, to rouse enthusiasm,* etc.

EUPHEMISM, EUPHUISM. The former applies to a delicate word or expression substituted for an indelicate or offensive word or expression; the latter refers to an affected use of words or language.

EXPECT. Incorrectly used for *suppose, imagine, suspect.* It means *to look forward to.*

Wrong: I *expect* so.
Right: I *imagine* so.
Right: I *expect* to go to Florida.

EXTANT, EXTENT. The former means *not destroyed or lost;* the latter, *measure.*

EXTRA. Incorrectly used for *unusually.*

Wrong: This flour is ground *extra* fine.
Right: This flour is ground *unusually* fine.

F

FAKER, FAKIR. The former means *a swindler, one who fakes;* the latter, *a Mohammedan ascetic or mendicant priest.*

FARTHER, FURTHER. Use *farther* to indicate *greater distance or remoteness* and *further* to express *moreover, in addition to.*

FELLOW. Colloquial for *man, person, sweetheart.*

FEWER, LESS. In modern usage *fewer* is used with reference to *number; less* is used with reference to *quantity* or *degree.* Say "*fewer* people," not "*less* people."

FIRSTLY. Prefer *first* with reference to items in a series. *Secondly, thirdly,* etc. are acceptable but *second, third,* etc. are rapidly displacing the longer terms.

FIX. This word means *to make fast, secure, set or place firmly.* Do not use in the sense of *repair, mend.* The word is also used colloquially in the sense of *condition, predicament, situation.*

Colloq.: He is in a *bad fix.*
Better: He is in a *serious predicament.*

FOREGO, FORGO. The former means *to go before, precede;* the latter, *to abstain from.*

FORMER, LATTER. Used with reference to two persons or things previously mentioned.

FORMERLY, FORMALLY. The first means *at a former time;* the second, *in a formal manner.*

FUNNY. Means *laugh-provoking, droll, comical.* Do not use in the sense of *queer, odd, remarkable.*

G

GENTLEMAN, LADY. Use to describe only persons of good breeding.

GET. Do not use for *be, be able to, may, come, become.*

GOOD, WELL. *Good* is an adjective. Do not use as an adverb: "He plays the piano *well* (not *good*)."

GOT. Means *obtained, secured.* Unnecessary in the sense of having: "Have you a bicycle? (not *got*)." In the sense of *must* it is colloquial.

Colloq.: I *have got* to go.
Better: I *must* go.

GOTTEN. An older form of the past participle of *get.*

GUERRILLA, GORILLA. The former refers to *irregular warfare* or one who participates in it; the latter, *an ape.*

GUESS. Means *conjecture, hit upon at random.* Do not use in the sense of *think, suppose.*

H

HAD HAVE. A vulgarism for *had:* "I wish I *had* gone (not *had have*)."

HAD OUGHT. Never use in speech or writing.

Wrong: I *had ought* to do that.
Right: I *ought* to have done that.
Or: I *ought* to do that.

HEALTHY, HEALTHFUL. Frequently confused. *Healthy* means *possessed of health; healthful* means *health giving.* Thus, "He has a *healthy* appearance," but "This city has a *healthful* climate."

HEAPS, HEAP. Do not use for *much, a great deal, many.*

HOME, TO HOME. Say "He was not *at* home (not *home*, or *to home*)."

HOMEY. A provincialism for *homelike.*

HONORABLE, REVEREND. Both should be written in full, preceded by *the* and followed by the full name: "The Honorable George Smith"; "The Reverend Thomas Matthews," or "The Reverend Mr. Matthews."

HOW COME? A vulgarism for *why.*

HUNG. One form of the past tense of *hang.* When speaking of the death penalty use *hanged* in preference to *hung.*

HYPOCRITICAL, HYPERCRITICAL. The former means *deceitful;* the latter, *excessively critical.*

I

IF. *Whether* is preferred after verbs of *seeing, learning, doubting, asking,* etc.

Right: I doubt *if* I shall go.
Preferable: I doubt *whether* I shall go.

ILLEGIBLE, UNREADABLE. The former means *difficult to read;* the latter, *not suitable for reading.*

IN, INTO. *In* means *within; into* refers to the act of entering or motion toward, as "He was *in* the room," but "He walked *into* the room."

IN BACK OF. Do not use for *behind, at the back of.*

INCREDIBLE, INCREDULOUS. The former has the meaning of *unbelievable;* the latter, *skeptical.*

INDICT, INDITE. The first means *charge with a crime;* the second, *to write.*

INFER, IMPLY. Frequently confused. *Infer* means *to derive by induction or deduction; imply* means *to express indirectly, insinuate.*

INFERIOR. Say *inferior to* and not *inferior than.*

INGENIOUS, INGENUOUS. The former means *having skill, intelligent;* the latter, *frank, candid,* or (sometimes) *naive.*

INSIDE OF. The *of* is unnecessary.

INTERSTATE, INTRASTATE. The former means *between states;* the latter, *within a state.*

INVITE. This is a verb and should never be used as a noun.

IT'S, ITS. The former is the contraction of *it is;* the latter expresses possession.

K

KIND OF A, SORT OF A. Omit *a. Kind of, sort of* is also used colloquially in the sense of *rather, somewhat, somehow.*

Colloq.: His wit is *sort of* dull.
Preferable: His wit is *rather* dull.

L

LAST, LATEST. Use *last* to indicate *definite finality* and *latest* to indicate *most recent but not necessarily final.*

LATER, LATTER. The former means *after something else in point of time;* the latter means *the second of two things previously mentioned.*

LAUNDERED. Not *laundried.*

LAY, LIE. *Lie* is an intransitive verb and means *to recline; lay* is a transitive verb and means *to put down.* The principal parts of these verbs are:

lie	lay	lain
lay	laid	laid

Right: *Lie* down and rest a bit.
Right: *Lay* the book on the table.

LEAVE, LET. Do not use *leave* for *let* as in the sentence "*Let* (not *leave*) them go."

LIKE, AS. *Like* should not introduce a subject and verb. Say "He acted *as if* (not *like*) he had never heard of the subject."

LIKE TO HAVE. Do not use in the sense of *almost, come near to*.

LOAN. Except when referring to a financial transaction do not use as a verb: "*Lend* (not *loan*) me the book."

LOSE, LOOSE. Frequently confused. *Lose* means *cease to have in possession; loose* means *not tight, to release*.

LOSE OUT, WIN OUT. Used in sports columns of newspapers, but should be avoided in all other writing.

LOT, LOTS OF. Do not use for *many* or *much*.

LOVELY. Has the meaning of *inspiring with love, lovable*, and should not be used loosely in the sense of *pleasant, delightful, interesting*, etc.

LUXURIANT, LUXURIOUS. The former means *superabundant in growth, profuse;* the latter, *costly indulgence in pleasures of the senses*.

M

MAD. Frequently misused for *angry*. The word means *insane*.

MAGNIFICENT. Overworked as a substitute for *excellent, good*, etc.

MATTER. Used vaguely for *subject, question, trouble, request*. Choose the more specific word.

MAY BE, MAYBE. The former is a verb; the latter, an adverb, meaning *perhaps*.

MEAN. Do not use for *irritable, vicious, ill-tempered, unkind*.

MESSRS., MISS, MR., MRS. These titles should never be used alone but must always be followed by the surname.

MIGHT OF. A vulgar corruption of *might have*.

MIGHTY. Do not use in the sense of *very*.

MOST, ALMOST. Do not use the former, which is the superlative of *much* or *many*, for the latter which is an adverb. "We went there *almost* (not *most*) every day."

N

NICE. Means *fastidious, precise, delicate*. Do not use for *pleasant, kind, admirable*.

NOHOW. A vulgarism. Say *anyhow, by no means*.

NOT A ONE. A colloquialism for *no one, not one*.

NOWHERE NEAR. Prefer *not nearly*.

NOWHERES. Preferable without the *s*.

O

OBSERVANCE, OBSERVATION. The former means *performance of rites;* the latter, *the act of observing*.

OFF OF, OFF FROM. The *of* and *from* are superfluous.

ON. Superfluous in such expressions as *continue on, later on*, etc.

OR. Should not be used with *neither*. Use *nor*.

ORAL, VERBAL. *Oral* means *by mouth;* verbal means *by word*.

ORDNANCE, ORDINANCE. The first means *artillery;* the second, *law* or *statute*.

OUT. Superfluous in such expressions as *lose out, win out*, etc.

OUT LOUD. Do not use for *aloud*.

OUTSIDE OF. Do not use for *except* or *aside from*.

OVER WITH. The *with* is superfluous.
Wrong: The contest is *over with*.
Right: The contest is *over*.

P

PAIR, SET. These are singulars, not plurals.

Right: One *pair* of shoes.
Wrong: Two *pair* of shoes.
Right: Two *pairs* of shoes.

PARTY, PERSON, INDIVIDUAL. *Party* refers to a group and, except in a purely legal sense, should never be used to designate a single person. *Individual* refers to a particular being. In all other cases use *person, man, woman*, etc.

PECUNIARY, FINANCIAL. The former refers to money; the latter, to scientific management of monetary affairs.

PEEVE. Do not use for *annoy, vex*, or *irritate*. The word means *to make resentful*.

PER CENT, PERCENTAGE. The former should be used only after a numeral. The latter, a noun, should be used to indicate a specified quantity.

PERSECUTE, PROSECUTE. The first means *to harass vengefully;* the second, *bring suit against at law*.

PHENOMENA. The plural of *phenomenon*. Do not use for *events, facts, occurrences*.

PHENOMENAL. Do not use for *remarkable*.

PHONE. Colloquial for *telephone*. Should be avoided.

PIECE. Do not use in the sense of *distance* as "He lives up the road *a piece*."

PLAN ON GOING. Say *plan to go*.

POORLY. Do not use for *ill*.

PRACTICAL, PRACTICABLE. The former means *useful;* the latter, *feasible, possible*.

PRINCIPAL, PRINCIPLE. The former means *occupying first place or rank;* the latter, *fundamental truth or law*.

PROPHECY, PROPHESY. The former means *a prediction;* the latter, *to predict*.

PROPOSAL, PROPOSITION. The former refers to *that which is brought forward for consideration;* the latter, *to an offer of terms*.

PROPOSE, PURPOSE. The former means *to bring forward* or *offer for consideration;* the latter, *design, end, to have an intention*.

PROVEN. Use *proved* as the past participle of *prove*.

PUT IN, PUT OVER, PUT ACROSS. Colloquial expressions, the first having the meaning of *devote, spend;* the last two, the meaning *to succeed despite opposition.* These colloquialisms should be avoided.

Q

QUALITY. Frequently used vaguely. The word means *attribute, peculiar power or property.*

QUITE. Do not use in the sense of *almost.* The word means *wholly, completely.*

QUITE A FEW. Colloquial for *a good many.*

Colloq.: He has *quite a few* friends.
Preferred: He has *a good many* friends.

R

RAISE, RISE. The former is a transitive verb and means *to cause to rise;* the latter is an intransitive verb and means *to ascend.* The principal parts of these verbs are:

raise	raised	raised
rise	rose	risen

Right: I *raise* the window.
Right: I *rise* at six o'clock.

Raise in the sense of *to rear, to bring up children* is a colloquialism to be avoided.

RARELY EVER. Use *rarely* alone or *hardly ever.*

REACTION. Do not use for *response, opinion, attitude.*

REAL. Do not use for *very.*

REASON IS BECAUSE. Use *that* instead of *because.*

RECKON. Means to *compute, count.* Do not use for *think, suppose.*

REMEMBER OF. *Of* is superfluous.

REPEAT AGAIN. *Again* is superfluous.

RESEARCH. Means *investigation.* Do not say "*research* work."

RESPECTFULLY, RESPECTIVELY. The former means *with respect;* the latter refers to a particular person or thing.

RIGHT. Colloquial Southern usage for *very. Right along, right away, right off* are colloquial for *continuously, immediately, at once.*

ROUT, ROUTE. The first means *put to flight, scoop out;* the second, *to send by a certain way.*

RUN. Do not use in the sense of *conduct, amount to.*

Wrong: He *runs* a men's shop.
Right: He *operates* a men's shop.
Wrong: What's the bill *run to?*
Right: How much does the bill *amount to?*

S

SAME, SAID, SUCH. Avoid the use of these words as pronouns. Prefer *it, this, that.*

SATISFIED. Do not use in the sense of *convinced, sure.*

SCARCELY. Never follow with *than* or a negative.

SELDOM EVER. Say *seldom if ever, seldom or never.*

SELF-CONFESS. The word *self* is superfluous. Obviously our misdeeds cannot be confessed by another.

SENSUOUS, SENSUAL. The first means *appealing to the senses;* the second, *pertaining to the grosser senses.*

SET, SIT. The former is a transitive verb and means *to place* or *put in position;* the latter is an intransitive verb and refers to the act of being in a sitting position. The principal parts of these verbs are:

set	set	set
sit	sat	sat

Right: The maid *set* the table.
Right: I *sat* in the balcony.

SEVERAL. Means *more than two* but not *many.*

SHALL, WILL. To express simple futurity use *shall* for the first person and *will* for the second or third. To express determination or promise use *will* for the first person and *shall* for the second or third.

SHAPE. Do not use for *condition, state, manner.*

SHOULD OF. A vulgar corruption of *should have.*

SHOW. Do not use for *opportunity.* Also a colloquialism for a *movie, drama, performance,* etc.

SICK, ILL. The former connotes *nausea.* Use the latter except in this sense.

SIGHT. Do not use for *much, a great many.*

SIMPLY. Means *in a simple manner.* Do not use for *really, very.*

SIZE UP. Slang for *estimate.*

SMART. Do not use for *intelligent.*

SOME. Do not use as an adverb. Say *somewhat.*

SOMEWAY. Prefer *somehow.*

SPECIE, SPECIES. The former refers to money; the latter means *kind* or *class* and is both singular and plural.

STATIONARY, STATIONERY. Frequently confused. The former means *fixed, not moving;* the latter refers to writing materials and their accessories.

Right: The star Polaris is *stationary.*
Right: We buy our letterheads at the *stationery* shop.

STATUE, STATURE, STATUTE. A *statue* is a *sculptured figure; stature* means *height; statute* means *law.*

STOP. Use *stay:* "Where did you *stay* (not *stop*) in Philadelphia?"

STRATA. Plural of *stratum* and should be used only with plural form of the verb.

SUPERIOR, BETTER. Do not confuse. The former means *higher or above in place, rank, excellence,* etc.; the latter, *having good qualities in greater degree.*

SUPERIOR THAN. Say *superior to.*

SURE AND, TRY AND. Say *sure to, try to.*

SURVIVE. Do not use for *live,* or *persist.*

SUSPICION. This is a noun and should never be used as a verb.

Wrong: I *suspicion* him of the theft.
Right: I *suspect* him of the theft.
Or: I place him under *suspicion* of theft.

T

TASTE OF. *Of* is superfluous in such expressions as "She *tasted* of it."

TASTY. Colloquial for *agreeable, attractive, of good taste, palatable.*

TERMED AS. *As* is superfluous.

TERRIBLE, TERRIBLY. These words imply *fear, awe, terror.* Do not use for *extremely, very.*

THAT WAY. Say *in that way:* "You must do it *in that way.*"

THIS HERE, THAT THERE, THESE HERE, THOSE THERE. The usage of *here* and *there* with these demonstratives is vulgar.

Vulgar: *This here* book is good.
Right: *This* book is good.
Vulgar: *That there* boy.
Right: *That* boy.

THROUGH. In the sense of *finished* it should be avoided.

Wrong: He is *through* with his music practice for today.
Right: He has *finished* his music practice for today.

TO MY KNOWLEDGE. Do not use for *in my opinion.*

TRANSPIRE. Means *to become known.* Do not use for *happen, occur.*

TWO FIRST, TWO LAST. Illogical expressions. Say first two, last two.

TYPE. Overworked for *kind, sort, variety.*

U

UGLY. Means *offensive to the eye.* Do not use for *ill-tempered, vicious.*

UMPIRE, EMPIRE. The first means *an arbiter;* the second, *a realm governed by an emperor.*

UNIQUE. Means *sole, unequaled.* Do not use for *odd, rare, unusual.*

UNMORAL, IMMORAL. *Unmoral* means *not involving morality; immoral* means *not moral.*

UP. Do not use with *divide, end, finish, fold, open, rest, settle,* or *write.* Correctly used with *dig, double, lay, plow, wake, hang,* etc.

UP-TO-DATE. Correct as an adverb. Prefer *modern* as an adjective.

V

VENAL, VENIAL. The former means *mercenary;* the latter, *pardonable.*

VOCATION, AVOCATION. The first means *a profession or calling;* the second, *a secondary interest.*

VULGAR. Do not use for *immodest,* or *indecent.* The word means both *common* and *unrefined* but has no relation to indecency.

W

WAIT ON. Means *to serve.* Do not use for *wait for.*

WAYS. Say *way:* "He lives a short *way* up the road."

WEIRD. Means *uncanny.* Do not use for *odd, strange.*

WHERE. Do not use for *that:* "I saw in the evening paper *that* you were chosen."

WHICH. Use *who* or *that* when referring to persons; use *which* when referring to animals or inanimate objects.

WHIP. The word means *to beat with a whip.* Do not use for *chastise,* or *defeat.*

WHOSE. This is the possessive case of *who,* not of *which.*

WILL, SHALL. See SHALL, WILL.

WIRE. A colloquialism for *telegraph, telegram.*

WITHOUT. Do not use for *unless.*

WOODS. Say *a wood.*

WORST KIND, SORT, WAY. Do not use for *very much.*

WOULD BETTER. Prefer *had better.*

WOULD OF. A vulgar corruption of *would have.*

WOULD RATHER. Say *had rather.*

WRITE UP. Slang for a *report, description, account.*

WRITER, THE WRITER. Affectation for *I.*

Y

YOU WAS. Say *you were.*

Representation of Numbers

1. Spell out every number of less than three digits when used in ordinary text matter.

The price was two dollars.
There were eighty-two boys and eighteen girls.

2. Where similar numbers occur in groups, do not use figures for some and spell out others. If the largest contains three or more digits, use figures for all.

The number of bushels produced during June, July, and August was 42, 89, and 127 respectively.

3. Use figures to express dimensions, degrees, distances, weights, measures, sums of money, etc., in mathematical or statistical text.

92 pounds 22 miles
45 caliber 16 feet
$1,000 32° F

4. Compound numerals of less than one hundred should be hyphenated.

eighty-four but fifteen hundred

5. Spell out round numbers of even units (100, 1,000, 10,000, etc.).

There were about five hundred present.
There were 550 present.

6. Do not begin a sentence with figures, even if similar figures are used elsewhere.

Two hundred and eighteen ships, 417 flags, and 86 uniforms.

7. Spell out numbers representing the time of day except when used with A.M., or P.M.

He left at eight.
The race starts at half-past two.
At 4:00 P.M. (omit *o'clock*).

8. Spell out the age of persons, places, or things.

She was twenty-six years old.
This vase is one hundred and fifty-six years old.
Chicago is more than one hundred years old.

9. Do not use *st, nd, rd, th* with the day of the month.

January 15, 1935, not January 15th, 1935.

Diction

Diction is the choice of words for the accurate, effective, and varied expression of thought and feeling in speech and writing.

While accepted usage varies from occasion to occasion, from one class of people to another, and according to differences in locality, yet logic and good taste demand the observance and practice of certain standards of good usage in formal writing and speech.

The following suggestions were formulated in accordance with these standards:

1. Do not use *archaic* or *obsolete* words.
   Archaic words are those peculiar to remote periods of time, such as *thou* for *you*, *forsooth* for *indeed*, etc.
   Obsolete words are those which have completely gone out of use. Most authorities do not condemn as obsolete any word used in a major literary work written since the Restoration (1660).

2. Do not use *provincialisms* in formal speech or writing. Such expressions, however, are permissible in conversation or informal writing.
   Provincialisms are words or expressions current in one section of a country but unknown or not used in the same sense elsewhere.
   Examples: *Varmint* for *vermin*, *cayuse* for *horse*, *calculate* for *think*, *plumb* for *completely*.

3. Never use *vulgarisms*.
   Vulgarisms are words or expressions characteristic of illiteracy.
   Examples: *Them flowers, where does he live at, to enthuse.*

4. Avoid *improprieties*.
   Improprieties are words or expressions correct in themselves but used either in an incorrect sense or in an incorrect function.

5. Do not use *colloquialisms* in formal speech or writing.
   Colloquialisms are words or expressions permissible in ordinary conversation or writing but not used in formal speech or writing.
   Examples: *Taxi, isn't, pal, backbone* for *taxicab, is not, friend, courage*.

6. Guard against affected or flowery language, too rigid adherence to bookish correctness, and a straining for accuracy which sometimes causes awkwardness.

7. Guard against *redundancy* and *tautology*.
   Redundancy is the use of grammatically superfluous words or phrases.
   Example: Come down off *of* the fence.
   Tautology is the repetition of synonymous words or expressions in close succession.
   Example: The day dawned clear and bright, *without a cloud in the sky*.

8. *Idiomatic* words and expressions are accepted as good form.
   An idiomatic word or expression is one which is peculiar to a language and sanctioned by long usage, although sometimes in violation of the rules of grammar.
   Examples: *Plan to go, at home, different from, as regards.*

9. Use words that express the exact thought or feeling you wish to convey.

In addition to their literal meaning (*denotation*) many words are possessed of color, atmosphere, and tone, all of which give to them fine shades of meaning and powers of suggestion (*connotation*) beyond those of other words having the same literal definition.

Consult your dictionary for the literal meaning of the word you wish to use. If the meaning of that particular word does not completely express your thought, or if it is weak, trite, or overworked, look it up in your thesaurus and choose from its synonyms the one most suitable to your subject, the occasion, reader, or auditor.

10. Choose words having easy and pleasant combinations of sounds.

The following suggestions will be found helpful: (a) avoid placing in close succession words that rhyme; (b) avoid the use of a too regular meter (singsong effect); (c) avoid like sounds in close succession, especially sibilants.

Remember, finally, that the monotonous repetition of certain words and phrases, the habitual use of slang, and deliberate smartness in writing or speaking are usually indicative of a lazy mind!

Every effort made toward better diction will aid mental alertness, outline ideas more sharply, and freshen and strengthen the powers of expression—all of which makes utilization of one's intelligence a keen delight.

Spelling

Misspelling is often due to mispronunciation. Learn carefully how to pronounce words and, generally speaking, the correct spelling of them will be easy.

Never write a word of which you are not certain of the spelling. Use your dictionary constantly.

General Spelling Rules.—The following rules are intended to provide a general guide to correct spelling and, though there are exceptions to them, they will be found adequate in most cases.

Suffixes.—A suffix is a letter or a syllable added at the end of a word to serve a derivative, formative, or inflectional function.

1. Words of one syllable and those accented on the last syllable if ending in one consonant preceded by one vowel, generally double the consonant when a suffix beginning with a vowel is added.

mad madder
prefer preferred

When the accent is given to a syllable other than the last, the doubling does not occur.

visit visited

When the addition of a suffix causes a shifting of the accent to a syllable other than the last, the consonant is not doubled.

prefer preference

2. In words ending with silent *e*, drop the *e* when adding a suffix beginning with a vowel.

glide gliding

When adding a suffix beginning with *a* or *o* to words ending in *ce* or *ge* retain the *e* to preserve the soft sound of the *c* or *g*.

service serviceable
courage courageous

3. In spelling words containing *ei* or *ie* remember the jingle:

Write *i* before *e*
Except after *c*
Or when sounded as *a*
As in *neighbor* and *weigh*.

relieve freight receive

4. When adding a suffix to a word ending in *y* preceded by a consonant, change the *y* to *i*.

lazy laziness

Verbs ending in *y* retain it when *ing* is added

play playing

The rule for changing *y* to *i* also applies to the forming of plurals except when the *y* is preceded by a vowel.

fly flies
play plays

Prefixes.—A prefix is a letter or syllable placed at the beginning of a word to modify its significance.

1. Words beginning with a consonant do not double that consonant when a prefix ending in a vowel is attached.

proficient *not* profficient

2. When a prefix ending with a consonant is added to a word beginning with a vowel, the consonant is not doubled.

disappoint *not* dissappoint

3. Prefixes ending with a consonant retain it when followed by a word beginning with a consonant.

addition *not* adition

Plurals

1. Nouns which do not end in *s* or *es* form their plurals by adding *s*.

bees cows
trains bricks
horses girls

2. Nouns ending with a sibilant (*s, sh, x, z*) form their plurals by adding *es*.

dresses taxes
fishes blazes

3. Nouns ending with *y* preceded by a consonant form their plurals by changing the *y* to *i* and adding *es*.

armies studies
factories follies

4. Nouns ending with *y* preceded by a vowel form their plurals by retaining the *y* and adding *s*.

plays jays
donkeys keys

5. Nouns ending in *o* preceded by a vowel form their plurals by adding *s*.

portfolios cameos
radios folios

6. Nouns ending with *o* preceded by a consonant add *s* or *es* to form the plural.

potatoes dynamos
Negroes solos
tomatoes pianos

7. The following are examples of surviving Old English irregular plurals:

geese swine
oxen sheep

8. Foreign words commonly used in the English language usually form their plurals in accordance with the language from which they were borrowed. The present tendency,

however, is to anglicize the pronunciation of the plural of such words.

alumna (feminine)
  alumnae (pronounced a-lum'ne)
alumnus (masculine)
  alumni (pronounced a-lum'ni)
basis
  bases (pronounced ba'ses)
focus
  foci (pronounced fo'si)

9. Compound nouns usually form their plurals by adding *s* or *es* to the governing word in the compound.

runners-up
daughters-in-law
courts-martial

If the compounded words are so closely associated as to form one word, the *s* or *es* is added to the end of the word.

bucketfuls
spoonfuls
basketfuls

Compound Words

1. Adjectives formed of two or more words and preceding the noun which they modify should be hyphenated.

well-known author   half-dead victim

Adjectives or adverbs in combined form should *not* be hyphenated when used *after* the word modified.

The new encyclopedia is strictly up to date.

2. When such words as *book*, *house*, *mill*, etc., are prefixed by a noun of one syllable, they form one word.

textbook	sawmill
smokehouse	cookbook

When the prefixed noun contains two syllables, use the hyphen.

sample-book	lumber-mill
power-house	powder-room

When the prefixed noun contains three or more syllables the two words are written separately.

policy book	chocolate mill
business house	etiquette book

3. Compound numerals of less than a hundred and more than twenty, when used as adjectives, should be hyphenated.

forty-seven	twenty-five
thirty-nine	fifty-six

When fractions are used as nouns, however, the hyphen is not used.

One sixth of the cotton was burned.

4. Words to which prefixes are attached are hyphenated only when such words begin with *w*, *y*, or the same vowel in which the prefix ends.

coeducation	intra-yearly
co-operation	tri-weekly
anti-idealist	pro-oceanic

5. Compound words retain the hyphen when absence of it might cause difficulty in reading or interpretation.

re-creation	recreation
twenty five-dollar bills	twenty-five dollar bills

6. The following words and phrases are written separately:

all right	good night
any one	some one
any time	some day
by and by	some way
every one	per cent

ABBREVIATIONS

Discrimination must be exercised in the use of abbreviations. Under normal circumstances do not abbreviate a word if the abbreviated form is difficult or puzzling to read.

1. Capitalize an abbreviation only if the unabbreviated word would be capitalized.

2. Titles preceding personal names should be spelled out except the following:
(a) Mr., Messrs., Mrs. before a name
(b) Esq., Sr., Jr., after a name
(c) Rev. and Hon., except in formal invitations and announcements when they are spelled out and preceded by *The*.
The Reverend Elwood Harbridge
The Honorable Harry S. Truman

3. Christian names should be spelled out except where they are abbreviated in a signature or from the author's choice.

George C. Armstrong
Geo. C. Armstrong

4. Do not abbreviate parts of geographic names except in tabular matter where space will not permit full spelling.

Port Arthur   Pt. Arthur

Note: *Saint* or *Saints* are always abbreviated when used before a name:

St. Mary's Church
SS. Peter and Paul

5. Abbreviate designations of weights and measures and symbols of measurements when these are preceded by a number.

3 yds.	6 gals.
4 hrs.	10 min.

Common Abbreviations

A. or Ans.—Answer.
A.A.A.—Agricultural Adjustment Administration.
A.A.A.G.—Acting Assistant Adjutant General.
A.A.G.—Assistant Adjutant General.
A.A.A.S.—American Association for the Advancement of Science.
A.A.P.S.—American Association for the Promotion of Science.
A.A.S.—*Academiæ Americanæ Socius*, Fellow of the American Academy (of Arts and Sciences).
A.A.S.S.—*Americanæ Antiquarianæ Societatis Socius*, Member of the American Antiquarian Society.
A.B.—Able-bodied seaman.
A.B.—*Artium Baccalaureus*, Bachelor of Arts.
A.B.C.F.M.—American Board of Commissioners for Foreign Missions.
Abl.—Ablative.
Abp.—Archbishop.
Abr.—Abridgement, or Abridged
A.B.S.—American Bible Society.
A.C.—Air Corps.
A.C.—Alternating Current.
Acad.—Academy.
Acad. Nat. Sci.—Academy of Natural Sciences.
Acc.—Accusative.
Acct.—Account.
A.C.S.—American Colonization Society.
A.D.—*Anno Domini*, in the year of the Lord.
A.D.C.—Aide-de-camp.
Adj.—Adjective.
Adj. or Adjt.—Adjutant.
Adjt. Gen.—Adjutant General.
Ad. lib.—*Ad libitum*, at pleasure.
Adm.—Admiral; Admiralty.
Admr.—Administrator.
Admx.—Administratrix.
Ad val.—*Ad valorem*, at (or on) the value.
Adv.—Adverb.
Advt.—Advertisement.
Aet.—*Aetatis*, of age; aged.
A.F.L.-C.I.O.—American Federation of Labor-Congress of Industrial Organizations.
Afr.—African.
A.G.—Adjutant General; Attorney General.
Agr.—Agriculture.
Agr. Dept.—Department of Agriculture.
A.G.S.S.—American Geographical and Statistical Society.
Agt.—Agent.
A.H.—*Anno Hegiræ*, in the year of the Hegira.
A.H.M.S.—American Home Missionary Society.
A.L.—American Legion.
Al.—Aluminum.
Ala.—Alabama.
A.L.A.—American Library Association.
Alas.—Alaska.
Alb.—Albany.
Alba.—Alberta.
Ald.—Alderman.
Alex.—Alexander.
Alf.—Alfred.
Alg.—Algebra.
Alt.—Altitude.
A.M.—*Ante meridiem*, before noon; morning.
A.M.—*Artium Magister*, Master of Arts.
A.M.A.—American Medical Association.
Am. Assn. Sci.—American Association for the Advancement of Science.
Amb.—Ambassador.
Amer.—American.
Amer. Acad.—American Academy.
A.M.E.Z.—African Methodist Episcopal Zion.
Amp.—Ampere.
Amt.—Amount.
An.—*Anno*, in the year.
An. A.C.—*Anno ante Christum*, in the year before Christ.
Anal.—Analysis.
Anat.—Anatomy.
Anc.—Ancient; Anciently.
Ang.-Sax.—Anglo-Saxon.
Anon.—Anonymous.
Ans.—Answer.
Ant., or Antiq.—Antiquities.
A.O.S.S.—*Americanæ Orientalis Societatis Socius*, Member of the American Oriental Society.
Ap.—Apostle; Appius.
Ap.—*Apud*, in writings of; as quoted by.
A.P.—Associated Press.
Apo.—Apogee.
Apoc.—Apocalypse.
Apocr.—Apocrypha.
App.—Appendix.
Apr.—April.
Apt.—Apartment.
Aq.—Water (*aqua*).
A.Q.M.—Assistant Quartermaster.
A.Q.M.G.—Assistant Quartermaster-General.
A.R.—*Anno regni*, year of the reign.
Arch.—Architect; Architecture.
Archd.—Archdeacon.
Arith.—Arithmetic.
Ariz.—Arizona.
Ark.—Arkansas.
Arr.—Arrive; Arrival.
A.R.S.S.—*Antiquariorum Regiæ Societatis Socius*, Fellow of the Royal Society of Antiquaries.
Art.—Article.
Artil.—Artillery.
A.-S.—Anglo-Saxon.
A.S., or Assist. Sec.—Assistant Secretary.
A.S.A.—American Statistical Association.
Ass., Assn.—Association.
Asst.—Assistant.
A.S.S.U.—American Sunday-School Union.
A.T.S.—American Tract Society.
Atty.—Attorney.
Atty. Gen.—Attorney General.
A.U.A.—American Unitarian Association.
A.U.C.—*Anno urbis conditæ*, or *ab urbe condita*, in the year from the building of the city (Rome).
Aug.—August.
Aust.—Austria; Austrian.
Auth. Ver., or A.V.—Authorized Version (of the Bible).
Av.—Average; Avenue.
Avdp.—Avoirdupois.
Ave.—Avenue.
Avoir.—Avoirdupois.
A.W.O.L.—Absent without leave.

B

B.—Born.
B.A.—Bachelor of Arts.
Bal.—Balance.
Bapt.—Baptist.
Bar.—Barometer.
Bart. or bt.—Baronet.
B.B.C.—British Broadcasting Corp.
Bbl.—Barrel.
B.C.—Before Christ; British Columbia.
B.C.L.—Bachelor of Civil Law.
B.D.—*Baccalaureus Divinitatis*, Bachelor of Divinity.
B.E.F.—British Expeditionary Force.
Belg.—Belgium.
Benj.—Benjamin.
Bib.—Bible; Biblical.
Biog.—Biography; Biographical.
Bldg.—Building.
B. LL.—Bachelor of Laws.
Bls.—Bales.
Blvd.—Boulevard.
B.M.—*Baccalaureus Medicinæ*, Bachelor of Medicine.
Bot.—Botany.
Bp.—Bishop.
B.P.O.E.—Benevolent and Protective Order of Elks.
Br.—British.
Braz.—Brazil; Brazilian.

Brig.—Brigade; Brigadier.
Brig. Gen.—Brigadier General.
Brit. Mus.—British Museum.
Bro.—Brother.
B.S.—Bachelor in the Sciences.
B.T.U.—British thermal unit.
Bulg.—Bulgaria.
Bush.—Bushel; Bushels.
B.W.I.—British West Indies.

C

C.—Cent.
C.—Consul.
C., or Cels.—Celsius's Scale for the thermometer.
C., or Cent.—*Centum*, a hundred; Century.
C., Ch., or Chap.—Chapter.
C.A.—Chief Accountant; Commissioner of Accounts.
C.A.A.—Civil Aeronautics Authority.
Cal.—California.
Calif.—California.
Can.—Canon.
Cant.—Canticles.
Cantab.—Of Cambridge (*Cantabrigiensis*).
Caps.—Capitals.
Capt.—Captain.
Capt.-Gen.—Captain-General.
Car.—Carat.
Card.—Cardinal.
Cash.—Cashier.
C.C.—County Commissioner; County Court.
C.C.—Cubic centimeter.
C.C.C.—Civilian Conservation Corps; Commodity Credit Corporation.
C.C.P.—Court of Common Pleas.
Cd.—Cadmium.
C.E.—Civil Engineer.
C.E.—Christian Endeavor (Young People's Society of).
Cel., or Celt.—Celtic.
Cent.—Centigrade, a scale of 100° from freezing to boiling.
Cert.—Certify.
Certif.—Certificate.
Cf.—Compare.
C.G.—Commissary General; Consul General; Coast Guard.
Ch.—Church; Chapter.
Chanc.—Chancellor.
Chap.—Chapter.
Chas.—Charles.
Chem.—Chemistry.
Chr.—Christ; Christian.
Chr.—Christopher.
Chron.—Chronicles.
Circ.—Circuit.
Cit.—Citation; Citizen.
C.J.—Chief Justice.
Cl.—Chlorine.
Clk.—Clerk.
Cm.—Centimeter.
C.M.T.C.—Citizens' Military Training Corps.
Co.—Company; County.
C.O.—Commanding officer.
C/O—Carried over; Care of.
Coch., or Cochl.—A spoonful (*cochleare*).
C.O.D.—Cash (or collect) on delivery.
C. of S.—Chief of Staff.
Col.—Colonel; Colossians.
Coll.—Collector; Colloquial; College; Collection.
Colo.—Colorado.
Com. Arr.—Committee of Arrangements.
Com.—Commerce; Committee; Commissioner; Commodore.
Com. & Nav.—Commerce and Navigation.
Comdg.—Commanding.
Comm.—Commentary.
Comp.—Compare; Comparative; Compound; Compounded.
Com. Ver.—Common Version.
Con.—*Contra*, against; in opposition.
Conch.—Conchology.
Confed.—Confederate.
Cong.—Congress.
Conj.—Conjunction.
Congl.—Congregational; Conglomerate.
Conn.—Connecticut.
Const.—Constable; Constitution.
Cor.—Corinthians.
Cor. Mem. — Corresponding Member.
Corp.—Corporal; Corporation.
Cor. Sec.—Corresponding Secretary.
C.P.—Common Pleas.
C.P.A.—Certified Public Accountant.
C.P.O.—Chief Petty Officer.
C.P.S.—*Custos Privati Sigilli*, Keeper of the Privy Seal.
Cr.—Chromium.
Cr.—Creditor; Credit.
C.R.—*Custos Rotulorum*, Keeper of the Rolls.
C.S.—Court of Sessions.
C.S.—Christian Science.
C.S.A.—Confederate States of America; Confederate States Army.
C.S.C.—Civil Service Commission.
C.S.D.—Doctor of Christian Science.
Csk.—Cask.
C.S.N.—Confederate States Navy.
Ct.—Court.
Cts.—Cents.
Cu.—Cubic.
Cur.—Currency.
C.W.—Canada West.
Cwt.—Hundredweight.
Cyc.—Cyclopedia.
C.Z.—Canal Zone.

D

D.—Died.
D.—Five Hundred.
D.—Penny; Pence (*denarius*).
D.A.—District Attorney.
Dan.—Daniel; Danish.
Dat.—Dative.
D.B. or Domesd. B.—Domesday-Book.
D.C.—District of Columbia.
D.C. Direct Current.
D.C.L.—Doctor of Civil Law.
D.C.S.—Deputy Clerk of Sessions.
D.D.—*Divinitatis Doctor*, Doctor of Divinity.
D.D.S.—Doctor of Dental Surgery.
Dea.—Deacon.
Dec.—December; Declination.
Dec. of Ind.—Declaration of Independence.
Def.—Definition.
Def., Deft.—Defendant.
Deg.—Degree; Degrees.
Del.—Delaware.
Del.—Delegate.
Dem.—Democrat; Democratic.
Dep.—Deputy.
Dept.—Department.
Deut.—Deuteronomy.
D.F.—Defender of the Faith.
D.H.—Dead-head.
Diam.—Diameter.
Dict.—Dictionary; Dictator.
Dim.—Diminutive.
Disc.—Discount.
Diss.—Dissertation.
Dist.—District.
Dist. Atty.—District Attorney.
Div.—Division.
D.L.O.—Dead-Letter Office.
D.M.—Doctor of Music.
Do.—*Ditto*, the same.
Doc.—Document.
Dols.—Dollars.
D.O.M.—*Deo optimo maximo*, to God, the best, the greatest.
Doz.—Dozen.
Dpt.—Department.
Dr.—Debtor; Doctor.
Dr.—Drams; Drachms.
D.Sc.—Doctor of Science.
D.S.M.—Distinguished Service Medal.
D.S.T.—Daylight Saving Time.
D.S.O.—Distinguished Service Order.
Duo.—Duodecimo, twelve folds.
D.V.—*Deo volente*, God willing.
Dwt.—Pennyweight.
Dyn.—Dynamics.

E

E.—East.
Eccl.—Ecclesiastes.
Ecclus.—Ecclesiasticus.
E.D.—Eastern District.

Ed.—Editor; Edition.
Edm.—Edmund.
Edw.—Edward.
E.E.—Electrical Engineer.
E.G.—*Exempli gratia*, for example.
E.I.—East Indies or East India.
E.I.B.—Export-Import Bank.
Eliz.—Elizabeth.
E. Lon.—East longitude.
E.M.—Mining Engineer.
Emp.—Emperor; Empress.
Encyc.—Encyclopedia.
E.N.E.—East-northeast.
Eng.—England; English.
Eng. Dept.—Department of Engineers.
Ent., Entom.—Entomology.
Env. Ext.—Envoy Extraordinary.
E.o.w.—Every other week.
Ep.—Epistle.
Eph.—Ephesians; Ephraim.
Epis.—Episcopal.
E.R.A.—Emergency Relief Administration.
Esd.—Esdras.
E.S.E.—East-southeast.
Esq.—Esquire.
Esth.—Esther.
E.T.—English Translation.
Et. al.—*Et alii*, and others.
Etc., or &c.—*Et cæteri, et cæteræ, et cætera*, and others; and so forth.
Eth.—Ethiopic; Ethiopian.
Et. seq.—*Et sequentia*, and what follows.
Etym.—Etymology.
E.U.—Evangelical Union.
Ex.—Example.
Ex.—Exodus.
Exc.—Excellency; Exception.
Exch.—Exchequer; Exchange.
Ex. Doc.—Executive Document.
Exec. Com.—Executive Committee.
Execx.—Executrix.
Ex. gr.—For example (*exempli gratia*).
Exod.—Exodus.
Exr. or Exec.—Executor.
Ez.—Ezra.
Ezek.—Ezekiel.

F

F. and A.M.—Free and Accepted Masons.
F., or Fahr.—Fahrenheit (thermometer).
F.A.S.—Fellow of the Antiquarian Society.
F.B.I.—Federal Bureau of Investigation.
F.B.S.—Fellow of the Botanical Society.
F.C.—Free Church of Scotland.
Fcap. or fcp.—Foolscap.
F.C.C.—Federal Communications Commission.
F.C.S.—Fellow of the Chemical Society.
F.D.I.C.—Federal Deposit Insurance Corporation.
Feb.—February.
Fec.—*Fecit*, he did it.
Fed.—Federal.
Fem.—Feminine.
Ff.—Following.
F.F.M.C.—Federal Farm Mortgage Corporation.
F.F.V.—First Families of Virginia.
F.G.S.—Fellow of the Geological Society.
F.H.A.—Federal Housing Administration.
F.H.S.—Fellow of the Horticultural Society.
Fig.—Figure.
Fin.—Finland.
Finn.—Finnish.
Fir.—Firkin.
Fla.—Florida.
F.L.B.—Federal Land Banks.
F.M.—Field Marshal.
F.O.—Field Officer; Foreign Office.
F.O.B.—Free on Board.
F.O.E.—Fraternal Order of Eagles.
Fol.—Folio.
For.—Foreign.
F.P.C.—Federal Power Commission.
F.P.S.—Fellow of the Philological Society.
Fr.—France; French.
Fr.—From.
F.R.A.S.—Fellow of the Royal Astronomical Society.
F.R.B.—Federal Reserve Board.
Fred.—Frederick.
Fr. E.—French ells.
Fr., Frs.—Franc; francs.
F.R.G.S.—Fellow of the Royal Geographical Society.
Fri.—Friday.
F.R.S.—Fellow of the Royal Society.
F.S.A.—Fellow of the Society of Arts, or of Antiquaries.
F.S.S.—Fellow of the Statistical Society.
Ft.—Foot; Feet; Fort.
F.T.C.—Federal Trade Commission.
Fth.—Fathom.
Fur.—Furlong.

G

Ga.—Georgia.
G.A.—General Assembly.
Gal.—Galatians; Gallon.
G.A.R.—Grand Army of the Republic.
G.B.—Great Britain.
G.B. & I.—Great Britain and Ireland.
G.C.—Grand Chapter; Grand Conductor.
G.D.—Grand Duke; Grand Duchess.
G.E.—Grand Encampment.
Gen.—Genesis; General.
Gen.—Genus; Genera; Genealogy.
Gent.—Gentleman.
Geo.—George.
Geog.—Geography.
Geol.—Geology.
Geom.—Geometry.
Ger.—German; Germany.
G.H.Q.—General Headquarters.
Gl.—*Glossa*, a gloss.
G.L.—Grand Lodge.
G.M.—Grand Master.
G.O.—General Order.
G.O.P.—Grand Old Party, name for Republican Party.
Goth.—Gothic.
Gov.—Governor.
Gov. Gen.—Governor General.
Govt.—Government.
G.P.O.—General Post Office.
G.R.—*Georgius Rex*, King George.
Gr.—Greek; Gross.
Gr., Grs.—Grain; Grains.
Grad.—Graduated.
Gram.—Grammar.
Gro.—Gross.
G.S.—Grand Secretary; Grand Sentinel; Grand Scribe.
G.T.—Good Templars; Grand Tyler.

H

H.A.—*Hoc anno*, this year.
Hab.—Habakkuk.
Hab. corp.—*Habeas corpus*, you may have the body.
Hag.—Haggai.
Hants.—Hampshire.
H.C.L.—High Cost of Living.
Hdqrs.—Headquarters.
H.E.—*Hoc est*, that is, or this is.
Heb.—Hebrews.
Her.—Heraldry.
Hg.—*Hydrargyrum*, mercury.
H.H.—His or Her Highness; His Holiness (the Pope).
Hhd.—Hogshead.
H.I.—Hawaiian Islands.
Hind.—Hindu; Hindustan; Hindustanee.
Hist.—History.
H.J.S.—*Hic jacet sepultus*, here lies buried.
H.M.—His Majesty.
H.M.P.—*Hoc monumentum posuit*, erected this monument.
H.M.S.—His or Her Majesty's Ship.
H.O.L.C.—Home Owners' Loan Corporation.
Holl.—Holland.
Hon.—Honorable.
Hort.—Horticulture.
Hos.—Hosea.

H.P.—Horsepower; Half pay.
Hr.—Hour.
H.R.—House of Representatives.
H.R.E.—Holy Roman Empire.
H.R.H.—His Royal Highness.
H.R.I.P.—*Hic requiescat in pace*, here rests in peace.
H.S.—*Hic situs*, here lies.
H.T.—*Hoc titulum*, this title; *hoc tituli*, in or under this title.
Hund.—Hundred.
Hung.—Hungarian.
Hyd.—Hydrostatics.
Hypoth.—Hypothesis; Hypothetical.

I

I.—Island.
Ia.—Iowa.
Ib., or ibid.—*Ibidem*, in the same place.
I.C.C.—Interstate Commerce Commission.
Icel.—Iceland; Icelandic.
Ich.—Ichthyology.
Icon. Encyc.—Iconographic Encyclopedia.
I.C.S.—Indian Civil Service.
Id.—*Idem*, the same.
Id.—The Ides (*Idus*).
Ida.—Idaho.
I.E.—*Id est*, that is.
I.H.S.—Jesus the Savior of Men (*Jesus Hominum Salvator*).
Ill.—Illinois.
I.L.O.—International Labor Organization.
Imp.—Imperative; Imperfect.
Imp.—Imperial; Emperor (*Imperator*).
In.—Inch; Inches.
In.—Indium.
Inc.—Incorporated.
Incog.—*Incognito*, unknown.
I.N.D.—*In nomine Dei*, in the name of God.
Ind.—Index; Indiana.
Indef.—Indefinite.
Inf.—*Infra*, beneath, or below.
In f.—*In fine*, at the end of the title, law, or paragraph quoted.
Inhab.—Inhabitant.
In lim.—*In limine*, at the outset.
In loc.—*In loco*, in the place; on the passage.
In pr.—*In principia*, in the beginning and before the first paragraph of a law.
Ins.—Inspector; Insulated; Insurance.
Inst.—Instant, of this month; Institutes.
Inst.—Institute; Institution.
In sum.—*In summa*, in the summary.
Int.—Interest.
Interj.—Interjection.
In trans.—*In transitu*, on the passage.
Int. Dept.—Department of the Interior.
Int. Rev.—Internal Revenue.
Introd.—Introduction.
I.O.F.—Independent Order of Foresters.
Ion.—Ionic.
I.O.O.F.—Independent Order of Odd Fellows.
I.O.R.M.—Improved Order of Red Men.
I.O.U.—I owe you.
Ipecac.—Ipecacuanha.
I.Q.—Intelligence quotient.
Ire.—Ireland.
Is., Isa.—Isaiah.
Is., Isl.—Island.
I.T.—Inner Temple.
It.—Italy.
Ital.—Italic; Italian.
I.W.—Isle of Wight.
I.W.W.—Industrial Workers of the World.

J

J.—Justice, or Judge.
J.A.—Judge Advocate.
J.A.G.—Judge Advocate General.
Jam.—Jamaica.
Jan.—January.
Jas.—James.
J.C.D.—*Juris Civilis Doctor*, Doctor of Civil Law.
Jer.—Jeremiah.
JJ.—Justices.
Jno.—John.
Jona.—Jonathan.
Jos.—Joseph.
Josh.—Joshua.
J.P.—Justice of the Peace.
J. Prob.—Judge of Probate.
Jr., or Jun.—Junior.
J.U.D., J.V.D.—*Juris Utriusque Doctor*, Doctor of both laws (of the Canon and the Civil Law).
Jud.—Judicial.
Jud.—Judith.
Judg.—Judges.
Judge Adv.—Judge Advocate.
Jul. Per.—Julian Period.
Just.—Justinian.

K

K.—King.
Kal.—The Kalends (*Kalendæ*).
Kans.—Kansas.
K.G.—Knight of the Garter.
Kg., Kgs.—Keg; Kegs.
Kil.—Kilometer.
Kilo.—Kilogram.
Kingd.—Kingdom.
K.K.K.—Ku Klux Klan.
K.M.—Knight of Malta.
Knick.—Knickerbocker.
Knt. or Kt.—Knight.
K. of C.—Knights of Columbus.
K. of P.—Knights of Pythias.
K.P.—Kitchen Police.
Kt.—Knight.
K.T.—Knight Templar.
Kw.—Kilowatt.
Ky.—Kentucky.

L

L.—*Liber*, book; Lake.
L., £, or l.—*Libra* or *libræ*, pound or pounds sterling.
La.—Louisiana.
Lam.—Lamentations.
Lang.—Language.
Lat.—Latitude; Latin.
Lb., or lb.—*Libra*, or *libræ*. pound or pounds in weight.
L.C.L.—Less than carload lot.
Ld.—Lord.
Leg.—Legate.
Legis.—Legislature.
Lev.—Leviticus.
Lex.—Lexicon.
L.G.—Life Guards.
L.H.D.—Doctor of Humanities.
L.I.—Long Island.
Lib.—*Liber*, book.
Lieut.—Lieutenant.
Lieut. Col.—Lieutenant Colonel.
Lieut Gen.—Lieutenant General.
Lieut. Gov.—Lieutenant Governor.
Lin.—Lineal.
Linn.—Linnaeus; Linnaean.
Liq.—Liquor; Liquid.
Lit.—Literally; Literature.
Lith.—Lithuanian.
L. Lat.—Low Latin; Law Latin.
LL.B.—*Legum Baccalaureus*, Bachelor of Laws.
LL.D.—*Legum Doctor*, Doctor of Laws.
LL.M.—Master of Laws.
Loc. cit.—*Loco citato*, in the place cited.
Lon.—Longitude.
L.O.O.M.—Loyal Order of Moose.
L.S.D.—Pounds, shillings, and pence.
Lt.—Lieutenant.
Ltd.—Limited.
Lv.—Leave.

M

M.—Married.
M.—Mile.
M.—*Meridies*, noon.
M.—*Mille*, a thousand.
M., or Mons.—Monsieur.
M.A.—Master of Arts.
M.A.—Military Academy.
Macc.—Maccabees.
Mad.—Madam.
Mag.—Magazine.
Maj.—Major.
Maj. Gen.—Major General.
Mal.—Malachi.
Man.—Manitoba.

Mar.—March.
March.—Marchioness.
Marg.—Margin.
Masc.—Masculine.
Mass.—Massachusetts.
Math.—Mathematics; Mathematician.
Matt.—Matthew.
Max.—Maxim; Maximum.
M.B.—*Medicinæ Baccalaureus*, Bachelor of Medicine.
M.B.—*Musicæ Baccalaureus*, Bachelor of Music.
M.B.A.—Master of Business Administration.
M.C.—Member of Congress; Master of Ceremonies; Master Commandant.
Md.—Maryland.
M.D.—*Medicinæ Doctor*, Doctor of Medicine.
Mdpn.—Midshipman.
Me.—Maine.
M.E.—Methodist Episcopal; Military or Mechanical Engineer.
Mech.—Mechanic; Mechanical.
Med.—Medicine.
Mem.—Memorandum.
Mem.—*Memento*, remember.
Memo.—Memorandum.
Messrs., or MM.—Messieurs; Gentlemen.
Met.—Metaphysics.
Metal.—Metallurgy.
Meteor.—Meteorology.
Meth.—Methodist.
Mex.—Mexico, or Mexican.
Mfd.—Manufactured.
Mfg.—Manufacturing.
Mfr.—Manufacturer.
Mic.—Micah.
Mich.—Michaelmas; Michigan.
Mil.—Military.
Min.—Mineralogy.
Min.—Minute.
Minn.—Minnesota.
Min. Plen.—Minister Plenipotentiary.
Miss.—Mississippi.
Mlle.—Mademoiselle.
MM.—Messieurs; Gentlemen.
Mme.—Madame.
Mn.—Manganese.
M.N.A.S.—Member of the National Academy of Sciences.
Mo.—Month; Missouri.
M.O.—Money Order.
Mod.—Modern.
Mon.—Monday.
Mons.—Monsieur; Sir.
Mont.—Montana.
Morn.—Morning.
Mos.—Months.
M.P.—Member of Parliament; Member of Police; Methodist Protestant; Military Police.
M.P.E.—Master of Physical Education.
M.P.H.—Miles per Hour.
Mr.—Mister.
M.R.A.S.—Member of the Royal Asiatic Society; Member of the Royal Academy of Science.
Mrs.—Mistress.
M.S.—*Memoriæ sacrum*, Sacred to the memory.
M.S.—Master of the Sciences.
MS.—*Manuscriptum*, manuscript.
Msgr.—Monsignor.
MSS.—Manuscripts.
Mt.—Mount, or mountain.
Mus. B.—Bachelor of Music.
Mus. D.—Doctor of Music.
M.W.—Most Worthy; Most Worshipful.
M.W.A.—Modern Woodmen of America.
M.W.G.M.—Most Worthy Grand Master; Most Worshipful Grand Master.
M.W.P.—Most Worthy Patriarch.
Myth.—Mythology.

N

N.—North; Number; Noun; Neuter.
N.—Note.
N.A.—North America.
Nah.—Nahum.
N.A.S.—National Academy of Sciences.
Nat.—Natural.
Nat. Hist.—Natural History.
Nat. Ord.—Natural Order.
Naut.—Nautical.
Naut. Alm.—Nautical Almanac.
N.B.—North Britain.
N.B.—New Brunswick; North British.
N.B.—*Nota bene*, mark well; take notice.
N.C.—North Carolina.
N.C.O.—Noncommissioned Officer.
N. Dak.—North Dakota.
N.E.—New England; Northeast.
N.E.A.—National Education Association.
Neb.—Nebraska.
Neh.—Nehemiah.
N.e.i.—*Non est inventus*, he is not found.
Neth.—Netherlands.
Neut.—Neuter (gender).
Nev.—Nevada.
Newf.—Newfoundland.
New Test., or N.T.—New Testament.
N.F.—Newfoundland.
N.G.—New Granada; Noble Grand; No Good.
N.H.—New Hampshire.
Ni. pri.—*Nisi prius*, no protest.
N.J.—New Jersey.
N. l.—*Non liquet*, it does not appear.
N. lat.—North latitude.
N.L.R.B.—National Labor Relations Board.
N.M.—New Mexico.
N. Mex.—New Mexico.
N.N.E.—North Northeast.
N.N.W.—North Northwest.
N.O.—New Orleans.
No.—*Numero*, number.
Nol. Pros.—*Nolle prosequi*, unwilling to proceed.
Nom., or nom.—Nominative.
Noncom.—Noncommissioned officer.
Non cul.—*Non culpabilis*, Not guilty.
Non obst.—*Non obstante*, notwithstanding.
Non pros.—*Non prosequitur*, he does not prosecute.
Non seq.—*Non sequitur*, it does not follow.
Nos.—Numbers.
Nov.—November.
N.P.—Notary Public.
N.S.—New Style (after 1752); Nova Scotia.
N.S.J.C.—Our Savior Jesus Christ (*Noster Salvator Jesus Christus*).
N.S.P.C.A.—National Society for the Prevention of Cruelty to Animals.
N.S.P.C.C.—National Society for the Prevention of Cruelty to Children.
N.T.—New Testament.
Num.—Numbers; Numeral.
N.V.—New Version.
N.V.M.—Nativity of the Virgin Mary.
N.W.—Northwest.
N.W.T.—Northwest Territory.
N.Y.—New York.
N.Y.C.—New York City.
N.Z.—New Zealand.

O

O.—Ohio; Ontario.
Ob.—*Obiit*, he or she died.
Obad.—Obadiah.
Obs.—Obsolete; Observatory; Observation.
Obt., or Obdt.—Obedient.
Oct., or 8vo.—Octavo, eight pages.
Oct.—October.
O.D.—Officer of the Day; Olive Drab.
O.E.S.—Order of the Eastern Star.
O.-F.—Odd-Fellow, or Odd-Fellows.
O.G.—Outside guardian.
Okla.—Oklahoma.
Old Test., or O.T.—Old Testament.
Olym.—Olympiad.
O.M.—Old Measurement.
Ont.—Ontario.
Opt.—Optics.
Ore., Oreg.—Oregon.

Orig.—Originally.
Ornith.—Ornithology.
Os.—Osmium.
O.T.—Old Testament.
O.T.C.—Officers' Training Camp.
Oxf.—Oxford.
Oxon.—*Oxonia, Oxonii,* Oxford.
Oz.—Ounce.

P

P.—*Pondere,* by weight.
P., or p.—Page; Part; Participle.
Pa.—Pennsylvania.
Pal.—Palaeontology.
Par.—Paragraph.
Par. Pas.—Parallel passage.
Parl.—Parliament.
Pat. Off.—Patent Office.
Pathol.—Pathology.
P.A.U.—Pan American Union.
Payt.—Payment.
P.B.—Primitive Baptist.
P.C.—Past Commander.
Pd.—Paid.
P.E.—Protestant Episcopal.
P.E.I.—Prince Edward Island.
Penn., Penna.—Pennsylvania.
Pent.—Pentecost.
Per, or pr.—By the, or per lb.
Per an.—*Per annum,* by the year.
Per cent.—*Per centum,* by the hundred.
Peruv.—Peruvian.
Pet.—Peter; Petrine.
P.G.—Past Grand.
Phar.—Pharmacy.
Ph.B.—*Philosophiæ Baccalaureus,* Bachelor of Philosophy.
Ph.D.—*Philosophiæ Doctor,* Doctor of Philosophy.
Phil.—Philip; Philippians; Philosophy; Philemon.
Phila.—Philadelphia.
Philem.—Philemon.
Philom.—*Philomathes,* a lover of learning.
Philomath.—*Philomathematicus* a lover of the mathematics.
Phren.—Phrenology.
P.I.—Philippine Islands.
Pinx., or pxt.—*Pinxit,* he (she) painted it.
Pk.—Park.
Pl., or Plur.—Plural.
Plff.—Plaintiff.
Plupf.—Pluperfect.
P.M.—*Post meridiem,* afternoon, evening.
P.M.—Postmaster; Passed Midshipman.
P.M.G.—Postmaster-General.
P.O.—Post-Office.
P. of H.—Patrons of Husbandry.
Pop.—Population.
Port.—Portugal, or Portuguese.
P.P.—Parish priest.
Pp., or pp.—Pages.
PP.—*Patres,* Fathers.
Pph.—Pamphlet.
P.Q.—Province of Quebec.
P.R.—Prize Ring; Puerto Rico; Proportional Representation; the Roman People (*Populus Romanus*).
P.R.C.—*Post Romam conditam,* from the building of Rome.
Preb.—Prebend.
Pref.—Preface.
Pref.—Preferred.
Prep.—Preposition.
Pres.—President.
Presb.—Presbyterian.
Prin.—Principally.
Prob.—Problem.
Proc.—Proceedings.
Prof.—Professor.
Pron.—Pronoun; Pronunciation.
Prop.—Proposition.
Prot.—Protestant.
Pro tem.—*Pro tempore,* for the time being.
Prot. Epis.—Protestant Episcopal.
Prov.—Proverbs; Provost.
Prov.—Province.
Prox.—*Proximo,* next (month).
P.R.S.—President of the Royal Society.
Prs.—Pairs.
Prus.—Prussia; Prussian.
P.S.—*Post scriptum,* Postscript.
P.S.—Privy Seal.
Ps.—Psalm, or Psalms.
Pt.—Part; Pint; Payment; Point; Port.
Pt.—Platinum.
P.T.A.—Parent-Teacher Association.
P.T.O.—Please turn over.
Pub.—Publisher; Publication; Published; Public.
Pub. Doc.—Public Documents.
Pvt.—Private.
P.W.D.—Public Works Department.
Pwt.—Pennyweight; Pennyweights.

Q

Q.—*Quasi,* as it were; almost.
Q.—Queen.
Q.—Question.
Q.e.—*Quod est,* which is.
Q.e.d.—*Quod erat demonstrandum,* which was to be proved.
Q.e.f.—*Quod erat faciendum,* which was to be done.
Q.e.i.—*Quod erat inveniendum,* which was to be found out.
Q.l.—*Quantum libet,* as much as you please.
Q.M.—Quartermaster.
Qm.—*Quomodo,* how; by what means.
Q.M.C.—Quartermaster Corps.
Q.M.G. — Quartermaster-General.
Q.p., or q.pl.—*Quantum placet,* as much as you please.
Qr.—Quarter.
Q.S.—Quarter Sessions.
Q.s.—*Quantum sufficit,* sufficient quantity.
Qt.—Quart.
Qu., or qy.—*Quaere,* inquire; query.
Quar.—Quarterly.
Que.—Quebec.
Ques.—Question.
Q.v.—*Quod vide,* which see; *quantum vis,* as much as you will.

R

R.—*Recipe,* take.
R.—*Regina,* Queen.
R.—River; Rood; Rod; Rabbi; Republican.
R.A.—Royal Academy; Royal Academician; Rear Admiral.
R.C.—Roman Catholic; Red Cross.
RC.—*Rescriptum,* a counterpart.
Rd.—Road.
R.E.—Reformed Episcopal.
R.E.—Royal Engineers.
R.E.A.—Rural Electrification Administration.
Rec.—Recipe; Recorder.
Recd.—Received.
Rec. Sec.—Recording Secretary.
Rect.—Rector; Receipt.
Ref.—Reformed; Reformation; Reference.
Ref. Ch.—Reformed Church.
Reg.—Register; Regular.
Reg. Prof.—Regius Professor.
Regr.—Registrar.
Regt.—Regiment.
Rel.—Religion.
Rep.—Representative; Reporter.
Repts.—Reports.
Retd.—Returned.
Rev.—Reverend; Revelation (Book of); Review; Revenue; Revise.
R.F.C.—Reconstruction Finance Corporation; Royal Flying Corps.
R.F.D.—Rural Free Delivery.
R.H.—Royal Highness.
Rhet.—Rhetoric.
R.H.S.—Royal Humane Society; Royal Historical Society.
R.I.—Rhode Island.
R.I.H.S.—Rhode Island Historical Society.
R.M.—Royal Marines; Royal Mail.
R.N.—Royal Navy; Registered Nurse.
R.N.R.—Royal Navy Reserve.
Ro.—*Recto,* right-hand page.
Robt.—Robert.
Rom.—Romans (Epistle to the).

Rom. Cath.—Roman Catholic.
R.O.T.C.—Reserve Officers' Training Corps.
R.P.—Reformed Presbyterian.
R.P.—*Regius Professor*, the King's Professor.
R.P.M.—Revolutions per minute.
R.R.—Railroad.
R.R. Sta.—Railroad Station.
R.S.—Recording Secretary; Revised Statutes.
Rs.—*Responsus*, to answer; Rupees.
R.S.A.—Royal Society of Antiquaries; Royal Scottish Academy.
R.S.V.P.—*Répondez, s'il vous plaît*, answer, if you please.
Rt. Hon.—Right Honorable.
Rt. Rev.—Right Reverend.
Rt. Wpful.—Right Worshipful.
Russ.—Russia; Russian.
R.V.—Revised Version.
R.W.—Right Worthy.
R.W.D.G.M.—Right Worshipful Deputy Grand Master.
R.W.G.R.—Right Worthy Grand Representative.
R.W.G.S.—Right Worthy Grand Secretary.
R.W.G.T.—Right Worthy Grand Treasurer; Right Worshipful Grand Templar.
R.W.G.W.—Right Worthy Grand Warden.
R.W.J.G.W.—Right Worshipful Junior Grand Warden.
R.W.S.G.W.—Right Worshipful Senior Grand Warden.
Ry.—Railway.

S

S.—*Solidus*, a shilling.
S.—South; Saint; Scribe; Sulphur; Sunday; Sun; Series.
S.A.—Salvation Army.
S.A.—South America; South Australia.
S.a.—*Secundum artem*, according to art.
S.A.E.—Society of Automotive Engineers.
S. Afr.—South Africa.
Sam.—Samuel.
Sansc., or Sansk.—Sanscrit, or Sanskrit.
S.A.R.—Sons of American Revolution.
S.A.S.—*Societatis Antiquariorum Socius*, Fellow of the Society of Antiquaries.
Sask.—Saskatchewan.
Sat.—Saturday.
Sax.—Saxon; Saxony.
Sax. Chron.—Saxon Chronicle.
S.C.—South Carolina; Signal Corps.
Sc.—*Sculpsit*, he (or she) engraved it.
Sc., or scil.—*Scilicet*, namely.
Sc.B.—Bachelor of Science.
Schol.—*Scholium*, a note.
Schr.—Schooner.
Scot.—Scottish; Scotland.
Scr.—Scruple.
Scrip.—Scripture.
Sculp.—*Sculpsit*, he (or she) engraved it.
S.D.—*Salutem dicit*, sends health.
S.D.—South Dakota.
S.E.—Southeast.
Sec.—Secretary; Second.
S.E.C.—Securities and Exchange Commission.
Sec. Leg.—Secretary of Legation.
Sec. leg.—*Secundum legem*, according to law.
Sec. reg.—*Secundum regulam*, according to rule.
Sect.—Section.
Sem.—*Semble*, it seems.
Sem.—Seminary.
Sen.—Senate; Senator; Senior.
Sept.—September; Septuagint.
Seq.—*Sequentia*, following; *sequitur*, it follows.
Ser.—Series.
Serg.—Sergeant.
Serg.-Maj.—Sergeant-Major.
Sess.—Session.
S.G.—Solicitor-General.
Sgt.—Sergeant.
Shak.—Shakespeare.
S.H.S.—*Societatis Historiae Socius*, Fellow of the Historical Society.
S.I.—Staten Island.
Sic—Doubtful; Literally.
Sing.—Singular.
S.Isl.—Sandwich Islands.
S.J.—Society of Jesus.
S. lat.—South latitude.
S.M.—State Militia; Short Meter; Sergeant-Major; Sons of Malta.
Soc. Isl.—Society Islands.
Sol.—Solomon; Solution.
Sol.-Gen.—Solicitor-General.
Sp.—Spain; Spanish.
S.P.A.S.—*Societatis Philosophicae Americanae Socius*, Member of the American Philosophical Society.
S.P.C.A.—Society for the Prevention of Cruelty to Animals.
S.P.C.C.—Society for the Prevention of Cruelty to Children.
S.P.G.—Society for the Propagation of the Gospel.
Sp. gr.—Specific gravity.
S.P.Q.R.—*Senatus Populusque Romanus*, the Senate and people of Rome.
Sq. ft.—Square foot, or square feet.
Sq. in.—Square inch, or inches.
Sq. m.—Square mile, or miles.
Sq. yd.—Square yard.
Sr.—Senior; Señor (Spanish for Mr.)
Sra.—Señora (Spanish for Mrs.)
S.R.I.—*Sacrum Romanum Imperium*, Holy Roman Empire.
S.R.O.—Standing Room Only.
Srta.—Señorita (Spanish for Miss).
S.S.—Sunday-school; Steamship.
SS.—Saints.
SS., or ss.—*Scilicet*, to wit.
S.S.E.—South-southeast.
S.S.W.—South-southwest.
St.—Saint; Street; Strait.
Stat.—Statute.
S.T.B.—Bachelor of Sacred Theology.
S.T.D.—*Sacrae Theologiae Doctor*, Doctor of Divinity.
Str.—Steamer.
Subj.—Subjunctive.
Subst.—Substantive.
Sun., or Sund.—Sunday.
Sup.—Supreme.
Sup.—Supplement; Superfine.
Supt.—Superintendent.
Surg.—Surgeon; Surgery.
Surg.-Gen.—Surgeon-General.
Surv.—Surveyor.
Surv.-Gen.—Surveyor-General.
S.v.—*Sub verbo*, under the word or title.
S.W.—Southwest.
Sw.—Swiss.
Swe.—Sweden; Swedish; Swedenborg; Swedenborgian.
Switz.—Switzerland.
Syn.—Synonym; Synonymous.
Syr.—Syriac.

T

T., or tom.—Tome, volume.
Tab.—Table; Tabular.
Tan.—Tangent.
T.E.—Topographical Engineers.
Tenn.—Tennessee.
Ter.—Territory; Terrace.
Tex.—Texas.
Th., or Thurs.—Thursday.
T.H.—Territory of Hawaii.
Th.D.—Doctor of Theology.
Theo.—Theodore.
Theol.—Theology; Theological.
Theoph.—Theophilus.
Thess.—Thessalonians.
Thos.—Thomas.
Thur., Thurs.—Thursday.
Tim.—Timothy.
Tit.—Titus.
T.O.—Turn over.
Tob.—Tobit.
Topog.—Topography; Topographical.
Tp.—Township.
Tr.—Transpose; Translator; Translation; Trustee.
Trans.—Translator; Translation; Transactions; Transpose.

Treas.—Treasurer.
Trin.—Trinity.
Tues., or Tu.—Tuesday.
T.V.A.—Tenessee Valley Authority.
Typ.—Typographer.

U

U.—Union.
U.B.—United Brethren.
U.C.—*Urbe condita*, year of Rome.
U.J.C.—*Utriusque Juris Doctor*, Doctor of both Laws.
U.K.—United Kingdom.
Ult.—*Ultimo*, last; of the last month.
Unit.—Unitarian.
Univ.—University.
Univt.—Universalist.
U.P.—United Presbyterian; United Press.
U.S.—United States.
U.s.—*Ut supra*, or *uti supra*, as above.
U.S.A.—United States Army.
U.S.A.—United States of America.
U.S.C.G.—United States Coast Guard.
U.S.M.—United States Mail.
U.S.M.—United States Marines.
U.S.M.A.—United States Military Academy.
U.S.M.C.—United States Marine Corps; United States Maritime Commission.
U.S.M.H.S.—United States Marine Hospital Service.
U.S.N.—United States Navy.
U.S.N.A.—United States Naval Academy.
U.S.S.—United States Senate; United States Ship.
U.S.S.R.—Union of Soviet Socialist Republics.
Ut.—Utah.

V

V.—Village.
V., or vid.—*Vide*, see.
V.—Violin.
V., or vs.—*Versus*, against; *Versiculo*, in such a verse.
Va.—Virginia.
Val.—Value.
Vat.—Vatican.
V.C.—Victoria Cross; Vice-Chairman; Vice-Chancellor.
V.D.L.—Van Diemen's Land.
Ven.—Venerable.
Ver.—Verse.
Vet.—Veteran; Veterinary.
V.F.W.—Veterans of Foreign Wars.
V.G.—Vicar General.
V.I.—Virgin Islands.
Vice-Pres., or V.P.—Vice-President.
Vic., Vict.—Victoria.
Visc.—Viscount.
Viz., or vl.—*Videlicet*, to wit; namely; that is to say.
Vo.—*Verso*, left-hand page.
Vol.—Volume.
V.P.—Vice-President.
V.S.—Veterinary Surgeon.
Vs.—Versus.
Vt.—Vermont.
Vul.—Vulgate (Version).

W

W.—West.
Wash.—Washington.
W.B.M.—Woman's Board of Missions.
W.C.A.—Woman's Christian Association.
W.C.T.U.—Women's Christian Temperance Union.
Wed.—Wednesday.
Wf.—Wrong font.
W.I.—West Indies.
Wis.—Wisconsin.
Wisd.—Wisdom (Book of).
Wk.—Week.
W.M.—Worshipful Master.
Wm.—William.
W.M.S.—Wesleyan Missionary Society.
W.N.C.T.U.—Woman's National Christian Temperance Union.
W.N.W.—West-northwest.
W.S.W.—West-southwest.
Wt.—Weight.
W.Va.—West Virginia.
Wyo., Wy.—Wyoming.

X

X., or Xt.—Christ.
Xmas., or Xm.—Christmas.
Xn., or Xtian.—Christian.
Xnty., or Xty.—Christianity.

Y

Y.—Young Men's Christian Association.
Yd.—Yard.
Y.M.C.A.—Young Men's Christian Association.
Y.M.C.U.—Young Men's Christian Union.
Y.M.H.A.—Young Men's Hebrew Association.
Y.P.S.C.E.—Young People's Society of Christian Endeavor.
Yr.—Year.
Yrs.—Years; Yours.
Y.W.—Young Women's Christian Association.
Y.W.C.A.—Young Women's Christian Association.
Y.W.H.A.—Young Women's Hebrew Association.

Z

Zach.—Zachary.
Zech.—Zechariah.
Zeph.—Zephaniah.
Zn.—Zinc.
Zool.—Zoölogy.

BASIC REFERENCE WORKS

Samuel Johnson, famous English lexicographer, once said, "Knowledge is of two kinds. We know a subject ourselves, or we know where we can find information upon it." This distinction is especially pertinent today, when the world's store of knowledge is so vast that no individual can hope to possess it. Our best guides to the fields of knowledge unfamiliar to us are reference works; with them we should be as familiar as a mariner is with compass and sextant.

Almost all libraries have the more important reference works, which are usually kept separate from other books. Probably the best way to learn about a subject is to consult several general encyclopedias. The encyclopedia article gives a valuable, general, comprehensive outline of the subject, and usually provides a preliminary bibliography. More specialized reference works may then be consulted; these in turn will list books and articles in the special field being investigated. It should be remembered that reference works, although valuable guides, usually deal only in a general way with a subject, and should not be regarded as final authorities. For more detailed, and probably more authoritative information, students should consult works which deal with the specific questions they are investigating.

The student should also become acquainted with the reference works which treat of language and its use. A familiarity with these books enriches one's knowledge.

In various specialized fields there are also valuable reference works which the students should consult. Some of the most important of these have been selected.

ENCYCLOPEDIAS

American Peoples Encyclopedia.
Compton's Encyclopedia.
Encyclopedia Americana.
Encyclopaedia Britannica.
Encyclopedia International.
New Book of Knowledge.
World Book Encyclopedia.

DICTIONARIES

American College Encyclopedic Dictionary.
New Century Dictionary.
Oxford English Dictionary.
Shorter Oxford English Dictionary.
Webster's Columbia Concise Dictionary.
Webster's Columbia Encyclopedic Dictionary.
Webster's Columbia Reference Dictionary.
Webster's New International Dictionary.

SPECIAL DICTIONARIES

Craigie, Sir William and Hulbert, James R. *Dictionary of American English on Historic Principles.*
Fernald, J. C. *English Synonyms and Antonyms.*
Fowler, H. W. *A Dictionary of Modern English Usage.*
Roget, P. M. *Thesaurus of English Words and Phrases.*

BIOGRAPHICAL DICTIONARIES

Current Biography.
Dictionary of American Biography.
Dictionary of National Biography (British).
Webster's Biographical Dictionary.
Who's Who (British).
Who's Who in America.

YEARBOOKS AND REFERENCES FOR CURRENT EVENTS

American Peoples Encyclopedia Yearbook.
Americana Annual.
Britannica Book of the Year.
Congressional Record.
New International Year Book.
New York Times Index.
Statesman's Year-Book.
Times Official Index (London).
World Almanac.

PERIODICAL INDEXES

International Index to Periodicals.
Reader's Guide to Periodical Literature.

SPECIAL REFERENCE WORKS

Bartlett, John. *Familiar Quotations.*
Book Review Digest.
Brewer, E. C. *Dictionary of Phrase and Fable.*
Cambridge Ancient History.
Cambridge History of American Literature.
Cambridge History of English Literature.
Cambridge Medieval History.
Cambridge Modern History.
Catholic Encyclopedia.
Encyclopedia of Religion and Ethics.
Encyclopedia of the Social Sciences.
Grove's Dictionary of Music and Musicians.
Jewish Encyclopedia.
Stevenson, Burton. *The Home Book of Quotations.*
University of Knowledge.

WRITING TO SELL

MARKETS

Writing is a business like any other. Unless employed as a staff writer, the professional writer is his own employer, office force, and efficiency expert. He is familiar with the various markets for written material, since in order to achieve success he must sell to those markets. Roughly, they may be divided into the book publishers, the smooth-paper magazines, the pulp-paper magazines, the newspapers and syndicates, the trade journals and house organs.

Book publishers form a very distinct class. They are looking for material of suitable length for publication in book form. They seldom constitute a profitable market for the beginner, who usually finds it wiser in the long run to concentrate on shorter pieces of writing, any one of which does not represent a great investment of time. Later he may work up to the novel and the long nonfiction work.

The magazines published on smooth paper are termed "slicks" by the writers. They include *The Saturday Evening Post, McCalls, Cosmopolitan*, etc. They print chiefly the work of established fiction authors and prominent writers of nonfiction. The pay is very good, but the volume and quality of competition leave little opportunity for the beginner. Nevertheless, since some of these magazines are found on every newsstand and in many homes, they receive a very large number of manuscripts from unknowns—manuscripts which would have a much better chance in less prominent markets.

The magazines printed on pulp paper—"pulps" in writers' parlance—publish fiction almost exclusively. They buy love stories and detective stories, tales of mystery and adventure, particularly in its "western" variety. But each "pulp" publishes only one kind of story. A magazine may be wholly devoted to adventure stories about aviators, or tales based on future scientific developments—"science fiction." A rapid-fire style, easy to read, with shrewd, terse characterizations is desired.

The newspapers pay relatively low rates to unknown outsiders. Most of their material is gathered and written by paid employees. Nevertheless they will sometimes accept interesting items from outsiders. Small newspapers particularly may be developed into a valuable market by the enterprising writer. The syndicates furnish material for newspapers and magazines. Some of them use only established authors. But others, which supply stories and articles to rural newspapers and small periodicals, are willing to accept material from unknowns. True, the pay is small, but the competition is not so keen and a matured style is not essential.

Trade journals are periodicals devoted to a single business or profession. Much of their material is written on contract. Still they should not be neglected by the author who has or is willing to gain the necessary specialized knowledge. House organs are the publications of single business firms, intended for circulation among employees, customers, or agents. Because they are little known, they sometimes offer interesting opportunities. It must be remembered that even the large newsstand does not give a true picture of writers' markets. Tiny periodicals and amateur magazines never appear on the newsstand. Many of these latter do not pay for the material they publish, but they should not therefore be invariably shunned by the writer. Merely to have a story or article published is a heartening achievement, psychologically valuable to the beginner.

Reaching the Market.—In view of the confusing multiplicity of markets and the burdensome amount of work involved in selling, the writer can sometimes profitably avail himself of the services of an agent. An agent is a professional salesman of written material. He accepts stories and articles from a writer and receives from the writer a commission (almost invariably ten per cent) on anything he sells. A good agent has a wide knowledge of markets and, more important, he knows the condition of markets from month to month—which ones are actively buying, the sort of material for which there is a special call, the top price that can be asked and obtained for a certain manuscript in a certain market, etc. He is also personally acquainted with a number of editors, though this does not mean that an editor will buy everything an agent recommends. He understands publishers' contracts and is able to protect an author's rights effectively. Since his business office is usually located in New York, the chief publishing center, he can rapidly submit manuscripts to a large number of buyers. Unquestionably there are certain classes of writers for whom an agent's services are very valuable; among them may be mentioned the established author who wishes to be relieved of business responsibilities, the writer who dislikes and shirks the task of selling, and the beginner who is personally acquainted with an energetic agent. But certain possible disadvantages must be noted. An agent may not push the work of a beginner as energetically as might the writer himself. An agent may not be interested in sending material to the cheapest markets, since his commission would be trifling. Finally, an agent may be a considerable expense. In this connection it should be remembered that a good agent seldom charges a fee for reading a manuscript; he tries to make money *with* rather than *out* of a writer; he does not engage in the conduct of correspondence courses in writing; he is a salesman, not a teacher—although he is often able to give valuable advice to the authors whom he sponsors. Beyond this, the question of whether or not to employ an agent is one which each individual author must decide for himself.

Specific information about markets, the names and addresses of periodicals, type of material used, and rates paid, can be obtained in publishers' directories and in the magazines published especially for writers, such as *The Writer* and *Writer's Market*.

Study markets carefully and shrewdly. Write to fit the needs of markets, or at least try to find the markets in which your style of product has the best chance. A thorough search frequently will reveal a possible market for material that seems at first glance impossible to sell.

Fiction

The story that will sell is a story people like to read. Most people do not like to read about unpleasant subjects. Since they identify themselves with the hero or heroine, they do not like to read stories in which those characters come to grief or end up in a state of bafflement or bewilderment. This is not to say that the reader dislikes reading about struggles, difficulties, clashes of will and character. On the contrary, those are the very things he delights to read about. But he also wants things to come out well—or at least definitely—in the end. He demands a clean-cut finish. The story of failure and disillusionment has its place in literature, but the success story is easier to sell. Like it or not, the writer usually must cater to the daydreams and hidden ambitions of his readers.

The story that will sell is a story people can believe—at least while they are reading it. It need not be consistently realistic, but no single event in the story should strain the reader's credulity. Fantastic and improbable things may happen, but the reader's credulity must first be aroused by the proper suggestions and atmospheric touches. The motivation of the characters is especially important. Their problems must be easy to grasp, their reactions natural. The reader must be able to put himself in their place and feel that their emotions are genuine, their actions necessary.

Most stories can be reduced to a very simple formula: A. one or more characters want to attain a certain goal; B. obstacles arise which seem to make the attainment of the goal impossible; C. the obstacles are overcome (usually by the direct efforts of the characters involved) and the goal reached. For example, a young man falls in love with his employer's daughter; the employer makes their marriage contingent on the young man's selling a large insurance policy to a miserly millionaire; the young man manages to sell the policy and he and the girl are united. This particular plot is trite and outworn. Nevertheless it illustrates the essential elements. Obviously its story-interest would depend largely on the cleverness of the device by which the young man sold the policy. He might rescue the millionaire's grandchild from drowning. He might learn that the millionaire was a stamp-collector and find a rare stamp for him. He might make a bet with the millionaire. Or the girl might solve the problem instead of the young man. There is no end to the possible variations.

This basic plot-structure (goal-obstacle-success) can be applied to stories of all types. In the detective story it takes the form of: A. problem as to who committed a murder; B. false clues and misleading evidence; C. discovery of who committed the murder. In the outdoor story it is a man's struggle with and overcoming of the forces of nature. The formula fits the tale of two thwarted lovers and the story of a man's struggle to become reconciled with his God.

It must be remembered, however, that most successful stories do not use the simplest form of the A.B.C. formula. There are usually several obstacles, one giving rise to another. The obstacle may often take the form of an individual—the villain. One of the obstacles may come as a sudden surprise when the goal is almost in sight; a new character may enter the story, giving the plot a radical turn. This surprise element is especially useful and almost essential in lifting the reader's interest midway in the narrative. Or one of the characters may be a doubtful quantity, so that the reader does not know until the end whether he is an ally of the hero or an obstacle. In general, the most interesting struggles are those which depend on the clash of personalities. Readers like interesting, human characters with failings as well as good points.

All of which boils down to one essential consideration: the writer must keep the reader constantly in mind when he creates his story. He must keep the reader interested all the way.

Nonfiction

The writer of nonfiction has certain definite advantages over the fictionist. His market is, if anything, larger, and interesting subject matter can compensate to a considerable degree for defects in style. His work is based solidly on fact. If he comes across certain facts which he thinks make a story worth telling, there is a good chance that editors and readers will be of the same opinion. Human interest is his keynote. True-life happenings, the experiences of people who pursue unusual occupations or have been in out-of-the-way places—these are his stock in trade. Unless he has special aptitudes or advantages, he should avoid the more abstract and controversial subjects, such as politics, economics, and the like. He can find his subject matter within the range of his own experience. And he can readily expand the scope of his experience by making more acquaintances, seeing more of the city or district in which he lives, following up unusual stories which he hears at second hand—in short, imitating the practices of the competent free-lance reporter.

This does not mean that the nonfiction writer should neglect to read periodicals and books. On the contrary, he should make every effort to gauge the needs of the publications to which he is attempting to sell, and to keep up with and ahead of public taste. Moreover, reading may provide him with valuable clues and hints. Material supplied by newspapers and national publications may be reslanted to fit the needs of a lesser market. Dry scientific and scholarly articles may hide a good story. The writer should attempt to capitalize on his own interests and hobbies, develop them into specialties.

Although subject matter is the chief concern of the nonfiction writer, an interesting narrative style will add greatly to the marketability of his articles. Clarity is paramount. Obscure statements and hazy explanations should be avoided. The reader should be led along by easy stages. Each paragraph should satisfy a part of his curiosity and at the same time arouse his interest further. The first sentence should not tell the whole story. The writer should canvass the main points of interest in his subject and then space them out evenly through his article, neither packed at the beginning nor delayed until the end. If this practice is followed, the whole article gains in effectiveness.

Many poorly-written articles are published merely because the subject matter is interesting. If the writer combines interesting subject matter with an effective terse style of narration, he will find a market.

Important Points

Adapt your style and material to the market to which you are attempting to sell. Read the various publications of that market; they are your blueprints. Study the information given in the writers' magazines. Become familiar with editors' likes and dislikes. Learn which subjects are favored and which tabooed. The magazine market is roughly divided into groups of magazines of similar policy. A story rejected by one magazine can usually be offered for sale to half a dozen others with some hope of acceptance. Watch for new markets opening up. They will need more material and will be more likely to take the work of unknown authors.

Keep ahead of public taste. Don't just rewrite the stories which appeared in last month's magazines. They are dead wood. Strive for novelty. This does not mean that an editor will accept material violating the policy and special taboos of his publication. It does mean that editors are looking for new angles and new variants on old themes.

Take particular pains to make the beginnings of your stories or articles interesting. If the first paragraph sets a problem and suggests fascinating possibilities, the reader will be eager to go on. If the first paragraph is dull, even though later material is very exciting, the reader may go no further. A good story or article may fail because the writer did not give sufficient thought to catching the reader's interest. A story in the modern style begins with action, not with a long description of the characters and background.

If possible, type your manuscripts on regular typing paper ($8\frac{1}{2}$ by 11 inches). Double space the lines. Type only on one side of the paper. Leave wide margins. Do not crowd the pages. Most magazines will not return unwanted manuscripts unless they are accompanied by a self addressed envelope with the required amount of postage already affixed. Manuscripts of any size are best sent flat in a large envelope. Small manuscripts may be folded and sent in a business-size envelope. They should not be rolled. Bulky manuscripts may be sent more economically by express, with enclosed directions that they be returned to you by express, collect. Do not address manuscripts to "The Editor"; it will not procure them additional attention. It is usually unnecessary to write an explanatory letter. Manuscripts whose form violates these rules are at a disadvantage.

Above all, keep on writing! Don't be worried by rejection slips. Most successful authors spend five to ten years receiving nothing much else. There are a hundred reasons because of which a good story or article may be rejected. It may accidentally duplicate material already purchased. It may be submitted at a time when the market is slack, the editor buying little or nothing. Most magazines can buy only six or eight stories a month—a tiny fraction of the total material submitted. So don't let feelings of despondency interfere with your writing. An author is a poor judge of the quality of his own product. He may do some of his best work when he feels he is doing his worst. Inspiration is a rather rare commodity. You cannot depend on it. Set yourself definite working hours and keep them, whether or not inspiration comes. If you really want to write for a living, the effort will be worth while.

PROOFREADING AND PROOFREADER'S MARKS

The common marks used by proofreaders and typesetters are listed and illustrated here. These marks, used universally, provide the best means of indicating corrections and changes clearly and quickly. However, if the writer feels the slightest doubt of his ability to make clear his intentions, he can write on the margin a brief note to the typesetter, explaining precisely what he wants done.

After a piece of writing is set in type, proofs are pulled and sent to the author for correction or approval. Usually the proofs are galleys, long sheets equal to a little more than three pages of an ordinary book. Each galley represents a heavy tray of metal at the typesetter's, and any change in the proof must be duplicated in the type itself.

When the original manuscript was set in type, the typesetter read each line of the manuscript, word for word, and transcribed it. When the corrected galleys go back to the typesetter so that the type can be made to correspond with the amended galleys, the typesetter does not read them. He looks only at the margins. Any correction not clearly marked outside the type area will be ignored.

ꝺ	Delete
stet	Let it stand unchanged
^at this	Insert marginal copy^point
out-see copy	Out—see copy./text missing
#	Insert wordspace
⁐	Close up sp ace
‿	Less space here
eq#	Equalize word spacing
¶	Start paragraph. ¶Here
no ¶	No paragraph. Run in preceding paragraph
□	Indent one em
[	Move to left
]	Move to right
⌐	Move up
⌴	Move down
=	Straighten line
‖	Align type on left / Align type on right
9	Turn inverted letter [—word, line]
wf	Type is from wrong font
×	Replace defective type
⊥	Push down this "work-up"
tr	Transpose letters (words or)
Compositor (sp)	(Comp.) spell out
ꝺ?	Query to authoress
⁀	Use ligature [fitting]
❛	Insert apostrophe [Johns]
[/]	—brackets ^See copy^
⊙	—colon^
❜	—comma^
|em|	—em dash^
|en|	—en dash [1948^1950]
hr#	—HAIR SPACES between letters
=/	—hyphen [a man^of^war]
?/	—interrogation point [Thus]
ld	—lead (place two points of spacing) between lines
❞	—quotation mark ["quotes]
(/)	—parentheses^called "parens"^
⊙	—period^
;/	—semicolon^
bf	Reset in boldface, **thus**
caps	—capitals [or (ring) word]
ital	—italic, *thus*
lc	—LOWER CASE, thus
rom	—(roman) thus
sc	—small caps, THUS
C+sc	—caps and small caps, As HERE
C̲	Substitute a capital Letter
¢	—lower Case letter

Proofreaders' marks with copy-marking demonstrated

MUSICAL SIGNS AND ABBREVIATIONS

𝄞 *The sign of the treble clef.* It represents the S of *Sol* (G). The second line from the bottom is the G above middle C.

𝄢 *The sign of the bass clef.* It represents the F of *Fa* (F). The fourth line from the bottom is the F below middle C.

𝄐 *Fermate.* Indicates a long pause on a note or rest.

♯ *Sharp.* Indicates a note is to be played a half step higher than written.

♭ *Flat.* Indicates a note is to be played a half step lower than written.

♮ *Natural.* Indicates a note previously sharped or flatted is to be played as written.

𝄪 *Double sharp.* Indicates a note is to be played two half steps higher than written.

♭♭ *Double flat.* Indicates a note is to be played two half steps lower than written.

♮♯ *Single sharp.* Indicates a note previously double-sharped is to be played one half step lower.

♮♭ *Single flat.* Indicates a note previously double-flatted is to be played a half step higher.

𝄴 *Common time.* A signature mark indicating that what follows is to be played with four quarter notes to the measure.

4/4, 4/2 *Rhythm marks.* They indicate the number of notes per measure.

∾ *Turn.* An embellishment.

Written Played

tr~~ *Trill.* An embellishment.

Written Played

Mordent. An embellishment.

Written Played

Crescendo. Gradual increase of tone.

Decrescendo. Gradually softer.

Segno. A sign marking the beginning or end of a passage to be repeated.

Double bar. Placed at the beginning or end of a passage, it indicates the marked section is to be repeated.

Notes:

Whole note (*semi-breve*); half note (*minim*); quarter note (*crotchet*); eighth note (*quaver*); sixteenth note (*semi-quaver*); thirty-second note (*demisemi-quaver*); sixty-fourth note (*hemidemi-semi-quaver*).

Rests:

Whole; half; quarter; eighth; sixteenth; thirty-second; sixty-fourth.

Accel. Accelerando. Gradually increasing speed.

Ad lib. Ad libitum. To be rendered freely, as the performer pleases.

And. Andante. Moderately slow.

A tem. A tempo. In time.

Cresc. Crescendo. Gradually increasing volume.

D.C. Da capo. From the beginning: return to beginning of composition and repeat to double bar marked *fine*.

Dim. Diminuendo. Gradual decrease of volume.

f. Forte. Loudly, strongly.

ff. Fortissimo. Very loud.

fz. Sforzando. As loud as possible.

fp. Forte-piano. Loud, then soft.

Leg. Legato. In a smooth gliding manner.

marc. Marcato. With emphasis.

mf. Mezzo-forte. Moderately loud.

M.M. Maelzel's metronome. Found at the beginning of a composition, together with the number of metronome beats per minute at which the piece is to be played, e.g., M.M. 80, or 80 quarter notes per minute.

mp. Mezzo-piano. Moderately soft.

Ott. Ottava. An octave. *Ottava alta*: to be played an octave higher than written. *Ottava bassa*, to be played an octave lower.

p. Piano. Softly.

pf. Piano-forte. Soft, then loud.

pp. Pianissimo. Very soft.

ppp. Pianissimo. As softly as possible.

pizz. Pizzicato. Direction to violinists to pluck the string with the fingers.

Rall. Rallentando. Becoming gradually slower.

Sost. Sostenuto. Sustained: prolonging the tone for the full duration indicated.

Trem. Tremolando. Tremblingly; a note or chord played with great rapidity, so as to produce such an effect.

EFFECTIVE PUBLIC SPEAKING

The most pleasing style of public speaking and the one most characteristic of the twentieth century, is the conversational. Amplification systems have made it unnecessary for the speaker on the rostrum to develop a voice sufficiently loud and carrying to "reach the last row." The radio has made the quiet easy way of talking seem the natural thing, and has in addition brought into existence a class of radio speakers who deliberately cultivate a low, rapid, well-modulated voice and avoid all sounds involving explosive or windy expulsions of breath. The resonant, full-throated utterances of the old-school actor and the fervent political orator have by gradual stages come to have an artificial and almost insincere sound. Their style was well suited to the needs of pre-radio civilization. It had several points in its favor and was decidedly more difficult to master, requiring as it did the vocal equipment of an opera singer. But there is no question that it is being replaced by the conversational style, which achieves effectiveness in a simpler and easier way.

The basis of an effective modern manner of speaking is good conversational ability. The latter is not, however, a very common attribute. Many socially successful people are not in the strictest sense of the word good conversationalists. They talk in half-sentences and phrases, seldom say more than a few words at one time. They use a surprisingly small vocabulary. They are jocular, witty, proficient at repartee—in short, good mixers. But they find themselves in difficulties as soon as they have to talk connectedly for two consecutive minutes. Without the stimulus of replies, questions, and comments, their source of inspiration dries up.

The person who wants to become an effective public speaker will find it helpful to cultivate a more extended conversational style. He should try to express his thoughts fully, rather than hint at them with brief phrases. He should acquire the not-so-common habit of talking in sentences. This is good mental discipline as well. Most people talk vaguely because their thoughts are vague, their opinions uncertain and ill-defined. An abbreviated, cryptic style of speech helps cover up this condition. Fuller expression brings it into the open and forces the individual to think and to think clearly. Some sort of logical structure becomes necessary. Certain ideas and phrases must be subordinated. Others must be emphasized. In short, the individual finds himself acquiring the ability to talk in the connected, smooth-flowing way that characterizes the successful public speaker. Arguments are particularly helpful, since they encourage the marshaling of ideas in a persuasive order, building up to the final capstone. The telling of anecdotes, jokes, and stories is also useful, requiring a dramatic, well-timed style of delivery. In short, conversation provides a valuable field of practice.

The individual who has developed conversational ability has no reason to feel frightened when he rises to address a group. All that is expected of him is a somewhat more extended effort. For this he may find notes helpful, usually just a few indications of main points, so that he will not wander too far from his subject; or the notes may be greater in number, and he may refer to them more often. One particular value in notes is that they provide a new starting-point if the speaker happens to lose the thread of his discourse or find himself at a momentary loss for words. Some speakers go even farther and write their speeches out beforehand. This involves a great deal of extra work and is apt to create a somewhat labored, though possibly more coherent, effect; it is nevertheless frequently advisable for persons who are called upon to speak but rarely, or who have to expound very complex subjects. Certainly all speakers, whether or not they use notes or speak from a written manuscript, should rehearse their talks beforehand. Friends or family sometimes provide a good audience for such a rehearsal, their presence encouraging a conversational delivery. Practice is just as essential for the speaker as for the singer or pianist. If he goes for a few days without sessions of extended talking, he will find himself becoming less glib. Sentences will not flow smoothly and effortlessly. He will begin to hesitate and make false starts. The only remedy for such faults is continual practice of one sort or another.

Little advice of real value can be given the speaker as to his physical behavior on the platform or its equivalent. Old schools of oratory placed great emphasis on gestures, and developed complicated systems of movement to emphasize various attitudes and emotions—the clenched fist to indicate defiance, the palm pushed out to symbolize rejection, the finger pointed at an imaginary adversary, etc. These are practically useless for the modern speaker, who should carry his body easily and employ only such gestures as occur naturally in the course of any conversation. If he speaks naturally and devotes real thought to what he is saying, his body will take care of itself. Audiences never resent nervous mannerisms on the part of the speaker, if what he says is interesting. Anything that is natural is not offensive. The speaker should not be afraid of pausing in order to think out a point before making his next statement. There is no need for him to pour out words in a steady flow, like some sort of machine. Many beginners, in fact, talk too fast. The experienced speaker pauses after key statements, in order that they will sink into the consciousness of his listeners. He gives his audience ample time to appreciate his arguments. If they laugh at his jokes, he does not cut in on their laughter. He is a past master in the art of timing.

Despite the thoroughness of a speaker's preparations, it is not always easy for him to maintain a natural, straightforward attitude toward his listeners. They tend to dissolve into a sea of impersonal faces and he senses only an excruciating social pressure. He becomes embarrassed and finds the utterance of each word painful. There is an easy and almost infallible remedy for this difficulty. It consists of looking at the audience as individuals. Instead of talking to the whole audience at once, the speaker concentrates on single persons, notes their expressions, looks them in the eye, tries to make them nod or smile. He establishes a personal contact. His listeners are gratified by this device and the speaker gains a great advantage. He has transformed the difficult problem of persuading or amusing an impersonal group into the easy problem of persuading or amusing single individuals. Without conscious effort, his manner of talking becomes conversational, intimate, and convincing.

SECRETARIES' GUIDE AND MANUAL OF INFORMATION

SHORTHAND : TYPING : FILING BY ALPHABET : LETTER WRITING OFFICE ROUTINE : POSTAL INFORMATION : WEIGHTS AND MEASURES BUSINESS ETIQUETTE : THE SUCCESSFUL SECRETARY SUCCESS IN YOUR JOB

SHORTHAND

The modern business concern desires its office workers to be versatile, and frequently encourages versatility by shifting individuals from one kind of work to another, thus making it easier to handle emergency situations and also preparing the individual worker for promotion. A good working knowledge of shorthand and typing is always a valuable asset, even in a position which does not directly involve secretarial or stenographic duties. It cannot be too strongly emphasized, therefore, that the time taken in learning shorthand and typing is well spent and will repay the student many times over. Even a little knowledge of the fundamentals is better than none at all.

Without knowing it, most office workers make use of a kind of simplified shorthand. That is, they learn to use abbreviations in noting down memorandums and making outlines for their own personal use. A few letters are made to stand for a word, and unessential words are eliminated. Shorthand carries this process a great deal further, by using an alphabet of marks, in which curving lines stand for syllables and words, and in which the particular curve and slant of each line and the position of each dot has a meaning. The accompanying illustration shows the characteristic shorthand alphabet. It is included through the courtesy of the Gregg Publishing Company. It is beyond the scope of this section to attempt a course of instruction on the subject of shorthand; that belongs to the schools and colleges of business.

THE ALPHABET OF GREGG SHORTHAND

CONSONANTS

Written forward:

K G R L N M T D TH (or)

Written downward:

P B F V CH J S (or) SH

H NG NK

VOWELS

ă ĭ ŏ ŭ

ä ĕ aw o͝o

ā ē ō ōō

DIPHTHONGS

	Composed of		Composed of
ū	ē-ōō as in *unit*	*oi*	aw-ē as in *oil*
ow	ä-ōō as in *owl*	*ī*	ä-ē as in *isle*

BLENDED CONSONANTS

The consonants are so arranged that two strokes joining with an obtuse or blunt angle may assume the form of a large curve, thus:

ten, den — ent, end — def-v, tive

tem, dem — emt, emd — jent-d, pent-d

TYPING

With typing the situation is somewhat different. Today the typewriter has become an instrument of general use, neither confined to the office, nor requiring a highly skilled operator. This is because it is fairly easy for anyone to attain moderate proficiency in handling the machine. Of course, very speedy, accurate typing can only be accomplished by use of the "touch" system, which requires a rather long period of instruction. But very speedy typing is usually needed only for copy work. The demands of the average person are satisfied if he learns to type with sufficient speed to keep up with the words and sentences formulated in his mind. This is generally not difficult.

It is possible to attain a satisfactory degree of efficiency on the typewriter by the "sight" system without losing the time or going to the expense of mastering the elaborate touch system. In fact, any intelligent person in a few weeks can acquire such skill as would require many months by the touch system. With a typewriter in every office and in many homes, there is a real need for the simple exercises included in the following paragraphs. Sight typewriting is the system universally used by so-called one-finger artists. In our system, however, we recommend right from the beginning the use of two fingers, the first and second on each hand. Later on as your skill increases you may bring into use the third and fourth digits.

The keyboards of all standard typewriters are identical and when you have mastered one you have mastered all. All keys to the right-hand side of the keyboard are struck with either the first or second finger of the right hand; all the keys to the left-hand side of the keyboard with the first and second fingers of the left hand. The space bar should always be operated with the thumb, and the shift keys, back spacer or tabulating keys with the little fingers, thus leaving the first two fingers free for the actual typing.

Exercise 1.—Fill one whole page with the word "them."

"t" is struck with the first finger of the left hand.

"h" is struck with the first finger of the right hand.

"e" is struck with the second finger of the left hand.

"m" is struck with the first finger of the right hand.

This exercise is put here for two reasons. In the first place the first three letters, "the" are used more than any other word in the English language. Secondly, it will introduce that important principle of typewriting, the alternate hand movement.

Exercise 2.—Copy each of the following words three hundred times: then, these, theme, there, those, think.

This exercise introduces the principle of using one finger to strike two or three times in succession (se and ese).

Exercise 3.—Copy "they" three hundred times, and "that" three hundred times. Then fill up an entire page with the words, "they think that," and another whole page with the words "they think that those think." Be sure to strike the space bar after each word.

Exercise 4.—Write the first three letters of the alphabet "abc" one hundred times. Then add the next letter "a b c d" and write the combination one hundred times. Keep adding one letter in this manner until you have written the entire alphabet one hundred times.

Exercise 5.—The following sentence contains all the letters of the alphabet:

"The big brown fox jumped quickly over the lazy dog's back."

Write the first word 100 times, the first two words 100 times, the first three words 100 times and so on until you have written the whole sentence 100 times.

Exercise 6.—Here is another sentence that contains every letter of the alphabet:

"Wafting zephyrs quickly vexed Jumbo."

Copy this sentence the same as in exercise 5.

Capitals, Figures, Punctuation Marks, and Symbols.—Capital letters are made by pushing down the shift key with the little finger and then striking the letter required with one

Standard typewritter keyboard

of the other fingers. The standard keyboard provides a special row of keys for all the figures except 1, which is formed by the small "l" or by the capital "I." Punctuation marks and symbols, with the exception of commas and periods, are also made on most machines by depressing the shift key.

Exercise 7.—Copy each of the following exercises two hundred times:

Harold James Theodore Walter
Loren William Meyers
1 2 3 4 5 6 7 8 9 0
26 341 8674 95216
2000 Bu. wheat @ $1.57\frac{3}{8}$

SPEED.—Now that you have mastered the keyboard it is time to try for speed. Although almost any will serve the purpose, the following practice sentence is suggested: "Now is the time for all men to come to the aid of the party." Copy this sentence at least 100 times every day until you are able to run off sixty words a minute with ease and accuracy. It is also good practice to write your personal letters on the typewriter, to copy interesting items from newspapers and magazines, always holding in your memory as many words as possible while copying. You will be astonished to learn what rapid progress you can make in this way.

FILING BY ALPHABET

Alphabetizing is the basis of the filing systems used in all business offices. Although the systems in ordinary use differ in details, all are based upon the same general rules. These rules are given below. It is important to remember that occasionally offices have developed systems which depart from standard practice in some respects.

Alphabetical Arrangement

Arrange words, or proper names, according to the order of their first, second, third letters, etc., carrying the process far enough to place the words in correct alphabetical order. For example:

NOT ARRANGED	ALPHABETICALLY ARRANGED
Smithers	Smith
Smythe	Smithers
Smith	Smythe

NOT ARRANGED	ALPHABETICALLY ARRANGED
Abrams	Abarbanell
Abrahams	Abrahams
Abarbanell	Abrams
Bankhead	Bangs
Bangs	Bankhead
Davisson	Davidson
Davidson	Davisson
Slotkowsky	Schmidt
Slotkowski	Schultz
Schultz	Schulze
Schulze	Slotkowski
Schmidt	Slotkowsky
Winters	Stone
Witherspoon	Wallace
Wallace	Winters
Stone	Witherspoon

File the names of persons according to (1) surname, (2) given name, (3) middle names or middle initials. For example:

Edward H. Bangs should be filed as *Bangs, Edward H.*

Alternative Spellings

When the same name is spelled in more than one way, enter each spelling in the file and cross-refer each spelling to its alternatives.

Miller; *see also* Mueller, Muller.
Mueller; *see also* Miller, Muller.
Muller; *see also* Miller, Mueller.

Titles and Degrees

Professional titles and *academic degrees* are placed last, in parentheses ( ), and are not considered in alphabetizing.

NOT ARRANGED	ALPHABETICALLY ARRANGED
Col. John Quincy Jefferson	Edwards, Anthony (Prof.)
Rev. Edward Holmes	Holmes, Edward (Rev.)
Prof. Anthony Edwards	Jefferson, John Quincy (Col.)
C. Arbuthnot McGuire, PhD.	McGuire, C. Arbuthnot (Ph.D.)

Titles of nobility are usually treated as part of the person's name.

INCORRECT	CORRECT
Astor, Nancy (Lady)	Astor, Lady Nancy
Nordenskjöld, Nils (Baron)	Nordenskjöld, Baron Nils

When the title of nobility differs from the person's name, it is usually necessary to cross-refer to a listing by titles.

Buchan, John; *see* Tweedsmuir, Baron
Baldwin, Stanley; *see* Baldwin of Bewdley, Earl of
Disraeli, Benjamin; *see* Beaconsfield, Earl of
Wellesley, Arthur; *see* Wellington, Duke of

When several individuals have the same surname, and first names beginning with the same letter, the names of those individuals whose first names are represented by initials are listed first, followed by the spelled-out names in alphabetical order.

NOT ARRANGED	ALPHABETICALLY ARRANGED
Herman Hitchens	Hitchens, H.
Herbert Hitchens	Hitchens, H. M.
H. McDougal Hitchens	Hitchens, H. McDougal
Henry Hitchens	Hitchens, Harold Montessori
H. Hitchens	Hitchens, Henry
H. M. Hitchens	Hitchens, Herbert
Harold Montessori Hitchens	Hitchens, Herman
Reginald Tracy	Tracy, R. P.
R. P. Tracy	Tracy, Reginald

In general, such prefixes as *da, de, von, van, Mac, Mc, O'*, etc., are treated as the first syllable of the surname, and apostrophes are not considered. This rule is observed in English, but it does not obtain in many other languages. In doubtful cases, usage must be the guide; and cross-references are often necessary.

NOT ARRANGED	ALPHABETICALLY ARRANGED
Robert La Chance	D'Artagnan, Raoul
Alfred von Tirpitz	De Forest, Lee
Jan van Rebeck	De Grey, Lord
Bernardo O'Higgins	de MacMahon, Marie
Marie de MacMahon	de Saavedra, Angelo
Raoul D'Artagnan	La Chance, Robert
Lee De Forest	O'Higgins, Bernardo
Lord De Grey	van Rebeck, Jan
Angelo de Saavedra	von Tirpitz, Alfred

Classify compound or hyphenated names by the first part of the compound.

NOT ARRANGED	ALPHABETICALLY ARRANGED
Sir Johnston Forbes-Robertson	Byng-Enfield, Stephen
Stephen Byng-Enfield	Forbes-Robertson, Sir Johnston
Nikolai Rimsky-Korsakov	Rimsky-Korsakov, Nikolai
Ernestine Schumann-Heink	Schumann-Heink, Ernestine

Names of Organizations

In general, the names of businesses, societies, etc., are alphabetized as printed. Be sure the name used is correct, as set forth in the charter of incorporation. There are many exceptions to the rule for institutional names, the most important of which are given below. If confusion is likely to arise, cross-references should be used.

NOT ARRANGED	ALPHABETICALLY ARRANGED
Smith and Wesson	American Tobacco Company
Oppenheimer Casing Company	Crown-Zellerbach Paper Company
General Cigar Company	General Cigar Company
American Tobacco Company	Lake Superior Piling Company
Crown-Zellerbach Paper Company	Northwestern Foundry Company
Lake Superior Piling Company	Oppenheimer Casing Company
West Virginia Pulp and Paper Company	Smith and Wesson
Northwestern Foundry Company	West Virginia Pulp and Paper Company

Ampersands (that is, the figure "&"), when correctly a part of the name, should not be written out.

Brown & Jones should not be written as *Brown and Jones.*

When *and* is spelled out in the name, the ampersand should not be used.

Jones and Brown should not be written as *Jones & Brown.*

Note that when such words as *American Northwestern, Lake,* and *West* occur in corporate or institutional names, they are considered in alphabetizing. Compound words which are sometimes written as two words (northwestern—north western), are always arranged as though written in the compounded form.

When the name of an institution contains the name of an individual, the individual's name determines the alphebetical classification for filing purposes.

NOT ARRANGED	ALPHABETICALLY ARRANGED
Barron G. Collier Corporation	Collier, Barron G., Corporation
George E. Davies Foundation	Davies, George E., Foundation
L. C. Smith and Corona Typewriters, Inc.	Smith, L. C., and Corona Typewriters, Inc.

The, when it occurs at the beginning of a corporate or institutional name, is placed in parentheses at the end of the name. When it occurs elsewhere in the name it is disregarded entirely.

The Bussert-Koffler and Leiber Company of Detroit should be classified as:

Bussert-Koffler and Leiber Company of Detroit, (The)

And is similarly ignored. The instance above is properly classified as though it read:

Bussert-Koffler . . . Leiber Company . . . Detroit.

Notice that the hyphenated form *Bussert-Koffler* is treated as one word. Compounds not formed of the names of persons are treated in the same manner.

NOT ARRANGED	ALPHABETICALLY ARRANGED
Smart and Daniels	Eat-and-Drink, Inc.
While-U-Wait Pressers	Small Arms Manufacturing Company, (The)
Eat-and-Drink, Inc.	Smart-Cut Clothiers, Inc.
Smart-Cut Clothiers, Inc.	Smart and Daniels
Whitman and Kane	While-U-Wait Pressers
The Small Arms Manufacturing Company	Whitman and Kane

The suffix, 's, attached to the name of an individual within an institutional name, is sometimes ignored. When it is ignored, this type of classification results:

Foster's American Shoe Company
Foster, Lee and Company
Foster, Mark, Corp.
Foster's Shoe Store
Foster's Tailor Shop
Foster and Young, Inc.

Some organizations prefer to group the possessive forms separately, after the group of names without apostrophes. In such cases, this type of arrangement results:

Goldberg and Company
Goldberg, Max, and Company
Goldberg and Nathan, Inc.
Goldberg's Market
Goldberg's Meat Market
Goldberg's Shoe Store

The numbers in a name should be treated as though they were spelled out.

NOT ARRANGED	ALPHABETICALLY ARRANGED
4-Deuces Club	Eighteenth National Bank
2222 Elm Street Building Corporation	Four-Deuces Club
18th National Bank	Twenty-two twenty-two Elm Street Building Corporation

When several organizations have the same name, arrange them alphabetically by their locations, considering the town first:

Economy Chevrolet Company,
Fostoria, Ohio
Economy Chevrolet Company,
Newmarket, Indiana
Economy Chevrolet Company,
Newmarket, Wyoming

Names of Government Agencies

The names of government subdivisions and officials are alphabetized under the customary English name of the government.

"Sverige," the official name in Swedish for Sweden, would be "Sweden" in an American file or index.

Where it is necessary to refer to a subdivision within the government or to an individual officer, the subdivisions are detailed in descending order, beginning with the most important.

The *Chief of the Bureau of Public Roads of the U. S. Department of Agriculture* should be filed as:

United States Government
Agriculture, Department of,
Public Roads, Bureau of,
. . . ., Chief.

United States Government is the customary heading for agencies of the U. S. Government. Other examples:

U. S. Agricultural Marketing Service should be filed as:

United States Government
Agriculture, Department of,
Agricultural Marketing Service.

U. S. Employment Service should be filed as:

United States Government
Commerce, Department of,
Employment Service.

The *Canadian Bureau of Parks and Forests* should be filed as:

Dominion of Canada
Mines and Resources, Department of,
Parks and Forests, Bureau of.

The *Bureau of Transportation of the City of Chicago* should be filed as:

Chicago, City of,
Transportation, Bureau of.

LETTER WRITING

The Importance of Good Business Letters

Few secretarial tasks are so important or consume so much time as the writing of business letters. Some secretaries are expected merely to transcribe the letters dictated to them, with due attention to correctness and appearance; others have the additional responsibility of determining the wording of letters. Since secretaries are judged largely by the quality of their letters, they should become thoroughly familiar both with the effective use of English, and with correct business-letter usage in the arrangement of parts, spelling, punctuation, and related subjects treated in this office manual.

Secretaries will sense the importance of this phase of their work when they realize that every letter reveals the character and personality of the organization which sends it. If the letter is intelligently composed and carefully typewritten, it adds to the recipient's respect for the organization, and in the long run to the esteem upon which a company's reputation and good will are based. The business letter thus has a role much like that of a firm's personal representative, who may impart either very favorable or extremely unfavorable impressions of his organization. The successful representative takes pains both to dress well and to approach his clients in a correctly trained manner. It rests with the secretary to see that the letter produces the proper effect by being suitably worded and neatly written.

The importance of excellent business letters is increased by the permanence of the impression they produce. In modern business establishments all correspondence is kept on file, at least until it becomes certain that it will no longer be needed. In this way a letter may serve for a long time as a point of contact between organizations and individuals. Every time the executive reviews a file of correspondence, he experiences again the pleasant or unpleasant impressions which the letters produced when first received. Time expended in the careful preparation of letters is therefore time well invested.

As suggested, the duties of the secretary in the writing of letters vary widely according to the individual situation. Some executives make a practice of indicating the gist of the letter in a few general sentences, and require the secretary to clothe their ideas in appropriate words. The secretary should have a practical knowledge of writing methods to perform such a task successfully; and the person who has this ability is an indispensable and highly valued assistant. Other executives dictate the letter in full. Some resent the change of a word or a punctuation mark as unwarranted presumption, and expect the secretary only to typewrite the letter exactly as dictated, putting the parts in proper order and spacing the materials correctly on the page. But with either method of work the secretary who is perfectly informed in letter-writing usages will achieve the most satisfactory results.

The Language of Business Letters

Letters are of two main kinds: business letters and social letters. The letters which a secretary in a business office prepares are nearly all of the first kind. In social correspondence between friends a good deal of latitude is permitted in the choice of words and the arrangements of parts, but in the business letter it is necessary to follow conventional usage with greater strictness. The body of the business letter, however, sometimes offers scope for individuality of treatment, but business letters may not use slang and the freedom of treatment which are acceptable in letters between friends. Both business and social letters require the observance of good grammar and correct punctuation at all times.

In general terms, the most effective business letters are those which succeed best in combining cordiality with dignity. Such letters convey to the reader a sense of the sincerity and friendliness of the writer, and promote the objectives with which the letter is sent. Cordiality in business letters, however, degenerates into effusiveness if used to excess, sounding hollow and defeating its purpose of making the recipient desirous of cooperating with the writer.

The tone which business letters strive to achieve naturally varies according to the nature of the correspondence, and the social relationship between the writer and the reader. Courtesy and correctness are essential in all business correspondence, but the general tone will vary somewhat with the type of letter, depending upon whether an order for merchandise, a recommendation, a letter of information, an adjustment, or a sales letter is being written. An application for employment or a communication to an important governmental official is necessarily more formal and respectful than the ordinary business letter. Each sort of letter has a particular objective, and each should use the language and arrangement best suited for its attainment. Correspondence between people who have had a long business association in which an element of friendship may have entered usually is not as dignified and formal as correspondence between people who are communicating for the first time.

TRITE EXPRESSIONS.—The message of the letter should be expressed in simple and natural terms. There are dozens of conventional phrases which have become so hackneyed that they have ceased to have any meaning, while others are unduly brief. Both types should be avoided entirely, since they destroy the clarity of the letter and make it seem old-fashioned. A business letter should resemble neither a telegram nor an engraved invitation to tea. Hence it should not contain telescoped expressions like "the 15th inst." and "in re," or effusions of pretended gratitude such as "your esteemed favor" and "thanking you in advance." Instead, brevity should be the result of clear thinking and avoidance of repetition. Courtesy should pervade the message as a whole, rather than being injected here and there by the use of a trite phrase.

Below are listed some of the trite and objectionable phrases which should be avoided in modern business letters in the interest of concise and unaffected expression. Besides the ones listed, there are many others of a similar character which the alert person will learn to detect and avoid.

ADVISE. Should not be used in the sense of *tell*, or *inform*.

AND OBLIGE. Not in good taste.

APPRECIATE. Means *to judge* or *estimate correctly*. Should not be used for *like*, *thank you for*, *feel kindly toward you for*, etc.

AS PER. A correct phrase is *according to*.

AT HAND. Trite.

ATTACHED FIND. If it is attached, it will be found. It is better to say *attached is*.

ATTACHED HERETO. *Hereto* is superfluous.

BEG, OR BEG LEAVE. Trite, overworked, and useless.

BEG TO STATE, ADVISE, INFORM, ACKNOWLEDGE. To *beg* means to ask something for nothing. These expressions should be avoided.

CONTENTS CAREFULLY NOTED. One is expected to notice the contents of letters carefully. It is a waste of time to tell the correspondent that this has been done.

DICTATED BUT NOT READ. The letter of a correspondent who uses this expression ought to be returned with the notation "Received but not read."

ESTEEMED FAVOR. Only people are *esteemed* and a *favor* is a kindness.

FURTHER COMMANDS. This term is hackneyed.

HAND YOU. How can anything be handed to another in a letter? *Send you is* preferable.

HEREWITH. Superfluous. *Enclose* means as much as *enclose herewith*.

HOPING TO HEAR FROM YOU. This is usually taken for granted.

I HAVE BEFORE ME YOUR LETTER. The correspondent doesn't care where his letter is if it is given proper attention.

IN DUE COURSE. This is too indefinite.

IN RE. A Latin term meaning "concerning," or "in the matter of." Should not be used except in legal writing.

IN REPLY WISH TO STATE. This statement is a waste of time.

INST. An antiquated term for *this month*.

KIND, KINDLY. Overworked and trite.

PERMIT ME TO SAY. This is a needless prefix to an expression of opinion.

PROPOSITION. Business slang. It is better to say *proposal*, or *undertaking*.

PROX. The proper term is *next month*.

RECENT DATE. Letter should be referred to either by the exact date or the subject or by both.

SAME. Should not be used as a pronoun except in legal documents.

THANKING YOU IN ADVANCE. It is presumptuous to assume a request will be granted.

THE WRITER. The pronoun *I* is better because more direct.

THIS IS IN REPLY TO. Perfectly obvious from the contents of the letter.

ULT. A poor way of saying *last month*.

WISH TO SAY. Overworked, meaningless, and trite.

Five Essentials of Business-Letter English

The language used in every business letter, regardless of type, must contain five qualities which are indispensable in effective correspondence. These are:

1. Clearness
2. Conciseness
3. Completeness
4. Courtesy
5. Correctness

The writer who keeps these "Five C's" constantly in mind while composing the letter will find his task greatly simplified. Also, in reviewing the letter after it is drafted, he can estimate the value of his work according to the presence or absence of these qualities. The "Five C's" are the hallmarks of good modern correspondence, for their use distinguishes progressive letter-writing of the present from that of the past.

CLEARNESS.—A letter is first of all a message to a reader. If the reader does not grasp this message easily and thoroughly, the letter has failed in its purpose, no matter how correct its form or how attractive its appearance may be. Consequently the writer must make sure that the letter conveys a message in unmistakable terms.

Clarity in letters can be achieved by following a very simple yet important procedure. Before beginning the composition of the letter the writer must determine definitely what he wishes to say—whether or not he will order the materials, supply the information, give the recommendation, or do whatever else the reader has requested. If one waits until the actual writing of the letter to make these decisions, ambiguity and indecisiveness are almost certain to result. Although such a caution may appear obvious and needless, many letters are begun before the writers know what they are going to say.

After this first step, which is a matter of individual consideration for each case at hand, the writer must find the best words for expressing the message determined upon. Clearness in the actual writing is attained by care in the selection of words, and in the punctuation, the length and arrangement of sentences, and the paragraphing. It is important to avoid vague words or those subject to misinterpretation. Sentences should be as direct as possible, not weighed down by a burden of parenthetical expressions, subordinate clauses, or participial phrases. In addition, sentences in a business letter should be reasonably brief, though too many very short sentences in succession give an undesirable staccato effect. Both vocabulary and sentence structure must be adapted to the intelligence and education of the reader: greater simplicity is obviously required in a letter to a farmer or a housewife than in one to an editor or an instructor. The principles of good paragraphing must also be observed, so that each topic or group of related topics occupies a paragraph by itself.

CONCISENESS.—The man of business has so many claims on his limited time that he welcomes methods which conserve his working hours and energy. The best business letters, therefore, are those which enable him to grasp their message with the greatest ease and rapidity. Clearness in words and grammatical structure are means to this end; another is conciseness. Conciseness in writing consists in the omission of unessential matter, and the avoidance of repetition and of unduly lengthy modes of expression. It should be noted, however, that concise writing need not be incomplete nor discourteous writing. Really essential facts must not be overlooked, and the brusqueness which would result from the deletion of all expressions of cordiality and good will is undesirable. Without the usual pronouns and articles the language becomes clipped and telegraphic, as in the following instance, "Received yours of 29th ult."

The letter writer can find no better way to train himself in conciseness than to review his completed letters and note the number of phrases, words, and even whole sentences which could be left out without impairing the meaning of the whole.

COMPLETENESS.—The completeness of the message should never be sacrificed in an exaggerated effort to achieve brevity of expression. Every item which is essential must find its place in the letter, for omission of important details is likely to cause confusion. The writer's best way of working to avoid this difficulty is to check over the items he intends to mention before the letter is begun, making sure that he has in mind all the needed details and no more. The letter should be read through after it is written, to see if it complies with the requirements of completeness. If something has been forgotten, the letter should probably be rewritten, since details tacked on in a postscript are an admission that the letter was inexpertly drafted in the first place.

COURTESY.—Every successful business organization shows great courtesy in personal contacts with individuals and other companies, for much of its success depends on the esteem of its clients and associates. Courtesy in business letters is no less essential, especially in view of the permanence of written words.

There is a great difference, however, between true courtesy, which consistently takes into account the problems, needs, and feelings of the reader, and sham courtesy. The latter expresses itself in resounding phrases which do not truly represent the sentiments of the writer. Furthermore, exaggerated expressions of thanks and esteem are in poor taste, even if they are sincere.

Courtesy depends in part on a properly chosen salutation and complimentary close, but to a much greater degree on the language in the body of the letter. True consideration rests in the acts of the individual or company, but whether these favor or disfavor the reader's interests, they must be communicated in courteous terms. With skill, even collection letters or refusals to grant charge accounts can be stated with a minimum of chagrin to the reader. Business letters of this type should show respect for the dignity and character of the recipient, and should avoid imputing bad faith to him. Sarcasm and abuse should never appear in business letters of any kind, since they brand the writer as ill-bred, and antagonize the reader.

CORRECTNESS.—Correctness in the business letter is a requirement so absolute that without it the time spent in drafting a clear, well-phrased, and courteous message is hardly worth while, for a letter which contains errors in formal details furnishes but a sorry impression of the intelligence and character of the individual or firm which sends it. A carefully worded but carelessly transcribed letter is as ineffectual as a well-informed speaker with a severe stammer: neither the letter nor the speaker can win the favorable attention which the quality of their message deserves.

After the letter is composed, but before it is typewritten, it should be checked for its correctness in the following particulars: (1) grammar, (2) spelling, (3) capitalization, (4) punctuation, (5) the form of numerical expressions, (6) abbreviations. When it is ascertained that the letter is correct in these usages, it should be typewritten with care, that errors of fact do not creep in, and in accordance with the rules for spacing and the order of parts found in the following pages.

The Form of Business Letters

The letter's neat and pleasing appearance, like its correctness in details, enhances the value of skillful phrasing and offsets to some degree the bad effects of clumsy expression. Furthermore, clear-cut paragraph separations and proper spacing of the materials on the page permit quicker assimilation of the contents. Likewise, paper of good quality and a well-designed letterhead reflect credit on the writer.

The sheets of paper most commonly used in commercial correspondence, and those which best accommodate the business letter of average length are approximately 8½" x 11", though smaller sizes are used for some purposes. Most business stationery has an engraved or printed letterhead at the top of the sheet, bearing the name and address of the company. This letterhead should be well proportioned and should use faces of type which combine well. The typewriter ribbon should be black and must be fresh enough to make a clear imprint.

Carelessness in making erasures may produce smudges on the page which are hard to remove. These smudges can be avoided by use of a celluloid cutout which exposes only the letter or word to be erased. Typographical errors should not be struck over with the correct letter; instead the error should be carefully erased and the proper symbol typed in its place. Since it is difficult to insert the correction in exactly the right spot when the page has been removed from the typewriter and then replaced, it is best to read the letter over for errors before taking it out of the machine.

Few business letters run longer than one page. When they do, however, the bottom of the first sheet must not be crowded. The typist should never crowd a page to avoid using a second. The second sheet should bear the name of the reader, the page number, and the date, thus:

Mr. Ralph C. Roberts Page 2 June 30, 1963

Letterhead stationery is preferably not used for any pages after the first. Instead, plain paper should be used, of the same color and quality as the first page.

Carbon copies should be made of all letters, as a matter of course, and promptly filed. This practice makes the review of correspondence an easy matter, and is therefore essential in the smooth running of the office.

SPACING.—Proper spacing of the materials on the page has a great effect on the letter's legibility and attractiveness. The letter should be approximately centered on the page, but with the upper and left-hand margins slightly wider than the lower and right-hand margins. If the letter occupies a full page or more, the upper and left-hand margins should be not less than 1½ inches wide, and the lower and right-hand margins not less than 1 inch wide. A shorter letter will require wider margins, but these should maintain the same proportions. The length of the lines also varies according to the length of the letter. A letter of 100 words or less presents the best appearance if the lines are about 40 characters long (counting both letters and the spaces between words). A letter containing from 100 to 150 words should have 50-character lines; one of more than 150 words should have 60-character lines. If the typewriter used has "elite" type (that is, type which measures 12 characters to the inch), letters exceeding 200 words in length should have 70-character lines; but if the typewriter has larger type than this, a line of 70 characters will be too long for the minimum margins of 1½ inch and 1 inch. Before the transcription of the letter is begun the typist should make an approximate estimate of its length and set the typewriter's margin guides accordingly.

The length of the letter determines not only the preferable width of the lines, but also the vertical spacing. If the letter is a very brief one, it is likely to appear lost in a sea of white paper. This may be avoided by increasing the number of blank lines between the various parts of the letter, so as to expand it vertically on the page. The area which the letter covers on the page may also be increased by double-spacing.

BLOCK AND INDENTED STYLES.—The left-hand margins of the various parts of the letter may follow either of two styles, known as block style and indented style. In block style, which is perhaps the more common in modern usage, each line of the address or the heading is flush on the left with the lines above and below. The following is an example of block style:

501 Shelby Street
Northfield, Vermont
June 30, 1963

Mr. Ralph C. Roberts
831 North Stacy Place
Jonesborough, Texas

In indented style each line begins a little more to the right than the line above it, thus:

501 Shelby Street
    Northfield, Vermont
        June 30, 1963

Mr. Ralph C. Roberts
    831 North Stacy Place
        Jonesborough, Texas

The application of block and indented styles to the paragraphs of the letter, and to the signature are explained in the sections BODY, p. 205, and SIGNATURE, p. 206.

OPEN AND CLOSED PUNCTUATION.—Two styles of punctuation are also acceptable. These are "open punctuation" and "closed punctuation." The first of these is much used at the present time. It uses no punctuation marks at the ends of lines except to indicate that a word is abbreviated. In "closed punctuation" the suitable punctuation marks close each line. It should be noted, however, that these distinctions of style do not apply to the body of the letter, which is always punctuated according to the rules applying to other types of writing. Furthermore, even in open punctuation it is customary to follow the salutation with a colon, and the complimentary close with a comma.

The foregoing examples of block and indented style have "open punctuation." The following is an example of "closed punctuation" applied to heading, address, salutation, and complimentary close:

501 North Shelby Street,
Northfield, Vermont,
June 30, 1963

Mr. Ralph C. Roberts,
831 North Stacy Place,
Jonesborough, Texas.

Dear Mr. Roberts:

(Body of the letter)

Very truly yours,

Whichever method of punctuation and indention is used must be applied consistently throughout the entire letter except the body. If the heading is in indented style with closed punctuation, the address and the complimentary close must follow the same form. The addresses on the envelope must also be uniform in treatment with the letter inside.

The Parts of Business Letters

Besides the envelope, the business letter consists of six main parts, usually found in the following order: (1) heading, (2) the inside address or introduction, (3) the salutation, (4) the body, (5) the complimentary close, (6) the signature.

HEADING.—The heading consists of the name and address of the individual or organization, and the date. Most companies use letterhead stationery which has the name and the address at the top of the sheet. To complete the heading the date must be added. It may be placed either at the top beneath the letterhead, or, according to more conservative practice, a little below the letterhead but to the right, so that it is even with the right-hand margin of the body of the letter to follow. If letterhead stationery is not used, the entire heading should be typed in the upper right-hand corner, and should contain street address, city, state, and date in the order given.

Figures should not be used for the month or two digits for the year. No letters such as "st," "rd," or "th," should follow the day of the month. Correct and incorrect forms of the date line are illustrated as follows:

INCORRECT
April 17, '60
12/11/60
January 6th, 1960
September 23rd, 1960

CORRECT
April 17, 1960
December 11, 1960
January 6, 1960
September 23, 1960

Correct methods for date lines on letterhead stationery:

(Printed Letterhead)

August 3, 1963

or

(Printed Letterhead)

August 3, 1963

Heading typewritten on plain stationery, extending to right-hand margin of letter:

119 Falk Street
Oak Center, Ohio
January 23, 1963

INSIDE ADDRESS.—The inside address or introduction of the letter follows the same form as the address on the envelope. It should contain the name, street address, city, and state of the person to whom the letter is sent. Usually the name occupies the first line, the street address the second, and the city and state the third. If the name of the company is given to which the individual addressed belongs, this occupies the second line, all succeeding lines being pushed down. Sometimes the company itself is addressed, in which case the company name forms the first line. The name of a well-known office building or hotel sometimes supplements or replaces the street address.

The business title of the individual, indicating the position he holds in an organization, always follows the name, either on the same line or on the line below. The only words which precede the name are such terms of respect as "Mr.," "Mrs.," or "Miss," and the titles showing professional standing, like "Dr.," "Professor," and "The Reverend." Exceptions to this practice which may occur in addressing people of elevated position are listed under FORMS OF ADDRESS FOR GOVERNMENT AND ECCLESIASTICAL OFFICIALS, p. 210. The term "Esq.," which is used for lawyers in England, and occasionally used in a general sense in the United States, always follows the name. In this case no title precedes the name. Two titles are not used for a single name.

The following examples illustrate correct and incorrect forms for the name line of the inside address:

INCORRECT

Treasurer Richard Wilts
Dr. Harold Coombs, M.D.
Mayor John Adams
Mr. Samuel Slaughter, Esq.
or
Mr. Samuel Slaughter, Attorney
Bursar James McCabe

CORRECT—

Mr. Richard Wilts, Treasurer
Dr. Harold Coombs
or
Harold Coombs, M.D.
The Honorable John Adams
Mr. Samuel Slaughter
or
Samuel Slaughter, Esq.
or
Samuel Slaughter, Attorney
Mr. James McCabe, Bursar

The following are the various acceptable forms for the complete inside address, using both open and closed punctuation, and indented and block style in margins. Use the same style on envelope.

Mr. Roscoe Blair, Registrar
Municipal College of Fine Arts
1711 North Main Street
Pikesville, Tennessee
or
Mr. Roscoe Blair
Registrar, Municipal College of Fine Arts
1711 North Main Street
Pikesville, Tennessee

Economy Fuel Company
1181 Cross Street
Birmingham, Alabama

Mr. Harrison J. Watts, Vice President,
Economy Fuel Company,
1181 Cross Street,
Birmingham, Alabama.
or
Mr. Harrison J. Watts,
Vice President, Economy Fuel Company,
1181 Cross Street,
Birmingham, Alabama.

Clarence Morton, Esq.,
1216 King's Place,
Manchester, England.

Miss Clair Bellingham,
Fulton Hotel,
1200 Broadway,
New York, N.Y.

The Reverend Albert Thwing, Secretary
Universal Gospel Society
Terminals Building
Washburn, Ohio

The preceding examples show the variety of ways in which the inside address may be treated. In friendly correspondence it is usually omitted entirely, so that the salutation directly follows the heading. In government correspondence and some very formal letters the inside address is frequently placed below the signature, at the lower left-half corner of the page. The usual practice, however, is one of those indicated above.

SALUTATION.—The salutation marks the formal opening of the letter after the sender's and reader's addresses have been written. It begins at the left-hand margin, usually two spaces below the inside address, from which it is thus separated. It is followed by a colon, or in friendly letters by a comma. Users of the open punctuation system sometimes use no punctuation mark after the salutation, but the use of the colon is more general.

The choice of the salutation depends on the relationship between the writer and the reader of the letter. In ordinary business correspondence, moderately dignified salutations are desirable, unless the relationship has developed into a warmly personal one, when considerable informality is permissible. Special forms of address are used in writing to government officials; these are listed in FORMS OF ADDRESS FOR GOVERNMENT AND ECCLESIASTICAL OFFICIALS, p. 210.

The salutations suitable for various situations are as follows:

For addressing a company—
Gentlemen: (formal or informal)

For addressing a group of women—
Ladies: (formal or informal)
Mesdames: (formal)

For addressing an individual—
My dear Mr. O'Hara: (formal)
My dear Miss Foster: (formal)
Dear Sir: (moderately informal)
Dear Madam: (moderately informal)
Dear Mr. O'Hara: (moderately informal)
Dear Miss Foster: (moderately informal)

For addressing close acquaintances, and rarely used in business correspondence—
Dear Tom, (:) (very informal)
Dear Beatrice, (:) (very informal)
Dear O'Hara, (:) (very informal)

The writer should observe that the word "dear" in a salutation is capitalized only if it is the first word in the phrase. All other words used in salutations are capitalized wherever they occur. The only abbreviations used in salutations are "Mr.," "Mrs.," "Dr.," and "Rev."

A letter addressed directly to an organization as such should use the salutation "Gentlemen." However, if the writer wishes the matter to receive the attention of a particular individual in the firm, this is accomplished by the phrase "Attention of Mr.——," written either on the same line as the salutation, or else below it to the right, *thus:*

Simmons and Tate, Inc.
803 Clinton Court
New York, N. Y.

Gentlemen: Attention of Mr. John Harris

or thus:

Simmons and Tate, Inc.
803 Clinton Court
New York, N. Y.

Gentlemen:
Attention of Mr. John Harris

Body.—The body of the letter is the portion which contains the message. It begins one or two lines below the salutation.

There are two methods of typing the body: double-spaced and single-spaced. The choice of one or the other depends on the preference of the individual or firm, as well as on the amount of material in the letter, which affects the spacing. Materials intended to be printed, however, should always be double-spaced, to facilitate the work of the editor and the compositor.

If the body is double-spaced, the beginning of each paragraph must be indented so as to be clearly marked off from neighboring paragraphs. Paragraph divisions are made still more evident by leaving one or two blank lines between paragraphs, in addition to the indention at the beginning. However, the use of blank lines is optional in double-spaced matter.

If the body of the letter is single-spaced, paragraphs may begin flush with the left-hand margin, or indentions may be used if preferred. In either case the paragraphs must be separated from one another by one or more blank lines between them.

The block style of paragraphing is particularly suitable when the heading and the inside address are blocked. But when these parts of the letter are put in indented style, indented paragraph beginnings achieve a desirable effect of uniformity.

Regardless of the method of punctuation employed in the heading and inside address, the body of the letter must be punctuated in conformity with the punctuation rules in this book.

Following are four examples of the different ways the body of the letter may be spaced on the letterhead:

Double-spaced indented paragraphs with no blank lines between them:

Double-spaced indented paragraphs with blank line between them:

Single-spaced indented paragraphs with blank line between them:

Single-spaced paragraphs in block style, with blank line between them:

If the body of the letter contains an address for the information of the reader, it is helpful to make this stand out prominently for convenience in reference. This may be accomplished by putting it in the same form as the inside address of the letter, but centered on the page, as in this example:

> For additional details we advise you to communicate with America's foremost authority in this field:
>
> Dr. Franz A. Heiden
> 193 Wall Street
> New York, N.Y.
>
> We feel confident he can furnish the information you require.

COMPLIMENTARY CLOSE.—The complimentary close is a formal expression of regard with which the writer takes leave of the reader. It follows the body of the letter, occupying a line by itself, two or more lines below the last line of the body. It should begin at the middle of the page, or slightly to the right of the middle.

The use of a particular phrase for the complimentary close, like the salutation, depends on the relationship between the sender and the receiver. The complimentary close should be consistent with the salutation in the degree of its formality.

The most frequently encountered complimentary closes for business correspondence are as follows:

Respectfully yours, (very formal, and used principally for government officials and people in superior positions)
Very truly yours, (moderately formal)
Yours very truly, (moderately formal)
Yours truly, (moderately formal)
Sincerely yours, (informal; most used in business correspondence between well-acquainted persons)
Cordially yours, (informal; most used in business correspondence between well-acquainted persons)

The complimentary closes of friendly letters are less subject to rule than those of business letters, many being devised by the writer. In some friendly letters the complimentary close is omitted.

The complimentary close should have only its first letter capitalized, and should contain no abbreviations. It should not be attached to the preceding sentence or follow such stereotyped expressions as "I beg to remain," "Believe me to be," and "Hoping for a prompt reply I am . . ." It is usually followed by a comma, even when open punctuation is used, though it is sometimes omitted in the latter case.

SIGNATURE.—The signature of the business letter contains the name of the individual, the name of the organization, or both. Sometimes the position of the individual in the organization is also included.

The signature is typewritten from two to several lines below the complimentary close, the number of blank lines depending on the need of compressing or expanding the materials on the page. If the inside address follows block style, the one or more lines of the signature are lined up evenly under the complimentary close; but if the inside address follows indented style, it is preferable to begin the signature a little to the right of the complimentary close, with additional indentions for each succeeding line.

Complimentary close and signature in block style:

> Very truly yours,
>
> ECONOMY FUEL COMPANY
> (Signature)
> Harrison J. Watts, Vice President

Complimentary close and signature in indented style:

> Very truly yours,
>
> ECONOMY FUEL COMPANY
>   (Signature)
>   Harrison J. Watts, Vice President

If the signer of the letter wishes to indicate that he is writing as an individual, his name should precede the firm name; but if he is writing merely as a representative of the firm, the firm name should precede.

When letterhead paper is used, the firm name is often omitted from the signature. The firm name in the signature, when included, is sometimes written in capital letters to give it prominence.

It is necessary that the reader should know the exact name of the individual writing the letter, so that his reply may reach the proper person. Since the scrawl with which names are sometimes written in signatures is confusing, it is courteous to have the name of the person typewritten below the handwritten signature. It is also helpful to the reader to know the writer's position in the firm. This may be added after the typewritten personal name, either on the same line or on the next line below. The statement of position should not be added to the handwritten signature, however.

Alternative methods of indicating official position:

(Handwritten signature)

Roscoe J. Blair, Registrar
or
(Handwritten signature)
Roscoe J. Blair
Registrar

An individual should always sign his name the same way in all business correspondence. The first and middle names may be either written in full or written as initials only. A woman may wish to indicate whether she is married or single. If she is single, the word (Miss) may precede her signature; if she is married the word "Mrs." in parentheses may precede the signature, or her married name may be typewritten beneath the signature as shown below:

(Miss) Francis K. Graham
(Mrs.) Alice C. White
or
Alice C. White
(Mrs. John White)

Neither the handwritten nor the typewritten portions of the signature should contain personal titles such as "Mr.," "Rev.," "Dr.," or "Professor"; or academic degrees such as "M.A.," "Ph.D.," or "LL.D." The only exception to this rule is the use in parentheses of a title indicating the marital status of a woman, as noted in the previous paragraph and shown in the example above.

Three additional letter parts which require consideration, though they do not appear in all business letters, are the postscript, the identification letters, and the notice of enclosure.

POSTSCRIPT.—Postscripts are seldom used in well-written business letters, since their use is an evidence of confused thinking on the part of the composer of the letter, who only remembered to include an essential detail after the letter was typewritten. If the postscript is necessary, however, it should be added several lines below the signature, preceded by the letters "P.S."

IDENTIFICATION LETTERS.—The identification letters are the initials of the writer of the letter, and those of the secretary who transcribed it. The initials of the writer always come first. Identification letters are placed in the lower left-hand corner of the page, on one line or on two, and in any of the following forms:

RJMcM/EMP MDE AK,SED
PEQ:ls GF

NOTICE OF ENCLOSURE.—The notice of enclosure informs the reader that something additional to the text of the letter is enclosed within the envelope, and must be looked for. The words "Encl." or "Enclosure" are written in the lower left-hand corner, just below the identification letters. If there is more than one enclosure, the number should be stated, as:

RJMcM/EMP
Enclosures (3)

ENVELOPE.—The envelope should be clean, carefully typed, and well spaced, because it comes first to the attention of the reader and may give him a favorable or unfavorable impression of the contents.

For business letters both the sender's and the receiver's addresses should appear on the face of the envelope, though in writing friendly letters the return address is sometimes placed on the back flap. Most business letters use letterhead envelopes with the sender's return address in the upper left-hand corner; on plain envelopes this information is typewritten in the same location.

The address to which the letter is being sent (also called the superscription), should begin about halfway down the envelope, and slightly to the left of the middle. It should usually contain the same information as the inside address, with which it should be uniform in using the block or indented style. The name of the county may be added after the name of the community if the latter is small or little-known. Abbreviations should be avoided whenever possible, since "Va." and "Pa.," and "Mass.," "Miss.," and "Minn." are easily confused.

If the address is in an office building or hotel, the number of the room or suite may

Skeleton Envelope Form

__________ (Printed Letterhead
__________ or
__________ Typewritten Return Address)

____
____
____

__________ (Room or Suite No. if any)

Skeleton Business Letter Form

(Single-spaced and in indented style, with closed punctuation)

__________,
__________,
__________. TYPEWRITTEN HEADING

__________,
__________,
__________. INSIDE ADDRESS

__________: SALUTATION

__________ BODY

__________, COMPLIMENTARY CLOSE
__________, SIGNATURE

____/____ IDENTIFICATION LETTERS
__________. NOTICE OF ENCL.

Skeleton Business Letter Form

(Single-spaced and in block style with open punctuation)

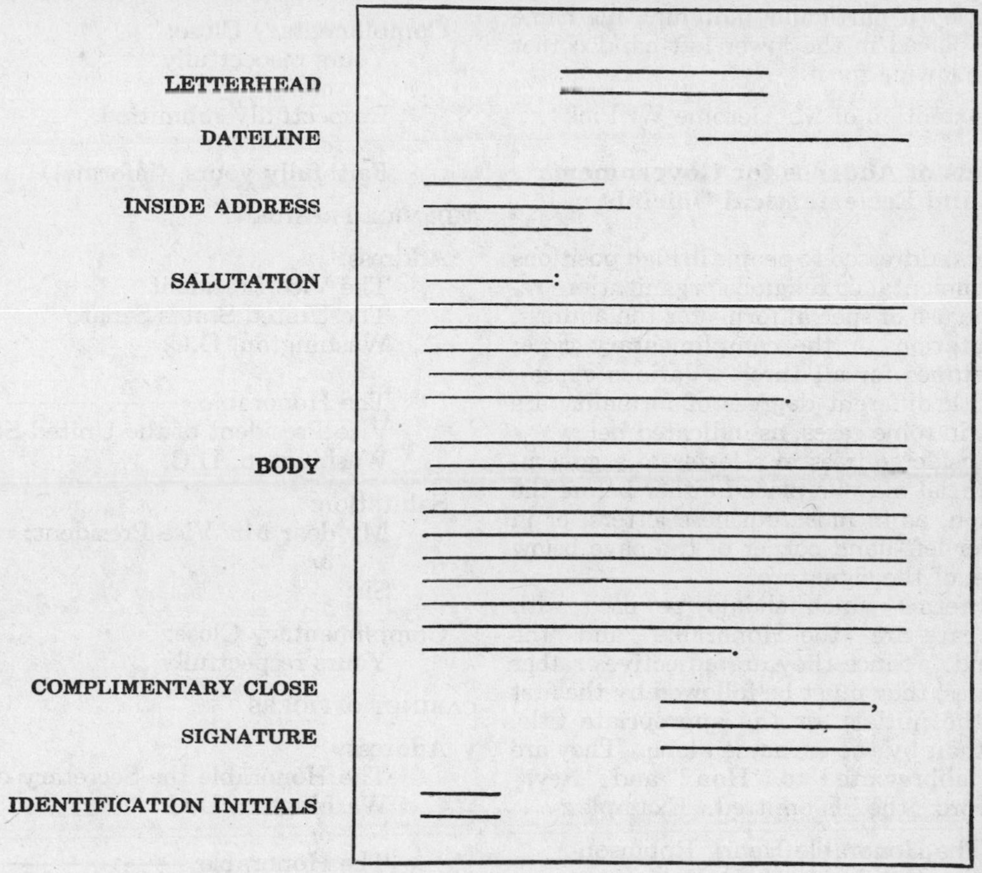

LETTERHEAD

DATELINE

INSIDE ADDRESS

SALUTATION :

BODY

COMPLIMENTARY CLOSE ,

SIGNATURE

IDENTIFICATION INITIALS

Skeleton Envelope Form

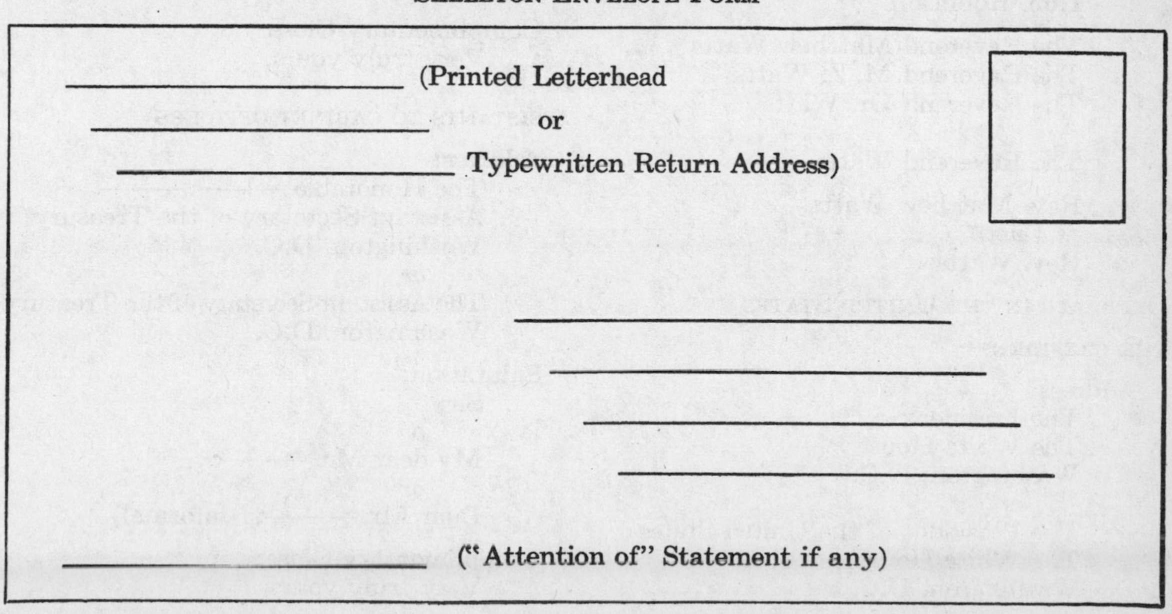

(Printed Letterhead

or

Typewritten Return Address)

("Attention of" Statement if any)

be placed in the lower left-hand corner of the envelope, as:

Room 1271 Suite 37

When the letter is addressed directly to an organization, but the writer wishes it to be received by a particular indiviual, his name may be placed in the lower left-hand corner in the following form:

Attention of Mr. Jerome W. Pick

Forms of Address for Government and Ecclesiastical Officials

Letters addressed to people in high positions in governmental or religious organizations require the use of special forms for the address, the salutation, or the complimentary close; or sometimes for all three. Various expressions with different degrees of formality are possible in some cases, as indicated below.

The inside address in a letter to a government official may be placed either before the salutation, as in most business letters, or in the lower left-hand corner of the page below the level of the signature.

Two terms which should be used with special care are "the Honorable" and "the Reverend." Since they are adjectives rather than titles, they must be followed by the first name, the initials, or the appropriate title, rather than by the surname alone. They are usually abbreviated to "Hon." and "Rev." if the word "the" is omitted. Examples:

The Honorable Henry Robinson
The Honorable H. F. Robinson
The Honorable Mr. Robinson
not
The Honorable Robinson

Hon. H. F. Robinson
not
Hon. Robinson

The Reverend Matthew Watts
The Reverend M. Z. Watts
The Reverend Dr. Watts
not
The Reverend Watts

Rev. Matthew Watts
not
Rev. Watts

Officials in the United States

THE PRESIDENT

Address:
The President
The White House
Washington, D.C.
or
The President of the United States
The White House
Washington, D.C.

Salutation:
Sir:
or
Mr. President:
or
To the President:

Complimentary Close:
Yours respectfully,
or
Respectfully submitted,
or
Faithfully yours, (informal)

THE VICE PRESIDENT

Address:
The Vice President
The United States Senate
Washington, D.C.
or
The Honorable ——— ———
Vice President of the United States
Washington, D.C.

Salutation:
My dear Mr. Vice President:
or
Sir:

Complimentary Close:
Yours respectfully,

CABINET OFFICERS

Address:
The Honorable the Secretary of State
Washington, D.C.
or
The Honorable ——— ———
Secretary of State (of War, etc.)
Washington, D.C.

Salutation:
Sir:
or
My dear Mr. Secretary:

Complimentary Close:
Very truly yours,

ASSISTANTS TO CABINET OFFICERS

Address:
The Honorable ——— ———
Assistant Secretary of the Treasury
Washington, D.C.
or
The Assistant Secretary of the Treasury
Washington, D.C.

Salutation:
Sir:
or
My dear Mr. ———:
or
Dear Mr. ———: (informal)

Complimentary Close:
Very truly yours,

THE SECRETARY TO THE PRESIDENT

Address:
The Secretary to the President
Washington, D.C.
or
The Honorable ——— ———
Secretary to the President
Washington, D.C.

Salutation:
Dear Mr. Secretary:
or
Dear Mr. ———: (informal)

Complimentary Close:
Very truly yours,

JUSTICE OF THE SUPREME COURT

Address:
The Honorable ——— ———
Chief (or Associate) Justice of the Supreme Court
Washington, D.C.
or
Mr. Justice ———
Washington, D.C.

Salutation:
Mr. Justice:
or
My dear Mr. Justice:
or
My dear Justice ———: (informal

Complimentary Close:
Very truly yours,

UNITED STATES SENATOR

Address:
The Honorable ——— ———
United States Senate
Washington, D.C.

Salutation:
Sir:
or
My dear Mr. Senator:
or
My dear Senator ———: (informal)

Complimentary Close:
Very truly yours,

UNITED STATES CONGRESSMAN

Address:
The Honorable ——— ———
House of Representatives
Washington, D.C.

Salutation:
Sir:
or
Dear Sir:
or
My dear Mr. ———: (informal)

Complimentary Close:
Very truly yours,

GOVERNOR OF A STATE

Address:
The Honorable the Governor of ———
(State Capitol, State)
or
The Honorable ——— ———
Governor of ———
(State Capitol, State)

Salutation:
Sir:
or
My dear Governor ———: (informal)

Complimentary Close:
Very truly yours,

STATE SENATOR

Address:
The Honorable ——— ———
The State Senate
(State Capitol, State)

Salutation:
Sir:
or
My dear Senator ———: (informal)

Complimentary Close:
Very truly yours,

STATE ASSEMBLYMAN

Address:
The Honorable ——— ———
Member of the Assembly
(State Capitol, State)

Salutation:
Dear Sir:
or
My dear Mr. ———: (informal)

Complimentary Close:
Very truly yours,

MAYOR

Address:
The Honorable ——— ———
Mayor of the City of ———
(City, State)
or
The Mayor of the City of ———
(City, State)

Salutation:
Sir:
or
My dear Mr. Mayor:
or
Dear Mayor ———: (informal)

Complimentary Close:
Very truly yours,
or
Respectfully yours,

Diplomatic Officials

UNITED STATES AMBASSADOR

Address:
His Excellency
The American Ambassador
(City or country where stationed)
or
The Honorable ——— ———
American Ambassador
(City and country where stationed)

Salutation:
Sir:
or
Your Excellency
or
My dear Mr. Ambassador:

Complimentary Close:
Respectfully yours,

UNITED STATES CONSUL

Address:
To the American Consul at ————
or
Mr. ——— ———
United States Consul at ————

Salutation:
Dear Sir:

Complimentary Close:
Very truly yours,

Roman Catholic Church Officials

CARDINAL

Address:
His Eminence Cardinal ———
or
His Eminence Francis Cardinal ———

Salutation:
My Lord Cardinal:
or
Your Eminence:

Complimentary Close:
Respectfully yours,

ARCHBISHOP

Address:
The Most Reverend Archbishop of ———
or
His Excellency, the Archbishop of ———

Salutation:
Most Reverend Archbishop:
or
Your Excellency:
or
Dear Archbishop ———: (informal)

Complimentary Close:
Respectfully yours,

BISHOP

Address:
The Most Reverend ———, Bishop of ———
or
The Most Reverend Bishop ————

Salutation:
Your Excellency:
or
Dear Bishop ———: (informal)

Complimentary Close:
Respectfully yours,

MONSIGNOR

Address:
The Right Reverend Monsignor ———

Salutation:
Right Reverend Sir:

Complimentary Close:
Respectfully yours,

PRIEST (SECULAR)

Address:
The Reverend ——— ——— (followed by initials of degree)

Salutation:
Reverend Sir:
or
Dear Sir:
or
Dear Father ———: (informal)

Complimentary Close:
Respectfully yours,

Protestant and Jewish Ecclesiastical Officials

PROTESTANT EPISCOPAL BISHOP

Address:
To the Right Reverend ———, Bishop of ———

Salutation:
Right Reverend and Dear Sir:
or
Dear Bishop ———: (informal)

Complimentary Close:
Sincerely yours,

PROTESTANT CLERGYMAN

Address:
The Reverend ——— ———
or, if a Doctor of Divinity
Rev. Dr. ——— ———

Salutation:
Dear Sir:
or
Reverend Sir:
or
Dear Mr. (*or* Doctor) ———:

Complimentary Close:
Respectfully yours,
or
Sincerely yours,

RABBI

Address:
Rabbi ——— ———
or
The Reverend ——— ———
or
Rev. ——— ———

Salutation:
Reverend Sir:
or
Dear Sir:
or
Dear Rabbi ———: (informal)

Complimentary Close:
Respectfully yours,
or
Sincerely yours,

OFFICE ROUTINE

An effective office routine is based on common sense. It is no different from the routine used by a clear thinking and efficient individual in his personal affairs, except that it has greater scope and is adapted to the needs of a business and the workers who compose it. An orderly individual makes memoranda of approaching tasks and appointments, keeps a careful watch on bills, money orders, and bank statements, files away important letters, documents, and receipts in such a fashion that he can find them again easily, makes careful plans before traveling, and in general tries to dispatch the business of life with a minimum of bother and error. The same is true of an efficient office. Time is a precious commodity, and hours saved from routine can be devoted effectually to more important efforts.

This does not mean that all office routines are perfect. In some there is considerable hampering red tape and "system for system's sake." In others carelessness and laxity are conspicuous. It *does* mean, however, that an effective routine is intelligible to anyone who has common sense and is acquainted with the business in question. If things are done in a certain way, there is usually a sound reason. If certain rules are enforced and precautions taken, they are usually necessary. If a person wishes to understand any phase of office routine, he should try to determine the reason for it. Naturally a new worker will have to follow some routines blindly until he gets a chance to think them out. In the long run common-sense understanding makes for a better worker than does automatic, unreasoned obedience. This is especially true for the secretary, from whom a considerable degree of initiative is frequently expected.

There is, of course, considerable variation in method from office to office. Each business has its own individual problems, and each executive his own ideas about efficiency. Nevertheless, business organizations have many general principles of operation in common. They are all part of the same economic order, and the laws of common sense hold true for all of them.

The Secretary's Work

The secretary is an important figure in modern business. She performs a variety of duties, many of them demanding independent thought and decision. Her treatment of callers and handling of business letters help to establish the tone of a firm. She is to a large degree responsible for the smooth functioning of the executive or executives to whom she may be specially assigned. Her position is that of an important minor hub, around which the wheels of office routine revolve.

The secretary, although she must usually be a good stenographer, is much more than that. The stenographer takes dictation in shorthand and transcribes it on the typewriter into the characters of the alphabet; to be able to do this, she must in addition be an expert typist. She is judged by her reliability, accuracy, and speed. Her work, though essential, is decidedly limited when compared to that of the secretary.

The term secretary is a flexible one. It is applied to the general stenographic assistant and receptionist of the individual executive or professional man—in short, the private secretary. Such a secretary may sometimes be shared between two or more executives, performing like services for each. In committees, institutions, clubs, and other nonbusiness organizations the term secretary is frequently applied to an important individual who performs all the actual work attendant on executing orders and decrees. This is in some ways similar to the secretary in the small office, who may be responsible for all office routine, or to the general secretary of a large office, who may have some of the duties of an office manager.

There are certain types of work which the business-office secretary will almost certainly be called upon to perform. These are (1) the opening and sorting of incoming mail; (2) the taking of dictation; (3) the transcription of shorthand; (4) the dispatch of outgoing mail; (5) the filing of letters and other materials; (6) the making of appointments; (7)

the handling of callers and of telephone calls; (8) running errands. But there are many other types of work which the secretary may be called upon to learn and execute, among them the following: (1) the arrangement, in part, of her employer's schedule; (2) reading mail and drafting replies to routine letters; (3) organization and management of one or more filing systems and indexes; (4) clipping newspapers; (5) interviewing callers; (6) planning itineraries; (7) ordering office supplies; (8) handling petty cash, stamps, etc.; (9) making bank deposits; (10) writing checks and paying bills; (11) checking bank statements.

Few secretaries have to perform all these duties. Some, on the other hand, may be expected to handle these and more. There is no listing all possible duties, since each business may have special ones attached to it. The secretary attempting to master her job and improve her efficiency has three reliable guides: the instructions of her employer, her experience, and her common sense. This section is intended as an introduction to those secretarial duties which are common to many offices. For a general discussion of the personality qualifications of the secretary, the reader is referred to the sections THE SUCCESSFUL SECRETARY, p. 228, and ETIQUETTE FOR BUSINESS MEN AND WOMEN, p. 224.

Adjusting to a New Job

When the secretary is acquainting herself with the routine of a new position, it is a good idea for her to make a list of all tasks required, with memoranda of detailed procedures involved in the more important work. Just as her employer has a daily schedule, which it may become her duty to arrange, so she ought to keep a similar daily schedule for herself, with reminders of future work, etc. She should also make a list of essential telephone numbers, and of the names of individuals and firms with which her employer comes in contact. Naturally many of these things will soon become a part of her memory, but lists are very helpful in the beginning.

Good work cannot be done in unpleasant or uncomfortable surroundings. The responsibility for such matters lies chiefly with the employer. Nevertheless, the new secretary should keep her desk neat and clean, try to obtain a swivel chair and adjust it to the most comfortable height, seek to avoid stuffy atmosphere and draughts, and do whatever else she is able in order to improve her working conditions. Her employer should appreciate this, since it increases her efficiency.

The following outline of the duties of the secretary is arranged for convenience in the order in which the tasks might ordinarily occur during the day.

The Executive's Schedule

The working hours of the modern executive must be apportioned carefully if he is to discharge his duties efficiently and advance the interests of his firm. For this purpose a series of written memoranda, entered on a desk pad or file cards, is much more reliable than memory. Many secretaries are responsible for such memoranda, and all secretaries should become familiar with the system their employer uses.

The executive's schedule contains two types of entries: (1) reminders of daily appointments and other important non-routine business; (2) "ticklers" or reminders that preparations should be made for matters that are coming up shortly, such as taxes or bills requiring payment, conferences at which a report or set of suggestions will have to be produced, or interviews necessitating special preparation. A "tickler"—so-called because it is intended to jog or "tickle" the memory—is entered on the schedule a suitable number of days before the coming event to which it refers. If it is taken care of, it is crossed off the schedule. If not, a similar entry is made for the following day, and so on until it is taken care of. Naturally reminders and ticklers are usually both entered on the same schedule, since they are closely related.

Whether such entries are made on desk pads, index cards, or in folders depends on their number and complexity. In any case the executive almost always keeps a desk pad, frequently divided into sections for each hour of the working day, on which both he and the secretary enter his daily appointments. Such a pad is handy to use, allowing appointments to be entered at the moment they are made. Tickler entries may also be made on the desk pad, but are usually kept on a separate pad or set of cards.

Too often the sheets of desk pads are torn off and discarded. As these sheets are a valuable record, some form of desk pad should be used which allows the sheets to be turned under or to one side from day to day.

The secretary often finds it advisable to keep a desk pad of her own, on which are entered those things she has been delegated to do and the things of which she is to remind her employer. The competent secretary has the knack of writing entries in a form which is clear and concise. It is unnecessary, for example, to preface each entry with the phrase "Remember to . . ." But no entry should be so brief as to be puzzling when referred to again after a few hours or days.

A tickler file consists of a set of cards, usually about thirty in number, one for each day of the month. At the end of each day, the card for that day is taken out and filed elsewhere, after the entries have either been crossed off or transferred to the card for the following day. At the same time a new card is added at the end of the file, thus keeping the number of cards in the file constant.

Another type of tickler file consists of a set of folders, again one for each day. Each folder contains notations of coming events and the documents such as tax bills, inventory forms, letters, etc., which bear on them. This is a convenient system for the executive, permitting him to lay his hands on the pertinent documents without delay, whenever he has a spare moment in which he can cast his thoughts ahead.

Handling Incoming Mail

In a small organization one person may open and sort all the mail. In a large organization mail for executives may be handled only by their secretaries. In either case, it is essential the mail be opened in such a way that there is little chance of tearing the contents or of throwing away enclosures with the envelopes. When the contents have been shaken away from the end to be opened, the envelope is slit with a paper knife. After the contents have been removed, the envelope may be cut on three sides and the interior examined to prevent the loss of enclosures, which should be clipped to the covering letter, if that has not already been done by the sender.

An entire delivery of mail should be opened at one time. When the letters have been opened, the next task is to sort them according to the nature of their contents. The custom of the office will determine the precise method of sorting, just as it will decide whether the secretary is to open letters marked "personal" or "confidential." As a rule advertisements and circulars are grouped together, orders are collected into another group, and routine correspondence is placed in a category by itself. Personal mail and letters requiring special handling are segregated from all other groups.

In a small office the secretary who opens the mail ordinarily distributes it among the individuals concerned. In a large office where the secretary is serving one executive, all the mail is placed on his desk, arranged according to the order of its importance, with the most urgent business at the top. Ordinarily the circulars and advertisements, being least important, would be placed at the bottom.

Some secretaries may be required to read incoming mail carefully, underline important matters to bring them to the executive's attention, and answer routine letters.

Taking Dictation

Success in taking dictation depends on a thorough knowledge of shorthand and English, but the ability of the stenographer and the person giving dictation to work together smoothly is also of vital importance. The stenographer—or secretary doing stenographic work—should behave in a manner that is tactful, thoughtful, courteous, and businesslike. She should sit facing the person giving dictation, her notebook supported on the desk or some other firm surface. Most business men do not like to dictate to a person whose attention seems to be concentrated elsewhere. Neither do they like to have their flow of thought interrupted by a person who habitually anticipates words or constantly interrupts. The competent stenographer shows an intelligent interest in the executive's words. In taking fast dictation she learns to concentrate separately on each word spoken, waiting for a pause before reviewing their meaning.

The secretary prepares to take dictation as soon as she has finished opening and sorting the mail. Notebooks and sharpened pencils should always be kept in the same, readily accessible place, so that there will be no delay in reporting for dictation. Several pencils should be taken into the executive's office, so that the breaking of a pencil point cannot cause loss of time. Filled pages in the notebook should be fastened together with a rubber band, so that the proper beginning page can be found immediately. Notes and notebooks should always be conspicuously dated, in order that quick reference can be made to past dictation—something the executive may frequently desire to do. Most offices require all stenographers to keep a file of their filled notebooks for at least one year. Even when this is not an office rule, it is a good practice, since stenographers' notebooks are a valuable record of past business transactions.

If, when taking dictation, the stenographer misses words or finds them confused, she may call attention to the matter by repeating the last word or phrase spoken. Or she may mark uncertain portions of her notes, and ask questions about them when the piece of dictation is finished. Pauses during dictation may be utilized in adding to and completing notes, and in reading through those which have been taken. Such readings help to fix the meaning of the notes and make the task of transcription easier. If a visitor enters the room and the executive breaks off dictating, it is customary for the stenographer to leave, unless specifically requested to remain.

Special attention should be given during dictation to dates, numbers, and unfamiliar names. Accuracy being essential, the person giving dictation should allow the stenographer time to write these out in full.

If the dictation is too rapid, it is perfectly

permissible for the secretary to request a more moderate pace. Most executives prefer such requests and questions about wording to the alternative presented by spoiled stationary and time wasted through enforced retyping.

Transcribing Shorthand

No system of shorthand is infallible in practice. Therefore shorthand notes cannot be transcribed automatically. Constant exercise of thought and judgment is necessary. It is a good idea to read each letter quickly before beginning to type it, in order to get a general idea of the contents. Then each sentence should be read for meaning and consistency before being typed out. This avoids erasures. It is wise to check dates and names against either enclosures or previous correspondence. Meaningless or ridiculous sentences should not be written in, but questioned; otherwise retyping will obviously be necessary. Doubtful material should be questioned, or at least indicated by a light-penciled question mark in the margin. The extent to which the stenographer may correct or improve wording depends entirely on the office and executive. In any case, she should watch out for excessive verbiage and words awkwardly repeated, since many dictators when groping for words tend to throw in unnecessary phrases.

In doing transcription, immediate attention should be given to telegrams, special instructions, and the like. Such notes should be prominently marked to distinguish them from the others. Telegrams should be transcribed and sent before letters are transcribed.

The transcriber should not hesitate to consult the dictionary and other authoritative works when in doubt. It is essential that the letter be cast in a proper form and effectively arranged on the page, and that the rules of proper spelling and good English be followed. For information on the form, arrangement, style, and content of business letters, the reader is referred to the section LETTER WRITING, p. 198; for grammar and construction, to the section MODERN ENGLISH USAGE, p. 155.

Unless otherwise instructed, the transcriber should always make at least one carbon copy of each letter, usually for filing with correspondence. Sometimes additional carbon copies will be needed, especially in the case of orders, instructions, etc. If more than four carbon copies are to be made, a typewriter with a hard platen should be used; otherwise the lower carbons will not be legible.

Before submitting letters for signature, the transcriber should assure herself that they are true copies of the shorthand notes, and that the typing is mechanically correct. The work of a good typist differs radically from that of an amateur. In addition to speed, it shows accuracy, uniformity of impression (all the characters being struck with equal force, so that they are alike in degree of blackness), and a pleasing arrangement of lines and margins.

Copy Typing

It is always possible to make mistakes when transcribing shorthand notes or in interpreting the words of a person giving dictation, but in copying materials already typed or printed the secretary is expected to do a perfect job. There is no excuse for mistaking definite words and characters.

Since such copies are usually of documents, contracts, letters received, and the like, absolute accuracy is essential. Copies should always be headed by the word "Copy" in parentheses, and any signatures should be preceded by "signed," also in parentheses. Unless the secretary is instructed otherwise, all apparent errors in the original should be copied faithfully. It is a common practice, however, to place an asterisk (*) after such errors and, at the bottom of the page, another asterisk, followed by a footnote explaining that the error occurs in the original. In the most strict variety of this work, such as that performed in legal offices, it may be necessary to copy line for line and page for page. All copy typing should be proofread against the original for errors.

Typing clean copies of rough drafts made by someone in the firm is quite a different matter, and the secretary is usually permitted to make corrections in spelling and grammar. If the meaning of some phrase cannot be determined, she should not hesitate to consult the writer.

Drafting Letters

In some offices it is part of the secretary's job to prepare replies to routine letters. She should learn to decide quickly which letters are routine and which are not. Her answers should be clearly reasoned and to the point. The general instructions contained in the section LETTER WRITING, p. 198, should be followed. According to the common procedure, she submits her replies to her employer for reading or signature at the same time that she shows him the incoming letters. This arrangement saves time.

Handling Outgoing Mail

Presuming that the letter has been typed and read, and the envelope typed, there are still certain precautions that the secretary should automatically take. She should make sure that the address on the envelope is identical with that given in the heading of the letter. She should assure herself that the letter has been signed. Finally, she should glance through the letter to ascertain what enclosures there are supposed to be, and then check the enclosures accordingly.

The letter should be neatly folded in such a way that it occupies most of the envelope but leaves ample space for opening the letter without danger of tearing the contents. Small supplementary folds made at the last minute have an ugly and untidy appearance. There is no excuse for them. The secretary should determine beforehand the most graceful way of folding all sizes of paper used in her office. Enclosures should usually be clipped to the letter, in order to avoid being lost. If pressure must be applied in sealing an envelope, it is advisable to place a sheet of paper over the flap, in order to avoid smudges. The stamp should be affixed securely, after it is checked for correct value.

To expedite business transactions, it is important that letters be mailed promptly. The accomplished secretary knows the times at which letters are collected from the box used by her office, and plans the mailing of batches of letters accordingly. If speed is essential, letters may be sent straight to the main post-office, and letters or packages may be sent direct to local destinations by messenger.

Detailed information on postal regulations, methods, and rates is contained in the section POSTAL INFORMATION, p. 221, to which the reader is referred.

Filing Systems

In an efficient office, all materials pertaining to business transactions are made readily available for reference by a suitable filing system. The backbone of the system is almost always a correspondence file, consisting of folders, one for each separate firm or individual with whom there are business dealings—customers, creditors, manufacturers, advertising agencies, etc. Each folder contains letters received from the firm in question, carbon copies of letters sent in reply, and other pertinent documents, such as advertising matter and reports on interviews and conferences. The contents of each folder are arranged in the order of their dates, and therefore tell a complete, coherent story of vital importance to a business man wishing to review for one purpose or another the stages in a set of transactions.

The secretary may be responsible for keeping such a file in order and up to date. In any case it will be necessary for her to file carbon copies of the letters which she has written for her employer. She may frequently be called upon to find material in the files.

The arrangement of items (folders, in the case of the correspondence file) is almost always alphabetical. There is a detailed discussion of this method in the section FILING BY ALPHABET, p. 196. Other arrangements include the geographical, in which firms are grouped by regions, a method convenient for sales campaigns and distributions; the numerical; and the Dewey Decimal Classification, familiar in libraries. The two latter methods are seldom used in business offices.

Cardboard guides are used to separate the folders in a file. These guides bear identification tabs, facilitating the locating of material. It is more convenient to file material in front of the guide referring to it, but the system of filing *behind* the guides is still used in many offices.

A large file is generally accompanied by a card index, in which each folder is represented by a corresponding card bearing the name of the firm or individual. If a firm is known by several different names, or different forms of the same name, there are cross reference cards; as, for example, "Corrugated Box and Fiberboard, Inc. Look under: Midwestern Corrugated Box and Fiberboard" or "Antiquarian Society of America. See American Antiquarian Society." Similar cross-reference cards would be used if the correspondence for two related firms happened to be filed in the same folder. Use of an index does away with time wasted in long searches through the bulkier files. For a small file, however, an index is seldom worth the time taken in maintaining it.

There are many supplementary files and indexes used in business offices. These may include mailing lists, lists of customers and prospective customers, files of newspapers and magazine clippings, legal documents, receipts, orders, employee records, indexes of references to books, and the like. In large offices each executive maintains an individual file of matters pertaining to his special province, and this file is usually kept in order by his private secretary.

A mailing list of any size is best kept on a series of cards, one for each firm or individual, rather than on typewritten sheets. Then names can be added to or dropped from the list without the need for a lengthy retyping and without disturbing the convenient alphabetical order. For similar reasons, card indexes of the names of customers and "prospects" are advisable. These may also be classified according to the item in which the customer is most interested, cards of a different color being used for this purpose; for example, a firm dealing in hardware might list purchasers of kitchen utensils on green cards, purchasers of tools on yellow cards, general purchasers on white cards, etc. Then if a special sales campaign for one type of product were undertaken, the appropriate cards could quickly be removed from the file.

There are certain general suggestions as to efficient filing:

(1) A file or index is only valuable if kept up to date. Otherwise it is a source of error and confusion. When a firm changes its name or address, a new card should be made out immediately, and correspondence transferred to a new folder.

(2) Care should be taken to list firms according to their complete, official name.

(3) If there is doubt as to where an item should most properly be filed, the quickest thing to do is to file it arbitrarily in one place and then make out a number of cross-reference cards.

(4) Preliminary to being filed, material may be kept in a general "suspense folder." However, the contents of the suspense folder should be filed at the earliest possible date; otherwise it will quickly become larger than the file itself. Instead of a single suspense folder, several may be used, one for each type of material, thus allowing for a certain amount of preliminary filing.

(5) In a large firm it is generally advisable for employees taking material from the files to sign a note to that effect, thus guarding against the loss of folders and making it easy to locate materials temporarily out of the files. If a folder is to be kept out for some time, it should be replaced with an "out card" the same size as the folder, thus quickly indicating to another searcher that the material has not been lost or filed elsewhere.

(6) Letters and other related papers are less bulky if stapled rather than clipped together.

(7) Bulky material, such as catalogues, samples, and pamphlets, should be kept in a separate file or case, with cross-reference cards indicating the location.

(8) The drawers of a filing cabinet should be kept closed when not in immediate use, and locked when the office is empty.

(9) The materials most frequently referred to should be kept where most easily reached, usually in the upper file-drawers rather than in those next to the floor.

(10) If several different folder files are in use in an office, it is well to mark the folders constituting each file with tabs of the same color, thus preventing folders from being returned to the wrong file.

The Treatment of Callers

It is the secretary's duty to learn the nature of the caller's business. Having learned it, she must decide on the basis of her past experience whether it is such as to be of interest to her employer and whether to send the caller in at once or make an appointment for him to see her employer at some other time. In many cases she may have to consult with her employer before arriving at a decision.

Many employers wish their secretaries to act as buffers between them and callers they are unable or unwilling to see. Secretaries in this rather uncomfortable position are required to exercise a good deal of tact and patience. A secretary who can perform such a difficult task well, and who, in addition, can transact business with routine callers without referring them to her employer at all, is a very great asset to a business. There is a further discussion of these problems in the section ETIQUETTE FOR BUSINESS MEN AND WOMEN, p. 224.

Many offices keep a daily list of callers, each entry ordinarily including the name of the caller, his business connections, and the errand on which he called. The lists are usually filed and retained as a semi-permanent record. Even when office rules do not require such a list to be kept, some secretaries make them because they are of value as records of transactions and because they serve to acquaint the secretary with the people who frequent the office.

The handling of telephone calls is essentially the same as the handling of callers. In both cases the secretary's duty is to learn the caller's business in as brief and courteous a way as possible, and then to refer the call in the manner determined by her experience. A cheerful voice creates a good impression. If a call must be kept waiting for some time before being answered by the person to whom it is referred, it is a good idea for the secretary to make occasional reassuring remarks so that the caller will not feel he has been forgotten or slighted. It is a good practice to keep a list of telephone calls similar to the list of those who call in person.

Appointments and Itineraries

In addition to scheduling her employer's day at the office, the secretary may be required to make arrangements for his time spent outside the office—visits to other firms, extended trips for the purpose of sales and conferences, and the like. For this purpose it is desirable that she have a good working knowledge of local transportation facilities, general traveling conditions, and her employer's personal preferences in such matters. Naturally she should consult him when in doubt, but if she performs her task sensibly and efficiently, he may come to rely greatly on her judgment.

In making appointments, courtesy and the dignity of her firm are important considerations. Where possible, appointments should be definite rather than tentative, and arranged by one phone call rather than several. This makes for efficient routine. It often proves advisable to combine business and social dates, as by having the meeting include a luncheon. There are certain hours of the working day during which an executive can best afford to be absent from the office; such hours, often those of the afternoon, are most suitable for outside appointments. Before leaving for his appointment he will usually want to refresh his mind by going over recent correspondence with the person he is going to meet. Therefore the appropriate folder should be on hand, together with notes on plans or proposals which he may wish to discuss. It is often a part of the secretary's duties to bring such matters to his attention.

The preparing of an itinerary for an extended trip is a more complicated task, usually involving the purchase of railroad or airway tickets, making hotel reservations, and making appointments in advance by letter or telegram. The secretary will need to rely to a considerable extent on the advice of travel bureaus, though she should always adopt an arrangement suited to her employer's preferences and convenience. It is wise for her to have timetables on hand, though great care should be taken to renew these whenever there is a change of schedules; otherwise they will prove a source of error. In general, all arrangements should be checked on by telephone or letter. Hotel reservations may be made by letter. The accomplished secretary familiarizes herself with the travel and hotel facilities in those regions to which her employer's business interests are apt to carry him.

In planning itineraries economy of time and movement is essential. If several cities are to be visited, appointments should be made in such an order as to involve the least amount of traveling; here a knowledge of the geography of the locality is essential.

After the itinerary has been planned, it should be drawn up on paper. A brief one may indicate only the hours of arrival and departure for each day, along with information as to the name of the railroad line, the station, and number of the car in which reservation has been made. Railroads and airways will furnish such an itinerary made out in full. A more complete itinerary indicates hotel reservations, time and place of appointments, names of individuals to be met, notes on matters to be discussed, plans and suggestions, subsidiary matters to be taken up if there is time available, local transportation arrangements, etc. Such an itinerary is chiefly for the convenience of the traveler, but copies should always be kept at the home office. Then it will be possible to get in touch with the traveler if any important instructions or periodic reports are to be forwarded to him.

The secretary may pack for the traveler a special folder containing such office supplies as blank letterhead paper, plain paper, notebooks, pencils, etc., if there will be occasion to use them.

Care of Office Equipment

Secretaries are not usually mechanics, and they are not expected to repair their own typewriters. They are, however, supposed to clean and oil them in accordance with the manufacturer's instructions. The ability of the secretary to turn out good work depends on her remembering to change the ribbon of her machine and to clean its type whenever necessary. The care of office equipment involves covering typewriters, adding machines, etc., at the end of the working day, and dusting desks and office equipment at regular intervals. The interior portions of typewriters may be dusted effectively with a narrow, long-handled brush.

The secretary is often, among other things, her employer's business housekeeper. In many offices the appearance of his desk is as much her responsibility as is the taking of his dictation. However, she should never rearrange his desk without determining whether that is agreeable to him.

Ordering Supplies

It may be part of the secretary's duties to order minor office supplies from an outside dealer. These usually include: paper bearing the firm's letterhead; blank sheets of the same size, color, and quality, for the pages of letters following the first; carbon paper; second sheets for carbon copies; envelopes, both blank and with the firm's name and address; stamps; postcards; stenographic notebooks; memorandum pads; index cards; file folders; labels; tabs; bank deposit slips; pencils; pens; erasers for pencil, ink, and typewriter; clips; staples; pins; typewriter ribbons; oil for typewriter; paste; transparent mending tape; etc.

The secretary may also have the responsibility of holding the petty cash box and keeping the petty cash account. In a large office she is more often required to requisition supplies from another department of the organization. In either case, it is her business to see that the quantities on hand are always adequate. Supplies should never be ordered in such quantities, however, that they deteriorate before use. Most typewriter ribbons rot, and certain kinds of white paper turn yellow with age. These items in particular should not be ordered unless there is reasonable certainty of their being used within a fairly short time. The secretary should keep a list of all supplies being used and note down impending shortages. All supplies should be orderly arranged in the proper cabinets.

Bank Accounts

The handling of a bank account involves three chief operations: (1) making deposits; (2) writing checks and paying bills; (3) checking bank statements.

The bank book should always be taken to the bank when a deposit is to be made. If for some reason it is necessary to leave the bank book in the office, a duplicate deposit slip should be made out by the secretary and initialed by the teller. This slip should be preserved by the secretary until it is possible to have the deposit entered in the bank book. All deposits should be entered in the stub of the check book so that the officials of the company may always be able to ascertain the exact bank balance.

One method of endorsing checks should be adopted and maintained. This is the rule in almost all business offices.

When possible, bills should be paid by check. When this is impossible, a receipt should be obtained for the cash disbursed. All offices have a procedure of verifying bills before paying them. These procedures always embrace verification of quantity, quality, and specifications; the checking of credit allowances and discounts; and the checking of the arithmetic of the bill.

When, on or shortly after the first of the month, the canceled checks for the previous month are returned, the secretary should go over them carefully. The checking of a bank statement involves these processes:

(1) The checks as returned should be checked against the stubs in the book. This is an elementary precaution against forgery.

(2) The deposit items on the bank statement should be checked against the deposit items in the bank book. Bank book and bank statement should agree.

(3) The canceled checks should agree with the withdrawal items on the bank statement.

(4) By subtracting the total of the checks from the total of the deposit items, a figure is arrived at which should equal the current bank balance.

(5) Checks issued in one month and not presented until after the first of the following month are always a nuisance to bookkeepers and cashiers. It is perfectly permissible to ask that checks outstanding for a long time be deposited.

The Large Office

The routine of a large office has certain special characteristics setting it off from that of a small office. As a result of the difference in size, the number of tasks are multiplied. The proper carrying out of such a complex routine is far beyond the powers of one secretary of general ability, or even several. Specialization is essential, each employee concentrating on a few steps in a highly complicated process. Even the work of the private secretary is usually limited to that entailed in serving one executive or a small group in a specialized field.

This specialization, though inescapable, brings up certain difficulties seldom found in small offices. Greater dependence must be placed on a carefully-thought-out and foolproof routine. It becomes impossible for one person to oversee and coordinate everything. Yet the specialized office worker performing only one task has difficulty in understanding the function of his work and seeing it in the proper perspective, and when tasks are performed by many individuals instead of one or two, there is a correspondingly greater chance for misunderstanding, error, and confusion.

To offset this disadvantage, many large offices make a practice of shifting workers from one task to another, so that they will gain a greater understanding of the whole routine and be better able to detect errors. Some workers resent being assigned to new tasks, disliking the added mental effort involved and thinking it merely a matter of whim. Actually they should welcome such opportunities and look upon them as training for promotion. This is even more true when individuals are shifted from department to department, spending a certain amount of time in production work, advertising, merchandising, sales work, and distribution. Such varied training is a frequent preliminary to advancement. The wider your knowledge, the better are your chances for promotion.

It must always be remembered that the large modern office should be an adjusting mechanism between the other departments, which have a less flexible sort of work and must struggle with external factors—the production department with machines and materials, the distribution department with transportation facilities, the sales department with general business conditions and consumers' demands. Unfortunately some office administrations consider that their job is to exercise authority and direct the activities of all other departments. This mistaken authoritarianism is largely an inheritance from the days of smaller businesses, when one or a few individuals personally supervised all activities. The efficient modern office administration coordinates activities, smooths out difficulties, avoids inter-departmental difficulties, and in all ways acts as an adjusting mechanism. Therefore the more flexible the individual worker is and the better he is acquainted with other jobs besides his own, the better he will be able to serve his employer and himself.

POSTAL INFORMATION

The proficient office worker should know how to make use of the facilities of the United States mails intelligently and economically. The sources of postal loss should be understood, in order that they may be avoided. A good working knowledge of the classification and rates of postage is essential.

Through its thousands of postoffices and rural routes it is estimated that the U.S. Postal Department handles billions of pieces of mail every year. With this immense volume of business it is hardly necessary to point out that losses do occur. Valuable letters and parcels disappear, and occasional delays cause inconvenience and damage. By far the greatest loss occurs as a direct result of carelessness and ignorance on the part of the users of the mails.

Hundreds of millions of letters are mailed every year that require special examination and re-addressing by postoffice clerks before they can be delivered. The Dead Letter Office receives many tens of millions of letters every year. It is impossible to compute the annual indirect loss occasioned by wrongly addressed parcels and letters, and resulting in misunderstandings in business and money matters, failure to complete deals or keep appointments.

It is estimated by the federal Post Office Department that hundreds of thousands of letters bearing no address whatsoever are received every year in the Division of Dead Letters and its several branches. This represents an actual waste of thousands of dollars in postage stamps alone, not to mention the value of their contents. It does not include the carloads of letters and parcels which never reach their destination because of insufficient or incorrect addressing.

The total of postage stamps found loose in the mails would amount to hundreds of thousands yearly. Carelessness in affixing the stamps is responsible for most of this loss. By reason of insecure wrapping hundreds of thousands of articles of merchandise are found loose in the mails every year, and sent to the postoffices at the respective division headquarters of the Railway Mail Service. These articles include everything from jewelry to tires.

The Dead Letter Office returns what it can, but the carelessness which misdirects letters is likely to record no return address, with the result that millions of letters are destroyed and thousands of dollars worth of property is sold at auction.

To avoid losses of this kind it is well to keep in mind the following suggestions:

a) Always write "Transient" or "General Delivery" on mail matter for persons not permanently located in the city addressed.

b) Be sure that name and address is given in full with street and number, postoffice box, or R.F.D. address, plus zip code.

c) Owing to the fact that in some states there is more than one town of the same or nearly the same name, it is sometimes advisable to give the county.

d) Abbreviation of state names is encouraged by the postoffice when used in connection with zip codes.

e) It is essential that mail be properly prepared for mailing. See that letters are properly sealed and parcels securely wrapped.

Ignorance of postal regulations can result in many other types of loss. Sometimes, for example, an extensive advertising campaign is launched involving the expenditure of thousands of dollars, only to be held up as violating some one of the numerous postal regulations. Occasionally an advertising agency will overlook the postal requirements when preparing circulars and other matter for mailing, with the result that a higher rate of postage must be paid than was originally intended. Postal authorities report that millions of letters and parcels pass through their hands every year which could just as well go in another class at a lower rate.

First Class

To this class of domestic mail belongs all matter wholly or partly in writing, whether handwritten or typewritten, sealed or unsealed. Matter containing any writing whatsoever (except the sender's card enclosed in a parcel) must be sent at the first-class rate. Also mail sealed against inspection belongs to the first class unless printed labels giving permission for inspection and nature of contents are attached.

Second Class

This class includes newspapers and periodicals.

Third Class

Circulars, photographs, books (i.e., trade or commercial literature) and catalogues, other printed matter (except newspapers and periodicals, which are second class) and merchandise belong to this class. Third class is limited to unsealed matter weighing less than 16 ounces.

Fourth Class, or Parcel Post

Merchandise, printed matter, and all other matter not embraced in the first and second classes may be sent via parcel post.

Between First Class Post Offices (except to and from Alaska and Hawaii). *The Limit of Weight* is 40 Pounds. *Limit of Size* 72 Inches in Length and Girth Combined.

Special Rate for Books. A special rate is applicable to books for general circulation (literature). This classification does not include advertising literature in book form or books furthering the commercial interests of a particular group, as banking reports, trade annuals, etc. The package must bear the words "Special Fourth Class Rate—Books."

The Limit of Size is 100 inches in length and girth combined. The length is determined by measuring the greatest distance in a straight line between the ends (but not around the parcel), while its girth is the distance around the parcel at its thickest part.

The Limit of Weight is 70 pounds.

Special Delivery

To insure prompt handling of mail and a delivery earlier than that provided by the usual carrier, mail should be sent special delivery. Such mail will be delivered by special messenger if it is received at the post office of destination between 7 a.m. and 9 p.m.; if it is received before 6 p.m. Sunday, it will be delivered on Sunday.

If money or other valuables are sent by special delivery, they should be insured, or better, registered.

Special Handling

Parcel-post packages requiring special handling, such as those containing eggs, day-old chicks, etc., will receive the speediest handling and transportation practicable on payment of a special fee. The special-handling charge does not include special delivery.

Registered Mail

First, second, and third-class matter (and parcel-post, if sealed and mailed at the first-class rate) may be registered by paying a fee in addition to the regular postage. Mail which should be registered rather than insured:

1) Money, if checks or money orders are not available.
2) Valuable papers.
3) Articles of unusual value.
4) Articles for which a return receipt is desired, showing delivery.
5) Articles or letters for which a return receipt is requested showing address where delivered.
6) Letters which are to be delivered to addressee in person.

Indemnity up to $10,000 may be obtained.

Receipts for registered mail should be retained until the sender is certain that the mail has been received. If the matter is not delivered within a reasonable time, a request should be made at the post office to trace it.

Insurance

Third and fourth-class mail may be insured against loss or damage by payment of a fee in addition to the regular postage. First and second-class matter, with some exceptions, cannot be insured, but must be registered.

C.O.D.

Mail may be sent C.O.D. in order to make collection on an article through the Post Office Department. This applies to sealed as well as to unsealed third and fourth-class mail. On a single C.O.D. package not more than $200 may be collected. The fee on C.O.D. mail includes insurance or registration (depending upon the class).

Money Orders

Money should not be transmitted by mail. To prevent loss or theft, money orders, issued in amounts up to $100, should be used. Receipts for money orders should be kept until the money orders have been cashed.

Air Mail Service

Any matter which is accepted in the ordinary mail may be sent via air mail if it is not subject to damage by freezing. Matter sent by air must be marked "AIR MAIL" and may be deposited in any mail box. Ordinary postage stamps may be used, although special air mail stamps are issued by the government.

On air mail the limit of weight is 70 pounds and the limit of size, 100 inches in length and girth combined.

The fees for registration, insurance, special delivery, and C.O.D. are the same as for regular mail.

TABLE OF WEIGHTS AND MEASURES

Avoirdupois Weight

(Used in the United States, Great Britain and other English-speaking countries for weighing goods other than such small items as drugs, rare metals, precious stones, etc.)

16 drams = 1 ounce (oz.)
16 ounces, or 7,000 grains = 1 pound (lb.)
25 pounds (in U. S.) = 1 quarter (qr.)
28 pounds (in Great Britain) = 1 quarter
4 quarters of 25 pounds = 1 short, or U. S., hundredweight (cwt.)

4 quarters of 28 pounds = 1 long, or British, hundredweight (cwt.)
20 short hundredweights (2,000 pounds) = 1 short ton
20 long hundredweights (2,240 pounds) = 1 long ton

Linear Measure

12 lines = 1 inch (in.)
12 inches = 1 foot (ft.)
3 feet = 1 yard (yd.)
$5\frac{1}{2}$ yards or $16\frac{1}{2}$ feet = 1 rod (rd.)
40 rods = 1 furlong (fur.)
8 furlongs, or 5,280 feet = 1 land or statute mile

Square Measure

144 square inches (sq. in.) = 1 square foot (sq. ft.)
9 square feet = 1 square yard (sq. yd.)
$30\frac{1}{4}$ square yards, or $272\frac{1}{4}$ square feet = 1 square rod (sq. rd.)
160 square rods, or 43,560 square feet = 1 acre (a.)
640 acres = 1 square mile (sq. mi.)

In the United States, a square mile of public land is known legally as a *section.* Thirty-six sections, when arranged in a square 6 miles by 6 miles, form a *township.* In some states and counties the *township* is an administrative or taxing division.

Cubic Measure

1,728 cubic inches (cu. in.) = 1 cubic foot (cu. ft.)
27 cubic feet = 1 cubic yard (cu. yd.)

Liquid Measure

4 gills (gi.) = 1 pint (pt.)
2 pints = 1 quart (qt.)
4 quarts = 1 gallon (gal.)
$31\frac{1}{2}$ gallons = 1 barrel (bbl.)
2 barrels = 1 hogshead (hhd.)

The U. S. gallon is equal to .833 imperial gallon, or British gallon.

Dry Measure

2 pints (pt.) = 1 quart (qt.)
4 quarts = 1 gallon (gal.)
2 gallons or 8 quarts = 1 peck (pk.)
4 pecks = 1 bushel (bu.)
8 bushels = 1 quarter (qr.)

The Metric System

The metric system was developed in France, but it is now used everywhere for scientific purposes. It is the prevailing commercial system in most of the countries of continental Europe and has been officially adopted in Latin America. The basic units of the system are the *gram*, a measure of weight, the *meter*, a measure of distance, and the *liter*, a measure of volume. By combining these basic units with the following prefixes, fractional and multiple units are obtained, as *milligram, centigram, decigram*, etc.

milli- = one thousandth (.001)
centi- = one hundredth (.01)
deci- = one tenth (.1)
deca- = ten
hecto- = one hundred
kilo- = one thousand
myria- = ten thousand

Weight

The gram is the fundamental unit of weight, and is defined as one one-thousandth of the weight of a certain platinum-iridium bar kept at the International Bureau of Weights and Measures at Sèvres.

10 milligrams (mg.) = 1 centigram (cg.)
10 centigrams = 1 decigram (dg.)
10 decigrams = 1 gram (gr.)
10 grams = 1 decagram (dcg.)
10 decagrams = 1 hectogram (hg.)
10 hectograms = 1 kilogram (kg.)
10 kilograms = 1 myriagram (myg.)
10 myriagrams = 1 quintal (q.)
10 quintals = 1 metric ton (1,000,000 grams)

Linear Measure

10 millimeters (mm.) = 1 centimeter (cm.)
10 centimeters (cm.) = 1 decimeter (dm.)
10 decimeters = 1 meter (m.)
10 meters = 1 decameter (dcm.)
10 decameters = 1 hectometer (hm.)
10 hectometers = 1 kilometer (km.)
10 kilometers = 1 myriameter (10,000 meters)

Area or Surface Measure

100 square millimeters (mm^2, or sq. mm.) = 1 square centimeter (cm^2, or sq. cm.)
100 square centimeters = 1 square decimeter (dm^2, or sq. dm.)
100 square decimeters = 1 square meter (sq. m., or m^2)
100 square meters = 1 square decameter (dcm^2, or sq. dcm.)
100 square decameters = 1 square hectometer (hm^2, or sq. hm.), or hectare
100 hectares = 1 square kilometer (km^2, or sq. km.), or myriare
100 square kilometers = 1 square myriameter (sq. mym., or mym^2)

Volume or Liquid Measure

1,000 cubic millimeters (mm^3, or cu. mm.) = 1 cubic centimeter (cm^3, or cu. cm.)
1,000 cubic centimeters = 1 cubic decimeter (dm^3, or cu. dm.)
1,000 cubic decimeters = 1 cubic meter (m^3, or cu. m.), or 1 stere
1,000 cubic meters = 1 cubic decameter (dcm^3, or cu. dcm.)
1,000 cubic decameters = 1 cubic hectometer (hm^3, or cu. hm.)
1,000 cubic hectometers = 1 cubic kilometer (km^3, or cu. km.)
1,000 cubic kilometers = 1 cubic myriameter (mym^3, or cu. mym.)

Capacity Measure

10 milliliters (ml.) = 1 centiliter (cl.)
10 centiliters = 1 deciliter (dl.)
10 deciliters = 1 liter (l.)
10 liters = 1 decaliter (dcl.)
10 decaliters = 1 hectoliter (hl.)
10 hectoliters = 1 kiloliter (kl.)
10 kiloliters = 1 myrialiter (myl.)

Equivalents

1 meter = 39.37 inches
1 kilometer = 3,280.83 feet, or .62137 mile
1 cubic centimeter = .06102 cubic inch
1 liter = 1.0567 U. S. liquid quarts, or .908 U. S. dry quart
1 gram = 15.432 grains
1 decagram = .3527 ounce avoirdupois
1 kilogram = 2.2046 pounds avoirdupois
907.18 kilograms = 1 short ton
1,016.05 kilograms = 1 long ton
1 foot = 30.48 centimeters; 1 surveyors' chain = 20.117 meters; 1 engineers' chain = 30.48 meters.
1 square foot = 929.03 square centimeters; 1 acre = 4,046.87 square meters; 1 square mile = 2.59 square kilometers.

Apothecaries' Weight

(Used in weighing drugs and medicines.)
20 grains (gr.) = 1 scruple (℈)
3 scruples = 1 dram (ʒ)
8 drams = 1 ounce (℥)
12 ounces, or 5,760 grains = 1 pound (lb.)

Apothecaries' Liquid Measure

(Used in the United States in measuring liquid drugs and medicines.)
60 minims (m.) = 1 fluid dram (fʒ)
8 fluid drams = 1 fluid ounce (f℥)
16 fluid ounces = 1 pint (O.)
8 pints = 1 gallon (Cong. or C.)

Angular Measure

(Used in measuring distances on the circumference of a circle or sphere.)
60 seconds (″) = 1 minute (′)
60 minutes = 1 degree (°)
90 degrees = 1 quadrant, or right angle
360 degrees = 1 circumference

Land Measure

9 square feet (sq. ft.) = 1 square yard (sq. yd.)
30¼ square yards, or 272¼ square feet = 1 square rod (sq. rd.)
40 square rods = 1 rood (r.)
4 roods, or 160 square rods = 1 acre (a.)
640 acres = 1 square mile (sq. mi.)

Surveyors' Measure

7.92 inches = 1 link (li.)
100 links, or 66 feet = 1 surveyor's or Gunter's chain
80 chains = 1 mile
or
12 inches = 1 link (li.)
100 links (or feet) = 1 engineers' or Ramsden's chain

Nautical Measure

(Used in measuring distances and depths at sea.)
6 feet = 1 fathom
100 fathoms, or 120 fathoms = 1 cable-length
1,000 fathoms = 1 nautical mile

The length given above for the nautical mile is commonly used, but it is not the official length. In the United States the nautical mile is officially 6,080.27 feet, or one minute of a great circle on the earth. In Great Britain the nautical mile is officially 6,080 feet.

ETIQUETTE FOR BUSINESS MEN AND WOMEN

Streamlined Courtesy

Business etiquette is courtesy adjusted to meet requirements of speed and efficiency. That is what distinguishes it from general social etiquette, which is largely an etiquette of leisure. At parties and other friendly gatherings there is sufficient time for the exchange of pleasant formalities and other indications of mutual affability. But in the world of business, such courtesies are trimmed down to a convenient minimum.

Downright incivility and lack of consideration are no more excusable in the office than at home or in public. The plea of "business" does not justify rudeness or offensive impersonality of behavior. Courtesy unembroidered is courtesy nevertheless. And an office in which an atmosphere of friendliness and mutual consideration prevails is far preferable to the frigid temple of unadulterated "efficiency" in which both employers and employees are lifeless robots.

On the other hand it must be remembered that during office hours business men and women are workers. Unlike persons attending a social function, their time is not their own. This fundamental fact determines the nature of business etiquette.

Salutations

Elaborate greetings are obviously inappropriate for fellow workers who meet every day. A simple "Good morning" is sufficient, and even this is often dispensed with after work has begun. If the meeting takes place on the way to work a more informal and extended greeting is common. The same general rule holds good for closing time. For example, if employees chance to leave the office at the same moment, they will exchange "Good nights," but it is neither necessary nor advisable for each worker to take formal leave of every other worker. Repeated greetings become meaningless and develop an artificial and hollow sound. Fellow workers take their daily meetings for granted.

An accurate knowledge and use of the names of individuals, however, is essential in the business world. A business man should know the names of all staff members with whom he is apt to come in contact. This is partly a matter of courtesy; every person likes the sound of his own name. But it also makes for efficiency by preventing hesitation and confusion.

In the matter of names a certain formality is frequently desirable and may be absolutely required in some concerns. Individuals who call each other by the first name outside working hours, frequently find it advisable to address each other by their last names while at work, especially if they are of the opposite sex. There is of course a great deal of variation in this practice from office to office, but it must be remembered that coworkers are meeting as employees and not as friends. Outside the office the reverse holds true. The fact that two people are employed by the same firm is no reason for added formality when they meet at a social gathering. Friendships between superiors and subordinates, it is true, may give rise to special problems. The transition from friendly sociability to polite impersonality is not an easy one, and rules of etiquette provide no ready-made solutions to problems of personal relations. They must be solved by the individuals involved.

Greetings addressed to superiors by subordinates require greater formality. In many concerns they are omitted altogether, particularly if the difference in status is considerable. Much depends on the attitude of the superior, who is in the best position to take the initiative. The employee must be guided by his behavior. It is assumed that the executive's time is especially valuable, and therefore greetings and remarks ought not to be addressed to him if he seems at all preoccupied. There is no hard and fast rule. A company president who invariably says "Good morning" to the elevator operator may be quite startled to hear himself similarly addressed by one of his clerks. The good executive, however, shows a more general affability and solicitude; he tries to avoid being curt, crusty, or "formidable," knowing that his position is no excuse for rudeness.

Working Together

Any person attempting to concentrate on a job has a right to expect that he will not be interrupted unnecessarily. Therefore those who work in an office should think twice before breaking in on the thoughts of their deskmates. Interruptions are particularly taboo if it is obvious that the person is performing a complicated task or thinking out a difficult problem. In such cases the interruption, even though necessary, should be delayed if possible until the person comes to a natural stopping point. Similarly, one should knock before entering a private office.

The same rule holds when two persons are talking and the third approaches them to make a request or deliver some special instructions. Naturally too much hesitation is as bad as too little, since it is apt to slow up important matters. The business man or woman should cultivate a nice discrimination in approaching fellow workers who are occupied. In giving or transmitting orders, brevity and directness are advisable. The employee, unless he is a temperamental specialist, is not a stranger who must be artfully persuaded to do the tasks assigned him. The capable employer, it is true, knows how to phrase orders pleasantly, but he does not temporize. Requests, such as those made between departments or individuals of equal status, are a different matter and require a more tactful approach; here the elements of cooperation and mutual consideration should be stressed.

Most concerns discourage conversation on personal matters and many forbid it outright. The overly talkative worker makes it difficult for others to concentrate on their work. In some businesses a great deal of conversation is necessary, but it should be conducted in such a way as not to disturb any third person.

This also applies to telephone conversations. Some people unconsciously develop an unnaturally loud and strained telephone-voice. Nervous mannerisms, mumblings, and fidgetings are also very distracting. To counteract them, habits of poise and grace should be cultivated.

It is customary to introduce a newcomer to all those with whom he or she will come in contact, thus facilitating future cooperation and helping create a friendly atmosphere. Such introductions may take the form: "Mr. Jameson—Mr. Edwards, the production manager. Mr. Jameson is going to work with us in the advertising department." Introductions aid in orienting the new employee, provided they are not so numerous as to be confusing.

The new employee should usually let others take the initiative in establishing further acquaintance. He should not attempt to press too quickly into the circles of office friendship. However, he should not be overly retiring. Aggressiveness and straightforwardness are at a premium in modern business.

In many offices collections are taken up to buy presents for departing employees, etc. Such collections should not be made obligatory, and should be limited to individuals acquainted with the employee for whom the present is intended. Good judgment and discretion are necessary in handling the matter. Some firms forbid the practice.

The Visitor in the Office

Any commercial or industrial enterprise depends for its success on the attitude of the public and of other business concerns. Representatives of those two social groups are therefore treated with consideration and tact. The trained receptionist is direct without being brusque, cordial but not effusive. She greets the visitor with a "Good morning" or "Good afternoon," as the case may be, and then waits for him to state his name and occupation. She is especially careful to discover whether or not he has an appointment. If the information is not volunteered, she politely requests it. Then she promptly transmits this information to the proper person. If it is necessary for the visitor to wait, she invites him to be seated and shows solicitude for his comfort and convenience. Hers is the responsibility for seeing that the firm creates a good impression. She must also prevent pointless interviews and wasted time. Her manner toward the visitor should create a dual impression: first, that she understands his point of view and will do her best to expedite his business; second, that her firm is efficient in its methods and that the time of her superiors is valuable. She is quick to size up visitors, as that may help her employers decide whether or not to grant an interview, but she is extremely cautious about judging visitors herself merely by their appearance; she knows that important people do not always look or act important.

The receptionist must also have a good working knowledge of the organization of her firm, in order to direct visitors to the proper official or department. She makes it her business to learn the names of visitors, particularly those who come frequently; such knowledge increases her efficiency and adds an intimate charm to her greeting. She is careful to shield higher executives from inquiries or requests that could be appropriately handled by subordinates. Finally, if the visitor cannot be granted an interview, she does her best to lighten his disappointment and send him away in a good humor. She should be careful, however, in promising future interviews or putting people off with vaguely hopeful suggestions. Sometimes this may be required, but in the long run such temporizing will tend to make both her and her firm unpopular. Frankness and sincerity pay in dealing with the outsider.

A visitor, on the other hand, should cooperate by being precise in stating his business. It sometimes saves time to send in a business card, with or without a written message.

A different type of visitor is the personal friend of the employer or employee. Such a person must be treated with similar cordiality and directness by the receptionist. Business men and women, however, should not encourage their friends and relatives to visit them during working hours, as such meetings frequently cause embarrassing interruptions.

Appointments and Interviews

Punctuality is essential in the business world. There is no such thing as being "fashionably late." The business man plans his day with strict regard for economy of time and efficiency. An appointment broken or delayed often results in the upsetting of important plans. If an appointment must be broken, notification should be given at the earliest possible moment. Such notification should be accompanied by an explanation and statement of regrets.

The person granting interviews, on the other hand, should attempt to fulfill them punctually. If the business man is wise, he will not use his importance as an excuse for keeping visitors waiting. A crowded reception room may add to his prestige in a superficial way, but it may also be interpreted as a sign of inefficiency and rudeness. Naturally, the person who seeks an interview without previous appointment must expect to wait.

The handling of an interview depends to a

considerable degree on the business man's personal judgment. It is up to him to decide whether to be brief and terse, or engaging and conversational. In either case, a few pleasant remarks take little time and put the visitor at ease.

The person seeking an interview, such as a salesman, will respect the value of the business man's time, if he hopes to create a good impression. He will also select a convenient hour for making his calls, and avoid visiting people when he knows they are at their busiest.

A clear conversational voice is important in interviews, and even more important in telephone conversations. Good enunciation and a well-modulated tone are not only essential to accurate understanding, but also constitute a courteous compliment to the listener. Slurring of words is especially to be avoided, since facial expression and gesture cannot help out. The secretary and switchboard operator should strive not to develop a sing-song intonation.

Personal Appearance

The attire of the business man should be simple and neat, though usually not too conservative or sober. A dark suit, white shirt, and "quiet" necktie are always appropriate. Considerable depends on the nature of the firm. Some companies prefer to create a slightly old-fashioned, conservative, and "reliable" impression. Others find it helpful to cultivate an air of being very fashionable and up-to-date. The newcomer should guide himself by observation, remembering that, whatever his position, he is in a sense a representative of his firm. Observation will also determine matters of behavior. In some offices, for example, men may remove their coats and vests. In others this is never done, and a thin suit-coat of dark material may be desirable. Smoking is prohibited in some offices. Even when permitted, it is wise for the subordinate employee not to indulge unless he is absolutely sure he will not offend some superior with strict ideas about smoking. In matters such as this the junior clerk should not guide himself by the behavior of the privileged executive.

While the clothes of the business woman should not be clinging, bright-hued party dresses, she should also avoid excessive severity and mannishness. Any simple dress which avoids such extremes is appropriate. Some business women frequently wear spectator-sports costumes or gracefully tailored suits with effect, but good taste does not depend on expensiveness; costly dresses are inappropriate in the office. White collars and cuffs generally create a favorable impression. Well-groomed hair is essential and a judicious use of make-up always advisable. A pretty and charming woman, neatly dressed, is an asset to any office.

The Woman in Business

No longer are a large number of employments closed to the woman. Indeed, many occupations and types of position have become her special province. Her place in the world of commerce and industry is established. Just as she need no longer imitate the severity of men's clothing, so she need not attempt to pattern herself after the business man in other ways. Within the limits of business practice she is free to express her femininity and follow the bent of her personality.

A married woman may use her maiden name in business if she considers that desirable. Or she may use her married name; as *Jean Arlan Kennedy*; or her married title; as, *Mrs. Ralph Kennedy*. If a widow, she generally retains her married title. If a divorcee, she may use her husband's surname; as, *Jean Kennedy*; or her maiden name; *Jean Arlan*. She may not use her married title. In either case she may prefix *Miss* or *Mrs.* to her name. Only a married woman, using her married title, regularly prefixes *Mrs.* to her name. If *Mrs.* is used in other cases, it should be enclosed in parentheses; as *(Mrs.) Jean Kennedy*. The same rule holds good for *Miss*; as *(Miss) Jean Arlan*.

The ambitious business woman wants to be treated as a worker, and not as someone requiring special assistance and personal concessions. The courtesy granted her should be sufficient to satisfy the respect accorded her sex, but not so much as to emphasize and underline her femininity. Elaborate drawing-room manners are out of place in business.

Men are not expected to remove their hats when a woman enters the elevator, or see to it that she is always allowed to enter and leave the car first. Such courtesies would make for considerable delays, particularly in the morning and at closing time, when the elevator is apt to be very crowded. In a crowded elevator, too, there is hardly room for a man to hold his hat conveniently at his side. When the car is not crowded, women are generally allowed to precede, though here again an executive or someone who is hurrying for a legitimate reason may go first. The same holds true in the matter of passing through doors, though all individuals are expected to hold the door open for those following. Similarly, a man seated in an office is not expected to rise when a woman speaks to him.

Business in Public

Business is not limited to the office or to office hours. It is also transacted at lunches and dinners, in clubs and locker rooms; it is greatly affected by contacts made at various social gatherings. The advice "Don't mix business with pleasure" is, fortunately or unfortunately, only half true. It would be nearer the truth to say, "If you do mix business with pleasure, be sure the mixture is a pleasant one, and agreeable to the person to whom it is offered." The average business man doesn't put his work out of his mind the minute he leaves the office, any more than the author forgets the book he is writing or the scientist the experiment he is conducting. No matter how frequently shop talk is decried, most people like to talk it. The man who refuses to consider business at social gatherings may be setting himself unnecessary obstacles.

But it must always be remembered that business topics do not take precedence at friendly meetings, as they do at the office. Courtesy requires that they be introduced naturally into conversation, and that mention of them cease if they seem uninteresting to individuals present. This is an important point. The salesman who takes a customer to lunch and then uses the opportunity to bombard him with an interminable salestalk, shows rudeness and very often spoils his own chances as well. The same is true of the executive who lectures on efficiency at a company dinner or gives orders to an employee he meets on a holiday. At social gatherings business conversation cannot be conducted in an abrupt, cut-and-dried manner. It must be pleasantly colored with wit and anecdote, dressed in party clothes, made vivid and interesting. The experienced business man or woman understands the proper technique. A casual word or two, an amusing story, mention of a new idea, a stimulating suggestion, a serious conversation only if the listener is obviously receptive—that's how it's done.

In short, business outside office hours must be conducted according to the rules of general social etiquette.

The salesclerk is in a special position, having to deal with the public constantly and still adhere to a business routine. The customer often behaves with a brusqueness and lack of consideration to which the clerk cannot safely reply in kind. According to modern sales methods, the guiding principle "The customer is always right" must generally be followed, whether the customer is courteous or not.

Flexibility

There are two chief ideas behind the concept of etiquette: mutual consideration, and respect for custom. This is as true for business etiquette as for any other. Some customs are almost universal; others differ from place to place. A department store is very different from a broker's office, and behavior suitable for a newspaper office is out of place in a bank. The business man or woman must follow the maxim "When in Rome, do as the Romans do"—only being very sure not to "outdo the Romans," that is, to show so much facile enthusiasm and over-ready complaisance as to lose dignity and character. Mutual consideration is impossible, however, without mutual understanding. In order to please a person and avoid offending him, one must know his likes and dislikes, his behavior patterns. And no two persons are alike.

This does not mean that a great deal of business etiquette cannot be applied at all times and places. There are certain standards of behavior which almost all civilized business men are expected to live up to. It does mean, however, that etiquette divorced from human understanding is a cold and lifeless routine. If it is to become a warm reality, distinguishing its possessor, it must be tempered with fine tact and breadth of sympathy. It is in this respect that flexibility of behavior in meeting new situations and individuals is essential.

THE SUCCESSFUL SECRETARY

The Secretarial Position

The secretary acts as a personal representative, responsible for the accurate conveying of information to her employer and the accurate issuing of his communications and instructions. The activities of the secretary may vary greatly from employer to employer, sometimes involving only intelligent execution of instructions and in other instances demanding considerable initiative and judgment. But the elements of tact and mediation are always apparent. This is inevitable in the modern world, where the interrelationships between business and public, and between business and business are constantly developing new ramifications. In present-day society the secretary plays an important role, and upon her efficiency depends much of the smooth functioning of the executive.

This does not imply that the secretary has superseded the executive, notwithstanding fictional or actual instances to the contrary. Most employers consider themselves competent to do their own thinking, and often resent any but the most subtly phrased of unsolicited or solicited suggestions, although they are quick to appreciate all assistance which lightens their tasks without challenging their authority. Secretaries who think for their employers, functioning as a kind of master mind behind a screen, are largely a product of twentieth-century fiction. The competent executive's appetite for argument and advice is usually well satisfied by conference with his colleagues and clients.

One of the most important qualifications of a proficient secretary is accuracy. It insures the employer against having to check and recheck small items in search of possible errors. It gives him a comfortable feeling of security. Having someone he can trust, he need not clog his mind with detail.

Accuracy is more a matter of self-discipline than education. A person widely read and highly educated may frequently be guilty of inaccuracies in his thinking and in the verbal or written expression of his thoughts, particularly if he makes a point of glibly rattling off answers to all questions in order to create an impression of brilliance and encyclopedic knowledge. The really accurate individual makes a very clear distinction between facts of which he is certain and notions about which he is vague or doubtful. He has schooled himself to trust and employ the former, and not to waste time trying to puzzle out the latter, especially when consultation of some recognized authority would quickly resolve his doubts.

A relatively small amount of information, organized with clarity and logic, is more valuable than a vast mass of opinions, suppositions, half-remembered rules and procedures, and other loose ends of education. The comparison is the same as that between a relatively small but well-trained body of soldiers and a huge army whose individual fighting men are poorly equipped, unorganized, and badly instructed. The first, if vigorously and strategically employed, will defeat the second. The accurate mind, for that matter, is like a clearly-drawn military map, in which special attention is given to key points and important objectives. It may also be likened to a carefully arranged index, which makes information available in the shortest possible time.

Accuracy need not and should not, however, involve constant recourse to authorities, whether they be books, persons, or information agencies. Such recourse can become a pernicious habit, subtly undermining the individual's confidence in his every belief and assertion, until the spelling of the simplest word or the recalling of the most familiar telephone number awakens overwhelming doubts. The competent secretary does not let such unreasonable worries get the upper hand. She not only knows, but she knows that she knows. Moreover, in consulting authorities, she seeks not only to find an answer for the immediate problem, but also, time permitting, to imprint on her own mind the information so gained, provided it seems apt to be useful a second time and is of such a nature as to be readily learned. Such intelligent use of authorities is in itself an education, rapidly building up a skeleton framework of key facts, into which further information can easily be inserted. Knowledge, if so organized, begets knowledge, since interrelated facts provide clues to each other, and are much more easily recalled than isolated facts.

It is difficult to exaggerate the importance for the secretary of such a skeleton framework, including such fields as spelling, grammar, and usage, frequently-used addresses and telephone numbers, recognized form of letters, proper methods of indexing and filing, regulations on mailing and expressing, the names and faces of individuals and their personality, occupation, and degree of importance, office procedure both general and specific, arrangement of interviews and appointments, and the like. The executive, specialist, or scholar can and very often should forget matters of detail in order to devote his mind more completely and effectively to larger issues. Indeed, it is for this very reason that he employs a secretary. He desires to be left with as free a hand as possible, depending on his secretary to handle all minor matters with intelligence, decision, and discretion. This division of labor, when properly carried out by both parties, is a very effective one.

The secretary should never, except when absolutely unavoidable, question the employer on matters of detail. Such questioning amounts to a confession that she doesn't know her job, and is especially irritating to him because it forces him to cudgel his brains over the very problems of which he wishes to be relieved.

In matters of knowledge and accuracy the requirements of the stenographer are similar to those of the secretary, save that the activities of the former are necessarily limited to a narrower field. Shorthand and typing are usually the sole occupations of the stenographer. To the secretary they are an alphabet, a language which she is able to employ with great facility in the accomplishment of her wider and more varied duties.

The duties of the secretary are not only more complicated and numerous than those of the stenographer; they involve greater responsibility, flexibility, and a significant personal element. The stenographer works with words; the secretary with people.

In this connection the quality of restraint or unobtrusiveness, though not pre-eminent, is especially characteristic and undeniably important. The successful secretary does not obviously impose her personality on her surroundings, but has a way of shading into the background. She cultivates a soft but distinct voice, a quiet but capable manner. Her style of dressing is pleasing to the eye but usually simple and neat, neither overly feminine nor mannish, and above all, suited to the type of establishment in which she is working. Tact and discretion are habitual to her. She is self-effacing—but never hesitant or shy, for she knows that such tactics are out of place in the office, immediately making her a bother rather than a help. When present at conferences and interviews, she maintains a thoroughly impersonal attitude, which facilitates matters and avoids embarrassment. She manages to do this without seeming in the least bored or aloof.

The nature of the secretarial function puts an unusually great premium on discretion and restraint. Inevitably the secretary comes to know a great many matters concerning the firm and employer for whom she is working, many of them confidential. Her position as a personal representative makes it dangerously easy to pass on private information about her immediate employer to the staff, and about members of the staff to her employer. Both of these activities can easily become unethical, damaging, and serious. The accomplished secretary avoids them; by establishing a reputation for discretion, she gains the co-operation of her colleagues. She also makes it possible for her employer to think, talk, plan, and thrash matters out freely, without feeling a constant need for caution in her presence and a constant fear of possible ridicule being circulated subsequently. She becomes a kind of business confidant. In so doing, she advances her status greatly and is better able to play her proper role, which is that of trusted assistant, leaving her employer free to consider major problems.

Ease and Efficiency

The personal qualities of a successful secretary cannot be dissected out of her personality and each discussed by itself, for actually they are all interdependent. For example, accuracy, knowledge, self-discipline, and confidence go hand in hand; one cannot exist without at least something of the others. In the successful personality all qualities are well integrated.

The same is true of ease and efficiency. It is difficult to do things easily without doing them efficiently, and it is difficult to be truly efficient if nervous and tense. Naturally, a person cannot relax while learning a new job. At such times the mind is constantly active—learning, experimenting, testing, watching itself for errors. Even at such a time too much tenseness represents energy wasted. Once the groundwork of the job is learned, it is possible to devote more time to doing it smoothly. Matters of routine become a habit, and the mind is free for other considerations.

The professional dancer performs with a wonderful display of ease and poise. Each turn and gesture is the epitome of grace. Movements that have taken literally years to learn and which are utterly beyond the powers of untrained muscles, are performed in such an effortless manner that the spectator often feels certain a child could duplicate them. But the dancer's performance is comparatively simple in one sense. She is executing a predetermined routine and seldom need adjust herself suddenly to new circumstances. But in the swift-changing world of business, surprises are the rule. The secretary, whose tasks are usually so multitudinous that her work—like all "woman's work"—is never done, must be ready to meet all kinds of demands on her time. Correspondence to be read, letters to be typed, incoming and outgoing telephone calls, dictation, arranging of appointments and conferences, inquiries and instructions—all may descend upon her at once, as if specially designed to confuse and confound her. Nevertheless, she is expected to handle them all dexterously and without losing her poise.

The efficient secretary is busy but never preoccupied. She shifts smoothly from one job to another; does not hesitate, since she knows which action takes precedence over another. When the telephone rings, she does not desperately attempt to finish several lines of typing before answering it—nor does she necessarily break off nervously in the middle of a word. By rigorous self-discipline she has taught herself to leave a piece of work in the middle and come back to it with a minimum loss of time in hunting for loose ends. If she is called upon to do so many things at once that she begins to forget some of them—and that can happen to the most efficient secretary—she takes care of the most pressing matters first and then turns her attention to the others, asking questions if necessary.

Such efficiency is largely a matter of following a routine, and an effective and time-saving routine comprises two chief elements: efficient habits and the ability to make plans. Habit is what enables an individual to perform a task with a minimum of conscious thought. Any action which is repeated a sufficient number of times becomes a habit: walking is a habit; dancing or typing may become habits. Saying "Good morning" to certain individuals and walking down one side of a street rather than another are matters of habit. But habits are not necessarily efficient. In learning to use the typewriter, for example, the "hunt and peck" system can become just as much a habit as the touch system. A stenographer may learn to consult the dictionary automatically when confronted by an unfamiliar word, but she may also learn to become so dependent on the dictionary as seriously to limit her ability; both are habits. Invariably saying "Hello" when answering the telephone may become a habit, although the word "Hello" is usually a waste of time, since it tells nothing and must be immediately followed by an explanation as to who is saying "Hello." In short, habit alone is not enough. Before allowing any action to become habitual, it is well to ask, "Is it an efficient and smooth-flowing action, performed in the fewest number of moves? Will it be an asset to my personality, or just an unnecessary burden? Is it a short-cut, or the long way around?" Thoughts, too, can become as habitual as actions: the mind develops its stereotyped patterns, which may be either helps or hindrances. In these matters, every person must be his own efficiency expert. Business and secretarial schools, of course, inculcate into the individual a groundwork of efficient habits, but the work does not end there. Every time a new routine is learned or an old routine is changed, careful thought must be devoted to habit-building. Question it thoroughly as to its advantages and disadvantages.

The ability to make plans—the other element of an effective routine—demands clear thinking. Every executive has some way of arranging his day's work and that of his secretary. The first hour of the morning may be devoted to reading and answering correspondence; then interviews may be held with members of the staff, followed by interviews with salesmen and other outsiders, and so on, each task being handled at a definite time. But there is no such thing as a foolproof and unalterable routine. Interruptions of all sorts are always coming up. Pressing matters must be given a special time-allotment or shoved ahead. The day's routine must be rearranged again and again. Much of the responsibility for this falls on the secretary, and particularly such difficult tasks as postponing interviews without hurting feelings, and seeing that essential business is handled by an employer deep in conference. To plan a routine calls only for careful deliberation, but to break a routine and replace it with a new one on the spur of the moment demands ingenuity and quick thinking.

Dealing with People

The good secretary is well liked. Visitors to the office recall her courteous, cheerful manner, her intelligent considerateness, her smile. Fellow employees value her helpful cooperation and the little favors she is able to grant them. As for her employer, he depends on her in a hundred different ways, not only in business dealings but sometimes in social matters as well. It is part of her job to create a good impression, establish and maintain friendly relations. Her corner of the office shows a touch of color, literally as well as figuratively.

The business world moves at high speed and in quick tempo. The office building hums with activity. Executives are drawn together by a complex web of letters, telephone calls, conversations, agreements. Transactions are set underway whose success depends on the swift and efficient functioning of each employee, from the highest to the most subordinate. In this fast-moving world, confusions, misunderstandings, delays, and other manifestations of poor cooperation prove costly. Yet it is all too easy for an individual to develop a hurried, nervous tempo of working, no more efficient than a burst of speed by a high-powered auto in heavy traffic. Obviously, whatever makes for greater smoothness in personal relations and functioning is very important.

The secretary is a vital part of this swift-moving scene; yet her position enables her to obtain a perspective of the entire picture. And since she is largely a mediator, she is in a good position to work for smoothness. She can make it easier for people to cooperate. She can do her bit to keep those with whom she comes in contact in good humor, soften their disappointments, increase their enthusiasm. She can do her best to smooth over difficulties, lessen intra-office jealousies, and avoid gaining the reputation of gossip and office spy.

The good secretary has developed the qualities of ease and efficiency and is therefore able to relax to a certain degree during her work; and by doing this she makes it easier for others to relax. She does not "fight against" her job, wasting time in worry and bitterness, but makes her work a part of her life. She promotes a similarly healthy attitude in others.

To be able to do all this, the secretary must be expert at personal relations. Now a great deal has been written about the art of handling people. Psychologists, authors, homespun philosophers, and "business experts" of varying intelligence and ability have told the world how to make "friends," conciliate enemies, and develop an irresistible personality. Their copious advice can usually be reduced to one central principle: namely, that any human being is somewhat egotistical and likes to feel important. Therefore, he likes the sound of his own name; he likes to be reminded of his success and good points; he likes to be remembered and to feel that people have affection for him; he likes compliments, provided they are not too obviously flattering; he likes to think that his ideas and suggestions receive serious attention, etc. He does not like to remember his failures and failings; he does not like to admit he's wrong or give up an untenable position in argument, unless there is a graceful "out"; he dislikes cleverness in others and fears sarcasm; he is jealous of success; he does not like to be forgotten, etc. All this is, of course, very true, as the secretary who understands anything of human nature is well aware; and she must also know how to make use of her knowledge. However, a human being is more than a self-centered, jealous child, and there is a limit to the use that can be made of methods for handling people which are based largely on flattery, facile enthusiasm, and general heartiness. Sincerity, courtesy, and unforced human interest—natural rather than artificial qualities—are more important.

Another important consideration is that all individuals are different. They do not conform to type—"rich man, poor man, beggarman, thief,"—or some more sophisticated set of categories. Each has his own quirks and idiosyncracies. The methods that work with one will not necessarily work with another. The good secretary is a student of individual human nature, and learns more than names and faces and occupations. She discovers the things that please and displease the people with whom she comes in contact; she comes to know their strong and weak points. Above all, she studies the personality of her employer with a concentrated interest. His habits in giving dictation; his attitude toward salesmen; his tendencies to hurry through certain matters and linger over others, are all matters of importance to her. She discovers the extent to which he desires her to make changes in the form of his letters, or rearrange materials on his desk. This study is for the most part a silent one, conducted by observation rather than questions, yet it is of vital importance. For it enables the secretary to handle her work in the way her employer would like to see it handled, and by adjusting her personality to his, to serve her employer most satisfactorily.

SUCCESS IN YOUR JOB

There are people who get ahead without pushing and without making a fuss. They do their work smoothly and easily. Obstacles are unable to hold them back for long. Promotion comes to them naturally. They take new responsibilities in stride. It seems as if Fortune were always smiling on them.

Those are the people who know the secret of getting along with their work.

It is possible for a person to fight his job without being aware of the fact. He may think he is putting forth a great deal of effort, more than should be required of him. Actually, he grudges every particle of energy he is forced to expend. Old assignments bore him. New assignments seem like an imposition. He is irritated by his co-workers and superiors. Everything rasps his nerves. As a result, he goes down to business each morning feeling like a man who is about to encounter an old enemy.

Yet there is nothing fundamentally lacking in such a person. Watch him when he is busy with a hobby, or conversing with a friend, or reading a book on some favorite subject, or otherwise amusing himself. At such times he seems a different person. His face lights up. He forgets himself and the fatigue that weighed on him during working hours. Ideas come to him thick and fast. If something happens to interest him especially, he is willing to sit up half the night discussing it or working on it. His mind and body begin to function as they were intended to, as they are always capable of functioning.

No, there is nothing fundamentally lacking in such a person—but there *is* something vitally wrong in the relationship between him and his job. It is as if he had built a wall between his job and his true self.

Work, of course, is not the same thing as play. There are many jobs which have disagreeable, arduous, and boresome aspects. But—and here is the important thing—all jobs have some interesting aspects. There are friendships with fellow employees and superiors to be cemented and extended. There are opportunities to increase efficiency, make improvements in technique. Finally, if a person looks beyond the seemingly narrow limits of his own special job, a whole new world opens up for him. He begins to learn the work of those around and above him. He increases his knowledge of the business as a whole. He sees his own job as one unit in a mighty chain of productive activity, and because of this broader vision his job acquires a new glamour.

The enterprising and successful individual gets into his job, lets it take hold of him. He does not dole out energy like a miser. He does not isolate himself from his fellow workers. He tackles his work as if it were an exciting game (and it is an exciting game for those who know the secret). He does more than he is told. He gives his interests free rein. Whenever he gets a chance, he satisfies his curiosity about other aspects of the business. He is genuinely loyal for the simple reason that he really likes his work. He can't help working smoothly, since his alert, forward-looking attitude makes it easy for him to forget petty irritations and grievances. He studies his own job in relation to those of others. As a result he is ready, like the understudy of a theatrical star, to step into a bigger part.

When an opportunity for advancement is open, the boss is on the lookout for someone who can competently perform the more responsible job, and he naturally turns to the person in whom he has confidence. The enterprising and forward-looking individual builds himself a reputation for ability, integrity, and dependability. He qualifies himself through study, experience, and application, so that he is prepared to go ahead and fill the better job.

Such a person is truly alive. Beyond all else, he knows the deep satisfaction of using the energy that is in him and, giving freely and eagerly of himself, the rich happiness of effort well spent that makes life worth living.

DICTIONARY OF

BUSINESS LAW FOR LAYMEN

INTRODUCTION

According to an old adage, the man who attempts to be his own lawyer has a fool for his client. There is, no doubt, a great deal of truth in that statement, and it is not the purpose of this book to enable a man to act as his own lawyer. In order to conduct his business intelligently, however, it is necessary for the layman to understand some of the principles of the laws which govern his rights and duties toward those with whom he deals. Never has this been more true than at present. In the course of his daily living, the average citizen is constantly coming into contact with the law and with legal problems.

It is to meet this need of a practical knowledge of the law on the part of the individual that this section is intended. BUSINESS LAW FOR THE LAYMAN, in convenient *dictionary* form, contains up-to-date information on practically every branch of the law and covers all recent legislation with reference to bankruptcy, wages and hours, and the relationship of employer to employee. It also includes a complete set of the most commonly used legal forms.

In brief, this section contains an accurate, concise statement of the law, as it affects the average layman and business man, and should prove invaluable as a ready reference handbook and guide.

EXPLANATION OF TERMS

1. DEFINITION OF TERMS.—*Statute* refers to the laws passed by Congress and the several state legislatures. The term *common law* refers to that body of law and jurisprudence which was originated, developed, and formulated in England prior to the time of the Colonial settlements in North America, and which has become the law in most of the United States, except where it has been abrogated by statute. An *action* is a suit or case which one party brings against another in court.

2. COMMON LAW.—In a large measure the common law establishes the rules and regulations under which we live. Legal decisions are precedents which must be followed in other cases of the same general nature. In cases involving similar facts, the lower courts are bound by decisions of the higher courts. The Federal Courts in a particular state must follow the decisions of the Supreme and Appellate Courts of that state, except in cases involving the interpretation of the constitution and laws of the United States or on questions which are purely procedural. The courts in one state are not bound by the decisions of a court in another state. Of course the common-law decision may be set aside by statute or modified when it no longer applies to present conditions.

3. LAW AND EQUITY.—These two terms appear frequently in the following pages and are quite generally misunderstood. The word *law* signifies a rule of action either written or unwritten. *Equity* rather looks to the substance than to the form. When an act is *equi-*

table it may be just, even though it has no foundation in the law. Formerly separate courts existed to try cases in equity. The modern tendency is to combine law and equity and to give judges the power to try both law and equity cases. See EQUITABLE REMEDIES and LEGAL REMEDIES.)

4. CIVIL LAW AND CRIMINAL LAW.—The difference between civil and criminal law is not always understood. Criminal law may be defined as the law dealing with offenses against the people. The acts that are crimes are clearly defined by statute and the cases are prosecuted by public officers. Civil law takes in all law not criminal in nature. Wrongful acts may be subject to both criminal and civil actions. If a man steals an automobile, he has committed a crime against the state, and at the same time the person robbed has a civil action against him for the loss. (See TORTS.)

5. CLASSES OF COURTS.—There are four main classes of courts in each of the states. The first are the courts which have jurisdiction over petty criminal offenses and in which minor suits are brought. Second, there are the courts of general jurisdiction, in which more important suits are brought. Next are the Appellate Courts, and finally, there is the Supreme Court, or court of last resort, which reviews decisions of lower courts.

Of course the judicial system varies widely in the different states. For example, the Illinois law provides for Justice of the Peace Courts, which are limited to minor cases. Next comes the County Court, one in each county, which has special and limited jurisdiction. Then there is the Circuit Court, which is the general court of original jurisdiction. Following the Circuit Court come the courts of review, first the State Appellate Court, and at the top, the State Supreme Court. Besides these courts, the larger counties have special courts to hear probate cases and the like. Cities with a population of 50,000 or more have municipal courts with jurisdiction over cases confined to the city.

6. FEDERAL COURTS.—There are three classes of Federal Courts. The lowest is called the District Court, taking its name from the fact that the country as a whole is divided into districts, with one court for each district. Next is the Circuit Court of Appeals, to which appeals from the District Court are taken. And finally, there is the United States Supreme Court, in which appeals may be sought from decisions of the Courts of Appeal and from the Supreme Courts of the several states and in certain criminal cases direct from the Federal District Courts. Upon application made in proper form this court decides whether or not it will review a particular case.

7. BASIS OF APPEALS.—No court will review the decision of a lower court unless the application is founded on errors in the former proceedings. Thus the proof of wrongful admission of or refusal to admit proper evidence in the former trial would be sufficient to obtain a rehearing.

8. EVIDENCE.—Evidence includes all means and ways by which the truth of an alleged fact is established or disproved. *Direct evidence* is the testimony of a witness or written documents and records, which are competent, relevant, and material to the issues joined and which, if believed, prove the existence of the fact in issue without any inference. *Circumstantial evidence* is a chain of facts or circumstances, all tending, when connected up, to establish a logical inference or conclusion that such fact does exist.

LAW DICTIONARY

Acknowledgment of Deeds, Mortgages and Releases

All deeds, mortgages, releases, and other documents relating to or affecting real estate must be acknowledged before an officer authorized by law to take acknowledgments. Chattel mortgages must also be so acknowledged. Notaries public, justices of the peace, masters in chancery, and judges and clerks of courts of record having a seal are authorized to take acknowledgments in most cases.

The laws of some states require the acknowledgment to show, in cases where an instrument is signed by both husband and wife, that the wife signed out of the presence of her husband. Many states also require that where an acknowledgment is taken before a Notary Public, the date of the expiration of his commission must be shown.

Form 1, for Chattel Mortgages

STATE OF ILLINOIS,)
KANE COUNTY) ss.

I, John Richard, a Justice of the Peace in the Town of Dundee, in and for the said County, do hereby certify that this mortgage was duly acknowledged before me by the above named ...., the grantor therein named, and entered by me this 17th day of July, 19....

Witness my hand and seal.

(Seal)

JOHN RICHARD,
Justice of the Peace.

Form 2, for Releases

STATE OF ILLINOIS,)
COUNTY OF DU PAGE) ss.

I, John Smith, a Notary Public in and for said County, and in the State aforesaid do hereby certify that James Y. Scammon, who is personally known to me to be the same person whose name

...d to the foregoing instrument, appeared before me this day in person and acknowledged that he signed, sealed, and delivered the instrument as his free and voluntary act for the uses and purposes therein set forth.

Given under my hand and Notarial Seal this ...th day of May, 19.....

(Notarial Seal)

JOHN SMITH,
Notary Public.

Form 3, for Mortgages and Deeds

STATE OF ILLINOIS,)
COUNTY OF DU PAGE) ss.

I, John Smith, a Notary Public in and for said County in the State aforesaid, do hereby certify that Samuel P. Smith and Sarah E. Smith, his wife, who are personally known to me to be the same persons whose names are subscribed to the foregoing instruments, appeared before me this day in person and acknowledged that they signed, sealed, and delivered said instrument as their free and voluntary act for the uses and purposes therein set forth, including a release and waiver of all rights under and by virtue of the homestead exemption laws of this State.

Given under my hand and Notarial Seal this first day of January, A.D. 19.....

(Notarial Seal)

JOHN SMITH,
Notary Public.

Form 4, General and Short Form

STATE OF....................,)
COUNTY OF ....) ss.

On the ....day of .... in the year one thousand nine hundred and ....., before me personally came (names of both parties), who are known to me to be the individuals described in, and who executed, the foregoing instrument, and acknowledged that they executed the same.

(Signature.)

Affidavits

1. DEFINITION.—An affidavit is a voluntary statement reduced to writing and sworn to or affirmed before an officer legally empowered to administer it. Affidavits are not testimony in courts of law, because the makers cannot be cross-examined; but a person who makes a false affidavit may be punished for perjury.

2. FORM.—The following is a common form and with certain modifications can be made to apply to most cases.

Common Form of Affidavit

STATE OF ILLINOIS,)
COUNTY OF HENRY) ss.

John Jones being duly sworn on his oath states that he is well acquainted with the handwriting of Daniel Seitz, one of the subscribing witnesses to the deed hereto attached; that affiant has frequently seen him write and knows his signature; that he believes that the name of the said Daniel Seitz, signed in the said deed, is in the handwriting of the said Daniel Seitz, and further affiant says not.

(Signed)
JOHN JONES

Subscribed and sworn to before me this 28th day of February, A.D. 19.....

E. M. SCHWARTZ,
Notary Public.

Agency

1. DEFINITIONS.—Agency is the relation between two or more persons by which one person (the agent) represents another (the principal) in the transaction of lawful acts or business. Agents are of two kinds, general and special. A *General Agent* is authorized to represent the principal in all of his business, or in all business of a particular kind. A *Special Agent* is authorized to do a specific thing, as sell a farm, buy a house, or transact some special business for the principal.

2. WHO MAY ACT AS PRINCIPAL AND AGENT.—Any person who is able to act for himself, may act as principal. This excludes a lunatic, an alien enemy, or any other person incapable of contracting. On the other hand, any person who is competent to act in his own right, and who is of sound mind and understanding, may act as an agent. Husband and wife may act for each other, except where prevented by the statutes of the particular state. A person unable to contract on his own account, such as a person under age, may sometimes act as an agent. Anyone except a lunatic, imbecile, or infant of tender years may be an agent. Corporations often act as agents.

3. AUTHORITY, HOW GIVEN.—The authority of an agent may be constituted in three ways: By deed under seal, by writing, or by mere word. Express authority is given to an agent by what is called a power of attorney. If the authority is to execute a writing under seal and acknowledged, the power of attorney must be likewise under seal and acknowledged. In a few states, however, this rule has been changed by statute. An agent to sell land, or to do any important business, where he is required to make contracts, draw or sign notes, drafts, or checks, should be appointed by a carefully drawn legal document. The general rule with respect to the liability of a principal for unauthorized acts of his agent is that the principal is liable to third persons for any acts done by the agent for the principal in the course of his duties and within the actual or apparent scope of his agency. Agency may be implied from previous dealings and transactions between the parties. If the principal has held a person out as an agent he will be bound by his acts, even though as a matter of fact the agent had no express authority to represent him. The acts or contracts of an agent made

beyond the scope of his authority may be ratified by the principal and when so ratified are binding on the latter.

4. AGENT'S RESPONSIBILITY.—An agent concealing his principal is himself responsible, and if acting fraudulently or deceitfully, is himself responsible to third parties. He cannot appoint a substitute or delegate his authority to another, without consent of his principal. If an agent embezzles his principal's property, it may be reclaimed if it can be identified or distinctly traced. An agent employed to sell property cannot buy it himself, or if employed to purchase property, cannot buy from himself.

5. PRINCIPAL'S LIABILITY.—The principal is liable to the third person for the negligence or unskillfulness of the agent, when he is acting in the fulfillment of the agency business. The principal is liable for all acts of his agent within the scope of his agency, but money paid by an agent can be recovered by the principal, if it has been paid by mistake. The knowledge of the agent relating to the business of the agency is binding upon the principal, and notice to an agent as to matters relating to the agency is notice to the principal.

6. AUTHORITY MAY BE REVOKED.—The authority of an agent may be terminated: First, by the express revocation thereof by the principal. Second, by renunciation of such power by the agent. Third, by the death of the principal. Fourth, by the expiration of the time within which the agent was to perform the acts which were to be done by him, or by his having completed and fully performed the commission and closed the business which he was to transact. Fifth, by the sale of the subject matter of the agency. Sixth, by the insanity of either principal or agent. Seventh, by the bankruptcy of the principal or the agent. A revocation of authority takes effect, so far as the agent is concerned, when he receives notice thereof; so far as the third persons are concerned, when they receive notice of such revocation. Personal notice or its equivalent is required, and is sufficient, to those who have dealt with the agent. Advertising the fact would be sufficient as to all others. Without a sufficient notice of the revocation, a contract made in good faith with the agent after revocation will bind the principal the same as before.

7. SPECIAL RULES OF AGENCY.—An agent cannot delegate his powers to another without the consent of the principal, unless the act to be done is a minor service, or one requiring no personal ability or skill. Both principal and agent are liable if the persons with whom the agent is transacting business do not know of the agency relationship. An agent can receive no personal profit from a transaction.

8. CAUTION.—Persons dealing with agents who are strangers should be very careful to ascertain that the agent has authority to transact business in hand. In all transactions in regard to real estate the authority of the agent should be in writing, signed by the owner of the property, in order to be binding upon him. In all cases of doubt as to the authority of an agent or the extent of his authority, it would be wise to require of the agent a written proof of his agency and the extent of his authority.

9. POWER OF ATTORNEY.—Whenever it becomes necessary to delegate to an agent the power to sign notes, checks, or other legal documents, it is advisable to grant such powers in a written document. Such document is usually called a Power of Attorney. It should be signed by the principal and witnessed, and should set forth exactly and explicitly what the attorney or agent has power to do, and if the agent is to deal in real estate, it is sometimes required by law, and, in any event always advisable, that such Power of Attorney be under seal.

Power of Attorney, General Form

KNOW ALL MEN BY THESE PRESENTS, That I, James L. Binton, of Naperville, County of Du Page, and State of Illinois, have made, constituted and appointed, and BY THESE PRESENTS do make, constitute and appoint, Chas. A. Lerch true and lawful attorney for me and in my name, place and stead, (here state the purpose for which the power is given), giving and granting unto my said attorney full power and authority to do and perform all and every act and thing whatsoever, requisite and necessary to be done in and about the premises, as fully, to all intents and purposes, as I might or could do if personally present, with all power of substitution and revocation, hereby ratifying and confirming all that my said attorney or his substitute shall lawfully do or cause to be done by virtue thereof.

IN WITNESS WHEREOF, I have hereunto set my hand and seal the 2nd day of January, one thousand nine hundred ....

Signed, Sealed and Delivered
in Presence of

....

JAMES L. BINTON. (Seal.)

To be properly acknowledged before an officer, the same as a deed according to the law of the State.

Proxy or Power of Attorney to Vote

Know all men by these presents: That I, David E. Hughes, do hereby constitute and appoint C. A. Brown my true and lawful attorney, for me and in my name, place and stead, to vote as my proxy and representative at the .... meeting of the stockholders of the ...., a corporation, and at any adjournment of said meeting, all of the .... shares of the capital stock of said corporation standing in my name on the books of said corporation, as fully and amply as I could or might do were I personally present; with full power of substitution and revocation.

Witness my hand and seal at Aurora, Illinois, this 26th day of June, A.D. 19.....

E. R. Zemmer. (Seal.)

Revocation of Power of Attorney

Whereas, I, Sylvester Jones of Aurora, County of Kane, and State of Illinois, did on the tenth day of June, 19...., by my letter or power of attorney appoint John C. Cook of Chicago my true and lawful attorney, for me and in my name to (here state in precise language what he was authorized to do) as by the said power of attorney, reference thereunto being had, will fully appear;

Therefore, know all men by these presents, That I, Sylvester Jones, aforesaid, have revoked and recalled the said power of attorney, and by these presents do revoke and recall all power and authority thereby given to the said John C. Cook.

Given this tenth day of October, 19.....

Signed and sealed in presence of ....

Sylvester Jones. (Seal.)

Agreement to Purchase Land

1. Must Be in Writing.—An agreement to purchase real estate must be in writing, and should be signed by both buyer and seller. The writing need not mention the amount to be paid for the land. It should be signed in ink, but is not invalid if signed with a lead pencil or even with a rubber stamp. The entire contract need not be on the same sheet of paper, and it sometimes happens that two or more sheets of paper constitute the contract, as in cases where the agreement to purchase land is completed through correspondence between the two parties.

2. Exceptions.—There are some exceptions to the rule that an agreement to purchase real estate is not enforceable unless in writing. For example, if A sells a piece of property to B and receives the purchase price, and without a written agreement allows B to take possession of the property, and if B makes valuable and lasting improvements on the property, the courts will compel A to give B a deed to the property.

3. A Common Misunderstanding.—It is quite generally believed that, if a purchaser makes an oral agreement to purchase land and pays part of the purchase price, he can compel the seller to give him a deed to the real estate. This is not the law. The purchaser, however, can compel the seller to return the money he has paid.

4. Options.—An option is a contract by which the owner of property agrees with the other party that he shall have the right to purchase the property at a fixed price within a certain time. For example A agrees to sell a piece of property to B at a certain price within a certain period of time, for which B gives A a valuable consideration. B must either exercise his option and purchase the property within the time limit, or forfeit his consideration. All options must be in writing. If no time limit is fixed in the agreement, the option must be exercised within a reasonable time.

5. Transferring of Title.—In most real estate contracts the seller agrees to furnish the buyer with a good and merchantable title. He also agrees to transfer title to the property by a Warranty Deed, which warrants the title in him and the buyer against any loss which might be occasioned by defects in the title. A purchaser should always insist that the contract provide that the seller is to furnish and deliver a merchantable title. The contract generally requires the seller to furnish, also, evidence that he has good title. This is done by producing either an Abstract, Guaranty Policy, or Torrens Certificate, showing good title in the seller.

6. Abstract of Title.—An abstract is a statement in substance of what appears in the public records affecting the title to the land in question from the time it was owned by the government down to date. The public records are searched and the matters shown therein. An abstract will show all transfers, mortgages, judgments, tax sales, liens of all kinds, court proceedings and everything of record affecting the title to the property. These abstracts are prepared by private concerns or individuals known as abstract companies or abstracters. To determine whether or not the seller's title is good, the purchaser should have the abstract examined by an attorney competent to pass upon the law of real property. This examination by an attorney will reveal the validity or merchantability of the title. The objections to a clear title may be simple or exceedingly complex, and require the services of a competent attorney in that field. Usually the seller pays all of the expenses incidental to bringing the abstract down to date. The purchaser generally pays the examination fee.

7. Title Insurance or Guaranty Policy.—Under this system the title company issues a policy guaranteeing the holder of the policy against any loss he might sustain by reason of any defect in the title, whether of record or otherwise, existing before or at the time of the issuance of the policy. This system is becoming more popular in cities because of the demand for facilities to expedite real estate transactions and also because of the protective feature.

8. Torrens System.—The Torrens System is a system providing for the registration of land titles in such a manner that, when the title is once registered, a certificate of the registrar of titles will show the exact condition

of the title. In order to register a title under this system, it is necessary that a court proceeding be had first in which the decree of the court settles and establishes the title. After this has been done, the registrar of titles will issue an official certificate which will show who has title to the land, and what defects, if any, appear in his title. After the title to a particular parcel of property has been so registered, all subsequent transactions affecting the title to that property must be filed with the registrar of titles, and are noted upon the certificate of title. This enables a purchaser to determine the true state of the title by merely examining the certificate of the registrar. The purpose of the system is to simplify the transfer of real estate, and it is now in force in a number of states.

Agreement for Sale of Land

This agreement, made and entered into this .... day of .... by and between ...., party of the first part, and ...., party of the second part, witnesseth:

1. The said party of the first part, for and in consideration of the sum of $........ to be paid as hereinafter provided, hereby agrees to sell unto the party of the second part the following described tract of land:

[Description]

2. The said party of the second part hereby agrees to purchase said premises at said consideration of $........., and to pay the same as follows: (set out terms of payment).

3. The said party of the first part, upon receiving the final payment mentioned above, shall execute and deliver to the said party of the second part, or to his assigns, a duly acknowledged Warranty Deed, conveying to him or them the fee simple title to said premises, free and clear from all incumbrance.

In witness whereof the said parties have hereunto set their hands and seals the day and year first above written.

Form of Option

For and in consideration of the sum of .... dollars to me in hand paid, the receipt whereof is hereby acknowledged, I hereby grant unto .... an option for ...... days from the ...... day of .... 19...., to purchase for the sum of .... dollars, the following described lands situated in the County of .... and State of ....:

[Insert description of property],

upon the following terms and conditions: [insert terms of sale], said .... to signify his intention to take or reject the same by due notice in writing within the time above specified, and a failure to serve such notice within the time specified shall terminate this option without further action, time being the essence of this agreement.

In case said notice shall be served in due time, then thirty days shall be given in which to examine abstract or other evidence of title, and close the sale.

Auctioneer

1. Definition.—An auctioneer is a person employed to sell property to the highest bidder at public sale.

2. Agent for Both Buyer and Seller.—An auctioneer is the exclusive agent of the owner until he accepts the purchaser's bid and knocks down the property to him. On accepting the bid the auctioneer becomes the agent of the purchaser also, and thus represents both parties.

3. Completion of the Sale.—A sale by auction is completed when the auctioneer announces its completion by the fall of the hammer, or in any other customary manner. Until such announcement is made, the auctioneer may withdraw the property from sale unless the sale has been advertised to be without reserve. Any bidder may also withdraw his bid at any time before the fall of the hammer.

4. Responsibility of Auctioneer.—Authority to sell property does not imply power to sell at auction. Thus a purchaser buying goods from an auctioneer, when he knows the auctioneer has no authority to sell them, acquires no title to the property thus purchased. The seller or owner is not bound by any statements by the auctioneer. An auctioneer must accept the most favorable bid. He cannot refuse to accept legitimate bids. He is justified, however, in rejecting the bids of insane or drunken persons, minors, trustees of the property, and persons who refuse to comply with the terms of the sale.

5. Things an Auctioneer Cannot Do.—An auctioneer is not permitted to delegate his duties to another, except minor or incidental duties. He cannot act contrary to the wishes and instructions of the owners in any matters relating to the details of the sale. He may not permit a bidder to withdraw his bid after its acceptance, without the consent of the owner. He cannot sell the property to himself, or employ another to bid it in for him. He is not permitted to sell at private sale contrary to the owner's instructions.

Automobile

1. The Right to Use the Highways.—The public has a right to use the public roads to travel and transport property. Drivers of automobiles have an equal right on the highways with other vehicles, but they do not have any greater right. All have the same rights and the same restrictions. The courts hold that all travelers have equal right to use the highways. Thus, a pedestrian has the same right as the driver of an automobile. The state cannot exclude non-residents from the public roads, or place greater restrictions or burdens on non-resident motorists than those imposed on its own citizens.

2. Parking.—In the absence of any city ordinance or statutory regulation an automobile may be left at the side of the road after shutting off the engine and setting the brakes. However, an automobile so left after dark must be properly lighted.

3. License.—The several states issue licenses to the owners of automobiles, motorcycles, and trucks, permitting them to use the public highways. Many cities require a municipal license. Such a license is neither a contract nor a tax. It is simply a privilege, and as such does not pass to a purchaser of the vehicle and may be revoked for any good reason.

4. The Law with Reference to Rented Vehicles.—Suppose A rents his automobile to B for a certain consideration. The law will not hold A responsible for the negligent acts of B even if B is an unskilled driver. On the other hand if A knew when he rented the car that B was an immature child or of low mentality, or under the influence of alcohol, the courts would hold him responsible. If the owner lends his car with a chauffeur, he will be held liable for the negligent acts of the chauffeur. In case of damage to the rented car, the renter is liable only if it can be proved that he did not exercise ordinary prudence and care. Should the renter sell the car without the owner's authority, the owner can recover even from an innocent purchaser. The owner of an automobile is entitled to a fair compensation for its use, even if no definite sum is agreed upon, and he can collect a reasonable hire if his automobile is used by another without his knowledge or consent. Criminal liability also is attached to the unlawful use of another's automobile.

5. The Speed of Automobiles along a public road is regulated by law. Some state laws prescribe the maximum rates of speed for the business district, residence district, and country. A municipality has the right to modify the speed laws in accordance with local requirements. Courts of most states hold that it is the duty of a driver on a public highway to have his car under control and to operate it at a reasonable rate of speed, having regard to the traffic and other conditions. He must so operate it as to avoid endangering the life or limb of any person or the safety of anyone's property.

6. The Laws of the Road are intended to prevent collisions and accidents. 1. Vehicles approaching each other from opposite directions are required to pass each other on the right. If, therefore, two automobiles collide in a street which is wide enough for safe passage, the driver on the wrong side of the road is responsible for the other driver's injury, provided, of course, the other was not himself guilty of negligence. 2. Each driver must pass on his right side of the center of the traveled road. This applies even when the road is covered with snow, to side roads, and to roads under construction. 3. It is the duty of every driver to exercise reasonable care in avoiding accidents or injuries to others. This rule applies just as strongly when the driver's car is on the right side of the road. 4. At street intersections it is customary to allow the right of way to the vehicle approaching from the right and, in many states and municipalities, this rule has been embodied in the statutes and ordinances. 5. It is the duty of the driver to keep his car under control at all times. 6. If one willfully or negligently drives a car on a street or road at an unlawful speed, thereby killing another, he may be guilty of homicide. 7. The driver of a car may be charged with negligence if, without warning to others, he suddenly changes the course of his direction or backs his car.

7. The Fitness of the Driver.—The driver of an automobile should be physically and mentally fit. A man who is subject to fainting spells or epileptic attacks has no right to drive a car upon the public highway. The same rule applies to one with defective eyesight, but it has been held that proper eyeglasses may restore the competency of the driver. No person should ever attempt to drive an automobile while intoxicated, thereby endangering the lives of others.

8. The Chauffeur's Liability.—As a general rule the owner is liable for the acts of his chauffeur, provided the chauffeur is acting within the scope of the owner's business. However, should the chauffeur use the car without the consent or knowledge of the owner, or should he be using it for his own business and without the owner's consent, the owner is not liable for the driver's acts. The same rule applies when the owner's son uses the parent's car without his knowledge or consent. If the car is run with his knowledge by a member of his family, or for the convenience of other members of the family, the parent may be liable for the negligent acts of the driver. Most states require a chauffeur to take out a license.

9. Minor.—The statutes of most states forbid children under a certain age to drive automobiles. The ages vary in different states. The owner of a car, therefore, who allows a child to operate it, may be held responsible for accident or injury resulting from the child's negligence.

10. The Chauffeur's Rights.—A chauffeur may recover damages from his employer for injury received while operating the car, provided that the employer is in some way responsible for the injury. On the other hand, if his injury was due to a defective part, he could not recover from his employer, unless it so happened that the employer knew of the defect and the chauffeur did not. If a chauf-

feur should be injured while riding in a car driven by the owner, the chauffeur could recover for injuries sustained due to the owner's negligence.

11. THE OWNER'S INJURY.—If the owner of a car be injured in any way through the wrongful acts or negligence of his chauffeur, the chauffeur may be held liable.

12. GARAGE KEEPER.—A garage keeper is bound to exercise reasonable care with reference to vehicles entrusted to him. The owner of a car is not liable to third parties for the negligence of the garage keeper or his employees in the care and operation of his automobile. If a garage keeper or his employee operates an automobile the garage keeper is liable for any damage done to the car or to third persons. A public garage, while not considered a public nuisance, is subject to public regulations as to location, odors, noise and fire hazards. A garage keeper is entitled to a reasonable compensation for storage of a car or for repairs which he has been instructed to make. He is not liable for fire damage to the automobile, unless the fire is caused by his own negligence or that of his employees. He is liable for theft, if he failed to use reasonable precautions to guard against it.

13. USED AUTOMOBILES.—There are two points to keep in mind when purchasing a second-hand automobile. Such automobiles are usually sold "as is" and the motorist often complains when he finds the car is not in perfect running order. If the cylinders prove to be scored or the bearings are loose, the purchaser has no redress at law. The law presumes that if any warranty was made, it would have been reduced to writing in the form of a contract.

14. BILL OF SALE.—Statutes in most states require that a bill of sale be given, and the purchaser should be careful to see that the statute is complied with. The bill of sale should be drawn in accordance with the laws of the state where the purchase is made. The following form will answer the purpose in most of the states:

Bill of Sale

Know all men by these presents, that I (here insert name and address of party selling the car) in the county of ...., state of ...., in consideration of (here insert amount of money to be paid party selling by party buying) dollars this day to me in hand paid, do hereby grant, sell, transfer and deliver unto the said (here insert name of party buying) the following goods and chattels, to-wit: (Then insert name of automobile, its model, the engine number and the car number, also the type of car, its color, together with any other information which will help to identify it); to have and to hold said goods and chattels to the said (name of purchaser), his executors, administrators and assigns to their use forever.

I hereby covenant with the said grantee that I am the lawful owner of the said goods and chattels; that they are free and clear from all incumbrances; that I have good right to sell the same and that I will warrant and defend the same against the lawful claims and demands of all persons.

In witness whereof, I, the said (name of party selling) hereunto set my hand and seal the ...... day of ...., 19.....

Signature of party selling ....Seal

15. IN CASE OF ACCIDENTS.—Accidents will happen in spite of the most careful driving. If you happen to be in an accident, here are a few things to remember:

a. Do not drive away without reporting the facts to the police or nearest police station, or without giving your name, address, and license number to the other party involved. Leaving the scene of an accident may constitute a crime punishable by fine or imprisonment.
b. Be sure to get the name and address of the other party, or if he drives away, his license number.
c. Get the names and addresses of all persons who witnessed the accident, or saw the results of it, including all injured persons.
d. Try to visualize just how it happened, remember your own position and that of the other party, both before and after the accident, and note carefully the wheel marks on the road or pavement.
e. Be calm and courteous. Do not admit that you are in the wrong or accuse the other party.
f. Do not make immediate settlement or offer to do so, or incur any expense except for necessary medical relief.

Bailment

1. DEFINITIONS.—A *Bailment* is a delivery of a thing in trust for some special object or purpose, with the understanding, expressed or implied, that the person receiving it shall return it when that purpose has been fulfilled. A *Bailor* is one who makes a bailment or delivers goods to a bailee. A *Bailee* is a person who receives goods of another to hold according to the purpose of delivery.

2. BAILOR AND BAILEE.—To create this relation the property must be delivered to the bailee. Thus if A takes his car to a public garage to remain over night, the garage owner becomes a bailee for hire. The contract of bailment also exists when a man takes a suit of clothes to a tailor shop to be altered, or when a farmer takes a load of oats to a mill to be ground.

3. THE LAW WITH REFERENCE TO LOST PROPERTY.—The finder of lost property is entitled to keep it until the owner is found,

and the general rule is that the finder has good title to it against everyone but the true owner. Usually the law provides the necessary steps to be taken in the case of lost property. The finder must make an honest effort to locate the owner. Failing in this, he may retain the property and maintain his rights as against all others. Should the true owner appear, the finder has no lien on the property, unless a reward has been offered for its return.

The finder does not always take title to the article found. The article must actually have been lost, not merely laid down or aside voluntarily, and forgotten. Thus, if a woman lay down a package in a department store, the owner of the store is the proper custodian, rather than the finder.

4. THE BAILEE'S RESPONSIBILITY.—A bailee can, provided the limitation is not in violation of law or public policy and does not excuse him from negligence or fraud on his part, limit his liability by agreement. He becomes the custodian of the goods and is generally required to exert reasonable care against accident or loss. As a rule he cannot be held responsible for loss resulting from the nature of the goods stored. For example if a truck load of fruit arrives at a cold storage plant, the owner is not responsible for any loss due to the condition of the fruit when it arrived. On the other hand, if an employee of the storage company negligently allows the goods to spoil, the owner of the fruit can recover from the storage company.

Suppose your bank grants you the privilege of keeping a strongbox in the bank building without making any charge therefor. The bank, of course, is not bound to exercise as much care as a regular safety deposit company, but it is required to take reasonable precaution, as much care as it uses to protect its own property. Suppose the cashier steals the box. Would the bank be liable to you for the loss? If the bank exercised reasonable care, and if the cashier were a long-trusted employee against whom there was no cause for suspicion, the bank would not be responsible for the loss.

5. THE BAILEE'S DUTY.—The bailee is usually a keeper only. However, if he is keeping livestock, he must supply the food necessary to the animals' good condition. Milch cows must be properly milked; and in case of sickness animals must be given proper medical care and attention. In every case the bailee is required to exercise reasonable care for the goods in the bailment.

Bankruptcy

1. THE BANKRUPTCY ACT.—The Constitution of the United States grants to Congress the power to make uniform laws on the subject of bankruptcy. The Bankruptcy Act of 1938, popularly known as the Chandler Act, now contains the law on this subject.

2. COURTS.—The Act gives jurisdiction in bankruptcy cases to the district courts of the United States and of the territories and possessions to which the Act applies, and to the District Court of the United States for the District of Columbia.

3. BANKRUPTS.—Bankrupts are of two classes, voluntary and involuntary. Voluntary bankrupts are those who are declared bankrupt upon their own petitions. Under the new Act, any person (or corporation) owing debts, except a municipal, railroad, insurance, or banking corporation or a building and loan association, is entitled to the benefits of the Act as a voluntary bankrupt. Involuntary bankrupts are those who are declared bankrupt by the proper courts, and who have committed one or more of the acts of bankruptcy hereinafter specified. Any natural person, and any corporation except a building and loan association, a municipal, railroad, insurance, or banking corporation, owing debts to the amount of $1,000 or over, may be adjudged an involuntary bankrupt.

4. ACTS OF BANKRUPTCY.—As stated in the preceding paragraph, before a person can become an involuntary bankrupt, it is necessary for the petitioning creditors to show that he has committed an act of bankruptcy. The Bankruptcy Act specifically defines what constitutes an act of bankruptcy. A person has committed an act of bankruptcy when he has:

a. Conveyed, transferred, concealed, removed, or permitted to be concealed or removed any part of his property, with intent to hinder, delay, or defraud his creditors or any of them; or

b. Transferred, while insolvent, any portion of his property to one or more of his creditors with intent to prefer such creditor over his other creditors; or

c. Suffered or permitted, while insolvent, any creditor to obtain a lien upon any of his property through legal proceedings, and not having vacated or discharged such lien within thirty days from the date thereof or at least five days before the date set for any sale or other disposition of such property; or

d. Made a general assignment for the benefit of his creditors; or

e. While insolvent or unable to pay his debts as they mature, procured, permitted, or suffered voluntarily or involuntarily the appointment of a receiver or trustee to take charge of his property; or

f. Admitted in writing his inability to pay his debts and his willingness to be adjudged a bankrupt.

5. FILING A VOLUNTARY PETITION.—Any person who is entitled to the benefits of the

Bankruptcy Act and wishes to avail himself of the same should file his petition, in duplicate, with the clerk of the court in the district where he has had his principal place of business, or resided, or has had his domicile for the preceding six months, or for a longer portion of the preceding six months than in any other jurisdiction. He must also file, with the petition, a schedule, under oath and in triplicate, setting forth: the names of his creditors and their residences if known, the amount due each, and what security they hold, if any; a description of the petitioner's property, showing its nature, location and value; and his claim for legal exemptions, if any. The judge then hears the petition, and either adjudicates the petitioner bankrupt or dismisses the petition.

6. Filing an Involuntary Petition.—Where a person owing debts to the amount of $1,000 has committed one or more of the acts of bankruptcy enumerated above and does not belong to one of the classes excluded by the Act (as wage earners and farmers), a petition to have such person adjudged a bankrupt may be filed by three or more creditors who have provable claims against him, fixed as to liability and liquidated as to amount, which amount in the aggregate, in excess of the value of securities held by them, to $500 or over; or if all of the creditors of such person are less than twelve in number, then the petition may be filed by one of such creditors whose claims equal such amount. The petition must be filed in triplicate with the clerk of the court and must include the following information and allegations: the name of the alleged bankrupt; that he has had his principal place of business within the district for a longer portion of the six months immediately preceding the filing of the petition than in any other judicial district; that he owes debts to the amount of $1,000 and is not a wage earner or a farmer; the names and addresses of the petitioning creditors; that they have provable claims against said alleged bankrupt, fixed as to liability and liquidated as to amount, amounting in the aggregate, in excess of securities held by them, to $500 or over; the nature and amount of petitioner's claims; that within four months next preceding the filing of the petition, the alleged bankrupt committed an act of bankruptcy; and a statement as to what acts on his part are alleged to have constituted said act of bankruptcy. The petition must also be duly signed and verified. Upon the filing of the petition, together with a filing fee of $30, the clerk will issue a subpoena to the alleged bankrupt, returnable within ten days. When the alleged bankrupt has been served with the subpoena and a copy of the petition, he is required to file his answer within five days after the return day. If it is necessary, the court may appoint a receiver to take charge of the alleged bankrupt's property to prevent loss.

7. Hearing in Involuntary Proceedings.—If the alleged bankrupt fails to appear and plead within the time allowed, the court will either adjudicate him bankrupt or dismiss the petition. If the alleged bankrupt wishes to deny any of the matters set out in the petition, he may do so by filing his sworn answer within the time allowed by law. The matter will then be set down for hearing, and on the day set the petitioners must either prove the allegations in their petition or the court will dismiss it on motion of the alleged bankrupt. If they do prove them, the court will proceed to enter the order of adjudication. Within five days after the order adjudging him bankrupt, the bankrupt is required to file schedules of his creditors and property similar to those filed by a voluntary bankrupt.

8. Statement of Affairs.—The law also requires a bankrupt to file in triplicate with the court at least five days prior to the first meeting of his creditors, a statement of his affairs in such form as may be prescribed by the Supreme Court. The purpose of this provision is to furnish helpful information to the creditors and trustee to assist them in administering the bankrupt's affairs as well as in their examination of the bankrupt.

9. First Meeting of Creditors.—After adjudication, that is, the order of court finding a person to be bankrupt, the procedure with reference to voluntary and involuntary bankrupts is the same. The court causes the first meeting of creditors to be held not less than ten nor more than thirty days after adjudication. The meeting is held at the county seat of the county in which the bankrupt had his principal place of business, resided, or had his domicile; or if that place would be manifestly inconvenient, the court may designate a more convenient place for the meeting. The judge or referee presides. He may allow or disallow claims presented there, and is required publicly to examine the bankrupt. He may also permit the creditors to examine him. At this meeting the creditors appoint a trustee, who is to act as their representative and take charge of the bankrupt's property. Relatives of the bankrupt, and, where the bankrupt is a corporation, its stockholders, officers, and members of its board of directors, are not allowed to vote. The new Act provides that the creditors may also appoint a committee of three or more creditors, which committee may consult and advise the trustee in connection with the administration of the estate. The bankrupt must be present at the first meeting of creditors.

10. Subsequent Meetings.—The law provides that the court shall call a meeting of creditors whenever one-fourth or more in number of those who have proved their claims

shall file a written request for a meeting. Whenever the affairs of the bankrupt's estate are ready to be closed, the court orders a final meeting of creditors. A case in which there are no assets may be closed without such final meeting.

11. VOTING AT MEETINGS.—Matters submitted to creditors at their meetings are passed upon by majority vote in number and amount of claims of all creditors whose claims have been allowed and who are present. However, creditors holding claims which are secured or have priority are not entitled to vote in respect to such claims, and such claims are not counted in computing either the number of creditors or the amount of their claims, except in cases where the amounts of such claims exceed the values of such securities and priorities, and then only for such excess. The new Act also provides that claims of $50 or less shall not be counted in computing the number of creditors voting or present at meetings, but shall be counted in computing the amount.

12. PROOF OF CLAIMS.—In order to share in any dividends which may be paid to creditors out of the property of the bankrupt, it is necessary for a creditor to file his claim in court or with the referee within six months after the first date set for the first meeting of creditors, to prove it and have it allowed by the court. The law requires that a proof of claim be filed, consisting of a statement under oath in writing and signed by the creditor, setting forth the claim; the consideration therefor; whether any, and if so, what securities are held therefor; whether any, and if so, what payments have been made thereon; and that the claim is justly owing from the bankrupt to the creditor. If the claim is founded upon an instrument in writing, such as a promissory note, such instrument, unless lost or stolen, shall be filed with the proof of claim. If such instrument has been lost or stolen, a sworn statement of such fact and the circumstances of such loss or destruction must be filed with the claim. After the claim has been allowed, such instrument may be withdrawn by permission of court upon substitution of copies.

Claims so properly presented, if liquidated claims, are allowed unless objected to by parties in interest or by the court. If objected to, they are set down for hearing before the court or referee.

Only fixed and liquidated claims and claims provable in law or equity are provable in bankruptcy. Contingent claims are not provable.

13. DISCHARGE OF BANKRUPT.—Under the present Bankruptcy Act, it is not necessary for an individual who has been adjudged bankrupt to make application for his discharge in bankruptcy. The act provides that the adjudication shall operate as an application for discharge. This is not true with reference to corporations, however. A bankrupt corporation may file an application for discharge within six months after its adjudication. In the case of individuals, the law now provides that after the bankrupt has been examined, either at the first meeting of creditors or at a meeting specially called for that purpose, the court shall enter an order fixing the time for the filing of objections to the bankrupt's discharge, that notice of said order shall be given to all parties in interest, and that at the expiration of the time fixed, if no objection has been filed, the court shall discharge the bankrupt. The effect of a discharge in bankruptcy is to release the bankrupt from all of his provable debts except the following (1) taxes; (2) liabilities for obtaining money by false pretenses, or for willful and malicious injuries to the person or property of another, or for alimony due or to become due, or for maintenance or support of wife or child, or for seduction, or for breach of promise of marriage accompanied by seduction, or for criminal conversation; (3) debts not scheduled in time for proof and allowance, with the name of the creditor, if known to the bankrupt, unless such creditor had notice or actual knowledge of the proceedings in bankruptcy; (4) liabilities created by his fraud, embezzlement, misappropriation or defalcation while acting as an officer or in any fiduciary capacity; (5) wages earned within three months before the date of commencement of the proceedings in bankruptcy due to workmen, servants, clerks, or traveling or city salesmen, on salary or commission basis, whole or part time, whether or not selling exclusively for the bankrupt; (6) debts for moneys of an employee received or retained by his employer to secure the faithful performance by the employee of the terms of a contract of employment.

14. COMPOSITIONS.—After a bankrupt has filed the schedule of his property and list of his creditors and has been examined in open court or at a meeting of creditors, he may, if he desires, offer terms of composition. That is, he offers to make immediate payment of a certain proportion of each claim provided the creditor will release him from the balance. This is, of course, precisely what happens by operation of law if the bankruptcy proceeding is carried to a conclusion, but a composition is often more desirable because it can be carried out at once, thus dispensing with a good many of the costs of longer proceedings, and preserving the estate in cases where the property is of a nature that will deteriorate or accumulate expense during a delay. Then, too, if the composition is confirmed by the court the debtor is spared some of the ignominy of having gone through bankruptcy

and received a discharge. Before being filed in court the composition must have been accepted in writing by a majority in number of all creditors whose claims have been allowed, which number must also represent a majority in amount of such claims. When the application for confirmation of the composition is filed in court, the money necessary to carry the composition into effect, together with that necessary to pay all debts which have priority, and to pay the costs of the proceedings which have already taken place, must be deposited in such place as shall be designated by and subject to the order of the judge. If the judge is then satisfied at a hearing that the composition is for the best interests of the creditors and is offered by the bankrupt in good faith, he will confirm it and dismiss the case after each creditor has received his share of the money set aside by the bankrupt as a consideration for the composition. The confirmation of a composition has the same effect as a discharge in that it releases all debts of the bankrupt that would be released by a discharge in regular form.

Bonds

1. DEFINITION.—A bond is defined to be an obligation in writing under seal. It is a form of contract which is almost infinite in variety. The parties to the bond are the obligor and the obligee, the former being the one who makes the promise and the latter the person to whom the promise is made.

2. A SIMPLE BOND is an instrument promising payment of money at a certain time, and generally bears interest at the rate specified in the bond. Nearly all corporate and municipal bonds are of this character and contain no condition except for the payment of the amount of the bond at a certain time and place with a certain specified rate of interest. Frequently interest coupons are attached to the original bond, providing for the payment of the several installments of interest as they come due.

The following is the form commonly in use for such bonds:

UNITED STATES OF AMERICA.
JEFFERSON CITY, STATE OF MISSOURI.
RENEWAL SCHOOL BOND.
INTEREST 6 PER CENT, PAYABLE SEMI-ANNUALLY

The Board of Education of the City of Jefferson, County of Cole, and State of Missouri, being legally organized under and pursuant to an act of the General Assembly of the State of Missouri entitled "An act to revise and amend the Laws in relation to Public Schools in Cities, Towns and Villages," approved April 26th, 19...., for value received promise to pay to the bearer ten years after the date hereof ONE THOUSAND DOLLARS at the St. Louis National Bank, in the City of St. Louis, Missouri, together with interest thereon at the rate of Six per centum per annum from the date hereof, which interest shall be payable semi-annually at said St. Louis National Bank in the City of St. Louis, Missouri, on the surrender of the proper interest coupons hereto attached. This bond shall be redeemable at the pleasure of the said Board of Education of the City of Jefferson at any time after the expiration of Five years from the date hereof, and is issued under and pursuant to an act of the General Assembly of the State of Missouri, entitled "An Act to authorize Boards of Education to issue renewal funding School Bonds to be sold or exchanged for the purpose of meeting and paying matured or maturing bonded indebtedness of school districts and for levying special tax to pay the bonded indebtedness of school districts," approved April 11th, 19.....

In Testimony Whereof: the said Board of Education has caused this bond to be signed by the President, countersigned by the Secretary, authenticated by the seal of said Board of Education and attested by the Clerk of the County Court of said County of Cole, with the seal of said Court affixed this First day of July, 19.....

JOHN JONES, President.
WM. SMITH, Secretary.
GEO. SMILEY, Clerk County Court.

3. BONDS OF PUBLIC OFFICIALS conditioned for the faithful performance of their duties are of almost infinite variety and in common use. All state, county, town and city officers having in their hands moneys or funds of any character belonging to such corporation are required to give bonds for the proper performance of the duties of their office. The following form of a bond of city treasurer can be used with a few slight changes for almost any office:

KNOW ALL MEN BY THESE PRESENTS, That we, John Jones, Henry Smith, and Charles Marshall of the City of Naperville, County of Du Page, and State of Illinois, are held and firmly bound unto the City of Naperville in the penal sum of Twenty Thousand ($20,000) Dollars, for the payment of which, well and truly to be made, we bind ourselves, our heirs, executors, and administrators jointly and firmly by these presents.

Witness our hands and seals this 14th day of July, 19.....

The condition of the above obligation is such that whereas the said John Jones has been duly elected to the office of City Treasurer of the City of Naperville; Now if the said John Jones shall faithfully perform all the duties of said office and shall account for and pay over all moneys that may come into his hands as such Treasurer, according to law and the ordinances of said City and the order and direction of the city council of said City, then this obligation to be void, otherwise to remain in full force and effect.

JOHN JONES. [Seal.]
HENRY SMITH. [Seal.]
CHARLES MARSHALL. [Seal.]

4. OFFICERS OF CORPORATIONS are often

required to give bonds for the faithful performance of their duties. The following form can be used for nearly all such bonds:

KNOW ALL MEN BY THESE PRESENTS, That we, James Lord, John Williams, and Charles Smith, are held and firmly bound unto the Naperville Manufacturing Company, a corporation duly organized under the laws of the State of Illinois, in the penal sum of Ten Thousand ($10,000) Dollars, good and lawful money of the United States, for the payment of which, well and truly to be made to said corporation or its assigns, we bind ourselves jointly and severally.

Witness our hands and seals this 14th day of July, 19. . . .

The condition of the above obligation is such that whereas the said James Lord has been elected President of the Naperville Manufacturing Company; Now Therefore, if the said James Lord shall well and truly perform the duties of his said office and shall account for and pay over all moneys that shall come into his hands as such President, and do all required of him by the by-laws of said corporation now in force or hereafter enacted, and obey all orders given him by the board of directors of said corporation, then this obligation shall be void, otherwise to remain in full force and effect.

JAMES LORD. [Seal.]
JOHN WILLIAMS. [Seal.]
CHARLES SMITH. [Seal.]

5. INDEMNIFYING BONDS.—Bonds are also frequently given to indemnify persons who incur liability for another in nearly all walks of life. The following form may be used:

KNOW ALL MEN BY THESE PRESENTS, That William Marsh, Principal, and John Henry, Surety, are held and firmly bound unto John Jones in the penal sum of One Hundred ($100) Dollars, lawful money of the United States, for the payment of which, well and truly to be made, we bind ourselves, our heirs, executors, and administrators, jointly, severally and firmly by these presents.

Witness our hands and seals this 1st day of June, A.D. 19. . . . .

The condition of the above obligation is such that whereas the said John Jones has been surety for the above William Marsh on his note for One Thousand Dollars ($1000) payable to the order of Charles William, due in one year from the date hereof, with interest at the rate of 6 per cent per annum.

Now, Therefore, if the said William Marsh shall well and truly pay the said note with all interest thereon when the same comes due and shall from time to time and at all times hereafter save, keep harmless and indemnify the said John Jones of and from all actions, suits, costs, charges, damages, and expenses whatsoever, including attorney's fees, which shall or may at any time hereafter happen or come to him for any reason, by reason of his becoming surety on said note, then this obligation to be void, otherwise to remain in full force and effect.

WILLIAM MARSH, [Seal.]
JOHN HENRY. [Seal.]

6. EXECUTOR'S BOND.—Executors, administrators, guardians, and conservators are required to enter into bonds to be approved by the proper court before they are allowed to enter upon their duties as such. The forms for such bonds, however, vary in the different states.

Broker

1. DEFINITIONS.—A broker is a person who transacts business for another, commonly in stocks, bills, notes, shipping, insurance, real estate, pawned goods, merchandise, etc., using the name of the principal. He does not have custody of the property. Brokerage is the fee charged by a broker for transacting business.

2. WHY BROKERS ARE EMPLOYED.—Brokers are often employed to transact business or to negotiate bargains between different individuals. By specializing in a single line or a limited number of lines of business, they acquire a knowledge and skill that an average merchant does not possess. It is often advantageous for large firms to employ brokers to buy their raw material. In large cities brokers are extensively employed. The business of brokerage is regulated largely by the customs of the trade.

3. A BROKER'S LIABILITY.—A broker usually has no special property in the goods he sells. If he does not disclose the principal's name he is liable to the same extent as other agents. He must serve faithfully and cannot act for both parties in the same transaction without the consent and knowledge of both. Neither can he delegate his powers without the principal's assent. He is bound to obey the express instructions of his principal, and to keep accurate accounts of his transactions.

4. A BROKER'S COMPENSATION.—Usually a broker's compensation is a commission or percentage of the value of the thing sold or exchanged. If the amount of the compensation is not fixed, the custom of the trade rules. A broker is entitled to a reasonable compensation for his services.

5. A REAL ESTATE BROKER must act for his principal alone. He is employed to negotiate sales and exchanges of land, and often has such additional duties as renting real estate, collecting rent, and procuring loans. To gain his commission on the sale he must produce a customer who is ready, able and willing to accept and live up to the terms of the sale. A property owner cannot avoid paying the commission or brokerage by selling the property himself, or at a lower price than he listed with the broker.

6. PAWNBROKERS.—The business of a pawnbroker, the rate of interest he may charge, and the sale of pawned goods are usually regulated by law. A license is usually required

and the business is always subject to regulation and control. Suppose A takes a watch to a pawnbroker who advances him $20.00. A, or his assignee, or the purchaser of the pawn ticket, may redeem it within the fixed time, or even beyond that time, if the pawnbroker has not exercised his right to sell the watch. A pawner has the right to assign or sell his interest in the watch. If A fails to redeem the watch, the pawnbroker can usually hold him for any deficiency after the watch is sold.

Carriers

1. Definitions.—A carrier is a person or company that undertakes, or whose business it is, to carry persons or merchandise for hire. Carriers are of two kinds, private and common. A *Private Carrier* is one who carries only occasionally, and not as a public business. Such a carrier need not serve all who wish to employ him, but is liable for negligence in transporting the goods he accepts. A *Common Carrier* is one whose regular business it is to carry goods or passengers from place to place for all persons who elect to employ and pay him.

2. Examples.—A private carrier is usually an individual who, without being engaged in such business as a public employment, carries merchandise from one point to another for a consideration. He is bound to exercise such care of the property as a man of ordinary intelligence would of his own property. Examples of common carriers are railroad companies, steamship companies, streetcar companies, taxicab companies, truckmen, and express companies, who hold themselves out to carry goods or passengers from one place to another, for all persons who offer to employ them.

3. Responsibility.—Common carriers are generally responsible for all loss and damage caused by transportation from whatever cause, except the act of God or of the public enemy, and they are bound to carry all goods which are offered them, provided such goods come within the class of articles they hold themselves out to carry. The carrier is not responsible for losses occurring from natural causes, such as frosts, fermentation, or natural decay of perishable articles, or the necessary and natural wear in the course of transportation, provided it exercises all reasonable care to have the loss or deterioration as little as practical.

4. Act of God.—The term "Act of God" is generally held to mean such casualties as occur without human intervention. Great floods, electrical storms, tornadoes, and earthquakes have been held to come within this classification.

5. Loss by Fire.—The carrier is liable for any and all loss occasioned by accidental fire.

6. Perishable Goods.—Carriers are not responsible for loss to fruits that decay in their possession through no fault of theirs or for goods shipped in defective boxes, such as glassware not properly packed and other articles that are easily broken. Goods must be properly packed in order to make the carrier responsible.

7. Bill of Lading.—Bill of lading is the receipt given by the common carrier to the owner of the goods desiring to have the same shipped, and should contain a description of the quantity, the marks on the merchandise, the name of the shipper or the person sending the goods, and the consignee, the name of the person to whom the goods are shipped, place of departure and place of discharge of the goods and the price of freight, and also weight of the separate packages and the number of the car in which the same were shipped.

8. Equal Liability.—Railroad Companies and other carriers who allow express companies to carry parcels and packages on their cars or other vehicles are liable as the common carriers for all damages which occur, without regard to the contract between them and such express company.

9. Baggage.—In the transportation of the baggage of passengers the liability of the carrier for loss to the same is the same as in case of transportation of goods for hire, and in case of loss the carrier must make it good.

10. When Liability Begins and Ends.—The responsibility of the common carrier begins upon the delivery of the goods for immediate transportation. A delivery at the usual place of receiving freight or to the employee of the company in the usual course of business is sufficient. The responsibility of the carrier as such terminates after the arrival of the goods at their destination and sufficient time has elapsed thereafter for the owner to have received them during business hours. After the expiration of such time the responsibility of the carrier is simply that of a warehouseman and he is required only to keep the goods with ordinary care.

11. Limitation of Liability.—A carrier can limit his liability by contract, unless forbidden by statute. Thus a bill of lading given as a receipt for a freight or express shipment, or a receipt given a passenger limiting the amount of the carrier's liability on his baggage is considered binding by the courts, and relieves the carrier of additional liability. The general rule is that a carrier may relieve himself from all liability except for loss or damage caused by his own negligence.

12. The Passenger's Rights.—The law requires common carriers to carry all passengers who pay the required fare, and who are in a sufficiently intelligent condition to travel. The carrier must exercise great care

in transporting passengers and is liable for injury due to the carrier's negligence. If the passenger was himself negligent and contributed to his own injury, he cannot as a rule hold the carrier liable. Although a sleeping-car company is not a common carrier, it is liable for negligence in failing to protect the passengers from theft or from injury resulting from the negligence of its own employees or agents.

13. Different Lines.—Where goods are accepted for shipment to points beyond the line of the carrier to whom they are first delivered, such carrier is responsible for the delivery of the goods at their destination. The law now provides under such circumstances the carrier shall be liable for any loss or injury occurring during the shipment whether on its own line or that of the connecting carrier.

14. Demurrage is the sum charged by transportation companies for the non-removal of goods from their cars within the time fixed by the rules of the companies. The rules of a large number of railroad companies require that the car be unloaded within twenty-four hours after its arrival at the destination and a fixed rate of demurrage for each twenty-four hours of delay after the expiration of the usual time for unloading is imposed on the persons to whom goods are shipped.

15. The Carrier's Rights.—The carrier is entitled to a reasonable compensation for his services, and may demand payment in advance. The shipper is liable for freight, unless the carrier agrees to look exclusively to some other party; or after delivery the carrier may recover the amount of freight from the consignee. But freight may be collected only for the goods actually delivered, unless the delivery be prevented by the owner, or it be agreed that freight shall be payable regardless of losses by the way. The carrier also has a lien on the goods for his freight and advances on such goods, and may refuse to deliver until such charges be paid. This lien has priority over the owner's right of stoppage in transit, and the claims of the general creditors of the owner or consignee. A carrier by water also has a lien for salvage, and for customs duties advanced on imported goods.

16. Telegraph and Telephone Companies are not common carriers and may therefore establish reasonable regulation for the transmission of messages. Like common carriers, however, they are required to serve all who apply and offer to pay the charges, and are liable for damages when messages are not sent promptly and accurately. They come within the classification of public service corporations, and are subject to legislative regulation and control as to kind of service to be rendered and rates.

Chattel Mortgage

1. Definition.—A chattel mortgage is an instrument by which the owner conveys conditional title to personal property to secure the payment of a debt or the performance of a contract or other obligation. It is a pledge that the debt will be paid. Any personal property that may be sold may be mortgaged, such as livestock, machinery, farm implements, life-insurance policies, corporation stock, and crops. The *mortgagor* is the person who conveys the property. The *mortgagee* is the person to whom the transfer is made.

2. Form of Mortgage.—The usual form of a chattel mortgage is a bill of sale with the conditional clause stating the terms of the loan, and that on the mortgagor's failure to pay, the mortgagee may take possession of the property. Any person competent to make a contract, or his agent, may make a chattel mortgage. Partners or joint tenants may mortgage jointly on their individual interests. A corporation may also mortgage its personal property.

Chattel mortgages are usually given to secure notes in the same way in which real estate mortgages are given to secure notes. Greater strictness, however, is required in the acknowledgment, docketing, and recording of chattel mortgages than in the case of real estate mortgages. A chattel mortgage must be acknowledged before a justice of the peace or some other person authorized by law to take acknowledgments.

3. Describing the Property.—The property mortgaged must be described clearly enough to enable third persons to identify it, but this is determined largely by the nature of the chattels. "All" articles in a stated place is generally a valid description.

4. Foreclosure.—When the mortgagor fails to pay his debt, the right of the mortgagee to proceed in taking the property is regulated by law. In most chattel mortgages a clause is included permitting the mortgagee to seize and sell the property should the mortgagor fail to make payment.

5. General Principles.—A chattel mortgage remains in effect as between the parties themselves until it is released or becomes barred by what is known as the statute of limitations. However, in order to preserve its validity as against creditors of the mortgagor and subsequent purchasers, it must be refiled or renewed periodically. The periods vary in different states. They are generally from one to three years. To sell property covered by a chattel mortgage for a valuable consideration without notifying the purchaser of the existence of the mortgage is a criminal offense. Statutes in a few states provide that notes secured by chattel mortgages must show on their face that they are secured by

chattel mortgages, or they are absolutely void; and that defense which the maker of the note secured by chattel mortgage could make against the original payee, is good against the note in the hands of an indorsee, even though indorsed before maturity. In other states, chattel mortgages on household goods must be signed by both the mortgagor and his wife. (See MORTGAGE.)

Chattel Mortgage with Power of Sale

Know all men by these presents, that I, A. B., in consideration of the sum of $........ paid by C. D., have bargained and sold, and by these presents do hereby sell and convey to said C.D., the following goods and chattels, to wit: (describe the articles mortgaged, or refer to them as the goods and chattels mentioned in the schedule hereto annexed), and which are now in my possession.

Whereas, the said A.B. is justly indebted to C.D. in the sum of $........, payable on the ...... day of ...., 19...., with interest at six per cent from the ...... day of .... 19...., (upon a promissory note of even date herewith, or for goods sold and delivered).

Now the condition of the above obligation is such that if the said A.B. shall well and truly pay said C.D. said sum of money and interest when the same shall become due, then this conveyance shall be void, otherwise to remain in full force and effect. It is also agreed that said A.B. may retain possession of the said mortgaged property until said debt become due. But if default be made in the payment of said sum or any part thereof, the said C.D. and his assigns are hereby authorized to sell said goods and chattels, or so much thereof as will be necessary to satisfy the amount then due, together with the cost and expenses incurred by reason of said default.

(Signed) A. B.

In the presence of E. F.

Mortgage on Goods and Chattels, Another Form

Know all men by these presents, that A. B., residing at ...., of the first part, for securing the payment of the ...., hereinafter mentioned, and in consideration of the sum of $1, to .... in hand paid, at or before the execution and delivery of these presents, by C. D., of the second part, the receipt whereof is hereby acknowledged, has (have) granted, bargained, sold, and assigned, and by these presents does (do) grant, bargain, sell, and assign unto the said party (parties) of the second part, all ....now remaining and being ....

To have and to hold, all and singular, the goods and chattels above bargained and sold, or intended so to be, unto the said party (parties) of the second part, ...executors, administrators, and assigns forever. And the said party (parties) of the first part, for .... heirs, executors, and administrators, all and singular, the said goods and chattels above bargained and sold unto the said party (parties) of the second part, ... executors, administrators, and assigns, against the said party (parties) of the first part, and against all and every person or persons whomsoever shall and will warrant, and by these presents forever defend.

Upon condition, that if the said party (parties) of the first part shall and does (do) well and truly pay, or cause to be paid, unto the said party (parties) of the second part, ... executors, administrators, or assigns, the sum of ...., then these presents and everything herein contained shall cease and be void. And the said party (parties) of the first part, for .... executors, administrators, and assigns, does (do) covenant and agree to and with the said party (parties) of the second part, ... executors, administrators, and assigns, to make punctual payment of the money hereby secured .... And in case default shall be made in payment of the said sum above mentioned, or in case the said party (parties) of the second part shall sooner choose to demand the said goods and chattels, it shall and may be lawful for, and the said party (parties) of the first part does (do) hereby authorize and empower the said party (parties) of the second part, ... executors, administrators, and assigns, with the aid and assistance of any person or persons, to enter and come into and upon the dwelling-house and premises of the said party (parties) of the first part, and in such other place or places as the said goods and chattels are or may be held or placed, and take and carry away the said goods and chattels to sell and dispose of the same for the best price they can obtain, at either public or private sale, and out of the money to retain and pay the said sum above mentioned, with the interest and all expenses and charges thereon, rendering the overplus (if any) unto the said party (parties) of the first part, ... executors, administrators, and assigns. And until default be made in the payment of the aforesaid sum of money, the said party (parties) of the first part to remain and continue in quiet and peaceable possession of the said goods and chattels, and the full and free enjoyment of the same, unless the said party (parties) of the second part, ...executors, administrators, or assigns, shall sooner choose to demand the same; and until such demand be made, the possession of the said party (parties) of the first part shall be deemed the possession of an agent or servant, for the sole benefit and advantage of his principal, the said party (parties) of the second part.

In witness whereof, the said party (parties) of the first part, has (have) hereunto set .... hand(s) and seal(s) this .... day of ...., 19.....

Sealed and delivered in the presence of ......

..........County of ....ss.:

On this ...... day of ...., 19...., before me came ...., to me known to be the person(s) described in and who executed the foregoing instrument, and .... acknowledged that he (they) executed the same.

Notice of Sale under Chattel Mortgage

Notice is hereby given that by virtue of a chattel mortgage, dated on the ...... day of ...., 19...., and duly filed in the office of the county clerk of .... county, ... on the ...... day of ...., 19...., in book ...., of ...., on page ...., and executed by A. B. to C. D. to secure the payment of the sum of $.........., and upon which there is now due the sum of $........... Default having been made in the payment of said sum, and no suit or other proceeding at law having been instituted to recover said debt or any part thereof, therefore, I will sell the property therein described, viz: (here describe the articles substantially as in the mortgage) at public auction to the highest bidder, for cash, at ......, in the (city, town, or precinct) of ...., in ....county, on the ...... day of ...., at one o'clock P.M. of said date.

C. D.
Mortgagee.

Dated ...., ..., 19....

Assignment of Mortgage

This instrument, made this ...... day of ...., 19...., between ...., of the first part, and ...., of the second part, witnesseth: That the party (parties) of the first part, for a good and valuable consideration, to .... in hand paid by the party (parties) of the second part, has (have) sold, assigned, transferred, and conveyed, and does (do) hereby sell, assign, transfer, and convey to the party (parties) of the second part, a certain mortgage bearing date the ...... day of ...., 19...., made by ...., recorded in the clerk's office of .... county in book .... of mortgages, at page ......, on the ...... day of ...., 19...., at ...... o'clock ....m., together with the bond accompanying said mortgage, and therein referred to, and all sums of money due and to grow due thereon. And the party (parties) of the first part hereby covenant that there is .... due on the said bond and mortgage the sum of ....

In witness whereof, the party (parties) of the first part has (have) hereunto set .... hand(s) and seal(s) the day and year first above written.

Citizenship

1. Definition.—A citizen is a member of a state or nation who enjoys political rights and is entitled to public protection. Citizenship, therefore, carries with it the duty of allegiance to the government and the right of protection from it.

2. General Principles.—A citizen residing in any of the several states owes an allegiance both to the United States and to the state, and may demand protection from each government. A citizen residing in the District of Columbia is a citizen of the United States only. A citizen's ordinary rights are protected by the state government.

All persons born or naturalized in the United States and subject to its jurisdiction or persons born abroad of American parents are citizens of the United States. Formerly a woman took the citizenship of her husband upon marriage. Now marriage does not affect the American citizenship of the wife unless she chooses to renounce it. Neither does naturalization of the husband operate to confer citizenship upon the wife.

3. Naturalization.—In order to be naturalized, an alien must follow the forms prescribed by law. His entry into the country must have been lawful, and he must furnish a certificate showing the time, place, and manner of his arrival. He must declare on oath, before the clerk of an authorized court in the district in which he resides, his intention of becoming a citizen of the United States and of residing here permanently, and he must renounce all allegiance to any foreign power. Not less than two nor more than seven years after he has made such declaration of intention, he must file his petition for admission to citizenship. He must declare on oath in open court that he will support and defend the Constitution of the United States, and renounce allegiance to any foreign power. The law also requires that no alien shall be admitted to citizenship unless immediately preceding the date of his petition he has resided continuously within the United States for at least five years, and within the county where he resided when he filed his petition for at least six months. Naturalization of the parent confers citizenship on his minor children if they reside in the United States at the time or subsequently begin to reside here permanently.

4. Aliens' Rights.—Aliens have the right to hold and transfer title to real estate. At common law they are entitled to purchase, own, and sell personal property, engage in business and to make contracts or wills. In return they must obey the laws of the land in which they reside.

Contracts

1. Definitions.—A contract is a mutual agreement between two or more competent parties for a valuable consideration to do or not to do a particular thing. A *Simple Contract* may or may not be in writing and requires no seal. A *Specialty* is a contract in writing which does require a seal to the signatures. An *Executed Contract* is completed; an *Executory Contract* is one still to be executed or completed. An *Express Contract* is a contract actually made between two or more parties; an *Implied Contract*, as the name suggests, is one in which some of the provisions or the entire agreement must be implied from previous agreements, from existing customs, or from the acts of the parties.

2. Requirements.—A contract must have:

a. Two or more competent parties,
b. Legal subject matter,
c. Consideration, and
d. Assent of the parties. There cannot be a contract when any of these are wanting.

THE FORM OF THE CONTRACT

3. In many written contracts the parties are referred to as "party of the first part," "party of the second part," according to the order in which their names first appear. It does not matter which name is written first.

4. A written contract begins with a statement of the date, the names of the parties, and their places of residence. Then appears a statement of the consideration, followed by a full statement of all that the first party agrees to do, and all that the second party agrees to do.

5. Next appears a statement of the penalties or forfeitures in case either party does not faithfully and fully perform, or offer to perform, his part of the agreement.

6. The contract ends with the signatures of the parties and their seals and the signatures of witnesses. (A seal is simply the mark of a pen around the word "seal," written after the signature, or the word "seal" in parentheses printed or typewritten on the form.)

7. Competent lawyers should be employed in the drafting of a contract.

8. Errors in grammar or spelling do not affect the legality of the agreement.

9. If the language should be obscure on certain points, the court will try to determine the intent of the parties when they entered into the agreement, providing the intent can be gathered from the terms of the instrument itself. It is of the utmost importance that the terms of the contract be specifically and explicitly stated. Competent attorneys should be employed.

10. When an agreement is written it must all be in writing. It cannot be partly written and partly oral.

THE VITAL PART OF A CONTRACT—CONSIDERATION

11. Definition.—A consideration is the thing which induces a party to make a contract. It is the substantial cause or reason inducing the parties to enter into an agreement.

12. A Sufficient Consideration.—The law does not require that the consideration should be a good or bad bargain. As long as something is done or suffered by either party, always providing it is not illegal, the consideration is good. The smallest consideration is sufficient to make it legal. The value of the consideration is generally unimportant.

13. A Valuable Consideration.—A valuable consideration is one which is equal to money or may be translated into monetary terms. It is sometimes defined as "money or its equivalent."

14. A Good Consideration.—A good consideration is one which is based upon love, gratitude or esteem, or blood relationship. A good consideration is not sufficient unless the agreement has to be performed by one or both parties.

15. Immoral Consideration.—All considerations which are immoral are consequently illegal, and contracts based upon them are generally void.

THE LAW GOVERNING ALL KINDS OF CONTRACTS

16. An intentional alteration of a contract in a material part, by one party without the consent of the other, after its execution, discharges the other party from his obligations under the contract.

17. A contract made by a minor is not binding upon him, yet he can hold the party with whom he contracts, to all the conditions of the contract.

18. A fraudulent contract may be binding on the party guilty of fraud, although not laying any obligation on the part of the party acting in good faith.

19. A contract for the sale or purchase of personal property over a certain amount—ranging from $30 to $500 in the different states—must be in writing.

20. A contract which cannot be performed within a year must be in writing.

21. If no time of payment is stated in the contract, payment must be made on the delivery of the goods.

22. A contract totally restraining the exercise of a man's trade or profession is void, but one restraining him in any particular place is not void.

23. An offer or proposal, which includes the essential parts of a contract, becomes a contract as soon as accepted. Generally the acceptance must be at the time of receiving the offer. The offer may be withdrawn at any time before it has been accepted. Offers may be made and accepted within a reasonable time by word of mouth, telephone, telegraph, or mail.

24. A contract required by law to be in writing cannot be changed by verbal agreement.

25. A contract cannot be rescinded except by consent of both parties unless one party has given the other legal grounds to rescind, such as default, fraud, etc.

26. A contract binding in the place where it is made is binding everywhere, but courts of one state will not enforce contracts made in another state where to do so would be in violation of the statutes or public policy of their own state.

27. Each party to an agreement or contract should retain a signed copy.

28. While signatures or contracts written with a pencil are valid in law, it is always safer to write them in ink.

CONTRACTS THAT ARE NOT LAWFUL

29. A contract to commit a breach of peace.
30. An agreement for immoral purposes.
31. An agreement procured by threats, violence, or fraud.
32. Wagers or bets (cannot be collected by law).
33. Interest at rates higher than the maximum rate fixed by law cannot be collected.
34. A contract with an intoxicated person, lunatic, or minor (cannot be enforced by the other party).
35. A contract in violation of a statute in the state in which it is made.
36. An agreement to prevent competition on a sale under an execution.
37. An agreement to prohibit the carrying on of a trade throughout the state.
38. Where consent to an agreement is given by mistake, such agreement cannot be enforced.
39. The right to vote or hold a public office cannot be sold by contract.
40. A contract without a consideration, such as a promise to make a gift, cannot be enforced.
41. Two or more persons cannot intentionally make a contract to willfully injure a third person.
42. Contracts for concealing felony or violating public trust, for bribery and extortion, are prohibited.
43. Useless things cannot become the subject of a contract, such as agreeing not to go out of the house for a month.
44. A verbal release without payment or satisfaction for the debt is not good. Release must be under seal, unless made for some new consideration.
45. If two parts of a contract are in direct conflict with each other, the former part holds good in preference to the latter.
46. Contracts in which there is misrepresentation or concealment of material facts cannot be enforced by the party guilty of such misrepresentation or concealment.
47. If a thing contracted for is not in existence at the time of making the contract (as in a case where parties contract for the purchase and sale of a horse not knowing that the horse is dead at the time) the contract is not valid.
48. If a person agrees to serve as a laborer or clerk, he cannot be compelled to fulfill his agreement; damages, however, can be recovered for a failure to perform.
49. An agreement with a thief to drop a criminal prosecution, in consideration of his bringing back the goods and paying all damages, is not good, and will be no bar to a future prosecution.
50. Guardians, trustees, executors, administrators, or attorneys cannot take advantage of those for whom they act by becoming parties to contracts in which the persons for whom they are acting are interested.

51. Quasi Contracts.—A quasi contract may be defined as a contract implied in law, or in the nature of a contract. It is a legal obligation resulting from some direct or indirect benefit accruing to one party from the other without any express agreement on the part of the first. The law, nevertheless, compels him to pay. For example:

a. One who has reason to believe that payment for goods tendered is expected, must not accept them unless he intends to pay for them. If he accepts the goods, he can be compelled to pay for them.
b. A man employed under the promise of good wages or division of profits is entitled to fair treatment, even though such an arrangement is no contract at all.
c. Money paid on an illegal contract or on one which is void because of non-existence of the property, may be recovered.
d. If an express company delivers valuable goods to the wrong party, the company can recover from the person who wrongfully accepted them.
e. If, on account of a mistake, a man pays his grocery bill twice for the same period, he can recover.
f. Action to recover can be brought against a man who sells property not his own, or which proves to be worthless.
g. All these questions hinge on the presence or absence of consideration in the agreement.
h. Such liability is imposed regardless of consent, as distinguished from a contract implied *in fact*, which is an actual contract, and based on presumed intent or consent.

52. Statute of Frauds.—In every state there is a statute called the statute of frauds which provides that certain contracts must be in writing to bind the parties. Thus:

a. Agreements for the sale of real estate are unenforceable unless they are in writing.
b. A contract for the sale of goods for more than a certain amount, which amount varies in different states, must be in writing or there must be actual delivery and acceptance of the goods or part payment therefor.
c. A contract must be in writing to charge the defendant upon any special promise to answer for the debt, default, or miscarriage of another person or to charge any executor or administrator upon any special promise to answer any debt or damages out of his own estate.

d. A written contract is necessary to charge any person upon any agreement made upon consideration of marriage, or upon any agreement that is not to be performed within the space of one year from the making thereof.

DAMAGES FOR VIOLATION OF CONTRACT

53. A statute which provides no penalties for the lawbreaker is merely the expression of a wish, or the giving of advice. Similarly the contract must be binding on both parties. This element of mutual obligation is the very essence of a contract.

54. Where no actual loss has been sustained by the violation of a contract, the plaintiff is entitled to nominal damages only. Thus, A contracted to drill a well for B and to complete same within a specified time or forfeit $1000.00, said amount being intended not as an assessment of the damages which would probably be actually sustained, but to secure the performance of the contract by the imposition of a penalty. The courts will not compel A to pay the $1000.00 damages unless his failure to complete the well has actually meant a loss of $1000.00 to B. They will, however, permit B to recover from A such damages as he actually sustained as a result of A's failure to complete the well within the specified time.

55. Expected profits on speculations in real property cannot be recovered in case of a violation of contract.

56. Failure on the part of the seller to convey real estate or deliver personal property according to agreement entitles the plaintiff to recover damages or to sue for specific performance of the contract.

57. In case of loss of goods by a common carrier the plaintiff is entitled to the value of the goods where they were to be delivered, less the freight on such goods.

58. If a party contracts to employ another for a certain time, at a specified compensation, and discharges him, without cause, before the expiration of the time, the employee can obtain judgment for the full amount of wages for the entire unexpired balance of the time, provided he is unable to secure employment in the same line of work, after making an earnest effort to do so. Should he obtain work at a lower wage he can collect the difference.

59. To prevent lawsuits and disputes the amount of damages for the violation of contracts is sometimes fixed by the parties themselves by inserting in the contract some such provision as the following:

AND IT IS FURTHER AGREED that the party that shall fail to perform this agreement on his part shall pay to the other the full sum of (here state amount), as liquidated damages.

General Form of Agreement

This agreement, made and entered into this ...... day of ...., 19...., by and between Clarence Ranck of Aurora, County of Kane, State of Illinois, party of the first part, and Charles Vandersall of Columbus, Ohio, party of the second part, witnesseth:

In consideration of (insert consideration), it is agreed between the parties hereto as follows:

Said party of the first part agrees (insert agreement of party of the first part).

Said party of the second part agrees (insert agreement of the party of the second part).

In witness whereof the said parties have hereunto set their hands and seals the day and year first above written.

CLARENCE RANCK (Seal)
CHARLES VANDERSALL (Seal)

Copyright

1. DEFINITION.—A copyright is the exclusive right to reproduce, publish, and sell a literary or artistic work. Under the United States Copyright Law, a copyright may be granted for the following classes of material:

(a) Books, including collections, anthologies, and encyclopedias;
(b) Magazines and newspapers;
(c) Lectures, sermons, or other addresses for oral delivery;
(d) Dramatic and musical-dramatic compositions;
(e) Musical compositions;
(f) Maps;
(g) Works of art, including models and designs;
(h) Reproductions of works of art;
(i) Scientific or technical drawings or plastic work;
(j) Photographs;
(k) Prints and pictorial illustrations;
(l) Motion-picture photoplays;
(m) Other motion pictures.

Copyrights can also be secured on compilations, abridgments, arrangements, or adaptations, whether of non-copyrightable material or, with the permission of the copyright holder, of material that has been copyrighted already. Republished works that include new material are also copyrightable.

2. HOW TO OBTAIN.—To secure a copyright on a work which is to be reproduced for sale or public distribution, the work should be published with a copyright notice, which may be in the following form:

Copyright, 1960, by
JONES, SMITH, AND COMPANY

On maps, photographs, pictures, and other works where it is difficult to place a complete copyright notice, the letter C enclosed in a circle, ©, is used; it must be accompanied by a symbol or mark of the owner of the copyright, and his name must appear elsewhere on the work.

After publication of the work, two copies of the best edition (or one copy in the case of a work by a foreign citizen and published first in another country) should be sent to the Copyright Office, Washington, D.C., with an application for registration.

Books by American authors and proprietors or alien authors and proprietors domiciled within the United States must be accompanied by an affidavit stating that the typesetting, printing, and binding were done in the United States.

Forms for the affidavit and application for registration are supplied by the Copyright Office upon request.

3. FEES.—The fee for registration of a published work is $4; payment of this sum also entitles one to a certificate under seal of the Copyright Office.

The charge for the renewal of a copyright is $2. Copyrights may be assigned to other persons.

4. HOW TO OBTAIN COPYRIGHT FOR OTHER ARTICLES.—A copyright may also be obtained on certain works not published or reproduced for sale by filing an application for registration; the fee is $4. It should be accompanied by one manuscript of the work, if it is a lecture, sermon, address, or dramatic or musical composition; by one print, for copyright of a photograph not intended for general circulation; and by a photograph or reproduction in the case of works of art and scientific or technical drawings or plastic works. To obtain a copyright on a motion-picture photoplay not published or for sale, the application for registration must be accompanied by the title, description, and a print from each scene or act.

An application for registration of another type of motion picture must be accompanied by the title, description, and two prints from different sections of the picture.

5. DURATION OF COPYRIGHT.—A copyright is valid for 28 years and may be renewed for the same length of time; provided application for renewal is made and registered within one year prior to the expiration of the original term of copyright. It cannot be renewed again. If an author is not living, his copyright may be renewed by the widow or widower, or his children. If none of these are living the executors have the right of renewal; and if there is no will the copyright may be renewed by the next of kin. The person to whom a copyright has been assigned may also renew it, at the expiration of the original 28-year period.

6. PRINTS AND LABELS.—Copyrights may be taken out on prints and labels for advertising purposes. They must be published first with a notice of copyright. Application for registration should then be filed by the owner or author. These copyrights are also effective for 28 years and may be renewed for a similar period.

7. UNIVERSAL COPYRIGHT.—The United States is a party to the Universal Copyright Convention that became effective in September 1955. There are over forty contracting states to this convention.

Under the terms of the agreement each state provides for the protection of the rights of authors and other copyright owners in literary, scientific, and artistic works, including writings, music, drama, cinematographic works, paintings, engravings, and sculpture. Works first published in any member nation will generally get the same protection in other member nations as they afford their own nationals. The copyright symbol © accompanied by the name of the copyright owner and the date of publication is sufficient to obtain protection for the work in any country that is a party to the Universal Copyright Convention.

Foreign works need not fulfill the United States requirement of deposit and registration if they are first published in a country party to the Universal Copyright Convention or if they are written by nationals of any of the contracting states.

Applications for registration of claims to copyright are filed with the Register of Copyrights, Library of Congress, Washington 25, D.C. These application forms as well as information circulars covering the various subjects are furnished free upon request to the Register of Copyrights. Proposed changes to the copyright law, by the Subcommittee on Patents, Trademarks, and Copyrights of the Senate Committee on the Judiciary, may be obtained from the U.S. Government Printing Office.

Corporations

1. DEFINITION.—A corporation is a group of persons empowered to act as a single individual, and treated by the law as such in many respects.

2. KINDS OF CORPORATIONS.—Corporations known as *Business Corporations* are the most common. *Public Corporations* are agencies of the government. Railroad corporations, and other public service corporations, though performing a public service, are nevertheless *Private Corporations*. Then there are *Religious, Charitable* and *Beneficial Corporations*, usually organized for beneficial purposes, not for profit. *Quasi Corporations*, such as school districts, resemble corporations in some ways. They can own and manage real estate, make contracts, sue and be sued like any other corporation. A *Close Corporation* is one where

the capital stock or ownership is confined to one family or distinct group of individuals.

3. FORMATION OF CORPORATION.—The formation of a corporation involves numerous legal questions, and should never be attempted without the services of a competent corporation lawyer. In most states the first step after having a certain amount of stock subscribed and paid for is to file with the Secretary of the state a statement giving name, object, amount of capital stock, amount of stock paid for, location of office, and duration of the proposed corporation. The charter is then issued and a meeting of stockholders is called to elect directors. State laws vary, but usually three or more individuals may form a corporation. Corporations created in one state may transact any lawful business in another state, and they can acquire and transfer property as individuals, provided they comply with the law of the state in which they do business and obtain a license to do business there.

4. LIFE OF A CORPORATION.—A corporation exists until the expiration of its charter unless it fails or is discontinued for other good reasons. Most charters are now perpetual. The stockholder's rights may pass from one to another by sale or by inheritance.

5. CAPITAL STOCK.—Corporations generally have assets composed of money, real estate, buildings, machinery, patents, copyrights, etc. Capital stock is divided into parts called shares, and the owners of the shares are called stockholders. By this method of promotion the necessary money for the enterprise may be collected from many different sources, and unlike a partnership the individual stockholders are not personally liable for the debts of the corporation. In large measure these facts account for the great popularity of the corporate form of organization. Corporations may increase or decrease the amount of their capital stock, provided the change is made in good faith, without intent to defraud.

6. WHO MAY SUBSCRIBE FOR STOCK.—Anyone capable of making a contract may subscribe for the stock of a corporation. Minors are excluded. Where fictitious subscriptions are used to induce others to buy, the purchaser may refuse to pay his subscription. If already paid for he may recover the money, or he may keep the stock and sue for damages. The selling of subscriptions to stock is now very strictly regulated by statute.

7. THE STOCK CERTIFICATE is a written statement of the number and par value of the shares to which the holder is entitled. In other words, it is the evidence of ownership. A stockholder may prove ownership even though a certificate has never been issued him. When the capital stock of a corporation is increased each shareholder usually has the right to purchase a portion of the new stock before it can be offered for sale to outsiders.

8. PREFERRED STOCK.—This kind of stock takes preference over the ordinary or common stock of a corporation. The holders of preferred stock are entitled to a stated percentage annually out of the net earnings of the corporation before a dividend can be declared on the common stock, or to some other preference set out in the certificate. Preference, rather than actual payment, is guaranteed. Holders of preferred stock usually have the right to vote at any stockholders' meeting on the same basis as the holders of common stock. In some states the law requires that each share of stock have equal voting rights with every other share.

9. COMMON STOCK is the ordinary stock of a corporation. The holders are entitled to all the rights incident to their ownership.

10. TRANSFER OF STOCK.—This is provided for by statute. Usually the seller must assign the certificate to the transferee, execute a power of attorney, and deliver the certificate to the company for cancellation. The transfer agent then issues a new certificate to the purchaser.

11. A SUBSCRIPTION FOR STOCK is a contract and must be in writing. An agent cannot refuse to receive a subscription from a competent person, nor can he release a subscriber or alter the terms of the contract. The subscriber must inform himself as to his obligations and cannot evade payment unless he can prove fraud.

12. THE SHAREHOLDER'S LIABILITY.—As stated previously, a corporation differs from a partnership in that the shareholders in a corporation are liable only for the amount of stock they own. Each member of a partnership is liable for all the debts of the firm. However, in the case of National Banks the shareholders are liable for double the amount of their holdings in case the bank fails, if that much more is required to pay the debts. The amount of a stockholder's liability is fixed by statute. A stockholder in any corporation is liable for the full amount of his stock, whether paid in full or not.

13. RECEIVERSHIP.—When a corporation fails, a receiver is sometimes appointed by the court to take charge of its affairs. The receiver has the power to convert the property into cash, levy and collect assessments from the shareholders, where authorized by law, and pay dividends to the creditors, as in the case of bankruptcy proceedings. The receiver may be an individual, a group of individuals, or a trust company.

14. MANAGEMENT.—The power of a corporation rests in its members or individual stockholders—except as restricted or limited by law. Unless the charter or state laws alter the case, policies are determined by a majority vote; usually a shareholder has as many votes as he has shares in the corporation. The

right to vote in a stockholders' meeting is determined by the stock record of ownership as of the date of meeting, or on the date the books are closed prior to the meeting. The bylaws of the corporation generally fix the time for the closing of the books. A stockholder has the right to vote even if no certificate has been issued to him. He may vote in person or by proxy. An executor or trustee may vote the stock of the estate.

15. MEETINGS.—The statutes or the bylaws of a corporation usually prescribe the manner in which meetings are to be called, and the bylaws fix the time and place of meetings. Should the proper officer fail to call a meeting at the required time, the meeting may lawfully be held later, and if he should refuse to issue the proper notice, he may be compelled by mandamus proceedings to do so. *Regular Meetings* are held in the manner set forth by the charter or bylaws, and the object of the meeting need not be stated in the notice. On the other hand, special meetings may be called at any time on proper authority, but the notice must state the object of the meeting, and no other business may be there transacted. Any authorized meeting may be adjourned from time to time or from day to day, and the adjournments must be considered as the same meeting. Even if a meeting is illegally called it becomes a valid meeting by ratification of the proper official or by the shareholders. Notice of meeting is sent to whoever has the right to vote the stock.

16. DIRECTORS.—Management of a corporation is vested in the directors. Most corporations delegate managerial powers to directors who are elected either by a majority vote of the shareholders, or by a cumulative system of voting in states in which such system is used. Their powers are established by statute, charter, or bylaws. As a rule they have general supervision over the business of the corporation. Their authority may be delegated to committees, corporate officials, or individuals. Thus the president, the secretary, the treasurer, and other officers and committees of the corporation are chosen by the board of directors to act in the capacity of agents, in administering its affairs. A director may not act for the corporation individually, but his unauthorized acts would bind the corporation if subsequently ratified. A director may not act both for the corporation and for himself in the same transaction. Unless otherwise provided, directors are not entitled to compensation for their services.

17. THE DIRECTORS' LIABILITY.—The directors of a company are liable to the company and to shareholders and outsiders for negligence, fraud, or for acts committed outside the scope of their authority. These are questions of fact to be determined by the courts. The directors of a corporation are personally liable for its debts if it can be proved that they incurred the obligations knowing that the corporation was insolvent. They have been held personally, jointly, and severally liable as partners, for debts of the corporation contracted in a state in which the company was found to have been doing business without having taken out a license.

18. THE OFFICERS of a corporation are usually the president, vice-president, secretary, and treasurer chosen by, and often from, the board of directors. The ordinary rules of agency govern their powers and duties.

The President is the chief executive officer and usually presides at meetings of the Board of Directors.

The vice-president takes over the duties of the president when, for any reason, the latter is unable to perform them. Quite frequently there are numerous vice-presidents assigned to different duties.

The secretary is the keeper of the records and the chief clerk of the corporation. He usually has the custody of the corporate seal.

The treasurer has charge of the corporation's finances. He is usually under bond for the faithful performance of his duties.

19. DIVIDENDS.—A dividend is a payment to the shareholders out of the net profits of the corporation. It may be in actual cash, in property or in additional stock. When stock is selling above par on the exchange, corporations sometimes grant shareholders the right to purchase additional stock at par instead of declaring a cash stock dividend. The law will not permit the payment of dividends out of capital, or from borrowed money, without the consent of the stockholders, and the directors would be liable for such a fraudulent payment. Furthermore, illegally paid dividends may be recovered for the benefit of creditors. The net profit of a corporation is an asset, and not secure against creditors unless, or until, the money has been declared as a dividend. When the dividend has been legally declared payable, no action can be brought by creditors to stop its payment. The directors must act in good faith, but they cannot be compelled to pay dividends when they do not deem it advisable to do so. The courts hold that dividends must be general on all stock of the same class, so that each shareholder in that class will receive his just share, and that the dividends shall be paid to the owner as determined by the books of the company.

20. LIABILITIES OF A CORPORATION.—Through its agents or servants a corporation can be guilty of slander, libel, false representation, trespass, or negligence, and can be sued accordingly.

21. THE SHAREHOLDER'S RIGHTS.—A shareholder has the right to inspect the company's books at any reasonable time for any proper purpose. Furthermore, he may employ an expert accountant to go through the records if he has reason to believe that the affairs of the company are not being handled properly.

General Proxy

Know all men by these presents, that I, ..., the undersigned, do hereby constitute and appoint .... my attorney and agent (with power of substitution for me and in my name, place and stead) to vote as my proxy for the election of directors and upon all matters that may be considered at the annual meeting of the stockholders of the .... company, to be held at its office at the city of .... of the county of ...., state of ...., on the .... day of ...., 19...., at .... o'clock ...M., or any adjournment thereof, according to the number of votes I should be entitled to vote if I were personally present at said meeting, hereby revoking all former proxies by me made and given.

In witness whereof, I have hereunto set my hand and seal this ...... day of ...., 19.....

Witness:

.... (Signature)

Revocation of Proxy

Know all men by these presents, that I, the undersigned, do hereby revoke and annul a certain proxy by me given to .... (or, any and all proxies or powers of attorney heretofore given by me) authorizing and empowering the said .... to represent me and to vote in my name and stead and to act for me in any way whatsoever at any meeting or meetings of the stockholders of the .... company.

In witness whereof, I have hereunto set my hand and seal this ...... day of ...., 19....

(Witnessed.) (Signed.)

Criminal Law and Procedure

1. DEFINITION.—A crime is an act in violation of some existing prohibitory statute and the common morality of the country. An individual cannot compromise a criminal wrong, for crime is a matter for the State to settle. Crimes may be classified as felonies, or more serious offenses; and misdemeanors, or less serious offenses; but the distinction is largely an arbitrary one.

2. BURDEN OF PROOF.—The burden of proof is upon the State. In other words a person accused of a crime is presumed to be innocent until the contrary is proved. The verdict of the jury must be unanimous to convict. If any doubt remains in the minds of the jury, after hearing all the evidence, it is its duty to acquit the defendant, and once acquitted, a prisoner cannot be brought to trial a second time for the same offense in the same jurisdiction.

3. DEFENSES.—Two defenses which are often raised are the defense of insanity and that of self-defense. A person who cannot distinguish right from wrong is insane and cannot be held responsible for his acts, but the insanity must be proved. Also, a person may defend his person, family, or property and may use such force as is necessary. If he can show that the act was committed in self-defense, he is guilty of no crime.

4. CONFESSION.—A legal confession must be voluntary and free from all compulsion, either physical or mental. Third-degree methods are unlawful, and a confession procured by the use of threats or violence has no standing in court.

5. TRIAL BY JURY.—A person accused of a crime is guaranteed the right to a fair and impartial trial by a jury of twelve, and the right to be represented by a competent lawyer. The trial must occur in the county where the crime was committed unless a "change of venue" is granted. The defendant is entitled to a change of venue if it can be proved that on account of prejudice on the part of the judge or jury the accused could not there receive a fair trial.

6. HABEAS CORPUS.—A writ of habeas corpus is sometimes issued by the court to prevent people from being unlawfully deprived of their liberty. The prisoner is brought before the court and is released unless cause can be shown for his detention. This is a fundamental right under the Constitution.

7. CRIMINAL PROCEDURE.—The first step in criminal procedure is generally the issuing of a warrant by a justice of the peace or other judicial officer. When arrested the accused is either placed in custody, or, if he can furnish a satisfactory bond, he is released on bail awaiting trial. If the offense is a misdemeanor the case is usually tried and settled before the justice. If it is a felony, the justice holds a preliminary trial, certifying his findings to the grand jury. Acting in an investigating capacity, the grand jury may indict the accused, and the case is tried on its merits in the regular criminal court. If the grand jury fails to indict, the charge may be dropped on account of insufficient evidence.

Criminal Law in Brief

8. ADULTERY.—In many of the states, it is a crime for any married man and woman not married to each other to live together openly as man and wife.

9. ACCESSORY TO THE CRIME.—Any person assisting another to commit a crime or to escape from the scene of the crime is equally guilty with the principal.

10. Assault and Battery.—A person who threatens, or attempts to strike, another person is guilty of assault, even though the threat is not followed by actual battery. Assault becomes battery when injury is actually done. The slightest unlawful touching may be battery.

11. Bribery consists in the offering or giving of money or other valuable consideration to a public officer or one performing a public duty, as an inducement for him to commit an unlawful act. The giver and the receiver of the bribe are equally guilty.

12. Bigamy.—A person having more than one husband or wife at one time is guilty of the crime of bigamy.

13. Burglary consists in the unlawful breaking into and entering of the building of another with the intent to commit a crime.

14. Bail means the sureties who bind themselves to have the accused present in court when required for trial.

15. Contempt of Court.—Any attempt to obstruct justice or to injure the dignity of the court is punishable by the action of the court.

16. Conspiracy.—When two or more persons agree to do an unlawful act, the agreement is called a conspiracy, and is in itself a crime.

17. Embezzlement is the wrongful appropriation and use of the personal property of another person by one to whom it has been voluntarily turned over for some lawful use.

18. Extortion is the asking and accepting of unlawful fees by a public officer.

19. False Pretense.—It is a criminal offense to obtain money or other things of value by the false or fraudulent representation of a past or existing fact.

20. Fornication is illicit sexual intercourse other than adultery, as that between unmarried persons. It is punishable in some states.

21. Forgery is the false making, or the material alteration, of a written instrument, contract, or any other legal paper with intent to defraud.

22. Larceny is the unlawful appropriation and use of a person's property. It differs from embezzlement in that the original taking is unlawful.

23. Manslaughter is the unlawful killing of a human being without malice or premeditation.

24. Mayhem is the act of maiming, disfiguring, or cutting away any part of the human body.

25. Murder is the unlawful taking of a human life with malice and premeditation.

26. Malicious Mischief is a crime which consists of the willful and intentional injury of another's property.

27. Offenses on the High Seas are tried by the country under whose flag the ship is sailing.

28. Perjury is the false swearing of a person under oath. A person inducing another to perjure himself is equally guilty.

29. Rape.—It is a felony to have sexual intercourse with a girl or woman without her consent.

30. Robbery is stealing property from another by force and intimidation. It is a felony punishable by imprisonment in the penitentiary.

31. Seduction.—To have intercourse with a woman of chaste reputation through false promises of marriage is a crime.

32. Stolen Property.—It is a crime to buy, receive, or conceal stolen property with the intent not to return it to the rightful owner. When buying property, demand proof of the ownership.

33. Treason.—It is treason to make war against, or to assist the enemies of, the existing government. It is punishable by death. A foreigner, owing no allegiance to the government, cannot be guilty of treason.

34. Unlawful Assembly.—It is a criminal offense for two or more persons to assemble in contemplation of some unlawful act.

Deeds

1. Definitions.—A deed is a written document, under seal, conveying real estate. There are two kinds of deeds in general use: warranty deeds and quitclaim deeds. Any person of legal age, competent to transact business and owning real estate, may convey it by deed. The seller is called the *grantor*, the buyer the *grantee*.

2. A Warranty Deed is one in which the seller or grantor warrants the title to be good, and agrees to defend the same against all parties. Such a deed usually provides:

(a) That the seller has a right to convey the real estate; (b) that he is the owner of the land mentioned in the deed; (c) that the land is free and clear from all former and other grants, bargains, sales, liens, taxes, assessments, and encumbrances of any kind: (d) and that the purchaser will have quiet enjoyment of the real estate; that is, that he will not be put out of possession by anyone having superior title. If it afterwards develops that the grantor did not have the right to sell, or if the grantee discovers an encumbrance on the land, or if he has any trouble about the title, the purchaser has a good cause of action against the seller.

3. A Quitclaim Deed conveys only what interest the grantor may have in the property. This form of deed is often given by one whose title to the real estate may be defective. The

seller conveys only whatever interest he may have. A quitclaim deed contains no warranties.

4. General Principles.—

a. Deeds must be written, typewritten, or printed.

b. The names of the parties and places of residence are generally written first.

c. The property must be fully described. The description should be by bounds, or by divisions of United States surveys, or by subdivisions into blocks and lots, as shown on the records in the county recorder's office.

d. The deed must express a consideration, and be signed and sealed by the grantor or grantors. A deed without consideration is void.

e. Numbers should always be written in words followed by figures in parentheses, thus, Two Hundred Dollars ($200.00).

f. If the grantor is married, both he and his wife should join in the deed, and it should be executed and acknowledged by both.

g. The acknowledgment of a deed can be made only before persons authorized by law to take the same, such as justices of the peace, notaries, masters in chancery, and judges and clerks of the courts.

h. The deed takes effect upon its delivery to the person authorized to receive it, and should be recorded at once.

i. After the signing and acknowledgment of a deed the parties have no right to make the slightest alteration.

j. Never purchase real estate without a careful examination of the title by a trusted attorney.

k. Always procure an abstract of title or guaranty policy before advancing money or signing a contract for purchase of land or lots.

l. A deed in which a mistake has been made can be corrected in all cases of fraud or accident.

m. In investigating the title to real estate, the attorney is bound to make a careful examination of the records and report the facts and his conclusions with respect to the condition of the title, and is liable for any injury resulting from his negligence.

n. A deed is considered recorded as soon as it reaches the recording officer, who generally notes upon it the day, hour, and minute when it was received by him.

o. If the land is a gift and no price is paid for it, it is customary to insert "in consideration of one dollar and other good and valuable considerations."

Form of Warranty Deed

Know all men by these presents, that we .... and ...., husband and wife, in consideration of the sum of $...... in hand paid, do hereby grant, bargain, sell and convey to ...., of .... county, ..., the following described real estate situated in the county of ...., and state of .... to wit: (describe premises), to have and to hold to his heirs and assigns forever. Together with all of the tenements, hereditaments, and appurtenances thereto belonging. And we hereby covenant with said .... that we are lawfully seized of said premises; that they are free from incumbrances; that we have good right and lawful authority to sell the same, and we covenant to warrant and defend the same against the lawful claims of all persons whosoever. And the said ...., hereby relinquishes her right of dower in said premises.

In witness whereof we have hereunto set our hands and seals this ...... day of ...., 19....

In presence of .... (Seal)
.... (Seal)

State of ....
.... County.

....
....

On this ...... day of ...., 19...., before me, a notary public in and for said county, personally came the above named .... and ...., his wife, who are known to me to be the identical persons whose names are affixed to the above deed as grantors, and severally acknowledge the instrument to be their voluntary act, and deed.

In witness whereof I have hereunto set my hand the day and year above written.

....
Notary Public

N. B. Statutes in many states provide for a short form which may be used in place of the above and has the same effect.

Form of Quitclaim Deed

The grantor (here insert name or names of grantor or grantors and place or places of residence), of the city of ...., for the consideration of (here insert consideration), convey and quitclaim to (here insert name or names of grantee or grantees) all interest in the following described real estate (here insert description), situated in the county of .... in the state of ....

Dated this ...... day of ...., A.D., 19....

.... (Seal)

N. B. Use same form of acknowledgment as that shown for warranty deeds above.

Dower

1. Definition.—*Dower* is the provision which the law makes for the support of a

widow out of her deceased husband's estate. Unless modified by statute this interest consists of the use for life of one-third of her husband's land after his death. During the husband's life, the law protects the wife's interest by prohibiting the sale of real estate unless she joins with him in signing the deed. If the property is sold and she does not sign the deed, she still has her dower right in the property. The interest which a husband acquires in the land belonging to his wife after her death is called *curtesy*. In some states the term "curtesy" has been abolished and the word "dower" is substituted, so that the latter term applies to the interest of either the husband or the wife in the land of the deceased spouse.

2. General Principles.—(a) The dower right is regulated by widely differing statutes in the several states. (b) If the land is subject to a mortgage which was signed by the wife along with her husband, or a prior lien, the wife cannot get possession until the encumbrance has been removed. (c) A woman may release her dower right by signing with her husband a deed for the conveyance of the real estate. (d) A husband can will his wife a certain amount in place of her dower, but the wife can claim the dower instead if she prefers it. (e) The widow is usually entitled to administer the estate of her deceased husband. (f) Dower exists in growing crops and trees, and also in mines and quarries opened during the husband's lifetime. (g) The widow of a partner is entitled to her dower in partnership land after payment of all debts of the partnership. (h) A legal marriage is necessary to sustain a dower estate. An absolute divorce divests the wife of her dower if the divorce was granted to the husband by reason of the wife's misconduct. (i) Dower is assigned to the widow either by direction of the court or by agreement. (j) Dower may be barred by a marriage settlement or agreement made before marriage.

Drunkenness

1. Both the civil and criminal courts are frequently called upon to rule on cases in which one of the parties involved was intoxicated.

2. In Civil Cases the courts have recognized cases in which intoxication was an excuse for repudiating a contract. The mental condition must be taken into consideration, especially where a man has become utterly incompetent or insane as a result of his intemperate habits. As we have seen before, such a man cannot make a contract. If one is visibly intoxicated, the contract could be declared void on the ground that the other party must have realized his condition. The element of fraud enters if one party deliberately induced the condition of the other. However, if the intoxicated party ratifies the agreement when sober, or fails to repudiate it, he would be legally bound by it.

3. In Criminal Cases the courts hold that one who voluntarily becomes intoxicated cannot claim his intoxication as an excuse for his criminal acts. Yet in all such cases the facts must show intent to commit the crime before there can be any conviction. This aspect has been brought up in many cases where the defendant was so drunk that he entered the wrong house, or carried off the property of others, or slandered the reputation of another.

4. General Principles.—(a) It is the duty of those who deal with an intoxicated person to take his condition into consideration. (b) A sober party must exercise a reasonable degree of care to avoid injury to a drunken individual. (c) A railroad company is also bound to take into account the helpless condition of its passenger, and to exercise reasonable care in keeping him out of danger. (d) Drunkenness is not a legal excuse for the commission of a crime, but sometimes it is evidence of the absence of malice.

Employer and Employee

1. Explanation.—The term employee refers to a person who is hired by a *contract of service* to perform certain duties for another person called the *employer*.

2. Kinds of Contracts.—There are two types of general employment contracts. (a) Contracts to do some particular thing such as to buy and sell stocks or provisions, or collect accounts. (b) Contracts to do whatever the employer may direct. Farm hands, domestic servants, and clerks belong to this class. Such contracts are frequently verbal, or even only implied, rather than written.

3. Compensation.—If no agreement has been made beforehand the employee is entitled to the wages usually paid for such service. If the employee leaves because of insufficient food, ill-treatment, or disabling sickness, he is entitled to pay for the time he worked.

4. Duties of Employee.—The employee is expected to perform faithfully the services for which he contracted for the entire term or period of service. In many cases, as in those of workers employed by the day or hour, this period of service may be very short. Courts frequently hold that if he leaves before expiration of time, he can claim no pay for the work done. Some judges have held, however, that even in this case the employee is entitled to pay for work done, less what the employer lost by necessity of paying higher wages to the employee's successor, or what he lost by the employee's failing to perform his contract. The employee is bound to take

reasonable care of the property in his care, and is liable for any loss or injury to it when due to his negligence.

5. Discharge.—An employee may be discharged at the end of his contract without any cause or previous notice. If he is discharged without good cause before the termination of his agreement, however, he is entitled to pay for the whole period, provided he has first made an earnest attempt to secure other employment in the same kind of work. If he gets work at lower wages, he is entitled to the difference. If his pay is equal to, or higher than, the former rate, he can not collect. If, however, the discharge is on account of incapacity, dishonesty, or misconduct, he is not entitled to any pay for the unexpired period. Frequently a person is hired for a month, or for a year, at the termination of which the work continues. In such cases the law presumes a new contract on the same terms.

6. Liability of Employer.—An employer's liability is of two kinds: (a) liability for the acts of his employees, and (b) liability for the injury or death of his employees.

7. Liability for Acts of Employee.—The employer is liable for the wrongful acts of his employee producing injury to others, provided the acts are done in the course of the ordinary employment. Thus a railroad company is liable to passengers for negligence of conductors and engineers.

8. Workmen's Compensation.—Workmen's compensation acts have largely provided new remedies to take the place of the employee's right to sue his employer for injuries incurred in the course of his employment. Under these acts liability is generally imposed upon the employer without regard to the question as to whether or not the employer was at fault, and payments are made as insurance rather than as damages.

9. Who is Entitled to Compensation.—Any person employed by a contract of service who is under the control of the employer while at work at the machine or other device from which the injury arose is entitled to compensation. Previous physical condition is not considered in determining the amount.

10. Who is Excluded.—The workmen's compensation acts differ in the several states. The Federal act protects persons employed by the United States and workmen engaged in interstate commerce. While it is difficult to give a general rule, the following are excluded from the benefits in most states, and in others the compensation is optional:

a. Minors and apprentices.
b. Farm laborers.
c. Domestic servants.
d. Casual employees.
e. Independent contractors.
f. Public officers.

11. Dependents.—The law also provides that the compensation be paid to dependents in case of death. Payments may be made only to actual dependents or to partial dependents in accordance with the degree of dependency. These include widows, children, step-children, illegitimate children, adopted children, or a dependent parent.

12. Payments.—The compensation acts provide for payments to the injured or his dependents in case of partial incapacity, permanent incapacity, or death, in amounts depending on the earning power of the injured at the time of the accident. Maximum and minimum amounts are usually specified.

13. Insurance.—The compensation laws are rigidly enforced, and to protect themselves, employers often take out liability insurance on the life and health of each employee. Then, when an accident occurs, the insurance company assumes all liability and relieves the employer of any claims which might be made under the workmen's compensation law. This method of limiting liability is provided for in the laws of all the states. The cost of such insurance is based on the size of the payroll and the nature of the employment. It ranges from a purely nominal figure for office work to a rather high rate for the more hazardous occupations.

14. Variations.—It is impossible in a brief space to attempt an explanation of the workmen's compensation laws in the different states. In some states deductions are made for contributory negligence, and in others awards are fixed for specific injuries, and in almost every state there can be found numerous variations.

15. Sources of Information.—Copies of the compensation and liability statutes may be secured free of charge by writing to the Secretary of State of the state for which information is desired. He should be addressed at the state capital. Owing to the technical nature of the subject, however, it is always a good plan to ask an insurance adviser to explain the duties and obligations under the law.

Assignment of Wages

For a valuable consideration to me in hand paid by .... of .... the receipt whereof is hereby acknowledged, I do hereby transfer, assign and set over to the said ...., his heirs, executors, administrators, or assigns, all salary or wages, and claims for salary or wages, due or to become due from .... & Company, or from any other person or persons, firm, copartnership, company, corporation, organization or official by whom I am now or may hereafter become employed, at any time before the expiration of .... years from the date hereof.

I do hereby constitute irrevocably the said ...., his heirs, executors, administrators or assigns, my attorney, in my name to take all legal mesures which may be proper or necessary for the complete recovery and employment of the claim hereby assigned, and I hereby authorize, empower and direct the said .... & Company, or any one by whom I may be employed as above, to pay the said demand and claim for wages or salary to the said ...., his executors, administrators or assigns, and hereby authorize and empower him or them to receipt for the same in my name.

Dated at .... this ...... day, 19.....

16. THE FAIR LABOR STANDARDS ACT.—In 1938 Congress enacted the Fair Labor Standards Act which set a minimum wage and maximum work week for employees engaged in interstate commerce or in the production of goods for commerce. Because of the broad interpretation by the Supreme Court of the Federal Government's constitutional power to regulate interstate commerce, this act has a widespread effect on employment.

There are also provisions in the Act restricting the employment of children. Children under eighteen years of age may not engage in hazardous occupations. Children under sixteen years may work for their parents in non-mining or non-manufacturing occupations. Children between the ages of fourteen and sixteen years may work at non-mining and non-manufacturing occupations after school hours and under conditions which will not affect their health or well-being.

The Fair Labor Standards Act is administered by the Wage and Hour Division of the United States Department of Labor at Washington, D.C. Many of the states have similar legislation affecting employment conditions among employees working in business wholly within the state.

17. THE NATIONAL LABOR RELATIONS ACT AND LABOR-MANAGEMENT RELATIONS ACT.—The National Labor Relations Act, known as "The Wagner Act," has given employees the legal right to organize and bargain collectively with their employer without interference or coercion by the employer. The National Labor Relations Board enforces the Act and may, upon request of the employer or employees, hold an election to determine the union which shall act as bargaining agent. The Board may prohibit the employer from using unfair labor practices and may, after proper hearing, compel the reinstatement of a former employee discharged because of union activities. The Act has been amended by the Labor-Management Relations Act, known as the Taft-Hartley Act, which has added such things as prohibitions against unfair labor practices by employees. Some states have legislation patterned after these Acts.

18. THE NORRIS-LA GUARDIA ACT.—Another Federal act affecting employer-employee relationships is the Norris-La Guardia Act, which restricts the power of the Federal Courts to issue injunctions in labor disputes, although these restrictions have been eased somewhat by the Taft-Hartley Act, and prohibits them from enforcing "yellow dog" contracts. A "yellow dog" contract is one by which the employee, as a condition of his employment, agrees to withdraw from, or refrain from joining, a labor organization. Some states have similar laws affecting their own courts.

19. THE SOCIAL SECURITY ACT.—The two phases of the Social Security Act that are most important to employer and employee are: (1) that which sets up a permanent system of old-age benefits, and (2) that which promotes the enactment of permanent unemployment insurance systems by the states. The old-age benefit system is administered by the Federal Government, and to support the plan, employer and employee pay a tax based on the size of the employee's wage, which the employer must remit to the Federal treasury. When the employee reaches 65, his monthly benefit payments begin and their amount is calculated with reference to the total tax he has paid over his years of work. These benefit provisions apply to all classes of persons within the Act, and should not be confused with old-age pensions to needy persons.

The Act attempts to induce the states to enact and administer unemployment insurance systems. The employer must pay a tax on his total payroll into the Federal treasury. If the state has an unemployment insurance act which meets the standards set up by Congress, the Federal Government will grant money to the state to help pay the cost of the insurance. The employer may also deduct up to 90 per cent of the Federal tax to pay the state unemployment insurance tax.

Other sections of the Social Security Act provide for Federal grants to the states for maternal and child welfare, for public health work, and for aid to the blind, the needy aged, and dependent children.

Equitable Remedies

1. DEFINITIONS.—A *remedy* is the legal means employed to enforce a right or redress an injury. Suppose A has purchased an automobile from B who refused to deliver it. In a court of equity A could compel B to deliver the car and this would be an *equitable remedy*. In a court of law A could recover damages for the loss he had sustained through B's refusal to deliver the automobile, and this would be a *legal remedy*.

2. THE COMMON REMEDY.—Relief in equity is often sought to compel a person to execute

a contract which he has made. It quite frequently happens that a seller regrets his action after the contract has been made. The court of equity will compel him to deliver the property, provided that the law gives the purchaser no adequate remedy. When an article has a peculiar sentimental value, when it is of rare value like an heirloom, or when it is an article which cannot be easily purchased in the open market, the one party can compel the other to fulfill his contract. Ordinarily, the buyer of articles like cattle, lumber, dry goods, hardware, etc., has only the legal remedy to recover damages.

3. EQUITY WILL ENFORCE AGREEMENTS OR GRANT RELIEF:—

a. When legal remedies (or damages) would be inadequate.
b. When the seller of a business agrees not to enter into competition with the buyer.
c. When an employee agrees not to disclose the trade secrets of his employer.
d. When a tenant threatens or attempts to injure the real estate of the landlord.
e. When an established patent has been infringed.
f. In many other similar cases which would be too numerous to mention here.

4. EQUITY WILL NOT ENFORCE AGREEMENTS OR GRANT RELIEF:—

a. When the law has an adequate remedy.
b. When the goods contracted for can be readily purchased in the open market.
c. To force a person to perform his contract to render personal services.
d. When the contract in question is one where one party agrees to lend money to the other.
e. When there is a contract to form a partnership.
f. When such agreement would be in restraint of trade, would create a monopoly, or would be illegal for any other reason.

5. INJUNCTIONS.—Relief in equity is often brought about by the means of an injunction. An *injunction* is a restraining order issued by a court of equity on petition of the injured party. If the need is great the court will immediately issue a temporary injunction which orders the injuring party to do, or not to do, certain things, and fixes the time for a hearing. At this hearing, which is fixed within a reasonable time, and which is conducted like any ordinary trial, the court decides whether the injunction will be dissolved or whether it will be made permanent. Injunctions came into especial prominence through their use against labor unions during strikes. Injunctions were issued and upheld enjoining the members of labor unions from picketing, or otherwise preventing other workers from taking their places. Legislation has curbed the use of injunctions against labor groups although they are still legal in some cases.

Exemptions

1. DEFINITIONS.—A homestead is the abode or dwelling house of a family landowner and includes a specific amount of the adjacent land, varying in the different states. Exemption laws are defined as laws for the purpose of protecting those who are unable to pay their debts without causing distress to themselves and their families.

2. GENERAL PRINCIPLES.—(a) The laws in some states provide that a person can waive his exemption rights in a promissory note or other written contract. (b) The laws of other states provide that exemptions cannot be waived. In nearly all the states an exemption in wages cannot be waived. A legal homestead is generally in one piece, but it may be divided by a road and in some states may consist of several distinct pieces. (c) A homestead is exempt from all debts except taxes, although in some states it is not exempt from pre-existing liens, fines for public offenses, and similar debts. (d) A person who is the head of a family, within the legal meaning of the term, is generally entitled to homestead exemption. This right survives to the husband or the wife in case of death, or to the surviving children until they come of age. (e) In divorce cases the wife ceases to be a member of the family and thus loses her homestead right unless reserved in the decree. (f) Desertion of the husband by the wife does not destroy his homestead right but does destroy hers. (g) A homestead may be sold or mortgaged regardless of the claims of creditors.

Guaranty

1. *A guaranty* is a written promise that a person will perform some duty or contract, or answer for the payment of some debt, in case of the failure of another person.

2. The person who guarantees the faithfulness of another is called the guarantor.

3. The guarantee or creditor is the person to whom the pledge is made.

4. A guaranty must be in writing.

5. A guaranty, to be binding, must be for a consideration.

6. A guaranty must be accepted in order for it to become a contract, and the guarantor must have notice of its acceptance within a reasonable time.

7. A guarantor, after paying the debt, can become the legally recognized creditor of the person for whom he was guarantor.

FORMS OF GUARANTY

Guaranty on Back of a Note

Fort Scott, Kansas, Oct. 12, 19.....

For value received, I hereby guarantee the payment of the within note.

JAMES GLOVER.

Guaranty for Payment of a Bill

Dayton, Ohio, Aug. 30, 19....

W. Reinke, Esq.
Dear Sir:

I hereby guarantee the payment of any bill or bills of merchandise Mr. John A. Dahlem may purchase from you, the amount of this guaranty not to exceed five hundred dollars ($500), and to expire at the end of three months from date.

CHAS. ADAMS.

Guaranty of a Debt Already Incurred

St. Louis, Mo., July 10, 19.....

Messrs. H. E. Bechtel & Co., West Salem.
Gentlemen:

In consideration of one dollar and other good and valuable considerations paid me by yourselves, the receipt of which I hereby acknowledge, I guarantee that the debt of four hundred dollars ($400) now owing to you by Ira J. Ferry shall be paid at maturity.

W. A. PIPER.

Husband and Wife

1. MARRIAGE is a civil contract. Marriage licenses are required by all the states, and many restrictions have been thrown around the issuing of such licenses within recent years. Marriages between whites and Negroes, between whites and Indians, and between whites and Chinese, are forbidden in various states. Unlike other contracts, marriage cannot be terminated by the consent of both parties.

2. CONTRACT TO MARRY IN THE FUTURE.—Mutual promise by a man and a woman to marry at some future day constitutes a valid contract in some states.

3. A MARRIAGE CONTRACT.—A marriage is a civil contract, and is entered into by the consent of the parties. If a man says to a woman, "Will you marry me?" or words to that effect, and she says "Yes," or words that imply an affirmative answer, it is, by law, an agreement or promise of marriage, and both parties are legally held to carry out in good faith the promise thus made.

4. BREACH OF PROMISE.—If either party refuses to carry out the contract, he or she is guilty of breach of promise, and in some states the other party may recover damages. It is not very often that the man sues the woman, though he has an equal right to do so if she fails to make good her promise. In several states, however, suits for breach of promise are now outlawed.

5. NECESSARY PROOF.—Generally in case of a lawsuit for breach of promise, there are no direct witnesses, as people usually become engaged without the presence of a third party. The engagement may be implied from the conduct of the party sued.

6. IMPLIED EVIDENCE.—In states where suit for breach of promise is recognized, a promise of marriage may be implied from circumstances such as constant visits, presents, or open declaration of the parties, their reception by the parents or friends as an engaged couple, without any objections from the party being sued.

7. EXCUSES FOR BREAKING THE PROMISE.—A refusal to marry may be justified on the ground of the bad character or conduct of the other party; poor health of either party is sometimes a good excuse, but not generally. If the woman were a widow, or a divorcee, and concealed this fact from the man, this justifies a refusal on his part to marry.

8. TIME OF MARRIAGE.—When a man promises to marry a woman without stating any special time, the law may hold him guilty of breach of promise unless he is ready to fulfill his engagement within a reasonable time; five years was held in one instance to be an unreasonable time.

9. WHEN A PROMISE IS NOT BINDING.—If either party is underage, he or she is not bound by promise to marry and the law will excuse the party underage.

10. SEDUCTION.—Seduction of a woman under promise of marriage and subsequent refusal on the man's part to marry, subjects him to damages in a civil action and often to criminal liability as well.

11. SEPARATION.—The law allows agreements between husband and wife in which they agree to live separately. This does not in any way abolish her rights in his estate unless the contract so specifies.

12. DIVORCE.—Divorces are of two kinds: namely, (a) absolute divorces, and (b) judicial separation, generally known as separate maintenance. The word as now commonly used has the former meaning. In the case of an absolute divorce the marriage is ended and the parties become single. A judicial separation is a limited divorce in which the court gives one party the right to live separately from the other. The decree of divorce usually makes provision for the payment of alimony, for the custody and support of the children, if there are any, and for the settlement of property rights between the parties. The divorce laws of the several states vary, although most states recognize and respect the laws of the other states. It is possible, however, to be legally married in one state but considered an adulterer in another; for children to be regarded as legitimate in one state and illegitimate in another.

13. AUTHORITY OF WIFE LIVING APART

FROM HUSBAND TO BIND HIM.—Whether or not the person who supplies a wife with necessaries has knowledge at the time of her husband's provision for her support, the presumption of a wife's authority to pledge her husband's credit is negatived by the fact of their living apart, and the tradesman who supplies her under such circumstances upon the credit of her husband, and without his express sanction or approval, does so at his own peril. In order to charge her husband with the cost of supplies furnished her he must show that they were not only of the kind usually regarded as "necessaries," but that in consequence of the inadequacy of the husband's provision, they were actually required for the wife's proper support, commensurate with his means and her station in the community.

14. PROPERTY RIGHTS OF MARRIED WOMEN.—One of the marked evidences of the growth of true civilization in the United States is the enactment by nearly all the states of legislative provisions for the benefit of married women. These laws vary greatly in the different states, and there are frequent changes, but all tend toward the releasing of woman from her former condition of absolute dependence upon her husband. By the old common law a married woman had few rights. She was subject to the authority of her husband, and he could rule over her. This condition has now been changed, however, and the rights of married women are recognized by every court. All property owned by the wife before marriage, or received after marriage and held as her separate property, can be sold and transferred without the consent of her husband except his rights of dower or curtesy in her real estate. If a husband fails to make provision for the support of his wife, the law will compel him to furnish her proper support if he has sufficient means.

15. GENERAL PRINCIPLES REGARDING THE MARRIAGE CONTRACT.—(a) There must be a serious agreement or mutual assent of both parties. (b) A marriage may be declared void because of fraud, incompetence of one of the parties, or the fact that one of the parties is underage. (c) The minimum age at which marriage can legally be contracted varies from state to state. With consent of parents or guardians, the minimum age in several states is 18 for men and 16 for women; in states under common law the ages are 14 and 12, respectively. Without such consent, the minimum age is frequently 21 for men and 18 for women, although there are numerous exceptions. (d) A marriage is not void simply because it has been improperly performed or licensed, but the officials responsible are liable. (e) At common law a wife is solely responsible for her crimes unless they were committed in her husband's presence, in which case coercion on the part of the husband is presumed. In many states this law has been changed so that the husband is responsible only when he participated in the crime, unless coercion is proved. (f) A married man can sue for the alienation of his wife's affections. In some states the wife has a similar right. Suits for alienation of affections are now prohibited by the laws of a number of states. (g) Either husband or wife may act as the agent for the other party. (h) The husband is not responsible for the debts or wrongs of his wife unless, of course, the debts are necessary for the support of the family. (i) The husband must provide a home, and support and protect his wife and children. His duty to protect his family carries with it all the rights of "self defense." (j) He must maintain law and order in his household, and may use force in preventing a member of his family from committing a crime. (k) A wife is required to care for the house and family. She cannot be forced to go into business or enter any gainful occupation. (l) The husband must support his wife, and she can pledge his credit for articles necessary to sustain life and maintain her social position.

Innkeeper

1. DEFINITION.—An innkeeper is one who keeps a public house for the reception and entertainment of travelers.

2. GAINING ADMISSION TO AN INN OR HOTEL.—An innkeeper is required to accomodate all comers with the following exceptions which vary in different states:

(a) He may exclude anyone if he has no accommodations.
(b) He may exclude those who do not come at a suitable time or in a proper manner.
(c) He must exclude certain persons such as criminals and thieves.
(d) He may refuse admission to those he believes would disturb the peace and safety of his guests.
(e) He can expel any guest who does disturb the peace and safety of his other guests.

If he refuses to provide reasonable and proper accommodations, he is liable. He need not provide any particular room. If he operates a garage or stable in connection with the inn, he is under the same obligation to receive and care for the automobiles or horses of his guests.

3. THE INNKEEPER'S LIABILITY.—The law fixes the liability and responsibility of an innkeeper:

(a) An innkeeper is responsible for the loss or damage to a guest's baggage committed to his care unless such loss is caused by an act of God, a public enemy, or neglect or fault of the owner of the baggage.

(b) In most states innkeepers are relieved from liability for loss by fire unless the fire is caused by the negligence of the innkeeper or his servants.

(c) An innkeeper is liable for goods of a guest if they were stolen by the innkeeper's servants, by another guest, or by an outsider. However, he is not liable if the loss was due to the negligence of the owner.

(d) The innkeeper is bound to secure honest and trustworthy employees.

(e) If two guests occupy the same room, the innkeeper can be held responsible if a theft is committed by one against the other.

4. Liens.—An innkeeper has a lien on a guest's baggage or other property left in his care, to secure the payment for the accommodations.

5. Regulations.—An innkeeper may make regulations for the observance of his guests in order to protect their property. Thus he may limit his liability somewhat by notifying the guests that he is not responsible for the loss of valuable articles unless they are deposited with him. Such regulations will bind the guest if brought to his notice.

6. Lodging and Boarding Houses.—The keepers of lodging or boarding houses do not come under the same head as innkeepers as far as the law is concerned. They are not required to accommodate all who may apply. They are not liable for refusing to accommodate all comers.

Insurance

A. FIRE INSURANCE

1. Definition.—Fire insurance is indemnity against loss by fire. It is now generally furnished by large stock companies or by mutual companies.

2. Mutual Companies are generally established by statute and provide for the payment of losses by pro rata assessment upon the policy-holders, who constitute the stockholders, and who manage the affairs of the company. Some of these mutual companies require a small premium paid in advance, which, unless unusual losses occur, is enough to pay all the losses for the year. Others simply require a small fee to pay for the expense of making the survey and issuing the policy. All of them, however, in case of loss, make an assessment pro rata upon the policy-holders to pay the same.

3. Stock Insurance Companies.—The insurance business of private corporations is carried on for profit.

4. Underwriters' Associations.—The stock fire insurance companies all submit complete underwriting and loss figures to the National Board of Underwriters, which, in addition to acting as a clearing house and as statisticians for such information, also supervises common services to the public such as fire protection, information, and grading. There are also local agents' boards and state associations operating to promote uniformity of service and contract. Fire insurance rates are usually established by rating bureaus which are administered and paid for by a majority of companies doing business in the state or locality. Rates are usually adhered to by all agents either by common agreement or as directed by state law. Specific rates are published for mercantile houses, warehouses, business and manufacturing buildings. Rates by classes are used for dwellings, small apartment houses, farms, and similar property.

5. The Purpose of Fire Insurance.—Fire insurance is a means of distributing the cost of damages caused by fire. A fund is supplied by the payment of premiums, from which the insurance company agrees to pay the loss in case of fire.

6. Classification.—In order that each person thus protected from loss may contribute the proper amount to this fund, a system of classification has been worked out, whereby the premium rate has been established. This classification is based on the probability of fire. The National Board of Fire Underwriters, having the reports of the various insurance companies, knows the probable number of fires and the value of the property involved. Statistics show that a certain percentage of residences, barns, schools, merchandise, etc., will be burned each year. Also that buildings of one type of construction are more likely to burn than those of some other type of construction. Population, water pressure, fire department, building contents, and many other elements are taken into consideration by the rating bureau in determining the rate each person must pay for insurance.

7. Reducing the Rate.—When you pay your premium, you can judge, by the rate you pay, what the experience of the insurance companies has been with regard to similar property, with similar conditions. If the rate is high, find out just what factors make it high. Then you may be able to make such changes or take such precautions that your rate will be reduced.

8. Who Has An Insurable Interest.—In order to be indemnified against loss the insured must have an interest in the property or goods insured, both at the time the insurance is issued and at the time of the loss. Thus the following may be insured:

a. A bailee (one who receives goods of another to hold).
b. A consignee (one to whom property is consigned or shipped).
c. A mortgagee (one who holds a mortgage on real or personal property).
d. An assignee (one to whom property is assigned).
e. A warehouseman.
f. An executor or an administrator.
g. A landlord.
h. A tenant.
i. The holder of a lien on property.
j. An agent who has the custody or care of the principal's property.

All these as well as many others, have what is called an insurable interest. If all insurable interests in a property are not noted on the policy at the time of loss, the company is not liable to the party having an interest which is not so noted.

9. THE INSURANCE POLICY IS A CONTRACT between the insurance company and the insured, by which the first party insures the property of the second party against loss by fire. The consideration, or premium, is usually paid when the policy is issued, although it may be charged on account or paid by check or note. The contract becomes binding and valid when the policy is properly executed. Actual delivery of the policy to the insured is not necessary. Thus if a loss occurs after the duly executed policy is in the hands of the insurance company's agent, but before it has been delivered to the insured, the company must pay the loss. A preliminary contract is sometimes made, in which case the risk begins immediately upon the signing, even though such contract be dated several days before the policy is actually issued. Most local agents have authority to protect an applicant for insurance against loss for a period of 5 to 30 days preceding acceptance of the risk by the company.

10. CANCELLATION.—A fire insurance contract, like any other contract, may be canceled by mutual agreement, but unless otherwise stated in the policy the company cannot cancel the contract without the consent of the policyholder.

11. GENERAL PRINCIPLES.—

a. The property insured, and the terms of the contract, must be clearly defined.
b. If the written part of the policy contradicts the printed sections, the written part will hold.
c. Clerical or typographical errors may usually be corrected when discovered.
d. The insurance on the building covers those things which have become a part of it, but does not include fixtures or surrounding sheds or buildings.
e. Misrepresentation or fraud on the part of the insured renders the insurance policy null and void.
f. If a policyholder secures additional fire insurance on his property without the consent of the insurance company, his former policy becomes void. Most policies today, however, consent to the writing of additional insurance on the property by other companies and in case of loss the liability is pro-rated.
g. In addition to the actual fire loss most policies cover damage by water used to put out the fire, damage to goods while being removed to avoid fire, and damage from an explosion caused by fire.
h. An insurance company is not responsible for goods stolen while they are being removed during a fire.
i. An ordinary policy of insurance does not usually insure against lightning, but lightning clauses will be attached to nearly all policies if requested at the time of issue.
j. The insurance company is not relieved from liability by the carelessness of the policyholder, yet the insured is bound to take reasonable care to prevent fire.
k. In a total loss the insurance company is liable for the full value of the property, provided that this value does not exceed the amount of the insurance. In a partial loss the company is liable only for the actual loss.
l. In an open policy the amount of the insurer's liability is not fixed until after the loss. In a valued policy the maximum liability for a total loss is fixed.
m. In order to calculate the approximate loss on merchandise in case of fire, the value of the following items should be ascertained: the most recent inventory; invoices for goods bought subsequent to that inventory; freight and dray bills on same; credit memorandums for merchandise returned; production department payrolls; appreciation in value of goods since purchase. These items should be added together and from their sum should be subtracted the sum of the following items: outgoing charges, representing goods sold since the last inventory; depreciation in value of goods since purchase; salvage, or market value of goods not destroyed. The remainder gives the approximate value of goods destroyed, for which insurance compensation can be obtained.

B. LIFE INSURANCE

12. DEFINITION.—Life insurance is a contract whereby the insurer agrees, on the payment of a fixed premium, to pay a certain

sum of money to the insured when he reaches a certain age, or to his beneficiaries at his death. Thus it is possible for a man to insure his productive ability for the amount of money it would be worth to him if he were to survive his expected time. (See table of expectancy below.)

AMERICAN EXPERIENCE TABLE OF MORTALITY

13.—The approximate number of years the average person may expect to live at different ages is shown in the following table:

Age years	*Expectation of Life years*	*Age years*	*Expectation of Life years*
10	48.7	53	18.7
11	48.0	54	18.0
12	47.4	55	17.4
13	46.8	56	16.7
14	46.1	57	16.0
15	45.5	58	15.3
16	44.8	59	14.7
17	44.1	60	14.1
18	43.5	61	13.4
19	42.8	62	12.8
20	42.2	63	12.2
21	41.5	64	11.6
22	40.8	65	11.1
23	40.1	66	10.5
24	39.4	67	10.0
25	38.8	68	9.4
26	38.1	69	8.9
27	37.4	70	8.4
28	36.7	71	8.0
29	36.0	72	7.5
30	35.3	73	7.1
31	34.6	74	6.6
32	33.9	75	6.2
33	33.2	76	5.8
34	32.5	77	5.4
35	31.7	78	5.1
36	31.0	79	4.7
37	30.3	80	4.3
38	29.6	81	4.0
39	28.9	82	3.7
40	28.1	83	3.3
41	27.4	84	3.0
42	26.7	85	2.7
43	26.0	86	2.4
44	25.2	87	2.1
45	24.5	88	1.9
46	23.8	89	1.6
47	23.0	90	1.4
48	22.3	91	1.1
49	21.6	92	.9
50	20.9	93	.8
51	20.2	94	.6
52	19.4	95	.5

14. Applications.—Nearly all companies require applications for life insurance to be in writing, and they are usually accompanied by the report of a medical examination made by the local medical examiner of the company. These applications are forwarded to the home office, and if they pass the head medical examiner, the policy is issued to the insured and the application is made a part of the policy. Any false statement contained therein which is material to the risk will vitiate the policy, and applicants for insurance should be careful to see that all questions are fully and truthfully answered. The moral hazard involved is also carefully considered by the insuring company. Most life insurance policies provide that the insurance shall not be in force until the first premium is paid, and most policies are now incontestable after the payment of a certain number of premiums. By the laws of all states, in case default is made in the payment of premium after a certain number of full premiums have been paid, the policyholder may have the option to select any one of the following nonforfeiture provisions:

a. Cash surrender value.
b. Reduced paid-up insurance.
c. Term insurance for the full face amount of the policy.

15. The Policy.—The usual clauses contained in life insurance policies are these: That the insurance ceases unless the premiums are promptly paid; that the company shall be exempt if, within two years after the issuance of the policy, the insured commits suicide whether sane or insane, or if death shall come by the hands of justice for a violation of law; that agents are not authorized to alter or discharge any part of the contract; that assignments of the policy shall not take effect until notice thereof shall be received by the company at its home office; that after two years the policy will be incontestable except for fraud or non-payment of premium. All policies also provide for a 30 or 31 day period of grace after the due date for payment of premiums.

16. Insurable Interest.—In order for an insurance policy to be valid the person taking out the policy must have an insurable interest in the subject matter of the insurance, that is, one who would suffer loss, financial or otherwise, on the happening of the event insured against. However, such a person may name any beneficiary, although companies hesitate to approve applications for life insurance where the named beneficiary has no such interest. The relationship of uncle or aunt and nephew or niece, or that of cousins is generally not sufficient unless other circumstances show an insurable interest.

17. Kinds of Policies.—There are many kinds of life insurance policies. Among the more common are the following:

a. *Ordinary Life Policy* in which premiums are paid during life and in which the face value of the policy is payable at death. This is the simplest and lowest-premium form of life insurance.

b. *Limited Payment Plan.*—The face value of the policy is payable only at death, and premiums are payable only for a limited period of years, or until death if it occurs within that period.

c. *Endowment Policy.*—The insurance company agrees to pay a fixed sum at the end of a fixed term of years, or at death, if it occurs before the expiration of the term, provided a fixed premium is paid during the entire term.

d. *Convertible Term Policy* insures against death for a limited term of years, and may be converted into any other form of insurance, without medical examination, within a stated period.

e. *Income Agreements* may be issued on any of the other plans, with a provision that the face value of the policy is to be paid in monthly installments instead of in a lump sum.

18. General Principles:

a. Unless forbidden by statute, a life insurance policy may be assigned to one having an insurable interest, or to a person without such an interest, provided that the assignment is made in good faith. An assignment is often made for the benefit of creditors, or as security for the payment of a debt.

b. A contract for insurance does not take effect until it has been approved by the company, and the insured has paid the first premium.

c. A general agent can bind his principal even against the express terms of the policy provided that the insured was not negligent in failing to advise himself concerning the terms.

d. A life insurance contract may be void on account of a mistake in issuing it, on account of violation of statute, on account of fraud by either party, or if the policy is contrary to public policy.

e. Words or figures written or printed on the margin or on the back of the policy, or on a slip attached to the policy, must be considered as an integral part of the agreement.

f. The payment of premiums to an agent will bind the company, unless the insured has received notice to the contrary.

g. A policy may be canceled by mutual agreement and the insured is then entitled to the surrender value of the policy or any other nonforfeiture option contained therein.

C. OTHER FORMS OF INSURANCE

19. Accident Insurance may be secured against all kinds of accidents. Upon payment of small premiums, policies may be had insuring against accident from one day to ten years, for any reasonable amount. The rates generally depend upon the occupation of the insured.

20. Marine Insurance.—Marine insurance is governed largely by the same rules that control fire insurance. This form of insurance may include all casualties resulting from unusual or violent actions of the elements, foundering at sea, grounding, collision, fire, perils of war, rests and restraints, jettison, and any other perils, losses, or misfortunes of the sea.

21. Fraternal Insurance.—This is one of the oldest forms of insurance, originating with the ancient secret societies. Originally the societies assumed an obligation to pay sick and death benefits to their members. Today there are numerous societies that issue standard life insurance policies, with a fixed premium rate and a limited amount of insurance payable at death.

22. Industrial Insurance.—Many large business organizations issue this form of insurance for the benefit of their employees. The amounts are usually small and the weekly or monthly payments are deducted from the wages of the insured.

23. Other Kinds of Insurance include employers' liability, public liability, tornado, explosion, health, hospital, automobile, burglary, fraud, insolvency, and loss through bad debts. Almost every kind of risk imaginable may be covered by insurance.

Assignment of Policy of Insurance

Know all men by these presents, that I, ... of the village of ...., for and in consideration of ...., to me in hand paid by .... of the same place, the receipt whereof is hereby acknowledged, have sold, assigned, transferred, and set over, and by these presents do sell, assign, transfer, and set over, unto the said .... the policy of insurance known as policy No. .... of the .... Insurance Company, and all sum and sums of money, interest, benefit, and advantage whatsoever, now due, or hereafter to arise, or to be had or made by virtue thereof, to have and to hold the same unto the said .... and his assigns forever.

In witness whereof, I have hereto affixed my hand this 20th day of June, 19.....
(Acknowledgment.) (Name)

International Law

1. Definitions.—International law is the body of rules designed to govern the conduct of nations toward one another. It includes

customs and usages that have grown up among nations and have become generally accepted by them; and the enactments contained in treaties and conventions. International law is intended to do for nations what the domestic law does for individuals.

2. Treaties.—Much international law is embodied in treaties. A treaty is an agreement between two or more nations to adjust differences or to govern future conduct. Treaties are sometimes made for a limited period of years, but a treaty made by one administration is binding upon the following administration.

3. Representatives.—Ambassadors are the authorized diplomatic representatives of nations. They are immune from civil or criminal liability, but may be tried for crime by their home governments. A consul is a commercial representative sent by one nation to another to aid in the establishment and maintenance of trade relations between the nations, and to look after the interests of the citizens or subjects of his country. He is personally liable for his actions.

4. General Principles. There are certain well established principles of international law, which provide as follows:

a. One nation cannot interfere with the internal affairs of another.

b. Crimes committed on the high seas are under the jurisdiction of the nation under whose flag the ship sails.

c. The property of alien enemies is subject to confiscation.

d. A neutral country must be fair and impartial in its relations with warring nations.

e. It is a violation of international law for a warring nation to fight on, or cross the territory of, a neutral power.

f. It is also a violation of international law to carry the necessary finished goods or materials of warfare to a combatant nation.

g. A fugitive criminal cannot be brought back from another nation unless the terms of the treaty between the two nations so provide.

h. Confiscation is the penalty for attempting to violate a blockade in time of war.

5. Passports.—A passport is a document granted by the government to a citizen, enabling him to travel to other countries. (See Passports.)

Lease

1. Definitions.—The phrase *landlord and tenant* is used to denote the relationship which exists by virtue of a contract expressed or implied between two or more persons for the possession or occupancy of lands or tenements either for a definite period or at will. The *landlord* or *lessor* is the person who lets the land or premises. The *tenant* or *lessee* is the one who occupies the land or premises. The *lease* is the contract between the two.

2. Leases Should Be in Writing.—Leases which are to run for more than a year or which are not to be performed within a year must be in writing, or they are invalid. Leases for a year or less and which can be performed within a year are valid even if not in writing. To avoid misunderstandings, disputes, and possible litigation it is always best, however, that the lease be in writing and signed by both parties, regardless of the length of the term.

3. Leases for Life are those which are terminated by death either of the lessee or of some other person living at the date of the lease. Unless such leases contain covenants to the contrary, the life tenant or the lessee is required to pay all taxes on the premises and keep the same in repair.

4. Leases for Years.—The lessor, unless it is otherwise expressly provided in the lease, is under obligation to see that his tenant's possession is not disturbed by any title paramount to the landlord's. He is not required to make repairs unless he agrees to do so in the lease, nor is there an implied contract on his part that the premises are fit for the purpose for which they are let. He must pay all the taxes regularly levied and assessed against said premises and keep the buildings on said premises insured at his own expense if he desires to carry insurance.

5. Implied Agreement by Tenant.—Where there is no agreement to the contrary, the tenant is bound to take possession of the premises, take ordinary care of the same, keep them in a tenantable condition, and make repairs made necessary by his negligence, but he need not make repairs made necessary by ordinary wear and tear or inevitable accident.

If the premises leased be a farm, he is also required to cultivate the same in the manner required of good husbandry. He must not commit waste, alter buildings or fences, and must surrender up the premises at the end of his term in as good condition as when entered upon originally, ordinary wear and tear excepted. He is not required to pay taxes or keep buildings insured, but must pay the stipulated rent at the time it becomes due by the terms of his lease. If no time is specified in his lease, then the rent is due at the end of the term. He may sublet the premises or assign the lease unless it contains provisions to the contrary.

If he places permanent improvements upon the premises which are so attached to the buildings or land that they cannot be removed without injury to the buildings or land, he has no right to remove the same unless his lease so provides. He may remove trade fixtures, provided they are removed from the premises before the expiration of his lease.

6. COMMON PROVISIONS OF A LEASE.—Most leases provide for the yielding up of the possession of the premises at the end of the term without notice, in as good condition as when they were entered upon by the lessee, loss by fire, inevitable accident, and ordinary wear excepted. There is frequently a provision against subletting or assigning the lease, and a clause stating that in case of non-payment of rent, or failure to perform any of the covenants of the lease, the lessor shall have the right to terminate the lease and recover possession of the premises.

Farm leases usually provide, in addition to the stipulations mentioned above, that the tenant shall keep the fruit and ornamental trees, vines, and shrubbery free from injury by stock, plowing, or otherwise; that the lessee will draw out the manure and spread it on the premises; that no straw shall be sold or removed from the premises during the term or at its termination; that the tenant will keep the buildings and fences in repair, the landlord to furnish necessary material; that the landlord may do fall plowing on the stubble ground after the grain has been removed therefrom, and that he may enter for the purpose of making repairs, viewing the premises, and sowing timothy seed. Sometimes the landlord covenants to make all new fences, to furnish water, and to carry out other provisions which may be inserted in the lease.

7. TERMINATION OF LEASE.—Under the strict rules of the common law the landlord might terminate the lease for non-payment of rent, but in order to do so it was necessary for him to go upon the premises and make a demand for the exact amount of rent due upon the very day that the rent came due, and a failure to do this waived the right to obtain forfeiture. This strict rule of the common law has been modified in nearly all the states so that it is no longer necessary to make a demand for the rent on the day the rent comes due. Instead of this, most of the states provide that before the landlord shall declare a forfeiture, a demand in writing, for the amount of rent due, shall be served upon the tenant, and he be notified that in case he fails to pay the rent within a fixed time, generally five or ten days, the landlord will elect to terminate his lease. In such cases the tenant has until the end of the last day fixed in the notice to pay the rent and prevent the forfeiture. The statutes of the various states also provide that in case of breaches of other agreements contained in the lease, notice of such breaches and intention of the landlord to terminate the lease shall be served upon the tenant.

8. TERMINATION OF TENANCY FROM YEAR TO YEAR AND MONTH TO MONTH.—Where a tenant has a lease for a year, and at the end of his term remains in possession of the property without a new agreement, the law construes this to be a leasing from year to year, and such tenancy at common law could be terminated only by either party's giving the other six months' notice prior to the end of any year. This notice has been changed by a statute in Illinois to sixty days prior to the end of any year, and a shorter time has been fixed in other states. A tenant who has a lease on property for one or more months and who remains on the property after the termination of his lease, is termed a tenant from month to month, and such tenancy can be terminated only by either party giving the other party thirty days' notice. A tenancy from month to month may also be created by agreement. A tenancy at will is one which can be terminated at any time by either party.

9. DEMAND.—It is a general rule, subject to few exceptions, that in order to get possession of property where the original occupancy by the tenant was lawful, either a notice to quit or a demand for possession is necessary on the part of the owner before commencing proceedings to get possession.

10. SECURING POSSESSION.—When a lease has been terminated either by its term or by notice, and the landlord is entitled to possession, the most common method of recovering possession is to commence an action of forcible entry and detainer against the tenant for the possession of the premises. This may be done by filing a complaint and having a summons issued. If the possession of the tenant was lawful at the time of its beginning, the landlord has no right to dispossess him forcibly, and if he does so, it is at his peril. Taking possession by force may subject the landlord to an action for damages. Leases sometimes contain clauses stating that where a forfeiture has taken place the landlord shall have the right to take possession of the premises leased, by force if necessary. Such provisions, however, cannot be enforced and do not justify the landlord in using force. The only legal course for the landlord is to begin an action, obtain a judgment for possession, and have the constable or sheriff put him in legal possession.

11. DISTRESS FOR RENT.—An effective method of collecting rent is by distress warrant. This is a warrant issued by the landlord to some third person, authorizing and empowering such third person to levy said warrant upon any personal property of the tenant for the satisfaction of the rent. A very important advantage of this remedy is that it enables the landlord to seize the personal property of the tenant without delay. This process is of very ancient origin. As used here the term personal property means property other than real estate. The statutes of most of the states

provide for this remedy, and the mode of procedure is generally prescribed by the statute. In general, it is the duty of the officer, as soon as the levy is made, to file with a justice of the peace or with the clerk of the court an inventory of the property levied upon, together with a copy of his warrant, and usually a summons is issued.

12. Time of Levy.—Under the common law the tenant had all of the day on which the rent came due to make payment, and a distress warrant could not be levied until the day after the rent came due. In some states, however, in case the tenant sells or attempts to dispose of the crop grown upon the premises, thereby endangering the landlord's lien for his rent, a distress warrant may be levied before the rent comes due. The person making the levy should be careful not to levy on more property than is necessary in order to satisfy the rent due, otherwise he may be liable to the tenant for making an excessive levy.

13. Landlord's Lien.—Under the common law the landlord had no lien upon the property of the tenant until a distress warrant was actually levied upon the property of the tenant. Most of the states, however, now provide that the landlord shall have a lien upon all the crops grown upon the leased premises until the rent for the year in which said crop was grown has been paid, and this lien is ahead of all other liens, even though another legal claim may have been levied upon such crops. The landlord's lien is paramount until the rent is satisfied. The usual method of enforcing the lien of the landlord is by distress warrant.

The Courts Have Held:—

(a) Unless the tenant makes a specific agreement relieving himself, he is liable for the rent of the building on the land leased, after the building has burned down, just as if he were still occupying it.

(b) When the terms of a lease are in doubt, the courts endeavor to ascertain the intention of the parties from the lease itself and from the circumstances under which it was made.

(c) The term of a lease expiring on a specified day continues through the whole of that day.

(d) When the tenant continues to occupy the premises without the consent of the landlord after the expiration of the lease, the landlord may treat him either as a trespasser or as a tenant for another term.

(e) A lease may be made to take effect at some future date.

(f) A lease must clearly define the property, but no special form or wording is necessary.

(g) Valid leases may be made by minors, married women, corporations, executors, administrators, or trustees, subject to certain restrictions. However, there is always uncertainty in a contract with a minor.

(h) A lease for an unlawful purpose is generally held to be void.

(i) As in other contracts, if the printed and the written parts of a lease do not agree, the written part will usually hold.

(j) The lease of a private house is not a warranty that it is fit to be occupied.

(k) When a landlord agrees to keep the building in repair and fails to do so, the tenant's remedy is to sue for damages. He may not continue to occupy the premises and refuse to pay rent.

(l) When a tenant is evicted he is excused from the payment of rent for any time after his eviction. Any act by the landlord which renders the property unfit for, or impossible of, occupancy is an eviction.

(m) If land is rented on shares the relation of landlord and tenant usually exists even if the rent is to be paid in produce instead of cash.

(n) The landlord is liable for injuries caused by defective stairways, open elevator shafts, or other dangerous conditions which exist in the parts of a rented building which are under his control.

Short Form of Lease

THIS INDENTURE, made this sixth day of April, 19. . . ., between JOHN PARKS, as lessor, and J. B. MOULTON, as lessee, WITNESSETH: That the lessor has this day leased to the lessee the premises known as number 142 Archer Street, in the City of Chicago and State of Illinois, to be occupied by the lessee as a residence (or insert any other purpose for which building is leased) only, for and during the term commencing on the first day of May, 19. . . ., and ending on the thirtieth day of April, 19. . . ., upon the terms and conditions hereinafter set forth; and in consideration of said demise and the covenants and agreements hereinafter set forth, it is covenanted and agreed as follows:

First.—The lessee shall pay to the lessor at the office of the lessor as rent for said leased premises for said term the sum of Six Hundred Dollars ($600.00) payable in advance in equal monthly installments upon the first day of each and every month during the term hereof.

Second.—The lessee has examined said premises prior to and as a condition precedent to his acceptance and the execution hereof and is satisfied with the physical condition thereof, and the lessee's taking possession thereof shall be conclusive evidence of the lessee's receipt thereof in good order and repair, except as otherwise specified herein, and the lessee agrees to keep said premises and the appurtenances thereto in a clean, sightly, and healthy condition and in good repair, and to yield back said premises to the lessor upon the termination of this lease, whether such termination shall occur by expiration of the term hereof or in any other manner whatever, in the same condition of cleanliness, sightliness and repair as at the date of the execution hereof, loss by fire or other casualty, and ordinary wear and tear excepted.

THIRD.—The lessee agrees to pay the water tax charged against said premises when due.

FOURTH.—The lessee agrees to allow the lessor free access to the leased premises for the purpose of examining or exhibiting the same, or making any needful repairs or alterations of said premises which the lessor may see fit to make: also to allow to be placed upon said premises at all times during the term hereof "For Sale" and "To Rent" signs and not to interfere with the same.

FIFTH.—The lessee agrees not to assign this lease, nor sublet said leased premises, or any part thereof, without the written consent of the lessor endorsed hereon.

SIXTH.—In case said leased premises shall be vacated during said term the lessor may take immediate possession thereof for the remainder of the term and in his discretion relet the same and apply the proceeds upon this lease, the lessee to remain liable for the unpaid balance of the rent.

SEVENTH.—The failure of the lessee to perform the foregoing covenants, or any of them, shall constitute a forfeiture of all of the lessee's rights under this lease and the further occupancy by the lessee of said leased premises after such forfeiture shall be deemed and taken as a forcible detainer of such premises by the lessee, and the lessor may, without notice, re-enter and take possession thereof, with or without force, and with or without legal process, evict and dispossess the lessee from and of said leased premises.

EIGHTH.—The foregoing covenants, and the terms and conditions of this lease, shall inure to the benefit of and be binding upon the respective heirs, devisees, personal representatives, successors, and assigns of the parties hereto, except as herein otherwise provided.

Witness the hands and seals of the parties hereto, the day and the year first above written.

JOHN PARKS [SEAL]

....

Lessor

J. B. MOULTON [SEAL]

....

Lessee

Legal Remedies

1. DEFINITION.—As we have already seen, a *remedy* is a legal means employed to enforce a right or redress an injury. For example, suppose A and B enter into a binding contract for the purchase and sale of land. If A, the seller, refuses to live up to his contract, B can sue A for the damages he sustained through A's refusal to sell the land. This would be a *legal remedy*. In a court of equity B could compel A to sell him the land and that would be an *equitable remedy*.

2. STEPS NECESSARY TO SECURE A LEGAL REMEDY.—When one party to a contract has a legal cause of action against the other, he brings suit as follows:

(a) B files a complaint against A, stating the agreement and giving the facts of A's failure to fulfill his contract, and the loss resulting to B from such violation.

(b) A is summoned to appear in court to answer the charge and the court is asked to render judgment against A for the damage resulting from A's refusal to fulfill the contract, and also for the costs.

(c) The case is then tried, and if judgment is rendered against A, the court empowers the sheriff to levy on any property A may have above statutory exemptions, sell it, and turn the proceeds over to B for the damages awarded, returning any surplus to A.

3. VARIOUS KINDS OF ACTIONS.—The common-law forms of action have been abolished in most states, but similar actions are allowed by the codes which have supplanted the common-law forms of action. The following is a list of actions, for the most part designated and defined as they were at common law:

(a) *Complaint* is the general name used in many states for the pleading used to institute any legal action.

(b) *Ejectment* is a form of action to determine the title to land and right of possession.

(c) *Habeas Corpus* is an action or writ used to recover a person's liberty from illegal restraint.

(d) *Libel* is an action brought to collect damages for any malicious writing tending to injure the business or reputation of the plaintiff.

(e) *Mandamus* is an action to compel someone to do some specific thing pertaining to his office or duty.

(f) *Quo warranto* is a writ used to recover an office or a franchise from the person or corporation in possession of it.

(g) *Replevin* is a form of action for the recovery of the possession of specific personal property.

(h) *Slander* is an action to collect damages for malicious defamation by word of mouth.

(i) *Tort* is an action to recover damages for a private or civil wrong or injury arising independent of any contract.

License

1. DEFINITIONS.—A license is a right or permission granted by competent authority to a person, giving him the right to do something which otherwise he would not have the right to do. The *licensor* is the one who grants the license. The *licensee* is the one to whom the license is issued.

2. KINDS OF LICENSES.—Licenses are of almost infinite variety and are issued not only by the federal government, but by states, counties, cities, towns, and villages. They may be issued to manufacturers or

dealers in certain articles, such as tobacco or liquor, to proprietors of amusement places, peddlers, transportation companies, chauffeurs, automobile owners, itinerant merchants, and cab drivers. Such licenses are issued under what is known as the police power of the state.

3. ILLEGAL LICENSES.—Cities sometimes require the payment of a local license by salesmen or canvassers who are taking orders for goods to be shipped from another state at some future time. The supreme court has held such a license requirement as in restraint of interstate commerce, and therefore, illegal.

4. MARRIAGE LICENSES.—All states require a marriage license. The person who performs the ceremony is required by law to note the fact of the marriage on the face of the license, and to return it to the county recorder for record.

Lien

1. A LIEN is a legal claim upon property for the payment of a debt. It is the right to hold possession of property until some claim against the owner has been satisfied.

2. POSSESSION is always necessary to create a lien, except in case of mortgages and judgments and statutory liens such as mechanic's liens. The lien simply permits the holding of the property in question until the debt is satisfied. The property cannot be sold without the consent of the owner, except by order of the court.

3. LAW.—The existence of a lien does not prevent the party entitled to it from collecting the debt or claim by taking it into court.

4. PARTIES ENTITLED TO LIENS.—Warehousemen, carpenters, tailors, dyers, millers, printers, etc., or any persons who perform labor or advance money on property or goods of another, usually have a lien on that property or those goods until all charges are paid.

5. HOTEL KEEPERS have a lien on the baggage of the guests whom they have accommodated.

6. COMMON CARRIERS have a lien on goods carried for transportation charges.

7. AGENTS have a lien on goods of their principals for money advanced.

8. HOW TO HOLD THE LIEN.—Do not give up possession of the property until the debt is paid.

9. REAL PROPERTY.—If the debt is on a house, barn or other real property, file a lien on the whole property, and have it recorded in the county recorder's office. The claim then partakes of the nature of a mortgage.

10. MECHANIC'S LIEN.—Nearly all the states permit liens designed to protect certain classes of individuals, who furnish material and labor for the erection, construction, repair, and improvement of buildings. The method of securing these liens and enforcing them varies so widely in the different states that it is almost impossible to give such a statement as will cover all states. The courts have construed such laws very strictly, and in order to entitle a person to such lien the provisions of the law granting the same must be strictly complied with. Individuals desiring to avail themselves of these statutes should consult a lawyer and have him prepare the necessary papers. The following form is the one commonly in use in the State of Illinois:

Form of Mechanic's Lien

STATE OF ILLINOIS)
) SS.
COUNTY OF DU PAGE)

IN THE OFFICE OF THE CLERK
OF THE
CIRCUIT COURT, DU PAGE COUNTY,
ILLINOIS

Julius Warren)
vs.) Claim for Lien
Martin Smith)

The Claimant, JULIUS WARREN, of the City of Wheaton, County of Du Page, State of Illinois, hereby files a Claim for Lien against Martin Smith of Du Page County, Illinois, and states:

That on the first day of October, 19...., said Martin Smith was the owner of the following described land, to wit: Lot two (2) in Block three (3) of the original town of Hinsdale, in the County of Du Page and State of Illinois.

That on the first day of October, 19...., the Claimant made a contract with said owner to furnish labor and materials for the building to be erected on said land for the sum of Seven Hundred Fifty Dollars ($750.00), and on the 23rd day of October, 19...., completed all work required to be done by said contract.

That said owner is entitled to credits on account thereof totaling $250.00, leaving due, unpaid and owing to the Claimant on account thereof, after allowing all credits, the balance of Five Hundred Dollars ($500.00), for which, with interest, the Claimant claims a lien on said land and improvements.

JULIUS WARREN

....

STATE OF ILLINOIS)
) SS.
COUNTY OF DU PAGE)

Julius Warren, being first duly sworn, on oath deposes and says, That he is the above named Claimant, that he has read the foregoing Claim for Lien, knows the contents thereof, and that all the statements therein contained are true.

JULIUS WARREN

....

Subscribed and sworn to before me
this 1st day of November, 19....

GEORGE JOHNSON

....

Notary Public

(Seal)

Mortgage

1. DEFINITION.—A mortgage is a conveyance of property, either real or personal, given to secure the payment of a debt. When the debt is paid the mortgage becomes void and is released. The person who mortgages his property is called the *mortgagor*. The person to whom the mortgage is given is the *mortgagee*.

2. REQUIREMENTS.—All real estate mortgages must be in writing, and under seal unless the seal has been abolished by statute. The instrument must clearly state the amount of the debt and the day on which it falls due. The property must be clearly described. The mortgage must then be acknowledged before the proper public official and properly recorded in the county records. The mortgagor usually gives a bond or note as evidence of the indebtedness, stating on its face that it is secured by a mortgage of the same date.

3. POSSESSION OF THE PROPERTY generally remains with the mortgagor. The mortgagor also receives all rents and profits from the property, and pays all taxes and other expenses.

4. IMPROVEMENTS TO THE PROPERTY.—If a mortgagor erects buildings on mortgaged land and the mortgage is foreclosed, the mortgagee in taking possession gets all these additions. If the mortgagee erects buildings and the mortgagor thereafter redeems his land, he gets the buildings without paying for them.

5. ASSIGNMENT.—A mortgagee can transfer, sell, or assign his mortgage at any time regardless of the wishes of the mortgagor. On the other hand, if the mortgagor wishes to sell his real estate he must sell subject to the mortgage. In other words, he can do nothing to invalidate the mortgagee's security.

6. INSURANCE.—The property may be insured by both parties. In case of loss by fire the holder of the mortgage can collect the insurance which he had on the property. Practically all mortgages now contain provisions requiring the mortgagor to keep the property properly insured. The insurance policy contains a clause showing the name of the mortgagee or trustee and providing for his protection in case of loss by fire; and the policy itself is usually held by the mortgagee.

7. FORECLOSURE.—A foreclosure is a legal proceeding to sell the property mortgaged to satisfy the debt. If the property is sold to satisfy the debt, the mortgagor has a right to purchase it. The following steps are necessary for a foreclosure:

(a) Application to a court.
(b) A hearing by the court.
(c) Referring to a master in chancery or a referee.
(d) Advertising the property.
(e) Public sale to the highest bidder.
(f) Deeding the property to the purchaser.
(g) Paying the money due to the mortgagee.
(h) Returning any surplus to the mortgagor.

8. REDEMPTION.—Formerly, a mortgagor could redeem his land only before or when the debt became due, but further time is now given. This right to redeem is called a right in equity to redeem, or an equity of redemption. The redemption period varies in different states according to statutes. This right to redeem is considered of so much importance that no party is permitted to lose it even by his own agreement. Even though the mortgagor agrees in the most positive terms to forfeit his equity of redemption, the law disregards such agreement and gives the debtor full time to redeem his property.

9. GENERAL PRINCIPLES:—

a. A mortgage may be made to cover future advances.
b. As the county records are public and may be examined by anyone, the injured party alone is responsible if he buys, or lends money on, a piece of property without first making certain that there are no encumbrances on it.
c. The law assumes that the mortgage contract covers all the agreements concerning the payment of the debt and the return of the property. The courts, therefore, ignore other agreements made at the same time. Later agreements, however, will hold if based on valid consideration.
d. Several mortgages may be made on the same piece of real estate. The one recorded first has the first lien.
e. A creditor cannot compel payment of the mortgage before it is due. Neither can the debtor compel the creditor to accept the payment before it is due.
f. If after a foreclosure there is any deficit due the mortgagee, the mortgagor is still liable. (See CHATTEL MORTGAGE.)
g. A trust deed serves the same purpose as a real estate mortgage but conveys the property to a third party as trustee to hold title for the mortgagee, instead of conveying title direct to the mortgagee himself.

Assignment of Mortgage by Endorsement

KNOW ALL MEN BY THESE PRESENTS, That I, Henry Betzoid, the within named Mortgagee, for a consideration of eight hundred dollars ($800.00), hereby sell, assign, transfer, and set over unto E. B. Newman, his heirs and assigns, the within named instrument of mortgage, and all the real estate, with appurtenances therein mentioned and described, and the promissory note, debts, and claims thereby secured, to have and to hold the same forever, subject to the conditions therein contained.

In witness whereof the party of the first part has hereunto set his hand and seal this third day of March, in the year of our Lord nineteen hundred and .....

Sealed and delivered in the presence of
E. E. Hawthorne
(Most states no longer require this attestation.)

HENRY BETZOID. [Seal]

Form of Release

KNOW ALL MEN BY THESE PRESENTS, That I, James Y. Scammon, of the County of Cook, and State of Illinois, for and in consideration of one dollar, to me in hand paid, and for other good and valuable considerations, the receipt whereof is hereby confessed, do hereby grant, bargain, remise, convey, release, and quitclaim unto Samuel P. Smith and Sarah E. Smith, of the County of Du Page and State of Illinois, all the right, title, interest, claim, or demand whatsoever I may have acquired in, through or by a certain indenture or mortgage deed, bearing date the first day of January, A.D. 19...., and recorded in the recorder's office of Du Page County, Illinois, in book 25 of mortgages, page 100, in and to the premises situated in the ..... of ......, in said county of .... and in said mortgage deed described as follows, to wit: [description] and which said deed was made to secure two certain promissory notes, bearing even date with said deed, for the sum of twenty-five hundred dollars.

Witness my hand and seal this 28th day of February, A.D. 19.....

JAMES Y. SCAMMON. [Seal]

10. A TRUST DEED is a deed to a piece of real estate held by a third party in trust as security for a note. This deed is very extensively used because it takes the place of a mortgage deed and renders the note negotiable. States frequently have statutory forms for trust deeds, and where such forms exist it is advisable to use them.

Form of Trust Deed

This deed, made this .... day of ...., 19...., between .... of ...., county of .... and state of ...., of the one part, and .... of ...., and .... of ...., of the other part, witnesseth, that the party of the first part doth grant unto the parties of the second part the following property, to wit:

(Insert description of property)

in trust, to secure to .... of ...., in the state of .... the payment of ..... dollars in .... years from this date, with interest at .... per cent per annum thereon, according to a promissory note made by the party of the first part to said .... for said sum.

In event that default shall be made in the payment of the above-mentioned sum as it becomes due and payable, then the trustees, or either of them, on being required so to do by ...., his executors, administrators, or assigns, shall sell the property hereby conveyed. And it is covenanted and agreed between the parties aforesaid that in case of a sale the same shall be made after first advertising the time, place, and terms thereof for ...... days in some newspaper published in the said county of ...., and upon the following terms, to wit: for cash as to so much of the proceeds as may be necessary to defray the expenses of executing this trust, the fees for drawing and recording this deed, if then unpaid, and to discharge the amount of money then payable upon said note; and if there be any residue of such purchase money, the same shall be made payable at such time, and be secured in such manner, as ...., his executors, administrators, or assigns, shall prescribe and direct, or in case of his or their failure to give such direction, at such time and in such manner as the trustees, or either of them, shall think fit. The party of the first part covenants to pay all taxes, assessments, dues, and charges upon the said property hereby conveyed so long as he or his heirs or assigns shall hold the same, and hereby waives the benefit of all homestead exemptions as to the debt secured by this deed.

If no default shall be made in the payment of the above-mentioned debt, then, upon the request of the party of the first part, a good and sufficient deed of release shall be executed to him at his own proper costs.

Witness, the hand .... and seal .... of said Grantor this ...... day of ...., A.D., 19.....

.... [Seal]
.... [Seal]

Municipal Corporations

1. DEFINITION.—A municipal corporation is a corporation formed to carry on the work of government in a town or city. Its charter is granted by the State and it possesses only such powers as the State confers upon it, and no others.

2. POWERS.—A city government is usually given the power:

a. to make its own laws or ordinances with reference to matters over which its charter gives it jurisdiction,
b. to enforce its laws,
c. to control all matters and things within its corporate boundaries within the limits fixed by its charter,
d. to issue bonds.

3. OFFICERS OF A MUNICIPAL CORPORATION.—The mayor is usually the chief executive, the Board of Aldermen the lawmaking body, of a municipality. The titles of these officers vary widely, however, in the different states. Under the commission form of government the above offices are held by a commission of three or five men, who have complete charge of the business of city government. The judicial power is usually vested in the

police magistrate's court, or in larger cities in the municipal court. These are courts of limited jurisdiction only, however, and their jurisdiction does not supersede or conflict with that of the courts of the county in which they are situated.

4. WRONGFUL ACTS OF OFFICERS.—The city is not responsible for damage for injuries to persons or property caused in the execution of a governmental duty. But what is considered a governmental duty is a question that has been the source of much litigation. The city is not liable for false arrest, false imprisonment, or assaults by police officers. If any wrongful act is committed by an officer while acting in his official capacity, he is liable personally.

5. THE CITY'S DUTY.—It is the duty of the city government to provide and maintain safe and passable streets and highways, maintain police and fire protection, and provide for the general safety and welfare of its citizens.

6. LIABILITY.—If the city fails to maintain safe and passable streets, the city is liable for damages resulting to those rightfully upon the streets, provided the city had notice that the streets were unsafe and not passable, and failed to exercise reasonable care to make the streets safe. It is almost universally held that a city is not liable for loss or injury resulting from failure to maintain proper police and fire protection.

7. POLICE POWER OF CITIES.—The police power of a city extends to the city limits and a reasonable distance beyond the city limits in certain instances. The police magistrate, sometimes called the recorder, sits in a court having jurisdiction equal to that of a justice of the peace. The police magistrate and the police officers are bound to enforce the laws of the city, called ordinances. An officer may arrest a person:

a. When a wrongful act is committed in his presence.
b. Upon a valid warrant.
c. Upon suspicion, when well grounded and in good faith, no warrant then being necessary.

8. SCHOOLS.—The schools of a city are usually controlled by a board of education. This board has control and supervision over teachers, students, buildings, and all other matters pertaining to public education.

9. PUBLIC SERVICE CORPORATIONS.—Any corporation furnishing the public as a whole a service or commodity is called a public service corporation. Its activities are as a rule controlled and supervised by a public service commission having the power to fix prices and regulate many of the activities of the corporations that affect the public.

Negotiable Instruments

1. DEFINITION.—A *negotiable instrument* is any paper that may be transferred by endorsement or delivery in such a way as to give the person receiving it the right to bring a suit thereon in his own name. The person who promises to pay is called the *maker* or *drawer*, and the one to whom he promises is called the *payee*.

2. KINDS OF NEGOTIABLE INSTRUMENTS.—Almost every written contract or agreement to pay money is negotiable, in the sense that the owner can sell it to a third person who can enforce it against the maker. However, in the more strict sense of the word there are three common forms of negotiable paper, namely, checks, notes, and bills of exchange or drafts.

3. FORM OF NEGOTIABLE INSTRUMENTS.—The law does not require negotiable instruments to be in any prescribed form. However, certain things are necessary in all checks, notes, or bills of exchange to make them negotiable:

a. The instrument must be in writing.
b. It must be signed by the maker or drawer.
c. It must contain a promise or order to pay.
d. The promise or order must be unconditional.
e. The promise or order must be a promise or order to pay a certain sum in money.
f. The instrument must be payable on demand or at a fixed or determinable time in the future.
g. The instrument must be payable to the order of some person, or to bearer.
h. If the instrument is addressed to a drawee, as would be the case if it were a bill of exchange or draft, the drawee must be named or otherwise indicated in the instrument with reasonable certainty.

4. CONSIDERATION.—While it is not always necessary to express any consideration in negotiable paper, it is safer to do so. When an instrument is in the hands of an innocent third party, the law assumes a valuable consideration. The words "for value received" usually appear on promissory notes.

5. PROTEST.—A protest of a note, check, or draft is a formal statement by a notary public that the paper was presented for payment and was refused. The costs are added to the instrument.

6. NEGOTIABILITY.—The words "to bearer," or "to the order of," or words of like effect, render a paper negotiable. Any person capable of making a contract is capable of making a negotiable instrument. A person who receives a negotiable instrument under the conditions hereinafter mentioned becomes

what is known as a "holder in due course," and certain defenses which might have been raised against the original holder cannot be raised against him. He must have taken the instrument under the following conditions: (1) The instrument must be complete and regular on its face. (2) It must not have been overdue, and the holder must not have known it was previously dishonored if such were the fact. (3) He must have taken it in good faith and paid value for it. (4) At the time he took it he must have had no notice of any infirmity in the instrument or defect in the title of the person negotiating it to him.

A. NOTES

7. Definitions.—A *note* is a simple written promise to pay a certain sum at a certain time to a person named therein. An *individual promissory note* is a note in which one party promises to pay another a certain sum of money at a specified time. A *joint promissory note* is the same as an individual note except that it is signed by two or more parties, all of whom are liable jointly but not severally. In a *joint and several promissory note* two or more parties severally and separately agree to pay a certain sum at a specified time, and each signer is responsible for the whole amount. Statutes in many states provide that all joint obligations shall be held to be joint and several.

8. Transferring Notes.—The following rules govern the transferring of notes:

a. Instruments payable to bearer may be transferred by delivery, payable to order by endorsement.
b. An endorser is a person who writes his name on the back of a note or other instrument.
c. Endorsement in blank is an endorsement which does not mention the name of the person in whose favor it is made.
d. The endorser is liable for the payment of a note if the maker fails to meet it and the endorser is properly notified.
e. An endorser who is compelled to pay a note has a claim against the maker and against each endorser whose name appears above his own.
f. An endorser to whose order a note is drawn or endorsed can transfer it without becoming liable for its payment by writing the words "without recourse" over his signature on the back.

9. Collecting Notes.—

a. A note destroyed by mistake or accident can be collected upon proof of loss.
b. Money paid by mistake must be refunded.
c. If no time is specified the note is payable on demand.
d. The day of maturity is the day on which a note becomes legally due.
e. In finding the day of maturity, actual days must be counted if the note falls due a specific number of days after the day on which it was drawn, but months are counted when the note falls due a specific number of months after the day on which it was drawn.
f. Negotiable paper to bearer or endorsed in blank, which has been lost or stolen, cannot be collected by the finder or thief, but a holder who innocently receives it in good faith before maturity for value received can hold it against the owner's claims.
g. A note made in one state, payable in another, must be governed by the laws of that state in which it is to be paid.
h. Demand for payment of a note must be made upon the day of maturity and at the place named. If no place is specified, it is payable at the maker's place of business or at his residence. In most of the states, when a note falls due on a Sunday or legal holiday, by statute the maker is given until the following day to pay the same.
i. An extension of the time of a note by the holder, releases sureties and endorsers, unless consent to such extension has been given by the endorsers or sureties.
j. Upon presentment for payment and refusal by the maker at maturity, in order to hold the endorser, notice of default must be given to the endorser immediately.

10. Payment of Notes.—All the parties who have endorsed a note are liable for the full amount, but only one satisfaction can be recovered. In certain cases notes are unenforceable, especially when held by the original payee. Among such cases are the following:

a. A note given by one who is not of age, unless the minor ratified it after becoming of age.
b. A note made by an intoxicated person.
c. A note given by one who cannot write, and not witnessed at the time.
d. A note obtained by duress, by putting the maker in fear of illegal imprisonment, or by threats that would lead an ordinary person to fear injury to his person, his reputation, or his property.
e. A note obtained by fraud.
f. A note given for illegal consideration.
g. One who receives a note knowing it to have defects has no better right to collect it than the one from whom he received it.

h. If a person at the time of taking a note has notice that it is void because of fraud or for any other reason, he cannot collect it.

Forms of Note

Negotiable by Endorsement

$375.00 Naperville, Ill., Oct. 7, 19. . . ,

For value received, one year after date I promise to pay to the order of J. L. Nichols the sum of Three Hundred and Seventy-Five Dollars with interest at six per cent from date until paid.

J. R. PRICE.

Negotiable without Endorsement

$100.00 Cleveland, O., Aug. 1, 19. . . . .

Ninety days after date I promise to pay to bearer, One Hundred Dollars, value received.

E. M. KECK.

Not Negotiable

$100.00 Chicago, Ill., Dec. 10, 19. . . . .

Sixty days after date I promise to pay Geo. C. Dixon One Hundred Dollars, value received.

EUGENE LANSING.

A Corporation Note

$200.00 Augusta, Me., Mar. 18, 19. . . . .

Nine months after date, the Granite Stone Company, a corporation, promises to pay S. A. Chilton, or order, Two Hundred Dollars, with interest at six per cent. Value received.

Attest: I. K. Dawes, Secretary.

GRANITE STONE COMPANY.
O. R. Phillips, President

N.B.—If corporation notes are drawn and signed in the above manner, the officers are not personally liable.

Collateral Note

$500.00 Mendota, Tex., Sept. 25, 19. . . . .

Sixty days after date, for value received, I promise to pay to the order of T. J. Boyd, the sum of Five Hundred Dollars, with interest at the rate of six per cent per annum after date, having deposited United States Bonds of the face value of Six Hundred Dollars, which I authorize the holder of this Note, upon the non-performance of this promise at maturity, to sell, at public or private sale, without further notice, and to apply proceeds, or as much thereof as may be necessary to the payment of this Note, and all necessary expenses and charges, holding myself responsible for any deficiency.

W. W. STRATTON.

Judgment Note

$2,000.00 Philadelphia, Pa., Jan. 4, 19. . . . .

Six months after date, for value received, I promise to pay to the order of J. W. Krasley Two Thousand Dollars, with interest at the rate of 6 per cent per annum, after maturity, until paid.

And to secure the payment of said amount I hereby authorize any attorney of any court of record to appear for me in such court, in term time or vacation, at any time after maturity, to waive a jury trial and confess judgment, without process, in favor of the holder of the note, for such amount as may appear to be paid thereon, together with costs and five per centum attorney's fees, and to waive and release all errors which may intervene on any such proceedings, and consent to immediate execution upon such judgment; hereby ratifying and confirming all my said attorney may do by virtue hereof.

GEORGE W. BAIRD.

Payable at Bank

$440.00 Chicago, Ill., Oct. 10, 19. . . . .

Two years after date, for value received, I promise to pay T. M. Culver, or order, Four Hundred Forty Dollars at Second National Bank, with interest at six per cent per annum.

CHARLES HEARN.

On Demand

$25.67 Kansas City, Mo., Oct. 12, 19. . . .

On demand I promise to pay to the order of J. T. Connor, Twenty-Five 67-100 Dollars. Value received, with interest at six per cent.

A. H. SIMPSON.

N.B.—This note answers the same purpose as a note written one day after date.

Joint Note

$200.00 Lisle, Ill., Jan. 1, 19. . . . .

One year from date, we promise to pay D. F. Shaw, or order, Two Hundred Dollars. Value received. Interest at six per cent.

J. LEWIS BEAN.
B. A. WHITE.

Joint and Several Note

$2,000.00 Ottawa, Ont., Nov. 25, 19. . . . .

Ten months after date, we, or either of us, promise to pay Maggie Patterson Two Thousand Dollars, value received. Interest at five per cent.

J. C. HARDY.
R. E. WOOD.

Principal and Surety Note

New York, N.Y., Sept. 21, 19. . . . .

For value received, on or before July 27, 19. . . ., I promise to pay to the order of John Jackson, Six Hundred Dollars. Interest at five per cent.

W. J. SHAW, Principal.
THOS. RODDEN, Surety.

N.B.—The general form of a principal and surety note is for the principal to properly sign the note and the surety to endorse it.

A Note by One Who Cannot Write

$49.50 Cleveland, Ohio, Mar. 20, 19. . . . .

One year after date, I promise to pay N. Bowker, or order, Forty-Nine 50-100 Dollars, with interest at five per cent. Value received.

H. A. Starr. Witness. his
JOHN x ROURKE.
mark

N.B.—A note made by a person who cannot write should always be witnessed by a disinterested person.

My Own Order

New Orleans, La., July 20, 19.....

For value received, I promise to pay, sixty days after date, to my own order, Two Hundred Dollars, with interest at eight per cent.

A. S. BARNARD.

N.B.—A note may be drawn to the maker's own order, with his endorsement in favor of the creditor.

Note Secured by a Mortgage

$1,000.00 Chicago, Ill., April 15, 19.....

Six months after date I promise to pay to John Williams $1,000.00 with interest at six per cent.

This note is secured by a mortgage of even date herewith from Robert Jones to John Williams.

ROBERT JONES.

B. CHECKS

11. DEFINITIONS.—A check is an order drawn upon a bank, payable on demand. The person who writes the check is the *drawer*, the bank on which the check is drawn is called the *drawee*, the person to whom the check is made payable is called the *payee*.

12. SIGNATURE.—A check must be properly signed by the drawer or his duly authorized agent. A signature made on behalf of the drawer by another person is valid if authorized. It should, of course, be written in ink, but a signature made with a pencil or rubber stamp is valid if intended as a signature.

13. PRESENTATION.—A check must be presented for payment within a reasonable time after its issue, or the drawer will be discharged from liability thereon to the extent of the loss caused by the delay; and it is generally held that one day after the receipt of the check is a reasonable time to present or forward the same for presentation.

14. THE AGREEMENT TO PAY is between the bank and the depositor. For this reason a check, of itself, does not operate as an assignment of any part of the funds to the credit of the drawer with the bank. Consequently, should the bank refuse to pay the check, the holder cannot bring action against the bank, unless or until the bank has accepted or certified the check. On the other hand, if the bank fails to fulfill its contract with the depositor he has a just cause of action against the bank. Should the bank refuse to honor a customer's check owing to an employee's mistake in bookkeeping, the bank could be held responsible for any loss resulting therefrom.

15. CERTIFYING A CHECK.—A certification of a check by the bank is equivalent to an acceptance, and discharges the drawer and all the endorsers preceding the holder who secures the certification. When a check is presented to a bank for this purpose, the bank charges the drawer's account with the amount, so that as far as the drawer and the bank are concerned the check has actually been paid. Therefore, if a certified check is not presented at his bank for payment and is returned to the drawer, it should not be destroyed but should be redeposited as cash.

16. STOPPING PAYMENT.—The drawer of the check may order the bank to stop payment on a check before it is presented. The bank is required to follow these instructions and is liable for any loss resulting from failure to do so.

17. FORGED CHECKS.—The law insists that the banker exercise the greatest care in paying the checks of customers. If the signature has been forged or the amount of the check altered, the bank is liable for any improper payment. The drawer of the check must also use every precaution to prevent alterations. He should write in a way to avoid confusing the banker who is to pay the check. The bank is not responsible for any loss caused by negligence on the part of the drawer in making out the check.

18. VITAL POINTS ON CHECKS.—A check is not due until presented. It is negotiable. It has no days of grace. Giving a check is not payment of an indebtedness, unless the check is paid, or unless it is accepted as payment. The death of the drawer of the check before it is presented to the bank renders the check null and void. The amount of the check should always be written out in words as well as in figures. If a raised check is paid by the bank, the bank can charge the depositor only the amount for which he drew the check, unless the raising of the check was made possible by the carelessness of the drawer. In that case the drawer would be responsible for the loss.

If you write a check for a stranger who needs identification at your bank, have him endorse the check in your presence and under his indorsement write "Endorsement above guaranteed," signing your name. He can then usually cash the check without further identification, by signing his name again in the presence of the banker.

C. DRAFTS

19. DEFINITION.—A *draft* is a written order by one person on another for the payment of a specified sum of money to a designated third person. The one who writes the draft is called the *drawer*, the one on whom it is written, the *drawee*, and the one to whom it is to be paid, the *payee*.

20. KINDS OF DRAFTS.—Drafts may be made payable at sight, on demand, at a cer-

tain time after date, or after sight. A *sight draft* or *demand draft* is drawn by one person on another and is payable when presented. *Time drafts* are similar to sight drafts, but are payable a certain number of days after presentation. A *Bill of Exchange* is an unconditional order in writing addressed by one person to another, signed by the person giving it, requiring the person to whom it is addressed to pay on demand or at a fixed or determinable future time a certain sum of money to order or to bearer. The term includes drafts and checks.

21. ACCEPTANCE.—Sight and demand drafts are presented for payment only. Time drafts require acceptance by the party against whom they are drawn in order to bind him. The usual method of acceptance is to write across the face of the draft in red ink the word "accepted," followed by the date and the signature of the drawee. Should the person on whom the draft is drawn die before it was accepted, it should be presented to his legal representative for acceptance.

22. GENERAL PRINCIPLES:—

a. When either acceptance or payment is refused, the draft may be protested like any note or check.

b. Drafts are negotiable both before and after acceptance.

Forms of Draft

Bank Draft

$100. State of Illinois, May 10, 19.....
The First National Bank of Naperville. Pay to the order of F. A. Lueben, One Hundred Dollars.
To Union National Bank. W. L. HETZ, Cashier.
Chicago, Ill.

Demand Draft

$100. Troy Grove, Ill., Aug. 1, 19.....
On demand pay to the order of Frank Myers at the Mendota First National Bank, One Hundred Dollars.
Value received.
To Charles Lerch, A. S. HUDSON.
Mendota, Ill.

Sight Draft

$500. Naperville, Tenn., July 10, 19.....
At sight pay to the order of C. Parman, Five Hundred Dollars, and charge to the account of
To Jessee Lerch, H. H. ZEMMER.
Meriden, Ill.

Time Draft

$450.30 Ottawa, Fla., July 5, 19.....
Ten days from date pay to J. L. Nichols, or order, Four Hundred Fifty 30-100 Dollars. Value received.
To Alvin Brown, C. E. LAMALE.
Ottawa, Fla.

D. ENDORSEMENTS

23. DEFINITION.—An endorsement is a writing on the back of a negotiable instrument for the purpose of transferring the title or ownership from one person to another. The writing may be in pen or pencil upon any part of the instrument or upon a paper attached thereto. It consists ordinarily of the payee's signature and that of other holders, if any.

24. HOW TO ENDORSE.—Write across the back of the paper (not lengthwise) near the left end. Always endorse a check or note exactly as your name appears on the face. If the check is payable to F. Black, do not write Frank Black. If your name is misspelled, endorse first as it appears on the face and then write your correct signature underneath; no written explanation is necessary; banks are familiar with this practice. The same rules govern the endorsement of notes, drafts, and other written instruments. A check or other instrument may be endorsed and title thereby transferred many times. Each endorser is liable to those who endorse after him.

25. KINDS OF ENDORSEMENTS:—

An *endorsement in blank* is made when the payee simply signs his name in the proper place (across the left end of the reverse) without any statement of conditions. Such a note or check is negotiable without further endorsement. Endorsement in blank is commonly used when a check is deposited or cashed at a bank. It should not be used when there is danger of the check's being lost or stolen.

An *endorsement in full* or *special endorsement* consists of writing the name of the person to whom, or to whose order, the money is to be paid, followed by the payee's signature. For example: "Pay to F. Black or order, J. Jones"; when endorsed in this form, the check cannot be cashed until F. Black endorses it.

In a *qualified endorsement* the endorser relieves himself of any liability in connection with the instrument, by writing above his signature the words "Without recourse"; thus, "Without recourse, J. Jones."

A *restrictive endorsement* limits the payment of the note, bill, or check. The endorser writes "pay to F. Black only," or "for deposit in the First National Bank," signing his name underneath. A check or other instrument so endorsed cannot be further negotiated by the person or bank receiving it. Restrictive endorsement is a wise precaution when there is danger of a negotiable instrument being lost or stolen after endorsement.

A *conditional endorsement* is one directing payment only upon the performance of a certain condition. The endorser's liability is thereby limited. For example, "Pay to the order of F. Black unless he previously receives the amount from my agent, J. Jones." Neither the original character of the note nor its negotiability is affected by such an endorsement. It may affect, however, the title of the one to whom it is transferred.

Endorsement by an agent is made in the following form: "J. Jones, by H. Smith, his agent." In this manner the agent endorses for his principal.

In a *guaranteed endorsement* one party guarantees payment on a note for another party. He writes above his signature "I hereby guarantee payment of this note," or words of like effect. He is then absolutely liable for the amount due by the terms of the note in case the maker fails to pay. In effect, he becomes a co-maker.

E. "IOU"

26. An IOU is not a promissory note, and is not negotiable. It is evidence of a debt due by virtue of a previous contract. The following is an example:

Chicago, Ill., June 4, 1940

Mr. A. O. Rogers,
IOU Sixty Dollars ($60.00).

W. G. Allen.

F. DUE BILLS

27. A due bill is not payable to order, nor is it assignable by mere endorsement. It is simply the acknowledgment of a debt; yet it may be transferred. It may be payable in money, in merchandise, or in services.

Due bills do not draw interest unless so specified.

$125.00 Chicago, Aug. 14, 19.....

Due Henry Harrington, for value received, One Hundred and Twenty-Five dollars with interest at six per cent.

Q. Yinzer.

On Demand

$250.00 Naperville, Ill., July 1, 19.....

Due E. E. Miller, on demand, Two Hundred Fifty Dollars in goods from my store, for value received.

A. T. Hanson.

In Merchandise

$1,000.00 Lincoln, Neb., Nov. 1, 19.....

Due R. William, One Thousand Dollars, payable in wheat at market price, on the first day of January, 19.....

Charles Schuerer.

G. RECEIPTS

28. A receipt is an acknowledgment in writing that a certain sum of money or thing has been received by the party giving and signing the same.

29. A complete receipt requires the following statements: that a payment has been received; the date of the payment; the amount of article received; from whom received, and if for another, on whose behalf payment is made; to what debt or purpose it is to be applied; the signature of the person receiving the property, and if for another, on whose behalf it was received.

30. If the giving and taking of receipts were more generally practiced in business transactions, less trouble, fewer lawsuits, and the saving of thousands of dollars would result.

31. If payment is made upon account, upon a special debt, or in full, it should be so stated in the receipt.

32. When an agent signs a receipt, he should sign his principal's name and then write his name underneath as agent.

33. It is not necessary to take a receipt on paying a note, draft, or other instrument indorsed by the payee, because the instrument itself becomes a receipt.

34. If a receipt is obtained through fraud, or given under error or mistake, it is void.

Receipt for Payment on Account

$250.00 Naperville, Ill., July 6, 19.....

Received of J. L. Nichols, Two Hundred and Fifty Dollars on account.

J. K. Rohmer.

Receipt for Settlement of an Account

Joliet, Ill., March 20, 19.....

Received of Thomas Rourke, Two Hundred and Twenty 14-100 Dollars, in full settlement of account to date.

C. S. Selby.

Receipt in Full of All Demands

Meriden, Conn., Jan. 14, 19.....

Received of C. F. Hetche, One Thousand Dollars, in full of all demands to date.

O. N. Obright.

Receipt for a Particular Bill

Brooklyn, N.Y., Aug. 1, 19.....

Received of Morris Cliggitt, Four Hundred Dollars, in payment for a bill of Merchandise.

R. Zachman.

Receipt for Rent

Snyder, Tex., Mar. 20, 19.....

Received of L. Heininger, Forty Dollars in full for one month's rent, for month ending April 20, 19...., for residence at 44 Olive Street.

J. Lewis Bean.

Receipt for a Note

Received, Buffalo, March 6, 19...., from Messrs. Taylor & Co., their note of this date, at three months, our favor, for Twelve Hundred and

Twenty Dollars; which, when paid, will be in full of account rendered to 1st instant.

$1,220.00. C. H. OLIVER.

Receipt for Services

Lemont, Ill., July 23, 19.....

Received of Samuel Lynn, Forty-four Dollars, in full for services to date.

$44.00 DANIEL FURBUSH.

Receipt for Money Advanced on a Contract

$500.00 Chicago, Ill., May 10, 19.....

Received of Arthur Kahl the sum of Five Hundred Dollars, part payment on contract to build for him a house at No. 1439 Perry St., Chicago.

CARL DIENST.

Receipt for Interest Due on a Mortgage

$75.00 Chicago, August 1, 19.....

Received of G. A. Caton, Seventy-five Dollars, in full of six months' interest due this day, on his note to me dated August 1st, 19...., for Two Thousand Five Hundred Dollars, secured by mortgage on property at 1430 Maple Street, Chicago.

EDWARD TRONT.

Notaries Public

1. THE OFFICE AND ITS FUNCTIONS.—The office of notary public as it exists in the several states today is the outgrowth of various practices traceable to the Roman Empire. Anciently merely a scribe, the power and duties of the notary have been amplified by legislative enactments to meet the needs of changing conditions and a growing civilization. His commission is granted upon representation of his capacity and integrity. In accepting office the notary contracts the obligation to fill it intelligently and honestly.

2. DEFINITION.—A notary public is a state officer whose function is to attest and certify, by his hand and official seal, various documents, in order to give them authenticity in other jurisdictions, to take acknowledgments of deeds and other conveyances and instruments, and to certify the same; and to perform other official acts, the power to do which is conferred by statutory enactment.

3. CLASSIFICATION OF FUNCTIONS.—As a general rule the functions of a notary are ministerial, not judicial. They are confined to the civil, as distinguished from the criminal, branch of the law, and consist for the most part in protesting inland and foreign bills of exchange and promissory notes, authenticating their dishonor by the refusal of the drawee or payee to accept or pay them on presentation or when due; the authentication of transfers or conveyances of property, and other documents required by law to be authenticated; administering oaths and affirmations as to correctness of accounts; the taking of depositions under the rules and instructions of the courts when cases are pending; and the taking of affidavits as to the truth of statements made in legal papers for use in proceedings before courts of civil or maritime jurisdiction.

4. DEFINITION OF FUNCTIONS.—The term *protest* as applied to commercial paper means the taking of such steps as are required to charge or fix liability upon one secondarily liable, such as an endorser. As applied to the notarial act, it means a declaration made in writing by a notary public after doing the acts certified, that the bill or note to which it relates was, on the day it became due, presented for payment, and that payment was refused. To *authenticate* a document means for a notary to certify under his hand and seal of office with a notice of the date and in most states the expiration of his commission, such facts as the law requires to give the document operative effect. A *deposition* is the testimony of a witness taken down in writing, under oath or affirmation before a notary public, and usually subscribed by the witness, pursuant to special authority granted by a court after notice to the adverse party. It is authenticated by the notary. An *affidavit* is a voluntary statement, formally reduced to writing and sworn to or affirmed and subscribed before a notary public. An *acknowledgment* is an oral declaration or admission made by one who has executed a document, made before a notary public or other officer authorized by law to take acknowledgments, to the effect that the execution is his act and deed.

The written certificate endorsed on the document by the officer taking the acknowledgment, certifying to the facts of the same, is sometimes referred to as "an acknowledgment." The function of an acknowledgment is two-fold—to authorize the document to be given in evidence without further proof of its execution, and to entitle it to be recorded. A notary's *certificate of acknowledgment* is not part of its execution, but only evidence of it. At least six essential facts must appear in a certificate of acknowledgment: (1) the designation of the officer making the certificate; (2) the name of the person making the acknowledgment, and that he or she personally appeared before the officer; (3) that there was an acknowledgment; (4) that the person who made the acknowledgment was identified as the one who executed the instrument; (5) that such identity was personally known or proved by the officer taking the acknowledgment; (6) the day and year when the acknowledgment was made. An *oath* is an outward pledge, given by the person taking it, that his attestation or promise is made under an immediate sense of his responsibility to God.

5. FORM AND MANNER OF ADMINISTERING

OATHS, AFFIDAVITS, AND AFFIRMATIONS.—The customary and approved manner of administering an oath or taking an affidavit is to have the person making the same raise his hand and swear by the everliving God. There should be at least some manifestation that the officer and the person taking the oath understand the nature of their undertaking; a mere mental process is not sufficient. In many states the form and manner of taking an oath are prescribed by law.

Any person who desires may in lieu of an oath or affidavit take and subscribe or assent to an affirmation, which is administered by the officer repeating the words, "You do solemnly, sincerely and truly declare and affirm that," etc., "and so you do affirm." It is not unusual to ask the question, "Do you swear or affirm" rather than to wait for the deponent to express his desire. A strict and solemn compliance with these forms is important. Any person who willfully and falsely swears or affirms to any material matter is guilty of perjury. The average citizen is inclined to attach only such importance and solemnity to these acts as the officer administering them shows. To perform these acts in a perfunctory manner is to deprive them of their intended value, and in some instances to encourage perjury.

6. FORM OF AFFIDAVIT OR AFFIRMATION:—

State of Pennsylvania,)
) SS.
County of Philadelphia.)

Allen B. White, being duly sworn (or affirmed), according to law, deposes and says (or in case of affirmation, in lieu of "deposes and says" insert "affirms and declares") that he is the person who executed the foregoing instrument (or if by an officer or agent of a corporation, insert in lieu of "he is the person," etc., the following: "he is the [name of office] of the [name of corporation] above named, that he has authority from it to make this affidavit [or affirmation] in its behalf); and that the facts therein set forth are true to the best of his (add "and its" where made by officer or agent for corporation) knowledge, information and belief.

Sworn (or affirmed) and subscribed before me this 22nd
day of November, A.D. 19....

ALLEN B. WHITE.

[Seal] C. D. BLACK.
Stamp com. expires.

7. FORM OF ACKNOWLEDGMENT RECOMMENDED BY AMERICAN BAR ASSOCIATION—BY SINGLE PERSON OR BY HUSBAND AND WIFE:—

STATE OF ....)
SS.
COUNTY OF ....)

On this .... day of ...., 19...., before me, the subscriber (here insert title of officer), personally appeared A. B. (and C. B., his wife, if so), to me known to be the person (or persons) described in and who executed the foregoing instrument, and acknowledged that he (she or they) executed the same as his (her or their) free act and deed.

[Seal] (Signature and title), etc.

Parent and Child

1. ANCIENT AUTHORITY.—In past ages the father was by custom considered an absolute monarch of the home. In the oriental countries of today the same custom still prevails; modern progress and modern ideas, however, have changed old customs, and the authority of the parent in civilized countries has been considerably limited by law.

2. RIGHTS OF PARENTS.—The parent has the right of control over his child, and has all reasonable authority to enforce obedience. As long as the parent treats his child properly, no one has a right to interfere with his authority, or take the child away and retain him against the wishes of the parent.

3. A RUNAWAY CHILD.—A child has no right to leave home without permission of the parent, and should a child run away he can be brought back by force. If relatives or other parties keep him and refuse to give him up, the parent by legal process can obtain possession of his child, unless it can be shown that the father is brutal, or is not a fit person, on account of drunkenness or other causes, to take proper care of his child.

4. PUNISHMENT OF CHILDREN.—A parent has a right to punish his minor child, provided he is not guilty of cruelty or brutality, which are crimes punishable by severe legal penalties. The parent must be reasonable in his punishment, and in no way injure the health of the child.

5. RIGHTS TO EARNINGS.—A parent is entitled to all the earnings of his minor child. If the child should refuse to turn over his earnings to the parent, the employer of the child may be notified, and be compelled to pay the parent only.

6. SPECIAL RIGHTS.—The parent may, however, free his child from all obligations to himself and allow the child to collect his own wages for himself. When a parent thus makes public such a declaration, he cannot thereafter collect the child's wages.

7. THE PROPERTY OF THE CHILD.—A parent may control the earnings of the child, yet he has no control of the property belonging to the child, acquired either by gift or by legacy, or in any other way. If a parent should appropriate his child's property, it would be just as criminal in the eyes of the law as stealing.

8. PARENT'S OBLIGATION TO SUPPORT.—Parents are legally held for the support of their minor children. The fact that a child

has property does not relieve the parent from the support of his child; he, however, can apply to court and get permission to use a part, or all, of the income of the property for the child's support.

9. ILLEGITIMATE CHILDREN.—It is a parent's duty to support an illegitimate child. Such a child has legally no father, but his putative father, as he is called, may be compelled to furnish the child with reasonable support, so that it shall not become a burden upon the community. All children born in wedlock are legitimate, unless it is proved that the husband could not possibly be the father. The adultery of the wife cannot affect the legitimacy of the child. It is presumed to be that of the husband. It makes no difference how soon after marriage the child is born. A child born the same day as the marriage, if subsequent to the ceremony, is legitimate unless there is reason for believing that the husband is not the actual father.

10. EFFECT OF ILLEGITIMACY.—The only important legal effect of illegitimacy is that the child cannot generally inherit property from his father. He may, of course, take a legacy given to him by his putative father's will, but if there is no will, he generally cannot inherit. An illegitimate child usually inherits from his mother even though there are legitimate children.

11. CHILDREN'S OBLIGATIONS.—Where the parents or grandparents are unable to support themselves, in many states the child is legally held for their support and care.

12. CRIMES.—A parent cannot be held for crimes committed by his minor child. If a child commits a premeditated crime, he is personally liable.

13. GUARDIAN,—If a child has no parents living, a guardian may be appointed, or if he has arrived at a certain age, varying in different states, he may petition the court for the appointment of his own guardian, who will in a legal sense exercise the prerogative of a parent.

14. CONTRACTS WITH A MINOR.—A contract made by a minor is valid if it is for necessities. Just what constitutes a necessity depends on the circumstances and is a matter for the jury to decide. If a minor contracts for other things, the contract is not always void, but may be avoided by the minor. Even though a minor fraudulently represents himself to be of age and makes a contract for goods, the seller cannot recover on the contract. His only remedy is an action of deceit. A minor who has a parent or guardian cannot make a contract even for necessities. But if the minor receives and retains such articles with the permission of the parent or guardian, the parent or guardian will be deemed to have ratified the contract and will be held personally liable. If the parent or guardian is unwilling to provide the necessities he can be compelled to do so by the courts.

Parliamentary Law

1. PARLIAMENTARY RULES.—In every community it is necessary to hold public meetings from time to time, and in order to expedite the proceedings of such meetings, as well as to settle matters of dispute, it is necessary that rules of procedure be adopted. In order to be able to take an intelligent interest and part in such meetings, it is essential that young and old be informed on the most important points of parliamentary rules.

2. RULES OF PARLIAMENTARY LAW.—The following rules and suggestions will be found helpful in conducting public meetings:

a. The chairman selected should be a person of maturity and one held in respect and confidence.

b. To address the meeting permission must be obtained from the chairman by rising and saying: "Mr. President" or "Mr. Chairman."

c. No speaker should be interrupted unless his remarks are out of order, when he should be called to order by the chair. If the chairman fails to call him to order, any member may do so.

d. The proper way to make a motion is to say: "Mr. Chairman, I move that (here state motion)."

e. When a motion is presented to the meeting and seconded, it should be stated or read by the secretary or chairman.

f. After debate, the motion should be put to the meeting, the chairman announcing the result.

g. A speaker is "out of order" when he is speaking of matters and things foreign to the issue before the house.

h. Any violation of rules must be recognized and checked by the presiding officer.

i. When a member is called to order by the president, he should take his seat, unless he is permitted to explain.

j. Any ruling of the chairman may be appealed and decided by a vote.

k. It is the privilege of any member to call for the yeas and nays and thus put on record the vote of every member.

l. The chairman is the servant, not the master, of the house. To get rid of an undesirable chairman, the house may refuse to do any business, or may adjourn.

m. A motion to adjourn is always in order and is not debatable.

3. OVER THREE HUNDRED POINTS OF ORDER.—Trace up each reference on the next page, and then look up the corresponding numbers which give information bearing on the point in question.

Forms in which questions may be put...	28, 29, 30, 31, 32
Questions of precedence of questions.	19, 20, 21, 22, 23, 24, 25, 26, 27
Motion to withdraw a motion	1, 5, 7, 9, 13, 14, 16
To take up a question out of its proper order	1, 5, 7, 9, 12, 14, 16
Motion to take from the table	1, 5, 7, 11, 12, 14, 16
Motion to suspend the rules	3, 5, 8, 10, 13, 14, 16
To substitute in the nature of an amendment	3, 5, 8, 9, 13, 14, 16
Motion to make subject a special order......	3, 5, 8, 9, 12, 14, 16
Question whether subject shall be discussed	1, 5, 7, 9, 12, 15, 17
Motion that committee do not rise.........	1, 5, 7, 10, 13, 14, 16
Motion to refer a question	3, 6, 8, 10, 13, 14, 16
Motion to reconsider an undebatable question	1, 5, 7, 10, 13, 14, 18
Motion to reconsider a debatable question..	3, 6, 7, 10, 13, 14, 16
Reading papers.......	1, 5, 7, 9, 13, 14, 16
Questions of privilege..	3, 5, 8, 9, 13, 14, 16
Questions touching priority of business....	1, 5, 8, 9, 13, 14, 16
Motion for previous question	1, 5, 7, 9, 13, 14, 16
Motion to postpone indefinitely	3, 6, 7, 9, 13, 14, 16
Motion to postpone to a definite time.......	4, 5, 8, 9, 13, 14, 16
Motion for the orders of the day..........	1, 5, 7, 9, 13, 15, 17
Objection to consideration of question....	1, 5, 7, 9, 12, 15, 17
Motion to limit debate on question........	1, 5, 8, 9, 12, 14, 16
Motion to lay on the table	1, 5, 7, 11, 13, 14, 16
Leave to continue speaking after indecorum.	1, 5, 7, 9, 13, 14, 16
Motion to extend limits of debate on question	1, 5, 8, 9, 13, 14, 16
Motion to commit.....	3, 6, 8, 9, 13, 14, 16
Motion to close debate on question........	1, 5, 8, 9, 12, 14, 16
Call to order.........	1, 5, 7, 9, 13, 15, 17
Motion to appeal from Speaker's decision generally	3, 5, 7, 9, 13, 14, 17
Motion to appeal from Speaker's decision re indecorum.......	1, 5, 8, 9, 13, 14, 17
Motion to amend the rules	3, 5, 8, 9, 12, 14, 16
Motion to amend an amendment	3, 5, 7, 9, 13, 14, 16
Motion to amend......	3, 5, 8, 9, 13, 14, 16
Motion to determine time to which to adjourn	2, 5, 8, 9, 13, 14, 16
Motion to adjourn.....	1, 5, 7, 10, 13, 14, 16

POINTS OF ORDER

1. Question undebatable; sometimes remarks tacitly allowed.
2. Undebatable if another question is before the assembly.
3. Debatable question.
4. Limited debate only on propriety of postponement.
5. Does not allow reference to main question.
6. Opens the main question to debate.
7. Cannot be amended.
8. May be amended.
9. Can be reconsidered.
10. Cannot be reconsidered.
11. An affirmative vote on this question cannot be reconsidered.
12. Requires two-thirds vote, unless special rules have been enacted.
13. Simple majority suffices to determine the question.
14. Motion must be seconded.
15. Does not require to be seconded.
16. Not in order when another has the floor.
17. Always in order though another may have the floor.
18. May be moved and entered on the record when another has the floor, but the business then before the assembly may not be put aside. The motion must be made by one who voted with the prevailing side, and on the same day the original vote was taken.
19. Fixing the time to which an adjournment may be made; ranks first.
20. To adjourn without limitation; second.
21. Motion for the Orders of the Day; third.
22. Motion to lay on the table; fourth.
23. Motion for the previous question; fifth.
24. Motion to postpone definitely; sixth.
25. Motion to commit; seventh.
26. Motion to amend; eighth.
27. Motion to postpone indefinitely; ninth.
28. On motion to strike out words, "Shall the words stand as part of the motion?" unless a majority sustains the words they are struck out.
29. On motion for previous question the form to be observed is: "Shall the main question be now put?" This, if carried, ends debate.
30. On an appeal from the chair's decision, "Shall the decision be sustained as the ruling of the house?" the chair is usually sustained.
31. A motion for Orders of the Day is put in the following form: "Will the house now proceed to the Orders of the Day?" This, if carried, supersedes intervening motions.
32. When an objection is raised to considering question, "Shall the question be considered?" objection may be made by any member before debate has commenced, but not subsequently.

Partnership

1. DEFINITION.—The Uniform Partnership Act defines a partnership as "an association of two or more persons to carry on as co-owners a business for profit."

2. KINDS OF PARTNERSHIP.—A *general partnership* is one in which the partners agree to enter into a certain business without limita-

tion or condition. There may also be a partnership in a single transaction, such as to buy and sell a single oil lease. An *implied partnership* is one in which one party acts in such a way as to lead outsiders to believe that partnership actually exists. In a *special* or *limited* partnership there may be general partners with unlimited liability and special partners with limited liability.

3. KINDS OF PARTNER.—A *general partner* is one who is generally known as a partner and whose liability is not limited. A *secret partner* is one who is not openly declared as a partner. A *silent partner* takes no active part in the business but shares in the profits, losses, and liabilities. A *nominal partner* is held out as a partner without sharing in the profits or losses of the business although he may be active in it.

4. FORMING A PARTNERSHIP.—A partnership is formed by an agreement, usually in writing, though it may be oral. Any persons competent to transact business in their own names may become partners. Partners often have separate fields of endeavor, each doing the work for which he is best fitted. The article of agreement should specify the division of profits and losses and should be very carefully drawn. In the absence of any written agreement the law assumes that the partners share profits and losses equally. A partnership may hold both real and personal property.

5. LIABILITY.—Each partner is a general agent and has full authority to act for the partnership. Not only common property, but also all the private property of each partner may be taken to satisfy the debts of the firm. A partner cannot make the firm responsible for his separate or private debt, nor bind the firm by entering into engagements unconnected with, or foreign to, the partnership. The authority of a partner usually extends to the making or endorsing of negotiable paper, and to all transactions fairly connected with the business. A person who, after due care, lends money to one of a partnership firm for the firm, can hold the firm liable, although the money is fraudulently appropriated by the partner to his own use. An illegal contract made by one partner will not bind the partnership.

6. HOW TO AVOID LIABILITY.—In order to avoid individual liability in transacting business, the partners may form a corporation or a limited liability partnership. The latter consists of two or more general partners and also special partners, whose contribution and liability are made known to the public. These special partners are liable only for the amount of capital they advanced.

7. DISSOLUTION.—There are numerous ways in which a partnership may be dissolved, as follows:

a. Any partner, upon due notice to others, may withdraw at any time provided no specific date for the dissolution of the partnership is mentioned in the articles of agreement. There is some authority, however, to the effect that the power to withdraw should be exercised in a good faith so as not to prejudice the other partners. The retiring partner should notify the public of his retirement in order to relieve himself from future liability.

b. The partnership may be dissolved by mutual consent.

c. The death of one of the partners automatically dissolves the partnership.

d. The taking in of a new partner constitutes a new partnership. This is usually a matter of reorganization and the new partnership may or may not assume liabilities of the old firm.

e. The insanity or bankruptcy of one of the partners ends the partnership.

f. A court may dissolve a partnership for any good reason such as incapacity, drunkenness, or fraud.

g. The expiration of the time specified in the articles of partnership acts as a dissolution.

8. LIQUIDATION.—In case of failure the assets of the partnership must be used to pay the debts of the partnership, the assets of the partners to pay their personal debts. If in either case any property remains, the partnership property is applied on the personal debts, and the partners' personal property must go towards the partnership debts. The affairs of the insolvent partnership are usually placed in the hands of one of the partners, subject to control of the court, or turned over to a receiver appointed by the court, either of whom has the right to liquidate the affairs of the partnership.

ARTICLES OF CO-PARTNERSHIP

ARTICLES OF AGREEMENT, made ....., 19...., between .... and ....

The said parties hereby agree to become copartners, under the firm name of ...., and as such partners to carry on together the business of buying and selling all sorts of dry goods, at .... street, in the city of ....

The said .... agrees to contribute two thousand dollars ($2,000) to the capital of said firm; and the said .... agrees to contribute one thousand dollars ($1,000) to the same; the sum of $2,500 of said capital to be expended in the purchase of a stock in trade.

The said .... shall have exclusive charge of all the buying for the firm.

All the net profits arising out of the business shall be divided in the following proportions, two-thirds to the said .... and one-third to the said ....

Each partner shall devote all his time, attention, and efforts to the said business.

Neither partner shall, without the consent of the other in writing, sign any bond, bill or note as surety, or otherwise become obligated as security for any other person.

Witness the hands and seals of the parties hereto, this .... day of .... A.D., 19.....

..........................[Seal]

..........................[Seal]

AGREEMENT TO DISSOLVE PARTNERSHIP

We, the undersigned, do mutually agree that the within mentioned partnership be, and the same is, hereby dissolved, except for the purpose of final liquidation and settlement of the business thereof, and upon such settlement wholly to cease and determine.

Witness our hands and seals this .... day of .... nineteen hundred and ....

Signed, Sealed and Delivered
in Presence of

....

....

(Most states do not require this attestation)

..........................[Seal]

..........................[Seal]

Passports

1. Passports are issued by the United States Department of State for the purpose of providing citizens and nationals who are traveling abroad with documentary evidence identifying them as entitled to the protection afforded such persons. Some countries require a visa, that is, a stamp of approval, to be affixed to the passport by the consulate of the country to be visited. Other countries do not insist on this formality. Some countries that do not require visas ask visitors making a short stay to fill out tourist cards.

The United States government does not issue passports for travel to Communist-controlled parts of China, Korea, or Vietnam or to Albania or Cuba unless special circumstances prevail that require travel to either Albania or Cuba.

2. An application for a passport must be executed before a clerk of a Federal court or a state court authorized to accept applications or before an agent of the Passport Office, Department of State. Passport agents are located in Boston, Chicago, Honolulu, Los Angeles, Miami, New Orleans, New York, San Francisco, Seattle, and Washington, D.C.

3. To obtain a passport, a native-born citizen must submit a birth certificate or baptismal certificate or a certified copy of the record of baptism. If these are not available, he may submit secondary evidence.

No witness is required if proof of identity is sufficient. Otherwise a witness must take oath that he has known the applicant for over two years.

A person claiming U.S. citizenship through birth abroad must present consular report of birth, birth certificate, certificate of citizenship, or evidence of parent's citizenship.

A married woman must submit evidence of citizenship and also evidence of marriage under certain conditions. Special regulations govern women married prior to 1922:

a. An American woman who was married to a native American citizen prior to September 22, 1922, may submit evidence of either her own or her husband's American citizenship. One married to a naturalized American citizen prior to September 22, 1922, must submit evidence of her husband's naturalization.

b. An American woman who lost American citizenship by marriage to an alien, but who alleges that after the termination of the marital relation and prior to September 22, 1922, she resumed American citizenship, must submit evidence that she was an American citizen at the time of marriage. If the marital relation is alleged to have been terminated by divorce, a certified copy of the decree of court granting the absolute divorce should be submitted. A legal separation or an interlocutory decree of divorce does not terminate marriage.

c. An American woman who was married to an American citizen or to an alien on or after September 22, 1922, must submit evidence of her own citizenship.

d. An alien woman eligible to naturalization who was married to an American citizen prior to September 22, 1922, must submit evidence of her husband's American citizenship.

4. A person who claims American citizenship by naturalization must submit with his application a certificate of naturalization.

5. A person who claims citizenship by the naturalization of husband or parent must submit with application for a passport the naturalization certificate of the husband or parent.

6. An alien leaving the United States must request passport facilities from his home government. He must have a permit from his local Collector of Internal Revenue. If he wishes to return to the United States, he should request a re-entry permit from the Immigration and Naturalization Service.

7. Persons traveling because of a contract with the U.S. government must submit letters from their employer stating their position and the purpose of travel.

8. Persons of military draft age may receive passports but should inform their draft boards of their whereabouts.

PHOTOGRAPHS

9. Two recently taken photographs (duplicates) must be submitted of each person named in application, one affixed to the application, the other, signed by the applicant, must accompany the application unattached. A group photograph should be used when a wife, or wife and children, are included in one application. Photographs must be full face, on thin paper, with a light background, and not over 3 x 3 inches nor less than 2½ by 2½ inches in size. Photographs printed on photographic paper the back of which is glazed, will not adhere to passports and therefore will not be accepted.

FEES

10. A passport costs $9. A fee of $1 is added when the passport is executed by a passport agent or by a clerk of a Federal court. A state court may charge $2. A person on official business need not pay the passport fee if he has a sponsoring letter. Emergency clearance costs $2 at all agencies except those in New York City, where it is $1. Emergency service fee after working hours is $10 in addition to the passport fee.

VALIDITY AND RENEWAL OF PASSPORTS

11. A passport issued prior to Sept. 14, 1959, was valid for two years unless limited. It could be renewed for two years for $5. Applications for renewal could be made one and one-half years from the date of original issue.

Passports issued on and after Sept. 14, 1959, are valid for three years, unless limited, and may be renewed for two years for $5. Application for renewal should be made after two and one-half years after original issue.

12. If a passport is lost, the U.S. Department of State should be notified. If it is lost abroad, the owner should report the loss to the U.S. Consul.

HEALTH REQUIREMENTS

13. A valid smallpox vaccination certificate issued within three years must be shown by all persons entering the United States.

Valid vaccination certificates are required from persons arriving from cholera-infected areas within five days. Similar certificates are required from persons arriving from yellow fever-infected areas within six days and destined for receptive areas in the United States.

Vaccinations should be recorded on International Certificates of Vaccination. The smallpox and cholera vaccination certificates should be stamped by the local or state health office.

ADDITIONAL INFORMATION

14. A naturalized American citizen who visits his homeland may be subject to military service and other regulations there. The U.S. State Department recommends that such a naturalized citizen get specific information from the consulate of the country of origin before departure.

15. A British citizen who becomes a naturalized American citizen is considered a British citizen by the British government until he makes a formal renunciation of British nationality before the British authorities.

16. A French citizen wishing to become an American citizen is required by French law to have French authorization any time within fifteen years of his enrollment in the army unless he has been exempted, has a final discharge, or is over military age, or unless he has fulfilled his military obligations in the U.S. Army during World War I and World War II. An American woman who marries a Frenchman acquires French nationality unless prior to her marriage she declines it.

17. For Israel there are two types of visas, visitors' visas and immigration visas. A visitor's visa is limited to three months and may be renewed. An immigration visa must be obtained by a person who wishes to live in Israel permanently. Such a person must give military service if a male between 18 and 49 inclusive or if a female between 18 and 38 inclusive. Authorization must be obtained from the Ministry of Defense if the person wishes to leave the country before completing military service. Jews who have immigration visas acquire Israeli nationality automatically unless they disavow any intention to a consul of Israel or to the Israeli government.

18. An American citizen who voluntarily joins a foreign army loses his American citizenship unless he has the written consent of the U.S. government to do so.

19. Each returning resident of the United States, whether a citizen or not, may bring free of duty merchandise for personal use worth a maximum of $100. Members of a family may pool their exemptions if they live in the same household and travel together. The exemption cannot be claimed more often than once in thirty-one days.

20. Articles purchased abroad and intended to be gifts may be shipped to the United States before or after the return of the U.S. resident. They must be addressed to him or to him in care of some other person and declared in customs. Also, free entry is permitted for bona fide gifts not exceeding $10 in value and sent to persons in the U.S.

Patents

1. Definition.—As here used the word patent is defined to mean the granting by the United States to inventors for limited time the exclusive right to the use, manufacture, and sale of their own inventions. The instrument by which this privilege is confirmed to the inventor is called the "letters patent" and is issued in the name of the United States of America under the seal of the Patent Office and is signed by the Secretary of the Interior, and countersigned by the Commissioner of Patents.

2. Items Patentable.—The law provides that "Any person who has invented or discovered any new and useful art, machine, manufacture, or composition of matter, or any new and useful improvement thereof, or who has invented or discovered and asexually reproduced any distinct and new variety of plant, other than a tuber-propagated plant, not known or used by others in this country before his invention or discovery thereof, and not patented or described in any printed publication in this or any foreign country before his invention or discovery thereof, for more than one year prior to his application, and not patented in a country foreign to the United States . . . more than twelve months before his application, and not in public use or on sale in the United States for more than one year prior to his application, unless the same is proved to have been abandoned, may, upon payment of the fees required by law, and other due proceedings had, obtain a patent."

3. Foreign Patent Not a Bar.—A person is not debarred from receiving a patent for his invention or discovery by reason of its first having been patented in a foreign country unless his application for the foreign patent was filed more than twelve months prior to his filing of the application in the United States. In the case of patenting designs, the interval is limited to six months.

4. Duration of Patent.—A patent is good for seventeen years, but now cannot be extended except by act of Congress. Inventions previously patented in a foreign country must expire at the same time that the foreign patent expires, but in no case shall they be extended more than seventeen years.

5. How Secured.—The method of securing patents is by petition, which must be in writing addressed to the Commissioner of Patents, and must state the name and residence of the petitioner requesting the granting of a patent, designate by title the invention sought to be patented, and contain a reference to the specifications of the invention. It must be signed by the applicant and attested by two witnesses. An alien may obtain a patent on the same terms as a citizen.

6. Specifications.—The specifications above referred to are a written description of the invention or discovery, and the manner of making, constructing, composing, and using the same, and they are required to be in such full, clear, concise, and exact terms as to enable any person skilled in the art or science to which the invention or discovery appertains, to make, construct, compose, and use the same. The inventor or discoverer must point out in particular how his invention or discovery is different from others in the same line.

The specifications and claims should be written on but one side of the paper and signed by the applicant. All interlineations and erasures should be avoided.

7. The Oath.—The applicant for a patent must make oath or affirmation that he verily believes himself to be the first and original discoverer of the art, machine, manufacture, composition, other article, or improvement for which he solicits a patent; that he does not know and does not believe that the same was ever before known or used. In addition he should state of what country he is a citizen and where he resides, and whether he is a sole or joint inventor.

The oath should be sworn to before a notary public or some other officer authorized to administer oaths and having an official seal.

8. Drawings.—The applicant for patent is required also to furnish drawing of his invention whenever the nature of the case admits. Drawings must be signed by the inventor and must be attested by two witnesses; they must show every feature of the invention covered by the claims. When the invention is an improvement on some old machine, a drawing must exhibit in one or more views the invention itself disconnected from the old structure, and also in another view so much of the old structure as will suffice to show the connection of the invention therewith.

9. Material.—Drawings must be made upon pure white, calendered, smooth, bristol board of three-sheet thickness. India ink alone must be used. Sheets must be exactly ten by fifteen inches in size. Drawings must be made with pen only, and must be absolutely black. Drawings must be made with the fewest lines possible consistent with clearness.

The scale to which a drawing is made must be large enough to show the mechanism without crowding.

10. Signature of the inventor should be placed at the lower right-hand corner of each sheet of drawing and two attesting witnesses should sign at the lower left-hand corner. Drawings should be rolled for transmission to the patent office. The drawings must never be folded.

11. MODEL.—A model must be furnished when required by the commissioner.

12. SPECIMENS must be furnished when required by the commissioner.

13. ATTORNEYS.—The practice of the Patent Office allows the applicant to retain an attorney and when the petition is prosecuted by an attorney a power of attorney should be included in the petition. In ordinary cases it is always best to retain some experienced patent attorney to prosecute the application.

14. CAVEATS.—Formerly an inventor could file a caveat setting forth the object and distinguishing characteristics of his invention and asking protection for his right until he had finished his invention. This operated for one year. This law was repealed in 1910, so that the only way an inventor can secure any form of federal protection on his patent is by applying for letters patent.

15. FEES.—The schedule of fees and prices of publications can be had on application to the Commissioner of Patents, Washington, D.C. For any other information concerning patents an inquiry should be addressed to the Commissioner of Patents.

16. PRELIMINARY EXAMINATIONS.—An applicant for a patent may often save considerable expense by having a preliminary examination made of the patents allowed by the Patent Office, to determine whether or not the invention has been patented by somebody else. This examination cannot be made by the Commissioner or any one of his office, but patent attorneys will make the examination for a small fee.

17. ASSIGNMENTS.—Patents may be assigned in whole or in part, and the right to manufacture, sell, and use the patent in any county, state, township, or other district may be granted by the holder of the patent. All such assignments or transfers should be in writing, and are void unless recorded in the Patent Office within three months from their date.

18. FOREIGN PATENTS.—Contrasted with most foreign countries the cost of a patent is very low in the United States and the law is liberal in allowing the inventor to exploit it. The patent will remain protected even though the invention is not manufactured at all. Some European countries will protect patents only as long as the articles are actually manufactured within their own borders, and as long as the taxes are paid. In the United States foreigners can have their inventions patented without manufacturing them here, and without any taxes whatever.

Payment

1. LEGAL TENDER.—In all agreements the payment is to be made in cash unless otherwise stipulated. Since 1933 all coins and currencies of the United States, including Federal Reserve notes, are legal tender for all debts. The United States, however, has ordered that gold coins and certificates payable in gold be exchanged at the Treasury for silver and silver certificates. Any provision in an obligation which calls for payment in gold is against public policy and may be discharged by payment in legal tender.

2. CHECKS.—In modern times checks are given and received in payment of debts. Legally, however, a check is not payment until it is cashed. In other words, a check is a conditional payment and if the check is not honored, the creditor can sue on the check. He can also sue any of the endorsers whose names appear on the check. But if the holder of the check does not present it for payment within a reasonable time and the bank on which it is drawn fails, he must suffer the loss caused by the delay.

3. NOTES.—A note given in payment for a debt, may or may not cancel the debt. If the parties intended the note as actual payment the debtor cannot sue on the original debt; he must sue to recover on the note itself. This is a question of the facts in the case, to be determined by the court.

4. APPLYING PAYMENT WHEN THERE IS MORE THAN ONE DEBT.—If a debtor owes more than one debt to the same creditor, he can apply his payments in any way he sees fit. If he fails to do so, the creditor can make the application, and if neither does so, the law applies the payment first to interest due and the balance to the oldest debt. A signer on a note may insist that payment be applied first to the debt on which he is surety.

5. RECEIPTS.—A receipt for a debt is regarded on its face as evidence of payment. This evidence, however, is not conclusive and can sometimes be contradicted by other evidence. For example, suppose "A" gave "B" a receipt for $20.00 and afterwards discovered that the bill "B" had given him was a counterfeit. "A" could introduce evidence to prove fraud and thus invalidate the receipt. A contract embodied in a receipt without seal or consideration is not binding, but if there is a valuable consideration, or if the instrument is under seal, such a contract would be as lawful as any other.

Prescriptive Rights or Easements to Title

1. DEFINITION.—A prescriptive right is a right acquired by use and time and allowed by law.

2. A RIGHT OF WAY.—A person may acquire a permanent right of way over another's land by passing over that land to his own land for a period of time fixed by law. This right of way cannot be acquired against a minor or

against any one who is incapable of defending his possessions. A person attempting to establish such a right of way can be stopped by appropriate legal action.

3. A WAY OF NECESSITY.—Sometimes a person sells a part of his farm which is not located on the road. The law allows the purchaser the right to enter and leave the premises, and such a right is called "a way of necessity." He must exercise reasonable care in selecting his road to the main road, and this road ultimately becomes part of the title to the property.

4. RESTRICTIONS.—The law prescribes restrictions on the use of a right of way or a way of necessity. Thus the purchaser of the farm away from the road could not subdivide it and transfer his right of way to others without permission of the real owner of the way. However, more than one person can claim a right of way. A tenant can never acquire a right of way beyond the duration of his lease.

5. BUILDING RIGHTS.—

a. The owner of a building has no action against one who cuts off his light, air, or view by erecting a building on adjacent land, unless the right has been expressly acquired. The right to light, air, and unobstructed view may sometimes be acquired by deed or by presumption. If the owner has acquired such a right he loses it by tearing down the building and erecting a new one.

b. A person has the right to the lateral support of his land. If, therefore, a neighbor excavates in an unreasonable manner and a building consequently falls down, the owner has an action against the neighbor and any excavator hired by him.

6. WATER RIGHTS.—

a. The water which runs through a person's land may legally be held back for a short time to furnish water power, or it may be used for any other reasonable purpose.

b. Neither a person nor a municipality may dump impurities or sewage into a stream, making the water unfit for use below.

c. As a general rule ditches or obstructions may not be dug either to hinder or to hasten the flow of water from one person's land to another in other than the natural way.

d. A riparian owner has the right to cut and sell ice which forms over the portion of the bed of the stream which he owns, provided he does not interfere with the rights of other owners.

e. A person digging a well cannot be held for cutting off his neighbor's water supply, unless it can be proved that he acted maliciously.

Professional Men

1. DOCTORS.—A doctor or physician is a person who has (1) been educated in the science of medicine and surgery, (2) been graduated from a medical college, (3) passed the state medical examination, and (4) been licensed by the state to practice his profession.

2. CONFIDENTIAL DISCLOSURES.—It frequently happens that a doctor is called upon to give expert testimony in a civil or criminal case. He is not, however, required or permitted to divulge on the witness stand any confidential statement or information obtained in his professional relationship with his patient.

3. LIABILITY.—A doctor is not legally liable for the success or failure of his treatment in the absence of an express contract. He is required to exercise the greatest care, diligence, and skill in his work, and can be held criminally liable only for carelessness and gross inefficiency. The crime of malpractice consists of any injurious or improper treatment.

4. LAWYERS.—A lawyer is a person who has (1) been educated in the science of law, (2) been graduated from a law school (in some states), and (3) passed the state bar examination. Every man is entitled by law to have a lawyer represent him in his trial, but the court will furnish the services of a lawyer only in criminal cases.

5. CONFIDENTIAL DISCLOSURES.—What has already been said about the confidential relationship existing between doctors and patients, applies even more strongly to attorneys and their clients. The matters spoken of between them are confidential and no law can force the lawyer to divulge them on the witness stand.

6. LIENS.—An attorney has a lien for the payment of his fee on all documents, moneys and other things coming into his possession.

7. LIABILITY.—A lawyer cannot be held liable for the failure of his case unless he did not exercise reasonable care and judgment.

Sale and Transfer of Property

1. DEFINITION.—A sale is the exchange of property for a consideration called the *price*, which is either to be paid at once or at some future date. An agreement to sell at a future date is called an *executory sale*. A present sale is called an *executed sale*. A sale may be made either in writing or orally.

2. WHAT CONSTITUTES A SALE.—

a. Sales are based on mutual agreement.

b. Either the thing sold must exist at the time of the sale or there must be reason to believe that it will be in existence and in possession of the seller. For example: If a man sold a horse for $100 and the horse died before the actual time of the sale the transaction would not be a sale.

c. Grain or other produce not yet sowed or planted can be sold because the seller may reasonably expect a crop. Machinery or other manufactured goods may be sold before they are made and the seller can be held to perform his part of the contract as though the articles actually existed at the time of the sale.
d. The thing sold must be specified and set apart as the property of the buyer in order to complete the sale.
e. When nothing is said as to the time of payment when the sale is made, the law presumes that the property must be paid for before the purchaser can secure possession. If credit is agreed upon, the buyer is entitled to immediate possession.
f. When goods are sold "on sale or return" the title passes to the purchaser immediately, but may go back to the seller if the goods are returned within the time specified in the agreement.
g. If goods are sold on approval, the title passes to the buyer when he signifies his approval or when he keeps them beyond the time set for their return.
h. When no price is fixed in the agreement, the purchaser must pay a reasonable price.
i. Goods are often sold and shipped subject to bill of lading, that is, payment is not made until the goods are delivered. Thus the seller controls the property until it is paid for, although the title may pass to the buyer.

3. STATUTE OF FRAUDS.—The Uniform Sales Act provides that a contract to sell $500.00 worth of goods or more, cannot be enforced:

a. unless the purchaser advances a sum of money to bind the bargain, or
b. unless the purchaser accepts a part of the goods, or
c. unless the contract is in writing.

This rule, of course, does not apply when the goods sold are to be manufactured especially for the buyer and would not be readily salable to others.

4. RELIEVING THE BUYER.—The buyer's obligation is limited in various ways. For instance, the contract may be voided:

a. if the goods purchased have been damaged or destroyed before delivery;
b. if in his own opinion the goods are not satisfactory.

5. WARRANTIES.—When goods are sold there are certain warranties by the seller which may be either expressed or implied. Any statement made by the seller tending to induce the buyer to purchase is an express warranty. In every sale there are implied warranties, (1) that the seller has the title to the property, and (2) that the goods will correspond with the description or sample. Any defects which can be seen in property when sold do not relieve the buyer from meeting his contract though he claims that he did not see the defects. The law does not furnish eyes for the purchaser of property. But defects in property which cannot be seen and of which the seller makes no statement release the buyer from his contract

6. THE BULK SALES LAW is a part of the law of many states. It provides that when a stock of goods or merchandise is sold, transferred or consigned in bulk, the seller's creditors must be notified in writing a certain number of days before the sale is completed. Thus when a merchant sells his merchandise in bulk, the buyer should keep the following considerations in mind: First, he should demand a bill of sale. Second, he should either demand an affidavit from the seller that he has notified the creditors, or secure a sworn list of the creditors and notify them himself. This law applies to corporations, partnerships, and individuals; and any attempt to evade its provisions carries with it a penalty of a fine, a year's imprisonment, or both. If the creditors are not properly notified they can hold the purchaser liable for the debts.

7. STOCK MARKET SPECULATION.—Trading in stocks, grains, and cotton, together with the buying and selling of futures, is now largely regulated by statute. A contract of this kind which involves the actual delivery of property is perfectly legal, even if at the time the sale was made, the seller did not own the property sold. However, when no exchange of property is ever contemplated and the parties merely propose to effect a settlement based on the market changes, the contract is not legal.

Form of Bill of Sale

KNOW ALL MEN BY THESE PRESENTS, That I, ... of ...., County ...., in consideration of six hundred ($600) dollars to me in hand paid by .... of the same place, the receipt of which is hereby acknowledged, do hereby grant, sell, assign, transfer, and deliver unto the said ...., his heirs and assigns, the following goods and chattels, to wit:

Four Yearling Heifers, at $50.00 each	$200.00
30 head of Sheep, at $4.00 each....	120.00
Five sets of Harness, at $20.00 each	100.00
Two Farm Wagons, at $35.00 each.	70.00
One Corn Planter, at $20.00.......	20.00
Six Plows, at $15.00 each.........	90.00

To have and to hold all of the said goods and chattels to the said ...., his heirs and assigns forever. And I do hereby covenant to and with the said .... that I am the legal owner of said goods and chattels; that they are free and clear from all other and prior sales and incumbrances; that I have good right to sell and convey the same as aforesaid, and that in the peaceable possession of the said .... I will forever warrant and defend the same against the lawful claims and demands of all persons whomsoever.

In witness whereof I have hereunto set my hand and seal this 29th day of June, A.D. 19....

In the presence of

....

....

(Signed) .... [Seal]

Note: In selling or buying automobiles, especially used cars, it is always wise to insert the name of the machine, its model, the engine number, the car number, also the type of car, its color, and any other information which will help to identify it.

Shipping

1. Registration.—The law requires all ships flying the United States flag to be registered. A ship engaged in foreign trade must be *registered* with the collector of customs in the district in which her home port is situated. This formality is called *enrollment* in the case of large ships engaged in coastwise or internal commerce, and *license* for smaller ships.

2. Ownership.—Vessels may be owned by individuals, partnerships, or corporations, and the ownership may be acquired either by purchase or construction. If several individuals own a ship, they are tenants in common where there is no other relation between the part owners of a vessel than that arising out of joint ownership. Each part owner has his share of the profits and expenses, and no one individual can bind the others except for the necessary maintenance of the ship. When a partnership or corporation owns a vessel, the ordinary rules of corporations and partnership apply.

3. Sale.—The owner of a ship can sell or mortgage his interest at any time, but in order to effect a good title against third parties the contract should be in writing. If a ship is sold while it is at sea, the buyer takes it subject to all contracts made by the master before learning of the sale. In all other cases the buyer is not liable for repairs made or supplies furnished previous to the sale.

4. Maritime Loans.—In cases of great emergency, for example when a ship is in a foreign port without funds to purchase necessary supplies, a master can secure a maritime loan, in which the vessel is put up as security. If the vessel fails to reach home, the lender loses his money, but in the event of a safe arrival, he has the boat as security and can hold the master personally. Such a contract calls for a high rate of interest but is perfectly legal. The technical name for the contract is "contract of bottomry."

5. The Master of a vessel is the chief officer. The law gives him authority to bind the owners for necessary repairs or supplies. He must render accurate accounts of his actions and money received, but his first duty is to the passengers and the crew. He has the power to regulate their actions in any manner which is necessary to their safety, comfort, and good order. If on account of illness, insanity, or other reason, the master is unable to perform his duties properly, they pass to the lower officers in the order of their rank.

6. The Seamen.—Statutes and maritime law generally require the execution of shipping papers between the master and the seamen before starting on a voyage to a foreign country or from one state to another. These articles must specify:

a. the exact nature of the voyage.
b. the destination.
c. the duration.
d. the amount of wages to be paid each seaman.

If shipping articles are not properly executed, or if the master violates the contract, the seaman can leave the ship and recover the highest rate of wages, his expenses home, and damages. On the other hand a seaman may be discharged for reasons which show him to be unfit for the service or to be trusted in the vessel, such as:

a. long continued disobedience.
b. drunkenness.
c. incapacity (due to his own conduct).

7. Courts of Admiralty have jurisdiction over all maritime contracts, torts, injuries, or offenses.

Statutes of Limitation

1. Definition.—A statute of limitation is a law which specifies the time in which debts or actions are outlawed. All states have such laws providing different periods of time, varying from one to twenty years, within which legal actions must be brought, before the courts are closed to them.

2. The Time Begins to Run as soon as the debt is incurred or, in accounts, from the date of the last purchase or from the time of the injury complained of. The debt may be renewed by a partial payment of principal or interest, or by a written acknowledgment in a note or paper, with an expressed willingness to pay indicated.

Torts or Wrongs

1. Definition.—A tort is a private or civil wrong or injury arising independent of contract. The proper remedy is an action for damages.

2. Torts and Crimes.—There is a distinction between torts and crimes. If a wrongful act violates a private right it is a tort; if it violates a public right it is a crime. Very frequently the wrongful act is in violation of both private and public rights. In such cases, even if the wrong-doer makes personal restitution or settlement with the person wronged, the state still has the right to punish the wrong-doer for the crime. Suppose A steals $500 from B who finds it out and succeeds in getting A to return the money. "A" has still committed a crime against the public and can be punished as the law provides.

3. Violation of Contract.—Contracts frequently contain clauses fixing the amount of damages for breach of the contract. Such a clause is called a "liquidated damages" clause. If the clause is reasonable and does not amount to a penalty, it will be upheld by the courts

4. Assault and Battery.—A person who intentionally invades the person of another by physical contact (or puts him in apprehension of an invasion of his person by threat of immediate physical contact) without such person's consent, and not in reasonable defense of person or other interest, and not in the performance of some duty imposed by law, or the exercise of some privilege by reason of the relation of the parties, is liable in damages. A successful assault becomes a battery when the injury is actually done.

a. Every person is entitled by law to liberty, security of life, and security of his property.
b. Mere words do not constitute an assault.
c. The wrong consists not so much in the actual striking of the person as in the manner and spirit of the act.
d. Accidental injury is not a battery.
e. A blow unlawfully aimed at one person but striking another is a battery.
f. Reasonable methods of self defense may be employed in resisting a battery and in defending a member of one's family, or property.
g. A school teacher has the right to require obedience to reasonable rules, and proper attention to his authority, and to inflict punishment for disobedience. Hence, reasonable punishment, having in mind the age, size, and physical condition of the pupil, is not a battery.

5. Defamation.—A defamation is a false and malicious imputation of bad character or reputation either by slander or by libel.

a. Every person has a right to his good reputation.
b. Every person is assumed to have a good reputation until the contrary is proved.
c. Slander is oral defamation.
d. Libel is defamation in writing or printing.

6. Slander.—In simple words this tort consists of speaking words in another's hearing which injure a third person's reputation. The United States Supreme Court has classified slanderous words which are objectionable:

a. Words falsely spoken of a person which impute to the party the commission of some criminal offense involving moral turpitude for which the party, if the charge is true, may be indicted and punished.
b. Words falsely spoken of a person which impute that the party is infected with some infectious disease, which, if the charge is true, would exclude the party from society.
c. Defamatory words spoken of a party which impute to the party unfitness to perform the duties of an office or employment for profit, or the want of integrity in the discharge of the duties of such an office or employment.
d. Defamatory words falsely spoken of a party which prejudice such party in his or her profession or trade.
e. Defamatory words falsely spoken of a person, which, though not in themselves actionable, occasion the party special damage.

7. Libel.—It is even more dangerous to defame a person's character in writing. Many words when written or printed are libelous, which if spoken would not be slanderous without proof of special injury.

a. The owners of books and newspapers generally are liable for the publication of libelous matter, though made without their knowledge and even against their orders.
b. Newsdealers are immune from any liability for selling or displaying newspapers or magazines which contain libelous matter, providing such dealers have no knowledge of the libelous matter.
c. In order to hold the editor or proprietor of the printing plant it must be proved that the libelous matter could be recognized by an intelligent person as libel.

8. The Defenses are given below:

a. The truth of the charge generally is a complete defense against an action for damages. Statutes, however, sometimes require that not only must the words be true, but they must be uttered in good faith.

b. A privileged communication, such as what is said or written in a judicial proceeding or in a legitimate newspaper report thereof, is not held to be libelous matter. This privilege extends to the heads of the executive departments of government. Statements rendered by mercantile agencies, and the reports of many semi-public societies are also conditionally privileged.

c. Fair comment is still another defense. The conduct of public men is held to be a proper matter for public discussion, so long as the writer keeps within the bounds of an honest intention to discharge a duty to the public, and does not make the occasion a mere cover for false allegations. The same rule applies to newspaper reports of literary or artistic productions offered to the public.

9. False Imprisonment is a crime and the person unlawfully imprisoned has a civil action for damages. The defense may be that the officer was clothed with the proper authority, and in the case of parent and child, guardian and ward, or teacher and pupil it may be shown that the alleged wrongdoer was acting within his duty.

10. Malicious Prosecution is another wrong. This is the malicious instituting of suit without probable cause, and both the malice and the lack of probable cause must be proved. A suit to recover for this wrong cannot be commenced before the alleged malicious prosecution has come to an end. That the party acted on the advice of his attorney after a full and fair disclosure of the facts is a good defense.

11. Conspiracy.—A conspiracy is a combination of two or more persons to accomplish an unlawful end which is injurious to another. Thus a trade union may lawfully agree that they will stop work, or that they will not work with certain other laborers, but they commit a wrong as soon as they interfere with the liberty of others. Employers combined to use unlawful methods to exclude a certain class of workmen, are also guilty of a wrong. An agreement among manufacturers that they will all operate as the majority agree may be a conspiracy in restraint of trade.

12. Religious Liberty is guaranteed to every man by the constitution. The law does not interfere with religious societies unless they wrongfully expel a member or otherwise break the laws.

13. Search and Seizure.—It is unlawful to search private premises unless a search warrant has been issued by proper authority. It is a criminal offense to open another's letters, or to retain or pry into them. The Federal and state constitutions protect persons against unreasonable searches and seizures.

14. Nuisances.—A nuisance is anything wrongfully done or permitted which injures or annoys another in the enjoyment of his legal rights. Below is a list of some of the nuisances subject to an action in tort:

a. To remove or weaken the lateral support of the adjoining land.
b. To mine or tunnel under another's land without providing suitable support.
c. To extend buildings over another's land.
d. To allow filthy deposits to accumulate on one's property.
e. To deposit refuse in a stream of water.
f. To erect a dam, backing up the water to injure the land of another.
g. To use or care for explosives, loaded weapons, or dangerous machines in a negligent manner.
h. To conduct a place of business or amusement, or engage in any activity, in a way that will materially interfere with the ordinary physical comfort of others.
i. To allow poisonous or offensive materials to remain in a place where they may cause injury to others.
j. To put or allow a heavy article or substance to remain where it is likely to fall and injure persons or property.
k. To erect, operate, and maintain electrical appliances without reasonable care in proportion to their danger.
l. For a state, county, or municipality to allow defects in streets, highways, or sidewalks which result in injury to persons or property.

Trademarks

1. Definition.—A trademark is an emblem or symbol to designate the goods of a merchant or manufacturer.

2. Registration.—The owner of a trademark may have it registered in the U.S. Patent Office and thus acquire the right to keep others from using it.

3. Steps Necessary to Secure Registration.—The first step is to file or sign an application addressed to the Commissioner of Patents. This must include:

a. the name, domicile, location, and citizenship of applicant.
b. description of the goods for which trademark is used.
c. method of affixing trademark.
d. length of time the trademark has been used.
e. description of trademark.
f. drawing and specimens of the trademark.

The next step is the payment of the sum of $25.00 for registration.

4. Register.—There are two registers of the U.S. Patent Office on which trademarks may be registered. To be registered on the Principal Register, the trademark must be coined, arbitrary, fanciful, or suggestive; these are usually called technical marks. If the trademark is merely descriptive of goods or their regional origin or is primarily a surname, it is placed on the Supplemental Register.

5. Length of Time a Trademark Is Protected.—The registration of a trademark remains in force for twenty years. It may be renewed for a period of twenty years if it is still used in trade regulated by the U.S. Congress. The fee for renewal is $25.00. A trademark may be canceled or surrendered. It is canceled if within one year next preceding the expiration of six years from the date of registration the applicant fails to file an affidavit that he is using the mark or showing reason for nonuse. Unless the affidavit is filed, the registration is canceled after six years.

6. Restrictions.—The law has placed certain restrictions on the registration of trademarks. For example, it is impossible to register a trademark if:

a. it comprises immoral, deceptive, or scandalous matter;
b. it contains matter that may disparage or falsely suggest a connection with persons living or dead;
c. it contains matter that may disparage or falsely suggest a connection with institutions, beliefs, or national symbols;
d. it consists of, or includes, the flag or coat of arms or other insignia of the United States, any state, municipality, or foreign nation;
e. it uses, without his consent, the portrait, signature, or name of a living person, or those of a deceased president of the United States without consent of his widow.

7. Registration of Other Marks.—The law provides for the registration of service marks, certification marks, and collective marks. A service mark is defined as a mark "used in the sale or advertising of services to identify the services of one person and distinguish them from the services of others." A certification mark is used to certify origin or quality of goods; an example is a union label. A collective mark is used by an association, such as a cooperative.

8. Additional Information.—A pamphlet, *General Information Concerning Trademarks,* is available from the U.S. Patent Office, Washington 25, D.C. It describes the way applications and drawings are to be prepared and gives sample forms for applications. The *Official Gazette* contains information on trademarks registered, renewed, or published for opposition.

Vicious Animals

1. The Owner's Responsibility.—The owners of vicious animals are responsible for any injuries they may cause while running at large. If a dog annoys travelers on a public road by scaring horses or frightening children, the owner is responsible in damages to the injured party. The owner of a vicious bull or stallion is required to exercise the greatest care in protecting the public from injury. If a person on a social or business errand is injured by a savage animal on the premises of the owner, the owner is responsible.

2. Trespassers.—These rules do not apply to trespassers who know the dangerous nature of the animal.

3. Domestic Animals.—The owner of domestic animals is responsible in case injury results because of his own negligence. On the other hand, if the animals trespass on a neighbor's land, they cannot be injured or killed by the neighbor. He has a legal remedy, however, and can collect damages.

4. Fence Laws.—In certain sections of the country there are open lands where cattle and other animals are allowed to graze at will. The owners of cultivated land are there required to provide their own protection against the animals. Most states, however, have stock laws providing that animals must be kept within an enclosure, and if damage results, the owner of the animals is responsible.

Wills

1. Definitions.—A *will* or *testament* is generally a written instrument making disposition of a person's property, to take effect after his death. A *testator* is the maker of a will when the same is made by a male person; if a female, the maker is called a *testatrix.* A *codicil* is an addition or alteration of a part of an executed will. A *legacy* is a gift or bequest of money or personal property by will. The person to whom it is given is called a *legatee,* and if the gift consists of the remainder of the property after paying all debts and other legacies he is called the *residuary legatee.* A person to whom real estate is given is called a *devisee.* An *executor* is a male person named in the will to whom is entrusted the duty of administrating the estate of the testator according to the provisions of the will. If the will names a female person, she is called the *executrix.* An *administrator* is the male person appointed by the court to administer the estate of a deceased person who did not have

a will or if the party named in the will is incompetent or refuses to act. If the party appointed by the court is a female person, she is called the *administratrix*.

2. WHO MAY MAKE A WILL.—All persons are competent to make a will except infants, persons of unsound mind, and idiots. In like manner any person who is competent to make a will can appoint his own executor. If the person so appointed is legally competent to transact business, the court will confirm the appointment if he lives within the jurisdiction of the court.

3. KINDS OF WILLS.—There are two kinds of wills, written and unwritten. An unwritten will is called *nuncupative*. Such a will might be made by a soldier in active service or a sailor at sea, and depends upon proof of the persons hearing it.

4. REQUIREMENTS:—

a. A will should be written.
b. A will should be dated.
c. Testator should sign his name in full, by mark if necessary.
d. It should be witnessed by two or more disinterested parties, the number of witnesses varying according to statutes.
e. It is not necessary that the witnesses should know the contents of the will. It is generally necessary that the testator acknowledge to them that it is his will, sign it in their presence, and request them to sign as witnesses in his presence and in the presence of each other.
f. The wishes of the testator should be fully and clearly expressed in the will.
g. No exact form of words is necessary to make a will.
h. In writing wills simple language should be used. Statements concerning every provision or condition of the will should be fully and plainly made.
i. A will is valid even if written with a lead pencil.
j. A will to be effective in matters pertaining to real estate must be executed according to the laws of the state in which the real estate is located. This requirement is generally in regard to the number of witnesses to a will. Care should be exercised to dispose of all the property belonging to the person making a will. In order to accomplish this, a will should have a clause, "all the rest, residue, and remainder of my estate, I give" etc., or "all the rest, residue, and remainder of my estate shall be divided into the following parts, $\frac{1}{3}$ to ......, $\frac{1}{6}$ to ......," etc.
k Personal property may be conveyed in accordance with the law of the state in which the testator resides.
l. If trust provisions or limited estates are to be provided for in a will, it is best to have the will drawn by a competent lawyer, as these provisions are very technical, and may result in much litigation if not carefully drawn.
m. Generally a person does not need to give his property or any part of it to his children, but mention of the names of all the children is evidence of the testator's competency.

5. CODICILS.—The same principles apply to a codicil as to a will. It must be signed in the presence of witnesses.

6. MARRIED WOMEN.—A wife is entitled to a certain portion of her husband's property called the *dower*. If the will does not provide that amount for her, she can have it set aside and claim her dower right.

7. WHEN IS A WILL SET ASIDE?—

a. When it can be proved that the testator was feeble-minded or lacking in mental capacity.
b. When the testator revokes it before death. It is usually destroyed.
c. When the property devised has been disposed of during the testator's lifetime.

8. GENERAL PRINCIPLES:—

a. Any person may be a devisee or a legatee, including married women, minors, or corporations.
b. Testator's property is primarily liable for testator's debts and funeral expenses, which must be paid before any part of it can be distributed to legatees.
c. A will has no force or effect until after testator's death.
d. The last will annuls all former wills.
e. A will takes effect from the day of the testator's death.
f. All matters pertaining to wills and inheritances are handled by the court having probate jurisdiction.

FORM OF WILL

A will to be valid must be in writing and signed at the end by the testator in the presence of at least two witnesses (in some jurisdictions the requirement is three witnesses), who must all be present when the testator signs his name to the will, and the witnesses must also sign their names as such witnesses in the presence of each other and in the presence of the testator. If the will is written on more than one single sheet it is a wise precaution for the testator and all of the witnesses to sign their names on the margin of each sheet.

Will Form

I, ..., residing in ...., in the County of ...., and State of ...., being of sound mind and disposing memory do make, ordain, publish, and declare this to be my Last Will and Testament, hereby revoking all former Wills and Codicils by me made.

[Here insert all bequests and instructions]

Lastly, I make, constitute, and appoint .... to be the executor (trix) of this my Last Will and Testament.

IN WITNESS WHEREOF, I have hereunto subscribed my name and affixed my seal the ...... day of ...., in the year of Our Lord, One Thousand Nine Hundred and ....[Seal]

Testator's Signature.

This instrument was on the day of the date hereof, signed, published, and declared by the said testator .... to be his (her) Last Will and Testament in the presence of us who at his (her) request have subscribed our names hereto as witnesses, in his (her) presence, and in the presence of each other.

[Witnesses' names and addresses]

INFORMATION FOR EXECUTORS AND ADMINISTRATORS

An executor is named in a will to execute that will and settle the estate. If the will does not name an executor, or if named, he will not or cannot act, the Probate Court (in some states called the Surrogate, in others Orphans', Court) appoints an "administrator with the will annexed." If a person dies without leaving a will, the court appoints an administrator, whose duty is the same as that of an executor, except that he, having no will of the deceased, distributes the property as the law directs.

The duties of an executor are: First: To see that the deceased is suitably buried, avoiding unreasonable expense if the estate is insolvent. Second: To offer the will for probate, or proving; to conform to the laws of his state and rules of the court, the clerk of which will give full instructions. Third: To make and return to the court within required time an inventory of the property. Real estate lying in another state need not be inventoried, for that must be administered upon in the state where it lies; but personal property situated in another state should be inventoried. If the real estate is encumbered, it should be described. Fourth: To collect the property, pay the debts and dispose of the remainder as the law and will, or either, directs. Generally the debts should be paid as follows: 1. Funeral expenses. 2. Expenses of last sickness. 3. Debts due the United States. 4. Debts due the state. 5. Claims of creditors. Fifth: To render the accounts as directed by the court.

The law provides that the widow of the intestate shall be the first entitled to act as administrator; next, the nearest of kin who are competent; next, any creditor who will accept the trust; and lastly, any other suitable person.

Executors and administrators are required to take an official oath; also to give bond, which is usually for double the amount of the estate.

Generally speaking, any blanks for probate may be secured from the clerk of the court having probate jurisdiction.

CYCLOPEDIA OF
BUSINESS AND FINANCE

MONEY AND BANKING : INFORMATION FOR SHIPPERS : CREDITS AND COLLECTIONS : BOOKKEEPING : BUSINESS ARITHMETIC

MONEY AND BANKING

Under a banking system such as that in the United States where hundreds of millions of dollars change hands every day, it is only natural that huge losses occur. Some of them are direct—actual monetary losses in dollars and cents. Others are indirect, resulting in the loss of reputation, the lowering of credit standings, or the inability to grasp an opportunity when it presents itself. Most of them could be prevented.

Banking Losses

Banking losses are of two kinds: those due to carelessness and those resulting from ignorance of ordinary banking laws and customs. If every individual were as careful about money matters as he should be, and if he knew and understood the fundamental principles of money and banking, losses would be much smaller than they are.

Losses Due to Carelessness

Let us consider first of all the careless things people do in connection with their banking business. How do they write checks? How do they endorse them? How do they handle canceled vouchers? What about overdrafts? Why is it that some people have no bank account whatever? These and countless other questions must be considered if we are to avoid unnecessary loss.

Every banker knows that at least 50% of the checks passing through his hands could be raised or altered by the clumsiest amateur. The only reason more of them are not changed is that there are not more dishonest people in the world.

Liability

Many persons believe that after making out a check payable to a firm or individual, writing in the amount, and affixing the signature, their responsibility ceases. But such is not law. One of the decisions of the Supreme Court of the United States reads: "Your bank is responsible for the signature on your check, but not for what is written in the body of the check, and money paid in good faith and without negligence on an altered check, cannot be recovered by the maker thereof." *Espey* vs. *Cinni Bank*, 18 Wall, U. S. 118.

How Checks Are Altered

There are several methods by which a dishonest man can alter a check to his personal advantage. In the first place there are simple pen changes, which include many combinations that can be made by a careful study of the handwriting. For example, one to eight—one to eighty—one hundred to eight hundred—one thousand to eight thousand, etc. The employees of a bank are not mind readers and will consequently pay the check if there is no evidence of fraud.

It is a comparatively simple matter to apply an acid and wipe off every written word or figure except the signature on a common white check. On colored checks the fine lines of the signature are covered up until after the acid bath, leaving the check perfectly white. Any convenient name and amount may then be written in. Even when safety paper (so called) is used, checks are altered every day. The professional check raiser has considerable knowledge of chemicals enabling him to alter checks, drafts, letters of credit, and registered bonds. He is also something of an artist. For instance, if the payee's name on a safety check is to be changed, he delicately traces out the name with his acid, and then with a fine camel's hair brush he can restore the most delicate tints, leaving a perfect safety check for his own purposes. Thus no bank safety paper is a protection against him.

The largest percentage of loss from altered checks occurs from changing the payee's name. Large checks are seldom raised, but the payee's name is changed to "bearer" or "cash." Many names permit of changing by adding a letter or a syllable, or a few pen strokes. Thus, F. C. AHRENS is changed to F. C. AHRENSON by simply adding the letters "on."

CHECK PROTECTORS

The first mechanical device for protecting the amount of checks was one which crimped the paper over the numerical amount of the check. This was followed by a machine which punched the numerical amount of the check through the paper. Next came the machine stamping the words "Not over $000 dollars." Check-protecting manufacturers then produced a great variety of machines which wrote or stamped the amount in words in colored ink, as well as machines which stamped the amount in numerals. Such machines were generally accepted as insurance against alteration, and are still so considered by many people.

The skill of the criminal, however, kept pace with the inventive genius of the manufacturer. He soon learned that it was a simple matter to iron out the crimped surface of the check and to paste on little discs of paper or apply tinted chalk when the check was perforated. In the case of machines which stamped the words "Not more than $000" in indelible ink he discovered a means of erasing the indelible ink and stamping in a greater amount by the aid of a similar device. With the invention of an instrument which broke up and disturbed the surface of the paper the criminal was forced to seek another method of fraud and he found it in the practice of changing the payee's name to bearer or to cash. Because of the fact that these check protectors do not permit of writing a large amount, the professional criminal cleverly devised the scheme of taking a small check reading:

THIRTY-FOUR DOLLARS FIFTY CENTS

and writing a larger amount above these words on a similar machine so that the check reads:

ONE THOUSAND NINE HUNDRED AND
THIRTY-FOUR DOLLARS FIFTY CENTS

The paying teller can see at a glance that it would be impossible to write the whole amount on one line so he pays the check without questioning it.

The modern check protector accomplishes three things. First, it macerates the amount line and prints the amount in indelible ink into this broken paper surface. In the second place, it prints the words at such an angle that the very largest amounts can all be written on one line and in the proper place. And finally, it so macerates the payee's name that it cannot be successfully altered to bearer, cash, or another name.

Rules for Writing Checks

a. A check should be made payable "to the order of" a specific person, never to bearer.

b. Write figures plainly with ink, never with pencil.

c. Be sure that the amount in figures corresponds with the written amount. The bank will always pay the written amount.

d. Write the amount of the check as far to the left as possible so that no additional words or figures can be inserted.

e. Fill in the space remaining with a heavy black line so that nothing can be added.

f. Exercise the utmost care in writing and handing out checks. The person who carelessly draws a check must stand any loss which may occur through its alteration.

g. Remember that a check is your order to the bank *to pay out money*, and that it is necessary for the bank to know *without question* when, to whom, and how much it shall pay.

h. Use the best known mechanical methods of protecting your check against alteration.

The habit of endorsing checks in blank should be discouraged for more than one reason. If you endorse a check by simply signing your name across the back of it, that endorsement has the effect of making the check payable to any holder, or to the bearer. If it is lost or stolen, it is as valuable to the finder or thief as the actual currency would be. Many business men make a practice of endorsing their checks in blank and carrying them to the bank for deposit. Suppose there is a hold-up or that in the excitement of an accident or a fire on the way to the bank, the checks disappear. The unfortunate owner has little chance of getting the money back. Again by endorsing a check you vouch for its genuineness in every respect. Thus, if you endorse in blank and permit the check to come into the hands of a forger who afterward raises the amount, you have made yourself liable for the larger amount. Always endorse a check payable to some specific person or firm. If the checks are intended for deposit, write across the back the words: "For Deposit in First National Bank" or "For Deposit Only" and sign your name.

KEEPING RECORDS

When a man puts money into a bank, his deposits and withdrawals are all carefully recorded by an efficient system of modern bookkeeping. However, the individual does not always exercise the same great care in keeping his own accounts. As a result he allows his account to be overdrawn, injuring his credit with the bank, or he issues checks when he has no money in the bank thus lowering his credit standing with his creditors.

One check coming back marked "Not sufficient funds" will do more damage to a man's credit than a dozen past due accounts and may destroy a commercial reputation it has taken years to establish.

A depositor should call at the bank for his statement and vouchers every month. He should also check the bank statement with his own check book in order to avoid errors, detect strange checks, and save confusion and loss of time.

The following practices should be observed:

a. Always keep a correct record, on the stubs of your check book, of all deposits and checks.

b. See that you receive all checks charged to you on the bank statement, and arrange them in order.

c. Check off stubs for all checks returned with your statement, also verify deposits shown in your pass book with those shown on the statement.

d. To the balance shown on the last stub used on which this statement is balanced, add the amounts of all checks shown on the *unchecked stubs*, that is, the amount of outstanding or unpaid checks.

e. The total should agree with the balance shown by the bank. Report any differences immediately.

Value of a Bank Account

Although the number of bank accounts in the United States averages more than one for every person in the country yet there are thousands of people who do not take advantage of the convenience and safety which banks offer for the handling of money. There are four distinct ways in which the man who has no bank account is likely to lose. In the first place, when a check, a pass book, a certificate of deposit, or a bank draft is lost or stolen, the owner has some chance to recover, but when the cash is gone, it is usually gone forever. Secondly, the lack of a bank account naturally leads to a lack of credit. The man without enough money to warrant a bank account has a decided limit placed on his buying power. Thirdly, the man who has no banking acquaintance is always subject to inconvenience and delay when he wishes to cash a check or a bank draft sent to him from another person. And, in the last place, it very often happens that a young man going into business is denied the financial help he needs from the bank for the single reason that he is unable to show any satisfactory savings balance or other visible evidence of his character and habits. Thus the man who has no bank account runs the grave risk of losing money, credit, time, and opportunity.

The holder of a check should present it for payment within a reasonable time after he receives it. He may keep it as long as he pleases, but if in the meantime the bank fails, he cannot demand payment again from the maker. The law provides that the check should be presented at the bank for payment or forwarded by mail for collection on the same day it is received or not later than the day following. Again, a man's death automatically stops payment on all his outstanding checks. In other words, if a man dies before you have deposited his check, the bank will refuse to cash it and you will be obliged to wait for your money until his estate is settled. It is a matter of safety, therefore, to deposit all checks without any unreasonable delay.

It is sometimes desirable for two persons to deposit money in their joint names, payable to either or both signatures. A joint account of man and wife subject to withdrawals by either during their lifetime, and by the survivor in event of the death of the other, is often a very wise arrangement. But in those states having an inheritance tax it may not be generally known that if one party to a joint account dies, the other is not permitted to draw out the money until the state treasurer or other authority has been notified of the death, and given his consent to the withdrawal. The same laws govern the actions of a bank or trust company having in its possession a safety deposit box of a deceased person. This box may not be removed or opened by friends or relatives until the proper state official has checked its contents and given his release. Thus it frequently happens that at a time when ready funds are most needed, the cumbersome processes of the law cause uncertainty and delay.

Functions of a Bank

To many individuals, a bank is nothing more than an elaborately furnished building with a lot of dignified individuals sitting around at mahogany desks, trying to look wise, and an immense safety vault filled with gold and currency. To many others, a bank is merely a convenient place in which to get a check cashed. Few really understand the internal organization of a bank, or know its real functions. As a result of this lack of understanding, the banks are unable to perform the services they otherwise might. Here briefly are the real functions of a bank:

a. To provide a safe place for the custody of money and other valuables.

b. To lend money for legitimate purposes.

c. To facilitate the transmission of funds by drafts, or bills of exchange.

d. To encourage thrift.

e. To act in an advisory capacity on matters of an economic or financial nature.

A banker primarily is a dealer in money. He borrows of one party and lends to another. The difference between the terms at which he borrows and those at which he lends, forms the source of his profit. By this means he draws into active operation those small sums of money which were previously unproductive in the hands of private individuals, and at the same time furnishes accommodation to those in need of additional capital for carrying on their commercial transactions. Anything that the banker can do to encourage thrift and improve methods of business among his customers, automatically increases his deposits and swells his profits. In banking, therefore, as in any other business, real service means success, not only for the bank individually, but for the community it serves.

A bank, therefore, means a place where you can leave your money in safety; a place in which to borrow money if you need it for some legitimate purpose; a place where you can purchase a draft or bill of exchange that will be legal tender in every country in the world; a place to learn the advantages of saving; and a place to turn to when you are in need of information, advice, or assistance in your business affairs.

Federal Reserve System

The Federal Reserve System consists of twelve regional Federal Reserve banks. All national banks are required to become members of the system; state banks may, if eligible. The member banks form the capital stock of their district Reserve bank by subscribing six per cent of their capital, three per cent of which is paid in; they receive a six per cent dividend on the stock which they hold in the Federal Reserve Bank. The system is controlled by a Federal Reserve Board with supervisory powers, and by boards of directors for the regional banks.

The chief purpose of the Federal Reserve System is to accumulate a reserve that can be used as a basis for loans in time of temporary or seasonal need. Each member bank deposits a part of its deposits in its district Reserve Bank, and can borrow from the Reserve Bank to satisfy changes in currency and credit demand. Loans made by member banks may be discounted and sent to the Federal Reserve Bank, where they are rediscounted on the basis of the member bank's collateral notes. The notes may not be lent for investment purposes or for trading in any securities other than those of the United States government. By raising or lowering the rediscount rate, the district bank attempts to regulate the flow of credit. The Reserve Banks also attempt to regulate credit by purchases and sales of government securities and other paper in the open market.

Bank Statements

Many people who have no knowledge of accounting, feel that they can not understand a bank statement, and therefore pay no attention to it. This is a mistake. Every person who has money on deposit, either in a savings or checking account ought to know the condition of his bank, and how its condition compares with that of other banks. Below is a simple statement of a moderate-sized national bank, together with an analysis of the various items:

Resources

Cash on Hand and Due from Banks	$201,568.71	
Loans and Discounts	964,393.37	
Bonds and Other Securities	500,050.00	
Banking House...	50,000.00	
Stock in Federal Reserve Bank..	7,500.00	
		$1,723,512.08

Liabilities

Capital Stock....	$200,000.00	
Surplus	50,000.00	
Undivided Profits.	22,197.25	
Demand and Time Deposits	1,224,179.21	
Rediscounts and Money Borrowed	225,000.00	
Reserve for Taxes and Interest....	2,135.62	
		$1,723,512.08

By resources is meant what the bank owns. Let us consider each resource as it appears:

Cash on Hand and Due from Banks

This item represents the actual cash on hand in the bank, the money which the bank has on deposit with the Federal Reserve or correspondent banks, and checks deposited for collection which are drawn on other banks. Banks usually keep a considerable sum on deposit with other banks, in order that they may draw drafts against that money, when necessary.

Loans and Discounts

This represents the value of the promissory notes of the firms or individuals who have borrowed money from the bank. The interest from the loans constitutes the main source of the bank's income. When you apply for a loan your request is passed on by the officers of the bank or a discount committee appointed for that purpose, whose business it is to see that the bank is properly safeguarded in giving you the money.

Bonds and Other Securities

This sum represents the value of such bonds or other securities as the bank has invested in. High grade bonds make a very desirable investment for surplus funds because of their safety and because they can be sold advantageously on short notice, at a price quoted every day. Bonds of the United States government, bonds of large industrial corporations, and state and municipal securities are also held, in varying amounts.

Banking House

Under this head there is included the cost of the ground, building, furniture and fixtures used by the bank in carrying on its transactions. This is valuable property owned by the bank.

Stock in Federal Reserve Bank

All member banks in the Federal Reserve System must own a block of stock in their district reserve bank, equal to 6% of their combined capital and surplus.

Liabilities

By liabilities we mean the things that the bank owes. Every dollar paid into the bank immediately becomes a liability. The earnings belong to the stockholders, hence are liabilities. A deposit of money is recorded as a resource, but it really belongs to the depositor and must be included among the liabilities. In this particular statement the liabilities of the bank are shown under six different headings:

Capital Stock

When a bank is organized the stockholders pay in a certain amount of money to protect the depositors. This is called the capital or the capital stock of the bank. It is shown as a liability, because the bank is indebted to the stockholders for what money they pay in. In other words, the stockholders are the owners of the bank. If, however, the bank fails or is unable to pay its depositors, the capital may be used. In addition the stockholders in national banks and in some state banks are personally liable for an equal amount, if it is needed to pay the debts. Deposits are now insured up to a certain amount by the Federal Deposit Insurance Corporation.

Surplus

A national bank is required by law to accumulate from its profits a fund which will equal 20% of its capital. This is called the surplus fund. Many banks of course accumulate a fund much larger than 20% of their capital. The surplus is also a liability because it belongs to the shareholders, but it remains in the bank as part of the working capital.

Undivided Profits

The undivided profits account represents earnings which have neither been added to the surplus nor paid out in dividends. The size of this account varies with the earnings and when it is large enough, it is transferred to the surplus account. A well managed bank never pays out all its profits in dividends.

Demand and Time Deposits

Money deposited with a bank in a checking account is a demand deposit. The savings accounts on which interest is paid are time deposits. The bank owes its patrons for all these deposits and must be prepared to meet their demands.

Rediscounts and Money Borrowed

It frequently happens that a bank must borrow money from other banks in order to accommodate its customers. This is done by putting up good security as collateral for the loan, or in the case of a member bank in the Federal Reserve System, by rediscounting commercial paper as explained above. These loans being debts owed by the bank must be shown as direct or contingent liabilities.

Reserve for Taxes and Interest

Instead of carrying a large sum of money as undivided profits, most banks set up a reserve fund for the payment of taxes, interest, bad debts and other necessary expenditures. As the payments are made, they are charged against this account. Thus the bank avoids creating a wrong impression in the published statements it makes.

The law requires banks to submit statements to the proper authorities and to publish them regularly in local newspapers. This is in addition to the official examination to which all banks are subject by national or state bank examiners, clearing house officials, or reserve bank examiners. The published statements, if fully understood, will give depositors an accurate idea of the standing of their bank. By learning to read between the lines you will soon discover that what at first appears to be only a formidable and uninteresting column of figures, is in reality very simple and instructive.

CREDITS AND COLLECTIONS

Many businesses find it essential to do their customers the convenience and courtesy of extending them credit. However, the question of when and how to extend credit and how and when to collect overdue accounts, presents some difficulties. The firm that is haphazard, thoughtless, and over-generous in extending credit finds itself overwhelmed by bad debts. Suspiciousness, reluctance, and stinginess, on the other hand, offend reputable customers and break down good will.

The aim of every business man should be to keep his losses as near the zero point as possible without needlessly limiting sales. In order to accomplish this result, a person of good judgment must be in charge of and responsible for credits. In large concerns there is a credit man. In the vast majority of cases, however, this duty falls on the shoulders of the proprietor himself, or on one of the officers of the corporation. Slipshod methods of extending credit should never be permitted. They sap the very life blood of the business.

Sources of Credit Information

Where the trade is local the man in charge of credits needs to know all there is to know about the character, habits, and financial condition of the purchasers. Theoretically the same thing ought to be true when a house sells its goods over an extended territory, but for practical purposes he must content himself with such general information as is available, coupled with an exact knowledge of the general financial situation in the territory covered. Every possible effort should be made to learn the particular hazards and peculiarities of the customer's business. On the other hand the credit man must be thoroughly familiar with stock on hand, production costs, and all the operative details of his own business. In addition to all these other considerations, a familiarity with the laws of finance, collection, exemption, bankruptcy, and commercial paper is absolutely essential.

How is the credit man to obtain all this vital information? Government reports show up the light and dark spots in the general financial condition of different parts of the country. And as for the reputation, habits, and financial standing of individual customers, the credit man has four different sources of information open to him, namely: the mercantile agencies, local banks, trade reports, and salesmen's reports.

The mercantile agencies attempt to show the net worth and the credit standing of every corporation, partnership, or individual doing business. While their reports are not always accurate and must be qualified by past experience and other available information, they nevertheless are an invaluable source of credit information, and give business men a great inducement to keep their commercial records clean. It must always be remembered, however, that changes in personnel, location, and credit standing, change in these listings at the rate of well over 50% every year.

Many business houses prefer to get their credit information from local sources, such as the bankers or the attorneys in the customer's city. These are always valuable to verify the reports of the mercantile agencies, but as sources of original information they are not always reliable. Delay, partiality, enmity, inaccuracy, or indifference in answering the requests for information, result far too frequently. Most banks refuse to give out credit ratings unless the individual happens to be one of its own customers.

Credit men in the same or allied lines of business often exchange credit information. Manufacturers of certain products sometimes form an association and co-operate in the manufacture and sale of their goods. The members of such an organization are always glad to exchange credit information. Some of these even go so far as to maintain what is known as a black list containing the name and address of firms which are not reliable, and every credit man has a copy of that list.

Firms which employ salesmen to sell their products are in a position to get definite and reliable information on their customers. The salesman makes frequent visits, becomes acquainted with the customer, knows his reputation, observes his method of transacting business and is able to supply first hand reports not only on the customers, but on the general condition of the trade in the city and surrounding country. It does not pay to depend altogether on his reports, however, because his zeal for increased commissions might lead him to ignore the usual danger signals.

Methods of Collecting Accounts

The granting of credit automatically gives rise to the problem of collecting overdue accounts. Even though every reasonable effort is made to secure accurate credit ratings, there will be slow or doubtful accounts. In a vigorous, forward-looking business this is inevitable, since customers are trusted and given the benefit of the doubt wherever possible.

When an account is not paid, it is unwise to resort to law—often a tedious and expensive process—or to forceful, unfriendly methods of dunning, except as a last resource. Every possible concession must be made to avoid litigation, if there seems to be any possibility of a friendly settlement and continued business relations. Non-payment of accounts is by no means evidence of intent to defraud on the part of the debtor. All sorts of everyday reasons may be responsible—temporary financial reverses, lost or misplaced letters, misunderstanding, inaccuracy on the part of a salesman, forgetfulness, or merely a kind of laziness in business matters. This should be taken into consideration. Tact and consideration turn many doubtful accounts into reliable and valuable ones.

The statement should be sent when the account becomes due and payable, not on the 1st and 15th of the month. It should be enclosed in a friendly letter calling attention to the maturity of the bill and making it clear that a remittance is expected. Many customers must be educated to the fact that payments must be met promptly at maturity in order to maintain a good commercial rating. After allowing a week or ten days for a reply, a second collection letter should be sent courteously calling to the attention of the debtor his failure to pay. As many as four such letters may be sent. The latter may be given a more forceful tone, but all should be short and friendly, though not temporizing. They should convince the debtor of the writer's sincerity, get under his skin without being offensive. Threats are inadvisable at this point.

If several collection letters do not induce a reply, there is little hope of a friendly adjustment.

It is at this point that a sight draft is valuable. Formerly when a merchant refused to honor a sight draft, he found that such action lowered his credit standing. This is not always true today because many firms make it a positive rule never to pay sight drafts. The presentation of such a draft, particularly in a small town, where everybody knows all about the affairs of everybody else, is likely to bring some results. If possible it is always more satisfactory to draw the draft through the debtor's own bank.

After the sight draft has been drawn and refused it may be advisable to send the collection to a Justice of the Peace, or to the debtor's local bank, either of whose charges will not exceed 10%. On the other hand an attorney may be able to effect a prompt settlement, his charge depending on the amount of the claim. Collection agencies using a series of letters threatening suit or attachment proceedings, or public advertisement, are often effective, but it must be understood that such a system does away with the last hope of future business.

In order to begin suit to enforce a civil debt a complaint is filed stating the facts upon which the action is founded. The court then summons the debtor to appear and answer the charges, and the case is tried upon its merits. If judgment is rendered in favor of the creditor, the sheriff attaches, seizes, and sells enough of the debtor's property to satisfy the judgment. Either before or after the judgment is actually rendered, the creditor may cause to be issued a writ of garnishment or a writ of attachment. The former attaches money or property of the debtor in the possession of a third party while the latter authorizes the sheriff to seize the debtor's property in case he is about to leave the State, abscond, or is a non-resident. Bond is necessary in both cases to indemnify the debtor against loss caused by a wrongful suit.

Recourse to law is seldom advisable unless the account is a large one, and all other efforts have failed. Proper care in extending credit. and a good collection system are worth more to a business than a hundred judgments.

INFORMATION FOR SHIPPERS

The carelessness and ignorance of the shippers and receivers of freight are responsible for a great annual loss of time and money.

In shipping freight one should comply with the following instructions:

a. See that each item is carefully checked in packing.

b. Use the utmost care in nailing, sealing, or tying the shipping case.

c. Mark the case plainly, showing name and address of both shipper and consignee.

d. Make out a uniform bill of lading in clear, legible form, and deliver to the transportation company.

Great care must be taken in accepting freight to avoid misunderstanding.

a. Remove freight promptly to avoid congestion and storage charges.

b. Examine all freight before giving a receipt to the company.

c. In case of any visible damage or loss, the agent should write a description of it on the freight bill.

d. In case of invisible damage or loss, notify the carrier's agent to come immediately and verify your claim.

e. Notify the freight agent in writing if you intend to store the cases without checking until some later date.

f. If merchandise does not check with invoice, or if it is received in damaged condition, file a claim immediately with the transportation company and notify the shipper.

Filing a Freight Claim

The law allows nine months after date of delivery in which to file a claim on damaged merchandise, and nine months for non-delivery of shipments after a reasonable time has elapsed. The documents required are:

a. The original paid freight bill.
b. The original invoice or certified copy.
c. The original bill of lading or memo.

On shipments damaged beyond repair or entirely lost, full invoice value plus freight should be claimed. An effort should be made to dispose of the damaged merchandise and allow credit for it on the claim. This in no way invalidates the claim. All correspondence should be answered promptly, quoting the file reference and furnishing all available information. The carrier's investigation may take from thirty to ninety days. In tracing claims, patience is essential. In making a claim against an express company, the procedure is practically the same. The invoice or copy thereof, and copy of original express receipt are the necessary documents. The Postal Department has a standard form to be filled in and signed when making claim for lost or damaged parcel post packages.

Rates and Classifications

It is very important for a shipper to consult the published rate. He cannot always depend on the statement of the carrier's agents. If the agent quotes an incorrect rate, the shipper is liable for the published rate. According to law the published rates are common documents, and carriers cannot charge any other rate. Ignorance of this law leads to many losses. A manufacturer may put in a bid on a certain order, and agree to pay all transportation charges. He may get the order, but in making shipment discover that he is compelled to pay a higher rate, which will wipe out his expected profit. On the other hand, he may figure the cost too high, and the order will go to his competitor, who makes it his business to consult the legal published rate.

Months or even years afterwards a shipper may learn to his sorrow that his merchandise has been moving under a wrong rate and be compelled to pay the difference.

According to law, a shipper must make it his business to know the correct freight classifications. He should do so for financial reasons as well. It is the duty of the traffic man to know the principal classifications, and the cheapest rate under each for his goods. He should describe the shipment in the exact language of the classification, avoiding the use of trade names. Frequently there are changes to lower freight costs by finding the best designation in each classification. Thus the rates differ for goods crated and uncrated, in packages or in bulk, set up or shipped flat, the saving running as high as 50 or 75% in many instances.

Losses to be Avoided

When goods are improperly routed or sent to a wrong destination owing to the shipper's error in making out the shipping ticket or bill of lading, the shipper must pay the excess freight. This is always true when the bill of lading is made out incorrectly and usually so when there is an error in shipping ticket, because of the fact that the carrier relies on the accuracy of the shipping ticket to expedite the shipment. Because of such mistakes, shipments are frequently billed to another town of the same name in another state or in an entirely different section of the country, and the difference in the cost of freight is a considerable item.

A railroad allows forty-eight hours after official notice of arrival of cars in which to unload. An unloaded car standing longer than this is subject to a demurrage charge, listed in the published rates. No charge is made for Sundays, holidays, or days on which it rains to any extent. The charge is a just one, and the receivers of freight should empty cars promptly for two reasons: first to avoid paying the demurrage charge; and second, to release cars, enabling the carrier to reduce his fixed charges, and thus ultimately reduce the cost of transportation.

The following certificate must appear on shipping orders and bills of lading when goods are shipped in fiber boxes:

The fiber boxes used for this shipment conform to the specifications set forth in the boxmaker's certificate thereon, and all other requirements of Rule 41 of the Consolidated Freight Classifications.

Failure to do this may cost the shipper or his customer 20% more in freight charges.

BOOKKEEPING

Bookkeeping is the art of recording business transactions in a regular and systematic manner; in a sense it is a branch of mathematics based on certain accepted rules and principles. A set of books properly kept tells a story of profits and losses, a story essential to the successful functioning of any business firm. Systems of bookkeeping differ greatly. In a small business the system may be very simple and readily learned. In a large business it is exceedingly complex. Years can be spent at high schools, business and commercial schools, colleges and universities in detailed study of the art of bookkeeping and the more general field of accounting. This does not mean that there is anything mysterious about the art, but only that it has many ramifications. Like other business methods, it is based on common sense.

There are two fundamental systems of bookkeeping: single entry and double entry. The distinction between them is based on the idea that every business transaction may be viewed from two aspects. From one aspect it is a gain; from the other, a loss. For example, when a sale is made, money is received and goods are lost. Similarly, when a purchase is made, goods are received and money is paid out. In single-entry bookkeeping, only one of these aspects is taken account of, and only one entry is made for each transaction; this system is analogous to that of a simple cash book, in which the only entries are those for money received and money paid out. In double-entry bookkeeping, on the other hand, two entries, identical in value, are made for each transaction, the one a debit, the other a credit. Debit entries are made when assets are increased, or when liabilities or proprietorship is decreased. Credit entries are made when assets are decreased, or when liability or proprietorship is increased. Further explanation of these terms will be found in the section "bookkeeping terms," following.

Single-entry bookkeeping involves less clerical work and is sometimes suitable for small businesses. But double-entry bookkeeping provides an invaluable check against errors, since the sum of the debits should always equal the sum of the credits; in other words, the books should balance.

There are three principal kinds of books used in double-entry bookkeeping: the books of first entry or journals; the ledger or ledgers; and the auxiliary books or subsidiary ledgers. Books of first entry include the day book or journal, cash book, sales book, and voucher register. Transactions are first recorded in these books and later transferred to the ledger. The latter operation is known as posting. The ledger is the most important and essential of all the books.

The auxiliary books, or subsidiary ledgers, are used to facilitate the grouping of related accounts, such as accounts receivable, in a separate book in order to relieve the general ledger of a mass of detail. The most important of the auxiliary books are the accounts-receivable ledger, the accounts-payable ledger, and the inventory record.

Intelligent, accurate bookkeeping is obviously essential to the success of a firm. It serves many purposes besides the main one of recording the status of a business and analyzing the reasons for its success or failure. It makes it possible for a firm to obtain credit, since when credit is desired a correct statement of financial condition must be furnished. It may be of great service as evidence in legal disputes. Finally, it enables a firm to meet competition intelligently by showing what merchandise costs, what selling and overhead expenses are, and what percentage must be added to make sales profitable.

Bookkeeping Terms

The following terms, arranged alphabetically, consist chiefly of types of accounts and types of entries. Particular attention is given to the question of where and how various entries are made.

Accounts Payable.—These are accounts owed others. Credit the general ledger account under that title with the total of all such accounts, and debit or charge it with all that has been paid on them during the month. The balance must agree with the sum of the individual balances of the accounts owed.

Accounts Receivable.—These are accounts of persons or individuals in debt to the firm in question. Debit the general ledger account under that heading with the total of all charges against these accounts during the month, and credit it with all payments and allowances made on said accounts. The balance must agree with the sum of the balance of the individual accounts and represents an asset.

Accrued Expenses.—Accrued expenses, such as interest payable, salaries or wages payable, etc., should be charged to these respective accounts at the end of the accounting period, in order to show correctly the amount of unpaid earnings at this time, and credited when paid.

Accrued Interest Receivable.—Where interest has accrued but is not yet payable on notes and other commercial paper, due from others, charge this account with the amount, and credit the interest account. When the interest is received it is credited to "accrued interest receivable."

Allowances.—Discount taken contrary to terms, but allowed, returned merchandise, etc., are debited to the terms account, and credited to the account of the firm in question.

Assets or Resources.—A resource or asset is anything of value owned by the firm from which cash can be realized. Examples of assets are cash, merchandise, buildings, real estate, store fixtures and furniture, notes receivable, accounts receivable, etc.

Balance Sheet.—This is a statement showing the financial condition of a business at a particular time. The assets or resources are arranged in one group; and the liabilities in another. The difference between the totals of the two groups gives the net worth of the business. The title of the statement should be clearly stated and include the name of the business enterprise and the date on which the statement was made.

Cash.—This is a title used to designate money. Under it is included currency, bank drafts, checks, express and postal money orders. Cash is debited when received and credited when paid out. The difference shows the cash on hand which is an asset.

Cash Book.—This book is used for recording all cash transactions. One section is usually set aside to record cash received, and the other to record cash paid out. If the business is large, separate books are kept for receipts and disbursements. The footings in these books are posted to the general ledger accounts at the end of the accounting period.

Day Book and Journal.—Formerly these two books were kept separately and entries made in the day book were arranged by debits and credits in the journal before posting to the ledger. Now the two books are consolidated into one, preferably called a "journal," and the entries arranged for posting by debits and credits, followed by a short explanation of the transaction. The ordinary two-column journal may be used, with the left hand column for the debit and the right hand column for the credit, but in order to save time and work in posting, special journals of four, six, eight and more columns are often prepared.

Deferred Charges.—Insurance and other similar expense items paid ahead or beyond the date of closing the books are entitled to a credit for that portion of the premium on the unexpired time. This credit is entered on the credit side of insurance accounts and the difference charged to profit and loss. After closing the books this account will be brought forward to the debit side as an asset and appears as such in the financial statement. Office supplies, packing material on hand, etc., also come under this head.

Depreciation.—Property such as buildings, machinery, tools, store and office fixtures, depreciates from year to year by reason of wear and tear and obsolescence. In the course of time it becomes entirely worthless and must be replaced. Provision is made for such replacement by setting up a reserve-for-depreciation account. The percentage or amount to be charged off each year depends upon the estimated life or length of usefulness of the asset. Accounts and bills receivable are also subject to shrinkage in value when some of them are found worthless and uncollectable, and a reserve must be provided for bad debts. The amount of reserve is based on the past experience of the company.

Equipment.—Store, office, and delivery equipment represent an investment. Charge store equipment with such items as counters, shelving, scales, measures, etc.; office equipment with such office furniture as desks, safes, letter files, etc.; delivery equipment with trucks, wagons, horses, harness, etc. Repairs for these should not be charged to any of these accounts; they are an expense. A reasonable amount should always be charged off annually for the depreciation of equipment.

Expenses.—Under this title are generally included such items as rent, salaries, office supplies, fuel, light, postage, etc. If it is desired to show these items in detail, separate accounts may be opened for each one in the ledger. Expense accounts are finally included in the profit and loss account.

Ledger.—The ledger is the book of final entry, collecting and classifying from the books of original entry, all debits and credits having the same name under the one heading, called an account, by a process termed posting. In large business several ledgers or divisions of ledgers are used, viz.: general ledger, purchase ledger, and sales ledger, the latter two carrying controlling accounts on the general ledger. In a small business only one ledger is used. It may, however, be divided into three sections: (1) *general accounts*, (2) *accounts receivable*, (3) *accounts payable*. With the present loose-leaf ledger method this division can be easily made, and by arranging the accounts under each division in alphabetical order, the necessity for a separate index is avoided.

Liabilities.—A liability is an obligation owed by the firm in question, such as notes payable or any personal account.

Losses and Gains.—An account shows a loss if the thing it represents has cost more than it has produced; a gain if it has produced more than it cost.

Merchandise.—This is the general term for all goods and wares dealt in or carried in stock by an active business concern. A merchandise account may be opened and debited with all goods bought and credited with all the proceeds from goods sold. The value of goods on hand unsold added to the proceeds from sales, less the cost, shows the profit on the goods sold. However, if the cost exceeds the other two items, the goods were sold at a loss. The inventory of goods on hand is always an asset. Sometimes, for the purpose of showing profits and losses in greater detail, separate accounts are opened with such commodities as "flour," "potatoes," "apples," "corn," etc., instead of including all under "merchandise."

Monthly Summary of Business.—A monthly summary of purchases, sales, expenses, and ratios is often useful. It may be arranged with columns for these various headings with the figures taken from the ledger. Each month the figures for that month should be recorded so that the record will give the total for each month from the first of the year to date. The sum of these monthly totals will be the record of totals for the year.

Notes Payable.—These are notes, or written obligations, which others hold, for which the firm must pay a certain amount when due. Credit this account with all notes given to trade creditors, or trade acceptances and time drafts accepted in their favor, and charge the account as they are paid. The balance of the account shows obligations outstanding.

Notes Receivable.—These are other persons' notes or written obligations, for which, when due, the payment of a specific sum is expected. Charge this account with all notes, time drafts, and trade acceptances held against others, and credit it when paid or otherwise disposed of. The balance will show the sum of the unpaid items, which is an asset.

Personal Accounts. Persons are debited when they get into debt to the firm, and when the firm gets out of their debt. Persons are credited when the firm gets into their debt, and when they get out of debt to the firm.

Profit and Loss Statement.—This financial statement is second in importance only to the balance sheet. Its main difference is that it reflects the results of operations between two particular dates as distinguished from the financial condition at a particular time. The accounts used in making up this statement are the sales, purchases, and expense accounts. In other words, all accounts which cannot be classified as assets, liabilities, or net worth are used in the profit and loss statement.

Property.—Property is debited under such titles as merchandise, real estate, cash, etc., when it comes into the firm's possession. It is credited when it goes out of the firm's possession.

Proprietorship.—This account, occasionally called the proprietor's capital account, represents the proprietor's net capital. The account is debited for his liabilities assumed by the business, for all amounts drawn by him from the business, for his private use, and for his net loss if any. It is credited for the amount of his investment on commencing business, for all later investments, and for his net gain, if any. The balance of the account is his net capital at the time of closing.

Purchases Account.—Modern practice is introducing the purchases account in place of the debit to merchandise. All merchandise purchased is debited or charged to purchase account. If accounts for freight, drayage, expressage, etc., on merchandise are kept separately, their totals should finally be charged into this account also. Credit the account with any merchandise returned to the seller or any discounts or allowances for defects, etc. The balance of the account is transferred to the debit of a "trading account."

Reserves.—Part of the profits of a concern may be retained in the business to provide funds for certain future needs as for the payment of fixed debts or business extensions, depreciation, bad debts, income taxes, etc. The sum set aside for such purposes is taken out of and charged to the surplus account, and credited to the reserve set up for that special purpose.

Resources and Liabilities.—An account shows a resource, if it represents property on hand or a debt owed to the firm; a liability, if it represents a debt owed by the firm. The excess in an account showing either a resource or a loss will always be on the debit side and the excess showing either a liability or a gain on the credit side.

Sales Account.—Credit it with the total sales of all merchandise as shown by the sales book, sales tickets, or whatever method is used for recording sales. Merchandise returned by customers, whether for cash or credit, should be charged or debited at selling price to this account. The difference in the account, the net sales, is transferred to the "trading account."

Sales Book.—This is a book in which all the merchandise sales are recorded. The personal accounts charged therein should be posted daily and the total sales may be carried forward until the end of the month and then posted in one entry to the credit of a sales account in the ledger. Where sales and credit tickets are used instead of a sales book, they may be sorted at the close of the day, charging the total cash receipts to cash, crediting sales to the accounts of their respective customers, and crediting the total sales to the sales account. When goods are returned, sales accounts must be charged with them and the customer's account credited.

Trading Account.—This account shows the inventory of merchandise at the opening of business, is charged with purchases and sales allowances, and credited with sales. The inventory at closing is then credited and the balance shows the gross profit on trading. This gross profit is then transferred as a credit to the profit and loss account, and the inventory brought down for a new balance.

Trial Balance.—The trial balance is taken to ascertain the equality of the debits and credits as posted in the ledger. It is nothing more nor less than a copy of the accounts or their balances, and if the footings of the debits and credits do not agree there is an error in posting. The trial balance is not an absolute proof of correctness, but if the footings are equal the work is generally regarded as correct.

Locating Errors in Double-Entry Bookkeeping

When trial balance totals do not agree it is certain that one or more errors have been made somewhere, but there is no single rule or combination of rules with which such errors can at once be located outside of a careful review of the entire work. However, the following hints and suggestions may be of service and help in locating them.

A large difference between the debit and credit totals of a trial balance usually indicates an omission of some item or account. See if all the accounts or balances of accounts have been included in the trial balance. If an amount has been omitted in posting, the trial balance also will be out of balance by that much. Look for such an unchecked amount in the books from which postings were made.

An amount posted to the wrong side of the ledger will throw the trial balance just twice that amount out of balance. If the difference is divisible by 2, look for half of that amount on the side with the smaller totals in the books from which postings were made and see if such an amount was posted to the other side of the ledger account. The cash and accounts-receivable balance can never be on the credit side, nor the accounts-payable balance on the debit side of the account.

If the difference between the debit and credit totals be 1, or in round numbers, as 10, 100, 1,000, the error very likely results from wrong addition or subtraction. Check the additions of the trial balance and if the error is not found there, check those of the ledger also. Where ledger balances only are entered in the trial balance, an error may have been made in finding the difference between the two sides of an account. If an error is in the cents column only, the columns to the left need not be re-added.

If the difference is divisible by 9 the error may rest in a transposition of figures, as for instance 57 posted as 75 causing a difference of 18, or 735 posted as 537 causing a difference of 198, both of which are divisible by 9. Errors of transposition are difficult to find; however, if the difference consists of less than three figures such as 9, 18, 27, etc., a one-column transposition may have caused the error. Divide this difference by 9; if the quotient is 1, the difference between the two transposed figures is also 1; if 2 or 3 the difference between the transposed figures is likewise 2 or 3. When the difference lies between 99 and 1,000, the error may be due to a two-column transposition. Here the middle figure of the error is always a 9, as for instance 981 written as 189 results in an error of 792. Dividing the two outside figures of the difference (72) by 9, the quotient 8 is also the difference between the two transposed figures (9 and 1).

Another common type of error results from a transplacement or "slide." Figures are transplaced when some or all of the digits of a number are moved one or more places to the right or left without any change in their order; for instance 327 written as 32.70 or 3.27. The first is a one-column, the second a two-column slide. The error caused by a one-column slide is always divisible by nine, a two-column by 99, a three-column by 999, etc. Such division, disregarding decimals, always gives the figures whose transplacement has caused the error. The error caused by writing 327 as 32.70 is 294.30 which divided by 9 produces 327; or 327 written as 3.27 causes a difference of 323.73 which divided by 99 produces 327.

Legal Points in Bookkeeping

Occasions may sometimes arise in which the books of a firm become of importance in courts of law. Only records of original entry are accepted as evidence in court, especially the day book and journal, as evidence of sale and delivery of goods or work done. For this reason, as well as for many others, the time to make an entry or charge against the purchaser of goods or for work done is when the goods are ready for delivery, or the work has been completed. Entries to be admissable as evidence, should be made by the proper person, and without erasure, alterations, or interlineations. Mistakes should be corrected by marking the wrong entry void, and then making a correct entry. All accounts must be itemized and no general charge can be considered as evidence, unless it lists the separate items.

If A guarantees that he will see that B will pay a certain bill of goods, then the goods must be charged to A and not to B in order to hold A responsible; but if A guarantees the account of B, if the account is for some date of the past, the guarantee must be in writing.

To collect a debt on the evidence of book accounts from a person in a distant place, a copy of the account should be made out and accompanied by an affidavit, setting forth that the account is correctly taken from the book or records of original entries; that the charges were made at or about the same time of their respective dates; that the goods were sold and delivered at or about the time the charges were made; that the charges are correct and the accounts just; and that the person named is not entitled to any credit not mentioned in the account. The affidavit should be sworn to before a magistrate, commissioner or notary public. This obviates the trouble of producing or sending the books.

BUSINESS ARITHMETIC

This section is hardly intended to be an exhaustive study of business arithmetic; nor does it attempt to touch upon the theoretical abstractions of arithmetic. The inclusion of material has been guided by the practical needs of everyday business problems: problems involving fractions, decimals, percentage, interest, discounts and measurements. The principles of these arithmetical processes will be given, as well as such other aids as will be helpful.

The four fundamental operations of arithmetic—addition, subtraction, multiplication, and division—are familiar to everyone. The underlying principle of these operations is that *only similar quantities* can be added, subtracted, multiplied or divided. Thus, one can add *5 hats* and *3 hats*, for instance, and get *8 hats;* but one cannot add *5 hats* and *3 oranges*, because they are dissimilar quantities.

Addition

Addition is the process of uniting two or more numbers in one total called a *sum.* The sign used to indicate this process is called *plus* (+): $6 + 3 = 9$. To add rapidly it is best to group mentally the numbers in a column of figures, so that they total 8, 9, 10, 12, or some other convenient sum.

6	2	82
3	5	31
8	3	25
2	6	49
9	4	36
1	1	12
6	3	60
9	8	89
44	32	384

Accuracy is more important than speed in arithmetic. Of the various methods by which the correctness of an addition may be checked, these two are the simplest: (1) If the column of figures has been added from top to bottom, then re-add starting at the bottom and going upward; if the results obtained by both methods are the same, the answer is probably correct. (2) Re-add the column of figures, omitting the top row of figures from the addition, and subtract this sum from the first result obtained; if the difference between these two sums is equal to the top row of figures omitted from the second addition, then the answer is probably correct. By applying this method to the above column, for instance, omitting the *82*, one obtains the sum of *302*, which when subtracted from *384* leaves *82*.

Subtraction

Subtraction is the operation of finding the difference between two numbers. The larger number or the one from which the subtraction is being made, is called the *minuend*, the smaller number is called the *subtrahend*, and the result is called the *remainder*. The sign used to indicate this process is called *minus* (−). In subtraction, the smaller number is always taken from the larger one; the reverse is impossible except algebraically. Thus 6 can be subtracted from 10, but 10 cannot be subtracted from 6. To check the correctness of a result in subtraction, add the remainder to the subtrahend, and if the sum is equal to the minuend the answer is correct. Thus:

		Check
Selling Price	\$831.50	\$207.35
Cost	624.15	624.15
Profit	\$207.35	\$831.50

Multiplication

Multiplication is the process by which any given number or quantity may be augmented any number of times by a short method of addition. The number to be multiplied is called the *multiplicand*, the number by which it is multiplied is called the *multiplier*, and the result is called the *product*. The sign used to indicate multiplication is called *times* (×).

Of the many short cuts in this process, the multiplication table, which should be learned by heart, is one of the most helpful. Another short method is multiplying by 10, 100, 1000, etc. simply by adding the ciphers to the multiplicand. Thus, in 100 × 15, add the two zeros to the 15, and the product is 1500; in 1000 × 24, add the three zeros to the 24 and the product is 24,000, etc. If the number to the left of the ciphers in the multiplier is something other than 1 (as 40, 1600, 23,000) then multiply by that number and add the ciphers to the product.

23000	82
12	1600
46	492
23	82
276000	131200

If the multiplier is 9, 99, 999, etc., multiply by 10, or 100, or 1000 and subtract the multiplicand from the product. Thus, in 48 × 99 take 48 times 100, or 4800, and subtract 48:

$$48 \times 100 = 4800 - 48 = 4752.$$

If the multiplier is 11, 101, 1001, etc., multiply by 10, 100, or 1000 and add the multiplicand to the product. Thus, in 16 × 101 take 16 times 100, or 1600, add 16:

$$16 \times 100 = 1600 + 16 = 1616.$$

To check the results of multiplication, divide the product by the multiplier, and if the quotient is equal to the multiplicand, then the answer is probably correct. The following will serve as an illustration of a multiplication and check:

82	82
16	16/1312
492	128
82	32
1312	32

Division

Division is the process of determining the number of times one number is contained in another. The number to be divided is called the *dividend*, the number by which it is divided is the *divisor*, and the result is the *quotient*. If the solution does not come out to an even number the fractional part left over is called the *remainder*. The sign used to indicate division is ÷.

In general, there are two methods of division: (1) *short* division, where the steps in the process are done mentally (usually with a divisor of 10 or less); (2) *long* division, where all steps in the process are written out. Thus $6432 \div 8 = 804$ is an illustration of short division. Long division is illustrated by the following:

$$\begin{array}{r} 815\frac{67}{85} \\ 85\overline{)69312} \\ \underline{680} \\ 134 \\ \underline{85} \\ 492 \\ \underline{425} \\ 67 \end{array}$$

To check, multiply the quotient by the divisor (adding the remainder, if any, to the product), and if the product equals the dividend, the result is correct.

For numbers which are a power of 10, (100, 1000, 10,000) this short method is helpful: beginning at the right, cross out as many figures in the dividend as there are zeros in the divisor; the figures in the dividend, other than crossed out zeros, constitute the remainder.

$$16\not{0} \div 1\not{0} = 16$$
$$62\not{8}\not{5}\not{1} \div 1\not{0}\not{0}\not{0} = 62\,\frac{851}{1000}.$$

For numbers which are a multiple of 10 (30, 50, 200, etc.) proceed as above, dividing what is left by the remaining figure in the divisor.

$$15\not{0} \div 3\not{0} = \frac{15}{3} = 5$$

$$860\not{1}\not{3} \div 2\not{0}\not{0} = \frac{860}{2} + \frac{13}{200} = 430\,\frac{13}{200}.$$

Fractions

Fractions are parts of a whole expressed numerically. The number in a fraction written below the line is the *denominator*; the one written above the line is the *numerator*; both together are called the *terms* of a fraction. If the numerator of a fraction is less than the denominator, as $\frac{4}{5}, \frac{3}{10}, \frac{7}{8}$, it is a *proper* fraction. If the numerator is equal to, or exceeds, the denominator, as $\frac{4}{4}, \frac{6}{4}, \frac{7}{2}$, it is an *improper* fraction. If the fraction expresses a whole number and a fractional part, as $1\frac{3}{4}, 2\frac{5}{7}, 3\frac{3}{5}$, it is a *mixed number*.

Fractions are capable of being added, subtracted, multiplied and divided. It is frequently expedient, and a time saver, to reduce fractions to their lowest terms or to find their least common denominator before starting any one of these processes. For this a knowledge of factoring and cancellation is necessary. *Factoring* is the process of finding the smallest numbers (prime numbers) which are the divisors of a larger number. Thus 2 and 3 are the *prime factors* of 6 because they are the smallest numbers which, when multiplied together, equal 6; 2 and 2 and 2 are the prime factors of 8; 4 and 3 the prime factors of 12, etc. The following rules will be found helpful in factoring:

Two will divide evenly any even number.

Three will divide evenly any number the sum of whose digits is divisible by 3. Thus 3 will divide evenly 813 because 12, the sum of $8 + 1 + 3$, is evenly divisible by 3.

Four will divide evenly any number whose last two digits on the right form a figure divisible by 4. Thus, 4 will evenly divide 69,816 because 16, the last two digits, is evenly divisible by 4.

Five will divide evenly any number ending in 0 or 5.

Six will divide evenly any even number the sum of whose digits is divisible by 3. Thus 6 will divide evenly 2616 because 15, the sum of $2 + 6 + 1 + 6$, is divisible by 3.

Eight will divide evenly any number whose last three digits on the right make a figure divisible by 8. Thus, 8 will divide evenly 23,624 because 624, the last three digits, is evenly divisible by 8.

Nine will divide evenly any number the sum of whose digits is divisible by 9. Thus 9 will divide evenly 32,193 because 18, the sum of $3 + 2 + 1 + 9 + 3$, is evenly divisible by 9.

Ten will divide evenly any number ending in 0.

Cancellation is the process of eliminating a common factor in both the numerator and denominator of a fraction. It is most useful in multiplying and dividing fractions, and in reducing a fraction to its lowest terms. For instance, the result $\frac{\overset{26}{\not{52}} \times \overset{3}{\not{18}}}{\underset{2}{\not{12}}} = 78$ is obtained by determining that 6, a common factor of 12 and 18, divides into those numbers 2 and 3 times respectively. Two, a factor of 52, divides into this number 26 times. Multiplying 26 by 3, 78 is obtained.

An improper fraction can be changed to a whole number or mixed number by dividing the numerator by the denominator. Thus, the improper fraction $\frac{6}{2}$ is converted to the whole number 3 simply by dividing 6 by 2; likewise, $\frac{7}{2}$ is converted to the mixed number 3½ by dividing 7 by 2. To change 3½ (a mixed number) back to $\frac{7}{2}$ (an improper fraction) multiply 3 (the whole number) by 2 (the denominator of the fraction ½) and add 1 (the numerator of the fraction ½) to the product, retaining 2 as the denominator of the newly created fraction. Thus,

$$\frac{3 \times 2 + 1}{2} = \frac{7}{2}.$$

Addition of Fractions and Mixed Numbers

If the fractions to be added have the same denominator, add the numerators, write this sum over the denominator, and reduce to lowest terms, if necessary. Thus, $\frac{1}{5} + \frac{2}{5} = \frac{3}{5}$; similarly, $\frac{1}{6} + \frac{5}{6} = \frac{\not 6}{\not 6} = 1$.

If the fractions to be added do not have the same denominator, find the least common denominator, divide it by the denominator of each fraction, multiply the results by the respective numerators and write the new figures over the common denominator; add the numerators, and reduce to lowest terms. The least common denominator, 8, is divided by 2, and the result, 4, multiplied by 1. Similarly, it is divided by 4, and the result, 2, multiplied by 3, producing 6. Adding these newly obtained numerators, one arrives at $\frac{17}{8}$, which reduces to $2\frac{1}{8}$.

$$\begin{array}{c|l} \frac{1}{2} & \frac{4}{8} \\ \frac{3}{4} & \frac{6}{8} \\ \frac{7}{8} & \frac{7}{8} \\ \hline & \frac{17}{8} = 2\frac{1}{8} \end{array}$$

If mixed numbers are to be added, add the fractions first, then the whole numbers, and finally combine the two sums.

$$\begin{array}{c|l} 1\frac{5}{8} & \frac{15}{24} \\ 2\frac{3}{4} & \frac{18}{24} \\ 6\frac{2}{3} & \frac{16}{24} \\ \hline 9 & \frac{\not 49}{24} = 2\frac{1}{24} \\ 2\frac{1}{24} & \\ \hline 11\frac{1}{24} & \end{array}$$

The fractional part is done as in the example, so that $\frac{49}{24}$, which reduces to $2\frac{1}{24}$, is obtained. Adding the whole numbers, 9 is obtained, to which is added $2\frac{1}{24}$, producing the final result of $11\frac{1}{24}$.

Subtraction of Fractions and Mixed Numbers

If the fractions to be subtracted have the same denominator, subtract the numerators, write this remainder over the denominator, and reduce to lowest terms, if necessary.

Thus, $\frac{2}{6} - \frac{1}{6} = \frac{1}{6}$; similarly, $\frac{5}{6} - \frac{1}{6} = \frac{\not 4}{\not 6} = \frac{2}{3}$.

If the fractions to be subtracted do not have the same denominator, the steps followed are the same as in addition except that the new numerators are subtracted instead of added.

$$\begin{array}{c|l} \frac{3}{6} & \frac{6}{12} \\ \frac{1}{4} & \frac{3}{12} \\ \hline & \frac{\not 3}{\not 12} = \frac{1}{4}. \end{array}$$

If mixed numbers are to be subtracted, first subtract the fractions, borrowing 1 from the whole number if necessary, then subtract the whole numbers, and finally combine the two.

The least common denominator, 8, when divided by 4 and multiplied by 3 produces 6. Subtracting, $\frac{1}{8}$ is obtained. Subtracting the whole numbers, 3 is obtained, which is combined with $\frac{1}{8}$, giving the final result of $3\frac{1}{8}$.

$$\begin{array}{c|l} 4\frac{3}{4} & \frac{6}{8} \\ 1\frac{5}{8} & \frac{5}{8} \\ \hline & \frac{1}{8} \end{array}$$

$$\begin{array}{c|l} \overset{3}{\not 4}\frac{2}{3} & \frac{8}{12} + \frac{12}{12} = \frac{20}{12} \\ 1\frac{3}{4} & \frac{9}{12} \\ \hline 2\frac{11}{12} & \frac{11}{12} \end{array}$$

The solution is the same as in the preceding problem, except that 9 could not be subtracted from 8, a smaller number. Hence, 1, or $\frac{12}{12}$, was borrowed from the whole number 4, and added to $\frac{8}{12}$, giving $\frac{20}{12}$, from which $\frac{9}{12}$ is subtracted. Then 1 from 3 is subtracted, giving 2, which is combined with $\frac{11}{12}$.

Multiplication of Fractions and Whole Numbers

If fractions are to be multiplied, cancel where possible, then write the product of the numerators over the product of the denominators, and reduce to lowest terms if necessary.

Thus, $\frac{\overset{1}{\cancel{2}}}{3} \times \frac{1}{\underset{3}{\cancel{6}}} = \frac{1}{9}$; similarly, $\frac{1}{3} \times \frac{2}{5} = \frac{2}{15}$.

If mixed numbers are to be multiplied, change the mixed numbers to improper fractions, cancel where possible, then write the product of the numerators over the product of the denominators, and reduce to lowest terms if necessary.

Thus, $8\frac{3}{5} \times 6\frac{1}{4} = \frac{43}{\underset{1}{\cancel{5}}} \times \frac{\overset{5}{\cancel{25}}}{4} = \frac{215}{4} = 53\frac{3}{4}$;

similarly, $4\frac{9}{10} \times 5\frac{3}{7} = \frac{\overset{7}{\cancel{49}}}{\underset{5}{\cancel{10}}} \times \frac{\overset{19}{\cancel{38}}}{\underset{1}{\cancel{7}}} = \frac{133}{5} = 26\frac{3}{5}$.

If a whole number and a fraction are to be multiplied, cancel where possible, multiply the whole number by the numerator, and divide by the denominator.

Thus, $\overset{49}{\cancel{343}} \times \frac{3}{\underset{1}{\cancel{7}}} = 147$;

similarly, $\overset{125}{\cancel{250}} \times \frac{3}{\underset{2}{\cancel{4}}} = \frac{375}{2} = 187\frac{1}{2}$.

Division of Fractions and Mixed Numbers

If fractions are to be divided, invert the divisor, cancel where possible, and proceed as in multiplication.

Thus, $\frac{5}{6} \div \frac{3}{4} = \frac{5}{\underset{3}{\cancel{6}}} \times \frac{\overset{2}{\cancel{4}}}{3} = \frac{10}{9} = 1\frac{1}{9}$;

similarly, $\frac{2}{3} \div \frac{1}{3} = \frac{2}{\cancel{3}} \times \frac{\cancel{3}}{1} = 2$.

If mixed numbers are to be divided, change these to improper fractions, invert the divisor, cancel where possible, and proceed as in multiplication.

Thus, $3\frac{5}{7} \div 8\frac{2}{5} = \frac{26}{7} \div \frac{42}{5} = \frac{\overset{13}{\cancel{26}}}{7} \times \frac{5}{\underset{21}{\cancel{42}}} = \frac{65}{147}$;

similarly,

$$6\frac{1}{2} \div 5\frac{1}{5} = \frac{13}{2} \div \frac{26}{5} = \frac{\overset{1}{\cancel{13}}}{2} \times \frac{5}{\underset{2}{\cancel{26}}} = \frac{5}{4} = 1\frac{1}{4}.$$

If a whole number and a fraction are to be divided, invert the divisor, cancel where possible, and proceed, as in multiplication.

Thus, $69816 \div \frac{4}{5} = \overset{17454}{\cancel{69816}} \times \frac{5}{\cancel{4}} = 87270$;

similarly,

$$840 \div 5\frac{3}{5} = 840 \div \frac{28}{5} = \overset{30}{\cancel{840}} \times \frac{5}{\underset{1}{\cancel{28}}} = 150.$$

Decimals

A fraction can be written in one of two ways: As a common fraction, or as a decimal (also called decimal fraction). Thus, the common fraction $\frac{7}{10}$ can also be expressed decimally as .7 (to avoid confusion a zero is sometimes placed to the left of the decimal point, as 0.7); the common fraction $\frac{7}{100}$ can also be expressed decimally as .07; $\frac{7}{1000}$ as .007; $\frac{7}{10{,}000}$ as .0007, etc. From this it can be seen that in a common fraction the denominator is always written, whereas in a decimal the denominator is represented by a period or decimal point, which is placed to the left of the numerator ($\frac{7}{10} = .7$). The size of the denominator in a decimal fraction is always determined by the number of figures to the right of the decimal point. Thus, one decimal place represents tenths; two decimal places represent hundredths; three decimal places represent thousandths; four decimal places represent ten-thousandths, five decimal places represent hundred-thousandths, etc.

To change a fraction to a decimal, divide the numerator by the denominator, placing a decimal to the right of the numerator and adding as many zeros as necessary to bring out the division evenly or approximately. Thus, $\frac{1}{4}$, for instance, is converted to a decimal in the following manner:

$\frac{1}{4} = 4\overset{.25}{\overline{)1.00}}$; similarly, $\frac{2}{3} = 3\overset{.66\frac{2}{3}}{\overline{)2.00}}$.

To change a decimal to a fraction, drop the decimal point, write in a denominator with as many zeros as there are figures to the right of the decimal, and reduce to lowest terms. Thus .875, for instance, is converted to a fraction as follows:

$$.875 = \frac{\overset{7}{\overset{\cancel{35}}{\cancel{875}}}}{\underset{8}{\underset{\cancel{40}}{\cancel{1000}}}} = \frac{7}{8};$$

$$\text{similarly, } .66\frac{2}{3} = \frac{66\frac{2}{3}}{100} = \frac{20\cancel{0}}{30\cancel{0}} = \frac{2}{3}.$$

The $\frac{200}{300}$ is obtained by multiplying the numerator and denominator by 3.)

Addition of Decimals

To add a column of decimals, arrange the figures so that the decimal points are placed one directly under the other, and proceed as in ordinary addition.

```
 $69.20        84.691
  17.84         7.02
   5.31        35.1
  23.65         0.0921
  14.78         3.1416
 -------      --------
$130.78       130.0447
```

Subtraction of Decimals

To subtract decimals, arrange the figures so that the decimal points are placed one directly under another, and proceed as in ordinary subtraction.

```
$16.95        16.83
  3.22        12.0914
------        -------
$13.73         4.7386
```

(In subtracting 12.0914 from 16.83, zeros were added mentally so that it became 16.8300. This can be done because the addition of zeros to the last number of a decimal does not alter its value.)

Multiplication of Decimals

To multiply decimals, proceed as in ordinary multiplication, count the number of decimal places in the multiplier and multiplicand, and point off as many in the product, starting at the right and moving toward the left.

```
  4.56         3.1416
   8.3           .05
 -----        --------
 1368         0.157080
3648
------
37.848
```

Division of Decimals

To divide a decimal by a whole number, place the decimal point on the quotient line, directly above the decimal point in the dividend, and proceed as in ordinary division. If the answer is not even, carry out to at least two decimal places.

```
     .46             30.12
 15/6.90          23/692.76
    60               69
     90                27
     90                23
                        46
                        46
```

To divide a decimal by a decimal, move the decimal point in the divisor to the extreme right, move it as many places to the right in the dividend as it was moved in the divisor, and proceed as in ordinary division. For example, to divide 8.5116 by 2.46, the decimal point must first be moved two places to the right in the divisor, changing that number from 2.46 to the whole number 246; then it must be moved an equal number of places in the dividend, changing that number from 8.5116 to 851.16.

```
       3.46
246/851.16
    738
    1131
     984
     1476
     1476
```

To divide a whole number by a decimal, move the decimal point in the divisor to the extreme right, add as many zeros to the dividend as the decimal point was moved places in the divisor, putting a decimal point after the last of these zeros, and proceed as in ordinary division, carrying out to two decimal places if the answer is not even. For example, to divide 6248 by 1.25 the decimal point must first be moved two places to the right in the divisor, changing that number from 1.25 to the whole number 125. The decimal point having been moved two places in the divisor, two zeros must now be added to the dividend, changing that number from 6248 to 624800

```
       4998.4
125/624800.0
    500
    1248
    1125
     1230
     1125
      1050
      1000
        500
        500
```

Since the result 4998 still left a fractional part, the latter was eliminated by carrying out to one more decimal place, giving the even answer 4998.4.

Percentage

Percentage is the expression of numbers in terms of hundredths. The sign used to indicate this process is called *per cent* (%). The number upon which the per cent is calculated is the *base*; the amount of the per cent is the *rate*; and the result of the calculation made with the base and the rate is called the *percentage*. For example, in 2% of \$125 = \$2.50, 2% is the rate, \$125 is the base, and \$2.50 the percentage.

If the base and the rate are known, divide the rate by 100 and then multiply the one by the other to find the percentage. Thus to find 8% of \$240 multiply one hundredth part of the rate (.08) by the base (\$240).

```
 $240   (base)
   .08  (rate)
$19.20  (percentage).
```

To find the rate when the base and percentage are known, divide the percentage by the base. Thus, if \$100 yielded a return of \$4.00, what was the rate of return?

$$\frac{(\text{percentage})\ \$4.00}{(\text{base})\ \$\ 100} = .04 \text{ or } 4\% \text{ (rate)}.$$

To find the base when the percentage and rate are known, divide the percentage by one hundredth part of the rate. Thus, if 4% yielded a return of \$4.00, how much money was invested?

$$\frac{(\text{percentage})\ \$4.00}{(\text{rate})\ .04} = \$100 \text{ (base)}.$$

Where b = base, r = rate, and % = percentage, these three principles may be expressed with the following formulas:

$$(1)\quad b \times \frac{r}{100} = \%$$

$$(2)\quad \frac{\%}{b} = \frac{r}{100}$$

$$(3)\quad \frac{\%}{\frac{r}{100}} = b$$

The following table of percentages and their fractional equivalents, because of their frequent use, should be memorized.

$12\frac{1}{2}\% = \frac{1}{8}$	$16\frac{2}{3}\% = \frac{1}{6}$
$25\% = \frac{1}{4}$	$33\frac{1}{3}\% = \frac{1}{3}$
$37\frac{1}{2}\% = \frac{3}{8}$	$66\frac{2}{3}\% = \frac{2}{3}$
$50\% = \frac{1}{2}$	$83\frac{1}{3}\% = \frac{5}{6}$
$62\frac{1}{2}\% = \frac{5}{8}$	$20\% = \frac{1}{5}$
$75\% = \frac{3}{4}$	$40\% = \frac{2}{5}$
$87\frac{1}{2}\% = \frac{7}{8}$	$60\% = \frac{3}{5}$
$8\frac{1}{3}\% = \frac{1}{12}$	$80\% = \frac{4}{5}$

Interest

Interest is the amount of money earned by, or paid for, the use of a sum of money called the *principal*. The *rate* is the per cent of interest charged or paid for the use of the money. In the calculation of simple interest a year consists of 360 days, or of 12 months of 30 days each. Unless otherwise specified interest is always calculated on the basis of one year. Where I stands for interest, P for principal, R for rate, and T for time, the method of finding the interest on any principal can be expressed by the following formula:

$$I = P \times \frac{R}{100} \times T$$

This formula will always work, whether the time be expressed in terms of years, months, or days. The following examples will serve as illustration of usual and alternate methods of solution.

(1) Find the interest on \$835 at 6% for 3 years.

```
(1)   $835   (P)                        (2)   $835
        .06  (R)                                .18
     $50.10  (int. for 1 yr.)                  6680
          3  (T)                                835
    $150.30  (int. for 3 yrs.)              $150.30
```

In this solution, since 6% for 3 yrs. amounts to 18%, the principal is multiplied by .18.

(2) Find the interest on \$276 at 6% for 5 months.

(1) \$276 (P)
.06 (R)
\$16.56 (int. for 1 yr.)

$$(2)\quad \frac{\overset{23}{\$27\!\!\!/6\!\!\!/} \times .06 \times 5}{1\!\!\!/2\!\!\!/} = \$6.90$$

$$(3)\quad \frac{\overset{.23}{\$2.7\!\!\!/6\!\!\!/} \times 6 \times 5}{1\!\!\!/2\!\!\!/} = \$6.90$$

$$(T)\quad \frac{5}{1\!\!\!/2\!\!\!/} \times \overset{1.38}{1\!\!\!/6.5\!\!\!/6\!\!\!/} = \$6.90 \text{ (int. for 5 mos.)}.$$

In solution 3, by dividing \$276 by 100, yielding \$2.76, the .06 immediately changes to the whole number 6.

(3) Find the interest on \$496 at 8% for 45 days.

(1) \$496 (P)
.08 (R)
\$39.68 (int. for 1 yr.)

$$(2)\quad \frac{\overset{62}{\$49\!\!\!/6\!\!\!/} \times .08 \times 4\!\!\!/5\!\!\!/}{\underset{8}{3\!\!\!/6\!\!\!/0\!\!\!/}} = \$4.96$$

$$(3)\quad \frac{\overset{.62}{\$4.9\!\!\!/6\!\!\!/} \times 8 \times 4\!\!\!/5\!\!\!/}{\underset{8}{3\!\!\!/6\!\!\!/0\!\!\!/}} = \$4.96$$

$$(T)\quad \frac{4\!\!\!/5\!\!\!/}{3\!\!\!/6\!\!\!/0\!\!\!/} \times \overset{4.96}{3\!\!\!/9.6\!\!\!/8\!\!\!/} = \$4.96 \text{ (int. for 45 days)}.$$

Shorter Methods for Computing Simple Interest

To find the interest at 6% for 60 days, point off two places from the right on the principal. For example, the interest on $635 at 6% for 60 days is $6.35. By bearing this principle in mind, the interest at 6% for any number of days can be quickly found.

(1) Find the interest on $345 at 6% for 45 days.

$345 = $3.45 (int. for 60 days)

$$\frac{\overset{3}{\cancel{45}}}{\underset{4}{\cancel{60}}} \times \$3.45 = \frac{10.35}{4} = \$2.5875$$

or $2.59 (int. for 45 days).

Since the interest was for a period of less than 60 days, the fractional part of 60 or $\frac{45}{60}$, had to be multiplied by $3.45 in order to find the interest for 45 days, resulting in $2.5875 or $2.59. If an interest problem does not come out even after the second decimal, carry it out to two more decimal places, and if the third number after the decimal point in the answer is 5 or more, add 1 to the result.

(2) Find the interest on $725 at 6% for 75 days.

$725 = $7.25 (int. for 60 days)

$$\frac{\overset{5}{\cancel{75}}}{\underset{4}{\cancel{60}}} \times 7.25 = \frac{\$36.25}{4} = \$9.0625$$

or $9.06 (int. for 75 days).

To find the interest for 60 days at a rate other than 6%, the following rules will be found helpful.

At 2%, since this is $\frac{1}{3}$ of 6, take $\frac{1}{3}$ of the interest at 6%.
At 3%, since this is $\frac{1}{2}$ of 6, take $\frac{1}{2}$ of the interest at 6%.
At 4%, since this is $\frac{1}{3}$ less than 6, subtract $\frac{1}{3}$ of the interest at 6%.
At 5%, since this is $\frac{1}{6}$ less than 6, subtract $\frac{1}{6}$ of the interest at 6%.
At 7%, since this is $\frac{1}{6}$ more than 6, add $\frac{1}{6}$ of the interest at 6%.
At 8%, since this is $\frac{1}{3}$ more than 6, add $\frac{1}{3}$ of the interest at 6%.
At 9%, since this is $\frac{1}{2}$ more than 6%, add $\frac{1}{2}$ of the interest at 6%.
At 10%, since this is 4% more than 6%, add 4% to that at 6%.

Banker's interest is the same as simple interest except that the exact number of days must be counted instead of using a 30-day month. For example, what would be the banker's interest on $858 at 6% from March 1 to May 9?

Days in March............31
Days in April............30
Days in May..............9
70

$858 = $8.58 (int. for 60 days)

$$\frac{\cancel{70}}{\cancel{60}} \times \$8.58 = \$10.01 \text{ (int. for 70 days).}$$

(1.43 written above)

Compound Interest

Compound interest differs from simple interest in that the interest at the end of the year is added to the principal, and each succeeding year's interest calculated on the basis of interest plus principal. For example, what is the compound interest on $2500 for 3 years at 4%?

$2500	$2600	$2704
.04	.04	.04
$100.00 (int. for 1 yr.)	$104.00 (int. for 2nd yr.)	$108.16 (int. for 3rd yr.)

$2704.00
108.16
$2812.16 (int. plus prin. for 3rd yr.)

Discount

Discount is the interest paid to a bank for converting commercial papers such as drafts, promissory notes, etc., into cash before their date of maturity. This is often called a *bank discount*. The *face* of a note or draft is the value of the paper (*i.e.*, the total amount of money involved) minus interest. The *value* or *amount*, of a note or draft is what the paper is worth at the date of maturity. The *proceeds* of a note or draft are the value, less all charges. The *discount period* is the time (figured in days) between the date of discount and the date of maturity.

The bank discount and proceeds of a commercial paper are found by determining the value of the paper and the bank discount, and subtracting the bank discount from the value. For example, What are the proceeds of a note for $8200 dated May 3, due in 3 months, and discounted by the bank on June 2 at 5%?

Note due August 3

30–2 = 28 days in June
31 days in July
3 days in Aug.
62 days = discount period at 5%

Face of note	= $8200.00
Bank discount on $8200 for 62 days	= 70.61
Proceeds	= $8129.39

Measurements

In business, the two measurements most frequently used are that of area or surface, a two-dimensional product expressed in terms of square inches, square feet, or square yards; and that of volume, a three-dimensional product expressed in terms of cubic inches, cubic feet, or cubic yards.

To find the area of a square or rectangle multiply the length by the width. For instance, How much linoleum is needed to cover a floor 15 feet long and 18 feet wide? Multiply 18 by 15 to get the answer.

To find the area of a triangle, multiply the product of the base and the height, or altitude, by $\frac{1}{2}$. (The altitude of a triangle is a perpendicular dropped from the vertex to the base.) For instance, what is the area of a triangle with an altitude of 5 feet 3 inches and a base of 9 feet 4 inches?

$$\frac{5\frac{1}{4} \times 9\frac{1}{3}}{2} = \frac{\frac{\overset{7}{\cancel{21}}}{\cancel{4}} \times \frac{\overset{7}{\cancel{28}}}{\cancel{3}}}{2} = \frac{49}{2} = 24\tfrac{1}{2} \text{ sq. ft.}$$

(It is best to work with a uniform unit of measurement. Hence, since $\frac{3}{12} = \frac{1}{4}$ of a foot, and $\frac{4}{12} = \frac{1}{3}$ of a foot, 5 feet 3 inches is changed to $5\frac{1}{4}$ feet and 9 feet 4 inches to $9\frac{1}{3}$ feet.)

To find the area of a circle, divide the product of the circumference and diameter by 4. The circumference of a circle is obtained by multiplying the diameter by *pi* which equals 3.14159 or about $3\frac{1}{7}$. For example, what is the area of a circle having a diameter of 5 feet?

$$\begin{array}{r} 3.14159 \text{ (pi)} \\ 5 \text{(diameter)} \\ \hline 15.70795 = \text{circumference} \end{array}$$

$$\frac{15.70795 \times 5}{4} = \frac{78.53975}{4} = 19.635 \text{ sq. ft.} = \text{area}$$

To find the volume of a solid, multiply the length by the width by the height. For example, what is the volume of air in a room that is 12 feet high, 10 feet wide, and 14 feet long?

$$12 \times 10 \times 14 = 1680 \text{ cubic feet.}$$

To find the number of board feet in lumber, multiply the length by the width by the thickness. If the board is less than 1 inch thick, consider it as a full inch; if more than 1 inch thick, use exact dimensions. For example, how many board feet are in a piece of wood 20 feet long, 3 feet wide, and $\frac{3}{4}$ of an inch thick?

$$20 \times 3 \times 1 = 60 \text{ board feet.}$$

PERPETUAL CALENDAR

This calendar will give you the day of the week on which a date falls during the two centuries from 1901 to the year 2100. To locate the day, first look at the proper year in the list below. A letter follows this year which indicates the calendar in use during that year.

1901	C	1930	D	1959	E	1988	M	2017	A	2046	B	2075	C
1902	D	1931	E	1960	M	1989	A	2018	B	2047	C	2076	K
1903	E	1932	M	1961	A	1990	B	2019	C	2048	K	2077	F
1904	M	1933	A	1962	B	1991	C	2020	K	2049	F	2078	G
1905	A	1934	B	1963	C	1992	K	2021	F	2050	G	2079	A
1906	B	1935	C	1964	K	1993	F	2022	G	2051	A	2080	I
1907	C	1936	K	1965	F	1994	G	2023	A	2052	I	2081	D
1908	K	1937	F	1966	G	1995	A	2024	I	2053	D	2082	E
1909	F	1938	G	1967	A	1996	I	2025	D	2054	E	2083	F
1910	G	1939	A	1968	I	1997	D	2026	E	2055	F	2084	N
1911	A	1940	I	1969	D	1998	E	2027	F	2056	N	2085	B
1912	I	1941	D	1970	E	1999	F	2028	N	2057	B	2086	C
1913	D	1942	E	1971	F	2000	N	2029	B	2058	C	2087	D
1914	E	1943	F	1972	N	2001	B	2030	C	2059	D	2088	L
1915	F	1944	N	1973	B	2002	C	2031	D	2060	L	2089	G
1916	N	1945	B	1974	C	2003	D	2032	L	2061	G	2090	A
1917	B	1946	C	1975	D	2004	L	2033	G	2062	A	2091	B
1918	C	1947	D	1976	L	2005	G	2034	A	2063	B	2092	J
1919	D	1948	L	1977	G	2006	A	2035	B	2064	J	2093	E
1920	L	1949	G	1978	A	2007	B	2036	J	2065	E	2094	F
1921	G	1950	A	1979	B	2008	J	2037	E	2066	F	2095	G
1922	A	1951	B	1980	J	2009	E	2038	F	2067	G	2096	H
1923	B	1952	J	1981	E	2010	F	2039	G	2068	H	2097	C
1924	J	1953	E	1982	F	2011	G	2040	H	2069	C	2098	D
1925	E	1954	F	1983	G	2012	H	2041	C	2070	D	2099	E
1926	F	1955	G	1984	H	2013	C	2042	D	2071	E	2100	F
1927	G	1956	H	1985	C	2014	D	2043	E	2072	M		
1928	H	1957	C	1986	D	2015	E	2044	M	2073	A		
1929	C	1958	D	1987	E	2016	M	2045	A	2074	B		

A

JANUARY	MAY	SEPTEMBER
S M T W T F S 1 2 3 4 5 6 7 8 9 10 11 12 13 14 15 16 17 18 19 20 21 22 23 24 25 26 27 28 29 30 31	S M T W T F S 1 2 3 4 5 6 7 8 9 10 11 12 13 14 15 16 17 18 19 20 21 22 23 24 25 26 27 28 29 30 31	S M T W T F S 1 2 3 4 5 6 7 8 9 10 11 12 13 14 15 16 17 18 19 20 21 22 23 24 25 26 27 28 29 30
FEBRUARY	**JUNE**	**OCTOBER**
S M T W T F S 1 2 3 4 5 6 7 8 9 10 11 12 13 14 15 16 17 18 19 20 21 22 23 24 25 26 27 28	S M T W T F S 1 2 3 4 5 6 7 8 9 10 11 12 13 14 15 16 17 18 19 20 21 22 23 24 25 26 27 28 29 30	S M T W T F S 1 2 3 4 5 6 7 8 9 10 11 12 13 14 15 16 17 18 19 20 21 22 23 24 25 26 27 28 29 30 31
MARCH	**JULY**	**NOVEMBER**
S M T W T F S 1 2 3 4 5 6 7 8 9 10 11 12 13 14 15 16 17 18 19 20 21 22 23 24 25 26 27 28 29 30 31	S M T W T F S 1 2 3 4 5 6 7 8 9 10 11 12 13 14 15 16 17 18 19 20 21 22 23 24 25 26 27 28 29 30 31	S M T W T F S 1 2 3 4 5 6 7 8 9 10 11 12 13 14 15 16 17 18 19 20 21 22 23 24 25 26 27 28 29 30
APRIL	**AUGUST**	**DECEMBER**
S M T W T F S 1 2 3 4 5 6 7 8 9 10 11 12 13 14 15 16 17 18 19 20 21 22 23 24 25 26 27 28 29 30	S M T W T F S 1 2 3 4 5 6 7 8 9 10 11 12 13 14 15 16 17 18 19 20 21 22 23 24 25 26 27 28 29 30 31	S M T W T F S 1 2 3 4 5 6 7 8 9 10 11 12 13 14 15 16 17 18 19 20 21 22 23 24 25 26 27 28 29 30 31

B

JANUARY	MAY	SEPTEMBER
S M T W T F S 1 2 3 4 5 6 7 8 9 10 11 12 13 14 15 16 17 18 19 20 21 22 23 24 25 26 27 28 29 30 31	S M T W T F S 1 2 3 4 5 6 7 8 9 10 11 12 13 14 15 16 17 18 19 20 21 22 23 24 25 26 27 28 29 30 31	S M T W T F S 1 2 3 4 5 6 7 8 9 10 11 12 13 14 15 16 17 18 19 20 21 22 23 24 25 26 27 28 29 30
FEBRUARY	**JUNE**	**OCTOBER**
S M T W T F S 1 2 3 4 5 6 7 8 9 10 11 12 13 14 15 16 17 18 19 20 21 22 23 24 25 26 27 28	S M T W T F S 1 2 3 4 5 6 7 8 9 10 11 12 13 14 15 16 17 18 19 20 21 22 23 24 25 26 27 28 29 30	S M T W T F S 1 2 3 4 5 6 7 8 9 10 11 12 13 14 15 16 17 18 19 20 21 22 23 24 25 26 27 28 29 30 31
MARCH	**JULY**	**NOVEMBER**
S M T W T F S 1 2 3 4 5 6 7 8 9 10 11 12 13 14 15 16 17 18 19 20 21 22 23 24 25 26 27 28 29 30 31	S M T W T F S 1 2 3 4 5 6 7 8 9 10 11 12 13 14 15 16 17 18 19 20 21 22 23 24 25 26 27 28 29 30 31	S M T W T F S 1 2 3 4 5 6 7 8 9 10 11 12 13 14 15 16 17 18 19 20 21 22 23 24 25 26 27 28 29 30
APRIL	**AUGUST**	**DECEMBER**
S M T W T F S 1 2 3 4 5 6 7 8 9 10 11 12 13 14 15 16 17 18 19 20 21 22 23 24 25 26 27 28 29 30	S M T W T F S 1 2 3 4 5 6 7 8 9 10 11 12 13 14 15 16 17 18 19 20 21 22 23 24 25 26 27 28 29 30 31	S M T W T F S 1 2 3 4 5 6 7 8 9 10 11 12 13 14 15 16 17 18 19 20 21 22 23 24 25 26 27 28 29 30 31

C

JANUARY	MAY	SEPTEMBER
S M T W T F S 1 2 3 4 5 6 7 8 9 10 11 12 13 14 15 16 17 18 19 20 21 22 23 24 25 26 27 28 29 30 31	S M T W T F S 1 2 3 4 5 6 7 8 9 10 11 12 13 14 15 16 17 18 19 20 21 22 23 24 25 26 27 28 29 30 31	S M T W T F S 1 2 3 4 5 6 7 8 9 10 11 12 13 14 15 16 17 18 19 20 21 22 23 24 25 26 27 28 29 30
FEBRUARY	**JUNE**	**OCTOBER**
S M T W T F S 1 2 3 4 5 6 7 8 9 10 11 12 13 14 15 16 17 18 19 20 21 22 23 24 25 26 27 28	S M T W T F S 1 2 3 4 5 6 7 8 9 10 11 12 13 14 15 16 17 18 19 20 21 22 23 24 25 26 27 28 29 30	S M T W T F S 1 2 3 4 5 6 7 8 9 10 11 12 13 14 15 16 17 18 19 20 21 22 23 24 25 26 27 28 29 30 31
MARCH	**JULY**	**NOVEMBER**
S M T W T F S 1 2 3 4 5 6 7 8 9 10 11 12 13 14 15 16 17 18 19 20 21 22 23 24 25 26 27 28 29 30 31	S M T W T F S 1 2 3 4 5 6 7 8 9 10 11 12 13 14 15 16 17 18 19 20 21 22 23 24 25 26 27 28 29 30 31	S M T W T F S 1 2 3 4 5 6 7 8 9 10 11 12 13 14 15 16 17 18 19 20 21 22 23 24 25 26 27 28 29 30
APRIL	**AUGUST**	**DECEMBER**
S M T W T F S 1 2 3 4 5 6 7 8 9 10 11 12 13 14 15 16 17 18 19 20 21 22 23 24 25 26 27 28 29 30	S M T W T F S 1 2 3 4 5 6 7 8 9 10 11 12 13 14 15 16 17 18 19 20 21 22 23 24 25 26 27 28 29 30 31	S M T W T F S 1 2 3 4 5 6 7 8 9 10 11 12 13 14 15 16 17 18 19 20 21 22 23 24 25 26 27 28 29 30 31

D

JANUARY	MAY	SEPTEMBER
S M T W T F S 1 2 3 4 5 6 7 8 9 10 11 12 13 14 15 16 17 18 19 20 21 22 23 24 25 26 27 28 29 30 31	S M T W T F S 1 2 3 4 5 6 7 8 9 10 11 12 13 14 15 16 17 18 19 20 21 22 23 24 25 26 27 28 29 30 31	S M T W T F S 1 2 3 4 5 6 7 8 9 10 11 12 13 14 15 16 17 18 19 20 21 22 23 24 25 26 27 28 29 30
FEBRUARY	**JUNE**	**OCTOBER**
S M T W T F S 1 2 3 4 5 6 7 8 9 10 11 12 13 14 15 16 17 18 19 20 21 22 23 24 25 26 27 28	S M T W T F S 1 2 3 4 5 6 7 8 9 10 11 12 13 14 15 16 17 18 19 20 21 22 23 24 25 26 27 28 29 30	S M T W T F S 1 2 3 4 5 6 7 8 9 10 11 12 13 14 15 16 17 18 19 20 21 22 23 24 25 26 27 28 29 30 31
MARCH	**JULY**	**NOVEMBER**
S M T W T F S 1 2 3 4 5 6 7 8 9 10 11 12 13 14 15 16 17 18 19 20 21 22 23 24 25 26 27 28 29 30 31	S M T W T F S 1 2 3 4 5 6 7 8 9 10 11 12 13 14 15 16 17 18 19 20 21 22 23 24 25 26 27 28 29 30 31	S M T W T F S 1 2 3 4 5 6 7 8 9 10 11 12 13 14 15 16 17 18 19 20 21 22 23 24 25 26 27 28 29 30
APRIL	**AUGUST**	**DECEMBER**
S M T W T F S 1 2 3 4 5 6 7 8 9 10 11 12 13 14 15 16 17 18 19 20 21 22 23 24 25 26 27 28 29 30	S M T W T F S 1 2 3 4 5 6 7 8 9 10 11 12 13 14 15 16 17 18 19 20 21 22 23 24 25 26 27 28 29 30 31	S M T W T F S 1 2 3 4 5 6 7 8 9 10 11 12 13 14 15 16 17 18 19 20 21 22 23 24 25 26 27 28 29 30 31

E

JANUARY	MAY	SEPTEMBER
S M T W T F S 1 2 3 4 5 6 7 8 9 10 11 12 13 14 15 16 17 18 19 20 21 22 23 24 25 26 27 28 29 30 31	S M T W T F S 1 2 3 4 5 6 7 8 9 10 11 12 13 14 15 16 17 18 19 20 21 22 23 24 25 26 27 28 29 30 31	S M T W T F S 1 2 3 4 5 6 7 8 9 10 11 12 13 14 15 16 17 18 19 20 21 22 23 24 25 26 27 28 29 30
FEBRUARY	**JUNE**	**OCTOBER**
S M T W T F S 1 2 3 4 5 6 7 8 9 10 11 12 13 14 15 16 17 18 19 20 21 22 23 24 25 26 27 28	S M T W T F S 1 2 3 4 5 6 7 8 9 10 11 12 13 14 15 16 17 18 19 20 21 22 23 24 25 26 27 28 29 30	S M T W T F S 1 2 3 4 5 6 7 8 9 10 11 12 13 14 15 16 17 18 19 20 21 22 23 24 25 26 27 28 29 30 31
MARCH	**JULY**	**NOVEMBER**
S M T W T F S 1 2 3 4 5 6 7 8 9 10 11 12 13 14 15 16 17 18 19 20 21 22 23 24 25 26 27 28 29 30 31	S M T W T F S 1 2 3 4 5 6 7 8 9 10 11 12 13 14 15 16 17 18 19 20 21 22 23 24 25 26 27 28 29 30 31	S M T W T F S 1 2 3 4 5 6 7 8 9 10 11 12 13 14 15 16 17 18 19 20 21 22 23 24 25 26 27 28 29 30
APRIL	**AUGUST**	**DECEMBER**
S M T W T F S 1 2 3 4 5 6 7 8 9 10 11 12 13 14 15 16 17 18 19 20 21 22 23 24 25 26 27 28 29 30	S M T W T F S 1 2 3 4 5 6 7 8 9 10 11 12 13 14 15 16 17 18 19 20 21 22 23 24 25 26 27 28 29 30 31	S M T W T F S 1 2 3 4 5 6 7 8 9 10 11 12 13 14 15 16 17 18 19 20 21 22 23 24 25 26 27 28 29 30 31

F

JANUARY	MAY	SEPTEMBER
S M T W T F S 1 2 3 4 5 6 7 8 9 10 11 12 13 14 15 16 17 18 19 20 21 22 23 24 25 26 27 28 29 30 31	S M T W T F S 1 2 3 4 5 6 7 8 9 10 11 12 13 14 15 16 17 18 19 20 21 22 23 24 25 26 27 28 29 30 31	S M T W T F S 1 2 3 4 5 6 7 8 9 10 11 12 13 14 15 16 17 18 19 20 21 22 23 24 25 26 27 28 29 30
FEBRUARY	**JUNE**	**OCTOBER**
S M T W T F S 1 2 3 4 5 6 7 8 9 10 11 12 13 14 15 16 17 18 19 20 21 22 23 24 25 26 27 28	S M T W T F S 1 2 3 4 5 6 7 8 9 10 11 12 13 14 15 16 17 18 19 20 21 22 23 24 25 26 27 28 29 30	S M T W T F S 1 2 3 4 5 6 7 8 9 10 11 12 13 14 15 16 17 18 19 20 21 22 23 24 25 26 27 28 29 30 31
MARCH	**JULY**	**NOVEMBER**
S M T W T F S 1 2 3 4 5 6 7 8 9 10 11 12 13 14 15 16 17 18 19 20 21 22 23 24 25 26 27 28 29 30 31	S M T W T F S 1 2 3 4 5 6 7 8 9 10 11 12 13 14 15 16 17 18 19 20 21 22 23 24 25 26 27 28 29 30 31	S M T W T F S 1 2 3 4 5 6 7 8 9 10 11 12 13 14 15 16 17 18 19 20 21 22 23 24 25 26 27 28 29 30
APRIL	**AUGUST**	**DECEMBER**
S M T W T F S 1 2 3 4 5 6 7 8 9 10 11 12 13 14 15 16 17 18 19 20 21 22 23 24 25 26 27 28 29 30	S M T W T F S 1 2 3 4 5 6 7 8 9 10 11 12 13 14 15 16 17 18 19 20 21 22 23 24 25 26 27 28 29 30 31	S M T W T F S 1 2 3 4 5 6 7 8 9 10 11 12 13 14 15 16 17 18 19 20 21 22 23 24 25 26 27 28 29 30 31

G

JANUARY	MAY	SEPTEMBER
S M T W T F S 1 2 3 4 5 6 7 8 9 10 11 12 13 14 15 16 17 18 19 20 21 22 23 24 25 26 27 28 29 30 31	S M T W T F S 1 2 3 4 5 6 7 8 9 10 11 12 13 14 15 16 17 18 19 20 21 22 23 24 25 26 27 28 29 30 31	S M T W T F S 1 2 3 4 5 6 7 8 9 10 11 12 13 14 15 16 17 18 19 20 21 22 23 24 25 26 27 28 29 30
FEBRUARY	**JUNE**	**OCTOBER**
S M T W T F S 1 2 3 4 5 6 7 8 9 10 11 12 13 14 15 16 17 18 19 20 21 22 23 24 25 26 27 28	S M T W T F S 1 2 3 4 5 6 7 8 9 10 11 12 13 14 15 16 17 18 19 20 21 22 23 24 25 26 27 28 29 30	S M T W T F S 1 2 3 4 5 6 7 8 9 10 11 12 13 14 15 16 17 18 19 20 21 22 23 24 25 26 27 28 29 30 31
MARCH	**JULY**	**NOVEMBER**
S M T W T F S 1 2 3 4 5 6 7 8 9 10 11 12 13 14 15 16 17 18 19 20 21 22 23 24 25 26 27 28 29 30 31	S M T W T F S 1 2 3 4 5 6 7 8 9 10 11 12 13 14 15 16 17 18 19 20 21 22 23 24 25 26 27 28 29 30 31	S M T W T F S 1 2 3 4 5 6 7 8 9 10 11 12 13 14 15 16 17 18 19 20 21 22 23 24 25 26 27 28 29 30
APRIL	**AUGUST**	**DECEMBER**
S M T W T F S 1 2 3 4 5 6 7 8 9 10 11 12 13 14 15 16 17 18 19 20 21 22 23 24 25 26 27 28 29 30	S M T W T F S 1 2 3 4 5 6 7 8 9 10 11 12 13 14 15 16 17 18 19 20 21 22 23 24 25 26 27 28 29 30 31	S M T W T F S 1 2 3 4 5 6 7 8 9 10 11 12 13 14 15 16 17 18 19 20 21 22 23 24 25 26 27 28 29 30 31

H

JANUARY	MAY	SEPTEMBER
S M T W T F S 1 2 3 4 5 6 7 8 9 10 11 12 13 14 15 16 17 18 19 20 21 22 23 24 25 26 27 28 29 30 31	S M T W T F S 1 2 3 4 5 6 7 8 9 10 11 12 13 14 15 16 17 18 19 20 21 22 23 24 25 26 27 28 29 30 31	S M T W T F S 1 2 3 4 5 6 7 8 9 10 11 12 13 14 15 16 17 18 19 20 21 22 23 24 25 26 27 28 29 30
FEBRUARY	**JUNE**	**OCTOBER**
S M T W T F S 1 2 3 4 5 6 7 8 9 10 11 12 13 14 15 16 17 18 19 20 21 22 23 24 25 26 27 28 29	S M T W T F S 1 2 3 4 5 6 7 8 9 10 11 12 13 14 15 16 17 18 19 20 21 22 23 24 25 26 27 28 29 30	S M T W T F S 1 2 3 4 5 6 7 8 9 10 11 12 13 14 15 16 17 18 19 20 21 22 23 24 25 26 27 28 29 30 31
MARCH	**JULY**	**NOVEMBER**
S M T W T F S 1 2 3 4 5 6 7 8 9 10 11 12 13 14 15 16 17 18 19 20 21 22 23 24 25 26 27 28 29 30 31	S M T W T F S 1 2 3 4 5 6 7 8 9 10 11 12 13 14 15 16 17 18 19 20 21 22 23 24 25 26 27 28 29 30 31	S M T W T F S 1 2 3 4 5 6 7 8 9 10 11 12 13 14 15 16 17 18 19 20 21 22 23 24 25 26 27 28 29 30
APRIL	**AUGUST**	**DECEMBER**
S M T W T F S 1 2 3 4 5 6 7 8 9 10 11 12 13 14 15 16 17 18 19 20 21 22 23 24 25 26 27 28 29 30	S M T W T F S 1 2 3 4 5 6 7 8 9 10 11 12 13 14 15 16 17 18 19 20 21 22 23 24 25 26 27 28 29 30 31	S M T W T F S 1 2 3 4 5 6 7 8 9 10 11 12 13 14 15 16 17 18 19 20 21 22 23 24 25 26 27 28 29 30 31

I

JANUARY	MAY	SEPTEMBER
S M T W T F S 1 2 3 4 5 6 7 8 9 10 11 12 13 14 15 16 17 18 19 20 21 22 23 24 25 26 27 28 29 30 31	S M T W T F S 1 2 3 4 5 6 7 8 9 10 11 12 13 14 15 16 17 18 19 20 21 22 23 24 25 26 27 28 29 30 31	S M T W T F S 1 2 3 4 5 6 7 8 9 10 11 12 13 14 15 16 17 18 19 20 21 22 23 24 25 26 27 28 29 30
FEBRUARY	**JUNE**	**OCTOBER**
S M T W T F S 1 2 3 4 5 6 7 8 9 10 11 12 13 14 15 16 17 18 19 20 21 22 23 24 25 26 27 28 29	S M T W T F S 1 2 3 4 5 6 7 8 9 10 11 12 13 14 15 16 17 18 19 20 21 22 23 24 25 26 27 28 29 30	S M T W T F S 1 2 3 4 5 6 7 8 9 10 11 12 13 14 15 16 17 18 19 20 21 22 23 24 25 26 27 28 29 30 31
MARCH	**JULY**	**NOVEMBER**
S M T W T F S 1 2 3 4 5 6 7 8 9 10 11 12 13 14 15 16 17 18 19 20 21 22 23 24 25 26 27 28 29 30 31	S M T W T F S 1 2 3 4 5 6 7 8 9 10 11 12 13 14 15 16 17 18 19 20 21 22 23 24 25 26 27 28 29 30 31	S M T W T F S 1 2 3 4 5 6 7 8 9 10 11 12 13 14 15 16 17 18 19 20 21 22 23 24 25 26 27 28 29 30
APRIL	**AUGUST**	**DECEMBER**
S M T W T F S 1 2 3 4 5 6 7 8 9 10 11 12 13 14 15 16 17 18 19 20 21 22 23 24 25 26 27 28 29 30	S M T W T F S 1 2 3 4 5 6 7 8 9 10 11 12 13 14 15 16 17 18 19 20 21 22 23 24 25 26 27 28 29 30 31	S M T W T F S 1 2 3 4 5 6 7 8 9 10 11 12 13 14 15 16 17 18 19 20 21 22 23 24 25 26 27 28 29 30 31

J

JANUARY	MAY	SEPTEMBER
S M T W T F S 1 2 3 4 5 6 7 8 9 10 11 12 13 14 15 16 17 18 19 20 21 22 23 24 25 26 27 28 29 30 31	S M T W T F S 1 2 3 4 5 6 7 8 9 10 11 12 13 14 15 16 17 18 19 20 21 22 23 24 25 26 27 28 29 30 31	S M T W T F S 1 2 3 4 5 6 7 8 9 10 11 12 13 14 15 16 17 18 19 20 21 22 23 24 25 26 27 28 29 30
FEBRUARY	**JUNE**	**OCTOBER**
S M T W T F S 1 2 3 4 5 6 7 8 9 10 11 12 13 14 15 16 17 18 19 20 21 22 23 24 25 26 27 28 29	S M T W T F S 1 2 3 4 5 6 7 8 9 10 11 12 13 14 15 16 17 18 19 20 21 22 23 24 25 26 27 28 29 30	S M T W T F S 1 2 3 4 5 6 7 8 9 10 11 12 13 14 15 16 17 18 19 20 21 22 23 24 25 26 27 28 29 30 31
MARCH	**JULY**	**NOVEMBER**
S M T W T F S 1 2 3 4 5 6 7 8 9 10 11 12 13 14 15 16 17 18 19 20 21 22 23 24 25 26 27 28 29 30 31	S M T W T F S 1 2 3 4 5 6 7 8 9 10 11 12 13 14 15 16 17 18 19 20 21 22 23 24 25 26 27 28 29 30 31	S M T W T F S 1 2 3 4 5 6 7 8 9 10 11 12 13 14 15 16 17 18 19 20 21 22 23 24 25 26 27 28 29 30
APRIL	**AUGUST**	**DECEMBER**
S M T W T F S 1 2 3 4 5 6 7 8 9 10 11 12 13 14 15 16 17 18 19 20 21 22 23 24 25 26 27 28 29 30	S M T W T F S 1 2 3 4 5 6 7 8 9 10 11 12 13 14 15 16 17 18 19 20 21 22 23 24 25 26 27 28 29 30 31	S M T W T F S 1 2 3 4 5 6 7 8 9 10 11 12 13 14 15 16 17 18 19 20 21 22 23 24 25 26 27 28 29 30 31

K

JANUARY	MAY	SEPTEMBER
S M T W T F S 1 2 3 4 5 6 7 8 9 10 11 12 13 14 15 16 17 18 19 20 21 22 23 24 25 26 27 28 29 30 31	S M T W T F S 1 2 3 4 5 6 7 8 9 10 11 12 13 14 15 16 17 18 19 20 21 22 23 24 25 26 27 28 29 30 31	S M T W T F S 1 2 3 4 5 6 7 8 9 10 11 12 13 14 15 16 17 18 19 20 21 22 23 24 25 26 27 28 29 30
FEBRUARY	**JUNE**	**OCTOBER**
S M T W T F S 1 2 3 4 5 6 7 8 9 10 11 12 13 14 15 16 17 18 19 20 21 22 23 24 25 26 27 28 29	S M T W T F S 1 2 3 4 5 6 7 8 9 10 11 12 13 14 15 16 17 18 19 20 21 22 23 24 25 26 27 28 29 30	S M T W T F S 1 2 3 4 5 6 7 8 9 10 11 12 13 14 15 16 17 18 19 20 21 22 23 24 25 26 27 28 29 30 31
MARCH	**JULY**	**NOVEMBER**
S M T W T F S 1 2 3 4 5 6 7 8 9 10 11 12 13 14 15 16 17 18 19 20 21 22 23 24 25 26 27 28 29 30 31	S M T W T F S 1 2 3 4 5 6 7 8 9 10 11 12 13 14 15 16 17 18 19 20 21 22 23 24 25 26 27 28 29 30 31	S M T W T F S 1 2 3 4 5 6 7 8 9 10 11 12 13 14 15 16 17 18 19 20 21 22 23 24 25 26 27 28 29 30
APRIL	**AUGUST**	**DECEMBER**
S M T W T F S 1 2 3 4 5 6 7 8 9 10 11 12 13 14 15 16 17 18 19 20 21 22 23 24 25 26 27 28 29 30	S M T W T F S 1 2 3 4 5 6 7 8 9 10 11 12 13 14 15 16 17 18 19 20 21 22 23 24 25 26 27 28 29 30 31	S M T W T F S 1 2 3 4 5 6 7 8 9 10 11 12 13 14 15 16 17 18 19 20 21 22 23 24 25 26 27 28 29 30 31

L

JANUARY	MAY	SEPTEMBER
S M T W T F S 1 2 3 4 5 6 7 8 9 10 11 12 13 14 15 16 17 18 19 20 21 22 23 24 25 26 27 28 29 30 31	S M T W T F S 1 2 3 4 5 6 7 8 9 10 11 12 13 14 15 16 17 18 19 20 21 22 23 24 25 26 27 28 29 30 31	S M T W T F S 1 2 3 4 5 6 7 8 9 10 11 12 13 14 15 16 17 18 19 20 21 22 23 24 25 26 27 28 29 30
FEBRUARY	**JUNE**	**OCTOBER**
S M T W T F S 1 2 3 4 5 6 7 8 9 10 11 12 13 14 15 16 17 18 19 20 21 22 23 24 25 26 27 28 29	S M T W T F S 1 2 3 4 5 6 7 8 9 10 11 12 13 14 15 16 17 18 19 20 21 22 23 24 25 26 27 28 29 30	S M T W T F S 1 2 3 4 5 6 7 8 9 10 11 12 13 14 15 16 17 18 19 20 21 22 23 24 25 26 27 28 29 30 31
MARCH	**JULY**	**NOVEMBER**
S M T W T F S 1 2 3 4 5 6 7 8 9 10 11 12 13 14 15 16 17 18 19 20 21 22 23 24 25 26 27 28 29 30 31	S M T W T F S 1 2 3 4 5 6 7 8 9 10 11 12 13 14 15 16 17 18 19 20 21 22 23 24 25 26 27 28 29 30 31	S M T W T F S 1 2 3 4 5 6 7 8 9 10 11 12 13 14 15 16 17 18 19 20 21 22 23 24 25 26 27 28 29 30
APRIL	**AUGUST**	**DECEMBER**
S M T W T F S 1 2 3 4 5 6 7 8 9 10 11 12 13 14 15 16 17 18 19 20 21 22 23 24 25 26 27 28 29 30	S M T W T F S 1 2 3 4 5 6 7 8 9 10 11 12 13 14 15 16 17 18 19 20 21 22 23 24 25 26 27 28 29 30 31	S M T W T F S 1 2 3 4 5 6 7 8 9 10 11 12 13 14 15 16 17 18 19 20 21 22 23 24 25 26 27 28 29 30 31

M

JANUARY	MAY	SEPTEMBER
S M T W T F S 1 2 3 4 5 6 7 8 9 10 11 12 13 14 15 16 17 18 19 20 21 22 23 24 25 26 27 28 29 30 31	S M T W T F S 1 2 3 4 5 6 7 8 9 10 11 12 13 14 15 16 17 18 19 20 21 22 23 24 25 26 27 28 29 30 31	S M T W T F S 1 2 3 4 5 6 7 8 9 10 11 12 13 14 15 16 17 18 19 20 21 22 23 24 25 26 27 28 29 30
FEBRUARY	**JUNE**	**OCTOBER**
S M T W T F S 1 2 3 4 5 6 7 8 9 10 11 12 13 14 15 16 17 18 19 20 21 22 23 24 25 26 27 28 29	S M T W T F S 1 2 3 4 5 6 7 8 9 10 11 12 13 14 15 16 17 18 19 20 21 22 23 24 25 26 27 28 29 30	S M T W T F S 1 2 3 4 5 6 7 8 9 10 11 12 13 14 15 16 17 18 19 20 21 22 23 24 25 26 27 28 29 30 31
MARCH	**JULY**	**NOVEMBER**
S M T W T F S 1 2 3 4 5 6 7 8 9 10 11 12 13 14 15 16 17 18 19 20 21 22 23 24 25 26 27 28 29 30 31	S M T W T F S 1 2 3 4 5 6 7 8 9 10 11 12 13 14 15 16 17 18 19 20 21 22 23 24 25 26 27 28 29 30 31	S M T W T F S 1 2 3 4 5 6 7 8 9 10 11 12 13 14 15 16 17 18 19 20 21 22 23 24 25 26 27 28 29 30
APRIL	**AUGUST**	**DECEMBER**
S M T W T F S 1 2 3 4 5 6 7 8 9 10 11 12 13 14 15 16 17 18 19 20 21 22 23 24 25 26 27 28 29 30	S M T W T F S 1 2 3 4 5 6 7 8 9 10 11 12 13 14 15 16 17 18 19 20 21 22 23 24 25 26 27 28 29 30 31	S M T W T F S 1 2 3 4 5 6 7 8 9 10 11 12 13 14 15 16 17 18 19 20 21 22 23 24 25 26 27 28 29 30 31

N

JANUARY	MAY	SEPTEMBER
S M T W T F S 1 2 3 4 5 6 7 8 9 10 11 12 13 14 15 16 17 18 19 20 21 22 23 24 25 26 27 28 29 30 31	S M T W T F S 1 2 3 4 5 6 7 8 9 10 11 12 13 14 15 16 17 18 19 20 21 22 23 24 25 26 27 28 29 30 31	S M T W T F S 1 2 3 4 5 6 7 8 9 10 11 12 13 14 15 16 17 18 19 20 21 22 23 24 25 26 27 28 29 30
FEBRUARY	**JUNE**	**OCTOBER**
S M T W T F S 1 2 3 4 5 6 7 8 9 10 11 12 13 14 15 16 17 18 19 20 21 22 23 24 25 26 27 28 29	S M T W T F S 1 2 3 4 5 6 7 8 9 10 11 12 13 14 15 16 17 18 19 20 21 22 23 24 25 26 27 28 29 30	S M T W T F S 1 2 3 4 5 6 7 8 9 10 11 12 13 14 15 16 17 18 19 20 21 22 23 24 25 26 27 28 29 30 31
MARCH	**JULY**	**NOVEMBER**
S M T W T F S 1 2 3 4 5 6 7 8 9 10 11 12 13 14 15 16 17 18 19 20 21 22 23 24 25 26 27 28 29 30 31	S M T W T F S 1 2 3 4 5 6 7 8 9 10 11 12 13 14 15 16 17 18 19 20 21 22 23 24 25 26 27 28 29 30 31	S M T W T F S 1 2 3 4 5 6 7 8 9 10 11 12 13 14 15 16 17 18 19 20 21 22 23 24 25 26 27 28 29 30
APRIL	**AUGUST**	**DECEMBER**
S M T W T F S 1 2 3 4 5 6 7 8 9 10 11 12 13 14 15 16 17 18 19 20 21 22 23 24 25 26 27 28 29 30	S M T W T F S 1 2 3 4 5 6 7 8 9 10 11 12 13 14 15 16 17 18 19 20 21 22 23 24 25 26 27 28 29 30 31	S M T W T F S 1 2 3 4 5 6 7 8 9 10 11 12 13 14 15 16 17 18 19 20 21 22 23 24 25 26 27 28 29 30 31

2,000 NAMES AND THEIR MEANINGS

A Practical Guide for Parents and All Others Interested in Better Naming

by ALEXANDER McQUEEN

Using this dictionary, you can interpret the names of over a hundred million Americans. This may sound like an amazing statement, but it is true. Almost everyone in the United States and Canada bears a name that is listed and explained in this dictionary.

So here they are—names by the thousands. Most of them are desirable names; many of them are good enough; a few of them had better not be used. But even the less desirable ones are interesting. This whole business of naming is interesting. From very ancient times fathers and mothers have given careful thought to the names they chose for their little ones, and grown-ups have changed their own names for many different reasons.

Every name has a more or less definite meaning. This is true even of artificial names, made up of sounds that someone thought were pleasing. Such names begin by meaning nothing, but they soon acquire a meaning from the mind and character of the person wearing them.

Every name in this book has been traced to its original language and has been interpreted carefully according to the rules and customs of that language. Some of the conventional meanings, copied by one writer from another for centuries, have been discarded; they were based on mistakes, and repetition has failed to make them true.

When you hand this dictionary to a friend, he or she will probably turn right to the name lists. Soon you may hear remarks such as "Oh, I don't like this one!" That's just as it should be. Nobody will like all the names. But with over 2,000 to choose from, it should be possible to satisfy all tastes.

As you look through the name lists, you may come across some surprises, not all of them welcome. It is disappointing to find that *Claudia* means "lame," *Cecilia* "blind," *Blaine* "lean," *Caleb* "a dog," *Calvin* "bald," and *Portia* "something to do with pigs." However, as these names have occurred in history, they have often acquired new values, based not on the meaning of the words but on the character of the people who bore them. If these new values are important enough, you may decide to forget the original meanings and use the names again.

In the work on this dictionary many problems were encountered. Sometimes a name would be found that seemed to have two entirely opposite meanings, for example, the name *Casimir*. That name was a poser. It has been interpreted as "preacher of peace" and also as "disturber of peace." The first is based on a verb starting with *kaz*, meaning "preach, command"; the second, on a verb starting with the same three letters but meaning "hinder, spoil." In both cases the *mir* means peace. Now what would you do in a case like that? Perhaps we have here a three-way choice: (1) the peaceful meaning, (2) the warlike meaning, (3) both meanings at once, on the theory that real and lasting peace is sometimes gained only by fighting enemies who come, as recorded by Jeremiah, "saying peace, peace, when there is no peace."

Fortunately, not all names are as paradoxical as *Casimir*. With the aid of 500 dictionaries and 40 years of study in the field of personal names, over 2,000 names were traced to their sources.

ABBREVIATIONS USED IN THIS DICTIONARY OF NAMES

In the lists of names the language indicated by the abbreviation is usually the earliest source of the name. The name itself may be French, German, or Swedish, but if, for example, the abbreviation is (H), the earliest traceable origin is Hebrew.

Ar Arabic
Aram Aramaic
Armen Armenian
Assyr Assyrian
Eg Egyptian
F French
Fin Finnish
Gr Greek
H Hebrew
Hg Hungarian
Icel Icelandic
Ir Irish
J Japanese
K Keltic (shared among Irish, Gaelic, Welsh, Breton)
L Latin
Lith Lithuanian
OE Old English (same as Anglo-Saxon)
OF Old French
Pers Persian
Port Portuguese
Rum Rumanian
Rus Russian
Scan Scandinavian (*See also* T.)
Skt Sanskrit
Sl Slavic (Czech, Russian, Polish)
Sp Spanish
T Teutonic (properly includes Old English and Scandinavian)
W Welsh
dim. diminutive (suggests smallness but dim. form sometimes longer than original)
var. variant, variation
fem. feminine
masc. masculine

THE IMPORTANCE OF NAMING

"The giving of names is no small matter, nor should it be left to chance or to persons of mean abilities." . . . . . SOCRATES

WHY DOES IT MATTER?

The naming of an infant is of more than passing importance because it brings to parents the privilege and duty of bestowing upon their child something that will distinguish it from others and will represent it in a fitting and honorable manner.

Sometimes the baby does not get all the consideration it deserves in this matter of providing it with a permanent name; sometimes it even receives a name that will prove a handicap in later life. As a rule, however, parents are eager to choose desirable names for their offspring, and it is to help such parents that this work was designed.

MOTHER'S OPPORTUNITY

The mother—God bless her—often has the last word when it comes to naming her little ones. And if she should say, "I don't care what you call him, so long as it's Arthur," wisdom might suggest a graceful surrender on the part of the father and all other persons interested in solving the family problem, for if any one person is to make the decision unaided, it should by all means be the one who has already done so much by consecrating herself to the duties of motherhood and whose judgment is guided by the light of mother love.

HOW TO FIND A GOOD NAME

A wise mother is usually willing to listen to anyone who has constructive suggestions about the welfare of her babies. To aid her in making the vital decision, seven rules of naming have been devised. These rules, explained in detail on the following pages, are as follows:

1. The name should be worthy.
2. It should have a good meaning.
3. It should be original.
4. It should be easy to pronounce.
5. It should be distinctive.
6. It should fit the family name.
7. It should indicate the sex.

WHAT IS A WORTHY NAME?

Rule One says that the name should be worthy. It should be based upon the dictates not only of affection but of sound judgment. If the child is regarded as a gift of God, it is worth naming well.

Careful research is employed and large sums of money are expended in the selection or invention of names for new articles of commerce, the idea being to establish a name that will not only identify the article but protect it and represent it creditably. Wise parents are learning to exercise similar care and to confer names that will be a pride and an inspiration to their children. An enthusiast for better naming recently covered the ground rather completely when he exhorted parents to "give your children names indicative of what you would have them be—in this world and in the world to come—and at the same time bear in mind the practical, everyday value of a well-chosen name." It will not be so hard to find common-sense names that measure up to these requirements if we keep in mind the hints embodied in the seven rules.

BIBLE NAMES

The thought might occur to some readers that a simple way to insure the adoption of a "good" name would be to confine their choice to names recorded in the Scriptures. It is true that many Bible names are beautiful and expressive, but good taste must prevail in this as in all other matters. If some of the longer or less familiar scriptural names are given, their careless use may result in drawing ridicule upon the bearer of the name or upon its sacred source. This is true of some names containing rare or unusual sounds and of names that lend themselves easily to distortion or punning. This point should not be unduly stressed, but it may be illustrated by several names that by reason of their inherent holiness should be kept beyond the likelihood of unseemly treatment: *Hezekiah*, meaning "strength of the Lord"; *Eliphalet*, "God of salvation"; *Bezaleel*, "in the shadow of God."

WORTHY AND UNWORTHY NAMES

A good name will inspire respect in the minds of others because of its pleasant sound or associations, and it will inspire in its owner pride and the desire to be really worthy of it. As specimens of names that can hardly be called worthy in this sense we may mention such names as *Quintus*, *Sextus*, *Septimus*, and *Octavius*, which are merely numbers meaning "fifth," "sixth," "seventh," and "eighth." Such arithmetical terms, usually not employed until the fifth child comes, might almost suggest that the accumulating of a family has become a bore.

WHY DOES THE MEANING MATTER?

According to Rule Two, the name should have a good meaning or at least a pleasant or harmless association. The reason for this will be apparent to most readers, but there are some considerations in naming that are often overlooked. Few parents would call a child *Judas* (a name of good meaning but tragic or sad association) or *Benoni* ("son of my sorrow"), but many have inflicted on their innocent babes the names of battles or of political events of passing interest. An infant receives its name when it is helpless; parents should be considerate and should refrain from wishing anything onto their child that might cause embarrassment later.

FAMOUS NAMES

If family names happen to be those of famous persons, such as Shakespeare, Lincoln, or Nightingale, the children are not helped by calling them *William*, *Abraham*, or *Florence*. When they grow up they will not want to be annoyed, in season and out, by the empty remarks of people who pay more attention to the name than to the person.

SOME GOOD NAMES NOT FAVORED

It is by some people deemed wise to avoid the use of certain very good names that, on account of our strange modern sense of humor, have come to be regarded as effeminate. Of these we might mention *Percival*, *Algernon*, *Cecil*, and *Reginald*—all of them really splendid names. Perhaps a remote origin of their disrepute may be found in the contemptuous attitude of the rugged Anglo-Saxons toward their somewhat dandified Norman conquerors.

WATCH THE INITIALS

The initials of a name should not form unpleasing or undignified words. *Martin Ulysses Taylor* is sure to be nicknamed "Mutt," and *Sydney Alfred Lee* will doubtless be known as "Sally."

HUMOR IN NAMING

In naming there is no place for humor. Life is real, life is earnest; naming is a serious, though not necessarily cheerless, affair. Of course, there have been cases where parents have purposely given funny names to their children—for example, when a first child was called *Peter* and the second child *Re-peater*, and when the father of a large and expensive family insisted on naming one of the boys *Bill* "because he came on the first of the month." Many other cases could be quoted—some of them so absurd as to be hardly believable—but sensible parents will not want to follow such examples, and it is perhaps just as well not to give any more of them here.

WHY NOT USE IMAGINATION?

Rule Three suggests that the name should be as original as possible without being eccentric. A certain article of furniture we call *chair;* another article of furniture we call *stool*. They are not the same, but they are both designed to sit upon and are near enough alike to be classed as first cousins. Mark you—they are similar but named differently. Now we come to two men. One of them is rich and fat and fair and slow and stupid; the other is poor and thin and dark and quick and intelligent. And we call one of them *John*, and the other—*John*. Altogether dissimilar, but named alike. This is simply another way of stating that human beings are named with less variety and imagination than inanimate objects—less discrimination in naming the lords of creation than in naming stocks and stones.

An ideal condition would be for every individual to have a name indicating not only his character but his place and function in society; but as such exactness is hardly possible this side of eternity, we have to be satisfied with a very limited assortment of names, unless we are bold enough to invent new ones for the babies.

In ancient times the giving of made-up or invented names was an ordinary occurrence. In the Old Testament we are told "And Adam called his wife's name *Eve* ("life"), because she was the mother of all living." "And Abraham called the name of his son that was born unto him . . . *Isaac*"; this name referred to the laughter, both of disbelief and joy, that preceded and followed the birth of the son of the patriarch's old age.

HOW TO INVENT NAMES

Invent really means "find," and the new names of which we are speaking are the easiest things in the world to find if parents will only use their powers of reflection and observation. For example, if the coming of a baby girl is connected in the parents' mind with some notable act of Providence, it is not nessary to follow the example of our Puritan predecessors and call the child *The Lord Will Provide;* the idea can be expressed beautifully and adequately in the name *Provida* (pronounced "proveeda"), which someone has already invented and used. With imagination and common sense it is possible to invent excellent names.

NEW NAMES FOR NEW CHILDREN

While the motive of this book is by no means

that of supplanting all traditional and time-honored names, it is written with the idea that every baby, even at birth, has an identity of its own, which can be fittingly recognized by giving it a new name or a new combination of names.

SOUND AND SPELLING

Rule Four suggests that the name should be easy to pronounce by persons of average education. This rule may not be as important as the others; however, if several names seem equally attractive, it is well to choose one easy to pronounce. It is sometimes wise to avoid trouble from the start by making the spelling fit the pronunciation. In a name like *Phoebe*, for instance, the silent *o* may just as well be dropped, for it serves only to remind scholars that the name used to be pronounced "Foiby."

FOREIGN NAMES

When for some reason it is deemed necessary to use a name from a language quite unlike our own (such as the Polish language), a change in spelling will often help. For example, the Polish *cz* can be changed to *ch; sz* can be changed to *sh;* and other unusual combinations can be simplified.

VARIATIONS

Difference in pronunciation is not always a sign of incorrectness. Take the name *Viola;* Shakespearean students and actors accent the first syllable and pronounce the *i* as in *vine*. Others, with equal correctness, call it "Vee-o-la," with stress on the *o*.

When pronouncing unfamiliar names listed in this dictionary, it will usually be safe to give the vowels their Italian sounds.

"COMMON" PROPER NAMES

According to Rule Five, the name should be easily distinguishable from names of others in the same family or community. Centuries ago a newly converted monarch in eastern Europe caused his subjects to be baptized in batches. All in a given batch received the same Christian name—hundreds of Johns, hundreds of Thomases, hundreds of Marys, Ruths, and so forth. A study of some of our modern city directories, on the pages devoted to certain well-known surnames, might lead us to suppose that this labor-saving custom still prevails. Go into any large assemblage, such as a baseball crowd, and shout "Jack!" or "Bill!" You will probably be amazed at the number of men and boys who will turn immediately to respond to your call.

THE USE OF *JUNIOR*

The custom of naming after parents and relatives has been a potent factor in the duplication—indeed, multiplication—of the same name in a community. While it has seemed natural, especially in the case of sons, to give the name of a parent, the practice is attended with some real difficulties in modern times. Modern young men begin to "cut a figure" in the world early in life, occupying a prominent place in business and social activities. The use of the suffix *Junior* is often overlooked. Father and son (sometimes even grandpa!) are constantly opening one another's letters, and occasions for confusion and embarrassment are multiplied. More than one case is on record in which a son has voluntarily dropped one of his two given names merely to avoid such inconveniences.

DYNASTIC NAMES

John Brown I, John Brown II, John Brown III—here we have one attempt to overcome the trouble caused by copying the parent's name. But it does not deserve encouragement in our progressive and individualistic age. All things considered, it is better not to give children exactly the same names as their parents or other relatives. A child ought not to be an exact duplicate (mental, moral, or spiritual) of its parents. It should be better, and its name ought not to tie it too definitely to the limitations of the past.

ANOTHER HINT

If the reason for naming after a certain person seems to be weighty (expectation of a legacy, for instance!) it is sometimes possible to compromise satisfactorily by substituting a modification for the original name, for instance, *Anita* for *Anna; Jean* for *John; Georgette* or *Georgia* for *Georgina;* and so forth.

DUPLICATE INITIALS

The choice of names with the same initials should be avoided, especially in the case of brothers. Similar names or similar initials cause particular confusion when applied to twins, as for instance in the case of two privates in the same Ohio regiment in World War I who had been christened *Iden A. Brown* and *Aden I. Brown*. The similarity caused them an unlimited amount of trouble in their business transactions.

LONG NAMES

In the search for distinctiveness it is well to avoid the giving of many names to one child. Properly chosen, two names are plenty. In fact, one is enough if it is a good name and serves well to identify its bearer. An extreme example is recorded in the case of a Portuguese princess born early in the 19th century, who was christened *Maria Jose Beatrix Joanna Eulalie Leopoldina Adelaide Isabel Carlotta Michaela Raphaela Gabriela Francisca Paula Inez Sophia Joaquina Theresa Benedicta Bernarda*—a total of 20 names and 141 letters. This young lady would have been popular in ancient Greece or Rome, where fashionable young men were in the habit of pledging their sweetheart's health in as many cups of wine as there were letters in her name.

Prominent men often drop one or more of their names to add distinction or help the rhythm, as, for example, *Charles* (*John Huffham*) *Dickens* and (*Thomas*) *Woodrow Wilson*.

HOW TO HELP THE FAMILY NAME

Rule Six dictates that the given name ought to fit the family name or, at least, not clash with it.

A distinctive given name is of great service to a person with a common family name. The word *common* is used here merely to indicate such names as Smith, Brown, Jones, Robinson, and Johnson, which for historical reasons are borne by many thousands of families. When the Johnson parents name their baby *John*, they are simply piling up trouble for his grown-up life, in the shape of wrongly delivered letters, vexatious errors and delays, and general difficulty in keeping his identity clear in the public mind. In one eastern city alone there are more than 300 John Johnsons.

Family names draw honor and renown from the lives and behavior of their owners; therefore, all such names—however derived, pronounced, or spelled—may be counted honorable and satisfactory. Some people, however, bear names that they consider awkward or undignified, and they can usually improve the effect of such names, in the case of their children, by a careful choice of given names.

AMERICAN NAMES

All names, no matter what their origin, might be regarded as American names. But in an English-speaking nation there is an inclination to class as foreign such names as do not have an Anglo-Saxon sound. There are many exceptions, of course. Hundreds of continental European names have become household words in our midst; but the fact remains that certain names look or sound strange to the average modern American.

FOREIGN FAMILY NAMES

A safe plan with foreign family names is to use simple given names that fit the family name and to take care to choose names reasonably familiar in the New World. One thing is certain: We ought never to make such unnatural combinations as *Denis Schultz* or *Fritz De la Rue*.

SHORT NAMES

Short family names are often helped by the use of given names with two or more syllables. To use two familiar examples from legal language, how much better *Richard Roe* sounds than *John Doe! Tom Brown* may be a good enough name, but it lacks distinction and originality. *Hilary Brown* or *Theodore Brown* are combinations that set off the surname much better. They save the name from being very ordinary and, at the same time, are not elaborate enough to be considered eccentric. A glance at the Brown, Smith, or Jones section of any large city directory will show the force of this argument.

LONG NAMES

On the other hand, if the surname is long, it is better to avoid a long given name. *Sophonsiba Cunningham* and *Cornelius J. Langenbrenner* would sound better as *Rita Cunningham* and *Otto*, or *David*, *Langenbrenner*.

HE OR SHE?

According to Rule Seven, the name should indicate the sex of the child. There is no law to compel the giving of masculine names to boys and feminine names to girls. Even in ancient times some men were named *Mehetabel* and some women were named *Gomer*. In Latin countries the sex is sometimes disregarded, and boys may receive the name of a female saint if they are born on her name day. In the United States there have sometimes been men named *Florence*, either after the city or from a family name, and such names as *Marion* and *Marian* are applied indiscriminately to infants of both sexes.

When one considers the wide material to choose from (more than 2,000 names in this dictionary alone), it seems a pity to give children names that are not immediately recognized as masculine or feminine when written or pronounced.

HERE'S TO THE MOTHERS!

But after all these *do*'s and *don't*s and warnings, we come back to where we started—to the good judgment and loving care of the mothers. Here's to the mothers! May they name their infants as they please—and may they please to accept this dictionary in the friendly spirit in which it is offered.

FAVORITE NAMES AND THEIR MEANINGS

Dear names,
And thousand others throng to me! . . . RUPERT BROOKE

During the writing of this dictionary, which is based on long years of study and research, an interesting discovery was made: Of the more than 2,000 names in our list, two dozen of them would include the names of about a third of the population of the United States. Those names, in the order of their estimated popularity, are: (for girls) Mary, Elizabeth, Barbara, Dorothy, Helen, Margaret, Ruth, Virginia, Jean, Frances, Nancy, and Patricia; (for boys) John, William, Charles, James, George, Robert, Thomas, Henry, Peter, Joseph, Edward, and Samuel. The author decided to take those 24 names, plus some other frequently used names, and write a few words about the meaning of each of them. Following are the descriptions of those favorite names for girls and boys. For convenience, the names in each list have been arranged in alphabetical order.

GIRLS

Alice is derived from Teutonic names based on *Adal-* or *Adel-*, meaning "noble." It has sometimes been translated "noble cheer," but the German *Adelheid* suggests that it means "nobility." Variations of the popular name are *Adelaide*, *Adeline*, *Adela*, and *Adeliza*.

Anna, in 50 or more forms, is from the Hebrew *Hannah*, relating to "grace, mercy." It was the name of the mother of Samuel. Variations include *Nan*, *Anka* (Serbian), and *Panni* (Hungarian).

Barbara is usually interpreted as meaning "a stranger." It is of Greek origin, and the theory is that the ancient Greeks thought the speech of foreigners sounded like *bar-bar-bar*. Such language, they said, was "barbaric," and the people who spoke it were "barbarians." If one of the babbling strangers happened to be a woman and pretty, she too was a "barbarian," but the word then took on a friendlier meaning. When uttered by men, it might even turn into some pet name, such as *Barbara*. It's as simple as that.

An early form of the name in England and America was *Barbary*, now heard only in a few traditional ballads. Popular modern variants are *Babs* and *Babbie*.

Bernice is a Greek name meaning "bringing victory." The *nice* refers to "victory." In Greek it is spelled *nike;* in military aviation a nike jet is a victory jet. The soldiers rhyme *nike* with *Mikey*, but the final syllable in *Bernice* should rhyme with *lease*.

Carol, if derived from Greek, means "a song of joy." It is associated also with the word *choral* and with dancing, for in ancient times singing and dancing often went together. However, *Carol* and *Caroline* are also forms of the Teutonic name *Charles*, which means "a man." To avoid calling a feminine Carol a man, the interpretation "strong, vigorous" is used.

Dolores means "sorrow" or "sorrows." The name is usually associated with "Our Lady of Sorrows." It is popular in all the Latin countries and is spelled in many ways.

Doris is one of the familiar *Dor-* names that come from the Greek word for "a gift." Examples are *Dora*, *Dorea*, *Dorothy*. The last-named means "gift of God" and is reversed in *Theodora*, with the same meaning. Doris is sometimes regarded as a "gift" name, but it is really the name of a district in ancient Greece, so *Doris* might mean simply "a Dorian." Doris in mythology was a daughter of Oceanus. When *Doris* is derived from the Lithuanian language, it means "noble, courageous."

Dorothy is another name of Greek origin. It means "gift of God," the same as *Theodora*. In each case the *theo* part stands for "God" and the *dora* for "gift."

Once upon a time, three or four centuries ago, a little girl gave this name to her most valued possession, a toy baby. But *Dorothy* was hard to say, and the child was content to say "*Dolly*." That's how we got one of our most popular names. Dolls have been "dollies" ever since, and many Dorothys have been described as "dolls."

Edith is a Teutonic name. The *ed* in the name (as in *Edward*, *Edgar*, *Edmund*) means "rich." The *-ith* is from an old word meaning "gift." So *Edith* means "rich gift."

Elizabeth is another name that needs some explanation. In the list it is rendered simply as "worshiper of God." This is the general meaning of the name. In its original Hebrew form, *Elisheva*, it contains the idea of an oath and of the number seven. *Eli* refers to God; *sheva* to an oath or seven. In ancient times seven and an oath were related because they both typified completion and consecration. A covenant was completed by the swearing of an oath. Seven was regarded as a most holy number, indicating fullness; it is so regarded to this day. Learned Hebrew scholars have given several interpretations of this name: "God of the seven," "oath of my God," "God is her oath." All of them suggest a dedication to the worship of God.

There are many variations of *Elizabeth*, all the way from the Estonian *Elts* in one syllable to the Russian *Yelissaveta* in five. Some of the more usable variants are found in this dictionary.

Evelyn is sometimes regarded as a variant of *Eve*, but it really comes from a Keltic word meaning "pleasant, agreeable." In some cases it has been related to the Latin *avellana*, the filbert or hazelnut, possibly accounting for the modern popularity of *Hazel* as a girl's name. The spelling of the name varies a good deal—*Evolyn*, *Evelina*, and so forth. Occasionally the name *Evelyn* is given to a man.

Florence and its other forms, such as *Flora*, *Florrie*, *Flo*, and *Flossie*, simply mean "flourishing." Some men have been named *Florence*, perhaps after a masculine saint or from the city of that name.

Frances means "free." *France*, the name of a great nation, is really of Teutonic origin and is probably related to a group of ancient words beginning with the sound *fr-* and meaning "love, joy, frolicking, freedom, and peace." What a book could be written on *Frances* and *Frank* and their origins! Variants of *Frances* include *Francesca*, *Francina*, *Fanchon*, and many others in our list of names.

Gertrude means "spear-maiden." It is one of the many battle-names invented long ago. *Ger* occurs in many names with the meaning of "spear"; it appears as *gar* in the name of the garfish. *Gertrude* has a number of variations and diminutives, including the familiar *Trudy*, *Trudchen* (German), *Traudl* (Bavarian), *Trudje* (Dutch), *Truta* (Estonian), and *Giertrude* (Polish).

Harriet is the feminine form of *Harry* or *Henry*. *Harry* is interpreted as "master of the home," so Harriet would be "mistress of the home."

Helen is another Greek name, derived from a word meaning "sunlight." It is one of the most popular feminine names of modern times; indeed, it has been popular in many lands through the centuries. Its fame has been extended by many noted ladies, including Helen of Troy, St. Helena, Elaine of the Round Table, and countless others. We have it in such variants as *Eleanor*, *Eleonore*, *Elinor*, and even *Alienor*, also *Leonore*, *Lenore*, *Eileen*, *Ellen*, *Nelly*, and a score of related forms. They all share their origin with *Helios*, the name of the Greek sun god, and with *heliotrope*, a plant reputed to turn (*tropein*) with the sun.

Irene means "peace." The name has grown steadily in popularity in the 20th century. This word, from the Greek *eirene*, used as a greeting, corresponds to the Hebrew *shalom*. In Palestine, in the 1st century A.D., the two greetings were often interchangeable.

Jean is one of the countless feminine variations of *John*, and therefore it means "the Lord is gracious." In French this form is masculine, with *Jeanne* for the feminine. Some of the principal variants are *Johanna*, *Joan* (properly one syllable), *Jenny*, *Janet*, *Juanita*. Others will be found in the list of names. Reference is also suggested to our little essay on the name *John*.

Josephine is the feminine of *Joseph*, which is explained at length in the stories about men's names. Its general meaning is "addition" or "increase."

Katharine is a Greek name with about a hundred variations, all the way from English *Kate* to Russian *Ekaterina*. They all mean "pure." Some unusual forms are *Kadi* (Bavarian), *Tri* (Swiss, using the middle of the name only), *Kasia* (Polish), *Katelik* (Breton), *Kaatje* (Dutch), *Gaton* (French), and *Karin* (Swedish).

Lois is sometimes mistakenly regarded as a variant of *Louis* or *Louise*, but it is really a Greek New Testament name, usually translated "better, agreeable."

Louise is a popular name in what is loosely termed the Western world. Like *Ludwig* and *Louis*, it is a warlike name, generally given the meaning "famous in battle." The first syllable stands for "fame"; *-wig* refers to "battle."

Lucille and its variant forms are derived from *Lux*, the Latin word for "light" (as of the sun). It occurs as *Lucy*, *Lucia*, *Lucinda*, *Lucienne*, *Luciana*, and so forth.

Margaret is a "pearl," at least according to her name in Greek. The name, in one form or another, is known in many countries. It can be as long as ten letters, the Italian *Margherita*, or as short as three, the Scottish *Meg*. From its first syllable are derived forms like *Meg* and *Madge;* from its ending, the Estonian name *Kret*. Its 60 or more variants include *Maisie*, *Maggie*, *Peggy*, *Meta*, *Greta*, *Gretel*, *Gretchen*, *Rita*, and even an inelegant and somewhat rare English form, *Gritty*.

Mary, like the correspondingly important masculine name *John*, is of Hebrew origin. It first occurred in the form of *Miriam*. In Exod. 15:20 is the familiar account of how "Miriam the prophetess, the sister of Aaron, took a timbrel in her hand" and led the women of Israel, with timbrels and dances, in a song of thanksgiving for deliverance from the Egyptians.

In one form or another, *Mary* is a name revered by Christian, Jew, and Moslem. Various meanings have been assigned to it, most of them without proper foundation. Some were suggested by great and good men in the days before language study had become a science. One ingenious guess followed another, with all lovers of the name *Mary* veering away from the fact that its original meaning was not a pleasant one. Let us face the facts; perhaps they're not so dreadful, after all.

This Hebrew name, *Miriam*, became *Mariam* in the Greek language and *Maria* in Latin, whence our *Mary*. In its original Hebrew the name indicated "rebellion, bitterness." One form of the name, *Mara*, appears in the first chapter of Ruth, where Naomi says, "Call me not Naomi, call me Mara; for the Almighty hath dealt very bitterly with me." The Israelites could not drink of the waters of the brook Marah for they were *mariym*, that is, "bitter."

But even bitterness can lead to good. And once again Hebrew shows the way. For the word meaning "bitter" is related to *mor*, meaning "myrrh." Myrrh indeed is bitter; but when it is used for perfume or incense, it is sweet. Myrrh is also used in worship for anointing and in medicine for healing. So within the obvious translation, "bitterness," there is preserved a sense of sweetness. In any case, this is a name of scriptural origin and of profound importance.

In Ireland about a fifth of the women are named *Mary*, sometimes spelled in the Gaelic fashion, *Maire*. Another form, not used in christening, is *Muire*, reserved exclusively for the Blessed Virgin Mary. Many variants will be found in the list in this dictionary.

Mildred means "mild counsel." It is of Old English origin and has been interpreted "mild threatener," because an early form was spelled *Mildthryth*. Modern researchers, however, trace the second syllable from Old English *raed*, meaning "advice, counsel."

Nancy, a variant of *Hannah*, is of Hebrew origin and means "grace, mercy." In its original form the name was pronounced *Kha-nah*, with some stress on the second syllable. As one nation after another adopted it, changes took place; it now exists in many forms, 70 or more, ranging from *Ann* to *Annushka*. Popular forms are *Anna*, *Annette*, and *Anita*.

Patricia means "a patrician, a noble lady." It is, of course, the feminine form of *Patrick*, famed for its connection with the patron saint of Ireland. The original patricians were descended from the *patres*, or fathers of their country, Rome. Our modern Patricias share with Patrick the nickname of *Pat*.

Phyllis is a Greek name meaning "green leaf, green foliage." The name was used by oldtime poets as typifying a rustic sweetheart.

Rose is a popular name in many lands because of the beauty of the rose, in bud or in full bloom. Several variations are given in our alphabetical list, all with the simple floral interpretation. However, in ancient times the rose was used as an emblem of love in its purest form—the lasting love in happy marriages.

Ruth is interpreted as "beauty." It comes from a Hebrew word meaning "appearance, vision (understood to be a vision of beauty)." The original Ruth, whose touching story is told in the Bible book bearing her name, was an ancestress of King David.

It might be well to note that the name *Ruth* can also be drawn from another source, for the word in English signifies "compassion, sorrow for the misfortunes of another." We speak of a heartless person as one who is ruthless; for one who is merciful, we can properly use the word *ruthful*.

From the Hebrew, *beauty*—from Old English, extending back into Icelandic, *compassion*—and both of them are joined in the name *Ruth*.

Sarah (meaning "princess") was the name of the wife of Abraham. She was originally named *Sarai*. Some writers have supposed this to mean "contentious," because of her long childlessness. Perhaps a better theory is that *Sarai* meant "my princess" and that the new name, *Sarah*, with the letter *h* taken from the most holy name, *Jehovah*, was conferred because of the promise that she was to be the mother of nations. Thus she was ordained to be a princess par excellence, without the limiting pronoun *my*. Of the many variants of this name the most popular is *Sally*.

Sylvia, described by Shakespeare in his *Two Gentlemen of Verona* as kind and fair and generally desirable, bore a name that has been given to many modern girls. Latin in origin, it means "one who lives in the woods," or a "forester." A diminutive is *Sylvie*.

Virginia is often related to the colony and state of Virginia, named after Elizabeth, "The Virgin Queen," but it is really of another derivation. Even as *Virgil* was originally *Vergil*, *Virginia* was originally *Verginia*. *Ver* was the word for "springtime." Beaumont and Fletcher, oldtime poet-playwrights, sang of "Primrose, firstborn child of Ver, merry springtime's harbinger." So *Ver* meant "spring" even in our own language. Our vernal breeze is the refreshing breeze of springtime. The spirit of the name *Virginia* is the ideal of awakening life, of new beginnings, of re-creation.

BOYS

Abraham is an important name with a fascinating history. The founder of the Hebrew people was originally named *Abram* (*Ab*, "father"; *ram*, "height"), translated as "father of elevation" or "exalted father." But when he was ordained to be "a father of many nations" (Gen. 17:5), his name was changed to *Abraham*, which involved the addition of the letter *H* from the most holy name, *Jehovah*, *H* being regarded as neither vowel nor consonant but as the very breath of life.

Anthony is derived from the Latin *Antonius*. It has been translated as "deserving praise," also "beyond praise" or "inestimable." Variants are *Anton* (German, Russian), *Antonin* (Czech), *Antonino* (Italian), *Antonio* (Italian, Spanish), *Antoine* (French), *Anthonius* (Dutch), and *Antel* (Hungarian). The usual modern diminutive is *Tony*.

Charles, interpreted as meaning "manly, strong," really means "man." However, it was often used admiringly as a given name to signify "What a man!" Perhaps the most noted wearer of the name was Charles the Great, remembered by the Germans as Karl der Grosse and by the French as Charlemagne. In his day he ruled them both, which ought to give them something to agree about, for Frenchmen and Germans alike regard him as a national hero.

Our English word *churl*, meaning "one who is surly," was originally a form of *Charles*. *Charles* kept its high meaning, but *churl* came down in the world. Among other forms of the name are *Carl*, *Carlo*, *Karel*, and, in Irish, *Searlas*.

Clarence, like all *clar*-names, is derived from Latin *clarus*, "clear" or "bright." The name dates back to the 14th century, when the Norman family name *Clare* was amplified into *Clarence*. By the 16th century Clarence had become a baptismal name in England.

Donald is an ancient Keltic name meaning "world-mighty." Customary diminutives are *Don* and *Donnie*.

Edward means "rich guardian." *Ed* is from an Old English word for "wealth, property." *Ward* is "guard," just as *warranty* is "guarantee"; *w* and *gu* are often interchangeable. A glance at our dictionary list will show several other *Ed*-names. Sometimes *Ed* was considered to mean "blessed," as in *Edric*, presumably on the theory that blessings are spiritual riches.

Variations include *Eduard*, *Edoardo*, *Edvard*, and a score of others. Diminutives are *Eddie*, *Neddy*, *Ned*, and sometimes *Teddy;* but the last-named belongs properly to *Theodore*.

Elmer is a Teutonic name. An early form joined two words —*adel*, "noble," and *mar*, "fame." "Noble fame" is the usual modern interpretation. Elmer as a baptismal name has gained in popularity in the 20th century, especially in the United States.

Elvis is a variant of the Teutonic *Elvin*, meaning "elf-friend." Elves were supposed to be wise, so all *elv*- names carry a suggestion of "wisdom."

Eugene is a complimentary name, fashioned from two Greek words: *eu*, "good, well," and *genes*, "born." It brings to mind the science of eugenics, which concerns itself with the improvement of offspring. The customary diminutive is *Gene*.

George, which is of Greek origin, means "man of the earth," "man of the land," or "farmer." The *ge*- in this name means "earth," and the rest of the word means "to work, or till, the soil." The personal name in Greek is *Georgios*. The *ge*- element is found in our word *geography*, which has to do with the earth, and also in *geometry*, *geology*, *geophysics*, and many others.

In view of the fact that *George* can mean "farmer," it may be interesting to note that the nickname "Farmer George" was given to George III of England and to his great adversary, George Washington. Both men were keenly interested in farming. Washington was one of America's most progressive farmers; he read every farm book he could find, including one by Samuel Deans, of Massachusetts, entitled *The New England Farmer, or Georgical Dictionary*, where again we see the Greek *Georg*- used in its original sense.

There are more than 50 variations of the name, including *Jorge*, *Jurgen*, *Joris*, *Jerzy*, and *Egor*.

Henry suggests "real estate." It has been derived from two Teutonic origins, *Hagen-rich* and *Heimrich*. The first means "master of the enclosure," referring to the entire homestead or estate; the second means "master of the home," referring to the inside of the house. The two amount to just about the same thing; they hint that the man is boss. (But what about *Henrietta!*)

Like most other popular names, *Henry* comes in a variety of forms—all the way from shorties like English *Hal* and German *Hein* to the long-drawn out Italian *Arriguccio*. Familiar forms are the Dutch and Danish *Hendrik*, the French *Henri*, the Spanish and Portuguese *Enrique*, and the Italian *Enrico*.

Herbert is a Teutonic name meaning "bright warrior," the second syllable standing for "bright."

An early form was the Frankish name *Charibert*, later *Haribert*. The Norsemen used many *her-* or *har-* names.

Howard is a name of Teutonic origin, meaning "sword-guardian" (*Heoru-gard*). Some early forms of the name favor the theory that it sometimes had the general meaning of "steward." A familiar modern diminutive is *Howie*.

Hugh is a Teutonic name relating to "mind, thought, study." In other forms it is *Hugo* (Spanish, Portuguese) or *Ugo* (Italian). It is related to the modern name *Hubert*, meaning "bright mind."

Jacob, in Hebrew *Ya-a-kov*, means literally "one who takes hold by the heel" and so trips up his adversary. It is often translated "supplanter," which is virtually the same thing, for the Latin *supplantare* means "to slip something under the sole of another's foot," thus "to trip him up." A modern form of this name is *James*.

James is really a form of the Hebrew *Jacob*, meaning "a supplanter," one who trips another up or takes his place, as Jacob did when he was unfair to Esau, his brother. Esau spoke of this in his complaint, "Is not he rightly named Jacob? for he hath supplanted me these two times."

Best known in English-speaking lands as *James*, *Jim*, *Jimmy*, and *Jamie*, the name is *Seamus* (*Shamus*) in Irish and *Jacques* in French. In Spanish it is *Jayme*, *Diego*, and *Iago*. *Santiago*, name of several cities, means "Saint James."

John is the most important given name in the lands that we are pleased to call the civilized nations. In the United States, for instance, it is the name of one twenty-fifth of the entire male population.

If a good name is better than riches, *John* must be a very good name. In its original Hebrew form it means "the Lord is gracious" or "the Lord is merciful"; therefore, to the millions who bear the name, it should come as a sort of blessing. In the benediction "The Lord make his face to shine upon thee and be gracious unto thee," the word for "gracious" is related to an element in the name *John*. In Hebrew the name was *Yeho-khanan*, with some stress on the final syllable. The first part is a form of the name *Jehovah;* the second part is "gracious, merciful."

In different lands John has taken different forms, not all of them spelled with the letter *J;* for example, *Ain*, *Evan*, *Giovanni*, *Hansi*, *Ian*, *Ivan*, *Nuccio*, *Ohannes*, *Sean*, *Vanni*, *Yanos*, and *Zanni*. Under the letter *J* alone it is easy to collect scores of different John-names, such as the Persian *Jehan*, the Hungarian *Janos*, the Spanish *Juan*, the Dutch and Polish *Jan*, and some familiar American names we may never have connected with *John*. A good-sized book could be written on the name *John*, a name sacred in the past and inspiring in the present.

Joseph is a name with the general meaning of "addition" or "increase," and it is universally regarded as a name of good fortune. The use of this name in the Scriptures for one of the sons of Jacob is referred to in Gen. 30:24 where Rachel rejoiced, "And she called his name Joseph, and said, The Lord shall add to me another son." The other son was to be Benjamin; but the one who bore the name of addition was Joseph, pronounced in the original Hebrew *Yosef*. This simple form of the name is variously translated as "gathering," "addition," "increase," "he will add," and "whom may God increase." However, the name is sometimes given in a more complete form, pronounced *Yeho-sef*. Here the syllables *Yeho* are a clear indication of the most holy name, *Jehovah;* hence, the most impressive interpretation is "Jehovah shall add." In this complete form the name comes as a promise of blessing from the Almighty.

Variants are many. In Europe they include such diverse forms as *Jose*, *Giuseppe*, *Sepperl*, and *Ossip;* throughout the Arab world there are *Yussufs* by the hundred thousand, perhaps by the million, all happy to possess a name of good omen.

Laurence, in its various forms, is usually traced back to the Latin word *laurus*, "the laurel," and is assumed to mean "laurel-crowned." A popular nickname is Larry.

Martin, derived from the Latin *Martinus*, is connected with Mars and therefore is translated "warlike." Variants include *Martino* (Italian, Spanish), *Martinho* (Portuguese), *Martili* (Swiss), *Martijn* (Dutch), *Martoni* (Hungarian). Popular diminutives are *Marty* and *Mart*.

Michael is a Biblical name meaning "Who is like unto God," which may be taken as a question or an affirmation, in either case stressing the uniqueness of the deity. Three Hebrew words are involved: *Mi* ("*who*"), *kha* ("like"), and *El* ("God"). Variants are *Michel* (French), *Miguel* (Spanish), *Michail* (Russian), and *Mihaly* (Hungarian). Popular diminutives are *Mike*, *Mickey*, *Mikey*.

Nathan is Hebrew for "gift." *Nathaniel* means "gift of God" or "my gift is God." A popular modern diminutive is *Nat*.

Oliver is from *Oliva*, Latin for "olive," "olive tree," or "olive branch." Many children have been given names derived from this word, perhaps because the ancients believed the olive to be an emblem of love in its highest sense. The related idea of peace was established when a dove, as recorded in Gen. 8:11, brought an olive leaf to Noah.

Oscar is a name with two interpretations. When of Teutonic origin, it means "divine spear"; when of Keltic origin, it means "one who leaps forward in battle" or "a champion." In modern times there are no familiar variants of this name.

Peter is a name of prime importance in Christian lands. It is derived from the Greek *petra*, "a rock." It still means "a rock," but it is generally accepted as a symbol of firmness. In a theological sense Peter means "faith," especially the faith on which Christianity was founded. In John 1:42 it is written: "And when Jesus beheld him, he said, Thou art Simon, the son of Jona; thou shalt be called *Cephas*, which is by interpretation, a stone." As might be expected, this statement is full of meaning. The man's name had been *Simon*, which in Hebrew means "hearing" or "obedience." Naturally one has to hear before he can receive faith; therefore, he was first *Simon* and afterward *Peter*. The other name, *Cephas*, is simply the Aramaic word for "a rock," related to Hebrew *Kephah* with the same meaning.

Peter occurs in many languages, varying all the way from Swedish *Per* to Italian *Petruccio*, which latter is a modification of the customary *Pietro*. Perhaps the best known variant is the French *Pierre*.

Philip is a Greek name meaning a "lover of horses." The *phil* refers to "love"; *hip*, from the Greek *hippos*, means "horse." A hippodrome is a course where horses run. A hippopotamus is a horse of the river (Greek *potamos*).

Ralph, more correctly spelled *Ralf*, is a Teutonic name meaning "wolf," or, if it is considered a short form of *Randolph*, it means a "shield-wolf," referring to the wolf's head often featured at the center of a circular shield. In ancient times a wolf-name was honorable because of the strength of the animal. An old-fashioned variant is *Rafe*.

Raymond is a Teutonic name meaning "wise protection" (*ragin*, "counsel"; *mund*, "protection"). Variants include *Raimond* (French), *Raimondo* (Italian), and *Ramon* (Spanish). A modern diminutive is *Ray*.

Robert means "bright in fame." In ancient times it was made up of *hruod*, meaning "flame," and *percht*, or some such word, meaning "bright." Luckily for us, it was gradually worn down to *Robert*, which is easier to say. Modern variations include *Rupert*, *Bob*, and *Robin*. As *Roberta*, the name has been popular with the ladies, who have also borrowed *Robin*.

Samuel means "heard of God," or "asked for of God." It is the name of a great man who served Israel as judge, counselor, and prophet. When he was born, after his childless mother had prayed for offspring, "she called his name Samuel, because (she said) I have asked him of the Lord." The first part of the name refers to "hearing"; the ending, *El*, is the word for "God." It is so in many Hebrew names, as in *Gamaliel*, "reward of God," and *Bethel*, "house of God."

The "hearing" element in this name is suggested throughout the story of Samuel. When he was a small boy, serving in the temple, and the voice of God came to him in the night watches, he responded, "Speak, for thy servant heareth." When he became a man, his counsel was heard, though not always followed, by all Israel.

This name occurs in many languages without much variation in form. Sometimes it is heard in authentic Hebrew, *Sh'mu-el*, with a slight stress on the sacred closing syllable.

Stephen is derived from the Greek *stephanos*, "a crown," referring chiefly to the wreath of laurels or other leaves awarded to Greek youths for winning a contest. Some variants are *Etienne* (French), *Stefano* (Italian), *Esteban* (Spanish), and *Istvan* (Hungarian).

Thomas is a twin. That is to say, the name is derived from the Aramaic *Tama*, "twofold, twin," and perhaps earlier from the Hebrew *Tomim*, "twins." The Thomas of the Scriptures was sometimes called *Didymus*, a Greek name with the same meaning. His mind is said to have been as twofold as his name, causing him to be something of a skeptic—hence the expression "Doubting Thomas." *Thomas* is a good name, nevertheless, and has been borne by many famous men. Its familiar forms include *Tom* and *Tommy*, also the Scottish *Tam*, as in *Tam-o-Shanter*.

William is an important name in many languages. In the days of William the Conqueror and his son William Rufus, it became very popular. In 12th-century England there were almost seven times as many Williams as Johns.

In 1173 at a court feast of the English King Henry II, 120 knights were guests, all named William. In France in 1300 a chevalier named *Guillaume* visited Rouen on the 10th of January, the feast day of St. William. It is recorded that he invited all knights named *William* or *Guillaume* to dine with him, and 300 turned up. So it was a popular name in France as well.

Of Teutonic origin, the name is related to two Old English words, *Wil*, meaning "will, resolve," and *Helm*, meaning "helmet, defense." It can, therefore, be interpreted as meaning "resolute defense" or "resolute helmet."

The most popular short forms are *Will* and *Bill;* in Dutch the name is streamlined into *Willem*, which may then be reduced to *Wim*. In the Romance languages there are various forms spelled with *Gu-*; in the Slavic tongues there are some examples in *V*. A few usable variants are found in our list of names.

SOME POPULAR NAMES FOR GIRLS

The preceding pages present somewhat detailed discussions of the meanings of some favorite names for girls and boys. The following lists give the meanings of many other names. Often several variants of a name are given. It is interesting that most of these popular names come from the sacred languages—Hebrew, Greek, and Latin. This is not surprising, for names tend to be traditional, and many of the world's traditions were established when these three languages served most of the civilized nations. The meanings of the abbreviations used in the following list are given on the opening page of this Dictionary of Names.

Aasta (Scan)	Love
Abigail (H)	Father's joy
Acadia (American Indian)	Abundance
Ada (T)	Happy
Adah (H)	An ornament
Adelaide (T)	Of noble origin
Adele	
Adeline	
Adelot	Old French var. of Adeline
Adeva (T)	Rich gift
Adina (H)	Pleasant, adaptable
Adrienne (L)	From Adria in Italy
Afra (T)	Peaceful ruler
Agatha (Gr)	Good, kind
Agnes (Gr)	Pure, chaste; a lamb
Aileen (Gr)	Irish form of Helen
Aimée (L)	Beloved
Aina (Fin)	Always, ever
Aithne (Ir)	A command; also knowledge, discernment
Alaine (K)	Handsome, amiable
Alastrina	Keltic form of Alexandra
Alberta (T)	Nobly bright, illustrious
Alda (T)	Rich
Alena	Var. of Helen
Alethe (Gr)	Truth
Alethea	
Alexandra (Gr)	Helper
Alfreda (T)	Elf-counsel, wise
Alfrida	
Alice (T)	Noble cheer
Aline (T)	Noble
Alison	Keltic var. of Adelaide; also of Alexandra
Allene (K)	Bright, amiable, beautiful
Alma (Hg)	Apple
Alma (L)	Kind, indulgent
Almah (H)	Maiden
Almas (Ar)	A diamond
Almira (Ar)	Princess
Alodia (Gr)	Breton form of Alexandra
Althea (Gr)	Wholesome; a healer
Alva (L)	White
Alvina (T)	Loved by all
Amabel (L)	Lovable
Amalina (Skt)	Stainless, clean
Amana (H)	A confirmation, a covenant; trust
Amanda (L)	Loving
Amarantha (Gr)	Unfading, imperishable
Amaryllis (Gr)	With sparkling, twinkling eyes
Amata (L)	Beloved
Amelia (T)	Busy, energetic
Amina (Ar)	Faithful
Amy (L)	Beloved
Anastasia (Gr)	Resurrection, rebirth
Anatolia (Gr)	The sunrise
Andrea (Gr)	Fem. of Andrew
Andri	Dim. of Andrea
Angela (Gr)	Messenger, angel
Angeline	
Anika (Vei)	Very beautiful
Anita (H)	Dim. of Ann
Ann (H)	Grace, mercy
Anna	
Annabel (H-L)	Grace and beauty
Annabella	
Annabelle	
Anne (H)	Grace
Annetta	
Annette	
Annora	Var. of Arnthora
Antonia (L)	Deserving praise
Antoinette	
Apollonia (Gr)	Fem. form of Apollo
Arabella (L)	Beauty of the hearth; sometimes a var. of Arnbella
Arax (Assyr)	Lively, dashing, impetuous (ancient name of a famous river)
Areta (Gr)	Virtue
Ariadne (Gr)	Most pure, chaste
Arina (Fin)	Hearth, center of home
Arina	Russian form of Irene
Arita (Skt)	Praised
Arla (K)	Harvest home; ingathering of the harvest
Arleen (K)	A pledge
Arlene	
Arline	
Arnbella (T-L)	Eagle maiden
Arnthora (T)	Eagle of Thor
Arvida (Scan)	Eagle of the woods
Asta	Scandinavian dim. of Augusta
Astra (Gr)	Starlike
Astrid (Scan)	Loving
Astrild (Scan)	Love
Atara (H)	A crown, diadem
Athena (Gr)	Wisdom
Audrey (OE)	Noble counsel
Augusta (L)	Venerable
Aura (Gr)	Gentle breeze; a radiating influence
Aurelia (L)	Golden
Aurelle	
Aurora (L)	The dawn
Ava (L)	A bird
Avis	
Avon (K)	A river; intelligence

Name	Meaning
Avril (F)	Born in April
Ayamé (J)	Iris (the flower); pronounced *A-ya-mé*
Babette	Dim. of Barbara
Barbara (Gr)	Stranger
Bathsheba (H)	Daughter of an oath; sometimes used to mean the seventh daughter
Beata (L)	Blessed
Beatrice (L)	One who blesses or makes happy
Belita	Dim. of Bella
Bella (L)	Beautiful
Belle	
Belva (K)	Fair-spoken (Belva Lockwood was the second woman nominated for the United States presidency, 1884 and 1888. *See* **Victoria.**)
Benedetta (L)	Blessed
Benedicta	
Benita	
Berenice (Gr)	Bringing victory
Beriah (H)	A wonderful new creation
Berita (H)	Covenant
Berith	
Berna (T)	The bear; emblem of Bern,
Berne	Switzerland
Bernadette (T)	Brave as a bear
Bernadine	
Bernice	Var. of Berenice
Berta (T)	Bright
Bertha	
Beryl (Gr)	The jewel of Tarshish, typifying "truth with power"
Beth (H)	A house; also a dim. of Elizabeth
Bethel (H)	House of God
Betsey	Dims. of Elizabeth
Bette	
Bettina	
Betty	
Beulah (H)	Married
Beverly (OE)	Meadow of the beavers
Bianca (L)	White, fair
Binah (H)	Intelligence
Birgit (K)	Strength
Blanche (L)	White, fair
Blenda (T)	Dazzling
Blessing (T)	Benediction
Brenda (T)	A sword
Bridget (K)	Strength
Brigitta	Latinized forms of Bridget
Brita	
Brinna (K)	Visions, reveries
Bruna (T)	Of a dark complexion
Bryna (Scan)	Coat of mail
Camilla (L)	An assistant at sacred rites
Camille	
Candida (L)	White
Capitola (L)	From the ancient Capitol, adopted by the Romans as an emblem of eternity
Cara (L)	Dear, beloved
Carelia (T)	*See* **Carolina.**
Carina (L)	Dear, beloved
Carita	
Carla	Vars. of Carolina
Carline	
Carlotta	
Carmel (H)	A fruitful field
Carmela	
Carmen (L)	A song, a poem
Carmina (Ar)	Rosy
Carol (Gr)	A song of joy
Carolina (T)	Strong, vigorous; fem. forms
Caroline	of Charles
Carolyn	
Cassandra (Gr)	Helper of men
Catharine (Gr)	Pure
Catherine	
Cathleen	Vars. of Catharine (*See* **Kath-**
Cathlin	**leen.**)
Catriona	
Cecelia (L)	Blind
Cecile	
Celeste (L)	Heavenly
Celestine	
Celia	
Chara (L)	Dear, beloved
Charis (Gr)	Grace, a gift
Charity (L)	Charity, greatest of the virtues
Charlene (T)	Strong, vigorous; fem. forms
Charlotta	of Charles
Charlotte	
Chloe (Gr)	Springtime verdure
Christina (Gr)	Anointed, baptized
Christine	
Clara (L)	Bright, illustrious
Clarice	
Clarinda	
Clarissa	
Claudia (L)	Lame
Claudette	
Claudine	
Cleanthe (Gr)	Famous flower
Clemence (L)	Merciful
Clementine	
Cleo (Gr)	Famed, renowned
Cleona	
Cleone	
Clio (Gr)	One who celebrates or makes famous; name of the muse of epic poetry and history
Coela (W)	Trust, belief, credo
Colette	French dims. of Nicola
Colinette	
Colinda (Rum)	Christmas hymn
Colleen (Ir)	Irish word for "girl"; as a name, means "darling"
Columbia (L)	A dove
Constance (L)	Firm, dependable
Consuela (L)	Consolation
Consuelo	
Cora (Gr)	Maiden
Cora (K)	A choir, harmony
Coral (OF)	Cordial, warm-hearted
Coralie (Gr)	Coral pink
Cordelia (L)	Warm-hearted
Corinne (Gr)	Maiden
Cornelia (L)	Powerful (The horn, *cornu*, anciently typified the power of truth.)
Corona (L)	A crown, diadem
Corra (Ir)	Spear
Creda (L)	Faith

Name	Meaning
Cynthia (Gr)	The moon; Diana
Cyrilla (Gr)	Noble lady
Dagmar (T)	Joy of the Danes
Dagni (T)	Dawn
Dagny	
Daisy (OE)	From the flower poetically named *Day's eye*
Danna (J)	A parishioner, suppprter of the church
Daphne (Gr)	The laurel, the bay tree
Dara (H)	Pearl of wisdom
Dara (K)	An oak; emblem of eternity
Daria	Russian dim. of Dorothea
Davida (H)	Beloved
Davnet (Ir)	A poet
Dawn (T)	Enlightenment
Deborah (H)	The bee
Debra (H)	Dims of Deborah; also Ethiopian words for "mountain"
Devra	
Delia (Gr)	From the Isle of Delos
Delphine (Gr)	A priestess of the Delphic Apollo; a prophetess
Denise (Gr)	From Dionysus, Grecian god of wine
Dervilia (Ir-L)	True desire
Desirée (L)	Desired
Diana (L)	Goddess (of the moon and of hunting); emblem of faith
Diane	
Dinah (H)	Judgment
Diona (Gr)	Fem. form of Dis, an old name of Zeus
Dionetta	Fem. of Dion
Dionette	
Dolores (L)	Sorrows
Dominica (L)	Sunday's child
Donata (L)	A gift
Donetta	
Donette	
Donna (L)	A lady
Dora (Gr)	A gift
Dorcas (Gr)	A gazelle
Dorea (Gr)	A gift
Doris (Gr)	A gift
Doris (Lith)	Noble, courageous
Dorothea (Gr)	Gift of God
Dorothy	
Drusilla (K-L)	Strong
Duana (K)	Poet
Dulcia (L)	Sweet
Dulcie	
Easter (T)	The dawn; name of ancient goddess Eostra
Ebba (OE)	Ebb tide
Ebba (T)	Brave as a wild boar
Edda	Security
Edeva (T)	Rich gift
Edina (T)	Ancient name of Edinburgh, Scotland
Edith (T)	Rich gift
Edla (T)	Of noble origin
Edna (H)	Pleasure
Ednah	
Edrie (OE)	Blessed power
Edry	
Edwina (T)	Rich friend
Eevin (Ir)	Beautiful (name of a powerful banshee)
Eileen	An Irish form of Helen
Eithne (Ir)	A kernel, a heart
Elaine	Var. of Helen
Eleanor (Gr)	Light
Eleanora	
Eleonore	
Elinor	
Electa (L)	Chosen
Electra (Gr)	Amber-hued
Elfrieda (T)	Elf-counsel, wise
Elfrida	
Elfride	
Elise	Vars. of Elizabeth
Eliza	
Elizabeth (H)	Worshiper of God
Ella (OE)	Elfin, white, wise; sometimes a dim. of Helen
Ellen	Vars. of Helen
Ellin	
Elma (L)	Kind, amiable
Elmira (Ar)	Princess
Elna	Var. of Eleanor or of Helen
Eloisa (Fin)	Lively
Eloisa (T)	Vars. of Louisa
Eloise	
Elsa (T)	Noble cheer; sometimes dim. of Elizabeth
Else	
Elsbeth	Scottish var. of Elizabeth
Elsha	Irish dim. of Adelaide
Elsie	Dim. of Elizabeth
Elspeth	Scottish var. of Elizabeth
Elva (T)	Elflike, in the sense of being whimsical and wise
Elvina (OE)	Elf-friend; meaning wise friend
Elvira (L)	White
Emerentia (L)	Well-deserving
Emilia (L-T)	Industrious
Emilie	
Emily	
Emma (T)	An aunt, a nurse, a grandmother
Emunah (H)	Firmness, security, faith in God
Endrede (Scan)	Lone rider
Engelberta (T)	Bright angel
Enid (K)	Pure
Erasma (Gr)	Amiable
Erica (T)	Ever mighty
Erika	
Erma (T)	Renowned, honored
Erna (T)	An eagle; perception, understanding
Ernata (K)	Knowing
Ernestine (T)	Earnest, sincere
Eslin (Ir)	A dream
Esmerelda (Gr)	An emerald
Estelle (L)	A star
Esther (H)	A star
Estrella (L)	A star (Spanish form)
Etelka	Hungarian for Ethel
Ethel (T)	Noble
Ethelburga (T)	Noble fortress
Ethelreda (T)	Noble counsel
Eudocia (Gr)	Good will, approval
Eudokia	
Eudora (Gr)	Generous
Eudoxia (Gr)	Good repute, glory
Eugenia (Gr)	Well-born

Eula (Gr)	Speaking sweetly
Eulalia	
Eulalie	
Eunice (Gr)	Good victory
Euphemia (Gr)	Of good repute
Eva (H)	Life
Eve	
Evadne (Gr)	The pleasing one
Evaine	Old French form of Eve
Evangeline (Gr)	Bearer of good tidings
Evelina (K)	Agreeable
Evelyn	
Evolyn	
Faith (L)	Faith, one of the seven virtues
Fanchon (T)	Old French var. of Frances
Fanny	Var. of Frances
Fawn (T)	A young deer
Felice (L)	Happy
Felicia	
Fenella (K)	White-shouldered
Fia	Dim. of Sophia
Fidelia (L)	The faithful
Fingalla (K)	Fair stranger
Fiona (K)	White, fair
Flavia (L)	Yellow-haired
Flora (L)	A flower
Florence (L)	Flourishing
Frances (T)	Free
Francesca	
Francine	
Francisca	
Freda (T)	Peace
Frida	
Frieda	
Frederica (T)	Peaceful ruler
Freya (T)	Norse goddess of love
Gabriela (H)	Hero of God
Gabrielle	
Gael (K)	A highlander
Gail (H)	Joy
Gail (K)	Valor, virtue
Gale	
Galatea (Gr)	Milk-white
Gemma (L)	A gem
Geneva (L)	The juniper tree
Genevra	
Ginevra	
Genevieve (K)	White wave
Genoveffa	
Georgette (Gr)	Farmer, tiller of the soil
Georgia	
Georgiana	
Geraldine (T)	Firm spear
Gerda (T)	Enclosure, guard
Gertrude (T)	Spear-maiden
Gilberta (T)	Bright pledge
Gilda (K)	Servant of God
Gilian (L)	Soft-haired
Gillian	
Gladys (L)	Lame; Welsh form of Claudia; has acquired secondary meaning of "gladness"
Gleda (T)	Making glad
Glida (OE)	A skater, glider
Gloria (L)	Glory
Gloriana (L-H)	Glory and grace; Spenser's poetical name for Queen Elizabeth I
Godiva (T)	Gift of God
Grace (L)	Blessing, thanksgiving
Gracia	
Graine (K)	Loving
Grania	Latinized form of Graine
Gratia (L)	Thanksgiving
Grazia	
Greta	Dims. of Margaret
Gretchen	
Grete	
Gretel	
Guida (T)	A spear of wood
Guinevere (K)	White wave
Gunila (Scan)	Fighter
Gwen (W)	White, fair, pleasant, blissful
Gwenda	
Gwendolyn (W)	White-browed
Gwyneth (W)	Blessed state, bliss
Gwynfryd (W)	Happy mind
Hadassah (H)	Myrtle
Hagar (H)	Sojourner
Haidee (Gr)	Modest
Halima (Rum)	Legend, romance, myth
Halina	Slavic var. of Helen
Halley (T)	Holy
Halloween (T)	Eve of All Saints' Day, October 31
Haninah (H)	Grace, mercy
Hannah (H)	Grace, mercy
Hansine	Dim. of Johanna
Harriet	Var. of Henrietta
Hazel (T)	The hazel tree; emblem of beauty, from its colors, and of magic, from the use of its twigs
Heather (T)	Flower of the heath; emblem of wholesome beauty
Hebe (Gr)	Eternal youth
Hedda	Var. of Hedwig
Hedwig (T)	Success in war
Helen (Gr)	Light
Helena	
Helene	
Helga (Scan)	Holy, peaceful
Helma (OE)	Rudder
Helma (Scan)	Helmed warrior
Helmi (Fin)	Pearl
Heloise	Var. of Louisa
Henrietta (T)	Mistress of the home
Henriette	
Hephzibah (H)	My delight is in her
Hera (Gr)	The protector of marriage
Herma (Gr)	Messenger, spirit of communication; from Hermes, or Mercury
Hermia	
Hermione	
Herma (T)	Same as Irma
Hertha (T)	Devoted to hearth and home
Hester	Var. of Esther
Hestia (Gr)	Guardian of the hearth
Hilaria (L)	Cheerful
Hilda (T)	Battle, or leader in battle
Hildegarde (T)	Fighting protectress
Hinda (Pers)	From India
Holima (Mende)	Patience
Holly (T)	Emblem of Yuletide; deemed sacred by the Druids
Honora (L)	Honorable
Honoria	

Name	Meaning
Hope (T)	Hope; one of the seven virtues
Hortense (L)	A gardener
Hortensia	
Hulda (T)	Faithful, kind
Huldah (H)	A weasel (anciently thought to excel in wisdom)
Hypatia (Gr)	Excellent
Iana (H)	Gracious gift of the Lord
Ianthe (Gr)	A violet-colored flower
Ida (T)	Happy; also farseeing
Iduna (T)	Youth
Ileana	Rumanian form of Helen
Ilona	Hungarian form of Helen
Imogene (L)	Picture, image
Imrah (H)	A song, hymn
Ines	Portuguese var. of Agnes
Inez	Spanish var. of Agnes
Inga (T)	Fem. of Ing; said to mean "young"
Ingeborg (T)	Ing's defense; young defense
Ingrid (T)	Ing's fidelity; young fidelity
Iola	Breton form of Julia
Iolanthe (Gr)	The violet flower
Iona (Gr)	The violet
Ione	
Ione (H)	A dove
Ionia (Gr)	A bank of violets
Iphigenia (G)	Strong-born, mighty
Irene (Gr)	Peace
Irina	Russian form of Irene
Iris (Gr)	The rainbow
Irma (T)	Renowned, honored
Isabel (H)	Pure, virtuous
Isabella	
Isadora (Gr)	Gift of Isis
Isidora	
Isolde (K)	Vision of beauty
Ivona	Var. of Yvonne
Ivy (T)	Constancy; one of the emblems of Aphrodite, goddess of true love
Jacqueline	A supplanter; French fem. o Jacob
Jane (H)	Gracious gift of the Lord
Janet	
Janice	
Janna	
Jannica	
Jean (H)	Gracious gift of the Lord
Jeanne	
Jeannette	
Jennie	
Jenny	
Jensine	
Jennifer (K)	White wave
Jessica (H)	The Lord sees
Jessie (H)	The Lord is
Jill (L)	One of the many forms of Julia; has acquired meaning suggesting a happy wife (*See* **Jack.**)
Jillian (L)	Soft-haired
Joan (H)	Gracious gift of the Lord
Joanna	
Jocelyn (L)	Joyful
Johanna (H)	Gracious gift of the Lord
Jolivette (OF)	A joy, a pleasure

Name	Meaning
Josepha (H)	He shall add
Josephine	
Jovana	Var. of Johanna
Jovena (OF)	New, youthful
Joy (L)	Joyful, glad
Joyce	
Juana	Spanish forms of Joanna
Juanita	
Judith (H)	The praised
Julia (L)	Soft-haired; related to the month of July
Juliana	
Julie	
Julienne	
Juliet	
June (L)	Named for the month or for the goddess Juno
Juno	
Justina (L)	Just
Justine	
Karelia (T)	Var. of Carolina
Karen (Gr)	Pure
Karin	
Karine	
Katharine	
Kathryn	
Katrina	
Karitsa (Fin)	Lamb
Kathleen (Gr)	Pure; anciently in Ireland fem. of Cathal, battle-mighty
Keavy (Ir)	Gentleness, courtesy
Kelin (Ir)	Slender
Kenin (K)	Comely, mild, noble
Kereth (H)	A city
Keven (H)	A horn; emblem of power
Keziah (H)	The cassia tree
Kirsten	Vars. of Christina
Kirstin	
Kitty	Dim. of Catharine
Korene (Gr)	Maiden
Lana (L)	Wool; emblem of innocence
Latona (L)	In safekeeping
Laura (L)	Laurel-crowned
Laurel	
Laurine	
Leah (H)	Wearied
Leal (L)	True-hearted, faithful, honest
Leila (Ar)	Night; figuratively "dark beauty"
Lela	Var. of Leila
Lempi (Fin)	Love, affection
Lena	Dim. of Helen; also of Magdalena
Lenora (Gr)	Light
Lenore	
Leoline	Var. of Leonarda
Leona (L)	The lion
Leonarda (Gr-T)	Brave as a lion
Leonora (Gr)	Light
Leonore	
Letitia (L)	Gladness
Liana (L)	A bond
Libby	Dim. of Elizabeth
Liena (L)	A bond
Lila (Gr)	From the flower; when white, typifying purity; when brightly colored, magnificence
Lilian	
Lillie	
Lily	
Lina	Dim. of Carolina

Linda (Sp) Pretty
Linnea (T) Named for Linnaeus, famed Swedish botanist
Lisbeth A var. of Elizabeth
Livia Var. of Olivia
Lizzie Dim. of Elizabeth
Llyn (W) A lake
Loella Var. of Luella
Lois (Gr) Agreeable
Lola
Lolita Dims. of Carlotta
Lona Dim. of Apollonia
Lorena (L) The laurel
Loretta (L) Laurel, sign of victory
Lorna (OE) Lost (This pretty name, invented by R. D. Blackmore for his "lost" heroine in *Lorna Doone* (1869), has been popular ever since, doubly so because the lost heroine was found and happily married her finder.)
Lorraine (T) Famed in war
Lotta
Lottie Dims. of Charlotte
Louisa (T)
Louise Famous in battle
Lucia (L)
Lucille
Lucinda
Lucy Light
Lucretia (L) Profitable (if from *lucrum*); lightbringer (if from *lux*)
Ludmila (Sl) The people's love
Luella (L)
Luelle Loosing, setting free
Lula Dim. of Luella
Lulu (Ar) A pearl
Luna (L) The moon
Lydia (Gr) From Lydia in Asia Minor
Lynn (K-T) Sea, lake, pool, brook, or waterfall
Lyris (Gr) A lyre; harmony
Lysandra (Gr) Liberator

Mabel (L) Amiable
Madeleine
Madeline
Madelon Vars. of Magdalene
Madge Dim. of Margaret
Mae (L)
Maia
May
Maya Relating to the month of May
Mae
May Sometimes dims. of Mary
Mafka (Eg) Turquoise stone
Magda Dim. of Magdalene
Magdalena (H)
Magdalene Elevated
Magna (L) Great
Maira Ethiopian form of Mary
Maisie Scottish dim. of Margaret
Malvina (K) One who ministers
Mamie A dim. of Mary
Mana (Maori) Influence, authority
Manette
Manon French vars. of Mary
Manuela (H) God with us

Marcella (L)
Marcelle
Marcia Related to Mars, or war
Margaret (Gr)
Margaretta
Margery
Margherita
Margot
Marguerite
Marjorie A pearl
Maria
Marian
Marianne
Marietta
Mariette A few of the many forms of Mary
Marilyn
Marylin Dims. of Mary
Marina (L) Lover of the sea; "born at sea" according to Shakespeare (*Pericles* III,3); sometimes a var. of Mary
Marion Var. of Mary
Marith (H) A pasturing
Marlene Var. of Magdalene
Martha (Aram)
Marta Lady of the house
Mary (H) Bitterness; presumably a healing bitterness (The Hebrew source of this name is related to *myrrh*, used in worship for anointing, in medicine for healing.)
Mathilda (T)
Mathilde
Matilda Mighty in battle
Maud (T)
Maude Mighty in battle; actually a dim. of Mathilda
Maura (L)
Maureen
Maurine Moorish, dark
Maureen Sometimes an Irish dim. of Mary
Mavis (OE) Redwing, thrush
Maxine (L) Greatest
Melanie (G-F) Black, dark-haired
Melba (OE) From Melbourne in Australia; name adopted by a famous prima donna
Melinda (Gr) Sweet as honey
Melissa (Gr) Honeybee
Mennefer (Eg) Good abode, or good haven; ancient name of Memphis in Egypt
Mercedes (Sp) Favorings, rewards
Meredith (W) The noisy animation of the sea
Meri (Fin) The sea
Merle (L) A blackbird
Meta (Gr) Pearl; dim. of Margaret
Michaela (H) Who is like unto God?
Michal (H) A streamlet
Mignon (F) Darling, pretty one
Mila (Sl) Lovable, amiable
Milada Czech form of Mildred
Mildred (OE) Mild counsel
Millicent (Gothic) Capable, strong, holy
Millie
Milly Dims. of Emily or sometimes of Mildred
Mimi A dim. of Wilhelmina

Mina (T)	Remembrance, love; sometimes a dim. of Wilhelmina
Minella	Dim. of Wilhelmina
Minerva (L)	Daughter of wisdom
Minna (T)	Rembrance, love
Minnie	
Mira (Ar)	Myrrh
Miranda (L)	Admirable
Miriam	Original Hebrew form of
Miryam	Mary
Mizpah (H)	Watchtower; sign of a covenant
Moina (K)	Gentle
Moira	An Irish var. of Mary
Molly	One of the many vars. of Mary
Mona (K)	Noble
Mona (OE)	The moon
Monica (L)	Unequaled, alone
Mora (Ir)	Great
Morna (K)	Tender, beloved, hospitable
Muriel (Ar)	Myrrh
Myna (OE)	The moon
Myra (Ar)	Myrrh
Myrna (K)	Loving, fond
Myrrha (Ar-Gr)	Myrrh
Myrtle (L)	Loving (The myrtle tree was sacred to Venus.)
Nada (Sl)	Hope
Nadia	
Nadine	
Nahleen (Apache Indian)	Maiden
Naida (Gr)	A river nymph
Nalina (Skt)	A water lily
Nancy	Dims. of Ann
Nanette	
Nanon	
Naomi (H)	Pleasantness
Natalia (L)	Christmas
Natalie	
Natasha	
Nathalia	
Nathalie	
Nathania (H)	A gift
Nedda (T)	Rich guard
Nell	Vars. of Helen
Nella	
Nelle	
Nellie	
Nesta	Var. of Agnes
Nette	Dims. of Ann or of Antoinette
Nettie	
Neva (L)	Snowy
Nevada	
Neysa	Slavic forms of Agnes
Neza	
Nicola (Gr)	Victory of the people
Nicole	
Nicolette	
Nicoline	
Nidavah (H)	A freewill offering
Nila (Skt)	Dark blue; name of a famous mountain
Nina	Dims. of Hannah or Haninah
Ninette	
Ninon	
Nita	Dim. of Juanita
Noela (L)	Christmas
Nona (L)	The ninth
Nora (L)	Honor
Norah (H)	Venerable, august
Nordri (Scan)	The North
Noreen	Irish dims. of Nora
Norine	
Norma	Model, standard
Norna (Scan)	A spirit of destiny
Nova (L)	New
Novita	
Novomira (Sl)	New peace
Nuala (K)	White-shouldered
Nunila (L)	Little nun
Octavia (L)	The eighth
Oda (G-L-T)	Rich, happy
Odette	
Odile	
Odilia	
Olga (T)	Holy
Olive (L)	The olive tree; symbol of love,
Olivia	hence of peace
Oona (Ir)	Safety
Ophelia (Gr)	Help, service, benefit
Ora (L)	The seacoast
Orah (H)	Light
Oriana (L)	Golden one; a poetic name of Queen Elizabeth I
Orlata (K)	Golden lady
Orsola	Italian form of Ursula
Osa (T)	A goddess
Othilia (T)	Rich, happy, prosperous; pre-
Othillie	sumably fem. of Otho
Ottilia	
Ottillie	
Ouida	Var. of Louisa
Palma (L)	Palm leaf, emblem of victory
Pamela (Gr)	All honey
Pandora (Gr)	All-gifted
Pasca (H)	Eastertide, Passover
Patience (L)	Forbearance, endurance, perseverance; one of the seven virtues
Patricia (L)	A noble lady
Paula (L)	Little; sometimes used in the
Paulette	sense of modest
Paulina	
Pearl (L)	The "pearl of great price," emblem of truth
Peggy	A dim. of Margaret
Penelope (Gr)	A weaver
Pernel (Gr)	Dim. of Petra
Petra (Gr)	A rock; faith
Petrea	
Petronella	
Philadelphia (Gr)	Love of brethren
Philema (Gr)	A kiss
Philippa (Gr)	Lover of horses
Philomela (Gr)	Lover of song; also the nightingale
Phebe (Gr)	Shining; the moon
Phoebe	
Phillis (Gr)	Green foliage
Phyllis	
Polly	One of the many vars. of Mary
Portia (L)	Originally Porcia (related to pigs); changed by Shakespeare to mean a resourceful jurist

Priscilla (H) Of ancient lineage
Provida (L) Foreseeing, provident
Prudence (L) One of the seven virtues, often used as a name

Rachel (H) A ewe, emblem of gentleness
Rae (T) A roe, a deer; also sometimes a dim. of Rachel
Ragna (T) Counselor
Ramona (T) Wise protection
Raphaela (H) Healed of God
Rebecca (H) Alluring, captivating
Regina (L) A queen
Reina
Renata (L) Reborn
Renée
Reva (OF) A dreamer
Rhoda (Gr) A rose
Rhona (Gr) A river
Rhonda (W) Swift river
Rita A dim. of Margherita
Rita (Skt) Proper, right, honest
Roberta (T) Bright fame
Romola (G-L) A Roman; also strength, power
Rosa (L) Named after the flower rose;
Rosalie used by Roman lovers as a
Rose term of endearment
Rosalba (L) White rose
Rosalind (Modern L) Fair rose
Rosamund (Modern L) Rose of the world; also pure rose
Rosemary (L) "Rosemary, that's for remembrance" (Shakespeare)
Rosetta (L) Little rose
Rosita
Roshena (Pers) Dawn of day
Rowena (K) White skirt
Ruby (L) Red, a color symbolic of good and of love; the first gem in Aaron's breastplate
Rufina (L) Red
Runa (T) A poem or song of mystery
Ruth (H) Beauty
Ruth (Old Icel) Compassion, mercy

Sabina (L) Of the Sabines, an ancient Italian people
Sabrina (L) The Severn River
Sally Dim. of Sarah
Saloma (H) Peaceful
Salome
Sandra Dim. of Alexandra
Sara (H) Princess
Sarah
Sari Hungarian form of Sarah
Selena (Gr) The moon
Selene
Selina
Selema (Ar) Peaceful, wholesome
Selma
Serena (L) Even-tempered
Shalina (Skt) Modest, retiring
Shamira (H) A diamond
Sharada (Skt) Autumn
Sharman (Skt) Joy, bliss, delight, protection, safety
Sharon (H) A great and fertile plain
Sheila Irish form of Cecilia
Shirah (H) A song
Shirley (OE) Bright meadow
Sibyl (Gr) Prophetess
Sigfrid (T) Victorious peace
Signe (T) Victory increasing
Sigrid (T) Victorious counsel
Silma (Fin) The eye
Silvia (L) Forester
Siranush (Armen) Sweetheart
Siri Dim. of Sigrid
Slania (K) Health, integrity
Solveig (T) Dark power
Sonia Dims. of Sophia
Sonya
Sophia (Gr) Wisdom
Stella (L) Star
Stephania (Gr) Crown, wreath
Stephanie
Sulia (L) A Breton form of Julia
Susan (H) A lily
Susanna
Suzanne
Suzette
Svea (Scan) Sweden
Sylvia (L) Forester

Tacey (L) Be silent! (Lat., *tace*, Fr. *taisez-vous*) (Puritans hoped that a woman so named would hold her tongue.)
Tadia (Aram) Praise
Tamar (H) Palm tree
Tamara
Tania Dim. of Titania
Tanya
Tarina (Fin) Legend, story
Tekla (Gr) Divine fame
Teresa (Gr) Harvester
Teruah (H) Rejoicing, shouts of joy
Terumah (H) An offering to God
Tess Dims. of Theresa
Tessa
Tevra (L) From the Tiber River
Thalia (Gr) Blooming; the muse of joy
Thalna (Gr) Etruscan goddess of springtime and beauty
Thecla (Gr) Divine fame
Thekla
Theda Dim. of Theodora
Thelma (Gr) A nurse
Theodora (Gr) Gift of God
Theodosia
Theophania (Gr) Manifestation of God (especially the Christian Epiphany, January 6)
Theora Dim. of Theodora
Theresa (Gr) Harvester
Therese
Thirza (H) Pleasantness
Thyrza
Tirzah
Thora (T) Named after Thor, Norse god of Thursday and thunder
Thylda (OE) Patience
Thyra (Gr) A door
Thyra (T) Belonging to Tyr, the Norse war god, after whom Tuesday is named

Tifarah (H) Beauty, honor, glory
Titania (G-L) In safekeeping, sheltered
Titiana
Tova (H) Good
Tovia (H) Goodness of the Lord
Trin A dim. of Catharine
Triona A Keltic dim. of Catharine

Ula (K) A treasure; darling
Ulrica (T) Noble ruler
Una (L) Truth, constancy, oneness
Undine (L) Of the waves
Unelma (Fin) A dream
Uni Etruscan var. of Juno
Urania (Gr) Heavenly
Ursa (L) A bear
Ursula (L) Little bear
Uta (T) Rich, happy

Valborg (Scan) Coast defense
Valda (T) Powerful
Valencia (L) The strong
Valentia
Valeria
Valerie
Valeska (Sl) Ruling in glory
Valisa (Fin) Luminous, bright
Varda (Assyr) A rose
Varina Var. of Barbara
Veda (Skt) Knowledge
Velma Dim. of Wilhelmina
Venetia (L) From Venice
Vera (L) Truth
Vera (Sl) Faith
Verda (L) Fresh, vigorous
Vergilia (L) Of the springtime, flourishing
Verita (L) True
Verna (L) Born in springtime
Vernata
Verone Old French dim. of Veronique
Veronica (L-G) True image
Veronique
Veronica (Gr) Var. of Berenice
Vesta (L) Guardian of the sacred flame
Veva Dim. of Genevieve
Vevina (K) Melodious
Victoria (L) Victory (Victoria Woodhull was first woman nominated for U.S. presidency, 1872. *See* **Belva.**)
Victorine
Vida (H) Beloved
Vida (Sp) Life
Vida (Skt) Knowledge, discovery
Vieno (Fin) Mild, gentle
Viera (Sl) Faith
Vilma Hungarian dim. of Wilhelmina
Vinatta (Icel) Friendship
Vincentia (L) Victorious
Viola (L) The violet, emblem of modesty
Violet
Virginia (L) Relating to the springtime and to regeneration (originally spelled with *ver-*, Latin for "spring")
Virida (L) Fresh, vigorous
Viveka (Skt) Right judgment, discrimination
Vivia (L) Lively
Vivian
Vivien
Volita (L) Wished for

Walda (T-L) Powerful
Wanda (T) Wanderer
Wendy (T) Wanderer
Wertha (OE) Honor, worship
Wilhelmina (T) Helmet of resolution
Willa Dims. of Wilhelmina
Willette
Wilma
Winfrey (T) Friend of peace; also set free
Winifred (T) Friend of peace
Winona (American Indian) First-born daughter (name of Hiawatha's mother)
Wyn (OE) Joy, delight; also a friend
Wynne

Xenia (Gr) Hospitality

Yadah (H) He knows
Yana Var. of Joanna
Yarah (H) Honey
Yerusha (H) Inheritance, possession
Yolanda (Gr) The violet
Yolande
Ysolde (K) Vision of beauty
Yvette (T) Bow-bearer, archer
Yvonne

Zahra (Ar) Flower
Zandra Dim. of Alexandra
Zara Var. of Sarah
Zarifa (Ar) Graceful
Zenda (Pers) Interpreter
Zenia (Gr) Hospitality
Zimrah (H) Music
Ziona (H) Zion
Zita (Ital) A lass, a young girl; sometimes a dim. of Theresa
Zoe (Gr) Life
Zofia Slavic var. of Sophia
Zona (Gr) Harvester, from Terezona, a var. of Teresa; also a girdle
Zora (Sl) The dawn
Zosia Var. of Sophia

SOME POPULAR NAMES FOR BOYS

The following list gives the meanings of many popular names of boys. If you can memorize a few dozen of the meanings from this list and from the preceding list of girls' names, you are well on the way to becoming the life of the party, for you will find that nothing interests people more than hearing interpretations of their names. Included in these two lists are more than 2,000 names. If you should forget the meanings of a few names, you can always promise to come up with the answers "next time."

The abbreviations used in the lists are defined on the opening page of this Dictionary of Names.

Aaron (H) Lofty, high; inspired
Abel (H) A breath; anciently typified charity, love of the neighbor
Abiel (H) Father of strength
Abner (H) Father of light
Abraham (H) Father of a multitude
Abram (H) Father of height
Absalom (H) Father of peace
Adalbert (T) Nobly bright
Adam (H) Red earth
Adiel (H) Ornament of God
Adlai (H) Justice of the Lord
Adolf (T) Noble wolf
Adrian (L) From Adria in Italy
Adriel (H) Flock of God
Ahban (H) Brother of the wise, prudent
Aidan (Ir) Fire
Aimo (Fin) Able, strong, bold
Alan (K) Bright, clear, handsome, amiable, glorious
Alaric (T) Noble ruler
Alastair Irish form of Alexander
Alba (L) White, fair
Alban (L)
Alben (L)
Albin (L)
Albert (T) Nobly bright, illustrious
Aldhelm (OE) A veteran (old helmet)
Aldred (T) Old counselor
Aldwin (T) Old friend
Alec
Alex Dims. of Alexander
Alexander (Gr) Helper of men
Alexenor (Gr) Aiding man (name of a physician)
Alexis (Gr) Helper
Alfons (T) Eager for battle
Alfonse (T)
Alfonzo (T)
Alfred (T) Elf-counsel, wise
Algernon (OF) With whiskers or moustache
Allen Var. of Alan
Allon (H) An oak; emblem of eternity
Almeric (T) Worker
Almon (H) Hidden
Almu (Fin) Alms, charity
Alonzo Spanish var. of Alfons
Aloysius (T) Famous in war
Alphonse
Alphonzo Vars. of Alfons
Alvin (T) Loved by all
Alvy (Ir) A flock
Alwyn (T) Loved by all
Amadeus (L) Love of God
Aman (H) Artist, architect
Ambrose (Gr) Immortal
Amerigo (T) Worker
Amias English var. of Amadeus
Amos (H) A burden
Anastasius (Gr) Resurrection, rebirth
Anders Scandinavian form of Andrew
Andre (Gr)
Andreas (Gr)
Andrew (Gr) Manly
Aneurin (W) Man of integrity
Angelo (Gr) A messenger, angel
Angus (K) Unhesitating strength
Anlon (Ir) Great champion
Ansel (T)
Anselm (T) God's helmet; divine protection
Anthony (L)
Antoine (L)
Anton (L)
Antonio (L) Deserving praise
Apollo (Gr) The sun, both as lifegiver and destroyer
Aram (H) High, exalted
Aram (Pers) Rest, tranquillity
Aran (H) Wild goat
Arba (H) Foursquare, perfect, complete
Archibald (T) Holy prince
Ardal (K) High valor
Ari (H) A lion
Ariad (W) Singer, reciter
Arian (W) Silver
Ariel (H) Lion of God; also a consecrated hearth or altar
Arlo (K) Harvest home; ingathering of the harvest
Armand (T)
Armin (T) War-man
Armo (Fin) Grace, mercy
Arne (T) Eagle
Arnold (T) Strong as an eagle
Arnvid (Scan) Eagle of the woods; courageous
Arpad (H) A prop or support; a firm base
Artemas (Gr)
Artemus (Gr) Pure, entire
Arthol (K) High courage
Arthur (K) Brave as a bear; noble
Arve Dim. of Arnvid
Arvid (Scan) Eagle of the woods; courageous
Arving (T) An heir
Arvo (Fin) Value, worth, importance
Asa (H) Physician
Asaph (H) Collecting, ingathering, harvest

Asgard (Scan) Divine stronghold
Asher (H) Happy, blessed, delightful
Athol (K) A rocky ford
Aubert Old French var. of Albert
Aubrey (T) Ruler of spirits
August (L) Exalted, worthy of high re-
Augustine (L) spect
Augustus (L)
Aulius (Fin) Generosity
Austen Vars. of Augustine
Austin
Axel (Scan) Divine reward, divine success
Aylmer (T) Noble fame

Baldor (T) The bolder one; a hero
Baldwin (T) Bold in war
Baptist (Gr) A baptizer, or one baptized
Barent Dutch var. of Bernard
Barnabas (H) Son of consolation
Barnaby (H)
Barry (H) Dim. of Baruch, blessed
Barry (K) Straight-shooter
Bartholomew (H) Son of furrows
Baruch (H) Blessed
Basil (Gr) Kingly
Bayard (OF) Originally meaning "a bay-colored horse"; earned glory as the name of the "Chevalier without fear and without reproach"
Bela (H) Swallowing (his enemies); a victor
Bela Hungarian var. of Albert
Beltran Spanish var. of Bertram
Benedict (L) Blessed
Bengt Scandinavian var. of Benedict
Benito (L) Blessed
Benjamin (H) Son of the right hand; true, good, and powerful
Bennett Var. of Benedict
Beorn (OE) A bear
Bercan (K) Little spear
Bern (T) A bear; emblem of Bern in Switzerland
Bernard (T) Bold as a bear
Bernarr (T)
Bertel (T) Bright power; or sometimes a
Bertil (T) dim. of Bartholomew
Bertram (T) Bright raven
Bertrand (T) Bright shield; sometimes a var. of Bertram
Bion (Gr) Course of life, career
Birel (OE) A steward
Birger (Scan) Protector
Bjorn (T) A bear
Blaine (K) Lean, meager
Blair (K) A cleared plain; a battlefield
Booker (OE) An author; a scribe
Boris (Sl) A warrior
Boyd (K) Yellow-haired
Brent (OE) Lofty, steep
Brian (K) Strong
Bruce (OF) From Brus or Braose, ancient Norman castle and family
Bruno (T) Of a dark complexion
Bryan (K) Strong
Bryce (W) Quick, lively
Burton (T) A fortified farmstead
Burwood (T) A woodland fortress

Byrel (OE) A steward
Byrne (OE) A coat of mail
Byron (T) Cottager; sometimes from a place name in Normandy

Cadmar (K) Strong in battle
Cadmus (Gr) From the East
Cadwallader (W) Battle ruler
Caesar (L) Hairy
Cairn (K) A priest; a sacrificer; an ancient altar; a memorial pile of stones
Caleb (H) A dog
Calvert (OE) Calf-herd, herdsman
Calvin (L) Bald
Camille (L) An assistant in sacred rites
Camillus (L)
Camon (H) Field of standing wheat
Carey (K) A rock
Carl (T) Manly, strong, vigorous
Carlile (K) Camp of the legion
Carlisle (K)
Carlyle (K)
Carmi (H) Vinedresser
Carvell (Ir) Warrior, champion
Cashin (K) Curly
Casimir (Sl) Preacher of peace; also disturber of peace
Caspar (Pers) Treasurer
Cathal (Ir) Battle-mighty
Cather (Ir) Warrior
Cato (L) Sagacious, wise
Cecil (L) Blind
Cedric (K) Battle ruler
Cephas (Aram) A rock
Chaim (H) Life
Charles (T) Manly, strong, vigorous
Chauncey (OF) From Canci, near Amiens
Chester (L) A camp
Christopher (Gr) Christ-bearer
Clarence (L) Illustrious
Claude (L) Lame
Clement (L) Merciful
Cleon (Gr) Famed, renowned
Clifford (OE) From place name describing a steep descent and a river crossing
Clovis Early form of Louis
Cnud *See* **Knud.**
Cnut
Coel (W) Trust, belief, credo
Colar Old French dim. of Nicholas
Colbert (L) Fellow-freeman
Colgan (K) Dove
Colin Old French dim. of Nicholas
Colin (K) Dove
Colin (K) Whelp, young animal
Colon (L) A dove; also a colonist; real name of Christopher Columbus
Colon (T) From Cologne
Colum (L) A dove
Conall (K) Love, friendship; also fruitfulness, ear of wheat, guardian of childhood
Conan (K) Brave, strong-willed, wise
Congal (K) Gallantry, bravery
Conlan (K) A hero
Conrad (T) Bold counsel

Constant (L) Resolute, faithful
Constantine (L)
Coral (Gr) Coral pink
Coral (L) Cordial, hearty
Corbet (L) A raven
Cordell (L) From Cordelles in France
Cormac (K) Son of a chariot; a charioteer
Cornelius (L) Powerful (the horn, *cornu*, anciently typifying the power of truth)
Corry (Ir) A spear
Cosmo (Gr) Order
Craig (K) A rock
Cronan (Ir) Dark brown
Curtis (L) Courteous
Cuthbert (T) Notably bright
Cyril (Gr) Lordly, masterly
Cyrus (Pers) The sun

Damon (Gr) One who subdues
Dan (H) Judging, perceiving truth
Dana (Ir) Bold, intrepid
Dana (T) From Denmark
Daniel (H) My judge is God; figuratively, the spirit of all prophecy
Dard (H) Pearl of wisdom
Darell (OE) Darling
Daric (H) *See* **Derek.**
Daric (Pers) An ancient golden coin; tribute
Darius (Pers) Preserver, restrainer
Daron (W) The thunderer
Darrell (OF) From Arel, in Normandy
Darvin (T) Spear-friend, comrade
Daryl Var. of Darrell
David (H) Beloved
Dean (OE) A dene, or wooded valley
Delos (Gr) The Isle of Delos; ancient emblem of simple charity
Denis (Gr) Belonging to Dionysus, Grecian god of wine
Derek (H) A way, path, mode of life
Derick Dim. of Frederick or of Theodoric
Dermot (K) Independent
Derry (K) The oak; emblem of eternity
Derval (Ir) True desire
Desmond (Ir) From Desmond in Ireland
Dexter (L) Right hand
Dio (Gr) Excellent, godly
Diogenes (G) Child of Zeus; inspired by Zeus
Dion (Gr) Relating to Dionysus, Grecian god of wine
Dirck (T) People's ruler
Dirk (T)
Dominic (L) Sunday's child
Don (K) Brown-haired
Donal (K) World power
Donald (K)
Dongal (K) Dark stranger
Doniol (W) Gifted
Doral (Icel) Devoted to Thor
Dorin (Gr) A gift
Doron (Gr) A gift
Dothan (H) Wells of water
Douglas (K) Dark stream
Drew Dim. of Andrew
Duane (K) Poet

Dugal (K) Dark stranger
Duke (L) Leader
Duncan (K) Brown chief
Dunstan (T) Hill-stone
Durward (OE) Door-ward; door-guardian
Dwight (F) From Doyt, a place in Normandy
Dylan (W) The ocean

Eamon Irish form of Edmund
Earl (T) Nobleman, leader
Earle (T)
Eben (H) A stone
Ebenezer (H) Stone of help
Edan (K) Fire
Eden (H) Love, delight, pleasure
Edgar (T) Rich spear
Edmond (T) Rich protection
Edmund (T)
Edom (H) Red
Edric (OE) Blessed power
Edris (Ar) Study, meditation (Arabic name for Enoch)
Edward (T) Rich guard
Edwin (T) Rich friend
Egan (K) Fiery, ardent
Egbert (T) Awesomely bright
Egor Russian var. of George
Elliv (Scan) Everliving
Einar (T) Enduring warrior
Eivind (Scan) Lasting friend
Elam (H) Youth; also long duration, eternity
Eldred (T) Ancient counsel
Eldric (T) Ancient rule
Eleazer (H) Whom God helps
Eleos (Gr) Mercy, compassion
Eli (H) Ascent, high rank
Elias Greek form of Elijah
Eliezer (H) God is his help
Elijah (H) My God is the Lord
Eliot English dims. of Elijah
Elliot
Elishah (H) My God is salvation
Elmer (T) Noble fame
Elmo (Gr) Amiable
Elon (H) An oak; emblem of eternity
Elrad (T) Wise counsel
Elsdon (OE) Ellis' valley, Ellis being an English form of Elishah
Elvin (T) Elf-friend, meaning wise friend
Emanuel (H) God with us
Emery (T) Worker
Emory (T)
Emil (L-T) Industrious
Emile (L-T)
Emmett (OE) An ant; active, lively
Endrede (Scan) Lone rider
Enoch (H) Dedicated
Ensi (Fin) First, foremøst
Eoin An Irish form of John
Ephraim (H) Doubly fruitful; full of high thoughts
Eran (H) Watchful
Erard (K) Noble, exalted, distinguished
Erasmus (Gr) Amiable
Ercan (Ir) Rainbow

Erdman (T)	Earthman; husbandman, farmer
Eric (T)	Ever mighty
Erland (T)	Stranger, exile
Erlend (T)	
Erle (T)	Nobleman, leader
Ernan (Ir)	Knowing, experienced
Ernest (T)	Earnest, sincere
Ernin (Ir)	Knowing, experienced
Erno	Hungarian form of Ernest
Errol (L)	Wandering
Ervin (T)	War-friend, comrade
Erwin (T)	
Esau (H)	Hairy
Ethan (H)	Firmness, constancy
Ethelbert (T)	Nobly bright
Ethelred (T)	Noble counsel
Ettore	Italian form of Hector
Eudo (T)	Rich, happy
Eugene (Gr)	Well-born
Eustace (Gr)	Happy in harvest, rich in wheat (*eustakhus*)
Eustace (Gr)	Steadfast (*eustathes*)
Evald (T)	Ever powerful
Evan (W)	A youth
Everard (T)	Strong as a wild boar
Everett (T)	
Evert (T)	
Ewald (T)	Ever powerful
Ewan (W)	A youth
Ewen (W)	
Eyulf (T)	Island wolf
Eyvind (Scan)	Lasting friend
Ezekiel (H)	Strength of God
Fabian (L)	Bean grower
Farry (Ir)	Manly, forceful
Felan (Ir)	A young wolf
Felim (Ir)	Ever good
Felix (L)	Happy
Feodor	Slavic var. of Theodore
Ferdinand (T)	Adventurous life
Fergus (K)	Man's strength
Festus (L)	Belonging to a holiday
Finbar (K)	Fair head
Fingal (K)	Fair stranger
Finian (Ir)	Fair
Flavius (L)	Yellow-haired
Floyd (W)	Gray
Franchot (T)	Free
Francis (T)	Free
Frank (T)	
Franklin (T)	A freeman
Frederic (T)	Peaceful ruler
Frederick (T)	
Fritz	German dim. of Frederick
Gabriel (H)	My hero is God
Gad (H)	A troop; good fortune, good works
Gail (H)	Joy
Gail (K)	Valor, virtue
Gale (K)	
Galdor (OE)	A charm, a singing enchantment
Galen (Gr)	Calm, gentle
Gamaliel (H)	Reward of God
Garabed (Armen)	Leader, guide
Gareth (T)	Firm spear
Garth (T)	A gardener; also a field, enclosure
Garry (K)	A gardener
Garvey (T)	Spear of war
Garvin (T)	Spear-friend, comrade
Garwood (OE)	A spear, or javelin, with shaft of wood
Gaston (Gothic)	Hospitable
Gavin (K)	Battle hawk
Gene	Dim. of Eugene
Goeffrey (T)	God's peace
George (Gr)	Earthman; husbandman, farmer
Gerald (T)	Spear power
Gerard (T)	
Gerbert (T)	Spear-bright
Gerhard (T)	Spear power
Gerritt	Dutch form of Gerard
Gershom (H)	A stranger
Gideon (H)	Tree-feller; bold warrior
Gilbert (T)	Bright pledge, bright sacrifice
Giles (Gr)	Shield-bearer
Glen (K)	A valley
Glendower (W)	Deep water
Godfrey (T)	God's peace
Godwin (T)	Loved by God; also, good friend
Gomer (H)	Complete, consistent
Gordon (T)	Name of famous Scottish clan, "the Gay Gordons"; meaning uncertain
Graham (OE)	Gray suit of armor
Grant (L)	Great
Gregory (Gr)	A watchman
Griffith (W)	Reddish
Grover (T)	Grove-dweller
Guido (T)	A spear of wood
Gulian (OE)	Rejoicing
Gunnar (T)	Warrior
Gunther (T)	Warrior
Gustav (T)	Goth's staff
Gwyn (K)	White, fair
Guy (F)	Mistletoe
Guy (L)	Standard bearer, guide; also sometimes dim. of Guido
Gylian (OE)	Rejoicing
Haakon (T)	Of high birth
Haim	Var. of Khaim
Halvard (T)	Stone guard
Halvor (T)	
Halvord (T)	
Hamlet (T)	A little home
Hamnet (T)	
Harlan (T)	Warrior-land
Harold (T)	Army ruler
Harry (T)	Ruler of the home
Harvey (K)	Bitter
Harvey (T)	Warrior
Hasan (Ar)	Handsome
Healdon (OE)	One who holds fast, a preserver
Heber (H)	Companionship, fellowship
Hector (Gr)	Defender
Heinz (T)	Ruler of the home
Helmer (T)	Helmed warrior
Henry (T)	Ruler of the home
Herbert (T)	Bright warrior
Hereward (T)	Sword-guardian

Name	Meaning
Herman (T)	Warrior
Hernan	Spanish form of Ferdinand
Hilary (L)	Cheerful
Hildebrand (T)	Battle sword
Hildric (OE)	Battle power
Hilmar (T)	Battle renown
Hiram (H)	Noble, highborn
Hjalmar (T)	Helmed warrior
Hobart (T)	Bright mind
Holger (T)	Island spear
Homer (Gr)	A security, pledge
Horace (G-L)	Clear-sighted, perceptive
Hosea (H)	Salvation
Howard (T)	A steward, or a sword-guardian
Huard (T)	Mind-guardian, also a soul-guardian
Hubert (T)	Bright mind
Hugh (T)	Mind, thought, study
Hugo (T)	
Hulbert (T)	Bright mind
Humbert (T)	Bright support
Humphrey (T)	Support of peace
Hyman	Modern var. of Chaim

Name	Meaning
Ian	Scottish form of John
Idris (Ar)	Study, meditation (Arabic name for Enoch)
Ignatius (L)	Fiery
Igor (T)	Commander
Ija	Dim. of Elijah
Ilo (Fin)	Joy, delight
Immanuel (H)	God with us
Imre	Hungarian form of Emery
Ing (T)	Legendary ancestor of Scandinavian kings; said to mean "young"
Ingo (T)	
Ingve (T)	
Ion	Rumanian form of John
Ira (H)	Watchful
Irenaeus (Gr)	Peaceful
Irial (Ir)	Salutation, greeting
Irvin (T)	War friend, comrade
Irving (T)	
Irwin (T)	
Isaac (H)	Laughter
Isador (Gr)	Gift of Isis
Isidor (Gr)	
Isaiah (H)	Salvation of the Lord
Ishmael (H)	Heard of God
Israel (H)	A prince, or champion, of God
Issachar (H)	Reward, fair dealing
Ivan	Russian form of John
Ivar (T)	Archer, bow-bearer
Ivo (T)	Archer, bow-bearer
Ivor (T)	

Name	Meaning
Jack	A popular var. of John; also the traditional happy partner of Jill
Jacob (H)	Supplanter; one who overthrows
James	English form of Jacob
Jan	Var. of John
Januel (OF)	January
Japheth (H)	Enlargement, growth
Jared (H)	Descent
Jasha	Russian dim. of Jacob
Jason (Gr)	Healer
Jasper (Pers)	Treasurer
Jesper (Pers)	
Jean	French form of John
Jeffrey (T)	God's peace
Jenkin	Welsh dim. of John
Jens	Var. of John
Jeremiah (H)	Exalted of the Lord
Jeremy (H)	
Jeriel (H)	Founded by God
Jerome (Gr)	Holy name
Jesse (H)	The Lord is
Jethro (H)	Excellence
Jevan (W)	A youth
Joachim (H)	The Lord will establish
Joaquin (H)	
Joel (H)	The Lord is God
John (H)	The Lord is gracious, merciful
Jon (H)	
Jonah (H)	A dove
Jonas (H)	
Jonathan (H)	Gift of the Lord
Jordan (H)	Descending, flowing down
Joris	Dutch form of George
Joseph (H)	He shall add; also, spiritual progress
Joshua (H)	The Lord is salvation
Josiah (H)	Given of the Lord
Jovian (L)	Gay, jovial
Juan	Spanish form of John
Judah (H)	Praise, confessing, also love of God
Jules (L)	Downy-bearded, soft-haired
Julius (L)	
Junius (L)	Youthful
Justin (L)	Just
Justus (L)	
Juvenal (L)	Youthful

Name	Meaning
Kallio (Fin)	Rock, cliff, mountain
Karel (T)	Man, manly
Karl (T)	
Kaspar (Pers)	Treasurer
Keith (K)	Ancient Scottish place name, interpreted as woody, narrow, hilly, or windy
Kelan (Ir)	Slender
Kendal (T)	Valley of the Ken River
Kenneth (K)	Handsome
Kent (K)	A headland, hill
Kephas (Aram)	A rock
Kereth (H)	A city; also a pulpit
Kermit (K)	Dark armor
Kerry (K)	Dark
Kesniel (H)	God is my strength
Kevan (K)	Comely, mild, noble
Kevin (K)	
Khaim (H)	Life
Kian (Ir)	Ancient, distant
Kieran (Ir)	Black, or gray
Kilian (K)	Warlike
Kim	A Keltic var. of Simon
Kirk (Gr)	The church
Knud (T)	A knot, in the sense of being rugged, strong
Knute (T)	
Kolmas (Fin)	Third
Kolya	Slavic dim. of Nicholas
Koresh (Pers)	The sun
Kuno (T)	Bold
Kurt	Dim. of Conrad

Laban (H)	White
Lachlan (K)	A champion
Lael (H)	To God
Lambert (T)	Brightness of the land
Lance (L)	Spear, spearman
Lancelot (L)	Servant, follower
Laren	Keltic form of Laurence
Lars	Scandinavian forms of Laurence
Larz	
Laurence (L)	Laurel-crowned
Laurie (L)	
Lawrence (L)	
Leander (Gr)	Lion-man, brave
Lee (T)	A meadow
Leigh (T)	
Leif (T)	Successor, inheritor
Leighton (T)	Meadow-town
Lemuel (H)	(Dedicated) to God
Lenox (K)	From County Lennox, Scotland; original meaning, smooth river
Leo (Gr)	A lion
Leon (Gr)	
Leofric (T)	Beloved rule
Leonard (Gr-T)	Strong as a lion
Leopold (T)	The people's courage
Leroy (L)	The king
Lesley	Vars. of Lisle
Leslie	
Lester (L)	Camp of the Legion
Leicester (L)	
Levi (H)	Joining, lending; charity
Lewis	English form of Louis
Liam	Irish form of William
Lionel (Gr)	Lionlike
Lisle (L)	Of the Isle; a Norman name
Llewellyn (W)	Lionlike
Lloyd (W)	Gray
Loren	Var. of Laurence
Lorenzo	Italian form of Laurence
Lori	Swiss form of Laurence
Lorin	Var. of Laurence
Louis (T)	Famous in battle
Lucas (L)	Light
Lucian (L)	
Lucius (L)	
Ludwig (T)	Famous in battle
Luke (L)	Light
Lyndon (OE)	Lake-hill
Lynn (K-T)	Sea, lake, pool, brook, or waterfall
Lysander (Gr)	Liberator of men
Madoc (W)	Beneficent, goodly
Magnus (L)	Great
Mahlon (H)	Great infirmity
Mahon (Ir)	A bear
Malachi (H)	Messenger of the Lord
Malchos (Gr)	Ruling, reigning
Malchus (Gr)	
Malcolm (K)	Servant of Columb
Malvin (K)	One who ministers
Manas (K)	Might, power
Manasseh (H)	Forgetfulness, unselfishness
Mandel (Gr-L-T)	The almond
Manfred (T)	Mighty peace
Mano	Hungarian form of Emanuel
Manoah (H)	Rest
Manoel	Portuguese form of Emanuel

Manuel	Spanish form of Emanuel
Manus	Gaelic form of Magnus
Marcel	Dims. of Marco
Marcellus	
Marco (L)	Belonging to Mars; but sometimes from Latin *marculus*, a small hammer, or Keltic *marc*, a horse
Marcus (L)	
Mark (L)	
Mario	In Latin lands, a masc. form of Maria
Mario (L)	Related to Mars, the war god
Marion	A masc. form of Mary
Marius (L)	Related to Mars, the god of war
Marquis (T)	Defender of his country's borders
Marshall (OF)	Master of the horses
Martel (L)	A hammer
Martin (L)	Warlike
Marvin (T)	Famous friend
Maskil (H)	Song of wisdom
Mathan (H)	A gift
Mathon	An Old French form of Mathew
Matthew (H)	Gift of the Lord
Maurice (L)	Moorish, dark
Max (L)	Greatest
Maxim (L)	
Maximilian (L)	
Mayer	*See* Meir.
Mayor	
Megen (OE)	Strength
Meier (T)	Steward, farmer
Meier (H)	Shining, illustrious
Meir (H)	
Melchior (H)	King of light
Meldan (Ir)	Pleasant
Melville (L)	From Maleville in Normandy
Melvin (K)	One who ministers
Menahem (H)	Comforter
Mendel	Modern dim. of Menahem
Mentor (Gr)	Wise teacher and friend
Menwin (W)	Intelligent
Meredith (K)	Noisy animation of the sea
Merle (L)	A blackbird
Mervin (K)	Sea-friend
Mervyn (K)	
Merwyn (K)	
Meyer (T)	Steward, farmer
Michael (H)	Who is like unto God?
Milan (Sl)	Amiable
Miles (L)	Soldier
Milo (Gr)	Crusher (after Milo, famed Greek wrestler)
Miltiades (Gr)	Ruddy complexion
Milton (OE)	Mill town, or mill farmstead
Misha	Russian dim. of Michael
Mishael (H)	Who is what God is?
Montague (L)	From Montacute in Normandy
Moran (Ir)	Hairy
Morel (L)	Moorish, dark
Morgan (W)	Dweller by the sea
Mori (J)	Grove, wood, forest
Morley (OF)	From Morlaix, in Brittany
Morris (L)	Moorish, dark
Mortimer (L)	From Mortemer in Normandy (literally "dead sea," but probably means "still water")

Morvan (W)	Dweller by the sea
Morven (W)	
Morvin (W)	
Moses (H)	Taken out of the water; deliverance
Muhammad (Ar)	Praised
Mungo (K)	Amiable, kind
Murdoch (K)	Navigator
Murray (Ir)	A seaman
Mustafa (Ar)	Elect, chosen
Myron (Gr)	Aromatic ointment or fragrance
Naphtali (H)	Wrestling; resisting temptation
Nathan (H)	A gift
Nathaniel (H)	Gift of God
Neal (K)	A champion
Neil (K)	
Nedan (Sl)	Sunday's child
Nelson (Scan)	Son of a champion
Nestor (Gr)	One who remembers
Nevan (K)	Heavenly, blissful
Neville (L)	From Neuville, "new town," in Normandy
Nial (K)	A champion
Niel (K)	
Nicholas (Gr)	Victory of the people
Niels	Dims. of Nicholas
Niles	
Nils	
Nishan (Armen)	A mark, a sign
Noah (H)	Rest, comfort
Noel (L)	Christmas
Norbert (T)	Brightness from the North
Norman (T)	North man
Norris (T)	Norseman
Norval (T)	Northern power
Octavius (L)	The eighth
Odo (T)	Rich, happy
Oen (Welsh)	A lamb
Ogden (T)	Oak valley
Olaf (Scan)	Heir of his forefathers
Olav (Scan)	
Olan (OE)	The holly tree
Oliver (L)	The olive tree
Omar (H)	Eloquent
Omer (H)	A sheaf of wheat
Oraham	Aramaic form of Abraham
Oran (K)	Song, poem
Ordan (Ir)	Nobility, dignity; also generosity; music
Oren (H)	A pine tree
Oriel (H)	God is my light
Orlando (T)	Fame of the land
Ormond (T)	Defender of the treasure
Orson (L)	A bear
Orville (OF)	Golden town; or, in some cases, golden valley (*Orival*)
Osbert (T)	Divinely bright
Oscar (T)	Divine spear
Oscar (K)	A champion
Osmond (T)	Divine protection
Osmund (T)	
Osric (T)	Divine rule
Oswald (T)	Divine power
Oswin (T)	Divine friend
Othniel (H)	Lion of God
Otho (T)	Rich, happy
Otto (T)	
Otis (Gr)	One who hears
Owen (W)	A youth
Pascal (H)	Eastertide, Passover
Patrick (L)	Noble, patrician
Paul (L)	Little, perhaps in the sense of being modest
Percival (W)	Lance-friend, comrade
Percy (W)	
Peregrine (L)	Pilgrim, wanderer
Perkin	An English dim. of Peter
Perron	Old French var. of Peter
Perry	Dim. of Peregrine; also, rarely, of Peter
Pesach (H)	Passover
Peter (Gr)	A rock; faith
Phelim (Ir)	Ever good
Philemon (Gr)	Undivided love
Philip (Gr)	Lover of horses
Phoebus (Gr)	Shining; the sun
Pierce	English var. of Peter
Pierre	French form of Peter
Piers	English var. of Peter
Plato (Gr)	Broad-shouldered, powerful, of wide influence
Prescott (T)	Priest's dwelling
Preston (T)	Priest's domain
Prosper (L)	Fortunate
Quentin (L)	The fifth
Quintin (L)	
Quincy (L)	From Quincy in France
Ragnal (T)	Ruling power
Ragnar (T)	
Raham (H)	Merciful
Ralph (T)	Wolf or wolf-shield
Ramon	Spanish form of Raymond
Ramsay (T)	From Ramsay (ram's water
Ramsey (T)	or ram's island) in England
Ramus (Lith)	Peaceful
Ranald (T)	Ruling power
Randal (T)	Shield wolf
Randolph (T)	
Raphael (H)	Healed of God
Ray	Vars. of Roy
Rey	
Raymond (T)	Wise protection
Read (OE)	Red; also counsel, help
Redbert (T)	Bright counselor
Reginald (T)	Ruling power
Reinald (T)	Ruling power
Regnier (T)	Ruling power
Rembert (T)	Bright judgment
René (L)	Reborn
Reuben (H)	"Behold, a son"; also understanding
Reuel (H)	Friend of God
Reverdy (OF)	Joy, pleasure
Rex (L)	King
Richard (T)	Stern ruler
Robert (T)	Bright fame
Robin (T)	
Roderick (T)	Famous ruler
Rodney (T)	Famed new power
Roger (T)	Famous spear
Roland (T)	Fame of the land

Name	Meaning
Rolf	Dim. of Rudolph
Romano (G-L)	A Roman; also strength, power
Romney (K)	From the marsh
Ronald (T)	Ruling power
Ronan (Ir)	A young seal or sea-calf
Ross (T)	Horse
Rowan (Ir)	Red
Rowan (T)	The mountain ash
Roy (K)	Red
Roy (L)	A king
Rudolph (T)	Famed wolf
Rudyard (T)	A cleared field
Rufus (L)	Red
Runo (Fin)	A poem
Rupert (T)	Bright in fame
Russell (F)	A stream, a brook; or from Rosel in Normandy
Russell (L)	Of a reddish color
Samson (H)	Splendid sun
Samuel (H)	Heard of God
Sandor	Hungarian form of Alexander
Sanfrid (L-T)	Holy peace
Sasha	A Russian dim. of Alexander
Saul (H)	Asked for
Sean	Irish form of John; (pronounced *shawn*)
Sebastian (Gr)	Venerable
Septimus (L)	The seventh
Seth (H)	Appointed
Sextus (L)	The sixth
Selim (Ar)	Peaceful, wholesome
Selmar (H-T)	Peaceful
Seumas	Irish form of James; (pronounced *shamus*)
Seymour (L)	From St. Maur in Normandy
Shelley (T)	From a town in England called Shelly, meaning "shallow"
Shem (H)	Celebrated name
Sherman (OE)	A shear-man, a cutter; also a county overseer
Sherwin (T)	A swift runner, one who shears the wind; also a sheer (sincere) friend
Sheth (H)	Appointed
Sholem (H)	Peace
Sibert (T)	Conquering brightness
Sidney (L)	From St. Denis, or from Sathonay, France
Siegfried (T)	Victorious peace
Sigeric (OE)	Victorious
Sigmund (T)	Victorious protection
Sigurd (T)	Victory watchman
Silas (L)	Dweller in the woods
Silvan (L)	
Silvanus (L)	
Silvester (L)	
Simeon (H)	Hearing, obedience
Simon (H)	
Sinon (Ir)	Wise
Solomon (H)	Peaceful
Sonas (K)	Success, fortune, happiness
Spencer (L)	A steward
Spenser (L)	
Stacy	Dim. of Anastasius
Stanislaus (Sl)	Standing glory
Stanislav (Sl)	
Stanley (OE)	From the stony meadow
Stanton (OE)	Stone town
Stefan (Gr)	Crown, wreath
Stephen (Gr)	
Steven (Gr)	
Sterling (T)	Genuine, dependable
Stewart (OE)	A steward
Stuart (OE)	
Svante (T)	A young swan
Sven (T)	A rustic; a youth; a bachelor
Swain (T)	
Sydney	*See* **Sidney.**
Sylvan (L)	Dweller in the woods
Sylvanus (L)	
Sylvester (L)	
Taliesin (W)	Radiant brow; (pronounced *tal-yessin*)
Talvi (Fin)	Winter
Terence (Gr)	Soft, tender
Terry	Dim. of Terence, also of Theodoric
Thaddeus (Aram)	Praise, thanksgiving
Thady (Ir)	Poet, philosopher
Theobald (T)	People's power
Theodore (Gr)	Gift of God
Theodoric (T)	People's ruler
Theophilus (Gr)	Beloved of God
Theron (Gr)	A hunter
Thomas (H)	A twin
Thoris (Gothic)	Noble, courageous
Thoron (T)	Boldness
Thorvid (Scan)	Thor's wood
Thurston (T)	Thor's stone
Timothy (Gr)	God-fearing
Tito (L)	Safe, protected
Titus (L)	
Tobias (H)	Goodness of the Lord
Tony	Dim. of Anthony
Torkild (T)	Thor's kettle
Torvald (T)	Thor's power
Tracy (Gr)	Harvester
Tristam (L)	Sad
Tristram (L)	
Trystan (L)	
Trygve (T)	Constant, true
Tudor	Welsh form of Theodore
Turgal (Assyr)	Great chief
Turlo (Ir)	Resembling Thor
Tyrone (K)	Land of Owen
Tyrus (H-Gr)	A rock; also the city of Tyre
Uan (Ir)	A lamb
Ulmer (T)	From Ulm on the Danube
Ulric (T)	Noble ruler
Ulysses (L)	A Latin form of Greek Odysseus, traditionally meaning "hatred"
Urban (L)	Of the city; civil, polite
Uriel (H)	Light of God
Vahan (Armen)	A shield
Valdemar (T)	Power-renowned
Valentine (L)	Healthy, well
Valo (Fin)	The light
Vance (L)	One who keeps ahead
Vanya	A dim. of Ivan
Vartan (Armen)	Name of an Armenian hero; *vart* means "a rose"

Vathan (Gothic)	A leader
Vaughan (K)	Little
Vergil (L)	Of the springtime; flourishing
Virgil (L)	
Verne (L)	Born in springtime
Verner (T)	Protecting warrior
Vernon (L)	Of the springtime; flourishing
Vero (L)	True
Victor (L)	Conqueror
Vincent (L)	Conquering
Vivian (L)	Lively
Vivien (L)	
Vladimir (Sl)	Ruling in peace
Volmer (T)	Power-renowned
Waldemar (T)	Power-renowned
Walden (T)	Powerful
Waldo (T)	Powerful
Wallace (T)	Welshman
Walter (T)	Powerful warrior
Ward (T)	Guardian, or guarded
Warner (OE)	A game warden
Warner (T)	Protecting warrior
Warren (OE)	A game preserve
Warren (T)	A defense
Wayne (T)	A wagon; also a meadow
Wendel (T)	Wandering
Werner (T)	Protecting warrior
Wilbur (T)	Resolute protection
Wilfred (T)	Resolute peace
Wilfrid (T)	
Wilhelm (T)	Helmet of resolution
Willard (T)	A firm will
William (T)	Helmet of resolution
Willis (T)	Son of Will or of William
Wilmot (T)	Resolute courage
Wilram (T)	Welcome raven
Winfred (T)	Friend of peace
Winston (T)	Friendly stone
Wilfram (T)	Wolf-raven
Wyn (OE)	Joy, delight; also a friend
Wynne (OE)	
Xavier (Ar)	Conspicuous
Yon	Var. of John
Zabdiel (H)	Gift of God
Zadoc (H)	Just
Zavier (Ar)	Conspicuous
Zebulon (H)	Desire for home and marriage
Zerah (H)	Rising of light

NAMES OF THE UNITED STATES AND THEIR ORIGIN

The fifty states that comprise the United States of America have received their names from varied sources. Many of them were derived from proper names that were used to honor certain individuals. Others were American Indian words that described the land or the people of that particular area. Variations from the original words are frequently found, and in some instances the proper meaning or origin of the name is in dispute. The following list has been compiled by consulting a number of sources and using the most commonly accepted derivations and meanings.

STATE NAME	PROBABLE MEANING	DERIVATION	NICKNAME
ALABAMA		Indian; named for tribe of Creek Confederacy and tribal town	*Cotton*
ALASKA		Russian version of Aleut word for Alaska Peninsula	
ARIZONA	"*Little spring place*"	Spanish version of Pima Indian word meaning "spring"	*Grand Canyon*
ARKANSAS	"*South wind people*"	French version of name of Sioux Indian tribe	*Land of Opportunity*
CALIFORNIA		Supposedly named by the conquistadors for an imaginary island in a Spanish romantic novel	*Golden*
COLORADO	"*Red*"	Spanish; first given to the Colorado River	*Centennial*
CONNECTICUT	"*Long river place*"	Algonquian Indian	*Constitution*
DELAWARE		Named after colonial administrator Lord Delaware; also given to river and Indian tribe	*Diamond*
FLORIDA	"*Flowery*"	Spanish; given by Ponce de León on Easter Sunday (*pascua florida*)	*Sunshine*
GEORGIA		Neo-Latin; named for Kings George I and II by James E. Oglethorpe, colonial administrator	*Empire State of the South*
HAWAII	"*Homeland*"	Native word	*Aloha*
IDAHO	"*Salmon tribe*"	Shoshone Indian	*Gem*
ILLINOIS	"*Land of warriors*"	French version of Algonquian word *Illini*, meaning "warriors" or "men"; also given to river and tribe	*Prairie*
INDIANA		So called because Indians lived there	*Hoosier*
IOWA	"*One who puts to sleep*"	Sioux Indian; name also given to river and tribe	*Hawkeye*
KANSAS	"*South wind people*"	Sioux Indian	*Sunflower*

STATE NAME	PROBABLE MEANING	DERIVATION	NICKNAME
KENTUCKY	*"Plain"*	Indian	*Blue Grass*
LOUISIANA		Named for Louis XIV of France by Sieur de La Salle	*Pelican*
MAINE		French; after Mayne, a former province of France	*Pine Tree*
MARYLAND		Named after Queen Henrietta Maria of England, wife of Charles I	*Old Line*
MASSACHUSETTS	*"Large hill place"*	Indian; named for tribe in Massachusetts Bay area	*Bay*
MICHIGAN	*"Great water"*	Chippewa Indian	*Wolverine*
MINNESOTA	*"Cloudy water"*	Dakota Sioux Indian; also given to river	*Gopher*
MISSISSIPPI	*"Large river"*	Indian, probably Chippewa	*Magnolia*
MISSOURI	*"Canoeist"*	Algonquian Indian; also given to river and tribe	*Show Me*
MONTANA	*"Mountainous"*	Latin	*Treasure*
NEBRASKA	*"Flat, shallow"*	Omaha Indian; also given to river	*Beef*
NEVADA	*"Snowclad mountain"*	Spanish *sierra nevada*	*Silver*
NEW HAMPSHIRE		Named after Hampshire, England	*Granite*
NEW JERSEY		Named after Jersey Island, England	*Garden*
NEW MEXICO		Spanish *nuevo Mexico*, term applied by Spaniards in Mexico to land north and west of the Rio Grande	*Land of Enchantment*
NEW YORK		Named for James, duke of York, when the English took over the Dutch settlement of New Amsterdam	*Empire*
NORTH CAROLINA		Neo-Latin; named for Charles I and Charles II	*Tar Heel*
NORTH DAKOTA	*"Friend, ally"*	Sioux Indian	*Sioux*
OHIO	*"Magnificent, beautiful"*	Indian; name also given to river	*Buckeye*
OKLAHOMA	*"Red people"*	Choctaw Indian; name suggested by Chief Allen Wright, an Indian	*Sooner*
OREGON	*"Hurricane"*	Origin uncertain; name used by Indians for a river but may have come from the French *ouragan*, meaning "hurricane"	*Beaver*
PENNSYLVANIA	*"Penn's woodland"*	Neo-Latin *sylvania*; named in honor of Admiral William Penn, father of William Penn, the Quaker, who received the land from Charles II	*Keystone*
RHODE ISLAND		The island of Rhodes in the Mediterranean Sea	*Little Rhody*
SOUTH CAROLINA		Neo-Latin; named for Charles I and Charles II	*Palmetto*
SOUTH DAKOTA	*"Friend, ally"*	Sioux Indian	*Coyote*
TENNESSEE		Cherokee Indian	*Volunteer*
TEXAS	*"Hello, friend"*	Caddo Indian	*Lone Star*
UTAH	*"Higher up"*	Navajo Indian; also given to a Shoshone tribe called Utes	*Beehive*
VERMONT	*"Green mountains"*	French *vert* (green) and *mont* (mountain)	*Green Mountain*
VIRGINIA		Neo-Latin; named in honor of Elizabeth I, the Virgin Queen of England	*Old Dominion*
WASHINGTON		Named in honor of George Washington	*Evergreen*
WEST VIRGINIA		Same as derivation of *Virginia*	*Mountain*
WISCONSIN	*"Grassy place"*	Chippewa Indian	*Badger*
WYOMING	*"Large prairie place"*	Indian	*Equality*

NICKNAMES OF FAMOUS PEOPLE

Addisonian (The)
Washington Irving (1783-1859); essayist and historian

All Eyes
Daniel Webster (1782-1852); statesman and orator

American Carlyle
Ralph Waldo Emerson (1803-1882); poet and historian

American Louis Philippe
Millard Fillmore (1800-1874); 13th president of the United States

American Woodman
John James Audubon (1785-1851); naturalist and painter

America's First Gentleman
Chester Alan Arthur (1830-1886); 21st president of the United States

Angel of the Battlefield
Clara Barton (1821-1912); organized the American Red Cross

Artist of Damnation
Jonathan Edwards (1703-1758); theologian; preached vivid sermons on hell and damnation

Aunt Rachel
Rachel D. Jackson (1767-1828); wife of President Andrew Jackson

Babe Ruth
George Herman Ruth (1895-1948); professional baseball player

Bachelor President
James Buchanan (1791-1868); 15th president of the

United States; unmarried

Billy the Kid
William H. Bonney (1859-1881); outlaw

Boss (The)
Franklin Delano Roosevelt (1882-1945); 32d president of the United States

Boy General
George A. Custer (1839-1876); brigadier general of Union Army Volunteers at the age of 24

Brown Bomber
Joe Louis (1914-); professional boxer

Buffalo Bill
William F. Cody (1846-1917); U.S. plainsman and army scout; provided railroad construction camps with buffalo meat

Bull Moose
Theodore Roosevelt (1858-1919); 26th president of the United States

Cactus Jack
John Nance Garner (1868-); vice president of the United States, 1933-1941

Calamity Jane
Martha Jane Burke (1852-1903); frontierswoman

Cassius the Brashest
Cassius Clay (1942-); professional boxer

Centennial President
Benjamin Harrison (1833-1901); 23d president of the United States

Chief
Herbert Clark Hoover (1874-); 31st president of the United States

Children's Poet
Henry Wadsworth Longfellow (1807-1882); poet

Corduroy Killer
Bobby Fischer (1943-); international grand master of chess at 15; youngest player ever to earn the title

Cowboy Philosopher
Will Rogers (1879-1935); humorist and actor

Dark Horse President
Rutherford B. Hayes (1822-1893); 19th president of the United States

Diamond Jim
James Buchanan Brady (1856-1917); financier famed for his lavish display of jewelry

Dizzy Dean
Jay Hanna Dean (1911-); professional baseball player

Doughboy's General
Omar Bradley (1893-); U.S. general; prominent in World War II

Empire Builder
James Jerome Hill (1838-1916); railroad executive; played important role in the development of the Northwest

Era of Good Feeling President
James Monroe (1758-1831); 5th president of the United States

Father of His Country
George Washington (1732-1799); 1st president of the United States

Father of the American Navy
John Adams (1735-1826); 2d president of the United States; recommended establishment of the Navy Department

Father of the Constitution
James Madison (1751-1836); 4th president of the United States; one of the chief architects of the U.S. Constitution

Fighting Quaker
Nathanael Greene (1742-1786); Quaker; general in War of American Independence

First Dark Horse
James Knox Polk (1795-1849); 11th president of the United States

Gentleman Jim
James J. Corbett (1866-1933); professional boxer

Grandma Moses
Anna Mary Robertson Moses (1860-1961); painter who began her career at the age of 78

Great Commoner
William Jennings Bryan (1860-1925); political leader and orator

Great Emancipator
Abraham Lincoln (1809-1865); 16th president of the United States

Great White Chief
Theodore Roosevelt (1858-1919); 26th president of the United States

Grover the Good
Grover Cleveland (1837-1908); 22d president of the United States

Handsome Frank
Franklin Pierce (1804-1869); 14th president of the United States

Happy Chandler
Albert B. Chandler (1898-); governor of Kentucky and American baseball commissioner

Happy Warrior
Alfred E. Smith (1873-1944); Democratic presidential candidate in 1928

Hero of Fort Sumter
Pierre Gustave Toutant Beauregard (1818-1893); Confederate general in American Civil War; captured Fort Sumter

Hero of Manila
George Dewey (1837-1917); admiral who captured Manila during the Spanish-American War

His Accidency
John Tyler (1790-1862); 10th president of the United States

Holy Horatio
Horatio Alger (1834-1899); clergyman and writer

Honest Abe
Abraham Lincoln (1809-1865); 16th president of the United States

Hoosier Poet
James Whitcomb Riley (1849-1916); poet

Idol of Ohio
William McKinley (1843-1901); 25th president of the United States

Ike
Dwight D. Eisenhower (1890-); 34th president of the United States

Iron Man of Baseball
Henry Louis (Lou) Gehrig (1903-1941); professional baseball player

Johnny Appleseed
John Chapman (1775-1845); pioneer; wandered through what are now Ohio, Indiana, and Illinois planting apple seeds

Kid Gloves Harrison
Benjamin Harrison (1833-1901); 23d president of the United States

La Belle Américaine
Mrs. James Monroe (1768-1830); wife of President Monroe; popular with the French during her husband's ambassadorship in Paris

Light-Horse Harry
Henry Lee (1756-1818); cavalry officer in War of American Independence

Lippy
Leo Durocher (1906-); baseball club manager

Little Flower
Fiorello La Guardia (1882-1947); mayor of New York City, 1934-1945

Little Giant
Stephen A. Douglas (1813-1861); statesman and orator

Little Sure Shot
Annie Oakley (1860-1926); markswoman

Little Van
Martin Van Buren (1782-1862); 8th president of the United States

Log Cabin President
William Henry Harrison (1773-1841); 9th president of the United States

Lone Eagle
Charles A. Lindbergh (1902-); American aviator; made the first solo nonstop flight to Europe

Mad Anthony Wayne
Anthony Wayne (1745-1796); officer in War of American Independence

Manassa Mauler
Jack Dempsey (1895-); professional boxer; born at Manassa, Colo.

Man from Missouri
Harry S Truman (1884-); 33d president of the United States

Man of a Thousand Faces
Lon Chaney (1883-1930); actor

Man of Destiny
Grover Cleveland (1837-1908); 22d and 24th president of the United States

Man on Horseback
Theodore Roosevelt (1858-1919); 26th president of the United States

Man with the Golden Arm
Sandy Koufax (1935-); professional baseball player

March King
John Philip Sousa (1854-1932); bandmaster and composer

Molly Pitcher
Mary McCauley (1754-1832); heroine in War of American Independence; carried water to wounded soldiers

Moses of Her People
Harriet Tubman (1821-1913); abolitionist

Old Ace of Spades
Robert E. Lee (1807-1870); Confederate commander in American Civil War

Old Andy
Andrew Johnson (1808-1875); 17th president of the United States

Old Buck
James Buchanan (1791-1868); 15th president of the United States

Old Hickory
Andrew Jackson (1767-1845); 7th president of the United States

Old Man Eloquent
John Quincy Adams (1767-1848); 6th president of the United States

Old Rough and Ready
Zachary Taylor (1784-1850); 12th president of the United States

Old Stony Phiz
Daniel Webster (1782-1852); statesman and orator

Pathfinder
John Charles Frémont (1813-1890); explorer and army officer

Plant Wizard
Luther Burbank (1849-1926); horticulturist

Poor Richard
Benjamin Franklin (1706-1790); statesman, scientist, and author

Preacher President
James A. Garfield (1831-1881); 20th president of the United States; lay preacher in his church

Prince of Humorists
Mark Twain (Samuel Clemens) (1835-1910); humorist

Professor
Woodrow Wilson (1856-1924); 28th president of the United States

Purse
Franklin Pierce (1804-1869); 14th president of the United States

Railsplitter
Abraham Lincoln (1809-1865); 16th president of the United States

Rocky
Nelson A. Rockefeller (1908-); governor of New York

Sage of Monticello
Thomas Jefferson (1743-1826); 3d president of the United States

Second John
John Quincy Adams (1767-1848); 6th president of the United States; son of John Adams

Sergeant (The)
Alvin C. York (1887-); World War I hero

Silent Cal
Calvin Coolidge (1872-1933); 30th president of the United States

Silent Man
Ulysses S. Grant (1822-1885); 18th president of the United States

Stonewall Jackson
Thomas Jackson (1824-1863); Confederate general in American Civil War

Tippecanoe
William Henry Harrison (1773-1841); 9th president of the United States

Traitor (The)
Benedict Arnold (1741-1801); officer in War of American Independence; plotted with the British

Uncle Sam
Ulysses S. Grant (1822-1885); 18th president of the United States

Veep
Alben William Barkley (1877-1956); vice president of the United States, 1949-1953

Veto President
Andrew Johnson (1808-1875); 17th president of the United States

Vinegar Joe
Joseph W. Stilwell (1883-1946); commander of the U.S. 10th Army in the Pacific theater in World War II

Voice of the Revolution
Patrick Henry (1736-1799); American Revolutionary statesman

Wild Bill Hickok
James Butler Hickok (1837-1876); U.S. marshal

Yankee Clipper
Joseph Di Maggio (1914-); professional baseball player

The Story of America

IN PICTURES

Edited and Narrated by **E. DOUGLAS BRANCH, PH. D.**

Associate Editor **FRANKLIN J. MEINE, A.M.**

INTRODUCTION

This is a history of our country. It is told in words and pictures, dramatically and instructively.

As this panorama of American history unfolds, we find North America a wilderness sparsely dotted with Indian settlements; then suddenly come the peoples of western Europe, embarking upon a marvelous age of expansion. Spanish, then French, explorers bring dreams of mighty empire; a "New Netherland" is established on Manhattan Island. But our interest turns to English colonists establishing tenacious footholds on the Atlantic shore. We pause amidst colonial wars, where we first meet George Washington, Benjamin Franklin, Paul Revere, Patrick Henry, and other heroes who pass in pictorial review, while the Minute-men keep full their powder horns for the first battles of the American Revolution.

Pictures of war on sea and land pass by; and the curtain discloses a New Nation, symbolized not only by the festivities of Washington's inauguration but by the figure of Daniel Boone, leading a group braving the perils of an unknown and obdurate wilderness. We give particular attention to the frontier, productive of sturdy men impatient of restraint, impetuous of thought and action; we follow the westward march of the settlement of a continent. Transportation, too, offers vivid pictorial chapters—canoes, stagecoaches, "Tom Thumb" locomotives; rafts, steamboats; Model T's and flying machines. Grimly dramatic are the pages that show the cleavage between the sections, and the tragic assassination of Abraham Lincoln; but the profound beauty of the Gettysburg address is the more impressive because it is reproduced in Lincoln's own handwriting.

We follow the rise of invention from amusing-looking little models until it becomes a great force remaking the face of America. The "Wild West" lingers in many vivid, carefully selected pictures. The advancing pages carry us into scenes of the nation's tremendous economic and industrial development. Early sports pictures show us a people learning to play as well as work. Crises of war and depression years; boom years, new events in the dynamic drama of American life—all these carry us on our pictorial journey from the past into today.

The vitality of American art in delineating native historical subjects is attested by many reproductions within these covers. Among famous artists represented by original paintings are John Trumbull, Frederick Remington, John Steuart Curry, George Catlin, Jean L. G. Ferris, Allen True, Norman Price, Charles C. Nahl, Peter Frederick Rothermel, Robert Dudley, George Caleb Bingham, and Seth Eastman. The renowned Thomas Nast is among the caricaturists represented; reproductions from Currier and Ives lithographs reflect another popular school of American art.

Hundreds of pictures are reproduced in these pages; thousands more were examined. Famous art galleries extended gracious permission to use their American treasures. Included in these pages are reproductions from the Metropolitan Museum of Art, New York; the Pennsylvania Academy of Fine Arts, Philadelphia; the Corcoran Gallery of Art, Washington; the E. B. Crocker Art Gallery, Sacramento; the City Art Museum of St. Louis; the Museum of the City of New York. Several stereopticon paintings by Joseph Boggs Beale appear by arrangement with Modern Enterprises, Philadelphia. Emphasis has been placed upon the use of contemporary pictures and sketches of the American scene, as portrayed in periodicals, documents, and books.

Other historical societies and university libraries also permitted the use of their original paintings and rare plates. Among the depositaries of regional lore here represented are the Ancient and Honorable Artillery Company of Massachusetts; the Carpenters' Company of Philadelphia; the Denver Public Library; the Essex Institute of Salem, Mass.; the Sullivan Memorial Library of Temple University; the New York Historical Society; the Connecticut State Library; Washington University, St. Louis; the Illinois State Historical Library; the Wisconsin Historical Museum; the Maryland Historical Society; Colonial Williamsburg, Inc.; and the Nebraska State Historical Society.

The institutions and individuals who made pictures available for this book are too numerous to be listed in full. Such a list should in fairness include many sources from which pictures were secured that are not, for various editorial reasons, reproduced in these already abundant pages.

Particular acknowledgment, however, is more than due John S. Worley, curator and chairman of the Transportation Library of the University of Michigan; L. Hubbard Shattuck, executive director of the Chicago Historical Society; and Miss Barbara Boston, librarian of the Ayer Collection, the Newberry Library, Chicago. The editors have availed themselves of the discriminating taste of these authorities, who suggested and gave generous consent to the use of pictures in rare volumes, portfolios, and other scarce reproductions. The private collection of Mr. Franklin J. Meine, Americana expert, was made available; many magazine illustrations and rare prints are from that source.

DISCOVERY

NORSEMEN

"Foes are they fierce beyond other foes, and cunning as they are fierce; the sea is their school of war, and the storm their friend"—sang a Roman poet of the Norsemen. In the ninth century these bold Scandinavians displaced a group of Christian Irish colonists in Iceland, who had lived in quiet isolation for almost two centuries. In the tenth century Greenland was discovered by Eric the Red. But farther west than Greenland was, perhaps, the rim of the world, with terrifying supernatural beasts in wait for foolhardy mariners; perhaps a new and wonderful land. In about the year 1000 Leif Ericsson, son of Eric, decided to find out. Just where his Norsemen landed we do not know; probably on a shore of the Gulf of St. Lawrence. The Icelandic sagas call the region "Vinland," for its autumnal clusters of wild grapes. The Indians were so hostile that the colonists gave up and returned to Greenland. The drama of American history was but a dim prologue until, in 1492, a sailor from Genoa bearing the colors of Spain raised the curtain.

PHOTO JOSEPH BOGGS BEALE, MODERN GALLERIES, PHILADELPHIA

COLUMBUS

Christopher Columbus, born in 1451, was the son of a weaver. The sea lapped against the wharves near his home, and when he was but fourteen he was sailing before the mast. Coveted spices, drugs, and gems from the Orient reached Europe by overland routes that were tortuous and dangerous. But learned men knew that the world was round, and had made maps to demonstrate it. The imaginative Columbus put the two facts together: the Orient could be reached by a westward voyage! In 1492 Ferdinand and Isabella, sovereigns of Spain, undertook to pay for the venture. At sunrise, August 3, on the wharves of Palos, the last mass was celebrated for Columbus and the crews of his three ships. Into the "Sea of Darkness" they sailed, with three instruments for their direction: a compass, an astrolabe, and the stubborn courage of the Admiral. At 2 a.m., October 12, bright moonlight enabled a lookout to descry the sand cliffs of an island, now called Watling Island, in the Bahamas.

A PALISADED VILLAGE

In 1492 there were 1,153,000 Indians in the United States, an average of one Indian to every three square miles; but spaciousness does not exclude passions, greed, and pride. The Indian expected war, and was trained for it. In the South Atlantic region, typical villages were practically fortresses.

PHOTO NEWBERRY LIBRARY

DUGOUT CANOE

The Indian's main means of transportation was the great highways provided by nature—the rivers. Where deer and other large game were plentiful, Indians developed great skill in making canoes of skins and withes. Less privileged tribes used the boles of sturdy trees near the riverbanks.

PHOTO THE ART INSTITUTE OF CHICAGO

ALGONQUIN FISHING

The dawn of man in America was but a short while ago, as time is measured by the archeology of Asia and Europe. At some time more than twenty five thousand years in the past, came the first large bands of "red Mongoloids" from Siberia into Alaska, where they found the hunting good, and found in the warmer climates to the southward an invitation to further migrations. As the centuries advanced, two types of Indian culture developed: one that settled about the hearth, learned to raise maize and other vegetables, and to catch fish in the nearby streams. The other type was the nomadic culture of the Great Plains tribes, who hunted the big game animals for their principal food.

PHOTO THE ART INSTITUTE OF CHICAGO

EXPLORATION

DISCOVERY OF THE PACIFIC

Vasco Nunez de Balboa, a debt-ridden stowaway from San Domingo, became—through a combination of luck and character—commander of a little Spanish colony near the Isthmus of Panama. From the Indians he heard of a great sea but forty-five miles to the west; he led an expedition through the jungle and over the spine of the Cordilleras to find it. On September 29, 1513, into the surf of the immeasurably broad ocean before him, Balboa strode with drawn sword and lifted banner, claiming the sea and all its shores for the king of Spain. Westward, certainly, lay the Spice Islands; and this discovery stimulated exploration for a seaway around, or through, America. Ferdinand Magellan, a Portuguese, found the route in 1519-20, when the globe was circumnavigated for the first time. But hope persisted that there might be a shorter course from Europe to India than Magellan's route around the tip of South America; and the quest for the Northwest Passage was to add many chapters of courage and tragedy to the drama of American history.

CABOT'S LANDING

Spain became over-greedy in European politics; and as its prestige on the continent slipped away, France, England, and the Netherlands were stimulated to grasp colonial domains. John Cabot, Italian-born but in the service of the Merchant Adventurers of Bristol, England, received in 1496 royal authority to "sayle to all partes, Countreys, and Seas"; his ship, the *Matthew*, braved the North Atlantic in 1497. He discovered teeming codfisheries of the Grand Banks of Newfoundland, and somewhere along the shores ceremonially planted the ensign of St. George's Cross. The British flag had come to America.

DRAKE IN CALIFORNIA

In avid pursuit of the treasures and rumors brought from the New World by Spanish explorers and missionaries, Spain built a colonial empire in Latin and South America. This domain was extended into California. But the exploits of Sir Francis Drake, English Admiral, foreshadowed the passing of Spanish ascendency. As a privateer commissioned by Queen Elizabeth, he waylaid and plundered Spanish vessels in the Caribbean Sea. In 1577-79 he led a little fleet on a looting cruise around South America; on the California coast he made friends with the Indians and took possession in the name of the Queen.

ST. AUGUSTINE

Columbus and the navigators alertly following the wake of his caravels had discovered a new Land of Promise. "New Spain" spread its ambitious, grasping tentacles over most of Latin and South America; the names of Cortez and Pizarro head the list of zealots who brought a violent end to the Aztec and Inca kingdoms. But Spanish claims feathered far and indefinitely into North America. When Philip II learned that French Huguenots were about to set up a colony in Florida, he dispatched an able and ruthless naval commander, Pedro Menendez de Aviles, to extirpate the French and establish, instead, a Spanish settlement. Menendez did not fail. On September 6, 1565, he disembarked his colonists at the bay of St. Augustine. The town, although twice razed by English freebooters, may claim to be the first permanent settlement in the United States.

PHOTO NEWBERRY LIBRARY

DISCOVERY OF THE MISSISSIPPI

Excited by reports of much gold and silver in Florida, Hernando de Soto — a wealthy veteran of the Spanish conquest of the Inca kingdom—in 1539 financed and led a grandiose expedition which landed on the west coast of Florida and for four years wandered in quest of elusive riches. Near the Chickasaw Bluffs, Mississippi, in May, 1541, De Soto reached the east bank of the Father of Waters. Rafts were built, and the expedition continued its fruitless search into Arkansas and Oklahoma. Hunger, disease, and Indian hostility harried the party. A year later the discouraged leader died, and in the darkness of night—lest Indians know—was buried in the river which he had discovered.

COURTESY ANHEUSER-BUSCH INC., ST. LOUIS, MO.

THE LANDING AT JAMESTOWN

The permanent English Colonization of Virginia was effected by a joint-stock company. Gentlemen down on their luck, some released prisoners, some blacksmiths, orchard workers, and goldsmiths, were among the motley company who, on "the sixth and twentieth day of April [1607], descried the land of Virginia." The site chosen—Jamestown—was beautiful, but it was a malarial place and had ultimately to be abandoned. Meanwhile, the colonists made inept attempts to establish security in a new and wild environment. From the confusion emerged a strong leader, Captain John Smith. He learned of the native crops from the Indians, and set the colonists to work; he explored the streams inland, and did what he could to promote trade.

CROATOAN

England was not a great power when, in 1558, Elizabeth became queen; but the day of England's greatness was at hand. A new lusty, vigorous, ambitious national character was born. While Shakespeare, Marlowe, and others were writing matchless plays, merchants and mariners such as Sir John Hawkins, Martin Frobisher, Sir Humphrey Gilbert, and Sir Walter Raleigh were, in imagination translated into fact, penetrating far corners of the world. In 1587 Raleigh dispatched a colony to the land which—in honor of the Virgin Queen—he had named "Virginia." The settlement was made at Roanoke Island. Before the vessels sailed on the return to England, a girl-baby was born, on August 18—Virginia Dare, the first child of English parentage born in America. What happened to her, and to the adult colonists, no one can say. When a supply ship came in 1590, there was found only a sacked and ruined settlement; and, carved upon a tree, "Croatoan"—the name of a nearby island, where there were no signs of life.

CHAMPLAIN AND THE IROQUOIS

In the wake of Jacques Cartier, "the Columbus of French Canada," who made three voyages to the Gulf of St. Lawrence in search of a water passage to India, came Samuel de Champlain. Champlain gained his first knowledge of the New World as a mariner in the Caribbean. He was first to suggest a canal across the isthmus of Panama. In 1608 Champlain founded a trading post at the site of Quebec, and in the following year joined a war party of the Hurons which was marching southward to attack the formidable Iroquois. Champlain, with less than a handful of fellow Frenchmen, directed muskets at the enemy tribe, who had never before encountered gunfire. The Iroquois fled in fright; and the tradition is that because of this spectacular incident the powerful Iroquois Confederation hated and fought the French and their Indian allies. Actually, rivalry for control of the fur supply was the reason.

PHOTO CHICAGO HISTORICAL SOCIETY

Captain JOHN SMITH AND POCAHONTAS

John Smith, an excellent executive, explorer, and writer, liked to relate romantic stories about himself. One of these is the legend of his rescue by Pocahontas, a delightful incident that has become a part of our folklore. Pocahontas was the daughter of Powhatan, most powerful chieftain in Virginia. Whether or not she lifted a supplicating arm to save the neck of John Smith from the executioner's axe, she did marry another colonist, John Rolfe (first to cultivate tobacco), and went with her husband to England.

PHOTO CHICAGO HISTORICAL SOCIETY

DISCOVERY OF THE HUDSON

The people of Holland, with their cherished traditions of maritime commerce and sea warfare, were ready, when the Spanish yoke weakened at the beginning of the 17th century, to assume an affluent part in world trade. While the Dutch East India Company established Dutch prestige in one part of the world, an English navigator and explorer—Henry Hudson—was commissioned to seek the Northwest Passage. His ship, the *Half-Moon,* wandered far toward the Arctic, but on September 3, 1609, entered the lower bay of New York. Soon Hudson had found the great river which bears his name. The *Half-Moon* sailed up the stream as far as Albany. The Dutch claim to the region had been established, and Hollanders were soon crossing the sea to trade with the Hudson River tribes.

PHOTO COURTESY CHICAGO HISTORICAL SOCIETY

THE FOUNDING OF NEW ENGLAND

THE FIRST DECEMBER "No group of settlers in America was so ill-fitted by experience and equipment" (wrote the historian Morison) "to cope with the wilderness as this little band of peasants, city workers, and petty bourgeoisie; yet none came through more magnificently." Each head of a family had to build his own house on the lot assigned to him, while the rigors of winter hindered work; provisions were scanty and poor, and diseases engendered by want and exposure became prevalent.

LANDING OF THE PILGRIMS A constant theme of American history has been the search of the common man for liberty and security. This also meant, for the Pilgrims and Puritans, "to have the right worship of God, according to the simplicitie of the Gospell, without the admixture of men's inventions." The Pilgrim Fathers were a small band of humble—but stubborn!—folk in East Anglia, whose religious meetings were so interfered with that they decided to move to Leyden, Holland, in 1609. After ten years' exile they decided to seek a wilderness fastness where they could celebrate their own faith and use their own speech. A group of English merchants, acting under the Crown charter of the Virginia Company, financed the migration. At Plymouth, England, 102 passengers crowded into the *Mayflower*. For 65 days the little ship was buffeted by a turbulent ocean, until "they fell in with that land which is called Cape Cod, the which being made certainly knowne, they were not a little joyfull." While still aboard, the Pilgrims drafted and signed the historic Mayflower Compact, a pledge to abide by government as established by common consent. On Dec. 16, 1620, the Mayflower dropped anchor in Plymouth harbor. Plymouth Rock, the stepping-stone to shore, is preserved within a stately monument.

PHOTO ANCIENT AND HONORABLE ARTILLERY COMPANY OF MASSACHUSETTS

THE FIRST THANKSGIVING In November, 1621, Governor Bradford sent out hunters, "that so we might after a more speciall manner rejoice together after we had gathered the fruit of our labors." This was the origin of the Thanksgiving festival. The first harvest had been fair; Massasoit arrived with ninety other Indians, bringing more contributions for the three days' festival. Thanksgiving became a traditional New England holiday, nationally observed by Presidential proclamation in 1789, and made an annual holiday by President Lincoln in 1863.

PHOTO COURTESY PILGRIM SOCIETY

PILGRIMS GOING TO CHURCH

PHOTO NEW YORK PUBLIC LIBRARY

THE RED MAN'S WELCOME In March an Indian, Samoset, stalked boldly in among the colonists, greeting them with a few English words he had learned from voyagers on the Maine coast. He and other friendly Indians taught the Pilgrims how to plant corn and fertilize the fields with the alewives that swarmed in the brook. Samoset guided two delegates to Massasoit, chieftain of the region, to confirm a treaty of peace and friendship.

PHOTO CHICAGO HISTORICAL SOCIETY

OLD MANHATTAN

PURCHASE OF MANHATTAN

Peter Minuit, first governor of New Netherland, bought Manhattan Island from the Indians in 1626. A returning mariner reported: "Our people there are of good courage and live peaceably. . . . They have bought the island Manhattes from the wild men for the value of sixty guilders." But, quaintly, the twenty-four dollars' worth of trinkets in exchange for the title was given to the Canarsie Indians, who might be described as visitors from Brooklyn; and Minuit had to make a later payment to the tribe that was actually resident. Life in New Amsterdam under Minuit and his successors is rollickingly described in Washington Irving's "Diedrich Knickerbocker's *History of New York*."

PHOTO TITLE GUARANTEE AND TRUST CO., NEW YORK

FORT AMSTERDAM

The first settlement in New Netherland was made at Fort Orange (now Albany) in 1624; it became a depot of the fur trade. But the southern tip of Manhattan, commanding the great harbor at the mouth of the Hudson, was of the highest strategic importance. Here, in 1626, came engineers from Holland to construct a fort. Within its rectangular stone walls permanent houses were built, replacing the thatched dwellings which had been the first abode of Manhattanites. Soon Manhattan had its first "skyline": the solid outlines of the fort; the flagstaff; the silhouette of a giant windmill; and the masts of trading ships.

PHOTO TITLE GUARANTEE AND TRUST CO., NEW YORK

THE CATTLE FAIR

The first cattle in New Amsterdam belonged to the Dutch West India Co. Each morning they were driven to the "Bouwerie," as the common was called. Just southwest of the Bowery was the Bowling Green, a level greensward where the burghers played at ninepins. As agriculture and dairying passed to individual initiative, Bowling Green became the site of a "cattle fair," where livestock was marketed; cheese, laces, and linens were sold by farmers' wives in their booths; Indian women brought basketwork and oddments of wood handicraft; and steins and staves added to the joys of bartering. These conclaves were predecessors of the "county fair" which became a colorful part of American rural life.

BROWN BROS. PHOTO

STUYVESANT'S WRATH

The last and mightiest Director-General of New Netherland was Peter Stuyvesant, a redoubtable curmudgeon, famous alike for his temper and for his wooden leg, encircled with silver bands and studded with shining brads. He annexed the Swedish colony of Delaware, ordered the thoroughfares of New Amsterdam to be laid out as streets and numbered, and did his best to get military and financial aid from Holland against the encroaching English. When English emissaries demanded the surrender of the colony, Stuyvesant "thrust a prodigious quid of tobacco into his left cheek, pulled up his galligaskins, hummed a hideous northwest ditty"—and wanted to fight.

SURRENDER Four English men-o'-war, under Colonel Richard Nicolls, sailed into the mouth of the Hudson in 1664. Fort Amsterdam was long out of repair, and Stuyvesant was short of powder. On September 6, at the Governor-General's "bouwerie" house, articles of surrender were signed: New Netherland and New Amsterdam were, henceforth, New York.

PHOTO COURTESY TITLE GUARANTEE AND TRUST CO., NEW YORK

JOHN ELIOT

While many of the New England clergy were concerned with theological controversy or political influence, the Rev. John Eliot of Roxbury became, in effect, the first missionary of the region. His life work was the conversion of the Indians; toward that aim he mastered their difficult language, preached to them in their own tongue, and wrote an *Indian Bible* (1663), the first Bible printed in America. One tribe which he converted was thenceforward known as the "Praying Indians."

PHOTO COURTESY CHICAGO HISTORICAL SOCIETY

ROGER WILLIAMS AMONG THE NARRAGANSETTS

The Pilgrim settlement was soon absorbed into the new and thriving Massachusetts Bay Colony, of which Boston was the center. Puritanism was rooted in belief in freedom of thought and liberty of conscience; but the ministers and magistrates who controlled Massachusetts Bay would not concede that these freedoms might extend farther than their own conclusions. Intolerance, therefore, became a dark aspect of Puritanism. One of the sufferers was Roger Williams, accused of heresy and sentenced to banishment. A ship was ready to carry him back to England when, on a stormy winter night, he fled and found shelter among the Indians. Next spring, 1636, Williams and five companions founded a settlement he named Providence. This was the origin of the colony of Rhode Island. Connecticut had been founded three years before, the result of the first westward migration of the New England settlers.

CULVER PHOTO

THE WITCHCRAFT DELUSION

Superstition is as old as humankind. In Puritan theology a beneficent supernatural influence attended the fortunes of the colonists; it is not surprising that when accidental and abnormal traits of some people—particularly of eccentric, aged folk—were not understood, the agency of Satan or his imps should be surmised. In 1688 a mischievous girl in Boston accused an old washer-woman of bewitching her, and simulated hysterical spasms when the woman was brought near; the poor crone was hanged. From this beginning sprang an epidemic which culminated in the New England witchcraft craze of 1692. Twenty innocent persons, and two dogs suspected of being witches' familiars, were hanged; several accused victims died awaiting trial; and 150 prisoners were released when, belatedly and ashamedly, the authorities came to their senses.

PHOTO COURTESY ESSEX INSTITUTE

THE CHARTER OAK

Connecticut was granted, in 1662, a charter so liberal that it was almost a grant of freedom. But King James II endeavored to annul this and other charters and create a "Dominion of New England" under one governor-general—Sir Edmund Andros. At the courthouse in Hartford in 1687, Andros demanded the surrender of the charter; but the lights were suddenly extinguished, and when they were relit the charter was gone. An ardent patriot had secreted it in the hollow of an old oak. High legal authority in England decided that since the charter had not been surrendered it remained in full force. The "Charter Oak" became a symbol of liberty. It fell in 1856, at the estimated age of one thousand years.

PHOTO COURTESY CONNECTICUT STATE LIBRARY

PENN'S TREATY WITH THE INDIANS

William Penn, a Quaker of prominent and influential family, was already connected with the two new colonies of East and West Jersey when, in 1681, King Charles II granted him a great tract of land which, the royal donor insisted, be named Pennsylvania. To Penn the new project was a "Holy Experiment," and liberal terms and extensive advertising soon attracted large numbers of settlers. To the Indians Penn wrote, "I have great Love and Regard towards you"; and under a great elm at Shackamaxon the Proprietor and the Indians entered into a treaty that was never infringed.

COURTESY PENNSYLVANIA ACADEMY OF THE FINE ARTS

THE SOUTHERN COLONIES

COTTON AND SLAVERY

Production of another staple crop, cotton, began in the West Indies and South Carolina, and gradually spread over the lower South, weaving a many-patterned fabric of aristocratic culture and ultimate tragedy. The first dark thread entered the woof in 1619, when a shipload of Negro slaves reached Virginia. Cotton production was particularly adapted to a system of large plantations using cheap, unskilled labor. In England the spinners and looms invented by Arkwright and Hargreaves inaugurated a wide expansion of the textile market; toward the close of the eighteenth century a young New Englander, Eli Whitney, was to invent a ginning machine that encouraged the production of cotton to the exclusion of almost every other crop in the South. Cotton became a tyrannical King.

PHOTO COURTESY WILLIAM L. CLEMENTS LIBRARY

THE SURRENDER OF JAMESTOWN

The Puritan Rebellion in England found scant sympathy in the southern colonies. Barbados, Bermuda, and Antigua refused to recognize Cromwell's government; the Virginia assembly denounced the execution of King Charles I and made it a treasonable offense to question the lawful succession of the Stuarts. A formidable fleet overawed the royalist colonies in the West Indies, and in March, 1652, sailed into the James River. Sir William Berkeley, governor of Virginia, and his fellow cavaliers prudently offered formal submission, and the affairs of the province were handed over to Parliamentary commissioners. The news of the fall of the Commonwealth and the accession of Charles II, in 1660, was hailed with joy in Virginia.

TOBACCO SHIPS ON THE JAMES

Tobacco, unknown in Europe, was a fascinating discovery of the first explorers. In Virginia, John Rolfe (who married Pocahontas) began, in 1612, experimental plantings with the Indian weed to develop a leaf suitable for export; his fellow colonists adopted tobacco as their chief product, and from Virginia the culture extended into Maryland and North Carolina. On the eve of the Revolution the yearly exports averaged a hundred million pounds. Because of the scarcity of metallic money, these three colonies used tobacco as currency; taxes and salaries were payable in the fragrant herb, and a traveler wrote of the Virginians: "Tobacco is their Meat, Drink, Clothing, and Money."

BUCCANEERS IN CHARLESTON

A roistering, if villainous, phase of colonial history was piracy — sometimes almost identical with privateering, licensed preying on enemy commerce. Most famed, probably, was Captain William Kidd, whose legendary treasure was in fact dug up and appropriated by Governor Bellomont of New York. In the middle of the 17th century, when the buccaneers numbered several thousand, the coasts of the West Indies offered secluded harbors and supply stations. The islets and inlets of South Carolina were also favored; Captain Teach ("Blackbeard") was the most notorious of the Carolina swashbucklers.

THE BEGINNINGS OF GEORGIA

James Edward Oglethorpe, distinguished soldier and philanthropist, founded Georgia as a haven for Englishmen imprisoned for debt, and for other unfortunates. Parliament appropriated moneys for this humanitarian plan. Oglethorpe led his first group of settlers to Savannah in 1733. Tomo, principal chieftain of the district, welcomed the colonists; and the youngest of the Thirteen Colonies had no Indian wars.

CULVER PHOTO

MARQUETTE ON THE MISSISSIPPI Louis Joliet, voyageur and prospector, was selected by the Governor of New France to explore the course of the Mississippi, which was supposed to flow into the "Sea of California." His companion was Jacques Marquette, a Jesuit missionary. From the Great Lakes into Green Bay, up the Fox River, and by portage to the Wisconsin River, they reached—June 17, 1673—the waters of the Mississippi. They descended the mighty stream as far as the Arkansas, when, satisfied that the Mississippi flowed into the Gulf of Mexico, they turned back. Entering the Illinois River, Marquette and Joliet made a portage to Lake Michigan at the site of Chicago, and returned to Quebec. Church and State had co-operated in an imperial enterprise which reached the heart of the American continent. COURTESY ANHEUSER-BUSCH INC., ST. LOUIS, MO.

LA SALLE CLAIMING LOUISIANA

The French in quest of furs from the Great Lakes region found themselves in competition with the Iroquois, a powerful confederacy dominating western New York and acting as middlemen to bring pelts to the Dutch at Fort Orange (Albany). It was not until 1678 that a party of Frenchmen braved the savage and vigilant tribes and discovered Niagara Falls. La Salle, Father Hennepin, and Tonti ("the Iron Hand") were the leaders. La Salle grasped the commercial and military importance of Niagara as a link with the West, recommended the construction of a fort there, and made plans for a great exploration of the unknown country beyond, to locate a chain of colonies that should tap the profits of the fur trade and extend the prestige of France. In 1679 he sailed the first ship on the Lakes, "Le Griffon"; and two winters later crossed the Chicago portage, followed the frozen Illlinois River by sledge, and reached the Mississippi on Feb. 6, 1682. Down the great river, he paused at the mouths of the Arkansas and Red Rivers, taking formal possession of the lands in the name of his king. On April 9, La Salle reached the delta; the river had been traced, for the first time, from its upper waters to the sea.

INDIAN CAMP As the French traders reached the farthest west of the Great Lakes and sought out the fur-bearing regions of Minnesota, they encountered Assiniboins and other tribes whose mode of life was both more spacious and careless than that of the eastern tribes. These Indians lived in skin lodges, tipis, that were easily dismantled, and moved their village sites in pursuit of their main subsistence, the buffalo.

PHOTO COURTESY NEWBERRY LIBRARY

VOYAGEURS Fur traders and missionaries were riding the ripples of inland lakes and streams almost before the wake of the explorers' canoes had subsided against the banks. Voyageurs soon formed a distinct class in Canada: sturdy fellows who lived on dried and salted meats, who made friends with the Indians, who followed beaver, mink, and otter into unknown streams, and developed songs and folk tales all their own.

PHOTO COURTESY TRANSPORTATION LIBRARY, UNIVERSITY OF MICHIGAN

STARVED ROCK There are hints that La Salle hoped to free himself from the entanglements of Canada and become governor of an independent realm in the Mississippi Valley. At Starved Rock, an imposing landmark on the Illinois River, in 1682 he built Fort St. Louis as a center of Indian trade. But political misfortunes overtook him. In 1687 La Salle was treacherously shot from ambush.

PHOTO COURTESY ILLINOIS STATE HISTORICAL LIBRARY

COLONIAL WARS

SIEGE OF LOUISBOURG

Neither French nor British were satisfied with their narrow perches on the rim of the continent; ambitions soared, and inevitably clashed. Time and again these British and French colonists crossed swords, sometimes in regional expeditions, sometimes as contingents of imperial wars. The most ambitious of colonial expeditions was the siege of Louisbourg in 1745. Louisbourg, "the Gibraltar of Canada," was a fortification on Cape Breton Island commanding the entrance to the Gulf of St. Lawrence. For the attack, Massachusetts raised 3,000 men; Connecticut and New Hampshire added 1,000; New York lent its heavy artillery. William Pepperell of Maine commanded the force, which landed before Louisbourg as English men-of-war ensured command of the sea. The fortress surrendered, after a prolonged bombardment, just as the Provincials were preparing an assault. But when emissaries met at a peace conference in 1748, Louisbourg was returned to France. The American colonists were bitterly disappointed. Another and more dramatic chapter in the struggle for supremacy in North America was inevitable.

BRADDOCK'S DEFEAT

The wedge of conflict between French and British ambitions was the hilly little triangle between the Monongahela and Allegheny rivers and their confluence into the Ohio. This, the site of Pittsburgh, was the gateway to the Middle West and the Mississippi Valley. Céloron de Bienville in 1749 buried six leaden tokens of French claims to the region. George Washington was in command of a tiny expedition of Virginians which sought, in 1754, to command the "golden triangle"; his force had to surrender, and through drizzling rain marched back to the mother colony. In 1755 General Braddock, a veteran British commander, was despatched with British regulars, later supplemented with colonial troops, for an expedition against the French in the Ohio Valley. From Maryland he marched slowly and arduously, building a road through the wilderness. But within a day's march of the Ohio his men were in column formation in a little valley flanked by dense woods; then the French and Indians struck. All Braddock's staff, except Washington, were disabled or killed. Braddock had scarcely ordered retreat before he fell mortally wounded. Within a year the Seven Years' War, between France and England, was being waged fiercely both in the Old World and the New.

WASHINGTON IN THE WEST

As part of a three-pronged campaign against the French, one prong of the British-Colonial campaign stretched toward Lake Champlain, one toward Niagara, and one toward the Forks of the Ohio, where the French had built a fort. The last-mentioned expedition was under the command of an energetic but irascible and invalided Scotsman, General Forbes. Washington had already distinguished himself among the Virginian troops which joined this expedition. Both by cleverness and courage he so impressed the commanding general that Washington was made a brigadier, and led the march which, on November 25, 1758, took possession of the smoking ruins of the French stronghold—Fort Duquesne—at the Forks. Fort Pitt was built on the smouldering site. Washington's imagination was excited by these western lands, and he planned to become a great landlord. But his military experience was preparation for a greater role.

U. S. SIGNAL CORPS PHOTO

THE ATTACK ON QUEBEC

PHOTO COURTESY NEWBERRY LIBRARY

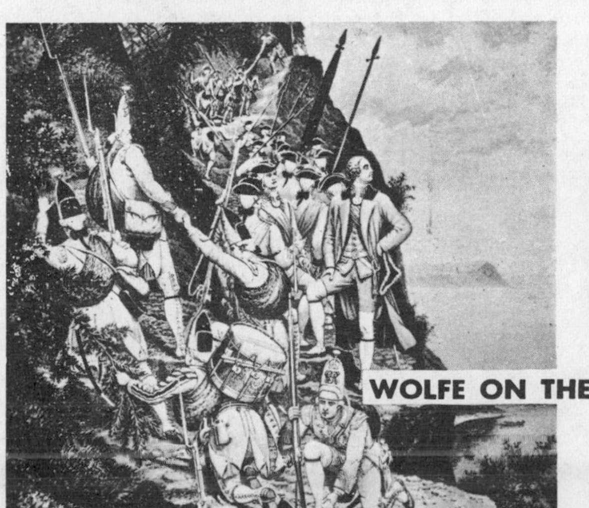

WOLFE ON THE HEIGHTS

After the victories of 1758 the British decided to strike at the very heart of New France—Quebec, high on a bluff overlooking the St. Lawrence. The French government was honeycombed with corruption, but the military commander, Montcalm, was a brave and honest man. Wolfe, the British general, was his peer, and had the larger army. The cliff was scaled; and on the Plains of Abraham beside the city the French-Canadian forces were routed after fierce fighting. Montcalm lost his life on the field of battle; and Wolfe, wounded, exclaimed with his last breath: "What, do they run already? Then I die happy!" With the Treaty of Paris in 1763, France ceded its title in the New World east of the Mississippi to England, and bestowed its claims to lands west of the great river (with New Orleans) upon Spain.

PHOTO JOSEPH BOGGS BEALE. MODERN GALLERIES, PHILADELPHIA

TWO GENTLEMEN

One was the tenth child of a good, hardworking "undistinguished" family. His father did not have the money to keep him in the Boston Grammar School, and Benjamin went to work when he was ten, as tallow chandler and soapmaker • One was born to the estate and expectations of a large plantation. In his impressionable years George was in contact with the courtly manners and leisurely enjoyments of the best English culture • One was printer, author, philanthropist, inventor, diplomat, philosopher, scientist • One was surveyor, soldier, commander, squire, planter, and first president of the United States • Both were statesmen. In the interests of Colonial liberties, of American dignity, of independence and international recognition, of the formation of a strong republican government, their paths of influence and action interwove again and again • Each was experienced in public affairs, and mature beyond his years, when the Peace Treaty of 1763 closed an era of external struggles for the Colonists, and began an era of internal growth, a firming of spirit leading inevitably into national unity. The twenty-five years until 1789 produced many great men; but Washington and Franklin are the names that children learn first and men esteem most.

When the time came for a convention to draw up the body of fundamental law for a United States of America, Washington was the presiding officer. He said that the purpose of the new Constitution was "to establish good order and government and to render the nation happy at home and respected abroad." Franklin, on the floor of the convention, was the conciliator whose prestige and personality calmed passions and compromised disputes. He said: "I cannot help expressing a wish that every member of the Convention . . . would with me, on this occasion, . . . to make manifest our unanimity, put his name to the instrument." • Their diversities of origin and training, their separate skills, the varied adversities each faced and overcame, and their meetings upon the ground of common achievement, are part of the meaning of America.

BREAKFAST!

FRANKLIN AS PRINTER'S DEVIL

PHOTO JOSEPH BOGGS BEALE. MODERN GALLERIES. PHILA.

FRANKLIN THE SCIENTIST

PHOTO JOSEPH BOGGS BEALE. MODERN GALLERIES. PHILA.

The story of Franklin's early years is best told by himself, in his ever-delightful *Autobiography*. Here is related his apprenticeship to his half-brother James, editor of the *New England Courier*; his persistent readings for self-improvement, and his first stealthy adventures as a writer; also, the quaint story of his first breakfast in Philadelphia—three bulky rolls for a penny, a meal that set his future wife to laughing at the amusing young stranger. Franklin's famous experiment with kite and iron key to demonstrate the identity of lightning and electricity was performed in 1752.

OLD WILLIAMSBURG CAPITOL Washington's first public office was as burgess in the Virginia Assembly, in 1759. The farming possibilities of his estates seemed more important to him, then, than politics; but successively re-elected, he faithfully shouldered his share of legislative duties. The capital of Virginia during this period was Williamsburg, also the economic, educational, and social center of the colony. This little metropolis was renowned for its attractive architecture. In recent years private endowments have made possible a great undertaking to restore and preserve Williamsburg in its eighteenth-century appearance.

PHOTO COURTESY COLONIAL WILLIAMSBURG, INC.

Washington married, in 1759, Martha Custis, and **MOUNT VERNON** established his household at Mount Vernon, on the south bank of the Potomac 16 miles below the city of Washington. Here he spent his most enjoyable years, supervising his farms and sharing the social diversions of the "First Families" of Virginia. At the close of the Revolution he returned to complete the improvement of buildings, gardens, and grounds into substantially the form they have today. The First President and his wife are interred here in the family vault.

PHOTO COURTESY METROPOLITAN MUSEUM OF ART

EVE OF THE REVOLUTION

"BOSTON TEA PARTY"

The powerful East India Company was granted a monopoly on all tea exported to the Colonies, and decided to sell its tea through its own agents, eliminating the independent merchants. This ill-considered step drove the mercantile classes into alliance with the political malcontents. Three tea-ships were moored in Boston harbor on the night of Dec. 16, 1773. A band of men disguised with Mohawk war-paint boarded the vessels and threw the tea overboard while a large crowd silently and eagerly watched. In Philadelphia the news set the Liberty Bell to ringing; there, as in New York and Charleston, tea cargoes were rejected. Chances for peaceful settlement of the difficulties between the Colonies and the mother country were mired at the bottom of Boston harbor.

CULVER PHOTO

PATRICK HENRY AT THE CONTINENTAL CONGRESS

Patrick Henry, of gifted and passionate tongue, was spokesman for the frontier folk of Virginia. When copies of the Stamp Act were circulated among the outraged burghers, Henry wrote a set of resolutions which demanded complete legislative independence for Virginia. It was then that he made his speech with the famous comparison: "Caesar had his Brutus—Charles the first, his Cromwell—and George the third—may profit by their example." As leader of a Committee of Correspondence, Henry did much to bring the discontent elements of each colony into a body ready for unified action if the need should come. He had been appointed a delegate to the Continental Congress when, to the Virginia Assembly on March 20, 1775, he declared "Give me liberty, or give me death." Henry was governor of Virginia for five terms, and took a decisive part in many phases of the Revolution.

PHOTO COURTESY AMERICAN TELEPHONE AND TELEGRAPH CO.

BURNING OF THE STAMPS

George Grenville, who became prime minister of England in 1763, was an honest and courageous man, but without tact. He demanded more revenue from the Colonies, and drew up a comprehensive scheme of taxation by stamp duties. But the Colonies were in no mood to submit to levies which did not originate in their own legislatures. "If taxes are laid upon us in any shape," demanded Samuel Adams in the Boston Town Meeting of May, 1764, "without our having a legal representation where they are laid, are we not reduc'd from the character of free subjects to the miserable state of tributary slaves?" The protest ran from Massachusetts to the South. Stamp distributors were treated roughly, and everywhere the stamps were seized and destroyed. Too late to quench the fires of independence, Parliament repealed the measure.

THE LIBERTY BELL

The year 1751 was the Golden Jubilee of William Penn's 1701 Charter of Privileges, which had given the colonial Assembly control of legislation and taxation. So the Assembly decided to get a resonant symbol for the anniversary, two thousand pounds of bronze cast by the most famous bell-founder of England. Isaac Norris suggested the motto emblazoned about the crown of the bell: PROCLAIM LIBERTY THROUGHOUT ALL THE LAND AND UNTO ALL THE INHABITANTS THEREOF. But perhaps the time was not quite ripe for liberty; for when the bell was hung in Independence Hall it cracked at the first stroke of the clapper. It was twice melted and remoulded by Philadelphia metal-workers. Soon its clarion summonings—for news good or bad, for public functionings, for occasions of ceremony—were part of the colonial democracy. In time its tones were to vibrate far beyond the horizons of Philadelphia.

PHOTO JOSEPH BOGGS BEALE, MODERN GALLERIES PHILA.

"BOSTON MASSACRE"

The scarlet uniforms of British troops quartered in Boston were an irritating reminder of royal control; and the pompous bearing of the "Beefeaters" rankled the Colonials. Pent-up feelings overflowed on March 5, 1770. A mob of rioters set upon a squad of soldiers. Some of the soldiers, without orders, fired into a crowd and killed five citizens. Indignation was so high that the Governor removed the troops to a fortress in Boston harbor.

THE CALL TO ARMS

"THE MIDNIGHT RIDE"

Paul Revere, silversmith, was one of the fifty earnest citizens who donned war-paint and feathers for the Boston Tea Party. As official courier for the Massachusetts Assembly to the Continental Congress, the fleeting Revere became a familiar sight to the countryside. On April 18, 1775, he rode from Boston to Concord to warn the patriots to move their military stores from Concord, lest the British seize the munitions. On this journey he arranged with "Colonel Conant and some other gentleman that, if the British went by water, we would show two lanthorns in the North Church steeple; and, if by land, one as a signal." Eleven o'clock two nights later was the zero hour, when he knew that the British were about to march. Under the very prows of the King's ships he rowed across the Charles River. On the opposite shore he began his celebrated ride to rouse the countryside. "Through the gloom and the light, the fate of a nation was riding that night."

MINUTE-MEN

The first members of the Revolutionary Army were the Minute-Men, a part of the militia pledged to respond to the call of duty at a moment's notice. Revere's warning was carried to the farmhouses and villages—the johnny-cakes were left untouched and the breakfast buttermilk hastily gulped as the men seized their breech-loaders and powder horns, and hastened to the Concord Road.

BATTLE OF LEXINGTON

The British detachment had not marched far from Boston when the ringing of village bells and the firing of muskets announced that their march to Concord would be opposed. Advance forces reached Lexington, early on April 19, to find a band of militiamen drawn up on the green. The British commander accosted them: "Disperse, you rebels—Damn you, throw down your arms and disperse!" The "Rebels" spontaneously fired. The engagement was short; it involved only a few hundred men. But blood was shed, and the story of the actual fight for freedom was begun.

THE SPIRIT OF '76

In this famous delineation of the Revolutionary spirit, three generations step sturdily forward: the little drummer-boy looking with happy confidence toward the old man, who has ageless youth in his eyes, and the wounded veteran of middle age piping the lilting cadence for the drums. The picture means, to Americans, that in any crisis citizens of whatever years will rise in defense of liberty.

BUNKER HILL

After the ordeals of the road back from Lexington, the British huddled safely under their guns on the Charles River. Soon they received large reinforcements from overseas. But, astonishingly, this trained and well-equipped army was cooped up in Boston by a little-organized mass of militia and armed civilians. This American "army" decided to build redoubts on the high ground overlooking Boston; but instead of pausing on Bunker Hill, impetuous officers passed on to a dangerously advanced position, Breed's Hill. Here the battle of June 17, 1775, was actually fought. General Gage and his Redcoats could easily have trapped the Colonial troops, by taking a narrow isthmus between the Charles and Mystic rivers. Instead, he chose to order a frontal assault on Breed's Hill. The third of three bloody assaults was successful, only because the Americans' ammunition had run out. The Colonists had no bayonets or other equipment for hand-to-hand fighting, and were driven toward Cambridge. Gage was disgraced, and Lord Howe replaced him as commander-in-chief of the army "in His Majesty's rebellious colonies in America."

PHOTO CHICAGO HISTORICAL SOCIETY

WASHINGTON AND HIS GENERALS

After the Battle of Bunker Hill, the Continental Congress took over the patriot forces in the name of all the Colonies; and the first American army was created. John Adams of Massachusetts nominated George Washington as commander-in-chief. On July 3, 1775, under a famous oak at Cambridge, Washington formally assumed command. Very slowly, against the free-and-easy tendencies of the volunteers, he shaped a military machine for the odds-end task confronting it. He had the aid of a group of Colonial officers, and of volunteer friends of liberty from overseas—including Lafayette of France, Von Steuben of Prussia, and Kosciusko of Poland.

PHOTO TITLE GUARANTEE AND TRUST CO., NEW YORK

THE MARTYR SPY

Nathan Hale, athletic young schoolmaster and social favorite, was just twenty when he became a captain in the Continental Army. He was with Washington's army when it marched from Boston to New York, where Lord Howe had established his Redcoats. Washington was in imperative need of information about the strength and designs of the enemy; Hale volunteered. Posing as a schoolmaster seeking a position, he sketched the British encampments and made valuable notes. Seized as a spy—betrayed, it is said, by a Tory cousin—he was condemned by Lord Howe without the formality of a trial. On the next morning—Sept. 22, 1776—as the noose was draped over his head, Nathan Hale made a farewell speech long remembered: "I only regret that I have but one life to lose for my country."

PHOTO JOSEPH BOGGS BEALE, MODERN GALLERIES, PHILA.

THE CAPTURE OF TICONDEROGA

The British post at Ticonderoga, upper gateway to the Hudson Valley, was a storehouse of heavy guns and ammunition. Benedict Arnold was hardly rested from the Battle of Lexington when he sought permission to make a quick march, fall upon the garrison at Ticonderoga before it was informed of the outbreak of war, and seize the cannon for the Colonials. Dividing command with Ethan Allen, whose "Green Mountain Boys" made up most of the expedition, Arnold reached the fort in the early morning of May 10, 1775, and quickly subdued the sleepy Redcoats. Next winter, the cannon of Ticonderoga were hauled on sledges over snow and frozen streams to Cambridge; Washington, greatly heartened, mounted the artillery on heights overlooking Boston. The British abandoned hopes of holding the city, and retired to Halifax to plan another campaign.

PHOTO FROM U. S. SIGNAL CORPS

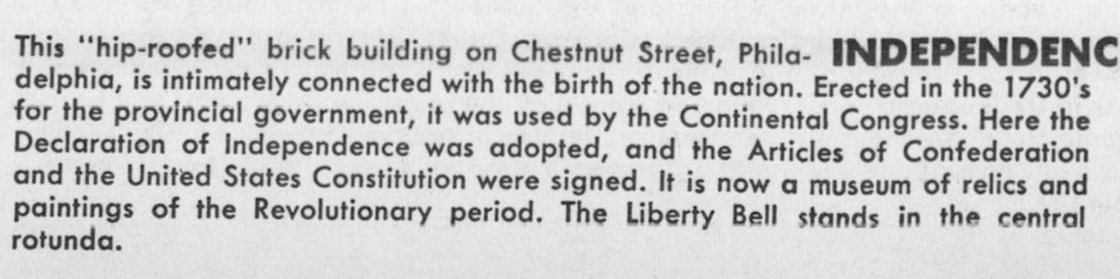

INDEPENDENCE HALL

This "hip-roofed" brick building on Chestnut Street, Philadelphia, is intimately connected with the birth of the nation. Erected in the 1730's for the provincial government, it was used by the Continental Congress. Here the Declaration of Independence was adopted, and the Articles of Confederation and the United States Constitution were signed. It is now a museum of relics and paintings of the Revolutionary period. The Liberty Bell stands in the central rotunda.

CROSSING THE DELAWARE Repulsed in New York, Washington led a dwindling American army in retreat through New Jersey and across the Delaware. The British army settled into winter quarters on the left bank of the river. The outpost at Trenton was occupied by German mercenaries ("Hessians"). Christmas night, 1776, was a storm of bitter sleet. Within the Hessian quarters, logs blazed on the fireplaces, and tankards of spirituous cheer were replenished again and again. A spy from the Pennsylvania shore sent a message that the Americans were launching an attack; but it was written in English, and Colonel Rahl, the commander, by that time could not have read a message in his native German. Washington's bold move across the Delaware was a spectacular success. "The hurry, fright, and confusion of the enemy," wrote Washington's aide, "was like which it shall be when the last trump shall sound." Rahl was mortally wounded; the Hessians were raked with musketry and steel, and surrendered. American hopes were revived in a dark hour.

PHOTO COURTESY CHICAGO HISTORICAL SOCIETY

THE BATTLE OF PRINCETON

To cancel out the reverse at Trenton, Lord Cornwallis hastened against the Americans. Washington's army was encamped in a precarious position near Trenton. The first skirmishes and artillery duels were so favorable to the British that, at nightfall, Cornwallis amiably decided to postpone the definitive engagement until morning. But in a maneuver of unparalleled audacity, Washington moved his men in a long circuit toward Princeton, so secretly that Cornwallis' outposts and night patrols detected nothing. Rallied by Washington and joined by new arrivals, the patriots drove the enemy from the field. The outgeneraled Cornwallis withdrew his army in feverish haste to protect his money-chests at New Brunswick. A British chronicler wrote sadly that "the moral effect of the past campaigns was in great measure cancelled, and the whole of the work, excepting the capture of New York, required to be done again."

PHOTO COURTESY CHICAGO HISTORICAL SOCIETY

CLARK AT VINCENNES

Detroit was the key post of British control of the fur trade and of the Indian tribes in the Old Northwest. "Hair-buyer" Hamilton (so called because he offered bounties to the Indians for frontiersmen's scalps) was commander, and instigated the dispatching of many Indian war parties against the frontier settlements. George Rogers Clark, a young Virginian who had cast his lot with the Kentucky pioneers, consulted Patrick Henry, then (1777) governor of Virginia. Clark had a plan for conquering the Northwest. In May, 1778, he took command of a volunteer force of little more than two hundred men. He captured the French towns in Illinois; took, lost, and recaptured Vincennes, in a heroic campaign over flooded prairies, and made Hamilton prisoner. Although Detroit was never attained, Clark retained control of most of the Old Northwest. So, in the peace treaty, Great Britain conceded to the new republic all the country between the Alleghenies and the Mississippi.

PHOTO COURTESY INDIANA HISTORICAL BUREAU

COURTESY CHICAGO HISTORICAL SOCIETY

VALLEY FORGE Lord Howe moved against Philadelphia, capital of the infant nation, and established his winter quarters for 1777 in the Quaker City. Washington was hard-pressed; his seasoned troops had largely been replaced with raw recruits. He withdrew his forces to Valley Forge, on the Schuylkill River. Negligence and mismanagement in the commissary and transport services almost destroyed the Continental Army in its winter encampment. Heavy snows and freezing weather in December, a January thaw which turned the roads into muck, and epidemic diseases that spread in the absence of medical supplies or of adequate clothing—these were elements in the dismal story of the winter of 1777-78. Washington emerged as the soul of the patriots' war. Never losing dignity or fortitude even in the gloomiest hours, he became to his troops, as to all Americans, the symbol of patient vigilance and serene moral courage.

FRANKLIN, THE DIPLOMAT

Before the formal declaration of independence, Benjamin Franklin headed a delegation from the Continental Congress which met with the British command to discuss peace proposals; in this painting the gentlemen at table are, left to right, Lord Howe, Franklin, John Adams, and Edward Rutledge. Franklin became the Revolution's ingenious and invaluable advocate in Europe. His popularity contributed much to the success of the mission—including also Silas Deane and Arthur Lee—which persuaded France, in 1778, to enter into treaties of commerce and alliance with the United States. Without French gold to replenish the Revolutionary coffers, and without the French navy in our coastal waters, the war in America might not have ended in 1781.

PHOTO COURTESY TITLE GUARANTEE AND TRUST CO., NEW YORK

THE PATRIOT WOMEN

In the Revolution, as in all wars, there was a heroine for every hero—most of them unsung, aiding the cause in subtle and gentle ways: a few like comets, inspiring valor in their menfolk by direct example. Margaret Corbin followed her husband when he joined the First Pennsylvania Artillery. In the midst of the battle of Fort Washington (1776) he was killed; Margaret leapt into his place, and loaded and sponged the cannon until she was severely wounded. Congress voted her "during her natural life, the one-half of the monthly pay drawn by a soldier; and now, one complete suit of cloaths." Another Revolutionary heroine was Mary Hays, beside her husband at the battle of Monmouth (1778). In the terrific heat of that June day "Molly" made numberless trips from a well to the battlefield, carrying water to the exhausted and wounded. When her husband fell, overcome by the heat, she took his place beside the cannon, and did an artilleryman's work ably and heroically for the rest of the battle. Tradition has Washington riding up to salute "Molly Pitcher."

PHOTO JOSEPH BOGGS BEALE COLLECTION, MODERN GALLERIES, PHILA.

"BONHOMME RICHARD" AND "SERAPIS"

The history of the Americans' naval successes is almost the story of John Paul Jones, a young Scotsman attracted to the Revolutionary cause. When in October, 1776, Congress determined the rank of naval captains, Jones was only eighteenth on the list. But within a short while he was on roving commands far into European waters, taking many British ships as prizes. On Sept. 23, 1779, Jones was proceeding up the east coast of England in his flagship, the *Bonhomme Richard*—a worn-out, converted India merchantman—when he encountered a British ship of war, the *Serapis*. Fierce exchanges of broadsides wreaked heavy slaughter on both vessels, and the little flagship was leaking badly. It was then that Jones answered the British demand to surrender: "I have not yet begun to fight." For two more hours the vessels were locked in battle, until the British flag was struck. Jones became internationally famous. After the Revolution he sought new glory as admiral in the Russian navy.

PHOTO COURTESY CHICAGO HISTORICAL SOCIETY

ANDRE'S DEATH WARRANT

General Benedict Arnold of the Continental Army fought gallantly for the patriots' cause in the first three years of the war. But frustrated personal ambitions twisted his brilliant mind, and he entered into negotiations with the enemy. Arnold demanded a large bribe for the betrayal of West Point, his command. Negotiator for the British was Major John Andre. After a secret meeting with Arnold, the young major changed his costume for a disguise and set out to carry the treasonable papers to British headquarters at New York. Andre was seized by provincial pickets, and the incriminating documents found in his stocking. Court-martialed, he was ordered to be hanged. Washington reluctantly refused to intercede, for according to the articles of war Andre became technically a spy when he donned a disguise. Benedict Arnold escaped into the British lines.

SURRENDER AT YORKTOWN

The South, scene of some of the fiercest conflicts of the war, was also the setting of the final engagement. General Nathanael Greene, taking command of the southern army in 1780, proved himself one of the greatest leaders of troops that America has produced. Lord Cornwallis with his army retired to the Virginia coast. De Grasse, admiral of the French fleet in the West Indies, offered Washington his cooperation. The commanding general saw his opportunity, and by marches of dazzling rapidity brought a combined French and American army of 16,000 men before Yorktown. Cornwallis' 8,000 troops were cut off from escape by sea as the French vessels sailed into Chesapeake Bay. On October 19, 1781, Cornwallis sent his sword to Washington; and the British troops stacked their arms while their band played *The World Turned Upside Down!* In Trumbull's painting General Lincoln, Washington's aide, is leading the dismounted British officers past the French (left) and American (right) staffs. The war was practically ended.

PHOTO COURTESY YALE UNIVERSITY ART GALLERY

THE NEW NATION

After several experimental years with a loosely knit, almost powerless government—under the Articles of Confederation—the States faced the necessity of contributing some of their sovereign prerogatives to the building of a firm national government, which could speak and act for all. To the Constitutional Convention at Philadelphia in 1787 came many able men. As their discussions proceeded behind closed doors, conflicting proposals were threshed into compromises; balances of power were delicately poised among the legislative, executive, and judicial departments; past experience with national weakness became a guide for the making of national strength. On September 15 the Constitution was accepted by delegates of all the States represented. Washington wrote: "The warmest friends and the best supporters the Constitution has, do not contend that it is free from imperfections; but . . . as there is a constitutional door open for it, the people (for it is with them to judge)" could decide on alterations and amendments when necessary. The cornerstone of the new nation had been laid. Gladstone, the great English statesman of the nineteenth century, considered the Constitution "the most wonderful work ever struck off at a given time by the brain and purpose of man."

RECEPTION The Constitution might have failed the test of ratification by a majority of the States, were it not that everyone welcomed the prospect of Washington as first president—everyone, that is, save Washington himself, who wanted only to be a country gentleman at Mount Vernon. He vowed: "The great Searcher of human hearts is my witness, that I have no wish which aspires beyond the humble and happy lot of living and dying a private citizen on my own farm." But the formal election was unanimous. Washington's trip to New York for the inauguration was a series of celebrations in every village along the way. At the Jersey shore of the Hudson he was escorted aboard a stately boat; innumerable decorated barges maneuvered about; the public rejoicing was deafening with its cannons, bells, and martial music. At the Manhattan wharf the steps were covered with crimson carpet. Washington mounted them with reluctance.

PHOTO COURTESY MUSEUM OF THE CITY OF NEW YORK

INAUGURAL The New York city hall had been remodeled into a suitable capitol by Pierre Charles L'Enfant (who was to design a magnificent city on the Potomac to be the permanent capital). Here Washington delivered his first inaugural address. It was short, and was not well spoken. The burden of responsibility was heavier than the red canopy that crowned the hall's platform. But as Alexander Hamilton had told him, "No other man can sufficiently unite the public opinion, or can give the requisite weight to the office, in the commencement of the government." The early years of his presidency were devoted to the establishment of sound precedents for enduring government. An immediate effect was the restoration of the national credit and the revival of business.

PHOTO COURTESY CHICAGO HISTORICAL SOCIETY

DANIEL BOONE At the outbreak of the Revolution the frontier of settlement was just beginning to top the Appalachians. By the end of Washington's administration Kentucky and Tennessee were full-fledged States, and Ohio was on the verge of admission. A distinctive combination of "backwoodsman" and leader was Daniel Boone, whose early hunting and exploring trips into the wilderness were so frequent that they blend into a general picture of venturesome youth. In the autumn of 1775 Boone led a band of pioneers into Kentucky. They followed the Wilderness Road past the many-hued forested slopes through the Cumberland Gap. The travelers were his North Carolina neighbors, whom he had persuaded to "pull up stakes" with him, for new homes in the rich new land. Indian dangers in the early years added only to the tenacity of the pioneers. A more democratic world was being created in the rugged conditions of the West. Its political influence was felt in the election of 1800, when it helped to defeat the aristocratic Easterner, John Adams, and to elect Thomas Jefferson president.

PHOTO FROM PAINTING BY GEORGE CALEB BINGHAM. COURTESY WASHINGTON UNIVERSITY, ST. LOUIS

Commerce, like politics, linked regions that were originally widely separated in customs and interests. As the eighteenth century merged into the nineteenth, turnpike and bridge companies flourished. Shares of these enterprises offered the first important opportunity for stock trading in America. This view of the Frederick Road before the Fairview Inn, near Baltimore, suggests the abundance and variety of inland trade and travel.

PHOTO COURTESY MARYLAND HISTORICAL SOCIETY

COURTESY ANHEUSER-BUSCH INC., ST. LOUIS, MO.

LEWIS AND CLARK Jefferson, alert to expand the frontiers of all fields of knowledge, ordered a scientific expedition to explore the vast, scarcely known realm of Louisiana, which in 1803 became American. As its leader he placed his private secretary, Captain Meriwether Lewis—"brave, prudent, habituated to the woods, familiar with Indian manners and character; of courage undaunted." Sharing command of the great venture, at Lewis's invitation, was William Clark, a keen frontiersman, younger brother of George Rogers Clark. On May 14, 1804, the party of 45 men assembled near St. Louis, and (wrote Clark) "proceeded on under a Jentle brease up the Missourie." By flatboat and keelboat the expedition ascended the river—toiling over sandbars and around snags, harassed by "ticks and musquiters"; meeting Indians and distributing trinkets and medals; keeping daily journals that were to become wonderbooks in the literature of exploration. At the Mandan villages in North Dakota the party made winter camp. Next spring they followed the upper Missouri in canoes. With them now was Sacajawea, the "Bird Woman," of great help as the expedition reached suspicious tribes of the farther West. From the sources of the Missouri the snow-capped Rockies loomed ahead. On horses bought from the Shoshones the party pushed over the Continental Divide on a difficult, blizzard-whipped trail. The explorers finally reached the Columbia River; and on November 7, 1805, gazed upon the Pacific Ocean. The return journey ended at St. Louis in autumn, 1806. A great epic in human achievement had been written.

BROWN BROS. PHOTO

THE BURR-HAMILTON DUEL In the formative years of the republic, strong conflicts between principles of government, and between ambitious personalities, were inevitable. The most notable "war of ideas" was between Jefferson, favoring a liberal democracy, and Alexander Hamilton, who wished a centralized national authority. Less dignified was the clash between Hamilton and Aaron Burr. Hamilton called his opponent "a dangerous man and one who ought not to be trusted with the reins of government." Burr at last declared, "These things must have an end." At Weehawken, on a July morning in 1804, each man fired once; Burr's bullet reached its mark. It was a grievous day in American history; but the vicious code of dueling lingered in some sections.

PHOTO JOSEPH BOGGS BEALE, MODERN GALLERIES, PHILA.

"DECATUR AND THE ALGERINE" The young republic followed the custom of European nations in paying annual tributes to the piratical states of the Barbary Coast—Morocco, Algiers, Tripoli, and Tunis— for the unmolested passage of its merchantmen through the Mediterranean. But Tripoli seized several American vessels in 1801, and forced a naval war. United States men-o'-war under Captain Edward Preble blockaded the Tripolitan coast. The daring exploits of Stephen Decatur added drama to the victory. Tripoli agreed in 1805 to make no more demands for tribute. But a second expedition under Decatur, ten years later, was needed before all the Barbary states agreed never to bother an American ship.

THE LOUISIANA PURCHASE As the tide of population flowed westward, states and territories were created between the Allegheny Mountains and the Mississippi. Free navigation of the Mississippi became essential to the national commerce. As long as lax and decadent Spain possessed the mouth of the river, western produce could reach the Gulf of Mexico by treaty agreements or by discreet bribery. But in 1800 Louisiana was transferred to France, where Napoleon was imperial and militant master. The West might become a pawn in the impending war between France and England. Jefferson, himself alarmed, and impelled by an aroused people, sent negotiators to Napoleon to see if a little land on both banks of the lower Mississippi might not be bought. The astonished commissioners were offered the whole of Louisiana, 560,000,000 acres, for $15,000,000. The Purchase of 1803 added to American sovereignty more land than was embraced in all the original thirteen states. At New Orleans, the Stars and Stripes were raised with impressive ceremony.

PHOTO COURTESY CHICAGO HISTORICAL SOCIETY

EASTERN TRAVELWAYS

THE ERIE CANAL Canals as an improved method of inland navigation had been a fascinating subject since George Washington, in 1785, had become president of a corporation which hoped to achieve a waterway connection between the Potomac and the Ohio. The years 1817-37 were a booming "Canal Era" for investors and for engineers. Many useful canals were built as civic or industrial enterprises. Progenitor of the boom was the Erie Canal. De Witt Clinton of New York identified himself with the vision of a canal from the Hudson River to the Great Lakes. After years of effort, State funds were granted in 1817. In the fall of 1825 this miracle of commercial expansion was achieved. For the formal celebration a patriotically bedecked canal-boat left Buffalo, bearing Clinton and other notables; passed through a continuous ovation as it proceeded to Albany and was towed on to New York City. Here Clinton poured a cask of Lake Erie water into the Atlantic, to symbolize the "marriage of the waters." This waterway into the West was of immeasurable benefit to the State and the nation.

MAUCH CHUNK "Documents Tending to Prove the Superior Advantages of Rail-ways and Steam-carriages" was the imposing title of a book in 1812. John Stevens, a pioneer steamboat builder, wrote it. His friends considered him ingenious but addle-pated. The first railroads had no anticipation of steam power, but used horses or stationary engines to draw the carts along the rails, and were for mining or industrial uses. Longest was the Mauch Chunk railway, nine miles, built in 1827, an inclined plane from anthracite mines to the Lehigh River docks. Mules pulled the empty carts up the grooves to the mine entrance; then rode down in style, on a flatcar behind the coal-laden cars descending by gravity. Stevens built and operated a steam locomotive on his own estate in 1825; but he was a bit ahead of the times.

PHOTO COURTESY NEWBERRY LIBRARY

The "coach and four" of the eighteenth-century British squire became a public conveyance in America, with an added seat to permit nine passengers to squeeze into the box. Early coaches were springless, because rough roads snapped the coils; light in bulk and oval in shape, for better luck in crossing the bridgeless streams. The most famous type was the Concord coach, which became progressively sturdier as roads were improved. Concords provided the genteel mode of travel on the National Road, built from Cumberland, Maryland, to Wheeling, Virginia, in 1815-1818; and they followed the westward march to the Pacific shore.

PHOTO COURTESY TRANSPORTATION LIBRARY, UNIV. OF MICHIGAN

THE "CLERMONT" Fifteen steamboats had been built when the keel was laid for the *Clermont,* first commercially successful steamboat. The snub-nosed side-wheeler began its memorable voyage up the Hudson from New York to Albany on August 17, 1807, and returned in five days. Its actual running speed was nearly five miles an hour. "Fulton's Folly" was a success, and insured the introduction and continued operation of steamboats on other rivers and in coastwise waters. Robert Fulton, his financial backer Robert Livingston, and their contractor Nicholas Roosevelt, in 1811 built the first steamboat to navigate the Ohio and Mississippi rivers.

PHOTO COURTESY TRANSPORTATION LIBRARY, UNIV. OF MICHIGAN

DOWN RIVER

"FLOATING DOWN THE RIVER ON THE O-HI-O"

By 1810 a million people had settled in the Western territories; the paths of their coming and of their commerce were the river highways. Emigrants brought their families and goods by wagon and pack horse to the riverbank at Pittsburgh or at one of the towns on the Monongahela. Each year hundreds of newly built flatboats made a one-way journey down the Ohio; they were the standard craft of the settlers, and at the end of the voyage were broken up for the use or sale of their lumber. They were usually built of green-oak plank fastened by wooden pins to a timber frame, and calked with tar. Other types of vessels—all propelled by paddle, oar, or sweep, and occasionally by sails—plied the twisting highway into the New West. Down the river also went an endless variety of freight and provisions. Some flatboats that reached New Orleans fought their way back up the river with cargoes of sugar and molasses; but these were few, for it took thirty men three months to push and tow a flatboat against the current from New Orleans to Cairo.

COURTESY TRANSPORTATION LIBRARY, UNIVERSITY OF MICHIGAN

CAVE-IN-ROCK

Banditry and river piracy added violent colors to the panorama of the flatboat era. At Cave-in-Rock, on the northern bank of the lower Ohio, was an inn whose promise of rest and drink decoyed travelers into a den of shrouded crime. Boats were hailed to the banks, and seized by robber gangs hidden in the brush. Sometimes boats were scuttled or wrecked in surprise attacks; boarders appropriated the goods and killed the crews. On the Mississippi were other lairs. Such overland roads as the Natchez Trace, from Nashville to Natchez, also had deadly traps for the unwary.

PHOTO COURTESY NEWBERRY LIBRARY

COURTESY TRANSPORTATION LIBRARY, UNIVERSITY OF MICH.

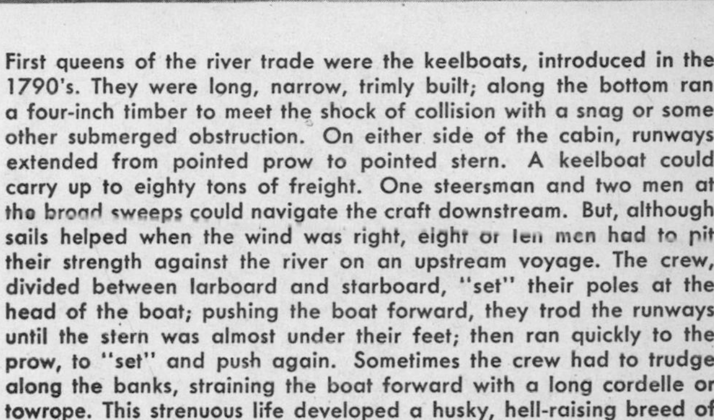

First queens of the river trade were the keelboats, introduced in the 1790's. They were long, narrow, trimly built; along the bottom ran a four-inch timber to meet the shock of collision with a snag or some other submerged obstruction. On either side of the cabin, runways extended from pointed prow to pointed stern. A keelboat could carry up to eighty tons of freight. One steersman and two men at the broad sweeps could navigate the craft downstream. But, although sails helped when the wind was right, eight or ten men had to pit their strength against the river on an upstream voyage. The crew, divided between larboard and starboard, "set" their poles at the head of the boat; pushing the boat forward, they trod the runways until the stern was almost under their feet; then ran quickly to the prow, to "set" and push again. Sometimes the crew had to trudge along the banks, straining the boat forward with a long cordelle or towrope. This strenuous life developed a husky, hell-raising breed of keelboatmen ("half horse, half alligator," they boasted).

KEELBOAT

COURTESY FRANKLIN J. MEINE

RIVER STEAMBOAT Zadok Cramer's *Navigator,* the classic handbook of the river pilots, announced in 1811: "There is now on foot a new mode of navigating our western waters. This is with boats propelled by the power of steam. A boat of this kind is now on the stocks at Pittsburgh, of 138 feet, calculated for 300 or 400 tons burden. It will be a novel sight!" More than novel—the success of this first Western steamboat, the *New Orleans,* was a portentous event in the development of the Mississippi Valley. Stately and palatial side-wheelers were developed for the wide Mississippi; stern-wheelers of light draft plied the tributaries. The paddle-wheelers swept downstream at ten to twelve miles an hour, upstream at six; keelboats and other craft could not compete with them. New Orleans in 1814 wonderingly witnessed 21 steamboat arrivals. In 1819 there were 191; in 1833 more than 1,200 steamboat cargoes were unloaded; and by 1840 the steamboats had made New Orleans the fourth port of the world.

LEVEE SCENE AT ST. LOUIS

COURTESY ANHEUSER-BUSCH INC., ST. LOUIS, MO.

WAR OF 1812

THE BATTLE OF TIPPECANOE

As a last attempt to stay the white advance into the Ohio Valley, a tribal confederation was organized by the chieftain Tecumseh and his brother "the Prophet," a religious mystic. But frenzy was no match for muskets. Governor William Henry Harrison determined to anticipate Tecumseh's blows at the frontier settlements by striking first. After a furious battle near their campsite on Tippecanoe Creek, Indiana, in the dawn of November 7, 1811, the Indians withdrew. Soon the Indian troubles in the Old Northwest were merged into an international struggle. It was known that the Indians were receiving arms and ammunition from British agents in Canada. British interference with American commerce on the high seas, and occasional impressment of American sailors on the high seas, added mercantile grievances to frontier protests. By a close vote on June 18, 1812, Congress declared war against Great Britain.

PHOTO COURTESY CHICAGO HISTORICAL SOCIETY

THE FLAG

The War of 1812 emphasized the meaning of the breeze-rippled standard as a symbol of national pride and integrity. On June 14, 1777, the Continental Congress had resolved: "That the flag of the thirteen United States be thirteen stripes, alternate red and white, that the union be thirteen stars, white in a blue field representing a new constellation." Other stars were added as new states were admitted. Pleasant legend has it that Betsy Ross, who conducted an upholstery shop in Philadelphia, made the first Stars and Stripes, following instructions by George Washington and his friends—and, for want of other material in that war-torn year of 1777, slashing her own petticoat for the crimson bands. We do know that the American flag received its first salute from a foreign power as it flew from John Paul Jones's *Ranger* in a French harbor in February, 1778. Before a one-room clapboard schoolhouse in the village of Colerain, Massachusetts, in 1812, began the flag-raising ceremony which has become traditional in free schools.

THE BURNING OF WASHINGTON

The nation was ill-prepared for war. Popular feeling was divided; the army was inadequate and poorly trained, and its generals proved incompetent in active combat. A series of disasters on land was climaxed when, on August 24, 1814, British forces captured and burned Washington. The Capitol, the White House, most other public buildings, and many civilian establishments were put to the torch.

PHOTO JOSEPH BOGGS BEALE, MODERN GALLERIES, PHILA.

"THUS BE IT EVER"

A young lawyer of Baltimore happened to be detained aboard a British man-o'-war while, through the night, the British bombarded a little fortress in Baltimore harbor. The morning's first beams disclosed a splash of color Francis Scott Key had not dared expect: over the ramparts of Fort McHenry a precious bit of muslin, with broad stripes and bright stars, was still streaming. He scribbled four verses on the back of an envelope. The next day they were printed on a handbill, and a week later appeared in a Baltimore newspaper. In the elation of a moment America's timeless anthem, "The Star-Spangled Banner," had been created.

PHOTO JOSEPH BOGGS BEALE, MODERN GALLERIES, PHILA.

THE BATTLE OF LAKE ERIE

Almost literally hewing his vessels from the forests around Lake Erie, Oliver Hazard Perry in 1813 was building, assembling, equipping, officering, and manning a fleet to challenge British control of the Great Lakes. His three brigs and six schooners were ready in August. The *Lawrence* headed the line. The opposing fleets converged in battle on September 9. Perry's flagship, the *Lawrence*, bore the brunt of the British attack for three hours; then through dangerous fire Perry was rowed to another vessel. Now, with a change of wind in their favor, the American ships blazed raking cannonades. Perry sent a laconic message: "We have met the enemy and they are ours."

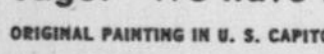

ORIGINAL PAINTING IN U. S. CAPITOL

BATTLE OF NEW ORLEANS

Whenever a report of world news reaches us the instant that our informant is speaking into a little device several thousand miles away, we may forget that words have not always moved on wings. On Christmas Eve, 1814, two related things happened. Near New Orleans, detachments of American and British armies, drawing their lines for a great battle, met in a stubborn skirmish. At Ghent, Belgium, British and American commissioners signed a treaty of peace. But how could Andrew Jackson and Sir Edward Pakenham, the opposing commanders at New Orleans, know that? A New England ship captain hurried home, under all the sail his vessel could carry, with the news. New York papers printed "Extras" with the good tidings on the night of February 11—and the Lower Mississippi had to wait for several days more! Meanwhile, on January 8, the British army of 6,000 men made a frontal assault on New Orleans' hastily prepared defenses of cotton bales and cypress logs. Jackson's volleys were intense and deadly. When the depleted lines of the British regulars reeled back for the last time, more than 2,000 dead and wounded lay on the field. The American loss was but 71. General Pakenham and 82 other officers were among those buried next day as the roll of muffled drums brought an end to the fighting on land. This magnificent victory added much to General Jackson's stature with the common people; fourteen years later he became their president.

CULVER PHOTO

THE "CONSTITUTION"

The *Constitution,* the first vessel authorized by Congress after the Revolution, was to be a full-rigged ship "superior to any European frigate." Design, woodwork, ironwork, canvas, cables, and all were of the best; as was exhorted for a sister ship, "Sons of Freedom! Let every man in possession of a white oak tree be ambitious to make the name of America respected among the nations of the world. Your largest and longest trees are wanted, and the arms of them for knees and rising timber. . . ." The *Constitution* slid down the ways at Boston in October, 1797. She was the Commodore's flagship in an undeclared naval "war" with France, and again in the war against the Barbary pirates. Victorious in several sea duels in the War of 1812, the *Constitution* became a symbol of American "hearts of oak." Ordered broken up in 1830, she was saved by a wave of public protest; and is today a floating historical museum.

"OLD IRONSIDES"

Captain Isaac Hull of the *Constitution* was in August, 1812, cruising along the sea lanes near the Grand Banks of Newfoundland, watching for British merchantmen. But he encountered worthier game—the *Guerrière,* British man-o'-war. The *Constitution* with its 55 guns was somewhat the superior ship; but the British navy, after its great victories in the European wars, felt well-nigh invincible, and the *Guerrière* offered battle. At range so close that for a while the *Guerrière*'s bowsprit was fouled in the *Constitution*'s mizzen-rigging, the ships exchanged thirty minutes of raking fire. Then, with all her masts shot away and her gunports rolling under water, the *Guerrière* surrendered. This was the first important naval victory of the war. In the height of the engagement a sailor, seeing a shot rebound from the *Constitution*'s stout hull, shouted, "Huzza, her sides are made of iron!" And so the ship acquired its nickname.

PHOTO COURTESY CHICAGO HISTORICAL SOCIETY

THE RIVER FRONT OF NEW ORLEANS AFTER THE WAR OF 1812

THE FUR TRADE

UPSTREAM Fur traders and trappers—Scots, French-Canadians, Americans—pushed into the crannies of the Great Lakes country. Their main quest was for beaver, whose double thickness of fur was very fashionable for both coats and hats. The trappers waded into the icy streams, sinking their traps under the water level so as not to leave the scent of their hands on the iron. Traders met Indian tribes, to barter for the winter's catch of beaver, otter, mink, raccoon, etc., with their stores of knives, hatchets, awls, needles, fishhooks, kettles, cloths, blankets, beads, ornaments, guns, whiskey, tobacco. Indians found it easier to get their necessities from the white traders than to keep up their old handicrafts; but they were nearly always in debt to the traders. This picturesque, colorful frontier of the fur traders was always in motion, seeking new regions of abundant game to replace those it had depleted.

DETROIT IN 1820 Earliest capital of the Great Lakes fur trade was Detroit, where every year the Indians gathered with the traders to sell their pelts, collect their goods for the coming season—and get royally drunk. Expansion of American activity after the War of 1812 pushed the trading center to scenic Michilimackinac Island, at the "crossroads" of Lakes Huron, Michigan, and Superior. For this longer distance the American Fur Company chartered the *Walk-in-the-Water*, first steamboat on the Lakes. The difficulties of its construction, in 1818, show that the Lakes were isolated inland seas until the Erie Canal was built. The *Walk-in-the-Water*'s engine, made in New York City, was carried in sloops to Albany and thence hauled overland to Buffalo by four-horse teams; it took more than a month to transport the machinery and parts to the waiting hull at Buffalo. Although capital of Michigan Territory, Detroit in 1820 was merely a sprawling village.

COURTESY WISCONSIN HISTORICAL MUSEUM

THE "YELLOWSTONE" John Jacob Astor attempted to challenge the great fur-trading companies of Canada; his American Fur Company was planned to operate on a continental scale. The Astoria Expeditions—overland and by sea to the mouth of the Columbia—failed of lasting results because of the outbreak of the War of 1812. Ten years later the powerful "AMF" (as their bales and goods-boxes were stamped) invaded the Rocky Mountain trade. Fort Union was established at the head of navigation on the Missouri. The Company's steamboat *Yellowstone* was the first one seen on the upper Missouri. It reached Fort Pierre, North Dakota, on its maiden voyage in 1831. The next year, when it pushed on to Fort Union, an alert passenger was the artist George Catlin, whose brush fixed in spirited permanence the appearance and customs of the Plains Indians.

COURTESY NEWBERRY LIBRARY

COURTESY NEWBERRY LIBRARY

BELLEVUE Oldest settlements in the West were, typically, of military and fur-trading origin. These causes interlocked, for imperial diplomacy and Indian trade proceeded hand in hand. Detroit, Vincennes, and Kaskaskia are examples. Again, as fur interests reached into the Upper Mississippi and Missouri regions, the traders' stockades became the roots of towns. Bellevue, an American Fur Company outpost on the Missouri, was the first permanent white settlement in Nebraska. This restful picture shows the beginnings of homemaking.

FORT LARAMIE Near the confluence of the Laramie and North Platte rivers, in the land of the Cheyenne and the Sioux, Fort Laramie was the most important trading post on the Overland Trail. When the fur trade declined, the fort was purchased by the government and occupied by the army.

FROM PAINTING BY ALFRED J. MILLER; IN THE COLLECTION OF MRS. CLYDE PORTER; COURTEST COOPERATION PUB. CO., NEW YORK

COMANCHE WARRIOR As conquistadores from Mexico extended their stock ranches into Texas and Arizona, the Indians learned the value of the horses which these arrogant newcomers brought. Strays grazed on the fenceless range; and there were inviting corrals to be raided in the moonlight. The Plains Indian changed his way of life and became a mounted hunter, a mobile warrior. The Comanches in particular became superb horsemen. They claimed western Texas as part of a vast domain; their raiding parties made a bloody barrier to frontier settlement. The invention of the six-shooter and the establishment of the Texas Rangers were needed to hold them in check.

COURTESY NEWBERRY LIBRARY

SAM HOUSTON Mexico became independent of Spain in 1823. A Connecticut Yankee, Moses Austin, was convinced that the time for speculation in Texas lands was ripe; and his son Stephen brought many American colonists into the Mexican province. The seat of government—Mexico City—was far from Texas; conditions were chaotic; and the nationalities did not blend. The Texans declared their independence. Their leader in the field was Sam Houston, a man born to leadership on the rugged frontier and uncomfortable anywhere else. Of Ulster Scot ancestry; an adopted member of the Cherokees; a governor of Tennessee; an Indian trader in Texas; commander-in-chief in the Texas Revolution, and president of the Lone Star Republic—Sam Houston was a towering figure. When Texas joined the Confederacy he said: "I would not see wrong inflicted on the North or the South, but I am for the Union, without any 'if' in the case."

COURTESY NEWBERRY LIBRARY

THE ALAMO An Anglo-Texan detachment of about 150 men was at San Antonio when a Mexican army of several thousand, under General Santa Anna, arrived. Santa Anna called himself "the Napoleon of the West," and had ordered that no prisoners be taken alive. The Texans could have withdrawn, but that was not in their character. Within the stout adobe walls of Alamo Mission, they answered a demand for surrender with a cannon shot and: "Our flag still proudly waves from the wall. Victory or death!" On the thirteenth day of battle the Alamo's mortar crumbled. All the defenders died. Mexican losses were about 750. "Remember the Alamo!" became the cry of the Texan troops.

BROWN BROTHERS PHOTO

SURRENDER OF SANTA ANNA Houston's army, outnumbered, retreated into southeast Texas. Most of the population had fled their villages and plantations, toward the Louisiana border. Santa Anna's forces pressed through charred towns for their confidently anticipated victory. But at the San Jacinto River, Houston's men were screened by trees as the Mexican army marched into a shallow ravine. When the Texan charge began, there was no shelter for the enemy troops save a marsh, where hundreds were bogged to await destruction. Houston was among the very few Texans wounded. Santa Anna signed armistice terms in return for a promise of safe conduct back to Mexico. Texas became an independent nation for nine years, 1836-1845; then accepted annexation into the United States.

BROWN BROTHERS PHOTO

FORT ON THE WESTERN BORDER Frontier forts were various stockades built by the settlers, in common, for protection against Indian raids; army outposts; gathering places for fur traders and buffalo hunters; and far-flung links in the commerce of freighters' caravans. Some, as in this picture, were built of well-chinked logs. Others were built of thick adobe walls. Bent's Fort, on the upper Arkansas, became the outstanding trading post of the Southwest.

COURTESY NEWBERRY LIBRARY

BREAKING OF THE PRAIRIE

THE GOOD EARTH The "patient ox," first power machine of the ancient farmer, came with the settlers to the Atlantic seaboard. In the meadows, and in the clearings laboriously shaped from the forest, were heard the lowings of cattle and the drivers' calls remembered from centuries of European tillage. Oxen pulled the covered wagons across the Appalachians; their strength was a fulcrum of pioneer husbandry, and their flesh provided subsistence when there was need. On the prairies of the Middle West frontiersmen found new conditions—a glacier-spread soil unobstructed by rocks and, amazingly, "No stumps to plow around!" Tough grass-roots formed a protective armor over the rich loam. Farmers needed new implements to link with the oxen for the sod-breaking, and inventors provided them. The great prairie-breaking plow was developed, with its wooden moldboard strengthened with iron strips. John Deere improved upon this with a steel moldboard which would not become caked with the thick earth. Straining processions of oxen, plows, and the men at the handles, carved the sod into furrows as straight as the township lines of the Public Land surveys.

THE SHEAVES IN THE BARN At harvest-time through the centuries, the down-beat of the flails against the wheat-beards was an exciting and exhausting rhythm. On comparatively larger farms horses clopped upon the grain strewn on the threshing floor. A Yankee invented a threshing machine operated by a horse-powered tread-mill; its iron teeth on a whipping cylinder shook the grain from the straw and winnowed the chaff. Itinerant workers appeared, to earn a few dollars in the hurried season of threshing against their need for money to begin homesteading. Women provided large and lavish meals for the men sweating to bring in the crops at the brief moment of their right ripeness.

"THE SETTLER'S FIRST HOME IN THE WEST"

THE YANKEE PEDDLER

His laden wagon jolting over the country roads, came the peddler to the farmhouse door. He brought an assortment of "Yankee notions" from small factories in the East, tinware, watches, Bibles, fabrics, gadgets for the kitchen—and sometimes, dark rumor had it, wooden nutmegs and clocks without works. The peddler was a shrewd character; he had to be, for the farm-kitchen sugarbowl usually held but little money, and barter was a frequent mode of trade. His coming was both an economic and social event; for with his novelties and necessities the peddler also brought news. Often, too, he was a lively hand with the fiddle, and paid for his night's lodging with fireside gayety.

CULVER PHOTO

McCORMICK'S REAPER The primitive sickle for cutting grain was succeeded by a heavy hand-swung cradle, which was merely a scythe with parallel wooden bars. Such slow methods were not for the expanding homesteads—and expansive ambitions—of the nineteenth century. Obed Hussey patented a practical, if clumsy, reaping machine in 1833. A farmer's son in the Valley of Virginia, working independently, thought out the principles of the modern reaper; put it to tests in the field that delighted the neighboring farmers; and secured his patent in 1834. The young inventor, Cyrus H. McCormick, had a keen sense of business promotion and organization. He established his second factory in Chicago, potential center of the national granary; devised new merchandising methods; and steadily improved his machines.

PHOTO INTERNATIONAL HARVESTER CO.

INDIANS OF THE PLAINS

PIEGAN INDIAN ENCAMPMENT In the vast expanses of the trans-Mississippi West lived the Plains Indians—Sioux, Pawnee, Cheyenne, Arapaho, Blackfoot, and other tribes. While each claimed a particular, if vague, domain, they followed the migrations of the great game animals; this meant that for half a year the tribes were nomadic — abandoning the tame, scanty life of the maize-grower for the vigorous, exciting life of the hunter. Then the tribal "home" became a cavalcade, pitching its skin tepees at night where watercourse and shelter invited, and ready to move at will. In the 1830's the United States thought that the Great Plains region was useless to white men; so it was confirmed in many treaties as the permanent home of the Indian. Tribes east of the Mississippi were transferred to Buffalo Land.

PHOTO COURTESY NEWBERRY LIBRARY

MANDAN BULL DANCE
The pursuit of the buffalo had to be successful if the Plains Indian was to live. Dances and ceremonies developed to invoke the assistance of the gods of luck in the chase, and to appease the ghost-spirits of the slain buffalo. Imaginative myths also clustered about this magnificent beast. The highest secret society of the Mandans, the Bull Cult, had an elaborate ritual of mimic warfare between buffalo and Indian. Other tribal dances mirrored the rhythm and hazards of wilderness life.

PHOTO COURTESY NEWBERRY LIBRARY

BUFFALO HUNT Over the broad grasslands grazed uncounted millions of buffalo. They were the mainstay of life for the Plains Indians, supplying food; skins for tepees, clothing, shields, harness; sinews for bowstrings, thread, and ropes; bone for arrowheads, needles, awls; thick winter pelts for the fur trade. But the hunting of the buffalo demanded courage and dexterity; the huge shaggy beasts, when brought to bay, could charge and gore with deadly ferocity.

PHOTO COURTESY NEWBERRY LIBRARY

SIOUX BALL GAME This ancient game was called by the Indians "ball and racket." The early French *habitants* in the St. Lawrence Valley found the natives playing it, and adopted the sport for themselves under the name *la crosse*. Indians relished gambling games; they played with knucklebones, with hoops and poles, and wagered on arrows shot at a target. Little girls played "house" with miniature furniture; and future braves had whip tops, darts, and other toys.

FROM ORIGINAL PAINTING BY SETH EASTMAN, COURTESY CORCORAN GALLERY OF ART

THE ODOR OF DEATH Some poets and other writers have sighed for a lost "golden age" when the Noble Savage lived in peaceful communion with nature until the white man came with his ruthless, destructive ways. That is a sentimental delusion. Tribe warred with tribe; personal bravery in battle won distinction, but scalps taken by ambush and treachery made just as good a display when they were hung on poles outside the brave's tepee. The artist Carl Bodmer was at Fort Mackenzie when two rival tribes, coming there to trade, decided they preferred to kill each other. The whites within the stockade were powerless to stop the bloody fray.

PHOTO COURTESY NEWBERRY LIBRARY

WESTERN TRAILS

PHOTO FROM MURAL BY ALLEN TRUE IN THE DENVER PUBLIC LIBRARY

INDIANS ATTACKING A CARAVAN

COURTESY CHICAGO, BURLINGTON & QUINCY RAILROAD

THE OREGON TRAIL Oregon was an international frontier; but the region seemed to have no likely use save for its furs, and after the War of 1812 Great Britain and the United States agreed upon a joint "occupation." William Cullen Bryant in his poem "Thanatopsis" made stately reference to

> . . . the continuous woods
> Where rolls the Oregon and hears no sound
> Save his own dashings—

but the river soon heard the splash of missionaries boats. Devout pioneers of the Word, living in Indian villages, discovered the merits of the land. Letters to home folk told of the fertile soil, the heavy forests, the rivers abounding in salmon, and the rapids that were potential millsites. The native wealth of Oregon resembled, or exceeded, the favored regions that had tempted the pioneer over the Appalachians. It seemed the ideal combination of earth, wood, and water. In the 1840's the flood of pioneers over the Oregon Trail began. Explorers' journals and travelers' guidebooks charted the way from the Missouri River and up the Platte, over the Rockies through the South Pass, and on through the forbidding difficulties of the Snake River country and the Blue Mountains. The emigrants gathered on the western bank of the Missouri in the early spring, to take advantage of the fresh grasses for their livestock and to allow all possible time for the 2,000 mile journey—"the greatest trek of recorded history." They traveled in caravans, for the Indians naturally resented the ever-increasing flood of wagons across their hunting grounds. Travel in the 1840's and 1850's was so heavy that the Oregon Trail became a deeply rutted way, so grooved that hundreds of miles of it could still be traced generations after the last covered wagon had passed over it. The day of the agricultural settler had come to the Far West—over a pathway whose hardships and dangers were a test of spirit and endurance. In 1846 the Oregon country was divided between the United States and Canada at the present line.

COURTESY ANHEUSER-BUSCH INC., ST. LOUIS, MO.

"THE COMMERCE OF THE PRAIRIES" Santa Fé, founded in 1609, was the capital and only town of New Mexico. It was the gateway to a strange country of sandswept plains with no vegetation but cacti; of colorful mesas with weirdly eroded rock formations; of aboriginal Indian cities built into cliffsides; of the great cleft of the Colorado River. To Santa Fé, which had some precious metals to export and horses, burros, beaver skins, and buffalo robes to exchange, came Mexican traders from Chihuahua, and occasionally French traders from the Mississippi Valley. But this early trade was scant; the lonely city was supplied with most of its goods by mule trains on a roundabout and dangerous route from Vera Cruz, 1,500 miles away. Trade with Americans was prohibited until Mexico flared into revolution in 1821. Then began the husky days of the Santa Fé trade. William Becknell was first to mark out the Santa Fé Trail from the Missouri River; his pack trains brought goods that sold ten to twenty times over St. Louis prices. From Franklin (then Independence, and finally Kansas City), the course followed the prairie divide between the tributaries of the Kansas and the Arkansas; then followed the Arkansas to the tenacious mountain barriers of its upper reaches, turning south to the little metropolis. Becknell on his second journey, 1822, introduced wagons; and the prairie schooner became the standard carrier of the trade. Flourishing until the Mexican government stopped it on the eve of war with the United States, the trade remained a characteristically frontier enterprise; each merchant was "on his own," perhaps risking his entire capital on a single expedition. But at Council Grove, where the Trail edged into dangerous Indian country, the traders assembled into a caravan—electing trail captains and lieutenants. "Upon encamping" (explained Josiah Gregg, author of the classic story of the Santa Fé Trail), "the wagons are formed into a hollow square, constituting at once an enclosure for the animals when needed, and a fortification against the Indians. Not to embarrass the cattle-pen, the camp fires are laid outside of the wagons. Outside also the travelers spread their beds of buffalo robes and blankets." But there arrived a day of clamorous rejoicings and whipcrackings—when faces were washed and hair slicked back for the benefit of the señoritas, and wits were sharpened for dealings with the Santa Fé merchants.

INDEPENDENCE ROCK, NOTED LANDMARK ON THE OVERLAND TRAIL

COURTESY CLARENCE S. JACKSON

"PILGRIMS OF THE PLAINS"

THE YEAR OF DECISION

MORMON EMIGRANTS IN A STORM

A mystic revelation announced in western New York (a region so subject to religious revivals it was known as "the Burnt-over Ground") began an amazing movement across the face of America. Mormon doctrines conflicted with the frontier spirit of democracy. Mormon bands seeking a permanent location for their "kingdom of Zion" found no welcome in the sparsely settled counties of Ohio, Missouri, or Illinois. The assassination of their first prophet, Joseph Smith, indicated that their "temple" must be planted in a wilderness where a new society could be built unmolested. Brigham Young led the exodus to the Salt Lake Valley, one of the most successful colonizing movements in our history. The first expedition left Council Bluffs, Iowa, in the spring of 1847, and marked out the Mormon Trail. Once established in the subarid region which Young's vigorous, practical leadership was to transform into a "garden of the desert," the Mormons pursued a vigorous immigration policy. Some of the converts could not afford wagons; and handcart brigades attempted the journey. Two such companies encountered dire hardship as they were caught in the early winter storms.

PHOTO COURTESY NEWBERRY LIBRARY

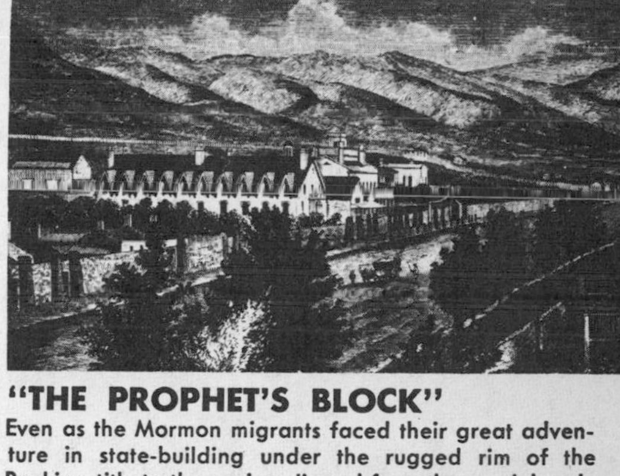

"THE PROPHET'S BLOCK"

Even as the Mormon migrants faced their great adventure in state-building under the rugged rim of the Rockies, title to the region slipped from the weak hands of Mexico to the firm grasp of the United States. But plans were not altered. Isolation in the desert environment proved as effective a spur to co-operate as persecution had been in the Middle West. Young sent groups to occupy the well-watered valleys in a chain of outposts against the Indians and to set the form for irrigation of the Salt Lake plain. The main settlement rose from adobe houses into a well-planned assemblage of brick and lumber dwellings and public buildings. The "Prophet's Block" was liberally planned to accommodate Brigham Young's ever-expanding family. A traveler in 1850 reported of the Mormons: "Their admirable system of combining labor, while each has his own property, and conducting the irrigating canals to supply the want of rain, the complete reign of good neighborhood, form themes of admiration for the stranger coming from the dark and sterile recesses of the mountain gorges into the flourishing valley."

PHOTO COURTESY NEWBERRY LIBRARY

PHOTO COURTESY CHICAGO HISTORICAL SOCIETY

"READING THE NEWS" OF THE MEXICAN WAR

A popular phrase among ambitious, confident Americans was "Manifest Destiny"; it implied that the domain of the United States must surely extend from ocean to ocean, and to unlimited bounds south and north. Annexation of California was the immediate desire; but Mexico, however weak, was sulking, and so resented the annexation of Texas in 1845 that its diplomatic representatives were recalled from Washington. A border fray on the Rio Grande provided reason for the United States to declare war in the spring of 1846. Most American troops were volunteers, who signed for the service during the emotional excitement of mass meetings and speech making. Their valor, as events proved, more than made up for their lack of training. The people at home first argued at fever heat over the justification for the war; then were hungry for news of how their boys were getting along. Arrival of the latest newspaper was a community event.

THE STORMING OF CHAPULTEPEC

The key to Mexico City was Chapultepec, a rocky eminence crowned with stone buildings. American batteries rained shells upon the lofty castle; but a defeated nation was making its last stand, with the pick of its troops. Attacking columns scaled the walls; on September 13, 1847, the citadel surrendered. With the formal entry of the American troops into the capital next day, the war was practically ended. Mexico received some monetary compensation, but gave up two-fifths of its territory: California and much of Arizona, New Mexico, Nevada, Utah, and Colorado became part of the United States. The American nation was now, more than ever, the custodian of an empire. But difficult problems were acquired along with this domain; important was the question of the extension of slavery.

CULVER PHOTO

THE LANDING AT VERA CRUZ

General Winfield Scott ("Old Fuss and Feathers") was the most able general of the war; and he had with him "our graduated cadets," the West Pointers. Against him were Mexican troops in greater numbers and the bulwarks of towering, steep-terraced mountains which invaders had to scale. Other difficulties were the poor organization of the American army, with shortages of transports, supplies, money, and of trained men in every field. But the navy and merchant marine provided invaluable support. Vera Cruz, besieged, surrendered in March, 1847; and Scott, fearing the yellow fever of the shorelands more than the enemy, hurried his troops to the mountains on the march to the Mexican capital.

THE RAILROAD

"The locomotive's coming,
With a clatter and a roar;
We all shall see it presently,
Or possibly before!"

THE "STOURBRIDGE LION"

The first steam locomotive on a commercial line in America was a seven-ton monster, the *Stourbridge Lion*, built in England. It was put in service on the Delaware and Hudson tracks between Carbondale and Honesdale, Pa., in 1829. The *Stourbridge Lion* weighed four tons more than the specifications called for; and its first trip was its last, as the engineer bravely drove it over trestles which trembled under its weight, over rails which barely supported that one triumphal trip. A similarly harrowing adventure occurred in 1848, when a Boston and Maine train made a special journey at the fantastic rate of a mile a minute; and a daring reporter in the passenger car "ventured to look out the window, and in the cloud of dust and soot which rose astonishingly in the rear, saw the strap-iron rails curling up in snakeheads amidst the cadavers of ducks and chickens from farms adjacent to the right of way."

PHOTO COURTESY TRANSPORTATION LIBRARY, UNIVERSITY OF MICHIGAN

THE "TOM THUMB"

The Baltimore and Ohio, chartered in 1827, was the first railroad constructed in America with the definite aim of carrying both passengers and freight. Charles Carroll, only living signer of the Declaration of Independence when the road was ceremonially begun, lifted the first shovelful of earth—a link between the birth-cries of the United States and its powerful maturity. The first section, thirteen miles from Baltimore to Ellicott's Mills, Maryland, was opened in May, 1830. Peter Cooper built a tiny locomotive aptly christened *Tom Thumb*. Gentlemen of wagering instinct staged a challenge race between the locomotive and a horse, August 28, 1830. The horse won when the locomotive slipped a belt; but Dobbin's success was only momentary. Soon all opposition to the railroad was smothered in public acclaim for the new mode of travel.

PHOTO FROM PAINTING BY H. D. STITT, COURTESY BALTIMORE AND OHIO RAILROAD

THE "DE WITT CLINTON"

The primary link in the great New York Central system was a seventeen-mile road between Albany and Schenectady. Horses were the first motive power; but in April, 1831, arrived a locomotive built at a West Point foundry and named after the father of the Erie Canal—De Witt Clinton. The train had its gala inaugural in August, pulling three passenger cars. The travelers had scant comfort; for the wood-burning locomotive threw sparks and soot in a fiery, grimy rain. Canal men and turnpike owners along the way feared the railroad, and tried all legal and other means to hinder its development.

PHOTO COURTESY TRANSPORTATION LIBRARY, UNIVERSITY OF MICHIGAN

EXPRESS PASSENGER LOCOMOTIVE, 1856

Each locomotive had its own name in the 1850's; this view shows the *Sagua la Grande*, typical of the best engines. It is an eight-wheeler American type locomotive—with diamond smokestack, high drivers, and burnished metalwork—a triumphant little Titan in blue steel, brass, and lacquer. The cab is probably of teakwood. The engineer, not the railroad, owned the headlight and decorated its translucent sides in accordance with the flowery taste of the times.

PHOTO COURTESY CHICAGO HISTORICAL SOCIETY

"BELLOWS FALLS, FIVE MINUTES!"

A train arrives at a little Vermont town. The year is 1849; the locomotive, with its wide funnel smokestack tapering over the boiler, brings the coaches to the crossroad. The carriage horses are panicky; the dogs are barking their happy excitement; the people are saluting the most romantic of the miracles of transportation. The friendly salute continues to this day: workmen beside the track wave to the passengers inside the speeding train, and their communal hail is returned. In 1849 the outside mechanics—the side rods, crossheads, eccentrics, the counterbalanced driving wheels—were symbols of strength, of driving power that excited the boyish and the adult imagination. That power is multiplied now, although hidden under the aluminum hoods of streamliners.

PHOTO COURTESY TRANSPORTATION LIBRARY, UNIVERSITY OF MICHIGAN

GROWTH OF A CITY

"How was it," asked the poet Edgar Lee Masters, "that Chicago, the great city, arose by Lake Michigan, amid the rich soil of Illinois, after countless centuries of no sound, save the blowing of wind, and the cry of gulls and wolves, and the shouts of Indians in play or in battle?"

In all parts of the world the growth of a city is dependent upon the progress of agriculture, industry, and commerce. (A political capital, such as Washington, expands as farm, factory, ship, and railroad require greater encouragement or regulation.) And practically all great cities are on navigable waters—that is not a coincidence. Where Lake Michigan and the "Checagou" River met, a city had to be.

FORT DEARBORN IN 1816

Soldiers came in 1803 to build a fort at the mouth of the Chicago River. As they toiled, Indians drew near to watch; whatever their thoughts then, some of those Indians were to join in the Fort Dearborn Massacre of August 15, 1812. In that calamity the garrison had already surrendered and evacuated the fort when they were ambushed and destroyed; even the white families' children were scalped. Chicago was reoccupied and a second Fort Dearborn erected in 1816. Some Indians lingered in Chicago and the vicinity until 1833, when a treaty banishing them was finally signed. An English traveler at the council wrote, "The pale light of the east hardly lighted up the dark and painted lineaments of the poor Indians. My heart bled for them in their desolation and decline." Chicagoans' hearts did not bleed.

EARLY CHICAGO

The first settler of Chicago was a strange man, Point de Saible, a far wanderer from his native Santo Domingo. In 1779 he built a log cabin on the riverbank near the Lake, residing there with only sea gulls and occasional Indians for company. He traded with the natives for furs. By 1803 there were but three more cabins; Canadian fur traders had built them. The site, Wolf Point, had changed but little thirty years later, the approximate date of this view.

CHICAGO'S FIRST SHIPMENT OF GRAIN, 1839

After boom years of land speculation and canal promotion came the nationwide panic of 1837. That year, wrote a Chicagoan, "will ever be remembered as the era of protested notes; it was the harvest of the notary and the lawyer—the year of wrath for the mercantile, producing, and laboring interests. . . . Artificial enterprises had failed, but nature was still the same." And nature's products now revived the city's trade. Farms in the near-by regions offered a surplus of foodstuffs to be shipped East. The muddy roads of Chicago echoed with the lowing of cattle and grunting of hogs as the droves were brought to the slaughterhouses. Commission dealers appeared. Vacant lots were filled with the encampments of wagoners bringing in the golden grain. Shipmasts rocked and steamboat engines puffed. No town on the western Lakes could now compete with Chicago.

THE CHICAGO RIVER, 1865

Chicago grew up, politically, when it was host to the Republican convention of 1860, which nominated Abraham Lincoln. The Civil War was both an emotional challenge and an economic tonic. Chicago still called itself "the Garden City," with exaggerated local pride. Michigan Avenue, the leading residential street, was a succession of three-story stone mansions with front yard spaces of grass and flowers. On the crowded river, tugs whistled by day and by night as they directed the bustle of commerce. The city could boast of its business structures and railroad terminals. It had an opera house in 1865, planned more parks, a medical college, a historical society. "Though men may make cities, cities also make men."

ALL PHOTOS COURTESY CHICAGO HISTORICAL SOCIETY

DOWNTOWN CHICAGO, 1865

THE GOLD RUSH

THE ARGONAUTS

James Marshall built a sawmill at Coloma, California; but he calculated badly, and placed the flutter wheel too low. A tailrace had to be dug in the obstructing bar; and on January 24, 1848, glancing at the loosened gravel, Marshall found a gold nugget. The secret could not be kept long; it spread down the Pacific coast; then leaped like wildfire to the East. Tales came of fortunes made from the stream beds of the Sierra Nevada, merely by separating the golden grains from the sand in a common washbowl. Soon pastoral California's drowsy existence was shaken by a fortune-hungry horde. It seemed as if the world were chanting an adaptation of Stephen Foster's "Oh! Susanna":

"Oh! California,
That's the land for me;
I'm off for Sacramento
With my washbowl on my knee . . ."

Workmen dropped tools, pioneer farmers abandoned their clearings, clerks left their desks, and ministers, their pulpits—in the rush for California's bounty. This picture shows rocker, pan, sluice, flume, and a "long tom" bringing down water to soften the dry rock.

STRIKING IT RICH

"Requited toil! Eureka! Look!
And read within those eyes
Their speaking luster, as they dwell
Upon the glittering prize!"

"SUNDAY MORNING AT THE MINES"

A practically womanless society, the mining country had its turbulent, hard-drinking, gun-firing aspects. The man with the rattlesnake (and snakebite cure!) and the sturdy patriarch with his Bible, represent a conflict common to the individualistic frontier. Good hard fun was one thing; but claim jumpers and highwaymen presented problems that had to be met by homemade laws—and by "necktie parties."

FROM THE ORIGINAL PAINTING BY CHARLES C. NAHL;
COURTESY E. B. CROCKER ART GALLERY, SACRAMENTO

A LOAD OF "PAY DIRT" FOR THE SMELTER

While the independent miner, with his lucky poke of nuggets and flecks, remained a romantic figure, large companies entered the field. These organizations, sometimes backed by British capital, brought expensive equipment to retain the smaller dust that was lost by primitive methods. California gold was of great importance to the North in the Civil War; its timely flow strengthened the nerves of trade and helped sustain the market for government bonds.

SHAFTS INTO THE ROCK

When the likeliest finds of free gold in the gravel beds of the mountain streams had been made, it was necessary to burrow into the hillsides in quest of the bedrock veins. This scene is of mining in Colorado in the 1860's; but its maze of mine openings suggests how the Sacramento and San Joaquin valleys were pitted by the horde of hopeful adventurers who came to California in the wake of the Forty-Niners.

BY SEA TO CALIFORNIA

From Atlantic ports boats of many descriptions—the fleetest clipper ships as well as lumbering freighters hastily scrubbed up for passenger service—carried emigrants to the new El Dorado. The first Pacific Mail ship had set out from New York, in ballast, in October of 1848, when the East had not yet learned of the gold discoveries. It sailed the lengthy route through the Strait of Magellan. When she reached the western shore of Panama on January 30, the crew was amazed to find 1,500 Americans, who had crossed the Isthmus and were clamorous for passage the rest of the way. More than 400 of them packed the ship to the rails—$1,000 for a steerage ticket, anything to get to California! Unscrupulous shipowners frequently sold tickets for full passage to California via the Panama route, without bothering to provide a ship for the voyage up the west coast.

PHOTO COURTESY CHICAGO HISTORICAL SOCIETY

CALIFORNIA
AGENCY OFFICE.

Persons who wish to secure a passage to California will do well to call on the subscriber, who has opened an office for the express accommodation of persons wishing to embark f... the

GOLD REGIONS.

He is employed by several Companies for the convenience of those wishing to secure passage. The ships are of the first class, being well victualled and ventilated, and commanded by experienced navigators.

Persons from the Country desiring information in regard to securing a passage can write to the subscriber by mail, at

CLARKE'S
GENERAL AGENCY OFFICE,
78 ANN STREET,
(A few doors from Blackstone Street.)

Life Insurance effected on the most advantageous terms and with surety.

Propeller Power Presses, 142 Washington St., Boston.

PASS IN THE SIERRA NEVADA

More than three-fifths of the gold seekers followed an overland trail. Guidebooks were hastened into print—such as *California Gold Regions, with a Full Account of Its Mineral Resources; How to Get There and What to Take; the Expense, the Time, and the Various Routes, Etc.*—but many of the emigrants had neither the money nor the patience to prepare adequately for the arduous journey. From the Snake River Valley the Overland Trail, turning away from the already well-worn Oregon Trail, followed the Humboldt River. A traveler in 1850 made note of this repellent country: "Numerous graves of emigrants are here scattered along by the wayside, and the effluvia of dead animals fill the surrounding atmosphere." But the most difficult stretch was ahead—the crossing of the Sierra Nevada. It was in these mountains that the Donner Party was entrapped by winter snows in 1846 and suffered indescribable hardships; only by cannibalism did the survivors escape starvation until rescue parties reached them.

COURTESY NEWBE

THE PONY EXPRESS

A romantic interlude in the story of transcontinental transportation was the Pony Express. From St. Joseph, Missouri, along a central route, it strung a line of stations about fifteen miles apart. Fleet, wiry Indian ponies were purchased; young, courageous, lightweight riders were hired. On April 3, 1860, a Pony Express messenger left cheering crowds at San Francisco, while another galloped away from St. Joseph. The run to San Francisco was made in 8 days. The line was like a giant relay, with seventy-five ponies being used in each direction. At each station the rider was allowed but two minutes to transfer saddlebags to a fresh mount and speed the mail on its way. Only urgent mail justified the high rate—five dollars a half ounce. But costs of operation were ruinous; and when in the autumn of 1861 a telegraph line reached across the West, the Pony Express passed into limbo.

INDIAN ATTACK ON THE OVERLAND MAIL

Mail for California usually went by boat, until in 1857 Congress agreed to subsidize a stagecoach route. John Butterfield's Concord coaches, on semiweekly trips, left St. Louis on a wide southward swoop toward El Paso, and over the comparatively level desert route reached California in twenty-five days. With the outbreak of the Civil War the overland mail was transferred to the central route, in Union-controlled territory, and was made a daily service. Stagecoach lines were extended into Oregon and Montana, and sometimes had spirited encounters with Indians or outlaws. Mark Twain celebrated the stage driver as "the lion of the road."

COURTESY ANHEUSER-BUSCH INC., ST. LOUIS, MO.

"PIKES PEAK OR BUST!"

California's placer boom days were repeated in the 1860's in Nevada and Montana. Strikes of precious metals in the Nevada mountains opened up the world's most famous silver mine, the Comstock Lode. Virginia City set new records for riotousness—where "Groups of keen speculators were huddled around the corners; rough customers, with red and blue flannel shirts, were straggling with specimens of croppings in their hands. Monte-dealers, thieves, and cut-throats were mingling miscellaneously in the dense crowds gathered around the bars." Gold discoveries in the Pikes Peak country brought a rush estimated at 100,000 men—an overwhelming, disorganized procession, in light wagons and heavy prairie schooners; on horseback, leading pack mules; men afoot, pulling handcarts and pushing wheelbarrows. Denver was founded. But the rush was premature, and many of the fortune seekers returned home with bitter comment about the "Pikes Peak humbug."

PHOTO COURTESY NEWBERRY LIBRARY

PROGRESS OF THE NORTH

"TIMBER!" In pre-Colonial America was the most magnificent forest stand in the world—nearly nine million acres of virgin timber. The edge of this forest has constantly retreated westward. Farmers cleared the land, burning the logs just to get them out of the way. Log cabins were succeeded by frame houses—more and more wood to feed the demands of civilization. As the cut was reduced in New England, the sawdust trail of the loggers reached New York and Pennsylvania. On the eve of the Civil War, the vast forest stands of Michigan felt the invader's axe. Noisy sawmills were pungent with the smell of uncured lumber; mess tables groaned with the huge quantities of food that the hardy lumberjacks demanded. The lumbering frontier created its own mythical hero, Paul Bunyan.

COURTESY TRANSPORTATION LIBRARY, UNIVERSITY OF MICHIGAN

HENRY STEPHENS'
WHITE PINE LUMBER MILLS AND YARD.

DIGGING AND LOADING COAL Water power contributed much to make New England the region in which factory industry was first centered. But water power was not dependable throughout the year and, until the invention of the electric dynamo, was very much limited in the amount of work it could do. Industry, with its increasing needs, turned to the practical uses of coal. The anthracite fields of eastern Pennsylvania and the great bituminous veins of the Appalachians became the mainstays of industrial power. Mines burrowed far into the earth, making black shafts where husky men worked like tireless cave-dwellers.

FILLING THE FURNACE The Indians knew nothing of iron; but the colonists were building little blast furnaces and forges, operated by charcoal, in the first years of settlement. At the eve of the Revolution the colonies had more ironworks, and were producing more pig and bar iron, than England and Wales combined. Nails, iron piping, and cast-iron stoves were typical products. The growth of commerce and shipbuilding in New England stimulated the industry; cannon, shot, anchors, distillery vats, barrel hoops, were in demand. As anthracite fuel gradually replaced charcoal, eastern Pennsylvania became the principal manufacturing region; across the Alleghenies, the blast furnaces of Pittsburgh were rolling their bituminous smoke over the hills. The "age of invention" produced a great expansion of the iron industry—for steam engines, agricultural implements, heavy machinery, and household gadgets. Steel was used only for cutlery and the finer grades of tools until new processes, after the Civil War, revolutionized the industry.

CLIPPER SHIP
When competition for the rich prizes of Oriental trade became keen, New England shipyards gave the world the highest development of the sailing ship in speed and beauty. "Clip," in Americanese, means a fast gait; and the slender, high-rigged vessels of the 1850's were paced for speed records that are yet unbroken. Eighteen clippers made passages from New York or Boston to San Francisco in less than one hundred days; the *Flying Cloud,* built by Donald McKay, on her maiden voyage made the great swing in eighty-nine days. The poet John Masefield saluted "These splendid ships, each with her grace, her glory," for their "Beauty in hardest action, beauty indeed." COURTESY TRANSPORTATION LIBRARY, UNIVERSITY OF MICH.

A GUSHER Indians knew some places in western New York and the Ohio Valley where oil bubbled to the surface; they skimmed it off in blankets, and used it as liniment and medicine. Proprietary advertisements in American newspapers of the 1850's proclaimed (with testimonials!) the marvelous virtues of "Seneca Oil" or Kier's Petroleum. Kerosene and petroleum became fashionable illuminants, replacing candles and sperm oil. In 1858 a former railway conductor, E. L. Drake, with two helpers experienced in drilling for artesian water and for salt brine, began the experiment of drilling for petroleum. Their well was near Titusville, in northwestern Pennsylvania. On August 27, 1859, they "struck oil." Oil Creek, a worked-over lumbering region, was besieged by hopeful multitudes. A new industry was born, in a quick frenzy of drilling and speculation. The story of petroleum as fuel for internal combustion engines, and as an explosive agent in world politics, was beginning.

PHOTO COURTESY NEWBERRY LIBRARY.

THE AGE OF INVENTION

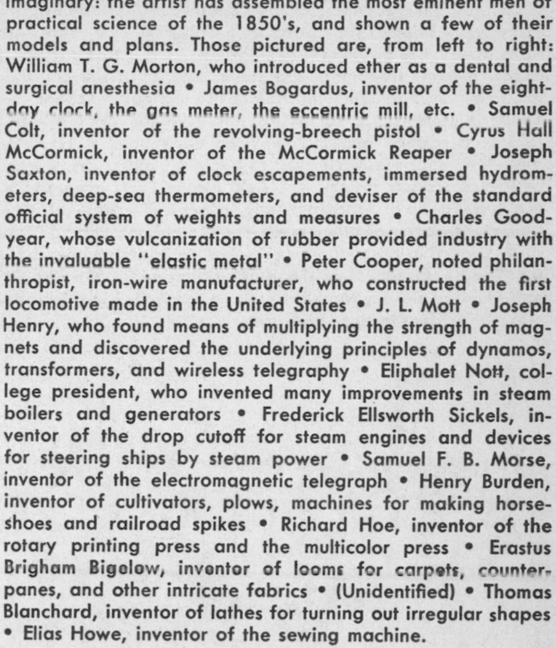

"THE CONGRESS OF INVENTORS" What a conclave of keen wits this would have been! But the picture is imaginary: the artist has assembled the most eminent men of practical science of the 1850's, and shown a few of their models and plans. Those pictured are, from left to right: William T. G. Morton, who introduced ether as a dental and surgical anesthesia • James Bogardus, inventor of the eight-day clock, the gas meter, the eccentric mill, etc. • Samuel Colt, inventor of the revolving-breech pistol • Cyrus Hall McCormick, inventor of the McCormick Reaper • Joseph Saxton, inventor of clock escapements, immersed hydrometers, deep-sea thermometers, and deviser of the standard official system of weights and measures • Charles Goodyear, whose vulcanization of rubber provided industry with the invaluable "elastic metal" • Peter Cooper, noted philanthropist, iron-wire manufacturer, who constructed the first locomotive made in the United States • J. L. Mott • Joseph Henry, who found means of multiplying the strength of magnets and discovered the underlying principles of dynamos, transformers, and wireless telegraphy • Eliphalet Nott, college president, who invented many improvements in steam boilers and generators • Frederick Ellsworth Sickels, inventor of the drop cutoff for steam engines and devices for steering ships by steam power • Samuel F. B. Morse, inventor of the electromagnetic telegraph • Henry Burden, inventor of cultivators, plows, machines for making horseshoes and railroad spikes • Richard Hoe, inventor of the rotary printing press and the multicolor press • Erastus Brigham Bigelow, inventor of looms for carpets, counterpanes, and other intricate fabrics • (Unidentified) • Thomas Blanchard, inventor of lathes for turning out irregular shapes • Elias Howe, inventor of the sewing machine.

"Invention and improvement are prolific, and beget more of their kind. The present progress is rapid." Benjamin Franklin was an old man when he wrote that; but he was quickened by the thrill of his foreknowledge that the day of great mechanical inventions was at its dawn. The expansive distances of America called forth vigorous, brilliant answers to the problems of transportation. The tradition of equal opportunity for all directed ambitious men to new routes of industrial development. And the abundant, varied resources of the western world challenged men with scientific knowledge to utilize these materials in improving the practical affairs of life. The characteristic American scientist was, therefore, less a theorist and more the practical inventor.

THE TYPEWRITER was another American invention. It was merely the toy of ingenious men, however, until after the Civil War. A woman no longer had to be "wife, schoolteacher, or old maid." The machine tapped out an invitation to her to enter the business world.

THE SEWING MACHINE was the life work of Elias Howe, who made his first smooth-running machine in 1845. The first uses of the instrument were industrial, in textile and shoe factories. The old system of "farming out" sewing work to be done in the home was doomed. The rise of the ready-made clothing industry was made possible by the sewing machine. The device came but slowly into private homes; this Singer model of 1851 is a pioneer.

PHOTO COURTESY SINGER MANUFACTURING CO.

COMPLETION OF THE ATLANTIC CABLE

The success **THE TRANSATLANTIC TELEGRAPH** of Morse's telegraph, which transmitted its first message ("What hath God wrought!") on the experimental line between Washington and Baltimore in 1844, inspired further developments of the electrical miracle. Cyrus Field thought: "Why not lay a cable across the Atlantic itself!" In August, 1858, after arduous labor and many disappointments, the laying was completed. The first message came from England: "Glory to God in the highest, on earth peace, goodwill to men!" Not until 1866, however, was continuous transmission achieved.

PHOTO COURTESY METROPOLITAN MUSEUM OF ART

THE OLD SOUTH

PICKING COTTON

Dominant in the economy of the South was the fluffy white fiber of the cotton boll. Tobacco, rice, and sugar plantations were allies of the cotton kingdom. "The entire society, white and black, master, freedman and slave, lawyer in the courthouse town preacher on the circuit, teacher in the log cabin school," were influenced in pocketbook, social life, and political views, by the all-important crop. Cotton growing required continuous work of a sort that unskilled labor was well able to perform; and slavery was the basis of the plantation system. The field hands lived in quarters, received regular rations of food (typically, a peck of cornmeal, three or four pounds of bacon or other meat, some molasses and salt) and clothes, and labored in gangs under their owner or an overseer. They envied the "house servants" in the planter's mansion. Geography and climate limited slavery largely to the cotton belt; but this, in the 1850's, was not evident to fiery partisans.

BALES OF RICHES: THE NEW ORLEANS WHARF

The steamboat made New Orleans the commercial emporium of the Mississippi Valley. The river packets brought from the Midwest the foodstuffs, machinery, and many other necessities which the South — committed to the one-crop system of plantation economy—required; and ocean-going vessels transported Southern produce to the Atlantic seaboard or to England. Cotton was King; by 1860 the annual crop was 5,000,000 bales, and represented two-thirds of the entire exports of the United States. The English textile industry demanded huge quantities of raw cotton; and when the price in Liverpool went up, "there was a grand minuet in the mansion house, more pork and pone in the slave cabins." But Southern prosperity was more superficial than real.

PHOTO COURTESY TRANSPORTATION LIBRARY, UNIVERSITY OF MICHIGAN

THE LOUISIANA SUGAR HARVEST

American colonists got their sugar and molasses from the West Indies. Until Louisiana was purchased in 1803, the only sugar made within the United States was from maple sap, for household use and frontier trading. But in the hot, moist climate of the lower Mississippi, sugar-cane culture thrived. New Orleans became the center of the trade, and in 1850 was boasting the largest sugar refineries in the world. Slave labor seemed necessary for the grueling work of the humid, but fragrant, cane fields.

THE COMPROMISE OF 1850

When California in 1850 applied for admission as a free state, proslavery interests were alarmed at the prospect of being denied the new and fertile lands which the wasteful plantation system demanded. Other factional animosities became involved with the major issue, the extension of slavery. The South voiced a strong, emotional feeling of insecurity; secession from the Union was threatened. Three venerable "giants" of the Senate made their last great speeches: Henry Clay, with an elaborate plan to reconcile the various conflicting interests; John C. Calhoun, defiantly, bitterly stating the demands of Southern extremists; Daniel Webster, pleading for the compromise, for all concessions that would help preserve the Union. (In Rothermel's painting, Clay is addressing the Senate; Webster rests with palm on cheek; Calhoun's white head is near the presiding officer's chair.) The compromises were enacted, although antislavery sentiment was outraged by a stringent Fugitive Slave law. Most significant was a speech by Senator William H. Seward (seated, extreme left) declaring, "There is a higher law than the Constitution"—the law of God.

PHOTO COURTESY CHICAGO HISTORICAL SOCIETY

A SLAVE AUCTION

As the plantation belt expanded westward, the demand for slave labor was much increased. At the same time slavery was becoming less profitable in the worn-out tobacco lands of the upper South; and professional traders did a lively business in transplanting slaves for resale in Nashville, New Orleans, or in Texas. Virginia "exported" about 220,000 slaves between 1830 and 1860. Negroes dreaded being sold "down the river," for new masters were often harsh and the trade broke up slaves' families. A young backwoodsman from Illinois, Abraham Lincoln, voyaged to New Orleans with a flatboat of produce; on seeing a slave auction in the Crescent City, it is said, he vowed that if he ever had a chance to strike at the institution of slavery, he would "hit it hard."

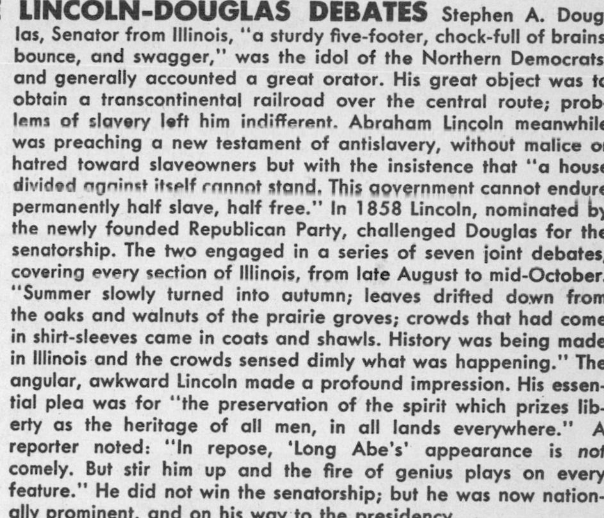

THE LINCOLN-DOUGLAS DEBATES Stephen A. Douglas, Senator from Illinois, "a sturdy five-footer, chock-full of brains, bounce, and swagger," was the idol of the Northern Democrats, and generally accounted a great orator. His great object was to obtain a transcontinental railroad over the central route; problems of slavery left him indifferent. Abraham Lincoln meanwhile was preaching a new testament of antislavery, without malice or hatred toward slaveowners but with the insistence that "a house divided against itself cannot stand. This government cannot endure permanently half slave, half free." In 1858 Lincoln, nominated by the newly founded Republican Party, challenged Douglas for the senatorship. The two engaged in a series of seven joint debates, covering every section of Illinois, from late August to mid-October. "Summer slowly turned into autumn; leaves drifted down from the oaks and walnuts of the prairie groves; crowds that had come in shirt-sleeves came in coats and shawls. History was being made in Illinois and the crowds sensed dimly what was happening." The angular, awkward Lincoln made a profound impression. His essential plea was for "the preservation of the spirit which prizes liberty as the heritage of all men, in all lands everywhere." A reporter noted: "In repose, 'Long Abe's' appearance is *not* comely. But stir him up and the fire of genius plays on every feature." He did not win the senatorship; but he was now nationally prominent, and on his way to the presidency.

PHOTO BROWN BROTHERS

"COUNTY ELECTION"
Crowds, speeches, cider, candidates' cards, mumblety-peg, and the faithful hound blend into Bingham's painting of the Great American Voter exercising his sovereign rights—proudly avowing his choices in the open air, before the days of the secret ballot. Interest in the election of 1860 brought out a record vote.

PHOTO COURTESY CHICAGO HISTORICAL SOCIETY

"THE RAIL SPLITTER"
When the Republican national convention met at the Wigwam, Chicago, Abraham Lincoln was a "dark horse" candidate. Some shrewd maneuvers of his friends helped him to win the nomination. Fence rails were exhibited which Lincoln presumably had split in the prairie days when he was doing many odd jobs to make a living. In this unfriendly cartoon Lincoln is being "supported" by a Negro symbolizing the antislavery vote, and by Horace Greeley, editor of the *New York Tribune*. The Negro says, "Dis nigger strong and willin', but it's awful hard work to carry Old Massa Abe on nothing but this 'ere rail!" Lincoln isn't comfortable: "It is true I have split Rails, but I begin to feel as if *this* Rail would split me; it's the hardest stick I ever straddled." Greeley is the strategist: "We can prove that you have split rails, and that will ensure your election to the Presidency." The Rail proved an effective campaign symbol of Lincoln's closeness to the common man.

PHOTO COURTESY CHICAGO HISTORICAL SOCIETY

THE INAUGURAL PROCESSION, MARCH 4, 1861 The new president was well aware how ominous were the times: seven states had already seceded, and others were threatening disunion. Friends persuaded Lincoln to pass secretly through Baltimore to circumvent a plot for his assassination. Inauguration Day was sunny; and as he rode to the unfinished Capitol, Lincoln's heart was warmly conciliatory. He said to all sections: "We must not be enemies. Though passion may have strained, it must not break our bonds of affection." But a realistic contemporary observed: "The cement in the national house is beginning to crack."

"THE MAN OF DOOM" John Brown, who had seen his sons killed by proslavery ruffians in Kansas, startled a nation whose nerves were already overwrought, by a spectacular, foolhardy raid upon the government arsenal at Harpers Ferry, Virginia, in 1859. He had only eighteen followers, but his fanatical expectation was that the slaves would revolt and use the ammunition against their masters. The news spread consternation through the South; the "irrepressible conflict" had come at last! Brown was hanged for treason by the state of Virginia. His last written message was: "I, John Brown, am now quite certain that the crimes of this guilty land will never be purged away but with blood."

THE CABINET OF THE CONFEDERACY

"To us"—wrote Jefferson Davis, in behalf of his fellow slaveowners—"it became a necessity to transfer our domestic institutions from hostile to friendly hands, and we have acted accordingly." Disunion was, in March of 1861, not a threat but a fact. A constitution for the "Confederate States of America" was adopted; and Davis, a Mississippian and West Point graduate who had served his country distinctively in the Mexican War, was elected president. Alexander H. Stephens of Georgia was elected vice-president. Stephens declared: "The corner-stone of our new government rests upon the truth that Negro slavery is . . . a natural and normal condition." Davis assembled a cabinet in which mediocre and able men were strangely mixed. In this picture are, left to right: Stephen R. Mallory, Secretary of the Navy; Judah P. Benjamin, Attorney General (later to become Secretary of War and Secretary of State); L. P. Walker, Secretary of War; Davis; General Lee; John H. Reagan, Postmaster General; Charles G. Memminger, Secretary of the Treasury; and Robert Toombs, Secretary of State. Richmond was named the capital of the Confederate government.

PHOTO COURTESY CHICAGO HISTORICAL SOCIETY

LEE AND "TRAVELER"

Robert E. Lee of Virginia, colonel in the United States Army, faced a grave and difficult choice in the spring of 1861. He was not a slaveholder, did not believe in secession; but when Virginia joined the Confederacy, he decided that his first allegiance was due his state. Lee became commander of the Confederate "Army of Northern Virginia." Students of military history have called him the greatest American strategist. Lee never had a force comparable in numbers, artillery, or equipment to the opposing armies; yet his record of stubborn defense and substantial victories sustained the hopes of the Confederacy. His white horse "Traveler" became a symbol of the admiration Lee commanded.

PHOTO COURTESY CHICAGO HISTORICAL SOCIETY

THE BOMBARDMENT

THE FIRST SHOT IN REPLY

FORT SUMTER

Along the South Atlantic coast and the Gulf of Mexico, the national government had a chain of fortifications, to ensure the defense of important sounds and harbors. Unlike Buchanan, President Lincoln decided to defend the sovereign claim of the United States to these forts. Against Fort Pickens, off Pensacola, the first shots of the Civil War were fired by Florida troops on January 8, 1861. On a sand bar in the center of Charleston harbor was Fort Sumter, occupied by meager Federal forces under Major Robert Anderson. Their ammunition was unfused; many of the guns lacked carriages or recoils; the food stores were low. Should the government maintain its occupation of this "pillbox on a sandspit" as a symbol of the indissolubility of the Union? Lincoln decided yes; but that provisions only—no shells, no reinforcements—should be sent. The provisions never reached Fort Sumter. The Secretary of State of the Confederacy warned his colleagues: "The firing on that fort will inaugurate a civil war greater than any the world has ever seen." But at dawn, April 12, General Beauregard's South Carolina troops began the bombardment of the fort. Thirty-four hours later the little garrison surrendered. There was no choice. Lincoln received the news with: "I shall meet blow by blow." The president's arch opponent, Stephen A. Douglas, came to him with outstretched hands, "The Union," he said, "must be defended at all hazards. . . . There can be but two parties, the party of patriots and the party of traitors."

THE BATTLE OF BULL RUN

"On to Richmond!" thundered editors, ministers, and public speakers in the early summer of 1861. "Have we not two men to our enemy's one? What dullards and laggards our generals must be to delay for a day or an hour!" Everyone expected a short war. Lincoln's first call for volunteers asked enlistment for ninety days only. Public optimism overrode the sober judgment of Winfield Scott, venerable hero of the Mexican War and commander in chief of the Federal armies; and Irwin McDowell, field commander. Bull Run is a stream a few miles south of Alexandria, Virginia. Here, on July 21, two raw, confused armies blundered into battle. Young men who had volunteered almost as a lark suddenly met the zing of bullets and the iron of bayonets; the Federal regulars could not check the panic. While the dead were being counted, headlines awoke the North to the sober realization that the War would be tedious, bloody, costly. "One Southerner is worth five Yankees" was, for the moment, the exultant cry south of the Potomac.

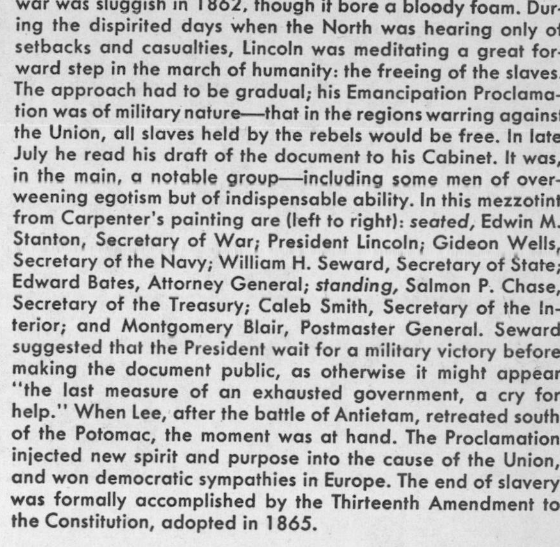

THE EMANCIPATION PROCLAMATION The tide of war was sluggish in 1862, though it bore a bloody foam. During the dispirited days when the North was hearing only of setbacks and casualties, Lincoln was meditating a great forward step in the march of humanity: the freeing of the slaves. The approach had to be gradual; his Emancipation Proclamation was of military nature—that in the regions warring against the Union, all slaves held by the rebels would be free. In late July he read his draft of the document to his Cabinet. It was, in the main, a notable group—including some men of overweening egotism but of indispensable ability. In this mezzotint from Carpenter's painting are (left to right): *seated,* Edwin M. Stanton, Secretary of War; President Lincoln; Gideon Wells, Secretary of the Navy; William H. Seward, Secretary of State; Edward Bates, Attorney General; *standing,* Salmon P. Chase, Secretary of the Treasury; Caleb Smith, Secretary of the Interior; and Montgomery Blair, Postmaster General. Seward suggested that the President wait for a military victory before making the document public, as otherwise it might appear "the last measure of an exhausted government, a cry for help." When Lee, after the battle of Antietam, retreated south of the Potomac, the moment was at hand. The Proclamation injected new spirit and purpose into the cause of the Union, and won democratic sympathies in Europe. The end of slavery was formally accomplished by the Thirteenth Amendment to the Constitution, adopted in 1865.

PHOTO COURTESY CHICAGO HISTORICAL SOCIETY

BARBARA FRITCHIE

The Confederates were on the march in the autumn of 1862; and "Stonewall" Jackson was in the vanguard as the Southern troops reached Frederick, Maryland. A valiant unionist of ninety-six summers, with a small American flag in her hand, defied the invaders:

"She leaned far out on the window-sill,
And shook it forth with a royal will"—

and Jackson, the gentleman, bade his men:

"'Who touches a hair of yon gray head
Dies like a dog! March on!' he said."

Whittier made a charming poem of the legend.

"HOME ON FURLOUGH"

McCLELLAN AT ANTIETAM In mid-September, 1862, Lee's army crossed the Potomac into Maryland and took stand for battle at a little creek called Antietam. General McClellan's Federal army had the advantage in position and numbers, and won a technical victory in an intense, day-long battle. However, overcautiousness, the dread incubus of the Union command, won in the night; and Lee's battered army, which might have been crushed, escaped—to prolong the war for more than two years. The North was hungry for victories; and the news of Antietam was welcome drink to parched hopes.

"MONITOR" AND "MERRIMAC"

The Federal navy, speedily rebuilt and expanded from a handful of obsolete vessels, had a tremendous duty to perform: the blockading of 3,000 miles of Southern coast line. It fulfilled the task with a surprising degree of success. A desperate innovation of the war was the protection of vessels with heavy iron casements. Such a Confederate vessel was the reconverted steam frigàte *Merrimac.* In March, 1862, she encountered a strange "cheese-box on a raft"—the *Monitor,* built by John Ericsson, noted engineer. Both ships suffered in an indecisive combat; the *Merrimac* so badly that, a few weeks later, she had to be blown up. The era of the wooden ship had come to a dramatic close; war and commerce alike now demanded new materials and new designs.

The greatest battle of the war was fought at Gettysburg, Pennsylvania, in the first three days of July, 1863. This was on Union soil; and it was meet that the Federal dead have their final resting place where they had fallen. The National Soldiers' Cemetery was created. On November 19, 1863, the sanctuary was dedicated. Edward Everett of Massachusetts, a distinguished scholar and orator, made the principal address—two hours of it, in the classic mold. Then a weary but inspired man, the President, spoke for two minutes. Those two minutes reverberate in the heart of humanity.

THE GETTYSBURG ADDRESS IN LINCOLN'S HANDWRITING

Four score and seven years ago our fathers brought forth upon this continent, a new nation, conceived in Liberty, and dedicated to the proposition that all men are created equal.

Now we are engaged in a great civil war, testing whether that nation, or any nation so conceived, and so dedicated, can long endure. We are met on a great battle-field of that war. We have come to dedicate a portion of that field, as a final resting place for those who here gave their lives, that that nation might live. It is altogether fitting and proper that we should do this.

But, in a larger sense, we can not dedicate— we can not consecrate— we can not hallow— this ground. The brave men, living and dead, who struggled here, have consecrated it, far above our poor power to add or detract. The world will little note, nor long remember, what we say here, but it can never forget what they did here. It is for us, the living, rather, to be dedicated here to the unfinished work which they who fought here, have, thus far, so nobly advanced. It is rather for us to be here dedicated to the great task remaining before us— that from these honored dead we take increased devotion to that cause for which they here gave the last full measure of devotion— that we here highly resolve that these dead shall not have died in vain— that this nation, under God, shall have a new birth of freedom— and that, government of the people, by the people, for the people, shall not perish from the earth.

"THE CAPTAIN WITH THE MIGHTY HEART"

"The most is due to the soldier who takes his life in his hands and goes to fight the battles of his country. In what is contributed to him when he passes to and fro, and in what is contributed to him when he is sick and wounded, in whatever shape it comes, whether from the fair and tender hand of woman, or from any other source, it is much. But there is still that which is of as much value to him in continual reminders that while he is absent he is yet remembered by the loved ones at home."

Abraham Lincoln, 1864

LINCOLN IN THE FIELD

Lincoln was truly Commander in Chief of the armed forces, exercising—when need was—powers much in excess of the Constitutional peacetime powers of the President. On the soil of battle he saw the dead in blue and gray, lying huddled and silent. He pardoned deserters. He talked to privates as an understanding friend. This photograph was taken by Matthew Brady, pioneer in his art, whose 3,500 photographs of Civil War battles, scenes, and men are a priceless record. With Lincoln are General McClernand, right, and Allan Pinkerton, left, who organized and directed the Secret Service of the war.

CEMETERY HILL

On the decisive third day of the battle of Gettysburg, the Confederate command of General Pickett made a valiant charge to take the highest slope of the rolling battleground. His 4,500 men advanced over half a mile against withering artillery and musket fire; scarcely a fourth returned. The ambitious Confederate invasion of the North was checked. Lee's army retreated, leaving—or carrying in field ambulances—20,000 casualties. The Federal loss was even greater.

CAPTURE OF NEW ORLEANS

Control of the Mississippi was necessary for Federal success in the West. As in the early days of the Republic when Spanish and French imperialism were feared, New Orleans was the key to the problem. Commander David Farragut was entrusted with the capture of the greatest seaport of the South. Two forts protected New Orleans; and athwart the river the Confederates stretched a barrier of cypress logs and heavy schooners. But Farragut's fleet of wooden vessels steamed up the river, bombarded the forts into silence, snapped the chains of the barrier boom, and beat off the Confederate fire-boats. "Don't flinch from that fire, boys!" shouted Farragut. "There is hotter fire than that for those who don't do their duty!" On April 26, 1862, the American flag again waved over New Orleans.

SHERIDAN'S RIDE

Phil Sheridan, impetuous young commander of cavalry, in 1864 was given orders to lay waste the fertile Valley of Virginia. Grant told him: "Take everything—horses, mules, cattle, food, and forage; and such as cannot be consumed, destroy. Make the Valley so that a crow flying over the country would need to carry his rations." And ruthlessly Sheridan razed the slopes of the Shenandoah. But Confederate troops came in strength, hammering Sheridan's army while the general was resting at Winchester, twenty miles from the field of battle. When the news was brought him, Sheridan rode to the scene at breakneck speed. Defeat was changed into decisive victory. The event was a remarkable exhibit of personal magnetism.

PHOTO COURTESY CHICAGO HISTORICAL SOCIETY

THE RAMPARTS OF VICKSBURG

While Union commanders in the Eastern field were making a dreary story of indecision, tragic losses, and forfeited opportunities, in the Mississippi Valley a strong man was forging stubbornly to public notice. Troops under Ulysses Simpson Grant were winning battles. Vicksburg, apparently impregnable on its steep escarpment above the river, had to be taken if Admiral Farragut's work at New Orleans was to be completed and the Mississippi be wholly under Federal control. In one of the boldest movements in modern warfare, Grant approached the Confederate citadel from its back door. Too strong to be taken by assault, Vicksburg was besieged. On July 4, 1863, the garrison surrendered; and the Confederacy was cleft in two.

PHOTO COURTESY CHICAGO HISTORICAL SOCIETY

GRANT IN THE FIELD

In the spring of 1864 Grant was called to the post of commander-in-chief. This photograph shows Grant flanked by General Rawlins *(left)* and Colonel Bowers *(right)*.

SHERMAN'S MARCH TO THE SEA

General William T. Sherman carried the Union banner in a series of brilliant successes; he marched into Atlanta on September 2, 1864. Of vivid and daring imagination, Sherman conceived the plan of marching across Georgia to Savannah, destroying the food supplies on which Lee's army largely depended. As his veterans marched, they cut a swath of devastation sixty miles wide; a holiday of destruction and pillage, designed not only to reduce Southern resources but also to break the will of the people to continue the struggle. Sherman had no illusions about the nature of war. Years later he addressed an audience: "There is many a boy here today who looks on war as all glory; but, boys, it is all hell. You can bear this warning voice to generations yet to come." Sherman's army reached the sea at Savannah on December 21, and turned northward, leaving "a track as bare and blackened as fire leaves on the prairies." Little was left of the dream of a Confederate States of America.

PHOTO COURTESY CHICAGO HISTORICAL SOCIETY

LEE'S SURRENDER

The day was Palm Sunday, April 9, 1865. At a farmhouse on the edge of Appomattox village, ninety-five miles west of Richmond, Lee and Grant met for the first time since they had fought side by side in the Mexican War. Jefferson Davis was a fugitive; Richmond was in Union hands. The Confederacy's Army of Northern Virginia was entrapped. Its troops had breakfasted that morning on parched corn, men and horses having the same food. "There is nothing left for me to do," Lee told his officers, "but to go and see General Grant, and I would rather die a thousand deaths." Grant's terms of surrender were generous. Union gunners made ready to fire a salute of national triumph, but Grant silenced them. He spoke: "The war is over; the rebels are our countrymen again."

Walt Whitman "saw as in noiseless dreams hundreds of battle-flags, Borne through the smoke of the battles and pierc'd with missiles . . . And at last but a few shreds left on the staffs, (and all in silence,) And the staffs all splinter'd and broken."

ALL PHOTOS COURTESY CHICAGO HISTORICAL SOCIETY

THE TOLL

In the course of the Civil War some 3,000,000 men, from North and South, were in war service—the young, the strong, the physically fit, carrying the heavy load and braving the blackness. "They were a host proven in valor and sacrifice," wrote Carl Sandburg. Killed in action or dead from wounds and disease were 620,000 Americans. Some—as the Confederate officer in the picture—were brought home. Others were buried in trenches with mass markers. The President wrote to a widow who had lost five sons: "I feel how weak and fruitless must be any word of mine which should attempt to beguile you from the grief of a loss so overwhelming. But I cannot refrain from tendering you the consolation that may be found in the thanks of the republic they died to save. I pray that our Heavenly Father may assuage the anguish of your bereavement, and leave you only the cherished memory of the loved and lost, and the solemn pride that must be yours to have laid so costly a sacrifice upon the altar of freedom. Yours very sincerely and respectfully, A. LINCOLN."

THE SCHEMER

John Wilkes Booth was a Shakespearean actor, of the declamatory, "scenery-chewing" type once much admired. Extravagant and headstrong in private life, he relished the role of conspirator, planning to wrest victory for his "South" by such a coup as the kidnaping and abduction of Lincoln and cabinet officers. The downfall of the Confederacy drove him to frenzied ingenuity: the plot to assassinate the President. Carl Sandburg wrote of him, "His own Southern heroes almost universally repudiated him as a madman or a snake, one who fought foul. And he was that . . . with a brain that was a haunted house of monsters of vanity, of vampires and bats of hallucination."

ASSASSINATION

The President dreamed (and he spoke of it at next day's cabinet meeting, Good Friday, April 14, 1865) of "a vague sense of floating—floating away on some vast and indistinct expanse, toward an unknown shore." The cabinet expressed sympathy with Lincoln's kindly feeling toward the vanquished South, and with his hearty desire to restore peace and safety everywhere. An amusing play, *Our American Cousin*, was to be presented at Ford's Opera House that evening. Lincoln was weary; but he had promised to attend. A young lady in the audience jotted a note: "The president is in yonder private box so handsomely decked with silken flags festooned over a picture of George Washington. How sociable it seems! . . . Everyone has been so jubilant for days that they laugh and shout at every clownish witticism." But shortly laughter was drenched in pandemonium. Booth's plans were at the instant of terrible maturity. He fired; leapt to the stage, shouting "The South is avenged!" and escaped. Lincoln lingered in dying, for a few unconscious hours. The nation was benumbed with grief. Secretary Stanton said, "Now he belongs to the ages."

THE DEATH OF LINCOLN

RECONSTRUCTION

Hearing the news of Lincoln's assassination, a Confederate leader exclaimed, "God help us! If that is true, it is the worst blow that has yet been struck the South." So it proved. Andrew Johnson, ill-fitted for the high office which Lincoln's death had thrust upon him, wished to carry out Lincoln's policy of leniency and conciliation. But he could not control Congress, dominated by a radical group who believed that ex-Confederates were incorrigible, that the South must be held under an iron yoke. For ten years their harsh doctrines prevailed. Carpetbaggers (Northerners who went south after the war for purposes of political profit), scalawags (Southern "poor whites" who joined in the plunder), and freedmen were supported in their control of the South by Federal troops. The first sketch shows the Southern "Colonel" being booted from the polls, disfranchised because of his Confederate service. In 1877 President Hayes withdrew the troops. The second sketch shows a carpetbagger, his opportunities for graft at an end, being kicked toward the first train north—with even the Negro jubilant.

A "NEW SOUTH"

The old plantation regime was gone forever, and the great estates of the Southland were broken up into small farms. The returning veterans turned courageously to the tasks of economic reconstruction. "Fields bloomed white with cotton bolls; houses, roads, and fences were repaired; the wandering Negro returned to his farm, a tenant now." By 1880 the cotton crop surpassed that of 1860. Increased attention was paid to other products, so that in time the total value of the minor crops outstripped that of cotton. But the chief distinction between the Old South and the New was the rise of industry and manufactures. Most notable was the growth of the textile industry, which in the Carolinas and Georgia took full advantage of proximity to raw material and water power, cheap labor and low taxes. "If we have lost the victory in the field of fight," declared a Carolina editor, "we can win it back in the workshop, in the factory, in an improved agriculture, in our mines and in our schoolhouses."

KU-KLUX KLAN

Most galling to Southern people was the active participation of Negroes in politics. Inexperienced Negro voters lent themselves to exploitation by unprincipled men; and state governments of the Reconstruction Era were characterized by extravagance and corruption. Clandestine societies using terroristic methods sprang up to combat these excesses. Most notorious was the "Invisible Empire of the South," commonly called the Ku-Klux Klan. Its members, clad in white robes and masks, rode through the countryside by night, burning crosses and trying to frighten the Negroes into relinquishing their right to vote. These secret societies, pledged to uphold "white supremacy," eventually became instruments of lawlessness and oppression. The government, in 1871, took measures to suppress the Ku-Klux Klan. The organization was subsequently revived and suppressed.

POLITICAL CIRCUS

The looting of Southern state treasuries under carpetbagger rule was matched in Northern and Western states. The wave of idealism had receded, leaving a backwash of cynical indifference to public or personal integrity. "Never before and only once since—after World War I—have public morals fallen to so low an ebb." Congressmen and even cabinet members were involved in scandals. In the cities the Boss and the Machine rose to positions of dominance. Contracts for public works, franchises for water, light, or street railways, even the licensing of a lowly pushcart peddler, offered opportunities for graft. Most notorious, but by no means unique, was the "Tweed Ring" in New York City, whose members grabbed $70,000,000 from the city treasury and gained another $100,000,000 in bribes. This powerful drawing by Thomas Nast, famous cartoonist of *Harper's Weekly*, who led the fight which ultimately broke up the Ring, shows the Tammany Tiger (symbol of the Democratic organization in New York) clawing the corpses of decent institutions while Nero ("Boss Tweed") and his henchmen relish the spectacle. Yet political corruption was only symptomatic of corruption in the business world. Like Alice in Wonderland when she ate the second cake, the nation was growing too fast.

TRANSCONTINENTAL RAILROADS

Transcontinental **"THE MARRIAGE OF THE RAILS"** railroads were advocated by farseeing men as early as the 1830's; Asa Whitney devoted his lifetime to agitating for a Pacific railway. Competing routes were advanced and surveyed; but the issue was deadlocked by sectional jealousy and party politics until the Civil War. President Lincoln signed the first Pacific Act on July 1, 1862. The Union Pacific was to build westward from Council Bluffs until it met the Central Pacific, authorized to build from Sacramento across the Sierras. The government promised liberal aid in land grants and loans. Even a New England Senator declared, "What are $75,000,000 or $100,000,000 in opening a railroad across the central region of this continent,that shall connect the people of the Atlantic and Pacific, and bind us together? As for the lands, we don't begrudge them." So was launched a magnificent epic of enterprise, of the progress of the rails, high above the waters of the American River in the Sierras; across the wide forks of the Platte and down the western slopes of the Wasatch Mountains, into the valley of the Latter-Day Saints. The month of April, 1869, witnessed the fastest track-laying in the history of railroading, as the Irish workmen of the Union Pacific approached within sight of the Chinese crews of the Central. On May 10 two special trains met ceremonially at Promontory Point, a few miles west of Ogden; they carried the directors and eminent guests, quantities of champagne, and the joyous congratulations of the nation. The "Last Tie" was of highly polished hardwood and bore a silver plate; the "Last Spike" was cast from twenty-dollar gold pieces and capped with a silver nugget; the ceremonial hammer was a silver mallet. "Magnetic bells" in the telegraph offices throughout the country rang as the operator at Promontory Point closed the circuit, announcing the moment when the continent was spanned with iron.

A CONVERSATION
May 10, 1869

What was it the Engines said,
Pilots touching—head to head,
Facing on the single track,
Half a world behind each back?

Said the Engine from the EAST:
"Those who work best talk the least . . .
Let these folks with champagne stuffing,
Not their Engines, do the *puffing.*
Listen! Where Atlantic beats
Shores of snow and summer heats;
Where the Indian autumn skies
Paint the woods with wampum dyes—
I have chased the flying sun,
Seeing all he looked upon,
Blessing all that he has blessed,
Nursing in my iron breast
All his vivifying heat,
All his clouds about my crest,
And before my flying feet
Every shadow must retreat."

Said the WESTERN Engine, "Phew!"
And a long, low whistle blew . . .
"You brag of your East! You do?
Why, *I* bring the East to *you!*
All the Orient, all Cathay,
Find through me the shortest way;
And the sun you follow here
Rises in my hemisphere . . .

"Yet today we shall not quarrel,
Just to show these folks this moral,
How two Engines—in their vision—
Once have met without collision."

That is what the Engines said,
Unreported and unread;
Spoken slightly through the nose,
With a whistle at the close.

BRET HARTE

LUNCH STOP!

JOSEPH BOGGS BEALE COLLECTION, MODERN GALLERIES, PHILA.

"HEAD O' TRACK," NORTHERN PACIFIC To link the navigation of the Great Lakes with the commerce of the Pacific, the Northern Pacific Railroad was chartered in 1864—its beginning to be at Duluth, on the tip of Lake Superior; and its western terminus at Tacoma, a site hewed from a forest of fir trees beside Puget Sound. Construction began in 1870; the road reached an Oregon connection in 1883, and was completed to Seattle four years later. Liberal government grants encouraged two other transcontinental lines—the Southern Pacific and the Santa Fe; the Great Northern was built entirely by private capital. The promotional story of these roads is one of "frenzied finance," stock manipulations, and battles for control between various groups of Wall Street "Titans." More important is the social story: the peopling of the West, the wide interchange of the products of nature and of skill.

SNOWBOUND IN THE SIERRAS

CHICAGO UNION STATION IN THE 1870's

THE WILD WEST

COURTESY ANHEUSER-BUSCH INC., ST. LOUIS, MO.

CUSTER'S LAST FIGHT Gold was discovered in the Black Hills of Dakota in 1874—on lands "permanently" reserved for the Sioux. But gold hunters rushed to the diggings. Not only were their treaty rights flouted; the Sioux, because of graft and negligence by the Indian agents, faced actual starvation for the winter of 1875-76. They left the reservation for a buffalo hunt; as they were joined by lawless braves from other tribes, a serious revolt seemed in the making. General George Custer with about 650 cavalrymen discovered the Indians encamped on the Little Big Horn River, June 25, and ordered a direct attack. It proved suicidal: an overwhelming force of Indians annihilated the army, perhaps because a major in charge of reinforcements "lost his head utterly at the critical moment." But Sitting Bull's Sioux could not maintain resistance. The march of the pioneers won, as always; Deadwood, in the heart of the hills, became the most exciting and picturesque town of the mining frontier.

SHOOTING BUFFALO FOR SPORT

The building of the Kansas Pacific and the Santa Fe into the Great Plains opened a new field for thrill seekers who didn't want danger: hunting the buffalo, associated with everything wild and daring, on a comfortable railway excursion. A Kansas Pacific handbill of 1868 advertised:

> "Buffaloes are so numerous along the road that they are shot from the cars nearly every day. All passengers can have refreshments on the cars at reasonable rates."

Professional hunters ruthlessly pursued the bison for their hides and furs, leaving the flesh to rot on the plains. In after years homesteaders picked up the whitened bones and sold them by the ton to button and fertilizer factories. The uncounted hordes of buffalo were reduced almost to extinction before the National Bison Society persuaded the government to set aside a protected range in Montana.

PHOTO COURTESY NEWBERRY LIBRARY

LAST CHANCE GULCH (HELENA, MONTANA)

California was the breeding ground of prospectors. Thence they wandered with their blankets and burros, their grubstakes and pans, over the trailless West; their seasoned eyes examined every odd-appearing boulder, and tried to trace every fragment of "float rock" back to the mother ledge. Across the Cascades into the inland country of the Far Northwest, and northward into British Columbia, the prospectors were the vanguard in new areas for exploitation and settlement. News of rich findings drew miners from Nevada and Colorado into Idaho and Montana. Alder Gulch, in western Montana, produced $30,000,000 in gold in three years; its main camp, Virginia City, had a population of 7,000 in 1864. Now Alder Gulch is a succession of "ghost towns." Last Chance Gulch, discovered in 1864, had its boom years and vigilance committees; rechristened Helena and made the capital of Montana, it passed its lusty ways along to the "copper town" of Butte.

COURTESY NORTHERN PACIFIC RAILWAYS

"FAMOUS AND FEARLESS"

In the center of this group, all dressed up for a studio photographer in 1873, is Buffalo Bill (William F. Cody) — sometime stage driver, Pony Express rider, army scout, and buffalo hunter for railway construction camps. By his remarkable exploits with the rifle in the latter occupation, he earned the nickname which shines in American legend. To the right is Texas Jack, a celebrated scout. The silken hair and flowing moustache belong to Wild Bill Hickok, quick-shooting marshal of several of the roughest frontier towns, noted marksman of a hundred lurid adventures. The three were united in a play, *The Scout of the Plains,* by Ned Buntline, author of many dime novels of Western locale. Buffalo Bill was the adventurous hero; the role of Texas Jack and Wild Bill was to jump on the stage just in time to rescue Cody from the burning stake and shout, "Now come on, you Redskins!" The poor Indians died several times each performance.

"THE DEADWOOD COACH"

First and most renowned of the Wild West shows—"an original American entertainment featuring exhibitions typical of the life of a cowboy, Indian, and soldier"—was Buffalo Bill's, a favorite of youths for many years. Buffalo Bill shot glass balls; trained horses were put through circusy routines; Annie Oakley, "Little Sure Shot," demonstrated marksmanship unexcelled in her sex; the "World's Rough Riders" galloped and bucked about the arena; Pawnee Bill brought his tamed buffalo for a mimic hunt, and in one season Sitting Bull stalked and scowled at the paleface customers. For the climax of this sensational bargain the Deadwood Coach, with a beautiful lady among its passengers, was attacked by Indians—then, Buffalo Bill to the rescue!

THE CATTLE COUNTRY

A TRAIL HERD

From Texas, realm of unfenced ranch life since Spanish times, the cattle industry expanded over open ranges as far north as Montana and Saskatchewan. The building of railroads into Kansas and Nebraska, and the discovery that lean Texas longhorn cattle became fat on the long grasses of the Great Plains, led to the beginning (in 1867) of the great cattle-drives in the glamorous era of the Cowboy. But however romantic Western movies and "pulp" fiction may be, life on the cattle trails contained much that was hard and tedious. In taking the herds for drives of seventy days or perhaps four months, there were swollen streams to cross; wild runs of cattle that had to be checked by few men, on tired mounts galloping perhaps in the dark; and much wearisome work. A driver's journal reads: "Worked all day in the River trying to make the Beeves swim and did not get one over. Had to go back to Prairie Sick and discouraged. Have *not* got the *Blues* but am in *Hel of a Fix*."

"PAINTING THE TOWN RED"

There were long, dusty weeks on the cattle trail, when black coffee and tepid water were the only drinks, and the one suggestion of woman was perhaps a treasured tintype carried behind the Bull Durham sack in the cowboy's shirt pocket. When the drive was over and wages were paid, human nature suggested some "whoopin' an' hollerin'." Whiskey straight, three-card monte, and some "tinsel and tawdry glitter" were the simple but exuberant attractions of the towns where the cattle-drive met the railroad. Ellsworth, Newton, Wichita, Dodge City, and Ogallala were among the wild and wooly cow-towns that became sedate agricultural centers in later years.

SHIPPING CATTLE TO EUROPE

Improved refrigeration methods and the growth of great slaughtering and meat-packing centers in the Middle West gradually wrought the extinction of the cattle boat, on which many a youngster worked his passage to Europe amid the aromas and mooings of the beeves.

"A DASH FOR TIMBER"

Indian dangers helped to make the Texas cowboy light-sleeping, quick-fingered, always wary. A Comanche raid somewhere on the Texas frontier could be anticipated each full moon; and Indians might attack a party of cowboys on the open range, with or without hope of plunder. "A snoring man was an abomination in the cow camp," related a cattleman; "if we cared for the life of such a man, we almost felt we had to guard him while he slept." For the first few years after the Civil War, Indian forays and ambushes were a menace to trail-driving. Sometimes the aggression was on the cowboys' part; to many of them the only good Indian was a dead Indian. With the slaughter of the buffalo herds, "Lo, the poor Indian!" became poor indeed; when he approached a trail herd, he was most likely to beg for an old steer and a little flour.

FROM ORIGINAL PAINTING BY FREDERICK REMINGTON, WASHINGTON UNIVERSITY COLLECTION; PHOTO COURTESY CITY ART MUSEUM, ST. LOUIS

A HOMESTEADER'S CABIN

Invading the open range, claiming tracts stubbornly athwart the cattle trails and fencing off water rights, came the "fool hoe-men," as cowboys called farmers. The land laws were on the side of the homesteader who could live on 160 acres, against the cattleman who needed unlimited space. A trail boss complained in 1884, "Now there is so much land taken up and fenced in that the trail for most of the way is little better than a crooked lane, and we have hard lines finding enough range to feed on. These fellows—the 'bone and sinew,' as politicians call them—have made farms, enclosed pastures, and fenced in water-holes till you can't rest; and I say, damn such bone and sinew!" As the fences spread and the free grass vanished, the lusty days ot the Cattle Kingdom drew to a close.

PHOTO COURTESY NEBRASKA STATE HISTORICAL SOCIETY

FARM AND HOME

FREE LAND

"Vote yourself a farm!" was a political slogan from the 1840's. The rich soil and grassy swells of the public domain seemed rightly to belong to the people. In 1862 Lincoln signed a Homestead Law, granting 160 acres of public land to anyone agreeing to cultivate it for five years. The basic features of the law are in force today, although the good lands have long since been claimed.

FROM ORIGINAL PAINTING BY JOHN STEUART CURRY; PHOTO COURTESY GENERAL LAND OFFICE, DEPT. OF THE INTERIOR

GRANGE MEETING IN A SCHOOLHOUSE

"To enhance the comforts and attractions of our homes" was a major purpose of the Patrons of Husbandry, a society for farmers and their wives. Each local unit was called a "Grange"; in 1875 there were 20,000 of them. The lodge, with its monthly meetings and picnics, lectures and entertainments, offered an escape from the loneliness and drudgery of the farm; and womenfolk especially were grateful for its social life. But farmers' thoughts were becoming grim. Droughts, insect pests, and plant diseases were bad enough; but worse was the fact that even a bumper crop brought the farmer little or no money. Interest rates were exorbitant; high tariffs protected the manufacturers; railroads and grain elevators were prospering with their arbitrary rates; retailers, wholesalers, and speculators in produce took their fat percentages—and the farmer, his pockets turned inside out, felt: "I pay for all!" The Grange turned from social to political and economic purposes, and became a force to be reckoned with. Agrarian discontent gave rise to a series of "third parties."

FARGO, NORTH DAKOTA, 1881

The unbroken, limitless land of the Great Plains drew pioneers from far and near. A typical pamphlet to attract emigrants proclaimed, on its title-page, North Dakota as "The Land of Golden Grain . . . The Lake-Gemmed, Breeze-Swept Empire of the New Northwest . . . Homes for the Homeless." When Hamlin Garland went to stake out a claim in Dakota, he found "trains swarming with immigrants from every country of the world haltingly creeping out upon the level lands. Norwegians, Swedes, Danes, Scotchmen, Englishmen, and Russians all mingled in this flood of land-seekers rolling toward the sundown plain. The street swarmed with boomers. All talk was of lots, of land." Speculators sought to assist destiny by making township plats with schools, churches, mills, department stores, all neatly located—dreams that sometimes came true.

A SOD HOUSE

Some homesteaders who came to the treeless plains of Kansas, Nebraska, and Dakota had money to buy, at the nearest railroad station, lumber for house-building. Poorer men built sod houses. The sward turned up by the breaking plow was matted and massed; out of this material, with no other tool than a spade, many a pioneer built his home. The wagon in this photograph has a load of sod blocks for repairing the roof. PHOTO COURTESY NEBRASKA STATE HISTORICAL SOCIETY

EMIGRANTS LANDING AT NEW YORK

After the Civil War, the stream of immigration from the Old World into the New swelled into a torrent. The traditional American policy (despite occasional "Nativist" agitations) was that of unrestricted admission to all who sought these shores. A popular ballad beckoned the poor of Europe:

> "Come along, come along, make no delay,
> Come from every nation, come from every way;
> Our lands are broad enough, don't be alarmed,
> For Uncle Sam is rich enough to give us all a farm."

And, although many immigrants clustered in cities and worked in industrial and unskilled trades, many accepted the all-too-rosy invitation to take up Western farmlands. Railroads, with millions of acres of Government-granted lands to dispose of, engaged in large-scale colonizing activities. Peoples from many lands were gathered into the great adventure of building a more democratic society; and most of them helped to build such a life for themselves and their children.

THE UNINVITED

THE CHICAGO FIRE

Sprawling Chicago had a population of 300,000 by 1871. Wooden houses, barns, and sidewalks . . . and so little provision for fire that even the roof of the water-pumping station was wooden! The summer and early autumn of 1871 were mercilessly hot and dry; the wind blew not off the Lake but from the burnt prairie. Perhaps, that evening of October 9, Mrs. O'Leary's cow kicked the kerosene lantern into the hay; perhaps a tramp fell asleep while his pipe was lit. The blaze began in a poor neighborhood, among shanties packed together like matchsticks; but soon the fire was no respecter of riches, and needed no bridges to cross the river. In the twenty-five hours of the red sky over Chicago an area of nearly four square miles was burned, including the business center of the city; 17,000 buildings were destroyed, and 100,000 people were homeless. The direct property loss was over $200,000,000; the loss of human lives, more than 300. But Chicago, like the fabled phoenix, rose brilliantly from its ashes.

THE ICEBOUND "JEANNETTE"

On to the North Pole! Lieutenant De Long was a good seaman and scientific officer; his vessel, the *Jeannette*, was a staunch old gunboat, double-timbered to buffet the Arctic seas; his crew was sturdy and loyal. With a crew of 33 officers and men, the *Jeannette* left San Francisco on July 8, 1879. But Bering Strait was scarcely passed when, on September 5, the vessel was caught in an ice pack. The Arctic drift carried the *Jeannette* far into the Siberian sea. On June 12, 1881, the ice floe parted, only to close again and crush the ship. The one hope for the men was to push southward by sledge and boat to the nearest Russian village. But all save two of the entire command succumbed to starvation and exposure. (The North Pole was ultimately discovered in 1909 by Robert Peary.)

THE ASSASSINATION OF GARFIELD

An erratic lawyer named Guiteau vainly importuned President James A. Garfield for a consular appointment. On July 2, 1881, as the President was passing through Pennsylvania Station in Washington, with Secretary of State Blaine as his only companion, Guiteau shot him down. The tragedy emphasized the disgracefully large part that the scramble for patronage had come to play in the political scene.

JOSEPH BOGGS BEALE COLLECTION. MODERN GALLERIES, PHILA.

THE HAYMARKET RIOT

What, an eight-hour day for laborers? Absurd! Conservative opinion was firm in 1886. Those who struck for shorter hours must be anarchists! In protest against the shooting of several workmen in a conflict between strikers and police, radical leaders called a mass meeting at Haymarket Square, Chicago, May 4. As a speaker raised his fist in an emphatic gesture, someone threw a bomb among the police; seven were killed, many injured. Was the raised fist a signal, part of a deadly plot? Public fears made an impartial investigation impossible. Eight alleged anarchists were sentenced to death; four were hanged. Governor Altgeld of Illinois pardoned the surviving prisoners, risking his political career to proclaim the trial unfair.

PHOTO COURTESY CHICAGO HISTORICAL SOCIETY

THE JOHNSTOWN FLOOD

High above the valley flats of Johnstown, Pennsylvania, was the Conemaugh Reservoir; its waters, held by an eighty-foot dam, were the private preserve of a group of Pittsburgh sportsmen. The rains came; the earthen walls of the dam yielded, May 31, 1889, inundating the Conemaugh Valley with a ruthless torrent of destruction. Fire and darkness added to the melee. Of Johnstown's 6,000 residents, 2,500 lives were lost; property losses totaled over $10,000,000. Generous aid poured in from all parts of the country. But why such a shoddy dam, without masonry, should have been permitted, was never investigated.

THE RISE OF SPORTS

The work-day was being shortened; a half holiday on Saturday became common. From the rush and whirl of city life, people turned to sports for re-invigoration. All classes took part in the new play life of the nation. The British ambassador said of Americans, "They make amusement into a business!"

CHAMPIONSHIP GAME AT ELYSIAN FIELDS, HOBOKEN

From "barn ball" and "one-old-cat," immemorial diversions of American lads, developed the sport which became the national game. Abner Doubleday suggested the diamond-shaped field and drew up rules in 1839; the swanky Knickerbocker Baseball Club of New York adopted the game as a pastime for the elite; soldiers of the Civil War played it in the intervals between campaigns. The Cincinnati Red Stockings, in 1869, became the first professional team. The first "world series" was played in 1884. Baseball became a favorite of paying spectators, while it was cherished by boys who asked only a baseball, a bat, and a vacant lot.

A "TEN-STRIKE" AT BOWLING

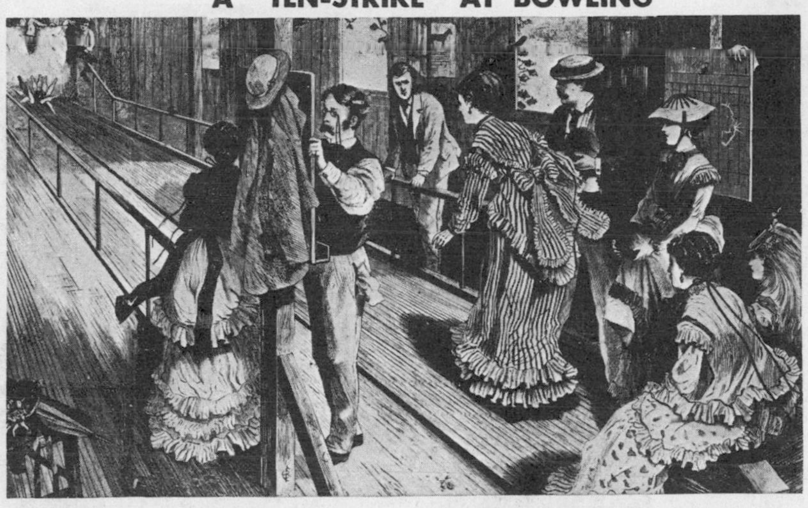

LADIES' DOUBLE-SCULL RACE

The first intercollegiate boat race was a Yale-Harvard contest in 1852. Professional scullers made amazing records in the 1870's; but rowing was essentially an amateur sport, and the gentle strokes of the fair sex added charm, if not skill, to rowing club regattas.

PRE-GIBSON GIRL IN TROUSERETTES

No sport attracted so many participants as did bicycling. The introduction in the 1880's of the "safety" bicycle, with wheels of equal height, and the replacement of solid rubber tires by pneumatic ones, produced a veritable craze. By 1893 a million bicycles were pedaling a merry course of healthful relaxation. The sport had a salutary effect in simplifying women's costume; and bicycle clubs were pioneers in the crusade for improved highways.

CENTRAL PARK IN WINTER

To rural pond, or New York's Central Park Lake—as the subsiding thermometer covered the water with a coat of firm crystal—came the crowd whose common bond was the glistening steel runner of the ice-skate. Spirits were filliped, the zest of life quickened, in the frosty air.

LAWN TENNIS

American tourists who found a new, attractive game in England brought racquets, nets, and balls in their return luggage; and introduced "lawn tennis" at Nahant, Newport, and other fashionable resorts. The staccato rhythm of swift service and return became a part of the American sports symphony. Ladies were not long content to remain on the sidelines. For obvious reasons, they preferred to play mixed doubles.

THE CHANGING SCENE

THE CHICAGO WORLD'S FAIR, 1893

The nation's progress in manufacturing since the Civil War (said an official report in 1902) was "probably the most rapid change in the methods of industry observable at any time in history." The nation's pride in its new accomplishments in many fields found expression in two great expositions. The first, held at Philadelphia in 1876, the centennial year of America's independence, boasted its "Machinery Hall," where entranced visitors could see a thousand articles manufactured before their very eyes. In 1890 Congress authorized the celebration of "the Four Hundredth Anniversary of the Discovery of America by Christopher Columbus, by holding an International Exhibition of Arts, Industries, Manufactures, and the Products of the soil, mines, and sea." The World's Columbian Exposition opened in Chicago in 1893, its 150 buildings arranged over 666 acres in Jackson Park. The principal halls were palaces of neoclassic architecture—the "White City." The many amusement features of the "Midway Plaisance" made the Fair a happy blend of fun with education.

PHOTO COURTESY CHICAGO HISTORICAL SOCIETY

HONOLULU RECEIVES THE NEWS OF ANNEXATION

Not grass skirts and yellow moons, but sandalwood and sugar cane, attracted American attention to Hawaii. Much capital was invested in developing the Sandwich Islands—investments endangered by political disturbances. The United States was interested also in the strategic value of Honolulu, queen of the Pacific, as a naval station, a halfway point between California and Asia. On July 7, 1898, Hawaii was annexed by joint resolution. (Japan protested the annexation.) The United States in the 1880's and 1890's asserted sovereignty over more than fifty other islands in the Pacific. "Manifest Destiny" was no longer bound by the continental shores.

"COXEY'S ARMY"

The Panic of 1893 brought widespread unemployment and distress. An Ohio reformer, Jacob S. Coxey, planned to arouse public and Congressional interest in relief measures by a "living petition"—a march of the unemployed to Washington. Coxey's parade reached Washington on May 1, 1894; but when he attempted to speak from the Capitol steps, Coxey was arrested. He protested bitterly: "Up these steps the lobbyists of trusts and corporations have passed unchallenged on their way to committee-rooms to which we, the representatives of the toiling wealth-producers, have been denied."

ALASKA Alaska was purchased by the United States from Russia in 1867, for $7,200,000. What was there save Esquimaux and reindeer, barren land under a glacial shield? The Secretary of State was derided for his extravagance, the purchase nicknamed "Seward's Folly." But in 1896 gold was discovered on the Klondike River. In 1897-99 more than 100,000 persons departed from Pacific ports for the new land of treasure. Against the winds of Chilkoot Pass (the scene of this picture) and White Pass, came miners. The region was made a Territory in 1912 and was voted statehood in 1958.

"LAND RUSH" The frontier was vanishing; its blended traditions of individualism and democracy were molded into the American character, but the horizonless vista of free lands and equal opportunity was broken and narrowed. A choice patch of land remained, which Westerners viewed hungrily—Oklahoma. The government tried, until 1889, to save Oklahoma for the Indians. When the legal barriers were raised, on April 22, thousands of homeseekers were at the borders. At high noon a trumpet blared; the restraining cordon of soldiers stepped aside, and thousands of people—afoot, on horseback, in carriages and buckboards—raced for their chosen sites. Oklahoma became a state in 1907. When Arizona and New Mexico were admitted in 1912, the states of the Union numbered forty-eight.

PHOTO COURTESY U. S. GENERAL LAND OFFICE, FROM PAINTING BY JOHN STEUART CURRY

THE GREAT EAST RIVER BRIDGE

Brooklyn Bridge, the first built between New York and Brooklyn, was opened in 1883. Thirteen years in construction, this majestic structure, over a mile in length, was the largest in the world.

COURTESY TRANSPORTATION LIBRARY, UNIVERSITY OF MICH.

CULVER PHOTO

"PROGRESS OF THE CENTURY"

This Currier & Ives print, a favorite wall decoration of proud Americans, was made in 1876. Had it been engraved a year later, the gentleman's office might have contained Alexander Graham Bell's epochal invention, the telephone — first put into practical use between Boston and Salem in 1877. In two more years, Thomas A. Edison further revolutionized the national scene by inventing the incandescent lamp. Some light on the role of invention is shown by Patent Office figures: About 62,000 patents were granted in the entire period before 1865; the number granted in the remainder of the century was nearly 640,000. Edison himself took out about 800 patents before 1900; he was hailed as the "Wizard" of electricity, the miracle man of practical invention. Edison is shown below, dictating his morning's correspondence into the invention he named the "phonograph."

BY PERMISSION CHARLES SCRIBNER'S SONS

"WHAT WE ARE COMING TO"!

A comic-weekly artist of 1895, inspired by the development of the skyscraper, has sketched a nightmarish version of the super-building of the future. Hydraulic and electric elevators were one factor—steel girder frames were another—in winging offices and apartments toward the skies. The City now had its focus, the cluster of towering business structures. A poet wrote: "All cities are mad; but the madness is gallant. All cities are beautiful; but the beauty is grim."

SPANISH-AMERICAN WAR

Newspaper headlines in the nineteenth century were usually small and conservative; but on February 16, 1898, they shouted boldly:

THE SINKING OF THE MAINE

2 OFFICERS, 251 MEN

APPALLING DEATH TOLL

CAUSE OF THE DISASTER A MYSTERY

—and a mystery the explosion of the *Maine*, a U. S. warship in Havana harbor, remains to this day. But this catastrophe, with a loss of 260 American lives, was the spark that ignited national resentment against the Spanish oppression of Cuba. War was declared on April 25.

PHOTO COURTESY CHICAGO HISTORICAL SOCIETY

BATTLE OF SAN JUAN The American army of regulars and volunteers sent to capture Cuba was a rough-and-tumble group who had to contend against—besides the Spanish foe—malaria, yellow fever, "embalmed beef" and shoddy clothing provided by unscrupulous contractors, inadequate communications, and the interference of political busybodies; but in actual combat they fought nobly. Theodore Roosevelt, lieutenant colonel of the Rough Riders, was a conspicuous, gallant leader. The annihilation of Admiral Cervera's Spanish fleet off Santiago on July 3, 1898, hastened the end of a one-sided war.

PHOTO JOSEPH BOGGS BEALE, MODERN ENTERPRISES, PHILADELPHIA

BATTLE IN THE JUNGLE American control of the Philippines was not easily established when the Spanish yoke was unleashed. Adherents of an independent Filipino republic resorted to a barbaric guerilla warfare, and were met in kind.

PHOTO JOSEPH BOGGS BEALE, MODERN ENTERPRISES, PHILADELPHIA

INVASION OF PUERTO RICO As almost an anticlimax to the conquest of Cuba, General Nelson A. Miles with but 3,000 troops landed on the southern coast of Puerto Rico and advanced over nearly impassable pathways of mud, water, and tangled undergrowth against the retiring Spaniards. The people of the island welcomed the coming of the Americans. Puerto Rico became a United States dependency.

BATTLE OF MANILA BAY On a Saturday afternoon when the Secretary of War was absent from his post, his energetic young Assistant Secretary — Theodore Roosevelt — cabled Commodore George Dewey, commander of the U. S. Asiatic Squadron: "Proceed at once to Philippine Islands. Commence operations at once against the Spanish fleet." Dewey asked himself: what would Farragut, his old admiral, do? *Attack*. His victory at Manila Bay was complete; in one day's action (May 1, 1898) all the Spanish ships were sunk or destroyed, and the shore batteries silenced. In taking the Philippines, the United States embarked upon a course of unforeseen responsibilities and consequences.

ASSASSINATION OF McKINLEY President William McKinley, who had reluctantly yielded to the clamor for war against Spain, believed ardently that the common good was derived from business prosperity, and furthered high protective tariffs with other conservative measures. His successful campaign slogan in the re-election campaign of 1900 was "A full dinner pail." But on September 6, 1901, at the Pan-American Exposition at Buffalo, McKinley was shot and mortally wounded by a crazed anarchist. He was the third President to die by an assassin's bullet. Theodore Roosevelt, who had been "sidetracked" into the vice-presidency as a political maneuver because of his liberal ardor, thus became President, and guided the nation into the expanding horizons of the Twentieth Century.

PHOTO BY BROWN BROTHERS

SAN FRANCISCO EARTHQUAKE On April 18, 1906, the rockbed underlying 450 miles of the California coastland was violently shaken. In this, the most serious disaster of its kind that has occurred in the United States, masonry crumbled and water mains were broken; San Francisco was the scene of an uncontrollable conflagration. The whole nation contributed to its rebuilding.

PHOTO BY BROWN BROTHERS

"FREE SILVER" Grover Cleveland, a sturdily independent President, wanted the American monetary system to remain anchored to the gold standard. But with the Panic of 1893, the country was gripped in the vise of deflation. From the mining states, with silver seeking a wider market, and from agricultural states where creditors seemed like a cloud of locusts to the harassed farmer, came demands for a more liberal economic structure. William J. Bryan, "the silver-tongued orator of the Platte," became their spokesman, but he was thrice defeated for the Presidency. To conservatives it seemed that Bryan and other liberals were traveling headlong into a financial abyss.

"EXCUSE MY DUST!" Jokes about the "horseless carriage" were current almost as soon as the internal-combustion gasoline engine as a propulsive agent became practicable. Horses shied at the phenomenon, and passers-by stared; as one awed Chinese said, "No pushee, no pullee; but go like hellee allee samee." The social changes in the wake of the first uncertainly chugging automobile were momentous.

PHOTO JOSEPH BOGGS BEALE, MODERN ENTERPRISES, PHILADELPHIA

PUSHCART ROW "The Shame of the Cities" was a theme of writers in the 1900's. Public conscience was awakened to the social waste of crowded and unkempt slums.

PHOTO COURTESY NEWBERRY LIBRARY, CHICAGO

KITTY HAWK

Flight in heavier-than-air machines was an aspiration of mankind that may be traced even to Greek mythology. Numberless inventors had vainly preceded two bicycle mechanics of Dayton, Ohio—Orville and Wilbur Wright—whose plane was first to make a sustained and free flight. The place was a sand beach near the fishing village of Kitty Hawk, N. C.; the day, Dec. 17, 1903; the power, a four-cylinder gasoline engine with a maximum of twelve horsepower! The trial flight covered 852 feet, taking 59 seconds. Power and the machine extended their dominion into the skies.

INTERNATIONAL NEWS PHOTO

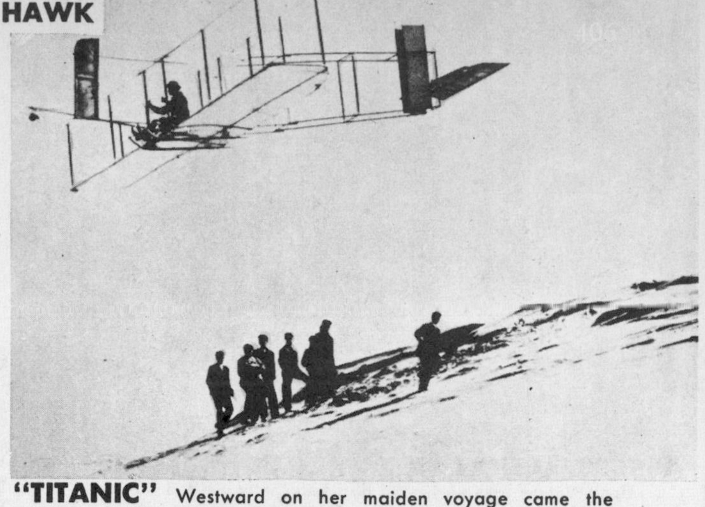

THE "TITANIC"

Westward on her maiden voyage came the proud White Star luxury liner, the *Titanic*, the largest ship then built—and supposedly unsinkable. Off Newfoundland, at about midnight of April 14, 1912, the vessel struck an iceberg; 1,517 persons, many of them Americans, were lost.

ACME PHOTO FROM PAINTING BY WILLY STOEWER

THE MOTOR CAR

The Ford Motor Company started business in 1903 with a capital of $28,000. (In this picture Henry Ford is at the "wheel" of an early model.) The automobile industry was emerging from the experimental 1890's into a period of intense activity and popular enthusiasm. As manufacturers standardized parts and perfected assembly-line techniques, prices were slashed and the installment plan of car purchasing was introduced. The automobile became part of the normal equipment of American life.

BROWN BROS. PHOTO

PHOTO BROWN BROTHERS

FRANCISCO VILLA

Depredations against American life and property on both sides of the border by insurgent "Villistas" prompted President Wilson to order a punitive expedition, in 1916. General Pershing's force advanced 400 miles into Mexico, but failed to capture the redoubtable bandit.

THE PANAMA CANAL

The United States had long been interested in an interoceanic canal across the Isthmus of Panama, or through the lakes of Nicaragua—for military emergency as well as to facilitate commerce between its far-flung coasts. In 1903 the newly created Republic of Panama accepted $250,000 in cash and $250,000 annually in return for the Canal Zone, ten miles wide. Construction began in 1906; the canal was completed in 1914, at a total cost of $350,000,000. Extremely difficult problems of engineering and sanitation were surmounted; "it is" said James Bryce, "the greatest liberty man has ever taken with nature!"

THE "EASTLAND" DISASTER

On the morning of July 24, 1915, employes of a Chicago industrial plant poured across the gangplank to the decks of the excursion steamer *Eastland*. It was a jolly, jostling crowd, about to take its annual all-day picnic. Suddenly the boat listed from its moorings; rolled and rocked; and capsized. Within five minutes, in the Chicago River at the center of the city, 812 persons died.

WORLD WAR I

SINKING OF THE "LUSITANIA" Deep-lying forces had divided the nations of Europe into two armed camps, when on June 28, 1914, a political assassination in a little Balkan country changed the continent into the most destructive battleground mankind had yet known. Could the United States best aid in achieving a lasting peace for all nations by staying out of the war, or by co-operation with the Allies? As it turned out, Germany's policy of unrestricted submarine warfare left America small choice. On May 7, 1915, the British liner *Lusitania,* sailing from New York, was torpedoed without warning. Nearly 1,200 lives were lost, including 124 Americans.

ACME PHOTO

By spring, 1917, **PRESIDENT WILSON'S WAR MESSAGE** it was evident that the government's valiant efforts to preserve both neutrality and our national honor were foredoomed. Wilson addressed Congress on April 2: "We shall fight for the things which we have always carried nearest our hearts, for democracy, for the right of those who submit to authority to have a voice in their own Governments, for a universal dominion of right." Four days later Congress overwhelmingly voted a declaration of war against Germany—a "war to end wars."

ACME PHOTO

THE A. E. F. ARRIVES
General John J. Pershing, selected to command the American Expeditionary Forces, reached France in June, 1917. (In this photograph Pershing and his staff are being greeted by Marshal Foch.) Soon came divisions of the U. S. Army, for hasty training on French soil with the assistance of veteran allied officers. Their presence had bracing psychological effects on the weary British and French, in the months before troops were arriving in hosts. Before the armistice was signed, nearly 2,100,000 U. S. troops were overseas.

PRESS ASSOCIATION PHOTO

Convinced against his idealistic will, as the thunders of war echoed from Europe, President Wilson in 1916 advocated a program of preparedness. Congress authorized a great increase in the regular army, with the introduction of military instruction in schools and colleges. Posters and speakers urged enlistments. But when the United States entered the war, conscription was necessary. "There is a universal obligation to serve," said the President.

PAUL'S PHOTOS, CHICAGO

WOMEN IN WHITE Alert in peacetime to soften the disastrous effects of earthquake, fire, and flood, in the war emergency the Red Cross attained new heights of service. It trained great numbers of nurses and directed their work abroad; organized base hospitals, recruited ambulance companies, and at home undertook social programs in and about the training camps. To the Red Cross the American people contributed, in twenty-one months, $400,000,000—"by far the largest voluntary gifts of money, of hand and heart, ever contributed purely for the relief of human suffering." Scarcely less important was the work of other volunteer agencies.

COURTESY TYLER COLLECTION, TEMPLE UNIVERSITY

CONVOY! The U. S. Navy had a twofold task: to help cripple German sea power, and to convoy troops and supplies across 3,000 miles of ocean. These tasks, with British co-operation, were performed vigorously. During the war months the number of vessels in commission increased from less than 200 to more than 2,000. Over 7,000,000 tons of supplies—everything from sewing kits to locomotives—were transported for the A. E. F.

LIBERTY LOANS

Publicity campaigns such as America had never seen maintained the people's ardent willingness to contribute the huge sums necessary for the war. Five bond issues—four Liberty Loans and a fifth, floated after the armistice, the Victory Loan—secured $20,500,000,000, about the cost of the United States' war establishment. The sum represented an expenditure of more than $1,000,000 an hour on the war. In addition, government loans to the Allies represented almost $500,000 an hour, nearly all in the form of credit for purchase of foodstuffs and supplies in the United States.

PHOTO COURTESY TYLER COLLECTION, TEMPLE UNIVERSITY

MARCHING TO THE FRONT

The Central Powers under General von Ludendorff launched a smashing offensive in the spring of 1918. Germany transferred her finest troops to the Western front, marshaling all her resources in a desperate bid for victory before the American army could be assembled. But United States troops were rushed to critical points, and won their honors in furious fighting at Aisne, Cantigny, Belleau Wood, Montlevon, and other memorable battlefields.

BROWN BROS. PHOTO

"CALAMITY JANE"

This U. S. mortar, aptly named after a cigar-smoking lady of the Dakota frontier famed alike for profanity and marksmanship, fired the last shot on the Western European front, at 10:59:59 a.m., November 11, 1918. The armistice had begun. The issues of world security were removed from the theater of war to conference chambers and hotel rooms.

PAUL'S PHOTOS, CHICAGO

MOVING UP

The Allied counteroffensive which began in July, 1918, regained burnt-over ground lost in the early months of the war and speeded the destruction of German morale. St. Mihiel, the Meuse-Argonne, and Sedan were salients of American advance.

U. S. SIGNAL CORPS PHOTO

PEACE!

Thanks to the error of a news service, the American people enjoyed two "armistices"—November 8 and, correctly, 11. Delight, frenzied and solemn, was more than ample for two days' celebration. This view is of a New York street.

ACME PHOTO

AMERICAN OUTPOST IN RUSSIA

After the armistice, several thousand U. S. troops remained in Europe as part of the Allied Army of Occupation, which crossed the Rhine for police duties in Germany. Other detachments joined an Allied expedition to aid anticommunist movements in Russia, and fought a few minor engagements in the near-Arctic wastes. They were withdrawn in 1920.

PAUL'S PHOTOS, CHICAGO

THE NINETEENTH AMENDMENT

Women played their full part as civilian reinforcements of the war effort; and thousands saw service abroad, as army nurses and ambulance drivers, as canteen workers and entertainers. The old arguments about the "frailty" and domestic sphere of the sex were discredited. Militant suffragists paraded to rally public opinion. The "Susan B. Anthony" amendment was passed by Congress in 1919, and ratified by the states in time for women to vote in the national election of 1920.

HISTORICAL PICTURES SERVICE, CHICAGO

FIRST ACROSS THE OCEAN

As the motorcar, adapted into an armored tank, became an engine of warfare, so did World War I introduce the airplane to the destructive purposes in which it was to become terribly effective. Improved construction of planes increased fuel carrying capacity; as the radius of flight widened, the conquest of the Atlantic became a fascinating probability. Three seaplanes designed by Glenn Curtiss and built by the U. S. Navy (hence called "NC" boats) started across the Atlantic from Newfoundland in May, 1919. Two were forced down by fog; but the other, the NC-4, making scheduled stops at the Azores and at Lisbon, reached England to complete the first transatlantic flight. Later in 1919 two Englishmen, Alcock and Brown, flying from Newfoundland to Ireland, made the first nonstop journey.

PRESS ASSOCIATION PHOTO

"SPIRIT OF ST. LOUIS"

A New York merchant, Raymond Orteig, offered a $25,000 prize for the first nonstop flight from New York to Paris. Three attempts at the prize had ended in disaster, and a fourth entry was dawdling on a New York runway when, on the morning of May 20, 1927, Charles A. Lindbergh took wing for Le Bourget, airport of the French capital. Lindbergh was then an air-mail pilot, with a reserve captain's commission in the army air corps. He had been toughened in the art of flying by experience as a "barnstormer," one who did hair-raising stunts to attract crowds to circuses or real-estate promotions. His epochal venture was financed by St. Louis businessmen, for whom Lindbergh named his new monoplane *Spirit of St. Louis*. "I'll carry extra gasoline instead of another man," he said; and made the first one-man crossing of the Atlantic by air, in 33½ hours nonstop flying time. America was hungry for a hero in the summer of 1927; and it greeted Lindbergh with a flush of enthusiasm it has shown for few men. The influence of aviation was marked; and "people began to talk about traveling by air as if they had always been accustomed to it as a means of getting around."

INTERNATIONAL NEWSREEL PHOTO

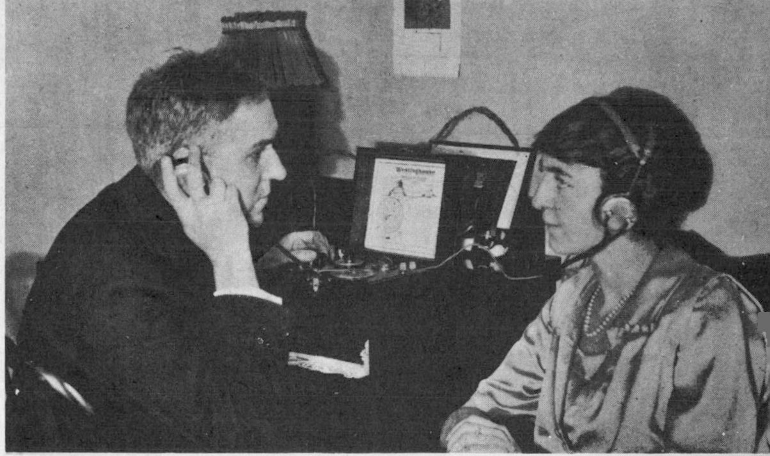

THE RADIO

"Harding wins!" The voice came mysteriously through the air, on the very night of the election—from KDKA, Pittsburgh, November 2, 1920, in the first regularly scheduled broadcast. Perhaps one hundred people possessed receiving sets then. From maritime, commercial, and military use, radio was amplifying its scope to bring the public entertainment, adventure, and instruction. Its growth was phenomenal: from crystal receivers to regenerative sets to superheterodynes to neutrodynes; from earphones to loudspeakers of progressive efficiency; from the concern of amateur experimentalists into a huge business. The air was so cluttered in 1927 that the Federal Radio Commission was created to assume control. The potential listening audience in 1928 was 35,000,000; in 1944, about 90,000,000.

BROWN BROS. PHOTO

FAREWELL! AND HAIL! Another social experiment of the 1920's—the "noble experiment," as President Hoover called prohibition—was not successful. The Eighteenth Amendment was highly controversial in its effects, and after thirteen years of attempted enforcement was canceled by the Twenty-first Amendment. In this photograph a New York *bon vivant* is awaiting, by special wire, the flash of the instant of repeal.

ACME PHOTO

DOWN—AND UP

So, in its characteristic slang, **"WALL STREET LAYS AN EGG!"** a theatrical weekly headlined the sudden crash of financial values on October 29, 1929. (This photograph is of Wall Street, New York, on that day.) The nation had been basking in the illusion of eternal opulence; the awakening was as if a realistic Joshua had snapped his fingers and shut off the sun. Inflated credits, fat dividends, high prices, good wages —where were they? with forfeited installment furniture, unredeemed pledges, unclaimed jewelry, lapsed memberships in the country club and the fraternal order, the wilted gardenia, and the foreclosed home! "Prosperity is just around the corner," was the desperate thesis of the President; and millions of federal dollars were poured into corporations that were already discharging employes and slashing wages to weather the storm. But in Pittsburgh men fought for sleeping space under the bridgeheads; in New York the Battery was a sunless if sunny park for thousands who had nowhere else to go; in Chicago men beat away pigeons to get the peanuts scattered on the sidewalk. There were many improvised villages squatting near city dumps. A surprising number of hotel guests fell from upper windows. An ironical little book with grisly illustrations, *Thirty-One Ways to Commit Suicide,* was a best seller. What had happened to the American Dream?

INTERNATIONAL NEWS PHOTO

SOCIAL UNREST

Workers with shrinking pay envelopes—or without work to do—became group-conscious. A sprinkling of avowedly Communist agitators was pepper in the pot. Among other demonstrations were two "Hunger Marches" to Washington, and a wave of strikes. In midsummer of 1932 twenty thousand needy war veterans gathered in Washington to urge cash payment of their service certificates; they were dispersed by army tanks and gas bombs.

ACME PHOTO

"THE CHIEF"

Conservatives in politics were strangely insensitive to the rumblings of the common people as the election of 1932 drew near. President Hoover, renominated, declared, "The grass will grow in the streets of a hundred cities, a thousand towns," if his opponent were elected. That opponent was Franklin D. Roosevelt, charging that big business interests had been favored as against the "forgotten man," and promising to inaugurate a "new deal." Roosevelt carried the country in a landslide. To millions of Americans the most important event of the decade was his inauguration on March 4, 1933. Chief Justice Charles E. Hughes administered the oath. Then began an era of far-reaching social and economic change.

ACME PHOTO

MEN IN THE MAKING

Boxcars are not ideal homes for youth. Young men and girls roaming the country in a vain search for employment were likely recruits for crime. As one helpful measure, the Civilian Conservation Corps was instituted. Young men between 17 and 28 voluntarily enrolled; the greater part of their pay went to their dependent families. "Given opportunities of schooling in their moments of leisure," as Dr. Schlesinger relates, "they carried on an extensive work of protecting the nation's natural resources—draining marshlands, building bridges and erosion dams, planting trees, fighting forest fires, and combating the ravages of insects and plant diseases." The National Youth Administration enabled moneyless students to complete their college courses.

ACME PHOTO

TO THOSE WHO HAVEN'T President Roosevelt proclaimed it a national responsibility to see that no one starved; and children were not forgotten. Surplus farm produce was distributed to provide healthier diets for millions of low-income families. Free school lunches were prepared for three million youngsters. Children who came to school breakfastless eagerly awaited the noon hour. States co-operated to furnish milk at a penny—or nothing—a bottle.

U. S. D. A. PHOTO BY KILLIAN

"DUST BOWL" Heat seethed over the Great Plains in the mid-1930's. Potatoes were shriveled nubbins in the baked ground. Corn was hardly knee-high when the blades browned. And over the flatlands a southeast wind carried blanketing waves of grit, dust, and poverty. The wagon is buried, the farm deserted, the trees whipped of their leaves. John Steinbeck wrote an attention-compelling novel, *The Grapes of Wrath,* about the "Okies" driven from the Dust Bowl to seek a fugitive living in California.

INTERNATIONAL NEWS PHOTO

No meteorologist can predict the orbit of a tropical storm on the **HURRICANE** rampage. The whirling cones of destruction, born usually in the Caribbean in late summer, most commonly strike somewhere on the Gulf Coast or dissipate their evil energies at sea. But in September, 1938, a vagrant storm reached New England, killed five hundred people, uprooted trees a century old, and left a wide swath of havoc. This view is of the waterfront at New London, Connecticut.

INTERNATIONAL NEWS PHOTO

DEATH OF A DIRIGIBLE

The German zeppelin *Hindenburg,* about to complete its twelfth westward voyage across the Atlantic, nosed gently against the mooring mast at Lakehurst, New Jersey, on the rainy evening of May 6, 1937. In an instant the airship was a blazing inferno. Thirty-six of the 97 passengers and crew were cremated in the seething wreckage.

INTERNATIONAL NEWS PHOTO

Foremost in **FARTHEST SOUTH** exploring the frozen world of the South Pole, past the periphery of the seals and penguins into regions where the crunch of a man's snowshoe was—save for the tumble of an avalanche — the first sound ever made, was Richard E. Byrd, American naval commander. Byrd flew over the South Pole (discovered by Amundsen in 1911) on November 29, 1929. He led three expeditions into the Antarctic. This view is of a warm afternoon in "Little America," main base of Byrd's expedition of 1933. (The warmth is inside!)

OFFICIAL PHOTO U. S. ANTARCTIC SERVICE

A "MAIN STREET" IN 1937 Rampages of the Mississippi and its tributaries — with highest water in 1927, 1936, and 1937—emphasized the failure of engineers and of dollars to cope with the most unpredictable of nature's forces: water. Down the deforested banks of the upper streams, rain and melted snow rushed too freely for the security of townsfolk along the rivers. Protection against flood was a national problem.

Congress authorized, in 1928, the Boulder Can- **MAN-MADE NIAGARA** yon project for thrusting a dam across the Colorado River at the Arizona-Nevada border—to insure flood control, provide water for irrigation, and furnish electric power to the Southwestern States. In 1936 an electrical impulse released by President Roosevelt sent 3,600,000 cubic feet of water a minute tumbling through gigantic Boulder Dam. Even more ambitious constructions followed—the great Bonneville and Grand Coulee dams, on the Columbia River, to provide irrigation and electric power in the Far Northwest.

ACME PHOTO

PREPARE!

"THE BIG FOUR"

Allied military successes were not the only reason that caused Germany to sue for peace in 1918. Another was President Wilson's "Fourteen Points" for a peace program, including moderation in dealing with the vanquished nations. Wilson spoke of "the voices of humanity that are in the air. They insist that the war shall not end in vindictive action of any kind; that no nation or people shall be robbed or punished because the irresponsible rulers of a single country have themselves done deep and irreparable wrongs." The Peace Conference at Versailles, January–May, 1919, was dominated by four statesmen: *(left to right)* Orlando, Lloyd George, Clemenceau, and Wilson — representing Italy, England, France, and the United States. But the completed treaty was vindictive rather than constructive. It bred discords and animosities. A desperate Germany turned for leadership to a hysterical little mongrel; Hitler's craft directed the building of another war machine, and his insane egotism became the national malady. On September 1, 1939, World War II began as German bombing planes sowed death over Poland. What price victory in 1919? And what, again, would be the role of the United States?

BROWN BROS. PHOTO

COURTESY PRESS ASSOCIATION, INC.

LAUNCHING THE "WASHINGTON"

President Roosevelt early recognized that Nazi ambitions were not restricted to Europe, but extended to world domination. Congress and the nation, however, were reluctant to acknowledge the danger, although a poll of public opinion showed that seventy per cent of the people favored supporting Britain and France by every means "short of war." A program of armed preparedness was accepted. Congress voted the largest peacetime naval appropriations in our history. In May, 1940, the 35,000-ton U.S.S. *Washington* slid majestically down the ways of the Philadelphia Navy Yard. It was America's first new battleship in nineteen years.

ENGINES OF PEACE AND WAR

Congress in 1940 appropriated $18,000,000,000 for rearmament. Substantial orders from the Allies for weapons, airplanes, and other manufactures also put new stresses upon American industry, and hastened the retooling of factories for military purposes. Industrial leaders hoped to maintain civilian production too. This picture suggests the transitional phases of 1940-41: farm tractors are on the shipping lines to the left, and Diesel-motored armored tanks on the flatcars and platforms to the right.

PHOTO COURTESY INTERNATIONAL HARVESTER CO.

SELECTIVE SERVICE

Congress enacted, in September, 1940, our first conscription measure in time of peace. It provided for registration of all men between 21 and 36, and for selecting annually by lot 900,000 of these young men for a year's military training. Their area of service was to be limited to the Western Hemisphere or United States possessions elsewhere. On registration day, October 16, about 16,500,000 men presented themselves. Their great number, and the prevailing sense of suspense as to their future, made the occasion memorable. On October 29, as President Roosevelt looked on, Secretary of War Stimson drew the first capsule of the draft lottery—Number 158.

ACME PHOTO

CO-OPERATION

"Somewhere at sea" in August, 1941, President Roosevelt and Prime Minister Churchill met in an epochal series of conferences. (Also in the picture are, standing, *left to right:* Harry Hopkins, Roosevelt's close friend and advisor; W. Averill Harriman, Lend-Lease co-ordinator in London; Admiral King, commander of the U.S. Atlantic Fleet; General Marshall, U.S. Army chief of staff; General Dill, chief of the British Imperial Staff; Admiral Stark and Admiral Pound, chiefs of U.S. and British naval operations.) The two leaders discussed the problems of the nations fighting aggression, and issued an "Atlantic Charter" of general principles for reconstructing the world after the final destruction of the Nazi menace.

ACME PHOTO

WORLD WAR II

AMERICAN TROOPS "DOWN UNDER"

The spectacular Japanese success had swept over the Indo-China peninsula, from Singapore over the East Indies, to islands of the South Pacific, and was threatening Australia. Then General Douglas MacArthur, having escaped from doomed Bataan at the order of his Commander-in-Chief, reached Melbourne and was named supreme commander of Allied forces in the Southwest Pacific. Convoy ships came, bearing thousands of American soldiers and tons of war materials.

ACME PHOTO

THE U.S.S. "WEST VIRGINIA," PEARL HARBOR

While Japanese diplomats were blandly talking to the Secretary of State in Washington, Japan launched a sudden and treacherous attack on American military bases in the Philippines and Hawaii. The nation was just beginning, that winter, to marshal its resources against possible danger, meanwhile lending half an ear to a loud minority of isolationists proclaiming that no danger existed. But in the dawn of Sunday morning, December 7, 1941, the Japanese bomber and torpedo planes caught the army and navy "off the alert," wreaking such damage that for months full details of the catastrophe were withheld. In one savage moment the United States had been jolted into the conflict.

ACME PHOTO

DECLARATION OF WAR

Japan declared war on the United States on December 7; next day President Roosevelt read a war message to Congress: "Hostilities exist. There is no blinking at the fact that our people, our territory, and our interests are in grave danger. With confidence in our armed forces—with the unbounding determination of our people—we will gain the inevitable triumph—so help us God." On December 11 Germany and Italy joined their Axis partner by declaring war against the United States. Roosevelt said: "The long-known and the long-expected has thus taken place. The forces endeavoring to enslave the entire world are now moving toward this hemisphere." Central and South American countries swelled the total of the United Nations.

PRESS ASSOCIATION PHOTO

INTRODUCING THE RATION BOOK

Most of the "home folks" cheerfully accepted, as an unavoidable inconvenience of the global war, restrictions on their purchases of gasoline, shoes, and foods suitable for shipment overseas. Rationing programs began in the summer of 1942. Tires, typewriters, and certain other items were made available for civilian use only when "priority" claims were justified.

ACME PHOTO

A BEACHHEAD IN THE SOLOMONS

Vigorous counterattacks by Allied troops in the summer of 1942 halted the rush of the "brown devils" toward Australia; dramatic successes at sea and in the air marked the turning point of the war of the Pacific, as the Japanese invaders were gradually forced on the defensive. In the picture of a war which strangely combined the newest in mechanical weapons and the highest in individual courage, jeeps and barges lined the sandy beach of Guadalcanal as U. S. Marines effected a landing.

ACME PHOTO

CONQUEST: NORTH AFRICA

Casablanca, an old Portuguese fishing village, was just a dot on the map of Morocco until November, 1942; its French officials were timid folk, not knowing where their best interests might lie. The Allies settled that, with a vast armada pouring men and supplies into North Africa. The Battle of the Desert was desperate for many months; but in May, 1943, the Allies, with air supremacy won at last, seized the two principal Tunisian cities, Tunis and Bizerte. The Axis dream of African empire was at an abrupt end; and the Allies had secure bases for the next step in their global strategy, the invasion of continental Europe from the Mediterranean—into the domain of the drooping peacock, Mussolini.

ACME PHOTO

PHOTO BRITISH COMBINE, LTD.

ALONG THE BURMA ROAD

The Burma Road, only highway connecting Free China with the southern seas, was improved and traffic speeded by American engineers. Relief trucks are seen here after unloading American materials for Chinese troops, at a way station along "China's lifeline." The arrival in China during 1941 of an increasing flow of American planes, with American instructors to train Chinese pilots, was another contribution to a courageous people. But this aid was necessarily little. America was vigilantly watching the Germans—almost forgetting the Japanese. The day of stunning surprise was at hand.

FRANCE RECLAIMED

D-day, D-hour—when? The Nazi hierarchy, the Nazi radio, guessed frantically at the place and the timing of the long-awaited Allied invasion of western Europe. The grim, decisive moment came in the wee small hours of June 6, 1944. The place was the Normandy peninsula; the route circled Cherbourg, important port on the Channel. Pouring from their landing craft, American troops closed in; Cherbourg, within a few days—after desperate slugging matches between eager doughboys and Nazis who were under orders to stand and fight or be shot—was in Allied hands. Through the deep-water dock facilities of Cherbourg poured supplies, men and more men; ahead, southward and eastward, arrows of destiny pointed the course of victory.

U. S. SIGNAL CORPS PHOTO, FROM ACME

THE BANNER AT IWO JIMA

With the Navy and Marines spearheading valiant counterthrusts to recover the vast Pacific territory seized by Japan in the first six months of the war, progress was sure but costly. Tarawa, Okinawa, Saipan, were won at great price. But in the wake of a decisive naval victory General MacArthur's army entered flaming, razed Manila. The island footsteps to Japan itself were within reach. Tiny Iwo Jima was striped with enemy airstrips that were strategically essential. For this volcanic cinder Marines slogged forward over the bodies of other Marines. The flag was raised with infinite pride and infinite sadness.

ACME PHOTO

THE GIANTS

Pipe, cigarette, and cigar *(left to right)*: they met, Stalin, Roosevelt, and Churchill, in far-off Teheran, late in 1943. They were the three men in whose hands the freedom of the world was cupped. With them were the ranking military strategists of three nations. In this history-making meeting, there was no time for enunciation of grand principles; the occasion called for deliberate, bedrock plans for destruction of the enemies of civilization. The world wondered what happened at Teheran, for words from the three leaders were scant. As history unfolded in 1944, it knew: *planned action!*

11TH AIR FORCE PHOTO, FROM ACME

THE NEW "BIG THREE"

Death came to "the Chief"; and as the cortege passed, oldsters wept beside teen-agers who had known no President but Roosevelt. At Potsdam in August, a new "Big Three" met: an energetic President out of the Middle West, Harry S. Truman; Clement R. Attlee, new Labor Party Prime Minister of Great Britain; and the indefatigable Stalin. The Potsdam Declaration of 1945 summarized the agreements of the "Big Three" on Allied policy in conquered Germany. Zones of occupation wiped out German central government, but Germany was to have been treated as a single economic unit although divided into military sections. However, as the zonal governments became actualities, it was found that Soviet Russia made no effort to live up to its promises at the conference. INTERNATIONAL NEWS PHOTO

JAPANESE SURRENDER The ceremony on the U.S.S. *Missouri* on September 3, 1945, brought to an end Japan's dream of world domination. The Emperor, regarded by the Japanese as a god, stepped into the role of a private citizen. Executive power in Japan was vested in General MacArthur, Supreme Commander of the Allied Powers. Under his guidance, the Japanese took their first steps on the path to democratic government. OFFICIAL PHOTO U.S. NAVY

WAR CRIMES TRIALS

War trials as a permanent record of atrocities and war guilt were conducted in the Far East as well as in Europe for both civilians and military personnel under the jurisdiction of the United Nations War Crimes Commission. The United States and its allies held over 2,000 trials in Europe and Asia from 1945 to 1948. ACME

UNITED NATIONS ASSEMBLY

The U.S., as a leader in the formation of the United Nations in 1945, became a prime mover in the effort to establish world peace and extend democratic methods. The nation which after World War I had found many reasons to vote against membership in the League of Nations now accepted world leadership in a plan for co-operative security. OFFICIAL PHOTO UNITED NATIONS

THE MARSHALL PLAN TO AID EUROPE

The Economic Co-operation Administration (ECA) was created by Congress in 1948. Called the Marshall Plan because it was first proposed by Secretary of State George C. Marshall in 1947, it aided foreign recovery through the granting of loans, equipment, and food to European and Asiatic countries. Its purpose was to stabilize the economic, social, and political structure of the world so that a democratic rehabilitation could occur that would prevent the spread of communism. Its aims were vital to the U.S. ACME

ISRAEL IS RECOGNIZED The Republic of Israel, formed in 1948, fulfilled the Jewish dream of a homeland. Immediate recognition was extended to the new nation; Dr. Chaim Weizman, its first head, was greeted by President Truman. INTERNATIONAL NEWS PHOTO

THE PROBLEM OF ATOMIC POWER

The atomic bomb, which hastened the surrender of the Japanese, was demonstrated at Bikini in July, 1946, by the United States, sole possessor of this powerful weapon. The frightful effects of this man-made explosion and continued experiments with the atom raised new questions about the control of atomic power—its extent, its nature, its effects, and its possible future significance in peace and war. Its discovery led to the invention of the hydrogen bomb, a weapon 1,000 times more powerful. JOINT ARMY—NAVY TASK FORCE ONE PHOTO

MIDCENTURY

KOREAN CONFLICT

In a surprise attack launched on June 25, 1950, North Korean armed forces invaded South Korea in an effort to unify Korea by force. The United States and other non-Communist countries went immediately to South Korea's aid, and they remained in the country three years, until a truce was effected. However, the truce did not bring lasting peace. Years later skirmishes were still occurring along the 38th parallel.

UPI

PUERTO RICO

After over 400 years of foreign rule, the island of Puerto Rico was granted the right to elect hei own government, and in 1952 she became the first overseas commonwealth of the United States. Voting home rule on March 3, Puerto Ricans ratified their new constitution. The United States could not repeal the island's laws nor appoint the island's auditors and Supreme Court justices. Luis Muñoz-Marín was elected governor of the new commonwealth, which was to be autonomous but associated with the United States. Puerto Ricans celebrated their Constitution Day on July 25, 1952, the 54th anniversary of the landing of United States troops on the island.

WIDE WORLD

HYDROGEN BOMB

On Nov. 16, 1952, the U.S. Atomic Energy Commission announced the successful testing of its first hydrogen bomb. The test island near Eniwetok was destroyed

USAF PHOTO

UNITED STATES AIR FORCE

At the time of World War I the United States so underestimated the importance of airpower that the country ranked 14th in air strength among the powers of the world. However, by midcentury that situation had changed, and the United States had become a leader in commercial, civil, and military aviation. Jet airliners were widely used in scheduled airline transportation; private planes were bought by individuals for business and for pleasure. The nation's X-15 rocket plane was flown at 4,105 miles per hour to break world speed records for manned winged aircraft. In recognition of the importance of airpower, the United States established near Colorado Springs, Colo., its Air Force Academy, the newest of the nation's service academies. It offers a bachelor of science degree and a second lieutenant's commission in the Regular Air Force.

USAF PHOTO

SCHOOL DESEGREGATION

A most important domestic problem confronting the United States after the midcentury was the elimination of discrimination against U.S. Negroes. This problem became a major issue in 1954 when the U.S. Supreme Court unanimously ruled segregation of public schools unconstitutional. Militant Negroes and whites then launched a many-pronged attack on discrimination in all its forms. Their goal was equal opportunity for all in employment, voting, housing, education, and public accommodations; they staged boycotts, rent strikes, sit-ins, and freedom marches to achieve that end. Their efforts were intense (on Aug. 28, 1963, some 200,000 staged a march on Washington), but change came slowly; near the end of the decade after the Supreme Court decision only about 8 percent of the Negro pupils in the South were in desegregated schools. However, change did come, as the story of Little Rock proves: When Negro students entered Central High School in 1957, they were accompanied by U.S. soldiers (left); in 1960, they entered the school freely.

UPI

WIDE WORLD

ATOMIC SUBMARINE

The launching of the world's first atomic-powered submarine by the U.S. Navy on Jan. 21, 1954, was a milestone in the harnessing of nuclear energy for military and industrial uses. In 1958 and 1959 the nuclear submarines *Nautilus* and *Skate* became the first ships to make underwater crossings of the North Pole. In the Atlantic Ocean in 1960 the first Polaris ballistic missile launched from a submerged submarine hit its target 1,200 miles away.

OFFICIAL U.S. NAVY PHOTO

TRANSOCEANIC TELEPHONE

One-way transoceanic telephone service was made possible in 1955 with the laying of the first of a pair of underwater cables from England to the United States and Canada. The vessel (left) used in the operation was specially fitted to handle up to 1,800 nautical miles of deep-sea cable. In 1957 the first transpacific cable was laid from California to Hawaii; it was the world's longest underwater cable, extending 2,400 miles. In 1959 a second pair of transatlantic cables was laid, this time between Newfoundland and France.

A. T. & T.

FIFTY STATES

After earlier bills providing for statehood had been defeated, Alaska and Hawaii joined the Union in 1959. Alaska achieved statehood on January 3; Hawaii, on August 21. With their joining they became the 49th and 50th states of the United States, and the United States thus embraced the last of its territories. Two new stars were added to the U.S. flag, which had not been redesigned since Arizona became the 48th state in 1912.

SUMMIT CONFERENCE

In July, 1955 Premier Bulganin of the U.S.S.R., President Eisenhower of the U.S., Premier Faure of France, and Prime Minister Eden of the U.K. met at Geneva, Switzerland in an effort to lessen the tensions of the Cold War. But the meeting's friendly spirit was short lived.

UPI

WIEN ALASKA AIRLINES PHOTO

CANADIAN RELATIONS

In 1961 the United States and Canada completed at Clear, Alaska, the second station of their Ballistic Missile Early Warning System (BMEWS) for their common defense. In 1963, however, relations between the two countries became strained when Canada resented the U.S. mandate that Canada accept nuclear warheads. The dispute led to the fall of the conservative Diefenbaker government and to the election of Liberal party leader Lester Pearson. Prime Minister Pearson maintained that Canada was morally bound to accept the nuclear warheads, and he agreed to receive them for missiles already installed.

RCA ELECTRONIC AGE

SATELLITES

Earth satellites launched by the United States and by the U.S.S.R. proved valuable in gathering scientific data, in relaying transatlantic telephone conversations, in aiding in weather forecasting, and in the intercontinental transmission of news copy. On Aug. 12, 1960, the U.S. launched Echo 1, the world's first communications satellite. President Eisenhower listened to a recording of his voice that was bounced off the satellite.

UPI

MISSILES To protect itself against enemy attack, the United States employs a variety of ballistic missiles operative on land, at sea, and in the air. The first successful test firing of the U.S. Atlas intercontinental ballistic missile (range, 6,000 miles) was made on Dec. 17, 1957. Since that time ICBM's with greater ranges have been developed.

USAF PHOTO

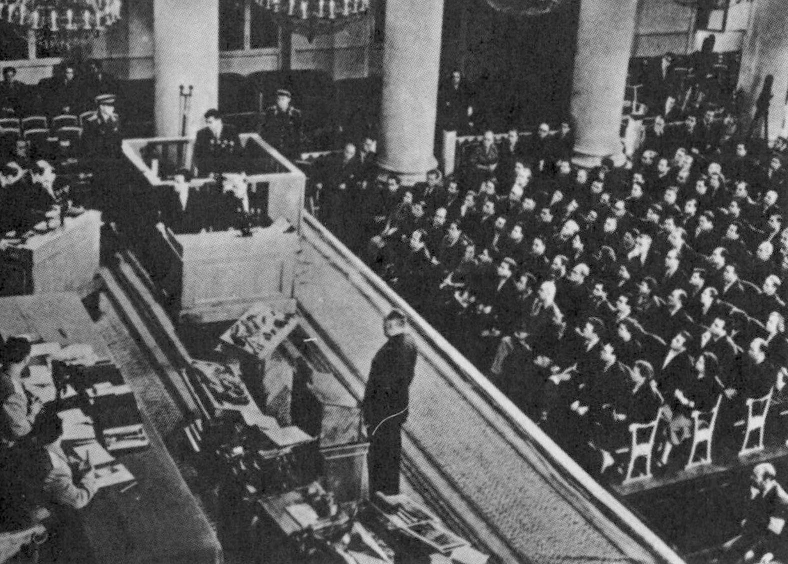

FRANCIS POWERS' TRIAL

On May 1, 1960, Francis Gary Powers, pilot of an American U-2 reconnaissance plane, was shot down by a Soviet rocket as he flew over the Soviet Union. His capture had international repercussions: the collapse of the 1960 East-West summit conference and the cancellation of President Eisenhower's proposed visit to the Soviet Union. On August 19 Powers was found guilty of espionage and was sentenced to ten years' detention. However, on Feb. 10, 1962, he was released in exchange for Rudolph Abel, a Soviet espionage prisoner. After testifying before the Senate Armed Services Committee on Mar. 6, 1962, Powers was cleared of charges that he had cooperated unduly with the Soviet Union.

WIDE WORLD

TELEVISION To listen to an event as it is occurring in a distant city became possible with the advent of radio. To listen to and to look at that event became possible with the advent of television. A television system was first proposed by the German Paul Nipkow in 1884, but successful demonstrations of it were not made until the early 1920's. The first commercial broadcast was produced in New York in 1941; by 1961 nearly 57 million television sets were in use. The first transatlantic television hookup was made in 1962 after the launching of Telstar, the first television communications satellite. In 1963 Telstar made possible a discussion among four world leaders (below, left to right): Dwight Eisenhower of the United States, Anthony Eden (Lord Avon) of England, Jean Monnet of France, and Heinrich von Brentano of West Germany (not shown).

CBS TELEVISION NETWORK

POPULATION

According to the 1960 census, the population of the United States made a record ten-year gain as it increased from 151 million to 180 million. In 1790, when the first census was taken, only 1 in 20 persons lived in a city; in 1960, only 1 in 13 persons lived on a farm. In 1960, Negro migration from South to North increased an average of 12,000 per month; persons of foreign stock living in the United States numbered 34 million; school enrollment reached 48 million. As the number of Americans moving to western states increased (California's population alone rose 5 million), the center of population shifted, and the obelisk marking that center was moved from Olney, Ill., to Centralia, Ill. The projected population for 1970 was 214 million.

WIDE WORLD

NASA PHOTO

SPACE EXPLORATION In the years following the Soviet launching of Sputnik in 1957, the U.S.S.R. and the United States made extraordinary advances in space exploration. The U.S.S.R. launched the first man in space in April, 1961; the U.S. launched John H. Glenn in *Friendship 7* in February, 1962. A few years earlier the Soviet satellite Lunik III had photographed the far side of the moon; in 1962 the American interplanetary probe Mariner II passed within 22,000 miles of Venus and successfully transmitted radiometric data to earth. The Soviets sent the first woman in space in 1963. In America, preparations were being made for a two-man space flight and a three-man lunar landing. After the lunar landing Mars was to be the goal, as man became more confident of his ability to achieve feats once thought impossible.

AUTOMATION, the technique of replacing a manually controlled process by an electronically controlled process, brought such radical improvements in industry that the post–World War II period was termed the second industrial revolution. At the same time, however, one serious drawback resulted—the widespread unemployment of workers in automated industries. To combat this effect many companies instituted retraining programs whereby workers could learn new skills.

PHOTO, DU PONT

UPI

KENNEDY INAUGURATED

Chief Justice Earl Warren administered the oath of office to John Fitzgerald Kennedy, 35th president of the United States, on Jan. 20, 1961. Kennedy, the Democratic candidate, had defeated Vice President Richard M. Nixon, the Republican candidate, in one of the closest presidential elections in the nation's history.

NATION'S HIGHWAYS

Because 90 percent of all U.S. intercity travel is done by automobile, the federal government began in 1956 to construct a network of interstate highways. The goal is the completion of 41,000 miles by 1972, when nearly 100 million vehicles will be traveling 1,000 billion miles. Although the network will constitute only 1.2 percent of the nation's highway mileage, its divided lanes will carry 25 percent of the highway traffic. As the New Jersey Turnpike (right) illustrates, streamlined design makes this possible.

PHOTO, TONY LINCK, CITIES SERVICE OIL CO.

PEACE CORPS

PEACE CORPS In 1961, by executive order, President Kennedy created the Peace Corps, an agency whose purpose is to provide educational and technical assistance to newly developing countries. Volunteers are selected for a two-year period of service, including a three-month period of orientation to the country's language and culture. Within two years nearly 5,000 Americans were serving in 47 countries.

UPI

CUBA

After the 1959 Cuban revolution, the U.S. broke diplomatic relations with Cuba. In 1962, after the Bay of Pigs invasion, the U.S.S.R. sent missiles to Castro. The U.S. established a blockade of vessels carrying offensive weapons. On Oct. 28, 1962, Khrushchev ordered the missile bases dismantled. In December, 1962, President Kennedy received the battle flag of about 1,000 invasion prisoners freed by Castro.

UPI

ALLIANCE FOR PROGRESS,

an organization of 20 American republics including the United States, was formed in August, 1961, to promote economic and social reform in Latin America. One of the programs executed by the Alliance was the financing of low-cost housing. In 1962 Teodoro Moscoso (left), coordinator of the Alliance, and Floyd Baird, vice-president of World Homes, arranged for a loan to help Colombia house 475 families.

PRESIDENT JOHN FITZGERALD KENNEDY was assassinated in Dallas, Tex., on Nov. 22, 1963, by a 24-year-old political radical, Lee Harvey Oswald. About two hours after the assassination, Lyndon Baines Johnson was sworn in as President of the United States by Federal Judge Sarch T. Hughes. Three days later requiem mass was celebrated for the assassinated President in Washington, D.C. The widow, Jacqueline Kennedy, stood with their two children, Caroline and John Fitzgerald, Jr., in front of Senator Edward Kennedy, Attorney General Robert Kennedy, and other members of the immediate family as the President's remains were carried from the church. John, who was three years old that day, stepped forward and saluted as his father's coffin passed. In the solemn procession to the final resting place of the President in Arlington National Cemetery, former Vice President Johnson walked, despite Secret Service objections, unprotected, in company with the Kennedy family, dignitaries, and heads of state from around the world.

UPI

THE JOHNSON ADMINISTRATION

UPI

Lyndon Johnson, assuming office after President Kennedy's assassination, was elected in 1964, with Hubert Humphrey as his vice president. Johnson's 1965 decision to commit U.S. troops to active combat in South Vietnam overshadowed his entire administration. He declared War on Poverty and began his Great Society program. Congress passed his comprehensive Civil and Voting Rights legislation. The Economic Opportunity Act of 1964 created Head Start, the Job Corps, and VISTA (Volunteers in Service to America). Federal aid was given to elementary and high schools, more scholarships were offered to the poor, and a Teacher Corps was formed. Immigration and consumer protection legislation was passed. Added to the Cabinet were a Department of Housing and Urban Affairs and a Department of Transportation. In 1965 Medicare was established to give health insurance to the aged. Federal income taxes were reduced in 1964, but in 1968 a 10 percent temporary surtax was enacted. To ease U.S.-U.S.S.R. Cold War tensions a multi-nation treaty to halt the spread of nuclear weapons was drawn up. Johnson met with Soviet Premier Aleksei Kosygin at Glassboro, N.J., in 1967. A total bombing halt over North Vietnam in October, 1968, led to Paris Peace talks between the U.S., North Vietnam, the Communist-led Vietcong, and South Vietnam. Under Johnson the economy reached its longest period of sustained prosperity and unemployment dropped to the lowest rate since the Korean War. Inflation developed as prices, bank interest rates, and budget deficits rose.

THE PUEBLO INCIDENT

The U.S.S. *Pueblo* Navy intelligence ship, seized by North Korea, Jan. 23, 1968, off its eastern coast, was accused of operating illegally within Korean waters. The ship remained in North Korean custody until the 82 surviving crew members (one had died) were released Dec. 22, 1968, after the U.S. signed a "solemn apology," publicly repudiated as false. A Navy court found Commander Lloyd Bucher innocent of violating Naval regulations.

PHOTOS, DEPARTMENT OF DEFENSE

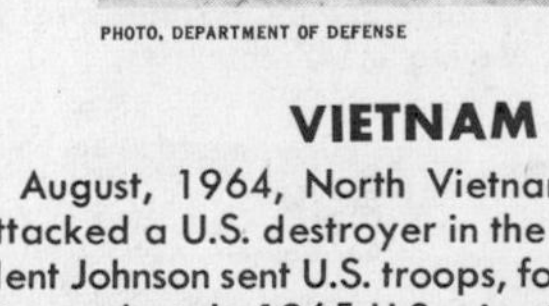

PHOTO, DEPARTMENT OF DEFENSE

VIETNAM

In August, 1964, North Vietnamese torpedo boats attacked a U.S. destroyer in the Gulf of Tonkin. President Johnson sent U.S. troops, formerly only advisors, into combat. In 1965 U.S. air attacks on North Vietnam began. Fighting increased during the 1968 Lunar cease-fire. Vietcong now infiltrated South Vietnamese cities as well as rural areas. In March, 1968, bombing over North Vietnam was de-escalated, and in May peace talks began in Paris between the U.S. and North Vietnam. Later it was agreed that the National Liberation Front and South Vietnam join the talks. After weeks of haggling, talks began but fighting continued. On Apr. 30, 1970, during the Nixon administration, U.S. and South Vietnamese forces entered Cambodia to clear enemy sanctuaries. U.S. units then withdrew to South Vietnam. As South Vietnamese troops became more effective, thousands of G.I.'s were able to return home.

UPI

CIVIL RIGHTS MOVEMENT

Negroes and white sympathizers continued demonstrations for equal rights for Negroes throughout the United States in the 1960's; the goals of the movement were improved education, nondiscriminatory voter registration, equal opportunity in employment, and open occupancy in housing. Martin Luther King (above), winner of the Nobel peace prize, led groups in nonviolent direct-action demonstrations.

MARCH ON WASHINGTON

Ralph David Abernathy, succeeding Martin Luther King, Jr., as president of the Southern Christian Leadership Conference, continued King's plans to lead a Poor People's March into Washington, D.C. It began May 11, 1968. Some 3,000 people of all races lived in "Resurrection City," a ghetto of plywood shanties. Participants held marches on the Capitol and met with legislators. Their success was hampered by conflict among their leaders, infiltrators intent on violence, lack of funds, and vagueness on specific goals. They won some concessions: Increased funds for emergency food and other anti-poverty programs; and the largest annual Indian aid appropriation in history. Government also enlisted private industry in efforts to train hard-core unemployed workers.

UPI

MARTIN LUTHER KING, JR., Civil Rights advocate of nonviolence, was assassinated April 4, 1968, in Memphis, Tenn. Dignitaries and poor people mourned as a mule team, symbolic of his devotion to the poor, carried the coffin through Atlanta. His death sparked riots in cities throughout the nation. The most serious were in Chicago, Washington, D.C., Baltimore, and Kansas City, Mo. Forty-six persons died; 45 million dollars property damage was suffered. James Earl Ray, an escaped convict, was tried, convicted, and sentenced to 99 years imprisonment for the murder.

UPI

UPI

STUDENT UNREST in the 1960's resulted in demonstrations at more than 100 colleges and universities. Dissenters included revolutionaries intent on destroying the system, students protesting the gap between the ideals of democracy and the conditions of American life, and war protesters. Some sought greater Black recognition. Others demanded a voice in policymaking. Some segments of society promised reform, but others doubted the ideals of the college generation.

UPI

ROBERT F. KENNEDY, U.S. Senator from N.Y., was assassinated in Los Angeles moments after claiming victory in California's 1968 Democratic presidential primary. A man of courage and compassion, Kennedy had promoted the causes of black people, American Indians, and other minority groups. Sirhan B. Sirhan, a Jordanian immigrant who opposed Kennedy's support for Israel, was tried for the murder and sentenced to death.

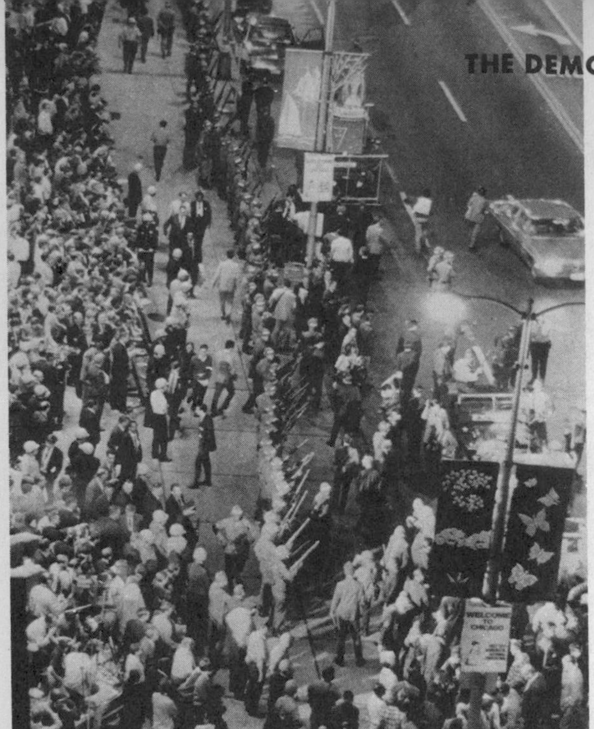

UPI

THE DEMOCRATIC CONVENTION OF 1968

was held in Chicago amid a background of violence and bitterness. Youthful anti-war demonstrators provoked police to attack, bringing charges of police brutality. Illinois National Guardsmen were stationed in front of the convention headquarters hotel (left). Vice president Hubert H. Humphrey was nominated on the first ballot and chose Senator Edmund S. Muskie of Maine as his running mate. Humphrey's allegiance to President Johnson's policy on Vietnam, an issue that drew stormy debate, plus the havoc of the Chicago demonstrations split the Democratic party.

UPI

RICHARD MILHOUS NIXON was elected 37th president of the United States on the Republican ticket, defeating Democrat Hubert Humphrey by a narrow margin. Spiro T. Agnew, governor of Maryland, became vice-president. Despite early indications that votes for third party candidate George Wallace might throw the election to the House of Representatives, Wallace won only 13 percent of the total votes cast.

HACKENSACK, N.J., RECORD

POLLUTION is caused by pollen, dust, combustion by-products, pesticides, radioactive fallout, bacteria, and other sources of contamination. It has become a national problem that requires meaningful programs and cooperation of all citizens in carrying them through. Air pollution is a major problem of cities and industrial areas (left and below). Among its causes are the burning of coal and oil and the automobile emission of pollutants. Some restrictions and controls have been instituted to protect the atmosphere. Pure water, necessary for domestic, recreational, and industrial uses, has been affected by bacteria unable to oxidize organic wastes, chemicals, suspended solids that smother breeding beds and purifying organisms, and mineral nutrients that promote the growth of algae and unwanted plants. Solutions include sewage treatment plants, increased dilution of industrial waste, and other efforts to furnish reuse of water.

SAN FRANCISCO NEWS COLL. BULLETIN

CHICAGO HOUSING AUTHORITY

URBAN PROBLEMS. In 1968 70 percent of the people of the U.S. lived in metropolitan areas that comprised 1 percent of the nation's total land. City problems increased with the influx of population until an urban crisis developed and solutions had to be found if the cities were to survive. Among city problems were air pollution, transportation, auto congestion, housing shortages, poverty, crime, high living costs, racial strife, and schools. Although a lack of funds delayed action on some of the issues, social rather than financial dilemmas prevented other issues from being resolved. Urban renewal and housing development needs were being met by replacing slum dwellings with low-rent public housing (above), mortgage financing at below-market rates, and developing new towns. The creation of the Department of Housing and Urban Development in 1966 and the establishment of the Model Cities Program were two attempts by government to give financial and technical aid through pre-planning.

RANGER 7 SPACECRAFT took excellent photographs of the moon's surface in July, 1964, and provided the first precise record. The photograph above, left, showing the Sea of Clouds area, was taken at a distance of 34 miles from the moon. Above, right, is a photograph of Ranger 7 before its flight. The possibility of moon exploration was further advanced in 1966 when Surveyor 1 made a soft landing on the moon and relayed photographs of the moon's surface and in 1967 when Surveyor 3, equipped with a mechanical scoop, sent photographs of its diggings. These space flights were preliminaries to the three-phase program to place man on the moon and bring him back safely: Mercury, during which techniques of manned orbital flight were developed; Gemini, during which manned flights, earth orbits, and rendezvous with other space ships were achieved; and Apollo, with final preparations for landing men on the moon.

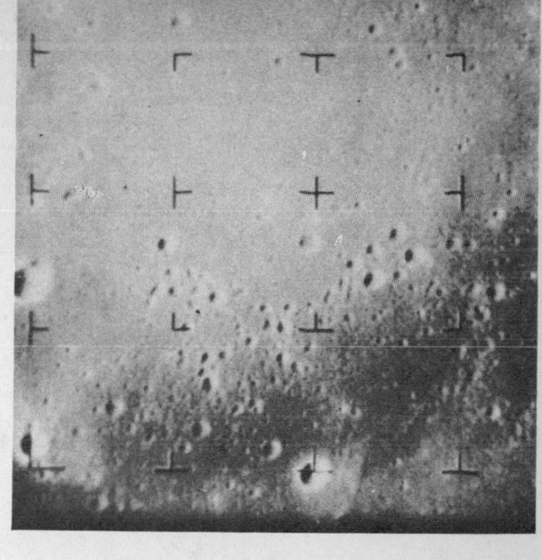

SPACE EXPLORATION

THE APOLLO PROGRAM was the last stage in the U.S. program to land men on the moon. It began manned testing of spacecraft systems with the flight of Apollo 7, Oct. 11–22, 1968. Apollo 8, launched Dec. 21, 1968, was the first manned space flight to orbit the moon. As they emerged from behind the moon, the astronauts took the first photographs of the earth as it rose above the lunar horizon (left). Apollo 9, flown March 3–13, 1969, tested the complete spaceship and the lunar module, the vehicle designed to land men on the moon. During Apollo 10, flown May 18–26, 1969, two astronauts detached from the command module (above, right) and orbited the lunar module within 47,000 feet of the moon, scouting landing sites for the Apollo 11 landing.

APOLLO 11 blasted off from Cape Kennedy, Florida, on July 16, 1969, to land the first men on the moon. On July 20, while Michael Collins (center) kept the mother ship *Columbia* in lunar orbit, Neil A. Armstrong (left) and Edwin E. Aldrin, Jr. (right) landed the lunar module *Eagle* near the Sea of Tranquillity. Armstrong said, as he first stepped onto the moon, "That's one small step for a man, one giant leap for mankind." As millions viewed the moon scene via live television broadcasts, Aldrin joined Armstrong outside the craft. They left on the moon a memorial plaque engraved in part, "We came in peace for all mankind." During the 2¼-hour moon walk the men deployed a United States flag, spoke with President Nixon, set up experiments, and collected lunar samples. On July 21 they headed for home and splashed down on July 24. During six subsequent Apollo moon missions, many experiments were conducted, including deep-space extravehicular activities, the launching of a lunar satellite from the command module, and the testing of lunar roving vehicles.

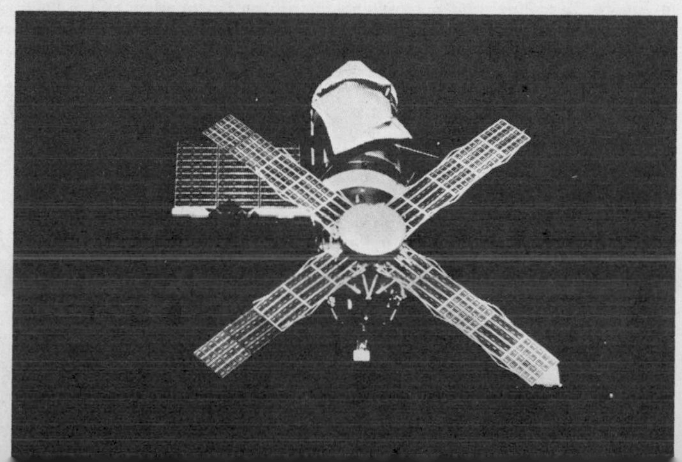

SKYLAB

In the Skylab program, the manned space project which followed the Apollo missions, the United States orbited and manned its first space station. The program's objectives included examining man's adaptability to space over long periods of time, determining the importance of having experiments and instruments monitored by men in space, studying the durability of equipment in space, and investigating both the sun and the earth. The space station was launched in May, 1973, but it suffered severe damage to its heat control shield and energy supply units. Astronauts Charles Conrad, Jr., Joseph P. Kerwin, and Paul J. Weitz were sent up to repair the damage. They successfully completed the repairs, proving that men were essential to the effectiveness of space missions. Twice again in 1973 crews were launched into space to dock with the Skylab space station and conduct experiments on board. The *Skylab 3* crew completed man's longest journey in space, lasting 84 days, and this mission brought to a close the successful Skylab program.

SUCCESSFUL DIPLOMATIC INITIATIVES were the hallmark of President Richard Nixon's first term of office and contributed to his landslide victory in the 1972 election. The first of these diplomatic moves was Nixon's visit to the People's Republic of China in February, 1972. For years U.S. relations with China had been marked by hostility and suspicion. This pattern was broken by Nixon's historic trip, the purpose of which was to improve relations with China and discuss issues of mutual concern. At the end of the visit, a joint communique was issued which called for increased U.S.-China contacts and eventual withdrawal of U.S. troops from Taiwan. Nixon's meetings with Chairman Mao Tse-tung and Premier Chou En-lai opened the door to a new U.S. Asian policy.

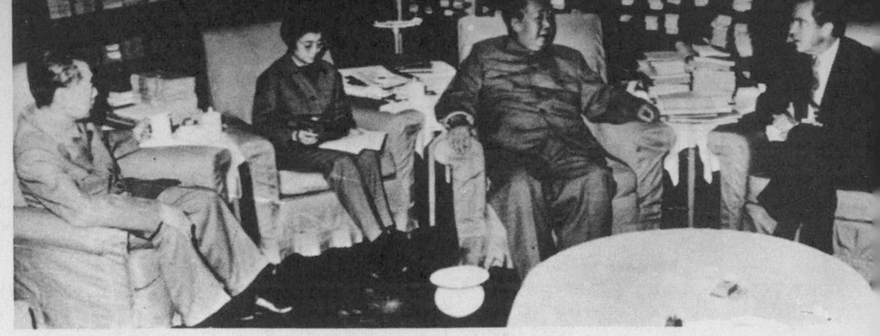

WIDE WORLD

WIDE WORLD

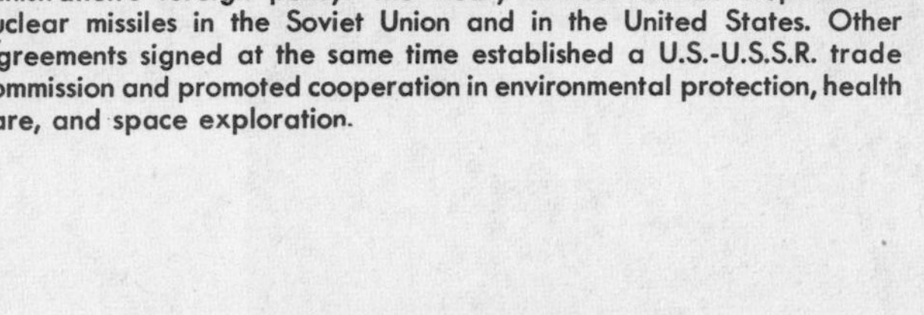

ARMS AGREEMENT IN MOSCOW

The Strategic Arms Limitation Talks treaty, signed in Moscow in May, 1972, by President Nixon and Soviet Communist Party chairman Leonid Brezhnev, was a second important accomplishment of the Nixon administration's foreign policy. The treaty limited the development of nuclear missiles in the Soviet Union and in the United States. Other agreements signed at the same time established a U.S.-U.S.S.R. trade commission and promoted cooperation in environmental protection, health care, and space exploration.

VIETNAM CEASE-FIRE

The cease-fire agreement in the Vietnam war was another achievement of the Nixon administration in the arena of foreign policy. The agreement was signed on January 27, 1973, following months of secret negotiations between Dr. Henry Kissinger, special assistant to President Nixon; Le Duc Tho, chief negotiator for North Vietnam (both shown at right initialing the agreement); and President Nguyen Van Thieu of South Vietnam. The accord called for a cessation of fighting, withdrawal of U.S. troops, and the prompt return of prisoners of war. Americans were relieved that active U.S. participation in the long and costly war had finally come to an end. In spite of the cease-fire agreement, however, civil war continued in Vietnam.

WIDE WORLD

WIDE WORLD

THE WATERGATE SCANDAL severely marred the image of the executive branch during Nixon's second term in office. The scandal first erupted in June, 1972, with the arrest and subsequent conviction of several men, two of whom were former White House aides and one an official of the Committee to Reelect the President, who had broken into the Democratic National Headquarters in Washington, D.C. As FBI, Justice Department, and Senate Committee investigators (left) delved into the break-in, it became apparent that other key members of the White House staff, and possibly the president himself, may have participated in or approved of this and other illegal campaign activities and tried to conceal information from investigators. Investigations were slowed by the president's refusal to turn over all evidence requested by the Justice Department's special prosecutor and by the Senate Committee, and a constitutional crisis on the question of the limits of executive powers and privileges seemed imminent. In May, 1974, the House Judiciary Committee formally opened its inquiry into possible grounds for impeachment of President Nixon. In August, 1974, Nixon resigned.

AGNEW RESIGNS

Also damaging to the executive branch was the resignation of Vice-President Spiro Agnew in October, 1973. Agnew stepped down from office rather than face indictment on charges of tax evasion, acceptance of bribes, and involvement in other illegal activities. Representative Gerald Ford of Michigan (right) became the new vice-president. When Nixon resigned, Ford became the thirty-eighth president.

Afghanistan

Albania

FLAGS OF THE WORLD

The proportions and colors of some of the flags represented on these pages are different from the specifications of individual nations. These changes were made for the sake of uniformity in presentation.

Algeria

Andorra

Argentina

Australia

Austria

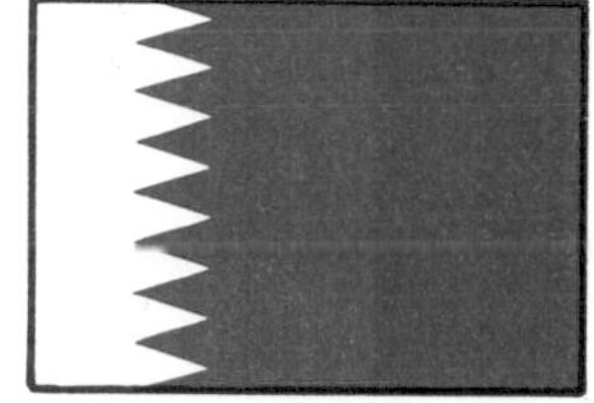
Bahrain

Bangladesh

Barbados

Belgium

Bhutan

Bolivia

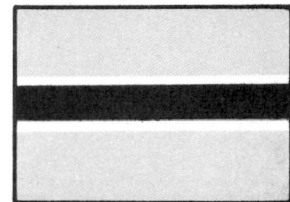

Botswana

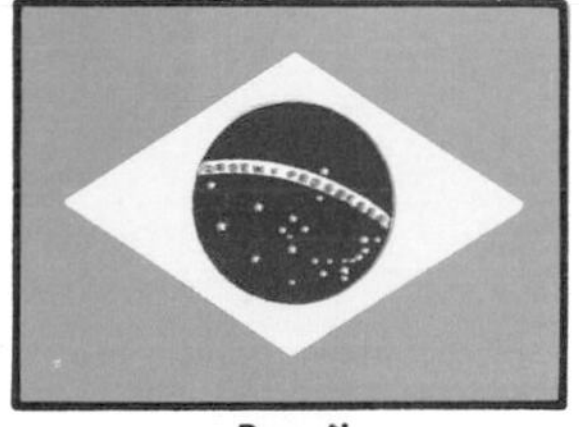
Brazil

Bulgaria

Burma

Burundi

Cameroon

Canada

Central African Republic

Chad

Chile

China (Nationalist)

China (People's Republic)

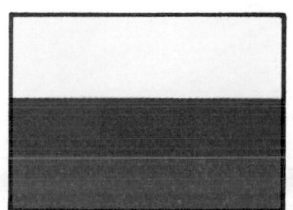

Colombia

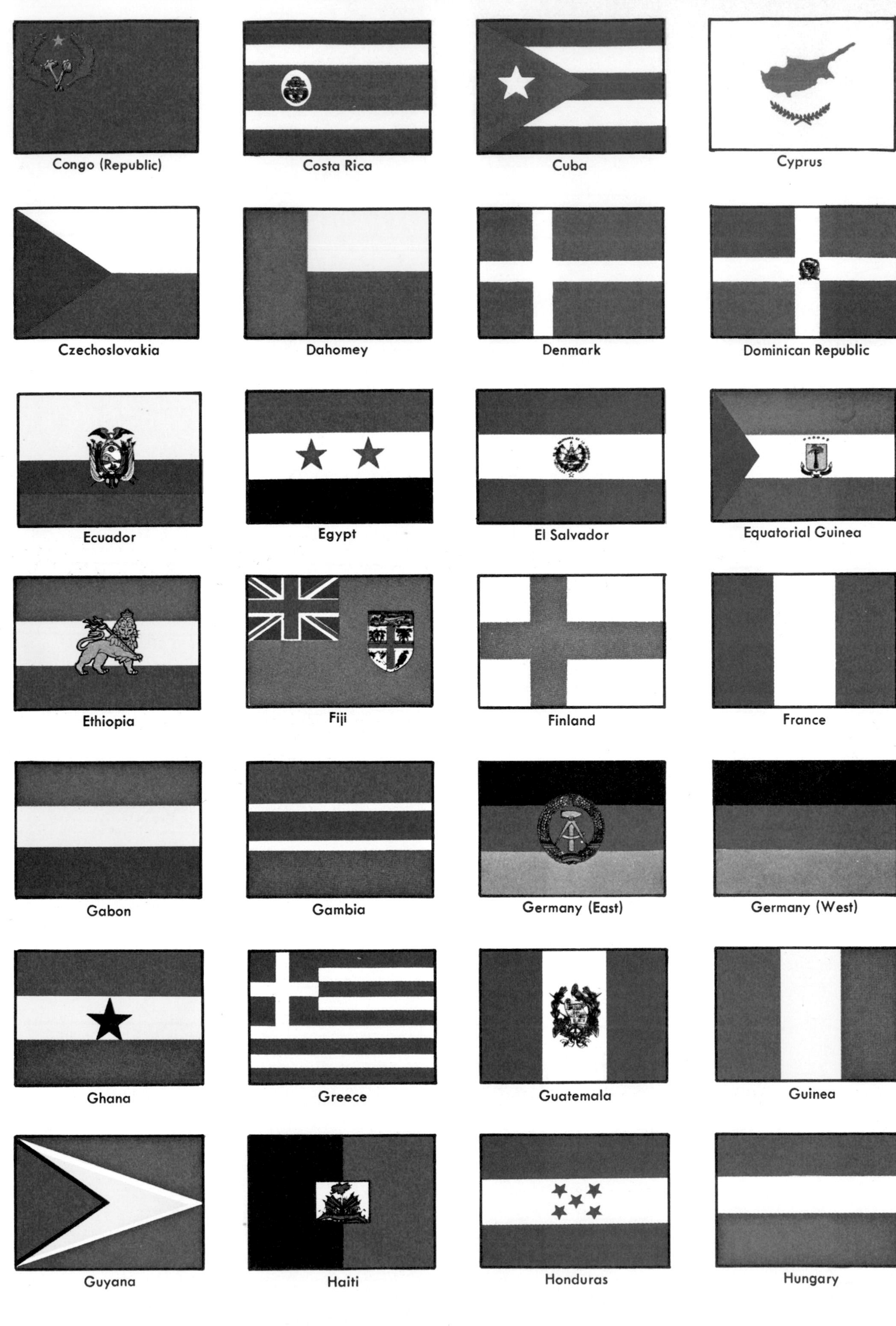
Congo (Republic)
Costa Rica
Cuba
Cyprus
Czechoslovakia
Dahomey
Denmark
Dominican Republic
Ecuador
Egypt
El Salvador
Equatorial Guinea
Ethiopia
Fiji
Finland
France
Gabon
Gambia
Germany (East)
Germany (West)
Ghana
Greece
Guatemala
Guinea
Guyana
Haiti
Honduras
Hungary

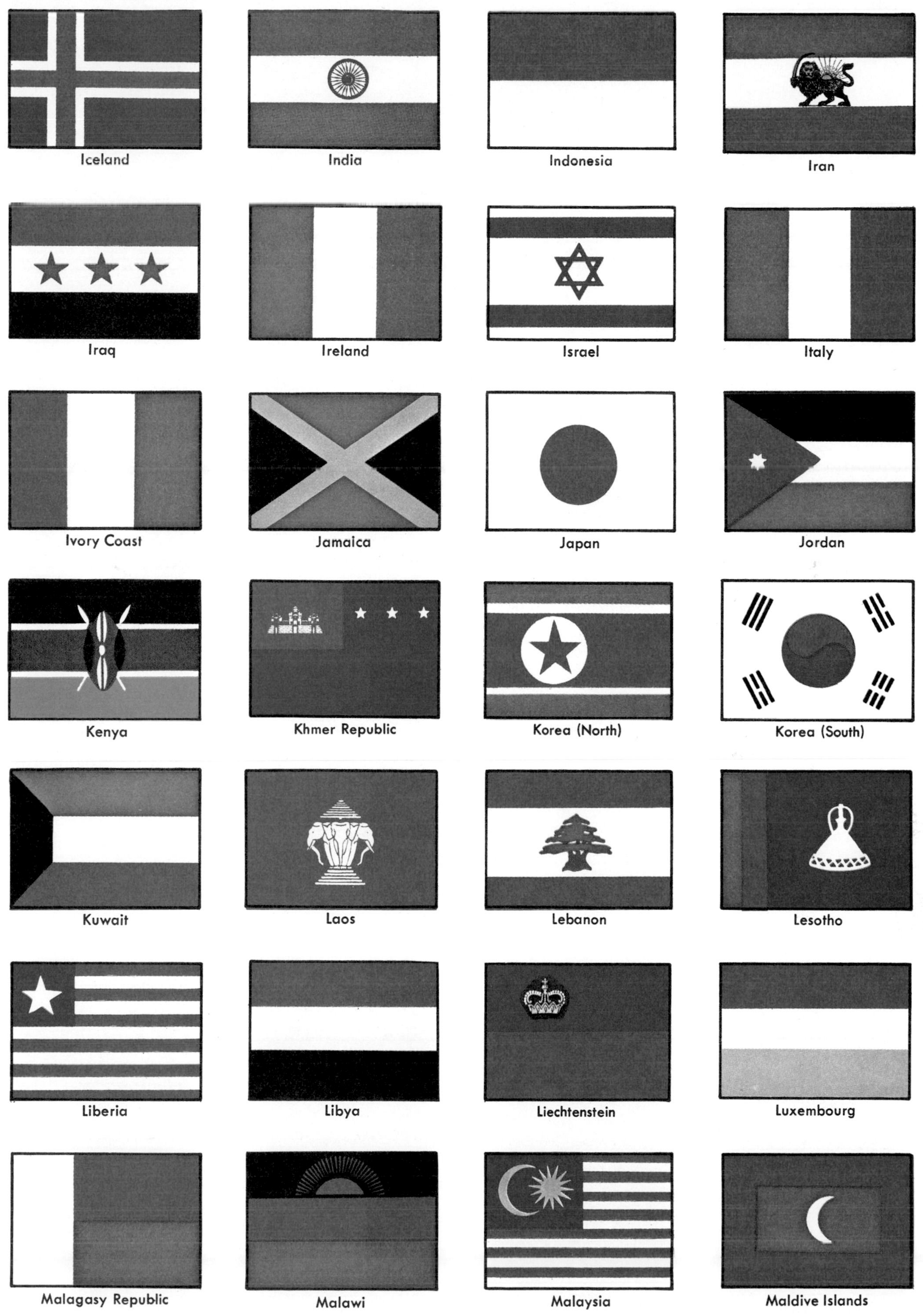
Iceland
India
Indonesia
Iran
Iraq
Ireland
Israel
Italy
Ivory Coast
Jamaica
Japan
Jordan
Kenya
Khmer Republic
Korea (North)
Korea (South)
Kuwait
Laos
Lebanon
Lesotho
Liberia
Libya
Liechtenstein
Luxembourg
Malagasy Republic
Malawi
Malaysia
Maldive Islands

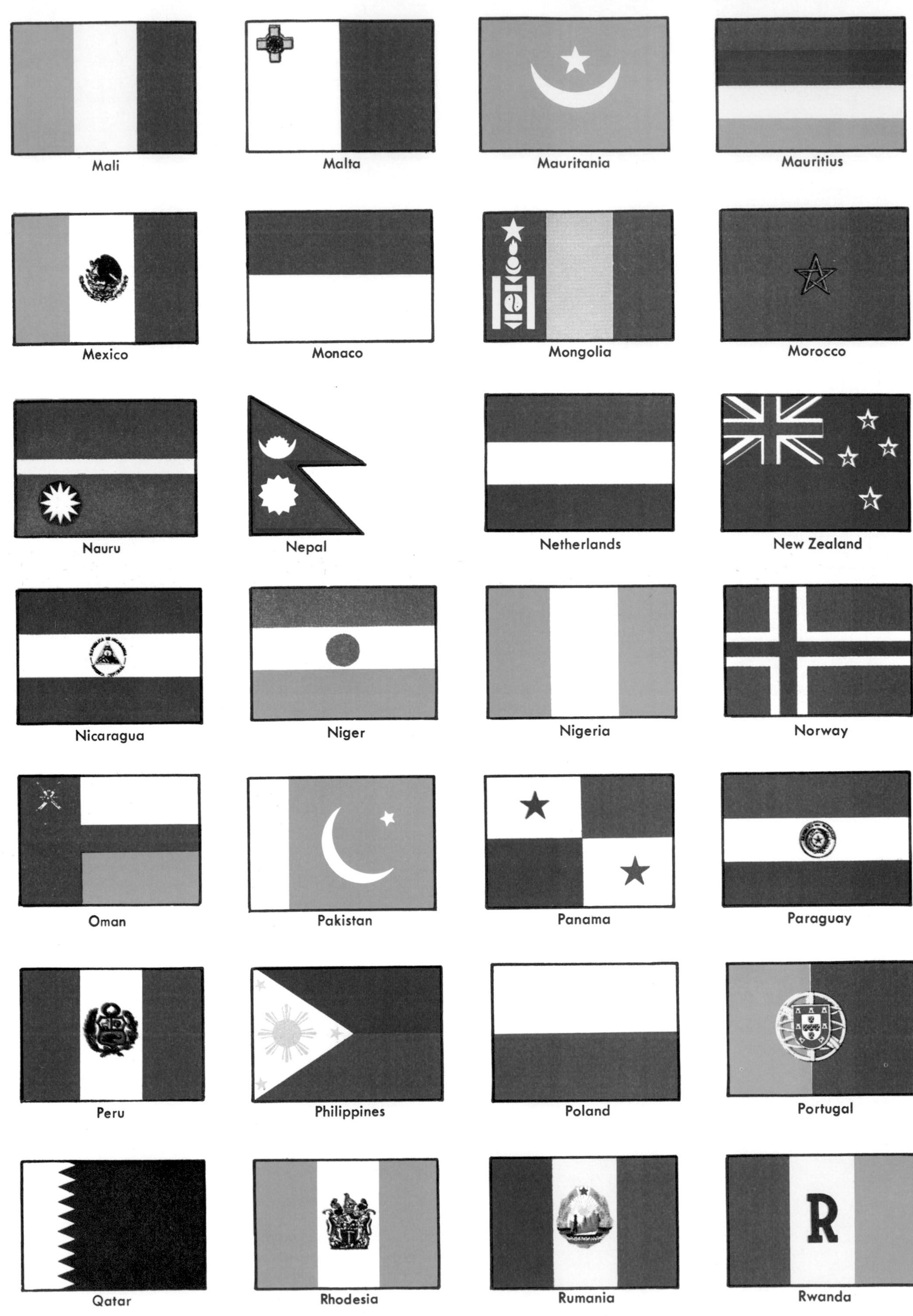

Mali
Malta
Mauritania
Mauritius
Mexico
Monaco
Mongolia
Morocco
Nauru
Nepal
Netherlands
New Zealand
Nicaragua
Niger
Nigeria
Norway
Oman
Pakistan
Panama
Paraguay
Peru
Philippines
Poland
Portugal
Qatar
Rhodesia
Rumania
Rwanda

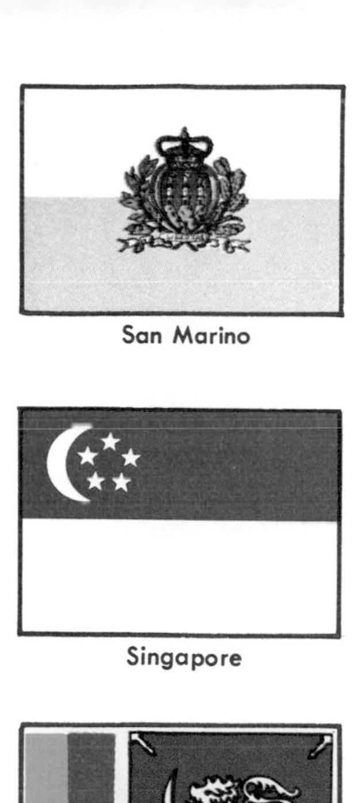

San Marino

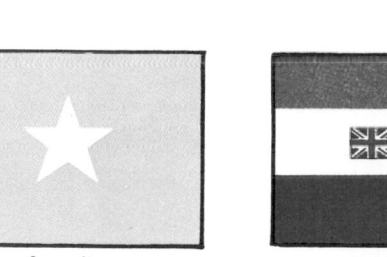

Saudi Arabia

Senegal

Sierra Leone

Singapore

Somalia

South Africa

Spain

Sri Lanka

Sudan

Swaziland

Sweden

Switzerland

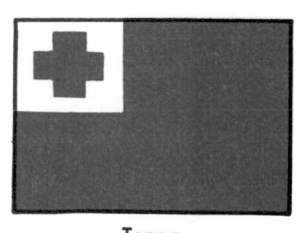

Syria

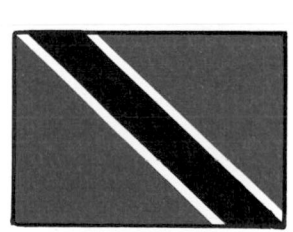

Tanzania

Thailand

Togo

Tonga

Trinidad and Tobago

Tunisia

Turkey

Uganda

Union of Soviet Socialist Republics

United Arab Emirates

United Kingdom

United States of America

Upper Volta

Uruguay

Vatican City

Venezuela

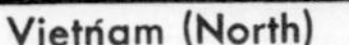
Vietnam (North)

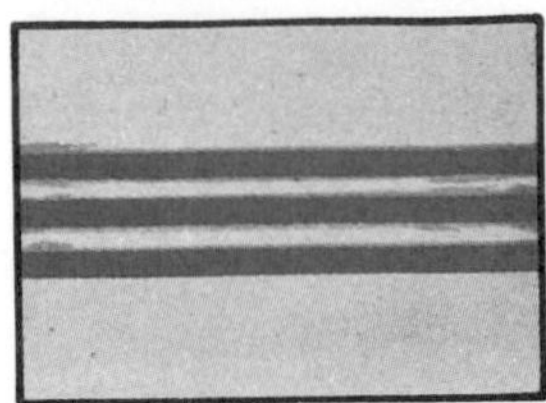
Vietnam (South)

Western Samoa

Yemen

Yemen (Peoples)

Yugoslavia

Zaire

Zambia

Flag of the United States of America

(A) Grand Union Flag
1775? – 1777

(B) National Flag
1775? – 1800

(C) Ensign and Jack
1775? – 1776

(D) National Flag
June 1777 – April 1795

(E) Bennington Flag
16 Aug. 1777

(F) National Flag
June 1777 – April 1795

(G) National Flag
May 1795 – Juy 1818

(H) National Flag
July 1818 – Sept. 1818

THE UNITED STATES FLAG

The first United States flag was the Grand Union flag (A), which appeared on January 1, 1776, as the banner of the American forces. Like the British Red ensign, the Grand Union flag had 13 alternate red and white stripes and the Union Jack as a canton. This flag was never officially adopted and other patterns emerged (B, C). After the Declaration of Independence, the Union Jack was considered an inappropriate symbol, so the Continental Congress called for a flag of 13 alternate red and white stripes and a blue canton with 13 stars. Evidence indicates that the original Stars and Stripes was designed by Francis Hopkinson, a signer of the Declaration. Most flags of this era display the stars in a circle (D), but some show the stars in a semicircle (E), or in a horizontal arrangement (F).

That Betsy Ross sewed the original Stars and Stripes was first asserted by her grandson, William J. Canby, on March 14, 1870. He reported that George Washington, Robert Morse, and George Ross came to her upholstery shop, showed her a design, and asked her to make the flag. This story has long been regarded as authentic, but there is no documentary evidence to support it.

In 1794, Congress voted to add two stripes and two stars to the flag (G), in recognition of the admission of Vermont and Kentucky to the Union. As the country expanded, the addition of a star and stripe for each admitted state became unfeasible. In 1818, Congress voted to return to the 13 alternate red and white stripes for the original colonies and to add one star for each state as it was admitted to the Union (H). After 1912, whenever a new state was admitted, the new design of the flag was established by executive order. The current flag contains 50 stars; the 49th represents Alaska and was added on July 4, 1959; the 50th represents Hawaii and was added on July 4, 1960.

THE FLAGS OF THE CONFEDERACY

The first flag to become a recognized symbol of the Confederate alliance was the Bonnie Blue Flag with its one central star against a field of blue (I). On March 4, 1861, the Confederate States revealed the Stars and Bars (J); it had three alternate red and white stripes and a blue canton bearing seven white stars. Most patterns showed the stars arranged in a circle with or without a star in the center. The flag eventually had 13 stars, one for each Confederate state (K).

Because of similarities between the Stars and Bars and the Union Flag, the Southern states adopted a new battle flag in July, 1861 (L). Although it was unofficial and never adopted by the Confederate government, the Battle Flag became the most popular symbol of the Confederacy.

In 1863 the Confederate Congress sought to adopt a new official banner because the Stars and Bars was modeled after the United States flag and because it had never been officially recognized. On May 1 the Congress revealed a pure white flag with the Battle Flag as a canton (M). Known as the Stainless Banner, it soon fell into disfavor because it soiled too easily and because it resembled a flag of truce. This flag was replaced on March 4, 1865, by a new flag that was slightly different in proportions and had a red stripe across the fly (N). Only a few of these flags were made however, because the war ended shortly after the banner was adopted.

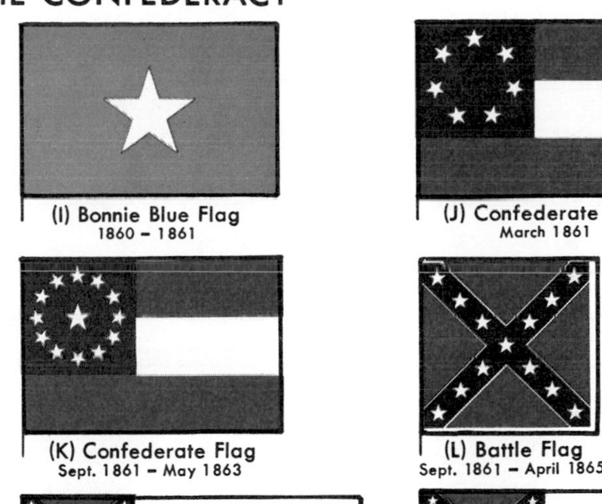

(I) Bonnie Blue Flag
1860 – 1861

(J) Confederate Flag
March 1861

(K) Confederate Flag
Sept. 1861 – May 1863

(L) Battle Flag
Sept. 1861 – April 1865

(M) Confederate Flag
May 1863 – March 1865

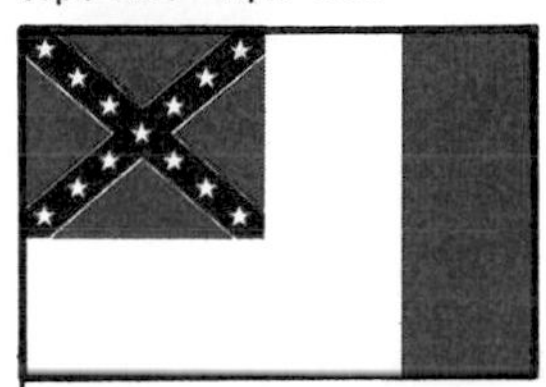

(N) Confederate Flag
March 1865 – April 1865

FLAGS OF STATES, TERRITORIES, AND COMMONWEALTHS

Alabama

Alaska

Arizona

Arkansas

California

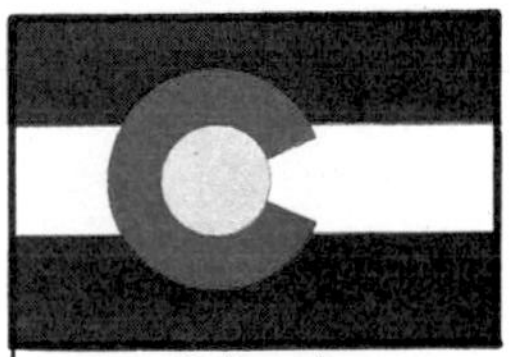

Colorado

Connecticut

Delaware

District of Columbia

Florida

Georgia

Guam

Hawaii

Idaho

Illinois

Indiana

Iowa

Kansas

Kentucky

Louisiana

Maine
Maryland
Massachusetts
Michigan
Minnesota
Mississippi
Missouri
Montana
Nebraska
Nevada
New Hampshire
New Jersey
New Mexico
New York
North Carolina
North Dakota
Ohio
OKLAHOMA
Oklahoma
STATE OF OREGON
1859
Oregon
Pennsylvania
Puerto Rico
Rhode Island
South Carolina
South Dakota
Tennessee
Texas
Utah
Vermont
Virginia
V
I
Virgin Islands
Washington
West Virginia
Wisconsin
Wyoming

PRESIDENTS of the UNITED STATES

The president is the chief executive of the United States. His office was originally established in 1789 to overcome the disadvantages of a weak central government. It has since become the most powerful political office in the country.

Under present statutes, an elected president is guaranteed at least one four-year term in office. He may be elected to two full terms and may serve a maximum of ten years if he started during his predecessor's term. Although exempt from all court actions while president, he may be impeached, and removed from office if convicted.

The duties and powers of the president, as delineated in the Constitution, are checked and balanced by the judicial and legislative branches of government. As chief executive he enforces federal legislation and supervises administrative agencies. These responsibilities are actually delegated to department heads, who are chosen by the president and approved by the Senate. The president also appoints judicial officials and foreign diplomats. He participates in the nation's lawmaking process by supporting certain laws and vetoing those laws passed by Congress which he feels would not be in the nation's best interest. As commander in chief of the armed forces, he assigns military commissions and directs the national war defense. He also has the power, subject to Senate approval, to negotiate foreign treaties.

George Washington (1732-1799)

Term 1789-1797, FIRST PRESIDENT

The high courage and strong but disciplined will of George Washington brought endurance and purpose to the cause of American independence. The son of a planter, he was born on the frontier of Virginia. His schooling, inspired by his half-brother Lawrence and by family friends, consisted largely of mathematics and military skills. At sixteen he was earning his own living as a surveyor. At twenty-one he had completed a hazardous mission through the wilderness to the Ohio country. Other important military and civic activities rapidly followed. In 1759 he married Martha Custis and began the extensive development of the Mount Vernon estate. Armed conflict called him in 1775 to the command of the Continental Army. Throughout the long and difficult struggle which followed, Washington held the ragged, unpaid, and hungry soldiers together until final victory came. From a well-deserved retirement he was called to preside at the Constitutional Convention. Unanimously chosen the first President of the United States, unanimously reelected, he declined a third term. In 1798, Washington was appointed Lieutenant-General of the U.S. armies. He died at Mount Vernon, regarded as a successful general, a fine statesman, and an inspiring leader who became "first in the hearts of his countrymen."

John Adams (1735-1826)

Term 1797-1801, SECOND PRESIDENT

John Adams was one of the most learned of the public men of his day. He had been sent to Harvard College to prepare for the ministry; but upon graduation, he chose the law for his career. In 1764 he married Abigail Smith, a brilliant and capable woman, who, in her own right, became one of the famous characters of American history. Noteworthy success came to John Adams in law and in civic affairs. In the troubled time of 1771 he won a seat in the Massachusetts Assembly. Deep concern about Colonial grievances inspired his leadership against the mother country. No one saw more clearly than he that the logical outcome of resistance would be war and independence. The fervent patriotism of John Adams gave direction to the Continental Congress, certainty to the Declaration of Independence—and resulted in his selection to represent the United States abroad. He negotiated a loan from Holland, participated in making a favorable peace, and served as the first minister to Great Britain. In 1788 John Adams returned from Europe in time to have his ability, distinction, and achievement rewarded with the vice-presidency of the United States, the first man to be so honored. As a candidate of the Federalist party, he defeated Thomas Jefferson in 1796, and became the only man to serve eight years as Vice-President and then to become President.

Thomas Jefferson (1743-1826)

Term 1801-1809, THIRD PRESIDENT

Thomas Jefferson's estimate of his own greatest achievements is indicated by the simple epitaph he asked to be inscribed on his tomb: "Here was buried Thomas Jefferson, Author of the Declaration of American Independence, of the Statute of Virginia for Religious Freedom, and Father of the University of Virginia." Jefferson was born in Albemarle County, Virginia, the son of a frontiersman and of Jane Randolph of the prominent Virginia Randolphs. From his mother and his classical education at the College of William and Mary he acquired the social graces and tastes of quality which gave distinguished charm to his personality; but the wisdom of his philosophy and the practicality of his politics were outgrowths of the frontier democracy of his childhood. Jefferson was probably the most versatile leader of his time. Skilled in horsemanship, music, drawing, mathematics, architecture, writing, education, farm management, law, and diplomacy, he had a genius for using these varied abilities to strengthen his own leadership and to improve the public welfare. It was Jefferson's sense of the need for security and expansion which helped in obtaining approval of the treaty for the purchase of Louisiana, and thus laid the basis for the future greatness of the United States. Jefferson retired at 65 and devoted himself largely to establishing the University of Virginia.

James Madison (1751-1836)

Term 1809-1817, FOURTH PRESIDENT

James Madison was preparing for the ministry, shortly after his graduation from Princeton, when the need for public leadership sought him out to head the Orange County Committee on Public Safety. His father owned a large estate in Orange County, Virginia, although James had been born at Port Conway in King George County some few miles away. The stirring demands of the Revolutionary period and the first years of the new Republic found expression in Madison's constructive skill, drafted to help write the state constitution of Virginia. He was twice elected as member of the state legislature and he was chosen a delegate to the Continental Congress and the Constitutional Convention. In the writing of the federal Constitution, and in the struggle over its ratification, Madison reached the peak of his public achievement. He earned the title, "Father of the Constitution." No man did more to perfect the instrument itself or to obtain its acceptance. Madison did all that he could to prevent the War of 1812. Ironically, his opponents called it, "Mr. Madison's War." Despite his genius at constitution-making, Madison had no genuine liking for the political arena, and welcomed retirement to his beautiful home, "Montpelier," in Orange County. Here he enjoyed his books and farming until his death at the age of eighty-five.

James Monroe (1758-1831)

Term 1817-1825, FIFTH PRESIDENT

James Monroe was the fourth Virginian to become President of the United States. He was born in Westmoreland County, the son of a planter of modest means. His college career at William and Mary was interrupted by his enlistment in the Colonial Army. After the war, Monroe turned to the practice of law and was soon immersed in politics. He represented his native state in the Assembly, in the Continental Congress, and in the United States Senate. President Washington appointed him minister to France; and, on his return, he was elected governor of Virginia. Under President Madison he served as Secretary of State and as Secretary of War. Few men have been better qualified by training and experience for the national presidency to which he was elected by the Democratic-Republican party in 1816. There was no opposition to his re-election four years later. The chief events of Monroe's administration were the pronouncement of the independent position of the Western Hemisphere (later to become famous as the Monroe Doctrine), the Anglo-American peace pledge over the Canadian border, the Florida Purchase from Spain, and the Missouri Compromise. He died in New York City at the age of seventy-three—five years after his retirement from a life of devoted service to his country.

John Quincy Adams (1767-1848)

Term 1825-1829, SIXTH PRESIDENT

John Adams was a great American, but perhaps in both learning and achievement his son, John Quincy Adams, surpassed him. The younger Adams received his early education in Europe. Exceptionally brilliant, he was secretary to the United States minister to Russia at fourteen. Later he was graduated from Harvard, and soon gained admission to the Massachusetts bar. President Washington appointed him minister to Holland; then, in turn, he became minister to Prussia, England, and Russia. Before going to Berlin, he married Louisa Johnson, whose father was the United States Consul in London. In 1814 Adams was one of the commissioners who negotiated the peace with Great Britain at Ghent, bringing to an end the War of 1812. Under President Monroe, Adams became a bold and successful Secretary of State. Adams' ideas prompted the National-Republican party to select him as its nominee in 1824. The election failed to return a majority, and Adams was chosen President by the House of Representatives. Adams sought to improve governmental efficiency and to extend foreign commerce. His concept of public service has been rarely, if ever, surpassed. He was more interested in being right and in the general good than he was in gaining popularity and in extending political patronage.

Andrew Jackson (1767-1845)

Term 1829-1837, SEVENTH PRESIDENT

Already a renowned Indian fighter, General Andrew Jackson emerged a national hero from the amazing victory of American frontiersmen over British regulars at New Orleans in 1815. In 1780, at the age of thirteen, he had fought the British in the Battle of Hanging Rock. An orphan at seventeen, he began the study of law, and was admitted to practice three years later. Within a year he was appointed prosecuting attorney for the western part of North Carolina (now Tennessee). He moved to Nashville, and in 1791 married Rachel Robards. One of the framers of Tennessee's constitution, he became, in quick succession, United States Representative and Senator, and judge of the Supreme Court of Tennessee. Impulsive and headstrong, his flaming energy carried him into quarrels, duels, and political conflicts. The western frontier was seething with reaction against the "aristocratic" leadership of the East; and "Old Hickory" was the ideal border captain to lead the way to the White House, which he reached in 1828. "Jacksonian Democracy" was a political triumph for the "common man." It developed the "spoils system," strengthened the federal government over the states, and ended the United States Bank. Retiring after two terms to his beloved estate, "The Hermitage," near Nashville, he continued to influence his party until his death.

Martin Van Buren (1782-1862)

Term 1837-1841, EIGHTH PRESIDENT

Martin Van Buren was the first president born a citizen of the United States. At the age of fourteen, he began the study of law while serving as office boy to the village lawyer at Kinderhook, New York, his native town. His interest in politics began even earlier, and by the age of eighteen he was an active party worker. Twice he was elected to the New York Senate; in 1821 he entered the United States Senate; for two months in 1829 he was governor of New York, but resigned to enter the Cabinet of President Jackson. Van Buren's vigorous support of Andrew Jackson in 1828 was rewarded with appointment as Secretary of State. Two years later he was chosen Vice-President. His loyalty and his political skill endeared him to President Jackson in such measure that Van Buren was selected to inherit the presidential mantle, which he received in the election of 1836. One of the most significant accomplishments of the period of his presidency was the creation of the independent treasury system. Martin Van Buren wrestled unsuccessfully with the reaction from the extremes of Jacksonian democracy. The Jackson inheritance proved too heavy a burden; and with other difficulties, it combined to prevent Van Buren's re-election. His interest in politics, however, continued for many years.

William Henry Harrison (1773-1841)

Term 1841, NINTH PRESIDENT

The father of William Henry Harrison was a Virginian of prominent social position who served as governor of his state. He lived at Berkeley, in Charles City County, Virginia, where his son, William, was born. Young Harrison attended Hampden-Sidney College, and later studied medicine in Philadelphia; in 1791 he enlisted in the United States Army. He became a staff officer for General Wayne in the campaigns against the Indians of the Northwest Territory. Briefly he served as Secretary of the Northwest Territory and as a delegate from the Territory to the national Congress. From 1801 to 1812 he was governor of Indiana Territory. In this position he won acclaim as an Indian fighter, particularly for his victory at Tippecanoe. In the War of 1812 Harrison became a major-general in full command of the Northwest frontier. After the War of 1812, he served in both houses of the Congress, in the Ohio Senate, and as minister to Colombia. The Whigs persuaded Harrison to be their candidate in 1840 with John Tyler, another Virginian, as his running mate. "Tippecanoe and Tyler too" won an overwhelming victory in the log cabin and hard cider campaign. President Harrison died of pneumonia one month after his inauguration. His grandson, Benjamin Harrison, also became President.

John Tyler (1790-1862)

Term 1841-1845, TENTH PRESIDENT

John Tyler became President by succession, at President Harrison's death, one month after the inauguration. Like Harrison, he was born in Charles City County of Virginia; and his father, like Harrison's, had been governor of Virginia. Young Tyler was graduated from William and Mary College at seventeen. At twenty-one he was a member of the state legislature. Later he represented Virginia in both houses of the Congress, with an intervening term as governor of his state. Consistently John Tyler opposed policies which strengthened the national government at the expense of the states. Although a Democrat, Tyler's forceful opposition to "Jacksonianism" had, in the eyes of the Whigs, made him appear desirable for the vice-presidency. They had not thought of the possibility of dealing with him as the President. Tyler's independent nature was shown in his decision to be President in the fullest sense and not merely a substitute as provided in the Constitution; thereby he set a precedent that has become the rule. His administration was marked by controversies with Congress, and by a trend toward territorial expansion; Texas was annexed shortly before the end of his term. Tyler's first wife died when he was in office; in June, 1844, twenty-one months later, he remarried.

James K. Polk (1795-1849)

Term 1845-1849, ELEVENTH PRESIDENT

An important issue in the campaign of 1844 was westward expansion, and closely bound up with it was the problem of the extension of slavery. Van Buren was the popular Democratic nominee for the presidency until he spoke against annexation. James Knox Polk, little known nationally, had received some mention for the vice-presidency; but it was his support of annexation which brought him the chance to be nominated and to be elected President. His administration became famous for the addition of Texas, California, New Mexico, Utah, Nevada, and the western part of Colorado to the United States; the "Oregon question" was also settled. Polk was born in Mecklenburg County, North Carolina. In 1806 the family moved to Tennessee. After Polk had been graduated from the University of North Carolina in 1818 at the head of his class, he returned to Tennessee and began preparation in the law. Attracted to politics, Polk soon became a member of the state legislature. In 1824 he was elected to the Congress, and in 1835 he became Speaker of the House—the only Speaker ever to reach the presidency. He retired from the Congress in 1839, was for one term governor of Tennessee, and in 1844 emerged as the successful "dark horse" candidate for President. In 1824 he married Sarah Childress.

Zachary Taylor (1784-1850)

Term 1849-1850, TWELFTH PRESIDENT

A few months after his birth in Orange County, Virginia, Zachary Taylor was taken by his parents by ox-cart to the Kentucky frontier. His boyhood was spent in the country near Louisville. An early desire to become a soldier was realized in 1808 when he joined the regular army. In the War of 1812 Taylor served with distinction. His brilliant defense of Fort Benjamin Harrison against a large force of Indians won him much acclaim. Later he led important commands against the Indians in Illinois and in Florida. By 1845 Taylor was a brigadier-general and in command of the troublesome Southwest. Ordered to the Rio Grande, he was attacked by the Mexicans; but he quickly won the battles of Palo Alto and Resaca de la Palma. Later, against heavy odds, he inspired his men to the new victory of Buena Vista. "Old Rough and Ready," as his soldiers admiringly called him, was a popular hero by 1848; and the Whigs chose him for their presidential candidate. An honest soldier, with no political ambitions or obligations, he protested against the "spoils system." It seemed that he might ease the tensions between the North and the South when suddenly, on July 4, 1850, he was stricken with fever and died five days later—a little more than a year and four months after his inauguration.

Millard Fillmore (1800-1874)

Term 1850-1853, THIRTEENTH PRESIDENT

Millard Fillmore came to the presidency by the accident of President Taylor's death. His political life was a familiar pattern. State-wide success as a lawyer and terms in the New York state legislature and the national Congress placed him high in the councils of the Whig party. Fillmore came from a humble farm family of Cayuga County, New York. As a youth he was apprenticed to a clothier, but he rebelled and studied law instead. He worked for eight years as a clerk in a law office. This different apprenticeship prepared him for the New York bar and fitted him to become a partner in a prominent Buffalo firm. Fillmore's political competitors were men of unusual gifts in oratory when debating skill was at its political peak. Perhaps it was the rivalry among such masters as Clay, Calhoun, and Webster which played a part in giving lesser men an inning of recognition. The highly controversial Compromise of 1850 received Fillmore's support, although President Taylor had opposed it. President Fillmore also signed the Fugitive Slave Law, which further fired the controversy. President Fillmore failed to obtain renomination from the waning Whig party and never again held high political office; he spent the remainder of his life at his home in Buffalo, New York, where he was chancellor at the University of Buffalo.

Franklin Pierce (1804-1869)

Term 1853-1857, FOURTEENTH PRESIDENT

When the Whigs nominated General Scott for the presidency in 1852, the Democrats sought a rival candidate, experienced in politics—with military glamour, and with political appeal to both Northern and Southern Democrats. Franklin Pierce qualified as the successful nominee. Pierce was born at Hillsborough, New Hampshire, and was graduated from Bowdoin College, Maine, in the class of 1824, one class ahead of Longfellow and Hawthorne. Pierce studied law, gained admission to the bar in 1827, and two years later was a member of the New Hampshire legislature. In 1833 he was sent to the House of Representatives at Washington, and in 1837 he entered the Senate. When war was declared with Mexico, Pierce volunteered as a private, but was commissioned as a colonel. His political background, pleasing personality, and steady application brought rapid promotion; and he emerged from the war a brigadier-general. The Pierce administration made the Gadsden Purchase from Mexico, opened up Japanese ports to American traders, furthered plans for the first railroad across the continent to the Pacific, and approved the Kansas-Nebraska Bill—an act which brought the question of slavery extension squarely before the people. Franklin Pierce failed to satisfy his own party and was not renominated.

James Buchanan (1791-1868)

Term 1857-1861, FIFTEENTH PRESIDENT

James Buchanan was born in southwestern Pennsylvania near Mercersburg. In his sixteenth year he entered Dickinson College. After his graduation, he studied law and was admitted to the bar at the age of twenty-one. While serving in the War of 1812, he was elected to the Pennsylvania legislature; and thus he began a long life of public service, including membership in both houses of the national Congress. He started his political career as a Federalist, but soon switched to the Democrats. He was President Polk's Secretary of State; and President Pierce made him minister to Great Britain. Three times his name was placed before national nominating conventions as a candidate for the presidency, and in 1856 he was nominated and elected. Slavery and states' rights became flaming questions during his administration. Although he was convinced that slavery was morally wrong, he believed that, under the Constitution, he could not interfere with slavery or prevent secession. Buchanan's administration has been held as inadequate in a time of great crisis. Four Cabinet members resigned, partly in protest against his do-nothing policy. Before a new President could take over the faltering ship of state, South Carolina had seceded, the Confederacy was founded, and war loomed between the North and South.

Abraham Lincoln (1809-1865)

Term 1861-1865, SIXTEENTH PRESIDENT

Whenever men speak of great leaders, the name of Abraham Lincoln is heard. No national leader has come from more humble beginnings, and none has achieved a more revered memory. Born in a log cabin, he was tested and trained by the rough, frontier life of Kentucky and Indiana. He had almost no formal schooling, but he was a devoted student of people and of the books that he could buy or borrow. In 1831 he settled in New Salem, Illinois. In turn, he was store-keeper, postmaster, and surveyor—earning the high regard of his neighbors as "Honest Abe." Already marked for leadership, Lincoln moved to Springfield in 1837 and began the practice of law. He was elected to the state legislature, became successful as a circuit-riding lawyer, and served for one term as Representative in Congress. Lincoln's loyalty to the Union inspired his belief that the nation could not endure "half slave and half free." As the Republican candidate for Senator, he opposed the extension of slavery in the famous debates with Stephen A. Douglas. He lost the election, but he won a national renown which elected him President in 1860. War followed his inauguration. Confusion and disaster endangered the Union cause, but Lincoln's courage and faith surmounted all obstacles. Five days after Lee's surrender, Lincoln was shot by John Wilkes Booth.

Andrew Johnson (1808-1875)

Term 1865-1869, SEVENTEENTH PRESIDENT

At the age of ten Andrew Johnson was apprenticed to a tailor. At that time he could neither read nor write. When he was eighteen, he left his birthplace, Raleigh, North Carolina—settling at Greenville in eastern Tennessee. The following year he married Eliza McCardle, who had a good education, and she began at once to teach her husband reading, writing, and arithmetic. Johnson became interested in politics as a Jacksonian Democrat. In 1830 he was elected mayor of Greenville; then, for several years he was a member of the state legislature; in 1843 he was sent to the House of Representatives at Washington; in 1853 he became governor of Tennessee; and in 1857 he entered the United States Senate where he advocated and secured passage of a homestead bill which President Buchanan vetoed. Although a sincere Southerner, he could not accept secession. He placed his faith and his devotion in the Union. This action separated him from the South and Lincoln appointed him military governor of Tennessee. Two years later he was chosen Vice-President. Lincoln's death thrust Johnson into a situation for which he seemed unfitted, but possibly no more so than were his associates. Politics led to impeachment proceedings; these failed, but Johnson was not renominated. Seven years later he was returned to the Senate.

Ulysses Simpson Grant (1822-1885)

Term 1869-1877, EIGHTEENTH PRESIDENT

Ulysses Simpson Grant was born at Point Pleasant, Clermont County, Ohio. He attended school and worked on his father's farm until, at the age of seventeen, he entered the Military Academy at West Point. Soon after his graduation, Grant took part in every important battle of the Mexican War, except Buena Vista; and he was twice cited for gallantry. In 1854 he resigned his captain's commission, and the next seven years saw Grant a dismal failure at farming, at selling real estate, and at clerking—the latter in his brother's store at Galena, Illinois. When war began in 1861, the Governor of Illinois put Grant to work at drilling recruits. Eight months later he was a major-general with brilliant victories to his credit. The North had found the military leader who could save the Union. The Republican party selected the victorious Grant for its candidate in 1868. Having no interest in politics, he reluctantly accepted the presidential honor which a grateful people awarded him. Grant's administration faced complex problems of reconstruction in the South, serious questions of national finance, and important matters in foreign policy. Despite difficulties, disagreements, and dissatisfactions, the Republicans returned him for a second term. He married Julia T. Dent of St. Louis, Missouri. He died at Mt. McGregor, New York, after a long illness.

Rutherford B. Hayes (1822-1893)

Term 1877-1881, NINETEENTH PRESIDENT

The war record of Rutherford Birchard Hayes, distinctive with brave exploits and topped in 1865 by a major-general's rank, gave him great prestige in his native state of Ohio. The state Republicans persuaded him to become a Congressman; and in 1867 he was elected Governor of Ohio. In 1875 he was chosen Governor for a third term, the first man in Ohio to gain this honor. The resulting acclaim brought to him national recognition and the Republican nomination for the presidency. In the campaign of 1876 he defeated Samuel J. Tilden by one electoral vote in a disputed election. His administration was peaceful and honorable. He fought for an improved civil service; and he opposed political patronage. Rutherford Hayes was unusually well educated. His first schooling was received from his widowed mother in the town of Delaware, Ohio. A kindly uncle sent him to a Connecticut academy and later to Kenyon College. At twenty he was graduated as the valedictorian and the youngest member of his class. He entered the Harvard University Law School, finished the course in two years, and in 1845 began the practice of law in Fremont, Ohio. Hayes married Lucy Ware Webb in 1852. They had seven sons and one daughter. He died at his Spiegel Grove estate in Fremont, Ohio, and was buried in Spiegel Grove State Park.

James Abram Garfield (1831-1881)

Term 1881, TWENTIETH PRESIDENT

Like most of the national leaders James A. Garfield came from sturdy pioneer stock. A Puritan ancestor was one of the founders of Watertown, Massachusetts, in 1630. His father, Abraham Garfield, moved to Ohio 200 years later, settling in Cuyahoga County—where James was born. His father died when James was two. His mother and older brother assured him a good education. Life was hard on the frontier, and James helped to earn his own way by working at various jobs. He taught country school, attended Geauga Seminary, and then worked his way through Williams College, graduating with honors. Returning to Hiram, Ohio, he taught school, preached sermons, made political speeches, studied law, became principal of the Eclectic Institute at Hiram, and was admitted to the bar. When the war between the states broke out, Garfield received a commission and served so well that he attained the rank of major-general. While still in service, he was elected to the Congress as Representative from his Ohio district. In 1880 Republican factions, after much difficulty in selecting candidates, compromised by nominating Garfield for President, with Chester A. Arthur as his running mate. On July 2, a few months after his inauguration, the President was fatally shot by Charles Guiteau.

Chester Alan Arthur (1830-1886)

Term 1881-1885, TWENTY-FIRST PRESIDENT

The choice of Chester A. Arthur in 1880 as nominee for the vice-presidency was the result of a settlement between two Republican factions. Thus, the incident of compromise plus the accident of President Garfield's death brought Arthur to the presidency. As Collector of the Port of New York, Arthur opposed President Hayes' attempt to bring his office, with its many small jobs, under the civil service, and he was removed from office by the President. The solemn obligations of the presidency changed Arthur's attitudes and actions. He served with ability and distinction. His old political associates were surprised as he now supported civil service reform and put the welfare of the country above party ambitions. By these actions he lost the support of his own political group, and he was not renominated. Arthur was born at Fairfield, Vermont, the eldest son of Reverend William Arthur. His school days began at Union Village in Washington County. At the age of eighteen he was graduated from Union College. He taught school while he studied law, became principal of an academy, and in 1853 he was admitted to the New York bar. Professional success came rapidly. During the war between the states, Arthur served as quartermaster-general of the New York State Militia and recruited and prepared troops for the front.

Grover Cleveland (1837-1908)

Terms 1885-1889, 1893-1897, TWENTY-SECOND PRESIDENT AND TWENTY-FOURTH PRESIDENT

Grover Cleveland's birthplace was Caldwell, New Jersey. Later the family moved to Fayetteville, New York, where Grover attended the village school. At sixteen his father's death forced him to earn his own way. He studied law in Buffalo, New York, and was admitted to practice in 1859. Cleveland's political career started with his appointment as assistant district attorney of Erie County, and shortly afterward he was elected sheriff. The citizens of Buffalo were seeking a courageous and honest mayor to end a long period of political corruption. The Democrats nominated Cleveland, and to the surprise of the political bosses he was elected. Cleveland's zeal for good government was rewarded further by his election in 1882 to the New York governorship. In 1884 a national recognition of his merit swept him into the Democratic nomination and the nation's highest office. In 1886 he became the first President to be married in the White House. His bride was Frances Folsom. Cleveland's strength within the party gained him the Democratic renomination in 1888, but the Republicans won the election. The Democrats chose him again in 1892, many independent voters came to his support, and he won easily. His honesty and unwavering courage were ably applied to his office.

Benjamin Harrison (1833-1901)

Term 1889-1893, TWENTY-THIRD PRESIDENT

Benjamin was the second Harrison to become President. His grandfather, William Henry Harrison, was ninth President of the United States, and his great-grandfather, Benjamin Harrison, was a governor of Virginia. His father, John Scott Harrison, was a member of the Congress for four years. Benjamin Harrison was born at North Bend, Ohio, where he attended school until he was fourteen. In 1852 he was graduated from Miami University. The next year he married Miss Caroline Scott, and in 1854 he was admitted to the bar, and settled in Indianapolis, Indiana. When war came, Harrison was active in recruiting the Seventieth Indiana Regiment of Volunteers. He served in the western campaigns; and in 1865 was mustered out a brigadier-general. He was defeated for the governorship of Indiana in 1876. He became United States Senator in 1881, but he was not reelected to the legislature. The Republicans, searching for a candidate with good political traditions, preferably from the Middle West, found Harrison to be the right man, and he defeated Cleveland in the election of 1888. Benjamin Harrison was the fourth general to become President since 1868. Under Harrison's administration six states were admitted to the Union: South Dakota, North Dakota, Montana, and Washington in 1889; and Idaho and Wyoming in 1890.

William McKinley (1843-1901)

Term 1897-1901, TWENTY-FIFTH PRESIDENT

William McKinley was the third President to be assassinated. Shot by an anarchist, Leon Czolgosz, September 6, 1901, at the Pan-American Exposition, Buffalo, New York, he died eight days later. The McKinley family lived at Niles, Ohio, when William was born. At seventeen he entered Allegheny College at Meadville, Pennsylvania. Later he taught school, then enlisted in the Twenty-third Ohio Volunteers. In four years of war he rose to the rank of major and was cited for gallantry by President Lincoln. On his return from the war, he completed a law course, married Miss Ida Saxton, and settled in Canton, Ohio, to practice his profession. As the prosecuting attorney of Stark County in 1869, he began a long and honorable career in the public service. From 1876 until 1891 he served in the national House of Representatives; then he was twice elected governor of Ohio. McKinley's staunch Republican record, as well as his support of a high tariff and of the gold standard, won popularity for him among the Republicans. He was nominated and elected President in the campaign of 1896. His administration was distinguished by victory in the Spanish-American War, annexation of Hawaii, and acquisition of the Philippines, Puerto Rico, and Guam. In 1900 McKinley was elected to a second term.

Theodore Roosevelt (1858-1919)

Term 1901-1909, TWENTY-SIXTH PRESIDENT

Theodore Roosevelt was born in New York City, where his ancestors, of Dutch origin, had lived since 1644. During his childhood Theodore was afflicted with asthma and near-sightedness. By unusual tenacity of purpose and effort, he overcame his physical handicaps, and at eighteen entered Harvard University, graduating in 1880. In 1882 he turned to politics, and with Republican party aid, he was elected to the New York legislature. Two years later he suddenly lost both his mother and his young wife. His health was not equal to this double tragedy, and he sought the curative qualities of a Dakota ranch. Returning to New York in 1886, he again threw his energy into politics and served as civil service commissioner and police commissioner of New York City. When the Spanish War came, he was the Assistant Secretary of the Navy, a post he resigned to organize the 1st U. S. Cavalry (Roosevelt's Rough Riders). In 1898 he was elected governor of New York; in 1900 popular approval of his attacks upon unfair practices increased his political strength and brought him the vice-presidency; in 1901 McKinley's assassination made him President; and in 1904 he was elected President. His term was noted for "trust busting," vigorous foreign policy, and for the Panama Canal Project. In 1912 he ran for President, but was defeated.

William Howard Taft (1857-1930)

Term 1909-1913, TWENTY-SEVENTH PRESIDENT

Nine years as Chief Justice of the Supreme Court and four years as Chief Executive of the United States made William Howard Taft the only American who has been chief of both judicial and executive branches of the national government. His father, a Superior Court judge, a Secretary of War, and an Attorney-General, set a pattern which his son exceeded. William became a judge of the Superior Court in Cincinnati (his native city), a United States Solicitor-General for President Harrison, and a Secretary of War for President Theodore Roosevelt. Taft was also a Federal Circuit judge and a Professor of Law in Yale University. In 1900 he was appointed Civil Governor of the Philippines and in 1906 took temporary charge of affairs in Cuba. In 1908 he was elected President, but the famous Republican split spelled defeat for him in 1912. Though Taft's administration was a stormy one, he was personally well-liked. He was notably successful as a lawyer, jurist, and public administrator. The postal savings bank and the parcel post system were created in his term; and the Sixteenth and Seventeenth Amendments were passed by the Congress. He was well educated, graduating from Yale University with high honors in 1878 and from the Cincinnati Law School in 1880. In 1886 he married Helen Herron.

Woodrow Wilson (1856-1924)

Term 1913-1921, TWENTY-EIGHTH PRESIDENT

Staunton, Virginia, was the birthplace of Thomas Woodrow Wilson, the eighth Virginian to become President. Young Wilson's early schooling was irregular, but a cultured home formed his character with wisdom and refinement. He was graduated from Princeton in 1879; and two years later he received a law degree at the University of Virignia. A zest for learning and for teaching led him into further study at Johns Hopkins University. Teaching positions at Bryn Mawr College and at Wesleyan and Princeton Universities followed. In 1902 he was chosen president of Princeton and served until 1910. From 1911 to 1913 he was governor of New Jersey. The Democrats, looking for a candidate of liberal views, selected Wilson as their leader in the 1912 campaign and the Taft-Roosevelt feud insured a Democratic victory. In Wilson's first term important legislation affected banking, trusts, tariff, labor, and income taxation. Wilson's personal strength and his sincere attempts to avert war won his re-election in 1916. Despite Wilson's efforts the inevitable war came, and he was compelled to give leadership for the great task of victory. As a world leader his fourteen points formed a basis for peace, and he insisted upon the acceptance of the League of Nations. which the United States, alone of the great nations, rejected.

Warren Gamaliel Harding (1865-1923)

Term 1921-1923, TWENTY-NINTH PRESIDENT

Warren Harding, the seventh President from Ohio, was born on a farm near the village of Corsica. As a boy he learned the printer's trade in a small shop at Caledonia, Ohio. For a time young Warren attended Ohio Central College, but a newspaper job at Marion lured him away from school and into a lifetime of newspaper work. Failing, by his Republican activities, to please his Democratic employer, Harding gained independence by purchasing the *Marion Star,* an enterprise which became a major success. From 1900 to 1904 he served in the Ohio State Senate, but he was defeated for the governorship in 1910. Ohio sent him to the United States Senate in 1915. The Republicans in 1920 were deadlocked over presidential candidates until some ardent Ohioans, supported by a small bloc of Senators and a few party leaders, manipulated a triumph for Warren Harding. The chief campaign issue was the acceptance of the League of Nations, but those who opposed it, or wished reservations, won out. Harding's distinguished appearance, genial nature, and political experience forecast a normal administration; but instead came such things as the "Teapot Dome" affair and the President's tragic death. Two unworthy Cabinet members were the chief figures in the Teapot Dome oil scandal.

Calvin Coolidge (1872-1933)

Term 1923-1929, THIRTIETH PRESIDENT

The news of Harding's death came to Calvin Coolidge in the little farmhouse at Plymouth, Vermont, where he was born. His father, a local justice, administered the oath of office to the new President by the light of a kerosene lamp. After a boyhood combining farm life with good schooling, Calvin entered Amherst College. He was graduated with honors in 1895. On leaving college, he began to read law in Northampton, Massachusetts, and two years later he was admitted to practice. In 1905 he married Grace A. Goodhue, who was to become one of the best liked of the White House hostesses. Coolidge served Massachusetts in both houses of the legislature and then became governor in 1919. The vigorous words and effective actions which Coolidge as governor applied to the Boston police strike rang favorably throughout the country. He was re-elected governor by a large majority; and he was at once proposed for the presidency, which he was to gain later by way of the vice-presidency. Coolidge brought native forthrightness, sparse utterance, and a thrifty economy to the White House. Drastic reduction of expenditures followed in all departments of the government. With rare political courage he vetoed a soldiers' bonus bill. Elected in his own right, in 1924, Coolidge declined renomination in 1927.

Herbert Clark Hoover (1874-1964)

Term 1929-1933, THIRTY-FIRST PRESIDENT

At nine years of age Herbert Hoover was left an orphan in his native village of West Branch, Iowa. Herbert went to live with his Quaker uncle in Oregon. He worked at various jobs, attended night school, and was admitted to Leland Stanford University, where he studied geology and mining. After several years of hard experience Hoover became chief engineer for a mining company in Australia. Then he was director-general of mines for the Chinese government, and soon thereafter he filled assignments the world over as a mining expert. When World War I began, Hoover was made chairman of the American Relief Commission in Belgium. In 1917 he was appointed Food Administrator for the United States. After the Armistice he became head of the European Economic Council and gave several years to the relief of distressed peoples. In 1921 when Hoover accepted the Secretary of Commerce post, he was probably the most favorably known American throughout the world. The American public continued to think well of him, electing him President in 1928. His term started smoothly, but was soon overwhelmed by world-wide depression and panic. His administration was blamed for the disaster, causing his defeat in 1932. Hoover was one of the most honored of presidents, receiving many honorary degrees in his lifetime.

Franklin Delano Roosevelt (1882-1945)

Term 1933-1945, THIRTY-SECOND PRESIDENT

Franklin D. Roosevelt, a fifth cousin of Theodore Roosevelt, was born at Hyde Park, New York. Privately tutored until fourteen, he prepared for college at Groton Academy. In 1904 he was graduated from Harvard and then attended Columbia University Law School, during which time he married Anna Eleanor Roosevelt. He was already interested in politics, and in 1910 was elected to the state senate on the Democratic ticket. Roosevelt was appointed Assistant Secretary of the Navy in 1913, serving until 1920, resigning to accept the nomination for Vice-President. Shortly after the Democratic defeat, he was stricken with infantile paralysis; but persistent treatment plus heroic courage permitted him to return to political activity. He carried on to be elected governor of New York for two terms, a record which brought him the presidential nomination in the depression year of 1932. New social legislation followed. Roosevelt was renominated and re-elected in 1936; in 1940 (the first third term); and for a fourth term in 1944. Long threatening war broke on December 7, 1941. Roosevelt met with Churchill to discuss global war's demands and later held further conferences with Churchill and Soviet Premier Stalin to outline postwar policies. Roosevelt died suddenly, April 12, 1945.

Harry S Truman (1884-1972)

Term 1945-1953, THIRTY-THIRD PRESIDENT

Harry S Truman was the seventh Vice-President to receive the presidential mantle by the constitutional provision of immediate succession. He accepted the heavy obligations of the presidency with courage and with resolution to successfully complete the plans already made for Allied victory. Before his election to the vice-presidency, Truman was, for ten years, a member of the United States Senate. He won commendation for his work as the chairman of a Senate committee on defense expenditures. Harry Truman spent the early years of his life on a farm near his birthplace, Lamar, Missouri. He combined farming with schooling, including music lessons, and was graduated from the Independence, Missouri, high school. He held jobs as a drugstore clerk, railroad timekeeper, bank clerk, and haberdasher. Entering World War I as a private, he became captain of a battery of field artillery and saw action in the famous battles of St. Mihiel and Meuse-Argonne. Truman, elected president in 1948, had to deal with the problems of postwar recovery, of the "Cold War," and of rearmament and the economic dislocations caused by it. He led opposition to the spread of communism in Europe with the Marshall Plan and in Asia with the signing in 1951 of the Pacific Pact and the Japanese Peace Treaty. He declined to be a candidate in 1952.

Dwight David Eisenhower (1890-1969)

Term 1953-1961, THIRTY-FOURTH PRESIDENT

The second graduate of West Point to become President, Dwight David Eisenhower was born in Denison, Tex. He was graduated from the United States Military Academy in 1915 and the following year married Mamie Geneva Doud. He was a member of Gen. Douglas MacArthur's staff, 1933-39. Having advanced rapidly in rank prior to U.S. entry in World War II he was supreme commander of the Allied forces in the North Africa invasion of 1942. As supreme commander of the Allied Expeditionary Forces, he directed the landing on the Normandy beaches. In December, 1944, he was made General of the Army, the highest military rank. He served as commander of the U.S. Occupation Forces in Germany. After serving as Chief of Staff, 1945-48, he retired from military service to become president of Columbia University. In 1950 he accepted a new post as supreme commander of NATO forces, but soon resigned to become the Republican presidential candidate in 1952. He was elected President the same year. Seeking re-election in 1956, the President campaigned on a platform of continued "Peace and Prosperity," and won a large majority of the popular vote and an overwhelming majority in the electoral college. During his second term, 1961, Eisenhower was the oldest—70 years 3 months—U.S. President in history.

John Fitzgerald Kennedy (1917-1963)
Term 1961-1963, THIRTY-FIFTH PRESIDENT

John Fitzgerald Kennedy, the second-youngest man to become President, was born in Brookline, Mass. He graduated *cum laude* from Harvard in 1940, and the following year enlisted in the U.S. Navy, and served with distinction throughout World War II. Entering politics in 1946 after a brief but highly successful career in journalism, he was elected on the Democratic ticket from the Eleventh District of Massachusetts to the House of Representatives; re-election followed in 1948 and 1950. In 1952, after a vigorous campaign, he was elected senator from Massachusetts, defeating the incumbent Republican, Henry Cabot Lodge, Jr., whom Kennedy was again to oppose and defeat in the 1960 presidential election, in which Lodge was Richard Nixon's Republican vice presidential running mate. The year 1956 saw the publication of Kennedy's best-selling, Pulitzer prize-winning *Profiles in Courage;* it also saw the youthful Massachusetts senator capture the political limelight by nearly winning the Democratic vice-presidential nomination. In 1958 he was re-elected senator. At the Democratic National Convention in July, 1960, he was the overwhelming choice of the assembled delegates, who gave him the nomination on the first ballot. He was elected President the following November. On November 22, 1963, he was assassinated.

Lyndon Baines Johnson (1908 1973)
Term 1963-1969, THIRTY-SIXTH PRESIDENT

Lyndon Baines Johnson was born near Stonewall, Tex. Supporting himself at Southwest Texas State Teachers College by doing janitorial work, he was graduated with a B.S. in 1930. From 1932 to 1935 he served as secretary to Representative Richard M. Kleberg of Texas. In 1934 he was married to Claudia Alta Taylor. After a year in law school and a year as state director of the National Youth Administration of Texas, he was elected to the U.S. House of Representatives, where he served five terms interrupted only by a tour of duty with the U.S. Navy in World War II. Elected to the U.S. Senate in 1943, he became in 1953 the youngest Senate party leader in U.S. history. As Vice-President in the Kennedy administration, he was an important governmental representative abroad. He also became chairman of the National Aeronautics and Space Council. On Nov. 22, 1963, after President Kennedy's assassination, Johnson was sworn in as President at Dallas, Tex. He was elected President in 1964. During his administration, Congress passed a number of bills that he had requested to support his Great Society program, such as Medicare, antipoverty legislation, civil rights, and aid to education. In foreign affairs, the role of the United States in Vietnam became a subject of controversy. In 1968 he declined to run for re-election.

Richard Milhous Nixon (1913-)
Term 1969-1974, THIRTY-SEVENTH PRESIDENT

Richard Milhous Nixon, born in Yorba Linda, Calif., received his education in Whittier College and Duke University Law School. After serving in the Navy during World War II he was elected, in 1946, to Congress, where he was catapulted to fame by his handling of the Chambers-Hiss case. In 1950 he moved to the Senate and in 1952 was elected Vice-President. He narrowly lost the 1960 presidential election to Kennedy and returned to California where, in 1962, he was badly defeated in the election for governor. He recovered from the defeat and, in 1968, was elected to the presidency. He was re-elected in 1972 by one of the largest majorities in the nation's history. Nixon's presidency was marked by strong achievements in foreign affairs: détente with Russia and China, termination of U.S. participation in the Vietnam war, truce in the Middle East. But at home his administration collapsed: his Vice-President, Spiro Agnew, resigned in disgrace, and, as the Watergate Scandal unfolded, twenty-eight of his aides were either convicted or indicted for criminal offenses. When, in 1974, further revelations showed his own part in the scandal and impeachment and conviction seemed certain, Nixon became the first President in the history of the United States to resign. His resignation became effective on August 9, and he was succeeded in office by his Vice-President.

Gerald Rudolph Ford (1913-)
Term 1974-1977, THIRTY-EIGHTH PRESIDENT

Gerald Rudolph Ford was born in Omaha, Neb. and christened Leslie Lynch King. His name was changed two years later when his mother remarried. Ford graduated from the University of Michigan in 1935 and, supporting himself as a football and boxing coach, continued his studies at Yale Law School, from which he was graduated in the top third of his class in 1941. He then practiced law in Grand Rapids, Mich.—with a four-year interruption while he served in the Navy during World War II—until he was elected to the House of Representatives from Michigan's Fifth District in 1948. Shortly before that election he met and married Elizabeth Bloomer. He was returned to Congress in six succeeding elections, never with less than 60 percent of the vote. In 1951 he was assigned to the House Appropriations Committee and in 1965 defeated Charles Halleck for the position of House Minority Leader. He defines his political philosophy as that of "... a conservative in fiscal affairs, a moderate in domestic affairs, and a liberal in foreign policy." At the urging of his wife, he had decided to retire from politics by 1976, but in 1973, upon Spiro Agnew's resignation, he was appointed Vice-President by Richard Nixon, and in 1974, when Nixon himself resigned, Gerald Ford assumed the office of the presidency.

James Earl (Jimmy) Carter, Jr. (1924-)
Term 1977-1981, THIRTY-NINTH PRESIDENT

Jimmy Carter was born and grew up in Plains, Georgia. He attended Georgia Southwestern College and the Georgia Institute of Technology in 1941 and 1942 and then entered the U.S. Naval Academy in Annapolis, graduating in 1946. Carter remained in the Navy until 1953. During his naval career he worked with Adm. Hyman Rickover whose influence on him was, according to Carter's autobiography, perhaps second only to that of his parents. Carter left the Navy in 1953 as a lieutenant. After his father's death in 1953, Carter entered the family business and became a successful peanut farmer. He had married Rosalynn Smith of Plains in 1947 and they had three sons and one daughter. In Plains, Carter became active in community affairs and local politics. In 1962, he won a seat in the state senate. Carter had a liberal voting record during his two senate terms. In 1966, he ran for governor of Georgia against segregationist Lester Maddox. Carter lost but ran again in 1970, this time winning both the primary and the general election. Carter began to broaden his political base in 1974 when he traveled as Democratic Party national campaign coordinator for the 1974 elections. He gained national notice in 1976 by intense campaigning, won the Democratic nomination, and finally defeated Gerald Ford in a closely fought race.

Ronald Wilson Reagan (1911-)
Term 1981- , FORTIETH PRESIDENT

Ronald Wilson Reagan, the only former actor to become President, was born in Tampico, Illinois. He received his education from Eureka College, graduating in 1932, became a radio sports announcer that same year in Davenport, Iowa. In 1937, while covering a sports assignment, he came to the attention of a Warner Brothers agent who gave him a screen test and signed him to a movie contract. Over the next several years he appeared in numerous pictures. His acting career was interrupted during World War II when he served in the Army Air Corps making training films. After the war, while continuing his work in the entertainment industry, he became increasingly involved in politics. Although at first active in many liberal political organizations, he soon became fearful of Communist subversion and moved to the right testifying before the House Un-American Activities Committee in 1947 on Communist influence in the movie industry. After 1965, he devoted full time to politics. In 1966 he campaigned for the governorship of California and beat Democratic incumbent Edmund G. Brown. In 1968 he made an unsuccessful bid for the Republican presidential nomination but was easily reelected Governor in 1970. He tried for the presidential nomination again in 1976 but again was unsuccessful. Finally in 1980, after intense campaigning, he won the nomination and went on to defeat Jimmy Carter, winning a large majority of the popular vote and an overwhelming majority in the electoral college.

NOMINATING CONVENTIONS

Every four years and during the summer preceding the presidential election, each major political party holds a national nominating convention to choose its presidential and vice-presidential candidate. Also adopted at this time are the party platforms and the rules governing the national party organization. The candidates are chosen by delegates who are selected from each state. About two-thirds of the states select their delegations at party conventions, while the remaining one-third select their delegates through primary votes.

National political conventions originated out of necessity and dissatisfaction with the old method of choosing a presidential candidate. Prior to the election of James Monroe in 1816, presidential nominations were made at informal party caucuses. During the Monroe administration, however, organized political parties, as they existed in the past, collapsed. The breakdown was most evident in the hotly contested election of 1824 when four candidates independently sought the office of the presidency. As a result of this election, political leaders came to realize the need for a party system that would enable them to form the alliances necessary to capture the presidency. After the election of Andrew Jackson in 1828, party lines became more defined, and in 1832 opposition parties met for the first time at national party conventions to prepare for the presidential elections. Since then, all candidates elected to the office of the presidency have been chosen from the two major political parties.

Today, political aspirants for their party's nomination may prove their merit by entering primary elections prior to the convention. By successfully campaigning in a given primary election, the perspective nominee may accumulate the necessary delegation commitments to aid in securing his nomination at the convention. These elections also serve to focus national attention on the nominees.

Although current nominating procedures of the two major political parties are similar, some variations exist. For example, in the Republican convention, each delegate is allowed to cast his vote as he chooses, while in the Democratic convention, a modified "unit vote" rule is imposed. Under this method, some states must cast their votes as a unit if instructed to do so by their state conventions, while other states allow their delegates to cast their votes individually if they were elected in the state primary. Another difference concerns the number of votes needed by a candidate to win his party's nomination. The Republicans have always required their candidate to gain a simple majority. This was not true for the Democrats until the 1936 convention. Before then, a candidate needed a two-thirds majority to win the nomination.

Balloting continues in each convention until one presidential nominee has received a simple majority. Although prolonged balloting is unusual, there have been some exceptions. In Democratic conventions 46 ballots were required in 1912, 44 in 1920, and 103 in 1924. The Republicans have been more successful in choosing their candidates on fewer ballots. Delegates often use their ballots for political maneuvering. They may cast their ballots for a candidate who cannot win in order to prevent another from winning, or they may withhold their ballots at first, only to release them later and thus show a candidate gaining strength. Most of the time, however, a given candidate is nominated on the first ballot.

Once the presidential nominee has been selected, delegates cast their ballot for a vice-presidential candidate. This ballot is usually perfunctory, as delegates as a rule unanimously endorse the running mate selected by the presidential nominee. After the vice-president is nominated the task of the convention is complete.

THE ELECTORAL COLLEGE

The electoral method of choosing the president was adopted by the Constitutional Convention on September 7, 1787. Other methods were discussed and debated but eventually rejected because they failed to engender adequate support. One method suggested that Congress choose the president. However, a deadlock resulted over the distribution of congressional voting power; that is, whether it should be by joint ballot or whether each state should have a single vote. The impasse was resolved by the complete rejection of the legislative electoral method. Another method suggested that the president be chosen by the direct vote of the people. This method had been discussed before and twice defeated when brought to a vote. Few delegates felt the nation was sufficiently mature to entrust the choice of a president directly to the people. The method finally accepted after many compromises was the intermediate elector plan. Under this plan the president would be chosen by representative electors from each state. The actual procedure for choosing electors is stated in Article II, Section I of the Constitution:

> Each state shall appoint, in such manner as the legislature thereof may direct, a number of electors, equal to the whole number of senators and representatives to which the state may be entitled in the Congress: but no senator or representative, or person holding an office of trust or profit under the United States, shall be appointed an elector.

It was not decided how the state legislatures should select their electors until September 13, 1788 when the Continental Congress directed the states to individually determine the selection of their electors. The actual duties of the electors are redefined in the twelfth amendment to the Constitution which was adopted on September 24, 1804:

> The Electors shall meet in their respective states, and vote by ballot for President and Vice-President, one of whom, at least, shall not be an inhabitant of the same state with themselves; they shall name in their ballots the person voted for as President, and in distinct ballots the person voted for as Vice-President, and they shall make distinct lists of all persons voted for as President, and of all persons voted for as Vice-President, and of the number of votes for each, which lists they shall sign and certify, and transmit sealed to the seat of the government of the United States, directed to the President of the Senate;—The President of the Senate shall, in the presence of the Senate and House of Representatives, open all the certificates and the votes shall then be counted;—The person having the greatest number of votes for President, shall be the President, if such number be a majority of the whole number of Electors appointed; and if no person has such majority, then from the persons having the highest numbers not exceeding three on the list of those voted for as President, the House of Representatives shall choose immediately, by ballot, the President. But in choosing the President, the votes shall be taken by states, the representation from each state having one vote; a quorum for this purpose shall consist of a member or members from two-thirds of the states, and a majority of all the states shall be necessary to a choice. . . . The person having the greatest number of votes as Vice-President, shall be the Vice-President, if such number be a majority of the whole number of Electors appointed, and if no person have a majority, then from the two highest numbers on the list, the Senate shall choose the Vice-President; a quorum for the purpose shall consist of two-thirds of the whole number of Senators, and a majority of the whole number shall be necessary to a choice. But no person constitutionally ineligible to the office of President shall be eligible to that of Vice-President of the United States.

The electoral plan was adopted because it offered something to each faction: the large states received representation of electors according to the size of their population; the small states got equal voting rights in contingent elections if the majority of electors failed to choose a president; those advocating States' rights were acknowledged by allowing the state legislature the right to select electors as they saw fit; and those favoring a direct popular vote got at least an approximation of a direct vote if the electors reflected the popular will.

Today, most states nominate their electors at the individual party conventions. After the popular presidential election, the designated party electors meet when the electoral college convenes and formally vote for the candidate with the greatest popular vote in their respective states. A given state's entire electoral vote goes to the candidate with the greatest popular vote.

The present electoral college consists of 538 votes: 435 correspond to the number of representatives in the House of Representatives; 100 represent the number of senators; and 3 represent the number for the District of Columbia. The votes are apportioned as follows:

State	Votes	State	Votes	State	Votes
Alabama	9	Kentucky	9	North Dakota	3
Alaska	3	Louisiana	10	Ohio	25
Arizona	6	Maine	4	Oklahoma	8
Arkansas	6	Maryland	10	Oregon	6
California	45	Massachusetts	14	Pennsylvania	27
Colorado	7	Michigan	21	Rhode Island	4
Connecticut	8	Minnesota	10	South Carolina	8
Delaware	3	Mississipi	7	South Dakota	4
District of Columbia	3	Missouri	12	Tennessee	10
Florida	17	Montana	4	Texas	26
Georgia	12	Nebraska	5	Utah	4
Hawaii	4	Nevada	3	Vermont	3
Idaho	4	New Hampshire	4	Virginia	12
Illinois	26	New Jersey	17	Washington	9
Indiana	13	New Mexico	4	West Virginia	6
Iowa	8	New York	41	Wisconsin	11
Kansas	7	North Carolina	13	Wyoming	3

PRESIDENTS OF THE UNITED STATES

Name	Held Office	From State	Born	Died	Brithplace	Party	Vice-President
1. GEORGE WASHINGTON	1789-1797	Va.	1732	1799	Westmoreland Co., Va.	Fed.	JOHN ADAMS
2. JOHN ADAMS	1797-1801	Mass.	1735	1826	Quincy, Mass.	Fed.	THOMAS JEFFERSON
3. THOMAS JEFFERSON	1801-1809	Va.	1743	1826	Shadwell, Va.	Rep.[1]	AARON BURR GEORGE CLINTON
4. JAMES MADISON	1809-1817	Va.	1751	1836	Port Conway, Va.	Rep.[1]	GEORGE CLINTON
5. JAMES MONROE	1817-1825	Va.	1758	1831	Westmoreland Co., Va.	Rep.[1]	DANIEL D. TOMPKINS
6. JOHN QUINCY ADAMS	1825-1829	Mass.	1767	1848	Quincy, Mass.	Rep.[1]	JOHN C. CALHOUN
7. ANDREW JACKSON	1829-1837	Tenn.	1767	1845	New Lancaster Co., S.C.	Dem.	JOHN C. CALHOUN MARTIN VAN BUREN
8. MARTIN VAN BUREN	1837-1841	N.Y.	1782	1862	Kinderhook, N.Y.	Dem.	RICHARD M. JOHNSON
9. WILLIAM HENRY HARRISON	1841	Ohio	1773	1841	Berkeley, Va.	Whig	JOHN TYLER
10. JOHN TYLER	1841-1845	Va.	1790	1862	Greenway, Va.	Whig	
11. JAMES KNOX POLK	1845-1849	Tenn.	1795	1849	Mecklenburg Co., N.C.	Dem.	GEORGE M. DALLAS
12. ZACHARY TAYLOR	1849-1850	La.	1784	1850	Orange Co., Va.	Whig	MILLARD FILLMORE
13. MILLARD FILLMORE	1850-1853	N.Y.	1800	1874	Cayuga Co., N.Y.	Whig	
14. FRANKLIN PIERCE	1853-1857	N.H.	1804	1869	Hillsboro, N.H.	Dem.	WILLIAM R. KING
15. JAMES BUCHANAN	1857-1861	Pa.	1791	1868	Mercersburg, Pa.	Dem	JOHN C. BRECKINRIDGE
16. ABRAHAM LINCOLN	1861-1865	Ill.	1809	1865	Hardin Co., Ky.	Rep.[2]	HANNIBAL HAMLIN ANDREW JOHNSON
17. ANDREW JOHNSON	1865-1869	Tenn.	1808	1875	Raleigh, N.C.	Dem.[2]	
18. ULYSSES SIMPSON GRANT	1869-1877	Ill.	1822	1885	Point Pleasant, Ohio	Rep.	SCHUYLER COLFAX HENRY WILSON
19. RUTHERFORD BIRCHARD HAYES	1877-1881	Ohio	1822	1893	Delaware, Ohio	Rep.	WILLIAM A. WHEELER
20. JAMES ABRAM GARFIELD	1881	Ohio	1831	1881	Orange, Ohio	Rep.	CHESTER A. ARTHUR
21. CHESTER ALAN ARTHUR	1881-1885	N.Y.	1830	1886	Fairfield, Vt.	Rep.	
22. GROVER CLEVELAND	1885-1889	N.Y.	1837	1908	Caldwell, N.J.	Dem.	THOMAS A. HENDRICKS
23. BENJAMIN HARRISON	1889-1893	Ind.	1833	1901	North Bend, Ohio	Rep.	LEVI P. MORTON
24. GROVER CLEVELAND	1893-1897						ADLAI E. STEVENSON
25. WILLIAM McKINLEY	1897-1901	Ohio	1843	1901	Niles, Ohio	Rep.	GARRET A. HOBART THEODORE ROOSEVELT
26. THEODORE ROOSEVELT	1901-1909	N.Y.	1858	1919	New York, N.Y.	Rep.	CHARLES W. FAIRBANKS
27. WILLIAM HOWARD TAFT	1909-1913	Ohio	1857	1930	Cincinnati, Ohio	Rep.	JAMES S. SHERMAN
28. WOODROW WILSON	1913-1921	N.J.	1856	1924	Staunton, Va.	Dem.	THOMAS R. MARSHALL
29. WARREN GAMALIEL HARDING	1921-1923	Ohio	1865	1923	Blooming Grove, Ohio	Rep.	CALVIN COOLIDGE
30. CALVIN COOLIDGE	1923-1929	Mass.	1872	1933	Plymouth, Vt.	Rep.	CHARLES G. DAWES
31. HERBERT CLARK HOOVER	1929-1933	Calif.	1874	1964	West Branch, Iowa	Rep.	CHARLES CURTIS
32. FRANKLIN DELANO ROOSEVELT	1933-1945	N.Y.	1882	1945	Hyde Park, N.Y.	Dem.	JOHN N. GARNER HENRY A. WALLACE HARRY S TRUMAN
33. HARRY S TRUMAN	1945-1953	Mo.	1884	1972	Lamar, Mo.	Dem.	ALBEN W. BARKLEY
34. DWIGHT DAVID EISENHOWER	1953-1961	N.Y.	1890	1969	Denison, Texas	Rep.	RICHARD M. NIXON
35. JOHN FITZGERALD KENNEDY	1961-1963	Mass.	1917	1963	Brookline, Mass.	Dem.	LYNDON B. JOHNSON
36. LYNDON BAINES JOHNSON	1963-1969	Texas	1908	1973	Johnson City, Texas	Dem.	HUBERT H. HUMPHREY
37. RICHARD MILHOUS NIXON	1969-1974	N.Y.	1913		Yorba Linda, Calif.	Rep.	SPIRO T. AGNEW[3] GERALD R. FORD
38. GERALD RUDOLPH FORD	1974-1977	Mich.	1913		Omaha, Neb.	Rep.	NELSON ROCKEFELLER
39. JAMES EARL CARTER, JR.	1977-1981	Ga.	1924		Plains, Ga.	Dem.	WALTER F. MONDALE
40. RONALD WILSON REAGAN	1981-	Calif.	1911		Tampico, Ill.	Rep.	GEORGE BUSH

1. Now the Democratic party 2. Candidate of the National Union Party (1864) and elected on that ticket 3. Resigned October 10, 1973